DIRECTORY OF AMERICAN SCHOLARS

DIRECTORY OF AMERICAN SCHOLARS

TENTH EDITION

VOLUME II

ENGLISH, SPEECH, & DRAMA

Caryn E. Klebba, Editor

GALE GROUP

THOMSON LEARNING

Detroit • New York • San Diego • San Francisco
Boston • New Haven, Conn. • Waterville, Maine
London • Munich

Caryn E. Klebba, *Editor*

Jason B. Baldwin, *Assistant Editor*

Contributing Editors: Alex Alviar, Claire M. Campana, Eric Hoss, Chris Lopez, Christine Maurer, Jenai Mynatt, Jaime E. Noce, Kathleen E. Maki Potts, Amanda C. Quick

Lynne Maday, *Contributor*

Erin E. Braun, *Managing Editor*

Ralph Wiazowski, *Programmer/Analyst*
Venus Little, *Manager, Database Applications, Technical Support Services*

Dorothy Maki, *Manufacturing Manager*
Evi Seoud, *Production Manager*
NeKita McKee, *Buyer*

Data Capture Specialists: Nikkita Bankston, Cynthia A. Jones, Frances L. Monroe

Mike Logusz, *Graphic Artist*

ISBN: 0-7876-5008-0 (Volume 1)
ISBN: 0-7876-5009-9 (Volume 2)
ISBN: 0-7876-5010-2 (Volume 3)
ISBN: 0-7876-5011-0 (Volume 4)
ISBN: 0-7876-5012-9 (Volume 5)
ISBN: 0-7876-5013-7 (Volume 6)
ISBN: 0-7876-5007-2 (set)
ISSN: 0070-5101

Printed in the United States of America
Published in the United States by Gale Group

CONTENTS

PREFACE

First published in 1942 under the auspices of the American Council of Learned Societies, the *Directory of American Scholars* remains the foremost biographical reference to American humanities scholars. With the tenth edition, the Gale Group has added social science scholars, recognizing the close relationship of the social sciences to the humanities.

The directory is arranged for convenient use in five subject volumes: Volume I: History, Archaeology, and Area Studies; Volume II: English, Speech, and Drama; Volume III: Foreign Languages, Linguistics, and Philology; Volume IV: Philosophy, Religion, and Law; Volume V: Psychology, Sociology, and Education. Each volume of biographical listings contains a geographic index. Volume VI contains an alphabetical index, a discipline index, an institutional index and a cumulative geographic index of scholars listed in the first five volumes.

The tenth edition of the *Directory of American Scholars* profiles more than 30,000 United States and Canadian scholars currently active in teaching, research, and/or publishing. The names of entrants were obtained from a variety of sources, including former entrants, academic deans, or citations in professional journals. In most cases, nominees received a questionnaire to complete, and selection for inclusion was made based on the following criteria:

1. Achievement, by reason of experience and training, of a stature in scholarly work equivalent to that associated with the doctoral degree, coupled with current activity in such work;

or

2. Achievement as evidenced by publication of scholarly works;

or

3. Attainment of a position of substantial responsibility by reason of achievement as outlined in (1) and (2).

Enhancements to the tenth edition include the addition of the fifth subject volume, Volume V: Psychology, Sociology, and Education, and the renaming of Volume I to better reflect the disciplines covered within. An outline of the major disciplines within the social sciences and humanities has been added to each volume to assist in locating scholars associated with disciplines related to, but not named outright in the titles of the individual volumes. Please see page ix for this information. Those individuals involved in multiple fields are listed in all appropriate volumes.

The tenth edition of the *Directory of American Scholars* is produced by fully automated methods. Limitations in the printing method have made it necessary to omit most diacritics.

Individual entries can include: place and year of birth, *primary discipline(s), vital statistics, education, honorary degrees, past and present professional experience, concurrent positions, *membership in international, national and regional societies, honors and awards, *research interest, *publications, postal mailing and electronic mailing addresses. Elements preceded by an asterisk are limited as to the number of items included. If an entrant exceeded these limitations, the editors selected the most recent information. Biographies received in the offices of the Gale Group after the editorial deadline were included in an abbreviated manner whenever possible.

The editors have made every effort to include material as accurately and completely as possible within the confines of format and scope. However, the publishers do not assume and hereby disclaim any liability to any party for any loss or damage caused by errors or omissions in the *Directory of American Scholars*, whether such errors or omissions result from negligence, accident, or any other cause.

Thanks are expressed to those who contributed information and submitted nominations for the new edition. Many societies provided membership lists for the research process and published announcements in their journals or newsletters, and their help is appreciated.

Comments and suggestions regarding any aspect of the tenth edition are invited and should be addressed to The Editors, *Directory of American Scholars*, Gale Group, 27500 Drake Road, Farmington Hills, MI 48333-3535.

MAJOR HUMANITIES & SOCIAL SCIENCE DISCIPLINES

Volume I: History, Archaeology, & Area Studies

Aesthetics
Architecture
Archaeology
Area Studies
Art
Art History
Assyriology
Community Studies
Community Planning
Demography
Geography
History
International Studies
Urban Studies
Western Civilization

Volume II: English, Speech, & Drama

Advertising
Audiology
Bibliography
Cinema
Classical Literature
Communications
Composition (Language Arts)
Creative Writing
Drama
English Literature
Film Studies
Journalism
Library Science
Literary Theory
Literature
Marketing
Mass Communication
Media Studies
Music
Music History
Musicology
Performing Arts
Poetry
Rhetoric
Speech Communication
Speech-Language Pathology
Theater Studies

Volume III: Foreign Languages, Linguistics, & Philology

Classical Languages
Comparative Literature
Foreign Languages
Foreign Literature Studies
Linguistics
Modern Languages
Philology
Romance Languages
Translation

Volume IV: Philosophy, Religion, & Law

Accounting
Business Administration
Corrections
Criminal Justice
Criminology
Economics
Epistemology
Ethics
Evangelism
Forensic Sciences
Government
Homiletics
International Relations
Missiology
Philosophy
Political Science
Public Affairs
Religious Studies
Statistics

Volume V: Psychology, Sociology, & Education

Adult Education
Anthropology
Behavioral Sciences
Child Development
Clinical Psychology
Counseling
Culture Studies
Education
Ethnology
Folklore
Gender Studies
Gerontology
Health Studies
Human Development
Language Education
Psychology
Social Work
Sociology
Women's Studies

ABBREVIATIONS

AAAS American Association for the Advancement of Science
AAUP American Association of University Professors
abnorm abnormal
acad academia, academic, academica, academie, academique, academy
accad accademia
acct account, accountant, accounting
acoust acoustical, accounstic(s)
adj adjunct, adjutant
actg acting
activ activities, activity
addn addition(s), additional
AID Agency for International Development
adjust adjust
admin administration, administrative
adminr administrator(s)
admis admissions
adv advisor(s), advisory
advan advance(d), advancement
advert advertisement, advertising
aerodyn aerodynamic(s)
aeronaut aeronautic(s), aeronautical
aesthet aesthetics
affil affiliate(s), affiliation
agr agricultural, agriculture
agt agent
AFB Air Force Base
AHA American Historical Association
akad akademi, akademia
Ala Alabama
Algem algemeen, algemen
allergol allergological, allergology
allgem allgemein, allgemeine, allgemeinen
Alta Alberta
Am America, Americain, American, Americana, Americano, Amerika, Amerikaansch, Amerikaner, Amerikanisch, Amerikansk
anal analysis, analytic, analytical
analog analogue
anat anatomic, anatomical, anatomy
ann annal(s)
anthrop anthropological, anthropology
anthropom anthropometric, anthropometrical, anthropometry
antiq antiquaire(s), antiquarian, antiquary(ies), antiquities
app appoint, appointed, appointment
appl applied
appln application
approx approximate, approximately
Apr April
apt apartment(s)
arbit arbitration
arch archiv, archiva, archive(s), archivio, archivo
archaeol archaeological, archaeology
archaol archaologie, archaologisch
archeol archeological, archeologie, archeologique, archeology
archit architectural, architecture
Arg Argentina, Argentine
Ariz Arizona
Ark Arkansas
asn association
asoc asociacion
assoc(s) associate(s), associated
asst assistant
Assyriol Assyriology
astrodyn astrodynamics
astron astronomical, astronomy
astronaut astronautical, astronautics
astronr astronomer
attend attendant, attending
atty attorney
audiol audiology
Aug August
auth author(s)
AV audiovisual
ave avenue

b born
BC British Columbia
bd board
behav behavior, behavioral, behaviour, behavioural
Bibl Biblical, Biblique
bibliog bibliografia, bibliographic, bibligraphical, bibliography(ies)
bibliogr bibliographer
bibliot biblioteca, bibliotec, bibliotek, bibliotheca, bibliothek, bibliothequeca
biog biographical, biography
biol biological, biology
bk(s) books
bldg building
blvd boulevard
bol boletim, boletin
boll bollettino
bor borough
bot botanical, botany
br branch
Brit Britain, British
Bro(s) Brother(s)
bull bulletin
bur bureau
bus business
BWI British West Indies

c children
Calif California
Can Canada, Canadian, Canadien, Canadienne
cand candidate
cartog cartografic, cartographical, cartography
cartogra cartographer
Cath Catholic, Catholique
CBS Columbia Broadcasting System
cent central
Cent Am Central America
cert certificat, certificate, certified
chap chapter
chem chermical, chemistry
chg charge
chemn chairman
Cie Compagnie
cient cientifica, cientifico
class classical
clin(s) clinic(s)
Co Companies, Company, County
coauth coauth
co-dir co-director
co-ed co-editor
co-educ co-educational
col(s) colegio, college(s), collegiate
collab collaboration, collaborative, collaborating, collaborator
Colo Colorado
Comdr Commander
com commerce, commercial
commun communication(s)
comn(s) commission(s)
comnr commissioner
comp comparative, comparee
compos composition(s)
comput computer, computing
comt committee
conf conference
cong congress
Conn Connecticut

conserv conservacion,conservation, conservatoire, conservatory
consol consolidated, consolidation
const constitution, constitutional
construct construction
consult consultant, consulting
contemp contemporary
contrib contribute, contribution
contribur contributor
conv convention
coop cooperation, cooperative
coord coordinating, coordination
coordr coordinator
corresp corresponding
Corp Corporation
coun council, counsel, counseling
counr councillor, counselor
criminol criminology
Ct Court
ctr center
cult cultra, cultural, culturale, culture
cur curator
curric curriculum
cybernet cybernetics
CZ Canal Zone
Czeck Czechoslovakia

DC District of Columbia
Dec December
Del Delaware
deleg delegate, delegations
demog demographic, demography
demonstr demonstrator
dent dental, dentistry
dep deputy
dept department
Deut Deutsch, Deutschland
develop development
diag diagnosis, diagnostic
dialectol dialectology
dig digest
dipl diploma, diploma, diplomate, diplome
dir director(s), directory directory
Diss Abstr Dissertation Abstracts
dist district
distrib distributive
distribr distributors
div division, divorced
doc document, documentation
Dom Dominion
Dr Doctor, Drive
Drs Doctroandus

e east
ecol ecological, ecology
econ economic(s), economical, economy
ed edicion, edition, editor, editorial, edizione
educ education, educational
educr educator(s)
Egyptol Egyptology
elec electric, electrical, electricity electrical
elem elementary
emer emeriti, emeritus
encour encouragement
encycl encyclopedia
employ employment
Eng England
environ environment, environmental
EPDA Education Professions Development Act
equip equipment
ERIC Educational Resources Information Center
ESEA Elementary & Secondary Education Act

espec especially
estab established, establishment
estud estudante, estudas, estudianet, estudio(s), estudo(s)
ethnog ethnographical, ethnography
ethnol ethnological, ethnology
Europ European
eval evaluation
evangel evangelical
eve evening
exam examination
examr examiner
except exceptional
exec executive(s)
exeg exegesis(es), exegetic, exegetical, exegetics
exhib exhibition(s)
exp experiment, experimental, experimentation
exped expedition(s)
explor exploration(s)
expos exposition
exten extension

fac faculties, faculty
facil facilities, facility
Feb February
fed federal
fedn federation
fel(s) fellow(s), fellowship(s)
filol filologia, filologico
filos filosofia, filosofico
Fla Florida
FLES Foreign Languages in the Elementary Schools
for foreign
forsch forschung, forschungen
found foundation
Fr Francais(s), French
Ft Fort

Ga Georgia
gen general, generale
geneal genealogical, genealogy
genoot genootschap
geod geodesy, geodetic
geog geografia, geografico, geographer(s), geographic, geographie, geographical, geography
geogr geographer
geol geologic, geological, geology
geophys geophysical
Ger German, Germanic, Germanisch, Germany
Ges gesellschaft
gov governing, governors
govt government
grad graduate
Gr Brit Great Britain
guid guidance
gym gymnasium

handbk(s) handbooks
Hawaii
Hisp Hispanic, Hispanico, Hispano
hist historie, historia, historial, historic, historica, historical, historique, historische, history
histol histology, histological
Hoshsch Hoshschule
hon honorable, honorary
hosp(s) hospital(s)
hq headquarters
HumRRO Human Resources Research Office
hwy highway

Ill Illinois

illum illuminating, illumination
illus illustrate, illustration
illusr illustrator
imp imperial
improv improvement
Inc Incorporated
incl include, included, includes, including
Ind Indiana
indust(s) industrial, industry(ies)
infor information
inst institut, instritute(s), institution(s), instituto
instnl institutional, institutionalized
instr instruction, instructor(s)
instruct instructional
int internacional, international, internazionale
intel intelligence
introd introduction
invest investigacion, investiganda, investigation, investigative
investr investigator
ist istituto
Ital Italia, Italian, Italiana, Italiano, Italica, Italien, Italienisch, Italienne, Italy

J Journal
Jan January
jour journal, journalism
jr junior
jurisp jurisprudence
juv juvenile(s)

Kans Kansas
Koninki koninklijk
Ky Kentucky

La Louisiana
lab laboratorie, laboratorio, laboratorium, laboratory(ies)
lang language(s)
lect lecture(s)
lectr lecturer
legis legislacion, legislatief, legislation, legislative, legislativo, legislature, legislazione
lett letter(s), lettera, letteraria, letterature, lettere
lib liberal
libr libary(ies), librerio
librn librarian(s)
lic license, lecencia
ling linguistic(s), linguistica, linguistique
lit liteary, literatur, literatura, literature, littera, literature
Ltd Limited

m married
mach machine(s), machinery
mag magazine
Man Manitoba
Mar March
Mariol Mariological, Mariology
Mass Massachusetts
mat matematica, matematiche, matematico, matematik
math mathematics, mathematical, mathematics, mathematik, mathematique(s), mathematisch
Md Maryland
mech mechanical
med medical, medicine
Mediter Mediterranean
mem member, memoirs, memorial
ment mental, mentally

metrop metropolitan
Mex Mexican, Mexicano, Mexico
mfg manufacturing
mfr manufacture, manufacturer
mgr manager(s)
mgt management
Mich Michigan
mid middle
mil military
Minn Minnesota
Miss Mississippi
mitt mitteilung
mkt market, marketing
MLA Modern Language Association of America
Mo Missouri
mod modern,moderna, moderne, moderno
monatsh monatsheft(e)
monatsschr monatsschrift
monogr monograph
Mont Montana
morphol morphologica, morphologie, morphology
mt mount, mountain(s)
munic municipal
mus museum(s)
musicol musicological, musicology

n north
nac nacional
NASA National Aeronautics & Space Administration
nat nationaal, national, nationale, nationalis, naturalized
NATO North Atlantic Treaty Organization
naz nazionale
NB New Brunswick
NC North Carolina
MCTE National Council of Teachers of English
NDak North Dakota
NDEA National Defense Education Act
NEA National Education Association
Nebr Nebraska
Ned Nederland, Nederlandsch
Nev Nevada
Neth Netherlands
Nfld Newfoundland
NH New Hampshire
NJ New Jersey
NMex New Mexico
no number
nonres nonresident
norm normal, normale
Norweg Norwegian
Nov November
NS Nova Scotia
NSW New South Wales
NT Northwest Territories
numis numismatic, numismatico, numismatique
NY New York
NZ New Zealand

occas occasional
occup occupation, occupational
Oct October
Ohio
OEEC Organization for European Economic Cooperation
off office, officer(s), official(s)
Okla Oklahoma
Ont Ontario
oper operation(s), operational, operative
ord ordnance
Ore Oregon
orgn organization, organizational
orient oriental, orientale, orientalist, orientalia
ornithol ornithological, ornithology

Pa Pennsylvania
Pac Pacific
paleontol paleontological, paleontology
PanAm Pan American
pedag pedagogia, pedagogic, pedagogical, pedagogico,
pedagogoie, pedagogik, pedagogique, pedagogy
Pei Prince Edward Island
penol penological, penology
phenomenol phenomenological, phenomenologie, phenomenology
philol philologica, philological, philologie, philologisch,
philology
philos philosophia, philosophic, philosophical, philosophie,
philosophique, philosophisch, philosophical, philosohpy,
philosozophia
photog photographic, photography
photogr photographer(s)
phys physical
pkwy parkway
pl place
polit politica, political, politicas, politico, politics,
politek, politike, politique, politsch, politisk
polytech polytechnic
pop population
Pontif Pontifical
Port Portugal, Portuguese
postgrad postgraduate
PR Puerto Rico
pract practice
prehist prehistoric
prep preparation, preparatory
pres president
Presby Presbyterian
preserv preservation
prev prevention, preventive
prin principal(s)
prob problem(s)
probtn probation
proc proceding
prod production
prof professional, professor, professorial
prog program(s), programmed, programming
proj project, projective
prom promotion
prov province, provincial
psychiat psychiatria, psychiatric, psychiatrica, psychiatrie,
psychiatrique, psychiatrisch, psychiatry
psychol psychological
pt point
pub pub, publique
publ publication(s), published, publisher(s), publishing
pvt private

qm quartermaster
quad quaderni
qual qualitative, quality
quart quarterly
Que Quebec

rd road
RD Rural Delivery, Rural Free Delivery
Rural Free Delivery
rec record(s), recording
rech recherche
redevelop redevelopment
ref reference
regist register, registered, registration
registr registrar
rehabil rehabilitation
rel(s) relacion, relation(s), relative, relazione
relig religion, religious
rep representative
repub republic
req requirement(s)
res research, reserve
rev review, revised, revista, revue
rhet rhetoric, rhetorical
RI Rhode Island
Rt Right
Rte Route
Russ Russian
rwy railway

s south
SAfrica South Africa
SAm South America, South American
Sask Saskatchewan
SC South Carolina
Scand Scandinavian
sch(s) school(s)
scholar scholarship
sci science(s), scientia, scientific, scientifico, scientifique,
scienza
SDak South Dakota
SEATO Southeast Asia Treaty Organization
sec secondary
sect section
secy secretary
sem seminaire, seminar, seminario, seminary
sen senator, sneatorial
Sept September
ser serial, series
serv service(s)
soc social, sociedad, sociedade, societa, societas, societate,
societe, societet, society(ies)
soc sci social science(s)
sociol sociological, sociology
Span Spanish
spec special
sq square
sr senior
sr sister
St Saint, Street
sta station
statist statistical, statistics
Ste Sainte, Suite
struct structural, structure(s)
subcomt subcommittee
subj subject
substa substa
super superieur, superior, superiore
suppl supplement, supplementary
supt superintendent
supv supervising, supervision
supvr supervisor
supvry supervisory
surg surgical, surgery
surv survey
Swed Swedish
Switz Switzerland
symp symposium
syst system, systematic

tech technic(s), technica, technical, technicky, techniczny,
techniek, technik, technika, technikum, technique, technisch
technol technologic, technological, technologicke,
technologico, technologiczny, technologie, technologika,

technologique, technologisch, technology
tecnol technologia, technologica, technologico
tel telegraph(s), telephone
temp temporary
Tenn Tennessee
Terr Terrace
teol teologia, teologico
Tex Texas
textbk textbook(s)
theol theological, theologie, theologique, theologisch, theology
theoret theoretic(al)
ther therapy
trans transactions
transp transportation
transl translation, translator(s)
treas treasurer, treasury
trop tropical
TV television
twp township

u und
UAR United Arab Republic
UK United Kingdom
UN United Nations
unemploy unemployment
UNESCO United Nations Educational, Scientific & Cultural Organization
UNICEF United Nations Children's Fund
univ(s) universidad, universite, university(ies)
UNRRA United Nations Relief & Rehabilitation Administration
UNRWA United Nations Relief & Works Agency
USA United States of America
US United States
USPHS United States Public Health Service
USSR Union of Soviet Socialist Republics
Utah

Va Virginia
var various
veg vegetable(s), vegetation
ver vereeniging, verein, vereingt, vereinigung
vet veteran, veterinarian, veterinary
VI Virgin Islands
vis visiting
voc vocational
vocab vocabulary
vol(s) volume(s), voluntary, volunteer(s)
vchmn vice chairman
vpres vice president
Vt Vermont

w west
Wash Washington
wetensch wetenschappelijk, wetenschappen
WHO World Health Organization
WI West Indies
wid widow, widowed, widower
Wis Wisconsin
wiss wissenschaft(en), wissenschaftliche(e)
WVa West Virginia
Wyo Wyoming

yearbk yearbook(s)
YMCA Young Men's Christian Association
YMHA Young Men's Hebrew Association
YWCA Young Women's Christian Association
YWHA Young Women's Hebrew Association

z zeitschrift

Biographies

A

AANERUD, REBECCA J.
PERSONAL Born 10/16/1961, Buffalo, NY, m, 1982, 1 child **DISCIPLINE** WOMEN STUDIES, ENGLISH **EDUCATION** Univ Wash, BA, 90; MA, 93; PhD, 98. **CAREER** Instr to lectr, Univ Wash, 98-. **HONORS AND AWARDS** Phi Beta Kappa, 90; Doman Award for Excellence in Teaching, 97; Robert R and Mary Roberts Waltz Grad Fel, 97. **MEMBERSHIPS** MLA, Am Studies Asn, Nat Women Studies Asn. **RESEARCH** Critical Race Theory, Feminist Theory, US American Literature and Culture, Globalization, Film/television theory, Cultural Studies. **SELECTED PUBLICATIONS** Auth, "Fictions of Whiteness: Speaking the Names of Whiteness in US Literature," Essays in Soc and Cult Criticism, ed Ruth Frankenberg, (Duke Univ Pr, 97); auth, "Now More than Ever: James Baldwin and the Critique of White Liberalism," James Baldwin Now, ed Dwight McBride, (NY Univ Pr, 99); auth, "Thinking Again: This bridge called My back and the Challenge to Whiteness," This Bridge We Call Home, ed AnaLouise Keating and Gloria Anzaludua, Routledge, (forthcoming). **CONTACT ADDRESS** Dept Women Studies, Univ of Washington, PO Box 354345, Seattle, WA 98195. **EMAIL** raan@u.washington.edu

AARSLEFF, HANS
PERSONAL Born 07/19/1925, Denmark **DISCIPLINE** ENGLISH **EDUCATION** Univ Copenhagen, BA, 45; Univ Minn, MA, 54, PhD, 60. **CAREER** From instr to assoc prof English, 56-72; prof, English, Princeton Univ, 72-98. **HONORS AND AWARDS** Jr fel coun humanities, Princeton Univ, 62; Am Coun Learned Soc fel, 64-65, 72-73; NEH fel, 75-76; fel Am Acad of Arts and Sci, 94; Howard T. Behrman Awd for Distinguished Achievement in the Hum, Princeton Univ, 94. **MEMBERSHIPS** Am Philos Soc; Royal Danish Acad of Sci and Lett; bd of eds, 79- , Bd of Dir, 81, J of the Hist of Ideas; Adv Bd, 88- , Hist of the Human Sci. **RESEARCH** History of doctrines about the nature and study of language and of the philosophy of language since the Renaissance; Locke; Leibniz; Condillac; Diderot; Herder; Breal. **SELECTED PUBLICATIONS** Auth, The Study of Language in England 1780-1860, 67; auth, From Locke to Saussure, Essays on the Study of Language and Intellectual History, 82; auth, Descartes and Augustine on Genesis, Language and the Angels, in Leibniz and Adam, 93; auth, Locke's Influence, in Cambridge Companion to Locke, 94; auth, Language and Thought in the 17th and 18th Centuries, in Chicago Ling Soc, 96; auth, Herder's Cartesian Ursprung vs Condillac's Expressivist Essai, Philosophies and the Language Sciences: a Historical Perspective in honour of Lia Formigari, 96; auth, "The rise and decline of Adam and his Ursprache in seventeenth-century Thought, in The Language of Adam/Die Sprache Adams, (99); auth, Introduction to translation of Condillac, (Essay on the Origin of Human Knowledge, 01). **CONTACT ADDRESS** Dept of English, Princeton Univ, McCosh 22, Princeton, NJ 08544-1016.

ABBOTT, ANTHONY S.
PERSONAL Born 01/07/1935, San Francisco, CA, m, 1960, 3 children **DISCIPLINE** ENGLISH **EDUCATION** Princeton Univ, AB, 57; Harvard Univ, PhD(English), 61. **CAREER** Instr English, Bates Col, 61-64; asst prof, 64-67, assoc prof, 67-80, Prof English, Davidson Col, 80- **MEMBERSHIPS** MLA; Soc Relig Higher Educ. **RESEARCH** Modern drama; history of English drama; American literature; creative writing. **SELECTED PUBLICATIONS** Auth, Shaw and Christianity, Seabury, 56; auth, Shaw and Christianity, 65; auth, The Vital Lie: Reality and Illusion in Modern Drama, 89; auth, The Girl in the Yellow Raincoat, 89; auth, A Small Thing Like a, 93; auth, The Search for Wonder in the Cradle of the World, 00. **CONTACT ADDRESS** Dept of English, Davidson Col, PO Box 1719, Davidson, NC 28036-1719. **EMAIL** toabbott@davidson.edu

ABBOTT, CRAIG STEPHENS
PERSONAL Born 11/23/1941, Washington, DC **DISCIPLINE** AMERICAN LITERATURE **EDUCATION** Tex A&M Univ, BA, 64, MA, 66; Univ Tex, Austin, PhD(English), 73. **CAREER** Asst prof, 73-78, assoc prof English, Northern Ill Univ, 78-85, prof, 85-, Assoc ed, Anal & Enumerative Bibliog, 77-98. **MEMBERSHIPS** Bibliog Soc Am; MLA; Soc Textual Scholar. **RESEARCH** Modern poetry; bibliography. **SELECTED PUBLICATIONS** Auth, Marianne Moore: A Descriptive Bibliography, Univ Pittsburgh, 77; auth, Marianne Moore: A Reference Guide, G K Hall, 78, John Crowe Ransom, Whitston, 99; Co-auth, An Introduction to Bibliographical and Textual Studies, MLA, 85, 89, 99. **CONTACT ADDRESS** Dept of English, No Illinois Univ, 1425 W Lincoln Hwy, De Kalb, IL 60115-2825. **EMAIL** cabbott@niu.edu

ABBOTT, H. PORTER
PERSONAL Born Baltimore, MD, m, 1966, 2 children **DISCIPLINE** ENGLISH LITERATURE **EDUCATION** Univ Toronto, PhD, 66; PhD, 68. **CAREER** Prof, Univ Calif, Santa Barbara. **SELECTED PUBLICATIONS** Auth, The Fiction of Samuel Beckett: Form and Effect, Univ California Press, 73; Diary Fiction: Writing as Action, Cornell Univ Press, 84; "Writing and Conversion: Conrad's Modernism Autobiography," Yale Jour of Criticism, 92; "Beginning Again: The Post-Narrative Art of Texts for Nothing and How It Is," The Cambridge Companion to Beckett, Cambridge, 93; "Character and Modernism: Reading Woolf Writing Woolf," New Lit Hist, 93; Beckett Writing Beckett: The Author in the Autograph, Cornell Univ Press, 96; auth, Extratextual Intelligence, New Literary History, 97; auth, Samuel Beckett and the Arts of Time, in Samuel Beckett and the Arts, 99; auth, The Evolution of the Storied Mind, Narrative, 00. **CONTACT ADDRESS** Dept of Eng, Univ of California, Santa Barbara, Santa Barbara, CA 93106-7150. **EMAIL** pabbott@humanitas.ucsb.edu

ABEL, RICHARD OWEN
PERSONAL Born 08/20/1941, Canton, OH, m, 1970 **DISCIPLINE** CINEMA STUDIES, COMPARATIVE LITERATURE **EDUCATION** Utah State Univ, BA, 63; Univ Southern Calif, MA, 65, PhD(comp lit), 70. **CAREER** Teaching asst comp lit, Univ Southern Calif, 65, teaching asst English, 65-66 & 66-67; instr English, 67-68; from instr to assoc prof, 68-80, prof English, Drake Univ, 80-, dir Cult Studies Prog, 90-93, dir Ctr for the Humanities, 96-00. **HONORS AND AWARDS** Theatre Library Asn Awd for best book on recorded performance, 85, 95; Jay Leyda Prize in Cinema Studies, 89; SCS Katherine Singer Kovacs Awd for best essay in cinema studies, 95-97, 98; NEH Fel for Col Teachers, 83-84; ACLS Res Fel, 86; Nat Humanities Ctr Fel, 88-89; John Simon Guggenheim Memorial Fel, 93-94; Ellis and Nell Levitt Dist Prof of Engl; Special Commendation, 99; KRASZNA-KAUS Moving Image Book Awd. **MEMBERSHIPS** MLA, Soc Cinema Studies, Demtor. **RESEARCH** Early Cinema, French Silent Cinema, American Silent Cinema. **SELECTED PUBLICATIONS** Auth, French Cinema: The First Wave, 1915-1929, Princeton, 84; French Film Theory and Criticism, 1907-1939: A History/Anthology, 2 vols, Princeton, 88; The Cin Goes to Town: French Cinema, 1896-1914, Calif, 94; ed, "Silent Film," in Depth of Field, series, Rutgers, 94; auth, The Red Rooster Scare Making Cinema American, 1900-1910, Calif, 99. **CONTACT ADDRESS** Dept of English, Drake Univ, 2507 University Ave, Des Moines, IA 50311-4505. **EMAIL** richard.abel@drake.edu

ABELMAN, ROBERT
PERSONAL Born 12/11/1955, New York, m **DISCIPLINE** BROADCASTING, MEDIA CRITICISM, PUBLIC RELATIONS **EDUCATION** MI State Univ, MA; Univ TX, PhD. **CAREER** Comm, Cleveland St Univ. **HONORS AND AWARDS** Mensa ed and Res Awd for Excellence, 99-00; Listed Top 100 Res in the Field of Communications Studies 1915-1995; Communications Monographs, 99; Listed as on of the Most Prolific Telecommunicaiton Scholar Roster, 85-95; **RESEARCH** Children and Television, broadcast history, religious broadcasting. **SELECTED PUBLICATIONS** Auth, Reclaiming the Wasteland: TV & Gifted Children, Hampton Press, 95; co-auth, Television and the Exceptional Child: A Forgotten Audience, Lawrence Erlbaum & Assoc, 92; Religious Television: Controversies and Conclusions, Ablex, 90. **CONTACT ADDRESS** Dept of Commun, Cleveland State Univ, 83 E 24th St, Cleveland, OH 44115. **EMAIL** r.abelman@csuohio.edu

ABELOVE, HENRY
PERSONAL Born 01/18/1945, Montgomery, AL, s **DISCIPLINE** ENGLISH **EDUCATION** Harvard Col, AB, 66; Yale Univ, PhD, 78. **CAREER** Instr to asst prof, Wesleyan Univ, 72-79; vis assoc prof, Brown Univ, 90; assoc prof, Wesleyan Univ, 79-90; distinguished vis prof, Univ Albta, 95; prof and prog dir, Wesleyan Univ, 91-. **HONORS AND AWARDS** John Simon Guggenheim Found Fel, 95-96; Fel, NEH, 95-96; Award for Excellence in Teaching, Wesleyan Univ, 95; Lambda Literary Prize, 93. **MEMBERSHIPS** MLA; Am Hist Asn; Am Studies Asn; Am Soc for Eighteenth-Century Studies; The Johnsonians; The Hume Soc; Eighteenth-Century Scottish Studies Soc. **RESEARCH** Eighteenth-Century Anglophone cultures; Lesbian/Gay/Queer history and literature. **SELECTED PUBLICATIONS** Auth, The Evangelist of Desire: John Wesley and the Methodists, 90; co-ed, The Lesbian and Gay Studies Reader, 93. **CONTACT ADDRESS** Ctr for the Humanities, Wesleyan Univ, Center for the Humanities, Middletown, CT 06457. **EMAIL** habelove@wesleyan.edu

ABERNETHY, CECIL EMORY
PERSONAL Born 04/08/1908, Charleston, SC, m, 1940, 1 child **DISCIPLINE** ENGLISH **EDUCATION** Birmingham-Southern Col, AB, 30; Univ NC, Chapel Hill, AM, 35; Vanderbilt Univ, PhD, 40. **CAREER** Instr English, high sch, Ala, 31-35; teaching fel, Vanderbilt Univ, 35-37; instr English, Univ Ala, 37-38; from instr to prof, 39-76, emer prof English, Birmingham-Southern Col, 76-. **MEMBERSHIPS** English Asn Gt Brit; Renaissance Soc Am; AAUP. **CONTACT ADDRESS** Dept English, Sonoma State Univ, 1801 E Cotati Ave, Rohnert Park, CA 94928-3609.

ABERNETHY, FRANCIS EDWARD
PERSONAL Born 12/03/1925, Altus, OK, m, 1948, 5 children **DISCIPLINE** ENGLISH **EDUCATION** Stephen F Austin State Col, BA, 49; La State Univ, MA, 51, PhD, 56. **CAREER** From asst prof to assoc prof English, Lamar State Col Tech, 56-65; Prof English, Stephen F Austin State Univ, 65-, Lamar State Col Tech res grant, 59-63; resident grants res folklore, 59-68. **MEMBERSHIPS** Am Folklore Soc; SCent Renaissance Conf; SCent Mod Lang Asn; Asn Mex Cave Studies. **RESEARCH** Folklore; Renaissance drama; east Texas history. **SELECTED PUBLICATIONS** Auth, Social Protest Literature, 1485-1558, La State Univ, 62; Tales From the Big Thicket, Univ Tex, 66; J Frank Dobie, Steck-Vaughn Co, 67; The East Texas Communal Hunt, Publ Tex Folklore Soc, 71; ed & contribr, Observations and Reflections, Encino, 72. **CONTACT ADDRESS** Dept of English, Stephen F. Austin State Univ, Nacogdoches, TX 75962.

ABINADER, ELMAZ
DISCIPLINE CREATIVE WRITING **EDUCATION** Univ Pittsburgh, BA, 74; Columbia Univ, MFA, 78; Univ Nebr, PhD, 85. **CAREER** Assoc prof; Mills Col, 93-. **RESEARCH** Creative writing; fiction and non-fiction. **SELECTED PUBLICATIONS** Auth, The Children of the Roojme, A Family's Journey from Lebanon, Madison, WI: Univ Wis Press, 97; The Children of the Roojme, A Family's Journey, NY: W.W. Norton & Co, 91; Looking for Our Lives, A Writer's Perspective on American Literature, Al Majal, 94; Beyond the Veil and Yemen can Wait, Metro, 93; Here, I'm an Arab; There, an American. The New York Times, 91; poetry, Anthologies: Reflections on a Gift of Watermelon Pickle, Eds Dunning and Lueders, NY: Scott Foresman, 94; Grape Leaves: A Century of Arab American Poetry, Salt Lake City: Univ Utah Press, 88; All My Grandmothers Could Sing, Lincoln, Nebr: Free Rein Press, 84; mag, Footworks: Paterson Lit Rev, Living with Opposition, Arabic Mus, Letters from Home, 94. **CONTACT ADDRESS** Dept of English, Mills Col, 5000 MacArthur Blvd, Oakland, CA 94613-1301. **EMAIL** moses@mills.edu

ABNER, JULIE LAMAY
DISCIPLINE ENGLISH **EDUCATION** Victor Valley Col, AV, 88; Calif State Univ, BA, 90; MA, 92, Union Inst, PhD, 98. **CAREER** Instr, Crafton Hills Col, 94-95; instr, San Bernardino Valley Col, 96-97; instr to asst prof, Chaffey Col, 97-. **HONORS AND AWARDS** Chair, Calif Indian Conf, 00-. **MEMBERSHIPS** MLA; Assoc for the Study of Am Indian Lit; NCTE; Col Comp and Commun; Nat Assoc for Ethnic Studies; Assoc for Am Indian Prof; Nat Indian Educ Assoc. **RESEARCH** Composition, American Indian Studies, Shakespeare, Collaborative Writing, Humanities and Cultural Studies, Ethnic and Gender Studies. **SELECTED PUBLICATIONS** Auth, "Gambling on Reservations", "East Los Angeles", "Blowout", Encyclopedia of Multiculturalism, Salem (Pasadena), 93; coauth, "I Defy Analysis: A Conversation with Gerald Vizenor", Studies in Am Indian Lit, (Fall 93): 43-51; coauth, "N. Scott Momaday: Native American Storyteller" and "Hollywood Paradigm and Cultural Stereotype: Captain Jack, the Modoc Wars, Drumbeat, and Indians in Mid-Century Film", New Ethnic American Literature and Arts: An Encyclopedia, Garland, (94); auth, "Diane Glancy", Dictionary of Literary Biography: Native American Writers, 97; auth, "Composition and Indian Literatures", Alternative Rhetorics, eds Sibylle Gruber and Laura Gray-Rosendale, Univ of Ariz Pr, 99; auth, "Composition", Petroglyphs: Quarterly Newsletter of the Mojave Inst of Arts I.2, (Winter 99); auth, "Pedagogy and American Indian Literatures", Col English, (forthcoming); auth, "Louis Owens", Studies in American Indian Lit, (99). **CONTACT ADDRESS** Sch Arts & Humanities, Chaffey Col, 5885 Haven Ave, Alta Loma, CA 91737-3002.

ABRAHAM, DANIEL
PERSONAL Born 08/22/1968, Middletown, NY, s **DISCIPLINE** MUSICOLOGY **EDUCATION** Univ Mass, BM, 90; Univ Md, MM, 95; PhD, 01. **CAREER** Grad tchg asst, Univ Md, 94-98; vis prof mus, George Washington Univ, 98-99. **HONORS AND AWARDS** Conducting Fel, Ore Bach Festival,97; Irving Lowens Awd for Student Musicol Res, 96; Daniel Palmery Prize for Performance & Scholarship in 18th Century Music. **MEMBERSHIPS** Am Musicol Soc; Soc 17th Century Mus; Am Bach Soc; Sonneck Soc Am Mus; Hist Brass Soc. **RESEARCH** 18th Century Music; Handel Music in Society; Performance Practice; Music of Bach and Handel; Computer Application in Musicology; Choral Music. **SELECTED PUBLICATIONS** Auth, In Tuneful Muses: A Tribute to Henry Purcell,Univ Md, 95. **CONTACT ADDRESS** Dept Performing Arts, American Univ, 4400 Mass Ave., Washington, DC 20014. **EMAIL** dabraham@wam.umd.edu

ABRAHAM, JULIE L.
DISCIPLINE ENGLISH LANGUAGE AND LITERATURE **EDUCATION** Columbia Univ, PhD, 89. **CAREER** Assoc prof Eng/Women's Studies. **RESEARCH** Modern British literature; women's literature; feminist literary theory. **SELECTED PUBLICATIONS** Auth, Are Girls Necessary?: Lesbian Writing and Modern Histories. **CONTACT ADDRESS** English Dept, Emory Univ, 1380 Oxford Rd NE, Atlanta, GA 30322-1950.

ABRAMS, MEYER HOWARD
PERSONAL Born 07/23/1912, Long Branch, NJ, m, 1937, 2 children **DISCIPLINE** ENGLISH LITERATURE **EDUCATION** Harvard Univ, AB, 34, AM, 37, PhD, 40. **CAREER** Instr, Harvard Univ, 38-42, res assoc, 42-45; from asst prof to prof English, 45-61, Whiton Prof, 61-73, Class of 1916 Prof, 73-83, prof emeritus, 83- , Cornell Univ; Rockefeller Found fel, 46-47; Ford Found fel, 53; Fulbright scholar, Royal Univ Malta & Cambridge Univ, 54; hon mem fac, Royal Univ Malta, 54-; Guggenheim fels, 58 & 60; Roache lectr, Ind Univ, 63; Alexander lectr, Univ Toronto, 64; adv ed, W W Norton & Co; mem, English Inst; mem, exec coun, MLA, 61-64; fel, Ctr Advan Studies Behav Sci, 67-68; Ewing lectr, Univ Calif, Los Angeles, 75; hon sr fel, Sch Critical Studies, Cornell Univ, 76-; mem Founders Group, Nat Humanities Ctr, 76-; vis fel, All Souls Col, Oxford Univ, 77; Cecil & Ida Green lectr, Univ BC, 80. **HONORS AND AWARDS** Gauss Prize, 53; James Russell Lowell Prize, MLA, 72; Am Acad award in Humanistic Stud, 84; Am Acad Inst Arts and Letters award, 90; littd, univ rochester, 78, northwestern univ, 81 & univ chicago, 82. **MEMBERSHIPS** MLA; fel Am Philos Soc; fel Am Acad Arts & Sci; corresp fel, British Academy. **RESEARCH** History of literature; literary criticism; European romanticism. **SELECTED PUBLICATIONS** Auth, The Mirror and the Lamp, Oxford, 53; auth, The Milk of Paradise, 34, 2nd ed, 70; Glossary of Literary Terms, Harcourt Brace, 57, 7th ed, 98; ed, The Poetry of Pope, Holt, 58; ed, The Romantic Poets: Modern Essays in Criticism, Oxford Univ, 60; ed, The Norton Anthology of English Literature, 62, 7th ed, 99 & auth, Natural Supernaturalism: Tradition and revolution in Romantic literature, 71, Norton; Coauth & ed, Wordsworth: A Collection of Critical Essays, Prentice-Hall, 72; co-ed, Wordsworth's Prelude, 1799-1850, Norton, 78; auth, The Correspondent Breeze: Essays on English Romanticism, Norton, 84; auth, Doing Things with Texts: Essays in Criticism and Critical Theory, Norton, 89. **CONTACT ADDRESS** Dept of English, Cornell Univ, Ithaca, NY 14853. **EMAIL** mha5@cornell.edu

ABUDU, GABRIEL
PERSONAL Born, Ghana, m, 2 children **DISCIPLINE** LITERATURE **EDUCATION** Univ Ghana, BA; Queen's Univ, Canada, MA; Temple Univ, PhD. **MEMBERSHIPS** MLA; Col Lang Assoc; Am Assoc of Teachers of Span and Port; Afro-Latin Am Res Assoc; Assoc of the Afro-Hispanic Rev. **RESEARCH** Twentieth-century Cuban poetry. **SELECTED PUBLICATIONS** Areas: Nancy Morejon. **CONTACT ADDRESS** Dept of English and Humanities, York Col, Pennsylvania, York, PA 17405-7199. **EMAIL** gabudu@ycp.edu

ACHBERGER, KAREN RIPP
PERSONAL Born 04/10/1943, Madison, WI, w, 1975, 2 children **DISCIPLINE** GERMAN LANGUGAGE AND LITERATURE, FILM STUDIES **EDUCATION** Univ Wis-Madison, BS, 67, MA, 68, PhD(Ger lit), 75. **CAREER** Asst prof, Univ Ore, 74-79; Asst Prof to Assoc Prof to Prof of Ger, St Olaf Col, 79-. **HONORS AND AWARDS** NEH, 94-95; ACLS, 84-85; Sr. Fulbright Fel, 81. **MEMBERSHIPS** MLA; Am Asn Teachers Ger; German Studies Assn; Women in Ger; Int Brecht Soc. **RESEARCH** Contemporary German women writers; Ingeborg Bachmann; postwar German Literature 20th Century; Austrian Literature. **SELECTED PUBLICATIONS** Auth, A multidisciplinary synthesis in teaching German culture and civilization, Pac Northwest Coun Foreign Lang Proc, 76; coauth, Irmtraud Morgner's Gospel of Valeska, New Ger Critique, 78; auth, Ingeborg Bachmann's Homberg Libretto: Kleist between humanism and existentialism, Mod Austrian Lit, 79; GDR women's fiction of the 1970's: The emergence of feminism within socialism, E Cent Europe, 79; Literatur als Libretto: Das deutsche Opernbuch seit 1945 Heidelberg, Winter 80; Bachmann und die Bibel: Gomorrah als weibliche Schopfungsgeschichte, Derdunkle Schatten, Locker, Vienna, 82; co-transl (with Friedrich Achberger), Morgner, White Easter, The Duel Shoes & The Rope, Wolter, I have married again, In: German Feminism, State Univ NY Press, 84; Understanding Ingeborg Bachmann. Understanding Modern European and Latin American Literature, James Hardin, ed, Columbia: U South Carolina Press, 95; Boesartig liebevoll' den Menschen zugetan, Humor in Ingeborg Bachmanns Todesarten-Projekt, Essays zu Ingeborg Bachmanns Todesarten-Projekt, Monika Albrecht and Dirk Gottsche, eds, Munster: Konigshausen & Neumann, 98. **CONTACT ADDRESS** 1520 St Olaf Ave, Northfield, MN 55057-1099. **EMAIL** krach@stolaf.edu

ACHINSTEIN, SHARON
PERSONAL Born 06/15/1963, Baltimore, MD, m **DISCIPLINE** ENGLISH **EDUCATION** Harvard Univ, BA, 85; Princeton Univ, PhD, 90. **CAREER** Asst Prof to Assoc Prof, NW Univ, 89-98; Assoc Prof, Univ Md, 99-. **HONORS AND AWARDS** Hanfield Awd; Milton Soc of Am, 94. **RESEARCH** 17th Century literature. **CONTACT ADDRESS** Dept Eng, Univ of Maryland, Col Park, 3101 Susquehanna Hall, College Park, MD 20742-8800.

ACKER, PAUL
DISCIPLINE OLD AND MIDDLE ENGLISH LITERATURE **EDUCATION** Brown Univ, PhD. **CAREER** Assoc prof, St Louis Univ, **SELECTED PUBLICATIONS** Transl, The Saga of the People of Floi and Valla-Ljot's Saga in The Complete Sagas of Icelanders, Leifur Eriksson, 97; auth, Revising Oral Theory: Formulaic Composition in Old English and Old Icelandic Verse, Garland, 98; auth, "An Unedited Middle English Religious Lyrics (IMEVS 250.3) in Plimpton MS Ass.2" Notes and Queries, 99. **CONTACT ADDRESS** Dept of English, Saint Louis Univ, 221 N Grand Blvd, Saint Louis, MO 63103. **EMAIL** ackerpl@slu.edu

ADAMS, BARBARA
PERSONAL Born 03/23/1932, New York, NY, w, 1952, 4 children **DISCIPLINE** ENGLISH **EDUCATION** SUNY, BS, 62; MA, 70; NYork Univ, PhD, 81. **CAREER** Prof, Pace Univ, 84-. **HONORS AND AWARDS** First Prize, Fiction Contest, 99. **MEMBERSHIPS** PEN; Poets and Writers; Poetry Soc of Am. **RESEARCH** Modern American Poetry and Fiction; Memoir. **SELECTED PUBLICATIONS** Auth, The Enemy Self: Poetry and Criticism of Laura Riding, UMI Res Press, 90; auth, Hapax Legomena, Edwin Mellen Press, 90. **CONTACT ADDRESS** Dept Eng, Pace Univ, New York, 1 Pace Plaza, New York, NY 10038-1502. **EMAIL** bbadams@fsinter.net

ADAMS, BARRY BANFIELD
PERSONAL Born 08/31/1935, Boston, MA, m, 1962, 2 children **DISCIPLINE** ENGLISH **EDUCATION** Boston Col, BA, 57; Univ NC, MA, 59, PhD(English), 63. **CAREER** From instr to assoc prof, 63-75, chmn dept, 70-76, Prof English, Cornell Univ, 75- **MEMBERSHIPS** MLA; Renaissance Soc Am. **RESEARCH** Middle and Renaissance English literature. **SELECTED PUBLICATIONS** Ed, John Bale's King Johan, Huntington Libr, 68; auth, The prudence of Prince Escalus, ELH, 3/68; The audiences of The Spanish Tragedy, J English & Ger Philol, 69; Orsino and the Spirit of Love (in Shakespeare's Twelfth Night), Shakespeare Quart, 78. **CONTACT ADDRESS** Dept of English, Cornell Univ, 252 Goldwin Smith Hall, Ithaca, NY 14853-0001. **EMAIL** bba1@cornell.edu

ADAMS, CHARLES H.
PERSONAL Born 11/01/1954, New York, NY, m, 2 children **DISCIPLINE** AMERICAN LITERATURE **EDUCATION** Univ Va, PhD. **CAREER** English and Lit, Univ Ark, Assoc dean for Instructional Programs and International Programs. **HONORS AND AWARDS** Chair dept. **SELECTED PUBLICATIONS** Auth, 'By Sartain Laws': Cooper's Sea Fiction and The Red Rover, Studies Am Fiction, 88; Versions of Revision: Conflict and Community in the American Canon, Kenyon Rev, 91; History and the Literary Imagination in Hawthorne's 'Chiefly About War-Matters', English Studies, 93; Reading Ecologically: Language and Play in Bartram's Travels", Southern Quart, 94; The Guardian of the Law: Authority and Identity in James Fenimore Cooper, Penn State, 91. **CONTACT ADDRESS** Col of Arts & Sciences, Univ of Arkansas, Fayetteville, Fayetteville, AR 72701. **EMAIL** cadams@uark.edu

ADAMS, DALE TALMADGE
PERSONAL Born 10/30/1937, Freeport, TX, m, 1960, 3 children **DISCIPLINE** ENGLISH **EDUCATION** N Tex State Univ, BS, 60; BA, 64; MA, 65; Univ Tex, PhD, 76. **CAREER** Prof, Lee Col, 65-. **MEMBERSHIPS** MLA, NCTE, CCCC, TYCA, TYCA-SW. **RESEARCH** Film. **CONTACT ADDRESS** Dept English, Lee Col, Texas, PO Box 818, Baytown, TX 77522-0818. **EMAIL** dadams@lee.edu

ADAMS, ELSIE B.
PERSONAL Born 08/11/1932, Atoka, OK, m, 1980, 2 children **DISCIPLINE** ENGLISH **EDUCATION** Univ Okla, BS, 53, MA, 59, PhD(English), 66. **CAREER** Instr English, Northeastern Okla A&M Jr Col, 53-54; teacher, high sch, Okla, 55-56; from asst prof to assoc prof English, Wis State Univ, Whitewater, 66-71; from asst prof to assoc prof, 71-77, Prof English, San Diego State Univ, 77-94; Assoc Dean, Col Arts & Letts, 75-78; Prof Emeritus 94-. **HONORS AND AWARDS** Phi Beta Kappa **RESEARCH** Bernard Shaw; female studies; Victorian literature. **SELECTED PUBLICATIONS** Auth, Bernard Shaws pre-Raphaelite drama, PMLA, 66; No exit: An explication of Kiplings A Wayside Comedy, English Lit Transition, 68; Gissings allegorical House of Cobwebs, Studies Short Fiction, spring 70; co-ed, Up Against the Wall, Mother .. On Womens Liberation, Glencoe, 71; auth, Israel Zangwill, Twayne, 71; Bernard Shaw and the Aesthetes, Ohio State Univ, 71; Feminism and Female Stereotypes in Shaw, Shaw Rev, 74; Shaw's Ladies, Shaw Rev, 80; auth, G.B. Shaw: An Annotated Bibliography of Writings About Him, Northern Illinois Univ Pr, 87; auth, Critical Essays on George Bernard Shaw, G.K. Hall, 91. **CONTACT ADDRESS** Dept of English & Comp Lit, San Diego State Univ, San Diego, CA 92102. **EMAIL** ebadams@mail.sdsu.edu

ADAMS, GEORGE ROY
PERSONAL Born 11/23/1928, Lime Springs, IA, m, 1959, 3 children **DISCIPLINE** ENGLISH, LINGUISTICS **EDUCATION** Univ Okla, BA, 52, PhD, 61. **CAREER** Instr English, Boston Univ, 61-63; asst prof, Harpur Col, State Univ NY Binghamton, 63-66; assoc prof, 66-76, prof English, Univ Wis, Whitewater, 76-. **MEMBERSHIPS** MLA; Mediaeval Acad Am. **RESEARCH** Medieval literary esthetic; medieval drama; history of the English language. **SELECTED PUBLICATIONS** Auth, Paul Goodman, Twayne; Chaucer's Shipman's Tale, Explicator, 66; coauth, Good and Bad Fridays and May 3 in Chaucer, English Lang Notes, 66; Chauntecleer's Paradise Lost and Regained, Mediaeval Studies, 67. **CONTACT ADDRESS** Dept of English, Univ of Wisconsin, Whitewater, 800 W Main, Whitewater, WI 53190-1790.

ADAMS, KATHERINE L.
DISCIPLINE INTERPERSONAL COMMUNICATION **EDUCATION** Univ UT, PhD. **CAREER** Instr, Grad coordr, Calif State Univ; assoc ed, Western J of Commun; assoc ed, Women's Stud in Commun. **SELECTED PUBLICATIONS** Auth, Aubrey Fisher's Interpersonal Communication: A Pragmatic Approach Textbook, 2nd ed; authored several instructor's manuals in interpersonal and small group communication. **CONTACT ADDRESS** California State Univ, Fresno, Fresno, CA 93740.

ADAMS, KIMBERLY V.
DISCIPLINE 19TH-CENTURY BRITISH LITERATURE, BRITISH AND AMERICAN NOVEL, WOMEN'S STUDIES **EDUCATION** Harvard Univ, PhD. **CAREER** Instr, Rutgers, State Univ NJ, Camden Col of Arts and Sci. **HONORS AND AWARDS** Provost's Tchg Excellence Awd, 93. **RESEARCH** Feminist symbol. **SELECTED PUBLICATIONS** Auth, Feminine Godhead, Feminist Symbol: The Madonna in the Work of Ludwig Feuerbach, Anna Jameson, Margaret Fuller, and George Eliot, J of Feminist Stud in Relig; The Madonna and Margaret Fuller, Women's Stud. **CONTACT ADDRESS** Rutgers, The State Univ of New Jersey, New Brunswick, Camden Col of Arts and Sci, New Brunswick, NJ 08903-2101.

ADAMS, LESLIE KENNEDY
DISCIPLINE ENGLISH, PROFESSIONAL WRITING **EDUCATION** Houston Baptist Univ, BA, 86, MA, 87; Tx A & M Univ, Col Station, PhD, 95. **CAREER** Grad teaching asst, 87-90, Tx A & M Univ; instr to asst prof, 90-, Houston Baptist Univ. **MEMBERSHIPS** Col English Assoc; Houston World Aff Coun; Nat Coun Teachers of English; Popular Culture Assoc. **RESEARCH** Vietnam War lit & film; war lit. **SELECTED PUBLICATIONS** Auth, Father She Never Knew Still Influences Her Work, Houston Chronicle, 95. **CONTACT ADDRESS** Dept of Lang, Houston Baptist Univ, 7502 Fondren Rd, Houston, TX 77074. **EMAIL** ladams@hbu.edu

ADAMS, LYNN
PERSONAL Born 11/12/1957, Coral Gables, FL, s **DISCIPLINE** COMMUNICATION **EDUCATION** Fla State Univ, BS, 79; MS, 80; Univ Tenn, PhD, 93. **CAREER** Asst Prof, SW Mo State Univ, 92-96; Asst Prof, Radford Univ, 96-. **MEMBERSHIPS** ASHA, SHAV. **RESEARCH** Autism. **CONTACT ADDRESS** Dept Comm Disorders, Radford Univ, PO Box 6961, Radford, VA 24142-6961.

ADAMS, MICHAEL F.
PERSONAL Born 03/25/1948, Montgomery, AL, m, 1969, 2 children **DISCIPLINE** COMMUNICATION **EDUCATION** Lipscomb Col, BA, 70; Ohio St Univ, MA, 71; PhD, 73. **CAREER** Pres & prof Polit Comm, Univ Ga, 97-; pres & prof Government, Centre Col, 89-97; vice-pres Univ Affairs & prof Polit Comm, Pepperdine Univ, 82-89; Staff, Gov Lamar Alexander, 80-82; Chief of Senator Staff, Howard H Baker Jr, 75-79; asst prof Comm, Ohio St Univ, 73-75. **HONORS AND AWARDS** CASE Circle of Excellence Awd, 96, 97; Knight Found Awd for Nat Pres Leadership, 96; Grand Gold Awd from CASE, 87; CASE Nat Alumni Prog Top Speaker; IABC Bronze Quill Awd; NSPRA Awd of Excellence; CASE Nat Assembly Chair, 88; Ohio St Univ Fel, Highest Academic Honor; Grand Gold Public Relations for Persian Gulf Educ Day. **MEMBERSHIPS** Nat Assoc Independent Col & Univ Chmn, 95-96; Chair, on Am Coun Educ, 98-00; Assoc of Presidents of Independent Col & Univ Bd of Dir, 92-95; Nat Collegiate Athletic Assoc Vice Chair, 95-96; S Assoc Col & Schs Exec Coun, 94-99; S Assoc Col & Schs Chair, 97-; Rhodes Scholar Selection Comt Ga St Chair, 97-. **RESEARCH** Southern Politics; mens media and politics. **SELECTED PUBLICATIONS** Inspiration by Instruction, Atlanta Constitution, 98; The Inaugural Address of the 21st President, Univ Ga, 98; "The State of the University Address, Univ Ga, 98; The Advancement President in the Liberal Arts College, The Advancement President And the Academy: Profiles in Institutional Leadership, ACE, 97. **CONTACT ADDRESS** Dept of political Communications, Univ of Georgia, 570 Prince Ave, Athens, GA 30601. **EMAIL** presuga@arches.uga.edu

ADAMS, PERCY GUY
PERSONAL Born 12/16/1914, Beeville, TX **DISCIPLINE** ENGLISH **EDUCATION** Tex Col Arts & Indust, AB, 33; Univ Tex, AM, 37, PhD, 46. **CAREER** Tutor English, Univ Tex, 41-43; instr, Ohio State Univ, 46-48; from asst prof to prof, Univ Tenn, 48-66; prof, La State Univ, Baton Rouge, 66-70; Prof English, Univ Tenn, Knoxville, 70-, Fulbright lectr, Univs Aix-Marseille & Grenoble, France, 58-59; gen ed, Great travel books, Dover Publ, Inc, 65-; Nat Endowment Humanities sr fel, 76-77. **HONORS AND AWARDS** Chancelor's Scholar of the Year, Univ Tenn, Knoxville, 77. **MEMBERSHIPS** Comp Lit Asn; Soc Hist Discoveries; Soc Southern Lit; MLA; NCTE. **RESEARCH** Eighteenth century and comparative literature. **SELECTED PUBLICATIONS** Auth, Travelers and Travel Liars: 1660-1800, Univ Calif, 62; Historical importance of assonance to poets, PMLA, 73; Epic tradition and the novel, Southern Rev, 73; Faulkner and French literature, Proc Comp Lit Symp, 73; European Renaissance literature and the discovery of America, Comp Lit Studies, 76; Graces of Harmony: Alliteration, Assocance, and Consonance in Eighteenth-Century Poetry, Univ Ga, 77; Seventeenth- and Eighteenth- century travel literature: A survey of recent approaches, Tex Studies Lang & Lit, 78; The achievement of James Cook and his associates in perspective, In: Exploration in Alaska: Captain Cook Commemorative Lectures (1978), 80. **CONTACT ADDRESS** Dept of English, Univ of Tennessee, Knoxville, Knoxville, TN 37916.

ADAMS, RACHEL
DISCIPLINE 19TH- AND 20TH-CENTURY AMERICAN LITERATURE **EDUCATION** Univ Calif-Berkeley, BA, 90; Univ Mich, MA, 92; Univ Calif, Santa Barbara, PhD, 97. **CAREER** Prof. **HONORS AND AWARDS** Mng ed, Camera Obscura: Feminism, Culture, and Media Studies. **SELECTED PUBLICATIONS** Pub(s), Freakery: Cultural Spectacles of the Extraordinary Body; The Black Female Body; Mich Quart. **CONTACT ADDRESS** Dept of Eng, Columbia Col, New York, 2960 Broadway, New York, NY 10027-6902.

ADAMS, STEPHEN J.
PERSONAL Born 07/20/1948, Madison, WI, m, 1974 **DISCIPLINE** ENGLISH **EDUCATION** Univ Minn, BA, 70, MA, 74, PhD, 79. **CAREER** Asst prof, Vir Polytech Inst, 79-86; asst prof, assoc prof, prof, Univ Minn, 86-. **HONORS AND AWARDS** Vir Hist Soc Mellon Res Fel, 98; Vir Cen for Human Res Fel, 89; NEH Col Teach Fel, 83-84; Horace T. Morse-Univ Minn Alum Asn Awd for Outst Contrib to Undergrad Edu, 00; UMD Stud Asn Outst Fac Awd, 96-97; UMD CLA Teach Awd, 95; UMD Access Cen Outst Fac Awd, 94; VPI and SU Alum Awd for Teach Excel, 86. **MEMBERSHIPS** MLA, ALSMLA, MMLA, Thoreau Soc, Asn for Stud Lit and Environ, ASA, MAASA, NCTE, Art Cult Nature. **RESEARCH** 19th-century American literature; depictions of American landscape; gothic literature. **SELECTED PUBLICATIONS** Auth, "The Heroic and Mock Heroic in Harlan Ellison's 'Harlequin,'" Extrapolation (85); auth, "Returning to the Land," Human Edu (89); auth, "Fish in Water, Weightlifters in Pink Rooms: Landscapes, Environments, and Learning in the Humanities," Human Edu (90); auth, "Quick Before It Dries: Setting the Pattern for Active Participation from Day One," Inst Dev (91); auth, "The Luminist Walt Whitman," Am Poetry (85); auth, "'That Tidiness We Always Look for in Woman': Margaret Fuller's Summer on the Lakes and Romantic Aesthetics" (Vir Univ Press, 87); co-auth, "Thoreau's Diet at Walden," in Studies in the American Renaissance (Vir Univ Press, 90); auth, "The Genres of a Week on the Concord and Merrimack Rivers" in Approaches to Teaching Thoreau, ed. Richard J. Schneider (MLA, 96); co-auth, Revising Mythologies: the Composition of Thoreau's Major Works (Vir Univ Press, 88); auth, "The Best and Worst Country in the World" in Perspectives on the Early Virginia Landscape (Vir UP, 00). **CONTACT ADDRESS** Eng Dept, Univ of Minnesota, Duluth, 10 University Dr, Duluth, MN 55812. **EMAIL** sadams@umn.edu

ADAMS, SUSAN S.
PERSONAL Born 04/17/1943, Chicago, IL, m, 1985, 2 children **DISCIPLINE** LITERATURE **EDUCATION** Univ Cincinnati, BA, 64; BS, 65; MA, 67; PhD, 75. **CAREER** Grad Teaching Asst to lecturer, Univ Cincinnati, 65-77; asst prof to prof, N Ky Univ, 83-. **HONORS AND AWARDS** Fac Awd, N Ky Univ Alumni Asn, 98; Ky Humaties Scholar, 00; Who's Who Among America's Teachers; Phi Beta Kappa; Sigma Tau Delta; alpha Lamba Delta. **MEMBERSHIPS** Ky Philol Asn, S Atl Mod Lang Asn, Popular Culture & Am Culture Asn of the South, Nat Women's Studies Asn. **RESEARCH** Contemporary Women Writers, especially American women writers of the South **SELECTED PUBLICATIONS** Auth, Moving On: The Heroines of Shirley Ann Grau, Anne Tyler, & Gail Godwin, Bowling Green, OH: Popular Press, 96; auth, In Common Cause: The 'Conservative' Frances Trollope & The 'Radical' Frances Wright, Bowling Green, OH: Popular Press, 93; co-ed, The Story of the Pewter Basin & Other Occasional Writings, TIS Pub: bloomington, 81. **CONTACT ADDRESS** Dept Lang & Lit, No Kentucky Univ, 1 N Ky Univ, Newport, KY 41099-0001. **EMAIL** adamsss@nku.edu

ADAMS, TIMOTHY D.
PERSONAL Born 12/11/1943, Monterey, CA, m, 1966, 1 child **DISCIPLINE** ENGLISH; AMERICAN LITERATURE **EDUCATION** Columbia, BS, 68; Texas, MA, 70; Emory Univ, PhD, 78. **CAREER** Instr, 72-75, Old Dominion Univ; asst prof, 79-81, Univ Ark; asst prof, 81-82, McMurry Col; asst prof, 82-84, assoc prof, 86-91; prof, 91- , W VA Univ. **MEMBERSHIPS** Mod Lang Asn. **SELECTED PUBLICATIONS** Ed, Autobiography, Photography, and Narrative, Mod Fiction Stud, 94; auth, Life Writing and Light Writing: Photography in Autobiography, Mod Fiction Studies, 94; coed, Terms of Identity: Essays on the Theoretical Terminology of Lifewriting, a/b: Auto/Biography Stud, 95; Deafness and Deftness in CODA Autobiography: Ruth Sidransky's In Silence and Lou Ann Walkers A Loss for Words, Biog, 97; Running in the Family: Photography and Autobiography in the Memoirs of Michael and Christopher Ondaatje, Biog Creation, Presses Univ de Rennes, 97; Photography and Ventriloquy in Paul Auster's The Invention of Solitude, True Relations: Essays on Autobiography and the Postmodern, Greenwood Press, 98; auth, Light Writing and Life Writing: Photography in Autobiography, Univ NC Press, 99. **CONTACT ADDRESS** English Dept, West Virginia Univ, Morgantown, PO Box 6296, Morgantown, WV 26506-6296. **EMAIL** tadams@wvu.edu

ADAMS, TYRONE L.
DISCIPLINE COMMUNICATIONS **EDUCATION** St Petersburg Jr Col, Assoc, 88; Univ Fla, BA, 90; Fla State Univ, MA, 92, PhD, 95. **CAREER** Asst Dir, Forensics, Fla State Univ, 90-93; Tchg Asssoc, Fla State Univ, 90-93; Fel, Fla State Univ, 93-95; Asst Prof, Univ Ark, 92-. **HONORS AND AWARDS** Chair, Speech Comm Major Assessment Comt; Ed, Am Comm Jour, 96-. **SELECTED PUBLICATIONS** Coauth, Empowerment as Semantic Strategy in the 1992 Presidential Elections: The Bush Campaign Targets Minority Constituencies, Spectrum, 92; The Terror-rhetoric Genre: Exploring Aristotelian Foundations for Violence as Persuasive Text, Jour Comm studies, 94; The Emerging Role of the World-Wide-Web in Forensics: On Computer-mediated Research and Community Development, Forensic, 96; 'Follow the Yellow Brick Road:' Using Diffusion of Innovations Theory to Enrich Virtual Organizations in Cyberspace, S Comm Journal, 97; Making Sense of the 1994 Right-wing Revolution in the United States, Speaker & Gavel, 97. **CONTACT ADDRESS** Univ of Arkansas, Monticello, BOX 3458, Monticello, AR 71656. **EMAIL** ADAMS@UAMONT.EDU

ADAMSON, JOSEPH
DISCIPLINE ENGLISH LITERATURE **EDUCATION** Trent Univ, BA; Univ Toronto, MA, PhD. **RESEARCH** Literary theory; Northrop Frye; comparative lit; American lit; mod lyric poetry. **SELECTED PUBLICATIONS** Auth, Melville, Shame, and the Evil Eye: A Psychoanalytic Reading, 97; auth, Northrop Frye: A Visionary Life, 93; auth, Wounded Fiction: Modern Poetry and Deconstruction, 88. **CONTACT ADDRESS** English Dept, McMaster Univ, 1280 Main St W, Hamilton, ON, Canada L8S 4L9. **EMAIL** adamsonj@mcmaster.ca

ADAMSON, LYNDA G.
PERSONAL Born 08/22/1945, NC, m, 1971, 2 children **DISCIPLINE** ENGLISH **EDUCATION** Univ NC, Chapel Hill, BA, 67, MAT, 68; Univ Md, PhD, 81. **CAREER** Prof, Prince Georges Community Col, 69-, chair, English Dept, coordr, Travel Study Prog, 85-93. **HONORS AND AWARDS** Nat Endowment for the Humanities grant, 89; Fac Excellence Awd for Teaching, 95; Md Public Schs grant, 96-97; grant, Am Library Asn and Md Humanities Coun, 99. **MEMBERSHIPS** Int Res in Children's Lit Asn, Int Bd on Books. **RESEARCH** Historical fiction. **SELECTED PUBLICATIONS** Auth, A Reference Guide to Historical Fiction for Children and Young Adults, Westport, CT: Greenwood Press (87); auth, Recreating the Past: A Guide to American and World Historical Fiction for Children and Young Adults, Westport, CT: Greenwood Press (94); auth, Literature Connections to World History, 7-12, Englewood, CO: Libraries Unlimited (98); auth, Literature Connections to World History, K-6, Englewood, CO: Libraries Unlimited (98); auth, Literature Connections to American History, 7-12, Englewood, CO: Libraries Unlimited (98); auth, Literature Connections to American History, 7-12, Englewood, CO: Libraries Unlimited (98); auth, Notable Women in World History: A Guide to Biographies and Autobiographies, Westport, CT: Greenwood Press (98); auth, World Historical Fiction for Adults and Young Adults, Phoenix, AZ: Oryx Press (99); auth, American Historical Fiction Novels for Adults and Young Adults, Phoenix, AZ: Oryx Press (99); auth, Notable Women in World History: A Guide to Biographies and Autobiographies, Westport, CT: Greenwood Press (99). **CONTACT ADDRESS** Dept English, Prince George's Comm Col, 301 Largo Rd, Upper Marlboro, MD 20774-2109. **EMAIL** lgadamson@cs.com

ADELMAN, GARY S.
PERSONAL Born 07/01/1935, Brooklyn, NY, m **DISCIPLINE** ENGLISH **EDUCATION** Univ Mich, BA, 57; Columbia Univ, MA, 58; PhD, 63. **CAREER** Prof, 93-, Univ Ill Urbana. **SELECTED PUBLICATIONS** Auth, Political Poems, The Depot Press (Urbana, IL), 68; auth, Honey Out of Stone., Doubleday (Garden City, NY), 70; auth, Heart of Darkness: Search for the Unconscious, Twayne Books (Boston: G. K. Hall), 87: auth, Anna Karenina: The Bitterness of Ecstasy, (Twayne Books Boston: G. K. Hall), 90; auth, Snow of–Fire: Symbolic Meaning in 'The Rainbow' and 'Women in Love', Garland Publishing, Inc (NY), 91; auth, Jude the Obscure: A Paradise of Despair, Twayne Books (NY, Macmillan), 92; auth, "Retelling Dostoyevsky: Literary Responses and Other Observations." Bucknell University Press, forthcoming; auth, "Reading Dostoyevsky Post-Holocaust." Shofar 14 (96): 85-115; auth, "Disrobing Dostoyevsky's Grand Inquisitor: The Hidden Legacy of Christian Anti-Semitism in The Brothers Karamazov," The Comparatist (00); auth, "Stalking Stavrogin: J. M. Coetzee's The Master of Petersburg and the writing of The Possessed," J Modern Lit (00); auth, "The Man Who Rode Away: What Lawrence Means to Today's Readers," Tri-quarterly (forthcoming); auth, "Naming the Unnamable in Beckett's Trilogy," Tri-quarterly (forthcoming); auth, "Doubles on the Rocks: Kazuo Ishiguru's The Unconsoled," Critique (forthcoming). **CONTACT ADDRESS** Dept English, Univ of Illinois, Urbana-Champaign, 608 South Wright St, Urbana, IL 61801-3613. **EMAIL** gadelman@uiuc.edu

ADELMAN, JANET ANN
PERSONAL Born 01/28/1941, Mt. Kisco, NY, m, 1976, 2 children **DISCIPLINE** ENGLISH LITERATURE **EDUCATION** Smith Col, BA, 62; Yale Univ, MA, 66, MPhil, 67, PhD(English), 69. **CAREER** Acting asst prof English, 68-70, asst prof, 70-72, assoc prof, 72-81, Prof English, Univ Calif, Berkeley, 81-, Chair, 99. **HONORS AND AWARDS** Am Coun

Learned Socs study fel, 76-77; Guggenheim Fel, 80-81. **MEMBERSHIPS** MLA; Shakespeare Asn Am; Interdisciplinary Member, San Francisco Psychoanalytic Inst; Renaissance Society of America. **RESEARCH** Shakespeare; English Renaissance narrative poetry; psychoanalytic criticism. **SELECTED PUBLICATIONS** Auth, Anger's my meat: Feeding, dependency, and aggression in Coriolanus, In: Shakespeare's Pattern of Excelling Nature, Univ Del, 78; Male Bonding in Shakespeare's Comedies, In: Shakespeare's Rough Magic: Renaissance Essays in Honor of C.L. Barber, Univ Del Press, 85; This Is and Is Not Cressid: The Characterization of Cressida, In: The (M)other Tongue: Essays in Feminist Psychoanalytic Interpretation, Cornell Univ Press, 85; Born of a Woman: Fantasies of Maternal Power in Macbeth, In: Cannibals, Witches, and Divorce: Estranging the Renaissance, Selected Papers from the English Inst, 85, 11th ed, The Johns Hopkins Univ Press, 87; Bed Tricks: On Marriage as the End of Comedy in All's Well That Ends Well and Measure for Measure, In: Shakespeare's Personality, Univ Calif Press, 89; She, Dying, Gave It Me: Dead Mothers and Dying Wives in Othello, In: Hebrew University Studies in Literature and the Arts: Essays in Honour of Ruth Nevo, 91; Suffocating Mothers: Fantasies of Maternal Origin in Shakespeare, Hamlet to the Tempest, Routledge, 92; Iago's Alter Ego: Race as Projection in Othello, Shakespeare Quart, 97; Making Defect Perfection: Shakespeare and the One-Sex Model, In: Enacting Gender on the English Renaissance Stage, Univ Ill Press, 98. **CONTACT ADDRESS** Dept of English, Univ of California, Berkeley, 322 Wheeler Hall, Berkeley, CA 94720-1030. **EMAIL** adelman@uclink4.berkeley.edu

ADELMAN, MARA

DISCIPLINE COMMUNICATIONS **EDUCATION** UCLA, BA, 72; CA State Univ, San Diego, MA, 80; Univ WA, PhD, 86. **CAREER** Comm, Seattle Univ. **HONORS AND AWARDS** Nat Jesuit Book Award, 99; NCA Applied Communication Book Award, 99. **MEMBERSHIPS** Speech Commun Asn; Int Commun Asn; Int Network of Personal Relationship. **RESEARCH** Commun and Comt; Retail and Service Interactions; Social Support Systems; Cross-cultural Commun; Expatriation; Dating Services; Sexual Commun. **SELECTED PUBLICATIONS** Auth, Social support and AIDS, J for AIDS and Publ Policy, 4, 90; Cross-cultural adjustment: A theoretical perspective and social support, Int J of Intercultural Relations, 12, 88; Healthy passions: Safe sex and play, AIDS: A communication perspective, Hillsdale, NJ: Lawrence Erlbaum Assoc(s), 92; Rituals of adversity and remembering: The role of possessions for persons and community living with AIDS, Advances in consumer research Vol 19, Provo, UT: Asn for Consumer Res, 91; coauth, The Fragile Community: Living Together with AIDS, Laawrence Erlbaum Assoc(s), Publishers; 97; Beyond language: Cross-cultural communication for English as a second language 2nd ed, Englewood Cliffs, NJ: Prentice-Hall, 93; Communicating social support, Newbury Park, CA: Sage, 87; Communication Practices in the Social Construction of Health in an AIDS Residence, J Hea Psychol, Vol 1, 3, 96; Formal intermediaries in the marriage market: A typology and review, J of Marriage and the Family, 54, 92; Mediated channels for mate seeking: A solution to involuntary singlehood, Critical Studies in Mass Communication, 8, 91; The pilgrim must embark: Creating and sustaining community in a residential facility for persons living with AIDS, Gp communication in context: Studies of natural gps, Hillsdale, NJ: Lawrence Erlbaum Assoc(s), 94; Market metaphors for meeting mates, Research in Consumer Behavior, Vol 6, London, England: JAI Press, 93; Building community life: Understanding individual, gp, and organizational processes, Handbook for assisted living, Chicago: Bonaventure House, 93; Beyond smiling: Social support and the service provider, Frontiers in service quality, Newbury Park, CA: Sage, 93; Two views on the consumption of mating and dating, Advances in consumer res, Vol 18, Provo, UT: Asn for Consumer Res, 91; video producer, Safe-sex talk, 88; video coproducer, The pilgrim must embark: Living in community, Annandale, VA: Speech Communication Association's Applied Communication Series, 91; rev(s), AIDS and the hospice community, Contemp Psychol, 38, 93; Life, liberty and the pursuit of health care: Multi- disciplinary perspectives on sustaining health in later life, Contemp Psychol, 37, 92; Beyond Consumption: Retail at the Edge, video and study guide, 00; Untold Tales From the Field: Living the Autoethnographic Life in an AIDS Residence, in Qualitative Research: Applications in Organizational Life, 01. **CONTACT ADDRESS** Dept of Commun, Seattle Univ, 900 Broadway, Seattle, WA 98122-4460. **EMAIL** mara@seattleu.edu

ADICKES, SANDRA ELAINE

PERSONAL Born 07/14/1933, New York, NY, s, 3 children **DISCIPLINE** ENGLISH; AMERICAN LITERATURE **EDUCATION** Douglas Col, BA, 54; Hunter Col, MA, 64; NYork Univ, PhD, 77 **CAREER** Secy and TV Prod Asst, 54-60; teacher, NYork Pubic High Schools, 60-72; asst prof, City Univ NYork, 72-88; prof, Winona State Univ, 88-98. **MEMBERSHIPS** Mod Lang Asn; Popular Cult Asn. **RESEARCH** American Women Political Writers and Activist **SELECTED PUBLICATIONS** Auth, The Social Quest, 91; auth, Legends of Good Women (novel), 92; auth, To Be Young Was Very Heaven: Women in New York Before the First World War, 97. **CONTACT ADDRESS** 19 Davids Ct., Dayton, NJ 08810-1302. **EMAIL** sadickes@eudoramail.com

ADICKS, RICHARD R.

PERSONAL Born 08/19/1932, Lake City, FL, m, 1959, 1 child **DISCIPLINE** ENGLISH **EDUCATION** Univ Fla, BAE, 54, MA, 59; Tulane Univ, PhD(English), 65. **CAREER** Teacher high schs, Fla, 56-58 & 59-61; instr English, Rollins Col, 61-63; asst prof, Ga Inst Technol, 65-68; from asst prof to assoc prof, 68-74, prof English, Univ Cent Fla, 74-99; Fulbright lectr, Africa University, 97-98; prof emer, 99-. **MEMBERSHIPS** Col English Asn; ALSC. **RESEARCH** Victorian literature; comparative literature. **SELECTED PUBLICATIONS** Auth, The sea-fight episode in Song of Myself, Walt Whitman Rev, 3/67; The Lily Maid and the Scarlet Sleeve, Univ Rev, 10/67; The unconsecrated Eucharist in Dubliners, Studies in Short Fiction, spring 68; Conrad and the politics of morality, Bull Asn Can Humanities, fall 72; coauth, Oviedo! Biography of a Town, private publ, 79 & 92; A Court for Owls, Pineapple Press, 89. **CONTACT ADDRESS** PO Box 620367, Oviedo, FL 32762. **EMAIL** adicks@pegasus.cc.ucf.edu

ADISA, OPAL P.

PERSONAL Born 11/06/1954, Kingston, Jamaica, s, 3 children **DISCIPLINE** ETHNIC LITERATURE STUDIES **EDUCATION** CUNY, Hunter Col, BA, 75; San Francisco State Univ, MA, 81; MA, 86; Univ Calif Berkeley, PhD, 92. **CAREER** Vis prof, Univ Calif Berkeley, 94-96; assoc prof to prof, Calif Col of Arts and Crafts, 93-. **HONORS AND AWARDS** Pushcart Prize, 87; Phi Beta Kappa; PEN Oakland/Josephine Miles Literary Awd, 92; Honoree of Literary Women, 94; Caribbean Writer Summer Inst Recipient, Univ of Miami, 95; Canute A Broadhurst Prize, 96; Distinguished Writer, Middle Atlantic Writers Assoc, 98. **MEMBERSHIPS** ACWWS; CPITS; CAFRA; NAES; NWU; MELUS; WILPF. **SELECTED PUBLICATIONS** Auth, Bake-Face and Other Guava Stories, Kelsey St Pr, (Berkeley), 86; coauth, Traveling Women, Jukebox Pr, (Oakland, CA), 89; auth, Tamarind and Mango Women, Sister Vision Pr, (Toronto), 92; auth, It Begins With Tears", Heinemann, (England), 97; auth, "I Must Write What I Know So I'll Know I've Known It All Along", The Woman, The Writer and Caribbean Society, ed Helen Pyne-Timothy, Center for Afro-Am Studies Pub, (98): 102-117; auth, "My First Lesson in Sex", Postcolonialism and Autobiography, eds Alfred Hornung and Ernstpete Ruhe, Rodopi, (Amsterdam, 98): 192-195; auth, "Children Must Be Seen and Heard", Voice, Memory, Ashes, ed Jacob Ross and Joan Anim-Addo, Mango Pub, (99): 25-42; auth, Leaf-of-Life, Jukebox Pr, 99; auth, Until Judgement Comes, (forthcoming). **CONTACT ADDRESS** Dept Humanities and Sci, California Col of Arts and Crafts, Oakland, 5212 Broadway, Oakland, CA 94618-1426. **EMAIL** opalpro@aol.com

ADKIN, NEIL

PERSONAL Born 07/04/1954, Hull, England, s **DISCIPLINE** CLASSICS **EDUCATION** Univ Col Oxford, BA, 76 (1st class), MA, 80; Univ Glasgow, PhD, 82. **CAREER** Thesaurus Linguae Latinae fel, Bayerische Akademie der Wissenschaften, 76-79; temporary lect in Medieval Latin, Univ Liverpool, 81-82; Univ Res fel, Univ Liverpool, 83-86; asst through assoc prof of Classics, Univ NE-Lincoln, 86-. **HONORS AND AWARDS** Hertford, De Paravicini, Ireland and Craven Scholarships, 73; Col of Arts and Sciences Awd for Outstanding Teaching, 90. **MEMBERSHIPS** APA. **SELECTED PUBLICATIONS** Author of 142 articles on Patristic, Medieval, and Renaissance Latin, principally Jerome, Walter of Chatillon, and Erasmus. **CONTACT ADDRESS** Dept Classics, Univ of Nebraska, Lincoln, 237 Andrews Hall, PO Box 880337, Lincoln, NE 68588-0337. **EMAIL** nadkin1@unl.edu

ADKINS, ARTHUR WILLIAM HOPE

PERSONAL Born 10/17/1929, Leicester, England, m, 1961, 2 children **DISCIPLINE** CLASSICS; PHILOSOPHY **EDUCATION** Oxford Univ, BA, 52, MA, 55, DPhil, 57. **CAREER** Asst lectr Latin humanities, Univ Glasgow, 54-56; lectr Greek, Bedford Col, Univ London, 56-61; fel class lang & lit, Exeter Col, Oxford, 61-65; prof classics, Univ Reading, 66-74; chmn, Dept Classics, 75-80, prof Greek, philos & early Christian lit, Univ Chicago, 74- ; vis sr fel classics Soc Humanities, Cornell Univ, 69-70. **MEMBERSHIPS** Soc Promotion Hellenic Studies; Class Asn Gt Brit; Am Philol Asn; Am Philos Asn; Asn Ancient Historians. **RESEARCH** Greek philosophy; Greek thought and religion; Greek literature. **SELECTED PUBLICATIONS** Auth, Merit and Responsibility: A Study in Greek Values, Clarendon, Oxford, 60; contribr, Greek religion, In: Historia Religionum Handbook for the History of Religions, Leiden, Brill, 69; auth, From the Many to the One: A Study of Personality and Views of Human Nature in the Context of Ancient Greek Society, Values and Beliefs, Constable, London & Cornell Univ, 70; Moral Values and Political Behavior in Ancient Greece, Chatto & Windus, London & Clark Irwin, Toronto, 72; Paralysis and Akrasia in Eth Nic 1102b16 ff, Am J Philos, Vol 97, 62-64; Polupragmosune and minding one's own business: A study in Greek social and political values, CP, 76; Callinus 1 and Tyrtaeus 10 as poetry, HSCP, 77; Lucretius I, 137 ff and the problems of writing Versus Latini, Phoenix, 77; auth, Poetic Craft in the Early Greek Elegists, Univ Chicago, 85; Ethics with Aristotle, Classical Philol, Vol 0088, 93; rev, Hybris- A Study in the Values of Honor and Shame in Ancient Greece, Class Jour, Vol 0090, 95; rev, Aidos - The Psychology and Ethics of Honor and Shame in Ancient Greek Literature, Class Jour, Vol 0090, 95. **CONTACT ADDRESS** Dept of Classics, Univ of Chicago, 1050 E 59th St, Chicago, IL 60637. **EMAIL** eadkins@midway.chicago.edu

ADLER, BRIAN UNGAR

PERSONAL Born 05/28/1957, El Paso, TX, m, 1988, 2 children **DISCIPLINE** AMERICAN LITERATURE **EDUCATION** Univ SC, BA, 78; Univ Ga, MA, 84; Univ Tenn, PhD, 88. **CAREER** Asst prof to assoc prof and prog co-ord, Marian Col, 89-94; prof to prog dir, Valdosta Univ, 94-. **HONORS AND AWARDS** Chancellor's Award, 95; Prof of the Year Award, 92; Provost's Ed Fel, 88; Davis Ed Fel, 84. **MEMBERSHIPS** Asn of Am Col and Univ; Nat Acad Advising Asn; MLA: Asn for the Study of Lit and Environ; Nat Col Honors Coun; S Reg Honors Coun; Bernard Malamud Soc; C.G. Jung Soc. **RESEARCH** Literature of War; Jungian Criticism; Nature Writing. **SELECTED PUBLICATIONS** Auth, "Akedah and Community in the 'The Magic Barrel'," Studies in Am Jewish Lit, (91): 187-197; auth, "Weeping by the Waters of Babylon: The Dystopian Vision in Twentieth Century Literature and Art," Nat Honors Report, (95): 36-38; auth, "Electronic Enhancements to Learning, Or A Neo-Luddite Word of Caution?" Nat Honors Report, (97): 43-49; auth, "Engaging First-Year Honors Students by Using The New York Times," in Using National Newspapers in the College Classroom: Resources to Improve Teaching and Learning. The First-Year Experience and Students in Transition, (Univ SC, 99), 55-56; auth, "Etheridge Knight," in Encyclopedia of American Literature, (Continuum Press, 99), 632-633; auth, "Yusef Komunyakaa," in Encyclopedia of American Literature, (Continuum Press, 99), 635-636; auth, "Mordecai Noah," in Encyclopedia of American War Literature, Greenwood Press, 00. **CONTACT ADDRESS** Dept English, Valdosta State Univ, 1500 N Patterson St, Valdosta, GA 31698-0100. **EMAIL** badler@valdosta.edu

ADLER, THOMAS PETER

PERSONAL Born 01/03/1943, Cleveland, OH, m, 1968, 2 children **DISCIPLINE** ENGLISH & AMERICAN LITERATURE **EDUCATION** Boston Col, AB, 64, AM, 66; Univ Ill, Urbana, PhD(English), 70. **CAREER** Asst prof, 70-75, from assoc prof to prof English, Purdue Univ, West Lafayette, 75-83, asst head dept, 80-83; assoc dean grad school, 84-88; assoc dean Lib Arts, 88-95; interim dean Lib Arts, 95-97; head English, 97-. **HONORS AND AWARDS** Phi Beta Kappa . **MEMBERSHIPS** MLA; NCTE; Midwest MLA; O'Neill Soc; Pinter Soc. **RESEARCH** Modern British and Am drama. **SELECTED PUBLICATIONS** Auth, Robert Anderson, Twayne, 78; auth, Mirror on the Stage: The Pulitzer Plays as an Approach to American Drama, Purdue Press, 87; auth, A Streetcar Named Desire: The Moth and the Lantern, G.K. Hall, 90; auth, American Drama, 1940-1960: A Critical History, Twayne Macmillian, 94. **CONTACT ADDRESS** Dept of English, Purdue Univ, West Lafayette, West Lafayette, IN 47907-1356. **EMAIL** tadler@purdue.edu

ADOLPH, ROBERT

PERSONAL Born 02/15/1936, Cambridge, MA, m, 1958, 3 children **DISCIPLINE** ENGLISH **EDUCATION** Williams Col, BA, 57; Univ Mich, MA, 58; Harvard Univ, PhD(English), 64. **CAREER** From instr to asst prof English, Mass Inst Technol, 61-67; Assoc Prof Humanities & English, York Univ, 68-, Dir, Graduate Programme in Interdisciplinary Studies, 76-79, 82-83. **MEMBERSHIPS** MLA; Can Asn Univ Teachers; Can Asn Am Studies (treas, 71-73). **RESEARCH** Seventeenth century English literature; nineteenth and twentieth century prose fiction. **SELECTED PUBLICATIONS** Auth, The Rise of Modern Prose Style, Cambridge: MIT Press, 68; auth, "Does Style Mean Anything Anymore?" CEA Critic (76): 7-10; auth, "On the Possibility of a History or Prose Style," Style, (81): 435-50; auth, "Marginality and After' The Making of Modern American Fiction," Canadian Review of American Studies, (83): 481-87; auth, "Apocalypse Then and Now: History, Myth, and the American Imagination," Canadian Review of American Studies, (87): 279-86; auth, "The Skydome Effect," In Not a Sentimental Journey, Goderich Ontario: Gumbyfield Press, 90; auth, "Whitman, Tocqueville and the Language of Democracy," In the Delegated Intellect: Emersonian Essays in Literature Science and the Arts, Lang, (95): 65-88; auth, "La Riforma Della Prosa," In La Storia delta civil & letteraria inglese Turin, Italy: U.T.E.T., (95): 773-796; auth, "Francis Bacon E La Storia Dello Stile in Prosa," In La Storia delta civil & letteraria inglese Turin, Italy: U.T.E.T, (95): 753-771; ed, Canadian Review of American Studies, Vol 27, 3, 97. **CONTACT ADDRESS** Div of Humanities, York Univ, 232 Vanier, Toronto, ON, Canada M3J 1P3. **EMAIL** adolph@yorku.ca

ADRIAN, DARYL B.

PERSONAL Born 09/24/1933, Hutchinson, KS, m, 1953, 3 children **DISCIPLINE** ENGLISH, LITERATURE **EDUCATION** Tabor Col, AB, 55; KS State Tchrs Col, MA, 61; Univ MT, Columbia, PhD, 67. **CAREER** Educ therapist, Menninger Found, Topeka, KS, 57-63; lectr Eng, Washburn Univ, 62-63; instr, Univ MO, Columbia, 61-62 & 63-67; from asst prof to assoc prof Eng, 67-76, admin asst chmn dept, 69-76, Prof Eng, Ball State Univ, 76-, Chmn Dept, 76-85; Exec Dir, Nat Coun Relig & Pub Educ, 75-84. **HONORS AND AWARDS** 1988-97: Eleven Outstanding Fac Tchg Awds, Eng Dept, Honors Col,

Blue Key, Golden Key, Mortar Board; Outstanding Fac Adv Awds, Eng Dept. **MEMBERSHIPS** MLA; Conf Christianity & Lit; Midwest Mod Lang Asn; John Steinbeck Soc Am; Milton Soc Am. **RESEARCH** Seventeenth and eighteenth century Brit lit, espec Milton; relig and lit; John Steinbeck; Medieval drama; John Donne's Holy Sonnets; Eng internships. **SELECTED PUBLICATIONS** Ed, John Bunyan's Pilgrim's Progress, Airmont, 69; auth, Humanities and the arts: nonfiction before 1900, In: Encounter With Books: A Guide to Reading, Intervarsity, 70; Steinbecks new image of American and Americans, Steinbeck Quart, fall 70; A comparative school curriculum and the study of religion, Relig Educ, 7-8/72. **CONTACT ADDRESS** Dept of Eng, Ball State Univ, 2000 W University, Muncie, IN 47306-0002. **EMAIL** dadrian@gw.bsu.edu

AERS, DAVID
DISCIPLINE ENGLISH LITERATURE **EDUCATION** Univ York, PhD. **CAREER** Engl, Duke Univ. **RESEARCH** Late medieval and early mod lit, relig and cult in Engl. **SELECTED PUBLICATIONS** Auth, Piers Plowman and Christian Allegory, Arnold, 75; Chaucer, Langland and the Creative Imagination, Routledge, 80; Chaucer, Harvester, 83; , Community, Gender and Individual Identity, 1360-1430, Routledge, 88; ed, Medieval Literature: Criticism, Ideology, History, Harvester, 86; Culture and History, 1350-1600, Wayne State, 92; auth, Powers of the Holy, PA State UP, 96; auth, Faith, Ethics and the Church 1360-1409, Brener, 00; ed, Medieval Literature and Historical Inquiry , Brener, 00. **CONTACT ADDRESS** Eng Dept, Duke Univ, Durham, NC 27708.

AFIFI, WALID A.
DISCIPLINE INTERPERSONAL COMMUNICATION **EDUCATION** Univ Iowa, BA, 90; Univ Ariz, MA, 92; PhD, 96. **CAREER** Asst prof, Univ of Del, 95-98; asst prof, Penn State Univ, 98-. **HONORS AND AWARDS** Grad Col fel, Univ Ariz, 92; grad regist scholar Univ Ariz, 92-94; res trng fel, Univ Ariz, 95, Outstanding prof, Univ Del, 95. **MEMBERSHIPS** Mem, Speech Commun Assn, 90-; Intl Commun Assn, 90-; Intl Network on Personal Relationships, 91-; Intl Soce Stud Personal Relationships, 94-; Nat Coun on Family Rel(s), 94-. **RESEARCH** How our goals fluctuate in relationships, and how that fluctuation is affected by the expecttions we hold; physician-patient interactions. **SELECTED PUBLICATIONS** Coauth, "Mass media in the Middle East: A comprehensive reference guide, in Y.R. Kamalipour & H. Mowlana, eds., (Westport: Greenwood Publishing Group, 94): 160-172; coauth, "What parents don't know: taboo topics and topic avoidance in parent-child relationships, in T.J. Socha and G. Stamp, eds., (Hillsdale: Lawrence Erlbaum, 95): 219-245; coauth, "We never talk about tht: A comparison of cross-sex friendships and dating relationships on uncertainty and topic avoidance, Personal Relationships, 5, (98): 255-272; coauth, "Communicative responses to jealousy as a function of self-esteem and relationship maintenance goals: A test of Bryson's dual motivation model, Communication Reports, 11, (98): 111-122; coauth, "Some things are better left unsaid II: Topic avoidance in friendships, Communication Quarterly, 36, (98): 213-249; coauth, "The use and interpretation of affection displays in a public setting: relationship and sex differences, Journal of Social and Personal Relationships, Journal of Social and Personal Relationships, 16, (99): 9-38; coauth, "The role fo Cnversational involvement in decptive interpersonal interaction, Personality and Social Psychology Bulletin, 25, (99): 669-685; coauth, "Toward a goalori-ented approach for understanding strategic communicative responses to jealousy, Western Journal of Communication, 63, (99): 216-248; auth, "Harming the ones we love; Relational Attachment and perceived consequences as predictors of safe-sex behavior, Journal of Sex Research, 36, (99): 198-206; coauth, "Motivations underlying topic avoidance in close relationships, in S. Petronio, ed., (Mahwah, NJ: Lawrence Erlbaum, 00). **CONTACT ADDRESS** Dept of Speech Commun, Pennsylvania State Univ, Univ Park, University Park, PA 16802-5201. **EMAIL** w-afifi@psu.edu

AGEE, RICHARD J.
PERSONAL Born 05/02/1953, Oakland, CA **DISCIPLINE** MUSIC HISTORY **EDUCATION** Univ Calif Berkeley, BA, 76; Princeton, MFA, 78, PhD, 82. **CAREER** 1978-82, Asst instr, Princeton, 78-82; vis asst prof, Reed Col, 82-83; asst prof, 83-90, assoc prof, 90-97, prof,Colorado Col, 97-. **HONORS AND AWARDS** Fulbright fel, Italy, 78-79; Gladys Krieble Delmas Grant, Venice; Am Coun Learned Soc Grant-in-Aid, res at Civico Museo Bibliografico Musicale in Bologna and the Biblioteka Jagiellonska in Krakow, 87. Am Coun Learned Soc Grant-in-Aid (hon), Harvard, 86; NEH, Bologna and Modena, Italy, 85. **MEMBERSHIPS** Am Musicol Soc; Col Mus Asn. **RESEARCH** Italian Renaissance music printing; Italian madrigal; chant in the Renaissance. **SELECTED PUBLICATIONS** Auth, The Venetian Privilege and Music-Printing in the Sixteenth Century, in Early Music History: Studies in Medieval and Early Modern Music,83, p1-42; Ruberto Strozzi and the Early Madrigal, in Jour Am Musicol Soc, vol 36, 83, p1-17; Filippo Strozzi and the Early Madrigal, in Jour Am Musicol Soc, vol 38, 85, p227-37; A Venetian Music Printing Contract and Edition Size in the Sixteenth Century, in Studi Musicali, Rome, 86, p59-65; coauth, La Stampa della Musica Nova di Willaert, in the Rivista Italiana di Musicologia, Brandeis Univ, 89, p219-305; Studies in Medieval and Early Modern Music, 96, p1-58; A Costanzo Festa's Counterpoints on a Cantus Firmus,Madison, Wis, A-R Editions, Inc, 97; Costanzo Festa's Gradus ad Parnassum, in Early Music History: The Gardano Music Printing Firms, 1569-1611, Univ Rochester Press, 98. **CONTACT ADDRESS** Music Dept, Colorado Col, Colorado Springs, CO 80903. **EMAIL** ragee@ColoradoCollege.edu

AGGELER, GEOFFREY DONOVAN
PERSONAL Born 09/26/1939, Berkeley, CA, m, 1962, 3 children **DISCIPLINE** ENGLISH **EDUCATION** Univ CA, Davis, BA, 61, MA, 63, PhD, 66. **CAREER** Lectr Eng, CA State Polytech Col, 63-64; asst prof, Can Serv Col Royal Rds, 66-69; from asst prof to assoc prof, 69-75, Prof eng, Univ UT, 75. **HONORS AND AWARDS** Phi Beta Kappa (hon), 98. **MEMBERSHIPS** Marlowe Soc Am; Shakespear Asn Am; Asn Lit Scholars & Critics. **RESEARCH** Eng Renaissance drama; twentieth century Brit fiction; hist of ideas. **SELECTED PUBLICATIONS** Auth, Anthony Burgess: The Artist as Novelist, Univ AL, 79; Faust in the Labyrinth, Mod Fiction Studies, autumn 81; Ed, Critical Essays on Anthony burgess, G K Hall, 86; The Eschatological Crux in The Spanish Tragedy, JEGP, 7/87; Hamlet and the Stoic Sage, Hamlet Studies, summer 87; Confessions of Jimmy Ringo, Dutton, 87; Neostoicism and the English Protest Conscience, Renaissance and Reformation, summer 90; Good Pity in King lear, Neophilologus, 4/93; Ben Jonson's Justice Overdo and Joseph Hall's Good Magistrate, Engl Studies, 9/95; Nobler in the Mind: The Stoic-Skeptic Dialectic in English Renaissance tragedy, Assoc Univ Presses, 98. **CONTACT ADDRESS** Dept of Eng, Univ of Utah, 3500 LNCO, Salt Lake City, UT 84112-8916. **EMAIL** geoffrey.aggeler@m.cc.utah.edu

AGOSTA, LUCIEN
PERSONAL Born 07/10/1948, Donaldson, LA, s **DISCIPLINE** ENGLISH **EDUCATION** La State Univ, BA, 70; Univ Tex Austin, MA, 71; PhD, 77. **CAREER** Assoc prof and dir of composition, Kans State Univ, 77-87; prof, Calif State Univ, 87-. **HONORS AND AWARDS** Outstanding Teacher, Col of Arts & Letters, Calif State Univ, 99-00. **RESEARCH** Children's literature, 19th century British literature. **SELECTED PUBLICATIONS** Auth, Howard Pyle, Twayne Pub, 87; auth, E.B. White: The Children's Books, Twayne Pub, 95. **CONTACT ADDRESS** Dept English, California State Univ, Sacramento, 6000 J St, Sacramento, CA 95819-2605.

AGUIRRE, ROBERT D.
PERSONAL Born 10/03/1961, Redwood City, CA, m **DISCIPLINE** ENGLISH **EDUCATION** UC Santa Barbara, BA, 83; Harvard, MA, 85; PhD, 90. **CAREER** Asst prof, Univ Calif, Los Angeles, 90-97; asst prof, Wayne State Univ, 97-. **HONORS AND AWARDS** Andrew E. Mellon Post-doctoral Fel, John Carter Brown Library. **MEMBERSHIPS** MLA. **RESEARCH** 19th century British and American literature. **SELECTED PUBLICATIONS** Auth, Richard Rodriguez's Days of Obligation, Gale Group (Farmington Hills, MI), 99; auth, Latin American Literature and its Times, Gale Group (Farmington Hills, MI), 99. **CONTACT ADDRESS** Dept English, Wayne State Univ, 51 W Warren Ave, Detroit, MI 48201-1305. **EMAIL** r.aguirre@wayne.edu

AHEARN, KERRY
DISCIPLINE SHORT STORY, CONTEMPORARY FICTION, AMERICAN LITERATURE **EDUCATION** Stanford Univ, BA, 67; Ohio Univ, MA, 68, PhD, 74. **CAREER** Engl, Oregon St Univ. **SELECTED PUBLICATIONS** Auth, 'Et In Arcadia Excrementum': Pastoral, Kitsch, and Philip Roth's The Great American Novel, Aethlon 94; Rural and Urban: Places in Oregon Literature, Ore Hum, 94. **CONTACT ADDRESS** Oregon State Univ, Corvallis, OR 97331-4501. **EMAIL** kahearn@orst.edu

AHEARN, W. BARRY
PERSONAL Born 01/29/1950, Montague City, MA, m, 1983, 1 child **DISCIPLINE** ENGLISH **EDUCATION** Trinity Col, BA, 73; Johns Hopkins Univ, MA, 75; PhD, 78. **CAREER** Asst prof, Manhattan Col, 79-80; asst prof to prof, Tulane Univ, 82-. **HONORS AND AWARDS** NEH, 92; ACLS grant, 85. **MEMBERSHIPS** Mod Lang Asn; Ezra Pound Soc. **RESEARCH** Modern language association, Ezra Pound Society. **SELECTED PUBLICATIONS** Auth, William Carlos Williams and Alterity, (94); auth, Zukofsky's "A": An Introduction, (83). **CONTACT ADDRESS** Dept English, Tulane Univ, 6823 Saint Charles Ave, New Orleans, LA 70118-5665. **EMAIL** ahearn@mailhost.tcs.tulane.edu

AHMADI, SHAHWALI
PERSONAL Born 12/06/1964, Kabul, Afghanistan, m, 1999 **DISCIPLINE** LITERATURE, PERSIAN, NEAR EASTERN STUDIES **EDUCATION** Calif State Univ Hayward, BA, 87; Univ Calif Los Angeles, MA, 91; PhD, 97. **CAREER** Lectr, Univ Vir, 96-00; asst prof, Univ Calif Berkeley, 00-. **HONORS AND AWARDS** FLAS Fel; Chancellor's Awd. **MEMBERSHIPS** MLA; MESA. **RESEARCH** Literary theory and criticism. **SELECTED PUBLICATIONS** Ed, Critique and Vision: An Afghan Journal of Culture, Politics and History. **CONTACT ADDRESS** English Dept, Univ of California, Berkeley, 250 Barrows Hall, Berkeley, CA 94720-0001. **EMAIL** ahmadi@socrates.berkeley.edu

AHRENSDORF, PETER J.
DISCIPLINE CLASSICS **EDUCATION** Yale Univ, BA; Univ Chicago, PhD. **CAREER** Assoc prof pol sci and hum, Davidson Col, 89-. **RESEARCH** Plato and Thucydides; Thomas Pangle; theories of international rel(s) in the hist of polit philos. **SELECTED PUBLICATIONS** Auth, The Death of Socrates and the Life of Philosophy: An Interpretation of Plato's Phaedo, SUNY, 95. **CONTACT ADDRESS** Davidson Col, 102 N Main St, PO Box 1719, Davidson, NC 28036. **EMAIL** peahrensdorf@davidson.edu

AIKEN, RALPH
DISCIPLINE ENGLISH **EDUCATION** Williams Col, BA; MA; Duke Univ. **CAREER** Prof, Sweet Briar Col. **RESEARCH** Women and lit; Restoration and 18th century lit; and mod drama. **SELECTED PUBLICATIONS** Auth, articles on 19th century women novelists as well as Renaissance poetry. **CONTACT ADDRESS** Sweet Briar Col, Sweet Briar, VA 24595.

AIKEN, SUSAN HARDY
PERSONAL Born 11/04/1943, Brooklyn, NY, m, 2 children **DISCIPLINE** ENGLISH **EDUCATION** Furman Univ, BA, 64, Duke Univ, MA, 66, PhD, 71. **CAREER** Instr Eng, Univ GA, 66-69; adj asst prof, State Univ NY, Stony Brook, 70-71; asst prof, Suffolk Community Col, 72-73; asst prof, 73-77, assoc prof, 78-89, prof eng, Univ AZ, 90, Univ Distinguised Prof, 98. **HONORS AND AWARDS** Ford Found fel, 64-65; Woodrow Wilson/Duke Univ fel, 65-66, Duke Univ fel, 69-70; Phi Beta Kappa, 71; Co-PI, NEH Curriculum Integration grant, Univ AZ, 84; Mortar Board Citation for Distinguished Acad Achievement, 85; Univ AZ Found Creative Tchg Awd, 85; Women's Studies Advisory Coun Res Grant, 87, 90; Provost's Tchg Awd, Univ AZ, 88; Burlington Northern Found Acad Excellence Awd, 88; Steinfeld Found Res Grant, 89; Univ AZ Res Grant, 90; Guest lectr tour, Univ Copenhagen, Univ Aarhus and Univ Odense, Denmark, 91; Inaugural Scholarly Address, Karen Blixen Museet, Rungstedlund, Denmark, 91; NEH Interpretive Res Grant, 91-93; Univ Distinguished Prof, 98. **MEMBERSHIPS** MLA; Nat Women's Studies Asn. **RESEARCH** Nineteenth and Twentieth Century Brit and Am lit and cult; Isak Dinesen/Karen Blixen; Gender theory. **SELECTED PUBLICATIONS** Co-ed, Changing Our Minds: Feminist Transformations of Knowledge, SUNY Press, 88; Auth, Isak Dinesen and the Engendering of Narrative, Univ Chicago Press, 90; Dialogues/Dialogi: Literary and Cultural Exchanges Between (Ex)Soviet and American Women, Duke Univ Press, 94; Co-ed, Making Worlds: Gender, Metaphor, Materiality, Univ AZ Press, 98; Auth articles and bk chap on nineteenth- and twentieth-century lit, feminist theory, photography. **CONTACT ADDRESS** Dept of Eng, Univ of Arizona, Tucson, AZ 85721. **EMAIL** sha@u.arizona.edu

AITKEN, JOAN EVELYN
PERSONAL Born 11/23/1947, Detroit, MI, m, 1974, 2 children **DISCIPLINE** COMMUNICATION STUDIES **EDUCATION** Mich State Univ, BA, 69; Univ Ark, MA, 72 & 85. **CAREER** Univ Mo at Columbia; St Louis Community Col; Univ Ark; Univ La Lafayette; prof, Univ of Mo Kansas City, 87-. **HONORS AND AWARDS** Outstanding Teaching Awd, Col Alumni. **MEMBERSHIPS** Orgn for the Study of Commun, Lang, & Gender, Nat Commun Asn. **RESEARCH** E-Relationships (online) and Communication (CMC), Communication Education, Interpersonal and Intrapersonal Communication. **SELECTED PUBLICATIONS** Auth, Intrapersonal Communication Processes; ed, Speech Communication Teacher. **CONTACT ADDRESS** Dept Commun, Univ of Missouri, Kansas City, 5100 Rockhill Rd, Kansas City, MO 64110-2446.

AKE, DAVID
PERSONAL Born 05/11/1961, New Haven, CT **DISCIPLINE** MUSICOLOGY **EDUCATION** Calif Inst Arts, MFA, 87; UCLA, MA, 96. **CAREER** Asst prof mus, Univ Nevada-Reno, 99-. **HONORS AND AWARDS** Ki Mantle Hood Prize, Soc for Ethnomusico Southern Calif Chap, 97, 98. **MEMBERSHIPS** Am Musicol Soc; Soc for Ethnomusicol; Sonneck Soc; Broadcast Mus, Inc (BMI). **RESEARCH** Popular Music,twentieth-century music,jazz. **SELECTED PUBLICATIONS** Book Review of Music Grooves by Charles Keil and Steven Feld, Am Mus, vol 15, No 2, Summer 97, p252-4; Re-Masculating Jazz: Ornette Coleman, Lonely Woman, and the New York Jazz Scene in the Late 1950s, Am Mus, vol 16, No 1, Spring 98, p25-44; Louis Jordan, in Encyclopaedia Britannica (CD-ROM version), 98. **CONTACT ADDRESS** Music Dept, Univ of Nevada, Reno, Reno, NV 89577-0049. **EMAIL** dake@unr.nevada.edu

AKRIGG, GEORGE P. V.
PERSONAL Born 08/13/1913, Calgary, AB, Canada **DISCIPLINE** ENGLISH LITERATURE **EDUCATION** Univ BC, BA, 37, MA, 40; Univ Calif Berkeley, PhD, 44. **CAREER** Prof, 58-79, Prof Emer English, Univ BC, 79-. **MEMBERSHIPS** MLA. **SELECTED PUBLICATIONS** Auth, Jacobean Pageant or the Court of King James I, 62; auth, Shakespeare and the Earl of Southampton, 68; coauth, 1001 British Columbia Place Names, 69; coauth, British Columbia Chronicle 1778-1846, 75; coauth, British Columbia Chronicle 1847-1871, 77;

coauth, British Columbia Place Names, 86; ed, Letters of King James VI & I, 84; ed, H.M.S. 'Virago' in the Pacific 1851-1955, 92. **CONTACT ADDRESS** Dept English, Univ of British Columbia, 2329 W Mall, Vancouver, BC, Canada V6T 124.

ALAIMO, STACY
DISCIPLINE AMERICAN LITERATURE **EDUCATION** Gustavus Adolphus, BA, 85; Univ Wis, MA, 86; Certificate in Critical Interpretive Theory, Univ Ill, 93; PhD, 94. **CAREER** Assoc prof, Univ Tex at Arlington. **MEMBERSHIPS** MLA, NWSA, ASLE, SSAWW, MELUS. **RESEARCH** Feminist Theory, Cultural Studies, Multicultural American Literature, Theories of Nature & Environment. **SELECTED PUBLICATIONS** Auth, Undomesticated Ground: Recasting Nature as Feminist Space, Cornell Univ Pr, 00. **CONTACT ADDRESS** Dept English, Univ of Texas, Arlington, PO Box 19035, Arlington, TX 76019. **EMAIL** stacya@utarlg.uta.edu

ALAYA, FLAVIA M.
PERSONAL Born 05/16/1935, New Rochelle, NY, m, 1993, 3 children **DISCIPLINE** ENGLISH AND LITERATURE **EDUCATION** Barnard Col, Columbia Univ, BA, 56; Columbia Univ, MA, 60; Columbia Univ, PhD, 65. **CAREER** Instr, eng, Univ NC, 59-60; lectr, Barnard Col, 60-62; lectr, Hunter Col, 62-66; instr to asst prof, NY Univ, 66-71; assoc prof, 71-73, prof, 74-80, eng & comp lit & dir sch of Intercultural Studies, Ramapo Col; prof, lit & cultural hist, sch of soc sci, Ramapo Col, 80-. **HONORS AND AWARDS** Fulbright, 57-58; Guggenheim fel, 74-75; NEH, 85; Kress Found fel, 97; Dodge Found writing fel, 97. **MEMBERSHIPS** MLA; Northeast Victorian Studies Asn; Nat Trust for Hist Pres; Ital Amer Writers Asn. **RESEARCH** Nineteenth-twentieth century cultural history (Europe and America); Literature of national and cultural identity; Italy in Victorian literature; Eliz Barrett & Robert Browning; South African literature; Space and place; Historic preservation; History of Paterson, NJ; Women in literature; Women's autobiographies; Ital-Amer literature. **SELECTED PUBLICATIONS** auth, Jour Hist Ideas; auth, Victorian Poetry; articles, Browning Inst Studies; Ramapo papers; auth, William Sharp: Fiona Macleod: a Study in Later Victorian Cosmopolitanism, Harvard, 70; auth, Gaetano Federici: The Artist as Historian, Passaic County Hist Soc, 80; auth, Silk & Sandstone: the Story of Catholina Lambert and Hist Castle, Passaic County Hist Soc, 84. **CONTACT ADDRESS** School of Social Science, Ramapo Col of New Jersey, 505 Ramapo Valley Rd, Mahwah, NJ 07430. **EMAIL** falaya@ramapo.edu

ALBERTI, JOHN
DISCIPLINE ENGLISH **EDUCATION** Univ Southern Calif, BA, 81; Univ Calif Los Angeles, MA, 84; PhD, 89. **CAREER** Lectr, Univ Calif at Los Angeles, 89-91; assoc prof, Northern Ky Univ, 91-. **MEMBERSHIPS** MLA, NCTE. **RESEARCH** American Culture, Media Studies, Composition, Literary Theory. **SELECTED PUBLICATIONS** Ed, The Canon in the Classroom: Pedagogical Implications of Canon Revision in American Literature, Garland, 95. **CONTACT ADDRESS** Dept Lang & Lit, No Kentucky Univ, Newport, KY 41099-0001. **EMAIL** alberti@nku.edu

ALBERTINI, VIRGIL
PERSONAL Born 04/01/1932, Frontenac, KS, m, 1960 **DISCIPLINE** ENGLISH **EDUCATION** Kans State Col, Pittsburg, BSEd, 53, MS, 60; Univ Tulsa, PhD, 74. **CAREER** Teacher, high schs, Kans, 54-60 & prep sch, Calif, 60-61; instr, 65-68, from asst prof to assoc prof English, 68-74, Prof English, Northwest MO State Univ, 74- **HONORS AND AWARDS** English Dept Prof of the Year, 3 different years; Northwest's Turret Awd Recipient for outstanding academic and athletic contributions, 95. **MEMBERSHIPS** NCTE; Cather Soc; ALAN; WLA. **RESEARCH** Nineteenth century American literature; Willa Cather; American literary naturalism; young adult literature. **SELECTED PUBLICATIONS** Auth, Towers in the Northwest, 1956-1980, Univ Wyo Press, 80; 35 articles in professional journals on American and British authors, 15 on Willa Cather. **CONTACT ADDRESS** Dept of English, 800 University Dr, Maryville, MO 64468-6015. **EMAIL** lujack@acad.nwmissouri.edu

ALBIN, CRAIG D.
PERSONAL Born 04/09/1961, West Plains, MO, s **DISCIPLINE** ENGLISH **EDUCATION** Oral Roberts Univ, BA, 83; Southwest Mo State Univ, MA, 84; Univ Mo, PhD, 98. **CAREER** Asst Prof to Assoc Prof, Southwest Mo State Univ, 90-. **HONORS AND AWARDS** Excellence in Teaching, Mo Governor's Awd. **MEMBERSHIPS** Nat Council of Teachers of English. **RESEARCH** Southern fiction, Ozark literature and culture. **SELECTED PUBLICATIONS** Auth, "In Search of the spirit's One Home': A Reading of Annie Dillard's Pilgrim at tinker Creek," Journal of the American Studies Association of Texas, (89): 71-78; auth, "A Ray of Relation: Transcendental Echoes in Annie Dillard's Pilgrim at Tinker Creek," Journal of the American Studies Association of Texas, (92): 17-31; auth, "Luck," Mark Twain Encyclopedia, (93): 475; auth, "T.DeWitt Talmadge," Mark Twain Encyclopedia, (93): 726; auth, "Theodore Watts-Dunton," Mark Twain encyclopedia, (93): 777-778; auth, "You've Been a Dam Fool, Mary. You Always Was!," Mark Twain Encyclopedia, (93): 801-802; auth, "The Prairie States," Walt Whitman: An Encyclopedia, (98): 538-539; auth, "The American West," Walt Whitman: An Encyclopedia, (98): 765-766; rev, of "The conscience of the Autobiographer," by John Barbour, Christian Century, (93): 830; rev, of "West Plains As I Knew It," by Robert Neathery, Ozarks Mountaineer, (95): 16. **CONTACT ADDRESS** Dept Arts, Southwest Missouri State Univ, Springfield, 128 Garfield Ave, West Plains, MO 65775-2715.

ALBRECHT, WILBUR T.
DISCIPLINE ROMANTIC POETS AND ESSAYISTS **EDUCATION** Brown Univ, BA, 60; Johns Hopkins Univ, MA, 61; Univ PA, 70. **CAREER** Instr, Drexel Univ, 64-67; prof, 67-. **RESEARCH** William Morris and the pre-Raphaelites. **SELECTED PUBLICATIONS** Publ, Profiles of the Monthly Rev, The Scots Rev, Eng Rev, The Lit Rev in Vol 1, Brit Lit Per. **CONTACT ADDRESS** Dept of Eng, Colgate Univ, 13 Oak Dr., Hamilton, NY 13346.

ALBRIGHT, ANN COOPER
DISCIPLINE DANCE **EDUCATION** Bryn Mawr Col, BA, 81; Temple Univ, MFA, 83; NYork Univ, PhD, 91. **CAREER** Assoc prof, Oberlin Coll, 90. **HONORS AND AWARDS** Individual Artist Awds, Ohio Arts Council in Dance Criticism **RESEARCH** Dancing and cultural theory. **SELECTED PUBLICATIONS** Au, Choreographing Difference: the Body and Identity in Comtemporary Dance, Weslyn Univ Press, 97. **CONTACT ADDRESS** Oberlin Col, Oberlin, OH 44074.

ALBRIGHT, DANIEL
PERSONAL Born 10/29/1945, Chicago, IL, m, 1977, 1 child **DISCIPLINE** ENGLISH **EDUCATION** Rice Univ, BA, 67; Yale Univ, MPhil, 69, PhD, 70. **CAREER** Asst to full prof, Univ Va, 70-86; visiting prof, Univ Munich, 86-87; Prof of English, 87-, Richard L. Turner Prof of Humanities, Univ Rochester, 95-. **HONORS AND AWARDS** Phi Beta Kappa, 66; NEH fel, 73; Guggenheim fel, 76. **MEMBERSHIPS** MLA. **RESEARCH** Modernism in music, literature, visual arts, and sciences. **SELECTED PUBLICATIONS** Auth, Quantum Poetics: Yeats, Pound, Eliot, and the Science of Modernism, Cambridge Univ Press, 97; Discrepancies Between Literary and Psychological Models of the Self, The Remembering Self: Construction and Accuracy in the Self-Narrative, Cambridge Univ Press, 94; Yeats and the Avant-garde, The Recorder, 94; Yeats and Science Fiction, Bullan: An Irish Studies J, 96; Beckett at the Bowling Alley, Contemporary Lit, 97; An Opera with No Acts: Four Saints in Three Acts, Southern Rev, 97; ed, W.B. Yeats: The Poems, J.M. Dent and Sons, 90 & 94. **CONTACT ADDRESS** Dept of English, Univ of Rochester, 121 Van Voorlis Rd., Pittsford, NY 14539.

ALEMAN, JESSE
PERSONAL Born 06/07/1968, Selma, CA, s **DISCIPLINE** ENGLISH **EDUCATION** Calif State Univ Fresno, BA, 91; MA, 94; Univ Kans, PhD, 99. **CAREER** Asst prof, Univ NMex, 99-. **HONORS AND AWARDS** NEH, 00; Julia M. Keleher Teaching Awd, 00. **MEMBERSHIPS** MLA; CMELUS; STPCA. **RESEARCH** 19th-century American literature; Mexican American war; Mexican American literature. **SELECTED PUBLICATIONS** Auth, "Chicano Novelist Discourse: Dialogizing the Corrido Critical Paradigm," MELUS 23 (98): 49-64; auth, "Novelizing National Discourses: History, Romance, and Land in Maria Amparo Aviz de Burton's 'The Squatter and the Don,'" in Recovering the U. S. Hispanic Literary Heritage, eds. Maria Herreva-Sobek, Virginia Sanchevkorrel (Houston: Arte Pub, 00): 38-49. **CONTACT ADDRESS** English Dept, Univ of New Mexico, Albuquerque, 217 Humanities Bldg, Albuquerque, NM 87131-0001. **EMAIL** jman@unm.edu

ALEXANDER, BRYAN
PERSONAL Born New York, NY, m, 1993, 2 children **DISCIPLINE** ENGLISH **EDUCATION** Univ Mich, BA, 90; MA, 91; PhD, 97. **CAREER** Asst prof, Centenary Col, 97-. **HONORS AND AWARDS** Pacesetter Awd, 99, 00; Humanities Chair Endowment, 99-01. **MEMBERSHIPS** MLA, Soc for Utopian Studies, Am Soc for Eighteenth-Century Studies. **RESEARCH** 18th Century British Literature, Critical Theory, The Gothe, Cyberculture, Literature of War. **SELECTED PUBLICATIONS** Auth, "Jameson's Adams and the Problem of Utopia," Utopian Studies 9.2, (98); auth, "Cybergoths," Minjadle, (00). **CONTACT ADDRESS** Dept Eng, Centenary Col, PO Box 41188, Shreveport, LA 71134-1188. **EMAIL** balexand@centenary.edu

ALEXANDER, DENNIS C.
PERSONAL Born 08/15/1941 **DISCIPLINE** COMMUNICATION STUDIES **EDUCATION** Ohio State Univ, PhD, 69. **CAREER** Assoc prof. **MEMBERSHIPS** Western States Commun Asn; Nat Commun Asn; Soc Study Symbolic Interaction. **RESEARCH** Political Communication **SELECTED PUBLICATIONS** Auth, Communication as History and Evolution: Comparing Contextualism and Symbolic Interactionism, Context, 96. **CONTACT ADDRESS** Dept of Communication, Univ of Utah, 255 South Central Campus Dr, Rm 2400, Salt Lake City, UT 84112. **EMAIL** dennis.alexander@m.cc.utah.edu

ALEXANDER, EDWARD
PERSONAL Born 12/28/1936, Brooklyn, NY, m, 1958, 2 children **DISCIPLINE** ENGLISH LITERATURE **EDUCATION** Columbia Univ, AB, 57; Univ Minn, AM, 59; PhD, 63. **CAREER** Instr to prof, Univ of Wash, 60-; vis prof, Hebrew Univ, Tel-Aviv Univ, Memphis Univ. **HONORS AND AWARDS** Phi Beta Kappa; ACLS Fel; Guggenheim Fel; Fulbright Fel. **MEMBERSHIPS** Nat Assoc of Scholars; Assoc of Lit Scholars and Critics. **RESEARCH** Victorian Literature; Modern Jewish Literature. **SELECTED PUBLICATIONS** Auth, Mathew Arnold and John Stuart Mill, 65; auth, Matthew Arnold, John Ruskin and the Modern Temper, 73; coauth, The Resonance of Dust, 79; auth, Isaac Bashevis Singer, 80; auth, The Jewish Idea and Its Enemies, 87; auth, The Holocaust and the War of Ideas, 94; auth, The Jewish Wars: Reflections By One of the Belligerents, 96; auth, Irving Howe - Socialist, Critic, Jew, 98. **CONTACT ADDRESS** Dept English, Univ of Washington, PO Box 354330, Seattle, WA 98195-4330. **EMAIL** eaengl@washington.edu

ALEXANDER, ESTELLA CONWILL
PERSONAL Born 01/19/1949, Louisville, KY **DISCIPLINE** ENGLISH **EDUCATION** Univ of Louisville, BA 1975, MA 1976; Univ of IA, PhD 1984. **CAREER** Univ of Iowa, instructor/director of black poetry 1976-79; Grinnell Coll, asst prof 1979-80; KY State Univ, prof of English; poet, currently. **HONORS AND AWARDS** Recording Motion Grace Gospel Recordings 1983; KY Arts Council Grant 1986; Art Grant KY Foundation for Women 1986. **CONTACT ADDRESS** Dept of English, Hunter Col, CUNY, 695 Park Ave, New York, NY 10021.

ALEXANDER, JONATHAN F.
PERSONAL Born 10/02/1967, New Orleans, LA **DISCIPLINE** ENGLISH, WOMEN'S STUDIES **EDUCATION** La State Univ, BA, 89; MA, 91, PhD, 93. **CAREER** Lectr, Univ of S Colo, 94-98; asst prof, Univ of Cincinnati, 98-. **HONORS AND AWARDS** Harvey Milk Awd; Who's Who Among Am Teachers, 98, 00; Kairos Hypertext of the Year Awd, 98; Jonas B. Hebberhoffer Awd. **MEMBERSHIPS** MLA, NCTE, Popular Cult Assoc of Am. **RESEARCH** Writing Pedagogy, Computers and Composition, Sexuality Studies, Media Studies. **SELECTED PUBLICATIONS** Auth, "Out of the Closet and Into the Network: Sexual Orientation and the Computerized Classroom," Computers and Composition, (97); coauth, "The Pedagogy of Marking: Sexual Orientation in the Classroom," Feminist Teacher, (97); coauth, "Teacher Involvement and Transformative Power on a Gender Issues Discussion List," Meeting the Challenge: Innovative Feminist Pedagogues in Action, (99); auth, "Hypertext and Queer Theory," Kairos, (98); auth, "Beyond Identity: The Search for Queer Values and Community," Jour of Gay, Lesbian and Bisexual Identity, (01); auth, "Homo-pages and Queer Sites: Studying the Construction and Representation of Queer Identities on the World Wide Web," Int Jour of Sexuality and Gender Studies, forthcoming. **CONTACT ADDRESS** Univ of Cincinnati, PO Box 210205, Cincinnati, OH 45221. **EMAIL** jamma@fuse.net

ALEXANDER, LYNN M.
PERSONAL Born 08/05/1956, Bemidji, MN **DISCIPLINE** ENGLISH, LITERATURE **EDUCATION** Phillips Univ, BA, 79; Univ Tulsa, MA, 81; PhD, 86. **CAREER** Asst prof, Upper Iowa Univ, 86-89; vis lectr, Keele Univ, 88; asst prof to assoc prof to prof to chmn, Univ Tenn Martin, 89-. **HONORS AND AWARDS** NEH, 90; Outstanding Educr, 97; Phi Kappa Phi. **MEMBERSHIPS** Victorian Inst; MVSA; RSVP; MLA; SCMLA; ADE; NWSA; SAMLA; NABS; TPA. **RESEARCH** Victorian studies; the novel, British and American; women's studies; literary theory. **SELECTED PUBLICATIONS** Auth, "Seamstresses, Dressmakers, and Milliners," in Victorian Britain: An Encyclopedia, ed. Sally Mitchell. (Garland, 88); auth, "Following the Thread: Dickens and the Seamstress," Victorian Newsletter (91): 1-7; co-ed, The Slaughter-House of Mammon: Social Protest Literature, Locust Hill Pr, 92; auth, "Transcending Gender: Industrial Literature by Nineteenth-Century American Women," Studies Humanities (93): 107-14; auth, "End of the Domestic Idyll: Literature," in Keeping the Victorian House, ed. Vanessa Dickerson (Garland, 95): 291-311; auth, "Creating a Hero: The Male Ambiguity in Nineteenth-Century British Women's Novels," Pre-Text (97); auth, "Ethel Sedgwick," in Dictionary of Literary Biography: Late-Victorian and Edwardian British Novelists, 1890-1918, Vol 197 (98): 264-268; auth, "Creating Protest Fiction," Tulsa Studies Women's Lit 18 (99): 29-38; auth, "Signifying Sex: Gloria Naylor's Bailey's Cafe and Western Biblical Tradition," in He Said, She Says: An RSVP to the Male Text, eds. Sarah Appleton Aguiar, Mica Howe (Fairleigh Dickinson Univ Pr, 01); auth, "Victorian Illustrators and Illustration," in Victorian Literary Cultures: A Critical Companion to the Nineteenth-Century Novel, eds. William Baker, Kenneth Womeck (Greenwood Pr, 02). **CONTACT ADDRESS** Humanities Dept, Univ of Tennessee, Martin, 131 Humanities, Martin, TN 38238. **EMAIL** lalexand@utm.edu

ALEXANDER, MEENA
PERSONAL Born 02/17/1951, Allahabzd, India, m, 1979, 2 children **DISCIPLINE** ENGLISH **EDUCATION** Khartoum

Univ, BA, 69; Nottingham Univ, PhD, 73. **CAREER** Prof, CUNY Hunter Col. **HONORS AND AWARDS** Awards from NEH, Arts Coun of England, ACLS, the Lila Wallace Found, the Altrusa Int Found, Nat Coun for Res on Women, NY State coun on the Arts, and NY Found for the Arts; vis fel, Sorbonne; Frances Wayland Collegium Lectr, Brown Univ; Writer in Residence, Ctr for Am Culture Studies at Columbia Univ; Univ Grants Comn Fel, Kerala Univ; Writer in Residence, Nat Univ of Singapore; Fel at the MacDowell Colony. **MEMBERSHIPS** MLA, PEN, Am Ctr. **RESEARCH** Questions of Migratar & Mewny. **SELECTED PUBLICATIONS** Auth, Night-Scene, The Garden, Red Dust, 92; auth, preface for Blood into Ink: South Asian and Middle Eastern Women Write War, Westview Press, 94; auth, River and Bridge, Rupa, 95 & TSAR Press, 96; auth, preface for Cast Me Out if You Will: Selected Writings of Lalithambika Antherjanam, Feminist Press, 98; auth, Notebook, 99. **CONTACT ADDRESS** Dept English, Hunter Col, CUNY, 695 Park Ave, New York, NY 10021-5024. **EMAIL** malexander@gc.cuny.edu

ALEXANDER, PAMELA
PERSONAL Born 04/02/1948, Natick, MA, m, 1998 **DISCIPLINE** CREATIVE WRITING, POETRY **EDUCATION** Bates Col, BA, 70; Univ Iowa, MFA, 73. **CAREER** Writer in Residence, MIT, 84-97; Assoc Prof, Oberlin Col, 97-. **HONORS AND AWARDS** Yale Younger Poet, 84; Bunting Fel, Radcliffe Col, 85; Iowa Prize, 96. **MEMBERSHIPS** Acad Am Poets, PSA, AWP. **SELECTED PUBLICATIONS** Auth, Navigable Waterways, Yale Univ Pr, 85; auth, Commonwealth of Wings, Wesleyan Univ Pr, 91; auth, Inland, Univ Iowa Pr, 97. **CONTACT ADDRESS** Dept Creative Writing, Oberlin Col, 135 W Lorain St, Oberlin, OH 44074-1053. **EMAIL** pamela.alexander@oberlin.edu

ALEXANDER, SANDRA CARLTON
PERSONAL Born 07/26/1947, Warsaw, NC, m, 1970, 2 children **DISCIPLINE** AMERICAN LITERATURE, RHETORIC **EDUCATION** NC A&T State Univ, BA, 69; Harvard Univ, MA, 70; Univ Pittsburgh, PhD(English), 76. **CAREER** Instr English, Coppin State Col, 73-74; from asst prof to prof, NC A&T State Univ, 74-. **HONORS AND AWARDS** NC Arts Coun Writers Fel, 92 **MEMBERSHIPS** Col Lang Asn. **RESEARCH** The life and works of Arna Bontemps; developing composition skills. **SELECTED PUBLICATIONS** Auth, Black Butterflies: Stories of the South in Transition, 94. **CONTACT ADDRESS** Dept of English, No Carolina Agr and Tech State Univ, 1601 E Market St, Greensboro, NC 27401-3209.

ALGEO, JOHN T.
PERSONAL Born 11/12/1930, St. Louis, MO, m, 1958, 2 children **DISCIPLINE** ENGLISH **EDUCATION** Univ of Miami, BEd, 55; Univ of Fla, MA, 57, PhD, 60. **CAREER** Instr, Fla State Univ, 59-61; asst prof, 61-66, assoc prof, 66-70, asst dean of the Grad School & dir of prog in Linguistics, 69-71, prof, Univ of Fla, 70-71; Prof, 71-88, Dir of prog in Linguistics, 74-79, Head, Dept of English, 75-79, Alumni Found Distinguished Prof of English, 88-94, Prof Emeritus, Univ of Ga, 94-; exchange prof, Univ of Erlangen, 85; Honorary Res Fel, Univ ClL London, Univ of London, 86-. **HONORS AND AWARDS** Phi Beta Kappa; Phi Kappa Phi; Fulbright Sr Res Scholar, Univ Col London, 86-87; Guggenheim Fel, 86-87; Univ of Ga Alumni Found Distinguished Prof, 88-94. **MEMBERSHIPS** Am Dialect Soc; Am Name Soc; Dictionary Soc of North Am; Int Asn of Univ Prof of English; Int Linguistic Asn; Int Phonetic Asn; Linguistic Soc of Am; MLA; Philological Soc. **RESEARCH** British-American linguistic differences; lexicography; neology; usage. **SELECTED PUBLICATIONS** Coauth, The Origins and Development of the English Language, Harcourt Brace Jovanovich, 93; auth, Fifty Years Among the New Words: A Dictionary of Neologisms 1941-1991, Cambridge UP, 91; Eigo no kigen to hattatsu, Bunkashobouhakubunsha, 91; British and American Biases in English Dictionaries, Cultures, Ideologies, and the Dictionary: Studies in Honor of Ladislav Zgusta, Niemeyer, 95; Having a Look at the Expanded Predicate, The Verb in Contemporary English: Theory and Description, Cambridge Univ Press, 95; Ther American Language and Its British Dialect, SECOL Rev, 95; American and British Words, Words: Proceedings of an Int Symposium, 96; Spanish Loanwords in English by 1900, Spanish Loanwords in the English Language: A Tendency towards Hegemony Reversal, Mouton de Gruyter, 96. **CONTACT ADDRESS** English Dept, Univ of Georgia, Athens, GA 30602.

ALI, SCHARI M.
PERSONAL Born 04/30/1948, Detroit, MI, m, 1986 **DISCIPLINE** ENGLISH **EDUCATION** Wayne State Univ, BA, 70; MA, 77; Univ Mich, PhD, 89. **CAREER** Prof, Wayne State Univ, 78-89; Prof, Oakland Community Col, 89-. **HONORS AND AWARDS** Outstanding Fac Awd, Oakland Community Col, 93; Teacher of the Year, Univ Tex, 93; Auset Awd, Eastern Mich Univ, 94. **MEMBERSHIPS** Asn for the Study of Classical African Civilization, Nat Educ Asn, Asn for the Study of Afro-Am Life and Hist. **RESEARCH** Linguistics, ancient Egyptian language and spirituality, philosophy, Twentieth-Century literature. **SELECTED PUBLICATIONS** Auth, Moments in Time (poetry); auth, Out of Egypt: The Spirituality of Ancient Kemet; auth, Ankhba: The Life of the Soul. **CONTACT ADDRESS** Dept English, Oakland Comm Col, 27055 Orchard Lake Rd, Farmington Hills, MI 48334-4556.

ALISKY, MARVIN HOWARD
PERSONAL Born 03/12/1923, Kansas City, MO, m, 1955, 2 children **DISCIPLINE** JOURNALISM, POLITICAL SCIENCE **EDUCATION** Univ TX, Austin, BA (liberal arts, political science & journalism combined), 46, MA (journalism), 47, PhD (political science, specifically Latin American politics), 53. **CAREER** NBC News correspondent in TX, 47, in Mexico, 48-49, Argentina-Uraguay, 49-50; asst prof journalism TV & govt, IN Univ, 53-57; assoc prof journalism and political science, AZ State Univ, 57-60; chemn, Mass Communications Dept, ASU, 57-65, prof political science, 60-90; founder, dir ASU Center for Latin American Studies, ASU, 65-72; once-a-month columnist, AZ Republic (Phoenix daily), 79-81; once-a-month columnist with Phoenix Gazette, 81-83; nationally syndicated columnist on Latin Am, NCI syndicate 81-84; lectr, US Information Agency, summers, Universities Mexico, Nicaragua, Costa Rica, Uruguay, Argentina, and Chile, 83-88; researcher, Latin Am Center in Beijing, China, 86, and in Soviet Union (Moscow and Leningrad) with World Media Asn, 89; columnist, editorial pages, East Valley Tribune, 98-. **HONORS AND AWARDS** Bd member (White House appointment), Fulbright Comm on Foreign Scholarships, 84-89; Envoy to UNESCO (4 month interim), 60; AZ-MEX Comm bd, 75-85; Town Hall fel, AZ Academy, 81-90. **MEMBERSHIPS** Life member, Sigma Delta Chi (Soc of Professional Journalists); Am Political Science Asn; Western Political Science Asn; assoc member, Inter-Am Press Asn, 63-98; consultant, Liga de Municipios, State of Sonora, Mexico. **RESEARCH** Latin Am public life, govts, and mass media. **SELECTED PUBLICATIONS** Auth, Uraguay: Contemporary Survey, Praeger, 69; Political Forces in Latin America, Wadsworth Press, 70; Historical Dictionary of Peru, Scarecrow Press, 79; Latin America Media: Guidance and Sensorship, IA State Press, 81; coauth with James Katz, Andres Ross, & Richard Latham, Arms Production in Developing Countries, Lexington Books, 84; coauth with S H Surlin, W C Soderlung, Mass Media and the Caribbean, Gordon & Breach, 90; auth, Historical Dictionary of Mexico, Scarecrow Press, 81, 2nd ed, 00. **CONTACT ADDRESS** 44 W Palmdale, Tempe, AZ 85282-2139.

ALLABACK, STEVE
DISCIPLINE AMERICAN LITERATURE **EDUCATION** Univ Wash, PhD, 66. **CAREER** Prof, Eng, Univ Calif, Santa Barbara. **RESEARCH** Writing of fiction. **SELECTED PUBLICATIONS** Auth, Alexander Solzhenitsyn, Warner, 79; Guide to the Journals of George and Anna Ticknor, Dartmouth Col Lib, 78. **CONTACT ADDRESS** Dept of Eng, Univ of California, Santa Barbara, Santa Barbara, CA 93106-7150. **EMAIL** steveall@humanitas.ucsb.edu

ALLEGREZZA, WILLIAM
PERSONAL Born 08/12/1974, Jackson, MS, m **DISCIPLINE** ENGLISH **EDUCATION** Univ Dallas, BA, 96; La State Univ, MA, 97. **CAREER** Columbia Col, 00; Ind Univ NW, 00-01. **MEMBERSHIPS** MLA, ACLA, M/MLA. **RESEARCH** Contemporary American and Italian Poetry, American Literature, Medieval Italian Literature. **CONTACT ADDRESS** 5535 S Everett Ave, Apt 1W, Chicago, IL 60637-5027. **EMAIL** alegr5@attglobal.net

ALLEN, BRENDA J.
DISCIPLINE COMMUNCATION STUDIES **EDUCATION** Case Western Reserve Univ, BA; Howard Univ, MA, PhD. **CAREER** Assoc prof. **HONORS AND AWARDS** Tchr Recognition Awd. **MEMBERSHIPS** Black Student Asn. **RESEARCH** Organizational communication; computer mediated communication. **SELECTED PUBLICATIONS** Auth, Black womanhood and feminist standpoints, 98; Sapphire and Sappho: Allies in authenticity, 97; Gender and computer-mediated communication, 95; Diversity and organizational communication, Jour Applied Commun Res, 95; co-auth, Vocabularies of motives in a crisis of academic leadership: Hell hath no fury, 97. **CONTACT ADDRESS** Dept of Communication, Univ of Colorado, Boulder, Boulder, CO 80309. **EMAIL** Brenda.J.Allen@Colorado.edu

ALLEN, CAROLYN J.
DISCIPLINE ENGLISH **EDUCATION** Univ Wash, BA, 65; Claremont Grad School, MA, 67; Univ Minn, PhD, 72. **CAREER** Lectr to instr, Alaska Methodist Univ, 67-70; asst prof to prof, Univ of Wash, 72-. **HONORS AND AWARDS** Distinguished Teaching Awd, Alaska Methodist Univ, 69; NEH Grant, 80 90; Univ of Wash Distinguished Teaching Awd, 80; Provost's Grant, 90-91; Hilliard/NEH Vis Prof, 91. **MEMBERSHIPS** MLA; CELJ. **RESEARCH** 20th Century Writers, women and gender studies, comtemporary literary and cultural theory, sexuality studies, theories of affect and emotion. **SELECTED PUBLICATIONS** Coauth, "The Gendered Context of Reading", Gender and Soc 4.4 (90): 534-552; Auth, "Sexual Narrative in the Fiction of Djuna Barnes", Sexual Practice, Textual Theory, eds Susan J. Wolfe and Julia Penelope, Basil Blackwell, (93): 184-198; auth, "The Erotics of Nora's Narrative in Djuna Barnes Nightwood", Signs: J of Women in Culture and Soc 19.1, (93): 177-200; auth, "Death and Dreams in John Haines Winter News", A Wilderness of vision: the work of John Haines, eds Kevin Walzer and Kevin Bezher, Story Line Pr, 96; auth, "Desire, Design and Debris: The Submerged Narrative of John Hawkes Recent Trilogy", Critical Essays on John Hawkes, ed Stanley Trachtenberg, G.K. Hall (NY, 92): 163-175; auth, "Louise Rosenblatt and Theories of Reader Response", The Experience of Reading: Louise Rosenblatt and Reader-response Theory, ed John Clifford, Heinemann, (NY, 91): 15-22; auth, "Editing Signs at the Borders", Yale J of Criticism, Winter 98; coauth, "Signs: Moving Forward in Provocative Times", Signs 21.3 (96); auth, Following Djuna: women Lovers and the Erotics of Loss, Ind Univ Pr, 96; coed, Provoking Feminisms, Univ of Chicago Pr, 00. **CONTACT ADDRESS** Dept English, Univ of Washington, PO Box 354330, Seattle, WA 98195-4330.

ALLEN, CHRIS
PERSONAL m, 2 children **DISCIPLINE** JOURNALISM AND BROADCASTING **EDUCATION** Iowa State Univ, BA, MA; Univ Mo, PhD, 96. **CAREER** Asst prof, Univ NDak, 87-92; instr, Univ Nebr, Omaha, 96-. **MEMBERSHIPS** Membership ch, Radio-TV Div, Asn for Educ in Jour and Mass Commun. **RESEARCH** Broadcast history. **CONTACT ADDRESS** Dept of Communication, Univ of Nebraska, Omaha, Omaha, NE 68182. **EMAIL** cwallen@cwis.unomaha.edu

ALLEN, CRAIG MITCHELL
PERSONAL Born 02/06/1954, Portland, OR, m, 1990, 1 child **DISCIPLINE** MASS COMMUNICATION **EDUCATION** Linfield Col, BA, 76; Univ OR, MA, 77; OH Univ, PhD, 89. **CAREER** News dir, KAPP-TV, 78-80; news dir, KRDO, 81-82; asst news mgr, KMGH-TV, 82-84; news manager, KHQ-TV, 84-85. **HONORS AND AWARDS** Choice Awd, 94; Sigma Delta Chi Awd, 96; Canadian Embassy Teaching fel, 97. **MEMBERSHIPS** Radio-Television News Directors Asn; Int Commun Asn. **RESEARCH** International communication. **SELECTED PUBLICATIONS** Auth, Our First Television Candidate: Ike Over Stephenson, Journalism Quart, summer 88; Robert Montgomery Presents: Hollywood Debut in the Eisenhower White House, J of Broadcasting and Electronic Media, fall 91; Eisenhower's Congressional Defeat of 1956: Limitations of Television and the GOP, Presidential Studies Quart, spring 92; News Conference on TV: Ike-Age Politics Revisited, Journalism Quart, spring 93; Eisenhower and the Mass Media: Peace, Prosperity, and Prime Time TV, Univ NC Press, 93; When the News is You, US Dept of Interior, 94; Priorities of General Managers and News Directors in Anchor Hiring: Extending the Business-Journalism Dialectic to the Executive Suite, J of Media Economics, autumn 95; Exploring Newsroom Views About Consultants in Local TV: The Effect of Work Roles and Socialization, J of Broadcasting and Electronic Media, fall 96. **CONTACT ADDRESS** Stauffer Hall, Arizona State Univ, Tempe, AZ 85287-1305. **EMAIL** craig.allen@asu.edu

ALLEN, GILBERT BRUCE
PERSONAL Born 01/01/1951, Rockville Centre, NY, m, 1974 **DISCIPLINE** ENGLISH & AMERICAN POETRY **EDUCATION** Cornell Univ, BA, 72, MFA, 74, PhD(English & Am poetry), 77. **CAREER** Instr, Cornell Univ, 75-77; from asst prof to assoc prof, 77-89; prof English, Furman Univ, 89-; asst ed, Epoch, 72-77. **HONORS AND AWARDS** Amon Liner Awd, 84; William Wordsworth Awd, 89; Rainmaker Awd, 90; David Ray Awd, 94; Robert Penn Warren Awd, 94, 95; Porter Fleming Awd, 95; SC Fiction Proj Prize, 87, 89, 92, 98. **MEMBERSHIPS** South Atlantic Mod Lang Asn; NCTE; Poetry Soc of Am. **RESEARCH** Modern poetry; creative writing. **SELECTED PUBLICATIONS** Auth, Edward Thomas and Wilfred Owen: Sixty years after, Postscript, 83; Measuring the Mainstream, Southern Humanities Rev, 83; Heraclitean Dithering: The Criticism and Metacriticism of Stanley Fish, Furman Studies, 12/85; The Arc of a New Covenant: The Idea of the Reader in A.R. Ammons' poems, Pembroke Mag, 86; Canon Fodder: Models for Writers in an Especially Difficult Age, NMex Humanities Rev, 89; Millay and Modernism, Critical Essays on Edna St. Vincent Millay, 94; Dabney Stuart, Contemporary Poets, Dramatists, Essayists, and Novelists of the South, 94; Passionate Detachment in the Lyrics of Jeffers and Yeats, Robinson Jeffers and a Galaxy of Writers, 95; The Night the New Jesus Fell to Earth, Ga Rev, 95; auth, Dragonfly Tie, Poet Lore, 97; auth; The Bunker in the Parsley Fields, Ga Rev, 98; auth, Poor People, Southen Hum Rev, 99; In Everything: Poems 1972-1979, The Lotus Press, 82; Second Chances: Poems, Orchises Press, 91; Commandments at Eleven: Poems, Orchises Press, 94; co-ed, 45/96: The Ninety-Six Sampler of South Carolina Poetry, Ninety-Six Press, 94. **CONTACT ADDRESS** English Dept, Furman Univ, 3300 Poinsett Hwy, Greenville, SC 29613-0438. **EMAIL** gil.allen@furman.edu

ALLEN, HARRIETTE LOUISE
PERSONAL Born 10/24/1943, Savannah, GA, d **DISCIPLINE** ENGLISH **EDUCATION** Fisk Univ, BA 1964; Univ of Wis, MST 1972; George Peabody Col for Tchrs Vanderbilt Univ, PhD English Educ 1980. **CAREER** S America Columbia, foreign exchange tchr of english, 64-65; Chicago Bd of Educ, spanish resource consult, 65-68; WI State Univ, asst proj dir tutorial prog 70-72; Fisk Univ, poet-storyteller 73-; Univ TN, poet-in-residence 77-79; TN State Univ, asst prof of comm, 79-; State of TN, ambassador of letters, 79-. **HONORS AND AWARDS** 1st Black to receive Gov Spotlight Awd; 1st Black poet to be read into the Congressional Record; 1st poet to be

pub in Attica Rebirth Newspaper of Attica Prison. **MEMBERSHIPS** Mem Alpha Kappa Alpha; Natl Theatre Assn; Black Theatre Assn SCETC; Natl Assn for Preservation & Perpetuation of Storytelling; Theta Alpha Phi Hon Forensic Frat; GA Soc of Poets; Natl Soc Pub Poets; Originator of Ballad Folk Theatre Art; star Jubas Jubilee Folktale Traveling Ensemble Co; 1st black storyteller at Natl Storytelling Fest Jonesboro TN. **SELECTED PUBLICATIONS** Auth, "Genesis & Jubas Folk Games". **CONTACT ADDRESS** State of Tennessee, #35 Legislative Plz, Nashville, TN 37219.

ALLEN, JULIA M.
PERSONAL Born 03/15/1947, Portland, OR **DISCIPLINE** ENGLISH **EDUCATION** Univ Calif Riverside, BA, 69; Portland State Univ, MA, 76; Univ Tex Austin, PhD, 88. **CAREER** Instr, Portland State Univ, 77-85; asst instr, Univ Tex Austin, 84-87; acad coordinator, Univ Calif Irvine, 88-90; assoc prof, Sonoma State Univ, 90-. **HONORS AND AWARDS** Fel, Univ Tex Austin, 87-88; Episcopal Women's Hist Res Grant. **MEMBERSHIPS** MLA, NCTE, Rhetoric Soc of Am, Coun of Writing Prog Admin, Nat Women's Studies Assoc, Soc for Critical Exchange. **RESEARCH** History of rhetoric. **SELECTED PUBLICATIONS** Auth, "Dear Comrade: Marian Wharton of The People's College of Fort Scott, Kansas, 1914-1917," Women's Studies Quart, (94); coauth, "Discursive Strategies for Social Change: An Alternative Rhetoric of Argument," Rhetoric Rev, (95); auth, "The Uses and Problems of a 'Manly' Rhetoric: Mary Wollstonecraft's Adaptation of Hugh Blair's Lectures in her two Vindications," Listening to Their Voices; The Rhetorical Activities of Historical Women, ed Molly Meijer Wertheimer, (97); auth, "That Accursed Aesopian Language: Prosecutorial Framing of Linguistic Evidence in US V Fost, 1949," Rhetoric and Public Affairs, (01). **CONTACT ADDRESS** Sonoma State Univ, 1801 E Cotati Ave, Rohnert Pk, CA 94928. **EMAIL** jallen47@earthlink.net

ALLEN, M. AUSTIN
DISCIPLINE FILM **EDUCATION** Univ CA Berkley, BA; Ohio Univ, MA, PhD. **CAREER** Assoc prof, Communications, Cleveland State Univ. **SELECTED PUBLICATIONS** Auth, Claiming open spaces, 86. **CONTACT ADDRESS** Commun Dept, Cleveland State Univ, 1983 E 24th St, Cleveland, OH 44115. **EMAIL** a.allen@csuohio.edu

ALLEN, MARK
PERSONAL Born 08/13/1952, Green Bay, WI, m, 1982 **DISCIPLINE** ENGLISH, LITERATURE **EDUCATION** St Norbert Col, BA; AR State Univ, MA; Univ IL at Champaign-Urbana, PhD. **CAREER** Assoc prof; taught at, Univ IL, AR State Univ & UTSA; taught in, UTSA London Semr Prog, 94; bibliogr, New Chaucer Soc; des & moderator, Online Chaucer Bibliog. **HONORS AND AWARDS** TX System's Chancellor's Coun Outstanding Tchg Awd, 90; UTSA President's Distinguished Teaching Award, 00; contrib, annotated bibliog for eng stud cd-rom. **RESEARCH** Medieval lit and cult; Chaucer; Arthurian lit, the hist of the Eng lang; fantasy lit; technol applications in the hum. **SELECTED PUBLICATIONS** Coauth, The Essential Chaucer: An Annotated Bibliography of Major Modern Studies, G K Hall, 87; articles in, Stud in the Age of Chaucer, S Cent Rev, Arthurian Interpretations & Lit Onomastics Stud; auth, "Mirth and Bourgeois Masculinity in Chaucer's Host," in Masculinities in Chaucer, ed. Peter G. Beidler (Boydell and Brewer, 98), 1-12. **CONTACT ADDRESS** Col of Fine Arts and Hum, Univ of Texas, San Antonio, 6900 N Loop 1604 W, San Antonio, TX 78249. **EMAIL** mallen@lonestar.utsa.edu

ALLEN, MYRIA
DISCIPLINE COMMUNICATIONS **EDUCATION** Univ Ky, BA, MA, PhD. **CAREER** Univ Ark **SELECTED PUBLICATIONS** Coauth, Broadcasting's silent majority: Departmental influence on perceptions and conflict, Journalism Quart, 88, Gender differences in perceptions of work: Limited access to decision-making power and supervisory support, Women's Studies Comm, 90; The impact of new technology on employees: A guide to consultants. Consultation, Int Jour, 90; A decade of organizational communication research: Journal articles 1980-1991, Comm Yearbook, 92; Communication and organizational commitment: Perceived organizational support as a mediating factor, Comm Quart, 92; Legimation endeavors: Impression management strategies used by an organization in crisis, Comm Monographs, 94; Communication variables shaping perceived organizational support, Western Jour Comm, 95; The relationship between communication, affect states, and voluntary turnover intentions, Southern Comm Jour, 96; Employee impression management strategy use when discussing their organization's public image. Jour Public Relations Res, 96; Total Quality Management, organizational commitment, perceived organizational support, and intraorganizational communication. Management Comm Quart, 97. **CONTACT ADDRESS** Univ of Arkansas, Fayetteville, Fayetteville, AR 72701. **EMAIL** myria@comp.uark.edu

ALLENTUCK, MARCIA EPSTEIN
PERSONAL Born 06/08/1928, Manhattan, NY, m, 1949, 1 child **DISCIPLINE** ENGLISH **EDUCATION** NYork Univ, BA, 48; Columbia Univ, PhD, 64. **CAREER** Lectr English, Columbia Univ, 55-57 & Hunter Col, 57-59; from lectr to prof English, City Col NY, 59-88; prof Hist of Art, 74-88, prof emer, 88- , Grad Ctr, CUNY; Am Asn Univ Women Morrison fel, Huntington Libr, 58-59; Howard fel, Brown Univ, 66-67; Am Philos Soc res grant, 66-67; Huntington Libr fel, 68; Nat Transl Ctr fel, Univ Tex, 68-69; Chapelbrook Found fel, 70-71; sr res fel, Dumbarton Oaks, Harvard Univ, 72-73; sr res fel, Nat Endowment for Humanities, 73-74; vis fel, Wolfson Col, Oxford Univ, 74-; Brit Acad fel, Newberry Libr, 80; res fel, Schlesingen Libr, Radcliffe Col, Harvard Univ, 82; Swann res fel, 89-90. **HONORS AND AWARDS** Sussman Mem Medal, 46; hon MA, Oxon, 74. **MEMBERSHIPS** Fel Royal Soc of Arts London; Brit Soc Aesthet; MLA; Milton Soc Am; Augustan Reprint Soc. **RESEARCH** History of ideas; comparative literature; aesthetics. **SELECTED PUBLICATIONS** Auth, The works of Henry Needler, Augustan Reprint Soc, 61; Expression, aesthetic science and information theory, Proc Fifth Int Cong Aesthet, Amsterdam, 64; Fuseli and Lavater: Physiognomonical theory and the enlightenment, In: Studies on Voltaire and the Eighteenth Century, Lounz, 67; Isaac Balshevis Şinger, Southern Ill Univ, 69; John Graham's System & Dialetics in modern art, Johns Hopkins Univ, 71; Fuseli and Herder, J Hist Ideas, 1/74. **CONTACT ADDRESS** 5 W 86th St Apt 12B, New York, NY 10024-3665.

ALLERT, BEATE I.
PERSONAL Born 01/05/1954, Stuttgart, Germany, m, 1997 **DISCIPLINE** LITERATURE **EDUCATION** Univ Tubingen, BA, 76; Univ Calif, MA, 85; PhD, 87. **CAREER** Teaching Asst, Univ Calif, 76-83; Instr, Mills Col, 84; Instr, Mt Holyoke Col, 84-85; Asst Prof, Mt Holyoke Col, 85-91; From Asst Prof to Assoc Prof, Purdue Univ, 91-. **HONORS AND AWARDS** Mt Holyoke Sabbatical Fel, 88-89; Mellon Grant; NEH Fel, 84; Summer XL Res Found Grant, Purdue Univ, 92; Fac Res Grant, Purdue Univ, 94-95. **MEMBERSHIPS** ACTFL, AATG, ASECS, GSA, GSNA, IAPL, IHS, Int Lessing Soc, JPG, MLA, N Am Soc for the Study of Romanticism, SLS, WIG. **RESEARCH** Enlightenment, classicism, romanticism, 18th 19th and 20th-Century cultural studies, literary theory, metaphor theory, visual theory, optics, semiotics, feminisms, modes of perception, literature and visual arts. **SELECTED PUBLICATIONS** Auth, "Lessing, Novalis, Schiller: Romantisierung und Medienspiel," Ethik un Asthetik: Werke und Werte in der Literatur vom 18, Peter Lang Publ (95): 223-233; auth, "Text-Image-Relations: Seeing and Antiocular Discourse in Berkeley, Jean Paul and Goethe," Trans of the Ninth Int Cong on the Enlightenment: Actes du congres int des Lumieres, Voltaire Found (96): 789-792; auth, "About a Burning Building in Eco and Lessing, or: How to Process Messages," Lessing Yearbk 29 (97): 57-86; auth, "Mannerism," The Feminist Encycl of Ger Lit, Greenwood Pr (97): 299-300; auth, "Mystical Female Figures," The Feminist Encycl of Ger Lit, Greenwood Pr (97): 342-343; auth, "Semiotics," The Feminist Encycl of Ger Lit, Greenwood Pr (97): 477-479; auth, "Theorizing Visual Language in George Berkeley and Jean Paul," Studies in Eighteenth-Century Cult 27 (98): 307-342. **CONTACT ADDRESS** Dept Lang & Lit, Purdue Univ, West Lafayette, Stanley Coulter Hall, West Lafayette, IN 47907. **EMAIL** allert@purdue.edu

ALLEY, HENRY MELTON
PERSONAL Born 01/27/1945, Seattle, WA **DISCIPLINE** ENGLISH, LITERATURE **EDUCATION** Stanford Univ, BA, 67; Cornell Univ, MA, 69; PhD, 71. **CAREER** Assoc prof, Col Ozarks, 72-75; assoc prof, Univ Idaho, 75-82; prof, Univ Ore Honors Col, 82-. **HONORS AND AWARDS** Phi Beta Kappa; Distinguished Teaching Fac Achievement Awd, Univ Ore. **MEMBERSHIPS** AWP; MLA. **RESEARCH** George Eliot; creative writing; prose; fiction. **SELECTED PUBLICATIONS** Auth, Through Glass, 79; auth, The Lattice, 86; auth, Umbrella of Glass, 88; auth, The Guest for Anominity: The Novels of George Eliot, 97. **CONTACT ADDRESS** English Dept, Univ of Oregon, Eugene, OR 97403-1205. **EMAIL** halley@coregon.edu

ALLISON, JONATHAN
PERSONAL Born 05/08/1958, Belfast, North Ireland, m, 1999, 2 children **DISCIPLINE** ENGLISH LITERATURE **EDUCATION** Queen's Univ, BA, 80; PGCE, 81; Univ Mich, MA, 83; PhD, 88. **CAREER** Asst prof to assoc prof, Univ of Ky, 88-. **HONORS AND AWARDS** Vis Fel, Inst of Advan Studies in Humanities, Edinburgh Univ, Scotland, 96. **MEMBERSHIPS** MLA, S Atlantic Mod Lang Assoc; Am Conf for Irish Studies. **RESEARCH** Modern British and Irish Literature. **SELECTED PUBLICATIONS** Ed, Yeat's Political Identities, Univ of Mich Pr, 96; auth, Patrick Kavanagh: A Reference Guide, G.K. Hall, 96. **CONTACT ADDRESS** Dept English, Univ of Kentucky, 1215 Patterson Tower, Lexington, KY 40506-0001. **EMAIL** jalliso@pop.uky.edu

ALLMAN, EILEEN JORGE
PERSONAL Born 06/22/1940, Mt. Vernon, NY, m, 1962, 1 child **DISCIPLINE** RENAISSANCE LITERATURE **EDUCATION** City Univ New York, BA, 61; Syracuse Univ, MA, 67, PhD, 73. **CAREER** Assoc prof, 70-98 Herbert H Lehman Col, CUNY **MEMBERSHIPS** MLA; Shakespeare Soc; Malone Soc. **RESEARCH** Jacobean tragedy; Shakespeare; Spenser. **SELECTED PUBLICATIONS** Auth, Player-King and Adversary: Two Faces of Play in Shakespeare, La St Univ Press, 81; auth, Jacobean Revenge Tragedy and the Politics of Virtue, Univ Delaware Press, 99. **CONTACT ADDRESS** 28 Frances Dr, Katonah, NY 10536. **EMAIL** allmanej@cs.com

ALLMAN, WILLIAM ARTHUR
PERSONAL Born 06/10/1924, Tiffin, OH, w, 1950, 3 children **DISCIPLINE** THEATRE ARTS, SPEECH, FILM STUDIES **EDUCATION** Heidelberg Col, BA, 49; Oh Univ, MA, 51; Oh State Univ, PhD, 60. **CAREER** Teacher & dir drama, High Sch, Ohio, 51-53; asst prof English & theatre arts, Ohio Northern Univ, 53-55; from asst prof to assoc prof speech & theatre, 55-77, dir drama, 55-81, prof speech & theatre, Baldwin-Wallace Col, 77-98. **HONORS AND AWARDS** Lifetime Achievement; Award from Cleveland Critics, 81; Grindstone (Person-of-the-Year) Award, in Berea, 83; Continuing Education Award from B-W Students, 87; Theatre Named in His Honor, Baldwin-Wallace Col, 98; Founder & Managing Dir of the Berea Summer Theatre, 57-96. **MEMBERSHIPS** Nat Theatre Conf; Theta Alpha Phi, Ohio Com Theatre Assoc, Ohio Theatre Alliance. **RESEARCH** Interpretative reading; theatre; films. **CONTACT ADDRESS** 625 Riverside Ave, Haverhill, MA 01830. **EMAIL** biga7@aol.com

ALLMENDINGER, BLAKE
PERSONAL Born 04/02/1959, Lawton, OK, s **DISCIPLINE** ENGLISH **EDUCATION** Harvard Univ, AB, 81; Oxford Univ, MA, 83; Univ Pa, PhD, 89. **CAREER** Asst prof, 89-95, ASSOC PROF, UNIV CALIF, LOS ANGELES, 95-. **HONORS AND AWARDS** Ahmanson/Getty fel, 93-94. **RESEARCH** Lit, pop cult Am West **SELECTED PUBLICATIONS** Co-ed, Over the Edge: Remapping the American WEst, Univ Calif Press, 98; auth, Ten Most Wanted: The New Western Literature, Routledge, 98; auth, The Cowboy: Representations of Labor in an American Work Culture, Oxford Univ Press, 92. **CONTACT ADDRESS** Dept of English, Univ of California, Los Angeles, Box 90095-1930, Los Angeles, CA 90095-1530. **EMAIL** allmendi@humnet.ucla.edu

ALPERT, JULIE
PERSONAL Born 03/29/1955, San Francisco, CA, m, 1 child **DISCIPLINE** ENGLISH **EDUCATION** Univ Calif Davis, BA; Columbia Univ, MA **CAREER** Teacher, ACHNA, Spain, 86-87; teaching fel, Harvard Univ, 87; teacher, UCSB, 88-89; assoc, prof, Santa Barbara City Col, 89-. **MEMBERSHIPS** TESOL **RESEARCH** Adult second language acquisition. **CONTACT ADDRESS** Dept English As A Second Lang, Santa Barbara City Col, 721 Cliff Dr, Santa Barbara, CA 93109-2312.

ALSEN, EBERHARD
PERSONAL Born 10/26/1939, Nuremberg, Germany, m, 1986, 6 children **DISCIPLINE** AMERICAN LITERATURE **EDUCATION** Univ Bonn, Germany, BA, 62; Ind Univ, MA, 65, PhD, 67. **CAREER** Asst prof, 66-69, Univ Minn; assoc prof, prof, 69-98, SUNY, Cortland. **HONORS AND AWARDS** Fulbright Prof, 75-76, 81-82, Univ Tubingen; vis prof, 93-95, Univ Trier. **MEMBERSHIPS** MLA. **RESEARCH** Contemporary Amer Fiction. **SELECTED PUBLICATIONS** Auth, Salinger's Glass Stone's as a Composite Novel, Whitston, 83; auth, American Short Stories on Film: Bartleby, Langenscheidt, 86; auth, Romantic Postmodernism in Am Fiction, Rodopi, 96; auth, Norman Mailer, Contemp Jew Am Novelist, Greenwood, 97; auth, Ernest J. Gtaines, Toni Morrison, Contemp African-Am Novelist, Greenwood, 98; ed, The New Romanticism: A Collection of Critical Essays, Garland, 00. **CONTACT ADDRESS** Dept of English, SUNY, Col at Cortland, Cortland, NY 13045. **EMAIL** ebalsen@twcny.rr.com

ALTEGOER, DIANA B.
DISCIPLINE EARLY ENGLISH LITERATURE **EDUCATION** Vassar Col, BA, 84; Oxford Univ, MA, 87, PhD, 93. **CAREER** Engl, Old Dominion Univ. **RESEARCH** Shakespeare, Renaissance non-dramatic literature. **SELECTED PUBLICATIONS** Areas: Baconian science and English Renaissance culture. **CONTACT ADDRESS** Old Dominion Univ, 4100 Powhatan Ave, BAL 442, Norfolk, VA 23058. **EMAIL** DAltegoer@odu.edu

ALTER, JUDY
PERSONAL Born 07/22/1938, Chicago, IL, d, 4 children **DISCIPLINE** ENGLISH **EDUCATION** Univ Chica, BA, 61; Trumen St Univ, MeD, 64; Texas Christ Univ, PhD, 70. **CAREER** Dir Pub Rel, Univ N Texas Heal Sci Cen, 78-80; Editor, TCU Press, 82-86; Dir, TCU Press, 87-. **HONORS AND AWARDS** Spur Awd Best West Novel; West Hert Wrangler Awds Nat Cowboy Hall of Fame; Texas Inst of Letters Best Juvenile. **MEMBERSHIPS** TX Inst Of Letters; West Writ of Am; Women Writ the West. **RESEARCH** Women in the American west. **SELECTED PUBLICATIONS** Auth, Beauty Pagents: Tiaras, Roses and Runways, Franklin Watts (Danbury, CT), 97; auth, Amusement Parks: Rollercoasters, Ferris Wheels and Cotton Candy, Franklin Watts (Danbury, CT), 97; auth, Meet Me at the Fair: County, State, and World Fairs and Exhibitions, Frankling Watts (Danbury, CT), 97; auth, Sam Houston, Grolier Inc (Danbury, CT), 97; auth, Wild West Shows: Rough Riders

and Sure Shots, Franklin Watts (Danbury CT), 97; auth, Cissie Palmer, Franklin Watts (Danbury, CT), 98; auth, The Sante Fe Trail, Grolier Inc. (Danbury, CT), 98; auth, Extraordinary Women of the American West, Children's Press (Danbury, CT), 99; coauth, Legend, Leisure (NY), 99; auth, Governor Ann Richards of Texas, Franklin Watts (NY), forthcoming. **CONTACT ADDRESS** TCU Press, Box 298300, Fort Worth, TX 76129. **EMAIL** j.alter@tcu.edu

ALTIERI, CHARLES F.
PERSONAL Born 11/11/1942, New York, NY, m, 1993, 2 children **DISCIPLINE** ENGLISH LITERATURE **EDUCATION** LeMoyne Col, AB, 64; Univ NC, Chapel Hill, PhD, 69. **CAREER** SUNY Buffalo, 68-75; Univ Washington, 76-92; Univ Calif, Berkeley, 93-. **HONORS AND AWARDS** NEH Summer Fel, 80; Guggenheim Fel, 80-81, Ctr for Advanced Study in Behav Sci. **MEMBERSHIPS** MLA, IAPL. **RESEARCH** 20th century American poetry, philosophy and the arts. **SELECTED PUBLICATIONS** Auth, Act and Quality; auth, Enlarging the Temple; auth, Self and Sensibility in Contemporary American Poetry; auth, Painterly Abstraction in Modernist American Poetry; auth, Subjective Agency. **CONTACT ADDRESS** Dept English, Univ of California, Berkeley, 322 Wheeler Hall, Berkeley, CA 94720. **EMAIL** altieri@uclink4.berkeley.edu

ALTMAN, RICK (CHARLES FREDERICK)
PERSONAL Born 01/09/1945, De Ridder, LA, m, 1967, 1 child **DISCIPLINE** FRENCH LITERATURE; CINEMA **EDUCATION** Duke Univ, AB & MA, 66; Yale Univ, PhD, 71. **CAREER** Fulbright-Hayes fel and lectr, Am studies, Univ Paris X, Nanterre, 70-71; asst prof French and comp lit, Bryn Mawr Col, 71-74; asst prof French, 74-77; assoc prof French and comp lit, 77-82; assoc prof Film, French and Comp Lit, Univ Iowa, 82-86; prof French & Film, 86-99; fel, Cornell Univ Soc for Hum, 74-75; dir, Paris Film Ctr, 80-81; vis prof, Univ Paris III-Censier, 80-81; prof, Cinema & Comp Lit, 99-; vis prof, Univ de Provence, 96; dir, The Living Nickelodion, 99-. **HONORS AND AWARDS** Russell B Nye Prize, Jour Pop Cult, 80; French nat. Decoration, Chevalier de L'Ordre des Palmes Academiques, 84; Soc for Cinema Studies prize, 84; French film critics award for best film book publ. in 1992, 92; NEW Fel, 90-91; Soc for Cinema Studies 2000 Katherine S. Kovacs prize for best film book published in 1999. **MEMBERSHIPS** MLA; SCS; Domitor. **RESEARCH** Narrative; 12th century Western culture; Film. **SELECTED PUBLICATIONS** Auth, "A Semantic/Syntactic Approach to Film Genre," Cenema J 23, no. 3 (Spring 84): 6-18; auth, The American Film Musical, Ind Univ Pr (Bloomington), 87; auth, The Video Connection: Integrating Video into Language Teaching, Houghton Mifflin (Boston), 88; auth, "Dickens, Griffith, and Film Theory Today," South Atlantic Q 88, no 2 (Spring 89): 321-59; ed, Sound Theory/Sound Practice, Routledge/Am Film Inst (NYork), 92; ed, "The State of Sound Studies," ispec issue of IRIS 27 (99); co-ed, "Global Experiments in Early Synchronous Sound," spec issue of Film Hist, 11:4 (99); auth, "Film Sound--All of It," IRIS 27 (99): 31-48; auth, Film/Genre, Ind Univ Pr & British Film Inst (Bloomington & London), 99; co-ed, The Sounds of Early Cinema, Ind Univ Pr (Bloomington), forthcoming. **CONTACT ADDRESS** Dept of Cinema & Comp Lit, Univ of Iowa, Iowa City, IA 52242. **EMAIL** rick-altman@uiowa.edu

ALTON, ANNE
PERSONAL Born, Canada **DISCIPLINE** ENGLISH **EDUCATION** Univ Calgary, BA, 85; MA, 87; Univ Toronto, PhD, 95. **CAREER** Asst prof, Central Mich Univ, 97-. **HONORS AND AWARDS** Hon Res Assoc, Univ of Sydney, Australia; Univ of Toronto Open Doctoral Fel. **MEMBERSHIPS** Bronte Soc; ChLA; Friends of Osborne & Lillian H. Smith Collections; IRSCL; MLA. **RESEARCH** Victorian Literature, Children's and Young Adult Literature, The Novel and the Picture Book, Louisa May Alcott, Charlotte Bronte, L.M. Montgomery, Maurice Sendak, Anthony Browne. **SELECTED PUBLICATIONS** Auth, "Education in Victorian Fact and Fiction: Kay-Shuttleworth and Dickens's Hard Times", Dickens Quarterly 9.1 (92): 67-80; auth, "Books in the Novels of Charlotte Bronte", Bronte Soc Transactions 21.7, (96): 265-74; auth, "John Knowles' A Separate Peace" and "Chaim Potok's The Chosen", Exploring Novels, Gale Res, 97; auth, "Changing the World: A Profile of Writer JoAnne James", Can Children's Lit 85, (97): 31-40; auth, "Bring the child in you out to play!: Children's Entertainment: Drama, Song, and Dance", Can Children's Lit 90, (98): 17-27. **CONTACT ADDRESS** Dept English, Central Michigan Univ, 100 W Preston Rd, Mount Pleasant, MI 48859-0001. **EMAIL** anne.alton@cmich.edu

ALVEY, RICHARD GERALD
PERSONAL Born 11/08/1935, Evansville, IN, m, 1967 **DISCIPLINE** FOLKLORISTICS, ENGLISH **EDUCATION** Univ Ky, BA, 69, MSLA, 70; Univ Pa, AM, 71, PhD(folkloristics), 74. **CAREER** Asst prof, 74-80, assoc prof folklore, Univ KY, 80-. **HONORS AND AWARDS** Mem, Coun on Exp Educ, 74-; Nat Endowment Humanities res grant, 76. **MEMBERSHIPS** Am Folklore Soc; Folklore Soc (British); Appalachian Studies Conf, 78; Asn Folklorists in South; Int Soc for Folk Narrative Res; bd mem, Appalachian Studies Conf, 78-. **RESEARCH** Folkloristics; Appalachian studies, regional studies; English. **SELECTED PUBLICATIONS** Auth, Phillips Barry and Anglo-American Folksong Scholarship, J Folklore Inst, 73; Folk beliefs about food & eating in Kentucky, Ky Hospitality, 76; A second look at the secondary ballad, Southern Folklore Quart, 78; Coyote tales, Enzyklopadie des Marchen **CONTACT ADDRESS** Dept of English, Univ of Kentucky, 500 S Limestone St, Lexington, KY 40506-0003.

AMABILE, GEORGE
PERSONAL Born 05/29/1936, Jersey City, NJ **DISCIPLINE** ENGLISH **EDUCATION** Amherst Col, AB, 57; Univ Minn, MA, 61; Univ Conn, PhD, 69. **CAREER** Lectr to assoc prof, 63-86, prof Eng, Univ Manitoba, 87-. **HONORS AND AWARDS** Hunter Prize; Anna Von Helmholz Phelan Prize, Univ Minn, 61; Can Coun grants, 68, 81-82, 95-96; Can Authors Asn Nat Prize Poetry, 83. **MEMBERSHIPS** W Can Publ Asn; League Can Poets. **RESEARCH** Canadian writing, Contemporary Poetry and modern lit. **SELECTED PUBLICATIONS** Auth, Blood Ties, 72; auth, Open Country, 76; auth, Flower and Song, 77; auth, Ideas of Shelter, 81; auth, The Presence of Fire, 82; auth, Four of a Kind 94; auth, Rumors of Paradise/Rumors of War, 95; co-founder & ed, The Far Point; ed, Northern Light; past ed, The Ivory Tower; past ed, The Penny Paper. **CONTACT ADDRESS** Dept of English, Univ of Manitoba, Winnipeg, MB, Canada R3T 2N2. **EMAIL** gamabile@home.com

AMASON, PATRICIA
PERSONAL Born 03/16/1957, El Dorado, AR, m, 1995, 1 child **DISCIPLINE** INTERPERSONAL COMMUNICATION **EDUCATION** Univ Ark, BSE, 80; Univ Ky, MA, 83; Purdue Univ, PhD, 93. **CAREER** Comm Stu, Univ Ark **HONORS AND AWARDS** Named "Favorite Teacher" by staff of Reid and Futrall Residence Halls, Univ of Ark, 99; recipient of outstanding teacher award from Chi Omega Sorority, Univ of Ark, 98-99; Nominee for Master Teacher Award, Univ of Ark, 98-99; Charles and Nadine Baum Teaching grant, Univ of Ark, 98; Undergraduate Res Fel, Sci Information Liason Office-SILO udnergraduate res fel prog, 96-97, 98-99; Top paper, Applied Commun Division, annual convention of the Southern States Commun Asn, 97; Top Three Paper, Applied Commun Division, annual convention of the Southern States Commun Asn, 99; Teacher of the Year, Dept of Commun, Univ of Ark, 95-96; Outstanding Fac Mem, Univ of Ark Panhellenic Council, 95; Teaching Incentive grant, Fulbright College of Arts and Sciences, Univ of Ark, 95; Finalist for the Outstanding Young Teacher Award, Central States Comm Asn, 94; Fac Res Grant, Univ of Tulsa, 89; Top Paper, Instructional and Developmental Division, Int Commun Asn, 86; Top Four Paper, Commun and Aging Commision, Speech Commun Asn, 86; Teacher of the Year Award, Huntsville High School, 81. **MEMBERSHIPS** Nat Commun Asn; Southern States Commun Asn. **RESEARCH** Influence of social cognition on the production of supportive messages and perceptions of sources of social support in organizational, dyadic, and family contexts. **SELECTED PUBLICATIONS** Coauth, "Popular, Rejected, and Supportive Preadolescents: Social Cognitive and Communicative Characteristics," in Communication Yearbook 10, ed. M.L. McLaughlin (Beverly Hills, Calif, Sage, 87); coauth, "Preadolescent Support Networks: Social-cognitive and Communicative Characteristics of Natural "Peer Counselors", Jour Thought 22 (87): 31-37; coauth, "Intraorganizational Communication, Perceived Organizational Support and Gender," Sex Roles 37 (97): 955-977; coauth, "Gender Differences in the Relationship Between Social Support and Hispanic Emotional Acculturative Stress," Communciation Studies 49 (98): 139-157; coauth, "Social Support and Acculturative Stress in the Multicultural Workplace," Journal of Applied Communication 27 (99); coauth, "Family and Medical Leave Act: Its Communcative Impact on Families and Employers," Communication Law Review 4 (00); coauth, "Intercultural Communicaiton Between Health Care Providers: An Exploration of Intercultural Communication Effectiveness, Cultural Sensitivity, Stress and Anxiety," Health Communication, forthcoming; auth, "Picking and Choosing the Text for the Family Communication Course: Selecting Among a Wealth of Opinions," Journal of Family Communication, forthcoming; coauth, "Relationship Stagnation: Does Calling it Quits Have to be so Painful?" in Readings in Gendered Context, ed. P. Backlund and M.R. Williams (Wadsworth, Belmont, Calif, forthcoming). **CONTACT ADDRESS** Univ of Arkansas, Fayetteville, Fayetteville, AR 72701. **EMAIL** pamason@uark.edu

AMATO, PHILIP P.
DISCIPLINE COMMUNICATION AND COMPUTER APPLICATIONS **EDUCATION** Emerson Col, BA, MA; MI State Univ, PhD. **CAREER** Com, Emerson Col. **SELECTED PUBLICATIONS** Auth, Organizational Patterns and Strategies in Speech Communication, Amato & Ecroyd, 75; Actuarial Mathematics of Finance, Satake, Amato and Gilligan, 94; A Summary of Statistical Inference, Satake, Amato and Hanssou, 94; Mathematical Reasoning: Sets, Logic and Probability, Satake and Amato, 97. **CONTACT ADDRESS** Emerson Col, 100 Beacon Street, Boston, MA 02116-1596.

AMBERG, ANTHONY
PERSONAL Born 03/19/1936, Chicago, IL **DISCIPLINE** ENGLISH **EDUCATION** Univ Chicago AB, 57; AB, 59; AM, 62. **CAREER** Lectr, Roosevelt Univ, 69-. **HONORS AND AWARDS** Phi Beta Kappa, Univ Chicago, 59; Woodrow Wilson Fel, Univ Chicago, 59. **MEMBERSHIPS** Soc for Theatre Res, Am Soc for Eighteenth-Century Studies. **RESEARCH** Edward Moore (1712-1757), British drama and theatre; Eighteenth-Century, British drama and theatre: Nineteenth-Century. **SELECTED PUBLICATIONS** Auth, "Moore's 'Gamester' on the London Stage 1771-1871," Theatre Notebook, 40 (86): 55-60, 144; auth, "The Gamester: A Century of Performances," Theatre REs Int, 15 (90): 105-125; auth, "Opie's 'Gamester': Fancy Picture or Performance Painting?" Apollo, 142 (95): 46-48; auth, Moore, Edward. "The Foundling": A Comedy and "The Gamester": A Tragedy, Univ Del Pr (Newark, NJ), 96. **CONTACT ADDRESS** Dept English, Roosevelt Univ, 430 S Michigan Ave, Chicago, IL 60605.

AMES, CHRISTOPHER
PERSONAL Born 11/21/1956, Teaneck, NJ, m **DISCIPLINE** ENGLISH **EDUCATION** Univ Tex, BA, 78; Stanford Univ, PhD, 84. **CAREER** Dept chair, Thatcher Sch, 84-86; prof and dept chair, Agnes Scott Col, 86-01; provost, Oglethorpe Univ, 01-. **HONORS AND AWARDS** Phi Beta Kappa; Choice Outstanding Acad Book Awd; Fleur Cowles Humanities Fel for Res; Haynes Found Fel, Huntington Libr; Danforth Found Grad Fel. **MEMBERSHIPS** MLA: Soc for the Study of Narrative Lit. **RESEARCH** Parties and festivity in literature; James Joyce; Hollywood in American culture; Hollywood novel; Liberal Arts in Higher Education; Postmodernist Literature. **SELECTED PUBLICATIONS** Auth, "Coover's Comedy of Conflicting Fictional Codes," Critique: Studies in Contemporary Fiction, 90; auth, "Power and the Obscene Word: Discourses of Extremity in Gravity's Rainbow," Contemporary Literature, 90; auth, "The Modernist Canon Narrative: Woolf's Between the Acts and Joyce's 'Oxen of the Sun'," Twentieth Century Lit, 91; auth, "Restoring the Black Man's Lethal Weapon: Race and Sexuality in Contemporary Cop Films," J of Popular Film and Television, 92; auth, "Modernism and Tradition: The Legacies of Belatedness," in Defining Modernism, 93; auth, "Carnivalesque Comedy in Between the Acts," Twentieth Century Lit; auth, "Shakespeare's Grave: The British Hollywood Novel," Twentieth Century Lit; auth, "Movies About the Movies: Hollywood Reflected," Univ Press of Ky, 97. **CONTACT ADDRESS** Dept English, Agnes Scott Col, 141 E College Ave, Atlanta, GA 30030. **EMAIL** cames@agnesscott.edu

AMES, FRANK
PERSONAL Born 04/14/1955, Denver, CO, m, 1974, 2 children **DISCIPLINE** BIBLICAL STUDIES, HEBREW BIBLE, LIBRARY SCIENCE **EDUCATION** Western Bible Col, BS, 77; Denver Sem, MDiv, 80; Univ Denver, MA, 81; PhD, 98. **CAREER** Adj instr, Denver Sem, 81-83; lib, Western Bib Col, 83-85; act dean, 85-89; asst dean, Colo Christ Col, 89-92; dean, assoc prof, Sch Bib Stud, Colo Christ Univ, 92-97; lib, prof, 97-. **HONORS AND AWARDS** Student Gov Asn Awd; Hebrew Fel. **MEMBERSHIPS** SBL; AAR. **RESEARCH** Social world of the Bible. **SELECTED PUBLICATIONS** Auth, "Levirate Marriage," in the New Intl Dictionary of Old Testament Theology and Exegesis, Zondervan, 97. **CONTACT ADDRESS** Dept Bible Studies, Colorado Christian Univ, 180 S Garrison St, Denver, CO 80226-1053. **EMAIL** fames@ccu.edu

AMOS, MARK ADDISON
DISCIPLINE LITERATURE **EDUCATION** Cornell Univ, AB, 81; Univ Miami, MA, 87; Duke Univ, PhD, 94. **CAREER** Grad instr, Univ of Miami, 85-86; asst, Univ Miami, 86-87; ed, Fuqua Sch Bus, 90; assoc coord, Duke Univ, 93; wrtg coord/instr, Duke Univ, 88-94; vis asst prof, Bates Col, 94-95; asst prof, Wilkes 96-98; asst prof Southern Ill Univ. **HONORS AND AWARDS** Tchg scholar, Univ of Miami, 85-87; outstanding tchg asst, Univ Miami, 87; master's thesis awaded distinction, Univ Miami, 87; Univ travel fel(s), Univ Miami, 88-94; tchg fel, Am Asn Col(s) Jr, 91-92; res fel(s), Duke Univ, 92-94; curriculum wrtg grant, 97; res fel, 97-98; fel, 97-98. **MEMBERSHIPS** Medieval Acad of Am; Early Bk Soc; MLA; Medieval Feminist Asn. **RESEARCH** Middle English literature and culture; Continental Medieval literatures and cultures; Medieval reading practices and early book production; Representations of class relations; Issues of representation; Gender studies; Literature and identity; Critical theory. **SELECTED PUBLICATIONS** Auth, "Rev, William Caxton and English Literary Culture, by N F Blake," Chaucer Yearbook 3, 96; auth, "Rev. Courtliness and Literature in Medieval England," in Studies in the Age of Chaucer, ed. David Burnley (99); auth, "'Cum Nimio Cachinno:' The Politics of Participation in the Boy Bishop Feast and the Benediktbeurn Ludus de Nativitate," The European Studies Journal 17.2, 18.1 (00-01): 99-114. **CONTACT ADDRESS** Dept. of Eng, So Illinois Univ, Carbondale, Southern Illinois University, Carbondale, IL 62901-4503. **EMAIL** maamos@siu.edu

AMSTUTZ, MARGARET A.
PERSONAL Born 05/22/1967, Knoxville, TN **DISCIPLINE** ENGLISH **EDUCATION** Centre Col, AB, 89; Washington Univ St Louis, MA, 92. **CAREER** Asst to Pres, Centre Col, 89-

91; TA, Washington Univ St Louis, 92-97; proj consult, pub dir, prog officer, Mo Humanities Coun, 92-97; asst to pres, Univ Ga, 97-. **HONORS AND AWARDS** Phi Beta Kappa; WashingtonUniv Hurst Fel, 97. **MEMBERSHIPS** NAPAHE, MLA. **RESEARCH** 19th-Century American Literature **SELECTED PUBLICATIONS** Auth, "Sarah Orne Jewett," Am Nat Biog, (Oxford Univ Pr, 98). **CONTACT ADDRESS** Office of the Pres, Univ of Georgia, Admin Bldg, Athens, GA 30606. **EMAIL** mamstutz@arches.uga.edu

ANATOL, GISELLE L.
DISCIPLINE ENGLISH **EDUCATION** Yale Univ, BA, 92; Univ Pa, MA, 94, PhD, 98. **CAREER** Instr, Univ Pa, 93-97; asst prof, Univ Kans, 98-. **HONORS AND AWARDS** Andrew W. Mellon Dissertation Fel, 96-97; Irene Diamond Dissertation Fel, Leadership Alliance, 97-98. **MEMBERSHIPS** ALA; ASA; MLA; Asn of Caribbean Women Writers and Scholars. **RESEARCH** Caribbean and African-American literature. **SELECTED PUBLICATIONS** Auth, dis, Mother Countries, Motherlands, & Mother Love: Representations of Motherhood in 20th-Century Caribbean Women's Literature. **CONTACT ADDRESS** Dept of English, Univ of Kansas, Lawrence, 3114 Wescoe Hall, Lawrence, KS 66045. **EMAIL** ganatol@falcon.cc.ukans.edu

ANDERSON, CAROLYN M.
PERSONAL Born 01/11/1939, Cleveland, OH, m, 1965, 2 children **DISCIPLINE** COMMUNICATION STUDIES **EDUCATION** Univ of Detroit, BA, 85; Wayne State Univ, MA, 88; Kent State Univ, PhD, 92. **CAREER** Adj prof, Univ of Detroit, 87-88; tchg fel, Kent State Univ, 88-91; vis asst prof, John Carroll Univ, 91-94; vis asst prof, Univ of Akron, 94-95; assoc prof, Univ of Akron, 95- . **HONORS AND AWARDS** Kent State Grad Student Outstanding Tchg Awd, 89/90; ICA Awd Outstanding Grad Tchr, 89, 90. **MEMBERSHIPS** Nat Commun Asn; Central States Commun Asn. **RESEARCH** Hea Commun; Small Group Commun; Organizational Commun. **SELECTED PUBLICATIONS** Coauth, Nonverbal Behavior and rapport during nurse-practitioner-patient interviews, Mich Asn of Speech Commun Jour, 29, 94; Why employees speak to bosses and coworkers: Motives, gender, and organizational satisfaction, Jour of Bus Commun, 32, 95; Communication traits: A cross-generation investigation, Commun Res Reports, 13, 96; Argumentativeness and verbal aggressiveness, Jour of Social Behavior & Personality, 11; 96; The relationship between perceived understanding and self-disclosure in the sibling relationships, Commun Res Reports, 14, 97; Verbal aggression in sibling relationships, Commun Quarterly, 45, 97; Aggressive communication traits: How similar are young adults and their parents in argumentativeness, assertiveness, and verbal aggression, Western Jour of Commun, 61, 97; Reliability, separation of factors, and sex differences on the assertiveness-responsiveness measure: A Chinese sample, Commun Res Reports, 14, 97; Verbal aggression: A study of the relationship berween communication traits and feelings about a verbally aggressive television show, Commun Res Reports, 14, 97; The cognitive flexibility scale: Three validity studies, Commun Reports, 11, 98; Motives for communicating with family and friends: A Chinese Study, The Howard Jour of Commun, 9, 98; auth, The Handbook of group communication: Theory & research (Thousand Oaks, CA: Sage Publications, 99), 139-163; auth, Let's Talk: A cognitive skills approach to interpersonal communication, Dubuque, IA: Kendall/Hunt, 00. **CONTACT ADDRESS** Dept of Communication, Univ of Akron, Akron, OH 44325-1003. **EMAIL** canders@uakron.edu

ANDERSON, CELIA CATLETT
DISCIPLINE CHILDREN'S LITERATURE **EDUCATION** Univ CT, MA; Univ RI, PhD. **CAREER** Eng Dept, Eastern Conn State Univ **SELECTED PUBLICATIONS** Coauth, Nonsense Literature for Children: From Aesop to Seuss. **CONTACT ADDRESS** Eastern Connecticut State Univ, 83 Windham Street, Willimantic, CT 06226. **EMAIL** ANDERSONC@ECSU.CTSTATEU.EDU

ANDERSON, CHRIS
DISCIPLINE CREATIVE NONFICTION, WRITING AND READING **EDUCATION** Gonzaga Univ Univ, BA, 77, MA, 79; Univ Wash, PhD, 83. **CAREER** Engl, Oregon St Univ. **SELECTED PUBLICATIONS** Auth, Style as Argument: Contemporary American Nonfiction. Southern Ill Univ Press, 87; Free/Style: A Direct Approach to Writing. Houghton-Mifflin, 92. Edge Effects: Notes from an Oregon Forest. Univ Iowa Press, 93; Coauth, Forest of Voices: Reading and Writing the Environment, Mayfield, 95. **CONTACT ADDRESS** Oregon State Univ, Corvallis, OR 97331-4501. **EMAIL** canderson@orst.edu

ANDERSON, EARL ROBERT
PERSONAL Born 09/16/1943, Virginia, MN, m, 1967, 2 children **DISCIPLINE** POETRY **EDUCATION** Univ Minn, BA, 65; Univ Ore, MA, 67, PhD, 70. **CAREER** Asst prof, 70-74, assoc prof Eng, Cleveland State Univ, 74-. **MEMBERSHIPS** Medieval Acad Am; MLA. **RESEARCH** Old English poetry; Middle English poetry. **SELECTED PUBLICATIONS** Auth, Cynewolf: Style, Structure and Theme on His Poetry, Fairleigh Dickinson University Press, 98. **CONTACT ADDRESS** Dept of English, Cleveland State Univ, 1983 E 24th St, Cleveland, OH 44115-2440. **EMAIL** anderson_earl@hotmail.com

ANDERSON, ERIC GARY
PERSONAL Born 03/13/1960, Plainfield, NJ **DISCIPLINE** AMERICAN INDIAN LITERATURE **CAREER** Teaching asst and lectr, Rutgers Univ, 82-93; lectr, Univ of Pa, 94; vis lectr, Rutgers Univ, 94-95; asst prof, Okla State Univ, 95-. **HONORS AND AWARDS** Okla Found for the Humanities Res Grant, 96; Dean's Incentive Grant, 96-97; Dean's Incentive Grant, 97-98; Elected Assoc Fel, Center for Great Plains Studies, Univ of Nebr, 97-; Oklah Found for the Humanities Res Grant, 98. **MEMBERSHIPS** Asn for the Study of Am Indian Literatures; Wordcraft Circle of Native Writers and Storytellers (Non-Native Voting Member); Modern Lang Asn; South Central modren Lang Asn; AM Studies Asn; Western Lit Asn; Multi-Ethnic Literatures of the United States. **RESEARCH** Late 19th and American Indian literature; 20th century American literature. **SELECTED PUBLICATIONS** Rev, of Mark Wigley, The Architecture of Deconstruction: Derrida's Haunt, MIT Press, (93); auth, "Manifest Dentistry, or Teachnig Oral Narrative in McTeague and Old Man Coyote," in Tricksterism in Turn-of-the-Century American Literature: A Multicultural Perspective, UP of New England, (94): 61-78; auth, "The Literature of Oklaahoma," Louisiana State UP, (forthcoming); rev, of The Oxford History of World Cinema, National Forum: Phi Kappa Phi Journal, (Oxford UP, 97): 50-51; rev, of The Secret Life of John C. Van Dyke: Selected Letters (U of Nevada P, 98): 167-168; auth, "Drivving the Red Road; Powwow Highway," in Hollywood's Indian: Th ePortrayal of Native Americans in Film, (UP of Kentucky, 98): 137-152; rev, on Arnold Krupat, The Turn to the Native, (U of Nebr), and Kathleen Donovan, Feminist Readings of Native American Literatue, (U of Ariz P), Am Indian Quarterly, 99; auth, American Indiain Literature and the Southwest: Contexts and Dispositions, Austin: The Univ of Tex Press, 99; auth, "States of Being in the Dark: Removal and Survival in Linda Hogan's Mean Spirit," Great Plains Quarterly, (00): 55-67; auth, "Situating American Indian Poetry: Place, Community, and the Question of Genre," Soiccited for Speak to Me Words: Essays on Contemporary American Indain Poetry, U of Ariz P, 01. **CONTACT ADDRESS** Dept of Eng, Oklahoma State Univ, Stillwater, 205 Morrill Hall, Stillwater, OK 74078-4069. **EMAIL** ericg@osuunx.uss.okstate.edu

ANDERSON, FLOYD D.
PERSONAL Born 04/07/1940, Pocatello, ID, d, 1 child **DISCIPLINE** COMMUNICATION STUDIES **EDUCATION** Idaho State Univ, BA; Univ Kans, MA; Univ Ill, PhD. **CAREER** Prof. **HONORS AND AWARDS** Past President, Eastern Communication Association; 2 National Endowment for the Humanities Fellowships; 86 Chair; Committee of Scholars; Eastern Communication Association. **MEMBERSHIPS** Eastern Commun Asn; National Communication Ass; Kenneth Burke Society; Internation Society for the History of Rhetoric; American Branch. **RESEARCH** Contemporary Rhetroical Theory; History of Rhetoric; Public Address. **SELECTED PUBLICATIONS** Auth, pubs on rhetorical theory and criticism. **CONTACT ADDRESS** Dept of Communication, SUNY, Col at Brockport, Brockport, NY 14420. **EMAIL** fanderso@po.brockport.edu

ANDERSON, GORDON A.
PERSONAL Born 01/16/1947, Rockford, IL, m, 1970, 3 children **DISCIPLINE** LIBRARY SCIENCE, EUROPEAN STUDIES **EDUCATION** Iowa, BA, 70; Univ S Calif, MA, 75; Iowa, MLS, 80; Kansas, MA, 81. **CAREER** Slavic and Ger lang Cataloger, Univ of Nebr Libr, Lincoln, 81-84; Head, Slavic Dept, Univ of Kans Libr, Lawrence, 85-93; Ref Librn and Europe Studies Bibliogr, Univ of Kans Libr, Lawrence, 94-. **MEMBERSHIPS** Am Asn for Advancement of Slavic Studies, Western Europ Studies Sect, Asn od Col and Res Libr, Am Libr Asn. **RESEARCH** Central European Publishing, European History. **CONTACT ADDRESS** Univ of Kansas, Lawrence, 350 Watson Library, Lawrence, KS 66045-2800. **EMAIL** ganderson@ukans.edu

ANDERSON, GREG
PERSONAL Born 10/24/1962, Weston Super Mare, England **DISCIPLINE** CLASSICS; HISTORY **EDUCATION** Univ of Newcastle UK, BA, 86; Univ of London UK, MA, 88; Yale Univ PhD, 97. **CAREER** Asst Prof, 97-98, Elmira College; Asst Prof, 98-, Univ of IL, Chicago. **MEMBERSHIPS** APA **RESEARCH** Ancient Grecian to ancient greek political & cultural history, sports history, nationalism. **SELECTED PUBLICATIONS** Auth, The Athenian Experiment: Building a New Kind of Political Community in Ancient Attica, 508-490 B.C.", Ann Arbor, Univ of Mich Press, forthcoming; Alcmeonid Homelands Political Exile and the Unification of Attica, in: Historia, forthcoming; Games for Heros, Greek Athletics and the Invention of the Olympic Tradition, in: Report of the Yale-Smithsonian Annual Seminar on Material Culture, 97. **CONTACT ADDRESS** Dept of History, Univ of Illinois, Chicago, 601 S Morgan St, Chicago, IL 60607-7109. **EMAIL** gregand@uic.edu

ANDERSON, JAMES C., JR.
PERSONAL Born 04/15/1951, Malden, MA, m, 1978, 2 children **DISCIPLINE** CLASSICS **EDUCATION** Colo Col, BA, 73; Univ NC, Chapel Hill, MA, 76, PhD, 80. **CAREER** From asst prof to assoc prof to prof, 80-, Univ Ga; Mellon prof in charge, Intercollegiate Ctr Classical Stud, Rome, 93-94; dir, Classical Summer Sch Am Acad, Rome, 92-94. **HONORS AND AWARDS** Josiah Meigs Prof, 99-; Gen S. Beaver Tchg Prof, 96-99; NEH Fel Col Tchrs, 94-95; NEH Summer Stipend, 83; Fel Am Acad Rome, 78-79; Thomas J. Watson Fel, 73-74; Phi Beta Kappa, 73; fel, 78-79, am acad rome; thomas j. watson fel, 73-74, greece, britain; phi beta kappa, 73. **MEMBERSHIPS** Archaeol Inst Am; Soc of Architectureal Historians; Soc Fel Am Acad, Rome; Classical Assoc Middle West and South. **RESEARCH** Roman archaeology; Roman art and architecture; Latin Epigraphy. **SELECTED PUBLICATIONS** Auth, Historical Topography of the Imperial Fora, 84; auth, Roman Brick Stamps: The Thomas Ashby Collection, 91; auth, Roman Architecture and Society, 97. **CONTACT ADDRESS** Dept of Classics, Univ of Georgia, Park Hall, Athens, GA 30602-6203. **EMAIL** janderso@arches.uga.edu

ANDERSON, JUDITH H.
PERSONAL Born 04/21/1940, Worcester, MA, w, 1971 **DISCIPLINE** ENGLISH **EDUCATION** Radcliffe Col, AB, 61; Yale Univ, MA, 62; PhD, 65. **CAREER** Instructor, Cornell Univ, 64-66; Asst Prof, Cornell Univ, 66-72; Visiting Lecturer, Yale Univ, 73; Visiting Asst, Prof, Univ of Michigan, 73-74; Assoc Prof, Indiana Univ, 74-79; Prof, Indiana Univ, 79-99; Chancellors Prof, Indiana Univ, 99. **HONORS AND AWARDS** Nat Endowment for the Humanities Sr Res Fel; Huntington Library-NEH Fel; Fel; Falger Library; Nat Humanities Ctr Fel; Woman Scholar Awd; Teaching Excellence Recognition Awd; Chancellors Professorship; Mayers Found Fel, Dulin Fel; Outstanding Woman Scholar Awd. **MEMBERSHIPS** MLA; Int Spenser Soc; Renaissance Soc of Am; Shakespeare Assoc of Am; Phi Beta Kappa; Milton Soc; AAVP. **RESEARCH** Renaissance/early modern literature, esp., Spenser, Donnie, Milton; intellectual and cultural history; theories of texts and language; allegory and metaphor. **SELECTED PUBLICATIONS** Auth, The Growth of a Personal Voice, Yale, 76; auth, Biographical Truth: The Representation of Historical Persons in Tudor-Stuart Writing, Yale UP, 84; Words Thaf Matter, Stanford, 96; ed, Will's Vision of Pers Plowon, with Elizabeth Kirk; Ed, Spenser's Life and the Subject of Biography, with Donald Cheney & David Richardson; auth, "Narrative Reflections: Re-envisaging the Poet in The Canterbury Tales and The Faerie Queene," in Refiguring Chaucer in the Renaissance, ed. Theresa M. Krier, (U of Florida P, 98), 87-105; auth, "Translating Investments: The Metaphoricity of Language, 2 Henry IV, and Hamlet," Texas Studies in Literature and Language 40 (98): 231-67; auth, "Better a Mischief than an inconvenience: The saiyng self in Spenser's View, or, How many meanings can stand on the head of a proverb?" in Worldmaking Spenser: Explorations in the Early Modern Age' ed. Patrick Cheney and Lauren Silberman (U of Kentucky P, 99.) **CONTACT ADDRESS** Dept English, Indiana Univ, Bloomington, 442 Ballantine Hall, 1020 E Kirkwood Ave, Bloomington, IN 47405-7103. **EMAIL** anders@indiana.edu

ANDERSON, LAURIE
DISCIPLINE LITERATURE **EDUCATION** Univ Maine, BA, 65; Mich State, MA, 69, Univ Pacific, MA, 71. **CAREER** US Peace Corps, 65-67; Chair, Mizpah E Caroline Islands, 71-72; Chair, Am Girls Col, Turkey, 72-76; chair, Suomi Col, 76-. **HONORS AND AWARDS** NEH Summer Sem and Inst (6). **MEMBERSHIPS** MLA; Hemingway Soc. **RESEARCH** Hemingway, Commonwealth Literature. **SELECTED PUBLICATIONS** Auth, Hunting Hemingway's Trout; auth, Heikki Heikkinen and Other Stories; auth, Children of the Kaleva; auth, Small Winter Wars. **CONTACT ADDRESS** Dept Lang and Lit, Suomi Col, 601 Quincy St, Hancock, MI 49930-1832.

ANDERSON, LINDA
PERSONAL Born Minneapolis, MN **DISCIPLINE** ENGLISH **EDUCATION** Univ Mn, PhD, 84 **CAREER** Assoc prof, Va Tech. **HONORS AND AWARDS** Col of Arts & Sci Cert of Teaching Excellence, 93-94 **MEMBERSHIPS** Shakespeare Soc of Amer; Int Shakespeare Soc; Renaissance Soc of Amer; SAMLA; SCMLA; SE Renaissance Conf. **RESEARCH** Shakespeare; Renaissance lit; pop culture. **SELECTED PUBLICATIONS** Auth, A Kind of Wild Justice: Revenge in Shakespeare's Comedies, Univ Del Press, 87; auth, Every Good Servant Does Not All Commands: Shakespeare's Servants and the Duty to Disobey, Upstart Crow, 92; art, What Movie Are We Watching Here: Cinematic Quotation in Recent Hollywood Films, Literature and Film in the Historical Dimension: Selected Papers from the Fifteenth Florida State University Conference on Literature and Film, Univ Press Fl, 94; auth, A Losing Office: Shakespeare's Use of Messengers, Upstart Crow, 97; art, Oh Dear Jesus It Is Female: Monster as Mother/Mother as Monster in Stephen King's It, Imagining the Worth: Stephen King and the Representation of Women, Greenwood Press, 98; auth, If Both My Sons Were on the Gallows, I Would Sign: Oppression of Children in Beaumont's The Knight of the Burning Pestle, Ilha do Desterro, Brazil, 98. **CONTACT ADDRESS** Dept of English, Virginia Polytech Inst and State Univ, Blacksburg, VA 24061-0112. **EMAIL** lianders@vt.edu

ANDERSON, MICHAEL JOHN
PERSONAL Born 05/30/1967, London, England, m, 1993 **DISCIPLINE** CLASSICAL LANGUAGES; LITERATURE **EDUCATION** Princeton Univ, AB, 89; Univ Oxford, DPhil, 94. **CAREER** Vis asst prof, Univ Oregon, 93/94; Mellon post-doctoral fel in humanities, Columbia Univ 94-96; asst prof, Yale Univ, 97- . **HONORS AND AWARDS** Fulbright Sch for study in Freiburg, GER, 89/90; Marshall Scholarship for study in Oxford, ENG, 90-93. **MEMBERSHIPS** APA **RESEARCH** Greek literature; Greek art. **SELECTED PUBLICATIONS** The Fall of Troy in Early Greek Poetry and Art, 97; The Sophrosyne of Persinna and the Romantic Strategy of Heliodorus' Aethiopica, Classical Philology, 97. **CONTACT ADDRESS** Dept of Classics, Yale Univ, New Haven, CT 06520-8266. **EMAIL** michael.j.anderson@yale.edu

ANDERSON, ROLAND F.
PERSONAL Born 09/19/1928, London, England, m, 1994 **DISCIPLINE** ENGLISH **EDUCATION** Univ Brit Colum, BA, 57; Univ Wis, MA, 58; Univ Toronto, PhD, 61. **CAREER** TA, Univ of Toronto, 60-61; asst prof, Univ of Albta, 61-65; lectr, Massey Univ, NZ, 65-68; asst prof to prof, Univ of Albta, 68-; lectr, Pa State Univ, 95-. **HONORS AND AWARDS** Univ of Toronto Fel, 58-59; Can Coun Fel, 59-60. **MEMBERSHIPS** MLA, Am Assoc of Australian Lit Studies. **RESEARCH** Australian and New Zealand literature and culture. **SELECTED PUBLICATIONS** Auth, "An Invisible Country and Commonwealth Literature," Assoc of Commonwealth Lang & Lit Studies Bulletin 4.5, (77); auth, "The Rise and Fall of the Man Alone," Ariel: Rev of Int English Lit, 16.4, (85). **CONTACT ADDRESS** Dept English, Pennsylvania State Univ, Univ Park, 712 Franklin St, State College, PA 16803. **EMAIL** rfa2@psu.edu

ANDERSON, STEVE
PERSONAL Born 05/16/1943, Leachville, AR, m, 1968, 2 children **DISCIPLINE** FILM **EDUCATION** Univ of Missouri, PhD. **CAREER** Northern Montana College, UALR **HONORS AND AWARDS** Chair, eng dept; Ed, Technical Reader. **SELECTED PUBLICATIONS** Auth, American Expedition, Beloit Fiction Jour; Caesura, Beloit Fiction Jour; Skin, Beloit Fiction Jour; Forgiveness, Vietnam Generation; Strack, Perimeter Light. **CONTACT ADDRESS** Univ of Arkansas, Little Rock, 2801 S University Ave., Little Rock, AR 72204-1099. **EMAIL** wsanderson@ualr.edu

ANDERSON, STEVEN D.
PERSONAL Born 12/14/1954, Dawson, MN, m, 1979, 3 children **DISCIPLINE** MASS COMMUNICATION **EDUCATION** ST. Cloud State Univ, BA, 78; Univ Denver, MA, 85; PhD, 89. **CAREER** Asst Prof, Va Tech, 89-94; Asst Prof, Univ of Wis, River Falls, 94-95; Asst Prof, Utah State Univ, 95-97; Asst Prof, Univ of Okla, 97-00; Assoc Prof, James Madison Univ, 00-. **HONORS AND AWARDS** Cert of Teaching Excellence, Va Tech. **MEMBERSHIPS** Broadcast Educ Asn, Asn for Educ in Jour and Mass Commun, Nat Press Photographers Asn. **RESEARCH** Multimedia, Communication technology, Broadcast News. **SELECTED PUBLICATIONS** Coauth, "A Convergent Validity Model of Emergent Leadership in Groups," Small Group Res 22-3 (Aug 91); auth, "The Development of a Class in Electronic News Gathering," Feedback 34-1 (Winter 93); auth, "Keeping the Best and Brightest: Stations Must Improve Intern Programs to Attract Serious Students," Television Broadcast (Sep 95); auth, "Is Lawsuit Broadcast Intern's Last Stand?," Television Broadcast (Sep 96); coauth, "Multimedia Adoption in BEA Member Scholars," Feedback 37-4 (Fall 96); auth, "Internet Radio," in Historical Dictionary of American Radio, ed. Donald G. Godfrey and Frederic A. Leigh (Greenwood Press, 98); auth, "Internet Radio, KOA Radio and Broadcast Education Association," in Encyclopedia of Radio, ed. Christopher H. Sterling (Fitzroy Dearborn Publ, forthcoming, 01). **CONTACT ADDRESS** Sch of Media Arts and Design, James Madison Univ, MSC #6804, Harrisonburg, VA 22807.

ANDERSON, THOMAS JEFFERSON
PERSONAL Born 08/17/1928, Coutesville, PA, m **DISCIPLINE** MUSIC **EDUCATION** West Virginia State Col, BMus, 50; Penn State Univ, MEd, 51; Univ Iowa, PhD, 58. **CAREER** Instr, W Va State Col, 55-56; prof & ch of Dept, Langston Univ, 58-63; composer-in-res, Atlanta Symphony Orchestra, 69-71; Danforth vis prof, Morehouse co, 71-72; Hill dist vis prof, Univ Minn, 90; dist vis prof, Calif State Univ-Chico, 99; composer-in-residence, Northwestern Univ, Apr 92, Apr 97; vis King/Chavez/Parks prof, univ Mich, Mar 93; composer-in-res, Ohio State Univ, May 94; assoc, Nat Human Ctr, Res Triangle Pk, 96-97; Prof Music & Ch of Dept, 72-80, Austin Fletcher Prof Music, 78-90, Prof Emer, Tufts Univ, 90- . **HONORS AND AWARDS** Fellow, MacDowell Colony, 1960-83; fellow, Yhaddo 1970-77; Copley Foundation Awd, 1964; Fromm Foundation Awd, 1964-71; Phi Beta Kappa, honorary member, 1977; over 50 published compositions; artistic residency, University of Salvador, 1988; 60th Birthday Concert, Videmus, Harvard University, 1989; fellow, John Simon Guggenheim Foundation, 1989; bd mem, Harvard Musical Assn, 1989. **MEMBERSHIPS** Founder/president, Black Music Caucus MENC; board member, Elma Lewis School of Fine Arts, 1975-; advisory bd, Meet The Composer, 1980; chair, Comm of the Status of Minorities, College Music Society, 1976-80; Music Council the Arts & Humanities 1978-81; Harvard Musical Assn, 1976-; St Botolph Club, 1980. **CONTACT ADDRESS** 111 Cameron Glen Dr, Chapel Hill, NC 27516-2333.

ANDERSON, WILLIAM SCOVIL
PERSONAL Born 09/16/1927, Brookline, MA, m, 1983, 5 children **DISCIPLINE** CLASSICS **EDUCATION** Yale Univ, BA, 50, PhD, 54; Cambridge Univ, BA, 52, MA, 56. **CAREER** Instr classics, Yale Univ, 55-60; from asst prof to assoc prof Latin, 60-65, chmn dept classics, 70-73, Prof Latin & Comp Lit Univ CA, Berkeley, 65-; prof in charge, Intercol Ctr Class Studies, Rome, 67-68; ed Vergilius, 65; res prof, Univ Melbourne, 84; Robson Lectr, Victoria Col, Toronto, 87; Blegen Res Prof, Vassar Col, 89-90; Vis Distinguished Prof, FL State Univ, 95. **HONORS AND AWARDS** Prix de Rome, 54; Morse fel, 59; Am Coun Learned Soc grant to deliver lect at Int Cong Satire, Rostock, Ger, 65; Nat Endowment Hum sr fel, 73-74; classicist-in-residence, Am Acad, Rome, 73-74. **MEMBERSHIPS** Am Philol Asn (pres, 77); Soc Relig Higher Educ; Philol Asn Pac Coast. **RESEARCH** Roman satire and comedy; Vergil; Ovid. **SELECTED PUBLICATIONS** Auth, The Art of the Aeneid, Prentice-Hall, 69; Ovid's Metamorphoses: Books 6-10, Univ OK, 72, Books 1-5, Univ OK, 96; Ovidius, Metamorphoses, Leipzig: Teubner, 77; Essays on Roman Satire, Princeton Univ, 82; Barbarian Play: Plautus' Roman Comedy, Toronto, 93. **CONTACT ADDRESS** Dept of Class, Univ of California, Berkeley, 7212 Dwinelle Hall, Berkeley, CA 94720-2521. **EMAIL** wsa@socrates.berkeley.edu

ANDO, CLIFFORD
PERSONAL Born 05/03/1969, Philadelphia, PA **DISCIPLINE** CLASSICAL STUDIES **EDUCATION** Univ Mich, PhD, 96. **CAREER** Asst prof, York Univ, 96-98; asst prof, Univ of Southern Calif, 98-. **HONORS AND AWARDS** Fel, Am Coun of Learned Soc. **MEMBERSHIPS** Am Philol Asn; North Am Patristics Soc. **RESEARCH** Roman history; Latin and Greek historiography. **SELECTED PUBLICATIONS** Auth, "Pagan Apologetics and Christian Intolerance in the Ages of Themistius and Augustine" in J of Early Christian Studies, 96; "Tacticus, Annales VI: Beginning and End" in Am J of Philol, 97; auth, "Was Rome a polis?, Classical Antiquity, 99; auth, "Imperial ideology and provincial loyalty in the Roman Empire," Berkeley: Univ of Calif Press, 00; auth, "Signs, idols and the incarnation in Augustinian metaphysics," Representations, 01. **CONTACT ADDRESS** Classics Dept, Univ of So California, Taper Hall 224, Los Angeles, CA 90089-0352. **EMAIL** cando@usc.edu

ANDREA, BERNADETTE D.
DISCIPLINE ENGLISH LITERATURE **EDUCATION** Univ Calgary, BA, 89; MA, 90; Cornell Univ, MA, 93; PhD, 96. **CAREER** Asst prof, W Va Univ, 96-98; asst prof, Univ Tex San Antonio, 98-. **HONORS AND AWARDS** Univ of Calgary, Scholarship, 84, 87-88, 89-90; Fac of Humanities Gold Medal, 89; Governor General's Gold Medal, Altenate Winner, Univ of Calgary, 90; Beatrice Brown Awd, Cornell Univ, 93; Clark Distinguished Teaching Awd, 93, Mellon Fel, 93-95, 99-00; SSHRC Fel, 90-94, 95-96; Senate Grant, W Va Univ, 97; Folger Inst Grant, 98; Riggle Fel, 98; Dean's Circle Res Grant, 99; Clark Libr Fel, 00; NEH Grant, 01. **MEMBERSHIPS** MLA, Renaissance Soc of Am, Soc for the Study of Early Modern Women. **RESEARCH** Renaissance Studies, Women's Studies, Literary and Cultural Theory. **SELECTED PUBLICATIONS** Auth, "Properly Speaking: Publishing Women in Seventeenth-Century England," Diss Abstracts Int 56.11:4404 (96): auth, "Early Modern Women, 'Race', and (Post)Colonial Writing," ARIEL 27, (96): 127-49; auth, "Columbus in Istanbul: Ottoman Mappings of the 'New World,'" and "Space, Place, and Signs in Early Modern Studies," Genre: Forms of Discourse and Culture 30, (97): 135-65, 1-9; ed, Space, Place and Signs in Early Modern Studies 30.1, 97; auth, "Black Skin, The Queen's Masques: Africanist Ambivalence and Feminine Author(ity) in the Masques of Blackness and Beauty," Eng Lit Renaissance 29.2 (99): 246-81; auth, "Teaching (Early Modern Women's) Writing," Teaching Tudor and Stuart Women Writers, eds Susanna Woods and Margaret Hannay, MLA, (NY, 00): 266-70; auth, "Coming Out in Margaret Cavendish's Closet Dramas," In-between: Essays and Studies in Literary Criticism 9, (00): 205-18; auth, "Pamphilia's Cabinet: Gendered Authorship and Empire in Lady Mary Worth's 'Urania,'" ELH 68 (01): 335-58. **CONTACT ADDRESS** Dept English, Univ of Texas, San Antonio, 6900 N Loop 1604 W, San Antonio, TX 78249-0643. **EMAIL** bandrea@utsa.edu

ANDREAS, JAMES, SR.
PERSONAL m, 1976, 4 children **DISCIPLINE** ENGLISH LITERATURE **EDUCATION** Vanderbilt Univ, PhD, 73. **CAREER** Dept Eng, Clemson Univ; Prof Emeritus, English, Clemson Univ. **HONORS AND AWARDS** Phi Beta Kappa, 65; ed, the upstart crow: a shakespeare jour; dir, clemson shakespeare festival and sc shakespeare collaborative. **RESEARCH** Medieval and Renaissance literature and African American Literature. **SELECTED PUBLICATIONS** Auth, Othello's African American Progeny in Materialist Shakespeare: A History, Verso Press, 95; For O, the hobbyhorse is dead: Hamlet and the Death of Carnival, Renaissance Papers, SE Renaissance Conf, 97; Newe Science from Olde Bokes: A Bakhtinian Approach to the Summoner's Tale in Casebook on the Canterbury Tales, Macmillan, 97; auth, Chancer's Defense of the Vulgar Tongue, in Time, Memory and the Verbal Arts, 98; auth, Signifying on Shakespeare: Gloria Naylor's Mama Day in Shakespeare and 99; auth, In Love With Shakespeare, in World book Yearbook, 00. **CONTACT ADDRESS** Clemson Univ, 611 Strode, Clemson, SC 29634. **EMAIL** asjames@clemson.edu

ANDREWS, LARRY RAY
PERSONAL Born 08/09/1940, Greencastle, IN, m, 1961, 4 children **DISCIPLINE** ENGLISH; COMPARATIVE LITERATURE **EDUCATION** Ohio State Univ, BA, 62; Rutgers Univ, PhD(comp lit), 71. **CAREER** Instr English, Univ SC, 66-69; asst prof, 69-78, Assoc Prof English, Kent State Univ, 78-, Dean, Honors Col, 93-. **MEMBERSHIPS** Col Lang Asn. **RESEARCH** European romanticism; Russian-Western literary relations in 19th century; African American women's fiction. **SELECTED PUBLICATIONS** Auth, D V Venevitinov: A sketch of his life and works, Russ Lit Triquart, 74; Dostevskij and Hugos Le Dernier Jour d'un Condamne, Comp Lit, 77; The Spatial Imagery of Oblomovism, Neophilologus, 88; Black Sisterhood in Gloria Naylor's Novels, CLAS, 89; Hugo's Gilliatt and Leskov's Golovan: Two Eccentric Folk-Epic Heroes, Comp Lit, 94. **CONTACT ADDRESS** Honors Col, Kent State Univ, PO Box 5190, Kent, OH 44242-0001. **EMAIL** landrews@kent.edu

ANDRIA, MARCO
DISCIPLINE COMMUNCATION STUDIES **EDUCATION** Aston Univ, PhD. **CAREER** Asst prof. **SELECTED PUBLICATIONS** Co-auth, Face-to-Face: Interpersonal Communication in the Workplace, Prentice Hall, 94; Peter Gzowski: An Electric Life, ECW, 94; Music of Our Times: Eight Canadian Singer-Songwriters, Lorimer, 90. **CONTACT ADDRESS** Dept Communcation Studies, Athabasca Univ, 1 University Dr, Athabasca, AB, Canada T9S 3A3. **EMAIL** marco@cs.athabascau.ca

ANGELOU, MAYA
PERSONAL Born 04/04/1928, St. Louis, MO, d **DISCIPLINE** LITERATURE, HISTORY **CAREER** Author, poet, playwright, stage and screen producer, director, actress, 54-; Southern Christian Leadership Conference, coordinator, 59-60; Arab Observer Egypt, associate editor, 61-62; University of Ghana, asst administrator, 63-66; African Review, editor, 64-66; California State University, Wichita State University, visiting professor; Wake Forest Univ, Department of Humanities, Reynolds Prof of Am Studies, 74-. **HONORS AND AWARDS** 32 Honorary Degrees; Pulitzer Prize Nomination, "Just Give Me A Cool Drink of Water 'fore I Diiie," 1972; Tony Awd Nomination, "Look Away," 1975; Ladies Home Journal, one of the Women of the Year in Communications, 1976; Emmy Awd Nomination, Performance, "Roots," 1977; Distingushed Woman of North Carolina, 1992; Essence Magazine, Woman of the Year, 1992; Horatio Alger Awd, 1992; Women In Film, Crystal Awd, 1992; American Academy of Achievement, Golden Plate Awd, 1990; Horatio Alger Awds Dinner Chairman, 1993; National Society for the Prevention of Cruelty to Children, London, England, NSPCC Maya Angelou CPT and Family Centre, London, England, center dedication, June 20, 1991; NAACP, Image Awd, Literary Work, Nonfiction, 1998. **MEMBERSHIPS** American Federation of Television & Radio Artists; board of trustees, American Film Institute, 1975-; Directors Guild; Actors' Equity; Women's Prison Assn. **SELECTED PUBLICATIONS** Author, works include: I Know Why the Caged Bird Sings, 1970; Just Give Me A Cool Drink of Water 'Fore I Die, 1971; Gather Together in My Name, 1974; Oh Pray My Wings Are Gonna Fit Me Well, 1975; Singin & Swingin & Getting Merry Like Christmas, 1976; And Still I Rise, 1978; The Heart of a Woman, 1981; Shaker, Why Don't You Sing? 1983; All God's Children Need Traveling Shoes, 1986; Mrs Flowers: A Moment of Friendship, 1986; Wouldn't Take Nothing for My Journey Now, Random, 1993; poems: Maya Angelou, 1986; Now Sheba Sings the Song, 1987; I Shall Not Be Moved, Random House, 1990; plays include: Cabraret for Freedom, 1960; The Least of These, 1966; Ajax, 1974; And Still I Rise, 1976; screenplays include: Georgia Georgia, 1972; All Day Long, 1974; PBS-TV Documentaries: "Who Cares About Kids" "Kindred Spirits," KERA-TV, Dallas, TX; "Rainbow In The Clouds," series, host, writer, WTVS-TV, Detroit, MI; "To The Contrary," Maryland Public Television; lecturer: Nancy Hanks Lecture, American Council for the Arts, 1990; contributing writer: "Brewster Place," mini-series, HARPO Productions; panelist: Institute for the Study of Human Systems, Zermatt, Switzerland, 1990; lyricist: "King Now," theatrical project, London, England; has appeared in numerous plays and TV productions as both an actress and singer; wrote and presented a poem for President Clinton's Swearing-In Ceremonies, 1993; Down in the Delta, director; named UNICEF National Ambassador, 1996. **CONTACT ADDRESS** Dept of Humanities, Wake Forest Univ, PO Box 7314, Winston-Salem, NC 27109.

ANGYAL, ANDREW J.
PERSONAL Born 04/21/1946, Mineola, NY, m, 1971, 2 children **DISCIPLINE** ENGLISH & AMERICAN LITERA-

TURE; ENVIRONMENTAL STUDIES **EDUCATION** Queens Col, NYork, BA, 68; Yale Univ, MAR, 72; Duke Univ, PhD (English), 76. **CAREER** Instr English, New Haven Col, 69-70; master English & drama, South Kent Sch, 70-72; grad tutor English, Duke Univ, 74-76; prof English, Elon Col 76-, publ affairs officer US Environ Protection Agency, 72-74; partic polit sci, Duke fac fels in Commun Policy, 76; Fulbright lectr, Louis Kossuth Univ, Debrecen, Hungary, 86; Piedmont Independent Col Asn vis prof at Guilford Col, 88. **HONORS AND AWARDS** NY State Regents Grad Teaching Fel, 68; Tuition Scholar, Yale Univ, 68-70; Grad Tutorship, Duke Univ, 74-76; Grad Res Grant, Duke Univ, 75; Elon Col Fac Res Grants, 78-86; Weymouth House Writer-in-Residence, Southern Pines, NC, 80; Fulbright Lecturer in Am Lit (Hungary), 86; Fel in Eastern European Studies, Appalachian Humanities Prog, Appalachian State Univ, 90-91; Vassar Col Summer NEH Inst on The Environmental Imagination, 97. **MEMBERSHIPS** Soc for Study Southern Lit; Conf on Christianity & Lit; NAS; ALSC; PAC. **RESEARCH** American literature; textual and bibliographic studies; science and literature; natural history; environmental studies. **SELECTED PUBLICATIONS** Coauth, Some Early Frost Imitations of Poe, Poe Studies, 6/76; auth, Robert Frost's Poetry Before 1913: A Checklist, Proof 5: Yearbk Am Bibliog & Textual Studies, 5/77; Wallace Stevens' Sunday Morning as Secular Belief, Christianity & Lit, 10/79; Literary Politics and the Shaping of the Frost Poetic Canon, SC Rev, 4/80; Loren Eiseley, G K Hall, 83; Lewis Thomas, G K Hall, 89; Wendell Berry, Twayne, 95; From Swedenborg to William James: The Shaping of Frost's Religious Beliefs, Robert Frost Rev, Fall 94; The Complex Fate of Being an American: The African-American Essayist and the Quest for an Identity, CLA J, 9/93; Loren Eiseley's Immense Journey: The Making of a Literary Naturalist, The Lit of Sci. Univ Ga Press, 93. **CONTACT ADDRESS** Dept of English, Elon Col, Box 2245, Elon College, NC 27244. **EMAIL** angyal@elon.edu

ANKENY, REBECCA T.

PERSONAL Born 12/17/1956, Wichita, KS, m, 1975, 2 children **DISCIPLINE** ENGLISH **EDUCATION** George Fox Col, BA, 77; Univ Ore. MA, 82; PhD, 86. **CAREER** Asst Prof, Westmont Col, 86-88; Asst Prof to Assoc Prof, George Fox Col, 88-96. **HONORS AND AWARDS** Grad Teaching Fel, 80-86; Burlington Northern Excellence in Teaching Awd, 91. **MEMBERSHIPS** Nat Coun of Teachers of English, Intl Asn for the Fantastic in the arts. **RESEARCH** George MacDonald, William Blake, Muriel Spark. **SELECTED PUBLICATIONS** Auth, "Endings and Meanings," in George MacDonald's The Portent, The Story, the Teller, and the Audience in George MacDonald's Fiction, Edwin Mellen Press, 00. **CONTACT ADDRESS** Dept Lit, George Fox Univ, 414 N Meridian St, Newberg, OR 97132-2625. **EMAIL** bankeny@georgefox.edu

ANSPAUGH, KELLY C.

PERSONAL Born 03/12/1960, Lima, OH, s **DISCIPLINE** ENGLISH **EDUCATION** Univ Wis-Madison, PhD, 92 **CAREER** LECTR, OHIO STATE UNIV-LIMA, 92-. **RESEARCH** Modern British literature, the novel. **SELECTED PUBLICATIONS** Auth, "The Partially Purged: Beckett's 'The Calmative' as Anti-Comedy," Can Jour of Irish Studies, 96; auth, " 'When Lovely Wooman Stoops to Conk Him'": Virginia Woolf in Finnegans Wake," Joyce Studies Annual, 96; auth, "Getting Even with Uncle Ez: Wyndham Lewis's 'Doppelganger," Jour of Modern Lit, 95; auth, "'Faith, Hope, and - what was it?': Beckett Reading Joyce Reading Dante," Jour of Beckett Studies, 96; auth, "The Metempsychosis of Ajax: Leopold Bloom as Excremental Hero," Moderna Sprak, 96; auth, "'Delenda Est Bloomsbury': Wyndham Lewis Blasts Virginia Woolf," Wyndham Lewis Annual, 96; auth, "James Joyce, Wyndham Lewis, and the High Modern Grotesque," in Literature and the Grotesque, 95, Rodopi Press; auth, "Ulysses Upon Ajax: Joyce, Harington, and the Question of Cloacal Imperialism," South Atlantic Rev, 95; auth, "Repression or Suppression? Freud's Interpretation of the Dream of Irma's Injection," The Psychoanalytic Rev, 95; auth, "Dante on his Head: Conrad's Heart of Darkness," Conradiana, 95; auth, "Reading the Intertext in Jonathan Swift's 'A Panegyrick on the Dean," Essays in Lit, 95; auth, "Blasting the Bombardier: Another Look at Lewis, Joyce, and Woolf," Twentieth Century Lit, 94; auth, "How Butt Shot the Chamber Pot: Finnegans Wake II.3," James Joyce Quarterly, 94; auth, "Powers of Ordure: James Joyce and the Excremental Vision(s)," Mosaic, 94; auth, "'Three Mortal Hour[i]s: Female Gothic in Joyce's 'The Dead,'" Studies in Short Fiction, 94; auth, "Illustrating 'Mark Time's Finist Joke,'" Thalia: Studies in Lit Humor, 95; auth, "'Bung Goes the Enemay': Wyndham Lewis and the Uses of Disgust," Mattoid, 94; auth, "The Innocent Eye? E. W. Kemble's Illustrations to Adventures of Huckleberry Finn," American Literary Realism, 93; auth, "Circe Resartus: William Browne of Tavistock's Circe and Ulysses Masque and To the Lighthouse," Virginia Woolf: Reading the Renaissance, 99. **CONTACT ADDRESS** Ohio State Univ, Lima, 4240 Campus Dr, Lima, OH 45804. **EMAIL** Anspaugh.2@osu.edu

ANSTENDIG, LINDA

PERSONAL Born 12/28/1941, Brooklyn, NY, m, 1962, 2 children **DISCIPLINE** ENGLISH, COMMUNICATION **EDUCATION** Conn Col, BA, 62; Harvard Univ, MAT, 64; Col New Rochelle, MSEd, 76; Columbia Teachers Col, EDD, 89. **CAREER** Prof of English/Commun, Pace Univ, 89-. **HONORS AND AWARDS** NEH grants recipient. **MEMBERSHIPS** Col English Asn, Modern Lang Asn, Nat Coun of Teachers of English, Am Asn of Higher Educ, Am Asn of Univ Profs, Westchester Coun of English Educators, Coun of Writing Prog Admin. **RESEARCH** Writing and technology across the curriculum. **SELECTED PUBLICATIONS** Auth, "Building Critical Thinking into a Freshman Writing Class," in Thinking Creatically, ed K. Johnson, Int Soc of General Semantics (91); coauth with David Hicks, Writing Through Literature, Prentice-Hall (96); rev of Jane Maher, Mina Shaughnessy: Her Life and Work, Urbana, Il: NCTE (97); coauth with Eugene Richie, Guide for Writing and Technology Across the Curriculum: A Resource for Professors and Student Assistants, Pace Univ (98); auth, "Democratizing the Classroom: Students Responding to Each Other," in Generative Tensions: When Learning is Linked through the Web, Washington, DC: Asn of Am Cols and Univs (98); coauth, "Web Research and Hypermedia: Tools for Engaged Learning," J on Excellence in Col Teaching, Vol 9, No 2 (99); coauth with Eugene Richie, "Memoir, Technology, and Research: Public Spaces for Students and Senior Citizens in Service Learning," Academic Exchange Quart (winter 2000). **CONTACT ADDRESS** Dept Lit/Commun, Pace Univ, Pleasantville, 861 Bedford Rd, Pleasantville, NY 10570-2700. **EMAIL** lanstendig@pace.edu

ANTHES, SUSAN H.

PERSONAL Born 11/03/1944, Manitowac, WI, m, 1966, 2 children **DISCIPLINE** LIBRARY SCIENCE **EDUCATION** Univ Wis, BA, 66, MA, 67. **CAREER** Librn, Univ Wis Law Libry, 67-68; asst librn, Univ Miami, 68-71; asst librn, Pa State Univ, 71-81; asst librn, 71-91; librn, 81-91, assoc dir, 91-, Univ Colo Boulder. **MEMBERSHIPS** Am Libr Asn; Colo Libr Asn; Asn Col & Res Libr. **RESEARCH** Management in libraries; women in libraries. **SELECTED PUBLICATIONS** Coauth, art, The Collaborative Course: Innovative Teaching and Learning, 91; auth, art, A Potpourri of Practical Ideas from ACRL'S 6th National Conference: Administration, 92; coauth, art, Incorporating Information Literacy into the Core Curriculum, 92; auth, art, Outreach, Promotion and Bibliographic Instruction, 93; auth, art, Report on LAMA Preconference, 97. **CONTACT ADDRESS** 1631 Gillaspie Dr, Boulder, CO 80303. **EMAIL** susan.anthes@colorado.edu

ANTHONY, BOOKER T.

PERSONAL Born 08/28/1958, Scotland Neck, NC, m, 1992, 2 children **DISCIPLINE** ENGLISH **EDUCATION** St. Augustine's Col, BA, 80; Ohio State Univ, MA, 82; PhD, 88. **CAREER** Assoc prof, Fayetteville State Univ, 86. **HONORS AND AWARDS** Harvard Univ Management Develop Prof, 95. **MEMBERSHIPS** Nat Assoc of Presidential Assts; Col Lang Assoc. **RESEARCH** American Literature, Fiction of Ernest J. Gaines, the Bible and Literature. **SELECTED PUBLICATIONS** Rev, of "A Lesson Before Dying" by Ernest J. Gaines, CLA Journal 37 (Dec 93): 235-252; auth, "Assessing Writing through Common Examinations and Student Portfolios", in Assessment in Practice, ed Trudy Banta, Jossey-Bass, 96. **CONTACT ADDRESS** Dept English, Fayetteville State Univ, 1200 Murchison Rd, Fayetteville, NC 28301-4252. **EMAIL** banthony@uncfu.edu

ANTHONY, GERALDINE

PERSONAL Born Brooklyn, NY **DISCIPLINE** ENGLISH **EDUCATION** Mt St Vincent Univ, BA, 51; St John's Univ, MA, 56, PhD, 63. **CAREER** Tchr, Mt St Vincent Acad, 63-65; asst prof, 65-71, assoc prof, 71-77, prof, 77-87, chair, 83-86, Prof Emer English, Mt St Vincent Univ 87-. **HONORS AND AWARDS** Fel Journalism, Wall St. J, 65; post-doc fel, Mod Drama, Columbia Univ, 69. **SELECTED PUBLICATIONS** Ed, Profiles in Canadian Drama, 77; ed, Canadian Theatre History, 80; ed, Canadian Theatre and Drama, 90-92. **CONTACT ADDRESS** Dept of English, Mount Saint Vincent Univ, 106 Shore Dr, Halifax, NS, Canada B4A 2E1.

ANTOKOLETZ, ELLIOTT MAXIM

PERSONAL Born 08/03/1942, Jersey City, NJ, m, 1972, 1 child **DISCIPLINE** MUSICOLOGY **EDUCATION** Juilliard Sch Music, 60-65; Hunter Col CUNY, AB, 68; MA, 70; CUNY, PhD, 75. **CAREER** Lectr, Chamber Music, Queens Coll CUNY, 73-76; Prof, Musicol, Univ TX-Austin, 76-. **HONORS AND AWARDS** Bela Bartok Memorial Plaque and Diploma, Hungarian Government, 81; Ph.D. Alumni Awd, Univ of New York, 87. **MEMBERSHIPS** Queens Coll String Quartet; Am Musicol Soc; Sonneck Soc; Coll Music Soc; Int Music Soc. **RESEARCH** Bela Bartock, 20th century music. **SELECTED PUBLICATIONS** The Music of Be'la Barto'k, Univ Calif Press, 84; Bela Bartok Memorial Plaque and Diploma, Hungarian Government, 81; Be'la Barto'k: A Guide to Research, Garland Press, 88; Twentieth Century Music, Prentice Hall, 97; Bartok Perspectives, Oxford Univ Press, 00. **CONTACT ADDRESS** School of Music, Univ of Texas, Austin, Austin, TX 78712. **EMAIL** antokoletz@mail.utexas.edu

ANTON, COREY

DISCIPLINE COMMUNICATIONS **EDUCATION** Univ Wisc, BA, 91; Ill State Univ, MS, 94; Purdue Univ, PhD, 98. **CAREER** Teaching Asst Ill State Univ, 92-94; Teaching Asst Purdue Univ, 94-98; Asst Prof, Grand Valley State Univ, 98-. **HONORS AND AWARDS** Alan H Monroe Scholar, Purdue Univ, 98; Purdue Res Foundation summer Grant, 97; Phi Kappa Phi, 98. **MEMBERSHIPS** Nat Comm Asn, Semiotic Soc of Am **RESEARCH** Communication theory; Phenomenology; Rhetoric. **SELECTED PUBLICATIONS** Auth, "Beyond the Constitutive/Representational Dichotomy: The Phenomenological Notion of Intentionality," Communication Theory, (99): 26-57; auth, "About talk: The Category of Talk-Reflexive Words," Semiotics, (98): 193-212; auth, "Concerning speech: Heidegger and Performative Intentionality," Philosophy and Rhetoric, (98): 131-144; auth, "On speaking: A Phenomenological Recovering of a Forgotten Sense," Philosophy and Rhetoric, (97): 176-189; auth, "References and Suggested Further Readings," in Pieces: Toward a Revisioning of Communication/Life, Ablex Pub, 97; auth, Selfhood and Authenticity, SUNY Press, in press; auth, "Beyond Theoretical Ethics: Bakhtinian anti-Theoreticism" Human Studies, in press; auth, "Transparency and Opacity: A Brief Phenomenology of Message Flesh," in communicating Differences; Phenomenology and Communicative Praxis, Rowman and Littlefield, in press. **CONTACT ADDRESS** Dept Comm, Grand Valley State Univ, 1 Campus Dr, Allendale, MI 49401-9401. **EMAIL** antonc@gvsu.edu

ANTONUCCI, MICHAEL A.

PERSONAL Born 02/28/1966 **DISCIPLINE** ENGLISH **EDUCATION** Brown Univ, BA, 88; Emory Univ, MA, 95; PhD, 00. **CAREER** Lectr, Univ Ill Chicago, 00-. **HONORS AND AWARDS** Emory Dean's Teaching Fel; Artist's Res, Nat Park Serv, Exemplary Syllabus, Univ Ill, 00. **MEMBERSHIPS** MLA; CAAR; MeLUS. **RESEARCH** African American Poetry; Blues; Jazz; African American Literature; American Contemporary Poetry (20th Century); American Race Ritual. **SELECTED PUBLICATIONS** Auth, "The ? Impulse of Mitchell S. Harper's Poetry," in Celebrating Harper, Univ Ill Press, forthcoming; ref, of "Reading Race in American Poetry: An Area of ACT," by Aldon Lynn Nielsen, African Am Rev, forthcoming; auth "The Map and the Territory: An Interview with Michael S. Harper, African Am Rev. **CONTACT ADDRESS** 2745 N Francisco, no 2, Chicago, IL 60647. **EMAIL** manton@uic.edu

ANTUSH, JOHN V.

PERSONAL Born 11/05/1932, Tacoma, WA, m, 1968, 3 children **DISCIPLINE** ENGLISH **EDUCATION** Gonzaga Univ, AB, 56; MA, 59; Stanford, PhD, 67. **CAREER** Teach fel, Stanford Univ, 61-63; Fordham Univ, 64-. **HONORS AND AWARDS** Woodrow Wilson Diss Fel; Fordham Fel, 67, 76, 89, 95; Fulbright Awd. **SELECTED PUBLICATIONS** Ed, Simpson Street and Other Plays: by Edward Gallardo, Arte Publico Press (Univ Houston), 90; ed, Recent Puerto Rican Theatre: Five Plays from New York, Arte Publico Press (Univ Houston), 91; ed, Nuestro New York: An Anthology of Puerto Rican Plays, Penguin (NY), 94; auth, "The New Puerto Rican in the Plays of Edward Gallardo," SCAPR NL 11 (90): 1-5; auth, "The American Experience in Puerto Rican Drama/The Puerto Rican Experience in American Drama," Sarpasso J Carib Stud 7 (91): 40-45; auth, "Rene Marques' The Oxcart: Revolutionizing Drama of the Americans," SCAPR NL 12 (92): 2; auth, "Roberto Rodriguez Buarez: Transcultural Catalyst of Puerto Rican Drama," J Am Drama Thea 4 (92): 42-53; auth, "Editing the Bilingual Text at Cross-Cultural Purposes," TEXT 6 (94); auth, "The Academic Politics and Commercial Possibilities of Publishing Puerto Rican Plays in New York," Multi Rev 3 (94); auth, "The Internal Third World Voice and Postcolonial Literature: Rene Marques's The Oxcart," in Staging Difference: Cultural Pluralism in American Theater and Drama, ed. Marc Maufort (Peter Lang Pub: NY, 95); auth, "The New York Puerto Rican Playwrights of New York," forthcoming. **CONTACT ADDRESS** Dept English, Fordham Univ, 441 East Fordham Rd, Bronx, NY 10458-5149.

ANWAR, WASEEM

PERSONAL Born 03/15/1956, Rawalandi, Pakistan, m, 1988, 2 children **DISCIPLINE** ENGLISH **EDUCATION** Punjab Univ, MA, 78; MPhil, 94; Allama Iqbal Open Univ, Islamabad, Dipteil, 91; Ind Univ Pa, PhD, 01. **CAREER** Lectr, Govt Col, 80-84, Pakistan; lectr to asst prof, FC Col, Pakistan, 84-89; assoc prof, Punjab Public Serv Comm, 94; TA, Ind Univ of Pa, 99-01. **HONORS AND AWARDS** Fulbright Fel, 95-99; Phi Kappa Phi, 00. **MEMBERSHIPS** MLA, SALA, Phi Kappa Phi. **RESEARCH** African American Literature, Post Colonial Literature, Modern/Postmodern Drama, Feminist Theories. **SELECTED PUBLICATIONS** Rev, of "Theatre and Feminist Aesthetics," by Karem Laughlin and "Contemporary African American Women Playwrights," by Danna A Williams, Studies in the Humanities 27.2, (00); auth, "Histories of Censorship: Psychosemiots of Silence in the Plays of Suzan-Lori Parks," SORAC, (in press); auth, "Transcribing Resistance: Cartographies of Struggling Bodies and Minds in Mahasweta Devi's 'Imaginary Maps,'" S Asian Rev, 01. **CONTACT ADDRESS** Dept English, Indiana Univ of Pennsylvania, 263 Kareem Block, c/o Major Javaid Anwar, Allama Iqbal Town, Lahore, Pakistan. **EMAIL** miaaon@hotmail.com

AOKI, ERIC
DISCIPLINE COMMUNICATION STUDIES **EDUCATION** Calif State Univ Fresno, BA, MA; Univ Wash, PhD. **CAREER** Prof. **RESEARCH** Intercultural communication; interpersonal communication; ethnography of communication. **SELECTED PUBLICATIONS** Auth, Passages of Guilt, Interrace Magazine. **CONTACT ADDRESS** Speech Communication Dept, Colorado State Univ, 202 Eddy Bldg, Fort Collins, CO 80523-1783. **EMAIL** akoi@vines.colostate.edu

APPEL, ALFRED, JR.
DISCIPLINE ENGLISH **EDUCATION** Columbia Univ, PhD. **CAREER** Dept Eng, Northwestern Univ **SELECTED PUBLICATIONS** Auth, Nabokov's Dark Cinema, 74; Signs of Life: a work on American photography and popular culture of the past five decades, 83; The Art of Celebration: The Expression of Joy in 20th Century Art, Literature, Photography and Music, Knopf, 92; rev ed, The Annotated Lolita. **CONTACT ADDRESS** Dept of English, Northwestern Univ, 1801 Hinman, Evanston, IL 60208.

APPELBAUM, ROBERT
PERSONAL Born 02/02/1952, New York, NY, 1 child **DISCIPLINE** ENGLISH **EDUCATION** Univ Chicago, BA, 75; Univ Calif Berkeley, PhD, 97. **CAREER** Vis asst prof, Univ of Cincinnati, 97-99; vis asst prof, Univ Ala Birmingham, 99-00; fel, Univ San Diego, 00-. **HONORS AND AWARDS** Mellon Found Fel, 92, 93-94; Bancroft Libr Fel, 92-93; Eugenio Battisti Awd, 97; Univ of Cincinnati Res Coun Awd, 98; NEH, 99, 00; Newberry Libr, 00, Folger Shakespeare Libr, 00-01. **MEMBERSHIPS** MLA, GEMCS. **RESEARCH** Early Modern Cultural Studies, British literature to 1744, Sahakespeare and Milton, Culture, Literature and Food. **SELECTED PUBLICATIONS** Auth, "Utopian Dubrovnik, 1659: An English Fantasy," Utopian Studies, (96); auth, "Tip-toeing to the Apocalypse: Herbert, Milton, and the Modern Sense of Time," George Herbert Jour, (96); auth, "Standing to the Wall: The Pressures of Masculinity in Romeo and Juliet," Shakespeare Quart, (97); auth, "'O Power': Gerrard Winstanley and the Limits of Communist Poetics," Prose Studies, (99); auth, "War and Peace in the Lepanto of James VI and I," Mod Philol, (00); auth, "Aguecheek's Beef," Textual Practice, (00); auth, "Newe Bokes of Cookerie," JEMCS, (01); auth, "Belch's Hiccup: Disturbances of the Appetite in twelfth Night," Textus, (forthcoming); auth, Literature and Utopian Politics in Seventeenth-Century England, Cambridge Univ Pr, (forthcoming). **CONTACT ADDRESS** Dept English, Univ of San Diego, 5998 Alcala Pk, San Diego, CA 92110. **EMAIL** appel@sandiego.edu

APPLEGATE, JOHN A.
DISCIPLINE SPEECH, LANGUAGE **EDUCATION** Muskingum Col, BA, 66; Oh Univ, MA, 68; Kent State Univ, PhD, 84. **CAREER** Speech pathologist, W Hartford Pub Sch, 68-70; Instructor, Murray State Univ, 70-77; Teaching Fel, Kent State Univ, 77-80; Prof, Truman State Univ, 80-. **MEMBERSHIPS** Am Speech Lang Hearing Asn; MO Speech Lang Hearing Asn. **RESEARCH** Voice; Fluency disorders. **CONTACT ADDRESS** Dept Comm Disorders, Truman State Univ, Kirksville, MO 63501. **EMAIL** jaa@truman.edu

APPLEWHITE, JAMES W.
PERSONAL Born 08/08/1935, Wilson City, NC, m, 1956, 3 children **DISCIPLINE** ENGLISH LITERATURE **EDUCATION** Duke Univ, PhD, 69. **CAREER** Prof, Duke Univ. **HONORS AND AWARDS** Guggenheim Fel; AWP Poetry Awd, Princeton Series of Contemp Poets. **MEMBERSHIPS** Fel of Southern Writers. **SELECTED PUBLICATIONS** Auth, Wordswor Seas and Inland Journeys: Landscape and Consciousness fth to Roethke, Ga, 85; River Writing: An Eno Journal, Princeton, 88; Daytime and Starlight, LSU, 97; pubs on modern Am poetry; southern lit, and modernist and postmodernist aesthet poetry and visual art. **CONTACT ADDRESS** Eng Dept, Duke Univ, Durham, NC 27706.

APPLEYARD, JOSEPH A.
PERSONAL Born 05/09/1931, Malden, MA **DISCIPLINE** ENGLISH **EDUCATION** Boston Col, AB, 53; Weston Col, PhL, 58; Harvard Uniy, PhD, 64; Faculteit SJ, Maastricht, Netherlands, STL, 67. **CAREER** From asst prof to assoc prof Eng, 67-91, prof eng, Boston Col, 91-, chmn dept, 79-, Dir, Col of Arts and Sci honors prog, 87-97, vpres, Univ mission and ministry, 98. **RESEARCH** Nineteenth and twentieth century Eng lit; lit criticism and theory. **SELECTED PUBLICATIONS** Auth, Coleridge's Philosophy of Literature, Harvard Univ, 65; Becoming a Reader, Cambridge Univ, 90. **CONTACT ADDRESS** Boston Col, Chestnut Hill, 140 Commonwealth Ave, Chestnut Hill, MA 02467-3800. **EMAIL** jospeh.appleyard@bc.edu

APSELOFF, MARILYN FAIN
PERSONAL Born 03/18/1934, Attleboro, MA, m, 1956, 4 children **DISCIPLINE** CHILDREN'S LITERATURE, AMERICAN LITERATURE **EDUCATION** Univ Cincinnati, BA, 56, MA, 57. **CAREER** From instr to prof Children's Lit, Kent State Univ, 68-. **HONORS AND AWARDS** Children's Lit Assoc Honor BK, 90 for Nonsense Lit for Children. **MEMBERSHIPS** Children's Lit Asn (pres-elect, 78-79). **RESEARCH** 20 th Century humorous books for children; whaling wives and children at sea. **SELECTED PUBLICATIONS** Auth, Virginia Hamilton: Ohio Explorer in the World of Imagination, State Libr Ohio, 78; Monograph, Virginia Hamilton: Ohio Explorer in the World of Imagination, State Libr Ohio, 78; Old Wine in New Bottles: Adult Poetry for Children, Children's Lit Educ, winter 79; Tom Thumb in Academia, The New Era, 5-6/81; They Wrote for Children Too, Greenwood, 89; Elizabeth George Speare, Twayne, 91; Nonsense Literature for Children with Celia C Anderson, Shoestring Press, 89. **CONTACT ADDRESS** Dept of English, Kent State Univ, PO Box 5190, Kent, OH 44242-0001. **EMAIL** mapselof@kent.edu

APTER, RONNIE
PERSONAL Born 06/04/1943, Hartford, CT, m, 1967, 2 children **DISCIPLINE** ENGLISH **EDUCATION** Sarah Lawrence Col, BA, 65; NY Univ, MA, 67; Fordham Univ, PhD, 80. **CAREER** From Asst Prof to Prof, Cent Mich Univ, 86-. **HONORS AND AWARDS** Thomas Wolfe Poetry Awd, NY Univ, 67; NEH Grant, Princeton Univ, 86. **MEMBERSHIPS** ALTA, ATA, ICLS, LSSWMR, MLA. **RESEARCH** Translation, word-music relations. **SELECTED PUBLICATIONS** Transl, Reader's Digest Bible for Children: Timeless Stories from the Old and New Testaments, Readers Dig Young Families Publ/ Joshua Morris Publ, 95; auth, A Bilingual Edition of the Love Songs of Bernart de Ventadorn in Occitan and English: Sugar and Salt, The Edwin Mellen Pr (New York/Ontario/Wales), 99. **CONTACT ADDRESS** Dept English, Central Michigan Univ, 100 W Preston Rd, Mount Pleasant, MI 48859-0001. **EMAIL** ronnie.apter@cmich.edu

ARAC, JONATHAN
PERSONAL Born 04/04/1945, New York, NY **DISCIPLINE** ENGLISH **EDUCATION** Harvard Univ, BA, 67; AM, 68; PhD, 74. **CAREER** Teaching Fel, Harvard Univ, 69-70; jr fel, Harvard Univ, 70-73; asst prof, Princeton Univ, 73-79; from assoc prof to prof, Univ Ill, 79-86; prof, Duke Univ, 86-87; prof, Columbia Univ, 87-90; prof, Univ Pittsburgh, 89-; Drue Heinz Vis Acad, Oxford Univ, 00; Avalon Distinguished Vis Prof, Northwestern Univ, 00. **HONORS AND AWARDS** Phi Beta Kappa, 66; Woodrow Wilson Fel, 67; Fel, Am Coun of Learned Soc, 78-79; grant, NEH Div of Educ, 84; NEH Fel, 86-87 & 94-95; USIA Acad Specialist Grant, 93; Chancellor's Distinguished Res Awd, 98; Fel, Ctr for Advanced Study in Behav Sci, 00-01. **SELECTED PUBLICATIONS** Auth, Commissioned Sprits: The Shaping of Social Motion in Dickens, Carlyle, Melville and Hawthorne, Columbia Univ Pr, 79; auth, Critical Genealogies: Historical Situations for Postmodern Literary Studies, Columbia Univ Pr, 87; auth, "Narrative Forms", Prose Writings, 1820-1865, Cambridge Hist of Am Lit, ed Sacvan Bercovitch, Cambridge Univ Pr, (95): 605-777; auth, "Huckleberry Finn as Idol and Target: The Functions of Criticism in Our Time, Project on Am Writers, Univ of Wis Pr, 97; ed, The Yale Critics: Deconstruction In America, Univ of Minn Pr, 83; ed, Postmodernism and Politics, Theory and Hist of Lit, Vol 28; Univ of Minn Pr, 86; ed, After Foucault: Humanistic Knowledge, Postmodern Challenges, Rutgers Univ Pr, 88; coed, Consequences of Theory, Johns Hopkins Univ Pr, 90; coed, Macropolitics of Nineteenth-Century Literature: Nationalism, Exoticism, Imperialism, Univ of Pa Pr, 91. **CONTACT ADDRESS** Dept English, Univ of Pittsburgh, 58 Cathedral of Learning, Pittsburgh, PA 15260-6100. **EMAIL** jarac@pitt.edu

ARAM, DOROTHY M.
DISCIPLINE COMMUNICATION DISORDERS **EDUCATION** Northwestern Univ, BS, MA; Case Western Univ, PhD. **CAREER** Com, Emerson Col. **SELECTED PUBLICATIONS** Auth, Diagnosis of Speech and Lang Disorders; Child Lang Disorders. **CONTACT ADDRESS** Emerson Col, 100 Beacon Street, Boston, MA 02116-1596.

ARATA, STEPHEN D.
PERSONAL Born 08/03/1958, Philadelphia, PA, m, 1982, 2 children **DISCIPLINE** ENGLISH **EDUCATION** Col of William and Mary, BA, 80; MA, 82; Univ of Chicago, PhD, 90. **CAREER** Asst to assoc prof, Univ Va, 90-. **HONORS AND AWARDS** William Rainey Harper Fel, 88-89; Mrs Giles Whiting Fel, 88-89; Marc Perry Galler Prize, 90; ACLS Fel, 93-94; Alumni Teaching Award, 96; Fulbright Fel, 99; Sesquicentennial Associateship, Center for Adv Studies, 02. **MEMBERSHIPS** MLA, Mod Studies Asn, Victorians Inst, William Morris Soc, Powys Soc of N Am. **RESEARCH** 19th and 20th Century British Literature and Culture, Narrative Theory, History of the Novel, S Asian Writing in English. **SELECTED PUBLICATIONS** Auth, Fictions of Loss in the Victorian Fin de Siecle, Cambridge Univ Pr, 96. **CONTACT ADDRESS** Dept English, Univ of Virginia, Bryan Hall 219, PO Box 22904-4121, Charlottesville, VA 22904-4121. **EMAIL** sda2e@virginia.edu

ARAUJO, LUISA
PERSONAL Born 05/20/1965, Portugal, m, 1985, 2 children **DISCIPLINE** ENGLISH **EDUCATION** Univ Del, BA, 90; MA, 93; PhD, 00. **CAREER** Adj, Rutgers Univ, 95-97; asst prof, William Paterson Univ, 98-. **HONORS AND AWARDS** Women of the Year Excellence Awd, 93. **MEMBERSHIPS** NCTE; ACEI; AATSP; IRA. **RESEARCH** Emergent Literacy, Reading, ESL, and World Languages. **SELECTED PUBLICATIONS** Auth, Pre-service teachers as literacy mediators during children's play, ERIC Document, 96; auth, O Bom Barqueiro", Hispania 82.3 (99): 527-528; coauth, World Languages Curriculum Standards Alignment Manual, Corn Assoc, (forthcoming). **CONTACT ADDRESS** Dept Curric and Instr, William Paterson Col of New Jersey, 300 Pompton Rd, Wayne, NJ 07470.

ARAVAMUNDAN, SRINIVAS
DISCIPLINE ENGLISH **EDUCATION** Loyola Univ, BA, 84; Purdue Univ, MA, 86; Cornell Univ, MA, 88; PhD, 91. **CAREER** Asst prof, Univ Utah, 91-96; asst prof to assoc prof, Univ Wash, 96-00; assoc prof, Duke Univ, 00-. **HONORS AND AWARDS** Outstanding Book Awd, MLA, 00. **MEMBERSHIPS** MLA; ASECS. **RESEARCH** 18th-century Britain and France; colonialism; post colonialism; literary theory. **SELECTED PUBLICATIONS** Auth, Tropicopolitans: Colonization and Agency 1688-1804, Duke Univ Pr, 99; auth, Slavery, Abolition and Emancipation: Writings of the British Romantic Period, Pickering and Chetto, 99. **CONTACT ADDRESS** English Dept, Duke Univ, PO Box 90015, Durham, NC 27708. **EMAIL** srinivas@duke.edu

ARCANA, JUDITH
DISCIPLINE ENGLISH LITERATURE **EDUCATION** Northwestern Univ, BA; Univ Ill, MA; Univ Chicago, PhD. **CAREER** Lectr. **RESEARCH** Women's studies; improvisational theater performance; radical health care; magic and the old religion. **SELECTED PUBLICATIONS** Auth, Mamababy, 95; The Body of A Goddess, 95; My Father's Prostrate Gland, Sojourner, 94; The Book of Daniel, 94; Abortion is a Motherhood Issue, 94. **CONTACT ADDRESS** Union Inst, 440 E McMillan St., Cincinnati, OH 45206-1925.

ARCHIBALD, ELIZABETH F.
DISCIPLINE MEDIEVAL; EARLY RENAISSANCE LITERATURE **EDUCATION** Univ Cambridge, MA; Yale Univ, PhD. **CAREER** Assoc prof **SELECTED PUBLICATIONS** Auth, Apollonius of Tyre: Medieval and Renaissance Themes and Variations, Boydell & Brewer, 91; co-ed, A Companion to Malory, Boydell & Brewer, 96. **CONTACT ADDRESS** Dept of English, Univ of Victoria, Clearihue Bldg, Rm D333, PO Box 3070, Victoria, BC, Canada V8W 3W1. **EMAIL** efa@uvic.ca

AREHOLE, S.
PERSONAL Born 10/19/1957, India, m, 1988, 3 children **DISCIPLINE** COMMUNICATION DISORDER **EDUCATION** Univ Texas Dallas, PhD 86. **CAREER** Univ of SW Louisiana, assoc prof, prof, 87-. **HONORS AND AWARDS** CDRC Audiology fel, Hathorne-BORSF Endowed Prof, 99. **MEMBERSHIPS** ASLHA; AAS; AAA. **RESEARCH** Auditory electrophysiology and Central auditory processing. **SELECTED PUBLICATIONS** Auth, Auditory evoked potentials in low-achieving gifted adolescents, coauth, Roeper Rev; Central auditory processing abilities of low-achieving gifted adolescents, coauth, Jour of Secondary Gifted EDU , 98; Clarification: Masking level differences with GSI-10 audiometer, Amer Jour of Audiology, 98; Identification and assessment of hearing-impaired infants and toddlers, coauth, in: F. Billeaud, ed, Communication disorders in infants and toddlers: Assessment and management. Reading MA, Andover Med Pub, 98; Objective assessment of central auditory processing disorder, Jour of Indian Speech and Hearing Assoc, 98; Cerumen management and audiology practice: Attitudes among otolaryngologists and Audiologists, coauth, Nat Stud Speech Lang and Hearing Jour, 96; A preliminary study of the relationship between long latency response and learning disorder, Brit Jour of Audiology, 95; auth, Auditory evoked potentials in low-achieving gifted adolescents, Arehole, S, & Rigo, T.G, Roeper Review, Vol 22, 51-56. **CONTACT ADDRESS** Dept of Communication Disorders, Univ of Southwestern Louisiana, PO Box 43170, Lafayette, LA 70506. **EMAIL** sxa3201@louisiana.edu

ARENBERG, NANCY
DISCIPLINE EPISTOLARY FICTION **EDUCATION** Grinnell Col, BA, 82; Univ Ill, MA, 89; Univ Ariz, PhD, 96. **CAREER** English and Lit, Univ Ark. **SELECTED PUBLICATIONS** Area: seventeenth- and eighteenth-century French literature. **CONTACT ADDRESS** Univ of Arkansas, Fayetteville, Fayetteville, AR 72701.

ARIETI, JAMES ALEXANDER
PERSONAL Born 05/12/1948, New York, NY, m, 1976, 2 children **DISCIPLINE** CLASSICS, HISTORY **EDUCATION** Grinnell Col, BA, 69; Stanford Univ, MA, 72, PhD(classics), 72. **CAREER** Asst prof classics, Stanford Univ, 73-74; asst prof, Pa State Univ, 74-75; asst prof classics & hist, Cornell Col, 75-77; asst prof, 78-81, assoc prof, 81-88, prof classics, Hampden-Sydney Col, 88-95, Thompson Prof Classics, 95-; asst bibliographer ling, MLA, 74-75; NEH fel, classics, 77-78; chemn bd & sr fel, Hesperis Inst for Humanistic Studies, 77-. **HONORS AND AWARDS** Phi Beta Kappa, 69; Woodrow Wilson fel, 69; Mettauer Reseach Award, 86, 97; John Temple-

ton Prize for Science & Religion, 96. **MEMBERSHIPS** Am Philol Asn; Class Asn of Middle West & South; VA Classical Asn. **RESEARCH** Ancient historiography and philosophy; ancient literary criticism; Septuagint. **SELECTED PUBLICATIONS** Auth, The Vocabulary of Septuagint Amos, J Biblical Lit, 74; Nudity in Greek Athletics, Class World, 75; coauth, The Dating of Longinus, Studia Classica, 75; co-ed, MLA Int Bibliography, In; 1974 Vol III, MLA, 76; contrib, Two Studies in Latin Phonology, Studia Ling et Philol, 76; coauth, Love Can Be Found, Harcourt Brace Jovanovich, 77; auth, Empedocles in Rome: Rape and the Roman Ethos, Clio, 81; A Herodotean Source for Rasselas, Note & Queries, 81; coauth, Longinus on the Sublime, Edwin Meller pub, 85; co-ed, Hamartia: The Concept of Error in the Western Tradition, Edwin Mellen Pub, 83; auth, Interpreting Plato: The Dialogues as Drama, Rowman & Littlefield, 91; Discourses on the First Book of Herodotus, Littlefield Adams Books, 95; numerous articles and reviews. **CONTACT ADDRESS** Dept of Classics, Hampden-Sydney Col, Hampden-Sydney, VA 23943. **EMAIL** jarieti@email.hsc.edu

ARLIN, MARY I.
PERSONAL Born 06/26/1939, Lyons, NY **DISCIPLINE** MUSIC THEORY **EDUCATION** Ithaca Col, BS; Univ Ind, PhD. **CAREER** Prof. **MEMBERSHIPS** Soc Music Theory; Am Viola Soc; Music Theory Soc NYork State; Phi Kappa Lamda; Phi Kappa Phi. **RESEARCH** History of theory; Pedagogy of theory. **SELECTED PUBLICATIONS** Auth, Interval Tutor: A Computer Program for Ear Training; auth, Frustrating Fundamentals: A Computer Program for Theory, Pendragon; auth, Esquisse de l'histoire de l'harmonie: An English-Language Translation of the Francois-Joseph Fitis History of Harmony, Pendragon; co-auth, Music Sources, Prentice Hall, 89; auth, Supplement, Sightsinging I and II, Lyceum; auth, Source Book, Theory 1 (6th ed), Lyceum. **CONTACT ADDRESS** School of Music, Ithaca Col, Ithaca, NY 14850-7240. **EMAIL** arlin@ithaca.edu

ARLISS, LAURIE
DISCIPLINE COMMUNICATION STUDIES **EDUCATION** SUNY-Cortland Univ, BA, MA; SUNY Buffalo Univ, PhD. **CAREER** Assoc prof. **SELECTED PUBLICATIONS** Auth, pubs on gender and communication and family communication. **CONTACT ADDRESS** Dept of Speech Communication, Ithaca Col, 100 Job Hall, Ithaca, NY 14850.

ARMER, ALAN A.
PERSONAL Born 07/07/1922, Los Angeles, CA, m, 1949, 4 children **DISCIPLINE** SPEECH, DRAMA **EDUCATION** Stanford Univ, BA; Univ Calif at Los Angeles, MA. **CAREER** Wrote, produced, or directed over 350 network TV shows; prof, Calif State Univ at Northridge. **HONORS AND AWARDS** Emmy Awd; Distinguished Teaching Awd; Mystery Writers Awd; Western Writers Awd; Producers Guild Awd; TV Guide Awd. **MEMBERSHIPS** Directors Guild of Am, Television Academy, Producers Guild of Am. **RESEARCH** The Nature of Creativity. **SELECTED PUBLICATIONS** Auth, Directing TV and Film, Wadsworth Publ; auth, Writing the Screenplay, Wadsworth Publ. **CONTACT ADDRESS** Dept Television/Radio/Film, California State Univ, Northridge, 18111 Nordhoff St, Northridge, CA 91330-0001. **EMAIL** aaarmer@aol.com

ARMSTRONG, DIANNE
DISCIPLINE ENGLISH **EDUCATION** Univ Southern Calif, MA, 90; PhD, 92. **CAREER** Instr, Univ of Calif, 84-87; instr, Calif State Univ, 86-91; lectr, Univ of Southern Calif, 92-93; instr, Santa Barbara City Col, 93-94; instr, Ventura Col, 96-. **HONORS AND AWARDS** Teaching Commendation, Univ of Calif, 87; Instr of the Year, Ventura Col, 96-97. **MEMBERSHIPS** NCTE; Philological Assoc of the Pacific Coast; MLA; Conf on Col Composition and Commun; Soc for the Study of Narrative Lit. **SELECTED PUBLICATIONS** Auth, "The Myth of Cronus: Cannibal and Sign in Robinson Crusoe", Eighteenth-Century Fiction 4.3, (92): 207-20; auth, "Twain's Jim: Uncle Remus Redux?", Nineteenth-Century Studies 9, (95): 65-84; auth, "Pragmatics", Encycl of Rhetoric and Composition, ed Theresa Enos, Garland, (NY/ London), 96. **CONTACT ADDRESS** Dept Lib Arts, Ventura Col, 4667 Telegraph Rd, Ventura, CA 93003-3872. **EMAIL** dianneO@aol.com

ARNASON, DAVID E.
DISCIPLINE ENGLISH LITERATURE **EDUCATION** Univ Manitoba, MA; Univ New Brunswick, PhD. **CAREER** Prof; Head, Dept of Eng. **HONORS AND AWARDS** Ed, Jour Can Fiction; ed, Macmillan Themes Can Lit; ed, Nineteenth Century Can Stories; ed, Turnstone Press. **RESEARCH** Canadian lit, prairie fiction. **SELECTED PUBLICATIONS** Auth, Marsh Burning; The Icelanders; Piece of Advice; The Circus Performer's Bar; The Happiest Man in the World; The Pagan Wall; Skragg; The New Icelanders; The Dragon and The Drygoods Princess; If Pigs Could Fly; 50 Stories and a Piece of Advice. **CONTACT ADDRESS** Dept of English, Univ of Manitoba, Winnipeg, MB, Canada R3T 2N2. **EMAIL** arnasn@cc.umanitoba.ca

ARNER, ROBERT DAVID
PERSONAL Born 01/17/1943, Lehighton, PA, 2 children **DISCIPLINE** AMERICAN LITERATURE **EDUCATION** Kutztown State Col, BS, 64; PA State Univ, MA, 66, PhD(English), 70. **CAREER** From instr to asst prof English, Cent Mich Univ, 68-71; from asst prof to assoc prof, 71-75, PROF ENGLISH, UNIV CINCINNATI, 75-; Mem int bibliog comt, MLA, 68-; Fred Harris Daniels fel, Am Antiq Soc, 75; Henry E Huntington fel, Huntington Libr, 75; MEMLA/AAS fel, 91. **MEMBERSHIPS** MLA; SAMLA. **RESEARCH** Early American literature; 19th century American literature; American humor. **SELECTED PUBLICATIONS** Auth, Hawthorne and Jones Very: Two Dimensions of Satire in Egotism: Or, the Bosom Serpent, New England Quart, 6/69; Ebenezer Cooke's The Sot-Weed factor: The Structure of Satire, Southern Lit J, fall 71; Pastoral Patterns in William Bartram's Travels, Tenn Studies Lit, 73; Literature to 1800, Am Lit Scholarship, 74-77; Westover and the Wilderness: William Byrd's Images of Virginia, Southern Lit J, 75; Kate Chopin, La Studies, 75; The Romance of Roanoke: Virginia Dare and the Lost Colony in American Literature, 1585-1970, Southern Lit J, 78; James Thurber: An Introduction, Nat Endowment for Humanities Proj Ohio Cult, Ohio State Libr, 80; Dobson's Encyclopedia: The Publisher, Text, and Publication of America's First Britannica, Univ PA, 91; Historical Essay on Charles Brockden Brown's Alcuin and Stephen Calvert, Kent SUP, 86; Thomas Dobson's American Edition of the Encyclopedia Britannica, Voltaire Studies, no 315, 94; Thomas Dobson's Rolling Mill for Copper: A Note on the Publisher of the Encyclopedia, PMHB, 94. **CONTACT ADDRESS** Dept of English, Univ of Cincinnati, P O Box 210069, Cincinnati, OH 45221-0069. **EMAIL** robert.arner@uc.edu

ARNESON, PAT
DISCIPLINE INTERPERSONAL COMMUNICATION **EDUCATION** OH Univ, PhD, 87. **CAREER** Prof, Univ Northern CO. **MEMBERSHIPS** CO Speech Commun Asn; Western States Commun Asn; Nat Commun Asn. **RESEARCH** Interpersonal commun; qualitative research methods. **SELECTED PUBLICATIONS** Auth, Sacred Dimensions of the shaman's web. Integrative Explorations, J of Cult and Consciousness, 4(1), 97; coauth, Interpersonal communication ethics and the limits of individualism, The Electronic J of Commun/La Rev Electronique de Commun, 6(4), 96; Educational Assessment as invitation for dialogue, J of the Asn for Commun Admin, 79, 97. **CONTACT ADDRESS** Univ of No Colorado, Greeley, CO 80639.

ARNETT, RONALD C.
PERSONAL Born 03/10/1952, Fort Wayne, IN, m, 1972, 2 children **DISCIPLINE** COMMUNICATION STUDIES **EDUCATION** Manchester Col, BS, 74; Ohio Univ, MA, 75; PhD, 77; Bethany Theol Seminary, MDiv, 83. **CAREER** Asst to Assoc Prof, St. Cloud State Univ, 77-84; Assoc Prof, Marquette Univ, 84-87; Prof, Manchester Col, 90-93; Prof and Chair, Duquesne Univ, 93-. **HONORS AND AWARDS** Article of the Year Awd, Religious commun Asn, 99; Top competitive Paper Awd, Nat Commun Asn, 97; Patron Saint for Saturday Col Commencement, Duquesne Univ, 97; Outstanding Alumnus, Ohio Univ, 96. **MEMBERSHIPS** Intl Commun Asn, Nat Commun Asn, Speech Commun Asn of Penn, Cen States Commun Asn, Ind Commun Asn, Relig Speech Commun Asn, Consortium on Peace Res, Educ and Development, Phi Kappa Phi. **RESEARCH** Interpersonal Communication, The Philosophy of Communication, Communication administration, Theology, peace studies and communication and english. **SELECTED PUBLICATIONS** Auth, Dialogical Civility in a Cynical Age: Community, Hope, and Interpersonal Relationship, Univ New York Press, 99; auth, "Metaphorical Guidance: Administration as Building and Renovation," Journal of Educational Administration, 99; auth, "Organizational Ethical Standards and Organizational Commitment," Journal of Business Ethics, (99): 289-300; auth, "Departmental Excellence: Constituencies in Tension," ACA Bulletin, (99): 19; auth, "Review--'Between Jerusalem and Athens: Ethical Perspectives on Culture, Religion, and Psychotherapy," Mennonite Quarterly Review, (99): 142; auth, "The Praxis of Narrative Assessment: Communication Competence in an Information Age," Journal of the Association for Communication Administration, (98): 44-58; auth, "Interpersonal Praxis: The Interplay of Religious Narrative, Historicality and Metaphor," Journal of Communication and Religion, 98; auth, "Educational Assessment as Invitation for Dialogue," Journal of the Association for Communication Administration, (97): 81-94. **CONTACT ADDRESS** Dept Commun, Duquesne Univ, 600 Forbes Ave, Pittsburgh, PA 15282-0001. **EMAIL** arnett@duq.edu

ARNEZ, NANCY L.
PERSONAL Born 07/06/1928, Baltimore, MD, d **DISCIPLINE** ENGLISH **EDUCATION** Morgan State Col, AB 1949; Columbia Univ, MA 1954, EdD 1958; Harvard Univ, post doctoral 1962; Loyola Col, 1965. **CAREER** Baltimore Pub Sch, English tchr, 49-58, dept head 58-62; Morgan State Coll, dir student teaching, 62-66; Northeastern IL Univ, assoc prof/asst dir Cntr for Inner City Studies, 66-69, prof/dir Cntr for Inner City Studies, 69-74, co-founder, Cultural Linguistic, Follow Through Early Childhood CICS, 69-74; Howard Univ School of Educ, acting dean, 75, assoc dean, 74-, dept chairperson, 80-86, professor, 86-. **HONORS AND AWARDS** Assn of African History Serv Awd 1972; Alpha Kappa Alpha Sor Serv Awd 1971; Appointed Hon Citizen of Compton, CA 1972; Howard Univ distinguished faculty research awd 1983; 4th place in the international competition for Phi Delta Kappa's biennial awd for outstanding research 1985. **MEMBERSHIPS** Congress of African People 1968-70; Amer Assn of School Admin 1968-87; Black Child Devel Inst DC 1971-74; Assn of African Historians Chicago 1972; Assn of the Study of Afro-Amer Life & Hist 1972-77; mem African Heritage Studies Assn, bd of dir membership sec 1973-77; Natl Alliance of Black Sch Educators 1973-; Amer Assn of Sch Admin Resolutions Comm 1973-75; African Information Cntr Catalyst Chicago 1973-77; bd of dir DuSable Museum Chicago 1973-74; mem Black Women's Comm Devel Found DC 1974; Amer Assn of Coll Tchrs of Educ 1977; Natl Council of Negro Women 1977; mem Phi Delta Kappa Howard Univ Chap 1974-, editorial bd 1975-78; Journal of Negro Education, editorial bd 1975-80; AASA Professor, editorial bd 1981-84; NABSE Newsbrief, editor 1984-86;mem DC Alliance of Black School Educator 1984-, pres 1986-88. **SELECTED PUBLICATIONS** 180 publications. **CONTACT ADDRESS** Howard Univ, 2400 6th St, NW, Washington, DC 20059.

ARONSON, ARNOLD
PERSONAL Born 03/08/1948, Morristown, NJ, m, 1988, 1 child **DISCIPLINE** PERFORMING ARTS **EDUCATION** Rutgers Univ, BA, 69; New York Univ, MA, 75, PhD, 77. **CAREER** From asst to assoc prof, Univ Va, 76-84; vis assoc prof, Cornell Univ, 84-85; vis assoc prof, Univ Del, 85-86; assoc prof, Univ Mich, 86-90; CUNY prof, Hunter Col, 90-91; prof, Columbia Univ. **HONORS AND AWARDS** Chemn, Univ Mich, 87-90; chemn, Hunter Col, 90-91, chemn, Columbia Univ, 91-98. **MEMBERSHIPS** Int Org of Scenographers, Theatre Archit, and Technicians; Am Soc for Theatre Res; US Inst for Theatre Tech. **RESEARCH** Theatre Hist. **SELECTED PUBLICATIONS** Auth, The History and Theory of Environmental Scenography, 81; auth, American Set Design, 85; auth, Theatre Technology and the Shifting Aesthetic, 97; auth, The Scenography of Chekhov's Plays, 99; auth, Am Avant-Garde Theatre, 00; **CONTACT ADDRESS** Div of Theatre, Columbia Univ, 2960 Broadway, 601 Dodge Hall-MC 1807, New York, NY 10027. **EMAIL** apay@columbia.edu

ARTHUR, GWEN
PERSONAL Born 02/05/1953, Charleston, SC, m, 1991 **DISCIPLINE** COMMUNICATION; LIBRARY SERVICE **EDUCATION** Wesleyan Univ, BA, 75; Columbia Univ, MLS, 82; Univ Pa Philadelphia, 90. **CAREER** Co-ord to bibliogr, Temple Univ, 85-91; head, Bowling Green St Univ, 91-95; head, Trinity Col, 95-96; head, Trinity Col, 96-99; dir, Clark Univ Libraries, 99- . **HONORS AND AWARDS** Cum laude, Wesleyan Univ; Beta Phi Mu, Columbia Univ. **MEMBERSHIPS** Amer Libr Assoc; Assoc of Col & Res Libr; Libr Admin & Mgmt Assoc; Ref & User Svc Assoc. **RESEARCH** Library personnel issues; electronic ref & collections; soc sci librarianship. **SELECTED PUBLICATIONS** Auth, Using Video for Reference Staff Training and Development: A Selective Bibliography, Ref Svc Rev, 92; 90's Alternatives for Library Staff Development, paper, Acad Libr Assoc Oh Annual Conf, 93; Customer Service Training in Academic Libraries, J of Acad Librarianship, 94; The Graying of Librarianship: Implications for Academic Library Managers, J of Acad Librarianship, 98. **CONTACT ADDRESS** Clark Univ, 53 Elm St., Worcester, MA 01609-2518. **EMAIL** garthur@clarku.edu

ARTHUR, THOMAS H.
PERSONAL Born 01/04/1937, Chicago, IL, m, 1976, 4 children **DISCIPLINE** DRAMA **EDUCATION** Northwestern Univ, BS (general speech), 59; IN Univ, MA (theatre), 69, PhD (Am Studies), 73. **CAREER** Teaching asst in acting, directing, and oral interpretation, IN Univ, 65-68; adjunct lect in Theatre Hist, IL Wesleyan Univ, 72-73; asst prof, IL State Univ, 69-73; assoc prof, 73-80, prof, Center for Dance & Theatre, 85-86 & Dept of Commun Arts, 80-85, prof, School of Theatre & Dance, James Madison Univ, Harisonburg, VA, 86-. **HONORS AND AWARDS** Honorable mention, Russell B Nye Awd, 81-82; selection of directorial work for the ACTF Southeast Regional Am Col Theatre Festival, Greensboro, NC, and Clemson, SC, 98; invited appearance of directing work, The Roadhouse Theatre for Contemporary Art, Erie, PA, 92; selection of producing work, ACTRF, Radford, VA, 92, and at ACTF Nat Festival at Kennedy Space Center; invitation/financing to write South African Theatre J Reviews ofm 92 Grahamstown Theatre Festival plays; James Madison Univ nomination for State Coun of Higher Ed in VA Outstanding Fac Awd, 93, 95; US Information Agency Arts Am Consultant, Naples, Italy, Nov 95, Budapest, Hungary, March 94, Finland, Nov 89, and South Africa, June/July, 89; biography found in numerous publications. **MEMBERSHIPS** Am Soc for Theatre Res; Am Asn for Univ Prof; Asn for Theatre in Higher Ed; Black Theatre Network; Int Fed for Theatre Res; Nat Asn of Schools of Ed; Southeastern Theatre Conference; Speech Commun of Am; VA Theatre Asn. **SELECTED PUBLICATIONS** Auth, Review of Athol Fugard's My Children! My Africa! in Theatre J, May 90; Spaghetti Westerns and American Football: The Extraordinary Life of Actor Woody Strode, Encore Mag, May 90; Review of Method Acting: Three Generations of an American Acting Style by Steve

Vineberg, Dramatics, Oct 91; Looking for My Relatives: The Political Implications of Family in Selected Works of Athol Fugard and August Wilson, SATJ, Sept 92; review of Deon Opperman's Women in the Wings at the 1992 Grahamstown Nat Theatre Festival, Theatre J, May 93; The 1994 Grahamstown Festival, co-auth by Michael D Arthur, South African Theatre J, Sept 94; review of David Edgar's Pentecost in Stages section of Theatre Insight, co-auth by Kathleen G Arthur, fall 96; the Heritage of Paul Reinhardt, Theatre Design and Technology, summer 98; Female Interpretations of Ibsen on Broadway, 1896-1947: Minnie Maddern Fiske, Alla Nazimova and Eva Le Galliene, Contemporary Approaches to Ibsen, Scandanavian Univ Press, fall 98; numerous other publications. **CONTACT ADDRESS** School of Theatre and Dance, James Madison Univ, Harrisonburg, VA 22807. **EMAIL** arthurth@jmu.edu

ARZOOMANIAN, RALPH SARKIS
PERSONAL Born 01/23/1937, Providence, RI, m, 1957, 4 children **DISCIPLINE** DRAMA **EDUCATION** Boston Univ, BA, 61; Iowa Univ, MA, 63, PhD(drama), 65. **CAREER** Fel, Yale Univ, 65-66; instr theatre, Hunter Col, 66-71; asst prof, 71-80, assoc prof Speech & Theatre, Herbert H Lehman Col, 80-. **SELECTED PUBLICATIONS** Auth, The Coop (play), Prompt Theatre Mag, London, 6/68; Four Plays, Aranat Press; The Tack Room, published in Best American Short Plays, 92-93. **CONTACT ADDRESS** Dept of Speech & Theatre, Lehman Col, CUNY, 250 Bedford Park W, Bronx, NY 10468-1527.

ASHBY, CLIFFORD
PERSONAL Born 06/11/1925, Effingham, IL, m, 1950, 2 children **DISCIPLINE** THEATRE **EDUCATION** State Univ IA, BA, 50; Univ HI, MA, 53; Stanford Univ, PhD, 63. **CAREER** Asst prof drama, Univ Pac, 53-54; instr, Univ FL, 54-57; asst prof, Univ NE, 61-63; assoc prof theatre, 63-67, res grant, 68, Prof Theatre, TX Tech Univ, 67-89, emeritus, 89-. **MEMBERSHIPS** Am Soc Theatre Res; Am Inst of Archaeology; Int Federation for Theatre Res. **RESEARCH** Classical Greek Theatre; Popular Theatre; Playwrighting. **SELECTED PUBLICATIONS** Auth, "The Siting of Greek Theatres," Theatre Research International 16 (91): 181-201; auth, "Undiscovered Europe: An American in Albania," Wall Street Journal (17 September 91): A14; auth, "Did the Greeks Really Get to the Theater Before Dawn--Three Days Running?," Theatre Research International 17 (92): 2-7; auth, Performance Sites of the Ancient World: A Photographic Survey, Emmett Publishing, 93; auth, "Theatrical Adventure on the Mississippi," Theatre Hist Studies, vol 14 (94): 1-4; The Three Actor Rule, Theatre Res Int, vol 20 (95): 183-188; auth, "Harley Sadler" and "Tent Show," in The New Handbook of Texas (Texas State Historical Asn, 96); auth, "Henry Miller" and "Harley Sadler," in American National Biography, 97; auth, "The Playwright and the 'Dramateur,'" Dramatists Guild Quarterly (98); auth, Classical Greek Theatre: New Vision of an Old Subject, Univ of Iowa Press (Iowa City), 00. **CONTACT ADDRESS** Texas Tech Univ, Lubbock, TX 79410. **EMAIL** ashcliff@aol.com

ASHDOWN, PAUL GEORGE
PERSONAL Born 07/26/1944, New York, NY, m, 1975, 1 child **DISCIPLINE** JOURNALISM **EDUCATION** Univ Fla, BA, 66, MA, 69; Bowling Green St Univ, PhD, 75. **CAREER** United Press International, 69-70; inst, Univ Toledo, 71-75; asst prof, Western Ky Univ; prof, Univ Tenn, 77-. **HONORS AND AWARDS** Fulbright-Hays Gra, 95; Fac Res Gran, 89; Outstanding Faculty Member, Univ Tenn Col of Commun, 83 & 92; Joseph Sbuttoni Key, 85; Faculty Res Awd, 86; Univ Tenn Nat Alumni Assn Outstanding Teacher Awd, 91; Univ Tenn Chancellor's Teacher-Scholar, 95-97; Robert Foster Cherry Awd for Great Teachers, 98; Alexander Prize, 00. **MEMBERSHIPS** Amer Jour Historians Assn; Soc of Professional Journalists. **RESEARCH** Journalism as literature; Journalism history. **SELECTED PUBLICATIONS** Co-ed, Morbid Curiosity and the Mass Media: Proceedings of a Symposium, Gannett Found, 84; ed, James Agee: Selected Journalism, Univ Tenn, 85; WTVJ's Miami Crime War: A Television Crusade, Floridia Historical Quart, 80; A Profile of the Press in the Republic of Ireland in 4th Ann Communs Res Symposium, Univ Tenn, 81; Sherlock Holmes Makes a Dodge Commercial in Cats, Chocolate, Clowns & Other Amusing, Interesting and Useful Subjects Covered by Newsletters, Dembner Books, 82; Ireland in World Press Encycl, Facts on File 82; Seattle 1962: Seattle's World's Fair (Century 21 Exposition in Historical Dict of the World's Fairs and Expositions, 1851-1988, Greenwood, 90; James Agee & Ernest Hemingway in A Sourcebook of Amer Lit Jour: Representative Writers in an Emerging Genre, Greenwood, 92; Prophet from Highland Avenue: James Agee's Visionary Journalism in James Agee: Reconsideration, Univ Tenn, 92; Journalism and the Telepathic Planet in Journ & Journ Educ in a Free Society, Comenius Univ, 93 (also pub in Slovak); A Key to the Attic, foreword to Knoxville's Secret History, Scruffy City Pub, 95; James Agee in Encycl Americana, Grolier, 96; Ron Rosenbaum, Joan Didion & Samuel Lover in American Literary Journalists, 1945-95, Dict of Lit Biog, Bruccoli Clark Layman, 97 & 98; The Battle of Johnsonville in Tenn Encycl of History & Culture, Tenn Historical Soc, 98; Joan Didion and Salvador, P.J. O'Rourke, & Hunter Thompson, in Dictionary of Political Communication, 99; T.S. Matthews & Thomas Willis White in Amer Nat Biog, Oxford, 99; That Delicate Flying Foot: South Florida as a Region and Metaphor in Regions & Regionalism in North America and Europe, Univ Bonn, in press; Forget Being Trendy--Dullness is Editor's Fate: Newspapers Will Always Thrive with the Trivia of Everyday Life, Bulletin of Amer Soc of Newspaper Eds, Apr. 95; American Journeys and General Washington's Ghost, Vital Speeches of the Day, Nov 94; Glimpses of India, Tenn Alumnus, Summer 96; Tovenarij in de Mediawereld, De Journalist, Apr 18, 97; Everything Changes in a Century, Ed & Pub, May 17, 97; "Technointellectual in Cyberspace," The Independent Scholar, 99-00; "From Public Intellectuals to Technointellectuals," Soundings, an Interdisciplinary J, spring/summer 99. **CONTACT ADDRESS** Sch of Journalism, Univ of Tennessee, Knoxville, 330 Communications Bldg, Knoxville, TN 37996-0330. **EMAIL** pashdown@UTK.edu

ASHLEY, LEONARD R. N.
PERSONAL Born 12/05/1928, Miami, FL **DISCIPLINE** ENGLISH, LINGUISTICS **EDUCATION** McGill Univ, BA, 49, MA, 50; Princeton Univ, AM, 53, PhD, 56. **CAREER** Instr, 53-55, Univ Utah; instr, 55-56, Royal Can Air Force, London; 2nd asst to air hist, 56-58; instr, 58-61, Univ Rochester; from instr to assoc prof, 61-72, prof, 72-, prof emeritus, 95-, Brooklyn Col; res grants, Univ Utah, 55 & Univ Rochester, 60; lectr, 61-, New Sch Social Res; Brooklyn Col fac res grant, 68; contrib ed, Papertexts, Simon & Schuster & Washington Sq Press; consult, Harper & Row & Oxford Univ Press; exec bd, Amer Name Soc; ed bd, 65-99, reviewer, Bibliotheque d' Humanisme et Renaissance, Geneva; co-ed, 97, 99, 01 Goelinguistics; Pres, Amer Soc of Geolinguistics, 91-. **HONORS AND AWARDS** Shakespeare Gold Medal, 49; hon, LHD, 98. **MEMBERSHIPS** MLA; Am Name Soc (pres, 79, 87); Int Conf Gen Semantics; NY Acad of Sci; Intl Linguistics Assn, secretary 80-82; Amer Soc of Geolinguistics, pres, 85, 91-; Am Dialect Soc. **RESEARCH** English drama; English language, especially onomastics and geolinguistics; English nondramatic literature. **SELECTED PUBLICATIONS** Auth, The Complete Book of Superstition, Prophecy, and Luck, Barricade Bks, 95; auth, The Complete Book of Magic and Witchcraft, Barricade Bks, 95; auth, The Complete Book of Devils and Demons, Barricade Bks, 96; auth, The Complete Book of Devil's Disciples, Barricade Bks, 96; auth, The Complete Book of Spells, Curses and Magical Recipes, Barricade Bks, 97; auth, The Complete Book of Vampires, Barricade Bks, 98; auth, The Complete Book of Ghosts and Poltergeists, 99; auth, George Alfred Henty and the Victorian Mind, Internet Scholar pub, 98; auth, Turkey: Names and Naming Practices, Univ Press of America, 01. **CONTACT ADDRESS** Dept of English, Brooklyn Col, CUNY, Brooklyn, NY 11210.

ASHWORTH, SUZANNE M.
PERSONAL Born 11/13/1970, Champaign, IL, m, 1995, 2 children **DISCIPLINE** ENGLISH **EDUCATION** Miami Univ, MA, 92; Penn State Univ, MA, 94, PhD, 00. **CAREER** Vis asst prof, Denison Univ, 00-01; vis asst prof, Wittenberg Univ, 01-02. **HONORS AND AWARDS** Sparks Fel, 98; Phillip Young Awd, 98; Lib Arts Dis Grnt, 97; Lib Arts Outs Teach Awd, 96; Phi Kappa Phi. **MEMBERSHIPS** SSAWW, SHARP, MLA. **RESEARCH** History of reading; literary celebrity; fan letters; popular culture studies; gender studies. **SELECTED PUBLICATIONS** Auth, "The Conduct of Reading: Susan Warner's The Wide, Wide World, Conduct Literature, and Protocols of Female Reading in Antebellum America," Legacy (00); auth, "Reading on Walden Pond and the Transfiguration of American Manhood," ESQ (forthcoming). **CONTACT ADDRESS** Eng Dept, Wittenberg Univ, Springfield, OH 43085. **EMAIL** smashworth@mindspring.com

ASKEW, TIMOTHY
DISCIPLINE ENGLISH LITERATURE **EDUCATION** Emory Univ, PhD. **CAREER** Dept Eng, Clark Atlanta Univ **RESEARCH** Early and 19th Century American literature, Southern literature, Autobiography, and Black Studies. **SELECTED PUBLICATIONS** Auth, Abbeville Road. **CONTACT ADDRESS** Clark Atlanta Univ, 223 James P Brawley Dr, SW, Atlanta, GA 30314.

ASMIS, ELIZABETH
DISCIPLINE CLASSICS **EDUCATION** Univ Toronto, BA, 62; Yale Univ, MA, 66, PhD, 70. **CAREER** Lectr, McGill Univ, 63-65; res asst, British Museum, 66-68; asst prof, Cornell Univ, 70-79; Assoc prof, Univ Chicago, 79-94; Prof, Univ Chicago, 94-. **HONORS AND AWARDS** Woodrow Wilson Fel; Phi Beta Kappa Fel; NEH Fel; ed, clas philol. **SELECTED PUBLICATIONS** Auth, Epicurus' Scientific Method, Cornell Univ Press, 84; auth, Asclepiades Rediscovered?, Class Philol, 93; auth, Philodemus on Censorship, Moral Utility, and Formalism in Poetry, Philodemus and Poetry: Poetic THeory and Practice in Lucretius, Philodemus and Horace, 95; auth, Epicurean Semiotics, Knowledge Through Signs, Ancient Semiotic Theoris and Practices, 95; The Stoics on Women, Ancient Philos and Feminism, 96. **CONTACT ADDRESS** Dept of Classics, Univ of Chicago, 1050 E 59th St, Chicago, IL 60637. **EMAIL** e-asmis@uchicago.edu

ASPINALL, DANA E.
PERSONAL Born 10/18/1961, Lewiston, MN, m, 1997 **DISCIPLINE** ENGLISH **EDUCATION** Univ Mn at Fort Kent, 84; Univ SC, MA, 87; Univ CT, PhD, 96. **CAREER** Asst prof, Univ of Montevallo, 96-98; asst prof, Assumption Col, 98-. **MEMBERSHIPS** Sixteenth Century Studies, Shakespeare Asn Am. **RESEARCH** 17th century dramatic reception/adaptation. **SELECTED PUBLICATIONS** Auth, " 'I wol thee telle al plat': Poetic Influence and Chaucer's Pardoner," Miss Studies in English 11 & 12 (93-96): 230-242; auth, "The Role of Folk Humor in Seventeenth-Century Receptions of Beaumont's 'The Knight of the Burning Pestle' Philol Quart76.2 (spring 97): 169-192; rev, of John Ford, 'Tis Pity Sh'e a Whore, ed Simon Barker, London & New York: Routledge (97), in Sixteenth Century J 30.1 (spring 99): 265-266; rev, Johnathan Gil Harris, Foreign Bodeis and the Body Politic: Discourses of Social Pathology in Early Modern England, Cambridge and New York: Cambridge Univ Press (98), in Sixteenth Century J 30.2 (summer 99): 510-511; auth, "William Francis Butler," in Barbara Brothers & Julia Gergits, eds, Dictionary of Literary Biography 166 (British Travel Writers, 1837-1875), (98): 12-128; auth, "Ethel Mannin," in Barbara Brothers & Julia Gergits, eds, Dictionary of Literary Biography, 195 (British Travel Writers, 1910-1939), (98): 216-234; auth, "Robert Armin, Shakespeare's Fool," in Vicki Janik, ed, Fools and Jesters in Literature, Art, and History: A Bio-Bibliographical Sourcebook, Westport, CT: Greenwood Pubs (98): 41-49; auth, "Thomas Blount," in Edward Malone, ed, Dictionary of Literary Biography (Seventeenth- and Eighteenth-Century English Rhetoricians), (forthcoming); ed, The Taming of the Shrew: Critical Essays and Theater Reviews, New York: Garland Pubs (Shakespeare Criticism series, vol 19, gen ed, Philip Kolin) (forthcoming); ed, Amey Hayward, Females Legacy, Brookfield, VT: Ashgate (The Early Modern Englishwoman, Series II, Printed Writings 1640-1700; gen eds Betty Travitsky and Patrick Cullen) (forthcoming). **CONTACT ADDRESS** Dept English, Assumption Col, PO Box 15005, Worcester, MA 01615-0005. **EMAIL** dasinal@assumption.edu

ASPIZ, HAROLD
PERSONAL Born 06/19/1921, St. Louis, MO, m, 1952, 1 child **DISCIPLINE** ENGLISH, AMERICAN LITERATURE **EDUCATION** Univ CA, Los Angeles, BA, 43, MA, 44, PhD(English), 49. **CAREER** Asst prof English, Lewis & Clark Col, 50-51; res technican & statistician, Div Hwy, State Bd Equalization, CA, 52-58; from asst prof to Prof English, CA State Univ, Long Beach, 58-, CA State Univ, Long Beach res fel, 65 & 81. **MEMBERSHIPS** MLA; Philol Asn Pac Coast; Melville Soc. **RESEARCH** Nineteenth century literature and popular culture; Walt Whitman; literary realism. **SELECTED PUBLICATIONS** Auth, Educating the Kosmos: There was a child went forth, Am Quart, winter 66; Phrenologizing the whale, Nineteenth-Century Fiction, 6/68; A reading of Whitman's Faces, Walt Whitman Rev, 6/73; An early feminist tribute to Whitman, Am Lit, 11/79; The lurch of the torpedo-fish: Electrical concepts in Billy Budd, ESQ, 3rd Quarter, 80; Walt Whitman and the Body Beautiful, Univ Ill Press, 80. **CONTACT ADDRESS** Dept of English, California State Univ, Long Beach, 6101 E Seventh St, Long Beach, CA 90840.

ASTINGTON, JOHN H.
PERSONAL Born 01/20/1945, Stockport, England **DISCIPLINE** ENGLISH, DRAMA **EDUCATION** Univ Leeds, BA, 66; McMaster Univ, MA, 67; Univ Toronto, PhD, 74. **CAREER** Lectr, 71-75, asst prof, 75-78, assoc prof Eng, Univ Toronto, 78-. **HONORS AND AWARDS** Can Coun doctoral fel; Ont grad fel; SSHRCC res grants; Folger Libr fel (Washington, DC). **MEMBERSHIPS** Am Soc Theater Res; Shakespeare Asn Am; Int Shakespeare Asn; The Malone Soc. **RESEARCH** The printed image in England, 1450-1700; Shakespeare staging. **SELECTED PUBLICATIONS** Auth, English Court Theatre 1558-1642, Cambridge, 99; auth, Deviceful Settings: The English Renaissance Emblem and its Contexts, New York, 99; auth, The Emblem Tradition and the Low Countries, Turnhout, 99; auth, Other Voices, Other Views: Expanding th eCnon in English Renaissance Studies, Newark, DE, 99; auth, The Performance Text, Ottawa, 99; auth, Fortune; All is but Fortune, Washington, 00. **CONTACT ADDRESS** Erindale Col, Univ of Toronto, 3359 Mississauga Rd N, Mississauga, ON, Canada L5L 1C6. **EMAIL** asting@credit.erin.utoronto.ca

ASTROFF, ROBERTA J.
PERSONAL Born 05/31/1953, New York, NY **DISCIPLINE** LIBRARY SCIENCE **EDUCATION** Univ Rochester, BA, 75; NYork Univ, MA, 81; Univ Il Urbana-Champaign, PhD, 86; Ind Univ, MLS, 98. **CAREER** Asst prof Univ Wi Madison, 86-90; asst prof, Univ Pittsburgh, 90-97; librn, Penn St Univ, 98-. **MEMBERSHIPS** ALA; SALALM; ASIS. **RESEARCH** Humanities & new technologies; global studies. **SELECTED PUBLICATIONS** Auth, Spanish Gold: Stereotypes, Ideology and the Construction of a U S Latino Market, Howard J of Commun, 89; The Politics and Political Economics of Language, Media Develop, 92; Advertising, Anthropology, and Cultural Brokers: A Research Report, in Global and Multi-National Advertising, Lawrence Erlbaum Assoc 94; Capital's Cultural Study, in Buy This Book, Routledge, 97; coauth, Cultural Identity, Civil Society, and Mass Communication in Catalonia, in Information Society and Civil Society: The Changing World Order, Purdue Univ Press, 94. **CONTACT ADDRESS** Arts &

Humanities Libr, Pennsylvania State Univ, Univ Park, E502 Paterno Library, University Park, PA 16802. **EMAIL** r4a@psulias.psu.edu

ATHANASON, ARTHUR NICHOLAS

PERSONAL Born 08/17/1937, Pensacola, FL, s **DISCIPLINE** ENGLISH **EDUCATION** Univ Fla, BA, 59; Yale Univ, MFA, 62; Pa State Univ, PhD, 72. **CAREER** Instr, George Washington Univ, 65-66; instr to prof, Mich State Univ, 70-. **HONORS AND AWARDS** Leopold Schepp Found Fel, 68-69; Amoco Found Excellence in Teaching Awd, 93. **MEMBERSHIPS** MLA, Assoc of Lit Scholars and Critics. **RESEARCH** Modern American Drama, Modern British Drama, Recent British Drama. **SELECTED PUBLICATIONS** Auth, "The Mousetrap Phenomenon," Armchair Detective 12, (79): 152-157; auth, "John Osborne" and "Agatha Christie," Dict of Lit Biog V 13: Brit Dramatists Since World War II, ed Stanley Weintraub, (Detroit: Bruccoli-Clark, 82): 371-393, 119-118; auth, "John Osborne," Concise Dict of Brit Lit Biog, ed David Marshall James, (Detroit: Bruccoli-Clark, 92): 231-254; auth, "Endgame: The Ashbin Play," Twayne's Masterwork Studies No 109, ed Robert Lecker, (NY: Twayne Publ, 93); auth, "Murder Most Civilized: The Stage Thrillers of Frederick Knott," Shaw and Other Matters: A Festschrift in Tribute to Prof Stanley Weintraub, (Cranbury, NJ: Assoc Univ Pr, 98). **CONTACT ADDRESS** Dept English, Michigan State Univ, 201 Morrill Hall, East Lansing, MI 48824-1036. **EMAIL** athanaso@pilot.msu.edu

ATHANASSAKIS, APOSTOLOS N.

PERSONAL Born 09/20/1938, Astrochorion, Arta, Greece, d, 2 children **DISCIPLINE** CLASSICAL LINGUISTICS, GREEK POETRY **EDUCATION** Univ Pa, PhD, 65. **CAREER** Prof, Class Ling, Univ Calif, Santa Barbara. **HONORS AND AWARDS** Nat Board of Lecturers for the Bicentennial, 74-76; NEH Fellow, 76-77; Fulbright Professor to Iceland, 77; Guggenheim Fellow, 87-88. **SELECTED PUBLICATIONS** Transl, introd, text, Via Sancti Pachomii, Scholars' Press, 75; Transl, introd, comment, The Homeric Hymns, Johns Hopkins Univ Press, 76; Transl, text, The Orphic Hymns, Scholar's Press, 77; Transl, introd, Hesiod: Theogony, Works and Days, Shield, Johns Hopkins Univ Press, 88; ed, Essays on Hesiod, Vol I, Ramus 21, 92; Essays on Hesiod, Vol II, Ramus 21, 93; auth, The Life of St. George of Choceba, coauth, Tim Vivian, Catholic Scholars Press, 93; auth, The Life of St. Anthony, coauth, Tim Vivian, Catholic Scholars Press, 98. **CONTACT ADDRESS** Dept of Classics, Univ of California, Santa Barbara, Santa Barbara, CA 93106-7150. **EMAIL** gmangold@humanitas.ucsb.edu

ATKIN, DAVID J.

PERSONAL Born 12/12/1960, Lansing, MI, m, 1986, 2 children **DISCIPLINE** TELECOMMUNICATIONS, MASS COMMUNICATION THEORY **EDUCATION** Univ CA, Berkley, AB; MI State Univ, MA, PhD. **CAREER** Prof Internship dir, asst ch, Cleveland State Univ. **HONORS AND AWARDS** Krieghbaum "Under 40" Awd, AESMC, 99; Distinguished Univ Scholar, 00. **MEMBERSHIPS** AESMC, ICA, BEA. **RESEARCH** New Com Tech Adoption and Uses; Com Policy. **SELECTED PUBLICATIONS** Auth, Government Ambivalence Towards Telephone Regulation: Using past as prologue in the videodialtone debate, Commun Law Jour, 1, 96; Local and long distance telephony, Commun Tech, Focal Press, 96; Assessing uses of the information superhighway for commun and consumer needs, Hong Kong Econ Jour, 94. **CONTACT ADDRESS** Commun Dept, Cleveland State Univ, 83 E 24th St, Cleveland, OH 44115. **EMAIL** d.atkin@csuohio.edu

ATKINS, STEPHEN E.

PERSONAL Born 01/29/1941, Columbia, MO, m, 1966, 2 children **DISCIPLINE** POLITICAL SCIENCE, LIBRARY SCIENCE **EDUCATION** Univ Missouri, Columbia, BA, 63, MA, 64; Univ Iowa, PhD, 76, MA, 83. **CAREER** Monograph cataloger, Library, Univ Iowa, 74-89; polit sci subject specialist, Library, Univ Ill, Urbana-Champaign, 83-89; head, collection dev, 89-97, Asst Univ Librn, 97- Texas A & M Univ. **HONORS AND AWARDS** Phi Eta Sigma; Peace Awd, ALA, 92; **MEMBERSHIPS** ALA; ACRL; LAMA. **RESEARCH** International security issues; arms control and disarmament; terrorism; atomic energy; academic library history. **SELECTED PUBLICATIONS** Auth, The Academic Library in the American University, ALA, 91; auth, Terrorism: A Reference Handbook, ABC-CLIO, 92; auth, A Historical Encyclopedia of Atomic Energy, Greenwood, 99. **CONTACT ADDRESS** 716 Royal Adelaide Dr, College Station, TX 77845. **EMAIL** s-atkins@tamu.edu

ATKINSON, COLIN B.

DISCIPLINE ENGLISH LANGUAGE; LITERATURE **EDUCATION** McGill, BEng; Sir George Williams, BA; Columbia, MA; NY Univ, PhD, 71. **CAREER** Assoc prof. **RESEARCH** Victorian period; women's studies; the drama. **SELECTED PUBLICATIONS** Pub (s), Sydney Owenson, Lady Morgan; Maria Edgeworth; attitudes to death in nineteenth-century American parlour songs; and the place of Thomas Bentley and Anne Wheathill in the devotional tradition of women in Renaissance England. **CONTACT ADDRESS** Dept of English Language and Literature, Univ of Windsor, 401 Sunset Ave, Windsor, ON, Canada N9B 3P4. **EMAIL** p68@uwindsor.ca

ATKINSON, JAMES BLAKELY

PERSONAL Born 11/24/1934, Honolulu, HI, m, 1970, 1 child **DISCIPLINE** ENGLISH & COMPARATIVE LITERATURE **EDUCATION** Swarthmore Col, AB, 56; Columbia Univ, MA, 61, PhD(English & comp lit), 68. **CAREER** Asst prof English, Dartmouth Col, 66-73, fac fel, 71; Asst Prof English, Earlham Col, 73-. **MEMBERSHIPS** MLA; Renaissance Soc Am; AAUP. **RESEARCH** Literature of the Renaissance in Europe and England; the novel. **SELECTED PUBLICATIONS** Transl, Mandrou Duby's A History of French Civilization, Random, 65; auth, Montaigne and Naivete, Romanic Rev, 73; Naivete and Modernity: The French Renaissance Battle for a Literary Vernacular, J Hist Ideas, 74; ed & translr, Machiavelli's The Prince, Bobbs-Merrill, 75; Changing Attitudes to Death, 19th-Century Parlor Songs as Consolation Literature, Can Rev of Am Studies, vol 23, 93; with Anne Wheathill, A 'Handfull of Holesome Through Homelie Hearbs' 1584, The First English Gentlewomans Prayer Book, Sixteenth Century J, vol 27, 96; Machiavellian Rhetoric-From the Counterreformation to Milton, with V. Kahn, Renaissance Quart, vol 50, 97. **CONTACT ADDRESS** 115 S 17th St, Richmond, IN 47374.

ATKINSON, MICHAEL

PERSONAL Born 07/02/1942, Midland, TX **DISCIPLINE** LITERARY THEORY, ARCHETYPAL PSYCHOLOGY & LITERATURE **EDUCATION** Rice Univ, BA, 64; PA State Univ, MA, 67, PhD(English), 70. **CAREER** Assoc Prof English, Univ Cincinnati, 70-. **MEMBERSHIPS** MLA; AAUP; Midwest Mod Lang Asn; Popular Culture Asn. **RESEARCH** American renaissance; contemporary poetics. **SELECTED PUBLICATIONS** Auth, Collective Preconscious & Found Footage Film as an Inexhaustable Source of the Underground, Film Comment, Vol 29, 1993; Genuine B-Noir & Films of Director James B. Harris, Sight and Sound, Vol 3, 1993; Ousmane Sembene & The Film Director and African Cinema-We-Are-No-Longer-In-The-Era-of-Prophets, Film Comment, Vol 29, 1993; Between Worlds & Surrealists, Film and Hathaway, Henry 'Peter Ibbetson', Film Comment, Vol 29, 1993; The 'Tattooed Woman in Heavens Flower Shop', MI Quart Rev, Vol 32, 1993; Head Case & Arnaud Desplechin La 'Sentinelle', Film Comment, Vol 29, 1993; 'Airfield', Literary Rev, Vol 36, 1993; The 'Mask', wirh C. Russell, Sight and Sound, Vol 4, 1994; The Night Countries of the Brothers Quay & Film Directors, Film Comment, Vol 30, 1994; 'Highway Patrolman', with A. Cox, Film Comment, Vol 30, 1994; 'Death and the Compass', Film Comment, Vol 30, 1994; Regulation of Science by Peer Review, Studies in Hist and Philos of Sciencs, Vol 25, 1994; Crossing ther Frontiers--with Everyone from Psychos to Scholars Hitting the Highway, Has the Road Movie Found New Wheels, Sight and Sound, Vol 4, 1994; The Faber Book of Movie Verse, with P. French and K. Wlaschin, Film Comment, Vol 30, 1994; The 'Paper', with R. Howard, Sight and Sound, Vol 4, 1994; A 'Perfect World', with C. Eastwood, Sight and Sound, Vol 4, 1994; Son of Apes & 'Planet of the Apes' Film Serials, Film Comment, Vol 31, 1995; Delirious Inventions--Why Have Comics and Cartoons from 'Popeye' Onwards So Often Been Translated into Live Action Movies, Sight and Sound, Vol 5, 1995; 'Jefferson in Paris', with J. Ivory, Sight and Sound, Vol 5, 1995; Earthly Creatures & Peter Jackson Horror Film "Heavenly Creatures', Film Comment, Vol 0031, 1995; The 'Specialist', with L. Llosa, Sight and Sound, Vol 5, 1995; 'Tommy Boy', with P. Segal, Sight and Sound, Vol 5, 1995; 'Beach Red' -, with C. Wilde, Film Comment, Vol 32, 1996; Naked Prey--The Cinema of Cornel Wilde, Introduction & Conclusions, Vol 32, 1996; 'Aeon Flux', Film Comment, Vol 32, 1996; Songs of Crushed Love--TheCinema of Stanley Kwan, Film Comment, Vol 32, 1996; 'No Blade of Grass', with C. Wilde, Film Comment, Vol 32, 1996; Best of 96 & Movies, Film Comment, Vol 33, 1997; 'Lumiere et Compagnie', with S. Moon, Film Comment, Vol 33, 1997. **CONTACT ADDRESS** Dept of English, Univ of Cincinnati, P O Box 210069, Cincinnati, OH 45221-0069.

ATLAS, MARILYN JUDITH

DISCIPLINE ENGLISH **EDUCATION** Univ Ill, BS, 72; Univ Ill, AB, 73; Univ Ill, AM, 73; Mich State Univ, PhD, 79. **CAREER** Adv, Univ Ill, Col of Arts and Sciences, 72-74; grad asst, Mich State Univ, Dept of English, 74-78; instr and asst prof, Mich State Univ, Dept of Am Thought and Lang, 78-80; dir, Ohio Univ, Women's Studies, 80-82; asst prof, Ohio Univ, 80-84; vis prof, De La Salle Univ, Philippines, 85; assoc prof, Ohio Univ, 84-97. **HONORS AND AWARDS** Best Feminist Res Awd, Women's Studies Program, Ohio Univ; Winner of the Excellence-in-Teaching Citation, Mich State Univ; Phi Beta Kappa; Phi Kappa Phi; Psi Chi; Kappa Delta Pi. **MEMBERSHIPS** Soc for the Study of Midwestern Lit; Am Culture Asn. **RESEARCH** Early Am lit; Am Renaissance; Am Modernism; contemporary lit; women's lit; ethnic lit; Jewish lit; literary hist; literary theory; canon formation. **SELECTED PUBLICATIONS** Auth, "Toni Morrison's Beloved and the Critics", in Midwestern Miscellany 18, 90; auth, "Tone and Technology in Harriet Monroe's 'The Turbine'", in MidAmerica 22, 95; auth, "Cracked Psyches and Verba Putty: Geography and Integrity in Toni Morrison's Jazz", in Midwestern Miscellany 4, 96; auth, "The Roles of Chicago in the Careers of Ellen Van Volkenburg and Maurice Browne", in MidAmerica 23, 96. **CONTACT ADDRESS** Department of English, Ohio Univ, Athens, OH 45701.

ATON, JAMES M.

PERSONAL Born 08/14/1949, Louisville, KY, s, 1 child **DISCIPLINE** ENGLISH **EDUCATION** Spring Hill Col, BA, 71; Univ of Ky, MA, 77; Ohio Univ, PhD, 81. **CAREER** Prof of English, Southern Utah Univ, 80-. **HONORS AND AWARDS** Distinguished Educator Awd, Southern Utah Univ; fulbright lectr, Indonesia, 89-90, China, 97-98. **MEMBERSHIPS** Am Soc of Environmental Hist; Utah State Historical Soc; Western Hist Asn. **RESEARCH** Environmental history of the Colorado plateau. **SELECTED PUBLICATIONS** Auth, "Stalking Henry Thoreau," South Dakota Review, 84; auth, John Wesley Powell, Dictionary of Lit Bio: Nineteenth-Century Western Am Writers Vol 186, Gale Res, 97; The River, The Ditch and The Volcano: Bluff, 1879-1884, Blue Mountain Shadows, 93; Us vs. Them: John Wesley Powell and Western Water Issues, Akademika, 90; Inventing: The Major, His Admirers and Cash Register Dams in the Colorado River Basin, SUSC Distinguished Fac Lectr, 88, reprinted by Five Quail Books, 94; An Interview With Barry Lopez, Western Am Lit, 86; auth, Rive Flowing from the Sunrise: An Environmental History of The lower San Juan, with Robert S. McPherson, USU Press, 00. **CONTACT ADDRESS** Dept of Lang and Lit, So Utah Univ, Cedar City, UT 84720. **EMAIL** aton@suu.edu

ATTEBERY, BRIAN

DISCIPLINE ENGLISH LITERATURE **EDUCATION** Brown Univ, PhD, 79. **CAREER** Prof. **RESEARCH** Fantasy and science fiction; folklore; American studies theory and methodology. **SELECTED PUBLICATIONS** Auth, The Fantasy Tradition in American Literature; Strategies of Fantasy; co-auth, The Norton Book of Science Fiction. **CONTACT ADDRESS** Dept of English and Philosophy, Idaho State Univ, Pocatello, ID 83209. **EMAIL** attebria@isu.edu

ATTEBERY, JENNIFER

DISCIPLINE ENGLISH LITERATURE **EDUCATION** Ind Univ, PhD, 85. **CAREER** Prof. **RESEARCH** Swedish and Swedish-American culture and history. **SELECTED PUBLICATIONS** Auth, Building Idaho: An Architectural History; Building with Logs: Western Log Construction in Context. **CONTACT ADDRESS** Dept of English and Philosophy, Idaho State Univ, Pocatello, ID 83209. **EMAIL** attejenn@isu.edu

ATTEBERY, LOUIE WAYNE

PERSONAL Born 08/14/1927, Weiser, ID, m, 1947, 2 children **DISCIPLINE** ENGLISH & AMERICAN LITERATURE, FOLKLORE **EDUCATION** Col ID, BA, 50; Univ Mont, MA, 51; Univ Denver, PhD, 61. **CAREER** Teacher English, Middleton High Sch, ID, 49-50, Payette High Sch, 51-52, Nyssa High Sch, Ore, 52-55 & East High Sch, Denver, 55-61, chmn dept, 61; from asst prof to assoc prof, 61-69, chmn dept, 68-73 & 76-78, Prof English, Col of ID, 69-98, prof emer, 98-; Prin lectr, Summer Inst Am Studies, 63-70, dir, 66-70; Bruern fel, Univ Leeds, 71-72; consult, EXPO 74, acting vice pres for acad affairs, 83-84. **MEMBERSHIPS** Western Lit Asn; Western Hist Asn; Am Folklore Soc. **RESEARCH** The epistemology of Western American literature; the cement truck urban belief tale; the Oregon cowboy: a continuing search for authenticity. **SELECTED PUBLICATIONS** Auth, Governor jokes, Southern Folklore Quart, 12/69; The American West and the Archetypal Orphan, Western Am Lit, fall 70; It was a DeSoto, J Am Folklore, 10-12/70; The Fiddle Tune: An American Artifact, Readings in Am Folklore, 79; auth, The College of Idaho: A Centennial History, The College of Idaho, 91; auth, Sheepmay safely Graze, Univ of Idaho, 93; auth, The Most of What we Spend: A Biography of Robert L. Hendren, Jr., West Shore Press, 97; auth, Albertson College of Idaho: The Second Hundred Years, Albertson College of Idaho, 99; auth, J.R. Simplot: A Billion the Hard Way, Caxton Press, 00. **CONTACT ADDRESS** Dept of English, Albertson Col of Idaho, Caldwell, ID 83605. **EMAIL** lattebery@albertson.edu

ATTIAS, BERNARDO

DISCIPLINE COMMUNICATIONS **EDUCATION** Northwestern Univ, BS, 88; Univ Iowa, PhD, 97. **CAREER** Instr to Teaching Asst, Univ Iowa, 89-92; Adj Asst Prof, Temple Univ, 94; Asst Prof, Calif State Univ, 94-. **HONORS AND AWARDS** Creative Activity Awd, Calif State Univ, 97-98; Res Stipend, School of Comm, Health, and Human Services, 96; Intl Res support Grant, 95; Affirmative Action Fac Development Prog, 95; Scholarly Presentations Awd, Univ Iowa, 93, 92, 91; Iowa Res Fel, 92-93; Top Four Papers in Rhetorical Criticism, Central States comm Asn, 91; Iowa Teaching Fel, Univ Iowa, 89-92. **RESEARCH** Cultural Studies; Media Studies; Rhetorical Studies; History of Sexuality; Political Economy. **SELECTED PUBLICATIONS** Auth, "Toward a Cartography of Internal Third Worlds," in Understanding Development in the era of Globalization, Chicago, forthcoming; auth, "Cocaine," in the St. James encyclopedia of Popular Culture, St. James Press, 99; auth, "To Each its Own Sexes: Towards a rhetorical Understanding of Molecular revolution," in Deleuze and Guattari: New Mappings in Politics/Philosophy/Culture, Univ Minn Press, 98; rev, of "Framer Framed" by Trinh T Minh-ha, Iowa Journal of cultural Studies, 93. **CONTACT ADDRESS** Dept Speech Comm, California State Univ, Northridge, 18111 Nordhoff St, Northridge, CA 91330-0001. **EMAIL** bernardo.attias@csun.edu

ATTRIDGE, DEREK
DISCIPLINE ENGLISH LANGUAGE AND LITERATURE **EDUCATION** Natal Univ, BA; Cambridge Univ, BA; PhD. **CAREER** Dist vis prof English. **RESEARCH** British and Irish modernism; poetic form and performance; literary theory; South African writing. **SELECTED PUBLICATIONS** Auth, Poetic Rhythm: An Introduction, Cambridge, 95; auth, Peculiar Language: Literature as Difference from the Renaissance to James Joyce Cornell, 88; The Rhythms of English Poetry Longman, 82; Well-weighed Syllables: Elizabethan Verse in Classical Metres , Cambridge, 74; ed, Acts of Literature by Jacques Derrida, Routledge, 92; The Cambridge Companion to James Joyce, Cambridge, 90; co-ed, Writing South Africa: Literatue, Apartheid, and Democracy, Cambridge, 98; Post-structuralist Joyce: Essays from the French, Cambridge, 84; The Linguistics of Writing: Arguments between Literature and Language, Routledge, 88; Post-structuralism and the Question of History, Cambridge, 87. **CONTACT ADDRESS** Dept of English, Rutgers, The State Univ of New Jersey, New Brunswick, 510 George St, Murray Hall, New Brunswick, NJ 08901-1167.

ATWILL, WILLIAM D.
DISCIPLINE 19TH- AND 20TH-CENTURY AMERICAN LITERATURE **EDUCATION** Univ S Fla, BA; Fla Atlantic Univ, MA; Duke Univ, PhD. **CAREER** Assoc prof, Univ NC, Wilmington. **RESEARCH** Contemporary postmodern fiction and literary nonfiction from 1945 to the present. **SELECTED PUBLICATIONS** Auth, Fire and Power: The American Space Program as Postmodern Narrative, Univ Ga Press, 94. **CONTACT ADDRESS** Univ of No Carolina, Wilmington, Morton Hall, Wilmington, NC 28403-3297. **EMAIL** atwillw@uncwil.edu

ATWOOD, MARGARET
PERSONAL Born Ottawa, ON, Canada **DISCIPLINE** AUTHOR, POET **EDUCATION** Victoria Col, Univ Toronto, BA, 61; Radcliffe Col, AM, 62. **CAREER** Lectr, English, Univ BC, 64-65; instr, Univ Alta, 69-70; asst prof, York Univ, 71-72; Writer-In-Residence, Univ Toronto, 72-73; MFA Hon Ch, Univ Alabama, 85; Berg Ch, New York Univ, 86; Writer-In-Residence, Macquarie Univ, Australia, 87; Writer-In-Residence, Trinity Univ, San Antonio, Tex, 89. **HONORS AND AWARDS** Gov Gen Awd, 66, 86; Guggenheim Fel, 81; Companion Order Can, 81; Order Ont, 90; Trillium Awd Excellence Ont, 94; Commonwealth Writers' Prize Can & Caribbean Region, 94; Chevalier dans l'Ordre des Arts et des Lettres, Govt France, 94; Sunday Times Awd Literary Excellence, 94; DLitt, Trent Univ, 73; DLitt, Queen's Univ, 74; DLitt, Smith Col, MA, 82; DLitt, Univ Toronto, 83; DLitt, Univ Waterloo, 85; DLitt, Univ Guelph, 85; DLitt, Mount Holyoke Col, 85; DLitt, Univ Toronto, 87; DLitt, Univ de Montreal, 91; DLitt, Univ Leeds, 94. **MEMBERSHIPS** Writers' Union Can; PEN. **SELECTED PUBLICATIONS** Auth, The Circle Game, 64; auth, The Edible Woman, 69; auth, Surfacing, 72; auth, Lady Oracle, 76; auth, Life Before Man, 79; auth, Bodily Harm, 81; auth, The Handmaid's Tale, 85; auth, Cat's Eye, 88; auth, The Robber Bride, 93; auth, Alias Grace, 96. **CONTACT ADDRESS** McClelland & Stewart, 481 University Ave, Ste 900, Toronto, ON, Canada M5G 2E9.

AUBREY, JAMES R.
PERSONAL Born 12/03/1945, Kittanning, PA, w, 1968, 2 children **DISCIPLINE** ENGLISH **EDUCATION** Univ Wash, PhD, 79. **CAREER** Prof, Metrop State Col Denver, 89- . **MEMBERSHIPS** MLA **RESEARCH** British literature. **SELECTED PUBLICATIONS** Auth, John Fowles: A Reference Companion, 91; auth, John Fowles and Nature: Fourteen Perspectives on Landscape, 99. **CONTACT ADDRESS** 2337 Ash St., Denver, CO 80207. **EMAIL** aubreyj@mscd.edu

AUERBACH, JONATHAN
PERSONAL Born 02/07/1954, Denver, CO, m, 1983, 1 child **DISCIPLINE** ENGLISH **EDUCATION** Univ Calif, BA, 76; Johns Hopkins Univ, MA, 78; PhD, 84. **CAREER** From Asst Prof to Prof, Univ Md, 84-. **HONORS AND AWARDS** Fulbright Lect, 90; Fel, Dartmouth Col, 93; Fel Huntington Libr, 94. **MEMBERSHIPS** MLA, ASA. **RESEARCH** Nineteenth-Century and early twentieth-century American culture, early cinema. **SELECTED PUBLICATIONS** Auth, The Romance of Failure: First-Person Fictions of Poe, Hawthorne and James, Oxford Univ Pr, 89; auth, "Black Like Me, or How the Other Half Lives," in Proceedings of the 13th Conf of the Portuguese Assoc of Anglo-Am Studies (94): 81-91; auth, "'The Nation Organized': Utopian Impotence in Edward Bellamy's 'Looking Backward'," Am Lit Hist, vol 6, no 1 (94): 24-47; auth, "'Congested Mails': Buck and Jack's 'Call'," Am Lit, vol 67, no 1 (95): 51-76; auth, Male Call: Becoming Jack London, Duke University Pr, 96; auth, Jack London, Northland Ser, Penguin Pr, 97; auth, "McKinley at Home: How Early American Cinema Made News," Am Quart, vol 51, no 4 (99): 792-832; auth, "Debut de siecle, debut de carriere: Comment John Griffith Chaney devint Jack London," Europe, no 844 (99): 28-39; auth, American Studies Today: Conference Proceedings Co-Editor Nguyen Lien, Vietnam Nat Univ (Hanoi, Vietnam), 00; auth, "Chasing Film Narration: Repetition, Recursion and the Body in Early Cinema," Critical Inquiry (forthcoming). **CONTACT ADDRESS** Dept English, Univ of Maryland, Col Park, 3101 Susquehanna Hill, College Park, MD 20742-8800. **EMAIL** ja44@umail.umd.edu

AUFDERHEIDE, PATRICIA
PERSONAL Born Bad Canstratt, Germany, m, 2 children **DISCIPLINE** MASS COMMUNICATION **EDUCATION** Univ Minn, BA, MA, PhD. **CAREER** Prof, Am Univ. **HONORS AND AWARDS** Phi Beta Kappa; john simon guggenheim memorial fel; fulbright res fel, brazil. **MEMBERSHIPS** International Communication, ASN, Assoc for Educ in Journalism nad Mass Comm. **RESEARCH** Communication Policy, media literacy, cultural studies. **SELECTED PUBLICATIONS** Auth, Anwar Sadat; contrib auth, Seeing Through Movies; Watching Television: Voices of Dissent, theMedia; assoc ed, Black Film Rev; st ed, Am Film Mag; ed, Beyond PC: Toward a Politics of Understanding and Latin American Vision; auth, Communication Policy and the Public Interest: The Telecommunications Act of 1996, 99; auth, The Daily Planet, 00. **CONTACT ADDRESS** American Univ, 4400 Massachusetts Ave, Washington, DC 20016.

AUGUST, EUGENE R.
PERSONAL Born 10/19/1935, Jersey City, NJ, m, 1964, 2 children **DISCIPLINE** ENGLISH **EDUCATION** Rutgers Univ, AB, 58; Univ Conn, MA, 60; Univ Pittsburgh, PhD(English), 65. **CAREER** Asst English, Univ Conn, 58-60; from instr to asst prof, carnegie-Mellon Univ, 62-66; from asst prof to assoc prof, Univ Dayton, 66-74 vis assoc prof, Univ Hawaii, Manoa, 74-75; prof English, Univ Dayton, 76-, Nat Endowment for Humanities younger humanist fel, 73-74. **MEMBERSHIPS** NAS, ALSC, AMSA. **RESEARCH** Victorian literature; Divine Comeedies; Men's Studies. **SELECTED PUBLICATIONS** Auth, The Growth of the Windhover, PMLA, 10/67; ed, The Nigger Question & The Negro Question, 71, AMH Publ; Mill's Autobiography as Philosophic Commedia, Victorian Poetry, summer 73; Mill as Sage: The Essay on Bentham, PMLA, 1/74; auth, John Stuart Mill: A Mind at Large, Charles Scribner's Sons, 75; The Only Happy Ending: Divine Comedies in Western Literature, Bull Midwest; Modern Language Association, Vol 14, spring 81; Amours de Voyage and Matthew Arnold in Love, Victorian Newsletter, fall 81; The New Men's Studies, Libraries Unlim, 95. **CONTACT ADDRESS** Dept of English, Univ of Dayton, 300 College Park, Dayton, OH 45469-1520. **EMAIL** august@checkor.hm.udayton.edu

AUKSI, PETER
PERSONAL Born 12/01/1942, Estonia, m, 1975 **DISCIPLINE** ENGLISH LITERATURE **EDUCATION** Univ Toronto, BA, 65; Oxford Univ, BA, 67, MA, 70; Harvard Univ, AM, 68, PhD(English lit), 71. **CAREER** Asst prof, 71-80, Assoc Prof English, Univ Western Ont, 80-. **RESEARCH** Renaissance, influence of the Reformation, rhetoric, stylistics. **SELECTED PUBLICATIONS** Auth, Christian Plain Style: The Evolution of a Spiritual Ideal, 95. **CONTACT ADDRESS** English Dept, Univ of Western Ontario, University College, London, ON, Canada NGA3K7. **EMAIL** pauksi@julian.uwo.ca

AULT, C. THOMAS
PERSONAL Born 08/07/1936, Moline, IL, s **DISCIPLINE** THEATRE **EDUCATION** Univ Mich, BA, 65; MA, 67; PhD, 83. **CAREER** Lect, Univ Mich, 83-84; asst prof, Centenary Col La, 84-86; Asst Prof, Univ Penn, 88-. **HONORS AND AWARDS** Merit Sabbatical, IUP, 96; ACTF, Meritorious Achsets; 7th Regional UCTA, best set, 85; INDO-US Subcommission Gr, Smithsonian Inst, 86-87; Fulbright gr, Am Inst of Indian Studies, 96; Disting Fac Awd for Res, Ind Univ of Pa, 00. **MEMBERSHIPS** So for Theatre Res (Eng); Am Soc for Theatre Res; Asn for Asian Perform; Renaissance Soc of NAm; Am Asn of Ital Studies. **RESEARCH** Theaters and theatrical machines. **SELECTED PUBLICATIONS** Auth, "Hawks and Handsaws: Shakespeare's 'Hamlet'," The Explicator vol 49, no 4, 91; auth, "Tonight 'Amar Singh Rthore': Marwari Khyal in Transition," Asian Theatre J vol 8, no 2, 92; auth, "Architecture in the Baroque Age of Theatre," Theatre Design & Tech vol 8, no 2, 92; auth, "Fracesco Piranesi's Reconstruction of the Ancient Theatre at Herculanium," Theatre Design & Tech vol 30, no 2, 94; auth, "Tessins's Notes on Baroque Theatre at Villa Contarini-1688," Theatre Hist Studies, vol 14, 94; auth, "The Queen's Cavern: A Sanskrit Theatre of Ancient Khalinga, Second Century BC India," Theatre Design & Tech, Winter 96; auth, "Leone Battista Alberti on Theatre Architecture," Theatre Design & Tech, Winter 97; auth, "Classical Humanist Drama in Transition: The First Phase of Renaissance Theatre in Ferrara," Theatre Ann, 98; auth, Gods, Heroes and Villains: The Theatre of Rahasthan, DK Printworld Ltd (New Dehli), in press 00. **CONTACT ADDRESS** Dept of Theatre, Indiana Univ of Pennsylvania, 103-B Waller Hall, Indiana, PA 15701. **EMAIL** ctault@grove.iup.edu

AUSTEN, ZELDA
DISCIPLINE VICTORIAN PERIOD, ENGLISH NOVEL **EDUCATION** SUNY, Stony Brook, PhD. **CAREER** Prof, Long Island Univ, C.W. Post Campus. **SELECTED PUBLICATIONS** Auth, Oliver Twist: A Divided View; Why Feminist Critics are Angry at George Eliot; The Ant and the Grasshopper: William Morris and Oscar Wilde in the Eighties; Factories and Fairy Palaces: The Response of Dickens and Other to the Industrial Revolution. **CONTACT ADDRESS** Long Island Univ, C.W. Post, Brookville, NY 11548-1300.

AUSTERN, LINDA
PERSONAL Born 02/20/1957, Pittsburgh, PA, m **DISCIPLINE** MUSICOLOGY **EDUCATION** Univ Pittsburgh, BA, 77; Univ Chicago, PhD, 84. **CAREER** Cornell Univ, vis fel, 84-86; Allegheny Col, vis asst prof, 86-87; Univ New Haven, vis asst prof, 87-88; Radcliffe Col, Harvard Univ, Bunting fel, 88-89; Univ of Notre Dame, asst prof, 89-95; Univ Notre Dame, assoc prof, tenure, 95; Univ Iowa, vis assoc prof, 97; Folger Shakespeare Libr NEH long-term fel, 97-98 Newberry Libr, 87; Scholar-in-Residence, 98-99. **HONORS AND AWARDS** Newberry Libr Short-Term Resident Fel, 87 Andrew W Mellon Fel to Harvard Univ, 88-89 (turned down); Fel, Bunting Inst of Radcliffe Col, 88-89; Am Council of Learned Societies Travel Grant, 90; Folger Shakespeare Libr NEH Fel, 97-98; NEH Fel for Col Teachers, 97-98; ACLS Fel, 98; Brit Acad Vis Fel, 98. **MEMBERSHIPS** Am Musicol Soc; Int Musicol Soc; Renaissance Soc Am; Royal Musical Asn; Shakespeare Asn Am; Soc for Emblem Studies; Soc for 17th-Century Music; Soc for the Study of Early Mod Women; **RESEARCH** Music, gender and sexuality; music in early mod England; 17th-century opera; music in early mod science and medicine; emblematics; cult criticism of European & N Am musics; Shakespearean drama. **SELECTED PUBLICATIONS** 'Alluring the Auditorie to Effeminacie:' Music and the Idea of the Feminine in Early Modern England, Music & Letters 74, 93; Music and the English Controversy Over Women, in Cecilia Reclaimed: Feminist Perspectives on Gender and Music, ed Susan Cook and Judy Tsou, Univ Ill Press, 94; 'No Women Are Indeed': The Bouy Actor as Vocal Seductress in English Renaissance Drama, in Embodied Voices: Female Vocality in Western Culture, ed Leslie Dunn & Nancy Jones, Cambridge Univ Press, 94; 'The Conceit of the Minde': Music, Medicine and Mental Process in Early Modern England, Irish Musical Studies 4, 96; 'Foreign Conceits and Wand'ring Devices': The Erotic as Exotic, in The Exotic in Western Music, ed Jonathan Bellman, Northeastern Univ Press, 98; Nature, Culture, Myth and the Musician in Early Modern England, J Am Musicol Soc 51, 98; 'For, Love's a Good Musician': Performance, Audition and Erotic Disorders in Early Modern Europe, in Musical Quarterly, 98; 'No Pill's Gonna Cure My Ill': Erotic Melancholy and Traditions of Musical Healing in the Modern West, in Musical Healing in Cultural Contexts, ed Penelope Gouk, Ashgate Publ, 98; Musical Treatments for Lovesickness: The Early Modern Heritage, in Music as Medicine: The History of Music Therapy Since Antiquity, Variorum/Scolar Press, 98; The Siren, the Muse, and the God of Love: Music and Gender in Seventeenth-Century English Emblem Books, J Musicol Res; My Mother Musicke, in Mothers and Others: The Caregiver Figure in Early Modern Europe, ed Naomi Miller and Naomi Yavneh. **CONTACT ADDRESS** Newberry Library, 60 West Walton St, Chicago, IL 60610-3380. **EMAIL** austern@calumet.purdue.edu

AUSTIN, BOBBY WILLIAM
PERSONAL Born 12/29/1944, Bowling Green, KY, m **DISCIPLINE** LITERATURE **EDUCATION** Western Kentucky Univ, BA 1966; Fisk Univ, MA 1968; McMaster Univ, PhD 1972; Harvard Univ, Diploma 1986. **CAREER** Univ of DC, exec asst to the pres; Georgetown Univ, asst prof 1971-72; Dept of Soc Georgetown summer term, chmn 1972; The Urban League Review Natl Urban League, editor; UDC Bd Vis Team Creative Prod Black Amer Folklore NETA-WASH PBS, pol spec & spec asst; pres Austin & Assoc. **HONORS AND AWARDS** Kellogg Natl Fellow. **MEMBERSHIPS** Mem Natl Council for Accrdttn of Tchr Edn; mem Amer Soc Assn; Groves Conf on Marriage & the Family; Alpha Phi Alpha Frat; Natl Cong of Black Professionals; mem VOICE Inc; mem Alphi Phi Omega Natl Serv Fraternity; Peoples Congregational Church; Hannover Project, Germany; Academic Council on the UN Systems; Global Co-Operation for a Better World; UN Assn, DC Chapter **SELECTED PUBLICATIONS** Author of numerous publications; paper presented at the Assn for the Study of Afro-Amer Life & History New York, 1973; published Natl Black Opinion ACRA Inc 1977. **CONTACT ADDRESS** Austin & Associates, 6611 16th St NW, Washington, DC 20012.

AUSTIN, GAYLE M.
DISCIPLINE THEATRE HISTORY **EDUCATION** CUNY, PhD. **CAREER** Instr, Hunter Col; instr, Univ SC; assoc prof, Ga State Univ; exec dir, Southeast Playwrights Proj, 87-89. **SELECTED PUBLICATIONS** Auth, The Madwoman in the Spotlight: Plays of Maria Irene Fornes, in Making a Spectacle, Univ Mich Press, 89; The Exchange of Women and Male Homosocial Desire in Miller's 'Death of a Salesman' and Hellman's 'Another Part of the Forest,' in Feminist Rereadings of Modern American Drama, Fairleigh Dickinson UP, 89; Feminist Theories for Dramatic Criticism, Univ Mich Press, 90; Resisting the Birth Mark: Subverting Hawthorne in a Feminist Theory Play, in Upstaging Big Daddy: Directing Theater as if Gender and Race Matter, Univ Mich Press, 93. **CONTACT ADDRESS** Georgia State Univ, Atlanta, GA 30303. **EMAIL** jougma@panther.gsu.edu

AUSTIN, J. NORMAN
PERSONAL Born 05/20/1937, Anshun, China, s **DISCIPLINE** CLASSICS **EDUCATION** Univ of Toronto, BA, 58; Univ of Calif, MA, 60, PhD, 65 **CAREER** Lect, 64-65, Oakland Univ MI; Asst Prof, 65-66, Univ S CA; Assoc Prof, 66-76,

Univ of CA, Los Angeles; Aurelio Prof, 76-78, Boston Univ; Prof, 78-80, Univ MA Amherst **HONORS AND AWARDS** John S Guggenheim Fel, 74-75; Jnr Fel, Center for Hellenic Studies, 68-69 **MEMBERSHIPS** Am Philol Assoc; Am Assoc of Univ Profs **RESEARCH** Homer; Archaic Greek Culture & Literature; Comparative Literature **SELECTED PUBLICATIONS** Auth, Archery at the Dark of the Moon Poetic Problems in Homer's Odyssey, Univ of CA Press, 75; auth, Meaning and Being in Myth, Penn State Univ Pr, 90; auth, Helen of Troy and her Shameless Phantom, Cornell Univ Pr, 94. **CONTACT ADDRESS** Dept of Classics, Univ of Arizona, 2939 E Third St, Tucson, AZ 85716. **EMAIL** naustin@u.arizona.edu

AUSTIN, LINDA
DISCIPLINE VICTORIAN STUDIES **EDUCATION** Rochester, PhD, 86. **CAREER** Engl, Okla St Univ. **SELECTED PUBLICATIONS** Auth, The Practical Ruskin: Economics and Audience in the Late Work, Johns Hopkins, 91. **CONTACT ADDRESS** Oklahoma State Univ, Stillwater, 101 Whitehurst Hall, Stillwater, OK 74078.

AUSTIN, MICHAEL
DISCIPLINE ENGLISH **EDUCATION** Brigham Young Univ, BA, 90, MA, 92; Univ CA at Santa Barbara, PhD, 97. **CAREER** Asst prof, Shepherd Col, 97-; tchg assoc, Writing Prog, Univ CA at Santa Barbara, 97; tchg asst-instr, Univ CA,at Santa Barbara, 92-97; tchg assoc, Univ CA at Santa Barbara, 95; tchg asst, Brigham Young Univ, 90-92. **MEMBERSHIPS** MLA; Northeastern Soc for 18th-Century Stud; AAUP. **RESEARCH** Hist of criticism; hist of rhetoric; contemp critical theory, lit of the Bible. **SELECTED PUBLICATIONS** Auth, Saul and the Social Contract: Constructions of 1 Samuel 8-11 in Cowley's Davideis and Defoe's Jure Divino, Papers on Lang and Lit 32 4, 96; Marxist Criticism, textbk Chap, The Critical Experience, Dubuque, Iowa: Kendall/Hunt, 94; Saul Bellow and the Absent Woman Syndrome: Traces of India in Leaving the Yellow House, Saul Bellow J 11 2/12 1, 93-94; The Genesis of the Speaking Subject in Mr Sammler's Planet, Saul Bellow J 10 2, 92. **CONTACT ADDRESS** Dept of Eng and Mod Lang, Shepherd Col, Shepherdstown, WV 25443. **EMAIL** maustin@shepherd.wvnet.edu

AUTER, PHILIP J.
DISCIPLINE COMMUNICATION **EDUCATION** Ga State Univ, BA, 85; Univ Ga, MA, 87; Univ Ky, PhD, 92. **CAREER** Asst prof. **RESEARCH** Uses and gratifications of television programming and computer services; computer mediated communication; parasocial interaction; effects of message production techniques on audience interaction, interest, involvement, and mood; history of television. **SELECTED PUBLICATIONS** Auth, A Fine Mess: A Look at the Effects of Colorization on Audience Interaction With a Comedy Program, 97; TV that talks back: An experimental validation of a parasocial interaction scale, 92; Analysis of the ratings for television comedy programs 1950-1959: The end of "Berlesque", 90; coauth, The challenge of developing online courses, 98; When characters speak directly to viewers: Breaking the fourth wall in entertainment television, 97; DuMont: The original fourth television network, 95; Buying from a friend: A content analysis of two teleshopping programs, 93. **CONTACT ADDRESS** Univ of West Florida, 11000 Univ PKWY, Pensacola, FL 32514. **EMAIL** pauter@uwf.edu

AVERY, HARRY COSTAS
PERSONAL Born 04/09/1930, Philadelphia, PA, m, 1962, 4 children **DISCIPLINE** CLASSICS **EDUCATION** Univ PA, AB, 53; Univ IL, MA, 56; Princeton Univ, PhD, 59. **CAREER** Instr Greek, Bryn Mawr Col, 59-61; from asst prof to assoc prof classics, Univ TX, Austin, 61-67; Prof Classics & Chmn Dept, Univ Pittsburgh, 67-, Jr fel, Ctr Hellenic Studies, 63-64; chmn adv coun, Comt Sch Class Studies, Am Acad Rome, 70-73, trustee, 75-78; vis res prof Greek hist & lit, Am Sch Class Studies Athens, 71-72, mem exec comt, Managing Comt, 72-76. **HONORS AND AWARDS** Bromberg Awd, Univ TX, 66. **MEMBERSHIPS** Am Philol Asn; Soc Promotion Hellenic Studies; Archaeol Inst Am. **RESEARCH** Greek history and literature; Roman history. **SELECTED PUBLICATIONS** Auth, Euripides' Heracleidai, 71 & Herodotus' Picture of Cyrus, 72, Am J Philol; Herodotus 6.112.2, Trans Am Philol Asn, 72; Themes in Thucydides' Account of the Sicilian Expedition, Hermes, 73; Sophocles' Political Career, Historia, 73; The Three Hundred at Thasos, 411 BC, Class Philol, 78; A Lost Episode in Caesar Civil War, Hermes-Zeitschrift Fur Klassische Philologie, Vol 121, 93; Glaucus, A God, 'Iliad' Zeta-128-143 & Homer, Hermes-Zeitschrift Fur Klassische Philologie, Vol 122, 94. **CONTACT ADDRESS** Dept of Classics, Univ of Pittsburgh, Pittsburgh, PA 51260.

AVINS, STYRA
PERSONAL Born New York, NY, m, 1963, 2 children **DISCIPLINE** MUSIC HISTORY **EDUCATION** City Col of NYork, BA, 59; Juilliard Sch of Music, BS, 59; Manhattan Sch of Music, MM, 63. **CAREER** Mem, Seoul Symphony, Am Symphony Orchestra, NY City Opera Orchestra, 60-69; fac mem, United Nations Int Sch, 80-90; mem of Queens Symphony Orchestra, 80-; assoc prof, Drew U. Grad Sch, 95-; cellist, The Cameo Trio; artistic dir, Community Chamber Concerts of NY and NJ. **HONORS AND AWARDS** Royal Philharmonic Soc Awd, High Commendation, 98; Phi Beta Kappa, 57. **MEMBERSHIPS** Am Brahms Soc; Violoncello Soc; Am Musicological Soc; Johannes Brahms Gesellschaft Int. Vereinigung e.V.; Oesterreichische Brahms Gesellschaft; AF of M Fedn of Musicians, Local 802; Bohemians (NYC); Gessellschaft zur Forderund des Brahms-Inst Lubeck. **RESEARCH** Documents relating to life and work of Johannes Brahms and his circle; Women musicians in the Brahms circle; Sir Georg Henschel and his American, English and German careers; 19th century performance practice as it relates to the music of Brahms. **SELECTED PUBLICATIONS** Auth, Brahms the Cellist, in Newsletter of the Violoncello Soc, summer and fall, 92; A Jolly End to My Summer: Gustav Wendt and the Clarinet Sonatas, in Newsletter of the Am Brahms Soc, vol. IX, 199?; The Young Brahms: Another View, Newsletter of the Am Brahms Soc, vol. XI, no. 2, 93; An Undeniable Gift, in The Strad Mag, Oct. 96; Johannes Brahms: Life and Letters, 97; Oxford Companion to Music, forthcoming. **CONTACT ADDRESS** 941 Ironbridge Rd, New Jersey, NJ 08802. **EMAIL** savins@drew.edu

AVOTINS, IVARS
PERSONAL Born 11/16/1931, Riga, Latvia, m, 1967 **DISCIPLINE** CLASSICS **EDUCATION** Univ Toronto, BA, 59; Harvard Univ, PhD, 68. **CAREER** Lectr, asst prof, Univ W Ontario, 62-66; asst prof, Univ Calif, Berkeley, 68-70; assoc prof, prof, Univ W Ontario, 70- . **RESEARCH** Epicurus and Lucretius; the second Sophistic; Greek legal language in the Roman Empire. **SELECTED PUBLICATIONS** Auth, Index to the Lives of the Sophists of Philostratus, 78; Index in Eunapii, 83; On the Greek of the Code of Justinian, 89; On the Greek of the Novels of Justinian, 92. **CONTACT ADDRESS** Dept of Classical Studies, Univ of Western Ontario, Rm 420, Talbot College, London, ON, Canada N6A 3K7.

AVRAM, WESLEY D.
PERSONAL Born 03/21/1959, Detroit, MI **DISCIPLINE** RHETORICAL STUDIES **EDUCATION** Princeton Theolog Seminary, Mdiv, 84; Northwestern Univ, PhD, 94 **CAREER** Lctr Relig & Rhetoric, Col Chaplain, Bates Col, 90-96; Res Fel, Yale Univ Divinity School, 93-94; Senior Pastor, First Presbyterian Church, 97-00; Clement-Menhl Asst Prof of Communications, Yale Univ Div Sch, 00-. **HONORS AND AWARDS** Team Teaching Grant, Louisville Inst, 97; Summer Seminar Grant, Ntl Endowment Humanities, 95; Res Fel, Yale Univ Divinity School, 93; Presiden't Fel, Northwestern Univ, 85; Roberts Preaching Prize, Princeton Theolog Seminary, 83; Graduate Study Fel, Princeton Theolog Seminary, 84; Alfred P. Klausler Preaching Awd, 99. **MEMBERSHIPS** Ntl Comm Assoc; Amer Acad Relig **RESEARCH** Philosophical Theology; Rhetorical Studies; Technology and Culture **SELECTED PUBLICATIONS** "Mother Teresa, Princess Di, and the Media," New Oxford Rev, 97; "On the Priority of 'Ethics' in Emmanuel Levinas," Jrnl Religious Ethics, 96; "Chaplaincy at the Present Moment," Still Small Voice, 92; auth, "Jury Duty in the New Realm," Christian Ministry, 999): 20-22. **CONTACT ADDRESS** Divinity School, Yale Univ, 409 Prospect St., New Haven, CT 06511. **EMAIL** wda@mac.com

AXELRAD, ARTHUR MARVIN
PERSONAL Born 08/26/1934, New York, NY **DISCIPLINE** ENGLISH LITERATURE **EDUCATION** Brooklyn Col, BA, 55; NYork Univ, MA, 57, PhD, 62. **CAREER** Asst, Sch Com, NY Univ, 55-57; asst prof English, UT State Univ, 61-64; assoc prof, 64-72, Prof English, CA State Univ, Long Beach, 72-, Assoc ed in charge abstr, Seventeenth-Century News, 57-65; Woodrow Wilson rep, 68-; Danforth fel liaison officer, 68-. **HONORS AND AWARDS** Founders' Day Distinguished Scholar Awd, NY Univ, 63. **MEMBERSHIPS** Milton Soc Am; Int Arthurian Soc. **RESEARCH** English Renaissance, especially Milton; medieval, especially Arthurian literature. **SELECTED PUBLICATIONS** Co-ed, The Prose of John Milton, NY Univ, 67; contribr, Milton Encyclopedia, Univ Wis. **CONTACT ADDRESS** Dept of English, California State Univ, Fullerton, Fullerton, CA 92634.

AXELROD, STEVEN GOULD
PERSONAL Born 05/15/1944, Los Angeles, CA, m, 1966, 1 child **DISCIPLINE** AMERICAN AND MODERN LITERATURE **EDUCATION** Univ Calif, Los Angeles, AB, 66, MA, 69, PhD, 72. **CAREER** Asst prof English, Univ Mo, St Louis, 72-73; vis assoc prof English, 78-79, Univ Colo, Boulder; asst prof, 73-78, prof English, 86-, dir Composition, 86-90,; chmn English dept, 92-96, Univ Calif, Riverside. **HONORS AND AWARDS** Pulitzer Prize nominee; Distinguished Teaching Awd; Chair in Teaching Excellence. **MEMBERSHIPS** MLA; PAMLA; CEA; Am Studies Assn; NCTE. **RESEARCH** American literature; Modern literature; poetry. **SELECTED PUBLICATIONS** Auth, Robert Lowell: Life and Art, Princeton Univ, 78; coauth, Robert Lowell: A Reference Guide, G K Hall, 82; co-ed, Robert Lowell Essays on the Poetry, Cambridge, 86; auth, Sylvia Plath: The Wound & The cure of Words, Johns Hopkins UP, 90; ed, Critical Essays on William Carlos Williams, G K Hall, 95; ed, The Critical Response to Robert Lowell, Greenwood, 99; co-ed, Anthology of American Poetry, Rutgers, forthcoming; auth, 40 articles. **CONTACT ADDRESS** Dept of English, Univ of California, Riverside, 900 University Ave, Riverside, CA 92521-0323. **EMAIL** steven.axelrod@ucr.edu

AXTON, WILLIAM F.
PERSONAL Born 09/24/1926, Louisville, KY, m, 1951, 3 children **DISCIPLINE** ENGLISH LITERATURE **EDUCATION** Yale Univ, AB, 48; Univ Louisville, MA, 51; Princeton Univ, PhD, 61. **CAREER** Instr English, Miami Univ, 52-53 & Brown Univ, 57-61; from asst prof to assoc prof, Univ KY, 61-67; assoc prof, 67-69, chmn dept, 71-74, Prof English, Univ Louisville, 69-, Assoc ed, Dickens Studies Ann, 68-; rev ed, Dickens Newslett, 69-71, prod ed, 75-; pres, Dickens Soc, 72. **MEMBERSHIPS** MLA; Victorian Soc; Dickens Soc; Victorian Soc Am; Browning Soc. **RESEARCH** Nineteenth century art and architecture; Dickens; Victorian aesthetics. **SELECTED PUBLICATIONS CONTACT ADDRESS** Dept of English, Univ of Louisville, Louisville, KY 40208.

AYCOCK, ROY E.
PERSONAL Born 04/11/1926, Greenville, SC **DISCIPLINE** ENGLISH **EDUCATION** Furman Univ, BA, 49; Univ NC, MA, 52, PhD, 60. **CAREER** Instr English, Auburn Univ, 52-54 & Ga Inst Technol, 54-57; assoc prof, 60-64, Prof English, Old Dominion Univ, 64-. **MEMBERSHIPS** MLA; Renaissance Soc Am; Shakespeare Asn Am. **RESEARCH** Shakespeare, Milton and Conne; 16th and 17th centuries; metaphysical poetry. **SELECTED PUBLICATIONS** Auth, Gray's-Inn Journal, Yearbk English Studies, 72; Shakespeare, Boito and Verdi, Musical Quart, 10/72; Dual Progression in Richard III, SAtlantic Bull; George Herbert and the Passion Week, Rivista Di Storia E Letteratura Religiosa, Vol 31, 95. **CONTACT ADDRESS** Dept of English, Old Dominion Univ, Norfolk, VA 23508.

AYCOCK, WENDELL M.
DISCIPLINE ENGLISH AND COMPARATIVE LITERATURE **EDUCATION** Univ SC, PhD, 69. **CAREER** Prof, chp, dept Eng, TX Tech Univ, 90-97; bibliogr, Stud in Short Fiction; assoc dean of The Graduate School, Tex Tech Univ, 00-. **HONORS AND AWARDS** Two Fulbright grants; NEH grant; Mellon grant. **RESEARCH** Short story. **SELECTED PUBLICATIONS** Ed or co-ed eighteen volumes coming from the Comparative Literature Symposium project at Texas Tech, produced 20th-Century Short Story Explication, New Ser, Vol II. **CONTACT ADDRESS** Texas Tech Univ, Lubbock, TX 79409-5015. **EMAIL** W.Aycock@ttu.edu

AZZARA, CHRISTOPHER D.
DISCIPLINE MUSIC **EDUCATION** George Mason University, BM; Eastman Sch Music, MM, PhD. **CAREER** Prof, Hartt Sch Music, 91-. **RESEARCH** Improvisatio; instrumental music education; jazz studies-piano arranging; measurement and evaluation in music; music learning theory; music technology, & music learning. **SELECTED PUBLICATIONS** Auth, Creativity In Improvisation; Jump Right In: The Instrumental Series; ed, Concert Selections for Winds and Percussion. **CONTACT ADDRESS** Hartt Sch Music, Univ of Hartford, 200 Bloomfield Ave, West Hartford, CT 06117.

B

BABB, GENIE
DISCIPLINE LITERATURE **EDUCATION** Brown Univ, PhD. **CAREER** Univ Alaska. **SELECTED PUBLICATIONS** Area: Two Old Women. **CONTACT ADDRESS** Univ of Alaska, Anchorage, 3211 Providence Dr., Anchorage, AK 99508.

BABB, VALERIE M.
PERSONAL Born 05/06/1955, New York, NY **DISCIPLINE** ENGLISH **EDUCATION** Queens Col, City Univ of NYork, BA, 77; State Univ of NYork at Buffalo, MA, 81; PhD, 81. **CAREER** Georgetown Univ, Washington DC, asst prof, associate professor, professor, currently. **HONORS AND AWARDS** Award for Academic Excellence, Seek Program, City Univ of New York, 1985; MT. Zion United Methodist Church Award for "Black Georgetown Remembered: A Documentary Video," 1989. **SELECTED PUBLICATIONS** Book: Whiteness Visible: The Meaning of Whiteness in American Literature & Culture, NYU Press, 1998. **CONTACT ADDRESS** Dept of English, Georgetown Univ, PO Box Box 571131, Washington, DC 20057-1131.

BABCOCK, ROBERT
PERSONAL Born 10/17/1958, Marion, IN, m, 1979, 2 children **DISCIPLINE** CLASSICS **EDUCATION** La State Univ, BA, 78; Duke Univ, MA, 81; PHD, 83. **CAREER** Asst Prof, 84-86, Miss St Univ; Asst Prof, 87, Bucknell Univ; Cur/Lect, 87, Yale Univ **HONORS AND AWARDS** Alexander von Humbolt Fellow, 84; Comite Internationale de Paleographielitve, 98 **MEMBERSHIPS** Am Philolol Assoc; Medieval Acad of Am; Am Soc of Papyrologists **RESEARCH** Classical Transmission **SELECTED PUBLICATIONS** Auth, Reconstructing a Medieval Library, New Haven, 93; coauth, Learning from the Greeks, New Haven, 94; ed, The Rosenthal Collection of Printed Books with Manuscript Annotations, New Haven, 97. **CONTACT ADDRESS** Beinecke Library, PO Box 208240, New Haven, CT 06520-8240. **EMAIL** robert.babcock@yale.edu

BABCOCK, WILLIAM
DISCIPLINE MASS COMMUNICATION STUDIES **EDUCATION** S Ill Univ, PhD. **CAREER** Assoc prof, Journ, Univ Minn. **HONORS AND AWARDS** Ed, Christian Sci Monitor. **SELECTED PUBLICATIONS** Co-auth, Three Major U.S. Newspapers' Content and President Kennedy's Press Conference Statements Regarding Space Exploration and Technology, Pres Studies Quarterly, 83; Reagan Inauguration, Hostages Release, or Both? Publications Time, Ownership, and Circulation Size as Factors in Daily Newspaper Editorial Decisions, Newspaper Res J, 82. **CONTACT ADDRESS** School of Jour, Univ of Minnesota, Twin Cities, 206 Church St SE, 210 Murphy Hall, Minneapolis, MN 55455. **EMAIL** babco001@umn.edu

BABIN, JAMES L.
DISCIPLINE AMERICAN LITERATURE **EDUCATION** Duke Univ, PhD, 70. **CAREER** Assoc prof, La State Univ; assoc ed, Henry James Rev, 79-. **RESEARCH** Voegelinian essays in American literature; 19th and 20th century religion and literature; the place of writers in American (modern) society. **SELECTED PUBLICATIONS** Auth, Melville's Billy Budd, in Explicator, 81; Captain Graveling in Melville's Billy Budd, in Explicator, 84; coed, The Nature of the Law and Related Writings, 91. **CONTACT ADDRESS** Dept of Eng, Louisiana State Univ, 212B Allen Hall, Baton Rouge, LA 70803. **EMAIL** jbabin@lsu.edu

BABROW, AUSTIN S.
PERSONAL Born 08/31/1954, NY, m, 2 children **DISCIPLINE** HEALTH COMMUNICATION, PERSUASION **EDUCATION** Univ Ill, PhD, 86. **CAREER** Assoc prof, Purdue Univ. **SELECTED PUBLICATIONS** Auth, The many meanings of "uncertainty" in illness: Toward a systematic accounting, Babrow, A. S., Kasch, C. R., & Ford, L A., Health Communication 10 (98): 1-24; auth, Colloquy: Developing multiple-process theories of communication, Babrow, A. S., Human Communication Research 25 (98): 152-155; auth, Dialysis patients' preferences for family-based advance care planning. Annals of Internal Medicine, Hines, S. C., Glover, J. J., Holley, J. L., Babrow, A. S., Badzek, L. A., & Moss, A. H., 130 (99): 825-828; auth, From "reducing" to "coping with" uncertainty: Reconceptualizing the central challenge in breast self-exams. Social Science & Medicine, Babrow, A. S., & Kline, K. N., 00. **CONTACT ADDRESS** Dept of Commun, Purdue Univ, West Lafayette, 1366 Lib Arts & Educ Bldg 2114, West Lafayette, IN 47907-1080. **EMAIL** ababrow@sla.purdue.edu

BACH, REBECCA ANN
DISCIPLINE SHAKESPEARE AND EARLY MODERN ENGLISH LITERATURE **EDUCATION** Univ PA, PhD. **CAREER** Dept Eng, Univ Ala **SELECTED PUBLICATIONS** Articles, Studies Eng Lit 1500-1900, Medieval & Renaissance Drama Eng, and Race, Ethnicity and Power in the Renaissance. **CONTACT ADDRESS** Univ of Alabama, Birmingham, 1400 University Blvd, Birmingham, AL 35294-1150.

BACKSCHEIDER, PAULA R.
PERSONAL Born 03/31/1943, Brownsville, TN, m, 1964, 2 children **DISCIPLINE** ENGLISH LITERATURE **EDUCATION** Purdue Univ, PhD, 72. **CAREER** Asst prof, Rollins Coll; asst prof, assoc prof, prof, Roswell Burrows Prof, Univ Rochester; prof, Auburn Univ; Stevens Philpot Eminent Scholar. **HONORS AND AWARDS** British Council Prize for best Book in the Humanities, 90; Guggenheim, NEH, ACLS, Inst for Advanced Studies Edinburgh. **MEMBERSHIPS** MLA; ASECS; SEASECS; NEASECS, AAUP. **RESEARCH** Eighteenth-Century British Lit; Feminist Criticism; Biography. **SELECTED PUBLICATIONS** Auth, Daniel Defoe: His Life, 89; Spectacular Politics: Theatrical Power and Mass Culture in Early Modern England, 93; coauth, Popular Fiction by Women, 1660-1730: An Anthology, 96; auth, Reflections on Biography, 99. **CONTACT ADDRESS** Dept of Eng, Auburn Univ, Auburn, AL 36849. **EMAIL** pkrb@eng.auburn.edu

BACON, HELEN HAZARD
PERSONAL Born 03/09/1919, Berkeley, CA **DISCIPLINE** CLASSICAL LANGUAGES & LITERATURE **EDUCATION** Bryn Mawr Col, BA, 40, PhD(classics), 55. **CAREER** Instr Greek & English, Bryn Mawr Col, 46-48, instr Greek, 48-49; instr classics, Woman's Col, 51-52; from instr to assoc prof, Smith Col, 53-61; assoc prof, 61-65, Prof Classics, Barnard Col, Columbia Univ, 65-, Mem, Col Bd Latin Comt, 61-64; Am Asn Univ Women Founders fel, 63-64; mem fac, Bread Loaf Sch English, Vt, summers 66, 68, 73 & 75; scholar-in-residence, Am Acad in Rome, 68-69; Blegen Distinguished vis res prof, Vassar, fall 79; consult Latin lang & scholar, Comt Physicians Overseeing Translation of 16th Century Latin Medieval Text, 73-. **HONORS AND AWARDS** DLitt, Middlebury Col, 70. **MEMBERSHIPS** Am Philol Asn; Archaeol Inst Am. **RESEARCH** Greek tragedy; Plato; ancient romances. **SELECTED PUBLICATIONS** Auth, Socrates crowned, Va Quart Rev, 59; Barbarians in Greek Tragedy, Yale Univ, 61; The Shield of Eteocles, Arion, 64; Woman's Two Faces: Sophocles' View of Woman's Relation to the Tragedy of Oedipus and His Family, Sci & Psychoanal, 66; co-transl, Aeschylus' Seven against Thebes, Oxford Univ, 73; auth, In-and Out-door Schoolings Robert Frost and the Classics, Am Scholar, 74; For Girls: From Birches to Wild Grapes, Yale Rev, 77; Aeschylus and Early Tragedy, In: Ancient Writers: Greece, Scribner's, 82; The Chorus in Greek Life and Drama, Arion-A Journal of Humanities and the Classics, Vol 3, 95. **CONTACT ADDRESS** Dept of Greek & Latin, Barnard Col, New York, NY 10027.

BACON, ROGER L.
PERSONAL Born 10/23/1939, Boise, ID, m, 1965, 5 children **DISCIPLINE** ENGLISH **EDUCATION** Univ Ore, BA, 64; MA, 65; Univ Ut, PhD, 72; Univ Ut Cultural Found Educ, PhD, 76; Univ Wash, post-doctorate, 82. **CAREER** Asst prof, Southern Ore Univ, 65-69; assoc prof, Northern Ariz Univ, 72-; intern dir, pre-law advisor, & coord of technical writing prof, Northern Ariz Univ, 72-; Chaplain & Colonel, U.S. Airforce (retired); teaching fel & vis prof, Univ Ut; vis prof, Univ Wash. **HONORS AND AWARDS** Phi Kappa Phi. **MEMBERSHIPS** Soc for Technical Commun, Asn of Teachers of Technical Writing, Research Officer's Orgn. **RESEARCH** Readability Measures of Professional Writing, Christina's Story/Poem Collecting, Environmental Writing in Government and Industry. **SELECTED PUBLICATIONS** Coauth, How to Write Quality E. A.'s and E. I. S.'s, Shipley Associates, 78; contribur, Franklin Covery Style Guide, 97. **CONTACT ADDRESS** Dept English, No Arizona Univ, Box 6032, Flagstaff, AZ 86011-0001. **EMAIL** roger.bacon@nau.edu

BADAL, JAMES J.
PERSONAL Born 02/09/1943, Cleveland, OH **DISCIPLINE** ENGLISH **EDUCATION** Western Reserve Univ, BA, 65; MA, 67; Case Western Reserve Univ, PhD, 75. **CAREER** Asst prof, Westminster Col, 69-75; asst prof, Ursuline Col, 77-80; asst prof, Cuyahoga Cmty Col, 80-. **RESEARCH** Liberal arts, music. **SELECTED PUBLICATIONS** Auth, Recording the Classics: Maestros Music and Technology, Kent State Univ Press, 96. **CONTACT ADDRESS** Dept Humanities & Soc Sci, Cuyahoga Comm Col, Eastern, 4250 Richmond Rd, Highland Hills, OH 44122-6104. **EMAIL** james.badal@tri-c.cc.oh.us

BADIAN, ERNST
PERSONAL Born 08/08/1925, Vienna, Austria, m, 1950, 2 children **DISCIPLINE** HISTORY, CLASSICAL STUDIES **EDUCATION** Univ NZ, BA, 45; MA, 46; Oxford Univ, BA, 50; MA, 54; DPhil, 56; Victoria Univ, Wellington, LitD, 62. **CAREER** Jr lectr classics, Victoria Univ Wellington, 47-48; asst lectr classics & ancient hist, Univ Sheffield, 52-54; lectr classics, Univ Durham, 54-65; prof ancient hist, Univ Leeds, 65-69; prof classics & hist, SUNY Buffalo, 69-71; prof hist, Harvard Univ, 71-82; John Moors Cabot Prof Hist, Harvard Univ, 82-98; John Moors Cabot Prof Hist Emer, Harvard Univ, 98-. **HONORS AND AWARDS** Conington Prize, Oxford Univ, 59, for Foreign Clientelae; Fel Brit Acad, Am Acad Arts & Scis, Am Numismatic Soc; corresp mem, Austrian Acad Scis, German Archaeol Inst; for mem, Finnish Acad Scis; hon mem, Soc Prom Roman Studies; hon Fel, Univ Col, Oxford; Austrian Cross of Hon in Sci & Art, 99; fel, Am Coun Learned Socs 72, 82; Leverhulme Fel, 73; Guggenheim Fel, 84; vis mem, Inst Adv Study, Princeton, fall 80, fall 92; fel, Nat Hum Ctr, 88; Hon LitD, Macquarie Univ, 93, Univ Canterbury, 99. **MEMBERSHIPS** Mem, Am Philol Asn, Asn Ancient Historians, Class Asn Can, UK Class Asn, Soc Prom Hellenic Studies, Virgil Soc. **RESEARCH** Alexander the Great; Roman Republic; Achaemenid Persia. **SELECTED PUBLICATIONS** Auth, Foreign Clientelae 264-270 BC, 58; auth, Studies in Greek and Roman History, 64; ed, Polybius, 66; ed, Ancient Society and Institutions, 66; auth, Roman Imperialism in the Late Republic, 67; auth Publicans and Sinners, 72; ed, "Sir Ronald Syme," Roman Papers Vols 1-2 (79); auth, From Plataea to Potidaea, 93; auth, Zoellner und Suender, 97; Ed, Am J Ancient Hist, 76-00. **CONTACT ADDRESS** Dept of Hist, Harvard Univ, Robinson Hall, Cambridge, MA 02138.

BAENDER, PAUL
PERSONAL Born 12/01/1926, Alameda, CA, m, 1957, 3 children **DISCIPLINE** AMERICAN LITERATURE **EDUCATION** Univ CA, Berkeley, AB, 49, MA, 52, PhD, 56. **CAREER** Instr English, Univ Chicago, 56-60; from asst prof to assoc prof, 60-68; Prof English, Univ Iowa, 68-. **MEMBERSHIPS** Midwest Mod Lang Asn. **RESEARCH** Nineteenth century American literature; Mark Twain; bibliography. **SELECTED PUBLICATIONS** Co-ed, Mark Twain's Roughing It, 72, ed, What is Man? and Other Philosophical Writings of Mark Twain, 73 & co-ed, Mark Twain's Adventures of Tom Sawyer, 80, Univ CA; Alias Macfarlane-Who in L was L, Resources fro Am Literary Study, Vol 19, 93. **CONTACT ADDRESS** Dept of English, Univ of Iowa, Iowa City, IA 52242.

BAER, JOEL H.
PERSONAL Born 10/05/1938, New York, NY, m, 1981, 1 child **DISCIPLINE** ENGLISH **EDUCATION** NY Univ, BA, 60; Princeton Univ, MA, 70; PhD, 70. **CAREER** Instr, Wash & Lee Univ, 62-64; assoc prof, Macalester Col, 66-. **HONORS AND AWARDS** Clifford Prize, Am Soc for Eighteenth-Century Studies, 82. **MEMBERSHIPS** Am Soc of Eighteenth-Century Studies. **RESEARCH** Satire, The Novel, Piracy in Eighteenth-Century Life and Fiction. **SELECTED PUBLICATIONS** Auth, "'The Complicated Plot of Piracy': Aspects of English Criminal Law and the Image of the Pirate in Defoe," The Eighteenth Century 23 (82): 3-26; auth, "Captain John Avery and the Anatomy of a Mutiny," Eighteenth-Century Life 18 (94): 1-26; auth, "Bold Captain Avery in the Privy Council: Early Variants of a Broadside Ballad from the Pepys Collection," Folk Music J 7 (95): 4-26; auth, "William Dampier at the Crossroads: New Light on the 'Missing Years,' 1691-1697," Int J of Maritime Hist 8 (96): 1-21; auth, "Penelope Aubin and the Pirates of Madagascar: Biographical Notes and Documents," Eighteenth-Century Women 1 (00). **CONTACT ADDRESS** Dept English, Macalester Col, 1600 Grand Ave, Saint Paul, MN 55105-1801. **EMAIL** baer@macalester.edu

BAER, WILLIAM
PERSONAL Born 12/29/1948, Geneva, NY, m, 1987, 2 children **DISCIPLINE** ENGLISH LITERATURE **EDUCATION** Rutgers, BA; NY Univ, MA; Univ SC, PhD; Johns Hopkins Univ, MA; Univ S Calif. **CAREER** Fulbright prof, Portugal; prof. **HONORS AND AWARDS** T S Eliot prize in poetry; Jack Nicholson Screen Wrtg Awd; Arts fel, NEA. **SELECTED PUBLICATIONS** Founding ed, and pub(s), The Formalist; auth, Conversations with Derek Walcott; The Unfortunates; Elia Kazan: Interviews. **CONTACT ADDRESS** Dept of Eng, Univ of Evansville, 1800 Lincoln Ave, Evansville, IN 47714. **EMAIL** wb4@evansville.edu

BAETZHOLD, HOWARD GEORGE
PERSONAL Born 01/01/1923, Buffalo, NY, m, 1950, 2 children **DISCIPLINE** ENGLISH **EDUCATION** Brown Univ, AB, 44, AM, 48; Univ Wis, PhD(English & Am lit), 53. **CAREER** From asst dir to dir vet col, Brown Univ, 47-49, admis officer, 48-50; teaching asst 50-51; asst to the assoc dean, Col Lett & Sci, Univ WI, 51-53; from asst prof to assoc prof, 53-57, prof, 67-81, Rebecca Clifton Reader Prof & Head Dept English, Butler Univ, 81-88, Univ IA & US Off Educ res grant for work on Iowa-CA Ed of Writings of Mark Twain, Univ CA, Berkeley, NY Pub Libr, Yale Univ, Princeton Univ & Univ VA, 65-66; Am Coun Learned Soc grant-in-aid, Univ CA, Berkeley, 67; Rebecca Clinton Reade prof emer, 88-; vis prof, Univ of Delaware, summer 63; Am Philosopical Soc grant-in-aid, Univ CA, Berkeley, 58. **HONORS AND AWARDS** Scholar's Library of the Modern Lang Assoc inclusion, 70; nominated as one of the " most distinguished books fo the year" by Indiana Univ Comt for Indiana Authors Day, 71; Who's Who Among Indiana Scholars, 84; Who's Who in Am, 43rd ed, 84-85; Butler Univ Fel, 86, 87; " Sagamore of the Wabash" Indiana Governor Robert D. Orr, 88; " Howard Baetzhold Day" Mayor William H Hudnut, 88; Advisory Bd of Mark Twain Encyclopedia, 89; John S Tuckey Memorial Res Fel, Elmira Col Ctr for Mark Twain Studies, Quarry Farm, 90; Consultant for Sam Clemens and Mark Twain, 93; " Mark Twain Biog" : Prospect and Prospect:" panel , Am Lit Assn Conv, Baltimore,95; Honary lifetime member of the Mark Twain Circle of Am, 95. **MEMBERSHIPS** Am Assoc of Univ Prof, Assoc of Dept of English, Col English Assoc, Modern Laug Assoc of Am, Am Lit Section, Modern Lang Assn, Mark Twain Circle of Am. **RESEARCH** Nineteenth Century American Literature, especially works of Mark Twain: 19th Century Anglo-American literary relations; Twentieth century American Literature. **SELECTED PUBLICATIONS** Auth, Course of Composition of Mark Twain's A Connecticut Yankee, Am Lit, 5/61; What was the Model for Martin Chuzzlewit's Eden?, Dickinson, 9/59; Mark Twain and John Bull: The British Connection, IN Univ, 70; Found: Mark Twain's Lost Sweetheart, Am Lit, 11/72; Mark Twain on Scientific Investigation: Contemporary Allusions in Some Learned Fables for Good Old Boys and Girls, In: Literature and Ideas in America: Essays in Memory of Harry Hayden Clark, OH Univ, 75; Of Detectives and Their Derring-do: The Genesis of Mark Twain's The Stolen White Elephant, Studies Am Humor, 76; Our Famous Guest, Mark-Twain in Vienna, with C. Dolmetsch, Am Lit, Vol 66, 94. **CONTACT ADDRESS** Dept of English, Butler Univ, Indianapolis, IN 46208.

BAGDIKIAN, BEN HAIG
PERSONAL Born 01/30/1920, Marash, Turkey, m, 1983, 2 children **DISCIPLINE** JOURNALISM **EDUCATION** Clark Univ, AB, 41. **CAREER** Corresp, Providence, RI J & Bull, 47-61; contrib ed, Sat Eve Post, 62-67; proj dir news media, Rand, 68-69; asst managing ed nat, Wash Post, 70-72; Prof and Dean Jour, Univ CA, Berkeley, 77-90, John Simon Guggenheim Found fel, 62. **HONORS AND AWARDS** LHD, Brown Univ, 61; Lit, Clark Univ, 63, LHD, URI, Peabody Awd, 51, Ala, Madison Awd **MEMBERSHIPS** Mellet Fund for Free & Responsible Press (pres, 66-76); Nat Prison Proj; Soc Sci Res Coun. **RESEARCH** Journalism; media structures; criminal justice. **SELECTED PUBLICATIONS** Ed, Man's Contracting World in an Expanding Universe, Brown Univ, 60; auth, In the Midst of Plenty, Beacon, 64; The Information Machines, Harper, 70; The Shame of the Prisons, Simon & Schuster, 72; The Effete Conspriacy, 72 & Caged, 76, Harper; The 'Media Monopoly" & Adapted From the Preface to the Recently Published 6th-Edition of the Book, Television Quart, Vol 28, 97. **CONTACT ADDRESS** 25 Stonewall Road, Berkeley, CA 94705. **EMAIL** benmar@uclink4.berkeley.edu

BAGLEY, MARY
PERSONAL Born 03/11/1958, St Louis, MO, s, 2 children **DISCIPLINE** ENGLISH **EDUCATION** Univ Missouri, BA;

Univ Missouri, MA; St. Louis Univ, PhD. **CAREER** Teaching Fellow, Univ of Mo-St. Louis, 80-82; instr, St. Louis Univ, 83-85; Vis Lecturer, Southern Illinois Univ-Edwardsville, 83-87. **HONORS AND AWARDS** SLCC Outstanding Teaching Awd; William Barnaby Faherty Awd. **MEMBERSHIPS** MLA; Theatre Historical Society; Sigma Tan Delta; NCTE. **RESEARCH** Willa Cather; Contemporary American Literature. **SELECTED PUBLICATIONS** Auth, The Front Row; auth, Business Communication; auth, Handbook for Professional & Academic Writing; auth, The Art of Writing Well; auth, Professional Writing Types; auth, Selected Redings in 19th & 20th Cent lit (ed.); auth, Poetics of Realism; auth, Willa Cather's Myths. **CONTACT ADDRESS** Dept Humanities, Missouri Baptist Col, 1 College Park Dr, Saint Louis, MO 63141-8660. **EMAIL** bagley@mobap.edu

BAHK, C. M.
DISCIPLINE COMMUNICATION **EDUCATION** Michigan State Univ, PhD, 94. **CAREER** Asst prof, Univ of Cincinnati, 95-. **HONORS AND AWARDS** Phillip K. Tompkins Awd for Outstanding Research, SUNY at Albany. **MEMBERSHIPS** NCA, ICA, BEA. **RESEARCH** Mass media effects; intercultural interaction; health and environmental communication. **SELECTED PUBLICATIONS** Art, Descriptions of Sexual Content and Ratings of Movie Preference, Psychological Reports, 98; art, The Impact of Presence Versus Absence of Negative Consequences in Dramatic Portrayals of Alcohol Drinking, J of Alcohol and Drug Education, 97; auth, Interpersonal and Perceptions of Same-Sex and Opposite-Sex Friendships in the United States and Korea, Interpersonal Communication in Friend and Mate Relationships, SUNY Press, 93; coauth, The Relationship of Empathy to Comforting Behavior Following Film Exposure, Communication Research, 93. **CONTACT ADDRESS** Dept of Communication, Univ of Cincinnati, Univ of Cincinnati, Cincinnati, OH 45221-0184. **EMAIL** bahkcm@uc.edu

BAILEY, RICHARD WELD
PERSONAL Born 10/26/1939, Pontiac, MI, m, 1960, 2 children **DISCIPLINE** ENGLISH **EDUCATION** Dartmouth Col, AB, 61; Univ Conn, MA, 63; PhD, 66. **CAREER** From asst prof to prof, English, Univ Mich, Ann Arbor, 76-; trustee, Washtenaw Community Col, 75-. **HONORS AND AWARDS** Rackham Fac Fel 67, 75; ACLS Grant for Computer-Oriented Res in the Humanities, 68; Res Fel, Off of Res dmin, Univ Mich, 70; ACLS Grant-in-Aid Fel, Inst for Advanced Stud in the Humanities, Univ of Edinburgh, 71; Proj Dir, Early Mod English Dictionary Proj, supported by the Nat Endowment for the Humanities, 71-73, 75; Co-Proj Dir, Int Conf on the Semiotics of Art, 78; Co-Proj Dir, Prog to Improve Student Writing, the Ford Found, 78-80; Proj Dir, Colloquium on English Lexicography, Nat Endowment for the Humanitites, 85; Distinguished Fac Achievement Awd, U-M, 89; Fel for Univ Teachers, Nat Endowment for the Humanitites, 91-92; Regent's Awd for Distinguished Public Service, 92; U-M Press Book Awd, 93, 98; Mich Humanities Fel, 97. **MEMBERSHIPS** NCTE; MLA; Ling Soc Am; Asn Comput & Humanities; Am Dialect Soc; Dictionary Soc North Am. **RESEARCH** Stylistics; dialectology; computational lexicography; history of English. **SELECTED PUBLICATIONS** Co-ed, English Stylistics: A Bibliography, Mass Inst Technol, 68; auth, Statistics and Style, Am Elsevier, 69; auth, Varieties of Present-Day English, Macmillan, 73; auth, Michigan Early Modern English Materials, Xerox Univ Microfilms, 75; ed, Early Modern English, Georg Olms Verlag, 78; co-ed, The Sign: Semiotics Around the World, Mich Slavic Pub(s), 78; auth, English as a World Language, Univ Mich Press, 82; ed, Computing in the Humanities, North-Holland, 82; assoc ed, The Oxford Companion to the English Language, Oxford and New York: Oxford Univ Press, 92; auth, Nineteenth-Century English, Ann Arbor: Univ Mich Press, 96; auth, Images of English: A Cultural History of the Language, Ann Arbor, Univ Mich Press 91, Cambridge Univ Press, 92. **CONTACT ADDRESS** Dept of English, Univ of Michigan, Ann Arbor, 505 S State St, Ann Arbor, MI 48109-1003. **EMAIL** rwbailey@umich.edu

BAILEY, TERENCE
DISCIPLINE MUSIC **EDUCATION** Univ Wash, PhD, 68. **CAREER** Prof, Univ of Western Ontario. **HONORS AND AWARDS** Fel, Royal Soc Can. **RESEARCH** Ambrosian chant; music and Liturgy of the Latin Church; medieval modal theory; musical paleography; text/music relationships in the Middle Ages and Renaissance. **SELECTED PUBLICATIONS** Auth, Commemoratio Brevis, Introduction, Critical Edition and Study, Ottawa: The Univ of Ottawa Press, 79; auth, The Ambrosian Cantus, Edition and Introductroy Study, Ottawa: The Institute of Mediaeval Music, 87; auth, "Milanese Melodic Tropes," Journal of the Plainsong and Mediaeval Music Soc 11, (90): 1-12; auth, "Word Painting and the Romantic Interpretation of Chant," in Beyond the Moon: Fetschrift Luther Dittmer, (Ottawa: The Institute of Medieval Music, 90): 1-15; auth, "An Ancient Psalmody without Antiphons in the Ambrosian Ferial Office," Revista de Musicologia 16/2, (93): 873-82; Antiphon and Psalm in the Ambrosian Office, Ottawa: The Institute of Mediaeval Music, 94; auth, "Ambrosianischer Gesang," "Mailand," in Musik in Geschichte und Gegenwart, (Kasssel: Barenreiter, 96). **CONTACT ADDRESS** Dept of Music, Univ of Western Ontario, London, ON, Canada N6A 5B8. **EMAIL** tbailey@julian.uwo.ca

BAILEY, THOMAS CULLEN
PERSONAL Born 11/29/1940, m, 1990, 4 children **DISCIPLINE** ENGLISH & AMERICAN LITERATURE **EDUCATION** Oberlin Col, BA, 62; Univ MO, MA, 64; WA Univ, Ph-D(English), 74. **CAREER** Instr English, Westminster Col, 64-66; Prof English, Western MI Univ, 70-, Nat Endowment Humanities fel Am autobiog, Dartmouth Col, 75-76. **MEMBERSHIPS** MLA, WLA, UCOA, ASLE. **RESEARCH** Autobiography; John Clare's poems; Mark Twain, Nature writing. **SELECTED PUBLICATIONS** Auth, Ecotone, Wayfaring on the Margins, with F. Krall, Women's Studies-An Interdisciplinary J, Vol 25, 96; auth, chapt, Earthly Words, Univ of Mich Press, 94 " John McPhee the Making of a Meta-Naturalist."; auth, chapt, Rick Bass Univ of Utah Press, 00, " Ricks Bass's Winter: Self-Revelations in a Cold Chive". **CONTACT ADDRESS** Provosts Office, Western Michigan Univ, Kalamazoo, MI 49008. **EMAIL** bailey@wmich.edu

BAILLY, JACQUES A.
PERSONAL Born 01/28/1966, Salt Lake City, UT **DISCIPLINE** CLASSICS **EDUCATION** Brown Univ, BA, 88; Cornell Univ, PhD, 97. **CAREER** Lectr, Colby Col, 96-97; lectr, 97-98, asst prof, 98- , Univ Vermont. **HONORS AND AWARDS** Fulbright award, 88-90; Jakob K Javits Scholarship, 91-95. **MEMBERSHIPS** APA. **RESEARCH** Ancient philosophy; philology. **CONTACT ADDRESS** Dept of Classics, Univ of Vermont, 481 Main St, Burlington, VT 05401. **EMAIL** jbailly@zoo.uvm.edu

BAIRD, JOHN D.
PERSONAL Born 05/09/1941, Glasgow, Scotland **DISCIPLINE** ENGLISH LITERATURE **EDUCATION** St Andrews Univ, MA, 63; McMaster Univ, MA, 64; Princeton Univ, MA, 67, PhD, 70. **CAREER** Fac mem, 67-81, Prof English Lit, Victoria Col & Univ Toronto, 81-, dir grad stud, 85-89, assoc dean hum, School of Grad Stud, 92-95. **RESEARCH** Richard Watson 1737-1816; poetry of battle; William Cowper; Thomas Gray. **SELECTED PUBLICATIONS** Co-ed, The Poems of William Cowper, 80-95; auth, "Criminal Elements: Fielding's Jonathan Wild," in M.L. Friedland, (Toronto, 91), 76-94; auth, Divorce and Matrimonial Causes: An Aspect of Hard Times Victorian Studies, 77. **CONTACT ADDRESS** Victoria Col, Univ of Toronto, Toronto, ON, Canada M5S 1K7. **EMAIL** john.baird@utoronto.ca

BAKER, BARBARA A.
DISCIPLINE ENGLISH **EDUCATION** Univ Pitt, BA, 91; Auburn Univ, MA, 93; PhD, 99. **CAREER** Grad teaching asst, Auburn Univ, 91-97; instr to asst prof, Tuskegee Univ, 97-. **HONORS AND AWARDS** Co-Dir NEH; **MEMBERSHIPS** CBMR; Charles Chenutt Asn; MLA; SSSL; SAMLA. **RESEARCH** The African American vernacular tradition; manifestations of the blues aesthetics in American literature. **SELECTED PUBLICATIONS** Auth, "The Aesthetics of Thug Life in the Music of the Vernacular Tradition: Representations of Resilience and the Justifiable Homicide," Black Arts Quart (01); auth, "George Washington Harris," "Albert Murray," "Lewis Nordan," "Phillis Berry," A Biographical Guide to Alabama Literature, Univ Ala Pr; auth, "The Blues," A Companion to Southern Literature, Univ Ala Pr. **CONTACT ADDRESS** English Dept, Tuskegee Univ, Tuskegee, AL 36088. **EMAIL** bakerbar@tusk.edu

BAKER, BEULAH PEARL
PERSONAL Born Baton Rouge, LA **DISCIPLINE** LITERATURE **EDUCATION** Spring Arbor Col, BA, 67; Mich State Univ, MA, 69, PhD, 76. **CAREER** Prof English lit, John Wesley Col, 69-79; prof English & chair dept English, Taylor Univ, 79-. **HONORS AND AWARDS** NEH grant; Teaching Excellence and Campus Leadership Awd, 95. **MEMBERSHIPS** Conf Christianity & Lit; MLA; Col English Asn; MMLA. **RESEARCH** Modern and post-modern poetry, especially William Carlos Williams; African literature. **SELECTED PUBLICATIONS** Auth, reviews in CCL Journal. **CONTACT ADDRESS** Dept of English, Taylor Univ, Upland, 236 W Reade Ave, Upland, IN 46989-1002. **EMAIL** BLBaker@TaylorU.edu

BAKER, C. EDWIN
PERSONAL Born 05/28/1947, Nashville, TN **DISCIPLINE** CONSTITUTIONAL LAW, LEGAL PHILOSOPHY, MASS MEDIA **EDUCATION** Stanford Univ, BA, 69; Yale Univ, JD, 72. **CAREER** Asst prof, Univ Toledo, 72-75; asst prof, Univ Ore, 75-79, assoc prof, 79-81 & prof, 81-82; Prof Law, Univ Pa, 82-, Fel, Harvard Univ, 74-75; vis prof law, Univ Tex, 80 & Univ Pa, 81-82; Staff Atty, ACLU, NY, 87-88; Fel, Shorentein Barone Ctr, Kennedy Sch Govt, Harvard, 92; vis prof, Cornell Univ, 93; Vis Lombard Prof, Kennedy Sch Govt, Harvard Univ, 93; vis prof, Univ of Chicago, 00. **RESEARCH** Mass media; constitutional law. **SELECTED PUBLICATIONS** Auth, Human Liberty and Freedom of Speech, Oxford Univ 89; Advertising and a Democratic Press, Princeton, 94; author of numerous journal articles. **CONTACT ADDRESS** Law Sch, Univ of Pennsylvania, 3400 Chestnut St, Philadelphia, PA 19104-6204. **EMAIL** ebaker@law.upenn.edu

BAKER, CHRISTOPHER P.
PERSONAL Born 09/07/1946, Ypsilanti, MI, m, 1 child **DISCIPLINE** ENGLISH **EDUCATION** St. Lawrence Univ, BA, 68; Univ NC, Chapel Hill, MA, 70, PhD, 74. **CAREER** Inst to full prof, Lamar Univ, 76-94; Head, langs/lit/drama, 94-98, prof Eng, 98-, Armstrong Atlantic ST UNIV. **HONORS AND AWARDS** R.A. Law Shakespeare award, Conference of Col Tchrs of Eng in TX, 87; Am Council on Edu Fel, 88-89. **MEMBERSHIPS** MLA; South Central Renaissance Conf; Southern Comp Lit Assoc; Sicteenth Century Studies Conf; Renaissance Soc of Am. **RESEARCH** English Renaissance literature; Christianity and literature. **SELECTED PUBLICATIONS** Auth, Spenser and 'The City in the Sea,' Poe Studies, 1972; auth, Francis Davison and Guilpin's Satire III, Etudes Anglaises, 78; auth, The Dead Art of 'The Dead', English Studies, 82; auth, Francis Bacon and the Technology of Style, Technical Writing Teacher, 83; auth, The Christian Contect of Falstaff's 'Finer End,' Explorations in Renaissance Culture, vol. XII, 86; auth, The Alchemist and Shakespeare's Sonnet 129, Notes and Queries, 93; auth, Frost's 'After Apple-Picking' as Hypnagogic Vision, The Robert Frost Review, 94; auth, A Prayer Book Allusion in 2HenryIV, Notes and Queries, 96; auth, Shakespeare's Hamlet, 1.5.23, Explicator, 96; auth, Arnold's 'To A Friend' and Sidney's Astrophil and Stella, Victorian Poetry, 99; ed, Absolutism and the Scientific Revolution: 1600-1720, Greenwood Press, forthcoming. **CONTACT ADDRESS** Armstrong Atlantic State Univ, 11935 Abercorn St, Savannah, GA 31419. **EMAIL** bakerchr@armstrong.edu

BAKER, DAVID
PERSONAL Born 08/17/1963, Washington, DC, m, 1991, 2 children **DISCIPLINE** ENGLISH **EDUCATION** Bennington Col, BA, 86; Columbia Univ, PhD, 94. **CAREER** Vis Asst Prof, Univ of Miss, 94-95; Asst Prof, Rutgers Univ Newark, 95-. **HONORS AND AWARDS** Writing Dissertation Fel, 92-93. **MEMBERSHIPS** MLA, Renaissance Soc of Am. **RESEARCH** Renaissance humanism. **SELECTED PUBLICATIONS** Auth, "Topical Utopias: radicalizing Humanism in Sixteenth-Century England," Studies in English Lit (Winter 96); auth, "Cavalier Shakespeare: The 1640 Poems of John Benson," Studies in Philology (Spring 98); auth, Divulging Utopia: Radical Humanism in Sixteenth-Century England, The Univ of Mass Press, 99. **CONTACT ADDRESS** Dept English, Rutgers, The State Univ of New Jersey, Newark, 180 University Ave, Newark, NJ 07102-1803.

BAKER, DAVID ANTHONY
PERSONAL Born 12/27/1954, Bangor, ME, m, 1987, 1 child **DISCIPLINE** ENGLISH **EDUCATION** Cent Mo State Univ, BSE, 76, MA, 77; Univ Ut, PhD, 83. **CAREER** Ed, Kenyou Rev; Chr Creative Writing & Prof English, Denison Univ; NEA fel; Oh Arts Coun fel; Guggenheim Fel. **HONORS AND AWARDS** Soc Midland Auth Book Awd, Ohioana Poetry Awd. **MEMBERSHIPS** AWD; MLA; Poets and Writers; Academy of Am Poets. **RESEARCH** American poetry; Poetics. **SELECTED PUBLICATIONS** Auth Laws of the Land, Ahsahta/Boise State Univ, 81; Haunts, Cleveland State Univ Poetry Ctr, 85; Sweet Home, Saturday Night, Ar, 91; After the Reunion, Ar, 94; Meter in English: A Critical Engagement, Ar, 96; The Truth about Small Towns, Univ Ar Press, 98; auth, Heresy and the Ideal: On Contemporary Poetry, Ar, 00; auth, Changeable Thunder, Ar, 01. **CONTACT ADDRESS** Dept of English, Denison Univ, Granville, OH 43023. **EMAIL** baker@denison.edu

BAKER, DELBERT WAYNE
PERSONAL Born 01/25/1953, Oakland, CA, m **DISCIPLINE** JOURNALISM **EDUCATION** Oakwood Coll, Huntsville, AL, BA (cum laude), 1975; Andrews Univ Seminary, Berrien Springs, MI, MDiv (with honors), 1978; Howard Univ, Washington, DC, PhD, 1992. **CAREER** Pastor in MI, VA, OH, 75-85; Messsage Magazine, Hagerstown, MD, editor-in-chief, 85-92; Howard Univ, instructor, 90-91; Consultant, 90-; Loma Linda Univ, Asst to the Pres, Dir of Diversity, Assoc Prof, 92-. **HONORS AND AWARDS** Alumnus of the Year, Oakwood Coll, 1985; Editorial Journalism Awds, Editors Intl, 1988-90. **MEMBERSHIPS** Bd mem, San Mars Children's Home, 1986-89; bd mem, bd of dir, Oakwood Coll, 1985-; bd mem, Human Relations Council General Conference of Seventh-day Adventist Church, 1987-; Clergy's Black Caucus, 1985-; contributor video, Africa Continent of Explosive Growth, 1987; bd mem, Review & Herald Pub Assn, 1985-; board member, Loma Linda University; chairman, Diversity Advisory Committee. **SELECTED PUBLICATIONS** Author of four books: The Unknown Prophet, 1986; From Exile to Prime Minister, 1988; Profiles of Service, 1990; Communication and Change in Religious Organization, 1992. **CONTACT ADDRESS** Office of Diversity, Loma Linda Univ, Magan Hall, Rm 103, Loma Linda, CA 92350.

BAKER, DENISE NOWAKOWSKI
PERSONAL Born 04/23/1946, Detroit, MI, m, 1970, 1 child **DISCIPLINE** ENGLISH **EDUCATION** Univ Mich, BA, 68; Univ Calif, Santa Barbara, MA, 70; Univ Va, PhD(English), 75. **CAREER** Asst prof to prof, Univ NC, Greensboro, 75-. **HONORS AND AWARDS** Fel, Southeastern Inst Medieval & Renaissance Studies, summer 78. **MEMBERSHIPS** Medieval

Acad Am, MLA. **RESEARCH** Medieval literature; medieval mystics; Julian of Norwich; Langland's Piers Plowman. **SELECTED PUBLICATIONS** Auth, The Priesthood of Genius: A Study of the Medieval Tradition, Speculum, 4/76; From Plowing to Penitence: Piers Plowman and Fourteenth Century Theology, Speculum, 10/80; Julian of Norwich's Showings: From Vision to Book, Princeton Univ Press, 94. **CONTACT ADDRESS** Dept of English, Univ of No Carolina, Greensboro, 1000 Spring Garden, Greensboro, NC 27402-0001. **EMAIL** dnbaker@uncg.edu

BAKER, DONALD C.
PERSONAL Born 12/12/1928, Jonesboro, AR, m, 1952, 4 children **DISCIPLINE** ENGLISH MEDIEVAL LITERATURE **EDUCATION** AR State Col, AB, 49; Univ MS, MA, 50; Univ OK, PhD, 54. **CAREER** Instr English compos, Univ OK, 52-53 & Agr & Mech Col TX, 53-55; asst prof English lit, State Univ SD, 55-57; assoc prof, Univ MS, 57-62; assoc prof, 62-68, Prof English, Univ CO, Boulder, 68- Fulbright lectr, Finland, 61-62. **MEMBERSHIPS** MLA; Mediaeval Acad Am; Renaissance Soc Am. **RESEARCH** Middle English; Old English; Renaissance literature. **SELECTED PUBLICATIONS** **CONTACT ADDRESS** Dept of English, Univ of Colorado, Boulder, Boulder, CO 80302.

BAKER, DONALD WHITELAW
PERSONAL Born 01/30/1923, Boston, MA, m, 1945, 2 children **DISCIPLINE** ENGLISH LITERATURE **EDUCATION** Brown Univ, AB, 47, AM, 49, PhD(English), 55. **CAREER** Instr English, Brown Univ, 48-52; from asst prof to prof English, 53-76, dir drama, 54-59, Milligan Prof English Lit & Shakespeare, Wabash Col, 76-, Poet in Residence, 63-, Dir, New Writers Awards Prog, Great Lakes Col Asn, 76-. **MEMBERSHIPS** MLA; NCTE. **RESEARCH** English novel; modern fiction; creative writing. **SELECTED PUBLICATIONS** Auth, Three Poets, 7/67, Five Poets, 12/67 & The Poetry of James Dickey, 3/68, Poetry; Twelve Hawks, Sugar Creek Poetry Ser, 74; Topical Utopias, Radicalizing Humanism in 16th-Century England, Studies in English Literature 1500-1900, Vol 36, 96. **CONTACT ADDRESS** Dept of English Lit, Wabash Col, Crawfordsville, IN 47933.

BAKER, HOUSTON A.
PERSONAL Born 03/22/1943, Louisville, KY, m, 1 child **DISCIPLINE** AFRICAN AMERICAN LITERATURE **EDUCATION** Howard Univ, BA, 65; Univ Calif, Los Angeles, MA, 66, PhD, 68. **CAREER** Instr, Howard Univ, 66; Instr, 68-69, Asst prof, 69-70, Yale; Assoc prof and mem of Ctr for Adv Studies, 70-73, prof, 73-74, Univ VA; Dir of Afro Amer studies 74-77, prof, 77-99, Univ Pa; Dir, Ctr for the Study of Black Lit and Culture, 87-99; prof, Duke Univ, 99-. **HONORS AND AWARDS** Legion of Honor Chapel of the Four Chaplains (Philadelphia Commun Service Awd), 81; Christian R. And Mary F. Lindback Found Awd for Dist Teaching (Univ PA), 84; Alum Awd for for Dist Achievement in Lit and the Humanities, Howard Univ, 85; Outstanding Alum Awd of Howard Univ, 85; Dist Writer of the year, Mid Atlantic Writers Assoc, 86; Creative Scholarship Awd College Lang Assoc of Amer for Afro Amer Poetics, 88; PA Governors Awd for Excellence in the Humanities, 90; Fullbright 50th Anniv Dist Fel to Brazil, Council for Intl Exchange of Scholars, 96. **MEMBERSHIPS** English Inst Brd of Supervisors 89-91; MLA second vp 90-91, first vp 91-92, pres 92; School of Criticism and Theory, Cornell Univ, sr. Fel. **RESEARCH** Afro Amer Lit; Literary and cultural studies; Post Colonial studies; Psychoanalytic expressive cultural theory; Autobiography. **SELECTED PUBLICATIONS** Auth, Workings of the Spirit: A Poetics of Afro-American Women's Writing, 91; Black Studies, Rap and the Academy, 93; coed, Black British Cultural Studies: A Reader, 96; auth, Blues, Ideology and Afro-American Literature; auth, Modernism and the Harlem Renaissance; auth, Critical Memory, Univ of Ga Press, forthcoming; auth, Turning South Again: Rethinking Modernism/Rereading Booker T., Duke Univ Press, forthcoming. **CONTACT ADDRESS** Dept of English, Duke Univ, 302 Allen, Box 90014, Durham, NC 27708. **EMAIL** bakerh@acpub.duke.edu

BAKER, J. ROBERT
DISCIPLINE ENGLISH LITERATURE **EDUCATION** Univ Notre Dame, AB; MA; PhD. **CAREER** Prof, Fairmont State Col, 94-. **RESEARCH** Compos and lit; computer tech in the classroom; world lit; world novel; Southern lit; bible as lit. **SELECTED PUBLICATIONS** Coauth, CD-ROM hypertext on Malcolm X. **CONTACT ADDRESS** Dept of English, Fairmont State Col, 1201 Locust Ave, Fairmont, WV 26554. **EMAIL** jbaker@mail.fscwv.edu

BAKER, MOIRA
DISCIPLINE ENGLISH LITERATURE **EDUCATION** Col St Rose, BA magna cum laude, 73; Univ Notre Dame, MA, 76, PhD, 82. **CAREER** Rector. Lewis Hall, 78-82, adj asst prof, Univ Notre Dame, 82-86; asst to assoc prof, 86-97, prof Radford Univ, 97-. **HONORS AND AWARDS** Univ first-yr fel, Univ Notre Dame, 74; univ dissertation yr fel, Univ Notre Dame, 81; NOVUS Awd, Conf for the Advan of Early Stud, 87; Omicron Delta Kappa, Nat Honor Soc, 89; fac prof and develop leave, Radford Univ, 97. **MEMBERSHIPS** Int Virginia Woolf Soc; Nat Coun of Tchr of Eng; Philol Asn of the Carolinas; South-Atlantic Mod Lang Asn; Southeastern Women's Stud Asn; South-Cent Renaissance Asn; VA Asn of Tchr of Eng. **SELECTED PUBLICATIONS** Auth, 'This Gift of Celestial Honey': A (W)rite of Passage to Renaissance Studies, Eric ED 295 214, 88; At Home in the Contra War, Notre Dame Mag 18.1, 89; 'The Dichotomiz'd Carriage of all our Sermons': Satiric Structure in the Sermons of Thomas Adams, Eng Renaissance Prose 3.1, 89; (En)Gendering Change: One Woman's Voice and the Traditional Canon, VA Eng Bull 40.2, 90; 'The Uncanny Stranger on Display': The Female Body in Sixteenth- and Seventeenth-Century Love Poetry, South-Atlantic Rev 56.2, 91; Mentoring as Teaching and Learning, ERIC ED 358 459, 93; Thomas Adams, in Dictionary of Literary Biography: British Prose Writers of the Early Seventeenth Century, Vol 151, ed Clayton D. Lein, Gale, 95; 'What is English?': Developing a Senior 'Capstone' Course for the English Major, ERIC ED 411 512, 97. **CONTACT ADDRESS** Radford Univ, Radford, VA 24142. **EMAIL** mpbaker@runet.edu

BAKER, ROBERT SAMUEL
PERSONAL Born 01/11/1940, St. Catharines, ON, Canada, m, 1968 **DISCIPLINE** ENGLISH LITERATURE **EDUCATION** Univ Western Ont, BA, 67, MA, 69; Univ IL, Urbana, PhD(English), 72. **CAREER** Instr English, Univ Western Ont, 68-69; asst prof, 72-77, Assoc Prof English, Univ WI-Madison, 77-. **HONORS AND AWARDS** Chancellorio Awd for Excellence in Teaching, 81. **MEMBERSHIPS** MLA. **RESEARCH** Romantic and Victorian poetry; modern British literature; philosophy of history. **SELECTED PUBLICATIONS** Auth, Gabriel Nash's House of Strange Idols: Aestheticism in The Tragic Muse, Tex Studies Lit & Lang, spring 73; Sanctuary and Dungeon: The Imagery of Sentimentalism in Meredith's Diana of the Crossways, Tex Studies Lit & Lang, summer 76; Imagination and Literacy in Dicken's Our Mutual Friend, Criticism, winter 76; Faun and Satyr: Meredith's Theory of Comedy and The Egoist, Mosaic, 76; ; Romantic Onanism in Patrick White's The Vivisector, TX Studies Lit & Lang, summer 79; The Dark Historic Page: Social Satire and HIstoricism in the Novels of Aldovs Huxley, Univ WI Press, 82; auth, Aldovs Huxley's Brave New World: Science, History and Dystopia, 91; Aldous Huxley, History and Science Betweeen the Wars, Clio-A J of Lit Hist and the Philos of Hist, Vol 25, 96; History and Periodization-Introduction, Clio-A J of Lit Hist and the Philos of Hist, Vol 26, 97; ed, The Collected Essays of Aldovs Huxley, Ivan Dee Press, 00; Aldous Huxley's Brave New World: Science, History, and Dystopia, 1991. **CONTACT ADDRESS** Dept of English, Univ of Wisconsin, Madison, 600 North Park St, Madison, WI 53706-1403.

BAKER, ROBERT SAMUEL
PERSONAL Born 09/30/1926, Weed, CA, 3 children **DISCIPLINE** ENGLISH **EDUCATION** Pac Univ, BA, 53; Univ Chicago, MA, 56. **CAREER** Instr, 57-60, Asst Prof Humanities, or Col Educ, 60-, Fulbright teachers grant, Univ Trieste, 64-66. **MEMBERSHIPS** NCTE; MLA. **RESEARCH** Contemporary and comparative literature; translation theory. **SELECTED PUBLICATIONS** Auth, People Get Hooked, Commentary, 3/63; Italo Svevo and the Limits of Marriage, In: Essays on Italo Svevo, Univ Tulsa, 68; co-ed, The Wor(l)d on Wheels: Reading/Thinking/Writing About the Automobile in America, Allyn & Bacon, 72. **CONTACT ADDRESS** Dept of Humanities, Univ of Oregon, Monmouth, OR 97361.

BAKER, STUART EDDY
PERSONAL Born 08/13/1938, Albuquerque, NM **DISCIPLINE** DRAMATIC THEORY & CRITICISM **EDUCATION** New York Univ, BS, 62; City Univ New York, PhD(theatre), 77. **CAREER** Adj lectr theatre hist, Hunter Col, 72-75; asst prof, 77-82, Assoc Prof Theatre & Drama, FL State Univ, 82-. **MEMBERSHIPS** Am Theatre Asn. **SELECTED PUBLICATIONS** Auth, Georges Feydeau and the Aesthetics of Farce, UMI Res Press, 81. **CONTACT ADDRESS** Sch of Theatre, Florida State Univ, 600 W College Ave, Tallahassee, FL 32306-1096.

BAKER, TERRI M.
PERSONAL Born 01/26/1948, Durant, OK, m, 1978, 1 child **DISCIPLINE** ENGLISH **EDUCATION** Southeastern Okla State Univ, BA, 69; Univ Ut, MA, 74; La State Univ, PhD, 81. **CAREER** Mus Professional, 82-84; Adj Prof, Tulsa Community Col, 81-87; Prof, Northeastern State Univ, 87-. **HONORS AND AWARDS** Fac of the Year Awd, Northeastern State Univ, 99. **MEMBERSHIPS** Word Craft Circle, Popular Cult Asn, Asn for the Study of Lit and the Environ. **RESEARCH** Native American literature. **SELECTED PUBLICATIONS** Co-ed, Seminary Leaves: A Northeastern State University Anthology, 98; auth, Bois d'arc in Little Dixie," Pig Iron Pr, forthcoming. **CONTACT ADDRESS** Dept English, Northeastern State Univ, 600 N Grand Ave, Tahlequah, OK 74464-2301. **EMAIL** bakert@nsuok.edu

BAKER, TRACEY
DISCIPLINE RHETORIC AND COMPOSITION **EDUCATION** Purdue Univ, PhD, 84. **CAREER** Dept Eng, Univ Ala **SELECTED PUBLICATIONS** Coauth, Writing and Synthesis: A Multicultural Approach, HarperCollins, 93. **CONTACT ADDRESS** Univ of Alabama, Birmingham, 1400 University Blvd, Birmingham, AL 35294-1150.

BAKER, WILLIAM
PERSONAL Born 07/06/1944, Shipston, Warwickshire, United Kingdom, m, 1969, 2 children **DISCIPLINE** ENGLISH **EDUCATION** Univ Sussex, BA, 66; London Univ, MPhil, 69; PhD, 74; Loughborough Univ, MLS, 87. **CAREER** Lectr, City Literary Inst, 67-71; lectr, Ben-Gurion Univ, 71-77; lectr, Univ of Kent, 77-78; lectr, West Midlands Col of Higher Educ, 78-85; housemaster, Clifton Col, 86-89; assoc prof to prof, Northern IL Univ, 89-. **HONORS AND AWARDS** British Acad Res Awd, 81; NIU Grants, 91, 95, 90-92; Ball Brothers Fel, 93; Fel, Bibliographical Soc of Am, 94-95; Am Philos Soc Grant, 97; Awd, Luso-am Develop Found, 98; URAP Awd, 99. **MEMBERSHIPS** MLA; SHARP. **RESEARCH** Victorian Novel, bibliography, textual studies, editing letters, Shakespeare. **SELECTED PUBLICATIONS** Auth, The Early History of the London Library, Edwin Mellen Pr, 92; auth, The Letters of George Henry Lewes, Univ of Victoria, 95; auth, "15 Unpublished Letters from John Blackwood and Joseph Munt Langford to GH Lewes and George Eliot", Victorians Inst J 25, (97): 203-209; coauth, "Recent Works in Critical Theory", Style 31.4 (97); 569-701; auth, "Wilkie Collins's Last Romance: The Challenges and Opportunities of Editing His Letters", Australasian Victorian Studies J 3.2 (98): 86-94; auth, "The Victorian Novel" and "Bibliography and Textual Criticism", YEWS, Vol 77, ed PJ Kitson et al, English Assoc, (Oxford, 96); coauth, Recent Work in Critical Theory, 1989-1995: An Annotated Bibliography, Greenwood Pr, (Westport), 96; coauth, "Recent Work in Critical Theory", Style 32.4, (98): 535-679; coed, The Letters of Wilkie Colllins, Macmillan, (London), 99; ed, The Letters of George Henry Lewes, volume 3 with new letters by George Eliot, Univ of Victoria, 99; auth, "The Chicago School" and "British New Criticism", Edinburgh Encycl of Post-'War Lit Criticism and Theory, ed J Wolfreys, Edinburgh Univ Pr, (forthcoming). **CONTACT ADDRESS** Dept English, No Illinois Univ, 1425 W Lincoln Hwy, Dekalb, IL 60115-2828. **EMAIL** wbaker@niu.edu

BAKERMAN, JANE SCHNABEL
PERSONAL Born 07/04/1931, Gary, IN, m, 1971 **DISCIPLINE** AMERICAN LITERATURE, POPULAR CULTURE **EDUCATION** Hanover Col, AB, 53; Univ IL, MA, 59. **CAREER** Teacher English, William A Wirt High Sch, Gary, Ind, 53-57; assoc prof, WV Wesleyan Col, 59-64; Assoc Prof English, IN State Univ, 64-, Consult, Guide to Am Women Writers, Frederick Ungar Publ, 77- & Twentieth Century Crime and Mystery Writers, St James Press, 80. **MEMBERSHIPS** AAUP; MLA; Popular Cult Asn; Nat Women's Studies Asn; NCTE. **RESEARCH** American literature; feminist studies; mystery-detective fiction. **SELECTED PUBLICATIONS** Contribr to numerous journals, 72- **CONTACT ADDRESS** Dept of English & Jour, Indiana State Univ, Terre Haute, IN 47809.

BAKISH, DAVID JOSEPH
PERSONAL Born 05/15/1937, New York, NY **DISCIPLINE** ENGLISH LITERATURE AND COMPOSITION **EDUCATION** Bucknell Univ, BA, 59, MA, 63; Univ Del, PhD(English), 71. **CAREER** Instr English, Mt Pleasant High Sch, Wilmington, Del, 63-66; grad asst, Univ Del, 66-68; asst prof, Trenton State Col, NJ, 68-71; asst prof, 71-79, ASSOC PROF ENGLISH & HUMANITIES, MEDGAR EVERS COL, CITY UNIV NEW YORK, 79- **MEMBERSHIPS** MLA; Popular Cult Asn; Am Studies Asn; Col Lang Asn; Media Educr Asn. **RESEARCH** Afro-American literature; modern American literature, with the emphasis on drama. **SELECTED PUBLICATIONS** Auth, Underground in an ambiguous dream world, Studies Black Lit, 2, autumn 71; Richard Wright, Ungar, 73; Imamu Amiri Baraka (Le Roi Jones) & Chester Himes, In: Encycl World Lit 20th Century, Vol 4, Ungar, 75, rev ed, 81; coauth, Afro-American Fiction, 1853-1976, Gale, 79; Black American short fiction: A comprehensive bibliography of collections, Studies Short Fiction, fall 79. **CONTACT ADDRESS** 415 W 57th St, New York, NY 10019.

BAKKER, BAREND H.
PERSONAL Born 09/12/1934, Hilversum, Netherlands **DISCIPLINE** LITERATURE **EDUCATION** Univ Toronto, BA, 56, MA, 58, PhD, 68. **CAREER** Lectr, Wilfrid Laurier Univ, 59-60; instr, Univ Toronto, 60-63; lectr, Ind Univ, 64-65; asst prof, 65-70, assoc prof, 70-75, dir, Zola Res Prog, 73-95, Prof French York Univ, 75-95 (RETIRED), Prin Investr & Sr Ed, The Zola Res Proj, 76-95; vis fel, Wolfson Col, Cambridge, 83; vis prof Waseda Univ (Tokyo), Aichi Univ (Nagoya), Univ Kyoto, 85; vis prof, Univ Calif Santa Barbara, 87. **HONORS AND AWARDS** Can Coun fel, 66-68, 72-73. **MEMBERSHIPS** MLA; Asn Profs Fre Univ & Cols Can; Societe litteraire des Amis d'Emile Zola. **RESEARCH** Emile Zola **SELECTED PUBLICATIONS** Auth, Naturalisme pas mort, Lettres inedites de Paul Alexis a Emile Zola 1871-1900, 71; ed, Emile Zola: Correspondence, vols 1-10, 78-95. **CONTACT ADDRESS** 12 De Vere Gardens, Toronto, ON, Canada M5M 3E5.

BAKKER, JAN
PERSONAL Born 01/27/1936, New York, NY **DISCIPLINE** AMERICAN LITERATURE, TECHNICAL WRITING **EDUCATION** Univ VA, BA, 58, MA, 61; Univ TN, PhD (English), 75. **CAREER** Instr English, Clemson Univ, 60-62 & Memphis

State Univ, 62-63; asst prof, Armstrong State Col, 67-68; lectr, Univ MD, 68-72; asst prof, 77-80, Assoc Prof English, UT State Univ, 80-, UT State Univ fac res grant, 78; consult ed, Children's Literature; Fulbright vis prof, Univ Gadjah Mada, Indonesia, 80-81. **MEMBERSHIPS** MLA; Children's Lit Asn; Soc for Study Southern Lit; Am Studies Asn; Western Lit Asn. **RESEARCH** American literature; old south; children's literature. **SELECTED PUBLICATIONS** Auth, A List of the Juvenile Literature in the Hughes Public Library, Rugby, Tennessee, Children's Lit, 76; Time and Timelessness in Images of the Old South: Pastoral in John Pendleton Kennedy's Swallow Barn and Horse-Shoe Robinson, Tenn Studies in Lit, 79; Parallel Water Journeys into the American Eden in John Davis's The First Settlers of Virginia and F Scott Fitzgerald's The Great Gatsby, Early Am Lit, 81; Summer Reading at Woodlands: A Juvenile Library of the Old South, Children's Lit, 81; .. The Bold Atmosphere of Mrs Hentz' and Others: Fast food and Feminine Rebelliousness in Some Rmances of the Old South, J Popular Cult ; coauth, The Ruskin Experiment, Stonehill; Twist of Sentiment in Antebellum Southern Romance, Southern Literary J, Vol 26, 93. **CONTACT ADDRESS** Dept of English, Utah State Univ, 3200 University Blvd, Logan, UT 84322-3200.

BALAKIAN, PETER
DISCIPLINE AMERICAN POETRY, POETRY WRITING **EDUCATION** Bucknell Univ, BA, 73, Brown Univ, PhD, 80. **CAREER** Donald M. and Constance H. Rebar Prof of the Humanities in the dept of English, Colgate Univ. **HONORS AND AWARDS** Guggenheim Fel; PEN/Martha Albrand Prize for Memoir, 98; New Jersey Coun for the Humanities Book Awd; Anahit Literary Prize. **RESEARCH** Am poetry, genocide studies, peace studies, Armenian lit and cult. **SELECTED PUBLICATIONS** Auth, Father Fisheye, Sheep Meadow Press, 79; Sad Days of Light, Sheep Meadow Press, 83; Reply From Wilderness Island, Sheep Meadow Press, 88; Dyer's Thistle, Carnegie Mellon, 96; auth, Black Dog of Fate, a Memoir, Basil Books, 97; auth, June-tree, New and Selected Poems, Harper Collins, forthcoming; (critical): Theodore Roethke's Far Fields-(La State UP, 89; ed, Graham House Rev, Colgate UP. **CONTACT ADDRESS** Dept of Eng, Colgate Univ, 13 Oak Dr., Hamilton, NY 13346.

BALDO, JONATHAN
PERSONAL Born 06/01/1953, Evanston, IL, m, 1981, 2 children **DISCIPLINE** ENGLISH **EDUCATION** SUNY at Buffalo, PhD. **CAREER** Assoc prof; taught at, SUNY, Buffalo & Univ FL. **HONORS AND AWARDS** ACLS senior fel, winner of open submissions competition , Shakespeare Assoc of Am, and Int Shakespearean Assoc. **RESEARCH** Contemp literary theory; soc hist, Renaissance Literature and Culture, 20th Century Literature and Culture, Cultural Studies. **SELECTED PUBLICATIONS** Publ on, Shakespeare, Shelley, Keats, Balzac, Kafka, Walter Benjamin, Garcia Marquez & Ingmar Bergman. **CONTACT ADDRESS** Dept of Humanities, Eastman School of Music, 26 Gibbs St, Rochester, NY 14604. **EMAIL** anoj@mail.rochester.edu

BALDWIN, ARMINTA TUCKER
PERSONAL Born 02/15/1939, West Union, WV, d, 1 child **DISCIPLINE** ENGLISH LITERATURE **EDUCATION** Glenville State Col, BA, 60; WVa Univ, MA, 62. **CAREER** Asst English, WVa Univ, 60-62; instr, Alderson-Broaddus Col, 62-66; assoc prof, 66-75, Prof English & Dept Chmn, WVA Wesleyan Col, 75-, Teacher of humanities fed grant, 73 **HONORS AND AWARDS** Outstanding Young Women of WVa, 70; Community Council Outstanding Fac Awd, 98. **MEMBERSHIPS** AAUP; NCTE; Nat Coun Publ Adv **RESEARCH** Women's literature. **SELECTED PUBLICATIONS** Auth, Keats & Shelley, WVEA Bulletin. **CONTACT ADDRESS** Dept of English, West Virginia Wesleyan Col, 59 College Ave, Buckhannon, WV 26201-2699. **EMAIL** baldwin@wvwc.edu

BALDWIN, DEAN
PERSONAL Born 08/18/1942, Buffalo, NY, m, 1964, 2 children **DISCIPLINE** ENGLISH LITERATURE **EDUCATION** Capital Univ, BA, 64; Ohio State Univ, MA, 66; Ohio State Univ, PhD, 72. **CAREER** Central Missouri State Col, 66-67; Yankton Col, 67-69, 72-75; Penn State Erie, 75 -. **HONORS AND AWARDS** Coun of Fel Res Awd; NWPCTE Distinguished Service Awd; PCEA Outstanding Service Awd. **MEMBERSHIPS** Pennsylvania Col English Asn; Asn of Literary Scholars and Critics; NCTE, Col English Asn; MLA. **RESEARCH** British short story; Shakespeare. **SELECTED PUBLICATIONS** Auth, "H.E. Bates", in Critical Survey of Long Fiction, Salem Press, 83; auth, "Atmosphere in the Short Stories of H.E. Bates", in Short Story Criticism, Gale Research, 93; auth, "The British Short Story in the 1950's", in The English Short Story: 1945-, 85; auth, H.E. Bates: A Literary Life, Selinsgrove: Susquehanna UP, 87; auth, V.S. Pritchett, Twayne, 87; auth, "Sylvia Townsend Warner", in An Encyclopedia of British Women Writers, Garland, 88; auth, Virginia Woolf: a Study of Short Fiction, Twayne, 89; coauth, The Short Story in English: Britain and North America, Scarecrow Press, 94; auth, Introduction, in British Short Fiction Writers 1945-1980, Gale Research, 94; auth, "John Wain", in British Short Fiction Writers, Gale Research, 94; ed, British short Fiction Writers, 1945-1980, Gale Research, 94; auth, "H.E. Bates: the Poacher", in Recharting the Thirties, Susquehanna Press, 96; auth, Riverside Anthology of Short Fiction: Convention and Innovation, Houghton Mifflin, 97; coauth, Instructors Manual, Riverside Anthology of Short Fiction, Houghton Mifflin, 97; auth, "Sylvia Townsend Warner", in Women Writers of Great Britain and Europe, An Encyclopedia, Garland, 97; auth, "Mary Wesley, An Encyclopedia of British Women Writers," rev. ed, Rutgers Univ Press, 98. **CONTACT ADDRESS** The Behiend College, Pennsylvania State Univ, Erie, The Behrend Col, Station Rd., Erie, PA 16563. **EMAIL** dxb11@psu.edu

BALDWIN, JOHN R.
DISCIPLINE COMMUNICATION; RELIGIOUS STUDIES **EDUCATION** Abilene Christian Univ, Masters, 91; Ariz State Univ, PhD, 94. **CAREER** Asst prof, Ill State Univ, 94-. **HONORS AND AWARDS** Ralph E. Cooley Awd, top intercultural paper, nat conf of the Speech Commun Assn. **MEMBERSHIPS** Nat Commun Assn, Cent States Commun Assn, Int Network on Personal Rels, Soc for Int Educ, Training and Res. **RESEARCH** Intergroup/Intercultural commun; relationships; issues of tolerance. **SELECTED PUBLICATIONS** Co-auth, An African American communication perspective, Intercultural communication: A reader, Wadsworth, 7th ed, 140-147, 94; co-auth, Definitions of culture: Conceptualizations from five disciplines, Urban Studies Ctr, Ariz State Univ, 94; auth, Lost and Found: Ethics in intercultural/interethnic communication studies, Seeking understanding of communication, language and gender, CyberSpace, 94; co-auth, The layered perspective of cultural (in)tolerance(s): The roots of a multidisciplinary approach, Intercultural Communication Theory, Sage, 59-90, 95; Book review, Understudied relationships: Off the beaten track, ISSPR Bulletin: Official News Journal of the International Society for the Study of Personal Relationships, 16-18, 96; co-auth, An African American Communication Perspective, Intercultural communication: A reader, Wadsworth, 8th ed, 147-154, 97; co-auth, Family culture and relationship differences as a source of intercultural communication, Readings in cultural contexts, Mayfield, 335-344, 98; co-auth, Layers and holograms: A new look at prejudice, Communication of Prejudice, Sage, 57-84, 98; Auth, Tolerancee/intolerance: A historical and multidisciplinary view of prejudice, Communication of Prejudice, Sage, 24-56, 98. **CONTACT ADDRESS** Dept of Commun, Illinois State Univ, Ill State Univ, PO Box 4480, Normal, IL 61790-4480. **EMAIL** jrbaldw@ilstu.edu

BALES, KENT
PERSONAL Born 06/19/1936, Anthony, KS, m, 1958, 2 children **DISCIPLINE** ENGLISH **EDUCATION** Yale Univ, BA, 58; San Jose State Col, MA, 63; Univ CA, Berkeley, PhD, 67. **CAREER** Instr Eng, Menlo Sch & Col, 58-63; actg instr, Univ CA, Berkeley, 67; asst prof, 67-71, assoc prof, 71-82, prof eng, Univ MN, Minneapolis, 81, Ch, Eng Dept, Univ MN, 83-88, Vis Scholar, Inst Lit Sci, Budapest, 73-74 & 81; Fulbright lectr, Budapest, 80, res fel 88-89. **MEMBERSHIPS** MLA; Am Comp Lit Asn; Am Studies Asn; Midwest Mod Lang Asn. **RESEARCH** Am lit; lit and the other arts; comp studies in romanticism and the nineteenth century. **SELECTED PUBLICATIONS** Auth, The Blithedale Romance: Coverdale's mean and subversive egotism, Bucknell Rev, 73; The allegory and the radical romantic ethic of The Blithedale Romance, Am Lit, 74; Fishing the ambivalence, or, a reading of Trout Fishing in America, Western Humanities Rev, 75; Factors determining the translation of American Belles-Lettres into Hungarian, 1945-1973, Slavonic & E Europ Rev, 76; Hawthorne's prefaces and Romantic perspectivism, 77 & Sexual exploitation and the fall from natural virtue in Rappaccini's garden, 78, ESQ; O Henry, American Writers, suppl II, part I, Scribner's, 81; Pictures, Signs, and Stereotypes in Hawthorne's Meditations on the Origins of American Culture, In: The Origins and Originality of American Culture (Tibor Frank, ed), Akademiai Kiado, 84; From Emigre to Ethnic: Form, Subject, and Audience in Emigrant Hungarian Writing, In: The European Emigrant Experience in the USA (Walter Holbling and Reinhold Wagnleitner, ed), Gunter Narr Verlag, 92; Walt Whitman's Daughter, or Postcolonial Self-Transformation in the Fiction of Bharati Mukherjee, In: Daughters of Restlessness: Women's Literature at the End of the Millennium (Coelsch-Foisner, et al, ed), winter 98. **CONTACT ADDRESS** Dept of Eng, Univ of Minnesota, Twin Cities, 207 Church St S E, Minneapolis, MN 55455-0156. **EMAIL** bales@tc.umn.edu

BALL, BO
PERSONAL Born 04/17/1937, Davenport, VA, m **DISCIPLINE** ENGLISH **EDUCATION** Va Univ, BA, 61; Duke Univ, MA, 62; Univ Ky, PhD, 68. **CAREER** Eastern Ky Univ, 66-68; Agnes Scott Col, 68-. **HONORS AND AWARDS** Woodrow Wilson Fel, 61; two pushcart Prizes. **SELECTED PUBLICATIONS** Auth, Appalachian Patterns: Eleven Short Stories, Independence Press, 88. **CONTACT ADDRESS** Dept English, Agnes Scott Col, 141 E College Ave, Decatur, GA 30030-3770.

BALL, ROBERT J.
PERSONAL Born 11/04/1941, New York, NY **DISCIPLINE** CLASSICS **EDUCATION** Queens Col, BA, 62; Tufts Univ, MA, 63; Columbia Univ, PhD(class), 71. **CAREER** Asst prof, 71-76, assoc prof, 76-83, prof class, Univ Hawaii, 83-. **HONORS AND AWARDS** Excellence in Teaching Awd, Am Philol Asn; Regents' Medal for Excellence in Teaching, Univ Hawaii. **MEMBERSHIPS** Am Philol Asn. **RESEARCH** Latin poetry; Latin pedagogy; history of classical scholarship. **SELECTED PUBLICATIONS** Auth, Tibullus the Elegist: A Critical Survey, Vandenhoeck & Ruprecht, 83; ed, The Classical Papers of Gilbert Highet, Columbia Univ Press, 83; auth, Reading Classical Latin: A Reasonable Approach (2nd ed), McGraw-Hill, 97; auth, Reading Classical Latin: The Second Year (2nd ed), McGraw-Hill, 98; ed, The Unpublished Lectures of Gilbert Highet, Peter Lang Pub, 98. **CONTACT ADDRESS** Dept Europ Lang & Lit, Univ of Hawaii, Manoa, 1890 E West Rd, Honolulu, HI 96822-2318. **EMAIL** rball@hawaii.edu

BALLSTADT, CARL P. A.
PERSONAL Born 12/28/1931, Sault Ste. Marie, ON, Canada **DISCIPLINE** ENGLISH **EDUCATION** Univ Western Ont, BA, 57, MA, 59; Univ London, PhD, 65. **CAREER** Tchr, Sault Ste Marie schs, 53-57, 59-60; fac mem, Univ Sask, 62-66; fac mem, Guelph Univ, 66-67; fac mem, 67-86, Prof to Prof Emer, English, McMaster Univ, 86-. **MEMBERSHIPS** Bibliog Soc Can. **SELECTED PUBLICATIONS** Auth, The Search for English Canadian Literature, 75; auth, Catherine Parr Traill and Her Works, 83; coauth, Susanna Moodie: Letters of a Lifetime, 85; coauth, Letters of Love and Duty: The Correspondence of Susanna and John Moodie, 93; coauth, I Bless You In My Heart: Selected Correspondence of Catherine Parr Traill, 96; ed, Roughing it in the Bush (Susanna Moodie), 88; ed, Major John Richardson: A Selection of Reviews and Criticism, 72; co-ed, Forest and Other Gleanings: The Fugitive Writings of Catherine Parr Traill, 94; contribur, Dictionary Canadian Biography. **CONTACT ADDRESS** Dept of English, McMaster Univ, 1280 Main St West, 321 Chester New Hall, Hamilton, ON, Canada L8S 4L8.

BALSAMO, ANNE
DISCIPLINE MEDIA **EDUCATION** Univ Ill, Urbana-Champaign, PhD, 91. **CAREER** Assoc prof, dir, Grad Stud, Ga Inst of Technol; researcher, Xerox Palo Alto Res Ctr. **RESEARCH** The development of new media genres. **SELECTED PUBLICATIONS** Auth, Technologies of the Gendered Body, Duke UP, 96. **CONTACT ADDRESS** XEROX Palo Alto Res Ctr, 3333 Coyote Hill Rd, Palo Alto, CA 94304.

BALUTANSKY, KATHLEEN M.
PERSONAL Born 12/17/1954, Phaeton, Haiti, m, 1989, 1 child **DISCIPLINE** ENGLISH **EDUCATION** Goshen Col, BA, 76; Univ Notre Dame, MA, 78, PhD, 84. **CAREER** Asst Prof, Univ Va, 88-92; Assoc Prof, St Michael's Col, 92-. **HONORS AND AWARDS** Carter G Woodson Inst, Post-doctoral Fellow, 82-84; Ford Foundation, Post-doctoral Fellow, 91-92. **MEMBERSHIPS** Asn of Carib Women Writers & Sch; Asn of Carib Stud; Haitian StudAsn **RESEARCH** Post-colonial theory, hist and memory in Haiti **SELECTED PUBLICATIONS** Auth, the novels of Alex La Guma: The Representationa of a Political Conflict, 90; Auth, Houses of the People and Houses of the Spirit: An Interview with Marilene Phipps, Callaloo, 18.2, 419-26, 95; auth, Surviving Tokenism, Concerns, 2.2, 41-46, 95; auth, "Creolite in Question: caliban in Maryse Conde's Traversee de la mangrove," Penser la creolite, Paris: Karthala, (95), 101-111; auth, " Redefining Femal Indentity in Conteporary Anglohone and Francophone Caribbean Womens's Fiction," vol III of a Comparative Hist of Lit in the Carivvean, Philadelphia: John Benjamins Pub Comp, (97), 267-282; auth, The Muse Speaks A New Tongue: New Perspectives on Language and Identity in Haitian American Women's Texts, MaComere, 1, 115-133, 98; co-ed, Representing Caribbean Creolization: Reflections on the Dynamics of Language and Literature, Univ Press of Fla, 98. **CONTACT ADDRESS** Dept of English, Saint Michael's Col, Colchester, VT 05439. **EMAIL** kbalutansky@smcvt.edu

BAMFORD, KAREN V.
PERSONAL Born Toronto, ON, Canada, m, 1988, 2 children **DISCIPLINE** ENGLISH **EDUCATION** Queen's Univ, BA, 78; Univ of Toronto, MA, 87; PhD, 93. **CAREER** Instr, McMaster Univ, 91-93; assoc prof, Mt Allison Univ, 93-. **HONORS AND AWARDS** Paul Pare Teaching Award, 01. **MEMBERSHIPS** ACCUTE, MLA, Can Soc for Renaissance Studies, Shakespeare Soc of Am. **RESEARCH** English Renaissance drama, Canadian Shakespeare. **SELECTED PUBLICATIONS** Auth, Sexual Violence on the Jacobean Stage, St Martin's, 00. **CONTACT ADDRESS** Mount Allison Univ, 165 York St, Sackville, NB, Canada E4L 1G9. **EMAIL** kbanford@mta.ca

BANBURY, HORACE
PERSONAL Born 03/26/1941, Jamaica, m, 1985 **DISCIPLINE** COMMUNICATIONS **EDUCATION** Fordham Univ, BS, 66; MS, 69. **CAREER** Lectr, John Jay Col of Criminal Justice, 70-; adj instr, John Jay Col, 71-75; instr, Marymount Manhattan Col, 74-75; instr, Col of New Rochelle, 78-83; adj assoc prof, Pace Univ, 78-86. **HONORS AND AWARDS** Jam Fraternal Org Creative Arts Awd, 85; Fac Awd, John Jay Col, 91; Serv Awd, John Jay Col, 95; Grant, CUNY, 93-94; Phi Delta Kappa. **MEMBERSHIPS** Col Eng Assoc; Int Reading Assoc; Jamaica Reading Assoc; NY City Art Teachers Assoc; Assoc

of African Am Caribbean Artists. **SELECTED PUBLICATIONS** Ed, Building Bridges: An Anthology of Multi-Cultural Readings, Ginn Pr, 89; ed, The Accommodating Reader, McGraw-Hill, 92; auth, "An Interview with Carl Davis", Routes Mag 4.10, (94); coauth, "Art, Crafts and Memorabilia", Routes Mag 3.21 (94); auth, "Haitian Art: A Galaxy of Images", Class Mag 16.2 (95). **CONTACT ADDRESS** Dept Commun, John Jay Col of Criminal Justice, CUNY, 445 West 59th St, New York, NY 10019-1104.

BAND, ARNOLD J.
PERSONAL Born 10/20/1929, Boston, MA, m, 1954, 2 children **DISCIPLINE** LITERATURE **EDUCATION** Harvard Univ, AB, 51, MA, 54, PhD(comp lit), 59; Hebrew Col, Boston, MHL, 51. **CAREER** Teaching fel humanities, Harvard Col, 54-58; asst Greek & Hebrew, Brandeis Univ, 58-59; from asst prof to assoc prof, 59-68, Prof Hebrew, Univ Calif, Los Angeles, 68-, Asst prof, Hebrew Col, Boston, 57-59; Am Philos Soc grant, 62; Am Coun Learned Soc-Cos Sci Res Coun joint grant, Mid East, 62; mem, Near Eastern Ctr, Univ Calif, Los Angeles, 62; Warburg fel, Hebrew Univ, Israel, 62; mem, Exam Comt Col Bd Hebrew Achievement Test, 63-68; fel, Inst Creative Arts, Univ CA, 66-67. **MEMBERSHIPS** MLA; Am Philol Asn: Nat Asn Prof Hebrew; Pen Club; Am Comp Lit Asn. **RESEARCH** Modern Hebrew literature; comedy. **SELECTED PUBLICATIONS CONTACT ADDRESS** Dept of Near Eastern Lang, Univ of California, Los Angeles, Los Angeles, CA 90024.

BANET-WEISER, SARAH
DISCIPLINE COMMUNICATION **EDUCATION** Univ CA, San Diego, BA, 89, MA, 90, PhD, 95. **CAREER** Lectr, Univ Southern CA, 97-98; lectr, UCLA, 94-96 & Univ CA, San Diego, 95-; postdoctoral res fel, Univ CA Hum Res Inst, 96-97. **RESEARCH** Feminist theory and politics; media studies; race and sexuality; contemp Am cult; nationalism; popular cult, qualitative methods. **SELECTED PUBLICATIONS** Auth, Crowning Identities: Performing Nationalism, Femininity, and Race in US Beauty Pageants, Univ Calif Press, 98; Fade to White: Racial Politics and the Troubled Reign of Vanessa Williams in Women Transforming Politics, NY UP, 97; Viva La Hispanidad: Constructions of National Identity, Femininity, and Ethnicity in Beauty Pageants, in Minority Discourses, Cultural Productions: Theories, Texts, and Contexts, Univ Calif Press, 98; Fade to White: Race, Nation and the Miss America Pageant, Ctr Feminist Res, Univ Southern Calif, 97 & Miss America/Miss Universe: Gender, Race and Nation in Televised Beauty Pageants, Int Commun Asn, 97, Montreal, Can; rev, Figures of Beauty, Figures of Nation: Global Contests of Femininity Amer Quart, Vol 50, 98. **CONTACT ADDRESS** Annenberg School for Commun, Univ of So California, University Park Campus, Los Angeles, CA 90089. **EMAIL** sbanet@usc.edu

BANK, ROSEMARIE KATHERINE
PERSONAL Born 10/19/1942, Chicago, IL, m, 1970 **DISCIPLINE** THEATRE **EDUCATION** IN Univ, BA, 64; Univ IA, MA, 70, PhD(Theatre), 72. **CAREER** Instr theatre, Grinnell Col, IA, 70-71; asst prof, IL State Univ, 72-75; asst prof theatre, Purdue Univ, 76-80; prof, Kent State Univ, 84-. **MEMBERSHIPS** Am Theatre Asn; Am Soc Theatre Res; Speech Commun Asn; AAUP. **RESEARCH** 19th century American theatre history and drama; melodrama; the frontier play, image of women. **SELECTED PUBLICATIONS** Auth, Theatre Culture in America, 1825-1860, Cambridge UP, 97. **CONTACT ADDRESS** Dept Theatre & Dance, Kent State Univ, PO Box 5190, Kent, OH 44242-0001. **EMAIL** rbank@kent.edu

BANKOWSKY, RICHARD JAMES
PERSONAL Born 11/25/1928, Wallington, NJ, m, 1952, 3 children **DISCIPLINE** CREATIVE WRITING **EDUCATION** Yale Univ, BA, 52; Columbia Univ, MA, 54. **CAREER** From instr to assoc prof, 59-67, Prof English, Calif State Univ, Sacramento, 67-, Nat Inst Arts & Lett grant, 63; Rockefeller Found grant, 68 **RESEARCH** Writing novels **SELECTED PUBLICATIONS** Auth, A Glass Rose, 58, After Pentecost, 61, On a Dark Night, 64 & The Pale Criminals, 67, Random; The Barbarians at the Gates, Little, 72 **CONTACT ADDRESS** Dept of English, California State Univ, Sacramento, 6000 J St, Sacramento, CA 95819-2694.

BANNON, CYNTHIA J.
DISCIPLINE CLASSICAL STUDIES **EDUCATION** Harvard Univ, AB, 84; Univ Mich, PhD, 91. **CAREER** Asst prof, Intercollegiate Center for Class Studies, Rome, 96-97; asst prof, Ind Univ, Bloomington. **RESEARCH** Roman law; Latin prose style and grammar; rhetoric; history. **SELECTED PUBLICATIONS** Auth, The Brothers of Romulus, Princeton, 97. **CONTACT ADDRESS** Dept of Classical Studies, Indiana Univ, Bloomington, 1020 E Kirkwood Ave, 547 Ballantine Hall, Bloomington, IN 47405. **EMAIL** cbannon@indiana.edu

BANTA, MARTHA
PERSONAL Born 05/11/1928, Muncie, IN, s **DISCIPLINE** ENGLISH **EDUCATION** Indiana Univ, BA, 50, PhD, 64. **CAREER** Asst prof, Univ Calif, Santa Barbara, 64-70; assoc prof, 70-74, prof, 74-83, Univ Wash; prof, 83-98, Univ Calif Los Angeles. **HONORS AND AWARDS** Pres, Am Stud Asn; ed, PMLA; NEH fel; Guggenheim fel. **MEMBERSHIPS** MLA; Am Stud Asn. **RESEARCH** American literature and culture; art history. **SELECTED PUBLICATIONS** Ed and introd, Edith Wharton, The House of Mirth, Oxford, 94; auth, The Ghostly Gothic of Wharton's Everyday World, Am Lit Realism, 94; auth, The Three New Yorks: Topographical Narratives and Cultural Texts, Am Lit Hist, 95; auth, The Razor, The Pistol, and The Ideology of Race Etiquette, in Kartiganer, ed, Faulkner and Ideology: Essays from the Nineteenth Annual Yoknapatawpha Conference, Mississippi, 95; auth, The Excluded Seven: Practice of Omission/Aesthetics of Refusal, in McWhirter, ed, Henry James and the Construction of Authorship, Stanford, 95; auth, Strange Deserts: Hotels, Hospitals, Country Clubs, Prisons and the City of Brotherly Love, Henry James Rev, 96; auth, Being a Begonia in a Man's World, in, Rowe, ed, New Essays on The Education of Henry James, Cambridge, 96; auth, Men, Women, and the American Way, in The Cambridge Companion to Henry James, 97. **CONTACT ADDRESS** Dept of English, Univ of California, Los Angeles, Los Angeles, CA 90095. **EMAIL** banta@ucla.edu

BAR, FRANCOIS
DISCIPLINE COMMUNICATIONS **CAREER** Sr res fel Berkeley Roundtable Int Econ (BRIE), Univ CA Berkeley; sr fel, San Diego Supercomput Ctr; asst prof, Standford Univ, present; dir net res, Stanford Comput IndusProj (SCIP), present. **HONORS AND AWARDS** Adv coun, CompuMentor; ed bd Comms & Strats, IDATE; adv comm, prog sci, tech, soc, Stanford Univ. **RESEARCH** Comp telecommun policy; economic, strategic and soc dimensions of computer networking, new media and the internet. **SELECTED PUBLICATIONS** Auth, Intelligent Manufacturing in the Global Information Economy in The Transition to a Global Economy: Challenges for United States and the World, 20th Century Fund, 95; Information Networks and Competitive Advantage: Issues for Government Policy and Corporate Strategy, Int Jour Tech Mgmt; coauth, From Welfare to Innovation: Toward a New Rationale for Universal Service, The Information Society, 98; Islands in the Bit-stream: Mapping the NII Interoperability Debate--BRIE Working Paper #79, UC-Berkeley, 95; Reseaux CAO-CFAO et Reseaux Fournisseurs/Clients: Recherche sur la Mise en Place de l'Usine Integree, a partir d'une Etude Comparative France-Etats Unis dans l'Industrie Automobile, Rapport au Ministere de la Recherche, Universite de Paris-XIII, 93. **CONTACT ADDRESS** Stanford Univ, McClatchy Hall, Room 344, Stanford, CA 94305. **EMAIL** fbar@leland.stanford.edu

BARASCH, FRANCES K.
PERSONAL Born 04/10/1928, New York, NY, m, 1952, 3 children **DISCIPLINE** ENGLISH **EDUCATION** Brooklyn Col, BA, 49; NYork Univ, MA, 52, PhD(english), 64. **CAREER** Prof, City Univ of NYork. **HONORS AND AWARDS** NYU Grad Sch of Arts and Sci Alumni Certificate of Honor; NYU Alumni Federation Sesquicentennial Crystal Awd, 82; NYU Alumni Meritorious Service Awd, 83; Nat Endowment for the Humanities, 86; AFT Women's Rights Committee Living the Legacy award, 98. **MEMBERSHIPS** Shakespeasre Asn of Am; Modern Language Asn. **RESEARCH** Medieval and Renaissance literature and art; the grotesque; Commedia dell'Arte. **SELECTED PUBLICATIONS** Auth, Norwich Cathedral: The Bauchun Chapel Legend of the Accused Queen, in The Early Drama, Art, and Music Rev, 93; auth, The Bayeux Painting and Shakespearean Improvisation, Shakespeare Bul, 93; auth, He's for a Iigge, or a Tale of Baudry in Shakespeare Bul, 95; auth, Castiliano Vulgo Revisited, Shakespeare Newsl, 96; auth, "Shakespeare and Comedienne Art," in Shakespeare and Italy (99); auth, "Shakespeare and the Italians," in Shakespeare Int Yearbk (99); auth, Theatrical Prints: Zany, Pantalone, and the Elizabethans, On Page and Stage, 00. **CONTACT ADDRESS** Baruch Col, CUNY, Lexington Ave, New York, NY 10010. **EMAIL** fbarasch@aol.com

BARBA, HARRY
PERSONAL Born 06/17/1922, Bristol, CT, m, 1965, 2 children **DISCIPLINE** ENGLISH, WRITING **EDUCATION** Bates Col, AB, 44; Harvard Univ, MA, 51; Univ Iowa, MFA, 60, PhD, 63. **CAREER** Instr, 47, Wilkes Col; instr, 47-49, Univ Conn, Hartford; instr, 59-63, Univ Iowa; from asst prof to assoc prof, 63-68, Skidmore Col, fac res fels, 65-67; prof & dir, 68-70, Marshall Univ; res & writing, 70-, Fulbright prof, 63-64, Damascus Univ; ed consult, Bantam Bks, Inc, 67 & Macmillan, 72; mem staff, Writers Conf; publ, Harian Press, NY & WVa; dir & consult, Spa Writers & Educ Conf, 67-73; speaker & reader, NY State Coun on Arts, 71-76; dist vis lectr & consult writing comt, SUNY, Albany, 77-78. **HONORS AND AWARDS** Yaddo residence fel, 50; Fel, Univ of Iowa, 61-62; Skidmore res, grantee, 65-68; Univ Benedeum grantee, 69; Macdowell Colony residence fel, 70; Arts grantee, 71; Recipient certificate of merit Dictionary Int Biograpyh, 74; Guggenheim fel, 89-90; Man of Year Awd, 96-97; World's Hall of Fame in Lit, 97-; **MEMBERSHIPS** Auth League Am; MLA; Col English Assn; PEN Club; Poets & Writers. **RESEARCH** Creative and expository writing; interdisciplinary studies; the writing arts and American studies. **SELECTED PUBLICATIONS** Auth, Teaching in Your Own Write, 70; auth, The Case for Socially Functional Education, 73; auth, One of A Kind--The Many Faces & Voices of America, 76; auth, The Day the World Went Sane, 79; auth, What's Cooking in Congress? A Congressional Smorgasbord of Recipes, 79; auth, According to Everyman, 81; auth, The Gospel According to Everyman, Harian, 81; auth, Round Trip to Byzantium, 85; auth, When the Deep Purple Falls, 85; auth, Mona Lisa Smiles, 93. **CONTACT ADDRESS** 47 Hyde Blvd, Ballston Spa, NY 12020.

BARBARESE, J. T.
PERSONAL Born Philadelphia, PA **DISCIPLINE** ENGLISH **EDUCATION** Temple Univ, MA, 81; PhD, 94. **CAREER** Instr, Friends Select Sch, 84-93; Prof, Rutgers Univ, 93-. **MEMBERSHIPS** AWP, MLA **SELECTED PUBLICATIONS** Auth, "The Voice in the Workshop," Mid-Am Rev, 4 (84): 84-92; auth, Under the Blue Moon, Poems, Univ Ga Pr (Athens, GA), 85; auth, "The Measure of the Eye: The Inadequacies of a Critical Metaphor," Semeiotica, 58 (86): 315-328; auth, New Science, Poems, Univ Ga Pr (Athens, GA), 89; auth, "Landscapes of the American Psyche," The Sewanee Rev, 100 (92): 599-626; auth, "Ezra Pound's Imagist Aesthetics: Lustra to Mauberley," in The Columbia Hist of Am Poetry (NY: Columbia Univ Pr, 93); auth, "Hart Crane's Difficult Passage," in The Columbia His of Am Poetry (NY: Columbia Univ Pr, 93; auth, "Dramas of Naming in Coleridge," Studies in English Lit, 37.4 (97): 673-698; auth, "The Contemporaneity of Homer's Odyssey," The Sewanee Rev, CVII.2 (99): 275-283; auth, "Who Needs Palgrave?" Victorian Poetry (99); auth, "The children of Herakles," in Euripedes, 4, (Philadelphia, PA: Univ Pa Pr), 99. **CONTACT ADDRESS** Dept English, Rutgers, The State Univ of New Jersey, Camden, 311 N 5th St, Camden, NJ 08102-1405. **EMAIL** barbares@crab.rutgers,edu

BARBER, MARGARET
DISCIPLINE COMPOSITION, ADVANCED COMPOSITION, SHAKESPEARE, WORLD LITERATURE **EDUCATION** TX Christian Univ, BA, 64, MA, 66, PhD, 77. **CAREER** Asst prof, Univ of Southern CO. **RESEARCH** Computer assisted compos; Shakespeare's Macbeth; women in early world lit; the novel; Lafcadio Hearn; ecofeminist theory. **SELECTED PUBLICATIONS** Publ on, artistic develop of Lafcadio Hearn. **CONTACT ADDRESS** Dept of Eng, Univ of So Colorado, 2200 Bonforte Blvd, Pueblo, CO 81001-4901. **EMAIL** Barber@meteor.uscolo.edu

BARBERA, ANDRE
PERSONAL Born 05/24/1950, New London, CT, m, 1970, 3 children **DISCIPLINE** MUSICOLOGY **EDUCATION** Wesleyan Univ, BA, 74; Univ NC, PhD, 80. **CAREER** Tutor, St John's Col, Annapolis, 90-; St. Vincent de Paul Soc of Annapolis, Inc., 93-; Pres, 97-. **HONORS AND AWARDS** The Am Counc of Learned Soc Grant, 87; Nat Endow Human Grant, 83, 86, 87; Newberry Library Grant, Chicago, 78. **MEMBERSHIPS** Am Musicol Soc. **RESEARCH** History of jazz; history of music theory; non-Euclidean geometry. **SELECTED PUBLICATIONS** Republic 530C - 531C: Another Look at Plato and the Pythagoreans, Am Jour Philology 102, 81, 395-410; Interpreting an Arithmetical Error in Boethius's De Institutione Musica, iii 14-16, Arch int d'hist des sciences 31, 81, 26-41; Octave Species, Jour Musicol 3, 84, 229-241; The Consonant Eleventh and the Expansion of the Musical Tetractys: A Study of Ancient Pythagoreanism, Jour Mus Theory 28, 84, 191-223; Placing Sectio canonis in Historical and Philosophical Contexts, Jour Hellenic Stud 104, 84, 157-161; Recent Studies in Ancient Music and Ancient Music Theory, Jour Am Musicol Soc 43, 90, 353-367; Music Theory and its Sources: Antiquity and the Middle Ages, Univ Notre Dame Press, 90; The Euclidean Division of the Canon: Greek and Latin Sources, Univ Nebr Press, 91; New and Revived Approaches to Text Criticism in Early Music Theory, Jour Musicol 9, 91, 57-73; George Gershwin and Jazz, The Gershwin Style, Oxford Univ Press, 98; auth, The Role of Translation in the Transmission and Reception of Musical Culture, Atti del XIV Congresso della Societa Internazionale di Musicologia: Trasmissione e recezione delle forme di cultura musicale, vol. II, Study Sessions, Ed. Angelo Pompilio, Donatella Restani, Lorenzo Bianconi, F. Alberto Gallo, Turin: EDT/Musica, 90, pp. 153-169; auth, Gregorian Chant and the Melodies of the Troubadours: A Comparison of Transmission, 1983 NEH Institute Resource Book for the Teaching of Medieval Civilization, Ed. Howell Chickering, Amherst, Mass.: Five Colleges, Inc., 84, pp. 211-215i; auth, Arithmetic and Geometric Divisions of the Tetrachore, The Journal of Music Theory 21, 77: 294-323; auth, Choruses of Revolt in Verdi's Operas of the 1840s, The Journal of Fine Arts 1, 77: 32-60. **CONTACT ADDRESS** St. John's Col, Maryland, Annapolis, MD 21404. **EMAIL** c-barbera@sjca.edu

BARBERA, JACK VINCENT
PERSONAL Born 07/18/1945, Rockville Centre, NY **DISCIPLINE** CONTEMPORARY LITERATURE, FILM **EDUCATION** Univ Chicago, AB, 68, AM, 69, PhD, 76. **CAREER** Instr humanities, Roosevelt Univ, 74-75; asst prof English, 76-83, assoc prof English, 83-87, prof English, 87-, English, Univ Miss, 76-. **HONORS AND AWARDS** DeWitt Wallace/Readers Digest/MacDowell Colony Fel 81. **MEMBERSHIPS** MLA; Ed Bd 20th Century Lit. **RESEARCH** Modern poetry; film criticism; American literature. **SELECTED PUBLICATIONS** Ed, Special Athol Fugard issue of Twentieth Century Literature, 93; Auth Introduction and Fugard as Director: An In-

terview with the Cast of Boesman and Lena, 20th Century Lit, 93; Entries on August Wilson, Ma Rainey's Black Bottom, Fences, and Two Trains Running, Identities and Issues in Literature, David Peck, ed, Salem Press, CA, 97; The Emotion of Multitude and David Rabe's Streamers, Am Drama, 97; MWP: John Crews, MS Writers Page; Fugard's Valley Song, The Nation, 96; auth, " Strangers in the Night: Three Interior Dramatic Monologues by Tennessee Williams," Southern Quarterly 38, Fall 99: 71-80. **CONTACT ADDRESS** Dept English, Univ of Mississippi, University, MS 38677-9999. **EMAIL** jvbarber@olemiss.edu

BARBOUR, ALTON BRADFORD

PERSONAL Born 10/13/1933, San Diego, CA, m, 1996, 4 children **DISCIPLINE** COMMUNICATIONS **EDUCATION** Univ Northern Colo, BA, 56; Univ Denver, MA, 61, PhD, 68. **CAREER** Instr, 65, asst prof, 68, assoc prof, 73, prof, 77, chemn 80-98, Univ Denver. **HONORS AND AWARDS** Intellectual Freedom Awd, Nat Council Tchrs English, 97; Hannah Weiner Dist Prof Serv Awd, Am Soc Psychodrama and group Psychotherapy, 97; trainer, educ practitioner certification, 78, am board examiners. **MEMBERSHIPS** Nat Commun Asn; Colo Lang Art Soc; Am Soc Psychodrama and Group Psychotherapy. **RESEARCH** Action methods in communication education. **SELECTED PUBLICATIONS** Auth, art, The Process of Becoming, 97; auth, art, The Train from Cheyenne: A Message from the Chair, 98; auth, art, A Rationale for Nonclinical Certification, 98; auth, art, On the Question of Professionalism: A Message from the Chair, 98; auth, art, Round Up the Usual Suspects: A Message from the Chair, 99. **CONTACT ADDRESS** Dept of Human Communications Studies, Univ of Denver, 2199 S Univ Blvd, Denver, CO 80208. **EMAIL** abarbour@dn.edu

BARBOUR, BRIAN MICHAEL

PERSONAL Born 07/26/1943, Lorain, OH, m, 1968, 3 children **DISCIPLINE** ENGLISH & AMERICAN LITERATURE **EDUCATION** Univ Notre Dame, BA, 65; Kent State Univ, MA, 66, PhD(English), 69. **CAREER** Asst prof, 69-74, assoc prof, 74-78, Prof English, Providence Col, 78-, Dir Am Studies, 81-85; Chemn English, 86-88; dir Development of Western Civilization, 94; Ed, Providence Studies in Western Studies in Western Civilization, 95. **HONORS AND AWARDS** Vis Fel, St Edmund's Coll, Cambridge, 93-. **MEMBERSHIPS** Melville Soc Am; Fel of Catholic Scholars; Natl Assoc of Scholars; Assn of Literary Scholars & Critics. **RESEARCH** Am lit since 17th Century; 19th & 20th Century English Lit; Cambridge English; C S Lewis, Solzhenitsyn. **SELECTED PUBLICATIONS** Ed, American Transcendentalism: An Anthology of Criticism, Univ Notre Dame, 73; auth, The Great Gatsby, and the American Past, Southern Review, 73; Emerson's Poetic Prose, Mod Lang Quart, 74; Poe and Tradition, Southern Lit J, 78; ed, Benjamin Franklin: A Collection of Critical Essays, Prentice-Hall, 78; auth, "'Between Two Worlds': The Structure of the Argument in 'Tintern Abbey'," Nineteenth Century Literature 48 (93): 147-68; Gaining Upon Certainty: Selected Literary Criticism of Rene Fortin, Providence College, 95; Lewis and Cambridge, Modern Philology, 99. **CONTACT ADDRESS** Dept of English, Providence Col, 549 River Ave, Providence, RI 02918-0002. **EMAIL** bbarbour@providence.edu

BARBOUR, JOHN D.

PERSONAL Born 08/08/1951, Kalamazoo, MI, m, 1978, 2 children **DISCIPLINE** RELIGION AND LITERATURE **EDUCATION** Oberlin Col, BA, 73; Univ Chicago Divinity Sch, MA, 75; PhD, 81. **CAREER** Prof & Chemn of Dept of Relig, St Olaf Col. **SELECTED PUBLICATIONS** Auth, Tragedy as a Critique of Virtue, 84; auth, The Conscience of the Autobiographer, 92; auth, Versions of Deconversion: Autobiography and the Loss of Faith, 94. **CONTACT ADDRESS** Dept Relig, St. Olaf Col, 1520 Saint Olaf Ave, Northfield, MN 55057-1574.

BARBOUR, PAULA LOUISE

PERSONAL Born 03/07/1949, Portland, ME, m, 1979 **DISCIPLINE** SEVENTEENTH CENTURY ENGLISH LITERATURE, WOMEN'S STUDIES **EDUCATION** Tufts Univ, BA, 71; Yale Univ, MA, 72, MPhil, 74, PhD(English), 75. **CAREER** ASST PROF ENGLISH, FLA STATE UNIV, 75-, Coordr, Woman's Studies Prog, Fla State Univ, 76-77 & 79-80; dir, Merit & Achievement Scholars Prog, 80-85; dir, Honors and Scholars Prog, FSU, 85-93; assistant in English, English Dept, FSU, 93-. **RESEARCH** Seventeenth-century English drama; women's studies (literature written before 1750). **CONTACT ADDRESS** Dept of English, Florida State Univ, Box 1580, Tallahassee, FL 32306-1580. **EMAIL** pbarbour@english.fsu.edu

BARBOUR, RICHMOND

DISCIPLINE RENAISSANCE **EDUCATION** Stanford Univ Univ, BA, 70; Univ Calif, Berkley, PhD, 90. **CAREER** Engl, Oregon St Univ. **SELECTED PUBLICATIONS** Auth, The Elizabethan Jonson in Print,"Criticism, 92; 'When I Acted Young Antinous': Boy-Actors and the Erotics of Jonsonian Theater, PMLA, 95. **CONTACT ADDRESS** Oregon State Univ, Corvallis, OR 97331-4501. **EMAIL** rbarbour@orst.edu

BARDEN, THOMAS

PERSONAL Born 08/05/1946, Richmond, VA, s, 1981, 3 children **DISCIPLINE** ENGLISH **EDUCATION** Univ of Va, BA, 68; MA, 72; PhD, 75. **CAREER** Asst Prof, Univ of VA, 75-76; Asst to Full Prof, Univ of Toledo, 76-91; Dir of Amer Studies Program, Univ of Toledo, 91-95; Dir of Graduate Studies, Dept of English, Univ of Toledo, 95-99; Assoc Dean for the Humanities, College of Arts & Sciences, Univ of Toledo, 99-. **HONORS AND AWARDS** Fulbright Senior Lecturer, 93-94, Univ of Wales, Swansea; UT Faculty Research Awd, 92. **MEMBERSHIPS** Amer Folklore Society; Council of Colleges of Arts & Sciences. **RESEARCH** Modern Literature; Amer Studies; Folk Narrative; Folklore and Literature. **SELECTED PUBLICATIONS** Auth, "An Annotated Listing of the Virginia WPA Folklore, (Norwood), Pennsylvania: Norwood Editions, 79; auth, "The Masopust: A Czech-American Shrovetide Festival," Midwestern Journal of Language and Folklore, 8, No. 1, 82, 48-54; auth, Flesh on the Bones of the Past: The Folk Art of Halsey Rinehart," Wisconsin Academy Review, 30, No. 2, Spring, 1984, 69-62; auth, "Tobacco Culture in Southwest Wisconsin: Ethnicity and Change in a Traditional Labor Practic," Midwestern Jornal of Language and Folklore, 12, No. 1, Spring, 86, 24-37; auth, "A Reaction to Studying and Documenting Toledo's Hungarian Ethnic Traditions," in 19087 Educational Comment, Univ of Toledo: College of Education, Winter, 87, 43-47; auth, "Passing the time in Muscoda," The National Story Telling Journal, 4, No. 2, Spring, 87, 4-8; auth, "John Millington Synge's In the Shadow of the Glen; a Study and Evaluation," in Masterplots of Modern Drama II, Pasadena, California: Salem Press, 92, 815-19; auth, "The WPA Collection of Virginia Folk Legends," Virginia Cavalcade, 41, No. 3, Winter, 92, 100-111; auth, "Contemporary Legends of American Soldiers in the Vietnam War," Fabula: Journal of Folktale Studies 36, (Gottingen, Germany) Autumn Issue, 4, 95, 29-51; auth, "Entries at "Anecdote," "Cadence Chant," "Juke Joint," "Arthur Kyle Davis, Jr., and "Vietnam War" in American Folklore: An Encyclopedia, ed. Jan H. Brunvand, New York: Norton, 96 **CONTACT ADDRESS** Col of Arts and Sci, Univ of Toledo, 2801 West Bancroft St., Toledo, OH 43606-3328. **EMAIL** tbarden@uoft02.utoledo.edu

BAREISS, WARREN J.

PERSONAL Born 11/08/1962, Pennsylvania, PA, m, 1990 **DISCIPLINE** MASS COMMUNICATION **EDUCATION** IN Univ, PhD, 96. **CAREER** Asst prof, 96-98, Shorter Col; asst prof, South Dakota St Univ, 98- . **MEMBERSHIPS** Intl Comm Asn **RESEARCH** Telemedicine; noncommercial media; community identity; radio drama history. **SELECTED PUBLICATIONS** Auth, The Life of Riley/Goodyear Playhouse/Original Amateur Hour, Encycl of TV, Fitzroy Dearborn, 97; auth, Suspense/Sustaining Prog, Hist Dist of Amer Radio, Greenwood Press, 97. **CONTACT ADDRESS** 20566 469th Ave., Brookings, SD 57006. **EMAIL** warren_bareiss@sdstate.edu

BARFIELD, RAY

PERSONAL Born 09/06/1939, Thomasville, GA **DISCIPLINE** ENGLISH LITERATURE **EDUCATION** Univ Tenn, PhD, 69. **CAREER** Dept Eng, Clemson Univ **RESEARCH** Shakespeare, popular culture, and writing. **SELECTED PUBLICATIONS** Auth, Listening to Radio 1920-1950, Praeger, 96; coauth, Business Communications, Barron, 92. **CONTACT ADDRESS** Clemson Univ, 813 Strode, Clemson, SC 29634. **EMAIL** brayfor@clemson.edu

BARGE, J. KEVIN

PERSONAL Born 08/08/1959, San Jose, CA, m, 1998 **DISCIPLINE** COMMUNICATIONS STUDIES **EDUCATION** Milliken Univ, BA, 81; Univ Kansas, MA, 85, PhD, 86. **CAREER** Assoc prof, Baylor Univ, 85-. **HONORS AND AWARDS** Baylor Univ Centennial Awd; Outstanding Univ Prof, Baylor Univ, 92. **MEMBERSHIPS** Natl Commun Assn; Central States Commun Assn. **RESEARCH** Leadership in organizations; public dialogue. **SELECTED PUBLICATIONS** Auth, Leadership: Communications Skills for Organizations and Groups, 94; auth, "On Doing Appealing Work in Group Communication," Communication Studies, vol 45, 94; auth, "Putting Leadership Back to Work," Management Communication Quarterly, vol 8, 94; co-ed, Managing Group Life: Communicating in Decision-making Groups, 97. **CONTACT ADDRESS** Dept of Communication Studies, Castellaw Communications Center, Baylor Univ, Waco, 143 Castellaw, Waco, TX 76798. **EMAIL** kevin_barge@baylor.edu

BARGE, LAURA I.

PERSONAL Born 09/25/1933, Macon, MS, m, 1951, 3 children **DISCIPLINE** ENGLISH **EDUCATION** Miss State Univ, BA, 71; MA, 75; Univ Ala, PhD, 86. **CAREER** Asst prof to chmn, Belhaven Col, 91-96; adj prof, Miss State Univ, 96-. **HONORS AND AWARDS** Fac Alpha Theta Teaching Awds, 95, 96; Grad Res Fel, 75, 80. **MEMBERSHIPS** Nat Sec Conf Christ Literature; ALSC; NAS. **RESEARCH** British novelist playwright Samuel Beckett; Bible as literature; works and writings of Renee Girard. **SELECTED PUBLICATIONS** Auth, "An Elizabeth Spencer Checklist, 1948-1976," Miss Quart (76); auth, "Coloured Images in the Black Dark: Samuel Beckett's Later Fiction," PMLA (77); auth, "Life and Death in Beckett's Four Stories," S Atlan Quart (78); auth, "Beckett's Skull Cliff in 'La Falaise,'" Roma Notes (84); auth, God, the Quest, the Hero: Thematic Structures in Beckett's Fiction, Chapel Hill, 88; auth, " Beckett's Metaphysics and Christian Thought," Christ Scholar rev (90); auth, "Job's Travail of Creation in Hopkin's Poetry," Cithara (91); auth, "Changing Forms of the Pastoral in Southern Poetry," S Lit J (93); auth, "Renee Girard's Categories of Scapegoats and Literature of the South," Christ Literature (01); auth, " Out of Ireland: Revisionist Strategies in Beckett's drama," Comp Dram (01). **CONTACT ADDRESS** PO Box 72, Macon, MS 39341-0072. **EMAIL** lbarge@ebicom.net

BARKER, THOMAS T.

DISCIPLINE ENGLISH LITERATURE **EDUCATION** Univ TX, Austin, PhD, 80. **CAREER** Assoc prof, TX Tech Univ. **RESEARCH** Computer documentation. **SELECTED PUBLICATIONS** Auth, Writing Software Documentation; ed, Perspectives on Software Documentation. **CONTACT ADDRESS** Texas Tech Univ, Lubbock, TX 79409-5015. **EMAIL** TBarker@ttu.edu

BARKER, WENDY

PERSONAL Born 09/22/1942, Summit, ND, d, 1 child **DISCIPLINE** LITERATURE **EDUCATION** AR State Univ, BA, MA; Univ CA at Davis, PhD. **CAREER** Prof; taught at, Univ CA at Davis & AR State Univ; Rockefeller Foun Residency, Bellagio Stud and Conf Ctr, 94; organized, ch & presented, papers on panels on var Am writers at Mod Lan Asn meetings. **HONORS AND AWARDS** Mary Elinore Smith Poetry Prize, ed(s) of The Am Scholar, 91; won the Ithaca House Poetry Series competition, 90; NEA fel, 86; 3 UTSA Fac Res Awd(s);UTSA President's Distinguished Achievement Awd for Tchg Excellence. **MEMBERSHIPS** PEN, TIL, MLA. **RESEARCH** Creative writing-poetry; 19th and 20th-century Am lit; 20th-century Brit poetry; lit by women; poetry; mod poetry, translation. **SELECTED PUBLICATIONS** Auth, bk of poems, Winter Chickens, Corona Publ Comp, 90; Let the Ice Speak, Ithaca House Bks, Greenfield Rev Press, 91; Lunacy of Light: Emily Dickinson and the Experience of Metaphor, Southern IL UP, 87; co-ed, a collection of essays on the poetry of Ruth Stone, The House Is Made of Poetry, Southern IL UP, 96; Eve Remembers, Aark Arts Publ, London, 96; Way of Whiteness, Wings Pr, 00. **CONTACT ADDRESS** Col of Fine Arts and Hum, Univ of Texas, San Antonio, 6900 N Loop 1604 W, San Antonio, TX 78249. **EMAIL** wbarker@lonestar.utsa.edu

BARKLEY, HEATHER S.

DISCIPLINE ENGLISH LITERATURE **EDUCATION** Yale Univ, PhD. **CAREER** Asst prof, TX Tech Univ. **RESEARCH** Anglo-Saxon lang and lit; the Old Irish Saga. **SELECTED PUBLICATIONS** Ed with the Yale Editions of the Papers of James Boswell. **CONTACT ADDRESS** Dept English, Texas Tech Univ, PO Box 43091, Lubbock, TX 79409-3091. **EMAIL** cbhsb@ttacs.ttu.edu

BARLOW, JUDITH ELLEN

PERSONAL Born 08/21/1946, Bronx, NY **DISCIPLINE** AMERICAN LITERATURE, MODERN DRAMA **EDUCATION** Cornell Univ, AB, 68; Univ Pa, AM, 70, PhD, 75. **CAREER** Instr, Univ PA, 71-72; lectr, 73-75, asst prof, 75-82, assoc prof eng, State Univ NY, Albany, 82-95, Prof, 95-, Adj prof women's studies, State Univ NY, Albany, 80-82, adj assoc prof, 82-; Assoc ed, Theatre Survey, 80. **HONORS AND AWARDS** Collins Fel, Univ Albany, SUNY, 97; Pres Awd Excellence in Acade Service, Univ Albany, SUNY, 91; State of NY & UPP Excellence Awd, 91; Pres Awd for Excellence in Teaching, Univ Albany, SUNY, 83. **MEMBERSHIPS** MLA; Nat Women's Studies Asn; Eugene O'Neill Soc; Intl Women Playrights; assoc Theatre in Higher Edu. **RESEARCH** Am women playwrights; Eugene O'Neill. **SELECTED PUBLICATIONS** Auth, Semantic satiation and the semantic differential, Cornell J Social Rel, 10/66; coauth, Distinctive features in the pluralization rules of English speakers, Lang & Speech, 1-3/68; auth, Long Day's Journey into Night: From early notes to finished play, Mod Drama, 3/79; ed, Plays by American women: The early years, Avon, 81; auth, Plays by American Women 1930-1960, Applause Books, 94; Final Acts: The Creation of Three Late O'Neill Plays, Univ GA Press, 85; Plays by American Women 1900-1930, Applause Books, 85. **CONTACT ADDRESS** Eng Dept, SUNY, Albany, 1400 Washington Ave, Albany, NY 12222-1000. **EMAIL** jbarlow@albany.edu

BARLOW, WILLIAM

DISCIPLINE RADIO PRODUCTION, HISTORY OF BROADCASTING **EDUCATION** Univ Southern Calif, PhD. **CAREER** Prof. **RESEARCH** World music. **SELECTED PUBLICATIONS** Auth, bk and numerous publ on, history of Black music and radio. **CONTACT ADDRESS** School of Communications, Howard Univ, 2400 Sixth St NW, Washington, DC 20059.

BARNARD, SYLVIA

PERSONAL Born Greenfield, MA, s, 1 child **DISCIPLINE** CLASSICS **EDUCATION** Cambridge Univ, BA, 62; MA, 67; Yale Univ, MA, 63; PhD, 66. **CAREER** Asst prof, Kenyon Col,

66-67; asst to prof, State Univ of NY, 67-. **MEMBERSHIPS** Am Philological Asn, Am Inst of Arch. **RESEARCH** Women in Antiquity. **SELECTED PUBLICATIONS** Auth, "Hellenistic Women Poets," Classical Journal, 78; auth, Ante, Poet of Children and Animals, in Rose di Pieria, 91; auth, "The Matres of Roman Britain," Archaeological Journal, 85; auth, Cornelia and the Women of her Family, 90. **CONTACT ADDRESS** Sept Classics, SUNY at Albany, 1400 Wash Ave, Albany, NY 12222-10000. **EMAIL** sbarnard@csc.albany.edu

BARNES, DANIEL RAMON
PERSONAL Born 05/16/1940, Fillmore, NY, m, 1989, 4 children **DISCIPLINE** AMERICAN LITERATURE, FOLKLORE **EDUCATION** St Bonaventure Univ, BA, 62; Univ KS, MA, 66; Univ KY, PhD(English), 70. **CAREER** From instr to asst prof, 68-73, Assoc Prof English, OH State Univ, Columbus, 73-, Consult, Smithsonian Inst Festival of Am Folklore, 71; Asst Prof, 73-95; ed, Motif: Int Newslett Res in Folklore & Lit, 81-; Emeritus Prof, 95-, Visiting Prof, Oberlin College, 97, Ohio U, 98-99. **HONORS AND AWARDS** Invited as 1985 Nordic Institute Lecturer In Folklore; elected Folklore Fel, Finnish Acad Sci and Letters, 90. **MEMBERSHIPS** MLA; Am Folklore Soc; Asn Anthrop Study of Play; Int Soc Folk Narrative Res; Folklore Soc Britain. **RESEARCH** Nineteenth century American literature; folklore and literature; folklore and folklife. **SELECTED PUBLICATIONS** Auth, Ford and the Slaughtered Saints: A New Reading of The Good Soldier, Mod Fiction Studies, summer 68; Folktale Morphology and the Structure of Beowulf, Speculum, 70; Physical Fact and Folklore: Hawthorne's Egotism, or the Bosom Serpent, Am Lit, 71; The Bosom Serpent: A Legend in American Literature and Culture, J Am Folklore, 72; Toward the Establishment of Principles for the Study of Folklore and Lliterature, Southern Folklore Quart, 79; Telling it Slant: Emily Dickinson and the Proverb, Genre, summer 79; auth, "Interpreting Urban Legends," ARV: Sccandinavian Yearbook of Folklore, 84. **CONTACT ADDRESS** Dept of English, Ohio State Univ, Columbus, 164 W 17th Ave, Columbus, OH 43210-1326.

BARNES, DOROTHY
PERSONAL Born 02/22/1954, Brooklyn, NY, d, 1 child **DISCIPLINE** ENGLISH **EDUCATION** Tuskegee Inst, BA, 78; NC A&T St Univ, MA, 87; Howard Univ, PhD, 92. **CAREER** Assoc Prof, Gettysburg Col, 92-. **HONORS AND AWARDS** Sigma Tau Delta; All Am Scholar, 90-91; NEH Res Fel, 93; NEH Summer Stipend, 94. **MEMBERSHIPS** MLA, ALA, CLA, Toni Morrison Soc, Charles Chesnutt Soc. **RESEARCH** Toni Morrison, Jim Crow era writers, Arthur R Daves, American literature, African literature, women's literature. **SELECTED PUBLICATIONS** Auth, "I'd Rather Be a Lamppost in Chicago: Richard Wright and the Chicago Renaissance," Langston Hughes Rev (96); auth, "Arthur A Schomburg," The Oxford Companion to African-Am Lit, Oxford UP (96); auth, "Harriet Tubman," The Oxford Companion to African-Am Lit, Oxford UP (96); auth, "The Bottom of Heaven: Myth, Metaphor and Memory in Toni Morrison's Reconstructed South," Studies in the Lit Imagination (98); auth, "The Elephant and the Race Problem," Callaloo (98); auth, "Reading Paradise: Racing the Future," Envisioning Paradise: Toni Morrison's Art and Imagination (Princeton UP (99). **CONTACT ADDRESS** Dept English, Gettysburg Col, 300 N Washington St, Gettysburg, PA 17325-1400. **EMAIL** dbarnes@gettysburg.edu

BARNES, JIM WEAVER
PERSONAL Born 12/22/1933, Summerfield, OK **DISCIPLINE** COMPARATIVE LITERATURE, CREATIVE WRITING **EDUCATION** Southeast Oklahoma State Univ, BA, 64; Univ Ark, Fayetteville, MA, 66, PhD, 72. **CAREER** Instr English, Northeastern Okla State Univ, 65-68; prof comp lit, 70-, ed, The Chariton Review, Truman State Univ, 76-; Nat Endowment for the Arts creative writing fel, 78; Rockefeller Found Bellagio Fel, 90; Sr Fulbright to Switzerland, 93-94; Akademie Schloss Solitude Fel, 98. **HONORS AND AWARDS** Transl Prize Summons and Sign, Columbia Univ, 80; The Am Book Awd, 98. **MEMBERSHIPS** Coord Coun of Lit Mags; MLA. **RESEARCH** Twentieth century fiction and poetry; creative writing. **SELECTED PUBLICATIONS** Auth, On Native Ground, University of Oklahoma Press, 97; auth, Paris, University of Illinois Press, 97. **CONTACT ADDRESS** Div of Lang & Lit, Truman State Univ, 100 E Normal St, Kirksville, MO 63501-4221. **EMAIL** jbarnes@truman.edu

BARNES, RONALD EDGAR
PERSONAL Born 03/12/1930, Minneapolis, MN, m, 1954 **DISCIPLINE** DRAMATIC LITERATURE **EDUCATION** Univ Minn, BA, 51; Stanford Univ, PhD(Drama), 63. **CAREER** From instr to asst prof Drama, Mills Col, 57-65; assoc prof, 56-69, prof Drama & chmn dept, Calif State Univ, San Bernardino, 70-88; retired, 97. **MEMBERSHIPS** US Inst Theatre Technol; CA Theatre Assn; Southern CA Theatre Assn. **RESEARCH** Dramatic analysis; theatre architecture. **SELECTED PUBLICATIONS** Auth, The Dramatic Comedy of William Somerser Maugham, Mouton, 68. **CONTACT ADDRESS** Dept of Drama, California State Univ, San Bernardino, 5500 University Pky, San Bernardino, CA 92407-7500. **EMAIL** rbarnes@wiley.csusb.edu

BARNES, SUE
PERSONAL Born 04/26/1951, Trenton, NJ, m, 1997 **DISCIPLINE** COMMUNICATIONS **EDUCATION** Pratt Inst, BFA 73; NYork Univ, MFA 75, PhD 95. **CAREER** Fordham Univ, digi med spec, assoc ch, asst prof, 96 to 98-; Marymont Manhattan College, adj prof, asst prof, 84-96; Fashion Inst Tech, SUNY, adj prof, 88-97, comp tchr, 90-94; Pratt Manhattan, vis inst, 88-90; Cen for the Media arts, inst, 84-88. **HONORS AND AWARDS** McGannon Gnt; Ames Gnt, 97&98; Best Paper Awd; SUNY Fac Gnt; Innovations Using Pagemaker winner. **MEMBERSHIPS** MEA; IEEECS; ACM; NJCA; NYSCA; ECA; NCA; ICA. **RESEARCH** Computer Mediated Communication; Visual Comm; Digital Comm; Comp and EDU ; Hist of Comp and Digital Media. **SELECTED PUBLICATIONS** Are Computers Defining Our Culture? The NJ Jour of Comm, 98; Developing a Concept of Self in Cyberspace Communities, in: The Emerging Cyberculture: Literacy, Paradigm and Paradox, eds, Stephanie Gibson and Ollie O. Oviedo, Hampton Press, 99; Education and Technology: A cultural Faustian Bargain, Jour of Sci Tech Soc, 99; Ethical issues for a Virtual self, in: Law@Virtual Space, eds, Gary Gumbert and Susan Drucker, Hampton Press, 99 Auth, Online Connections: Internet Interpersonal Relationships, Hampton Press, 00. **CONTACT ADDRESS** Dept of Comm and Media Studies, Fordham Univ, 441 E Fordham Rd, Bronx, NY 10458. **EMAIL** barnes@fordham.edu

BARNES, TIMOTHY DAVID
PERSONAL Born 03/13/1942, Yorkshire, England, m, 1965, 3 children **DISCIPLINE** CLASSICS, HISTORY **EDUCATION** Oxford Univ, BA, 64, MA, 67, DPhil, 70. **CAREER** Jr res fel classics, Queen's Col, Oxford, 66-70; from asst prof to assoc prof, Univ Col, Toronto, 70-76; assoc chmn grad studies, 79-83, Prof Classics Univ Toronto, 76-. **HONORS AND AWARDS** Conington Prize, Oxford Univ, 74. **MEMBERSHIPS** Am Philol Asn; Can Class Asn; Am Soc Papyrologists; Am Asn Ancient Historians; Soc Promotion Roman Studies. **RESEARCH** Hist, lit, culture and religions of Roman Empire from Augustus to the sixth century, Theodosian Code, Early Christian Hagiography. **SELECTED PUBLICATIONS** Auth, Athanasius and Constantius, Theology and Politics in the Constantinian Empire, Harvard UP, 93; auth, From Eusebius to Augustine, Selected papers 1982-1993, Aldershot: Varorium Reprints, 94; auth, "The Sources of the Historia Augusta 1967-1992," Historae Augustae Colloquium Maceratense, (95): 1-28; auth, "Statistics and the Conversion of the Roman Aristocracy," Journal of Roman Studies 85, (95): 135-147; auth, "Emperors, Panegyrics, Prefects, Provinces and Palaces," Journal of Roman Archaeology 9, 96; auth, Representation and Reality in Ammianus Marcellinus, book being prepared for submission to Cornell UP. **CONTACT ADDRESS** Dept of Classics, Univ of Toronto, 97 St George St, Toronto, ON, Canada M5S 2E8. **EMAIL** tbarnes@chass.utoronto.ca

BARNETT, LOUISE
DISCIPLINE AMERICAN LITERATURE, NATIVE AMERICAN LITERATURE **EDUCATION** Univ NC, BA; Bryn Mawr, MA, PhD **CAREER** Prof Eng, Rutgers, The State Univ NJ. **RESEARCH** 19th Century American Culture. **SELECTED PUBLICATIONS** Auth, The Ignoble Savage: American Literary Racism; Touched by Fire: the Life, Death, and Mythic Afterlife of George Armstrong Custer; Authority and Speech: Language, Society, and Self in the American Novel; auth, Ungentlemanly Acts: The Army's Notorious Incest Trial. **CONTACT ADDRESS** Dept of Eng, Rutgers, The State Univ of New Jersey, New Brunswick, Murray Hall 510 George St, New Brunswick, NJ 08903. **EMAIL** lk_barnett@acad.fandm.edu

BARNEY, STEPHEN ALLEN
PERSONAL Born 10/10/1942, Rocky Mount, NC, m, 1962, 2 children **DISCIPLINE** ENGLISH LITERATURE, MEDIEVAL STUDIES **EDUCATION** Univ Va, BA, 64; Harvard Univ, AM, 65, PhD, 69. **CAREER** From asst prof to assoc prof English, Yale Univ, 68-78; vis assoc prof English, Univ VA, 78; Prof English, Univ CA, Irvine, 79-98, prof emer, 98-. **HONORS AND AWARDS** Wilson Prize, UVA, 64; Phi Beta Kappa; Woodrow Wilson Fel, 64-65; Kent Fel, 65-68; Elliott Prize, Mediaeval Acad Am, 72; Morse Fel, Yale, 72-73; Am Coun of Learned Societies Fel, 76; Nat Endowment for the Humanities, Res Tools Grant, 79-81; Guggenheim Fel, 86-87; UC Humanities Res Inst Fel, 90, 94; Nat Endowment for the Humanities, Interpretive Res Grant, 92-97; UC President's Res Fel in the Humanities, 94; UCI Humanities Associates Teaching Awd, 98. **MEMBERSHIPS** MLA; Mediaeval Acad Am; Early English Text Soc; New Chaucer Soc. **RESEARCH** Chaucer; Medieval Latin allegorical dictionaries; textual criticism. **SELECTED PUBLICATIONS** Auth, Word-Hoard: An Introduction to Old English Vocabulary, Yale Univ Press, 77; auth, Allegories of History, Allegories of Love, Archon, 78; ed, Chaucer's Troilus: Essays in Criticism, Archon, 80; ed, Chaucer, Troilus and Criseyde, In The Riverside Chaucer, 87; ed, Annotation and Its Texts, Oxford Univ Press, 91; auth, Studies in Troilus: Chaucer's Text, Meter, and Diction, Colleagues Press, 93; co-ed, Contradictions: From Beowulf to Chaucer, Selected Studies of Larry D. Benson, Scolar Press, 95. **CONTACT ADDRESS** 667 Tumbleweed Circle, Incline Village, NV 89451. **EMAIL** sbarney@uci.edu

BARNHISEL, GREGORY P.
PERSONAL Born 12/07/1969, Portland, OR, m, 2001 **DISCIPLINE** AMERICAN LITERATURE **EDUCATION** Reed Col, BA, 92; NY Univ, MA, 95; Univ Tex Austin, PhD. **CAREER** Asst prof, Southwestern Univ, 98-00; vis asst prof, Tex Lutheran Univ, 98-99, 00-01; director, Univ of SCal, 01-. **HONORS AND AWARDS** Univ Tex Diss Fel. **MEMBERSHIPS** MLA. **RESEARCH** Ezra Pound, Cultural history of modernism, US Cultural diplomacy in the Cold War, Reconstruction and the publishing industry, Contemporary political rhetoric, advertising, public relations. **SELECTED PUBLICATIONS** Auth, "Hitch Your Wagon to a Star: The Square $ Series and Ezra Pound," Papers of the Bibliog Soc of Am 92.3, (98); auth, "Instructor's manual," Good Reasons with Contemporary Arguments, ed Lester Faigley and Jack Selzer, (Allyn and Bacon, 00); auth, "Marketing Modernism in America during the Great War," World War I and the Cultures of Modernity, ed Mackaman and Mays, (Univ Pr of Miss, 00); rev of "Pound/ Cummings, " Paideuma 23.2-3, (00); auth, "James Laughlin and Ezra Pound: The Publisher as Spin Doctor," Paideuma, forthcoming. **EMAIL** gbarnhisel@yahoo.com

BARNOUW, ERIK
PERSONAL Born 06/23/1908, The Hague, Netherlands, m, 1939, 3 children **DISCIPLINE** DRAMATIC ARTS **EDUCATION** Princeton Univ, AB, 29. **CAREER** Writer, dir & producer, 31-42; script ed, Nat Broadcasting Co, 42-44; consult, Secy War, 44; supvr ed unit, armed forces radio serv, US War Dept, 44-45; asst prof in charge courses in TV, radio & film, 46-53, ed, Ctr for Mass Commun, Univ Press, 49-72, from assoc prof to prof, 53-73, Emer Prof Dramatic Arts, Columbia Univ, 73-, Consult, US Pub Health Serv, 48-51; Fulbright grant, India, 61-62; Guggenheim fel, 67; J D Rockefeller III Fund fel, Asia, 72; Woodrow Wilson fel, Smithsonian Inst, 76; film & TV specialist, Libr Cong, 77-78; chief, Motion Picture, Broadcasting and Recorded Sound Div, Libr Cong, 78-81. **HONORS AND AWARDS** Gavel Awd, Am Bar Asn, 59; Bancroft Prize, Columbia Univ, 71; Preceptor Awd, San Francisco State Col, 71; George Polk Awd, Long Island Univ, 72; Silver Dragon Awd, Cracow Film Festival, 72; Film Libr Quart Bk Awd, 80. **MEMBERSHIPS** Auth League Am (secy, 49-53); Soc Am Historians; Soc Cinema Studies. **RESEARCH** Documentary film; television. **SELECTED PUBLICATIONS** Auth, A Tower in Babel, 66, The Golden Web, 68, The Image Empire, 70, Documentary: A History of the Non-Fiction Film, 74, Tube of Plenty: The Evolution of American Television, 75, The Sponsor: Notes on a Modern Potentate, 78, coauth, Indian Film, 2nd ed, 80 & auth, The Magician and the Cinema, 81, Oxford Univ. **CONTACT ADDRESS** Columbia Univ, New York, NY 10027.

BARNUM, CAROL
PERSONAL m **DISCIPLINE** COMMUNICATION STUDIES **EDUCATION** Univ NC, BA; GA State Univ, MA, PhD. **CAREER** Prof tech commun, So Polytech State Univ, 79-. **HONORS AND AWARDS** Phi Beta Kappa **MEMBERSHIPS** Soc Tech Commun. **SELECTED PUBLICATIONS** Auth, publ(s) on tech or prof commun. **CONTACT ADDRESS** Hum and Tech Commun Dept, So Polytech State Univ, S Marietta Pkwy, PO Box 1100, Marietta, GA 30060. **EMAIL** cbarnum@spsu.edu

BAROLSKY, PAUL
PERSONAL Born 07/13/1941, Paterson, NJ, m, 1966, 2 children **DISCIPLINE** ART HISTORY, LITERARY CRITICISM **EDUCATION** Middlebury Col, BA, 63; Harvard Univ, MA, 64, PhD(Art hist), 69. **CAREER** Asst prof, Cornell Univ, 68-69; Commonwealth Prof Art Hist, Univ VA, 69-. **RESEARCH** Italian Renaissance art and literature. **SELECTED PUBLICATIONS** Michelanglo's Nose, Penn State, 90; Why Mona Lisa Smiles, Penn State, 91; Giotto's Father, Penn State, 92; The Faun in the Garden, Penn State, 94; Fables of Art, VA Quart Rev, Vol 71, 95; A Very Brief History of Art From Narcissus to Picasso, Classical J, Vol 90, 95; The Visionary Experience of Renaissance Art, Word & Image, Vol 11, 95; Johannes Vermeer, with A. K. Wheelock, VA Quart Rev, Vol 72, 96; Flesh and the Ideal-Winckelman and the Origins of Art History, with A. Potts, Classical J, Vol 91, 96; The Fable of Failure in Modern Art, VA Quart Rev, Vol 73, 97. **CONTACT ADDRESS** Dept of Art, Univ of Virginia, 102 Fayerweather, Charlottesville, VA 22903. **EMAIL** pb4r@virginia.edu

BARON, CAROL K.
PERSONAL Born New York, NY, w, 1963, 2 children **DISCIPLINE** MUSIC **EDUCATION** Graduate Ctr of the City Univ of NYork, PhD, 87. **CAREER** Adjunct lectr, York Col, 74-75; adjunct lectr, Hunter Col, 78-80; adjunct prof, Adelphi Univ, 80-82; exec dir, Bach Area Group Asn, Bach Aria Festival and Inst at the Univ Stony Brook, 80-97. **HONORS AND AWARDS** Travel grant, American Council of Learned Societies; Alfred P. Sloan Fel; ASCAP Deems Taylor Awd. **MEMBERSHIPS** Am Musicology Soc; Soc for Music Theory; Sonneck Soc. **RESEARCH** Music of Charles Ives; late 19th century/early 20th century American culture; music of J.S. Bach; religious trends in 17th and early 18th century Germany. **SELECTED PUBLICATIONS** Auth, Dating the Music of Charles Ives: Facts and Fictions, in Perspectives of New Music

28, 90; auth, Meaning in the Music of Charles Ives, in Metaphor - A Musical Dimension, Australian Studies in the History, Philosophy and Social Studies of Music, 91; auth, George Ives's Essay on Music Theory: An Introduction and An Annotated Edition, in American Music, 92; auth, Larry Starr. A Union of Diversities: Style in the Music of Charles Ives, in Notes, 93; auth, At the Cutting Edge: Three American Theorists at the End of the Nineteenth Century, in International Journal of Musicology 2, 93; auth, What Motivated Charles Ives's search for Time Past, in The Musical Quart 78/2, 94; auth, "New Sources for Ives Studies: An Annotated Catalogue," in ISAM Bulletin, 00; auth, "Father knew (and filled me up with) Bach": Bach and ives -- Affinities in Lines and Spaces, In Bach Perspectives 5, 01. **CONTACT ADDRESS** 321 Melbourne Rd, Great Neck, NY 11021. **EMAIL** cbaron@ms.cc.sunysb.edu

BARON, DENNIS
PERSONAL Born 05/09/1944, New York, NY, m, 1979, 3 children **DISCIPLINE** ENGLISH **EDUCATION** Brandeis Univ, BA, 65; Columbia Univ, MA, 68; Univ Mich, PhD, 71. **CAREER** Assoc Prof to prof to dir to head, Univ Ill, 84-. **HONORS AND AWARDS** NEH Fel, 89; Fulbright Fel, 78-79; pmla advisory committee; mla delegate assembly. **MEMBERSHIPS** MLA; NCTE; LSA; ADS. **RESEARCH** Literacy and technology; language legislation & linguistic rights; history of English language. **SELECTED PUBLICATIONS** Grammar and Good Taste: Reforming the American Language, 82; Grammar and Gender, 86; Declining Grammar and Other Essays on English Vocabulary, 89; The English-Only Question: An Official Language for Americans?, 90; Guide to Home Language Repair, 94. **CONTACT ADDRESS** Dept of English, Univ of Illinois, Urbana-Champaign, 608 S Wright St, Urbana, IL 61801. **EMAIL** debaron@uiuc.edu

BARON, F. XAVIER
PERSONAL Born 07/29/1941, Springfield, MO, s, 3 children **DISCIPLINE** MEDIEVAL & ENGLISH LITERATURE **EDUCATION** Mo State Univ, BA, 63; Univ Iowa, MA, 65, PhD(English), 69. **CAREER** Asst prof, 69-74, assoc prof English, Univ Wis, Milwaukee, 74-, exec dir, Milwaukee Humanities Prog, 78-79, consult, Ital-Am Hist Asn, Chicago Proj, 77-78, Visiting Prof, Giessen Univ, 83-88, Visiting Prof, Univ of Wisconsin London Program, 82,83,94. **HONORS AND AWARDS** Nat Endowment for Humanities younger humanist fel, 71-72. **MEMBERSHIPS** Int Arthurian Soc; MLA; Midwest Mod Lang Asn; Int Courtly Lit Soc (secy-treas, 77-). **RESEARCH** Medieval Arthurian literature; Chaucer and Middle English literature; London in literature and art. **SELECTED PUBLICATIONS** Auth, Mother and Son in Sir Perceval of Galles, Papers Lang & lit, 72; Visual Presentation in Beroul's Tristan, 72 & Love in Chretien's Charrette: Reversed Values and Isolation, 73, Mod Lang Quart; coauth, Amour Courtois, The Medieval Ideal of Love: A Bibliography, Univ Louisville, 73; auth, Chaucer's Troilus and self-renunciation in love, Papers Lang & Lit, 74; Medieval Arthurian Motifs in the Modernist Art and Poetry of David Jones, In: Studies in Medievalism IV: Medievalism in England, Boydell and Brewer, 92; Medieval Traditions in the English Renaissance: John Stow's Portrayal of London in 1603, In: Medieval and Renaissance Texts & Studies, Binghamton, NY, 94; Washington Irving, In: American Travel Writers, 1776-1864, Dictionary of Literary Biography, vol 183, Gale Res, 97; William Dean Howells, In: American Travel Writers, 1850-1915 [1920], Dictionary of Literary Biography, vol 189, Gale Res, 98; auth, London 1066-1914: Literary Sources and Documents, 3 volumes, Helm Information, Ltd, 97; auth, London in Art and Poetry, 1660-1798, in Proceddings of The 7th Northern Plains Conference on Early British Literature, Northern Univ Press, 99; auth, J.R.R. Tolkien, Dictionary of World Biography, The Modern Era, Salem Press, 99; auth, Impressionist London in the Novels of George Gissing in Essays in Honour of Raimumd, Borgmeier, Wissenschaftlichen Verlag, 00; auth, London in Art, 1603-1992: Art History Sources and Documents, 2 volumes, Helm Information, Ltd, 01. **CONTACT ADDRESS** Dept of English, Univ of Wisconsin, Milwaukee, PO Box 413, Milwaukee, WI 53201-0413. **EMAIL** fxbaron@uwn.edu

BARON, JAMES
PERSONAL Born 11/21/1942 **DISCIPLINE** CLASSICAL STUDIES **EDUCATION** Catholic Univ Am, AB, 64; Univ Minn, MA, 67, PhD, 72. **CAREER** Tchg asst, 66-69; tchg assoc, 69-70, Univ Minn; asst prof, Macalester Col, St Paul, Minn, 70-71; asst prof, Concordia Col, Moorehead, Minn, 70-71; asst prof, Col William and Mary in Va, 71-76; assoc prof, 76- & ept ch, 83-89 & 91-92. **RESEARCH** Augustan poetry; classical tradition in film; Scandinavian literature. **SELECTED PUBLICATIONS** Auth, Drag Humor in Aristophanes Comedies, Class Asn Mid W and S, 90; Direct Address to the Audience in the Films of Ingmar Bergman: A Classical Device Radically Transformed, Inaugural Meeting Int Soc for the Class Tradition, Boston, 91; The Orpheus Myth in the Early Films of Ingmar Bergman, CAMWS Southern Sect Meeting, Richmond, 92; Horatii Carmina I.37.17-20: Citus Venator: Homo aut Canis, Class Asn Mid W and S, Atlanta Georgia, 94; Bergman's Cries and Whispers, a Masterpiece of Classical Architecture, Soc Advancement for Scand Study, Davenport, 94; Alliteration and Other Sound Effects in Seneca's Tragedies, Class Asn Mid W and S, Southern Section, Chapel Hill, NC, 94; Willa Cather's Alexandra Bergson: Aeneas on the Nebraska Prairie, Class Asn Mid W and S, Omaha, 95 & A Child of Soil Reads Catullus, Horace, and Vergil, Amer Philol Asn, San Diego, 95; rev, Persona: the Transcendent Image, Scand Stud, vol 60, 98. **CONTACT ADDRESS** Dept of Classical Studies, Col of William and Mary, Morton Hall, PO Box 8795, Williamsburg, VA 23187-8795. **EMAIL** jrbaro@facstaff.wm.edu

BARON, JOHN H.
PERSONAL Born 05/07/1936, Milwaukee, WI, m, 1973, 3 children **DISCIPLINE** MUSICOLOGY **EDUCATION** Brandeis Univ, PhD, 67; Harvard Univ, MA, 59, BA, 58 **CAREER** From prof to Schawe prof, 69-, Tulane Univ. **MEMBERSHIPS** Am Musicol Soc **RESEARCH** Jewish music; New Orleans Music; chamber music. **SELECTED PUBLICATIONS** Auth, Ballet des Fees de forest de Saint Germain, New York: Dance Perspectives No. 62, 75; auth, Chamber Music, Garland Pr (NYork), 87; auth, Baroque Music, Garland Pr (NYork), 92; coauth, The Remarkable mrs. Beach, Warren, MI: Harmonie Park Press, 94; auth, A History of Chamber Music, Stuyvesant, NY, Pendragon Press, 98. **CONTACT ADDRESS** Dept of Music, Tulane Univ, New Orleans, LA 70118-5683. **EMAIL** caccini@tulane.edu

BARON, MARY K.
DISCIPLINE ENGLISH, PEDOGOGY, WRITING **EDUCATION** Brandeis Univ, AB, 69; Univ Mich, Ann Arbor, AM, 71; Univ Ill-Urbana, PhD, 73. **CAREER** Asst prof, Tufts Univ, 73-75; asst prof, Hartwich Col, 76-78; assoc prof, Univ Alaska, Fairbanks, 80-84, prof, 85-87; prof, Univ North Fla, 87-. **HONORS AND AWARDS** Hopwood, poetry, 71; Mellon Teaching, 85; Teaching Incentive Awd, 98. **MEMBERSHIPS** NCTE. **RESEARCH** Teaching of writing, adolescent literature, poetry. **SELECTED PUBLICATIONS** Auth, Letters for the New England Dead (poems), David Godens Pubs, Boston (96); auth, Wheat Among Bones (poems), Sheep Meadow Press, NY (80). **CONTACT ADDRESS** Dept English & Langs, Univ of No Florida, 4567 St Johns Bluff Rd S, Jacksonville, FL 32224-2646. **EMAIL** mbaron@unf.edu

BARR, ALAN PHILIP
PERSONAL Born 11/25/1938, Brooklyn, NY, m, 2 children **DISCIPLINE** ENGLISH **EDUCATION** Mass Inst Technol, BA, 59; Univ Rochester, PhD, 63. **CAREER** From instr to asst prof English, Wayne State Univ, 63-68; from asst prof to assoc prof, 68-76, Prof English, Ind Univ Northwest, 76-; Dept ch. **RESEARCH** Victorian literature; modern drama; film. **SELECTED PUBLICATIONS** Auth, Diabolonian pundit: G B S as critic, Shaw Rev, 68; The paradise behind 1983, Eng Miscellany, 68; Cervantes' probing of reality & psychological realism in Don Quixote, Lit & Psychol, 68; Victorian Stage Pulpiteer: Bernard Shaw's Crusade, 73; ed, The Major Prose of Thomas Henry Huxley, Univ Ga Press, 97; ed and contribr, Thomas Henry Huxley's Place in Science and Letters: Centenary Essays, Univ Ga Press, 97; ed, Modern Women Playwrights of Wurope, Oxford Univ Press, 01; author of numerous journal articles. **CONTACT ADDRESS** Dept of English, Indiana Univ, Northwest, 3400 Broadway, Gary, IN 46408-1101. **EMAIL** abarr@iunhaw1.iun.indiana.edu

BARR, JEANINE R.
PERSONAL Born 05/15/1941, Toledo, OH, m, 1981 **DISCIPLINE** COMMUNICATON **EDUCATION** OH Univ, BFA, 63; Miami of OH, MA, 67; Univ MD, PhD, 94. **CAREER** Instr, SUNY, Albany; asst prof to assoc prof, York Col of PA, 70-. **HONORS AND AWARDS** NIH grant, summer 80. **MEMBERSHIPS** Nat Commun Asn; Pi Kappa Delta. **RESEARCH** Communication in recovery from addiction; forensics. **SELECTED PUBLICATIONS** Co-auth, Communication in Recovery; misc articles on addiction, recovery, and forensics. **CONTACT ADDRESS** Dept of Commun, York Col, Pennsylvania, York, PA 17403. **EMAIL** jbarr@eagle.ycp.edu

BARR, MARLEEN SANDRA
PERSONAL Born 03/01/1953, New York, NY **DISCIPLINE** WOMEN & LITERATURE **EDUCATION** State Univ NYork Albany, BA, 74; Univ MI, MA, 75; State Univ NYork Buffalo, PhD(English), 79. **CAREER** Asst Prof English, VA Polytech Inst & State Univ, 79-, Consult, Educ Testing Serv, 82 & Coun Wis Writers Annual Awards Competition, 82. **MEMBERSHIPS** MLA; Northeast Mod Lang Asn; Popular Cult Asn. **RESEARCH** Science fiction studies; contemporary American literature. **SELECTED PUBLICATIONS** Ed, Future Females: A Critical Anthology, Bowling Green Univ, Popular Press, 81; contribr, The Feminine Eye, 82, Frederick Ungar Co; auth, Science Fiction and the Fact of Women's Repressed Creativity, Extrapolation, spring 82; A Nerw Species-Gender and Science in Science-Fiction, with R. Roberts, Science-Fiction Studies, Vol 20, 93. **CONTACT ADDRESS** Dept English, Virginia Polytech Inst and State Univ, Blacksburg, VA 24061. **EMAIL** mbarr@vt.edu

BARRET, HAROLD
PERSONAL Born 03/20/1925, Heladsburg, CA, m, 1948, 4 children **DISCIPLINE** RHETORIC, SPEECH COMMUNICATION **EDUCATION** Univ Pac, BA, 49; MA, 52; Univ Ore, PhD 62. **CAREER** Teacher, Lodi High Sch, Lodi, CA; 50-54; instr, Compton Coll, 54-59; instr, Univ Ore, 59-61; asst prof, S Ore Univ, 61-63; prof, Calif State Univ, 63-92. **HONORS AND AWARDS** Outstanding fac mem, Ore Univ, 63; outstanding prof, Calif State Univ, 82. **MEMBERSHIPS** Nat Commun Asn; Western Speech Commun Asn; World Commun Asn. **RESEARCH** Rhetorical interaction; Narcissism and defensiveness, communication. **SELECTED PUBLICATIONS** Auth, Rhetoric and Civility, 91; Speaking in America, 93; Maintaining the Self in Communication, 98. **CONTACT ADDRESS** 33 S Modoc Ave, Medford, OR 97504. **EMAIL** oldrhetor@aol.com

BARRETT, EILEEN
PERSONAL Born 05/06/1952, Middleton, NY **DISCIPLINE** LITERATURE **EDUCATION** Boston Col, BA, 74; PhD, 87. **CAREER** Lectr, Boston Col, 82-87; from lectr to prof & interim dir, CSU Hayward, 87-. **HONORS AND AWARDS** Co-Winner of Twentieth Century Lit Prize in Lit Criticism, 87. **MEMBERSHIPS** Modern Lang Asn, Int Virginia Woolf Soc. **RESEARCH** American women writers, Virginia Woolf feminist theory, lesbian literature, James Baldwin. **SELECTED PUBLICATIONS** Co-ed, American Women Writers: Diverse Voices in Prose Since 1845, St Martins Press (New York), 92; auth, "Septimus and Shadrack: Woolf and Morrison Envision the Madness of War," in Emerging Perspectives, eds. Mark Hussey and Vara Neverow Pace Univ Press, 94): 26-32; auth, "DeCamping Sally Potter's Orlando," in Re:Reading, Re: Writing, Re:Teaching Virginia Woolf: Selected Papers from the Forth Annual Virginia Woolf Conference, eds. Eileen Barrett and Patricia Cramer (Pace Univ Press, 95): 197-199; co-ed, Re: Reading, Re:Writing, Re:Teaching Virginia Woolf: Selected Papers from the Forth Annual Virginia Woolf Conference, Pace Univ Press (NY), 95; co-ed, Virginia Woolf: Texts and Contexts: Selected Papers from the Fifth Annual Virginia Woolf Conference, Pace Univ Press (NY), 96; co-ed, Virginia Woolf: Lesbian Readings, New York Univ Press, 97; auth, "Unmasking Lesbian Passion: The Inverted World of Mrs. Dalloway," Virginia Woolf: Lesbian Readings (New York Univ Press, 97): 146-164; auth, "Introduction: Lesbian Intersections," Virginia Woolf: Lesbian Readings (New York Univ Press, 97): 3-9; auth, "Woolf's Lesbian Erotics of the Soul," Virginia Woolf and Her Influences: Selected Papers from the Seventh Annual Virginia Woolf Conference (Pace Univ Press, 98): 111-116; auth, "The Language of Fabric in "To the Lighthouse,"" in Approaches to Teaching Woolf's TO THE LIGHTHOUSE, eds. Beth Rigel Daugherty and Mary Beth Pringle (forthcoming). **CONTACT ADDRESS** Dept English, California State Univ, Hayward, 25800 Carlos Bee Blvd, Hayward, CA 94542-3001. **EMAIL** ebarrett@csuhayward.edu

BARRETT, JANICE M.
PERSONAL Born 08/03/1944, Boston, MA, w, 1 child **DISCIPLINE** COMMUNICATIONS **EDUCATION** Boston Col, BS, 66; Boston Univ, MS, 80; Harvard Univ, MEd, 90; EdD, 96. **CAREER** Director Comm, Nathaniel Hawthorne Col, 91-92; Director Comm, Regis Col, 92-94; Asst Prof, Boston Univ, 94-; Co-Chair and Instr, Harvard Univ, 96-. **HONORS AND AWARDS** Doctoral Student Awd, Harvard Grad School, 89-90; Editor's Choice Awd, IVLA, 98; Third Prize Winner, Intl Asn of Bus Comm, 99; Board Member, Peace Studies and Conflict Resolution Commission, 98. **MEMBERSHIPS** Am Asn for Educ Res, Am Asn for Higher Learning, Askwith Symposium Committee, Asn for Educ in Journalism and Mass Comm, Asn of Indep Col and Univ of Mass, Coun for Advancement and Support of Educ, Harvard Club, Harvard Faculty Club, Harvard Higher Educ Student Asn, Intl Comm Asn, Intl Visual Literacy Asn, Nat Educ Asn, Mass Teachers Asn, Nat Comm Asn, Wellesley Col Club. **RESEARCH** Political Communications, Media Relations, New Technologies and Communication. **SELECTED PUBLICATIONS** Auth, "The Changing Dynamics of New Technologie and Media Relations: Perspectives from Journalists and Public Relations Practitioners," IABC Res Foundation, (99): 53-118; ed, Media and American Democracy Curriculum Compendium, Harvard Univ Press, 99; auth, "Education and the Media," The Boston Globe, Aug12/99; auth, "Computer Focused Communication: Challenges for the Contemporary Organization," in The International Journal of Telematics and Informatics, (99); auth, "Congressman Joe Kennedy's withdrawal from Public Office: A Case Study in Media Ethics and Visual Images," in Visual Literacy in an Information Age: Aspects of Vision in an Increasingly Technological Global Community, 99; auth, "Channel One TV Equipment: Reports About its Use in Massachusetts Schools," in Connecting with the Community: Exploring Resources for Visual Learning and Expression, 98; auth, "Participants Provide Mixed Reports About Learning from Channel One," in Journalism and Mass Communication Educator, 98; auth, "Administration Changes Shape," Ed Lines, (90): 5-6; auth, "Barriers to Face: Margaret Marshall on the Importance of Women's Colleges," Regis Today, (94): 15. **CONTACT ADDRESS** Dept Mass Comm, Boston Univ, 640 Commonwealth Ave, Boston, MA 02215-2422.

BARROS, CAROLYN
DISCIPLINE ENGLISH **EDUCATION** Univ TX at Arlington, BA, 76; TX Christian Univ, Med, 78; Univ TX at Dallas, PhD, 84. **CAREER** Assoc prof, Univ TX at Arlington, 96 & asst prof, 90 & 96; Dir, UTA Honors Prog, 95-; assoc dean, asst

dean, asst to the dean, Col Liberal Arts, UTA, 77-90; dept ser, 95-96, ch, Hermann Lect Ser Comt; mem, Fac Search Comt, Rhetoric and Compos Div, Brit Lit Div & Grad Stud Comt; prior dept ser, interim dir, Freshman Engl; ch, Freshman Engl Comt, Hermann Lect Ser Comt, GTA Selection Comt & Comp Acquisition Comt; mem, Fac Search Comt, KA Porter Lect Ser, Fac Adv Comt, Res Enhancement Comt, Rhetoric and Compos Div, Brit Lit Div, Grad Stud Comt, Freshman Engl Comt & Travel Comt; lectr, Sigma Tau Delta Engl Honors Soc; Judge, Freshman Writing Contest; invited lect, Sigma Tau Delta, UTA, 94; Hermann Lecte Ser, UTA, 93; TCJC Cornerstone Prog, NEH Symp, Fort Worth, 91; Class Asn, Tulane Univ, New Orleans, 88; Conf Freshman Yr, Dallas, 87. **HONORS AND AWARDS** UTA Summer Stipend, $3,000, 96; Nat Collegiate Hon Coun Portz Grant, $500; NEH Summer Seminar Grant, 88; NEH Higher Educ Grant, $392,000, 85-87. **MEMBERSHIPS** Nat Collegiate Honors Coun; Great Plains Honors Coun; Cole Conf on Compos and Commun; Soc Lit, Science & Technol; MLA; S Cent MLA; Nat Coun Tchrs Eng; Conf Col Tchrs Eng. **RESEARCH** Rhetoric of Caroline Herschelis autobiography; autobiography of Gertrude Stein. **SELECTED PUBLICATIONS** Auth, Figura, Persona, Dynamis: Autobiography and Change, Biog 15 1, 92; Discourse Topics and the Problem of the Big Text and the Little Text, Readerly/Writerly Texts Vol 3, 95; The Literate Mind: Readers, 3 Vol(s), Dubuque, Kendal Hunt, 90; coauth, The Literate Mind, Second Edition, Dubuque, Kendal Hunt, 90. With Thomas E. Porter and Harry Reeder. **CONTACT ADDRESS** Dept of Eng, Univ of Texas, Arlington, PO Box 19035, Arlington, TX 76019. **EMAIL** barros@utarlg.uta.edu

BARRY, BARBARA R.

PERSONAL Born 06/02/1949, London, England, m, 1984, 2 children **DISCIPLINE** VISUAL AND PERFORMING ARTS **EDUCATION** Univ London Goldsmith's, PhD, 82. **CAREER** Dept Visual Perf Arts, 7 yrs, Clark Univ; fac, 10 yrs, Radcliffe College; Chair, 10 yrs, Longy Sch of Music. **MEMBERSHIPS** SMT; NECMT. **RESEARCH** 19TH Century Music; Beethoven; Mahler. **SELECTED PUBLICATIONS** Auth, Inversional Symmetry in the Magic Flute, Opera J, 97; The Spider's Stratagem: The Motif of Masking, in, Don Giovanni, Opera J, 96; Recycling the End of the Leibquartett: Models Meaning and Propriety, in: Beethoven's Quarter in B-Flat Major Opus 130, J Musicology, 95. **CONTACT ADDRESS** Dept of Visual & Performing Arts, Clark Univ, 950 Main St, Worcester, MA 01610.

BARRY, JACKSON GRANVILLE

PERSONAL Born 11/04/1926, Boston, MA, m, 1956, 1 child **DISCIPLINE** ENGLISH **EDUCATION** Yale Univ, BA, 50; Columbia Univ, MA, 51; Western Reserve Univ, MFA, 62, PhD(drama-aesthet), 63. **CAREER** Instr drama, DeCordova Mus, 53-56; instr, Smith Col, 58-61; asst prof humanities, Univ Miami, 63-64; asst prof drama, Villanova Univ, 64-67; assoc prof theatre arts, State Univ NY, Stony Brook, 67-70; assoc prof to PROF ENGLISH, UNIV MD, COLLEGE PARK, 70-, dir Graduate Studies, 79-84. **HONORS AND AWARDS** Ed bd, Am J of Semiotics. **MEMBERSHIPS** MLA;Medieval and Renaissance Drama Soc; Semiotic Soc Am; Linguistic Soc Am. **RESEARCH** Medieval and renaissance literature; semiotics and cognition. **SELECTED PUBLICATIONS** Auth, Dramatic Structure: The Shaping of Experience, Univ CA, 70; Art, Culture, and the Semiotics of Meaning, St Martin's, 98; articles in: Shakespeare Quart, Ed Theatre J, Language and Style, Ariel, Quart J Speech, Papers on Language and Literature, Am J Semiotics, Poetics Yoday, Interdisciplinary J Germanic Linguistics and Semiotic Analysis. **CONTACT ADDRESS** Dept English, Univ of Maryland, Col Park, 3101 Susquehanna Hall, College Park, MD 20742. **EMAIL** jb19@umail.umd.edu

BARRY, MARILYN H.

PERSONAL Born 02/23/1942, Centralia, WA, m, 1987, 4 children **DISCIPLINE** LITERATURE **EDUCATION** San Diego State Col, BA, 64; Mills Col, MA, 65; Univ Ore, DArts, 79. **CAREER** Teacher, Stafford High Sch, 65-66; instr, Chico State Col, 67-69; adj lectr, Calif State Univ, 78-87; adj instr, Wenatchee Valley Col, 89-94; adj instr, Univ of Alaska, 94; adj instr to prof, Alaska Pacific Univ, 93-. **HONORS AND AWARDS** Outstanding Teaching Awd, APU, 95, 99, 00; Outstanding Serv Awd, APU, 00. **MEMBERSHIPS** NCTE, Alaska Coun of Teachers of English, Am Guild of Organists, Assoc of Teachers of Eng Grammar, Coun on Col Composition. **RESEARCH** Writing pedagogy, Writing for Discourse Communities. **SELECTED PUBLICATIONS** Coauth, "Digging In: Dynamics of Assessing General University Competencies by Portfolio," Portfolio Standard: How Students Can Show Us What They Know and Are Able to Do, ed Bonnie S. Sunstein and Jonathan H. Lovell, Heinemann, (NB: Portsmouth, 00). **CONTACT ADDRESS** Dept Lib Studies, Alaska Pacific Univ, 4101 University Dr, Anchorage, AK 99508. **EMAIL** mbarry@alaskapacific.edu

BARRY, MICHAEL

DISCIPLINE AMERICAN LITERATURE **EDUCATION** Loyola Univ, BA; SUNY Buffalo, PhD. **CAREER** Instr, Turkey; People's Republic of China; asst prof, 94-. **RESEARCH** Relationship of ideology and aesthetics, literary components of liberation struggles. **SELECTED PUBLICATIONS** Pub(s), articles on Robert Penn Warren, John Steinbeck, and James Welch. **CONTACT ADDRESS** Dept of Eng, Univ of Detroit Mercy, 4001 W McNichols Rd, PO BOX 19900, Detroit, MI 48219-0900. **EMAIL** mbarry@libarts.udmercy.edu

BARSAM, RICHARD

PERSONAL Born Los Angeles **DISCIPLINE** FILM STUDIES **EDUCATION** Univ Southern Calif, PhD. **CAREER** Prof; Hunter Col, 94-; past consult, PBS for Films of Persuasion; Amer Film Inst/PBS for America in the Movies; CBS for Leni Riefenstahl & Camera Three prog; consult, Metropolitan Mus Art/J. Paul Getty Mus Proj for Art on Film and Video; Chancellor's staff as Univ dean for Fac and Res, CUNY, 84-88 & Univ dean Exec Search and Eval, 88-91; provost, Pratt Inst, 91-93. **HONORS AND AWARDS** Co-foundeer, baccalaureate and grad prog in Cinema Stud, Richmond Col-CUNY; organized, CUNY Film Fac. **MEMBERSHIPS** Past chem, CUNY Film Fac; exec coun, Soc for Cinema Stud; bd ed, Advisers Hist Amern Cinema; ed bo, Cinema J & adv panels, Nat Endowment for the Humanities; Nat Endowment for the Arts Panel for Support for Young Film Critics; dir, NEH Summer Sem for Cole Teachers in Nonfiction Film and the Realist Aesthet, 81. **SELECTED PUBLICATIONS** Auth, Nonfiction Film: A Critical History, Dutton, 73, rev and expanded ed, Ind UP, 92; The Vision of Robert Flaherty: The Artist as Myth and Filmmaker, IUP, 88; A Peaceable Kingdom: The Shaker Abecedarius, Viking, 78; In the Dark: A Primer for the Movies, Viking, 77; Filmguide to Triumph of the Will, IUP, 75; Nonfiction Film Theory and Criticism, Dutton, 75. **CONTACT ADDRESS** Dept of Film and Media Studies, Hunter Col, CUNY, 695 Park Ave, New York, NY 10021.

BARSKY, ROBERT

DISCIPLINE ENGLISH LITERATURE **EDUCATION** Univ Brandeis; BA; McGill Univ, MA; PhD. **CAREER** Assoc prof, Univ of Western Ontario; assoc ed, Sub-Stance; founder and coed, Discours social/Social Discourse; ed bd, Dialogism. **RESEARCH** Literary theory; legal studies; argumentation; discourse analysis; social discourse theory; sociocriticism; cross-cultural communication; Mikhail Bakhtin; 19th and 20th century literature; refugee studies. **SELECTED PUBLICATIONS** Co-ed, Bakhtin and Otherness, 91; Constructing a Productive Other: Discourse Theory and the Convention Refugee Hearing, John Benjamins, 94; auth, Noam Chomsky and His Milieus, 96; auth, Arguing and Justifying: Assessing Convention Refugee Choices of Moment, motive, and Host Country, 96; Introduction a la theorie litteraire, Quebec, 96; transl, Passion and the Philosopher, (97); Noam Chomsky: A Life of Dissent, MIT, 97; auth, Arguing and Justifying, 98. **CONTACT ADDRESS** Dept of English, Western Ontario Univ, 1151 Richmond St, Suite 2, London, ON, Canada N6A5B8. **EMAIL** rbarsky@atsjulian.uwo.ca

BARTEL, LEE R.

PERSONAL Born 04/04/1948, Steinbach, MB, Canada **DISCIPLINE** MUSIC EDUCATION **EDUCATION** Univ Man, BA, 73, MEd, 84; Brandon Univ, BMus, 75; Univ Ill, PhD, 88. **CAREER** High sch & univ mus tchr, 69-76; prof & mus dept ch, Steinbach Bible Col, 75-85; dir develop, 86-87, assoc prof & ch music education, Univ Toronto, 87-, founder & dir, Can Mus Educ Res Ctr, 89-. **MEMBERSHIPS** Am Educ Res Asn; Can Univ Mus Soc; Int Soc Mus Educ; Mus Educ Nat Conf; Ont Mus Educ Asn. **RESEARCH** Research methods, evaluation, social psychology, choral music, and alternative methods in secondary music. **SELECTED PUBLICATIONS** Coauth, A Guide to Provincial Music Curriculum Documents since 1980, 93; coauth, Get Into Guitar, 73; ed, A College Looks Forward, 87; ed, Research Perspectives on Music Education (monograph ser); ed, Can J Res Mus Educ, 93-. **CONTACT ADDRESS** Music Educ Div, Univ of Toronto, Toronto, ON, Canada M5S 1A1. **EMAIL** lbartel@eps.utoronto.ca

BARTH, J. ROBERT

PERSONAL Born 02/23/1931, Buffalo, NY **DISCIPLINE** ENGLISH **EDUCATION** Bellarmine Col, AB, 54; Fordham Univ, MA, 56; WoodstockCol, STB, 61; STL, 62; Harvard Univ, PhD, 67. **CAREER** Asst prof, Canisius Col, 67-70; asst prof, Harvard Univ, 70-74; assoc prof to prof, 74-88; vis prof, dean, prof, Boston Col, 85-. **HONORS AND AWARDS** Dexter Fel, 67; Howard Mumford Jones Prize, 67; NEH Summer Stipend, 69; ACLS Grant, 70, 76, 84; Harvard Fac Res Grant, 73; Purple Chalk Teaching Award, 81; Curators Publ Award, 88. **MEMBERSHIPS** MLA, Wordsworth-Coleridge Asn, Keats-Shelley Asn, N Am Soc for the Study of Romanticism, Conf of Christianity and Lit, AAUP. **RESEARCH** British Romantic literature, religion and literature. **SELECTED PUBLICATIONS** Auth, Coleridge and Christian Doctrine, Harvard Univ Pr, 69; ed, Religious Perspectives in Faulkner's Fiction: Yoknapatawpha and Beyond, Univ Nore Dame Pr, 72; auth, the Symbolic Imagination: Coleridge and the Romantic Tradition, Princeton Univ Pr, 77; auth, Coleridge and the Power of Love, Univ Mo Pr, 88; coed, Coleridge, Keats, and the Imagination: Romanticism and Adam's Dream, Univ Mo Pr, 90. **CONTACT ADDRESS** Dept English, Boston Col, Chestnut Hill, Chestnut Hill, MA 02467. **EMAIL** robert.barth@bc.edu

BARTLET, M. ELIZABETH C.

DISCIPLINE MUSICOLOGY **EDUCATION** Univ Chicago, PhD. **CAREER** Musicol prof, Duke Univ. **HONORS AND AWARDS** ALCS; NEH; Am Philos Soc fels. **SELECTED PUBLICATIONS** Auth, publ(s) on 18th and 19th century French opera, music during the French Revolution, Rossini's Guillaume Tell, Rameau. **CONTACT ADDRESS** Dept of Music, Duke Univ, Mary Duke Biddle Music Bldg, Durham, NC 27708-0665. **EMAIL** mecb@duke.edu

BARTLETT, CYNTHIA L.

DISCIPLINE ADULT NEUROGENIC COMMUNICATION DISORDERS **EDUCATION** IN Univ, BA, MA; Univ Pittsburgh, PhD. **CAREER** Assoc prof and grad prog dir, Emerson Col. **CONTACT ADDRESS** Dept of Commun Sciences and Disorders, Emerson Col, 216 Tremont St, Boston, MA 02116-1596. **EMAIL** cynthia_barlett@emerson.edu

BARTLETT, LEE

DISCIPLINE CREATIVE WRITING, POETRY AND AMERICAN LITERATURE **EDUCATION** Univ Calif, Berkeley, BA; Univ Calif, Davis, PhD, 79. **CAREER** Instr, Univ Nmex, 81-. **SELECTED PUBLICATIONS** Auth, The Greenhouse Effect, Lords of Language; auth, Kenneth Rexroth/James Laughlin: Selected Letters, W.W. Norton; auth, Letters to Christopher, Black Sparrow Press; auth, The Sun is But a Morning Star: Studies in West Coast Poetry and Poetics, Univ of New Mexico Press; auth, Talking Poetry; Conversations in the Workshop with Contemporary Poets, Univ of New Mexico; auth, William Everson: The Life of Brother Antoninus, New Directions. **CONTACT ADDRESS** Dept of English, Univ of New Mexico, Albuquerque, Albuquerque, NM 87131.

BARTON, GAY

PERSONAL Born Wharton, TX **DISCIPLINE** ENGLISH **EDUCATION** Abilene Christian Col, BA, 68; Abilene Christian Univ, MA, 90; Baylor Univ, PhD, 99. **CAREER** Asst Prof, Abilene Christian Univ, 99-; Editorial Assist, Baylor Univ, 95-98; Teaching Asst, Abilene Christian Univ, 88; Graduate Asst, Abilene Christian Univ, Sept 87-May 88; Secondary Teacher, Nhowe Secondary School, 68-69. **HONORS AND AWARDS** Baylor: Christian Scholar Fel, 95-98; Baylor: Cornelia Smith Graduate Scholarship, 98. **MEMBERSHIPS** Modern Language Association, MLA; Society for the Study of Multi-Ethnic Literature of the United States, MEUS; American Association for Higher Education, AAHE; Conference on Christianity & Literature, CCL; Conference of College Teachers of English, CCTE; **RESEARCH** 20th Century American Women Novelists; Native American Novelists. **SELECTED PUBLICATIONS** Auth, Amativeness, and Even Animality: A Whitman/Chopin Dialogue on Female Sexuality, A Whitman/Chopin Dialogue on Female Sexuality," Journal of the American Studies Association of Texas 27, 96: 1-18; auth, "Chopin, Kate," "Quicksand Years," Song of Prudence," Walt Whitman: An Encyclopedia, edited by J.R. LeMaster and Donald D. Kummings, New York: Garland, 98; auth, "Child Vision in the Fantasy of George MacDonald," In Nursery Realms: Children in the Worlds of Science Fiction, Fantasy, and Horror, edited by Gary Westfahl and George Slusseer, Athens: Univ of Georgia Press, 99; Coauth, A Reader's Guide to the Novels of Louise Erdrich, Co-author, Peter G. Beidler, Columbia, Missouri: Univ of Missouri Press, 99; auth, "Chopin, Kate," American National Biography, edited by John A. Garraty, 20 vol, Cary, North Carolina: Oxford University Press, 99; auth, Family Connections and Characterization in Erdrich's North Dakota Sequence," In Approaches to Teaching the Works of Louise Erdrich, edited by Connie A. Jacobs and James Forthcoming, 00. **CONTACT ADDRESS** Dept English, Abilene Christian Univ, Acu Box 28252, Abilene, TX 79669-0001. **EMAIL** bartong@acu.edu

BARTON, MIKE ALAN

PERSONAL Born 09/30/1940, Wichita, KS, m, 1964, 1 child **DISCIPLINE** THEATRE HISTORY, DRAMATIC LITERATURE **EDUCATION** Kans State Teachers Col, BA, 61, MS, 66; Ind Univ, PhD(theatre hist), 71. **CAREER** Prof actor, New York City, 61-62; instr speech, Kans State Teachers Col, 65-66; instr theatre, Univ Omaha, 66-68; asst, Ind Univ, Bloomington, 68-71; prof Theatre, Drake Univ, 71-. **RESEARCH** Nineteenth century theatre history; film history. **SELECTED PUBLICATIONS** Auth, Silent films: High camp or genuine art, Advance, 11/72; Aline Bernstein, In: Notable American Women, Harvard Univ, 78. **CONTACT ADDRESS** Dept of Theatre Arts, Drake Univ, 2507 University Ave, Des Moines, IA 50311-4505. **EMAIL** mike.barton@drake.edu

BARTOW, CHARLES L.

PERSONAL Born 11/03/1937, Somerville, NJ, m, 1964, 3 children **DISCIPLINE** SPEECH **EDUCATION** Mich State Univ, AB, 58; Princeton Theol Sem, BD, 63; Mich State Univ, MA, 64; NYork Univ, PhD, 71. **CAREER** Asst prof, Princeton Theol Sem, 63-71; asst prof, Mansfield State Univ, 71-74; pastor, Presby Church of Deep Run, 74-80; assoc prof, San Francisco Theol Sem/Grad Theol Union, 80-84; prof, 84-91; prof, Princeton Theol Sem, 91- . **HONORS AND AWARDS** Honors graduate, Mich State Univ; Book of the Year Awd, The Relig Speech Commun Asoc, 80; Book of the Year Awd, The Religious Communication Assoc, 98. **MEMBERSHIPS** Relig

Commun Asoc; Acad of Homiletics; Nat Commun Asoc; Societas Homiletica; Assoc of Practical Theology. **RESEARCH** Rhetorical and performance criticism in Scriptural hermeneutics and preaching; oral interpretation of poetry and Biblical literature; speech arts and liturgical praxis. **SELECTED PUBLICATIONS** Auth, The Preeching Moment: A Guide to Sermon Delivery, 80, 95; auth, Effective Speech Communication in Leading Worship, 88; auth, Sermon Delivery, A Concise Encyclopedia of Preaching, 95; auth, Who Says the Song? Practical Hermeneutics as Humble Performance, Princeton Sem Bull, 96; auth, Just Now: Aimee Semple McPherson's Performance and Preaching of Jesus, J Commun and Relig, 97; auth, God's Human Speech: A Practical Theology of Proclamation, 97; auth, "Sonnet in Remberance of Pan American Flight 103," in The Dawn of Inspiration, (99); auth, "Sonnet in Honor of a Man of God," Princeton Seminary Bulletin, (00). **CONTACT ADDRESS** Princeton Theol Sem, 64 Mercer St, PO Box 821, Princeton, NJ 08542-0803. **EMAIL** charles.bartow@ptsem.edu

BARTSCH, SHADI
PERSONAL Born 03/17/1966, London, England, m, 2000 **DISCIPLINE** LATIN LITERATURE OF THE EARLY EMPIRE, CULTURAL THEORY AND INTERPRETATION, HISTORY OF CLASSICAL RHETORIC, THE ANCIENT NOVEL **EDUCATION** Princeton Univ, BA (summa cum laude), 87; Harvard Univ, in PhD prog, 87-89, then as exchange scholar at the Univ CA, Berkeley, 88-89; Univ CA, Berkeley, MA, Latin, 89, PhD (Classics), 91. **CAREER** Acting asst prof, Classics and Rhetoric, Univ CA, Berkeley, 91-92, asst prof, 92-95, assoc prof, 95-98; vis assoc prof, Classics, Univ Chicago, Jan-June, 98, prof, Classics and the Committee on the History of Culture, Univ Chicago, July 98-; ed bd, Representations, 97-98; ed bd, Classical Philology, 98-; editor-in-chief, Classical Philology, 00-. **HONORS AND AWARDS** Mellon fel in the Humanities, Harvard Univ, 87-89; Berkeley fel, Univ CA, Berkeley, 89-91; Richardson Prize for Trans into Latin, Univ CA, Berkeley, 90; Honorary P S Allen Junior Res fel, Corpus Christi, Oxford, 90; Humanities Res fel, Univ CA, Berkeley, 95-96; George Walsh Memorial Lecturer, Univ Chicago, 98; Jackson Knight Lecturer, Exeter 00; Quantrell Awd, Chicago, 00; ACLS Fellow, 99-00. **MEMBERSHIPS** APA; adv committee for APA 1998; adv committee for ICAN 2000; coordinator, Workshop on Ancient Societies, Univ Chicago, 98-99. **SELECTED PUBLICATIONS** Auth, Decoding the Ancient Novel: The Reader and the Role of Description in Heliodorus and Achilles Tatius, Princeton Univ Press, 89; Actors in the Audience: Theatricality and Doublespeak from Nero to Hadrian, Harvard Univ Press, 94; Ideology in Cold Blood: A Reading of Lubcan's Civil War, Harvard Univ Press, 98; review, V Rudich, Dissidence and Literature under Nero: The Prince of Rhetoricization, in the Times Literary Supp, March 27, 98; Ars and the Man: The Politics of Art in Vergil's Aeneid, Classical Philology, forthcoming 98; The Philosopher as Narcissus: Knowing Oneself in Classical Antiquity, in Robert S Nelson, ed, Seeing as Others Saw: Visuality Before and Beyond the Renaissance, Cambridge Univ Press, 00; ed with Tom Sloan, Oxford Encyclopedia of Rhetoric, Oxford Univ Press, forthcoming; auth, The Cult of the Trope: Hermeneutics and the Classics in the Middle Ages, Princeton Univ Press, forthcoming; The Mirror of Philosophy: Specularity, Sexuality, and Self-Knowledge in the Roman Empire, forthcoming; numerous other articles, reviews, papers, and publications. **CONTACT ADDRESS** Dept of Classics, Univ of Chicago, 1010 E 59th St, Chicago, IL 60637. **EMAIL** sbartsch@midway.uchicago.edu

BARUCH, ELAINE HOFFMAN
PERSONAL Born New York, NY, 1 child **DISCIPLINE** ENGLISH, WOMEN'S STUDIES **EDUCATION** Queens Col, NYork, BA, 54; Radcliffe Col, MAT, 55; Columbia Univ, PhD(English, comp lit), 66. **CAREER** Lectr English, Queens Col, NY, 60-62 from instr to asst prof, 67-77, Assoc Prof English to prof emer, York Col, NY, 78-, Gen ed, Women's Studies Ser, Everett/Edwards Cassette Curric, 74-. **MEMBERSHIPS** MLA. **RESEARCH** Seventeenth century. **SELECTED PUBLICATIONS CONTACT ADDRESS** Dept of English, York Col, CUNY, 150-14 Jamaica Ave, Jamaica, NY 11451.

BARUSHOK, JAMES WILLIAM
PERSONAL Born 02/26/1929, Chicago, IL, m, 1952, 3 children **DISCIPLINE** SPEECH **EDUCATION** Northwestern Univ, BA, 51, MA, 52; Mich State Univ, PhD(theatre), 66. **CAREER** Instr speech, Wright Jr Col, 54-56; from instr to assoc prof, Univ Maine, 56-68; Chmn Dept Speech, Northeastern Ill Univ, 68-, Maine fine arts rep, New Eng Ctr Continuing Educ, 66-68; Kellog Found fel, 81-82. **MEMBERSHIPS** Speech Commun Asn; Am Educ Theatre Asn; Am Acad Polit & Soc Sci. **RESEARCH** History of theatre; sociology of the community theatre; dramatic theory. **SELECTED PUBLICATIONS** auth, Lost prodigy: community theatre, Players, 9/69. **CONTACT ADDRESS** Dept of Speech, Northeastern Illinois Univ, 5500 N St Louis Ave, Chicago, IL 60625-4625.

BASHIR, ANTHONY S.
DISCIPLINE ADULT NEUROGENIC COMMUNICATION DISORDERS **EDUCATION** Northwestern Univ, BS, MS, PhD. **CAREER** Com, Emerson Col. **HONORS AND AWARDS** Fel, Am Speech-Lang-Hearing Asn. **SELECTED PUBLICATIONS** Areas: Learning Disabilities and Lang Disorders. **CONTACT ADDRESS** Emerson Col, 100 Beacon Street, Boston, MA 02116-1596.

BASS, EBEN E.
PERSONAL Born 06/12/1924, Willimantic, CT, m, 1957 **DISCIPLINE** ENGLISH **EDUCATION** Univ CT, BA, 48, MA, 50; Univ Pittsburgh, PhD(English), 61. **CAREER** Asst instr English, OH State Univ, 54-56; from asst prof to prof, Geneva Col, 56-72, Prof English & Chmn Dept, Slippery Rock State Col, 72-. **MEMBERSHIPS** MLA; NCTE. **RESEARCH** Henry James and modern novel; English Romantic and Victorian writers. **SELECTED PUBLICATIONS** Auth, Dramatic scene and The Awkward Age, PMLA, 3/64; The Verbal Failure of Lord Jim, Col English, 3/65; The Fourth Element in Ode to the West Wind, Papers Lang & Lit, fall 67; The Languages of 'Losing Battles', Studies in Am Fiction, Vol 21, 93. **CONTACT ADDRESS** Dept of English, Slippery Rock Univ of Pennsylvania, Slippery Rock, PA 16057.

BASSAN, MAURICE
PERSONAL Born 04/22/1929, New York, NY, m, 1960, 2 children **DISCIPLINE** AMERICAN LITERATURE **EDUCATION** New York Univ, BA, 51, MA, 52; Univ CA, Berkeley, PhD, 61. **CAREER** Instr English, Univ AZ, 58-60 & Univ NC, 61-63; from asst prof to assoc prof, 63-72, prof eng, San Francisco State Univ, 72, Lectr, Univ CA, Exten, Japan, 53-54; asst, Univ Calif, Berkeley, 55-58. **HONORS AND AWARDS** Fulbright lectr, Univ Valladolid, Spain, 67-68. **MEMBERSHIPS** MLA; Am Studies Asn; Hawthorne Soc; Stephen Crane Soc. **RESEARCH** Stephen Crane; late 19th century Am fiction; Am poetic traditions. **SELECTED PUBLICATIONS** Auth, Chaucer's Cursed Monk, Mediaeval Studies, 62; Flannery O'Connor's way, Renascence, 63; Some new perspectives on Stephen Crane's fiction, Studia Neophilologica, 63; ed, Stephen Crane's Maggie: Text and Context, Wadsworth, 66; Stephen Crane: A Collection of Critical Essays, Prentice-Hall, 67; auth, Hawthorne's Son, Ohio State Univ, 69; The True West Tales of Sam Shepard and Stephen Crane, American Literary Realism 28, 96. **CONTACT ADDRESS** Dept of Eng, San Francisco State Univ, 1600 Holloway Ave, San Francisco, CA 94132-1740. **EMAIL** mbasson@sfsu.edu

BASSETT, CHARLES WALKER
PERSONAL Born 07/07/1932, Aberdeen, SD, m, 1956, 2 children **DISCIPLINE** AMERICAN LITERATURE & STUDIES **EDUCATION** Univ SDak, AB, 54, MA, 56; Univ Kans, PhD(-English), 64. **CAREER** From instr to asst prof English, Univ Pa, 64-69; asst prof, 69-74, assoc prof, 74-80, prof English, Colby Col, 80-, chrm, dept of English, 87-89, Colby Col, dir AM studies, 71-96, Univ Pa fac res grant, 68; humanities grants, Colby Col, 78 & 79, Mellon grant, 79 & 83. **HONORS AND AWARDS** Mary C. Turpie Awd, Am Stud Asn; Senior Class Teaching Awd, 93, 97. **MEMBERSHIPS** Am Studies Asn; MLA. **RESEARCH** American fiction; American history. **SELECTED PUBLICATIONS** Auth, Katahdin, Wachusett, and Kilimanjaro: The symbolic mountains of Thoreau and Hemingway, Thoreau J, 4/71; O'Hara's roots (43 part ser), weekly in Pottsville Republican, Pa, 71-72; Undergraduate and graduate American studies programs in the US: A survey, Am Quart, 8/75; Naturalism revisited: The case of John O'Hara, Colby Libr Quart, 12/75; John O'Hara and The Noble Experiment: The use of alcohol in Appointment in Samarra, winter 78-79, John O'Hara: Irishman and American, 8/79 & O'Hara and history, 12/81, John O'Hara J; John O'Hara, In: Vol IX, Part 2, Dict of Literary Biography, 81. **CONTACT ADDRESS** Dept of English, Colby Col, 150 Mayflower Hill, Waterville, ME 04901-4799. **EMAIL** cwbasset@colby.edu

BASSETT, JOHN E.
PERSONAL Born 05/12/1942, Washington, DC, m, 1964, 2 children **DISCIPLINE** ENGLISH **EDUCATION** Ohio Wesleyan Univ, BA 63, MA 66; Col of Rochester, PhD 70. **CAREER** Wayne State Univ, asst prof, assoc prof, 70-84; N Carolina State Univ, prof, Dept hd, 84-93; Case Western Reserve Univ, prof, dean, 93-00; Pres, Clark Univ, 00-. **MEMBERSHIPS** MLA; SAMLA; SSSL; Phi Beta Kappa Assoc. **RESEARCH** American Lit; Faulkner; Twain; Sherwood Anderson. **SELECTED PUBLICATIONS** Auth, Wherefore This Southern Literature?, A Critical Tradition, 97; auth, Harlem in Review: The Critical Reaction to Black Amer Writers, 1920-1939, 1992; auth, A Heart of Ideality in My Realism, and other essays on Howells and Twain, 91; auth, Visions and Revisions, Essays on Faulkner, 89. **CONTACT ADDRESS** Clark Univ, Worcester, MA 01610. **EMAIL** jbassett@clarku.edu

BASWELL, CHRISTOPHER C.
DISCIPLINE ENGLISH **EDUCATION** Oberlin Col, BA, 75; Yale Univ, PhD, 83. **CAREER** Maitre asst, Univ Geneva, 81-84; asst prof to prof, Barnard Col, 84-00; prof, UCLA, 00-. **HONORS AND AWARDS** Am Coun of Learned Soc Fel, 87; NEH Fel, 88; Fel, Nat Humanities Ctr, 93-94; Beatrice White Prize of the English Asn, 98. **MEMBERSHIPS** MLA; Medieval Acad of Am. **RESEARCH** Classical tradition in the Middle Ages and Renaissance; Culture of the book; Dynastic and imperial narrative; Paleography and codicology; Contemporary poetry. **SELECTED PUBLICATIONS** Auth, "Talking Back to the Text: Marginal Voices in Medieval Secular Literature," in The Uses of Manuscripts in Literary Studies: Essays in Memory of Judson Boyce Allen, (Kalamazoo, 92), 121-160; auth, "Men in the Roman d'Eneas: The Construction of Empire," in Medieval Masculinities: Regarding Men in the Middle Ages, (Univ Minn Press, 94), 149-168; auth, Virgil in Medieval England: Figuring the "Aeneid" from the Twelfth Century to Chaucer, Cambridge Univ Press, 95; auth, "Troy Book : How Lydgate Translates Chaucer into Latin," in Translation Theory and Practice in the Middle Ages, (Kalamazoo, 97), 215-237; co-ed, The Longman anthology of British Literature, Addison Wesley Longman, 98; auth, "Latiitas," in Cambridge History of Medieval English Literature, (Cambridge Univ Press, 99), 122-151; auth, "Marvels of translation and crises of transition in the Romances of Antiquity," in The Cambridge Companion to Medieval Romance, (Cambridge Univ Press, 00), 29-44. **CONTACT ADDRESS** Dept English, Univ of California, Los Angeles, 2225 Rolfe, Box 951530, Los Angeles, CA 90095-1530. **EMAIL** baswell@humnet.ucla.edu

BATE, WALTER JACKSON
PERSONAL Born 05/22/1918, Mankato, MN **DISCIPLINE** ENGLISH **EDUCATION** Harvard Univ, AB, 39, AM, 40, PhD, 42. **CAREER** From asst prof to prof English, 46-62, Lowell prof, 62-79, Kingsley Porter Univ Prof Humanities, Harvard Univ, 79-. **HONORS AND AWARDS** Christian Gauss Prizes, 56, 64 & 70; Pulitzer Prize, 64 & 78; Nat Book Awd, 78; littd, in univ, 69, merrimac col, 70, univ chicago, 73; lhd, boston col, 71, fordham univ, 78. **MEMBERSHIPS** Am Acad Arts & Sci; Am Philos Soc. **RESEARCH** Eighteenth and 19th century English literature. **SELECTED PUBLICATIONS** Auth, Criticism: Major Texts, Harcourt, 52; Achievement of Samuel Johnson, Oxford Univ, 55; Prefaces to Criticism, Doubleday, 59; Yale Edition of Johnson, Vols 2-5, Yale Univ, 60-68; John Keats, Harvard Univ, 68; Coleridge, Macmillan, 68; The Burden of the Past and the English Poet, Harvard Univ,0; Samuel Johnson, Harcourt, 77. **CONTACT ADDRESS** Harvard Univ, 3 Warren House, Cambridge, MA 02138.

BATES, BENJAMIN J.
PERSONAL Born 01/25/1954, Chillicothee, OH, s **DISCIPLINE** COMMUNICATIONS **EDUCATION** Pomona Col, BA, 76; Univ of Wis, Madison, MS, 78; Univ of Wis, Stevens Point, MA, 81; Univ of Mich, PhD, 86. **CAREER** Teaching/res asst, Univ of Wis, Madison, 76-78; grad asst, Univ of Wis, Stevens Point, 80-81; teaching/res asst, Univ of Mich, 81-85; instr, Rutgers Univ, 85-86; lectr, Univ of Calif, Santa Barbara, 86-88; visiting asst prof, Mich State Univ, 88-89; visiting lectr, The Chinese Univ of Hong Kong, 92-93; asst prof, Texas Tech Univ, 89-94; dir, Inst for Commun Res, 89-94; ASST PROF, 94-96, ASSOC PROF, 96-, UNIV OF TENN, KNOXVILLE. **HONORS AND AWARDS** Col of Commun Fac Res Awd, Univ of Tenn, 95-96; Awd for Acad Excellence, Univ of Wis, Stevens Point, 81; Grant, NEC Infor Industry Univ Fac Grant Prog, 89, 90, 91, 92, 93, & 94; Leo Burnet Scholar Awd, Univ of Mich, 82; Fac Res Grant, Univ of Calif, Santa Barbara, 87; Fac Grant, Nat Cable Television Asn, 92; Fac Grant for 1995 Global Infor Infrastructure ComForum, 95; Fac Grant for IEC Commun Forum at Supercomm 98, IEC Infor Industry Fac Grant Prog, 98; Res Grant, Nat Asn of Broadcasters, 96; Fac Grant, Int Radio and Television Soc Found, 97. **RESEARCH** Telecom systems; economics; policy; new media systems. **SELECTED PUBLICATIONS** Coauth, The New World of Democratic Telecommunications: FidoNet as an Example of Horizontal Information Networks, Southwestern Mass Commun J, 93; coauth, Bypassing the Gateways: International News in the CNN WORLD REPORT, Commun Res Reports, 93; coauth, Political Distrust in Hong Kong: News Media Use and Political Beliefs Regarding the 1997 Transition, Asian J of Commun, 95; coauth, The Economic Basis for Radio Deregulation, J of Media Economics, forthcoming; coauth, Creating New Relations: The Internet in Central and Eastern Europe, Cyberimperialism: Global Relations in the New Electronic Frontier, Greenwood, forthcoming; auth, Concentration in Local Television Markets, J of Media Economics, 93; auth, Learning from the Evolution of Telecommunications in the Developed World, Telecommun and Development in China, Hampton Press, 97; auth, Valuation of Media Properties, Media Economics: A Reader, Lawrence Erlbaum Assocs, 93; auth, Introduction: Special Issue on the Economic Impact of the 1996 Telecommunications Act, J of Media Economics, 98; auth, Valuation of Media Properties, Media Economics: A Reader, Second Edition, Lawrence Erlbaum Assocs, forthcoming. **CONTACT ADDRESS** Dept of Broadcasting, College of Communications, Univ of Tennessee, Knoxville, 333 Communications, Knoxville, TN 37996-0333. **EMAIL** bjbates@utk.edu

BATES, MILTON JAMES
PERSONAL Born 06/04/1945, Warrensburg, MO, m, 1972, 2 children **DISCIPLINE** ENGLISH LITERATURE **EDUCATION** St. Louis Univ, BA, 68; Univ of Calif, Berkeley, MA, 72, PhD, 77. **CAREER** Asst prof, Eng, Williams Col, 75-81; asst prof, Eng, Marquette Univ, 81-86; assoc prof, Marquette Univ, 86-90; Prof, Marquette Univ, 91-. **HONORS AND AWARDS** Am Coun of Learned Soc Fel, 80, 86; Nat Endowment for the Hum Summer Stipend, 85; Guggenheim Fel, 89; Fulbright Dist Lectureship, 00. **MEMBERSHIPS** Wallace Ste-

vens Soc. **RESEARCH** Wallace Stevens; William Faulkner; Vietnam War literature; American nature writing. **SELECTED PUBLICATIONS** auth, Wallace Stevens: A Mythology of Self, Univ of Calif Pr, 85; ed, Sur Plusieurs Beaux Sujects: Wallace Stevens' Commonplace Book, Stanford Univ Pr, 89; ed, Opus Posthumous, Alfred A. Knopf, 89; auth, The Wars We Took to Vietnam: Cultural Conflict and Storytelling, Univ of Calif Pr, 96. **CONTACT ADDRESS** Dept of English, Marquette Univ, PO Box 1881, Milwaukee, WI 53201-1881. **EMAIL** Milton.Bates@marquette.edu

BATES, SCOTT

PERSONAL Born 06/13/1923, Evanston, IL, m, 1948, 4 children **DISCIPLINE** FRENCH, FILM **EDUCATION** Carleton Col, BA, 47; Univ Wis, MA, 48, PhD(French), 54. **CAREER** Asst prof, 54-64, Prof French Lang & Lit, Univ of The South, 64-, Ed, Ecol Papers, 70-72. **RESEARCH** Modern French poetry; modern English and American poetry; Film and Theatre. **SELECTED PUBLICATIONS** Auth, Guillaume Apollinaire, Twayne, 67 Rev. ed., 89; ed, Poems of War Resistance, Grossman, 69; Petit glossaire des mots libres d'Apollinaire, Sewanee, 75; The ABC of Radical Ecology, Highlander, 82; Lupo's Fables, 83; Merry Greenpeace, 95; Songs for the Queen of the Animals, 97; The Zyx of Political Sex, Highlander, 99; Ed, Poems of Protect for the Year, 00, War Resisters League, 00. **CONTACT ADDRESS** Dept of Lang & Lit, Univ of the South, P O Box 1263, Sewanee, TN 37383-1000. **EMAIL** sbates@seraphl.sewanee.edu

BATESON, MARY CATHERINE

PERSONAL Born 12/08/1939, New York, NY, m, 1960, 1 child **DISCIPLINE** ANTHROPOLOGY, ENGLISH **EDUCATION** Radcliffe Col, BA, 60; Harvard Univ, PhD, 63. **CAREER** Instr, Harvard Univ, 63-66; asst to assoc prof, Ateneo de Manila Univ, 66-68; sr res fel, Brandeis Univ, 68-69; assoc prof, Northeastern Univ, 69-71; vis lectr, Univ Tehran, 72-74; vis prof, Northeastern Univ, 74-75; prof, Damavand Col, 75-77; dean of social sci and humanities, Univ Northern Iran, 77-79; vis scholar, Harvard Univ, 79-80; prof, Amherst Col, 80-86; dean of fac, Amherst Col, 80-83; vis prof, Spelman Col, 96; Guggenheim fel, 87-88, fieldwork in Israel, 89, Clarence J. Robinson prof, George Mason Univ, 87- ; schlr-in-res, Radcliffe Inst for Adv Studies, Harvard Univ, 00-01. **MEMBERSHIPS** Amer Anthrop Asn; Lindisfarne Asn; Authors Guild, PEN. **SELECTED PUBLICATIONS** Co-ed, Approaches to Semiotics: Indiana University Conference on Paralinguistics and Kinesics, Moulton, 64; auth, Structural Continuity in Poetry: A Linguistic Study of Five Pre-Islamic Odes, Moulton, 70; auth, Our Own Metaphor: A Personal Account of a Conference on the Effects of Conscious Purpose on Human Adaptation, Knopf, 72, 2nd ed, Smithsonian Pr Paperback, 91; auth, With a Daughter's Eye: A Memoir of Margaret Mead and Gregory Bateson, Morrow, 84; co-auth, Angels Fear: Towards an Epistemology of the Sacred, Macmillan, 87; co-auth, Thinking AIDS, Addison-Wesley, 88; auth, Composing a Life, Atlantic Monthly Pr, 89; auth, Peripheral Visions: Learning Along the Way, HarperCollins, 94; auth, Full Circles, Overlaping Lives: Culture and Generation in Transition, Random House, 00. **CONTACT ADDRESS** Dept of Anthrop & English, George Mason Univ, Fairfax, 201 East Bldg, Fairfax, VA 22030-4444. **EMAIL** mcatb@attglobal.net

BATTEIGER, RICHARD P.

DISCIPLINE EARLY BRITISH LITERATURE **EDUCATION** Univ Fla, PhD, 70. **CAREER** Engl, Okla St Univ. **HONORS AND AWARDS** Prog dir, Composition & Rhetoric. **SELECTED PUBLICATIONS** Area: whether direct instruction in grammar improves student writing. **CONTACT ADDRESS** Oklahoma State Univ, Stillwater, 101 Whitehurst Hall, Stillwater, OK 74078.

BATTERSBY, JAMES L.

PERSONAL Born 08/24/1936, Pawtucket, RI, m, 1990, 1 child **DISCIPLINE** ENGLISH LITERATURE, CRITICAL THEORY **EDUCATION** Univ VT, BSEd, 61; Cornell Univ, MA, 62, PhD(English lit), 65. **CAREER** Asst prof English lit, Univ CA, Berkeley, 65-70; assoc prof, 70-82, Prof English, OH State Univ, 82-. **HONORS AND AWARDS** Phi Beta Kappa; Phi Kappa Phi; Kappa Delta Pi; Woodrow Wilson Fel; Samuel S. Fels Fel; Kidder Medal. **MEMBERSHIPS** MLA; Am Soc 18th Century Studies; Midwest Mod Lang Asn. **RESEARCH** Samuel Johnson; 18th century English literature; modern critical theory. **SELECTED PUBLICATIONS** Auth, Typical Folly: Evaluating Student Performance in Higher Education, Nat Coun Teachers English, 73; auth, Rational Praise and natural Lamentation: Johnson, Lycides and Principles of Criticism, 80; auth, Elder Olson: An Annotated Bibliography, 83; auth, Paradigms Regained: Pluralism and the Practice of Criticism, 91; auth, Reason and the Nature of Texts, 96. **CONTACT ADDRESS** Dept of English, Ohio State Univ, Columbus, Columbus, OH 43210. **EMAIL** batterj@msn.com

BATTESTIN, MARTIN CAREY

PERSONAL Born 03/25/1930, New York, NY, m, 1952, 2 children **DISCIPLINE** ENGLISH LITERATURE **EDUCATION** Princeton Univ, BA, 52, PhD(English), 58. **CAREER** From instr to asst prof English, Wesleyan Univ, 56-61; from asst prof to prof, 61-75, William R Kenan, Jr Prof English, Univ VA, 75-, Am Coun Learned Soc fel, 60-61 & 67; Guggenheim fel, 64-65; adv ed, Eighteenth Century Studies & Studies in the Novel, 67-; vis prof, Rice Univ, 67-68; adv ed, Studies in English Lit, 68-; hon res fel, Univ Col, Univ London, 70-71; Sesquicentennial res fel, Univ VA, 70-71; Coun Humanities sr fel, Princeton Univ, 71; assoc Clare Hall, Cambridge Univ, 72; Am Coun Learned Socs fel, 72; Nat Endowment for Humanities fel, 75 & 79; mem, Ctr Advan Studies, Univ VA, 75-76. **MEMBERSHIPS** MLA; Acad Lit Studies; Am Soc 18th Century Studies; Int Asn Univ Prof English; Johnsonians. **RESEARCH** Eighteenth century literature and the arts: The British novel, especially Henry Fielding. **SELECTED PUBLICATIONS** Auth, The Moral Basis of Fielding's Art, Wesleyan Univ, 59; ed, Fielding's Joseph Andrews and Shamela, Houghton, 61; Fielding's Joseph Andrews, Clarendon & Wesleyan Univ, 67; auth, Henry Fielding, In: New Cambridge Bibliography of English Literature, Cambridge Univ, 71; co-ed, Fielding's Tom Jones, Clarendon & Wesleyan Univ, 74; auth, The Providence of Wit: Aspects of Form in Augustan Literature and the Arts, Clarendon, 74; ed, Fielding's Amelia, Clarendon & Wesleyan Univ, 82; ed., British Novelists, 1660-1800, Gale Research Co. 85; ed., Henry Fielding: A Life, Routledge, 89; ed., New Essays by Fielding: His Contributions to the Craftsman (1734-39) and Other Early Journalism, Univ Press, Virginia, 89; ed., with C.T. Probyn, Correspondence of Henry and Sarah Fielding, Clarendon, 93; ed., Augustan Subjects: Essays in Honor of martin C. Battestin (Newark: Univ of Delaware Press, 97; auth, New Essays by Fielding: His Contributions to the Craftsman (1734-39) and Other Early Journalism, Univ Press of Virginia, 89. **CONTACT ADDRESS** Dept of English, Univ of Virginia, 1832 Westview Rd., Charlottesville, VA 22903. **EMAIL** mcb9g@virginia.edu

BAUCOM, IAN

DISCIPLINE ENGLISH LITERATURE **EDUCATION** Duke Univ, PhD. **CAREER** Prof, Duke Univ. **RESEARCH** Twentieth century Brit Lit and Cult; African and Black Atlantic lit(s). **SELECTED PUBLICATIONS** Auth, publ(s) on colonial and postmodern nostalgia; theories of nationhood; postimperial melancholy in Research in African lit; mod fiction. **CONTACT ADDRESS** Eng Dept, Duke Univ, Durham, NC 27706.

BAUER, MARGARET D.

PERSONAL Born 02/24/1963, Franklin, LA, d **DISCIPLINE** ENGLISH **EDUCATION** La State Univ, BA, 85; Univ Southwestern La, MA, 87; Univ Tenn, PhD, 93. **CAREER** Vis asst prof, Texas A & M Univ, 93-95; vis asst prof, Wabash Col, 95-96; asst prof, East Carolina Univ, 96-. **MEMBERSHIPS** MLA, SAMLA, SSSL. **RESEARCH** Southern literature; American literature; African-American literature; women's literature. **SELECTED PUBLICATIONS** Auth, " 'Put your heart in the land': A Intertextual Reading of Gone with the Wind and Barren Ground," Ellen Glasgow: New Perspectives, ed Dorothy M. Scura, Tenn Studies in Literature Series, Knoxville: Univ of Tenn Press (95): 162-82; auth, "Ellen Gilchrist's False Eden: The New Orleans Stories of In the Land of Dreamy Dreams," Xavier Rev, 16 (96): 88-107; auth, "Armand Aubigny, Still Passing After All These Years: The Narrative Voice and Historical Context of 'Desiree's Baby'," Critical Essays on Kate Chopin, ed Alica Hall Petry, New York: Hall (96): 161-83; auth, auth, "Ishmael's Reading of The Great White Whale: A Prophecy of the Second Coming," Logos 1.4 (98): 145-77; auth, " 'I have sinned in that I have betrayed the innocent blood': Quentin's Recognition of His Guilt," Southern Lit J, 32.1 (99); auth, "When a Convent Seems the Only Viable Choice: Questionable Callings in Stories by Alice Dunbar-Nelson, Alice Walker, and Louise Erdich," Critical Essays on Alice Walker, ed Ikenna Dieke, New York: Greenwood (999): 45-54; auth, The Fiction of Ellen Gilchrist, Gainesville: Univ Press of Fla (99). **CONTACT ADDRESS** Dept English, East Carolina Univ, 1000 E 5th St, Greenville, NC 27858-2502. **EMAIL** BauerM@mail.ecu.edu

BAUER, OTTO FRANK

PERSONAL Born 12/01/1931, Elgin, IL, m, 1956, 2 children **DISCIPLINE** COMMUNICATION, SEMANTICS **EDUCATION** Northwestern Univ, BS, 53, MA, 55, PhD, 59. **CAREER** From instr to asst prof English, US Air Force Acad, 59-61; from instr to prof speech, 61-71, dir grad admis & fels, 65-69, asst dean grad sch, 67-69, asst vpres, 70-71, Bowling Green State Univ; vchancellor, Univ Wis, Parkside, 71-76, actg chancellor, 74-75, prof commun, 71-79; vchancellor acad affairs, 79-94, prof commun, 78-, vchancellor emeritus, 95, Univ Neb, Omaha; Midwest Forensic Asn res grant, 66-67; Am Coun Educ fel, Univ Calif, Berkeley, 69-70; spec asst to chancellor & vis prof commun arts, Univ Wis, Madison, 76-77. **MEMBERSHIPS** Am Forensic Asn; Speech Commun Asn. **RESEARCH** Semantics; debate; political campaigning. **SELECTED PUBLICATIONS** Auth, Fundamentals of Debate: Theory and Practice, Scott, 66; art, Student trust at Berkeley, Educ Rec, 71; art, Relational Abstracting and the Structural Differential, Research Designs in General Semantics, Gordon & Breach, 72; art, The Early Debates, Commun Asn Pac, 7/77; art, State Government Trust of Higher Education in Wisconsin, fall 79; auth, Lower Moments in Higher Education, Rockbrook Press, 97. **CONTACT ADDRESS** Dept of Communications, 6001 Dodge St, Omaha, NE 68182-0002. **EMAIL** obauer@cwis.unomaha.edu

BAUER, RALPH R.

PERSONAL Born 08/06/1965, Nuremberg, Germany **DISCIPLINE** ENGLISH, LITERATURE **EDUCATION** Univ Erlangen, BA, 91; Mich St, MA, 93; PhD, 97. **CAREER** Instr, Mich St, 92-97; asst prof, Yale, 97-98; asst prof, Univ Maryland, 98-. **HONORS AND AWARDS** Mich State Univ, Fel, 95; John Carter Brown Lib, Fel, 97; Univ Maryland, Fel, 00; Richard Beale Davis Prize for Best Article, Early Am Lit, 95. **MEMBERSHIPS** SEA; MLA; ASA. **RESEARCH** Literature of the early Americas. **SELECTED PUBLICATIONS** Auth, "Imperial History, Captivity, and Creole Identity in Francisco Nunez de Pineda y Bascundn's Cautiverio Feliz," Col Lat Am Rev (98); auth, "The Emerson/Nietzsche Connection in Europe, 1920-1990," ESQ (98); auth, "Creole Identities in Colonial Space: Mary White Rowlandson and Francisco Nunez de Pineda y Bascundn" Am Lit (97); guest ed, Locations of Culture: Identity, Home, Theory, Cent Rev (98); auth, "John Eliot, the Praying Indian and the Rhetoric of a New England Errand," Zeitschrift fur Anglistik und Amerikanistik (96); auth, "Between Repression and Transgression: Rousseau's Confessions and Charles Brockden Brown's Wieland," ATQ (96); auth, "Millennium's Darker Side: the Missionary Utopias of Franciscan New Spain and Puritan New England," in Finding Colonial Americas, eds. Carla Mulford and David Shieds (NJ: Univ Del Press, 01); auth, "Criticism on the Boundary: Postcoloniality and the 'Worlding' of Literature" Cent Rev (98); auth, The Principle End of the Plantation': The Praying Indian and the Politics of a New England Colonial Identity, in The American Nation, National Identity, Nationalism, ed. Knud Krakau, Stud in North Am (97). **CONTACT ADDRESS** Eng Dept., Univ of Maryland, Col Park, College Park, MD 20742. **EMAIL** rb227@umail.umd.edu

BAUERLEIN, MARK

DISCIPLINE ENGLISH LANGUAGE AND LITERATURE **EDUCATION** Univ Calif Los Angles, PhD, 88. **CAREER** Prof **RESEARCH** 19th-century American literature; critical theory. **SELECTED PUBLICATIONS** Auth, Literary Criticism: An Autopsy; The Pragmatic Mind: Explorations in the Psychology of Belief; Whitman and the American Idiom. **CONTACT ADDRESS** English Dept, Emory Univ, 1380 Oxford Rd NE, Atlanta, GA 30322-1950. **EMAIL** engmb@emory.edu

BAULAND, PETER MAX

PERSONAL Born 12/19/1932, Ulm, Germany, m, 1961, 2 children **DISCIPLINE** ENGLISH, DRAMA, FILM **EDUCATION** Univ Pa, BA, 53, MA, 55, PhD, 64. **CAREER** Instr English, Lafayette Col, 57-58; from instr to asst prof, Drexel Inst, 59-64; asst prof, 64-69, chmn comp lit, 70-71, assoc prof English, Univ Mich, Ann Arbor, 69-, NEH fel, 69; Rackham res grant, 69, fac res fel, 77; Fulbright lectr & vis prof drama, Univ Munich, 71-72 & 79-80. **MEMBERSHIPS** Midwest Mod Lang Asn. **RESEARCH** Modern drama; film; comparative literature, especially German and English. **SELECTED PUBLICATIONS** Auth, The Hooded Eagle: Modern German Drama on the New York Stage, Syracuse Univ, 68; co-ed, The Tradition of the Theatre, Allyn & Bacon, 71; auth, chap, In: Modernes Amerikanisches Drama/Modern American Drama, Vandenhoeck & Ruprechet, for Univ Tubingen, Gottingen & Zurich, 73; transl, The judge's wife(novella), In: The Little Comedy and Other Stories, Ungar, 78; auth & transl, Gerhart Hauptmann's Before Daybreak: A Translation and an Introduction, Univ NC, 78. **CONTACT ADDRESS** Dept of English, Univ of Michigan, Ann Arbor, 505 S State St, Ann Arbor, MI 48109-1003. **EMAIL** pbauland@umich.edu

BAUMBACH, JONATHAN

PERSONAL Born 07/05/1933, New York, NY, d, 4 children **DISCIPLINE** ENGLISH, FILM STUDIES **EDUCATION** Brooklyn Col, AB, 55; Columbia Univ, MFA, 56; Stanford Univ, PhD(English & Am lit), 61. **CAREER** Asst prof English, Ohio State Univ, 61-64; dir writing, NY Univ, 64-66; assoc prof, 66-70, Prof English, Brooklyn Col, 71-, Mem bd dirs, Teachers & Writers Collaborative, 66-; vis prof English, Tufts Univ, 70-71; movie critic, Partisan Rev, 73-; Guggenheim fel, 78; vis prof creative writing, Univ Wash, Seattle, 78. **HONORS AND AWARDS** Nat Endowment of the Arts, 70; Guggenheim Fel, 79. **MEMBERSHIPS** Int PEN Club; Nat Soc Film Critics. **RESEARCH** American novel; cinema. **SELECTED PUBLICATIONS** Auth, The Landscape of Nightmare: Studies in Contemporary American Nove, NY Univ & Peter Owen, London, 65; A Man to Conjure With, Randon & Gollanez, London, 65; What Comes Next, Harper, 68; Reruns (novel), 74, Babble (novel), 76 & co-ed, Statements II: New Fiction, 77, Fiction Collective/Braziller; auth, Chez Charlotte, Emily FC, 79; auth, The Return of Service, stories, 79; auth, Seven Wives, novel, 84, FC2, 99; auth, The Life and Times of Major Fiction, stories, FC, 87; auth, My Father More or Less, novel, Fc2, 89; auth, Separate Hours, novel, fc2, 90; auth, Detours, novel, 98. **CONTACT ADDRESS** Brooklyn Col, CUNY, Brooklyn, NY 11210. **EMAIL** jquarte@panix.com

BAUMLIN, JAMES S.

DISCIPLINE RENAISSANCE AND SEVENTEENTH-CENTURY LITERATURE **EDUCATION** Georgetown Univ, BA, 77; Brown Univ, PhD, 83. **CAREER** Southwest Tex State Univ **HONORS AND AWARDS** Nat Excellence Eng Awd;

SMSU Found Fac Achievement Awd Outstanding Sch; dir, grad studies eng. **SELECTED PUBLICATIONS** Auth, John Donne and the Rhetorics of Renaissance Discourse, Univ Miss Press, 91; Coed, Ethos: New Essays in Rhetorical and Critical Theory, SMU Press, 94. **CONTACT ADDRESS** Southwest Missouri State Univ, Springfield, 901 S. National, Ste. 50, Springfield, MO 65804-0094.

BAUMLIN, TITA FRENCH
DISCIPLINE BRITISH DRAMA **EDUCATION** TX Christian Univ, BA, 76; Southern Methodist Univ, MA, 81; TX Christian Univ, PhD, 85. **CAREER** Southwest Tex State Univ **HONORS AND AWARDS** Ed, Explorations in Renaissance Cult. **SELECTED PUBLICATIONS** Coed, Ethos: New Essays in Rhetorical and Critical Theory, SMU Press, 94; Instructors' Manual for The HarperCollins World Reader sections on Medieval Europe, Early Modern Europe, and Modern Europe, HarperCollins, 94; coed, New Views on Jungian Literary theory, SUNY, forthcoming. **CONTACT ADDRESS** Dept of English, Southwest Missouri State Univ, Springfield, 901 S. National, Springfield, MO 65804. **EMAIL** titabaumlin@smsu.edu

BAUMWOLL, DENNIS
PERSONAL Born 07/08/1932, New York, NY, m, 1956, 4 children **DISCIPLINE** ENGLISH **EDUCATION** Univ Okla, BA, 54, MA, 58, PhD(English), 64. **CAREER** Instr English, Boston Univ, 62-65; from instr to asst prof, 65-72, assoc prof, 72-79, PROF ENGLISH, BUCKNELL UNIV, 79-, Ed consult, Bucknell Rev, 65-; consult, Pa Dept Pub Instr, 67; coordr acad enrichment prog, US Penitentiary, Lewisburg, 67- **MEMBERSHIPS** MLA; Teachers of English to Speakers of Other Lang. **RESEARCH** The novel as genre; modern fiction; English as a second language. **SELECTED PUBLICATIONS** Coauth, Advanced Reading and Writing, Holt, 65, 2nd ed, 78. **CONTACT ADDRESS** Dept of English, Bucknell Univ, Lewisburg, PA 17837-2029. **EMAIL** baumwoll@bucknell.edu

BAUSCHINGER, SIGRID ELISABETH
PERSONAL Born 11/02/1934, Frankfurt, Germany, s **DISCIPLINE** MODERN GERMAN LITERATURE **EDUCATION** Univ Frankfurt, Dr Phil. **CAREER** Instr Ger, Oberlin Col, 62-64, asst prof, 64-68; asst prof, 68-71, assoc prof, 71-79, head dept, 76-79, Prof Ger, Univ Mass, Amherst, 79. **HONORS AND AWARDS** Franz Rosenzweig Res Center for Ger-Jewish Lit and Cult Hist fel, 93; Am Asn Tchr(s) Ger hon mem, 95. **MEMBERSHIPS** MLA **RESEARCH** Twentieth century Ger lit; lit of exile; Ger-Jewish lit. **SELECTED PUBLICATIONS** Contribr, Psychologie in der Literaturwissenschaft, Lothar Stiehm, Heidelberg, 71 & Gedichte der Menschheitsdammerung, Albin Fink, Munchen, 71; coauth, Elementary German, Van Nostrand Rineholt, 71; coauth & co-ed, Amerika in der Deutschen Literatur, Reclam, 75; auth, Else Lasker-Schuler, Ihr Werk und ihre Zeit, Lothar Stiehm, Heidelberg, 80; co-ed, Amherster Kolloquien zur Deutschen Literatur, 81-00; auth, Die Posaune der Reform, Francke, Bern, 89-; ed, Ich habe elucas zu sagen, Annette Kolb 1860-1967, Diederichs, Munchen, 93; auth, engl. The Trumpet of Reform, Camden House, Columbia , SC, 99. **CONTACT ADDRESS** Dept of Ger, Univ of Massachusetts, Amherst, Herter Hall, Amherst, MA 01003-0002. **EMAIL** bauschin@german.umass.edu

BAXTER, GISELE
PERSONAL Born 11/01/1958, Digby, NS, Canada, s **DISCIPLINE** ENGLISH **EDUCATION** Mount St Vincent Univ, BA, 79; Dalhousie Univ, MA, 82; PhD, 90. **HONORS AND AWARDS** Killam Doc Fel, 88-90; Fel, SSHRC, 89-90. **RESEARCH** Modern and contemporary fiction; Popular culture. **CONTACT ADDRESS** Dept English, Univ of British Columbia, 397-1873 E Mall, Vancouver, BC, Canada V6T 1Z1. **EMAIL** gmb@interchange.ubc.ca

BAXTER, HAROLD J.
DISCIPLINE ENGLISH **EDUCATION** Houghton Col, BA, 66; Evangelical Sch Theol, BD, 69; Eastern Baptist Sem, ThM, 71; Old Dominion, MA, 80; FL State Univ, PhD, 83. **CAREER** Relig, Trinity Int Univ. **SELECTED PUBLICATIONS** Auth, Shadows and Fog. **CONTACT ADDRESS** Col of Arts and Sciences, Trinity Intl Univ, Col of Arts and Sciences, 2065 Half Day Road, Deerfield, IL 60015.

BAXTER-MOORE, NICK
DISCIPLINE COMMUNICATIONS **EDUCATION** Univ Manchester, BA; London Sch of Econ, MSc; Carleton Univ, PhD. **CAREER** Prof, Brock Univ. **RESEARCH** Nationalism and national identity; politics and popular culture/popular music; creation and dissemination of societal myth. **SELECTED PUBLICATIONS** Co-auth, Politics in Canada: Culture, Institutions, Behaviour and Public Policy, Prentice-Hall Can, 86; Studying Politics: An Introduction to Argument and Analysis, Copp Clark Longman, 94; auth, Ideology or Pragmatism?, The politics and management of the Mulroney government's privatization programme, Brit Jour Can Stud, 92. **CONTACT ADDRESS** Dept of Politics, Brock Univ, 500 Glenridge Ave, Saint Catharines, ON, Canada L2S 3A1. **EMAIL** nbaxterm@spartan.ac.BrockU.CA

BAY, LIBBY
PERSONAL Born 12/22/1932, New York, NY, m, 1955, 2 children **DISCIPLINE** ENGLISH **EDUCATION** Hunter Col, BA, 54; Univ Chicago, MA, 55. **CAREER** Lectr English, Brooklyn Col, 57-61 & Hunter Col, 61-65; Prof English. Rockland Commun Col, 75-93, Dept Chmn, 65-93, Chair, Humanities Div, 93-. **HONORS AND AWARDS** Phi Beta Kappa, 54; Penfield fel, NY Univ, 55-57; Chancellor's Awd Excellence in Teaching, State Univ NY, 73; Nat Endowment for Humanities grant, proj dir interdisciplinary humanities, 74-75; Mellon fel, 80-81, 85-86; Header Coll Hall of Fame, 88; East/West Inst Fel, Spring 90; NCCCA Awd for Most Outstanding Chair in NE, 93; Woman of the Year Awd, Rockland AAWN, 98; NYU Fac Network Judgement, 00. **MEMBERSHIPS** NCTE; MLA; Asn Departments Teachers English; 4 C's; TYCA. **RESEARCH** Composition and rhetoric; contemporary American literature; modern adaptations of classical themes; women's literature. **SELECTED PUBLICATIONS** Auth, Towards uniformity in grading, 77 & Counterparting: Teaching through modern responses, 78, Eric; Save the tiger: Strategies for literature enrollment, Community Col Rev, 6/78; Peer Critiquing, Insight, 82; Honors programs in community colleges, NCCJ J, 77; Rerouting a Career, ADE, 93. **CONTACT ADDRESS** Rockland Comm Col, 145 College Rd, Suffern, NY 10901-3611. **EMAIL** lbay@sunyrockland.edu

BAYLESS, OVID LYNDAL
PERSONAL Born 07/20/1931, Duncan, OK, m, 1953, 3 children **DISCIPLINE** SPEECH; COMMUNICATION **EDUCATION** Baylor Univ, BA, 53; MA, 59; Univ Denver, PhD, 65. **CAREER** Instr, broadcasting workshop, Baylor Univ, 59; instr English, US Air Force Acad, 62-63, asst prof tech writing & speech, 65-67, assoc prof advan compos & speech, 67-74, deputy dir instr technol, 68-74; prof speech commun & chmn dept speech commun & dramatic arts, Ark State Univ, 74- **MEMBERSHIPS** Speech Commun Asn; Am Forensic Asn; Int Commun Asn; Broadcast Educ Asn. **RESEARCH** Group problem-solving; persuasion; broadcasting. **SELECTED PUBLICATIONS** Auth, The American Forces Vietnam Network, J Broadcasting, 69; The Oral History Program, 69 & Television as a Demonstration Tool, 69, Educ TV. **CONTACT ADDRESS** Arkansas State Univ, PO Drawer 396, State University, AR 72467-0369. **EMAIL** obayless@aztec.astate.edu

BAYM, NINA
PERSONAL Born 06/14/1936, Princeton, NJ, m, 1971, 2 children **DISCIPLINE** ENGLISH **EDUCATION** Cornell Univ, BA, 57; Harvard Univ, MA, 58, PhD(English), 63. **CAREER** Asst English, Univ Calif, Berkeley, 62-63; at Univ Ill since 63, from instr to assoc prof, 63-76, assoc head dept, 71-75, prof English, 72-, dir Sch Humanities, 76-87; Jubilee prof Lib Arts and Sciences, 87; Swanlund Endowd chair, 97-; Cen for Adv Study prof, 97; Guggenheim fel, 75-76; Nat Endowment for Humanities fel, 82-83. **MEMBERSHIPS** MLA; Am Studies Asn; hon fel Am Asn Univ Women; Nathaniel Hawthorne Asn; Robert Frost Soc. **RESEARCH** American literature; American fiction women writers, gender issues, sociology of anthorship & canon-formation. **SELECTED PUBLICATIONS** Auth, Women in Cooper's Leatherstocking Tales, Am Quart, 71; The erotic motif in Herman Melville's Clarel, Tex Studies, 74; Revision and thematic change in The Portrait of a Lady, Mod Fiction Studies, 76; The Shape of Hawthorne's Career, 76 & Woman's Fiction: A Guide to Novels By and About Women in America 1820-1870, 78, Cornell Univ; Melville's quarrel with fiction, PMLA, 79; Melodramas of Beset Manhood: How theories of American fiction exclude women authors, Am Quart, 81; Nathaniel Hawthorne and his mother, Am Lit, 82; auth, Novels, Readers and Reviewers: Responses to Fiction in Antebellum America, 84; auth, Feminism and American Literary History: Essays, 92; American Women Writers and the Work of History, 95. **CONTACT ADDRESS** Dept of English, Univ of Illinois, Urbana-Champaign, 608 S Wright St, Urbana, IL 61801-3613. **EMAIL** baymnina@uiuc.edu

BAZARGAN, SUSAN
PERSONAL Born Tehran, Iran, d, 3 children **DISCIPLINE** ENGLISH LITERATURE **EDUCATION** DePauw Univ, BA, 68; Univ Wash, MA, 79, PhD, 84. **CAREER** Part-time Instr, Mashad Univ , 69-78; Tchg Asst, Univ WA, 80-82; Predoctoral Tchg Ass, Univ WA, 82-84; Acting asst prof, Univ WA, 84-95; Assoc prof, Eastern IL Univ, 85-93; Prof, Eastern IL Univ, 93-. **HONORS AND AWARDS** Robert Heilman Awd; Jessie J. Atkinson Awd, 79; Robert Heilman Dissertation Awd, 84; EIU Pres Summer Res Awds, 85, 89; EIU Fac Excellence Awd Res, 90; EIU Fac Res Awd, 94; NEH Independant Study Grant, 95; NEH Inst, 98; Scholar-in-resident, Zurich James Joyce Found, 99-00. **MEMBERSHIPS** Virginia Woolf Soc; James Joyce Found, ACIS; SCE; MLA. **RESEARCH** Twentieth-Century British and Irish Literature, Critical Theory. **SELECTED PUBLICATIONS** Auth, "Oxen of the Sun: Maternity, Language and History," James Joyce Quart, 85; The Headings in 'Aeolus': Cinematographic View, James Joyce Quart, 86; "Representation and Ideology in 'The Real Thing'," Henry James Rev, 91; coed, Image and Ideology in Modernist/Postmodernist Discourse, SUNY Press, 91; Mapping Gibralter: Colonialism, Time, and Narrative in "Penelope', Molly Blooms: A Polylogue on 'Penelope', 94; auth, "W.B. Yeats, Autobiography and Colonialism" in Yeats: An Annual of Critical and Textual Studies, vol 13 (97); auth, "The Book of Punishment: Lists in the Cyclops Episode", James Joyce Quart 35 (98). **CONTACT ADDRESS** Eastern Illinois Univ, 600 Lincoln Ave, Charleston, IL 61920-3099. **EMAIL** cfsxb@eiu.edu

BAZERMAN, CHARLES
PERSONAL Born 06/30/1945, Brooklyn, NY, m, 1972, 1 child **DISCIPLINE** WRITING & RHETORIC **EDUCATION** Brandeis Univ, MA, 68; PhD, 71. **CAREER** Prof, Baruch Col, 71-90; vis prof, Nat Univ of Singapore, 86-86; prof, Ga Inst of Technol, 90-94; prof, Univ of Calif at Santa Barbara, 94-; Watson Distinguished Vis Prof, Univ of Comisville, 97; Knight Distinguished Vis Scholar, Cornell Univ, 99. **HONORS AND AWARDS** Best Book in Tech & Sci Writing, NCTE, 90; Best Book, Am Medical Writers' Asn, 90; Best Scholarly Book in Hist of Sci and Technol, Am Asn of Pub, 99. **MEMBERSHIPS** NCTE, CCC, AERA, Hist of Sci Soc, Soc for Hist of Technol. **RESEARCH** Rhetorical Theory, Writing Across the Curriculum, Rhetoric of Science and Technology, Teaching of Writing. **SELECTED PUBLICATIONS** Auth, The Informed Writer: using Sources in the Disciplines, Houghton Mifflin (Boston, MA), 81, 85, 89, 92, & 95; auth, The Informed Reader: Contemporary Issues in the Disciplines, Houghton Mifflin (Boston, MA), 89; co-ed, Textual Dynamics of the Professions, Univ of Wis Press (Madison, WI), 91; auth, Shaping Written Knowledge: The Genre and Activity of the Experimental Article in Science, Univ of Wis Press (Madison, WI), 91; auth, Constructing Experience, Southern Ill Univ Press, 94; auth, Involved: Writing for College, Writing for Yourself, Houghton Mifflin, 97; auth, The Languages of Edison's Light, MIT Press, 99. **CONTACT ADDRESS** Dept Educ, Univ of California, Santa Barbara, 552 Univ Blvd, Santa Barbara, CA 93106. **EMAIL** bazerman@education.ucsb.edu

BAZIN, NANCY TOPPING
PERSONAL Born 11/05/1934, Pittsburgh, PA, m, 1992, 6 children **DISCIPLINE** ENGLISH, FRENCH **EDUCATION** Ohio Wesleyan Univ, BA, 56; Middlebury Grad School of French, MA, 58; Stanford Univ, PhD, 69 **CAREER** Eminent Scholar, Old Dominion Univ, 96-; prof, Old Dominion Univ, 84-; assoc prof, Old Dominion Univ, 78-84; Chair, Dept Eng, Old Dominion Univ, 85-89; dir, Women's Studies, Old Dominion Univ, 78-85 **HONORS AND AWARDS** Winner, 2nd Annual Charles O and Elisabeth C Burgess Faculty Res and Creativity Awd, 96; Resident Fel, Center for the Humanities of the Virginia Foundation for the Humanities and Public Policy, 95; Outstanding Faculty Awd, State Council Higher Education Virginia, 94; Ball Brothers Res Found Fel, 94; Phi Kappa Phi, 88; Sigma Tau Delta, 88; Phi Beta Kappa, 55; Mortar Board, 55; Kappa Delta Pi, 56 **MEMBERSHIPS** Modern Lang Assoc; African Lit Assoc; Ntl Women's Studies Assoc; Virginia Woolf Soc; Doris Lessing Soc **RESEARCH** 20th Century Writers **SELECTED PUBLICATIONS** Auth, Virginia Woolf and the Androgynous Vision, Rutgers, 73; coed, Conversations with Nadine Gordimer, Univ Miss, 90; auth, "Venturing into Feminist Consciousness: Two Protagonists from the Fiction of Buchi Emecheta and Bessie Head," Critical Perspectives on Buchi Emecheta, 96 **CONTACT ADDRESS** 4005 Gosnold Ave, Norfolk, VA 23508-2917. **EMAIL** nbazin@odw.edu

BEAL, REBECCA S.
DISCIPLINE ENGLISH **EDUCATION** Westmount Col, AB, 74; Univ Chicago, MA, 76; Univ Tex Austin, PhD, 82. **CAREER** Vis Instr, Rice Univ, 82-83; asst prof to prof, Univ of Scranton, 83-. **HONORS AND AWARDS** NEH Fel, 90; Grant, Univ of Scranton, 93. **MEMBERSHIPS** MLA, Dante Soc of Am, Int Arthurian Soc, Medieval Acad of Am, New Chaucer Soc. **RESEARCH** Dante, Chaucer, Endings in Medieval Literature, Medieval Arthuriana. **SELECTED PUBLICATIONS** Auth, "Grace Abounding to the Chief of Sinners: John Bunyan's Pauline Epistle," Studies in Eng Lit 21, (81): 147-60; auth, "Dante Among Thieves: Soteriological Allegory in the Seventh Bolgia (Inferno XXIV-XXV)," Mediaevalia (83): 101-123; auth, "Beatrice as Apocalyptic Woman in the Sun: Paradiso X-XI," Dante Studies 103, (85): 57-78; auth, "Dante in the Labyrinth," Mediaevalia 13 (87): 227-45; auth, "Bonaventure, Dante, and the Apocalyptic Woman Clothed With the Sun (Paradiso XI-XIII)," Dante Studies 114, (96): 209-28; auth, "Ending in the Middle: Closure, Openness, and significance in Embedded Medieval Narratives," Annali d'Italianistica 18, (00): 175-198. **CONTACT ADDRESS** 719 N Irving Ave, Scranton, PA 18510-1822. **EMAIL** bealr1@scranton.edu

BEALE, WALTER HENRY
PERSONAL Born 01/15/1945, Roseboro, NC, m, 1968, 1 child **DISCIPLINE** RHETORIC, ENGLISH LANGUAGE & LITERATURE **EDUCATION** Wake Forest Col, BA, 67; Univ MI, MA, 68, PhD, 71. **CAREER** Asst prof, 71-76, assoc prof English 76-86, prof English, 86-, Dean Col Arts Sci 90-, Univ NC, Greensboro, 76-. **MEMBERSHIPS** MLA; NCTE; Rhet Soc; Mediaeval Acad Am. **RESEARCH** Rhetorical theory and criticism; discourse theory; medieval literature. **SELECTED PUBLICATIONS** Auth, Walter Hilton and the concept of 'medlid lyf,' Am Benediction Rev, 75; Old and Middle English Poetry to 1500, Gale Res Co, 76; On rhetoric and poetry: John Donne's The Prohibition, Quart J Speech, 76; Rhetorical performating discourse: A new theory of epideictic, Philos & Rhet, 78; Rhet-

oric in the old English verse paragraph, Neuphilologische Mitteilungen, 79; Real Writing: Argumentation, Relflection, Information, & Stylistic Options, 82, Scott Foresman; A Pragmatic Theory of Discourse, S Il Press, 87. **CONTACT ADDRESS** Dept English, Univ of No Carolina, Greensboro, 105 Foust Bldg, Greensboro, NC 27412. **EMAIL** WHBeale@HAMLET.uncg.edu

BEAN, BOBBY
PERSONAL Born 01/15/1951, Houlka, MS, m, 1974 **DISCIPLINE** LIBRARY SCIENCE **EDUCATION** Southeast Missouri State University, BSE, 1974; Southern Illinois University, MSE, 1979, EDS, 1981; Lael University, EDD,1983; Atlanta University, MSLS, 1987; Interdenominational Theological Center, MDiv, 1989; Univ of Sarasota, EDD, candidate, 1998. **CAREER** Sikeston Public School, high school librarian assistant, 72-73; East St Louis Public School, 6th grade teacher, 74-82, junior high math teacher, 82-83, junior high librarian, 83-87; Atlanta Public School, John Hope Elementary, Media Specialist, 88-; Atlanta Univ Center, RW Woodruff Lib, Ref Librarian, 88-; Interdenominational Theology Center, Instructor, 92-. **HONORS AND AWARDS** American Biographical Institute, Research Board Advisor, 1990; Those Who Excel, School Media Service, Honorable Mention, 1987; ABI, Distinguished Leadership Awd. **MEMBERSHIPS** ITC, Dean's List, 1988-89; United Negro College Fund Scholarship, 1989; Theta Phi, 1989; Atlanta University, Beta Phi Mu Library Science Honor Fraternity, 1987; American Library Assn; Georgia Library Assn; American Assn of School Librarians; Georgia Chaplain Assn. **CONTACT ADDRESS** Dept Relig, Interdenominational Theol Ctr, 700 MLK Jr Dr SW, Atlanta, GA 30314-4143.

BEAN, JUDITH M.
PERSONAL Born 01/01/1945 **DISCIPLINE** ENGLISH, WOMEN'S STUDIES **EDUCATION** Sam Houston State Univ, BA, 62; MA, 88; Texas A and M Univ, PhD, 92. **CAREER** Lectr, Texas A and M Univ, 92-93; vis prof, Prairie View A and M Univ, 93-94; assoc prof, Tex Woman's Univ, 94-. **HONORS AND AWARDS** Who's Who Among America's Teachers, 96, 98. **MEMBERSHIPS** MLA, Margaret Fuller Soc, Ling Asn of the SW, Soc for the Study of Am Women Writers, CCC. **RESEARCH** American Women's Literature, Women's Discourse and Rhetoric, Sociolinguistics. **SELECTED PUBLICATIONS** Auth, "The Evolution of the Inchoatives 'Go to' and 'Get to,'" SECOL Rev, 91; auth, "Gender, Politeness and Discourse Management in Same-sex and Cross-sex Opinion-Poll Interviews," Jour of Pragmatics (92); auth, "True Grit and All the Rest: The Expression of Regional and Individual Identity in Molly Ivin's Discourse," Southwestern Am Lit, (93); coauth, "Workplace Reasons for Saying You're Sorry: Discourse Management and Apology," Discourse Processes, (94); auth, "Texts From Conversation: Margaret Fuller's Influence on Emerson," Studies in the Am Renaissance, (94); auth, "Conversations as Rhetoric in Margaret Fuller's Woman in the Nineteenth Century," In Her Own Voice: Nineteenth-Century American Women Essayists, (97); coauth, "Self-Expression and Linguistic Variation," Language in Society, (97); auth, "A Presence Among Us: Margaret Fuller's Place in nineteenth-Century Oratorical Culture," Fuller's Cultural Critique: Her Age and Legacy, (98); auth, "Margaret Fuller and Julia Ward Howe: A Woman-to-Woman Influence," (99); coed, Margaret Fuller, Critic: Writings from the New York Tribune, 1844-1846, 00. **CONTACT ADDRESS** Dept English, Speech and For Lang, Texas Woman's Univ, Denton, TX 76204-5829. **EMAIL** jbean@twu.edu

BEASLEY, JERRY CARR
PERSONAL Born 09/15/1940, Nashville, TN, m, 1966, 2 children **DISCIPLINE** ENGLISH LITERATURE **EDUCATION** George Peabody Col, BA, 63; Univ KS, MA, 67; Northwestern Univ, PhD(English), 71. **CAREER** Asst prof, 69-74, assoc prof, 74-81, Prof English, Univ DE, 81-, Assoc Chmn Dept, 77-, Nat Endowment for Humanities summer grant, 77. **MEMBERSHIPS** MLA; Am Soc 18th Century Studies. **RESEARCH** English novel, 18th and 19th centuries. **SELECTED PUBLICATIONS** Auth, Fanny Burney and Jane Austen's Pride and Prejudice, English Miscellany, 73; English fiction in the 1740's: Some glances at the major minor novels, Studies Novel, fall 73; The role of Tom Pinch in Martin Chuzzlewit, Ariel, 74; co-ed, The Novel in England, 1700-1775, Garland Publ, 74-75; auth, Romance and the new novels of Richardson, Fielding, and Smollett, Studies English Lit, summer 76; English Fiction, 1660-1800, Gale Res Co, 78; Portraits of a Monster: Robert Walpole and Early English Prose Fiction, Eighteenth Century Studies, summer 81; Novels of the 1740's, Univ Ga Press, 82. **CONTACT ADDRESS** Dept of English, Univ of Delaware, Newark, DE 19711.

BEASLEY, VANESSA B.
DISCIPLINE RHETORICAL THEORY **EDUCATION** Univ Tex, PhD. **CAREER** Asst prof, Texsa A&M Univ. **SELECTED PUBLICATIONS** Publ in, Political Commun & The Encycl Of Television. **CONTACT ADDRESS** Dept of Speech Communication, Texas A&M Univ, Col Station, College Station, TX 77843-4234. **EMAIL** csnidow@tamu.edu

BEATIE, BRUCE A.
PERSONAL Born 03/04/1935, Oakland, CA, m, 1990, 2 children **DISCIPLINE** MEDIEVAL, FOLK, AND POPULAR LITERATURE **EDUCATION** Univ Calif, Berkeley, AB, 59; Univ Colo, MA, 60; Harvard Univ, PhD(comp lit), 67. **CAREER** Asst prof Ger, Univ Colo, 64-67, asst prof Ger & comp lit, 67-68; assoc prof, Univ Rochester, 68-70; chmn, Dept Mod Lang, 70-77, Prof Ger,Cleveland State Univ, 70-88, Prof Comp & Medieval Studies, 89-. **HONORS AND AWARDS** Germanistic Society of Am, fel, 63-64; Nat Endowment for Humanities younger scholar fel, 70. **MEMBERSHIPS** Midwest MLA; AAUP, Sci Fiction Res Assoc, Int Arthurian Soc. **RESEARCH** Medieval comparative literature; popular and traditional narrative; folklore. **SELECTED PUBLICATIONS** Auth, Arthurian films and Arthurian texts: problems of reception and comprehension, Arthurian Interpretations, Spring 88; Arthur C. Clarke and the alien encounter: The background of Childhood's End, Extrapolation, Spring 89; E.E. Smith, In: Twentieth Century Science Fiction Writers, 3rd ed, St. James, 91; The broken quest: the Perceval romances of Chretien de Troyes and Eric Rohmer, In: The Arthurian Revival: Essays on Form, Tradition, and Transformation, Garland, 92; coauth, Reflected images in two Mexican poems of 1957: Piedra de sol by Octavio Paz and Misterios gozosos by Rosario Castellanos, Revista / Review Interamericana 26, 96; author of several other articles. **CONTACT ADDRESS** Dept of Mod Lang, Cleveland State Univ, 1983 E 24th St, Cleveland, OH 44115-2440. **EMAIL** b.beatie@popmail.csuohio.edu

BEATTIE, THOMAS CHARLES
PERSONAL Born 02/07/1938, St. Johns, MI, m, 1962 **DISCIPLINE** ENGLISH LANGUAGE & LITERATURE **EDUCATION** MI State Univ, BA, 60; Univ PA, MA, 61; Univ MI Ann Arbor, PhD, 68. **CAREER** Tchg fel Eng, Univ MI, 63-68; asst prof, 68-76, assoc prof, 76-80, prof eng, & chmn dept, Hartwick Col, 78-93, assoc dean, Acad Affairs, 94. **MEMBERSHIPS** MLA; Col Eng Asn. **RESEARCH** Novel; Jane Austen; 18th century Eng lit; Toni Morrison. **SELECTED PUBLICATIONS** Writing Competency: A Handbook, 79; Moments of Meaning Dearly Achieved: Virginia Woolf's Sense of an Ending, Mod Fiction Studies, 86. **CONTACT ADDRESS** Office of Acad Affairs, Hartwick Col, Oneonta, NY 13820-4020. **EMAIL** beattiet@hartwick.edu

BEATTY, MICHAEL
DISCIPLINE INTERPERSONAL AND ORGANIZATIONAL COMMUNICATION **EDUCATION** Univ MO, BS; Cent MO State Univ, MA; OH State Univ, PhD. **CAREER** Prof, Communication, Univ Mo-St Louis. **SELECTED PUBLICATIONS** Co-auth, Personality and Communication: Trait Perspectives, Hampton Press, 97; Trait Verbal Aggressiveness and the Appropriateness and Effectiveness of Fathers' Interaction Plans, Commun Quart, 96; auth, Thinking Quantitatively, An Integrated Approach to Communication Theory and Research, Hillsdale, NJ: Erlbaum, 96. **CONTACT ADDRESS** Commun Dept, Univ of Missouri, St. Louis, 8001 Natural Bridge Rd, Saint Louis, MO 63121. **EMAIL** beatty@umsl.edu

BEATY, FREDERICK L.
PERSONAL Born 10/22/1926, New Braunfels, TX, m, 1955, 2 children **DISCIPLINE** ENGLISH **EDUCATION** Univ TX, BA, 46; Harvard Univ, AM, 48, PhD, 52; Oxford Univ, BLitt, 50. **CAREER** Instr English, Cornell Univ, 54-55; from instr to assoc prof, 55-69, Prof English, Ind Univ, Bloomington, 69-91. **MEMBERSHIPS** Keats-Shelley Asn. **RESEARCH** Romantic period of English literature; Evelyn Waugh. **SELECTED PUBLICATIONS** Ed, The Lloyd-Manning Letters, IN Univ, 57; auth, Byron and Story of Francesca de Rimini, PMLA, 60; Mrs Radcliffe's Fading Gleam, Philo Quart, 63; Harlequin Don Juan, J English & Ger Philol, 68; Byron on Malthus, Keats Shelley J, 69; Light From Heaven: Love in British Romantic Literature, Northern IL Univ, 71; Byron's Longbow and Strongbow, Studies English Lit, 72; Byron's Imitations of Juvenal and Persius, SIR, 76; auth, "Byron on Joanna Southcott," Keats-Shelley J (77); auth, Byron the Satirist, Northern Ill Univ, 85; auth, "Evelyn Waugh and Lance Sieveking," Papers on Lang and Lit (89); auth, The Ironic World of Evelyn Waugh, Northern Ill Univ, 92. **CONTACT ADDRESS** Dept of English, Indiana Univ, Bloomington, Bloomington, IN 47405.

BEATY, JEROME
DISCIPLINE ENGLISH LANGUAGE AND LITERATURE **EDUCATION** Univ Ill, PhD, 56. **CAREER** Prof **RESEARCH** Victorian literature; poetics; the theory of the novel. **SELECTED PUBLICATIONS** Auth, Misreading Jane Eyre: A Postformalist Paradigm; coauth, Poetry: From Statement to Meaning; "Middlemarch" from Notebook to Novel; ed, Norton Introduction to the Short Novel; Norton Introduction to Fiction; Norton Introduction to Literature; New Worlds of Literature; Villette; Middlemarch. **CONTACT ADDRESS** Emory Univ, 1364 Clifton Rd NE, Atlanta, GA 30322-1950.

BEAUFORT, ANNE
DISCIPLINE ENGLISH **EDUCATION** Wheaton Col, BA, 69; Purdue Univ, MA, 71; Stanford Univ, PhD, 95. **CAREER** Teacher, Prince Georges County, Md, 69; instr, Purdue Univ, 69-71; teacher, Crouch Elem School, 71-72; teacher, Shaker Heights Jr High, 72-73; teacher, Cleveland Adult School, 74; instr, Contra Costa Col, 76; instr, Chabor Col, 76-79; pub rel manager, Pacific Bell, 81-89; adj prof, St. Mary's Col, 84-86; adj prof, Golden Gate Univ, 86-88; sr Trainer, Octel Commun Corp, 89-90; prof officer, Stanford Univ 91-92; cons, Stanford Univ, 91-92; TA, supervisor, Stanford Univ, 92-93; adj fac, Dominican Col, 93-94; adj fac, St. Mary's Col, 94-95; asst prof, Am Univ, 95-. **HONORS AND AWARDS** Cindy Gold Awd, United Way of Am Gold Awd, San Francisco Int Asn of Business, 85-86; Fel, Stanford Univ, 90-94; Spencer Found Fel, 94-95; Am Univ Res Awd, 95-96; CAS Mellon Res Grant, Am Univ, 96-97; Am Univ Res Awd, 97-98; CAS Mellon Fund Grant, Am Univ, 98-99. **MEMBERSHIPS** AERA; WPA Coun; NCTE; MLA. **RESEARCH** Post-secondary writing instruction, advanced writing literacy. **CONTACT ADDRESS** Prog in Writing and Rhetoric, SUNY, Stony Brook, 196 Humanities, Stony Brook, NY 11794-5350.

BEAVERS, MYRTLE B.
PERSONAL Born 04/21/1934, Page, OK, m, 1953, 3 children **DISCIPLINE** ENGLISH LITERATURE **EDUCATION** Okaloosa-Walton Community Col, AA, 72; Univ West FL, BA, 74, MA, 76; FL State Univ, PhD (English Lit), 94. **CAREER** Teacher, Ft. Walton Beach High School, 74-84; Prof, Okaloosa-Walton Community Col, 84-, chair, Communications Dept, 94-97. **HONORS AND AWARDS** Bert and Ruth Davis Awd for Outstanding Dissertation in British Literature for the Year 94-95. **RESEARCH** Thomas Hardy; Charles Dickens; 19th century British lit. **SELECTED PUBLICATIONS** Auth, book review of Boston Mountain Tales: Stories from a Cherokee Family by Glenn J. Twist, Greenfield Rev Press, 97, for the Am Indian Culture and Res Jour published by the Am Indian Studies Center of UCLA. **CONTACT ADDRESS** 712 Harbor Lane, Destin, FL 32541-1806. **EMAIL** beaversm@owcc.net

BEBOUT, LINDA J.
DISCIPLINE ENGLISH LANGUAGE; LITERATURE **EDUCATION** Central, BA; San Francisco State Univ, MSc; Cornell, PhD, 77. **CAREER** Asst prof **RESEARCH** Teaching of second-language vocabulary and the usage of gender-related terms in popular culture, such as in song lyrics. **SELECTED PUBLICATIONS** Pub (s), usage of gender-related words in English; language; language disorders and cross cultural attitudes toward them & teaching and learning English as a Second Language. **CONTACT ADDRESS** Dept of English Language and Literature, Univ of Windsor, 401 Sunset Ave, Windsor, ON, Canada N9B 3P4. **EMAIL** ljb@uwindsor.ca

BECHTEL, JUDITH A.
PERSONAL Born 06/12/1938, Cleveland, OH, d, 2 children **DISCIPLINE** LITERATURE **EDUCATION** Ohio Wesleyan, BA, 60; Univ Cincinnati, MA, 68; PhD, 78. **CAREER** Instr, Univ of Cincinnati, 69-72; Asst Prof, Ohio Col of Appl Sci, 72-79; Asst Prof and Dir of Composition, Northern Ky Univ, 79-86; Dir of Women's Studies, Northern Ky Univ, 86-93; Prof, Northern Ky Univ, 86-. **HONORS AND AWARDS** Phi Beta Kappa. **RESEARCH** Autobiography, Women's Literature, Rhetoric. **SELECTED PUBLICATIONS** Coauth, Reading in the Content Areas: Science, NEA (Washington DC), 80; auth, Improving Writing and Learning: A Handbook for Teachers in All Classes, Allyn and Bacon (Boston), 85; auth, "Why Teaching Writing Always Brings Up Questions of Equity," in Teaching Writing: Pedagogy and Questions of Equity, ed. Gillian Overing and Cynthia Caywood (Albany Univ Press, 86); auth, "McCrackin on Support, Conscience, and the Search of Truth," New Lifestyles 6-2 (spring 87): 2-3; coauth, "Building the Beloved Community: Maurice McCrackin's Life for Peace and Civil Rights, Temple Univ Press (Philadelphia), 91; co-ed, Mentors, Models, and Mothers: A Community Writing Project, Morris Publ Co (Lincoln), 97. **CONTACT ADDRESS** Dept Lang and Lit, No Kentucky Univ, Newport, KY 41099-0001. **EMAIL** Bechtel@nku.edu

BECK, ANN R.
DISCIPLINE SPEECH-LANGUAGE PATHOLOGY **EDUCATION** Southern Ill Univ, BS, 73, MS, 75; Univ Ill, PhD, 81. **CAREER** Clinical speech-language pathologist, Veterans Administration Medical Center, Danville, Ill, 75-86; clinical speech-language pathologist, Danville School District #118, Danville, Ill, 87-92; assoc prof, Ill State Univ, 92-. **HONORS AND AWARDS** Univ Teaching Initiative Awd, Ill State Univ. **MEMBERSHIPS** Am Speech-Language -Hearing Asn, Int Soc AAC, US Soc AAC, Ill Speech-Language-Hearing Asn, ASHA's Speech Interest Division #12 Augmentative and Alternative Commun (AAC). **RESEARCH** Augmentative and alternative communication, aphasia, school-based issues. **SELECTED PUBLICATIONS** Coauth with M. Dennis, "Attitudes of children toward a similar-aged peer who uses AAC," Augmentative and Alternative Commun, 12, (96): 78-87; coauth with C. Pirovano, "Facilitated communicator's performance on a task of receptive language," J of Autism and Developmental Disorders, 26 (96): 497-512; auth, "Language assessment methods used by speech-language pathologist for three age groups of children," J of Children's Commun Develop, 17 (96): 47-62; coauth with M. Dennis, "Speech-language pathologists' and teachers' perceptions of classroom-based interventions," Language, Speech, and Hearing Services in Schools, 28 (97): 146-

152; auth, Engaging Student Interest, The insider's guide to teaching at Illinois State University, Normal, Ill: Center for the Advancement of Teaching (98-99); coauth with H. Fritz, "Can people who have aphasia learn iconic codes? Augmentative and Alternative Commun, 14 (98): 184-196; coauth with J. Thompson, Assistive technology competencies and skills for teachers: Book 3-Technologies for Communication, Ill State Univ: Univ Communs (99); coauth with H. Fritz, A. Keller, and M. Dennis, "Attitudes of school-aged children toward their peers who use AAC," Augmentative and Alternative Commun, 16 (2000): 13-26. **CONTACT ADDRESS** Dept Speech Pathology & Audio, Illinois State Univ, 204 Fairchild Hall, Campus Box 4720, Normal, IL 61790-4720. **EMAIL** arbeck@ilstu.edu

BECK, CHARLOTTE H.
PERSONAL Born 07/15/1937, Nashville, TN, m, 1958, 2 children **DISCIPLINE** LITERATURE **EDUCATION** Univ Tenn, BM, 59; MA, 63; PhD, 72. **CAREER** TA, Univ Tenn, 62-63; instr to prof, Maryville Col, 66-01. **HONORS AND AWARDS** NEH Fel, 90; James Still Fel, UK, 86-91; Appalachian Col Asn Fel, 98-99; Beinecke Res Fel, 01. **MEMBERSHIPS** MLA, SAMLA, Robert Penn Warren Circle, Flannery O'Connor Soc, Katherine Anne Porter Soc. **RESEARCH** Robert Penn Warren's literary criticism, Southern poetry and fiction of the 1930s-1950s. **SELECTED PUBLICATIONS** Auth, Worlds and Lives: The Poetry of Randall Jarrell, Assoc Fac Pr, 83; auth, "Randall Jarrell and the Sweet Uses of Persona," S Atlantic Rev, (85); auth, "Randall Jarrell and Gerard Manley Hopkins: A Case of Acknowledged Superiority," Hopkins Among the Poets, ed Richard R Giles, (Int Hopkins Monograph Series, 85); auth, "Away from the Anxiety of Influence; Allen Tate and Randall Jarrell," The Vanderbilt Tradition: Essays in Honor of Thomas Daniel Young, ed Mark Royden Winchell, (La State Univ Pr, 91); auth, "The Postmodernism of Robert Penn Warren," To Love So Well the World: A Festschrift in Honor of Robert Penn Warren, ed Dennis L Weeks, (Peter Lang, 92); auth, "Solely the Southern Review: A Significant Moment in the Poetic Apprenticeship of John Berryman," Recovering Berryman: Essays on a Poet, ed Kelly and Lathrop, (Univ Mich Pr, 93); coauth, "Stanley Fish Was My Reader: Cleanth Brooks, the New Criticism, and Reader-Response Theory," The New Criticism and Contemporary Literary Theory, (Garland Pr, 95); auth, "Warren Scholarship at the Crossroads," Miss Quart, (95); auth, "Caroline Gordon and Flannery O'Connor: An Enabling Anxiety of Influence," Flannery O'Connor Bull, (98); auth, The Fugitive Legacy: A Critical History, La State Univ Pr, 01. **EMAIL** candrbeck@prodigy.net

BECK, ROGER L.
PERSONAL Born 01/11/1937, London, England **DISCIPLINE** CLASSICS **EDUCATION** New Col, Oxford Univ, BA, 61; Univ Ill, MA, 63, PhD, 71. **CAREER** Lectr, Univ Man, 63-64; lectr, Univ Col, Univ Toronto, 64-65; asst prof, 68 to prof Classics, Erindale Col, Univ Toronto; prof emer. **MEMBERSHIPS** Class Asn Can (secy 77-79); Am Philol Asn. **RESEARCH** Petronius and the ancient novel; the cult of Mithras. **SELECTED PUBLICATIONS** Auth, "Cosmic models: some uses of hellenistic science in Roman religion", in T.D. Barnes, The Sciences in Greco-Roman Society, (95); coauth, "The mysteries of Mithras", in J.S. Kloppenborg and S.G. Wilson, Voluntary Associations in the Ancient World, (96); auth, "Myster religions, aretalogy and the ancient novel," in G. Schmeling, The Novel in Antiquity, (96); auth, "Mithras" and "Astrology" in Hornblower and Spawforth, Oxford Classical Dictionary, (96); auth, "The Mysteries of Mithras: a new account of their genesis," Journal of Roman Studies 88, (98): 115-28. **CONTACT ADDRESS** Erindale Col, Univ of Toronto, 97 St. George St, Toronto, ON, Canada M5S 2E8. **EMAIL** rbeck@credit.erin.utoronto.ca

BECKER, ANDREW S.
PERSONAL Born 09/12/1959, Taungayi, Burma, m, 1987, 3 children **DISCIPLINE** CLASSICS **EDUCATION** Univ Mich, BA, 82; Cambridge Univ, BA, 84; MA, 88; Univ NCar, PhD, 88. **CAREER** Asst to Assoc Prof, Va Tech, 88-. **HONORS AND AWARDS** Cert of Teaching Excellence, VA Tech; Phi Beta Kappa; Phillips Prize; Countess Martmengo Cesaresco Awd; Pogue Fel. **MEMBERSHIPS** Am Philol Asn; Classical Asn of MidWest & S Emerson Soc **RESEARCH** Ancient and Modern Literature and Literary Theories; Epic; Ecphrasis; Pedagogy. **CONTACT ADDRESS** Dept For Lang, Virginia Polytech Inst and State Univ, 100 VA Tech, Blacksburg, VA 24061-0001. **EMAIL** andrew.becker@vt.edu

BECKER, JOHN
DISCIPLINE ENGLISH LITERATURE **EDUCATION** Yale Univ, PhD. **CAREER** Fac, Fairleigh Dickinson Univ. **RESEARCH** Am lit, literary theory, and the Bible as lit. **SELECTED PUBLICATIONS** Auth, Hawthorne's Historical Allegory, Kennikat, 71; Worldview, The Literary Review, and Ethics and International Affairs in College English. **CONTACT ADDRESS** Fairleigh Dickinson Univ, Teaneck-Hackensack, 1000 River Rd, Teaneck, NJ 07666.

BECKER, LLOYD GEORGE
PERSONAL Born 12/07/1942, Brooklyn, NY, m, 1995, 2 children **DISCIPLINE** AMERICAN LITERATURE & STUDIES **EDUCATION** Col William & Mary, AB, 64; State Univ NYork Buffalo, MA, 68, PhD, 80. **CAREER** Instr, 67-69, asst prof, 69-73, assoc prof, 73-78, prof eng, Suffolk County Community Col, 78. **HONORS AND AWARDS** NEH Summer Res Grant, 92. **MEMBERSHIPS** Am Lit Asn; Asn Lit Scholars & Critics; Western Lit Asn; Ralph Waldo Emerson Soc; Melville Soc; Mark Twain Circle; Jack London Soc. **RESEARCH** 19th Century Lit & Painting; Western Am Lit, esp. contemp fiction; Mythology. **SELECTED PUBLICATIONS** Auth, William Sidney Mount's Transparent Summer Morning, In: Paumanok Rising, Street Press, 80; Scenes of the Familiar, Emblems of the Eternal: Cultural Contexts of Shepherd Alonzo Mount, The Long Island Hist Jour, fall 90; Ken Nunn's Pomsra Queen, Western Am Lit, Aug. 94. **CONTACT ADDRESS** 533 College Rd, Selden, NY 11784. **EMAIL** becker1@sunysuffolk.edu

BECKMAN, RICHARD
PERSONAL Born 01/11/1932, New York, NY, m, 1952, 2 children **DISCIPLINE** ENGLISH LITERATURE **EDUCATION** Columbia Univ, BA, 53; Univ Rochester, MA, 54; Johns Hopkins Univ, PhD, 62. **CAREER** Instr English, Univ MD, 57-62; asst prof, 62-68, Assoc Prof to Prof Emer English, Temple Univ, 68-. **MEMBERSHIPS** MLA. **RESEARCH** English Romantic and Victorian literature. **CONTACT ADDRESS** Dept of English, Temple Univ, Philadelphia, PA 19122. **EMAIL** beckman@vm.temple.edu

BECKSON, KARL
PERSONAL Born 02/04/1926, New York, NY, m, 1957, 2 children **DISCIPLINE** ENGLISH **EDUCATION** Univ of Ariz, BA, 49; Columbia Univ, MA, 52; PhD, 59. **CAREER** Lectr, Columbia and Hunter Col, 56-59; instr, Fairleigh Dickinson Univ, 60-61; instr to prof, Brooklyn Col, 61-. **HONORS AND AWARDS** Mellon Fel, UCLA, 78; NEH Fel, 89-90. **MEMBERSHIPS** MLA; Oscar Wilde Soc; 1890's Soc. **RESEARCH** Late 19th, early 20th Century British Literature. **SELECTED PUBLICATIONS** Auth, London in the 1890s: A Cultural History, W.W. Norton, (London, NY), 95; coauth, "A Newly Discovered Lyric by Oscar Wilde", Times Literary Supplement, (London) Feb 95; ed, "I Can Resist Everything except Temptation" and other Quotations from Oscar Wilde, Columbia Univ Pr, (NY), 97; coauth, "Wilde as Poet", in Cambridge Companion to Oscar Wilde, ed Peter Raby, Cambridge Univ Pr, (97): 57-68; auth, "Oscar Wilde and the Religion of Art", The Wildean: J of the Oscar Wilde Soc, 12 (98): 25-29; auth, "Lady Jane Francesca Elgee Wilde", in Victorian Women Poets, ed William B. Thesing, Gale Res Co. (98): 298-305; coed, "The Yellow Book and Beyond: Selected Letters of Henry Harland to John Lane", Eng. Lit in Transition 1880-1920 41.1, (99): 401-32; auth, "Oscar Wilde and the Green Carnation", Eng Lit in Transition 1880-1920 43.3 (00); coed, Poems and Poems in Prose, Vol 1, Complete Works of Oscar Wilde, eds Russell Jackson and Ian Small, Oxford Univ Pr, 00. **CONTACT ADDRESS** Dept English, Brooklyn Col, CUNY, 2901 Bedford Ave, Brooklyn, NY 11210-2813.

BECKWITH, JOHN
PERSONAL Born 03/09/1927, Victoria, BC, Canada **DISCIPLINE** HISTORY OF MUSIC **EDUCATION** Victoria Col, 44-45; Royal Conserv Music, 45-50; Univ Toronto, MusB, 47, MusM, 61. **CAREER** Lectr, 55-61, asst prof 61-66, assoc prof, 66-70, dean, 70-77, Prof Music, Univ Toronto (RETIRED), 70-90; dir, Inst Can Music, 84-90; assoc ed, Can Music J, 57-62. **HONORS AND AWARDS** Can Music Coun Annual medal, 72; MusD (honoris causa), Mt Allison Univ, 74; Univ Toronto Sesquicentennial Awd, 77; MusD (honoris causa), McGill Univ, 78; Can Music Coun Composer Year, 85; mem, Order Can, 87; Richard S. Hill Awd, US Music Libr Asn, 90; Toronto Arts Awd, 94; Mus D (honoris causa), Univ Guelph, 95; diplome d'honneur, Can Conf Arts, 96. **MEMBERSHIPS** Can Musical Heritage Soc; Toronto Musicians Asn; Can League Composers; Sonneck Soc Am Music. **SELECTED PUBLICATIONS** Auth, Music Papers, 97; ed, Canadian Composers study ser, 75-90; ed, The Canadian Musical Heritage, vol 5, Hymn Tunes, 86, vol 18, Oratoria and Cantata Excerpts, 95; co-ed, The Modern Composer and His World, 61; co-ed, Contemporary Canadian Composers, 75; co-ed, Musical Canada, 88; contribur, Dictionary of Contemporary Music, 74; Can consult & contribur, The New Grove, 80; contribur & exec bd mem, Encyclopedia of Music in Canada, 81, 93. **CONTACT ADDRESS** Fac of Music, Univ of Toronto, Toronto, ON, Canada M5S 1A1.

BECKWITH, SARAH
DISCIPLINE ENGLISH LITERATURE **EDUCATION** Univ London, PhD, 92. **CAREER** Prof, Duke Univ. **RESEARCH** Middle Eng relig(s). **SELECTED PUBLICATIONS** Auth, Christ's Body: Identity, Religion and Society in Medieval English Writing, Routledge, 93; publ(s) on lit anchoritism, medieval theatre; sacramental cult. **CONTACT ADDRESS** Dept English, Duke Univ, 316 Allen Bldg., Box 90015, Durham, NC 27708. **EMAIL** sarah.beckwith@duke.edu

BEDFORD, BONNIE C.
PERSONAL Born 03/23/1953, Bradford, PA, s, 1 child **DISCIPLINE** CONTEMPORARY DRAMA AND FICTION; CREATIVE WRITING **EDUCATION** Waynesburg Col, BA; SUNY,Binghamton, MA, PhD. **CAREER** Tchg asst, SUNY; asst prof; assoc prof of Eng, Wilkes Univ. **HONORS AND AWARDS** Finalist Sundance Institutes Film Dev program for SNIPER; Semi-finalist Sundance Institute's Film Dev program. **MEMBERSHIPS** Mem, Dramatists Guild; Author's League of Am; Assn Theatre in Higher Edu; Assoc Wrtg Prog; Nat Coun tThr(s) Eng; Delta Kappa Gamma. **RESEARCH** Screenwriting, contemporary fiction, drama. **SELECTED PUBLICATIONS** Auth, Sniper, play, produced at Wilkes Univ, and T. Schreiber Studio, NYC. **CONTACT ADDRESS** Dept of Eng, Wilkes Univ, 170 S Franklin St, Wilkes-Barre, PA 18766. **EMAIL** bedford@wilkes.edu

BEDNARZ, JAMES P.
DISCIPLINE RENAISSANCE, SHAKESPEARE, CRITICAL THEORY **EDUCATION** Columbia Univ, PhD. **CAREER** Prof, Long Island Univ, C.W. Post Campus. **SELECTED PUBLICATIONS** Auth, Representing Jonson: Histriomastix and the Origin of the Poets' War; Ralegh in Spenser's Historical Allegory; Imitations of Spenser in A Midsummer Night's Dream; The Dual Nature of Paul Klee's Symbolic Language. **CONTACT ADDRESS** Long Island Univ, C.W. Post, Brookville, NY 11548-1300.

BEEBE, STEVEN A.
PERSONAL Born 09/19/1950, Independence, MO, m, 1974, 2 children **DISCIPLINE** COMMUNICATION **EDUCATION** Central Mo State Univ, BS, 72; Central Mo State Univ, MA, 73; Univ Mo, PhD, 76. **CAREER** From Asst Prof to Prof, Southwest Tex State Univ, 89-. **HONORS AND AWARDS** Teaching Excellence Awd, Southwest Tex State Univ, 88; Outstanding Commun Prof in Am, Nat Speaker's Assoc, 96; Outstanding Int Progs Adminr, Southwest Tex State Univ, 97; Commun Assessment Awd, Nat Commun Assoc, 98. **MEMBERSHIPS** Nat Commun Assoc, Assoc for Commun Admin, Int Commun Assoc, Central States Commun Assoc, Southern States Commun Assoc, Florida Speech Commun Assoc, Texas Speech Commun Assoc. **RESEARCH** Group communication, communication training, instructional communication, communication competence. **SELECTED PUBLICATIONS** Coauth, "Emotional Response and Learning: Explaining Affinity Seeking Behaviors in the Classroom," Resources in Educ, 372 (95); coauth, Interpersonal Communication: Relating to Others, Can Ed, Allyn and Bacon (Ontario, Can), 97; coauth, "Speech Communication in Russia," Commun Educ, 47 (98): 261-273; auth, "International Communication Education," in Commun Admin Handbk (Hillsdale, NJ: Earlbaum, 99); coed, Interpersonal Communication: Relating to Others, 2nd Ed, Allyn and Bacon (Boston, MA), 99; coauth, Public Speaking: An Audience-Centered Approach, 4th Ed, Allyn and Bacon (Boston, MA), forthcoming. **CONTACT ADDRESS** Dept Commun, Southwest Texas State Univ, San Marcos, TX 78666. **EMAIL** sb03@swt.edu

BEENE, LYNN DIANNE
PERSONAL Born 12/12/1946, Sarasota, FL, m, 1971 **DISCIPLINE** LANGUAGE AND RHETORIC, PROFESSIONAL WRITING, CONTEMPORARY FICTION **EDUCATION** Univ Ark, BA, 69; MA, 73; Univ Kans, PhD, 81. **CAREER** From asst prof to prof, Univ NMex, 81-. **HONORS AND AWARDS** Outstanding Teacher Awd, Univ Kans, 79; Endowment Fel, Univ Kans, 77; Presidential Recognition Awd, Univ NMex, 83; Awd of Excellence, 90. **MEMBERSHIPS** ADS, MLA, NSWA, NCTE. **RESEARCH** Rhetoric of science writing, contemporary fiction/genre fiction, pragmatics and discourse analysis. **SELECTED PUBLICATIONS** Coauth, The Riverside Handbook of Grammar and Rhetoric, Houghton Miffin Co (Boston, MA), 92; auth, "John le Carre," Twayne English Auth Series, G K Hall (Boston, MA), 92; auth, "William Wilkie Collins," in The Dict of Lit Biog (Columbia, SC: Bruccoli Clark Layman, 96), 58-76; auth, "John le Carre: Post-War Literatures in English" (96): 1-18; auth, Guide to British Prose Explication: Nineteenth & Twentieth Century, G K Hall (Boston, MA), 97; auth, "John Le Carre," Mystery & Suspense Writers: The Lit of Crime, Detection and Espionage, vol 1, Charles Scribner's Sons Publ (New York, NY), 98. **CONTACT ADDRESS** Dept English, Univ of New Mexico, Albuquerque, 1 University Campus, Albuquerque, NM 87131-0001. **EMAIL** lbeene@unm.edu

BEEVI, MARIAM
PERSONAL s **DISCIPLINE** LITERATURE, WOMEN'S STUDIES **EDUCATION** Univ Calif Irvine, BA, 94; MA, 96; PhD, 00. **MEMBERSHIPS** MLA, AAAS, AAS. **RESEARCH** Diaspora, Visual Studies, Psychoanalysis, Sexuality. **SELECTED PUBLICATIONS** Auth, "The Passing of Literary Traditions: The Figure of the Woman from Vietnamese Nationalism to Vietnamese American Transnationalism," Amerasia Jour 23.2 (97): 27-53. **CONTACT ADDRESS** Dept English, Univ of California, Irvine, 435 Hum Instructional Bldg, Irvine, CA 92697-0001. **EMAIL** mbeeri@uci.edu

BEGIEBING, ROBERT J.
PERSONAL Born 11/18/1946, Adams, MA, m, 1968, 2 children **DISCIPLINE** ENGLISH **EDUCATION** Norwich Univ, BA, 68; Boston Col, MA, 70; Univ NH, PhD, 77. **CAREER** Instr, Univ Ky Extension Prog, 70-71; Tchng Asst, 72-76, Assoc & Asst Prof, 77-84, Full Prof, 84-, New Hampshire Col.

HONORS AND AWARDS Who's Who Am Col & Univ; Dissertation Fellow, Univ NH, 76-77; Artist opportunity grant, NH Coun on the Arts, 93; Lila Wallace, Readers Dig Artist Fellow to the Am Antiquarian Soc, 96; coord of hum & eng language & lit, nh col, 94-96. **MEMBERSHIPS** MLA; AWP; Authors Guild. **RESEARCH** Nature writing; modern American & British literature. **SELECTED PUBLICATIONS** Auth, Acts of Regeneration: Allegory and Archetype in the Works of Norman Mailer, Univ Mo Press, 81; auth, Toward a New Synthesis: John Fowles, John Gardner, and Norman Mailer, Univ Rochester Press, 89; co-auth, The Literature of Nature: The British and American Traditions, Plexus Publishers, 90; auth, The Strange Death of Mistress Coffin, Algonquin Books, 91, 96; Auth, The adventures of Allegra Sullerton, UPNE, 99. **CONTACT ADDRESS** Dept of English, New Hampshire Col, 2500 N River Rd, Manchester, NH 03124. **EMAIL** rbegiebi@minerva.nhc.edu

BEGNAL, MICHAEL HENRY
DISCIPLINE MODERN ENGLISH & COMPARATIVE LITERATURE **EDUCATION** Univ Conn, BA, 61; Pa State Univ, MA, 63; Univ Wash, PhD, 68. **CAREER** Instr English, Colgate Univ, 63-65; assoc prof, English & comp lit, 68-80, prof Eng & comp lit, 80-, PA State Univ; prof Am lit, Charles Univ Prague, 73-74 & 75-76. **RESEARCH** James Joyce; Irish literature; modern literature; beat generation. **SELECTED PUBLICATIONS** Auth, Joseph Sheridan LeFanu, 71; auth, Narrator and Character in Finnegans Wake, Bucknell Univ, 74; co-ed & contribr, A Conceptual Guide to Finnegans Wake, Pa State Univ, 74; auth, Dreamscheme: Narrative and Voice in Finnegans Wake, Syracuse U Press, 88; auth, On Miracle Ground: Essays on the Fiction of Lawrence Durrell, Bucknell, 90. **CONTACT ADDRESS** Dept of English, Pennsylvania State Univ, Univ Park, 117 Burrowes Bldg, University Park, PA 16802-6200. **EMAIL** mhb3@psu.edu

BEHAGUE, GERARD
DISCIPLINE MUSIC, LATIN AMERICAN MUSIC, ETHNOMUSICOLOGY **EDUCATION** Tulane Univ, PhD. **CAREER** Prof; Virginia Murchison Regents prof; ed, Lat Am Music Rev; ch, Music Dept, 80-89. **HONORS AND AWARDS** Helped develop, grad prog in ethnomusicol; founder & ed, Lat Am Music Rev, 80-. **MEMBERSHIPS** Former pres, Soc for Ethnomusicol & ed, its J, 70s. **RESEARCH** Musical traditions of Latin Am and the Span Caribbean. **SELECTED PUBLICATIONS** Publ on, var aspects of Lat Am music. **CONTACT ADDRESS** School of Music, Univ of Texas, Austin, W 25th, Austin, TX 78712. **EMAIL** gbehaque@mail.utexas.edu

BEHDAD, ALI
PERSONAL Born 05/22/1961, Iran **DISCIPLINE** LITERATURE **EDUCATION** Univ Calif Berkeley, BA, 83; Univ Mich, MA, PhD, 90. **CAREER** Asst prof, Univ Rochester, 90-93; assoc prof, UCLA, 93- . **HONORS AND AWARDS** Rockham Fel, Univ Mich, 89-90; HRI Fel, Irvine, 97; UC President's Fel, 99-00. **MEMBERSHIPS** MLA; MESA. **RESEARCH** US nationalism & immigration, postcolonial lit & theory, travel literature. **SELECTED PUBLICATIONS** Auth, Belated Travelers: Orientalism in the Age of Colonial Dissolution, Duke Univ Press, 94; Ins and Outs: Producing Delinquency at the Border, J of Chicano Stud, 98; Postcolonial Belatedness and Cultural Politics, Duke Univ Press, 98; global Disjunctures, Diasporic Differences, and the New World (Dis)Order, Blackwell, 98; Orientalist or Orienteur? Antoin Sevruguin and the Margin of Photography, Sackler Gallery Series, 99. **CONTACT ADDRESS** English Dept, Univ of California, Los Angeles, Los Angeles, CA 90095. **EMAIL** behdad@humnet.ucla.edu

BEHRENDT, STEPHEN C.
PERSONAL Born 01/01/1947, Marinette, WI, m, 1969, 1 child **DISCIPLINE** ENGLISH LITERATURE **EDUCATION** Univ Wis, BA, 69, PhD(English), 74; Eastern Ky Univ, MA, 70. **CAREER** Vis asst prof English, Univ Minn, 75-77; instr English, Elizabethtown Col, 77-80; asst prof English, Univ Nebr, 80-, Am Philos Soc res grant, 78; Nat Endowment for Humanities summer sem, 79. **MEMBERSHIPS** MLA; Am Soc Eighteenth Century Studies; Midwest Mod Lang Asn. **RESEARCH** William Blake; English Romanticism, particularly Shelley; interrelations among the arts. **SELECTED PUBLICATIONS** Auth, Bright pilgrimage: William Blake's designs for L'Allegro and Il Penseroso, Milton Studies, 75; Blake's illustrations to Milton's Nativity Ode, Philol Quart, Winter 76; The polished artifact: Some observations on imitative criticism, Genre, Spring 77; The mental contest: Blake's Comus designs, Blake Studies, 78; The worst disease: Blake's Tiriel, Colby Libr Quart, 79; A Vocabulary of Lineaments: Blake and the Language of Art, Blake Studies (in press); The Exoteric Species: The Popular Idiom in Shelley's Poetry, Genre (in press); The Moment of Explosion: Blake and the Illustration of Milton, Univ Nebr Press, 83; A Step in the Dark, Mid-List Press, 96; Royal Mourning and Regency Culture: Elegies and Memorials of Princess Charlotte, Macmillan, 97; Romanticism, Radicalism, and the Press, Wayne State Univ Press, 97. **CONTACT ADDRESS** Dept of English, Univ of Nebraska, Lincoln, PO Box 880333, Lincoln, NE 68588-0333. **EMAIL** sbehrend@unlinfo.unl.edu

BEIDLER, PETER GRANT
PERSONAL Born 03/13/1940, Bethlehem, PA, m, 1963, 4 children **DISCIPLINE** ENGLISH & AMERICAN LITERATURE, AMERICAN INDIAN STUDIES **EDUCATION** Earlham Col, BA, 62; Lehigh Univ, MA, 65, PhD(English), 68. **CAREER** From asst prof to prof, 68-78, Lucy G Moses Dist Prof English, Lehigh Univ, 78-; NEH fel anthrop, Univ AZ, 73-74. **HONORS AND AWARDS** CASE Nat Prof of the Year, 83; Lindback Teaching Awd, 71, 94. **MEMBERSHIPS** MLA; Asn Study of Am Indian Lit. **RESEARCH** Chaucer; American Indian literature; Medieval literature. **SELECTED PUBLICATIONS** Auth, Fig Tree John, An Indian in Fact and Fiction, Univ AZ Press, 77; with Marion F Egge, The American Indian in Short Fiction: An Annotated Bibliography, Scarecrow Press, 79; John Gower's Literary Transformations in the Confessio Amantis, Univ Press Am, 82; Distinguished Teachers on Effective Teaching: Observations on Effective Teaching by College Professors Recognized by the Council for Advancment and Support of Education, Jossey-Bass, Pubs, 86; Ghosts, Demons, and Henry James: The Turn of the Screw at the Turn of the Century, Univ MO Press, 89; Writing Matters, McGraw-Hill, 90, Macmillan, 92; Henry James, The Turn of the Screw: Text and Five Contemporary Critical Essays, Bedford Books of St Martin's Press, 95; Geoffrey Chaucer, The Wife of Bath: Complete, Authoritative Text with Biographical and Historical Contexts, Critical History, and Essays from Five Contemporary Critical Perspectives, Bedford Books of St Martin's Press, 96; The Wife of Bath's Prologue and Tale: An Annotated Bibliography, with Elizabeth M. Biebel, Univ Toronto Press, 98; Masculinities in Chaucer, Boydell & Brewer, 98; auth, A Reader's Guide to the Novels of Louise Erdrich, with Gay Barton, Univ of MO Press, 99; auth, The Native American in Short Ficiton in the Saturday Evening Post, with Marion F. Egge, Scarecrow Press of the Univ Press of America, 00. **CONTACT ADDRESS** Dept English, Lehigh Univ, 35 Sayre Dr, Bethlehem, PA 18015-3076. **EMAIL** pgb1@lehigh.edu

BEJA, MORRIS
PERSONAL Born 07/18/1935, New York, NY, m, 1990, 2 children **DISCIPLINE** ENGLISH **EDUCATION** City Col NYork, BA, 57; Columbia Univ, MA, 58; Cornell Univ, PhD(English), 63 **CAREER** From instr to assoc prof, 61-71, Prof English, Ohio State Univ, 71-, chair, 83-94; Ohio State Univ res grants, 65, 68, 71, 75 & 78; Fulbright lectr Am lit, Univ Thessaloniki, 65-66; Develop Fund fac fel, 68; Fulbright vis prof English, Univ Col, Dublin, 72-73; Guggenheim fel, 72-73; ed, James Joyce Found Newslett, 77-. **HONORS AND AWARDS** Alumni Distinguished Teaching Awd, 82 **MEMBERSHIPS** MLA; Am Conf Irish Studies; Intl James Joyce Found; Intl Virginia Woolf Soc **RESEARCH** Modern fiction, Anglo-Irish literature, film **SELECTED PUBLICATIONS** Co-ed, Samuel Beckett: Humanistic Perspectives, Ohio State Univ Press, 83; ed, Critical Essays on Virginia Woolf, G K Hall, 85; co-ed, James Joyce: The Centennial Symposium, Univ Ill Press, 86; co-ed, Coping with Joyce: Essays from the Copenhagen Symposium, Ohio State Univ Press, 89; auth, Epiphany in the Modern Novel, Univ of Wash Press, 71; auth, Film and Literature, Longman, 79; auth, Joyce, The Artist Manque, and Indeterminancy: A Lecture and an Essay, pamphlet, Princess Grace Irish Libr Lectr, Colin Smyth, 89; auth, James Joyce: A Literary Life, Ohio State Univ Press, Macmillan, London, Gill & Macmillan, Dublin, 92; ed, Perspectives on Orson Welles, G K Hall, 95; co-ed, Joyce in the Hibernian Metropolis: Essays, Ohio State Univ Press, 96; ed, Virginia Woolf, Mrs Dalloway, Basil Blackwell, 96. **CONTACT ADDRESS** Dept of English, Ohio State Univ, Columbus, 164 W 17th Ave, Columbus, OH 43210-1326. **EMAIL** beja.1@osu.edu

BEJEL, EMILIO
PERSONAL Born, Cuba **DISCIPLINE** SPANISH, SPANISH AMERICAN LITERATURE **EDUCATION** Univ Miami, BA, 67; Flor State Univ, MA, 69; PhD, 70. **CAREER** Asst prof, 71-75, assoc prof, 75-80, prof, 80-82, Fairfield Univ; assoc prof, 82-84, prof, 84-91, Univ Fla; prof, Univ Colo, 91-. **HONORS AND AWARDS** Yale Vis Fel; NEH; Lilly Found Fel; Lit Guild Frst Prize; Phi Delta Pi. **MEMBERSHIPS** MLA; LASA. **RESEARCH** Contemporary Spanish American literature; Cuban literature and culture. **SELECTED PUBLICATIONS** Auth, Buero Vallejo: lo moral, lo social y lo metafisico, Inst de Estudios Superiores (Montevideo), 72; auth, Literatura de Nuestra America: Estudios de literatura cubana e hispanoamericana, Cen Invest Ling Lit Univ Veracruzana (Xalapa), 83; coauth, La subversion de la semiotica: Analisis estructural de textos hispanicos, Hispamerica (Gaithersburg), 88; auth, Jose' Lezama Lima: Poet of the Image, Univ Press Flor (Gainesville), 90; auth, Escribir en Cuba: Entrevistas con escritoires cubanos, 1979-89, Univ Puerto Rico (San Juan), 91. **CONTACT ADDRESS** Dept Spanish, Portuguese, Univ of Colorado, Boulder, PO Box 278, Boulder, CO 80309-0278. **EMAIL** bejel@spot.colorado.edu

BELASCO, SUSAN
PERSONAL Born 06/25/1950, Pittsburgh, PA **DISCIPLINE** ENGLISH **EDUCATION** Baylor Univ, BA, 72; Baylor Univ, MA, 74; Univ Leicester, MA, 83; Tex A&M Univ, PhD, 87. **CAREER** Instr, McLennan Community Col, 76-87; Asst Prof, Allegheny Col, 87-92; Assoc Prof, Calif St Univ, 92-94; Assoc Prof, Univ Tulsa, 94-00; Prof, Univ Nebr, 00-. **HONORS AND AWARDS** Rotary Found Fel. **MEMBERSHIPS** MLA, RSAP, SSAWW, NCTE, SHARP. **RESEARCH** Nineteenth-Century American literature and culture. **SELECTED PUBLICATIONS** Co-ed, Periodical Literature in Nineteenth-Century America, UP of Va (Charlottesville), 95; ed and introduction, Ruth Hall, by Fanny Fern, Penguin Books (New York, NY), 96; co-ed, Approaches to Teaching 'Uncle Tom's Cabin,' Mod Lang Asn (New York, NY), 00; auth, Constructing Literacies: A Harcourt Reader for College Writers, Harcourt Brace Publ (New York, NY), 00; **CONTACT ADDRESS** Dept English, Univ of Nebraska, Lincoln, 227 Andrews Hall, Lincoln, NE 68588-0333. **EMAIL** sbelasco@unl.edu

BELIFIORE, ELIZABETH S.
PERSONAL Born 06/21/1944, Austin, TX, m, 1966, 1 child **DISCIPLINE** CLASSICAL STUDIES **EDUCATION** Barnard Col, BA, 66; Univ Calif Los Angeles, MA, 72; PhD, 78. **CAREER** Asst prof, Scripps Col, 79-80; asst prof to prof, Univ Minn, 80-. **HONORS AND AWARDS** Fel, ACLS, 87-88; Fel, NEH, 88. **MEMBERSHIPS** Am Philol Asn; Class Asn of the Mid W and S; Women's Class Caucus; Soc for Ancient Greek Philos **RESEARCH** Ancient Philosophy; Greek tragedy. **SELECTED PUBLICATIONS** Auth, Tragic Pleasures: Aristotle on Plot and Emotion, Princeton Univ Press, 92; auth, "Aristotle and Iphigenia," in Essays on Aristotle's Poetics, (Princeton Univ Press, 92),359-377; auth, "Harming Friends: Reciprocity in Greek Tragedy," in Reciprocity in Ancient Greece, (Oxford Univ Press, 98), 139-158; auth, Murder Among Friends: Violation of Philia in Greek Tragedy, Oxford Univ Press, 00. **CONTACT ADDRESS** Dept Class and Near E Studies, Univ of Minnesota, Twin Cities, 9 Pleasant St SE, 305 Folwell Hall, Minneapolis, MN 55455. **EMAIL** esb@tc.umn.edu

BELL, BERNARD W.
DISCIPLINE ENGLISH **EDUCATION** Howard Univ, BA, 62, MA, 66; Univ MA, Amherst, PhD, 70. **CAREER** Teaching asst, Howard Univ, Washington, DC, 62-63; res asst, Prof Sterling Brown, summer 63; teacher, Calvin Coolidge High School, Washington, DC, 63-67; teaching asst, Univ MA, 67-68; teacher, Upward Bound Project, Univ MA, summer 68, 69, 71; lect/asst prof, Dept of English, Univ MA, Amherst, Sept 69- Feb 75; lect, Dept of Afro-Am Studies, Smith Col, Northampton, MA, Jan-June 73; vis prof, Dept of English, Clark Univ, Worcester, MA, Jan-June 72, Sept 73-Jan 74; lect, Inst of Afro-Am Culture, Univ IA, June 74; vis lect, Dept of English, Univ of Freiburg, West Germany, Sept 74-Aug 75; lect, Dept of English, Padagogische Hochschule, Freiburg, West Germany, 75; vis lect, Dept of English, Williams Col, Williamstown, MA, 79; Sr Fulbright Scholar, Univ of Coimbra, Portugal, 82-83; assoc prof, Dept of English, Univ MA, Amherst, 75-87; vis prof, Dept of Black Studies, Amherst Col, 88-89; prof, Dept of English, Univ MA, Amherst, 87-91; prof, Dept of English, PA State Univ, University Park, 91-; Sr Fulbright lect, Univ of Salamanca, Spain, Jan-June 96. **HONORS AND AWARDS** NDEA Fel, 65, 68-69; Phi Kappa Phi Honors, 69; NEH fel, 72-73; Col Lang Asn Creative Book Prize for The Afro-American Novel and Its Tradition, 89; Sr Fulbright-Hays Scholar: Univ of Coimbra, Portugal, Oct 82-July 83; Univ of Salamanca, Spain, Jan-June 96. **MEMBERSHIPS** Am Studies Asn, 88-; Multi-Ethnic Lit of the US Soc, 88-; Northeast Modern Lang Asn, 71-73; Modern Lang Asn, 71-78, 87-, delegate assembly, 95-97, exec comm div of Black Am lit and Culture, 95-; Col Lang Asn, 71-; Nat Coun of Teachers of English, 97. **RESEARCH** African Am studies; Am realism; modern British and Am novel; Jean Toomer; William Faulkner; Mark Twain; Vernacular Theory. **SELECTED PUBLICATIONS** Ed, Modern and Contemporary Afro-American Poetry, Allyn and Bacon, 74; auth, The Folk Roots of Contemporary Afro-American Poetry, Broadside Press, 74; The Afro-American Novel and Its Tradition, Univ MA Press, 87; guest ed, Clarence Major Special Issue, African Am Rev, 94; co-ed, Contemporary Literature in the African Diaspora, Univ of Salamanca, 97; co-ed, Call and Response: The African American Literary Tradition, Houghton Mifflin, 97; co-ed, W. E. B. DuBois on Race and Culture, Routledge, 97; more than 50 essays, articles, and reviews in such journals and periodicals as The MA Rev, Black World, The World and I, Commonwealth, College Lang Asn J, Phylon, Mark Twain J, MI Quart Rev, and Am Dialog. **CONTACT ADDRESS** Dept of English, Pennsylvania State Univ, Univ Park, 39 Burrowes, State College, PA 16801. **EMAIL** bwb4@psu.edu

BELL, ILONA
DISCIPLINE ENGLISH **EDUCATION** Harvard Univ, BA, 69; Boston Col, PhD, 77. **CAREER** Prof, Williams Col. **HONORS AND AWARDS** Mary Ingraham Bunting Fel; Nat Endow for the Huimanities Fel; Mellon Grant for Faculty Dev; Francis C. Oakley Center for the Humanities and Soc Sci Fel; Am Coun of Learned Soc, fel for Recent Ph D Recipients **MEMBERSHIPS** John Donne Soc, Milton Soc, Shakespearre Assoc of Am, Soc for the Study of Earyl Modern Women. **RESEARCH** The poetry, politics, and practice of Elizabethan Courtship; Renaissance Women; Elizabeth I, John Donne; Shakespeare's sonnets and "A Lovers's Complaint" **SELECTED PUBLICATIONS** Auth, "Under ye rage of a hott sonn & yr eyes: John Donne's Love Letters to Ann More," The Eagle and the Dove: Essays Reassessing John Donne, (86), 25-52; auth, Elizabeth I--A woman, and (if that be not enough) an unmarried Virgin; Polit Rhetoric, Power, and Renaissance Women, 95; auth," What if

it be a she, The Riddle of Donne's Curse," John Donne's desire of more: The Subject of Anne More Donne in His Poetry, (96), 106-139; auth, "Elizabethan Love Poetry and the Femal Lyric Audience," Representing Women in Renaissance England, (Univ of Missouri Press, 97), 76-92; auth, Elizabethan Women and the Poetry of Courtship, Cambridge Univ Press, 98; auth, a Lover's Complaint--A Conclusion to Shakespeare's Sonnets, Critical Essays, 98; auth, "Courting Anne More," John Donne Journal 19, (00); auth, "A Letter sent by the Maydens of London-- In Defense of their Lawful Liberty," Women, Writing, and the Reprodiuction of Culture in Tudor and Stuart Britain, Syracuse Univ Press, 00; auth, Elizabeth I and the Politics of Elizabethan Courtship, (forthcoming). **CONTACT ADDRESS** Dept of English, Williams Col, Stetson d-20, Williamstown, MA 01267. **EMAIL** ibell@williams.edu

BELL, KIMBERLY
DISCIPLINE COMPOSITION **EDUCATION** Vanderbilt Univ, PhD, 72. **CAREER** Dept Eng, Clemson Univ **RESEARCH** Composition and writing. **SELECTED PUBLICATIONS** Auth, Resolving the Dichotomy Between Academic Discourse and Expressive Writing in High School and First-Year College Courses, Tenn Eng Jour, 97. **CONTACT ADDRESS** Clemson Univ, 507 Strode, Clemson, SC 29634.

BELL, ROSEANN P.
PERSONAL Born 05/02/1945, Atlanta, GA, d **DISCIPLINE** ENGLISH **EDUCATION** Howard University, BA, 1966; Emory University, MA (cum laude), 1970, PhD (cum laude), 1974. **CAREER** US Civil Service Commission, typist, 64-66; Atlanta Public School System, instructor, 66-70; various/part-time teaching positions; freelance editor of education manuscripts, 70-; Spelman College, asst prof, 70-; Atlanta Voice Newspaper, columnist, 71; Cornell Univ, Afro-American Studies Dept, asst prof; Univ of Mississippi, Dept of English, prof, currently. **HONORS AND AWARDS** Emory University, scholarship winner, 1968-70; Natl Institute of Humanities Fellowship, 1971-73; Natl Fellowships Fund Fellowship, Ford Foundation, 1973-74. **SELECTED PUBLICATIONS** Numerous articles. **CONTACT ADDRESS** Dept of English, Univ of Mississippi, University, MS 38677-9701.

BELL, STEVEN
DISCIPLINE MODERN SPANISH AMERICAN LITERATURE **EDUCATION** Univ Kans, BA, 77; Univ Ky, MA, 79; Univ Kans, PhD, 84. **CAREER** English and Lit, Univ Ark. **SELECTED PUBLICATIONS** Ed & coauth, Critical Theory, Cultural Politics, 93. **CONTACT ADDRESS** Univ of Arkansas, Fayetteville, Fayetteville, AR 72701.

BELL, VEREEN M.
DISCIPLINE MODERN POETRY AND FICTION, CRITICAL THEORY **EDUCATION** Duke Univ, PhD. **CAREER** Instr, Vanderbilt Univ. **SELECTED PUBLICATIONS** Published books on Robert Lowell, Cormac McCarthy, and W. B. Yeats. **CONTACT ADDRESS** Vanderbilt Univ, Nashville, TN 37203-1727.

BELL-METEREAU, REBECCA
DISCIPLINE FILM AND PROSE FICTION **EDUCATION** IN Univ, BA, MA, PhD. **CAREER** Southwest Tex State Univ **SELECTED PUBLICATIONS** Auth, Hollywood Androgyny; Writing With:(New Directions in Teaching, Learning, and Research); Essays in Women Worldwalkers: New Dimensions of Science Fiction and Fantasy; Cultural Conflicts in Contemporary Literature; Deciding Our Future: Technological Imperatives for Educations. **CONTACT ADDRESS** Southwest Texas State Univ, 601 University Dr, San Marcos, TX 78666-4604.

BELLAMY, JOE DAVID
PERSONAL Born 12/29/1941, Cincinnati, OH, m, 1964, 2 children **DISCIPLINE** ENGLISH LITERATURE **EDUCATION** Antioch Col, BA, 64; Univ Iowa, MFA, 69. **CAREER** Asst col ed, Antioch col, 65-67; from instr to asst prof English, Mansfield State Col, 69-72; asst prof, 72-74, assoc prof, 74-80, Prof English, St Lawrence Univ, 80-, Publ & ed, Fiction Int, 72-; Breadloaf scholar, Bridgeman Award, Middlebury Col, 73; dir, Ann Fiction Int-St Lawrence Univ Writer's Conf, 74-80; consult ed, Short Fiction Ser, Univ Ill Press, 74-; Nat Endowment Humanities grant, Brown Univ, 74. **HONORS AND AWARDS** Fels Awd ed, Coord Coun Lit Mag, 76. **MEMBERSHIPS** MLA; Northeast Mod Lang Asn; AAUP; Coord Coun Lit Mag, (pres, 79-81). **RESEARCH** Formal innovation in contemporary fiction. **SELECTED PUBLICATIONS** Auth, 'Atomic Love', NAmer Rev, Vol 0278, 93; Literary Politics, Frohnmayer, 5 Sex Acts, Wild Thing, the Nea, and Me, Antioch Rev, Vol 0052, 94. **CONTACT ADDRESS** Dept of English, St. Lawrence Univ, Canton, NY 13617-1499.

BELLMAN, JONATHAN
PERSONAL Born 08/15/1957, Fresno, CA, m, 1 child **DISCIPLINE** MUSICOLOGY **EDUCATION** Univ Calif, BA, 79; Univ Ill, MM, 82; Stanford Univ, DMA, 90. **CAREER** Asst prof, Univ Richmond, 90-92; assoc prof, Univ N Colo, 93-. **RESEARCH** Music style; Hungarian-Gypsy music; Musical exoticism; Chopin; 19th-century music; Piano performance practices; Rock music. **SELECTED PUBLICATIONS** Auth, The Style Hongrois in the Music of Western Europe, 93; ed, The Exotic in Western Music, 98, Northeastern Univ; auth, "A Short Guide to Writing About Music," Longman, 00. **CONTACT ADDRESS** School of Music, Univ of No Colorado, Greeley, CO 80639. **EMAIL** jdbellm@bentley.unco.edu

BELLMAN, SAMUEL IRVING
PERSONAL Born 09/28/1926, El Paso, TX, m, 1952, 2 children **DISCIPLINE** ENGLISH **EDUCATION** Univ Tex, BA, 47; Wayne Univ, MA, 51; Ohio State Univ, PhD, 55. **CAREER** Teaching asst, Ohio State Univ, 53-54, asst instr, 54-55; instr English, Fresno State Col, 55-57; asst prof, Calif State Polytech Col, San Luis Obispo, 57-59; from asst prof to assoc prof, 59-66, prof, 66-96, prof emer, English, Calif State Polytech Univ, Pomona, 96- ; Vis exchange prof Am lit, Portsmouth Polytech, Eng, 75-76. **RESEARCH** Modern Amer literature; poetics; literary criticism. **SELECTED PUBLICATIONS** Ed, College Experience, 62 & Survey and Forecast, 66, Chandler Publ; auth, Marjorie Kinnan Rawlings, Twayne, 74; auth, Constance Mayfield Rourke, GK Hall & Twayne, 81; auth, "Where the West Begins: Constance Rourke's Images of Her Own Frontierland," in Women & Western American Literture, ed Helen W. Stauffer & Susan J. Rosowski (Whitson Pub, 82); auth, "Popular Writers in the Modern Age: Constance Rourke, Pearl Buck, Marjorie Kinnan Rawlings, and Margaret Mitchell," in American Women Writers: Bibliographical Essays, ed Maurice Duke, Jackson R. Bryer, & M. Thomas Inge (Greenwood Pr, 83); auth, "Mars and Venus in the Groves of Academe," in Short Story, vol 2 (Spring 94); auth, "Barbara Pym," in Encycl of British Humorists, vol 2, ed Steven H Gale (Garland Pub, 96); auth, "School for Courtship," Women & Lang, vol 20 (Spring 97). **CONTACT ADDRESS** 1012 Lake Forest Dr, Claremont, CA 91711. **EMAIL** sibellman@csupomona.edu

BELLO, RICHARD S.
PERSONAL Born 02/15/1955, Baton Rouge, LA **DISCIPLINE** SPEECH COMMUNICATION **EDUCATION** Louisiana State Univ, BA, 77; MA, 79; PhD, 99. **CAREER** Instr, Tex AM Univ, 83-84; asst prof, Nichols State Univ, 84-. **HONORS AND AWARDS** Phi Beta Kappa; Mu Sigma Rho; Pi Sigma Alpha. **MEMBERSHIPS** SSCA; NCA. **RESEARCH** Language in interpersonal and public communication; equivocation; interpretation of message. **SELECTED PUBLICATIONS** Auth, "A Burkeian Analysis of the 'Political Correctness' Confrontation in Higher Education," Southern Comm J 61 (96); auth, "The Contemporary Rise of Louisiana Voices and Other Neo-Chautauqua's: A Return to Oral Performance," Text and Perform Quart 17 (97); co auth, "Judicial Tests for Distinguishing Statements of Fact from Statements of Opinion: An Empirical Examination," Southwestern Mass Comm J 15 (99); auth, "Determinates of Equivocation: The Influence of Situational Formality, Interaction Phase, and Ambiguity Tolerance," Comm Res 27 (00). **CONTACT ADDRESS** Dept Performing Arts, Nicholls State Univ, 906 East 1st Street, Thibodaux, LA 70310-0001. **EMAIL** spcd-rsb@mail.nich.edu

BELLOW, SAUL
PERSONAL Born 06/10/1915, Lachine, PQ, Canada, m, 1989, 4 children **DISCIPLINE** WRITER **EDUCATION** Northwestern Univ, BS, 37; **HONORS AND AWARDS** Nobel Prize, 76; Pulitzer Prize; three National Book Awards. **SELECTED PUBLICATIONS** The Dangling Man, 44; The Victim, 47; Henderson the Rain King, 59; Herzog, 64; Humbolt's Gift, 74; auth, The Dean's December, 82; auth, More Die of Heartbreak, 87; auth, A Case of Love, 92; auth, The Actual, 97; auth, Ravelstein, 00. **CONTACT ADDRESS** Boston Univ, 745 Commonwealth Ave, Boston, MA 02215. **EMAIL** wlautzen@bu.edu

BELTON, JOHN
DISCIPLINE ENGLISH LANGUAGE AND LITERATURE **EDUCATION** Columbia Univ, BA; Harvard Univ, MA; PhD. **CAREER** Prof **RESEARCH** Film theory; cultural studies. **SELECTED PUBLICATIONS** Auth, Widescreen Cinema; auth, America Cinema/American Culture. **CONTACT ADDRESS** Dept of English, Rutgers, The State Univ of New Jersey, New Brunswick, 510 George St, Murray Hall, New Brunswick, NJ 08901-1167.

BEN-ZVI, LINDA
DISCIPLINE ENGLISH LITERATURE **EDUCATION** Boston Univ, BA; NYork Univ, MA, Univ Okla, PhD. **CAREER** Prof. **RESEARCH** Modern drama; women playwrights; women's studies. **SELECTED PUBLICATIONS** Auth, pubs on modern drama; works of Samuel Beckett. **CONTACT ADDRESS** Dept of English, Colorado State Univ, Fort Collins, CO 80523-1773. **EMAIL** lbenzvi@vines.colostate.edu

BENARDETE, JANE
PERSONAL Born Columbus, OH, m, 1961, 2 children **DISCIPLINE** ENGLISH & AMERICAN LITERATURE **EDUCATION** Radcliffe Col, AB, 52, AM, 54, PhD(Hist of Am civilization), 58. **CAREER** Instr hist & lit, Harvard Univ, 58-61; asst prof English, Northeastern Univ, 61-65; asst prof, 65-71, assoc prof, 71-; prof English, Hunter Col, 82-00. **HONORS AND AWARDS** City Univ New York grants, 71, 80. **MEMBERSHIPS** Am Studies Asn. **RESEARCH** American literature, especially 19th century. **SELECTED PUBLICATIONS** Ed, Crumbling Idols, Harvard Univ, 60; auth, Huckleberry Finn and the Nature of Fiction, Mass Rev, Spring 68; ed, American Realism, Putnam, 72; ed, Companions of Our Youth, Ungar, 80. **CONTACT ADDRESS** 31 W 12th St, New York, NY 10011.

BENARDETE, SETH GABRIEL
PERSONAL Born 04/04/1930, New York, NY, m, 1960, 2 children **DISCIPLINE** CLASSICS **EDUCATION** Univ Chicago, BA, 49, MA, 53, PhD, 55. **CAREER** Teaching intern Greek & humanities, St John's Col, Md, 55-57; jr fel, Harvard Univ, 57-60; asst prof Greek & Latin, Brandeis Univ, 60-65; assoc prof, 65-76, prof classics, NY Univ, 76-, vis lectr philos, Grad Fac, New Sch Social Res, 65-; Nat Endowment for Humanities sr fel, 72. **HONORS AND AWARDS** D Litt, Adelphi, 89. **RESEARCH** Greek poetry and philosophy. **SELECTED PUBLICATIONS** Transl, Aeschylus II,The Persians and The Suppliant Maidens, Univ Chicago, 56; Herodotean Inquiries, M Nijhoff, 69; The Being of the Beautiful, Univ Chicago, 84; The Rhetoric of Morality & Philosophy, Univ Chicago, 91; Socrates Second Sailing, Univ Chicago, 89; The Tradegy & Comedy of Life, Univ Chicago, 93; The Bow & the Lyre, Rauman & Littlefield, 97; Sacred Transgressions, St Augustine's Press, 98; auth, the Argument of the Action, Univ Chicago, 00; auth, Plato's "Laus": The Discovery of Being, Univ Chicago, 00. **CONTACT ADDRESS** Dept of Classics, New York Univ, 25 Waverly Pl, New York, NY 10003-6701. **EMAIL** sb5@isq.nyu.edu

BENARIO, HERBERT W.
PERSONAL Born 07/21/1929, New York, NY, m, 1957, 2 children **DISCIPLINE** CLASSICS **EDUCATION** City Col New York, BA, 48; Columbia Univ, MA, 49; Johns Hopkins Univ, PhD(classics), 51. **CAREER** Instr Greek & Latin, Columbia Univ, 53-58; asst prof classics, Sweet Briar Col, 58-60; from asst prof to assoc prof, 60-67, chmn dept, 68-73 & 76-78, Prof Classics, Emory Univ, 67-, Mem Latin achievement test comt, Col Entrance Exam Bd, 63-66; fel, Southeastern Inst Medieval & Renaissance Stud, 65; consult, Nat Endowment for Humanities, 71 & 72; Am Coun Learned Soc fel, 78. **HONORS AND AWARDS** Ovation from Class Asn Midwest & South, 79. **MEMBERSHIPS** Am Philol Asn; Vergilian Soc Am (pres, 80-82); Class Soc Am Acad Rome (pres, 65); Archaeol Inst Am; Class Asn Midwest & South (pres, 71-72). **RESEARCH** Latin literature; Roman history; Roman monuments and topography. **SELECTED PUBLICATIONS** Auth, Christians and Pagans in Roman Britain, Classical World, Vol 0086, 92; Roman Papers, Vol 6, Vol 7, Classical J, Vol 0087, 92; Tacitus and Commotus in 'Ann 13.56'/, Historia-Zeitschrift Fur Alte Geschichte, Vol 0043, 94; Roman Towns in Britain, Classical World, Vol 0087, 94; Tacitus and Commotus in 'Ann 13.56'/, Historia Zeitschrift Fur Alte Geschichte, Vol 0043, 94; Recent Work on Tacitus 1984-1993, Classical World, Vol 0089, 95; Camws the Classical Assoc of the Middle West andSouth--the 9th Decade, Classical J, Vol 0091, 96; Academic Tributes to 97, Classical J, Vol 0093, 97. **CONTACT ADDRESS** Dept of Classics, Emory Univ, Atlanta, GA 30322.

BENDER, BERT
PERSONAL Born 01/29/1938, Cape Girardeau, MO, m, 1982, 1 child **DISCIPLINE** ENGLISH **EDUCATION** Univ Wash, BA, 60; Univ Calif Irvine, PhD, 73. **RESEARCH** Mid-19th to mid-20th Century American writers. **SELECTED PUBLICATIONS** Auth, The Descent of Love: Darwin and the Theory of Sexual Selection in American Fiction, 1871-1926, 96; auth, Evolution and the Sex Problem: Soundings of Life and Love in American Fiction During the Eclipse of Darwinism, 02. **CONTACT ADDRESS** Dept English, Arizona State Univ, MC 0302, Tempe, AZ 85287.

BENDER, CAROL
DISCIPLINE RHETORIC AND MODERN AMERICAN LITERATURE **EDUCATION** Mich State Univ, PhD. **CAREER** Prof, Chair of the Dept, Alma Col. **HONORS AND AWARDS** Sears-Roebuck Tchg Excellence Awd; Outstanding Fac Mem in Hum Awd; Lee Posey Awd for Teaching Excellence. **MEMBERSHIPS** MLA, CCCC, NCTE. **RESEARCH** Women's and African-American literature. **SELECTED PUBLICATIONS** Her articles have appeared in Lang and Style, Lang Arts J of Mich, Beyond Bindings and Boundaries several Masterplots reference works; Concerns; Gloria Naylor: Strategy and Techniques, Magic and Myth. **CONTACT ADDRESS** Alma Col, Alma, MI 48801. **EMAIL** bender@alma.edu

BENDER, EILEEN TEPER
PERSONAL Born 12/01/1935, Madison, WI, m, 1956, 3 children **DISCIPLINE** AMERICAN LITERATURE, MODERN FICTION, WOMEN'S STUDIES **EDUCATION** Northwestern Univ, BSJ, 56; Notre Dame Univ, PhD(English), 77. **CAREER** Assoc lectr English, Ind Univ, South Bend, 66-68, dir grant & spec proj, 76-78, asst chair Arts & Sci, 78-80, actg chair, 80; asst instr English, Yale Univ, 72-73; Asst Prof English, Notre Dame UNIV, 80-85; Prof English, IN Univ South Bend, 85; Mem adv bd, Danforth Found Grad Fel Prog, 78-81;

mem, Ind Comt for Humanities, 78-82; selection comt, Rhodes Scholar Prog, 79-82; consult, Young Fel Sem, Carnegie Corp, 80; selection comt, Charlotte Newcombe Fel Prog, 81-84; Academic Advisor to the Pres, IN, 89-95. **HONORS AND AWARDS** Faculty Colloquium on Excellence in Teaching, (FACET), 89; IU Sylvia Bowman Awd, 95; Lundquist Facutly Fellow, IUSB, 95; Carnegie Prof of the Year, 99. **MEMBERSHIPS** Soc Values Higher Educ; MLA; Danforth Asn; AAHE. **RESEARCH** Contemporary Amer novelists; modern English and Amer women writers; post contemporary narrative strategies; Nature American Literature. **SELECTED PUBLICATIONS** Auth, Hist As Womans Game, 'Bellefleur' As Texte De Jouissance, Soundings, Vol 0076, 93. **CONTACT ADDRESS** Indiana Univ, South Bend, South Bend, IN 46634-7111. **EMAIL** ebender@iusb.edu

BENDER, HENRY V.
PERSONAL Born 05/23/1945, Teaneck, NJ, m, 1973, 3 children **DISCIPLINE** CLASSICS **EDUCATION** Fordham Univ, AB, 67; Pa State Univ, MA, 68; Rutgers Univ, PhD, 87. **CAREER** Dept Chair, St Joseph's Preparatory Sch, 69-98; Adj Prof, St Joseph's Univ, 81-; Adj Prof, Villanova Univ, 85-; Dept Chair, Hill Sch, 98-; Adj Prof, Rutgers Univ, 93-96. **HONORS AND AWARDS** Pres Fel, 63-67; Nat Defense Fel, Bryn Mawr, 68-70; Fulbright Fel, Am Acad Rome, 84; Fel, NEH, 88, 92, 98; Ignatian Awd for Teaching, St Joseph's Preparatory Sch, 88; Adv Placement Teacher Recognition Awd, 94; alumnus of the Year, St Joseph's Preparatory Sch, 97. **MEMBERSHIPS** Class Asn of the Atlantic States; Class Asn of N Eng; Class Asn of the Midwestern States; Am Philol Asn; Philadelphia Class Soc; NJ Class Soc; Pa Class Asn; Nat Asn of Indep Sch; Intl Tour Managers Asn. **RESEARCH** Classical architecture and typography in Renaissance settings; Roman topography and Augustan Age Literature. **SELECTED PUBLICATIONS** Contrib, The World of Roman Costume, Univ Wis Press, 90; co-auth, Catullus for the AP, Bolchazy-Carducci, 97; auth, A Horace Reader, Focus Press, 98. **CONTACT ADDRESS** Dept Humanities, Hill Sch, 717 E High St, Pottstown, PA 19464. **EMAIL** hbender@thehill.org

BENDER, NATHAN E.
PERSONAL Born 09/29/1957, Amherst, OH, s **DISCIPLINE** ANTHROPOLOGY, LIBRARY SCIENCE **EDUCATION** Ohio State Univ, BA, 80; Univ Wash, MA, 83; Kent State Univ, MLS, 86. **CAREER** Libr Western Hist Collections, Univ Okla, 86-89; Head, spec collections, Mont State Univ Librs, 89-94; curator, head spec collections, WV Univ Librs, 94-97; curator, McCracken Res Libr, Buffalo Bill Hist Ctr, 97-. **MEMBERSHIPS** Am Library Asn, Soc of Am Archivists, Am Indian Library Asn, Am Folklore Soc. **RESEARCH** The American Native Press, Native American syllabaries, Wester American folklore and literature, history of technology, archaeology, western frontier photographers. **SELECTED PUBLICATIONS** Auth, "A Bibliographic Note on the Siwinowe Kesibwe," Native Pr Res Journal 4 (87): 25-27; auth, "The Moccasin, Songs of the Navajo Sea and the Cult Archaeology of Harry E. Miller," Native Pr Res Journal 9 (89): 1-10; auth, "The Library Division of the Western History Collections," in American Indian Resource Materials in the Western History Collections, Univ of Oklahoma, ed. Donald L. DeWitt, Univ of Oklahoma Pr, 90; auth, "Libraries Celebrate the Western States Centennials, 1989-90," coauth with Gregg Sapp, Public Libraries Quarterly, 91; auth, "Cherokee Shorthand: As Derived from Pitman Shorthand and in Relation to the Dot-Notation Variant of the Sac and Fox Syllabary," American Indian Culture and Res Journal, 91. **CONTACT ADDRESS** McCracken Research Library, Buffalo Bill Histol Ctr, 720 Sheridan Ave, Cody, WY 82414. **EMAIL** nbender@bbhc.org

BENDER, ROBERT M.
PERSONAL Born 03/15/1936, Chicago, IL, m, 1986, 5 children **DISCIPLINE** ENGLISH **EDUCATION** Univ Mich, PhD, 63. **CAREER** Prof; mem, Women Stud fac, Faculty Liaison, Information and Access Technology Services; adv bd, Univ Mo Inst Instruct technol. **HONORS AND AWARDS** Led the effort, Univ Mo comput-mediated writing into the classroom. **SELECTED PUBLICATIONS** Ed, The Sonnet, Simon & Schuster, 87; auth essays on, topics relating to Shakespeare, modern drama & women writers. **CONTACT ADDRESS** Dept of English, Univ of Missouri, Columbia, 107 Lowry, Columbia, MO 65211. **EMAIL** benderr@missouri.edu

BENIGER, JAMES R.
PERSONAL m, 1984, 2 children **DISCIPLINE** COMMUNICATIONS AND SOCIOLOGY **EDUCATION** Harvard Univ, BA; Univ CA at Berkeley, MS, MA, PhD. **CAREER** Assoc prof, Univ Southern CA, 85-; res asst, Bureau Soc Sci Res, WA; lectr, UC-Berkeley; asst prof, Princeton Univ & vis assnt prof, Yale Univ. past consult, Off Technol Assessment, US Cong. **HONORS AND AWARDS** Asn Am Publ award; Phi Kappa Phi Fac Recognition Awd; NY Times Bk Rev, Notable Paperback Yr, 89; Nat Newspaper Fund fel. **MEMBERSHIPS** Past mem ed bd, Publ Opinion Quart, J Commun, Critical Stud in Mass Commun, Commun Theory & Knowledge; past assoce ed, Commun Res & auth, Far Afield; past bd, Overseers Gen Soc Survey, NORC, Univ Chicago & 2 yr elected terms, publ ch & sec-treas, Am Asn Publ Opinion Res. **SELECTED PUBLICATIONS** Auth, The Control Revolution: Technological and Economic Origins of the Information Society, Harvard UP, 86 & Trafficking in Drug Users: Professional Exchange Networks in the Control of Deviance, Cambridge UP, hardcover, 83 & paperback, 84; publ on, technol & soc change, mass media and publ opinion, popular cult & the arts. **CONTACT ADDRESS** Annenberg School for Commun, Univ of So California, University Park Campus, Los Angeles, CA 90089.

BENIS, TOBY RUTH
DISCIPLINE BRITISH ROMANTICISM **EDUCATION** Columbia Univ, PhD. **CAREER** Asst prof, St Louis Univ. **SELECTED PUBLICATIONS** Auth, Epic, Sir James Mackintosh, Encyclopedia Romanticism, Garland, 92; Martha Ray's Face: Life During Wartime in Lyrical Ballads, Criticism, 97; auth, Romanticism on the Road: the Marginal Gains of Wordsworth's Homeless, Macmillan/St. Martins, 00. **CONTACT ADDRESS** Dept of English, Saint Louis Univ, 221 N Grand Blvd, Saint Louis, MO 63103. **EMAIL** benistr@slu.edu

BENKE, ROBIN PAUL
PERSONAL Born 01/30/1953, Trinidad, West Indies, s **DISCIPLINE** LIBRARY SCIENCE **EDUCATION** Hampden-Sydney Col, BA, 75; Peabody Col, Vanderbilt Univ, MLS, 78. **CAREER** Reference librn, 78-88, dir of lib, 88-, Univ. Va's College at Wise. **HONORS AND AWARDS** Clinch Valley Col Outstanding Service Awd, 98; Univ Va Harrison Awd, 98; Henson Student Life Awd, 99; Va Educ Media Asn Media Educator of the Year-Higher Educ, 96; Beta Phi Mu; Kappa Delta Pi. **MEMBERSHIPS** ALA; ACRL; AAUP; Va Lib Asn; Va Educ Media Asn. **RESEARCH** College librarianship; school media librarianship. **CONTACT ADDRESS** PO Box 1519, Wise, VA 24293. **EMAIL** rbenke@virginia.edu

BENKENDORF, RAY R.
PERSONAL Born 05/04/1935, Saginaw, MI, m, 1979 **DISCIPLINE** RHETORICAL COMMUNICATION **EDUCATION** Univ MN, PhD, 86. **CAREER** Prof Speech Commun, 65-71, Chaffey Col, Alta Loma; adj asst prof, 68-71, Calif St Univ; prof, 71-, Southwestern Col, Chula Vista, CA; tchng assoc, 80-81, Univ Minn. **HONORS AND AWARDS** Alpha Psi Omega; Pi Kappa Delta; Phi Kappa Phi; Blue Key; Dean's List; NDEAS Grad fel, San Jose St Univ, 67; Who's Who Among Am Tchrs, 97. **MEMBERSHIPS** Nat Commun Asn; Western Commun Asn; Cent St Commun Asn; Int Commun Asn; Kenneth Burke Soc; Rhetoric Soc of Am; Int Soc for the Hist of Rhetoric; Int Churchill Soc. **RESEARCH** Classical rhetorical theory and contemporary rhetorical criticism. **SELECTED PUBLICATIONS** Ed bd, Communication Education, 76-82; ed advisor, J of the Am Forensic Asn, 77-79; ed bd, Moments in Rhetoric, Univ Minn Press, 75-77; NCA, recent res contrib & res panel chmn, Flowing Upward How the Basic Course Influences Theory, San Antonio, TX, 95; NCA res, chmn, Employing Burkeian Theory in the Construction of Social Reality, San Diego, CA, 96; NCA res, chmn, Burkeian Criticism and Its Utility Into the Investigation of Social Movements, Chicago, IL, 97; NCA, res, chmn, Burke and Clinton: Modern or Postmodern?, NY, 98. **CONTACT ADDRESS** Rhetoric and Commun Studies, Southwestern Col, California, Chula Vista, CA 92910.

BENNETT, ALMA
DISCIPLINE ENGLISH LITERATURE **EDUCATION** Univ Tex, PhD, 91. **CAREER** Dept Eng, Clemson Univ **RESEARCH** Interdisciplinary humanities; 20th-century American & British literature. **SELECTED PUBLICATIONS** Auth, Mary Gordon, United States Authors Series, Twayne/Simon and Schuster, 96; Featured Event: Ethel Smyth and Argento/ Woolf Recital and Freshwater, Virginia Woolf and the Arts: Selected Papers from the Sixth Annual Virginia Woolf Conference, Pace Univ Press, 97; Conversations with Mary Gordon, SC Rev, 95; Mary Gordon; American Writers Series, Scribner's, 96; Pound and the Malatestan Territory: A 1994 Update, Paideuma, 95; The Persistent Presence: Mathematical Language in Literature, Mathematical Connections, 94; coauth, A Selected Discography of Works by Ethel Smyth (1858-44) on Compact Disc, Virginia Woolf and the Arts: Selected Papers from the Sixth Annual Virginia Woolf Conference, Pace UP, 97. **CONTACT ADDRESS** Clemson Univ, 604 Strode, Clemson, SC 29634. **EMAIL** balma@clemson.edu

BENNETT, BARBARA A.
PERSONAL Born 07/08/1959 **DISCIPLINE** ENGLISH **EDUCATION** Ariz State Univ, PhD, 94. **CAREER** Asst prof, Marian Col, 95-97; asst prof, Ga Southwestern State Univ, 97-99; asst prof, Wake Forest Univ, 99-. **MEMBERSHIPS** SAMPLA, MLA, SSSL. **RESEARCH** 20th Century American Literature, Southern Literature, Women's Studies, Ecofeminism. **SELECTED PUBLICATIONS** Auth, Comic Visions, Female Voices: Contemporary Women Novelists and Southern Humor, LSU Pr, 98; auth, Understanding Jill McCorkle, USC Pr, 01. **CONTACT ADDRESS** Dept English, Wake Forest Univ, Winston-Salem, NC 27109. **EMAIL** bennetb@wfu.edu

BENNETT, BETTY T.
DISCIPLINE LITERATURE **EDUCATION** NYork Univ, PhD. **CAREER** Prof, Am Univ. **HONORS AND AWARDS** . **RESEARCH** Romanticism. **SELECTED PUBLICATIONS** Auth, Mary Diana Dods: A Gentleman and a Scholar, co-ed, Mary Shelley Reader; ed, Letters of Mary Wollstonecroft Shelley. **CONTACT ADDRESS** American Univ, 4400 Massachusetts Ave, Washington, DC 20016.

BENNETT, CARL D.
PERSONAL Born 07/22/1917, Waycross, GA, m, 1942, 3 children **DISCIPLINE** ENGLISH **EDUCATION** Emory Univ, BA, 40, MA, 44, PhD, 62. **CAREER** Instr English, WGA Col, 41-42; asst prof, Wesleyan Col, 44-47; assoc prof, 47-59; prof English, 59-82, chemn Afro-Asian Cultures, 63-67, chemn Hum & Fine Arts Div, 73-78, dist prof English, 82-88, Dist prof English Emer, 88- , St Andrews Presby Col; vis prof Mercer Univ, 48, Seinan Gakuin Univ, Japan, 80-81. **HONORS AND AWARDS** Fulbright-Hays grant, 64; NEH sem, 78. **MEMBERSHIPS** MLA; S Atlantic Mod Lang Asn; AAUP. **RESEARCH** American and English literature; Afro-American and non-Western literatures. **SELECTED PUBLICATIONS** Articles on ethics, on Booth Tarkington, Joseph Conrad, Thomas Hardy, Dorothy Richardson, Ruth Prawer Jhabvala, and Thomas Pynchon; a book of Joseph Conrad. **CONTACT ADDRESS** St. Andrews Presbyterian Col, Laurinburg, NC 28352. **EMAIL** bennettc@tartan.sapc.edu

BENNETT, JAMES RICHARD
PERSONAL Born 03/15/1932, Harrison, AR, m, 1951, 2 children **DISCIPLINE** ENGLISH LITERATURE **EDUCATION** Univ Ark, BA, 53, MA, 54; Stanford Univ, PhD(English, humanities), 61. **CAREER** From instr to asst prof English, Mont State Univ, 60-62; asst prof, Western Wash State Col, 62-65; from asst prof to assoc prof, 65-69, Prof English, Univ Ark, Fayetteville, 69-, Chmn Humanities Prog, 75-, Co-ed, Style, 67-; Fulbright lectr, Yugoslavia, 68-69; mem deleg assembly, MLA, 78-80. **MEMBERSHIPS** NCTE; MLA; Rhetoric Soc Am; Am Civil Liberties Union. **RESEARCH** Nineteenth century literature; style; literature and film. **SELECTED PUBLICATIONS** Auth, English Prose Style, Chandler, 71; Style, S Atlantic Mod Lang Bull, 71; Shelley, Keats-Shelley J, 74; Tzvetan Todorov, Bucknell Rev, 74; Resistance museums, Mankind, 75; Literary style, Symp Rhet, 75; Stylistics checklist, Style, 76 & 77. **CONTACT ADDRESS** Dept of English, Univ of Arkansas, Fayetteville, Fayetteville, AR 72701-1202.

BENNETT, JOHN
PERSONAL Born 03/12/1920, Pittsfield, MA, m, 1960, 2 children **DISCIPLINE** ENGLISH & AMERICAN LITERATURE **EDUCATION** Oberlin Col, BA, 47; Univ wis, MA, 50, PhD, 56. **CAREER** Instr English, Ind Univ, 53-58; asst prof, Beloit Col, 58-59; from assoc prof to prof, Rockford Col, 59-68, chmn dept, 60-68; prof, 68-70, Bernard H Pennings Distinguished Prof English, St Norbert Col, 70-, Poet in-Residence, 79-, Consult commun, Air War Col, Maxwell AFB, Ala, 51; ed, Beloit Poetry J, 58-72; mem fac adv comt, Ill Bd Higher Educ, 62-68. **HONORS AND AWARDS** Devins Mem Awd, 70; Soc Midland Auth Poetry Awd, 71 & 78. **MEMBERSHIPS** Melville Soc; Acad Am Poets. **RESEARCH** Herman Melville; modern poetry; creative writing. **SELECTED PUBLICATIONS** Auth, The Struck Leviathan, Univ Mo, 70; Griefs and Exultation, 70 & Knights and Squires, 72, St Norbert; Poems from a Christian enclave, Anglican Theol Rev, 76; Echoes From the Peaceable Kingdom, Eerdmans, 78; Seeds of Mustard, Seed of Tare, 79 & Fire in the Dust, 80, Houghton Col Press; Beyond the Compass Rose, Midwestern Writers Publ House, 82. **CONTACT ADDRESS** 526 Karen Lane, Green Bay, WI 54301.

BENNETT, PAULA
PERSONAL Born 12/30/1936, Brookline, MA, d, 2 children **DISCIPLINE** LITERATURE **EDUCATION** Columbia Univ, PhD, 70. **CAREER** Prof, 91-, Southern IL Univ; board member, Legacy; A Jour of Am Women Writers. **HONORS AND AWARDS** NEH Amer Antiquarian Soc, 96-97; Phi Beta Kappa; Bunting Fel Radcliff Col, 96-97. **MEMBERSHIPS** MLA; ASA; ALA; SSAWW; NEMLA. **RESEARCH** Emily Dickinson; 19th Cent Amer Womens Poetry. **SELECTED PUBLICATIONS** Auth, Emily Dickinson: Woman Poet Harvester P (Hemel Hempstead, England), 90; auth, "Critical Clitoridectomy Female Sexual Imagery and Feminist Psychoanalytic Theory," Jour of Women I Culture and Soc (93); auth, "The Descent of the Angel: Interrogating Domestic Ideology in American Women's Poetry 1858-1890," American Literary History 7 (95): 591-610; coed, Solitary Pleasures The Historical Literary and Artistic Discourses of Autoeroticism, Routledge (NYork), 95; auth, Not Just Filler Not Just Sentimental Womens Poetry in American Victorian Periodicals 1860-1900, in: Period Lit in the Nineteenth Cent Amer, 95; auth, Nineteenth-century American Women Poets: An Anthology, Blackwell Publishers (Oxford), 97; auth, "Phillis Wheatley's Vocation and the Paradox of the 'Afric Muse,'" PMLA (98): 64-76; auth, Palace-Burner: the Selected Poetry of Sarah Piatt, Univ of Ill P (Champaign-Urbana), 01. **CONTACT ADDRESS** English Dept, So Illinois Univ, Carbondale, Carbondale, IL 62901. **EMAIL** pbernat@aol.com

BENNETT, ROBERT E.
PERSONAL Born 11/07/1942, Des Moines, IA, p, 1986 **DISCIPLINE** CLASSICS **EDUCATION** Trinity Col, BA, 64;

Yale Univ, MA, 65; PhD, 70. **CAREER** Vis instr, Trinity Col, 66; instr to prof, acad dean, assoc prov, Trinity Col, 67-. **HONORS AND AWARDS** Woodrow Wilson Fel, 64-67; Am School Athens, 66; Ford-Mellon Grants, 70, 71, 72; NEH, 75-76; Mellon Grant, 00-01. **MEMBERSHIPS** Assoc of Ancient Hist, Am Philol Assoc, OH Class Conf, Class Assoc of the Middle West and South, Women's Class Caucus, Great Lakes Col Assoc. **RESEARCH** Ancient Religion, Gender in Antiquity, Plutarch, the Cappadocian Fathers. **SELECTED PUBLICATIONS** Auth, "Let His Children Be Waifs and Beggars: On Reading the Psalms," Gambier Jour, (96); auth, "Classical Influence in Mary Shelley's 'Frankenstein,'" Humanitias, (96); auth, "Homosexuality in the Gilded Age," Dict of the Gilded Age, (01); coauth, "Can Men Learn to Float," Men at Church, ed Philip Culburtson, Fortpress Pr, (01). **CONTACT ADDRESS** Dept History, Kenyon Col, Ascension Hall 11, Gambier, OH 43022. **EMAIL** bennett4@kenyon.edu

BENNETT, RONALD
PERSONAL Born 10/11/1946, Rigby, ID, m, 1965, 6 children **DISCIPLINE** ENGLISH **EDUCATION** Brigham Young Univ, BA; Idaho State Univ, MA. **CAREER** Dept of Communication Chairman, Ricks Col; Coordinator of Journalism, Ricks Col. **HONORS AND AWARDS** Idaho Journalism Teacher of the Year; Dow Jones Newspaper Fund Distinguished Teacher. **MEMBERSHIPS** College Media Advisors; Journalism Education Association. **RESEARCH** Integrated newsroom concept. **SELECTED PUBLICATIONS** Auth, Adviser Update articles; auth, Scholastic News Service. **CONTACT ADDRESS** Dept Comunication, Ricks Col, 525 S Center St, Rexburg, ID 83460-0001. **EMAIL** bennettr@ricks.edu

BENOIT, RAYMOND
DISCIPLINE ROMANTICISM **EDUCATION** Univ OR, PhD. **CAREER** Prof, St. Louis Univ. **SELECTED PUBLICATIONS** Auth, Single Nature's Double Name: The Collectedness of the Conflicting in British and American Romanticism, Mouton, 73; An Unpublished Note from Edwin Arlington Robinson to Stewart Beach, ANQ: Quart Jour Short Articles, Notes, & Rev, 93; Young Goodman Brown': The Second Time Around, The Nathaniel Hawthorne Rev, 93; The Existential Intuition of Flannery O'Connor in The Violent Bear it Away, Notes Comp Lit, 93; 'Moss-Picking': An Undergraduate Theme of Theodore Roethke, Eng Lang Notes, 96; Irving's 'The Legend of Sleepy Hollow', Explicator, 96; 'My Estrangement from Nature': An Undergraduate Theme of Theodore Roethke, ANQ: Quart Jour Short Articles, Notes, & Rev, 98; auth, "Poe's 'The Fall of the House of Usher.'" The Explicator 58(00): 79-81; auth, '"A Dolphin's at My Door': Unpublished Lines by Theodore Roethke." ANQ: A Quarterly Journal of Short Articles, Notes, and Reviews 14 (01): 40-44. **CONTACT ADDRESS** Dept of English, Saint Louis Univ, 221 N Grand Blvd, Saint Louis, MO 63103. **EMAIL** benoitr@slu.edu

BENOIT, WILLIAM L.
PERSONAL Born 03/17/1953, New Castle, IN, m, 1974, 1 child **DISCIPLINE** COMMUNICATION **EDUCATION** Ball State Univ, BS, 75; Central Mich Univ, MA, 76; Wayne State Univ, PhD, 75. **CAREER** Fac, Bowling State Green Univ; fac, Miami Univ; prof, Univ of Mo. **HONORS AND AWARDS** Outstanding Academic Book; Gold Chalk Graduate Teaching Awd. **MEMBERSHIPS** Nat Commun Assoc; Int Commun Assoc; Am Forensic Assoc. **RESEARCH** Rhetorical theory & criticism; political communication, persuasion. **SELECTED PUBLICATIONS** Auth, Account, excuses, apologies: A theory of image restoration discourse, State Univ of NY Press, 95; co-auth, Candidates in conflict: Persuasive attack and defense in the 1992 presidential debates, University of Alabama Press, 96; co-auth, Effects of ideology and presidential debate watching on attitudes and knowledge, Argumentation & Advocacy, vol 34, 163-72, 98; auth, Merchants of Death: Persuasive defenses by the tobacco industry, Argument in a time of change: Definition, frameworks, and critiques, Speech Commun Assoc, 220-25, 98.co-auth, Campaign 96: A functional analysis of acclaiming, attacking, and defending, (in press); auth, Seeing Spots: A functional analysis of presidential television advertising, 1952-1996. **CONTACT ADDRESS** Commun Dept, Univ of Missouri, Columbia, 115 Switzler Hall, Columbia, MO 65211. **EMAIL** benoitw@missouri.edu

BENREMOUGA, KARIMA
DISCIPLINE COMMUNICATION STUDIES **EDUCATION** Univ Algiers, BA, 84; Univ Kans, MA, 87, PhD, 95. **CAREER** Adj prof, Univ of Kans, 96, 97; asst prof, Emporia State Univ, 95-97; instructional technology specialist dir, St. Mary's Col of Md, 98; coord, Univ of Houston; adj fac, Univ of Houston, 98-. **HONORS AND AWARDS** Fullbright-Hays Fac Res Abroad Program, 96. **RESEARCH** French language and culture; Arabic language and culture; Language methodology; Computer assisted language learning. **SELECTED PUBLICATIONS** Auth, "The Redesign of English as a Second Language (ESL) and Bilingual Programs," KFLA Bulletin, 96; auth, "Introduction to Distance Learning," MidTESOL Newsletter, 97; auth, "The LEO Lab: Student and Teacher Training" in Technology-Enhanced Learning Envirronments, ed. Elizabeth Hanson-Smith, TESOL Publications, 00. **CONTACT ADDRESS** Dept of Modern & Classical Languages, Univ of Houston, 4800 Calhoun Rd, Houston, TX 77204. **EMAIL** Kbenremouga@uh.edu

BENSELER, DAVID P.
PERSONAL Born 01/10/1940, Baltimore, MD, m, 1985, 4 children **DISCIPLINE** LITERARY THEORY **EDUCATION** Western Washington Univ, BA, 64; Univ of Oregon, MA, 66; Eberhard-Karls-Univ, Graduate Study, 67-68; Univ of Oregon, PhD,71. **CAREER** Inst,, Univ of Oregon, 68-69; Asst Prof, Washington State Univ, 69-74; Assoc Prof, Washington State Univ, 74-77; Admin Fel, Washington, DC 76-77; Prof, Chair, Ohio State Univ, 77-85; Prof, Ohio State Univ, 85-87, 88-91; Vis Prof, New Mexico State Univ, 89; Chair, Case Western Univ, 91-98; Prof, Case Western Univ, 91-99; Prof, Case Western Univ, 99-. **HONORS AND AWARDS** Elected to Delta Phi Alpha, National German Honorary , April 63; Recipient, Fulbright Graduate Fel, 67-68; Recipient , Fulbright Fel to Tubingen , Germany, 67-68; Elected to Sigma Kappa Phi, National Foreign Language Teachers, 75; Pro Lingua Awd, Washington Assoc of Foreign Language Teachers, Oct, 75 ; Publications Awd, Ohio Foreign Language Assoc, 85; Recipient, Bundesverdienstkrenz I. Klasse (Meritorious Service Cross, First Class, of the Federal Government of Germany) , 85; Distinguished Vis Prof of Foreign Languages, United States Military Academy , West Point, NY, 87-88; Army Commendation Medal for Distinguished Civilian Service, United States Military Academy, West Point, NY, 88; Distinguished Vis Prof of Foreign Languages, New Mexico State Univ, Las Cruces, 89; Eminent Scholar Awd, Ohio State Univ, 90; Louis D Beaumont Univ Prof of the Humanities, Case Western Reserve Univ, 91; Elected toe Phi Sigma Iota, International Foreign Language Honorary, 92; Alumni Fel, Western Washington Univ, Bellingham, 93; Editor of the Modern Language Journal, 80-93; Mortar Board " Top Prof" Awd , Case Western Reserve Univ, 97; Journal of Language for International Business, 9 (98); Max Kade Foundation Grant t, Case Western Univ , 98; First Emile B de Sauze Professor of Modern Languages and Literatures, Case Western Reserve Univ, 98. **MEMBERSHIPS** American Assoc of Teachers of German; American Assoc of University Prof,; American Assoc of University Sup and Coord of Foreign Language Progs; American Council on the Teaching of Foreign Language; American Goethe Society; Assoc of Progs and Depts of Comparative Lit,; Bibliographical Society of America,; German Studies Assoc; The Lessing Society; Modern Language Assoc of America; Society for German-American Studies. **RESEARCH** Modern German Culture, Drama, Novelle, German Folklore and Tales; History of the Profession, Bibliography, Methodology, Graduate and Undergraduate Progs in Gemanics. **SELECTED PUBLICATIONS** Auth, Second Language Teaching 76: Proceedings of the Pacific Northwest Council Foreign Languages, 28, ii, Corvallis, OR: PNCFL, 78; auth, Teaching the Basics in te Foreign Language Classroom: Options and Strategies, Skokie, IL National Textbook, 79;coauth, Intensive Foreign Language Courses, Language in Education: Theory and Practice 18, Arlington, VA: Center for Applied Linguistics, 79; coauth, Teaching German in America; Prolegomena to a History, German Studies in The United States 6, Madison: Univ of Wisconsin Press, 88; coauth, Directory of Foreign Language Teacher Preparation in the United States; The Modern Language Journal 64 (80) through 77 (93); 56 Quarterly issues (14 vols); auth, The Dynamics of Language Program Direction, Yearbook an Coordinators 4, Boston: Heinle, 93; coauth, A Comprehensive Index to The Modern Language Journal: 1916-1991. Electronic/ CD- ROM Version, Oxford & Boston: Blackwell, 00; coauth, Teaching German in Twentieth-Century America, German Studies in the United States Madison: Univ of Wisconsin Press, forthcoming, 00. **CONTACT ADDRESS** Case Western Reserve Univ, 10900 Euclid Ave, Cleveland, OH 44106. **EMAIL** dpb5@po.cwru.edu

BENSMAN, MARVIN R.
PERSONAL Born 09/18/1937, Two Rivers, WI, m, 1965, 2 children **DISCIPLINE** COMMUNICATION **EDUCATION** Univ of Wis, BS, 60; MS, 64; PhD, 69. **CAREER** Teacher, Western High School, 60-62; Teacher Northern High School, 62-63; TA, Univ of Wis, 64-67; instr, Univ of Ver, 67-69; asst prof, Univ of Memphis, 69-. **HONORS AND AWARDS** Intellectual Property Awd, Univ of Memphis, 81; Cert of Special Merit in Prog, Intl Radio and TV Soc, 85. **MEMBERSHIPS** Broadcast Ed Assoc; Cable Regulatory Board. **RESEARCH** Communication and Entertainment Law, History of Electronic Media, Archiving and Collection of Radio Programs. **SELECTED PUBLICATIONS** Auth, Broadcast Regulation: Selected Cases and Decisions, Univ Pr of Am, 83; auth, "Victor H. Laughter: Radio Pioneer", Tenn Speech Commun Jour, 85; auth, Broadcast/Cable Regulation, Univ Pr of Am, 90; auth, "Radio Broadcast Programming for Research and Teaching", Jour of Radio Studies, 93; auth, The Beginning of Broadcast Regulation in the Twentieth Century, McFarland Pub, 00. **CONTACT ADDRESS** Dept Commun, Univ of Memphis, 3706 Alumni St, Memphis, TN 38152-0001. **EMAIL** mbensman@memphis.edu

BENSON, JACKSON J.
PERSONAL Born 09/02/1930, San Francisco, CA, m, 1960, 2 children **DISCIPLINE** CONTEMPORARY AMERICAN LITERATURE **EDUCATION** Stanford Univ, AB, 52; San Francisco State Univ, MA, 56; Univ Southern Calif, PhD(English), 66. **CAREER** Assoc prof English, Orange Coast Col, 56-66; from asst prof to assoc prof, 66-72, Prof Am Lit to Prof Emer, San Diego State Univ, 72-, Consult, San Diego City Schs, 67-68. **HONORS AND AWARDS** Nat Endowment for Humanities grant, 70; Am Philos Soc grant, 71; Nat Endowment for Humanities fel, 78-79. **MEMBERSHIPS** MLA; Am Stud Asn. **RESEARCH** Ernest Hemingway; John Steinbeck. **CONTACT ADDRESS** Dept of English and Comp Lit, San Diego State Univ, 5500 Campanile Dr, San Diego, CA 92182-8140. **EMAIL** benson2@mail.sdsu.edu

BENSON, LARRY DEAN
PERSONAL Born 06/20/1929, SD, m, 1951, 4 children **DISCIPLINE** ENGLISH **EDUCATION** Univ Calif, Berkeley, AB, 54, MA, 56, PhD, 59 Hon Degree: MA, Harvard Univ, 65. **CAREER** From instr to assoc prof, 59-69, Prof English, Harvard Univ, 69-, Asst ed, Speculum, 66- **MEMBERSHIPS** Mediaeval Acad Am; Int Arthurian Soc. **RESEARCH** Old and middle English literature. **SELECTED PUBLICATIONS** Auth, Art and Tradition in Sir Gawain and the Green Knight, Rutgers Univ, 65; The literary character of Anglo-Saxon formulaic verse, PMLA, 10/66; The pagan coloring of Beowulf, In: Old English Poetry, Brown Univ, 67; The originality of Beowulf, In: The Interpretation of Narrative: Theory and Practice, Harvard Univ, 70; co-ed, The Literary Context of Chaucer's Fabliaux, 71 & ed, King Arthur's Death, The Middle English Alliterative Morte Arthure and Stanzaic Morte Arthur, 74, Bobbs; ed, The Learned and the Lewed, 75 & auth, Malory's Morte D'Arthur, 76, Harvard Univ; ed The Riverside Chaucer, 87. **CONTACT ADDRESS** Libr, Harvard Univ, 271 Widener Lib, Cambridge, MA 02138-3800. **EMAIL** ldb@wjh.harvard.edu

BENSON, MARY E.
PERSONAL Born 07/24/1943, Washington, PA, m, 1998 **DISCIPLINE** ENGLISH **EDUCATION** Westminster Col, BA, 65; Miami Univ, MA, 69; PhD, 75. **CAREER** Teacher, Berlin-Brothersvalley Schools, 65-67; instr to asst prof, Behrend Col of the Pa State Univ, 70-81; assoc prof to prof, Tarkio Col, 81-91; prof, Avila Col, 91-. **HONORS AND AWARDS** NDEA Fel, 67-70; Excellence in Teaching Awd, Tario Col, Who's Who in Am. **MEMBERSHIPS** MLA, NCTE, Col English Assoc. **RESEARCH** 19th and 20th Century American Literature, Middle English Literature, Linguistics. **SELECTED PUBLICATIONS** Auth, "An Existential Everyman," Philol Papers 27, (80); auth, "The Good, the Bad, and the Ugly: A Study of Malory's Women," Mid-Hudson Lang Stud, (82). **CONTACT ADDRESS** Avila Col, 11901 Wornall Rd, Kansas City, MO 64145. **EMAIL** bensonme@mail.avila.edu

BENSON, RICHARD LEE
PERSONAL Born 12/12/1930, Brawley, CA, m, 1958, 5 children **DISCIPLINE** DRAMA, SPEECH **EDUCATION** Univ Calif, Los Angeles, BA, 58; Univ Ill, Urbana, MA, 62, PhD(-theatre), 68. **CAREER** From instr to asst prof drama, Beloit Col, 62-69; Prof Speech & Theatre Arts & Chmn Dept, Eastern KY Univ, 69-. **MEMBERSHIPS** Speech Commun Asn. **RESEARCH** Shakespearean promptbooks; Amer theatre history. **SELECTED PUBLICATIONS** Auth, A Tribute to Bowman, TCI, Vol 0027, 93. **CONTACT ADDRESS** Dept of Speech & Theatre Arts, Eastern Kentucky Univ, Richmond, KY 40475.

BENSON, THOMAS W.
PERSONAL Born 01/25/1937, Abington, PA, m, 1960, 2 children **DISCIPLINE** SPEECH **EDUCATION** Hamilton Col, AB, 58; Cornell Univ, MA, 61, PhD, 66; John F. Kenndy School of Government, Harvard Univ, 00. **CAREER** 63-71, SUNY, Buffalo NY; 71-, Edwin Erle Sparks Prof of Rhetoric, 90-, Penn St Univ. **HONORS AND AWARDS** Eastern Comm Asn Scholar, 82-83; Robert A Kibler Mem Awd, Speech Comm Asn, 83; Meritorious Svc Awd, Eastern Comm Asn, 87; Dist Res Fel, Eastern Comm Asn, 98; Presidential Citation, Natl Comm Asn, 97; Douglas Ehninger Dist Rhetorical Scholar Awd, Natl Comm Asn, 97; Dist Scholar Awd, Natl Comm Asn, 97; Shorenstein Fel, 99; Mentor Awd, Comm Assoc, 00. **MEMBERSHIPS** Speech Comm Asn; Intl Comm Asn; Eastern Comm Asn; Rhetoric Soc of Amer; Speech Comm Asn of PA; Univ Film and Video Asn; Soc for Cinema Studies; Intl Soc for the History of Rhetoric, Nat Comm Assoc. **RESEARCH** Rhetorical theory and criticism; political comm; media criticism. **SELECTED PUBLICATIONS** Ed, Communication Quarterly, 76-78; auth, Speech Communication in the 20th Century, S Illionois Univ Press, 85; auth, Quarteryl Journal of Speech, 87-89; auth, Reality Fictions, with Carolyn Anderson, S Illinois Ulniv Press, 89; coauth, Put Down the camera and Pick up the Shovel An Interview with John Marshall: The Cinema of John Marshall, Academic Pub, 93; auth, rhetorical Structure and Primate in Critical Questions Invention Creativity and the Criticism of Disourse and Media, St Martins, 94; auth, Longinus On the Sublime, Encylepdia of Rhetoric and Composition, Garland, 96; auth, forward to Donn Abbott Rhetoric in the New World, Univ of SC Press, 96; auth, Desktop demos New Communication Technologies and the Future of the Rhetorical Presidecy, beyond the Rhetorical Prsidency, TX A&M Univ Press, 96; auth, Rhetoric and Community, 97; auth, Review of Communication , 99-. **CONTACT ADDRESS** Pennsylvania State Univ, Univ Park, 227 Sparks Building, University Park, PA 16802. **EMAIL** t3b@psu.edu

BENSTOCK, SHARI
PERSONAL Born 12/04/1944, San Diego, CA, s, 1 child **DISCIPLINE** ENGLISH **EDUCATION** Drake University, BA, 67, Drake University, MA, 70, Kent State University, PhD, 75. **CAREER** Inst, Dept English, Drake University, 70-72; teaching fel, Dept English, Kent State University, 72-74; admin asst to head, Dept of Polit Sci, 75-77, Admin Assoc, Med Schol Prog, Col Med, University IL at Urbana-Champaign; fel, Am Asn Univ Women, 81-82; associate prof English, Univ Tulsa, 82-86, dir, Tulsa Ctr for the Study of Women's Lit, 82-86; assoc prof, 86-87, prof, English and Women's Studies, Univ Miami, 88-, founding dir, Women's Studies Program, 87-90, chair, Dept English, 96-; Lamont Prof, Union Col, Spring 93; Assoc Dean, Univ of Miami, 00-. **HONORS AND AWARDS** Fel, Asn Univ Women, 81-82; Univ Ill, Res Bd, 81; Univ Tulsa Res Grants, 84, 85; Univ Miami Summer Res Grants, 88, 89, 95; Humanities Res Ctr, Univ Texas, Austin, 89; Rockefeller Found Fel, Bellagio Study Ctr, 90; Ball Brothers Fel, Ind Univ, 91; Donald C. Gallop Fel, Yale Univ, 91; NEH Sr Fel, 93-94; Phi Kappa Phi; Golden Key Honor Soc. **MEMBERSHIPS** Mod Lang Asn; Am Studies Asn; James Joyce Int Found; Int Comp Lit Asn; Am Asn Univ Women; MLA Women's Caucus; Edith Wharton Soc; Virginia Woolf Soc. **RESEARCH** Expatriate studies; gender studies; modernism; biography; autobiography. **SELECTED PUBLICATIONS** Coauth, Who's He When He's at Home: a James Joyce Directory, Univ Ill Press, 80; ed, Feminist Issues in Literary Scholarship, Ind Univ Press, 87; auth, Women of the Left Bank: Paris, 1900-1940, Univ Tex Press, 86; auth, Textualizing the Feminine: On the Limits of Genre, Univ Okla Press, 91; ed, Edith Wharton: The House of Mirth, St Martin's Press, 93; auth, No Gifts from Chance: A Biography of Edith Wharton, Charles Scribner's Sons, 94; co-ed, On Fashion, Rutgers Univ Press, 94; author of numerous articles and other publications. **CONTACT ADDRESS** Dept English, Univ of Miami, Coral Gables, FL 33124. **EMAIL** sbenstock@umiami.iv.miami.edu

BENTLEY, D. M. R.
PERSONAL Born 08/14/1947, Kitale, Kenya, m, 1972, 3 children **DISCIPLINE** ENGLISH **EDUCATION** Univ Victoria, BA, 69; Dalhousie Univ, MA, 70; Univ London, PhD, 74; Carleton Univ, MA, 75. **CAREER** Asst prof to prof, Univ Western Ont, 76-. **HONORS AND AWARDS** Fel, Royal Soc of Arts; Fel, Royal Soc of Canada; Pleva Medal for Teaching, Univ W Ont; 3M Fel for Excellence in Teaching and Instructional Develop. **MEMBERSHIPS** Asn of Can Col and Univ Teachers of English; Asn of Can and Quebec Lit. **RESEARCH** Victorian literature; Canadian literature; Pre-Raphaelites and Pre-Raphaelitism; Ecocriticism; Memory; Kenyan literature; Urbanism. **SELECTED PUBLICATIONS** Auth, The Gay, Grey Moose: Essays on the Ecologies and Mythologies of Canadian Poetry, 1690-1990; auth, Mimic Fires: Accounts of Early Long Poems on Canada; auth, Mnemographia Canadensis: Essays on Memory, Community and Environment in Canada; ed, Early Long Poems on Canada; ed, The Essays and Reviews of Archibald Lampman; ed, The Letters of Bliss Carman to Margaret Lawrence. **CONTACT ADDRESS** Dept of English, Univ Western Ont, University College, London, ON, Canada N6A 3K7. **EMAIL** dbentley@julian.uwo.ca

BENTLEY, ERIC
PERSONAL Born 09/14/1916, England, m, 2 children **DISCIPLINE** DRAMA, COMPARATIVE LITERATURE **EDUCATION** Oxford Univ, BA, 38, BLitt, 39; Yale Univ, PhD, 41. **CAREER** Matthews prof dramatic lit, Columbia Univ, 54-69; Cornell Prof Theatre, State Univ NY Buffalo, 77-82, Guggenheim fel, 48-49 & 67-68; Charles Eliot Norton prof poetry, Harvard Univ, 60-61; ed, Works of Brecht, Grove Press, 60-67; Ford Found artist in residence, Berlin, 64-65. **HONORS AND AWARDS** Longview Awd, 60; George Nathan Prize, 67; Obie, 78; inducted into the Theatre Hall of Fame, New York, 98; dfa, univ wis, 75; dlitt, univ east anglia, uk, 79. **MEMBERSHIPS** Fel Am Acad Arts & Sci; PEN Club; Am Acad of Arts and Letters; **RESEARCH** Literary record albums; poetry and songs. **SELECTED PUBLICATIONS** Auth, The Life of the Drama, 64; The Theatre of Commitment, 67; Theatre of War, 72; The Recantation, 72; Are You Now Or Have You Ever Been, 72; Rallying Cries, Three Plays, New Repub Bks, 77; Lord Alfred's Lover (play), Can Theatre ,Rev, 78; The Brecht Commentaries, Grove Press, 81; auth, The Kleist Variations, 81; auth, Monstrous Martyrdoms, 85; auth, Bentley on Brecht, 98. **CONTACT ADDRESS** 194 Riverside Dr, Ste 4E, New York, NY 10025-7259.

BENTMAN, RAYMOND
PERSONAL Born 07/09/1925, Philadelphia, PA, 2 children **DISCIPLINE** ENGLISH LITERATURE **EDUCATION** Kenyon Col, BA, 50; Univ Pa, MA, 51; Yale Univ, PhD , 61. **CAREER** Instr English, Univ Mich, 59-60 and Univ NC, 60-61; from instr to assoc prof, 61-70, Prof English, Temple Univ, 70-, Am Philos Soc grant-in-aid, 68. **MEMBERSHIPS** MLA. **RESEARCH** Satire; 18th century British literature. **SELECTED PUBLICATIONS** Auth, Robert Burns' use of Scottish diction, In: From Sensibility to Ramanticism, Oxford Univ, 66; Satiric structure and tone in the conclusion of Gulliver's Travels, Studies English Lit, 71; Robert Burns' declining fame, Studies Romanticism, 72; ed, The Methodist, ARS, 72; The Poetry of Robert Burns, Houghton, 72. **CONTACT ADDRESS** Dept of English, Temple Univ, Philadelphia, PA 19118.

BENTON, ROBERT MILTON
PERSONAL Born 07/06/1932, Braidwood, IL, m, 1956 **DISCIPLINE** ENGLISH **EDUCATION** Trinity Univ, BA, 54; Univ Colo, MA, 63, PhD (English), 67. **CAREER** Teaching assoc English, Univ Colo, 63-66, instr, 66-67; from asst prof to assoc prof, 67-77, Prof English, Cent Wash Univ, 77-. **MEMBERSHIPS** MLA; John Steinbeck Soc Am; Pac Northwest Am Studies Asn; Western Lit Asn. **RESEARCH** Colonial American literature; environmental literature; John Steinbeck. **SELECTED PUBLICATIONS** Auth, Edward Taylor's use of his text, Am Lit, 3/67; Annotated list of Puritan sermons, Bull NY Libr, 5/70; The ecological nature of Cannery Row, In: Steinbeck: Man & His Work, 71; John Winthrops and scientific thought, Early Am Lit, winter 73; The long valley, In: A Study Guide to Steinbeck, 74; Scientific point of view in Steinbeck, Steinbeck Quart, fall 74; The preachers, In: Am Literature, 1764-1789: The Review Years, 77; Edward Abbey's antiheroes, In: Westerning Experience in America, 77. **CONTACT ADDRESS** Dept of English, Central Washington Univ, Ellensburg, WA 98926.

BERAN, CAROL L.
PERSONAL Born 01/29/1944, Brooklyn, NY, m, 1968, 2 children **DISCIPLINE** ENGLISH **EDUCATION** Susquehanna Univ, BA, 66; Johns Hopkins Univ, MAT, 67; Univ Calif, Berkeley, PhD, 77. **CAREER** Prof Eng, St Mary's Col, 77- . **HONORS AND AWARDS** Can Embassy St Fel Awd, 91-92. **MEMBERSHIPS** Asn for Can Stud in the US; Western Soc Sci Asn; Margaret Atwood Soc; Margaret Laurence Soc; Soc for the Study of Narrative Lit. **RESEARCH** Canadian literature. **SELECTED PUBLICATIONS** Auth, Living over the Abyss: Margaret Atwood's Life Before Man, ECW Press, 93; auth, The End of the World and Other Things, in Wilson, ed, Approaches to Teaching Atwood's The Handmaid's Tale; auth, The Studhorse Man: Translating the Boundaries of Text, Great Plains Q; auth, Intertexts of Margaret Atwood's Life Before Man, Am Rev of Can Stud; auth, Functional Ethnicity in Atwood's Life Before Man, Essays on Can Writing; auth, George, Leda, and a Poured Concrete Balcony: A Study of Three Aspects of the Evolution of Lady Oracle, Can Lit. **CONTACT ADDRESS** Saint Mary's Col, California, PO Box 4336, Moraga, CA 94575-4336. **EMAIL** cberan@stmarys-ca.edu

BERETS, RALPH ADOLPH
PERSONAL Born 00/00/1939, Amersfoort, Netherlands, m, 1963, 3 children **DISCIPLINE** MODERN FICTION, FILM **EDUCATION** Univ Mich, BA & MA, 63, PhD(English), 69. **CAREER** Lectr Engineering English, Univ Mich, 69-70; Asst Prof Film, Kansas City Art Inst, 71-76; Asst Prof, 70-76, assoc prof English, Univ Mo Kansas City 76-, Chm English Dept 89-99. **MEMBERSHIPS** MLA; Midwest Mod Lang Asn; ACA; Nat Coun, Teachers of English; Asn of Dept of English; Am Film Inst; Popular Culture Asn. **RESEARCH** Comparative literature; modern fiction; film; film and the law; ethics and the humanities; the literature of death and dying; from fiction into film; screenwriting; contemporary novel. **SELECTED PUBLICATIONS** Auth, The Magus: A Study in the Creation of a Personal Myth, Twentieth Century Lit, 4/73.; Van Eyck's The Just Judges in Camus' The Fall, Res Studies, 6/74; John Fowles, An Overview, Reader's Encycl of English Lit, 75; Repudiation and Reality Instruction in Saul Bellow's Fiction, Centennial Rev, Winter 76; Why Is There So Much Violence in Contemporary Films?, J of the Producers Guild of Am, 76; Saul Bellow, Contemporary Lit Criticism, Gale Research, X, 79; Changing Images of Justice in American Films, Legal Studies forum, XX, 96; From Real to Reel: The Depiction of Lawyers in Film, Legal Studies Forum, 97; Seeing the Holocaust Through Recent Films, publ on CD-ROM in the 1996 issue of ISSEI Journal, MIT Univ Press, 98; author of numerous other published articles. **CONTACT ADDRESS** Dept of English, Univ of Missouri, Kansas City, 5100 Rockhill Rd., Kansas City, MO 64110-2499. **EMAIL** rberets@umkc.edu

BERG, DAVID M.
DISCIPLINE INFLUENCE OF MASS COMMUNICATION ON CONTEMPORARY SOCIETY **EDUCATION** Minn, PhD, 63. **CAREER** Prof, Purdue Univ. **RESEARCH** The way in which media affect traditional forms of public communication such as political speaking. **SELECTED PUBLICATIONS** Auth, Rhetoric, reality, and mass media, Quart J of Speech, 72; coauth, Crisis management and the paradigm case, Rhetorical and Critical Approaches to Public Relations, Erlbaum, 92. **CONTACT ADDRESS** Dept of Commun, Purdue Univ, West Lafayette, 1366 Liberal Arts, Ed Bldg 2114, West Lafayette, IN 47907-1366. **EMAIL** dberg@sla.purdue.edu

BERG, MAGGIE
DISCIPLINE ENGLISH LITERATURE **EDUCATION** Oxford Univ, DPhil. **CAREER** Dept Eng, Queen's Univ **HONORS AND AWARDS** Alumni Teaching Awd, 98. **RESEARCH** Victorian literature; literary theory; feminist theory. **SELECTED PUBLICATIONS** Auth, Jane Eyre: Portrait of a Life, G.K. Hall, 87; Escaping the Cave: Luce Irigaray and Her Feminist Critics, 88; Luce Irigaray and the 'Contradictions' of Poststructuralism and Feminism, J Women Cult Soc, 91; auth, "Signs: Journal of Women in Culture and Society," 17, no. 1, Autumn 91, 80-91; Wuthering Heights: The Writing in the Margin, G.K. Hall, 96. **CONTACT ADDRESS** English Dept, Queen's Univ at Kingston, Kingston, ON, Canada K7L N6. **EMAIL** bergm@qsilver.queensu.ca

BERGER, ARTHUR A.
PERSONAL Born 01/03/1933, Boston, MA, m, 1961, 2 children **DISCIPLINE** COMMUNICATIONS **EDUCATION** Univ of Mass, BA, 54; Univ of Iowa, MA, 56; Univ of Minn, PhD, 65. **CAREER** English and Am studies, 60-65; Fulbright lectr, Univ of Milan, 63-64; vis prof, Annenberg School for Commun, Univ of Southern Calif, 84-85; Prof, San Francisco State Univ, 65-. **HONORS AND AWARDS** Fulbright, 63-64. **RESEARCH** Communication; American culture; media criticism; cultural studies; popular culture; semiotics; humor. **SELECTED PUBLICATIONS** Auth, Blind Men & Elephants: Perspectives on Humor, Transaction, 95; Cultural Criticism: A Primer of Key Concepts, SAGE, 95; Essentials of Mass Communication Theory, SAGE, 95; Manufacturing Desire: Media, Popular Culture & Everyday Life, Transaction 96; The Genius of the Jewish Joke, Jason Aronson, 97; Bloom's Morning, Westview/Harper Collins, 97; The Art of Comedy Writing, Transaction 97; Postmortem for a Postmodernist, AltaMira, 97; The Postmodern Presence, AltaMira, 98; auth, Media and Communication Research methods, Sage, 00; Jewish Jesters, Hamoton, 00; auth, AOS, FADS and Consumer Culture, Rownan & Littlefield, 00; auth, Die Laughing, Juniverge.com, 00. **CONTACT ADDRESS** Dept of Broadcast and Electronic Communication Arts, San Francisco State univ, San Francisco, CA 94132. **EMAIL** aberger@sfsu.edu

BERGER, SIDNEY L.
PERSONAL Born 01/25/1936, New York, NY, m, 1963, 2 children **DISCIPLINE** THEATRE **EDUCATION** Brooklyn Col, BA, 57; Univ Ks, MA, 60, PhD, 64; **CAREER** Asst instr, Univ Ks, 58-63; asst prof to assoc prof, Mich St Univ, 64-69; prof, dir, Univ Houston, 69- . **HONORS AND AWARDS** All-Univ res grants, 67, 68; tour awards to Asia, Greenland, Iceland, Europe, Amer Theatre Assoc, Dept of Defense, 60, 63, 68, 72, 85; Nat Theatre Conf; Silver Awd, Houston Int Film Festival, 89, 93; Outstanding Accomplishments in the Arts, 89, 93; Who's Who. **MEMBERSHIPS** Amer Theatre Assoc; Houston Coal for the Arts; Theatre & Film Prof Adv Bd, Univ Ks. **SELECTED PUBLICATIONS** Auth, Sweeney Todd, opera cues, 84; The Great Globe Itself, standpoints, 88; Contemporary American Theatre, standpoints, 89; coauth, The Theatre Team, 97; coed, The Playwright Versus the Director, Greenwood Press, 94;. **CONTACT ADDRESS** 4711 Imogene, Houston, TX 77096.

BERGER, THOMAS LELAND
PERSONAL Born 03/26/1941, Oak Park, IL, 3 children **DISCIPLINE** ENGLISH LITERATURE, DRAMA **EDUCATION** Dartmouth Col, BA, 63; Duke Univ, MA, 67, PhD (English), 69. **CAREER** Instr English, Univ NC, Chapel Hill, 69-70; fel Macalester Col, 70-71; asst prof, 71-76, assoc prof, 76-80, Prof English, St Lawrence Univ, 80-, Fac, Col Level Exam Prog, NY State Educ Dept. **MEMBERSHIPS** MLA; Shakespeare Asn Am; Renaissance Soc Am; Malone Soc. **RESEARCH** English Renaissance drama; bibliography and textual criticism. **SELECTED PUBLICATIONS** Auth, Petrarchan fortress of The Changeling, Renaissance Papers, 69; Index of Characters in English Renaissance Drama, Microcard Ed, 75; The Printing of Henry V, QI, The Library, 1: 114-125; Thomas Dekker's Blurt Master Constable, 1602, Austria, 80; Variants in the Quarto of Shakespeare's 2 Henry IV, The Library, 3: 109-118. **CONTACT ADDRESS** Dept of English, St. Lawrence Univ, Canton, NY 13617-1499.

BERGERON, DAVID M.
PERSONAL Born 02/08/1938, Alexandria, LA, w, 1966 **DISCIPLINE** ENGLISH **EDUCATION** La Col, BA, 60; Vanderbilt Univ, MA, 62, PhD, 64. **CAREER** Asst prof, Eng, Univ Louisville, 64-68; assoc prof, Eng, Univ New Orleans, 68-76; Prof, Eng, Univ Kansas, 76-. **HONORS AND AWARDS** Woodrow Wilson Fel, 60; ACLS Fel, 68-69; Folger Shakespeare Libr, summer Fel ACLS, Grant-in-Aid, 76; Brit Acad Grant, 99. **MEMBERSHIPS** Shakespeare Asn of Am; Renaissance Soc Am; Mod Lang Asn. **RESEARCH** Shakespeare, Renaissance drama; British history (Stuarts). **SELECTED PUBLICATIONS** Auth, Shakespeare: A Study and Research Guide, 95; Reading and Writing in Shakespeare, 96; King James and Letters of Homoerotic Desire, 99; auth, Practicing Renaissance Scholarship, 00. **CONTACT ADDRESS** Dept of English, Univ of Kansas, Lawrence, Lawrence, KS 66045. **EMAIL** bergeron@kuhub.cc.ukans.edu

BERGGREN, PAULA S.
PERSONAL Born 07/10/1942, New York, NY, m, 1968 **DISCIPLINE** ENGLISH RENAISSANCE LITERATURE, ENGLISH POETRY & DRAMA, WORLD LITERATURE **EDUCATION** Barnard Col, AB, 63; Yale Univ, MA, 64, PhD(English), 67. **CAREER** Asst prof English, Yale Univ, 67-72; asst prof, 72-80, assoc prof 81-86; prof English 86- Baruch Col, 81-86. **HONORS AND AWARDS** Recipient of Presidential Awd for Distinguished Service, May 98; Nominated for Presidential Awd for Distinguished Service, 97, 95; Inducted as Honorary Member, Golden Key National Honor Society, Fall,

96. **MEMBERSHIPS** MLA. **RESEARCH** Teaching world literature; Jacobean drama; female image in English and American literature. **SELECTED PUBLICATIONS** Auth, A lost soul: Work without hope, Awakening, Regionalism and Female Imagination, Spring 77; Womanish' mankind: Four Jacobean Heroines, Int J Women's Studies, 7/78 & 8/78; The wound in the thigh: The persistance of parody in Shakespeare's 1 Henry IV, Iowa English Bull, Fall 78; Spatial imagery in Webster's tragedies, Studies English Lit, Spring 80; The woman's part: Female sexuality as power in Shakespeare's plays, In: The Woman's Part: Feminist Criticism of Shakespeare, Univ Ill Press, 80; auth, "A prodigious thing: The Jacobean heroine in male disguise," Philol Quart; 62 Summer 83: 383-402, Published by The University of Iowa; auth, "For what we lack,/We laugh': Incompletion and The Two Noble Kinsmen," Modern Language Studies, 14 fall 84: 3-17; auth, "Imitari is Nothing': A Shakespearean Complex Word," Texas Studies in Literature and Language, 26, Spring 84: 94-127. Published by University of Texas Press; auth, "From a God to a bull': Shakespeare's Slumming Jove," Classical and Modern Literature, 5, Summer 85: 277-91, Published by CML, Inc., Terre Haute, Indiana; with the eds, "Teaching with The Norton Anthology of World Masterpieces: The Western Tradition, 7th edition, 2 vols New York: W.W. Norton, 99, Volume I: 220 pages; Volume II: 337 pages; Teaching with the Norton Anthology of World Masterpieces, Expanded Edition in One Volume, New York: W W Norton, 97; ed, "Teaching with auth, "Teaching Hamlet in a Global Literature Survey: Linking Elizabethan England and Ming China," The MLA Approaches to Teaching Hamlet, edited by Bernice W. Kliman, Forthcoming, 00-01. **CONTACT ADDRESS** Dept of English, Baruch Col, CUNY, 17 Lexington Ave, New York, NY 10010-5518. **EMAIL** paula_berggren@baruch.cuny.edu

BERGMAN, DAVID L.

PERSONAL Born 03/13/1950, Fitchburg, MA, s **DISCIPLINE** ENGLISH **EDUCATION** Kenyon Col, AB, 72; Johns Hopkins Univ, MA, 74; PhD, 77. **CAREER** Prof, Towson Univ. **HONORS AND AWARDS** Gaiety Transfigured, Outstanding Book in the Field of Human Rights, Gustavus Myers Center for the Study of Human Rights, 92; Gaiety Transfigured, Oustanding Academic Book 1993, Choice, 93; 1996-97 Vice Versa Awd for Excellence in the Gay and Lesbian Press, 1st place, Best Entertainment Feature for "Apprectiation: Allen Ginsburg," 98. **MEMBERSHIPS** MLA **RESEARCH** American poetry; American gay literature. **SELECTED PUBLICATIONS** Ed, Men on Men 5: Best Gay Short Fiction, 94; ed, The Burning Library: Essays, 94; ed, Men on Men 6: Best New Gay Fiction, 96; auth, Heroic Measures, 98; ed, Men on Men 7: Best New Gay Fiction, 98. **CONTACT ADDRESS** English Dept., Towson State Univ, Towson, MD 21252. **EMAIL** dbergman@towson.edu

BERGMANN, FRANK

PERSONAL Born 01/20/1941, Markneukirchen, Germany, m, 4 children **DISCIPLINE** AMERICAN & COMPARATIVE LITERATURE **EDUCATION** Univ AR, MA, 66; Eberhard-Karls-Universitaet Tuebingen, GER, DPhil(Am lit), 69. **CAREER** Instr lang, KS Wesleyan Univ, 65-66; Wiss asst Am lit, Am Studies Dept at Tuebingen, WGer, 66-68 & Univ Frankfurt, WGer, 68-69; asst prof English & Ger, 69-73, chm div humanities, 73-76, assoc prof, 73-79, prof English & Ger, Utica Col, Syracuse Univ, 79-, assoc dean for humanities, 91-96, assoc dean for arts and sciences, 96-00, acting dean of the fac, 98; mem, vis comt mod foreign lang & lit, Lehigh Univ, 74-78; member, fac ed comt, Syracuse Univ Press, 94-98; series ed, New York Classics reprints, Syracuse Univ Press, 86-; member, nat screening comt for Fulbright graduate study awards to Germany, 95-96, 99-. **HONORS AND AWARDS** Valedictorian, Neues Gymnasium, Ravensburg, 61; Fulbright scholarship to Hamilton Col, 61-62; Dr Phil, Magna Cum Laude, 69; Distinguished Teaching Awd, Utica Col, 85; Clark Res Awd, Utica Col, 94. **MEMBERSHIPS** ALSC; Cooper Soc; Arthur Miller Soc; MLA; NYSHA. **RESEARCH** American literature 1861-1914; literature of upstate New York; fairy tales and literary fantasy. **SELECTED PUBLICATIONS** Auth, The Worthy Gentleman of Democracy: John William De Forest and the American Dream, Carl Winter Univ, Heidelberg, Ger, 71; Robert Grant, Twayne Publ, 82; ed and auth, Upstate Literature: Essays in Memory of Thomas F O'Donnell, Syracuse Univ Press, 85 (John Ben Snow manuscript prize; certificate of merit, Regional Conference of Hist Agencies, NY State). **CONTACT ADDRESS** Div Arts and Sciences, Utica Col of Syracuse Univ, 1600 Burrstone Rd, Utica, NY 13502-4892. **EMAIL** fbergmann@utica.ucsu.edu

BERGMANN, LINDA S.

PERSONAL Born 11/12/1950, Syracuse, NY, 1 child **DISCIPLINE** COMPOSITION, AMERICAN LITERATURE **EDUCATION** Oberlin Col, BA, 72; Univ Chicago, MA, 73, PhD, 83. **CAREER** Nonfiction ed, Chicago Rev, 78-80; ed consult, Deltak, Inc, Oak Brook, Ill, 79-80; instr/tutor/tchg asst, 75-89, Columbia Col Chicago, Loyola Univ Chicago, Ind Univ Northwest, Univ Chicago; asst prof, dir, writing, Hiram Col, 89-91; asst prof, dir, writing across curric, Ill Inst Technol, 91-96; assoc prof, dir, writing across curric, Univ Mo, Rolla, 96-; ed bd, ISLE: Interdisciplinary Stud in Lit and Environ; ed bd, J of Midwest MLA. **HONORS AND AWARDS** NEH summer sem, 90; Fac Serv Awd, African Am Stud's Asn, Hiram Col, 91; Fac summer res grant, Ill Inst Technol, 92; Ethics Across Curric fel, Ill Inst Technol, 92; NEH summer stipend, 93; Booz-Allen & Hamilton Awd for Excellence in Tchg and Serv, Ill Inst Technol, 95; Florence Howe Awd, Women's Caucus for Mod Lang, 96. **MEMBERSHIPS** MLA; Midwest MLA; Soc for Lit and Sci; Asn for Stud of Lit and Environ; NCTE; Conf on Col Compos and Commun; Coun of Writing Prog Adminr; Women's Caucus for Mod Lang; Hist of Sci Soc; Soc for Critical Exchange. **RESEARCH** Elizabeth Agassiz. **SELECTED PUBLICATIONS** Auth, Academic Discourse and Academic Service: Composition vs. WAC in the Academy, ERIC Clearinghouse on Reading, Eng, and Commun Skills microfiche, Mar 94; Plagiarism in the Composition Classroom, in The Council Chronicle, NCTE, Vol 3, No 5, Je 94; Exploration and Discovery and Popular Science, in Bibliography of the Relations of Literature and Science, Configurations, Vols 1, 93, 2, 94, 3, 95; A Troubled Marriage of Discourses: Science Writing and Travel Narrative in Louis and Elizabeth Agassiz's A Journey in Brazil, J of Am Cult, 18, 95; Epic, Parody, and National Identity: George Washington in Nineteenth-Century American Humor, Stud in Am Humor, NS 3, No 2, 95; Funny Papers: Initiation and Subversion in First Year Writing, J of Tchg Writing 15.1, 96; Oedipus in Steerage: On the Pain of the Adjunct, in Dossier on Shared Borders, Contested Boundaries: Part-Time Faculty, Others, and the Profession, The Journal of the Midwest Modern Language Association, 30, 1-2, 97: 46-50; auth, Widows, Hacks, and Biographers: The Voice of Professionalism in Elizabeth Agassiz's Louis Agassiz: His Life and Correspondence, A/B: Auto/Biography Studies 12.1, 97: 1-21; auth, Elizabeth Agassiz, In American Travel Writers, 1850-1915, ed. James Schramer and Donald Ross, Dictionary of Literary Biography, 189, Detroit: Gale Research, 98, 12-17; auth, Missionary Projects and Anthropological Accounts: Ethics and Conflict in Writing Across the Curriculum, in Foregrounding Ethical Awareness in Composition and English Studies, ed. Sheryl I. Fontaine and Susan Hunter, Portsmouth, NH: Heinemann, 98, 144-159; auth, Women of Letters: Personal Narrative in Public and Private Voices, In The Personal Narrative: Writing Ourselves as teachers and Scholars, ed. Gil Haroian-Guerin, Portland, Maine: Calendar Island Press, 99, 88-101; auth, Addressing Gender Issues in the Engineering Classroom, with Connie Meinholdt and Susan Murray, Feminist Teacher 12, 99: 169-183; auth, Problem -Posting Learning in the Computer Writing Classroom, with Lucas P. Niiler, In Interactive Learning: Vignettes from America's Most Wired Campuses, ed, David G. Brown, Bolton, MA: Anker, 00, 229-232; auth, WAC and the Ethos of Engineering: Conflict and Accommodation, Forthcoming in Language and Learning Across the Disciplines. **CONTACT ADDRESS** Dept of Eng, Univ of Missouri, Rolla, Rolla, MO 65409. **EMAIL** bergmann@umr.edu

BERGQUIST, PETER

PERSONAL Born 08/05/1930, Sacramento, CA, m, 1956, 2 children **DISCIPLINE** MUSICOLOGY **EDUCATION** Mannes Col Music, NYork, BS, 58; Columbia Univ, MA, 60, PhD, 64. **CAREER** From asst prof to assoc prof, 64-73, prof music, Sch Music, Univ OR, 73-95, Emer, 95. **HONORS AND AWARDS** Ersted Distinguished Tchg Awd, Univ OR, 73; Fulbright Sr Res Grant, Germany, 85; DAAD study grant, 92; ACLS travel grant, 95; NEH publ grant, 94-98. **MEMBERSHIPS** Am Musicol Soc; Col Music Soc; Music Libr Asn; AAUP; Soc Music Theory. **RESEARCH** Renaissance music and music theory; Late Romantic music, Schenkerian analysis. **SELECTED PUBLICATIONS** Auth, Mode and Polyphony around 1500: Theory and practice, Vol I, Music Forum, 67; transl, Pietro Aaron, Toscanello in Musica, (1523, 1529), Colo Col Music, 70; auth, The first movement of Mahler's Symphony No 10: An analysis and examination of the sketches, Vol V, Music Forum, 80; eight articles on 16th century music and musicians, In: New Grove's Dictionary of Music and Musicians, 80; The poems of Orlando di Lasso's Prophetiae Sibylarum and their sources, J Am Musicol Soc, Vol 32, 79; ed, Orlando di Lasso, two motet cycles on readings from the Prophet Job, In: Recent Researches in the Music of the Renaissance, 83; ed, Orlando di Lasso, The Seven Penitential Psalms and Laudate Dominum de caelis, In: Recent Researches/Renaissance, 90; Orlando di Lassos Nunc dimittis-Vertonungen, Musik in Bayern, 86; Why did Orlando di Lasso not publish his posthumous motets?, Festschrift fur Horst Leuchtmann, Tutzing, Hans Schneider, 93; The anonymous propers in Munich Mss 32 and 76: Are they previously unknown works by Orlando di Lasso, Acta Musicologica, 93; ed, Orlando di Lasso, Samtliche Werke neue Reihe, vol 22, Lamentationes Jeremiae Prophetae, 92, vol 23, Offizien und Messproprien, 93, vol 24, Musik fur die Officia, 93, vol 25, Litaneien und Falsibordoni, 93; The modality of Lasso's compositions in A Minor, Orlando di Lasso in der Musikgeschichte, Verl der Bayer Akad der Wissensch, 96; ed, Orlando di Lasso, The Complete Motets, In: Recent Researches/Renaissance, 1995-; 12 vol; ed, Orlando Di Lasso Studies, Cambridge Univ Press, 99. **CONTACT ADDRESS** Sch of Music, Univ of Oregon, Eugene, OR 97403-1205. **EMAIL** pbergq@darkwing.uoregon.edu

BERGSTROM, MARK

DISCIPLINE COMMUNICATION STUDIES **EDUCATION** Univ Okla, PhD, 95. **CAREER** Asst prof. **MEMBERSHIPS** Int Commun Asn; Northwest Commun Asn; Nat Commun Asn; Western Nat Commun Asn. **SELECTED PUBLICATIONS** Coauth, Cohort differences in interpersonal conflict: Implications for the older patient-younger care provider interaction, Health Commun, 96; The institutionalized elderly: Interactive implications of long-term care, Erlbaum, 96. **CONTACT ADDRESS** Dept of Communication, Univ of Utah, 100 S 1350 E, Salt Lake City, UT 84112. **EMAIL** Bergstrom@admin.comm.utah.edu

BERKELEY, DAVID SHELLEY

PERSONAL Born Pittsburgh, PA, m, 1943 **DISCIPLINE** ENGLISH LITERATURE **EDUCATION** Juniata Col, AB, 38; Harvard Univ, AM, 41, PhD , 49. **CAREER** From instr to assoc prof English, 48-60, chmn grad English studies, 69-76, Prof English, Okla State Univ, 60-, Vis prof, Univ Okla, 65. **MEMBERSHIPS** MLA; SCent Mod Lang Asn; Milton Soc Am. **RESEARCH** Milton; Shakespeare; Restoration drama. **SELECTED PUBLICATIONS** Auth, Through the Telescope of Typology, What Adam Should Have Done, Milton Quart, Vol 0026, 92. **CONTACT ADDRESS** Dept of English, Oklahoma State Univ, Stillwater, Stillwater, OK 74074.

BERKHOUT, CARL T.

PERSONAL Born 08/28/1944, St Charles, IL, s **DISCIPLINE** ENGLISH, LIBRARY SCIENCE **EDUCATION** Benedictine Col, BA, 66; Marquette Univ, MA, 68; Univ Notre Dame, PhD, 75. **CAREER** Instr, Marquette Univ, 68-69; curator to asst prof, Univ Notre Dame, 73-79; asst prof, Univ Dallas, 79-82; asst prof to assoc prof, Univ Ariz, 82-86-. **MEMBERSHIPS** MAA; MLA; MAP; ACMRS; ISAS. **RESEARCH** Old English language and literature; bibliography; palaeography and cardiology. **SELECTED PUBLICATIONS** Auth, "The Pedigree of Laurence Nowell the Antiquary," English Lang Notes 23 (85): 15-26; auth, "The Parkerian Legacy of a Scheide Manuscript: William of Malmesbury's Gesta Regum Anglorum," Prince Univ Lib Chronicles 55 (94): 277-86; "The Published Writings of R. I. Page," in Runes and Runic Inscriptions, ed. David Parsons (Woodbridge/Suffolk/Rochester: Boydell, 95): 339-46; auth, "Laurence Nowell (1530-1570)," in Medieval Scholarship: Biographical Studies on the Formation of a Discipline, ed. Helen Damico (NYork/London: Garland, 98): 3-17; auth, "William Lambarde and Old English," Notes Query 47 (00): 415-20; auth, "The Old English Inscription Attributed to Roger Ascham," Notes Query 47 (00): 420-23; auth, "Gabriel Harvey's Lost Aristotle," Notes Query 47 (00): 432-33; auth, "Old English Bibliography," Old English Newsletter (77-00). **CONTACT ADDRESS** English Dept, Univ of Arizona, Tucson, AZ 85721-0001. **EMAIL** ctb@uarizonza.edu

BERKMAN, LEONARD

PERSONAL Born 07/21/1938, New York, NY, m, 1962, 2 children **DISCIPLINE** THEATRE **EDUCATION** Columbia Univ, BA, 60; Yale Univ, MFA, 63, DFA(Playwriting, Dramatic Lit & Criticism), 70. **CAREER** Instr English, Univ Tex, El Paso, 63-64; instr Playwriting, Univ Mass, 68-69; asst prof Theatre & Speech, 69-78, assoc prof Theatre, Smith Col, 78-83; prof, 83-94; Anne Hesseltine Hoyt prof of Theatre, 94. **HONORS AND AWARDS** Smith College Disting Teacher Awd, 92; Charis Medal for Teaching, 94. **RESEARCH** Nineteenth and 20th century European drama; American drama; Afro-American and African drama; Latino and Latin American Drama; Canadian Drama; Australian Drama. **SELECTED PUBLICATIONS** Auth,Two Demon Plays, an Broadcasting Corp, 73; Off-off-off Broadway, in Massachusetts, Magic Dust, Winter 78; Voila! Rape in Technicolor, Smith, 2/78; Jane Addams Mem Theatre, Chicago, 3/78; Til the Beatles reunite, WTTT, 3/79; Sleeping Through the End of the World: The Plays and Poems of Rochelle Owens, Parnaussus, Spring 82; All Ears, To Let My Ideas Transform in Upstaging Big Daddy, 93; I Won't Go See A Play Called A Parent's Worst Nightmare, NY Stage & Film Co, Poughkeepsie, NY, 95; Quits, NYU Experimental Theatre Wing, NYC, 98; Quits, Smith, 99; On Irene Formes in Conducting A Life 00; Completely Dead, Thornes Gallery Theatre, 00; More Enterprise in Walking Naked in Theatre In Crisis, 00. **CONTACT ADDRESS** Dept Theatre, Smith Col, 98 Green St, Northampton, MA 01063-0001. **EMAIL** lberkman@sophia.smith.edu

BERKOVE, LAWRENCE IVAN

PERSONAL Born 01/08/1930, Rochester, NY, m, 1967, 3 children **DISCIPLINE** ENGLISH & AMERICAN LITERATURE **EDUCATION** Univ Ill, AB, 51; Univ Minn, MA, 53; Univ Pa, PhD, 62. **CAREER** Asst instr, Univ Pa, 57-58 & 60-61; instr English, Skidmore Col, 58-60; instr, DePaul Univ, Pa, 61-62; from instr to asst prof English lit, Colo Col, 62-64; from asst prof to assoc prof English lit, 64-74, prof & am lit, Univ Mich, Dearborn, 74-. **HONORS AND AWARDS** Nat Endowment for Humanities proj develop grant, 75; consult, Nat Endowment for Humanities grant to Am Univ, 78-79; vis prof English & Am lit, Rikkyo Univ, Tokyo, Japan, 82-83; Pres, UM-Dearborn chap of AAUP, 94-97; Pres, Jack London Soc, 00-02. **MEMBERSHIPS** MLA; Midwest Mod Lang Asn; Col English Asn; Am Studies Asn; AAUP. **RESEARCH** American literature of the nineteenth and early twentieth centuries; American studies; religious influences on literature; Am Assn of Univ Profs; MLA; Col English Assn. **SELECTED PUBLICATIONS** Auth, The poor players of Huckleberry Finn, Papers Mich Acad Sci, Arts & Lett, 68; Henry James and Sir Walter

Scott: A virtuous attachment?, Studies Scottish Lit, 80; The free man of color in The Grandissimes and works by Harris and Mark Twain, Southern Quart, summer 80; ed & introd, Ambrose Bierce: Skepticism and Dissent: Selected Journalism from 1898-1901, Ann Arbor: Delmas, 80; A strange adventure: The story behind a Bierce tale, Am Lit Realism, spring 81; The heart has its reasons: Ambrose Bierce's successful failure at Philosophy, In: Critical Essays on Ambrose Bierce, G K Hall, 82; Dan De Quille, auth, The Fighting Horse of the Stanislaus, ed. Lawrence I. Berkove, Iowa City, U of Iowa, P, 90; The Sorceress of Attu, ed with intro Lawrence I Berkove, Dearborn, MI, Univ of Michigan-Dearborn, 94; Critical Essays on Kate Chopin, ed, Alice Hall Petry, NY, GK Hall, 96; auth, A Gramma of Dissent: Flatland, Newman, and the Theology of Probability, Victorian Studies, Winter, 96; auth, The Myth of Hope: Jack London's The Red One, in Re-reading Jack London, ed. Jeanne Reesman, Stanford UP, 96; auth, An Irregular Correspondent: The European Travel Letters of Joe Goodman Mark Twain Journal, fall 97; auth, Reasoning as we go: The Flaved Logic of Young Goodman Brown, Nathaniel Hawthorne Review, Spring 98; auth, Connecticut Yankee: Twain's Other Masterpiece in Making Mark Twain Work in the Classroom, ed. James Leonard, Durham, Duke UP, 99. **CONTACT ADDRESS** Dept of Humanities, Univ of Michigan, Dearborn, 4901 Evergreen Rd, Dearborn, MI 48128-1491. **EMAIL** lberkove@umd.umich.edu

BERKOWITZ, GERALD MARTIN

PERSONAL Born 01/11/1942, New York, NY **DISCIPLINE** ENGLISH AND AMERICAN LITERATURE **EDUCATION** Columbia Univ, BA, 63, MA, 64; Ind Univ, MA, 67, PhD (English), 69. **CAREER** Instr, Univ Southern Calif, 67-69 & asst prof, 69-71; asst prof, 71-78, Assoc Prof English, Northern Ill Univ, 78- **RESEARCH** Contemporary British and American drama; Shakespeare; theatre and film. **SELECTED PUBLICATIONS** Auth, Realism and the American Dramatic Tradition, Mod Drama, Vol 0040, 97; Get the Guests, Psychoanalysis, Modern American Drama, and the Audience, Mod Drama, Vol 0038, 95; Staging Depth, Oneill, Eugene and the Politics of Psychological Discourse, Mod Drama, Vol 0039, 96. **CONTACT ADDRESS** Dept English, No Illinois Univ, 1425 W Lincoln Hwy, De Kalb, IL 60115-2825.

BERLAND, KEVIN JOEL

PERSONAL Born 12/06/1947, Chicago, IL, 3 children **DISCIPLINE** ENGLISH **EDUCATION** Carleton Univ, BA, 75; MA, 77; McMaster Univ, PhD, 84. **CAREER** Assoc prof, Pa State, 88-. **HONORS AND AWARDS** Can Coun Res Fel. **MEMBERSHIPS** Am Soc for Eighteenth Century Studies; Eighteenth Century Ireland Soc; Int Soc for the Classical Tradition; Int Soc for Eighteenth Century Studies; Int Soc for Intellectual Hist. **RESEARCH** Early-modern English Literature, 18th-century anglo-Irish Literature, early modern historiography of ancient philosophy, Socrates in European letters, early modern appropriations of ancient authority, physiognomy, 18th-century poetry. **SELECTED PUBLICATIONS** Auth, "Dialogue into drama: Socrates in 18th-century verse dramas",Themes in Drama, Cambridge Univ Pr, 12 (90): 127-41; auth, "Didactic, Cathechetical, or Obstretricious: Socrates and 18th-Century Dialogue", in Compendious Conversations: Essays on Eighteenth-Century Dialogue, (Peter Lang, Frankfurt, 92), 93-104; auth, "Reading character in the face: Lavater, Socrates, and physiognomy", Word and Image 9.3, (93): 252-69; auth, "Frances Moore Brooke" and Frances Chamberlaine Sheridan" in Eighteenth-Century Anglo-Am Women Novelists: A Critical Ref Guide, ed Doreen Alvarez Saar and Mary Anne Schofield, G.K. Hall, Prentice Hall int, (NY, London, 96): 18-43; auth, "The Bangorian Controversy", Edmund Burke (1729-1797)" and "William Law (1686-1761)", in Britain in the Hanoverian Age 1714: An Encycl, ed Gerald Newman, Garland (NY, 77); auth, "The Marks of Character: Physiology and Physiognomy in Dryden's Absalom and Achitophel", Philol Quart, 76.3 (97): 193-218; auth, "The Air of a Porter: Lichtenberg and Lavater Test Physiognomy by Looking at Dr. Johnson", The Age of Johnson 10 (99): 219-230; coauth, "William Byrd's Scriblerian Stories", Scriblerian 32, 2/32 (99): 231-34; auth, "William Byrd's Sexual Lexicography", Eighteenth-Century Life, 23.1 (99): 1-11; auth, "The Paradise Garden and the Imaginary East: Alterity and Reflexivity in Brit Orientalist Romances", Eighteenth-Century Novel 2, 00; coed, The Commonplace Book of William Byrd II of Westover, Univ of NC Pr, (Chapel Hill) (forthcoming). **CONTACT ADDRESS** Dept English, Pennsylvania State Univ, Shenango, 147 Shenango Ave, Sharon, PA 16146-1597. **EMAIL** bcj@psu.edu

BERLEY, MARC

PERSONAL Born 04/14/1963, New York, NY, m, 1997 **DISCIPLINE** ENGLISH **EDUCATION** Columbia Col, BA, BA; Columbia Univ, MA; 88; PhD, 93. **CAREER** Precept, Columbia Univ, 88-93; vis asst prof, Lawrence Univ, 93-94; vis asst prof, Rutgers Univ, 95-96; adj prof, Columbia Univ, 96-98; asst prof, Barnard Col, 00-. **HONORS AND AWARDS** Pres Fel, Columbia Univ, 89-93; Teach fel, Columbia Univ, 88. **MEMBERSHIPS** MSA; SAA; RSA. **RESEARCH** 17th-cen British literature; Shakespeare; Milton; renaissance literature. **SELECTED PUBLICATIONS** Auth, "Milton's Earthy Grossness: Music and the Condition of the Poet in 'L'Allegro' and 'Il Penseroso,"' Milton Stud 30 (93); auth, "Jessica's Belmont Blues: Music and Merriment in The Merchant of Venice," in Opening the Borders (Univ Del Press, 99); auth, After the Heavenly Tune: English Poetry and the Aspiration to Song (Duquesne UP, 00). **CONTACT ADDRESS** Eng Dept., Barnard Col, 3009 Broadway, New York, NY 10027. **EMAIL** msb@columbia.edu

BERLIN, NETTA

DISCIPLINE LATIN AND GREEK LANGUAGE AND LITERATURE **EDUCATION** Wellesley Col, BA, 84; Univ MI, MA, 88, PhD, 93. **CAREER** Asst prof, 93-, Tulane Univ. **RESEARCH** Epic poetry, mythology, ancient literary criticism. **SELECTED PUBLICATIONS** Auth, War and Remembrance: Aeneid 12.554-60, and Aeneas' Memory of Troy, Amer Jour Philol 119, 98. **CONTACT ADDRESS** Dept of Class Stud, Tulane Univ, 6823 St Charles Ave, New Orleans, LA 70118. **EMAIL** nberlin@mailhost.tcs.tulane.edu

BERLIN, NORMAND

PERSONAL Born 12/06/1931, New York, NY, m, 1956, 2 children **DISCIPLINE** ENGLISH **EDUCATION** NYork Univ, BA, 53; Columbia Univ, MA, 56; Univ CA, Berkeley, PhD(Eng), 64. **CAREER** From instr to asst prof Eng, McGill Univ, 61-65; from asst prof to assoc prof, 65-74, Prof Eng, Univ MA, Amherst, 74-95; Emer 95-. **HONORS AND AWARDS** Distinguished Tchr Awd, Univ MA, 76, Hum Res Fel, 89; Bronze Medal for Outstanding Work on O'Neil, 95. **RESEARCH** Shakespeare; Elizabethan and Jacobean drama; mod drama. **SELECTED PUBLICATIONS** Auth, The Base String: The Underworld in Elizabethan Drama, Fairleigh Dickinson Univ, 68; Thomas Sackville, Twayne, 74; The Secret Cause: A Discussion of Tragedy, Univ Mass Press, 81; Eugene O'Neil, Macmillan, London & Grove Press, 82; O'Neill's Shakespeare, Michigan, 93. **CONTACT ADDRESS** Dept of English, Univ of Massachusetts, Amherst, Amherst, MA 01002. **EMAIL** nberlin@english.umass.edu

BERLIND, BRUCE

PERSONAL Born 07/17/1926, Brooklyn, NY, m, 1954, 5 children **DISCIPLINE** ENGLISH **EDUCATION** Princeton Univ, BA, 47; Johns Hopkins Univ, MA, 50, PhD , 58. **CAREER** From instr to assoc prof, 54-66, chmn dept, 67-72, prof, 66-80, Charles A Dana Prof English and Chmn Dept, Colgate Univ, 80-, US Info Serv lectr, Ger, 63; vis assoc prof, Univ Rochester, 66; mem Hungarian PEN Transl Prog, Budapest, 77 and 79. **MEMBERSHIPS** MLA; AAUP; Poetry Soc Am. **RESEARCH** Contemporary American poetry; translation. **SELECTED PUBLICATIONS** Auth, Poetry and Politics, Am Poetry Rev, Vol 0022, 93; Meaning of Fragment, Fragment of Meaning, Poetry, Vol 0168, 96. **CONTACT ADDRESS** Dept of English, Colgate Univ, Hamilton, NY 13346.

BERLINER, TODD

PERSONAL Born 12/11/1964, Los Angeles, CA, m, 1995, 2 children **DISCIPLINE** FILM STUDIES **EDUCATION** Univ of CA, Berkeley, PhD, 96, MA, 91, AB, 86 **CAREER** Asst Prof, 96-, Univ of NC **MEMBERSHIPS** Soc for Cinema Studies, Unvi Film and Video Assoc. **RESEARCH** Am Film; Hollywood films of the 1970's; Film genres; John Cassavetes. **SELECTED PUBLICATIONS** Auth, Hollywood Movie Dialogue and the 'Real Realism' of John Cassavetes, Film Quarterly, vol. 52, no.3, (99); auth, " The Genre Film as Booby Trap: Seventies Genre Bending and The Frenh connetion," Cinema Journal 40:3, (01). **CONTACT ADDRESS** Wilmington, NC 28401. **EMAIL** berlinert@uncwil.edu

BERMAN, AVIS

PERSONAL Born 06/29/1949, Hartford, CT **DISCIPLINE** ENGLISH **EDUCATION** Bucknell Univ, BA (magna cum laude), English, 71; Rutgers Univ, MA, English literature, 74. **CAREER** Writer and art historian, 78-; oral historian, Archs of Amer Art, Mark Rothko Found, Estate of Stuart Davis, Pollock-Krasner House and Study Center, 80-90; guest lecturer, various universities and museums, 83-; dir, Archs of Amer Art, Oral History Program, 87-92; consult, New York Studio School of Drawing, Painting, and Sculpture, and the Pollock-Krasner House and Study Center, 91-93; consult, Addison Gallery of Amer Art, 91-96; consult, The Andy Warhol Gallery of Amer Art, 93-94; consult, Metropolitan Museum of Art Archs, 93-94; consult, Museum of Modern Art Arch, 96-97; Collector, Archs of Am Art, 99-. **HONORS AND AWARDS** Res grants, John Sloan Memorial Found; Fellowship for Independent Study and Res, NEH; Grant-in-Aid, Amer Coun of Learned Societies; fellowships, Andrew W. Mellon; grant, Soc for the Preservation of Amer Modernists Publication **MEMBERSHIPS** Author's Guild; Natl Coalition of Independent Scholars; Intl Assn of Art Critics, Amer Section, bd of dirs, 93-98, membership chair, 94-98. **RESEARCH** American art, 1890-1950; museum history; women in the museum world; history of taste; James McNeill Whistler. **SELECTED PUBLICATIONS** Auth, Rebels on Eighth Street: Juliana Force and the Whitney Museum of American Art, 90; contrib, Addison Gallery of American Art: 65 Years, 96; auth, "Ursula von Rydingsvard," Dictionary of Women Artists, 97; contrib, Brassai: The Eyes of Paris, 98; "Remembering Leger, Champion of Nuts and Bolts," New York Times, 8 Feb, 98; "Ursula von Rydingsvard, Sculpts Metaphors in Wood," Smithsonian Magazine, May 98; ed, The Artist's Voices Talks with Seventeen, Modern Artists, 99. **CONTACT ADDRESS** 407 E 91st St, Apt 3A, New York, NY 10128. **EMAIL** avisberman@aol.com

BERNARD, CLAUDIE

PERSONAL Born 04/10/1955, Bourg. De. Peage, France, m, 1987, 2 children **DISCIPLINE** LITERATURE **EDUCATION** Ecole Normale Superieure, Paris; French Doctorate, Univ de Paris, 79; Princeton Univ, PhD, 83. **CAREER** Asst Prof, Columbia Univ, 83-89; Assoc Prof, Columbia Univ, 89-92; Assoc Prof, New York Univ, 92-; tenure 96. **RESEARCH** Nineteenth-Century French Literature and history of ideas. **SELECTED PUBLICATIONS** Auth, Le Chouan romanesque, Balzac, Barbey d' Aurevilly, Hugo, Presses Univ de France, 89; Le Passe recompose, le roman historique francais au dix-neuvieme siecle, Paris: Hachette, 96. **CONTACT ADDRESS** Dept French, New York Univ, 19 Univ Pl, New York, NY 10003-4556. **EMAIL** cb1@is.nyu.edu

BERNARD, J. W.

PERSONAL Born 06/27/1951, Portsmouth, NH, m, 1984, 1 child **DISCIPLINE** MUSIC **EDUCATION** Harvard Univ, BA 72; Yale Univ, PhD 77. **CAREER** Univ Washington, prof 87-; previously at Yale Univ and Amherst College, 25 years teaching experience. **HONORS AND AWARDS** Morse Fel; Young Sch Awd; Paul Sacher Foun. **MEMBERSHIPS** SMT; AMS. **RESEARCH** Theory and analysis of 20th century music; the history of music theory 1700 to present; theory and aesthetics of art and music. **SELECTED PUBLICATIONS** Auth, The Music of Edgard Varese, Yale Univ Pr (New Haven), 87; auth, "Elliott Carter and the Modern Meaning of Time," The Musical Quart (95); auth, "Poem as Non-Verbal Text: Elliott Carter's Concerto for Orchestra and St John Perse's Vents," in Analytical Strategies and Musical Interpretation, ed. Craig Ayrey and Mark Everist (Cambridge Univ Press, 96); auth, Music Theory in Concept and Practice, Univ Rochester Press, 97; Elliott Carter: Collected Essays and Lectures, Rochester Univ Press, 97; "Tonal Traditions in Art Music since 1960," in The Cambridge History of American Music, ed. David Nicholls (Cambridge Univ Press, 98); "Chord Collection and Set in Twentieth-Century Theory," in Music Theory in Concept Practice, ed David Nicholls (Cambridge Univ Press, 98); "Listening to Zappa," in Contemporary Music Rev, spec issue, ed. John Covach and Walter Everett, 00; "The Musical World(s?) of Frank Zappa: Some Observations of His 'Crossover' Pieces," in Expression in Pop-Rock Music, ed. Walter Everett (Garland Publishing, 00); "Feldman's Painters," in The New York Schools of Visual Art and Music, ed. Steven Johnson (Garland Publishing, 01). **CONTACT ADDRESS** School of Music, Univ of Washington, 353450, Seattle, WA 98195. **EMAIL** jbernard@u.washington.edu

BERNARD, JOHN

PERSONAL Born 11/26/1935, Baltimore, MD, m, 1961, 4 children **DISCIPLINE** ENGLISH LITERATURE **EDUCATION** Harvard Col, AB, 57; Harvard Graduate Sch, MAT, 59; Univ Minn, PhD, 70. **CAREER** Instr to asst prof, Wash Univ, 67-78; assoc prof to prof, Univ Houston, 79-. **HONORS AND AWARDS** NEH Fel, 72-73, 81, 82, 88, 90; Univ Hosuton Teaching Excellence Award, 83; Univ Houston/Houston City Coun Fac Excellence Award, 90. **MEMBERSHIPS** MLA, Renaissance Soc of Am. **RESEARCH** Renaissance reader reception and book production; humanism and popular writing, Pietro Aretino. **SELECTED PUBLICATIONS** Auth, "To Constancie Confin'de: The Poetics of Shakespeare's Sonnets," PMLA, (79); auth, "Spenserian Pastoral and the Amoretti," ELH, (80); ed, Vergil at 2000: Commemorative Essays on the Poet and His Influence, AMS Pr, 86; auth, "Realism and Closure in the Heptameron: Marguerite de Navarre and Boccaccio," Mod Lang Rev, (89); auth, "Sexual Oppression and Social Justice in Marguerite de Navarre's Heptameron," Jour of Medieval and Renaissance Studies, (89); auth, "Ceremonies of Innocence: Pastoralism in the Poetry of Edmund Spenser, Cambridge Univ Pr, 89; auth, "Montaigne and Writing: Diversion and Subjectification in the Essais," Montaigne Studies, (91); auth, "Theatricality and Textuality The Example of Othello," New Lit Hist, (95); auth, "Spenser, Spenser and Hayden, Huntington Libr Quart, (99); auth, "Formiamo un cortegian: Castiglione and the Aims of Writing," Mod Lang Notes, (00). **CONTACT ADDRESS** Univ of Houston, Houston, TX 77204-2090. **EMAIL** jbernard@uh.edu

BERNARD, KENNETH

PERSONAL Born 05/07/1930, Brooklyn, NY, m, 1952, 3 children **DISCIPLINE** ENGLISH **EDUCATION** City Col NYork, BA, 53; Columbia Univ, MA, 56, PhD , 62. **CAREER** From instr to assoc prof, 59-71, Prof English, Long Island Univ, 71-, Guggenheim Found fel playwriting, 72-73; NY State Creative Artists Pub Serv Grant playwriting, 72-73; NY 73-74, consult, 74-75, grant fiction, 76; Rockefeller grant playwriting, 75; consult, Mass Arts and Humanities Found, 75, Wis Arts Bd, 75 and Md Arts Coun, 78; Nat Endowment for Arts grant fiction, 78; asst ed, Confrontation. **HONORS AND AWARDS** Arvon Poetry Prize, 80. **MEMBERSHIPS** PEN Club. **RESEARCH** Dramatic writing. **SELECTED PUBLICATIONS** Auth, Unbalancing Acts--Foundations or a Theater, Am Book Rev, Vol 0015, 93; Pinter the Homecoming, Explicator, Vol 0052, 94. **CONTACT ADDRESS** Dept of English, Long Island Univ, Brooklyn, One University Plaza, Brooklyn, NY 11201. **EMAIL** Kenneth.Bernard@liu.edu

BERNE, STANLEY
PERSONAL Born 06/08/1923, New York, NY, m, 1952 **DISCIPLINE** ENGLISH **EDUCATION** Rutgers Univ, BS, 51; NYork Univ, MA, 52. **CAREER** Asst prof, 63-67, assoc prof, 68-82, Res Assoc Prof English, Ctr for Advan Professional Studies and Res, Eastern NMex Univ, 82-, Guest lectr, Univ of Americas, 65 and Univ SDak, 68; res grants, Eastern NMex Univ, 66-73; pres, Am-Can Publ Inc, 76-; co-producer, co-host, PBS TV Series, Future Writing Today, 80. **MEMBERSHIPS** Comt Small Mags, Eds & Publ; Rio Grande Writers Asn; Western Independent Publ. **RESEARCH** Contemporary novel and short story; aesthetics and criticism. **SELECTED PUBLICATIONS** Auth, Looking for a Lost House, Ploughshares, Vol 0020, 94. **CONTACT ADDRESS** Dept of English, Eastern New Mexico Univ, Portales, Portales, NM 88130.

BERNSTEIN, CAROL L.
PERSONAL Born 02/09/1933, New York, NY, m, 1955, 4 children **DISCIPLINE** ENGLISH, COMPARATIVE LITERATURE **EDUCATION** Swarthmore Col, BA, 54; Yale Univ, MA, 56, PhD(English), 61 **CAREER** Instr English, Hebrew Univ, Israel, 57-58; lectr, Albertus Magnus Col, 65; vis lectr English & Am lit Hebrew Univ, Israel, 65-66; lectr English, Univ Pa, 67-69, asst prof, 69-74; lectr, 74-76, assoc prof, 76-90, Prof English, Bryn Mawr Col, 90-, Prof Comp Lit, 93-. **HONORS AND AWARDS** Phi Beta Kappa; Ford and Pew Found grants; NEH summer stipend; Fairbank Prof Humanitities, 92-97; Mary E Garrett Alumnae Prof English, 97-. **MEMBERSHIPS** MLA; ACLA **RESEARCH** Nineteenth and twentieth century literature; narrative theory; Walter Benjamin and theories of the sublime; psychoanalyic theory and literary criticism; cultural memory. **SELECTED PUBLICATIONS** Auth, Precarious Enchantment: A Reading of Meredith's Poetry, Cath Univ Am Press, 79; The Celebration of Scandal: Toward the Sublime in Victorian Urban Fiction, Penn State Univ Press, 91. **CONTACT ADDRESS** Dept of English, Bryn Mawr Col, 101 N Merion Ave, Bryn Mawr, PA 19010-2899. **EMAIL** cbernste@brynmawr.edu

BERNSTEIN, CHARLES
PERSONAL Born 04/04/1950, New York, NY, m, 1977, 2 children **DISCIPLINE** ENGLISH, POETRY **EDUCATION** Harvard Col, AB, 72. **CAREER** Vis lectr, Univ Calif, San Diego, 87; vis prof, Queens Col, City Univ of NY, 88; fac mem/series coordr, Wolfson Center for Nat Affairs, New Sch for Soc Res, 88; lectr, Princeton Univ, 89, 90; Butler Prof (vis), Dept English, State Univ of NY, Buffalo, 89; vis prof, City Col, CUNY, 98; David Gray Prof of Poetry and Letters, Dept English, State Univ of NY, Buffalo, Dir, Poetics Prog, assoc mem, Prog in Comparative Lit, 90-. **HONORS AND AWARDS** William Lyon McKenzie King Fel, Simon Fraser Univ, 73; NEA Creative Writing Fel, 80; John Simon Guggenheim Memorial Fel, 85; Univ Auckland Found Fel, 86; NY Found for the Arts Fel, 90, 95; Roy Harvey Pearce/Archive for New Poetry Prize, Univ of Calif, San Diego, 99. **SELECTED PUBLICATIONS** Auth, Islets/Irritations, NY: Roof Books (92, rpt of Jordan Davies, 83); auth, Content's Dream: Essays 1975-1984, Los Angeles: Sun & Moon Press (86, 94); auth, The Sophist, Los Angeles: Sun & Moon Press (87); auth, Rough Trades, Los Angeles: Sun & Moon Press (91); auth, A Poetics, Cambridge: Harvard Univ Press (92); co-ed with Hank Lazer, Modern Contemporary Poetics, Univ Ala Press (98-); ed, ed, 99 Poets/1999: An International Poetics Symposium, a special issue of boundary 2; Close Listening: Poetry and the Performed Word, Oxford Univ Press (98); auth, My Way: Speeches and Poems, Chicago: Univ of Chicago Press (99); auth, Republics of Reality: 1975-1995, Los Angeles: Sun & Moon Press (2000). **CONTACT ADDRESS** Poetics Prog, Dept of English, SUNY, Buffalo, 438 Clemens Hall, Box 604610, Buffalo, MY 14260-4610. **EMAIL** bernstei@bway.net

BERNSTEIN, JANE
PERSONAL Born 06/10/1949, Brooklyn, NY, d, 2 children **DISCIPLINE** ENGLISH **EDUCATION** NYork Univ, BA, 67; Columbia Univ, MFA, 77. **CAREER** Assoc Prof, Carnegie Mellon Univ. **HONORS AND AWARDS** Fel, NEH, 82-83; 00-01. **MEMBERSHIPS** WGA; PEN; AWP. **RESEARCH** Writer **SELECTED PUBLICATIONS** Auth, "Making Rachel big," New York Times Magazine, (94): 20; auth, "Taking Care," Creative Nonfiction, (95): 67-76; auth, "The Silent Struggle," Self, (96): 122-125; auth, "How and Why," Creative Nonficiton, (96): 35-40; auth, "On Regret," The Sun, (96): 15-18; auth, "Healing Rituals for Miscarriage," Self, (97): 130, 139-140; auth, Bereft--A Sister's Story, North Point Press, 00. **CONTACT ADDRESS** Dept Eng, Carnegie Mellon Univ, 5000 Forbes Ave, Pittsburgh, PA 15213-3815. **EMAIL** janebern@andrew.cmu.edu

BERNSTEIN, LAWRENCE F.
PERSONAL Born 03/25/1939, New York, NY, m, 1965 **DISCIPLINE** MUSICOLOGY **EDUCATION** Hofstra Univ, BS, 60; NYork Univ, PhD (musicol), 69. **CAREER** From instr to asst prof music and humanities, Univ Chicago, 65-70; assoc prof, 70-80, Prof Music, Univ PA, 80- **HONORS AND AWARDS** Alfred Einstein prize of the Am Musicological Society, 74; National Endowment for the Humanities fel, 78; Am Philosophical Society grant, 83; Guggenheim fel, 87. **MEMBERSHIPS** Am Musicol Soc; Int Musicol Soc; Music Libr Asn; AAUP. **RESEARCH** French secular music of the Renaissance; eighteenth century symphony; stylistic analysis. **SELECTED PUBLICATIONS** Auth, Ma Bouche Rit Et Mon Coeur Pleure--A Chanson A 5 Attributed to Josquin Desprez, J Musicol, Vol 0012, 94. **CONTACT ADDRESS** Dept of Music, Univ of Pennsylvania, Philadelphia, PA 19174. **EMAIL** lbernste@sas.upenn.edu

BERNSTEIN, MARK H.
PERSONAL Born 03/19/1948, New York, NY, s **DISCIPLINE** CLASSICS, PHILOSOPHY **EDUCATION** CUNY, 69; Univ Calif, Santa Barbara, PhD, 82. **CAREER** Cis Asst Prof, Wesleyan Univ, 82-83; From Asst Prof to Prof, Univ Tex, 83-. **HONORS AND AWARDS** 2 NEH Fels, Res Develop Awd. **MEMBERSHIPS** APA, SSPP **RESEARCH** Applied ethics, animal ethics, metaphysics, free will. **SELECTED PUBLICATIONS** Auth, Fatalism, Univ Nebr Pr, 92; auth, On Moral Considerability, Oxford UP, 98. **CONTACT ADDRESS** Dept Classics & Philos, Univ of Texas, San Antonio, 6900 N Loop 1604 W, San Antonio, TX 78249-1130. **EMAIL** markb@10.com

BERNSTEIN, MATTHEW H.
PERSONAL Born 06/11/1958, New York, NY, m, 1980, 2 children **DISCIPLINE** FILM STUDIES **EDUCATION** Univ Wisc, Madison, BA, 80; PhD, 87; Columbia Univ, MFA, 82. **CAREER** Lectr, 88-89, asst prof, 89-95, assoc prof, 95-, film stud, Emory Univ. **HONORS AND AWARDS** NEH fel, 89, res grant, 97-99; Emory Univ res grants, 90, 91, 93, 94. **MEMBERSHIPS** Soc for Cinema Stud; Univ Film and Video Asn. **RESEARCH** Am film industry; classical Hollywood cinema; film comedy; Japanese film; post-war European film; documentary film; African-Americans and film. **SELECTED PUBLICATIONS** Co-ed, "Visions of the East: orientalism in Film", Rutgers Univ Press, 97; co-ed, "Movie-going Metropolis," Special Issue of Atlanta History 43, no. 2, 99; auth, "Model Criminals: Visual Style in Bonnie and Clyde," Arthur Penn's Bonnie nd Clyde, Cambridge Univ Press, (99): 101-126; auth, "Selznick's March: Gone With the Wind Comes to White Atlanta," Atlanta History 43, no. 2, (99): 7-33; co-ed, "Floating Triumphantly: The American Critics on Titanic," Titanic: Anatomy of a Blockbuster, Rutgers Univ Press, (99): 14-28; auth, "Perfecting the New Gangster: Writing Bonnie nd Clyde," Film Quarterly 53, no. 4, (00): 16-31; co-ed, "High and Low: Art Cinema and Pulp Fiction in Yokohama Harbor," Film Adaptation, Rutgers Univ Press, (00): 172-189; ed, Controlling Hollywood: Censorship and Regulation in the Studio Era, Rutgers Univ Press, 00; auth, Walter Wanger, Hollywood Independent, Univ of Minn Press, 00. **CONTACT ADDRESS** Dept of Film Studies, Emory Univ, Atlanta, GA 30322. **EMAIL** mbernst@emory.edu

BERRY, BOYD MCCULLOCH
PERSONAL Born 05/29/1939, Chicago, IL, 2 children **DISCIPLINE** ENGLISH LITERATURE, RENAISSANCE **EDUCATION** Harvard Univ, BA, 61; Univ Mich, MA, 62, PhD (English), 66. **CAREER** Asst prof English, Ind Univ, 66-74; vis lectr, Ife Univ, Nigeria, 70-71; Assoc Prof English, VA Commonwealth Univ, 74-. **MEMBERSHIPS** MLA; Milton Soc Am. **RESEARCH** John Milton; 16th and 17th century prose and poetry. **SELECTED PUBLICATIONS** Auth, On looking at Madmen and Specialists, Pan-African J, 72; Puritan soldiers in Paradise Lost, Mod Lang Quart, 74; The first English pediatricians and Tudor attitudes toward childhood, J Hist of Ideas, 74; Process of Speech: Puritan Religious Writing and Paradise Lost, Johns Hopkins Univ, 76. **CONTACT ADDRESS** Dept of English, Virginia Commonwealth Univ, Richmond, VA 23284. **EMAIL** bberry@vcu.edu

BERRY, EDWARD I.
DISCIPLINE RENAISSANCE LITERATURE **EDUCATION** Wesleyan Col, BA; Univ Calif, Berkeley, MA, PhD. **CAREER** Prof. **HONORS AND AWARDS** Fulbright fel, 69-70. **RESEARCH** Shakespeare; Sidney. **SELECTED PUBLICATIONS** Auth, Patterns of Decay: Shakespeare's Early Histories, Va UP, 75; Shakespeare's Comic Rites, Cambridge UP, 84; Japanese translation, Univ Nagoya Press, 89; co-ed, True Rites and Maimed Rites, Univ Ill Press, 92; The Making of Sir Philip Sidney, U of Toronto P, 98. **CONTACT ADDRESS** Dept of English, Univ of Victoria, PO Box 3070, Victoria, BC, Canada V8W 3W1. **EMAIL** eberry@uvic.ca

BERRY, HERBERT
PERSONAL Born 05/09/1922, New York, NY, m, 1948, 4 children **DISCIPLINE** ENGLISH **EDUCATION** Furman Univ, BA, 47; Univ Nebr, MA, 48; Univ Colo, PhD (English), 53. **CAREER** Instr English, Univ Nebr, 50-51; asst prof, Univ Omaha, 51-55; assoc prof and head dept, Doane Col, 55-58; from asst prof to assoc prof, Univ Western Ont, 59-67; prof Eng Univ, Sask, 67- **MEMBERSHIPS** MLA; Renaissance Soc Am. **RESEARCH** English literature of the 16th and 17th centuries. **SELECTED PUBLICATIONS** Auth, The Noble Science, Delaware UP, 91. **CONTACT ADDRESS** 320 Arts Tower, 9 Campus Dr, Saskatoon, SK, Canada S7N 5A5.

BERRY, MARGARET
PERSONAL Born Greensboro, NC **DISCIPLINE** ENGLISH, SOUTH ASIAN STUDIES **EDUCATION** St Joseph Col, BA, 44; Cath Univ, Am, MA, 50; St Johns Univ, NYork, PhD (English), 56; Univ Pa, MA, 68. **CAREER** From instr to assoc prof English, St Joseph Col, 54-65; Assoc Prof English, John Carroll Univ, 65-, Ford Found Asian studies grant, 63-64; NDEA fel S Asia studies, 67-68; Danforth assoc, 72; vis res scholar, Univ Mysore, fall 73; vis lectr, Univ Madurai, fall 73; fac fel, John Carroll Univ, 73. **MEMBERSHIPS** Asn Asian Studies; AAUP. **RESEARCH** Literary criticism of the English Catholic revival; Indian fiction in English. **SELECTED PUBLICATIONS CONTACT ADDRESS** Dept of English, John Carroll Univ, 20700 N Park Blvd, Cleveland, OH 44118.

BERRY, RALPH M.
PERSONAL Born 11/14/1947, Atlanta, GA, m, 1988 **DISCIPLINE** ENGLISH **EDUCATION** Furman Univ, BA, 70; Wesley Seminary at Am Univ, MTS, 74; Univ Iowa, MFA, 80, PhD, 85. **CAREER** Lectr, Univ de Tours (France), 85; Asst Prof, 86-91, Assoc Prof, Fla State Univ, 91-98, Prof, Florida State Univ, 99-. **HONORS AND AWARDS** Fulbright Jr. Lectr, 85; Fiction Collective Award, 84; Honorable Mention Pushcart Prize, 91-92; Fla Individual Artist Grant, 88-89, 95-96. **MEMBERSHIPS** MLA; AWP. **RESEARCH** 20th century literature; philosophy and literature. **SELECTED PUBLICATIONS** Auth, What Is a Narrative Convention?, Narrative, 95; In Which Henry James Strikes Bedrock, Philos & Lit, 97; Leonardo's Horse, 97; auth, Dictionary of Modern Anguish, 00. **CONTACT ADDRESS** English Dept, Florida State Univ, Tallahassee, FL 32306-1580. **EMAIL** rberry@english.fsu.edu

BERS, VICTOR
PERSONAL Born 08/30/1944, Providence, RI, m, 1966, 2 children **DISCIPLINE** CLASSICS **EDUCATION** Chicago Univ, AB, 66; Oxford Univ, BA, 68; Harvard Univ, PhD, 72. **CAREER** Lectr to prof, 72-, Yale Univ. **MEMBERSHIPS** APA **RESEARCH** Greek literature, especially tragedy; Greek stylistics. **SELECTED PUBLICATIONS** Auth, Enallage and Greek Style, Leiden, 74; auth, Greek Poetic Syntax in the Classical Age, New Haven, 84; auth, Speech in Speech: Studies in Incorporated Oration Recta in Attic Drama and Oratory, Langham, MD, 97. **CONTACT ADDRESS** Dept of Classics, Yale Univ, Box 8266, New Haven, CT 06520-8266. **EMAIL** victor.bers@yale.edu

BERST, CHARLES A.
PERSONAL Born 09/30/1932, Seattle, WA, m, 1962, 2 children **DISCIPLINE** ENGLISH **EDUCATION** Univ Wash, BA, 55, PhD, 65. **CAREER** Asst prof, Univ Alberta, 65-67; from asst to assoc prof, 67-81, prof, 81-94, prof emeritus, 94-, Univ Calif Los Angeles; chemn Col of Lett and Sci Fac, 77-81, vice chemn & chemn, Fac Senate, 87-89, UCLA. **HONORS AND AWARDS** Univ Wash, PhD (hon), 65; UCLA Distinguished Tchg Awd, 87; UCLA Univ Service Awd, 91. **MEMBERSHIPS** MLA. **RESEARCH** Bernard Shaw; modern drama; drama and religion **SELECTED PUBLICATIONS** Auth, Bernard Shaw and the Art of Drama, Univ Ill, 73; ed, Shaw and Religion, Penn State, 81; auth, As Kingfishers Catch Fire: The Saints and Poetics of Shaw and T.S. Eliot, in Dukore, ed, 1992: Shaw and the Last Hundred Years, Penn State, 94; auth, Pygmalion: Shaw's Spin on Myth and Cinderella, Twayne, 95; auth, Superman Theater: Gusts, Galumphs, and Grumps, in Laurence, Unpublished Shaw, Penn State, 96; auth, New Theatres for Old, in Innes, ed, The Cambridge Companion to Shaw, Cambridge, 98. **CONTACT ADDRESS** Dept of English, Univ of California, Los Angeles, Los Angeles, CA 90095. **EMAIL** berst@humnet.ucla.edu

BERTELSEN, DALE A.
DISCIPLINE SPEECH COMMUNICATION **EDUCATION** Penn State Univ, MA, 85; PhD, 89. **CAREER** Asst prof, 88-93, assoc prof, 93-96, PROF, 96-, BLOOMSBURG UNIV; Emerging Scholar Award, 93, a nd Distinguished Serv Award, 96, from Kenneth Burke Soc; E L Hunt Scholar Award, 97; Distinguished tchg fel, 97, and Distinguished Serv Award, 98 from E Commun Asn. **MEMBERSHIPS** Nat Commun Asn; E Commun Asn; Speech Commun Asn of PA; Sppech Commun Asn of PR; Kenneth Burke Soc. **RESEARCH** Media criticism; Rhetorical criticism. **SELECTED PUBLICATIONS** Auth Media Form and Government: Democracy as an Archetypal Image in the Electronic Age, Commun Quart, 92; Kenneth Burke's Conception of Reality: The Process of Transformation and its Implic ations for Thetorical Criticism, Extensions of the Burkeian System, Univ Alabama Press, 93; Sophistry, Epistemology, and the Media Context, Philos and Rhetoric, 93; coauth Analyzing Media: Communication Technologies as Symbolic and Cognitive Systems, Guilford Publ, 96. **CONTACT ADDRESS** Dept of Commun Studies & Theatre Arts, Bloomsburg Univ of Pennsylvania, 400 E 2nd St, Bloomsburg, PA 17815-1301. **EMAIL** dberte@planetx.bloomu.edu

BERTELSEN, LANCE
PERSONAL Born 10/24/1947, Inglewood, CA, d, 2 children **DISCIPLINE** ENGLISH LITERATURE, EIGHTEENTH CENTURY ENGLISH CULTURE **EDUCATION** Dartmouth Col, AB, 69; Univ WA, PhD(English), 79. **CAREER** Asst prof,

79-85, assoc prof English, Univ Tex, Austin, 86-, assoc ch, 94-97. **HONORS AND AWARDS** Fel, Nat Humanities center, 83; fel, Yale Center for British Art, 84; TX Inst of Letters O. Henry Awd, 90; URI Fac Res assignment, 91; Frank C. Erwin Centennial Honors Prof, 94; Dean's Fel, 97; President's Associates Teaching Awd, 00. **MEMBERSHIPS** Am Soc 18th Century Studies; S Cent Am Soc 18th Century Studies. **RESEARCH** Fielding; WWII. **SELECTED PUBLICATIONS** Auth, Ireland, temple, and the Origins of the Drapier, Papers on Lang & Lit, 77; The Smollettian View of life, Novel, 78; David Garrick and English painting, 18th Century Studies, 78; Have at you all: Or, Bonnell Thornton's Journalism, Huntington Libr Quart, 81; New Information on a Brush for the Sign Painters, Eighteenth-Century Life, 7, 82; The Interior Structures of Hogarth's Marriage a la Mode, Art History, 6, 83; the Crab: An Unpublished Poem by Charles Churchill, Philol Quart, 63, 84; Jane Austen's Miniatures: Painting, Drawing, and the Novels, Modern lang Quart, 4, 84; The Nonsense Club: Literature and Popular Culture, 1749-1764, Oxford: Clarendon Press, 86; The Significance of the 1731 Revisions to The Fall of Mortimer, Restoration and Eighteenth-Century Theatre Res, 2nd ser, 2, winter 87; Icons on Two, J of Popular Culture, 22, spring 89; San Pietro and the Art of War, Southeast Rev, 74, 89; How Texas Won the Second World War, SE Rev, 76, 91; Journalism, Carnival, and Jubilate Agno, ELH, 59, 92; Committed by Justice Fielding, Eighteenth-Century Studies, 30, 97; auth, Henry Fielding at Work: Magistrate, Businessman, Writer, St. Martins Press, New York, 00. **CONTACT ADDRESS** Dept English, Univ of Texas, Austin, 0 Univ of TX, Austin, TX 78712-1026. **EMAIL** lberte@uts.cc.utexas.edu

BERTHOFF, ANN EVANS
PERSONAL Born 02/13/1924, New York, NY, m, 1949, 2 children **DISCIPLINE** ENGLISH, SEMIOTICS **EDUCATION** Cornell Col, Iowa, AB, 45; Radcliffe Col, AM, 48. **CAREER** Instr English, Bradford Jr Col, 48-51, Bryn Mawr Col, 51-62 and Haverford Col, 63-65; lectr, Swarthmore Col, 65-67; assoc prof, 70-78, Prof English, Univ Mass, Boston, 78-87, prof emer, 88; Mem, NCTE Comn on Compos, 78-81; consult, WNET/Channel 13, 79- and Bread Loaf Sch English, 80; dir, Nat Endowment for Humanities Summer Sem, 80. **HONORS AND AWARDS** Randolph Vis Distinguished Prof, Vassar Col, 89-90; Exemplar CCCC, 98. **MEMBERSHIPS** NCTE; Conf Col Compos and Commun; Col English Asn; New England Col English Asn (pres, 77-78); MLA. **RESEARCH** English pedagogy; philosophy of language; Renaissance poetry. **SELECTED PUBLICATIONS** Auth, The Resolved Soul: A Study of Marvell's Major Poems, Princeton Univ Press, 70; auth, " Remembering Paulo Freire," Journal of Advanced Composition, 17. 87; ed, Richards on Rhetoric, Oxford Univ Press, 91; auth, " Walker Percy's Castaway," Sewanee Rev, Vol 0102, 94; auth, " A Semiotic Journey Across the Field of Geist," Semiotica, 119-3/4, 98; auth, The Mysterious Barricades: Language and Its Limits, Univ of Toronto Press, 99; auth, " Reclaming the Active Mind," College English, Vol61, 99; auth, " Susanne K Langer and 'the odyssey of the mind,' Seminotica, 128-1/2,00. **CONTACT ADDRESS** 14 Thoreau St, Concord, MA 01742.

BERTHOFF, WARNER BEMENT
PERSONAL Born 01/22/1925, Oberlin, OH, m, 1949, 2 children **DISCIPLINE** ENGLISH **EDUCATION** Harvard Univ, BA, 47, MA, 49, PhD, 54. **CAREER** Tchng fel, 49-51, Harvard Univ; from asst prof to prof, 51-67, Bryn Mawr Col; prof Eng,67-90, Harvard Univ; Fulbright fel, vis prof, 57-58, Univ Catania; vis prof, Univ Warsaw, 63; vis prof, Univ Minn, 61; vis prof, Univ Calif, Berkeley, 62-63; Guggenheim fel, 68-69; sr fel, Soc for Human, 75-76, Cornell; Wilson Ctr fel, 84. **MEMBERSHIPS** Melville Soc. **SELECTED PUBLICATIONS** Auth, Literature and the Continuances of Virtue, Princeton Univ, 86; auth, Hart Crane: A Reintroduction, Minn, 89; auth, American Trajectories: Authors and Readings, 1790-1970, Penn St, 94. **CONTACT ADDRESS** Harvard Univ, Widener 446, Cambridge, MA 02138.

BERTHOLD, DENNIS A.
PERSONAL Born 10/29/1942, Los Angeles, CA, m, 1984, 1 child **DISCIPLINE** ENGLISH **EDUCATION** Univ Calif, Riverside, BA, 64; MA, 66; Univ of Wisc, Madison, PhD, 72. **CAREER** Instr, Savannah State Col, 66-68; instr, Univ Wisc Stevens Point, 71-72; prof, Tex A&M Univ, 72-. **HONORS AND AWARDS** NEH Summer Stipends, 74, 87; Tex A&M Distinguished Achievement Awd in Teaching, 77; NEH Res Fel, 80-81; Vis prof, Univ of Zagreb, Croatia, 88. **MEMBERSHIPS** MLA; ASA; SCMLA; Melville Soc; Hawthorne Soc. **RESEARCH** 19th Century American Literature, particularly Herman Melville, literary iconography, sea literature. **SELECTED PUBLICATIONS** Couth, Dear Brother Walt: The Letters of Thomas Jefferson Whitman, 84; auth, "Charles Brockden Brown, Edgar Huntley and the Origins of the American Picturesque", William & Mary Quarterly, 84; coauth, Hawthorne's American Travel Sketches, 89; auth, "Melville, Garibaldi, and the Medusa of Revolution", Am Lit Hist, 97; auth, "Class Acts: Melville's The Two Temples and The Astor Place Riots", Am Lit, 99. **CONTACT ADDRESS** Dept English, Texas A&M Univ, Col Station, 1 Texas A&M Univ, College Station, TX 77843-4227. **EMAIL** d-berthold@tamu.edu

BERTMAN, STEPHEN
PERSONAL Born 07/20/1937, New York, NY, m, 1968, 2 children **DISCIPLINE** CLASSICS **EDUCATION** NYork Univ, BA, 59; Brandeis Univ, MA, 60; Columbia, PhD, 65. **CAREER** Asst prof, Fla State Univ, 63-67; Prof, Univ Windsor, 67-. **HONORS AND AWARDS** Phi Beta Kappa; Eta Sigma Phi; Alumni Awd Exc, Univ Teaching, Univ Windsor. **MEMBERSHIPS** Amer Philol Asn; Archaeol Inst Amer; Class Asn Mid W & S; World Future Soc; Soc Psychol Study Soc Issues. **RESEARCH** The impact of time and speed on cultural values and memory. **SELECTED PUBLICATIONS** auth, Art and the Romans, 75; The Conflict of Generations in Ancient Greece and Rome, 76; Doorways Through Time: The Romance of Archaeology, 86; Hyperculture: The Human Cost of Speed, 98; Cultural Amnesia: America's Future and the Crisis of Memory, 00. **CONTACT ADDRESS** 5459 Piccadilly Circle N, West Bloomfield, MI 48322.

BEST, MICHAEL R.
DISCIPLINE RENAISSANCE DRAMA **EDUCATION** Univ Adelaide, BA, PhD. **CAREER** Prof; dept ch, Univ of Victoria. **HONORS AND AWARDS** Co-ord ed, Internet Shakespeare Editions; Cmpt Software: Shakespeare's Life and Times, Intellimation: Santa Barbara, CA, 91; hypertext program for the Macintosh, Version 2.1, 92; version 3.0 for CD ROM, 94; Shakespeare dir, a program for blocking scenes from Shakespeare's plays, Intellimation: Santa Barbara, CA, 94. **RESEARCH** Shakespeare; electronic texts; computer-assisted learning. **SELECTED PUBLICATIONS** Co-ed, The Book of Secrets of Albertus Magnus, Clarendon, 73; auth, A Lost Glitter: Letters between South Australia and the Western Australian Goldfields, 1895-97, Wakefield Press, 86; Shakespeare I: Power and Justice, Open Lrng Inst BC, 85; Shakespeare II: Freedom and Restraint in Love (Text: Open Learning Institute of B.C., 1986)ed, Gervase Markham, The English Housewife, McGill-Queen's UP, 86; internet pub(s), Internet Shakespeare Editions, texts of 32 plays in original spelling; articles for EMLS and Text/Technology. **CONTACT ADDRESS** Dept of English, Univ of Victoria, PO Box 3070, Victoria, BC, Canada V8W 3W1. **EMAIL** mbest1@uvic.ca

BETHEL, ELIZABETH RAUH
PERSONAL Born 08/27/1942, Grosse Pointe, MI **DISCIPLINE** SOCIOLOGY; COMMUNICATION **EDUCATION** Univ Oklahoma, PhD, 74. **CAREER** Lander Univ, prof, sociol, 74-; Univ Madras, Fulbright lectr, 90. **MEMBERSHIPS** ASA; SSS; NWU. **RESEARCH** African Am Culture; Southern US Culture; Global Ethnic Culture. **SELECTED PUBLICATIONS** Black Communities, in Neil Larry Schumsky, ed, American Cities and Suburbs: An Encyclopedia, Clio, pub 98; Journals and Voices: Mosaics of Community, in Documenting Cultural Diversity in the Resurgent American South, in: Margaret R Dittemore and Fred J Hay, eds, Am Lib Asn, 97; AIDS: Readings on a Global Crisis, Allyn and Bacon, 95; numerous other pub. **CONTACT ADDRESS** Dept Sociology, Lander Univ, Greenwood, SC 29646. **EMAIL** ebethel@lander.edu

BETT, RICHARD
PERSONAL Born 06/10/1957, London, England, m, 1986 **DISCIPLINE** CLASSICS AND PHILOSOPHY **EDUCATION** Oxford Univ, BA, 80; UC Berkley, PhD, 86. **CAREER** Asst Prof, Univ TX at Arlington, 86-91; Asst Prof, Johns Hopkins Univ, 00; 91-94; Assoc Prof, 94-, Sec Appt in Classics, 96-; Acting Exec Dir, APA, 00; Prof, 00-. **HONORS AND AWARDS** Fel Center for Hellenic Stud, Washington DC 94-95. **MEMBERSHIPS** APA; Soc for Ancient Greek Phil; North Amer Nietzsche Soc **RESEARCH** Ancient Greek philosophy, especially Greek skepticism. **SELECTED PUBLICATIONS** Art, Scepticism and Everyday Attitudes in Ancient and Modern Philosophy, Metaphilosophy, 93; art, What Did Pyrrho Think about the Nature of the Divine and the Good, Phronesis, 94; art, Aristocleson Timon on Pyrrho the Text it Logic and its Credibility, Oxford Stud in Ancient Phil, 94; auth, Sextus Against the Ethicists Scepticism, Relativisim or Both, Apeiron, 94; art, Hellenistic Essays Translated, Papers in Hellenistic Phil, 96; Entries in Encyl of Class Philos, 97; auth, Sextus Empiricus, Against the Ethicists (Adversus Mathematicos XI): Introduction, Translation and Commentary, (Oxford: Clarendon Press, 97); auth, Pyrrho, his Antecedents and his Legacy (Oxford: Clarendon Press) forthcoming. **CONTACT ADDRESS** Dept of Philosophy, Johns Hopkins Univ, Baltimore, Gilman Hall, Baltimore, MD 21218-2890. **EMAIL** bett_r@jhunix.hcf.jhu.edu

BETTAGERE, RAMESH N.
DISCIPLINE COMMUNICATION SCIENCES AND DISORDERS **EDUCATION** Mysore Univ, India, BSc, 70; Karnatak Univ, India, MA, 76; Baylor Univ, MS, 86, Ohio Univ, PhD, 97. **CAREER** Dir, A.P. Ear, Nose and Throat Hosp, India, 71-74; instr, Gujarath Univ, India, 76-85; couns, Richmond Fel for Mental Welfare, Eng, 85-86; speech pathologist, Tex Dept of Mental Health, 86-90; grad assoc, Ohio Univ, 93-97; assoc prof, SE La Univ, 97-. **HONORS AND AWARDS** Phi Kappa Phi; Travel Fel, ASHA, 95. **MEMBERSHIPS** Am Acad of Audiol; ASHA; La Speech-Lang-Hearing Assoc. **RESEARCH** Speech and hearing sciences, diagnostic audiology, computer applications in speech and hearing and psychological applications in speech and hearing. **SELECTED PUBLICATIONS** Auth, "Silent world of the deaf-mute child", Akashavani 11 (80): 34-37; coauth, "Group psychotherapy with adult stutterers" Indian Jof Clinical Psychol 9 (82): 125-129; auth, "Presumed sudden idiopathic hearing loss: Some observations", Mental Health Rev 2.2 (84): 103-109; coauth "Effect of stimulus familiarity on magnitude-estimation scaling of different languages", Jof the Acoustical Soc of Am, (95): coauth "Effects of prematurity on the language development of Hispanic infants", Infant Toddler Intervention: The Transdisciplinary J5.3 (95): 219-231; coauth, "Synthetic speech intelligibility under several experimental conditions" Augmentative and Alternative Commun 11 (95): 113-117; coauth, "Language familiarity in magnitude-estimation scaling of loudness by young adults", Perceptual and Motor Skills 80 (95): 419-423; coauth, "Magnitude estimation scaling of computerized (digitized) speech under different listening conditions", Perceptual and Motor Skills 88 (99): 1362-1378; auth, "Assessment of intelligibility of digitized speech by young adults under different listening conditions", Jof the Acoustical Soc of Am 106.4 (99): 2272; auth, "Intelligibility of digitized speech in background environmental noise", Behavior Res Methods, Instruments and Computers (forthcoming). **CONTACT ADDRESS** Dept Spec Educ, Southeastern Louisiana Univ, 500 Western Ave, Hammond, LA 70402-0001. **EMAIL** rbettagere@selu.edu

BETZ, MARK W.
PERSONAL Born 11/14/1965, Winnipeg, MB, Canada **DISCIPLINE** FILM STUDIES **EDUCATION** Univ Man, BA, 86; MA, 94; Univ Rochester, MA, 94; PhD, 99. **CAREER** Instr, Univ Man, 88-89; instr, Univ Rochester, 91-95; instr, George Eastman House, 97-98; asst prof, Univ Albta, 99-01; lectr, King's Col London, 01-. **HONORS AND AWARDS** Univ Man Fel, 88; Film Studies Prog, Univ Rochester, 95-97. **MEMBERSHIPS** SCS; MLA; FSAC. **RESEARCH** Post-World War II cinema; non-Western and alternative cinemas; history and historiography; contemporary film theory. **SELECTED PUBLICATIONS** Auth, "Film History, Film Genre, and Their Discontents: The Case of the Omnibus Film," Moving Image (01); auth, "The Name Above the (Sub)Title: Internationalism, Coproduction, and the Polyglot European Art Cinema," Camera Obscura (01). **CONTACT ADDRESS** Film Study Dept, Univ of London, Strand, London, England WC2R 2LS. **EMAIL** mark.betz@kcl.ac.uk

BETZ, PAUL F.
DISCIPLINE ENGLISH LITERATURE **EDUCATION** La Salle Col, BA; Cornell Univ, MA, PhD. **CAREER** Prof. **SELECTED PUBLICATIONS** Auth, British Romantic Art, 90; Pictures for a Revolution: Ten Contemporary Images, 92; Romantic Archaeologies, 95. **CONTACT ADDRESS** English Dept, Georgetown Univ, 37th and O St, Washington, DC 20057.

BEVINGTON, DAVID M.
PERSONAL Born 05/13/1931, New York, NY, m, 1953, 4 children **DISCIPLINE** ENGLISH **EDUCATION** Harvard Univ, BA, 52; MA, 57; PhD 59. **CAREER** Instr Eng, Harvard Univ, 59-61; from asst prof to prof, Univ Va, 61-68; prof eng, Univ Chicago, 68-. Guggenheim fel, 64-65 & 81-82. **HONORS AND AWARDS** Phi Beta Kappa, bk prize, Univ VA, 63; Guggenheim fel, 64-65; Quantrell tchg award, 79; sec guggenheim award, 81-82; Awarded Doctor of Humane Letters, Wittenberg Univ, 99. **MEMBERSHIPS** MLA; Medieval Acad Am; Renaissance Soc Am; Shakespeare Asn Am; Malone Soc; Am academ arts sci; Am Pilos soc. **RESEARCH** Late medieval and Renaissance Eng Drama. **SELECTED PUBLICATIONS** Auth, From Mankind to Marlowe, Harvard Univ, 62; ed, Shakespeare's 1 Henry V1, Penguin, 67; Twentieth-Century Interpretations of Hamlet, Prentice-Hall, 68; auth, Tudor Drama and Politics, Harvard Univ, 68; ed, Medieval Drama, 75; Shakespeare, Pattern of Excelling Nature, 78; compiler, Bibliography of Shakespeare, 78; ed, The Complete Works of Shakespeare, 80,88,92,97; The Bantam Shakespeare, compl, 29 vols, Bantam, 88; ed, The Revels Student Series; ed, The Revels Series; ed, a new edition of Ben Jonson. **CONTACT ADDRESS** Dept of Eng, Univ of Chicago, 1010 E 59th St, Chicago, IL 60637-1512. **EMAIL** bevi@midway.uchicago.edu

BEWELL, ALAN J.
PERSONAL Born 01/28/1951, Calgary, AB, Canada **DISCIPLINE** ENGLISH **EDUCATION** Simon Fraser Univ, BA, 77; Univ Calif Irvine, MA, 78; PhD, 83. **CAREER** Asst prof, Yale Univ, 83-88; asst prof to assoc prof to ed to assoc chmn to prof, Univ Toronto, 88-. **HONORS AND AWARDS** SSHRC, 92, 94, 01; Connaught Fac Grant, 88; Morse Fel, Yale Univ, 87; Dean's Award Excellence, Univ Toronto, 97; Keats-Shelley Asn Prize, 92. **MEMBERSHIPS** NASSR; ASECS; MLA; ACCU. **RESEARCH** British romanticism; 18th and 19th century literature; literature and science; literature and history of medicine; British colonialism. **SELECTED PUBLICATIONS** Auth, Wordsworth and the Enlightenment: Nature, Man, and Society in the Experimental Poetry, Yale Univ Pr, 89; ed, Medicine and the West Indian Slave Trade, Pickering/Chatto, 99; auth, Romanticism and Colonial Disease, John Hopkins Univ Pr, 99. **CONTACT ADDRESS** English Dept, Univ of Toronto, Toronto, ON, Canada M5S 1A1. **EMAIL** a.bewell@utoronto.ca

BEYEA, MARION

PERSONAL Born Saint John, NB, Canada **DISCIPLINE** ARCHIVIST **EDUCATION** Univ NB, BA, 67. **CAREER** Manuscript archiv, Arch Ont, 67-75; archiv, Anglican Ch Can, 75-78; Prov Archivist, Prov Arch NB 78-. **MEMBERSHIPS** Can Coun Archv; Asn Can Archv; Coun Archv NB; Anglican Diocese Fredericton. **SELECTED PUBLICATIONS** Auth, The Professional Associations and the Formation of the Canadian Archival System in Janus, 87; auth, Technology, Industry and the Archival Heritage, Possibilities and Needs in Janus, 92; ed, Archives Bulletin, 73-75. **CONTACT ADDRESS** Prov Archives of New Brunswick, PO Box 6000, Fredericton, NB, Canada E3B 5H1. **EMAIL** marion.beyea@gov.nb.ca

BEYER, DAVID W.

PERSONAL Born 10/03/1949, Sioux Falls, SD, s **DISCIPLINE** MUSIC EDUCATION **EDUCATION** North Tex State Univ, MME, 72. **CAREER** Independent scholar, bibl chronol, unaffiliated, San Diego/Newport Beach, Calif. **MEMBERSHIPS** Soc of Bibl Lit. **RESEARCH** Biblical chronology; Josephus studies. **SELECTED PUBLICATIONS** Auth, Josephus Reexamined: Unraveling the Twenty-second Year of Tiberius, Chronos Kairos Christos II, Vardaman, Mercer Univ Press, 98; auth, Finegan's Reliance on Early Manuscript Discoveries of Beyer, 284, 292, 301, Handbook of Biblical Chronology, Hendrickson Publ, 98. **CONTACT ADDRESS** 204 N. El Camino Real E-401, Encinitas, CA 92024.

BEZANSON, MARK

PERSONAL Born 11/06/1943, Providence, RI, m, 1994 **DISCIPLINE** FILM, COMMUNICATION, LITERATURE **EDUCATION** Rutgers Univ, BA, 67; MA, 74. **CAREER** Peace Corps Teacher, Zarzes Col Secondaire, Tunis, 67; Peace Corps Teacher, Bourguiba Inst, Tunis, 68; Instr, Rutgers Univ, 70-72; Assoc Prof, Raritan Valley Community Col, 75-. **HONORS AND AWARDS** Presidential "E" Awd Intercultural Studies. **MEMBERSHIPS** AET, NARS. **RESEARCH** Film Studies, Communication Studies, Teaching as an Art. **SELECTED PUBLICATIONS** Auth, Girl in the Hairy Paw Modern American Novel and the Movies, 78; auth, "Wallace and King;" auth, Berger and Penn's West: visions and revisions. **CONTACT ADDRESS** Dept Humanities, Raritan Valley Comm Col, PO Box 3300, Somerville, NJ 08876-1265.

BIALOSTOSKY, DON

PERSONAL Born 05/11/1947, Portland, OR, m, 1966, 3 children **DISCIPLINE** ENGLISH **EDUCATION** Univ Chicago, AB, 69, MA, 73, PhD, 77. **CAREER** Lect, Univ Chicago, 73-75; vis instr, English, Univ UT, 75-77; asst prof, English, Univ WA, 77-83; assoc prof, English, 83-87, assoc prof, Comparative Lit, SUNY, Stony Brook, 87; prof English, Univ Toledo, 87-92, Distinguished Univ Prof of English, 92-93; Prof, English, PA State Univ, 93-, Head, Dept of English, 95-. **HONORS AND AWARDS** Presidential Scholar, 65; Nat Merit Scholar, 65; Phi Bata Kappa, 68; Danforth fel, 69; R. S. Crane Awd for writing on literary subjects, 74; NEH summer study grant, 78; ACLS grant for recent recipient of the PhD, 79; ACLS travel award, 85; Univ Toledo Summer Fac Res Awd, 88, 89, 91; OH Bd of Regents Challenge grant in rhetorical theory (principal author), 89-95; Univ Toledo Outstanding Fac Res Awd, 91; Univ Toledo Col of Arts & Sciences Exceptional Merit Awd, 91; res and grad studies award for preparation of Rhetorical Traditions and British Romantic Literature, 93; EGO Awd for Outstanding Teacher (shared with one other fac member), 94; Charles W. Kneupper Awd for Outstanding Contrib to Rhetoric Soc Quart, shared with 3 others, 95; CIC Academic Leadership fel, 98-99. **MEMBERSHIPS** Modern Lang Asn; Asn for Depts of English; Nat Coun of Teachers of English; Conference on Col Composition and Communication; Soc for Critical Exchange; Soc for the Study of Narrative Lit; Rhetoric Soc of Am; Am Soc for the Hist of Rhetoric; Am Asn of Univ Profs. **RESEARCH** Hist and theory of rhetoric; literary theory; British Romantic poetry; William Wordsworth; Mikhail Bakhtin. **SELECTED PUBLICATIONS** Auth, Making Tales. The Poetics of Wordsworth's Narrative Experiments, Univ Chicago Press, 84; Wordsworth, Dialogics, and the Practice of Criticism, Cambridge Univ Press, 92; Bakhtin and the Future of Rhetorical Criticism: A Response to Halasek and Bernard-Donals, Rhetoric Soc Quart 22, 92, Booth, Bakhtin, and the Culture of Criticism, Rhetoric and Pluralism: Legacies of Wayne Booth, Columbus OH State Univ Press, 95; Metaphors Critics Live By: Property, Names, and Colleagues in the Critical Archive, MN Rev, March 95; Antilogics, Dialogics, and Sophistic Social Psychology: Michael Billig's Reinvention of Bakhtin from Protagorean Rhetoric, Rhetoric, Pragmatism, Sophistry, ed Steven Mailloux, Cambridge Univ Press, 95; numerous other publications. **CONTACT ADDRESS** Dept of English, Pennsylvania State Univ, Univ Park, University Park, PA 16802. **EMAIL** dhb1@psu.edu

BIBB, T. CLIFFORD

PERSONAL Born 10/29/1938, Montgomery, AL, s, 4 children **DISCIPLINE** ENGLISH **EDUCATION** Ala State Univ, BS 60, MEd 61; Northwestern Univ, PhD 73. **CAREER** Rust Coll, chair English dept 1961-65; Daniel Payne Coll, chair English dept 1965-67; Miles Coll, English coord 1967-71; Northwestern Univ, English supr 1971-72; AL State Univ, chair advancement studies and dir four year plus curriculum prog. **HONORS AND AWARDS** Choir Dir/Singer in "The Long Walk Home", starring Whoopi Goldbert & Sissy Spacek. **MEMBERSHIPS** Dir upward prog Northwestern Univ 1972-73; commiss, composition NCTE 1973-76; sec Peterson-Bibb Lodge 762 1974-; fac adv Alpha Phi Alpha 1981-; exec comm NCTE 1983-88; exec sec & bd mem Central Montgomery Optimists 1984-86; desoto commiss State of AL 1986-95; National Council of Teachers of Eng, 1991-93; newsletter editor, AL Assn for Dev Ed, 1992-95; table leader (ETS), Ed Testing Service for APT/ENG, 1994-; Alabama State Council on The Arts, 1992-; NAT Council of Ed Opportunity Assn, 1992-; Natl Assn for Developmental Educ (NADE), pres-elect, 1997-98, pres, 1998-99. **CONTACT ADDRESS** Chair, Advancement Studies, Alabama State Univ, PO Box 234, Montgomery, AL 36101-0271. **EMAIL** tcbibb@asunet.alasu.edu

BICKNELL, JOHN W.

PERSONAL Born 01/22/1913, Mansfield, MA, m, 1936, 7 children **DISCIPLINE** ENGLISH **EDUCATION** Hamilton Col, BS, 35, MA, 36; Cornell Univ, PhD, 50. **CAREER** Instr English, St Lawrence Univ, 37-43; instr, Cornell Univ, 50-54; from assoc prof to prof, 54-78, chmn dept, 57-71, convener, Grad Prog English, 62-76, actg dean, Grad Sch, 67-69, Emer Prof English, Drew Univ, 78-. **HONORS AND AWARDS** Phi Kappa Phi. **MEMBERSHIPS** MLA; Northeast Victorian Studies; Conf Brit Studies. **RESEARCH** Victorian literature; the history of intellectual history; Sir Leslie Stephen. **SELECTED PUBLICATIONS** Auth, "Leslie Stephen's English Thought in the 18th C: A Tract for its Times," Victorian Studies 6 (62); ed, "The Wasteland of F. Scott Fitzgerald," in F. Scott Fitzgerald (Eble, 73); ed, "Mr. Ramsay was Young Once," in Virginia Woolf & Bloombury (Marcus, 87); auth, "The Unbelievers," Victorian Press Writers A Guide to Research (MLA, 74); Selected Letters of Leslie Stephen, 2 vols, Macmillan, Ohio State, 96; **CONTACT ADDRESS** Dept of English, Drew Univ, Madison, NJ 07940. **EMAIL** jmbicknell@acadia.net

BIEGANOWSKI, RONALD

PERSONAL Born 05/23/1941, Milwaukee, WI **DISCIPLINE** ENGLISH, THEOLOGY **EDUCATION** St Louis Univ, AB, 65, MA, 66, PhL, 66; Jesuit Sch Theol, Berkeley, STM, 72; Fordham Univ, PhD (English), 77. **CAREER** Instr English, Marquette High Sch, Milwaukee, 66-69; lectr, Univ of San Francisco; Asst Prof English, Marquette Univ, 76-81, Dir, Honors Prog, 81-93; Dir, Alumni Ministry, 93-96; Adjunct Asst Prof of English, 97-. **HONORS AND AWARDS** NDEA, Univ of the Pacific, 68; NDEA, Univ of New Hampshire, 68; NDEA, Loyola Col, Baltimore, 68; Am Philos Soc (Frost's Reading of Bergson's Creative Evolution), 81. **MEMBERSHIPS** Mod Lang Asn; Am Lit Secion/Mod Lang Asn; Christianity and Lit; Robert Frost Soc. **RESEARCH** Robert Frost; modern American poetry; modern American fiction. **SELECTED PUBLICATIONS** Auth, "Robert Frost's New Hampshire: Realm Not Region," Literature and Belief 2 (82): 83-92; auth, "Robert Frost's Annotations to Henri Bergson's Creative Evolution," Resources for American Literary Study 13 (83): 184-93; auth, "Robert Frost's Sense of Choice in Mountain Interval," College Literature 11 (84): 258-68; auth, "James Baldwin's Vision of Otherness in 'Sonny's Blues' and Giovanni's Room," College Language Association Journal 32 (88): 69-80; auth, "The Self-Consuming Narrator in Poe's Ligeia and Usher," American Literature 60 (88): 175-87; auth, "Robert Frost's A Boy's Will and Henri Bergson's Creative Evolution," The South Carolina Review 21 (88): 9-16; rev, "Robert Frost's Emergent Design: The Truth of The Self In-between Belief and Unbelief Johannes Kjorven," in Journal of Modern Literature 15 (Fall 88): 332-3; rev, "Bergson and American Culture: The Worlds of Willa Cather and Wallace Stevens Tom Quirk," in International Studies in Philosophy 23 (91): 141-2; rev, Robert Frost's "Star in a Stone Boat: A Grammar of Belief," Edward Ingebretsen, S.J. in Theological Studies 57 (March 96): 194; rev, Robert Frost's "Road Taken," Robert F. Fleissner in The Robert Frost Review, (97): 87-8. **CONTACT ADDRESS** Dept of English, Marquette Univ, Milwaukee, WI 53201. **EMAIL** ron.bieganowski@marquette.edu

BIEN, PETER ADOLPH

PERSONAL Born 05/28/1930, New York, NY, m, 1955, 3 children **DISCIPLINE** ENGLISH **EDUCATION** Haverford Col, BA, 52; Columbia Univ, MA, 57; PhD, 61. **CAREER** Lectr Eng, Columbia Univ, 59-60; from instr to prof, Dartmouth Col, 61-69, T & H Geisel Third Century prof hum, 74-79. Hon fel Greek, Univ Birmingham, 70-71 & 75; vis prof, Harvard Univ, 83; Beebe prof in the Art of Writing, 89-97; prof emer, 97-; Melborne Univ, 83 Unive of thessalouiki, 96,00, Princeton Univ, 00. **HONORS AND AWARDS** E Harris Harbison Awd, Danforth Found, 68. **MEMBERSHIPS** MLA; Mod Greek Studies Asn. **RESEARCH** Mod Brit and Greek lit. **SELECTED PUBLICATIONS** Transl, Nikos Kazantzakis, The Last Temptation of Christ, 60, Saint Francis, 62 & Report to Greco, 65, Simon & Schuster; auth, L P Hartley, Chatto and Windus, 63; Nikos Kazantzakis, Columbia Univ, 72; Kazantzakis and the Linguistic Revolution in Greek literature, Princeton Univ, 72; transl, S Myrivilis, Life in the Tomb, Univ Press New England, 77; auth, Antithesis and Synthesis in the poetry of Yannis Ritsos, Kedros, Athens, 80; coauth, Demotic Greek II: O Iptamenos Thalamos, Univ Press New England, 82; auth, Three Generations of Greek Writers: Introductions to Cavafy, Kazantzakis, Ritsos, Efstathiadis, 83; auth, Kazantzakis: Politics of the Spirit, Princeton Univ, 89; Nikos Kazantkazis: Novelist, Duckworth, 89; coauth, God's Struggler: Religion in the Writings of Nikos Kazantzakis, Mercer Univ, 96; co ed, In Stillness There Is Fullness, Pendle Hill, 00. **CONTACT ADDRESS** Dept of English, Dartmouth Col, Hanover, NH 03755-3533. **EMAIL** peter.bien@dartmouth.edu

BIER, JESSE

PERSONAL Born 07/18/1925, Hoboken, NJ, m, 1950, 3 children **DISCIPLINE** ENGLISH **EDUCATION** Bucknell Univ, AB, 49; Princeton Univ, AM, 52, PhD (English), 56. **CAREER** Instr English lang and lit, Univ Colo, 52-55; from instr to assoc prof, 55-63, Prof English, Univ Mont, 63- Fulbright prof Am lit and civilization, Univs Lyon and Clermont, 57-58; vis lectr English, Bucknell Univ, 65-66; chair in Am lit, Univ Lausanne, 71-72; vis prof humanities, San Diego State Col, summer, 71; Can Govt study grant, 79. **HONORS AND AWARDS** Native Son Writer Awd in Fiction, NJ State Teachers Asn, 65. **MEMBERSHIPS** Hon mem Mark Twain Soc; hon mem Am Humor Soc. **RESEARCH** American literature; creative writing; education. **SELECTED PUBLICATIONS** Auth, Enter Tainment and Exit Tainment--Literature and Sub Literature, Thalia Stud Lit Humor, Vol 0015, 95. **CONTACT ADDRESS** Wildcat Rd, Missoula, MT 59801.

BIESECKER, BARBARA

PERSONAL Born 06/12/1959, Addington Heights, IL, s **DISCIPLINE** RHETORIC & COMMNICATION STUDIES **EDUCATION** Univ Pittsburgh, PhD, 89. **CAREER** Assoc prof, Univ Iowa, 91- . **MEMBERSHIPS** NCA **RESEARCH** Rhetorical theory and criticism, visual rhetorics, feminist theory and criticism **SELECTED PUBLICATIONS** co-auth with James P. McDaniel, The Irruptive Possibilities of the Other, The Encyclopedia of Rhetoric, 95; co-auth with Susan Biesecker, Gerald Mast, James McDaniel, A Genealogy of Oratory, The Encylopedia of Rhetoric, 95; auth, Addressing Postmodernity: Kenneth Burke, Rhetoric, and a Theory of Social Change, Studies in Rhetoric and Communication, 97; auth, Rhetoric and the 'New' Psychoanalysis: What's the Real Problem? or Framing the Problem of the Real, Quartelry Jour of Speech, 98; auth, Rhetorical Ventriloquism: Fantasy and/as National Identity, Proceedings of the Tenth SCA/AFA Conference on Argumentation, 98. **CONTACT ADDRESS** Rhetoric Dept, Univ of Iowa, Iowa City, IA 52240. **EMAIL** bbieseck@blue.weeg.uiowa.edu

BIESTER, JAMES

DISCIPLINE ENGLISH **EDUCATION** Stanford Univ, BA, 82; Columbia Univ, MA, 84,MPhil, 86, PhD, 90. **CAREER** Assoc prof; dir, grad prog(s). **RESEARCH** Early modern literature and culture; history of literary theory; history of rhetoric; modern poetry. **SELECTED PUBLICATIONS** Auth, Lyric Wonder: Rhetoric and Wit in Renaissance English Poetry, Cornell UP, 97; Admirable Wit: Deinotes and the Rise and Fall of Lyric Wonder, Rhetorica 14.3, 96; Nothing seene: Fear, Imagination, and Conscience in Fulke Greville's Caelica 100, Hellas 7.2, 96. **CONTACT ADDRESS** Dept of English, Loyola Univ, Chicago, 6525 N. Sheridan Rd., Chicago, IL 60626. **EMAIL** jbieste@wpo.it.luc.edu

BILES, ZACHARY P.

PERSONAL Born 12/15/1968, Philadelphia, PA, m, 1997, 1 child **DISCIPLINE** CLASSICS **EDUCATION** Univ Maryland, BA, 92; Univ Col, MA, 95, PhD, 99. **CAREER** Lectr, Univ Col, 99-00; asst prof, Univ Ore, 00-01; asst prof, Davidson Col, 01-. **HONORS AND AWARDS** Norlin Fel, 98-99. **MEMBERSHIPS** APA; CAMS. **RESEARCH** Aristophanes and Attic comedy; ancient scholarship; Greek culture. **SELECTED PUBLICATIONS** Auth, "Eratosthenes on Plato Comicus: Didaskaliae or Parabasis?," Zeits fur Papyro and Epigra (99). **CONTACT ADDRESS** Dept of Classics, Univ of Oregon, Eugene, OR 97403. **EMAIL** biles@darkwing.uoregon.edu

BILLICK, DAVID JOSEPH

PERSONAL Born 05/19/1947, Toledo, OH, m, 1973 **DISCIPLINE** SPANISH LITERATURE BIBLIOGRAPHY **EDUCATION** Univ Toledo, BA, 69, MA, 71; Univ Iowa, PhD (Span), 76. **CAREER** Instr, Univ Iowa, 76-77; asst prof Span, Rutgers Univ, 77-80; Assoc Ed, Hispania, 76-, Libr Asst, Univ Mich, 81- **MEMBERSHIPS** Am Asn Teachers Span and Port; MLA; Nat Womens Studies Asn; Am Libr Asn. **RESEARCH** Women in Hispanic literature; Jose de Espronceda; 19th century Spanish literature. **SELECTED PUBLICATIONS** Auth, Bibliography of Publications on the Comedia 1991-1992, Bull Comediantes, Vol 0044, 92. **CONTACT ADDRESS** Grad Libr Ref Dept, Univ of Michigan, Ann Arbor, Ann Arbor, MI 48109.

BILODEAU, BRENDA

PERSONAL Born 08/12/1964, Sacramento, CA, d **DISCIPLINE** ENGLISH **EDUCATION** Tex Tech Univ, BA, 94; E NMex Univ, MA, 97. **CAREER** Ed advisor, Virgo Pub; instr, E NMex Univ; prof, Mesa Community Col. **HONORS AND AWARDS** Teaching and Writing Scholar, E NMex Univ. **MEMBERSHIPS** Nat Coun Teachers of English; Am Asn of

Community & Jr Colleges. **RESEARCH** Early Twentieth-Century American Literature, agriculture, downtown, and urban architecture. **SELECTED PUBLICATIONS** Auth, "Farming/Ranching," Horse Professional. **CONTACT ADDRESS** Dept English, Mesa Comm Col, 1833 W Southern Ave, Mesa, AZ 85202-4822. **EMAIL** bilodeau@mail.mc.maricopa.edu

BILSON, MALCOLM
PERSONAL Born 10/24/1935, Los Angeles, CA, m, 1961, 2 children **DISCIPLINE** MUSIC **EDUCATION** Vienna State Acad, Reifezeugnis, 59; Paris, Licena Libre, Ecole Normale de Musique, 60; Urbana, DMA, 68; Bard Col, Hon Doct, 91. **CAREER** Frederick J. Whiton prof; **HONORS AND AWARDS** Fulbright fel, Vienna, 57-59; Harriet Hale Woolley fel, Paris, 59-60. **MEMBERSHIPS** Amer Musicol Soc; Early Music Am; ed bd, Early Mus Mag London; ed bd, Piano and Keyboard Mag, US; Amer Acad Arts and Sci. **RESEARCH** Music of the late 18th and early 19th centuries; performance practice; problems of notation and execution; instruments; aesthetics. **SELECTED PUBLICATIONS** Auth, Beethoven and the Piano, Clavier Magazine, Vol 22, 83; Execution and Expression in Mozart's Sonata in E-flat, K. 282, Early Music Mag, 92; Do We Know How to Read Urtext Editions, Piano and Keyboard Mag, 95. **CONTACT ADDRESS** Dept of Music, Cornell Univ, 104 Lincoln Hall, Ithaca, NY 14853. **EMAIL** mb68@cornell.edu

BING, JANET M.
PERSONAL Born 01/18/1937, Oak Park, IL, m, 1985, 1 child **DISCIPLINE** ENGLISH **EDUCATION** Coe Col, BA, 59; Stanford Univ, MA, 60; Univ Mass, PhD, 79. **CAREER** Textbook writer, Berlitz Int, 80-81; asst prof, Univ of Minn, 81-82; asst prof to prof, Old Dominion Univ, 81-. **HONORS AND AWARDS** Phi Beta Kappa; Phi Kappa Phi; Stern Awd, 95; TABI Awd, 98. **MEMBERSHIPS** Ling Soc of Am; TESOL; Southeastern Conf on Ling. **RESEARCH** Language and gender, phonology. **SELECTED PUBLICATIONS** Coauth, Cross-Cultural Studies Manual for Afghanistan Training Programs, Peace Corps (Washington, D.C.), 67; auth, Aspects of English Prosody, Garland Press (New York, NY), 85; auth, GrammarGuide: English Grammar in Context, Prentice-Hall Regents (New York, NY), 89; coauth, "The Question of Questions: Beyond Binary Thinking", in Rethinking Language and Gender Research: Theory and Practice (96), 1-30; coed, Rethinking Language and Gender Research: Theory and Practice, Longman (NY), 96; coauth, "Talking Past Each Other about Sexual Harassment", Discourse and Soc 8 (97): 293-311; coauth, "Nobody's Listening: A Frame analysis of the Ebonics Debate", Secol Rev 22 (98): 1-20; coauth, "Forum: What are the Responsibilities of Feminist Academic Publishers", Women & Lang, (99): 4-23; auth, "Brain sex: How the media reports and distorts brain research" Women and Lang 22 (99): 4-12. **CONTACT ADDRESS** Dept English, Old Dominion Univ, Norfolk, VA 23529. **EMAIL** jbing@odu.edu

BIRD, DELORES
PERSONAL Born 12/06/1942, Chattanooga, TN, 1 child **DISCIPLINE** LITERATURE **EDUCATION** Boston Univ, BA, 67; Univ Hartford, MA, 74; Univ Mass, PhD, 78. **CAREER** From Instr to Prof, Cape Cod Community Col, 77-. **HONORS AND AWARDS** Phi Beta Kappa, Boston Univ. **MEMBERSHIPS** Emily Dickinson Int Soc, Ralph Waldo Emerson Soc, Thoreau Soc, Hawthorne Soc. **RESEARCH** 19th-Century American literature. **SELECTED PUBLICATIONS** Auth, Early Encounters: Native Americans and Europeans in New England from the Papers of W. Sears Nickerson, Mich St UP (East Lansing, MI), 95; auth, "Introduction," Inside Out: The Poetry of George Hoar, Sullwold Pr (94); ed, Land Ho!--1920, A Seaman's Story of the Mayflower: Her Construction, Her Navigation and Her first Landfall," Mich St UP (East Lansing, MI), 97. **CONTACT ADDRESS** Dept Lang & Lit, Cape Cod Comm Col, 2240 Iyanough Rd, West Barnstable, MA 02668-1532. **EMAIL** dbird@capecod.mass.edu

BIRD, HAROLD WESLEY
PERSONAL Born 08/23/1937, Nottingham, England, m, 1962, 2 children **DISCIPLINE** ANCIENT HISTORY AND LITERATURE **EDUCATION** Cambridge Univ, BA, 60, dipl, 61, MA, 64; McMaster Univ, MA, 63; Univ Toronto, PhD (Greek and Roman hist), 72. **CAREER** Head Latin Dept, Salt Fleet High Sch, Ont, 63-64; from lectr to asst prof classics, Univ NB, 64-67; from asst prof to assoc prof, 69-75, Prof Classics, Univ Windsor, 75-, Head, Dept Class and Mod Lang, 82- **MEMBERSHIPS** Class Asn Can; Am Asn Ancient Historians. **RESEARCH** Roman imperial history; history of the late Roman Republic; Roman historiography. **SELECTED PUBLICATIONS** Auth, Julian and Aurelius Victor--Did Victor Receive the Governorship of Pannonia Secunda for Writing De Caesaribus, Latomus, Vol 0055, 96. **CONTACT ADDRESS** Dept of Class Studies, Univ of Windsor, Windsor, ON, Canada N9B 3P4. **EMAIL** hbird@uwindsor.ca

BIRD, ROGER A.
PERSONAL Born 05/02/1938, Toronto, ON, Canada **DISCIPLINE** JOURNALISM **EDUCATION** Carleton Univ, BA, 61; Univ Minn, MA, 63, PhD, 69. **CAREER** Journ, vars publs, 65-68; asst prof Eng, Sir George Williams Univ, 68-74; Assoc Prof Journalism, Carleton Univ, 74-. **MEMBERSHIPS** Can Commun Asn; Asn Stud Can Radio & TV; Can Asn Journ; fel, Royal Can Geog Soc. **SELECTED PUBLICATIONS** Auth, The End of News, 97; ed, Documents of Canadian Broadcasting, 88; ed adv comt, Can Geog mag. **CONTACT ADDRESS** Journalism Dept., Carleton Univ, 1125 Colonel By Dr, Ottawa, ON, Canada K1S 5B6. **EMAIL** roger_bird@carleton.ca

BIRDSALL, ERIC
PERSONAL Born 06/28/1944, Glendale, CA, m, 1964, 1 child **DISCIPLINE** ENGLISH **EDUCATION** Johns Hopkins Univ, PhD, 76. **CAREER** Instr English, Salem Community Col, 74-75; instr, Penn State Univ, Shenango Valley, 75-76; assoc prof, Penn State Univ, Shenango Valley, 76-84; assoc prof, Penn State Univ, Shenango Valley, 84-87; prof English, Univ Akron, 87-; head, Dept of English, Univ Akron, 87-94. **HONORS AND AWARDS** Soc Res Grants, Am Philosophical Soc; award in the Humanities, Penn State Univ. **MEMBERSHIPS** Wordsworth-Coleridge Asn; North Am Soc for the Study of Romanticism. **RESEARCH** English and Am Romanticism; Wordsworth. **SELECTED PUBLICATIONS** Ed, Descriptive Sketches, Cornell Univ Press, 84; coauth, Writing on the Job: A Guide for Nurse Managers, Wiley, 86; auth, "Nature and Society in Descriptive Sketches", in Mod Philology 84, 86; auth, "Unmerited Contempt, Undeserved Praise: More on Wordsworth's Earliest Reviews", in The Wordsworth Circle 17, 86; auth, "Interpreting Henry James: Bogdanovich's Daisy Miller", in Literature/Film Quart 22, 94. **CONTACT ADDRESS** Department of English, Univ of Akron, Akron, OH 44313. **EMAIL** birdsall@vakron.edu

BIRENBAUM, HARVEY
PERSONAL Born 07/08/1936, Philadelphia, PA, m, 1963, 2 children **DISCIPLINE** ENGLISH **EDUCATION** Antioch Col, BA, 58; Yale Univ, MA, 59; PhD, 63. **CAREER** Prof, San Jose State Univ, 65-. **HONORS AND AWARDS** Woodrow Wilson Fel, 58-62; NEH Fel, 84-85. **SELECTED PUBLICATIONS** Auth, Stoic in Love: Convention and Self in the Poetry of Wyatt, Univ Microfilms (Ann Arbor), 81; auth, Tragedy and Innocence, Univ Pr of Am (Washington, DC), 82; auth, Myth and Mind, Univ Pr of Am (Lanham, MD), 88; auth, The Art of our Necessities: Form and Consciousness in Shakespeare, Peter Lang Pub, (Bern and NY), 89; auth, Between Blake and Nietzsche, Bucknell Univ Pr, (Lewisburg, PA), 92; auth, The Happy Critic: A Serious but not Solemn Guide to Thinking and Writing About Literature, Mayfield Pub Co, (Mountain View, CA), 97. **CONTACT ADDRESS** Dept English, San Jose State Univ, 1 Washington Sq, San Jose, CA 95192-0001.

BIRNBAUM, MILTON
PERSONAL Born 06/01/1919, Poland, m, 1950, 1 child **DISCIPLINE** ENGLISH **EDUCATION** City Col NYork, AB, 42; NYork Univ, MA, 48; PhD, 56. **CAREER** Instr to asst prof to assoc prof to dept chmn to dean, American Inter Col, 48-96; vis lectr, Holyoke Col, 61-64; vis prof, St Hyacinth Col Sem, 72-73. **HONORS AND AWARDS** NYork State Regents Scholar; Phi Beta Kappa; Jewish Acad Arts Sci, NYU Found Awd; D. Litt, Am Inter Col, 96. **MEMBERSHIPS** MLA; Phi Beta Kappa; AAS. **RESEARCH** British novel between World Wars; American romanticism; literature; philosophy and religion; 20th-century American novel. **SELECTED PUBLICATIONS** Auth, Aldous Huxley's Quest for Values, U Tenn Pr, 71; intro, An Encyclopedia of Pacifism, Garland, 72; auth, "The Drift of College English in the Last Three Years," Col English1 (74); auth, "Politics and Character in Point Counter Point," Study Nov, (77); auth, "Ernest Hemingway Read Anew," Mod Age, (79); auth, "Herman Melville: Forever Cotemporary," World and I (91); auth, "The Aging Process: A Literary Perspective," World and I, (95). **CONTACT ADDRESS** 132 Groveland St, Springfield, MA 01108-2935.

BIRNS, NICHOLAS B.
PERSONAL Born 05/30/1965, New York, NY **DISCIPLINE** LITERATURE **EDUCATION** Columbia Univ, BA, 88; NY Univ, PhD, 92. **CAREER** Vis asst prof, W Conn State Univ, 92-93; faculty, New School Univ, 95-. **HONORS AND AWARDS** NY Univ Fel, 88; Univ of Newcastle Fel, 01. **MEMBERSHIPS** mla, samla, Assoc Int des etuces quebecoises, Ivor Gurney Soc, Willa Cather Soc, Guild of Scholars of the Episcopal Church, Powys Soc, Anthony Powell Soc, Conf for Christianity and Lit, Am Assoc of Australian Lit Studies. **RESEARCH** American literature, Australian literature, modern British literature, religion and literature, postcolonial theory. **SELECTED PUBLICATIONS** Auth, "Secrets of the Birth of Time: The Rhetoric of Cultural Origins in Alastor and Mont Blanc," Studies in Romanticism 32.3 (93); auth, "Beyond Metafiction: Placing John Barth," Ariz Quart 49.2 (93): 113-136; auth, "The Trojan Myth: Postmodern Reverberations," Exemplaria: A Jour of Theory in Medieval and Renaissance Studies, (93); auth, "Telling Inside fromOutside: Or, Who Really Killed Laura Palmer," Lit/Film Quart, (93); auth, "Indefinite Desires: Love and the Search for Truth in the Fiction of Gerald Murnane," Southerly, (95); auth, "In Our Bodies: Incarnate History in Les Murray," Counterbalancing Light: Essays on the Poetry of Les Murray, ed Carmel Gaffney, Kardoorair Pr, (97); auth, "Weird White: Allusion and Literary History in The Twyborn Affair," Zeitschrift fur Anglistik und Amerikanistik, (Germany, 97); auth, " May in September: Australian Literature as Anglophone Alternatives," Australian Studies, (01); auth, "Octavia Butler: Fashioning Alien Constructs," Hollins Critic, (01); auth, "Guessing Theocritus: Le Bas's Poems, Rereading, and Classicism in the School Scenes of Anthony Powell's 'A Question of Upbringing,'" Proceedings of the Anthony Powell Conf, (01). **CONTACT ADDRESS** New Sch for Social Research, 205 E Tenth St, New York, NY 10003. **EMAIL** birnsn@newschool.edu

BISCHOFF, JOAN
PERSONAL Born 03/20/1943, Orange, NJ, m, 1992, 3 children **DISCIPLINE** ENGLISH **EDUCATION** E Stroud State Col, BS, 65; Lehigh Univ, MA, 71; PhD, 75. **CAREER** Teach, Pa, NJ Sch, 65-70; teach asst, Lehigh Univ, 70-74; adj prof, NHam Com Col, 75; instr, asst prof, assoc prof, Slip Rock Univ, 75-87; adj prof, Col St Fran, 88; adj prof, Lehigh Univ, 88; assoc prof, Univ Wis, 88-94; prof, 94-. **HONORS AND AWARDS** Chan Awd; UWS Fac Dev Gnt, 89, 90, 91, 92. **MEMBERSHIPS** MLA; TAUWP. **RESEARCH** Work of Toni Morrison; Twentieth-century American authors and their work. **SELECTED PUBLICATIONS** Auth, "Views and Reviews: An Annotated Bibliography (on Ken Kesey)," Lex Sci 13 (77): 93-103; auth, "The Novels of Toni Morrison: Studies in Thwarted Sensitivity," Stud Black Lit 6 (75): 21-23; auth, "The Creative Project: A Wordless Response to Literature," Wis Eng J 32 (89): 81-83; auth, "John Hawkes' Horses of the Apocalypse," Notes Contemp Lit 6 (76):12-14; auth, "Fellow Rebels: Annie Dillard and Maxine Hong Kingston," Eng J 78 (89): 62-67; auth, "Annie Dillard," in Contemporary Literary Criticism (Detroit: Gale Research, 99). **CONTACT ADDRESS** Dept Language, Literature, Univ of Wisconsin, Superior, PO Box 200, Superior, WI 54880-4500. **EMAIL** jbischof@staff.uwsuper.edu

BISHOP, ALLAN
DISCIPLINE ENGLISH LITERATURE **EDUCATION** Rhodes Univ, BA; Oxford Univ, MA, PhD. **RESEARCH** WWI literature; literature of peace and war; modern British novel. **SELECTED PUBLICATIONS** Ed, Joyce Cary, Selected Essays, 76; ed, Vera Brittain, Chronicle of Youth, 81; ed, Vera Brittain, Chronicle of Friendship, 86. **CONTACT ADDRESS** English Dept, McMaster Univ, 1280 Main St W, Hamilton, ON, Canada L8S 4L9. **EMAIL** bishop@mcmaster.ca

BISHOP, JONATHAN P.
PERSONAL Born 10/27/1927, Paris, France, d, 3 children **DISCIPLINE** ENGLISH **EDUCATION** Harvard, AB, 50, PhD, 56. **CAREER** Amherst, 54-57; Univ Calif, Los Angeles, 57-61; Cornell Univ, 61-99. **RESEARCH** American literature, religious studies. **SELECTED PUBLICATIONS** Auth, Some Bodies, Macon, GA: Mercer Univ Press (92); auth, In Time, Ithaca, NY: McBooks (99). **CONTACT ADDRESS** Dept English, Cornell Univ, 252 Golwin Smith Hall, Ithaca, NY 14853-3201.

BISHOP, THOMAS G.
PERSONAL Born 06/19/1960, Melbourne, Australia **DISCIPLINE** RENAISSANCE AND EARLY MODERN LITERATURE **EDUCATION** Univ Melbourne, BA; Yale Univ, PhD. **CAREER** English, Case Western Reserve Univ. **HONORS AND AWARDS** Dir, Baker-Nord Ctr Hum. **MEMBERSHIPS** MLA, SAA, AAALS. **RESEARCH** Shakespeare; colonial & post-colonial lit. **SELECTED PUBLICATIONS** Auth, Shakespeare and the Theater of Wonder. **CONTACT ADDRESS** Case Western Reserve Univ, 10900 Euclid Ave, Cleveland, OH 44106. **EMAIL** tgb2@po.cwru.edu

BISHOP, WENDY
PERSONAL Born 01/13/1953, Japan, m, 2000, 2 children **DISCIPLINE** ENGLISH **EDUCATION** Univ Calif Davis, MA, 76; MA, 79; Ind Univ Pa, PhD, 88. **CAREER** Prof, Fla State Univ. **HONORS AND AWARDS** Joseph Henry Jackson Awd, 80; Palanquin Pr Chapbook Awd, 97; William and Kingman Page Chapbook Awd, 98. **SELECTED PUBLICATIONS** Auth, Touching Liliana, Jumping Cholla Pr, 98; auth, Mid-Passage, Nightshade Pr, 98; My 47 Lives, Palanquin Pr, 98; auth, Ethnographic Writing Research - Writing It Down, Writing It Up, and Reading It, Boynton/Cool Heinemann, 99; auth, Thirteen Ways of Looking for a Poem: A Guide to Writing Poetry, Longman, 00; coauth, Metro: A Sourcebook for Writing Creatively, Longman, 00; auth, The Subject is Reading, Boynton/Cook, 00; auth, In Praise of Pedagogy: Poems and Flash Fiction on Teaching, Calendar Islands Pr, 00, auth, The Process Reader, McGraw Hill, 00. **CONTACT ADDRESS** Dept English, Florida State Univ, PO Box 3061580, Tallahassee, FL 32306-1580. **EMAIL** wbishop@english.fsu.edu

BITTENBENDER, J. CHRISTOPHER
DISCIPLINE TWENTIETH CENTURY, EIGHTEENTH CENTURY, AND MEDIEVAL BRITISH LITERATURE **EDUCATION** Univ St Andrews, PhD. **CAREER** Eastern Col **HONORS AND AWARDS** Ed, Janus, Running Press Book Publ. **SELECTED PUBLICATIONS** Areas: James Kelman, Robert Crawford, and Robert Burns. **CONTACT ADDRESS** Eastern Col, 1300 Eagle Rd, Saint Davids, PA 19087-3696.

BITTRICH, LOUIS EDWARD
PERSONAL Born 11/04/1937, Omaha, NE, m, 1961, 2 children **DISCIPLINE** COMPARATIVE LITERATURE, THEATRE **EDUCATION** Gustavus Adolphus Col, BA, 59; Bowling Green State Univ, MA, 60; Univ NCar, PhD, 67; Southwest Tex State Univ, MA, 85. **CAREER** Instr English & dir theatre, Tex Lutheran Col, 60-62; instr English, Gustavus Adolphus Col, 62-63; asst prof, Winthrop Col, 65-66; asst prof, Gustavus Adolphus Col, 66-67; assoc prof, 67-79, prof English, 79-, chmn dept, 67-95, prof theatre, 95-, chmn dept, Texas Lutheran Col. **HONORS AND AWARDS** Ford Found fel, 65; Exchange prof humanities, Winthrop Col, 65-66. **MEMBERSHIPS** MLA. **RESEARCH** Comparative literature and the arts, especially theatre production. **SELECTED PUBLICATIONS** Auth, Alchemy vindicated in our age, Cresset, 4/72. **CONTACT ADDRESS** Dept of Theatre, Texas Lutheran Univ, 1000 W Court St, Seguin, TX 78155-5978. **EMAIL** lbittrich@tlu.edu

BIVONA, DANIEL E.
PERSONAL Born 02/08/1952, Stamford, CT, m, 1979, 3 children **DISCIPLINE** ENGLISH **EDUCATION** Univ Conn, BA, 74; Northeastern Univ, MA, 79; Brown Univ, PhD, 87. **CAREER** Asst Prof, RI Col, 87-88; Asst Prof, Univ Pa, 88-95; Asst Prof, Rowan Univ, 95-96; Asst Prof to Assoc Prof and Chair, Ariz State Univ, 96-. **HONORS AND AWARDS** Fel, Brown Univ, 80-81. **MEMBERSHIPS** MLA; P Coast Brit Studies Asn; Interdisciplinary Nineteenth-Century Studies Asn; Asn of Dept of English. **RESEARCH** Nineteenth-Century British Studies; Imperialism and Culture; The Novel; Cultural Studies; Literary Theory. **SELECTED PUBLICATIONS** Auth, Desire and Contradiction: Imperial Visions and Domestic debates in Victorian Literature, Manchester UP, 90; auth, "Conrad's Bureaucrats: Agency, Bureaucracy, and the Problem of Intention," Novel, 93; auth, "Playing the Muslim: Sir Richard Burton's Pilgrimage and 'Negative' Cultural Identity," Borders of Culture, Margins of Identity, 93; auth, "The Erotic Politics of Indirect Rule: T.E. Lawrence's 'Voluntary Slavery'," Prose Studies, 97; auth, British Imperial Literature, 1870-1940: Writing and the Administration of Empire, Cambridge UP, 98. **CONTACT ADDRESS** Dept English, Arizona State Univ, Box 870302, Tempe, AZ 85287-0302. **EMAIL** dbivona@asu.edu

BIZZELL, PATRICIA L.
PERSONAL Born 11/03/1948, Chicago, IL, m, 1977, 2 children **DISCIPLINE** ENGLISH LITERATURE **EDUCATION** Wellesley Col, BA, 70; Rutgers Univ, PhD, 75 **CAREER** Asst prof, Rutgers, 75-78; asst prof, Holy Cross, 78-81; assoc prof, Holy Cross,, 81-88; dir, Writing Programs, Holy Cross, 81-94; dir, College Honors Program, 94-98; prof, Holy Cross, 88- **HONORS AND AWARDS** Ntl Council Teachers of English Outstanding Book Awd, 92 **MEMBERSHIPS** Modern Lang Assoc; Ntl Council Teachers English; Conf Col Composition and Comm; Amer Assoc Univ Professors; Speech Comm Assoc; Council Writing Program Admin; Rhetoric Soc Amer **RESEARCH** American Literature, composition studies, history and theory of rhetoric. **SELECTED PUBLICATIONS** Coauth, The Bedford Bibliography for Teachers of Writing, St Martin, 96; coauth, Negotiating Difference: Readings in Multicultural American Rhetoric, St Martin, 95; auth, Academic Discourse and Critical Consciousness, Univ Pitt, 92 **CONTACT ADDRESS** English Dept, Holy Cross Col, Worcester, MA 01610. **EMAIL** pbizzwel@holycross.edu

BJERKEN, XAK
DISCIPLINE MUSIC **EDUCATION** Univ Calif at Los Angeles, BA, 89; Peabody Conserv Music, MM, 91, DMA, 94. **CAREER** Lectr. **HONORS AND AWARDS** Second place, Harrison Winter Concerto Competition, Peabody Conserv, 92; Winner of all undergrad performance awards, Univ Calif, Los Angeles, 86-89; Dean's Gold Medal; founding mem, florestan trio now taliesin trio, 95 & third millenium music, 94. **RESEARCH** 20th-century music; Messiaen and post-WWII Eastern Europeans. **SELECTED PUBLICATIONS** Auth, Chopin's Harmony, Preston-Whitelaw, Ltd, 95; CD-ROM discussing Chopin's harmony, with over 50 excerpts from his piano music. **CONTACT ADDRESS** Dept of Music, Cornell Univ, 104 Lincoln Hall, Ithaca, NY 14853. **EMAIL** xb10@cornell.edu

BJORK, ROBERT E.
PERSONAL Born 02/19/1949, Virginia, MN **DISCIPLINE** MEDIEVAL LITERATURE **CAREER** Adj lectr to prof, Ariz State Univ, 79-. **HONORS AND AWARDS** Transl Prize, Am-Scandinavian Found, 87; Hon Mention, John Nicholas Brown Prize, 89. **MEMBERSHIPS** MLA, Medieval Acad of Am, Int Soc of anglo-Saxonists, Soc for Advan of Scandinavian Study, Am-Scandinavian Found. **RESEARCH** Old and Middle English literature, Old Norse literature, modern Scandinavian literature. **SELECTED PUBLICATIONS** Ed, Sources and Analogues of Old English Poetry II: The Major Germanic and Celtic Texts in Translation, DS Brewer, 83; auth, The Old English Verse Saints Lives: A Study in Direct Discourse and the Iconography of Style, Univ of Toronto Pr, 85; auth, Jitsurei ni yoru igaku Eigo ronbun no kakikata: bunsho kosei no pointo, Mejikaru Byushi, (Tokyo), 87; transl, land of Wooden Gods, Univ of Nbr Pr, 89; transl, People of the Dawn, Univ Nebr Pr, 90; transl, Sacrifical Smoke, Univ Nebr Pr, 91; transl, Only a Mother by Ivar Lo-Johannson, Univ Nebr Pr, 91; ed, Cynewulf: Basic Readings, Garland, 96; coed, A Beowulf Handbook, Univ Nebr Pr, 97; ed, The Oxford Dictionary of the Middle Ages, Oxford Univ Pr, (forthcoming). **CONTACT ADDRESS** Ariz Center for Medieval and Renaissance Studies, Arizona State Univ, Tempe, AZ 85287-2301. **EMAIL** robert.bjork@asu.edu

BLACK, DANIEL
DISCIPLINE ENGLISH LITERATURE **EDUCATION** Temple Univ, PhD, 93. **CAREER** Joint fac Eng and African/African Am Studies. **RESEARCH** Black male studies and Africana Literary traditions. **SELECTED PUBLICATIONS** Auth, Dismantling Manhood, 96. **CONTACT ADDRESS** Clark Atlanta Univ, 223 James P Brawley Dr, SW, Atlanta, GA 30314.

BLACK, EDWIN
PERSONAL Born 10/26/1929, Houston, TX, m, 1979 **DISCIPLINE** RHETORIC **EDUCATION** Univ Houston, BS, 51; Cornell Univ, MA, 53, PhD, 62. **CAREER** Instr/asst prof of English, Washington Univ, 56-61; vis prof, Univ Calif-Berkeley, 64; vis prof, Univ Minn, 67; vis prof, Calif State Univ, 69 & 72; vis prof, Univ Calif-Davis, 78 & 88; asst prof/prof of Speech, Univ Pittsburgh, 61-67; prof of commun arts, 67-94, Prof Emeritus, Univ Wis-Madison, 94-. **HONORS AND AWARDS** Speech Commun Asn Book Award, 66; Speech Asn Monograph Award, 89. **MEMBERSHIPS** Nat Commun Asn. **RESEARCH** Rhetorical criticism. **SELECTED PUBLICATIONS** Auth, Rhetorical Questions: Studies of Public Discourse, Univ of Chicago Press, 92; Gettysburg and Silence, Quart J of Speech, 94; The Invention of Nixon, Beyond the Rhetorical Presidency, Tx A&M Univ Press, 96; The Aesthetics of Rhetoric, American Style, Rhetoric and Political Culture: Interpreting Am Public Discourse, Mich State Univ Press, 97; The Prospect of Rhetoric: Twenty-Five Years Later, Making and Unmaking the Prospects for Rhetoric, Lawrence Erlbaum Assocs Inc, 97. **CONTACT ADDRESS** 3326 Valley Creek Cr., Middleton, WI 53526-1988. **EMAIL** e-black@msn.com

BLACK, LENDLEY C.
DISCIPLINE COMMUNICATION STUDIES **EDUCATION** Univ Tennessee, BA; Univ Conn, MA; Univ Kans, PhD. **CAREER** Prof, 82-. **SELECTED PUBLICATIONS** Auth, pubs on Russian theatre and drama; Michael Chekhov. **CONTACT ADDRESS** Div of Communcation and Theatre Arts, Emporia State Univ, 1200 Commercial St, Emporia, KS 66801-5087. **EMAIL** blacklen@esumail.emporia.edu

BLACK, NANCY BREMILLER
PERSONAL Born 11/12/1941, Norristown, PA, m, 1964, 2 children **DISCIPLINE** ENGLISH; COMPARATIVE LITERATURE **EDUCATION** Vassar Col, BA, 63; Univ Pa, MA, 64; Columbia Univ, PhD(English), 71. **CAREER** Lectr English, City Col New York, 71-72; from instr to Assoc Prof, 72-95, Prof English, Brooklyn Col, 95-. **HONORS AND AWARDS** Shaughnessy scholar, 81-82. **MEMBERSHIPS** MLA; Mediaeval Acad Am. **RESEARCH** Medieval comparative literature. **SELECTED PUBLICATIONS** Co-ed, White on Red: Images of the American Indian, Kennikat, 76; ed and transl, The Perilious Cemetary, Garland, 94; auth, "Woman as Savior: The Virgin Mary and the Empress of Rome in Gautier de Coinci's Miracles, Romanic Review 88.4, (97): 503-17; auth, "The Politics of Romance in Jean Maillart's Roman du Comte d'Anjou," French Studies 51.2 (97): 129-37; auth, "Language of the Illustrations of Chretien de Troyes's Le Chevalier au Lion Yvain," Studies in Iconography 15 (93): 45-75. **CONTACT ADDRESS** Dept of English, Brooklyn Col, CUNY, 2900 Bedford Ave, Brooklyn, NY 11210-2813.

BLACK, STEPHEN AMES
PERSONAL Born 08/31/1935, Los Angeles, CA, m, 1980, 1 child **DISCIPLINE** AMERICAN LITERATURE **EDUCATION** Calif State Col, Los Angeles, BA, 60, MA, 61; Univ Wash, PhD(English), 64. **CAREER** Asst prof English, Monmouth Col, 64-66; asst prof, 66-69, assoc prof, 69-74, Prof English, Simon Fraser Univ, 74-00, Can Coun leave fel, 74-75; affil instr, Seattle Psychoanalytic Inst, 75-; prof emer, Simon Fraser Univ, 74-00. **MEMBERSHIPS** MLA. **RESEARCH** Am Lit, 1850-1960, Lit and Psychoanalysis, Shakespearean Tragedy, Greek Tragedy. **SELECTED PUBLICATIONS** Auth, Whitman's Journeys into Chaos: A Psychoanalytic Study of the Poetic Process. **CONTACT ADDRESS** Dept of English, Simon Fraser Univ, 8888 Univ Dr, Burnaby, BC, Canada V5A 1S6. **EMAIL** sblack@sfu.ca

BLACK, STEVE
PERSONAL Born 12/12/1959, Huntsville, AL, m, 1980, 1 child **DISCIPLINE** LIBRARY SCIENCE **EDUCATION** Fla State, BA, 82; Univ Va, M.Ed, 87; SUNY, MLS, 93. **CAREER** Librn, Col Saint Rose, 95-. **RESEARCH** Economics of scholarly publications. **SELECTED PUBLICATIONS** Auth, Journal Collection Analysis at A Liberal Arts College, 97; auth, "An Assessment of Social Sciences Coverage by Four Prominent Full-Text Online Aggregated Journal Packages," Library Collections, Acquisitions, and Technical Services 23(4) (99); auth, "Obstacles to Teaching Novice Researchers How to Evaluate the Quality of World Wide Web Resources," in All That Glitters: Prospectiong for Information in the Changing Library World, ed.Steven Vincent and Sue K. Norman (Stamford, CT: JAI Press, 99); auth, "Scholarly Articles Online, or How Do I Know it this Article is Scholarly, and Why Should I Care?" in Critical Thinking and the Web: Teaching Users to Evaluate Internet Resources, ed. T.E. Jacobson (Pittsburgh: Library Instruction Publications, 00). **CONTACT ADDRESS** 10352 Duanesburg Rd, Quaker Street, NY 12141. **EMAIL** blacks@rosnet.strose.edu

BLACKBURN, ALEXANDER
PERSONAL Born 09/06/1929, Durham, NC, m, 1975, 3 children **DISCIPLINE** ENGLISH **EDUCATION** Yale Univ, BA, 51; Univ North Carolina, MA, 56; Cambridge Univ, PhD, 63. **CAREER** Instr, Hampden-Sydney Col, 59-60; instr, Univ Penn, 63-65; lectr, Univ Maryland, Euro Div, 67-72; from asst prof to prof emer, Univ Colorado at Colorado Springs, 74-95. **HONORS AND AWARDS** Fac book awd, UCCS, 93; Chancellor's Awd, 94; ed in chief, writers' forum, 74-95. **MEMBERSHIPS** RMMLA; Colo Auth League; PEN Ctr West; Writers Guild. **RESEARCH** Fiction. **SELECTED PUBLICATIONS** Auth, The Myth of the Picaro, 79; auth, The Cold War of Kitty Pentecost, 79; ed, The Interior Country: Stories of the Modern West, 87; auth, A Sunrise Brighter Still: The Visionary Novels of Frank Waters, 91; ed, Higher Elevations: Stories from the West, 93; auth, Suddenly a Mortal Splendor, 95; auth, Creative Spirit: Essays on Literature, Imagination, and The New World of Consciousness, 00. **CONTACT ADDRESS** 6030 Twin Rock Ct, Colorado Springs, CO 80918.

BLACKBURN, THOMAS
PERSONAL Born 05/28/1932, m, 2 children **DISCIPLINE** ENGLISH **EDUCATION** Amherst Col, BA, 54; Oxford Univ, MA, 60; Stanford Univ, PhD, 63. **CAREER** Actg instr, Stanford Univ, 58-61; instr, Swarthmore Col, 61-63; vis lctr, Bryn Mawr Col, 68; asst prof, Swarthmore Col, 63-69; to assoc prof, 69-75; to chr Eng dept, 74-75; to dean 75-81; to prof 83-85; to dir undergrad wrtg assocs prog, 85-; to Centennial prof Engl, 92-. **HONORS AND AWARDS** Grant, Folger Shakespeare Inst, 88 and 90; ACLS Fellow, 65-66; NLA grant, Sloan Foundation, 87; res grants, Swarthmore Col, 93, 88-89, 81-82, 74-75, 70. **MEMBERSHIPS** MLA; Renaissance Soc Am; Milton Soc Am; Shakespeare Assoc Am; Nat Coun Tchrs Eng; Conf Col Comp Comm. **SELECTED PUBLICATIONS** Auth, Shakespeare in the Electronic Classroom, Shakespeare and the Classroom, 95; Lycidas: Eternity As Artifice, Milton Studies, 91; Carnal Rhetoric: Milton's Iconoclasm and the Poetics of Desire, Renaissance Quart, 97; The Ashland Shakespeare Festival, Shakespeare and the Classroom, 95; Shakespeare and the Changing Curriculum, Shakespeare and the Classroom, 93; John Milton in The Poetic Birth: Milton's Poems of 1645 by CWRD Moseley, and John Milton: Political Writings, Rev Engl Studies, 93. **CONTACT ADDRESS** Swarthmore Col, 500 College Ave, Swarthmore, PA 19081-1397. **EMAIL** tblackb1@swarthmore.edu

BLACKMORE, ROBERT LONG
PERSONAL Born 09/13/1919, Akron, NY, m, 1941, 2 children **DISCIPLINE** ENGLISH **EDUCATION** Colgate Univ, BA, 41, MA, 61; Syracuse Univ, PhD(English), 65. **CAREER** From instr to assoc prof, 60-70, chmn dept, 72-75, actg dir humanities, 75, 77-78, provost & dean of fac, 79-80, prof English, 70- , prof emeritus, Colgate Univ; Dir, Colgate Univ Press, 64-; ed, Powys Newslett, 70- **MEMBERSHIPS** MLA. **RESEARCH** Nineteenth-century British literature; Georgian literature: creative writing. **SELECTED PUBLICATIONS** Auth, Introduction to Blackmore's Lorna Doone, Everyman's Libr, London, 66; Introduction to John Cowper Powys' Autobiography, Macdonald, London, 67; ed, Introduction to Blackmore's Springhaven, Everyman's Libr, 69; Advice to a Young Poet: Llewelyn Powys, Fairleigh Dickinson, 69; John Cowper Powys' An Englishman Upstate, Village, London, 74; auth, Powys to Knight, C Woolf, London, 82. **CONTACT ADDRESS** 21 University Ave, Hamilton, NY 13346.

BLACKSTONE, MARY A.
PERSONAL Born Ellsworth, ME **DISCIPLINE** ENGLISH **EDUCATION** Univ Maine, BA, 71; Univ Brunswick, MA, 73, PhD, 78. **CAREER** Lectr, Univ Toronto, 79-81; asst prof, Washington & Jefferson Col, 81-82; coordr grad stud drama, Univ Alberta, 87-90; asst prof, 82-87, Assoc Prof Theatre, Univ Regina 90-, Dean Fine Arts 90-. **HONORS AND AWARDS** Maine/NB scholar, 69-70; REED post-doctoral fel, Univ Toronto. **MEMBERSHIPS** Can Asn Fine Arts Deans; Int Coun Fine Arts Deans; Am Soc Theatre Res; Int Shakespeare Asn. **SELECTED PUBLICATIONS** Auth, Robin Hood and the Friar, 81. **CONTACT ADDRESS** Faculty of Theatre Arts, Univ of Regina, Regina, SK, Canada S4S OA2. **EMAIL** mary.blackstone@uregina.ca

BLACKWELL, MARILYN JOHNS
PERSONAL Born 08/01/1948, Cincinnati, OH, m, 1980 **DISCIPLINE** SCANDINAVIAN LITERATURE, FILM **EDUCATION** Univ Wis, BA, 70; Univ Wash, MA, 73, PhD(Scand lit),

76. **CAREER** Lectr, Univ BC, 75-77; Asst Prof, Univ VA, 77-; Assoc Prof. **HONORS AND AWARDS** Mellon fac fel, Harvard Univ, 81-82. **MEMBERSHIPS** Soc Advan Scand Studies; MLA. **RESEARCH** 19th and 20th century drama and prose; feminist criticism; film. **SELECTED PUBLICATIONS** Auth, Structures of Influence: Comparative Approaches to August Strindberg, 81; auth, C.J.L. Almqvist and Romantic Irony: The Aesthetics of Self-Consciiousness, 83; auth, Persona: The Transcendent Image, 86; auth, Gender and Representation in the films of Ingmar Bergman, 97. **CONTACT ADDRESS** Dept Germanic Languages and Literatures, Ohio State Univ, 1841 Millikin Rd, 320 Cunz Hall, Columbus, OH 43210. **EMAIL** blackwell.4@osu.edu

BLACKWOOD, ROY E.
PERSONAL Born 03/17/1944, Rochester, PA, m, 1980, 2 children **DISCIPLINE** COMMUNICATION **EDUCATION** US Marine Corps Commun Sch, 63-64; Univ AK, 67-68; Cleveland State Univ, BA, 72; Cornell Univ, MA, 75, PhD, 81. **CAREER** Commun Specialist, US Marine Corps, 63-67; manag ed, Polar Star, Univ AK, 67-68; reporter/photog, Daily News, Anchorage, AK, 68-69; freelance writer, 69-72; tchg asst, 72-73, news writer, 73-74, commun specialist, 74-78, Cornell Univ; commun specialist, Univ IL, 78-82; asst prof, 82-87, assoc prof, 87, Bemidji State Univ; foreign expert, journalism, Liaoning Univ, 88-89; assoc prof 89-91, prof, 91-, Bemidji State Univ; vis prof, Chulalongkorn Univ, 93-94; chair, Mass Commun, 97-; Balkan Scholar, American Univ in Bulgaria, 99-00. **HONORS AND AWARDS** Univ Merit Awd, 84; Nat Tchg Awd, 87; Study Tour Chinese Media, 87, US Academics; Fulbright Travel Grant, 90; Freedom Forum Sem, 91. **MEMBERSHIPS** Asn Educ Journalism and Mass Commun; Int Commun Asn; Canadian Commun Asn; Midwest Asn Canadian Studies. **RESEARCH** Treatment of US in Thai and Chinese press; treatment of US in Canadian editorial cartoons; international content of US and Canadian newsphotos; sex and race roles in newspaper photos. **SELECTED PUBLICATIONS** Auth, "The Content of News Photos: Roles Portrayed by Men and Women," Jour Quart, 83; "Using PC's As A Front-End Network to Produce A College Newspaper," Coll Media Rev, 86; "International News Photos in US and Canadian Papers," Jour Quart, 87; "Ronbo and the Peanut Farmer in Canadian Editorial Cartoons," Jour Quart, 89; "Great Walls: Barriers to Journalism Research in the People's Republic of China," Am Jour, 90. **CONTACT ADDRESS** Dept of Mass Communication, Bemidji State Univ, Bemidji, MN 56601. **EMAIL** rblackwood@bemidjistate.edu

BLAIR, CAROLE
DISCIPLINE COMMUNICATION **EDUCATION** Univ Iowa, BA, 77; MA, 79; Pa State Univ, PhD, 83. **CAREER** Lectr, Univ of Calif Davis, 82-83; asst prof, Univ of Md, 84; lectr, Calif State Univ Hayward, 85-86; asst prof, Calif State Univ, Sacramento, 86-89; asst prof to prof, Univ of Calif Davis, 89-; Director, UCD Washington Center, 00-. **HONORS AND AWARDS** Golden Anniversary Monograph Awd, Nat Commun Assoc, 92-93; Fel, Univ of Calif, 95; Outstanding Article Awd, Org for the Study of Commun, Lang and Gender, 95; Outstanding Mentor Awd, Univ of Calif Davis, 99. **MEMBERSHIPS** Am Studies Assoc; Int Commun Assoc; Nat Commun Assoc; Nat Counc on Pub Hist; Org for the Study of Commun, Lang and Gender, Rhetoric Soc of Am; Soc of Archit Hist; Western States Commun Assoc. **RESEARCH** American commemorative art, public art, rhetoric and cultural studies. **SELECTED PUBLICATIONS** Coed, Friedrich Nietzsche on Rhetoric and Language, Oxford Univ Pr, (NY), 89; coauth, "Public Memorializing in Postmodernity: The Vietnam Veterans Memorial as Prototype", Quarterly J of Speech 77, (91): 263-88; auth, "Contested Histories of Rhetoric: The Politics of Preservation, Progress, and Change", Quarterly J of Speech 78, (92): 403-428; coauth, "Disciplining the Feminine", Quarterly J of Speech 80, (94): 383-409; coed, Critical Questions: Invention, Creativity, and the Criticism of Discourse and Media, St. Martin's Pr, (NY), 94; auth, "Symbolic Action and Discourse: The Convergent/Divergent Views of Kenneth Burke and Michel Foucault", Kenneth Burke and Contemporary European Thought: Rhetoric in Transition, ed Bernard L. Brock, Univ of Ala Pr, (Tuscaloosa, 95): 119-65; coauth, "Commemorating in the Theme Park Zone: Reading the Astronauts Memorial", At the Intersection: Cultural Studies and Rhetorical Studies, ed Thomas Rosteck, Guildford, (NY, 99): 29-83; auth, "Contemporary U.S. Memorial Sites as Exemplars of Rhetoric's Materiality", Rhetorical Bodies, ed Jack Selzer and Sharon Crowley, Univ of Wisc Pr, (Madison, 99): 16-57; coauth, "Reproducing Civil Rights Tactics: The Rhetorical Performances of the Civil Rights Memorial", Rhetoric Soc Quarterly 00. **CONTACT ADDRESS** Dept Am Studies, Univ of California, Davis, 2301M St, Fifth Flr, Washington Center, Washington, DC 20037. **EMAIL** cblair@ucdavis.edu

BLAIR, JOHN
DISCIPLINE ENGLISH **EDUCATION** FL State Univ, BA, MA; Tulane Univ, PhD. **CAREER** Southwest Tex State Univ **SELECTED PUBLICATIONS** Auth, A Landscape of Darkness; Bright Angel. **CONTACT ADDRESS** Southwest Texas State Univ, 601 University Dr, San Marcos, TX 78666-4604.

BLAIR, P.
PERSONAL Born 10/18/1951, Pittsburgh, PA, m, 1984, 1 child **DISCIPLINE** ENGLISH **EDUCATION** St Vincent Col, BA, 73; Duquesne Univ, MA, 80; Univ Iowa, PhD, 89. **CAREER** Prof of English, Univ of Pittsburgh, 81-83; Prof of English, Waynesburgh Col, 89-90; Adjunct Prof of English, Washington & Jefferson Col, 93-96; Adjunct Prof of English, Georgetown Univ, 98-00. **HONORS AND AWARDS** Washington Prize for Poetry, 99, Defined Providence Press Chapbook Contest, 98, PA Council on the Arts Fellowship for Poetry, 95. **RESEARCH** William Carlos Williams Contemporary Poetry-Gerald Stern, Philip Levine, George Oppen. **SELECTED PUBLICATIONS** Auth, Last Heat Poems; auth, Furnace Greens. **CONTACT ADDRESS** Dept English, Georgetown Univ, PO Box 571131, Washington, DC 20057-1131. **EMAIL** erg5h@virginia.edu

BLAIR, REBECCA S.
PERSONAL Born 03/26/1958, Terre Haute, IN, m, 1989 **DISCIPLINE** ENGLISH **EDUCATION** Univ Indianapolis, BA, 80; Univ Ill, MA, 82; Ind Univ, MA, 86; PhD, 88. **CAREER** Teaching fel to assoc instr, Ind Univ, 82-88; vis prof, Webster Univ, 88-89; assoc prof to dir to dept chmn, Westminster Col, 89-99; assoc prof, Univ Indianapolis, 00-. **HONORS AND AWARDS** Who's Who Am Women, Midwest, 98, 99, 00; Buschman Fac Awd, 97; Fac Mem of Yr Awd, 96; Outstanding Fac Mem, 92; Kellogg Found Fel, 90. **MEMBERSHIPS** MLA; MMLA; WPA; NCTE; CCC; ASA; NCRW; AAUP. **RESEARCH** 19th century American literature and culture; Rhetoric; Composition; religion and literature; gender and culture. **SELECTED PUBLICATIONS** Auth, "Ring Larder," in Encycl of American Humorists, ed. Steven H. Gale (NYork: Garland, 88); auth, "Pattern Analysis," in Reaching Adult Learners With Whole Language, eds. Tirza Kroeker, Margaret Heinrichs (NYork: Richard C. Owen Pub, 93); auth, "The Westminster Writing Assessment Program: A Model for Small Colleges," Con Col Comp Comm (94); auth, "Portfolio Literacy's: Responding to a Changing Environment," Con Col Comp Comm (95). **CONTACT ADDRESS** 5704 Stafford Castle Ln, Apt 1215, Indianapolis, IN 46250-5614. **EMAIL** sblair@uindy.edu

BLAISDELL, ROBERT EHLER
PERSONAL Born 11/19/1959, Houston, TX, m, 1991, 2 children **DISCIPLINE** LITERATURE **EDUCATION** Univ Calif-Santa Barbara, BA, 81, MA, 84, PhD, 88. **CAREER** Tchg asst, 83-88, tchg assoc, 88, lectr, 88-92, Col Creative Stud & English Dept, Univ Cal-Santa Barbara; adj asst prof, Borough of Manhattan Comm Col, CUNY, 93-95; adj asst prof, Jersey City State Col, 96; asst prof, DeVry Inst, 96-97; substitute asst prof, 97-98, Asst Prof, 98- , Kingsborough Comm Col, CUNY; Prog Dir Journal ism Program. **HONORS AND AWARDS** Awd for Innovative and Creative Teaching, DeVry Inst, 97. **RESEARCH** D H Lawrence; Leo Tolstoy. **SELECTED PUBLICATIONS** Rev, Janice Radway's A Feeling for Books, Am Book Rev, 98; rev, Martha C. Nussbaum's Cultivating Humanity, Am Book Rev, 98; auth, The Boy's Coach, Teaching and Learning: The Journal of Natural Inquiry, 98; Teaching Jamaica Kincaid's 'Putting Myself Together' College Teaching, 98; How Do You Know When You're in Love? , The Teachers & Writers Guide to William Carlos Williams, 98; My Antonia, Spectrum, 98; Hercules for Young Readers, Classical World, 98; Tolstoy, the Writing Teacher, Teaching and Learning Literature, 98; rev, Emmanuel Bove's A Winter's Journal, Am Book Rev, 99; auth, Sensational von Kleist: Using His Stories, Classics in the Classroom: Using Great Literature to Teach Writing, 99; ed, introduction Tolstoy as Teacher: Leo Tolstoy's Writings on Education, Teachers & Writers Collaborative, 00; ed, Great Speeches by Native Americans, Dover, 00; rev, And Still We Rise by Mile Corwin, NY Times Book Revew. **CONTACT ADDRESS** 401 W 118th St, No.33, New York, NY 10027. **EMAIL** rblaisdell@kbcc.cuny.edu

BLAISE, C.
PERSONAL Born 04/10/1940, Fargo, ND **DISCIPLINE** CREATIVE WRITING **EDUCATION** Denison Univ, BA, 61, PhD(hon), 79; Univ Iowa, MFA, 64. **CAREER** Prof, Concordia Univ, 66-78; prof, York Univ, 78-80; prof, Skidmore Col, 80-81, 82-83; writer-in-residence, David Thompson Univ Ctr, 83; writer-in-residence, Emory Univ, 85; adj prof, Columbia Univ, 86; vis prof, 81-82, DIR, INTERNATIONAL WRITING PROG, UNIV IOWA, 90-. **HONORS AND AWARDS** Can Coun grants; Guggenheim fel, NEA grant. **MEMBERSHIPS** PEN. **SELECTED PUBLICATIONS** Auth, A North American Education, 73; auth, Tribal Justice, 74; auth, Lunar Attractions, 78; auth, Lusts, 83; auth, Resident Alien, 86; auth, Man and His World, 92; auth, I Had a Father, 93; coauth, Days and Nights in Calcutta, 77; coauth The Sorrow and the Terror, 97; co-ed, Here and Now, 77; co-ed, Best Canadian Stories, 78, 79, 80. **CONTACT ADDRESS** Dept English, Univ of California, Berkeley, 322 Wheeler Hall, Berkeley, CA, 94720-1030.

BLAKE, JAMES JOSEPH
PERSONAL Born 04/29/1939, New York, NY **DISCIPLINE** ENGLISH & IRISH LITERATURE **EDUCATION** Manhattan Col, BA, 62; NYork Univ, MA, 64, PhD, 79 **CAREER** From instr to assoc prof, 65-78, Prof English, Nassau Community Col, 78-, Sr bibliogr Irish Gaelic lit res, Celtic Lit Sect Head, MLA, 78-; broadcaster, Weekly hour prog in Spoken Irish, WFUV FM, Fordham Univ, 79-; adj prof, Irish lit, undergraduate, 88-95, graduate 91-95, NY Univ, Sch Arts and Science; adj lectr Irish-Gaelic, John Jay Col, 80-81; adj assoc prof mod Irish, Queens Col, 82; secy, Sub-Comt Irish Lang, Am Comt Irish Studies, 82-83. **HONORS AND AWARDS** Fulbright fel, Trinity Col, Dublin, Ireland, 69-70. **MEMBERSHIPS** MLA; Am Irish Studies; Exec comt Am Conf Irish Studies, 93-95; Exec comt, Columbia Univ Seminar Irish Studies, 85-; Vpres, North Am Asn Celtic Lang Teachers, 98-99. **RESEARCH** William Butler Yeats; Irish Gaelic; Ireland's literary Renaissance in both English and Irish. **SELECTED PUBLICATIONS** Ed, Eire-Ireland: A Jour Irish Studies (quart), 86-90; Irish Lang ed, New Hibernia Rev (quart), 96-; consult ed, Jour Celtic Lang Learning (annual), 95-; auth, Irish in education and the media, Eire-Ireland, winter 94; Irish language cultural communities, Eire-Ireland, summer 95; The Irish language today: The enhanced public presence of Irish, New Hibernia Rev, summer 97; Beal Feirste (Belfast): An Irish language community, New Hibernia Rev, winter 97; auth, "Language Policy and Planning in Ireland," New Hibernia Rev (98); auth, "Irish Language Theatre in the 1990s: Slogadh to Tielifis na Gaeilge," New Hibernia Rev (99); auth, "Irish Gaelic and Scottish Gaelic Today," New Hibernia Rev (00). **CONTACT ADDRESS** Nassau Comm Col, Garden City, NY 11530-6793. **EMAIL** blakejsdb@aol.com

BLAKE, RICHARD
PERSONAL Born 02/21/1939, New York, NY, s **DISCIPLINE** FILM STUDIES **EDUCATION** Fordham, MA, 65; Northwestern, PhD, 72 **CAREER** Ed, 71-85, America Magazine; visiting prof, 85-87, Georgetown Univ; prof, 87-96, Le Moyne Coll; prof, 96-, Boston Coll. **HONORS AND AWARDS** Jesuit Chair, Georgetown, 85-86; Gasson Chair Boston Coll, 96-98. **MEMBERSHIPS** Soc for Cinema Studies **RESEARCH** Religious Imagination in Film **SELECTED PUBLICATIONS** Woody Auth, Allen Profane and Sacred, Scarecrow, 95; Redeemed in Blood, The Sacramental Universe of Martin Scorsese, in Journal of Popular Film & Television, Sring 96; Igmar Bergman's Post-Christian God: Silent, Absent and Female, Religion and the Arts, Spring 97; Frank Capra: It's a Dangerous Life, Boston College Magazine, Summer 98; Afterimage: Catholic Imagination in American Film, Loyola Press, 00. **CONTACT ADDRESS** Fine Arts Dept, Devlin Hall, Boston Col, Chestnut Hill, Chestnut Hill, MA 02467. **EMAIL** blakeri@bc.edu

BLAKE, ROBERT GRADY
PERSONAL Born 03/06/1934, Charlotte, NC, m, 1965, 2 children **DISCIPLINE** ENGLISH **EDUCATION** Harvard Univ, AB, 56; Duke Univ, MA, 59, PhD(English), 68. **CAREER** Asst prof English, Stetson Univ, 59-62; assoc prof, Morris Harvey Col, 64-68, acting chemn dept, 65-68; chemn dept, 68-77, William S Long Prof English, Elon Col, 68-, Lilly scholar, Duke Univ, 77-78. **MEMBERSHIPS** Phi Beta Kappa; Alpha Chi (honorary); Phi Kappa Phi (honorary); Sigma Tau Delta; Omicron Delta Kappa; Phi Theta Kappa. **RESEARCH** Periodicals of the 19th century; Victorian literature, especially poetry; 19th century poetry reviews. **SELECTED PUBLICATIONS** The Edinburgh Magazine, or Literary Miscellany, In: British Literary Magazines; "Algernon Charles Swinburne, A E Housman, and Sociological Approaches to Poetry," in Critical Survey of Poetry; The Taming of the Shrew and Titus Andronicus, Masterplots: Twentieth Anniversary Revised Second Edition; Hershel Baker, Walter Jackson Bate, and Lionel Stevenson in Dictionary of Lit Bio; A C Swinburne, The St James Guide to Bio; auth, "A.E. Housman," "Henrik Ibsen," "Christopher Marlowe," "William Makepeace Thackery," "Socrates," "Sophocles," in Cyclopedia of World Authors (Salem Press, 97). **CONTACT ADDRESS** Dept of English, Elon Col, Elon College, NC 27244. **EMAIL** Robert.Blake@elon.edu

BLANCH, ROBERT JAMES
PERSONAL Born 02/17/1938, Brooklyn, NY, s, 1961, 5 children **DISCIPLINE** MEDIEVAL LITERATURE **EDUCATION** Col Holy Cross, AB, 59; Northeastern Univ, MA, 61; State Univ NYork, Buffalo, PhD(English), 67. **CAREER** Instr English, Northeastern Univ, 61-62; instr, Newman Prep Sch, Boston, 62-63; instr, State Univ NY, Buffalo, 63-66; asst prof, Canisius Col, 66-67; asst prof, Bentley Col Acct and Finance, 67-68; assoc prof, 68-78, Prof English, Northeastern Univ, 78-. **MEMBERSHIPS** MLA. **RESEARCH** The works of the Pearl Poet; Chaucer; courtly love literature. **SELECTED PUBLICATIONS** Auth, the Name and Fame of Gawain in 'Sir Gawain and the Green Knight,' Studia Neophilologica, Vol 0064, 92; 'rev, Sir Gawain and the Green Knight' - a Dual-Language Version, Speculum-J of Medieval Stud, Vol 0068, 93; The Current State of 'Sir Gawain and the Green Knight' Criticism, Chaucer Rev, Vol 0027, 93; 'rev, Sir Gawain and the Green Knight' and the Idea of Righteousness, J of Eng and Ger Philol, Vol 0093, 94. **CONTACT ADDRESS** Dept of English, Northeastern Univ, 360 Huntington Ave, Boston, MA 02115-5000.

BLANCHARD, ROBERT O.
DISCIPLINE COMMUNICATIONS **EDUCATION** Northwestern Univ, BSJ, 55-57, MSJ, 57-58; Syracuse Univ, PhD, 66. **CAREER** Tchg asst, Northwestern Univ, 58-59; tchg asst, Syracuse Univ, 61-63; asst to the dean, Syracuse Univ, 63-64;

asst prof, Am Univ, 65-66; ch, asst, assoc, full prof, Am Univ, 66-77; founting dean, prof, Am Univ, 77-78; dir, prof, PA tate Univ, 78-82; ch, dept prof, 82-92; prof, ch, 92-. **HONORS AND AWARDS** Curriculum consult, Southwestern, Xavier, Univ S Dakota, Evansville, Denison, Wichita State, St Michael's, Hofstra, S Ill, Linfield Col, Bradley, Univ Ariz, Ursinus Col, Bradley Univ, 86-; founding ed, Southwestern Mass Commun Jour, 85-88; columnist, The Marquise, 95-. **MEMBERSHIPS** Repr, Assn Commun Admin, 88-93; VP, 80-81, pres, 81-82, Am Assn Sch(s) and Dept(s) of Jour; Mem, Assn Commun Admin; Assn Edu in Jour and Mass Commun. **RESEARCH** Italian Humanism; Renaissance Literature **SELECTED PUBLICATIONS** Auth, Congress and the News Media, Hastings House, 74; Newspaper missed significant issues on city elections, council action, San Antonio Exprcss-Ncws, 97; The disintegration of professional integrity, Jour Edu, First Amendment Imperative, and the Changing Mctia Marketplacc, 97; co-auth, Mission Staternents, Outcomes, and the New Liberal Arts, Assessing Communicatwn, A Handbook for Media, Speech, and Theater L Erlbaum, 94; Beyond the Media Workshop, Fccdback, 94; Thoughts on Ehrlich's 'Newcomer: Fccdback, 94; The Undergraduate Communication, Colloquia: Theory Anyone? Fecdback, 94; Assessing media education in an integrated communication program, Media Edu Assessment Handbook, L Earlbaum, 97. **CONTACT ADDRESS** Dept of Commun, Trinity Univ, 715 Stadium Dr, San Antonio, TX 78212.

BLANCHARD, SCOTT
PERSONAL Born 12/30/1955, m, 2 children **DISCIPLINE** SHAKESPEARE; RENAISSANCE STUDIES **EDUCATION** Columbia Univ, PhD. **CAREER** Engl, Col Misericordia **RESEARCH** Italian Lumanism; Renaissance Literature. **SELECTED PUBLICATIONS** Area: Renaissance satire; auth, "Italian Humanism." **CONTACT ADDRESS** Col Misericordia, 301 Lake St., Dallas, PA 18612-1098. **EMAIL** sblancha@miseri.edu

BLANK, DAVID L.
DISCIPLINE CLASSICS **EDUCATION** Yale Univ, BA, 74; Amer Sch of Class Stud, 74-75; Princeton Univ, MA, 77; Univ Bonn, grad stud, 77-78; Princeton Univ, PhD, 80. **CAREER** Vis asst prof, UCLA, 80-82; asst prof, UCLA, 82-86; lehrauftrag, Freie-Univ Berlin, 89; assoc prof, UCLA, 86-95; Prof, Ch, UCLA, 95-. **HONORS AND AWARDS** ITT-Fulbright fel, Greece, 74-75; Paul Elmer More fel, Princeton, 75-76, 78-79; Deutscher Akademischer Austauschdienst Stipendium, Ger, 77-78; Whiting res fel, Princeton, 79-80; Alexander-von-Humboldt fel, Berlin, 88-89. **SELECTED PUBLICATIONS** Auth, "Analogy, Anomaly, and Apollonius," Companions to Ancient Thought, 3: Philos of Lang, Cambridge 94; "Philodemus on the Technicity of Rhetoric, Philodemus On Poetry," Oxford, 94; "Diogenes of Babylon and the Kritikoi in Philodemus: A Preliminary Suggestion," Cronache Ercolanesi 20, 93; "Stop or Spirant: A Note on the Division of Nonvocal and Semivocal Elements," Glotta 94; Rev, Stefania N. Pieri, Platone. Gorgia, Ancient Philos, 94; Catherine Atherton, The Stoics on Ambiguity, Philos Rev, 94; Ammonius, Commentary on On Interpretation, Vol 1, London, Duckworth, 95. **CONTACT ADDRESS** Univ of California, Los Angeles, PO Box 951436, Los Angeles, CA 90095-1436.

BLANK, G. KIM
DISCIPLINE ENGLISH LITERATURE **EDUCATION** Univ Simon Fraser, BA; Univ Wales, MA; Univ Southampton, PhD. **CAREER** Prof; dir, Eng grad stud. **RESEARCH** Romantic poetry; critical approaches; professional writing; canonization. **SELECTED PUBLICATIONS** Auth, Wordsworth's Influence on Shelley: A Study of Poetic Authority, Macmillan, St. Martin's; Influence and Resistance in Nineteenth-Century English Poetry, Macmillan, St. Martin's; Wordsworth and Feeling: The Poetry of an Adult Child, Fairleigh Dickensen UP, Assoc UP; co-ed, The New Shelley: Later Twentieth-Century Views, Margot Louis, Macmillan, St. Martin's. **CONTACT ADDRESS** Dept of English, Univ of Victoria, PO Box 3070, Victoria, BC, Canada V8W 3W1. **EMAIL** gkblank@uvic.ca

BLANK, PAULA CARIN
PERSONAL Born 05/04/1959, NJ, m, 1986, 1 child **DISCIPLINE** ENGLISH **EDUCATION** Wesleyan Univ, BA, 81; Harvard Univ, MA, 85' PhD, 91. **CAREER** Asst prof, Hofstra Univ, 91-92; asst prof to assoc prof, Col William Mary, 92-. **HONORS AND AWARDS** Whiting Fel, 90-91; ACLS Fel, 94-95; NEH, 01-02. **MEMBERSHIPS** MLA. **RESEARCH** Renaissance English language and literature; early modern linguistics; politics of language. **SELECTED PUBLICATIONS** Auth, "Comparing Sappho to Philaenis: John Donne's 'Homopoetics,'" PMLA (95); auth, Broken English Dialects and the Politics of Language in Renaissance Writings, Routledge, 96. **CONTACT ADDRESS** English Dept, Col of William and Mary, PO Box 8795, Williamsburg, VA 23187-8795. **EMAIL** pcblank@wm.edu

BLANSFIELD, KAREN C.
PERSONAL Born Wilmington, DE **DISCIPLINE** DRAMATIC ART **EDUCATION** ECar Univ, BA; MA; Univ NCar Chapel Hill, PhD. **CAREER** Lectr, ECar Univ, 76-82; Instr to asst prof, Univ NCar Chapel Hill, 86-. **HONORS AND AWARDS** Ford Found Teaching Fel; Alpha Phi Gama. **MEMBERSHIPS** SAMLA, MLA, SCMLA, Mod Drama Asn, Asn for Theatre in Higher Educ, Rocky Mt MLA, Am Theatre and Drama Soc. **RESEARCH** Modern British Drama, Irish Drama, Federal Theatre Project. **SELECTED PUBLICATIONS** Auth, Three Lives: Kafka, James Agee, Montaigne," Threepenny Rev, (86); auth, Cheap Rooms and Restless Hearts: A Study of Formula in the Urban Tales of William Sydney Porter, Popular Pr, 88; auth, "Woody Allen and the Comic Tradition in America," Studies in Am Humor, (88); auth, "Artistic and Social Dimensions of Black Culture in the 'Voodoo Macbeth,'" Jour of Am Drama and Theatre, (92); auth, "Michael Frayn and the World of Work," S Atlantic Rev, (95); auth, "Michael Frayn," British Playwrights 1956-1995: A Research and Production Sourcebook, ed William W Demastes, (96); auth, "Porter and the Popular Tradition in Literature," Short Stories for Students, (Gale Publ, 97); auth, "Woody's Alice and Ayckbourn's Susan: A Tale of Two Women," Wood Allen: A Casebook, ed Kimball King, (01). **CONTACT ADDRESS** Univ of No Carolina, Chapel Hill, 217 Center for Dramatic Art, CB 3230, Chapel Hill, NC 27599-3230. **EMAIL** karenb@email.unc.edu

BLASING, MUTLU KONUK
PERSONAL Born 06/27/1944, Istanbul, Turkey, m, 1965, 1 child **DISCIPLINE** ENGLISH **EDUCATION** Col of William and Mary, BA, 69; Brown Univ, PhD, 74. **CAREER** Lectr, Eng, Univ Mass, 74-76; asst prof, Eng, Pomona Col, 77-79; **HONORS AND AWARDS** Postdoctoral fel, U Mass, 74-76. **RESEARCH** American poetry; translation of poetry. **SELECTED PUBLICATIONS** Auth, The Art of Life, Texas, 77; auth, American Poetry, Yale, 87; auth, Politics and Form in Postmodern Poetry, Cambridge, 95. **CONTACT ADDRESS** English Dept, Brown Univ, PO Box 1852, Providence, RI 02912. **EMAIL** mutlu_blasing@brown.edu

BLATT, STEPHEN J.
DISCIPLINE INTERPERSONAL COMMUNICATION **EDUCATION** Morehead State Univ, BA, 64; Ohio Univ, MA, 67; PhD, 70. **CAREER** Assoc prof, 71-. **RESEARCH** The use of small groups in classroom management strategies. **SELECTED PUBLICATIONS** Publ, Midwestern Edu Researcher, 95; Rev of Higher Edu, 96. **CONTACT ADDRESS** Dept of Commun, Univ of Dayton, 300 Col Park, Dayton, OH 75062. **EMAIL** Sblatt@Udayton.edu

BLAU, HERBERT
PERSONAL Born 05/03/1926, Brooklyn, NY, m, 1981, 4 children **DISCIPLINE** ENGLISH; COMPARATIVE LITERATURE **EDUCATION** NYork Univ, BchE, 47; Stanford Univ, MA, 49, PhD, 54. **CAREER** From asst prof to prof, San Francisco State Univ, 50-65; co-found and co-dir, The Actor's Workshop of San Francisco, 52-65; co-dir, Repertory Theater of Lincoln Ctr, NY, 65-67; prof, City Univ of NY, 67-68; provost and dean, School of Theater and Dance, Calif Inst of the Arts, 68-71; found and artistic dir, KRAKEN theatre, 71-81; prof of the Arts and dir of Inter-Arts Prog, Oberlin Col, 72-74; dean, div of Arts and Hums, Univ of Md, 74-76; prof, Univ of Md, 76-78; prof, Univ of Wis, 78-84; disting. prof, Univ of Wis, 84-00; ed and adv bds, Performing Arts J, Discourse, Theater J, Assaph, World Encycl of Contemp Theatre, Mod Int Drama, Jour of Beckett Studies, Contemp Dramatists, The Drama Rev, Arts in Soc. **HONORS AND AWARDS** Ford Found fel, 59; President's Disting. Serv Awd, 65; Guggenheim fels, 62, 77; Camargo Found fel, 84; George Nathan Awd for Dramatic Criticism; Sen fel for Independant Study/Res, Nat Endowment for Hums, 84; Nat Endowment for Hums grant, 81, 83, 87, 90; The Kenyon Rev prize for literary excellence, 93. **SELECTED PUBLICATIONS** Auth, The Impossible Theater: A Manifesto, 64; Blooded Thought: Occasions of Theater, 82; Take Up the Bodies: Theater at the Vanishing Point, 82; The Eye of Prey: Subversions of the Postmodern, 87; The Audience, 90; Universals of Performance; or, Amortizing Play, By Means of Performance: Intercult Studies of Theater and Ritual, ed R. Schechner and W. Appel, 90; The Oversight of Ceaseless Eyes, Around the Absurd: Essays on Modern and Postmodern Drama, ed E. Brater and R. Cohn, 91; Quaquaquaqua: The Babel of Beckett, The World of Beckett, ed J. Smith, Psychiatry and Humanities, vol 12, 91; The Surpassing Body, The Drama Rev 35.2, 91; Readymade Desire, Confronting Tennessee Williams? A Streetcar Named Desire: Essays in Critical Pluralism, ed P.C. Kolin, 92; To All Appearances: Ideology and Performance, 92; Nothing in Itself: Complexions of Fashion, 99; Sails of the Herring Fleet: Essays on Beckett, 00; The Prospect Before Us, Discourse 14.2, 92; Ideology, Performance, and the Illusions of Demystification, Crit Theory and Performance, ed J.G. Reinelt and J. Roach, 92; Spacing Out in the American Theater, The Kenyon Rev 14.2, 93; A Valediction: Chills and Fever, Mourning, and the Vanities of the Sublime, Performing Arts Jour 16.1, 94; Rhetorics of the Body: Do You Smell a Fault?, Cult Artifacts and the Production of Meaning: The Page, the Image and the Body, ed. M. Ezell and K. O'Brien O'Keefe, 94; Fantasia and Simulacra: Subtext of a Syllabus for the Arts in America, The Kenyon Rev 16.2, 94; Flat-Out Vision, Fugitive Images: From Photography to Video, ed P. Petro, 95; coed, Performance Issue(s): Happenings, Body, Spectacle, Discourse 14.2, 92. **CONTACT ADDRESS** Dept of English, Univ of Washington, Seattle, WA 98195-3765.

BLAU, SHERIDAN
DISCIPLINE ENGLISH LITERATURE **EDUCATION** Brandeis Univ, PhD, 67. **CAREER** Lectr, Eng, Univ Calif, Santa Barbara. **RESEARCH** Seventeenth-century lit; Rhet and compos; Eng educ. **SELECTED PUBLICATIONS** Auth, numerous articles on Milton, Herbert, Renaissance thought, the development of literacy, the teaching of composition and literature, theory of the composing process. **CONTACT ADDRESS** Dept of English, Univ of California, Santa Barbara, Santa Barbara, CA 93106-7150. **EMAIL** blau@education.ucsb.edu

BLAYDES, SOPHIA BOYATZIES
PERSONAL Born 10/16/1933, Rochester, NY, m, 1961, 2 children **DISCIPLINE** ENGLISH AND AMERICAN LITERATURE **EDUCATION** Univ Rochester, BA, 55; Ind Univ, Bloomington, MA, 58, PhD(English), 62. **CAREER** From instr to asst prof Am lit, Mich State Univ, 62-65; from asst prof to assoc prof English and Am lit, 66-77, Prof English, WVA Univ, 77-, Folger res fel, 81; chaif fac Senate, 90-91, Prog Coordinator for retired and senior fac, 94-, pres, Carolinas symposium for Butes Studie, 90-91; co-dir, Literary Discussion Group for Senior Citizens, 78-; fac for Elderhosld, 85, 87, 88, 90, 94; mem Central Exec Comm Folger Inst, 92-99; Bd of Advisors WVU, 90-91; rep Advisory Coun to Bd of Trustee, 93-99, mem Bd of Trustees, 98-99; State del to 95, White House Conf on Aging, 95. **MEMBERSHIPS** Am Soc 18th Century Studies; MLA; English Inst; NCTE. **RESEARCH** Eighteenth-century poetry; Restoration and eighteenth-century drama; biography and autobiography. **SELECTED PUBLICATIONS** Auth, Christopher Smart as a Poet of His Time: Re-appraisal, Mouton, The Hague, 66; auth, The McCarthy-Army hearings: History as drama, J English Teachings Tech, fall 75; Cordelia: Loss of insolence, Stuides Humanitues, 10/76; Literary allusions as satire in Simon Asay's Butley, Midwest Quart, summer 77; Metaphors of life and death in the poetry of Plath Levertov, Dalhousie Rev, fall 77; coauth, Sir William Davenant, Tawayne, 81; The poetry of the Duchess of Newcastle: Apyram of praise, Bull W Va Asn Col English Teachers, 81; auth, Su William Davenart: an Annotated Bibliograph, 86. **CONTACT ADDRESS** Dept of English, West Virginia Univ, Morgantown, PO Box 6296, Morgantown, WV 26506-6296. **EMAIL** sblayde@wvu.edu

BLAZEK, RONALD DAVID
PERSONAL Born 06/13/1936, Chicago, IL, m, 1960, 2 children **DISCIPLINE** LIBRARY SCIENCE **EDUCATION** B.Ed. Chicago Teachers College, 58, M.Ed., Chicago Teachers College, 61, M.S.,Univ of Illinois, 65, PhD., Univ of Illinois, 71. **CAREER** Teacher-Librarian, Chicago Public School System, 58-64, Head Library Circulation Dept, Chicago Teachers College, 65-68, Asst Prof, Chicago State Univ, 68-71, Assoc Prof, Florida State Univ, 71-80, Prof, Florida State Univ, 81. **HONORS AND AWARDS** Oustanding Senior, Chicago Teachers College, Beta Phi Mu-National Hogan Fraternity, Univ of Illinois, Outstanding Academic Book Awds, Choice Magazine, 94, 95, Florida Assoc Travfour, Honor Roll, 96. **MEMBERSHIPS** American Library Association, Assoc for Library and Information Sci Educ, Southeastern Library Assoc, Florida Library Assoc. **RESEARCH** Reference/Info Services, Bibliography , Library Hist **SELECTED PUBLICATIONS** United States Hist: A Selective Guide to Information Sources, 1st edition, with Anna H Perrault, Libraries Unlimited, 94; The Humanities: A Selective Guide to Information Sources, 3rd with Elizabeth Aversa, Libraries Unlimited, 88; 4th edition, with Elizabeth Aversa, Libraries Unlimited, 94; The Humanities CD: An Electronic Guide to Information Sources, Libraries Unlimited, 95; Term Paper Resource Guide to 20th Century United States History, with Bob Muccigrosso and Theresa Maggio, Grenwood Press, 98; The Humanities: A Selective Guide to Information Sources, 5th edition, with Elizabeth Aversa, Libraries Unlimited, 00; Information Needs of the Rural Physician: A Descriptive Study, with Cheryl Dee, Medical Library Assoc Bulletin, 93; The Role of the School Library Media Specialist in a Literature-Based Reading Program, with Kay Bishop, School Media Quarterly, 94; The Nature of a Disscipline: A Bibliometric Study of Communication with Some Comparisons to Library Reference/Information Work, with Joan Dick, The Reference Librarian, 95, Transforming Library Services Through Action Research; with Anna Perrault, Florida Libraries, 97; coauth, "Management Characteristics and Employee Stress and Burnout as Reported in the Periodical "Lit of Business," J of Business and Finance Librarianship, 97; auth, Management Characteristics and Employee Stress and Burnout as Reported in the Periodical Literature of Business, Jouranl of Business and Finance Libraniaship, with Darlene Parrish, 97; auth, George Burmell Utley Am Nat Bibliography, Oxford Univ Press, 98; auth, "George Buxwell Utley," in Am Nat Bibliography, Oxford Univ Pr, 98; The Humanities: A Selective Guide to Information Sources, 5th edition, with Elizabeth Aversa, Libraries Unlimited, 00. **CONTACT ADDRESS** School of Library Science, Florida State Univ, Tallahassee, FL 32306. **EMAIL** blazek@lis.fsu.edu

BLAZEKOVIC, ZDRAVKO
PERSONAL Born 05/13/1956, Zagreb, Croatia **DISCIPLINE** MUSICOLOGY **EDUCATION** Acad Mus, Zagreb, Croatia, BA, 80, MA, 83; City Univ NYork, MPhil, 91, PhD, 97. **CAREER** Editor, RILM Abstracts of Mus Lit, NY, 87- ; Assoc dir, 91-98, dir, 98- , Res Ctr Mus Iconography; Ed, RIdIM/RCMI

newsletter, 89-97, Art in Mus, 98- ; US Corresp, Hrvatsko Slovo, 96- ; Area ed, Die Musik in Geschichte und Gegenwart, 2nd ed, Kassel, Ger, 95- ; res asst, Inst Musicol Res, Croatian Acad Sci and Arts, 81. **MEMBERSHIPS** Int Asn Mus Libr, Archives and Document Ctr; Int Musicol Soc; Croatian Musicol Soc; Int Coun Trad Mus. **RESEARCH** History of Croatian music; music iconography; music in medieval astrological thoughts; social history of music. **SELECTED PUBLICATIONS** Music in Zagreb between Croatian, Hungarian and Austrian politics, Hist Euro Ideas XVI/4-6, 93; Horns in a Bag, or, Disparity of Parallel Musical Histories among the South Slavs, The Consortium on Revolutionary Europe, 1750-1850: Proceedings, 1992. Talahasee, Fla State Univ; Inst on Napoleon and the French Rev, 93, 107-116; Franz von Suppe und Dalmatien, Studien zur Musikwissenschaft XLIII 94, 249-268; Political Implications of the Croatian Opera in the Nineteenth-Century, Music Cultures in Contact: Convergences and Collisions, Sydney, Gordon and Breach, Currency Press, 94, 48-58; Due musicisti nella Pannonia del primo Ottocento: Djuro Arnold e Johann Petrus Haibel, Danubio: Una civilta musicale. VI: Croazia, Serbia, Bulgaria, Romania, Monfalcone: Teatro Communale, 94, 47-64; Salonsko Kolo: Dance of Nineteenth-Century Croatian Ballrooms, Dance res: The jour Soc for Dance Res XII/2, 94, 114-126; Origins of Modern Croatian Music, 1770-1830, Jour Croatian stud XXXIV-XXXV, 93-94, 75-97; Coauth, European Fiction Facts or Music, Hist of Euro Ideas XX/1-3, Jan 95, 461-467; Coauth, Jakob Petrus Haibel (1762-1826) and His Sixteen Newly-Discovered Masses from Djakovo, Off-Mozart: Musical culture and the Kleinmeister of Central Europe, 1750-1820, Zagreb, Hrvatsko muzikolosko drustvo, 95, 67-75; Music autographs in the Nikola Udina Algarotti Collection in Zagreb (circa 1740-1838), Current musicol 57, 95, 127-164; Indian decans, Arabic interpretations, European images, European iconography east and west: Selected papers of the Szeged international conference June 9-12, 1993, Leiden, E.J. Brill, 96, 225-235; Jugoslavien, Die Musik in Geschichte und Gegenwart: Allgemeine Enzyklopodie der Musik, Sachteil 4, Kassel, Barenreiter, Stuttgart: Metzler, 96; Anonymous vs. onymous, or When will Croatian musicology remember an unknown composer, Studia musicologica Academiae Scientiarum Hungaricae XXXVII/2-4, 96, 217-230; Orgelbildung: Kroatien und Montenegro, Die Musik in Geschichte und Gegenwart: Allgemeine Enzyklopadie der Musik, Sachteil 7, Kassel, Barenreiter; Stuttgart: Metzler, 97; Ed, Music and Politics in Post-Communist Europe, The European Legacy: Toward New Paradigms II/1, Mar 97, 133-159; Coauth, Serbien und Montenegro, Die Musik in Geschichte und Gegenwart: Allgemeine Enzyklopadie der Musik, Sachteil 8, Kassel: Barenreiter; Stuttgart: Metzler, 98; The shadow of politics on the north Croatian music of the nineteenth century, Music, politics, and war: Views from Croatia, Zagreb: Zavod za etnologiju and folklore res, 98, 65-78. **CONTACT ADDRESS** City Univ, 33 W 42nd St, New York, NY 10036. **EMAIL** zblazeko@email.gc.cuny.edu

BLEDSOE, ROBERT TERRELL
PERSONAL Born 11/14/1944, Monticello, AR **DISCIPLINE** VICTORIAN LITERATURE **EDUCATION** Harvard Univ, BA, 66; Univ Kent, Canterbury, MA, 67; Princeton Univ, PhD, 71. **CAREER** Asst prof, 71-77, assoc prof English 77-91; prof English, 91-, Univ TX, El Paso, 77-. **MEMBERSHIPS** MLA; Res Soc for Victorian Per; Dickens Fel. **RESEARCH** 19th Century literature; 19th Century musical journalism. **SELECTED PUBLICATIONS** Auth, Sibi Constet: The goddess of Castlewood and the goddess of Walcote, Studies in Novel, summer 73; Pendennis and the power of sentimentality: A study of motherly love, Publ Mod Lang Asn Am, 10/76; Kubrick's Vanity Fair, Rocky Mountain Rev Lang & Lit, spring 77; Dickens and Chorley, Dickensian, fall 79; A reconsideration of the virgin of Villette, Women & Lit, 80; Vanity fair and singing, Studies in Novel, summer 81; Dickens and Opera, Dickens Stud Ann, 90; contrib Grove Dictionnary of Opera, 92; An Oxford Companion to Dickens, 98; H F Chorley: Victorian Journalist, Ashgate Press, 98; Contrib, Dictionary of National Biography, 01; Contrib, New Grove Dictionary of Music, 01. **CONTACT ADDRESS** Dept English, Univ of Texas, El Paso, 500 W University Ave, El Paso, TX 79968-0001. **EMAIL** rbledsoe@utep.edu

BLEDSTEIN, ADRIEN
PERSONAL Born 03/04/1939, Los Angeles, CA, m, 1959, 2 children **DISCIPLINE** HISTORY; ENGLISH **EDUCATION** Univ California at Los Angeles, BA, 60; Teaching Certificate, 61. **CAREER** KAM Isiah Israel Congregation, Chicago, 30 years. **MEMBERSHIPS** SBL; Chicago Soc for Biblical Research **RESEARCH** Bible and ancient near Eastern lit. **SELECTED PUBLICATIONS** Auth, Was Eve Cursed (Or Did a Woman Write Genesis), Bible Review, 93; Are Women Cursed in Genesis 3.16, A Feminist Companion to Genesis, 93; Binder, Trickster, Heel and Hairy-man: Re-reading Genesis 27 as a Trickster Tale Told by a Woman, A Feminist Companion to Genesis, 93; Is Judges a Woman's Satire of Men Who Play God, A Feminist Companion to Judges, 93; Female Companionships: If the Book of Ruth Were Written by a Woman, A Feminist Companion to Ruth, 93; Dr. Tamar, Bible Review, 95; Tamar and the Coat of Many Colors, A Feminist Companion to Samuel and Kings II, forthcoming. **CONTACT ADDRESS** 5459 S. Hyde Pk. Blvd., Chicago, IL 60615-5801. **EMAIL** ajb@icanbreathe.com

BLEETH, KENNETH ALAN
PERSONAL Born 03/12/1942, New York, NY **DISCIPLINE** MEDIEVAL LITERATURE **EDUCATION** Harvard Univ, AB, 63, AM, 65, PhD(English), 69. **CAREER** Asst prof, Boston Univ, 69-77; lectr, Univ Calif, Santa Barbara, 77-79; asst prof English, Conn Col, 79-83; from assoc prof to prof, 83-93; Nat Endowment for Humanities younger humanist fel, 73-74. **MEMBERSHIPS** MLA; Medieval Acad Am. **RESEARCH** Middle English poetry, especially Chaucer. **SELECTED PUBLICATIONS** Auth, Juliana, 647-652, Medium Aevum, 69; Narrator and landscape in the Commedia, Dante Studies, 70; The image of paradise in the Merchant's Tale, Harvard English Studies, 74; The rocks in the Franklin's tale of Ovid's Medea, Am Notes & Queries, 82; auth, Joseph's Doubting of Mary and the Conclusion of the Merchant's Tale, Chaucer Review, 21, 86, 59-67; The Rocks and the Garden: The Limits of Illusion in Chaucer's Franklin's Tale, English Studies, 93; auth, The Imitation David: Plagiarism, Collaborationm and the Making of a Gay Literary Tradition in Daid Leavitt's The Trem Paper Artists, PMLA, 00. **CONTACT ADDRESS** Dept of English, Connecticut Col, 270 Mohegan Ave, New London, CT 06320-4125. **EMAIL** kable@conncoll.edu

BLEICH, DAVID
PERSONAL Born New York City, NY, 1 child **DISCIPLINE** ENGLISH **EDUCATION** NYork Univ, PhD. **CAREER** Prof; Taught at, NY Univ, IN Univ & Simon Fraser Univ. **HONORS AND AWARDS** ACLS study fel, Res Ctr for Mental Hea NY Univ. **MEMBERSHIPS** MLA, AAA, NCTE, CCCC, AERA. **RESEARCH** Lang; lit; literacy; tchg; feminist critique of knowledge. **SELECTED PUBLICATIONS** Auth, Readings and Feelings, Subjective Criticism, Utopia: The Psychology of a Cultural Fantasy & The Double Perspective: Language, Literacy and Social Relations; auth, Know and Tell: A Writing; ed, Writing With: New Directions in Collaborative Teaching, Learning, and Research, Collaboration and Change in the Academy; articles on, Morrison, Kafka, literary theory, teaching, curriculum, collaboration & academi c ideology; auth, Pedagogy of Dis closure, Genre and Membership. **CONTACT ADDRESS** Dept of Eng, Univ of Rochester, Rochester, NY 14627. **EMAIL** dblh@mail.rochester.edu

BLEISCH, PAMELA
DISCIPLINE CLASSICAL STUDIES **EDUCATION** Brown Univ, BA, 83; Univ Chicago, MA, 85; Univ Calif, PhD, 94. **CAREER** Asst prof, Univ Georg, 94-99; asst prof, Boston Univ, 99-. **HONORS AND AWARDS** Univ Georg Res Found Grnt, 98; Univ Georg Hum Cen Fel, 95-96; Luckman Dis Fel, 92-93; Connell Fel, 91-92; Chancellor's Fel, 85-86; Grad Div Stip, 84; J. Hatten Col Teach Hon Awd, 97; Lilly Teach Fel, 96-97; Luckman Dist Teach Awd, 91-92. **MEMBERSHIPS** APA; Vergilian Soc; WCC. **RESEARCH** Latin literature; the Augustan Age; Hellenistic poetry; gender in antiquity. **SELECTED PUBLICATIONS** Auth, "The Empty Tomb at Rhoeteum: Deiphobus and the Problem of the Past," Class Ant (99); auth, "Altars Altered: the Alexandrian Tradition of Etymological Wordplay," Am J Philo (98); auth, "On Choosing a Spouse," Am J Philo (96); auth, "Nisus' Choice: Bovillae at Aeneid," Class Qtly (01); auth, "Silence is Golden: Simonides, Callimachus, and Augustan Panegyric at the close of Horace Carm," Quad Urb di Cult Class (01). **CONTACT ADDRESS** Dept Classical Studies, Boston Univ, 745 Commonwealth Ave, Boston, MA 02215.

BLESSINGTON, FRANCIS C.
PERSONAL Born 05/21/1942, Boston, MA, m, 2 children **DISCIPLINE** ENGLISH **EDUCATION** Boston Col, AB, 63; Northeastern Univ, MA, 66; Boston Univ, PhD, 67; AM, 73; PhD, 72. **CAREER** Prof, Northeastern Univ. **SELECTED PUBLICATIONS** Auth, Wolf Howl, Univ Mo Press, 00; auth, "Is There a Lyric Center," The Sewanee Review, (99): 216-226; auth, "Paradise Lost and the Apotheosis of the Suppliant," Arion 3rd series, (98): 83-97; auth, Euripides: The Bacchae and Aristophanes: The Frogs, Crofts Classics, 93; auth, Lorenzo de' Medici, Univ Press of America, 92; auth, "Heroic Eve," in Shaping the short Essay, Harper Collins, (91): 203-207; auth, Paradise Lost: Ideal and Tragic Epic, 88; auth, Lantskip, Dublin, 87; auth, The Motive for Metaphor: Essays on Modern Poetry in Honor of Samuel French Morse, Northeastern Univ Press, 83. **CONTACT ADDRESS** Dept English, Northeastern Univ, 360 Huntington Ave, Boston, MA 02115-5005. **EMAIL** blessington@neu.edu

BLEWETT, DAVID
DISCIPLINE ENGLISH LITERATURE **EDUCATION** Univ Manitoba, BA; MA; Univ Toronto, PhD. **RESEARCH** Eighteenth century English literature; literary illustration; Bloomsbury Group. **SELECTED PUBLICATIONS** Auth, Defoe's Art of Fiction, 79; ed, Defoe's Roxana, 79; auth, Fielding's Amelia, 87; auth, Moll Flanders, 89. **CONTACT ADDRESS** English Dept, McMaster Univ, 1280 Main St W, Hamilton, ON, Canada L8S 4L9. **EMAIL** blewett@mcmaster.ca

BLIQUEZ, LAWRENCE J.
PERSONAL Born 06/12/1941, Des Moines, IA, m, 1969, 2 children **DISCIPLINE** CLASSICS **EDUCATION** St Mary's Coll Calif, BA, 63; Stanford Univ, MA, 65; PhD, 68. **CAREER** Asst prof, San Francisco State Coll, 66-69; asst prof Univ Wash Seattle, 69-77; assoc prof, 77-85; prof, Univ Wash Seattle, 85-. **HONORS AND AWARDS** Jr Fel, Center for Hellenic Studies, 77-78; Distinguished Teaching Awd, Univ Wash, 77-78. **MEMBERSHIPS** APA; Soc for Ancient Med. **RESEARCH** Greek and Roman Minor Objects, surgical instruments. **SELECTED PUBLICATIONS** Auth, Roman Surgical Instruments and Other Minor Objectsin the Nat Archaeol Museum of Naples, 94. **CONTACT ADDRESS** Dept of Classics, Univ of Washington, Box 353110, Seattle, WA 98195. **EMAIL** lbliquez@u.washington.edu

BLISS, LEE
DISCIPLINE RENAISSANCE LITERATURE **EDUCATION** Univ Calif, Berkeley, PhD, 72. **CAREER** Prof, Eng, Univ Calif, Santa Barbara. **HONORS AND AWARDS** NEH/Folger Shakespeare Library Fel, 92-93. **MEMBERSHIPS** SAA, RSA, Malone Soc, MLA. **RESEARCH** Shakespearean and non-Shakespearean Renaissance drama; Modern drama. **SELECTED PUBLICATIONS** Auth, The World's Perspective: John Webster and the Jacobean Drama, Rutgers Univ, 83; Francis Beaumont, Twayne, 87; pub(s), articles on Shakespeare, Webster, Chapman, Beaumont, Fletcher, Renaissance dramatic genres, and sixteenth- and seventeenth-century retellings of the Griselda story; auth, New Cambridge Shaakespeare edn. of Coriolanus, 00. **CONTACT ADDRESS** Dept of Eng, Univ of California, Santa Barbara, Santa Barbara, CA 93106-7150. **EMAIL** lbliss@humanitas.ucsb.edu

BLOCH, CHANA
PERSONAL Born 03/15/1940, New York, NY, d, 1969, 2 children **DISCIPLINE** ENGLISH LITERATURE **EDUCATION** Cornell Univ, BA, 61; Brandeis Univ, MA, 63 & 65; Univ Calif, Berkeley, PhD, 75. **CAREER** Instr, Hebrew Univ, Jerusalem, 64-67; instr, 73-75, asst prof, 75-80, assoc prof, 81-87, chair Dept English, 86-89, Prof English Lit, Mills Col, 87-, W M Keck Prof English, 96-99, dir, creative writing prog, 93-; Graves Award fel study & writing, 76-77; NEH fel, 80. **HONORS AND AWARDS** Discovery Awd (poetry), 74; Transl Awd, Columbia Univ Transl Center, 78; Book of the Year Awd, Conf on Christianity & Lit, 86; Writers Exchange Awd, Poets & Writers, 88; Felix Pollak Prize, Poetry, 98. **MEMBERSHIPS** MLA; PSA; ALTA; ALSC. **RESEARCH** George Herbert; The Bible; The Song of Songs; contemporary poetry; translation. **SELECTED PUBLICATIONS** Transl, "Yiddish poems by Glatstein, Sutzkever, Zeitlin," in A Treasury of Yiddish Poetry, 69; transl, "The Riddle," by Isaac Bashevis Singer, Playboy, 70, also in A Friend of Kafka, 70; A Dress of Fire: Selected Poetry of Dahlia Ravikoritch, Menard Press, London, 76, Sheep Meadow Press, 78; The Secrets of the Tribe (poems), Sheep Meadow Press, 81; Spelling the Word: George Herbert and the Bible, Univ Calif Press, 85; co-ed & transl, Selected Poems of Yehuda Amichai, Harper & Row, 86, rev and expanded ed, Univ Calif Press, 96; co-ed & transl, The Window: New & Selected Poems of Dahlia Ravikovitch, Sheep Meadow Press, 89; The Past Keeps Changing (poems), Sheep Meadow Press, 92; cotransl, The Song of Songs: A New Translation with an Introduction and Commentary, Random House, 95, paperbk ed, Univ Calif Press, 98; Mrs Dumpty (poems), Univ Wis Press, 98; cotransl, Open Closed Open, Harcourt, 00. **CONTACT ADDRESS** Dept of English, Mills Col, 5000 MacArthur Blvd, Oakland, CA 94613-1000. **EMAIL** chana@mills.edu

BLOCK, GEOFFREY
PERSONAL Born 05/07/1948, Oakland, CA, m, 1982, 2 children **DISCIPLINE** MUSIC HISTORY **EDUCATION** UCLA, BA 70; Harvard Univ, MA, 73, PhD, 79. **CAREER** The Thacher Sch, Dir of Music, 77-80, Univ of Puget Sound, 80-present, prof of Music Hist. **HONORS AND AWARDS** Fulbright Fel 75-76, Washington Commission for the hum: Inquiring Mind Scholar 85-87, National Endowment for the Hum, 90-91, Univ of Puget Sound Regester Lectr, 99, General Ed, Yal Broadway Masters. **MEMBERSHIPS** Am Musicological Soc; Soc for Am Music. **RESEARCH** Beethoven Mozart Ives Am musical theater. **SELECTED PUBLICATIONS** Enchanted Evenings: The Broadway Musical from Show Boat to Sondheim, Oxford Univ Press, 97; Ives: Piano Sonata No. 2 (Concord, MA, 1840-1860), Cambridge Univ Press, 96); co-ed, Charles Ives and the Classical Tradition, New Haven: Yal Univ Press, 96; Charles Ives, A Biobibliography, Greenwood Press, 88; Articles in Ives Studies, Cambridge Univ Press, 98; Journal of the Royal Musical Association, 96; The Journal of Musicology, 93; Mozart-Jahrbuch 91, 92; Beethoven's Compositional Process, Univ of NE, 91; The Opera Quarterly, 90; The Musical Quarterly, 89; Beethoven Essays, Harvard Univ Press, 84. **CONTACT ADDRESS** Music Dept, Univ of Puget Sound, 1500 N. Warner, Tacoma, WA 98416. **EMAIL** Block@ups.edu

BLOCK, STEVEN
PERSONAL Born 11/05/1952, New York, NY, m, 1977, 7 children **DISCIPLINE** COMPOSITION THEORY **EDUCATION** Univ Pitts, PhD, 81. **CAREER** Asst Prof, 87-89, Northeastern IL Univ; Asst Prof, Assoc Prof, 89 to 95-, Univ New Mexico. **HONORS AND AWARDS** Teach Achiev Alumni Fac Awd; UNM Schl Awd. **MEMBERSHIPS** AMT; ACA. **RESEARCH** 20th Century Music and Music Theory; Free Jazz; Non-Western Music. **SELECTED PUBLICATIONS**

Auth, Bemsha Swing: The Transformation of a Bebop Classic to Free Jazz, Music Theory Spectrum, 97; Vector Products and Intervallic Weighting, J Music Theory, 94; Organized Sound, Annual Rev of Jazz Studies, 93. **CONTACT ADDRESS** Dept of Music, Univ of New Mexico, Albuquerque, Albuquerque, NM 87031. **EMAIL** sblock@unm.edu

BLODGETT, HARRIET H.
PERSONAL Born 09/04/1932, New York, NY, m, 1955, 1 child **DISCIPLINE** ENGLISH **EDUCATION** Queens Col, BA, 54; Univ Chicago, MA, 56, Univ Calif, PhD, 68. **CAREER** Prof, Calif St. U., Stanislaus, Dept of Eng, 98; Assoc Prof, Calif St. U, Stanislaus, Dept of Eng, 94-98; Asst Prof, Calif St. U, Stanislaus, Dept of Eng, 92-94; Lecturer, Calif St. U, Stanislaus, Dept of Eng, 88; Literature Bd. Of Kresge Col and Crown Col Core Program; Lecuturer, UC Davis (UCD), Program in Comparative Lit, 86-87; Lecturer, UC Irvine, Dept of English and Comp Lit, 85-86; Lecturer, Calif St. U., Sacramento, Depts of Eng and of Humanities, also Women's Studies, 82-87; Lecturer, UCD, Program in Comparative Lit, 79-85; Asst Prof (vis), Univ of Oregon, Dept of English, 78-79; Lecturer, Calif St. U., Chico Dept of English, 72-73; instr, Sacramento City Col, Dept of English, 68-69. **HONORS AND AWARDS** Awarded Modern Literature Asn (MLA); Independent Scholar Prize for Best Book 89; Visiting Scholar, Institute for Research on Women and Gender, Stanford Univ, 83. **MEMBERSHIPS** Phi Beta Kappa; Phi Kappa Phi; Assoc of Literary Scholars and Critics. **RESEARCH** British Women Writiers including Diarists noneuropean women writers. **SELECTED PUBLICATIONS** Auth, ""Patterns of Reality: Elizabeth Bowen's Novels," The Hague: Mouton, 75; auth, "Capacious Hold-All: An Anthology of Englishwomen's Diary Writings, ed, H. Blodgett," Chalottsville and Lon: Univ of Press of VA, 91; auth, "As The Englishwoman's Diary, London: Fourth Estate, 92; auth, "Centuries of Female Days: Englishwomen's Private Diaries," New Brunswick, NJ: Rutgers; UP, 88, reissue 91; also Gloucester, England: Alan Sutton, 89; auth, "Is the Angel in the House Immortal?" Virginia Woolf Miscellany, No. 45, Spring 95: 6; auth, "Preserving the Moment in the Diary of Margaret Fountaine," Inscribing the Daily: Critical Essays on Women's Diaries, ed, S. Bunkers and C. Huff, Amherst: U MA Press 96, 156-168; rev, "Writing Selves: Contemporary Feminist Autobiography, by Jeanne Perreault, U of Minnesota Press, 55 in Biography 19, Fall 96: 435-37; auth, "Realism Reconstructed: The Death of the Heart," California State Univ, Stanislaus, Journal of Research, 1, 96:16-23; auth, "A Mystery Concerning George Eliot's Life," George Eliot--George Henry Lewes Studies nos. 32-33, September 97: 70-72; auth, "Food for Thought in Virginia Woolf's Novels," Woolf Studies Annual 3, 97:45-60; auth, "In Cambridge Guide to Women's Writing in English," ed. Lorna sage, Cambridge: Cambridge UP, 99, Essay entries on Diaries and Journals, The Diary of Fanny Burney, Margaret Fountaine, Margaret Hoby, Sarah Macnaughtan, Ellen Weeton, **CONTACT ADDRESS** Dept English, California State Univ, Stanislaus, 801 West Monte Vista Ave, Turlock, CA 95382-0256. **EMAIL** blodgett@athena.csustan.edu

BLOOM, ABIGAIL BURNHAM
PERSONAL m, 2 children **DISCIPLINE** LITERATURE **EDUCATION** Boston Univ, BA, 73; Univ Mich, MA, 75; New York Univ, PhD, 89 **CAREER** Managing ed, Victorian Literature and Culture, 92-; adjunct instr, New School Univ, 96- **MEMBERSHIPS** MLA; NEMLA; MMLA; NVSA **RESEARCH** Victorian Literature **SELECTED PUBLICATIONS** Ed, "Anne Thackeray Ritchie," Cambridge Bibliography of English Literature, 99; ed, "Nineteenth Century British Women Writers," Greenwood, 00; auth, "Transcendence through Incongruity: The Background of Humor in Carlyle's Sartor Resartus," The Victorian Comic Spirit, ed Jennifer Wagner-Lawlor, Ashgate, 00; auth, "Portraits and Photographs of the Carlyles," "The Poetry of Jane Carlyle" and "Carlyle's Humor," The Carlyle Encyclopedia, forthcoming. **CONTACT ADDRESS** 54 Riverside Dr., 15-D, New York, NY 10024-6553. **EMAIL** abigail.bloom@nyu.edu

BLOOM, HAROLD
PERSONAL Born 07/11/1930, New York, NY, m, 1958, 2 children **DISCIPLINE** ENGLISH AND AMERICAN LITERATURE **EDUCATION** Cornell Univ, BA, 51; Yale Univ, PhD, 55. **CAREER** From instr to prof English, 55-74, William Clyde DeVane prof humanities, 74-77; Prof, Humanities, Yake Univ, 77-; lectr, Hebrew Univ, 59; Sterling Prof of Humanities at Yale and Berg Prof of English at NYU. **HONORS AND AWARDS** John Addison Porter Prize, 56; Morse fel, Yale Univ, 58-59; Guggenheim fel, 62-63; sr vis fel, Cornell Soc Humanities, 68-69; Melville Cane Awd, Poetry Soc Am, 71; Morton Daunen Zabel Awd, Am Acad Arts and Lett, 82; A MacArthur Fellowship, The Charles Eliot Norton Professorship of Poetry at Harvard The Gold Medal For Criticism from the American Acad of Art and honorary degrees from Rome and Bozo Ana; littd, boston col, 73; lhd, yeshiva univ, 76. **MEMBERSHIPS** Am Acad Arts & Lett. **RESEARCH** English Romantic and Victorian poetry; theory of poetic influence, British and American poetry from the later 18th century to the present day. **SELECTED PUBLICATIONS** Auth, Operation Shylock--A Confession, NY Rev Bk(s), Vol 0040, 93; Bloom,Harold Interviewed By Wachtel,Eleanor, Queens Quart, Vol 0102, 95; Feminism As The Love Of Reading, Raritan Quarterly Rev; auth, The Anxiety of Influence, 73; auth, The Book of J 90; auth, The Western Canon Shakespeare: The Invention of the Human, 98; auth, How To Read and Why, 00. **CONTACT ADDRESS** Yale Univ, PO Box 208302, New Haven, CT 06520-8302.

BLOOM, LYNN Z.
PERSONAL Born 01/11/1934, Ann Arbor, MI, m, 1958, 2 children **DISCIPLINE** ENGLISH **EDUCATION** Univ Mich, BA, 56, MA, 57, PhD, 63. **CAREER** Asst prof to assoc prof, Butler Univ, 70-74; assoc prof, Univ NM, 75-78; assoc prof, 76-83, dir writing, 78-83, Col Wm & Mary; prof, 82-90, dept head, 82-83, Va Commonwealth Univ; Prof English, Aetna Chair Writing, Univ Conn, 88-. **HONORS AND AWARDS** Nat Counc Teachers Eng, 97-98; Aetna Chair of Writing, Univ Conn, 88-; U. S. Dept Ag, 96-99; NEH, 79-81, 84, 86-87; Board of Trustees Distinguished Prof, 00-. **MEMBERSHIPS** Phi Beta Kappa; Mod Lang Asn; Nat Counc Teachers. **RESEARCH** Creative nonfiction; composition studies; autobiography; essays; women writers. **SELECTED PUBLICATIONS** Co-ed, Composition in the 21st Century: Crisis and Change, S Ill Univ Press, 96; ed, Forbidden Family: A Wartime Memoir of the Philippines, 1941-45, Univ Wis Press, 89, 98; auth, Subverting the Academic Masterplot, in Narration as Knowledge, Heinemann, 98; auth, Composition Studies as a Creative At: Teaching, Writing, Scholarship, Administration, Utah State Univ Press, 98; auth, The Essay Canon, Col Eng, March 99; auth, Fact and Artifact: Writing Nonfiction, Harcourt, 85, reprint, Blair/Prentice Hall, 94; ed, The Essay Connection: Readings for Writers, Heath, 84, 88, 91, 95, Houghton Mifflin, 98, 01. **CONTACT ADDRESS** Dept Eng, U-25, Univ of Connecticut, Storrs, Storrs, CT 06268-1025. **EMAIL** Lbloom@uconnvm.uconn.edu

BLOOM, MELANIE
DISCIPLINE INTERCULTURAL COMMUNICATION, INTERPERSONAL COMMUNICATION **EDUCATION** OH Univ, PhD. **CAREER** Instr, ch, Acad Senate, CA State Univ. **RESEARCH** Cult differences in the learning styles of cultural groups represented at CSU Fresno. **SELECTED PUBLICATIONS** Auth, Sex Differences in Ethical Systems, Commun Quart, 90. **CONTACT ADDRESS** California State Univ, Fresno, Fresno, CA 93740.

BLOOM, ROBERT
PERSONAL Born 05/28/1930, Brooklyn, NY, m, 1953, 3 children **DISCIPLINE** ENGLISH LITERATURE **EDUCATION** NYork Univ, BA, 51; Columbia Univ, MA, 52; Univ Mich, PhD, 60. **CAREER** Instr English, Univ Mich, 58-60; from asst prof to assoc prof, 60-73, Prof English, Univ Calif, Berkeley, 73-, Bruern fel Am lit, Univ Leeds & Fulbright travel grant, Eng, 63-64; humanities res fel, Univ Calif, Berkeley, 67-68, humanities res prof, 79. **MEMBERSHIPS** MLA. **RESEARCH** Modern British and American literature; literary criticism. **SELECTED PUBLICATIONS** Auth, The Indeterminate World: A Study of the Novels of Joyce Cary, Univ of Pennsylvania Press, 62; auth, Anatomics of Epotism: A Reading of the Last Novels of H.G. Wells, Univ of Nebraska Press, 77. **CONTACT ADDRESS** Dept of Eng, Univ of California, Berkeley, Berkeley, CA 94720.

BLOOMER, W. MARTIN
DISCIPLINE CLASSICS **EDUCATION** BA, 82; MA, 83; MPhil, 84; Yale Univ, PhD, 87. **CAREER** Asst prof, Stanford Univ. **RESEARCH** Latin lit; ancient rhetoric; ancient historiography. **SELECTED PUBLICATIONS** Auth, Valerius Maximus and the Rhetoric of the New Nobility, 92; The Superlative Nomoi of Herodotus's Histories, 93; A Preface to the History of Declamation: Whose Speech? Whose History?, 96; Latinity and Literary Society at Rome, 97. **CONTACT ADDRESS** Stanford Univ, Bldg 20, Main Quad, Stanford, CA 94305.

BLOOMFIELD, ELISABETH M.
PERSONAL Born 10/01/1960, Le Puy, France, m, 1993 **DISCIPLINE** LITERATURE, FRENCH **EDUCATION** Sorbonne Univ, BA, 82; MA, 83; Univ Calif San Diego, PhD, 00. **CAREER** Lectr, John Hopkins Univ, 96-00; asst prof, Univ Ky, 00-. **MEMBERSHIPS** MLA. **RESEARCH** 20th-century literature and criticism; poetry. **SELECTED PUBLICATIONS** Auth, "The Impossible Sacrifice of Poetry, Bataille and the Critiques of Sacrifice," Diac 26 (96): 86-96; auth, "Reminiscence de Proust," MLN 113 (98): 757-779. **CONTACT ADDRESS** 130 University Ave, Lexington, KY 40503-1032. **EMAIL** earno2@pop.uky.edu

BLOOMFIELD, SUSANNE GEORGE
PERSONAL Born 03/06/1947, Minden, NE, m, 1999, 2 children **DISCIPLINE** AMERICAN LITERATURE **EDUCATION** Univ Nebr, Lincoln, doctorate, 88. **CAREER** Prof of English, Univ Nebr, Kearney. **HONORS AND AWARDS** Pratt Heins Awd for Teaching; Susan Koppleman Awd, Mari Sandoz Awd. **MEMBERSHIPS** Nat pres, Western Lit Asn; fel, Ctr for Great Plains Stud; bd dir, Willa Cather Pioneer Mem and Educ Found; Nebr Hum Speaker's Bur. **RESEARCH** 19th century American Literature, autobiography/biography, Western Am Lit. **SELECTED PUBLICATIONS** Auth, The Adventures of The Woman Homesteader: The Life and Letters of Elinore Pruitt Stewart, Univ Nebr Press, 92; ed, Wellsprings: Poems by Six Nebraska Poets, Univ Nebr, Kearney, 95; coed, The Platte River: An Atlas of the Big Bend Region, Univ Nebr, Kearney, 93; auth, Kat M. Cleary: A Literary Life with Selected Works, Univ of Nebr Pr, 97; coed, A Prairie Mosaic; An Atlas of Central Nebraska's Land, Culture and Nature, 00. **CONTACT ADDRESS** Univ of Nebraska, Kearney, Kearney, NE 68849. **EMAIL** bloomfields@unk.edu

BLOT, DAVID
PERSONAL Born 05/13/1941, White Plains, NY, m, 1994, 3 children **DISCIPLINE** ENGLISH **EDUCATION** Catholic Univ, BA, 65; Columbia Univ, MA, 75; Fordham Univ, PhD, 91. **CAREER** Assoc, Counseling Learning Inst, 78-; assoc prof, Bronx Community Col, CUNY, 89-. **HONORS AND AWARDS** Grant, Bronx Community Col, 99. **MEMBERSHIPS** CUNY ESL Council. **RESEARCH** How students learn, the relationship of counseling to learning. **SELECTED PUBLICATIONS** Auth, Starting Lines, Heinle & Heinle Pub; auth, Write From the Start, Heinle & Heinle Pub; auth, Put It in Writing, Heinle & Heinle Pub. **CONTACT ADDRESS** Dept English, Bronx Comm Col, CUNY, 2155 University Ave, Bronx, NY 10453-2804.

BLOTNER, JOSEPH LEO
PERSONAL Born 06/21/1923, Plainfield, NJ, m, 1946, 3 children **DISCIPLINE** ENGLISH **EDUCATION** Drew Univ, BA, 47; Northwestern Univ, MA, 47; Univ Pa, PhD, 51. **CAREER** Instr English, Univ Idaho, 53-55; from asst prof to assoc prof, Univ Va, 55-68; prof, Univ NC, Chapel Hill, 68-71; prof English, 72-93, Prof English Emer, 93- , Univ Mich, Ann Arbor, 72-, Fulbright lectr Am lit, Univ Copenhagen, 58-59 & 63-64; Guggenheim fels, 64-65 & 67-68; William Faulkner lectr, Univ Miss, 77; res scholar, Rockefeller Bellagio Ctr, 79; vis prof, Trinity Col, 62, Univ Ariz, 82, & Univ Rome, 84; Off Fr Legion Hon, 97; Am Philos Soc fel; Am Coun Learned Soc fel; NEH fel; Univ NC Chapel Hill, D.Litt., 00. **MEMBERSHIPS** MLA; Am Lit Group; Soc Studies Southern Lit. **RESEARCH** Modern American and British literature; the novel. **SELECTED PUBLICATIONS** Auth, The Political Novel, Doubleday, 55; Fiction of J D Salinger, Univ Pittsburgh, 59; coauth, Faulkner in the University, 59 & auth, William Faulkner's Library: A Catalogue, 64, Univ Va; The Modern American Political Novel: 1900-1960, Univ Tex, 66; Faulkner: A Biography (2 vols), 74 & Selected Letters of William Faulkner, 77, Random; Uncollected Stories of William Faulkner, Random House, 79; coed William Faulkner: Novels 1930-1935, 85, Novels 1936-1940, 90, Novels 1942-1954, 94; auth Robert Penn Warren: A Biography , 97. **CONTACT ADDRESS** 108 Bedford Pl, Charlottesville, VA 22903. **EMAIL** jblotner@aol.com

BLOUIN, LENORA P.
PERSONAL Born 07/07/1941, Seattle, WA, s **DISCIPLINE** LIBRARIAN-REFERENCE **EDUCATION** MA, 72; MLS, 74 **CAREER** Retired in 1996 after 23 years as professional librarian; Senior librarian, head of reference, 86-96, San Jose Public Library. **MEMBERSHIPS** Natl Coalition of Independent Scholars; Modern Language Assoc. **RESEARCH** Bibliography **SELECTED PUBLICATIONS** Auth, May Sarton: A Bibliography, Scarecrow Pr, 78; auth, The Independent Scholar, Some Further Comments on Library Research for Independent Scholars, summer 97; Puckerbrush Review, A Dose of Muses, summer/fall 97, Giving Away, winter/spring 98; The Independent Scholar, Independent Research on May Sarton, winter 97-98; auth, May Sarton: A Revised Bibliography, Scarecrow Pr, 00. **CONTACT ADDRESS** 4571 Madoc Way, San Jose, CA 95130. **EMAIL** Blcknblu@ix.netcom.com

BLOUNT, MARCELLUS
DISCIPLINE AMERICAN AND AFRICAN-AMERICAN LITERARY AND CULTURAL STUDIES **EDUCATION** Williams Col, BA, 80; Yale Univ, PhD, 87. **CAREER** English and Lit, Columbia Univ **HONORS AND AWARDS** Stephen H. Tyng Grant; res fel carter g. woodson inst; vis fel wesleyan's ctr afro-am studies; rockefeller fel ctr study black lit & cult. **SELECTED PUBLICATIONS** Coauth, In a Broken Tongue: Rediscovering African-American Poetry. **CONTACT ADDRESS** Columbia Univ, 2960 Broadway, New York, NY 10027-6902.

BLOXAM, M. JENNIFER
DISCIPLINE MUSIC **EDUCATION** Yale Univ, PhD. **CAREER** Assoc prof, Williams Col, 86. **HONORS AND AWARDS** NEH; Martha Baird Rockefeller Fund & Fulbright Found. **RESEARCH** Exegesis and narrative in medieval and Renaissance music and the arts; musical borrowing; compositional process; the cultural context of music. **SELECTED PUBLICATIONS** Publ on late medieval plainsong and sacred polyphony, J Amer Musicological Soc, Early Mus Hist, J Musicol; Plainsong in the Age of Polyphony, Cambridge, 92; Hearing the Motet, Oxford, 96; Continuities and Transformations in Musical Culture, 1450-1500, Oxford, 96; publ on, Haydn in The Haydn Yearbk; contribur, to the new ed of Musik in Geschichte und Gegenwart, rev ed, The New Grove Dictionary of Music and Musicians. **CONTACT ADDRESS** Music Dept, Williams Col, 54 Chapin Hall Dr., Williamstown, MA 01267.

BLUES, THOMAS
PERSONAL Born 06/16/1936, Detroit, MI, m, 1958, 2 children **DISCIPLINE** ENGLISH **EDUCATION** Univ Mich, BA, 58; Univ Iowa, MA, 60, PhD(English), 66. **CAREER** Asst prof, 65-70, Assoc Prof English, Univ KY, 70-, Fulbright lectr, Univ Warsaw, 71-72. **MEMBERSHIPS** MLA; Am Studies Asn. **RESEARCH** American literature 1860 to present; Black literature. **SELECTED PUBLICATIONS** Auth, The strategy of compromise in Mark Twain's boy books, Mod Fiction Studies, spring 68; Mark Twain and the Community, Univ Ky, 70; The moral structure of Catch-22, Studies in Novel, spring 71; Is There Life After Baseball?: Philip Roth's The Great American Novel, Am Studies, spring 81. **CONTACT ADDRESS** Dept of English, Univ of Kentucky, 500 S Limestone St, Lexington, KY 40506-0003.

BLUESTEIN, GENE
PERSONAL Born 05/01/1928, Bronx, NY, m, 1949, 4 children **DISCIPLINE** AMERICAN LITERATURE **EDUCATION** Brooklyn Col, BA, 50; Univ Minn, MA, 53, PhD(Am studies), 60. **CAREER** From instr to asst prof English, Mich State Univ, 59-63; from asst prof to assoc prof, 63-71, Prof English, Calif State Univ, Fresno, 71-, Carnegie Found fel, 57-58; James J Hill Family Found fel, 58; Calif State Cols & Univs fel, 67; Fulbright-Hays lectr, Helsinki Univ, 67-68. **MEMBERSHIPS** Philol Asn Pac Coast. **RESEARCH** American studies; folklore; American literature. **SELECTED PUBLICATIONS** Auth, The Strzegowa Ghetto--Holocaust Memorial Book Honoring The Victims Of Nazi Persecutions--The Way It Began, Yiddish, Vol 0010, 96. **CONTACT ADDRESS** Dept of English, California State Univ, Fresno, Fresno, CA 93710.

BLUME, DONALD THOMAS
PERSONAL Born 05/25/1964, Hartford, CT, s **DISCIPLINE** LITERATURE **EDUCATION** Case W Reserve Univ, BA, 87; Univ Del, MA, 89; Fla State Univ, PhD, 00. **CAREER** Asst prof, Central Conn State Univ, 00-01. **MEMBERSHIPS** MLA; ALA; Frank Norris Soc; W. D. Howells Soc. **RESEARCH** Ambrose Bierce; American literature between 1865 and 1914; Virginia Woolf and George Mallory, Leslie Stephen and 19th-century British mountaineering. **SELECTED PUBLICATIONS** Auth, Ambrose Bierce's Civilians and Soldiers in Context: A Critical Study, Kent State UP, (forthcoming). **CONTACT ADDRESS** 400 Trout Brook Dr, West Hartford, CT 06110-1034. **EMAIL** rcblume@snet.net

BLUMENTHAL, ANNA
PERSONAL Born 02/07/1952, Providence, RI, d, 1 child **DISCIPLINE** ENGLISH; AMERICAN LITERATURE **EDUCATION** Univ Rochester, BA, 74; Wash Univ-St Louis, MA, 76; PhD, 86. **CAREER** Asst prof, Morris Brown Col, 89-93; asst prof, 93-97, assoc prof, 97- , Morehouse Col. **HONORS AND AWARDS** Who's Who in Am; Who's Who in the S & SW; Fac Res Network Schol, 99. **MEMBERSHIPS** MLA **RESEARCH** American literature. **SELECTED PUBLICATIONS** Auth, "The Ambivalence of Stance in Edwin Arlington Robinson's Early Poems and Letters," Style 23.1, pp 87-112, (89); authy, "Edwin Arlington Robinson's 'Tilbury Town' Poems and William James," The Dalhousie Rev 71.4, pp 411-437, (91/92); co-auth, "From 'Participant' Stance to 'Spectator' Stance in African American Letters", The Negro Educ Rev 48.1-2, pp 71-80, (97); auth, "'Joe urner's Come and Gone': Sacrificial Rites and the Rebirth of the Self" Postscript 15: pp53-65, (98). **CONTACT ADDRESS** Dept English, Morehouse Col, 830 Westview Dr SW, Atlanta, GA 30314-3773. **EMAIL** ablument@morehouse.edu

BLUMENTHAL, EILEEN
DISCIPLINE THEATER HISTORY AND CRITICISM **EDUCATION** Brown Univ, BA, MA; Yale, PhD. **CAREER** Instr, Rutgers, The State Univ NJ, Univ Col-Camden; consult, Nat Endowment for the Arts. **HONORS AND AWARDS** Woodrow Wilson fel, 68; Kent (Danforth) fel, 74; Guggenheim fel, 88; George Jean Nathan Awd for Dramatic Criticism, 89; Asian Cult Coun grant, 90; Soc Sci Res Coun grant, 90; NEH fel, 92; Rockefeller Found Bellagio Residency, 93. **RESEARCH** The royal performing arts of Cambodia. **SELECTED PUBLICATIONS** Auth, Joseph Chaikin, Cambridge UP, 84. **CONTACT ADDRESS** Dept of Theater Arts, Rutgers, The State Univ of New Jersey, New Brunswick, 33 Livingston Ave, New Brunswick, NJ 08901-1959. **EMAIL** msomvill@rci.rutgers.edu

BLYN, ROBIN
DISCIPLINE CONTEMPORARY FICTION **EDUCATION** Temple Univ, MA; Univ Wash, PhD. **CAREER** Instr, 97-. **RESEARCH** Influence of spectacle culture on the twentieth-century experiments in the novel. **SELECTED PUBLICATIONS** Auth, Memory Under Reconstruction: Beloved and the Fugitive Past, Ariz Quart; Freak Fictions: Kafka, Barnes and the Modern Spectacle. **CONTACT ADDRESS** Dept of Eng, Westfield State Col, 577 Western Ave., Westfield, MA 01085.

BLYTHE, STUART
DISCIPLINE TECHNOLOGY AND WRITING **EDUCATION** Purdue Univ, BA, 86; Univ Ill, MA, 90; Purdue Univ, PhD, 97. **CAREER** Grad instr, Univ Ill, 87-89; Part-time instr, Purdue Univ, 89-92; Grad instr, Purdue Univ, 92-97; Asst prof, W Ky Univ, 97-99; asst prof, Ind Univ-Purdue Univ, Fort Wayne, 99-. **HONORS AND AWARDS** Phi Beta Kappa, Nat Writing Ctrs Asn Dissertation Fell, 96; Purdue Research Found Summer Res Grant, 96; Excellence Tchg Bus Writing, 94-96; Golden Key Nat Honor Soc; Sigma Tau Delta. **MEMBERSHIPS** Nat Counc Tchs Eng; Conference Col Composition & Comm; Asn Tchs of Technical Writing; MLA; Nat Writing Ctrs Asn; Alliance Computers & Writing; Ky Coun of Tchs Eng. **RESEARCH** Professional and technical writing with a particular focus on pedagogy. **SELECTED PUBLICATIONS** Auth, Toward Usable OWLs: Incorporating Usability Methods into Writing Center Research; Wiring the Center, Univ Utah Press, 98; Technology in the Writing Center: Strategies for Implementation & Maintenance, Nat Writing Ctrs Asn, 98; Writing Centers + Networked Computers = ? Thinking About Computer Technology and Writing Center Practice, Writing Ctr Jour, 97; Coauth, A Discussion on Collaborative Design Methods for Collaborative Online Spaces Nat Writing Ctrs Asn. **CONTACT ADDRESS** Dept of English and Ling, Indiana Univ-Purdue Univ, Fort Wayne, 2101 E Coliseum Blvd, Classroom Med Bldg 117, Fort Wayne, IN 46805. **EMAIL** blythes@ipfw.edu

BOARDMAN, KATHY
DISCIPLINE ENGLISH AND AMERICAN LITERATURE **EDUCATION** Univ Nebr, BA, 69; Univ Wash, MA, 70; Univ Nebr, Lincoln, PhD, 92. **CAREER** Instr, dir, Core Writing prog, Univ Nev, Reno. **RESEARCH** Western American writers. **SELECTED PUBLICATIONS** His essays on autobiographical writing and western American writers have appeared in scholarly journals and special-interest newsletters. **CONTACT ADDRESS** Dept of Eng, Univ of Nevada, Reno, Reno, NV 89557. **EMAIL** kab@unr.edu

BOATWRIGHT, MARY T.
PERSONAL Born 04/16/1952, VA, m, 1981, 2 children **DISCIPLINE** CLASSICS **EDUCATION** Stanford Univ, BA, 73; Univ per Stranieri Perugia, Laurea voto ottimo, 74; Univ of Mich, MA, 75, PhD, 80. **CAREER** ICCS, grad Asst, 76-77, Duke Univ; A W Mellon Asst Prof, Asst Prof, Assoc Prof, Prof 79-, Chmn dept Classics 79-99, ICCS Rome; A W Mellon Prof in charge, 92-93. **HONORS AND AWARDS** Phi Beta Kappa, Borso di Studio, Duke Endowment Awd Excellence in Teaching, G A & E G Howard Found Fel, NEH Fel. **MEMBERSHIPS** APA, AIA, SPRS, AAH, SFAAR. **RESEARCH** Social & cultural history during the Imperial Roman period, Roman women, Roman cities. **SELECTED PUBLICATIONS** Auth, Hadrian and the Cities of the Roman Empire, Princeton Univ Press, 00; co-ed, The Shapes of City Life in Rome and Pompeii, Essays in Honor of L Richardson Jr on the Occasion of his Retirement, Caratzas, 00; auth, Hadrian and the City of Rome, Princeton Univ Press, 97; auth, Imperial Women of the Early Second Century A C, Amer J of Philology, 91; Hadrian and Italian Cities, Chiron, 89. **CONTACT ADDRESS** Dept of Classical Studies, Duke Univ, Durham, NC 27708-0103. **EMAIL** tboat@duke.edu

BOBBITT, CURTIS W.
PERSONAL Born 12/12/1951, Muncie, IN, s **DISCIPLINE** ENGLISH **EDUCATION** Ind Univ, BA, 74; MS, 76; Ball State Univ, PhD, 89. **CAREER** Teacher, Connerville High School, 74-77; Instructor, Ball State Univ, 82-87; Prof, Univ Great Falls, 87-. **HONORS AND AWARDS** Fac Merit Development Awd, 96; Learn and Serve Fac Fel, 89, **MEMBERSHIPS** Nat Coun of Teachers of English, Mod Lang Asn, Intl Soc of Technol in Educ, Asn for Supervision and Curriculum Development, Am Asn of Univ Prof, Teachers and Writers Collaborative, Nat Writing Project. **CONTACT ADDRESS** School of Hist, Lang and Lit, Univ of Great Falls, 1301 20th St S, Great Falls, MT 59405-4934. **EMAIL** cbobbitt@ugf.edu

BOBINSKI, GEORGE SYLVAN
PERSONAL Born 10/24/1929, Cleveland, OH, m, 1953, 2 children **DISCIPLINE** LIBRARY AND INFORMATION SCIENCE, HISTORY **EDUCATION** Case Western Univ, BA, 51, MLS, 55; Univ of Mich, MA, 61, PhD, 66. **CAREER** Ref asst, Cleveland Pub Libr, 54-55; asst dir, Royal Oak Pub Libr, 55-59; dir of libraries, SUNY Col at Cortland, NY, 60-67; asst dean/assoc prof, Sch of Libr Sci, Univ of Ky, 67-70; Dean and Prof, Sch of Infor and Libr Studies, Univ at Buffalo, 70-99; Prof, 99-. **HONORS AND AWARDS** Beta Phi Mu Int Libr Sci Hon Soc; Fulbright Sch Lectr, Univ of Warsaw, 77; Vis Sch, Jagiellonian Univ-Krakow, 92, 97; Meritorious Medal, 97. **MEMBERSHIPS** Am Libr Asn; Asn for Libr and Infor Sci Educ. **RESEARCH** History of Libraries; Library Education; Comparative Librarianship-Poland. **SELECTED PUBLICATIONS** auth, Carnegie Libraries: Their History and Impact on American Public Library Developments, ALA, 69; auth, Dictionary of American Library Biography, Libraries Unlimited, 78; auth, "The Golden Age of American Librarianship 1945-1970," Wilson Libr Bull, 84; ed, "Current and Future Trends in Library and Information Science, " Libr Trends; auth, "Carnegie Libraries: Their Current and Future Status," Public Libraries, 92; "Libraries in the Democratic Process," Jagiellonian Press, 95. **CONTACT ADDRESS** Sch of Infor and Libr Studies, SUNY, Buffalo, Buffalo, NY 14260. **EMAIL** bobinski@acsu.buffalo.edu

BOCHIN, HAL WILLIAM
PERSONAL Born 02/23/1942, Cleveland, OH, m, 1975, 1 child **DISCIPLINE** SPEECH COMMUNICATION **EDUCATION** John Carroll Univ, BA, 64; Univ Wis-Madison, MA, 67; IN Univ, Bloomington, PhD(speech), 70. **CAREER** Asst prof, 69-75, assoc prof, 75-77, Prof Speech Commun & Dir Forensics, CA State Univ, Fresno, 78-. **HONORS AND AWARDS** Meritorious Performance Awds, 88, 90; Outstanding Prof, 97. **MEMBERSHIPS** Am Forensics Asn; Nat Commun Asn. **RESEARCH** History of American public address; argumentation; rhetorical criticism. **SELECTED PUBLICATIONS** Auth, Caleb B Smith's opposition to the Mexican War, Ind Mag Hist, 6/73; Controlling Land Use: Issues & Evidence, Alan, 75; contribr, American broadcasting: A source book on the history of radio and TV, Hastings House, 75; coauth, The San Francisco simulation, Commun Educ, 3/77; auth, Law Enforcement: Issues & Evidence, Alan, 77; coauth, with Michael A. Weatherson, Hiram Johnson: A Bio-Bibliography, Greenwood Press, 88; auth, Richard Nixon: Rhetorical Strategist, Greenwood Press, 90; President Nixon's First Inaugural Address, in Halford Ryan, ed, The Inaugural Addresses of Twentieth Century American Presidents, Praeger, 93; Richard Milhous Nixon, in Halford Ryan, ed, U. S. Presidents as Orators, Greenwood Press, 95; coauth, with Michael A. Weatherson, Hiram Johnson: Political Revivalist, Univ Press of Am, 95; auth, Marcus Moziah Garvey, in Richard Leeman, ed, African-American Orators: A Bio-Critical Sourcebook, Greenwood, 96; President Clinton's First Inaugural Address, in Lloyd Rohler, ed, Great Speeches for Criticism and Analysis, Alistair Press, 97. **CONTACT ADDRESS** Dept of Commun, California State Univ, Fresno, 5201 N Maple, Fresno, CA 93740-9739. **EMAIL** halb@csufresno.edu

BOCK, CAROL A.
DISCIPLINE 19TH-CENTURY BRITISH LITERATURE **EDUCATION** Univ Wis, Madison, PhD. **CAREER** Assoc prof, Univ Minn, Duluth. **SELECTED PUBLICATIONS** Auth, Charlotte Bronte and the Storyteller's Audience, Univ Iowa Press, 92. **CONTACT ADDRESS** Dept of English, Univ of Minnesota, Duluth, Duluth, MN 55812-2496. **EMAIL** cbock@d.umn.edu

BOCK, MARTIN F.
DISCIPLINE MODERN ENGLISH, IRISH AND AMERICAN LITERATURE **EDUCATION** Univ Wis, Madison, PhD. **CAREER** Assoc prof, Univ Minn, Duluth. **SELECTED PUBLICATIONS** Auth, Crossing the Shadow-line: The Literature of Estrangement,Ohio State UP, 89. **CONTACT ADDRESS** Dept of Eng, Univ of Minnesota, Duluth, Duluth, MN 55812-2496.

BODDEWYN, JEAN J.
PERSONAL Born 02/03/1929, Brussels, Belgium, m, 1979, 3 children **DISCIPLINE** MANAGEMENT AND STRATEGY, BUSINESS AND SOCIETY, AND MARKETING **EDUCATION** Univ Louvain, Belgium, commercial eng, 51; Univ Ore, MBA, 52; Univ Wash, PhD, Bus Admin. **CAREER** Galeries Anspach, Belgian dept store, market res and systems anal, 52-55; Jantzen Inc, time and motion study, 55-57; Univ Portland Ore, asst prof bus admin, 57-64; NY Univ, full prof of intl bus, 64-73; Baruch Col CUNY, full prof of intl bus, 73-. **HONORS AND AWARDS** Fulbright scholar, 51-52; fel, Acad of Mgt, 74; fel, Acad of Intl Bus, 80; fel, Intl Acad Mgt, 81. **MEMBERSHIPS** Acad Intl Bus; Acad Mgt; Europ Intl Bus Acad; Intl Asn for Bus and Soc. **RESEARCH** International regulation and self-regulation of advertising; International standardization of marketing policies; Political behavior of business firms at home and abroad. **SELECTED PUBLICATIONS** Auth, Global Perspectives on Advertising Self-Regulation, Westport, CT, Quorum Books, 92; papers in prof jour, American Marketing in the European Union: Standardization's Uneven Progress in 1973-1993, with Robert Grosse, Europ Jour of Marketing, 29, 12, 23-42, 95; The Legitimacy of International-Business Political Behavior, The Intl Trade Jour, 9, 1, 143-161, spring, 95; articles, Cigarette Advertising Bans and Cigarette Consumption: The Flawed Policy Connection, Intl Jour of Advert, 13, 4, 325-345, 94; The Taxation of Advertising: A Review of Current Issues, Jour of Current Issues & Res in Advert, 16, 1, 1-13, spring, 94; The Domain of International Management, Journal of International Management, 99; International-Business Research: Beyond Deja Vu, Management International Review 39, 99; with Jacques Picard and Robert Grosse, Centralization and Autonomy in International-Marketing Decision Making: A Longitudinal Study (1973-1993) of U.S. MNEs in the European Union, Journal of Global Marketing, 12, 98; chapters in books, Is International Business a Distinct Field of Inquiry?, in B. Toyne and D. W. Nigh, International Business: Institutions and the Dissemination of Knowledge, Columbia, SC, Univ SC Press, 17-23, 97; The Conceptual Domain of International Business: Territory, Boundaries, and Levels, in B. Toyne and D. W. Nigh, International Business Inquiry: An Emerging Vision, Columbia, SC, Univ SC Press, 50-61, 101-102, 97; Political Resources and Markets in International Business: Beyond Porter's Generic Strategies, in A. M. Rugman and A. Verbeke, Global Competition: Beyond the Three Generics, Research in Global Strategic Management, vol 4, Greenwich, CT, JAI Press, 83-99, 93; articles, Centralization and Autonomy in International-Marketing Decision Making: A Longitudinal Study (1973-1993) of U.S.

MNEs in the European Union, Journal of Global Marketing, 98, with Jacques Picard and Robert Grosse; The Domain of International Management, Journal of International Management, 5, 99; International Business Research: Beyond Deja Vu, Management International Review, 99. **CONTACT ADDRESS** 372 Fifth Ave., Apt 9K, New York, NY 10018. **EMAIL** jjmsbodde@aol.com

BODE, ROBERT FRANCIS

PERSONAL Born 10/14/1944, Baltimore, MD **DISCIPLINE** ENGLISH LITERATURE **EDUCATION** Loyola Col, BS, 66; Univ SC, MA, 69; PhD, 70. **CAREER** Asst prof, 70-76, Assoc Prof Eng, Tenn Technol Univ, 76-88, Prof 88-, Chairperson, Dept of English, 95-. **MEMBERSHIPS** S Atlantic Mod Lang Asn; Southeastern Am Soc Eighteenth Cent Studies. **RESEARCH** Seventeenth century British drama; metaphysical poetry, Chaucer. **SELECTED PUBLICATIONS** Auth, A Back-To-The-Future--Formation Plus Back-Formation And The Etymology Of Contraption, Amer Speech, Vol 0068, 93. **CONTACT ADDRESS** Dept of English, Tennessee Tech Univ, Cookeville, TN 38505. **EMAIL** rbode@tntech.edu

BODEL, JOHN

PERSONAL Born 01/25/1957, Sharon, CT, m, 1979, 2 children **DISCIPLINE** CLASSICS **EDUCATION** Princeton Univ, BA, 78; Univ Mich, MA, 79, PhD, 84. **CAREER** Asst dir, 83, co dir, 91, 95, Am Acad Rome; asst prof to assoc prof, 84-92; Harvard Univ; vist asst prof, Brown Univ, 92-93; dir to assoc prof to chemn to prof, 94-, Rutgers Univ. **HONORS AND AWARDS** NEH Res Fel, 93; Fel, 82-83, trustee, 99-01, Am Acad Rome; Pres, Am Society of Greek and Latin Epigraphy, 98-00; Dir, US Epigraphy Project, 95-. **RESEARCH** Latin epigraphy; Latin literature; Roman history. **SELECTED PUBLICATIONS** Auth, Roman Brick Stamps in the Kelsey Museum, 83; auth, Graveyards and Groves: A Study of the Lex Lucerina, 94; auth, art, Monumental Villas and Villa Monuments, 97; coauth, Greek and Latin Inscriptions in the USA: A Checklist, 97; auth, ed, Epigraphic Evidence: Ancient Hist from Inscriptions, 00. **CONTACT ADDRESS** Dept of Classics, Rutgers, The State Univ of New Jersey, New Brunswick, 131 George St, New Brunswick, NJ 08901-1414. **EMAIL** bodel@rci.rutgers.edu

BODI, SONIA

PERSONAL Born 06/24/1940, Chicago, IL, m, 1966, 3 children **DISCIPLINE** LIBRARY SCIENCE **EDUCATION** Augustana Col, BA, 62; Univ Edinburgh, Scot, 60-61; Dominican Univ, MALS, 77; Northwestern Univ, MA, 86. **CAREER** Teach, Gemini Jr. HS, Niles, 62-64; teach, Nagoya Intl Sch, Nagoya, Japan,64-65; teach, Old Orchard Jr. HS, Skokie, 65-67; teach, Northwest Church Play Sch, Chicago, IL, 71-75; ref lib, Wilmette Pub Library, Wilmette, IL, 77-79; ref lib, Kendall Col, Evanston, IL, 79-81; prof, North Park Univ, 81-; Hd ref lib, 81-96; lib dir, 96-; div chair, 88-99. **HONORS AND AWARDS** Phi Beta MU; Best Res Pap Awd, IACRL, 98; Top Twenty Pub Art, ALA, 95. **MEMBERSHIPS** CLSBD; CCIC-CMP; IACRL; ILA; ACRL; ALA; Pres, Lincolnwood Bd Edu. **RESEARCH** Bibliographic Instruction in academic libraries. **SELECTED PUBLICATIONS** Auth, "Relevance in Library Instruction: The Pursuit," Coll Res Libraries 45 (84): 59-65; auth, "Critical Thinking and Bibliographic Instruction: The Relationship," J Academic Librarianship 14 (88): 150-153; auth, "Teaching Effectiveness and Bibliographic Instruction: The Relevance of Learning Styles," Coll Res Libraries 51(90): 113-119; auth, "Collaborating with Faculty in Teaching Critical Thinking; The Role of Librarians," Res Strategies 10 (92): 69-72; auth, "Propaganda or Scholarship: How Librarians Can Help Students Tell the Difference," J Academic Librarianship. 21 (95): 21-25; "Ethics and Information Technology: Some Principles to Guide Students," J Academic Librarianship. 24 (98): 459-463. **CONTACT ADDRESS** Dept Library, No Park Univ, 3225 West Foster Ave, Chicago, IL 60625. **EMAIL** sbodi@northpark.edu

BODLING, KURT A.

DISCIPLINE HISTORICAL THEOLOGY, LIBRARY SCIENCE **EDUCATION** Concordia Col, AA, 74; Concordia Sen Col, BA, 76; Concordia Sem, MDiv, 80, MST, 86; Univ Ill, MS; Fordham Univ, PhD cand. **CAREER** Ref, res asst, 81-86; asst dir, ref svcs, 86-87, Concordia Hist Inst; free-lance ed, Concordia Pub, 88-89; assoc lib, Winterthur Mus, 90-91; dean, spiritual life, 95-96, COL ARCH, 93- , asst prof, 91-98, ASSOC PROF, RELIG, 98-, DIR LIBR SVCS, 91-, CONCORDIA COL. **HONORS AND AWARDS** Beta Phi Mu. **MEMBERSHIPS** Soc of Am Archivists, Am Library Society, Asn of Col and Res Libraries. **RESEARCH** Am Lutheran History; Religious History of Am. **CONTACT ADDRESS** Concordia Col, New York, 171 White Plains Rd., Bronxville, NY 10708.

BODO, MURRAY

PERSONAL Born 06/10/1937, Gallup, NM, s **DISCIPLINE** ENGLISH **EDUCATION** St Anthony Novitiate, 55-56; profession of solemn vows, 56-60, BA, Duns Scotus Col, 59; ed for & ordination to the Priesthood, St Leonard Col, 60-64; Xavier Univ, MA, 67; Univ of Cincinnati, doctoral in English, 92-. **CAREER** Internship, St Boniface Parish, 64-65; English teacher, St Francis High School Seminary, 65-77; Provincial Board, Franciscan Province of St John the Baptist, 76-79; staff, Assisi Summer Pilgrimages, 76-88; prof, chair of English dept, dir of Young Friars, Duns Scotus Col, 77-79; instr, English, Chatfield Col, 87-92; ASST PROF OF ENGLISH, WERITER IN RESIDENCE, THOMAS MORE COL, 91-. **HONORS AND AWARDS** Cincinnati Editors' Awd, 79; 3rd Prize for Poetry, Catholic Press Asn, 84; Belly of the Whale Awd, 91. **MEMBERSHIPS** Acad of Am Poets and Franciscan Acad. **RESEARCH** Franciscana and Medieval Poetry. **SELECTED PUBLICATIONS** Auth, Transcribing the Life of The Little Priest, Provincial Chronicle, 98; auth, The Dalai Lama Visits Merton's Home, St Anthony Messenger, 97; auth, Followers of Francis: Fray Angelico Chaves, St Anthony Messenger, 96; coauth, The Basilica of St Francis, The Cord, 96; auth, A Retreat with Francis and Clare of Assisi, St Anthony Messenger Press, 96; auth, The Threefold Way of St. Eramis, Paulist Press, 00; auth, Poetry as Prayer: Denise Levertoo, Pauline Books, 01; auth, St. Francis' Office of the Passion, Messagero Press, Milano/Franciscan Institute; auth, "Signatures of Grace: Catholic Writers on the Sacraments," Holy Orders, (Dutton/Penguin, 00); auth, "Fray Angelico Chavez, Poet, Priest, and Artist," The Frances of Fray Angelico Chavez, (Univ of New Mexico Press, 00). **CONTACT ADDRESS** 1723 Pleasant St., Cincinnati, OH 45210. **EMAIL** mbodo51278@aol.com

BODON, JEAN

PERSONAL Born 11/05/1949, Paris, France, m, 1994, 1 child **DISCIPLINE** FILM & TELEVISION **EDUCATION** Birmingham S Col, BA, 73; Univ Ala, MA, 76; Fla State Univ, PhD, 83. **CAREER** Film dir, Hidden Fears, 93; film producer, Seven Sundays, 95. **HONORS AND AWARDS** Gold Star, Brussels Festival; Telly Awd. **MEMBERSHIPS** Dir Guild Am; Soc des Realisateurs de Films. **RESEARCH** Cinema **SELECTED PUBLICATIONS** Auth, Cinema: An Introduction, 98; auth, Essays on Chaplin, 85. **CONTACT ADDRESS** 2845 Thornhill Rd, Apt 121B, Birmingham, AL 35213. **EMAIL** bodon@uab.edu

BOEGEHOLD, ALAN

PERSONAL Born 03/21/1927, Detroit, MI, m, 1954, 4 children **DISCIPLINE** CLASSICS **EDUCATION** Univ MI, AB, 50; Harvard Univ, AM, 54, PhD, 58. **CAREER** Instr, asst prof dept classics, Champaign-Urbana, 57-60; from asst prof to prof dept classics, Brown Univ, 60; dir summer session Amer Sch Classical Studies Athens, 63, 64, 74, 80, vis prof, 68-69; dir Ancient studies program Brown Univ, 85-91, chmn dept classics, 66-71, acting chmn, 73-74; visiting lectr hist Harvard Univ, 67; visiting prof classics Yale Univ, 71, Univ CA, Berkeley, 78; mem com to evaluate dept classics Swarthmore Coll, 72, Univ VA, 82, 88, coms humanities and hist Yale Univ Coun, 82-87; interim pres, vp and sec Nargansett Soc Archaeol Inst Am; vice chmn mng com Am Sch Classical Studies,85-90, chmn, 90-98. **HONORS AND AWARDS** Thomas Day Seymour fel Amer Sch Classical Studies Athens, 55-56; Rsch fel, 74-75; Rsch fel Agora Excavations, 80-81; Charles Eliot Norton fel Amer Sch Classical Sudies Athens; Howard fel, 56-57; grantee Amer Coun Learned Socs, 80-81. **MEMBERSHIPS** Active ACLU; Amnesty Internat; Providence Athenaeum; Mass Audubon Soc; Common Cause **RESEARCH** Greek History, Literature, and Art. **SELECTED PUBLICATIONS** Ed, Athenian Identity and Civic Ideology, 93; auth, ed, Agora XXVIII, Law Courts at Athens, 95; auth, When A Gesture Was Expected, 99. **CONTACT ADDRESS** Dept of Classics, Brown Univ, 48 College Hill St, Providence, RI 02912-9079.

BOGEL, FREDRIC V.

PERSONAL Born 07/18/1943, Newark, NJ, m, 1996, 3 children **DISCIPLINE** ENGLISH **EDUCATION** Dartmouth Col, AB, 65; Yale Univ, PhD, 71. **CAREER** Instr, Conn Col, 69-81; vis prof to prof, Cornell Univ, 81-; distinguished vis prof, Cornell Col, 95. **HONORS AND AWARDS** Stephen and Margery Russell Distinguished Teaching Awd, 00; Nominated, Stephen H. Weiss Pres Fell, 94, 99; Paramount Prof Awd, 92, 93; Soc Humanities Fel, Cornell Univ, 89-90; James L. Clifford Prize, 83; FIPSE Grant, Conn Col , 80. **RESEARCH** 18th-century British and American literature; critical theory. **SELECTED PUBLICATIONS** Auth, Acts of Knowledge: Pope's Later Poems, Associated Univ Pr (Lewisburg, Pa), 81; auth, Lit and Insubstantiality in Later Eighteenth-Century England, Princeton Univ Pr, 84; auth, "Did you once see Johnson plain?: Reflections on Boswell's Life and the State of Eighteenth-Century Studies," in Boswell's Life of Johnson: New Questions, New Answers, ed. John A Vance (Ga: Univ of Ga Pr, 85): 73-93; co-ed, "Understanding Prose," in Teaching Prose: A Guide for Writing Instructors, eds. Fredric V. Bogel, Katherine K. Gottschalk (NY: W. W. Norton, 88): 155-215; co-ed, "Teaching Prose: A Guide for Writing Instructors, W. W. Norton (NYork), 88; auth, "The Dream of My Brother": An Essay on Johnson's Authority (Victoria, Brit Colum: Univ Victoria Mono, 90); auth, The Difference Satire Makes: Rhetoric and Reading from Johnson to Byron, Cornell Univ Pr, 01. **CONTACT ADDRESS** PO Box 420, Aurora, NY 13026-0420. **EMAIL** fvb1@cornell.edu

BOGUS, DIANE ADAMZ

PERSONAL Born 01/22/1946, Chicago, IL, m, 1989 **DISCIPLINE** AMERICAN LITERATURE **EDUCATION** Stillman Coll Tuscaloosa AL, BA 1968; Syracuse Univ Syracuse NYork, MA 1969; Miami Univ Oxford OH, PhD 1988; Univ of Hawaii, PhD, parapsychology, 1998. **CAREER** LA Southwest Coll, instructor, 76-81; Miami U, instructor, 81-84; WIM Publications, author, 71-, founder, 79-, publisher; California State Univ, Stanislaus Turlock, CA, prof of American literature, 86-90; De-Anza College, Cupertino, CA, instructor, 90-. **HONORS AND AWARDS** Honored by Art & Music Dept Trenton Public Lib 1983; works adapted into CA State Univ Archives 1982; nominated for Pulitzer Prize, Sapphire's Sampler 1982; nominated for Lambda Literary Awd for The Chant of the Women of Magdalena; Black Writer's Awd from Peninsula Book Club, 1992; Woman of Achievement Awd, 1997. **MEMBERSHIPS** Mem Delta Sigma Theta Sorority 1965-; mem Nat Tchrs of Engl 1981-; mem Feminist Writer's Guild 1980-; mem COSMEP Independent Publishers 1975-; board member, Multicultural Publishers Exchange, 1989-92. **CONTACT ADDRESS** WIM Publications, PO Box 2087, Cupertino, CA 95015.

BOIARSKY, CAROLYN

PERSONAL Born 05/31/1942, Philadelphia, PA, 1 child **DISCIPLINE** ENGLISH **EDUCATION** Georgia State Univ, PhD, 84; Loyola Univ, Los Angeles, MA, 71; Univ Penn, BA, 63. **CAREER** Assoc Prof of English, Purdue Univ Columet, 95-; Instr, Illinois Central Col, 90-93; Asst Prof of English, Illinois State Univ, 84-90. **HONORS AND AWARDS** Frank R. Smith Outstanding Journal Article Awd, 98. **MEMBERSHIPS** NCTE; Society of Technical Communications; IEEE/PCS. **RESEARCH** Technical Communication; Transfer of Information; Writing in the Workplace. **SELECTED PUBLICATIONS** Auth, "Technical Writing: Contexts, Audiences, Communities," Published by Allyn & Bacon; auth, "Writing from the Workplace: Documents, Models, Cases," Published by Allyn & Bacon; auth, "The Art of Workplace Writing," Published by Boynitor/Cook. **CONTACT ADDRESS** Dept English & Philosophy, Purdue Univ, Calumet, 2233 171st St, Hammond, IN 46323.

BOLCHAZY, LADISLAUS J.

PERSONAL Born 06/07/1937, Slovakia, m, 1965, 1 child **DISCIPLINE** CLASSICS AND PHILOSOPHY **EDUCATION** St. Joseph's Col & Sem, NYork, BA, philos, 63; NYork Univ, MA, classics, 67; SUNY Albany, PhD, classics, 73. **CAREER** Latin/eng, Iona Prep, 64-65; Latin/eng, Sacred Heart High Sch, 62-64; instr, Siena Col, 66-67; asst prof, La Salette Col and Sem, 71-75; visiting asst prof, Millersville State Univ, 75-76; visiting asst prof, Loyola Univ of Chicago, 76-77; adjunct prof, Loyola Univ of Chicago, 79-; pres, Bolchazy-Carducci Publ Inc. **HONORS AND AWARDS** NEH summer inst, ancient hist, Univ Mich, 77; NEH summer sem, Sophocles and Thucydides, Cornell Univ, 76; teaching fel, State Univ of NY Albany, 67-71; res grants, Loyola Univ, spring and summer, 77. **MEMBERSHIPS** Amer Philol Asn. **RESEARCH** History of ethical & theological concepts; Stylometric analysis of language. **SELECTED PUBLICATIONS** Auth, Hospitality in Antiquity, Ares Publ, Chicago, 96; auth, A Concordance to Ausonius, George Olms, Hildesheim, 83; auth, The Coin-Iscriptions and Epigraphical Abbreviations of Imperial Rome, Ares Publ, 78; auth, A Concordance to the Utopia of St. Thomas More, Georg Olms, Hildesheim, 78; auth, Hospitality in Early Rome, Ares Publ, Chicago, 77. **CONTACT ADDRESS** Ladislaus J. Bolchazy, PhD, Bolchazy-Carducci Publishers, Inc, 1000 Brown St., No 101, Unit 101, Wauconda, IL 60084. **EMAIL** classics@bolchazy.com

BOLIN, JOHN SEELYE

PERSONAL Born 09/20/1943, Ft Bragg, NC, m, 1965, 1 child **DISCIPLINE** DRAMATIC LITERATURE, THEATRE HISTORY **EDUCATION** Kalamazoo Col, BA, 65; Univ MI, Ann Arbor, MA, 65, PhD, 70. **CAREER** Prof eng & theatre ,Berea Col, 70, dir repertory theatre festival, 81-83, Assoc dean Gen Educ, 89-94, Dean Fac, 98-; Mellon Found, Berea Col, Sabbatical fel, 77-78. **HONORS AND AWARDS** Kellog Nat Fel, 83-86; Canadian Embassy, Fac Res Grant, 94-95. **MEMBERSHIPS** AAUP; William Morris Soc; Asn Canadian Studies in U S; Midwestern Asn canadian Studies; KY Hum Coun, bd mem,, Asn Am Col and Univ, 94-98. **RESEARCH** Theatre aesthetics; theatre hist; criticism of drama. **SELECTED PUBLICATIONS** Auth, var rev & articles on Canadian Theatre and drama. **CONTACT ADDRESS** Dept of Eng, Berea Col, 101 Chestnut St, Berea, KY 40404-0003. **EMAIL** john_bolin@berea.edu

BOLING, BECKY

DISCIPLINE WOMEN WRITERS **EDUCATION** Northwestern State Univ, PhD. **CAREER** Literature, Carleton Col. **SELECTED PUBLICATIONS** Areas: Griselda Gambaro, Carlos Fuentes, Gabriel Garcia Marquez, Ana Lydia Vega, and Luisa Valenzuela. **CONTACT ADDRESS** Carleton Col, 100 S College St., Northfield, MN 55057-4016.

BOLSTERLI, MARGARET JONES

PERSONAL Born 05/10/1931, Watson, AR, 2 children **DISCIPLINE** ENGLISH, CULTURAL HISTORY **EDUCATION** Univ Ark, BA, 53; Wash Univ, MA, 53; Univ Minn, PhD(English), 67. **CAREER** Asst prof English, Augsburg Col, 67-68; Prof English, Univ Ark, 68-, Nat Endowment Humanities

Younger Humanist Award, 70-71; Ark Endowment Humanities grant, 80-81. **MEMBERSHIPS** MLA; SCent Mod Land Asn; Am Asn State & Local Hist. **RESEARCH** Nineteenth century Britain; the American south; women's studies. **SELECTED PUBLICATIONS** Auth, Porter,Katherine,Anne and Texas, Mod Fiction Stud, Vol 0038, 92; An Interview with Bolsterli,Margaret,Jones, Ark Hist Quart, Vol 0055, 96; Warren,Robert,Penn And The American Imagination--Mod Fiction Stud, Vol 0038, 92. **CONTACT ADDRESS** Dept of English, Univ of Arkansas, Fayetteville, Fayetteville, AR 72701.

BOLTON, JONATHAN W.
PERSONAL Born 12/21/1961, Binghamton, NY, m, 1989, 2 children **DISCIPLINE** ENGLISH **EDUCATION** Univ Miami, BBA, 84; CUNY Brooklyn Col, MA, 91; Univ Md, PhD, 96. **CAREER** Asst Prof to Assoc Prof, Auburn Univ, 96-. **HONORS AND AWARDS** Alice Geyer Dissertation Prize, Univ Md; S Atlantic Rev Essay Prize; Camp War Eagle Fac Honoree, Auburn Univ,; Cardinal Key Honor Soc Fac Honoree, Auburn Univ. **MEMBERSHIPS** S Atlantic MLA; D.H. Lawrence Soc; Lawrence Durrell Soc. **RESEARCH** Twentieth-Century British and Irish Literature; Poetry; Irish Studies; Culture Studies. **SELECTED PUBLICATIONS** Auth, "W.H. Auden's 'Hearing of harvests rotting in the valleys'," The Explicator, 94; co-auth, "Native American Scholars, Writers, and Professionals," in Facts on File, 94; auth, "The Historian with His Spade: Landscape and Historical Continuity in the Poetry of Bernard Spencer," J of Mod Lit, 95; auth, "Personal Landscape and the Poetry of the 1940s," Deus Loci, 96; auth, "Empire and Atonement: Geoffrey Hill's 'An Apology for the Revival of Christian Architecture in England'," contemporary Literature, 97; auth, Personal Landscapes: British Poets in Egypt during the Second World War, St Martins's Press, 97; auth, "Lines (In)formation: Anglophone Poetry of the Second World War," in World War II in Asia and the Pacific and the War's Aftermath, with General Themes: A Handbook of Literature and Research, 98; auth, "Irish Stew at the Cafe du Monde: Heterogeneity and the Emigre Experience in Paul Muldoon's 'Yarrow',: S Atlantic Rev, 99; auth, "Customary Rhythms: Seamus Heaney and the Rite of Poetry," Papers on Language and Literature, 01. **CONTACT ADDRESS** Dept English, Auburn Univ, 9030 Haley Center, Auburn, AL 36849. **EMAIL** boltojw@auburn.edu

BOLZ, BARBARA J.
DISCIPLINE COMMUNICATION **EDUCATION** Oakland Univ, BA; Wayne State Univ, MA, PhD. **CAREER** Prof, Univ Detroit Mercy, 89-. **HONORS AND AWARDS** Elizabeth Youngjohn Teaching awd, Wayne State Univ. **RESEARCH** Public speaking, public opinion, mass media, political campaign and organizational communication. **CONTACT ADDRESS** Dept of Communications, Univ of Detroit Mercy, 4001 W McNichols Rd, PO Box 19900, Detroit, MI 48219-0900. **EMAIL** BOLZBY@udmercy.edu

BOMBERGER, E. DOUGLAS
PERSONAL Born 11/15/1958, Lancaster, PA, m, 1982, 2 children **DISCIPLINE** HISTORICAL MUSICOLGY **EDUCATION** Univ of MD-Col Park, PhD, 91, Univ of NC-Chapel Hill, MM, 83, Goshen IN Col, BA, 81. **CAREER** Univ of HI-Manoa assoc prof, 98-, asst prof, 94-98 Ithaca Col asst prof, 92-94 Sweet Briar Col lectr, 89-90, Goshen Col asst prof, 83-87. **HONORS AND AWARDS** Deutscher Akademischer Austauschdienst fel, 90-91 Irving Lowens Student Research in Music Award, 88 Dean's Fel, Univ of MD, 87-89. **MEMBERSHIPS** Am Musicological Soc, ch, Capital Chapter, 93-94; Col Music Soc; Soc for Am Music; Am Liszt Soc. **RESEARCH** Am and Ger music of the late 19th century, hist and lit of the piano. **SELECTED PUBLICATIONS** Auth, "Opera in Context", ed. Mark A. Radice (Amadeus, 98), auth, Brainard's Biographies of American Music, (Greenwood 99); auth, Articles in "Piano Roles", ed. James Parakilas (Yale, 99); Musical Quarterly, Notes, American Music, etc. **CONTACT ADDRESS** Univ of Hawaii, Manoa, 2411 Dole Street, Honolulu, HI 96822. **EMAIL** edb@hawaii.edu

BONACCORSO, RICHARD L.
PERSONAL Born 04/15/1941, New York, NY, m, 1977, 2 children **DISCIPLINE** ENGLISH **EDUCATION** Villanova Univ, BA, 63; MA, 70; Univconn, PhD, 72. **CAREER** Eastern Conn State Col, 68-74; Prof, Central Conn State Univ, 75-. **MEMBERSHIPS** Am Conf for Irish Studies, Irish-American Cultural Inst. **RESEARCH** Modern Irish literature; The short story tradition. **SELECTED PUBLICATIONS** Auth, Sean O'Faolain's Irish vision, State Univ of New York Press, 87; auth, "Cork, paris, and the rule of the river: O'Faolain and Maupassant," Connecticut Review, (90): 35-38; auth, "The end of an Irish Lover's Quarrel," Irish Literary supplement, (91): 18; auth, "Back to 'foundry House': brian Friel and the short Story," Canadian Journal of Irish Studies, (91): 72-77; auth, "Seamus Heaney an the Integrity of Poetry," American Catholic, (95): 15-16; auth, "Not Noticing History: Two Tales by William Trevor," connecticut Review, (96): 21-27; auth, "Personal Devices: Two Representative Stories by Brian Friel," colby Quarterly, (96): 93-99; auth, Willim Trevor's Martyrs for Truth," studies in short Fiction, (97): 113-118; auth, "Love's Progress: Stories by William Trevor," Connecticut Review, (99): 17-24 **CONTACT ADDRESS** Dept English, Central Connecticut State Univ, 1615 Stanley St, New Britain, CT 06053-2439. **EMAIL** bonaccorsor@ccsu.edu

BONENFANT, JOSEPH
PERSONAL Born 04/29/1934, St-Narcisse Champlain, PQ, Canada, m, 1960, 2 children **DISCIPLINE** LITERATURE **EDUCATION** Univ Laval, BA, 57; Univ Montreal, LLL, 59; Univ Paris, DrUniv, 66. **CAREER** Teacher French, Latin and Greek, Col Brebeuf, Montreal, 59-63; Prof French Lit, Univ Sherbrooke, 66-, Co-ed, Ellipse, Writers in Transl, 69-; Consult, Can Coun Arts, 71- and Humanities Res Coun Can, 72- **RESEARCH** French critics; le mouvement litteraire dans les Cantons de l' Est: 1925-1950; subventionne par le Conseil des Arts du Canada. **SELECTED PUBLICATIONS** Auth, The Pragmatic Approach to Poetry, Etudes Litteraires, Vol 0025, 92. **CONTACT ADDRESS** Dept of French Studies Fac of Arts, Univ of Sherbrooke, Sherbrooke, QC, Canada J1K 2R1.

BONESTEEL, MARGARET D.
PERSONAL Born 10/02/1946, Beaver Falls, PA, s, 2 children **DISCIPLINE** ENGLISH, COMPOSITION **EDUCATION** Wittenberg Univ, AB, 68; Syracuse Univ, MS, 88; EdD, 94. **CAREER** Teacher, Liverpool Central Schools, 68-73; instr, SUNY Oswego, 73-74; writing consultant, instr, director, Syracuse Univ, 90-. **MEMBERSHIPS** NCTE, CCCC, AAHE, MLA, NACEP. **RESEARCH** Professional Development incentives and impact, Classroom communities. **SELECTED PUBLICATIONS** Coauth, "College Teaching: An Art or a Science?" Student ratings of Instruction: Issues for Improving Practice, ed J Franklin and M Theale, (San Francisco: Jossey Bass, 90). **CONTACT ADDRESS** Syracuse Univ, 400 Ostrom Ave, Syracuse, NY 13244-0001. **EMAIL** mdbonest@advance.syr.edu

BONGIE, CHRIS
PERSONAL Born 03/07/1960, Vancouver, BC, Canada **DISCIPLINE** ENGLISH, COMPARATIVE LITERATURE **EDUCATION** Univ Brit Columb, BA, 82; Stanford Univ, AM, 78; PhD, 82. **CAREER** Asst to assoc prof, director, Col of William and Mary, 94-. **HONORS AND AWARDS** Mellon Fel, 93-94; NEH Grant, 01-02. **RESEARCH** 19th and 20th Century French and Francophone literature, cultural studies, Victorian Literature. **SELECTED PUBLICATIONS** Auth, Exotic Memories: Literature, Colonialism, and the Fin de Siecle, Stanford Univ Pr, 91; auth, Islands and Exiles: The Creole Identities of Post/Colonial Literature, Stanford Univ Pr, 98. **CONTACT ADDRESS** Dept English, Col of William and Mary, Williamsburg, VA 23187-8795. **EMAIL** clbong@wm.edu

BONNER, THOMAS, JR.
PERSONAL Born 09/19/1942, New Orleans, LA, m, 1966, 2 children **DISCIPLINE** ENGLISH **EDUCATION** Tulane Univ, Phd; Tulane Univ, MA; Southeastern LA Univ, BA. **CAREER** Xavier Univ, prof; Xavier Review Journal, editor. **HONORS AND AWARDS** Dist vis prof, USAF; Henry C McBay Fel; Bush Excell in Tchg Awd; Andrew W Mellon Postdoctoral Fellow; exec com Soc for the study of Southern Lit; **MEMBERSHIPS** SO Cent Modern Lang Assoc, Pres, Exec Com Society for the Study of Southern Literature, Exec Com South Central Conference on Christianity and Literature. **RESEARCH** Southern lit and writers who have worked in New Orleans. **SELECTED PUBLICATIONS** Auth, William Faulkner: The William B. Wisdom Collection, 80; The Kate Chopin Companion, 88; editor of Above Ground, 93 and Immortelles, 95. **CONTACT ADDRESS** Dept of English, Xavier Univ, Louisiana, 25 W. Pk. Pl., New Orleans, LA 70125. **EMAIL** tbonner@xula.edu

BONNYMAN-STANLEY, ISABEL
PERSONAL Born 04/12/1943, Knoxville, TN, m, 1963, 3 children **DISCIPLINE** ENGLISH **EDUCATION** BA, 77, MA, 82, East Tennessee State Univ; Univ Tennessee, PhD, 90. **CAREER** Assoc Prof, English, 83-, East Tennessee State Univ. **MEMBERSHIPS** Modern language Association; Tennessee Philogical Association; Women in Higher Education in Tennessee; Sigma Tau Delta; Chi Omega. **RESEARCH** 19th and 20th Century British Literature; Women Writer and Women's Studies. **SELECTED PUBLICATIONS** Numerous short articles. **CONTACT ADDRESS** Dept of English, East Tennessee State Univ, Johnson City, TN 37614. **EMAIL** stanleyi@etsu.edu

BONO, BARBARA JANE
PERSONAL Born 08/08/1948, Poughkeepsie, NY, m, 1970, 1 child **DISCIPLINE** ENGLISH LITERATURE, HISTORY OF IDEAS **EDUCATION** Fordham Univ, AB, 70; Brown Univ, PhD, 78. **CAREER** Instr, 75-78, Asst Prof English, Univ Mich, Ann Arbor, 78-82; prof, 82-, dept chair, SUNY Buffalo. **HONORS AND AWARDS** Mellon Fel, Harvard Unic, 83-84; Junior Fel, Cornell Soc for the Humanities, 82-83; SUNY Chancellor's Awd for Excellence in Teaching, 89; NEH Summr Inst, 96; Milton Plesur Undergraduate Student Awd for Excellence in Teaching, 92-93. **MEMBERSHIPS** MLA; Renaissance Soc Am. **RESEARCH** Renaissance intellectual history; English and comparative literature; genre criticism. **SELECTED PUBLICATIONS** Auth, Literary Transvaluation from Vergilian Epic to Shakespearean Tragicomedy, Calif Pr, 84; auth, "Mixed Gender, Mixed Genre in Shakespeare's As You Like It," Rosalind, 92; auth, '"the chirf Knot of All the Discourse': The Maternal Subtext Tying Sidney's Arcadia to Shakespeare's King Lear," Gloriana's Face: Women, Public and Private, in the Englihs Renaissance, 92; auth, Medicine and Shakespeare in the English Renaissance, Lit Med, Vol 0012, 93; The Birth of Tragedy--Tragic Action in Julius Caesar, Engl Lit Renaissance, Vol 0024, 94; auth, "The Birth of Tragedy: Tragic Action in Julius Caesar," English Literary Renaissance 24 (94): 449-70. **CONTACT ADDRESS** Dept of English, SUNY, Buffalo, 306 Clemens Hall, PO Box 604610, Buffalo, NY 14260. **EMAIL** bbono@acsu.buffalo.edu

BOOKER, JOHN T.
DISCIPLINE NINETEENTH-CENTURY LITERATURE **EDUCATION** Univ MN, PhD. **CAREER** Assoc prof, Univ KS. **RESEARCH** French novel **SELECTED PUBLICATIONS** Publ(s), on Stendhal, Balzac, Constant, Gide, and Mauriac. **CONTACT ADDRESS** Dept of French and Italian, Univ of Kansas, Lawrence, Admin Building, Lawrence, KS 66045.

BOOKER, M. KEITH
DISCIPLINE MODERN BRITISH AND IRISH LITERATURE **EDUCATION** Univ Fla, PhD. **CAREER** English and Lit, Univ Ark. **SELECTED PUBLICATIONS** Auth, Literature and Domination: Sex, Knowledge, and Power in Modern Fiction, Fla, 93; Vargas Llosa among the Postmodernists, Fla, 94; Flann O'Brien, Bakhtin, and Menippean Satire, Syracuse, 95; Joyce, Bakhtin, and the Literary Tradition: Toward a Comparative Cultural Poetics, Mich, 96;), A Practical Introduction to Literary Theory and Criticism, Longman, 96; : Colonial Power, Colonial Texts: India in the Modern British Novel, Mich, 97. **CONTACT ADDRESS** Univ of Arkansas, Fayetteville, Fayetteville, AR 72701.

BOON, KEVIN A.
PERSONAL Born 10/13/1956, Tampa, FL, d **DISCIPLINE** ENGLISH, AMERICAN STUDIES **EDUCATION** Univ S Fla, BA, 83; MA, 91; PhD, 95. **CAREER** Instr, Univ S Fla, 95-96; instr, Univ Alabama, 96-97; asst prof, Maritime Col, SUNY, 97-00; asst prof, Pa State, 00-. **HONORS AND AWARDS** Hon Men, USF Fic Con; Eng Poetry Awd; Anspaugh Fic Awd; Flora Zbar Grad Teach Awd. **MEMBERSHIPS** NYCEA; MLA. **RESEARCH** 20th Century literature and culture; Kurt Vonnegut; Chaos Theory; Technology; Film; Science and Literature. **SELECTED PUBLICATIONS** Auth, Chaos Theory and the Interpretation of Literary Texts: The Case of Kurt Vonnegut, Edwin Mellon Press, 97; auth, An Interpretive Commentary on Virginia Woolf's The Waves, Edwin Mellon Press, 98; auth, Reading the Sea: New Essays on Sea Literature, Ft Schuyler Press, 99; auth, Absolute Zero, Ft Schuyler Press, 99; auth, At Millennium's End: New Essays on the Work of Kurt Vonnegut, SUNY Press, in press; auth, "Efrem Zimbalist, Sr," Scribner Encycl Am Lives v2 (98); auth, "In Defense of John Carpenter's Thing," Creat Screen Writ 44 (99): 66-74; auth, "Mrs Mallory's Mummified Dog," Lullwater Rev 6 (95): 35-43; auth, "Last Rites," Sandhill Rev (95): 14-17; auth, "Clean and Simple," Sandhill Rev (forthcoming); auth, "Railroad Men," Sandhill Rev (95); auth, "In the Corridors of the Cardiac Unit," Poetry Motel (98). **CONTACT ADDRESS** Dept Humanities, SUNY, Maritime Col, 6 Pennyfield Ave, Bronx, NY 10465-4127.

BOOS, FLORENCE SAUNDERS
PERSONAL Born 11/11/1943, Santa Barbara, CA, m, 1965, 1 child **DISCIPLINE** ENGLISH LITERATURE, WOMEN'S STUDIES **EDUCATION** Univ Mich, BA, 64; Harvard Univ, AM, 65; Univ Wis, PhD, 72. **CAREER** Instr English, Univ Sask, 70-71; asst prof, 73-77, assoc prof, 77-81, Prof English, Univ Iowa, 82-, Old Gold fel, Univ Iowa, 74 & 79, fac res grant, 75-76; bibliog, Women & Lit, 74-77, assoc ed, 75-80; Bunting fel, 80-81; Univ Iowa fac scholar, 81-84; Fulbright sr lectr, Univ Iceland, fall 85; NEH fel, Univ Iowa, summer 92. **HONORS AND AWARDS** Woodrow Wilson Nat fel, 64-65; Douglas Stuart fel, Queen's Univ, 66-67; Fac scholar award, Univ Iowa, 75, 90; Fac development assignment, Univ Iowa, 97. **MEMBERSHIPS** Midwest Victorian Studies Asn; MLA; Women's Caucus Mod Lang; Res Soc Victorian Periodicals; Hopkins Soc. **RESEARCH** Social and cultural history of Britain from the eighteenth century to the present; Victorian poetry. **SELECTED PUBLICATIONS** Auth, Catharine Macaulay's Letters on Education 1790: An Early Feminist Polemic, Univ Mich Papers Woman's Studies, No 2; The Poetry of Dante Gabriel Rossetti: A Critical and Source Study, Mouton, The Hague, 75, reprinted, in Nineteenth-Centruy Literature Criticism, Gale Res Co, 83; ed, Socialist Diary, Windhover Press, 81; The Juvenillia of William Morris, William Morris Soc, 82; ed, Bibliography of Women and Literature, 1975-80, 2 vol, Holmes and Meier, 88; ed & contrib, Socialism and the Literary Artistry of William Morris, Univ Mo Press, 90; The Design of William Morris's The Earthly Paradise, Edwin Mellen Press, 91; ed, & contrib, History and Community: Essays in Victorian Medievalism, Garland Publ, 92; guest ed, William Morris: 1896-1996, Victorian Poetry, winter 96; The Earthly Paradise by William Morris, vol I and II, Garland Publ, 00. **CONTACT**

ADDRESS Dept of English, The Univ of Iowa, 308 English Phil Bld, Iowa City, IA 52242-1492. **EMAIL** florence-boos@uiowa.edu

BOOSE, LYNDA E.

DISCIPLINE ENGLISH LITERATURE **EDUCATION** UCLA, PhD. **CAREER** Prof, Dartmouth Col. **RESEARCH** Shakespearean drama; Renaissance and women's lit. **SELECTED PUBLICATIONS** Auth, The Priest, the Slanderer, the Historian, and the Feminist; Eng Lit Ren, 95; The Taming of the Shrew, Good Husbandry, and Enclosure in Re-Reading Shakespeare, Cornell UP, 94; The Getting of a Lawful Race: Racial Discourse in Early Modern England and the Unrepresentable Black Woman in Women, 'Race,' and Writing in the Early Modern Period, Routledge, 94; co-ed, Daughters and Fathers,. The Johns Hopkins UP, 88, rptd 93. **CONTACT ADDRESS** Dartmouth Col, 3529 N Main St, #207, Hanover, NH 03755. **EMAIL** lynd.e.boose@dartmouth.edu

BOOTH, PHILIP

PERSONAL Born 10/08/1925, Hanover, NH, m, 1946, 3 children **DISCIPLINE** ENGLISH **EDUCATION** Dartmouth Col, AB, 48; Columbia Univ, AM, 49. **CAREER** Instr English, Bowdoin Col, 49-50; asst to dir admis, Dartmouth Col, 51-52, instr English, 53; from instr to asst prof, Wellesley Col, 54-61; assoc prof, 61-66, prof english, Syracuse Univ, 66-. **HONORS AND AWARDS** Hokin Prize, 55; Lamont Prize, 56; Saturday Rev poetry Awd, 57; Phi Beta Kappa Poet, Columbia Univ, 62; co-recipient, Emily Clark Balch Prize, 64; Nat Inst Arts and Lett Awd, 67; Theodore Roethke Prize, 70; Guggenheim fel, 58-59 and 65; Rockefeller Found fel, 68; Nat Endowment for Arts fel, 80; dlitt, colby col, 68. **MEMBERSHIPS** PEN Club; Acad Am Poets. **RESEARCH** Contemporary poetry; poetry workshops; the novel. **SELECTED PUBLICATIONS** Auth, Writing it Down--Poetry, 97; Rivers, Sam and the Rivbea Orchestra, Down Beat, 96; Identification, Shenandoah, 97; Seven States, Shenandoah, 96; Three Awakenings in New England, New England Rev Middlebury Ser, 94; A Dog Skin From Asthall, Intl J Osteoarchaeology,96; Sarasota Jazz Club--To Serve all Ages, Down Beat, 93; Letter to the Poetry Editor, Gray-Flannel Poets, Concord, Mass, Oct 7, 1957, Chicago Rev, 96; Key Views, Ga Rev, 95; March Again, Poetry, 93; Swinging at the Sandbox, Down Beat, 93; Drew, Kenny--Father and Son on 2 Pianos, Down Beat, 93; Ages, Poetry, 95; Outlook, Poetry, 93; Sentences, Am Poetry Rev, 94; Half Life, Am Poetry Rev, 94; Fog-Talk, Am Poetry Rev, 94; Talk about Walking, Am Poetry Rev, 94; Backcountry, Am Poetry Rev, 94; Nov Sun, Poetry, 93; Late Wakings, Ga Rev, 96; Coming to, Poetry, 96; Sixty Six, Am Poetry Rev, 94. **CONTACT ADDRESS** Box 330, Castine, ME 04421.

BOOTH, STEPHEN

PERSONAL Born 04/20/1933, New York, NY, m, 1959, 2 children **DISCIPLINE** ENGLISH, DRAMA, & VERSE **EDUCATION** Harvard Col, AB, 55; Cambridge Univ, Trinity Col, BA, 57, MA, 60; Harvard Univ, PhD(English), 64. **CAREER** From asst prof to assoc prof English, 62-74, prof English, Univ Calif, BerkeleY, 74-, Nat Endowment for Humanities fel, 68; Guggenheim Found fel, 70-71. **HONORS AND AWARDS** Marshall Scholar, Trinity College, Cambridge, 55-57; James Russell Lowell Prize for 1977, awarded 78 (for Shakespeare's Sonnets, ed with Commentary); Distinguished Teaching Awd, Univ of Ca, Berkeley, 82; Doctor of Humane Letters, Georgetown Univ, May 91; OBE (Office of the British Empire), July 95. **MEMBERSHIPS** MLA; Shakespeare Asn Am. **RESEARCH** Aesthetics; Shakespeare. **SELECTED PUBLICATIONS** Auth, An Essay on Shakespeare's Sonnets, Yale Univ, 69; The Book Called Holinshead's Chronicles, Bk Club San Francisco, 69; On the Value of Hamlet, In: Reinterpretations of Elizabethan Drama, Columbia Univ, 69; ed, Shakespeare's Sonnets, Yale Univ, 77; auth, Shakespeare at Valley Forge, Shakespeare Quart, 27, 231-42, 76; Syntax as Rhetoric in Richard II, in Mosaic, x.3, 87-103, 77; Speculation on Doubling in Shakespeare's Plays, in Shakespeare: The Theatrical Dimension, ed P.C. McGuire and D.A. Samuelson, New York, 79; Henry IV, Part Two and the Aesthetics of Failure, in Shakespeare Plays, ed V.L. Lee, Dubuque, 80; Exit Pursued by a Gentleman Born, in Shakespeare's Art from a Comparative Perspective, ed W.M. Aycock, pp 51-66, Lubbock, 81; Milton's "How soon hath time": A Colossus in a Cherrystone, ELH, 49, 449-67, with Jordan Flyer, 82; King Lear, Macbeth, Indefinition, & Tragedy, New Haven, 83; Poetic Richness: A Preliminary Audit, in Pacific Coast Philology, XIX, No 1-2, 68-78, 84; Twelfth Night, l.i: The Audience as Malvolio, in Shakespeare's Rough Magic: Renaissance Essays in Honor of C.L. Barber, ed Peter Erikson and Coppelia Kahn, pp. 149, Newark, Delaware, 85; The Shakespearean Actor as KamikazePilot, Shakespeare Quart, 36, 553-70, 85; The Function of Criticism at the Present Time and All Others, Shakespeare Quart, 41, 262-68, 90; Liking Julius Ceasar (pamphlet), Ashland, Oregon, 91; Close Readings Without Readings, in Shakespeare Reread: The Texts in New Contexts, ed Russ McDonald, pp 42-55, Ithaca: Cornell, 94; The Coherences of 1 Henry IV and of Hamlet, in Shakespeare Set Free: Teaching Hamlet and 1 Henry IV, ed Peggy O'Brian, pp 32-46, New York: Washington Square Press, 95; Shakespeare's Language and the Language of Shakespeare's Time, Shakespeare Survey 50, 1-17, 98; A Long, Dull Poem by William Shakespeare, Shakespeare Studies, 25, 229-37, 98; Precious Nonsense: The Gettysburg Address, Ben Johnson's Epitaphs on His Children, and Twelfth Night, Berkeley, 98. **CONTACT ADDRESS** Dept of English, Univ of California, Berkeley, 322 Wheeler Hall, Berkeley, CA 94720-1030.

BOOTH, WAYNE CLAYSON

PERSONAL Born 02/22/1921, American Fork, UT, m, 1946, 2 children **DISCIPLINE** ENGLISH LITERATURE **EDUCATION** Brigham Young Univ, AB, 44; Univ Chicago, AM, 47, PhD, 50. **CAREER** Instr, Univ Chicago, 47-50; asst prof English, Haverford Col, 50-53; prof and head dept, Earlham Col, 53-62; Pullman prof, 62-70, dean col, 64-69, chmn com ideas and methods, 73-75, Distinguished Serv Prof English, Univ Chicago, 70-, Fels, Ford fac, 52-53, Guggenheim, 56-57 and 69-70, Ind Univ, 62, Am Acad Arts and Sci, 72, Nat Endowment for Humanities, 75-76 and Rockefeller, 81-82; vis consult, US-SAfrica Leader Exchange Prog, 63; consult, Danforth Found, 63-69; mem bd trustees, Earlham Col, 65-75; co-ed, Critical Inquiry, 74- **HONORS AND AWARDS** Christian Gauss Awd, Phi Beta Kappa, 62; David H Russell Awd, NCTE, 66; Fel, Am Academic of Arts and Sci(s); Am Philosophical Soc; honorary degrees from thirteen colleges and universities; lld, rockford col, 65, st ambrose col, 71 and univ nh, 77. **MEMBERSHIPS** MLA; NCTE; Conf Col Compos and Commun; AAUP; Acad Lit Studies. **RESEARCH** Theory of literary criticism; 18th century English literature; theory and practice of rhetoric. **SELECTED PUBLICATIONS** Auth, The Rhetoric of Fiction, 61; auth, A Rhetoric of Irony and Modern Dogma and the Rhetoric of Assent, 74; auth, Critical Understanding: The Power and Limits of Pluralism, 79; coauth, The Harper and Row Reader, 84; auth, The Vocation of a Teacher and The Company we Keep: An Ethics of Fiction, 88; auth, The Art of Growing Older, 92; coauth, The Craft of Research, 95; auth , For the Love of It: Amateuring and Its Rivals, 99. **CONTACT ADDRESS** Dept of English, Univ of Chicago, Chicago, IL 60637.

BORCK, JIM SPRINGER

PERSONAL Born 08/16/1941, New Orleans, LA, m, 1977 **DISCIPLINE** ENGLISH LITERATURE **EDUCATION** Univ Fla, BA, 63; MA, 65; Univ Calif, Riverside, PhD (English), 69. **CAREER** Asst prof, 69-80, Prof English, LA State Univ, Baton Rouge, 80-. **HONORS AND AWARDS** Univ of Calif vis scholar, 77-78; NEH Improvement of Instruction grant, 80-81. **MEMBERSHIPS** MLA; SCent Mod Lang Asn. **RESEARCH** Eighteenth century Romantics; History of the book; Textual editing; Bibliography; Computer assisted scholarship. **SELECTED PUBLICATIONS** Auth, "Bunyan's Mr. Badman, Presented," Review (90); auth, "Wordsworth's 'The Prelude' and the Failure of Language," Essential Articles in Nineteenth-Century Criticism (Gale Research Inc., 92); auth, "Composed in Tears: The Clarissa Project," Studies in the Novel (95); auth, "An Appreciation of Donald Greene," The East-Central Intelligencer (97); project dir, The Clarissa Project, Samuel Richardson's Published Commentary on Clarissa, 1747-1765, 4 vols, 98; ed, The Eighteenth Century: A Current Bibliography. **CONTACT ADDRESS** Dept of English, Louisiana State Univ and A&M Col, Baton Rouge, LA 70803-0001. **EMAIL** eneccb@lsuvm.sncc.lsu.edu

BORDEN, DIANE M.

DISCIPLINE ENGLISH LITERATURE **EDUCATION** Lone Mountain Col, BA, 64; San Francisco State Univ, MA, 66; Univ CA, PhD, 71. **CAREER** Prof, Univ Pacific. **HONORS AND AWARDS** Graves Tchg Awd; UOP Spanos Tchg Awd. **SELECTED PUBLICATIONS** Auth, publ(s) on Bergman, De Sica, Bertolucci, Henry James, Wallace Stevens, Ezra Pound, Fassbinder, and Antonioni. **CONTACT ADDRESS** Eng Dept, Univ of the Pacific, Stockton, Pacific Ave, PO Box 3601, Stockton, CA 95211.

BORDEN, SANDRA L.

PERSONAL Born 11/07/1963, Argentina, m, 1986 **DISCIPLINE** MASS COMMUNICATION **EDUCATION** Univ of Mo, BJ, 85; Ohio State Univ, MA, 91; Indiana Univ, PhD, 97. **CAREER** Instr, Middle Tenn State Univ, 91-92; asst prof, Western Mich Univ, 96- . **HONORS AND AWARDS** Nom. for AEJMC Nafziger-White dissertation award. **MEMBERSHIPS** Asn for Educ in Jour & Mass Commun; Asn for Practical & Prof Ethics; Nat Commun Asn; Central States Commun Asn. **RESEARCH** Media ethics; Ethical discourse; Ethical decision making and organizational culture. **SELECTED PUBLICATIONS** Auth, Emphatic listening: The journalist's betrayal, Jour of Mass Media Ethics, 8 (4), 93; Gotcha! Deciding when sources are fair game, Jour of Mass Media Ethics, 10 (4), 96; Choice processes in a newspaper ethics case, Commun Monographs, 64, 97; Avoiding the pitfalls of case studies, Jour of Mass Media Ethics, 13 (1), 98; coauth, Deceiving sources, Journalism ethics: A reference handbook, eds E.D. Cohen and D. Elliott, 97; rev, Journalists and the community, Jour of Mass Media Ethics, 12 (3), 97. **CONTACT ADDRESS** Dept of Communication, Western Michigan Univ, 1201 Oliver St., Kalamazoo, MI 49008. **EMAIL** sandra.borden@wmich.edu

BOREN, JAMES LEWIS

PERSONAL Born 03/19/1941, Phoenix, AZ, m, 1971, 2 children **DISCIPLINE** ENGLISH LITERATURE **EDUCATION** San Francisco State Univ, BA, 65, Univ of Iowa, MA, 67, PhD(English), 70. **CAREER** Asst prof, 70-76, assoc prof English, Univ Ore, 76-. **HONORS AND AWARDS** Ersted Awd for Distinguished Teaching, Univ Ore, 77; Burlington Northern Foundation Faculty Achievement Awd for Distinguished Teaching, Univ Ore, 87; Arts and Sciences Distinguished Educator Awd, Univ of Oregon, 99. **MEMBERSHIPS** Mediaeval Acad Am; Medieval Asn Pacific; New Chaucer Soc. **RESEARCH** Old English and middle English literature; Chaucer. **SELECTED PUBLICATIONS** Auth, Form and meaning in Cynewulf's Fates of the Apostles, Papers Lang & Lit, 69; Alysoun of Bath and the Vulgate Perfect Wife, Neuphilologische Mitteilungen, 75; The Design of the Old English Deor, In: Anglo-Saxon Poetry, Univ Notre Dame, 75; Narrative design in the alliterative Morte Arthure, Philol Quart, 77. **CONTACT ADDRESS** Dept of English, Univ of Oregon, Eugene, OR 97403-1286. **EMAIL** jlboren@oregon.uoregon.edu

BORIS, EDNA Z.

PERSONAL Born 02/25/1943, New York, NY, m, 1964, 1 child **DISCIPLINE** ENGLISH **EDUCATION** Hunter Col, BA, 64; Ind Univ, Bloomington, MA, 66, PhD, 74. **CAREER** Assoc instr Eng, IN Univ, 67-68; inst, Shippensburg State Col, 71-72; adj assoc prof, 74-79, asst prof eng, La Guardia Col, 79-, Dir, Words-Worth Assoc; Coordr, writing courses for ABLE prog, Adelphi Univ, 78-80. **MEMBERSHIPS** Board of Trustees Belle Zeller Scholarship Trust Fund; Shaksper electronic conference; Assoc ed Shakespeare and the Classroom; AAUP Comt on Prof Ethics; MLA; Shakespeare Asn; Scribes. **RESEARCH** Shakespeare; business writing; law and lit. **SELECTED PUBLICATIONS** Auth, Pairing of business communications and word processing classes, Am Bus Commun Asn Bull, 9/76; The Tudor Constitution and Shakespeare's two tetralogies, Col Lit, fall 77; Shakespeare's English Kings, The People and the Law, Assoc Univ, 78; The interview in a business writing course, Am Bus Commun Asn Bull, 7/78; A final memo, Am Bus Commun Asn Bull, 3/79; And now it's time to write, Nat Law J, 10/12/81; Co-auth Test your legal writing skills, Docket Call, Am Bar Asn, Spring 82; Classroom minutes: A valuable teacing device, In: Improving college & university teaching, Spring 83; Resumes, resumes, resumes, a student handout, The Bulletin, Dec 91; Teaching Shakespeare: Non-traditional research topics, The Shakespeare Newsletter, Fall 92; A student role in syllabus planning, Exercise exchange, Spring 94; Mastering bibliographic form through collaborative learning, Collaborative learning: a sourcebook for higher education, vol 2, Nat Center on Postsecondary Teaching, Learning, and Assessment, 94; Sentence structure and sentence sense, Perspectives: Teaching legal research and writing, Spring 96; CRASS Summer of 1995, Shakespeare and the classroom, Spring 96; To soliloquize or not to soliloquize, Q/W/E/R/T/Y, Arts, Litteratures & Civilisations du Monde Anglophone, Univ of Pau, France, Oct 96; Sentence sense: We, our, us problems, Perspectives: Teaching legal research and writing, Spring 97. **CONTACT ADDRESS** Dept of Eng, LaGuardia Comm Col, 3110 Thomson Ave, Long Island City, NY 11101-3071. **EMAIL** 104757.652@compuserve.com

BORMANN, DENNIS ROBERT

PERSONAL Born 11/07/1935, Mitchell, SD, m, 1962, 2 children **DISCIPLINE** SPEECH COMMUNICATION, GERMAN **EDUCATION** Univ SDak, 57; Univ Iowa, MA, 59, PhD (speech, drama), 68. **CAREER** Asst prof Speech, Mankato State Col, 64-66; from instr to assoc prof, 66-77, interim chmn speech, 75-77, Prof Speech, Univ Nebr-Lincoln, 77-, Woods fac res fel, Univ Marburg, 73; comn int and intercultural speech commun, Speech Commun As, 77-79. **HONORS AND AWARDS** Fulbright Scholar, 57-58; Wood Fac Res Fel, 72; Maude Hammond Fling Res Fel, 84; George Holmes Res Fel, 89. **MEMBERSHIPS** Nat Commun Asn; AAUP; Phi Beta Kappa; Omicron Delta Kappa; Tau Kappa Alpha; Delta Phi Alpha. **RESEARCH** Rhetorical theory; German rhetoric and poetic; public address. **SELECTED PUBLICATIONS** Auth, "Some Common Sense about Campbell, Hume, and Reid," Quart J Speech 71 (85); auth, "George Campbell's Cura Prima on Eloquence," Quart J Speech, 75 (88); auth, The 6th Canon--Belletristic Rhetorical Theory and Its French Antecedents, Philos Rhet, Vol 0029, 96. **CONTACT ADDRESS** Dept of Speech Cummun, Univ of Nebraska, Lincoln, P O Box 880329, Lincoln, NE 68588-0329. **EMAIL** bormann@unlserve.unl.edu

BORNSTEIN, GEORGE J.

PERSONAL Born 08/25/1941, St Louis, MO, m, 1982, 3 children **DISCIPLINE** ENGLISH LITERATURE **EDUCATION** Harvard Univ, BA, 63; Princeton Univ, PhD, 66. **CAREER** Asst prof, MIT, 66-69; asst prof, Rutgers Univ, 69-70; assoc prof, Univ Mich, 70-75; prof; 75-. **HONORS AND AWARDS** ACLS Fel; NEH Fel; Guggenheim Fel; Teach Awd, Amoco Found; Rosenthal Res Awd. **MEMBERSHIPS** STS; MLA; ACIS. **RESEARCH** Modernist literature; Irish literature; modern poetry; editorial theory. **SELECTED PUBLICATIONS** Auth, Yeats and Shelley, 70; auth, Transformations of Romanticism in Yeats, Eliot, and Stevens, 76; auth, Poetic Remaking: The Art of Browning, Yeats, and Pound, 88; auth, Representing Modernist Texts, 91; ed, W. B. Yeats: The Early Poetry 87, 94; ed, The Iconic Page, 98. **CONTACT ADDRESS** Dept English, Univ of Michigan, Ann Arbor, 505 South State St, 3187 Angell Hall, Ann Arbor, MI 48109-1003. **EMAIL** georgeb@umich.edu

BOROFKA, DAVID
PERSONAL Born 12/07/1954, Los Angeles, CA, m, 1979, 2 children **DISCIPLINE** ENGLISH, CREATIVE WRITING **EDUCATION** Lewis & Clark Col, BA, 76; Univ Ala, MFA, 83. **CAREER** Instr, Reedley Col, 83-. **HONORS AND AWARDS** Miss Rev Editors Prize, 92; Carolina Quarterly's Charles B Wood Awd, 92; Iowa Short Fiction Awd, 96. **MEMBERSHIPS** AWP; MLA. **RESEARCH** Short Fiction. **SELECTED PUBLICATIONS** Auth, "Adagio, 1958", Shenandoah 46.4, (96): 90-106; auth, Hints of His Mortality, Univ of Iowa Pr, (Iowa City), 96; auth, "The Euphemism of Lethal Injection", Writing Voyage, ed, Thomas E Tyner, Wadsworth Pub, (Belmont, 96); auth, The Island, MacMurray & Beck, (Denver, CO), 97; auth, "Prayers and Miracles", Christian Century 114.36, (97)1194-1197; auth, "Nessun Dorma", Bellingham Rev 20.2 (97/98): 24-44; auth, "Business is Rotten", Northwest Rev 36.1 (98): 20-40; auth, "Underland", Things on Heaven and Earth, ed Harold Fickett, Paraclete Pr, (Cambridge, MA), 98; auth, "Monopoly", In the Groove 8, (99): 11-18; auth, "My Life as a Mystic", Image, (forthcoming). **CONTACT ADDRESS** Dept English and Lang, Reedley Col, 995 N Reed Ave, Reedley, CA 93654-2017. **EMAIL** dborofka@ix.netcom.com

BORSCH, FREDERICK HOUK
PERSONAL Born 09/13/1935, Chicago, IL, m, 1960, 3 children **DISCIPLINE** ENGLISH LITERATURE, THEOLOGY **EDUCATION** Princeton Univ, AB, 57; Oxford Univ, MA, 63; Univ Birmingham (UK), PhD, 66. **CAREER** Tutor, Queens Coll, Birmingham (UK), 63-66; assoc prof, Seabury-Western Theol Sem, 66-71; prof, General Theol Sem, 71-72; dean, prof, Church Div Sch of the Pacific, 72-81; dean of chapel, prof, Princeton Univ, 81-88; Bishop, Episcopal Diocese of Los Angeles, 00-. **MEMBERSHIPS** Am Acad Rel; Soc Bib Lit; Studiorum Novi Testamenti Soc; Phi Beta Kappa. **RESEARCH** New Testament theology and literature; early church history. **SELECTED PUBLICATIONS** Auth, The Son of Man in Myth and History, Westminster Press, 67; auth, The Christian and Gnostic Son of Man, SCM Press, 70; auth, God's Parable, Westminster Press, 77; auth, Introducing the Lessons of the Church Year, Seabury Press, 78; auth, Power in Weakness, Fortress Press, 83; ed, Anglicanism and the Bible, Morehouse-Barlow, 84; auth, Many Things in Parables, Fortress Press, 88; auth, Outrage and Hope, Trinity Press Int, 96. **CONTACT ADDRESS** Box 512164, Los Angeles, CA 90051-0164. **EMAIL** bishop@ladiocese.org

BOSCAGLI, MAURIZIA
DISCIPLINE ENGLISH LITERATURE **EDUCATION** Brown Univ, PhD, 90. **CAREER** Assoc Prof, Eng, Univ Calif, Santa Barbara. **RESEARCH** Gender stud and feminist theory; theories of subjectivity; Brit and Europe modernism; theories of mass cult. **SELECTED PUBLICATIONS** Auth, "A Moving Story: Masculine Tears and the Humanities of Televised Emotions," Discourse, 92-3; The Eye on the Flesh: Fashions of Masculinity in the Early Twentieth Century, Westview Press, 96; Translation of Toni Negri's Constituent Power, Univ Minn Press, 96; "The Squat, the Urn, the Tearoom, and the Designer Bathroom: Home to Class in Thatcher's England," Burning Down the House, Westview Press, 96; "Brushing Benjamin Against the Grain," Revising the Canon, Penn State, 96. **CONTACT ADDRESS** Dept of Eng, Univ of California, Santa Barbara, Santa Barbara, CA 93106-7150. **EMAIL** boscagli@humanitas.ucsb.edu

BOSE, SARIKA
PERSONAL Born 03/18/1965, Calcutta, India, s **DISCIPLINE** ENGLISH **EDUCATION** Univ BC, BA, 86; MA, 89; Univ Birmingham, PhD, 99. **CAREER** Teaching asst, Simon Fraser Univ, 96-98; lectr, Univ BC, 99-. **RESEARCH** Oscar Wilde and Drama; Late Nineteenth Century West End Drama; Late Nineteenth Century Women's Writing in Britain; Missionary Accounts; Domestic Space. **SELECTED PUBLICATIONS** Auth, "For Their Native Sisters: The Wesleyan Ladies' Auxiliary in India," in Faces of the Feminine in Early, Medieval and Modern Times, Oxford Univ Press, 00; auth, "Strength in Community," Can Children's Lit, (forthcoming). **CONTACT ADDRESS** Dept English, Univ of British Columbia, 397-1873 E Mall, Vancouver, BC, Canada V6T 1Z1. **EMAIL** sbose@interchange.ubc.ca

BOSMAJIAN, HAMIDA H.
DISCIPLINE ENGLISH **EDUCATION** Univ ID, BA; Univ CT, MA, PhD, 68. **CAREER** Prof, Seattle Univ. **MEMBERSHIPS** MLA, Children's Lit Asn. **SELECTED PUBLICATIONS** Auth, Psychoanalytic Criticism, The International Companion Encyclopedia of Children's Literature, NY: Routledge, 96; Memory and Desire In Sendak's Dear Mili, The Lion and the Unicorn, 19, 95; Mildred Taylor's Story of Cassie Logan: A Search for Law and Justice in a Racist Society, Children's Lit, 24, 96; The Anvil or the Crucible? Narrations of Youthful Experience in Nazi Germany, The Lion and the Unicorn, 13, 91. **CONTACT ADDRESS** Dept of Eng, Seattle Univ, 900 Broadway, 501 Casey, Seattle, WA 98122-4340. **EMAIL** bosmajia@seattleu.edu

BOSTDORFF, DENISE M.
PERSONAL Born 03/25/1959, Bowling Green, OH, m, 1987, 2 children **DISCIPLINE** COMMUNICATION **EDUCATION** Bowling Green State Univ, BA, 82; Univ Ill., MA, 83; Purdue Univ, PhD, 87. **CAREER** Vis asst prof, Purdue Univ, 87-88; from asst prof to assoc prof, Purdue Univ, 88-94; from asst prof to assoc prof, Col of Wooster, 94-. **HONORS AND AWARDS** B. Aubrey Fisher Outstanding Article Awd, Western States Commun Asn, 92; W. Charles Redding Awd for Excellence in Undergrad Tchg, Purdue Univ, 94; School of Liberal Arts Departmental Awd for Educat. Excellence, Purdue Univ, 94. **MEMBERSHIPS** Nat Commun Asn, Ctr for the Study of the Presidency; Central States Commun Asn. **RESEARCH** Anal of polit rhet, particularly presidential rhet, also rhet pertaining to vice presidents and first ladies. **SELECTED PUBLICATIONS** Auth, The Presidency and the Rhetoric of Foreign Crisis, 94; Clinton's Characteristic Issue Management Style: Caution, Conciliation, and Conflict Avoidance in The Case of Gays in the Military, The Clinton Presidency: Issues, Images, & Communication Strategies, ed Robert E. Denton, Jr., and Rachel L. Holloway, 96; Hillary Rodham Clinton and Elizabeth Dole as Running Mates in the 1996 Campaign: Parallels in the Rhetorical Constraints of First Ladies and Vice Presidents, The 1996 Presidential Campaign: A Communication Perspective, ed Robert E. Denton, Jr., 98; coauth, Idealism and Pragmatism in American Foreign Policy Rhetoric: The Case of John F. Kennedy and Vietnam, Presidential Studies Quarterly 24, 94; Values Advocacy: Enhancing Organizational Images, Deflecting Public Criticism, and Grounding Future Arguments, Public Relations Review 20, 94; The Presidency and the Promotion of Domestic Crisis: John Kennedy's Management of the 1962 Steel Crisis, Presidential Studies Quarterly 27, 97. **CONTACT ADDRESS** Dept of Communication, The Col of Wooster, 103 Wishart Hall, Wooster, OH 44691. **EMAIL** dbostdorff@acs.wooster.edu

BOSWELL, JACKSON CAMPBELL
PERSONAL Born 10/02/1934, Whiteville, NC, m, 1969 **DISCIPLINE** ENGLISH LITERATURE, AMERICAN STUDIES **EDUCATION** Univ NC, Chapel Hill, AB, 60, MA, 62; George Wash Univ, MPhil, 73, PhD, 74. **CAREER** Instr English, Col William & Mary, 62-63; Randolph-Macon Woman's Col, 63-65; asst prof, DC Teachers Col, 68-77; Prof English, Univ DC, 77-. **HONORS AND AWARDS** NEH Fel, Folger Shakespeare Libr, 78-79; Fulbright Fel, Brit Libr, Univ London, 81-82. **MEMBERSHIPS** Milton Soc Am; Col Lang Asn; Southeastern Renaissance Conf. **RESEARCH** Renaissance reputations of Chaucer, Dante, Petrarch, Cervantes and others; Am thought and culture; North Atlantic civilization. **SELECTED PUBLICATIONS** Contr, MLA International Bibliography, PMLA, 69-77; auth, Milton's Library, Garland, 75; auth, Register of Paul's Cross Sermons, Dovehouse, 89; auth, Sir Thomas More in the English Renaissance, MRTS, 94; auth, Dante's Fame in England, Delaware/AUP, 99. **CONTACT ADDRESS** Dept of English, Univ of District of Columbia, 4200 Connecticut N W, Washington, DC 20008-1175. **EMAIL** jboswell@udc.edu

BOTAN, CARL H.
DISCIPLINE PUBLIC RELATIONS **EDUCATION** Wayne State, PhD, 85. **CAREER** Assoc prof, Purdue Univ. **SELECTED PUBLICATIONS** Auth, Communication Work and Electronic Surveillance; A Model for Predicting Panoptic Effects, Commun Monogr; International Public Relations: Critique and Reformation, Pub Rel Rev, 92; coauth, Public Relations Theory, Erlbaum, 90; Investigating Communication and Interpreting Communication, Prentice-Hall, 92; A Human Nature Approach to Image and Ethics in International Public Relations, Pub Rel Res, 93. **CONTACT ADDRESS** Dept of Commun, Purdue Univ, West Lafayette, 1080 Schleman Hall, West Lafayette, IN 47907-1080. **EMAIL** cbotan@sla.purdue.edu

BOTTIGHEIMER, RUTH B.
PERSONAL Born 07/14/1939, Salem, NJ, m, 1960, 2 children **DISCIPLINE** ENGLISH **EDUCATION** Univ Calif, BA, 61; Univ Calif, MA, 64; State Univ NY (SUNY), DA, 81. **CAREER** Lectr, Princeton Univ, 81-84; From Asst Prof to Prof, State Univ NYork (SUNY), 84-. **HONORS AND AWARDS** Phi Beta Kappa; Fulbright Vis Fel, Clare Hall Cambridge; Vis Fel, Oxford Univ; Best Book, Children's Lit Asn, 96. **MEMBERSHIPS** Int Soc for Folk Narrative Res, Int Soc for Res in Children's Lit, Children's Lit Asn. **RESEARCH** Folk narrative, illustrations, historical children's literature. **SELECTED PUBLICATIONS** Auth, The Bible for Children: From the Age of Gutenberg to the Present, Yale UP (New Haven), 96; auth, "Fairytales About Fairytales," in Whelks Walk Rev 1.1 (98); 59-62; auth, "Illustration and Imagination," in Fellowship Prog Res Report, Int Inst for Children's Lit (99): 71-106; auth, "Fertility Control and the Birth of the Modern Fairytale Heroine," in Marvels and Tales 14.1 (00): 64-79; auth, Folklore and Gender, Zooni Publ, 99; auth, "Historical Authorship, Commercial Interest and National Attribution: L'Histoire du Vieux et du Nouveau Testament (forthcoming). **CONTACT ADDRESS** Dept English, SUNY, Stony Brook, Stony Brook, NY 11794-3355. **EMAIL** rbottigheime@notes.cc.sunysb.edu

BOUDREAU, GORDON V.
PERSONAL Born 05/17/1929, Marshall, MN, w, 1960, 7 children **DISCIPLINE** ENGLISH **EDUCATION** St Mary's Col, BA, 51; Marquette Univ, MA, 57; Ind Univ, PhD, 67. **CAREER** Instr, Marquette Univ, 57-60; teaching asst, Ind Univ, 60-63; asst prof to assoc prof to prof, LeMoyne Col, 63-94. **HONORS AND AWARDS** NEH, 77; Scholar of Year Awd, 91. **MEMBERSHIPS** MLA; Thoreau Soc; Melville Soc. **RESEARCH** Henry David Thoreau; Herman Melville; religion; literature. **SELECTED PUBLICATIONS** Auth, "Of Pale Ushers and Gothic Piles: Melville's Architectural Symbology," ESQ 18 (72): 67-82; auth, "H.D. Thoreau, William Gilpin, and the Metaphysical Ground of the Picturesque," Am Lit 45 (73): 357-69; auth, "'Remember thy Creator': Thoreau and St. Augustine," ESQ 19 (73): 149-60; auth, "Thoreau and Richard C. Trench: Conjectures on the Pickerel Passage of Walden," ESQ 20 (74): 117-24; auth, The Roots of Walden and the Tree of Life, Vanderbilt UP (Nashville), 90; auth, "'Here Lies . . . Rear-Admiral Van': Thoreau's Crowded Grave," New Eng Quart 56 (83): 523-37; auth, "Transcendental Sport: Hunting, Fishing, and Trapping in Walden," Thought 67 (92): 74-87; auth, "Sauntering after Sixty: Thoreau in the Elderhostel Program," in Approaches to Teaching Thoreau 's Walden and Other Works, ed. Richard J. Schneider (NY: MLA, 96): 192-98. **CONTACT ADDRESS** 306 Millen Dr, North Syracuse, NY 13212-2222. **EMAIL** gordy@dreamscape.com

BOULER, STEVEN W.
PERSONAL Born 03/12/1958, Montgomery, AL, m, 1993 **DISCIPLINE** LITERATURE, COMPOSITION **EDUCATION** Auburn Univ Montgomery, BA, 84; La State Univ, MA, 87; Univ Calif Santa Barbara, PhD. **CAREER** Instr, La State Univ, 87-89; instr, Auburn Univ Montgomery, 89-90; instr, Tuskegee Univ, 90-93; instr, Santa Fe Community Col, 93-94; instr, Col of Santa Fe, 93-94; instr, Ohlone Col, 95-97; lectr, Calif State Univ Hayward, 95-97; lectr, Cominican Col San Rafael, 96-98; TA, UCSB, 96-99; asst prof, Univ of Judaism, 00-. **HONORS AND AWARDS** Univ of Calif Fel, 97-98. **MEMBERSHIPS** MLA, Am Soc for Theatre Res, Samuel Johnson Soc of S Calif, Am Soc for 18th Century Studies, Int Samuel Johnson Soc, Calif Educ Theatre Assoc, Am Inst of Archit Students. **RESEARCH** 18th Century Theatre History and Literature, Samuel Johnson, Theatre Architecture, Performance Studies. **CONTACT ADDRESS** Univ of Judaism, 15600 Mulholland Dr, Bel Air, CA 90077-1599. **EMAIL** bouler@mindspring.com

BOURNE, LESLEY-ANNE
DISCIPLINE ENGLISH, CREATIVE WRITING **EDUCATION** York Univ, BA; Univ British Columbia, MFA, 89. **CAREER** Coord, Tchr Ctr, Senate Comm Enhancement, 90-92; Lectr Creative Writing, Univ Prince Edward Island 91-. **HONORS AND AWARDS** Bliss Carman Poetry Awd, Banff Ctr Arts, 86; Air Can Awd, Can Auth Asn, 94. **MEMBERSHIPS** League Can Poets. **SELECTED PUBLICATIONS** Auth, The Story of Pears, 90; auth, Skinny Girls, 93; auth, Field Day, 96. **CONTACT ADDRESS** Univ of Prince Edward Island, 550 University Ave, Charlottetown, PE, Canada C1A 4PS. **EMAIL** lbourne@upei.ca

BOUSON, J. BROOKS
DISCIPLINE ENGLISH **EDUCATION** Loyola Univ Chicago, PhD. **CAREER** Prof. **MEMBERSHIPS** Margaret Atwood Soc, Toni Morrison Soc, MLA, MMLA. **RESEARCH** Modern British literature; psychoanalysis and literature; emotions and literature; trauma and narrative; women's literature; history of feminist criticism. **SELECTED PUBLICATIONS** The Empathic Reader: A Study of the Narcissistic Character and the Drama of the Self, Univ Mass Press, 89; Auth, Brutal Choreographies: Oppositional Strategies and Narrative Design in the Novels of Margaret Atwood, Amherst: Univ Mass Press, 93; auth, "Biographical sketch," Contemporary Authors, vol 151, (96); auth, "Quiet as It's Kept: Shame and Truma in Toni Morrison's The Bluest Eye," Scenes of shame: Psychoanalysis, Shame, and Writing, Albay: SUNY Press, (99), 207-236; auth, "The Edible Woman's Refuasl to Consent to Feminity," Margaret Atwiid: Modern Critical Vews, Philadelphia: Chelsea House Pub, (00), 71-91; auth, "Biographical sketch," Who's Who in Am, 55th ed, 01; auth, The Misogyny of Patriarchal Culture in The Handmaid's Tale: Modern Critical Int, Philadelphia: Chelsea House Pub, 01; auth, You Nothing But Trash: White Trash Shame in Dorothy Allison's Bastard Out of Carolina," "Southern Lit J, Forthcoming; auth, Psychoanalytic Approaches, Shame, Truam, " Entries in a Tonie Morrison Encyclopedia, Westport Conn: Greenwood Press, Forthcoming; **CONTACT ADDRESS** Dept of English, Loyola Univ, Chicago, 6525 N. Sheridan Rd., Chicago, IL 60626. **EMAIL** jbouson@luc.edu

BOWDEN, BETSY
PERSONAL Born 01/30/1948, Grove City, PA, s **DISCIPLINE** MEDIEVAL LITERATURE, FOLKLORE **EDUCATION** UCLA, Berkeley, PhD. **CAREER** Ch, exec comt, Chaucer Div of MLA; prof of Eng, Rutgers, State Univ NJ, Camden Col of Arts and Sci. **SELECTED PUBLICATIONS** Auth, Performed Literature: Words and Music by Bob Dylan, Ind, 82; Chaucer Aloud: The Varieties of Textual Interpretation, Pa, 87; Listeners' Guide to Medieval English: A Discography, Garland,

88; ed, Eighteenth-Century Modernizations from the Canterbury Tales, Boydell & Brewer, 91. **CONTACT ADDRESS** Rutgers, The State Univ of New Jersey, Camden, Camden Col of Arts and Sci, Camden, NJ 08102-1405.

BOWDITCH, LOWELL
PERSONAL Born 12/13/1961, New York, NY **DISCIPLINE** CLASSICS **EDUCATION** Univ Calif, BA, 84; Brown Univ, MA, 89; PhD, 92. **CAREER** Asst Prof to Assoc Prof, Univ Ore, 93-. **MEMBERSHIPS** Am Philol Asn. **RESEARCH** Augustan Literature; Classics and Contemporary Poetry. **SELECTED PUBLICATIONS** Auth, Horace and the Gift Economy of Patronage, Univ Calif Press, 01. **CONTACT ADDRESS** Dept Class, Univ of Oregon, Dept Class, Eugene, OR 97403. **EMAIL** bowditch@oregon.uoregon.edu

BOWEN, BARBARA C.
PERSONAL Born 05/04/1937, England, m, 1963, 2 children **DISCIPLINE** LITERATURE **EDUCATION** Oxford Univ, BA, 58; MA, 62; Doctorat de l'Universite de Paris, 62. **CAREER** From instr to prof, Univ Ill, 62-87; prof, Vanderbilt Univ, 87-. **HONORS AND AWARDS** Guggenheim Fel, 74-75; NEH Summer Sem, 80 & 91; NEH Sr Fel, 81-82 & 88-89. **MEMBERSHIPS** Renaissance Soc of Am, Am Asn of Teachers of French. **RESEARCH** Rabelais, French Comic Theater, Renaissance Intellectual History. **SELECTED PUBLICATIONS** Auth, Enter Rabelais, Laughing, Vanderbilt Univ Press (Nashville, TN), 88; ed, One Hundred Renaissance Jokes: A Critical Anthology, Summa Pub (Birmingham, AL), 88. **CONTACT ADDRESS** Dept French & Ital, Vanderbilt Univ, PO Box 1647-B, Nashville, TN 37235-0001. **EMAIL** barbara.c.bown@vanderbilt.edu

BOWEN, ROGER
PERSONAL Born 11/03/1942, Cardiff, Wales **DISCIPLINE** ENGLISH LITERATURE **EDUCATION** Cambridge Univ, BA, Hons, 65; Simon Fraser Univ, MA, 68; Harvard Univ, PhD(English), 72. **CAREER** Asst prof, 72-77, from assoc prof to prof English, Univ Ariz, 77-96. **MEMBERSHIPS** MLA; H G Wells Soc; Philip Larkin Soc. **RESEARCH** Modern British poetry; modern British fiction; colonial & postcolonial lit. **SELECTED PUBLICATIONS** Auth, Confession and equilibrium: Robert Lowell's poetic development, Criticism, 69; A version of pastoral: E M Forster as country guardian, SAtlantic Quart, 76; Science, myth, and fiction in H G Wells's The Island of Dr Moreau, Studies Novel, 76; Philip Larkin's XX Poems: poet in transition, Iowa Rev, 77; Death, Failure, and survival in the poetry of Philip Larkin, Dalhousie Rev, 78; Native and exile: The poetry of Bernard Spencer, Malahat Rev, 1/79; The edge of a journey: Notes on Bernard Spencer, London Mag, 12/79 & 1/80; ed, Bernard Spencer: Collected Poems, Oxford Univ Press, 81; Orientalism and Empire in The Alexandria Quartet, Studies in the Literary Imagination, 91; Many Histories Deep: The Personal Landscape Poets in Egypt, 1940-1945, Associated Univ Pr, 95; Investing in Conrad, Investing in the Orient: Margaret Drabbie's 'The Gates of Ivory,' 20th Century Lit, fall 99. **CONTACT ADDRESS** Dept of English, Univ of Arizona, 1 University of Az, PO Box 210067, Tucson, AZ 85721-0001. **EMAIL** rbowen@u.arizona.edu

BOWERBANK, SYLVIA
DISCIPLINE ENGLISH LITERATURE **EDUCATION** McMaster Univ, BA, PhD; Simon Fraser, MA. **RESEARCH** 17th and 18th century English lit; cultural meaning of landscape literature; feminist theory and pedagogy; First-Nations writing; educational theory and the teaching of writing. **CONTACT ADDRESS** English Dept, McMaster Univ, 1280 Main St W, Hamilton, ON, Canada L8S 4L9. **EMAIL** bowerban@mcmaster.ca

BOWERS, BEGE K.
PERSONAL Born 08/19/1949, Nashville, TN, d **DISCIPLINE** ENGLISH **EDUCATION** Vanderbilt Univ, BA, 71; Univ Tenn, MACT, 73; PhD, 84. **CAREER** Teaching Asst, Knoxville, 72-75; Teaching Asst, Univ Tenn, 82-84; Asst Prof to Prof, Youngstown State Univ, 84-. **MEMBERSHIPS** Col English Asn, Asn of Teachers of Technical Writing, Soc for Technical Comm, NE Ohio Soc for Technical Comm, Conf on Col Composition and Comm, Mod Lang Asn, New Chaucer Soc, Phi Kappa Phi, Gould Soc Fac Committee **RESEARCH** Jay R Gould Award, Soc for Technical Comm, 99; Distinguished Service Award, Col English Asn, 96; Distinguished Prof Award for Public Service, Youngstown State Univ, 96; Grant, New Chaucer Soc, 93-94; NEH Summer Inst, Yale Univ, 91; Distinguished Prof Award for Excellence in Teaching, Youngstown State Univ. **SELECTED PUBLICATIONS** Ed, Internships in Technical Communication: A Guide for Students, Faculty Supervisors, and Internship Sponsors, Soc for Technical Comm, 91; ed, Reading and Writing Women's Lives: A Study of the Novel of Manners, UMI Research Press, 90; auth, "Samuel Warren," in British Reform Writers, 1732-1914. Dictionary of Literary Biography, Gale Research, 98; auth, "Florence Nightingale," in British Travel Writers, 1837-1875, Dictionary of Literary Biography, Gale Research, 96; auth, "Studies in the Age of Chaucer. **CONTACT ADDRESS** Dept English, Youngstown State Univ, 1 Univ Plaza, Youngstown, OH 44555-0001. **EMAIL** bkbowers@cc.ysu.edu

BOWERS, EDGAR
PERSONAL Born 03/02/1924, Rome, GA **DISCIPLINE** ENGLISH LITERATURE **EDUCATION** Univ NC, BA, 47; Stanford Univ, MA, 49, PhD(English), 53. **CAREER** Instr English, Duke Univ, 52-55; asst prof, Harpur Col, State Univ NY, 55-58; from asst prof to assoc prof, 58-67, Prof English, Univ Calif, Santa Barbara, 67-, Sewanee Rev fel, 54; Guggenheim fels, 59 & 69. **HONORS AND AWARDS** Ingram Merrill Found, 74; Brandeis Creative Arts, 79. **RESEARCH** English, American and French lyric poetry and literary criticism. **SELECTED PUBLICATIONS** Auth, Hawthorne and the Extremes of Character, Sewanee Rev, Vol 0102, 94; John, poetry, vol 0161, 93. **CONTACT ADDRESS** 1502 Miramar Beach, Santa Barbara, CA 93108.

BOWERS, JOHN M.
DISCIPLINE MEDIEVAL ENGLISH LITERATURE **EDUCATION** Duke Univ, BA, magna cum laude, 71; Univ Va, MA, 73; Oxford Univ, MPhil, 75; Univ Va, PhD, 78. **CAREER** Lectr, Univ Va, 78-80; asst prof, Hamilton Col, 80-82; asst prof, Princeton Univ, 84-87; assoc prof, 87-92, prof, 92-, chemn, Univ Nev, Las Vegas, 97-00; referee and rev, Stud in the Age of Chaucer, Yearbk of Langland Stud, Envoi, Medium Aevum, Exemplaria: J of Theory in Medieval and Renaissance Stud. **HONORS AND AWARDS** Andrew W Mellon postdoctoral fel, Calif Inst of Technol, 82-84; NEH grant, 85; NEH summer stipend, Huntington Libr, 86; vis fac assoc, Calif Inst of Technol, 87; NEH fac develop inst, UNLV, 88; Outstanding Teacher, Univ Nev, Las Vegas, 89; Distinguished Tchr, Southern Nev Tchr of Eng, 90; Rita Deanin Abbey Tchr of the Yr Awd, Univ Nev, Las Vegas, 90; NEH fel for Univ Tchr, 92-93; Outstanding Tchr of Eng, UNLV Alumni Asn, 95; NEH summer inst, Univ Colo, Boulder, 95; Tchr of the Yr Awd, Consolidated Stud Univ Nev, 96; Phi Kappa Phi, UNLV, 97; Rockefeller/Bellagio Fellow; Guggenheim Fellow. **MEMBERSHIPS** Medieval Acad of Am; Early Eng Text Soc; MLA; Southeastern Medieval Asn; New Chaucer Soc; John Gower Soc; Philol Asn of the Pacific Coast; Medieval Asn of the Pacific. **RESEARCH** The relationship between politics and medieval literature. **SELECTED PUBLICATIONS** Auth, Ordeals, Privacy, and the Lais of Marie de France, J of Medieval and Renaissance Stud 24, 94; Mankind and the Political Interests of Bury St. Edmunds, AEstel 2, 94; The Politics of Pearl, Exemplaria: J of Theory in Medieval and Renaissance Stud 7, 95; Piers Plowman's William Langland: Editing the Text, Writing the Author's Life, Yearbk of Langland Stud 9, 95; Chaste Marriage: Fashion and Texts at the Court of Richard II, Pacific Coast Philol 30, 95; Pearl in its Royal Setting: Ricardian Poetry Revisited, Stud in the Age of Chaucer 17, 95; auth, The Politics of "Pearl": Court Poetry in the Age of Richard II. **CONTACT ADDRESS** Dept of Eng, Univ of Nevada, Las Vegas, 4505 Maryland Pky, Las Vegas, NV 89154-5011. **EMAIL** bowers@nevada.edu

BOWERS, NEAL
PERSONAL Born 08/03/1948, Clarksville, TN, m, 1979 **DISCIPLINE** ENGLISH **EDUCATION** Austin Peay State Univ, BA, 70; MA, 71; Univ of Fla, PhD, 76. **CAREER** Prof to Distinguished prof, Iowa State Univ, 77-. **HONORS AND AWARDS** NEA Poetry Fel; Fredrick Bock Prize; Union League Aware. **MEMBERSHIPS** Modern Poetry Assoc. **RESEARCH** Contemporary American Poetry. **SELECTED PUBLICATIONS** Auth, Theodore Poethke: The Journey from I to Otherwise, Univ of Miss, 82; auth, James Dickey: The Poet as Pitchman, Univ of Miss, 85; auth, Words for the Taking: The Hunt for a Plagarist, W.W. Norton, 97. **CONTACT ADDRESS** Dept English, Iowa State Univ, 1 Iowa State Univ, Ames, IA 50011-2010. **EMAIL** nbowers@iastate.edu

BOWERS, PAUL
DISCIPLINE ENGLISH **EDUCATION** Univ Tulsa, BA; OK State Univ, M.A., PhD. **CAREER** English, Phillips Univ. **RESEARCH** Irish poetry and the writings of James Joyce. **SELECTED PUBLICATIONS** Auth, Taking Certain Measures, OK Best 97. **CONTACT ADDRESS** Div of Lang Arts, No Oklahoma Col, 100 South University Ave, PO Box 2300, Enid, OK 73702-2300. **EMAIL** pbowers@nocaxp.north-ok.edu

BOWMAN, LEONARD JOSEPH
PERSONAL Born 02/04/1941, Detroit, MI, m, 2 children **DISCIPLINE** RELIGION; LITERATURE **EDUCATION** Duns Scotus Col MI, BA 63; Univ Detroit, MA 67; Fordham Univ, PhD 73. **CAREER** Marycrest Intl Univ, prof 73-94, vpres acad dean 94-97; Col Notre Dame MD, vpres acd affs, 97-. **MEMBERSHIPS** AAUP **RESEARCH** Medieval Franciscan Spirituality; St. Bonaventure. **SELECTED PUBLICATIONS** Auth, A Retreat With St. Bonaventure, Element Books Ltd, 93. **CONTACT ADDRESS** Dept of Academic Affairs, Notre Dame Col, 4003 Roundtop Rd, Baltimore, MD 21218. **EMAIL** lbowman@udm.edu

BOWMAN, MARY RUTH
PERSONAL Born 05/13/1964, Fairfax, VA, s **DISCIPLINE** ENGLISH **EDUCATION** Col of William and Mary, AB, 86; Duke Univ, MA, 88; PhD, 93. **CAREER** Instr, Duke Univ, 89-93; lectr, Lord Fairfax Col, 94-95; asst prof, Pikeville Col, 95-97; vis asst prof, Shenandoah Univ, 97-98; asst prof, Univ Wisc, 98-. **HONORS AND AWARDS** John Lievsay Dissertation Fel, 92-93; James B. Duke Fel, 86-89; Phi Beta Kappa, 85. **MEMBERSHIPS** MLA; Midwest MLA; Nat Coun of Teachers of English; Spencer Soc; Milton Soc; Renaissance Soc of Am; New Chaucer Soc. **RESEARCH** Renaissance English and Italian literature, emphasis on romance, epic and lyric poetry. **SELECTED PUBLICATIONS** Auth, "She there as princess rained: Spencer's figure of Elizabeth," Renaissance Quart, (90): 509-528; auth, "Half as She Were Mad: Dorigen in the Male World of the Franklin's Tale," Chaucer Rev, (93): 239-251; auth, "Distressing Irena: Gender, Conquest, and Justice," in Book V of The Faerie Queens, forthcoming. **CONTACT ADDRESS** 217 Saint Paul St, Apt A, Stevens Point, WI 54481-2291. **EMAIL** mbowman@uwsp.edu

BOYD, ANNE E.
PERSONAL Born 09/13/1969, N Kansas City, MO, m, 2000 **DISCIPLINE** ENGLISH **EDUCATION** Univ Minn, BA, 91; Purdue Univ, MA, 94; PhD, 99. **CAREER** Teaching asst, Purdue Univ, 92-97; asst prof, Univ New Orleans, 99-. **HONORS AND AWARDS** Fac Grant, Univ New Orleans, 01, 00; Purdue Res Fel, 97-99; A. H. Ismail Award, 97; Chester Eisinger Award, 96. **MEMBERSHIPS** ALA; MLA; ASA; SSAWW; SAMLA; Constance Fenimore Woolson Soc. **RESEARCH** Nineteenth-century American literature and culture; women's literature; race relations. **SELECTED PUBLICATIONS** Auth, "Lifestyles, Social Trends and Fashions," in American Eras: The Reform Era and Eastern US Development, 1815-1850, ed. Gerald Prokopowicz (Detroit: Gale Res, 98); auth, "'What! Has She Got into the Atlantic?:' Women Writers, the Atlantic Monthly, and the Formation of the American Canon," Am Studies 39 (98): 5-36; rev, "Regions of Identity: The Construction of America in Women's Fiction, 1885-1914," by Kate McCullough, S Atlantic Rev 65 (00): 162-165; auth, "Anticipating James, Anticipating Grief: Constance Fenimore Woolson's 'Miss Grief,'" in Constance Fenimore Woolson's Nineteenth Century, ed. Victoria Brehm (Wayne State Univ Pr, 01). **CONTACT ADDRESS** English Dept, Univ of New Orleans, New Orleans, LA 70148. **EMAIL** aeboyd@uno.edu

BOYD, BARBARA WEIDEN
PERSONAL Born 03/31/1952, Bronx, NY, m, 1980, 1 child **DISCIPLINE** CLASSICAL STUDIES **EDUCATION** Manhattanville Col, BA, 74; Univ Mich, MA, 76. PhD, 80. **CAREER** Asst prof to prof, Bowdoin Col, 80- . **HONORS AND AWARDS** NEH Fel, 87-88. **MEMBERSHIPS** Am Philol Asn; Vergilian Soc; Class Asn of the Midwest & South; Class Assn of New England. **RESEARCH** Latin poetry, Vergil and Ovid; Augustan Rome; Republican Roman literature and society. **SELECTED PUBLICATIONS** Auth, Cydonea mala: Virgilian Word-Play and Allusion, in Harvard Studies in Class Philol, 83; auth, Tarpeia's Tomb: A Note on Propertius 4.4, in Am J of Philol, 84; auth, Parva seges satis est: The Landscape of Tibullan Elegy in 1.1. and 1.10, in Transactions of the Am Philol Asn, 84; auth, the Death of Corinna's Parrot Reconsidered: Poetry and Ovid's Amores, in the Class J, 87; auth, Propertius on the Banks of the Eurotas, in Class Q, 87; auth, Virtus Effeminata and Sallust's Sempronia, in Transactions of the Am Philol Asn, 97; auth, Non Hortamine Longo: An Ovidian "Correction of Virgil, in Am J of Philol, 90; auth, Vergil's Camilla and the Traditions of Catalogue and Ecphrasis, in Am J of Philol, 92; auth, Non enarrabile textum: Ecphrastic Trespass and Narrative Ambiguity in the Aeneid, in Vergilius, 95; auth, Bibliography for Ovid's Amores and Metamorphoses, in Teacher's Guide to Advanced Placement Courses in Latin, 95; auth, Changes in the 1999 Advanced Placement Examinations in Latin (Vergil and Latin Literature), in Class Outlook, 97; auth, Ovid's Literary Loves: Influence and Innovation in the Amores, Univ Michigan Pr, 97; auth, Pallas and Turnus: Selections from Vergil, Aeneid Books 10 and 12, Bolchazy-Carducci, 98. **CONTACT ADDRESS** Dept of Classics, Bowdoin Col, Brunswick, ME 04011. **EMAIL** bboyd@bowdoin.edu

BOYD, LINDA F. WHARTON
PERSONAL Born 04/21/1961, Baltimore, MD **DISCIPLINE** COMMUNICATION **EDUCATION** Univ of Pgh, BA 1972, MA 1975, PhD 1979. **CAREER** Howard Univ, asst prof 1979-85; Washington DC Office of the Mayor, communications specialist 1984-86; DC Department of Administrative Services, dir of public affairs 1986-88; DC Department of Recreation, director of communications, 88-92; The Wharton Group, Pres, 90-; Alcohol and Drug Abuse Services Administration, chief of criminal justice, 92-95; DC Dept of Human Svcs, Sr Asst, Dir of Policy and Communication, currently. **HONORS AND AWARDS** Outstanding Black Women's Awd Communication Arts Creative Enterprises 1974; Doctoral Honor's Seminar Prog Howard Univ Speech Comm 1977; Bethune Legacy Awd, Natl Council of Negro Women 1986; Natl Public Radio Documentary Awd 1985. **MEMBERSHIPS** Delta Sigma Theta Sor 1971-; exec treas Natl Speech Comm Assn Black Caucus 1975-; honorary bd mem, Pgh Black Theatre Dance Ensemble 1978-; bd mem, Natl Arts Prog Natl Council of Negro Women 1979-; consultant, NAACP Labor & Indus Sub-com on Comm; chairperson, Joint Chapter Event, Natl Coalition of 100 Black Women Inc. **SELECTED PUBLICATIONS** Auth, "Black Dance, It's Origin and Continuity," Minority Voices, 1977; advisor: "Stuff," children's program, NBC-TV, Washington, DC. **CONTACT ADDRESS** DC Dept of Health, 800 9th St SE, Washington, DC 20024.

BOYD, MELBA J.
PERSONAL Born 04/02/1950, Detroit, MI, d, 2 children **DISCIPLINE** ENGLISH **EDUCATION** Western Mich Univ, BA, 71; MA, 72; Univ Mich at Ann Arbor, Doctor Arts, 79. **CAREER** Grad asst, Western Mich Univ, 70-71; substitute teacher, Detroit Board of Educ, 71; asst ed, Broadside Pre, 72-76; english teacher, Cass Tech High Sch, 72; instr, Wayne County community Col, 72-79 & 80-82; english teacher, Eastside Street Academies, 74; instr, Shaw Col, 75-76; Instr, Wayne State Univ, 76-77; from grad asst to instr, Univ Mich, 78; curriculum specialist, W. I. C. Magnet Sch Project for the Gifted and Talented, 79-80; from vis prof to asst prof, Univ Iowa, 82-88; vis prof, Colgate Univ, 86; dir & assoc prof, Univ Mich at Flint, 89-; adj assoc prof, Univ Mich at Ann Arbor, 92-93; assoc prof, Africana Studies, 93-; assoc prof & chemn dept Africana Studies, Wayne State Univ, 96-; adj prof, Univ Mich Ctr for Afro-American and African Studies, 99. **HONORS AND AWARDS** Literature Awd, Nat Confr of Artists, 78; Individual Artist Awd, Mich Coun for the Arts, 81; Sr Fulbright Lectr, Univ Bremen, 83-84; Old Gold Summer Res Fel, Univ Iowa, 85, 87, & 88; Res and Publ Awd, Ohio State Univ, 89; Recognition for Major Contributions to African Am Culture, Soc of the Culturally Concerned, 90; Fac Res Grant, Univ Mich, 91-93; Minority/Women Summer Res Grant, Wayne State Univ, 94; Grant Awd, Mich Coun for the Arts, 94; Special Project Awd, Arts Found of Mich and the Detroit Coun of the Arts, 95-96; Outstanding Achievements in the Lit Arts, Frances E. W. Harper Lit Soc, 96. **MEMBERSHIPS** Collegium of African Am Res, Am Studies Asn. **RESEARCH** African American Poetry, African American Film, African American Biography. **SELECTED PUBLICATIONS** Auth, "Frances E. W. Harper's Legacy," Against the Current 10.1 (95); "Envisioning Freedom: Jazz, Film, Writing and the Reconstruction of American Thought," in The Canon in the Classroom: The Pedagogical Implications of Canon Revision in American Literature, ed. John Alberti (NY: Garland Publ, 95); auth, "Literacy in the Liberation of Bigger Thomas," in Approaches to Teaching Wright's Native Son, ed. James Miller (MLA, 96); auth, "Frances E. W. Harper," in Encyclopedia of American Poetry, ed. Eric Haralson (Chicago and London: Fitzroy Publ, 98); auth, "The Music in Poetry," in Sing the Sun Up: Creative Writing Ideas from African American Literature, ed. Lorenzo Thomas (NY: Teachers & Writers Collaborative, 98); auth, "Afro-Centrics, Afro-Elitists, and Afro-Eccentrics: The Polarization of Black Studies Since the Student Struggles of the Sixties," in Dispatches from the Ebony Tower, ed. Manning Marable (NY: Columbia Univ Pr, 00). **CONTACT ADDRESS** Dept of Africana Studies, Wayne State Univ, 51 W Warren, Detroit, MI 48202. **EMAIL** ab6993@wayne.edu

BOYER, DALE KENNETH
PERSONAL Born 04/06/1936, Baker, OR, m, 1959, 3 children **DISCIPLINE** ENGLISH & AMERICAN LITERATURE **EDUCATION** Univ Ore, BA, 58, MA, 63; Univ Mo-Columbia, PhD(English), 69. **CAREER** Instr English, Univ Mo-Columbia, 63-68; from instr to assoc prof, 68-76, prof English, Boise State Univ, 76-01, Co-ed, Ahsahta Press, Boise State Univ, 76-96; Retired 01. **HONORS AND AWARDS** Phi Beta Kappa, Univ Ore, 58; Phi Kappa Phi, Boise State Univ, 88. **RESEARCH** Brit Romantic poetry and essay; 20th century Am and Brit poetry; Victorian poetry and essay. **SELECTED PUBLICATIONS** Ed, Winter Constellations, 77, Stealing The Children, 78, To the Natural World, 80, Agna Negra, 81, Ahsahta Press; auth, Ten poets: A review, Western Am Lit, Vol XV, 80; The Clock of Moss, 83; Deer in the Haystacks, 84; Flights of the Harves-mare, 85; Underground, 86; Men at Work, 89; Sycamore Oriole, 91; The One Right Touch, 92; Each Thing We Know Has Changed Because We Know It, 94; Prayers for the Dead Ventriloquist, 95; The Ahsahta Anthology: Poetry of the American West, 96. **CONTACT ADDRESS** Dept of English, Boise State Univ, 1910 University Dr, Boise, ID 83725-0399.

BOYER, HORACE CLARENCE
PERSONAL Born 07/28/1935, Winter Park, FL, m **DISCIPLINE** MUSIC **EDUCATION** Bethune-Cookman College, BA, 1957; Eastman School of Music, University of Rochester, MA, 1964, PhD, 1973. **CAREER** Monroe High School, instructor 1957-58; Poinsett Elementary School, instructor, 60-63; Albany State College, asst professor, 64-65; University of Central Florida, asst professor, 72-73; University of Massachusetts Amherst, Dept of Music, professor, 73-. **HONORS AND AWARDS** Ford Foundation Fellow, Eastman School of Music, 1969-72; curator, Natl Museum of American History, Smithsonian, 1985-86; United Negro College Fund, Distinguished Scholar-at-Large, Fisk University, 1986-87. **MEMBERSHIPS** Vice Pres, A Better Chance, 1980-82; editorial board, Black Music Research Journal, 1980-83; vice president, Gospel Music Assn, 1983-84. **CONTACT ADDRESS** Dept of Music, Univ of Massachusetts, Amherst, Amherst, MA 01003-0041.

BOYER, JAY M.
PERSONAL Born 08/31/1947, Chicago, IL, m, 1977, 1 child **DISCIPLINE** ENGLISH **EDUCATION** St Louis Univ, BA, 69; SUNY Buffalo, MA, 71; PhD, 76. **CAREER** Prof, Ariz State Univ, 76-. **HONORS AND AWARDS** Ariz Prof of the Year, 95. **RESEARCH** Film; Literature. **SELECTED PUBLICATIONS** Auth, Ishmael Reed, Boise State Univ Press, 93; auth, Sidney Lumet, Mcmillan, 93; auth, Bob Rafelson: Hollywood Maverick, SS/Twayne Film Series, 96. **CONTACT ADDRESS** Dept English, Arizona State Univ, 3370 N Harden Rd, Scottsdale, AZ 85251. **EMAIL** J.Boyer@asu.edu

BOYERS, ROBERT
PERSONAL Born 11/09/1942, Brooklyn, NY, m, 1975, 3 children **DISCIPLINE** ENGLISH **EDUCATION** CUNY, Queens Col, BA, 63; NYU, MA, 65. **CAREER** Prof, Skidmore Col, 69-; Tisch prof, 95-; ed, Salmagundi mag, 65-; dir, NYork State Sum Writ Inst, 87-. **HONORS AND AWARDS** NIH, Sr Schl Awd, 80, 90; Rockefeller Found Awd, 80; Choice Awd, 85. **RESEARCH** 20th C art; literature; politics. **SELECTED PUBLICATIONS** Auth, Atrocity and Amnesia, 85; auth, After the Avant-Garde, 86; auth of essays in The New Republic, The Am Scholar, Partisan Rev, Dissent; Granta; auth of short stories in Parnassus, MI Quart Rev, Southwest Rev, 95-. **CONTACT ADDRESS** Dept English, Skidmore Col, Saratoga Springs, NY 12866. **EMAIL** rboyers@skidmore.edu

BOYLE, FRANK T.
PERSONAL Born 04/20/1959, Cleveland, OH, m, 1991, 2 children **DISCIPLINE** ENGLISH **EDUCATION** Columbia Col, NY, BA, 81; Trinity Col, Dublin, PhD, 89. **CAREER** Asst prof, Fordham Univ, 85-98; assoc prof, 98-; dept chair, 98-. **MEMBERSHIPS** ASECS; MLA; NY 18th C Sem. **RESEARCH** 18th C literature; travel writing; satire; literature; science. **SELECTED PUBLICATIONS** Auth, Swift as Nemesis: Modernity and Its Satirist, Stanford Univ Press (00). **CONTACT ADDRESS** Dept English, Fordham Univ, 441 East Fordham Rd, Bronx, NY 10458-5149. **EMAIL** ftboyle@fordham.edu

BOYLE, THOMAS CORAGHESSAN
PERSONAL Born 12/02/1948, m, 3 children **DISCIPLINE** ENGLISH HISTORY AND LITERATURE **EDUCATION** Suny Potsdam, BA, 68, Univ Iowa, MFA, 74, Univ Iowa, PhD, 77. **CAREER** Dir, 78-90, Found of Creative Writing Prog, 78, Asst Prof, Eng, 78-82, Assoc Prof, Eng, 82-86, Prof, Eng, 86, USC. **HONORS AND AWARDS** Coord Coun of Lit Mag Fiction Award, 77, Nat Endow for the Arts Grant, 77, St. Lawrence Award for Fiction, 80, Paris Rev, Aga Khan Prize for Fictin, 81, Nat Endow for the Arts Grant, 83, Paris Rev, John Train Humor Prize, 84, Commonwealth Club of Calif, Silver Medal for Lit, 86, Editors' Choice, NY Times Book Rev, 87, Guggenheim Fel, 88, PEN/Faulkner Award, 88, O'Henry Short Story Award, 88 and 89, Commonwealth Club of Calif Gold Medal for Lit, 88, Prix Passion publ prize, Fr, 89, PEN Ctr West Lit Prize, 89, Editors' Choice, NY Times Book Rev, 89, Doctor of Humane Letters hon degree, State Univ NY, 91, Howard D. Vursell Mem Award, Nat Acad of Arts and Letters, 93, Best Amer Stories, 97, Prix Medicis Etranger, Paris, 97. **MEMBERSHIPS** Mem, lit panel, Nat Endow for the Arts, 86-87. **SELECTED PUBLICATIONS** Auth, Descent of Man, Boston, Atlantic-Little, Brown, 79; auth, Water Music, Boston, Atlantic-Little, Brown, 82; auth, Budding Prospects, NY, Viking, 84; auth, Greasy Lake, NY, Viking, 85; auth, World's End, NY, Viking, 87, auth, If the River Was Whiskey, NY, Viking, 89; auth, East Is East, NY, Viking, 90; auth, The Road to Wellville, NY, Viking, 93; auth, Without A Hero, NY, Viking, 94; auth, The Tortilla Curtain, NY, Viking, 95; auth, Riven Rock, NY, Viking, 98; auth, T. C. Boyle Stories, NY, Viking, 98. **CONTACT ADDRESS** Dept of English, Univ of So California, Univ Park, THH 420, Los Angeles, CA 90089-03564.

BOYNTON, VICTORIA A.
PERSONAL Born 04/26/1950, Cleveland, OH, 1 child **DISCIPLINE** ENGLISH **EDUCATION** SUNY Binghamton, PhD, 95. **CAREER** Asst Prof, SUNY Cortland, 99-. **MEMBERSHIPS** NCTE, NEMLA, MLA. **SELECTED PUBLICATIONS** Auth, "Collaborative Power Sharing," The Compos Chronicle 6.1 (93): 6-8; auth, "Benefits of the Mock Trial in the College Classroom: Collaboration, Close Reading, Culture, and Conflict," The English Record 43.2 (93):11-16; auth, "Desire's Revision: Feminist Appropriation of Native American Traditional Stories," Mod Lang Studies 26.2 (Spring/Summer 96): 53-71; auth, "Kate Chopin," in Nineteenth-Century American Women Writers: A Bio-Bibliographical Critical Sourcebook, ed. Denise Knight (Greenwood Press, 97); auth, "Rhetoric and Feminism," in Theorizing Composition: A Critical Sourcebook of Theory and Scholarship in Contemporary Composition Studies, ed. Mary Lynch Kennedy (Greenwood Press, 97); co-ed, Tow Dozen Strategies for Using Writing in Amy Course, 98; coauth, "Nomadic Travels: An Interdisciplinary Transformation of Composition," Transformations (Fall 99); co-ed, The Cortland Composition Handbook, 99. **CONTACT ADDRESS** Dept English, SUNY, Col at Cortland, PO Box 2000, Cortland, NY 13045-0900.

BRACKEN, JAMES K.
PERSONAL Born 03/16/1952, Toledo, OH, m, 1973, 4 children **DISCIPLINE** LIBRARY AND INFORMATION SERVICES **EDUCATION** Univ of Toledo, BA, 73, MA, 76; Univ of SC, ML, 79, PhD, 83. **CAREER** Reader Services Librn, Knox Col, 79-85; humanities bibliographer, asst prof, Purdue Univ, 85-88; Head of Second Floor Maim Libr Imfor Servies, Prof, The Ohio State Univ, 88-. **HONORS AND AWARDS** Ameritech Prize, 92, Outstanding Service Awd, The Ohio State Univ, 95; OSU Office of Research Interdisciplinary Seed Grant, 93-94; U.S. Dept of Education Foreign Periodical Prog grant, 93-95. **RESEARCH** Bibliography; printing history. **SELECTED PUBLICATIONS** Auth, Literature, Humanities and the Library, Am Libr Asn, 93; Reference Works in British and American Literature, Libr Unlimited, 98; co-ed, The British Literary Book Trade 1700-1820 (Dictionary of Literary Biography Vol 154, Gale, 95; The British Literary Book Trade 1475-1700 (Dictionary of Literary Biography Vol 170), Gale, 96coauth, Telecommunications Research Resources: An Annotated Guide, Erlbaum, 95; Mass Communications Research Resources: An Annotated Guide, Erlbaum, 98. **CONTACT ADDRESS** Second Fl Main Libr Infor Services, Ohio State Univ, Columbus, 1858 Neil Ave Mall, Columbus, OH 43210-1286. **EMAIL** bracken.1@osu.edu

BRACKEN, PAMELA
DISCIPLINE ENGLISH **EDUCATION** Bethany Nazarene Col, BA, 81; Southern Nazarene Univ, MA, 86; Catholic Univ Am, PhD, 94. **CAREER** Assoc prof, Southern Nazarene Univ, 95-. **MEMBERSHIPS** Conf on Christianity & Lit; MLA; William Morris Soc of the US. **RESEARCH** Victorian literature; Alice Meynell; William Morris; Julia Margaret Cameron. **SELECTED PUBLICATIONS** Auth, art, The Art Worker' Guild, 93; auth, intro, notes, The Table Turned or Nupkins Awakened, 94; auth, art, About Suffering They Were Never Wrong: Reflections on the Oklahoma Bombing, 95; auth, art, Scenes of Cultural Life: George Eliot and the Clergy, 95; auth, art, Fire and Ice: Clashing Visions of Iceland in the Travel Narratives of William Morris and Sir Richard Burton, 96. **CONTACT ADDRESS** Dept of English, So Nazarene Univ, 6729 NW 39th Expy, Bethany, OK 73008. **EMAIL** pbracken@snu.edu

BRACKETT, DAVID
DISCIPLINE MUSIC HISTORY **EDUCATION** Univ CA Santa Cruz, BA; New Engl Conservatory, MM; Cornell Univ, DMA. **CAREER** Fac, Univ MI and Cornell Univ, vis asst prof, present. **HONORS AND AWARDS** Scholar/awds/fellows from Meet the Composer, Yaddo Artist's Colony, Pittsburgh New Music Festival, Cornell Coun Performing Arts, Cornell Univ, New Engl Conservatory; performances by the soc composers, pittsburgh new music festival, syracuse soc new music, cornell contemporary chamber players, and chiron new music. commissions by the harpur jazz ensemble and binghamton univ theater dept; sec/treas, us branch int assoc **MEMBERSHIPS** US branch Int Assoc Study Pop Music (IASPM). **RESEARCH** Compos; non-Western music; hist of popular music. **SELECTED PUBLICATIONS** Auth, Interpreting Popular Music, Cambridge UP, 95; articles/revs in The Journal Am Musicol Soc, Pop Music, Am Music, The Stanford Hum Rev, The Musical Quart, and Critical Quart. **CONTACT ADDRESS** Dept Music, SUNY, Binghamton, PO Box 6000, Binghamton, NY 13902-6000.

BRACKETT, MARY VIRGINIA
PERSONAL Born 04/07/1950, Fort Riley, KS, m, 1991, 3 children **DISCIPLINE** CREATIVE WRITING, ENGLISH, LITERATURE **EDUCATION** Univ Ark, BS, 78; Missouri S State Col, BA, BS, 89; Pitt State Univ, MA, 91; Univ Kan, PhD, 98. **CAREER** Adj instr, Pitt State Univ, 89-91; adj instr, Johns Cnty Comm Col, 91-94; teach asst, Univ Kan, 94-95; instr, Triton Col, 99-. **HONORS AND AWARDS** Ser Learn Res Grnt, Triton Col, 01; OK Hum Coun Res Grnt, 98; E Cen Univ Res Grnt, 98, 97; book, Elizabeth Cary: Writer of Conscience, rec for NYPL, 97. **MEMBERSHIPS** MLA, NCTE, ISA, SCBWI. **RESEARCH** Early women writers; Angie Debo: OK human rights activist. **SELECTED PUBLICATIONS** Auth, Elizabeth Cary: Writer of Conscience, Morgan Reyn, 96; auth, "Sharp Necessities," Women and Lang (96); auth, Classic Love and Romance Literature, ABC-CLIO, 99; auth, "Avoiding the Ambiguous: Mythic Archetypes in Peppermints in the Parlor," Mosaic (01); auth, "Putting the Flowers In," Arachne (00); auth, Jeff Bezos: a biography, Chelsea House, 00; auth, The Contingent Self: One Reading Life, Morgan Reyn, 01; auth, F. Scott Fitzgerald: a biography, Morgan Reyn, forthcoming; Steve Jobs: a biography, Enslow Pub, forthcoming; John Brown: a biography, Chelsea House, forthcoming. **CONTACT ADDRESS** Eng Dept., Triton Col, 2000 Fifth Ave, River Grove, IL 60171. **EMAIL** mbrackett@triton.cc.il.us

BRACY, WILLIAM
PERSONAL Born 03/25/1915, Rich Square, NC, m, 1962, 2 children **DISCIPLINE** ENGLISH **EDUCATION** Univ NC, Chapel Hill, AB, 36, MA, 39, PhD(English), 49. **CAREER** Asst, Univ NC, Chapel Hill, 39-42, part-time instr, 46-48, instr English, 48-49; asst prof, Univ Mo, Columbia, 49-54; Foyle res fel, Shakespeare Inst, Stratford-on-Avon, England, 53; asst ed humanities, Collier's Encycl, New York, 55-58; humanities ed & consult, Encycl Americana, 58-64; lectr English, City Col New York, 64-65; assoc prof, 65-68, acting chmn dept, 67-68, chmn, 69-71 & 77-80, Prof English, Beaver Col, 68-; Prof Emer, 85-. **RESEARCH** Shakespeare; Renaissance; English drama. **SELECTED PUBLICATIONS** Auth, The Merry Wives of Windsor: the History and Transmission of Shakespeare's Text, Univ Mo, 52; Doctor Faustus .. Analysis with Critical Commentary, 65 & coauth, Early English Drama ..

Middle Ages to the Early 17th Century, 66, Studies Master; articles for Collier's and Americana Encyclopedias; poetry; auth, Peerless Poet and Patron: Sonnets in the Shakespearean Made, Minerva Press (London), 01. **CONTACT ADDRESS** Dept of English, Beaver Col, Glenside, PA 19038.

BRADDOCK, ROBERT COOK
PERSONAL Born 05/31/1939, Mt Holly, NJ, m, 1962, 2 children **DISCIPLINE** ENGLISH & EARLY MODERN EUROPEAN HISTORY **EDUCATION** Middlebury Col, AB, 61; Northwestern Univ, MA, 63, PhD(hist), 71. **CAREER** From instr to asst prof, 70-75, chmn dept, 76-78, 96-98, assoc prof to prof Hist, Saginaw Valley State Univ, 75-. **HONORS AND AWARDS** Dist Fac Awd, State Univ Mich, 91; Fel of Early Mod Studies, Sixteenth Century Studies Conf, 98. **MEMBERSHIPS** AHA; Renaissance Soc Am; Conf Brit Studies. **RESEARCH** Administrative history especially early modern Europe; the court in Tudor-Stuart England; office holding. **SELECTED PUBLICATIONS** Auth, The Character and Composition of the Duke of Northumberland's Army, Albion VI, 74; The Rewards of Office-Holding in Tudor England, J Brit Studies XIV, 75; J. H. Plumb and the Whig Tradition, In: Recent Historians of Great Britain, Iowa State Univ Press, 90; contribr, Historical Dictionary of Tudor England, Greenwood Press, 91; Dict of National Biography, Oxford Univ Press, forthcoming; Reader's Guide to British History, Fitzroy-Dearborn Press, forthcoming. **CONTACT ADDRESS** Dept of Hist, Saginaw Valley State Univ, 7400 Bay Rd, University Center, MI 48710-0001. **EMAIL** rcbrad@svsu.edu

BRADFORD, CLINTON W.
PERSONAL Born 11/05/1909, Grapevine, AR, w, 1946, 2 children **DISCIPLINE** SPEECH COMMUNICATION **EDUCATION** Univ Arkansas, BA, 38; State Univ Iowa, MA, 41; Louisiana State Univ, PhD, 51. **CAREER** Prof Speech Commun, Louisiana State Univ, 51-73. **RESEARCH** Researching and writing histories of Bradford family and Warbritton family. **SELECTED PUBLICATIONS** Auth, Ministry for Retired Persons, Reily Memorial Univ Church, 87; auth, Elected Lay Leaders 1941--1991, 92. **CONTACT ADDRESS** 212 Amherst Ave, Baton Rouge, LA 70808-4603.

BRADLEY, DORIS P.
DISCIPLINE SPEECH **EDUCATION** Univ Pittsburgh, PhD, CCC-SLP. **CAREER** Served as VP, Am Speech-Lang-Hearing Asn. **RESEARCH** Lang disorders; cleft palate; organic speech disorders. **SELECTED PUBLICATIONS** Publ articles & bk Chaps in her spec areas. **CONTACT ADDRESS** Dept of Speech and Hearing Sci(s), Univ of So Mississippi, 2701 Hardy St, Hattiesburg, MS 39406.

BRADLEY, JACQUELINE
PERSONAL Born 01/02/1962, Dallas, TX, s **DISCIPLINE** ENGLISH **EDUCATION** Univ Tex, BA, 88; S Methodist Univ, MA, 93. **CAREER** Adj prof, Brookhaven Col, 93-; instr, SMU, 97-. **HONORS AND AWARDS** Who's Who Among Am Teachers, 89; Sigma Tau Delta, 93; Outstanding English Fac Member of the Year, Brookhaven Col, 98; HOPE Awd, SMU, 00. **MEMBERSHIPS** Nat Council of Teachers of English, Shakespeare Asn of Am, MLA. **RESEARCH** 19th & 20th century American literature, British & American Victorian literature, British renaissance literature. **SELECTED PUBLICATIONS** Auth, Joyce Carol Oates' Black Water and Diminishing Significance: Nameless, Wordless, Worthless. **CONTACT ADDRESS** Dept English, So Methodist Univ, PO Box 750001, Dallas, TX 75275-0001. **EMAIL** jdbradle@mail.smu.edu

BRADLEY, JAMES ROBERT
PERSONAL Born 03/28/1935, Philadelphia, PA, d, 4 children **DISCIPLINE** CLASSICS **EDUCATION** Trinity Col, CT, BA, 57; Harvard Univ, MA, 59, PhD(class philol), 68. **CAREER** Instr classics, Hobart & William Smith Cols, 60-62; asst prof, Univ NC, 67-70; asst prof classics,Trinity Col, 74-00, assoc prof classics, Trinity Col, CT, 74-. **MEMBERSHIPS** Am Philol Asn; Archaeol Inst Am. **RESEARCH** Greek and Latin literature; classical civilization. **SELECTED PUBLICATIONS** Auth, The Elegies of Sulpicia: An Introduction and Commentary, New Eng Class Newsletter and Jour, XXII, 159-164, May, 95; rev, Apuleius, Cupid and Psyche, New Eng Class Newsletter and Jour, XIX, May, 92; auth, Chinese New Year: Four Centuries Ago, New Eng Class Newsletter and Jour, XIX, 26-27, Dec, 91; auth, The Sources of Cornelius Nepos, Selected Lives, Garland Publ, 91; auth, All the Tea in China, Class Outlook, 68, Fall, 90; auth, Ovid, Ars 1.39-40: Making Tracks - Speed, Ritual or Art, Class World, 83, 100-101, 89; rev, Ars Amatoria I, New Eng Class Newsletter, XIV, Oct, 86; auth, The Sources of Cornelius Nepos: Selected Lives, NY and London, Garland Pub, 91. **CONTACT ADDRESS** Dept Classics, Trinity Col, Connecticut, 808 Main St, South Windsor, CT 06074. **EMAIL** james.bradley@mail.trincoll.edu

BRADLEY, JERRY W.
PERSONAL Born 08/24/1948, Jacksboro, TX, d **DISCIPLINE** ENGLISH **EDUCATION** Midwestern Univ, BA, 69; Tex Christian Univ, MA, 73; PhD, 75. **CAREER** Asst prof, Boston Univ, 75-76; assoc prof, New Mex Tech, 76-93; prof & dean of humanities, Ind Univ SE, 93-94; prof, W Tex A & M Univ, 94-. **HONORS AND AWARDS** Brit Lit Awd, 96; Hoe D. Thomas Scholar-Teacher of the Year, Tex Col English Asn, 00. **MEMBERSHIPS** Am Acad of Poets, Col English Asn, Conf of Col Teachers of English, Panhandle Council of Teachers of English, Popular Culture Asn, Rocky Mountain MLA, S Cent MLA, Tex Asn of Creative Writing. **RESEARCH** Modern British and American literature, southwestern studies. **SELECTED PUBLICATIONS** Auth, The Movement: British Poets of the 1950s, Twaynes English Authors Series, McMillan (NY), 93; coauth, Famous Writers of American Literature, Ashai Shuppansha (Tokyo), 97. **CONTACT ADDRESS** Dept English & Lang, West Texas A&M Univ, 2501 4th Ave, Canyon, TX 79016-0001. **EMAIL** jbradley@mail.wtamu.edu

BRADLEY, RITAMARY
PERSONAL Born 01/30/1916, Stuart, IA **DISCIPLINE** ENGLISH LITERATURE **EDUCATION** Marygrove Col, PhB, 38; St Louis Univ, MA, 45, PhD(English), 53. **CAREER** Head dept English, Marycrest Col, 45-56; asst exec secy, Sister Formation Conf, 61-64, ed, Sister Formation Bull, 54-64; distinguished res fel, Univ Minn, 64-65; Prof English, St Ambrose Col, 65-, Workshop philos in a tech cult, Cath Univ Am, 63; ed, 14th-Century English Mystics Newsletter, 75-; part-time fac mem, Inst Women Today, 77-. **HONORS AND AWARDS** LLD, Marquette Univ, 60; LHD, Fordham Univ, 60. **MEMBERSHIPS** MLA; Mediaeval Acad Am; Relig Educ Asn; Nat Coalition Am Nuns. **RESEARCH** Women in literature; English medieval mystics; women in religious history. **SELECTED PUBLICATIONS** Auth, The Ways of the Spirit--Underhill, Relig & Lit, vol 0024, 92; Modern Guide to the Ancient Quest for the Holy--Underhill, Relig & Lit, vol 0024, 92; The Ways of the Spirit--Underhill, Relig & Lit, vol 0024, 92; Underhill, Evelyn--Artist of the Infinite Life--Greene, Relig & Lit, vol 0024, 92; The Saint and the City--Micheline-De-Pesaro Died, 1356, Franciscan Tertiary, J Medieval Studies, vol 0069, 94; From Virile Woman to Womanchrist--Studies In Medieval Religion And Literature, J Medieval Studies, vol 0071, 96; From Virile Woman to Womanchrist--Studies In Medieval Religion And Literature, J Medieval Sutdies, vol 0071, 96. **CONTACT ADDRESS** Dept of English, St. Ambrose Univ, 518 W Locust St, Davenport, IA 52803-2898.

BRADY, LEO
PERSONAL Born 01/23/1917, Wheeling, WV, m, 1945, 8 children **DISCIPLINE** DRAMA **EDUCATION** Cath Univ Am, AB, 41, MA, 42. **CAREER** From assoc prof to Prof Speech & Drama, Cath Univ Am, 46- **MEMBERSHIPS** Am Theatre Asn. **RESEARCH** Dramatic Criticism; history of drama; aesthetics. **SELECTED PUBLICATIONS** Auth, Horatio, Southerly, vol 0054, 94; Antidote, Southerly, vol 0056, 96; Solstice, Westerly, vol 0042, 97; Donegal, Southerly, vol 0053, 93. **CONTACT ADDRESS** Dept of Drama, Catholic Univ of America, Washington, DC 20017.

BRADY, OWEN E.
PERSONAL Born 05/03/1946, Chicago, IL, m, 1971, 3 children **DISCIPLINE** DRAMATIC LITERATURE **EDUCATION** Ill Benedictine Col, BA, 68; Univ Notre Dame, MA, 70, PhD(English), 73. **CAREER** Instr English & humanities, Univ Notre Dame, 72-73; lectr English, Njala Univ Col, Univ Sierra Leone, WAfrica, 73-75; asst prof humanities, 75-81, assoc prof, 81-98, Dean Lib Studies, Clarkson Col, 82-94, Consult, Asn Depts English, summer, 80; res assoc, Inst Writing, Univ Iowa, 80-. **MEMBERSHIPS** NE MLA; Conf Col Compos & Commun. **RESEARCH** Performance criticism of drama; Shakespeare; Am drama; African Am Lit. **SELECTED PUBLICATIONS** Auth, Baraka's Experimental Death Unit # 1: Plan for (R)Evolution, Black Am Lit Forum, 75; Cult ritual and cultural conflict in LeRoi Jones' The Toilet, Educ Theatre J, 76; Wright's Lawd Today: The American dream festering in the sun, Col Lang Asn J, 78; LeRoi Jones' The Slave: A ritual of purgation, Black Lit in Rev, Obsidian, 78; Great Goodness of Life: Baraka's black bourgeoisie Blues, In: Imamu Amiri Baraka: A Collection of Critical Essays, Prentice-Hall, 78; contribr, Afro-American Literature: The Reconstruction of Instruction, MLA, 79; auth, Irony and sentiment: The delicate balance of the Guthrie Theater's 1979-80 Glass Menagerie, Tennessee Williams Newslett, 80; auth, Theodore Ward's Our Law: From the Slavery of Melodrama to the Freedom of Tragedy, Callaloo, 84; Blackness and the Unmanning of America in Dave Rabe's Streamers War, Literature, and the Arts, 97; 11 Theater Reviews in Theatre Journal, 79-95. **CONTACT ADDRESS** Ctr for Lib Studies, Clarkson Col, Box 5750, Potsdam, NY 13699-0000. **EMAIL** obrady@clvm.clarkson.edu

BRADY, ROBERT M.
PERSONAL Born 03/23/1952, Maxfield, KY, m, 2 children **DISCIPLINE** INTERPERSONAL COMMUNICATION **EDUCATION** Univ Mich, PhD. **CAREER** Comm Stu, Univ Ark **HONORS AND AWARDS** Fulbright Cols Outstanding Adv Awd; vice-chair. **SELECTED PUBLICATIONS** Articles, Jour Business Comm; Comm Monographs; Western Jour Comm; Jour Language Soc Psychol; Soc Behavior Personality. **CONTACT ADDRESS** Univ of Arkansas, Fayetteville, Fayetteville, AR 72701. **EMAIL** rbrady@uark.edu

BRAENDLIN, BONNIE HOOVER
PERSONAL Born 03/03/1940, Dickinson, ND, m, 1968, 1 child **DISCIPLINE** MODERN BRITISH & AMERICAN MINORITY LITERATURE **EDUCATION** Augustana Col, BA, 62; Univ Pittsburgh, MA, 65; Fla State Univ, PhD(English lit), 78. **CAREER** Instr English, Calif Lutheran Col, 65-68; vis asst prof, 81-82, Dir Freshman English, Fla State Univ, 82-, Ed newslett, Womens Caucus of SAtlantic Modern Lang Asn, 80-82. **MEMBERSHIPS** MLA; SAtlantic Modern Lang Asn; Soc Study of Multi-Ethnic Lit of the US; Col English Asn. **RESEARCH** The Bildungsroman; women's studies; modern novel. **SELECTED PUBLICATIONS** Auth, Noncanonical American Literature--Introduction, Cea Critic, vol 0055, 92. **CONTACT ADDRESS** Florida State Univ, 1915 Rhonda Dr, Tallahassee, FL 32303.

BRAILOW, DAVID GREGORY
PERSONAL Born 10/31/1950, Penn Yan, NY, m, 1991, 1 child **DISCIPLINE** RENAISSANCE LITERATURE, BRITISH NOVEL **EDUCATION** Amherst Col, BA, 72; Univ Ore, MA, 76, PhD, 79. **CAREER** Vis asst prof, Wake Forest Univ, 79-82; from asst to assoc to prof Eng, 82-, John Peter Smith prof of Eng, McKendree Coll, 95-. **HONORS AND AWARDS** Sears Foundatin Awd for Teaching Excellence and Campus Leadership, McKendree College, 89; NEH Summer Seminars and Institutes. **MEMBERSHIPS** Shakespeare Assn Am. **RESEARCH** Shakespeare in performance. **SELECTED PUBLICATIONS** Assoc ed, The Dictionary of British Literary Characters: The Eighteenth and Nineteenth Century Novel, Facts-on-File, 93; art, Twelfth Night Across the Continents: An Interview With Michael Pennington, Shakespeare Bulletin 14, 96; art, The Dream World of Richard II: Barbara Gaines Directs, Shakespeare Bulletin 14, 96; art, Authority and Interpretation: Hamlet at Shakespeare Repertory Theater, Essays in Theatre/Etudes theatrales, 98. **CONTACT ADDRESS** LLC Div, McKendree Col, 701 College Rd, Lebanon, IL 62254-1299. **EMAIL** dbrailow@atlas.mckendree.edu

BRAITHWAITE, DAWN O.
PERSONAL Born 01/13/1955, Chicago, IL, m, 1984 **DISCIPLINE** COMMUNICATION STUDIES **EDUCATION** Univ MN, Doctor of Philosophy, Speech-Communication, 88. **CAREER** Teaching assoc, 78-80, lect, dept commun, CA State Univ, Long Beach, 81-82; instr, div of the Humanities; Golden West Col, 79-82; lect, dept speech commun, CA State Univ, Fullerton, 80-82; instr, Univ MN, Continuing Ed for Women, 83-85; instr, Dept of Commun, The Col of St Catherine, 84; instr, Continuing Mangement Ed, Univ MN, 83-85; teaching assoc, dept of speech commun, 82-87, instr, dept speech & theatre, 85-87, asst prof, Univ MN, 88-89; dir graduate studies, dept commun studies, 89-92, asst prof, NM State Univ, 89-92; asst prof, dept commun studies, 92-96, affiliate fac member, Gerontology prog, 94-, interim dir, Gerontology prog, 96-97, assoc prof, dept of commun studies, 96-, AZ State Univ West; assoc prof, Dept Commun Studies, Univ NE-Lincoln, 98-, elected graduate fel, 98-, dir graduate studies, 99-2000. **HONORS AND AWARDS** Awd of Excellence in Teaching by a Graduate Student, Int Commun Asn, 85; elected fac Commencement speaker, Univ MN, Morris, 86; elected First Vice Pres of Western States Commun Asn, 98, to become Pres, 2000. **MEMBERSHIPS** Nat Commun Asn; Western States Commun Asn; Central States Commun Asn; Int Network on Personal Relationships; Int Soc for the Study of Personal Relationships; Phi Kappa Phi Honor Soc. **RESEARCH** Communication strategies of people with disabilities; relational identity: communication and the development of stepfamilies; commun rituals; commun of social support. **SELECTED PUBLICATIONS** Co-auth, with D Labrecque, Responding to the Americans with Disabilities Act: Contributions of Interpersonal Communication Research and Training, J of Applied Commun, 22, 94; with L A Baxter, "I Do" Again: The Relational Dialectics of Renewing Marriage Vows, J of Social and Personal Relationships, 12, 95; auth, Ritualized Embarrassment at "Coed" Wedding and Baby Showers, Commun Reports, 8, 95; co-auth, A Binding Tie: Supportive Communication of Family Kinkeepers, J of Applied Commun Res, 24, 96; with C Cumber, A Study of Perceptions and Understanding of Multiculturalism, Howard J of Commun, 7, 96; auth, "I Am a Person First": Different Perspectives on the Communication of Persons with Disabilities, in E B Ray, ed, Case Studies in Communication and Disenfranchisement: Applications to Social Health Issues, Lawrence Erlbaum Assocs, Pubs, 96; Persons First: Expanding Communicative Choices by Persons with Disabilities, in E B Ray, ed, Case Studies in Communication and Disenfranchisement: Social Health Issues and Implications, Lawrence Erlbaum Assocs, Pubs, 96; co-auth, with A L Harper and C A Braithwaite, Here?: Strategies for Teaching About Cultural Diversity in Non-Diverse Regions, J of Professional Studies, 4, 97; co-auth, with C A Braithwaite, Understanding Communication of Persons with Disabilities as Cultural Communication, in L A Samovar and R Porter, eds, Intercultural Communication: A Reader, 8th ed, earlier versions in 4-7th eds, Wadsworth Pub, 97; numerous other publications and several new works in press. **CONTACT ADDRESS** Communication Studies Dept, Univ of Nebraska, Lincoln, 424 Oldfather Hall, Lincoln, NE 68588-0329. **EMAIL** dbraithwaite@unl.edu

BRANCH, EDGAR MARQUESS
PERSONAL Born 03/21/1913, Chicago, IL, m, 1939, 3 children **DISCIPLINE** AMERICAN LITERATURE **EDUCA-**

TION Beloit Col, AB, 34; Univ Chicago, AM, 38, Univ Iowa, PhD, 41. **CAREER** From instr to prof English, 41-64, chmn dept, 59-64, res prof, 64-78, Emer Prof English & Res Assoc Am Lit, Miami Univ, 78-, Vis assoc prof, Univ Mo, 49; Nat Endowment for Humanities sr fel, 71-72, independent study, 76-77; Guggenheim Found Fel, 79. **HONORS AND AWARDS** Benjamin Harrison Medallion, Miami Univ, 78; Distinguished Serv Citation, Beloit Col, 79; Nancy Dasher Bk Awd, Col English Asn, 80. **MEMBERSHIPS** Soc Studies Southern Lit; MLA; Am Studies Asn; Soc Study Midwestern Lit; Western Lit Asn. **RESEARCH** Mark Twain; 19th century American literature; James T Farrell. **SELECTED PUBLICATIONS** Auth, Bixby-Vs-Carroll, New Light on Clemens, Sam Early River Career, Mark Twain J, vol 0030, 92. **CONTACT ADDRESS** Dept of English, Miami Univ, Oxford, OH 45056. **EMAIL** branchem@muohio.edu

BRANCH, MICHAEL
PERSONAL Born 12/06/1963, Wyandotte, MI, s **DISCIPLINE** AMERICAN LITERATURE **EDUCATION** Col William and Mary, BA, Univ Va, MA, PhD. **CAREER** Asst prof, Fla Int Univ, 93-95; asst prof to assoc prof, Univ of Nev Reno, 95-. **HONORS AND AWARDS** Phi Beta Kappa, 85; Governor's Fel, 89, 91; Golden Key Nat Honor Soc Distinguished Teacher Awd, 97; Fac Mentor, Senior Scholar Awd, 98, 00; **MEMBERSHIPS** MLA; Assoc for the Study of Lit and Environ; W Lit Assoc; Am Lit Assoc. **RESEARCH** Literature and Environment, Early American Literature, Environmental History, Textual Editing. **SELECTED PUBLICATIONS** Auth, "Marjory Stoneman Douglas: 1890-1998", ISLE 5.2 (98): 123-127; coauth, "A Place in the South, Appalachian Heritage 26.1 (98): 18-25; coed, The Height of Our Mountains: Nature Writing from Virgina's Blue Ridge Mountains and Shenandoah Valley, Johns Hopkins Univ Pr, (Baltimore and London), 98; coed Reading the Earth: New Directions in the Study of Literature and the Environment, Univ of Idaho Pr, (Moscow), 98; auth, "Cosmology in the Casino: Simulacra of Nature in the Interiorized Wilderness", in The Nature of Cities: Ecocriticism and Urban Environments, ed Michael Bennett and David W. Teague, Univ of Ariz Pr, 99, 277-298; auth, "Telling Nature's Story: John Muir and the Decentering of the Romantic Self, in John Muir in Historical Perspective, ed Sally M. Miller, Peter Lang Pub, 99, 99-122; ed, John Muir's Last Journey: South to the Amazon and East to Africa, Island Pr/Shearwater Books (Washington, DC) (forthcoming); auth, "Writing the Swamp: Marjory Stoneman Douglas and The Everglades: River of Grass" in Such News of the Land: American Women Nature Writers, dc Tom Edwards and Beth DeWolfe, Univ Pr of New England, (forthcoming) auth, "Jeremiad, Elegy, and the Yaak: Rick Bass and the Aesthetics of Anger and Grief", the Bard of the Yaak: Rick Bass, Writer and Environmental Activist, ed Alan Weltzien, Univ of Utah Pr, (forthcoming); auth, "Five Generations of Literary Coopers: Intergenerational Valuations of the Frontier", in Studies of Susan Fenimore Cooper, ed Rochelle Johnson and Alan Weltzien, Univ of Utah Pr, (forthcoming). **CONTACT ADDRESS** Dept English, Univ of Nevada, Reno, N Virginia Ave, Reno, NV 89557-0001. **EMAIL** mbranch@unr.edu

BRANDE, DAVID
DISCIPLINE ENGLISH LITERATURE **EDUCATION** Portland State Univ, BA, 85, MA, 88; Univ Wash, PhD, 95. **CAREER** Asst prof. **SELECTED PUBLICATIONS** Auth, The Business of Cyberpunk: Symbolic Economy and Ideology in William Gibson, Johns Hopkins Univ, 95; Making Yourself a Body without Organs: The Cartography of Pain in Kathy Acker's Don Quixote, 91. **CONTACT ADDRESS** Dept of Humanities, Illinois Inst of Tech, 3301 S Dearborn, Chicago, IL 60616. **EMAIL** dbrande@charlie.cns.iit.edu

BRANDLER, MARCIELLE
PERSONAL Born 06/27/1950, Riverside, CA, d **DISCIPLINE** ENGLISH, POETRY **EDUCATION** Univ Utah, BA, 81; Univ Southern Calif, MA, 94. **CAREER** Dir of Poetry Workshops at various Cols, schools, and writing centers since 86; teaching lit & English at los Angeles City Col, 88-, and others; also teacher of Grammar courses. **HONORS AND AWARDS** San Francisco Quart, Yearly Poetry Awd, Two Poetry Awds, 87; First Place in the Staff Division for poem, "Eden," in Mt. San Antonio Col Writers' Day Festival, 96. **MEMBERSHIPS** Calif Poets in the Schools, Calif Teacher's Asn, Literary Network, Luz en Arte y Literatura Int Bilingual Asn, Nueva Generacion Literatura, Int PEN. **RESEARCH** Online publishing and online education; literature and critical thinking. **SELECTED PUBLICATIONS** Auth, "The Breathing House," and "Lark in the High Desert," Revista/Review Interamericana, Puerto Rico; auth, "Inner Caf¤," Voices: New Poems of Life and Experience; auth, "Black School," Two Twenty-four Poetry Quart; auth, "I Met a Man," Haight Ashbury Lit J; auth, "America: At Your Service," and "Paladins of the Styx," The Forum: J of the Academic Senate for California Community Colleges; auth, "Monroe, Utah," Southern Calif Anthol, Univ Southern Calif; auth, "Upon Receiving an Invitation to a Memorial for Ken Saro-Wiwa," Ogoni's Agonies: Ken Saro-Wiwa and the Crisis in Nigeria, Africa, World Press, Inc; auth, "Eden," Wilderness of Dreams: California Poets in the Schools Statewide Anthol; auth, "Raven's Canyon," Hurakan: J of Contemporary Lit, Col of the Mainland. **CONTACT ADDRESS** English & Foreign Lang, Pasadena City Col, 1570 E Colorado Blvd, Pasadena, CA 91106-2003.

BRANDON, JAMES R.
PERSONAL Born 04/10/1927, St. Paul, MN, m, 1961, 1 child **DISCIPLINE** DRAMA **EDUCATION** Univ Wis, PhB, 48, MS, 49, PhD, 55. **CAREER** Instr drama & speech, Univ Conn, 50; asst cult attache, US Info Agency, Djakarta, 55-56, radio off, 56-57, Japanese lang off, Tokyo, 58-59, asst cult attache, 59-61; assoc prof drama, Mich State Univ, 61-67, prof theater, 67-68; Prof Theater, Univ Hawaii, 68-, Int Prog Mich State Univ-Ford Found res grant, Southeast Asia, 63-64; Fulbright Res Scholar grant, Japan, 66-68; Nat Endowment for Humanities sr fel, 71-72. **MEMBERSHIPS** Asia Soc; Japan Soc; Am Theatre Asn. **RESEARCH** Asian theatre. **SELECTED PUBLICATIONS CONTACT ADDRESS** Dept of Drama & Theatre, Univ of Hawaii, Manoa, 1770 E West Rd, Honolulu, HI 96822-2317.

BRANDT, BRUCE E.
PERSONAL Born 10/18/1946, Indianapolis, m, 1968, 2 children **DISCIPLINE** ENGLISH **EDUCATION** Univ Denver, BA, 69; MA, 71; Harvard Univ, PhD, 77. **CAREER** Prof, SDak State Univ, 79-01. **HONORS AND AWARDS** NEH Summer Sem, 86; OF Butler Found Awd, 92. **MEMBERSHIPS** Marlowe Soc of Am, MLA, MWMLA, Rocky Mtn MLA, Southeastern Renaissance Conf. **RESEARCH** English Renaissance Drama, especially Christopher Marlowe. **SELECTED PUBLICATIONS** Auth, "Marlowe's II Tamburlaine, v.I.86,103," Explicator 42.1 (83): 9-10; auth, "Marlowe's Helen and the Soul-in-the-Kiss Conceit," Philol Quart 64, (85): 118-121; auth, Christopher Marlowe and the Metaphysical Problem Play, Univ Salzburg, (Salzburg), 85; auth, "Shakespeare's The Rape of Lucrece: Argument, Text, and Interpretation," Proceedings of the First Dakotas Conf on Earlier Brit Lit, ed Jay Ruud, (Aberdeen: N State Univ Pr, 93): 22-32; auth, "Images of Christopher Marlowe in Recent Fiction," Proceedings of the Second Dakotas Conf on Early Brit Lit, ed John H Laflin, (Aberdeen: N State Univ Pr, 94): 47-57; auth, "Transformations: The Interplay of Source and Text in Marlowe's Hero and Leander and Dido, Queen of Carthage," Proceedings of the Sixth Northern Plains Conf on Earlier Brit Lit, ed Linda Kruckenberg and W Andrew Alexander, (Wayne State Col, 98); ed, Proceedings of the Third Dakotas Conference on Earlier Brit Lit, Dordt Col, 95; auth, Christopher Marlowe in the Eighties: An Annotated Bibliography of Marlowe Criticism from 1978 through 1989, Locust Hill Pr, (W Cornwall: CT, 92). **CONTACT ADDRESS** Dept English, So Dakota State Univ, PO Box 504, Brookings, SD 57007-1391. **EMAIL** bruce_brandt@sdstate.edu

BRANDT, DI
PERSONAL Born Winkler, MB, Canada **DISCIPLINE** ENGLISH **EDUCATION** Can Mennonite Bible Col, BTh, 72; Univ Toronto, MA, 76; Univ Man, BA, 75, PhD, 93. **CAREER** Writer, 83-, lectr, asst prof, Eng, Univ Winnipeg, 86-95; Writer in Residence, 95-96, Res Fel, Univ Alberta, 96-. **HONORS AND AWARDS** A.L. Wheeler Bk Prize, Univ Man, 75; Gerald Lampert Awd, 87; Patrick Mary Plunkett Memorial Scholar, Univ Man, 89; McNally Robinson Awd Man Bk of Year, 90; Nat Poetry Awd, Can Authors' Asn, 95. **MEMBERSHIPS** Writers' Union Can; PEN; League Can Poets; Man Writers' Guild. **SELECTED PUBLICATIONS** Auth, questions I asked my mother, 87; auth, mother, not mother, 92; auth, Wild Mother Dancing: Maternal Narrative in Canadian Literature, 93; auth, Jersualem, beloved, 95; auth, Dancing Naked: Narrative Strategies for Writing Across Centuries, 96. **CONTACT ADDRESS** Dept of English, Univ of Windsor, 401 Sunset Ave, Windsor, ON, Canada N9B 3P4.

BRANTLEY, JENNIFER
DISCIPLINE ENGLISH LITERATURE **EDUCATION** KS State Univ, MA; Univ NE Lincoln, PhD. **CAREER** Prof, Univ of WI. **RESEARCH** Women's lit; 20th century lit; poetry writing. **SELECTED PUBLICATIONS** Auth, pubs on Carson McCullers, Kate Chopin, and Anne Ellis. **CONTACT ADDRESS** Eng Dept., Univ of Wisconsin, River Falls, S 3rd St, PO Box 410, River Falls, WI 54022-5001.

BRANTLEY, WILLIAM
PERSONAL Born 08/15/1955, Atlanta, Ga, s **DISCIPLINE** ENGLISH **EDUCATION** Ga State Univ, BA, 77; MA, 81; Univ Wis, PhD, 91. **CAREER** Fel, Ga Inst of Tech 88-91; lecturer, Univ Calif, 91-92; asst prof to assoc prof, Middle Tenn State Univ, 92-. **HONORS AND AWARDS** Eudora Welty Awd, 92. **MEMBERSHIPS** Mod Lang Asn, Soc for the Study of Southern Lit, Katherine Anne Porter Soc. **RESEARCH** Modern American literature, Southern literature, Film criticism. **SELECTED PUBLICATIONS** Auth, Feminine Sense in Southern Memoir, Univ Press Miss, 93; auth, Conversations with Pauline Kael, Univ Press Miss, 96. **CONTACT ADDRESS** Dept English, Middle Tennessee State Univ, 1301 E Main St, Murfreesboro, TN 37132-0001. **EMAIL** wbrantle@frank.mtsu.edu

BRASCH, WALTER MILTON
PERSONAL Born 03/02/1945, San Diego, CA, m, 1983, 2 children **DISCIPLINE** JOURNALISM **EDUCATION** San Diego State Col, AB, 66; Ball State Univ, MA, 69; Ohio Univ, PhD, 74. **CAREER** Reporter-ed daily newspapers, Calif, Ind, Iowa & Ohio, 65-71; writer-producer, United Screen Artists & United TV Productions, 65-66 & 75-81; writer, Maushake Advert, 65-66 & 76-80; producer-writer, MID Productions, 71-74; copywriter/media advisor, Jackson-Walsh Advertising, L.A., 73-81; asst prof jour,Temple Univ, 74-76; corresp ed, Jour Hist, 75-; consult, Major Makers Video Productions, 76-80; writer, Weitzman polit pub rels; consult ed, Int J Creole Studies, 77-; prof jour, Bloomsburg Univ, 80-; writer-consult, K-Squared Productions, 95-. **HONORS AND AWARDS** Meritorious Achievement Medal, U.S. Coast Guard, 77; Flotilla Commanders Awd, 78; Creative Teaching Awd, Bloomsburg Univ, 81; Creative Arts Awd, 83; Director's Awd, Soc Professional Journalists, 92; Nat Freedom of Infor Awd, 94; finalist, column, Nat Soc of Newspaper Columnists, 96; Points of Excellence winner/alumni, San Diego State Univ, Col Arts & Letters, 97; silver medalist, editorial and opinion wirting, Int Asn of Business Communicators, 98; Scribendum Libros honor (honoris causa), Alpha Kappa Delta; Outstanding Advisor of a Col Publication, Nat Federation of Pr Women; 1st place, column, Spotlight Awds, Soc Prof Journalists, 00. **MEMBERSHIPS** Soc Prof Journalists; Anchors Guild; United Auto Workers/Nat Writers Union; Newspaper Guild; Nat Soc Newspaper Columnists; Penn Press Club; Penn Women's Press Asn. **RESEARCH** Media history; media and society; journalism. **SELECTED PUBLICATIONS** Auth, A Comprehensive Annotated Bibliography of Am Black English, LSYU Pr, 74; auth, Black English and the Mass Media, Univ Mass PR, 81, revised 84, auth, Columbia County Place Names, May fly, 82, revised, 98; auth, Cartoon Monickers, An Insight Into the Animation Industry, Bowling Green Univ Popular Pr, 83; coauth, The Press and the State, Sociohistorical and Contemporary Interpretations, Univ Pr of Am, 86; auth, A ZIM Self-Portrait, Associated Univ Presses, 88; auth, With Just Cause, Unionization of the Am Journalist, Univ Pr of Am, 91; auth, Forerunners of Revolution: Muckrackers and the Am Social Conscience, Univ Pr Am, 91; auth, Enquiring Minds and Space Aliens: Wandering Through the Mass Media and Popular Culture, Mayfly, 96; auth, Brer Rabbit, Uncle Remus, and the Cornfield Journalist: The Tale of Joel Chandler Harris, Mercer, 00. **CONTACT ADDRESS** Dept Jour, Bloomsburg Univ of Pennsylvania, 400 E 2nd St, Bloomsburg, PA 17815-1399. **EMAIL** brasch@planetx.bloomu.edu

BRASFIELD, JAMES
PERSONAL Born 01/19/1952, Savannah, GA, m, 1984, 1 child **DISCIPLINE** ENGLISH **EDUCATION** Armstrong-Atlantic State Univ, BA, 75; Columbia Univ, MFA, 79. **CAREER** Lectr, Pa State Univ, 87-. **HONORS AND AWARDS** Sr Fulbright Lectr, Ukraine, 93-94, 99; Am Asn for Ukranian Studies Transl Prize, 99; PEN Awd, 99; Pushcart Prize, 00. **RESEARCH** Poetry. **SELECTED PUBLICATIONS** Auth, Inheritance and Other Poems, Armstrong Col Pr, (Savannah, GA), 83; auth, "Poems", Anatomy: Raw, Elbow Pr, (Rochester, NY), 91; auth, "Poem", In the West of Ireland, Enright House, Ireland, 92; transl, From Three Worlds: New Writing from Ukraine, Zephyr Pr, (Sommerville, MS), 96; auth, "Poem", Family Portraits, Adam & Art, (Bellefonte, PA), 97; transl, The Selected Poems of Oleh Lysheha, Harvard Univ Pr, (Cambridge, MS), 99; transl, The Pushcart Prize XXIV, 2000, (Wainscott, NY). **CONTACT ADDRESS** Dept English, Pennsylvania State Univ, Univ Park, 117 Burrowes Bldg, University Park, PA 16802-6200. **EMAIL** jeb16@psu.edu

BRATER, ENOCH
PERSONAL Born 10/01/1946, New York, NY, m, 1973, 2 children **DISCIPLINE** ENGLISH & THEATER **EDUCATION** NYork Univ, BA, 65; Harvard Univ, AM, 67, PhD(English), 71. **CAREER** Managing dir, Loeb Drama Ctr, Harvard Univ, 70-71; asst prof drama, Univ Pa, 71-75, Prof, English and Theater, Univ Mich, 75-. **MEMBERSHIPS** MLA; ATHE. **RESEARCH** Samuel Beckett; British drama, 20th century; American drama. **SELECTED PUBLICATIONS** Auth, The Drama in the Text; auth, Beyond Mininalism; auth, Beckett at 80/Beckett in Context; auth, Why Beckett; auth, Feminine Focus; auth, The theatrical Gamut; auth, Around the Absurd; auth, Approaches to Teaching 'Waiting for Godot'; auth, The Theater: A Concise History (rev.ed.); auth, Arthur Miller's America; auth, The Stages of Arthur Miller. **CONTACT ADDRESS** Dept of English, Univ of Michigan, Ann Arbor, 505 S State St, Ann Arbor, MI 48109-1045. **EMAIL** enochb@umich.edu

BRAUDY, LEO
PERSONAL Born 06/11/1941, Philadelphia, PA, m, 1974, 2 children **DISCIPLINE** LITERATURE **EDUCATION** Swarthmore Col, BA, 63; Yale Univ, MA, 64, PhD, 67. **CAREER** Danforth tchng fel, 65-66, instr, 66-68, Yale Univ; asst prof, 68-70, assoc prof, 70-73, prof, 73-76, Columbia Univ; fac, 72, 73, Bread Loaf Schl; vis instr, 73, 74, vis prof, 75, Yale Univ; prof, 74-77, 79-80, Univ Calif, Santa Barbara; prof, 76-83, Johns Hopkins Univ; prof, 83-85, 98-, Leo S. Bing prof, 85-, univ prof, 98-, chmn, 83-86, 98-99, Univ So Calif. **RESEARCH** History of war, history of fame, 17th century English lit, film hist, theory & criticism, Amer popular cult. **CONTACT ADDRESS** Dept English, Univ of So California, Los Angeles, CA 90089-0354. **EMAIL** braudy@usc.edu

BRAUN, KAZIMIERZ
PERSONAL Born 06/29/1936, Mokrsko Dolne, Poland, m, 1962, 3 children **DISCIPLINE** THEATRE **EDUCATION** Poznan Univ, Poland, ML, 58; Theatre Academy, Warsaw, MFA, 62; Poznan Univ, PhD, 71; Wroclaw Univ, PhD, 75; Polish State Title: Prof, 92. **CAREER** Assoc prof, Wroclaw Univ, 74-85; assoc prof, Sch of Drama, Krakow, 78-85; vis prof, NYork Univ and Swarthmore Col, 85-86; Regents Prof, Univ of Calif, fall 86; Prof with Tenure, State Univ of NYork at Buffalo, 89-. **HONORS AND AWARDS** More than 30 artistic and scholarly Awds in Poland, USA, Canada, Germany, Spain, and Japan, including: Japanese Found Awd, 81; Guggenheim Found Awd, 90; Canadian Aurum Awd, 2000. **MEMBERSHIPS** Int Theatre Inst, PEN Club, Int Fedn for Theatre Res. **RESEARCH** Theatre history and theory. **SELECTED PUBLICATIONS** Auth, A History of Polish Theatre, 1939-1989: Spheres of Captivity and Freedom, Westport, Ct: Greenwood Press (96); auth, Essays on Polish Theater Artists, Warsaw: Semper (96, in Polish); auth, Introduction to Directing, Warsaw: Semper (98, in Polish); auth, Day of Witness, Bystom: 4K Pubs (99, in Polish); auth, Theatre Directing-Arts, Ethics, Creativity, Lewiston: Mellon Press (2000). **CONTACT ADDRESS** Theatre & Dance/ Alumni Complex #278, SUNY, Buffalo, PO Box 605030, Buffalo, NY 14260-0001. **EMAIL** kaz@acsu.buffalo.edu

BRAUNMULLER, A. R.
PERSONAL Born 11/25/1945, Plainfield, NJ **DISCIPLINE** ENGLISH LITERATURE **EDUCATION** Stanford Univ, BA, 67; Yale Univ, M Phil, 70, PhD (English), 71. **CAREER** Asst prof, Dept English, 71-76, assoc prof, Dept of English and Prog in Comparative Lit, 76-82, Prof, Dept of English and Prog of Comparative Lit, 82-; vis prof, Univ Zurich, 90; Dean, Undergrad and Intercollege Curricular Development, 90-. **HONORS AND AWARDS** Nat Merit Scholarship, 63-67; NDEA Title IV Fel, 67-70; Eastman Fel, Yale Univ, 70-71; Folger Shakespeare Library Fel, summer 70, 73; NEH, Younger Humanist, summer 72; Regent's Fac Fel, summer 75; Harvey L. Eby Awd for the Art of Teaching, UCLA, 80; Am Coun of Learned Socs Sr Fel, 85; Col of Letters and Science, UCLA, grant, 85; NEH-Folger Shakespeare Library Sr Fel, 88-89; Gold Shield Faculty Prize, UCLA, 94-96; dir, NEH-Folger Shakespears Libr seminar, 96; coun member, malone soc, 86-; vp, renaissance english text soc, 90-; co-ed, viator: medieval and renaissance studies; ed bd, shakespeare quart, 89-; assoc general ed, new cambridge shakespeare, 89-; trustee, shakespeare asn of am, 95-98; neh seminar leade **MEMBERSHIPS** Modern Lang Asn; Shakespeare Asn of Am; Malone Soc; Renaissance Soc of Am; Renaissance English Text Soc. **RESEARCH** Early modern British and European drama; early modern European art and collecting; Nineteenth- and Twentieth-century British and European drama. **SELECTED PUBLICATIONS** Auth, The Captive Lady (anonymous drama, c. 1622) Malone Society Reprints, Oxford Univ Press, 82; George Peele, G. K. Hall, 83; A Seventeenth-Century Letter-Book: A Facsimile Edition of Folger MS. V.a. 321 with Transcription, Introduction, and Commentary, Univ of DE Press & Assoc Univ Presses, 83; Early Shakespearean Tragedy and Its Contemporary Context: Cause and Emotion in Titus Andronicus, Richard III, and The Rape of Lucrece, in M. Bradbury and D. J. Palmer, eds, Shakespearean Tragedy, Stratford-upon-Avon Studies, 20, Edward Arnold, 84; Comedy from Shakespeare to Sheridan: Change and Continuity in the English and European Tradition: Essays in Honor of Eugene M. Waith, ed and with intro by A. J. Braunmuller and J. C. Bulman, Univ DE Press & Assoc Univ Presses, 86; William Shakespeare, King John, Oxford English Texts, Oxford Univ Press, 89; 'Second Means': Agent and Accessory in Elizabethan Drama, in C. E. McGee and L. Magnusson, eds, Elizabethan Theatre XI, Meany, 90; 'To the Globe I Rowed': John Holles sees A Game at Chess, English Literary Renaissance, 20, 90; The Cambridge Companion to English Renaissance Drama, ed with Michael Hattaway, Cambridge Univ Press, 90; Natural Fictions: George Chapman's Major Tragedies, Univ DE Press & Assoc Univ Presses, 92; William Shakespeare, Macbeth, New Cambridge Shakespeare, Cambridge Univ Press, 97. **CONTACT ADDRESS** Dept of English, Univ of California, Los Angeles, Box 951530, Los Angeles, CA 90095-1530. **EMAIL** barddoc@humnet.ucla.edu

BRAUS, IRA
DISCIPLINE MUSIC **EDUCATION** Oberlin Conservatory, BM; State Univ NYork, MM; Harvard Univ, PhD. **CAREER** Taaught at SUNY Oneonata, New England Conserv of music, Baters College; Prof, Hartt Sch Music, 97-. **SELECTED PUBLICATIONS** Auth, pubs in The History and Psychology of Music. **CONTACT ADDRESS** Hartt Sch Music, Univ of Hartford, 200 Bloomfield Ave, West Hartford, CT 06117. **EMAIL** braus@mail.hartford.edu

BREDBECK, GREGORY W.
DISCIPLINE ENGLISH LITERATURE **EDUCATION** Ohio State Univ, BA; Univ Pa, PhD. **CAREER** Prof, Art Hist, Univ Calif, Riverside. **HONORS AND AWARDS** Outstanding Acad Bk, 91-92. **RESEARCH** English Renaissance studies; Modern and postmodern gay male writing. **SELECTED PUBLICATIONS** Auth, Sodomy and Interpretation: Marlowe to Milton, Cornell Univ Press, 91; Milton's Ganymede: Negotiations of Homoerotic Tradition in Paradise Regained, PMLA, 91. **CONTACT ADDRESS** Dept of Eng, Univ of California, Riverside, 1156 Hinderaker Hall, Riverside, CA 92521-0209. **EMAIL** bredbeck@ucrac1.ucr.edu

BREDIN, MARIAN
DISCIPLINE COMMUNICATIONS **EDUCATION** Trent Univ, BA; Univ Leicester, MA; McGill Univ, PhD. **CAREER** Prof, Brock Univ. **RESEARCH** Cultural politics and cultural identity; minorities and media; aboriginal broadcasting in Canada; feminist cultural analysis. **SELECTED PUBLICATIONS** Auth, Histories of Appropriation: Territorial and Cultural Dispossessopm pf Aboriginal People in Canada, Appropriation and Re-Appropriation: the Return of Canadian Native Voices, Univ of Toronto, 97; Transforming Images: Communication Technologies and Cultural Identity in Nishnawbe- Aski, Cross-cultural Consumption, Routledge, 96; Ethnography and Communication: Approaches to Aboriginal Media, Can Jour Commun 18, 96. **CONTACT ADDRESS** Dept of Communications Studies, Brock Univ, 500 Glenridge Ave, Saint Catharines, ON, Canada L2S 3A1. **EMAIL** mbredin@spartan.ac.brocku.ca

BREEDEN, DAVID M.
PERSONAL Born 03/23/1958, Granite City, IL, m, 1983, 3 children **DISCIPLINE** ENGLISH **EDUCATION** Southern Ill Univ, BA; Univ Iowa Writer's Workshop, MFA; Univ Southern Miss, PhD. **CAREER** Asst prof, Ark State Univ, 88-91; prof, Schreiner Col, 91-. **HONORS AND AWARDS** The Margaret Hosler Awd for Excellence in Teaching. **MEMBERSHIPS** Am Lit Transl Asn, S Central MLA, PEN Ctr USA W, Sigma Tau Delta. **RESEARCH** Old English, Middle English, Prosody. **SELECTED PUBLICATIONS** Auth, Stuck to the Moon; auth, Another Number; transl, The Adventures of Beowulf; auth, Bringing Down the Tower. **CONTACT ADDRESS** Dept Liberal Arts, Schreiner Col, 2100 Memorial Blvd, Kerrville, TX 78028-5611. **EMAIL** dbreeden@schreiner.edu

BREEN, MARCUS
DISCIPLINE COMMUNICATION STUDIES **EDUCATION** Univ Queensland, BA; Australian Nat Univ, BLet; Victoria Univ Tech, PhD. **CAREER** Journalist, 81-90; fes fel, Ctr Int Res Communic, Info Techn, 90-94; consult, Dept State Dev, Victoria, Australia, 94- 96; ASST PROF, UNIV NC, CHAPEL HILL, 96-. **CONTACT ADDRESS** Dept of Communi Studies, Univ of No Carolina, Chapel Hill, 113 Bingham Hall, CB#3285, Chapel Hill, NC 27599-3285. **EMAIL** mbreen@email.unc.edu

BREITROSE, HENRY S.
DISCIPLINE COMMUNICATIONS **EDUCATION** Univ Wis, BA, 58; Northwestern Univ, MA 59; Stanford Univ, PhD, 66. **CAREER** Prof, 60, Stanford Univ. **HONORS AND AWARDS** NBC/BBC Europ Prod Unit, Thames TV; consult, Fr nat TV; consult, Nat Film Bd Can; consult, Asian Inst Broadcast Devel; consult, Corp Pub Broadcasting; found mem ed bd, Quart Rev Film Studies; found ed, Cambridge Studies Film; vpres CILECT, Int Assoc Film TV. **RESEARCH** Intellectual hist of the documentary idea. **SELECTED PUBLICATIONS** Auth, articles in film aesthetics/criticism and experimental attitude change and non-verbal commun in jour such as the Journal of Abnormal and Social Psychology and the Journal of Education Psychology. **CONTACT ADDRESS** Dept Commun, Stanford Univ, McClatchy Hall, Stanford, CA 94305-2050. **EMAIL** hbreit@leland.stanford.edu

BREMEN, BRIAN A.
PERSONAL Born 11/29/1952, Camden, NJ, 2 children **DISCIPLINE** ENGLISH **EDUCATION** Princeton Univ, AB, 75; PhD, 89. **CAREER** Instr, Peddie School, 75-84; asst instr to lectr, Princeton Univ, 86-90; asst to assoc prof, Univ Tex Austin, 90-. **HONORS AND AWARDS** Lib Arts Instr Tech Serv Awd, Univ Tex Austin, 00; Dean's Fel, Univ Tex Austin, 00-01; Harry Ransom Res Ctr Fel, 00-01; Tex Excellence Teaching Awd, 01. **MEMBERSHIPS** Am Lit Assoc, Am Studies Assoc, Coun of Ed of Learned Jour, Kenneth Burke Soc, MLA, Modernist Studies Assoc, William Carlos Williams Soc. **RESEARCH** 20th Century British and American Literature, Modernism, Pedagogy, American Literature, Computers and English Studies, Literature and Medicine, Pragmatism and Literature, Postmodernism, American Ethnogenesis, Literary Theory. **SELECTED PUBLICATIONS** Auth, "'He Was Too Scrupulous Always': A Re-examination of Joyce's 'The Sisters,'" James Joyce Quart, (84); auth, "'The Radiant Gist': 'The Poetry Hidden in the Prose' of William Carlos Williams's Paterson," Twentieth Century Lit, (86); auth, "Emerson, DuBois, and the 'Fate' of Black Folk," Am Literary Realism, 1870-1910, (92); auth, "Jean Toomer," Am Writers Supplement III, Macmillan Publ Co, (91); auth, William Carlos Williams and the Diagnostics of Culture, Oxford Univ Pr, (93). **CONTACT ADDRESS** Dept English, Univ of Texas, Austin, 807 W Lynn, No 117, Austin, TX 78703. **EMAIL** bremen@curly.cc.utexas.edu

BRENNAN, ANNE DENISE
DISCIPLINE 20TH CENTURY AMERICAN AND BRITISH LITERATURE **EDUCATION** St. Louis Univ, PhD, 88. **CAREER** Engl, Col Mt. St. Vincent **HONORS AND AWARDS** Enright Awd Tchg, 92; Higher Opportunity Prog Distinguished Serv Awd, 94; Sr. Magdalen Horsting Spec Awd- Sports Dept. CMSV, 96; Certificate Appreciation-Honors Track CMSV, 96; Honorary Student Life Staff mem, 98. **SELECTED PUBLICATIONS** Auth, Breaking the Ice: Some Highlights of the History of Humor. **CONTACT ADDRESS** Col of Mount Saint Vincent, 6301 Riverdale Ave, Riverdale, NY 10471.

BRENNAN, ANTHONY
DISCIPLINE ENGLISH LITERATURE **EDUCATION** Oxford Univ, BA; McMaster Univ, MA, PhD. **RESEARCH** Shakespeare; modern British drama. **SELECTED PUBLICATIONS** Auth, Onstage/Offstage Worlds in Shakespeare's Plays, 89; auth, Shakespeare's Dramatic Structures, 86; auth, Henry V: A New Critical Introduction, 92. **CONTACT ADDRESS** English Dept, McMaster Univ, 1280 Main St W, Hamilton, ON, Canada L8S 4L9. **EMAIL** abrennan@mcmaster.ca

BRENNAN, JOHN P.
PERSONAL Born 07/02/1942, Melrose, MA, d, 1966, 4 children **DISCIPLINE** ENGLISH **EDUCATION** Boston Col, BS, 63; Univ Calif, Davis, MA, 65, PhD, 67. **CAREER** Assoc English, Univ Calif, Davis, 66-67; asst prof, 67-86, Assoc Prof, English, Ind Univ-Purdue Univ, Ft Wayne, 86-, dir, Composition, 76-78, dir, Graduate Studies, 87-94. **HONORS AND AWARDS** IU summer fac fel, 69; IPFW summer fac fel, 76; NEH summer seminar, 78; Outstanding fac mem, Assisting Disabled Students, IPFW, 83-84; NEH summer inst, 90. **MEMBERSHIPS** AAUP; MLA; Mediaeval Acad Am; Sci Fiction Res Asn; NCTE. **RESEARCH** Chaucer; Old and Middle English literature; Greek and Latin classics; Folklore and traditional music; Science fiction. **SELECTED PUBLICATIONS** Coauth, Medieval manuscripts of Jerome Adversus Jovinianum, Manuscripta, 69; auth, Reflections on a gloss to the Prioress's tale from Jerome's Adversus Jovinianum, Studies Philol, 73; coauth, Anarchism and utopian tradition in The Dispossessed, in Writers of the 21st Century: Ursula K Leguin, Taplinger Publ, 79; auth, Troilas and Criseyde, English Lang Notes, 79; The mechanical chicken: Psyche and society in The Space Merchants, Extrapolation, 84; Administering Truth, Papers in Comparative Studies, 85. **CONTACT ADDRESS** Dept of English & Ling, Indiana Univ-Purdue Univ, Fort Wayne, 2101 Coliseum Blvd E, Fort Wayne, IN 46805-1499. **EMAIL** brennanj@ipfw.edu

BRENNAN, KIT
DISCIPLINE DRAMA **EDUCATION** MA, PhD, Queen's and the Univ Alberta. **CAREER** Assoc prof. **HONORS AND AWARDS** First prize, Can Nat Playwriting Competition, 94; Saskatchewan Writers' Guild lit award, 93; first prize, Dramatic GRAIN Competition, 92; cooord, bfa major in playwriting. **SELECTED PUBLICATIONS** Auth, Tiger's Heart, Scirocco Drama, 96; Spring Planting, Nuage Editions, 98; ed, Going It Alone: Plays by Women for Solo Performers, Nuage Editions, 97. **CONTACT ADDRESS** Dept of Theatre, Concordia Univ, Montreal, 7141 Sherbrooke St W, Montreal, QC, Canada H4B 1R6. **EMAIL** kbrennan@alcor.concordia.ca

BRENNAN, LINDA
PERSONAL Born 02/22/1961, Los Angeles, CA, s **DISCIPLINE** ACTING, VOICE, SPEECH, PSYCHOLOGY **EDUCATION** Calif State Univ, BA, 85; Brandeis Univ, MFA, 88; Antioch Univ, MA, 94. **CAREER** Chair, AM Acad of Dramatic Arts W Voice & Speech Dept; staff therapist, Verougo Mental Health; voice & dialect coach. **MEMBERSHIPS** Calif Asn of Marriage and Family Therapists, Screen Actors Guild, Voice and Speech Teachers Asn, Am Fedn of Television & Radio Artists. **CONTACT ADDRESS** Dept Drama, American Acad of Dramatic Arts, West, 600 Playhouse Alley, Pasadena, CA 91101-5218.

BRENNAN, MARY ALETHEA
PERSONAL Born 06/11/1909, Larksville, PA **DISCIPLINE** PHILOSOPHY, CLASSICS **EDUCATION** Col Mt St Vincent, BA, 30; Cath Univ Am, MA, 44, PhL, 48, PhD(philos), 50; Univ Freiburg & Univ Dublin, 62. **CAREER** Instr chem & math, Cathedral High Sch, New York, NY, 34-35, chem, 35-41, head dept, 41-43; instr chem & Latin, 44-45, asst prof Latin, 45-47, from instr to assoc prof philos, 50-76, Adj Assoc Prof Philos, Col Mt St Vincent, 76- **MEMBERSHIPS** Am Philos Soc; Am Cath Philos Asn; Metaphys Soc Am; Cath Class Asn (pres, 43-44). **RESEARCH** Science, especially chemistry. **SELECTED PUBLICATIONS** Auth, Religion, Law, and Power, the Making of Protestant Ireland, 1660-1760, Albion, Vol 0025, 93; Neither Kingdom Nor Nation in the Irish Quest For Constitutional-Rights, 1698-1800, Albion, Vol 0027, 95. **CONTACT ADDRESS** Dept of Philos, Col of Mount Saint Vincent, Mount View, CA 94039.

BRENNAN, MATTHEW C.
PERSONAL Born 01/18/1955, Richmond Heights, MO, m, 1994, 1 child **DISCIPLINE** ENGLISH **EDUCATION** Grinnell Col, AB, 77; Univ Minn, MA, 80; PhD, 84. **CAREER** Teaching Assoc, Univ of Minn, 78-82; Sr Ed, Gulle and Holmes Financial Learning, 82-84; Vis Asst Prof, Univ of Minn, 84-85; From Asst Prof to Prof, Ind State Univ, 85-. **HONORS AND AWARDS** Univ Res Grant, Ind State Univ, 91, 96; Arts Endowment Grants, Ind State Univ, 93, 98; Ind Arts Comn Master

Fel in Poetry, 94-95; Thomas Merton Ctr Prize in Poetry, 99. **MEMBERSHIPS** Wordsworth-Coleridge Asn, Indianapolis Writers' Center, Acad of Am Poetry, Inst for Evolutionary Psychology. **RESEARCH** Romanticism, Gothic, Literature and visual arts, Contemporary poetry. **SELECTED PUBLICATIONS** Auth, Wordsworth, Turner, and Romantic Landscapes, Camden House, 87; auth, Seeing in the Dark: Poems, Hawkleid Press, 93; auth, The Music of Exile, Coverdale Books, 94; auth, The Gothic Psyche, Camden House, 97. **CONTACT ADDRESS** Dept English, Indiana State Univ, 210 N 7th St, Root Hall, Terre Haute, IN 47809-0001. **EMAIL** M.Brennan@ Indstate.edu

BRENNAN, TIMOTHY A.
DISCIPLINE LITERATURE **EDUCATION** Univ Wis, BA, 76; Columbia Univ, MA, 91; Columbia Univ, PhD, 97. **CAREER** Asst Prof, Purdue Univ, 86-90; Vis Asst Prof, Univ Mich, 89-90; Asst Prof, St Univ NY (SUNY), 90-94; Vis Asst Prof, Rutgers Univ, 93-94; Assoc Prof, St Univ NY (SUNY), 94-97; Assoc Prof, Univ Minn, 98-. **HONORS AND AWARDS** ACLS Grant-in-Aid, 87; Sen Fel, Rutgers Univ, 93-94; Fel, Calif Humanities Res Inst, 90-91; Fulbright Fel, Berlin, 96-97; Sen Fel, Cornell Univ, 96-97; Swedish Inter-Country Grant, 98; McKnight Res Awd, 99; Univ Miami Grand-in-Aid, 99. **MEMBERSHIPS** MLA, Am Comparative Lit Asn, Int Asn for Philos & Lit, Latin Am Studies Asn, Teachers for a Democratic Cult. **RESEARCH** Twentieth-Century literary and cultural theory, European modernity and its relationship to the new world, the triangular relationship between the Caribbean, the United States and Britain, relations between literature, popular culture and cultural policy. **SELECTED PUBLICATIONS** Auth, "Race, Culture.. And Creed," Multiculturalism in Transit: Germany and the U S, Berghahn (98): 13-35; auth, "The Cultural Politics of Rushdie Criticism: All or Nothing," in Critical Essays on Salman Rushdie (New York: G K Hall, 99), 107-128; auth, "Cosmo-Americanism," 2B: A J of Ideas, 13 (98): 135-137; auth, "Poetry and Polemic," Race & Class 41 (99); auth, "The Organizational Imaginary," Cult Critique 43 (00); "The Illusion of a Future: Orientalism as Traveling Theory," Critical Inquiry (00) auth, "The Cuts of Language: The North/South of East/West," in Public Cult (forthcoming). **CONTACT ADDRESS** Dept Lit, Univ of Minnesota, Twin Cities, 9 Pleasant St SE, Minneapolis, MN 55455-0194. **EMAIL** brenn032@tc.umn.edu

BRESLIN, LINDA
DISCIPLINE COMPOSITION **EDUCATION** Cedar Crest Col, BA, 85; MA, 89, Lehigh Univ, PhD, 94. **CAREER** Teacher of Freshman Composition and Literature, Lehigh Univ, 87-94; Instr and Tutor of Reading and Writing, Northampton County Col, 92-94; Teacher of Composition, Johns Hopkins Univ, 92-97; Teacher of Rhetoric and Composition, Texas Tech University, Lubbock, TX, 94-98. **HONORS AND AWARDS** Pres of the Grad Student Coun, Lehigh Univ, 88-90; Grad Leadership Awd, Lehigh Univ, 90; Summer Res Grant from Lehigh Univ, 90; Vice Chair of Nat of Asn of Grad/Professional Students, 90-92; Who's Who Among Teachers in Am Universities and Colleges, 96, 97; Fac Senator, Texas Tech Univ, 96-98. **MEMBERSHIPS** Col Composition and Commun; MLA; Nat Coun of Teachers of English; The Alliance for Computers and Writing. **RESEARCH** Composition Theory; freshman and advanced composition, computer-assisted composition; business and technical writing; british and american survey. **SELECTED PUBLICATIONS** Ed, Approaches to Computer Classrooms: Learning from Practical Experience, SUNY Press, 93; auth, "Audience Defined Through Electronic Experience," Exercise Exchange, (93): 16-17; auth, "Computer-Aided Tutoring: New Ideas for the Writing Center," in Proceedings from the Ninth International Conference on Technology and Education (94); auth, "Electronic Conferencing: Expanding Beyond the LAN," in Computers and Texts (95); auth, "Networking Graduate Students toward Share Governance," Council of Graduate Studies Communicator (95); auth, "Rhetoric? Fun? You Bet," Statements, (98); auty, Editor, Administrative Problem-Solving for Writing Programs and Writing Centers, NCTE (99). **CONTACT ADDRESS** Dept of English, Texas Tech Univ, Mail Stop 3091, Lubbock, TX 79409-3091. **EMAIL** l_breslin@ yahoo.com

BRESLIN, PAUL
DISCIPLINE ENGLISH **EDUCATION** Haverford Col, BA; Univ Va, PhD. **CAREER** Prof, Northwestern Univ. **SELECTED PUBLICATIONS** Auth, The Psycho-Political Muse: American Poetry Since the Fifties, Chicago, 87; auth, You Are Here, TriQuarterly Books, 00; auth, Nobody's Nation: Reading Derek Walcott, Chicago, 01. **CONTACT ADDRESS** Dept of English, Northwestern Univ, Univ Hall 215, 1897 Sheridan Rd, Evanston, IL 60208. **EMAIL** p-breslin@northwestern.edu

BRESNAHAN, ROGER J. JIANG
PERSONAL Born 07/01/1943, Springfield, MA, m, 1970, 1 child **DISCIPLINE** LITERATURE, CULTURAL STUDIES **EDUCATION** Boston Col, BA, 67; New York Univ, MA 68; Univ Mass, PhD, 74. **CAREER** Asst prof, Voorhees Col, 74-76; Vis Lectr, Univ of the Philippines, 76-77; Chair, Vorhees Col, 77-78; prof, Mich State Univ, 78-. **HONORS AND AWARDS** Hon Life Mem, Col English Asn; Fulbright Senior Lectureship; Teacher-Scholar Awd, Mich State Univ; Trio Prog Teaching Awd, Mich State Univ. **MEMBERSHIPS** Assoc for Asian Studies; MLA; Soc for the Study of Midwestern Lit. **RESEARCH** Literature of Southeast Asia, especially Philippines, American Cultural Studies. **SELECTED PUBLICATIONS** Auth, Literature and Society, Manila, 77; auth, In time of Hesitation, Philippines, 81; auth, Conversations with Filipino Writers, Philippines, 90; auth, Angles of Vision, Philippines, 92. **CONTACT ADDRESS** Dept American Thought, Michigan State Univ, 277 Bessey Hall, East Lansing, MI 48824-1033. **EMAIL** bresnaha@msu.edu

BRETT, PHILIP
PERSONAL Born 10/17/1937, Edwinstowe, United Kingdom **DISCIPLINE** MUSIC **EDUCATION** BA, Cambridge 58, BMUS 61, MA, 62, PhD, 65. **CAREER** King's Col, fel, 63-66, asst lectr, 64-66; Dean 66-91; Univ of CA, asst prof, 66-71, assoc prof, 71-78, prof, 78-90; Univ of CA, Riverside, 91-. **HONORS AND AWARDS** Royal Insurance Company Fel and Fulbright Travel Awd, 62-63; The Archibald Davison Medal for Musicology (Harriet Cohen International Music Awds), 70; Am Council of Learned Soc Fel, 71-72; The Noah Greenberg Awd of the Am Musicological Soc, 80; Project Dir, The Byrd Edition, National Endowment for the Hum 80-82; Bd of the Am Musicological Soc, 84-86; Distinguished vis prof, Univ of Alberta, 85; Grammy nomination in the Best Class Choral Perfomance, 91; The Gay and Lesbian Study Group of the Am Musicological Soc Inst Philip Brett Awd, 96; BBC Proms lectr The Britten Era, 97. **MEMBERSHIPS** Am Musicological Soc, Royal Musical Assoc, Soc for Ethnomusicology. **RESEARCH** Eng music, textual criticism and ed, gay studies and queer theory, perfomativity. **SELECTED PUBLICATIONS** Ed, The Byrd Editiong, 76-; ed, Benjamin Britten: Peter Grimes, Cambridge Univ Press, 83; ed, Queering the Pitch: The New Gay and Lesbian Musicology; Crusing the Performative: Interventions into the Representation of Ethnicity, Nationality, and Sexuality, IN Univ Press, 95. **CONTACT ADDRESS** Univ of California, Riverside, Riverside, CA 92521-0325. **EMAIL** pbrett@mail.ucr.edu

BRETT, SALLY A.
DISCIPLINE ENGLISH LITERATURE **EDUCATION** FL State Univ, PhD. **CAREER** Adj asst prof pract eng, Duke Univ. **SELECTED PUBLICATIONS** Auth, publ(s) in American Women Writers, Ungar. **CONTACT ADDRESS** Eng Dept, Duke Univ, Durham, NC 27706.

BREWER, DANIEL
DISCIPLINE THE LITERATURE AND CULTURE OF THE ANCIEN REGIME AND ENLIGHTENMENT **EDUCATION** Johns Hopkins Univ, PhD. **CAREER** Instr, Univ Minn, Twin Cities. **MEMBERSHIPS** Am Soc for eighteenth-century studies; MLA. **RESEARCH** The reception and reinscription of Enlightenment in 19th- and 20th- century French literature, history, and philosophy. **SELECTED PUBLICATIONS** Auth, The Discourse of Enlightenment In Eighteenth-Century France, Cambridge, 93. **CONTACT ADDRESS** Univ of Minnesota, Twin Cities, 9 Pleasant St. SE, 260 Folwell Hall, Minneapolis, MN 55455. **EMAIL** dbrewer@umn.edu

BREWER, MARIA MINICH
DISCIPLINE 20TH-CENTURY NARRATIVE, THEATER, AND CULTURAL THEORY **EDUCATION** Yale Univ, PhD. **CAREER** Instr, Univ Minn, Twin Cities. **RESEARCH** Issues of survival and writing in the aftermath of World War II. **SELECTED PUBLICATIONS** Auth, Claude Simon: Narrativities Without Narrative, Univ Nebr Press, 95. **CONTACT ADDRESS** Univ of Minnesota, Twin Cities, 9 Pleasant St. SE, 350 Folwell Hall, Minneapolis, MN 55455. **EMAIL** mbrewer@ umn.edu

BREWSTER, GLEN
DISCIPLINE ENGLISH **EDUCATION** Univ Tenn, BA, MA; Duke Univ, PhD, 94. **CAREER** Asst Prof, Westfield State Col; Ex instr, Univ Tenn, Duke Univ, Auburn Univ, EC Univ. **HONORS AND AWARDS** John C.Hodges tchg excellence award, Univ Tenn, 94-95. **RESEARCH** Gender roles and refigurations in the poetry of William Blake. **SELECTED PUBLICATIONS** Publ, articles and rev(s), Nineteenth-Century Contexts, South Atlantic Rev, Proceedings of the Soc for the Interdisciplinary Study of Soc Imagery, NC Lit Rev, Southern Hum Rev, Am Studies Intl. **CONTACT ADDRESS** Dept of Engl, Westfield State Col, 577 Western Ave., Westfield, MA 01085. **EMAIL** gbrewster@wirdm.wsc.ma.edu

BREWTON, BUTLER E.
PERSONAL Born 02/07/1935, Spartanburg, SC, m **DISCIPLINE** ENGLISH **EDUCATION** Benedict, BA 1956; Montclair State, MA 1970; Rutgers, PhD 1978. **CAREER** Montclair State Coll, assoc prof, English, 70-. **HONORS AND AWARDS** NDEA fellow SC State Coll 1965. **MEMBERSHIPS** Consultant, McGraw Hill Intl Press 1972; poet NJ State Council on the Arts 1970-76; speaker NCTE Kansas City 1978. **SELECTED PUBLICATIONS** Poems: Tramp, Lady of the Evening, 5 PM, Discovered, Pattern, Barren, Southbound, Idol, Yesterday Hangs, The Custodial Hour, Democracy, The Kiss, For A Reprieve, Peach Orchard, Full Measure, At the General Store, We Children, 1992; Grandpa's, 1992; Rafters, 1992; auth, A Diploma Must Mean What It's Supposed to Mean, New York Times 1986; auth, South and Border States, The Literary Guide to the US; auth, Richard Wright's Thematic Treatment of Women, ERIC; ed, Modern Century Encyclopedia. **CONTACT ADDRESS** English Dept, Montclair State Univ, Upper Montclair, NJ 07043.

BRIER, PETER A.
PERSONAL Born 03/05/1935, Vienna, Austria, m, 1975, 2 children **DISCIPLINE** ENGLISH LITERATURE **EDUCATION** Yale Univ, BA, 56; Harvard Univ, MA, 58; Claremont Grad Sch & Occidental Col, PhD, 71. **CAREER** Instr English, Ark A&M State Col, 58-60; instr, Occidental Col, 65-68; from instr to asst prof, 69-75, assoc prof, 75-81, prof English, Calif State Univ, Los Angeles, 81-; Exchange prof, Maitre de Conf, Univ Clermont-Ferrand, 78-79, 99. **HONORS AND AWARDS** Outstanding Prof Awd, CSULA, 92-93. **MEMBERSHIPS** MLA; Philol Asn Pac Coast. **RESEARCH** English romantic writers; Charles Lamb; literary criticism. **SELECTED PUBLICATIONS** Auth, Acrostic to EB--an unpublished poem by Charles Lamb, English Lang Notes, 9/71; Dramatic characterization in the essays of Charles Lamb, Coranto, spring & summer 73; On teaching Coleridge, Pacific Coast Philol, 4/74; Reflections on Tintern Abbey, Wordsworth Circle, winter 74; Lamb, Dickens and the theatrical vision, Charles Lamb Bull, 4-7/75; The Ambulant mode: Pantomime and meaning in the prose of Charles Lamb, Huntington Libr Quart, 5/77; Caliban Reigns: Romantic theory and some contemporary fantasists, Denver Quart, spring 78; coauth (with Anthony Arthur), American Prose and Criticism, 1900-1950, A Guide to Information Sources, Vol 35, Gale Res Co, 81; Howard Mumford Jones and the Dynamics of Liberal Humanism, Univ Mo Press, 94. **CONTACT ADDRESS** Dept of English, California State Univ, Los Angeles, 5151 Rancho Castilla, Los Angeles, CA 90032-4202. **EMAIL** pbrien@yahoo.com

BRIGGS, JOHN
PERSONAL Born 01/08/1945, Detroit, MI, m, 1968 **DISCIPLINE** ENGLISH **EDUCATION** Wesleyan Univ, BA, 68; NYork Univ, MA, 72; The Union Inst, PhD, 81. **CAREER** Humanities Faculty, The New School for Social Research, 73-87; Adjunct English Dept Faculty, Merch College, 74-87; Assoc Prof of English, Journalism Coord, WCSU, 87-95; Prof of English, Journalism Coord, WCUS; 95, Adjunct faculty: Union Institute, Vermont College of Norwich Univ, 95-98; Asst Ed, Connecticut Review, 97; Co-Chair Dept of English, WCSU, 99; Univ Prof, CT State Univ, 00. **HONORS AND AWARDS** AAUP Res Awd, 91; George Herbert Awd for Poetry, 86. **MEMBERSHIPS** Am Asn of Univ Profs; Nat Writer's Union; Sci and Med Network; Am Soc for Aesthetics. **RESEARCH** Aesthetics, Science and the Arts, Creativity. **SELECTED PUBLICATIONS** Auth, "The Balm of Irony," in Voices on the Threshold of Tomorrow (Boston: Quest Books, 93); auth, "Alice in the Mirror of Art" in Lesi Carroll's Lost Quantum Diaries, ed. William Shanley (Frankfurt: Werner Locher, 98); auth, "Where's The poetry? Consciousness as the Flight of Three Blackbirds" in Advances in Consciousness Research, ed. Paavo Pylkkanen (Amsterdam: John Benjamins Publ, forthcoming); coauth, "Tim O'Brien's Ironic Aesthetic: What is the Nature of a True Story," in O'Brien Criticism, ed. Catherine Calloway (MI: Univ Mich Pr, forthcoming); coauth, Looking Glass Universe, Simon and Schuster, 94; auth, Fire in the Crucible: The Alchemy of Creative Genius, St. Martin's Press, 88; auth, Turbulent Mirror: An Illustrated Guide to Chaos Theory and the Science of Wholeness, Harper & Row, 89; auth, Metaphor, The Logic of Poetry. Revised edition (Pace Univ Press, 91). Orginally The Logic of Poetry, published by McGraw-Hill as a textbook in 74. Coauthored with Richard Monaco; auth, Fractals: The Patterns of Chaos, Simon & Schuster, Touchstone, 92; auth, Seven Life Lessons of Chaos, HarperCollins, 99. **CONTACT ADDRESS** Dept English, Western Connecticut State Univ, 181 White St, Danbury, CT 06810-6826. **EMAIL** briggsjp@wcsu.ctstateu.edu

BRIGGS, JOHN C.
DISCIPLINE RENAISSANCE LITERATURE AND SHAKESPEARE **EDUCATION** Harvard Univ, BA; Univ Chicago, PhD. **CAREER** Prof, Art Hist, Univ Calif, Riverside. **HONORS AND AWARDS** Thomas J Wilson award, 88; fac tchg award, 95-96; dir, basic wrtg prog; inland area wrtg proj. **RESEARCH** Phenomenon of Shakespearean persuasion and the nature of catharsis; Study of Lincoln's rhetoric. **SELECTED PUBLICATIONS** Auth, Francis Bacon and the Rhetoric of Nature, Harvard Univ Press, 88; Edifying Violence: Peter Elbow and the Pedagogical Paradox, Jour of Adv Comp, 98. **CONTACT ADDRESS** Dept of Eng, Univ of California, Riverside, 1156 Hinderaker Hall, Riverside, CA 92521-0209.

BRIGGS, WARD W.
PERSONAL Born 11/26/1945, Riverside, CA, s **DISCIPLINE** CLASSICS **EDUCATION** Wash & Lee Univ, AB, 67; Univ of NC, MA, 69, PhD, 74. **CAREER** Instr, Univ of SC, 73-74; from asst prof to prof, Univ of SC, 75-; visting scholar, Univ VA, 88; Carolina disting. prof of Classics and L. Fry Scudder prof of hum, 96- ; Mel Hill disting. prof, Hobart &

Wm. Smith Colleges, 92-93; Interim Assoc Provost, 96-97. **HONORS AND AWARDS** Phi Beta Kappa; Founders Awd, Confederate Lit Soc, 99. **MEMBERSHIPS** Am Philol Asn; Class Asn of Middle West and South, Am Class League; Institute for Advanced Study, Princton, 99-00. **RESEARCH** Hist of Class Scholarship; Latin lit of the Golden Age. **SELECTED PUBLICATIONS** Auth, Narrative and Simile, 79; Concordantia in Varronis Libros De Re Rustica, 83; Concordantia in Catonis Librum De Agri Cultura, 84; Soldier and Scholar: The Southern Papers of Basil Lanneau Gildeersleeve, 88; coed, Basil Lanneau Gildersleeve: An American Classicist, 86; Classical Scholarship: A Biog Encycl, 90; The Roosevelt Lects of Paul Shorey (1913-1914), 98; ed, The Letters of Basil Lanneau Gildersleeve, 87; Selected Classical Papers of Basil Lanneau Gildersleeve, 92; Biog Dictionary of North American Classicists, 94; Greek Authors, Dictionary of Lit Biog, vol 176, 97; Ancient Roman Auths, Dictionary of Lit Biog, 98. **CONTACT ADDRESS** Dept of French and Classics, Univ of So Carolina, Columbia, Columbia, SC 29208. **EMAIL** wardbriggs@sc.edu

BRIGHT, DAVID F.
PERSONAL Born 04/13/1942, Winnipeg, MB, Canada, m, 2 children **DISCIPLINE** CLASSICS **EDUCATION** Univ Manitoba, BA, 62; Univ Cincinnati, MA, 63 PhD, 67. **CAREER** Univ Manitoba, inst, 61-62; Univ Cincinnati, tchg fel, 63-67; Williams Col, asst prof, 67-70; Univ IL asst prof, assoc prof, prof, ch classics, acting dir, sch Hum, chemn dept classics, dir prog comp lit, acting dean, 70-89; Iowa State Univ, prof, dean of coll lib arts & sci, 89-91, Emory Univ, prof, vpres.arts & sci, dean Emory col, 91-. **HONORS AND AWARDS** Skuli Johnson Gold Medal, Univ Man Gold medallist, Woodrow Wilson Fel, Can Council Res fel, Semple Trav fell, Univ Cinci res fel, Elected Society of Fel, Amer Acad Rome, Delmas Found Schl, Phi Beta Kappa **MEMBERSHIPS** APA, CAMW&S, Vergilian Soc., AAHE **RESEARCH** Latin poetry; literature of late antiquity and early mediaeval literature. **SELECTED PUBLICATIONS** Auth, Haec mihi fingebam: Tibullus in His World, Leiden: Brill, 78; auth, Elaborate Disarray: The Nature of Statius' Silvae, Meisenheim, 80; auth, Classical Texts and their Traditions, Studies in Honor of C.R. Trahman, ed., D.F. Bright & E.S. Ramage, Chico CA: Scholars Press, 84; auth, The Miniature Epic in Vandal Africa, Norman: Univ Oklahoma Press, 87; Theory and Practice in the Vergilian cento, IL Class Stud, 84; auth, The Chronology of the Poems of Dracontius, Classica et Mediaevalia, forthcoming. **CONTACT ADDRESS** Dept of Classics, Emory Univ, N404 Callaway Center, Atlanta, GA 30322. **EMAIL** dbright@emory.edu

BRIND'AMOUR, LUCIE
DISCIPLINE LATE MEDIEVAL AND 16TH CENTURY, AND QUEBEC LITERATURE **EDUCATION** Univ Sherbrooke, B.A, 73; Univ Montreal, M.A, 75; PhD, 77. **CAREER** Assoc chair, Dept Fr and Italian, May 97-; acting chair, summers 97, 98; asst prof, 78-81; assoc prof, 81-, La State Univ. **HONORS AND AWARDS** Grant from the Professional Develeopment Fund Prog for Res in Quebec, Quebec government, summer 81; grant from the Center for French and Francophone Studies, LSU, summer 86. **SELECTED PUBLICATIONS** Auth, L'Archeologie du signe, Pontifical Isnt of Medieval Studies (Toronto), 83; auth, "Charles VIII a Rouen: l'image, le mot et le sens," in Semiotics Unfolding, ed. Tasso Borbe (Mouten, Berlin, 84), 775-782; auth, "Amour et litterature a la fin du Xve siecle: Michault Taillevent et Guillaume Cretin," Fifteenth Century Studies XII (Stuttgart, Akademisher Verlag, 87), 5-15; auth, "La tradition de l'amour courtois. L'Epoque de la Renaissance 1400-1600, " in A Comparative History of Literatures in European Languages sponsored by the Int Comparative Literature Asn (Budapest, Akademiai Kiado, 88), 446-459; auth, "Le plaidoye de l'amant doloreux: d'une plainte sans fin," Fifteenth Century Studies XIV (Stuttgart, Akademisher Verlag, 88). **CONTACT ADDRESS** Dept of Fr Grad Stud, Louisiana State Univ and A&M Col, Baton Rouge, LA 70803.

BRINK, JEAN R.
PERSONAL Born 07/02/1942, Frankfort, IN, w, 2 children **DISCIPLINE** ENGLISH RENAISSANCE LITERATURE **EDUCATION** Northwestern Univ, BA, 64; Harvard Univ, MA, 66; Univ Wis, MA, 66; PhD, 72. **CAREER** Dir, Ariz Ctr Medieval & Renaissance Studies, 81-94; Prof English, Ariz State Univ, 84- **HONORS AND AWARDS** Phi Beta Kappa, 64; Woodrow Wilson Fel, 64; Dean's Quality Teaching Awd, 78; Clark Libr Fel, 80; Newberry Libr Fel, 80; Huntingdon Libr Fel, 92; APS, 93; NEH Fel, 92, 95-96; Univ Res Awd, 96. **MEMBERSHIPS** Spenser Soc, IAUPE, MLA, Milton Soc, Biblio Soc, Soc for the Study of Early Mod Women, RSA, 16th Century Studies; Shakespeare Assoc. **RESEARCH** Edmund Spenser, biography and critical bibliography, the book trade; Michael Drayton's Elizabethan Bibliography. **SELECTED PUBLICATIONS** Auth, "Fortres of Fathers: An Unpublished Sixteenth-Century Manuscript Relating to Patristic Writing on the Eucharist," Sixteenth Century Jour 10, (79); auth, "Samuel Johnson and John Milton," Studies in English Lit 20, (80); auth, Michael Drayton Revisited, 90; auth, "Bathsua Reginald Makin: 'Most Learned Matron,'" Huntington Libr Quart 54, (91): 315-28; ed, Privileging Gender in Early Modern Britain, 93; auth, "Appropriating the Author of the Faerie Queene: Attribution of the View of the Present State of Ireland and A Brief Note of Ireland to Edmund Spenser," Sounds of Things Done . . . in Honor of SK Heninger, JR, ed Peter E Medine and Josephe A Wittreich, (97); auth, "Manuscript Culture Revisted," Sidney Jour 17, (99); auth, "Materialist History of the Publication of Spenser's Faerie Queene," RES, (forthcoming). **CONTACT ADDRESS** Dept English, Arizona State Univ, c/o Reader Services, Henry E Huntington Libr, San Marino, CA 91108. **EMAIL** jbrink@asu.edu

BRINKLEY, ELLEN H.
PERSONAL Born Charleston, WV, m, 2 children **DISCIPLINE** ENGLISH **EDUCATION** Univ Charleston, BA, 69; Western Mich Univ, MA.73; Mich State Univ, PhD, 91. **CAREER** Instr, Ohio Wesleyan Univ, 78-83; Teacher, Madeira High School, 83-86; Director, Third coast Writing Project, Western Mich Univ, 94-; Prof, Western Mich Univ 86-. **MEMBERSHIPS** Nat Coun of Teachers of English, Intl Reading Asn, Nat Coun Against Censorship, Conf on Col Composition and Comm, Conf on English Educ, Center for Expansion of Lang and Thinking, Mich for Pub Educ. **RESEARCH** Censorship; Public education advocacy; Teacher leadership; Composition; Writing assessment; Teaching writing, reading, literature; Religion and teaching English language arts. **SELECTED PUBLICATIONS** Auth, Caught Off Guard: Teachers Rethinking Controversy and Censorship, Boston, 99; auth, "Critical Literacy and Large-Scale Writing Assessment: The Michigan High School Proficiency Test," in The Literacy Connection, 99; auth, "What's Religion Got to Do with Attacks on Whole Language?," In Defense of Good Teaching: What Teachers Need to know About the 'Reading Wars', 98; auth, "Phonics, Whole language, and the Religious and Political Right," In Defense of Good Teaching: What Teachers Need to know About the 'Reading Wars', 98; auth, "Organizing for Political Action: Suggestions from Experience," In Defense of Good Teaching: What Teachers Need to know About the 'Reading Wars', 98; auth, "Believing in What's Possible, Taking Action to Make a Difference," Language Arts, (97): 537-544; auth, "Learning to Use Grammar with Precision Through Editing Conferences," Lessons to Share on Teaching Grammar in Context, Boynton/Cook, 97; auth, "Guidelines for the Professional Developments of Teachers of English Language Arts, 96; auth, "Rethinking Writing in the Classroom: Planning for Writing MEAP and Proficiency Tests," Language Arts Journal of Michigan, (95): 87-97; auth, "Faith in the Word: Examining Religious Right Attitudes about Texts," English Journal, (95): 91-98. **CONTACT ADDRESS** Dept English, Western Michigan Univ, 1201 Oliver St, Kalamazoo, MI 49008-3804. **EMAIL** ellen.brinkley@wmich.edu

BRISMAN, LESLIE
PERSONAL Born 05/22/1944, Brooklyn, NY, m, 1973, 2 children **DISCIPLINE** ENGLISH **EDUCATION** Columbia Col, AB, 65; Cornell Univ, MA, 66, PhD, 69. **CAREER** PROF ENGLISH, YALE UNIV, PRESENTLY **HONORS AND AWARDS** Morse fel, Yale, 73-74; Guggenheim fel, 76-77; National Endowment for the Humanities Seminars, 91, 93, 96, 99; Honorable Mention, The Conference on Christianity and Literature 1990 book Awd; The Sidonie Miskimin Clauss Prize for Teaching Excellence in the Humanities, 00. **SELECTED PUBLICATIONS** Auth, Milton's Poetry of Choice and Its Romantic Heirs, Ithaca, Cornell Univ Press, 73; auth, Romantic Origins, Ithaca, Cornell Univ Press, 78; auth, The Voice of Jacob: On the Composition of Genesis, Bloomington, Indiana Univ Press, 90; auth, Chosen People: The Intra-biblical Critique, forthcoming. **CONTACT ADDRESS** Dept of English, Yale Univ, New Haven, CT 06520-8302. **EMAIL** leslie.brisman@yale.edu

BRITTON, ALLEN PERDUE
PERSONAL Born 05/25/1914, Elgin, IL, m, 1938 **DISCIPLINE** MUSIC **EDUCATION** Univ Ill, BS, 37, MA, 39; Univ Mich, PhD(musicol), 49. **CAREER** Teacher, pub schs, ind, 38-41; instr music, Eastern Ill State Col, 41-43; dean, 69-79, Prof Music, Univ Mich, Ann Arbor, 49-, Emer Dean Sch Music, 79-, Ed, J Music Educ Nat Conf, 53-73; assoc dean sch music, Univ Mich, Ann Arbor, 60-68; mem overseas tours comt, United Serv Orgn-Dept Defense, 62-72; mem exec comt, Mus Am Music, 67-; mem bd trustees, interlochen Ctr Arts, 73-; ed, Am Music, 79-; mem bd dir, Univ Mich Musical Soc, 74- **MEMBERSHIPS** Am Musicol Soc; Am Studies Asn; Music Educ Nat Conf (pres, 60-62, vpres, 62-64); Sonneck Soc. **RESEARCH** Early American music. **SELECTED PUBLICATIONS** Auth, Easy instructor, 1798-1831, J Res Music Educ; Music in Early American public education, Nat Soc Study Educ, 58; Singing school movement in the United States, Cong Report, Int Musicol Soc, 61. **CONTACT ADDRESS** Sch of Music, Univ of Michigan, Ann Arbor, Ann Arbor, MI 48109.

BRKKILA, BETSY
DISCIPLINE ENGLISH **EDUCATION** UC, Berkeley, PhD. **CAREER** Prof, Northwestern Univ. **RESEARCH** 19th century American literature and culture. **SELECTED PUBLICATIONS** Auth, Walt Whitman Among the French: Poet and Myth, 80; Whitman the Political Poet, 89; The Wicked Sisters: Women Poets, Literary History, and Discord, 92; co-ed, Breaking Bounds: Whitman and American Cultural Studies; ed, Ezra Pound: The Contemporary Reviews, 94. **CONTACT ADDRESS** Dept of English, Northwestern Univ, 1801 Hinman, Evanston, IL 60208.

BROADHEAD, GLENN J.
DISCIPLINE TECHNICAL WRITING, RHETORIC AND COMPOSITION **EDUCATION** Univ Calif, PhD, 73. **CAREER** Prog dir, Technical Writing; Assoc prof, Okla State Univ. **HONORS AND AWARDS** NCTE res award. **RESEARCH** Style, composing processes, generative rhetoric, pedagogy in technical communication. **SELECTED PUBLICATIONS** Auth, Variables of Composition: Process and Product in a Business Setting. **CONTACT ADDRESS** Oklahoma State Univ, Stillwater, 101 Whitehurst Hall, Stillwater, OK 74078.

BROCK, DEWEY HEYWARD
PERSONAL Born 06/02/1941, Greenville, SC, m, 1963, 3 children **DISCIPLINE** ENGLISH & AMERICAN LITERATURE **EDUCATION** Newberry Col, AB, 63; Univ KS, MA, 65, PhD(Eng), 69. **CAREER** From instr to asst prof Eng, 68-75, asst dean, col arts & sci, 69, assoc prof, 76-80, dir, Ctr Sci & Cult & Prog Cult Biomed, 77-79, Prof Eng & Life & Health Sci, Univ Of DE, 81-; vis prof, Univ Essex, England, 81-82; Sr Assoc Dean, College of Arts and Science, 87-. **HONORS AND AWARDS** Am Council Learned Soc & Nat Sci Found Fel, Summer Inst Humanistic Computation, 70; fac res grant, Univ DE, 71, 75 & 81; nat bd consults, Nat Endowment for the Hum, 77-83; gen ed, Studies in Sci & Cult, 79-; assoc ed, Lit & Med , 80-; Nat Sci Found & Nat Endowment for Hum Educ Proj, 80; Am Philos Soc fel, 81-82 **MEMBERSHIPS** Council of Col(s) of Arts and Sci(s), Soc for Lit and Sci. **RESEARCH** Renaissance lit; lit and sci; Am lit. **SELECTED PUBLICATIONS** Coauth, Percy MacKaye: Community Drama and the Masque Tradition, Comp Drama, 72; auth, The Portrait of Abbott Samson in Past and Present: Carlyle and Jocelin of Brakelond, Eng Miscellany, 72; coauth, Ben Jonson: A Quadricentennial Bibliography, 1947-1972, Scarecrow, 74; Graham Greene and the Structure of Salvation, Renascence, 74; auth, Durrenmatt's Der Besuch der alten Dame: The Stage and Screen Adaptations, Lit/Film Quart, 76; Mirrors of Man's Life: The Masques of Ben Jonson and social order, Artes Liberales, 76; ed Ben Jonson: Works 1616, Scolar, 76; A Ben Jonson Companion, Indiana, 83; The Doctor as Dramatic Hero, Perspectives in Bio and Med, 91. **CONTACT ADDRESS** Dept of English, Univ of Delaware, Newark, DE 19716. **EMAIL** hbrock@udel.edu

BROCK, JAMES W.
PERSONAL Born 05/23/1919, Greensfork, IN, m, 1941, 3 children **DISCIPLINE** SPEECH **EDUCATION** Manchester Col, AB, 41; Northwestern Univ, MA, 42, PhD(theatre), 50. **CAREER** From instr to assoc prof speech, Albion Col, 45-55; asst prof commun skills, Mich State Univ, 55-56; asst prof speech, Univ Mich, 56-57; assoc prof, Fla State Univ, 57-58; from asst prof to assoc prof, 58-66, chmn dept, 66-69, prof, 66-80, Emer Prof Theatre, Calif State Univ, Northridge, 80-, Fac res grants, Calif State Univ, Northridge, 63-64, 65-68; Church Soc Col Work fel, 64-65. **MEMBERSHIPS** Nat Asn Arts & Humanities; Nat theatre Conf; Am theatre Asn. **RESEARCH** Elizabethan, religious and contemporary drama. **SELECTED PUBLICATIONS** **CONTACT ADDRESS** Dept of Law, Miami Univ, Oxford, OH 45056.

BROCKMAN, WILLIAM S.
PERSONAL Born 06/02/1950, Paterson, NJ, m, 1985, 2 children **DISCIPLINE** ENGLISH, LIBRARY SCIENCE **EDUCATION** Rutgers Univ, BA, 72, MLS, 77; Drew Univ, MA, 86. **CAREER** Ref librn, Rutgers Univ, 77; ref librn, Drew Univ, 77-89; ENG LIBRN, ASSOC PROF, UNIV ILL, URBANA-CHAMPAIGN, 89-. **MEMBERSHIPS** Am Library Assoc; MLA; Internet James Joyce Found. **RESEARCH** James Joyce, bibliography. **SELECTED PUBLICATIONS** Auth, "Current JJ Chedelist," James Joyce Quarterly. **CONTACT ADDRESS** Pennsylvania State Univ, Univ Park, W329 Pattee, University Park, PA 16802. **EMAIL** wsb10@psu.edu

BROCKMANN, STEPHEN
PERSONAL Born 09/04/1960, New York City, NY, S **DISCIPLINE** TWENTIETH CENTURY GERMAN LITERATURE AND CULTURE **EDUCATION** Univ Wisc, PhD, 89. **CAREER** Assoc Prof, German, Carnegie Mellon Univ. **HONORS AND AWARDS** Alexander Von Humboldt Foundation Fellowship, 99. **MEMBERSHIPS** German Studies Assoc; Am Assoc of Teachers of German; Modern Language Assoc of Am; American Assoc of Univ Professors. **RESEARCH** Literature and cultures of the Weimar Republic, Third Reich, German Democratic Republic, and Federal Republic of Germany. **SELECTED PUBLICATIONS** Co-ed, "New German Critique," Special Issue on German Unification, ed Anson Rabinbach, (91), N. 52; co-ed, Dancing on the Volcano: Essays on the Culture of the Weimar Republic, ed. Thomas Kniesche, Camden House, 94; Co-ed, Revisiting Zero Hour 1945: The Emergence of Postwar German Culture, ed. Frank Trommler, Am Inst Contemporary German Studies, 96; Literature and German Reunification, Cambridge Univ Pr, 99; co-ed, Heroes and Heroism in German Culture: Essays in Honor of Jrs and Hermand, ed James Stenkley, Rodopi, forthcoming 01. **CONTACT ADDRESS** Carnegie Mellon Univ, 5000 Forbes Ave, Pittsburgh, PA 15213.

BRODERICK, JOHN CARUTHERS
PERSONAL Born 09/06/1926, Memphis, TN, m, 1949, 2 children **DISCIPLINE** ENGLISH **EDUCATION** Southwestern at Memphis, AB, 48; Univ NC, MA, 49, PhD(English), 53. **CAREER** Instr English, Univ NC, 49-52; Univ Tex, 52-56, spec instr, 56-57; from asst prof to prof, Wake Forest Col, 57-65; specialist Am cult hist, 64-65, asst chief, 65-74, acting chief, 68, chief manuscript div, 75-79, Asst Librn Res Serv, Libr Cong, 79-, Vis prof, Univ Va, 59; Am Coun Learned Soc grant-in-aid, 62-63; adj prof English, George Washington Univ, 64-; vis prof English, Univ NC, 68; mem adv bd, Resources for Am Lit Studies, 70-; Coun Libr Resources fel, 71; advisory comt, US Senate Hist off, 76-; mem, Nat Hist Publ & Records Comn, 78-; gen ed, the Journal of Henry D Thoreau, Princeton Univ, 81- **MEMBERSHIPS** MLA; Soc Am Archivists; Bibliog Soc Am; Am Antiquarian Soc. **RESEARCH** Literature of 19th century New England; Thoreau's essays on government and society; American literary and historical manuscripts. **SELECTED PUBLICATIONS** Auth, The movement of Thoreau's prose, Am Lit, 61; Whitman the Poet, Wadsworth, 62; Emerson and Moorfield Storey: A lost journal found, Am Lit, 66; Emerson, Thoreau and transcendentalism, In: American Literary Scholarship (1967-1971): An Annual, Duke Univ, 69-73; American literary manuscripts, Resources for Am Lit Study, 76; coauth, Librarians of Congress, 1802-1974, Libr of Congr, 77. **CONTACT ADDRESS** Manuscript Div Libr of Cong, Washington, DC 20540.

BRODHEAD, GARRY
DISCIPLINE MUSIC THEORY **EDUCATION** Univ Pa, BA; Univ Ind, MM, PhD. **CAREER** Prof. **SELECTED PUBLICATIONS** Auth, pubs on qualitative time and structure in music. **CONTACT ADDRESS** Dept of Music History, Theory and Composition, Ithaca Col, 100 Job Hall, Ithaca, NY 14850. **EMAIL** gbrodhea@ithaca.edu

BROFMAN, MIKITA
PERSONAL Born 10/30/1966, Sheffield, England, s **DISCIPLINE** LITERATURE **EDUCATION** Oxford Univ, BA, 89; MA, 91; PhD, 94. **CAREER** Asst prof, E Mediterranean Univ, 93-94; asst prof, Univ E London, 94-98; asst prof, Ind Univ, 98-00; prof, Md Inst Col of Art, 00-. **HONORS AND AWARDS** Nielsen Scholar, Oxford Univ, 86-89; Br Acad Award, 90-94. **RESEARCH** Film; Popular culture; Psychoanalysis; Critical theory. **SELECTED PUBLICATIONS** Auth, Offensive Films, Greenwood Press, 97; auth, Meat is Murder, Creation Books, 98; auth, Hollywood Hex, Creation Books, 99; ed, Jack Nicholson, Creation Books, 00; ed, Car Crash Culture, St Martin's Palgrave, 02. **CONTACT ADDRESS** Dept English, Shippensburg Univ of Pennsylvania, Dauphin Humanities Center, Shippensburg, PA 17257. **EMAIL** mibrof@wharf

BROGAN, JACQUELINE V.
DISCIPLINE 20TH-CENTURY AMERICAN, LANGUAGE THEORY **EDUCATION** Southern Methodist Univ, BA, 74; MA, 75; Univ Texas, PhD, 82. **CAREER** Asst prof, Univ of Haw, 83-86; from asst prof to prof, Univ Notre Dame, 86-; vis prof, Univ of Lancaster, fall 94. **HONORS AND AWARDS** NEH fel. **MEMBERSHIPS** Elizabeth Bishop Soc; Am Lit Asn. **RESEARCH** The writing of poetry; the relations between poetry, politics, and ethics. **SELECTED PUBLICATIONS** Auth, Stevens and Simile: A Theory of Language; Part of the Climate: A Critical Anthology of American Cubist Poetry. **CONTACT ADDRESS** Dept of English, Univ of Notre Dame, 356 O'Shaughnessy Hall, Notre Dame, IN 46556. **EMAIL** jacqueline.v.brogan.2@nd.edu

BROKAW, JOHN W.
PERSONAL Born 09/17/1936, Phoenix, AZ, m, 1959, 2 children **DISCIPLINE** THEATRE, DRAMA **EDUCATION** Ariz State Univ, BA, 59; Univ Ariz, MA, 64; Ind Univ, PhD(theatre), 70. **CAREER** Teacher speech-drama, Phoenix High Schs, Ariz, 59-65; co-mgr, Ind Theatre Co, 66-68; from instr to asst prof, 68-74, from assoc prof Drama, Univ Tex, Austin, 74-88; consult, Oceana Publ Inc, 70-; Nat Endowment for Humanities fel, 73; prof, 98-01; prof emer, 01. **HONORS AND AWARDS** Teacher of the Year (Col of Fine Arts, Tex), 88, 96. **MEMBERSHIPS** Soc Theatre Res; Am Soc for Theatre Res. **RESEARCH** Anglo-American, Mexican and Chicano theatre, particularly in the 19th century. **SELECTED PUBLICATIONS** Ed, Thespis adorned, Tobin Found, 71; auth, A nineteenth century Mexican acting company--teatro de Iturbide: 1856-7, Latin Am Theatre Rev, 72; Wilson Barrett's papers: A theatrical legacy, Libr Chronicle, 74; Centro libre experimental de teatro y artistica, Educ Theatre J, 74; An inventory of gas lighting equipment in the Theatre Royal, Hull, 1877, Theatre Surv, 74; The repertory of a Mexican-American theatrical troupe: 1849-1924, Latin Am Theatre Rev, 74; A Mexican-American acting company: 1849-1924, 75 & Teatro Chicano: Some reflections, 77, Educ Theatre J; The London Stage, 1800-10, et, 88; contrib ed, The Adelphi Calendar, 1806-1850, 90; contrib ed, The Adelphi Calendar, 1851-1900, 93; auth, "History of the U.S. Air Force Police," serially, 92. **CONTACT ADDRESS** Dept of Drama, Univ of Texas, Austin, 5706 Trailridge Dr, Austin, TX 78731. **EMAIL** gael@mail.utexas.edu

BROMAN, PER F.
PERSONAL Born 07/26/1962, Norrkoping, Sweden, m, 1997 **DISCIPLINE** MUSICOLOGY **EDUCATION** Ingesund Col Mus, MA, 87; Royal Col Mus, Stockholm, Post-grad Dipl in Mus Theory, 92; McGill Univ, Montreal, MA, 98; Univ Gothenburg, PhD, 99. **CAREER** Asst prof, Swedish Conserv in Jakobstad, Finland, 87-88; lect, Orebro Univ, Sweden, Sch Mus, 91-93; asst prof, Lulea Univ Tech, Sweden, Sch Mus, 93-; ed, Internet publ, STM-Online, 98- ; mem, ed board for ex tempore: A Journal of Compositional and Theoretical Research in Music, 97-; asst prof, Butler Univ, 99-. **HONORS AND AWARDS** Carl-Allan Moberg Musicol Awd, 96; res fel, Univ Gothenburg, fac mus, 97-99. **MEMBERSHIPS** Am Musicol Soc; Soc Mus Theory; Col Mus Soc; Swedish Musicol Soc. **RESEARCH** Aesthetics; Historiography of Western Art Music; Scandinavian Art Music. **SELECTED PUBLICATIONS** Jan Sandstrom and Modernism, Nutida Musik, 37/4, 94, 51-58; Emperor's New Clothes: Performance Practice in the Late Twentieth Century, Journal of Swedish Musicological Society, 76-77, 94-95, 31-53; Paleomodernism, Neomodernism, Postmodernism and the Musical Life in Montreal, Nutida Musik, 38/3, 95, 3-13; A Musicological Debacle, Nutida Musik, 38/1, 95, 79-82; Richard Wagner's Die Meistersinger in Nurnberg: A Hidden anti-Semitic Plan? OV-Revyns Arsbok 1995-96, Stockholm, Operavannerna, 96, 20-22; Darmstadt on memory lane, Nutida Musik, 39, 2-3, 96, 82-84; Camp, Irony, (Neo) Avantgarde: Three Readings of the Gloria Movement from Sven-David Sandstrom's High Mass, Nutida Musik, 39, 2-3, 96, 33-38; Richard Wagners Antisemitism was also Apparent in his Operas, Svenska Dagbladet, May 14, 96; The Russian Folk Music's Importance for Stravinsky, Oxford Univ Press, 96, Svenska Dagbladet, Sept 18, 97; I am no longer sure what MUSIC, New Questions Demand New Answers: Recent Approaches in Musicology, Nutida Musik, 40/1, 97, 4-14; Pluralistic Perception, Token Musics, and Canon Formations: Memoirs from Darmstadt 1996, In the Plural: Institutions, Pluralism and Critical Self-Awareness in Contemporary Music, Copenhagen, Dept Musicol, Univ Copenhagen, 97, 49-53; The Compositions of Bengt Hambraeus, Crosscurrents and Counterpoints: Offerings in Honor of Bengt Hambraeus at 70, 255-66; The Writings of Bengt Hambraeus: A Selective Bibliography, Crosscurrents and Counterpoints: Offerings in Honor of Bengt Hambraeus at 70, 267-280; ed-in-chief, Crosscurrents and Counterpoints: Offerings in Honor of Bengt Hambraeus at 70, Gothenburg, Univ of Gothenburg, 98; The Idea of the Authentic Performance Is a Chimera, Svenska Dagbladet, Jan 29, 98; auth, Back to the Future: Towards an Aesthetic Theory of Bengt Hambraeus, Gothenburg, Univ Gothenburg, 99. **CONTACT ADDRESS** Butler Univ, 2625 N Meridian St, Apt 526, Indianapolis, IN 46208-7705. **EMAIL** pbroman@butler.edu

BROMMEL, BERNARD
PERSONAL Born 08/13/1930, Des Moines, IA, d, 6 children **DISCIPLINE** SPEECH, HISTORY **EDUCATION** IA Northern Univ, BA, 51; State Univ IA, MA, 55; IN Univ, PhD, 63; post doc, Family Inst, Northwestern univ, 83. **CAREER** Tchr, High Sch, IA, 51-54; Keokuk Sr High & Community Col, 54-59; assoc prof speech, IN State Univ, 59-67; prof & chmn dept, Univ ND, 67-71; prof speech, Northeastern IL Univ, 71-97, Mem bd dir, Eugene V Debs Found, 68-98; scholar in residence, Newberry Libr, 71-83; bd dir, Lakeview Mental Health Ctr & IL Labor Hist Soc, 71-91; priv psychotherapist, 80-00. **HONORS AND AWARDS** Best Biog Awd, Soc Midland Authors, 79. **MEMBERSHIPS** Speech Commun Asn; Cent States Speech Commun Asn; Int Commun Asn; Soc Midland Authors (pres, 82-83). **RESEARCH** Hist; speech; commun; family commun. **SELECTED PUBLICATIONS** Auth, Pacifist Speechmaking of Eugene V Debs, Quart J Speech, 66; Debs' Cooperative Commonwealth Movement, Labor Hist, fall 71; coauth, Vocalic Communication in Persuasion, Quart J Speech, 10/72; Eugene V Debs: Spokesman for Labor & Socialism, 78; (with K Galvin), Family Communication: Cohesion and change, 5th ed, 99. **CONTACT ADDRESS** Dept of Speech, Northeastern Illinois Univ, 5500 N St Louis Ave, Chicago, IL 60625-4625. **EMAIL** brnbrommel@aol.com

BROMWICH, DAVID
DISCIPLINE ENGLISH **EDUCATION** BA, 73, PhD, 77, Yale Univ. **CAREER** Instr, 77-78, Asst Prof, 78-83, Assoc Prof, 83-87, Mellon Prof, 87-88, Princeton Univ; Prof, 88-, Housum Prof, 95-, Yale Univ. **CONTACT ADDRESS** Dept of English, Yale Univ, New Haven, CT 06520-8302.

BROOK, BARRY SHELLEY
PERSONAL Born 11/01/1918, New York, NY, m, 1958, 2 children **DISCIPLINE** MUSICOLOGY **EDUCATION** City Col New York, BSS, 39; Columbia Univ, MA, 42; Univ Paris, DUniv, 59. **CAREER** Tutor music, 45-47, from instr to assoc prof, 48-66, Prof Musicol, Queens Col, NY, 66-; Exec Off, PHD Prog in Music, City Univ New York, 67-, Ford Found fel, 54-55; Fulbright res scholar, 58-59; adv ed col music, Holt, Rinehart & Winston, inc, 60-; mem, Nat Screening Comt, Fulbright awards in musicol, 60-63; Guggenheim fels, 61-62 & 66-67; Univ Club Educ Found res grant, 62; vis prof, Grad Sch Arts & Sci, NY Univ, 64-65; inst Musicol, Sorbonne, 67-68; Nat Endowment for Humanities grant to estab computerized bibliog of music lit, 67-68; ed, RILM Abstr, 67-; Martha Baird Rockefeller & Am Coun Learned Soc grants for RILM proj, 68; mem, Music Adv Screening Comt Sr Fulbright Awards, 68-70; chmn, Comn Mixte, Repertoire int Iconographie Musicale, 72- **HONORS AND AWARDS** Publ Awd, Nat Ctr Sci Res, 62; Dent Medal, Royal Musical Asn, 65; Chevalier, Order of Arts & Lett, France, 72. **MEMBERSHIPS** Am Musicol Soc; int Musicol Soc; Fr Musicol Soc; Belgian Musicol Soc; Royal Musical Asn. **RESEARCH** Music and aesthetics of the classical period; sociology of music; computer applications in musicology. **SELECTED PUBLICATIONS** Auth, On Reprinting Music and Books About Music in then and Now, Fontes Artis Musicae, Vol 0039, 92; The Symphonie Concertante in Its Musical and Sociological Bases/, Int Rev Aesthet and Sociol Mus Vol 0025, 94. **CONTACT ADDRESS** Ctr Mus Res & Documentat, Graduate Sch and Univ Ctr, CUNY, 50 Central Park West, New York, NY 10021.

BROOKER, JEWEL SPEARS
PERSONAL Born 06/13/1940, Jenkins, KY, m, 1962, 2 children **DISCIPLINE** MODERN BRITISH & AMERICAN LITERATURE **EDUCATION** Stetson Univ, BS, 62; Univ Fla, MA, 64; Univ SFla, PhD(English), 76. **CAREER** Postdoctoral Fel English, Yale Univ, 80-81 fel English, Yale Univ, 80-81; Prof Eckerd Col, 81-; Vis Scholar, Univ of Cambridge (English), 87; Vis Prof, Columbia Univ, 99; Vis Prof, Doshisha Univ, Kyoto, Japan, 92-94; Kahml Fel in Lit. Manuscripts, Harvard Univ, 99; John Adams Fel, Univ of London, 00. **HONORS AND AWARDS** Nat Endowment for Humanities fel, 80, 87; Sears-Roebuck Found Teaching Excellence and Campus Leadership Award, 89-90; SAMLA Prize, best scholarly essay, SAtlantic Mod Lang Asn, 93-94; grants from Knight Found, Liberty Fund, Fla Endowment for the Humanities. **MEMBERSHIPS** MLA; Int Asn Philos & Lit; Am Asn Advan Humanities. **RESEARCH** T S Eliot; T E Hulme and Irving Babbitt. **SELECTED PUBLICATIONS** Auth and ed, Approaches to Teaching Eliot's Poetry and Plays, Mod Lang Asn, 88; ed, The Placing of T.S. Eliot, Univ Mo Press, 91; coauth, Reading The Waste Land: Modernism and the Limits of Interpretation, Univ Mass Press, 90; auth, Mastery and Escape: T.S. Eliot and the Dialectic of Modernism, Univ Mass Press, 94; ed, Conversations with Denise Levertov, Univ Press of Miss, 98; T.S. Eliot and Our Turning World, Macmillan (forthcoming 98); author of numerous essays and reviews in scholarly journals. **CONTACT ADDRESS** Letters Collegium, Eckerd Col, 4200 54th Ave S, Saint Petersburg, FL 33711-0000. **EMAIL** jsbrooker@aol.com

BROOKS, A. RUSSELL
PERSONAL Born 05/19/1906, Montgomery, AL **DISCIPLINE** ENGLISH LITERATURE **EDUCATION** Morehouse Col, AB, 31; Univ Wis, AM, 34, PhD, 58. **CAREER** Instr English, Univ High Sch, Univ Atlanta, 32-33; prof & chmn, Agr & Tech Col NC, 34-44; prof, Morehouse Col, 46-60; Prof & Head Dept, KY State Col, 60-72; Retired. **MEMBERSHIPS** MLA; NCTE; Col Lang Asn. **RESEARCH** James Boswell; Afro-American literature. **SELECTED PUBLICATIONS** Auth, A Tribute to Daniel,Maggie,Crowne, Cla J-Coll Lang Asn, Vol 0037, 94. **CONTACT ADDRESS** Kentucky State Univ, 415 College Park Dr, Frankfort, KY 40601.

BROOKS, DWIGHT E.
PERSONAL Born 05/05/1955, Philadelphia, PA, m, 1991, 1 child **DISCIPLINE** COMMUNICATION STUDIES, MEDIA & CULTURAL STUDIES **EDUCATION** East Stoudsburg Univ, BA, 77; Ohio State Univ, MA, 79; Univ of Iowa, PhD, 91. **CAREER** Professional radio, commercial and noncommercial. **MEMBERSHIPS** Nat Commun Asn; Broadcast Ed Asn; Asn for Ed in Journalism & Mass Commun. **RESEARCH** Cultural studies; race, gender, & media; media programming; advertising & consumer culture. **SELECTED PUBLICATIONS** Auth, Magazine Advertising and Minorities, Hist of the Mass Media in the United States: An Encycl, Garland Pub, in press; auth, Black Magazines and National Advertising: An Historical Perspective, Hist of the Mass Media in the United States: An Encycl, Garland Pub, in press; auth, Space Traders, Media Criticism, and the Interpositional Communicative Strategy, Redings in Cultural Contexts, Mayfield Pub Co, 98; auth, Basic Cable Netowrk Programming, Broadcast/Cable Programming: Strategies and Practices, Wadsworth Pub, 96; auth, In Their Own Words: Advertisers' Construction of an African American Consumer Market, the World War II Era, The Howard J of Commun, 95; auth, Ebony and Our Consumer Culture, Afrian Am Forum, 95; coauth, Black Men in the Margins: Space Traders and the Interpositional Strategy Against B[l]acklash, Commun Studies, 96; couath, Research and Organizing Messages, Intro to Speech Commun, Waveland Press, 94. **CONTACT ADDRESS** Dept of Telecommunications, Univ of Georgia, Athens, GA 30602-3018. **EMAIL** debrooks@arches.uga.edu

BROSNAHAN, LEGER
PERSONAL Born 12/11/1929, Kansas City, MO, m, 1967, 2 children **DISCIPLINE** ENGLISH, LITERATURE, COMPOSITION, ESL **EDUCATION** Georgetown Univ, AB, 51; Harvard Univ, MA, 52; PhD, 58. **CAREER** Instr, Northwestern Univ, 57-61; asst prof, Univ of Hawaii-Manoa, 61-63; asst prof, Univ of Md at Col Park, 65-68; from assoc prof to prof, Ill State Univ, 68-. **MEMBERSHIPS** ALSC, NAS, MSA, AAUP, MLA. **RESEARCH** English Language, Literature, Composi-

tion, ESL, Comparative Medieval Literature. **SELECTED PUBLICATIONS** Auth, Around the World in English, Kenkyusha, 74; auth, Japanese and English Gesture, Taishukan, 88; auth, Chinese and English Gesture, BLCUP, 91; auth, Standard American English Behavior, Dongyang Munhuasa, 98. **CONTACT ADDRESS** Dept English, Illinois State Univ, 1 Campus PO Box 4240, Normal, IL 61790. **EMAIL** lnbrosna@ilstu.edu

BROTHERS, THOMAS
DISCIPLINE MUSIC **EDUCATION** Univ CA Berkeley, PhD. **CAREER** Musicol prof, Duke Univ. **RESEARCH** Music of the 14th, 15th and 16th centuries; African-Am music; jazz. **SELECTED PUBLICATIONS** Auth, publ(s) on Medieval and Renaissance music. **CONTACT ADDRESS** Dept of Music, Duke Univ, Mary Duke Biddle Music Bldg, Durham, NC 27706. **EMAIL** tdb@duke.edu

BROUGHTON, THOMAS ROBERT SHANNON
PERSONAL Born 02/17/1900, Corbetton, ON, Canada, m, 1931, 2 children **DISCIPLINE** CLASSICS, ANCIENT HISTORY **EDUCATION** Univ Toronto, AB, 21, MA, 22; Johns Hopkins Univ, PhD (Latin), 28. **CAREER** Instr Greek, Amherst Col, 26-27; assoc Latin, Bryn Mawr Col, 28-30, from assoc prof to prof, 30-65; Paddison prof class, 65-70, Emer Prof Classics, Univ NC, Chapel Hill, 70-, Vis prof, Johns Hopkins Univ, 38-40; Guggenheim fel, 45-46; Fulbright res grant, Italy, 51-52; prof in charge, Sch Classical Studies, Am Acad Rome, 59-61; vpres, int Fed Soc Classical Studies, 59-69; mem comt res libr, Am Coun Learned Soc, 67; ann mem, inst Advan Studies, 71-72. **HONORS AND AWARDS** Awd, Am Philol Asn, 53; lld, johns hopkins univ, 69, univ toronto, 71 & univ nc, chapel hill, 74. **MEMBERSHIPS** Am Acad Arts & Sci; AHA; Archaeol inst Am (hon vpres, 53-58); Am Philol Asn (pres, 54); Class Asn Can. **RESEARCH** Economic history of Rome; provinces of the Roman Empire; Roman constitutional history and politics. **SELECTED PUBLICATIONS** Auth, Dionysus and the History of Archaic Rome, Classical J, Vol 0088, 93. **CONTACT ADDRESS** Dept of Classics, Univ of No Carolina, Chapel Hill, Murphey Hall, Chapel Hill, NC 27514.

BROWN, A. PETER
PERSONAL Born 04/30/1943, Chicago, IL, m, 1968, 1 child **DISCIPLINE** HISTORICAL MUSICOLOGY **EDUCATION** Northwestern Univ, BME, 65, MM, 66, PhD(music), 70. **CAREER** Asst prof music, Univ Hawaii, 69-74; assoc prof, 74-81, Prof Musicol, Ind Univ, Sch Music, 81-, Am Coun Learned Soc fel Ordonez, 72-73; Guggenheim Found fel haydn, 78-79; NEH Col Teaching Sem Dir, 84. **HONORS AND AWARDS** Malin Awd for Excellence in the res and editing of choral music. **MEMBERSHIPS** Am Musicol Soc; int Musicol Soc; Music Libr Asn; Nat Acad Rec Arts & Sci. **RESEARCH** Viennese music 1730-1830; history of orchestral music; Joseph Haydn. **SELECTED PUBLICATIONS** Auth, Carlo d'Ordonemz: A Thematic Catalogue, Info Coordr, 78; contribr, Papers for Haydn Festival and Conference, 75, Norton, 81; The Symphonies of Carlo d'Ordonez, Haydn Yearbk, XII; Approaching Musicol Classicism, CMS Symposium, XX; Joseph Haydn and Leopoid Hofmannn's Street Songs, XXXIII & Notes on some Viennere copyists, XXXIV, Am Musicol Soc J; ed, Seven Symphonies of Carlo d'Ordonez, Garland, 79; String Quartest op 1 of Carlo d'Ordonez, A-R, 80; auth, Performing Haydn's the Creation, Indiana, 85; auth, Haydn's Keyboard Music, Indiana, 86; auth, Music Publisher Guera of Lyon, Information Coordinators, 87; ed, Haydn, The Creation, Oxford, 91 & 95; auth, The Symphonic Reputoire (5 Vols.) Vol. III, Indiana, 01. **CONTACT ADDRESS** Sch of Music, Indiana Univ, Bloomington, Bloomington, IN 47401. **EMAIL** brownap@indiana.edu

BROWN, ALAN K.
PERSONAL Born 12/21/1938, San Francisco, CA, m, 1971, 2 children **DISCIPLINE** ENGLISH **EDUCATION** Hamilton Col, BA, 56; Stanford Univ, PhD, 69. **CAREER** Instructor to Lecturer, Univ Ariz, 63-70; Assoc Prof to Prof, Ohio State Univ, 70-. **HONORS AND AWARDS** SE Medieval and Renaissance Summer Sem, 79; NEH Res Grant, 84-89. **MEMBERSHIPS** Medieval Soc of Am, Linguistic Soc of Am. **RESEARCH** Old English literature; Middle English literature; Early-medieval Latin glossaries; Pacific coast in late colonial Spanish history and explorations; environmental history of California. **SELECTED PUBLICATIONS** Auth, Old Irish Astol, Old English Lestel: The Common Etymology, Cambridge, 93 **CONTACT ADDRESS** Dept English, Ohio State Univ, Columbus, 164 W 17th Ave, Columbus, OH 43210-1326. **EMAIL** abrown+@osu.edu

BROWN, ALANNA KATHLEEN
PERSONAL Born 02/07/1944 **DISCIPLINE** ENGLISH LITERATURE **EDUCATION** Univ Calif, Santa Barbara, BA, 66, MA, 68, PhD(English), 74. **CAREER** Asst prof, 73-78, assoc prof English & asst dean Lett & Sci, Mont State Univ, 78-83, Nat Endowment Humanities fel in residence, 75-76; Danforth Assoc, 75; act dir, Univ Honor's Prog, 82-85; from assoc prof to prof English, 78-95, 95-. **HONORS AND AWARDS** Burlington Northern Teaching Awd for Excellence, 89; NEH Summer Stipend to work on Mourning Dove's Okanogan Sweat House, 94; Outstanding Teacher, Col of Letters & Sci, 96; Phi Kappa Phi Honor Society Western Region Distinguished Scholar, 98-01. **MEMBERSHIPS** MLA; Western Literature Assoc. **RESEARCH** Native American Literature & Victorian Literature. **SELECTED PUBLICATIONS** Auth, The Self and the other: George Meredith's The Egoist, Women and Violence in Literature, ed Kathleen Ackley, New York: Garland, 90; auth, Mourning Dove (Humishuma), Dictionary of Literary Biography: Native American Writers of the United States, Vol 175, ed, Kenneth M Roemer, Detroit, Washington, DC, London: Bruccoli Clark Layman, 97. **CONTACT ADDRESS** Dept of English, Montana State Univ, Bozeman, Bozeman, MT 59717-0001. **EMAIL** brown@english.montana.edu

BROWN, ARTHUR A.
PERSONAL Born 03/18/1955, New York, NY, m, 1985, 2 children **DISCIPLINE** ENGLISH **EDUCATION** Univ Calif, Berkeley, BA, 76; Univ N Mex, MA, 88; Univ Calif, Davis, PhD, 94. **CAREER** Asst prof, Univ Evansville, 95-. **HONORS AND AWARDS** Regents Fel, 92-93, Univ Calif, Davis. **MEMBERSHIPS** MLA **RESEARCH** American literature; narrative theory. **SELECTED PUBLICATIONS** Auth, art, Death and Telling in Poe's "The Imp of the Perverse," 94; auth, art, Benjy, the Reader, and Death: At the Fence in 'The Sound and the Fury,' 95; auth, art, Literature and the Impossiblity of Death: Poe's "Berenice," 96; auth, art, Henry James and Immortality: 'The Beast in the Jungle and Is There a Life After Death,' 98; auth, art, Ghosts and the Nature of Death in Literature: Henry James' 'Sir Edmund Orme,' 98. **CONTACT ADDRESS** Dept of English, Univ of Evansville, 1800 Lincoln Ave, Evansville, IN 47722. **EMAIL** ab48@evansville.edu

BROWN, BILL
PERSONAL Born 07/20/1957, Trenton, ND, m, 1985, 1 child **DISCIPLINE** ENGLISH **EDUCATION** Duke, BA; Stanford, PhD. **CAREER** Asst prof to prof, Univ of Chicago, 89-. **MEMBERSHIPS** Am Studies Assoc; MLA. **RESEARCH** 19th and 20th century American literature and cultural history, literary theory. **SELECTED PUBLICATIONS** Auth, The Material Unconscious: American Amusement, Stephen Crane and the Economies of Play, Harvard; auth, Reading the West, Bedford Books. **CONTACT ADDRESS** Dept English, Univ of Chicago, 5845 S Ellis Ave, Chicago, IL 60637-1476. **EMAIL** wlbrown@midway.uchicago.edu

BROWN, BRENDA
PERSONAL Born 08/30/1963, St Louis, IL, m, 1985, 3 children **DISCIPLINE** ENGLISH **EDUCATION** Univ N Tex, BA, 84; Univ Tex, MA, 86; Tex Christian Univ, PhD, 91. **CAREER** Assoc prof, Univ Sci and Arts Okla, 92-. **HONORS AND AWARDS** Sigma Tau Delta; Kappa Delta Pi; USAO Travel Grant, 93, 95-99; Regents Awd Scholar, 95, 96; Gladys Emerson Res Awd, 93-96, 99. **MEMBERSHIPS** CCCC; NCTE; SCMLA; OCTE; HEACO. **RESEARCH** Modern American Novel, American Literature, Rhetoric and Composition Theory. **SELECTED PUBLICATIONS** Auth, "Elizabeth Barrett Browning's Twentieth-Century Works", PMPA, (90): 16-20; auth, "Baby Talk", Out Near Phantom Hill, 90; auth, "The History and Application of the Toulmin Model", English in Tex 22, (91): 10-14; auth, "Home Truth: A Powerful, Understated Novel", Tex Books in Rev 7, (92): 11; auth, "Revisiting Revision", English in Tex 25.1 (93): 28-30; auth, "Elocution", Encycl of Rhetoric, 93; auth, "Call No Man Master", Tex Books in Rev (95): 25; auth, "English for Careers: Business, Professional, and Technical", Issues in Teaching Writing, (97): 204-206; auth, "War", Encycl of am Lit, 99. **CONTACT ADDRESS** Dept Humanities, Univ Sci and Arts Okla, PO Box 82345, Chickasha, OK 73018. **EMAIL** facbrownbr@usao.edu

BROWN, CAROLE ANN
PERSONAL Born 05/26/1936, New York, NY, m, 1956, 2 children **DISCIPLINE** ENGLISH **EDUCATION** Univ Minn, BA, 56, MA, 61, PhD(English), 65. **CAREER** Teaching asst English, Univ Minn, 57-60, from instr to asst prof, 61-74, assoc prof, 74-80, Prof, Hamline Univ, 80- **MEMBERSHIPS** MLA; NCTE; Conf Col Compos & Commun. **RESEARCH** Eighteenth century English literature; English Renaissance literature; modern novel. **SELECTED PUBLICATIONS** Auth, The art of the novel: Virginia Woolf's the Voyage Out, Virginia Woolf Quart, 77. **CONTACT ADDRESS** Dept of English, Hamline Univ, Saint Paul, MN 55101.

BROWN, DAN
DISCIPLINE COMMUNICATION STUDIES **EDUCATION** Univ Mass, PhD, 82. **CAREER** Assoc prof, 84-. **SELECTED PUBLICATIONS** Auth, pubs on learning from media; effects of television on family values; entertainment features in children's educational television; content and uses of pornography; humor in mass media and college teaching; public communication about the causes of disease. **CONTACT ADDRESS** Dept of Communication, East Tennessee State Univ, PO Box 70717, Johnson City, TN 37614-0717.

BROWN, GEORGE HARDIN
DISCIPLINE ENGLISH **EDUCATION** BA, 55; PhL, 56; Univ St Louis Univ, MA, 59; Univ Innsbruck, BD, 63; Harvard Univ, PhD, 71. **CAREER** Prof, Stanford Univ. **RESEARCH** Old and Middle Eng philology; post-classical Latin, espec Anglo-Latin; Latin and Medieval vernacular paleography. **SELECTED PUBLICATIONS** Auth, Bede the Venerable, 87; The Dynamics of Literacy in Anglo-Saxon England in The 94 Toller Lecture, John Rylands Lib; Bede the Educator, Jarrow Lecture, 96. **CONTACT ADDRESS** Stanford Univ, Bldg 20, Main Quad, Stanford, CA 94305.

BROWN, HARRY MATTHEW
PERSONAL Born 01/24/1921, Newark, OH, m, 1951, 4 children **DISCIPLINE** ENGLISH **EDUCATION** Malone Col, ThB, 45; Baldwin-Wallace Col, AB, 46; Western Reserve Univ, MA, 48, PhD(English), 55. **CAREER** Instr English, Baldwin-Wallace Col, 46-50; teaching fel, Western Reserve Univ, 50-53; asst prof, Shepherd Col, 53-56; from asst prof to assoc prof English, 56-63; intermediate instr, Calif State Polytech Col, 63-66; dean humanities & soc sci, 68-78, prof English, Midwestern State Univ, 66-. **HONORS AND AWARDS** Minnie Stevens Piper Prof, 81. **MEMBERSHIPS** MLA; NCTE; Am Bus Commun Asn; Conf Col Teachers English. **RESEARCH** American literature; poetry; literature and religion. **SELECTED PUBLICATIONS** Coauth, Readings for College Writers, 2nd ed, Ronald, 67; Patterns in Poetry, Scott-Foresman, 68; A Workbook for Writers, 4th ed, Van Nostrand, 70; auth, Thought-Patterns for Composition, Prentice-Hall, 76; The Contemporary College Writer, 2nd, Van Nostrand, 77; coauth, Practical English Workbook, Van Nostrand, 78; auth, How to Write, Holt, 78; Business Report Writing, Van Nostrand, 80. **CONTACT ADDRESS** Dept of English, Midwestern State Univ, 3410 Taft Blvd, Wichita Falls, TX 76308-2096.

BROWN, HOMER O.
PERSONAL Born, OK, m, 3 children **DISCIPLINE** ENGLISH LITERATURE, CRITICAL THEORY **EDUCATION** Univ Okla, BA, 59; John Hopkins Univ, MA, 64; PhD, 66. **CAREER** Asst prof, Columbia Univ, 66-71; assoc prov, SUNY Buff, 74-75; assoc prof, 71-79; prof, Univ Cal, Irvine, 79-. **HONORS AND AWARDS** HRIS Res Fel; SUNY Res Grant; Am Soc 18th Century Stud Best Essay; Univ Ill Res Fel; Fels Diss Fel. **MEMBERSHIPS** MLA. **RESEARCH** Transatlantic literature; 18th and 19th Century British and American Novel and Poetry. **SELECTED PUBLICATIONS** Auth, Institutions of the English Novel: from Defoe to Scott, Univ Penn Press (97); auth, James Joyce Early Fiction: The Biography of a Form, Case Western Res (73); auth, "The Institution of the English Novel: Defoe's Contribution," Novel: A Forum on Fiction 29 (96): 299-318; auth, "Why the Story of the Origin of the (English) Novel is an American Romance," in Cultural Institutions of the Novel, eds. Deidre Lynch, William Warner (Duke UP, 96); auth, "Of the Title og Things Real: Conflicting Stories," ELH: J Eng Lit Hist 55 (88): 917-54. **CONTACT ADDRESS** Dept English, Univ of California, Irvine, Irvine, CA 92697. **EMAIL** hobrown@uci.edu

BROWN, JAMES DALE
PERSONAL Born 04/28/1948, Spokane, WA **DISCIPLINE** AMERICAN LITERATURE, AUTOBIOGRAPHY **EDUCATION** Univ Wash, BA, 70, MA, 71; Univ Ore, PhD(English), 79. **CAREER** Instr English, Univ Ore, 79-80; Res & Writing, 81-, Fiction ed, Northwest Rev, 78; chief ed, Northwest Rev Bks, 81. **MEMBERSHIPS** Am Studies Asn; Assoc Writing Prog; MLA; Philol Asn Pac Coast. **RESEARCH** American autobiography; American writers in Europe; Science fiction and fantasy. **SELECTED PUBLICATIONS** Auth, Henry Miller: From the Everglades to China, Northwest Rev, 78; coauth, Dict of Literary Biography: Americans in Paris, 1920-1939, Gale, 79; auth, Jay Martin's biogrpahy, Mod Fiction Studies, 79-80; coauth, Dict of Literary Biography Yearbook: 1980, 81, Dict of Literary Biography Yearbook: 1981, 82 & Documentary Encyl of Literature, 82, Gale; ed, The Anthology of Eugene Writers, Northwest Rev Bks, 82. **CONTACT ADDRESS** Box 2921, Eugene, OR 97402.

BROWN, JARED
PERSONAL Born 12/03/1936, New York, NY, m, 1958, 2 children **DISCIPLINE** THEATER **EDUCATION** Ithaca Col, BA, 60; San Francisco St Col, MA, 62; Univ Minn, PhD, 67. **CAREER** Assoc prof, 65-78, prof, 79-89, acad dir, 79-80, Western Ill Univ; prof, dir, schl theatre arts, 89-, Ill Wesleyan Univ. **HONORS AND AWARDS** Dupont Awd for Teaching Excellence, 97; Chosen "Best Dir" by The Pantagraph, 91, 91, 94, 96; Summer Stipend, 88; Barnard Hewitt Awd, 87; Distinguished Fac Lectr, 86. **RESEARCH** Amer theatre history; dramatic theory. **SELECTED PUBLICATIONS** Auth, The Fabulous Lunts, Atheneum, 86; auth, Zero Mostel: A Biography, Atheneum, 89; auth, The Theatre in America during the revolution, Cambridge Univ Press, 95; auth, American National Biography, Oxford Univ Press, 99. **CONTACT ADDRESS** Sch of Theatre Arts, Illinois Wesleyan Univ, PO Box 2900, Bloomington, IL 61704-2900. **EMAIL** jbrown@titan.iwu.edu

BROWN, JESSIE LEMON
PERSONAL Born 05/15/1911, Columbia, SC, m **DISCIPLINE** ENGLISH **EDUCATION** Hampton Inst, BS, 34; Columbia Univ, MA, 45, EdD(English), 55. **CAREER** Teacher high sch, Va, 35-44; from instr to prof English, 44-70, dir spec proj upgrading & remediation, 65-70, dir div lang & lit, 67-70,

Old Dominion Prof Humanities & Dir Freshman Commun Ctr, Hampton Inst, 70-, Consult teaching English, Va Sec Schs, 58-63. **HONORS AND AWARDS** Lindback Distinguished Teaching Awd, 63-64. **MEMBERSHIPS** Col English Asn; Asn Higher Educ. **SELECTED PUBLICATIONS** Contribr, Communication in General Education, W C Brown, 60; auth, Identifying academic achievement, Va Teachers Asn Bull, 12/61; The road less traveled by--a message to college students, Negro Hist Bull, 3/64. **CONTACT ADDRESS** Dept of English, Hampton Univ, Hampton, VA 23368.

BROWN, JULIA PREWITT
PERSONAL Born 02/10/1948, St. Louis, MO, m, 4 children **DISCIPLINE** ENGLISH LITERATURE **EDUCATION** Barnard Col, BA, 70; Columbia Univ, MA, 71, PhD(English), 75. **CAREER** Asst prof, 74-90, prof English, Boston Univ, 90-. **HONORS AND AWARDS** Mellon Grant, Harvard Univ, 79. **MEMBERSHIPS** MLA; ALSC. **RESEARCH** English novel; Victorian literature; late 19th century aestheticism in England. **SELECTED PUBLICATIONS** Auth, Jane Austen's Novels: Social Change and Literary Form, Harvard Univ; Reader's Guide to 19th Century Novel, Macmillan; Cosmopolitan Criticism: Oscar Wilde's Philosophy of Art, Virginia. **CONTACT ADDRESS** 236 Bay State Rd., Boston, MA 02215-1403.

BROWN, LADY
PERSONAL Born 01/18/1941, Snyder, TX, m, 1964, 1 child **DISCIPLINE** COMPOSITION AND RHETORIC **EDUCATION** TX Tech Univ, PhD, 89. **CAREER** Lectr, dir, writing ctr, TX Tech Univ; exec bd, Alliance for Comput and Writing; ed bd, Writing Ctr J. **HONORS AND AWARDS** NWCA Outstanding Serv Awd, 94, Outstanding fac mem, Mortar Bd and Omicron Delta Kappa, TX Tech Univ, 95. **MEMBERSHIPS** Pres, Nat Writing Ctr Asn. **RESEARCH** Writing center theory and practice; computer-based writing instruction. **SELECTED PUBLICATIONS** Contrib biblir to the CCCC Bibliography of Composition and Rhetoric; auth, "Owls in theory and Practice: A Director's Perspective," Taking Flight with OWLS, Erlbaum. **CONTACT ADDRESS** Texas Tech Univ, Lubbock, TX 79409-5015. **EMAIL** L.Brown@ttu.edu

BROWN, LINDA BEATRICE
PERSONAL Born 03/14/1939, Akron, OH, m, 1985, 2 children **DISCIPLINE** ENGLISH LITERATURE, AFRICAN-AMERICAN LITERATURE, CREATIVE WRITING **EDUCATION** Bennett Col, BA, 61; Case Western Reserve, MA, 62; Union Inst, PhD, 80. **CAREER** Instr, Kent State Univ, 62-66; instr, Univ NC, Greensboro, 70-86; assoc prof, Guilford Col, 86-92; distinguished prof of Humanities, Bennett Col, 92-. **HONORS AND AWARDS** NC Coalition of the Arts Awd for Best Novel by Minority Writers, 80; grant for summer in residence at Headlands, CA from NC Arts Coun, 94. **MEMBERSHIPS** NC Writers Network, bd member; HELUS. **RESEARCH** African-American history. **SELECTED PUBLICATIONS** Auth, Rainbow 'Roun Mah Shoulder, novel; Crossing Over Jordan, novel. **CONTACT ADDRESS** Bennett Col, 900 E Washington St, Greensboro, NC 27401. **EMAIL** lbeatrice@aol.com

BROWN, LORRAINE ANNE
PERSONAL Born 04/03/1929, Grand Rapids, MI, m, 1951, 1 child **DISCIPLINE** ENGLISH, AMERICAN LITERATURE **EDUCATION** Univ Mich, BA, 52, MA, 61; Univ Md, PhD(Am lit), 68. **CAREER** Asst prof, 67-73, assoc prof, 74-80, Prof English, George Mason Univ, 80-; assoc dir, Fed Theatre Res Ctr, 76-78. **HONORS AND AWARDS** George Mason Univ res grant, 75; Nat Endowment for Humanities res grant, 76-78. **MEMBERSHIPS** MLA; SAtlantic Mod Lang Asn; Am Studies Asn; Am Theatre Asn; Women's Caucus Mod Lang Asn. **RESEARCH** Henrik Ibsen; Adrienne Kennedy; contemporary drama, American, English and continental. **SELECTED PUBLICATIONS** Auth, The characters are myself, Negro Educ Forum, fall 75; Swanhild and the Mermaid, Scand Studies, summer 75; coauth, FTP Scrapbook, New Repub Bks, 11/78; auth, Black Drama: Federal Theatre, Franklin (in press). **CONTACT ADDRESS** Dept of English, George Mason Univ, Fairfax, 4400 University Dr, Fairfax, VA 22030-4444. **EMAIL** lbrown@gmu.edu

BROWN, MARION MARSH
PERSONAL Born 07/22/1908, Brownville, NE, m, 1937, 1 child **DISCIPLINE** ENGLISH **EDUCATION** Nebr State Teachers Col, Peru, AB, 27; Univ Nebr, MA, 31. **CAREER** Teacher English, High Sch, Auburn, Nebr, 27-29; Nebr Sch Agr, Curtis, Nebr, 29-31; high sch, Wayne, Nebr, 31-32; Franklin, 32-33; instr English & jour, Nebr State Teachers Col, Peru, 33-37; instr English, Univ Nebr, Omaha, 45-51, from asst prof to prof, 52-68; Retired. **HONORS AND AWARDS** Distinguished Serv Awd, Nebr State Teachers Col, 79. **MEMBERSHIPS** Am Asn Univ Women; Nat League Am Pen Women. **RESEARCH** Semantics and linguistics; great Americans who make inspirational biographies for young people. **SELECTED PUBLICATIONS** Coauth, The Silent Storm, Abingdon, 63; auth, Stuart's Landing, Westminster, 68; coauth, Willa Cather: the Woman and her works, Scribner, 69; Marnie, Westminster, 71; auth, The Pauper Prince, Crescent, 73; The Brownville Story, Nebr State Hist Soc, 74; Only One Point of the Compass, Archer, 80; Homeward the Arrow's Flight, Abingdon, 80; Letters Home + Remarks on Reading of Personal Correspondence of Authors Deceased Father/, Harvard Libr Bull, Vol 4, 1993. **CONTACT ADDRESS** 2615 N 52nd St, Omaha, NE 68104.

BROWN, MARK W.
PERSONAL Born 09/20/1959, Birmingham, AL **DISCIPLINE** ENGLISH **EDUCATION** Samford Univ, BA, 81; Vanderbilt Univ, MA, 83; PhD, 89. **CAREER** Lectr, Vanderbilt Univ, 90-91; asst prof to prof, Jamestown Col, 91-. **MEMBERSHIPS** MLA. **RESEARCH** Modern British and American Poetry. **SELECTED PUBLICATIONS** Auth, "A Style So Worn and Bare: Pheidias, Praxiteles, and the 'Eros' of Robert Bridges," Dalhousie Rev, (93-94): auth, "Ivor Gurney and Edward Thomas: A Distinction," PN Rev, (95); auth, "Hopkins and Gurney Again," Studies: An Irish Quart Rev, (96); auth, "Music and Lyrics by Ivor Gurney," Ivor Gurney Soc Jour, (97). **CONTACT ADDRESS** Jamestown Col, 6021 College Lane, Jamestown, ND 58405. **EMAIL** brown@jc.edu

BROWN, MONKIA
PERSONAL Born 08/17/1950, Friedberg, Germany, m, 1974, 1 child **DISCIPLINE** ENGLISH **EDUCATION** Univ Ga, BA, 70; Duke Univ, MA, 73; PhD, 81. **CAREER** Teacher, DeKalb Co Schools, 70-71; Lecturer, Univ Munster, 75-77; Instructor, Winthrop Col, 80-82; Lecture to Prof, Univ NC, 82-. **HONORS AND AWARDS** Outstanding Teaching Awd, UNC, 97; NEH Summer Sem, 86, 92; NEH Summer Inst, 90. **MEMBERSHIPS** Nat Coun of Teachers of English, Mod Lang Asn, Col Conf on composition & comm, Col English Asn, Victorians Inst, 19th Century Studies Asn. **RESEARCH** Victorian fiction and criticism, 19th Century European literature and culture, Literature adaptations in film and music. **SELECTED PUBLICATIONS** Auth, "Joining the Critical conversation in a sophomore Literature Class," The CEA Critic, (99): 17-33; auth, "Film Music as sister Art: Adaptations of the Turn of the Screw," Mosaic: An Interdisciplinary Journal of Literature, (98): 61-81; auth, "Joseph Conrad," dictionary of Literary Biography. Short Fiction, 1880-1920: The romantic Tradition, Gale Research, 96; auth, "Reading Realist Literature: Madame Bovary in a Great books or World Literature Course," in Approaches to Teaching Flaubert's Madame Bovary, New York, 95; auth, "Thomas Carlyle" and "Johann Wolfgang von Goethe" in Research Guide to European Historical Biography, Beacham, 93; auth, "Literary Theory and Criticism," Romanticism: an Encyclopedia, Garland Pub, 92. **CONTACT ADDRESS** Dept English Theatre and Lang, Univ of No Carolina, Pembroke, Pembroke, NC 28372-1510.

BROWN, PEARL LEBLANC
PERSONAL Born 06/28/1936, Youngsville, LA, m, 1960, 1 child **DISCIPLINE** ENGLISH **EDUCATION** Univ Southwestern La, BA, 57; Univ Ark, MA, 58, PhD(English), 65. **CAREER** Instr English, Univ Southwestern La, 58-60; asst prof, St Mary's Col, Minn, 63-66; asst prof, 66-72, Assoc Prof English, Quinnipiac Col, 72-. **RESEARCH** Romantic poetry, especially Keats. **CONTACT ADDRESS** Dept of English, Quinnipiac Col, 275 Mt Carmel Ave, Hamden, CT 06518.

BROWN, ROBERT E.
PERSONAL Born 01/11/1945, New York, NY, d, 1 child **DISCIPLINE** ENGLISH; COMMUNICATIONS **EDUCATION** Univ Rochester, PhD, 66. **CAREER** Assoc prof, Salem State Col. **MEMBERSHIPS** Nat Commun Asn. **RESEARCH** Public Relations. **SELECTED PUBLICATIONS** Auth, Investor Relations Trends, Soc Sci Monitor, 1:2, 90; Senior Corporate Officer Perceptions About Communication, NY State Speech Jour, VII 1, 93; Congruence of Orientations Toward Public Relations: A Cross-Cultural Comparison of British and American Practicioners, World Commun Asn Jour, 22, 93; Communication Strategies of College Students: Winning a Public Relations Award, The Strategist, 97/98. **CONTACT ADDRESS** Dept of English, Salem State Col, 352 Lafayette Ave, Salem, MA 01970. **EMAIL** d28man@mindspring.com

BROWN, RUSSELL MORTON
PERSONAL Born 12/02/1942, Elizabeth City, NC, m, 1964, 1 child **DISCIPLINE** ENGLISH **EDUCATION** Univ St Thomas, Houston, BA, 65; State Univ NY Binghamton, MA, 68, PhD(English), 72. **CAREER** Instr English, State Univ NY, Binghamton, 68-69; asst prof, Lakehead Univ, 69-77; assoc prof Eng, Scarborough Col, Univ Toronto, 77-, Ed, Lakehead Univ Rev, 72-75; co-ed, Descant, 78-. **MEMBERSHIPS** MLA. **RESEARCH** Canadian prairie writing and culture its relationship to the emergence of postmodernism. **SELECTED PUBLICATIONS** Auth, Borderlines and Borderlands in English Canada: The Written Line, The Borderlands Project (Orono, ME), 90; coed, An Anthology of Canadian Literature in English, Oxford Univ Pr (Toronto, ON), 90; auth, "'The Same Old Story Once Again': Making Rain and Making Myth in Kroetsch's The Words of My Roaring," Open Letter 9th Ser (96): 129-46; auth, "Selves in Letters: Laurence, Purdy, and Laurence-Purdy," La Creation Biographique: Biographical Creation (97): 219-225. **CONTACT ADDRESS** Div of Humanities, Univ of Toronto, 1265 Military Trail, West Hill Scarborough, ON, Canada M1C-1A4. **EMAIL** rbrown@shass.utoronto.ca

BROWN, RUTH CHRISTIANI
PERSONAL Born 11/18/1917, Sidney, MT, m, 1938, 3 children **DISCIPLINE** ENGLISH LITERATURE **EDUCATION** Univ Mont, Ba, 39; Univ Tex, El Paso, MA, 62; Ariz State Univ, PhD(English), 71. **CAREER** Lectr English, Ariz State Univ, 62-65; asst prof, 66-80, Assoc Prof English, Calif State Univ, San Diego, 80-. **MEMBERSHIPS** AAUP; MLA; NCTE. **RESEARCH** Nineteenth century British novel; modern British novel. **SELECTED PUBLICATIONS** Auth, The role of Densher in The Wings of the Dove, Mod Spraak, 71; A precursory vision, Poland, 12/72; Nostromo: Women opposing the world, the flesh, and the devil, In: Proc Int Contrad Conf, H Mursia, Milan, 74. **CONTACT ADDRESS** Dept of English, San Diego State Univ, San Diego, CA 92115.

BROWN, STEPHEN JEFFRY
PERSONAL Born 03/30/1929, Moline, IL, m, 1969 **DISCIPLINE** ENGLISH LITERATURE **EDUCATION** Yale Univ, BA, 50, PhD(English), 59 Cambridge Univ, BA, 52. **CAREER** Instr English, Yale Univ, 57-60; asst prof, Swarthmore Col, 60-64; assoc prof, George Washington Univ, 64-68; assoc dean, 68-70, Prof English, George Mason Univ, 68-. **MEMBERSHIPS** MLA; Shakespeare Asn Am. **RESEARCH** English Renaissance drama and poetry; history, sociology and literature. **CONTACT ADDRESS** Dept of English, George Mason Univ, Fairfax, 4400 University Dr, Fairfax, VA 22030.

BROWN, STEVEN
PERSONAL Born 07/05/1952, Hayward, CA, s **DISCIPLINE** ENGLISH **EDUCATION** Univ Calif, BA, 74; San Diego State Univ, MA, 79; Univ Pittsburgh, PhD, 96. **CAREER** Instr to Staff Admin Univ Pittsburgh, 86-95; Instr to Asst Prof, Youngstown State Univ, 95-. **HONORS AND AWARDS** Master Teacher Awd, Youngstown State Univ, 97; Phi Beta Delta, 96. **MEMBERSHIPS** Teachers of English to Speakers of Other Lang, Am Asn for Applied Linguistics, Intl Reading Asn, Materials Development Asn, Nat Coun of Teachers of English, Ohio Teachers of English to Speakers of Other Lang. **RESEARCH** Foreign/second language reading and listening comprehension; Foreign/second language materials development. **SELECTED PUBLICATIONS** Co-auth, Understanding Language Structure, Interaction and Variation, Univ Mich Press, 00; co-auth, English Firsthand Beginners Course, Longman Pub, 00; ed, Journeys, Prentice Hall, 97-99; co-auth, English Firsthand Gold Edition, Longman Pub, 99; co-auth, Active Listening: Expanding Understanding through Content, Cambridge Univ Press, 96; co-auth, Active Listening: Introducing Skills for Understanding, Cambridge Univ Press, 95. **CONTACT ADDRESS** Dept English, Youngstown State Univ, 1 Univ Plaza, Youngstown, OH 44555-0001. **EMAIL** srbrown@cc.ysu.edu

BROWN, T. DENNIS
DISCIPLINE MUSIC **EDUCATION** Boston Univ, BM; Univ Mich, MM, PhD. **CAREER** Assoc prof, Univ Mass, Amherst, 77-. **SELECTED PUBLICATIONS** Auth, pubs in Music Edu J, Annual Jazz Rev, Percussive Notes, Instrumentalist, and Nat Asn Jazz Edu Res Papers. **CONTACT ADDRESS** Dept Music and Dance, Univ of Massachusetts, Amherst, Amherst, MA 01003. **EMAIL** tdbrown@music.umass.edu

BROWN, TERRY
DISCIPLINE ENGLISH LITERATURE **EDUCATION** VA Tech Univ, MA; Univ FL, PhD. **CAREER** Prof, Univ of WI; Asst Dean of Arts and Scis. **SELECTED PUBLICATIONS** Auth, pubs on women's studies, Virginia Woolf, Kathy Acker; sexuality; classroom pedag. **CONTACT ADDRESS** Eng Dept, Univ of Wisconsin, River Falls, 410 S 3rd St, River Falls, WI 54022. **EMAIL** terry.m.brown@uwrf.edu

BROWN, THOMAS H.
PERSONAL Born 01/03/1941, Granite Falls, MN, m, 1961, 3 children **DISCIPLINE** ENGLISH **EDUCATION** Western State Col, Colo, BA, 62; Ohio Univ, MA, 69; Univ Ga, PhD(-English), 73. **CAREER** Teacher English, Minneapolis Pub Schs, 64-68; instr, Univ Ga, 72-73; Asst Prof English, Univ Miss, 74-. **MEMBERSHIPS** NCTE; SCent Mod Lang Asn; Col English Asn. **RESEARCH** Colonial American literature of the South; medicine in history. **SELECTED PUBLICATIONS** Auth, The quest of Dante Gabriel Rosetti in the Blessed Damozel, Victorian Poetry, 72; Noah Webster and the medical profession, J AMA, 10/13/75; An introduction to Go Down, Moses (monogr), Miss Libr Comn, 76; Flannery O'Connor's use of eye imagery in Wise Blood, SCent Bull, 77; co-ed, Dimensions; Essays for Composition, Winthrop, 79. **CONTACT ADDRESS** Dept English, Univ of Alabama, Birmingham, 1530 3rd Ave S, Birmingham, AL 35294-0001.

BROWN-GUILLORY, ELIZABETH
PERSONAL Born 06/20/1954, Lake Charles, LA, m, 1983, 1 child **DISCIPLINE** ENGLISH **EDUCATION** Univ of Southwestern Louisiana, BA, English, 1975, MA, English, 1977; Florida State Univ, PhD, English, 1980. **CAREER** Univ of South Carolina, Spartanburg, asst profr of English, 80-82; Dillard Univ, asst prof of English, 82-88; Univ of Houston, prof of English, 98-. **HONORS AND AWARDS** UH Cooper Teaching Excellence Awd, 97; Sigma Tau Delta, Outstanding

Professor, 91 and 00; UH Coun of Ethic Organization Awd; Young Black Achievers of Houston Awd; Louisiana state wide competition, First Place Playwriting Awd, 85; The City of New Orleans Playwriting Awd, 83; Florida State Univ, Res Fel, 79. **MEMBERSHIPS** Southern Conf on Afro-Am Studies, Inc; Col Language Assoc; South Central Modern Language Assoc; Modern Lang Assoc; Int Women's Writing Guild; Am Soc for Theatre Res; Conf of Col Teachers of English of Texas; Black Theater Network; Assoc for Theatre in Higher Education. **SELECTED PUBLICATIONS** Editor: Wines in the Wilderness: Plays by African-American Women from the Harlem Renaissance to the Present, 1990; Editor: Women of Color: Mother-Daughter Relationships in 20th Century Literature, 1996; Author: Their Place on the Stage: Black Women Playwrights in America, 1988; playwright: Mam Phyllis, Snapshots of Broken Dolls, 1987; Bayou Relics, 1983; numerous others. **CONTACT ADDRESS** English Dept, Univ of Houston, 4800 Calhoun Rd, Houston, TX 77204-3012. **EMAIL** ebrown-guillory@utt.edu

BROWNE, DONALD R.
PERSONAL Born 03/13/1934, Detroit, MI, m, 1958, 3 children **DISCIPLINE** MASS COMMUNICATIONS **EDUCATION** Univ Mich, AB, 55, MA, 58, PhD(speech, polit sci), 61. **CAREER** Radio & TV off, US Inform Serv, 60-63; asst prof mass commun, Boston Univ, 63-65; speech, Purdue Univ, 65-66; assoc prof, 66-70, dir off int prog, 76-78, Prof Radio & TV, Univ Minn, Minneapolis, 70-; Off Int Prog res grant, Univ Minn, 67-68 & 70-, McMillan Fund travel grant, 70- & 72-; Fulbright-Hays vis prof, Am Univ Beirut, 73-74. **HONORS AND AWARDS** Outstanding Young Teacher Awd, Cent States Speech Asn, 68. **MEMBERSHIPS** Broadcast Educ Asn; Int Commun Asn; Asn Educ in Jour; Int Inst Commun. **RESEARCH** International broadcasting; comparative broadcasting and national development. **SELECTED PUBLICATIONS** **CONTACT ADDRESS** Dept of Speech, Univ of Minnesota, Twin Cities, 460 Folwell Hall 9 Pleasant St S.E., Minneapolis, MN 55455. **EMAIL** brown003@tc.umn.edu

BROWNE, RAY B.
PERSONAL Born 01/15/1922, Millport, AL, m, 1952, 3 children **DISCIPLINE** ENGLISH **EDUCATION** Univ Ala, AB, 43; Columbia Univ, MA, 47; Univ Calif, Los Angeles, PhD, 56. **CAREER** Instr English, Univ Nebr, 47-50, Univ Md, 56-60; assoc prof, Purdue Univ, 60-67; Prof Popular Cult & English, Bowling Green State Univ, 67-, Chmn Dept, 80-, Exec secy, Popular Cult Hall of Fame; ed, J Popular Cult. **MEMBERSHIPS** MLA; Popular Cult Asn (secy-treas); Am Studies Asn; Am Folklore Soc. **CONTACT ADDRESS** Popular Press, Bowling Green State Univ, Bowling Green, OH 43403. **EMAIL** rbrowne@bgnet.bgsu.edu

BROWNE, WILLIAM FRANCIS
PERSONAL Born 12/26/1935, Pittsburgh, PA, m, 1986, 4 children **DISCIPLINE** VICTORIAN LITERATURE **EDUCATION** Long Island Univ, BA, 69, MA, 71; City Univ New York, PhD, 79. **CAREER** Adj lectr Am lit & compos, 71-73, instr, Eng & Am lit & compos, 73-79, asst prof eng & Am lit & compos,assoc prof, 82-96, prof, 96-, Brooklyn Col, 71. **HONORS AND AWARDS** Book of the Year Award, 99. **RESEARCH** Victorian studies (Hardy, Gissing and Browning); Am studies (Melville, Twain, Wright and Browning). **SELECTED PUBLICATIONS** Auth, Gissing's Boinin Exile: spiritual distance between author and character, 4/79 & Gissing: The reluctant prophet, 4/80, Gissing Newslett; Two Kinds of Courage: Frederick Douglas and John Brown. **CONTACT ADDRESS** Dept Eng Am Lit, Brooklyn Col, CUNY, 2901 Bedford Ave, Brooklyn, NY 11210-2813. **EMAIL** wbrowne@catskill.net

BROWNING, JUDITH
PERSONAL m, 2 children **DISCIPLINE** RENAISSANCE LITERATURE, DRAMA, 19TH-20TH CENTURY WOMEN'S LITERATURE, COMPOS **EDUCATION** Northern AZ Univ, BS; Rutgers Univ, MA; Grad Theol Un, PhD. **CAREER** Prof, assoc dean, Sch of Liberal Stud & Pub Aff, ed, Golden Gate Univ Fac News, Golden Gate Univ. **HONORS AND AWARDS** Outstanding Tchg Award, Golden Gate Univ, 96. **MEMBERSHIPS** MLA. **SELECTED PUBLICATIONS** Auth of articles on Milton, Renaissance lit, and tchg of lit. **CONTACT ADDRESS** Golden Gate Univ, 536 Mission St, San Francisco, CA 94105-2968. **EMAIL** jbrowning@ggu.edu

BROWNING, MARK
PERSONAL Born 12/28/1962, Independence, MO, m, 1982, 4 children **DISCIPLINE** ENGLISH **EDUCATION** William Jewell Col, BA, 84; Univ Mo, MA, 88; Univ Kans, PhD, 96. **CAREER** From asst prof to assoc prof, Johnson County Community Col, 88-. **HONORS AND AWARDS** NISOD Teaching Excellence Awd; Burlington Northern Santa Fe Fac Achievement Awd. **MEMBERSHIPS** MLA, NCTE. **RESEARCH** Religious Formations of Racial Attitudes, Religious Rhetoric. **SELECTED PUBLICATIONS** Auth, Haunted by Waters: Fly-Fishing in North American Literature," Univ Ohio Press, 98; auth, "Your Logos Against Mine," dialogue: A J for Writing Specialists 6 (99): 8-13. **CONTACT ADDRESS** Dept Commun, Johnson County Comm Col, 12345 Col Blvd, Shawnee-Mission, KS 66210-1283. **EMAIL** mbrownin@jccc.net

BROWNLEY, MARTINE WATSON
PERSONAL Born 07/27/1947, Spartanburg, SC **DISCIPLINE** ENGLISH LITERATURE; WOMEN'S STUDIES **EDUCATION** Agnes Scott Col, BA, 69; Harvard Univ, AM, 71, PhD(English), 75. **CAREER** Goodrich C. White Prof of English and Winship Distinguished Res Prof, Emory Univ, 96-. **HONORS AND AWARDS** Recognition Awd, Am Asn Univ Women, 78; Fel for Univ Teachers, NEH, 88-89. **MEMBERSHIPS** MLA; Am Soc 18th Century Studies; Southeastern Am Soc 18th Century Studies. **RESEARCH** 17th & 18th century British literary historiographers; Women's studies. **SELECTED PUBLICATIONS** Ed., Mothering the Mind, Holmes & Meier, 84; Auth, Clarendon and the Rhetoric of Historical Form, U of Penn P, 85; ed., Women and Autobiography, Scholarly Resources, 99; auth, Deferrals of Domain: Contemporary Women Novelists and the State, St. Martin's P, 00. **CONTACT ADDRESS** Dept of English, Emory Univ, 537 Kilgo Cir N-317, Atlanta, GA 30322. **EMAIL** mbrown1@emory.edu

BROYLES, MICHAEL
DISCIPLINE MUSIC HISTORY, HISTORY **EDUCATION** Austin Coll, BA, 61; Univ Texas at Austin, MA, 64, PhD, 76. **CAREER** Prof, mus, Univ Maryland Baltimore; PROF, MUS & AM HIST, PENN STATE UNIV. **MEMBERSHIPS** Am Antiquarian Soc **SELECTED PUBLICATIONS** Auth, A Yankee Musician in Europe: The European Journals of Lowell Mason, UMI Research Press, 90; auth, "Music and Class Structure in Antebellum Boston," Jour of the Am Mus Soc, 91; auth, "Music of the Highest Class": Elitism and Populism in Antebellum Boston, Yale Univ Press. 92. **CONTACT ADDRESS** Sch of Mus, Pennsylvania State Univ, Univ Park, University Park, PA 16802. **EMAIL** broyles@psu.edu

BRUCCOLI, MATTHEW J.
PERSONAL Born 08/21/1931, New York, NY, m, 1957, 4 children **DISCIPLINE** ENGLISH **EDUCATION** Yale Univ, BA, 53; Univ of Va, MA, 56; PhD, 60. **CAREER** Asst prof to prof, Ohio State Univ, 61-69; prof, Univ of SC, 69-; Jefferies Prof, 76-. **HONORS AND AWARDS** NEH lectr, 97, 98; Thomas Cooper Medal, Univ of SC, 99. **RESEARCH** F. Scott Fitzgerald, Ernest Hemingway, Thomas Wolfe, John O'Hara, James Gould Cozzens, Bibliography, Literary biography, the profession of authorship. **SELECTED PUBLICATIONS** Coauth, Reader's Companion to F. Scott Fitzgerald's Tender Is the Night, Univ of SC Pr, (Columbia), 96; ed, The Only Thing That Counts: The Ernest Hemingway - Maxwell Perkins Correspondence, Scribners, (NY), 96; coed, F. Scott Fitzgerald on Authorship, Univ of SC Pr, (Columbia), 96; auth, F. Scott Fitzgerald Centenary Exhibition: The Matthew J. and Arlyn Bruccoli Collection, The Thomas Cooper Library, Univ of SC Pr, (Columbia), 96; coed, American Expatriate Writers: Paris in the Twenties, Gale, (Detroit), 97; ed, The Bad and the Beautiful, by Charles Schnee, S IL Univ Pr, (Carbondale), 98; auth, 150 Years of the American Short Story: An Exhibition Prepared by William R. Cagle and Matthew J. Bruccoli, Lilly Libr, Ind Univ, (Bloomington), 98; coed, Crux: The Letters of James Dickey, Knopf (NY), 99; ed, F. Scott Fitzgerald's The Great Gatsby: A Documentary Volume, Gale, (Detroit), 00. **CONTACT ADDRESS** Dept English, Univ of So Carolina, Columbia, Columbia, SC 29225. **EMAIL** bruccolim@gwm.sc.edu

BRUCE, ALEXANDER
PERSONAL Born Memphis, TN, m, 1991, 2 children **DISCIPLINE** ENGLISH **EDUCATION** Univ of the South, BA, 89; Univ GA, MA, 93; PhD, 97. **CAREER** Asst prof, Gordon col, 97-98; assist prof, Fla s col, 98-. **HONORS AND AWARDS** Nat endowment for the Humanities, W Mich Univ, 99; Outstanding Grad Student, Univ GA, 97; Sigma Tau Delta, Phi Kappa Phi. **RESEARCH** Pedagogy, Old and middle english language and literature. **SELECTED PUBLICATIONS** Auth, scyld and Scef: Expanding the Analogues, Garland Pub, (forthcoming); auth, "Strategies for Introducing Old and Middle English Language and Literature to Beginning students," studies in Medieval and renaissance Teaching, (99): 33-42; auth, "The Development of Orthographic Wh- in early Middle english," Journal of english Linguistics, (97): 97-101; auth, "Encouraging TA Development at a Research Institution: A Case Study of TA Mentoring in the Univ of Georgia's English Department," The Journal of Graduate Teaching Assistant Development, (97): 5-14; auth, "Clearing the air: black and White Assumptions and attitudes toward the Royal Crown Air Fresheners," Southern Folklore, (96): 25-40; auth, "The Questing Beast in Malory's Morte Darthur," Proceedings of the Patristic, medieval, and Renaissance Conference, (96): 133-142. **CONTACT ADDRESS** Dept Humanities, Florida So Col, 111 Lake Hollingsworth Dr, Lakeland, FL 33801-5607. **EMAIL** abruce@flsouthern.edu

BRUDER, KURT A.
PERSONAL Born 09/15/1961, Battle Creek, MI, m, 1998, 1 child **DISCIPLINE** COMMUNICATIONS **EDUCATION** Mich State Univ, MA, 87; Univ of Tex, Austin, PhD, 94; Tex Tech Univ, MEd, 98. **CAREER** Asst prof, Emerson College, 99-. **HONORS AND AWARDS** Fulbright scholar award, 96-97. **MEMBERSHIPS** Natl Commun Assoc; Int Commun Assoc. **RESEARCH** The interdependence of communicative practice and psychological experience. **SELECTED PUBLICATIONS** Auth, Monastic Blessing: Deconstructing and Reconstructing the Self, Symbolic Interaction, 98; auth, A Pragmatic for Human-Divine Relationship: An Examination of the Monastic Blessing Sequence, in J of Pragmatics, 98; auth, "A World in a Grain of Sand: Therapeutic Discourse or Making Much of Little Things," in Excavating the Taken-for-Granted: Essays in Language and Social Interaction, 00; coauth, Interactive Art Interpretation: How Viewers Make sense of Paintings in Conversation, 00. **CONTACT ADDRESS** Dept of Communications, Emerson Col, 120 Boylston, Boston, MA 02116. **EMAIL** kurt_bruder@emerson.edu

BRUFFEE, KENNETH ALLEN
PERSONAL Born 09/01/1934, Torrington, CT, m, 1976, 3 children **DISCIPLINE** ENGLISH **EDUCATION** Wesleyan Univ, BA, 56; Northwestern Univ, MA, 57, PhD(English), 64. **CAREER** Instr English, Univ Va, 62-65, Columbia Univ, 65-66; Brooklyn College from instr to assoc prof English, 66-75, dir, freshman writing prog, 70-74, chmn, MLA teaching writing div, 76, Prof English, Brooklyn Col, 76-, Fund Improv Post Sec Educ grant, 79-82; Dir, Scholars Program, 85-; Dir Honors Academy, 96-. **HONORS AND AWARDS** Wolfe Institute Research Fellowship, 91-92; NYU Faculty Resource Network Scholar in Residence, 98, 99, 00. **MEMBERSHIPS** MLA; NCTE. **RESEARCH** Elegiac romance; modern fiction; collaborative learning. **SELECTED PUBLICATIONS** Auth, A Short Course in Writing, Winthrop, 2nd ed, 80; The way out: A critical survey of innovations in college teaching, Col English, 72; The Brooklyn plan: Attaining intellectual growth through peer group tutoring, 78, The structure of knowledge and the future of liberal education, 81 & The social justification of belief, 82, Lib Educ; CLTV: Collaborative learning television, Educ Commun & Technol J, 82; A Comment on Social Constructionism and Literacy Studies + Response to Sullivan,Patricia,A. Review of 'Collaborative Learning'/, Col English, Vol 58, 1996; Comment on Issue on Teaching Literature/, PMLA-Publ Mod Lang Asn Am, Vol 112, 1997. **CONTACT ADDRESS** Dept of English, Brooklyn Col, CUNY, 2901 Bedford Ave, Brooklyn, NY 11210-2813. **EMAIL** kbruffee@brooklyn.cuny.edu

BRUNER, M. LANE
PERSONAL Born 07/25/1958, Kansas City, MO, m, 1984 **DISCIPLINE** SPEECH COMMUNICATION, RHETORICAL AND CRITICAL THEORY **EDUCATION** CA State Univ, Northridge, BA, 91; Louisiana State Univ, MA, 93; Univ Washington, PhD, 97. **CAREER** Asst prof of communication, Babson Coll. **HONORS AND AWARDS** Wilma Grimes Memorial Teaching Awd in Performance Studies, 94; MacFarlane Scholarship, Outstanding Humanities Graduate Student, 96. **MEMBERSHIPS** International Communication Assn; Natl Communication Assn; The Assn for the Study of Nationalities; Amer Soc for Hist of Rhetoric **RESEARCH** Rhetorical theory; collective identity construction and political memory; political theory; nationalism; critical theory. **SELECTED PUBLICATIONS** Auth, Producing Identities: Gender Problematization and Feminist Argumentation, Argumentation and Advocacy, Spring 96; Towards a Poststructural Rehetorical Critical Praxis: Foucault, Limit Work and Jenninger's Kristallnacht Address, Rhetorica, Spring 96; From Etnic of Nationalism to Strategic Multiculturalism: Shifting Strategies of Remembrance in the Quebecois Secessionist Movement, Javnost, fall 97; Strategies of Remembrance in Pre-Unification West Germany, Quarterly Journal of Speech, 00; auth, Rhetorics of the State: The Public Negotiation of Political Character in Germany, Russia, and Quebec, National Identities, 00. **CONTACT ADDRESS** History & Society Div, Babson Col, Babson Park, MA 02157. **EMAIL** bruner@babson.edu

BRUNING, STEPHEN D.
DISCIPLINE COMMUNICATION **EDUCATION** Ohio Univ, BSC, 87, MA, 88; Kent State Univ, PhD, 92. **CAREER** Assoc prof of commun, Ohio Univ; Tenure. **MEMBERSHIPS** NCA; AEJMC; ICA **RESEARCH** Public Relations. **SELECTED PUBLICATIONS** Coauth, Building Loyalty Through Community Relations, The Pub Rels Strategist, 3(2), 97; Community Relations and Loyalty: Toward a Relationship Theory of Public Relations, Bus Res Yearbook, 4, eds J. Biberman and A. Alkhafaji, 97; The Applicability of Interpersonal Relationship Dimensions to an Organizational Context: Toward a Theory of Relational Loyalty a Qualitative Approach, Acad of Managerial Communs Jour, 1, 97; Organizational-Public Relationships and Consumer Satisfaction: The Role of Relationships in the Satisfaction Mix, Commun Res Reports, 15(2), 98; Ten Guidelines for Effectively Managing the Organization-Public Relationship, Bus Res Yearbook, 5, eds J. Biberman and A. Alkhafaji, 98; Relationship Management in Public Relations: Dimensions of an Organization-Public Relationship, Public Relations Rev, 24, 98; The Media Audit: A Management Approach to Media Relations, Bus Res Yearbook, 5, eds J. Biberman and A. Alkhafaji, 98. **CONTACT ADDRESS** Dept of Communication, Capital Univ, 2199 E Main St, 118 Spielm, Columbus, OH 43209-3913. **EMAIL** sbruning@capital.edu

BRUNS, GERALD L.
PERSONAL Born 04/10/1938, Minneapolis, MN, m, 1986, 4 children **DISCIPLINE** ENGLISH **EDUCATION** Marquette Univ, BA, 60, MA, 62; Univ of VA, PhD, 66. **CAREER** Asst

Prof, 65-70, Ohio State Univ; Assoc Prof to Prof, 70-84, Univ of Iowa; Prof of Eng, William P. & Hazel B. White, 84-, Univ of Notre Dame. **HONORS AND AWARDS** Guggenheim Fellow; Fellow, Center for Advanced Stud, Hebrew Univ, Jerusalem; Fellow, Center for Advanced Stud in the Behavioral Sci, Stanford. **MEMBERSHIPS** MLA, APA, SPEP, Renaissance Soc Amer. **RESEARCH** Modern Drama; Henry James; Hermeneutics; Maurice Blanchot, Emmanuel Levinas; 20th Century Poetics; Anglo-Irish Literature. **SELECTED PUBLICATIONS** Auth, Tragic Thoughts at the End of Philosophy: Language, Literature and Ethical Theory, Northwestern Univ Press, 99; Maurice Blanchot, The Refusal of Philosophy, Johns Hopkins Univ Press, 97; Hermeneutics Ancient and Modern, Yale Univ Press, 92; Inventions, Writing, Textuality and Understanding in Literary History, Yale Univ Press, 82; Modern Poetry and the Idea of Language, Yale Univ Press, 74. **CONTACT ADDRESS** Dept of English, Univ of Notre Dame, Notre Dame, IN 46556. **EMAIL** Gerald.L.Bruns.1@nd.edu

BRUNSDALE, MITZI MALLARIAN
PERSONAL Born 05/16/1939, Fargo, ND, m, 1961, 3 children **DISCIPLINE** ENGLISH, COMPARATIVE LITERATURE **EDUCATION** NDak State Univ, BS, 59, lMS, 61; Univ NDak, PhD(English), 76. **CAREER** From asst prof to prof, Mayville State Univ, 76-; chair, div of communicaiton arts, publishers weekly, 96-; bk critic, Houston Post, Tex, 70-89; grant rev panelist, Nat Endowment for Humanities, 77-; chair, Humanities Coun, 80-, bk critic, The Armchair Detective, 96-, bk critic, Publishers Weekly, 98-. **RESEARCH** Early 20th century British literature; early 20th century European comparative literature; D H Lawrence. **SELECTED PUBLICATIONS** Auth, Lawrence and the Myth of Brynhild, Western Humanities Rev, autumn 77; The Effect of Mrs Rudolf Dircks' Translation of Schopenhauer's The Metaphysics of Love on D H Lawrence's Early Fiction, Rocky Mountain Rev Lang & Lit, spring 78; D H Lawrence and Raymond Otis: Brothers of Blood, NMex Humanities Rev, winter 78-79; The German Effect on D H Lawrence and his Works, 1885-1912, P L Verlag, Berne, 79; Alexander Solzhenitsy, In: The Encyclopedia of Short Fiction, 81, Boris Pasternak, In: The Encyclopedia of Short Fiction, 81 & D H Lawrence, In: A Critical Survey of Poetry, Salem Press; D H Lawrence's David: Drama as a Vehicle for Religious Prophecy, In: Themes in Drama V, Cambridge Univ Press, 82; Toward the Greater Day: Rilke, Lawrence, and Immortalilty, Comp Lit Sudies, 82; Sigrid Undset: Ch.. of Norway, Oxford: Berg, 88; Dorothy L. Sayers: Solving the Mystery of Wickedness, Oxford: Berg, 90; James Joyce: The Short Fiction, NY: Twayne, 93; James Herriot, NY: Twayne, 96; auth, A Student Companion to George Orwell, Westport, CT: Greenwood, 00. **CONTACT ADDRESS** Mayville State Univ, 330 3rd St NE, Mayville, ND 58257-1299. **EMAIL** Mitzi_brunsdale@mail.masu.nodak.edu

BRUNSON, MARTHA LUAN
PERSONAL Born 09/29/1931, Anna, IL, m, 1954, 4 children **DISCIPLINE** VICTORIAN & EIGHTEENTH CENTURY BRITISH LITERATURE **EDUCATION** Northwestern Univ, BSEd, 52; TX Tech Univ, MA, 58, PhD, 67. **CAREER** Tchr Eng & hist, Plainview Independent Sch Dist, TX, 53-56, Eng, Lubbock High Sch, 56-58; instr, Del Mar Col, 61-62, 64-65; from asst prof to assoc prof, 67-76, prof eng, Southwest TX State Univ, 76-, chmn dept, 72-83, assoc dean, Sch Lib Arts, 81-98, Pres, Asn Depts Eng 82. **MEMBERSHIPS** MLA; Col Eng Asn; NCTE. **RESEARCH** Thomas Hardy; Charles Dickens; Victorian women writers. **CONTACT ADDRESS** Dept of Eng, Southwest Texas State Univ, 601 Univ Dr, San Marcos, TX 78666-4685. **EMAIL** mb14@swt.edu

BRUSHWOOD, JOHN STUBBS
PERSONAL Born 01/23/1920, Glenns, VA, m, 1945, 2 children **DISCIPLINE** SPANISH AMERICAN LITERATURE **EDUCATION** Randolph-Macon Col, BA, 40; Univ Va, MA, 42; Columbia Univ, PhD, 50; DLitt, Randolph-Macon Col, 81. **CAREER** Instr Romance lang, Va Polytech Inst, 42-44; from instr to prof Span, Univ Mo, 46-67, chmn dept Romance lang, 53-57 & 58-59; Roy A Roberts Prof Emer Latin Am Lit, Univ Kans, 67-. **HONORS AND AWARDS** Fund Advan Educ fel, 51-52; Am Philos Soc grant, 57; Am Coun Learned Soc grant, 61; Soc Sci Res Coun grant, 71; Nat Endowment for Humanities, summer 76; Bellagio scholar in residence, 78. **MEMBERSHIPS** Midwest Mod Lang Asn (pres, 62-63); MLA; Am Asn Teachers Span & Port; Inst Int Lit Iberoam. **RESEARCH** Mexican literature; Spanish American novel **SELECTED PUBLICATIONS** Auth, Mexico in Its Novel: A Nation's Search for Identity, Univ Tex, 66; Enrique Gonzales Martinez, Twayne, 69; Los Ricos en la Prosa Mexicans, Diogenes, 70; Mexico en su Novela, Fondo Cult Economics, 73; The Spanish American Novel: A Twentieth Century Survey, Univ Tex, 75; Genteel Barbarism: New Readings of Nineteenth Century Spanish American Novels, Univ Nebr, 81; cotransl, The Precipice (Galindo), Univ Tex, 69; Don Goyo (Aguilera-Malta), Humana, 80. **CONTACT ADDRESS** Dept of Span and Port, Univ of Kansas, Lawrence, 2071 Wescoe Hall, Lawrence, KS 66044. **EMAIL** riopo@eagle.cc.ukans.edu

BRUSTEIN, ROBERT
PERSONAL Born 04/21/1927, Brooklyn, NY **DISCIPLINE** ENGLISH **EDUCATION** Amherst Col, BA, 48; Columbia Univ, MA, 50, PhD, 57; Dr Art, Bard Col, 81. **CAREER** Instr English, Cornell Univ, 55-56; drama, Vassar Col, 56-57; lectr, Drama Sch, Columbia Univ, 57-58, from asst prof to prof English, 58-66; prof English & dean sch drama, 66-79, artistic dir, Yale Univ Repertory Theatre, 66-79; Prof English, Harvard Univ, 79-, Art Dir, Am Rep Theatre, Loeb Drama Ctr, 79-, Drama critic, New Repub, 59-; Guggenheim fel, 61-62; Ford Found grant, 64-65; mem panel, Theatre Div, Nat Endowment for Arts, 70-72; drama critic, The Observer, London, 72-73; monthly contribr, New York Times, 72-; trustee, Sarah Lawrence Col, 73- mem panel, Nat Endowment for the Humanities, 74-75 & 81. **HONORS AND AWARDS** George Jean Nathan Awd, 62-63; George Polk Awd in Theatre Criticism, 64; Jersey City J Awd in Criticism, 65; American Academy of Arts and Letters Distinguished Service to the Arts, 97; Assoc for Theatre in Higher Education Career Achievement Awd, 00; dlitt, lawrence univ, 68 & amherst col, 72; lld, beloit col, 74. **MEMBERSHIPS** MLA; American Academy of Arts and Letters; American Academy of Arts and Sciences. **RESEARCH** Modern and classical drama; Elizabethan and Stuary drama. **SELECTED PUBLICATIONS** Auth, Madison Avenue villain, Partisan Rev, 62; Theatre of revolt, Atlantic Monthly, 64; Seasons of discontent, Simon & Schuster, 65; The Third Theatre, Knopf, 69; Revolution as Theatre: Notes on the New Radical Style, Liveright, 71; Cultural schizophrenia, New York Times Mag, 71; The Culture Watch: Essays on Theatre and Society, Knopf, 76; Can the show go on?, NY Times Mag, 77; Critical Movements, 80 & Making Scenes, 81, Ramdom House; Dumbocracy in America + Crypto-Maoist Roots of Political-Correctness/, Partisan Rev, Vol 60, 1993; The Theater of Guilt +/, New Theatre Quart, Vol 10, 1994; Cultural Politics and Coercive Philanthropy/, Partisan Rev, Vol 62, 1995; On Money + Money and the Theater/, Theater, Vol 27, 1996; auth, Cultural Calisthenics, Ivan R. Dee, 98. **CONTACT ADDRESS** Loeb Drama Ctr, Harvard Univ, 64 Brattle St, Cambridge, MA 02138. **EMAIL** etarvin@fas.harvard.edu

BRUSTER, DOUGLAS
DISCIPLINE ENGLISH, LITERATURE, DRAMA **EDUCATION** Univ NE, BA; Harvard Univ, MA, PhD. **CAREER** Asst prof; taught at, Harvard Univ & Univ Chicago. **HONORS AND AWARDS** NEH Fellowship. **MEMBERSHIPS** MLA, Shakespeare Asn, Ren Soc Am. **RESEARCH** Shakespeare and early mod drama; poetry of early mod Engl; 20th-century drama and film; critical theory. **SELECTED PUBLICATIONS** Auth, Drama and the Market in the Age of Shakespeare, Cambridge UP, 92; publ on, lit and cult of early mod Engl; auth, Quoting Shakespeare: Form and Culture in Early Modern England, Univ Nebr P, 00. **CONTACT ADDRESS** Dept of English, Univ of Texas, Austin, Austin, TX 78712. **EMAIL** bruster@mail.utexas.edu

BRYAN, FERALD J.
PERSONAL Born 07/09/1958, Covington, GA, d, 1 child **DISCIPLINE** COMMUNICATIONS **EDUCATION** Univ Vt, BA, 80; Northern Ill Univ, MA, 82; Univ Mo, PhD, 85. **CAREER** Teaching Asst, Northern Ill Univ, 80-82; Teaching Asst, Univ Mo, 82-85; Asst Prof, Mt Union Col, 85-88; Asst prof to Assoc prof, Northern Ill Univ, 88-. **HONORS AND AWARDS** Paul W Crawford Awd, Northern Ill Univ, 82; Outstanding Grad Student Teacher Awd, Univ Mo, 84; Who's Who among Grad Students, 85; Grant, Northern Ill Univ, 90, 91, 97; Grant, Hoover Presidential Library Asn, 94; **MEMBERSHIPS** Nat Comm Asn, Rhetoric Soc of Am, Center for the Study of the Presidency, Central States Comm Asn, Am Inst of Parliamentarians. **RESEARCH** History of American Public Address; Rhetorical Criticism and Metaphor; Presidential Rhetoric; Political Rhetoric in 19th and 20th Century America. **SELECTED PUBLICATIONS** Auth, Henry Grady or Tom Watson?: The Rhetorical Struggle for the New south, 1880-1890, Mercer Univ press, 94; co-ed, Contemporary American Speeches, Eighth Ed, Kendall Hunt, Pub, 97; co-ed, Contemporary American Speeches, Ninth Ed, Kendall Hunt, Pub, 00; auth, "Robert Kennedy, Joe McCarthy and the Greek Shipping crisis: a Study of American Foreign Policy Rhetoric," Presidential Studies Quarterly, (94)93-104; auth, "C-SPAN: A Key Resource for contemporary American Public Address, " C-SPAN Networks: Professor's Guide, (94): 9-10; auth, "Thomas Edward Watson," in American National Biography, Oxford Univ Press, 99 **CONTACT ADDRESS** Dept Comm, No Illinois Univ, 1425 W Lincoln Hwy, Dekalb, IL 60115-2828. **EMAIL** fbryan@niu.edu

BRYANT, JOHN
PERSONAL Born 12/08/1949, Austin, TX, m, 1975, 3 children **DISCIPLINE** ENGLISH **EDUCATION** Univ Chicago, AB, 71; AM, 72; PhD, 75. **CAREER** Asst prof, Widener Univ, 78-80; assoc prof, Pa State Univ, 80-86; prof, Hofstra Univ, 86-. **HONORS AND AWARDS** Fulbright Fel, Univ Genoa, 77-78; Lily Endowment Teaching Fel, 82-83; NEH Fel, 90. **MEMBERSHIPS** MLA; CELJ; ALA; Melville Soc. **RESEARCH** Herman Melville; Textual Scholarship. **SELECTED PUBLICATIONS** Auth, Melville and Repose, Oxford, 93; auth, Typee by Herman Melville, Penguin Am Classics, 96; auth, "Melville's Rose Poems," Ariz Quart, (97): 49-84; auth, Melville's Tales, Poems, and Other Writings, Random House, 02; auth, The Fluid Text, Univ Mich Press, 02. **CONTACT ADDRESS** Dept English, Hofstra Univ, 107 Calkins Hall, Hempstead, NY 11549-0001. **EMAIL** engjlb@hofstra.edu

BRYDON, DIANA
PERSONAL Born Hamilton, ON, Canada **DISCIPLINE** ENGLISH **EDUCATION** Univ Toronto, BA, 72, MA, 73; Australian Nat Univ, PhD, 77. **CAREER** Asst prof, 79-87, assoc prof, 87-89, Univ BC; assoc prof, 89-92, Prof English, Univ Guelph 92-. **HONORS AND AWARDS** George Drew Memorial Trust Fund Award; Distinguished Prof Tchr Award. **MEMBERSHIPS** Can Asn Commonwealth Lit & Lang Studs **RESEARCH** Comparative postcolonial literary; studies, especially Australian, Canadian and Caribbean; colonial and feminist literary theories. **SELECTED PUBLICATIONS** Ed, World Literature Written in English, 89-93; coauth, Christina Stead, 87; auth, Decolonising Fictions, 93; auth, Writing on Trial: Timothy Findley's Famous Last Words, 95. **CONTACT ADDRESS** Dept English, Univ of Western Ontario, Univ College, Rm 173, London, ON, Canada N6A3K7. **EMAIL** dbrydon@julian.uwo.ca

BRYER, JACKSON R.
PERSONAL Born 09/11/1937, New York, NY, m, 1988, 4 children **DISCIPLINE** ENGLISH **EDUCATION** Amherst Col, BA, 59; Columbia Univ, MA, 60; Univ Wisc, PhD, 65. **CAREER** Asst prof, Univ Maryland, 65-68; assoc prof, 68-72; prof, 72-. **HONORS AND AWARDS** NEH Grant; NEH Stp; APS trv Grant; GRBG, Sum Grant, Sem Grant; RCAH Fel; Co-Found Resources for Am Lit Stud. **MEMBERSHIPS** MLA; RALS; NMLA. **SELECTED PUBLICATIONS** Ed, The Playwright's Art: Conversations With Contemporary American Dramatists, Rutgers Univ Press (New Brunswick, NJ), 95; ed, New Essays on F. Scott Fitzgerald's Neglected Stories, Univ Missouri Press (Columbia), 96; ed, F Scott Fitzgerald at 100: Centenary Tributes by American Writers, Quill & Brush (Rockville, MD), 96; co-ed, French Connections Hemingway and Fitzgerald Abroad, St. Martin's Press (NY), 98; auth, "Thornton Wilder at 100: His Achievement and His Legacy." in Thornton Wilder: New Essays, eds. Martin Blank, Dalma Hunyadi Brunauer, David Garrett Izzo (West Cornwall, CT: Locust Hill Press, 99): 3-20; auth, "An Interview with Neil Simon." in Neil Simon: A casebook, ed. Gary Konas (NY: Garland, 97); ed, "Neil Simon" and "Lanford Wilson," in The Playwright's Art: Conversations With Contemporary American Dramatists (New Brunswick, NJ: Rutgers Univ Press, 95): 221-40 and 277-96; auth, "Torches of Fury: The Correspondence of Scott and Zelda Fitzgerald," in American Literary Dimensions: Poems and Essays in Honor of Melvin I Friedman, eds. Ben Siegel, Jay L Halio (Newark: Univ Delaware Press, 99); auth, History from the Brown-Forman Classics in Context Festival at Actors Theatre of Louisville, Smith and Kraus (Lyme, NH) 00: 333-50. **CONTACT ADDRESS** Dept English, Univ of Maryland, Col Park, 3101 Susquehanna Hall, College Park, MD 20642-8800. **EMAIL** jb92@umail.umd.edu

BRYSON, NORMAN
PERSONAL Born 08/04/1949, Glasgow, Scotland, m, 1988, 1 child **DISCIPLINE** LITERATURE **EDUCATION** Cambridge Univ, MA, 70, PhD, 77. **CAREER** Fel of King's Col, Cambrige Univ, 77-88; prof of visual and cultural studies, Univ of Rochester, 88-90; Prof of art hist, Harvard Univ, 90-. **HONORS AND AWARDS** Getty Res Fel, 98-99; Guggenheim Fel, 98-99. **RESEARCH** Modern art history and cultural studies. **SELECTED PUBLICATIONS** Auth, Word and Image: French Painting of the Ancien Resime, Cambridge Univ Press, 81; Tradition and Desire: From David to Delacroix, Cambridge Univ Press, 83; Vision and Painting: The Logic of the Gaze, Yale Univ Press, 84; Looking at the Overlooked: Four Essays on Still Life Painting, Harvard Univ Press, 91. **CONTACT ADDRESS** Dept of Fine Arts, Harvard Univ, 485 Broadway, Cambridge, MA 02138. **EMAIL** bryson@fas.harvard.edu

BRYSON, RALPH J.
PERSONAL Born 09/10/1922, Cincinnati, OH, s **DISCIPLINE** ENGLISH **EDUCATION** Univ Cincinnati, BS 1947; Univ Cincinnati, MS 1950; OH State Univ, PhD 1953. **CAREER** So Univ, instr English, 49; Miles Coll, instr English, 49-50; AL State Univ, assoc prof English, 53-62; prof & dept head, 62-75, chmn div of humanities, 75-77, prof of English, 77-; Univ of AL, adjunct prof, 87. **HONORS AND AWARDS** Dexter Ave King Memorial Baptist Church; Outstanding Journalistic Contributions & Achievement Kappa Alpha Psi; Outstanding Men of Yr & Montgomery; Cited Outstanding OH State Univ Graduate in They Came & They Conquered; Bryson Endowed Scholarships Established at University Cin'ti & Ohio State University, 1995; 56th Recipient of the Elder Watson Diggs Awd, 72nd Grand Chapter elected grand historian, 73rd Grand Chapt, Kappa Alpha Psi, 1997. **MEMBERSHIPS** Pres Assn Coll English Tchrs AL; AL Council Tchrs English Exec Bd; Nat Council Tchrs English; Modern Language Assn; S Atlantic MLA; Coll Language Assn; Conf Coll Composition & Communication; Phi Delta Kappa; Lectr Author & Consult; Kappa Alpha Psi; Editor Column Books & Such; chmn Nat Achievement Commn; officer, mem Province Bd Dir; Am Bridge Assn; chmn exec bd & sectional vice pres, Montgomery Seminar Arts; bd of trustees, Museum Fine Arts Assn; Alabama

Writers' Forum, bd of dirs. **CONTACT ADDRESS** English Dept, Alabama State Univ, 915 S Jackson St, Montgomery, AL 36101-0271.

BUCCO, MARTIN

PERSONAL Born 12/03/1929, Newark, NJ, m, 1956, 1 child **DISCIPLINE** ENGLISH LITERATURE **EDUCATION** Highlands Univ, BA; Columbia Univ, MA, Univ Mo, PhD. **CAREER** Prof. **HONORS AND AWARDS** Nat Endowment grants; Honors Prof, Colorado State Univ; STERN Distinguished Prof, Colorado State Univ; Willard O. Eddy Distinguished Teacher, Colorado State Univ. **MEMBERSHIPS** Western Lit Asn; Sinclair Lewis Soc. **RESEARCH** American literary realism; American criticism. **SELECTED PUBLICATIONS** Auth, pubs on Frank Waters, Wilbur, Daniel Steele, E.W. Howe, Rene Wellek, and Sinclair Lewis. **CONTACT ADDRESS** Dept of English, Colorado State Univ, Fort Collins, CO 80523.

BUCCOLA, REGINA M.

PERSONAL Born 06/17/1969, Louisville, KY **DISCIPLINE** ENGLISH **EDUCATION** Bellermine Univ, BA, 91; Univ Ken, MA, 94; Univ Ill, PhD, 00. **CAREER** Teach asst, Univ Ken, 91-94; teach asst, dir's asst, Univ Ill, 94-00; asst prof, Roosevelt Univ, 00-. **HONORS AND AWARDS** NEH, 01; Woodrow Wilson Pract Grnt, 99; Wilson Wyatt Fel, 94; Frederick Stern Awd Excel Teach, 98; Chanc Ser Awd, Univ Ill, 98. **MEMBERSHIPS** MLA; RSA; SSEMW. **RESEARCH** Early modern drama; feminist, literary and performance theory; 20th-century women's drama and poetry. **SELECTED PUBLICATIONS** Auth, "Salem," Sparrowgrass Poet For (95); auth, "Scarecrow," New Grow Arts Rev (94); auth, "Area Code," and "Postage Stamp," Reflections (94); auth, "A Place for Everything," "Household Appliances," and "Valley Girl" Aries (01); auth, "Megan Terry: 'The Mother of Feminist Theater,'" in The American Berserk (Red Hen Press, 01); auth, "'He Made Me a Hole!': Gender Bending, Sexual Desire and the Representation of sexual violence," in Tortilleras: Hispanic and Latina Lesbian Expression (Temple UP, 01). **CONTACT ADDRESS** Eng Dept, Roosevelt Univ, 430 S Michigan Ave, Chicago, IL 60605. **EMAIL** rbuccola@roosevelt.edu

BUCHANAN, CARL J.

PERSONAL Born 07/03/1956, Wichita, KS, m, 1985, 1 child **DISCIPLINE** LITERATURE, WRITING, COMPOSITION **EDUCATION** Friends Univ, BA, 78; Kans State Univ, MA, 80; Univ Southern Miss, PhD, 82. **CAREER** Asst prof, Bilkent Univ, 92-94; Int Am Univ, Eng Chairman, 94-96; Am Univ Dubai, Lib Arts Chairman, 96-97; prog cons, Fatih Univ, 97; educ cons. Carroll Acad, 99-00; asst prof, Univ Tenn Martin, 00-. **MEMBERSHIPS** MLA, AWP. **RESEARCH** Poetry, Science Fiction, Fantasy, Mythology, Native American Literature, Creating Writing, Translating. **SELECTED PUBLICATIONS** Auth, RIPPER!, Univ SCar, 99. **CONTACT ADDRESS** Univ of Tennessee, Martin, Martin, TN 38238. **EMAIL** cbuchanan98@yahoo, com

BUCHANAN, DONNA A.

DISCIPLINE MUSIC **EDUCATION** Beloit Col, BA; Univ TX, PhD. **CAREER** Asst prof, 97-, Univ IL at Chicago. **RESEARCH** Musical styles of Bulgaria; music as symbolic commun; music in aesthetic syst; music and power rel(s); music and cosmology; and music and soc identity. **SELECTED PUBLICATIONS** Auth, Performing Democracy: Bulgarian Music and Musicians in Transition, 97; pubs in Ethnomusicology. **CONTACT ADDRESS** Dept of Music, Univ of Illinois, Urbana-Champaign, E Gregory Dr, PO Box 52, Champaign, IL 61820. **EMAIL** buchana1@uiuc.edu

BUCHANAN, RAYMOND W.

DISCIPLINE COMMUNICATION THEORY **EDUCATION** David Lipscomb Col, BA, 59; La State Univ, MA, 67, PhD, 70. **CAREER** Instr, Univ Ctr FL, 70-86; ch, 72-86; dir, Pepperdine's Florence, 89-91; prof, 86-. **HONORS AND AWARDS** Commun consult, high profile criminal trial FL v. Rolling, 93-94. **RESEARCH** Legal commun. **SELECTED PUBLICATIONS** Co-auth, Communication Strategies for Trial Attorneys. **CONTACT ADDRESS** Dept of Commun, Pepperdine Univ, 24255 Pacific Coast Hwy, Malibu, CA 90263. **EMAIL** rbuchana@pepperdine.edu

BUCK, ROBERT J.

PERSONAL Born 07/05/1926, Vermilion, AB, Canada **DISCIPLINE** CLASSICS **EDUCATION** Univ Alta, BA, 49; Univ Kentucky, MA, 50; Univ Cincinnati, PhD, 56. **CAREER** Asst prof, Univ Kentucky, 55-60; assoc prof, 60-66, head dept, 66-72, prof, 66-91, PROF EMER CLASSICS, UNIV ALTA, 91-; mng comt, Am Sch Classical Stud (Athens), 61-83. **HONORS AND AWARDS** Fel, Can Inst Rome, 76. **MEMBERSHIPS** Can Mediter Inst; Can Archaeol Inst Athens; Class Asn Can. **RESEARCH** Greek history; Greek and Roman archaeology. **SELECTED PUBLICATIONS** Auth, A History of Boetia, 79; coauth, The Excavations of San Giovanni di Ruoti, vol I 93, vol II 96. **CONTACT ADDRESS** Dept Hist and Classics, Univ of Alberta, Edmonton, AB, Canada T6G 2E5.

BUCKALEW, RONALD EUGENE

PERSONAL Born 07/29/1935, Wilmington, DE, m, 1958, 2 children **DISCIPLINE** ENGLISH **EDUCATION** Col Wooster, BA, 57; Univ Ill, MA, 59, PhD, 64. **CAREER** Tchg asst, Univ IL, Urbana, 59-61, 62-63; asst prof Eng, 63-74, assoc prof eng, PA State Univ, 74-97, Germanistic Soc Am fel, univ Minister, 61-62; LSA post dr, fel, UCLA, 66; consult, Allyn & Bacon, Inc, 65-68; co-ed, Gen Ling, 70-74; fel, Inst Arts & Humanistic Studies, PA State Univ, 76-77; res grantee, Am Coun Learned Soc, 76-77, Am Philos Soc, 76-77 & 78-79 & Nat Endowment for Hum, 79; assoc mem, Clare Hall, Cambridge Univ, 77-78 & 80-81, life mem; spec adv, Dict Old Eng, Ctr Medieval Studies, Univ Toronto, 77-78. **MEMBERSHIPS** MLA; Ling Soc Am; Mediaeval Acad Am; Early Eng Text Soc; AAUP. **RESEARCH** Eng linguistics, espec historical; Old Eng lang and lit, espec Beowulf and Aelfric; Chaucer. **SELECTED PUBLICATIONS** Auth, A phonological analysis of present-day standard English, Gen Ling, fall 72; Night lessons on language, In: A Conceptual Guide to Finnegans Wake, Pa State Univ, 73; Beowulf, lines 1766-1767: Odde for seoddan?, Neuphilologische Mitteilungen, summer 74; Leland's Transcript of Aelfric's Glossary, Anglo-Saxon England, Cambridge Univ, 78; Nowell, Lambarde, and Leland: The significance of Lawrence Nowell's transcript of Aelfric's Grammar and Glossary, In: Anglo-Saxon Scholarship: The First Three Centuries, G K Hall, 82; Attempts to Equalize Sex References in American English, Strani Jezici, 85; Latin in Old England, Research, Penn State, 86; co found, assoc ed, Anglo-Saxon manuscripts in microfiche. **CONTACT ADDRESS** Dept of Eng, Pennsylvania State Univ, Univ Park, 116 Burrowes Bldg, University Park, PA 16802-6200. **EMAIL** reb@psu.edu

BUCKLAND, ROSCOE LAWRENCE

PERSONAL Born 07/28/1918, Blackfoot, ID, m, 1941, 2 children **DISCIPLINE** ENGLISH, AMERICAN CIVILIZATION **EDUCATION** Univ Idaho, BA & MA, 48; State Univ Iowa, PhD(Am civilization), 55. **CAREER** Instr English, Wash State Col, 48-51; from asst prof to prof, Long Beach State Col, 55-70, chmn dept, 60-68; chmn dept, 70-78, Prof Lib Studies, Western Wash Univ, 70-, Asst, Univ Iowa, 52-55; lectr, Workers Educ Asn & Nat Arts Coun, Sydney, Australia, 68-69, Exchange Prof, Tokyo, Spring 85. **MEMBERSHIPS** Am Studies Asn; Brit Asn Am Studies; Am Cult Asn; Western Lit Asn; Am Folklore Asn. **RESEARCH** Australian and American frontier literature; American folklore; 19th century popular culture. **SELECTED PUBLICATIONS** Reviews in Western American Literature, 1967-1996; reviews in Studies in Short Fiction, 1969-1994; reviews in Pacific Northwest Quarterly, 1994; "Jack Hamlin: Bret Harte's Romantic Rogue," Western American Literature, Fall 73, reprinted in Short Story Criticism, Gale 1991; "Contrasting Views, Lynching in Two Western Stories," Wyoming Annals, Winter 93; Frederic Remington: The Writer, Twayne's U.S. Authors Series, 2000; papers read at Western American Literature annual conferences 1972-1999. **CONTACT ADDRESS** 1719 E Maple St, Apt 131, Bellingham, WA 98226.

BUCKLEY, JEROME HAMILTON

PERSONAL Born 08/30/1917, Toronto, ON, Canada, m, 1943, 3 children **DISCIPLINE** ENGLISH LITERATURE **EDUCATION** Univ Toronto, BA, 39; Harvard Univ, AM, 40, PhD, 42; Victoria Univ, DLItt, 97. **CAREER** From instr to prof English, Univ Wis, 42-54; vis assoc prof, Columbia Univ, 52-53, prof, 54-61; prof, 61-75, Gurney Prof English Lit, Harvard Univ, 75-, Emeritus, 87; Guggenheim fel, 46-47 & 64; vis prof, Univ Colo, 60 & Univ Hawaii, 69; Huntington Libr fel, 78; Nessima Lecturer, Doshisha Univ (Koyoto), 89. **HONORS AND AWARDS** Christian Gauss Awd, Phi Beta Kappa, 52. **MEMBERSHIPS** MLA; Tennyson Soc; Int Asn Univ Professors English; Am Acad Arts & Sci. **RESEARCH** Romantic and Victorian literature; intellectual history; autobiography. **SELECTED PUBLICATIONS** Auth, The Victorian Temper, Harvard Univ, 51; Tennyson, the Growth of a Poet, Harvard Univ, 60; ed, Poetry of the Victorian Period, Scott, 65; The Triumph of Time, Harvard Univ, 66; ed, The Pre-Raphaelites, Mod Libr, Random, 68; chap, In: The Victorian Poets, Harvard Univ, 68; auth, Season of Youth: Bildungsroman from Dickens to Golding, Harvard Univ, 74; ed, The Worlds of Victorian Ficition, Harvard, 75; Victorian Poets & Prose Writers, AHM, 77; auth, The Turning Key: Autobiography and the Subjective Impulse, Harvard, 84; auth, David Copperfield, Norton, 90; auth, Newman's Autobiography-Newman After a Hundred Years, ed Ian Ker nad alan G Hill, 90; auth, Tennyson and The Lyric in he Distance-Tennyson Seven Essays, ed Philip Collins, 92: High Victorian Culture - Morse,D/, Victorian Studies, Vol 37, 1993; The Victorians and Renaissance Italy - Fraser,H/, Albion, Vol 25, 1993; Tennyson and the Text, The Weaver Shuttle - Joseph,G/, Nineteenth-Century Lit, Vol 48, 1993; auth, Wordsworth and Tennyson: Columbia History of British Poetry, ed, Carl Woodring, 94; Annoying the Victorians - Kincaid,JR/, Nineteenth-Century Lit, Vol 50, 1995; Victorian Poetry - Poetry, Poetics, and Politics - Armstrong,I/, Albion, Vol 27, 1995. **CONTACT ADDRESS** Dept of English, Harvard Univ, Baker Center, Cambridge, MA 02138.

BUCKLEY, JOAN

PERSONAL Born Minneapolis, MN, m, 1957, 2 children **DISCIPLINE** ENGLISH LITERATURE **EDUCATION** St Olaf Col, BA; Univ Chicago, MA; Univ Iowa, PhD. **CAREER** Prof. **HONORS AND AWARDS** Lily Gyldenvand Prof of Communication. **MEMBERSHIPS** MLA, MMLA, CCCC, Delta Kappa Gamma, Phi Delta Kappa, Phi Beta Kappa, NAHA. **SELECTED PUBLICATIONS** Auth, Han Ola og Han Per; More Han Ola og Han Per. **CONTACT ADDRESS** English Dept, Concordia Col, Minnesota, 901 8th St S, Moorhead, MN 56562. **EMAIL** buckley@cord.edu

BUCKLEY, WILLIAM KERMIT

PERSONAL Born 11/14/1946, San Diego, CA, m, 1969, 1 child **DISCIPLINE** LITERARY CRITICISM, BRITISH LITERATURE **EDUCATION** Univ San Diego, BA, 69; San Diego State Univ, MA, 72, MA, 75; Miami Univ, PhD(English), 80. **CAREER** Instr Compos & Lit, San Diego State Univ, 71-72; instr, Reading Prog, Calif Community Cols, 72-74; instr & dir, Learning Skills, San Diego State Univ, 74-75; asst prof Compos & Lit, Hanover Col, 79-82; prof Compos & Lit, Ind Univ Northwest, 82-, co-ed & co-founder, Recovering Lit, 72-. **HONORS AND AWARDS** Best Chapbook of Poetry, 97, Who's Who in American Teaching, 00. **MEMBERSHIPS** Am Acad Poets. **RESEARCH** The life and works of Louis-Ferdinand Celine; the life and works of D H Lawrence. **SELECTED PUBLICATIONS** Coauth, Louis-Ferdinand Celine: Critical Essays, MacMillan, 86; Lady Chatterley's Lover, Loss and Hope, NY: Macmillan, 93; auth, By the Horses Before the Rains, 97; auth, 81 Mygrations, Fithian Press, 98; auth, Athena in Steeltown, Small Poetry Press, 99; auth, Lost Heartlands, Small Poetry Press, 00. **CONTACT ADDRESS** English Dept, Indiana Univ, Northwest, 3400 Broadway, Gary, IN 46408. **EMAIL** wbuckley@iun.haw1.in.edu

BUCKNELL, BRAD

DISCIPLINE ENGLISH LITERATURE **EDUCATION** Univ Alberta, BA; MA; Univ Toronto, PhD. **CAREER** Asst prof **RESEARCH** Modernism; postmodernism; philosophy of aesthetics; philosophy of music; cultural studies; African American literature; twentieth century Irish literature; contemporary British literature; computers and writing. **SELECTED PUBLICATIONS** Auth, pubs on Pater, Wilde, Pound, Stein, Joyce, and musical and literary relations. **CONTACT ADDRESS** Dept of English, Univ of Manitoba, Winnipeg, MB, Canada R3T 2N2. **EMAIL** bucknell@ms.umanitoba.ca

BUCKSTEAD, RICHARD C.

PERSONAL Born 03/17/1929, Viborg, SD, m, 1956, 4 children **DISCIPLINE** AMERICAN LITERATURE, ASIAN LITERATURE **EDUCATION** Yankton Col, BA, 50; Univ SDak, MA, 56; State Univ Iowa, PhD(English), 59. **CAREER** Instr English, Augustana Col, SDak, 57-58; asst prof, Southeast Mo State Col, 58-61; asst dean, 64-67, dir Asian studies, 71-73, asst prof to assoc prof, 61-80, prof English, St Olaf Col, 80-, Assoc Cols Midwest grant Asian studies, 67-68; vis prof, Chulalongkorn Univ Bangkok, 67-68. **MEMBERSHIPS** Asn Asian Studies. **RESEARCH** The novels of Yukio Mishima; Japanese prose; Chinese poetry. **SELECTED PUBLICATIONS** Auth, Kawabata and the Divided Self, China Printing, Taipei, 72; The meaning of symbol in Kawabata's Thousand Cranes, Tamkang Rev, Taipei, 11/72; The search for a symbol in Kawabata's Snow Country, 6/73 & The role of nature in Mishima's The Sound of Waves, 2/77, Asian Profile, Hong Kong; A conversation with a Master Luthier, The Strad, Kent, 5/77. **CONTACT ADDRESS** Dept of English, St. Olaf Col, 1520 St Olaf Ave, Northfield, MN 55057-1099. **EMAIL** buckster@stolaf.edu

BUDD, LOUIS JOHN

PERSONAL Born 08/26/1921, St. Louis, MO, m, 1945, 2 children **DISCIPLINE** ENGLISH **EDUCATION** Univ Mo, AB, 41, AM, 42; Univ Wis, PhD(English), 49. **CAREER** Instr English, Univ Mo, 42, 46; from instr to asst prof, Univ Ky, 49-52; from asst prof to assoc prof, 52-66, chmn dept, 73-79, Prof English, Duke Univ, 66-83, Guggenheim fel, 65-66; Fulbright-Hays lectr, Am Studies Res Ctr, Hyderabad, 67 & fall 72; managing ed, Am Lit, 79-; sr fel, Nat Endowment for Humanities, 79-80; JB Duke Prof, 83-91; Chm, ed, board, 86-91. **HONORS AND AWARDS** D Litt, U of Missouri, 88; D Lit, Elmira Col, 95; JB Hubbell Medal (MLA), 98 **MEMBERSHIPS** MLA; SAtlantic MLA; Am Humor Studies Asn (pres, 79); Am Assoc of Univ Prof (chap. Pres. 71-72); Mark Twain Circle of America (founding pres. 86-87). **RESEARCH** Mark Twain; realism and naturalism; American literary history, 1865-1920. **SELECTED PUBLICATIONS** Auth, Mark Twain: Social Philospher, 62; auth, Mark Twain in American Literary Scholarship: An Annual, 76-85; ed, A Listing and Selection of Newspaper and Magazine Interviews with S.L. Clemens, 77; auth, Critical Essays on Mark Twain, Vol 2, 82-83; auth, Our Mark Twain: The Making of His Public Personality, 83; auth, New Essays on "Adventures of Huckleberry Fin," 85; auth, Mark Twain: Collected Tales, Sketches, Speeches & Essays, 92; auth, Mark Twain: The Contemporary Reviews, 99. **CONTACT ADDRESS** Dept of English, Duke Univ, 314 Allen Bldg, Durham, NC 27708. **EMAIL** budd@duke.edu

BUDD, MICHAEL

PERSONAL Born 08/26/1944, Beloit, KS, m, 1982, 3 children **DISCIPLINE** FILM AND MEDIA STUDIES **EDUCATION** Univ Kans, BA, 66; Univ Iowa, PhD, 75. **CAREER** Asst prof,

Fla Atlantic Univ, 74-79; assoc prof, 79-84, prof, 84-; Chair, Fla Atlantic Univ, 83-87. **MEMBERSHIPS** Soc for Cinema Studies; Union for Democaratic Commun. **RESEARCH** Cultural Politics. **SELECTED PUBLICATIONS** Auth, The Cabinet of Dr. Caligari: Texts, Contexts, Histories, Rutgers, 90; coauth, Consuming Environments: Television and Commercial Culture, Rutgers, 99. **CONTACT ADDRESS** Dept Commun, Florida Atlantic Univ, PO Box 3091, Boca Raton, FL 33431-0991. **EMAIL** mbudd@fau.edu

BUDDS, MICHAEL J.
PERSONAL Born, IL **DISCIPLINE** MUSIC HISTORY AND LITERATURE **EDUCATION** Knox Col; Univ Iowa, PhD. **CAREER** Assoc prof & coordr, Music Hist and Lit, Univ Miss Columbia **HONORS AND AWARDS** William T. Kemper Fel for Excellence in Teaching. **RESEARCH** American music; history of African-American music; music in Victorian England. **SELECTED PUBLICATIONS** Auth, Jazz in the Sixties, 2nd ed, 90; coauth, Rock Recall: Readings in American Popular Music from the Emergence of Rock and Roll to the Demise of the Woodstock Nation, 93; ed, Source Readings in American Choral Music, 96; contribur, The New Grove Dictionary of American Music, the New Grove Dictionary of Jazz, Women & Music: A History. **CONTACT ADDRESS** Dept of Music, Univ of Missouri, Columbia, 140 Fine Arts Bldg, Columbia, MO 65211. **EMAIL** BuddsM@missouri.edu

BUDRA, PAUL VINCENT
PERSONAL Born 07/03/1967, Toronto, ON, Canada, m, 1984, 2 children **DISCIPLINE** ENGLISH **EDUCATION** Univ Toronto, BA, 79; MA, 80; PhD, 87. **CAREER** Asst prof to assoc prof, Simon Fraser Univ, 89-. **HONORS AND AWARDS** SSHRC Res Grant, 97; Woodsworth Resident Scholar, 91. **MEMBERSHIPS** SAA; PNRS; MLA. **RESEARCH** English renaissance literature; Shakespeare; 20th-century popular culture. **SELECTED PUBLICATIONS** Auth, A Mirror for Magistrates and the De Casibus Tradition, Univ Toronto Pr, 98; co-ed, Reflections on the Sequel, Univ Toronto Pr, 98. **CONTACT ADDRESS** English Dept, Simon Fraser Univ, Burnaby, BC, Canada V5A 1S6. **EMAIL** budra@sfu.ca

BUELL, FREDERICK HENDERSON
PERSONAL Born 11/17/1942, Bryn Mawr, PA, m, 1982, 2 children **DISCIPLINE** ENGLISH & AMERICAN LITERATURE **EDUCATION** Yale Univ, BA, 64; Cornell Univ, PhD, 69. **CAREER** From instr to asst prof, 69-74, assoc prof, 74-79, prof eng, Queens Col, 79. **HONORS AND AWARDS** NEA grant, 71; Yaddo Residency, 81; FIPSE grant, 87-90; New York Found for the Arts grant, 94; Excellence in Tchg Awd, 96; ACLS grant, 97-98. **MEMBERSHIPS** MLA **RESEARCH** 20th Century Am lit; globalization and cult; Am environmental writing. **SELECTED PUBLICATIONS** Auth, W H Auden As a Social Poet, Cornell Univ, 73; Sylvia Plath's Traditionalism, boundary 2, 76; To be quiet in the hands of the Marvelous: The poetry of A R Ammons, Iowa Rev, 77; The Non-Literary Style of American Poetry, Cornell Rev, 79; rev, "Conceptualizations of Contemporary Global Culture," Comparative Civilizations, 92; National Culture and the New Global System, Johns Hopkins, 94; Post Nationalist Nationalism, Am Quart, 98; auth, "Ashis Nandy and Globalist Discove," Dissemting Knowledges, Open Futures, 00. **CONTACT ADDRESS** Dept of Eng, Queens Col, CUNY, 6530 Kissena Blvd, Flushing, NY 11367-1597. **EMAIL** buell@warwick.net

BUELL, LAWRENCE I.
PERSONAL Born 06/11/1939, Bryn Mawr, PA, m, 1962, 2 children **DISCIPLINE** ENGLISH, LITERATURE, LANGUAGE **EDUCATION** Princeton Univ, AB, 61; Cornell Univ, PhD, 66. **CAREER** Instr, Turghai Univ, 63-65; asst prof to assoc prof to prof, Oberlin Col, 66-90; prof, Harvard, 90-. **HONORS AND AWARDS** Howard Found Fel; Woodrow Wilson Fel; Guggenheim Fel; NEH Fel. **MEMBERSHIPS** MLA; ASA. **RESEARCH** American literature and cultural history; environmental studies. **SELECTED PUBLICATIONS** Auth, Literary Transcendentalism: Style Belief in the American Renaissance, Cornell Univ Pr, 73; auth, New England Literary Culture: from Resolution to Renaissance, Cambridge Univ Pr, 86; auth, The Environmental Imagination: Thoreau, Nature Writing, and the Formation of American Culture, Harvard Univ Pr, 95; auth, Writing for an Endangered World: Literature, Culture and Environment in the US and Beyond, Harvard Univ Pr, 01. **CONTACT ADDRESS** English Dept, Harvard Univ, Cambridge, MA 02138. **EMAIL** lbuell@fac.harvard.edu

BUELOW, GEORGE JOHN
PERSONAL Born 03/31/1929, Chicago, IL **DISCIPLINE** MUSICOLOGY **EDUCATION** Chicago Musical Col, BM, 50, MM, 51; NYork Univ, PhD, 61. **CAREER** Instr music hist, Chicago Conserv Music, 59-61; assoc prof, Univ Calif, Riverside, 61-68; prof & chmn dept, Univ Ky, 68-69; prof music, coord chmn dept & dir grad studies, Rutgers Univ, New Brunswick, 69-77; Prof Musicol, Ind Univ Bloomington, 77-; Am ed, Acta Musicologica, 67-86; mem exec comt, The New Grove Dict Music & Musicians, 6th ed, 72-80; fac res fel, Rutgers State Univ, 74-75; gen ed, Studies in Musicol, Univ Microfilms Res Press, 77-90; co-chmn, Int Johann Mattheson Symp, Wolfenbuttel, Ger, 81; co-ed, New Mattheson Studies, Cambridge Univ Press, 83; ed comt, Documenta musicologica, 81-. **HONORS AND AWARDS** Fulbright scholar, Univ Hamburg, 54-55; Guggenheim fel, 67; The "Martin Bernstein" Lectr, NYU, 85. **MEMBERSHIPS** Am Musicol Soc; Int Musicol Soc; Gesellschaft fur Musikforschung; Am Bach Soc (pres 87-91); Am Handel Soc (vpres 89-91); Soc 17th Century Music. **RESEARCH** Baroque music and performance practices; the history of opera; the music of Richard Strauss. **SELECTED PUBLICATIONS** Ed & auth, Music and Society--The Late Baroque, Macmillan, 93; The Italian Influence in Heinichen's Der General-Bass in der Composition, Basler Jahrbuch fur Historische Musikpraxis 18, Amadeus, Basel, 94; co-ed, Musicology and Performance, Essays of Paul Henry Lang, Yale, New Haven, 97; author of numerous other articles and publications. **CONTACT ADDRESS** Sch of Music, Indiana Univ, Bloomington, 1 Indiana University, Bloomington, IN 47405. **EMAIL** buelow@indiana.edu

BUERKEL-ROTHFUSS, NANCY
PERSONAL Born 01/21/1951, Saginaw, MI, m, 1998, 1 child **DISCIPLINE** COMMUNICATION STUDIES **EDUCATION** Oakland Univ, BA, 73; Mich State Univ, MA, 75, PhD, 78. **CAREER** Asst prof, Univ Ky, 78-80; asst prof, 80-82, assoc prof, 82-86, full prof, 86- , Central Mich Univ. **HONORS AND AWARDS** Elected div chemn, Nat Commun Asn, 95-98 & 96-99. **MEMBERSHIPS** Nat Commun Asn; Int Commun Asn. **RESEARCH** Family communication; interpersonal communication; mass communication; instructional communication. **SELECTED PUBLICATIONS** Auth, Media, Sex and Adolescents; auth, Communication: Competencies and Contexts; auth, Understanding Family Communication. **CONTACT ADDRESS** Speech Communication & Drama Dept, Central Michigan Univ, 333 Moore Hall, Mount Pleasant, MI 48859. **EMAIL** wffcclady2@voyager.net

BUGGE, JOHN MICHAEL
PERSONAL Born 06/03/1941, Milwaukee, WI, m, 1966 **DISCIPLINE** MEDIEVAL ENGLISH LITERATURE **EDUCATION** Marquette Univ, BA, 63; Harvard Univ, MA, 66, PhD(English), 70. **CAREER** Asst prof, 68-76, assoc prof English, Emory Univ, 76-, men screening comt, Harbison Award for Distinguished Teaching, Danforth Found, 71-72, Grand Fels for Women, 72-74; Nat Endowment for Humanities Young Humanist fel, 73-74; Professor Emory Univ, 96-. **MEMBERSHIPS** MLA; Mediaeval Acad Am. **RESEARCH** Concepts of virginity and female sexuality in Medieval literature; the Medieval English alliterative tradition; Chaucer. **SELECTED PUBLICATIONS** Auth, Damyan's Wanton Clyket and an Ironic New Twiste to the Merchant's Tale, Annuale Mediaevale, 73; Rhyme as Onomatopoeia in The Dry Salvages, Papers Lang & Lit, 74; Virginitas: An Essay in the History of a Medieval Ideal, Nijhoff, 75; The Virgin Phoenix, Mediaeval Studies, 76; Tell-Tale Context: Two Notes on Biblical Quotation in The Canterbury Tales, Am Notes and Queries, 76; The Arthurian Tradition: Essays in Convergence, 88. **CONTACT ADDRESS** Dept of English, Emory Univ, Atlanta, GA 30322-0001. **EMAIL** engjmb@emory.edu

BUHLER, STEPHEN M.
PERSONAL Born 10/23/1954, Brooklyn, NY, m, 1983, 1 child **DISCIPLINE** ENGLISH **EDUCATION** Calif State Univ Long Beach, BA, 76; Univ Calif Los Angeles, MA, 83; PhD, 89. **CAREER** Instr, St Anthony HS, 76-84; teaching assoc, Univ Calif Los Angeles, 84-88; asst prof to assoc prof, Univ Nebr Lincoln, 89-. **HONORS AND AWARDS** Founder, Sweet Will and the Saucy Jacks; co-found, Bland John and the Miltones; Univ Calif Los Angeles Fel, 88-89; Folger Inst Fel, 92-94; NEH Fel, 93; Huntington Lib Fel, 96; Univ Nebr Lincoln Fel, 90, 96, 97. **MEMBERSHIPS** MSA; MLA; RSA; SAA; SSA. **RESEARCH** Early modern literary culture and its intersections with philosophy; performing arts; pedagogy. **SELECTED PUBLICATIONS** Auth, "Marsilio Ficino's 'De Stella Magorum' and Renaissance Views of Magi," Renaissance Quart 43 (90); auth, "Text, Eyes and Videotape: Screening Shakespeare Scripts," Shakespeare Quart 46 (95); auth, "No Spectre, No Scepter: The Agon of Materialist Thought in Shakespeare's 'Julius Caesar,'" English Lit Renaissance 26 (96); auth, "Preventing Wizards: The Magi in Milton's Nativity Ode," J English Ger Philos 96 (97); auth, "Double Takes: Branagh Gets to Hamlet," Post Script 17 (97); auth, "Counterpoint and Controversy: Milton and the Critiques of Polyphonic Music," Milton Studies 36 (98); auth, "Introducing Stage History to Students," in Teaching Shakespeare Through Performance, ed. Riggio (MLA, 99); auth, "Pre-Christian Apologetics in Spenser and Sidney," Spenser Studies 13 (99); auth, "Camp 'Richard III' and the Burdens of (Stage/Film) History," in Shakespeare Film, Fin de Siecle, eds. Burnett, Wray (Macmillan, 00); auth, Shakespeare in the Cinema: Ocular Proof, SUNY Pr, 01. **CONTACT ADDRESS** English Dept, Univ of Nebraska, Lincoln, Lincoln, NE 68588-0333. **EMAIL** sbuhler@unl.edu

BUITENHUIS, PETER M.
PERSONAL Born 12/08/1925, London, England, m, 1977, 7 children **DISCIPLINE** ENGLISH **EDUCATION** Jesus Col, Oxford, BA, 49, MA, 54; Yale Univ, PhD, 55. **CAREER** Instr, Univ Okla, 49-51; instr Am stud, Yale Univ, 54-59; asst to assoc prof, Univ Toronto, 59-66; vis prof, Univ Calif Berkeley, 66-67; prof, McGill Univ, 67-75; Prof and Chmn English, Simon Fraser Univ, 75-81; Prof Emer, 91. **HONORS AND AWARDS** Can Coun fel, 63-64; Am Coun Learned Soc fel, 72-73; SSHRC leave fel, 82-83, res grant, 91-94. **MEMBERSHIPS** Asn Can Stud; Can Asn Am Stud; Can Asn Univ Tchrs. **RESEARCH** Can and Am Lit; Writers and Propaganda. **SELECTED PUBLICATIONS** Auth, Hugh MacLennan, 68; auth, Viewpoints on Henry James' Portrait of a Lady, 68; ed, Selected Poems of E.J. Pratt, 69; ed, The Grasping Imagination: The American Writings of Henry James, 70; ed, The Restless Analyst: Essays by Henry James, 80; ed, The Great War of Words: British, American and Canadian Propaganda and Fiction 1914-1933, 87; co-ed, George Orwell: A Reassessment, 89; co-ed, The House of the Seven Gables: Severing Family and Colonial Ties, 91. **CONTACT ADDRESS** English Dept, Simon Fraser Univ, Burnaby, BC, Canada V5A 1S6. **EMAIL** peter_buitenhuis@sfu.ca

BUJA, MAUREEN
PERSONAL Born 10/30/1958, Pittsburgh, PA, m **DISCIPLINE** MUSICOLOGY **EDUCATION** Univ of IL, Urbana-Champaign, BA, 80; Univ of NC, Chapel Hill , MA, 82, PhD, 95; Columbia Univ MPHIL, 87. **CAREER** Professional managing ed, Stagebill, 97. **MEMBERSHIPS** MLA, IAML, AMS, RMA. **RESEARCH** Renaissance printing, Italian madrigals. **SELECTED PUBLICATIONS** Bks Vincenzo Ruffo The Italian Madrigal in the Sixteenth Century, vol 26, NY Garland Publ, 89, Introduction and Edition, Vincenzo Ruffo, Italian Renaissance Poetry, A First-Line Index to Petrarch, Ariosto, Tasso and Others, var articles, Essays in Honour of Donald Mitchell on His 70th Birthday. **CONTACT ADDRESS** Stagebill, 140 East 65th Str., New York, NY 10023. **EMAIL** mebuja@stagebill.com

BUKALSKI, PETER J.
PERSONAL Born 06/05/1941, Milwaukee, WI, m, 1971, 2 children **DISCIPLINE** FILM **EDUCATION** Univ Wis, Milwau, BA; Univ Wis, Madis, MA; Univ Cal, Los Ang, MFA; Ohio State Univ, PhD. **CAREER** Franklin Col, asst prof, 66-70; Wright State Univ, Dir motion pic stud, 70-73; Ohio State Univ, teach assoc, 73-75; SO IL Univ, Carbondale, chr, cine photog, 75-79; Am Film Inst, dir edu serv, 79-83; School Fine Arts Comm, Dean, 84-89; SO IL Univ, prof theat and dance, 89-. **HONORS AND AWARDS** Numerous teaching awards **MEMBERSHIPS** Univ Film Video Asn; Soc for Cine Stud; Univ Film Video Found; Am Mus Instr Soc; I **RESEARCH** Am film hist, 1927-1945; film edu; higher edu admin. **SELECTED PUBLICATIONS** Guide to Faculty Advancement: Annual Evaluation, Promotion and Tenure, Los Angeles, Univ Film and Video Asn, 00; "You've Got to Know the Territory: Six Principles of Academic Politics," UFVA Digest, 99; Oboe Making in the United States, A Laubin Inc, The Dble Reed, 90. **CONTACT ADDRESS** So Illinois Univ, Edwardsville, Dept Theater and Dance, Box 1777, Edwardsville, IL 62026. **EMAIL** pbukals@siue.edu

BULLARD, JOHN MOORE
PERSONAL Born 05/06/1932, Winston-Salem, NC **DISCIPLINE** BIBLICAL STUDIES; ENGLISH LANGUAGE AND LITERATURE **EDUCATION** AB, 53, AM, 55, UNC- Chapel Hill; Mdiv, 57, PhD, 62, Yale Univ. **CAREER** Asst in Instruction, Yale Univ, 57-62; Asst Prof, 61-65, Assoc Prof, 65-70, Albert C. Outler Prof, 70-, Chmn, Dept of Religion, 62-, Wofford Col. **HONORS AND AWARDS** Fund for the Study of the Great Religions grant to travel around the world and live 6 months in Indian, Colgate, Univ, 70-71; James Graduate Fel at Yale, 57-62; NEH Summer Senimars: Harvard, 82, Upenn, 86, Yale, 87; Dana Fel, Emory Univ, 89-90. **MEMBERSHIPS** Amer Acad of Religion; Soc of Biblical Lit; South Carolina Acad of Religion; New Bach Soc; Moravian Music Fdn. **RESEARCH** The Hymn as Literary form from ancient Sumerians to the Hebrew Psalter and beyond. **SELECTED PUBLICATIONS** Auth, Dictionary of Biblical Interpretation, ed. J.H. Hayes, Abingdon Press, 99; auth, Encyclopedia of the Ancient World, ed. C. Moose, Salem Press, CA, 00. **CONTACT ADDRESS** Dept of Religion, Wofford Col, 429 N. Church St., Spartanburg, SC 29303. **EMAIL** bullardjm@wofford.edu

BULLARD, TRUMAN
DISCIPLINE MUSIC **EDUCATION** Haverford Col, BA, 60; Harvard Univ, MA, 63; Univ Roch, Eastman Sch Music, PhD, 71. **CAREER** Music teach, Lakeside School, Seattle, WA, 63-65; Inst, 65, asst prof, 67, assoc prof, 71, PROF, 81-, DICKINSON COL; ADJ PROF MUSICOL, EASTMAN SCH MUSIC, 87-. **CONTACT ADDRESS** Music Dept, Dickinson Col, Carlisle, PA 17013-2896. **EMAIL** bullardt@dickinson.edu

BULLARO, GRACE RUSSO
PERSONAL Born Salarno, Italy **DISCIPLINE** ENGLISH **EDUCATION** CUNY City Col, BA, 71; SUNY Stony, MA, 89; PhD, 93. **CAREER** Teach asst, SUNY Stony, 88-92; adj asst prof, Nassau Com Col, 90-; adj asst prof, CUNY, Lehman Col, 91-; sub asst prof, CUNY, 98. **HONORS AND AWARDS** Who's Who in Am, World, Am Women, 00; Outstand People; Pres Awd; Phi Beta Kappa. **MEMBERSHIPS** MLA; NCTE; SPFA; Inst Fran¤ois. **SELECTED PUBLICATIONS** Auth, "Il

Piacere di Gabriele D'Annunzio: Nota critica a proposito del diano di Maria Ferres," Gradiva (91):140-143; auth, "Blade Runner: The Subversion and Redefinition of Categories," River Ouart 9 (93): 102-109; auth, "Rape and Conquest: Male Domination and the 'Natural Order' in Wertmuller's Swept Away," Ital Cult 13 (95): 309-321; auth, "Jean Genet: Gay Deceiver or Repressed Homosexual?" in Flowers and Revolution, ed. Barbara Read (London: Middlesex Univ Press, 97); auth, "The Political Education of a Bumpkin: The Emergence of Individualism and the Rejection of Marxism in Wertmuller's The Seduction of Mimi," Ital Cult 14 (99):351-36; auth, "'Man in Disorder' and Human Perfectibility in Wertmuller's Seven Beauties," Ital Cult 15 (97): 371-388; auth, "Racist Discourse in the Absence of Racial Difference in Wertmuller's 'Ciao Professore' ," Forum Ital (99). **CONTACT ADDRESS** Dept English, Lehman Col, CUNY, Bronx, NY 10468. **EMAIL** gracebullaro@msn.com

BULLER, JEFFREY L.
PERSONAL Born 09/09/1954, Milwaukee, WI, m, 1996, 2 children **DISCIPLINE** CLASSICS **EDUCATION** Univ Notre Dame, BA, 76; Univ Wis, MA, 77; PhD, 81. **CAREER** Asst prof to assoc prof, Loras Col, 81-90; assoc prof to prof, Ga S Univ, 90-97; asst to acting Dean, 90-. **HONORS AND AWARDS** Phi Beta Kappa; Phi Kappa Phi; Fulbright Fel (2). **MEMBERSHIPS** Am Philog Assoc; Classical Assoc of the Middle W and S; Wagner Soc of NY. **RESEARCH** Influence of classical literature on opera. **SELECTED PUBLICATIONS** Auth, "Looking Backwards: Baroque Opera and the Ending of the Orpheus Myth", Int J of the Class Tradition 1.3 ((5): 57-79; auth, "The Thematic Role of Stabreim in Richard Wagner's Der Ring des Nibelungen", Opera Quart 11.4 (95): 59-76; auth, Sleep in the Ring", Opera Quart, 12.2 (95): 3-22; auth, "The Messianic Hero in Wagner's Ring", Opera Quart, 13.2 (96): 21-38; auth, "From Clemtia Caesaris to La Clemenza di Tito", in Qui Miscuit Utile Dulci: Festschrift for Paul MacKendrick, Bolchazy-Charduzzi, (Wauconda, IL, 98), 69-85; auth, "Spectacle in the Ring", Opera Quart 14.4 (98): 41057; auth, "Ellen Faull: A Life in Song", Opera Quart (00). **CONTACT ADDRESS** Dept Hist, Georgia So Univ, PO Box 8054, Statesboro, GA 30460-1000. **EMAIL** jbuller@gasou.edu

BULLON-FERNANDEZ, MARIA
DISCIPLINE ENGLISH **EDUCATION** Univ Sevilla, BA, 89; Cornell Univ, PhD, 95. **CAREER** Eng, Seattle Univ. **MEMBERSHIPS** Medieval Acad Am; MLA; John Gower Soc; Soc Medieval Feminist Scholar; AEDEAN, Span Asn Anglo-North Am Stud; SELIM, Span Soc Medieval Engl Lang & Lit; ESSE, Europ Soc Stud Engl; New Chaucer Soc. **SELECTED PUBLICATIONS** Auth, Engendering Authority: Father and Daughter, State and Church in John Gower's Tale of Constance and Chaucer's Man of Law's Tale, in Revisioning Gower, 98; Confining the Daughter: Gower's 'Tale of Canace and Machaire' and the Polit of the Body, in Essays in Medieval Stud, 11, 94; Beyonde the water: Courtly and Religious Desire in Pearl, Stud in Philol, XCI 1, 94; Gower frente a las convenciones del amor cortes: el cuento de Rosiphelee y el papel social de la mujer en la Confessio Amantis, Actas del XV Congreso de AEDEAN, 91; La tentacion de Adan y Eva en la literatura inglesa de la Baja Edad Media: Caracterizacion alegorica, in ATLANTIS, 13 1-2, 91; collab, Caedmon y Beda: La traduccion del mensaje cristiano en la Inglaterra Anglosajona, Actas del XIV Congreso de AEDEAN, 90; rev, Estudio sobre Confessio Amantis de John Gower y su version castellana Confisyon del amante de Juan de Cuenca, Selim, 4, 95; auth, Fathers and Daughters in Gower's Confessio Amantis: Authority, Family, State, and Writing, Cambridge: DS Brewer, 00. **CONTACT ADDRESS** Dept of Eng, Seattle Univ, 900 Broadway, Seattle, WA 98122-4460. **EMAIL** bullon@seattleu.edu

BUMP, JEROME FRANCIS ANTHONY
PERSONAL Born 06/13/1943, Pine River, MN, m, 1998, 2 children **DISCIPLINE** ENGLISH LITERATURE, COMPARATIVE STUDIES **EDUCATION** Univ Minn, Minneapolis, BA, 65; Univ Calif, Berkeley, MA, 66, PhD(English), 72 **CAREER** Asst prof, 70-76, assoc prof, 76-85, Prof English, Univ Tex, Austin, 85-. **HONORS AND AWARDS** Nat Endowment for Humanities fel, 74. **MEMBERSHIPS** NCTE; Int Hopkins Asn **RESEARCH** Emotional intelligence; creativity; Victorian literature. **SELECTED PUBLICATIONS** Auth, 1 bk, 1 ed, 34 articles, 10chap, 1 ed letter, 1 bibliogr, 14 rev essays, 25 rev & 87 papers. **CONTACT ADDRESS** Dept of English, Univ of Texas, Austin, Austin, TX 78712-1164. **EMAIL** bump@mail.utexas.edu

BUNGE, NANCY LIDDELL
PERSONAL Born 05/13/1942, La Crosse, WI **DISCIPLINE** AMERICAN LITERATURE, ENGLISH LITERATURE **EDUCATION** Radcliffe Col, AB, 64; Univ Chicago, MA, 66; Univ Wis-Madison, PhD, 70. **CAREER** From instr to asst prof Am lit, George Washington Univ, 68-73; from Asst Prof to Assoc Prof, 73-84, prof Am thought & lang, Mich State Univ, 84-. **HONORS AND AWARDS** Teacher-Scholar Awd, Mich State Univ, 78; Sr Fulbright Lectr in Am Culture, Univ Vienna, 86-87; sr Fulbright lectr in Am lit, Free Univ of Brussels & the Univ of Ghent, 99-00. **MEMBERSHIPS** MLA; Midwest Mod Lang Asn. **RESEARCH** Writing. **SELECTED PUBLICATIONS** Interviewer & ed, Finding the Words: Conversations with Writers Who Teach, Swallow, 85; auth, Nathaniel Hawthorne: A Study of the Short Fiction, Twayne/Macmillan, 93. **CONTACT ADDRESS** Dept of Am Thought & Lang, Michigan State Univ, 229 Bessey Hall, East Lansing, MI 48824-1033. **EMAIL** bunge@pilot.msu.edu

BURBICK, JOAN
PERSONAL Born 06/20/1946, Chicago, IL, s, 1 child **DISCIPLINE** AMERICAN LITERATURE **EDUCATION** Brandeis, PhD. **CAREER** Prof, Washington State Univ. **HONORS AND AWARDS** Norman Foerster Awd, 86, Maita Sulton Weeks Fellow, Stauford Humanities Center, Edward R. Meyer Prof of Liberal Arts, 99, Louis E. and Stella G. Buchanau Prof of English. **RESEARCH** Nationalism and gender in the American West. **SELECTED PUBLICATIONS** Auth, Thoreau's Alternative History: Changing Perspectives on Nature, Culture, and Language, 87 & Healing the Republic: The Language of Health and the Culture of Nationalism in Nineteenth Century America, 94. **CONTACT ADDRESS** Dept of English, Washington State Univ, Pullman, WA 99164-5020. **EMAIL** burbick@wsu.edu

BURD, VAN AKIN
PERSONAL Born 04/19/1914, m, 1942, 1 child **DISCIPLINE** ENGLISH **EDUCATION** Univ Chicago, AB, 36; Stanford Univ, MA, 41; Univ Mich, PhD, 51. **CAREER** Teacher, pub schs, Mich, 36-40; teaching fel & jr instr English, Univ Mich, 46-51; prof, 51-74, chmn dept, 59-60, 61-63 & 65-68, res found fels, 55, 65, 68 & 73, prof, 73-79, Distinguished Emer Prof English, State Univ NY Col Cortland, 79-, Am Coun Learned Soc fel, 60-61, grant-in-aid, 68-69 & 78-79; Am Philos Soc grants-in-aid, 60, 68, 73 & 79; Delmus Found Venetian Studies grant-in-aid, 79. **MEMBERSHIPS** MLA; NCTE; Thoreau Soc; Turner Soc. **RESEARCH** Romantic and Victorian periods of English literature, especially John Ruskin. **SELECTED PUBLICATIONS** Ed, The Winnington Letters: The Correspondence of John Ruskin and M Bell, Harvard Univ, 69 & The Ruskin Family Letters, Cornell Univ, 73; auth, A new light on the writing of modern painters & Background to modern painters: The tradition and the Turner controversy, MLA Publ; Ruskin's quest for a theory of imagination, Mod Lang Quart; John Ruskin and Rose LaTouche, Oxford Univ, 79; Sharp,Frederick,James 1880-1957/, Bk Collector, Vol 44, 1995; Ruskin, Bembridge and Brantwood - The Growth of the Whitehouse-Collection - Dearden,JS/, Bk Collector, Vol 44, 1995. **CONTACT ADDRESS** Dept of English, SUNY, Col at Cortland, Cortland, NY 13045.

BURDE, EDGAR J.
PERSONAL Born 12/23/1930, New York, NY, m, 1963, 3 children **DISCIPLINE** ENGLISH **EDUCATION** Hobart Col, Geneva, NYork, BA, 53; Univ of Edinburgh, Scotland, postgrad English studies, 55-56; Univ Calif, Berkeley, MA, 63; Claremont Grad Sch, Calif, PhD(English), 69. **CAREER** Corporal, US Army, Germany, 53-55; Instr English, Univ Mont, Missoula, 63-64; instr English, Whitman Col, 64-66; asst prof English, Claremont Men's Col, 69-70; from asst prof to assoc prof, 70-86, prof English, State Univ Ny Col Plattsburgh, 76-00; prof emeritus, 00-. **MEMBERSHIPS** MLA; ALSC. **RESEARCH** Am Lit. **SELECTED PUBLICATIONS** Auth, The Ambassadors and the Double Vision of Henry James, Essays in Literature, Spring 77; Mark Twain: The Writer as Pilot, PMLA, Oct 78; Slavery and the Boys: Tom Sawyer and the Germ of Huck Finn, Am Lit Realism, Fall 91. **CONTACT ADDRESS** Dept of English, SUNY, Col at Plattsburgh, Plattsburgh, NY 12901. **EMAIL** ej.burde@plattsburgh.edu

BURDUCK, MICHAEL L.
PERSONAL Born 05/26/1955, New York, NY, m **DISCIPLINE** ENGLISH **EDUCATION** St Johns Univ, BA, 77; Eastern Kentucky Univ, 78; Univ Miss, PhD, 84. **CAREER** Prof, Tenn Tech Univ, 85-. **HONORS AND AWARDS** Fulbright Prof of Am Studies, Norway, 94-95. **MEMBERSHIPS** Poe Soc of Baltimore, Hawthorne Soc, Poe Studies Asn, Am Lit Section of MLA. **RESEARCH** Nineteenth Century Am literature, Poe, Gothic, Faulkner. **SELECTED PUBLICATIONS** Auth, Grim Phantasms: Fear in Poe's Short Fiction, Garland: New York, 92; auth, Usher's Forgotten Church? Edgar Allan Poe and Nineteenth Century American Catholicism, The Edgar Allan Poe Society: Baltimore, 00. **CONTACT ADDRESS** Dept English, Tennessee Tech Univ, 1000 N Dixie Ave, Cookeville, TN 38595-0001. **EMAIL** mburduck@tntech.edu

BURGCHARDT, CARL
DISCIPLINE COMMUNICATION STUDIES **EDUCATION** Pa State Univ, BA; Univ Wis, MA, PhD. **CAREER** Prof. **RESEARCH** Public speaking; rhetorical criticism. **SELECTED PUBLICATIONS** Auth, Readings in Rhetorical Criticism; Discovering Rhetorical Imprints: La Follette, 'Iago' and the Melodramatic Scenario, Quarterly J Speech, 85; Two Faces of American Communism: Pamphlet Rhetoric of the Third Period and the Popular Front, Quarterly J Speech, 80. **CONTACT ADDRESS** Speech Communication Dept, Colorado State Univ, Fort Collins, CO 80523. **EMAIL** cburgchardt@vines.colostate.edu

BURGESS, JONATHAN
PERSONAL Born 04/17/1960, Baltimore, MD, m, 1988, 2 children **DISCIPLINE** CLASSICS **EDUCATION** Univ Toronto, PhD, 95. **CAREER** Asst prof, classics, Univ Toronto, 95-. **HONORS AND AWARDS** Gov Gen Gold Medal, Univ Toronto, 95. **MEMBERSHIPS** APA; CAC; CAAS. **RESEARCH** Early Greek epic; mythology. **SELECTED PUBLICATIONS** Auth, The Death of Achilles, forthcoming. **CONTACT ADDRESS** Dept of Classics, Univ of Toronto, 97 St George St, Toronto, ON, Canada M5S 1A1. **EMAIL** jburgess@class.utoronto.ca

BURGESS, MICHAEL
PERSONAL Born 02/11/1948, Fukuoka, Japan, m, 1976, 2 children **DISCIPLINE** LIBRARY SCIENCE **EDUCATION** Gonzaga Univ, AB, 69; Univ S Calif, MS, 70. **CAREER** Dept Head, Calif State Univ, 70-. **HONORS AND AWARDS** Pilgrim Awd, 93; Lifetime Collector's Awd, 93. **MEMBERSHIPS** Am Libr Asn; Calif Libr Asn; Sci Fiction Res Asn; Intl Asn of the Fantastic in the Arts; Sci Fiction and Fantasy Writers of Am; Horror Writers of Am; Mystery Writers of Am; Calif Fac Asn. **RESEARCH** Fantastic literature; Bibliography; Eastern Orthodoxy; Paperback publishing; Historical fiction. **SELECTED PUBLICATIONS** Auth, Reference Guide to Science Fiction, Fantasy, and Horror, Libr Unlimited, 92; auth, Science Fiction and Fantasy Literature, Gale Res Co., 92; auth, The House of the Burgesses, Burgess & Wickizer, 94; auth, Lords Temporal and Lords Spiritual, Borgo Press, 95; co-auth, Codex Derynianus, Underwood Books, 98; auth, Katydid & Other Critters, Ariadne Press, 01. **CONTACT ADDRESS** Libr Admin, California State Univ, San Bernardino, 5500 Univ Pkwy, San Bernardino, CA 91407. **EMAIL** mburgess@csusb.edu

BURGOON, JUDEE
DISCIPLINE COMMUNICATION **EDUCATION** Iowa State Univ, BA, 70; Univ Illinois, MS, 72; West Virginia Univ, PhD, 74. **CAREER** Teach, HS, 70-71; Instr, Ill State Univ, 71-72; Instr, West Virginia Univ, 72-74; asst prof, Univ Florida, 74-77; vis asst prof, Mich State Univ, adj asst prof, Hunter Col, 77-78; asst prof, assoc prof, Mich State Univ, 78-83; vis schl, Harvard Univ, 89; fac, Univ Arizona, 86-94; prof, Univ Arizona, 84-. **HONORS AND AWARDS** Phi Kappa Phi; Outstand Yg Wom Am; Outstand Yg Teach; Teach Schl Awd; SBS Excell Teach; B Aubrey Fisher Ment Awd; ICD Top Four Paper; Charles H Woolbert Res Awd; ICD Top Three Paper; NCA Dist Schl. **SELECTED PUBLICATIONS** Auth, Expectancy approaches to language and attitudes, Sage Pub (Thousand Oaks, CA), forthcoming; coauth, Nonverbal communication: The unspoken dialogue, McGraw-Hill (NY), 96; coauth, Interpersonal adaptation: Dyadic interaction patterns, Cambridge Univ Press (NY), 95; coauth, Nonverbal communication: The unspoken dialogue McGraw-Hill (NY), 96; coauth, Expectancy approaches to language and attitudes, Sage (Thousand Oaks, CA), forthcoming; "Strategic behavior during deceptive conversation," J Lang Soc Psycho (in press); coauth, "Becoming mindful in and through interpersonal communication, " J Soc Issues (in press). **CONTACT ADDRESS** Dept Communication, Univ of Arizona, 1103 e Univ Blvd, Tucson, AZ 85721.

BURGOS, FERNANDO
PERSONAL Born Osorno, Chile **DISCIPLINE** LITERATURE **EDUCATION** Univ Chile, BA, 70; Univ Fla, PhD, 81. **CAREER** Asst prof Span Am Lit, Univ Chile, 71-76; grad asst, 76-80, res asst Span Am Lit, 78-80, Univ Fla; instr, Middlebury Col, 80 & 81; asst prof to prof, Univ Memphis, 81- . **HONORS AND AWARDS** Fel Vis Schol Prog Univ Chicago, 92; SPUR Awd, 94; Univ Memphis Recog Outstanding Res Activities. **MEMBERSHIPS** Assoc Int Hisp. **RESEARCH** Spanish-American literature. **SELECTED PUBLICATIONS** Auth, Antologia del cuento hispanoamericano. Mexico: Editorial Porrua, (91); ed, Esteban Echeverria, El matadero, Ensayos Esteticos y Prosas Varia de Esteban Echeverria, Nanover, NH: Ediciones del Norte, (92); auth, Vertientes de la Modernidad hispanoamericana. Caracas: Monte Avila Editores, (95); auth, Cuentos de Hispanoamerica en el siglo veinte. 3 vols. Madrid: Castalia, (97). **CONTACT ADDRESS** Dept For Lang, Univ of Memphis, 3706 Alumni St, Memphis, TN 38152-0001. **EMAIL** fburgos@memphis.edu

BURIAN, JARKA MARSANO
PERSONAL Born 03/10/1927, Passaic, NJ, m, 1951 **DISCIPLINE** DRAMATIC ART **EDUCATION** Rutgers Univ, BA, 49; Columbia Univ, MA, 50; Cornell Univ, PhD, 55. **CAREER** Instr English Cornell Univ, 54-55; from asst prof to assoc prof English, 55-63, chmn dept theatre, 71-74 & 77-78, prof, 63-93, prof emeritus, 93-, theater dept, SUNY Albany; vis assoc prof dramatic art, Univ Calif, Berkeley, 61-62; US State Dept specialist's lect grant, Czechoslovakia, fall 65; Inter-Univ Comt Travel Grants res grant, Czechoslovakia, 68-69; Int Res & Exchange Bd res grant, Czechoslovakia, 74-75, Poland & Hungary 82; Czech Republic, 93-94; producer & artistic dir, Arena Summer Theatre, Albany, 59 & 63-64, 66-68 & 72-73; NEH fel, 74; Fulbright res award, 82, 88. **MEMBERSHIPS** US Inst Theatre Technol; Am Soc Theatre Res; AAUP. **RESEARCH** Comparative literature; play production. **SELECTED PUBLICATIONS** Auth, The Scenography of Josef Svoboda, Middletown,

CT: Wesleyan Univ Press, (71): 1-202; auth, K H Hilar and the Early Twentieth Century Czech Theatre, Educ Thr J, 82; auth, Snoboda: Wagner, Wesleyan, 83; auth, Designing for the 90s, Cue Int, 89; auth, The Dark Era in Modern Czech Theatre: 1948-1950, Theatre Hist Stud, 95; auth, Two Women and Their Contribution to Contemporary Czech Scenography, Theatre Design and Technol, 96; auth, Laterna Magika as a Synthesis of Theatre and Film, Theatre Hist Stud, 97; auth, "Svoboda's Scenography for Faust: Evolution in the Use of Mirrors," Theatre Design and Ttechnology 34.5 (Fall 98): 34-41; auth, "Three Young Czech Directors," Slavic and East European Performance 19.1 (Spring 99): 14-31; auth, Modern Czech Theatre: Reflector and Conscience of a Nation, Iowa City, Iowa: University of Iowa Press, (00): 1-265. **CONTACT ADDRESS** Dept of Theatre, SUNY, Albany, 1400 Washington Ave, Albany, NY 12222.

BURKE, ALEXANDER J.
PERSONAL Born 04/24/1931, New York, NY, m, 1955, 7 children **DISCIPLINE** ENGLISH **EDUCATION** Holy Cross Col, BA, 53; Fordham Univ, MA, 55; Seminary Immaculate Conception, MA, 95; Fordham Univ, PhD, 95. **CAREER** Instr, Fordham Univ, 59-60; Prof, Hofstra Univ, 94-. **RESEARCH** Chaucer, gospel of John, Bible as literature, New Testament studies. **CONTACT ADDRESS** Dept English, Hofstra Univ, 1000 Fulton Ave, Hempstead, NY 11550-1030. **EMAIL** ajburkejr@aol.com

BURKE, JOHN J., JR
PERSONAL Born 05/04/1942, Buffalo, NY, m, 1969, 4 children **DISCIPLINE** ENGLISH **EDUCATION** Boston Col, AB, 67; Northwestern Univ, MA, 68; UCLA, PhD, 74. **CAREER** Teacher, Chicago, 68-69; fel and assoc, UCLA, 69-73; acting asst prof, UCSD, 73-74; asst prof to prof, Univ Ala, 74-. **HONORS AND AWARDS** Outstanding Commitment to Students, Col of Arts and Sci, 99; Morris L. Mayer Awd, Univ Ala, 97; Teaching Excellence, Univ Ala, 95; Burlington N Fac Achievement Awd, 91; Outstanding Commitment to Teaching Awd, Univ Ala, 83. **MEMBERSHIPS** ASECS; SEASECS; ECSSS; MLA; SAMLA. **RESEARCH** Johnson & Boswell; Sir Walter Scott; Shakespeare; The novel; Historiography; The epic in the 18th century. **SELECTED PUBLICATIONS** Auth, "Crime and Punishment in 1777: The Execution of the Reverend Dr. William Dodd and Its Impact upon His Contemporaries," in Executions and the British Experience, (McFarland, 90), 59-75; auth, "Johnson's Quarrel with Lord Chesterfield: The Originality of Boswell's Version," in New Light on Boswell, (Cambridge Univ Press, 91), 143-161; auth, "Talk, Dialogue, Conversation, and Other Kinds of Speech Acts in Boswell's 'Life of Johnson'," in Compendious Conversations, (Peter Lang, 92), 65-79; auth, "Filling in the Blanks of Shakespeare's Biography," S Atlantic Rev, (95): 101-112; auth, "Boswell and the Text of Johnson's Logia," Age of Johnson, (98): 25-46; auth, "The Homoerotic Subtext in Scott's Portrait of James I: the Question of Evidence," CLIO (00): 295-314. **CONTACT ADDRESS** Dept English, Univ of Alabama, Tuscaloosa, PO Box 870244, Tuscaloosa, AL 35487-0244. **EMAIL** jburke@english.as.ua.edu

BURKMAN, KATHERINE H.
PERSONAL Born 06/13/1934, Chicago, IL, m, 1965, 2 children **DISCIPLINE** ENGLISH, THEATRE **EDUCATION** Radcliffe Col, AB, 55: Univ Chicago, MA & cert educ, 56; Ohio State Univ, PhD(theatre), 68. **CAREER** Teacher English, Columbia high sch, 57-59; teacher, Fieldston high sch, Riverdale, NY, 59-63; promotion writer textbooks, Harcourt, Brace & World, 63-64; teaching asst rhet, Univ Iowa, 64-65; instr English, Butler Univ, 65-66; asst prof comp lit, 68-77, Assoc Prof English, Ohio State Univ, 77-95, Dir, Nat Endowment for Humanities grant, 69-70, 71-72; dir, The Collection, 69-73; Prof Emeritus, 95-. **MEMBERSHIPS** AAUP; Am Theatre Asn. **RESEARCH** Modern drama; uses of theatre in teaching literature; playwriting. **SELECTED PUBLICATIONS** Auth, Pinter's A slight ache as ritual, Mod Drama, winter 68; The Dramatic World of Harold Pinter: It's Basis in Ritual, Ohio State Univ, 71; co-ed, Drama Through Performance, Houghton, 77; auth, Literature Through Performance, Ohio Univ, 78; The Arrival of Godot: Ritual Pattern in Modern Drama Fairleigh Dickinson UP, 1986: Beckett 'Waiting for Godot'/, Theatre J, Vol 45, 1993; Pinter 'Old Times'/, Theatre J, Vol 46, 1994; Pinter,Harold - A Question of Timing - Regal,MS/, Mod Drama, Vol 39, 1996; coed, Staging the Page: The Web of Mysogyny in Modern Drama, Farileigh Dickinson UP, 1998. **CONTACT ADDRESS** Dept of English, Ohio State Univ, Columbus, 518 Denney Hall, Columbus, OH 43210. **EMAIL** burkman.2@osu.edu

BURKS, DON M.
DISCIPLINE RHETORICAL THEORY, THE RELATIONSHIPS AMONG RHETORIC, PHILOSOPHY, AND LITERA **EDUCATION** Univ Wis, PhD, 62. **CAREER** Assoc prof, Purdue Univ. **RESEARCH** The works of Kenneth Burke, Henry Johnstone, and Wayne Booth. **SELECTED PUBLICATIONS** Ed, Rhetoric, Philosophy and Literature: An Exploration, 78; Dramatic Irony, Collaboration, and Kenneth Burke's Theory of Form, Pre/Text, 85; Kenneth Burke: The agro-Bohemian Marxoid, Commun Stud, 91; coauth, Rhetorical sensitivity and social interaction, Commun Monogr, 72. **CONTACT ADDRESS** Dept of Commun, Purdue Univ, West Lafayette, 2115 Laeb, West Lafayette, IN 47907-1080. **EMAIL** dburks@sla.purdue.edu

BURLAND, MARGARET A. JEWETT
PERSONAL Born 04/10/1966, Cleveland, OH, m, 2000 **DISCIPLINE** LITERATURE **EDUCATION** Bryn Mawr Col, AB/MA, 88; Univ Chicago, PhD, 98. **CAREER** Lecturer, Univ of Chicago, 93-96; Asst Prof of French, Dartmouth Col, 98-. **HONORS AND AWARDS** Whiting Dissertation Year Fel, 97-98. **MEMBERSHIPS** Medieval Academy of America, International Arthurian Society, Society for Medieval Feminist Scholarship, Modern Language Assoc. **RESEARCH** Medieval French and Occitan Literature. **SELECTED PUBLICATIONS** Auth, "Remembering Ronevaux: Collective Identity and Literary Commentary in Medieval French and Occitan Versions of the Roland Legend,"(Univ of Chicago, 98). **CONTACT ADDRESS** Dept French & Italian, Dartmouth Col, 6087 Dartmouth Hall, Hanover, NH 03755-3511. **EMAIL** margaret.jewett@dartmouth.edu

BURLESON, BRANT R.
DISCIPLINE INTERPERSONAL COMMUNICATION **EDUCATION** Ill, PhD, 82. **CAREER** Prof, Purdue Univ. **RESEARCH** Social support; comforting; communication and emotion; philosophy of science. **SELECTED PUBLICATIONS** Auth, Comforting messages; Significance, approaches, and effects, Commun of Soc Support, 94; Thoughts about talk in romantic relationships; Similarity makes for attraction (and happiness, too), Commun Quart, 94; Personal relationships as a skilled accomplishment, Jour of Soc and Personal Relationships, 95; Men's and women's evaluations of communication skills in personal relationships: When sex differences make a difference-and when they don't, J of Soc and Personal Relationships, 96; The socialization of emotional support skills in childhood, Handbook of Soc Support and the Family, 96. **CONTACT ADDRESS** Dept of Commun, Purdue Univ, West Lafayette, 1366 Lib Arts & Educ Bldg 2114, West Lafayette, IN 47907-1366. **EMAIL** brantb@gte.net

BURLIN, ROBERT B.
PERSONAL Born 10/07/1928, Cleveland, OH **DISCIPLINE** ENGLISH **EDUCATION** Yale Univ, BA, 50, PhD(English), 56. **CAREER** Instr English, Yale Col, 55-59, Morse fel, 59-60; from asst prof to assoc prof English, 60-69, chmn dept, 68-75, Prof English, Bryn Mawr Col, 69-. **MEMBERSHIPS** MLA; Mediaeval Acad Am. **RESEARCH** Old and Middle English literature. **SELECTED PUBLICATIONS CONTACT ADDRESS** Dept of English, Bryn Mawr Col, Bryn Mawr, PA 19010.

BURLING, WILLIAM J.
PERSONAL Born 01/27/1949, Ladysmith, WI, m, 1980, 2 children **DISCIPLINE** ENGLISH LITERATURE **EDUCATION** Univ of Wis, BS, 72, MA, 74; Penn State Univ, PhD, 85. **CAREER** Instr, Univ of Wis, 74-77; instr, Northern Ill Univ, 78-79; asst prof, Auburn Univ, 85-89; ASSOC PROF TO PROF, SOUTHWEST MO STATE UNIV, 89-. **HONORS AND AWARDS** SMSU Found Excellence in Res Awd, 93. **MEMBERSHIPS** Am Soc of 18th Century Studies. **RESEARCH** English drama & theatre history, 1660-1843. **SELECTED PUBLICATIONS** Co-ed, The Plays of Colley Cibber, Fairleigh Dickinson Univ Press, 00; auth, Summer Theatre in London 1661-1820 and the Rise of the Little Haymarket Theatre, Fairleigh Dickinson Univ Press, 00; auth, A Checklist of New Plays and Entertainments on the London State 1700-1737, Fairleigh Dickinson Univ Press, 93; auth, A Preliminary Checklist and Finding Guide of the Correspondence of George Colman Jr, Bullt of Bibliog, 97; auth, British Plays 1697-1737: Premieres, Datings, Attributions, and publication Information, Studies in Bibliog, 89; auth, New Light on the Colley Cibber Canon: The Bulls and Bears and Damon and Phillida, Philolog Quart, 88; auth, Summer Theatre in London 1661-1694, Theatre Notebook XLII, 88; auth, A New Shadwell Letter, Modern Philol, 85; auth, Four More Lost Restoration Plays Found in Musical Sources, Music and Letters, 84; coauth, Theatrical Companies at the Little Haymarket Theatre 1720-1737, Essays in Theatre, 86. **CONTACT ADDRESS** Dept of English, Southwest Missouri State Univ, Springfield, 901 S National, Springfield, MO 65804. **EMAIL** wjb692f@mail.smsu.edu

BURLINGAME, LORI
DISCIPLINE NATIVE AMERICAN LITERATURE **EDUCATION** PhD. **CAREER** E Mich Univ **HONORS AND AWARDS** FIPSE, 94-95. **SELECTED PUBLICATIONS** Auth, The Voice of the Serpent: An Interview with Leslie Marmon Silko, ." Bookpress: Newspaper Lity Arts, 93; Cultural Survival in Runner in the Sun, Univ Okla Press, 96. **CONTACT ADDRESS** Eastern Michigan Univ, Ypsilanti, MI 48197. **EMAIL** Lori.Burlingame@online.emich.edu

BURNEKO, GUY
DISCIPLINE LITERATURE, PHILOSOPHY OF SCIENCE, EVOLUTION OF CONSCIOUSNESS **EDUCATION** Fordham Univ, BA; Univ AK, MA; Emory Univ, PhD. **CAREER** Assoc prof, dir, Grad Liberal Stud, Golden Gate Univ. **HONORS AND AWARDS** NEH fel, Claremont Grad Sch & Stanford Univ. **MEMBERSHIPS** Acad of Consciousness Stud, Princeton Univ. **SELECTED PUBLICATIONS** Auth of articles on intercultural and philosophical interpretation, philosophical hermeneutics, interdisciplinary and transdisciplinary educ, intuition and cult develop, and other topics. **CONTACT ADDRESS** Golden Gate Univ, San Francisco, CA 94105-2968.

BURNER, DAVID B.
PERSONAL Born 05/10/1937, Cornwall, NY, m, 1958, 2 children **DISCIPLINE** HISTORY, LITERATURE **EDUCATION** AB Hamilton Col, 58; PhD Columbia Univ, 65. **CAREER** Colby Col, 62-63; Oakland Univ, 63-67; SUNY, Stony Brook, 67-. **HONORS AND AWARDS** Guggenheim Fellowship; NYS Excellence Awd; Natl Hum Found. **MEMBERSHIPS** ASA; OAH; AHA. **RESEARCH** 20th century Am Poli. **SELECTED PUBLICATIONS** Making Peace with the 60s, Princeton Univ Press, 96; John F Kennedy and a New Generation, Little Brown, 89; Herbert Hoover: A Public Life, Alfred A Rucpt, 68; The Polotics of Provincialism: The Democratic Party in Transition, 1918-1932. **CONTACT ADDRESS** Dept Hist, SUNY, Stony Brook, Stony Brook, NY 11794. **EMAIL** DBBurner@AOL.com

BURNETT, ANN K.
PERSONAL Born Colorado Springs, CO, m, 1998, 1 child **DISCIPLINE** COMMUNICATION **EDUCATION** Colo Col, BA, 80; Univ of Northern Colo, MA, 81; Univ of Utah, PhD, 86. **CAREER** Teaching asst, Univ of Ariz and Univ of Northern Colo, 80-82; teaching asst, Univ of Utah, 83-88; asst prof, Vanderbilt Univ, 86-88; assoc prof, Univ of Nebr, 88-97; assoc prof, North Dakota State Univ, 97-. **HONORS AND AWARDS** Recognition Awd, UNL Parents' Asn/Teaching Coun, 90, 92, 94; Jaycee's Outstanding Young Professor Awd, 92; Col of Arts and Scis Distinguished Teaching Awd, 92; Walter Ulrich Awd, 93; Al Johnson Awd, Forensic Educator, 93; Chancellor's Awd for Outstanding Service to Students, 94. **MEMBERSHIPS** Nat Commun Asn; Am Bar Asn; Am Forensic Asn; Delta Sigma Rho-Tau Kappa Alpha; Western Commun Asn; North Dakota Speech and Theatre Asn. **RESEARCH** Jury decision making and courtroom communication; group decision making process. **SELECTED PUBLICATIONS** Auth, The verdict is in: A study of jury decision making factors, moment of personal decision, and jury deliberations - from the jurors' point of view, in Commun Quart, 38, 90; From attitudinal inherency to permutation standards: A survey of judging philosophies from the 1988 National Debate Tournament, in Argumentation and Advocacy, 27, 91; Good people speaking well: Delta Sigma Rho-Tau Kappa Alpha, in Argumentation and Advocacy, 33, 96; Mock trials, Cause of action, and Civil action,in Magill's Legal Guide, 99; Jury decision-making processes in the O.J. Simpson criminal and civil trials, book chap in book on O.J. Simpson trials, 99; coauth, Analysis of forensics program administration: What will the 1990s bring?, in Nat Forensics J, 10, 92; Radio and world maintenance: A root metaphor analysis of the Grand Ole Opry, 1948-1958, in J of Radio Studies, 1, 92; The role of forensics when departments/programs are targeted for elimination: A proposal to insure a 'call for support', in Nat Forensics J, 10, 93; Competitors' perceptions of questions in individual events rounds, in Nat Forensic J, 11, 93; Nonverbal involvement and sex: Effects on jury decision making, in J of Applied Commun, 22, 94; Coaching intercollegiate debate and raising a family: An analysis of perspectives from women in the trenches, in Nat Forensic J, 11, 94; The reason for decision in individual events: Its implementation and impact, in The Forensic Educator, 10, 95/96; The dark side of debate: The downfall of interpersonal relationships, in Speaker and Gavel, 35, 98. **CONTACT ADDRESS** Dept of Communication Studies, No Dakota State Univ, 321 Minard Hall, Fargo, ND 58105. **EMAIL** Ann_Burnett@ndsu.nodak.edu

BURNETT, ANNE PIPPIN
PERSONAL Born 10/10/1925, Salt Lake City, UT, m, 1960, 2 children **DISCIPLINE** CLASSICS **EDUCATION** Swarthmore Col, BA, 46; Columbia Univ, MA, 47; Univ Calif, Berkeley, PhD(ancient hist & classics), 53. **CAREER** Instr classics, Vassar Col, 57-58; asst prof, 61-66, assoc prof, 67-69, Prof Classics & Chmn Dept, Univ Chicago, 70-, Am Asn Univ Women traveling fel, Am Sch Class Studies Athens, 56-57; fel, Am Acad Rome, 58-59; grant, Am Philos Soc, 59-60; Am Coun Learned Soc fel, 68-69. **RESEARCH** Greek tragedy; Greek lyric poetry; Greek history. **SELECTED PUBLICATIONS CONTACT ADDRESS** Dept of Classics Div of Humanities, Univ of Chicago, Chicago, IL 60637.

BURNHAM, MICHELLE
PERSONAL Born 12/11/1962, Brooklyn, NY, m, 1991, 1 child **DISCIPLINE** ENGLISH **EDUCATION** Trinity Col, BA, 84; SUNY, Buffalo, MA, 91, PhD, 94. **CAREER** Asst prof, Auburn Univ, 94-97; ASST PROF, SANTA CLARA UNIV, 97-. **MEMBERSHIPS** MLS, SEA, ASA. **RESEARCH** Colonial American Literture 19th Century, American Literature, Native American Literature, Cultural Studies. **SELECTED PUBLICATIONS** Auth, Captivity and Sentiment, UPNE, 97. **CONTACT ADDRESS** Dept of English, Santa Clara Univ, Santa Clara, CA 95053. **EMAIL** mburnham@scu.edu

BURNIM, MELLONEE VICTORIA
PERSONAL Born 09/27/1950, Teague, TX, m **DISCIPLINE** MUSICOLOGY **EDUCATION** Northern Texas State University, BM (cum laude), music education, 1971; University of Wisconsin Madison, MM, African music ethnomusicology, 1976; Indiana University, PhD, ethnomusicology, 1980. **CAREER** Delay Middle School, director of choral music, 71-73; University of Wisconsin, research asst, 73, academic advisor, 73; Indiana Univ Bloomington, Afro-American Choral Ensemble, director, 76-82, Opera Theater, choral dir, 76, 80, Dept of Afro-American Studies, prof, currently. **HONORS AND AWARDS** Full Music Scholarship, NTSU, 1969-71; Natl Defense Foreign Language Fellow in Arabic, University of Wisconsin, 1973-74; fellow, Natl Fellowships Fund, University of Wisconsin & Indiana Unviersity, 1973-78; Eli Lilly Postdoctoral Teaching Fellow, 1984; alternate, Natl Research Council Postdoctoral Fellowship, Washington DC, 1984. **MEMBERSHIPS** Musical director, WTUI Bloomington, "Contemporary Black Gospel Music," 1979; Alpha Lambda Delta, 1968; Sigma Alpha Iota, NTSU, 1969; chapter vice pres, Mortar Board, NTSU, 1970-71; Pi Kappa Lambda, 1971. **SELECTED PUBLICATIONS** Musical director, video tapes 2-30 minutes, "The Life & Works of Undine S Moore," Afro-American Arts Institute, Indiana University, 1979. **CONTACT ADDRESS** Folklore and Ethnomusicology, Indiana Univ, Bloomington, 504 N Fess, Bloomington, IN 47405.

BURRIS, SIDNEY
DISCIPLINE CONTEMPORARY POETRY **EDUCATION** Univ Va, PhD. **CAREER** English and Lit, Univ Ark. **HONORS AND AWARDS** Dir, Fulbright Col Honors Studies. **SELECTED PUBLICATIONS** Auth, The Riot of Gorgeousness: The Poetry and Prose of Marianne Moore, Rev, 88; The Return of Eliot and the Discovery of Auden, Sewanee Rev, 91; An Empire of Poetry, Southern Rev, 91; Auden's Generalizations, Shenandoah, 93; A Day at the Races, Utah, 89; The Poetry of Resistance: Seamus Heaney and the Pastoral Tradition, Ohio Univ Press, 90. **CONTACT ADDRESS** Univ of Arkansas, Fayetteville, Fayetteville, AR 72701.

BURROUGHS, CATHERINE
PERSONAL Born 01/12/1958, Ann Arbor, MI, m, 1996, 1 child **DISCIPLINE** DRAMA, THEATRE **EDUCATION** Wake Forest Univ, BA, 80; Conn Col, MA, 83; Emory Univ, PhD, 88. **CAREER** Lectr, Cornell Univ, 97-00; Vis Assoc Prof, Wells Col, 97-. **HONORS AND AWARDS** Excellence in Teaching Awd, Emory Univ, 87; Acad of Am Poets Prize, Wake Forest Univ, 80; Phi Beta Kappa, Wake Forest Univ, 80; Midwest Fac Fel, Univ Chicago, 90-91; Andrew W Mellon Found Fel, Huntington Libr, 92; NEH Grant, 95. **MEMBERSHIPS** MLA, NASSR, ASTR, F. Scott Fitzgerald Soc, NWSA **RESEARCH** Drama and performance history, Joanna Baillie, women in British romantic theatre, feminist theatre theory. **SELECTED PUBLICATIONS** Auth, Closet Stages: Joanna Baillie and the Theater Theory of British Romantic Women Writers, Univ Pa Pr, 97; auth, "Joanna Baillie's Poetic Aesthetic: Passion and 'The Plain Order of Things'," Approaches to Teaching Brit Women Poets of the Romantic Period, MLA Pr (97): 135-140; auth, "Teaching the Theory and Practice of Women's Dramaturgy, Special Issue: Women Playwrights around 1800," Romanticism on the Net 12 (98); auth, "Hymen's 'Monkey Love': Female Sexual Initiation and 'The Concealed Francies (c 1645)'," Theatre J 51 (99): 21-31; auth, "'Be Good': Acting, Reader's Theatre and Oration in the Writing of Frances Anne Kemble," Romanticism and Women Poets: Opening the Doors of Reception, UP Ky (99): 125-143; auth, Women in British Romantic Theatre: Drama, Performance and Society 1790-1840, Cambridge UP, forthcoming. **CONTACT ADDRESS** Dept Humanities, Wells Col, PO Box 500, Aurora, NY 13026-0500. **EMAIL** cb64@cornell.edu

BURROWAY, JANET GAY
PERSONAL Born 09/21/1936, Tucson, AZ, m, 1993, 3 children **DISCIPLINE** ENGLISH **EDUCATION** Univ Ariz, 54-55; Barnard Col, AB, 58; Cambridge Univ, BA, 60; MA, 65; Yale Sch Drama, 60-61. **CAREER** Instr, Harpur Col, 61-62; lectr, Univ of Sussex, 65-70; assoc prof to Robert O. Lawson distinguished prof, Fla State Univ, 72-; fiction reviewer, Philadelphia Enquirer, 86-90; reviewer, NYork Times Book Rev, 91-; essay columist, New Letters: A Magazine of Writing and Art, 94-. **HONORS AND AWARDS** NEA fel, 76; Yaddo Residency Fel, 85 & 87; Lila Wallace-Reader's Digest Fel, 93-94; Carolyn Benton Cockefair Distinguished Writer-in-Residence, Univ of Mo, 95; Woodrow Wilson Vis Fel, Furman Univ, 95, Erskine Col, 97 and Drury Col, 99. **MEMBERSHIPS** Author's Guild. **SELECTED PUBLICATIONS** Auth, Descend Again, 60; auth, The Dancer From the Dance, 65; auth, Eyes, 66; auth, The Buzzards, 69; auth, The Truck on the Track, 70; auth, the Giant Jam Sandwich, 72; auth, Raw Silk, 77; auth, Opening Nights, 85; auth, Cutting Stone, 92. **CONTACT ADDRESS** Dept English, Florida State Univ, PO Box 3061580, Tallahassee, FL 32306-1580.

BURSK, CHRISTOPHER
PERSONAL Born 04/23/1943, Cambridge, MA, m, 1966, 3 children **DISCIPLINE** ENGLISH **EDUCATION** Boston Univ, PhD, 75; Warren Wilson Col, MFA, 87. **CAREER** Prof, Bucks County Community Col, 71-. **HONORS AND AWARDS** Guggenheim Fel; NEA Fel; PEW Fel. **SELECTED PUBLICATIONS** Auth, Cell Count, Tex Tech Univ Press; Auth, The One True Religion, Quart Rev. **CONTACT ADDRESS** Language and Literature Dept, Bucks County Comm Col, Swamp Rd, Newtown, PA 18940.

BURSTEIN, L. POUNDIE
PERSONAL Born New York, NY **DISCIPLINE** MUSIC THEORY **EDUCATION** CUNY, PhD. **CAREER** Prof; taught at, Mannes Col, Hunter Col, Graduate Ctr CUNY. **HONORS AND AWARDS** Distinguished Teacher Awd, New School. **RESEARCH** Schenkerian theory. **SELECTED PUBLICATIONS** Publ on music of, Haydn, Beethoven & Schubert, in Musical Quart, Theory and Practice, J Music Theory, and Music Analysis. **CONTACT ADDRESS** Dept of Music, Hunter Col, CUNY, 695 Park Ave, New York, NY 10021. **EMAIL** huntermust@aol.com

BURT, JOHN D.
DISCIPLINE ENGLISH **EDUCATION** Yale Univ, BS, 77; MA, 78; PhD, 83. **CAREER** Lectr, Univ Nev Reno, 79-80; TA, Yale Univ, 80-83; prof, Brandeis Univ, 83-. **HONORS AND AWARDS** Guggenheim Fel, 97; ACLS Fel, 97; Ambassador Prize, Eng Speaking Union, 98. **MEMBERSHIPS** MLA, Am Lit Assoc. **RESEARCH** American Poetry, American Romanticism. **SELECTED PUBLICATIONS** Auth, The Way Down, Princeton Univ Pr, 88; auth, Works on Port Hope, Johns Hopkins Univ Pr, 96; ed, The Collected Poems of Robert Penn Warren, 98. **CONTACT ADDRESS** Dept English, Brandeis Univ, Waltham, MA 02454. **EMAIL** burr@brandeis.edu

BURT, SUSAN MEREDITH
PERSONAL Born 09/15/1951, Los Angeles, CA, m, 1976, 2 children **DISCIPLINE** ENGLISH **EDUCATION** Bryn Mawr Col, BA, 73; Univ Ill, Urbana, MA, 79, PhD, 86. **CAREER** Asst prof English, Ill State Univ. **MEMBERSHIPS** Ling Soc of Am; Int Pragmatics Asn; TESOL. **RESEARCH** Intercultural conversation; code choice; language shift. **SELECTED PUBLICATIONS** Auth, Code Choice in Intercultural Conversation: Speech Accommodation Theory and Pragmatics, Pragmatics, 94; auth, Where Does Sociopragmatic Ambiguity Come From? Pragmatics and Lang Learning, 95; auth, Monolingual Children in a Bilingual Situation: Protest, Accommodation and Linguistic Creativity, Multilingua, 98. **CONTACT ADDRESS** Dept of English, Illinois State Univ, Campus Box 4240, Normal, IL 61790-4240. **EMAIL** smburt@ilstate.edu

BURTON, JOAN
PERSONAL Born Columbia, MO, m **DISCIPLINE** CLASSICAL STUDIES **EDUCATION** BA, 75, MA, 78, CPhil, 83, PhD, 88, Univ Calif, Berkeley. **CAREER** Actg instr, tchg assoc, classics, Univ Calif, Berkeley, 79-86; actg instr, classics, Univ Calif, Santa Cruz, 88; asst prof, 88-94, assoc prof, 94-, classics, chemn and assoc prof, comp lit, 98-, Trinity Univ. **HONORS AND AWARDS** Phi Beta Kappa, 74; dept citation class lang, 75; chancellor's fel, classics, 77-78, 80-81; John Rogers Fac Fel, 90-92. **MEMBERSHIPS** APA; Byzantine Stud Conf; Women's Class Caucus. **RESEARCH** Greek and Roman literature and culture; women's studies. **SELECTED PUBLICATIONS** Auth, The Function of the Symposium Theme in Theocritus' Idyll, Greek Roman, and Byzantine Stud, 92; auth, Why the Ancient Greeks Were Obsessed with Heroes and the Ancient Egyptians Were Not, Class Bull, 93; auth, Theocritus' Urban Mimes: Mobility, Gender and Patronage, Univ Calif, 95; auth, Women's Commensality in the Ancient Greek World, Greece and Rome, 98; auth, Reviving the Pagan Greek Novel in a Christian World, Greek,, Roman, and Byzantine Stud, 98. **CONTACT ADDRESS** Dept of Classical Studies, Trinity Univ, 715 Stadium Dr, San Antonio, TX 78212-7200.

BURWELL, ROSE MARIE
PERSONAL Born 03/12/1934, 6 children **DISCIPLINE** MODERN FICTION, FILM **EDUCATION** Augustana Col, IL, BA, 59; Univ IA, MA, 66, PhD, 69. **CAREER** Asst prof, 70-81, assoc prof, 81-94, prof eng, Northern IL Univ, 94, Consult, Nat Endowment for Hum, 77; coordr, Ill Humanities Coun Proj, Sheridan State Correctional Ctr, 77-78 & Dwight State Correctional Ctr, 78; vis lectr, Univ Col, Oxford, 80 & 81. **HONORS AND AWARDS** Kennedy Lib Fel, 91, 92 & 94; Princeton Univ Friends of Lib Fel, 96 & 97; Andrew Mellon Fel, Univ Tex Austin, 93. **MEMBERSHIPS** MLA; AAUP. **RESEARCH** Eng novel. **SELECTED PUBLICATIONS** Auth, A chronological catalogue of D H Lawrence's reading, spec issue D H Lawrence Rev, fall 70; A chronological catalogue of D H Lawrence's reading: addenda, D H Lawrence Rev, spring 73; Joyce Carol Oates and an old master: A garden of earthly depths, Critique, summer 73; Schopenhauer, Hardy and Lawrence: Toward a new understanding of Sons and lovers, Western Humanities Rev, summer 74; The process of individuation as narrative structure: Joyce Carol Oates' Do With Me What You Will, Critique, fall 75; With Shuddering Fall: Joyce Carol Oates first novel, Can Lit, summer 77; Wonderland: Paradigm of the psycho-historical mode in comtemporary American literature, Mosaic, fall 81; D H Lawrence's Reading, In: A D H Lawrence Handbook, Univ Manchester Press, 82; Hemingway's Garden of Eden: Protecting the Masculine Text, TSLL, summer 93; New Pieces in the Posthumous Hemingway Puzzle, Princeton Univ Lib Chronicle, autumn 94; Hemingway: The Postwar Years, The Posthumous Novels, Cambridge Univ Press, 96. **CONTACT ADDRESS** Dept of Eng, No Illinois Univ, 1425 W Lincoln Hwy, De Kalb, IL 60115-2825. **EMAIL** rmb39@interaccess.com

BURWICK, FREDERICK
PERSONAL Born 03/17/1936, Pomona, CA, m, 1969, 3 children **DISCIPLINE** ENGLISH **EDUCATION** Univ La Verne, BA, 59; Univ Wisc Madison, PhD, 65. **CAREER** Asst prof to prof, UCLA, 65-. **HONORS AND AWARDS** Fel, UC Humanities Res Inst, 91; Distinguished Scholar, Brit Acad, 92; Literary Distinction Awd, Frankfurt Germany, 92; Outstanding Book of the Year, Am Conf on Romanticism, 97; Distinguished Scholar, Keat-Shelley Asn, 98; Fac in Residence Awd, UCLA, 99-00. **MEMBERSHIPS** Am Soc for Eighteenth-Century Studies; Asn for Scottish Literary Studies; Friends of Dove Cottage; German Studies Asn; Goethe Soc of N Am; Interdisciplinary Nineteenth-Century Studies; Intl Vereinigung fur Germanistische Sprach und Literaturwissenschaft; Keats-Shelley Asn of Am; MLA; N Am Soc for the Study of Romanticism; Pac Ancient and Mod Lang Asn; Soc for Lit and Sci. **RESEARCH** Cognitive Science and Literature; Anglo-German Literary Relations; Romantic Drama. **SELECTED PUBLICATIONS** Auth, Illusion and the Drama: Critical Theory of the Enlightenment and Romantic Era, Penn State Univ Press, 91; co-ed, The Crisis in Modernism: Bergson and the Vitalist Controversy, Cambridge Univ Press, 92; co-ed, Reflecting Senses: Perception and Appearance in Literature, Cultural, and the Arts, De Gruyter, 95; auth, Poetic Madness and the Romantic Imagination, Penn State Univ Press, 96; co-ed, The Boydell Shakespeare Gallery, Peter Pomp, 96; co-ed, The Romantic Imagination in the Literature and Art of Germany and England, Rodopi8, 96; ed, The Works of Thomas De Quincey, Vol 3 and Vol 4, Pickering and Chatto, 00; auth, Thomas De Quincey: Knowledge and Power, Palgrave, 01; auth, Mimesis and its Romantic Reflections, Penn State Univ Press, 01. **CONTACT ADDRESS** Dept English, Univ of California, Los Angeles, 2225 Rolfe, Box 951530, Los Angeles, CA 90095-1530. **EMAIL** fburwick@humnet.ucla.edu

BUSBY, RUDOLPH E.
PERSONAL Born 11/01/1946, Beaumont, TX **DISCIPLINE** RHETORIC & COMMUNICATION THEORY, SPEECH COMMUNICATION **EDUCATION** Univ Houston, BA, 75, MA, 80, PhD, 83. **CAREER** Teaching asst, Univ Houston, 78-80; graduate teaching asst, Univ TX, 80; prof, San Francisco State Univ, 83-, campus coordinator, CA Pre-doctoral prof, 89-. **MEMBERSHIPS** Nat Commun Asn; Int Commun Asn. **RESEARCH** Rhetoric in cultural contexts. **SELECTED PUBLICATIONS** Auth, with R Majors, Basic Speech Communication: Principles and Practices, 89. **CONTACT ADDRESS** Dept of Commun Studies, San Francisco State Univ, 1600 Holloway Ave, San Francisco, CA 94132-1722. **EMAIL** rbusby@sfsu.edu

BUSCH, FREDERICK MATTHEW
PERSONAL Born 08/01/1941, Brooklyn, NY, m, 1963, 2 children **DISCIPLINE** AMERICAN & MODERN LITERATURE **EDUCATION** Muhlenberg Col, AB, 62; Columbia Univ, MA, 67. **CAREER** Writer, NAm Precis Syndicate, Inc, 64-65; assoc ed, Sch Mgt Mag, 65-66; prof English, Colgate Univ, 66-, NEA, 70; Fairchild Prof of Lit, 86, dir, Prog Creative Writing, Univ Iowa, 78-79; panelist. **HONORS AND AWARDS** Guggenheim, 81; Ingram Merrill, 82; Awd in Fiction, American Academy, 86; National Jewish Book Awd-- Fiction, 86; Pen/Malamud Awd for Distinction in Short Fiction, 91. **MEMBERSHIPS** AAUP, Writers Guild, Authors Guild, Pen. **RESEARCH** Fiction writing; modern American fiction; 19th century British fiction. **SELECTED PUBLICATIONS** Auth, I Wanted a Year Without Fall, 71 & Breathing Trouble, 73, Calder & Boyars, London; Hawkes: A Guide to His Fictions, Syracuse Univ, 73; Manual Labor, 74 & Domestic Particulars, 76, New Directions; The Mutual Friend, Harper & Row, 78; Rounds, FSG, 79; Hardwater Country, Knopf, 79; Take This Man, FSG, 81; Invisible Mending, Godine, 84; Too Late American Boyhood Blues, 84; Sometimes I Live in the Country, Godine, 86; Absent Friends, Knopf, 89; War Babies, New Directions, 89; Closong Arguments, Ticknor and Fields, 91; Long Way from Home, Ticknor and Fields, 93; The Children in the Woods, Ticknor, 94; Girls, Harmony, 97; A Dangerous Profession, St. Martins, 98; auth, The Night Inspector, Harmony, 99; auth, Don't Tell Anyone, Norton, 00. **CONTACT ADDRESS** Dept of English, Colgate Univ, 13 Oak Dr, Hamilton, NY 13346-1379. **EMAIL** fbusch@mail.colgate.edu

BUSH, HAROLD K.
PERSONAL Born 12/30/1956, Indianapolis, IN, m, 1989, 1 child **DISCIPLINE** AMERICAN LITERATURE **EDUCATION** Ind Univ, BA, 82; MS, 86; MA, 92; PhD, 95. **CAREER** Lectr, Mich State Univ, 95-98; asst prof, St Louis Univ, 98-. **HONORS AND AWARDS** Mellon Grants, 99, 2000; SLU 2000; Res Leave, 2001. **MEMBERSHIPS** ASA, Mark Twain Circle, Christianity and Lit. **RESEARCH** Mark Twain, American studies, American literature, Christianity and literature. **SELECTED PUBLICATIONS** Auth, "The Mythic Struggle Between East and West: Mark Twain's Speech at Whittier's 70th

Birthday Celebration and W. D. Howells's A Chance Acquaintance," Am Literary Realism, 27.2 (winter 95): 53-73; auth, "Structural America: The Persistence of Oppositional Paradigms in American Literary Theory," Col Lit 23.2 (June 96): 181-88; auth, "Acting Like Mark Twain: Performance in Nineteenth-Century American Culture," Am Quart (June 97): 404-13; auth, "Richard Henry Dana, Jr," Dictionary of Literary Biography: Travel Writers, 1800-1865, Detroit: Gale Res (98): 79-89; auth, " 'Our Great Confused West': redefining Mark Twain," Col English (Feb 98): 192-201; auth, " 'Absorbing' the Character: James Whitcomb Riley and Mark Twain's Theory of Performance," Am Lit Realism, 31.3 (spring 99): 31-47; auth, " 'Invisible Domains' and the Theological Turn in Recent American Literary Studies," Christianity & Lit, 49.1 (Autumn 99): 91-109; auth, American Declarations: Rebellion and Repentance in American Cultural History, Univ Ill Press (99); auth, "Remembering the Bomb: Hiroshima and the Culture Wars, 1946-1995," Mars Hill Rev, 49.1 (winter 2000); auth, "Robert Frost and Politics," The Robert Frost Encyclopedia, ed by John Zubizarreta and Nancy Tuten, Greenwood Press (forthcoming 2000); auth, "Mark Twain and American Religion," The Oxford Historical Guide to Mark Twain, ed Shelley Fisher Fishkin, Oxford Univ Press (forthcoming 2000). **CONTACT ADDRESS** Dept of English, Saint Louis Univ, Saint Louis, MO 63103. **EMAIL** bushhk@slu.edu

BUSH, SARGENT, JR.
PERSONAL Born 09/22/1937, Flemington, NJ, m, 1960, 2 children **DISCIPLINE** ENGLISH, AMERICAN LITERATURE **EDUCATION** Princeton Univ, AB, 59; Univ Iowa, MA, 64; PhD, 67. **CAREER** Wash & Lee Univ, Asst Prof, 67-71; Asst Prof, 71-73, Assoc Prof, 73-79, Prof, 79-, Ch, Dept Eng, 80-83, John Bascom Prof of Eng, 97-, Univ Wisc, Madison; Coll of Letters & Sci, Assoc Dean for Hum, 89-94. **HONORS AND AWARDS** Res fellow coop prog in the Hum, 69-70; ACLS, 74; Inst for res in the Hum, 78-79; Mass Hist Soc Fellow, 89-90; NEH Summer Stipends, 69, 86; Am Philos Soc Grants-in-Aid, 79, 97. **MEMBERSHIPS** Modern Lang Asn; Am Lit Asn; Asn for Documentary Editing; Cambridge Bibliographic Soc; Soc of Early Americanists; Am Stud Asn; Nathaniel Hawthorne Soc; Melville Soc; Thoreau Soc; SHARP. **RESEARCH** American literature, focus on 17th century Puritans. **SELECTED PUBLICATIONS** Coauth, Writings in England and Holland, 1626-1633, ed Thomas hooker, Harvard Theological Studies 28 (75); auth, The Writings of Thomas Hooker: Spiritual Adventure in Two Worlds, Univ of Wisc Press, 80; coauth, The Library of Emmanuel College, Cambridge, 1584-1637, with Carl J. Rasmussen, ed Sarah Kemble Knight, Cambridge Univ Press, 86; auth, Journal in Journeys in New Worlds: Early American Women's Narratives, ed William L. Andrews, Univ of Wisc Press, (90): 69-116; auth, Epistolary Counseling in the Puritan Movement: The Examples of John Cotton, Puritanism: Transatlantic Perspectives on a Seventeenth Century Anglo-American Faith, Mass Hist Soc, 127-147, 93; auth, After Coming Over: John Cotton, Peter Bulkeley, and Learned Discourse in the Wilderness, Stud in the Lit Imagination, 27, 7-21, 94; auth, The Correspondence of John Cotton, Univ NC Press, 99. **CONTACT ADDRESS** Dept English, Univ of Wisconsin, Madison, 600 N Park St, Madison, WI 53706. **EMAIL** sbush@facstaff.wisc.edu

BUSHNELL, JACK
DISCIPLINE ENGLISH LITERATURE **EDUCATION** Univ Colo, BA; Rutgers Univ, MA; PhD. **CAREER** Fac. **RESEARCH** British romanticism; 19th century British literature and culture. **SELECTED PUBLICATIONS** Auth, Circus of the Wolves, William Morrow; Sky Dancer, William Morrow; articles on Romantic and Victorian literature. **CONTACT ADDRESS** Dept of English, Univ of Wisconsin, Eau Claire, Hibbard Hall 431, PO Box 4004, Eau Claire, WI 54702-4004. **EMAIL** bushnejp@uwec.edu

BUSZA, ANDREW/ANDRZEJ
PERSONAL Born 11/17/1938, Krakow, Poland, m, 1962, 1 child **DISCIPLINE** ENGLISH **EDUCATION** Univ Col London, BA, 56; MA, 63. **CAREER** Teacher, Henry Thornton Grammar Sch London, 64-65; Instr to Assoc Prof, Univ BC, 65-; Vis Prof, Univ Nice, 77-78. **HONORS AND AWARDS** Fel, Univ London, 60-62; Fel, Can Coun, 69-71; Fel, SSHRC, 82-83; Res Grant, UBC, 80-89, 93, 95-97, 99; Koscielski Found Prize, 62. **MEMBERSHIPS** Intl Asn of Univ Prof of English; Joseph Conrad Soc; Joseph Conrad Soc of N AM; Polish Inst of Arts and Sci in Can. **RESEARCH** Life and Work of Joseph Conrad; European Modernism; Nineteenth-Century European Literature. **SELECTED PUBLICATIONS** Co-ed, Joseph Conrad, The Rover, OUP Worlds, Classics, 92; auth, "'Usque Ad Finem': Under Western Eyes, Lord Jim, and Conrad's Red Uncle", in Centennial Essays, Rodopi, Amsterdam, 00; auth, "Conrad's Rhetoric of Affirmation and the Moderns," Stanford Humanities Rev, 00. **CONTACT ADDRESS** Dept English, Univ of British Columbia, #397-1873 E Mall, Vancouver, BC, Canada V6T 1Z1. **EMAIL** abusza@interchange.ubc.ca

BUTLER, GERALD JOSEPH
PERSONAL Born 02/24/1942, San Francisco, CA, m, 1964, 3 children **DISCIPLINE** ENGLISH AND COMPARATIVE LITERATURE **EDUCATION** Univ Calif, Berkeley, AB, 63; Univ Wash, MA, 65, PhD(English), 68. **CAREER** Prof English, San Diego State Univ, 68-, Ed, Recovering Lit, 72-. **RESEARCH** Sex in literature; 18th century fiction; 20th century fiction. **SELECTED PUBLICATIONS** Auth, Arrows of desire, fall & winter, 74, Recovering Lit; Fielding's Unruly Novels; Making Fielding Novels Speak for Law-and-Order + Reply to Richter,David,Henry/, Eighteenth Century-Theory and Interpretation, Vol 37, 1996. **CONTACT ADDRESS** PO Box 805, Alpine, CA 92001. **EMAIL** butler1@mail.sdsu.edu

BUTLER, JAMES ALBERT
PERSONAL Born 05/18/1945, Pittsburgh, PA, d, 1967, 3 children **DISCIPLINE** ENGLISH & AMERICAN LITERATURE **EDUCATION** LaSalle Univ, BA, 67; Cornell Univ, MA, 70, PhD, 71. **CAREER** From asst prof to assoc prof, 71-78, prof English, LaSalle Univ, 78, from asst chmn to chmn dept English, 78-96,00- ; assoc ed, Four Quarters, 72-77 & 77-78; asst ed, The Cornell Wordsworth Series, 79-; assoc trustee, Wordsworth's Dove Cottage, 80-. **HONORS AND AWARDS** Amer Coun Learned Soc fel, 76-77; Lindback Awd, Distinguished Teaching, 80; NEH Fel, 83-84. **MEMBERSHIPS** MLA; AAUP. **RESEARCH** Wordsworth; English Romantic period; contemporary poetry. **SELECTED PUBLICATIONS** Ed, The Ruined Cottage and The Pedlar, by William Wordsworth, in The Cornell Wordsworth Series, Cornell Univ, 78; Lyrical Ballads, by William Wordsworth, in The Cornell Wordsworth Series, Cornell Univ, 92; auth, The Duty to Withhold the Facts: Family and Scholars on Wordsworth's French Daughter, in Princeton Univ Libr Chronicle, Winter 96; Tourist or Native Son: Wordsworth's Homecomings of 1799-1800, in Nineteenth Century Lit, 6/96; writer and producer, Charles Willson Peale at Belfield, film, 96; auth, Stepping Stones to the Future, in Charles Lamb Bull, 1/97; William and Dorothy Wordsworth, "Emma", and a German Translation in the Alfoxden Notebook, in Studies in Romanticism, Summer 97; Travel Writing, in A Companion to Romanticism, Blackwell's, 97; The Cornell Wordsworth Series, Wordsworth Circle, Summer 97. **CONTACT ADDRESS** Dept of English, La Salle Univ, 1900 W Olney Ave, Philadelphia, PA 19141-1199. **EMAIL** butler@lasalle.edu

BUTLER, KATHARINE G.
DISCIPLINE COMMUNICATION SCIENCES AND DISORDERS **EDUCATION** MI State Univ, PhD, 67. **CAREER** Res prof CCC-SLP. **HONORS AND AWARDS** Pres, Am Speech-Lang-Hearing Assoc, 96-. **RESEARCH** Lang acquisition and disorders; children's discourse acquisition, narrative mode of thought, and lang processing in the early years (0 to 5) among school aged children from culturally diverse populations. **SELECTED PUBLICATIONS** Ed, Language and Stuttering in Children: Perspectives on an Interrelationship, Topics Lang Disorders, 95; The New Narrative Landscape: Interface between Ability and Disability, Topics Lang Disorders, 95; Assessment Across Disorders: Perspectives, Practices, and Procedures, Aspen, 94. **CONTACT ADDRESS** Syracuse Univ, Syracuse, NY 13244.

BUTLER-EVANS, ELIOT
DISCIPLINE AFRICAN-AMERICAN LITERATURE **EDUCATION** Univ Calif, Santa Cruz, PhD, 87. **CAREER** Assoc Prof, Eng, Univ Calif, Santa Barbara. **RESEARCH** Marxist cult theory, narr theory and soc semiotics, gender and sexuality. **SELECTED PUBLICATIONS** Auth, Race, Gender, and Desire: Narrative Strategies in the Fiction of Toni Cade Bambara, Toni Morrison, and Alice Walker, Temple Univ Press, 89. **CONTACT ADDRESS** Dept of Eng, Univ of California, Santa Barbara, Santa Barbara, CA 93106-7150. **EMAIL** ebevans@humanitas.ucsb.edu

BUTSCHER, EDWARD
PERSONAL Born 09/30/1938, Flushing, NY, m, 1976 **DISCIPLINE** MODERN BRITISH & AMERICAN LITERATURE **EDUCATION** Queens Col, BA, 63; Long Island Univ, MA, 70. **CAREER** Teacher English, John Bowne, 71-, Ed, Univ Rev, 67-73; ed mem, NY Poets Cooperative, 73-81; contrib ed, Home Planet News, 76-; bd mem, Cross-Cult Commun, 76-; mem fac English, New Sch Social Res, 76-78; instr poetry, C W Posts Poetry Ctr, 78-80. **HONORS AND AWARDS** PSA's Melville Cane Award, 88. **MEMBERSHIPS** MLA; Authors' Guild; Cross-Cult Commun; Poets & Writers; Poetry Soc Am. **RESEARCH** Twentieth century British and American poetry; American literature (literary biography); contemporary British and American novel. **SELECTED PUBLICATIONS** Contribr, New American Poetry, McGraw-Hill, 73; co-ed, Group 74; NY Poets Coop, 75; auth, Sylvia Plath: Method and Madness & Poems About Silence, Seabury Press, 76; ed, Sylvia Plath: The Woman and the Work, Dodd, Mead, 77; auth, Adelaide Crapsey, Twayne, 79; Amagansett Cycle (poems), Cross-Cult, 80; contrbr, The Pure Clear Word: Poetry of James Wright, Univ Ill Press, 82; auth, Conrad Aiken: Poet of White Horse Vale, Univ of Georgia Press, 88; auth, Child in the House: Poems, Canio's Editions, 94. **CONTACT ADDRESS** 84-01 Main St, Jamaica, NY 11435.

BUTTE, GEORGE
PERSONAL Born 05/29/1947, Tulsa, OK, m, 1993, 2 children **DISCIPLINE** ENGLISH LITERATURE **EDUCATION** Univ Ariz, BA, 67; Oxford Univ, BPhil, 70; Johns Hopkins Univ, PhD(English lit), 73. **CAREER** From instr to prof English, Bishop Col, 70-74; prof English, Colo Col, 74-. **HONORS AND AWARDS** Woodrow Wilson Fel, 67; Rhodes Scholarship, 68. **MEMBERSHIPS** MLA. **RESEARCH** Nineteenth century British literature; film studies. **SELECTED PUBLICATIONS** Auth, numerous articles in SEL, Victorian Studies, Comparative Lit, The Hitchcock Annual, and the Oxford Trollope Companion; auth, Jane Austen's Business, ed. McMaster and Stoval, (London), 96. **CONTACT ADDRESS** Dept of English, Colorado Col, 14 E Cache La Poudre, Colorado Springs, CO 80903-3294.

BUTTERFIELD, BRADLEY J.
PERSONAL Born 11/12/1963, Philadelphia, PA, m, 2000 **DISCIPLINE** ENGLISH **EDUCATION** Univ Oregon, PhD, 98; Univ Oregon, MA, 92; Claremont Graduate School, MA, 89; Univ Redlands, BA, 86. **HONORS AND AWARDS** University of Oregon Graduate Teaching Fellow Awd for Outstanding Teaching, Spring 96; Owen Aldridge Awd for best graduate student essay in Comparative Literature, Spring 94; **MEMBERSHIPS** PMLA. **RESEARCH** Modern Western Literature and Philosophy; 20th Century American Lit. **SELECTED PUBLICATIONS** Auth, "Baudrillard's Primitivism and White Noise: 'The only avant-grade we've got' UnderCurrent: An Online Journal for the Analysis of the Present, No. 7," Feb 99; auth, "Ethical Value and Negative Aesthetics: Reconsidering the Baudrillard-Ballard Connection," PMLA, Jan 99: 64-77; auth, "Englightenment's Other in Patrick Suskind's Perfume: Adorno and the Ineffable Utopia of Modern Art," Comparative Literature Studies 32, 95: 401-418. **CONTACT ADDRESS** Dept English, Univ of Wisconsin, La Crosse, 426e North Hall, La Crosse, WI 54601-3742. **EMAIL** bbutter@mail.uwlax.edu

BUTTERFIELD, BRUCE A.
DISCIPLINE ENGLISH **EDUCATION** Knox Col, BA; Univ IL, MA; PhD, 74. **CAREER** Fac, Plattsburgh State Univ of NY. **HONORS AND AWARDS** Chancellor's Awd Excellence Tchg, 90. **RESEARCH** 20th century Brit, Am and Canadian fiction. **SELECTED PUBLICATIONS** Auth, publs about Canadian fiction; ed, Plattsburgh Studies in Humanities series. **CONTACT ADDRESS** SUNY, Col at Plattsburgh, 101 Broad St, Plattsburgh, NY 12901-2681.

BUTTERS, RONALD R.
PERSONAL Born 02/12/1940, Cedar Rapids, IA, d, 3 children **DISCIPLINE** ENGLISH **EDUCATION** Univ Iowa, BA, 62; Univ Iowa, PhD, 67. **CAREER** Asst prof, Duke Univ, 67-74; assoc prof, Duke Univ, 74-89; prof, Duke Univ, 89-. **MEMBERSHIPS** Amer Dialect Soc; Dictionary Soc of NC; Int Asn Forensic Linguists; Law and Soc Asn; Ling Soc of Amer. **RESEARCH** Structure of mod English and present-day usage; sociolinguistics; lexicography; lang and law. **SELECTED PUBLICATIONS** Auth, Dialectology and Sociolinguistic Theory, 96; What Did Cary Grant Know About Going Gay' and When Did He Know it?: On the Development of the Popular Term gay Homosexual', 98; What Is About to Take Place Is a Murder: Construing the Racist Subtext in a Small-Town Virginia Courtroom; Grammar; Auntie(-man)/tanti in the Caribbean and North America, 97; The Divergence Controversy Revisited, 96; Historical and Contemporary Distribution of Double Modals in English, 96; Two Notes: the Origin of jaywalking, 95; Free Speech and Academic Freedom, 95; If the Wages of Sin Are for Death: The Semantics and Pragmatics of a Statutory Ambiguity, 93. **CONTACT ADDRESS** PO Box 90018, Durham, NC 27708. **EMAIL** RonButters@aol.com

BUTTIGIEG, JOSEPH A.
DISCIPLINE MODERN BRITISH LITERATURE, LITERARY THEORY **EDUCATION** SUNY, Binghamton, PhD. **CAREER** William R. Kenan Jr. prof, Univ Notre Dame. **RESEARCH** The relationship between culture and politics; Antonio Gramsci. **SELECTED PUBLICATIONS** Auth, A Portrait of the Artist in Different Perspective; Antonio Gramsci's Triad: Culture, Politics, Intellectuals; ed, Criticism Without Boundaries. **CONTACT ADDRESS** Dept of English, Univ of Notre Dame, 356 O'Shaughnessy Hall, Notre Dame, IN 46556. **EMAIL** joseph.a.buttigieg.1@nd.edu

BUZZARD, KAREN S.
DISCIPLINE COMMUNICATION (INTERPERSONAL, GENDER, & MEDIA) **EDUCATION** Drury Col, BA, 71; Univ of Iowa, MA, 73; Univ of Wis, PhD, 85. **CAREER** Assoc prof, Northeastern Univ, 85-. **HONORS AND AWARDS** Stephen H. Coltrin Awd for Commun Excellence. **MEMBERSHIPS** Nat Commun Asn. **RESEARCH** Communication & gender; intimacy & communication; aging & communicating; communication & media rating. **SELECTED PUBLICATIONS** Auth, Chains of Gold: Marketing the Ratings & Rating the Markets, 90; auth, Electronic Media Ratings: Turning Audiences into Dollars & Sense, 92; auth, Holding Pattern: When Intimacy Alludes Us in Adulthood; Foundations of Intimate Communication (book proposal). **CONTACT ADDRESS** 81 Golden Ave., Medford, MA 02155. **EMAIL** kbuzzard@lynx.dac.neu.edu

BYARS, JACKIE L.
PERSONAL Born 01/05/1951, Harlingen, TX, m, 1983 **DISCIPLINE** FILM & TELEVISION STUDIES, AMERICAN CULTURE, WOMEN'S STUDIES **EDUCATION** Univ Tx at Austin, BA, 74, MA, 76, PhD, 83; Univ Calif School of Criticism & Theory, summer, 77; Inter-Univ Center for Film & Critical Studies, 80-81. **CAREER** Vis asst prof, 83-84, asst prof, Dept of Commun Arts, Univ Wis-Madison, 85-90; Andrew W. Mellon postdoctoral fel & lectr, Dept of the Hist of Art, Bryn Mawr Col, 84-85; asst prof, Dept of Radio-Television-Film, Tx Christian Univ, 90-91; vis asst prof, Dept of Commun, St. Mary's Col of Calif, 91-92; dir, women's studies prog, 94-97, Co-Dir, Film Studies Prog, 95-, Assoc Prof, Dept of Commun, Wayne State Univ, 92-. **MEMBERSHIPS** Soc for Cinema Studies; Union for Democratic Commun; Nat Commun Asn; Int Asn for Mass Commun Res. **RESEARCH** The representation of difference in mediated texts; the relation between corporate practices and screen representations; landcapes and communication. **SELECTED PUBLICATIONS** Auth, All That Hollywood Allows: Re-reading Gender in 1950s Melodrama, Univ of NC Press & Routledge, 91; The Prime of Ms. Kim Novak: Struggling Over the Feminine in the Star Image, The Other 50s: Interrogating Midcentury Am Icons, Univ of Ill Press, 97; Feminism, Psychoanalysis, and Female-Oriented Melodramas of the 1950s, Multiple Voices in Feminist Film Theory and Criticism, Univ of Minn Press, 93; Gazes/Voices/Power: Expanding Psychoanalysis for Feminist Film and Television Theory, Female Spectators: Looking at Film and Television, Verso, 88; Reading Feminine Discourse: Prime-Time Television in the U.S., Commun, 87; coauth, Telefeminism: The Lifetime Cable Channel, Critical Studies in Mass Commun, forthcoming; Once in a Lifetime: Narrowcasting to Women, Camera Obscura, May-Sept-Jan, 94-95; Reading Difference: The Characters at Frank's Place, Women Making Meaning: The New Feminist Scholar in Commun, Routledge, 92. **CONTACT ADDRESS** Dept of Commun, Wayne State Univ, 585 Manoogian Hall, Detroit, MI 48202. **EMAIL** jbyars@aol.com

BYERS, LORI
DISCIPLINE ORGANIZATIONAL COMMUNICATION **EDUCATION** PhD. **CAREER** Spalding Univ **SELECTED PUBLICATIONS** Auth chapter: Pearson and Nelson's text Understanding and Sharing: An Introduction to Speech Communication. **CONTACT ADDRESS** Spalding Univ, 851 S. Fourth St., Louisville, KY 40203-2188.

BYRD, R.
DISCIPLINE ENGLISH **EDUCATION** Shippensburg Univ, MA, 84; Univ Md, PhD, 96. **CAREER** Southern Adventist Univ, 98-. **MEMBERSHIPS** Sixteenth-century Scholars, MLA, NCTE. **RESEARCH** John Foxe, John Barbour, Religious Polemics, Sixteenth-century, Literary Theory, Hawthorne, Edmund Spenser, Richard Hooker, Christopher St German, Thomas Moore, Biography and Autobiography. **CONTACT ADDRESS** Dept English, Southern Adventist Univ, PO Box 370, Collegedale, TN 37315-0370.

BYRE, CALVIN S.
PERSONAL Born 11/22/1947, Appleton, MN, m, 1972 **DISCIPLINE** CLASSICAL LANGUAGES AND LITERATURES **EDUCATION** Univ Minn, BA, 69; Univ Chicago, PhD, 76; Rosary Col, MALS, 85. **CAREER** Asst prof/head of ref, Roosevelt Univ, 86-90; asst prof of bibliog and adjunct asst prof of classics, Univ Okla, 90-96; assoc prof of bibliog and adjunct assoc prof of classics, Univ Okla, 96-. **HONORS AND AWARDS** Phi Beta Kappa; Robert V. Cram Memorial Scholar in Classics, Univ Minn; Ford four-year fel, Univ Chicago. **MEMBERSHIPS** Amer Philol Asn; Classical Asn of the Middle West and South. **RESEARCH** Greek epic; Literary criticism. **SELECTED PUBLICATIONS** Auth, Suspense in the Phaeacian Episode of Apollonius' Argonautica, Ill Class Studes, 22, 65-73, 97; auth, On the Departure from Pagasae and the Passage of the Plactae in Apollonius, Argonautica, Mus Helveticum, 54, 106-114, 97; auth, The Killing of Apsyrtus in Apollonious Rhodius' Argonautica, Phoenix, 50, 3-16, 96; auth, Distant Encounters: The Prometheus and Phaethon Episodes in Apollonius' Argonautica, Amer Jour of Philol, 117, 275-283, 96; auth, The Rhetoric of Description in Odyssey 9.116-41, Odysseus and Goat Island, Class Jour, 89, 357-367, 94; auth, On the Description of the Harbor of Phorkys and the Cave of the Nymphs, Odyssey 13.96-112, Amer Jour of Philol, 115, 1-13, 94; auth, Narration, Description, and Theme in the Shield of Achilles, Class Jour, 88, 33-42, 92; auth, The Narrator's Addresses to the Narratee in Apollonius Rhodius' Argonautica, Transactions of the Amer Philol Asn, 121, 215-227, 91; auth, Penelope and the Suitors before Odysseus: Odyssey 18.158-303, Amer Jour of Philol, 109, 159-173, 88; auth, Per aspera (et arborem) ad astra. Ramifications of the Allegory of Arete in Quintus Smyrnaeus Posthomerica, 5, 49-68, Hermes, 110, 184-195, 82. **CONTACT ADDRESS** 1727 Bryant Cir., Norman, OK 73026. **EMAIL** cbyre@ou.edu

BZDYL, DONALD G.
DISCIPLINE ENGLISH LITERATURE **EDUCATION** Univ Ill, PhD, 77. **CAREER** Dept Eng, Clemson Univ **RESEARCH** Medieval studies, historical linguistics, and business communication. **SELECTED PUBLICATIONS** Auth, Juliana: Cynewulf's Dispellar of Delusio, Cyenwulf: Basic Readings, Garland, 96. **CONTACT ADDRESS** Dept English, Clemson Univ, 1 Clemson Univ, Clemson, SC 29634-0001. **EMAIL** bzdy609@clemson.edu

C

CABEZUT-ORTIZ, DELORES
PERSONAL Born 12/16/1948, Merced, CA, m, 1978, 2 children **DISCIPLINE** ENGLISH **EDUCATION** Merced Commun Col, AA, 67; Calif State Univ, Stanislaus, BA, 70; MA, 75. **CAREER** Instr, Merced Commun Col, English, 74-, chemn, Humanities Div, 97-. **HONORS AND AWARDS** Pres, Weaver Bd of Ed; Pres, Merced County Arts Coun. **MEMBERSHIPS** NEA, CTA, Merced County Arts Coun, Merced County Hist Soc, Calif Women for Agriculture, Calif Cattlemen's Asn. **RESEARCH** Local history. **SELECTED PUBLICATIONS** Auth, Merced County: A Golden Harvest; auth, Robert LeRoy Cooper: Early Cattle Trader; auth, Merced Falls: Early Industrial City. **CONTACT ADDRESS** Dept Humanities, Merced Col, 3600 M St, Merced, CA 95348-2806. **EMAIL** dcortiz@merced.cc.ca.us

CABLE, THOMAS MONROE
PERSONAL Born 06/17/1942, Conroe, TX, m, 1 child **DISCIPLINE** ENGLISH LANGUAGE & LINGUISTICS **EDUCATION** Yale Univ, BA, 64; Univ TX, PhD, 69. **CAREER** Asst prof Eng, Univ IL, Urbana-Champaign, 69-72; assoc prof Eng, 72-79, prof eng, Univ TX, Austin, 79, Blumberg Centennial Prof Eng, 84; Am Coun Learned Socs fel, 76-77; Fulbright, France, 80, 92. **HONORS AND AWARDS** TX Excellence Tchg Awd, Col of Lib Arts, 90. **MEMBERSHIPS** MLA; Medieval Acad Am; Ling Soc Am. **RESEARCH** Hist of Eng prosody; hist of the Eng lang; Old and Middle Eng lit. **SELECTED PUBLICATIONS** Auth, The Meter and Melody of Beowulf, Univ Ill, 74; coauth, A History of the English Language, Prentice-Hall, 3rd ed, 78, 4th ed, 93; The English Alliterative Tradition, Univ Penn, 91; A Companion to Baugh and Cable's History of the English Language, 2nd ed, Prentice-Hall, 93. **CONTACT ADDRESS** Dept of Eng, Univ of Texas, Austin, Austin, TX 78712-1164. **EMAIL** tcable@mail.utexas.edu

CACICEDO, ALBERTO JESUS
PERSONAL Born 01/05/1952, Cienfuegos, Cuba, m, 1980, 1 child **DISCIPLINE** ENGLISH LITERATURE AND COMPOSITION **EDUCATION** Pa State, BA, 74; Harvard, AM, 75; PhD, 82. **CAREER** Instr, Masbay Community Col, 82-85; asst prof, Blackburn Col, 85-89; asst prof to prof, Albright Col, 89-. **HONORS AND AWARDS** Lindback Distinguished Teaching Award. **MEMBERSHIPS** MLA, Shakespeare Asn of Am, Renaissance Soc of Am. **RESEARCH** Shakespeare, Milton, Dryden. **SELECTED PUBLICATIONS** Auth, "Seeing the King: Classical and Biblical Texts in Astraea Redux," SEL, (92): 407-27; auth, "Conversing, Looking, Loving: The Discourse of Reason in Paradise Lost," Cithara 32.2, (93): 13-38; auth, "She is fast my wife: Sex, Marriage, and Ducal Authority in Measure for Measure," Shakespeare Studies 23, (95): 187-209. **CONTACT ADDRESS** 11 Robeson St, Reading, PA 19604-2151. **EMAIL** alc@alb.edu

CAFFREY, RAYMOND T.
PERSONAL Born 04/27/1945, Elizabeth, NJ, m, 1966, 2 children **DISCIPLINE** ENGLISH **EDUCATION** St Charles Col, AA, 65; Seton Hall Univ, BA, 67; MA, 70; NYork Univ, PhD, 95. **CAREER** Adj instr, Kean Univ, 96-01. **MEMBERSHIPS** MLA; DH Lawrence Soc; NYU Bio Sem. **RESEARCH** D. H. Lawrence biography and paintings; Lady Chatterley's Lover; **SELECTED PUBLICATIONS** Auth, "Lady Chatterley's Lover: The Grove Pr Publication of the Unexpurgated Text," Lib Assoc Cour 20 (85); auth, "The Life of D. H. Lawrence 1923-1928:The Chatterley Years," (95); auth, "D. H. Lawrence's Impotence and Frieda's Affair with Angelo Ravagl," J DH Law Soc, Univ Hull, 98. **CONTACT ADDRESS** 7 Nickie Ct, Iselin, NJ 08830-2218. **EMAIL** raymondtcaffrey@earthlink.net

CAHILL, JANE
DISCIPLINE CLASSICAL MYTHOLOGY **EDUCATION** Leicester Univ, Eng, BA, 70; Univ W Ontario, MA, 71; Univ Brit Columbia, PhD, 76. **CAREER** Assoc prof **RESEARCH** Mythology and storytelling; history of words. **SELECTED PUBLICATIONS** Auth, Her Kind: Stories of Women from Greek Mythology, Broadview Press, 95. **CONTACT ADDRESS** Dept of Classics, Univ of Winnipeg, 515 Portage Ave, Winnipeg, MB, Canada R3B 2E9. **EMAIL** j-cahill@uwinnipeg.ca

CAHN, VICTOR L.
PERSONAL Born 09/07/1948, New York, NY, s **DISCIPLINE** ENGLISH **EDUCATION** Columbia Col, AB, 69; NYork Univ, MA, 73; PhD, 73. **CAREER** Instr, Mercersburg Acad, 69-71; Instr, Pomfret School 76-78; Instr, Phillips Exeter Acad, 78-80; Asst Prof, Bowdoin Col, 81-82; Asst Prof to Prof, Skidmore Col, 82-. **MEMBERSHIPS** MLA, Dramatists Guild. **RESEARCH** Shakespeare; Modern Drama. **SELECTED PUBLICATIONS** Auth, Beyond Absurdity: The Plays of Tom Stoppard, Fairleigh Dickinson Univ Press, 79; auth, The Heroes of Shakespeare's Tragedies, Peter Lang Pub, 88; auth, A Thinking Student's Guide to College, Christopher Pub House, 88; auth, Shakespeare the Playwright: A Companion to the Complete Tragedies, Histories, Comedies, and Romances, Greenwood Press, 91; auth, Gender and Power in the Plays of Harold Pinter, St Martin's Press, 93; auth, The Plays of Shakespeare: A Thematic Guide, Greenwood Press, forthcoming. **CONTACT ADDRESS** Dept English, Skidmore Col, 815 N Broadway, Saratoga Springs, NY 12866-1631.

CAI, DEBORAH A.
PERSONAL Born 07/31/1961, MI, m, 1986, 3 children **DISCIPLINE** COMMUNICATION **EDUCATION** Trinity Evangelical Divimity School, MA, 91; MI State Univ, PhD, 94. **CAREER** Vis prof, MI State Univ, East Lansing, 94-95; asst prof, Univ MD, College Park, 95-. **MEMBERSHIPS** Nat Commun Asn; Int Commun Asn; Am Asn of Chinese Studies. **RESEARCH** Intercultural commun; persuasian; negotiation & conflict management. **SELECTED PUBLICATIONS** Ed, with W Donahue, Communicating and Connecting: The Functions of Human Communication, Harcourt Brace College Pubs, 96; co-auth, with E L Fink, Social Influence, in W Donohue and D A Cai, eds, Communicating and Connecting: The Functions of Human Communication, Harcourt Brace College Pubs, 96; co-auth with M I Bresnahan, Gender and Aggression in the Recognition of Interruption, Discourse Processes, 21 (2), 96; co-auth with A Williams, H Ota, H Giles, H D Pierson, C Gallois, SA-H Ng, T-S Lim, E B Ryan, L Somera, J Maher, J Harwood, Young People's Beliefs About Intergenerational Communication: An Initial Cross-Cultural Comparison, Communication Res, 24, 97; co-auth with J I Rodriguez, Adjusting to Cultural Differences: The Intercultural Adaptation Model, Intercultural Communication Studies, VI (2), 97; with W A Donahue, Determinants of Facework in Intercultural Negotiation, Asian J of Commun, 7 (1), 97; auth, Difficulties of Doing Survey Research Across Cultures, in J Martin, T Nakayama, & L Flores, eds, Readings in Cultural Contexts, Mayfield, 97; co-auth with H Giles & K Noels, Intergenerational Communication in the People's Republic of China; Perceptions of Older and Younger Adults and Their Link to Mental Health, J of Applied Commun Res, 26 (1), 98; co-auth with M S Kim and H C Shin, Cultural Influences on the Preferred Forms of Requesting and Re-Requesting, Communication Monographs, 98; co-auth with L Drake, Intercultural Business Negotiation: A Communication Perspective, in M E Roloff, ed, Communication Yearbook 21, 98; author and co-author of numerous other articles and publications including one in press. **CONTACT ADDRESS** Dept of Commun, Univ of Maryland, Col Park, 2110 Skinner Bldg, College Park, MD 20742. **EMAIL** debcai@wam.umd.edu

CAILLER, BERNADETTE ANNE
PERSONAL Born 06/08/1941, Poitiers, France, w **DISCIPLINE** AFRICAN & CARIBBEAN LITERATURE **EDUCATION** Univ Poitiers, Lic es Lett, 61, Dipl d Etudes Superieures, 64; Univ Paris, Capes, 68; Cornell Univ, MA, 67, PhD(comp lit), 74. **CAREER** Asst prof, 74-79, Assoc Prof French, Univ Fla, 79-90; prof, 90-. **HONORS AND AWARDS** Certificat Maurice Cagnon, CIEF, La Fayette, LA, 99. **MEMBERSHIPS** African Lit Assn; Conseil Int d'Etudes Francophones; African Stu Assn; Int Comp Lit Assn. **RESEARCH** Interdisciplinary and Intertextual Studies. **SELECTED PUBLICATIONS** Auth, Proposition poetique, une lecture de l'oeuvre d'Aime Cesaire, Naaman, 76,; auth, Conquerants de la nuit nue: Edouard Glissant et l'H(h)istoire antillaise, Etudes Litteraires Francaises, vol 45, Gunter Narr Verlag, 88; co-ed, Toward Defining the African Aesthetic, Three Continents Press, 82; auth, If the Dead could only speak! Reflections on Texts by Niger, Hughes, an dFodeba, The Surreptitious Speech: Presence Africaine and the Politics of Otherness, 1947-1987, Univ Chicago, 92; auth, Creolization versus Francophonie. Language, Identity and Culture in the Works of Edouard Glissant, L'Heritage de Caliban, 92; auth, The Impossible Ecstasy: an Analysis of Valentin Y. Mudimbe's Dechirures, Research in African Literatures, 93; auth, Hitlerisme et enterprise coloniale 2: le cas Damas, French Cultural Studies, 94; auth, Si Marie-Madeleine se racontait: analyse d'une figure de Feux, Roman, Histoire et Mythe dans l'oeuvre de Marguerite Yourcenar, SIEY, 95; auth, La transgression creatrice d'Andree Chedid: Nefertiti ou le reve d'Akhnaton, Les memoires d'un scribe, Litteratures autobiographiques de la Francophonie, C.E.L.F.A., 96; auth, Interface between Fiction and Autobiography: From Shaba 2 to Les Corps glorieux, Canad Jour of African Stu, Vol 30, No 3, 96; auth, Totalite et Infini, alterite et rePation: d'Emmanuel Levinas a Edouard Glissant, in Les Poetiques d'edouard Glissant. Presses de Paris VI, Sorbonne, 99; auth, Reponse d'une Francaise de Floride a Lettres Algeriennes et Fis de la Laine, in Rachid Bondjedra, Une Poetique de la subversion, L'Harmattan, 99. **CONTACT ADDRESS** Dept of Romance Lang and Lit, Univ of Florida, PO Box 117405, Gainesville, FL 32611-7405. **EMAIL** cailler@rll.ufl.edu

CALARCO, N. JOSEPH
PERSONAL Born 03/19/1938, New York, NY, m, 1999, 2 children **DISCIPLINE** DRAMA **EDUCATION** Columbia Univ, AB, 59, MA, 62; Univ Minn, PhD(theatre), 66. **CA-**

REER Asst prof dramatic art, Univ Calif, Berkeley, 66-68; asst prof, 68-71, assoc prof, 71-78, prof theater, Wayne State Univ, 78- ; Mem bd dir fine arts sect, Mich Acad Sci Arts & Letters, 70-73; judge, Prof Actg Auditions, Theatre Commun Group, 74-75; chmn, Am Bicentennial Playwriting Competition, 74-76. **MEMBERSHIPS** Am Theatre Asn; Am Asn Univ Prof; Nat Acad TV Arts & Sci; Soc Stage Dir & Choreographers; Dramatists Guild. **RESEARCH** Directing; actor training; dramatic theory. **SELECTED PUBLICATIONS** Auth, Vision without compromise: Genet's The Screens, Drama Surv, spring 65; Tragedy as demonstration, Educ Theatre J, 10/66; Tragic Being: Apollo and Dionysus in Western Drama, Univ Minn, 68; contribr, Humanities and the Theatre, Am Theatre Asn, 73; auth, Production as criticism: Miller's The Crucible, Educ Theatre J, 10/77. **CONTACT ADDRESS** Univ Theatre, Wayne State Univ, 3225 Old Main St, Detroit, MI 48202-1303. **EMAIL** joecalarco@home.com

CALCAGNO, ANN
PERSONAL Born 11/14/1957, San Diego, CA, m, 1986, 2 children **DISCIPLINE** ENGLISH, CREATIVE WRITING **EDUCATION** Williams Col, BA, 79; Univ Mont, MFA, 84. **CAREER** Develop Writer, NW Univ, 84-88; adj, School of the Art Inst, 90-93; assoc prof, DePaul Univ, 93-. **HONORS AND AWARDS** Nat Endow Arts Fel; San Francisco Found Phelan Awd; IL Arts Counc Artists Fel; Ed choice Journeywoman Awd. **MEMBERSHIPS** Authors Guild; MLA; Poets & Writers, Assoc Writing Prog. **RESEARCH** Contemporary American Literature and Writing, Contemporary Italian Literature and Writing. **SELECTED PUBLICATIONS** Auth, Pray for Yourself, NW Univ Pr, 93; ed, Travelers Tales: Italy, O'Reilly Pub, 98. **CONTACT ADDRESS** Dept English, DePaul Univ, 802 W Belden, Chicago, IL 60614-3210.

CALDER, ROBERT L.
PERSONAL Born 04/03/1941, Moose Jaw, SK, Canada **DISCIPLINE** ENGLISH **EDUCATION** Univ Sask, BA, 64, MA, 65; Univ Leeds, PhD, 70. **CAREER** Instr to assoc prof, 65-81, dept head, 79-81, prof Eng, Univ Saskatchewan, 81-, assoc dean fine arts & hum, 81-84. **HONORS AND AWARDS** Gov Gen Lit Awd Non-fiction, 89. **SELECTED PUBLICATIONS** Auth, W. Somerset Maugham and the Quest for Freedom, 72; auth, Willie: The Life of W. Somerset Maugham, 89; coauth, Rider Pride: The Story of Canada's Best Loved Football Team, 85; co-ed, Time as a Human Resource, 91. **CONTACT ADDRESS** Dept of English, Univ of Saskatchewan, 320 Arts Tower, 9 Campus Dr, Saskatoon, SK, Canada S7N 5A5. **EMAIL** calderr@duke.usask.ca

CALDER, WILLIAM M., III
PERSONAL Born 09/03/1932, Brooklyn, NY, s **DISCIPLINE** CLASSICS **EDUCATION** Harvard Col, BA, 54, MA, 56; Univ of Chicago, PhD, 58. **CAREER** TA, Harvard Col, 55-56; TA, Univ of Chicago, 57-58; from instr to prof, Columbia Univ, 58-76; prof, Univ of Colorado Boulder, 76-88; prof of classics & comp lit, Univ of Illinois Urbana, 88-. **HONORS AND AWARDS** Erfurt Acad of Sci, Elected For Mem; Ger Acad Sci, Heinrich Schliemann Medallion; Univ of IL Urbana, A. O. Beckman Awd, Neubukow's Heinrich Schliemann Medallion, Alexander von Humbolat Prize Winner. **MEMBERSHIPS** SPHS London, SPRS London, CAE&W, EES, TM Gesell, ICC, ASGLE, AIA, APA, AAH, CAMS, GSA, ANS. **RESEARCH** Classic Greek lit; Greek and Roman pagan; hist of class scholarship; 19th and 20th cent in Eng, Ger, and US. **SELECTED PUBLICATIONS** Co-auth, Philology and Philosophy: The Letters of Hermann Diels to Theodor and Heinrich Gomperz, Hildesheim, 95; Lieber Prinz: Der Breifwechsel zwischen Hermann Diels und Ulrich von Wilamowitz-Moellendorf ,1869-1921, Hildesheim 95; Sed serviendum officio.. The Correspondence Between Ulrich von Wilamowitz-Moellendorff and Eduard Norden 1892-1931, Hildesheim, 97; Men in their Books: Studies in the Modern History of Classical Scholarship, Hildesheim, 98. **CONTACT ADDRESS** Dept of Classics, Univ of Illinois, Urbana-Champaign, 609 W Delaware Ave, Urbana, IL 61801. **EMAIL** wmcalder@uiuc.edu

CALDWELL, MARK LEONARD
PERSONAL Born 03/14/1946, Troy, NY **DISCIPLINE** ENGLISH LITERATURE **EDUCATION** Fordham Univ, BA, 67; Cambridge Univ, BA, 69; Harvard Univ, PhD, 73. **CAREER** Prof English, Fordham Univ, 89-. **MEMBERSHIPS** Authors Guild **RESEARCH** Literature of the English Renaissance, 1500-1660; science & literature, cultural studies. **SELECTED PUBLICATIONS** Auth, Sources and analogues of the Life of Sidney, Studies Philol, 7/77; Allegory: The Renaissance mode, ELH, winter 77; The Last Crusade: America's War on Consumption, 1862-1954, NY, Atheneum, 88; The Prose of Fulke Greville, Lord Brooke, NY, Garland, 87; A Short History of Rudeness, NY, Picador/St Martin's Press, 99, forthcoming. **CONTACT ADDRESS** Dept of English, Fordham Univ, 501 E Fordham Rd, New York, NY 10458-5191.

CALENDRILLO, LINDA T.
DISCIPLINE ENGLISH COMPOSITION AND LANGUAGE **EDUCATION** St John's Univ, BA, 73; Purdue Univ, MA, 75, PhD, 88. **CAREER** Undergraduate Asst, St. John's Univ, 69-73; fac, Purdue Univ, 73-79; fac, Ill State Univ, 80-82; fac, Indiana State Univ, 82-85; asst prof, Univ of South Alabama, 88-89; asst prof, Bradley Univ, 89-92; asst prof, Eastern Ill Univ, 92-99; asst prof, Dept of English, Western Kentucky Univ, 99-. **HONORS AND AWARDS** EIU 93-94 Awded Booth Library Fel, EIU, 94; EIU Fac Develop Mini-Grant, 94; EIU Col Arts & Hum Travel Grant NCTE, 95, 98; EIU Fac Excellence Awd Tchng, 95; EIU Disability Services Outstanding Assistance Recognition, 96; EIU Fac Achievement Awd Tchng, Service, & Publ, 97. **MEMBERSHIPS** Nat Coun of Teachers of English; Ill Asn Teachers English. **RESEARCH** Composition Theory and Pedagogy; History of Rhetoric; Basic Writing and Writing Centers; Writing Across the Curriculum Programs; Literary Area: Modern British Literature. **SELECTED PUBLICATIONS** Coauth, Atomistic Versus Holistic Evaluation of Student Essays, Notes from the National Testing Network in Writing, 91; Margaret Atwood, Beacham Publ, 92; Playing with Character, Plot, Scene: Strategies To Help Students Write More Creative Fiction, Ill Eng Bull, 92; Rethinking the Externalization of the Arts of Memory, Jour Evolutionary Psychol, 92; Xeroxing, Memory Loss, and Research Papers: What Can Teachers Do to Encourage the Use of Memory and Why Should They Bother?, Ill Eng Bull, 94; Review Essay of Frederick Reynolds' Rhetorical Memory and Delivery, Rhetoric Rev, 94; Memory, Encyclopedia of Rhetoric, Garland, 95; Mental Imagery, Psychology, and Rhetoric: An Examination of Recurring Problems, JAEPL, 95-96; Review Essay of Roy Fox's Language, Media, and Mind, JAEPL, 95-96; coauth, "Editors Message," and "Dedication to Alice G. Brand," The Journal of the Assembly for Expanded Perspectives on Learning, (98-99); auth, "Mining the Mother Lode of the Surreal," Journal of Evolutionary Psychology, forthcoming. **CONTACT ADDRESS** Dept of English, Western Kentucky Univ, 1 Big Red Way, Bowling Green, KY 42101. **EMAIL** linda.calendrillo@wku.edu

CALHOUN, RICHARD JAMES
PERSONAL Born 09/05/1926, Jackson, TN, m, 1954, 3 children **DISCIPLINE** ENGLISH **EDUCATION** George Peabody Col, BA, 48; Johns Hopkins Univ, MA, 50; Univ NC, PhD, 59. **CAREER** Jr instr, Johns Hopkins Univ, 48-50; instr English, Jacksonville State Col, 50-51; asst, Univ NC, 53-57; asst prof, Davidson Col, 58-61; from asst prof to prof, 61-69, Alumni Prof, Clemson Univ, 69-, Duke Univ-Univ NC Coop Prog Humanities fel, 64-65; co-ed periodical, SC Rev, 73-; Distinguished Alumni Prof Emer, 95-. **HONORS AND AWARDS** Fulbright-Hays lectr, Univ Ljubljana & Univ Sarajevo, 69-70; sr Fulbright lectr, Aarhus Univ & Odense Univ, Denmark, 75-76; Arts America lectr, Greece; USIA lectr, Europe, 90; Disitnguished retiring editor awards, Council Eds Learned Journals, 95; Honoree, Phil Assoc Carollinas, 95; Guest Prof and Sr Fulbright lectr Univ Vienna, Austria, 96. **MEMBERSHIPS** MLA; SAtlantic Mod Lang Asn; Soc Study Southern Lit. **RESEARCH** Contemporary poetry; southern American literature; American literature. **SELECTED PUBLICATIONS** Ed, The Autobiography of William J. Grayson, SC, 90; contrib, American Literary Scholarship, an annual, Duke, vols 1986-91/ contrib Galway Kinnell, Twayne, 93; auth, Simms--A Literary Life, Resources For Amer Lit Stud, Vol 0022, 96; contrib, Roads Not Taken, Rereading Robert Frost, Missouri, 01; contrib, Robert Frost Encyclopedia Greenwood, 01. **CONTACT ADDRESS** Dept of English, Clemson Univ, 6 Clover Dr, Chapel Hill, NC 27514. **EMAIL** rcalhoun@mindspring.com

CALHOUN, THOMAS O.
PERSONAL Born 03/01/1940, Pittsburgh, PA, m, 1 child **DISCIPLINE** ENGLISH **EDUCATION** Princeton Univ, AB, 62; Univ Pittsburgh, MA, 63; Univ Mich, PhD(English), 67. **CAREER** Instr English & classical lit, Univ Mich, 63-67; Asst Prof English & Comp Lit, Univ Del, 67-, Univ Mich fel, 67. **MEMBERSHIPS** MLA; Renaissance Soc Am; Milton Soc. **RESEARCH** Literature of the English Renaissance, 16th and 17th centuries; comparative literature; Petrarch. **SELECTED PUBLICATIONS CONTACT ADDRESS** Dept of English, Univ of Delaware, Newark, DE 19711.

CALLAGHAN, MICHAEL J.
PERSONAL Born 06/11/1948, London, UK, s **DISCIPLINE** ENGLISH **EDUCATION** St Charles Sem, BA, 71; MDiv, 75; Niagara Univ, MA, 81; NY Univ, PhD, 98. **CAREER** Pastor, Manoa Pa, 76-77; teacher, Warminster Pa, 78; teacher, St Joseph's Sem Princeton, 80; fac, St John's Univ, 85-. **HONORS AND AWARDS** Shannon Scholar, Intl Thomas Merton Soc, 97; Who's Who in Am Educ, 89. **MEMBERSHIPS** MLA; Nat Coun of Teachers of English; Medieval Acad of Am; Intl Thomas Merton Soc; St. John's Jazz ensemble; NY Rd Runners Club; Am Benedictine Acad. **SELECTED PUBLICATIONS** Auth, "It's Important to Me," The English Record; auth, "The Significance of Liturgical Feasts in Sir Gawain and the Green Knight," Hwaet!: Grad j of Medieval Studies, 91; auth, "The Influence of the English Mystics on Thomas Merton's Life and Writings," in Thomas Merton: Poet, Monk, Prophet, Papers from the 1998 Oakham Conf, Three Peaks Press, 98. **CONTACT ADDRESS** Col of Professional Studies, St. John's Univ, Dept English, Jamaica, NY 11439-0002.

CALLAHAN, JOHN FRANCIS
PERSONAL Born 12/31/1940, Meriden, CT, m, 1970, 1 child **DISCIPLINE** AMERICAN LITERATURE **EDUCATION** Univ Conn, BA, 63; Univ Ill, MA, 64, PhD(Am lit), 70. **CAREER** From instr to asst prof, 67-73, assoc prof, 73-80, Prof English, Lewis & Clark Col, 80-, Nat Endowment for Humanities younger humanist fel, 73-74. **MEMBERSHIPS** MLA; Am Lit Group, MLA; Northwest Am Studies Asn. **RESEARCH** The American novel; Black literature and history; 20th century Irish literature and history. **SELECTED PUBLICATIONS** Auth, Mckay,Claude, A Black Poets Struggle for Identity, Contemp Lit, Vol 0034, 93; Frequencies of Memory--A Eulogy for Ellison, Ralph, Waldo March 1, 1914 April 16, 94, Callaloo, Vol 0018, 95; Stealing The Fire--The Art and Protest of Baldwin, James, Contemp Lit, Vol 0034, 93; Fitzgerald, F.Scott Evolving American-Dream--The Pursuit of Happiness in Gatsby, Tender Is The Night, And The Last Tycoon, Twentieth Century Lit, Vol 0042, 96. **CONTACT ADDRESS** Dept of English, Lewis and Clark Col, 0615 SW Palatine Hill Rd, Portland, OR 97219-7879.

CALLANDER, MARILYN BERG
PERSONAL Born 09/05/1933, Jersey City, NJ, m, 1955, 3 children **DISCIPLINE** AMERICAN LITERATURE **EDUCATION** Beaver Col, BA, 55; Drew Univ, MPhil, 85; PhD, 87. **CAREER** Adj assoc prof, Drew Univ; Director, Drew-in-Nepal Prog; adv, Tribhuvan Univ, Kathmandu, Nepal. **HONORS AND AWARDS** Phi Beta Kappa; Fulbright Scholar 91, 92; Cert of Appreciation, Dept of State, 91. **MEMBERSHIPS** SVHE, NJCH, KJPT, Fulbright Assoc, Asia Soc, Southern Asia Inst. **RESEARCH** Comparative Folktales. **SELECTED PUBLICATIONS** Auth, Willa Cather and the Fairy Tale, UMI, (Ann Arbor, MI), 89. **CONTACT ADDRESS** 29 Still Hollow Rd, Lebanon, NJ 08833-4417. **EMAIL** mcallander@earthlink.net

CALLON, GORDON
PERSONAL Born 08/11/1945, Arvida, PQ, Canada, m, 1985 **DISCIPLINE** MUSIC **EDUCATION** MMA, McGill Univ, 71, BMUS, 89; DMA Univ of WA at Seattle, 84. **CAREER** Acadia Univ, 78-present: Assoc prof 84, Acadia Univ, 95-98: Dir, Sch of Music, Acadia Univ, 91-92,94-95: Actg Dir, Sch of Music Vancouver Community Col , found fac mem at VCC, Courtenay Youth Music Centre, summers 74-75; Univ of WA, 71-73 tchg asst: McGill Univ, 69-70, tchg asst. **HONORS AND AWARDS** Acadia Univ: Tchg Innovation Grant; 93-94, mem of group receiving award for develop of music/lang multimedia computer stations in teh lang lab; SSHRC Conference Grant; SSHRC General Grants 84-85, 91-92, Spring 93; Autumn 93; Research Fund Grants 89-90, 90-91, 93-94; Harvey T. Reid Summer Study Awards: 82,83. Canadian Music Centre: accepted as Assoc Composer, August 74; CBC/Canada Council Awards for Young Composers: Award Winner, 73-74; Univ of British Columbia: HR MacMillan Family Fel, 73-74: Univ of WA, Canada Council Doctoral Fel, 71-72, 72-73, offered 73-74, 76-77; McGill Univ Scholarship, 66-67, 67-68; Fac of Music Scholarships, 66-69; Gold Medal of the Minister of Educ, 69, Graduate Fac Spec Scholarship, 69-70; JW McConnell Memorial Fel, 70-71; Canada Council Arts Bursary 70-71, Southern IL Univ, mem, Phi Eta Sigma Hon Fraternity; Dean's List. **MEMBERSHIPS** Royal Musical Assoc. **RESEARCH** 17th Century Eng vocal music; computer applications in music, pedag applications of online research. **SELECTED PUBLICATIONS** Auth, "Songs with Theorbo," Journal of the Lute Society of America, (95), 15-51; ed, Nicholas Lanier: the Complete Works, Hereford: Seveinus Press, 97; auth, "Methodology in Music History for Undergraduate Music Majors at Acadia University: Music 2273," CAML Newsletter, (99), 20-24; ed, Baroque Music , (Wolfville: Acadia Univ, 00), 539. **CONTACT ADDRESS** Acadia Univ, Wolfville, NS, Canada B0P 1X0. **EMAIL** gordon.callon@acaduau.ca

CAMARGO, MARTIN J.
PERSONAL Born 07/23/1950, Flushing, NY, m, 1987 **DISCIPLINE** ENGLISH **EDUCATION** Princeton Univ, AB, 72; Univ of Illinois-Urbana/Champaign, MA, 73; PhD, 78. **CAREER** Visiting Asst Prof, Univ of Missouri, 78-79; Asst Prof, Univ of Alabama, 79-80; Asst Prof, Univ of Missouri, 80-85; Assoc Prof, 85-92; Prof 92-. **HONORS AND AWARDS** NEH Fellowship, 00; ACLS Fellowships, 84, 96-97; Alexander von Humboldt Fellowship, 87-88; Fulbright Fellowship, 74-75; William T. Kemper Fellowship for Teaching Excellence, 96. **MEMBERSHIPS** Modern Language Association; Medieval Academy of America; New Chancer Society; International Society for the History of Rhetoric; American Association of Univ Professors, etc. **RESEARCH** Medieval Rhetoric; Poetics; Middle English Genres; Chancer. **SELECTED PUBLICATIONS** Auth, "Books and Monographs: Medieval Rhetorics of Prose Composition," 95, auth, "The Middle English Verse Love Epistle," 91; auth, "Ars Dictaminis, Ars Dictandi," 91; auth, "Speculum," 84,99, auth, "Rhetorica," 98, 96, 98; auth, "Medieval Studies," 94; auth, "Traditio," 92. **CONTACT ADDRESS** Dept English, Univ of Missouri, Columbia, 107 Tate Hall, Columbia, MO 65211-1500. **EMAIL** camargom@missouri.edu

CAMERON, ELSPETH M.
PERSONAL Born 01/10/1943, Toronto, ON, Canada **DISCIPLINE** ENGLISH LITERATURE **EDUCATION** Univ BC, BA, 64; Univ NB, MA, 65; McGill Univ, PhD, 70. **CAREER** Prof, Eng, Concordia Univ, 70-77; coordr, Can Lit Lang, New Col, 80-90, Prof English to Prof Emer, Univ Toronto, 90-. **MEMBERSHIPS** Asn Can Stud; ACQL. **SELECTED PUBLICATIONS** Auth, Robertson Davies, 71; auth, Hugh MacLennan: A Writer's Life 81; ed, The Other Side of Hugh MacLennan: Selected Essays Old and New, 78; ed, Hugh MacLennan: 1982, 82; ed, Irving Layton: A Portrait, 85; ed, Robertson Davies: An Appreciation 91; ed, Earle Birney: A Life 94. **CONTACT ADDRESS** Dept of English, Univ of Toronto, 7 King's College Circle, Toronto, ON, Canada M5S 3K1. **EMAIL** cameron@chass.utoronto.ca

CAMERON, JOHN
PERSONAL Born 06/24/1930, Chicago, IL, d, 2 children **DISCIPLINE** ENGLISH **EDUCATION** Yale Univ, BA, 52, MA, 57, PhD, 63; Edinburgh Univ, dipl, 55. **CAREER** From instr to assoc prof, 58-70, prof English, Amherst Col, 70-. **HONORS AND AWARDS** MA, Amherst Col, 70. **MEMBERSHIPS** MLA; AAUP. **RESEARCH** Novel; film history and theory. **CONTACT ADDRESS** Dept of English, Amherst Col, Amherst, MA 01002-5003. **EMAIL** jacameron@amherst.edu

CAMERON, RUTH A.
PERSONAL Born 01/15/1929, Lisbon Falls, ME, m, 1950, 2 children **DISCIPLINE** ENGLISH LITERATURE **EDUCATION** Eastern Nazarene Col, BA; Boston Univ, MA, PhD. **CAREER** Eng Dept, Eastern Nazarene Col; First holder of Munro Chair of English Literature. **RESEARCH** Gerard Manley Hopkins. **SELECTED PUBLICATIONS** Auth, Meditations on Advent, 91. **CONTACT ADDRESS** Eastern Nazarene Col, 23 East Elm Ave, Quincy, MA 02170-2999. **EMAIL** cameronr@enc.edu

CAMERON, SHARON
PERSONAL Born 02/15/1947, Cleveland, OH **DISCIPLINE** ENGLISH & AMERICAN LITERATURE **EDUCATION** Bennington Col, BA, 68; Brandeis Univ, MA, 69, PhD(English & Am lit), 73. **CAREER** Asst prof English, Boston Univ, 72-76 & Univ Calif, Santa Barbara, 77-78; assoc prof, 78-80, Prof English, Johns Hopkins Univ, 81-, Fels, Nat Endow for Humanities, 79-80, Am Coun Learned Soc, 82 & Guggenheim, 82-83. **MEMBERSHIPS** MLA. **RESEARCH** American literature; lyric poetry; literary theory. **SELECTED PUBLICATIONS** Auth, The sense against calamity: Ideas of a self in three poems by Wallace Stevens, ELH, winter 76; A loaded gun: Dickinson and the dialectic of rage, PMLA, 5/78; Naming as history; Dickinson's poems of definition, Critical Inquiry, winter 78; Lyric Time: Dickinson and the Limits of Genre, 79 & The corporeal self: Allegories of our body, In: Melville and Hawthorne, Johns Hopkins Univ, 81; auth, The Way of Life by Abandonment: Emerson's Impersonal, Critical Inquiry, Fall 98; auth, Thinking of Henry James, Chicago, 89; auth, Choosing Not Choosing: Dickinson's Fascicles, Chicago, 92; Auth, Writing Nature; Henry Thoreau's Journal, Chicago; Beautiful Work; A Meditation on Pain, Duke, 00. **CONTACT ADDRESS** Dept of English, Johns Hopkins Univ, Baltimore, 3400 N Charles St, Baltimore, MD 21218-2680. **EMAIL** scameron@jhu.edu

CAMFIELD, GREGG
DISCIPLINE ENGLISH LITERATURE **EDUCATION** Brown Univ, AB, 80; Univ CA, 89. **CAREER** Prof, Univ Pacific. **HONORS AND AWARDS** Phi Beta Kappa, 80; NEH Focus Grant, 99-00; Graves Found fel, 00-01. **MEMBERSHIPS** MLA; AHSA; Mark Twain Circle. **RESEARCH** American literature up to 1910; intellectual history; literature humor; life and works of Mark Twain. **SELECTED PUBLICATIONS** Auth, Sentimental Twain: Samuel Clemens in the Maze of Moral Philosophy, 94; auth, Afterword to The Gilded Age in the Oxford Mark Twain, 96; auth, Necessary Madness: The Humor of Domesticity in 19th-c Am Lit, 97; auth, Argument of Beavis and Butt-head, I never saw anything of one so pathetic and funny! Humor in the Stories of Mary Wilkins Freeman, 99; auth, The Oxford Reader's Companion to Mark Twain, forthcoming 02. **CONTACT ADDRESS** English Dept, Univ of the Pacific, Stockton, Pacific Ave, PO Box 3601, Stockton, CA 95211. **EMAIL** gcamfiel@uop.edu

CAMINALS-HEATH, ROSER
PERSONAL Born 06/30/1956, Barcelona, Spain, m, 1981 **DISCIPLINE** ENGLISH LITERATURE **EDUCATION** Univ Barcelona, Spain, PhD, 86. **CAREER** Prof of Spanish & Chr Dept Foreign Languages, Hood Col. **HONORS AND AWARDS** 1st Prize Prose at Jocs Florals de la Diaspora, 98; Hodson fel. **MEMBERSHIPS** Am Assoc Tchr Span & Port; Am Lit Transl Asn; Assoc Writers Prog. **RESEARCH** Creative writing; Literary translation; XIXth and XXth Century Spanish fiction. **SELECTED PUBLICATIONS** transl The House of Ulloa: An English translation of the novel Los Pazos de Ulloa, Univ Ga Press, 92; Once Remembered, Twice Lived, Peter Lang, 93; Un Segle de Prodigis, Columna Ed, Barcelona, 95; Les Herbes Secretes, Pages Ed, Lleida, 98. **CONTACT ADDRESS** Dept of For Lang and Lit, Hood Col, 401 Rosemont Ave, Frederick, MD 21701. **EMAIL** rheath@hood.edu

CAMINERO-SANTANGELO, BYRON
PERSONAL Born 06/24/1961, New York, NY, m, 1991 **DISCIPLINE** ENGLISH **EDUCATION** Claremont McKenna Col, BA, 84; Univ of Calif at Irvine, MA, 87, PhD, 93. **CAREER** Lectr, Irvine Valley Col, 93-94; lectr, Calif State Univ, 94-95; tchg asst/assoc, 85-92, lectr, Univ of Calif at Irvine, 94-95; asst prof, DePaul Univ, 95-97; Asst Prof, Univ of Kans, 97-. **HONORS AND AWARDS** General Res Funded New Fac Awd, Univ of Kans; Fac Development Seminar Grant, DePaul Univ; Fac Career Development Awd, Postdoctoral Tchg Awd, Univ of Calif at Irvine; Dissertation Fel, Univ of Calif at Irvine Dept of English Humanities. **RESEARCH** 20th-Century British Lit; African fiction; postcolonial fiction and theory; critical theory. **SELECTED PUBLICATIONS** Auth, Neocolonialsim and the Betrayal Plot in A Grain of Wheat: Ngugi wa Thiong'o's Re-Vision of Under Western Eyes, Res in African Lit, 98; Story-teller in the Body of a Seaman: Joseph Conrad and the Rise of the Professions, Conradiana, 97; Testing for Truth: Joseph Conrad and the Ideology of the Examination, cLIO, 94; A Moral Dilemma: Ethics in Tess of the D'Urbervilles, English Studies, 94; The Pump-House Gang, An Encycl of Am Lit of the Sea and the Great Lakes, forthcoming. **CONTACT ADDRESS** 805 Missouri St, Lawrence, KS 66044. **EMAIL** bsantang@eagle.cc.ukans.edu

CAMINERO-SANTANGELO, MARTA
PERSONAL Born 12/19/1966, Quebec, PQ, Canada, m, 1991, 1 child **DISCIPLINE** ENGLISH **EDUCATION** Yale Univ, BA, 88; Univ Calif, MA, 91, PhD, 95. **CAREER** Asst prof English, DePaul Univ, 95-97; Asst Prof English, Univ Kansas, 97-. **HONORS AND AWARDS** Univ Kansas Provost's Fac Dev Grant; Ctr for Teach Excell Grant; Hall Ctr Teach Grant; univ calif, irvine chancellor's fel; pres diss fel; dorothy and donald strauss endowed diss fel. **MEMBERSHIPS** MELUS **RESEARCH** US Latinola lit, African-Am lit; US women's writing and feminist theory. **SELECTED PUBLICATIONS** Auth, "Multiple Personality and the Postmodern Subject: Theorizing Agency," in Literature/Interpretation/Theory, 96; "The Madwoman Can't Speak: Post-War Culture, Feminist Criticism, and Welty's 'June Recital,'" in Tulsa Studies in Women's Literature, 15.1,96; "Beyond Otherness: Negotiated Identities and Viramontes' 'The Cariboo Cafe'"in Jour of the Short Story in Eng, 96; "Beyond Otherness: Negotiated Identities and Viramontes' 'The Cariboo Cafe' in Women on the Edge: Ethnicity and Gender in Short Stories by Amican Women, 98; The Madwoman Can't Speak: Or Why Insanity Is Not Subversive, 98; auth, "Speaking for Others: Problems of Representation in the Novels of Julia Alvarez," Antipodas, 99; auth, "Contesting the Boundaries of 'Exile' Latinola Lit," World Lit Today, forthcoming. **CONTACT ADDRESS** English Dept, Univ of Kansas, Lawrence, 3114 Wescoe Hall, Lawrence, KS 66045. **EMAIL** camsan@eagle.cc.ukans.edu

CAMPBELL, C. JEAN
DISCIPLINE ITALIAN RENAISSANCE ART; ARCHITECTURE **EDUCATION** Univ of Toronto, Victoria University, Toronto, Ontario, Canada, BA, 84; Johns Hopkins Univ, MA, 86; Johns Hopkins Univ, PhD, 92. **CAREER** Assoc prof, Art, Emory Univ. **RESEARCH** art and poetry in early Renaissance Tuscany **SELECTED PUBLICATIONS** Auth, The Game of Courting and the Art of the Commune of San Gimignano, 1290-1320, Princeton: Princeton Univ Press, 98; auth, "The Lady in the Council Chamber: Diplomacy in Poetry in Simone Martini's Maesta," Word & Image vol. 14, no. 4, 98; auth, "Courtin, Harlotry and the Art of Gothic Ivory Carving," Gesta vol. 34, no. 1, 95 **CONTACT ADDRESS** Emory Univ, Atlanta, GA 30322-1950. **EMAIL** cjcampb@emory.edu

CAMPBELL, DAVID A.
PERSONAL Born 08/14/1927, Killywhan, Scotland, m, 1956, 3 children **DISCIPLINE** CLASSICS **EDUCATION** Glasgow Univ, MA, 48; Oxford Univ, BA, 53, MA, 67. **CAREER** Asst to sr lectr, Univ Bristol, 53-71; vis asst prof, Univ Toronto, 59-60; vis prof, Univ Texas Austin, 69-70; prof, 71-93, ch, 72-77, prof emer, Univ of Victoria, 93-. **MEMBERSHIPS** Am Philol Asn; Class Asn Can; Class Asn Pac NW; Class Asn Can W. **SELECTED PUBLICATIONS** Auth, Greek Lyric Poetry, 67, 2nd ed 82; auth, The Golden Lyre: The Themes of the Greek Lyric Poets, 83; auth, Greek Lyric, vols 1-5, 82-93; contribur, The Cambridge History of Classical Literature, vol 1, 85;Auth, The Fragments of Mimnermus--Text and Commentary, Jour Class Asn Can, Vol 0049, 95. **CONTACT ADDRESS** Dept of Greek and Roman Studies, Univ of Victoria, B409 Clearihue, PO Box 3045, Victoria, BC, Canada V8W 3P4.

CAMPBELL, DONNA
PERSONAL Born Watertown, NY, m **DISCIPLINE** ENGLISH, AMERICAN LITERATURE **EDUCATION** SUNY Albany, BA, 74; Univ Man, MA, 82; Univ Kans, MPhil, 90; PhD, 90. **CAREER** Instr, Buffalo State Col, 92-95; asst prof, Gonzaga Univ, 95-. **HONORS AND AWARDS** Phi Kappa Phi; Edwin M. Hopkins Scholar, 82, 83; Selden Lincoln Whitcomb Fel, 83; Kenneth Rockwell Scholar, 84; NE MLA - Ohio Pr Book Awd, 95. **MEMBERSHIPS** Am Lit Assoc; Am Studies Assoc; AIZEN; Stephen Crane Soc; Children's Lit Assoc; MLA; Pacific NW Am Studies Assoc; Edith Wharton Soc. **RESEARCH** Late 19th and early 20th century American literature, Literature of realism, naturalism, local color, Frank Norris, Edith Wharton, Sarah Irene Jewett, Rose Wilder Lane, Stephen Crane. **SELECTED PUBLICATIONS** Auth, "Sentimental Conventions and Self-Protection: Little Women and the Wide, Wide World", Legacy: A J of Am Women Writers 11.2 (94): 118-129; auth, "Frank Norris's Drama of a Broken Teacup: The Old Grannis-Miss Baker Plot in McTeague", Am Lit Realism 26.1 (93): 40-49; auth, "Edith Wharton and the Authoresses: The Critique of Local Color in Wharton's Early Fiction", Studies in Am Fiction 22 (94): 169-183; auth, "Rewriting the rose and lavender pages: Edith Wharton and Women's Local Color Fiction", Speaking the Other Self: New Essays on American Women Writers, ed Jeanne Campbell Ressman, Univ of Ga Pr, (Athens, 97): 263-277; auth, Resisting Regionalism: Gender and Naturalism in American Fiction, 1885-1915, Ohio Univ Pr, (Athens), 97; auth, "Edith Wharton: Critical Extracts", American Women Fiction Writers: 1900-1960; eds Harold Bloom, Chelsea House, (Philadelphia, 98); auth, "In Search of Local Color: Context, Controversy , and The Country of the Pointed Firs", Jewett and Her Contemporaries: Reshaping the Canon, eds Karen Kilcup and Thomas S Edwards, Univ of Fla Pr, (99): 63-76; auth, "Reading (theme)", "Self-denial/Self-control", and "Sentimentalism", The Louisa May Alcott Encycl, eds Gregory Eiselen and Anne Phillips, Greenwood (forthcoming); auth, "Wild Men and Dissenting Voices: Narrative Disruption in Little House on the Prairie, Great Plains Quarterly, (forthcoming). **CONTACT ADDRESS** Dept English, Gonzaga Univ, 520 E Boone Ave, Spokane, WA 99258-1774. **EMAIL** campbell@gonzaga.edu

CAMPBELL, ELIZABETH
DISCIPLINE NOVEL **EDUCATION** Univ Tenn, BA, 67; Univ Va, MA, 78; PhD, 83. **CAREER** Engl, Oregon St Univ. **RESEARCH** 19th-century Brit lit; George Eliot; Charles Dickens. **SELECTED PUBLICATIONS** Auth, Tess of the d'Urbervilles: Misfortune Is a Woman, Victorian Newsl, 89; Relative Truths: Teaching Middlemarch through Character: MLA approaches to Teaching 'Middlemarch', 90; Of Mothers and Merchants: Female Economics in Christina Rossetti's Goblin Market, Victorian Studies, 90; Minding the Wheel: Representations of Women's Time in Victorian Narrative, Rocky Mountain Rev Lang & Lit, 94; Great Expectations: Dickens and the Language of Fortune, Dickens Studies Annual, 95. **CONTACT ADDRESS** Oregon State Univ, Corvallis, OR 97331-4501. **EMAIL** ecampbell@.orst.edu

CAMPBELL, FELICIA F.
DISCIPLINE ENVIRONMENTAL LITERATURE, AMERICAN AND ENGLISH LITERATURE **EDUCATION** Univ Wis, Madison, BS, 54, MS, 57; USIU, San Diego, PhD, 73. **CAREER** Tchg asst, Univ Wis, Madison, 55-57, 59-61; instr, Wis State Col, 57-59; instr, 62-67, dir compos, 65-69, 94-97, asst prof, 67-73; co-dir, Environ Stud, 73-74, assoc prof, 73-93, prof, Univ Nev, Las Vegas, 94-; ed, Popular Cult Rev, 91-; adv ed, J of Popular Cult, Bowling Green State Univ, 93-. **HONORS AND AWARDS** Phi Lambda Alpha, 85; Morris Tchg Awd, 92. **MEMBERSHIPS** Pres, Nat Soc Prof, Univ Nev, Las Vegas, 74-75, 76; ch, Nev Governor's Comn on the Status of People, 75-77; exec dir, Far West Popular Cult Asn and Far West Am Cult Asn, 89-; pres, Popular Cult Asn, 93-95. **SELECTED PUBLICATIONS** Auth, Silver Screen, Shadow Play: The Tradition of the Wayang Kulit in The Year Of Living Dangerously, J of Popular Cult 28, No 1, 94; Frank Waters and Frank Bergon "Parallel Environmental Concerns", Stud in Frank Waters-X VI, 94; Nothing So Strange: The Atomic Scientist in Hilton and Waters, Stud in Frank Waters - XVII, 95; The Spell of the Sensuous in Frank Waters, Stud in Frank Waters - IX, 96. **CONTACT ADDRESS** Dept of Eng, Univ of Nevada, Las Vegas, 4505 Maryland Pky, PO Box 455011, Las Vegas, NV 89154-5011. **EMAIL** raksha@nevada.edu

CAMPBELL, J. LEE
PERSONAL Born 05/08/1960, Peoria, IL, m, 1994, 4 children **DISCIPLINE** COMPOSITION, PROFESSIONAL WRITING, AND LINGUISTICS **EDUCATION** Ill State Univ, BA, 81, MA, 83; Purdue Univ, PhD, 90. **CAREER** Asst prof Eng, 95-, adv, Eng to speakers of other lang endorsement, 95-, web site mgr, dept Eng, 97-, ed, fac Handbk, Valdosta State Univ, 95-; asst prof Eng, Henderson State Univ, 92-95; Asst prof Eng, Marquette U niv, 90-92. **MEMBERSHIPS** Nat Coun of Tchr of Eng; Conf on Col Compos and Commun; Mod Lang Asn; S Atlantic Mod Lang Asn; Soc for Tech Commun; Southeastern Conf on Ling; Rhet Soc of Am; Phi Kappa Phi. **RESEARCH** Applied linguistic theory; argumentation and rhetorical theory. **SELECTED PUBLICATIONS** Auth, 'It is as if a green bough were laid across the page': Thoreau on Eloquence, in Rhet Soc Quart, 90; An Applied Relevance Theory of the Making and Understanding of Rhetorical Arguments, in Lang and Commun, 92; Argument,in Encycl of Eng Stud and Lang Arts, 95. **CONTACT ADDRESS** Dept of Eng, Valdosta State Univ, 1500 N. Patterson St, Valdosta, GA 31698. **EMAIL** jlcampbe@valdosta.edu

CAMPBELL, JACKSON JUSTICE
PERSONAL Born 01/09/1920, Nowata, OK **DISCIPLINE** ENGLISH **EDUCATION** Yale Univ, AB, 41; Univ Pa, AM, 46; Yale Univ, PhD, 50. **CAREER** Asst instr, Univ Pa, 45-46;

from asst instr to instr, Yale Univ, 46-51; asst prof English, Univ Ill, 51-54; from asst prof to assoc prof, 54-64, Annan preceptor, Princeton Univ, 56-57; Prof English, Univ Ill, Urbana, 64- **MEMBERSHIPS** MLA; Mediaeval Acad Am; Early English Text Soc. **RESEARCH** Old English literature and language; Chaucer. **SELECTED PUBLICATIONS** Auth, The English Alliterative Tradition, Manuscripta, Vol 0036, 92. **CONTACT ADDRESS** Dept of English, Univ of Illinois, Urbana-Champaign, Urbana, IL 61801.

CAMPBELL, JANE
PERSONAL Born 06/04/1934, Parry Sound, ON, Canada, m, 1965 **DISCIPLINE** ENGLISH **EDUCATION** Queen's, BA, 56; Oxford, Mlitt,59; Toronto, PhD, 65. **CAREER** From lectr to asst prof, 61-68, Prof English to Prof Emer, Wilfrid Laurier Univ, 69-. **HONORS AND AWARDS** Can Coun res grant, 70-71; WLU Outstanding Tchr Awd, 86. **MEMBERSHIPS** Asn Can Univ Teachers English. **SELECTED PUBLICATIONS** Auth, Confecting Sugar: Narrative Theory and Practice in Antonia Byatt's Short Fiction; Everything: Gendered Transgression of Genre Boundaries in Sarah Ferguson's Autobiographies; Reaching Outwards: Versions of Reality in The Middle Ground; Both a Joke and a Victory: Humor as Narrative Strategy in Margaret Drabble's Fiction; The Hunger of the Imagination in A.S. Byatt's The Game. **CONTACT ADDRESS** Dept of English, Wilfrid Laurier Univ, 75 University Ave W, Waterloo, ON, Canada N2L 3C5.

CAMPBELL, SUEELLEN
DISCIPLINE ENGLISH LITERATURE **EDUCATION** Rice Univ, BA, Univ Va, MA, PhD. **CAREER** Prof, Colo State Univ. **SELECTED PUBLICATIONS** Auth, pubs on British Modernism; American environmental literature. **CONTACT ADDRESS** Dept of English, Colorado State Univ, Fort Collins, CO 80523-1773. **EMAIL** sueellen.campbell@colostate.edu

CAMPION, DANIEL R.
PERSONAL Born 08/23/1949, Oak Park, IL **DISCIPLINE** ENGLISH **EDUCATION** Univ Chicago, AB, 70; Univ Ill, MA, 75; Univ Iowa, PhD, 89. **CAREER** Indexer, Library Res Inc., 71-72; prod ed, Encycl Britannica, 72-74; TA, Univ of Ill, 74-76; ed asst, Follett Publ Co, 77-78; TA and res asst, Univ of Iowa, 78-84; test specialist, ACT, 94-. **HONORS AND AWARDS** Ill Arts Coun Lit Awd. **MEMBERSHIPS** Authors Guild, MLA, MWMLA, Soc for the Study of Midwestern Lit, Modern Poetry Assoc, Acad of Am Poets, NCTE. **RESEARCH** Contemporary poetry in English, the teaching of and assessment of achievement in English language arts, literary modernism, satire. **SELECTED PUBLICATIONS** Coed, Walt Whitman: The Measure of His Song, Holy Cow! Pr, 81; auth, "Eye of Glass, Eye of Truth: Surrealism in El Senor Presidente," Hispanic Jour, (81); auth, Peter De Vries and Surrealism, Bucknell Univ Pr, 95; auth, "Poetry Lost: When Periodicals Cast Out Verse," Writer's Chronicle, (01); auth, 'Peter De Vries," Dict of Midwestern Lit, (01). **CONTACT ADDRESS** ACT, 1700 E Rochester Ave, Iowa City, IA 52245. **EMAIL** campion@act.org

CAMURATI, MIREYA BEATRIZ
PERSONAL Born 08/17/1934, Buenos Aires **DISCIPLINE** SPANISH AMERICAN LITERATURE **EDUCATION** Univ Buenos Aires, Prof en Letras, 59; Univ Pittsburgh, PhD(Span Am lit), 70. **CAREER** Instr Span lang & lit, Univ Buenos Aires, 59-65, asst prof Span Am lit, 65-68; asst prof Span, IN Univ Northwest, 70-73; asst prof, 73-75, assoc prof Span Am lit, 75-80, Prof Spain AM Lit, State Univ NY Buffalo, 80-, prof Span Am lit, Univ Salvador, 64-68. **MEMBERSHIPS** MLA; Am Asn Teachers Span & Port; Inst Int Lit Iberoam; Int Asn Hispanists. **RESEARCH** Spanish American avant garde poetry; Spanish American modernismo; contemporary Spanish American novel. **SELECTED PUBLICATIONS** Auth, Funcion literaria del cuento intercalado en D Segundo Sombra, La voraegine y Cantaclaro, Rev Iberoam, 4-6/71; Blest Gana, Lukacs, y la novela historical Cuadernos Americanos, 11-12/74; Un capitulo de versificacion modernista: El poema de clausulas ritmicas, Bull Hispanique, 9-12/74; Una ojeada a la poesia concreta en Hispanoamerica: Dos precursores, y escasos epigonos, Cuadernos Hispanoamericanos, 2/76; La fabula en Hispanoamerica, Universidad Nacional Autonoma de Mexico, 78; Bifurcacion, multiplicacion, ficcion, Hispanofila, 1/79; Poesia y poetica de Vincente Huidobro, Fernando Garcia Cambeiro, Buenos Aires, 80; Enfoques, D C Heath, 80; Bioy Casares y el alegre trabajo de la inteligencia, Buenos Aires: Corregidor, 90. **CONTACT ADDRESS** Dept of Mod Lang & Lit, SUNY, Buffalo, P O Box 604620, Buffalo, NY 14260-4620.

CAMUS, RAOUL F.
PERSONAL Born 12/05/1930, Buffalo, NY, m, 1963, 3 children **DISCIPLINE** MUSIC **EDUCATION** Queens Col, CUNY, BA, 52; Columbia Univ, MA, 56; New York Univ, PhD, 69. **CAREER** Teacher of orchestral music, Newtown High School, 59-62; teacher of orchestral music, Queens Village Jr High School, 62-65; dir of bands, Martin Van Buren High School, 65-70; Adjunct Lectr, 69-70, Asst Prof, 70-75, Assoc Prof, 75-79, Prof, 79-95, Dept Chair, 83-86, Prof Emeritus, Queensborough Community Col, CUNY, 95-. **HONORS AND AWARDS** Queens Coun on the Arts Certificate of Appreciation, 75; PSC-CUNY Res award, 79-80, 80-81, & 86; Nat Endowment for the Humanities Fel, 79-80 & 82-83; Queens Col Choral Soc Silver Jubilee Awd, 84; Distinguished Service Awd, The Sonneck Soc for Am Music, 94; Fulbright Vis Prof, 95. **MEMBERSHIPS** Am Musicological Soc; Asn of Concert Bands; Col Band Dir Nat Asn; Int Military Music Soc; Int Soc for the Promotion and Investigation of Band Music; The Sonneck Soc; World Asn of Symphonic Bands and Ensembles. **RESEARCH** American music; wind bands; military music. **SELECTED PUBLICATIONS** Auth, American Wind and Percussion Music Vol 12: Three Centuries of American Music, G.K. Hall & Co, 92; Military Music of the American Revolution, Univ of NC Press, 76, Integrity Press, 93; Military Music in the United States Army Prior to 1834, Univ Microfilms, 69; Military Music and the Roots of the American Band Movement, New England Music: The Public Sphere 1600-1900, Boston Univ, 98; The American School Band Movement, Kongressbericht Mainz 1996, Alta Musica, Hans Schneider, 98; Some New Tools in Early American Band Research, Kongressbericht Abony/Ungarn 1994 Alta Musica, Hans Schneider, 96; Early American Wind and Cermemonial Music 1636-1836: Phase 2 of the National Tune Index, Notes, 96; The Early American Wind Band: Hautboys, Harmonies, and Janissaries, The Wind Ensemble and its Repertoire, Univ of Rochester Press, 94; Some Nineteenth-Century Band Journals, Festschrift zum 60. Geburtstag von Wolfgang Suppan, Hans Schneider, 93. **CONTACT ADDRESS** Dept of Music, Queensborough Comm Col, CUNY, Bayside, NY 11364. **EMAIL** rfcamus@rcn.com

CANADA, MARK A.
PERSONAL Born 08/21/1967, Indianapolis, IN, m, 1989, 2 children **DISCIPLINE** ENGLISH **EDUCATION** Ind Univ, BA, 89; Univ NCar Chapel Hill, MA, 94; PhD, 97. **CAREER** Asst prof, Univ NCar Pembroke, 97-. **HONORS AND AWARDS** Outstanding Teacher Award, UNCP. **MEMBERSHIPS** Phi Beta Kappa, Poe Studies Asn. **RESEARCH** Edgar Allan Poe, Banjamin Franklin, literature and journalism. **SELECTED PUBLICATIONS** Auth, "The Right Brain in Poe's Creative Process," Southern Quart, (98); auth, Vardis Fisher: An Essay in bibliography, Univ of Idaho Pr, 00; auth, "Flight in Fancy: Poe's Discovery of the Right Brain," Southern Lit Jour, (01). **CONTACT ADDRESS** English, Theatre and Lang., Univ of No Carolina, Pembroke, Pembroke, NC 28372-1510. **EMAIL** mark.canada@uncp.edu

CANARY, ROBERT HUGHES
PERSONAL Born 02/01/1939, Providence, RI, m, 1961, 2 children **DISCIPLINE** ENGLISH **EDUCATION** Denison Univ, BA, 60; Univ Chicago, MA, 62; PhD, 63. **CAREER** Asst prof English, San Diego Col, 63-66 & Grinnell Col, 66-68; assoc prof, Univ Hawaii, 68-70; assoc prof, 70-74, chmn, Div Humanities, 76-79, prof English, Univ Wis-Parkside, 74-, Chmn Div Humanities, 83-86, assoc ed, Catch Soc Am, 69-71; co-ed, Clio, J Lit Hist & Philos of Hist, 71-; assoc vice chanc 87-92; sec of fac, 93-98. **RESEARCH** American literature and popular culture; critical theory as applied to historiography; modern literature. **SELECTED PUBLICATIONS** The Cabell Scene, Revisionist, 77; co-ed, The Writing of History, Univ Wis, 78; auth, Robert Graves, Twayne, 80; auth, T.S. Eliot: The Poet and the Critics, Am Libr Asn Press, 82. **CONTACT ADDRESS** English Dept, Univ of Wisconsin, Parkside, Box 2000, Kenosha, WI 53141-2000. **EMAIL** canary@uwp.edu

CANCEL, ROBERT
PERSONAL Born 07/16/1950, Brooklyn, NY, m, 1973, 2 children **DISCIPLINE** AFRICAN LITERATURE **EDUCATION** State Univ NYork New Paltz, BS, 72; Univ Wis-Madison, MA, 77, PhD(African lang & lit), 81. **CAREER** Ed films, African Media Ctr, Mich State Univ, 78-80; Asst Prof African & Comp Lit, Dept Lit, Univ Calif, San Diego, 80- **MEMBERSHIPS** African Lit Asn; MLA. **RESEARCH** African oral narrative traditions, especially from the Tabwa people of Zambia; oral narrative traditions from the New World (Caribbean and the Americas); African and Caribbean written literatures in English, Spanish and Bantu languages **SELECTED PUBLICATIONS** **CONTACT ADDRESS** Dept of Lit D-007, Univ of California, San Diego, San Diego, La Jolla, CA 92039.

CANDIDO, JOSEPH D.
PERSONAL Born 05/05/1945, New Haven, CT, m, 1977, 2 children **DISCIPLINE** ENGLISH LITERATURE **EDUCATION** Colby Col, AB, 67; Univ of NH, MA, 72; Ind Univ, PhD, 77. **CAREER** Prof, Univ of Ark, 79-. **HONORS AND AWARDS** Huntington Libr Fel, 81; Master Teacher Awd, Univ of Ark, 89. **MEMBERSHIPS** Shakespeare Asn of Am; Int Shakespeare Asn; Malone Soc. **RESEARCH** Shakespeare, Drama. **SELECTED PUBLICATIONS** Auth, "Dining Out in Ephesus: Food in The Comedy of Errors," SEL, 90; auth, "Women and fooles break off your conference: Pope's Degradations and the Form of King John, Shakespeare's Histories," 95; auth, "Henry V: An Annotated Bibliography, Garland," 83; auth, "King John: the Critical Tradition," Athlone, 96; auth, Richard II, Henry IV, 1&2, and Henry V: An Annotated Bibliography of Shakespeare Studies, Pegasus, 99; auth, "Prefatory Matter(s) in the Shakespeare Editions of Nicholas Rowe and Alexander Pope," SP 97 (00): 210-218. **CONTACT ADDRESS** Dept English, Univ of Arkansas, Fayetteville, Fayetteville, AR 72701-1201. **EMAIL** candido@comp.uark.edu

CANFIELD, J. DOUGLAS
PERSONAL Born 02/04/1941, Washington, DC, m, 1963, 3 children **DISCIPLINE** ENGLISH & AMERICAN LITERATURE **EDUCATION** Univ Notre Dame, AB, 63; Yale Univ, MA, 64; Johns Hopkins Univ, MA, 66; Univ Fla, PhD, 69. **CAREER** Asst prof, UCLA, 69-74; assoc prof to regents prof, Univ Ariz, 74- **HONORS AND AWARDS** NEH Fel, 01-02; CASE, 93; Ariz Prof of the Year, Leicester and Kathryn Sherrill Creative Teaching Awd, Univ Ariz, 93; Fac Achievement Awd, Burlington Resources Found, 91; Five-Star Fac Awd, Univ Ariz, 84; Clark Libr Mellon Fel, 77; Folger Shakespeare Libr Fel, 76; NEH Fel, 75; Phi Beta Kappa. **MEMBERSHIPS** MLA; Am Soc for Eighteenth-Century Studies; Group for Early Mod Cultural Studies; Cormac McCarthy Soc. **RESEARCH** Restoration and early 18th Century English literature; Comparative baroque literature; Literature and culture of the American Southwest Borderlands; Faulkner. **SELECTED PUBLICATIONS** Co-ed, Cultural Readings of Restoration and Eighteenth-Century English Theater, Univ Ga Press, 95; auth, "The Classic Treatment of Don Juan in Tirso, Moliere, and Mozart: What Cultural Work Does it Perform?" Drama and Opera of the Enlightenment, (97): 42-64; auth, Tricksters and Estates: On the Ideology of Restoration Comedy, Univ Press Ky, 97; auth, Heroes and States : On the Ideology of Restoration Tragedy, Univ Press, Ky, 00; auth, Mavericks on the Border: The Early Southwest in Historical Fiction and Film, Univ Press Ky, 01; ed, The Broadview Anthology of Restoration and Early Eighteenth-Century English Drama, Broadview, 01. **CONTACT ADDRESS** Dept English, Univ of Arizona, 445 Modern Lang Bldg, PO Box 210067, Tucson, AZ 85721. **EMAIL** jdcanfie@u.arizona.edu

CANNON, GARLAND
PERSONAL Born 12/05/1924, Fort Worth, TX, m, 1947, 4 children **DISCIPLINE** ENGLISH **EDUCATION** Univ of Tex, BA, 47, PhD, 54; Stanford Univ, MA, 52 **CAREER** Instr, Univ of Hawaii, Honolulu, 49-52; instr, Univ of Tex, Austin, 52-54; instr, Univ of Mich, Ann Arbor, 54-55; asst prof, Univ of Calif, Berkeley, 55-56; acad dir, Am Univ Language Center, 56-57; asst prof, Univ of Fla, 57-58; visiting prof, Univ of PR, 58-59; asst prof, Columbia Univ, 59-62; dir, English language prog, Columbia Univ, 60-62; assoc prof, Northeastern Ill Univ, 62-63; assoc prof, Queens Col, CUNY, 63-66; ASSOC PROF, 66-68, PROF, 68-, TEXAS A&M UNIV; visiting prof, Univ of Mich, 70-71; visiting prof, Kuwait Univ, 79-81; visiting prof, Inst Teknologi Mara, 87; summer prof, Cambridge Univ, 80, Oxford Univ, 74, MIT, 69, Univ of Washington, 67. **HONORS AND AWARDS** Distinguished Achievement Awd, Tex A&M Univ, 72; Indian Govt Grantee, 84; Am Philos Asn grantee, 64, 66, & 74; Linguistic Soc of Am/Am Council Learned Socs grantee, 84. **MEMBERSHIPS** MLA; Am Dialect Soc; Dictionary Soc of North Am; South Asian Lit Asn. **SELECTED PUBLICATIONS** Auth, Sir William Jones, Orientalist: A Bibliography, 52; coauth, German Loanwords in English, 94; auth, Oriental Jones: The Life and Mind of Sir William Jones, 90; auth, Japanese Loanwords in English, 96; auth, Historical Change and English Word-Formation, 87; coauth, Arabic Loanwords in English, 94; ed, The Letters of Sir William Jones, 70; auth, Objects of Enquiry: The Life and Influences of Sire William Jones, 95. **CONTACT ADDRESS** Dept of English, Texas A&M Univ, Col Station, College Station, TX 77843. **EMAIL** g-cannon3@tamu.edu

CANNON, KEITH
DISCIPLINE COMMUNICATIONS **EDUCATION** Clemson Univ, BA; Univ Fla, MAJC; Tex A&M Univ, PhD. **CAREER** Assoc prof. **SELECTED PUBLICATIONS** Auth and ed, USA Today; Houston Chronicle. **CONTACT ADDRESS** Commun Dept, Wingate Univ, Campus Box 3059, Wingate, NC 28174. **EMAIL** kcannon@wingate.edu.

CANTOR, PAUL ARTHUR
PERSONAL Born 10/25/1945, Brooklyn, NY **DISCIPLINE** ENGLISH **EDUCATION** Harvard Univ, AB, 66, PhD(English), 71. **CAREER** Asst prof English, Harvard Univ, 71-77; assoc prof English, 77-85, prof English, Univ VA, 85-. **MEMBERSHIPS** ALSC; APSA; NAS. **RESEARCH** Renaissance literature, romantic literature. **SELECTED PUBLICATIONS** Auth, Shakespeare's Rome: Republic and Empire, Cornell Univ, 76; A Distorting Mirror: Shelley's The Cenci and Shakespearean Tragedy, In: Shakespeare: Aspects of Influence, Harvard Univ, 76; Shakespeare's The Tempest: The Wise Man as Hero, Shakespeare Quart, 80; Byron's Cain: A Romantic Version of the Fall, Kenyon Rev, 80; Prospero's Republic: The Politics of Shakespeare's The Tempest, In: Shakespeare as Political Thinker, Univ Dallas, 81; Friedrich Nietzsche: The Use and Abuse of Metaphor, In: Metaphor: Problems and Perspectives, Harvester Press, 82; Creature and Creator: Myth-making and English Romanticism, Cambridge Univ, 84; Shakespeare: Hamlet, Cambridge Univ, 89. **CONTACT ADDRESS** Dept English, Univ of Virginia, 219 Bryan Hall, Charlottesville, VA 22903. **EMAIL** pac2j@virginia.edu

CANTRELL, CAROL
DISCIPLINE ENGLISH LITERATURE **EDUCATION** Valparaiso Univ, BA; Northwestern Univ, PhD. **CAREER** Prof. **SELECTED PUBLICATIONS** Auth, pubs on Pound; femi-

nist theory. **CONTACT ADDRESS** Dept of English, Colorado State Univ, Fort Collins, CO 80523. **EMAIL** ccantrell@vines.colostate.edu

CANTRILL, JAMES G.
PERSONAL Born 11/06/1955, Seattle, WA, m, 1984 **DISCIPLINE** COMMUNICATION **EDUCATION** West Wash Univ, BA, 77; Humboldt State Univ, MA, 79; Univ of Ill, Urbana, PhD, 85. **CAREER** Iolani Sch, Hawaii, Fac member, Eng dept, 79-80; Parkland Community Col, Adjunct Fac, Champaign, Ill, 85; Univ of Ill-Urbana, visiting lecturer, Dir of Debate, 80-85; Emerson Col, Asst Prof, 85-86; Carroll Col, Gifted Stud Inst, Instructor, 85-86, Asst prof, 86-90; N Mich Univ, Outcomes Assessment Coord, 94-98; N Mich Univ, Prof, Commun & Perf Studs, 90-99. **HONORS AND AWARDS** Service Awd, Carrol Col, 90; Adv of the Month Awd, N Mich Univ, 91; Outstanding Fac Awd, N Mich Univ, 92; Fac Merit Awd, N Mich Univ, 91, 92, 93; nat recognition, intercol debate, 84, 85; nat discussion contest, 84, 85. **MEMBERSHIPS** Nat Commun Assoc; Soc of Environ Journalists. **RESEARCH** Environ commun; relational commun. **SELECTED PUBLICATIONS** Co-auth, Communication and Interpersonal Influence, Handbook of Interpersonal Communication, Sage, 94; Co-ed, The Conference on Communication and Our Environment, N Mich Univ Printing Svcs, 93; co-auth, co-ed, The Symbolic Earth: Discourse and Our Creation of the Environment, Univ Press of Ky, 96; co-auth, Gold, Yellowstone, and the Search for a Rhetorical Identity, Green Culture: Rhetorical Analyses of Environmental Discourse, Univ of Wisc Press, 96; co-auth, Environmental Perception and the Beartooth Alliance: Socioeconomic Struggles at the Grassroots, Proceedings of the 1995 Conference on Communication and Our Environment, Univ of Tenn Press, 97; co-auth, Cognition and Romantic Relationships, Sage, (in press). **CONTACT ADDRESS** Commun & Perf Studs, No Michigan Univ, 1401 Presque Isle Av, Marquette, MI 49855. **EMAIL** jcantril@nmu.edu

CAPE, ROBERT W., JR.
DISCIPLINE CLASSICS **EDUCATION** Uniz Ariz, BA, 83, MA, 85; UCLA, MA, 88, PhD, 91. **CAREER** Vis asst prof, Skidmore Col, 91-94; asst prof, Austin Col, 94-98; assoc prof, Austin Col, 98-. **HONORS AND AWARDS** Dir of Gender Studies, Austin Col, 95-. **MEMBERSHIPS** Am Philol Assoc; Nat Commun Assoc; Am Class League; Int Soc for the Hist of Rhet; Class Assoc of the Mid W & S. **RESEARCH** Cicero; ancient rhetoric; Roman literatukre & society; women in antiquity. **SELECTED PUBLICATIONS** Auth, The Rhetoric of Politics in Cicero's Fourth Catilinarian, Am J of Philol, 116.2, 155-177, 95; auth, Persuasive History: Roman Rhetoric and Historiography, Roman Eloquence: Rhetoric in Society and Literature, Routledge, 212-228, 97; auth, Roman Women in the History of Rhetoric and Oratory, Listening to Their Voices: The Rhetorical Activities of Historical Women, Univ SC Press, 112-132, 97. **CONTACT ADDRESS** Dept of Class & Mod Lang, Austin Col, Ste 61653, Sherman, TX 75090-4440. **EMAIL** rcape@austinc.edu

CAPPELLA, JOSEPH N.
PERSONAL Born 03/12/1947, Auburn, NY, m, 1947, 2 children **DISCIPLINE** COMMUNICATION **EDUCATION** LeMoyne Col, BS, 69; Mich State Univ, MS, PhD, 74. **CAREER** Univ of Wis, 74-90; Univ of Pa, 90-. **HONORS AND AWARDS** Fel, Int Commun Asn. **MEMBERSHIPS** Int Commun Asn; Soc for Experimental Social Psychology; Am Psychol Soc; Soc for Res in Child Development. **RESEARCH** Polit Commun; Persuasion and Attitudes; Nonverbal Commun. **SELECTED PUBLICATIONS** Auth, Multivariate Techniques in Human Communication Research, 80; Sequence and Pattern in Communcative Behavior, 85; Spiral of Cynicism, 97. **CONTACT ADDRESS** Annenberg School of Communication, Univ of Pennsylvania, 3620 Walnut St, Philadelphia, PA 19104-6220. **EMAIL** jcappella@POBox.Asc.Upenn.edu

CAPPS, JACK L.
PERSONAL Born 07/16/1926, Liberty, MO, m, 1953, 2 children **DISCIPLINE** ENGLISH **EDUCATION** US Mil Acad, BS, 48; Univ Pa, MA, 50, PhD, 63. **CAREER** From instr to assoc prof, 59-67, Prof English & Head Dept, US Mil Acad, 67-88, Chm adv bd, Concordance of Works William Faulkner 70-92; vis prof Am lit, Am Univ Beirut, 71-72; gen ed, Faulkner Concordance Series, 35 v, Univ Microfilms Int, 77-90; vis prof, Royal Mil Acad, Sandhurst, 80-81. **HONORS AND AWARDS** Educational Awd, John Brown Mem Asn, 77; Legion of Merit, 82; Brig Gen USA-ret, 88; Distinguished Service Medal, 88. **MEMBERSHIPS** AAUP; NCTE; MLA; Col Conf Compos & Commun. **RESEARCH** Nineteenth and 20th century American literature. **SELECTED PUBLICATIONS** Co-ed, Advanced Freshman English at West Point, Col Compos & Commun J, 5/63; auth, Emily Dickinson's Reading 1836-1886, Harvard, 66; co-ed, Benet's John Brown's Body, Holt, 68; Modern Education and the Military Academy, J Haile Selassie I Mil Acad, Ethiopia, 72; auth, Auxiliary Faulkner: Six New Volumes 1976-1977, Southern Lit J, fall 77; auth, Military Tradition, in, The Companion to Southern Literature, LSU, 00. **CONTACT ADDRESS** 210 Broadway, Hanover, PA 17331-2501.

CAPPS, RANDALL
PERSONAL Born 10/23/1936, Peytonsburg, KY, m, 1961, 2 children **DISCIPLINE** SPEECH **EDUCATION** KY Wesleyan Col, BA, 57; Western KY Univ, MA, 61; Univ VA, EdD, 70. **CAREER** From Instr to Asst Prof English & Speech, 62-68, Assoc Prof, 68-73, Prof Commun, Western KY Univ, 73-79, 82-87, 94, Asst to the Pres, 79-82, Dept Head Commun & Broadcasting, 87-94, Actg Head Dept, 68-70, Head Dept Commun & Theatre, 70-79; adjunct prof. **HONORS AND AWARDS** Univ Awd Res, 78. **MEMBERSHIPS** Int Commun Asn; Comn Am Parliamentary Procedure; Nat Commun Asn; pres, leadership stategies, 94-00. **RESEARCH** Public address; organizational communication; forensics. **SELECTED PUBLICATIONS** Auth, A History of Speech Education in Kentucky, Ky Asn Commun Arts, 72; The Rowan Story, Homestead, 76; Communication and Leadership, Sigma Nu Educ Found, 76; coauth, Speaking Out: Two Centuries of Kentucky Oratory, Hunter, 77; Fundamentals of Effective Speech Communication, Winthrop, 78; coauth, Communication for the Business and Professional Speaker, Macmillan, 81. **CONTACT ADDRESS** Dept of Commun, Western Kentucky Univ, P O Box 1529, Bowling Green, KY 42102.

CAPPUCCI, PAUL R.
PERSONAL Born 04/14/1968, New Haven, CT, m, 1993, 1 child **DISCIPLINE** ENGLISH **EDUCATION** King's Col, BA, 90; Col NJers, MA, 93; Drew Univ, MPhil, PhD, 98. **CAREER** Adj prof, Fairleigh Dickinson Univ, Drew Univ, Kean Univ, 94-99; asst prof, Col NJers, 99-00; asst prof, Georgian Ct Col, 00-. **MEMBERSHIPS** MLA; NMLA; PSA; WCWS. **RESEARCH** 19th-century and 20th-century American literature; American poetry; Civil war literature. **SELECTED PUBLICATIONS** Auth, "Wallace Stevens' 'God is Good. It is a Beautiful Night,'" Explication 55 (96): 33-34; auth, "Depicting the Oblique: Emily Dickinson's Poetic Response to the Civil War," Lit Arts 10 (98): 260-273; auth, "Negotiating the 1930's: William Carlos Williams's Struggle With Politics and Art on His Way to Paterson," J Image (99): 3-21. **CONTACT ADDRESS** 196 White Rd, Jackson, NJ 08527-5013. **EMAIL** cappuccip@georgian.edu

CAPTAIN, YVONNE
PERSONAL 1 child **DISCIPLINE** SPANISH LITERATURE & FILM **EDUCATION** Pitzer Col, BA, 73, Stanford Univ, PhD, 84. **CAREER** Asst prof to assoc prof, George Washington Univ, 84- ; pres, Phi Beta Delta Honors Soc, 97-99. **HONORS AND AWARDS** Dorothy Danforth-Compton Dissertation Fel, 83; Fel, Sch of Criticism & Theory, 86; Post-Doctoral Fel, 87; Phi Beta Delta Recognition Awd, 98. **MEMBERSHIPS** Phi Beta Delta Honors Soc for Int Scholars; Soc for Values in Higher Educ. **SELECTED PUBLICATIONS** Auth, The Culture of Fiction in the Works of Manuel Zapata Olivella, Univ of Mo Press, 93; El espiritu de la risa en el cuento de Ana Lydia Vega, Revista Iberoamericana, 93; Writing for the Future: Afro-Hispanicm in a Global, Critical Contest, Afro-Hispanic Rev, 94; The Poetics of the Quotidian in the Works of Nancy Morejon, in Singular Like a Bird, Howard Univ Press, 99; Manuel Zapata Olivella, in Encarta Africana, 99. **CONTACT ADDRESS** Dept of Romance Lang & Lit, The George Washington Univ, Washington, DC 20052. **EMAIL** ycaptain@gwu.edu

CAPUTI, ANTHONY FRANCIS
PERSONAL Born 12/22/1924, Buffalo, NY, m, 1948, 4 children **DISCIPLINE** ENGLISH **EDUCATION** Univ Buffalo, BA, 49, MA, 51; Cornell Univ, PhD, 56. **CAREER** Asst prof, 50-51, Univ Buffalo; from instr to assoc prof, 53-73, prof, 67-73, Cornell Univ; Fulbright res fel, 64-65; Guggenheim fel, 64-65; fel, Villa I Tatti, 64-65; NEH fel, 71-72. **RESEARCH** English Renaissance literature; British and American drama; modern British and American literature. **SELECTED PUBLICATIONS** Auth, John Marston, Satirist, Cornell Univ, 61; auth, The Shallows Of Modern Serious Drama, Mod Drama, 61; art, Scenic Design in Measure for Measure, J English & Ger Philol, 61; art, Anthony and Cleopatra: Tragedy Without Terror, Shakespeare Quart, 65; auth, Norton Anthology of Modern Drama, Norton, 66; auth, Masterworks of World Drama (6 vols), Heath, 68; auth, Loving Evie, Harper, 74; auth, Buffo, The Genius of Vulgar Comedy, Wayne St, 78; auth, Storms and Son, Atheneum, 85; auth, Pirandello and the Crisis of Modern Consciousness, Univ of Ill, 88; auth, Eight Modern Plays, Morton, 91. **CONTACT ADDRESS** Dept of English, Cornell Univ, Ithaca, NY 14850. **EMAIL** Afc3@Cornell.edu

CAPWELL, CHARLES
DISCIPLINE MUSIC **EDUCATION** Brown Univ, MA; Harvard Univ, PhD. **CAREER** Assoc prof, 77-, Univ IL Urbana Champaign. **RESEARCH** Music of India; music of Indonesia. **SELECTED PUBLICATIONS** Auth, The Music of the Bauls of Bengal; pubs on contemp and hist aspects of the music of India. **CONTACT ADDRESS** Dept of Music, Univ of Illinois, Urbana-Champaign, E Gregory Dr, PO Box 52, Champaign, IL 61820. **EMAIL** capwell@staff.uiuc.edu

CARAFIOL, PETER
DISCIPLINE AMERICAN LITERATURE AND THEORY **EDUCATION** Amherst Col, BA, 70; Claremont Grad Sch, MA, 72, PhD, 75. **CAREER** Prof, 90-; grad comm. **HONORS AND AWARDS** John Simon Guggenheim Mem Found fel, 94; NEH fel, 87; Sr Fulbright prof, Regensburg, Ger, 82-3. **SELECTED PUBLICATIONS** Auth, The American Ideal: Literary History as a Worldly Activity, Oxford Univ Press, 91; Transcendent Reason, Fa State, 82; ed, The American Renaissance: New Dimensions, 83; publ, articles, Am Lit, Am Lit Hist, Col Eng, ESQ. **CONTACT ADDRESS** Dept of Eng, Portland State Univ, PO Box 751, Portland, OR 97207-0751. **EMAIL** peter@nh1.nh.pdx.edu

CARAMAGNO, THOMAS C.
PERSONAL Born 02/16/1946, Los Angeles, CA, d **DISCIPLINE** ENGLISH **EDUCATION** Loyola Marymount Univ, MA, 70; MA, 75, Univ Calif at Los Angeles, PhD, 83. **CAREER** Asst prof, Univ of HI Manoa, 83-89; assoc prof, Univ of Nebr Lincoln. **HONORS AND AWARDS** Andrew W. Mellon Fel, Harvard Univ, 89-90; Fulbright Grant, Univ of Lisbon, Portugal, 99. **MEMBERSHIPS** Inst for the Psychol Study of the Arts. **RESEARCH** Critical theory, 20th Century literature, queer theory, psychoanalytic theory. **SELECTED PUBLICATIONS** Auth, The Flight of the Mind: Virginia Woolf's Art and Manic-Depressive Illness, Univ of Calif Pr, 92. **CONTACT ADDRESS** Dept English, Univ of Nebraska, Lincoln, PO Box 880333, Lincoln, NE 68588-0333. **EMAIL** hghoser@aol.com

CARAMELLO, CHARLES
PERSONAL Born 02/29/1948, Plymouth, MA, m, 1979, 1 child **DISCIPLINE** ENGLISH **EDUCATION** Wesleyan Univ, BA, 70; Univ Wis, Milwaukee, MA, 73, PhD, 78. **CAREER** Lectr, Univ Sorbonne, 75-76; vis fac, Wesleyan Univ, 82-83; asst prof to Prof English, 78-, dir of grad stud, dept of Eng, 94-98, Chair Eng Dept, 98-. **HONORS AND AWARDS** Res awards, Univ Md, 95, 86, 79; Andrew W. Mellon fel, Nat Humanities Ctr, 84-85; Andrew W. Mellon Postdoctoral fel Hum, Ctr for Human, Wesleyan Univ, 82-83; Frederick J. Hoffman Awd, Univ Wis, 78,72; Winchester Fel, Wesleyan Univ, 70. **MEMBERSHIPS** Am Lit Asn; Autobio Soc; Henry James Soc; Mod Lang Asn, MLA Am Lit Section. **RESEARCH** Modernism and postmodernism; 20th century American literature, autobiography and biography. **SELECTED PUBLICATIONS** Ed, Performance in Postmodern Culture, 77; auth, Silverless Mirrors: Book, Self, and Postmodern American Fiction, 83; auth, Henry James, Gertrude Stein, and the Biographical Act, 96. **CONTACT ADDRESS** Dept of English, Univ of Maryland, Col Park, 3101 Susquehanna Hall, College Park, MD 20742. **EMAIL** cc5@umail.umd.edu

CARBALLO, ROBERT
DISCIPLINE ENGLISH **EDUCATION** Univ Miami, BA, 72; Ma, 73; PhD, 86. **CAREER** Asst Prof to Full Prof, Millersville Univ, 88-. **HONORS AND AWARDS** Named in Who's Who Among Am Educators,00. **MEMBERSHIPS** EAPSU. **RESEARCH** The Victorian Age, Romanticism, Matthew Arnold, John Henry Newman, Drama Latino Studies. **SELECTED PUBLICATIONS** Auth, "Newman and the Rise of Modern Liberalism", Humanitas; auth, "Towards a Non-didactic Poetry of Dogma: Newman's 'Dream of Gerontius'" American Benedictine Review; auth, "Shakespearean Influences in Charles Brockden Brown's Wieland; Auth, "Cuban-American Folklore", Latino Encyclopedia; auth, "Matthew Arnold", Encyclopedia of the Essay; Auth, "Gilbert Keith Chesterton", Encyclopedia of Life Writing; auth, " The Poetry of Nicolas Guillen and the Forging of a National Identity", Review/Revista Interamericana; auth, "Gustavo Perez-Firmat's Next Year in Cuba and the Exile Experience as Formative of the Literary Imagination", Review/Revista Interamericana. **CONTACT ADDRESS** Dept English, Millersville Univ of Pennsylvania, PO Box 1002, Millersville, PA 17551-0302.

CARD, JAMES VAN DYCK
PERSONAL Born 04/14/1931, Montclair, NJ **DISCIPLINE** ENGLISH **EDUCATION** Rutgers Univ, BA, 53; Columbia Univ, MA, 57, PhD(James Joyce), 64. **CAREER** Lectr basic courses, Hunter Col, 61-62; instr, Washington & Jefferson Col, 63-64; vis asst prof 20th century Brit lit, Franklin & Marshall Col, 64-66; asst prof, 66-71, Assoc Prof 20th Century Brit Lit, Old Dominion Col, 71-. **MEMBERSHIPS** MLA; Southern MLA. **RESEARCH** Twentieth century British literature. **SELECTED PUBLICATIONS** Auth, In just proportion: Notes on final scene of Measure for Measure, Topic, spring 64. **CONTACT ADDRESS** Dept of English, Old Dominion Univ, Norfolk, VA 23508.

CARDACI, PAUL F.
DISCIPLINE ENGLISH LITERATURE **EDUCATION** Md Univ, BA, MA, PhD. **CAREER** Prof. **SELECTED PUBLICATIONS** Auth, Toward a Dialogical Method of Teaching, 85; Prose by Richare Lanham, 83; Trakl and Yevtushenki (rev), 80; The Seed of Revolt (rev), 77; His Life and Work (rev), 75; Dostoevsky's Underground as Symbol and Allusion, 74. **CONTACT ADDRESS** English Dept, Georgetown Univ, 37th and O St, Washington, DC 20057.

CARDAMONE, DONNA
PERSONAL Born 11/16/1937, Utica, NY, m, 1978, 1 child **DISCIPLINE** MUSICOLOGY **EDUCATION** Wells Coll, AB, 59; Harvard Univ, MA, 64, PhD, 72. **CAREER** Full Prof, 80-, Univ Minn, 69-; Fullbright Scholar; Am Coun Learned Soc Fel; Am Philos Soc Res Grant. **HONORS AND AWARDS** Am Asn Univ Women Diss Awd **MEMBERSHIPS** Am Musicol Soc; Int Musicol Soc; Renaissance Soc Am; Soc Ital di Musicol. **RESEARCH** 16th century Italian music; Music patronage in early modern Italy; Music printing in 16th century Italy; Women musicians in early modern Italy; Editing early music. **SELECTED PUBLICATIONS** Auth, The Prince of Salerno and the Dynamics of Oral Transmission in Songs of Political Exile, Acta Musicologica, 95; Lifting the Protective Veil of Anonymity: Woman as Composer-Performers, ca. 1300-1566, Women Composers: Music Through the Ages, Prentice Hall Int, 96; Orlando di Lasso and Pro-French Factions in Rome, Jaarboek van de Alamire Found, Antwerp, 96; The Salon as Marketplace in the 1550's: Patrons and Collectors of Orlando di Lasso's Secular Music, Orlando di Lasso Stud, Cambridge Univ Press, 99. **CONTACT ADDRESS** School of Music, Univ of Minnesota, Twin Cities, 2106 Fourth St, S, Ferguson H, Minneapolis, MN 55455. **EMAIL** jacks001@tc.umn.edu

CARDUCCI, ELEANOR
PERSONAL Born 12/05/1942, Mahanoy, PA, m, 1975, 1 child **DISCIPLINE** ENGLISH **EDUCATION** East Stroudsburg State Col, BS; Seton Hall Univ, MA; Rutgers Univ, PhD. **CAREER** Tchr, Dover Public Schools; assoc prof, English Educ, Centenary Col; Assoc Prof of English, Liberal Arts Coord, Sussex County Commun Col. **HONORS AND AWARDS** NJ Teaching and Leadership award; Sears Awd for teaching excellence and leadership; leadership award, Nat Chair Acad; Robert Kobat Awd for teaching excellence. **MEMBERSHIPS** Natl Coun of Tchrs of English; Phi Delta Kappa. **CONTACT ADDRESS** Sussex County Comm Col, College Hill, Newton, NJ 07860. **EMAIL** ecarducc@sussex.cc.nj.us

CARDUCCI, JANE
PERSONAL 2 children **DISCIPLINE** ENGLISH RENAISSANCE LITERATURE **EDUCATION** Colo Col, BA; Univ Nev, MA, PhD. **CAREER** Prof. **RESEARCH** Shakespeare, composition and pedagogy. **SELECTED PUBLICATIONS** Contribu, Lit and Psychology, Lang and Lit, Cahiers Elisabethians. **CONTACT ADDRESS** Winona State Univ, PO Box 5838, Winona, MN 55987-5838.

CAREY, CATHERINE
PERSONAL Born 02/14/1945, Ft Worth, TX, m, 1964, 3 children **DISCIPLINE** ENGLISH LITERATURE **EDUCATION** State Univ NYork, BA, 74; MA, 76; Univ Mass, PhD, 98. **CAREER** Teacher, Fairfax Co Public Schs, 78-95; Teaching Asst, Univ Mass, 91-98; Asst Prof, Univ Incarnate Word, 98-. **HONORS AND AWARDS** Superintendant's Awd; Career Level II Teacher; Nat Endowment for the Humanities Summer Seminar; Walker Gibson Prize. **MEMBERSHIPS** MLA, San Antonio/ Austin Psychoanalytic Soc, Virginia Woolf Soc, Northern Va Writing Proj. **RESEARCH** British female writers, feminist theory, object-relations theory. **SELECTED PUBLICATIONS** Rev, Sara Blachen Cohen: A Biographical Sketch; Rev, Violence to the Self: The Undoing of Precocity; Revs on Robert Coleg, Adrian Schwartz. **CONTACT ADDRESS** Dept Humanities & Fine Arts, Univ of the Incarnate Word, 4301 Broadway St, San Antonio, TX 78209-6318. **EMAIL** carey@universe.uiwtx.edu

CAREY-WEBB, ALLEN
DISCIPLINE ENGLISH **EDUCATION** Swathmore Col, BA, 79; Lewis and Clark Col, MA, 81; Univ Ore, MA, 88; PhD, 92. **CAREER** Tchr, West Linn High Sch, 80-86; Grad Tchg Asst, Univ Ore, 86-91; assoc prof, West Mich Univ, 92- . **HONORS AND AWARDS** Fac Res Grant, WMU, 93, 97; Hum Ctr Res Fel; Univ Ore Grad Student Res Awds, 89, 90. **MEMBERSHIPS** Asn Tchr Educators; MLA; Nat Coun Tch Engl; Mich Coun Tch Eng; Soc Crit Exchange. **SELECTED PUBLICATIONS** Auth, Teaching and Testimony: Rigoberta Mench and the North American Classroom, SUNY Press, 96. **CONTACT ADDRESS** Dept of Engl, Western Michigan Univ, Kalamazoo, MI 49008. **EMAIL** careywebb@wmich.edu

CARGILE, AARON C.
DISCIPLINE COMMUNICATION **EDUCATION** Univ Calif SB, PhD 96. **CAREER** Calif State Univ LB, asst prof, 96-. **MEMBERSHIPS** NCA; ICA. **RESEARCH** Intercultural/ Intergroup Communication **SELECTED PUBLICATIONS** Auth, Language Matters, in: L. Samovar, R. Porter, eds, Intercultural Comm: A Reader, Belmont CA; Wadsworth, in press; Language and Modes of Friendship: Verbal descriptions by Native Japanese, Howard Jour of Comm, in press; Language attitudes toward varieties of English: An Amer-Japanese context, coauth, Jour of Applied Comm Research, 98; rev, English with an Accent: Language ideology and discrimination in the US, Jour of Lang and Social Psychol, 98; Attitudes Toward Chinese-accented speech: An investigation in two contexts, Jour of Lang and Social Psychol, 97; auth, Understanding Language attitudes: Exploring listener affect and identity, coauth, Lang and Comm, 97; auth, Intercultural communication training: Review critique and a new theoretical framework, B. Burleson, ed, Comm Yearbook, Thousand Oaks CA, Sage, 96. **CONTACT ADDRESS** Dept of Communication Studies, California State Univ, Long Beach, 1250 N Bellflower Blvd, Long Beach, CA 90840-0006. **EMAIL** acargile@csulb.edu

CARINO, PETER A.
PERSONAL Born 11/16/1948, Paterson, NJ, m, 1992 **DISCIPLINE** ENGLISH **EDUCATION** William Patterson Col, BA, 77; Southern Ill Univ, MA, 79; Univ Ill, PhD, 84. **CAREER** From instr to prof, Ind State Univ, 83-; vis prof, Univ of Pisa, Spring 97. **HONORS AND AWARDS** Educ Excellence Awd, Ind State Univ, 93; East Central Writing Ctr Awd, 95; Nat Writing Ctr Asn Scholar Awd for Outstanding Serv, 95; Nat Writing Ctr Asn Scholar Awd for Best Article of 1997, 97. **MEMBERSHIPS** Nat Coun of Teachers of English, Nat Writing Ctr Asn, E Central Writing Ctr Asn, Soc for Am Baseball Res. **RESEARCH** American fiction, composition and rhetoric, writing centers, baseball literature, pedagogy. **SELECTED PUBLICATIONS** Auth, Basic Writing: Process and Purpose, 2nd Ed, Harper Collins (New York, NY), 95; auth, "Early Writing Centers: Toward a History," The Writing Ctr J, 15.2 (95): 16-27; auth, "Open Admissions and the Construction of Writing Center History: A Tale of Three models," The Writing Ctr J, 17.1 (96): 30-48; auth, "Computers and the Writing Center: A Cautionary History," in Wiring the Writing Ctr (Provo: Ut St UP, 98), 171-193; auth, "Writing Centers and Writing Programs: Local and Communal Politics," in The Polit of Writing Ctr (Portsmought, NH: Heinemann/Boynton Cook, forthcoming); auth, "Mark Twain, Westward Expansion, Immigrant Unrest: Baseball and American Growing Pains in Daryl Brock's 'If I Never Get Back'," Nine: A J of Baseball Hist and Soc Policy Perspective (forthcoming); auth, "Making Meaning in the Post-Modern Market: Teaching John Updike's 'A&P'," Teaching English in the Two-Year Col (forthcoming). **CONTACT ADDRESS** Dept English, Indiana State Univ, 210 N 7th St, Root Hall, Terre Haute, IN 47809-0001. **EMAIL** ejcarino@root.indstate.edu

CARKEET, DAVID CORYDON
PERSONAL Born 11/15/1946, Sonora, CA, m, 1975, 3 children **DISCIPLINE** ENGLISH **EDUCATION** Univ Calif, Davis, Ba, 68; Univ Wis, MA, 70; Ind Univ, PhD(English), 73. **CAREER** From Asst Prof to Assoc Prof, 73-86, Prof English, Univ MO, St Louis, 86-. **HONORS AND AWARDS** James D Phelan Awd, San Francisco Found, 76; O Henry Awd, Doubleday, 82. **RESEARCH** Fiction; English language. **SELECTED PUBLICATIONS** Auth, How critics write and how students write, Col English, 2/76; Old English correlatives: An exercise in internal syntactic reconstruction, Glossa, 76; Understanding syntactic errors in remedial writing, Col English, 3/77; Aspects of old English style, Lang and Style, 77; A new raising rule, Chicago Ling Soc, 77; The dialects in Huckleberry Finn, Am Lit, 11/79; Double negative, The Dial Press, 80; The source for the Arkansas gossips in Huckleberry Finn, Am Lit Realism, spring 81; The Greatest Slump of All Time, Harper and Row, 84; I Been There Before, Harper and Row, 85; The Full Catastrophe, Simon and Schuster, 90; The Error of Our Ways, Henry Holt, 97. **CONTACT ADDRESS** Dept of English, Univ of Missouri, St. Louis, 8001 Natural Bridge, Saint Louis, MO 63121-4499. **EMAIL** carkeet@umsl.edu

CARLSEN, JAMES CALDWELL
PERSONAL Born 02/11/1927, Pasco, WA, m, 1949, 4 children **DISCIPLINE** SYSTEMATIC MUSICOLOGY **EDUCATION** Whitworth Col, Wash, BA, 50; Univ Wash, MA, 58; Northwestern Univ, (music), 62. **CAREER** Teacher, Almira Pub Schs, 50-53 & Portland pub Schs, 53-54; assoc prof music theory & band dir, Whitworth Col, Wash, 54-63; assoc prof music theory & music educ, Univ conn, 63-67; Prof Syst Musicol & Music Educ, Univ Wash, 67-, Secy, Music Educ Res Coun, 68-70, chmn, 70-72; Fulbright-Hays Comn sr researcher, Staatliches Inst Musikforschung 73-74. **MEMBERSHIPS** Music Educ Nat Conf; Am Educ Res Asn; Int Soc Music Educ. **RESEARCH** Aural perception training; aural perception of music as a function of expectancy; physiologic effects of music. **SELECTED PUBLICATIONS** Auth, The Need to Know, 1994 Sr-Researcher-Award Acceptance Address, Jour Res Mus Edu, Vol 0042, 94. **CONTACT ADDRESS** Sch of Music, Univ of Washington, Seattle, WA 98195.

CARLSON, ERIC WALTER
PERSONAL Born 08/20/1910, Sweden, m, 1938, 3 children **DISCIPLINE** ENGLISH LITERATURE **EDUCATION** Boston Univ, BS, 32, AM, 36, PhD(English), 47. **CAREER** Instr English, Portland Jr Col, 34-36, Boston Univ, 38-41 & Babson Inst, 41-42; from instr to prof, 42-79, Emer Prof English, Univ Conn, 79- **MEMBERSHIPS** MLA; AAUP; Poe Studies Asn (pres, 73-78). **RESEARCH** American literature, especially from 1800 to present: symbolic and cultural values in literary criticism; Poe, Emerson and Dickinson. **SELECTED PUBLICATIONS** Auth, Poe, Edgar Allan--His Life and Legacy, Quart Jour Short Articles Notes and Rev(s), Vol 0007, 94; Poe, Edgar A.--Mournful and Never-Ending Remembrance, Quart Jour Short Articles Notes and Rev(s), Vol 0007, 94; Poe Pym--Critical Explorations, Quart Jour Short Articles Notes and Rev(s), Vol 0007, 94; Poe, Edgar Allan--Critical Assessments, Quart Jour Short Articles Notes and Rev(s), Vol 0007, 94. **CONTACT ADDRESS** Dept of English, Univ of Connecticut, Storrs, Storrs, CT 06268. **EMAIL** ecarlson@channel1.com

CARLSON, HARRY GILBERT
PERSONAL Born 09/27/1930, New York, NY, m, 1957 **DISCIPLINE** DRAMA & SPEECH **EDUCATION** Brooklyn Col, BA, 52; Ohio State Univ, MA, 55, PhD(theatre hist), 58. **CAREER** Instr drama & speech, Southwest Mo State Col, 57-59; asst prof, Valparaiso Univ, 59-61 & Northern Ill Univ, 61-64; assoc prof theatre & drama, Univ Ga, 64-66; assoc prof, 67-72, Prof Theatre & Drama, Queens Col, 72-, Prof Dance, 80-, Guggenheim Found fel, 66-67; City Univ NY Res Found grant, 70-71; mem theatre arts screening comt, Comt Int Exchange Persons, 68-71 & chmn, 71-72; Swedish Govt Travel grant, 76. **HONORS AND AWARDS** Translation, Arur Lundkvist Found, Sweden, 76. **MEMBERSHIPS** Am Theatre Asn; Soc Advan Scand Studies; Am-Scand Found; Stringberg Soc. **RESEARCH** Scandinavian drama and theatre; theatre history; translation. **SELECTED PUBLICATIONS** Auth, Lars Forssell--Poet in the Theatre, Scand Studies, 2/65; Dialogue at the Berliner Ensemble, Drama Rev, 1/67; ed & transl, Martin Lamm's August Stringberg, Blom, 71; co-ed & contribr, Handbook of Contemporary Drama, Crowell, 71; auth, The Odin Theatre in Holstebro, Am Scand Rev, 4/71; co-ed & contribr, Encyclopedia of World Drama, McGraw, 72; ed & contribr, The Unknown Strindberg, Scan Rev, 3/76. **CONTACT ADDRESS** Dept of Drama & Theatre, Queens Col, CUNY, 6530 Kissena Blvd, Flushing, NY 11367.

CARLSON, JULIE
DISCIPLINE ENGLISH LITERATURE **EDUCATION** Univ Chicago, PhD, 85. **CAREER** Assoc Prof, Eng, Univ Calif, Santa Barbara. **RESEARCH** British Romanticism; Drama theory. **SELECTED PUBLICATIONS** Auth, "Imposition of Form: Romantic Antitheatricalism and the Case Against Particular Women," ELH, 93; "Remorse for Jacobin Youth," Wordsworth Circle, 93; In the Theatre of Romanticism: Coleridge, Nationalism, Women, Cambridge Univ Press, 94; "Forever Young: Master Betty and the Queer Stage of Youth in English Romanticism," South Atlantic Quart, 96. **CONTACT ADDRESS** Dept of Eng, Univ of California, Santa Barbara, Santa Barbara, CA 93106-7150. **EMAIL** jcarlson@humanitas.ucsb.edu

CARLSON, KAY
PERSONAL Born Cambridge, ID, m, 1 child **DISCIPLINE** LIBRARY SCIENCE **EDUCATION** E OR St, BS; IN Univ, MLS **CAREER** Lib Dir, pres, Northwest Col; Lib Dir, Dull Knife Mem Col; Asst Libr, Umatilla Co Lib Dist; Asst Llib, Treasure Valley Comnty Col **HONORS AND AWARDS** Clayton Shepard Awd; Beta Phi Mu. **MEMBERSHIPS** Am Lib Asn; ACRL. **RESEARCH** Online searching; bibliographic instruction **CONTACT ADDRESS** Powell, WY 82435-9225. **EMAIL** carlsonk@nwc.cc.wy.us

CARLSON, MELVIN, JR.
PERSONAL Born 10/28/1942, Minot, ND, s **DISCIPLINE** ENGLISH LITERATURE, LIBRARY SCIENCE **EDUCATION** Olivet Nazarene Col, AB, 64; Univ of IL, MS, 66; Univ of MA, MA, 79; Columbia Univ, DLS, 89 **CAREER** Cataloger, 69-73, Univ of VT; Cataloger, 73-, Univ of MA **MEMBERSHIPS** Am Libr Sci **RESEARCH** Libr mgmt **CONTACT ADDRESS** PO Box 781, Amherst, MA 01004-0781. **EMAIL** melvinc@library.umass.edu

CARLSON, THOMAS CLARK
PERSONAL Born 05/13/1944, Elizabeth, NJ, m, 1970, 1 child **DISCIPLINE** AMERICAN LITERATURE **EDUCATION** Bucknell Univ, AB, 66; Rutgers Univ, New Brunswick, MA, 70, PhD(English), 71. **CAREER** Asst prof, 70-80, Assoc Prof English, Memphis State Univ, 80-, Asst bibliogeed, Poe Studies Asn, 72- **MEMBERSHIPS** MLA; Poe Studies Asn; Melville Soc; AAUP. **RESEARCH** Colonial American literature; Melville; 19th century American theatre. **SELECTED PUBLICATIONS** Auth, Who's afraid of Moby-Dick?, an approach to teaching Ishmael's autobiography, Interpretations: Studies in Lang & Lit, 11/73. **CONTACT ADDRESS** Dept of English, Univ of Memphis, 3706 Alumni St, Memphis, TN 38152-0001.

CARMICHAEL, CARL W.
PERSONAL Born 01/11/1940, PA, m, 1999, 3 children **DISCIPLINE** COMMUNICATION, COMMUNICATION ASPECTS OF AGING, SOCIAL LINGUISTICS **EDUCATION** Univ IA, PhD. **CAREER** Instr, CA State Univ. **RESEARCH** Critical thinking. **SELECTED PUBLICATIONS** Wrote a chapter on aging in a bk on Intercultural Commun; auth, Human Comm and the Aging Process. **CONTACT ADDRESS** California State Univ, Fresno, Fresno, CA 93740. **EMAIL** profcarl@aol.com

CARMICHAEL, SHELEIGH
PERSONAL Born 07/11/1953, San Antonio, TX, m, 1974, 2 children **DISCIPLINE** COMMUNICATION ARTS AND SCIENCES **EDUCATION** Univ Houston, BA, 78; Univ Hous-

ton, MA, 83. **CAREER** From Dir to Asst Prof, San Jacinto Col, 93-. **HONORS AND AWARDS** Minnie Stevens Piper Awd, 95; Nat Dir Awds, Kennedy Ctr-Am Col Theatre Festival, 95, 98, 00. **MEMBERSHIPS** TFA, TETA, TCCTA, TJCSTA, NISOD, KC/ACTF. **CONTACT ADDRESS** Dept Commun Arts & Sci, San Jacinto Col, South, 13735 Beamer Rd, Houston, TX 77089-6009. **EMAIL** scarmi@sjcd.cc.tx.us

CARMICHAEL, THOMAS
DISCIPLINE ENGLISH LITERATURE **EDUCATION** Guelph Univ, BA; Carleton Univ, MA; Univ Toronto, PhD. **MEMBERSHIPS** Canadian Asn of Am Studies, 99-01. **RESEARCH** Literary theory; narrative and the political unconscious; postmodernism; cultural theory; American studies. **SELECTED PUBLICATIONS** Co-ed, Constructive Criticism: The Human Sciences in the Age of Theory, Toronto, 95; contrib, Asia/Pacific as Space of Cultural Production, 95; contrib, Part Two: Reflections on the Sequel, 98; co-ed, Postmodern Times: A Critical Guide to the Contemporary, 00. **CONTACT ADDRESS** English Dept, Univ of Western Ontario, University College, London, ON, Canada NGA3K7. **EMAIL** tomc@julian.uwo.ca

CARMONA, VICENTE
DISCIPLINE 19TH AND 20TH CENTURY PENINSULAR LITERATURE **EDUCATION** UCLA, PhD, 95. **CAREER** Asst prof Span, undergrad adv, La State Univ. **RESEARCH** 19th and 20th century Peninsular literature; 20th century Latin American prose; literary theory. **SELECTED PUBLICATIONS** Auth, Federico Garcia Lorca: Dibujos, Ministerio de Cult, 86; El banquete del progreso en aquel Tiempo de silencio, Alba de Am, 95. **CONTACT ADDRESS** Dept of For Lang and Lit, Louisiana State Univ and A&M Col, 141 A Prescott Hall, Baton Rouge, LA 70803. **EMAIL** Carmona@Homer.forlang.lsu.edu

CARNELL, CORBIN SCOTT
PERSONAL Born 07/07/1929, Ormond Beach, FL, m, 1951, 4 children **DISCIPLINE** ENGLISH **EDUCATION** Wheaton Col, BA, 52; Columbia Univ, MA, 53; Univ FL, PhD, 60. **CAREER** Instr Eng, Bethany Col, WVA, 53-56; tchg assoc, 58-60, asst prof, 60-68, assoc prof, 68-76, prof eng, Univ FL, 76, Danforth Found regional selection chmn, 65-69, mem nat adv coun, Danforth Assoc Prog, 67-70. **MEMBERSHIPS** MLA; Conf Christianity & Lit (vpres, 64-65, pres, 74-77); Am Acad Relig. **RESEARCH** Contemp Am and Brit lit; hist of ideas, espec interrelationships of lit, philos and theol; film studies. **SELECTED PUBLICATIONS** Auth, Why sentimentality is wrong, Eternity, 11/67; C S Lewis on Eros as a means of grace, In: Imagination and the Spirit, 71 & ed & auth introd to A Slow, Soft River: 7 Stories by Lawrence Dorr, 73 & Bright Shadow of Reality: C S Lewis and the Feeling Intellect, 74, Eerdmans; coauth, Body-love and the city: a closer look at Sunday Bloody Sunday, Christianity and Literature, summer 75; Film-Going on Religious Ritual, Catalyst, 5/76; The Meaning of Masculine and Feminine in the Work of C S Lewis, Modern British Literature, 77; Ransom in C S Lewis' Perelandra as hero in transformation, Studies in the Literary Imagination, fall 81. **CONTACT ADDRESS** Dept of Eng, Univ of Florida, PO Box 117310, Gainesville, FL 32611-7310.

CARNEY, RAYMOND
PERSONAL Born 02/28/1947, Homestead, PA, m, 1972, 1 child **DISCIPLINE** AMERICAN LITERATURE, FILM **EDUCATION** Harvard Univ, BA, 69; Rutgers Univ, PhD(English), 78. **CAREER** Asst Prof Lit & Film, Middlebury Col, 78- **RESEARCH** Contemporary American film; contemporary criticism; Henry James. **SELECTED PUBLICATIONS** Contribr, John Ashbery, In: American Poets Since World War II, Gale, 80; A woman under the influence & Minnie and Moskowitz, In: Magills Survey of Cinema, Salem Press, 81; John Macdonald and Richard Matheson, In: American Science Fiction, Gale, 81; auth, Making the most of a mess, Ga Rev, fall 81; Film criticism, Raritan Rev, fall 81; contribr, Dreyers Ordet and Gertrud, In: Magills Survey of Cinema-Foreign Films, Salem Press, 82; John Cassavetes, In: American Screenwriter, Bruccoli-Clark, 82; auth, Critical impurity, The Chicago Rev, fall 82. **CONTACT ADDRESS** Dept of English, Middlebury Col, Middlebury, VT 05753.

CARNEY, VIRGINIA I.
PERSONAL Born 05/27/1941, Maryville, TN, m, 1963, 7 children **DISCIPLINE** ENGLISH, NATIVE STUDIES, WOMEN'S STUDIES **EDUCATION** Tenn Temple Univ, BA, 69; Cleveland State Community Col, AND, 78; Univ Alaska, MA, 90; Univ Ky, PhD, 00. **CAREER** Teacher, Nassau Christian Acad, 73-74; nurse, Bradley Mem Hosp, 78-80; nurse, Humana Hosp, 80-83; office nurse, 83-86; adj prof, Univ of Alaska, 90-93; TA, Univ of Ky, 93-97; asst prof, E Ky Univ, 98-. **HONORS AND AWARDS** S Reg Educ Board Diss Fel, 97-98; Scholars for the Dream Awd, 97; Ellershaw Awd, 98; Frances C. Allen Fel, 98; Fac Grant, E Ky Univ, 99-00; Chi Omega Outstanding Prof Awd, 00. **MEMBERSHIPS** Assoc for the Study of Am Indian Lit, Conf on Col Comp and Commun, MLA, NCTE, Wordcraft Circle of Native Writers and Storytellers. **RESEARCH** Letters and speeches of Eastern Band Cherokee Women, Black Indians. **SELECTED PUBLICATIONS** Auth, "These Are Our Mountains, Too!" Appalachian Heritage, (95); auth, "Cherokee/Appalachian Communities: Remembering the Pattern, Re-Spinning the Web," Jour of Appalachian Studies, (97); auth, "I Used to be a Hillbilly; Now I'm Appalachian," One Hundred Years of Appalachian Visions, Appalachian Imprints, (KY: Berea, 97); auth, "Native American Loanwords in American English," Wicazo SA Rev, (97); auth, Dancing on New Ground: The Life of Morningstar Conner, Unole Pr, (Wallingford, KY), 97; auth, "The Speeches of Nanye'hi (Nancy Ward) and Kitteuha," Speakers of the Eastern Woodlands, Greenwood Publ, (NY, 00); auth, "Irrepressible Voices: The As-Told-To Stories of Pretty Shield and Lee Maracle," Native Am Lit Strategies for the New Millennium, (01); auth, "A Time for Healing," The People Who Stayed Behind, (01). **CONTACT ADDRESS** Dept English, Eastern Kentucky Univ, 467 Case Annex, Richmond, KY 40475-3021. **EMAIL** engcarne@acs.eku.edu

CARNOCHAN, WALTER BLISS
PERSONAL Born 12/20/1930, New York, NY, m, 1979, 4 children **DISCIPLINE** ENGLISH LITERATURE **EDUCATION** Harvard Univ, AB, 53, AM, 57, PhD, 60. **CAREER** From instr to assoc prof, 60-73, chmn dept English, 71-73, vprovost & dean grad studies, 75-80, Prof English, Stanford Univ, 73-; Richard W. Lyman Prof of the Humanities 93-94; Richard W. Cyman Prof of the Humanities, emeritus, 94-. **MEMBERSHIPS** MLA **RESEARCH** Eighteenth century; American higher education. **SELECTED PUBLICATIONS** Auth, Hemuel Gulliver's Mirror for Man, 68; auth, Confinement and Flight: An Essay on English Literature of the Eighteenth Century, 77; auth, Gibbon's Solitude: the Inward World of the Historian, 87; auth, The Battleground of the Curriculum: Liberal Education and American Experience, 93; auth, Momentary Bliss: An American Memoir, 99. **CONTACT ADDRESS** Dept of English, Stanford Univ, Stanford, CA 94305. **EMAIL** hf.wbc@forsythe.stanford.edu

CARPENTER, CHARLES ALBERT
PERSONAL Born 06/08/1929, Hazleton, PA, m, 1950, 4 children **DISCIPLINE** ENGLISH, MODERN DRAMA **EDUCATION** Allegheny Col, BA, 51; Kent State Univ, MLS, 52; Cornell Univ, MA, 59, PhD(English), 63. **CAREER** From instr to asst prof English, Univ Del, 62-67; asst prof, 67-70, assoc prof, 70-81, Prof English, State Univ NY, Binghamton, 81- **RESEARCH** Theatre of the absurd; international bibliography of modern drama. **SELECTED PUBLICATIONS** Auth, Modern Drama Studies--An Annual Bibliog, Mod Drama, Vol 0036, 93. **CONTACT ADDRESS** Dept of English, SUNY, Binghamton, Binghamton, NY 13901.

CARPENTER, LYNETTE
PERSONAL Born 12/31/1951, Houston, TX, s **DISCIPLINE** ENGLISH **EDUCATION** Univ Tex, BA, 73; Ind Univ, MA, 75; PhD, 79. **CAREER** Asst Prof and Assoc Director, Univ Cincinnati, 80-89; Asst to Assoc Prof, Ohio Wesleyan Univ, 89-. **MEMBERSHIPS** Mod Lang Asn, Nat Women's Studies Asn, Authors Guild, Sisters in Crime. **RESEARCH** Women's supernatural literature. **SELECTED PUBLICATIONS** Auth, Haunting the House of Fiction; auth, The Cat Caliban Mystery Series, Berkley; auth, The Gilda Liberty Mystery Series, Ballantine. **CONTACT ADDRESS** Dept English, Ohio Wesleyan Univ, 61 S Sandusky St, Delaware, OH 43015-2333. **EMAIL** llcarpen@cc.owu.edu

CARPENTER, MARY
DISCIPLINE ENGLISH LITERATURE **EDUCATION** Brown Col, PhD. **CAREER** Dept Eng, Queen's Univ **RESEARCH** Victorian literature; literary theory; feminist, gender, and psychoanalytic theory; history of sexuality; women's writing. **SELECTED PUBLICATIONS** Auth, George Eliot and the Landscape of Time: Narrative Form and Protestant Apocalyptic History, Univ North Carolina Press, 86; auth, "The Trouble with Romola," in Thais E. Morgan, Victorian Sages & Cultural Discourse: Renegotiating Gender and Power, Rutgers UP, 90; auth, "Eat me, drink me, love me: The Consumable Female Body," in Christina Rossetti's Goblin Market, Victorian Poetry, 91; auth, "Representing Apocalypse: Sexual Politics and the Violence of Revelation," in Richard Dellamora, Postmodern Apocalypse: Theory and Cultural Practice at the End, Univ Pennsylvania Press, 95; auth, "Masquerade," in The Oxford Companion to Women's Writing in the United States, Oxford UP, 95; auth, "Female Grotesques: Ageism, Antifeminism, and Feminists on the Faculty, in Clark, Garner, Higonnet and Katrak," auth, The Phallus, Feminist Literary Theory, Garland, 96; Anti-feminism in the Academy, Routledge, 96. **CONTACT ADDRESS** English Dept, Queen's Univ at Kingston, Kingston, ON, Canada K7L 3N6. **EMAIL** carpentm@qsilver.queensu.ca

CARPENTER, SCOTT
DISCIPLINE LITERATURE OF THE EIGHTEENTH AND NINETEENTH CENTURIES **EDUCATION** Univ Wisc, PhD. **CAREER** Literature, Carleton Col. **SELECTED PUBLICATIONS** Auth, Acts of Fiction: Resistance and Resolution from Sade to Baudelaire, Penn State Univ Press. **CONTACT ADDRESS** Carleton Col, 100 S College St., Northfield, MN 55057-4016.

CARPENTER, WILLIAM MORTON
PERSONAL Born 10/31/1940, Cambridge, MA, s, 2 children **DISCIPLINE** ENGLISH **EDUCATION** Dartmouth Col, BA, 62; Univ Mn, PhD, 67. **CAREER** Asst prof English & Humanities, Univ Chicago, 67-73; mem fac Humanities, Col of the Atlantic, 73-, dean fac, 83-88. **HONORS AND AWARDS** Assoc Writing Prog, Poetry, 80; Samuel French Morse Prize 85; NEA Fel, 85. **MEMBERSHIPS** MLA. **RESEARCH** W B Yeats; modern poetry; creative writing. **SELECTED PUBLICATIONS** Auth, The Green Helmet poems and Yeats' myth of the Renaissance, Mod Philol, 8/69; The Hours of Morning, Univ Va, 81; Rain, Northeastern Univ, 85; Speaking Fire At Stones, Tilbury, 92; A Keeper of Sheep, Milkweed, 94. **CONTACT ADDRESS** Dept Humanities, Col of the Atlantic, 105 Eden St, Bar Harbor, ME 04609-1198. **EMAIL** carpenter@acadia.net

CARR, ROBIN
DISCIPLINE ENGLISH LITERATURE **EDUCATION** Ill State Univ, PhD, BA, MA; Univ Ill, PhD. **CAREER** Assoc prof. **RESEARCH** Literature for children and adolescents; language arts; traditional oral storytelling and poetry for children. **SELECTED PUBLICATIONS** Auth, pubs on death and dying in children's books, dialect in books for children and adolescents, language arts. **CONTACT ADDRESS** Dept of English, Illinois State Univ, Normal, IL 61761.

CARR, STEPHEN LEO
PERSONAL Born 11/09/1950, Brighton, MA, m, 1975, 2 children **DISCIPLINE** INTERDISCIPLINARY STUDIES, CRITICAL THEORY **EDUCATION** Williams Col, BA, 72; Univ Mich, MA, 73, PhD(English), 79. **CAREER** Vis instr, Carnegie-Mellon Univ, 77-79; asst prof English, 80-86, assoc prof, Univ Pittsburgh, 86-. **MEMBERSHIPS** MLA. **RESEARCH** Literature and the visual arts; literature and science. **SELECTED PUBLICATIONS** Auth, William Blake's print-making process in Jerusalem, J English Lit Hist, 80; Verbal-visual relationships: Zoffany's and Fuseli's illustrations of Macbeth, Art Hist, 80; The ideology of antithesis: science vs literature and the exemplary case of John Stuart Mill, Mod Lang Quart, 81; coauth, Seeing through Macbeth, Publ Mod Lang Asn, 81; auth, Visionary syntax: Non-tyrannical coherence and the style of Blake's visual art, 18th Century: Theory & Interpretation, 81; The rhetoric of argument in Berkeley's Siris, Univ Toronto Quart, 81. **CONTACT ADDRESS** Dept of English, Univ of Pittsburgh, 526 Cathedral/Learn, Pittsburgh, PA 15260-2504. **EMAIL** SCARR+@pitt.edu

CARR, STEVEN A.
PERSONAL Born 06/21/1964, Poughkeepsie, NY, s **DISCIPLINE** COMMUNICATION **EDUCATION** U Texas-Austin, PhD, 94; Northwestern U, MA, 87; U North Carolina-Chapel Hill, AB, 86. **CAREER** Vis Lecturer, Sam Houston State U; Asst Prof, Indiana U-Purdue U Fort Wayne, 94-. **HONORS AND AWARDS** Stephen H. Coltrin Awd for Communication Excellence, 98. **MEMBERSHIPS** UFVA; MLA; IAMCR; ICA; NCA;SCS **RESEARCH** Media History; Jewish Studies. **SELECTED PUBLICATIONS** Auth, "Hollywood and Anti-Semitism: A Cultural History, 1880-1941, New York: Cambridge UP, 01. **CONTACT ADDRESS** Dept Communication, Indiana Univ-Purdue Univ, Fort Wayne, 2101 East Coliseum Boulevard, Fort Wayne, IN 46805-1445. **EMAIL** carr@ipfw.edu

CARRIER, REBECCA
PERSONAL Born 01/06/1961, Boise, ID, m, 1 child **DISCIPLINE** COMMUNICATIONS **EDUCATION** Boise State Univ, BA, 88; Ind State Univ, MA, 90; Univ Ill, PhD, 98. **CAREER** Adj Prof, Ind State Univ, 89-90; Istructor, East Carolina Univ, 95-96; Instr, Ivy Tech State Col, 96-97; Asst Prof, Calif State Poly Univ, 97-. **HONORS AND AWARDS** Grant, Cal Poly Univ, 99, 97; Grant, East Carolina Univ, 96, 95; Fel, Univ Ill; Recognition of Teaching Excellence, Univ Ill; Phi Beta Kappa Nat Honor Soc. **MEMBERSHIPS** Asn for Educ in Journalism and Mass Comm, Intl Comm Asn, Nat Comm Asn, Comm Inst for On-Line Scholarship. **RESEARCH** Policy questions that focus on the social and political effects of mass media; International mass communication; New technologies. **SELECTED PUBLICATIONS** Auth, "On the electronic information frontier: Training the information poor in an age of unequal access," in The cyberspace ghetto: Race, class, gender and marginalization in cyberspace, Praeger Press, 98; auth, "Global news and domestic needs: reflections and adaptations of world information to national audiences," in News media and foreign relations: A multifaceted perspective, Ablex Press, 97; auth, "US policy considerations: The fine line between national security and international access to emerging communication technologies," Journal of International communication, (96): 331-332; auth, "global pictures, local stories: The beginning of Desert Storm as constructed by television news around the world," in Communication and the gulf War, Greenwood Press, 94; auth, "Chautauqua: Are media news spectacles perverting our political processes? Notes on recent Articles," Political communication, (93): 320-321; auth, Innovations in content analysis: applying content analytic techniques to new media; forthcoming; auth, Framing the president's affairs: a content analysis of how seven international newspapers covered the Clinton-Lewinsky scandal, forthcoming; auth, Preserving the

narrative structure of television news while conducting micro-level analyses: an alternative to traditional coding methods for television content analysis, forthcoming. **CONTACT ADDRESS** Dept Comm, California State Polytech Univ, Pomona, 3801 W Temple Ave, Pomona, CA 91768-2557. **EMAIL** racarrier@csupomona.edu

CARRIG, MARIA
DISCIPLINE ENGLISH **EDUCATION** Bryn Mawr Col, BA, 84; Yale Univ, MA, 88, PhD, 95. **CAREER** Asst prof. **RESEARCH** Shakespeare and Renaissance drama; commedia dell'arte; comic theory; origins of the novel; Renaissance philosophy. **SELECTED PUBLICATIONS** Auth, Pregnant Meanings: Sexuality, Skepticism and the Uses of Comic Language in Measure for Measure, The Comic Turn, Univ Fla Press, 97. **CONTACT ADDRESS** Dept of English, Loyola Univ, Chicago, 6525 N. Sheridan Rd., Chicago, IL 60626. **EMAIL** mcarrig@orion.it.luc.edu

CARRINGER, ROBERT L.
PERSONAL Born 05/12/1941, Knoxville, TN, m, 1968 **DISCIPLINE** FILM STUDIES, CULTURAL STUDIES, AMERICAN STUDIES **EDUCATION** Univ Tenn, AB, 62; Johns Hopkins Univ, MA, 64; Ind Univ, PhD, 70. **CAREER** Prof English & Film Studies, Univ Ill, Urbana, 70-, fel, Fac Study Second Discipline (Cognitive psychol), 90-91; assoc, Center for Advan Studies, 83-84; NEH res ed grant, 86-87; Getty Scholar, 96-97. **HONORS AND AWARDS** Undergrad Instr Awd, 79; Amoco Curric Develop Awd, 80; Distinguished Prof Awd, 85; Apple Computer Curric Innovation Awd, 88. **MEMBERSHIPS** Soc Cinema Studies; Univ Film Asn; Film Div, Mod Lang Asn; Film Studies Sect, Midwest Mod Lang Asn. **RESEARCH** American film; American Literature. **SELECTED PUBLICATIONS** Auth, Circumscription of space and the form of Poe's Arthur Gordon Pym, PMLA, 5/74; Citizen Kane, The Great Gatsby, and some conventions of American narrative, Critical Inquiry, winter 75; Rosebud, dead or alive, PMLA, 3/76; coauth, Ernst Lubitsch, G K Hall, 78; auth, The Scripts of Citizen Kane, Critical Inquiry, fall 78, ed, The Jazz Singer, Univ Wis, 79; auth, Orson Wells and Gregg Toland, Critical Inquiry, summer 82; ed, Citizen Kane, Criterion Laserdisc 84, rev ed, 92; auth, The Making of Citizen Kane, Univ Calif, 85, rev ed, 96; ed, The Magnificent Ambersons, Criterion Laserdisc, 84, rev ed, 92; auth, The Magnificent Ambersons: A Reconstruction, Univ Calif, 93; Designing Los Angeles: Richard Sylbert, Wide Angle, 98; Hollywood's LA, in Looking at Los Angeles, Getty, 00. **CONTACT ADDRESS** Dept of English, Univ of Illinois, Urbana-Champaign, 608 S Wright St, Urbana, IL 61801-3613. **EMAIL** fergus@uiuc.edu

CARRITHERS, GALE
DISCIPLINE ENGLISH RENAISSANCE, CULTURAL CRITICISM **EDUCATION** Yale, PhD, 60. **CAREER** Prof, former dept ch, La State Univ. **HONORS AND AWARDS** SUNY syst summer grants; Southern Reg Educ Bd, 86; Col of Arts and Sci summer grant; LSU Res Coun summer grants. **MEMBERSHIPS** Mem, MLA Comt on Careers, 80-84. **RESEARCH** Donne; Shakespeare. **SELECTED PUBLICATIONS** Auth, Donne at Sermons: A Christian Existential World, 72; City Comedy's Sardonic Hierarchy of Literacy, SEL, 89; Mumford, Tate, Eiseley: Watchers in the Night, 91; Eiseley and the Self as Search, Ariz Quart, 94; coauth, Milton and the Hermeneutic Journey, 94; Love, Power, Dust Royall, Gavelkinde, John Donne J, 95. **CONTACT ADDRESS** Dept of Eng, Louisiana State Univ and A&M Col, 229E Allen Hall, Baton Rouge, LA 70803.

CARROLL, LINDA M.
PERSONAL Born 07/29/1956, Sanford, ME, m, 1998, 1 child **DISCIPLINE** COMMUNICATIONS **EDUCATION** Univ Maine, BA, 79; Univ Maine, BS, 79; Columbia Univ, MS, 93; Columbia Univ, MPhil, 96. **CAREER** Adj Lectr, Pace Univ, 96-; Res Assoc, NYork Eye and Ear Infirmary, 98-; Adj Asst Prof, NYork Univ, 00-. **HONORS AND AWARDS** Miss Maine, 78; Feagin Scholar, Univ Tulsa; Wilder Fel, Columbia Univ; Phi Kappa Lambda; Kappa Delta Pi; Mu Alpha Sigma; ACE Awd, 95-96, 99; . **MEMBERSHIPS** ASHA, ASA, VASTA, NYSSSLHA. **RESEARCH** Voice physiology, vocal training, laryngeal aerodynamics. **SELECTED PUBLICATIONS** Coauth, "Singing Power Ratio: Quantitative Evaluation of Singing Voice Quality," J of Voice 10:3 (96): 228-235; auth, "Redirecting the Vocal Athlete: Hyperfunction in Singers and Actors," ASHA Voice and Voice Disorders 8:3 (98): 5-6; auth, "O Canto 'Belt' Broadway: Sera Que os Cantores da Broadway Conseguem Evitar Lesoes durante as Grandes Apresentacoes?" in Laringologia e Voz Hoje (Rio de Janiero: Revinter, 98); coauth, "The Singing Voice Specialist," in Vocal Health and Pedagogy (San Diego, CA: Singular Publ Group, 98); auth, "Application of Singing Techniques for the Treatment of Dysphonia," in Otolaryngologic Clinics of N Am (Philadelphia, PA: W B Saunders Co, 00); auth, "The Role of the Voice Specialist in Nonmedical Management of Benign Voice Disorders," in Diagnosis and Treatment of Voice Disorders, 2nd ed (New York: Igaku-Shoin Publ, 00). **CONTACT ADDRESS** Dept Commun, New York Univ, 424 W 49th St, Ste 1, New York, NY 10019. **EMAIL** lmcarroll@email,msn.com

CARROLL, WILLIAM
PERSONAL Born 01/04/1936, Brooklyn, NY, m, 1966 **DISCIPLINE** ENGLISH **EDUCATION** Harvard Univ, Cambridge MA, 1964; Norfolk State Coll, Norfolk VA, BA 1965; Temple Univ, Philadelphia PA, MA 1967; Univ of North Carolina, Chapel Hill NC, PhD 1978. **CAREER** Norfolk State Univ, Norfolk VA, instructor 1967-73, asst prof 1974-77, assoc prof 1978-95, prof, 95-. **HONORS AND AWARDS** Summer School Cooperative Scholarship, Harvard Univ, 1964; Teaching Fellowship, Univ of North Carolina, 1971. **MEMBERSHIPS** Mem Alpha Kappa Mu Natl Honor Society 1963-; mem Norfolk State Univ Alumni Assn 1965-; mem Coll Language Assn 1967-70, 1984-; mem Amer Assn of Univ Prof 1969-; vice pres Tidewater Fair Housing Inc 1969-70; mem Natl Council of Teachers of English 1975-86, 1988-; mem Sigma Tau Delta Intl Honor Society 1979-; mem NAACP 1982-; publicity dir Voter Registration 1982-84; mem United Council of Citizens & Civic Leagues 1982-; advisory board, Planned Parenthood of Southeastern Virginia, 1993; bd mem George Moses Horton Society; Middle Atlantic Writer's Assn, life mem, 1987-, vp, 1992-94. **SELECTED PUBLICATIONS** Co-author Rhetoric and Readings for Writing, 1981, Variations on Humankind: An Introduction to World Literature, 1990; author, "George Moses Horton," Dictionary of Literary Biography, 1986; contributor, Fifty More Southern Writers. **CONTACT ADDRESS** Professor, Norfolk State Univ, 2401 Corprew Ave, 205 Madison Communication Building, Norfolk, VA 23504.

CARROLL, WILLIAM DENNIS
PERSONAL Born 08/25/1940, Sydney, Australia, m, 1968, 3 children **DISCIPLINE** DRAMA **EDUCATION** Univ Sydney, BA, 62, MA, 66; Univ Hawaii, MFA, 65; Northwestern Univ, PhD, 69. **CAREER** From Asst Prof to Assoc Prof, 69-82, Prof, Theatre and Dance, Univ Haw, Manoa, 82-. **MEMBERSHIPS** Asn for Theatre in Higher Educ; Am Asn Australian Lit Studies. **RESEARCH** Australian and American theatre and drama; Finnish theatre. **SELECTED PUBLICATIONS** Ed, Kumu Kahua Plays, Univ Press Hawaii, 82; auth, Australian Contemporary Drama 1909-1982, Peter Lang, 85; David Mamet, In: Macmillan Modern Dramatists Series, Macmillan, 87; Australian Contemporary Drama, Currency Press, 2nd rev ed, 95; author of numerous articles, reviews, and book sections. **CONTACT ADDRESS** Dept Theatre & Dance, Univ of Hawaii, Manoa, 1770 E West Rd, Honolulu, HI 96822-2453. **EMAIL** carroll@hawaii.edu

CARRUTHERS, VIRGINIA
DISCIPLINE LITERATURE **EDUCATION** Duke Univ, PhD. **CAREER** Assoc prof, Univ Baltimore. **RESEARCH** Australian literature and film; Shakespeare. **SELECTED PUBLICATIONS** Ed, CEAMAGazine, Middle Atlantic Gp; Assoc ed, Deus Loci: The Lawrence Durrell Jour. **CONTACT ADDRESS** Commun Dept, Univ of Baltimore, 1420 N. Charles Street, Baltimore, MD 21201.

CARSON, LUKE
DISCIPLINE 19TH-20TH-CENTURY AMERICAN LITERATURE **EDUCATION** Univ McGill, BA; Univ Calif, LA, MA, PhD. **CAREER** Assoc prof; dir, Eng grad stud. **RESEARCH** Modern American poetry; critical theory; literary criticism. **SELECTED PUBLICATIONS** Auth, The Public Trust: Consumption and Depression in Gertrude Stein, Louis Zukofsky and Ezra Pound, Macmillan, 98; pub(s), articles, Sagetrieb, Mediations, Tex Stud in Lit and Lang. **CONTACT ADDRESS** Dept of English, Univ of Victoria, PO Box 3070, Victoria, BC, Canada V8W 3W1. **EMAIL** lcarson@uvic.ca

CARSON, MICHAEL
DISCIPLINE ENGLISH LITERATURE **EDUCATION** Ohio State Univ, PhD. **CAREER** Dept ch. **HONORS AND AWARDS** Poem, Words, nominated for the Pushcart Prize. **SELECTED PUBLICATIONS** Auth, Words, printed, Gulfstream; poems publ, Bitterroot, The Spoon River Anthology, The New Virginia Rev, The Beliot Jour, Anthology Of Hoosier Poets. **CONTACT ADDRESS** Dept of Eng, Univ of Evansville, 1800 Lincoln Ave, Evansville, IN 47714. **EMAIL** mc32@evansville.edu.

CARSON, WARREN JASON, JR.
PERSONAL Born 02/12/1953, Tryon, NC, s **DISCIPLINE** ENGLISH **EDUCATION** Univ of NC, AB 1974; Atlanta Univ, MA 1975; Univ of SC, Columbia, SC, PhD, 1990. **CAREER** Isothermal Community Coll, instructor, 75-76; Piedmont OIC, head of career prep div, 75-80; Rutledge Coll, dean for acad affairs, 80-84; Univ of SC at Spartanburg, prog dir, prof dept of English, 84-. **HONORS AND AWARDS** Church And Comm Awd 1984; Outstanding Teacher Awd Piedmont OIC 1980; Outstanding Teacher Awd Rutledge Clge 1982-83; Teacher of the Year, USC-Spartanburg, 1989; Amoco Outstanding Teacher Awd, Univ of SC, 1989; Governor's Distinguished Professor, SC Commission on Higher Education, Governor's Office, 1989. **MEMBERSHIPS** Pres Polk Cty NAACP 1976-; chrmn Mayor's Adv Task Force 1980-83; pres Tryon Schls PTA 1980-81; member, Polk Co (NC) Board of County Commissioners, 1986-88; member, City Council, Tryon, NC, 1989-; member, Polk Co Dept of Social Services, 1986-94; mem, Polk County Child Protection Team, 1993-. **CONTACT ADDRESS** English, Univ of So Carolina, Spartanburg, 800 University Way, Spartanburg, SC 29303.

CARTER, EVERETT
PERSONAL Born 04/28/1919, New York, NY, m, 1940, 2 children **DISCIPLINE** ENGLISH **EDUCATION** Univ Calif, Los Angeles, AB, 39, AM, 43, PhD, 47. **CAREER** Asst prof English, Claremont Col, 47-49 & Univ Calif, Berkeley, 49-57; assoc prof, 57-62, vchancellor, 59-62, spec asst to pres, 62-63, univ dean res, 63-66, Prof English, Univ Calif, Davis, 62-, Guggenheim fels, 52-53, 61-62; lectr, Salzburg Sem, Austria, 53; Fulbright fel, Univ Copenhagen, 54-55; vis lectr, Harvard Univ, 57-58; Fulbright lectr, 61-62; lectr, Asian Ctr Am Studies Hyderabad, 65; Fulbright lectr, Univ Strasbourg, 67-68; dir ctr studies, Univ Calif at Univ Bordeaux, 70-72 & 78-80; resident fel, Rockefeller Cult Ctr, Bellagio, 77; lectr, Sapporo-Cool Sem Am Studies, 81. **HONORS AND AWARDS** Nonfiction Gold Medal, Commonwealth Club, Calif, 54. **MEMBERSHIPS** MLA; Am Soc Composers, Authors & Publ; Am Studies Asn. **RESEARCH** American literature, especially fiction. **SELECTED PUBLICATIONS** Auth, Howells and the Age of Realism, 54; auth, The Am Idea, 77; auth, "Realists and Jews," Studies in American Fiction, Vol 0022, 94; auth, "Wilson,Edmund Refights the Civil-War--The Revision of Tourgee," Albion Novels, Amer Lit Realism 1870-1910, Vol 0029, 97. **CONTACT ADDRESS** Univ of California, Davis, 734 Hawthorn Lane, Davis, CA 95616.

CARTER, JOSEPH COLEMAN
PERSONAL Born 12/23/1941, New York, NY, 3 children **DISCIPLINE** CLASSICAL ARCHAEOLOGY, CLASSICS **EDUCATION** Amherst Col, BA, 63; Princeton Univ, MA, 67, PhD, 71. **CAREER** Asst prof, 71-76, prof class & class Archaeol, Univ TX Austin; Class Archaeol, Univ TX, Nat Endowment for Humanities younger humanist fel, 73-74; Am Coun Learned Soc fel, 79; NEH Fellowships, 88-89; Guggenheim Fellowships, 94-95. **HONORS AND AWARDS** James R. Wiseman Book, Awd Archaeological Institute of Am. **MEMBERSHIPS** Soc Promot Hellenic Studies; Archaeol Inst Am; Soc Promotion Roman Studies; Inst per la Storia della Magna Precia; Fellow Soc of An of London, 84. **RESEARCH** Excavation & research of Greek colonies on the Black Sea; Archaeological excavation, survey and research in Greek colonial S Haly. **SELECTED PUBLICATIONS** Auth, Relief sculpture from the Necropolis of Taranto, 74 & The Tomb of the Sire, 78, Am J Archaeol; The Sculpture of Taras, Philadelphia, 75; auth, The Chora of Metaponto: The Necropoleis, 97. **CONTACT ADDRESS** Dept of Class, Univ of Texas, Austin, Austin, TX 78712-1026. **EMAIL** j.carter@mail.utexas.edu

CARTER, LOCKE
DISCIPLINE RHETORIC AND COMPOSITION **EDUCATION** Univ TX, PhD, 97. **CAREER** Vis asst prof, TX Tech Univ; bd mem, Alliance for Comput and Writing; CEO, Daedalus Gp; sr ed, Labyrinth Publ. **HONORS AND AWARDS** Founder, Daedalus Gp, Inc. **RESEARCH** Theories of argumentation; hypertext. **SELECTED PUBLICATIONS** Auth, Daedalus Integrated Writing Environment, Composicion, McGraw-Hill; The Writer's Workshop, Addison-Wesley Longman. **CONTACT ADDRESS** Texas Tech Univ, Lubbock, TX 79409-5015. **EMAIL** L.Carter@ttu.edu

CARTER, MARVA GRIFFIN
PERSONAL Born 06/04/1947, Cleveland, OH, m, 1969, 1 child **DISCIPLINE** MUSIC **EDUCATION** Boston Cons of Music, BM, 68; N Eng Cons of Music, MM, 70; Boston Univ, MA, 75; Univ Ill, PhD, 88. **CAREER** Coord, Simmons Col, 73-77; Chair, Morris Brown Col, 89-93; Asst Dir Sch of Music, Ga State Univ, 93-96; Dir Grad Studies, Ga State Univ, 00-. **HONORS AND AWARDS** Intl Directory of Distinguished Leadership, 94; Outstanding Young Woman of Am, 76. **MEMBERSHIPS** Am Musicol Soc; Soc Am Music; Col Music Soc, Phi Kappa Lambda Psi. **RESEARCH** African American Musical Biography. **SELECTED PUBLICATIONS** Auth, "Noble Sissle," in The Encyclopedia of African-American Culture and History, Vol 5, (Macmillan Pub Co, 95), 2441; auth, "Francis Hall Johnson," in The Encyclopedia of African-American Culture and History, Vol 5, (Macmillan Pub Co, 95), 1456-1457; auth, "Will Marion Cook," in The Encyclopedia of African-American Culture and History, Vol 5, (Macmillan Pub Co, 95), 655-656; auth, "Robert Allen 'Bob' Cole," in The Encyclopedia of African-American Culture and History, Vol 5, (Macmillan Pub Co, 95), 605; auth, "Sidney Bechet," in The Encyclopedia of African-American Culture and History, Vol 5, (Macmillan Pub Co, 95), 299; auth, "Francis Hall Johnson," International Dictionary of Black composer, (Fitzroy Dearborn Pub, 99); auth, "Will Marion Cook," in International Dictionary of Black Composers, (Fitzroy Dearborn Pub, 99); auth, "The 'New Negro' Legacy of Will Marion Cook," Afro-Americans in New York Life and History, 99; auth, "Removing the Minstrel Mask in the Musicals of Will Marion Cook, Musical Quarterly, 00; auth, Swing Along: The Life and Music of Will Marion Cook, Oxford Univ Press, forthcoming. **CONTACT ADDRESS** Sch Music, Georgia State Univ, 3708 Cherry Ridge Blvd, Decatur, GA 30034. **EMAIL** musmgc@langate.gsu.edu

CARTER, MARVA GRIFFIN
DISCIPLINE MUSIC HISTORY AND LITERATURE **EDUCATION** Boston Conserv, Bachelor of Music; New Eng Conserv, Master of Music; Boston Univ, MA; Univ Ill, Urbana,

PhD. **CAREER** Asst prof to assoc prof, Ga State Univ. **RESEARCH** The music of the black church. **CONTACT ADDRESS** School of Music, Georgia State Univ, 117 Art and Music, Atlanta, GA 30303. **EMAIL** musmgc@panther.gsu.edu

CARTER, STEVEN RAY
PERSONAL Born 04/17/1942, Indianapolis, IN, m, 1976, 3 children **DISCIPLINE** ENGLISH **EDUCATION** Ohio State Univ, PhD 75, MA 67; Denison Univ, BA 64. **CAREER** Salem State Col, assoc prof, prof, 93 to 98-; Univ Puerto Rico, asst prof, assoc prof, prof, 82-94; Trenton State Col, ex prof, 91-92; Univ N C Wilmington, asst prof, 77-82; Univ Sassari Italy, Fulbright-Hays lectr, 76-77; Univ Akron, pt inst, 75-76; Ohio State Univ, tchg assoc, 72-75; Youngstown state Univ, inst, 68-70,72, 73. **HONORS AND AWARDS** Amer Bk Award; Geo Hendrick Award; Fulbright-Hays Jr Lectr; 2 NEH; Ford Foun Gnt; appeared in: who's who in the east; contemporary authors; the writer's directory. **MEMBERSHIPS** MLA **RESEARCH** African Amer Lit; contemp Amer lit; detective fiction; contemp sci-fi. **SELECTED PUBLICATIONS** Auth, James Jones, An American Orientalist Master, Univ IL Press, 98; Lorraine Hansberry, Amer Writers Supp, NY, Scribner's 97; Kathleen Collins, Woodie King Jr, Ted Shine, Richard Wesly and George C. Wolf, The Oxford Companion to African American Literature, eds, William L. Andrews, Frances Smith Foster and Trudier Harris, NY, Oxford Univ Press, 97; Adrienne Kennedy, The Oxford Companion to Women Writing in the US, eds, Cathy N. Davidson, Linda Wagner, NY, OUP, 95; Images of Men in Lorraine Hansberry's Writing, reprinted, Drama Criticism, Gale Research, Hansberry's Drama: Commitment Amid Complexity, Urbana IL, Univ IL Press, 91, pbk ed, New Amer Lib, NY, 93; Hansberry's Drama, reprinted, Black Literature Criticism, Gale Research, 93. **CONTACT ADDRESS** Dept of English, Salem State Col, Salem, MA 01970.

CARTER-SANBORN, KRISTIN
DISCIPLINE ENGLISH **EDUCATION** Stanford Univ, BA, 87; UCLA, PhD, 95. **CAREER** Asst prof. **RESEARCH** Cultural studies; US Latin American Studies; women's studies; feminist theory. **SELECTED PUBLICATIONS** Auth, We Murder Who We Were: Jasmine and the Violence of Identity in Subjects and Citizens: Nation, Race, and Gender from Oroonoko to Anita Hill. **CONTACT ADDRESS** Dept of English, Williams Col, Oakley Center, Williamstown, MA 01267. **EMAIL** kcarter@williams.edu

CARTWRIGHT, LISA
DISCIPLINE FILM AND MEDIA STUDIES, GENDER STUDIES **EDUCATION** Yale Univ, PhD. **CAREER** Assoc prof; taught at, Yale Univ. **HONORS AND AWARDS** Chicago Hum Inst Rockefeller fel; Univ Chicago Pembroke Ctr for Tchg and Res on Women fel & Brown Univ Alumna, Whitney Mus Am Art Independent Study Prog. **RESEARCH** Modernist modes of visual representation in US med sci. **SELECTED PUBLICATIONS** Auth, Screening the Body: Tracing Medicine's Visual Culture; co-ed, The Visible Woman: Imaging Technologies, Inscribing Science; articles on, film modernism and sci, med imag ing and gender, media and commun technol-(s) in health care & soc transformation through technol art and activism. **CONTACT ADDRESS** Dept of Eng, Univ of Rochester, 601 Elmwood Ave, Ste. 656, Rochester, NY 14642. **EMAIL** lisac@troi.cc.rochester.edu

CARTWRIGHT, MARGUERITE DORSEY
PERSONAL Born Boston, MA, w **DISCIPLINE** COMMUNICATIONS **EDUCATION** Boston Univ, BS, MS; NYork Univ, PhD 1948. **CAREER** Hunter Coll of the City Univ of NY, teacher, lecturer; communications, journalism other media; adv educ in foregin countries; Phelps Stokes Inst, rsch. **HONORS AND AWARDS** Phi Beta Kappa other scholarly hons & awds; Headliners Awd 1975; Highest Natl Awd of Women in Communications Inc; Awds from Ford Found, Links, various civic & professional groups; Amoris Alumna Pax Pope Paul VI; Knight Commander Order of African Redemption Rep of Liberia; Keys to Cities Wilmington Xenia Zurich; street name in Nigeria for serv to Univ of Nigeria; subj of various feature articles. **MEMBERSHIPS** Mem Provisional Council of Univ of Nigeria; served on various delegations & com; covered intl conf including Bandung Middle East African States African Peoples; state guest several Independence Celeb in Africa; mem Govs & Vice Pres Overseas Press Club of Amer bd mem Intl League for Human Rights & various civic orgns; mem UN Corres Assn; Women in Communications Inc; World Assn of Women Journalists & Writers other organs. **CONTACT ADDRESS** Phelps Stokes Inst, 10 East 87th St, New York, NY 10028.

CARUTH, CATHY
DISCIPLINE ENGLISH LANGUAGE AND LITERATURE **EDUCATION** Yale Univ, PhD, 88. **CAREER** Prof Eng/Dir comp lit prog. **RESEARCH** English and German Romanticism; trauma theory; psychoanalytic theory. **SELECTED PUBLICATIONS** Auth, Unclaimed Experience: Trauma, Narrative and History; co-ed/intro, Critical Encounters: Reference and Responsibility in Deconstructive Writing; Trauma: Explorations in Memory; Empirical Truths and Critical Fictions: Locke Wordsworth, Kant, Freud. **CONTACT ADDRESS** English Dept, Emory Univ, 1380 Oxford Rd NE, Atlanta, GA 30322-1950. **EMAIL** ccaruth@emory.edu

CARY, CECILE WILLIAMSON
PERSONAL Born 03/04/1938, Washington, DC, m, 1966, 3 children **DISCIPLINE** ENGLISH **EDUCATION** Macalester Col, BA, 59; Wash St. Louis Univ, MA, 64, PhD(English), 69. **CAREER** Instr English, Wayne State Univ, 64-67; from instr to asst prof, 67-72, assoc prof English, Wright State Univ, 72-. **HONORS AND AWARDS** Fulbright, 59-60. **MEMBERSHIPS** MLA. **RESEARCH** Renaissance English literature. **SELECTED PUBLICATIONS** Auth, Go break this lute: Music in Heywood's A Woman Killed with Kindness, Huntington Libr Quart, 74; Burlesque as a method of irony in Shakespeare's Troilus and All's Well, SMC, 75; It circumscribes us here: Hell in the Renaissance Stage, The Scenography of Hell, Kalamazoo: Med Institute Pub, 92. **CONTACT ADDRESS** Dept of English, Wright State Univ, Dayton, 3640 Colonel Glenn, Dayton, OH 45435-0002.

CASAGRANDE, PETER JOSEPH
PERSONAL Born 12/19/1938, Pen Argyl, PA, m, 1961, 5 children **DISCIPLINE** ENGLISH **EDUCATION** Gettysburg Col, BA, 60; Ind Univ, MA, 63, PhD(English), 67. **CAREER** Assoc chmn dept & chmn humanities, 71-72, dir, N Col, 72-73, dir honors, 73-75, from asst prof to Assoc Prof English, Univ Kans, 67-, Assoc Dean, Col Arts & Sci, 72, 91-00; Nat Endowment for Humanities fel, 73-74. **HONORS AND AWARDS** Outstanding Classroom Teacher Awd, 73-74; Outstanding Educator, Mortar Bd, 76 & 81. **MEMBERSHIPS** MLA; Midwestern MLA. **RESEARCH** Novels and poems of Thomas Hardy; novels of George Eliot; literary creativity. **SELECTED PUBLICATIONS** Auth, The shifted centre of altruism in Thomas Hardy's 'The Woodlanders,' English Lit Hist, 3/71; auth, Hardy's Wordsworth: A record and a commentary, English Lit Transition, 77; auth, A new view of Bathsheba Everdene, in Critical Views of Thomas Hardy, Macmillan, summer 78; co-auth, The name Henchard, Thomas Hardy Soc Rev, fall 78; auth, Unity in Hardy's Novels, Macmillan, 82; auth, Hardy's Influence on the Modern Novel, Macmillan, Barnes & Noble, 87; auth, 'tess of the D"Urbervilles": Unorthodox Beauty, Twayne, 92. **CONTACT ADDRESS** Dept of English, Univ of Kansas, Lawrence, Lawrence, KS 66044. **EMAIL** pjc@ukans.edu

CASAREGOLA, VINCENT
DISCIPLINE RHETORICAL THEORY **EDUCATION** Univ IA, PhD. **CAREER** Assoc prof, St Louis Univ, **HONORS AND AWARDS** Ed, IA Jour Lit Studies. **SELECTED PUBLICATIONS** Ed, IA Jour Lit Studies, coauth, Writing for Business and Industry, Univ Iowa, 89; auth, The Discourse of Values and the Literature of the Essay, Values and Public Life, Univ Press Am, 95; auth, "Unstable Elements: The Explosion of the Arcadia Project." Narrative Strategies in Early English Fiction, 95; coauth, "Minorities and Technology." In Encyclopedia of the Future, 95; Winged Visions: Using Images of Aviation and Space Technology in Teaching the Literature and Popular Culture of Modern America, Community Col Huma Rev, 95; auth, "Sir Philip Sidney." In Encyclopedia o Rhetoric, 96; auth, "Technical Communication." In Encyclopedia of Rhetoric, 96; auth, "Twentieth-Century Rhetoric" Encyclopedia of Rhetoric, 96; coauth, "Community and Information Networks in Hypermedia Culture," The Bulletin of Science, Technology, and Society, 97; auth, "Orality, Literacy, and Dialogue: Looking for the Origins of the Essay." Time, Memory, and The Verbal Arts: Essays on the Thought of Walter Ong, 98. **CONTACT ADDRESS** Dept of English, Saint Louis Univ, 221 N Grand Blvd, Saint Louis, MO 63103. **EMAIL** casarevg@slu.edu

CASE, ALISON
DISCIPLINE ENGLISH **EDUCATION** Oberlin, BA, 84; Cornell Univ, PhD, 91. **CAREER** Asst prof. **RESEARCH** Narrative in the 18th- and 19th-century British novel; Victorian women novelists; gender in Victorian poetry. **SELECTED PUBLICATIONS** Auth, Browning's 'Count Gismond': A Canvas for Projection; Tasting the Original Apple: Gender and the Struggle for Narrative Authority in Dracula; Gender and Narration in Aurora Leigh; Against Scott, the Anti-history of Dickens's Barnaby Rudge. **CONTACT ADDRESS** Dept of English, Williams Col, Stetson c-11, Williamstown, MA 01267. **EMAIL** acase@williams.edu

CASEY, ELLEN MILLER
PERSONAL Born 12/07/1941, Evanston, IL, m, 1965, 3 children **DISCIPLINE** ENGLISH LITERATURE **EDUCATION** Loyola Univ Chicago, BS, 62; Univ Iowa, MA, 63; Univ Wis-Madison, PhD(English), 69. **CAREER** Instr English, Mt Mary Col, 65-66; asst prof, 69-74, assoc prof, 74-81, prof English, Univ Scranton, 81-, Nat endowment for Humanities younger humanist fel, 74-75; Danforth Assoc, 81-86. **MEMBERSHIPS** MLA; AAUP; Dickens Soc; Res Soc Victorian Periodicals. **RESEARCH** The English novel; Victorian literature; literature and society. **SELECTED PUBLICATIONS** Auth, Vicrorian Censorship: Not Wisely but Too Well, Proceedings of the Sixth Nat Convention of the Popular Culture, compiled by Michael T. Marsden, Bowling Green State Univ Popular Press, 76; The Victorian Age, Victorian Studies Bull 4.3: 3, Sept 80; Junior Honors Seminar, Nat Col Honors Soc Newsletter, 8, fall 80; That Specially Trying Mode of Publication: Dickens as Editor of the Weekly Serial, Victorian Periodicals Rev, fall 81; Other People's Prudery: Mary Elizabeth Braddon, Sexuality and Victorian Literature, ed Don Richard Cox, Tennessee Studies in Lit, vol 27: 72-82, Knoxville: Univ Tenn Press, 84; In the Pages of the Athenaeum: Fiction in 1883, VPR 18.2: 57-72, summer 85; The Honors Project at Scranton U, The Nat Honors Report 6.4: 15-16, winter 85; Weekly Reviews of Fiction: The Athenaeum vs. the Spectator and the Saturday Review, VPR 23.1: 8-12, spring 90; Saturday Review, The 1890's: An Encyclopedia of British Literature, Art, and Culture, ed G.A. Cevasco,pp 530-531, NY: Garland, 93; The Novel, The 1890's: An Encyclopedia of British Literature, Art, and Culture, ed G.A. Cevasco, pp 439-440, NY: Garland, 93; John Churton Collins (1848-1908), The 1890's: An Encyclopedia of British Literature, Art, and Culture, ed G. A. Cevasco, pp 117-118, NY: Garland, 93; Our Transatlantic Cousins: The Battle over American Analytoc Novels in the Athenaeum, Studies in American Fiction 21.2: 237-249, autumn 93; Anthony Hope (Sir Anthony Hope Hawkins), Late-Victorian and Edwardian British Novelists: First Series, ed George M. Johnson, Dictionary of Literary Biography, 153, Detroit, Washington, D.C., London: Gale Research Inc, 95, 127-137; Hecht's More Light! More Light!, The Explicator 54.2: 113-115, winter 96; Edging Women Out?: Fiction Reviews in the Athenaeum, 1860-1900, Victorian Studies 39.2: 151-171, winter 96. **CONTACT ADDRESS** Dept of English, Univ of Scranton, 800 Linden St, Scranton, PA 18510-4044. **EMAIL** caseye1@uofs.edu

CASEY, JAMES GALLIGAMI
PERSONAL Born 01/23/1963, MA, m, 1987, 2 children **DISCIPLINE** LITERATURE **EDUCATION** Col Holy Cross, BA, 85; Univ Del, MA, 88; PhD, 91. **CAREER** Vis asst prof, Col Holy Cross, 92-00; vis assoc prof, Skidmore Col, 01-. **HONORS AND AWARDS** MLA Independent Scholar Prize. **MEMBERSHIPS** MLA; ASA; NCIS; SSAWW; SSNL. **RESEARCH** Modernism; feminism; leftist and working class aesthetics. **SELECTED PUBLICATIONS** Auth, Dos Passos and the Ideology of the Feminine, Cambridge Univ Pr, 98; auth, "Focus Left: Modernist Angst and the Proletarian Camera," (forthcoming); auth, "Realism, Modernism, and Proletarianism: Narrative and Ideology in the 1920s and 1030s," (forthcoming). **CONTACT ADDRESS** 228 Nelson Ave, Saratoga Springs, NY 12866-3419. **EMAIL** jcasey@skidmore.edu

CASEY, JOHN DUDLEY
PERSONAL Born 01/18/1939, Worcester, MA, m, 1982, 4 children **DISCIPLINE** HISTORY, LAW, AND LITERATURE **EDUCATION** Harvard Col, BA; Harvard Law School, LLB; Univ of Iowa, MFA. **CAREER** Prof of English, Univ of Va, 72-92. **HONORS AND AWARDS** Nat Board Awd for Fiction, 89. **MEMBERSHIPS** P.E.N. **SELECTED PUBLICATIONS** Auth, The Half-life of Happiness, 98; auth, Supper at the Black Pearl, 95; auth, Spartina, 89; auth, Testimony & Demeanor, 79; auth, An American Romance, 77. **CONTACT ADDRESS** Dept of English, Univ of Virginia, Bryant Hall, Charlottesville, VA 22904.

CASEY, MICHAEL W.
PERSONAL Born 05/14/1954, Kennett, MO, m, 1 child **DISCIPLINE** COMMUNICATION; RHETORIC **EDUCATION** Abilene Christian Univ, BA 76, MA 79; Univ Pitts, MA 81, PhD 86. **CAREER** Univ Maine, asst prof, 84-86; Pepperdine Univ, assoc prof, prof, 87-. **HONORS AND AWARDS** Outstanding Young Man of America. **MEMBERSHIPS** NCA; RCA; DCHS. **RESEARCH** Rhetoric; Religious Communication; Hist of Pacifism. **SELECTED PUBLICATIONS** Auth, Saddlebags City Streets Cyberspace: A History of Preaching in the Churches of Christ, Abilene, Abilene Christian U Press, 95; auth, The Closing of Cordell Christian College: A Microcosm of American Intolerance during World War I, Chronicles of Oklahoma, 98; auth, Villains and Heroes of the Great Depression: The Evolution of Father Charles E. Coughlin's Fantasy Themes, coauth, Jour of Radio Stud, 97; auth, Church's of Christ and World War II Civilian Public Service: A Pacifist Remnant, in: Theron Schlabach and Richard Hughes, eds, Proclaim Peace: Christian Pacifism from Unexpected Qtrs, U of IL Press, 97; auth, Government Surveillance of the Churches of Christ in World War I: An Episode of Free Speech Suppression, coauth, Free Speech YR Book, 96; auth, Driving Out the Money Changers: Radio Priest Charles E. Coughlin's Rhetorical Vision, coauth, The Jour of Comm and Religion, 96; auth, The Battle Over Hermeneutics in the Stone-Campbell Movement, 1800-1870, Lewiston, Edwin Mellen Press, 98; auth, The First Female Public Speakers in America (1630-1840): Searching for Egalitarian Christian Primitivism, The Jrnl of Comm and Rel, 00. **CONTACT ADDRESS** Dept of Communication, Pepperdine Univ, 24255 Pacific Coast Hwy, Malibu, CA 90263. **EMAIL** michael.casey@pepperdine.edu

CASINES, GISELA P.
PERSONAL Born 06/29/1951, Havana, Cuba, m **DISCIPLINE** BRITISH LITERATURE **EDUCATION** Fla Int Univ, BA, 73; Univ Fla, MA, 76; PhD, 82. **CAREER** Vis asst prof, to assoc dean, Fla Int Univ, 80-. **HONORS AND AWARDS** McKnight Minority Jr Fac Dev Prog Fel, 86-87. **MEMBERSHIPS** MLA, Assoc of 18th Century Studies, SE Assoc of 18th Century Studies, SAMLA, Coun of Col of Arts and Sci, Fla Assoc of Women in Educ. **RESEARCH** Restoration drama and

dramatic theory, Miami writers. **SELECTED PUBLICATIONS** Auth, "Private Sins, Public Penance: Poetic Justice in Some Restoration Plays with Spanish Sources," S Atlantic Rev 53.1, (88): 27-39; auth, "The Concept of Poetic Justice in Spanish Golden Age Literary Theory," Hispanofila 32.1 (89): 13-20; auth, "Guardians in Restoration Plays with Direct Spanish Dramatic Sources," Lamar Jour of the Humanities 14.1,2, (89): 51-60; auth, "Greater Miami," The Booklover's Guide to Florida, (Sarasota: Pineapple Pr, 92). **CONTACT ADDRESS** Arts and Sci, Florida Intl Univ, Dean's Office, Miami, FL 33199. **EMAIL** casinesgu@fiu.edu

CASMIR, FRED L.
PERSONAL Born 12/30/1928, Berlin, Germany, m, 1986, 2 children **DISCIPLINE** SPEECH AND COMMUNICATION **EDUCATION** David Lipscomb Col, BA, 50; Ohio State Univ, MA, 55, PhD, 61. **CAREER** Part-time Fac, East Los Angeles Col, 73-74; Part-time Fac to Assoc Prof, San Fernando Valley State Col, 61-73; Instr to Prof Commun, 56-94, dir, International Studies Major, Chmn, Pepperdine Univ, 89-94, 97-99; distinguished prof emer of International Commun Asn, National Commun Asn, Pepperdine Univ, 94-; assoc ed, editorial boards of Journal of Commun, Critical Studies in Mass Commun, 99-01. **HONORS AND AWARDS** Outstanding Teacher, Pepperdine Univ, 73; Second-place winner, national papers contest, Nat Asn Educ Broadcasters, 81; Teacher of the Year, Alumni Asn, Pepperdine Univ, 85; PRSSA, Outstanding Fac Advisor, 86; Outstanding Sr Interculturalist, Soc Intercultural Educ, Training and Res, Int, 87; Assoc, Sears-Roebuck Found Grant and Assoc Project for Asian Studies, Fac Development, Pepperdine Univ, 90-91; Fel, Irvine Found Grant, 93; recipient of several research grants from Pepperdine University and others. **MEMBERSHIPS** Nat Commun Asn; Pi Kappa Delta; Ger Speech Asn; Int Commun Asn; World Commun Asn; Western Speech Commun Asn. **SELECTED PUBLICATIONS** Ed, Building communication theories: A socio-cultural approach, Lawrence Erlbaum Assoc, 94; Communication in Eastern Europe: The role of history, culture and media in contemporary conflict, Lawrence Erlbaum Assoc, 95; auth, Foundations for the study of intercultural communication based on a third culture building model, Int J Intercultural Relations (in press); ed, Ethics in Intercultural and International Communication, Lawrence Erlbaum Assoc (97); auth and ed, of numerous other articles and publications. **CONTACT ADDRESS** Seaver Col, Pepperdine Univ, 24255 Pacific Coast Hwy, Malibu, CA 90263. **EMAIL** fcasmir@hotmail.edu

CASS, MICHAEL MCCONNELL
PERSONAL Born 07/01/1941, Macon, GA, m, 1965, 2 children **DISCIPLINE** AMERICAN LITERATURE & HISTORY **EDUCATION** University of the South, BA, 63; Emory Univ, PhD(Am Studies), 71. **CAREER** From instr to asst prof, 69-76, from assoc prof to prof Interdisciplinary Studies, Mercer Univ, 76-84; chmn, Lamar Mem Lec Comm, 92. **MEMBERSHIPS** SAtlantic Mod Lang Assn; Soc for the Study of Southern Lit. **RESEARCH** Southern literature; southern culture. **SELECTED PUBLICATIONS** Auth, Charles C Jones Jr and the lost cause, Ga Hist Quart, Summer 71; The South Will Rise Again, Anniversary & October Poem (poems), Southern Rev, Autumn 74; foreword to Lewis P Simpson's The Dispossessed Garden: Pastoral and History in Southern Literature, 74 & to Walter L Sullivan's A Requiem for the Renaissance: The State of Fiction in the Modern South, 75, Univ Ga Press; Joshua & Coming Back to Poetry (poems), World Order, Summer 75; At Home in the Dark, The Fairest Lass in All Christendom & The Lonesome End (poems), Southern Rev, Spring 77; Georgia Preacher (poem), Christian Century, 10/4/78; Survivors (poem), Christianity & Lit, Winter 79; foreword to Fred C. Hobson, Jr, The Writer in the Postmodern South, Athens, 91; to Jack Temple Kirby, The Counter-Cultural South, Athens, 96; auth, "Walker Percy," in Contemporary Southern Authors, ed Roger Matuz, St James Press, 98. **CONTACT ADDRESS** Interdisciplinary Studies, Mercer Univ, Macon, 1400 Coleman Ave, Macon, GA 31207-0003. **EMAIL** cass_mm@mercer.edu

CASSEL, SUSIE L.
PERSONAL Born 09/30/1966, Liberia, s **DISCIPLINE** ENGLISH **EDUCATION** Univ S Calif, BA, 86; BA, 87; Harvard Univ, MA, 88; Univ Calif, PhD, 96. **CAREER** Res Asst to Lecturer, Univ Calif, 93-95; Asst Prof, Calif State Univ, 96-. **HONORS AND AWARDS** Who's Who in Calif, 98-99; Who's Who of Am Women, 97-98; Who's Who in the West, 96-97; Grad Student of the Year, Univ Calif, 96. **MEMBERSHIPS** Mod Lang Asn, Asn Asia Am studies, San Diego Chinese Hist Soc, MELUS. **RESEARCH** Asian American identity politics and mixed race. **SELECTED PUBLICATIONS** Auth, "Pitfalls in Protocols," Hapa Issues Forum, 99; rev, of "The Wars We Took to Vietnam," by Milton J Bates, Journal of Asian American Studies, (98): 297-300; auth, "The Role of the Humanities within the corporate Model of Education," Education, 01; rev, of "The Very Inside: An Anthology of Writing by Asian and Pacific Islander Lesbian and Bisexual Women, MELUS, forthcoming; auth, "Eliza Ruhamah Scidmore," American National Biography, Oxford Univ Press, 99; auth, "Octavia Celeste W. LeVert," American National Biography, Oxford Univ Press, 99; co-auth, "Need Gratification and Brain dominance Serve as Nucleus for Transpersonal Psychology and biofeedback Use," Psychology, forthcoming. **CONTACT ADDRESS** Dept Arts & Sci, California State Univ, San Marcos, 333 S Twin Oaks Vlly, San Marcos, CA 92096-0001. **EMAIL** scassel@csusm.edu

CASSIDY, JANE W.
PERSONAL Born 05/29/1956, Palestine, TX, m, 1988, 1 child **DISCIPLINE** MUSIC **EDUCATION** Hartt Col of Music at the Univ of Hartford, BME, 78; Fla State Univ, MME, 85; Fla State Univ, PhD, 88. **CAREER** Music specialist, Putnum Public Schs, 78-84; GTA, Fla State Univ, 84-88; asst prof, Louisiana State Univ, 88-94; assoc prof, Louisiana State Univ, 94-present. **HONORS AND AWARDS** Phi Delta Kappa; Pi Kappa Lambda; Alpha Chi. **MEMBERSHIPS** Music Educators Nat Conf; Am Music Therapy Asn; Coun for Exceptional Children. **RESEARCH** Musical development and learning among children; music for special populations; teacher effectiveness. **SELECTED PUBLICATIONS** Auth, A comparison between student's self-observation and instructor observation of teacher intensity behaviors,Bull of the Coun for Res in Music Educ, 115, 93; auth, Effects of various sightseeing strategies on nonmusic majors' pitch accuracy,Jour of Res in Music Educ, 41, 93; coauth, The effect of music listening on physiological responses of premature infants in the NICU,Jour of Music Therapy, 22, 95; coauth, Verbal and operant responses of young children to vocal versus instrumental song performances, Jour of Res in Music Educ, 44, 97; coauth, Effects of music with video on responses of nonmusic majors: An exploratory study in Jour of Res in Music Educ, 44, 97; coauth, Nonmusic Majors' cognitive and affective responses to performance and programmatic music videos, Jour of Res in Music Educ, 35, 98; coauth, Presentation of aural stimuli to newborn and premature infants: An audiological perspective, in Jour of Music Therapy, 35, 98. **CONTACT ADDRESS** Sch of Music, Louisiana State Univ and A&M Col, Baton Rouge, LA 70803. **EMAIL** jcassid@lsu.edu

CASSIRER, THOMAS
PERSONAL Born 04/28/1923, Rome, Italy, m, 1948, 1 child **DISCIPLINE** FRENCH AND AFRICAN LITERATURE **EDUCATION** McGill Univ, BA, 45; Yale Univ, PhD(Fr & comp lit), 53. **CAREER** Asst prof French, Smith Col, 60-65; assoc prof, 65-69, Prof French & African Lit, Univ Mass, Amherst, 69-. **MEMBERSHIPS** MLA; Am Asn Teachers Fr; African Studies Asn. **RESEARCH** Eighteenth century French literature; modern African literature. **SELECTED PUBLICATIONS CONTACT ADDRESS** Dept of French & Italian, Univ of Massachusetts, Amherst, Amherst, MA 01002.

CASSIS, AWNY F.
PERSONAL Born 08/23/1934, Tahta, Egypt **DISCIPLINE** ENGLISH LITERATURE **EDUCATION** Ain Shams Univ (Cairo), BA, 54, DPE, 55; Trinity Col, Univ Dublin, PhD, 60. **CAREER** Lectr, Tchrs Trng Col (Egypt), 61; lectr, fac arts, Ain Shams Univ, 64; asst prof to prof, 68-94, dean arts & sci, 80-85, Prof Emer English, Univ Lethbridge, 95-. **RESEARCH** 20th century English literature; Graham Greene. **SELECTED PUBLICATIONS** Auth, The Twentieth Century English Novel: An Annotated Bibliography of Criticism, 77; auth, Graham Greene: An Annotated Bibliography of Criticism, 81; auth, Graham Greene, 94; auth, Graham Greene: Man of Paradox, 94. **CONTACT ADDRESS** Dept of English, Univ of Lethbridge, 4401 University Dr, Lethbridge, AB, Canada T1K 3M4.

CASSUTO, LEONARD
DISCIPLINE ENGLISH **EDUCATION** Columbia Univ, BA, 81; Harvard Univ, MA, 85; PhD, 89. **CAREER** Asst prof to assoc prof, Fordham Univ, 89-. **HONORS AND AWARDS** Fulbright Lectr, Tanzania, 96. **RESEARCH** American Literature, American Studies. **SELECTED PUBLICATIONS** Coed, Rereading Jack London, Stanford Univ Pr, 95; auth, The Inhuman Race: The Racial Grotesque in American Literature and Culture, Columbia Univ Pr 97; ed, Edgar Allan Poe: Literary Theory and Criticism, Dover 99. **CONTACT ADDRESS** English Dept, Fordham Univ, Line Center Campus, New York, NY 10023. **EMAIL** cassuto@fordham.edu

CASTELLANI, VICTOR
PERSONAL Born 02/14/1947, Brooklyn, NY, m, 1976, 2 children **DISCIPLINE** CLASSICS **EDUCATION** Fordham Univ, BA, 68; Princeton Univ, PhD, 71. **CAREER** Adj lectr, classics, Fordham Univ, 70-71; instr, 71-72, asst prof, 72-80, assoc prof, 80- , chemn 81-85, 89-98, Dept of Lang and Lit, Univ Denver. **HONORS AND AWARDS** Horace Acad, 65; Classic Prize, 66; Phi Beta Kappa, 67; Columbia Tchrs Col Book Awd, 67; NDEA, Princton fel, 68; Woodrow Wilson fel, 68; pres, Rocky Mtn MLN, 84; Awd for Outstanding Support, 93. **MEMBERSHIPS** Am Class League; Archaeol Inst Am; APA; Class Asn of Middle West and South; Pacific Ancient and Modern Lang Asn; Pro-Riesling Verein, Trier, Ger; Rocky Mountain MLA. **RESEARCH** Greek and Latin literature, especially epic and drama; ancient religion; comparative literature, especially narrative poetry, Dante, and drama, Ibsen; art and literature. **SELECTED PUBLICATIONS** Auth, Captive Captor Freed: The National Theater of Ancient Rome, Drama: Beitrage zum antiken Drama und seiner Rezeption, 95; auth, Flesh or Fish or What? Euripides' Orestes, Didaskalia: Ancient Theater Today, 95; auth, Athena and Friends: One Among the Greek Religions, in Dillon, ed, Religion in the Ancient World: New Themes and Approaches, Hakkert, 96; auth, Europa, Euripides, and the Differentiation of Europe, Jour of the Int Soc for the Study of European Ideas, 96; auth, Regulated European Wine: A View From Middle America, and, Classics at a Small University, Selected Proceedings of the 5th International Conference on ISSEI, 96; auth, After Stormy Seas Calm Once More I See: Reconciliation and Re-Moralization in Euripides, Jour of the Int Soc for Stud of European Ideas, 97; auth, Melpomene Polias: Athenian Tragedy and Politics in the Later Fifth Century, in Hillard, ed, Ancient History in a Modern University, vol 1, Eerdmans, 98; auth, Ibsen and the Return of Myth, in M. Deppermann, ed, Ibsen im europaischen Spannungsfeld zwischen Naturalismus und Symbolismus: Kongressakten der 8, Internationalen Ibsen-Konferenz, 98; auth, Beginnings of Ancient Greek History and Historiography, rev article, The European Legacy, 98; auth, Insignes Pietate? The Ancient Romans and Their Religious Life, rev article, The European Legacy, 99. **CONTACT ADDRESS** Dept of Languages and Literatures, Univ of Denver, Denver, CO 80208-2662. **EMAIL** vcastell@du.edu

CASTELLITTO, GEORGE
PERSONAL Born 07/02/1949, Jersey City, NJ, m, 1983 **DISCIPLINE** ENGLISH **EDUCATION** Fordham Univ, PhD, 84. **CAREER** Asst prof to prof, Felician Col, 88-, Dir, Grad English, 99-; ed, The J of Imagism, 96-. **HONORS AND AWARDS** Who's Who Among Am Teachers, 98, 2000. **MEMBERSHIPS** Modern Lang Asn, Wallace Stevens Soc, Asn Lit Scholars and Critics. **RESEARCH** American Imagist movement. **SELECTED PUBLICATIONS** Auth, "Imagism and Martin Scorsese: Images Suspended and Extended," Lit/Film Quart 26.1 (98); auth, "Imagism and Allen Ginsberg's Manhattan Locations: The Movement from Spatial Reality to Written Image," Colby Quart 35.2 (June 99); auth, "Willy Loman: The Tension Between Marxism and Capitalism," in The Salesman has a Birthday: Essays Celebrating the Fiftieth Anniversary of Arthur Miller's 'Death of a Salesman', Univ Press Am (2000). **CONTACT ADDRESS** dept Humanities, Felician Col, 262 S Main St, Lodi, NJ 07644-2117. **EMAIL** GEOCST@msn.com

CASTIGLIA, CHRISTOPHER
DISCIPLINE ENGLISH **EDUCATION** Amherst Col, BA; Columbia Univ, MA, PhD. **CAREER** Assoc prof. **RESEARCH** Antebellum American literature and culture; cultural Stud; gender Stud; Poststructuralist theory; popular culture. **SELECTED PUBLICATIONS** Auth, Bound and Determined: Captivity, Culture-Crossing, and White Womanhood from Mary Rowlandson to Patty Hearst, Chicago, 96; Captives in History: Susanna Rowsom's Reuben and Rachel, Redefining the Polit Novel; Rebel Without a Closet, Engendering Men; In Praise of Extra-vagant Women: Catharine Sedgwick and the Captivity Romance, Legacy, 90. **CONTACT ADDRESS** Dept of English, Loyola Univ, Chicago, 6525 N. Sheridan Rd., Chicago, IL 60626. **EMAIL** ccasti@luc.edu

CASTLE, TERRY
PERSONAL Born 10/18/1953, San Diego, CA **DISCIPLINE** ENGLISH **CAREER** Asst prof, English, 83-85, assoc prof, 85-87, Prof, Stanford Univ, 87-, Walter A. Haas Prof in the Humanities, 98. **HONORS AND AWARDS** Guggenheim fel, 88-89; nominated for the Lambda Literary Awd, 94 for The Apparitional Lesbian: Female Homosexuality and Modern Culture, Columbia Univ Press, 93, and selected as Breakthrough Book in Victorian Studies, Lingua Franca, Sept/Oct, 95, also Alternate Selection, Reader's Subscription Book Club, 94. **RESEARCH** 18th-20th century British lit; the hist of the novel; lit and sexuality; gay and lesbian lit. **SELECTED PUBLICATIONS** Auth, The Apparitional Lesbian: Female Homosexuality and Modern Culture, Columbia Univ Press, 93; Emma by Jane Austen, rev ed, with new intro, Oxford Univ Press, 95; In Praise of Brigitte Fassbaender, in Corinne Blackmer and Patricia J. Smith, eds, En Travesti: Women, Gender, Subversion, Opera, Columbia Univ Press, 95; The Female Thermometer: Eighteenth-Century Culture and the Invention of the Uncanny, Oxford Univ Press, 95, one of three books nominated for the PEN/Spielvogel-Diamonstein Award for the Art of the Essay, 96; Noel Coward and Radclyffe Hall: Kindred Spirits, Columbia Univ Press, 96; Women and Literary Criticism, in H. B. Nisbet and Claude Rawson, eds, The Cambridge History of Literary Criticism, Vol IV, Cambridge Univ Press, 97; The Mysteries of Udolpho by Ann Radcliffe, rev ed with new intro, Oxford Univ Press, 98; Masquerade, in International Encyclopedia of Dance, Univ CA Univ Press, forthcoming 98; Lesbian Aesthetics: A Historical View, in Michael Kelly, ed, Encyclopedia of Aesthetics, Oxford Univ Press, forthcoming; The Literature of Lesbianism: A Historical Anthology from Ariosto to Stonewall, Oxford Univ Press, in progress. **CONTACT ADDRESS** Dept of English, Stanford Univ, Stanford, CA 94305-2087.

CASTO-URIOS, JOSE
PERSONAL Born 12/04/1961, Montevideo, Uruguay, d **DISCIPLINE** LITERATURE, THEATER **EDUCATION** Univ San Marcos, BA, 88; Univ Pitt, MA, 91; PhD, 93. **CAREER** Assoc prof, Purdue Univ, Calmet. **HONORS AND AWARDS** Letras de Oro, Finalist, 93, 95. **MEMBERSHIPS** MLA; LASA. **RESEARCH** Contemporary literature and theater. **CONTACT ADDRESS** Dept Foreign Lang, Purdue Univ, Calumet, 2233 171st Street, Hammond, IN 46323.

CASTRONOVO, DAVID
PERSONAL Born 10/30/1945, Brooklyn, NY **DISCIPLINE** ENGLISH AND COMPARATIVE LITERATURE **EDUCATION** Brooklyn Col, BA, 67; Columbia Univ, MA, 68, PhD, 75. **CAREER** Adjunct asst prof, Brooklyn Col, 72-76; adjunct asst prof, Pace, 76-78, asst prof, 79-86, assoc prof, 86-88, prof of English, Pace Univ, NY, 88-. **HONORS AND AWARDS** Fac fel, Columbia Univ, 67-71; New York Times Notable Book (Edmund Wilson), 85. **MEMBERSHIPS** PEN; MLA. **RESEARCH** 19th and 20th century lit; social hist; literary criticism. **SELECTED PUBLICATIONS** Auth, Edmund Wilson, Frederick Ungar, 84; Thornton Wilder, Frederick Ungar, 86; The English Gentleman, Frederick Ungar, 87; The American Gentleman, Continuum, 91; From the Uncollected Edmund Wilson, ed and introduced with Janet Groth, OH Univ Press, 95; Richard Yates: Am American Realist, with Steven Goldleaf, Twayne/Macmillan, 96; Edmund Wilson Revisited, Twayne/ Macmillan, 98; auth, Encyclopedia of American Literature, 99; auth,"Ungar Encyclopedia of Literature in The 20th Century," in Scribner's Encyclopedia of American Lives (00). **CONTACT ADDRESS** Dept of English, Pace Univ, New York, 1 Pace Plaza, New York, NY 10038.

CATANO, JAMES
DISCIPLINE RHETORICAL AND CRITICAL THEORY, STYLISTICS **EDUCATION** Brown Univ, PhD, 80. **CAREER** Assoc prof, La State Univ. **HONORS AND AWARDS** Summer stipend, NEH, 83; grant, LSU CORE, 92. **RESEARCH** Gender theory; writing theory. **SELECTED PUBLICATIONS** Auth, Machines for the Garden, Writing Prog Admin, 83; Style and Stylistics, in Style, 85; Computer- Based Writing: Navigating the Fluid Text, in Col Compos and Commun, 85; Language, History, Style: Leo Spitzer and the Critical Tradition, 88; The Rhetoric of Masculinity: Origins, Institutions, and the Myth of the Self-Made Man, in Col Eng, 90; Stylistics, in Johns Hopkins Guide to Literary Criticism, 94. **CONTACT ADDRESS** Dept of Eng, Louisiana State Univ and A&M Col, 232C Allen Hall, Baton Rouge, LA 70803. **EMAIL** catano@ unix1.sncc.lsu.edu

CATRON, LOUIS E.
PERSONAL Born Springfield, IL, d, 1 child **DISCIPLINE** THEATRE, PLAYWRITING, DIRECTING **EDUCATION** Millikin Univ, AB, 58; Southern Ill Univ, MA, 59, PhD(-theatre), 66. **CAREER** Instr theatre & speech, Lincoln Col, 59-63; asst prof theatre, Ill State Univ, 64-65; assoc prof, 66-74, Prof Theatre, Col William & Mary, 74-, John Golden travel fel, 66; vis artist, Youngstown State Univ & Millikin Univ, 68. **HONORS AND AWARDS** Phi Beta Kappa, Outstanding Fac Awd; Commonwealth of Virginia. **MEMBERSHIPS** Am Theatre Asn; Speech Commun Asn. **RESEARCH** Theatre direction; history of the American theatre; history of war as depicted in fiction, especially dramatic literature. **SELECTED PUBLICATIONS** Auth, The Actions of Tigers, 66 & Lincoln at Springfield: January, 1859, 66, Southern Ill Univ; Centaur, Centaur! & The Rainbow Sign, 71, Col William & Mary; At a beetle's pace (play), 5/71, Where have all the lightning bugs gone (play), 11/71 & Touch the bluebird's song (play), 12/71, Dramatics; Where Have all the Lightning Bugs Gone, Touch the Bluebird's Song & At a Beetle's Pace (plays in book form), Samuel French, 72; The actions of tigers, One Act Publ Co, 73; auth, Writing, Producing, and Selling Your Play, Prentice Hall, 84; auth, The Director's Vision, Mayfield, 89; auth, Playwriting, Waveland Press, 90; auth, Overcoming Directorial Block About Blocking, Samuel French, 91; auth, The Elements of Playwriting, Macmillan, 93; auth, The Power of One: The Solo Play for Playwrights, Actors and Directors, Heinemann, 00. **CONTACT ADDRESS** Dept of Theatre & Speech, Col of William and Mary, Williamsburg, VA 23185. **EMAIL** lecatr@wm. edu

CATT, STEPHEN E.
DISCIPLINE COMMUNICATION STUDIES **EDUCATION** Univ Ariz, BA, MA; Univ Ohio, PhD. **CAREER** Prof. **HONORS AND AWARDS** Lib Arts Sci Tchg Awd. **SELECTED PUBLICATIONS** Auth, Fundamentals of Management: A Framework for Excellence. **CONTACT ADDRESS** Div of Communcation and Theatre Arts, Emporia State Univ, 1200 Commercial St, Emporia, KS 66801-5087. **EMAIL** cattstep@esumail.emporia.edu

CATTO, BONNIE A.
PERSONAL Born 04/19/1951, Boston, MA, m, 1975 **DISCIPLINE** CLASSICS **EDUCATION** Mt Holyoke Col, AB, 73; Univ Penn, MA, 76, PhD, 81. **CAREER** Vis lectr, Univ Mass Amherst, 78; instr, 78-81, asst prof, 81-87, assoc prof, 87-88, Mt Holyoke Col; vis assoc prof, Middlebury Col, 88-89; assoc prof, 89-97, prof, 97-, classics, Assumption Col. **HONORS AND AWARDS** Fully funded sabbatical, Assumption Col, 95-96; Sloan Found grant, 86; Phi Beta Kappa; Mary Lyon Scholar; Sarah Williston scholar. **MEMBERSHIPS** Amer Philol Asn; Archaeol Inst of Amer; Classical Asn of New England; Vergilian Soc; Pioneer Valley Classical Asn; Classical Asn of Mass. **RESEARCH** Lucretius; Ancient science; Vergil; Lyric & Elegiac poetry; Greek tragedy. **SELECTED PUBLICATIONS** Rev, Lucy Hutchinson's Translation of Lucretius: De Rerum Natura, The New England Classical Jour, 98; auth, Lucretius. Selections from De Rerum Natura, Bolchazy-Carducci Publ, 98; auth, Lucretian Light: Bacon's Debt to Lucretius and Epicurus, New England Classical Jour, 98; auth, The Wedding of Peleus and Thetis, Athenaze Newsletter, 97; auth, Selections from Lucretius' De Rerum Natura, The Classical Asn of New England, Short Greek and Latin Texts for Students, 96; rev, Musical Design in Sophoclean Theater, The New England Classical Jour, 96; auth, Duals, Athenaze Newsletter, 94; **CONTACT ADDRESS** Dept of Foreign Languages, Assumption Col, 500 Salisbury St., Worcester, MA 01609-1296. **EMAIL** bcatto@eve.assumption.edu

CAUGHIE, PAMELA L.
DISCIPLINE ENGLISH **EDUCATION** Univ Va, PhD, 87. **CAREER** Assoc prof; prof; dir of women's studies. **RESEARCH** Modernism, feminst, theory, literary theory, African-Am lit and theory, pedagogy. **SELECTED PUBLICATIONS** Auth, Virginia Woolf and Postmodernism: Literature in Quest and Question of Itself, Univ Ill Press, 91; articles, Let It Pass: Changing the Subject, Once Again, PMLA, 97; Passing as Pedagogy: Feminism in(to) Cultural Stud, in English Stud,Culture Stud, Univ Ill Press, 94; Making History, in Sandra M. Gilbert, Susan Gubar, and Feminist Literary History, Garland Publ, 93; auth, Passing and Pedagogy: The Dynamics of Responsibility, Univ of Illinois Press, 99; ed, Virginia Woolf in the Age of Mechanical Reproduction, Garland Publishing, 00. **CONTACT ADDRESS** Dept of English, Loyola Univ, Chicago, 6525 N. Sheridan Rd., Chicago, IL 60626. **EMAIL** pcaughi@luc.edu

CAVANAGH, SHEILA T.
DISCIPLINE ENGLISH LANGUAGE AND LITERATURE **EDUCATION** Brown Univ, PhD, 88. **CAREER** Assoc prof **RESEARCH** Renaissance literature; Shakespeare; literary criticism; feminist theory. **SELECTED PUBLICATIONS** Auth, Wanton Eyes and Chaste Desires: Female Sexuality in The Faerie Queene. **CONTACT ADDRESS** English Dept, Emory Univ, 1380 Oxford Rd NE, Atlanta, GA 30322-1950. **EMAIL** engstc@emory.edu

CAVER, CHRISTINE
DISCIPLINE AMERICAN FICTION **EDUCATION** Univ TX at San Antonio, BA; Univ TX at Austin, MA, PhD. **CAREER** Asst prof; taught at, Univ TX at Austin. **RESEARCH** Contemp Am fiction. **SELECTED PUBLICATIONS** Publ on res interest. **CONTACT ADDRESS** Col of Fine Arts and Hum, Univ of Texas, San Antonio, 6900 N Loop 1604 W, San Antonio, TX 78249.

CAWELTI, JOHN GEORGE
PERSONAL Born 12/31/1929, Evanston, IL, m, 1955, 5 children **DISCIPLINE** AMERICAN CIVILIZATION, MODERN & CONTEMPORARY LITERATURE **EDUCATION** Oberlin Col, BA, 51; State Univ Iowa, MA, 56, PhD(Am civilization), 60. **CAREER** From instr to asst prof humanities, Univ Chicago, 57-64, assoc prof English & humanities, 64-68, prof, 68-80, chmn comt gen studies in humanities, 70-75; Prof English, Univ KY, 80- **MEMBERSHIPS** Am Studies Asn; Popular Cult Asn. **RESEARCH** History of popular culture; literature and culture; American literature. **SELECTED PUBLICATIONS** Coauth, Sources of The American Republic, Scott, 61; auth, Form as cultural criticism in the work of Henry James, In: Literature and Society, Univ Nebr, 64; Apostles of the Self-Made Man, Univ Chicago, 65; American on display: The World's Fairs of 1876, 1893 and 1933, In: America and the Age of Industrialism, Free, 68; The Six-Gun Mistique, Bowling Green Popular, 70; A Focus on Bonnie and Clyde, Prentice-Hall, 73; Adventure, Mystery and Romance, Univ Chicago, 76. **CONTACT ADDRESS** Dept of English, Univ of Kentucky, 500 S Limestone St, Lexington, KY 40506-0003.

CAWS, MARY ANN
PERSONAL Born 09/10/1933, Wilmington, NC, m, 1952, 2 children **DISCIPLINE** FRENCH LITERATURE; ENGLISH LITERATURE; COMPARATIVE LITERATURE **EDUCATION** Bryn Mawr Col, BA, 54; Yale Univ, MA, 56; Univ Kans, PhD, 62. **CAREER** Vis asst prof French, Univ Kans, 64; from asst prof to assoc prof, 66-74, Prof Romance Lang, Hunter Col & Grad Ctr, City Univ New York, 74-, Exec Off Comp Lit Phd Prog, 76-, Asst ed, French Rev, 70-; Guggenheim fel, 72-73; Fulbright-Hays sr travel res scholar, 72-73; ed, Dada/ Surrealism, 72-; ed, Le Siecle eclate, 74; mem adv bd Western Europe, Fulbright-Hays Res Prog, 77-; Nat Endowment for Humanities fel, 79-80. **HONORS AND AWARDS** Guggenheim Fel, Fulbright Fel; NEH Sr Fel, NEH Summer Seminars; Phi Beta Kappa Vis Scholar; life mem of Clare Hall, Cambridge Univ; Getty Scholar; Rockefeller Found; Officier, Palmes Academiques. **MEMBERSHIPS** MLA, Asn Studies Dada & Surrealism, Am Asn Teachers Fr, Am Comp Lit Asn; Doctor of Humane Letters, Union Col, 83. **RESEARCH** Contemporary poetry; Dada and surrealism; poetics and literary theory translation. **SELECTED PUBLICATIONS** Auth, Robert Motherwell: What Art Holds, Columbia Univ Pr (New York), 95; auth, Carrington and Lytton/Alone Together, Cecil Woolf (London), 96; auth, Andre Breton, Revisited, Twayne (New York), 96; auth, The Surrealist Look: An Erotics of Encounter, MIT Pr (Cambridge), 97; auth, Surrealism and the Art of Display, Wexner Center, 97; auth, Bloomsbury and France: Art and Friends, Oxford Univ Pr, 99; auth, Picasso's Weeping Woman: The Life and Art of Dora Maar, Little Brown/Bulfinch, 00; ed, The Surrealist Painters and Poets, MIT Pr, (Cambridge), 01; ed, Manifesto: A Century of Isms., Univ of Nebr Pr (Lincoln), 01. **CONTACT ADDRESS** Ph.D. Program in French, Graduate Sch and Univ Ctr, CUNY, 365 Fifth Ave, New York, NY 10016. **EMAIL** cawsma@aol.com

CAYWOOD, CYNTHIA
PERSONAL Born 09/14/1952, KS, m, 1992, 3 children **DISCIPLINE** ENGLISH **EDUCATION** Univ Kansas, BA, 74; Univ Exeter (Eng), MA, 77; Duke Univ, PhD, 85. **CAREER** Asst prof to prof, Univ San Diego, 84- . **HONORS AND AWARDS** Rotary Int fel; James B. Duke fel; USD Davies Awd Teaching Exc. **MEMBERSHIPS** Am Soc 18th Century Student; Aphra Behn Soc; AAUP. **RESEARCH** 17th & 18th Century British drama. **SELECTED PUBLICATIONS** Auth, Teaching Writing: Pedagogy, Gender, & Equity, Gillian R. Overing; auth, Christmas Carol. **CONTACT ADDRESS** Dept English, Univ San Diego, 5998 Alcala Park, San Diego, CA 92110-2429. **EMAIL** ccaywood@acusd.edu

CAZEAUX, ISABELLE
PERSONAL Born 02/24/1926, New York, NY **DISCIPLINE** MUSICOLOGY **EDUCATION** Hunter Col, BA, 45; Smith Col, MA, 46; Ecole normale de musique, Paris, Licence d'Enseignement, 50; ConservaToire national de musique, Paris, Premiere medaille, 50; Columbia Univ, PhD, 61. **CAREER** Music & phonorecords cataloguer, New York Pub Libr, 57-63; Lectr, A.C. Dickerman Prof, Bryn Mawr col, 63-92; Musicology Fac, Manhattan Sch Mus, 69-82; vis prof, Rutgers Univ, Douglass Col, 78. **HONORS AND AWARDS** Libby van Arsdale Prize for Music, Hunter Col, 45; Fel, Smith Col, Columbia Univ, Inst Int Educ, 1941-59; grant from Martha Baird Rockefeller Fund Music, 1971-72; grant from Herman Goldman Foundation, 1980. **MEMBERSHIPS** Am Musicological Soc, Societe Francaise de Musicologie; Intl Musicological Soc, Mus Libr Asn, Nat Opera Assoc, Societe Theophile Gautier. **RESEARCH** French music: Renaissance & La Belle Epoque **SELECTED PUBLICATIONS** Auth, French Music in the Fifteenth and Sixteenth Centuries, Blackwell, Praeger, 75; Trans, The Memoirs of Philippe de Commynes, Univ SC Press, 69-73; co-ed, Anthologie de la chanson parisienne au XVI siecle; "One Does not Defend the Sum: Some Notes on Pladan and Wagner," in Music and Civilization, Norton, 84. **CONTACT ADDRESS** 415 East 72nd St., #5FE, New York, NY 10021.

CECCARELLI, LEAH M.
DISCIPLINE COMMUNICATION STUDIES; RHETORIC **EDUCATION** Northwestern Univ, PhD, 95. **CAREER** Instr, Loyola Univ, 93-93; asst prof, Pa State Univ, 94-96; asst prof, Univ of Wash, 96- . **HONORS AND AWARDS** Gerald R. Miller Dissertation Awd, Nat Commun Asn, 96; Golden Anniversary Monogr Awd, 99. **MEMBERSHIPS** Nat Commun Asn; Rhet Soc of Am; Am Asn for the Rhet of Sci and Tech. **RESEARCH** Rhet of Sci; Pub Address, Rhet Criticism. **SELECTED PUBLICATIONS** Auth, A Masterpiece in a New Genre: The Rhetorical Negotiation of Two Audiences in Schroedinger's What is Life?, Tech Commun Quart, 3, 94; A Rhetoric of Interdisciplinary Scientific Discourse: Textual Criticism of Dobzhansky's Genetics and the Origin of Species, Social Epistemology 9, 95; The Ends of Rhetoric: Aesthetic, Political, Epistemic, in: Making and Unmaking the Prospects for Rhetoric, 97; Polysemy: Multiple Meanings in Rhetorical Criticism, Quart Jour of Speech, 84, 98; Rhetorical Hermeneutics: Invention and Interpretation in the Age of Science, Rhet, 16, 97; Charles Alan Taylor, Defining Science: A Rhetoric or Demarcation, Quart Jour of Speech, 83, 97; auth, "Rhetorical Criticism and the Rhetoric of Science," Western J of Commun (in press); auth, Shaping Science with Rhetoric: The Cases of Dobzhansky, Shroedinger, and Wilson, Univ Chicago Press, in press. **CONTACT ADDRESS** Dept of Speech Communication, Univ of Washington, PO Box 353415, Seattle, WA 98195-3415. **EMAIL** cecc@u.washington.edu

CEDERSTROM, LORELEI S.
PERSONAL Born Milwaukee, WI **DISCIPLINE** ENGLISH **EDUCATION** Valparaiso Univ, BA, 59; Carleton Univ, MA, 68; Univ Manitoba, PhD, 78. **CAREER** Lectr, Univ Man, 75-78; asst prof, 79-86, assoc prof, 87-94, Prof English, Brandon Univ 94-. **MEMBERSHIPS** MLA; Can Asn Univ Tchrs. **SELECTED PUBLICATIONS** Auth, Fine Tuning the Feminine Psyche: Jungian Patterns in the Novels of Doris Lessing, 90; auth, Walt Whitman and the Imagists in Walt Whitman of Mickle Street: A Centennial Collection, 94; auth, The Great Mother in the Grapes of Wrath in Steinbeck & the Environment, 96. **CONTACT ADDRESS** Dept of English, Brandon Univ, 103 Clark Hall, Brandon, MB, Canada R7A 6A9.

CEGALA, DONALD JOSEPH
PERSONAL Born 08/03/1946, Buffalo, NY, m, 1967, 1 child **DISCIPLINE** COMMUNICATION **EDUCATION** Univ Wis-Madison, BA, 68; Purdue Univ, Lafayette, MA, 69; Fla State Univ, PhD, 72. **CAREER** Instr commun, Fla State Univ, 71-72; assoc prof 73-83, prof, Ohio State Univ, 83-, Chairperson consensus comt, Nat Proj on Speech Commun Competen-

cies Prekindergarten-12th Grade, 73-74. **MEMBERSHIPS** Nat Commun Asn, Int Commun Asn; Am Acad on Physician and Patient **RESEARCH** Doctor-patient communication; doctor and patient training in communication skills. **SELECTED PUBLICATIONS** Coath, A study of doctors' and patients' perceptions of information processing and communication competence during the medical interview, Health Commun, 7, 179-204, 95; coauth, Components of patients' and doctors' perceptions of communication competence during a primary care medical interview, Health Commun, 8, 1-28, 96; coauth, Provider-patient health communication research from a pateient-centered perspective, Health Commun, 9, 27-44, 97; auth, A Study of Doctors' and Patients' Patterns of Information Exchange and Relational Communication During a Primary Care Consultation: Implications for Communication Skills Training, Hour of Health Commun, 2, 169-194, 97. **CONTACT ADDRESS** Dept of Commun, Ohio State Univ, Columbus, 154 N Oval Hall, Columbus, OH 43210-1330. **EMAIL** cegala.1@osu.edu

CELLA, CHARLES RONALD
PERSONAL Born 06/16/1939, Frankfort, KY, m, 1962, 3 children **DISCIPLINE** AMERICAN LITERATURE **EDUCATION** Transylvania Col, BA, 61; Univ Ky, MA, 62 PhD, 68. **CAREER** Instr English, Eastern Ky Univ, 63-64; asst prof, 68-71, assoc prof, 71-80, Prof English, Murray State Univ, 80- **MEMBERSHIPS** MLA; Am Studies Asn; Popular Cult Asn. **RESEARCH** American novel; theories of realism in fiction; literature and other arts. **SELECTED PUBLICATIONS** Auth, Mary Johnston, G K Hall & Co, 81. **CONTACT ADDRESS** Dept of English, Murray State Univ, 7C Faculty Hall, Murray, KY 42071. **EMAIL** ron.cella@murraystate.edu

CENIZA, SHERRY
PERSONAL 2 children **DISCIPLINE** AMERICAN LITERATURE **EDUCATION** Univ of Iowa, PhD, 90. **CAREER** Assoc prof, Tex Tech Univ. **HONORS AND AWARDS** The Elizabeth Agee Prize, Univ of Ala Press, 96; Fulbright Scholar, Univ of Ghent, 96. **MEMBERSHIPS** Am Lit Asn; Walt Whitman Asn; Fulbright Asn. **RESEARCH** Walt Whitman, 19th century women reformers and writers, 19th century culture, contemporary American poetry. **SELECTED PUBLICATIONS** Auth, "Mr. Birmington," Col Engl 44 (82): 712-14; auth, "Interview with Nina Baym," Iowa J of Lit Studies 8 (87): 1-15; auth, "Walt Whitman and Abby Price," Walt Whitman Quart Rev 8 (89): 49-67; auth, "Whitman and Democratic Women," in Approaches to Teaching Whitman's Leaves Grass, ed. Donald D. Kummings (NY: MLA, 90), 153-58; auth, "Women's Letters to Walt Whitman: Some Corrections," Walt Whitman Quart Rev 9 (92): 142-47; auth, "'Being a woman, I wish to give my own view': Some Nineteenth-Century Women's Responses to the 1860 'Leaves of Grass,'" in Cambridge Companion to Walt Whitman, ed. Ezra Greenspan (NY: Cambridge Univ Press, 95), 110-134; auth, Walt Whitman and Nineteenth-Century Women Reformers, Univ of Ala Press, 98; auth, "Whitman's En Masse Aesthetics," in Walt Whitman 2000, ed. Liu Shusen and Ed Folsom (Beijing & Iowa City: Peking Univ Press & Univ of Iowa Press, forthcoming). **CONTACT ADDRESS** Dept of English, Texas Tech Univ, Lubbock, TX 79409-3091. **EMAIL** sceniza@ttacs.ttu.edu

CERASANO, SUSAN P.
DISCIPLINE THEATER HISTORY, SHAKESPEARE, RENAISSANCE LITERATURE **EDUCATION** W Chester State Col, BA, 75; Univ MI, MA, PhD, 76, 81. **CAREER** Assoc prof, Colgate Univ. **HONORS AND AWARDS** Hon fel, Univ Keele, Staffordshire, England; NEH grants, 88-89, 83; ACLS grant, 90; Rackham fel, Univ MI, 79-81. **MEMBERSHIPS** Mem, Mus London, 89-; ed bd, Shakespeare Studies, 93-. **RESEARCH** Renaissance theater hist and drama. **SELECTED PUBLICATIONS** Auth, Edward Alleyn: Elizabethan Acor, Jacobean Gentleman Dulwich Picture Gallery, London, 94; Gloriana's Face: Women, Public and Private in the English Renaissance, Harvester/Simon and Schuster, 92; Borrowed Robes, Costume Prices and the Drawing of Titus Andronicus, Shakespeare Studies, 94; Tamburlaine and Edward Alleyn's Ring, Shakespeare Studies, 94; Philip Henslowe, Simon Forman, and the Theatrical Community of the 1590's, Shakespeare Quart, 93. **CONTACT ADDRESS** Dept of Eng, Colgate Univ, 13 Oak Dr., Hamilton, NY 13346.

CERVO, NATHAN ANTHONY
PERSONAL Born 06/19/1930, New Haven, CT, m, 1964, 1 child **DISCIPLINE** ENGLISH LANGUAGE & LITERATURE **EDUCATION** Univ Conn, BA & MA, 54; Univ Toronto, PhD(English & philos), 59. **CAREER** Reader English, Univ Toronto, 56-57; instr, Boston Col, 58-59; asst prof, La State Univ, Baton Rouge, 60-61; from asst prof to assoc prof English & Dante, St Joseph Col, Conn, 61-66; asst prof English & Latin, Hartwick Col, 66-69; from assoc prof to prof, 70-77, Prof English, Franklin Pierce Col, 77-, Fulbright res fel, Univ Florence, 59-60; fel, Yale Univ, 63-65. **MEMBERSHIPS** MLA. **RESEARCH** The pre-Raphaelites; the aesthetes; Tennyson and Browning. **SELECTED PUBLICATIONS** Auth, Grey Riders of the Purple Sage, Explicator, Vol 0055, 97; Cool, I Faith and a Pans Face, the Social Unity of Shepherd and Flock in Browning Bishop Blougram Apology, Eng Lang Notes, Vol 0030, 93. **CONTACT ADDRESS** Dept of English Div of Humanities, Franklin Pierce Col, PO Box 60, Rindge, NH 03461-0060.

CEVASCO, GEORGE ANTHONY
PERSONAL Born 09/22/1924, Brooklyn, NY, m, 1954, 2 children **DISCIPLINE** ENGLISH **EDUCATION** St John's Univ, NYork, AB, 48; Columbia Univ, MA, 49. **CAREER** Instr English, Gannon Col, 51-52; from asst prof to assoc prof, Notre Dame Col, Staten Island, 52-55; asst dean, St John's Col, 65-69, asst prof, 55-71, Assoc Prof English, St John's Univ, NY, 71-, Lectr, Fordham Univ, 54-67; consult, Choice, 65-; abstractor, Abstr English Studies. **HONORS AND AWARDS** DLitt, Univ London. **MEMBERSHIPS** MLA; Am Soc Aesthet; Soc Huysmans; fel Royal Soc Arts. **RESEARCH** Life and works of J-K Huysmans; American grammar; aestheticism and decadence in British literature, 1870-1890. **SELECTED PUBLICATIONS** Auth, Salvador Dali; Master of Surrealism and Modern Art, 71 & Oscar Wilde, British Author, Poet and Wit, 72 & The Population Problem, 73, Samhar Press; New Words for You, Carillon Bks, 77; J-K Huyusmans: A Reference Guide, G K Hall, 80; auth, John Gray Twayne, 82; auth, Three Decadent Poets: Ernest Dowson, John Gray, Garland, 90; auth, Encyclopedia of British Literature, Art and Culture of The 1890's, Garland, 93; coauth, Biographical Dictionary of American and Canadian Naturalists and Environmentalists, Greenwood, 97. **CONTACT ADDRESS** Dept of English, St. John's Univ, Jamaica, NY 11432.

CHABORA, PAMELA
PERSONAL Born 12/21/1956, Portsmouth, VA, m, 1978, 1 child **DISCIPLINE** THEATRE **EDUCATION** Bera Col, BA, 78; Univ KY, MA, 88; Mich State Univ, PhD, 94. **CAREER** Lectr, Univ of Maine, 84-93; asst prof, Univ of Toledo, 93-96; asst prof, Univ of NH, 96-97; vis asst prof, Millersville Univ, 97-98; asst prof, Susquehanna Univ, 98-. **HONORS AND AWARDS** Moss Hart Nominee for Children's Theatre, 90; ACTF Meritorious Awd, 95, 98, 99; Univ NH Fel, 97; Degenstein Found Grant, 99. **MEMBERSHIPS** ATHE; ATME; DAEA; NETC; SETC; NEA; VASTA; NMTA; TAP; ACTF; AENA. **SELECTED PUBLICATIONS** Auth, "Introducing William Weiss' Mobile Voice", Vasta Pub, (95): director, "Six Characters in Search of an Author", Univ of Toledo, 95; auth, "Shifting Perspectives: A Multi-Media Approach to Sic Characters In Search of An Author", Theatre Topics, (97); auth, Guidelines for Evaluating the Teacher/Performer for Promotion and Tenure, 97; director, "Ghosts" by Ibsen, Rafters Theatre, Millersville Univ, 98; director, "women of Troy", Degenstein Center Theatre, Susquehanna Univ, 99; auth, "Emotion Training and The Mind/Body Connection: Alba Emoting and the Methods", The Method Reconsidered, ed David Krasner, St. Martin's Pr, (forthcoming). **CONTACT ADDRESS** Dept Commun Arts and Sci, Susquehanna Univ, 1 Susquehanna Univ, Selinsgrove, PA 17870-1001.

CHACE, WILLIAM M.
PERSONAL Born 09/03/1938, Newport News, VA, m, 1964, 2 children **DISCIPLINE** ENGLISH LANGUAGE AND LITERATURE **EDUCATION** Haverford Col, BA, 61; Univ Calif, Berkeley, MA, 63; Univ Calif, Ph.D, 68; Amherst Col, LLD, 90. **CAREER** Instr, Stillman Col, 63-64; Teaching Asst, Univ Calif, Berkeley, 64-66; Acting Instr, 67-68; Asst Prof, Univ Calif, 68-74; Assoc Prof, 74-80; Prof, 80; Assoc Dean, 81-85; Vice Provost, 81-88; Planning and Development, 85-88; Pres, Wesleyan Univ, 88-94, Emory Univ, 94-. **RESEARCH** Modern British and American literature. **SELECTED PUBLICATIONS** Ed, Justice Denied: The Black Man in White America, 70; auth, Making It New, 72; auth, James Joyce; A Collection of Critical Essays, 73; auth, The Political Identities o Ezra Pound and T.S. Eliot, 73; coauth, Lionel Trilling: Criticism and Politics, 80; auth, An Introduction to Literature, 85; auth, Graham Greene: A Revaluaton, 90. **CONTACT ADDRESS** English Dept, Emory Univ, 1380 Oxford Rd NE, Atlanta, GA 30322-1950. **EMAIL** mdearin@emory.edu

CHAFFEE, STEVEN H.
PERSONAL Born 08/21/1935, South Gate, CA, m, 1989, 4 children **DISCIPLINE** COMMUNICATION **EDUCATION** Univ Redlands, BA, 57; UCLA, MS, 62; Stanford Univ, PhD, 65. **CAREER** Dir Schl Jour Mass Comm, Univ WI Madison, 65-81; prof, Stanford Univ, 81-85; to chr 86-90; also to Janet M. Peck Prof Int Comm, 87; prof of commun and Rupe ch in Social Effects of Mass Commun, Univ of Calif, 99. **HONORS AND AWARDS** Elected a Fel of the International Commun Asn, 83; Recipient of the B. Aubrey Fisher mentorship award of the International Communication Asn, 92; Recipient of the Paul J. Deutschmann career res award of the Asn for Educ in Journalism and Mass Commun, 99; Recipient of the Murray Edelman award for research on political communication, Am Political Science Asn, 01; pres/fel, int comm assn; dir, inst comm res, 81-86. **MEMBERSHIPS** Asn fro Education in Journalism and Mass Commun; International Commun Asn; Am Political Sci Asn; International Soc for Political Psychology. **RESEARCH** Mass media effects; polit commun; adolescent develop; health commun; international commun; interpersonal and family commun; media institutions; research methodology; commun as an academic field; cognitive theories of commun. **SELECTED PUBLICATIONS** Auth, Political Communication, 76; Television and Human Behavior, 78; Handbook of Communication Science, 87; Communication Concepts 1: Explication, 91; To See Ourselves: Comparing Traditional Chinese and American Cultural Values, 94; and The Beginnings of Communication Study in America, 97; ed, "Brenda Dervin & Steven Chaffee, (forthcoming, 01); auth, Communication, a Different Kind of Horse Race: Essays Honoring Richard F. Carter, Hampton Press. **CONTACT ADDRESS** Dept Commun, Univ of California, Santa Barbara, Santa Barbara, CA 93106-4020. **EMAIL** chaffee@sscf.ucsb.edu

CHAMBERLIN, JOHN
DISCIPLINE PIERS PLOWMAN; ARTS OF DISCOURSE, ANCIENT; MODERN **EDUCATION** Haverford, BA; Toronto, MA, PhD. **CAREER** Asst Prof **SELECTED PUBLICATIONS** Auth, Increase and Multiply: Arts-of-Discourse Procedure in the Preaching of Donne, 76; What Makes Piers Plowman so hard to read?; The Rule of St. Benedict: The Abingdon Copy , 82; International Development Education in the English Classroom. **CONTACT ADDRESS** Dept English, Wilfrid Laurier Univ, 75 University Ave W, Waterloo, ON, Canada N2L 3C5. **EMAIL** jchamber@mach1.wlu.cas

CHAMBERS, ANTHONY HOOD
PERSONAL Born 07/01/1943, Pasadena, CA **DISCIPLINE** LITERATURE; LITERARY TRANSLATION **EDUCATION** Pomona Col, BA, 65; Stanford Univ, MA, 68; Univ Mich, PhD, 74. **CAREER** Asst Prof, 71-75, Arizona St Univ; prof, 75-98, Wesleyan Univ; prof, 98-, Arizona St Univ. **RESEARCH** Japanese lit; lit translation **SELECTED PUBLICATIONS** Auth, The Secret Window: Ideal Worlds in Tanizaki's Fiction **CONTACT ADDRESS** PO Box 870202, Tempe, AZ 85287-0202. **EMAIL** anthony.chambers@asu.edu

CHAMETZKY, JULES
PERSONAL Born 05/24/1928, Brooklyn, NY, m, 1953, 3 children **DISCIPLINE** ENGLISH **EDUCATION** Brooklyn Col, BA, 50; Univ Minn, MA, 52, PhD(English lit), 58. **CAREER** Instr English, Univ Minn, 54-56; instr humanities, Boston Univ, 56-58; from vis lectr to assoc prof, 58-69, Prof English, Univ Mass, Amherst, 69-, **HONORS AND AWARDS** Ed, Faulkner Studies, 53-54 & Mass Rev, 59-; Fulbright prof, Univ Tubingen, 62-63 & Univ Zagreb, 66-67; mem bd, dir, Coord Coun Lit Mag, 67-72; guest prof Am studies, Free Univ Berlin, 70-71, Freiburg, 76-77, Frankfurt Univ, 86, 92, Humboldt Univ, 94; Fulbright prof, Copenhagen, 98-99; Melus award for lifetime contribution to ethnic studies, 93. **MEMBERSHIPS** MLA; Am Studies Asn; Asn Lit Mag Am(pres, 65-67). **RESEARCH** Jewish American literature; literature of immigration and ethnicity; American realism. **SELECTED PUBLICATIONS** Co-ed, Black & White in American Culture, Viking, 71; auth, Regional Literature and Ethnic Realities, Antioch Rev, Fall 71; From HUAC to Watergate: Eric Bentley's Are You Now, Performance 7, fall 73; auth, "The Shelemiel as Post-Modern Hero," New Essays on Seize the Day, 98; From the Ghetto: The Fiction of Abraham Cahan, Univ Mass, 77; auth, Our Decentralized Literature, Univ Mass, 86. **CONTACT ADDRESS** 244 Amity St, Amherst, MA 01002. **EMAIL** jchamet@english.umass.edu

CHAMPION, LARRY STEPHEN
PERSONAL Born 04/27/1932, Shelby, NC, m, 1956, 3 children **DISCIPLINE** LITERATURE **EDUCATION** Davidson Col, AB, 54; Univ Va, MA, 55; Univ NC, PhD, 61. **CAREER** Instr English, Davidson Col, 55-56 & Univ NC, 59-60; from instr to assoc prof, 60-68, from asst head dept to assoc head, 67-71, Prof English, NC State Univ, 68-, Head Dept, 71-, Ed consult, Papers on Lang & **HONORS AND AWARDS** Outstanding Classroom Teacher Awd, NC State Univ, 70. **MEMBERSHIPS** MLA; NCTE; Renaissance Soc Am; Southeastern Renaissance Conf(pres, 78); SAtlantic Asn Dept English (pres, 74-75). **RESEARCH** Elizabethan and Jacobean drama, especially Shakespeare and Jonson; seventeenth century poetry, especially Herbert and Milton. **SELECTED PUBLICATIONS** Auth, Shakespearean Subversions--The Trickster and the Play-Text, Eng Stud, Vol 0075, 94; Politics, Plague, and Shakespeare Theater--The Stuart Years, Eng Stud, Vol 0075, 94; Misrepresentations--Shakespeare and the Materialists, Eng Stud, Vol 0076, 95; The Politics of Tragicomedy--Shakespeare and After, Eng Stud, Vol 0074, 93; Motives of Woe, Shakespeare and Female Complaint--Critical Anthology, Eng Stud, Vol 0074, 93; Shakespeare Reshaped 1606-1623, Eng Stud, Vol 0076, 95; Biblical References in Shakespeare Comedies, Shakespeare Quart, Vol 0046, 95; Shakespeare Reshaped 1606-1623, Eng Stud, Vol 0076, 95; The Subjectivity Effect in Western Literary Tradition--Essays Toward the Release of Shakespeare Will, Eng Stud, Vol 0074, 93. **CONTACT ADDRESS** Dept of English, No Carolina State Univ, 5320 Sendero Drive, Raleigh, NC 27212. **EMAIL** larrychampion@webtv.net

CHANCE, JANE
PERSONAL Born 10/26/1945, MO, m **DISCIPLINE** ENGLISH **EDUCATION** Purdue Univ, BA, 67; Univ Ill, AM, 68; PhD, 71. **CAREER** Lecturer to Asst Prof, Univ Sask, 71-73; Asst Prof to Prof, Rice Univ, 73-. **HONORS AND AWARDS** Fel, Coll Univ, London, 77-78; Dir, NEH Summer Seminar, 85; Disting Fac Teaching Awd, 95; Fel, Ctr for Study Cultures, 98; IMPACT Awd, Rice Univ, 98; Fac Rights Awd, 98. **MEMBERSHIPS** Mod Lang Asn; Scientia; Scn Hist Studies Inst for Adv Study. **SELECTED PUBLICATIONS** Ed, The Mythographic Art: Classical Fable and the Rise of the Vernacular in Early France and England, 90; auth, The Lord of the Rings: The

Mythology of Power, 92; auth, Medieval Mythography: From Roman North Africa to the School of Chartres, 94; auth, The Mythographic Chaucer: The Fabulation of Sexual Politics, 95; ed, The Assembly of Gods, 99; ed, Gender and Text in the Later Middle Ages, 96; ed, Medieval Mythography, Vol. 2: From the School of Chartres to the Court at Avignon, 1177-1350, 00; **CONTACT ADDRESS** Dept Eng, Rice Univ, 6100 Main St, Houston, TX 77005-1827. **EMAIL** jchance@rice.edu

CHANDLER, DANIEL ROSS
PERSONAL Born 07/22/1937, Wellston, OK **DISCIPLINE** SPEECH COMMUNICATION, RELIGION **EDUCATION** Univ Okla, BS, 59; Purdue Univ, MA, 65; Garrett Theol Sem, BD, 68; Ohio Univ, PhD(commun), 69. **CAREER** Asst prof speech, Cent Mich Univ, 69-70, State Univ NY, New Paltz, 70-71 & City Univ New York, 71-75; Asst Prof Commun, Rutgers Univ, New Brunswick, 76-, Asst pastor, Peoples Church of Chicago, 65-66; mem denominational affairs comt, Community Church of New York, 72-, John Haynes Scholar comt, 72-; vis fel, Princeton Univ, 74-75, 77, 79-80; res fel, Yale Univ, 74-75, 77 & 78; Marland fel, Union Theol Sem Columbia Univ, 75-76; vis scholar, New Sch for Social Res, 76-77. **MEMBERSHIPS** Nat Coalition Against Censorship; Speech Commun Asn; Speech Commun Asn Eastern States; Relig Speech Commun Asn; Acad Freedom Clearinghouse. **RESEARCH** Liberal religious movement in America; communication of mass movements; history and philosophy of freedom of speech. **SELECTED PUBLICATIONS** Auth, The Dawn of Religious Pluralism--Voices From the Worlds-Parliament-Of-Religions, 1893, Rel Hum, Vol 0027, 93; A Celebration of Humanism and Freethought, Rel Hum, Vol 0029, 95; Crimes of Perception--An Encyclopedia of Heresies and Heretics, Rel Hum, Vol 0029, 95; The American Radical, Rel Hum, Vol 0029, 95; 50 Days of Solitude, Rel Hum, Vol 0029, 95; Blavatsky, Madame Baboon, Rel Hum, Vol 0029, 95; Solitude--A Philosophical Encounter, Rel Hum, Vol 0029, 95; The Secularization of the Academy, Rel Hum, Vol 0028, 94; A Nation of Victims--The Decay of the American Character, Rel Hum, Vol 0028, 94; Pilgrimage Of Hope--100-Years of Global Interfaith Dialog, Rel Hum, Vol 0027, 93; A Fire in the Mind--The Life of Campbell, Joseph, Rel Hum, Vol 0027, 93; The Minds Sky--Human Intelligence in a Cosmic Context, Rel Hum, Vol 0027, 93; Holy Fire, Rel Hum, 0029, 95; An Aristocracy of Everyone--The Politics of Education and the Future of Education, Rel Hum, Vol 0028, 94; Paine, Thomas--Apostle of Freedom, Rel Hum, Vol 0029, 95; A Brief-History of American Culture, Rel Hum, Vol 0029, 95; American Religious Humanism, Rel Hum, Vol 0030, 96; America Alternative Religions, Rel Hum, Vol 0029, 95; Mapping American Culture, Rel Hum, Vol 0029, 95; Dewey,John--An Intellectual Portrait, Rel Hum, Vol 0029, 95; Same-Sex Unions in Premodern Europe, Rel Hum, Vol 0029, 95; Selling God--American Religion in the Marketplace of Culture, Rel Hum, Vol 0028, 94; The Evolution of Progress--The End of Economic-Growth and the Beginnings of Human Transformation, Rel Hum, Vol 0028, 94; Visions Of A Better World, Rel Hum, Vol 0028, 94; The Lambda Directory of Religion and Spirituality--Sources of Spiritual Support for Gay Men and Lesbians, Rel Hum, Vol 0029, 95; Cosmos Crumbling--American Reform and the Religious Imagination, Rel Hum, Vol 0028, 94; The Worlds-Parliament-of-Religions --The East/West Encounter, Chicago, 1893, Rel Hum, Vol 0029, 95; One Nation Under God--Religion in Contemporary American Society, Rel Hum, Vol 0028, 94; Notes From a Wayfarer--The Autobiography of Thielicke, Helmut, Rel Hum, Vol 0029, 95. **CONTACT ADDRESS** Dept of Commun, Rutgers, The State Univ of New Jersey, New Brunswick, New Brunswick, NJ 08903.

CHANDLER, WAYNE A.
PERSONAL Born 05/11/1965 **DISCIPLINE** ENGLISH **EDUCATION** NW Mo State Univ, BA, 94; MA, 94; Univ Ala, PhD, 00. **CAREER** Instr, SW Community College, 95-98; asst prof, NW Mo State Univ, 00-. **HONORS AND AWARDS** Award, NW Mo State Univ, 94-95; Letters of Commendation for Teaching, Univ of Ala, 98-99; Awd, Sigma Tau Delta, 99; Grant, Univ of Ala, 99; Buford Boone Fel, 99-00. **MEMBERSHIPS** MLA, SE Renaissance Conf. **RESEARCH** English Renaissance commendatory poetry, Shakespeare and other Renaissance drama, Renaissance authorial agency, reader-response theory. **SELECTED PUBLICATIONS** Auth, "Frankenstein's Many Readers," Extrapolation, (96); auth, "A Tragicomedy: Mary Wroth, John Fletcher, and Critical Reception," Renaissance Papers, (98); auth, "The Magic(s) of Steven Brust," Jour for the Fantastic in the Arts, (98); coauth, "An Epiphany at Owl Creek Bridge: Intimations of Immortalities in Ambrose Bierce's Fiction," Studies in Weird Fiction, (99). **CONTACT ADDRESS** Dept English, Northwest Missouri State Univ, Maryville, MO 64468. **EMAIL** chandlr@mail.nwmissour.edu

CHANG, BRIANKLE G.
PERSONAL Born 04/19/1954, Taipei, Taiwan **DISCIPLINE** COMMUNICATION **EDUCATION** Univ Il Champaign, PhD, 90 **CAREER** Assoc prof, Univ Ma, 93- **MEMBERSHIPS** ICA **RESEARCH** Cultural stud; philos of commun; theory & criticism. **SELECTED PUBLICATIONS** Auth, Deconstructing Communication: Subject, Representation and Economies of Exchange, Univ Minn Press, 96 **CONTACT ADDRESS** Dept of Commun, Univ of Massachusetts, Amherst, Machmer Hall 410, Amherst, MA 01003. **EMAIL** bchang@comm.umass.edu

CHANG, JOSEPH S.
PERSONAL Born 09/01/1935, Honolulu, HI, m, 1961, 5 children **DISCIPLINE** ENGLISH **EDUCATION** St Mary's Col (Calif), BA, 56; Univ Wis, MA, 60, PhD(English), 65. **CAREER** Asst prof English, Tulane Univ, 64-66; asst prof, 66-71, Assoc Prof English, Univ Wis-Milwaukee, 71-, Southeastern Inst Medieval & Renaissance Studies fel, 65. **RESEARCH** Shakespeare; Elizabethan drama; history of ideas in the Renaissance. **SELECTED PUBLICATIONS** Auth, A Class-Based Approach to Word Alignment, Computational Ling, Vol 0023, 97. **CONTACT ADDRESS** Dept English, Univ of Wisconsin, Milwaukee, PO Box 413, Milwaukee, WI 53201-0413.

CHANG, KANG-I S.
PERSONAL Born 02/21/1944, Beijing, China, m, 1968, 1 child **DISCIPLINE** CHINESE LITERATURE **EDUCATION** Tunghai Univ, BA, 66; Rutgers, MLS, 71; SDak State Univ, MA, 72; Princeton Univ, PhD, 78; Yale Univ, MA, 91. **CAREER** Vis asst prof, Tufts Univ, 79-80; curator, Gest Oriental Libr, Princeton Univ, 80-81; asst prof to prof, Yale Univ, 82-. **HONORS AND AWARDS** Ch'en Kuo-Fu Fel, 63; Sun Yet-Sen Fel, 66-68; Whiting Fel, 77-78; Most Distinguished Alumni, Taiwan, 92; Wu Found Conf Grant, 92-93; CCK Found Grant, 92-93; NEH Grant, 92-93; A Whitney Griswold Awd, 93-94; Judge, Int Col Debate, 95; Imp Scholarly Works Awd, 97. **MEMBERSHIPS** AAS, ACLS, MLA, ICLA, Yale-China. **RESEARCH** Literary Theory and Criticism, Canon Formation, Critical Theory in Hermeneutics. **SELECTED PUBLICATIONS** Auth, The Evolution of Chinese Tz'u Poetry, Princeton Univ Pr, 80; auth, Six Dynasties Poetry, Princeton Univ Pr, 86; auth, The late-Ming Poet Ch'en Tzu-Lung, Yale Univ Pr, 91; auth, Articles and Occasional Essays from Qianxue Studio, Yunchen, 94; coed, Writing Women in Late Imperial China, Stanford Univ Pr, 97; auth, Feminist Readings, Classical and Modern Perspectives, Lianhe Wenxue, 98; coed, Women Writers of Traditional China, Stanford Univ Pr, 99; auth, Reflections on Yale, Gender and Culture, Shanghai Wenyi, 00. **CONTACT ADDRESS** East Asian Lang & Lit, Yale Univ, PO Box 208236, New Haven, CT 06520-8236. **EMAIL** kang-I.chang@yale.edu

CHANG, TSAN-KUO
DISCIPLINE MASS COMMUNICATION STUDIES **EDUCATION** Nat Chengchi Univ, MA; Univ Tex Austin, PhD. **CAREER** Assoc prof. **RESEARCH** Mass media and foreign policy, sociology of news, international commun. **SELECTED PUBLICATIONS** Auth, The Press and China Policy: The Illusion of Sino-American Relations, 1950-1984, 93; co-auth, News as Social Knowledge in China: The Changing Worldview of Chinese National Media, J Commun, 94; Determinants of International News Coverage in the U.S. Media, Commun Res, 87; auth, All Countries Not Created Equal to Be News: World System and International Communication, Communication Res, 98; co-auth, From the United States with News and More: International Flow, Television Coverage and the World System, Gazette, 00. **CONTACT ADDRESS** Mass Communication Dept, Univ of Minnesota, Twin Cities, 111 Murphy Hall, 206 Church St SE, Minneapolis, MN 55455. **EMAIL** chang003@umn.edu

CHAPMAN, DAVID W.
PERSONAL Born 07/04/1954, Tulsa, OK, m, 1978, 2 children **DISCIPLINE** ENGLISH: RHETORIC AND COMPOSITION **EDUCATION** Univ Okla, BA, 76; Univ Tulsa, MA, 81; Texas Christian Univ, PhD, 85. **CAREER** Asst prof, Texas Tech Univ, 86-90; Assoc prof, Samford Univ, 90-95; prof, 95- ; dir, Writing Across the Curriculum, 90-95; assoc dean, Howard Col Arts & Sciences, 96 . **HONORS AND AWARDS** Phi Beta Kappa; Lichfield Poetry Awd; 83; Boswell Prize, 92. **MEMBERSHIPS** NCTE; CCCC; ATAC; WPA; ACTE; ACETA. **RESEARCH** Literary nonfiction; writing program administration; core curriculum; problem-based learning. **SELECTED PUBLICATIONS** Auth, Chapter, Encyclopedia of the Essay, 97; auth, Moral Essay, Encyclopedia of the Essay, 97; auth, George Orwell, Encyclopedia of the Essay, 97; auth, Problem-Based Learning and the Core Curriculum, PBL Insight, 98; WAC and the First-Yar Writing Course: Sellilng Ourselves Short, J Lang Learning Across the Disciplines, 98. **CONTACT ADDRESS** Samford Univ, Box 292260, Birmingham, AL 35229-2260. **EMAIL** dwchapma@samford.edu

CHAPMAN, MARY M.
PERSONAL Born 03/17/1962, Sault Ste Marie, ON, Canada **DISCIPLINE** ENGLISH **EDUCATION** Queen's Univ, BA; MA, 84; Cornell Univ, PhD, 92. **CAREER** Asst Prof to Assoc Prof, Univ Alta, 92-99; Assoc Prof, Univ BC, 99-. **HONORS AND AWARDS** Res Grant, Soc Sci and Humanities Res Coun of Can, 95-98 **MEMBERSHIPS** ASA; MLA; Can Asn of Am Studies; Can Asn of Univ Teachers of English. **SELECTED PUBLICATIONS** Co-ed, Sentimental Men: masculinity and the politics of affect in American Culture, Univ Calif Press, 99; ed, Ormond, or a Secret Witness, Broadview Press, 99 **CONTACT ADDRESS** Dept English, Univ of British Columbia, 397-1873 E Mall, Vancouver, BC, Canada V6T 1Z1. **EMAIL** marychap@interchange.ubc.ca

CHAPMAN, NORMAN
PERSONAL Born 05/13/1935, Brandon, Canada, s **DISCIPLINE** MUSIC **EDUCATION** Univ Kans, BMusic, 56; MMusic, 57; Case Western Reserve Univ, PhD, 73; Univ Memphis, MA, 81; MEd, 84. **CAREER** Rust Col, 74-. **HONORS AND AWARDS** Grants, NEH; Humanities Prof of the Year, Rust Col, 98-99. **MEMBERSHIPS** Nat Asn of Scholars. **RESEARCH** Music, Chamber Music, Chamber Music with Piano. **SELECTED PUBLICATIONS** Auth, "Treasury of Practice Devices," Clavier; auth, "Freedom at the Keyboard," Am Music Teacher; rev, of "Music in Canada," J of Res in Music Educ. **CONTACT ADDRESS** Dept Humanities, Rust col, 150 Rust Ave, Holly Springs, MS 38635-2330. **EMAIL** normanchapman@hotmail.com

CHAPMAN, VIRGINIA
DISCIPLINE COMMUNICATION **EDUCATION** Ball State Univ, BS, MA; IN Univ, PhD. **CAREER** Prof, Anderson Univ, 82. **SELECTED PUBLICATIONS** Wrote a unit for the bk Beyond Boundaries--Sex and Gender Diversity. **CONTACT ADDRESS** Anderson Univ, Anderson, IN 46012. **EMAIL** vchapman@anderson.edu

CHAPMAN, WAYNE K.
DISCIPLINE ENGLISH **EDUCATION** Portland State Univ, BS, 72; MA, 77; Wash State Univ, PhD, 88. **CAREER** Instr, Kans State Univ, 89-90; instr, Wash State Univ, 91; asst prof to prof, Clemson Univ, 91-. **HONORS AND AWARDS** Vis Fulbright Scholar, Univ London, 89-90; Harriet Holman Annual Awd, 97-98; Res Awd, Clemson Univ, 96-97; Innovation Fund Awd, Clemson Univ, 96; Fac Development Awd, Clemson Univ, 93-94; Andrew W. Mellon Foundation Fel, 91; fulbright Res Grant, 90. **RESEARCH** Victorian through twentieth-century British and Anglo-Irish literature especially poetry; American writers 1855 to present; Textual-genetic, bibliographic, stylistic, and interdisciplinary studies of literature and literary history; Poetry and poetics; W.B. Yeats and circle; Leonard and Virginia Woolf and Bloomsbury. **SELECTED PUBLICATIONS** Auth, Yeats and English Renaissance Literature, Macmillan Press, 91; auth, "Virginia Woolf's Contributions to Anonymous, Composite Reviews in The Nation and Athenaeum, 1924-1928," in Virginia Woolf and Her Influences: Selected Papers from the Seventh Annual Virginia Woolf Conference, (Pace Univ Press, 98), 63-69; co-ed, The Countess Cathleen: Manuscript Materials by W.B. Yeats, The Cornell Yeats Series, Vol 12, Cornell Univ Press, 99; auth, "Leonard Woolf, Cambridge, and the Art of the English Essay," in Virginia Woolf Turning the Centuries, (Pace UP 00), 215-222; auth, "W.B. and George Yeats: The Writing, Editing, and Dating of Yeat's Poems of the Mid-1920s and 1930s," Yeats Annual, Macmillan, forthcoming **CONTACT ADDRESS** Dept Eng, Clemson Univ, Clemson, SC 29634-1503. **EMAIL** cwayne@clemson.edu

CHAPPELL, FRED DAVIS
PERSONAL Born 05/28/1936, Canton, NC, m, 1959, 1 child **DISCIPLINE** ENGLISH **EDUCATION** Duke Univ, BA, 61, MA, 64. **CAREER** From instr to assoc prof, 64-70, prof English, Univ NC, Greensboro, 70-; Rockefeller Found grant, 67-68. **HONORS AND AWARDS** Awd in Lit, Nat Inst Arts & Letts, 68; Roanoke-Chowan Poetry Prize, 72, 75, 79, 80, 85, 89; Prix des Meilleur des Livres Etrangers, 72; Sir Walter Raleigh Prize, NC Hist Asn, 76; Oscar A Young Memorial Awd, 80; North Carolina Awd in Lit, 80; Zoe Kincaid Brockman Awd, 81; Bollingen Prize on Poetry, 85; Endowed Chair: The Burlington Industries Professorship, Univ NC, 87; Ragin-Rubin Awd, NC English Teachers Asn, 89; Thomas H Carter Essay Awd, Shenendoah Magazine, 91; World Fantasy Awd, Best Short Story, 92, 94; T S Eliot Prize, Ingersoll Found, 93; Aiken Taylor Awd in Poetry, 96; Best Novel, Southeastern Booksellers Asn, 99. **RESEARCH** Creative writing; 18th century literature; film. **SELECTED PUBLICATIONS** Auth, It is Time, Lord, Atheneum, 63; The Inkling, 65, Dagon, 68 & The Gaudy Place, 72, Harcourt; The World Between The Eyes, 71, River, 75 & Bloodfire, 78, LA State Univ Press; The Man Married Twice to Fire, Unicorn Press, 77; Awakening to Music, Briarpatch Press, 78; Wind Mountain, LA State Univ Press, 79; Earthsleep, LA State Univ Press, 80; Moments of Light, The New South Co, 80; Driftlake: A Leider Cycle, Mountain Press, 81; Midquest, LA State Univ Press, 81; Castle Tzingal, LA State Univ Press, 84;Source, LA State Univ Press, 85; I Am One of You Forever, LA State Univ Press, 85; The Fred Chappell Reader, St Martin's Press, 87; Brighten the Corner Where You Are, St Martin's Press, 89; First and Last Words, LA State Univ Press, 89; More Shapes Than One, St Martin's Press, 91; C: 100 Poems, LA State Univ Press, 93; Plow Naked: Selected Writings on Poetry, Univ MI Press, 93; Spring Garden: New and Selected Poems, LA State Univ Press, 95; Farewell, I'm Bound to Leave You, Picador USA, 96; Family Gathering, 00. **CONTACT ADDRESS** Dept English, Univ of No Carolina, Greensboro, 1000 Spring Garden, Greensboro, NC 27412-0001.

CHARI, V. K.
PERSONAL Born 11/28/1924, India, m, 1945, 2 children **DISCIPLINE** ENGLISH AND AMERICAN LITERATURE **EDUCATION** Banaras Hindu Univ, BA, 44, MA, 46, PhD(English), 50, dipl French, 65. **CAREER** Asst prof English, Govt

Educ Serv, Madhya Pradesh, India, 50-62; reader, Banaras Hindu Univ, 62-66; assoc prof, 66-74, Prof English, Carleton Univ, 74-, Fulbright fel, NY Univ, 59-60; vis prof, State Univ NY Col New Platz, 60-61; Can Coun res grant, 72-73; Can Coun res grant, 79-80. **RESEARCH** Literary theories in Sanskrit; modern and contemporary American and English poetry; Western and Indian literary aesthetics and criticism. **SELECTED PUBLICATIONS** Auth, Whitman in the Light of Vedantio Mysticism. **CONTACT ADDRESS** Dept of English, Carleton Univ, 1812 Dunton Tower, 1125 Colonel By Drive, Ottawa, ON, Canada K1S 5B6.

CHARNEY, MARK

PERSONAL Born 11/20/1956, Atlanta, GA, m, 1987, 2 children **DISCIPLINE** FILM, THEATER, ENGLISH LITERATURE **EDUCATION** Tulane Univ, PhD, 87. **CAREER** Dept Eng, Clemson Univ **HONORS AND AWARDS** Chair ACTF, region 4. **RESEARCH** Theater; contemporary literature; film. **SELECTED PUBLICATIONS** Auth, Beauty in the Beast: Technological Reanimation in the Contemporary Horror Film in Trajectories of the Fantastic: Selected Essays from the Fourteenth International Conference on the Fantastic in the Arts, Greenwood, 97; It's a Cold World Out There: Redefining the Family in Contemporary American Film, Beyond the Stars 5: Themes and Ideologies in American Popular Film, Bowling Green State Univ Popular Press, 96; auth, Barry Hannah, Twayne Publishers, 91; Schindler's List, Cambridge Press, forthcoming. **CONTACT ADDRESS** Clemson Univ, 607 Strode, Clemson, SC 29634. **EMAIL** cmark@clemson.edu

CHARNEY, MAURICE MYRON

PERSONAL Born 01/18/1929, Brooklyn, NY, m, 1954, 2 children **DISCIPLINE** ENGLISH **EDUCATION** Harvard Univ, AB, magna cum laude, 49; Princeton Univ, MA, 51, PhD(Eng), 52. **CAREER** Instr Eng, Hunter Col, 53-54; from instr to prof, 56-75, Distinguished Prof, Rutgers Univ, New Brunswick, 75-, Fulbright prof, Univ Bordeaux & Univ Nancy, 60-61; co-chmn, Am Civilization Sem, Columbia Univ, 77-79; vis prof, Concordia Univ, 81. **HONORS AND AWARDS** Medal of the City of Tours, 89; Pres, Acad of Lit Stud, 85-87; Pres, Shakespeare Asn of Am, 87-88. **MEMBERSHIPS** MLA; Malone Soc; Shakespeare Asn Am. **RESEARCH** Shakespeare and Elizabethan drama; hist and theory of the drama; theory of comedy. **SELECTED PUBLICATIONS** Auth, Shakespeare's Roman Plays, Harvard, 61; Shakespeare's Timon of Athens, New Am Libr, 65; Style in Hamlet, Princeton, 69; How to Read Shakespeare, McGraw, 71; coauth, The Language of Madwomen in Shakespeare and His Fellow Dramatists, Signs, 77; ed, Comedy: New Perspectives, NY Lit Forum, 78; auth, Comedy High and Low: An Introduction to the Experience of Comedy, Oxford Univ, 78; Sexual Fiction, Methven, 81; Joe Orton, Macmillian, 84; co-ed, The Psychoanalytic Study of Literature, Analytic Press, 85; ed, Classic Comedies, New AmLibrary, 85; ed, The Reader's Adviser, Vol 2, Bowker, 86; ed, Psychoanalytic Approaches to Literature and Film, Fairleigh Dickinson Univ-Press, 87; Hamlet's Fictions, Routledge, 88; Titus Andronicus, Harvester, 90; All of Shakespeare, Columbia Univ, 93; ed, Julius Caesar, Applause Books, 96. **CONTACT ADDRESS** Dept of English, Rutgers, The State Univ of New Jersey, New Brunswick, 510 George St, New Brunswick, NJ 08901-1167.

CHARTERS, ANN D.

PERSONAL Born 11/10/1936, Bridgeport, CT, m, 1959, 2 children **DISCIPLINE** ENGLISH **EDUCATION** Univ of Calif, Berkeley, BA, 57; Columbia Univ, MA, 60; PhD, 65. **CAREER** Fac, Colby Col, NH, 61-63; fac, Columbia Univ, 65-66; fac, NYork City Commun Col, 67-70; prof, Univ Conn, 74-; assoc dean, adj prof, Brown Univ, 89-90. **HONORS AND AWARDS** Phi Beta Kappa; Woodrow Wilson Fel, 58-59; Fulbright Prof, Uppsala Univ, SWE, 82 83. **MEMBERSHIPS** MLA; AAUP. **RESEARCH** Short story; Beat generation writers. **SELECTED PUBLICATIONS** Auth, Beats and Company, Doubleday (86); ed, The Portable Beat Reader, Viking Penguin (92); ed, Howls, Raps & Roars: Recordings of the San Francisco Poetry Renaissance, Fantasy Records (93); ed, The Kerouac Reader, Viking Penguin, 95; ed, Selected Letters of Jack Kerouac, 1940-1956, Viking Penguin, 95, Penguin (London), 96, Gallimard (Paris), 97, Mondadori (Milan), 97; auth, The Story and Its Writer, 5th Ed, St. Martin's Press, 98; auth, The American Story and Its Writer, St Martins Press, 00; auth, Selected Letters of Jack Kerouas, 1957-1969, Viking Penguin, 00. **CONTACT ADDRESS** Dept of English, Univ of Connecticut, Storrs, 337 Mansfield Rd, Unit 25, Storrs, CT 06269-1025.

CHARTIER, YVES

DISCIPLINE HISTORY OF MUSIC **EDUCATION** Univ Ottawa, BA, MA; Univ Paris, DU. **CAREER** Assoc prof, Univ Ottawa. **RESEARCH** Musicology (Middle Ages, Renaissance), aesthetics. **SELECTED PUBLICATIONS** Auth, L'Oeuvre musicale d'Hucbald de Saint-Amand, Mont real-Paris, Editions Bellarmin-Vrin, 94; Clavis opervm Hvcbaldi Elnonensis, Jour of Medieval Latin 4, 95; Les outils du musicologue, Dubuque, 91; coauth, Glossaire de Musique, Toronto, 90; ed, Georges MIGOT, Douze hymnes liturgiques, Paris, 87. **CONTACT ADDRESS** Dept of Music, Univ of Ottawa, PO Box 450 Stn A, Ottawa, ON, Canada K1N 6N5.

CHASE, KAREN S.

PERSONAL Born 10/16/1952, St Louis, MO, m, 1984, 2 children **DISCIPLINE** ENGLISH **EDUCATION** Univ Calif at Los Angeles, BA, 74; Stanford Univ, MA, 76; Stanford Univ, PhD, 79. **CAREER** Full Prof, Univ of VA; 79-. **HONORS AND AWARDS** Cavalier Chair for Distinguished Teaching **RESEARCH** Nineteenth-Century literature and culture. **SELECTED PUBLICATIONS** Auth, EROS and PSYCHE, Cambridge Landmarks Series: Middlemarch; auth, The Spectacle of Intimacy: A Public Life For The Victorian Family. **CONTACT ADDRESS** Dept English, Univ of Virginia, 219 Bryan Hall, Charlottesville, VA 22903. **EMAIL** ksc3j@virginia.edu

CHASE HANKINS, JUNE

PERSONAL Born 08/13/1944, Wichita Falls, TX, m, 1969, 1 child **DISCIPLINE** AFRICAN AMERICAN WOMEN NOVELISTS **EDUCATION** Southwestern Univ, BA, Univ AR, MA; TX A&M Univ, PhD. **CAREER** Southwest Tex State Univ **HONORS AND AWARDS** NEH Grant; Two NEH Summer Inst Grants. **MEMBERSHIPS** Soc for Tech Commun; Toni Morrison Soc. **RESEARCH** T. Morrison. **SELECTED PUBLICATIONS** Auth, Making Use of the Literacy Debate. **CONTACT ADDRESS** Southwest Texas State Univ, 601 University Dr, San Marcos, TX 78666-4604. **EMAIL** jh20@swt.edu

CHAVKIN, ALLAN

PERSONAL m, 1972, 1 child **DISCIPLINE** MODERN COMIC FICTION **EDUCATION** Dickinson Col, BA; Univ IL, MA, PhD. **CAREER** Southwest Tex State Univ **SELECTED PUBLICATIONS** Auth, Bellow's Alternative to the Wasteland: Romantic Theme and Form in Herzog, Studies Novel, 79; Ivan Karamazov's Rebellion and Bellow's The Victim, Papers Lang & Lit, 80; The Imagination as the Alternative to Sutpen's Design, Ariz Quart, 81; Suffering and the Wilhelm Reich's Theory of Character-Armoring in Bellow's Seize the Day, Essays Lit, 82; The Hollywood Thread & The First Draft of Bellow's Seize the Day, Studies Novel, 82; Fathers and Sons: 'Papa' Hemingway and Saul Bellow, Papers Lang & Lit , 83; Humboldt's Gift and the Romantic Imagination, Philol Quart, 83; The Problem of Suffering in the Fiction of Saul Bellow, Comp Lit Studies, 84; Saul Bellow in the 1980's: A Collection of Critical Essays, Mich State Univ Press, 89; Wordsworth and Modern Literature , MLA, 86; English Romanticism and the Modern Novel, AMS Press, 93; Bellow's Dire Prophecy, Centennial Rev , 89; Conversations with John Gardner, Univ Press Miss, 90; Saul Bellow's Visionary Project, Greenwood Press, 95; Mr. Sammler's War of the Planets, Greenwood Press, 95; The Dean's December and Blake's The Ghost of Abel, Saul Bellow Jour, 95; Conversations with Louise Erdrich and Michael Dorris, Univ Press Miss, 95; auth, The chippewa Landscape of Louise Erdrich, 99; auth, Leslie Marmon Siko's Ceremony: A Casebook, Oxford Univ Press, forthcoming. **CONTACT ADDRESS** Southwest Texas State Univ, 601 University Dr, San Marcos, TX 78666-4604. **EMAIL** aci0@swt.edu

CHAY, DEBORAH

DISCIPLINE ENGLISH LITERATURE **EDUCATION** Duke Univ, PhD, 92. **CAREER** Asst prof, Dartmouth Col. **RESEARCH** Eng and African lit; African Am Studies. **SELECTED PUBLICATIONS** Auth, Rereading Barbara Smith: Black Feminist Criticism and the Category of Experience, New Lit Hist, 93; Reconstructing Essentialism, Diacritics, 91. **CONTACT ADDRESS** Dartmouth Col, 3529 N Main St, #207, Hanover, NH 03755. **EMAIL** deborah.chay@dartmouth.edu

CHEAH, PHENG

DISCIPLINE ENGLISH **EDUCATION** Cornell Univ, PhD. **CAREER** Assoc prof, Northwestern Univ. **RESEARCH** Postcolonial literature and theory of Asia and Anglophone Africa. **SELECTED PUBLICATIONS** Coauth, Thinking Through the Body of the Law, Allen and Unwin, 96 & NY Univ Press, 96; Cosmopolitics: Thinking and Feeling Beyond the Nation, Minnesota Univ Press, 97. **CONTACT ADDRESS** Dept of English, Northwestern Univ, 1801 Hinman, Evanston, IL 60208. **EMAIL** p-cheah@northwestern.edu

CHECKETT, LAWRENCE

PERSONAL Born 11/28/1944, St Louis, MO, m, 1994, 3 children **DISCIPLINE** ENGLISH **EDUCATION** Univ Miss S Louis, BS, 72; Webster Univ, MA, 74. **CAREER** Instr to assoc prof, St Charles County Community Col, 92-. **HONORS AND AWARDS** Phi Kappa Phi Honor Soc. **MEMBERSHIPS** MCCA; TYCA; NCTE; CWA; M/MLA. **RESEARCH** Developmental Writing Instruction, Writing Across the Curriculum. **SELECTED PUBLICATIONS** Coauth, "The Write Start: Sentence to Paragraph", The Write Start: Paragraph to Essay" in Develop Writing Textb Series, Addison Wesley Longman. **CONTACT ADDRESS** Dept English, Saint Charles County Comm Col, PO Box 76975, Saint Peters, MO 63376-0092. **EMAIL** lcheckett@chuck.stchas.edu

CHELL, SAMUEL L.

DISCIPLINE ENGLISH LITERATURE AND COMPOSITION; FILM STUDIES; MUSIC **EDUCATION** Augustana Col, BA; Univ Ill, MA; Univ Wisc, PhD. **CAREER** English, Carthage Col, 68-. **HONORS AND AWARDS** Grants: National Endowment for the Humanities and the University of Chicago Midwest Faculty Seminar. **SELECTED PUBLICATIONS** Auth, The Dynamic Self: Browning's Poetry of Duration, 84. **CONTACT ADDRESS** Carthage Col, 2001 Alford Dr., Kenosha, WI 53140. **EMAIL** chells1@carthage.edu

CHELTE, JUDITH S.

PERSONAL Born 08/23/1951, Springfield, MA, m, 1982 **DISCIPLINE** ENGLISH **EDUCATION** Westfield State Col, BA, 73; Smith Col, MA, 74; Univ Mass, PhD, 94. **CAREER** Teacher, Chicopee Public Schools, 74-. **HONORS AND AWARDS** Cert, Nat Board of Prof Teaching Standards, 99; Paul Harris Recognition, 00. **MEMBERSHIPS** MLA, Chicopee Educ Assoc, Mass Teachers Assoc, NEA. **RESEARCH** Women in literature, minority women, voice, nonfiction (especially slave narratives and women's biolgraphy and autobiography), American literature. **SELECTED PUBLICATIONS** Auth, "What Should Be the Goals of American Literature Instruction in the Twenty-first Century?" The Leaflet: Jour of the New Eng Assoc of Teachers of Eng, 94.3; auth, "A Modern Transformation of a Literary Classic," This is Just to Say; NCTE Assembly on Am Lit, 5.1. **CONTACT ADDRESS** 63 Davenport St, Chicopee, MA 01013-2808. **EMAIL** chelte@massed.net

CHEN, CHIH-PING

PERSONAL Born 04/16/1960, Taiwan, s **DISCIPLINE** ENGLISH **EDUCATION** Nat Chengchi Univ, BA, 82; Nat Taiwan Univ, MA, 86; Univ Mass Amherst, PhD, 00. **CAREER** Teaching assoc, Univ Mass, 93-98; asst prof, Alma Col, 00-. **HONORS AND AWARDS** For Student Scholar, Univ Mass, 91-93; Robert E. Evans Grad Fel, Holyoke Cmty Col, 97. **MEMBERSHIPS** MLA; Interdisciplinary Nineteenth-Century Studies. **RESEARCH** British Victorian Culture and Literature; Post-Colonial Writers; Asian-American Literature. **SELECTED PUBLICATIONS** Trans, "A Good Man Is Hard to Find," by Flannery O'Connor, 90; Auth, "Essays on Shawn Wong and Lois-Ann Yamanaka," in Asian-American Novelists: A Bio-Bibliographical Critical Sourcebook, 00. **CONTACT ADDRESS** Dept English, Alma Col, 535 Wright Ave., Alma, MI 48801-1687. **EMAIL** chen@alma.edu

CHEN, GUO-MING

PERSONAL Born 06/30/1955, Taiwan, m, 1983, 2 children **DISCIPLINE** COMMUNICATION **EDUCATION** Chinese Cult Univ, BA, 77; Univ NMex, MA, 83; Kent State Univ, PhD, 87. **CAREER** Prof, Univ Rhode Island, 87-. **MEMBERSHIPS** NCA, ICA, ECA. **RESEARCH** Intercultural communication. **SELECTED PUBLICATIONS** Auth, Chinese Conflict Management and Resolution, Spec Issue of Intercult Commun Studies, 98; coauth, Foundations of Intercultural Communication, Allyn & Bacon (Needham Heights, MA), 98; auth, "Intercultural sensitivity: A Commentary," in Intercult Encounters (Englewood, CO: Morton, 98); auth, "A Chinese Model of Human Relationship Development," in Cross-Cult Commun E and W in the 90's (San Antonio, TX: Inst for Cross-Cult Res, 98); coauth, "A Review of the Concept of Intercultural Awareness," Human Commun 2 (99): 27-54; auth, "An Overview of Communication Theory and Research," Mass Commun Res 58 (99): 257-268; auth, Chinese Conflict Management in Intercultural Settings, Spec Issue of Intercult Commun Studies, 00; coauth, Communication and Global Society, Peter Lang Publ (New York), 00; coauth, "Intercultural Sensitivity," in Intercult Commun: A Reader (Belmont, CA: Wadsworth Pr, 00); auth, "Understanding the Chinese: A Harmony Theory of Chinese Communication," in The Handbk of Intercult Commun (Thousand Oaks, CA: Sage Publ, forthcoming). **CONTACT ADDRESS** Dept Commun, Univ of Rhode Island, Kingston, RI 02881. **EMAIL** gmchen@uri.edu

CHEN, NI

DISCIPLINE COMMUNICATION **EDUCATION** OH Univ, PhD. **CAREER** Instr, Towson Univ. **HONORS AND AWARDS** Life-long Distinguished Prof Award, Nanjing Normal Univ, PRC. **MEMBERSHIPS** PRSA **RESEARCH** Int and Comparative Public Relations **CONTACT ADDRESS** Towson State Univ, Towson, MD 21252-0001. **EMAIL** nchen@towson.edu

CHENEY, DONALD

PERSONAL Born 07/14/1932, Lowell, MA, m, 1956, 2 children **DISCIPLINE** ENGLISH, COMPARATIVE LITERATURE **EDUCATION** Yale Univ, BA, 54, MA, 57, PhD, 61. **CAREER** From instr to asst prof English, Yale Univ, 60-67; assoc prof, 67-75, Prof English, Univ Mass, Amherst, 75-, Morse fel, Yale Univ, 64-65; corresp ed, Spenser Newslett, 70-78, ed, 74-78; co-ed, Spenser Encycl, 79- **MEMBERSHIPS** MLA; Renaissance Soc Am; Spenser Soc; Milton Soc Am; ACLA. **RESEARCH** Renaissance poetry and drama. **SELECTED PUBLICATIONS** Auth, Gazing on Secret Sights--Spenser, Classical Imitation, and the Decorum of Vision, Jour Eng and Ger Philol, Vol 0092, 93. **CONTACT ADDRESS** Dept of English, Univ of Massachusetts, Amherst, Amherst, MA 01003-0002.

CHENEY, PATRICK

PERSONAL Born 07/24/1949, Great Falls, MT, m, 1974, 2 children **DISCIPLINE** ENGLISH **EDUCATION** Univ Mont, BA, 72; Univ Toronto, MA, 74, PhD, 79. **CAREER** From asst prof to prof English, comp lit, Pa State Univ, 80-. **HONORS AND AWARDS** Inst Arts, Hum Stud res fel, Pa State Univ, 87,95, 96, 97; Pa State Univ Fac Awd, 95, 96, 97, 00; Humanities Studies Term Fel, Inst Arts, 99-01; Mellon Issues in Interpretation Seminar, 00; vis res fel, Merton Col, Oxford, forthcoming; co-dir, the atist in an age of imperial culture careers in the early modern period, summer inst, 98; co-dir, the faerie queene in the world, 1596-1996. spenser among the disciplines, yale univ, 96; chair, prog comt, spenser at kalamazoo, medieval inst, 97 **MEMBERSHIPS** Mod Lang Asn; Renaissance Soc Am; Int Spenser Soc; Marlowe Soc Am. **RESEARCH** 16th, 17th cent Br lit, esp Spenser, Marlow, Shakespeare. **SELECTED PUBLICATIONS** Auth, Career Rivalry and the Writing of Counter-Nationhood: Ovid, Spenser, and Philomela in Marlowe's The Passionate Shepherd to His Love, ELH 65, 98; auth, Spenser's Famous Flight: A Renaissance Idea of a Literary Career, Univ Toronto Press, 93; auth, Marlowe's Counterfeit Profession: Ovid, Spenser, Counter-Nationhood, Univ Toronto Press, 97; auth, Thondring Word of Theatre: Marlowe, SPenser, and Renaissance ideas of a literary Career, in Marlowe, HIstory, and Sexuality: New Critical Essays on Christopher Malrowe, AMS Press, 98; co-ed, Worldmaking Spenser: Explorations in the Early Modern Age, Univ Press Ky, 00; co-ed, Approaches to Teaching Shorter Elizabethan Poetry, Mod Lang Asn, 00; auth, Spenser's Pastorals: The Shepheardes Calender and Colin Clouts Come Home Again, in The Cambridge Companion to Spenser, Cambridge Univ Press, forthcoming; auth, Recent Studies in Marlowe (1987- 1998), Eng Lit Renaissance, forthcoming; co-ed, Oxford Edition of the Collected Works of Edmund Spenser, forthcoming; auth, Teaching Spenser's Marriage Poetry: Amoretti, Epithalamion, Prothelamion, in Approaches to Teaching Shorter Elizabethan Poetry, Mod Lang Asn, forthcoming; auth, Materials, in Approaches to Teaching Shorter Elizabethan Poetry, NY: Mod Lang Asn, forthcoming; introduction, Worldmaking Spenser: Explorations in the Early Modern Age, Univ Press Ky, forthcoming. **CONTACT ADDRESS** Dept of English, Pennsylvania State Univ, Univ Park, University Park, PA 16802. **EMAIL** pgc2@psu.edu

CHENG, HONG

PERSONAL Born 01/08/1958, China, m, 1988, 1 child **DISCIPLINE** COMMUNICATION **EDUCATION** Taiyuan Normal Univ, BA, 81; Shanghai Int Studies Univ, MA, 88; Pa State Univ, PhD, 95. **CAREER** Asst Prof, Taiyuan Normal Univ, 81-86; Lectr, Shanghai Int Studies Univ, 88-90; Asst Prof, Bradley Univ, 94-. **HONORS AND AWARDS** Kappa Tau Alpha, Pa State Univ, 93; Fac Achievement Awd, Bradley univ, 97; Fel, Am Soc Newspaper Editors, 98; Phi Kappa Phi, Bradley Univ, 99; New Fac Achievement Awd, Bradley Univ, 99. **MEMBERSHIPS** AAA, Asn for Educ in Journ and Mass Commun, Ctr for Global Media Studies, CCA, ICA, Soc of Professional Journalists. **RESEARCH** International communication, intercultural communication, cross-social and cross-cultural studies of advertising and new news media. **SELECTED PUBLICATIONS** Coauth, "Cultural Values Reflected in Chinese and U S Television Commercials," J of Advert Res, 36 3 (96); coauth, "Foreign Advertising Agencies in China," Media Asia: An Asian Mass Commun Quart, 23 1 (96); auth, "Advertising in China: A Socialist Experiment," in Advert in Asia: Commun, Cult and Consumption (Ames, IA: Iowa St Univ Pr, 96); auth, "'Holding Up Half of the Sky'? A Sociocultural Comparison of Gender-Role Portrayals in Chinese and U S Advertising," Int J of Advert, 16 4 (97); auth, "Can We Report on the Real China? Enormous Social Change Sweeping Asian Giant Largely Ignored by Media as They Focus on Conflict," Quill, 85 10 (97); auth, "China: Advertising Yesterday and Today," in Int Advert: Realities and Myths (Thousand Oaks, CA: Sage Publ, 00): auth, "An Armchair Surfing of a New Global News Medium: The Web's Coverage of Hong Kong's Handover," Gazette, the Int J for Commun Studies, 62 5 (00). **CONTACT ADDRESS** Dept Commun, Bradley Univ, 1501 W Bradley Ave, Peoria, IL 61625-0001.

CHENG, MEILING

PERSONAL Born 12/15/1960, Taipei, Taiwan, m, 1990 **DISCIPLINE** THEATRE ARTS **EDUCATION** Nat Taiwan Univ, BA, 83; Yale Univ, MFA, 89; DFA, 93. **CAREER** Asst prof, Mount Holyoke Col, 93-94; asst to assoc prof, Univ of S Calif, 94-. **HONORS AND AWARDS** Award, Taiwan Univ, 80-83; Awd, Mount Holyoke Col, 94; Asian Cult Coun, Fel, 88-89; Mayer Found Fel, 87-88; Lord Mem Scholarship, 87-88; Bass Fel, 91-92; James H. Zumberge Res Fel, 99-00, USC/SCW Exposition Grant, 00; USC Arts Initiative Awd, 01. **MEMBERSHIPS** MLA, Performance Res, Assoc of Theatre in Higher Educ. **RESEARCH** Performance art, body art, avant-garde theatre, intermedia/cultural studies. **SELECTED PUBLICATIONS** Auth, "The American Chestnut by Karen Finley," Theatre Jour, (97); auth, "Sacred Naked Nature Girls," TheatreForum, (97); auth, "Monsters of Grace 1.0: A Digital Opera in Three Dimensions by Philip Glass and Robert Wilson," Theatre Jour, (98); auth, "Les Demoiselles d/L.A.: Sacred Naked Nature Girls Untitled Flesh," TDR, (98); auth, "The Speed of Darkness by Laurie Anderson," Theatre Jour, (99); auth, "Bob Flanagan's Body Double," The Artist's Body, ed Tracy Warr, Phaidon, (London, 00); auth, "Elia Arce's Performance Art: Transculturation, Feminism, Politicized Individualism," Text and Performance Quart 20.2, (00); auth, "Oguri and Renzoku," TheatreForum, (01); auth, "Cyborgs in Mutation: Osseus Labyrint's Alien Body Art," TDR 45.2, (01); auth, In Other Los Angeleses: Multicentric Performance Art, Univ of Calif Pr, forthcoming. **CONTACT ADDRESS** School of Theatre, Univ of So California, Los Angeles, CA 90089-0791. **EMAIL** meilingc@usc.edu

CHENG, SINKWAN

DISCIPLINE ENGLISH **EDUCATION** SUNY Buffalo, MA, 94; PhD, 95. **CAREER** Asst prof, Univ SDak, 95-96; res assoc, Univ Calif Irvine, 96-97; asst prof, Calif State Univ San Marcos, 97-99; prof, City Col NYork, 99-02. **MEMBERSHIPS** MLA; ALL; LSA; SSA; ACLA. **RESEARCH** @0th-century British and (post-) Colonial literature; interdisciplinary legal and cultural studies; literary and cultural theories; continental philosophy; political theory; European cultural and intellectual history. **SELECTED PUBLICATIONS** Auth, "From Fortuna to the Christian God: Gambling and the Calvinist Ethic," Am J Semiotics (93); auth, "Fantasizing the Jouissance of the Chinese (M-)Other: Amy Tan's Quest for Stardom in the Market of Neo-Racism," Savoir (97); rev, "Reading Seminar XI: Lacan's Four Fundamental Concepts of Psychoanalysis," J Psychol Culture Soc (97); auth, "Fremdworter as 'The Jews of Language' and Adorno's Politics of Exile," in Adorno, Culture, and Feminism, ed. Maggie O'Neill (London/NYork: Sage Pr, 99); auth, "Walter Benjamin," in Encycl Postmod (Routledge, 99); auth, "The Kingdom of Heaven vs. the Kingdom on Earth: Christianity and the Displacement of Africans in Black Anger," Jouvert (99); auth, "Subaltern Groups, Struggle for Recognition in the Twentieth Century, and the 'Objet a,'" (forthcoming); auth, "Crossing Desire and Drive in a Passage to India: The Subversion of British Colonial Law in the Twilight Zone of Double Vision," Lit Psychol (forthcoming); auth, "Psychoanalysis and Literature," Int Encycl of Psychoanalysis (Edinburgh, forthcoming). **CONTACT ADDRESS** English Dept, City Col, CUNY, W 138th St and Convent Ave, New York, NY 10031. **EMAIL** scheng@phantom.cct.ccny.edu

CHERCHI-USAI, PAOLO

DISCIPLINE ENGLISH **EDUCATION** Univ of Genoa, Italy, PhD. **CAREER** Adj prof & sr curator Motion Picture Dept, George Eastman House/Int Mus Photog and Film, Rochester, NY, taught at Int Sch for Film Restoration, Bologna. **HONORS AND AWARDS** Jean Vigo awd & Int al Film Guide awd; cofounder, domitor, int asn for the develop stud on early cinema. **MEMBERSHIPS** Co-dir, Silent Film Festival of Pordenone, Italy & bd directors, Int Fed Film Arch. **RESEARCH** Hist and aesthetics of film. **SELECTED PUBLICATIONS** Auth, Burning Passions: An Introduction to the Study of Silent Cinema, The Vitagraph Company of America 1897-1916; coauth, Silent Witnesses: Russian Films, 1908-1917; articles on, Lois Weber, early film pornography, pre-Technicolor techniques, Pastrone's hist epic Cabiria, Stanley Kubrick, film and archit, theory & methodology of film restoration; contribur, Sight & Sound, Film Hist, Iris & Hors Cadre; ed, Segnocinema, Griffithiana & J Film Preserv. **CONTACT ADDRESS** Dept of Eng, Univ of Rochester, 601 Elmwood Ave, Ste. 656, Rochester, NY 14642. **EMAIL** usai@uhura.cc.rochester.edu

CHERMAK, GAIL D.

PERSONAL Born 09/30/1950, New York, NY, s, 2 children **DISCIPLINE** SPEECH COMMUNICATION **EDUCATION** State Univ of NY, BA, 72; Ohio State Univ, MA, 73; PhD, 75. **CAREER** From assoc prof to prof and chair, Wash State Univ, 82-. **HONORS AND AWARDS** Phi Beta Kappa, 72; Kellogg Nat Fel, 86-89; Fulbright Scholar, 89-90; Edward R. Meyer Distinguished Prof of Speech and Hearing, Col of Lib Arts. **MEMBERSHIPS** Am Acad of Audiol, Int Soc of Audiology, Am Auditory Soc, Am Speech-Lang-Hearing Asn, Pan American Society of Audiology **RESEARCH** Central auditory processing disorders, international rehabilitation development. **SELECTED PUBLICATIONS** Auth, Handbook of Audiological Rehabilitation, Charles C. Thoms (Springfield, IL), 81; Auth, "A Helical Pursuit of Teaching as Leading," in Giving Voices to Songs Unsung, ed. S.E. Sutton (Ann Arbor, MI: Univ of Mich, 89): 55-59; auth, "Central Testing," in The Handbook of Pediatric Audiology, ed. S.E. Gerber (Washington, DC: Gallaudet UP, 96): 206-254; coauth, Central Auditory Processing Disorders: New Perspectives, Singular Publ Group (San Diego, CA), 97; auth, "Metacognitive Approach to Managing CAPD," in Central Auditory Processing Disorders: Mostly Management, eds. J.A. Katz, G.M. Masters and N.A. Stecker (Needham Hts, MA: Allyn & Bacon, 98): 49-61. **CONTACT ADDRESS** Dept Speech & Hearing Serv, Washington State Univ, 201 Daggy Hall, Pullman, WA 99164-2420. **EMAIL** chermak@wsu.edu

CHERNISS, MICHAEL DAVID

PERSONAL Born 04/07/1940, Los Angeles, CA **DISCIPLINE** ENGLISH **EDUCATION** Univ Calif, Berkeley, AB, 62, MA, 63, PhD(English), 66. **CAREER** From asst prof to assoc prof, 66-76, Prof English, Univ Kans, 76- **MEMBERSHIPS** MLA; Mediaeval Acad Am; New Chaucer Soc; Int Soc of Anglo-Saxonists **RESEARCH** Old and Middle English literature; continental medieval literature. **SELECTED PUBLICATIONS** Auth, Ingeld and Christ, Mouton, The Hague, 72; Boethian Apocalypse: Studies in Middle English Vision Poetry, Pilgrim Books, 97. **CONTACT ADDRESS** Dept of English, Univ of Kansas, Lawrence, Lawrence, KS 66045-0001.

CHERRY, CAROLINE LOCKETT

PERSONAL Born 06/16/1942, Washington, DC, d, 1968, 2 children **DISCIPLINE** ENGLISH LITERATURE **EDUCATION** Randolph-Macon Woman's Col, AB, 64; Univ NC, MA, 65, PhD(English Lit), 68. **CAREER** From asst prof to assoc prof, 68-78, prof English Lit, Eastern Col, PA, 78-, chmn Humanities Div, 72-; chmn English Dept, 88-. **HONORS AND AWARDS** Phi Beta Kappa; Lindback Awd for Distinguished Teaching. **MEMBERSHIPS** MLA. **RESEARCH** Renaissance; literature, Milton; film studies. **SELECTED PUBLICATIONS** Coauth, Contemporary Composition, Prentice-Hall, 70; auth, The Most Unvaluedest Purchase: Women in the Plays of Thomas Middleton, Univ Salzburg, 73. **CONTACT ADDRESS** Dept of English, Eastern Col, 1300 Eagle Rd, Saint Davids, PA 19087-3696. **EMAIL** ccherry@eastern.edu

CHERRY, CHARLES L.

PERSONAL Born 07/30/1942, Baltimore, MD, m, 1968 **DISCIPLINE** ENGLISH LITERATURE, HISTORY OF IDEAS **EDUCATION** Loyola Col, Md, BA, 64; Univ NC, Chapel Hill, MA, 66; PhD(English), 68. **CAREER** Asst prof, English, Univ NC, 65-68; asst prof, 68-77, dir honors prog, 72-77, assoc prof, 77-80, prof, English, Villinova Univ, 80-; assoc acad vp, 79-94; chmn, English dept, 96-; Commun consult, fed govt & ins indust, 71- . **HONORS AND AWARDS** Am Coun Educ fel & asst to pres of Univ Pa, 77-78; Cooper-Woods travel study grant, 77; Lilly found fel hist of sci, 80; T Wistar Brown fel, Haverford Col, 82-83; NEH & Amer Phil Soc res grants. **MEMBERSHIPS** MLA; NCTE, Friends Hist Asn. **RESEARCH** Hist of ideas; Brit Lit; written commun; Quaker hist. **SELECTED PUBLICATIONS** Coauth, Contemporary Composition, Prentice-Hall, 70; coauth, Write up the Ladder: A Communications Text, Goodyear, 76; auth, A Quiet Haven: Quakers, Moral Treatment and Asylum Reform, Fairleigh Dickinson Univ Pr, 89. **CONTACT ADDRESS** Dept of English, Villanova Univ, Villanova, PA 19085. **EMAIL** charles.cherry@villanova.edu

CHERRY, PAUL

PERSONAL Born 06/17/1934, Memphis, TN, m, 1963, 2 children **DISCIPLINE** MUSICOLOGY **EDUCATION** Duke, AB, 56; Eastman, MM, 58; Univ Colo, PhD, 80. **CAREER** Prof Mus, 40 years, 4 years prof. **HONORS AND AWARDS** Belbas-Larson Awd for Excellence in Teaching. **MEMBERSHIPS** Am Musicol Soc; Mus Union. **RESEARCH** Music of Darius Milhaud. **SELECTED PUBLICATIONS** Le Train bleu, rev of Darius Milhaud's ballet performed in Paris, Nov, 93; Etudes sur des themes liturgiques cu Comtat-Venaissin: A Hidden Mahzor in an Unknown String Auartet by Darious Milhaud; Two 'Unknown' String Quartets by Darius Milhaud; A Cornucopia of Quartets: The String Quartets of Darius Milhaud; Ten Seconds to a Terrific Tone; Helpful Hints for the High Register, Clarinet Pedagocical articles; auth, "Darius Milhaud's La Cheminee du Roi Rene and the Cavalcade d Amour," Study of music for original film score and revision for woodwind quintet. **CONTACT ADDRESS** Univ of So Dakota, Vermillion, Vermillion, SD 57069. **EMAIL** pcherry@usd.edu

CHESEBRO, JAMES W.

PERSONAL Born 06/24/1944, Minneapolis, MN, s **DISCIPLINE** COMMUNICATION **EDUCATION** Univ Minn, BA, 66; PhD, 72; Ill State Univ, MS, 67. **CAREER** Teaching asst, Ill State Univ, Normal, 66-67; instr, Concordia Col, Moorhead, Minn, 67-69; teaching assoc, Univ Minn, 69-72; vis prof, Univ Puerto Rico, fall 80; asst prof, Temple Univ, 72-76, assoc prof, 77-81; assoc prof, Queens Col of the City Univ of NY, 81-86, prof, 87-89; adjunct prof, George Mason Univ, 89-92; Dir of Educ Services, Nat Commun Asn; prof, Indiana State Univ, 92-. **HONORS AND AWARDS** Res Fel, NEH, 74; Distinguished Service Awd, Speech Commun Asn of Puerto Rico, 82l; Golden Anniversary Prize Fund Awd, Monograph Awd, Nat Commun Asn, 85; Everett Lee Hunt Scholar Awd, Eastern Commun Asn, 89; Jose De Diego Awd for Outstanding Service to SCAPR and to the Hispanic Community, Speech Commun Asn of Puerto Rico, 90; Distinguished Service Awd, Nat Kenneth Burke Soc, 93; President, Nat Commun Asn, 96-97; Everett Lee Hunt Awd for Outstanding Scholarship, Eastern Commun Asn, 97; Distinguished Teaching Fel, Eastern Commun Asn, 98; Life-Time Achievement Awd, Nat Kenneth Burke Soc, 99-. **MEMBERSHIPS** Nat Commun Asn, Int Commun Asn, Eastern Commun Asn, Speech Commun Asn of Puerto Rico, Southern States Commun Asn, Western States Commun Asn, Central States Commun Asn, Kenneth Burke Soc, NY State Speech Commun Asn, Asn for Educ in Journalism and Mass Commun, Asn for Commun Adminrs. **RESEARCH** Communication technologies; culture and media as symbolic systems; dramatic theories, methods, and criticism; media literacy; media technologies as communication and cognitive systems; methods of audience analysis and prediction; and communication research methods. **SELECTED PUBLICATIONS** Auth, Computer-Mediated Communication, Tuscaloosa, Ala: Univ Ala Press (89); auth, Extensions of the Burkeian System, Tuscaloosa, AL: Univ Ala

Press (93); auth, Analyzing Media, NY: Guilford (96); over 100 articles in communication journals such as Quart J of Speech, Commun Monographs, and Critical Studies in Mass Commun. **CONTACT ADDRESS** Dept Commun, Indiana State Univ, 323 Erickson Hall, Terre Haute, IN 47809-0001. **EMAIL** cmchese@ruby.indstate.edu

CHEUNG, KING-KOK
PERSONAL Born 01/11/1954, Hong Kong, m, 1 child **DISCIPLINE** ENGLISH **EDUCATION** Pepperdine Univ, BA, 75; MA, 76; Univ Calif Berkeley, PhD, 84. **CAREER** Asst prof, UCLA, 84-91; vis assoc prof, Harvard Univ, 91; vis assoc prof, Univ Kans, 97; assoc prof to prof and dir, UCLA, 91-; Fulbright prof, Univ Hong Kong, 00-01. **HONORS AND AWARDS** Fulbright Res Award, Univ Hong Kong; Fel, Stanford Univ, 95-96; Fel, Univ Calif, 91-92; Fel, Am Coun of Learned Soc Res, 87-88; Regents Fel, Univ Calif Berkeley, 81-83. **MEMBERSHIPS** MLA; MELUS. **RESEARCH** Comparative ethnic American literature; Asian American literature; Renaissance British literature. **SELECTED PUBLICATIONS** Auth, "The Woman Warrior versus The Chinaman Pacific: Must a Chinese American Critic Choose between Feminism and heroism?" in Conflicts in Feminism, (Routledge, 90), 234-251; auth, "Double-Telling: Intertextual Silence in Hisaye Yamamoto's Fiction," Am Literary Hist, (91): 277-293; auth, Articulate Silences: Hisaye Yamamoto, Maxine Hong Kingston, and Joy Kogawa, Cornell Univ Press, 93; ed, Seventeen Syllables. A volume in the Women Writers: Texts and Contexts series, Rutgers Univ Press, 94; ed, An Interethnic companion to Asian American Literature, Cambridge Univ Press, 97; ed, Words Matter: Conversations with Asian American Writers, Univ Hawaii Press, 00; auth, "Art, Spirituality, and the Ethic of Care: Alternative Expressions of Masculinity in Chinese American Literature," in Masculinity Studies and Feminist Theories, Columbia Univ Press, 01. **CONTACT ADDRESS** Dept English, Univ of California, Los Angeles, 2225 Rolfe, PO Box 951530, Los Angeles, CA 90095-1530. **EMAIL** cheung@humnet.ucla.edu

CHICHETTO, JAMES W.
PERSONAL Born 06/05/1941, Boston, MA, s **DISCIPLINE** WRITING, LITERATURE **EDUCATION** Stonehill Col, BA, 64; Holy Cross Col, MA, 68; Wesleyan Univ, MA, 78. **CAREER** Priest/educator, Peru, 68-72; instr & campus minister, Stonehill Col, 74-76; asst ed, Gargoyle, 76-82; asst ed, ed, & illustrator, The Conn Poetry Rev, 81-92; chaplain, Wheaton Col, 86-89; from instr to asst prof, Stone Hill Col, 92-. **HONORS AND AWARDS** General Electric Awd in Physics, 59; NEA grants, 81 & 83; Sri Chinmoy Poetry Awd, 86; Outstanding Service Awd, Stonehill Col, 97; Fel of Corporation, Stonehill Col, 98; Fel, World Lit Acad, 98; listed in Who's Who in U.S. Writers, Editors, and poets, 90-; listed in Marquis Who's Who, 00. **MEMBERSHIPS** Conn Lit Forum, Asn of Lit Critics and Scholars, Nat Coun of English Teachers, World Lit Acad, Holy Cross Hist Confr. **RESEARCH** Native American and American History, Epic Poetry, Physics, Drawing, Painting, Illustrating. **SELECTED PUBLICATIONS** Auth, "Homage to Father Edward Sorin," Conn Poetry Rev, 92 & 98; auth, "Night," Am Poets of the 90's, 93; auth, "Osceola Dream," Poem, 94; auth, "Gettysburg," Poem, 94; auth, "Bridge," E W Lit Rev, 94; auth, "Korean War Poem," in What Rough Beast, Poems at the End of the Century Anthology (Ashland Univ Press, 99). **CONTACT ADDRESS** Dept English, Stonehill Col, 320 Washington St, North Easton, MA 02357-7800.

CHILCOTE, WAYNE L.
PERSONAL Born 09/12/1945, Ft Oglethorpe, GA, m, 1980, 3 children **DISCIPLINE** ENGLISH, GEOGRAPHY **EDUCATION** Univ Tenn, BS, 71; E Tenn State. Univ, MA, 73. **CAREER** Res Asst, Univ of SC, 81-84; instr, Tusculun Col, 84-85; instr, Univ of Tenn, 85-86; instr, Piedmont Va Community Col, 86-89. Assoc Prof, Univ of SC Salkehatchie, 89-. **MEMBERSHIPS** SC Acad of Sci, Gamma Theta Upsilon, Tenn Alumni Relations Coun, Va Community Col Asn, SC Geog Alliance, SA Hist Asn. **RESEARCH** Southern Appalachian Culture, particulary music and religion, Geography/history of SC, interdisciplinary studies. **SELECTED PUBLICATIONS** Auth, "The Search for National Idendity: The U.S. in the Modern World. An Interdisciplinary Approach", The Proceedings of the South Carolina Historical Association (00): 43-50; auth, "The Evolution of Bluegrass Music from Appalachian Mountain Music", Highland Heritage, (74): 3-6. **CONTACT ADDRESS** Dept Humanities & Soc Sci, Univ of So Carolina, Salkehatchie Regional, PO Box 617, Allendale, SC 29810. **EMAIL** waynelc@yahoo.com

CHILDERS, JOSEPH W.
DISCIPLINE ENGLISH LITERATURE **EDUCATION** Univ Ark, BA, MA; Columbia Univ, PhD. **CAREER** Prof, Art Hist, Univ Calif, Riverside. **HONORS AND AWARDS** Fel, Amer Coun of Learned Soc, 92; assoc dir, uc riverside's ctr for ideas and soc, 96-97. **RESEARCH** Working-class and immigrant literature. **SELECTED PUBLICATIONS** Auth, Novel Possibilities: Fiction and the Formation of Early Victorian Culture, Univ Pa Press, 95; co-auth, The Columbia Dictionary of Modern Literary and Cultural Criticism, Columbia Univ Press, 95; Edwin Chadwick and the discursive formation of the Victorian working classes, Victorian Stud, 94; Class resistance and Victorian domesticity, Prose Stud, 94. **CONTACT ADDRESS** Dept of Eng, Univ of California, Riverside, 1156 Hinderaker Hall, Riverside, CA 92521-0209.

CHILTON, H. RANDOLPH
DISCIPLINE ENGLISH **EDUCATION** Stanford Univ, AB, 69; Univ Wis at Madison, MA, 74; PhD, 81. **CAREER** From asst prof to prof, Col/University of St Francis, 81-; chemn, Dept of English and For Lang, Col/University of St Francis. **HONORS AND AWARDS** Col of St Francis Teaching and Campus Leadership Awd, 91. **MEMBERSHIPS** MLA, MMLA, Asn for the Study of Lit and the Environment. **RESEARCH** Modern Poetry, Rhetoric and Lying, Post Colonialism and American Literature. **SELECTED PUBLICATIONS** Auth, "The Place of Being in the Poetry of George Opper," in George Opper: Man and Poet, ed. Burton Hatlen (The Nat Poetry Found, 81); auth, "Charles Rezmikoff: Objectivist Witness," in Charles Rezmikoff: Man and Poet, ed. Milton Hindus (The Nat Poetry Found, 84). **CONTACT ADDRESS** Dept English & For Lang, Univ of St. Francis, 500 Wilcox St, Joliet, IL 60435-6169. **EMAIL** rchilton@stfrancis.edu

CHINERY, MARY
PERSONAL Born 04/12/1964, Bayonne, NJ **DISCIPLINE** ENGLISH **EDUCATION** Georgian Ct Col, BA, 86; Northeastern Univ, MA, 88; Drew Univ, MPhil, 97; PhD. **CAREER** Instr, Ocean Co Col; 88; From Instr to Asst Prof, Georgian Ct Col, 89-. **HONORS AND AWARDS** Alpha Sigma Lambda, 97; Who's Who in Am Teachers, 97, 00. **MEMBERSHIPS** MLA, NEMLA, SEA, NJCEA. **RESEARCH** Willa Cather, Early American literature, American drama. **SELECTED PUBLICATIONS** Coauth, "Doctoral Degrees Earned by United States Women Religious 1907-1992," in Women Relig and the Intellectual Life: The N Am Achievement (San Francisco, CA: Int Scholars Publ, 96); rev, American Women Writers to 1800, by Sharon Karns, Transformations (98): 298-301; rev, Civil Tongues and Polite Letters in British America, by David Shields, Transformations (98): 298-301; auth, "Liminality in Willa Cather's 'Alexander's Bridge' and 'The Professor's House'." Willa Cather Pioneer Mem Newsletter (00): 58-62; auth," Willa Cather and the 'Santos' Tradition in 'Death Comes for the Archbishop'," Willa Cather on Mesa Verde and the Am Southwest, forthcoming. **CONTACT ADDRESS** Dept English, Georgian Court Col, 900 Lakewood Ave, Lakewood, NJ 08701-2600. **EMAIL** mchinery@georgian.edu

CHINITZ, DAVID
PERSONAL Born 11/19/1962, Brooklyn, NY, m, 1991, 2 children **DISCIPLINE** ENGLISH **EDUCATION** Columbia Univ, PhD 93; Brown Univ, MSc 85; Amherst Col, BA 84. **CAREER** Loyola Univ, asst prof 93 to 98; assoc prof, 98-; dir of Graduate Programs, 00-. **HONORS AND AWARDS** NEH **MEMBERSHIPS** MLA; Modernist Studies Asn; TS Eliot Soc; E E Cummings Soc. **RESEARCH** Moderinst poetry; poetry and culture. **SELECTED PUBLICATIONS** Auth, Cumming's Challenge to Academic Standards, 96; auth, "Dance, Little Lady: Poets Flappers and the Gendering of Jazz, Modernism Gender and Culture," Garland, 96; auth, Rejuvenation through Joy: Langston Hughes, Primitivism, and Jazz, ALH, 97; ed, Inventions of the March Hare, By T. S. Eliot, rev, ANQ, 98; auth, "A Jazz-Banjorine, Not a Lute: Eliot and Popular Music before The Waste Land," TS Eliot's Orchestra, Garland, 00; auth, "The Problem of Dullness: Eliot and the Lively Arts in the 1920's," T.S. Eliot and Our Turning World, Macmillan, 01; coed, Arm the paper arm: Kenneth Koch's Postmodern Comedy, The New York Sch Poets, NPF (forthcoming); auth, "Comedian of the Spirit: Kenneth Koch's Postmodern Pleasures," The New York Sch Poets, NPF (forthcoming). **CONTACT ADDRESS** Dept of English, Loyola Univ, Chicago, 6525 N Sheridan Rd, Chicago, IL 60626. **EMAIL** dchinit@luc.edu

CHINOY, HELEN KRICH
PERSONAL Born 09/25/1922, Newark, NJ, m, 1948, 2 children **DISCIPLINE** ENGLISH, THEATRE **EDUCATION** NYork Univ, BA, 43, MA, 45; Columbia Univ, PhD, 63. **CAREER** Instr English, NY Univ, 44-45 & Queens Col, 45, 50 & Newark Col, Rutgers Univ, 46-48; instr English, 52-55, theatre, Smith Col, 56-60; lectr English, Univ Leicester, 63-64; from lectr to assoc prof, 65-71, chmn dept theatre & speech, 68-71, prof theatre, 75-97, Prof Emeritus, Smith Col, 97-; Assoc ed, Theatre Jour, Publ Am Theatre Asn; Nat Endowment for Humnities fel, 79-80. **HONORS AND AWARDS** Emmy Awd, 89; Hoffman Eminent Scholar Chair in Theater, Fla State Univ, 90; Harold Clurman Prof, Hunter Col, 93. **MEMBERSHIPS** Nat Theatre Conf; fel Am Theatre Asn; Am Soc Theatre Res. **RESEARCH** History, theories and technicques of acting and directing; modern European and American drama and theater; Shakespearean staging, especially by modern directors. **SELECTED PUBLICATIONS** Coed, Actors on Acting, Crown, 49, rev ed, 70; coauth, Directors on Directing, Bobbs, 63; auth, The profession and the art: Directing 1860-1920, In: American Theatre: A Sum of its Parts, French, 71; Production and direction, In: Encycl Britannica; Reunion: A self portrait of the group theatre, Educ Theatre J, 12/76 & Am Theatre Asn, spring 77; Hallie Flanagan Davis, In: Notable American Women, Harvard Press, 80; auth, The Directory as Mythogog, Shakespeare Quarterly, Winter 76; coauth, Women in American Theatre, 81, 87; auth, Art Versus Business: The Role of Women in American Theatre, The Drama Review, June 80; auth, The Poetics of Politics, Some Ntes on Style and Craft in the Theatre of the Thirties, Theatre J, Dec 83. **CONTACT ADDRESS** 230 Crescent St, Northampton, MA 01060. **EMAIL** hchinoy@sophia.smith.edu

CHOW, KAREN
PERSONAL Born 06/20/1969, Weymouth, MA, s **DISCIPLINE** ENGLISH **EDUCATION** Univ So Calif, BS, 91; Univ Calif, Santa Barbara, MA, 93; PhD, 98. **CAREER** Asst Prof, Univ of Conn, 97-. **HONORS AND AWARDS** Phi Beta Kappa, 91; UCSB Fel, 91-96; Mike M. Masaoka Fel, JACL, 96-97; Summer Res Grant, Univ Conn, Res Found, 99. **MEMBERSHIPS** MLA; Asn of Asian Am Studies; East of Calif Asian Am Fac Asn; Am Studies Asn. **RESEARCH** Am Lit. **SELECTED PUBLICATIONS** Auth, "Hong Kong Americans," in Encycl of Multiculturalism (Marshall Cavendish, 94), 860-66; auth, "Wakako Yamauchi," in Ref Guide to Am Lit, Third Ed, ed Jim Kamp (London: St James Pr, 94), 940-41; auth, "The Woman Warrior," n Ref Guide to Am Lit, Third Ed, ed Jim Kamp (London: St James Pr, 94), 1058-59; auth, "Maxine Hong Kingston," n Ref Guide to Am Lit, Third Ed, ed Jim Kamp (London: St James Pr, 94), 494-96; auth, "Zora Neale Hurston," in Ref Guide to Engl & Am Writers, ed, Mark Dady-Hawkins (London: St James Pr, 96), 371-72; auth, "Asian American Literature," in Ref Guide to Engl & Am Writers, ed, Mark Dady-Hawkins (London: St James Pr, 96), 38-40; auth, "(E)Merging Chinese America: The Ethnopoetic Nature of Shawn Wong's 'Homebase'," J of Am Cult, forthcoming. **CONTACT ADDRESS** Dept of Eng, Univ of Connecticut, Storrs, U-25, Storrs, CT 06219-1025. **EMAIL** karen.chow@uconn.edu

CHRIST, CAROL TECLA
PERSONAL Born 05/21/1944, New York, NY **DISCIPLINE** ENGLISH **EDUCATION** Douglas Col, BA, 66; Yale Univ, MPhil, 69, PhD(English), 70. **CAREER** Asst prof, 70-76, Assoc Prof English, Univ Calif, Berkeley, 76-, Nat Endowment for Humanities res, 77. **RESEARCH** Victorian studies; women's studies. **SELECTED PUBLICATIONS** Auth, Browning Corpses--The Theme and Representation of the Dead in His Poetry, Victorian Poetry, Vol 0033, 95; The American-University and Womens Studies--Anniversary Lecture, Tulsa Stud in Womens Lit, Vol 0016, 97. **CONTACT ADDRESS** Dept of English, Univ of California, Berkeley, Berkeley, CA 94720-0001.

CHRIST, MATTHEW R.
DISCIPLINE CLASSICAL STUDIES **EDUCATION** Carleton Col, BA, 82; Princeton Univ, PhD, 87. **CAREER** Asst prof, Ind Univ, Bloomington. **RESEARCH** Greek Historiography; Athenian rhetoric and law; Athenian social history. **SELECTED PUBLICATIONS** Auth, Liturgy Avoidance and Antidosis in Classical Athens, 90; auth, Herodotean Kings and Historical Inquiry, 94; auth, The Litigious Athenian, Johns Hopkins Univ Press, 98. **CONTACT ADDRESS** Dept of Classical Studies, Indiana Univ, Bloomington, 1020 E Kirkwood Ave, 547 Ballantine Hall, Bloomington, IN 47405. **EMAIL** mrchrist@indiana.edu

CHRIST, WILLIAM G.
DISCIPLINE COMMUNICATION THEORY **EDUCATION** St Lawrence Univ, BA; Univ Wis-Madison, MA; Fla State Univ, PhD. **CAREER** Com, Trinity Univ. **RESEARCH** Audience analysis. **SELECTED PUBLICATIONS** Pub(s), children's stories. **CONTACT ADDRESS** Dept of Commun, Trinity Univ, 715 Stadium Dr, San Antonio, TX 78212.

CHRISTENSEN, GLENN
PERSONAL Born 08/15/1952, Mt Kisco, NY, s **DISCIPLINE** ENGLISH **EDUCATION** Iona Col, BA, 70; SUNY, MLS, 74; MA, 75; PhD, 79. **CAREER** Asst Prof, SUNY, 79-88; Asst Prof, Marquette Univ, 88-93; Asst Prof, Univ Wisc, 93-98; Asst Prof, Cardinal Strich Univ, 98-. **HONORS AND AWARDS** NEH Summer Sem and Inst Awd. **MEMBERSHIPS** Mod Lang Asn, Am Comparative Lit Asn, Shakespeare Asn of Am. **RESEARCH** 20th Century Fiction; Film Studies; Shakespeare; Chaucer; Comparative literature. **CONTACT ADDRESS** Dept English, Cardinal Stritch Col, 6801 N Yates Rd, Milwaukee, WI 53217-3945. **EMAIL** petergc@csd.uwm.edu

CHRISTENSEN, KERRY A.
DISCIPLINE CLASSICS **EDUCATION** Swarthmore Col, BA, 81; Princeton Univ, MA, 83; PhD, 93. **CAREER** Classics Dept, Williams Col **RESEARCH** Greek social and political history of the archaic era; Greek and Roman civic identity and models of leadership; ancient historiography; Greek cult and ritual. **SELECTED PUBLICATIONS** Auth, The Theseion: a Slave Refuge at Athens, Amer J Ancient Hist 9, 84; Solon's Mania: Forms of Public Discourse in Archaic Athens, Bryn Mawr Classics Colloquia, Bryn Mawr Col, 87-88; Kleisthenes, Ajax, and the Athenian Incorporation of Salamis, APA/AIA Annual Meeting, Atlanta, 94. **CONTACT ADDRESS** Classics Dept, Williams Col, Stetson Hall D28, Williamstown, MA 01267. **EMAIL** kchriste@williams.edu

CHRISTENSEN, LAIRD E.
PERSONAL Born 08/04/1960, Portland, OR **DISCIPLINE** ENGLISH, ENVIRONMENTAL STUDIES **EDUCATION** Keene State Col, BA, 91; Univ Ill, MA, 93; Univ Oreg, PhD, 99. **CAREER** Teaching fel, Univ Ill, 91-93; instr, Keene State Col, 93-94; instr, Franklin Pierce Col, 93-94; teaching fel, Univ Oreg, 94-99; vis instr, Alma Col, 99-00; asst prof, Green Mountain Col, 00-01. **MEMBERSHIPS** MLA, Am Lit Assoc, Assoc for the Study of Lit and the Environ. **RESEARCH** Ecological Literacy, Bioregional Writing, American Nature Poetry, Ecology and Religion, Native American Literatures, Mary Oliver, Gary Snyder, Wendell Berry. **SELECTED PUBLICATIONS** Auth, "Becoming Home," Ecotone: Jour of Environ Studies, (97); coed, The ASLE Collection of Syllabi in Literature and Environment, Assoc for the Study of Lit and Environ, 98; auth, "Not Exactly Like Heaven: theological Imperialism in The Surrounded," Studies in Am Ind Lit, (99); coauth, Recovering Pine River, WTW Publ, 00; auth, "Spirit Astir in the World: Wendell Berry's Sacramental Poetry," Renascence (00); auth, "The Pragmatic Mysticism of Mary Oliver, " Ecological Poetry: A Critical Introduction, (01). **CONTACT ADDRESS** Green Mountain Col, One College Cir, Poultney, VT 05764. **EMAIL** christensen1@greenmtn.edu

CHRISTENSEN, PAUL N.
PERSONAL Born 03/18/1943, West Reading, PA, m, 1969, 4 children **DISCIPLINE** AMERICAN LITERATURE **EDUCATION** Col William and Mary, BA, 67; Univ Cincinnati, MA, 70; Univ Pa, PhD, 75. **CAREER** Asst prof, Tex A&M Univ, 74-79; assoc prof, 79-83; prof, 83-. **HONORS AND AWARDS** NEH Poetry Fel; AAP Poetry First Prize; Dist Prof Awd; Best Short Fiction; Fulbright Sr Lectr, Austria, 89, Norway 96; Dist Prose Awd. **MEMBERSHIPS** TIL. **RESEARCH** American Poetry; Southwest life and literature; Bison history; Great Plains. **SELECTED PUBLICATIONS** Auth, The Complete Correspondence of Charles Olson and Edward Dahlberg, Paragon House, 90; auth, Minding the Underworld, Black Sparrow Press, 91; auth, West of the American Dream: An Encounter with Texas, Texas A&M UP, 00; auth, An American in Provence, forthcoming; auth, The Vectory, Cedarhouse Press, 78; auth, Signs of the Whelming, Latitudes Press, 81; auth, Weights & Measures, Univ Editions, 83; auth, Where Three Roads Meet, Cedarhouse/Open Theater, 96; auth, The News from Gran Quivira, forthcoming. **CONTACT ADDRESS** Dept English, Texas A&M Univ, Col Station, College Station, TX 77843-0001. **EMAIL** p-christensen@tamu.edu

CHRISTIAN, BARBARA T.
PERSONAL Born 12/12/1943, St. Thomas, VI, d, 1 child **DISCIPLINE** BRITISH AND AMERICAN LITERATURE **EDUCATION** Columbia Univ, PhD, British and Amer contemporary literature, 70. **CAREER** Lecturer, SEEK program, City Coll NY, 65-71; lecturer, English Dept, 71-72, asst prof, 72-78, chair, 78-83, assoc prof, 78-86, full prof, 86-, African Amer Studies, Univ Calif Berkeley. **HONORS AND AWARDS** Melus Awd for Contribution to Ethnic Studies and African Amer Studies Scholarship, 94; Louise Patterson Awd for Best Black Faculty, Univ Calif Berkeley, 95; contribution to black literary arts, Gwendolyn Brooks Center, 95; Phi Beta Kappa Awd for Distinguished Teaching, Northern California Chapter, 95; Amer Coun Learned Societies, 95-96; Fulbright, Center for Amer Studies, Ritsumeikan Univ, Summer Inst, 98. **MEMBERSHIPS** Modern Lang Assn; Toni Morrison Soc. **RESEARCH** African American literature; women's studies; multicultural studies. **SELECTED PUBLICATIONS** Ed, Norton Anthology of African American Literature, Contemporary Section, 96; auth, "Camouflaging Race and Gender," Representations, 96; coauth, Female Subjects in Black and White: Race, Psychoanalysis and Feminism, 97; auth, "Beloved: She's Ours," Narrative: Journal of the Society for the Study of Narrative Literature, Jan 97; auth, "Layered Rhythms: Toni Morrison and Virginia Woolf," in Reading Toni Morrison: Theoretical and Critical Approaches, 97. **CONTACT ADDRESS** Univ of California, Berkeley, 660 Barrows Hall, Berkeley, CA 94720. **EMAIL** bchristi@library.berkeley.edu

CHRISTIANS, CLIFFORD G.
PERSONAL Born 12/22/1939, Hull, IA, m, 1961, 3 children **DISCIPLINE** COMMUNICATIONS **EDUCATION** Univ of Ill-Urbana, PhD, 74. **CAREER** Res asst prof of commun, Univ of Ill-Urbana, 74-80; res assoc prof of commun, 80-87; res prof of commun, 87-; Dir, Inst of Commun Res, 87-. **HONORS AND AWARDS** Kappa Tau Alpha; Phi Kappa Phi; Univ of Ill Awd for Excellence in Undergraduate Teach; Pew Evangelical Schol. **MEMBERSHIPS** Assoc for Educ in J & Mass Commun; Int Commun Assoc; Int Assoc for Mass Commun Res; Nat Commun Assoc. **RESEARCH** Media ethics; philosophy of technology; Jacques Ellul; communication theory. **SELECTED PUBLICATIONS** Co-auth, Media Ethics: Cases and Moral Reasoning, Longman Inc., 83, 2nd ed, 87, 3rd ed, 91, 4th ed, 95, 5th ed, 98; co-auth, Good News: A Social Ethics of the Press, Oxford Univ Press, 93; co-auth, Communication Ethics and Universal Values, The Ethics of Being Communications Context, Sage, chap 1, 3-23, 93; co-auth, Role of the Media Ethics Course in the Education of Journalists, J Educ, 49:3, 20-26, 94; auth, The Naturalistic Fallacy in Contemporary Interactionist-Interpretive Research, Studs in Symbolic Interaction, vol 19, 125-130, 95; auth, Review Essay: Current Trends in Media Ethics, Eur J of Commun, 10:4, 545-558, 95; auth, The Problem of Universals in Communication Ethics, Javnost: The Public, 2:2, 59-69, 95; auth, Propaganda and the Technological System, Public Opinion and the Communication of Consent, Guilford Pubs, 156-174, 95; auth, Communication Ethics as the Basis of Genuine Democracy, The Democratization of Communication, Univ of Wales Press, 75-91, 95; auth, Cultures of Silence and Technological Development, Responsible Communication: Ethical Issues in Business, Industry, and the Professions, Hampton Press, 267-283, 96; co-auth, The Status of Ethics Instruction in Communication Departments, Commun Educ, 45:3, 236-243, 7/96; auth, Social Responsibility: Ethics and New Technologies, Ethics in Human Communication, Waveland Press, 4th ed, 321-335, 96; auth, Common Ground and Future Hopes, Images that Injure: Pictorial Sterotypes in the Media, Praeger, 237-243, 261-262, 96; auth, The Common Good and Universal Values, Mixed News: The Public/Civic/Communitarian Journalism Debate, Lawrence Erlbuam, 18-33, 97; auth, Chronology: Contemporary Ethical Issues, Journalism Ethics: A Reference Handbook, ABC-CLIO, 97; auth, Social Ethics and Mass Media Practice, Communication Ethics in an Age of Diversity, Univ of Ill Press, 187-205, 97; auth, Technology and Triadic Theories of Meditation, Rethinking Media, Religion, and Culture, Sage, 65-82, 97; auth, Critical Issues in Communication Ethics, Communication: Views from the Helm for the Twenty-First Centuiry, Allyn & Bacon, 270-275, 98; auth, The Sacredness of Life, Media Development, 45:2, 3-7, 98; auth, The Politics of Recognition, Nat Media Ethics and Law Conf Book, Univ of Minn Silha Ctr, 139-159, 98; auth, Media Ethics and the Technological Society, J of Mass Media Ethics, 13:2, 98. **CONTACT ADDRESS** 1002 W William St, Champaign, IL 61821. **EMAIL** cchrstns@uiuc.edu

CHRISTIANSEN, HOPE
DISCIPLINE MODERN SPANISH AMERICAN LITERATURE **EDUCATION** Kans State Univ, BA, 79, MA, 81; Univ Kans, PhD, 90. **CAREER** English and Lit, Univ Ark. **HONORS AND AWARDS** Fulbright Col Master Tchr Awd. **SELECTED PUBLICATIONS** Auth, "The Rhetoric of Self-Deprecation in Montaigne's Essais," Chimeres, 17, #2, 84; auth, "Writing and Vagabondage: Renee Nene nad Emma Bovary," Vol. XLIII, no. 1, Symposium, 94; auth, "Learning to See: Visual Education in," Les Egarements du coeur et de l'esprit, Studies on Voltaire and the Eighteenth Century, No. 319, 94; auth, The Theatre Industry in Nineteenth Century France by F.W. J. Hemmings, in French Rev, vol. II, 94; auth, "Two Simple Hearts: Balzac's Eugene and Flauberts' Felicite in Romance Quarterly 42.2, (95): 195-202; auth, The Theatre Industry in Nineteenth-Century France by F. W. J. Hemmings in Romance Quarterly 42.4, (95): 237-238; auth, Alekis de Tocqueville by Matthew Manchi in French Review 68, (95): 174-175; auth, Literature francaise du XIX Siecle by Arlette Michel, et. al. in French Review 69, (95): 1104-1105. **CONTACT ADDRESS** Univ of Arkansas, Fayetteville, 1402 E. Shadowridge, Fayetteville, AR 72701. **EMAIL** hopec@comp.uark.edu

CHRISTIANSEN, NANCY LEE
PERSONAL Born 07/07/1954, Glendale, CA, s **DISCIPLINE** ENGLISH **EDUCATION** Brigham Young Univ, BA, 78; MA, 83; Univ Calif at Los Angeles, PhD, 94. **CAREER** Lectr, Cal State Univ, 83-86; instr, Univ Calif, Los Angeles, 86-94; asst prof, BYU, 94-00. **HONORS AND AWARDS** Lily Bess Campbell Diss Fel. **MEMBERSHIPS** NCTE; CCC: RSA; ASHR; RMMRA; SAA; ISHR. **RESEARCH** Theories of language, reading composition and pedagogy in the British renaissance; Shakespeare's rhetorical practices; conjunction of rhetoric and ethics. **SELECTED PUBLICATIONS** Auth, "The Dialogue, the Frame and the Transfer: Three Metaphors as Heuristics for Good Reading," in Dialogues and Conversations, eds. Grant Boswell, Gary Hatch (Needham Hts, MA: Simon and Schuster, 96); auth, "Rhetoric as Character Fashioning: The Implications of Delivery's 'Places' in the British Renaissance," Rhetorical J 15 (97): 297-334; auth, "Synecdoche, Tropic Violence, and Shakespeare's Irritatio in Titus Andvorricus," Style (forthcoming). **CONTACT ADDRESS** Dept English, Brigham Young Univ, 1017 JKHB, Provo, UT 84602.

CHRISTIANSON, PAUL
DISCIPLINE ENGLISH LANGUAGE AND LITERATURE **EDUCATION** St Olaf, BA, 55; State Univ Iowa, MA, 56; Wash Univ, PhD, 64. **CAREER** Mildred Foss Thompson prof. **SELECTED PUBLICATIONS** Auth, books on medieval cult and lit. **CONTACT ADDRESS** Dept of Eng, The Col of Wooster, Wooster, OH 44691.

CHRISTIANSON, SCOTT
DISCIPLINE 20TH-CENTURY AMERICAN AND BRITISH LITERATURE, LITERARY THEORY AND CRITICISM **EDUCATION** Harvard Univ, MA, 74; Augustana Col, BA, 77; Univ NE, MA, 78; Univ MN, PhD, 86. **CAREER** Tchg assoc, Univ MN, 80-86; asst prof, Moorhead State Univ, 86-87; undergrad adv cord, 89-91, gard recruitment and admis cord, 89-91, mem, grad fac, 90-, assoc prof, 93-, ch, peace and world Security Stud minor prog, 93-94, assoc ch, dept Eng, 93-94, actg ch, dept Eng, Radford Univ, 94. **HONORS AND AWARDS** Grant, Col Arts and Sci, 92-93, grant, Ctr for Acad Enrichment Prog, 92-93, fac prof develop Leave, 95, fac adv of best res MA thesis award, Radford Univ, 97. **RESEARCH** T. S. Eliot. **SELECTED PUBLICATIONS** Auth, Rev of Narrative Chance: Postmodern Discourse on Native American Indian Literatures, ed Gerald Vizenor, Western Am Lit 29.2, 94; Talkin' Trash and Kickin' Butt: Sue Grafton's Hardboiled Feminism, in Feminism in Women's Detective Fiction, ed Glenwood Irons, Univ Toronto Press, 95; Ella Constance Sykes, in Dictionary of Literary Biography 174: British Travel Writers, 1876-1909, eds. Barbara Brothers and Julia Gergits, Gale Res, 97; The Eternal Return of T. S. Eliot, rev of Mastery and Escape, by Jewel Spears Brooker, Yeats Eliot Rev 14.3, 97. **CONTACT ADDRESS** Radford Univ, Radford, VA 24142. **EMAIL** schristi@runet.edu

CHRISTIE, N. BRADLEY
PERSONAL Born 05/23/1957, Durham, NC, m, 1980, 3 children **DISCIPLINE** ENGLISH **EDUCATION** Davidson Col, AB, 79; Univ Va, MA, 81; Duke Univ, PhD, 88; Erskine Theol Sem, MDiv, 99. **CAREER** Instr, Duke Univ, 83-87; Instr to Asst Prof, Stetson Univ, 88-91; Asst Prof to Prof, Erskine Col, 91-. **HONORS AND AWARDS** Who's Who in Am Educ, Andrew W Mellon Fel, Duke Univ, 87-88; Grad Tutorships, Duke Univ, 83-87; Thesis Honors, Davidson Col, 79; Omicron Delta Kappa; Alpha Psi Omega. **MEMBERSHIPS** Nat Coun of Teachers of English, Viet Nam Generation, Conf on Col composition and comm., SC Theater Asn. **SELECTED PUBLICATIONS** Auth, "Canonicity," in Viet Nam Generation: A Journal of Recent History and contemporary Issues, 97; auth, "Still a Vietnam Playwright After All These Years," in David Rabe: A casebook, Garland Pub, 91; auth, "Gay Wilson Allen," in Dictionary of Literary Biography, Gale, 91; auth, "Teaching Our Longest War: constructive Lessons From Vietnam," English Journal, 89; auth, "David Rabe's Theater of War and Remembering," I Search and Clear: Critical Responses to Selected Literature and films of the Vietnam War, Bowling Green State Univ Popular Press, 88 **CONTACT ADDRESS** Dept English, Erskine Col, PO Box 338, Due West, SC 29639-0338. **EMAIL** christie@erskine.edu

CHRISTOPHER, GEORGIA B.
PERSONAL Born Barnesville, GA **DISCIPLINE** RENAISSANCE ENGLISH LITERATURE **EDUCATION** Anges Scott Col, BA, 55; Yale Univ, MAT, 57, PhD(English), 66. **CAREER** Teacher English, Needham Broughton High Sch, Raleigh, NC, 57-59; instr, Mercer Univ, 59-62; asst prof, Univ NC, Chapel Hill, 66-71; assoc prof, Westhampton Col, Univ Richmond, 71-78, actg chmn dept, 73, prof English, 78-81; Assoc Prof, Emory Univ, 81-, Sr Folger fel, 75-76; Am Coun Learned Socs fel, 75-76. **MEMBERSHIPS** MLA; Milton Soc Am; SAtlantic Mod Lang Asn; Am Shakespeare Asn; Renaissance Soc Am. **RESEARCH** Milton; Renaissance; poetry and intellectual history. **SELECTED PUBLICATIONS** Auth, Subject and Macrosubject in l'Allegro and il Penseroso, Milton Stud, Vol 0028, 92. **CONTACT ADDRESS** Dept of English, Emory Univ, Atlanta, GA 30322.

CHU, FELIX T.
PERSONAL Born 02/27/1949, Taipei, Taiwan, m, 1975, 1 child **DISCIPLINE** LIBRARY SCIENCE **EDUCATION** Univ Wi Madison, BA, 72; Univ Iowa, MA, 73, 74, BA, 81; Il St Univ, PhD, 93. **CAREER** Cataloger, Univ Nb Lincoln, 75-78; librn, Univ Iowa, 79-80; data proc anal, Nb Dept of Revenue, 81-84; asst to dir, W Il Univ, 88; librn co coord, W Il Univ, 88- . **MEMBERSHIPS** Amer Libr Assoc; Il Libr Assoc. **RESEARCH** Interdepartmental commun in the libr; commun between librns & patrons or outside agencies; lateral relations; org structures; leadership & change, access to libr materials. **SELECTED PUBLICATIONS** Auth, Collaboration in a loosely coupled system: Librarian-faculty relations in collection develop, Libr & Infor Sci Res, 95; The freezing of dynamic knowledge, Technicalities, 96; Framing reference encounters, RQ, 96; The librarian-faculty relations in collection develop, J of Acad Librarianship, 97; Another look at staffing the reference desk, Col & Res Libr News, 97. **CONTACT ADDRESS** Univ Library, Western Illinois Univ, 1 University Cir, Macomb, IL 61455-1390. **EMAIL** f-chu@wiu.edu

CHU, MIKE S.
PERSONAL Born 09/16/1947, Taiwan, m, 1972, 3 children **DISCIPLINE** ENGLISH LITERATURE **EDUCATION** Univ Neb, MA; PhD, 85. **CAREER** Asst prof, Univ Neb, 85-88; asst prof, Univ Wis, 89; Col Du Page, 90-. **HONORS AND AWARDS** FSU, Schlp; UNL Regents Fel. **SELECTED PUBLICATIONS** Auth, The Town Crier, Crane Pub, 84; auth, Working American Idioms, Crane Pub, 86; auth, Sentence Combining, Bookman, 99. **CONTACT ADDRESS** Dept Communication Arts and Sciences, Col of DuPage, 425 22nd St, Glen Ellyn, IL 60137-6784.

CHUNG, YOUNSOOK NA
PERSONAL Born 08/19/1966, Seoul, Korea, m, 1992 **DISCIPLINE** ENGLISH **EDUCATION** Hankuk Univ, BA, 89; San Jose State Univ, MA, 92; Univ Nev, PhD, 00. **CAREER** Instr, Truckee Mea Community Col, 99; instr, Utah State Univ, 00-. **MEMBERSHIPS** MLA; KSMBAF; KSFSEL. **RESEARCH** Modern American fiction; feminism. **SELECTED PUBLICATIONS** Auth, "Bellow's Vision as a Bourgeois and Patriarchal

Humanist in Mr. Sammler's Planet," Study Mod Fict 7.2 (00); auth, "Bellow and Feminist Criticism," Fem Studies English Lit 8.2 (01). **CONTACT ADDRESS** English Dept, Utah State Univ, Logan, UT 84322. **EMAIL** ychung@english.usu.edu

CHURCH, DAN M.
PERSONAL Born 04/20/1939, NC, m, 1963, 2 children **DISCIPLINE** TWENTIETH-CENTURY THEATER AND FILM, TECHNOLOGY AND LANGUAGE ACQUISITION **EDUCATION** Wake Forest Col, BA, 61; Middlebury Col, MA, 62; Univ Wis, PhD, 68. **CAREER** Asst prof Fr, Antioch Col, 65-67; asst prof, 67-70; assoc prof, 70-01; dir, Vanderbilt-in-Fr, 74-76; dir, Workshop on the Quest Authoring Syst, 86; dir, Mellon Regional fac develop sem, 86; dir, lang lab, Vanderbilt Univ, 88-96; emeritus, 01. **MEMBERSHIPS** Comput Assisted Lang Instr Consortium; chemn, Courseware Develop Spec Interest Gp. **SELECTED PUBLICATIONS** Auth, Interactive Audio for Foreign-Language Learning, Lit & Ling Comp, V, 2; AndrQ Barsacq, Gaston Baty, and Roger Planchon, Theatrical Directors: A Biographical Dictionary, Greenwood Press, 94; rev, GramDef French, CALICO J, 98. **CONTACT ADDRESS** Vanderbilt Univ, 636 Timber Lane, Nashville, TN 37215. **EMAIL** dan.m.church@vanderbilt.edu

CHURCHILL, ROBERT J.
DISCIPLINE 19TH-CENTURY BRITISH LITERATURE, VICTORIAN STUDIES **EDUCATION** Creighton Univ, BA, 66, MA, 70; Univ NE-Lincoln, PhD, 79. **CAREER** Asst prof, Creighton Univ, 80-; past instr, Univ NE-Lincoln. **SELECTED PUBLICATIONS** Written on, Carlyle, Tennyson, Browning, Victorian Mysticism, Joseph Conrad, Eastern Literature & 19th-Century Travel-Adventure Narratives. **CONTACT ADDRESS** Dept of Eng, Creighton Univ, 2500 CA Plaza, CA 311, Omaha, NE 68178. **EMAIL** rchurch@creighton.edu

CHUSID, MARTIN
PERSONAL Born 08/19/1925, Brooklyn, NY, m, 1952, 1 child **DISCIPLINE** MUSIC HISTORY **EDUCATION** Univ Calif, Berkeley, AB, 50, AM, 55, PhD, 61. **CAREER** From instr to asst prof music hist, Univ Southern Calif, 59-63; assoc prof music, 63-68, chmn dept, 67-70, assoc dean grad sch arts & sci, 70-72, Prof Music, NY Univ, 68-, Dir Am Inst Verdi Studies, 76-, Am Coun Learned Socs sr fel, 74; mem screening comt music, Sr Fulbright-Hays Awards, 75-78, chmn, 77-78; Nat Endowment for Humanities grants, 77 & 77-79. **HONORS AND AWARDS** DHL, Centre Col Ky, 77. **MEMBERSHIPS** Am Musicol Soc; Int Musicol Soc; Int Music Libr Asn; Am Inst for Verdi Stud; Beethoven Soc; Am Schubert Inst. **RESEARCH** Music of Verdi, Schubert and Mozart. **SELECTED PUBLICATIONS** Auth, Schubert's overture for string quintet and Cherubini's overture to Faniska, J Am Musicol Soc, 62; Schubert's cyclic compositions of 1824, Acta Musicol, 64; The significance of D minor in Mozart's dramatic music, Mozart-Jahrbuch 1965-66, 67; auth & ed, Schubert's Symphony in B Minor (Unfinished): Essays in History and Analysis, a Critical Edition, Norton, 68, 2nd ed, 71; ed, Franz Schubert Streichquintette, Streichquartette vol.1, Neue Schubert-Ausgabe, Barenreiter, Ser VI, Vols II & III, 71 & 78; auth, Rigoletto and Monterone: A Study in Musical Dramaturgy, Report XI Congr, Int Musicol Soc, 72, Hansen, 74; A Catalog of Verdi's Operas, Boonin, 74; co-ed, A Verdi Companion, Norton, 79; ed, Rigoletto, The Works of Giuseppe Verdi, 83; Verdi's Middle Period, Univ Chicago 97; ed, A Companion to Schuberts " Schwanenqesang," Yale Univ Press, 00; ed, Schuberts " Schwanenqesang": Families of the Autograph and Sketches and a Reprint of the First Edition, Yale Univ Press, 00. **CONTACT ADDRESS** Dept of Music, New York Univ, 24 Waverly Pl, New York, NY 10003-6757. **EMAIL** mc4@is6.nyu.edu

CIANCIO, RALPH ARMANDO
PERSONAL Born 12/01/1929, Pittsburgh, PA, m, 1959, 3 children **DISCIPLINE** ENGLISH **EDUCATION** Duquesne Univ, AB, 57; Pa State Univ MA, 58; Univ Pittsburgh, PhD(English), 64. **CAREER** From instr to asst prof English, Carnegie-Mellon Univ, 59-65; from asst prof to assoc prof, 65-75, Prof, English, Skidmore Col, 76-, Chmn Dept, 80- **MEMBERSHIPS** MLA. **RESEARCH** American fiction; 20th century European novel. **SELECTED PUBLICATIONS** Auth, Richard Write, Eugene O'Neill, and The Beast in the skull, Modern Language Studies, Vol XXIII, No 3, Summer 98; auth, Laughing in Pain with Nathaniel West, Literature and the Grotesque, Rodophi Perspectives on Modern Literature, 15, 95; auth, Vico in Dixie, The Southern Literary Journal, Vol XXVIII, No 1, Univ NC, Chapel Hill, Fall, 95. **CONTACT ADDRESS** Dept of Eng, Skidmore Col, 815 N Broadway, Saratoga Springs, NY 12866-1698.

CIMA, GAY GIBSON
PERSONAL Born 11/18/1948, Falls City, NE, m, 1976, 2 children **DISCIPLINE** ENGLISH LITERATURE **EDUCATION** Univ Nebr, BA; Northwestern Univ, MA, Cornell Univ, PhD. **CAREER** Asst Prof, Univ Florida, Assoc, Univ Florida. **HONORS AND AWARDS** NEH, 98; Kahan Prize for best theatre article, 84. **MEMBERSHIPS** Asn for Theatre in Higher Educ; Am Soc for Theatre Res, Women and Theatre Prog. **RESEARCH** Feminist theatre. **SELECTED PUBLICATIONS** Auth, Performing Women: Female Characters, Male Playwrights; Modern Stage, Cornell, 93; auth, Conceived By Liberty: Maternal figures and Ninetenth-Century American Literature, Cornell Univ Press, 94; auth, " Bombshell," Body Politics and the Fictional Double, Indiana UP, 00; auth, " Cyber genetics," Genealogie und Genetik, series Einstein-bucher, Germany, 01; ed, Dale Bauer and Philip Gould, 01. **CONTACT ADDRESS** English Dept, Georgetown Univ, 4008 Turlington Hall, Washington, DC 20057.

CIRILLO, ALBERT
DISCIPLINE LITERATURE **EDUCATION** Johns Hopkins Univ, PhD. **CAREER** Mellon fel, Harvard, 90-91; co-ed, Gender and Theatre Series for Routledge; several res fel(s), Canada. **SELECTED PUBLICATIONS** Auth, essays on and is an authority on the Working Women: Their Social Identity in Victorian Culture, 91; George Bernard Shaw and the Socialist Theatre, 94; essays on, theatre history and popular culture in Victorian and Edwardian Engl; 16th & 17th century poetry. **CONTACT ADDRESS** Dept of English, Northwestern Univ, 1801 Hinman, Evanston, IL 60208. **EMAIL** acirillo@northwestern.edu

CIRRONE, STEVEN F.
PERSONAL Born 03/05/1969, Queens, NY **DISCIPLINE** ENGLISH **EDUCATION** SUNY Binghamton, BA, 91; Claremont Grad Sch, MA, 92; PhD, 97. **CAREER** Instr, Mt San Antonio Col, 92-94; instr, Heald Business Col, 94; assoc ed, QSF Mag, 97-00; instr, Harvey Milk Inst, 96-00; adj fac, City Col, 98-00; instr, Diablo Valley Col, 94-00; asst div chmn to assoc prof, Tidewater Community Col, 00-. **HONORS AND AWARDS** Claremont Grad Sch Fel, 92-95. **MEMBERSHIPS** MLA. **RESEARCH** Renaissance witchcraft and occult philosophy; Shakespeare and Marlowe; modern film. **SELECTED PUBLICATIONS** Auth, "The New Immigrants: A Detailed Look at the Immigrant Situation as it Affects Gays and Lesbians," QSF Mag 19 (98); auth, "Campus Intolerance: Special Report on Campus-Based Homophobia," QSF 20 (98); auth, "Anabolic Steroids and Human Growth Hormone: Are They Affective in Fighting Wasting?" QSF Mag 22 (99); auth, "Global Warning: An Investigative Report on the International Struggle for Gay Rights," QSF Mag 22 (99); auth, "A History Lesson," Harrington Pr, 01. **CONTACT ADDRESS** English Dept, Tidewater Comm Col, 300 Granby St, Norfolk, VA 23510. **EMAIL** tccirrs@tc.cc.va.us

CISSNA, KENNETH N.
PERSONAL Born 07/10/1948, San Francisco, CA, m, 1982, 2 children **DISCIPLINE** COMMUNICATION **EDUCATION** Humboldt Col, BA, 70; Southern IL Univ, MS, 71; Univ Denver, PhD, 75. **CAREER** Asst prof, St Louis Univ, 75-79; asst prof to prof, Univ of S Fla, 79-. **HONORS AND AWARDS** Alumni Prof Awd, Univ of S Fla, 81-82; Scholar of the Year, Fla Commun Assoc; Outstanding Book in Applied Commun, Speech Commun Assoc, 95; Member of Honor, Swedish Network for Confirmation Res, 96. **MEMBERSHIPS** Fla Commun Assoc; Int Commun Assoc; Nat Commun Assoc; Southern States Commun Assoc; United Fac of Fla. **RESEARCH** Applied Communication, Dialogic Communication, Interpersonal and Group Communication. **SELECTED PUBLICATIONS** Coed, The Reach of Dialogue: Confirmation, Voice and Community, Hampton Pr, (Cresskill, NJ), 94; coauth, "Communication and the Ground of Dialogue", The Reach of Dialogue: Confirmation, Voice, and Community, ed Rob Anderson, Kenneth N Dissna and Ronald C Arnett, Hampton Pr, (94): 9-30; ed, Applied Communication in the 21st Century, Lawrence Erlbaum Assoc, (Mahwah, NJ), 95; coauth, "Dialogue in Public: Looking Critically at the Buber-Rogers Dialogue", Martin Buber and the Human Science, SUNY Pr, (NY, 96): 191-206; auth, "Accuracy of Interpersonal Perception", Teaching about Culture, Ethnicity, and Diversity: Exercises and Planned Activities, ed Ted Singelis, Sage Pub, (Thousand Oaks, 97); 175-185; coauth, The Martin Buber-Carl Rogers Dialogue: A New Transcript with Commentary, SUNY Pr, (NY), 97; coauth, Moments of Meeting: Buber, Rogers, and the Potential for Public Dialogue, (forthcoming); auth, "Applied Communication Research in the 21st Century", J of Applied Commun Res 28.2, (forthcoming); coauth, "The Future of Dialogic Scholarship in Communication", Communication: Key Research in the Discipline, ed Sean Gilmore, (forthcoming). **CONTACT ADDRESS** Dept Commun, Univ of So Florida, 4202 E Fowler Ave, Tampa, FL 33620-9951. **EMAIL** kcissna@luna.cas.usf.edu

CITRON, MICHELLE
PERSONAL Born 10/25/1948, Boston, MA, p **DISCIPLINE** MEDIA ARTS, RADIO, FILM **EDUCATION** Univ Mass, BS, 70; Univ Wis Madison, MS, 71; PhD, 74. **CAREER** Asst prof, Temple Univ, 74-75; fac, Grand Val State Univ, 75-78; chmn to prof to cen dir to assoc dean, Northwestern Univ, 92-. **HONORS AND AWARDS** Ill Arts Council Fel, 85, 95; Van Zelst Res Prof, 92; Distinguished Prof Awd, 90; NEH, 86. **MEMBERSHIPS** SCS; UFVA; AIFVM; ISTSS. **RESEARCH** Narrative; directing. **SELECTED PUBLICATIONS** Auth, Parthenogenesis, (film) 75; auth, Daughter Rite, (film) 78; auth, What You Take for Granted, (film) 83; auth, Mother Rite, (video) 83; auth, As American as Apple Pie, (CD-ROM Narrative) 99; auth Home Movies and Other Necessary Fictions, Univ Minn Pr, 99; auth, Cocktails and Appetizers (CD-ROM Narrative) 01. **CONTACT ADDRESS** Media Dept, Northwestern Univ, 1905 Sheridan Rd, Evanston, IL 60208-0001. **EMAIL** citron@northwester.edu

CLACK, JERRY
PERSONAL Born 07/22/1926, New York, NY **DISCIPLINE** CLASSICS **EDUCATION** Univ Pittsburgh, PhD 62, MA 58; Princeton Univ, BA 46. **CAREER** Duquesne Univ, prof 68-; The March of Dimes Pittsburgh, dir 53-68; US Delegation to UNESCO, prog officer 46-67. **MEMBERSHIPS** APA; CAAS; PCA; CAP. **RESEARCH** Hellenistic poetry; Augustan literature. **SELECTED PUBLICATIONS** Auth, The Poems of Meleager, 94; The APA and Regional Associations: Transactions of the American Philological Association, 93; auth, Asclepiades of Samos and Leonidas of Tarentum: The Poems, 99. **CONTACT ADDRESS** Dept of Classic, Duquesne Univ, Pittsburgh, PA 15282. **EMAIL** clack@duq.edu

CLAIR, ROBIN P.
DISCIPLINE COMMUNICATIONS **EDUCATION** Kent State Univ, PhD, 90. **CAREER** Assoc prof, Purdue Univ. **HONORS AND AWARDS** Bk of the year award NCA (98-00) for Organizing Silence: A World of Possibilities; Golden Anniversary Awd NCA for Outstanding Research Article, 93. **MEMBERSHIPS** NCA; ICA. **RESEARCH** Studies organizational communication (socialization, sexual harassment, power and politics); how aesthetic theory, critica theory, feminist theory, and postcolonial theory can be applied to studies of organizational life. **SELECTED PUBLICATIONS** Auth, The Use of Framing Devices to Sequester Organizational Narratives: Hegemony and Harassment, Commun Monogr, 93; auth, The Political Nature of the Colloquialism, A Real Job: Implications for Organizational Socialization, Commun Monogr, 96; auth, Organizing Silence: A World of Possibilities, SUNY, 98. **CONTACT ADDRESS** Dept of Commun, Purdue Univ, West Lafayette, 1080 Schleman Hall, West Lafayette, IN 47907-1080. **EMAIL** rpclair@omni.cc.purdue.edu

CLANCY, JOSEPH P.
PERSONAL Born 03/08/1928, New York, NY, m, 1948, 5 children **DISCIPLINE** ENGLISH **EDUCATION** Fordham Univ, BA, MA, PhD. **CAREER** Instr, Fordham Col, 49-50; from asst prof to assoc prof, 50-65, Prof English, Marymount Manhattan Col, 65-, Chmn Dept, 50-, Am Philos Soc grant, 63 & 67; Nat Transl Ctr fel, 67. **MEMBERSHIPS** MLA. **RESEARCH** English drama to 1700; mediaeval Welsh poetry; 17th century English literature. **SELECTED PUBLICATIONS** **CONTACT ADDRESS** Dept of English, Marymount Manhattan Col, New York, NY 10021.

CLAPP-INTYRE, ALISA
PERSONAL Born 03/31/1967, Detroit, MI, m, 1996 **DISCIPLINE** ENGLISH **EDUCATION** Oakland Univ, BA, 89; Univ Ill Urbana-Champaign, MA, 91; PhD, 96. **CAREER** TA, Univ of Ill, 89-96; vis asst prof, DePauw Univ, 97-98; vis instr, Purdue Univ, 96-99; asst prof, Ind Univ E, 99-. **HONORS AND AWARDS** Pauline Gragg Fel, Univ Ill, 94-95; Outstanding TA Awd, Univ Ill, 95; William Winter Fel, Univ Ill, 95-96; Excellence in Teaching, Purdue Univ, 97; Fel, Ind Univ E, 00-01; Nominee, Horizon Teaching Awd, Ind Univ E, 01; Ind Univ Overseas Conf Fund Awd, 01. **MEMBERSHIPS** MLA, Midwest Victorian Studies Assoc, Children's Lit Assoc, TELL, Mich Acad of Sci, Arts and Letters. **RESEARCH** Victorian literature and music, Elizabeth Gaskell, George Eliot, Thomas Hardy, Alfred Lord Tennyson, Children's literature: Nancy Drew/Hardy Boys mysteries, Civil War Fiction, Environmental Picture Books, Writing/Teaching practices. **SELECTED PUBLICATIONS** Auth, "Texts Which Tell Another Story: Miscommunication in Elizabeth Gaskell's 'Mary Barton,'" Mich Acad 27.1 (95): 29-37; auth, "The Tenant of Patriarchal Culture: Anne Bronte's Problematic Female Artist," Mic Acad 28.2, (96): 113-122; auth, "The City, the Country, and Communities of Singing Women: Music in the Novels of Elizabeth Gaskell," Victorian Urban Settings: Essays on the Nineteenth-Century City and Its Contexts, ed Debra N Mancoff and DJ Trela, (NY, London: Garland, 96): 114-132; auth, "Dinah and the Secularization of Methodist Mymnody in Eliot's 'Adam Bede,'" Victorian Inst Jour 26, (98): 40-68; auth, "Marginalized Musical Interludes: Tennyson's Critique of Conventionality in 'The Princess,'" Victorian Poetry 38.2 (00): 227-248; auth, "The Indiana Interstate Case: Economics and Ethics Face Off," Bus Commun Quart 63.2 (00): 60-68; auth, "Three-Part Journaling in Introductory Writing and Literature Classes: More Work with More Rewards," Jour of Teaching and Learning website, (01); auth, Angelic Airs/Subversive Songs: Music as Cultural Discourse in the Victorian Novel and Society, Ohio Univ Pr, (forthcoming); auth, "Poetics of Sexuality and Liberality: Thomas Hardy's Poetry and the English Folk-Song Tradition," Nineteenth-Century Poetry and the Significance of Music, ed Phyllis Weliver, Ashgate Publ, forthcoming; auth, "Will Girls be Boys? Will Boys be Men? Re-visioning Gender and Age in the Nancy Drew and Hardy Boys Mystery Series," Learning to Listen in New Ways: Expanding the Literary Canon in Children's and Adolescent Literature, ed Darwin L Henderson and Jill P May, forthcoming. **CONTACT ADDRESS** Dept Humanities and Fine Arts, Indiana Univ, East, 2325 Chester Blvd, Richmond, IN 43774-1220. **EMAIL** aclappit@indiana.edu

CLARK, BASIL ALFRED
PERSONAL Born 07/19/1939, Prospect, ME, m, 1966, 2 children **DISCIPLINE** ENGLISH LITERATURE & LANGUAGE **EDUCATION** Bowdoin Col, AB, 60; Univ ME, MA, 69; OH State Univ, PhD, 75. **CAREER** From Asst Prof to Assoc Prof, 75-85, prof eng, Saginaw Valley State Univ, 85. **HONORS AND AWARDS** House Family Awd for Teacher Impact, Saginaw Valley State Univ, 91. **MEMBERSHIPS** MLA; NCTE. **RESEARCH** Medieval Brit lit. **SELECTED PUBLICATIONS** Heike Monogatari and Beowulf: A Comparative Study, Bull Shikoku Women's Univ 9.2, 90; auth, Saginaw Valley State University: The Early and Formative Years, 1963-1989, (Univ Ctr, MI) Saginaw Valley State Univ, 98. **CONTACT ADDRESS** Saginaw Valley State Univ, 7400 Bay Rd, University Center, MI 48710-0001. **EMAIL** baclark@svsu.edu

CLARK, BERTHA SMITH
PERSONAL Born 09/26/1943, Nashville, TN, m, 1973 **DISCIPLINE** SPEECH **EDUCATION** TN State Univ, BS (high distinction) 1964; George Peabody Clg for Tchrs, MA 1965; Natl Inst of Mental Hlth, Pre Doctoral Fellow 1978-80; Vanderbilt Univ, PhD 1982. **CAREER** Bill Wilkerson Hearing & Speech Center (BWHSC), head tchr OE #1 project, 65-70, speech pathologist, 65-78, 80-87; TN State Univ, supvr of clinical practicum, 69-78, 80-87; Mama Lere Parent Infant Home, Bill Wilkerson Hearing & Speech Center, parent-infant trainer, 82-86; Vanderbilt Univ, div of hearing and speech sciences, 70-87, adjunct asst prof, 87-98; Middle TN State Univ, prof, currently. **HONORS AND AWARDS** Honors grad Haynes HS 1960, TN St Univ 1964; predoctoral flwshp Natl Inst of Mental Hlth 1978-80; Honors of TSHA, In Speech, Language Hearing Assn 1988; Office of Education Trainee, Office of Education 1964-65; Fellow, Southern Education Foundation 1964. **MEMBERSHIPS** Board of dir League for the Hearing Impaired 1973-87, The Childrens House (A Montessori Preschool) 1984-86; advsry Cmt Early Devel & Assistance Project Kennedy Cntr 1984-88; co-chrprsn mem YWCA 1985; mem Delta Sigma Theta Sorority, Inc 1962-; admin comm, vice pres for educ TN Speech and Hearing Assn 1985-87; chairperson Cochlear Implant Scholarship Comm, 1985-86; mem Compton Scholarship Comm Vanderbilt Univ 1985-86; bd of dirs Peabody Alumni 1986-89; board of directors Bill Wilkerson Center 1990-95; board of directors Effective Advocacy for Citizens with Handicaps 1991-92; board of directors CFAW, MTSU 1991-. **CONTACT ADDRESS** Dept of Speech & Theatre, Middle Tennessee State Univ, Communication Disorders, Murfreesboro, TN 37132.

CLARK, BEVERLY LYON
PERSONAL Born 12/06/1948, Pittsfield, MA, m, 1969, 2 children **DISCIPLINE** ENGLISH **EDUCATION** Swarthmore Col, BA, 70; Brown Univ, PhD, 79. **CAREER** Lectr, asst prof, assoc prof, prof, Wheaton Col, 77-. **HONORS AND AWARDS** Phi Beta Kappa; NEH Fel; William C H and Elsie D Prentice Ch. **MEMBERSHIPS** MLA; CLA; IRSCL; AAUP. **RESEARCH** Children's literature; feminist theory; pedagogy; American literature. **SELECTED PUBLICATIONS** Auth, Regendering the School Story: Sassy Sissies and Tattling Tomboys Garland (NY), 96; coed, Critical Essays on Carson McCullers Hall (Boston), 96; coed, "Little Women" and the Feminist Imagination, Garland (NY), 99; coed, Girls, Boys, Books, Toys: Gender in Children's Literature and Culture, Johns Hopkins UP (Baltimore), 99; auth, "Domesticating the School Story, Regendering a Genre: Alcott's Little Men," New Literary History 26 (95): 325-44; coauth, "Reading Romance, Reading Ourselves," Centennial Rev 40 (96): 359-84; auth, "Kiddie Lit in Academe," Profession (96): 149-57; auth, "Man-books, Kiddie Lit, and Critical Distemper," Signal 87 (98): 196-202. **CONTACT ADDRESS** Dept English, Wheaton Col, Massachusetts, 26 E Main St, Norton, MA 02766-2311. **EMAIL** bclark@wheatonma.edu

CLARK, DAVID L.
DISCIPLINE ENGLISH LITERATURE **EDUCATION** Univ Western Ontario, BA, MA, PhD. **RESEARCH** Romantic poetry and prose; Romantic critical theory; Schelling and Nietzsche; contemp philos; critical theory. **SELECTED PUBLICATIONS** Co-ed, Intersections, 96; co-ed, New Romanticisms, 95. **CONTACT ADDRESS** English Dept, McMaster Univ, 1280 Main St W, Hamilton, ON, Canada L8S 4L9. **EMAIL** dclark@mcmaster.ca

CLARK, DAVID RIDGLEY
PERSONAL Born 09/17/1920, Seymour, CT, m, 1948, 4 children **DISCIPLINE** ENGLISH **EDUCATION** Wesleyan Univ, BA, 47; Yale Univ, MA, 50, PhD, 55. **CAREER** Instr Eng, Mohawk Col, 47; tchg fel, IN Univ, 48-50; instr, Univ MA, 51-56; lectr, Smith Col, 56-57; from asst prof to assoc prof, 58-65, chmn dept, 75-76, Prof Eng, Univ MA, 65-85; Emer Prof, Univ MA, Amherst, 85-; Saxton fel, 57; Bollingen Found grant-in-aid, 57; Am Philos Soc grant, 57, 77, 83; Mod Lang Asn, 58; Fulbright lectr, Univ Iceland, 60-61 & Univ Col, Dublin, 65-66; Nat Endowment for Hum proj grant, 69, 78; vis prof Eng, Univ Victoria, BC, 71-72; vis fel, Wolfson Col, Univ Cambridge, 78; vis prof & chmn, St. Mary's Col, Notre Dame, IN, 85-87; vis prof Williams Col, 89,90. **MEMBERSHIPS** MLA, Am Conf Irish Stud. **RESEARCH** W B Yeats and the mod lit of Ireland; the poetry of Hart Crane; late 19th and 20th century lit. **SELECTED PUBLICATIONS** Auth, The Texture of Hart Cranes's Poetry, Yale M.A. Thesis 1950;coauth, A Curious Quire, poems, Univ Mass, 62,67; Auth, W B Yeats and the Theatre of Desolate Reality, Dolmen, Dublin, 65, expanded ed. With Rosalind Clark, Washington, DC, Catholic Univ of America, 93; Dry Tree, 66 & co-ed, A Tower of Polished Black Stones, 71, Dolmen, Dublin; ed, Twentieth Century Interpretations of Murder in the Cathedral, Prentice-Hall, 71-; co-ed, Druid Craft: The Writing of the Shadowy Waters, Univ Mass, 71 & Dolmen, Dublin, 72; auth, Lyric Resonance: Yeats, Frost, Crane, Cummings, and others, Univ Mass, 72; That Black Day, Dolmen, 80; ed, Critical Essays on Hart Crane, G K Hall, 82; auth, Yeats at Songs and Chorusus, Colin Smythe Ltd & Univ Mass, 83; coed, W B Yeats and the Writing of Sopholcles' King Oedipus, Am Philos Soc, Philadelphia, 89; ed, W B Yeats The Winding Stair Manuscript Materials, Cornell, 95; auth, W B Yeats, Words For Music Perhaps, 2nd Other Poems, Manuscript, auth, Materials, Cornell, 99; auth, W B Yeats, The Plays, Collected Works, Scribners, 00, with Rosalinda Clark. **CONTACT ADDRESS** 481 Holgerson Rd, Sequim, WA 98382.

CLARK, EDWARD
PERSONAL Born 10/25/1923, Elyria, OH **DISCIPLINE** ENGLISH **EDUCATION** Miami Univ, AB, 49; Ind Univ, PhD(English), 55. **CAREER** Asst prof English, St Lawrence Univ, 55-61; assoc prof, 61-65, Prof English, Suffolk Univ, 65-, Fulbright lectr, Kiel Univ, 58-59. **MEMBERSHIPS** MLA; Col Lang Asn; AAUP. **RESEARCH** Leatherstocking tales of Fenimore Cooper; American and British novel; racial literature. **SELECTED PUBLICATIONS** Auth, Winesburg, Ohio: An interpretation, Die Neueren Sprachen, 59; Images of the Negro in the American novel, Jahrbuch fIr Amerikastudien, 60; Studying and teaching Afro-American literature, CLA, 72; The Harlem renaissance and today, Literatur in Wissenschaft und Unterricht, 75. **CONTACT ADDRESS** Dept of English, Suffolk Univ, Boston, MA 02114.

CLARK, EDWARD DEPRIEST, SR.
PERSONAL Born 05/24/1930, Wilmington, NC, d **DISCIPLINE** ENGLISH **EDUCATION** North Carolina A&T State University, Greensboro, NC, BS, 1948; NYork Univ, MA, 1955; Syracuse University, Syracuse, NYork, PhD, 1971. **CAREER** Union Point High School, Union Point, GA, English dept head, 48-51; Greensboro High School, Greensboro, GA, English dept head, 53-54; Emanuel County High School, Swainsboro, GA, English dept head, 54-57; Albany State College, Albany, GA, asst prof, English, 57-59; Southern University, Baton Rouge, LA, asst prof, English, 60-61; Fayetteville State University, Fayetteville, NC, assoc prof, chairman, 61-66, chairman, prof, English, 71-75; North Carolina State University, Raleigh, NC, assoc prof, English, 75-. **HONORS AND AWARDS** Outstanding Teacher Awd, 1989, elected to Academy of Outstanding Teachers, 1989, North Carolina State University; Alumni Outstanding Teacher Awd, North Carolina State University, 1989. **MEMBERSHIPS** Member, College Language Assn, 1961-; member, Modern Language Assn, 1961-; member, South Atlanta Modeern Language Assn, 1975-. **CONTACT ADDRESS** Professor, English, No Carolina Central Univ, Raleigh, NC 27602.

CLARK, GEORGE
DISCIPLINE ENGLISH LITERATURE **EDUCATION** Harvard Univ, PhD. **CAREER** Dept Eng, Queen's Univ **RESEARCH** Comparative studies in the early Middle Ages; characterization in early literature; representation of women in Old English and Norse-Icelandic literature. **SELECTED PUBLICATIONS** Auth, Beowulf, Twayne, 90; pubs on Beowulf, battle of Maldon, Old English poetry, Njals saga, the oral tradition, Robert Henryson, and Chaucer; auth, "The Hero and the Theme," in A Beowulf Handbook, Univ of Nebr Press, 97. **CONTACT ADDRESS** English Dept, Queen's Univ at Kingston, Kingston, ON, Canada K7L 3N6. **EMAIL** clarkg@post.queensu.ca

CLARK, GEORGE PEIRCE
PERSONAL Born 09/08/1915, Indianapolis, IN, m, 1946, 4 children **DISCIPLINE** ENGLISH AND AMERICAN LITERATURE **EDUCATION** Col Wooster, AB, 38; Yale Univ, PhD(English), 48. **CAREER** Asst prof English, Coe Col, 48-50; from asst prof to prof, Northern Ill Univ, 50-57; vis lectr, Univ Ill, 57-58; assoc prof, Mich State Univ, 59-60; cult affairs officer, US Info Agency, 60-67; prof & chmn dept, 67-81, Emer Prof English, Hanover Col, 81-, Ford fac fel, Harvard Univ, 53-54; Fulbright prof, Univ Mainz, 56-57. **MEMBERSHIPS** AAUP. **RESEARCH** Nineteenth-century American literature; Civil War history. **SELECTED PUBLICATIONS** Auth, Lakeside Toast, New Eng Rev-Middlebury Series, Vol 0016, 94; Mouthwash, New Eng Rev-Middlebury Series, Vol 0016, 94. **CONTACT ADDRESS** Hanover Col, PO Box 62, Hanover, IN 47243.

CLARK, IRA
PERSONAL Born 09/28/1940, Berkeley, CA, m, 1962, 2 children **DISCIPLINE** ENGLISH **EDUCATION** New Mexico State Univ, BA, 62; Northwestern Univ, MA, 63; Northwestern Univ, PhD. **CAREER** Lecturer, Univ of Maryland, Summer 67; Asst Prof, The Johns Hopkins Univ, 68-72; Assoc Prof, Univ of Florida, 72-83; Prof, Univ of Florida, 83-; Prof, Florida State Univ, State Univ System Abroad Program, Firenze, Fall 93. **HONORS AND AWARDS** NMSU Graduation "with highest honors;" Univ Tutorial Fellow, Northwestern Univ; Inland Steel Ryerson Foundation Fellow. **MEMBERSHIPS** Modern Language Assoc; South Atlantic MLA; National Council of Teachers of English; Florida College English Assoc; Renaissance Society of America; Southeastern Renaissance Society; Milton Society; United Faculty of Florida. **RESEARCH** Renaissance; Early Modern English Poetry; Milton; Tudor-Stuart Drama. **SELECTED PUBLICATIONS** Auth, "Milton and the Image of God," JEGP 68, 69: 422-31; auth, "Lord, in thee The beauty Lies in the Discover: Love Unknown and Reading Herbert," ELH, 39, 72: 560-84; auth, "Paradise Regained and the Gospel according to John," MP 71, 73: 1-16; auth, "Christ Revealed: The History of the Neotypological Lyric in the English Renaissance," Gainesville: Univ of Florida Press, 82; auth, "A Problem of Knowing Paradise in Paradise Lost," Milton Studies 27, 91: 183-207; auth, "Professional Playwrights: Massinger, Ford Shirley, & Brome," Lexington: Univ Press of Kentucky, 92; auth, "The Moral Art of Philip Massinger Lewisburg: Bucknell Univ Press, 93; auth, "Writing and Dueling in the English Renaissance," Medieval & Renaissance Drama in England 7, 95: 275-304; auth, "The Marital Double Standard in Tudor and Stuart Lives and Writing: Some Problems," Medieval & Renaissance Drama in England 9, 97: 34-55; auth, "Comic Violence on the Late Tudor-Early Stuart Stage: A Theory & an Application," Exemplaria, forthcoming 01. **CONTACT ADDRESS** Dept English, Univ of Florida, PO Box 117310, Gainesville, FL 32611-7310. **EMAIL** irac@english.ufl.edu

CLARK, JAMES ALFRED
PERSONAL Born 10/31/1954, Byrdstown, TN, d **DISCIPLINE** ENGLISH **EDUCATION** Vanderbilt Univ, BA, 76; Univ NCar, MA, 78; Univ Denver, PhD, 86. **CAREER** Instr, Auburn Univ, 86-87; asst prof, Univ Ga, 87-94; assoc prof, Barton Col, 94-. **HONORS AND AWARDS** Blumenthal Awd, 97; Harriett Arnow Awd, 90; Lilly Found Teaching Fel, 88-89; Alan Collins Scholar, 85; Randall Jarrell Scholar, 76-77. **MEMBERSHIPS** AWP; MLA; SAMLA; ASA; SSSL; AWA. **RESEARCH** Appalachian poetry; The Fugitives/Agrarians, poetic form; music; poetry. **SELECTED PUBLICATIONS** Auth, Dancing on Canaan's Ruins: Poems by Jim Clark, Eternal Delight Pub, 97; auth, Handiwork: Poems by Jim Clark, St Andrews Col Pr, 98; ed, The Selected Poems of Byron Herbert Reece, Univ Ga Pr, 01. **CONTACT ADDRESS** English Dept, Barton Col, PO Box 5250, Wilson, NC 27893. **EMAIL** jclark@barton.edu

CLARK, JAMES DRUMMOND
PERSONAL Born 03/01/1940, Lake Forest, IL, m, 1966, 1 child **DISCIPLINE** ENGLISH **EDUCATION** Colo Col, BA, 63; Univ Ariz, PhD, 67. **CAREER** Asst prof, 67-79, assoc prof Eng, Miami Univ, 79-. **MEMBERSHIPS** Malone Soc. **RESEARCH** Italian-English connections in early Elizabethan drama; Shakespearean comedy. **SELECTED PUBLICATIONS** Auth, The Bugbears: A Modernized Edition, Garland Publ, 79. **CONTACT ADDRESS** Dept of English, Miami Univ, 500 E High St, Oxford, OH 45056-1602. **EMAIL** clarkjd@muohio.edu

CLARK, JUSTUS KENT
PERSONAL Born 09/29/1917, Blue Creek, UT, m, 1939, 3 children **DISCIPLINE** ENGLISH **EDUCATION** Brigham Young Univ, AB, 39; Stanford Univ, PhD, 50. **CAREER** Instr, Stanford Univ, 42-43, 46-47; from instr to prof English, Calif Inst Technol, 47-86; prof emer, Calif Inst Technol, 86-. **RESEARCH** Eighteenth century English literature; 17th Century political history; Jonathan Swift; modern poetry. **SELECTED PUBLICATIONS** Auth, King's Agent, 58 & coauth, Dimensions in Drama, 64, Scribner; Goodwin Wharton (17th C biography), Oxford Univ Press, 85, Londo Sphere Press, 89. **CONTACT ADDRESS** Dept of English, California Inst of Tech, 101-40, Pasadena, CA 91125. **EMAIL** jkc@hss.caltech.edu

CLARK, KEVIN
PERSONAL Born 04/14/1950, New York, NY, m, 1983, 2 children **DISCIPLINE** ENGLISH **EDUCATION** Univ Fla, BA, 72; Univ Calif Davis, MA, 79; PhD, 86. **CAREER** Ricercatore, Univ Firenze, 85-86; lectr, Univ Calif Davis, 86-88; prof, Calif Polytech State Univ, 88-. **HONORS AND AWARDS** Charles Angoff Award, Lit Rev; Winner, State Street Press Chapbook Contest, 84; Fel, Bread Loaf Writer's Conf; Winner, Acad of Am Poets Contest, Univ Calif Davis, 80, 83. **MEMBERSHIPS** MLA; Assoc Writing Prog. **RESEARCH** Poetry writing; Modern and contemporary poetry; cw pedagogy. **SELECTED PUBLICATIONS** Auth, "Sandra McPherson," in Introduction to Poetry, Salem Press, 92; auth, "Learning to Read the Mother Tongue: On Sandra Gilbert's Blood Pressure," The Iowa Rev, 92; auth, "Stature," in The Point Where All Things Meet: Essays on Charles Wright, Oberlin Col Press, 94; auth, "The Wife's Went Bazook: Comedic Feminism in the Poetry of Ruth Stone," in The House is Made of Brick: The Poetry of Ruth Stone, S Ill Univ Press, 94; auth, "Study as Practice: On the Role of Creative Writing in the En-

glish Curriculum," in The Writer's Chronicle, 99; auth, "Privileging the Symbol: John Ashbery's 'A Wave'," Contemporary Lit Criticism, 00; auth, One of Us, Mille Grazie Press, 00; auth, In the Evening of No Warning, new Issues Press, 02. **CONTACT ADDRESS** Dept English, California Polytech State Univ, San Luis Obispo, 1959 Hays St, San Luis Obispo, CA 93405-2023. **EMAIL** kclark@calpoly.edu

CLARK, L. D.
PERSONAL Born 10/22/1922, Gainesville, TX, m, 1951 **DISCIPLINE** ENGLISH **EDUCATION** Columbia Univ, BA, 53, MA, 54, PhD(English), 63. **CAREER** Instr English, Agr & Mech Col Tex, 54-55; from instr to assoc prof, 55-70, Prof English, Univ Ariz, 70-, Vis prof, Univ Nice, 73-74; Nat Endowment for Humanities Text Materials fel, 78. **MEMBERSHIPS** MLA; D H Lawrence Soc. **RESEARCH** British literature of the 20th century, chiefly D H Lawrence. **SELECTED PUBLICATIONS** Auth, Gone Primitive--Savage Intellects, Modern Lives, D H Lawrence Rev, Vol 0023, 91; The Sense of an Ending in the Plumed Serpent, D H Lawrence Rev, Vol 0025, 94; The Risen Adam--Lawrence,D.H. Revistionist Typology, D H Lawrence Review, Vol 0024, 92. **CONTACT ADDRESS** Dept of English, Univ of Arizona, Tucson, AZ 85721.

CLARK, MARK E.
PERSONAL Born 09/10/1947, PA **DISCIPLINE** CLASSICS **EDUCATION** Univ NC, BA; Universitat Heidelberg, 73-74; Univ Minn, MA, 77; Ind Univ, PhD, 81. **CAREER** Honors Asst Prof to Assoc Prof, Univ southern Miss, 81-. **HONORS AND AWARDS** NEH grants, 94, 92, 88, 84, 82; Teaching Awd, Univ Southern Miss, 95; FIPSE grant, 86-90. **MEMBERSHIPS** Classical Asn of the Middle West and South, am Philol Asn. **RESEARCH** classics; Intellectual history; The classical tradition. **SELECTED PUBLICATIONS** Auth, "Hippocratic Medicine and Aristotelian Science in the Daemonum Investigatio Peripatetica of A. Caesalpino," bulletin of the History of Medicine (95): 527-41. **CONTACT ADDRESS** Dept History, Univ of So Mississippi, PO Box 5038, Hattiesburg, MS 39406-5038.

CLARK, PATRICIA
PERSONAL Born 10/26/1953, Evanston, IL **DISCIPLINE** LIBRARY AND INFORMATION SERVICES **EDUCATION** Northern IL Univ, BA, 75, MA, 89; IL State Univ, MS 94. **CAREER** Library Clerk II, 80-84, Library Technical Asst II, 84-90, Founders Memorial Library, Northern IL Univ; Library Systems Coord, IL Library Computer Systems Office, Univ IL, 90-91; Reference Librarian, 91-92, acting head, General Information & Reference, 92, Reference Librarian, General Reference & Documents, 92-93, System Development Librarian/Asst prof, Milner Library, IL State Univ, 93-95; Microcomputer and Instructional Technology Systems Coordinator/Asst Prof, 95-98, Assoc Dir, Systems/Asst Prof, Penrose Library, Univ Denver, 98-. **MEMBERSHIPS** ALA; ACRL; LITA; RUSA; NCA. **RESEARCH** Technology management. **SELECTED PUBLICATIONS** Auth, New Age Section in Magazines for Libraries, 8th ed, Bill Katz, ed; Natural Language & Probabilistic Retrieval, LITA Newsletter, 16 (4), fall 95; A Systematic Approach to Computer Skills Traning for Library Staff, CO Libraries, 322 (3); Disciplinary Structures on the Internet, Library Trends, 45 (2); with K. Messas, A. Cowgill, L. Jones, and L. Catalucci, Staff Training and Development, ARL SPEC Kit 224, Washington, DC, Asn of Res Libraries, 97; Building Community Through Staff Development Initiatives, Haworth Press, Technical Services Quart, 15 (4), forthcoming 98; numerous other publications and presentations. **CONTACT ADDRESS** Univ of Denver, 2150 E. Evans Ave., Denver, CO 80208-2007. **EMAIL** pcline@du.edu

CLARK, RAYMOND JOHN
PERSONAL Born 07/08/1941, Bristol, England, m, 1964, 3 children **DISCIPLINE** CLASSICS **EDUCATION** Univ Exeter, BA, 63, cert educ, 64, PhD(classics), 70. **CAREER** Assoc prof, 69-80, Prof Classics, Mem Univ Nfld, 80-, Can Coun leave fel, 76-77. **MEMBERSHIPS** Class Asn Can (vpres, 80-82); Vergilian Soc Am; Virgil Soc Eng; Am Philol Soc; Brit Class Asn. **RESEARCH** Greek and Latin epic, especially Homeric and Vergilian; classical religion, mythology and folklore, especially mortuary; pre-Socratic philosophy. **SELECTED PUBLICATIONS** Auth, Peter-of-Eboli, De Balneis Puteolanis--Manuscripts from the Aragonese-Scriptorium in Naples, Traditio-Stud in Ancient and Medieval Hist Thought and Rel, Vol 0045, 90; Giles-of-Viterbo on the Phlegraean-Fields--A Vergilian View, Phoenix-Jour Class Assn Can, Vol 0049, 95. **CONTACT ADDRESS** Dept of Classics, Mem Univ of Newfoundland, Saint John's, NF, Canada A1C 5S7. **EMAIL** rjclark@morgan.ucs.mun.ca

CLARK, SUZANNE
PERSONAL 2 children **DISCIPLINE** ENGLISH **EDUCATION** Univ Ore, BA, 61; MA, 65; Univ Calif Irvine, PhD, 80. **CAREER** Asst prof, Dickinson Col, 80-85; vis assoc prof, Western Wash Univ, 85-86; asst prof to assoc prof, Ore State Univ, 86-90; assoc prof to prof, Univ Ore, 90-. **HONORS AND AWARDS** CSWS Rockefeller Fel, 01. **MEMBERSHIPS** MLA; NCTE; MSA; WLA; PNASA. **RESEARCH** Modern literature; gender theory; rhetoric; cold war literature; the sentimental; the environment. **SELECTED PUBLICATIONS** Coauth, "Collaboration and Resistance," MLA (90); co-auth, "An Interview with Julia Kristeva and Cultural Strangeness and the Subject in Crisis," Discourse 13 (90); auth, "Discipline and Resistance: The Subjects of Writing and the Discourses of Instruction," Col Lit 18 (91); auth, Sentimental Modernism, Ind Univ Pr, 91; auth, "Rhetoric, Gender and the Critical: Is it Bad to Be Sentimental?" MLA (94); auth, "Uncanny Millay," in Millay at 100 (S Ill Univ Pr, 95); auth, "Julia Kristeva and The Woman as Rhetorician," in Reclaiming Rhetorica (Univ Pitt Pr, 95); auth, "Cold Warriors: The Nation and Literary Realism," Am Lit Realism (00); auth, Hemingway and Natural History, S Ill Univ Pr, 00. **CONTACT ADDRESS** English Dept, Univ of Oregon, Eugene, OR 97405. **EMAIL** sclark@oregon.uoregon.edu

CLARK, WALTER
PERSONAL Born 08/23/1952, Minneapolis, MN, m, 1 child **DISCIPLINE** MUSICOLOGY **EDUCATION** Univ California Los Angeles, PhD, 92 **CAREER** Prof Musicology, Univ Kansas, 93- **HONORS AND AWARDS** Fulbright to West Germany, 84-86; Del Amo Endowdowment Res Grant, 90-91; Res Grant, Prog Cult Coop between Spain's Ministry of Culture and U.S. universities, 95-96 **MEMBERSHIPS** Amer Musicol Soc; Sociedad Espanola de Musicolgia; Soc Ethnomusicology; Col Music Soc **RESEARCH** Music of Spain and Latin America, 1800 to present **SELECTED PUBLICATIONS** Isaac Albeniz: Portrait of a Romantic, Oxford, 99; Isaac Albeniz: A Guide to Research, Garland, 98 **CONTACT ADDRESS** Dept Music Dance, Univ of Kansas, Lawrence, 452 Murphy Hall, Lawrence, KS 66045. **EMAIL** wclark@lark.cc.ukans.edu

CLARK, WILLIAM BEDFORD
PERSONAL Born 01/23/1947, Oklahoma City, OK, m, 1972, 2 children **DISCIPLINE** ENGLISH, AMERICAN LITERATURE **EDUCATION** Univ Okla, BA, 69; La State Univ, MA, 71, PhD(English), 73. **CAREER** Instr English, La State Univ, 72-73; asst prof, NC A&T State Univ, 74-77; asst prof, 77-80, Assoc Prof English, 80-86, Prof of English, 86-, Tex A&M Univ; Nat Endowment for Humanities fel Afro-Am studies, Yale Univ, 73-74; Founding Ed, South Central Review, 84-87. **MEMBERSHIPS** MLA; SCentral Mod Lang Asn; Soc Study Southern Lit; Nat Asn Interdisciplinary Ethnic Studies; Conf Christianity & Lit. **RESEARCH** Southern literature; literature of the West; race and the literary imagination. **SELECTED PUBLICATIONS** Co-ed, Critical Essays on American Humor, G.K. Hall, 84; co-ed, Katherine Anne Porter and Texas, Texas A&M Press, 90; auth, The American Vision of Robert Penn Warren, Univ Pr of KY, 91; auth, Pilgrim in the Ruins--A Life of Percy, Walker, Sewanee Rev, Vol 0101, 93; In the Shadow of His Smile--Warren Quarrel with Emerson, Sewanee Rev, Vol 0102, 94; Souls Raised from the Dead, Sewanee Rev, Vol 0104, 96; Talking Animals, Medieval Latin Beast Poetry, 750-1150, Comp Lit Stud, Vol 0033, 96; The House of Percy--Honor, Melancholy, and Imagination in a Southern Family, Sewanee Rev, Vol 0105, 97; The Literary Percys--Family History, Gender, and the Southern Imagination, Sewanee Rev, Vol 0105, 97; Brooks, Cleanth and the Rise of Modern Criticism, Miss Quart, Vol 0050, 97; ed, Selected Letters of Robert Penn Warren, Louisiana State Univ Pr, Vol 1, (00), Vol II (01). **CONTACT ADDRESS** Dept of English, Texas A&M Univ, Col Station, 1 Texas A and M Univ, College Station, TX 77843. **EMAIL** wbclark@tamu.edu

CLARKE, BRUCE COOPER
PERSONAL Born 04/23/1950, Munich, Germany, m, 1977 **DISCIPLINE** LITERATURE AND SCIENCE **EDUCATION** Columbia Univ, BA, 74; State Univ NYork, Buffalo, PhD(English), 80. **CAREER** Instr, La State Univ, 80-82; asst prof to prof English, Tex Tech Univ, 82-. **HONORS AND AWARDS** Butler Dissertation Fel, SUNY/Buffalo, 79-80; Am Coun of Learned Soc Grant-in Aid, Dora Marsden and Modern Letters, 85; State Organized Res Seed Grant, Modernist Individualism, 87; Am Coun of Learned Soc Travel Grant for Inter Meetings, D.H. Lawrence and the Egoist Group, 90; Gloria Lyerla Memorial Res Travel Grant, The Allegory of Thermodynamics, 95; Harry Ransom Humanities Res Ctr Fel, Univ Tex, The Allegory of Thermodynamics, 96; Proj Dir, Texas Tech Univ Fund 2005 Seed Grant, Center for the Interaction of the Arts and Sciences, 96. **MEMBERSHIPS** MLA, SLS, MSA. **RESEARCH** Literature and Science, Modernism. **SELECTED PUBLICATIONS** Auth, Miss Lonelyhearts and the Detached Consciousness, 12/75 & Imagination's Glory the One, the Sexual Body: Contexts for Dejection: An Ode, 9/77, Paunch; Wordsworth's Departed Swans: Sublimation and Sublimity in Home at Grasmede, Studies in Romanticism, fall 80; auth multiple other essays; auth, The Body and the Text: Comparative Essays in Literature and Medicine, Tex Tech Univ Press, 90; Allegories of Writing: The Subject of Metamorphosis, State Univ of NY Press, 95; Dora Marsden and Early Modernism: Gender, Individualism, Science, Univ of Mich Press, 96. **CONTACT ADDRESS** Dept of English, Texas Tech Univ, Lubbock, TX 79409-3091. **EMAIL** bruno@ttu.edu

CLARKE, GEORGE E.
PERSONAL Born 02/12/1960, Windsor, NS, Canada **DISCIPLINE** LITERATURE **EDUCATION** Univ Waterloo, BA, 84; Dalhousie Univ, MA, 89; Queen's Univ, PhD, 93. **CAREER** Columnist, The Daily News (Halifax), 88-89; writer-in-residence, St Mary's Univ, 90; writer-in-residence, Selkirk Col, 91; tchg asst, 91-93, asst adj prof, Queen's Univ, 94; ASST PROF ENGLISH & CANADIAN STUD, DUKE UNIV, 94-; COLUMNIST, HALIFAX HERALD LTD, 92-. **HONORS AND AWARDS** Ont Arts Coun grant, 89; Can Coun grant, 90. **MEMBERSHIPS** MLA; Writers Fedn NS; Writers Union Can; League Can Poets; Black Cultur Soc NS. **SELECTED PUBLICATIONS** ed, Fire on the Water: An Anthology of Black Nova Scotian Literature, 2 vols, 91, 92; ed, Eyeing the North Star: Directions in African-Canadian Literature, 97; co-ed, Border Lines: Contemporary Poems in English, 95. **CONTACT ADDRESS** Dept of English, Duke Univ, Box 90015, Durham, NC 27708.

CLARKE, MICHAEL
DISCIPLINE ENGLISH **EDUCATION** Univ Ill at Chicago Circle, AB, 74, MA, 76; Univ Ill at Urbana-Champaign, PhD, 83. **CAREER** Assoc prof; dir writing prog, 94-; fac coun, 90-;ch; fac status comt, 93-; exec comt, 95-. **RESEARCH** Theory of the Novel; Feminist Theory; Victorian Novel; William Thackekray; the Brontes. **SELECTED PUBLICATIONS** Auth, Thackeray and Women, Northern Ill UP, 95; Thackeray's Barry Lyndon: An Irony Against Misogynists, reprint from TSLL,87, in Nineteenth-Century Literature Criticism, Gale Res Inc, 94; A Mystery Solved: Ainsworth's Criminal Romances Censured in Fraser's by J Hamilton Reynolds, not Thackeray, Victorian Periodicals Rev 23, 90; William Thackeray's Fiction and Caroline Norton's Biography: Narrative Matrix of Feminist Legal Reform, Dickens Stud Annual 18, 89. **CONTACT ADDRESS** Dept of English, Loyola Univ, Chicago, Crown Center for the Humanities, 6525 N Sheridan Rd, Chicago, IL 60626. **EMAIL** mclarke1@wpo.it.luc.edu

CLARKE, ROBERT F.
PERSONAL Born 06/20/1932, Newport News, VA, m, 1964, 2 children **DISCIPLINE** LIBRARY SCIENCE **EDUCATION** US Naval Acad, BS, 54; Rutgers Univ, MLS, 61; PhD, 63. **CAREER** Captain, US Air Force, 54-60; Dir Libr, US Public Health Serv, 62-84; Adjunct Instr, Nova Univ, 88; Sen Manager, Am Health Care Assoc., 87-88; Staff, Dade Co Libr, 90-92; Dir of Libr, City of Hileah, Fl, 92-95. **HONORS AND AWARDS** Beta Phi Tau; US Coast Guard Alumni Assoc. Awd; Feel, Rutgers Univ; Outstanding Serv Medal, US Public Health Serv. **MEMBERSHIPS** Am Libr Assoc., Special Libr Assoc., Ed libr Assoc., Correction Off Assoc. of the US Public Health Serv. **RESEARCH** Information transfer and dissemination. **SELECTED PUBLICATIONS** Auth, "Ralph R. Shaw" in Festscript (NJ: Scarecrow Pr, 67); US Govt Publ: Building Community Mental Health Through Research, Smoking and Health Bibliography, Smoking and Health Bibliographical Bulletin. **CONTACT ADDRESS** Dept Libr Sci, 10640 SW 129 Court, Miami, FL 33186-3545.

CLARKE, WILLIAM M.
DISCIPLINE GREEK AND ROMAN MYTHOLOGY, ROMAN EPIC **EDUCATION** Univ NC, PhD, 72. **CAREER** Assoc prof Classics, pres, Phi Beta Kappa, La State Univ. **RESEARCH** Greek poetry. **SELECTED PUBLICATIONS** Auth, The Manuscript of Straton's Musa puerilis, in GRBS 4, 76; Jewish Table Manners in the Cena Trimalcionis, in CJ 3, 92. **CONTACT ADDRESS** Dept of For Lang and Lit, Louisiana State Univ and A&M Col, 241 A Prescott Hall, Baton Rouge, LA 70803.

CLAUSEN, CHRISTOPHER
PERSONAL Born 05/14/1942, Richmond, VA, m, 1976 **DISCIPLINE** ENGLISH **EDUCATION** Earlham Co, BA, 64; Univ Chicago, PhD, 65; Queen's Univ, 72. **CAREER** Inst, Univ Hawaii, 65-66; asst prof, Concord COL, 66-68; lectr, Univ Guelph, 73; asst prof, 73-79, asso prof, 79-84, prof, 84-85, Va Polytech Inst & State Univ; PROF, PA STATE UNIV, 85-. **SELECTED PUBLICATIONS** Auth, The Place of Poetry, 81; auth, The Moral Imagination, 86; auth, My Life with President Kennedy, 94; auth, Faded Mosaic: The Emergence of Post-Cultural America, 00; plus many articles and essays. **CONTACT ADDRESS** Dept of English, Pennsylvania State Univ, Univ Park, University Park, PA 16802-6200. **EMAIL** cqc1@psu.edu

CLAUSS, JAMES
PERSONAL Born 09/01/1953, Scranton, OH, m, 1978, 3 children **DISCIPLINE** CLASSICAL STUDIES **EDUCATION** Univ Scranton, BA, 74; Fordham Univ, MA, 76; Univ Calif Berk, PhD, 83. **CAREER** Instr, asst prof, Creighton Univ, 83-84; asst prof, assoc prof, prof, Univ Wash, 84-. **HONORS AND AWARDS** Dist Teach Awd, 96. **MEMBERSHIPS** APA. **RESEARCH** Hellenistic poetry; Augustan poetry; Roman history and historiography; Roman topography; Greek and Roman literature in general. **SELECTED PUBLICATIONS** Auth, "Allusion and Structure in Horace Satire 2.1: the Callimachean Response," Trans Am Philo Asn 115 (85): 197-206; auth; "Lies and Allusions: the Addressee and the Date of Callimachus' Hymn to Zeus," Class Antiq 5 (86): 155-170, auth, "The Episode of the Lucian Farmers in Ovid's Metamorphoses," Harv Stud Class Philo 92 (88): 297-314; auth, "Vergil and the Euphrates Revisited," Am J Philo 109 (88): 309-320; auth, "The

Ignoble Consistency of M. Caelius Rufus," Athen 78 (90): 531-540; auth, "An Attic-speaking Crow on the Capitoline: A Literary Emigr from the Hecale," Zeits fur Papyr and Epig 96 (93): 167-173; auth, "A Delicate Foot on the Well-Worn Threshold: Paradoxical Imagery in Catullus 68b," Am J Philo 116 (95): 237-253; auth, "Domestici Hostes: the Nausicaa in Medea, the Catiline in Hannibal," Mater a Disc 39 (97): 165-185; auth, "The Best of the Argonauts," in The Redefinition of the Epic Hero in Book 1 of Apollonius' Argonautica (Univ Calif Press, 93); auth, Medea: Essays on Medea in Myth, Literature, Philosophy, and Art, Princeton UP, 97. **CONTACT ADDRESS** Dept of Classics, Univ of Washington, PO Box 353110, Seattle, WA 98195-3110.

CLAUSSEN, ERNEST NEAL
PERSONAL Born 08/15/1933, Petersburg, IL, m, 1961, 2 children **DISCIPLINE** SPEECH COMMUNICATION **EDUCATION** Ill State Univ, BS, 55; Southern Ill Univ, Carbondale, MA, 59, PhD(speech), 63. **CAREER** Instr speech & econ, Mendota High Sch, Ill, 55-56; asst prof speech, Colo State Col, 59-61; from asst prof to assoc prof, 63-71, assoc dean col lib arts & sci, 69-71, prof Speech, Bradley Univ, 71-. **HONORS AND AWARDS** The Harvard Awd, 89; Sanford Awd; 97 fror the Illinois Speech and Theatre Assoc. **MEMBERSHIPS** Speech Commun Asn; Rhetoric Soc Am. **RESEARCH** Rhetorical theory; rhetorical criticism; public communication. **SELECTED PUBLICATIONS** Auth, John Sharp Williams: Pacesetter for democratic keynoters, Southern Speech, 65; Hendrick B Wright and the nocturnal committee, Pa Mag Hist & Biog, 65; He kept us out of war: Martin H Glynn's keynote, Quart J Speech, 66; co-ed (with Karl R Wallace), John Lawson's Lectures Concerning Oratory, Southern Ill Univ Press, 72; Alben Barkley's rhetorical victory in 1948, Southern Speech Commun J, fall 79. **CONTACT ADDRESS** Dept of Speech Commun, Bradley Univ, 1501 W Bradley Ave, Peoria, IL 61625-0002. **EMAIL** claussen@bradley.edu

CLAY, JENNY STRAUSS
DISCIPLINE CLASSICAL STUDIES **EDUCATION** Univ Wash, PhD. **CAREER** Prof. **SELECTED PUBLICATIONS** Auth, Wrath of Athena, Princeton, 83; The Politics of Olympus, Princeton, 89; pubs on Greek and Roman poetry. **CONTACT ADDRESS** Dept of Classics, Univ of Virginia, Charlottesville, VA 22903. **EMAIL** jsc2t@virginia.edu

CLAYDON, MARGARET
PERSONAL Born 07/19/1923, New York, NY **DISCIPLINE** ENGLISH LANGUAGE & LITERATURE **EDUCATION** Trinity Col, DC, AB, 45; Cath Univ Am, MA, 53, PhD, 59. **CAREER** From instr to asst prof 52-59, pres, 59-75, prof Eng, Trinity Col, DC, 75-; vis lectr, Notre Dame Col, Scotland, 58-59; mem bd trustees, Mid States Assn, 65-72; mem bd dir, Nat Coun Independent Cols & Univs, 71-; trustee, Emmanuel Col, Mass, 72-; postdoctoral res fel, Yale Univ; guest resident fel, Timothy Dwight Col, Yale Univ, 75-76. **HONORS AND AWARDS** LHD, Georgetown Univ, 67, 71 & Cath Univ of Am, 75. **MEMBERSHIPS** Nat Cath Educ Assn. **RESEARCH** Renaissance English literature; metaphysical poets; classical literature. **SELECTED PUBLICATIONS** Auth, Richard Crashaw's paraphrases of the Vexilla Regis, Stabat Mater, Adoro Te, Lauda Sion, Dies Irae, O Gloriosa Domina, Cath Univ Am, 59. **CONTACT ADDRESS** Trinity Col, Washington, DC, 125 Michigan Ave NE, Washington, DC 20017-1090. **EMAIL** claydonm@trinitydc.edu

CLAYTON, JAY
DISCIPLINE LITERARY THEORY, 19TH CENTURY, ROMANTICISM, CONTEMPORARY LITERATURE **EDUCATION** Univ Va, PhD. **CAREER** Prof 93-; dir, grad stud, Vanderbilt Univ, 95-99. **HONORS AND AWARDS** Guggenhelm Fel, 99-00. **MEMBERSHIPS** Narrative Soc, Pres, 95-96; English Inst, Supervisor, 96-99. **SELECTED PUBLICATIONS** Auth, Romantic Vision and the Novel, 87; Influence and Intertextuality in Literary History, 91; The Pleasures of Babel, 93. **CONTACT ADDRESS** Vanderbilt Univ, Nashville, TN 37203-1727. **EMAIL** jay.clayton@vanderbilt.edu

CLAYTON, JOHN J.
PERSONAL Born 01/05/1935, New York, NY, m, 1956, 4 children **DISCIPLINE** FICTION WRITING, MODERN LITERATURE **EDUCATION** Columbia Univ, BA, 56; NYork Univ, MA, 59; Ind Univ, PhD(English & Am lit), 66. **CAREER** Instr English, Univ Victoria, BC, 62-63; lectr, Univ Md European Div, 63-64; asst prof humanities, Boston Univ, 64-69; assoc prof, 69-73, Prof Mod Lit & Creative Writing, Univ Mass, Amherst, 73-, Nat Endowment for Humanities fel, 80. **RESEARCH** Modern fiction; creative writing. **SELECTED PUBLICATIONS** Auth, Saul Bellow: In Defense of Man, Indiana University Press, 68; auth, What Are Friends For?, Little, Brown & Co. 79; auth, Bodies of the Rich, Univeristy of Illinois Press, 84; auth, Gestures of Healing: Anxiety and the Modern Novel, Amherst: University of Massachusetts Press, 91; auth, The Man I Never Wanted to Be, Permanent Press, 98. **CONTACT ADDRESS** Dept of English, Univ of Massachusetts, Amherst, Amherst, MA 01002.

CLAYTON, LAWRENCE RAY
PERSONAL Born 04/21/1938, San Antonio, TX, m, 1958, 2 children **DISCIPLINE** ENGLISH **EDUCATION** Ranger Junior Col, AA, 58; Stephen F. Austin State Univ, BS, 60; MEd, 64; North Tex State Univ, MA, 69; Tex Tech Univ, PhD, 74. **CAREER** Assoc prof to prof, Head of Dept, Hardin-Simmons Univ, 74-80, Dir, Nat Resources Inst, 90-92, Dean, Col of Arts and Sciences, 80-99, Dean, Col of Liberal Arts, 99-. **HONORS AND AWARDS** Phi Theta Kappa; Leadership Awd, Tex Joint Coun of Teachers of English, 89; Honors Recognition, Tex Tech Univ, 73; Phi Kappa Phi; Fac Member of the Year, Hardin-Simmons Univ, 88; Men of Achievement, 92, 96; Outstanding Alumnus, Ranger Jr Col, 76; Outstanding Alumnus, Dept of English, Tex Tech Univ, 88; Distinguished Alumnus, Dept of English, Univ North Tex, 90. **MEMBERSHIPS** Southwestern Am Lit Asn, Taylor Co Hist Comn, Tex Folklore Soc, Tex Joint Coun of Teachers of English, Western Lit Asn, West Tex Hist Asn, Tex/Southwest popular Culture Asn, Tex Cowboy Poets Asn. **RESEARCH** Folklore/folklife/literature of the Am West and Southwest, Am Fiction to 1920, History of the English language, Medieval British literature, war in literature and film. **SELECTED PUBLICATIONS** Ed, A Christmas Pudding, Abilene: Chestnut St Press (89, 95, 96, 97, 98, 99); co-ed with intro, Horsing Around: Contemporary Cowboy Humor, Detroit: Wayne State Univ Press (91), reprinted Lubbock: Tex Tech Univ Press (98); auth, "A Deer Hunter's Paen," Gray's Sorting J, 18, no 6 (Nov 93): 136; auth, Longhorn Legacy: Graves Peeler and the Texas Cattle Trade, Abilene: Cowboy Press (94), excerpted in Texas Longhorn Trails, 11, no 6-8 (99); ed, In Memorian: A Final Tribute to Watkins Reynolds Matthews by Some of His Friends, with photos by Sonja Clayton, Abilene: Cowboy Press of Abilene (97); auth, "All in a Day's Work for Three Cowboys," Tex Short Stories, ed Billy Bob Hill, Dallas: Browder Springs Press (97): 224-230; auth, Cowboys: Ranch Life Along the Clear Fork of the Brazos River, Austin: Eakin Press (97); coauth with Bob Green, Horses, Their Role on the J. R. Green Ranch, with photos by Sonja Clayton, Abilene: Hardin-Simmons Univ Press (98); coauth, Three Contemporary Ranch Women of Shackelford County: Mildred Palmer Diller, Doris Miller, and Sue Diller Balliew, photos by Sonja Clayton, Abilene: Cowboy Press of Abilene (99); auth, A History of Texas Music: Beginnings to 1950, Tex A & M Univ Press (in prep). **CONTACT ADDRESS** Dean, Col of Liberal Arts, Hardin-Simmons Univ, Box 16205, Abilene, TX 79698.

CLAYTON, TOM
PERSONAL Born 12/15/1932, New Ulm, MN, w, 1955, 4 children **DISCIPLINE** ENGLISH, CLASS & NEAR EASTERN STUDIES **EDUCATION** Univ Minn, BA, 54; Oxford Univ, DPhil, 60. **CAREER** Instr English, Yale Univ, 60-62; asst prof, Univ Calif, Los Angeles, 62-67, assoc prof, 67-68; assoc prof, 68-70, Prof English, Univ Minn, Minneapolis, 70-99, Prof Class & Near Eastern Studies, 80-, Chmn, Class Civilization Prog, 82-, Morse-Alumni Distinguished Teaching Prof Engl & Classical Studies, 93-; Am Coun Learned Soc grant, 62-63; fel, Inst for Humanities, Univ Calif, 66-67; assoc, Danforth Assoc Prog, 72-77; Guggenheim fel, 78-79; Bush fel, Univ Minn, 85-86; NEH award, Div Res Tools, 88; Regents Prof English, 99-. **HONORS AND AWARDS** Rhodes Scholar, Minn and Wadham College, Oxford, 54; Distinguished Teaching Awd, Col Lib Arts, Univ Minn, 71; Morse-Alumni Awd, Outstanding contrib undergrad educ, Univ Minn 82. **MEMBERSHIPS** Asn of Am Rhodes Scholars; Asn Literary Scholars and Critics; Renaissance English Text Soc; Int Shakespeare Asn; Shakespeare Asn Am. **RESEARCH** Shakespeare; literary criticism; earlier 17th Century English literature. **SELECTED PUBLICATIONS** Ed & auth, The Shakespearean Addition in the Books of Sir Thomas Moore, Ctr Shakespeare Studies, 69; ed & auth, The Non-Dramatic Works of Sir John Suckling, Clarendon, 71; ed & auth, Cavalier Poets, Oxford Univ, 78; auth, Is this the promis'd end?, Revision in the role of the King [himself], in The Division of the Kingdoms, Clarendon, 83; The texts and publishing vicissitudes of Peter Nichols's Passion Play, in The Library, 87; ed & auth, The Hamlet First Published (Q1, 1603), Univ Del, 92; That's she that was myself: Not-so-famous last words and some ends of Othello, Shakespeare Survey, 94; So our virtues lie in the interpretation of the time: Shakespeare's Coriolanus and Coriolanus, and Some Questions of Value, Ben Jonson J, 94; Who has no children in Macbeth?, in Festschrift for Marvin Rosenbert, Univ Del, 98 (forthcoming); So quick bright things come to confusion, or what else was A Midsummer's Night Dream about?, in Festschrift for Jay L Halio, 99. **CONTACT ADDRESS** Dept of English, Univ of Minnesota, Twin Cities, 207 Church St SE, Minneapolis, MN 55455-0134. **EMAIL** tsc@unm.edu

CLEARY, THOMAS R.
PERSONAL Born 05/23/1940, New York, NY, m, 1965, 3 children **DISCIPLINE** ENGLISH **EDUCATION** Queen's Col, CUNY, BA; Princeton Univ, MA, PhD. **CAREER** Instr English, Princeton Univ, 67-68; asst prof, 69-80, Assoc Prof English, Univ Victoria, BC, 80-. **MEMBERSHIPS** MLA; Johnson Soc Northwest (secy, 73-74); Am Soc Eighteenth-Century Studies. **RESEARCH** Restoration and 18th-century literature; the novel; history of criticism. **SELECTED PUBLICATIONS** Auth, Henry Fielding: Political Writer, Wilfrid Laurier UP, 84; auth, Time, Literature and the Arts: Essays in Honor of Samuel L. Macey, Eng Lit Stud, no 61, 95. **CONTACT ADDRESS** Dept of English, Univ of Victoria, PO Box 3070, Victoria, BC, Canada V8W 3W1. **EMAIL** trcleary@uvic.ca

CLEGG, CYNDIA SUSAN
PERSONAL Born 11/28/1946, Long Beach, CA, m, 1977, 1 child **DISCIPLINE** ENGLISH LITERATURE **EDUCATION** Univ Calif, Los Angeles, PhD, 76. **CAREER** Dir compos, 76-84, dist prof, English, 84- , Pepperdine Univ. **HONORS AND AWARDS** Br Acad fel, 91, 99; Mellon fel, Huntington Library, 92. **MEMBERSHIPS** MLA; Shakespeare Assoc of Am; Renaissance Soc of Am; Pacific Ancient and Mod Lang Assoc. **RESEARCH** Press censorship in early modern England; Shakespeare; Elizabethan historiography. **SELECTED PUBLICATIONS** Auth, Critical Reading and Writing Across the Disciplines, Holt, Rinehart & Winston, 88; coauth, Students Writing Across the Disciplines, Holt, Rinehart & Winston, 91; auth, Press Censorship in Elizabethan England, Cambridge, 97; auth, Ben Jonson and Censureship, Ben Jonson Jour, 97; auth, By the choise and invitation of al the realme: Richard II and Elizabethan Press Censorship, Shakespeare Quart, 97; auth, "Justice an Press Censorship in Book V of Spenser's Faerie Queene," Studies in Philol (98); auth, "Liberty License and Authority: Shakespeare and Press Censorship," in A Shakespeare Companion, ed, David Scott Kastan (Blackwells, 98); auth, "The History of the Book: An Undisciplined Discipline," Renaissance Q (01); auth, Press Censorship in Jacobean Englad, Cabridge Univ Pr, 01; auth, The Peacable and Prosperous Regiment of Blessed Queene Elisabeth: A Facsimile from Holinshed's Chronicles, Huntington Lib, 01. **CONTACT ADDRESS** Dept of Humanities, Pepperdine Univ, 24255 Pacific Coast Hwy, Malibu, CA 90263-4225. **EMAIL** cclegg@pepperdine.edu

CLEGHORN, CASSANDRA
DISCIPLINE ENGLISH **EDUCATION** Univ Calif, Santa Cruz, BA, 83; Yale Univ, PhD 95. **CAREER** Lectr & coordr, Williams Col Learning Technol Proj. **RESEARCH** American literature and cultural studies; theories of reading; contemporary poetry. **SELECTED PUBLICATIONS** Auth, Chivalric Sentimentalism: The Case of Dr Howe and Laura Bridgman, Sentimental and Men: Sentimentality and Masculinity in American Fiction and Culture. **CONTACT ADDRESS** Dept of English, Williams Col, Stetson 302, Williamstown, MA 01267. **EMAIL** ccleghorn@williams.edu

CLENDENNING, JOHN
PERSONAL Born 10/12/1934, Huntington, WV, d, 2 children **DISCIPLINE** AMERICAN LITERATURE & CIVILIZATION **EDUCATION** Calif State Univ, Los Angeles, BA, 57; Univ Iowa, MA, 58, PhD, 62. **CAREER** From instr to Prof English, CA State Univ, Northridge, 60-, Interim Assoc Dean, 97-98, chmn dept, 73-79; Am Coun Learned Soc study fel, 64-65 & fel, 68-69; Wesleyan Univ Ctr Advan Studies jr fel, 64-65; Guggenheim fel, 71-72; lectureship, Fulbright-Hays/Univ Athens, 77-78; mem delegate assembly, Mod Lang Asn, 78-80; pres, Stephen Crane Soc, 94-96. **HONORS AND AWARDS** Jerome Richfield Scholar, 96-97; Outstanding Prof, 96-97. **MEMBERSHIPS** MLA; Stephen Crane Soc. **RESEARCH** Philosophical themes in literature; American poetry. **SELECTED PUBLICATIONS** Auth, Cummings, comedy and criticism, Colo Quart, summer 63; Time, doubt and vision: Emerson and Eliot, Am Scholar, winter 66-67; Introd to Josiah Royce's The Feud of Oakfield Creek, 70; Letters of Josiah Royce, Univ Chicago, 70; The Life and Thought of Josiah Royce, Univ Wis, 85, rev ed 99; Stephen Crane and His Biographies, Am Lit Realism, 95. **CONTACT ADDRESS** Dept of English, California State Univ, Northridge, 18111 Nordhoff St, Northridge, CA 91330-8200. **EMAIL** john.clendenning@csun.edu

CLERC, CHARLES
PERSONAL 4 children **DISCIPLINE** ENGLISH **EDUCATION** Univ Iowa, PhD, 63. **CAREER** Instr Univ Iowa, 62-63; distinguished vis prof, Air Force Acad, 80-81; vis prof, Univ Bern, 89; asst prof to assoc prof to prof to dept chmn, Univ Pac, 70-. **HONORS AND AWARDS** Distinguished Teaching Awd, Univ Pacific, 80. **MEMBERSHIPS** MLA. **RESEARCH** Contemporary literature; modern American literature, with emphasis on the novel; the writing of fiction and drama. **SELECTED PUBLICATIONS** Auth, Seven Contemporary Short Novels, Scott Foresman, 69, 75, 82; auth, Approaches to Gravity's Rainbow, Ohio State Univ Pr, 83; auth, Stockton: Heart of the Valley, Windsor, 89; auth, The Y and Other Stories, Provine Pr, 97; auth, Mason and Dixon and Pynchor, Univ Pr Am, 00; auth, The Professor Who Changed My Life, Harmony House, 01. **CONTACT ADDRESS** 619 W Poplar St, Stockton, CA 95203-2339.

CLICK, J. WILLIAM
PERSONAL Born 04/22/1936, Huntington, IN, m, 1960, 2 children **DISCIPLINE** JOURNALISM **EDUCATION** Ball State Univ, AB, 58; Ohio Univ, MS, 59; Ohio State Univ, PhD, 77. **CAREER** Dir, Findlay Col, 59-60; Instr, Central Mich Univ, 60-65; Asst Prof, Ohio Univ, 65-83; Prof, La State Univ, 83-87; Prof, Winthrop Univ, 87-. **HONORS AND AWARDS** Medal of Merit, Soc for Collegiate Journalists, 79; Meritorious

Course Awd, Nat Univ Continuing Educ Asn, 80; Fac Serv Awd, Nat Univ Continuing Educ Asn, 80. **MEMBERSHIPS** Am Acad of Advert, Assoc. for Educ in Jour and Mass Commun, Soc of Professional Journalists, SC Pr Assoc., Assoc. of Commun Adminrs, Assoc. of Schs of Jour and Mass Commun. **RESEARCH** Magazine research, scholastic journalism, content analysis, audience effects, ethics. **SELECTED PUBLICATIONS** Auth, "Subscribers' Reaction to Redesign of the St Cloud Daily Times ," ANPA News Roes Report, no 32 (81); auth, "Reader Response to Front pages with Modular Format and Color," ANPA News Roes Report, no 35 (82); auth, "Principals Favor Discipline More than a Free Press," Jour Educ (88): 48-51; auth, "Educating for the First Amendment," Contemp Educ, vol 66, no 2 (95): 86-88; auth, Governing College Student Publications, College Media Advs, Inc, 2nd Ed, 94; auth, Magazine Editing and Production, Wm C Brown Publ (Dubuque, IA), 83, 86, 90, 94. **CONTACT ADDRESS** Dept Jour, Winthrop Univ, Rock Hill, SC 29732. **EMAIL** clickw@winthrop.edu

CLINES, RAYMOND H.
PERSONAL Born 07/19/1949, Tacoma, WA, m, 1991 **DISCIPLINE** ENGLISH **EDUCATION** Univ WA, BA, 71; Cen WA Univ, MA, 76; Univ RI, PhD, 86. **CAREER** Asst prof, Lander Univ, 84-85; asst prof, Eastern OR Univ, 85-87; prof, Jacksonville Univ, 87-. **HONORS AND AWARDS** Fulbright Schl, Thailand, 92. **MEMBERSHIPS** Nat Coun Teach Eng; ACA. **RESEARCH** Composition; Linguistics; English Pedagogy. **SELECTED PUBLICATIONS** Auth, Research Writing Simplified, Addison (NY), 92, 96, 99; auth, Read, Write, Research, Kendall Hunt (IA), 91, 96; auth, Guide to Rapid Revision Workbook, Macmillan (NY), 83, 89, 95. **CONTACT ADDRESS** Dept Humanities, Jacksonville Univ, 2800 University Blvd North, Jacksonville, FL 32211.

CLINTON, KEVIN
PERSONAL Born 09/29/1942, New York, NY, m, 1970, 2 children **DISCIPLINE** CLASSICS **EDUCATION** Boston Col, BA, 64; Johns Hopkins Univ, PhD, 69. **CAREER** Asst Prof Classics, St Louis Univ, 69-70; from Asst Prof to Assoc Prof, 70-81, Prof Classics, Cornell Univ, 81, Chmn Dept, 77-83; Vis Prof, Univ Calif-Berkeley, 86; mem, Inst for Advanced Study, 87-88; 99-00. **HONORS AND AWARDS** Am Coun Learned Soc fel, 75; Soc for Humanities fel, Cornell Univ, 76-77; spec res fel, Am Sch Class Studies, Athens, 83-84; Guggenheim Fel, 87-88; corresponding mem, Ger Archaeol Inst; NEH fel, 99-00. **MEMBERSHIPS** Am Philol Asn; Archaeol Inst Am. **RESEARCH** Greek religion, literature and institutions. **SELECTED PUBLICATIONS** Auth, Inscriptions from Eleusis, Arkhaiologike Ephemeris, 71; Apollo, Pan and Zeus, avengers of vultures: Agamemnon, 55-9, Am J Philol, 74; The Sacred Officials of the Eleusinian Mysteries, Am Philos Soc, 74; The Hymn to Zeus, Traditio, 79; A Law in the City Eleusinion Concerning the Mysteries, 80 & The Nature of the Late Fifth-Century Revision of the Athenian Law Code, Suppl 19, 80, Hesperia; Myth and Cult: The Iconography of the Eleusinian Hysterics, Stockholm, 92; The Thesmophorion in Central Athens and the Celebration of the Thesmophoria in Attica, Stockholm, 97. **CONTACT ADDRESS** Dept of Class, Cornell Univ, 120 Goldwin Smith, Ithaca, NY 14853-0001.

CLIVIO, GIANRENZO PIETRO
PERSONAL Born 01/18/1942, Turin, Italy **DISCIPLINE** LINGUISTICS, LITERATURE **EDUCATION** Univ Torino, Italy, BA, 62; Brandeis Univ, MA, 64; Harvard Univ, PhD (ling), 67. **CAREER** From asst prof to assoc prof, 68-77, prof Ital, Univ Toronto, 77-, Pres, Can Ctr Ital Cult & Educ, 77-81; pres, Nat Cong Ital Canadians, Ont Region, 80-; assoc ed, Can J Ital Studies, 81-; ed, Il Forneri, Bull Can Soc Ital Ling, 81- **MEMBERSHIPS** Am Asn Teachers Ital; Ling Asn US & Can; Int Soc Phonetic Sci; Can Soc Ital Ling (pres, 81-). **RESEARCH** Romance linguistics; sociolinguistics; Italian literature; romance philology, lang contact, bilingualism and lang acquisition, as well as dialectology. **SELECTED PUBLICATIONS** Auth, Observations on Poetic Texts by Borelli, Vittorio, Amedeo and On Settecento Piedemontese, Studi Piemontesi, Vol 0023, 94. **CONTACT ADDRESS** Dept of Ital Studies, Univ of Toronto, Toronto, ON, Canada M5S 1A1. **EMAIL** gclivio@chass.utoronto.ca

CLOGAN, PAUL MAURICE
PERSONAL Born 07/09/1934, Boston, MA, s, 3 children **DISCIPLINE** ENGLISH, COMPARATIVE LITERATURE **EDUCATION** Boston Col, AB, 56, MA, 57; St Michael's Col, PhL, 58; Univ Ill, PhD, 61; Pope John XXIII International, M.Div. 99. **CAREER** From instr to asst prof English, Duke Univ, 61-65; assoc prof English & comp lit, Case Western Reserve Univ, 65-72; adj prof, Cleveland State Univ, 71-72; prof English, Univ N TX, 72-99; prof emer English, Univ N Tex, 00. **HONORS AND AWARDS** Duke Found grant, 62-63; Am Coun Learned Soc fels, 62-64 & 71-72; sr Fulbright-Hays res fels, Italy, 65-66, Scuola Vaticana di Paleografia e Diplomatica, 66-67 & France, 78; Fulbright-Hays res fel; vis lectr, Univ Pisa, 65; Am Philos Soc grants, 65-67 & 69-70; US/UK cult exchange vis lectr, Univ Keele, 66; Bollingen Found & Prix de Rome fels, 66-67; fel, Am Acad Rome, 67; ed, Medievalia et Humanistica, 68-; mem steering comt, Asn Ctr Medieval & Renaissance Studies; Nat Endowment for Humanities fel, 70-71; vis mem, Inst Advan Study, NJ, 70 & 77; Univ N Tx; fac res grants, 72-75 & 80-81; vis lectr, Univ Tours, 78; MLA Mdeieval Exec Comt, 80-86; Deleg Assembly, 81-86; John Nicholas Brown Prize Comt, 81-83; Medieval Acad Am nominating comt, 75-76; U of N Tex Scholar of the Month, 88, 93; Cert of the U of N Tex Forum on Teaching and Learning, 95. **MEMBERSHIPS** MLA; Medieval Acad Am; Mod Humanities Res Asn; Ling Soc Am; Int Asn Univ Prof of English. **RESEARCH** Medieval literature and culture; history of the English language; literary theory. **SELECTED PUBLICATIONS** Auth, New Directions in Twelfth-Century Courtly Narrative, Mediaevistik, 90; auth, The Knight's Tale and the Ideology of the Roman Antique, Medievalia et Humanistica, 91; auth, The Imagery of the City of Thebes in The Knight's Tale, Typology and English Medieval Literature: Studies in Literary Imagination, 92; auth, Lydgate and the Roman Antique, 92; auth, Renaissance and Discovery: Imagination and Exploration, The Mutual Encounter of East and West, 1492-1992, 92; auth, Visions of Thebes in Medieval Literature, Force of Vision, Visions in History, 95; auth, Moral Discourse in the Trivium, Moral and Political Philosophies in the Middle Ages, 95; auth, Reading Status in the Renaissance, Acta Selecta Octavi Academiae Latinitati Fovendae, 95; auth, Imaging the City of Thebes in Fifteenth-Century England, Acta Conventus Neo-Latini Hafniensis, 94; Neo-Platoinic_Streak in the Statian Commentary of Fulgentius Planciades, Neoplatonisme et Philosophie Medievale, 97; auth, Italian Humanism in the court of King Robert of Anjou, Acta Conventus Neo-Latini Bariensis, 98. **CONTACT ADDRESS** Univ of No Texas, PO Box 2063, Waterville, ME 04903. **EMAIL** pclogan@ibm.net

CLOUD, DANA L.
PERSONAL Born 05/09/1964, Waco, TX, 1 child **DISCIPLINE** COMMUNICATION STUDIES **EDUCATION** PA State Univ, BA (English & telecomm), 86; Univ IA, MA (Rhetorical Studies), 89, PhD (Rhetorical Studies), 92. **CAREER** Res fel, Univ IA, Iowa City, 87, 92, teaching asst, 88-91; asst prof, Univ TX, Austin, 93-; summer res award, Univ Res Inst, 94; ed bd member, Western J of Comm, 95-; Col Comm Jamail grant, 96; special res grant, Univ TX, 97; ed bd member, Women's Studies in Communication, 97-; assoc ed, Quart J of Speech, 97-. **HONORS AND AWARDS** Nichols-Ehninger Awd in Rhetorical and Communication Theory, Speech Comm Asn, 94; B Aubrey Fisher Outstanding Article Awd, Western States Comm Asn, 95; National Communication Asn Karl Wallace Memorial Awd for Young Scholars in Rhetoric, 98; Dean's fel, Col Comm, Univ TX, spring 98. **SELECTED PUBLICATIONS** Auth, The Limits of Interpretation: Ambivalence and the Stereotype in Spenser: For Hire, Critical Studies in Mass Communication 9, 92; Materiality of Discourse as Oxymoron: A Challenge to Critical Rhetoric, Western J of Communication 58, 94; Hegemony of Concordance? The Rhetoric of Tokenism in Oprah Winfrey's Rags-to-Riches Biography, Critical Studies in Mass Comm 13, 96; Edwin Black, in Teresa Enos, ed, Encyclopedia of Rhetoric, 96; The Rhetoric of Family Values and the Public Sphere, Alta Conf on Argumanatation Proceedings, Speech Commm Asn, 96; Capitalism, Concordance, and Conservatism: Rejoinder to Condit, Critical Studies in Mass Comm 13, 97; Control and Consolation in American Politcs and Culture: Rhetorics of Therapy, Sage Press, 98; Queer Theory and Family Values, Transformation, 98; The Rhetoric of Family Values: Scapegoating, Utopia, and the Privatization of Social Responsibility, Western J of Comm, 98; Of Pancake Queens and Mother Dreams: The Failed Rhetoric of Maternal Utopia in Films of the 1930's, in Mother Daughter Communication: Voices from the Professions, forthcoming; several other book chapters, and two publications currently under review. **CONTACT ADDRESS** Speech Communication, Univ of Texas, Austin, CMA 7 112 A1105, Austin, TX 78712. **EMAIL** dcloud@mail.utexas.edu

CLOUGH, WULFSTAN
PERSONAL Born 04/19/1952, Wilmington, DE **DISCIPLINE** MEDIEVAL LITERATURE, FOLKLORE **EDUCATION** Univ Del, BA, 74; MA, 77; Univ Notre Dame, PhD, 84; St Vincent Sem, MDiv. **CAREER** Teaching asst, Univ Del, 75-77; teaching asst, Univ Notre Dame, 78-82; instr, Univ Del, 85-90; asst prof, St Vincent Col, 96-. **HONORS AND AWARDS** Ernest P. Dobson Awd, 99; Univ Notre Dame Res Fel, Teaching Fel, 78-82, 82-84; Univ Del, Teaching Fel, 75-77. **MEMBERSHIPS** MLA; CCL; NCTE; Mythopoeic Soc. **RESEARCH** Medieval and renaissance literature; myth and folklore; film; fantasy and science fiction. **SELECTED PUBLICATIONS** Co-ed, The Vercelli Homilies: Translations from the Anglo-Saxon, Univ Pr Am, 90; auth, "Oliier, Branagh, and the BBC: Three Henry V's on Film," Lit Conf (00); auth, "Einstein and Religion: What Do We Know?" ACTC Conf (forthcoming). **CONTACT ADDRESS** English Dept, Saint Vincent Col, Latrobe, PA 15650-2667. **EMAIL** wclough@stvincent.edu

CLOUGHERTY, ROBERT, JR.
PERSONAL Born 12/13/1960, Boston, MA, m, 5 children **DISCIPLINE** ENGLISH **EDUCATION** Villanova Univ, BA, 82; Tex Women's Univ, MA, 85; Univ Tulsa, PhD, 91. **CAREER** Asst Prof, Univ Nebr, 90-94; From Asst Prof to Assoc Prof, Tenn Technol Univ, 94-. **HONORS AND AWARDS** Fulbright Hays Sen Scholar, Univ Uppsala; English Speaking Union of Tulsa Res Grant, 89; Mary Major Crawford Outstanding Fac Member Awd, Univ Nebr, 91; UNK Summer Res Fel, 93; Mortar Board Outstanding Fac Member, Tenn Tech Univ, 95. **MEMBERSHIPS** Am Conf on Irish Studies, Int Asn for the Study of Irish Lit. **RESEARCH** Contemporary Irish literature, semiotics. **SELECTED PUBLICATIONS** Auth, "Ireland's Divided History: The Root of her Poetry," Etudes Irlandaises, 18.2 (93): 17-26; auth, "Who are We Neutral Against?: Patrick Kavanagh and the Irish National Emergency," Patrick Kavanagh, (Omaha: Creighton UP, 95), 72-84; auth, "Micheal Mac Liommoir," in Irish Playwrights 1880-1995: A Res and Prod Sourcebook (Westport: Greenwood, 97), 175-181; auth, "Voiceless Outsiders: Count Dracula as Bram Stoker," New Hibernia Rev (00). **CONTACT ADDRESS** Dept English, Tennessee Tech Univ, 1000 N Dixie Hwy, Cookeville, TN 38505-0001. **EMAIL** rclougherty@tntech.edu

CLOWERS, MARSHA L.
PERSONAL Born 04/25/1969, New Orleans, LA, s **DISCIPLINE** COMMUNICATION **EDUCATION** Arkansas State Univ, BS; Texas Tech, MA; Ohio Univ, PhD. **CAREER** Public Relations Agent, Senator M. Todd, 91; consult, Dept of Ed, Tx Tech Univ, 92; consult, Lubbock County Democratic Party, 92; Fordham Univ, 95-98; JOHN JAY COL OF CRIMINAL JUSTICE, 98-; ADJUNCT PROF, BEFORD HILLS CORRECTIONAL FACILITY, 98-. **HONORS AND AWARDS** First fac member appointed instr of the Fordham Freshman Symposium, 97; top four paper, Eastern Commun Asn convention, 97. **MEMBERSHIPS** NY State Commun Asn; Nat Commun Asn; Eastern Commun Asn. **RESEARCH** Health communication; criminology; incarcerated females. **SELECTED PUBLICATIONS** Coauth, Communication and Health, Commun and Health Outcomes, Hampton Press, 95; coauth, The Influences of Human Communication on Health Outcomes, Am Behavioral Sci, 94; coauth, An Examination of Communication Studies Department Curricula for Undergraduate Students and Areas of Growth in the Field, Tx Speech Commun J, 92; auth, Culture, Communication, and the Media: So What?, Iowa J of Commun, 97. **CONTACT ADDRESS** 1512 Schorr Pl, Apt 2A, Bronx, NY 10469. **EMAIL** mclowers@faculty.iiay.luny.edu

CLUBBE, JOHN
DISCIPLINE ENGLISH LITERATURE **EDUCATION** Columbia Col, BA, 59; Columbia Univ, MA, 60; PhD, 65; Sorbonne, Doctorat d'Universite, 61. **CAREER** Lectr, Columbia Univ, 62-63; lectr, City Col, 63-65; lectr, Univ of Munster, 65-66; asst to assoc prof, Duke Univ, 66-75; prof to prof emeritus, Univ of Ky, 75-. **HONORS AND AWARDS** NEH Fel, 71-72, 83-84; Guggenheim Fel, 75-76; Vis Scholar, Harvard Univ, 89-90; Distinguished Scholar, Keats-Shelley Assoc, 99. **MEMBERSHIPS** MLA, Keats-Shelley Assoc of Am, Midwest Victorian Assoc, W Am Lit Assoc, ASLE, Soc of Archit Hist, Napoleonic Alliance, Byron Soc. **RESEARCH** 19th Century English and American Literature (Byron, Napoleon, Carlyle, J.A. Froude, travelers to Cincinnati), Art, architecture and cities (Thomas Sully, Henry Farny, J.H. Sharp, Albert Bierstadt, Cincinnati and New York). **SELECTED PUBLICATIONS** Auth, Victorian Forerunner: The Later Career of Thomas Hood, Duke Univ Pr, (Durham, NC), 68; ed, Selected Poems of Thomas Hood, Harvard Univ Pr, (Cambridge, MA), 70; coed, The Collected Letters of Thomas and Jane Welsh Carlyle, Duke Univ Pr, (Durham, NC), 4vols, 70, 3 vols, 77, 2 vols, 81; ed, Two Reminiscences of Thomas Carlyle, Duke Univ Pr, (Durham, NC), 74; ed, Carlyle and His Contemporaries: Essays in Honor of Charles Richard Saunders, Duke Univ Pr, (Durham, NC), 76; ed, Froude's Life of Carlyle, Ohio State Univ Pr, (Columbus, OH), 79; coauth, English Romanticism: The Grounds of Belief, Macmillan, (London), 83; coauth, The English Romantic Poets: A Review of Research and Criticism, MLA, (NY), 85; coed, Victorian Perspectives: Six Essays, Macmillan, (London), 89; auth, Cincinnati Observed: Architecture and History, Ohio State Univ Pr, (Columbus, OH), 92. **CONTACT ADDRESS** 1266 Canyon Rd, Santa Fe, NM 87501-6128. **EMAIL** jclubbe@newmexico.com

CLUBBE, JOHN L. E.
PERSONAL Born 02/21/1938, New York, NY, s **DISCIPLINE** ENGLISH LITERATURE **EDUCATION** Columbia Col, AB, 59; Columbia Univ, MA, 60; PhD, 65. **CAREER** Lectr, Univ of Munster, Ger, 65-66; asst to assoc prof, Dulle Univ, 66-75; prof, Univ of Ky, 75-99; prof emeritus 99-. **HONORS AND AWARDS** NEH, 72-73, 83-84; Guggenheim, 75-76; Vis Scholar, Harvard Univ, 89-90. **RESEARCH** Romanticism, Byron, Victorian Literature, Carlyle, J.A. Froude, American culture, architecture, cities, the West. **SELECTED PUBLICATIONS** Auth, Cincinnati Observed: Architecture and History, 92. **CONTACT ADDRESS** Dept English, Univ of Kentucky, 500 S Limestone St, Lexington, KY 40506-0001.

CLUFF, RANDALL
PERSONAL Born 09/24/1951, Pheonix, AZ, m, 1979, 5 children **DISCIPLINE** ENGLISH **EDUCATION** Univ Tn, Knoxville, PhD, 97. **CAREER** Asst prof, chair, S Va Col, 97-. **MEMBERSHIPS** MLA; Melville Soc; SHARP. **RESEARCH** Melville; literary publishing history; American romanticism. **SELECTED PUBLICATIONS** Auth, John Greenleaf Whitti-

er, Oliver Cowdrey, Amer Nat Biog, Oxford UP, 99; auth, Andrew Jackson and Gansevoort Melville: Did the Old Hero Hear the Young Orator?, Melville Soc Extracts, 99. **CONTACT ADDRESS** So Virginia Univ, One College Hill Dr, Buena Vista, VA 24416. **EMAIL** rcluff@southernvirginia.edu

CLUM, JOHN M.
DISCIPLINE ENGLISH LITERATURE **EDUCATION** Princeton Univ, PhD **CAREER** Prof, Duke Univ. **RESEARCH** Twentieth century Brit and Am drama. **SELECTED PUBLICATIONS** Auth, Acting Gay: Male Homosexuality in Modern Drama, Columbia, 92; co-ed, Displacing Homophobia: Essays in Gay Male Literature and Culture, Duke, 89. **CONTACT ADDRESS** Eng Dept, Duke Univ, Durham, NC 27706. **EMAIL** jclum@acpub.duke.edu

COAKLEY, JEAN ALEXANDER
PERSONAL Born 07/27/1930, Croton-on-Hudson, NY, m, 1973, 5 children **DISCIPLINE** BRITISH LITERATURE **EDUCATION** Miami Univ, Ohio, BA, 71; MA, 72; PhD, 82. **CAREER** From asst prof to assoc prof, Miami Univ, Ohio, 82-, Ed, Charles F Kettering Found, 72-73, staff writer, 73-74. **MEMBERSHIPS** Int Arthurian Soc. **RESEARCH** Restoration drama and political literature; medieval metrical romances; mysteries. **SELECTED PUBLICATIONS** Auth, The School, Charles F. Kettering Found, 75; auth, The Learning Community, Charles F. Kettering Found, 75; auth, The Learning Environment, Charles F. Kettering Found, 75; ed, The Luckey Chance: A Critical Edition, Garland, 87; auth, "The Public Prints: The Newspaper in Anglo-American Culture, 1665-1740," Historian (94); auth, "Medieval Carlisle: The City and the Borders from the Late Eleventh to the Mid-Sixteenth Century," Historian (96); auth, "Comedy of Manners," in The Oxford Companion to Crime and Mystery Writing (NY: Oxford Univ Press, 99); auth, "C.L. Grace: Katherine Swinbrook, Fifteenth-Century Physician and Sleuth," in The Detective as Historian: History and Art in Historical Crime Fiction (Bowling Green State Univ Popular Press, 00). **CONTACT ADDRESS** Dept of English, Miami Univ, Oxford, OH 45056. **EMAIL** coakleja@muohio.edu

COALE, SAMUEL CHASE
PERSONAL Born 07/26/1943, Hartford, CT, m, 1972, 1 child **DISCIPLINE** ENGLISH, AMERICAN CIVILIZATION **EDUCATION** Trinity Col, Conn, AB, 65; Brown Univ, Am & PhD, 70. **CAREER** Instr Eng, 68-71, asst prof, 71-76, assoc prof, 76-81, asst dean, 78-80, prof eng & Am lit, Wheaton Col, 81, Co-Ch, Am hist & lit, 70, Wheaton res & travel grant, Wordsworth-Coleridge Conf, Engl, 72; Fulbright sr lectureship, Aristotelian Univ, Greece, 76-77, Universidade Federal de Minas Gerais, Brazil, 94; lectr, Engl, 72 & 96, Ann Poznan Am Cult Sem, Poland, 77, 78 & 79, India and Pakistan, 81, Sweden, 81, Czechoslovakia, 83-89, Israel and Egypt, 87, Pakistan, 90 & 93, Brazil, 90, Ygoslavia, 91, India, 94; Nat Endowment for Hum fel, 81-82; Teaching, Brazil at UFMG, 98; Prof, A. Howard Meneely, 00; Book reviewer for the Providence Journal; theatre and film reviewer for the East Side Monthly. **HONORS AND AWARDS** A Howard Meneely Prof Hum, Wheaton, 98; Awded the Faculty Appreciation Awd from the graduating class, 99. **MEMBERSHIPS** MLA; Northeast Mod Lang Asn; Hawthorne Soc; Poe Soc; Knight of Mark Twain. **RESEARCH** Mod Am lit; 19th century Am lit; Engromantic poets. **SELECTED PUBLICATIONS** Auth, Faulkner and the Southern Imagination, Grammata, Greece, 77; John Cheever, Ungar, 77; Hawthorne's American Notebooks: Contours of a haunted mind, Nathaniel Hawthorne J, 78; The Marble Faun: A frail structure of our own rearing, Essays in Lit, 80; Anthony Burgess, Ungar, 81; A Quality of Light: The fiction of Paul Theroux, Critique, 81; An interview with Anthony Burgess, In: The Ludic loves of Anthony Burgess, Mod Fiction Studies, 81; Into the Farther Darkness: The Manichean pastoralism of John Gardner, In: Critical Essays on John Gardner, Southern Ill Univ Press, 82; Didion's Disorder: An American Romancer's Art, Critique, 84; Paul Theroux, Twayne, 87; William Styron Revisited, Twayne, 91; The Scarlet Letter as Icon, ATQ, 92; Hawthorne's Black Veil: From Image to Icon, CEA Critic, 93; Red Noses, The Black Death, and AIDS: Cycles of Despair and Disease, Ill, 93; Spiritualism and Hawthorne's Romance: The Blithedale Theater as False Consciousness, Literature and Belief, 94; The Resurrection of Bullet Park: John Cheever's Curative Spell, Greenwood, 94; The Romance of Mesmerism: Hawthorne's Medium of Romance, Studies in the Am Renaissance, 94; Hillerman and Cross: The Re-Invention and Mythic (Re)-Modeling of the Poplar Mystery, Clues, 95; The Dark Domain of James Lee Burke: Mysteries within Mystery, Clues, 97; Mesmerism and Hawthorne: Mediums of American Romance, Alabama, 98; Blood Rites (a novel), Commonwealth, 98. **CONTACT ADDRESS** Dept of Eng & Am Lit, Wheaton Col, Massachusetts, 26 E Main St, Norton, MA 02766-2322. **EMAIL** samcoale@aol.com

COBB, JERRY
DISCIPLINE ENGLISH LITERATURE **EDUCATION** Gonzaga Univ, BA, 74; Univ WA, MA, 75, 81, Divinity Doctorate, 87. **CAREER** Instr, Seattle Univ. **MEMBERSHIPS** MLA; NCTE. **SELECTED PUBLICATIONS** Auth, The Ramsays as Dysfunctional Family in Woolf's To the Lighthouse. **CONTACT ADDRESS** Seattle Univ, Seattle, WA 98122-4460. **EMAIL** jcobb@seattleu.edu

COBLEY, EVELYN M.
DISCIPLINE ENGLISH LITERATURE **EDUCATION** Univ Utah, BA; Univ Brit Col, MA, PhD. **CAREER** Prof **HONORS AND AWARDS** Raymond-Klibansky Bk Prize, Aid to Schol Publ Prog, 93-94; post-dr fel, SSHRC, 83-84; res fel, SSHRC, 95-98. **RESEARCH** Critical theory; comparative literature; cultural studies; 20th-century British and American fiction. **SELECTED PUBLICATIONS** Auth, Representing War: Form and Ideology in First World War Narratives; pub(s), articles in Contemp Lit, Semiotic Inquiry, Can Rev of Comparative Lit, Jour of Narrative Tech, Style, Mosaic, Eng Stud in Can, Can Lit. **CONTACT ADDRESS** Dept of English, Univ of Victoria, PO Box 3070, Victoria, BC, Canada V8W 3W1. **EMAIL** ecobley@uvic.ca

COBURN, WILLIAM LEON
DISCIPLINE EIGHTEENTH CENTURY BRITISH LITERATURE, RHETORIC **EDUCATION** Univ NMex, BA, 65; Univ Calif, Davis, MA, 68, PhD, 69. **CAREER** Instr, Davis, 66-69; instr, 69-, dir, undergrad stud, dir, freshman compos, Univ Nev, Las Vegas, 80-81, 85-91; state dir, 69-71, judge, NCTE Achievement Awards, 94; dir, Southern Nev Writing Proj, 85-90. **HONORS AND AWARDS** NEH summer sem grant, 78; Outstanding Eng Tchr Awd, 83; Rita Dean Abbey Tchr of the Yr Awd, 94. **RESEARCH** Imitation and modeling in the teaching of writing and standards in grading. **SELECTED PUBLICATIONS** Auth, Notes of a Freshman Freshman Composition Director, J of Coun of Writing Prog Adminr, Spg, 82. **CONTACT ADDRESS** Dept of Eng, Univ of Nevada, Las Vegas, 4505 Maryland Pky, PO Box 455011, Las Vegas, NV 89154. **EMAIL** coburnw@nevada.edu

COCKRELL, DALE
PERSONAL Born 01/10/1947, Paducah, KY, m, 1986, 1 child **DISCIPLINE** MUSIC **EDUCATION** Univ Ill, BM, 71; MM, 83; PhD, 78. **CAREER** Asst prof, Middlebury Col; prof, Wm & Mary Col; prof, Vanderbilt Univ. **HONORS AND AWARDS** Irving Lowens Awd in Am Mus, 89; C. Hugh Holman Awd for Literary Scholarship, 97. **MEMBERSHIPS** Am Antiquarian Soc. **RESEARCH** 19th Century American Music. **SELECTED PUBLICATIONS** Auth, "The Hutchinson Family: 1841-45, or The Origins of Some Yankee Doodles," Inst for Stud in Am Mus Newsltr, vol XII/I, 82; auth, articles in The New Grove Dictionary of Music in America, 86; auth, "Of Gospel Hymns, Minstrel Shows, and Jubilee Choirs: Toward Some Black African Musics," Am Mus, 87; ed, Excelsior, Journals of the Hutchinson Family Singers, 1842-46, 89; coauth, History of Western Music, 91; auth, Il Pescaballo and Ten Nights in a Barroom, Nineteenth Century American Music Theatre, no 8, 94; auth, "Jim Crow: Demon of Disorder," Am Mus 14/2, 96; auth, "Callithumpans, Mummers, Maskers, and Minstrels: Blackface in the Streets of Jacksonian American," Theater Annual 49, 96; auth, "Hutchinson Family Singers," in Encycl of New Eng Cult (forthcoming); auth, "Demons of Disorder: Early Blackface Minstrels and Their World," Cambridge Studies in American Theatre and Drama, No. 8, 97; auth, "Popular Music in the United States: 1820-80," in The Universe of Music: A World History, vol 10 (forthcoming); auth, "Popular Music of the Parlor and Stage," Garland Encyclopedia of World Music, vol 8: North Am volume (forthcoming); auth, "Nineteenth Century Popular Music," The Cambridge History of American Music (forthcoming). **CONTACT ADDRESS** Blair Sch of Mus, Vanderbilt Univ, Nashville, TN 37212. **EMAIL** Dave.Cockrell@Vanderbilt.edu

CODY, RICHARD JOHN
PERSONAL Born 01/05/1929, London, England, m, 1995, 2 children **DISCIPLINE** ENGLISH **EDUCATION** London Univ, BA, 52; Univ Minn, MA, 58, PhD, 61. **CAREER** From instr to asst prof English, Univ Minn, 60-63; assoc prof, 63-68, col librn, 70-74, chmn dept, 71-73, prof English, Amherst Col, 68-. **HONORS AND AWARDS** MA, Amherst Col, 68. **RESEARCH** Renaissance; modern literature. **SELECTED PUBLICATIONS** Auth, The Landscape of the Mind: Pastoralism and Platonic Theory in Tasso's Aminta and Shakespeare's Early Comedies, Clarendon, 69; ed & contribr, Newsletter of the Friends of the Amherst College Library, 72-97. **CONTACT ADDRESS** Dept of English, Amherst Col, Amherst, MA 01002-5003.

COERS, DONALD V.
PERSONAL Born 06/02/1941, San Marcos, TX, m, 1966, 2 children **DISCIPLINE** ENGLISH **EDUCATION** Univ Tex at Austin, BA, 63, MA, 69; Tex A & M Univ, PhD, 74. **CAREER** Prof English, Sam Houston State Univ, 69-92; Coord of Grad Stud, 92-95; Assoc VP for Acad Affairs, 95-. **RESEARCH** John Steinbeck; Ebenezer Cook. **CONTACT ADDRESS** Academic Affairs, Sam Houston State Univ, Huntsville, TX 77341. **EMAIL** coers@shsu.edu

COFFIN, TRISTRAM POTTER
PERSONAL Born 02/13/1922, San Marino, CA, m, 1944, 4 children **DISCIPLINE** ENGLISH AND FORKLORE **EDUCATION** Haverford Col, BS, 43; Univ Pa, AM, 47, PhD, 49. **CAREER** From instr to assoc prof English, Denison Univ, 49-58; assoc prof English & folklore, 58-64, vdean, Grad Sch Arts & Sci, 65-68, prof English, 64-84, Prof Emer English and Folklore, Univ PA, 84- . **HONORS AND AWARDS** Guggenheim fel, 53. **MEMBERSHIPS** MLA; Am Folklore Soc (secy-treas, 60-65, 2nd vpres, 67-); Folklore Soc England. **RESEARCH** Anglo-American ballad; folk literature; American Indian and Negro. **SELECTED PUBLICATIONS** Auth, Index to the Journal of American Folklore, Univ Tex Press, 58; co-ed Folklore in America, 67; auth, Uncertain Glory, 71; auth, The Old Ball Game, 71; The Book of Christmas Folklore, Seabury, 73; co-ed, Folklore from the Working Folk of America, Doubleday Anchor, 73; auth, The Female Hero, Seabury, 75; The British Traditional Ballad in North America, Am Folklore Soc, 77; The Proper Book of Sexual Folklore, Seabury, 78; coauth, The Parade of Heroes, Doubleday Ancho, 78; Great Game for a Girl, Exposition, 80; co-ed, Folklore of the American Holidays, Editions I & II & III. **CONTACT ADDRESS** PO Box 509, Wakefield, RI 02880.

COFFLER, GAIL H.
PERSONAL Born 10/11/1939, Alton, IL, m, 1991, 4 children **DISCIPLINE** ENGLISH **EDUCATION** Southern Ill Univ, BA, 73; MA, 75; Univ Wis at Madison, PhD, 81. **CAREER** Grad teaching asst, Univ Wis, 75-81; Fulbright Lectr, Stuttgart Univ, 81-82; instr, Univ Kans at Lawrence, 82-85; prof, Suffolk Univ, 85-. **HONORS AND AWARDS** Newberry Libr Fel, Newberry Libr, 70-80; Harry Hayden Clark Prize in Am Lit, Univ Wis, 80; Fulbright Lectureship, Stuttgart Univ, 81-82. **MEMBERSHIPS** Melville Soc, MLA, Hawthorne Soc. **RESEARCH** Herman Melville, Nineteenth-century American Literature. **SELECTED PUBLICATIONS** Auth, Melville's Classical Allusions, Greenwood Press, 85; auth, "Classical Iconography in the Art of Billy Budd," in Melville and the Visual Arts (Kent State Univ, 92). **CONTACT ADDRESS** Dept English, Suffolk Univ, 8 Ashburton Place, Boston, MA 02108-2701.

COGSWELL, FREDERICK W.
PERSONAL Born 11/08/1917, East Centreville, NB, Canada **DISCIPLINE** LITERATURE **EDUCATION** Univ NB, BA, 49, MA, 50; Edinburgh Univ (IODE Scholar), PhD, 52; St. Francis Univ, Hon LLD, 82; King's Univ, DCL, 85; Mt Allison Univ, LLD, 88. **CAREER** Ed, The Fiddlehead lit mag, 52-66; prof, 52-83, prof emer, Univ NB, 83-; writer-in-residence, Scottish Arts Coun, 83-84. **HONORS AND AWARDS** Nuffield Fel, 59; Can Coun Sr Fel, 67; Order of Can, 81; Excellent Awd, NB Govt, 95. **MEMBERSHIPS** League Can Poets; Asn Can Publs; NB Writers Fedn. **RESEARCH** Canadian lit, the Romantics, and in Creative Writing. **SELECTED PUBLICATIONS** Auth, A Long Apprenticeship: Collected Poems, 80; Selected Poems, 82; Pearls, 83; The Complete Poems of Emile Nelligan, 83; Charles GD Roberts and His Works, 83; ed, An Atlantic Anthology, vol 1 83, vol 2 84; Meditations, 86; An Edge to Life, 87; Charles Mair and his Works, 88; The Best Notes Merge, 88; Black and White Tapestry, 89; co-ed & co-transl, Unfinished Dreams: Contemporary Poetry of Acadie, 90; Watching an Eagle, 91; When the Right Light Shines, 92; In Praise of Old Music, 92; In My Own Growing, 93; As I See It, 95; The Trouble With Light, 96; Folds, 97. **CONTACT ADDRESS** 31 Island View Dr, Douglas, NB, Canada E3A 7R7.

COHEN, DEREK M.
PERSONAL Born 09/24/1941, Pretoria, South Africa, m, 1998, 2 children **DISCIPLINE** ENGLISH, LITERATURE **EDUCATION** Rhodes, Grahamstown S Africa, BA, 64; Am Univ, MA, 68; NY Univ, PhD, 72. **CAREER** Prof, York Univ. **RESEARCH** Elizabethan and Jacobean drama. **SELECTED PUBLICATIONS** Auth, Shakespeare's Culture of violence, Macmillan; auth, The Politics of Shakespeare, Macmillan. **CONTACT ADDRESS** Dept English, York Univ, 4700 Keele St, Toronto, ON, Canada M3J 1P3. **EMAIL** derekc@yorku.ca

COHEN, EILEEN Z.
PERSONAL Born 12/15/1932, Baltimore, MD **DISCIPLINE** ENGLISH LITERATURE **EDUCATION** Univ Md, BS, 53, MA, 58, PhD(English lit), 65. **CAREER** From instr to asst prof English, Temple Univ, 61-68; from asst prof to assoc prof English lit, 68-77, Prof English, St Joseph's Col, 77-. **MEMBERSHIPS** Conf Brit Studies; Northeast Mod Lang Asn; MLA; Renaissance Soc Am; NCTE. **RESEARCH** Renaissance drama; 17th century poetry and prose; Shakespeare. **SELECTED PUBLICATIONS** Auth, The old arcadia: A treatise on moderation, Rev Belge de Philol et d'Hist, 68; Sir Philip Sidney as Ambassador, Hist Mag, Protestant Episcopal Church, 6/69; The visible solemnity; ceremony and order in Shakespeare and Hooker, Tex Study Lit & Lang, summer 70; Alex in wonderland, or Portnoy's complaint, Twentieth Century Lit, 7/71; Henry James's Governess--again, Four Quarters, summer 74; The role of Cassio in Othello, English Studies, 4/76; Virtue is Bold! The Bed-trick and Characterization in All's Well That End's Well and Measure for Measure, Philos Quart, 6/86; auth, "Shakespeare's Audience and Edgar's," The Upstart Crow (99); and misc. poems. **CONTACT ADDRESS** Dept of English, Saint Joseph's Univ, 5600 City Ave, Philadelphia, PA 19131-1376. **EMAIL** ecohen@sjc.edu

COHEN, JOSEPH
PERSONAL Born 04/27/1926, Central City, KY, w, 3 children **DISCIPLINE** ENGLISH **EDUCATION** Vanderbilt Univ,

BA, 49, MA, 51; Univ Tex, PhD(English), 55. **CAREER** Instr English, Univ Tex, 53-55; from instr to assoc prof, 55-75, asst dean, Col Arts & Sci, 57-58, assoc dean, 67-75, Prof English, Newcomb Col, Tulane Univ, 75-, Resident prof, Tulane-Newcomb jr yr in Gt Brit, 59-60, dir, 60-61; acad asst to dean, Newcomb Col, 61-67; assoc dir scholars & fels prog, Tulane Univ, 64-65, dir, 65-67, dir scholars prog, 67-68; contrib ed, J Higher Educ, 68-71; dir, Tulane Jewish Studies Prog, 81- **MEMBERSHIPS** MLA; Nat Col Honors Coun (pres, 70-71); SCent Mod Lang Asn; Asn Jewish Studies; Am Jewish Hist Soc. **RESEARCH** Contemporary literature, particularly British literature; 20th century war literature; Anglo-American Jewish literature. **SELECTED PUBLICATIONS** Auth, Vespers, So Hum Rev, Vol 0030, 96. **CONTACT ADDRESS** Tulane Univ, New Orleans, LA 70118.

COHEN, JUDITH
PERSONAL Born 12/09/1949, Montreal, PQ, Canada **DISCIPLINE** MUSIC, HISTORY **EDUCATION** McGill Univ, BA, 71; Concordia Univ, BFA, 75; Univ Montreal, MA, 80, PhD, 89; Univ Toronto BEd, 96. **CAREER** Pres, Can Soc Traditional Mus, 93-97; Adj Grad Fac Mus, York Univ. **HONORS AND AWARDS** Can Coun grants; SSHRCC grants. **MEMBERSHIPS** Iberian Ethnomusicol Soc; Europ Sem Ethnomusicol; Folklore Stud Asn Can; Int Coun Traditional Mus. **SELECTED PUBLICATIONS** Auth, Sonography of Judeo-Spanish Song in Jewish Folklore & Ethnol Rev, 93; auth, Women's Role in Judeo-Spanish Song in Active Voices, 95; auth, Pero la voz es muy educada in Hommage H.V. Sophia, 96. **CONTACT ADDRESS** 751 Euclid Ave, Toronto, ON, Canada M6G 2V3.

COHEN, MICHAEL MARTIN
PERSONAL Born 04/27/1943, Akron, OH, m, 1967, 2 children **DISCIPLINE** ENGLISH; LITERATURE **EDUCATION** Univ Ariz, AB, 65, MA, 67, PhD(English), 71. **CAREER** From instr to asst prof English, La State Univ, New Orleans, 70-76; from Asst Prof to Assoc Prof, 76-84, Prof English, Murray State Univ, 84-, Dept Chair, 94-98. **MEMBERSHIPS** MLA; SCent Mod Lang Asn; SAtlantic Mod Lang Asn; SCent Soc 18th Century Studies; Southeastern Atlantic Soc 18th Century Studies. **RESEARCH** 18th and 19th century English literature; Shakespeare; relationships between visual arts and literature; mystery fiction. **SELECTED PUBLICATIONS** Auth, coauth, The Poem in Question, Harcourt Brace Jovanovich, 83; Engaging English Art, Alabama, 87; Hamlet in My Mind's Eye, Georgia, 89; Sisters: Relation and Rescue in Nineteenth-Century British Novels and Paintings, Fairleigh Dickinson, 95; auth, Murder Most Fair: The Appeal of Mystery Fiction, Fairleigh Dickinson, 00. **CONTACT ADDRESS** Dept of English, Murray State Univ, 7C Faculty Hall, Murray, KY 42071. **EMAIL** michael.cohen@murraystate.edu

COHEN, MILTON
DISCIPLINE AMERICAN LITERATURE **EDUCATION** Syracuse Univ, PhD, 81. **CAREER** Assoc prof. **RESEARCH** 20th century American literature; modernist literature; painting and music. **SELECTED PUBLICATIONS** Auth, Fatal Symbiosis: Modernism and World War One, War Lit Arts, 96; The Futurist Exhibition of 1912: A Model of Prewar Modernism, Europ Studies Jour, 95; Fitzgerald's Third Regret: Intellectual Pretense and the Ghost of Edmund Wilson, Tex Studies Lit and Lang, 91; Subversive Pedagogies: Schoenberg's Theory of Harmony and Pound's A Few Don'ts by an Imagiste, Mosaic, 88; Poet and Painter: The Aesthetics of E.E. Cummings' Early Work, Wayne State Univ, 87. **CONTACT ADDRESS** Dept of Literature, Univ of Texas, Dallas, Richardson, TX 75083-0688. **EMAIL** mcohen@utdallas.edu

COHEN, PHILIP G.
PERSONAL Born 07/18/1954, Easton, PA, m, 1996, 4 children **DISCIPLINE** ENGLISH **EDUCATION** Am Univ, BA, 76; Univ S Calif, MA, 78; Univ Del, PhD, 84. **CAREER** Asst prof, Columbia Col, 84-85; asst prof, Marist Col, 85-86; asst prof to assoc prof, UT-Arlington, 86-; chair, 96-00; Dean, Grad Sch, 01-. **HONORS AND AWARDS** UT-Arlington Res Grant, 96; NEH Fel, 97. **MEMBERSHIPS** MLA, ALS, SAMLA, SCMLA, Soc for Study of S Lit, Soc for Textual Scholarship, Am Lit Assoc, William Faulkner Soc. **RESEARCH** William Faulkner, American Literature, Textual Scholarship and Editorial Theory. **SELECTED PUBLICATIONS** Auth, "Aesthetic Anomalies in Pudd'n'head Wilson," Studies in Am Fiction, (82); auth, "Balzac and Faulkner: The Influence of La Comedie humaine on Flags in the Dust and the Snopes Trilogy," Miss Quart, (84); coauth, ""Madame Bovary and Flags in the Dust: Flaubert's influence on Faulkner," Comp Lit Studies, (85); auth, "Faulkner's Introduction to The Sound and the Fury," Am Lit, (91); ed, Devils and Angels: Textual, Editing and Literary Theory, Virginia, 91; coauth, "Using Faulkner's Introduction to Teach The Sound and the Fury," Approach to Teaching The Sound and the Fury, (96); auth, "Textual Scholarship in the Classroom," TEXT, (97); ed, Texts and Textuality: Textual Instability, Theory and Interpretation, Garland, 97; auth, "A Authorial Revision, the Crisis of Masculinity, and Modernism," Renaissance and Mod Studies, (98); auth, "William Faulkner, the Crisis of Masculinity, and Textual Instability," Textual Studies and the Common Reader, (00). **CONTACT ADDRESS** Univ of Texas, Arlington, Box 19167, Arlington, TX 76013. **EMAIL** cohen@uta.edu

COHEN, RALPH ALAN
PERSONAL Born 09/07/1945, Columbia, SC, m, 1967, 3 children **DISCIPLINE** RENAISSANCE LITERATURE, FILM, SHAKESPEARE IN PERFORMANCE & TEACHING SHAKESPEARE **EDUCATION** Dartmouth Col, AB, 67; Duke Univ, MA, 70; PhD, 73; Georgetown Univ, DHL (honorary), 98. **CAREER** Asst prof, 73-78; assoc prof, 78-84; prof, James Madison Univ, 84-, Dominion Fel, 90-91; Duke Univ Fel, 67-69, Danforth Tchg Fel, 70-71; NEH Folger Inst, Shakespeare's Text in Action, 87, Seminar leader, 3/93; Master tchr, NEH Seminar, A Time to Think about Shakespeare, 6/89, Center for Renaissance and Shakespearean Staging Inst, summer 95; Proj dir, VA Found for the Hum and Public Policy, Bringing Shakespeare Home, 6/92, proj dir, Women on the Page and Stage, 7/94; cofounder, exec direcor, Shenandoah Shakespeare, 88-. **HONORS AND AWARDS** Duke Dissertation Travel Awd, 71; Va Found Grant, Film and the Polit Process, 75; JMU Summer Res Grant, 74, 77; JMU Admin Grant, 80; JMU Distinguished Tchg Awd, 84; Madison Scholar, 86; State Coun Higher Educ in VA, Outstanding Fac award, 87; JMU Eminent Prof, 87. **MEMBERSHIPS** AAUP; Malone Soc; Southeastern Renaissance Conf; MLA; Shakespeare Asn; Shakespeare Theatre Asn Am. **RESEARCH** Shakespeare and his contemporaries in performance. **SELECTED PUBLICATIONS** Auth, Reversal of Gender in Rape of the Lock, SAtlantic Bull, 72; auth, The Function of Setting in Eastward Ho, Renaissance Papers, 73; auth, Reading and Writing Movie Reviews in Freshman English, Freshman Eng News, 75; auth, The Importance of Setting in the Revision of Every Man in His Humour, English Lit Renaissance, 78; auth, Setting in Volpone, Renaissance Papers, 78; auth, Misdirection in A Midsummer Night's Dream and Bartholomew Fair, Renaissance Papers, 82; auth, Introduction to Shakespeare Quarterly, Edition on Teaching, summer 90; auth, Lighting effects in Macbeth, Renaissance Papers, 94; auth, "Looking for Cousin Ferdninand: Folio Stage Directions in Taming of the Shrew," in Textual Reformations, ed. Laurie Maquire and Thomas Berger (forthcoming); auth, Staging Comic Divinity: The Collision of High and Low in Antony and Cleopatra, Shakespeare Bull, summer 95; auth, Teaching the Early Comedies, Shakespeare's Sweet Thunder (Michael Collins, ed), Univ Del Press, 97; auth, Original staging and the Shakespeare classroom, Teaching Shakespeare, MLA, 98. **CONTACT ADDRESS** Dept of Eng, James Madison Univ, 800 S Main St, Harrisonburg, VA 22807-0002. **EMAIL** cohenra@jmu.edu

COHEN, SANDY
DISCIPLINE ENGLISH LITERATURE **EDUCATION** Miami Dade Jr Col, AA, 67; Fla Atlantic Univ, BA, 69; Auburn Univ, MA, 70; PhD, 72. **CAREER** Prof, Albany State Univ, 72-. **HONORS AND AWARDS** Research Excellence, Albany State Univ, 85; Fulbright, China, 91. **RESEARCH** Modern and Contemporary Literature of Australia, England and America. **SELECTED PUBLICATIONS** Auth, Norman Mailer's Novels, Rodopi; auth, Bernard Malamud and the Trial by Love, Radopi. **CONTACT ADDRESS** Dept English and Lang, Albany State Univ, 504 College Dr, Albany, GA 31705-2717. **EMAIL** scohen@asurams.edu

COHN, JAN
PERSONAL Born Cambridge, MA, m, 1969, 2 children **DISCIPLINE** ENGLISH **EDUCATION** Wellesley Col, BA, 55; Univ Toledo, MA, 61; Univ Mich, PhD, 64. **CAREER** Director, Carnegie-Mellon Univ, 73-79; dept chair, George-Mason Univ, 79-87; dean, Trinity Col, 87-94. **HONORS AND AWARDS** Phi Kappa Phi; ACLS Fel; NEH Jun Fel; Danforth Assoc; Funds for Excellence; Distinguished Fac Awd. **MEMBERSHIPS** Modern Lang Asn, Am Studies Asn, Popular Culture Asn, Am Culture Asn. **RESEARCH** American Literature, American Studies, Popular Culture. **SELECTED PUBLICATIONS** Auth, The Palace or the Poorhouse: The American House as a Cultural Symbol, Mich State Univ Press: East Lansing, 79; auth, Improbable Fiction: The Life of Mary Roberts Rinehart, Univ Pittsburgh Press: Pittsburgh, 80; auth, Romance and the Erotics of Property: Mass-Market Fiction for Women, Duke Univ Press: Durham, 88; auth, Creating America: George Horace Lorimer and "The Saturday Evening Post", Univ Pittsburgh Press: Pittsburgh, 89; auth, Covers of 'The Saturday Evening Post', Viking Studio Books: New York, 95. **CONTACT ADDRESS** Dept English, Trinity Col, Connecticut, 300 Summitt St, Hanford, CT 06106-3100.

COLATRELLA, CAROL
DISCIPLINE CULTURAL STUDY OF AMERICAN AND EUROPEAN LITERATURE **EDUCATION** Rutgers Univ, PhD, 87. **CAREER** Assoc prof, exec dir, Soc for Lit & Sci, Ga Inst of Technol. **RESEARCH** Herman Melville's fictions. **SELECTED PUBLICATIONS** Auth, Evolution, Sacrifice, and Narrative: Balzac, Zola, and Faulkner; coed, Cohesion and Dissent in America. **CONTACT ADDRESS** Sch of Lit, Commun & Cult, Georgia Inst of Tech, Skiles Cla, Atlanta, GA 30332. **EMAIL** carol.colatrella@lcc.gatech.edu

COLBOURN, FRANK E.
PERSONAL Born 07/05/1926, New Haven, CT, 4 children **DISCIPLINE** DEBATE **EDUCATION** Boston Univ, BSBA, 48, LLB, 50; Brooklyn Law Sch, SJD (magna cum laude), 56. **CAREER** Asst to secy, Household Finance Corp, Chicago, 50-52; real estate exec, F W Woolworth Co, New York City, 52-60; assoc prof, 60-65, Prof Speech Pace Univ, 65-, Debate Coach, 60-92, Pres NYC Chapt AAUP (4 terms); Adj prof speech grad sch, C W Post Col, Long Island Univ, 64-78; dir, Long Island Debate Inst, 65-81; lectr speech, Mercer Sch Theol, 66-70; dir, Pace Speech Assocs, 67-70; lectr, NY State Police Acad, Albany, 77-78; debate coach, US Merchant Marine Acad, Kings Point, 78-82; pres, Colbourn Commun Consults, Inc, 80-; Cert Instr in Critical Thinking and mem advisory bd, Straus Thinking and Learning Ctr, NYC. **MEMBERSHIPS** Eastern Forensic Asn; Speech Commun Asn; Am Forensic Asn; DSR; TKA. **RESEARCH** Problems in negotiation; interviewing; communication theory. **SELECTED PUBLICATIONS** Auth, Legal aspects of negotiation of long term leases for chain stores in shopping centers, Brooklyn Law Rev, 4/62 & 12/62; The art of debate, 71 & How to judge a debate, 75 (records), Listening Libr. **CONTACT ADDRESS** Speech Comm Studies, Pace Univ, New York, 1 Pace Plaza, New York, NY 10038-1598.

COLBY, ROBERT ALAN
PERSONAL Born 04/15/1920, Chicago, IL, m, 1947 **DISCIPLINE** ENGLISH, LIBRARY SCIENCE **EDUCATION** Univ Chicago, BA, 41, MA, 42, PhD(English), 49; Columbia Univ, MS, 53. **CAREER** Instr English, DePaul Univ, 46-47; instr English & speech, Ill Inst Technol, 47-49; asst prof English, Lake Forest Col, 49-51; lectr, Hunter Col, 51-53; head lang lit & arts div, Libr, Queens Col, NY, 53-64; assoc prof libr sci, Southern Conn State Col, 64-66; assoc prof, 66-69, Prof Libr Sci, Queens Col, NY, 69-, Asst ed, Wellesley Index to Victorian Periodicals, 77- Guggenheim fel, 78-79. **MEMBERSHIPS** MLA; Bibliog Soc Am; AAUP; Am Libr Asn; Asn Am Libr Schs; Victorian Soc Am. **RESEARCH** History of reading taste; history of books and printing; library history. **SELECTED PUBLICATIONS** Coauth, The Singular Anomaly: Mrs Oliphant and the Victorian Literary Marketplace, Archon, 66; auth, Fiction With a Purpose: Major and Minor Nineteenth Century Novels, Inc Univ, 67; contribr, European Authors, Wilson, 67 & Newman's Apologia Pro Vita Sua, Norton, 68; Thackeray's Canvass of Humanity: An Author and His Public, Ohio State Univ Press, 79; ed, William Makepeace Thackeray, Studies in The Novel, spring-summer 81. **CONTACT ADDRESS** Grad Sch Libr Info Studies, Queens Col, CUNY, 6530 Kissena Blvd, New York, NY 11367.

COLDIRON, ANNE E. B.
PERSONAL Born Greensboro, NC **DISCIPLINE** ENGLISH **EDUCATION** Univ Virginia, PhD, 96 **CAREER** Asst prof, 98-, Louisiana St Univ. **RESEARCH** Renaissance literature; poetics; comparative lit; Anglo-French literary relations; literary history & theory. **SELECTED PUBLICATIONS** Auth, "Translatio, Translation, and Charles of Orlean's Paroled Poetics," Exemplaria: A Journal of Theory in Medieval and Renaissance Studies 8.1 (96): 162-192; auth, "Charles of Orleans and Thomas Park's Copy of the Specimens of the Early English Poets," Notes and Queries 242.4 (97): 465-469; auth, "Sidney, Watson, and the 'Wrong Ways' to Renaissance Lyric Poetrics," Renaissance Papers 1997, ed. Trevor Howard-Hill and Philip Rollinson (Camden House Press, 97), 49-62; auth, "Review of Edmund Spenser's Amoretti and Epithalamion," in Sixteenth-Century Journal 30.2, ed. Kenneth J. Larsen (99), 582-584; auth, "Review of The End of the Middle Ages?," in Sixteenth-Century Journal 31.1, ed. John L. Watts (00), 282-283; auth, "Translation, Canons, and Cultural Capital," in Charles of Orleans in England, ed. Mary-Jo Arn (Woodbridge, UK, Boydell and Brewster Ltd., 00), 183-214. **CONTACT ADDRESS** English Dept, Louisiana State Univ and A&M Col, Baton Rouge, LA 70803. **EMAIL** acoldiron@lsu.edu

COLDWELL, JOAN
PERSONAL Born Huddersfield, England **DISCIPLINE** ENGLISH **EDUCATION** Univ London, BA, 58, MA, 60; Harvard Univ, PhD, 67. **CAREER** Asst prof, 60-72, Univ Victoria; prof, 72-96, Prof Emer, McMaster Univ, 96-. **HONORS AND AWARDS** Tchr Awd, McMaster Univ, 81-82; Tchr Awd, Confed Univ Fac Asn, 89; Woman of Year, Hamilton, 89. **MEMBERSHIPS** Can Res Inst Advan Women; Int Asn Stud Anglo-Irish Lit. **SELECTED PUBLICATIONS** Auth, Charles Lamb on Shakespeare, 78; auth, The Collected Poems of Anne Wilkinson, 90; auth, The Tightrope Walker: Autobiographical Writings of Anne Wilkinson, 92. **CONTACT ADDRESS** Dept of English, McMaster Univ, 1280 Main St West, 321 Chester New Hall, Hamilton, ON, Canada L8S 4L9. **EMAIL** coldwell@mcmail.cis.mcmaster.ca

COLE, DAVID WILLIAM
PERSONAL Born 02/16/1939, Worcester, MA, m, 1965, 2 children **DISCIPLINE** ENGLISH LITERATURE, COMPOSITION **EDUCATION** Oberlin Col, BA, 61; Syracuse Univ, MA, 63; Univ Wis-Madison, PhD(English), 70. **CAREER** Instr English, Univ Wis-Fox Valley, 65-66; from instr to asst prof, 68-73, assoc prof, 73-79, Prof English, Univ Wis Ctr-Baraboo-Sauk County, 79-, Wis Higher Educ Aids Bd grant, 71. **RESEARCH** Victorian and Edwardian literature and culture; modern drama; modern rhetoric. **SELECTED PUBLICATIONS** Auth, Shakespeare the Taming of the Shrew, Explicator, Vol 0053, 95; Conrad Heart of Darkness, Explicator, Vol 0054, 95.

CONTACT ADDRESS Dept of English, Univ of Wisconsin Ctr, Baraboo/Sauk County, 1006 Connie Rd, Box 320, Baraboo, WI 53913-1015.

COLE, EVE BROWNING
DISCIPLINE ANCIENT GREEK PHILOSOPHY, FEMINIST THEORY, ETHICS, CLASSICAL STUDIES **EDUCATION** Univ Fla, BA, 73; Univ Calif, San Diego, PhD; 79. **CAREER** Instr, Univ Denver; instr, Ohio State Univ; assoc prof, 84-, ch, Environ Stud adv bd, Univ Minn, Duluth. **RESEARCH** Ancient Greek philosophy; ethics. **SELECTED PUBLICATIONS** Auth, Philosophy and Feminist Criticism, Paragon, 93; coed, Explorations in Feminist Ethics: Theory and Practice, Ind UP, 88. **CONTACT ADDRESS** Univ of Minnesota, Duluth, Duluth, MN 55812-2496.

COLE, HOWARD CHANDLER
PERSONAL Born 05/09/1934, Oak Park, IL, m, 1961, 2 children **DISCIPLINE** ENGLISH LITERATURE **EDUCATION** Wheaton Col, Ill, BA, 56; Yale Univ, MA, 61, PhD, 63. **CAREER** From instr to asst prof, 62-70, assoc prof Eng, Univ Ill, Urbana, 70-81, prof Eng, Univ Ill, Urbana 81-. **MEMBERSHIPS** MLA; Midwest Mod Lang Asn; Renaissance Soc Am. **RESEARCH** Elizabethan romantic comedy; Italian and French backgrounds of Shakespearean comedy. **SELECTED PUBLICATIONS** Auth, The Christian context of Measure for Measure, Jour Eng & Ger Philol, 7/65; A Quest of Inquirie: Some Contexts of Tudor Literature, Bobbs, 73; Dramatic interplay in the Decameron, Mod Lang Notes, 1/75; The moral vision of As You Like It, Col Lit, winter, 76; Bernardo Accolti's Virginia: The uniqueness of Unico Aretino, Renaissance Drama, 79; The All's Well Story from Boccaccio to Shakespeare, Univ Ill Press, 81. **CONTACT ADDRESS** Univ of Illinois, Urbana-Champaign, 608 S Wright St, Urbana, IL 61801-3613.

COLE, JOHN Y., JR.
PERSONAL Born 07/30/1940, Ellensburg, WA, m, 1973 **DISCIPLINE** LIBRARIANSHIP **EDUCATION** Univ of Wash, BA, 62, MLS, 63; Johns Hopkins Univ, MLA, 66; George Washington Univ, PhD, 71. **CAREER** Libr of Congress, 66-; dir, Ctr for the Book, Libr of Congress, 77- . **HONORS AND AWARDS** ALA Lippincott Awd for contribution to the profession librarianship, 00. **MEMBERSHIPS** ALA, Am Stud Asn. **RESEARCH** History of books, reading, and libraries; history of the Library of Congress and its role in American culture and society. **SELECTED PUBLICATIONS** Auth, Jefferson's Legacy, 93; On These Walls, 95; The Library of Congress, 97. **CONTACT ADDRESS** Center for the Book, Library of Congress, Washington, DC 20540. **EMAIL** jcole@loc.gov

COLE, MIKE
PERSONAL Born 04/13/1938, Los Angeles, CA **DISCIPLINE** COMMUNICATIONS **EDUCATION** Univ Calif, Los Angeles, BA, 59; Ind Univ, PhD, 62. **CAREER** Asst prof, Yale Univ, 64-66; Assoc prof, Univ of Calif, 66-69; Assoc prof, The Rockefeller Univ, 69-75, Prof, 75-78; Coordr, Commun Prog, Univ of Calif, 78-81, Dir, Laboratory of Comparative Human Cognition, 78-89, 95-, Prof, 78-99; Guest Scientist, MRC Cognitive Development Unit, 86-87; Prof, Univ of Calif, 99. **HONORS AND AWARDS** Woodrow Wilson Fel, 59-60; Ford Found Foreign Area Fel, 60-62; U.S. State Dept grant, 66, 62-63; Behavioral Sci Awd Nyork Acad of Sci, 78; Fel, Japan Soc for the Promotion of Sci, 80; Herskovits Awd African Studies Asn, 82; James McKeen Catell Fund Awd, 86; Distinguished Contributions to Res and Development in Educ, Am Educ Res Asn, 88; Fel, Ctr for Advanced Study in the Behavioral Scis, 90-91; Sr Fel, The Spencer Found, 95-98; Honorary Doctorate, Copenhagen Univ, 96. **MEMBERSHIPS** Am Asn for the Advancement of Sci; Am Educ Res Asn; Am Psychol Asn; Psychonomic Soc; Am Anthropological Asn; Liberian Res Asn; Coun on Anthropology and Educ; Soc for Res in Child Dev; Nat Res Coun Comt. **RESEARCH** Elaboration of a mediational theory of mind; role of culture in human development. **SELECTED PUBLICATIONS** Co-auth, The Psychology of Literacy, Harvard, 81; auth, Cultural psychology: A once and future discipline, Harvard Univ Press, 96; co-ed Mind, culture and activity: Seminal papers from the Laboratory of Comparative Human Cognition, Cambridge Univ Press, 97; auth, Luia, Alexander Romanovich, The MIT encyclopedia of the cognitive sciences, Massachusetts Inst of Technology, 99; auth, Culture-free versus culture-based measures of cognition, The nature of cognition, The MIT Press, 99; auth, Bruner and Schofield on the cultural organization of learning, The Journal of the Learning Sciences, 99; auth, Computer mediation for learning and play, Journal of Adolescent & Adult Literacy, 99; Re-fusing anthropology and psychology, Bartlett, culture and cognition, Psychology Press, 00; auth, Socially shared cognition: System design and the organization of collaborative research, Theoretical foundations of learning environments, Erlbaum, 00. **CONTACT ADDRESS** Dept of Commun, Univ of California, San Diego, 9500 Gilman Dr, La Jolla, CA 92093. **EMAIL** mcole@weber.ucsd.edu

COLE, SUSAN LETZLER
PERSONAL Born 06/04/1940, Washington, DC, m, 1969 **DISCIPLINE** ENGLISH **EDUCATION** Duke Univ, BA, 62; Harvard Univ, MA, 63; PhD, 68. **CAREER** Prof, Albertus Magnus Col, 83- . **HONORS AND AWARDS** Woodrow Wilson Teach Fel, 62-63; Yale Vis Fac Fel, 78-79, 80-81; nom AAHE Fac Salute, 86. **MEMBERSHIPS** Shakespearean Assoc of Amer; MLA; NY Shakespeare Soc; Colum Univ Sem in Shakespeare. **RESEARCH** Shakespeare; theater rehearsal; tragedy in dramatic literature. **SELECTED PUBLICATIONS** Auth, Playwrights in Rehearsal, Routledge (NY & London, forthcoming). **CONTACT ADDRESS** Dept of English, Albertus Magnus Col, 137 Cottage St, Apt E-6, New Haven, CT 06511-2457.

COLEMAN, ARTHUR
PERSONAL Born 06/29/1924, New York, NY, m, 1946, 2 children **DISCIPLINE** AMERICAN LITERATURE **EDUCATION** NYork Univ, PhD. **CAREER** Prof, Long Island Univ, C.W. Post Campus; Bennett College, Iona College, Hofstra Univ. **SELECTED PUBLICATIONS** Auth, Sinclair Lewis: The Early Years, Epic and Romance Criticism; Hemingway's 'The Spanish Earth;' The Americanization of H. G. Wells; Sociocultural Inferences from the Practice of Naming America's Major League Ball Parks; A Case in Point and Petals on a Wet Black Bough; coauth, Drama Criticism; coauth, Annotated Bibliography of W.W.II Personal Narratives. **CONTACT ADDRESS** Long Island Univ, C.W. Post, Brookville, NY 11548-1300.

COLEMAN, DANIEL
DISCIPLINE ENGLISH LITERATURE **EDUCATION** Campion Co, BA; Regina, BEd, MA; Univ Alberta, PhD. **RESEARCH** English-Canadian lit; lit of migration; critical theory. **SELECTED PUBLICATIONS** Auth, Masculine Migrations: Reading the Postcolonial Male in 'New Canadian' Narrative, 98. **CONTACT ADDRESS** English Dept, McMaster Univ, 1280 Main St W, Hamilton, ON, Canada L8S 4L9. **EMAIL** dcoleman@mcmaster.ca

COLEMAN, EDWIN LEON, II
PERSONAL Born 03/17/1932, El Dorado, AR, m **DISCIPLINE** SPEECH **EDUCATION** City Coll of San Francisco, AA 1955; San Francisco State Univ, BA 1960, MA 1962; Univ of OR, PhD 1971. **CAREER** Melodyland Theatre, technician, 60; Chico State Univ, Speech Dept, asst prof, 63-66; Univ of OR Dept of English, dir, Folklore 1 Ethnic Program, currently; professional musician, currently. **HONORS AND AWARDS** Ford Fellow Educ Grant 1970; Danforth Assoc 1977-; Distinguished Black Faculty 1978; Outstanding Faculty Natl Mag OR Art Commission 1982; Frederick Douglass Scholarship Awd Natl Council of Black Studies 1986; University of Oregon, Charles S. Johnson Service Awd; NAACP Lifetime Achievement Awd. **MEMBERSHIPS** Bd Campus Interfaith Ministry 1975-; bd Sponsors Inc 1980-; bd Clergy & Laity Concerned 1980-; bd OR Arts Found 1981-84; pres OR Folklore Soc 1983-84; consul Natl Endowment for the Arts 1983-; Natl Humanities, faculty; mem Amer Folklore Soc; NAACP; Kappa Alpha Psi; Oregon Track Club; bd, Western States Arts Foundation. **CONTACT ADDRESS** Dept of English, Univ of Oregon, Eugene, OR 97403.

COLEMAN, JOYCE K.
PERSONAL Born 11/12/1949, Brooklyn, NY **DISCIPLINE** ENGLISH **EDUCATION** Barnard Col, BA, 71; Univ Tex, MA, 79; Univ Edinburgh, PhD, 93. **CAREER** From asst prof to assoc prof, Univ NDak, 94-; vis asst prof, Brown Univ, 00. **HONORS AND AWARDS** NEH, 97; Univ Tex Fel, 74-75; Univ Edin Fel, 89-91; APS Fel, 94; UCLA Cen Medi Renai Stud, 96. **MEMBERSHIPS** AAUP; EBS; ICLS; MAA; MCS; MLA; NCS; SMFS. **RESEARCH** Late medieval English and French reading practices: the public reading of secular literature. **SELECTED PUBLICATIONS** Auth, Public Reading and the Reading Public in Late Medieval England and France, Cambridge UP, 96; auth, "New Evidence about Sir Geoffrey Luttrell's Raid on Sempringham Priory, 1312," Brit Lib J (01); auth, "The Text Recontextualized in Performance: Deschamps' Prelection of Machaut's Voir Dit to the Count of Flanders," Viator (00); auth, "Interactive Parchment: The Theory and Practice of Medieval English Aurality," Yrbk Eng Stud (95); auth, "The Audible Caxton: Reading and Hearing in the Writings of England's First Publisher," Fifteenth-Cen Stud (90). **CONTACT ADDRESS** English Dept, Univ of No Dakota, PO Box 7209, Grand Forks, ND 58202. **EMAIL** joyce_coleman@und.nodak.edu

COLEMAN, MARK
DISCIPLINE ENGLISH **EDUCATION** Harvard Univ, BA; Cornell Univ, PhD. **CAREER** Fac, Cornell Univ to Northwestern Univ; to GA Col; to SUNY Potsdam. **RESEARCH** Eng lit (Restoration and 18th century, Renaissance, Romanticism); lit and the visual arts; graphic and literary satire; writing instruction; computer pedag in writing and lit; hypermedia. **SELECTED PUBLICATIONS** Auth, recent publ(s) have been in the application of computing tech to the tchg of writing and lit. **CONTACT ADDRESS** SUNY, Col at Potsdam, 44 Pierrepont Ave, 248 Morey , Potsdam, NY 13676. **EMAIL** scottja@potsdam

COLEMAN, ROBIN R.
PERSONAL Born Pittsburgh, PA, m, 1996 **DISCIPLINE** MASS COMMUNICATION **EDUCATION** Bowling Green State Univ, PhD, 96. **CAREER** Postdoctoral fel, Univ Pitts, 96-98; asst prof, NY Univ, 98- . **MEMBERSHIPS** Nat Commun Asn; Int Commun Asn. **RESEARCH** African Americans and mass media; reception study; media literacy. **SELECTED PUBLICATIONS** Auth African American Viewers and the Black Situation Comedy: Situating Racial Humor, Garland, 98. **CONTACT ADDRESS** 15 Washington Pl, 4J, New York, NY 10003. **EMAIL** robin.coleman@nyu.edu

COLEMAN, WILLIAM S. E.
PERSONAL Born 06/07/1926, m, 2 children **DISCIPLINE** DRAMA **EDUCATION** Slippery Rock State Col, BS, 49; Pa State Univ, MA, 53; Univ Pittsburgh, PhD(Theatre Hist), 65. **CAREER** Instr high sch, Pa, 49-52; asst prof Theatre, Speech & English, Slippery Rock State Col, 53-55; assoc prof & head dept, Glenville State Col, 55-63; asst prof Theatre & Speech, State Univ NY Buffalo, 65-66; prof Theatre Arts, Drake Univ, 66-, chmn, WVa State Comt Re-study Speech Teacher Educ, 61-62; mem planning comt, WVa Centennial Showboat, 62-63; dir, Loving Knife, NY Stage Co, 65; Danforth Teacher study grant, 63 & 64; State Univ NY Found res grant; guest lectr univs, mus & soc, Gt Brit, Italy & WGer. **HONORS AND AWARDS** Certif of Merit Awd, A Stranger to the Past, IMPA awards, 98; pres and founding mem Iowa Scriptwriters Alliance. **RESEARCH** London performances of The Merchant of Venice; William F Cody's performance career; American Indian Affairs. **SELECTED PUBLICATIONS** Auth, Found: An Author (play), The Playshop, 2/52; Planning for the Theatre, Univ Pittsburgh, 65; Post-restoration Shylocks prior to Macklin, Theatre Survey, 5/67; Buffalo Bill on stage, Players Mag, 12/71; coauth, Artand on an American campus, Oblique, 9/73; Buffalo Bill's Wild West (film script), 77 & Gods and Men in Ancient Greece (film script), 78, Perfection Form Co; William Shakespeare's King Lear, annotation, Perfection Forum, 97. **CONTACT ADDRESS** Dept of Theatre Arts, Drake Univ, 2507 University Ave, Des Moines, IA 50311-4505. **EMAIL** william.coleman@drake.edu

COLLETTE, CAROLYN PENNEY
PERSONAL Born 08/02/1945, Boston, MA, 2 children **DISCIPLINE** MEDIEVAL ENGLISH LITERATURE **EDUCATION** Mt Holyoke Col, AB, 67; Univ Mass, MA, 68, PhD, 71. **CAREER** From instr to asst prof English lit, 69-78, fac fel, 73-74, Assoc Prof English, Mt Holyoke Col, 78-. **HONORS AND AWARDS** Phi Beta Kappa, 67; Phi Kappa Phi; 69; Woodrow Wilson Fel, 67; NEH Summer Stipend, 76; Prof of English Lang and Lit, Alumnae Found at Mount Holyoke, 93. **MEMBERSHIPS** MLA; William Morris Soc; New Chaucer Soc; Int Courtly Lit Soc, vice pres, 95-98, pres, 98-2001. **RESEARCH** Old and Middle English literature; Gothic revival in England, 1750-1870. **SELECTED PUBLICATIONS** Auth, Milton's Psalm translations; petition and praise, Eng Lit Renaissance, fall 72; Lord John Manners' Old Nobility, Am Notes & Queries, 3/75; A Closer Look at Seinte Cecile's Special Vision, spring 76 & Sense and sensibility in The Prioress' Tale, fall 80, Chaucer Rev; several articles and reviews in literary journals and publications between 80 and 92; auth, Common Ground: Personal Writing and Public Discourse, with Richard Johnson, NY: Harper Collins, 93; Criseyde's Honor, Integrity and Public Identity in Chaucer's Courtly Romance, in Literary Aspects of Courtly Culture, ed Maddox and Sturm-Maddox, Cambridge: D. S. Brewer, 94; 'Peyntyng with Gret Cost': Virginia as Image in the Physician's Tale, Chaucer Yearbook, 94; Chaucer's Discourse of Mariology, in Art and Context in Late Medieval English Narrative, ed Robert Edwards, by D. S. Brewer, 94; Some Aestetic Implications of Multiplication of Species, Avista, 9, 95; Heeding the Counsel of Prudence: A Context for the Melibee, The Chaucer Rev, 29, 95; Finding Common Ground: A Guide to Personal, Professional and Public Writing, with Richard Johnson, 2nd ed, NY: Addison Wesley Longman, 97; and several works in progress. **CONTACT ADDRESS** Dept of English, Mount Holyoke Col, 50 College St, South Hadley, MA 01075-1461. **EMAIL** CCollett@MtHolyoke.edu

COLLEY, ANN C.
PERSONAL Born 01/09/1940, Bury, England, 1 child **DISCIPLINE** ENGLISH **EDUCATION** Unvi Chicago, PhD, 1983. **CAREER** Prof, Fisk Univ, 69-82; State Univ Col NY at Buffalo, 85- . **HONORS AND AWARDS** Sr Fulbright fel, Warsaw, Poland, 95-96; Am Philos Society Fellowship, 99; Sr Fulbright fel, Kieve Ukraine, 00. **MEMBERSHIPS** MLA; Northeast Victorian Studies Asoc; Tennyson Soc; Am Studies Asoc. **RESEARCH** Victorian literature and culture; words and images. **SELECTED PUBLICATIONS** Auth, Tennyson and Madness, 83; auth, The Search for Synthesis in Literature and Art, 90; auth, Edward Lear and the Critics, 93; auth, Robert Louis Stevenson and the Idea of Recollection, Victorian Lit and Cult, 97; auth, Writing Towards Home: The Landscape of Robert Louis Stevenson's A Child's Garden of Verses, Victorian Poetry, 97; auth, Ruskin and Turner's arrangements of Remberance', The Ruskin Gazette of the Ruskin Soc of London, 97; auth, Nostalgia and Recollection in Victorian Culture, 98; auth, Bodies and Mirrors: The Childhood Interiors of Ruskin, Pater, and Stevenson, Reading the Interior: Nineteenth Century Domestic Space, 99. **CONTACT ADDRESS** 332 Ashland Ave., Buffalo, NY 14222. **EMAIL** colleyac@buffalostate.edu

COLLEY, NATHANIEL S.
PERSONAL Born 06/08/1956, Sacramento, CA, d, 3 children **DISCIPLINE** THEATER **EDUCATION** University of Michigan, BA, 1977, Law School, JD, 1979; UC Davis, graduate study, anthropology. **CAREER** Colley-Lindsey & Colley, partner, 80; Sextus Productions (entertainment), partner, 74-; WCBN-FM Radio Station, general manager, 79, program director, 78, talk show host, 76-78, disc jockey, 74-76; Playwright, currently. **HONORS AND AWARDS** Natl Merit Scholarship Finalist, 1974. **MEMBERSHIPS** California Bar Assn, 1980; American Legion Boy's State CA, 1973; California Youth Senate, 1973; University of Michigan Assn of Black Communicators, 1974; vice pres, Sacramento NAACP Youth Council, 1973-74; natl bd dirs, NAACP 1972-75; Black Music Assn, 1979-. **SELECTED PUBLICATIONS** Playwright: "The Shoebox," Lorraine Hansberry Theatre; "A Sensitive Man,"; Moving Arts, LA Winner of 5 Dramalogue Awards; film: "The Abortion of Mary Williams,"; finalist "Showtime's Black Filmmaker Program," premiered on Showtime, 1998. **CONTACT ADDRESS** PO Box 741825, Los Angeles, CA 90004. **EMAIL** natcolley@earthlink.net

COLLIE, MICHAEL J.
PERSONAL Born 08/08/1929, Eastbourne, England **DISCIPLINE** ENGLISH, HISTORY OF SCIENCE **EDUCATION** St Catharine's Col, Cambridge Univ, MA, 56. **CAREER** Asst prof, Univ Man, 57; lectr, Univ Exeter, 61; assoc prof, Mt Allison Univ, 62; prof Eng, 65-90, dept ch, 67-69, dean grad stud, 69-73, Prof Emer, York Univ, 90-. **MEMBERSHIPS** Int Asn Univ Profs Eng; Mod Hum Res Asn; Bibliog Soc; Bibliog Soc Am; Asn Can Univ Tchrs Eng (pres, 68-69); Can Bibliog Soc; Soc Hist Sci; Geol Soc Am; Geol Soc London; Edinburgh Bibliog Soc. **SELECTED PUBLICATIONS** Auth, George Borrow Eccentric, 82; auth, George Borrow: A Bibliographical Study, 84; auth, George Gissing: A Bibliographical Study, 85; auth, Henry Maudsley: Victorian Psychiatrist, 88; auth, Huxley at Work, 91; auth, Murchison in Moray: the Geologist on Home Ground, 95; auth, George Gordon: A Catalogue of His Scientific Correspondence, 96. **CONTACT ADDRESS** Winters Col, York Univ, 4700 Keele St, Toronto, ON, Canada M3J 1P3.

COLLIER, CHERYL
DISCIPLINE AMERICAN LITERATURE **EDUCATION** Univ Ga, PhD, 94. **CAREER** Dept Eng, Clemson Univ **RESEARCH** American literature. **SELECTED PUBLICATIONS** Auth, Biographical essays on Amy Tan and Maragaret Walker in The Cyclopedia of World Authors; Introduction essay, The Langston Hughes Rev (Fall 95 issue). **CONTACT ADDRESS** Dept of Humanities, No Greenville Col, PO Box 1892, Tigerville, SC 29688-1892. **EMAIL** abramsc@clemson.edu

COLLINGTON, PHILLIP D.
PERSONAL Born 06/14/1968, Hamilton, ON, Canada, m, 1991, 2 children **DISCIPLINE** ENGLISH **EDUCATION** McMaster Univ, BA, 91; MA, 92; Univ Toronto, PhD, 98. **CAREER** Adj asst prof, Univ Windsor, 98-99; postdoctoral fel, Univ Mich Ann Arbor, 99-00; asst prof, Niagara Univ, 00-. **HONORS AND AWARDS** SSHRCC Doctoral Fel, 92-96, 99-00; Ont Grad Scholar, 91-92; Univ Toronto Open Doctoral Fel, 96-97; Heinz Kohut Mem Prize. **MEMBERSHIPS** MLA; NMLA; CRRS; CSRS; SAA. **RESEARCH** Shakespeare; English literature; drama and popular culture 1500-1700; cuckoldry and infidelity in English literature and popular culture; prison literature; and the representation of the confinement in English literature; post-Freudian psychoanalytic and its social historic approaches to literature; emblems, iconography and the visual arts; Anglo-French literary relations. **SELECTED PUBLICATIONS** Auth, "Slander to the State in The Culture of Slander in Early Modern England," English Lang Notes 37 (99): 76-86; auth, "Shame in Japan and the American South: Faulkner's Absalom, Absalom!" in Scenes of Shame: Psychoanalysis, Shame and Writing, eds. J. Adamson, H. Clark (Albany: SUNY Pr, 99): 167-87; auth, "'A Puppet-Play in Pictures:' Thomas Middleton's Emblematic Drama," in Other Voices Other Views: Expanding the Canon in English Renaissance Studies, eds. H. Ostovich, M. Silcox, G. Roebuck (Newark: Univ Del Pr/London: Assoc Univ Pr, 99): 91-131; auth, "It's A Mug's Game: A 'New' Portrait of Shakespeare and Jonson," Shakespeare Yearbk 9 (00): 1-18; auth, "'I Would Thy Husband Were Dead:' The Merry Wives of Windsor as Mock Domestic Tragedy," English Lit Renaissance 30 (00): 184-212. **CONTACT ADDRESS** English Dept, Niagara Univ, Lewiston, NY 14109-2035. **EMAIL** pdc@niagara.edu

COLLINS, CHRISTOPHER
PERSONAL Born 07/08/1936, Red Bank, NJ, m, 1968, 2 children **DISCIPLINE** POETIC THEORY, AMERICAN POETRY **EDUCATION** St Anselm's Col, BA, 58; Univ Calif, Berkeley, MA, 59; Columbia Univ, PhD, 64. **CAREER** Asst prof English, Nassau Community Col, 63-65; from asst prof to assoc prof & chmn dept, Borough of Manhattan Community Col, 65-68; assoc prof, 68-91, prof, NY Univ, ch, colloquim on Psychoaesthetics, 79-83, assoc dir, poetics instT, 81-85, Vis Scholar, Gonville & Caius Col, Cambridge Univ, 70. **HONORS AND AWARDS** Common Room, Gonville and Caius College, Cambridge, 71; Woodrow Wilson National Fel, 58. **MEMBERSHIPS** Conf Contemp Am Poetry; Northeastern Mod Lang Asn (secy, 78-79). **RESEARCH** Psychology of literature and rhetoric; American poetry and poetics **SELECTED PUBLICATIONS** Auth, The Act of Poetry, Random, 70; The Uses of Observation: Correspondential Vision in the Writings of Emerson, Thoreau, and Whitman, Mouton, The Hague, 71; Figure, ground, and open field, NY Quart, winter 71; transl & auth, introd, The Daphnis and Chloe of Longus, Imprint Soc, 72; If your drink is bitter, be wine, Nation, 5/72; Notes on prosody, In: The Logic of Poetry, Monaco & Briggs, 74; auth, Reading the Written Image: Verbal Play, Interpretation, and the Roots of Iconophobia, Penn State Press, 91; auth, The Poetics of the Mind's Eye: Literature and the Psychology of Imagination. Univ Penn, 91; auth, Authority Figures: Metaphoes of Mastery from the Iliad to the Apocalypse, Rowman and Littlefield, 96. **CONTACT ADDRESS** Dept of English, New York Univ, 19 University Pl, New York, NY 10003-4556. **EMAIL** cc3@nyu.edu

COLLINS, DAN STEAD
PERSONAL Born 12/05/1919, Williamsport, PA, m, 1955 **DISCIPLINE** ENGLISH **EDUCATION** Univ Pa, BS, 41; Univ NC, MA, 51, PhD, 60. **CAREER** Instr English, Univ Tenn, 46-47; part-time instr, Univ NC, 49-52; from instr to asst prof, 53-73, Assoc Prof English, Univ Mass, Amherst, 73-, Managing ed, English Lit Renaissance, 72-74, ed, 75, 77. **MEMBERSHIPS** Col English Asn; MLA; Renaissance Soc Am. **RESEARCH** Milton. **SELECTED PUBLICATIONS CONTACT ADDRESS** Dept of English, Univ of Massachusetts, Amherst, Amherst, MA 01003.

COLLINS, DEREK B.
PERSONAL Born 08/24/1965, Washington, DC, m, 1990, 2 children **DISCIPLINE** COMPARATIVE LIT; CLASSICS; FOLKLORE & MYTHOLOGY **EDUCATION** Univ CA, Los Angeles, MA, 91; Harvard Univ, PhD, 97. **CAREER** Asst Prof Classics, Univ Texas at Austin, 97-. **HONORS AND AWARDS** Nat Academy of Sciences, Ford Found, Doctoral Dissertation fel, 9/96--6/97. **MEMBERSHIPS** Am Philos Asn; Classical Asn of the Middle West and South; Am Folklore Soc. **RESEARCH** Greek lit; comparative lit (German); witchcraft. **SELECTED PUBLICATIONS** Trans, Greek selections in the Appendix to Claude Calame, The Craft of Poetic Speech in Ancient Greece, Cornell Univ Press, 95; auth, The Myth and Ritual of Ezili Freda in Hurston's Their Eyes Were Watching God, Western Folklore 55, 96; trans with J. Orion, Claude Calame, Young Women's Choruses in Ancient Greece: Their Morphology, Religious Role, and Social Functions, Lanham, MD, Rowman & Littlefield Pubs, 97; auth, Fatum, in the Dictionaire International des Termes Litteraitres, gen ed, Jean-Marie Grassin, A. Francke-Berne, Saur-Vg Pub, Berne, Munich, Paris, New York, 97; On the Aesthetics of the Deceiving Self in Nietzsche, Pindar, and Theognis, Nietzsche-Studien 26, 97; Review of Jacob Rabinowitz, The Rotting Goddess: The Origin of the Witch in Classical Antiquity, Scholia 7 (ns), 16, 98; Immortal Armor: The Concept of Alke in Archaic Greek Poetry, Lanham, MD, Rowman & Littlefield Pubs, 98; Hesiod and the Divine Voice of the Muses, Arethusa, forthcoming, 99. **CONTACT ADDRESS** Dept of Classical Studies, Univ of Michigan, Ann Arbor, 2160 Angell Hall, 435 S State St, Ann Arbor, MI 48109-1003. **EMAIL** dbcollin@umich.edu

COLLINS, JAMES M.
DISCIPLINE POSTMODERNISM, CULTURAL THEORY **EDUCATION** Univ Iowa, PhD. **CAREER** Assoc prof, Univ Notre Dame. **HONORS AND AWARDS** Mellon fel. **RESEARCH** Cultural life in the '90s. **SELECTED PUBLICATIONS** Auth, Uncommon Cultures: Popular Culture and Postmodernism; coed, Film Theory Goes to the Movies. **CONTACT ADDRESS** Dept of English, Univ of Notre Dame, 216 Decio Fac Hall, Notre Dame, IN 46556. **EMAIL** james.m.collins.3@nd.edu

COLLINS, K. K.
PERSONAL Born 09/15/1947, Union City, TN, m, 1970, 1 child **DISCIPLINE** ENGLISH LANGUAGE AND LITERATURE **EDUCATION** Col William & Mary, AB, 69; Vanderbilt Univ, PhD(English), 76. **CAREER** Lectr, 76-77, asst prof, 77-82, Assoc Prof English, Southern Ill Univ, Carbondale, 82-**HONORS AND AWARDS** Fel, Woodrow Wilson Diss, Nat Endowment Hum Summer, Mellon Sem; Sch of Criticism and Theory Sch; Am Philos Soc grant. **MEMBERSHIPS** MLA; Mod Humanities Res Asn; Dickens Soc. **RESEARCH** Nineteenth-century English literature; literature and philosophy; literature and science. **SELECTED PUBLICATIONS CONTACT ADDRESS** Dept of English, So Illinois Univ, Carbondale, Carbondale, IL 62901-4300. **EMAIL** kkcoll@siu.edu

COLLINS, MARTHA
PERSONAL Born 11/25/1940, Omaha, NE **DISCIPLINE** POETRY, AMERICAN LITERATURE **EDUCATION** Stanford Univ, AB, 62; Univ Iowa, MA, 65, PhD(English), 71. **CAREER** Asst prof English, Northeast Mo State Col, 65-66; instr, 66-71, asst prof, 71-75, assoc prof to PROF ENGLISH, UNIV MASS, BOSTON, 75-; PROF CREATIVE WRITING, OBERLIN COL, 97-. **MEMBERSHIPS** Assoc Writing Prog. **RESEARCH** Poetry; American literature; women's studies. **SELECTED PUBLICATIONS** Auth, The center of consciousness on stage: Henry James Confidence, Studies Am Fiction, 75; The self-conscious poet: The case of William Collins, ELH, 75; The narrator, the satellites, and the lady: Point of view in The Portrait of a Lady, Studies Novel, 76; The contents of discontent: A preface to some poems by Peter Klappert, Agni Rev, 78; ed, Critical Essays on Louise Bogan, G K Hall, 84. **CONTACT ADDRESS** Dept of English, Univ of Massachusetts, Boston, 100 Morrissey Blvd, Boston, MA 02125-3300.

COLLINS, MICHAEL J.
DISCIPLINE ENGLISH LITERATURE **EDUCATION** Fordham Univ, BA; Univ NYork, MA, PhD. **CAREER** Prof. **RESEARCH** Shakespeare; British theatre since 1950; Anglo-Welsh poetry. **SELECTED PUBLICATIONS** Auth, pubs on Shakespeare, Anglo- Welsh poetry, and American literature; ed, Shakespeare's Sweet Thunder: Essays on the Early Comedies, Delaware, 97. **CONTACT ADDRESS** English Dept, Georgetown Univ, 37th and O St, Washington, DC 20057.

COLLINS, RICHARD W.
PERSONAL Born 09/04/1952, Eugene, OR, m, 1992, 1 child **DISCIPLINE** ENGLISH **EDUCATION** Univ Ore, BA, 77; Univ Calif Irvine, MA, 79; PhD, 84. **CAREER** Asst prof, La State Univ, 82-92; assoc prof, Am Univ Bulgaria, 95-97; assoc prof, Xavier Univ, 97-. **HONORS AND AWARDS** Fulbright Sen Lectr, Univ Bucharest, 92-93; NSA Fel, Univ Wales, 84-85; NEH Summer Sem, Columbia, 83; Fulbright Hays Res Grant, UK, 8081; NEH Sch of Criticism and Theory, 79. **MEMBERSHIPS** MLA; SCMLA; Am Popular Culture Asn; Phi Bet Kappa. **RESEARCH** Victorian literature; 20th Century America; Romanian literature. **SELECTED PUBLICATIONS** Auth, Faute, Family and the Fiction of Confession, 99; auth, Andre: Codrescu's Mioritic Space, 99; auth, "The Ruins of Copain," in The Woman in White, 99; auth, Truth in Adversaries: Ridley Scott and Joseph Conrad, 00; auth, John Faute: A Literary Portrait, 00; auth, My Dear Miss Melineux, 00; auth, Concerning the Eccentricities of Ronald Firbank, 01; auth, Lafeadio Hesm in New Orleans, 01; auth, Marian's Moustache: Bearded Ladies, Hermaphrodities and Intersexual College, 01. **CONTACT ADDRESS** Dept English, Xavier Univ, Louisiana, 2800 Dauphine St, New Orleans, LA 70117-7847. **EMAIL** rnlcoll@bellsouth.net

COLLINS, ROBERT G.
PERSONAL Born 06/06/1926, Danbury, CT **DISCIPLINE** ENGLISH **EDUCATION** Miami Univ, Ohio, BA, 50, MA, 52; Univ Denver, PhD, 59. **CAREER** Ch grad Eng stud, Univ Man, 68-74; prof Eng, Univ Ottawa, 76-91; vis prof, Univ Kuwait, 94-97. **MEMBERSHIPS** MLA; Asn Can Univ Tchrs Eng; Bronte Soc; Kafka Soc Am; Conf Eds Learned J. **SELECTED PUBLICATIONS** Auth, Arch-Sinner: Branwell Bronte, 93; auth, E.J. Pratt, 88; auth, Tolerable Levels of Violence, 83; auth/comp, Critical Essays on John Cheever, 83. **CONTACT ADDRESS** 242 Elizabeth St, PO Box 522, Arnprior, ON, Canada K7S 3T8.

COLLINS, VICKI
DISCIPLINE HISTORY OF RHETORIC **EDUCATION** Wake Forest Univ, BA, 67; Duke Univ, MA, 68; Auburn Univ, PhD, 93. **CAREER** Engl, Oregon St Univ. **RESEARCH** 18th & 19th century Brit lit. **SELECTED PUBLICATIONS** Auth, Personality Type and Collaborative Writing. Collaborative Technical Writing: Theory and Practice Asn Tchrs Technical Writing, 89. **CONTACT ADDRESS** Oregon State Univ, Corvallis, OR 97331-4501. **EMAIL** vcollins@orst.edu

COLLISON, GARY L.
PERSONAL Born 01/17/1947, Lewistown, PA, m, 1969, 2 children **DISCIPLINE** ENGLISH **EDUCATION** Lehigh Univ, BA, 68; Bucknell Univ, MA, 71; Pa State Univ, PhD, 79. **CAREER** Prof, Pa State York, 75-. **HONORS AND AWARDS** Outstanding Book Awd, Gustavus Myers Ctr for Study of Bigotry and Racism, New York Univ, 97. **MEMBERSHIPS** Thoreau Soc, Ralph Waldo Emerson Soc, Asn for Gravestone Studies, Am Cult Asn, Am Lit Asn, Pa Ger Soc, York County Hist Soc. **RESEARCH** American transcendentalism, German American gravestones, underground railroad and black community history. **SELECTED PUBLICATIONS** Auth, "William Ellery Channing," in A Companion to American Thought, ed. Richard W. Fox and James T. Kloppenberg (Oxford UK and Cambridge MA: Blackwell, 95), 112-113; auth, "Theodore Parker," in Biographical Dictionary of Transcendentalism, ed. Wesley T. Mott (Westport, CT: Greenwood Press, 96), 196-199; auth, "Church of the Future," "Harvard Divinity School," "Higher Criticism," "Massachusetts Quarterly Review," in Encyclopedia of American Transcendentalism, ed. Wesley T. Mott (Westport, CT: Greenwood Press, 96), 30-31,79-80,81-82,114; auth, "Toward Democratic Vistas: Theodore Parker, Friendship, and Transcendentalism," in Emersonian Circles, ed. Wesley T. Mott and Robert Burkholder (Rochester: Univ of Emersonian Circles, 96), 161-180; auth, Shadrach Minkins: From Fugitive Slave to Citizen, Harvard Univ Press (Cambridge), 97; auth, "William Miller," in American National Biography (NY: Oxford Univ Press, 99), 520-521; coauth,

"Gravestones, Carvers and Ethnic Pride, " Stone in Am 112 (99): 22-23; auth, "Emerson and Antislavery," in A Historical Guide to Ralph Waldo Emerson, ed. Joel Myerson (NY: Oxford Univ Press, 00), 179-210. **CONTACT ADDRESS** Dept English, Pennsylvania State Univ, York, 1031 Edgecombe Rd, York, PA 17403. **EMAIL** glc@psu.edu

COLLMER, ROBERT GEORGE
PERSONAL Born 11/28/1926, Guatemala City, Guatemala, m, 1981, 2 children **DISCIPLINE** ENGLISH **EDUCATION** Baylor Univ, BA, 48, MA, 49; Univ Pa, PhD(English), 53. **CAREER** Asst instr English, Univ Pa, 49-52; from assoc prof to prof, Hardin-Simmons Univ, 54-61; prof & dean col, Wayland Baptist Univ, 61-66; Fulbright prof English & Am lit, Nat Univ Paraguay, 66-67; prof English, Tex Tech Univ, 67-73, dir grad studies, 69-70, acting chmn dept English, 70; prof English & chmn dept, 73-79, Dean Grad Studies & Res, Baylor Univ, 79-92, Smith-Mundt prof English & Am lit, Inst Technol, Mex, 58-60; Distinguished Prof, 92-97; Emeritus Distinguished Prof, 97-. **HONORS AND AWARDS** Southern Fel grant, 58; Fulbright Sr Res Award, Univ Leiden, Neth, 82. **MEMBERSHIPS** MLA; Renaissance Soc Am; SCent MLA; SCent Renaissance Conf (pres, 70-71). **RESEARCH** English literature of late Renaissance; Anglo-Dutch literary relations; Anglo-Hispanic literary relations. **SELECTED PUBLICATIONS** Auth, Grotius,Hugo--The Religiousness of the States of Holland and Westfriesland 1613--Dutch, English, Jour Church and State, Vol 0039, 97; Bunyan and His England, 1628-88, Durham Univ Jour, Vol 0085, 93. **CONTACT ADDRESS** Baylor Univ, Waco, Waco, TX 76798. **EMAIL** rcoll017@aol.com

COLTON, GLENN
DISCIPLINE MUSICOLOGY **EDUCATION** Memorial Univ Newfoundland, BM; McMaster Univ, MA; Univ Victoria, PhD. **CAREER** Dept Lang, Lakehead Univ **RESEARCH** Canadian music, nineteenth and twentieth-century music. **SELECTED PUBLICATIONS** Ed, Coulthard's second piano sonata; pub(s), numerous articles for, Can Univ Mus Rev; Fermata; Intl Alliance for Women in Mus Jour. **CONTACT ADDRESS** Dept of Music, Lakehead Univ, 955 Oliver Rd, Thunder Bay, ON, Canada P7B 5E1. **EMAIL** Glenn.Colton@lakeheadu.ca

COLTRANE, ROBERT
PERSONAL Born 11/21/1938, Hampton, VA, m, 1972, 2 children **DISCIPLINE** ENGLISH **EDUCATION** VA Military Inst, BA, 61; Univ of VA, MA, 62; PA St Univ, Phd, 92 **CAREER** Instr, 65-68, Old Dominion Univ; Dir PR, 69-83, Lock Haven Univ; Asst Prof, 83-93, Assoc Prof, 93-, Lock Haven Univ **MEMBERSHIPS** Int Theodore Dreiser Soc **RESEARCH** 20th Cent Am Poetry **SELECTED PUBLICATIONS** Auth, The Crafting of Dreiser's Twelve Men, Papers on Language & Literature, S IL Univ, 91 **CONTACT ADDRESS** Dept of English, Univ of Pennsylvania, Lock Haven, PA 17745. **EMAIL** rcoltran@eagle.1hup.edu

COLVERT, JAMES B.
PERSONAL Born 06/08/1921, Paris, TX, m, 1944, 2 children **DISCIPLINE** ENGLISH **EDUCATION** Henderson State Col, BA, 47; ETex State Univ, MA, 49; La State Univ, PhD(English), 53. **CAREER** From instr to asst prof English, Univ Tex, 53-57; asst prof, Univ Conn, 57-58; assoc prof, Univ Va, 59-68; head dept, 72-76, dir grad studies, 77-79, actg head dept, 79-80, Prof English, Univ GA, 68-. **RESEARCH** American literature. **SELECTED PUBLICATIONS** Auth, Day, Fred, Holland, Guiney, Louise, Imogen, and the Text of Crane,Stephen the Black Riders, Amer Lit Realism 1870-1910, Vol 0028, 96. **CONTACT ADDRESS** Dept of English, Univ of Georgia, Athens, GA 30601.

COLVIN, DANIEL LESTER
PERSONAL Born 03/10/1947, Amarillo, TX, m, 1969, 1 child **DISCIPLINE** ENGLISH LITERATURE **EDUCATION** Wheaton Col, BA, 69; Northwestern Univ, MA, 70, PhD(English), 76. **CAREER** Assoc prof, 72-80, assoc prof English, 80-86, prof English, Western Ill Univ, 86-. **HONORS AND AWARDS** NEH Inst, 95-96; NEH Summer Seminar, Univ of Mich, 77, Yale Univ, 88. **MEMBERSHIPS** MLA; Conf Christianity & Lit; AAUP; Shakespeare Asn of Am; Renaissance Soc of Am. **RESEARCH** Renaissance literary rhetoric; Christian literary criticism; theories of the pastoral; Shakespeare; The Bible as Literature. **SELECTED PUBLICATIONS** Auth, The Renaissance, Western Ill Univ, 78; Milton's Comus and the Pattern of Human Temptation, Christianity & Lit, 78; Measure for Measure: A Study Guide and Teacher's Handbook, Folger Shakespeare Libr Inst, 96; Francesco Petrarch, Magill's Survey of World Lit, Salem, 92; The How-to Guide to Ad Libbing Shakespeare, The Fight Master: Journal of the Soc of Am Fight Directors XIII, 90; That Abler Soule: Donne and the Poetic of Knowledge, Res Publica Litterarum, 83; Shakespeare's Measure for Measure: An interactive text (http://sterling, holy cross, edu/departments/theatre/projects/isp). **CONTACT ADDRESS** Dept of English, Western Illinois Univ, 1 University Cir, Macomb, IL 61455-1390. **EMAIL** DL-Colvin@wiu.edu

COLWELL, FREDERIC
DISCIPLINE ENGLISH LITERATURE **EDUCATION** Mich State Univ, PhD. **CAREER** Dept Eng, Queen's Univ **RESEARCH** Romantic poetry and art; psychoanalytic studies; Jungian psychology; travel literature of the 18th and 19th centuries; Richard Strauss. **SELECTED PUBLICATIONS** Auth, Rivermen: A Romantic Iconography of the River and the Source, McGill-Queen's Univ, 89; A Feast of Ashes, Oberon, 90; pubs on Romantic poetry and art. **CONTACT ADDRESS** Dept English, Queen's Univ at Kingston, Kingston, ON, Canada K7L 3N6.

COMENSOLI, VIVIANA
DISCIPLINE RENAISSANCE DRAMA **EDUCATION** Simon Fraser, BA, MA; British Columbia, PhD. **CAREER** Prof **RESEARCH** Renaissance drama, gender studies, genre. **SELECTED PUBLICATIONS** Auth, Household Business': Domestic Plays of Early Modern England, Univ Toronto, 96; Homophobia and the Regulation of Desire: A Psychoanalytic Reading of Marlowe's Edward II; Witchcraft and Domestic Tragedy in The Witch of Edmonton; Gender and Eloquence in Dekker's The Honest Whore, Part II. **CONTACT ADDRESS** Wilfrid Laurier Univ, 75 University Ave W, Waterloo, ON, Canada N2L 3C5. **EMAIL** vcomenso@wlu.ca

COMFORT, JUANITA R.
PERSONAL 2 children **DISCIPLINE** RHETORIC, COMPOSITION **EDUCATION** Old Dominion Univ, MA, BA; Ohio State Univ, PhD. **CAREER** Asst prof, English, Old Dominion Univ. **RESEARCH** Black feminist essays; rhetoric and culture; subjectivity and ethos. **SELECTED PUBLICATIONS** Auth, A Rheotric of 'Cultural Negotiation': toward an Ethos of Empowerment for African American Women Graduate Students, in Rhetoric, Cult Studies & Literacy, Hillsdale, LEA, 95; auth, "Becoming a Writerly Self: Col Writers Engaging Black Feminist Essays" Col Composition and Commun, 51:4 (June 00): 540-559; auth, "African Am Women's Rhetoric and the Culture of Eurocentric Scholarly Discourse," in Contrastive Rhetorics Revisited and Redefined, Erlbaum (Mahwah, New Jersey), in press. **CONTACT ADDRESS** Old Dominion Univ, BAL 205, Norfolk, VA 23529. **EMAIL** jcomfort@odu.edu

COMOR, EDWARD
PERSONAL Born Toronto, ON, Canada **DISCIPLINE** POLITICAL ECONOMY OF COMMUNICATION AND CULTURE **EDUCATION** Univ Toronto; BA; Univ Leeds, MA; York Univ, PhD. **CAREER** Prof, Am Univ. **HONORS AND AWARDS** Chair, Int Communication Section of the Int Studies Asn, 00-01. **MEMBERSHIPS** Int Studies Asn; Int Asn for Media and Communication Res; Int Communication Asn; Asn for Evolutionary Economics. **RESEARCH** United States foreign communication policy; The mediating role of free trade treaties and other international institutions; The political economic implications of the internet; auth, The Writings and methodology of Harold A. Innis. **SELECTED PUBLICATIONS** Ed/contribur, The Global Political Economy of Communications, St. Martin's Press, 94, 96; auth, Communication, Commerce and Power, St. Martin's Press, 98. **CONTACT ADDRESS** American Univ, 4400 Massachusetts Ave, Washington, DC 20016. **EMAIL** ecomor@american.edu

COMPRONE, JOSEPH JOHN
PERSONAL Born 03/11/1943, Lansdowne, PA, m, 1965, 1 child **DISCIPLINE** ENGLISH **EDUCATION** Springfield Col, BA, 65; Univ Mass, MA, 67, PhD(English), 70. **CAREER** Teaching asst English, Univ Mass, 66-69, asst dir freshman English, 68-69; asst prof English & coord compos, Univ Minn, Morris, 69-72; assoc prof English & dir freshman English, Univ Cincinnati, 72-76; prof English & dir compos, 76-81, Dir Grad Studies English, Univ Louisville, 81-, Freshman English consult; consult & rev, St Martin's Press, Houghton Mifflin & W Norton, 74-78. **MEMBERSHIPS** NCTE; Conf Col Compos & Commun; AAUP; MLA; Writing Prog Adminr (treas, 76-78). **RESEARCH** Literary theory and modern literature; rhetoric and composition; film and pedagogy. **SELECTED PUBLICATIONS** Auth, Where Do We Go Next in Writing Across the Curriculum, Col Composition and Commun, Vol 0044, 93. **CONTACT ADDRESS** Dept of English, Univ of Louisville, Louisville, KY 40208.

COMSTOCK, GEORGE ADOLPHE
PERSONAL Born 05/17/1932, Seattle, WA, d **DISCIPLINE** COMMUNICATIONS, SOCIAL PSYCHOLOGY **EDUCATION** Univ Wash, BA, 54; Stanford Univ, MA, 58, PhD(commun), 67. **CAREER** Asst prof jour, NY Univ, 67-68; social psychologist, Rand Corp, 68-70 & NIMH., 70-72; sr social psychologist, Rand Corp, 72-77; prof commun, S I Newhouse Sch Pub Commun, 77-79, S I Newhouse Chair Pub Commun, Syracuse Univ, 79- . **HONORS AND AWARDS** Sr sci adv, US Surgeon Gen Sci Adv Comt TV & Social Behavior, 70-72. **MEMBERSHIPS** Asn Educ Jour and Mass Commun; Am Asn Pub Opinion Res; Soc Psychol Study Social Issues. **RESEARCH** Behavioral effects of televised portrayals; influence of mass media on society. **SELECTED PUBLICATIONS** Co-ed, Media Content and Control, Vol I, Television and Social Learning, Vol II, Television and Adolescent Agressiveness, Vol III, Television in Day-to-day Life, Vol IV, Television's Effects: Further Explorations, Vol V, In: Television and Social Behavior, US Govt Printing Off, 72; coauth, Television and Human Behavior: The Research Horizon, Future and Present, & auth, Television and Human Behavior: The Key Studies, Rand Corp, 75; coauth, Television and Human Behavior, Columbia Univ, 78; auth, Television in America, 2nd ed, Sage, 91; auth, Evolution of American Television, Sage, 89; auth, Television and the American Child, Academic, 91; co-auth, Television: What's on, Who's Watching, and What It Means. **CONTACT ADDRESS** Pub Commun, Syracuse Univ, Syracuse, NY 13210.

CONACHER, DESMOND J.
PERSONAL Born 12/27/1918, Kingston, ON, Canada **DISCIPLINE** CLASSICS **EDUCATION** Queen's Univ, BA, 41, MA (Classics), 42; Univ Chicago, PhD (Greek Lang & Lit), 50; LLD(hon), Dalhousie Univ, 92; DLitt(hon), Univ Victoria, 93; LLD(hon), Queen's Univ, 95; LLD(hon), Univ Sask, 97. **CAREER** Lectr, Dalhousie Univ, 46-47; asst prof to assoc prof, Univ Sask, 47-58; assoc prof to prof, 58-84, dept head, 66-72, prof emer, Trinity Col, Univ Toronto, 84-, mem, sch grad stud, 84-90. **HONORS AND AWARDS** Fel, Royal Soc Can, 76. **MEMBERSHIPS** Class Asn Can; Am Philol Asn. **RESEARCH** Greek tragedy; Euripides; Aeschylus. **SELECTED PUBLICATIONS** Auth, Euripedean Drama, 67; auth, Aeschylus' 'Prometheus Bound': A Literary Study, 80; auth, Aeschylus' 'Oresteia': A Literary Commentary, 87; auth, Euripides' 'Alcestis': with Introduction, Translation and Commentary, 88; contribur, Sources of Dramatic Theory, vol 1, 91; contribur, Aeschylus: The Earlier Plays and Related Studies, 96. **CONTACT ADDRESS** Trinity Col, Univ of Toronto, 6 Hoskin Ave, 336 Larkin Bldg, Toronto, ON, Canada M5S 1H8. **EMAIL** djconacher@idirect.com

CONDON, WILLIAM
PERSONAL Born 03/28/1950, Athens, GA **DISCIPLINE** ENGLISH **EDUCATION** Univ of Ga, BA; Maimi Univ, MA; Brown, PhD. **CAREER** Assoc prof and dir, Wash State Univ. **HONORS AND AWARDS** Founding mem, Alliance for Comput and Writing. **MEMBERSHIPS** Past ch, Conf on Comput and Writing; mem, Exec Board, Coun of Writing Prog Adminrs; mem, WPA Consultant/Evaluator Panel. **RESEARCH** How portfolios contribute to writing across the curriculum and ways portfolios affect students' movement from one institution or school to another. **SELECTED PUBLICATIONS** Coauth, Portfolios in College Writing, 97; coauth, Writing the Information Highway, 97. **CONTACT ADDRESS** Dept of English, Washington State Univ, Avery 202, Pullman, WA 99164-5020. **EMAIL** bcondon@wsu.edu

CONGER, SYNDY MCMILLEN
PERSONAL Born 10/14/1942, Waterloo, IA, m, 1967 **DISCIPLINE** ENGLISH AND COMPARATIVE LITERATURE **EDUCATION** Univ Iowa, BA, 65; MA, 69; PhD, 76. **CAREER** Asst prof, 72-80, Assoc Prof, 80-84, Prof, English, 84-, ch, English & Journ Dept, Western Ill Univ, 98- . **HONORS AND AWARDS** Phi Beta Kappa, 64; Phi Kappa Phi, 82; Fulbright Fels (Germany), 73-74, 83-84; DAAD Fel, 82; NEH Summer Sem, 77, 81, 93; Newberry Library Fel, 89; ACLS travel grant, 89; Clifford Prize, Am Soc for 18th Century Studies, 86. **MEMBERSHIPS** MLA; Am Soc 18th Century Studies; N Am Soc for Study of Romanticism; NCTE **RESEARCH** Pros fiction; Gothic literature; 18th century Anglo-German literary relations; women's lit, 1680-1840. **SELECTED PUBLICATIONS** Auth, Matthew G. Lewis, Charles Robert Maturin, and the Germans, Arno Pr (New York, NY), 80; auth, "A German Ancestor for Mary Shelley's Monster: Kahlert, Schiller, and the Buried Treasure of Northanger Abbey," Philol Q 59; auth, "Hans Robert Jauss's 'Rezeptionsaesthetik' and England's Reception of Eighteenth Century German Literature," Eighteenth Century: Theory and Interpretation 22; auth, "Fellow Travellers: Eighteenth-Century Englishwomen and German Literature," Studies in Eighteenth Century Culture 14; auth, "The Sorrows of Young Charlotte: Werther's English Sisters 1785-1805," Goethe Yearbook 3; auth, "Another Secret of the Rue Morgue: Poe's Transformation of the 'Geisterseher' Motif," Studies in Short Fiction 24; auth, "Reading 'Lovers' Vows': Jane Austen's Reflections on English Sense andGerman Sensibility," Studies in Philol 85; auth, Mary Wollstonecraft and the Language of Sensibility, Fairleigh Dickinson Univ Pr, 94; auth, Prophecy and Sensibility: Mary Wollstonecraft in Frankenstein, 1650-1850: Ideas, Aesthetics, and Inquiries in the Early Modern Era,"AMS Pr, 97; auth, "Multivocality in Mary Shelley's Unfinished Biography of her Father," Europ Roman Rev 9. **CONTACT ADDRESS** Dept of English, Western Illinois Univ, 1 University Cir, Macomb, IL 61455-1390. **EMAIL** syndy_conger@ccmail.wiu.edu

CONLEY, KATHARINE
PERSONAL Born 08/10/1956, Washington, DC, m, 1997 **DISCIPLINE** LITERATURE, FRENCH **EDUCATION** Harvard Univ, BA, 79; Univ Colo, MA, 88; Univ Pa, MA, 90; PhD, 92. **CAREER** Asst prof to assoc prof, Dartmouth Col, 92-. **HONORS AND AWARDS** Whiting Found Travel Grant, 96; Jr Fac Fel, Dartmouth Col, 96; Burke Res Grant, Dartmouth Col, 92; Mellon Fel, 91-92. **MEMBERSHIPS** MLA; AATF; ACQS; WIF. **RESEARCH** Surrealism; Quebec fiction; writing by women. **SELECTED PUBLICATIONS** Auth, Automatic

Women, Nebr, 96; auth, Le Femme S'Entite: La Part du Feminin dans le Surrealisme, Pleine Marge, 98; auth, Robert Desnos pour l'am 2000, Gallimard, 00; auth, "Anamorphic Love: The Surrealist Poetry of Desire," in Desire Unbound, eds. Mundy, Ady (Tate Gallery, 01). **CONTACT ADDRESS** 334 Turnpike Rd, Norwich, VT 05055-9559. **EMAIL** katharine.conley@dartmouth.edu

CONLON, JOHN J.
PERSONAL Born 03/23/1945, Lowell, MA, m, 1973, 2 children **DISCIPLINE** ENGLISH **EDUCATION** Cath Univ, AB, 68; Tufts Univ, MA, 70, PhD, 74. **CAREER** Dir, Teacher Certification Prog and asst prof, 72-80, adjunct asst prof and asst dean, 80-83, assoc prof and assoc dean, 83-84, adjunct assoc prof and assoc dean, 84-90, lectr and assoc prof, Univ Mass, Boston, 90-. **HONORS AND AWARDS** Phi Beta Kappa; Woodrow Wilson Fel, 68; nomination: Univ Mass Chancellor's Distinguished Scholarship Awd, 83; Who's Who in the East, 92; Who's Who in Am Educ, 93; Dictionary of Int Biography, 94. **RESEARCH** Theatre: Elizabethan, 19th and 20th century. **SELECTED PUBLICATIONS** Auth, Walter Pater and the French Tradition, Bucknell Univ Press and Assoc Univ Presses (Lewisburg, PA and London), 82; auth, "Stanley Weintraub," in DLB, vol 111, American Literary Biographers, 2nd Series, ed Steven Serafin, (MI: Gale, 91), 285-299; auth, "The English Novel," in Critical Survey of Long Fiction: English Language Series, ed Frank N. Magill (91), 3779-3793; auth, "T. S. Eliot" in Magill's Survey of American Literature, ed F. N. Magill, (NY: Marshall Cavendish (91), 602-617; auth, "Appreciations (Pater)," "Walter Pater," "The Renaissance (Pater)," in The Eighteen-Nineties: An Encyclopedia, ed G. A. Cevasco, (NY: Garland, 93), 17-18, 453-454, 500-501; rev, of "Thomas Hardy on Stage," by Keith Wilson, ELT, 39:2 (96): 221-225; rev, of "Shaw, Lady Gregory, and the Abbey," by Laurence and Grene, ELT, 40:3 (97): 345-47; auth, "Literary Theory in the Age of Victoria," "Walter Pater," "Arthur Symons," in Encyclopedia of Literary Critics and Criticism, ed Chris Murray, (London: Fitzroy Dearborn, 99), 671-677, 829-832, 1071-1074. **CONTACT ADDRESS** Dept Theatre Arts, Univ of Massachusetts, Boston, 100 Morrissey Blvd, Dorchester, MA 02125-3300. **EMAIL** conlon@umb.edu

CONN, EARL LEWIS
PERSONAL Born 08/12/1927, Marion, IN, m, 1953, 6 children **DISCIPLINE** JOURNALISM **EDUCATION** Univ Ky, BA, 50; Ball State Univ, MS, 57; Ind Univ, Bloomington, DEd, 70. **CAREER** Staff writer, United Press, 50-51; wire ed, Chronicle-Tribune, Marion, Ind, 52-54; teacher jour & publ adv, Somerset High Sch, Ind, 54-57 & Richmond High Sch, 57-58; instr jour, Ball State Univ, 58-62; ed, Quaker Life, Friends United Meeting, 62-64; asst dir, Pub Info Serv, 64-65, from asst prof to assoc prof, 65-75, Prof Jour, 75-98, Dept Chair, 84-96, Dean, Col Of Commun, Infor, & Media, 96-98, Dean Emeritus, Ball State Univ, 98-. **HONORS AND AWARDS** Ind Jour Hall of Fame, 97; Ball State Jour Hall ot Fame, 97. **MEMBERSHIPS** Asn Educ in Jour; Oral Hist Asn; Soc Prof Journalists. **RESEARCH** Journalism history; media ethics; mass communications. **SELECTED PUBLICATIONS** Auth, Journalism 101 and the O.J. Trial, Ed & Publ, 11/11/95, and 5 Ind newspapers; Commotion over Court Ordered Ad, Ed & Publ, 4/27/96; Julie Andrews: Doing What She Loves, The Saturday Evening Post, May/June 96; Posthumous Victory, Ed & Publ, 2/28/97; author of numerous other articles. **CONTACT ADDRESS** Dept of Jour, Ball State Univ, 2000 W University, Muncie, IN 47306-0485. **EMAIL** 00elconn@bsu.edu

CONNELLY, MARK
PERSONAL Born 07/08/1951, Philadelphia, PA, s **DISCIPLINE** ENGLISH **EDUCATION** Carroll Col, BA, 73; Univ Wisc-Milwaukee, MA, 74, PhD, 84. **CAREER** Consult, Great Lakes Precision Products, 90-94; instr, Milwaukee Area Technical Col, 86-; Pres, Mark Connelly Productions, Inc, 2000-. **HONORS AND AWARDS** Annual Fiction Awd, Milwaukee Magazine, 82; First Place Annual Fiction Awd, Indiana Rev, 82. **MEMBERSHIPS** Modern Lang Asn, Irish Cultural and Heritage Center of Wisc, Treasurer. **RESEARCH** 19th and 20th century British and American literature, Irish Studies. **SELECTED PUBLICATIONS** Auth, The Diminished Self: Orwell and the Loss of Freedom, Duquesne Univ Press (87); auth, Orwell and Gissing, Peter Lang (97); auth, The Sundance Reader, Harcourt Col Pubs (97, 2nd ed, 2000); auth, The Sundance Writer, Harcourt Col Pubs (2000). **CONTACT ADDRESS** Dept English, Milwaukee Area Tech Col, 700 W State St, Milwaukee, WI 53233-1419'. **EMAIL** markconn@earthlink.net

CONNOLLY, JOY P. T.
PERSONAL Born 04/07/1970, Lowell, MA, s **DISCIPLINE** CLASSICS **EDUCATION** Princeton Univ, AB, 91; Univ Pa, MA, 95; PhD, 97. **CAREER** Asst prof, Univ Wash, 97-00; asst prof, Stanford Univ, 00-. **HONORS AND AWARDS** Simpson Center for the Humanities Fel, Univ Wash, 98; Fel, Stanford Univ, 99-00. **MEMBERSHIPS** Am Philol Asn; Class Asn of the Atlantic States. **RESEARCH** Greek and Roman rhetoric; Feminist theory; The ancient novel; Pastoral and elegy; Ancient education; Greek and Roman cultural relations. **SELECTED PUBLICATIONS** Auth, "Mastering corruption: constructions of identity in Roman oratory," in Women and Slaves in Greco-Roman Culture, 98; auth, "Asymptotes of pleasure: thoughts on the nature of Roman erotic elegy," Arethusa, (00): 71-98. **CONTACT ADDRESS** Dept Class, Stanford Univ, Main Quad, Bldg 20, Stanford, CA 94305-2080. **EMAIL** jptc@stanford.edu

CONNOLLY, THOMAS F.
PERSONAL Born 07/21/1960, Lynnfield, MA, m, 2000, 1 child **DISCIPLINE** ENGLISH **EDUCATION** Suffolk Univ BA, 83; Boston Univ MA, 86; Tufts Univ, PhD, 91. **CAREER** Mast lectr, Univ Ostrava, 86-95; asst prof, Suffolk Univ, 92-95; vis prof, Tufts Univ, 95, 00-; Fulbright prof, Univ Ostrava, 96-98; asst prof, Suffolk Univ, 98-; vis prof, Univ Ostrava, 99-. **HONORS AND AWARDS** Sr Fulbright Fel, 96-97; 97-98; Univ Ostrava Res Grnt, 96; US Info Agency Grnt, 96; Parliamentary Medal of the Czech Republic, 97. **MEMBERSHIPS** IFTR; ASTR; ALA; CSAS; Eugene O'Neill Soc. **RESEARCH** 19th-cen American theater; drama criticism; Central European culture; modern drama and theater historiography. **SELECTED PUBLICATIONS** Auth, George Jean Nathan and the Making of American Drama Criticism, Fairleigh Dickinson UP, 00; auth, British Aisles: Studies in English and Irish Drama and Theatre from Medieval Through Modern Times, Univ Ostrava Press, 98; contrb, Cambridge Guide to American Theatre, Cambridge UP, 93; contrb, Cassell Companion to 20th Century Theatre, Casswell, 01; contrb, International Dictionary of Theatre, St James, 92; contrb, Israel Horovitz: A Collection of Critical Essays, Greenwood, 94; contrb, Theatrical Spaces and Dramatic Places: The Reemergence of the Theatre Building in the Renaissance, Univ Ala, 96; contrb, Reflections on Ethival Values in Post(?) Modern American Literature, Univ Selesia Press, 00. **CONTACT ADDRESS** Eng Dept., Suffolk Univ, 41 Temple St, Boston, MA 02114. **EMAIL** tconnol@suffolk.edu

CONNOR, CAROLYN
PERSONAL Born 11/03/1943, Binghamton, NY, m, 1968, 2 children **DISCIPLINE** CLASSICS **EDUCATION** NY York Univ, PhD. **CAREER** Prof, Univ NC, Chapel Hill. **HONORS AND AWARDS** Hettleman Prize for Teaching and Scholarship, UNC-CH, 98. **MEMBERSHIPS** Medieval Acad of Am, Int Comt on Byzantine Studies Conf, Hagiography Soc, Col Art Assoc **RESEARCH** Byzantine art and civilization. **SELECTED PUBLICATIONS** Auth, Americans and the Unconscious, Oxford Univ, 86; auth, Religion and the Life Cycle, Fortress Press, 88; auth, Art and Miracles in Medieval Byzantium: The Crypt at Hosios Loukas and Its Frescoes, Princeton UP, 91; auth, New Perspectives on Byzantine Ivories, Gesta, Vol 30, 91; Hosios Loukas as a Victory Church, Greek, Roman and Byzantine Stud, Vol 33, 92; auth, Alternative Medicine and American Religious Life, Oxford Univ Press, 92; coauth, The Life and Miracles of Saint Luke of Steiris, A Translation and Commentary, Hellenic Col Orthodox Press, 94; auth, Naming the Antichrist, Oxford Univ Press, 95; auth, The Color of Ivory: Polychromy on Byzantive Ivories, Princeton Univ Press, 98; auth, Stairways to Heaven, Westview Press, 00. **CONTACT ADDRESS** Dept of Classics, Univ of No Carolina, Chapel Hill, CB#3145, Chapel Hill, NC 27599-3145. **EMAIL** clconnor@email.unc.edu

CONNOR, J. D.
PERSONAL Born 05/20/1970, Boston, MA, m, 1994, 1 child **DISCIPLINE** ENGLISH **EDUCATION** Harvard, BA, 92; Johns Hopkins, PhD, 00. **CAREER** Vis asst prof, Fordham, 00-01. **MEMBERSHIPS** MLA, ASA, SCS. **RESEARCH** Hollywood Cinema, Postwar American writing. **SELECTED PUBLICATIONS** Auth, "The Projections," Representations, (00). **EMAIL** connorjd@hotmail.com

CONNOR, JOAN
PERSONAL Born 01/21/1954, MA, d, 1 child **DISCIPLINE** ENGLISH **EDUCATION** Mount Holyoke Col, BA, 76; Middlebury Col, MA, 84; Vermont Col, MFA, 85. **CAREER** Workshop leader, Vt League of Writers, 94-95; Tutor, Okemo Mountain school, 94-95; Vis Prof to Asst Prof, Ohio Univ, 95-. **HONORS AND AWARDS** headlands Fel, 99; Philip Roth Fel, Buckness Univ, 95; Yaddo, 93; MacDowell colony, 92; The Richard Sullivan Prize, 99; Best of Vermont, ; John Simmons Awd, 97; The Ohio Writer contest, 96; Dark Valley Press Novella Chapbook competition, 95 **MEMBERSHIPS** AWP, Young Writers Inst. **RESEARCH** Hist Am Hucksters. **SELECTED PUBLICATIONS** auth, We Who Live Apart, Univ Mo Press, in press; auth, Here on Old Route 7, Univ Mo Press, in press; auth, "The Age of discovery," The spirit of Pregnancy, in press; auth, "Tolstoy's Daughter," women and Transitions anthology, in press; auth, "The Journalist," Millennium Watch anthology, in press; auth, "Baby, I'll Be Home for Halloween," Millennium Watch Anthology, in press; auth, "Florida," Timber Creek Review, 00; auth, "Writing the war Novel," Quarter After Eight, 99; auth, "And I Isolde," Arts and Letters, 099; auth, "The Parrot Man," The Journal, 00. **CONTACT ADDRESS** Dept English, Ohio Univ, 1 Ohio Univ, Athens, OH 45701-2942.

CONNOR, W. ROBERT
PERSONAL Born 08/30/1934, Worcester, MA, m, 1968, 2 children **DISCIPLINE** CLASSICS **EDUCATION** Hamilton Col, BA, 56; Princeton Univ, PhD, 61. **CAREER** Instr, Univ Mich, 60-63; asst prof to prof emeritus, Princeton Univ, 64-89; pres and dir, Nat Humanities Center, 89-. **HONORS AND AWARDS** Fulbright Fel, Univ Col Oxford, 56-57; Woodrow Wilson Fel; ACLS Fel; LHD Knox Col; LHD Hamilton Col; Behrman Award; Phi Beta Kappa. **MEMBERSHIPS** Am Philol Asn; Am Acad of Arts and Sci; Am Philos Soc. **RESEARCH** Athenian cultural history, classical period; Greek religion; Historiography. **SELECTED PUBLICATIONS** Auth, Thucydides, Princeton Univ Press, 84; auth, New Politicians of Fifth Century Athens, Princeton Press, 72. **CONTACT ADDRESS** Nat Humanities Center, 3017 Frank Perry Rd, Hillsborough, NC 27278. **EMAIL** connor@ga.unc.edu

CONOLLY, LEONARD W.
PERSONAL Born 09/13/1941, Walsall, England **DISCIPLINE** ENGLISH, DRAMA **EDUCATION** Univ Wales, BA, 63, PhD, 70; McMaster Univ, MA, 64. **CAREER** Instr, Univ Sask, 65-67; asst prof, 70-74, assoc prof, 74-79, prof, Univ Alta, 79-81; prof drama & dept ch, 81-86, acting dean arts, 86-87, vice pres acad, 88-92, acting vice pres acad, Univ Guelph, 92-93; pres & vice chancellor, 94-97, Prof English & Fellow, Catharine Parr Traill College, Trent Univ, 97-. **MEMBERSHIPS** Asn Can Theatre Res (pres, 77-79); Am Soc Theatre Res. **RESEARCH** English-Canadian drama; Canadian theatre history; censorship; 18th, 19th, and 20th century British theatre and drama, especially Shaw. **SELECTED PUBLICATIONS** Auth, The Censorship of English Drama 1737-1824, 76; coauth, English Canadian Theatre, 87; ed, Theatrical Touring and Founding in North America, 82; ed, Canadian Drama and the Critics, 87; co-ed, English Drama and Theatre 1800-1900, 78; co-ed, Nineteenth Century Theatre Research, 72-80; co-ed, Essays in Theatre, 82-89; co-ed, The Oxford Companion to Canadian Theatre, 89; co-ed, Bernard Shaw on Stage, 91; co-ed, The Encyclopedia of Post-Colonial Literatures in English, 94; gen ed, Selected Correspondence of Bernard Shaw; bd dir, World Encyclopedia of Contemporary Theatre (pres, 89-92). **CONTACT ADDRESS** Trent Univ, Catharine Parr Traill Col, Kerr House 205, Peterborough, ON, Canada K9J 7B8. **EMAIL** lconolly@trentu.ca

CONRAD, BRYCE D.
PERSONAL Born 09/09/1951, Palo Alto, CA, m, 1988, 2 children **DISCIPLINE** LITERATURE **EDUCATION** Univ Iowa, PhD, 88. **CAREER** Assoc prof, Tex Tech Univ; ed, William Carlos Williams Rev. **HONORS AND AWARDS** Fulbright scholar, 93-94. **MEMBERSHIPS** MLA; Fulbright Assoc; William Carlos Williams Soc. **RESEARCH** American modernism. **SELECTED PUBLICATIONS** Auth, Refiguring America: A Study of William Carlos Williams' In the American Grain. **CONTACT ADDRESS** Texas Tech Univ, Lubbock, TX 79409-3091. **EMAIL** bryce.conrad@ttu.edu

CONRAD, CHARLES R.
DISCIPLINE ORGANIZATIONAL COMMUNICATION, RHETORICAL THEORY **EDUCATION** Univ Kansas, PhD. **CAREER** Prof, Texas A&M Univ. **HONORS AND AWARDS** Southern Commun Journal's Outstanding Article Awd; Distinguished Tchg Awd, Asn Former Stud at Texas A&M Univ. **SELECTED PUBLICATIONS** Auth, Strategic Organizational Communication; ed, The Ethical Nexus; assoc ed, Quart J Speech. **CONTACT ADDRESS** Dept of Speech Communication, Texas A&M Univ, Col Station, College Station, TX 77843-4234.

CONRAD, KATHRYN A.
PERSONAL Born 07/03/1968, Grand Rapids, MI **DISCIPLINE** ENGLISH **EDUCATION** Univ Mich, BA, 90; Univ Pa, MA, 93; PhD, 96. **CAREER** Post-doctoral lectr, Univ Pa, 96-97; asst prof, 97-, Univ Ks. **HONORS AND AWARDS** NEH Younger Scholars Awd, 89; Jacob Javits Fel, 90; Nat Mellon Fel, 90-95; Dermot McGlinchey Awd for pioneering work in Irish stud, Irish Amer Cultural Inst, 95; ba with honors & high distinction; phi beta kappa. **MEMBERSHIPS** Modern Lang Assoc; Amer Conf for Irish Stud. **RESEARCH** Twentieth century Irish lit & culture; nationalism, sexuality, & gender. **SELECTED PUBLICATIONS** Coauth, Joyce and the Irish Body Politic: Sexuality and Colonization in Finnegans Wake, James Joyce Quart, 94; auth, Occupied Country: The Negotiation of Lesbianism in Irish Feminist Writing, Eire-Ireland, 96; coauth, Passing/Out: The Politics of Disclosure in Queer-Positive Pedagogy, Modern Lang Stud, 99; auth, Women Troubles, Queer Troubles: Gender, Sexuality, and the Politics of Selfhood in the Construction of the Northern Irish State, Reclaiming Gender: Transgressive Identities in Modern Ireland, St Martin's Press, 99. **CONTACT ADDRESS** Dept of English, Univ of Kansas, Lawrence, 2035 Wescoe Hall, Lawrence, KS 66044-2115. **EMAIL** kconrad@ukans.edu

CONSTANCE, JOSEPH
PERSONAL Born 04/16/1952, Montaul, MA, m, 1982, 2 children **DISCIPLINE** HISTORY, LIBRARY SCIENCE **EDUCATION** St. Michael's Col, BA (magna cum laude), 76; Univ VT, MA (Hist), 79; SUNY, Albany, MLS, 83; Boston Univ, PhD Candidate, 95-. **CAREER** Archivist and curator of Manuscripts, Soc of St. Edmund, Burlington, VT, 78-80; archivist and curator of Special Collections, Middle GA Hist Soc, Macon, 80-81; Univ archivist and curator of Rare Books, GA State Univ, Atlanta, 83-87; Head, Archives and Manuscripts Dept, John J. Burns Library of Special Collections, Chestnut

Hill, MA, 87-90; College Librarian, Saint Anselm Col, Manchester, NH, 90-. **SELECTED PUBLICATIONS** Auth, Time Management for Archivists, with Robert C. Dinwiddie in Provenance, fall 85; book reviewer for Library Journal, 83-. **CONTACT ADDRESS** Geisel Library, Saint Anselm Col, 87 St. Anselm Dr., Manchester, NH 03102-1323.

CONSTANTINOU, CONSTANTIA
DISCIPLINE MUSICOLOGY, LIBRARY SCIENCE **EDUCATION** CUNY, Queens College, BA, 87, MA, 91, MLS, 95. **CAREER** Asst, Avery Fisher Center for Multimedia, 91-92, ref assoc, 93, bibliog spec, 93, Elmer Bobst Libr, NY Univ; asst prof, act dir multimedia & elect svcs, CUNY, LaGuardia Community College, 95-96; dir, Arrigoni Libr, Iona Col, 96. **CONTACT ADDRESS** 36-54 Forest Ave, #3-R, Ridgewood, NY 11385. **EMAIL** cconstantinou@iona.edu

CONTE, JOSEPH
PERSONAL Born 05/22/1960, Newark, NJ, d **DISCIPLINE** ENGLISH **EDUCATION** Cornell Univ, BA, 82; Stanford Univ, PhD, 88. **CAREER** Asst prof, SUNY Buffalo, 88-92; assoc prof, 92-00. **HONORS AND AWARDS** Schl, Univ Siena, Italy, 81; Phi Beta Kappa, 81; Fel Human, 87-88; Fel, Lilly Found Teach, 91. **MEMBERSHIPS** MLA; NE MLA; ALA; SLS; Don Dehillo Soc; William Carlos Williams Soc; Wallace Stevens Soc. **RESEARCH** 20th C poetry and poetics; postmodern theory; postmodern fiction; Am literature. **SELECTED PUBLICATIONS** Auth, "Against the Calendar: Paul Blackburn's Journals" Sage 7 (88): 35-52; auth, "Seriality and the Contemporary Long Poem," Sagetrieb 11 (92): 35-45; auth, Unending Design: The Forms of Postmodern Poetry, Cornell Univ Press (Ithaca), 91; ed, Dictionary of Literary Biography 193: American Poets Since World War II, Gale Group (Detroit), 98; ed, Dictionary of Literary Biography 169: American Poets Since World War II, Gale Group (Detroit), 96; ed, Dictionary of Literary Biography 165: American Poets Since World War II, Gale Group (Detroit), 96; auth, Design and Debris: A Chaotics of Postmodern Fiction, Univ Alabama Press (Tuscaloosa), forthcoming; auth, "Natural Histories: Serial Form in the Later Poetry of Lorine Niedecker," in Loping Niedecker: Woman and Poet, ed. Jenny Penberthy (Orono, ME, Nat Poetry Found, 96), 345-60; auth. "The Smooth and the Striated: Compositional Texture in the Modem Long Poem," Modern Lang Studies 27 (97): 57-71. **CONTACT ADDRESS** Dept English, SUNY, Buffalo, PO Box 604610, Buffalo, NY 14260-4610. **EMAIL** jconte@acsu.buffalo.edu

CONWAY, GLENDA
PERSONAL Born 02/21/1953, Frankfort, KY, m, 1984, 2 children **DISCIPLINE** ENGLISH **EDUCATION** Univ Ky, BA, 75; MA, 79; Univ Louisville, PhD, 96. **CAREER** Asst Prof, Univ Montevallo, 96-. **HONORS AND AWARDS** Phi Kappa Phi, 97; Grad Dean's Citation, Univ Louisville, 97; Omicron Delta Kappa Hon Soc, 99. **MEMBERSHIPS** NCTE, CCCC, Southeastern Writing Ctr Asn, Nat Writing Ctr Asn. **RESEARCH** U S Supreme Court discouse, writing center theory and practice, composing processes of student writers. **SELECTED PUBLICATIONS** Auth, "What Are We Doing Today? Basic Writers Collaborating in a Computer Lab," Computers and Composition, 12 (95): 79-95; auth, "Judicial Constructions of Difference: The Supreme Court's Majority Opinions in Scot v Sandford and Bowers v Hardwick," Rhet, Cult Studies and Literacy: Selected Papers from the 1994 Conf of the Rhet Soc of Am, Lawrence Eribaum Assocs (95): 89-95; auth, "Reporting Writing Center Sessions to Faculty: Pedagogical and Ethical Considerations," Writing Lab Newsletter (98); auth, "Judging the Voice of the Law," Angelaki J of the Theoret Humanities, 4:1 (99): 159-172; auth, "Liberatory Tutoring in the Writing Center: It;'s Not Just for Radicals," Southern Discourse, 2:3 (99): 6-7, 10. **CONTACT ADDRESS** Dept English, Univ of Montevallo, PO Box 6000, Montevallo, AL 35115-6000. **EMAIL** conwayg@montevallo.edu

CONWELL, DAVID
PERSONAL Born 01/13/1959, Philadelphia, PA, m, 1992, 2 children **DISCIPLINE** CLASSICAL STUDIES **EDUCATION** Trinity Col, BA, 82; Univ Pa, PhD, 92. **CAREER** Instr, Baylor School, 95-. **HONORS AND AWARDS** NEH Teacher Exchange Fel, 97. **MEMBERSHIPS** Archaeol Inst of Am; Am Philol Asn; Classical Asn of the Midwest and South. **RESEARCH** Archaeology of Cyprus, Greece, and Italy; Ancient fortifications; Art history. **SELECTED PUBLICATIONS** Auth, "The White Poros Wall on the Athenian Pnyx: Character and Context," in The Pnyx in the Hist of Athens, 96; "Rediscovering the Athenian Long Walls," in Am School of Class Studies Newsletter, 95; "Topography and Toponyms between Athens and Piraeus," in J of Ancient Topography, 93. **CONTACT ADDRESS** Baylor School, P O Box 1337, Signal Mountain, TN 37377. **EMAIL** david_conwell@baylor.chattanooga.net

COOGAN, DAVID
DISCIPLINE ENGLISH LITERATURE **EDUCATION** State Univ NYork, PhD, 95. **CAREER** Instr. **SELECTED PUBLICATIONS** Auth, pubs in Computers and Composition. **CONTACT ADDRESS** Dept of Humanities, Illinois Inst of Tech, 3301 S Dearborn, Chicago, IL 60616. **EMAIL** coogan@charlie.cns.iit.edu

COOK, ELEANOR
PERSONAL Born Toronto, ON, Canada **DISCIPLINE** ENGLISH **EDUCATION** Univ Toronto, BA, 54, PhD, 67. **CAREER** Lectr, Univ BC, 58-59; asst prof to assoc prof, 67-84, Prof Victoria Col, Univ Toronto 85-. **HONORS AND AWARDS** Jr fel, Can Asn Women, 54; A.S.P. Woodhouse Thesis Prize, 68; Connaught fel, 94; Guggenheim fel, 94; Killiam fel, 95. **MEMBERSHIPS** Royal Soc Can; Massey Col. **SELECTED PUBLICATIONS** Auth, Browning's Lyrics: An Exploration, 74; auth, Centre and Labyrinth: Essays in Honour of Northrop Frye, 83; auth, Poetry, Word-Play and Word-War in Wallace Stevens, 88. **CONTACT ADDRESS** Dept of English, Victoria Col, Univ of Toronto, Toronto, ON, Canada M5S 3K1.

COOK, ELIZABETH HECKENDORN
DISCIPLINE EIGHTEENTH-CENTURY BRITISH AND FRENCH LITERATURE **EDUCATION** Stanford Univ, PhD, 90. **CAREER** Assoc Prof, Eng, Univ Calif, Santa Barbara. **RESEARCH** Intersection of natural history; Landscape aesthetics; Property law in the period 1789-1832. **SELECTED PUBLICATIONS** Auth, "The Limping Woman and the Public Sphere," Body and Text in the Eighteenth Century, Stanford Univ Press, 94; Epistolary Bodies: Gender and Genre in the Eighteenth-Century Republic of Letters, Stanford Univ Press, 96. **CONTACT ADDRESS** Dept of Eng, Univ of California, Santa Barbara, Santa Barbara, CA 93106-7150. **EMAIL** ecook@humanitas.ucsb.edu

COOK, ERWIN
PERSONAL Born 04/27/1957, Edinburgh, Scotland, 1 child **DISCIPLINE** CLASSICS **EDUCATION** Univ Calif, Berkeley, MA, 85, PhD, 90. **CAREER** Asst prof, Univ Texas, Austin, 90-93, 94-96; vis assoc prof, 93-94, assoc prof, Johns Hopkins, 97-, UT-Austin. **MEMBERSHIPS** Am Philol Asn; Classical Asn of the Midwest and South. **RESEARCH** Epic poetry, Greek religion, mythology, archaic Greek history. **SELECTED PUBLICATIONS** Auth, A Note on the Text of Sextus Empiricus, Adv. Math, Hermes, 91; auth, Ferrymen of Elysium and the Homeric Phaeacians, J of Indo-European Stud, 92; auth, Some Remarks on Odyssey 3.2 16-38, Class Philol, 94; auth, The Odyssey in Athens: Myths of Cultural Origins, Cornell, 95; auth, rev, Homer: His Art and His World, by Latacz, Bryn Mawr Class Rev, 96; auth, Heroism, Suffering and Change, Proceedings of a Conference Sponsored by the Smithsonian Institution and the Society for the Preservation of the Greek Heritage, 98; auth, Active and Passive Heroics in the Odyssey, Classical World 93:2 (99): 149-67; rev, The Returns of Odysseus: Colonization and Ethnicity, by I. Malkin, (Berkeley, 98), Bryn Mawr Class Rev 00. **CONTACT ADDRESS** Dept of Classics, Univ of Texas, Austin, 123 WAG, Austin, TX 78212. **EMAIL** efcook@mail.utexas.edu

COOK, JAMES WYATT
PERSONAL Born 09/08/1932, Hickman, KY, m, 1954, 3 children **DISCIPLINE** ENGLISH **EDUCATION** Wayne State Univ, BA, 54, PhD, 64; Univ Mich, MA, 55. **CAREER** From instr to assoc prof, 62-74, chmn dept, 71-77, Langbo Trustees' Prof English, Albion Col, 75-, Great Lakes Cols Asn grant, 64-66; Shell grant, 66; consult, Educ Methods Inc, 65-67 & Univ Mich Ctr Prog Instr Bus, 66-68; Carnegie Found & Great Lakes Cols grant, 67; pres, Validated Instr Assoc, 73-81; grad dean, Walden Univ, 75-77; Newberry fel, 77, 86, 89; Nat Endowment for Hum grant, 81; CRRS Fel, Pontifical Inst Medieval Studies Fel, Univ Toronto, 81-82; Founding Dir, Albion Col Prog, Venice, Italy, 98-99. **MEMBERSHIPS** MLA; Mediaeval Soc Am; ASECS, Ren. Soc Am. **RESEARCH** Petrarch; Medieval language and literature; Chaucer. **SELECTED PUBLICATIONS** Auth, Augustinian neurosis and therapy of orthodoxy, Universitas, Wayne State Univ, spring 64; Poetry: Method and Meaning, Educ Methods, 68; Chaucer's Canterbury Art: Echoes and Reflections, Writer's Workshop, Calcutta, 76; Helping the hard to serve, Can Jour of Spec Educ, 76; That she was out of all charitee: Point, counterpoint in Chaucer's Wife of Bath's Tale, Chaucer Rev, 78; Toward making a new English verse canzoniere, Yale Ital Studies, 80; Petrarch's mirrors of love and hell, Ital Cult, 82; transl and ed, The Autobiography of Lorenzo Di Medici, MRTS, 94; Petrarch's Songbook, MRTS, 95; Florentine Drama for Convent and Festival, Univ Chicago, 96; Founding dir, Albion col program in Venice Italy, 98 & 99. **CONTACT ADDRESS** Dept of English, Albion Col, 611 E Porter St, Albion, MI 49224-1831. **EMAIL** JCOOK@ALBION.EDU

COOK, SMALLEY MIKE
PERSONAL Born 03/10/1939, Chicago, IL **DISCIPLINE** THEATER **EDUCATION** Univ of Massachusetts, MA 1972; Union Grad Sch, PhD 1977. **CAREER** Image Alliance, Writer/Producer, 74-; Univ of Iowa, Prof of Drams, 87-. **MEMBERSHIPS** Consultant Chicago Urban League 1973-; consultant Chicago Dept of Cultural Affairs 1983-; founder Dramatic Arts Repertory Ensemble for Youth 1986-. **SELECTED PUBLICATIONS** Writer-producer "Drums of the Night Gods," staged, Los Angeles Cultural Ctr 1981; Goodman Theatre Chicago 1983, Chicago Cultural Ctr 1983; writer-producer "The Fire and the Storm" Lindblom Park Dist Chicago 1986. **CONTACT ADDRESS** Drama, Univ of Iowa, 303 English-Philosophy Bldg, Iowa City, IA 52242.

COOK, STEPHAN H.
DISCIPLINE ENGLISH **EDUCATION** Marquette Univ, PhD, 78. **CAREER** Instr, Marquette Univ, 73-75; lectr, Univ Calif, 78-80; prof, 96-. **HONORS AND AWARDS** Tchr yr, 86. **RESEARCH** Writing; art & lit; Eng romantic writers. **SELECTED PUBLICATIONS** Auth, Screenplaying: Seeing and Saying in Hart Crane, Santa Barbara Rev, 96; No Place for Paragraphs: The Correspondence Between Hart Crane and Waldo Frank, Whitston Press, 95; Purchasers of Heaven: Painting, Photography and Hart Crane, Iris Stud, 95; Peter Pan in Hell, Fac Dialogue, 87; Pulling Back the Water Ahead, Santa Barbara Rev, 93; Playing at the Father's Art, Santa Barbara Rev, 93; rev, Noah Ben Shea, The Word, Santa Barbara News Press, 95; Edward Brunner, Splendid Failure: Hart Crane & The Making of The Bridge, Christianity and Lit, 87; David Jasper, Coleridge as Poet and Religious Thinker, Christianity and Lit, 86. **CONTACT ADDRESS** Dept of Eng, Westmont Col, 955 La Paz Rd, Santa Barbara, CA 93108-1099.

COOK, SUSAN L.
PERSONAL Born 12/22/1949, Toledo, OH, s, 2 children **DISCIPLINE** HUMAN COMMUNICATIONS **EDUCATION** Univ Denver, PhD, 97. **CAREER** Adj Fac, Metro State Col of Denver, 93-; Asst Prof, James Madison Univ, 87-98; Asst Prof, Gonzaga Univ, 98-. **HONORS AND AWARDS** Cum laude (BA); All Am Schol (Master's Prog); Phi Kappa Gamma. **MEMBERSHIPS** NCA; ICA; STC; ATTW; ABC. **RESEARCH** Cognition and communication; technology and cognition. **SELECTED PUBLICATIONS** Coauth, The Failure to Communicate: Restructuring Telecommunications Based Services and our Perceptions about Them, Int Telecommunications Union: Telecom 95 - Technol Su Summit, 95; auth, The Psychological and Sociological Characteristics of E-mail, Regional Conf As Asn Bus Communicators, 96; Reflecting Upon the Rhetorical Concept of Inventio and Poster's Mode of Information, Regional Conf Int Commun Asn, 97; Coming Home to Orality: Oral Residue in an Online Dialogue Across Time, Regional Conf Nat Commun Asn, 97; Lessons We Have Learned About Persuasion: Hitler's Ten Steps for Persuading, Regional Conf Nat Commun Asn, 98. **CONTACT ADDRESS** Dept of Commun, Gonzaga Univ, 502 E Boone Ave, Spokane, WA 99258. **EMAIL** cook@calvin.gonzaga.edu

COOKE, THOMAS D.
PERSONAL Born 03/16/1933, Kansas City, MO, m, 1985, 2 children **DISCIPLINE** MEDIEVAL LITERATURE AND FILM **EDUCATION** Univ Pittsburgh, PhD, 70. **CAREER** Prof. **HONORS AND AWARDS** Mellon Fellom, ACLS & NEH grants. **RESEARCH** Comedy and tragedy with an emphasis on American movies; medieval literature; film; comedy and tragedy. **SELECTED PUBLICATIONS** Pub on, Old French fabliaux, Chaucer and 14th century lit; auth, Medieval fabliaux, miracles of the Virgin, tales. **CONTACT ADDRESS** Dept of English, Univ of Missouri, Columbia, 107 Tate Hall, Columbia, MO 65211. **EMAIL** cooked@pcisys.net

COOKS, LEDA M.
PERSONAL Born 08/15/1965, Lakeland, FL **DISCIPLINE** COMMUNICATION **EDUCATION** Ohio Univ, PhD, 93. **CAREER** Asst prof, 93-, Univ Ma. **HONORS AND AWARDS** Fulbright Res/Lect fel, Panama, 97. **MEMBERSHIPS** Nat Comm Asn; Int Asn for Conflict Management; Latin Am Stud Asn; Eastern Comm Asn; Oral Hist Asn. **RESEARCH** Intercultural communication; int training and development; commun ed. **SELECTED PUBLICATIONS** Coauth, A Phenomenological Inquiry into the Relationship Between Perceived Coolness and Interpersonal Competence, Interpretive Approaches to Interpersonal Communication, SUNY Press, 94;coauth, The Dilema of Ethics in the Field of Mediation, Mediation Quart, 12, 94; coauth, Teaching Dispute Mediation from a Communication Perspective: Exploring the Practice and the Paradoxes, Focus on Legal Stud, 9 (2), Am Bar Asn, 94; coauth, Gender and Power, Gender, Power & Comm in Human Relationships, Lawrence Erlbaum Assocs, 95; auth, Putting Mediation in Context, Negotiation J, 11, 95; coauth, Northern Exposure's Sense of Place: Constructing and Marginalizing the Matriarchal Community, Women's Stud in Communication, 18 (2), 95; coauth, Giving Voice to Sexual Harassment: Dialogues in the Aftermath of the Hill-Thomas Hearings, The Lynching of Language, Univ IL Press, 96; auth, Warriors, Wampum, Gaming and Glitter: Foxwoods Casino and the Representation of Post Modern Native Identity, Readings in Cultural Contexts, Mayfield Pub, 98. **CONTACT ADDRESS** Dept of Communications, Univ of Massachusetts, Amherst, 315 Machmer Hall, Amherst, MA 01003. **EMAIL** Leda@comm.umass.edu

COOLEY, DENNIS O.
PERSONAL Born 08/27/1944, Estevan, SK, Canada **DISCIPLINE** LITERATURE **EDUCATION** Univ Sask, BEd, 66, BA, 67, MA, 68; Univ Rochester, PhD, 71. **CAREER** Prof, St. John's Col, Univ Manitoba, 73-. **HONORS AND AWARDS** Olive Beatrice Stanton Awd for excellence in teaching; Univ of Manitoba Outreach Awd. **RESEARCH** Canadian and Am lit, especially contemporary poetry, poetics, prairie writing, and theory. **SELECTED PUBLICATIONS** Auth, Leaving, 80; auth, Fielding, 83; auth, Bloody Jack, 84; auth, Soul Searching, 87; auth, The Vernacular Muse, 87; auth, Dedications, 88; auth,

Goldfinger, 95; ed, Draft, 80; ed, RePlacing, 91; ed, Eli Mandel and His Works, 91; ed, Inscriptions: A Prairie Poetry Anthology, 92. **CONTACT ADDRESS** St. John's Col, Univ of Manitoba, Winnipeg, MB, Canada R3T 2M5. **EMAIL** dcooley@cc.umanitoba.ca

COOLEY, NICOLE R.

PERSONAL Born 10/01/1966, Iowa City, IA, m, 1994, 1 child **DISCIPLINE** ENGLISH AND CREATIVE WRITING **EDUCATION** Brown Univ, BA, 88; Univ IA, MFA, 90; Emory Univ, PhD, 96. **CAREER** Asst prof, Bucknell Univ, 97-99; asst prof, Queens Col, CUNY, 99-. **HONORS AND AWARDS** Grad Sch Fel, 90-94; NEA Grnt, 96; Creat Perf Arts Fel, 99; Pres Res Fel, 01; Walt Whitman Awd, 95. **MEMBERSHIPS** MLA. **RESEARCH** Twentieth C Am women writers, contemporary poetry. **SELECTED PUBLICATIONS** Auth, Resurrection, LSU P, 96; auth, Judy Garland, Ginger Love, Harper Collins, 98. **CONTACT ADDRESS** Eng Dept, Queens Col, CUNY, 65-30 Kissena Blvd, Flushing, NY 11367. **EMAIL** ncooley@qc.edu

COOLEY, PETER JOHN

PERSONAL Born 11/19/1940, Detroit, MI, m, 1965, 3 children **DISCIPLINE** POETRY **EDUCATION** Shimer Col, BA, 62; Univ Chicago, MA, 64; Univ Iowa, PhD, 70. **CAREER** Assoc prof creative writing, Univ Wis, Green Bay, 70-75; prof creative writing, Tulane Univ, 75-, Poetry ed, NAm Rev, 70-00. **HONORS AND AWARDS** Robert Frost Fellowship, Beidlorf Writers' Conf Fellowship, Division of the Arts, La. **MEMBERSHIPS** Poetry Soc Am; MLA; Assoc Writing Prog. **RESEARCH** Poetry writing. **SELECTED PUBLICATIONS** Auth, The Company of Strangers (poems), Univ Mo, 75; The Room Where Summer Ends (poems), Nightseasons, Carnegie-Mellon Univ, 79; The Van Gogh Notebooks (poems); Sacred Conversations (poems). **CONTACT ADDRESS** Dept of English, Tulane Univ, 6823 St Charles Ave, New Orleans, LA 70118-5698. **EMAIL** cooley@mailhost.tcs.tulane.edu

COOLEY, THOMAS WINFIELD

PERSONAL Born 06/24/1942, Gaffney, SC, m, 1989, 1 child **DISCIPLINE** AMERICAN LITERATURE, AMERICAN STUDIES **EDUCATION** Duke Univ, BA, 64; Ind Univ, Bloomington, MA, 68, PhD(English), 70. **CAREER** Asst prof, 70-79, Assoc Prof English, Ohio State Univ, 80-99; Prof of English, 00. **HONORS AND AWARDS** NEH Research grants; U.S. State Dept "Participant", Australia, New Zealand, and Taiwan; Exec Comnr of Am Lit Section of MLA. **MEMBERSHIPS** MLA. **RESEARCH** American literature; autobiography; psychology of narrative; composition. **SELECTED PUBLICATIONS** Auth, Educated Lives: The Rise of Modern Autobiography in America, Columbus: OSU Press, 76; auth, The Norton Sampler, New York: Norton 97; auth, The Norton Critical Edition of Huckleberry Finn, New York: Norton, 99; auth, The Ivory Leg in the Ebony Cabinet: Madness, Race, and Gender in Victorian America, Univ of MA Press, 01; auth, The Selected Letters of Sophia Hawthorne, Ohio State Univ Press; auth, American Literature, Twentieth-Century Literature, College Composition and Communication, Ohio History. **CONTACT ADDRESS** Dept of English, Ohio State Univ, Columbus, 164 W 17th Ave, Columbus, OH 43210-1326. **EMAIL** Cooley.1@osu.edu

COOLEY, TIMOTHY

PERSONAL Born 10/15/1962, Norfolk, VA **DISCIPLINE** ETHNOMUSICOLOGY **EDUCATION** Wheaton Conserv Music, Wheaton Col (Ill), B Mus, 85; Northwestern Univ, M Music, 87; Brown Univ, PhD, 99. **CAREER** Adjunct Instr, Rhode Island Col, 95-98; Lectr, Univ Cal, 98-. **HONORS AND AWARDS** Wilk Prize for Res in Polish Music, 97, for Authentic Troupes and Inauthentic Tropes; Polish Music Reference Center, Univ S Cal-Los Angeles; Graduate Fel, 97, Brown Univ, 97; James T Koetting Prize, 96, for Authenticity on Trial in Polish Contest Festivals; Northeast Chapter, Soc for Ethnomusicol Int Res and Exchanges Board: Individual Advanced Res Fel in Eastern Europ Studies, Poland, 94-95; Am Council of Learned Societies: Predissertation Travel Grant Program in Eastern European Studies, Poland, 1992, East European Language Training Grant, Poland, 1993; Polish Am Teachers Asn: Summer Sessions Scholarship, Jagiellonian Univ, Poland, 1993; Kosciuszko Found: Summer Sessions Scholarship, Jagiellonian Univ, Krakow, Poland, 1992, 2) Study Abroad Scholarship, Inst of Art, Polish Acad of Sciences, Warsaw, Poland, 1994, 3) Dissertation writing grant, 95-96; Pi Kappa Lambda, 87; Presser Scholar; Wheaton Col Conservatory, 84-85; Nat Asn of Teachers of Singing, First Place, performance competition, 84. **MEMBERSHIPS** Soc for Ethnomusicol; Am Musicol Soc; Int Coun for Traditional Music; Am Folklore Soc. **RESEARCH** Music cult Eastern Europe, Middle East, Oceania, Multicult Am, Ethnicity. **SELECTED PUBLICATIONS** Music of the Polish Tatra Mountain Gorale in Chicago, forthcoming; Am Musical Atlas, ed Jeff Todd Titon, Schirmer Books; United States of America, European-Am music, Polish, forthcoming, Janice Kleeman; In The New Grove Dictionary of Music and Musicians, rev ed; Macmillan; Authentic Troupes and Inauthentic Tropes, 98; Polish Music J, Online, 1(1), Univ S Cal; Shadows in the Field: An Introduction, 97; co-ed, In Shadows in the Field: New Perspectives for Fieldwork in Ethnomusicology, Oxford Univ Press; co-ed, Shadows in the Field: New Perspectives for Fieldwork in Ethnomusicology, 97, Oxford Univ Press; Dance, Ritual, and Music, 95; asst ed, Warsaw: Inst of Art, Polish Acad of Sciences; Fire in the Mountains: Polish Mountain Fiddle Music, v1, The Karol Stoch Band. CD with extensive notes, Shanachie Entertainment Corp, 97; Fire in the Mountains: Polish Mountain Fiddle Music, v2; The Great Highland Bands, CD with extensive notes, Shanachie Entertainment Corp, 97; Polish Village Music: Historic Polish-American Recordings 1927-1933, CD song transcriptions and translations, Arhoolie Productions, Inc, 95; auth, "Folk Festival as Modern Ritual in the Polish Tatra Mountains," The World of Music, 41, 3, (99): 31-55; auth, "Creating an 'Authentic' Folk Music of the Polish Tatras," in After Chopin: Essays in Polish Music, ed Maria Anna Harley, Polish Music History Series, Vol 6, forthcoming. **CONTACT ADDRESS** Dept of Music, Univ of California, Santa Barbara, Santa Barbara, CA 93106-6070. **EMAIL** cooley@humanitas.ucsb.edu

COOLIDGE, ARCHIBALD CARY, JR.

PERSONAL Born 06/09/1928, Oxford, England, m, 1951, 7 children **DISCIPLINE** ENGLISH **EDUCATION** Harvard Univ, BA, 51; Brown Univ, MA, 54, PhD, 56. **CAREER** Teacher, NY, 46-47; PROF, ENGLISH, UNIV OF IOWA, 74-. **HONORS AND AWARDS** Phi Beta Kappa. **RESEARCH** English novel; Greek drama; story form; English history. **SELECTED PUBLICATIONS** Auth, Beyond the Fatal Flaw: A Study of the Neglected Forms of Greek Drama, Maecenas Press, 80; auth, English Laws and American Problems, 95; auth, Charles Dickens as Serial Novelist, Iowa State Univ Press, 67; auth, A Theory of Story, Maecenas Press, 89; auth, Political Metaphors, Maecenas Press, 00. **CONTACT ADDRESS** Dept of English, Univ of Iowa, Iowa City, IA 52242. **EMAIL** archibald-coolidge@uiowa.edu

COOLIDGE, JOHN STANHOPE

PERSONAL Born 07/26/1926, Laramie, WY, m, 1964, 2 children **DISCIPLINE** ENGLISH AND COMPARATIVE LITERATURE **EDUCATION** Harvard Univ, BA, 49, MA, 51, PhD(English), 57. **CAREER** Instr English, Swarthmore Col, 56-60; asst prof, 60-67, assoc prof, 67-80, Prof English, Univ Calif, Berkeley, 80-, Huntington Libr grant-in-aid, 64-65. **MEMBERSHIPS** MLA; Renaissance Soc Am; NCTE. **RESEARCH** Puritanism and the Bible; influence of classical on later literature. **SELECTED PUBLICATIONS** Auth, Fielding and conservation of character, 5/60 & Marvell and Horace, 11/65, Mod Philol; Great things and small: The Virgilian progression, Comp Lit, winter 65. **CONTACT ADDRESS** Dept of English, Univ of California, Berkeley, Berkeley, CA 94720.

COONFIELD, W. A.

PERSONAL Born 01/22/1929, TX, m, 1951, 5 children **DISCIPLINE** ENGLISH, AMERICAN LITERATURE **EDUCATION** Univ NM, BA, 51; Univ Southern Cal, MS, 72; Cal State Univ, MA, 80; Columbia Pacific Univ, PhD, 84. **CAREER** Bus tech writer, 56-; instr, LA Pierce Col, 64-; instr, Sec LA United Sch Dist, 72-94. **MEMBERSHIPS** Soc Tech Writers Pub. **SELECTED PUBLICATIONS** Auth of company style manuals; sci and bus tech reports; tech proposals. **CONTACT ADDRESS** Dept English, Los Angeles Pierce Col, 6201 Winnetka Ave, Woodland Hills, CA 91371-0001.

COOPER, G. BURNS

PERSONAL Born Morristown, NJ, m **DISCIPLINE** ENGLISH **EDUCATION** Yale Univ, BA, 83; Univ Tex, MA, 86; PhD, 89. **CAREER** Visiting Asst Prof, Univ Ky, 89-90; Asst Prof, Univ Alaska, 90-97. **MEMBERSHIPS** Mod Lang Asn, Linguistic Soc of Am. **RESEARCH** Poetics; Intonation; Dialects. **SELECTED PUBLICATIONS** Auth, Mysterious Music: Rhythm and Free Verse, Stanford Univ Press, 98. **CONTACT ADDRESS** Dept English, Univ of Alaska, Fairbanks, PO Box 755720, Fairbanks, AK 99775-5720. **EMAIL** ffgbc@uaf.edu

COOPER, JOHN REX

PERSONAL Born 05/14/1932, Edmonton, AB, Canada, m, 1993, 2 children **DISCIPLINE** ENGLISH LITERATURE **EDUCATION** State Univ NYork, Albany, AB, 54; Yale Univ, MA, 57, PhD, 62. **CAREER** Inst, Lit and Humanities, Univ Chicago, 61-63; Asst Prof, Lit and Humanities, Univ Chicago, 63-67; Assoc Prof ,Lit and Humanities, Reed College, 67-70; Assoc Prof, English, Portland State Univ, 70-73; Prof, English, Portland State Univ, 73-00; Dept Head ,English, Portland State Univ, 81-88. **HONORS AND AWARDS** Kappa Phi Kappa **MEMBERSHIPS** AAUP **RESEARCH** Seventeenth century literature; Shakespeare; Metrical theory. **SELECTED PUBLICATIONS** Auth, The Art of the Compleat Angler, Duke Univ, 68; art, Shylock's humanity, Shakespeare Quart, 69; auth, Intonation and Iambic Pentameter, PLL, papers on language & literature, 97. **CONTACT ADDRESS** Dept of English, Portland State Univ, PO Box 751, Portland, OR 97207-0751. **EMAIL** cooperrohe@earthlink.net

COOPER, MARILYN MARIE

PERSONAL Born 07/19/1945, Detroit, MI **DISCIPLINE** LITERARY AND COMPOSITION THEORY **EDUCATION** Pa State Univ, BA, 67; Univ Mich, MA, 68; Univ Minn, PhD(-English), 80. **CAREER** Asst Prof English, Univ Southern Calif, 79-. **MEMBERSHIPS** MLA; Ling Soc Am; NCTE. **RESEARCH** Conversational behavior in contemporary drama; structure of expository texts; contemporary theory. **SELECTED PUBLICATIONS** Auth, Moments of Argument--Agonistic Inquiry and Confrontational Cooperation, Col Composition and Commun, Vol 0048, 97. **CONTACT ADDRESS** Dept of English, Univ of So California, Los Angeles, CA 90007.

COOPER, VIRGINIA W.

DISCIPLINE COMMUNICATIONS **EDUCATION** Univ Wash; PhD, 81. **CAREER** Dominion Univ. **MEMBERSHIPS** Speech Comm Asn; Int Comm Asn; World Comm Asn **SELECTED PUBLICATIONS** Auth, Participant and Observer Attribution of Affect in Interpersonal Communication: An Examination of Noncontent Verbal Behavior." Jour Nonverbal Behavior, 87; The Tactile Communication System: State of the Art and Research Perspectives, in Progress in Communication Sciences, Ablex Publ Corp, 88; The Measurement of Conflict Interaction Intensity: Observer and Participant Perceived Dimensions, Human Relations, 94; The Disguise of Self-Disclosure: The Relationship Ruse of a Soviet Spy, Jour Applied Com Res, 96. **CONTACT ADDRESS** Dept of Communication, Old Dominion Univ, 4100 Powhatan Ave, Norfolk, VA 23508.

COOREN, FRANCOIS

PERSONAL Born 11/10/1965, Lille, France, s **DISCIPLINE** COMMUNICATION **EDUCATION** Univ Lille, MA; Univ Montreal, PhD, 96. **CAREER** Res Asst Prof, Univ Cincinnati, 97-98; Asst Prof, SUNY, 98-. **HONORS AND AWARDS** W. Charles Redding Awds, Intl Comm Asn, 96. **MEMBERSHIPS** Intl Comm Asn, Nat Comm Asn, Intl Pragmatics Asn. **RESEARCH** Organizational communication, Semiotics, Rhetoric, Philosophy of Language. **SELECTED PUBLICATIONS** auth, "Toward a New Ideal Speech situation: A critique of Habermas' Reinterpretation of Speech Act Theory," Quarterly Journal of Speech, in press; auth, "Applying Socio-Semiotics to Organizational Communication. A New Approach," Management Communication Quarterly, (990: 294-304; auth, "The Procedural and Rhetorical Modes of the Organizing Dimension of Communication. Discursive Analysis of a Parliamentary Commission," Communication Review, (98): 65-101; auth, "Understanding the Distribution of Enablements and constraints in Computerized Settings: A socio-semiotic Analysis of Interobjectivity," Communication Review, (98): 125-164; auth, The Organizing Dimension of Communication, John Benjamins Pub, 00; auth, "Association and dissociation in an Ecological controversy: The Great Whale Case," in Technical communication, Deliberative Rhetoric, & Environmental Discourse, Ablex, 00; **CONTACT ADDRESS** Dept Comm, SUNY, 1400 Washington Ave, Albany, NY 12222-0100. **EMAIL** fcooren@csc.albany.edu

COPE, KEVIN

DISCIPLINE RESTORATION & 18TH C. SATIRE, BIBLIOGRAPHY, ENLIGHTENMENT PHILOSOPHICA **EDUCATION** Harvard, PhD, 80. **CAREER** Prof, La State Univ. **RESEARCH** Early modern era; John Locke; enlightenment philosophical texts. **SELECTED PUBLICATIONS** Auth, A Roman Commonwealth of Knowledge: Fragments of Belief and the Disbelieving Power of Didactic, Stud in 18th-Century Cult, 90; Conversations Containing Truth: Dialogues with Berkeley's Lying God, Man and Nature/L'Homme et la Nature, 90; Gothic Novel as Social Contract: Locke, Shaftesbury, and Walpole and the Casual Annexation of the Supernatural, The Age of Johnson, 90; Criteria of Certainty: Truth and Judgement in the English Enlightenment, 90; ed, Enlightening Allegory: Theory, Practice, and Contexts of Allegory in the Late Seventeenth and Eighteenth Centuries, 91; Compendious Conversations: The Method of Dialogue in the Early Enlightenment, 92. **CONTACT ADDRESS** Dept of Eng, Louisiana State Univ, 210J Allen Hall, Baton Rouge, LA 70803. **EMAIL** plushtoy@bellsouth.net

COPEK, PETER JOSEPH

PERSONAL Born 05/28/1945, Chicago, IL **DISCIPLINE** ENGLISH **EDUCATION** Loyola Univ, Chicago, BS, 67; Northwestern Univ, Chicago, MA, 69, PhD, 73. **CAREER** Asst prof, 72-77, assoc prof English, Ore State Univ, 77-; Dir, Ctr for the Humanities, 84-, fel, Rockefeller found, 75-76. **MEMBERSHIPS** MLA; Soc for Cinema Stud; Consortium for Humanities Ctrs and Inst. **RESEARCH** The English novel; literature and society; film. **CONTACT ADDRESS** Dept of English, Oregon State Univ, 238 Moreland Hall, Corvallis, OR 97331-5302. **EMAIL** peter.copek@orst.edu

COPELAND, DAVID ROBERT

PERSONAL Born 12/07/1960, Canada, s **DISCIPLINE** ENGLISH **EDUCATION** Univ Col Dublin, MA, 84; Univ Brit Colum, MFA, 86; Univ Toronto, PhD, 94. **CAREER** Lectr, Univ of Toronto, 95-98; lectr, Ryerson Polytechnic Univ, 97-01. **HONORS AND AWARDS** Bankson Mem Prize, Brissenden Scholarship, Univ Brit Colum. **MEMBERSHIPS** MLA, Assoc of Can Col and Univ. **RESEARCH** Modern British Literature, Postmodern American Literature, Children's Literature.

SELECTED PUBLICATIONS Auth, Reading and Translating Romance in Henry Green's 'Back', 00; auth, The Image of Childhood in Nightwood and Hayford Man, 01. **CONTACT ADDRESS** 232 Newton Dr, Willowdale, ON, Canada M2M 2P3.

COPELAND, ROBERT M.
PERSONAL Born 01/30/1945, Douglas, WY, m, 1966, 3 children **DISCIPLINE** MUSICOLOGY **EDUCATION** Geneva Col, BS, 66; Univ of Cincinnati, MMus, 70, PhD, 74. **CAREER** From asst prof to prof, Mid-Am Nazarene Col, 71-81; actg div hd, Mid-Am Nazarene Col, 80-81; prof, Geneva Col, 81-; prof of music and ch, dept of music, 77 vis lectr in music hist, Univ of KS, 83 vis prof of church music, reformed presbyterian theol seminary. **HONORS AND AWARDS** Fac Excellence in Scholarship Awd, 83-84 and 94-95 NDEA Fel, 68-71 NEH Summer Seminar, Univ of KS, 78. **MEMBERSHIPS** Am Musicological Soc; Sonneck Soc for Am Music; Soc for Ethnomusicology, Am Choral Dir Assoc; Am Assoc of Univ Profs. **RESEARCH** Am sacred music of the 18th-19th century; Parlor songs : Psalmody of the Refomation ; music historiography; music and musicians in fiction; the Holocaust and the arts. **SELECTED PUBLICATIONS** Sing Up: Learning Music for Worship, Pittsburgh, 73; Spare No Exertions, Pittsburgh, 86 Isaac Baker Woodbury, NJ, 95; Chapters in: Museums, Humanities and Educated Eyes, 82; Metrical Psalmody of the Covenanters, St. Louis, 77; articles, Musical Quarterly, Col Music Symposium; American Music; Notes; Christian Scholars Review, Reformed Worship. **CONTACT ADDRESS** Dept of Music, Geneva Col, 3200 Col Ave, Beaver Falls, PA 15010. **EMAIL** rmc@geneva.edu

COPJEC, JOAN
DISCIPLINE ENGLISH, COMPARATIVE LITERATURE, MEDIA STUDY **EDUCATION** Univ Wis, MA; Univ College Of London, Dipl.; New York Univ, PhD. **CAREER** Prof/Dir Ctr Study Psychoanalysis and Cult. **HONORS AND AWARDS** Fellow, Inst for Arch and Urban Studies; Fellow, Society for the Humanities, Cornell; Fellow, Center for Cultural Analysis of Contemporary Culture, Rutgers. **RESEARCH** Comp lit; cinema; lit criticism. **SELECTED PUBLICATIONS** Auth, Read My Desire: Lacan Against the Historicists, MIT, 94; ed, Jacques Lacan: Television, Norton, 90; Shades of Noir, Verso, 93; Radical Evil, Verso, 93; Supposing the Subject, Verso, 94; Giving Ground, Verso, 99. **CONTACT ADDRESS** Dept Comp Lit, SUNY, Buffalo, 639 Clemens Hall, Buffalo, NY 14260. **EMAIL** joancopjec@hotmail.com

COPPEDGE, WALTER RALEIGH
PERSONAL Born 01/18/1930, Morelia, Mexico, m, 1958, 1 child **DISCIPLINE** ENGLISH **EDUCATION** Univ Miss, BA, 52; Oxford Univ, BLitt, 58; Memphis State Univ, MA, 63; Ind Univ, PhD(English), 67. **CAREER** Asst prof English, Ala Col, 57-60; headmaster, Lausanne Sch Girls, Tenn, 60-66; pres, Col Charleston, 66-68; asst vpres acad affairs, 68-71, Prof English, VA Commonwealth Univ, 71-. **MEMBERSHIPS** Asn Am Rhodes Scholars; MLA. **SELECTED PUBLICATIONS** Auth, Mazursky Tempest, Something Rich, Something Strange, Lit-Film Quart, Vol 0021, 93. **CONTACT ADDRESS** 2014 Floyd Ave, Richmond, VA 23220.

COPPOLA, NANCY
DISCIPLINE COMMUNICATION **EDUCATION** Simmons Col, BA, 77; Syracuse Univ, MA, 80; DA, 83. **CAREER** Teaching Fel, Syracuse Univ, 79-83; Lecturer, Seton Hall Univ, 84-85; Special Lecturer to Asst Prof, NJ Inst of Technol, 84-. **HONORS AND AWARDS** Cable Awd for Programming Excellence, Advanced Professional and Technical Comm, 95; Excellence in Teaching Awd, NJ Inst of Technol, 94, Who's Who in Sci and Engineering, Who's Who in Am Educ, Directory of Pollution Prevention in Higher Educ: Fac and Programs, Who's Who in the World, Who's Who of Am Women. **MEMBERSHIPS** Soc for Technical Comm, IEEE Professional Comm Soc, Am computing Machinery, Asn of Teachers of Technical Writing, Coun for Programs in Technical and Scientific Comm, Mod Lang Asn. **RESEARCH** Theory and Practice of Technical Communication; Technical Communication and Environmental Rhetoric; Technology Enhanced Teaching and Learning; Technology Transfer and Technical Communication. **SELECTED PUBLICATIONS** Auth, Technical Communication, Deliberative Rhetoric, and Environmental Discourse: Connections and Directions, Ablex Pub, 00; auth, Environmental Protection: Solving Environmental Problems from Social Science and Humanities Perspectives, Hunt Pub, 97; auth, "Greening the Technological Curriculum: A Model for Environmental Literacy," The Journal of Technology Studies, (9): 39-46; auth, "Cognitive Characteristics of Web Developers: Creativity, Meaning Construction, and Problem Solving," WebNet Journal: Internet Technologies, Application, & Issues, forthcoming; auth, "Setting the Discourse Community: Tasks and Assessment for the New Technical Communication Service Course," Technical Communication Quarterly, (99): 249-267; auth, "Rhetorical Analysis of Stakeholders in Environmental Communication: A Model," Technical Communication Quarterly, (97): 9-24; auth, "Pollution Prevention Across the Technological Curriculum: An Interdisciplinary Case Approach," Bulletin of Science, Technology & Society, (94): 150-154; auth, "Grace Notes," Intro, (82): 3-13; auth, "Parties," Rectangle Magazine, (81): 17-25; auth, "Carl and His Dwarf," Syracuse Review, (79): 12-17. **CONTACT ADDRESS** Dept Humanities & Soc Sci, New Jersey Inst of Tech, 323 M L K Blvd, Newark, NJ 07102-1824. **EMAIL** coppola@adm.njit.edu

CORAL, LENORE
PERSONAL Born 01/30/1939, s **DISCIPLINE** MUSIC, LIBRARY SCIENCE **EDUCATION** Univ Chicago, MA; Univ London, PhD. **CAREER** Music librn and adj prof. **HONORS AND AWARDS** Fulbright, UK, 65-67; Citation, Music Libr Asn, 91; spec ach awd, Music Libr Asn, 95. **MEMBERSHIPS** Past pres, Music Libr Asn; pres, US Branch, Int Asn Music Libr, Arch and Doc Centre; dir, US-RILM Off. **RESEARCH** History of publishing and disseminating music. **SELECTED PUBLICATIONS** Auth, British Book Sale Catalogues 1676-1800: A Union List; auth, Towards the Bibliography of British Book Auction Catalogues, Papers of the Bibliog Soc Am, v. 89/4, 95; Evaluating the Conspectus Approach: Problems and Alternatives, in Collection Assessment in Music Libr, Canton, MA: Music Libr Asn, 94; Music Librarianship, in Careers in Music Librarianship, Canton, MA: Music Lib Asn, 90. **CONTACT ADDRESS** Music Librarian, Cornell Univ, Lincoln Hall, Ithaca, NY 14853-4101. **EMAIL** lfc1@cornell.edu

CORBEILL, ANTHONY
DISCIPLINE CLASSICAL LANGUAGES AND LITERATURE **EDUCATION** Univ MI, AB, 83; Univ CA, Berkeley, MA, 85, PhD, 90. **CAREER** Assoc prof, Univ KS. **HONORS AND AWARDS** APA fel, Thesaurus Linguae Latinae, Ger, 90-91; Rome Prize fel, Am Acad Rome, 94-95; adv coun, aar; contrib, tocs-in. **MEMBERSHIPS** Mem, Am Philol Assn; CAMWS; Am Class League; Soc of Fellows Am Acad Rome; outsanding acad book, Controlling Laughter. Polit Humor in the Late Roman Republic, Princeton, 97. **RESEARCH** Latin lit and Roman cult hist. **SELECTED PUBLICATIONS** Auth, Controlling Laughter. Political Humor in the Late Roman Republic, Princeton, 96; Deviant Diners in Roman Political Invective, Roman Sexualities, Princeton, 98. **CONTACT ADDRESS** Dept of Class, Univ of Kansas, Lawrence, Admin Building, Lawrence, KS 66045. **EMAIL** corbeill@ku.edu

CORBETT, JANICE
DISCIPLINE ENGLISH LANGUAGE AND LITERATURE **EDUCATION** B.A. Eastern College, M.S.(Comm), PhD (Eng), Temple Univ **CAREER** Fac, Delaware Valley Col, 96-. **HONORS AND AWARDS** Fellow, Rome Sem Art and Ideology; NEH fellow, UCLA; pub rel ed, staff writer, and dir. **RESEARCH** Eng wrting and compos. **SELECTED PUBLICATIONS** Auth, academic publ(s) in Perf Arts Jour, Tech Comms Jour, and JAISA. **CONTACT ADDRESS** Delaware Valley Col, 700 E Butler Ave, Doylestown, PA 18901-2697. **EMAIL** CorbettJ@devalcol.edu

CORDELL, ROSANNE M.
PERSONAL Born 07/06/1952, Fort Breckenridge, KY, m, 1973, 2 children **DISCIPLINE** LIBRARY SCIENCE- REFERENCE AND INSTRUCTION SERVICES **EDUCATION** IN Univ, South Bend, BS (Elementary Ed), 74, MS (Elementary Ed), 78; IN Univ, MLS (Library Science), 91. **CAREER** Head of Library Instruction, IN Univ, South Bend, 93-99, Head of Reference Services, 97-. **HONORS AND AWARDS** Teaching Excellence Recognition Awd, IN Univ, 97. **MEMBERSHIPS** Am Library Asn; Asn of College & Res Librarians; IN Library Federation. **RESEARCH** Library reference services; library instruction; intellectual freedom. **SELECTED PUBLICATIONS** Auth, review of Nicholas Givotovsky's An Introduction to the Issues and Applications of Interactive Multimedia for Information Specialists, Special Libraries Asn, 94, in Academic Library Book Review, 10 (2), Feb 95; Current Issues in Intellectual Freedom, series of five articles for AIME News, Jan - May 95, reprinted in IN Media J 18 (2), winter 96; Enhancing Library Instruction for At-Risk Students with Multimedia Presentations, IN Libraries 14 (2), 95; Enhancing Library Instruction with Multimedia Presentations, in New Ways of Learning the Library & Beyond: Papers and Session Materials Presented at the Twenty-Third National LOEX Library Instruction Conference, Pierian Press, 96, reprinted from IN Libraries 14 (2), 95; Intellectual Freedom Issues, quart column, IN Media J, 95-98; Intellectual Freedom Issues, monthly column, AIME News, 95-98; with Nancy A. Wootton, Institutional Policy Issues for Providing Public Internet Access, RSR Reference Services rev 24 (1), 96; with Nancy Wootton Colborn, Moving from Subjective to Objective Assessments of Your Instruction Program, RSR Reference Services Rev 26 (3-4), fall/winter 98; Determination of Whether Indiana School Library Personnel Use the Results of an Intellectual Freedom Survey to Self-Censor, submitted for pub. **CONTACT ADDRESS** Schurz Library, Indiana Univ, South Bend, PO Box 7111, South Bend, IN 46634. **EMAIL** rcordell@iusb.edu

CORE, GEORGE
PERSONAL Born 01/12/1939, Kansas City, MO, m, 1960, 4 children **DISCIPLINE** BRITISH AND AMERICAN LITERATURE **EDUCATION** Vanderbilt Univ, BA, 59, MA, 60; Univ NC, Chapel Hill, PhD(English), 71. **CAREER** Teaching asst, Univ NC, Chapel Hill, 65-66; instr English, Davidson Col, 66-68; asst prof English & sr ed, Univ Press, Univ Ga, 68-73; Ed, Sewanee Rev & Assoc Prof English, Univ of the South, 73-, Nat Endowment for Humanities Younger Humanist fel, 72-73, consult, 74- **MEMBERSHIPS** MLA; Soc Study South Lit (secy-treas, 73-76); SAtlantic Mod Lang Asn. **RESEARCH** Modern British and American fiction, especially Henry James; contemporary literary criticism; southern literary renaissance. **SELECTED PUBLICATIONS** Ed, Regionalism and Beyond: Essays of Randall Stewart, Vanderbilt Univ, 68; co-ed, The Southern Tradition at Bay, Arlington House, 68; ed, Southern Fiction Today, 69 & co-ed, K A Porter: A Critical Symposium, 69. Univ Ga; auth, Ordered life and the abysses of chaos: Parade's end, Southern Rev, summer 72; Henry James and the comedy of the New England conscience, In: The Comic Imagination in American Literature, Rutgers Univ, 73; The Literalists of the imagination: Southern New Critics and the Profession of Letters, La State Univ, 74; A naturalist looks at sentiment, Va Quart Rev, summer 77. **CONTACT ADDRESS** Dept of English, Univ of the South, Sewanee, TN 37375.

CORKIN, JANE
PERSONAL Born Boston, MA **DISCIPLINE** ARCHIVIST, PHOTOGRAPHY **EDUCATION** Queen's Univ, BA, 71. **CAREER** Asst, David Mirvish Gallery, 72-78; Owner, Jane Corkin Gallery 79-; consult, Nat Archs, Ottawa, 85; Adv, Sloane Museum, London, Eng, 88. **HONORS AND AWARDS** Women Who Make A Difference, 93; Toronto Branch Awd, Queen's Univ Alumni Asn, 95. **MEMBERSHIPS** Asn Int Photography Art Dealers; Power Plant Contemp Art Gallery; AGO; Art Bank. **SELECTED PUBLICATIONS** Auth, Twelve Canadians, Contemporary Canadian Photography, 81; auth, Margaret Bourke-White, Photographs, 88. **CONTACT ADDRESS** Jane Corkin Gallery, 179 John St, Ste 302, Toronto, ON, Canada M5T 1X4.

CORMAN, BRIAN
PERSONAL Born 02/23/1945, Chicago, IL, m, 1967, 1 child **DISCIPLINE** ENGLISH **EDUCATION** Univ Chicago, AB, 66, AM, 67, PhD(English), 71. **CAREER** Lectr, 70-71, asst prof, 71-76, Assoc Prof English, Univ Toronto, 76-, Can Coun leave fel, 75-76; Soc Sci & Humanities Res Counc Can fel, 81-82. **MEMBERSHIPS** Asn Can Univ Teachers English, MLA, Am Soc 18th Century Studies, Can Soc 18th Century Studies, Johnson Soc Cent Region. **RESEARCH** Eighteenth-century women novelists, the canon, and the history of the novel. **SELECTED PUBLICATIONS** Auth, Genre and Geneic Change in English Comedy 1660-1710, 93. **CONTACT ADDRESS** Dept of English, Univ of Toronto, 7 Kings Col Cir, Toronto, ON, Canada M5S 3K1. **EMAIL** bcorman@chass.utoronto.ca

CORNELIA, MARIE E.
DISCIPLINE 16TH-CENTURY ENGLISH LITERATURE, ELIZABETHAN-JACOBEAN DRAMA **EDUCATION** Fordham Univ, PhD. **CAREER** Evaluator, Mid States Asn; Assoc. Dean for Graduate Studies, Rutgers, State Univ NJ, Camden Col of Arts and Sci. **RESEARCH** Shakespeare, Donne, John Marston, Chaucer. **SELECTED PUBLICATIONS** Auth, The Function of the Masque in Jacobean Tragedy and Tragicomedy, Salzburg, 78. **CONTACT ADDRESS** Rutgers, The State Univ of New Jersey, New Brunswick, Camden Col of Arts and Sci, Camden, NJ 08102. **EMAIL** cornelia@camden.rutgers.edu

CORNIS-POPE, MARCEL H.
PERSONAL Born 02/14/1946, Arad, Romania, m, 1976, 3 children **DISCIPLINE** CONTEMPORARY LITERATURE AND CRITICISM **EDUCATION** Univ Cluj, BA, 68; MA, 68; Univ Timisoara, PhD, 79. **CAREER** Asst to assoc prof, Univ of Timisoara, 68-83; vis prof, Univ of Iowa, 86-87; assoc prof to prof, Va Commonwealth Univ, 88-. **HONORS AND AWARDS** Brit Coun Fel, 66, 71; Romanian Writers Awd, 75, 82; Fulbright Awd, 83-86; Andrew Mellon Fel, 87-88; Va Commonwealth Univ Awd, 91, 94; Phoenix Awd, 96; Fel, Netherlands Inst of Adv Studies, 99-00. **MEMBERSHIPS** MLA, Am Comp Lit Assoc, S Comp Lit Assoc, Int Assoc of Lit and Philos, Romanian-Am Acad, Soc for the Study of Narrative Lit. **RESEARCH** Critical and Cultural Theory, Nineteenth and twentieth-Century Anglo-American Literature, Comparative Literature, Postmodern Narratology, hypertextual reading and writing, Central European Literatures. **SELECTED PUBLICATIONS** Transl, Nine Stories, by J.D. Salinger, (Bucharest Univ, 71); transl, Look Homeward, Angel, by Thomas Wolfe, (Bucharest Univ, 77); transl, God Bless You Mr. Rosewater, by Kurt Vonnegut, (Bucharest Univ, 80); transl, Rebecca's Daughters, by Dylan Thomas, (Timisoara: Facla, 82); auth, Anatomy of the White Whale: A Poetics of the American Symbolic Romance, Bucharest Univ, 82; transl, One Flew Over the Cuckoo's Nest, by Ken Kesey, (Bucharest Univ, 83); auth, Hermeneutic Desire and Critical Rewriting: Narrative Interpretation in the Wake of Poststructuralism", St. Martin's, Macmillan (NY, London), 92; coed, 1995 Violence and Mediation in Contemporary Culture, SUNY Pr, (Albany, NY), 95; auth, The Unfinished Battles: Romanian Postmodernism Before and After 1989, Polirom (Iasi), 96; auth, Narrative Innovation and Cultural Rewriting in the Cold War Era and After, Palgrave (NY), 01. **CONTACT ADDRESS** Dept English, Virginia Commonwealth Univ, Chair's Office, Richmond, VA 23284-2005. **EMAIL** mcornis@vcu.edu

CORODIMAS, PETER
DISCIPLINE ENGLISH **EDUCATION** St Michaels Col, BA; John Carroll Univ, MA; OH State Univ, PhD, 71. **CAREER** Fac, Plattsburgh State Univ of NY. **RESEARCH** Contemp lit and creative writing. **SELECTED PUBLICATIONS** Auth, short stories in var magazines such as The Hudson Review, The New Yorker, and Redbook. **CONTACT ADDRESS** SUNY, Col at Plattsburgh, 101 Broad St, Plattsburgh, NY 12901-2681.

CORRALES, EDWIN
PERSONAL Born 02/22/1956, Costa Rica, d, 1 child **DISCIPLINE** HISTORY, LITERATURE **EDUCATION** Univ Costa Rica, BA Hist, 80; BA Soc Studies, 82; EdD, 81. **CAREER** Adj Prof, Ulster Co Community Col, 90-. **HONORS AND AWARDS** Essay Awd, Govt of Venezuela. **RESEARCH** Latin American Literature. **CONTACT ADDRESS** Dept Commun, Ulster Co Comm Col, Cottekill Rd, Stone Ridge, NY 12484. **EMAIL** corraleE@sunyulster.edu

CORRIGAN, KEVIN
PERSONAL Born 08/04/1948, United Kingdom, m, 1976, 4 children **DISCIPLINE** PHILOSOPHY; CLASSICS **EDUCATION** Lancaster, BA, 75; MA, 77, PhD, 80, Dalhousie **CAREER** Asst Prof, Col of Notre Dame, Saskatchewan, 82-86; Asst Prof, Assoc Prof, Full Prof, 86-, Dean, 91-, St. Thomas More Col, Univ of Saskatchewan. **RESEARCH** Philosophy; Classics; Ancient/Medieval Plato; Aristotle; Plotinus **SELECTED PUBLICATIONS** Auth, Plotinus Theory of Matter-Evil and the Question of Substance:Plato, Aristotle, and Alexander of Aphrodisias, 96. **CONTACT ADDRESS** 1437 College Dr., Saskatoon, SK, Canada S7N 0W6. **EMAIL** k.corrigan@usask.ca

CORRIGAN, MAUREEN
DISCIPLINE ENGLISH LITERATURE **EDUCATION** Fordham Univ, BA; Univ Pa, MA, PhD. **CAREER** Prof. **RESEARCH** 19th century British literature; women's literature; popular culture; detective fiction; contemporary American literature; Anglo-Irish literature. **SELECTED PUBLICATIONS** Auth, The Androgynous Strain: Robert B. Parker and the Feminization of the Hard- Boiled From", Mystery Writers, 98; Ruskin, Chesterton, and Gill, Chesterton Rev, 82; A Search for Right Relationships: The Twentieth-Century Medievalism of Eric Gill, 81. **CONTACT ADDRESS** English Dept, Georgetown Univ, 37th and O St, Washington, DC 20057.

CORRIGAN, VINCENT
PERSONAL Born 03/28/1945, Pittsburgh, PA, m, 1971, 2 children **DISCIPLINE** MUSICOLOGY **EDUCATION** Indiana Univ, PhD, 80 **CAREER** Prof, 73-. **MEMBERSHIPS** Am Musicol Soc; Medieval Acad of Am; Hagiography Soc. **RESEARCH** Medieval polyphony; music of troubadours and trouveres; early liturgies; harpsichord performance. **SELECTED PUBLICATIONS** Modal Transmutation in the 13th Century, Essays in Honor of Hans Tischler, ed David Halperin, Orbis Musicae Vol. XII, pp. 83-106; Music and Pilgrimage, The Pilgrimage to Compostela in the Middle Ages, ed Maryjane Dunn and Linda Kay Davidson, Garland Publ, 96; Modal Rhythm and the Interpretation of Trouvere Song, The Cultural meliue of the Troubadours and Trouveres, ed, Nancy Van Deusen, Musicol Studies LXII/1. Ottawa, Inst of Medieval Music, 94. **CONTACT ADDRESS** Col Musical Arts, Bowling Green State Univ, Bowling Green, OH 43403. **EMAIL** vcorrig@bgnet.bgsu.edu

COSGROVE, PETER
DISCIPLINE ENGLISH LITERATURE **EDUCATION** Columbia Univ, PhD, 89. **CAREER** Assoc prof, Dartmouth Col. **RESEARCH** Eng and Am lit. **SELECTED PUBLICATIONS** Undermining the Text: Edward Gibbon, Alexander Pope, and the Anti-Authenticating Footnote in Annotation and its Texts, Oxford UP, 91; Snapshots of the Absolute: Mediamachia in James Agee and Walker Evans's Let Us Now Praise Famous Men, Am Lit, 95; auth, The Circulation of Genres in Gibbon's Decline and Fall of the Roman Empire, ELH, 96; auth, "Edmund Burke, Gilles Deleuze, and the Subersive Masochism of the Image," ELH 66 (99): 405-437; auth, Impartial Stranger: History and Intertexuality in Gibbon's Decline and Fall of the Roman Empire, Univ of Delaware Press, 99. **CONTACT ADDRESS** Dept of English, Dartmouth Col, 6032 Sanborn House, Hanover, NH 03755. **EMAIL** Peter.W.Cosgrove@dartmouth.edu

COSTA, RICHARD HAUER
PERSONAL Born 07/05/1921, Philadelphia, PA, m, 1950, 1 child **DISCIPLINE** ENGLISH **EDUCATION** West Chester State Col, BS, 43; Syracuse Univ, MA, 50; Purdue Univ, PhD(-English), 69. **CAREER** Asst prof English & jour, Utica Col, 61-68, assoc prof English, 68-70; assoc prof, 70-73, Prof English, Tex A&M Univ, 73-, Ed & publ, Quartet Mag, 68-78; exec-secy & prog chair, SCent Mod Lang Asn, 75-81; chair lit panel, Tex Com Arts, 81-83. **HONORS AND AWARDS** Distinguished teaching award, Asn Former Students, Tex A&M Univ, 76. **MEMBERSHIPS** MLA; SCent Mod Lang Asn. **RESEARCH** British and continental modern fiction; H G Wells and Malcolm Lowry; the short story. **CONTACT ADDRESS** Dept of English, Texas A&M Univ, Col Station, Station, TX 77843. **EMAIL** richard-h-costa@tamu.edu

COSTANZO, WILLIAM VINCENT
PERSONAL Born 02/05/1945, Brooklyn, NY, m, 1973, 2 children **DISCIPLINE** ENGLISH, FILM **EDUCATION** Columbia Col, NYork, AB, 67, Columbia Univ, MA, 68, PhD(English), 78. **CAREER** Asst prof, 70-78, assoc prof,78-84, prof English and film, Westchester Community Col, 84-, Nat Endowment for Humanities educ grant, 78-79; adj instr, Teachers Col, Columbia Univ, 80-. **HONORS AND AWARDS** NEH fel, 81; 10M Softwar Grant, 88; Fac Excellence Awd, 90; NY State Chancellor's Awd, 82. **MEMBERSHIPS** MLA; NCTE; Joseph Conrad Soc Am. **RESEARCH** Modern British literature; film studies; composition; SCS. **SELECTED PUBLICATIONS** Auth, The French Version of Finnegans Wake: Translation, Adaptation, Recreation, James Joyce Quart, winter, 71; I Found it at the Movies: A Cinematic Approach to Teaching Writing Skills, Insight, 77; The Duellists: Transposing Conrad's fiction into film, Joseph Conrad Today, 4/79; Conrad's Visit to America, Conradiana, winter 81; Polanski in Wessex: Filming Hardy's Tess of the d'Urbervilles, In: Literature/Film Quart, summer 81; Reading the Movies, 92; The Electronic Text, 89; Double Exposure, 84. **CONTACT ADDRESS** Dept of English, Westchester Comm Col, 75 Grasslands Rd, Valhalla, NY 10595-1636. **EMAIL** wcostanzo@aol.com

COSTELLO, DONALD PAUL
PERSONAL Born 08/04/1931, Chicago, IL, m, 1952, 6 children **DISCIPLINE** AMERICAN STUDIES, DRAMA & FILM **EDUCATION** DePaul Univ, AB, 55; Univ Chicago, MA, 56, PhD, 62. **CAREER** Instr, Roosevelt Univ, 57-60 & Chicago City Jr Col, 58-59; from instr to assoc prof, 60-71, prof English, Univ Notre Dame, 71-, chmn Am studies & commun arts, 79-, soc relig higher educ fel, 64-65; consult, Educ Assoc, Inc for Proj Upward Bound, Wash, DC, 66-; consult/panelist, Nat Endowment for Humanities Lit & Fine Arts Panel, 77-. **MEMBERSHIPS** Soc Values Higher Educ; MLA. **RESEARCH** American literature; modern drama; cinema. **SELECTED PUBLICATIONS** Auth, The Language of The Catcher in the Rye, Am Speech, 10/59; art, Graham Greene and the Catholic Press, Renaissance, autumn 59; art, The Structure of the Turn of the Screw, Mod Lang Notes, 4/60; art, The Serpent's Eye: Shaw and the Cinema, Univ Notre Dame, 65; contribr, Black Man as Victim: The Drama of LeRoi Jones, Five Black Writers, New York Univ, 70; art, Counter-culture to Anti-culture: Woodstock, Easy Rider, and A Clockwork Orange, The Rev Polit, 10/72; art, Tennessee Williams' Fugitive Kind, Mod Drama, 5/72; art, Fellini's Road, Univ Notre Dame, 82. **CONTACT ADDRESS** Dept of English, Univ of Notre Dame, 356 Oshaugnessy Hall, Notre Dame, IN 46556.

COTTER, JAMES FINN
PERSONAL Born 07/05/1929, Boston, MA, m, 1960, 3 children **DISCIPLINE** ENGLISH LITERATURE, PHILOSOPHY **EDUCATION** Boston Col, AB, 54, MA, 55; Fordham Univ, MA, 58, PhD(English), 63. **CAREER** From instr to asst prof English, Fordham Univ, 60-63; assoc prof, 63-68, prof English, Mt St Mary Col, NY, 68-; Fulbright-Hays lectr, Univ Oran, 70-71. **MEMBERSHIPS** MLA; Conf Christianity & Lit; Dante Soc. **RESEARCH** Dante; Renaissance poetry; Sir Philip Sidney; Gerard Manley Hopkins. **SELECTED PUBLICATIONS** Auth, Visions of Christ in Dante's Divine Comedy, Nemla Studies, 83-84; Hopkins: The Wreck of the Deutschland, 28, The Explicator, 85; Apocalyptic Imagery in Hopkins That Nature is a Heraclitean Fire and of the Comfort of the Resurrections, Victorian Poetry, 86; Look at it loom there! The Image of the Wave in Hopkins' The Wreck of the Deutschland, The Hopkins Quart, 87; Dante and Christ: The Pilgrim as Beatus Vir, The Italian Quart, 88; The Book Within the Book in Medieval Illumination, Florilegium 12, 93; The Song of Songs in The Wreck of the Deutschland in GM Hopkins and Critical Discourse, AMS Press, 94; Augustine's Confessions and The Wreck of the Deutschland in Saving Beauty: Further Studies in Hopkins, Garland, 95; The Divine Comedy and the First Psalm in Dante: Summa Medievalis, Stony Brook: Forum Italicum, 95; auth, Hopkins and Job, Victorian Poetry, 95; auth, Hopkins and Augustine, Victorian Poetry, 01. **CONTACT ADDRESS** 330 Powell Ave, Newburgh, NY 12550-3412. **EMAIL** cotter@msmc.edu

COTTON, WILLIAM THEODORE
PERSONAL Born 07/14/1936, Manila, Philippines, d, 1 child **DISCIPLINE** ENGLISH LITERATURE **EDUCATION** Cornell Univ, BA, 58; Univ NMex, MA, 63, PhD(English), 74. **CAREER** Instr English, Univ NMex, 66-67; instr, 68-74, Asst Prof English, Loyola Univ of the South, 74-; Assoc Prof of English, 90; Dir, Univ Honors Program, 96-. **MEMBERSHIPS** MLA. **RESEARCH** English Renaissance literature, especially romance-epic; utopian literature. **SELECTED PUBLICATIONS** Auth, The Given and the Made--Strategies of Poetic Redefinition, New Orleans Rev, Vol 0022, 96; The Breaking of Style--Hopkins, Heaney, Dove, Graham, New Orleans Rev, Vol 0022, 96. **CONTACT ADDRESS** Dept of English, Loyola Univ, New Orleans, 6363 St Charles Ave, New Orleans, LA 70118-6195. **EMAIL** cotton@loyno.edu

COUCH, LEON W., III
PERSONAL Born 09/01/1970, Gainesville, FL, s **DISCIPLINE** MUSIC THEORY & ORGAN **EDUCATION** Organ Performance, MM, 95; ABD DMA Organ, PhD Theory. **CAREER** Asst prof Music **HONORS AND AWARDS** Various. **MEMBERSHIPS** Soc Music Theory; Am Musicol Soc; Int Computer Music Asn; Am Guild Organists; Soc for 17th Century Music. **RESEARCH** Performance & Theory; Pedagogy. **CONTACT ADDRESS** Dept Music, Luther Col, 700 College Dr., Decorah, IA 52101-1045. **EMAIL** profcouch@bigfoot.com

COUGHLIN, ROBERT M.
PERSONAL Born 06/11/1948, E Cleveland, OH, m, 1978, 3 children **DISCIPLINE** ENGLISH, POETRY **EDUCATION** Univ Notre Dame, AB, 70; Univ Cincinnati, MEd, 77; Ohio State Univ, PhD, 82. **CAREER** Berez Col, 82-88; Lakeland Community Col, 88-. **MEMBERSHIPS** Confr on Col Composition & Commun, Nat Confr of Teachers of English. **RESEARCH** Creative Writing. **SELECTED PUBLICATIONS** Coauth, Building the Beloved Community: Maurice McCrackin's Life for Peace and Civil Rights, Temple Univ Press, 91. **CONTACT ADDRESS** Dept English, Lakeland Comm Col, 770 Clocktower Dr, Willoughby, OH 44094-5198.

COULOMBE, JOSEPH L.
PERSONAL Born 12/05/1966, Lafayette, IN **DISCIPLINE** AMERICAN LITERATURE **EDUCATION** Univ St Thomas, BA, 89; Univ Del, MA, 98. **CAREER** Grad instr, Univ Del, 92-98; asst prof, Univ Tenn, 98-01; asst prof, Rowan Univ, 01-. **HONORS AND AWARDS** NEH, 99; Univ Del Dis Fel, 96; Phi Kappa Phi; Best Grad Teach Univ Del, 97-98; Who's Who Among Teach 00. **MEMBERSHIPS** MLA, WALA, AHA. **RESEARCH** Mark Twain and the American west, 19th C American literature, native American literature. **SELECTED PUBLICATIONS** Auth, "'To Destroy the Teacher': Walt Whitman and Martin Farquhar Tupper's 1851 Trip to America," Walt Whitman Qtly Rev (96); auth, "Man or Mannequin?: Selden in Edith Wharton's The House of Mirth," Edith Wharton Rev (96); auth, "Emerson Bennett," Dict of Lit Biog 202: Nineteenth-Cent Fict Writers (99); auth, "Mark Twain's Native Americans and the Repeated Racial Pattern in Adventures of Huckleberry Finn," Am Lit Realism (01); auth, "Go East, Young Man: Class Conflict and Degenerate Manhood in Mark Twain's Early Writings," West Am Lit (01). **CONTACT ADDRESS** Eng Dept, Rowan Univ, Bunce Hall, Glassboro, NJ 08028. **EMAIL** coulombe@rowan.edu

COUNCIL, NORMAN BRIGGS
PERSONAL Born 11/13/1936, Pensacola, FL, m, 1963, 2 children **DISCIPLINE** ENGLISH LITERATURE **EDUCATION** Univ of the South, BA, 58; Stanford Univ, MA, 64, PhD(English), 67. **CAREER** Instr English Lit, Univ Vt, 64-67; asst prof, Univ Calif, Santa Barbara, 67-76; chmn dept, 78-81, from assoc prof to prof English, Univ Utah, 76-93, dean, Col Humanities, 81-91, David P Gardner award, Univ Utah, 78-79. **MEMBERSHIPS** MLA. **RESEARCH** Shakespeare; Renaissance studies; Milton. **SELECTED PUBLICATIONS** Auth, Ben Jonson, Inigo Jones, and the transformation of Tudor Chivalry, J English Lit Hist, 47; Prince Hal: Mirror of success, Shakespeare Studies, 72; When Honour's at the Stake: Ideas of Honour in Shakespeare's Plays, Allen & Unwin, London, 73; O Dea Certe, Huntington Libr Quart, 76; L'Allegro Il Penseroso & the cycle of universal knowledge, Milton Studies, 76; Answering His Great Idean: The Fiction of Paradise Lost, Milton Studies, 96. **CONTACT ADDRESS** Dept of English, Univ of Utah, Langs & Commun Bldg, Salt Lake City, UT 84112-8916. **EMAIL** norman.council@m.cc.utah.edu

COUNTRYMAN, L. WM
PERSONAL Born 10/21/1941, Oklahoma City, OK, 1 child **DISCIPLINE** CLASSICS, NEW TESTAMENT **EDUCATION** Univ of Chicago, BA, 62, MA, 74, PhD, 77; General Theol Sem, STB, 65 **CAREER** Lect, 74-76, Univ of Chicago; Asst Prof, 76-79, SW Mission St Univ; Asst Prof, 79-83 TX Christ Univ; Prof, 83-pres, Church Div Sch of the Pac **HONORS AND AWARDS** Phi Beta Kappa **MEMBERSHIPS** Soc of Bibl Lit; Assoc of Anglican Bibl Schols; Soc for Study of Christian Spirituality **RESEARCH** Spirituality; Sexual Orientation **SELECTED PUBLICATIONS** Auth, The Rich Christian in the Church of the Early Empire, Edwin Mellen Press, 80; Auth, The Mystical Way in the Fourth Gospel, Crossing Over into God, Fortress Press, 87; Living on the Border of the Holy: The Priesthood of Humanity and the Priesthoods of the Church, Morehouse Publ, 99; Forgiven and Forgiving, Morehouse Publ, 98 **CONTACT ADDRESS** Church Divinity Sch of the Pacific, 2451 Ridge, Berkeley, CA 94709. **EMAIL** bcountryman@cdsp.edu

COUNTS, MICHAEL L.
DISCIPLINE THEATRE **EDUCATION** Pace Univ, BA; Hunter Col, MA; Grad Ctr CUNY, PhD. **CAREER** Assoc prof & dir, Harlequin Theatre, Lyon Col, 92. **RESEARCH** Acting; directing; theatre hist; theory and criticism. **SELECTED PUBLICATIONS** Auth, Coming Home: The Soldier's Return in Twentieth Century Drama, Peter Lang, NY, Bern, 88. **CONTACT ADDRESS** Dept of Theatre, Lyon Col, 2300 Highland Rd, PO Box 2317, Batesville, AR 72503. **EMAIL** mcounts@lyon.edu

COUPE, LYNDA
PERSONAL Born Mt Kisco, NY, m, 1985, 2 children **DISCIPLINE** LITERATURE **EDUCATION** Westchester Cmty Col, AA; Hunter Col, BA; MA; CUNY, MPhil; PhD. **CAREER** Adj Assoc Prof and Asst Dir, Pace Univ, 85-. **MEMBERSHIPS** MLA; NCTE; AAUW; Sigma Tau Delta; Kappa Delta Pi. **RESEARCH** Science and literature; Hunting and literature. **SELECTED PUBLICATIONS** Auth, "Daniel Boone and the Hunter/Farmer: Migration, Contemplation, and Progress," Westward Migration, forthcoming; auth, "Your New Best Friend: Email and Instant Intimacy," in Youth Tech, Stanford Univ Press, forthcoming; auth, Images of the Hunter in American Life and literature, Peter Lang Pub, forthcoming. **CONTACT ADDRESS** Dept Lit & Comm, Pace Univ, Pleasantville, 861 Bedford Rd, Pleasantville, NY 10570-2700. **EMAIL** lcoupe@pace.edu

COURAGE, RICHARD A.
PERSONAL Born 01/15/1946, Brooklyn, NY, m, 1969, 2 children **DISCIPLINE** ENGLISH EDUCATION **EDUCATION** Columbia Univ, PhD, 90 **CAREER** Assoc Prof English, Asst Chair English Dept, Westchester Community Coll, 90-. **HONORS AND AWARDS** State Univ NY Chancellor's Awd for Exc; Nat Inst forStaff & Org Dev. **MEMBERSHIPS** Nat Coun Teachers Eng; Hudson Valley Writing Proj; Mod Lang Asn. **RESEARCH** Literacy, African-Am lit. **SELECTED PUBLICATIONS** Auth, Dangerous Narrative, in College Composition and Commun, Feb 96; auth, Interaction of Public and Private Liteacies, in College Composition and Commun, Dec 93; auth, Basic Writing: End of a Frontier, in J Teaching Writing, Fall/Winter 90; auth, James Baldwin's Go Tell It on the Mountain: Voices of a People, in CLA J, june 89. **CONTACT ADDRESS** Westchester Comm Col, Valhalla, NY 10595. **EMAIL** rac46@aol.com

COURT, FRANKLIN EDWARD
PERSONAL Born 11/26/1939, Youngstown, OH, 2 children **DISCIPLINE** ENGLISH LITERATURE **EDUCATION** Youngstown State Univ, BA, 62; Univ Md, MA, 64; Kent State Univ, PhD(English), 69. **CAREER** Instr, Kent State Univ, 65-69; asst prof, 69-74, assoc prof, 74-80, Prof English, Northern Ill Univ, 80-99; prof emeritus, 99- . **HONORS AND AWARDS** Huntington Libr Res Fel, 93; Folger Inst travel grant, 95. **MEMBERSHIPS** MLA; Midwest Mod Lang Asn; ACIS **RESEARCH** Victorian literature; celtic studies. **SELECTED PUBLICATIONS** Auth, Walter Pater: An Annotated Bibliography of Writings About Him, Northern Ill Univ Press, 80; Pater and His Early Critics, Univ Victoria ELS Monograph Series, 80; Tale of Two Cities: Dickens, Revolution, and the Other, Victorian Newsletter, Fall 91; Institutionalizing English Literature: The Culture and Politics of Literary Study, 1750-1900, Stanford Univ Press, 92; Jeremy Bentham's Wager, the Game of Reading, and Westron Wind, Mosaic: J for the Interdisciplinary Study of Lit, 12/97; The Early Impact of Scottish Literary Teaching in North America, In: The Scottish Invention of English Literature: Origins and Development of a University Discipline, Cambridge Univ Press, 98; Clark's The Wind and the Snow of Winter and Celtic Oisin, Studies in Short Fiction, Spring 98; The Scottish Connection: The Rise of English Literary Study in Early Am, Syracuse Univ Press, 00. **CONTACT ADDRESS** Dept of English, No Illinois Univ, 1425 W Lincoln Hwy, De Kalb, IL 60115-2825. **EMAIL** fcourt@aol.com

COURTNEY, EDWARD
PERSONAL Born 03/22/1932, Belfast, Ireland, m, 1962, 2 children **DISCIPLINE** CLASSICS **EDUCATION** Trinity College Dublin, BA, 54; Christ Church Oxford, MA, 57. **CAREER** Lectr, Christ Church Oxford 55-59; Lectr 59-70, reader 70-77; Prof 77-82, Univ London King's College; Prof, 82-93, Stanford Univ; Gildersleeve Prof, classics, 93-, Univ Virginia. **MEMBERSHIPS** APA; CAMWS; CAV. **RESEARCH** Latin language and literature; Textual criticism and transmission of texts. **SELECTED PUBLICATIONS** Auth, Commentary on the Satires of Juvenal, 80; The Poems of Petronius, 91; The Fragmentary Latin Poets, 93; Musa Lapidaria, 95, Archaic Latin Prose, 99; texts edited; Valerius Flaccus, Argonatica, 70; coauth, Ovid, Fasti, 78, 4th edition, 97; auth, Juvenal, Satires, 84; Statins, Silvae, 90. **CONTACT ADDRESS** 1500 West Pines Dr, Charlottesville, VA 22901. **EMAIL** EC4S@virginia.edu

COURTNEY, RICHARD
PERSONAL Born 06/04/1927, Newmarket, England, m, 1952, 2 children **DISCIPLINE** DRAMA, EDUCATION **EDUCATION** Univ Leeds, BA, 51, dipl educ, 52. **CAREER** Sr lectr drama, Trent Park Col, Inst Educ, Univ London, 58-67; assoc prof, Univ Victoria, BC, 68-71; prof, Univ Calgary, 71-74; Prof Educ, Ont Inst Studies in Educ, 74-, Ed, Discussions in Develop Drama, Univ Calgary, 71-74; chmn, Nat Inquiry into Arts & Educ in Can, 75-80; vis fel, Melbourne State Col, 79. **HONORS AND AWARDS** Queen's Silver Jubilee Medal, 77. **MEMBERSHIPS** Fel Royal Soc Arts; Can Conf Arts (pres, 73-76); Can Child & Youth Drama Asn (pres, 70-72); Am Soc Aesthetics; Am Theatre Asn. **RESEARCH** Developmental drama, the relationship of enactment to philosophy, ethnology, education, psychology and sociology. **SELECTED PUBLICATIONS** Auth, Tree,Beerbohm and Knight,G.Wilson--Reply to Pearce,Brian, New Theatre Quart, Vol 0013, 97. **CONTACT ADDRESS** Dept of Curric, Ontario Inst for Studies in Education, Toronto, ON, Canada M5S 2L6.

COURTRIGHT, JOHN A.
PERSONAL Born 11/18/1948, m **DISCIPLINE** INTERPERSONAL COMMUNICATION **EDUCATION** Univ Iowa, BA, 71; MA, 73; PhD, 76. **CAREER** Res asst, Univ Iowa, 72-74; tchg asst, Univ Iowa, 74-76; instr, grad course in comp assisted statistical anal, Univ Iowa, 76; asst prof, Cleveland State Univ, 76-80; assoc prof, Cleveland State Univ, 80-85; asst dir, Comp Ctr, Cleveland State Univ, 83-86; prof, Cleveland State Univ, 85-86; prof, 86-; exec ed, Arts & Sci Newsletter, 92-96; ch, 86-. **HONORS AND AWARDS** Awd, Speech Commun Assn, 91; grant, 95; grant, UNIDEL Found, 97; assoc ed, mem, ed bd, commun res rpt, 96-99; ed referee, commun rpt, 96; assoc ed, mem ed bd, commun quart, 96-99; jour commun, 96-99; commun edu, 96-99. **RESEARCH** Multimedia presentation; statistics and environmental design. **SELECTED PUBLICATIONS** Co-auth, Commun Research Methods. Glenview, Scott, Foresman, 84; Inertial Forces and the Implementation of a Socio-Technical Systems Approach: A Commun Study, Org Sci, 95; Thinking Rationally About Nonprobability, Jour of Broadcasting and Electronic Media, 96; Communicating Online: A Guide to the Internet, Mayfield Publ Co, 98; The Mayfield Quick Guide to the Internet: For Communincations Students, Mayfield Publ Co, 98. **CONTACT ADDRESS** Dept of Commun, Univ of Delaware, 162 Ctr Mall, Newark, DE 19716.

COURTS, PATRICK LAWRENCE
PERSONAL Born 04/28/1944, Chicago, IL, m, 1969, 1 child **DISCIPLINE** ENGLISH EDUCATION, AMERICAN LITERATURE **EDUCATION** Chicago State Col, BS, 66; Mich State Univ, MA, 68, PhD(English), 71. **CAREER** Teacher English, Chicago Bd Educ, 66-68; instr, Mich State Univ, 68-71; asst prof, 71-75, assoc prof, 75-80, Prof English, State Univ NY Col Fredonia, 80- **MEMBERSHIPS** MLA; NCTE. **RESEARCH** Preparation of English Teachers for high school and college; teaching of composition and literature; subjective approaches to literature. **SELECTED PUBLICATIONS** Auth, Politicizing Literacy--Comment, Col Eng, Vol 0055, 93. **CONTACT ADDRESS** Dept of English, SUNY, Col at Fredonia, 1 Suny at Fredonia, Fredonia, NY 14063-1143.

COUTENAY, LYNN
PERSONAL Born 07/08/1943, Nashville, TN, d, 2 children **DISCIPLINE** ENGLISH; HISTORY; ART HISTORY **EDUCATION** Vassar Col, BA, 65; MA, PhD, 79, Univ of Wis-Madison. **CAREER** Visiting lectr, University of WI-Madison; lectr, sr lectr, 84-96, asst prof, 96-, University of WI-Whitewata. **HONORS AND AWARDS** Fel in humanities, Newberry Library, 90-91; NEH Cooperative Project Grant, 91; Honorary Fel in Art hist, 94-97; elected Fel of the Soc of Antiquaries (members by invitation only), 95; Who's Who Among America's Teachers, Natl Honor Students' nomination, 96; University of WI System Fel: Inst for research in the humanities, 98-99 **MEMBERSHIPS** Soc of Antiquairies; ICMA; AVISTA; CAA; Vernacular Architecture Group; RAI; AIA (USA). **RESEARCH** Medieval Architecture; historic carpentry; Roman architecture; late medieval social and cultural hist; hist of technology. **SELECTED PUBLICATIONS** Auth, The Westminster Hall Roof: A New Archaeological Source, British Archaeological Association Journal, 90; Architectural Technology up to the Scientific Revolution: The Art and Structure of Large-scale Buildings, 93; Scale and Scantling: Technological Issues in large-scale Timberwork of the High Middle Ages, in Technology and Resource Use in Medieval Europe, Cathedrals, the Mills, and Mines, Dec 97; The Engineering of Gothic Cathedrals, Studies in the History of Civil Engineering, Dec 11, 1997. **CONTACT ADDRESS** 3100 Lake Mendota Dr., #504, Madison, WI 53705. **EMAIL** hcourte@facstoff.wise.edu

COUTTS, BRIAN E.
PERSONAL Born 01/29/1948, Lethbridge, Canada, m, 1978, 1 child **DISCIPLINE** HISTORY, LIBRARY AND INFORMATION SCIENCE **EDUCATION** La State Univ, MLS, 83, Phd, 81. **CAREER** Hist bibliog, Fondren Libr, Rice Univ, 84-86; Coord, Collection Dev. Western Ky Univ, 87-90; PROF, HEAD, DEPT LIBRARY PUB SVCS, WESTERN KY UNIV, 91-. **HONORS AND AWARDS** Distinguished Research, Western Ky Univ, 91, 94; Outstanding Public Serv, 99; Louis Shores-Oryx Press Awd, ALA, 99. **MEMBERSHIPS** ALA, ACRL, La Hist. **RESEARCH** Colonial La hist, reference books publishing, hsitory of Belize. **SELECTED PUBLICATIONS** Auth, Belize, Clio Press, 93; auth, Reference Sources in History, 90, 2nd ed. 00; auth, Best Reference Sources of 1999, Libr J, Apr 15, 00; auth, Best Reference Websites of 1999, Libr J, apr 15, 00; auth, The Reference Revolution:Wired for the 90s, Libr J, Nov 15, 97; auth, Central America: From Civil Wars to Tourist Mecca, Libr J, Mar 1, 97. **CONTACT ADDRESS** Dept Libr Pub Svcs, Western Kentucky Univ, 1 Big Red Way, Bowling Green, KY 42101-3576. **EMAIL** brian.coutts@wku.edu

COVERT, JAMES THAYNE
PERSONAL Born 04/20/1932, Cimarron, KS, m, 1952, 6 children **DISCIPLINE** ENGLISH AND MODERN EUROPEAN HISTORY **EDUCATION** Univ Portland, BA, 59; Univ Ore, MA, 61, PhD(hist), 67. **CAREER** From instr to assoc prof hist, 61-71, chmn dept, 67-72, Prof Hist, Univ Portland, 71-97, Danforth assoc, 70- **HONORS AND AWARDS** Standard Oil Calif Leadership Awd, 57; Nat Asn Manufacturers' Presidential Awd, 58; Am Red Cross Recognition Awd for Vol Serv, 64; Culligan Fac Awd, 68 & Distinguished Prof Awd, 96, Univ Portland. **RESEARCH** Victorian and Edwardian England and England in the twentieth century; social, intellectual, political history. **SELECTED PUBLICATIONS** Auth, "Student Freedom in American Higher Education," edited with Louis Vacaro, New York: Teachers College Press, Columbia University, 69; auth, "A Point of Pride: The University of Portland Story," Portland: University of Portland Press, 76; auth, "Memory Makers: More than 100 Just-For-Fun Ways to Give Children Memories to Last a Lifetime," with Jan Smith, Portland: Frank Amato Publication, 88; auth, "Memoir of a Victorian Woman: Reflections of Louise Creighton, 1850-1936," Bloomington: Indiana University Press, 94; auth, "A Victorian Family as Seen through the Letters of Louise Creighton to her Mother, 1872-1880," Lewiston, NY: Edwin Mellen Press, 98; auth, "A Victorian Marriage: Mandell and Louise Creighton," London: The Hambledon Press, 01. **CONTACT ADDRESS** Dept of Hist, Univ of Portland, Portland, OR 97203. **EMAIL** covert@up.edu

COVINGTON, WILLIAM, JR.
PERSONAL Born 02/05/1954, Monroe, LA, s **DISCIPLINE** COMMUNICATION **EDUCATION** Bowling Green State Univ, PhD; Univ Louisiana, MA; BA. **CAREER** Asst Prof, Bridgewater State Col, 94; Graduate Fellow, Bowling Green State Univ, 93-94; Asst Prof, Huntington Col, 89-93; Asst Prof, Avila Col, 86-89 **HONORS AND AWARDS** Outstanding Young Men of America, U.S. Jaycees, 76; Who's Who in the Midwest, Marquis, 85. **MEMBERSHIPS** Communication Studies at Bridgewater State College, 94; Bowling Green State Univ, 93-94; Huntington College, 89-93; Avila College, 86-89. **RESEARCH** Systems Theory Applied to Television Station Management in the competitive Marketplace; Creativity and General Systems Theory; Creating the Person You're Becoming. **SELECTED PUBLICATIONS** Auth, Creativity and General Systems Theory, Universal Publishers (Parkland, FL), 98; Auth, Creativity the Person You're Becoming, Universal Publishers (Parkland, FL),99; auth, "Modeling Through Media Interviews", Speech Communication Teacher, 11 (96); auth, "Don't Overlook the Homefront: Ethical Dilemmas In Our Own Field", Media Ethics 9 (97); auth, "Management Principles Strategies Applicable at Broadcast Stations in Various Cultures", The Journal of Development Communication 9 (98); rev, "The Shortstop's Son," by Philip Martin, American Journalism 15 (Fall 98); rev, "The Highwaymen", by Ken Auletta, Journalism and Mass Communication Educator 54 (Winter 99); rev, "Media Career Guide," by James Seguin, Journalism and Mass Communication Quarterly 79 (Summer 99); rev, "America's Favorite Radio Station: WKRP in Cincinnati", by Michael B. Kassel, Journal of Radio Studies 6 (Autumn 99); rev, "The Voice of Business: Hill & Knowlton and Postwar Public Relations," Journal of Business Communication 37 (January 00). **CONTACT ADDRESS** Dept Communication Studies, Bridgewater State Col, 131 Summer St, Bridgewater, MA 02325-0001. **EMAIL** williamcovington@hotmail.com

COWAN, BAINARD
DISCIPLINE AMERICAN LITERATURE **EDUCATION** Yale, PhD, 75. **CAREER** Prof, La State Univ. **HONORS AND AWARDS** Newberry libr fel, 87-88; LEQSF Grant for Comp Lit, Inst and Colloquium, 92, 94, 96; NEH Higher Educ Grant, Comp Lit Inst, 94. **RESEARCH** World literatures and civilizations; science, technology, and literature; American lit in world context. **SELECTED PUBLICATIONS** Auth, Exiled Waters: Moby Dick and the Crisis of Allegory, 82; auth, Theorizing American Literature: Hegel, the Sign, and History, 91; auth, America Between Two Myths: Moby Dick as Epic, The Epic Cosmos, 92; auth, The Limits of Rationality: Oedipus the King, Class Texts and the Nature of Authority, 93; auth, The Nomos of Deleuze and Guattari: Emergent Holism in A Thousand Plateaus, Ann of Scholar, 96. **CONTACT ADDRESS** Dept of Eng, Louisiana State Univ, 229D Allen Hall, Baton Rouge, LA 70803. **EMAIL** encowa@lsu.edu

COWART, DAVID
PERSONAL Born 12/22/1947, Tuscaloosa, AL, 2 children **DISCIPLINE** ENGLISH **EDUCATION** Univ Ala, BA, 69; Ind Univ, MA, 71; Rutgers Univ, PhD, 77. **CAREER** Prof, Univ of SCar, 77-. **HONORS AND AWARDS** Amoco Outstanding Teaching Awd, 87; NEH, 90; Fulbright Fel, 92-93; 96-97; Michael J Mungo Teaching Awd, 95; Educ Found Res Awd, 95. **MEMBERSHIPS** MLA, SAMLA. **RESEARCH** Fiction in English after World War II. **SELECTED PUBLICATIONS** Auth, Thomas Pynchon: The Art of Allusion, S Ill Univ Pr, 80; auth, Arches and Light: The Fiction of John Gardner, S Ill Univ Pr, 83; auth, History and the Contemporary Novel, S Ill Univ Pr, 89; auth, "Faulkner and Joyce in Morrison's Song of Solomon," Am Lit, (90); auth, "Continuity and Growth: Pynchon's Vineland," Kenyon Rev, (90); auth, Literary Symbiosis: The Reconfigured Text in Twentieth-Century Writing, Univ of Ga Pr, 93; auth, "Significant, insignificant: Realist and Postmodernist Art in Hawke's Whistlejacket," Mod Fiction Studies, (95); auth, "Matriarchal Mythopoesis: Naylor's Mama Day," Philol

Quart, (98); auth, "The Luddite Vision: Mason & Dixon," Am Lit, (99); auth, Don DeLillo: The Physics of Language, 01. **CONTACT ADDRESS** Dept English, Univ of So Carolina, Columbia, 4109 MacGregor Dr, Columbia, SC 29206. **EMAIL** cowartd@gwm.sc.edu

COWASJEE, SAROS
PERSONAL Born 07/12/1931, Secundrabad, India **DISCIPLINE** ENGLISH **EDUCATION** St John's Col (Agra, India), BA, 51; Agra Col, MA, 55; Univ Leeds, PhD, 60. **CAREER** Asst ed, Times of India Press (Bombay), 61-63; instr, 63, prof, 71-95, PROF EMER ENGLISH, UNIV REGINA, 95-; res assoc, Univ Calif Berkeley, 70-71; vis prof, Univ Aarhus (Denmark), 75. **HONORS AND AWARDS** N Tata scholar postgrad stud, Leeds Univ; Can Coun leave fels. **MEMBERSHIPS** Asn Can Univ Tchrs Eng; Can Asn Commonwealth Lit & Lang Stud; Authors Guild India; Writers Union Can; Zorastrian. **RESEARCH** Indian and Anglo-Indian literature **SELECTED PUBLICATIONS** Auth, Sean O'Casey: The Man Behind the Plays, 63; auth, O'Casey, 66; auth, 'Coolie': An Assessment, 76; auth, So Many Freedoms: A Study of the Major Fiction of Mulk Raj Anand, 77; auth, Studies in Indian and Anglo-Indian Fiction, 93; ed, Author to Critic: The Letters of Mulk Raj Anand, 73; ed, Mulk Raj Anand: A Check-list, 79; ed, Modern Indian Fiction, 81; ed, Modern Indian Short Stories, 82; ed, Stories From the Raj, 82; ed, More Stories from the Raj and After, 86; ed, When the British Left, 87; ed, The Raj and After, 87; ed, Women Writers of the Raj: Short Fiction, 90; ed, Orphans of the Storm: Stories on the Partition of India, 95; ed, The Best Short Stories of Flora Annie Steel, 95; ed, The Oxford Anthology of Raj Stories, 98; ed, Arnold Publ Literature of the Raj series, 84-. **CONTACT ADDRESS** English Dept, Univ of Regina, Regina, SK, Canada S4S 0A2. **EMAIL** Saros.Cowasjee@uregina.ca

COWELL, PATTIE LEE
PERSONAL Born 03/10/1949, Auburn, WA **DISCIPLINE** ENGLISH **EDUCATION** Pacific Lutheran Univ, BA, 71; Univ Mass, MA, 73, PhD(English), 77. **CAREER** Teacher English, South Hadley High Sch, 72-74; teaching, Asst Rhetoric Prog, Univ Mass, 74-76; from instr to assoc prof, 77-86, Prof English, Colo State Univ, 86-, Chair, Women's Studies Interdisciplinary Program, 80-82, Admin Asst, Grad Sch, 82, Acting Dean, Grad Sch, 83-84, Acting Assoc Dean, Col of Arts, Humanities and Soc Sci, 86, Coordr of Grad Studies in English, 83-91; Ch, Dept of English, 91-; Ed Asst, Early Am Lit, 76; Field bibliographer in U.S. literature, MLA Int Bibliog, 82-98; Ed Board mem, Early Am Lit, 86-89; Advisory Board mem, Brown Univ Textbase of women Writers in English, 1350-1850, 89-. **HONORS AND AWARDS** Fac res Grant, Colo State Univ, 79; Dean's Award for Excellence, Col of Arts, Humanities and Soc Sci, CSU, 81; Dean's Schol Support Grant, CSU, 87; Professional Development Grant for Res Support, CSU, 89, 92, 95, 96; Cermak Award for Outstanding Graduate Advising, CSU, 91; Rockefeller Regional Schol, SW Inst for Res on Women, Univ Ariz, 91; Andrew W. Mellon Found Fel for research at the Library Company of Philadelphia, 96. **MEMBERSHIPS** MLA; NCTE; Women's Caucus Mod Lang; Rocky Mountain Mod Lang Asn. **RESEARCH** Early American literature; modern American fiction; cross-disciplinary perspectives on American culture. **SELECTED PUBLICATIONS** Auth, Introduction to Cotton Mather's Ornaments for the Daughters of Zion, Scholars' Facsimiles & Reprints, 78; Jane Colman Turell (1708-1735): Inclinations to poetry, 17th Century News, 78; Jane Colman Turell: A double birth, 13th Moon, 78; Women poets in pre-Revolutionary America, 1650-1735: A checklist, Bull Bibliog & Mag Notes, 79; seven entries, American Women Writers: A Critical Reference Guide (4 vols), Frederick Unger Publ, 79-82; Women Poets in Pre-Revolutionary America, 1650-1775, Whitston Publ Co, 81; Susanna Wright's verse epistle on the status of women in eighteenth-century America, Signs, 6: 795-800; Puritan women poets, In: A Companion to the Poetry of the Puritans, Pa State Univ Press, 85; co-ed, Critical Essays on Anne Bradstreet, G.K. Hall, 83; author of numerous articles, notes, and reviews. **CONTACT ADDRESS** Dept of English, Colorado State Univ, 3637 N Co Rd, 23 E, LaPorte, CO 80535. **EMAIL** pcowell@vines.colostate.edu

COWGILL, KENT
DISCIPLINE LITERATURE **EDUCATION** Univ Nebr, MA, PhD. **CAREER** Prof. **RESEARCH** Chaucer, classical mythology, American literature. **SELECTED PUBLICATIONS** Auth, The Cranberry Trail: Misfits, Dreamers, and Drifters on the Heartland Road, 96. **CONTACT ADDRESS** Winona State Univ, PO Box 5838, Winona, MN 55987-5838.

COX, DON RICHARD
PERSONAL Born 06/19/1943, Wichita, KS, m, 1976, 3 children **DISCIPLINE** VICTORIAN LITERATURE **EDUCATION** Wichita State Univ, BA, 66, MA, 68; Univ Mo, PhD(English), 75. **CAREER** Asst prof, 75-81, Assoc Prof English, Univ Tenn, 81-. **MEMBERSHIPS** MLA; SAtlantic Mod Lang Asn. **RESEARCH** Victorian novel. **SELECTED PUBLICATIONS** Coauth, Emblems of Reality, Glencoe Press, 73; auth, The vision of Robinson's Merlin, Colby Libr Quart, 74; Barbie and her playmates, J Pop Cult, 77; A world he never made: The decline of James T Farrell, Col Lang Asn, 79; The birds of Bleak House, Dickens Studies Newsletter, 80; co-ed, The Technical Reader, Holt, Rinehart & Winston, 80. **CONTACT ADDRESS** Dept English, Univ of Tennessee, Knoxville, Knoxville, TN 37996.

COX, E. SAM
PERSONAL Born 11/08/1947, Mountain Home, AK, m, 1967, 2 children **DISCIPLINE** COMMUNICATION **EDUCATION** Univ Ariz, PhD, 88. **CAREER** Asst, assoc prof, prof, comm, 85-, Central Mo St Univ. **HONORS AND AWARDS** Communicator Awds, ArlingtonTX, 98, hon men, PS Roadtrip - Electronic Field Trip #3. **MEMBERSHIPS** Natl Comm Assn; Amer Assn of Higher Ed. **RESEARCH** Technology & education; knowledge media; organizational communication. **SELECTED PUBLICATIONS** Auth, An Answer to The Call for Experimentation by the CEDA Assessment Conference: a Descriptive Study of a Peer-Judged Round, CEDA yearbk, 93; auth, A Reaction to Frank, and Horn and Underberg: An Assessment of Assessments, 20th Anniversary Assessment Conf Proc, Kendall/Hunt, 93; auth, The Officiated Approach to Return Tournament Debate to the Public Arena, Proc of Pi Kappa Delta Natl Develop Conf, 94; auth, The Need to Return Tournament Debate to the Public Arena, Pi Kappa Delta Natl Develop Conf, 94; coauth, Pi Kappa Delta as a Regulatory Agency for Competitive Debate: Toward Adapting and Adopting Officiated Debate, Pi Kappa Delta Natl Develop Conf, 95; coauth, The Value of Tournament Debating: An Analysis of Administrator's Views, Pi Kappa Delta Develop Conf, 95; auth, Toward Resolving the Debate Over Format: A Response to Panel Four, Pi Kappa Delta Develop Conf, 95; coauth, Pi Kappa Delta's Leadership Role in Competitive Debate: Toward Fairness, Civility and Accessibility, Forensic of Pi Kappa Delta, 80, 95; coauth, Valuing of Tournament Debate: Factors from Practitioners and Administrators, Forensic of Pi Kappa Delta, 80, 95; coauth, A Survey of the Entire CEDA Membership: Data for Decisions, J of Pragmatic Argumentation. **CONTACT ADDRESS** Central Missouri State Univ, Martin 136J, Warrensburg, MO 64093. **EMAIL** cox@cmsu1.cmsu.edu

COX, JOHN D.
PERSONAL Born 08/09/1945, Red Oak, IA, m, 1968, 3 children **DISCIPLINE** ENGLISH LANGUAGE & LITERATURE **EDUCATION** Hope Col, BA, 67; Univ Chicago, MA, 68, PhD, 75. **CAREER** Asst prof English, Westmont Col, 73-75; asst prof English, Univ Victoria, BC, 75-78; Mellon fac fel English, Harvard Univ, Cambridge, 78-79; prof English, Hope Col, 96-. **HONORS AND AWARDS** NEH fellowship, 85-86; NEH Summer Stipend, 93; Pew Fellowship, 95-96. **MEMBERSHIPS** MLA; Shakespeare Assn Am; Medieval & Renaissance Drama Soc. **RESEARCH** English Renaissance drama and poetry. **SELECTED PUBLICATIONS** Auth, Shakespeare and the Dramaturgy of Power, Princeton UP, 89; A New History of Early English Drama, Columbia UP, 97; auth, The Devil and the Sacred in English Drama, 1350-1642, Cambridge UP, 01; co-ed, Third Arden Edition of 3 Henry VI, 01. **CONTACT ADDRESS** Dept of English, Hope Col, Holland, MI 49423-3698. **EMAIL** cox@hope.edu

COX, ROBERT
PERSONAL Born 05/19/1937, Amarillo, TX, m, 1963, 4 children **DISCIPLINE** ENGLISH LITERATURE **EDUCATION** Northern AZ Univ, BA, 59; IN Univ, PhD, 65. **CAREER** Prof, Univ Pacific. **HONORS AND AWARDS** UOP Eberhardt Awd; Fulbright Jr Fellowship, 63-64; Fulbright Sr Fellowship (Honorary) 84-85. **MEMBERSHIPS** MLA, NCTE, LSA, Medieval Academy. **RESEARCH** Northern Europ lang(s); cult of the middle ages. **SELECTED PUBLICATIONS** Auth, pubs on Old English; Restoration drama; tchr educ. **CONTACT ADDRESS** Eng Dept, Univ of the Pacific, Stockton, 3601 Pacific Ave, PO Box 3601, Stockton, CA 95211. **EMAIL** rcox@uop.edu

COX, ROGER LINDSAY
PERSONAL Born 03/23/1931, Manson, IA, m, 1951, 4 children **DISCIPLINE** ENGLISH & COMPARATIVE LITERATURE **EDUCATION** Morningside Col, BA, 51; Univ Calif, Los Angeles, MA, 52; Columbia Univ, PhD, 61. **CAREER** Instr English, Bates Col, 58-61; from asst prof to assoc prof, DePauw Univ, 61-71; assoc prof, 71-75, Prof English, Univ Del, 75-, vis prof, Jean-Moulin Univ, Lyon, Fr, 93; **HONORS AND AWARDS** Great Lakes Cols Asn award, 67-68; Am Coun Learned Soc fel, 67-68; Andrew Mellon fel, Univ Pittsburgh, 69-70. **RESEARCH** Tragedy; Comedy; Shakespeare; the novel. **SELECTED PUBLICATIONS** Auth, Hamlet's Hamartia: Aristotle or St Paul?, Yale Rev, 66; Tragedy and the gospel narratives, Yale Rev, 68; Between Earth and Heaven: Shakespeare, Dostoevsky and the Meaning of Christian Tragedy, Holt, 69; The invented self: An essay on comedy, Soundings, summer 74; The structure of comedy, Thought, 3/75; Dostoevsky and the Ridiculous, Dostoevsky Studies, 80; Time and timelessness in Dostoevsky's fiction, Forum Int, fall 80; Stavrogin and Prince Hal, Canadian Slavonic Papers, 84; Kirillov, Stavrogin, and Suicide, Dostoevsky and the Human Condition after a Century, Greenwood Press, 86; Shakespeare's Comic Changes: The Time-Lapse Metaphor as Plot Device, Univ Georgia Press, 91. **CONTACT ADDRESS** 404 Vassar Dr, Newark, DE 19711. **EMAIL** ROGERLC@EROLS.COM

COX, SHELLY MARIE
PERSONAL Born 09/16/1948, Camden, NJ, s **DISCIPLINE** ENGLISH **EDUCATION** Univ of PA, BA, 70; Univ of Chicago, MA, 73; S IL Univ, MA, 81 **CAREER** Cataloger, 73-84, Librn, 85-, assoc prof, Southern Ill Univ. **MEMBERSHIPS** Am Libr Asn; Lawrence Durrell Soc **RESEARCH** Lawrence Durrell **SELECTED PUBLICATIONS** Auth, A Personal-Name Index to New Directions, Vol. 1-35. With a Historical Preface, Troy, NY, Whitston Publishing, 80 **CONTACT ADDRESS** Library Affairs, So Illinois Univ, Carbondale, Mailcode: 6632, Carbondale, IL 62901. **EMAIL** scox@lib.siu.edu

COX, STEPHEN D.
PERSONAL Born 01/12/1948, Niles, MI **DISCIPLINE** ENGLISH LITERATURE **EDUCATION** Univ Mich, BA, 72; Univ Calif, Los Angeles, MA, 73, PhD(English), 76 **CAREER** Lectr, 76-80, asst prof, 80-83, assoc prof, 83-92, Prof English, Dept Lit, Univ Calif, San Diego, 92-. **MEMBERSHIPS** Asn Literary Scholars & Critics; Am Soc for 18th Century Studies **RESEARCH** 18th century and romantic literature; Blake; classical liberalism; American religious history. **SELECTED PUBLICATIONS** Auth, The Stranger Within Thee: Concepts of the Self in Late Eighteenth Century Literature, Univ Pittsburgh Press, 80; Love and Logic: The Evolution of Blake's Thought, Univ Mich Press, 92; biogr intro, The God of the Machine, by Isabel Paterson, Transaction Publ, 93; Theory, Experience, and the American Religion, JETS, 93; The Two Liberalsims, Am Lit Hist, 94; The Devil's Reading List, Raritan, 96; The Titanic Story, Open Court Publ, 99. **CONTACT ADDRESS** Dept of Lit 0306, Univ of California, San Diego, 9500 Gilman Dr, La Jolla, CA 92093-0306. **EMAIL** sdcox@ucsd.edu

COYLE, MICHAEL GORDON
DISCIPLINE LITERARY AND CRITICAL THEORY **EDUCATION** Miami Univ, BA, 78; Univ VA, MA, 81, PhD, 86. **CAREER** Assoc prof, Colgate Univ, 86. **HONORS AND AWARDS** Ford Found grant, 89; President's fel, Univ VA, 85-86; Lily Dabney fel, Univ London, 82. **RESEARCH** Modernist lit and cult Hist. **SELECTED PUBLICATIONS** Auth, Ezra Pound, Popular Genres, and the Discourse of Culture Col Park: Pa State UP, 95; A Present with Innumerable Pasts: Postmodernity and the Tracing of Modernist Origins, Rev, Univ Va P, 96; Ezra Pound, Am Lit Scholar, Duke UP, 96. **CONTACT ADDRESS** Dept of Eng, Colgate Univ, 13 Oak Drive, Hamilton, NY 13346.

COYNE, STEPHEN
PERSONAL Born 05/08/1950, Salem, NJ, m, 1996, 2 children **DISCIPLINE** ENGLISH **EDUCATION** Catawba Col, BA, 72; Univ NC at Chapel Hill, MA, 76; Univ Denver, PhD, 88. **CAREER** Instr, Isothermal Community Col; teaching fel, Univ Denver, 84-87; assoc prof, Morningside Col, 88-. **HONORS AND AWARDS** NJ State Coun on the Arts Individual Artists Fel. **MEMBERSHIPS** MLA, Associated Writings Prog. **RESEARCH** Colonial Southern New Jersey. **SELECTED PUBLICATIONS** Auth, "Salvage," Am Short Fiction 5.20, (95); auth, "Sioux City," The Greensboro Rev 60, (96); auth, "Missing in Action," The Ga Rev, (96); auth, "Lost," The Southern Rev, (00); auth, "Steps," The Southern Rev, (00); auth, "Old Jazz," The Southern Rev, (00); auth, "Hunting country," The Southern Rev 36.1, (00); auth, "Scrambled Love," The Lit Rev (forthcoming). **CONTACT ADDRESS** Dept English, Morningside Col, 1501 Morningside Ave, Sioux City, IA 51106-1717. **EMAIL** sbc001@morningside.edu

CRABTREE, CLARIE
PERSONAL 2 children **DISCIPLINE** AMERICAN LITERATURE AND FOLKLORE **EDUCATION** Trinity Col, BA; Fordham Univ, MA; Wayne State Univ, PhD. **CAREER** Fulbright sr lectr, Romania, 94-95; Prof, 97-. **HONORS AND AWARDS** Dir, women's stud prog. **MEMBERSHIPS** MLA, Detroit Writers' Guild. **RESEARCH** William Faulkner. **SELECTED PUBLICATIONS** Pub(s), on Faulkner, and women writers sich as Erdrich, Hurston, and Toni Morrison. **CONTACT ADDRESS** Dept of Eng, Univ of Detroit Mercy, 4001 W McNichols Rd, PO BOX 19900, Detroit, MI 48219-0900. **EMAIL** crabtrec@udmercy.edu

CRABTREE, ROBBIN D.
PERSONAL Born 03/04/1960, CA **DISCIPLINE** COMMUNICATION **EDUCATION** Univ Minn, MA, 86, PhD, 92; Univ Cal, SB, BA, 82. **CAREER** Asst Prof, 93-, DCS, New Mexico State Univ; Asst Prof, 91-93, DePauw Univ; pub aff/host, 89-90, KUOM MN pub radio; grad teach Asst, 84-91, Univ Minn. **HONORS AND AWARDS** NM Dept Hlth Res Gnt; NMSU Res Gnt; LAS Con Awd; Pres Fac Gnt; BEA Harwood Diss Hon Men. **MEMBERSHIPS** ICA; NCA; WSCA; UDC. **RESEARCH** Intl Intercultural Communication, Development, Empowerment, the role of communication in social change. **SELECTED PUBLICATIONS** Auth, Communication and social change: Applied communication theory in service learning, in: Voices of Strong Democracy: Service Learning and Comm Stud, eds, B O Murphy, D Droge, AAHE, 98; Mutual Empowerment in cross-cultural participatory development and service learning: Lessons in comm and social justice form projects in El Salvador and Nicaragua, J Applied Comm

Res, 98; coauth, Communicating about emerging infectious diseases in the borderlands: Hantavirus education for rural border and migrant populations, in: Border Health: Res and Practice on the US-Mex Border, eds, J G Power, T Byrd, Thousand Oaks, Sage, 98; auth, Service learning and the liberal arts: Restructuring for integrated education, in: Restructuring for Integrative Edu: Multi Perspectives Multi Contexts, ed, TE Jennings, Westport CT, Bergin & Garvey, 97; coauth, Principles of Human Communication, Dubuque, Kendall/Hunt, 96. **CONTACT ADDRESS** Dept Comm Studies, New Mexico State Univ, Dept 3W, Las Cruces, NM 88003-8001. **EMAIL** crabtree@nmsu.edu

CRACROFT, RICHARD HOLTON
PERSONAL Born 06/28/1936, Salt Lake City, UT, m, 1959, 3 children **DISCIPLINE** AMERICAN LITERATURE **EDUCATION** Univ Utah, BA, 61, MA, 63; Univ Wis, PhD, 69. **CAREER** Prof English, Brigham Young Univ, 63-, Chmn Dept, 75-80, Dean, Col Humanities, 81-86; Assoc ed, Dialogue: A J of Mormon Thought, 69-73; res ed, Western Am Lit, 73-. **MEMBERSHIPS** Western Am Lit Asn; Rocky Mountain Mod Lang Asn; NCTE; MLA. **RESEARCH** Western American literature; Mark Twain; Mormon literature. **SELECTED PUBLICATIONS** Auth, The Big Sky: A B Guthrie's use of historical sources, Western Am Lit, fall 71; The gentle blasphemer: Mark Twain, holy scripture and the Book of Mormon, Brigham Young Univ Studies, winter 71; A pebble in the pool: Organic unity in Thomas Wolfe's You Can't Go Home Again, Mod Fiction Studies, winter 72; co-ed, A Believing People: Literature of the Latter-day Saints, Brigham Young Univ, 74, 79; 22 Young Mormon Writers, Commun Workshop, 75; auth, Provo Patriotic Reader, Brigham Young Univ, 76; coauth, Voices from the past, 80. **CONTACT ADDRESS** Dept of English, Brigham Young Univ, 3146 Jkhb, Provo, UT 84602-0002. **EMAIL** richard_cracroft@byu.edu

CRAFT, WILLIAM
DISCIPLINE LITERATURE OF THE RENAISSANCE AND REFORMATION **EDUCATION** Univ NC at Chapel Hill, MA, PhD. **CAREER** Newberry Libr Chicago fel; Amer Coun Educ fel; app 3-yr term, Undergrad dean. **SELECTED PUBLICATIONS** Auth, Labyrinth of Desire, 94. **CONTACT ADDRESS** Dept of English, Mount Saint Mary's Col and Sem, 16300 Old Emmitsburg Rd, Emmitsburg, MD 21727-7799. **EMAIL** craft@msmary.edu

CRAFTON, ROBERT E.
PERSONAL Born 08/26/1953, Baltimore, MD, m, 1981, 3 children **DISCIPLINE** ENGLISH **EDUCATION** Univ Del, BA, 75; Univ Va, MA, 77; Wash Univ, PhD, 90. **CAREER** Teacher, DeSmet Jesuit HS, 77-80; teaching asst, Wash Univ, 80-89; assoc prof to assoc dean, Lindenwood Col, 89-94; adj prof, Webster Univ, 96; asst prof, Slippery Rock Univ, 96-. **HONORS AND AWARDS** NEH Grant, 95; Wash Univ Fel, 84-85; Phi Beta Kappa. **MEMBERSHIPS** MLA; NCTE; CCCC; NAME. **RESEARCH** Cognitive mapping of Language and memory functions; curricular standards for public education; portfolio assessment. **SELECTED PUBLICATIONS** Auth, "Promises, Promises: Computer-Assisted Revision and Basic Writers," Computers/Compos (96); co-auth, "Mapping Language Function in the Brain: A Review of the Recent Literature," J Tech Writing Commun (00); auth, "Religiously," Ginger Hill (01); co-auth, "Thinking in Paragraphs: A Functional Magnetic Resonance Imaging Study," J Tech Writing Commun (in pr); co-auth, Mapping Cognitive Complexity: A MRI Comparison of Language and Mathematical Paradigms," J Tech Writing Commun (in pr). **CONTACT ADDRESS** English Dept, Slippery Rock Univ of Pennsylvania, 314 Spots World Cultures Bldg, Slippery Rock, PA 16057. **EMAIL** robert.crafton@sru.edu

CRAIG, CHRISTOPHER P.
DISCIPLINE CLASSICAL STUDIES **EDUCATION** Oberlin Col, AB, 74; Univ NC, PhD, 79. **CAREER** Instr, Stockley Inst, 83-84; Tchg fel, Univ NC, 78-79; instr, Univ Ca, 79-80; asst prof, 80-86, assoc prof, Univ Tenn, 86-. **HONORS AND AWARDS** Dir, Vergilian Soc Am, 85-93. **MEMBERSHIPS** Am Philol Asn; Archaeol Inst Am; Class Asn Middle W and S; Am Class League; Vergilian Soc Am; Tennessee Lang Tchr Asn; Tennessee Class Asn; Int Soc Hist Rhet; Am Soc Hist Rhet; Speech Commun Asn. **RESEARCH** Classical rhetoric and oratory; Cicero. **SELECTED PUBLICATIONS** Auth, "Cicero's Strategy of Embarrassment in the Speech for Plancius," Am Jour Philol, 90; auth, Form as Argument in Cicero's Speeches, Scholars, 93; auth, "Three Simple Questions for Teaching Cicero's First Catilinarian Oration," Class Jour, 93; auth, "Teaching Cicero's Speech for Caelius: What Enquiring Minds Want to Know," Class Jour, 95. **CONTACT ADDRESS** Dept of Classics, Univ of Tennessee, Knoxville, Knoxville, TN 37996-0413. **EMAIL** ccraig@utk.edu

CRAIG, GEORGE ARMOUR
PERSONAL Born 11/15/1914, Cleveland, OH, m, 1939, 2 children **DISCIPLINE** ENGLISH LITERATURE **EDUCATION** Amherst Col, AB, 37; Harvard Univ AM, 38, PhD, 47. **CAREER** Instr English, Harvard Univ, 38-40; from instr to assoc prof, 40-55, prof, 55-80, Kenan Prof English, Amherst Col, 80-, Vis lectr, Harvard Univ, 55-56. **MEMBERSHIPS** MLA. **RESEARCH** Seventeenth century English philosophy and literature; 19th century prose fiction. **CONTACT ADDRESS** Dept of English, Amherst Col, Amherst, MA 01002.

CRAIG, HERBERT EUGENE
PERSONAL Born 12/13/1946, Chardon, OH, m, 1995 **DISCIPLINE** LITERATURE, SPANISH **EDUCATION** Ohio State Univ, BA, 69; Univ Wis Madison, MA, 72; PhD, 83; Univ Ill, MA, 85. **CAREER** Asst prof, Bethany Col, 79-89; asst prof to assoc prof, Univ Nebr Kearney, 89-. **HONORS AND AWARDS** Phi Beta Kappa; Fulbright/Hays Fel, 76-77; NEH, 85; Res Grant, Univ Nebr, 97; Sab, Bethany Col, 85-86; Univ Nebr, 97-98. **MEMBERSHIPS** AATSP; MLA. **RESEARCH** Literary relation between Marcel Proust and Spanish America; Hispanic film; translation studies. **SELECTED PUBLICATIONS** Auth, "Proust y Mujica Lainez: La Memoria Asociativa," Cuadernos Hisp (84); auth, "Ideas de Ortega y Gasset Sobre la Novella Proustiana," Bulletin Hisp 88 (86); auth, "La Memoria Proustiana en Rayuela," Nueva Rev de Filol Hisp 37 (89); auth, "Proustian Time in Elamor en los Tiempos del Colera," Confluen 5 (90); auth, "Proustian in Spanish: The Old and New translations of Du Cote de Chez Swann," Platt Val Rev 23 (95); auth, "Proust en Espana y en Hispano-Americana: La Recepcion 1920-1929," Bulletin Hisp 101 (99). **CONTACT ADDRESS** 2111 9th Ave, Kearney, NE 68845-5016. **EMAIL** craigh@unk.edu

CRAIG, J. ROBERT
PERSONAL Born 12/21/1947, New Kensington, PA, m, 1971, 3 children **DISCIPLINE** RADIO, TELEVISION, FILM **EDUCATION** Clarion Univ of Pa, BSEd, 69; MS, 71; Univ of Mo, PhD, 81. **CAREER** NW Mo State Univ, 71-80; Central Mich Univ, 80-. **HONORS AND AWARDS** BCA Law & Reg Div paper competition winner, 96. **MEMBERSHIPS** Broadcast Educ Asn, Int Asn on Fantastic in Arts, Far W Popular Culture Asn, NEA. **RESEARCH** Film & Electronic Media Law. **SELECTED PUBLICATIONS** Auth, Auth, "On Visual Tropes as Expressions of the Psyche in Roman Polanski's The Tenant," J of the Fantastic in the Arts 9.2 (98); auth, "Reno v. American Civil Liberties Union: The First Amendment, Electronic Media, and the Internet Indecency Issue," Commun and the Law (June, 98); auth, "Trapping Simians in the Scottish Highlands: A Viewer Responds tot he Hitchcock MacGuffin in Terry Gilliam's 12 Monkeys," J of Evolutionary Psychol (98); coauth, "Three Viewers Viewing: A Viewer-Response Symposium on Jacob's Ladder," Literature/Film Quart 26.3 (98); coauth, "Implementing the FCC's Three-Hour Children's Television Rule: A First Look," Feedback (99); auth, "Special Effects and the Cult of Personality in Fantasy Film: Robert Zemeckis's Contact as Fantastic Reality," Popular Culture Rev (99); coauth, "Wreaking Vengeance: The Avenging Angel Motif in Spawn and The Crow," J of Evolutionary Psychol (00). **CONTACT ADDRESS** Dept Broadcast & Cinematic Art, Central Michigan Univ, 306 Moore Hall, Mount Pleasant, MI 48859-0001. **EMAIL** j.robert.craig@cmich.edu

CRAIG, ROBERT T.
PERSONAL Born 05/10/1947, Rochester, NY, m, 1979, 1 child **DISCIPLINE** COMMUNICATION **EDUCATION** Univ Wis-Madison, 69; Mich State Univ, MA, 70; PhD, 76. **CAREER** Asst prof, Pa State Univ, 76-79; asst prof, Univ Ill-Chicago, 79-81; asst/assoc prof, Temple Univ, 81-90; assoc prof, Univ Colo-Boulder, 90- . **HONORS AND AWARDS** Best Article Awd, Int Communication Asn, 00. **MEMBERSHIPS** Nat Commun Asoc; Int Commun Asoc; Western States Commun Asoc. **RESEARCH** Communication theory; language and social interaction. **SELECTED PUBLICATIONS** Auth, with K. Tracy, Grounded Practical Theory: The Case of Intellectual Discussion, Commun Theory, 95; auth, Practical Theory: A Reply to Sandelands, J for the Theory of Soc Behav, 96; auth, Practical-Theoretical Argumentation, Argumentation, 96; auth with D.A. Carlone, Growth and Transformation of Communication Studies in U.S. Higher Education: Towards Reinterpretation, Commun Educ, 98; auth, "Metadiscourse, Theory, and Practice," in Research in Language and Social Interation, 99; auth, "Communication Theory as a Field," in Communication Theory, 99. **CONTACT ADDRESS** Dept. of Communication, Univ of Colorado, Boulder, CB 270, Boulder, CO 80309-0279. **EMAIL** robert.craig@colorado.edu

CRAIGE, BETTY JEAN
PERSONAL Born 05/20/1946, Chicago, IL **DISCIPLINE** LITERATURE **EDUCATION** Pomona Col, BA, 68; Univ Washington, MA, 70, PhD, 74. **CAREER** Instr to prof, Univ Ga, 73-; dir, Center for Humanities & Arts, 93-; interim head of comparative lit, 97-99. **HONORS AND AWARDS** Honoratus Medal for Teaching, UGA Honors Prog, 87; Frederic W. Ness Book Awd, 89; co-winner, Ga Author of the Year Awd, 92; Univ Ga Alumni Soc Faculty Svc Awd, 94; dir, center for humanities & arts, 93- ; interim head of comparative lit, 97-99. **MEMBERSHIPS** Modern Lang Assoc; Amer Comparative Lit Assoc. **RESEARCH** Holism **SELECTED PUBLICATIONS** Auth, Lorca's Poet in New York: The Fall into Consciousness, Univ Press Ky, 77; Literary Relativity, Bucknell Univ Press, 82; Reconnection: Dualism to Holism in Literary Study, Univ of Ga Press, 88; Laying the Ladder Down: The Emergence of Cultural Holism, Univ Mass Pr, 92; America Patriotism in a Global Society, SUNY Press, 96. **CONTACT ADDRESS** Center for Humanities and Arts, Univ of Georgia, 164 Psychology Bldg., Athens, GA 30602. **EMAIL** bjcraige@uga.edu

CRAIN, PATRICIA
DISCIPLINE ENGLISH **EDUCATION** Bennington, BA, 70; Columbia Univ, MA, 89, PhD, 96. **CAREER** Asst prof of Eng, Univ of Minn. **MEMBERSHIPS** Am Antiquarian Soc **SELECTED PUBLICATIONS** Auth, "The Story of A: The Alphabetization of America from The New England Primer to the Scarlet Letter," Stanford Univ Press, 00. **CONTACT ADDRESS** Dept of Eng, Univ of Minnesota, Twin Cities, 207 Lind Hall Church St, SE, Minneapolis, MN 55455. **EMAIL** patcrain@umn.edu

CRAMER, OWEN C.
PERSONAL Born 12/01/1941, Tampa, FL, m, 1962, 4 children **DISCIPLINE** CLASSICS **EDUCATION** Oberlin Col, AB, 62; Univ Tex, PhD, 73. **CAREER** Instr to prof, Colo Col, 65-; vis prof, Univ Chicago, 87-88. **HONORS AND AWARDS** Woodrow Wilson Fel, 62. **MEMBERSHIPS** Am Philol Asn; Class Asn of the Middle W and S; Am Comparative Lit Asn; Mod Greek Studies Asn. **RESEARCH** Home; Greek historiography. **SELECTED PUBLICATIONS** Auth, "Speech and Silence in the Iliad," Class j, (76): 300-304; auth, "Ulysses the Good? What is the Formula at Od," Transactions of the Am Philol Asn, (74): 77-80. **CONTACT ADDRESS** Dept Class, Colo Col, 14 E Cache la Poudre St, Colorado Springs, CO 80903. **EMAIL** ocramer@coloradocollege.edu

CRANE, JON
DISCIPLINE COMMUNICATION STUDIES **EDUCATION** Univ IL, PhD, 91. **CAREER** Assoc prof, Univ NC, Charlotte. **SELECTED PUBLICATIONS** Auth, Terror and everyday life: Singular moments in the hist of horror film, Sage, 94. **CONTACT ADDRESS** Univ of No Carolina, Charlotte, Charlotte, NC 28223-0001.

CRANE, MILTON
PERSONAL Born 05/24/1917, Hartford, CT, m, 1940, 2 children **DISCIPLINE** ENGLISH AND AMERICAN LITERATURE **EDUCATION** Columbia Univ, AB, 37, AM, 38; Harvard Univ, AM, 41, PhD, 42. **CAREER** Instr English, Col William & Mary, 42-43 & Hunter Col, 44-47; asst prof, Univ Chicago, 47-52; res dir, US Dept State, 52-61, chief div res Brit Commonwealth, North & Cent Europe, 61-64; prof English lit, 64-76, Emer Prof English, George Washington Univ, 76-, Educ & res analyst, Off Strategic Serv, 43-45; assoc ed, Bantam Bk, Inc, 45-46; prof lectr, George Washington Univ, 55-61, 63. **MEMBERSHIPS** MLA; Shakespeare Asn Am. **RESEARCH** Shakespeare; George Bernard Shaw. **SELECTED PUBLICATIONS** Auth, They Hunt in Packs, Overland, Vol 0135, 94; Under the Bridge, Overland, Vol 0145, 96; A Dog Called Yesterday, Overland, Vol 0147, 97; How to Write the Perfect Suicide Note, Overland, Vol 0129, 92; The Race, Overland, Vol 0137, 94; Lullaby, Overland, Vol 0140, 95; The Ferryman, Meanjin, Vol 0054, 95. **CONTACT ADDRESS** Dept of English, The George Washington Univ, 2023 G St NW, Washington, DC 20006.

CRANE, SUSAN
DISCIPLINE ENGLISH LANGUAGE AND LITERATURE **EDUCATION** Univ Wisconsin, BA: Univ Calif Berkeley, MA; PhD. **CAREER** Prof **RESEARCH** Gender; cultural history; Medieval English and French literature. **SELECTED PUBLICATIONS** Auth, Insular Romance; auth, Gender and Romance in Chaucer's Canterbury Tales . **CONTACT ADDRESS** Dept of English, Rutgers, The State Univ of New Jersey, New Brunswick, 510 George St, Murray Hall, New Brunswick, NJ 08901-1167.

CRAUN, EDWIN DAVID
PERSONAL Born 03/17/1945, Riverside, CA, m, 1967, 2 children **DISCIPLINE** MEDIEVAL & RENAISSANCE POETRY & PROSE, ENGLISH & LATIN **EDUCATION** Wheaton Col, Ill, BA, 67; Princeton Univ, PhD, 71. **CAREER** From Asst Prof to Prof, 71-95, asst dean col, 78-81, Henry S. Fox, Jr. Prof English, Washington & Lee Univ, 95-. **HONORS AND AWARDS** Wheaton Col Scholastic Honor Soc, 67; Woodrow Wilson Fel, 67-69; Fel, SEastern Inst Medieval and Renaissance Studies, Summer 76; NEH Summer Seminars Program, 83, 89; NEH Fel for Col Teachers, 86-87; Mednick Memorial Fel, Va Found for Independent Colleges, Summer 90; Phi Beta Kappa, 92. **MEMBERSHIPS** MLA; Southeastern Med Asn; Med Acad Am; New Chaucer Soc. **RESEARCH** Medieval and Renaissance narrative poetry. **SELECTED PUBLICATIONS** Auth, Inordinata Locutio: Blasphemy in Pastoral Literature, 1200-1500, Traditio 29, 83; Blaspheming Her "Awin God": Cressid's Lamentatioun in Henryson's Testament, Studies in Philol 82, 85; Verbum Nuncius es Rationis: Augustinian Sign Theory in Medieval Pastoral Discourse on Deviant Speech, Augustinian Studies 20, 89; Most Sacred Vertue She: Reading Book V Alongside Aristotle and Thomas Aquinas on Justice, In: Approaches to Teaching Spenser's Faerie Queene, Mod Lang Asn, 94; Lies, Slander, and Obscenity in Medieval En-

glish Literature: Pastoral Rhetoric and the Deviant Speaker, Cambridge Studies in Medieval Literature 33, Cambridge Univ Press, 97. **CONTACT ADDRESS** Dept of English, Washington and Lee Univ, Lexington, VA 24450-2504. **EMAIL** craune@ulu.edu

CRAVEN, ALAN
DISCIPLINE ENGLISH **EDUCATION** Univ KS, AB, MA, PhD. **CAREER** Prof & dean, Col Fine Arts and Hum; 21 yrs dir, Div Engl, Classics, Philos & Commun; dean of the Col, 95-; taught at, Univ AR & Brandeis Univ. **RESEARCH** Bibl, renaissance lit, dramatic and non-dramatic; Shakespeare. **SELECTED PUBLICATIONS** Publ in, Engl Lang Notes, Papers of the Bibliog Soc of Amer, Stud in Bibliog, Shakespeare Quart. **CONTACT ADDRESS** Col of Fine Arts and Hum, Univ of Texas, San Antonio, 6900 N Loop 1604 W, San Antonio, TX 78249. **EMAIL** acraven@lonestar.utsa.edu

CRAWFORD, JERRY L.
PERSONAL Born 08/20/1934, Whittemore, IA, m, 1956, 3 children **DISCIPLINE** DRAMA **EDUCATION** Drake Univ, BFA, 56; Stanford Univ, MA, 57; Univ Iowa, PhD, 64. **CAREER** From instr to prof drama, 62-70, actg dean fac, 65-66, dean fac, 66-68, chmn dept speech & drama, 68-70, Prof Theatre Arts, 70-94, Prof Emer, 94- , Univ Nev, Las Vegas, 70- ; Dir Lit Sem, Utah Shakespearean Fest. Cedar City, UT, 88- . **HONORS AND AWARDS** Best New Play Awd, Southeastern Theatre Conf, 74; Gold Medallion, Am Oil Co, 77 & 80; Gov Nev Art Awd, State Nev, 82. **MEMBERSHIPS** Assoc Theatre Higuer Ed; Col Fel Am Theatre, 91- and Dean, Col Fel Am Theatre, 00-02; Dramatists Guild, 81- . **RESEARCH** Theory, technique and practice of playwriting; contemporary dramatic literature; acting and directing in the contemporary theatre. **SELECTED PUBLICATIONS** Auth, The auction tomorrow, Southeastern Theatre Conf J, fall 74; coauth, The Actor: In Person and in Style, 75 & 94; auth, The auction tomorrow (play), Judy Bayley Summer Repertory Theatre, Las Vegas, 76, The Corner Theatre, Baltimore, 77, Univ Theatre, Calif State Univ, Fresno, 77, Stockton Calif, 78 & Hartman Theatre, Stanford, Conn, 80; The passing of Corky Brewster (play), Circle Repertory Co, New York, 2-3/77; Halftime at the Superbowl (play), Playwrights unit Actors Studio, New York, 1/77; Those were the days they gave babies away with half a pound of tea (play), Meadows Playhouse, Las Vegas, 4/78; The Last President (play), St Clements Theatre, NY, 79 & UNLV, 81; Dance for Rain, Redmen, That Was Number 99 (play), Dramatics Mag, 4/82; The Brothers Silence, UNLV, 97; auth, The Dreamer, 98; auth, The Ball Turret Gunner, 98; auth, Rapid Robert Rap, 99; auth, Eniwetok, 99; auth, The Maven and the Ruse, 00. **CONTACT ADDRESS** Dept of Theatre Arts, Univ of Nevada, Las Vegas, Las Vegas, NV 89154. **EMAIL** bunnhoos@aol.com

CRAWFORD, JOHN W.
PERSONAL Born 09/02/1936, Ashdown, AR, m, 1962, 2 children **DISCIPLINE** ENGLISH LITERATURE **EDUCATION** TexarKansas Col, AA, 56; Quachita Col, BA, 59; Drake Univ, MSE, 62; Okla State Univ, EdD. **CAREER** Instr, Greene Co Schs, 59-62; Instr, Clinton Col, 62-66; Prof, Henderson State Univ, 67-97. **HONORS AND AWARDS** Sybil Nash Abrams Poetry Prize; SCCEA Teacher Awd; Ark PRA Merit Awd. **MEMBERSHIPS** CEA, South Central CEA, South Central MLA, Ark Philol Asn. **RESEARCH** English literature, Shakespearian studies, drama, American literature. **SELECTED PUBLICATIONS** Auth, Early Actresses of Shakespeare, Peter Lang Pr, 84; auth, Making the Connection, Mellen Poetry Pr, 89; auth, Wit, Wisdom and Learning of Shakespeare's Renaissance Women, Edwin Mellon Pr, 97. **CONTACT ADDRESS** Dept English & Lang, Henderson State Univ, PO Box 7813, Arkadelphia, AR 71999-0001.

CRAWFORD, RICHARD
PERSONAL Born 05/12/1935, Detroit, MI, m, 1967, 4 children **DISCIPLINE** MUSIC; MUSICOLOGY **EDUCATION** Univ Mich, BM, 58, MM, 59, PhD, 65. **CAREER** Asst prof, mus, Univ Mich; current, prof, Hans T. David Distinguished Univ. **HONORS AND AWARDS** Vincent H. Duckles Award; Otto Kinkeldey Award for Musical Excellence; Irving Lowens Award of the Soc for Am Music; Hon Mem; Am Musicol Soc. **MEMBERSHIPS** Am Antiquarian Soc; Am Acad of Arts and Scis. **RESEARCH** American music. **SELECTED PUBLICATIONS** Auth, Andrew Law: American Psalmodist, 68; auth, William Billings of Boston, 75; auth, The Core Repertory of Early American Pslamody, 84; co-ed & contribur, A Celebration of American Music, 90; auth, American Sacred Music Imprints, 1698-1810: A Bibliography, 90; coauth, Jazz Standards on Record, 1900-1942, 92; auth, The American Musical Landscape, 93; ed-in-chief, Music of the United States of America; auth, America's Musical Life: A History, 01; auth, An Introduction to America's Music, 01. **CONTACT ADDRESS** 1158 Baldwin St, Ann Arbor, MI 48104. **EMAIL** crawfish@umich.edu

CRAWSHAW, WILLIAM HENRY
DISCIPLINE GEORGIAN PERIODS OF BRITISH LITERATURE **EDUCATION** Univ FL, BA, 54; Univ Wales, MA, 59; Pa State Univ, PhD, 66. **CAREER** Prof, Colgate Univ, 63-. **RESEARCH** 18th century Brit lit. **SELECTED PUBLICATIONS** Publ, lit studies of US and Brit works in Studies, Burke & His Times, Conradiana, ESQ, DLB Mod Brit Playwrights, ANQ, Annual of Am Cult Studies; ed bd, Works of Joseph Conrad, Cambridge UP. **CONTACT ADDRESS** Dept of Eng, Colgate Univ, 13 Oak Drive, Hamilton, NY 13346.

CREAN, SUSAN M.
PERSONAL Born 02/14/1945, Toronto, ON, Canada **DISCIPLINE** WRITING **EDUCATION** Univ Toronto, BA, 67, MA, 69; Ecole du Louvre, Dipl, 69-70. **CAREER** Arts & tchg positions, 66-85; MacLean Hunter Ch, dept creative writing, Univ BC, 89-90; ch, Writer's Union Can, 91-92. **SELECTED PUBLICATIONS** Auth, Who's Afraid of Canadian Culture?, 76; auth, Newsworthy: The Lives of Media Women, 84; auth, In the Name of the Fathers: The Story Behind Child Custody, 88; auth, Writing Along Gender Lines, in Language in Her Eye, 90; auth, Culture, Gender and Power, in Changing Focus, 91; auth, Taking the Missionary Position, in Racism in Canada, 91; auth, Grace Hartman, A Woman For Her Time, 95; coauth, Deux pays pour vivre: un plaidoyer, 80; coauth, Two Nations: An Essay on the Culture and Politics of Canada and Quebec in a World of American Pre-eminence, 82. **CONTACT ADDRESS** 1916 W 11th Ave, Vancouver, BC, Canada V6J 2C6.

CREED, WALTER GENTRY
PERSONAL Born 12/30/1931, Philadelphia, PA, m, 1963, 2 children **DISCIPLINE** ENGLISH LITERATURE **EDUCATION** Univ Pa, BA, 60, MA, 61, PhD(English lit), 68. **CAREER** Instr English, Lafayette Col, 65-66, asst prof, 69; asst prof, 69-75, PROF ENGLISH, UNIV HAWAII, MANOA, 84-. **RESEARCH** Computers and writing; literature and science; critical theory. **SELECTED PUBLICATIONS** Auth, Pieces of the puzzle: The multiple-narrative structure of The Alexandria Quartet, Mosaic, winter 73; The whole pointless joke? Darley's search for truth in The Alexandria Quartet, Etudes Anglaises, 4-6/75; The Muse of Science and The Alexandria Quartet, Norwood Ed, 77; On reading Einstein, Four Quart, 1/79; Philosophy of science and theory of literary criticism: Some common problems, Philos Sci Asn, 1/80; The good soldier: Knowing and judging, English Lit Transition, 80; Is Einstein's work relevant to the study of literature?, In: After Einstein, Memphis State Univ Press, 81; Rene Wellek and Karl Popper on the Mode of Existence of Ideas in Literature and Science, J Hist Ideas, 49(1983); Writers Interact (software program). **CONTACT ADDRESS** Dept English, Univ of Hawaii, Manoa, 1733 Donaghho Rd, Honolulu, HI 96822-2368. **EMAIL** creed@hawaii.edu

CREW, H.
PERSONAL Born 07/07/1942, Grafton Flyford, England, m, 1964, 2 children **DISCIPLINE** COMMUNICATIONS **EDUCATION** Thomas A. Edison State Col, BA, 85; Rutgers, MLS, 87; PhD, 96. **CAREER** Asst prof, Kean Univ, 97-; grad coord, Master of Arts, Educ Media Specialist Prog, Dept of commun & Educ Services, Kean Univ, 99-. **MEMBERSHIPS** Am Libr Asn, Children's Lit Asn, USBBY. **RESEARCH** Literature for Youth. **SELECTED PUBLICATIONS** Coauth, "A Feminist Paradigm For Library and Information Science," Wilson Libr Bullet 68.2 (93) & J of Info, Commun, and Libr Sci, 2.1 (95): 89-95; auth, "Feminist Theories and the Voices of Mothers and Daughters in Selected African-American Literature For Young Adults," in African American Voices: Tradition, Transition, Transformation, ed. Karen Patricia Smith (Metuchan: Scarecrow, 94), 74-114; auth, "The Making of A Heroine: A Feminist Approach to the Representation of Heroines in Selected Historical Novels," in Mosaics of Meaning: Enhancing the Intellectual Life of Young People Through Story, ed. Kay E. Vandergrift (Lanham: Scarecrow, 95), 103-133; auth, "Kathryn Lasky," in Writers of Multicultural Fiction for Young Adults: A bio-Critical Sourcebook, ed. M. Daphne Kutzer (CT: Greenwood Press, 96), 227-234; auth, "Making Connections Across Differences: Multicultural Stories of Daughter Mother Relationships in Young Adult Novels," Voya 20.3 (97): 173-176; auth, "Feminist Theories of Adolescent Development: Implications for Young Adult Services in Libraries," J of Youth Services in Libraries Vol 10.4 (97): 405-417; auth, "Transforming the Hidden Curriculum: Gender and the School Library media Center," Knowledge Quest: J of the Am Asn of Sch Librarians 10.4 (98): 30-33; auth, "Richard Peck," in St James Guide to Young Adult Writers 2nd ed. (St James Press, 99); auth, "Kyoko Mori," St James Guide to Young Adult Writers 2nd ed. (St James Press, 99); auth, "Is It Really Mommie Dearest?: Daughter-Mother Relationships in young Adult Fiction, Scarecrow Press, 00. **CONTACT ADDRESS** Dept Commun Arts & Sci, Kean Col of New Jersey, 1000 Morris Ave, Union, NJ 07083. **EMAIL** hcrew@turbo.kean.edu

CREW, LOUIE
PERSONAL Born 12/09/1936, Anniston, AL, m, 1974 **DISCIPLINE** ENGLISH LITERATURE **EDUCATION** Baylor Univ, BA, 58; Auburn Univ, MA, 59; Univ of AL, PhD, 71. **CAREER** Assoc prof, Eng 94-; lectr, Acad Found, 92-94; assoc prof, Acad Found, 89-92; assoc prof, Claflin Col, 88-89; consult cmptr bus wrtg, Salme Ser, 87-88; lectr Eng, Chinese Univ Hong Kong, 84-87; vis for expert, Beijing 2d Inst For Langs, 83-84; assoc prof Eng, Univ WI, 79-84; assoc prof Eng, Ft Valley State Col, 73-79; prof Eng, Claflin Col, 71-73; acad dir, Exper Intl Living, 70-71; instr, Univ AL, 66-70; master Eng/Eng Hist, Penge Secon Mod Schl, 65-66; master Eng/Sacred Studies, Darlington Schl, 59-62. **RESEARCH** Computer software, literature, religion, gay/lesbian/bisexual issues. **SELECTED PUBLICATIONS** Auth, Autumn at Shum Shui Po, PBW, 97. Catherine Jordan's Prayer, Laughing Boy Rev, 97; Cruising, Stet Mag, 97; Death, Online Jour, 97; Ghost Houses, Switched/on Guenberg, 97; Gilded Nimbus, Vox Clamantis, 97; God, Bless Those Who Are Afraid, Prayers to Protest, 97; God's Flesh and Blood, Cz Mag, 97; I Believe in Fairies, The Exploding Chicken Fiasco, 97; auth, Loving Those on the Relig Right, Whosoever, 98; Let Us Now Praise Caustic Christians, More Light, 98. **CONTACT ADDRESS** Dept of Eng, Rutgers, The State Univ of New Jersey, Newark, 350 Dr Martin Luther King Jr Blvd, Hill Hall, Newark, NJ 07102-1801. **EMAIL** lcrew@newark.rutgers.edu

CREWE, JONATHAN V.
DISCIPLINE ENGLISH LITERATURE **EDUCATION** Univ Calif Berkeley, PhD, 80. **CAREER** Willard Prof drama and oratory; prof Eng and comp lit. **RESEARCH** Shakespearean and Renaissannce lit. **SELECTED PUBLICATIONS** Auth, Trials of Authorship: Anterior Forms and Poetic Reconstruction from Wyatt to Shakespeare, Univ Calif P, 90; Hidden Designs: The Critical Profession and Renaissance Literature, Methuen, 86; Unredeemed Rhetoric: Thomas Nashe and the Scandal of Authorship, Johns Hopkins UP, 82; Baby Killers, Differences, 95; In the Field of Dreams: Transvestism in Twelfth Night and The Crying Game, Representations, 95; Out of the Matrix: Shakespeare's Race-Writing, Yale Jour Crit, 95. **CONTACT ADDRESS** Dartmouth Col, 3529 N Main St, #207, Hanover, NH 03755.

CREWS, FREDERICK
PERSONAL Born 02/20/1933, Philadelphia, PA, m, 1959, 2 children **DISCIPLINE** ENGLISH **EDUCATION** Yale, BA, 55; Princeton Univ, PhD, 58. **CAREER** Instr to prof, 58-94, Chr Grad Stud, 88-92, Dept Chr, 92-94, prof emer, 94-, Univ Cal Berkeley, 58-; Fulbright lectr Italy, 61-62; ACLS Study Fel, 65-66; Guggenheim Fel, 70-71; Gayley Lectr Univ Cal, 74-75; Ward-Phillips Lectr Univ Notre Dame, 74-75; Short Term Fel Princeton Univ, 78; Dorothy T. Burstein Lectr UCLA, 84; Distinguished Tchg Award, UCB, 85; Frederick Ives Carpenter vis lectr Univ Chicago, 85; John Dewey Lectr, 87-88; Nina Mae Kellogg Lectr Portland State Univ, 89; Fac Res Lectr UCB, 91-92. **HONORS AND AWARDS** Natl Coun Arts & Hum Essay Prize, 68; Spielvogel-Diamonstein PEN Award, 92; Distinguished Teacher Award. **MEMBERSHIPS** Mod Lang Asn; False Memory Syndrome Found **RESEARCH** Modern British literature; American literature; Psychological theory; Cultural criticism. **SELECTED PUBLICATIONS** Auth, The Random House Handbook, Random House, 92; The Critics Bear It Away: American Fiction and the Academy, Random House, 92; coauth,The Borzoi Handbook Handbook for Writers, Knopf, 93; ed, Anthology of American Literature, Macmillan, 93; auth, The Memory Wars: Freud's Legacy in Dispute, Granta Press, 97; ed, Unauthorized Freud: Doubters Confront a Legend, Viking Press, 98. **CONTACT ADDRESS** 636 Vincente Ave, Berkeley, CA 94707-1524. **EMAIL** fredc@socrates.berkeley.edu

CRIBIORE, RAFFAELA
PERSONAL Born 03/27/1948, Varese, Italy, m, 1970, 2 children **DISCIPLINE** CLASSICS **EDUCATION** Universita Cattolica Milan, BA, 72; M Philos, 90; Columbia Univ, PhD, 93. **CAREER** Lectr, High School A Mosso Italy, 72-76; Scuola D'Italia NY, 79-85; tchg asst, Columbia Univ, 86-89; preceptor, 90; instr, 96, 97; res assoc, Columbia Univ, 96-; assoc curator of Papyri Rare Book and Manuscripts Library, 94-. **HONORS AND AWARDS** President's Fel, 86-89; Polychronis Fel, 89-90, Bd Dir of the Am Soc of Papyrologists, 95-98; Vis Comm to the Grad Fac of Political and Soc Sci, New School for Soc Res, 94-96. **RESEARCH** Greek and Latin Education; Greek Literature; Papyrology. **SELECTED PUBLICATIONS** Writing, Teachers, and Students in Graeco-Roman Egypt, 96. **CONTACT ADDRESS** 17 Sutton Pl, New York, NY 10022. **EMAIL** rc141@columbia.edu

CRISMORE, AVAN G.
PERSONAL Born 10/07/1929, Chicago, IL, m, 1949, 6 children **DISCIPLINE** ENGLISH, EDUCATION **EDUCATION** St. Francis Univ, BS, 64; MEd, 66; Univ IL, PhD, 85. **CAREER** Teacher, Norwell High School, 64-80; Dir, Univ of IL, 83; assoc to asst prof, Ind Univ Bloomington, 84; prof, Ind Univ Purdue Ft Wayne, 85-. **HONORS AND AWARDS** Who's Who Among Am Teachers; Int Student Org Awd for Teaching ESL. **MEMBERSHIPS** NCTE; Am Educ Res Assoc; Int Reading Assoc; Rhetoric Soc of Am; AILA. **RESEARCH** Visuals - 2 dimensional, Metadiscourse, Critical Thinking, English for Second Language-Controshire Rhetoric. **SELECTED PUBLICATIONS** Coauth, "On the reefs: The verbal and visual rhetoric of Darwin's other big theory", Rhetoric Soc Quarterly 21.2 (91): 11-25; rev, of "Writing: Invitation and Response" by Vincent Ruggeriero and Patrica Morgan, Focuses: Writing Theory and Practices 6.2 (93): 145-147; coauth, "Metadiscourse in persuasive writing: A study of texts written by American and Finnish university students", Written Commun 10.1 (93): 39-71;

coauth, "A quantitative contrastive study of metadiscourse: Problems in design and analysis of data", Papers and Studies in Contrastive Linguistics, Vol 28, ed J. Fisiak, Adam Mickiewicz Univ, (Poznam, Poland), (93): 137-151; auth, "Learning about metadiscourse", Encycl of English studies and language arts, Vol I, Nat Counc of Teachers of English, (93): 801-803; coauth, "Attitudes toward English in Malaysia", World Englishes 15.3 (96): 319-335; coauth, "Effects of hedges and gender on attitudes of readers in the United States toward material in a scientific textbook", Culture and Styles of Academic Discourse, ed A. Duszak, de Gruyeter, (Berlin/NY, 97): 222-247; coauth, "Hedges and readers: Effects on attitudes and learning", Hedging and Discourse: Approaches to the analysis of a pragmatic phenomenon in academic texts, eds R. Markkanen and H. Schroder, de Gruyter, (Berlin/NY), 97; coauth, "Collaborative learning in Malaysian postsecondary classrooms", TESOL J, 97; auth, "Visual Rhetoric in an Indiana University Foundation Annual Report", IU Center for Philanthropy working paper series, 98. **CONTACT ADDRESS** Dept English, Indiana Univ-Purdue Univ, Fort Wayne, 2010 E Coliseum Blvd, Fort Wayne, IN 46805-1445. **EMAIL** crismore@ipfw.edu

CROCKER, RICHARD LINCOLN
PERSONAL Born 02/17/1927, Roxbury, MA, m, 1948, 3 children **DISCIPLINE** HISTORY OF MUSIC **EDUCATION** Yale Univ, BA, 50, PhD(music), 57. **CAREER** From inst to asst prog, Yale Univ, 55-63; prof, Univ of CA at Berkeley, 63-94; chmn of dept, 75-78; prof emer, 94-; prof in grad studies, 95. **HONORS AND AWARDS** Alfred Einstein Mem Prize, Am Musicol Soc, 67; Guggenheim Fellowship, 69-70; Kinkeldey Award of the Am Musicological Soc, 78. **MEMBERSHIPS** Am Musicol Soc. **RESEARCH** Early Medieval music, sequences. **SELECTED PUBLICATIONS** Auth, History of Musical Style, McGraw-Hill, 66, reprint, Dover, 86; co-auth, Listening to Music, McGraw-Hill, 70; The Early Medieval Sequence, Univ of Calif Press, 77; co-ed & contrib, The Early Middle Ages to 1300, New Oxford History of Music, vol. II, 90; auth, Studies in Medieval Music Theory and the Early Sequence, 97; auth, Introduction to Gregorian Chant, Yale Univ Press, 00. **CONTACT ADDRESS** Dept of Music, Univ of California, Berkeley, Berkeley, CA 94720.

CROCKETT, BRYAN L.
PERSONAL Born 07/14/1954, Clinton, IA, m, 1978, 3 children **DISCIPLINE** ENGLISH **EDUCATION** Grinnell Col, BA, 76; Vanderbilt Univ, MA, 78; Univ Iowa, PhD, 91. **CAREER** Asst prof, Dept of English, Loyola Col, 91-97, assoc prof, 97-. **HONORS AND AWARDS** Nat Merit Scholar, 72-76; Outstanding Humanities Teacher Awd, Tenn Humanities Coun, 85; Eleven res grants, 86-200; Classical and Modern Lit Incentive Awd, 91. **MEMBERSHIPS** Shakespeare Asn of Am. **RESEARCH** Shakespeare; Renaissance drama and theology. **SELECTED PUBLICATIONS** Auth, The Play of Paradox: Stage and Sermon in Renaissance England, Univ of Pa Press (95); coauth with Gayla McGlamery, Instructor's Guide to The Norton Introduction to Literature, 6th ed, W. W. Norton & Col (95); auth, "Cicero, Ben Johnson, and the Puritans," Classical and Modern Lit, 15 (95): 375-376; auth, "The Act of Preaching and the Art of Prophesying," Sewanee Rev, 105 (97): 39-52; auth, "Thomas Playfere's Poetics of Preaching," in The English Sermon Revised, eds Peter McCullough and Lori Anne Ferrell, Manchester: Univ of Manchester Press (2000): 59-83. **CONTACT ADDRESS** dept English, Loyola Col, 4501 N Charles St, Baltimore, MD 21210-2601. **EMAIL** crockett@loyola.edu

CRONN-MILLS, DANIEL
PERSONAL Born 02/20/1964, Redwood Falls, MN, m, 1992, 1 child **DISCIPLINE** COMMUNICATION **EDUCATION** Univ Nebr, Lincoln, PhD, 95. **CAREER** Instr, Dept Speech Communication, Mankato State Univ, 92-95; asst prof, Mankato State Univ, 95-97; assoc prof, Minnesota State Univ, Mankato, 97-present. **HONORS AND AWARDS** Faculty Improvement Grant; Outstanding New Teacher of the Year, Central States Communication Asn; Arts and Humanities Res Mini-Grant; Mankato State Univ Found Special Projects Grant; nominated for Fac Appreciation Awd, Mankato State Univ. **MEMBERSHIPS** Am Forensic Asn; Central States Commun Asn; Commun and Theatre Asn of Minn; Delta Sigma Rho-Tau Kappa Alpha; Mid-American Forensic League; Minn Collegiate Forensic Asn; Nat Federation Interscholastic Speech and Debate Asn; Nat Forensic Asn; Religious Speech Commun Asn; Soc for the Scientific Study of Religion; National Commun Asn; Twin City Forensic League; Valley Forensic League. **RESEARCH** Investigating rhetorical process of organized religion from an historical and contemporary perspective; primarily involving Jehovah's Witnesses. Investigating current pragmatic and theoretical concerns in intercollegiate forensics. **SELECTED PUBLICATIONS** Co-auth, Book Review: Freedom of Speech in the Marketplace of Ideas (New York:NY), St. Martin's Press, 97; co-auth, The Status of speech communication instruction in Minnesota's technical colleges, CTAM, 98; auth, (Dis)empowering brothers and sisters: The rhetorical process of disfellowship by Jehovah's Witnesses, CTAM Journal, 99; auth, Reinventing Forensics for the 21st Century: A New Set of Individual Events, SpeakerPoints, online serial, 99; auth, A Qualitative Analysis of the Jehovah's Witnesses: The Rhetoric, Reality and Religion in the Watchtower Society (Lewiston, NY), Edwin Mellen Press, 99; co-auth, National sovereignty and communication technology: Can the two coexist?, In prodeedings of WebNet '99, in press. **CONTACT ADDRESS** Minnesota State Univ, Mankato, 230 Armstrong Hall, Mankato, MN 56001. **EMAIL** dmills@mnsu.edu

CROSKERY, MARGARET C.
PERSONAL Born 06/19/1961, Bellevue, WA, m, 1985 **DISCIPLINE** ENGLISH, LITERATURE **EDUCATION** Univ Va, BA, 83; MA, 95; PhD, 01. **CAREER** Teacher, Anacona Sch, 84-92; asst prof, Ohio N Univ, 99-. **HONORS AND AWARDS** Yalden-Thompson Res Fel, 97; NEH Summer Fel, 88, 90, 91. **MEMBERSHIPS** MLA; ASECS; CEAO; ALSC. **RESEARCH** 18th-century literature and culture; rise of the novel; novelist narrative. **SELECTED PUBLICATIONS** Auth, "Mothers Without Children, Unity Without Plot: Cranford's Radical Charm," Nineteenth Century Lit 52 (97); auth, "Masquing Desire: The Politics of Passion in Eliza Haywood's Fantomina," in Passionate Fictions of Eliza Haywood: Essays on Her Life and Work (00). **CONTACT ADDRESS** English Dept, Ohio No Univ, Ada, OH 45810. **EMAIL** m-croskery@onu.edu

CROSLAND, ANDREW TATE
PERSONAL Born 08/17/1944, San Francisco, CA, m, 1968, 1 child **DISCIPLINE** ENGLISH, COMPUTER SCIENCE **EDUCATION** Belmont Abbey Col, AB, 66; George Peabody Col, MA, 68; Univ SC, PhD(English), 76. **CAREER** Teacher English, math & sci, York Sch Dist 1, 66-67; from instr English to prof, Univ SC, Spartanburg, 68-; dir computer studies, 80-84; asst vice chancellor of academic affairs, Univ SC, Spartanburg, 84-91; assoc vice chancellor for academic affairs, 00-. **MEMBERSHIPS** MLA; Asn Lit & Ling computing; Soc Study Southern Lit; Asn Comput Mach; Asn Comput in Humanities. **RESEARCH** American literature; research tools; computer applications in the humanites. **SELECTED PUBLICATIONS** Ed, A Concordance to F Scott Fitzgerald's The Great Gatsby, 75 & A Concordance to the Complete Poetry of Stephen Crane, 75, Gale Res; auth, Sleeping and Waking: The Literary Reputation of The Great Gatsby, 1927-1944, 75 & The Great Gatsby and the Secret Agent, 75, Fitzgerald/Hemingway Ann; The Concordance and the Study of the Novel, Asn Lit & Ling Computing Bull, 75; The Concordance as an Aid in the Historical Study of Style, Style, 77; Sources for Fitzgerald's The Curious Case of Benjamin Button, Fitzgerald/Hemingway Ann, 79; The New Computer Science, SIGCSE Bull, 82; Alica Walker's Nineteen Fifty-Five: Fiction and Fact, ELN, 96; The Text of Zora Neale Hurston: A Caution, CLAJ, 94. **CONTACT ADDRESS** Dept English, Univ of So Carolina, Spartanburg, 800 University Way, Spartanburg, SC 29303-4932. **EMAIL** acrosland@gw.uscs.edu

CROSMAN, ROBERT
PERSONAL Born 02/18/1940, Chicago, IL, d, 1 child **DISCIPLINE** ENGLISH LITERATURE **EDUCATION** Univ Calif Berkeley, BA, 63; Columbia Univ, MA, 65, PhD, 71. **CAREER** Asst prof, 69-73, Williams Col; vis asst prof, 75-76, Trinity Col; lectr, 77-79, Tuft's Univ; fellow, 80-81, Boston Univ; vis lectr, 81-82, Rice Univ; instr, 82, MIT; asst prof to assoc prof, 85-, Univ Ak Anchorage. **HONORS AND AWARDS** Phi Beta Kappa, 62; Explicator Awd, 81; nat merit scholar, 57-61; harvard nat scholar, 57-61; w s ferguson hist essay prize, 59; phi beta kappa, 62; woodrow wilson fel, 63-64; columbia president's fel, 65; columbia col preceptorship, 66-68. **MEMBERSHIPS** MLA; Shakespeare Assoc of Amer. **RESEARCH** Shakespeare; reader response criticism; Milton. **SELECTED PUBLICATIONS** Auth, Reading Paradise Lost, Ind Univ Press, 80 **CONTACT ADDRESS** English Dept, Univ of Alaska, Anchorage, Anchorage, AK 99508. **EMAIL** afrc@uaa.alaska.edu

CROSS, GILBERT B.
PERSONAL Born 05/02/1939, Manchester, England, m, 1965, 2 children **DISCIPLINE** ENGLISH LITERATURE **EDUCATION** Manchester Univ, BA, 61; Univ London, cert educ, 62; Univ Louisville, MA, 65; Univ Mich, PhD, 71. **CAREER** Lectr Eng, Eastern Ky Univ, 65-66, Eastern Mich Univ, instr, 66-70, asst prof, 70-75, assoc prof, 75-80, Prof Eng, Eastern Mich Univ, 80-, Am Philos Soc grant, 78; Am Coun Learned Socs grant-in-aid, 78. **HONORS AND AWARDS** Barnard Hewitt Awd, 78. **MEMBERSHIPS** AAUP; Bronte Soc; Soc Theatre Res. **RESEARCH** Drama; Brontes; theatre. **SELECTED PUBLICATIONS** Coauth, Drury Lane Journal: Selections from the diaries of James Winston 1819-1827, Soc Theatre Res, 74; coauth (with A L Nelson), Aut Caesar, Aut Nullus: Edmund Kean's Articles of Agreement, 1825, 19th Century Theatre Res, autumn 74; auth, Next Week--East Lynne: Domestic Drama in Performance, Bucknell Univ Press, 77; coauth (with A L Nelson), A case of unassigned authorship: James Winston's Perseverance (1802), Educ Theatre J, 5/78; If These Be Truths, Farewell to Falsehoods: James Winston's Pedigree, Theatre Notebook, No 34, 80; auth, World Folktales: A Scribner Resource Collection, Scribner, 80; coauth, The Adelphi Theatre Calendar, Part I, 1806-1850, Greenwood, 90; coauth, The Adelphi Theatre Calendar, Part II, 1851-1900, Greenwood, 93. **CONTACT ADDRESS** Dept of Eng, Eastern Michigan Univ, 602M Pray Harrold, Ypsilanti, MI 48197-2201. **EMAIL** Eng_Cross@online.emich.edu

CROSSLEY, ROBERT THOMAS
PERSONAL Born 12/20/1945, Philadelphia, PA, m, 1974, 1 child **DISCIPLINE** ENGLISH LITERATURE **EDUCATION** Rockhurst Col, CIAB, 67; Univ Va, MA, 68, PhD, 72. **CAREER** Asst prof, 72-78, assoc prof, 79-87, prof, 87-, chmn Eng, 96-, Univ Mass, Boston. **HONORS AND AWARDS** Res Fel, NEH, 89-90, 00. **MEMBERSHIPS** Sci Fiction Res Asn. **RESEARCH** British science fiction; Utopian lit; lit executor Olaf Stapledon; Scientific and literary hist of Mars. **SELECTED PUBLICATIONS** Auth, H G Wells, Starmont, 86; auth, Talking Across the World, N England, 87; auth, Olaf Stapledon: Speaking for the Future, Syracuse, 94; auth, An Olaf Stapledon Reader, Syracuse, 97; auth, Imagining Apocalypse, 99; auth, Histories of the Future, 00; auth, The Massachusetts Review, 00. **CONTACT ADDRESS** English Dept, Univ of Massachusetts, Boston, 100 Morrissey Blvd, Boston, MA 02125-3300. **EMAIL** robert.crossley@umb.edu

CROW, CHARLES L.
PERSONAL Born 11/27/1940, Pomona, CA, m, 1965, 2 children **DISCIPLINE** ENGLISH **EDUCATION** Stanford, AB, 62; UC Berkeley, MA, 64; PhD, 71. **CAREER** From instr to prof emeritus, Bowling Green State Univ, 68-; vis prof, Univ of Salzburg, Austria, 81 & 85; fulbright lectr, Charles Univ, Czech Repub, 98; fulbright lectr, Univ of Ostrava, Czech Repub, 99. **HONORS AND AWARDS** Sr Fulbright Lectr, Czech Repub, 98-99. **MEMBERSHIPS** Am Lit Asn, W Lit Asn, Int Gothic Asn, Frank Norris Soc, Jack London Soc. **RESEARCH** Regional American literature, Western American literature, Gothic American literature, realists & naturalists. **SELECTED PUBLICATIONS** Co-ed, The Haunted Dusk: American Supernatural Fiction 1820-1920, Univ of Ga Press (Athens, GA), 83; co-ed, The Occult in America: The New Perspectives, Univ of Ill Press (Chicago, IL), 83; ed, American Gothic: An Anthology 1787-1916, Blackwell (Oxford), 99. **CONTACT ADDRESS** Dept English, Bowling Green State Univ, 1001 E Wooster St, Bowling Green, OH 43403-0001. **EMAIL** charleslcrow@yahoo.com

CROWELL, DOUGLAS E.
DISCIPLINE ENGLISH LITERATURE **EDUCATION** SUNY, Buffalo, PhD, 81. **CAREER** Assoc prof, TX Tech Univ. **HONORS AND AWARDS** Short-story award, TX Inst Lett; NEA Creative Writing fel grant. **SELECTED PUBLICATIONS** Publ fiction in jour(s) including Crazyhorse, Epoch, Fiction Int, Miss Rev, and New Directions; his stories have been anthologized in New Stories from the South and South by Southwest. **CONTACT ADDRESS** Texas Tech Univ, Lubbock, TX 79409-5015. **EMAIL** ykfdc@ttacs.ttu.edu

CROWL, SAMUEL
PERSONAL Born 10/09/1940, Toledo, OH, m, 1963, 2 children **DISCIPLINE** ENGLISH **EDUCATION** Hamilton College, AB, 62; Indiana Univ, PhD, 70. **CAREER** Asst Prof, Ohio Univ, 70-75; Assoc Prof, 75-80; Full Prof, 80-; Trustee Prof of English, 92-. **HONORS AND AWARDS** Univ Prof, Ohio Univ; Trustee Prof of English in 92. **MEMBERSHIPS** Modern Language Assoc; Shakespeare Assoc of Amer. **RESEARCH** Shakespeare; Shakespeare on Film; Shakespeare in Performance. **SELECTED PUBLICATIONS** Auth, "Shakespeare Observed: Studies in Performance on Stage and Screen, 92; auth, "Essays in Shakespeare and the Moving Image," The Cambridge Companion to Shakespeare on Film;" "Screening the Bard;" "Teaching Shakespeare Today." **CONTACT ADDRESS** Dept English, Ohio Univ, Athens, OH 45701-2942. **EMAIL** crowl@ohio.edu

CROWLEY, DAVID
DISCIPLINE COMMUNICATION STUDIES **EDUCATION** John Hopkins Univ, BA; Annenberg Univ, MA; McGill Univ, PhD. **CAREER** Assoc prof. **HONORS AND AWARDS** Gannett Found Grant, 85-86; SSHRC Res Grants, 82-83; 86-90. **RESEARCH** Hist and theory of communications; communications and info policy; socio technical approaches to communication; public consultation; res design. **SELECTED PUBLICATIONS** Auth, "Introduction to the New Edition," Harold Adams Innis, The Bias of Communication, Toronto: U of Toronto Press, 91; auth, Communications in History-Technology, Culture, Society, Longman, 91; auth, "Doing Things Electronically," Speical Ed on New Approaches to Communication Technology, Canadian Journal of Communication, vol. 19, no. 1, 94; auth, "Communications in Canada-Enduring Themes, Emerging Issues," in Goldie, Lambert, Lroimer Canada - Theoretical Discourse/Discours Thoriques, Asn for Canadian Stud, 94; auth, "Distance Research in Communiaction," Intermedia, vol. 22, no. 4, 95. **CONTACT ADDRESS** Dept Communications, McGill Univ, 845 Sherbrooke St, Montreal, QC, Canada H3A 2T5. **EMAIL** indc@musicb.mcgill.ca

CROWLEY, J. DONALD
DISCIPLINE AMERICAN LITERATURE AND 20TH CENTURY AMERICAN POETRY **EDUCATION** Ohio State Univ, PhD, 64. **CAREER** Prof to prof emer, Univ Mo, Columbia. **SELECTED PUBLICATIONS** Hist ed, Hawthorne's Major Tales and Sketches, Ohio St UP; ed, Robinson Crusoe, Oxford; co-ed, The Wings of the Dove, Norton; One Hundred Years of Huckleberry Finn, Mo UP & Critical Essays on Walk-

er Percy, GK Hall. **CONTACT ADDRESS** Dept of English, Univ of Missouri, Columbia, 222 Tate Hall, Columbia, MO 65211. **EMAIL** crowleyj@missouri.edu

CROWLEY, JOHN W.
PERSONAL Born 12/27/1945, New Haven, CT, d, 4 children **DISCIPLINE** ENGLISH & AMERICAN LITERATURE **EDUCATION** Yale Univ, BA, 67; Ind Univ, MA, 69, PhD, 70. **CAREER** Asst prof, 70-74, assoc prof, 74-79, prof, 79-, eng, Syracuse Univ; dir grad studies, 86-89, chemn, 89-92, dir humanities doctoral prog, 85-88, 96-, Syracuse Univ. **HONORS AND AWARDS** Phi Beta Kappa, 66. **RESEARCH** American literature, 1850-1950. **SELECTED PUBLICATIONS** Auth, George Cabot Lodge, Twayne Publ, 76; auth, The Black Heart's Truth: The Early Career of W. D. Howells, Univ NC Press, 85; auth, The Mask of Fiction: Essays on W. D. Howells, Univ Mass Press, 89; auth, The White Logic: Alcoholism and Gender in American Modernist Fiction, Univ Mass Press, 94; ed, George Cabot Lodge: Selected Fiction and Verse, John Colet, 76; ed, Henry Adams, The Life of George Cabot Lodge, Scholars' Facsimiles & Reprints, 78; co-ed, The Haunted Dusk: American Supernatural Fiction, 1820-1920, Univ Ga Press, 82; ed, New Essays in Winesburg, Ohio, Cambridge Univ Press, 90; ed, Roger Austen, Genteel Pagan: The Double Life of Charles Warren Stoddard, Univ Mass Press, 91; ed, Charles Jackson, The Sunnier Side, Syracuse Univ Press, 95; ed, W. D. Howells, The Rise of Silas Lapham, Oxford Univ Press, 96; ed, Drunkard's Progress: Narratives of Addiction, Despair and Recovery, Johns Hopkins Univ Press, 99; auth, The Dean of American Letters: The Late Career of William Dean Howells, Univ Mass Press, 99; auth, Bill W. and Mr. Wilson, Univ Mass Press, 00. **CONTACT ADDRESS** Dept. of English, Syracuse Univ, Syracuse, NY 13244-1170.

CROWLEY, JOSEPH P.
PERSONAL Born 02/27/1946, South Bend, IN, m, 1972, 5 children **DISCIPLINE** ENGLISH **EDUCATION** Univ Toronto, BA, 69; Univ NC Chapel Hill, PhD, 80. **CAREER** Asst prof, 80-98, assoc prof, 98-, Auburn Univ, Montgomery. **RESEARCH** Old Engl lang; glosses & additions to prayer bks; MS Royal 2 A xx; name stud; dialects. **CONTACT ADDRESS** Dept of English, Auburn Univ, Montgomery, PO Box 244023, Montgomery, AL 36124. **EMAIL** jcrowley@edla.aum.edu

CROWLEY, KELLEY M. WICKHAM
DISCIPLINE ENGLISH LITERATURE **EDUCATION** Georgetown Univ, BA; Univ Durham, MA; Cornell Univ, MA, PhD. **CAREER** Eng Dept, Georgetown Univ **RESEARCH** Old English and Early Middle English literature; intersections of physical and intellectual culture; archaeology of the British Isles; feminist gender theory; Anglo-Saxon architecture. **SELECTED PUBLICATIONS** Auth, La3amon's Narrative Innovations and Bakhtin's Theories, 94; pubs on archaeology for Year's Work in Old English. **CONTACT ADDRESS** English Dept, Georgetown Univ, 37th and O St, Washington, DC 20057.

CROWLEY, SUE MITCHELL
PERSONAL Born 10/31/1933, Columbus, OH, m, 1954, 2 children **DISCIPLINE** RELIGION AND LITERATURE **EDUCATION** St Mary's College Notre Dame, BA, cum laude 55; Ohio State Univ, MA, 68; Univ Iowa, course work for PhD. **CAREER** Instr, lectr, Asst Dir, 72 to 02, Univ Missouri; Instr, 82-84, Stephens College; lectr, Instr, 68-79, Univ Iowa; teacher, 67, Ursuline Acad. **HONORS AND AWARDS** Honors Teacher of the Year. **MEMBERSHIPS** AAR; MLA; Cen MO Colloquium on the Study of Religion. **RESEARCH** John Updike; Walker Percy; Robert Lowell; Toni Morrison. **CONTACT ADDRESS** 409 South Greenwood, Columbia, MO 65203.

CROZIER, ALICE COOPER
PERSONAL Born 06/29/1934, New York, NY, m, 1968, 2 children **DISCIPLINE** AMERICAN LITERATURE **EDUCATION** Radcliffe Col, BA, 56; Harvard Univ, PhD, 64. **CAREER** Instr English, Smith Col, 61-66; asst prof, 66-72, assoc prof English, Rutgers Univ, New Brusnwick 72-, Am Asn Univ Women fel, 64-65; Nat Endowment for Humanities fel, 71-72. **RESEARCH** American literature. **SELECTED PUBLICATIONS** Auth, The Novels of Harriet Beecher Stowe, Oxford Univ, 69. **CONTACT ADDRESS** Dept of English, Rutgers, The State Univ of New Jersey, New Brunswick, PO Box 5454, New Brunswick, NJ 08903. **EMAIL** acrozier@rci.rutgers.edu

CROZIER, LORNA
PERSONAL Born 05/24/1948, Swift Current, SK, Canada **DISCIPLINE** WRITING **EDUCATION** Univ Sask, BA, 69; Univ Alta, MA, 80. **CAREER** High sch Eng tchr, Sask, 72-77; creative writing tchr, Sask Summer Sch Arts, 77-81; dir comm, Dept Parks, Recreation & Culture, Govt Sask, 81-83; writer-in-residence, Regina Pub Libr, 84-85; instr, Banff Sch Fine Arts, 86-87; lectr, Univ Sask, 86-91; vis prof, 91-92, assoc prof, 92-96, prof writing, Univ Victoria, 96-; writer-in-residence, Univ Toronto, 89-90. **HONORS AND AWARDS** Sask Writers' Guild Poetry Awd, 84, 87; Nat Radio Awd, 87; Gov Gen Awd Poetry, 92; Can Authors' Asn Awd Poetry, 92; Pat Lowther Awd, 92, 95; Nat Mag Awd, Gold Medal Poetry, 95. **MEMBERSHIPS** Sask Writers' Guild; League Can Poets. **SELECTED PUBLICATIONS** Auth, Inside is the Sky, 76; auth, Crow's Black Joy, 78; auth, Humans and Other Beasts, 80; auth, The Weather, 83; auth, The Garden Going On Without Us, 85; auth, Angels of Silence, Angels of Flesh, 88; auth, Inventing the Hawk, 92; auth, Everything Arrives at the Light, 95; auth, A Saving Grace: The Collected Poems of Mrs. Bentley, 96; auth, What the Living Won't Let Go, 99; ed, Desire in Seven Voices, 99. **CONTACT ADDRESS** 1886 Cultra, Saanichton, BC, Canada V8M 1L7. **EMAIL** lcrozier@finearts.uvic.ca

CRUME, ALICE L.
PERSONAL Born 09/22/1944, Houston, TX, s **DISCIPLINE** COMMUNICATION STUDIES **EDUCATION** Carroll Col, BA; Univ Mont, MA; Bowling Green State Univ, PhD. **CAREER** Asst prof. **RESEARCH** Mediation training and ideology; Peer mediation/volunteer mediators; Conflict theories and conflict resolution practices. **SELECTED PUBLICATIONS** Auth, Conflict Resolution Through Communication, Burgess, 96; Ethics in Mediation, 96. **CONTACT ADDRESS** Dept of Communication, SUNY, Col at Brockport, Brockport, NY 14420. **EMAIL** acrume@po.brockport.edu

CRUMP, GAIL BRUCE
PERSONAL Born 04/05/1942, Kirksville, MO **DISCIPLINE** MODERN BRITISH & AMERICAN LITERATURE **EDUCATION** Turman State Univ, BA & BSEd, 64; Univ Ark, Fayetteville, MA, 65, PhD(English), 69. **CAREER** From asst prof to prof English, Cent Mo State Univ, 69-. **HONORS AND AWARDS** Nat Endowment for Humanities jr scholars grant, 76. **MEMBERSHIPS** MLA; AAUP; D H Lawrence Soc NAm; Soc Study Midwestern Lit; NCTE; Western Lit Asn; Popular Cult Asn; MMLA. **RESEARCH** Modern British and American fiction; modern drama; literature and film. **SELECTED PUBLICATIONS** Ed, Doctoral dissertations on D H Lawrence, 1931-1968: A bibliography, 70, auth, Gopher Prairie Orpapplewick? The Virgin and the Gipsy, as Film, 71 & Women in Love: Novel and Film, 71, D H Lawrence Rev; Wright Morris's One Day, Mid America, 76; D H Lawrence and the Immediate Present, D H Lawrence Rev, 77; The Novels of Wright Morris, Univ Nebr, 78; The Universe as Murder Mystery: Tom Stoppard's Jumpers, Contemp Lit, 79; auth, Transformations of Reality in R. M. Koster's Tinieblan Novels, Critique, 83; Art and Experience in Stoppard's The Real Thing, In: Tom Stoppard: A Casebook, 88; Lawrence's Rainbow and and Russell's Rainbow, D H Lawrence Rev, 89; Wright Morris: Author in Hiding, Western Am Lit, 90. **CONTACT ADDRESS** Dept of English, Central Missouri State Univ, Warrensburg, MO 64093-8888. **EMAIL** gbc8696@cmsu2.cmsu.edu

CRUMP, REBECCA
DISCIPLINE VICTORIAN POETRY, ROMANTIC POETRY, NINETEENTH-CENTURY BRITISH NOVEL **EDUCATION** Univ Tex, Austin, PhD, 70. **CAREER** Advis, undergrad prog, 96-, former assoc ch, codir, undergrad prog, dir, creative writing, prof, La State Univ. **HONORS AND AWARDS** ACLS summer grant, 72; NEH summer stipends, 74, 82; Guggenheim fel, 83-84; NEH senior fel, 87-88; LSU Found Distinguished Fac Awd, 91; Col of Arts & Sci Nicholson Awd, 96. **RESEARCH** Editing; bibliography. **SELECTED PUBLICATIONS** Auth, Christina Rossetti: A Reference Guide, 76; Charlotte and Emily Bronte, 1846-1915: A Reference Guide, 81; Charlotte and Emily Bronte, 1916-1954: A Reference Guide, 85; Charlotte and Emily Bronte, 1955-1983: A Reference Guide, 86; Order in Variety: Essays and Poems in Honor of Donald E. Stanford, 91; ed, Maude: Prose and Verse, Christina Rossetti, 76; The Complete Poems of Christina Rossetti: A Variorum Ed, 3 vols, 79-91. **CONTACT ADDRESS** Dept of Eng, Louisiana State Univ and A&M Col, 210B Allen Hall, Baton Rouge, LA 70803.

CRUPI, CHARLES WILLIAM
PERSONAL Born 04/06/1939, Wadsworth, OH, m, 1960, 3 children **DISCIPLINE** ENGLISH **EDUCATION** Harvard Univ, AB, 61; Univ Calif, Berkeley, MA, 63; Princeton Univ, PhD(English), 67. **CAREER** From instr to asst prof English, Princeton Univ, 66-74; assoc prof to prof English, Albion Col, 74-, chmn dept, 78-97; vis prof, Drew Univ, 73 & Stockholm Univ, 81. **MEMBERSHIPS** MLA; Mencken Soc; Soc Am Baseball Res; ARBA; SICULA. **RESEARCH** Shakespeare; Renaissance drama. **SELECTED PUBLICATIONS** Auth or coauth (with R Aiuto) of 6 plays, including: Mencken and Sara (play), Baltimore, 81; Robert Greene, Boston, 84. **CONTACT ADDRESS** Dept of English, Albion Col, 611 E Porter St, Albion, MI 49224-1831. **EMAIL** ccrupi@albion.edu

CUEVA, EDMUND
PERSONAL Born 10/26/1964, Esmeraldas, Ecuador, m, 1987 **DISCIPLINE** CLASSICS **EDUCATION** Univ S Fla, BA, 87; Univ Fla, MA, 89; Loyola Univ, MA 93; PhD, 95. **CAREER** Lecturer, Northwestern Univ, 91-92; Teaching Fel to Lecturer, Univ Chicago, 92-94; Vis Asst Prof, Xavier Univ, 94-96; Lecturer, Univ Cincinnati, Lecturer, 95-96; Asst Prof to Dept Chair, 96-. **HONORS AND AWARDS** Wheeler Grant, Xavier Univ , 99, 98; Publication Grant, Univ S Fla, 99; Nomination NEH Summer Fel, Xavier Univ, 97. **MEMBERSHIPS** Am Classical League, Am Philol Asn, Classical Asn of the Middle West and South, Eta Sigma Phi, Intl Plutarch Soc, Soc of Biblical Literature, Women's Classical Caucus. **SELECTED PUBLICATIONS** Co-ed, Humor in the Ancient World, Special issue of Classical Bulletin, forthcoming; co-auth, Longus: Text, Commentary and vocabulary, forthcoming; co-ed, Veritatis Amicitaeque Causa: Essays in Honor of Anna Lydia Motto and John R Clark, Bolchazy-Carducci Pub, 99; auth, "Art and Myth in Cupid and Psyche," in Veritatis Amicitiaeque Causa: Essays in Honor of Anna Lydia Motto and John R Clark, , Bolchazy-Carducci Pub, forthcoming; auth, "The state of Research on the ancient Novel," Classical Bulletin, (99)l; 47-59; auth, "The analogue of the Hero of Heliodorus' Aethiopica," Sylecta Classica, (98): 103-113; auth, Plutarch's Ariadne I Chariton's Chaereas and Callirhoe," American Journal of Philology, (96): 473-484; auth, "Anth. Pal. 14.34 and Achilles Tatius 2.14," Greek, Roman, and Byzantine Studies, (94): 281-288; auth, "Divine Indigestion: Ghosts, Cannibalism and the Ancient Novel," Classical Bulletin, forthcoming; auth, "Tacitean Necrologies," Journal of Ancient Civilizations, forthcoming. **CONTACT ADDRESS** Dept Classics, Xavier Univ, Ohio, 3800 Victory Pkwy, Cincinnati, OH 45207-1035.

CULATTA, BARBARA
DISCIPLINE COMMUNICATIVE DISORDERS **EDUCATION** Univ Pittsburgh, PhD. **CAREER** Prof; post-doctoral fel, Johns Hopkins Univ. **MEMBERSHIPS** Partners of the Am prog. **SELECTED PUBLICATIONS** Publ on, using play and story enactments in intervention contexts highlight these clinical practices; relationship between perceptual and linguistic deficits; lang difficulties in children with Spina Bifida & intervention practices within classroom contexts. **CONTACT ADDRESS** Dept of Communicative Disorders, Univ of Rhode Island, 8 Ranger Rd, Ste. 1, 116 Adams , Kingston, RI 02881-0807. **EMAIL** barb@uriacc.uri.edu

CULHAM, PHYLLIS
PERSONAL Born 06/22/1948, Junction City, KS, m, 1969, 1 child **DISCIPLINE** ANCIENT HISTORY, CLASSICAL LITERATURE **EDUCATION** Univ Kans, BA, 70; State Univ NYork Buffalo, MA, 72, PhD, 76. **CAREER** Lectr classics, Univ Calif, Irvine, 75-77; asst prof hist, Univ Ill, Chicago, 77-79; from Asst Prof to Assoc Prof, 79-91, prof hist, US Naval Acad, 91-. **HONORS AND AWARDS** NEH Curriculum Grant, 94. **MEMBERSHIPS** Asn Ancient Historians; Am Philol Asn. **RESEARCH** Roman bureaucratic history; Latin epigraphy. **SELECTED PUBLICATIONS** Auth, Classics: A Discipline and Profession in Crisis, 89; Seneca's on Favors, 95. **CONTACT ADDRESS** Dept of Hist, United States Naval Acad, Annapolis, MD 21402. **EMAIL** culham@nadn.navy.mil

CULIK, HUGH
DISCIPLINE ENGLISH LITERATURE **EDUCATION** Univ Mich, BA, MA; Wayne State Univ, PhD. **CAREER** Dept ch; dir, Wrtg Across the Curric. **SELECTED PUBLICATIONS** Co-ed, Post Identity; pub(s), short fiction. **CONTACT ADDRESS** Dept of Eng, Univ of Detroit Mercy, 4001 W McNichols Rd, PO BOX 19900, Detroit, MI 48219-0900. **EMAIL** hugh@libarts.udmercy.edu

CULLER, ARTHUR DWIGHT
PERSONAL Born 07/25/1917, McPherson, KS, m, 1941, 2 children **DISCIPLINE** ENGLISH **EDUCATION** Oberlin Col, AB, 38; Yale Univ, PhD(English), 41. **CAREER** Instr English, Cornell Univ, 41-42; from instr to asst prof, Yale Univ, 46-55; assoc prof, Univ Ill, 55-58; prof English, 58-86, Prof Emeritus, Yale Univ, 86-, chmn dept, 71-75; Fulbright res fel, England, 50-51; Guggenheim fel, 61-62 & 75; mem, PMLA Adv Comt, 71-74; Nat Endowment for Humanities res fel, 79-80. **HONORS AND AWARDS** DLitt. Merrimack Col, 72; Am Acad Arts & Scis, 86; Phi Beta Kappa; Explicator Literary Fdn Awd, 77. **MEMBERSHIPS** MLA. **RESEARCH** Victorian literature. **SELECTED PUBLICATIONS** Auth, Imperial Intellect, Yale Univ, 55; ed, Apologia Pro Vita Sua, 56 & Poetry and criticism of Matthew Arnold, 61, Houghton; auth, Imaginative Reason: The Poetry of Matthew Arnold, Yale, 66; The Poetry of Tennyson, Yale Univ, 77; auth, The Victorian Mirror of History, Yal, 86. **CONTACT ADDRESS** 200 Leeder Hill Dr., Apt 518, Hamden, CT 06517-2723.

CULROSS, JACK LEWIS
PERSONAL Born 06/04/1941, Rochester, NY, m, 1966, 2 children **DISCIPLINE** ENGLISH **EDUCATION** Spring Hill Col, BS, 63; La State Univ, Baton Rouge, MA, 66, PhD, 70. **CAREER** Instr English, La State Univ, 68-70; from Asst Prof to Assoc Prof, 70-80, Prof English, Eastern Ky Univ, 80-; Dean Acad Support & Undergrad Studies, 83-98. **RESEARCH** Victorian literature; literary criticism. **SELECTED PUBLICATIONS** Auth, Mary Barton: A Revaluation, Bull John Rylands Univ Libr Manchester 61, 78. **CONTACT ADDRESS** Office of the Dean, Undergrad Studies, Eastern Kentucky Univ, 521 Lancaster Ave, Richmond, KY 40475-3102. **EMAIL** gsoculro@acs.eku.edu

CUMBERLAND, SHARON L.
DISCIPLINE ENGLISH LITERATURE **EDUCATION** Coe Col, BA; Drake Univ, MA; CUNY, Doctorate, 94. **CAREER**

Instr, Seattle Univ. **MEMBERSHIPS** MLA; Soc for the Stud of Southern Lit; Popular Cult Asn; Acad of Am Poets; Poetry Soc of Am. **SELECTED PUBLICATIONS** Auth, Habit, What You Have, On Going In, Ploughshares, Apr, 94; The Rape of Sabine Women, Kalliope, 94; I Know I am Capable of Great Love, Laurel Rev, 94; Postulant, Smoke Offering, Ind Rev, Spg, 95; Before, Lipstick, Elberton Fling, Swing Alone, Westcoast, 95. **CONTACT ADDRESS** Seattle Univ, Seattle, WA 98122-4460. **EMAIL** slc@seattleu.edu

CUMMINGS, ANTHONY M.

PERSONAL Born 05/03/1951, Worcester, MA **DISCIPLINE** MUSICOLOGY **EDUCATION** BA, Williams Col, 73; MFA, Princeton Univ, 73; PhD, 80. **CAREER** Lectr in Music, Princeton Univ, 79-81, 82-83, 85-88; Dean of Admission, Princeton Univ, 83-88; Fulbright Scholar, Univ of Florence, 88-89; National Endowment for the Hum and Robert Lehman Found Fel, Villa I Tatti, The Harvard Univ Center for Italian Renaissance Studies, Florence, 89-90; Research Assoc, The Andrew W. Mellon Found, 90-92; Assoc prof of Music, Tulane Univ, and Dean of Tulane Col, 92-. **HONORS AND AWARDS** Fulbright Scholar, Univ of Florence, 88-89; National Endowment for the Hum and Robert Lehman Found Fel, Villa I Tatti, The Harvard Univ Center for Italian Renaissance Studies, Florence, 89-90; Trustee, Williams Col, 86-91; serve by invitation as rev of manuscripts for the Jour of Royal Musical Assoc, acad yr 90-91, and Renaissance Quarterly, 96-97; mem of a promotion and tenure commit at Haverford Col, 94-95; rev of proposals for funding from the National Endowment for the Hum, 95-96. **MEMBERSHIPS** Am Musicological Soc, Col Board, National Assoc of Col Admissions Counselors, Renaissance Soc of Am. **RESEARCH** Italian Renaissance hist and music, electronic infor tech. **SELECTED PUBLICATIONS** Auth, "The Motet, 1520-1640," The New Oxford History of Music, vol IV, Oxford Univ Press; Music in Renaissance Cities and Courts: Studies in Honor of Lewis Lockwood, co-ed, Harmonie Park Press, 96; "Mouton's and Palestrina's Sequence-Motet," A Conference on the Motet of the Middle Ages and Renaissance, Feb 13,-14, 1994, Washington Univ in St Louis; Univ Libraries and Scholarly Commun: A Study Prepared for the Andrew W. Mellon Found, with William G. Bowen, Richard H. Ekman, Laura O Lazarus, and Marcia L. Witte; Music for Medici Festivals, 1512-1537, Princeton Essays on the Arts, Princeton Univ Press, 92; "Gian Maria Giudeo, Sonatore del Liuto, and the Medici," Fontes Artis Musicae," "Gulio de Medici's Music Bks," Early Music History; "The Florentine Carnival of 1513," rev of Bernhard Meier, The Modes of Classical Vocal Polyphony, transl by Ellen S. Beebe, Broude Brothers Limited, 88, in Music and Letters; "The Transmission of Some Josquin Motets," Journal of the Royal Musical Assoc; "Ghiselin, and Alfonso II of Naples," with Allan W. Atlas, The Journal of Musicology; Collaborated on the production of the CD "Musica a Firenze al tempo di Lorenzo il Magnifico" (Music in Florence at the Time Lorenzo the Magnificent). **CONTACT ADDRESS** Tulane Univ, New Orleans, LA 70118-5698.

CUMMINGS, CRAIG

DISCIPLINE MUSIC THEORY **EDUCATION** Univ Ind, PhD. **CAREER** Assoc prof. **MEMBERSHIPS** Col Music Soc; Soc Music Theory. **SELECTED PUBLICATIONS** Auth, pubs on Schenkerian analysis, history of music theory, and music theory pedagogy. **CONTACT ADDRESS** Dept of Music History, Theory and Composition, Ithaca Col, 100 Job Hall, Ithaca, NY 14850. **EMAIL** cummings@ithaca.edu

CUMMINGS, PETER MARCH

PERSONAL Born 11/28/1941, Manchester, NH, m, 1965, 1 child **DISCIPLINE** ENGLISH LITERATURE **EDUCATION** Cornell Univ, BA, 63, Univ NC, Chapel Hill, MA, 64, PhD, 71. **CAREER** Lectr asst, Cornell Univ, 63-64; instr English Lit, Copenhagen Univ, 64-65; instr, Washington & Lee Univ, 68-69; asst prof, 70-76, assoc prof English, 76-82, Prof English & Comp Lit, Hobart & William Smith Cols, 82-. **HONORS AND AWARDS** Mellon Found grant, 79. **MEMBERSHIPS** AAUP; MLA. **RESEARCH** Renaissance poetry and drama; literary criticism. **SELECTED PUBLICATIONS** Coauth, 24 American Poets, Gad Copenhagen, 66; auth, Spenser's Amoretti as an allegory of love, Tex Studies Lang & Lit, 70; Northrop Frye and the necessary hybrid: Criticism as aesthetic humanism, In: The Quest for Imagination, Case Western Reserve Univ, 71; Bicycle story: Some theory and practice, Boston Phoenix, spring 74; Walt Whitman's Song of Myself and the History of the Future, Dansk Udsyn, 77; The Bicycle: History, Pyhsics, and Consciousness, Dansk Udsyn, 77; Bicycle Consciousness, Greenfield Rev Press, 79; Hearing in Hamlet: Poisoned Ears and the Psychopathology of Flawed Audition, Shakespeare Yearbook, 90; Violinmaking: An Alchemical Journal, Genre, 90; The Making of Meaning: Sex Words and Sex Acts in Shakespeare's Othello, The Gettysburg Rev, 90; The Alchemical Storm: Etymology, Wordplay, and New World Kairos in Shakespeare's The Tempest, The Upstart Crow, 92; Shakespeare's Bawdy Planet, The Sewanee Rev, 92; Learning to Read: The Heart of Liberal Arts Value, Liberal ed, 96; Verbal Energy in Shakespeare's Much Ado About Nothing, Shakespeare Yearbook, 97; Textuality and the Reader in Shakespeare's Non-Dramatic Poems, forthcoming in new journal, Shakespeare Studies, Moscow, 99; and auth of the following long poems: Hamlet at Sea, The Upstart Crow, 88; The Gasparo da Salo Viola, Notebook: A Little Magazine, 89; Shakespeare in Italy: Out of the Lost Years, Hobart and William Smith Cols, 89; Lear in the Country Near Dover, The Upstart Crow, 95; Kit on Will, The Upstart Crow, 97. **CONTACT ADDRESS** Dept of English, Hobart and William Smith Cols, 300 Pulteney St, Geneva, NY 14456-3382.

CUMMINGS, SHERWOOD

PERSONAL Born 03/05/1916, Weehawken, NJ, m, 1939, 2 children **DISCIPLINE** ENGLISH **EDUCATION** Univ Ill, BS, 38; Univ Wis, MA, 46, PhD(English), 51. **CAREER** Asst English, Univ Wis, 46-48; from instr to prof, Univ SDak, 48-63; assoc prof, 63-65, prof, 65-80, Emer Prof Am Lit, Calif State Univ, Fullerton, 80-, Vis prof, Univ Calif Berkeley, 60-61. **MEMBERSHIPS** MLA; Am Studies Asn; Am Lit Group. **RESEARCH** Mark Twain and science; American literature 1870-1910. **SELECTED PUBLICATIONS** Mark Twain's theory of realism, Studies in Am Humor, II, 209-221; A Conneticut Yankee in King Arthur's Court, In: Survey of Science Fiction Literature, Salem Press, 79. **CONTACT ADDRESS** California State Univ, Fullerton, Fullerton, CA 92634.

CUMMINS, W. JOSEPH

DISCIPLINE PHILOSOPHY; CLASSICS **EDUCATION** Xavier Univ, AB, 70; Emory Univ, MA, 71, PhD, 75; Univ Cincinnati, MA, 76, PhD, 89. **CAREER** Asst prof, Old Dominion Univ, 76-80; from asst prof to assoc prof, 84-, Grinnell Col. **RESEARCH** Greek and Roman philosophy; intellectual history **CONTACT ADDRESS** Dept of Philosophy, Grinnell Col, Grinnell, IA 50112. **EMAIL** cummins@grinnell.edu

CUMMINS, WALTER M.

PERSONAL Born 02/06/1936, Long Branch, NJ, m, 1981, 2 children **DISCIPLINE** ENGLISH **EDUCATION** Rutgers Univ, BA, 57; Univ Iowa, MA & MFA, 62, PhD(English), 65. **CAREER** Instr English, Univ Iowa, 62-65; from asst prof to assoc prof, 65-74, Prof English, Fairleigh Dickinson Univ, 74-; Ed-in-Chief, The Lit Rev, 84-. **HONORS AND AWARDS** NJ State Coun on the Arts Fel, 82. **SELECTED PUBLICATIONS** Auth, A Stranger to the Deed, 68 & Into Temptation, 68, Caravelle; co-ed, The Other Sides of Reality, Bryd & Fraser, 72; Witness (story collection), Samisdat, 75; Jantadeln and the reformation (story), Lit Rev, 77; coauth, Managing Management Climate, Lexington, 79; Kaiser-fraser (story), West Branch, 81; Where we live (story collection), Kans Quart, 83; Shifting Borders: East European Poetry of the eighties (edited collection), FDU Press, 93. **CONTACT ADDRESS** Dept of English, Fairleigh Dickinson Univ, Florham-Madison, 285 Madison Ave, Madison, NJ 07940-1099. **EMAIL** wcummins@worldnet.att.net

CUNNINGHAM, FRANK ROBERT

PERSONAL Born 08/15/1937, Philadelphia, PA **DISCIPLINE** ENGLISH, FILM STUDIES **EDUCATION** Villanova Univ, AB, 60, MA, 62; Lehigh Univ, PhD(English), 70. **CAREER** Instr English, Lehigh Univ, 66-68; asst prof, Franklin & Marshall Col, 68-69, Fordham Univ, 70-71 & Kans State Univ, 71-73; vis asst prof, San Jose State Univ, 73-76; Sen Fulbright lectr, Jagillonian Univ, Krakow, 76-77; assoc prof English, Univ SDak, 78-84, prof, 84-; vis fel, Princeton Univ, summer 81; vis fel, Univ of Calif, Berkeley, summer 84, 90; vis fel, Yale Univ, summer 99, 99-00. **HONORS AND AWARDS** NEH Summer Sem Fel, Yale Univ, 80; ed bd, Eugene O'Neill Rev, 89-; ed bd, Lit/Film Quart, 88-. **MEMBERSHIPS** Am Hist Asn; Eugene O'Neill Soc; Film Hist Lit Asn. **RESEARCH** 20th century American thought and literature, film. **SELECTED PUBLICATIONS** Auth, "Clifford Odets," in American Writers (Scribners, 81); auth, "Pascal's Wager and the Feminist Dilemma in Eric Rohmer's 'My Night at Maud's,'" in The Kingdom of Dreams (Fla State Univ Press, 87); auth, "Michael Gold," in Dictionary of American Biography (Scribners, 88); auth, Sidney Lumet: Film and Literary Vision, Univ Press of Ky, 91; auth, "Eugene O'Neill and Reality in America," in Realism and the American Dramatic Tradition (Univ of Ala Press, 96); auth, "The Sham of 'Measured Forms' in Melville's 'Billy Budd,'" J of Aesthetic Educ (00); auth, "F. Scott Fitzgerald and the Problem of Film Adaptation," Lit/Film Quart (00); auth, "A Newly Discovered Fourth Production of O'Neill's 'Lazarus Laughed,'" Eugene O'Neill Rev (00); auth, Sidney Lumet's 'Fail Safe,' Flick Bks, 01; auth, Sidney Lumet: Film and Literary Vision, 2nd ed, Univ of Ky Press, 01. **CONTACT ADDRESS** Dept of English, Univ of So Dakota, Vermillion, 414 E Clark St, Vermillion, SD 57069-2390.

CUNNINGHAM, KAREN

PERSONAL Born 10/09/1946, Woonsocket, RI, m, 1971 **DISCIPLINE** ENGLISH **EDUCATION** Sacramento State Col, BA, 69; San Francisco State Col, MA, 72; Univ CA, Santa Barbara, PhD, 85. **CAREER** Lectr, 85-87, Univ CA; Asst Prof, 87-93, Florida State Univ; Visiting Prof, spring 93, Princeton Univ; Assoc Prof, 93-present, Florida State Univ. **HONORS AND AWARDS** Princeton Univ, Shelby Cullom Davis Ctr for Hist Research Fel, spring 93; Florida State Univ, Univ Teaching Awd, 93-94; Dartmouth Coll, Sch of Criticism and Theory, Tuition Grant, summer 94; Florida State Univ, Teaching Incentive Program Awd, fall 94; Comnr, Florida Commission on the Status of Women, 95-present; Florida State Univ, Committee on Faculty Sabbaticals, one semester sabbatical, full support, fall 95; Florida State Univ, Committee on Faculty Research and Creativity, research grant, summer 96. **MEMBERSHIPS** Amer Assoc of Univ Women; Marlowe Soc of Amer; Modern Language Assoc; Renaissance Soc of Amer; Shakespeare Assoc of Amer; Soc for the Study of Early Modern Women; South Atlantic Modern Language Assoc; Women's Caucus of th south Atlantic Modern Language Assoc. **RESEARCH** Shakespeare; renaissance drama; cultural studies; law and literature. **SELECTED PUBLICATIONS** auth, Journal of Medieval and Renaissance Studies, A Spanish Heart in an english Body': The Ralegh Treason Trial and the Poetics of Proof, fall 92; Exemplaria: A Journal of Theory in Medieval and Renaissance Studies, She Learns As She Lies': Work and the Exemplary Female in English Early Modern Education, spring 95; Renaissance Drama, Female Fedelities on Trial: Proof in the Howard Attainder and Cymbeline, spring 96. **CONTACT ADDRESS** English Dept, Florida State Univ, 216 WJB, Tallahassee, FL 32306. **EMAIL** kcunning@english.fsu.edu

CUNNINGHAM, MERRILEE A.

PERSONAL Born 12/14/1943, Ft Benning, GA, m, 1966, 3 children **DISCIPLINE** ENGLISH **EDUCATION** Northwestern Univ, BA, 66; Marshall Univ, MA, 70; Vanderbilt Univ, PhD, 78. **CAREER** Instr, Peace Corp, 67-68; Instr, Vanderbilt Univ 71-73; Assoc Prof, Univ Houston, 78-. **HONORS AND AWARDS** Outstanding Teacher Awd, Univ Houston, 76, 90. **MEMBERSHIPS** MSA, RSA, PCSS. **RESEARCH** Renaissance non-dramatic literature, Renaissance dramatic literature. **SELECTED PUBLICATIONS** Auth, "The Paradox Regained in the Poetry of Elizabeth Bishop and the Work of Edward Hopper," Univ NC Pr (99). **CONTACT ADDRESS** Dept English, Univ of Houston, 1 Main St, Houston, TX 77002-1014. **EMAIL** cunningham@dt.uh.edu

CURLEY, MICHAEL JOSEPH

PERSONAL Born 12/23/1942, Hempstead, NY, 2 children **DISCIPLINE** MEDIEVAL LITERATURE, LATIN **EDUCATION** Fairfield Univ, BA, 64; Harvard Univ, MA, 65; Univ Chicago, PhD, 72. **CAREER** Prof Eng, dir Honors Prog, Univ Puget Sound, 71-; NEH fel classics, Univ Tex, Austin, 77-78; Am Coun Learned Soc fel Celtic, Harvard Univ, 79-80; Graves fel Celtic, Univ Wales, Aberystwyth, 82-83. **MEMBERSHIPS** Medieval Acad Am; Medieval Assn of Pac. **RESEARCH** Latin literature; palaeography; Celtic. **SELECTED PUBLICATIONS** Auth & trans, Physiologus, Univ of Texas Press, 79; auth & trans, Marie de France, Purgatory of Saint Patrick, Binghamton: Center for Medieval and Renaissance Texts, 93; auth, Geoffrey of Monmouth, New York: Macmillan, 94. **CONTACT ADDRESS** Honor's Program, Univ of Puget Sound, 1500 N Warner St, Tacoma, WA 98416-0005. **EMAIL** curley@ups.edu

CURLEY, STEPHEN J.

PERSONAL Born 03/03/1947, New York, NY, m, 1969, 3 children **DISCIPLINE** ENGLISH **EDUCATION** Fordham Univ, BA, 68; Rice Univ, PhD, 74. **CAREER** Teach English at Texas A&M Univ at Galveston, (TAMUG), 73-pres; Head, 85-97; Dept of General Academics, TAMUG, 77-80; 85-97. **HONORS AND AWARDS** Level Distinguised Achievement Awd in Teaching, Texas A&M University, 92; Most Effective Teacher of TAMUG, 88; Faculty/Staff Achievement Awd (TAMUG's Highest Awd), 87. **MEMBERSHIPS** Area Chair for Sea Literature; Popular Cullture Assoc/Amer Culture Assoc; Member; Texas Humanities Alliance; Texas Council for the Humanies; Representative, Accreditation Visiting Team; Southern Association of Colleges and Schools. **RESEARCH** Sea-related popular culture; War film. **SELECTED PUBLICATIONS** Auth, "Celluloid Wars: A Guide to Film and the American Experience of War," with Frank Wetta, Westport, CT: Greenwood, 92: 294; ed, "Living on the Edge: Collected Essays on Coastal Texas, Galveston: Texas A&M University at Galveston & Texas Committee for the Humanities, 89: 160; auth, "Searching High and Low for Culture," Texas Journal (Spring/Summer 1999): 54-57; auth, "Searching High and Low for Culture," Texas Journal (Spring/Summer 99): 54-57; autth, "The War and Film in the United States and Britain," World War II in Asia and the Pacific and the War's Aftermath, with General Themes, Ed. Loyd E. Lee, Westport: Greenwood, 98, 241-54; auth, "Texas Coast in Fiction," Our Coastal Experience, Ed., W. Wise, Gloucester: Coastal Society, 93: 817-24; auth, "The Texas Coastal Plan: Analysis of a Failure," Coastal Management, 18, 90: 1-14; auth, " War Film Bibliography," Journal of Popular Film & Television, 18, 90: 72-79; auth, "Managerial Theory and Teaching Writing: Get a Job," J Technical Writing and Communication, 12, 82: 57-67; auth, "Is the Teaching Writing Really Relevant?" J Technical Writing and Communication, 7, 77: 309-24. **CONTACT ADDRESS** Dept General Academics, Texas A&M Univ, Galveston, PO Box 1675, Galveston, TX 77553-1675. **EMAIL** curleys@tamug.tamu.edu

CURLEY, THOMAS MICHAEL

PERSONAL Born 05/22/1943, Waltham, MA, m, 1970, 3 children **DISCIPLINE** ENGLISH LITERATURE **EDUCATION** Boston Col, BS, 65; Harvard Univ, MA, 66, PhD(English), 70. **CAREER** Teaching asst English, Harvard Univ, 67-70; asst prof, Fordham Univ, 70-72; asst prof, 72-76, assoc prof, 76-81, Prof English, Bridgewater State Col, 81-, Harvard Univ Dexter

Travelling fel, 69; Am Bar Found fel legal hist & Friends of London House Found grant, 78; Woodrow Wilson fac develop grant, 79; Nat Endowment for Humanities summer grant, 80 & fel, 81; NEH fellow, 81, 92, 99 & 00. **HONORS AND AWARDS** Bridgewater Distinguished Service Awd, 79 & 81. **MEMBERSHIPS** MLA; Am Soc Eighteenth Century Studies; Northeast Mod Lang Asn. **RESEARCH** Eighteenth century English and Irish literature; travel literature; Anglo-American law and politics in literature. **SELECTED PUBLICATIONS** Auth, Samuel Johnson and the Age of Travel, 76; A Course of Lectures on the English Law by Sir Robert Chambers in Association with Samuel Johnson, 86; auth, Sir Robert Chambers: Law, Literature and Empire in the Age of Johnson, 98; auth, Johnson and the Irish: A Postcolonial Survey of the Irish Literary Renaissance in Imperial Great Britain, 00. **CONTACT ADDRESS** Dept of English, Bridgewater State Col, Bridgewater, MA 02324.

CURLIN, J.
PERSONAL Born 10/03/1960, El Paso, TX, m, 1987, 6 children **DISCIPLINE** ENGLISH **EDUCATION** Ouachita Baptist Univ, BA, 83; Univ Ark, MA, 85; Univ Mich, PhD, 93. **CAREER** Asst Prof, Univ Ark, 91-97; Asst Prof, Southwest Baptist Univ, 97-98; Asst Prof, Oauchita Baptist Univ, 98-. **HONORS AND AWARDS** Irene Samuel Awd, Milton Soc of Am, Distinguished Multiauthor. **MEMBERSHIPS** Milton Soc of Am. **RESEARCH** Milton, Seventeenth-Century literature, British and American poetry. **SELECTED PUBLICATIONS** Auth, "An Equal Poise of Hope and Fear: A Fraternal Harmony of Extremes," Arenas of Conflict: Milton and the Unfettered Mind, Susquehanna UP (Selinsgrove, PA), 97; auth, "'Is There no Temperate Region': Coopers Hill and the Call for Moderation," in Lit and the English Civil Wars, (Columbia: Univ Mo Pr, 99), 119-129. **CONTACT ADDRESS** Dept English, Ouachita Baptist Univ, 410 Ouachita Baptist St, Arkadelphia, AR 71998-0001. **EMAIL** curlinj@alpha, obu, edu

CURRAN, LEO C.
DISCIPLINE CLASSICS **EDUCATION** Oxford Univ, MA, 58; Yale Univ, BA; PhD, 61. **CAREER** Fac, 67-; to assoc prof emer, present, SUNY Buffalo. **HONORS AND AWARDS** Chancellor's Awd Excel Tchg, 80; found assoc ed, arethusa. **RESEARCH** Software for computer analysis of Latin lit and for Latin instruction; poetry of the late Republic and early Empire. **SELECTED PUBLICATIONS** Auth, Identification of Latin Poets by Sound, Syllecta Classica 2, 90; Identification of Latin Poets by Sound II, Syllecta Classica 3, 91. **CONTACT ADDRESS** Dept Classics, SUNY, Buffalo, 707 Clemens Hall, Buffalo, NY 14260. **EMAIL** lccurran@acsu.buffalo.edu

CURRAN, SONIA TERRIE
DISCIPLINE ENGLISH **EDUCATION** Univ Wis, PhD. **CAREER** Instr, 66-69, tchg asst, Youngstown State Univ, 70-73; instr, Univ Wis Extension Div, 73, asst to assoc prof, 73-, chemn, dept Eng, Providence Col , 76-78 & 92-96; annual evaluator, New Eng Assn of Sch and Col. **RESEARCH** Literary history of the English language. **SELECTED PUBLICATIONS** Auth, The Word Made Flesh: The Christian Aesthetic in Dorothy L. Sayers The Man Born to be King, As Her Wimsey Took Her: Critical Essays on the Work of Dorothy L. Sayers, Kent State Univ Press, 79; The Cultural Context of Chaucer's Canterbury Tales, Approaches to Teaching Chaucer'sCanterbury Tales, ed. by Joseph Gibaldi, MLA, 80. **CONTACT ADDRESS** Dept of English, Providence Col, Providence, RI 02918. **EMAIL** stcurran@providence.edu

CURRAN, STUART ALAN
PERSONAL Born 08/03/1940, Detroit, MI **DISCIPLINE** ENGLISH LITERATURE, ROMANTICISM **EDUCATION** Univ Mich, BA, 62, MA, 63; Harvard Univ, PhD(English), 67. **CAREER** From asst prof to assoc prof English, Univ Wis, Madison, 67-74; Prof English, Univ PA, 74-, Nat Endowment for Humanities jr fel Shelley, 70-71; John Simon Guggenheim Found fel, 73-74; ed, Keats-Shelley J, 80-93. **MEMBERSHIPS** MLA; Keats-Shelley Asn; Byron Soc; Int Asn Univ Prof English. **RESEARCH** English romanticism; Renaissance and romanticism; poetic genres. **SELECTED PUBLICATIONS** Auth, Shelley's CENCI: Scorpions Ringed with Fire, Princeton Univ, 70; ed, Le Bossu and Voltaire on the Epic, Scholars' Facsimiles, 70; co-ed, Blake's Sublime Allegory: Essays on The Four Zoas, Milton & Jerusalem, Univ Wis, 73; auth, Shelley's Annus Mirabilis: The Maturing of an Epic Vision, Huntington Libr, 75; auth, Poetic Form and British Romanticism, Oxford, 86; ed, The Poems of Charlotte Smith, Oxford, 93; ed, Cambridge Companion to British Romanticism, Cambridge, 93; co-ed, Shelley: Poet and Legislator of the World, Johns Hopkins, 96; ed, Mary Shelley, Valperga, Oxford, 97. **CONTACT ADDRESS** Dept of English, Univ of Pennsylvania, 3340 Walnut St, Philadelphia, PA 19104-6173. **EMAIL** curran@english.upenn.edu

CURRIE, WILLIAM W.
PERSONAL Born 09/24/1945, Midland, MI, s **DISCIPLINE** LIBRARY SCIENCE, ENGLISH **EDUCATION** Mich State Univ, BA, 68, MA, 76; W Mich Univ, MLS, 80 **CAREER** Librn Geol Survey Div, Mich Dept Nat Res, 77-78; Asst librn, 81-90, Librn, 90- , Firelands Col-Bowling Green State Univ. **HONORS AND AWARDS** Beta Phi Mu; Librn Hon Soc, 80. **MEMBERSHIPS** Am Libr Asn; Asn Col & Res Libr; Acad Libr Asn Ohio. **RESEARCH** Indexing and abstracting; Collection development. **SELECTED PUBLICATIONS** Auth, Annotated List of the Publications of the Mich Geological Survey, 1838-1977: Indexed by Author, Mineral and County, Mich Dept Nat Res, 78; The Inventory Process at a Two-Year Branch Campus Library, Comm & Jr Col Libr, 84; Evaluation of the Collection of a Two-Year Branch Campus by Using Textbook Citations, Comm & Jr Col Libr, 89. **CONTACT ADDRESS** 901 Rye Beach Rd, Huron, OH 44839. **EMAIL** wcurrie@bgnet.bgsu.edu

CURRY, ELIZABETH R.
PERSONAL Born 01/31/1934, Evanston, IL, w, 1958, 1 child **DISCIPLINE** ENGLISH **EDUCATION** Northwestern Univ, BA, 56; Univ Wis, PhD, 63. **CAREER** Prof, Slippery Rock Univ, 69-. **HONORS AND AWARDS** Bonbright Scholar; Advanced Knapp Fel; HFA Humanities Awd; Poetry Awds. **MEMBERSHIPS** APSCUF. **RESEARCH** Poetry, women's studies, art history, 20th-century British literature, Shakespeare. **SELECTED PUBLICATIONS** Auth, What Land Is This: A Book of Poems, Slippery Rock Pr (Slippery Rock, PA), 97. **CONTACT ADDRESS** Dept English, Slippery Rock Univ of Pennsylvania, 14 Maltby Dr, 314 SWC Bldg, Slippery Rock, PA 16057-1303.

CURTIN, MICHAEL
DISCIPLINE COMMUNICATIONS **EDUCATION** Brown Univ, AB, 77; Univ of Wis-Madison, MA, 86, PhD, 90. **CAREER** ASST PROF, DEPT OF TELECOMMUNICATIONS, 90-97, DIR, CULTURAL STUDIES PROGRAM, 94-, ASSOC PROF, DEPT OF COMMUN & CULTURE, IND UNIV, 97-; visiting scholar, Chinese Univ of Hong Kong, 97-98; lectr, Dept of Commun Arts, Univ of Wis, 89-90; producer, Wis Public Television, 87-90; Tokyo correspondent, National Public Radio, 82-84; producer, Youth News, 81-82; acting news dir, KPFA-FM, 80; reporter, KPFA-FM, 78-80; magazine freelance writer, 78-84. **HONORS AND AWARDS** Corecipient, Research fund, City Univ of Hong Kong, 98; corecip, Multidisciplinary Ventures Fund, 96; corecip, Funding for collaborative multimedia project involving Cultural Studies and the Res Center for Lang and Semiotic Studies, 95; Course Development Grants, Ind Univ, 95; corecip, Inter-Programs Research and Projects Grant; Charline Wackman Awd; Warren C. Price Awd; Wisconsin Alumni Research Foundation Fellow, University of Wis; Kaltenborn Foundation Awd; Corporation for Public Broadcasting, Public Radio Program Awd, 82; Champion Media Awd for Economic Understanding, 83; Gabriel Awd, 82. **MEMBERSHIPS** Ed Board, J of Critical Media Sciences; reviewer, J of Monographs, J of Commun, J of Asian Pacific Commun, Am Hist Rev, Am ethnologist, Cambridge Univ Press, Duke Univ Press. **RESEARCH** Cultural studies, globalization of media, media history, political economy of the culture industries, social implications of new media technologies, documentary. **SELECTED PUBLICATIONS** Auth, Redeeming the Wasteland: Television Documentary and Cold War Politics, Rutgers Univ Press, 95; auth, Packaging Reality: The Influence of Fictional Forms on the Early Development of Television Documentary 1955-1965, Journalism Monographs, 95; co-ed, Making and Selling Culture, Wesleyan Univ Press, 96; coed, The Revolution Wasn't Televised: Sixties Television and Social Conflict, Routledge, 97; coauth, Images of Trust, Economies of Suspicion: Hong Kong Media after 1997, Hist J of Film, Radio, and Television, 98; auth, Transgressive Imagery on Transnational Television, Con-temporary, 98. 18, no.2 (1998) **CONTACT ADDRESS** Dept of Commun and Culture, Indiana Univ, Bloomington, 809 E 7th St, Bloomington, IN 47405. **EMAIL** mcurtin@indiana.edu

CUSHMAN, STEPHEN B.
PERSONAL Born 12/17/1956, Norwalk, CT, m, 1982, 2 children **DISCIPLINE** ENGLISH **EDUCATION** Cornell Univ, BA, 78; Yale Univ, MA, 80; MPhil, 81; PhD, 82. **CAREER** From Asst Prof to Prof, Univ Va, 82-. **HONORS AND AWARDS** Phi Kappa Phi; Phi Beta Kappa; Fulbright Fel, Ionion Univ, 93; Omicron Delta Kappa, 94; Fel, Va Found Humanities, 97. **MEMBERSHIPS** MLA, William Carlos Williams Soc. **RESEARCH** American literature, poetry, the American Civil War. **SELECTED PUBLICATIONS** Auth, William Carlos Williams and the Meanings of Measure, Yale UP (New Haven, CT), 85; auth, Fictions of Form in American Poetry, Princeton UP (Princeton, NJ), 93; auth, Blue Pajamas (Poems), La St Univ Pr (Baton Rouge, LA), 98; auth, Bloody Promenade: Reflections on a Civil War Battle, UP of Va (Charlottesville, VA), 99. **CONTACT ADDRESS** Dept English, Univ of Virginia, 219 Bryan Hall, P O Box 400121, Charlottesville, VA 22904-4121. **EMAIL** sbc9g@virginia.edu

CUSICK, SUZANNE G.
DISCIPLINE MUSIC HISTORY **EDUCATION** Univ NC, PhD. **CAREER** Assoc prof, Dept Music, Va Univ **HONORS AND AWARDS** NEH Fel, 90-91. **RESEARCH** Feminist criticism; cultural history of 16th and 17th century European music; early opera; 19th century American popular music. **SELECTED PUBLICATIONS** Auth, Of Women, Music, and Power: A Model from Seicento Florence, Univ Ca, 93; Gendering Modern Music: Thoughts on the Monteverdi-Artusi Controversy, Jour Am Musicol Soc; 93; Thinking from Women's Lives: Francesca Caccini after 1627, 93; Feminist Theory, Music Theory, and the Mind-Body Problem, 93; 'And not one lady failed to shed a tear': Arianna's Lament and the Construction of Modern Womanhood, 94. **CONTACT ADDRESS** Dept of Music, Univ of Virginia, Cabell Hall No 113, PO Box 400176, Charlottesville, VA 22904-4176. **EMAIL** sgc5u@virginia.edu

CUTTER, PAUL F.
DISCIPLINE MUSIC HISTORY AND LITERATURE **EDUCATION** UCLA, BA; Harvard, MA; Princeton, MFA, PhD. **CAREER** Prof Mus, ch, Mus Hist and Lit, assoc dir, grad stud, TX Tech Univ. **HONORS AND AWARDS** TX Tech's President's Excellence in Tchg Awd, 88. **SELECTED PUBLICATIONS** Publ bks and articles on subjects ranging from Gregorian Chant to music in pioneer West Texas. **CONTACT ADDRESS** Texas Tech Univ, Lubbock, TX 79409-5015. **EMAIL** mspfc@ttacs.ttu.edu

CYGANOWSKI, CAROL K.
PERSONAL Born 04/12/1949, Chicago, IL, m, 1970, 1 child **DISCIPLINE** ENGLISH, AMERICAN LITERATURE **EDUCATION** Knox Col, BA, 69; Univ Chicago, MA, 70: PhD, 80. **CAREER** Instr, vis asst prof, Roosevelt Univ, 75-79; lectr, 81-84; instr, 84-86; asst prof, 86-90; WSP dir, 90-95; asp dir, 96-; pres, assoc prof, 90-; De Paul Univ. **HONORS AND AWARDS** Woodrow Wilson Fel; Ford Found Fel; De Paul Univ Human Fel. **MEMBERSHIPS** ASA; MLA; MMLA; BMROA. **RESEARCH** US publishing history; women writers; American drama. **SELECTED PUBLICATIONS** Auth, Magazine Editors and Professional Authors in 19th C America (Garland Press, 88). **CONTACT ADDRESS** Dept English, DePaul Univ, 2320 North Kenmore Ave, Chicago, IL 60614-3210. **EMAIL** ccyganow@condor.depaul.edu

CYR, MARY
PERSONAL Born Fargo, ND **DISCIPLINE** MUSIC, HISTORY **EDUCATION** Univ Calif, BA, 68, MA, 70, PhD, 75. **CAREER** Prof, McGill Univ, 76-92, dir grad studs, 91-92; prof & ch, Music, Univ Guelph, 92-. **HONORS AND AWARDS** Noah Greenberg Awd Excellence, Am Musicological Soc. **MEMBERSHIPS** Can Univ Music Soc; Early Music Soc; Am Musicological Soc. **SELECTED PUBLICATIONS** Auth, Performing Baroque Music, 92; auth, Violin Playing in Late Seventeenth-Century England: Baltzar, Matteis and Purcell in Performance Practice Review 8:1, 95. **CONTACT ADDRESS** Dept of Fine Art & Music, Univ of Guelph, Guelph, ON, Canada N1G 2W1. **EMAIL** mcyr@arts.uoguelph.ca

CYRUS, CYNTHIA
PERSONAL Born 09/02/1963, Seattle, WA, m, 1995, 2 children **DISCIPLINE** MUSIC **EDUCATION** Pomona Col, BA, 84; Univ NC Chapel Hill, MA, 87, PhD, 90. **CAREER** Vis asst prof, Univ Rochester, 91-92; vis asst prof, SUNY Stony Brook, 92- 94; asst prof, Vanderbilt Univ, 94- . **HONORS AND AWARDS** Univ Post-doctoral Fel, Oh St Univ, 90-91; Vanderbilt Univ Res Coun Grants, 95, 96; Distinguished Leadership Awd, 97; Vanderbilt Univ Res Scholar Fel, 00-01. **MEMBERSHIPS** Amer Musicol Soc; Int Machant Soc; Renaissance Soc; Medieval Acad. **RESEARCH** Medieval & Renaissance musical literacy; women & music; musical modeling in the 15th-16th centuries. **SELECTED PUBLICATIONS** Auth, Rereading Absence: Women in Medieval and Renaissance Music, Col Music Symp, 98; Women Owners and Women Readers: The Circulation of Music Books in the Late Medieval and Early Modern Eras, forthcoming; Obsessed with Death in Freiburg, Sewanee Medieval Stud, forthcoming; auth, De tous biens plaine: An edition of the Chanson Arrangements, Madison: A-R Editias, forthcoming. **CONTACT ADDRESS** Blair School of Music, Vanderbilt Univ, 2400 Blakemore Ave, Nashville, TN 37212. **EMAIL** cynthia.cyrus@vanderbilt.edu

CZERWINSKI, EDWARD J.
PERSONAL Born 06/06/1929, Erie, PA **DISCIPLINE** SLAVIC DRAMA AND THEATRE, COMPARATIVE LITERATURE **EDUCATION** Grove City Col, BA, 51; Pa State Univ, MA, 55; Univ Wis, MA, 64, PhD(Russ, Polish), 65. **CAREER** Instr English, Ga Tech, 57-59; asst prof English & drama, McNeese State Col, 59-60: assoc prof Russ & Polish lit, Univ Pittsburgh, 65-66; assoc prof Slavics & chmn dept, State Univ NY, Buffalo & Millard Fillmore Eve Div, 66-67; assoc prof Russ & Polish, Univ Kans, 67-70; Prof Russ & Comp Lit, State Univ NY Stony Brook, 70-, Chmn Comt Acad Exchange With Poland, 73-, Special ed & mem ed bd, Comp Drama; ed, Slavic & EEurop Theatre J. **HONORS AND AWARDS** Distinguished Teaching Awd, NY State Asn Foreign Lang Teachers, 75. **MEMBERSHIPS** MLA; Am Asn Teachers Slavic & EEurop Lang; Int Fedn Mod Lang & Lit; AAUP; Am Asn Advan Slavic Studies. **SELECTED PUBLICATIONS CONTACT ADDRESS** Dept of Ger & Slavic Lang, SUNY, Stony Brook, Stony Brook, NY 11790.

D

D'AVANZO, MARIO L.
PERSONAL Born 11/11/1931, New Britain, CT, d, 2 children **DISCIPLINE** ENGLISH **EDUCATION** Dartmouth Col, AB, 53; Trinity Col, Conn, MA, 54; Brown Univ, PhD(English), 63. **CAREER** From instr to assoc prof English, Providence Col, 60-68; assoc prof, 68-73, prof English, Queen's Col, 73-. **MEMBERSHIPS** MLA. **RESEARCH** English romantic poetry; American literature. **SELECTED PUBLICATIONS** Auth, Keats's Metaphors for the Poetic Imagination, Duke Univ, 67; Keats's and Vergil's underworlds: Source and meaning in Book II of Endymion, Keats-Shelley J, winter 67; King Francis, Lucrezia, and the figurative language of Andrea del Sarto, Tex Studies Lang & Lit, winter 68; The literary sources of My Kinsman, Major Molineaux: Shakespeare, Coleridge, Milton, Studies Short Fiction, spring 73; Fortitude and nature in Thoreau's Cape Cod, Esquire, 74; The Literary Art of the Bible: A Commentary, Am Press, 88; Robert Frost and the Romantics, Am Univ Press, 91. **CONTACT ADDRESS** Dept of English, Queens Col, CUNY, 6530 Kissena Blvd, Flushing, NY 11367-1597.

D'HEMECOURT, JULES
DISCIPLINE MASS COMMUNICATIONS **EDUCATION** Greenwich Univ, PhD, 91. **CAREER** Asst prof, La State Univ; atty; ling consult, MCI Telecommun. **SELECTED PUBLICATIONS** Auth, Breakfast TV, An Analysis of Morning Media, Ctr for Jour Stud, Gr Brit, 81; Feminization of Mass Communications in the Southern United States, Popular Cult Asn of the S; Am Cult Asn in the S, 90; Career Paths, Prof Communicator, Women in Commun mag, 94; coauth, Broadcast News English, 83. **CONTACT ADDRESS** The Manship Sch of Mass Commun, Louisiana State Univ and A&M Col, Baton Rouge, LA 70803. **EMAIL** jdhemec@unix1.sncc.lsu.edu

DABNEY, ROSS H.
DISCIPLINE ENGLISH **EDUCATION** Princeton Univ, AB; Harvard, PhD. **CAREER** Chr and prof Eng, Sweet Briar Col. **HONORS AND AWARDS** Consult ed, Dickens Studies Annual. **RESEARCH** Research focus on parents and children in the Eng novel. **SELECTED PUBLICATIONS** Auth, Love and Property in the Novels of Dickens. **CONTACT ADDRESS** Sweet Briar Col, Sweet Briar, VA 24595. **EMAIL** dabney@sbc.edu

DACE, LETITIA
DISCIPLINE DRAMATIC LITERATURE & WRITING **EDUCATION** Sweet Briar Col, BA, 63; Kans State Univ, MA, 67, PhD(English lit), 71. **CAREER** Instr speech & drama, Kans State Univ, 63-71; asst prof speech & drama & bus mgr dept, 71-74, assoc prof speech & drama & deputy chmn dept, John Jay Col Criminal Justice, 74-80, actg chmn dept, 78, chmn, 79-80; prof English & Drama & dean, Col of Arts & Sci; Univ Mass Dartmouth, 80-86; prof of English, 86-97; Chancelor Prof, 97-; asst ed, Shakespearean Res & Opportunities, 71-75; theatre critic, Soho Weekly News, 77-82, Other Stages, 78-82, The Villager, 82 & The Advocate, 82-. **HONORS AND AWARDS** Kans State Univ fac res awd, 69-70; Folger Shakespeare Libr Res Gr , 70; City Univ New York fac res awds, 72 & 73; ch, Maharam/Am Theatre Wing/Hewes theatre Design Awds, 84- ;NEH Summer Res Stipend, 87; Healey Res Gr, UMD Found, 95; UMD Scholar of the Yr Awd, 97; Innovation in Tchg Gr, UMD, 97; UMD Found Res Gr, 98. **MEMBERSHIPS** Am Soc Theatre Res; Theatre Libr Asn; Am Theatre Critics Asn; Outer Critics Circle; Drama Desk. **RESEARCH** Contemporary British drama; contemporary American drama; contemporary Jewish, women's, gay & African-American drama; modern drama. **SELECTED PUBLICATIONS** Auth, LeRoi Jones (Imamu Amiri Baraka), Nether Pr (London), 71; co-auth, The Theatre Student: Modern Theatre and Drama, Richards Rosen Pr (New York), 73; co-auth, Black American Writers, vol 2, St Martin's Pr (New York), 78; auth, "The Singular Careers of Tandy & Cronyn," Am Theatre I (Oct 84): 6: 10-15; auth, "From the Ridiculous to the Sublime," Theatre Crafts XX (March 86): 3: 34-37, 67-70; auth, "Who Wrote 'John Arden's' Plays?" in John Arden and Margaretta D'Arcy: A Casebook, ed Jonathan Wike (NY: Garland Pub, Inc, 95); auth, "On Langston Hughes: Pioneering Poet," Am Poetry Rev XXIV (Nov/Dec 95): 6: 35-58; auth, Langston Hughes: The Contemporary Reviews, Cambridge Univ Pr (Cambridge), 97; auth, "Designing Women," Back Stage (March 20, 98): 1, 30-33; auth, "Hewes on Hewes: ATCA's Founder in His Own Words, Part 1," Critics Q XII, 4 (Winter 00): 4-5, 12. **CONTACT ADDRESS** Engl Dept, Univ of Massachusetts, Dartmouth, 285 Old Westport Rd, North Dartmouth, MA 02747-2300. **EMAIL** tdace@umassd.edu

DADDARIO, GINA
DISCIPLINE COMMUNICATOIN STUDIES **EDUCATION** Univ NC, BA, 76; Univ Md, MA, 82; Univ Mass, PhD, 88. **CAREER** Prof. **SELECTED PUBLICATIONS** Auth, Women's Sports and Spectacle: Gendered Coverage and the Olympic Games. **CONTACT ADDRESS** Dept of Mass Communication, Shenandoah Univ, 1460 University Dr., Winchester, VA 22601.

DAHOOD, ROGER
PERSONAL Born 12/21/1942, New York, NY, m, 1980, 3 children **DISCIPLINE** ENGLISH LITERATURE **EDUCATION** Colgate Univ, BA, 64; Stanford Univ, MA, 67, PhD, 70. **CAREER** From asst prof to prof Eng, Univ Ariz, 70-. **MEMBERSHIPS** Int Arthurian Soc; Medieval Acad Am; Medieval Asn Pacific. **RESEARCH** Old and Middle Eng lit. **SELECTED PUBLICATIONS** Auth, Dubious readings in the French and Hale text of The Avowing of King Arthur, 71, A lexical puzzle in Ancrene Wisse, 78 & Four 13th century proverbs in MS Harley 47, 79, Notes & Queries; A Note on Beowulf, 1104-8a, Medium Aevum, 80; ed, The Avowing of King Arthur, 84; co-ed and transl, Ancrene Riwle: Introduction and part I, 84; Auth, Ancrene Wisse, the Katherine Group, and the Wohunge Group, In: Middle English Prose: A Critical Guide to Major Authors and Genres, 84; Four English Proverbs in the Hand of John Stow, Notes & Queries, 85; Design in Part I of Ancrene Riwle, Medium Aevum, 87; The Use of Coloured Initials and Other Division Markers in Early Versions of Ancrene Riwle, In: Medieval English Studies Presented to George Kane, 88; Variants of the Middle English Warning in William of Canterbury's Life of Becket, Parergon, 93; Hugh de Morville, William of Cantebury, and Anecdotal Evidence for English language History, Speculum 94; The Current State of Ancrene Wisse Group Studies, Medieval English Newsletter, 97. **CONTACT ADDRESS** Dept of Eng, Univ of Arizona, Mod Lang(s) Bldg, Tucson, AZ 85721-0001. **EMAIL** rdahood@u.arizona.edu

DAIGLE, LENNET J.
PERSONAL Born 01/28/1948, White Castle, LA, m, 3 children **DISCIPLINE** RENAISSANCE POETRY, COMPOSITION PEDAGOGY, THEORY, ONLINE LEARNING METHODOLOGY **EDUCATION** Univ Dallas, BA, 70; Univ SC Columbia, MA, 71; PhD 76. **CAREER** Chair, assoc prof, Coastal Georgia Comm Coll, 76-84; prof, Tunghai University, Taichung, Taiwan; 88-89; chair, assoc prof, Georgia Southwestern Coll State Univ, 84-90; hd, prof, North Georgia Coll State Univ; 90-96; dean, 95-. **HONORS AND AWARDS** Fulbright-Hayes Awd, Tunghai Univ, Taichung, Taiwan, 88-89; Gov Awd Human, 99. **MEMBERSHIPS** Georgia Human Coun (Board of Directors); AAHE; SMLA; Fulbright Asn; Asn Dept English. **RESEARCH** English Literature with a specialty in the English Renaissance. **SELECTED PUBLICATIONS** Auth, "Venus and Adonis: Some Traditional Contexts," Shakespeare Studies 18 (80); rpt, in Shakespearean Criticism 33, eds. Dana Barnes, Marie Lazzari (Gale Res, Detroit MI, 97), 330-339; coauth, Brief Workbook for Writers, Prentice Hall, Inc. (89); Various review articles in journals. **CONTACT ADDRESS** No Georgia Col and State Univ, 100 College Circle, Dahlonega, GA 30597-001. **EMAIL** ldaigle@ngcsu.edu

DAIGLE-WILLIAMSON, MARSHA A.
PERSONAL Born 06/16/1946, St John, ME, m, 1992 **DISCIPLINE** ENGLISH **EDUCATION** Col New Rochelle, BA, 66; Univ Wis, MA, 67; Univ Mich, PhD, 84. **CAREER** Instr, Washtenaw Community Col, 84-85; Adj Lectr, Univ Mich, 85; From Asst Prof to Prof, Spring Arbor Col, 85-. **HONORS AND AWARDS** Teaching Fel, Univ Mich, 67-71; Teaching Awds, Spring Arbor Col, 87, 89, 93, 99. **MEMBERSHIPS** Dante Soc, Int English Hon Soc. **RESEARCH** Dante, C S Lewis, Renaissance. **SELECTED PUBLICATIONS** Transl, Le desire et la tendresse (Paris: Fides et Laborares, 80): Sexual Desire and Love: Origins and History of the Christian Ethic of Sexuality and Marriage, by Eric Fuch, Seabury Pr (New York), 83; ed, The Ann Arbor Wedding Consultant, 85-87; auth, "Tradition and Lewis's Individual Talent," in Christian Scholar's Rev (98); ed, "A N Wilson," in Mod Authors, (99). **CONTACT ADDRESS** Dept English, Spring Arbor Col, 106 Main St, Spring Arbor, MI 49283. **EMAIL** marshadw@admin.arbor.edu

DAILEY, JOSEPH
DISCIPLINE ORGANIZATIONAL AND INTERPERSONAL COMMUNICATION **EDUCATION** Marquette Univ, MA; Univ Ill, PhD. **CAREER** Law, Caroll Col. **SELECTED PUBLICATIONS** Auth, The Reluctant Candidate: Dwight Eisenhower in 1951. **CONTACT ADDRESS** Carroll Col, Wisconsin, 100 N East Ave, Waukesha, WI 53186.

DAILEY, SHERON
PERSONAL Born 01/11/1940, Indianapolis, IN, m **DISCIPLINE** COMMUNICATIONS **EDUCATION** Wake Forest Univ, BA, 61; Univ Minn, MA, 63; PhD, 69. **CAREER** Prof, Ind State Univ, 65-. **HONORS AND AWARDS** Phi Beta Kappa; Phi Kappa Phi; Kenneth Burke Soc's Distinguished Serv Awd; Distinguished Prof Awd, Ind State Univ; ISU Res and Creativity Awd; Don Ecroyd Awd for Distinguished Teaching in Higher Educ, Nat Commun Asn; NCA Performance Studies Div Distinguished Serv Awd. **MEMBERSHIPS** NCA, Kenneth Burke Soc. **RESEARCH** Cross-cultural communication, cross-cultural poetics. **SELECTED PUBLICATIONS** Auth, "Grantsmanship: The Rules of the Game," in Lit in Performance, 1(81): 123-124; auth, "Reservations about a Creative Analog: Waiting for the Reviews," ACA Bulletin, Issue 48 (84): 58-61; feature ed, Lit in Performance: A J of Lit and Performing Art, 82-88; ed, Diversity: Celebration and Commitment, Nat Commun Asn Pr, (Annandale, VA), 97; ed, The Future of Performance Studies: Visions and Revisions, Nat Commun Asn Pr (Annandale, VA), 98. **CONTACT ADDRESS** Dept Commun, Indiana State Univ, 210 N 7th St, Terre Haute, IN 47809-0001.

DALE, HELEN
PERSONAL Born 02/06/1945, Chicago, IL, 2 children **DISCIPLINE** ENGLISH EDUCATION **EDUCATION** NYork Univ, MA; Univ Wis Madison, PhD. **CAREER** Fac. **HONORS AND AWARDS** Phi Beta Kappa; Promising Res Nat Awd, finalist; NCTE; Steve Cahir Awd for Outstanding Res in Writing--Am Ed Res Assoc. **RESEARCH** Composition theory; collaborative writing; ethics of qualitative research; the links between theory and practice for student teachers; collaborative self-study as reform in teacher education; high school/university literacy partnerships. **SELECTED PUBLICATIONS** Auth, Co-authoring in the Classroom: Creating an Environment for Effective Collaboration; auth, "Collaborative Wrinting Interactions in One Ninth-Grade Classroom," J of Educational Res 87.6, (94), 334-344; auth, "Dilemmas of Fidelity: Qualitative research in the Classroom," Ethics and representation in Qualitative Studies of Literacy, Urbana, IL: NCTE, (96), 77-94; auth, The Influence of Co-authoring on the Writing Process," J of teaching Writing 15.1, (96), 65-79; auth, "Letters of Intent: Collaborative Self-Study as Reform in Teacher Education," The Heart of the Matter: Teacher Ed Reform Perspectives and Possibilities, (98), 81-99; auth, "Creating Literacy Communities: high school/ University Partnerships," English J, (98), 53-58. **CONTACT ADDRESS** Dept of English, Univ of Wisconsin, Eau Claire, Hibbard Hall 412, PO Box 4004, Eau Claire, WI 54702-4004. **EMAIL** dalehn@uwec.edu

DALEY, KOOS W.
PERSONAL Born 03/11/1943, Utrecht, Netherlands, m, 1967, 2 children **DISCIPLINE** ENGLISH **EDUCATION** Univ Colo, BA, 80; MA, 85; PhD, 88. **CAREER** Asst Prof to Prof and Asst Dean, Adams State Col, 88-. **HONORS AND AWARDS** William B. Markward Endowment for Study in the Renaissance, 87-88; Fel, Univ Colo Grad Sch, 87-88; Phi Beta Kappa; Dissertation Awd, UCB Arts and Humanities, 89; Exemplary Teachers, ASC, 94, 95, 97, 00. **MEMBERSHIPS** John Donne Soc; Am Asn of Neth Studies; Can Asn for Neth Studies. **RESEARCH** The Dutch 17th century poet Constantijn Huygens; John Donne; Literary translations from Dutch into English. **SELECTED PUBLICATIONS** Auth, The Triple Foole, DeGraaf Pub, 90; trans, Holy Days, Mellen Poetry Press, 01. **CONTACT ADDRESS** Dept English, Adams State Col, 1901 Carroll St, Alamosa, CO 81101. **EMAIL** kwdaley@adams.edu

DALLINGER, JUDITH M.
PERSONAL Born 06/09/1953, IA, m, 1983, 2 children **DISCIPLINE** SPEECH COMMUNICATION **EDUCATION** Northwest Miss State Univ, BS, 74; Tex Christian Univ, MS, 76; Univ Nebr, PhD, 84. **CAREER** Fac mem, Western IL Univ, 81-. **HONORS AND AWARDS** Faculty Excellence Awd, Western IL Univ. **MEMBERSHIPS** Int. Commun Assoc; Nat Commun Assoc. **RESEARCH** Organizational communication, sex differences in communication, taking conflict personally. **SELECTED PUBLICATIONS** Coauth, "Personalizing and managing conflict", Int J of Conflict Management 6.3 (95): 273-289; coauth, "Perceiving and predicting the tendency to personalize arguments", Argumentation and Values, ed S. Jackson, (95): 434-438; auth, An Exploration of androgyny and rhetorical sensitivity: The connection of gender and communication style", Commun Reports 11.1 (98): 11-20; coauth, "Taking conflict personally, solidarity and relational satisfaction: Interrelationships with arguments", Argument in a time of change: Definition, frameworks, and critiques, ed J.F. Klumpp, Nat Commun Assoc, (Annandale, VA, 98): 90-96; coauth, "Assessment Day: Every which way but out", A collection of papers on self-study and institutional improvement, ed Van Kollenburg, Comm on Inst of Higher Educ of the N Central Assoc of Col and Schools (98): 182-184; coauth, "On the etiology of the rebuff phenomenon: Why are persuasive messages less polite after rebuffs?", Commun Studies 4, (98): 305-321; coauth, "Do you take conflict personally?", The 1999 training and performance sourcebook, ed M. Silberman, McGraw-Hill, (99): 157-172; coauth, "Assessing student knowledge of and attitudes toward the humanities", Col Teaching (forthcoming). **CONTACT ADDRESS** Dept Commun Arts & Sci, Western Illinois Univ, 1 University Circle, Macomb, IL 61455-1367. **EMAIL** mfjmd@wiu.edu

DALY, BRENDA O.
PERSONAL Born 06/27/1941, Hibbing, MN, d, 1 child **DISCIPLINE** ENGLISH **EDUCATION** Univ NDak, BA, 63; Mankato State Univ, MA, 78; Univ Minn, PhD, 85. **CAREER** Teacher, St. Olaf Col, Macalester Col, Univ of Minn, 64-87; thesis dir; POS comt; ch; teacher, Iowa State Univ, 87-. **HONORS AND AWARDS** Ruud Scholarship, Univ Minn, 82; Doctoral Dissertation Fellow, Univ Minn, 83-84; Aff Schol, Ctr for Adv Feminist Stud, Univ Minn, 86-88, 93-94; Res Salary Support, Iowa State Univ, 88; Fac Improvement Grant, Iowa State Univ, 90; Course Dev Grant, Iowa State Univ, 91; Res Incentive Grant, Iowa State Col of LAS, 93; Fac Improvement Leave, Iowa State Univ, 93; Fulbright Fellow to Norway (declined), 95; Proj, Aware Grant, Iowa State Univ Ctr for Tchng Excellence, 96; Fac Improvement Leave, Iowa State Univ, 97; Women's Studies Summer Grant, 99. **MEMBERSHIPS** Comt Member, POS Comt member; Nat Coun of Teachers of English; Modern Lang Asn, Midwest Modern Lang Asn; Nat Women's Studies Asn; Col English Asn; Nat Pop Culture Asn; Nat Education Asn; Am Lit Asn. **RESEARCH** Am women's narra-

tives; narrative theory; feminist theory; autobiographical criticism; pedagogy. **SELECTED PUBLICATIONS** Auth, Sexual Politics in Two Collections of Joyce Carol Oates's Short Fiction, Stud in Short Fic, 32, 83-93, 95; auth, Marriage as Emancipatory Metaphor: Women Wedded to Teaching and Writing in Joyce Carol Oates's Academic Fiction, Critique, 37:4, 270-88, 96; auth, Lavish Self-Divisions: The Novels of Joyce Carol Oates, Univ Press of Miss, 96; auth, Authoring a Life: A Woman's Survival in and Through Literary Studies, SUNY Press, 98; auth, Where is She Going, Where Are We Going, at Century's End? The Girl as Site of Cultural Conflict in Joyce Carol Oates's The Model, The Girl, St Martin's Press, 1-20, 98. **CONTACT ADDRESS** Dept of English, Iowa State Univ, Ames, IA 50011-1201.

DALY, ROBERT J.
PERSONAL Born 06/17/1943, Wayne County, OH, m, 1966, 2 children **DISCIPLINE** AMERICAN AND ENGLISH LITERATURE **EDUCATION** Univ Akron, BA, 65, MA, 67; Cornell Univ, PhD, 72. **CAREER** Instr English, Iowa State Univ, 67-69; asst prof, 73-77, assoc chmn dept, 80-81, assoc prof, 77-85, prof, 85-90, dist teaching prof, 90-, SUNY at Buffalo; Leverhulme fel England, The Leverhulme Trust, 72-73; consult & rev, Nat Endowment Humanities, Media Programs, 77-; vis prof, Cornell Univ, 80, & Chapman Col, 82. **HONORS AND AWARDS** Chancellor's Award for Excellence in Teaching, SUNY, 77; Guggenheim fel, 79-80. **MEMBERSHIPS** MLA. **RESEARCH** Early American literature; 17th-century English literature; modern American literature. **SELECTED PUBLICATIONS** Auth, God's Altar: The World and the Flesh in Puritan Poetry, Univ of Calif Press, 78; auth, "Transatlantic Perspectives: Founding Fictions in British-American Literature," Am Lit Hist 5 (93): 552-563; auth, "Powers of Humility and the Presence of Readers in Anne Bradstreet and Phillis Wheatley," Studies in Puritan Am Spirituality 4 (93): 1-23; auth, "'We Have Really No Country at All': Hawthorne's Reoccupations of History," Arachne 3 (96): 66-88; auth, "Anne Bradstreet," in American National Biography (NY: Am Council of Learned Soc, Oxford Univ Press, 99); auth, "Teaching Hope to Postmoderns, with Help from CS and Others," Catherine Maria Sedgwick Soc Newsletter 1 (99): 5-7; auth, "From Paradox and Aporia to Cultural Hybridization and Complex Adaptive Systems: New Theories and the Uses of Cooper at the Present Time," in James Fenimore Cooper: His Country and His Art, ed. Hugh C. MacDougall (NY: James Fenimore Cooper Soc, 99), 23-31. **CONTACT ADDRESS** Dept of English, SUNY, Buffalo, 306 Clemens Hall, Box 604610, Buffalo, NY 14260-4610. **EMAIL** rdaly@buffalo.edu

DALZELL, ALEXANDER
PERSONAL Born 05/08/1925, Belfast, Northern Ireland **DISCIPLINE** CLASSICS **EDUCATION** Trinity Col (Dublin), BA, 50, MA, 53, BLitt, 56. **CAREER** Lectr, Kings Col, Univ London, 51-53; lectr, Univ Sheffield, 53-54; lectr to prof, 54-88, dean arts, 68-73, vice provost, 72-79, acting provost, 73, 79, PROF EMER, TRINITY COL, UNIV TORONTO, 88-. **MEMBERSHIPS** Class Asn Can (pres 80-82); Am Philol Asn (mem publ comt), 81-84. **SELECTED PUBLICATIONS** Auth, The Criticism of Didactic Poetry, 96; contribur, Correspondence of Erasmus, vols 10 & 11, 92, 93; assoc ed/ed, Phoenix, 60-71; ed bd, Collected Works of Erasmus. **CONTACT ADDRESS** 344 Saunders St, Fredericton, NB, Canada E3B 1N8. **EMAIL** adalzell@nbnet.nb.ca

DAMERON, JOHN LASLEY
PERSONAL Born 07/29/1925, Burlington, NC, m, 1949, 2 children **DISCIPLINE** ENGLISH **EDUCATION** Univ NC, BS, 50, MA, 52; Univ Tenn, PhD(English), 62. **CAREER** Instr English, Emory & Henry Col, 53-55 & Univ Tenn, 58-59 & 61-62; from asst prof to assoc prof, 62-72, Prof English, Memphis State Univ, 72-, Nat Endowment Humanities grant, 67-68. **MEMBERSHIPS** MLA; Bibliog Soc Am; SAtlantic Mod Lang Asn; Cambridge Bibliog Soc; Poe Studies Asn (pres, 78-). **RESEARCH** Nineteenth century American and English literature; American authors, mid-19th century; bibliography of the criticism of Edgar Allan Poe. **SELECTED PUBLICATIONS** Auth, Melville and Scoresby on Whiteness--Moby-Dick by Melville,Herman and Scoresby,William Works on the Arctic and Whaling, Eng Stud, Vol 0074, 93; coauth, An Index to the Crritical Vocabulary of Blackwood's Edinburrgh Maagazine 1830-40, West Cornwall, CT, Locust Hill Press, 93; Poe Pym and Scoresby on Polar Cataracts, Resources for American Lit Stud, Vol 0021, 95; Simms, A Literary-Life, Miss Quart, Vol 0048, 95; auth, "Poe, Plagiarism, and Americn Periodicals", Poe Stud, Vol 30, 39-47. **CONTACT ADDRESS** Dept of English, Univ of Memphis, Memphis, TN 38152.

DAMES, NICHOLAS
DISCIPLINE ENGLISH LITERATURE **EDUCATION** Wash Univ, BA, 92; Harvard Univ, PhD, 98. **CAREER** Asst prof. **RESEARCH** Nineteenth-century British narrative and memory. **SELECTED PUBLICATIONS** Pub, on Charlotte Bronte. **CONTACT ADDRESS** Dept of Eng, Columbia Col, New York, 2960 Broadway, New York, NY 10027-6902.

DAMICO, HELEN
DISCIPLINE OLD AND MIDDLE ENGLISH LITERATURE **EDUCATION** NYork Univ, PhD, 80. **CAREER** Instr, Univ NMex, 81-. **SELECTED PUBLICATIONS** Ed, Medieval Scholarship: Biographical Studies on the Formation of a Discipline; Heroic Poetry in the Anglo-Saxon Period; New Readings on Women in Old English Literature. **CONTACT ADDRESS** Dept of English, Univ of New Mexico, Albuquerque, Albuquerque, NM 87131. **EMAIL** hdamico@umn.edu

DAMMERS, RICHARD H.
PERSONAL Born 05/27/1943, Passaic, NJ, m, 1968, 1 child **DISCIPLINE** ENGLISH LITERATURE **EDUCATION** Holy Cross Col, Mass, 65; Univ Va, MA, 66; Univ Notre Dame, PhD(English), 71. **CAREER** Instr English, Holy Cross Col, Mass, 66-67; asst prof, 71-76, Assoc Prof English, Ill State Univ, 76-; prof, english, 83-present. **HONORS AND AWARDS** Folger Shakespeare Libr fel. **MEMBERSHIPS** Am Soc 18th Century Studies. **RESEARCH** Restoration drama; 18th century literature. **SELECTED PUBLICATIONS** Auth, Richard Steele, 82. **CONTACT ADDRESS** Dept of English, Illinois State Univ, Normal, IL 61761.

DAMON, JOHN EDWARD
PERSONAL Born 10/26/1951, Fayetteville, AR, m, 1981, 2 children **DISCIPLINE** ENGLISH, MEDIEVAL LITERATURE **EDUCATION** Univ Ore, BA, 79; West Wash Univ, BA Edu, 84; Univ Ariz, MA, 89; PhD, 98. **CAREER** Asst prof, Univ Neb, 98-00. **HONORS AND AWARDS** Mary Major Crawford Awd, 99. **MEMBERSHIPS** MAA; New Chaucer Soc; ISAS; MAM; Hagiography Soc. **RESEARCH** Old and Middle English hagiography; Anglo-Saxon peace studies; Old and Middle English language and literature. **SELECTED PUBLICATIONS** Auth, "Seinte Cecile and Cristes owene knightes: Violence, Resignation and Resistance in The Second Nun's Tale," in Crossing Boundaries: Issues of Cultural and Individual Identity in the Middle Ages and Renaissance, ed. Sally McKee (Ariz Stud Middle Ages Renaissance, Turnhout, Belgium: Brepols, 99), 41-56; auth, "Anglo-Saxon Royal Saints: Leaders in Two Worlds," Plantagenet Conn 3 (95), 60-64; auth, "An Early Middle English Homily for the Common of an Apostle," Notes and Queries 40 (93), 10-11; auth, "Advisors for Peace in the Reign of Ethelred Unred," in Peace, Negotiation, and Reciprocity: Strategies of Co-existence in the Middle Ages and Renaissance, ed. Diane Wolfthal (Ariz Stud Middle Ages Renaissance, vol.4, Turnhout, Belgium: Brepols, 2000), 57-78; auth, "Sanctifying Anglo-Saxon Ealdormen: Lay Sainthood and the Rise of the Crusading Ideal," in "Via Crucis": Essays on Sources and Ideas in Memory of J E, Cross, ed. Thomas N. Hall, Thomas D. Hill, Charles D. Wright, forthcoming; auth, "Desecto Capite Perfido: Bodily Fragmentation and Reciprocal Violence in Anglo-Saxon England," in Exemplaria: A Journal of Theory in Medieval and Renaissance Studies 13, ed. R Alan Shoal (Univ Florida, Gainesville, forthcoming). **CONTACT ADDRESS** Dept English, Univ of Nebraska, Kearney, 905 West 25th St, Kearney, NE 68845-4238. **EMAIL** damonj@unk.edu

DAMON-BACH, LUCINDA
DISCIPLINE ENGLISH **EDUCATION** Univ California-Berkeley, BA, 81; Middlebury Col, MA, 85; MA, 85, PhD, 95, SUNY (Buffalo). **CAREER** Preceptor, Harvard Univ, 91-97; Adjunct Prof, Boston Col, 97-98; Asst Prof, Salem State Col, 98-99. **CONTACT ADDRESS** English Dept, Salem State Col, 352 Lafayette St, Salem, MA 01970. **EMAIL** lucinda.damonbach@salem.mass.edu

DAMROSCH, LEO
PERSONAL Born 09/14/1941, Manila, Philippines, m, 1983, 4 children **DISCIPLINE** ENGLISH LITERATURE **EDUCATION** Yale Univ, BA, 63; Cambridge Univ, MA, 66; Princeton Univ, PhD, 68. **CAREER** Asst prof to full prof, Eng, Univ Va, 68-83; prof, Univ Md, 83-89; Prof, Harvard Univ, 89-. **RESEARCH** 18th century British and French literature **SELECTED PUBLICATIONS** Auth, Symbol and Truth in Blake's Myth, Princeton Univ Press, 80; auth, God's Plot and Man's Stories: Studies in the Fictional Imagination from Milton to Fielding, Univ Chicago Press, 85; auth, The Imaginative World of Alexander Pope, Univ Calif Press, 87; Fictions of Reality in the Age of Hume and Johnson, Univ Wis Press, 89; auth, The Sorrows of the Quaker Jesus: James Nayler and the Puritan Crackdown on the Free Spirit, Harvard Univ Press, 96. **CONTACT ADDRESS** Barker Center, Harvard Univ, 12 Quincy St, Cambridge, MA 02138. **EMAIL** damrosch@fas.harvard.edu

DANBY, JUDD G.
PERSONAL Born 10/11/1966, Long Island, NY **DISCIPLINE** MUSIC COMPOSITION AND THEORY **EDUCATION** Rutgers Univ, BMus, 88; Univ Ill at Urbana-Champaign, MMus, 92; Univ Ill at Urbana-Champaign, AMusD, 98 **CAREER** Vis lectr music, Univ Ill at Urbana-Champaign, 95-97; vis prof music, Wabash Col, 98-99; BKT asst prof music, Wabash College, 99-. **MEMBERSHIPS** Am Music Ctr; Am Soc for Aesthetics; Broadcast Music, Inc.; Col Music Soc; Soc for Electro-Acoustic Music in the U.S.; Soc of Composers, Inc. **RESEARCH** Pitch-class set theory; twelve-tone/serial theory; Schenkerian analysis; the notion of form in music; perception and musical experience. **SELECTED PUBLICATIONS** Auth, Mirrors, for percussion quartet, Media Press; auth, The Piano's Stuck, for solo piano, Soundout Digital Press. **CONTACT ADDRESS** Fine Arts Center, Wabash Col, 301 W. Wabash, Crawford, IN 47933. **EMAIL** danbyj@wabash.edu

DANCE, DARYL CUMBER
PERSONAL Born 01/17/1938, Richmond, VA, m, 1958, 3 children **DISCIPLINE** ENGLISH **EDUCATION** VA State Coll, AB 1957, MA 1963; Univ of VA, PhD 1971. **CAREER** VA State Coll, asst prof of English, 62-72; VA Commonwealth Univ, asst prof of English, 72-78, assoc prof of English, 78-85; prof of English, 85-92; editorial advisor, Journal of West Indian Literature, 86-; University of California, Santa Barbara, visiting prof of African-American studies, 86-87; University of Richmond, prof English dept, 92-. **MEMBERSHIPS** Danforth Assoc 1964-; adv editor Black Amer Lit Forum 1978-. **SELECTED PUBLICATIONS** Auth, Shuckin' & Jivin', Folklore from Contemporary Black Americans, 1978; Fifty Caribbean Writers 1986; Long Gone The Mecklenburg Six & The Theme of Escape in Black Literature, 1987; New World Adams: Conversations with West Indian Writers, 1992; Honey, Hush! An Anthology of African American Women's Humor, 1998. **CONTACT ADDRESS** English, Univ of Richmond, Richmond, VA 23173. **EMAIL** ddance@richmond.edu

DANDRIDGE, RITA BERNICE
PERSONAL Born Richmond, VA **DISCIPLINE** ENGLISH AND AMERICAN LITERATURE **EDUCATION** Va Union Univ, BA, 61; Howard Univ, MA, 63, PhD(English), 70. **CAREER** Asst prof English lit, Morgan State Col, 64-71 & Univ Toledo, 71-74; assoc prof, 74-78, Prof English, Norfolk State Col, 78-. **MEMBERSHIPS** MLA; Col Lang Asn; Nat Coun Teachers English. **RESEARCH** Twentieth century Black literature, Black woman's novel and multi-ethnic literature. **SELECTED PUBLICATIONS CONTACT ADDRESS** Dept of English, Norfolk State Univ, 2401 Corprew Ave, Norfolk, VA 23504-3993.

DANE, JOSEPH A.
PERSONAL Born 09/29/1947, Portland, ME **DISCIPLINE** MEDIEVAL LITERATURE **EDUCATION** Bowdoin Col, BA, 69; Tulane Univ, MA, 76; Columbia Univ, PhD(comp lit), 79. **CAREER** Asst prof classics, Univ SDak, 79-80; asst prof English, Bowdoin Col, 81-82; Prof English, Univ Southern Calif, 82-, Nat Endowment for Humanities fel, 80-81. **MEMBERSHIPS** MLA; Mediaeval Acad. **SELECTED PUBLICATIONS** Auth, On the Shadowy Existence of the Medieval Pricking Wheel, Scriptorium, Vol 0050, 96; The Notions of Text and Variant in the Prologue to Chaucer Legend of Good Women--Ms,Gg, Lines 127-38, Papers of the Bibliographical Society of America, Vol 0087, 93; Queynte--Some Rime and Some Reason on a Chaucerian Pun, Jour Eng and Ger Phil, Vol 0095, 96; On Correctness--A Note on Some Press Variants in Thynne 1532 Edition of Chaucer, Lib, Vol 0017, 95; The Importance of Chaucer, Huntington Lib Quart, Vol 0056, 93; The Notion of Ring Composition in Classical and Medieval Studies--A Comment on Critical Method and Illusion, Neuphilologische Mitteilungen, Vol 0094, 93; Which-Is-The-Iustice-Which-Is-The-Theefe-Shakespeare--Variants of Transposition in the Text Of King Lear, Notes and Queries, Vol 0042, 95; On the Shadowy Existence of the Medieval Pricking Wheel, Scriptorium, Vol 0050, 96; What is a Text--Manuscripts, Literary Scholarship, Huntington Lib Quart, Vol 0058, 96; The Syntaxis-Recepta of Chaucer Prologue to the Millers Tale, Lines 3159-61, Eng Lang Notes, Vol 0031, 94; Bibliographical History Versus Bibliographical Evidence, the Plowmans Tale and Early Chaucer Editions, Bulletin John Rylands Univ Lib Manchester, Vol 0078, 96; Perfect Order and Perfected Order--The Evidence from Press-Variants of Early Seventeenth-Century Quartos, Papers Bibliog Soc Am, Vol 0090, 96; Who Is Buried in Chaucer Tomb--Prolegomena, Huntington Lib Quart, Vol 0057, 94. **CONTACT ADDRESS** Univ of So California, Los Angeles, CA 90089.

DANFORD, ROBERT E.
PERSONAL Born 01/18/1947, Kingsport, TN, m **DISCIPLINE** ENGLISH, LIBRARY SCIENCE **EDUCATION** ETSU, BS, 69; Univ Tn, MA, 71; MSLS, 73. **CAREER** Head of cataloging, 77-88, Wash & Lee Univ; librn, 88-96, Hartwich Col; libr dir, 96-, Widener Univ. **MEMBERSHIPS** ALA; ACRL; EDUCOM; CAUSES; ASIS. **RESEARCH** Inst organization; facilities mgmt & planning. **CONTACT ADDRESS** Wolfgram Mem, Widener Univ, Pennsylvania, Chester, PA 19013. **EMAIL** robert.e.danford@widener.edu

DANIEL, LEE A.
PERSONAL Born 11/17/1945, Dublin, TX, m, 1969, 3 children **DISCIPLINE** SPANISH AMERICAN LITERATURE **EDUCATION** Tarleton State Univ, BA, 68; Univ N Tex, MA, 72; Tex Tech Univ, PhD, 79. **CAREER** Lectr, Univ Ark, 79-80; asst prof, SW Okla State Univ, 80-85; prof, chair, Tex Christian Univ, 85-. **HONORS AND AWARDS** Phi Beta Delta, Finalist, Chancellor's Award for Distinguished Res; Nat Dir of Latin Americanists, 85; Mortar Board Preferred Prof, 88, 92, 94. **MEMBERSHIPS** MLA, SW Coun of Latin Am Studies. **RESEARCH** The imaginary town in Latin American

Literature, The Works of Rosa Maria Britton, The theatre of Sor Juana Ines de la Cruz. **SELECTED PUBLICATIONS** Auth, "Sor Juana's pentad of Carlosian Loas," Sor Juana Ines de la Cruz: Selected Studies, (89); auth, "El 'Dixie Gongorism' de joaquin Bestard y 'La obsesion de German Ortiga,'" Confluencia, (92); auth, "Sor Juana's Baroque Martyr-Auto, El martir del Sacramento, San Hermenegildo," Latin Am Theatre Rev, (94); aūth, The Los of Sor Juana Ines de la Cruz, York Pr, 94; ed, Cuentos de Beyhuale, York Pr, 94; auth, "Angustia y evasion en la narrativa de Rima de Vallbona," Revista de Filogia y Linguistica de la Universidad de Costa Rica, (95); auth, 'Influencia faulkneriana o experiencia mundovista': Las cronicas de Beyhuale y Maravillas," Confluencia (97); auth, "Mythical Worlds of Latin American Writers," Confluencia, (99); auth, "Entrevista a Rosa Mariqa Crespo de Britton," Mester, (00); auth, "El pueblo ficticio en la literatura mexicana: Una cartografia," Confluencia (01). **CONTACT ADDRESS** Span and Latin Am Studies, Texas Christian Univ, TCU Box 297220, Fort Worth, TX 76129. **EMAIL** 1.daniel@tcu.edu

DANIELL, BETH
DISCIPLINE ENGLISH LITERATURE **EDUCATION** Univ Tex, PhD, 86. **CAREER** Dept Eng, Clemson Univ **RESEARCH** Rhetoric, composition. **SELECTED PUBLICATIONS** Auth, Deena's Story: The Discourse of the Other, Jour Adv Comp, 96; A Communion of Friendship: Literacy, Orality, Voice, and Self Outside the Academy, Literacy Networks, 96; Composing (as) Power, College Comp and Comm, 94; Theory, Theory-Talk, and Composition, Writing Theory and Critical Theory, MLA, 94; coauth, Resisting Writing/Resisting Writing Teachers, The Subject is Writing, Boynton/Cook Heinemann, 93. **CONTACT ADDRESS** Clemson Univ, 608 Strode, Clemson, SC 29634. **EMAIL** dbeth@clemson.edu

DANIELS, LEANNE
DISCIPLINE MEDIA AND SOCIETY, MEDIA MANAGEMENT, AND INTERNATIONAL NEWS AND COMMUNICATI **EDUCATION** Ind Univ, PhD, 94. **CAREER** Asst prof, La State Univ. **RESEARCH** Media management; mass communication. **SELECTED PUBLICATIONS** Coauth, "Public Opinion on Investigative Reporting in the 1980s," Journalism Quarterly 69 (92): 146-155; auth, "Is News Superficial?" in Contemporary Media Issues, ed. David Sloan and Emily Erickson Hoff (Vision Press, 98); coauth, "Covering the Clinton-Lewinsky Story: Newsroom Decision-Makers Tell All," Southwestern Mass Communciation Journal (99). **CONTACT ADDRESS** The Manship Sch of Mass Commun, Louisiana State Univ and A&M Col, Baton Rouge, LA 70803. **EMAIL** ldaniel@lsu.edu

DANIELS, MARILYN
DISCIPLINE SPEECH COMMUNICATION **EDUCATION** NYork Univ, PhD, 89; Wm Paterson Col, MA, 80, BA, 79 **CAREER** Assoc Prof, 96-, Asst prof, 90-96, PA St Univ; Asst Prof, 89-90, Cent CT St Univ; Asst Prof, 87-88, Univ of Charleston **HONORS AND AWARDS** Matthews Awd for Excel in Res, 97; Campus Advisory Board Tch Awd, 96 **RESEARCH** Sign language **SELECTED PUBLICATIONS** Auth, Benedictine Roots in the Development of Deaf Education, Listening with the Heart, Bergin and Garvey, 97; The Dance in Christianity: A History of Religious Dance Through the Ages, Paulist Press, 81; auth, Dancing with Words: Signing for Hearing Children's Literacy, Bergin and Garvey, 00. **CONTACT ADDRESS** Pennsylvania State Univ, Worthington Scranton, Dunmore, PA 18512-1699. **EMAIL** mxd34@psu.edu

DANIELS, RICHARD
DISCIPLINE CREATIVE WRITING **EDUCATION** Ohio State Univ, BA, 64, MA, 66, PhD, 72. **CAREER** Engl, Oregon St Univ. **RESEARCH** Mid and old Eng lit & lang. **SELECTED PUBLICATIONS** Auth, Uxor Noah: A Raven or a Dove, Chaucer Rev, 79; Yirmiyahu Yovel's Spinoza and other Heretics, Minn Rev, 91; Complaint, Fiction Int, 91; Larry's Song, Minn Rev, 93; Dream House, Kanasa Quart, 93. **CONTACT ADDRESS** Oregon State Univ, Corvallis, OR 97331-4501. **EMAIL** rdaniels@orst.edu

DANIELSON, DENNIS R.
PERSONAL Born 05/08/1949, Victoria, BC, Canada, m, 1970, 4 children **DISCIPLINE** ENGLISH **EDUCATION** Univ Victoria, BA, 72; Univ Sussex, BA, 73; Stanford Univ, AM, 75; PhD, 79. **CAREER** Asst Prof to Assoc Prof, Univ Ottawa, 79-86; Assoc Prof to Prof, Univ BC, 86-. **HONORS AND AWARDS** Fel, Soc Sci and Humanities Res Coun, 75-79; Alexander von Humboldt Fel, 90-91; UBC Alumni Res Prize, 87. **MEMBERSHIPS** Milton Soc of Am; Can Sci Writers Asn; AAS. **RESEARCH** Milton; Literature and cosmology; History of astronomy. **SELECTED PUBLICATIONS** Co-ed, The Nondramatic Works of John Ford, MRTS, 91; ed, Cambridge Companion to Milton, 2nd ed, Perseus Pub, 99; auth, The Book of the Cosmos: Imagining the Universe from Heraclitus to Hawking, Perseus Pub, 00. **CONTACT ADDRESS** Dept English, Univ of British Columbia, 4086 Spruce St, Burnaby, BC, Canada V5G 1Y4. **EMAIL** danielso@interchange.ubc.ca

DANIELSON, LARRY W.
PERSONAL Born 08/08/1940, Lindsburg, KS, m, 1962, 2 children **DISCIPLINE** ENGLISH **EDUCATION** Bethany Col, BA; Ind Univ, MA, 68; PhD, 72. **CAREER** Univ Ill, 70-93; Western Ky Univ, 93-. **HONORS AND AWARDS** Teaching Awd, Univ Ill. **MEMBERSHIPS** Am Folklore Soc, Calif Folklore Soc. **RESEARCH** Ethnicity; Gender; Ritual/Custom. **CONTACT ADDRESS** Dept Mod Lang, Western Kentucky Univ, 1 Big Red Way St, Bowling Green, KY 42101.

DARBY, BARBARA
DISCIPLINE DRAMA, EIGHTEENTH-CENTURY LITERATURE **EDUCATION** Univ Lethbridge, AB, 88; Queen's Univ, MA, 89, PhD, 90-94. **CAREER** Asst prof, 98-99; part-time instr, 97-98; part-time instr, Mount Saint Vincent Univ, 95-97; adj asst prof, Queen's Univ, 94-95; tchg asst, Queen's Univ, 93-94; res asst, Queen's Univ, 91-92; tchg asst, Queen's Univ, 90-91; sessional instr, Univ Lethbridge, 89-90; tchg asst, Queen's Univ, 88-89; marking asst, Lethbridge Commun Col Learning Ctr, 88-89. **HONORS AND AWARDS** Postdoc fel, Soc Sci and Hum Res Coun of Can, 95-97; doc fel, Soc Sci and Hum Res Coun of Can, 90-94; Sir James Lougheed Grad award, Government of Alberta, 91-93; grad award, Queen's Univ, 88; gold medal, Univ Lethbridge Fac of Arts and Sci, 88; Louise B McKinney award, Government of Alberta, 97. **RESEARCH** Women writers, feminist theory, performance theory. **SELECTED PUBLICATIONS** Auth, Frances Burney, Dramatist: Gender, Performance, and the Late-Eighteenth-Century Stage, Univ Press of Ky, 97; Frances Burney's Dramatic Mothers, Eng Stud in Can, 97; "Tragedy, Feminism, and Frances Burney's Edwy and Elgiva," Jour of Dramatic Theory and Criticism, 97; "Bondage and Slavery in Eighteenth-Century Poetry by Women," Lumen 14, 95; Love, Chance, and the Arranged Marriage: Lady Mary Rewrites Marivaux, Restoration and Eighteenth-Century Theatre Research, 94. **CONTACT ADDRESS** Dept of Eng, Dalhousie Univ, Halifax, NS, Canada B3H 3J5. **EMAIL** bdarby@is.dal.ca

DARHOWER, MARTIN L.
PERSONAL Born 05/29/1969, Harrisburg, PA **DISCIPLINE** LINGUISTICS, ENGLISH **EDUCATION** Millersville Univ, BS, 92; MA, 94; Univ Pitts, PhD, 00. **CAREER** Adj instr, Harrisburg CC, 93-96; adj instr, Millersville Univ, 95-97; adj instr, Gettysburg Col, 94-97; teaching asst, Univ Pitts, 07-00; asst prof, Univ PR, 00-. **MEMBERSHIPS** AATSP; CALLICO; TESOL. **RESEARCH** Computer mediated communication; computer assisted language learning; second/foreign language pedagogy. **SELECTED PUBLICATIONS** Auth, "Some Interactional Features of Synchronous Computer Mediated Communication in the Intermediate L2 Class: A Sociocultural Case Study," CALICO J (01). **CONTACT ADDRESS** English Dept, Univ of Puerto Rico, Humacao Univ Col, Humacao, PR 00791. **EMAIL** markdarhower@aol.com

DARLING, GREGORY J.
PERSONAL Born 11/25/1948, Albany, NY, s **DISCIPLINE** ENGLISH **EDUCATION** Bowdoin Col, BA, 70; Columbia Univ Grad Sch Arts and Scis, MA, 82, PhD, 82; City Univ Grad Center, MPhil, 97; Grad Sch and Univ Center, City Univ New York, doctoral candidate, 90-. **CAREER** Adj asst prof, Baruch Col, 90-92; adj asst prof, Manhattan Col, 95-96; adj asst prof, St John's Univ, fall 95, fall 96; adj asst prof, John Jay Col of Criminal Justice, fall 92-; adj asst prof, Fordham Col, Lincoln Center, fall 97-. **HONORS AND AWARDS** Foreign Lang and Area Studies Fel, Federal Gov, 76-77, 77-78, 78-79; Teaching Asst, Columbia Univ Grad Sch, 79-80; President's Fel, Columbia Univ, 80-81; Whiting Fel, Columbia Univ, 81-82; Morton N. Cohen Diss Fel, CUNY Grad Sch, 99-2000. **RESEARCH** Composition and Rhetoric; Medieval Literature, particularly Old English, Old Irish and Middle Irish Literature; Romantic and Victorian Literature; World Religions; South Asian Literature and Religions-Hinduism and Buddhism. **SELECTED PUBLICATIONS** Auth, "Bhagavad Gita: Sri Aurobindo's Interoperation," Gnosis 1.1 (78); auth, "Vidya and Avidya in the Upanishads and in Shankara'a Vedanta," Gnosis 2.7-8 (79): 78-95; auth, An Evaluation of the Vedantic Critique of Buddhism, New Delhi, India: Motilal Banarsidass Pub Co (87); rev of P. J. Cosijn's Notes on Beowulf, translated by Bremmer, Van den Berg Johnson, Leeds Tests and Monographs, New Series 12 (91), in Envoi: A Review J of Medieval Lit 4.2; auth, "Feast or Fast: Orality in the Aislinge Meic Con Glinne," Proceedings: Northeast Regional Meeting of the Conference on Christianity and Literature, Nov 18, 95, Jane Collins and Sr M. Doretta Cornell, eds, Pleasantville, NY: Pace Univ (95): 45-53. **CONTACT ADDRESS** Dept English, John Jay Col of Criminal Justice, CUNY, 445 West 59th St, New York, NY 10019-1104.

DARSEY, JAMES
PERSONAL Born 01/11/1953, Sarasota, FL **DISCIPLINE** COMMUNICATION, RHETORIC STUDIES **EDUCATION** Fla State Univ, BA, 75; Purdue Univ, MA, 78; Univ Wisc, PhD, 85. **CAREER** Vis asst prof, Univ Iowa, 86-88; asst prof, Ohio State Univ, 88-95; from asst prof to assoc prof, Northern Ill State Univ, 95-00; assoc prof, Ga State Univ, 00-. **HONORS AND AWARDS** Diamond Anniversary Book Awd from Nat Commun Assoc, 98; James A. Winans/Herbert A. Wilchelns Mem Awd, Nat Commun Asn, 98; Marie Hochmuth Nichols Awd, Nat Commun Asn, 98; Outstanding Acad Bk Awd, Choice, 99. **MEMBERSHIPS** Nat Commun Assoc; Central States Commun assoc; Modern Lang Assoc; Int Assoc for the Study of Argumentation. **RESEARCH** Rhetorical criticism, critical methods, American public address, social movement rhetoric, gay rights rhetoric. **SELECTED PUBLICATIONS** Auth, "The Legend of Eugene Debs: Prophetic Ethos as Radical Argument," Quart J of Speech 74 (88): 434-452; auth, "From 'Gay is Good' to the Scourge of AIDS: The Evolution of Gay Liberation Rhetoric, 1977-1990," Commun Studies 42 (91): 43-66; auth, Die Non: Gay Liberation and the Rhetoric of Pure Tolerance, Queer Words/Queer Images: Communication and the Construction of Homosexuality, NY Univ Press, 45-76, 94; Must We All be Rhetorical Theorists?: An Anti-Democratic Inquiry, Western J of Commun, vol 58, 164-181, 94; auth, Joe McCarthy's Fantastic Moment, Commun Monographs, vol 62, 65-86, 95; auth, The Prophetic Tradition and Radical Rhetoric in America, NY Univ Press, 97; auth, The Voice of Exile: W. E.B. DuBois and the Quest for Culture, Rhetoric and Community: Case Studies in Unity and Fragmentation, Univ of SC Press, 98; auth, "Baldwin's Cosmopolitan Loneliness," in James Baldwin Now, ed. Dwight A. McBride (NY: NYork Univ Press, in press). **CONTACT ADDRESS** Dept of Commun, Georgia State Univ, 948D Park Place S, Atlanta, GA 30302-4038. **EMAIL** jdarsey@gsu.edu

DASH, IRENE GOLDEN
PERSONAL Born New York, NY, 2 children **DISCIPLINE** ENGLISH DRAMATIC LITERATURE, WOMEN'S STUDIES, AMERICAN THEATRE **EDUCATION** Beaver Col, BA; Columbia Univ, MA, PhD(English), 72. **CAREER** Lectr English, Queensborough Community Col, City Univ NY, 70-71; lectr, 72-74, Asst Prof English, Hunter Col, City Univ NY, 74-, Int corresp, World Shakepeare Bibliog, 81. **HONORS AND AWARDS** NEH Research Fellowship, 83-84; NEH Travel Grant 86; Folger Library Fellowship, 89-90; ACLS Travel Grant, 96; Lucius Littauer Grant, 96; Invited to Intl Shakespeare Conf, 94, 96, 98,00. **MEMBERSHIPS** Shakespeare Asn Am; Am Soc 18th Century Studies; Am Name Soc; NCTE; Am Soc Theatre Res. **RESEARCH** Shakespeare's women. **SELECTED PUBLICATIONS** Wooing, Wedding, & Power: Women in Shakespeare's Plays, Columbia VP, 81, paper 84; auth, Single-Sex Retreats in 2 Early-Modern Dramas--Shakespeare,William and Cavendish, Margaret--Loves Labors Lost and the Convent of Pleasure, Shakespeare Quart, Vol 0047, 96; Women's Worlds in Shakespear's Plays, Univ of Delaware Pr, 97; "Holiday, Judy." Jewish Women in America: An Historical Encyclopedia, Vol 1, Routledge, 97. **CONTACT ADDRESS** 161 W 16th St, New York, NY 10011. **EMAIL** idash1@aol.com

DATES, JANNETTE LAKE
PERSONAL Born Baltimore, MD, m, 1960, 4 children **DISCIPLINE** COMMUNICATIONS **EDUCATION** Coppin State College, BS; The Johns Hopkins Univ, MEd; Univ of Maryland at College Park, PhD. **CAREER** Baltimore City Public School System, classroom demonstration teacher, 58-63, televsion demonstration teacher, 64-69; Morgan State Coll and Goucher College, instructor, 70-72; Morgan State Univ, instructor, 72-77, coordinator of television projects, 73-80, asst prof, 77-80; Howard Univ, asst prof, 81-85, sequence coordinator, 81-85; Coppin State College, associate prof, 85-87, video production service dir, 85-87; Howard Univ School of Communications, associate dean, 87-92; Howard Univ, associate prof, 90-96; Prof, 96-; Howard Univ School of Communications, acting dean, 93-96, dean, 96-. **HONORS AND AWARDS** California State Univ at Dominquez Hills, Young, Gifted and Black Distinguished Resident Scholar, 1991; Freedom Forum Media Studies Center Fellowship, 1992; Gustavus Myer Awd, co-editor, best book on human rights, 1990. **MEMBERSHIPS** George F. Peabody Board of Dirs, Broadcast Educ Asn, Baltimore City Cable Television Commission, commissioner, 1979-81, education task force chairwoman, 1979-81; Baltimore Cable Access Corporation, pres, 1982-86, vice pres, 1986-88; Mayor's Cable Advisory Commission, education task force chairwoman, 1988-90, member, 1990-94. **SELECTED PUBLICATIONS** Co-author: Split Image: African Americans in the Mass Media, 1993; author: "African American TV Images Shaped By Others," Crisis magazine, December 1992; "Quantity, Not Quality, Suffices for Our TV Images," p 8, Sept 30-Oct 6, 1992; "This TV Season Will Be Blacker, But Will It Be Better?" September 13, 1992; reviewer: "A Review of the book Enlightened Racism," Journal of Broadcasting and Electronic Media, Fall 1993; "A Review of Said's Culture and Imperialism," Critical Studies in Mass Communications, Fall 1995. **CONTACT ADDRESS** Dean, School of Communications, Howard Univ, 525 Bryant St, NW, W2-203-G, Washington, VT 20059. **EMAIL** jdates@howard.edu

DAUGHERTY, GREGORY NEIL
DISCIPLINE CLASSICS **EDUCATION** Univ Richmond, BA, 70; Vanderbilt Univ, MA,75; PhD, 77. **CAREER** Instr, 76-78, asst prof, 78-84, assoc prof, 84-94, prof Class, Randolph-Macon Col, 94-; vis asst prof, Univ Richmond, 77, 91, 93; vis asst prof, Va Commonwealth Univ, 82, 85; vis assoc prof, Col William and Mary, 87. **HONORS AND AWARDS** Woodrow Wilson fel, Univ Richmond, 70; Fulbright scholar, Univ Pavia, Italy, 70-71; Thomas Branch Awd for Excellence in Tchg, Ran-

dolph-Macon Col, 78, 82; Fulbright grant, Italy, 79; NEH Summer Inst on Women in Antiquity, 83, Phi Beta Kappa, 70. **MEMBERSHIPS** Secy, Richmond Soc of the Archaeol Inst of Am, 82-95; mem, Va Dept of Educ, Lat Textbk Selection Comt, 84; consult, Va Dept of Educ, Standards of Lrng for Lat, 86-87.; Mem at Large, Exec Bd of the Class Asn of Va, 87-89; ed, Prospects Newsletter of the Nat Comt on Lat and Greek, 90-96; dir, Class Essay Contest, Class Asn of Va, 90-95; exec secy, Nat Comt on Lat and Greek, 91-93; mem, Joint Comt on Class in Am Educ, Am Philol Asn, 91-94; ch, Comt on Local Arrangements, Class Asn of the Midwest and S; mem, Final Rev Bd NEH Fel Prog for For Lang Tchr K-12, 94; ch, Membership Comt, Class Asn of the Midwest and S, 94-96; pres, For Lang Asn of Va, 95-96; secy-treas, Class Asn of the Midwest and S, 96-. **SELECTED PUBLICATIONS** Auth, Rev of John E. Stambaugh, The Ancient Roman City: The Johns Hopkins Univ Press 88, Class World 84.3, 91; Rev of Walter Ellis, Alcibiades. Classical Lives, Routledge, 89, Class World 84, 91; The Cohortes Vigilum and the Great Fire of 64 AD, Class J 87.3, 92; coauth, Preparation and Training for Teachers of Latin, Class J 86, 91. **CONTACT ADDRESS** Dept of Class, Randolph-Macon Col, Ashland, VA 23005-5505. **EMAIL** gdaugher@rmc.edu

DAUGHERTY, SARAH B.
PERSONAL Born 03/22/1949, Cleveland, OH, s **DISCIPLINE** ENGLISH **EDUCATION** Col Wooster, BA, 69; Univ Pa, AM, 70; Univ Pa, PhD, 73. **CAREER** Univ of Notre Dame, 73-80; State Univ, 80-82; Prof, Wichita State; 94. **HONORS AND AWARDS** Phi Beta Kappa, 69; Woodrow Wilson Fellow, 69; Phi Kappa Phi, 87. **MEMBERSHIPS** Modern Language Assoc; Amer Lit Assoc; Henry James Society; William Dean Howells Society; William Dean Howells Memorial Comt. **RESEARCH** 19th Century; Fiction; Criticism; Intellectual History **SELECTED PUBLICATIONS** Auth, "The Literary Criticism of Henry James, Ohio VP, 81; auth, The Henry James Review and American Literary Realism; rev, James Scholarship for America Literary Scholarship: An Annual," Duke VP. **CONTACT ADDRESS** Dept English, Wichita State Univ, 1845 Fairmount St, Wichita, KS 67260-0014.

DAUGHERTY, TRACY
PERSONAL Born 06/05/1955, Midland, TX, m, 2000 **DISCIPLINE** FICTION WRITING **EDUCATION** Southern Methodist Univ, BA, 76, MA, 83; Univ Houston, PhD, 85. **CAREER** Engl, Oregon St Univ. **SELECTED PUBLICATIONS** Auth, Desire Provoked, Random House, 87; auth, Low Rider, The New Yorker, 87; auth, Almost Barcalona, Gettysburg Rev, 95; The Woman in the Oil Field, SMU Press, 96; auth, What Falls Away, Norton, 96; auth, The Boy Orator, SMU Press, 99; auth, Comfort me with Apples, SMU Press, 01. **CONTACT ADDRESS** Oregon State Univ, Corvallis, OR 97331-4501. **EMAIL** tdaugherty@orst.edu

DAUGHTRY, PHILIP J.
PERSONAL Born 09/16/1942, Hexham, England, d, 2 children **DISCIPLINE** CREATIVE WRITING **EDUCATION** Univ Calif, Irvine, BA, 68, MFA, 71. **CAREER** Assoc prof, Santa Monica Col, 85-. **RESEARCH** Primitive art. **SELECTED PUBLICATIONS** Auth, The Stray Moon (poems); auth, Kid Migrado (poems); auth, Celtic Blood (poems); auth, "Hawk" (screenplay); author of plays and articles. **CONTACT ADDRESS** Dept English, Santa Monica Col, 1900 Pico Blvd, Santa Monica, CA 90405-1628. **EMAIL** PDaughtry@earthlink.net

DAUSE, CHARLES A.
DISCIPLINE COMMUNICATION STUDIES **EDUCATION** Muskingum Col, BA; Wayne State Univ, MA, PhD. **CAREER** Assoc dean, Liberal Arts; dir, Univ Adv and Acad Serv; assoc prof, Univ Detroit Mercy, 64-. **HONORS AND AWARDS** Developed & implemented, Acad Exploration Prog. **MEMBERSHIPS** Nat Acad Adv Asn. **RESEARCH** Public speaking, public opinion, mass media, political campaign and organizational communication. **SELECTED PUBLICATIONS** Coauth, Argumentation: Inquiry and Advocacy. **CONTACT ADDRESS** Dept of Communications, Univ of Detroit Mercy, 4001 W McNichols Rd, PO Box 19900, Detroit, MI 48219-0900. **EMAIL** DAUSECA@udmercy.edu

DAVENPORT, GUY MATTISON
PERSONAL Born 11/23/1927, Anderson, SC **DISCIPLINE** ENGLISH **EDUCATION** Duke Univ AB, 48; Oxford Univ, BLitt, 50; Harvard Univ, PhD, 61. **CAREER** Instr English, Washington Univ, 52-55; tutor, Harvard Univ, 57-60; asst prof, Haverford Col, 60-63; prof English, 63-90, PROF EMER, 90-, UNIV KY, 63- ; McArthur fel, 90-95. **HONORS AND AWARDS** Zabel Prize, Am Acad Arts & Lett, 81. **MEMBERSHIPS** Am Poetry Soc; William Carlos Williams Soc. **RESEARCH** Post 1910 American and European literature; Greek, archaic period; 19th century American and English intellectual history. **SELECTED PUBLICATIONS** Auth, The Intelligence of Louis Agassiz, Beacon, 64; Da Vinci's Bicycle, Johns Hopkins, 75; Archilochos, Sappho, Alkman, Univ Calif, 80; Geography and the Imagination, 81 & Eclogues, 81, North Point; Herakleitos and Diogenes, 81 & The Mimes of Herondas, 81, Grey Fox; Tatlin!, Johns Hopkins, 82; Apples and Pears, N Point, 84; The Drummer of the 11th North Devonshire Fusiliers, N Point, 90; Thasos and Ohio, N Point, 85; Every Force Evolves a Form, N Point, 87; Cities on Hills, UMI Press, 83; The Jules Verne Steam Balloon, n Point, 87; A Balthus Notebook, Ecco, 89; A Table of Green Fields, New Directions, 93; Seven Greeks, New directions, 95; Charles Burchfields Seasons, Chameleon, 94; The Drawings of Paul Cadmus, Rizzoli, 96; The Cardiff Team, New Directions, 95; Objects on a Table, Counterpoint, 98. **CONTACT ADDRESS** 621 Sayre Ave, Lexington, KY 40508.

DAVEY, FRANK W.
PERSONAL Born 04/19/1940, Vancouver, BC, Canada **DISCIPLINE** CANADIAN LITERATURE **EDUCATION** Univ BC, BA, 61, MA, 63; Univ S Calif, PhD, 68. **CAREER** Tchg asst, Univ BC, 61-63; lectr, Royal Roads Mil Col, 63-66; asst prof, 67-69, writer-in-residence, Sir George Williams Univ, 69-70; asst prof, 70-72, assoc prof, 72-80, prof English, York Univ, 80-90, dept ch, 85-90; Carl F. Klinck prof Canadian Literature, Univ Western Ont, 90-. **HONORS AND AWARDS** Can Coun grants/fels, 66, 71-73, 74-75; Dept Nat Defence Arts Res grant, 65, 66, 68; Writer's Choice Awd, 87. **MEMBERSHIPS** Can Asn Univ Tchrs; Asn Can Col Univ Tchrs Eng; Asn Can Que Lit. **RESEARCH** Canadian literature, discourse theory, narratology, canonicity, modernism, postmodernism, multiculturalism, Canadian cultural studies. **SELECTED PUBLICATIONS** Auth, Reading Canadian Reading, 88; auth, Post-National Arguments: The Politics of the Anglophone-Canadian Novel Since 1967, 93; auth, Reading "KIM" Right, 93; auth, Canadian Literary Power: Essays on Anglophone-Canadian Literary Conflict, 94; auth, Karla's Web: A Cultural Examination of the Mahaffy-French Murders, 94. **CONTACT ADDRESS** English Dept, Univ of Western Ontario, London, ON, Canada N6A 3K7. **EMAIL** fdavey@julian.uwo.ca

DAVID, ALFRED
PERSONAL Born 03/31/1929, Hamburg, Germany, m, 1968, 1 child **DISCIPLINE** ENGLISH **EDUCATION** Harvard Univ, AB, 51, AM, 54, PhD, 57. **CAREER** From instr to assoc prof, 58-68, Prof English, Ind Univ, Bloomington, 68-94. **HONORS AND AWARDS** Sheldon traveling fel, 57-58; Guggenheim & Fulbright fels, 67-68. **MEMBERSHIPS** Medieval Acad Am; New Chaucer Soc. **RESEARCH** Chaucer; medieval literature. **SELECTED PUBLICATIONS** Auth, The Strumbet Muse: Art and Morals in Chaucer's Poetry, 76; ed, George B. Pace, The Minor Poems, Part I, The Variorum Chaucer, 82; auth, The Middle Ages in the Norton Anthology of English Literature, 5th-7th editions, 86, 93, 99; auth, The Romaunt of the Rose in The Riverside Chaucer, 3rd edition, 87. **CONTACT ADDRESS** Dept of English, Indiana Univ, Bloomington, Bloomington, IN 47401. **EMAIL** aldavid@indiana.edu

DAVIDSON, ARNOLD E.
DISCIPLINE ENGLISH LITERATURE **EDUCATION** SUNY Binghamton, PhD, 77. **CAREER** Prof Can studies. **MEMBERSHIPS** MLA. **RESEARCH** Can and Brit fiction. **SELECTED PUBLICATIONS** Auth, Mordecai Richler, 83; Conrad's Endings, 84; JeanRhys, 85; Writing Against Silence: Joy Kogawa's Obasan, 93; CoyoteCountry: Fictions of the Canadian West,94; co-ed, The Art of Margaret Atwood, 81. **CONTACT ADDRESS** Eng Dept, Duke Univ, Durham, NC 27706.

DAVIDSON, CATHY N.
DISCIPLINE ENGLISH **EDUCATION** Elmhurst, BA, 70; SUNY-Binghamton, MA, 73, PhD, 74 **CAREER** Assoc, prof, Eng, Mich State Univ; current, DEVARNEY PROF ENG, DUKE UNIV; Vice Provost for Interdisciplinary Studies, Duke. **MEMBERSHIPS** Am Antiquarian Soc, Am Studies Asn, Modern Lang Asn. **RESEARCH** Am Fict. **SELECTED PUBLICATIONS** Co-ed, The Lost Tradition: Mothers and Daughters in Literature, 80; auth, The Experimental Fictions of Ambrose Bierce: Structuring the Ineffable, 84; auth, Revolution and the Word: The Rise of the Novel in America, 87; ed, Oxford University Press Early American Women Writers Series, editions of Charlotte Temple and Duloquita; Reading in the Americas: Literatures and Sonat Hastoz, Haphiers, 89 ; ed, with introd, Reading in America: Literature and Social History, Johns Hopkins Univ Press, 89 & 92; assoc ed, Columbia History of the American Name, 91; auth, The Book of Love: Writers and Their Love Letters, Pocket/Simon & Schuster, 92: Thirty-Six Views of Mt Fuji: On Finding Myself in Japan, Dutton-Signet, 93; co-ed, Oxford Companion to Women's Writing in the United States, Oxford Univ Press, 94; co-ed, Oxford Book of Women's Writing in the United States, 95; co-ed, Subjects and Citizens: Nation, Race and Gender from "Oroonoko" to Anita Hill, Duke Univ Press, 95; auth, Closing: The Life & Death of an American Factory, 98. **CONTACT ADDRESS** Dept of English, Duke Univ, Durham, NC 27706. **EMAIL** cathydavidson@duke.edu

DAVIDSON, CLIFFORD OSCAR
PERSONAL Born 10/29/1932, Faribault, MN, m, 1954 **DISCIPLINE** ENGLISH **EDUCATION** St Cloud State Univ, BS, 54; Wayne State Univ, MA, 61, PhD, 66. **CAREER** Instr Eng, Wayne State Univ, 61-65; from Asst Prof to Prof Eng, 65-89, Prof Eng & Medieval Studies, Western MI Univ, 89-, Co-ed, Comp Drama, Western MI Univ, 67-98, bd mem, Medieval Inst, 69-74, 75-78, 88-91, 93-96 & chmn, 76-77, 94-95; exec ed, Early Drama, Art & Music, 76. **HONORS AND AWARDS** Fac res grant, 67, 92, 95; res fel, 71, 74, 75, 77, 79, 81, 83, 85, 87, 89; Distinguished Schol Awd, Western MI Univ. **MEMBERSHIPS** Renaissance Soc Am; Medieval Acad Am; Malone Soc; Int Asn Univ Prof English; Int Soc for Study Medieval Drama; T.S. Eliot Soc; AAUP. **RESEARCH** Medieval and Renaissance drama; Eng lit of the late Middle Ages and Renaissance; iconography. **SELECTED PUBLICATIONS** Auth, On Tradition: Essays on the Use and Valuation of the Past, 92; ed, A Tretise of Miraclis Pleyinge, 93; The Iconography of Heaven, 94; Fools and Folly, 96; auth, Technology, Guilds, and Early English Drama, 97; coauth, Performing Medieval Music Drama, 98; auth, Baptism, the Three Enemies, and T.S. Eliot, Shaun Tyas, 99. **CONTACT ADDRESS** The Medieval Inst, Western Michigan Univ, 1201 Oliver St, Kalamazoo, MI 49008-3805. **EMAIL** davidson@wmich.edu

DAVIDSON, CYNTHIA A.
PERSONAL Born 06/13/1960, San Diego, CA **DISCIPLINE** WRITING **EDUCATION** Northeastern Ill Univ, BA, 83; MA, 89; Univ Ill, PhD, 97. **CAREER** TA, Northeastern Ill Univ, 87-89; adj fac, Triton Col, 89-90; col prep adj, Harold Washington Col, 90-91; TA to lectr, Univ of Ill, 91-98; lectr, SUNY, 98-. **HONORS AND AWARDS** Scholarship, Northeastern Ill Univ, 79-81; Salute to the Arts contest Winner, 90; Grant, SUNY, 99-00; Who's Who in Am, 00-01. **MEMBERSHIPS** MLA, Assoc Writing Prog, Sci Fiction Res Assoc, AAUW. **RESEARCH** Literature, Rhetoric, and Technology, Rhetoic and the Occult/New Age. **SELECTED PUBLICATIONS** Auth, "Union," Another Chicago Mag, (93); auth, "Water Mark," Wire, (93); auth, "Riveria's Golem, Haraway's Cyborg: Reading Neuromancer as Baudrillard's Simulation of Crisis," Sci-Fi Studies, (96); auth, "Creed," Tight, (98); auth, "Harold Jaffe: Seeking the (Black Hole) Sun," Electronic Book Review 10, (99); auth, "Some Thoughts on Style," How2/Forum/Style, (00); auth, "Ayson Hagy," Dict of Lit Biot 244, (01). **CONTACT ADDRESS** Prog in Writing and Rhetoric, SUNY, Stony Brook, 202 Humanities, Stony Brook, NY 11794. **EMAIL** cdavidson@ms.cc.sunysb.edu

DAVIDSON, HARRIET
DISCIPLINE MODERN POETRY, CONTEMPORARY AMERICAN POETRY, THE CIRTICISM OF POETRY **EDUCATION** Univ Tex, Austin, BA, Vanderbilt MA, PhD. **CAREER** Dir, Women's Stud prog, Rutgers, The State Univ NJ, Univ Col-Camden. **RESEARCH** Twentieth century literature; critical theory. **SELECTED PUBLICATIONS** Auth, T.S. Eliot and Hermeneutics: Absence and Interpretation in "The Waste Land". **CONTACT ADDRESS** Dept of Lit in Eng, Rutgers, The State Univ of New Jersey, New Brunswick, New Brunswick, NJ 08903. **EMAIL** hardav@rci.rutgers.edu

DAVIDSON, JOHN E.
PERSONAL Born 09/27/1960, Knoxville, TN, 2 children **DISCIPLINE** LITERATURE **EDUCATION** Univ South, BA, 82; Univ Iowa, MA, 90; Cornell Univ, PhD, 93. **CAREER** Assoc prof, OSU, 93-. **HONORS AND AWARDS** Fulbright Scholar; NEH Summer Grant. **MEMBERSHIPS** AATG; MLA; GSA. **RESEARCH** Film; literature; cultural theory. **SELECTED PUBLICATIONS** Auth, art, Hegemony and Cinematic Strategy, 96; auth, art, In der Fuhrer's Face: Undermining Reflections in and on Winfried Bonengel's Beruf Neonazi, 97; auth, art, Overcoming the Germany's Past(s) in Film since the Wende, 97; auth, Deterritorializiing the New German Cinema, 98; auth, art, Working for the Man, Whoever That May Be: The Vocation of Wolfgang Liebeneiner, 99. **CONTACT ADDRESS** Ohio State Univ, Columbus, 314 Cunz Hall, Columbus, OH 43210-1229. **EMAIL** davidson.92@osu.edu

DAVIDSON, ROBERTA
DISCIPLINE MEDIEVAL LITERATURE **EDUCATION** Sarah Lawrence Col, BA, 75; Princeton Univ, PhD, 86. **CAREER** Instr, Kenyon Col; reviewer, Tulas Stud in Woman Literature; Philosophy and Literature; asst prof-. **HONORS AND AWARDS** Co-founder, Whitman's Gender Stud Min. **RESEARCH** Medieval narratives of romance, spirituality and restriction. **SELECTED PUBLICATIONS** Auth, Cross-Dressing in Medieval Romance,Textual Bodies: Changing the Boundaries of Literary Representation, 97; I Have a Dream, PBS documentary. **CONTACT ADDRESS** Dept of Eng, Whitman Col, 345 Boyer Ave, Walla Walla, WA 99362-2038. **EMAIL** davidson@whitman.edu

DAVIES, GWENDOLYN
PERSONAL Born 02/12/1942, Halifax, NS, Canada **DISCIPLINE** ENGLISH **EDUCATION** Dalhousie Univ, BA, 63; Ont Col Educ, Univ Toronto Educ Cert, 64, 69; Univ Toronto, MA, 69; York Univ PhD, 80. **CAREER** Tchr, East York Col Inst, 63-67, 70-72; asst assoc, Centre d'etudes can, Univ Bordeaux, 74-75; asst to assoc prof, Mt Allison Univ, 76-88, assoc dir, Can studies, 80-81, dept head, 85-88; PROF ENGLISH, ACADIA UNIV, 88-, acting head, 91-92, head 94-; adj prof, Dalhousie Univ, 95-; W Stewart MacNutt Memorial Lectr, Univ NB, 92; vis prof Can stud, Univ London, 92-93; Dawson lectr, NS Tchrs Col, 95. **HONORS AND AWARDS** Acadia Asn Alumni Awd Excellence Tchg, 92; Canada 125 Medal, 93. **MEMBERSHIPS** Asn Can Stud (bd mem, 85-87); Can Asn

Chairs Eng, 86-89 (pres, 87-88); Can Inst Hist Microrepro, 90-93; Asn Can & Que Lit (vice-pres, 90-92); Bibliog Soc Can; Coun, Royal NS Hist Soc, 97-. **SELECTED PUBLICATIONS** Auth, The Mephibosheth Stepsure Letters by Thomas McCulloch, 90; auth, Studies in Maritime Literary History, 92; ed, Myth and Milieu, 93; co-ed, Canadian Poetry: From the Beginnings Through the First World War, 94; contribur, Dictionary of Canadian Biography/Dictionnaire biographique du Canada; adv bd, Routledge Encyclopedia of Post-Colonial Literatures, 88-92; adv bd, Newfoundland Studies, 94-99; adv bd, The Oxford Companion to Canadian Literature, 2nd ed, 95-97; ed bd, Canadian Literature, 96-. **CONTACT ADDRESS** English Dept, Acadia Univ, Wolfville, NS, Canada B0P 1X0. **EMAIL** Gwen.davies@acadiau.ca

DAVIS, ADAM B.
PERSONAL Born St Louis, MO, m, 1984, 4 children **DISCIPLINE** ENGLISH **EDUCATION** Univ Mich, BA, 83; Univ Mich, MA, 84; Univ Mo, PhD, 91. **CAREER** Guest prof, Albert Ludwigs Univ, 91-92; From asst prof to assoc prof , Truman State Univ, 91-. **HONORS AND AWARDS** Huggins Fel, Univ Mo; Hopwood and Cowden Prizes, Univ Mich; Alexander von Humboldt Fel. **MEMBERSHIPS** Medieval Acad of Am; AAUP; CCCC; NCTE; Mo Folklore Int Soc of Anglo Saxonists; Sigma Tau Delta; Phi Kappa Phi. **RESEARCH** Medieval, Linguistics, folklore, Literary Theory. **CONTACT ADDRESS** Dept Lang and Lit, Truman State Univ, 100 E Normal St, Kirksville, MO 63501-4200. **EMAIL** adavis@truman.edu

DAVIS, ALBERT J.
PERSONAL Born 06/23/1947, Houma, LA, m, 1994, 2 children **DISCIPLINE** ENGLISH, CREATIVE WRITING **EDUCATION** Nicholls State Univ, BA, 69; Colo State Univ, MA, 74. **CAREER** Distinguished Service Prof & Novelist in Residence, Nicholls State Univ. **HONORS AND AWARDS** John Z. Bennet Awd (poetry); Ione Burden Awd for the Novel. **MEMBERSHIPS** PEN Am Ctr, Assoc Writing Progs, Acad of Am Poets, Phi Kappa Phi, Nat Educ Asn. **SELECTED PUBLICATIONS** Auth, Leechtime, LSU Press, 89; auth, Marquis at Bay, LSU Press, 92; auth, What They Wrote on the Bath House Walls, Blue Heron Press, 90; auth, Virginia Patollt's Parish, La Lit Press, 99. **CONTACT ADDRESS** Dept Lang & Lit, Nicholls State Univ, 906 E 1st St, Thibodaux, LA 70310-0001. **EMAIL** engl-ajd@mail.nich.edu

DAVIS, CHARLES ROGER
PERSONAL Born 08/09/1943, Peoria, IL **DISCIPLINE** ENGLISH **EDUCATION** Yale Univ, BA, 65; Princeton Univ, MA, 69, PhD(English lang & lit), 73; Columbia Univ, MS, 72. **CAREER** NAm bibliogr, Univ Va Libr, 72-75; Bibliogr, Smith Col Libr, 75-, Corresp ed, Spenser Newslett, 75-79. **MEMBERSHIPS** MLA; Am Libr Asn; Renaissance Soc Am; Bibliogr Soc Eng; Bibliogr Soc Am. **RESEARCH** Renaissance poetry and prose; 18th century booktrade. **SELECTED PUBLICATIONS** Auth, The Poetics of Personification, Speculum-Jour Medieval Stud, Vol 0070, 95; King Arthurs Death--The Middle-English Stanzaic Morte Arthur and Alliterative Morte Arthur, Speculum-Jour Medieval Stud, Vol 0071, 96; Lancelot of the Laik and Sir Tristrem, Speculum-Jour Medieval Stud, Vol 0071, 96; The Shewings of Julian-Of-Norwich, Speculum-Jour Medieval Stud, Vol 0071, 96. **CONTACT ADDRESS** Library, Smith Col, Northampton, MA 01060.

DAVIS, CHERYL K.
PERSONAL Born 12/20/1971, East Machias, ME, s **DISCIPLINE** ENGLISH **EDUCATION** Cedarville Col, BA, 93; Univ Alaska, MA, 96; Ind Univ Pa, PhD, in progress. **CAREER** Univ Alaska, 96-98; Wayland Baptist Univ, 97-98; Cedarville Col, 98-. **HONORS AND AWARDS** Excellence in Teaching, Univ Iowa, 98. **MEMBERSHIPS** Nat Coun of Teachers of English, MLA. **RESEARCH** Composition Studies, Victorian Literature. **SELECTED PUBLICATIONS** Auth, Real Writing for Real Students, McGraw-Hill, 95. **CONTACT ADDRESS** Dept Lang & Lit, Cedarville Col, PO Box 601, Cedarville, OH 45314-0601. **EMAIL** davsc@cedarnet.cedarville.edu

DAVIS, CHRISTOPHER
PERSONAL Born 04/19/1960, Whitter, CA, s **DISCIPLINE** ENGLISH **EDUCATION** Syracuse Univ, BA in English, 83; Univ Iowa, MFA in Creative Writing, 85. **CAREER** Asst Prof, Murray State Univ, 87-89; Asst Prof, UNC Charlotte, 89-96; Assoc Prof, UNC Charlotte, 96-. **HONORS AND AWARDS** Teaching-Writing Fellow, Univ of Iowa, 83-85; Edith Shiffert Awd, Associated Writing Programs, 88. **MEMBERSHIPS** Associated Writing Programs. **RESEARCH** Poetry and related critical writing. **SELECTED PUBLICATIONS** Auth, "The Tyrant of the Past and the Slave of the Future, Texas Tech U Press, 89; auth, "The Patriot, Univ of Georgia Press, 98. **CONTACT ADDRESS** Dept English, Univ of No Carolina, Charlotte, 9201 University City Boulevard, Charlotte, NC 28223-0001. **EMAIL** dcdavis@email.uncc.edu

DAVIS, DALE W.
DISCIPLINE COMPARATIVE LITERATURE AND VICTORIAN LITERATURE **EDUCATION** Univ OK, PhD, 68. **CAREER** Assoc prof Eng, mem, grad fac, instr, Hum Stud, mem, Univ Honors Coun, dir, Bachelor of Gen Stud degree prog, TX Tech Univ. **RESEARCH** Interdisciplinary educ. **SELECTED PUBLICATIONS** Publ articles on Victorian lit, pedag, lit theory, and criticism, and co-auth a standard two-volume textbook on interdisciplinary hum--The Humanities in Western Culture (8th Edition). **CONTACT ADDRESS** Texas Tech Univ, Lubbock, TX 79409-5015. **EMAIL** ditdd@ttacs.ttu.edu

DAVIS, DAVID D.
PERSONAL Born 08/08/1956, Boston, MA, m, 1978, 2 children **DISCIPLINE** LIBRARY SCIENCE; HISTORY **EDUCATION** Catholic Univ Am, MSLIS, MS. **CAREER** Publ Libr, 82-88; Corp Libr, 88-94; Copyright Clearance Ctr, 94-. **MEMBERSHIPS** SLA **RESEARCH** Service quality; copyright; digital rights management (DRM) systems. **SELECTED PUBLICATIONS** Auth, "Copyright Dilemma," Computers in Libraries, 99; auth, "What DRM Means Today," Computers in Libraries, 01. **CONTACT ADDRESS** Copyright Clearance Ctr, 222 Rosewood Dr, Danvers, MA 01923. **EMAIL** ddavis@copyright.com

DAVIS, DONALD G., JR.
PERSONAL Born 12/06/1939, San Marcos, TX, m, 1969, 3 children **DISCIPLINE** LIBRARY SCIENCE, HISTORY **EDUCATION** UCLA, BA, 61; UC Berkeley, MA, 63, MLS, 64; Univ Ill, Champaign-Urbana, PhD, 72; Austin Presbyterian Theol Sem, MA, 96. **CAREER** Libry asst, UC Berkeley, 61-64; sen ref librn, Fresno State Col, 64-68; prof, Univ Tx Austin, 71-. **HONORS AND AWARDS** Beta Phi Mu; Phi Kappa Phi; HEA Title-B Fel; Newberry Libry Fel; Am Inst Indian Stud Fel; Berner-Nash Awd, Univ Ill; GLSIS; John P. Commons Tchg Fel, Univ Tex Austin; Beta Phi Mu, Golden Anniversary Awd, 99. **MEMBERSHIPS** Am Hist Asn; Am Libry Asn; Asn Bibliography Hist; Am Printing Hist Asn; Conference on Faith and Hist; Nat Asn Scholars; Org Am Hist; Tex Libry Asn; Tex State Hist Asn; American: History and Life; Annual Bibliography of the History of the Printed Book and Libraries. **RESEARCH** Hist of books and libraries; American library history; history of printing; Christian missions. **SELECTED PUBLICATIONS** Auth, Libraries & Culture, University of Texas Press, Quarterly Journal; auth, art, Problems in the Life of a University Librarian: Thomas James, 1600-1620, 70; auth, The Association of American Library Schools, 1915-1968: An Analytical History, 74; auth, art, Education for Librarianship, 76; auth, Reference Books in the Social Sciences and Humanities, 77; auth, art, The Status of Library History in India: A Report of an Informal Survey and a Selective Auth, Bibliographic Essay, 89; auth, American Library History: A Comprehensive Guide to the Literature, 89; auth, Encyclopedia of Library History, 94; auth, art, Destruction of Chinese Books in the Peking Siege of 1900, 97; auth, art, Arthur E. Bostwick and Chinese Library Development: A Chapter in International Cooperation, 98; auth, Library History Research in America,00. **CONTACT ADDRESS** Graduate School of Library and Information Science, Univ of Texas, Austin, Austin, TX 78712-1276. **EMAIL** dgdavis@gslis.utexas.edu

DAVIS, GREGSON
PERSONAL Born 10/20/1940, St. John's, Antigua, m, 1980, 4 children **DISCIPLINE** CLASSICS AND COMPARATIVE LITERATURE **EDUCATION** Harvard Univ, AB, 60; Univ Cal Berkeley, PhD, 68. **CAREER** Asst prof, Stanford Univ, 69-75; assoc prof, 75-85; prof, 85-89; prof, Cornell Univ, 89-94; prof, Duke Univ, 94- . **HONORS AND AWARDS** Latin Orator, Harvard Commencement, 60; Arthur D. Cory Travelling Fel, Harvard Univ, 61-63. **MEMBERSHIPS** Am Phil Asoc; MLA; Vergilian Soc; Caribbean Studies Asoc. **RESEARCH** Latin and Greek literature; Caribbean literature; rhetoric and poetics. **SELECTED PUBLICATIONS** Auth, Polyhymnia: The Rhetoric of Horatian Lyric Discourse, 91; auth, Desire and the Hunt in Ovid's Metamorphoses, The Burnett Lectures: A Quarter Century, 93; auth, Between Cultures: Toward a Redefinition of Liberal Education, African Studies and the Undergraduate Curriculum, 94; guest ed of spec issue, The Poetics of Derek Walcott: Intertextual Perspectives, South Atlantic Quart, 97; auth, Aime Cesaire, 97. **CONTACT ADDRESS** Dept. of Classical Studies, Duke Univ, 234A Allen Bldg., Durham, NC 27708-0103.

DAVIS, JACK L.
PERSONAL Born 08/13/1950, Wooster, OH **DISCIPLINE** CLASSICS **EDUCATION** Univ Akron, BA, 72; Univ Cincinnati, PhD, 77. **CAREER** Vis Fel, Fitzwilliam Col; Carl W. Blegen Chaired Prof, Univ Cincinnati, 93-; Asst prof, Univ Ill, 77-83; Assoc prof, 84-91; Prof, 91-93. **HONORS AND AWARDS** Silver Circle award, 82; AMOCO award, 82; Univ Scholar award, 85-87; Joanne Stolaroff Cotsen Prize; james rignall wheeler fel, eugene vanderpool fel. **MEMBERSHIPS** Archaeol Inst Am; Am Sch Classical Studies Athens; Institute for Aegean Prehistory; Archaeometry Comt; Nat Endowment Hum; Nat Hum Ctr. **SELECTED PUBLICATIONS** Co-ed, Papers in Cycladic Prehistory, UCLA, 79; auth, Period V, Meinz, 86; coauth, Landscape Archaeology as Long-Term History: Northern Keos in the Cycladic Islands, UCLA, 91; auth, Sandy Pylos: An Archaeological History from Nestor to Navarino, Univ of Tex Press, 98. **CONTACT ADDRESS** Dept of Classics, Univ of Cincinnati, PO Box 210226, Cincinnati, OH 45210-0226. **EMAIL** jack.davis@uc.edu

DAVIS, JAMES
DISCIPLINE ENGLISH, LITERATURE **EDUCATION** Ouachita Univ, BA; Univ Chicago, MA, Sch Int Training, MA, Univ Miss, PhD. **CAREER** English and Lit, Univ Ark. **SELECTED PUBLICATIONS** Rev ed, Language Learning. **CONTACT ADDRESS** Univ of Arkansas, Fayetteville, Fayetteville, AR 72701.

DAVIS, JANET
PERSONAL 2 children **DISCIPLINE** RHETORIC, MASS COMMUNICATION, AND HEALTH COMMUNICATION **EDUCATION** Bristol Univ, Eng, BA; Univ NE, MA; Univ IA, PhD. **CAREER** Instructor, Univ VA, 92-94; Assoc prof, 94-, Truman State Univ. **HONORS AND AWARDS** First Class hon(s), Bristol Univ; Outstanding grad student, Univ NE **MEMBERSHIPS** Mem, Nat Commun Assn; Cent States Commun Assn; Amer Soc Hist of Rhetoric; Rhetoric Soc Am; Hon Soc Phi Kappa Phi. **SELECTED PUBLICATIONS** Pub(s), area of class rhetoric; articles, Encycl Rhetoric and Composition, Garland, 96. **CONTACT ADDRESS** Div. Language & Literature, Truman State Univ, 100 E Normal St, Kirksville, MO 63501-4221. **EMAIL** FL06@Truman.edu

DAVIS, JED H.
PERSONAL Born 07/31/1921, Stillwater, MN, m, 1945, 3 children **DISCIPLINE** SPEECH; THEATRE **EDUCATION** Univ Minn, BA, 47, MA, 49, PhD, 58. **CAREER** Inst, 47-50, Asst prof, 50-53, Macalester Col; Asst Prof, Mich State Univ, 53-60; Vis Prof, Univ Minn, 66, 68; Vis Prof, Calif State Univ, Long Bch, 78; Asst Prof, 60-62, Assoc Prof, 62-65, Prof, Commun & Theatre, 65-86, Univ Kans; Prof Emeritus, Univ Kans, 87-. **HONORS AND AWARDS** AMOCO Gold Medallion, svc to ACTF Regional Festival, 73; Fellow of the Am Theatre Asn, 72; Photo Hangs in Portrait Gallery of Rarig Ctr, Univ Minn, 76; Kilty Kane, svc award, Kans Univ Theatre, 76; Kans Theatre Hall of Fame: Charter inductee, 80; Kans Univ Chancellor's Club Career Tchng Awd, 85; Campton Bell Awd, Am Asn of Theatre for Youth, 1987; Hon Fellow, Mid-Am Theatre Conf, 87; Dedicatory vol: Theatre for Young Audiences: Principles and Strategies for the Future; Medallion Awdee, Children's Theatre Found of Am, 98. **MEMBERSHIPS** Am Educ Theatre Asn (Am Col Theatre Festival Ch & Cent Comte, pres, 72); Children's Theatre Conf (pres, 63-65); Winifred Ward Schol Prog (ch, subcmte on Inst Cert, 80-82); ASSITEJ; Assoc of Kans Theatre (pres, 74-75); Lawrence Arts Commission (secy 74-76); Children's Theatre Found; Univ & Col Theatre Asn; Col of Fellows of the Am Theatre (dean, 90-92). **RESEARCH** Children's theatre; technical theatre; child development; theatre hist; hist of theatre org & theatre honoraries. **SELECTED PUBLICATIONS** Co-auth, Children's Theatre: Play Production for the Child Audience, Harper & Bros, 60, 63, 65, 68; auth, Prospectus for Research in Children's Theatre, Educ Theatre J, vol 13, 4, 274-277, 12/61; compiler & ed, A Directory of Children's Theatres in the United States, Am Educ Theatre Asn, 68; auth, Theatre for Children, Encycl Americana, vol 26, 621, 73; co-auth, Theatre, Children, and Youth, Anchorage Press, 82, 87; ed, foreword, afterword, Theatre Education: Mandate for Tomorrow, Anchorage Press, 85; ed, American Theatre Fellows: The First Thirty Years, Col of Fellows of the Am Theatre, 95. **CONTACT ADDRESS** 2602 Louisiana, Lawrence, KS 66046-4662.

DAVIS, JOHNETTA GARNER
PERSONAL Born 11/01/1939, Warrenton, VA **DISCIPLINE** COMMUNICATION SCIENCES AND DISORDERS **EDUCATION** Tchrs Coll, BS 1961; George Washington U, MA 1969; Howard U, PhD 1976 **CAREER** Speech pathologist, 61-68;Teachers Col, instructor, 69-71; Federal City College, assist prof, 70-71; Amer Speech & Hearing Assn, asst sec for prog dev, 71-72; assoc prof, prof, 72-78; Howard Univ, assoc dean, grad prof, 78-96, Washington DC Public Schools, Univ of Maryland, Col Park, Off of Grad Minority Educ, Assoc Dean of the Grad School and Dir, 93-. **HONORS AND AWARDS** Howard Univ, establishment of the Johnetta G Davis Awd for Best Mentor of Grad Students, 93; Grad Student Coun, Administrator of the Year, 1992, Distinguished Service Awds, 78-80, 82, 86, 88, 90; Outstanding faculty citation Students at DC Teachers Col, 71; Frederick Douglass Honor Soc Howard Univ Chap 74; Outstanding Yng Women in Am 76; Howard Univ, School of Commun, Outstanding Alumni Awd, 86; DC Teachers Col, Outstanding Junior Faculty Awd, 71; US Office of Education, Fel, 67; CCC-SP-L, Am Speech-Language Hearing Assn, certificate, 62. **MEMBERSHIPS** Washington, D.C. Chapter of The Society Inc., Potomac Chapter of Links Inc; American Speech-Language & Hearing Assn 1961-; DC Speech, Language and Hearing, 1963-; task force on intl grad educ Council of Grad Schs Task Force on Minority Education; board of directors Stoddard Bapt Home 1977-82; Sunday sch tchr Mt Sinai Bapt Ch 1977-82. **CONTACT ADDRESS** Graduate School, Univ of Maryland, Col Park, 2122 Lee Bldg, College Park, MD 20742-5121. **EMAIL** jgdavis@deans.umd.edu

DAVIS, KATIE CAMPBELL
PERSONAL Born 09/11/1936, Lumber City, GA, m **DISCIPLINE** COMMUNICATIONS **EDUCATION** TN State Univ, BA 1957; TN State Univ, MA 1968; Univ IL, PhD 1974. **CAREER** Norfolk State Univ, prof, speech, English, theatre arts, currently; teacher various public school since 51; communication consultant; spiritual, inspirational and motivational speaker. **HONORS AND AWARDS** National Consortium of Doctors' Perseverance Awd, 1992. **MEMBERSHIPS** Mem Speech Comm Assn; mem NAACP; Alpha Kappa Alpha Sorority; American Association of University Women. **CONTACT ADDRESS** Speech Commun, Norfolk State Univ, 2401 Corprew Ave, Norfolk, VA 23504.

DAVIS, KENNETH WALDRON
PERSONAL Born 06/15/1932, Holland, TX **DISCIPLINE** ENGLISH **EDUCATION** Tex Tech Col, BA, 54; Vanderbilt Univ, MA, 55, PhD, 63. **CAREER** From instr to assoc prof, 55-68, admin asst to dept head, 63, chmn sophomore English, 63-65, chmn grad studies, 65-69, Prof English, Tex Tech Univ, 68-94, Prof Emer, 94. **MEMBERSHIPS** MLA; NCTE; SCent Mod Lang Asn. **RESEARCH** English novel; 19th century English literature; literature of the English Renaissance. **SELECTED PUBLICATIONS** Auth, Dancing with the Devil, Jour Pop Cult, Vol 0030, 96; Careless Weeds--6 Texas Novellas, West Amer Lit, Vol 0029, 95. **CONTACT ADDRESS** Personnel Dept, Texas Tech Univ, 5302 31st, PO Box 1093, Lubbock, TX 79407-3518. **EMAIL** kdavis32@aol.com

DAVIS, LENNARD J.
PERSONAL Born 09/16/1949, NY, NY, m, 1978, 2 children **DISCIPLINE** LITERATURE **EDUCATION** Columbia Col, BA, 70; Columbia Univ, MA, 71; PhD, 76. **CAREER** Asst prof, Columbia Univ,77-85; asst prof, Brandeis Univ, 86-89; assoc prof, Univ Pa, 89-90; assoc prof, Hobart and William Smith, 91-92; prof, Binghamton Univ, 92-00; prof, head, Univ Ill Chicago, 00-. **HONORS AND AWARDS** Mellon Fel, 79-80; ACLS Fel, 85-86; John Carter Brown Libr Res Fel, 89-90; Fac Res Fel, Binghamton Univ, 93; Gustavus Myers Center Award, 96; Nat Book Critics Circle Nominee, 01. **MEMBERSHIPS** MLA. **RESEARCH** History of the Novel, Novel Theory, Marxist Theory, Cultural Studies, Disability Studies. **SELECTED PUBLICATIONS** Auth, Factual Fictions: The Origins of the English Novel, Columbia Univ Pr, 83; auth, Resisting Novels: Fiction and Ideology, Routledge, 87; coed, Left Politics and the Literary Profession, Columbia Univ Pr, 90; auth, Enforcing Normalcy: Disability, Deafness, and the Body, Verso, 95; ed, Disability Studies Reader, Routledge, 97; ed, Shall I Say a Kiss?: Courtship Letters of a Deaf Couple, 1936-1938, Gallaudet Univ Pr, 99; auth, My Sense of Silence: Memoir of a Childhood with Deafness, Univ Ill Pr, 00; auth, The Sonnets: A Novel, SUNY Pr, 01. **CONTACT ADDRESS** Univ of Illinois, Chicago, 601 S Morgan St, Chicago, IL 60607. **EMAIL** lendavis@uic.edu

DAVIS, MARIANNA WHITE
PERSONAL Born 01/08/1929, Philadelphia, PA, w **DISCIPLINE** ENGLISH **EDUCATION** SC State College, BA English 1949; NYork Univ, MA English 1953; Boston Univ, DEd English 1966. **CAREER** SC Pub Sch, tchr, 49-51, 55-56, 86-96; SC State Coll, asst prof, 56-64; Claflin Coll, prof, 66-69; Voorhees Coll, vis prof, 66-68; Boston Univ, vis prof, 67; Univ of TN, vis prof, 69; Benedict Coll, English prof & researcher, 69-82; Upward Bound Tufts Univ; Denmark Tech Coll, acting pres, 85-86; Davis & Assocs, pres, 80-; Northeastern Univ, African-American Literature Teacher Training Project, co-director, 92-94; Benedict College, special asst to the pres, 96-. **HONORS AND AWARDS** SC State Coll Alumni Scholarship; Crusade Scholar doctoral studies 1964-66; Outstanding educator of Amer 1970-71; IBM-UNCF Fellowships post doctoral studies 1971 & 1974; Pi Lambda Theta Travel Scholarship for study in Soviet Union 1973; Outstanding Educ Awd Kappa Alpha Psi Frat, Athens GA 1974; Contrib to Educ Awd SC Comm Affairs 1976; Educators Roundtable Awd 1976; Outstanding Cit Awd Omega Psi Phi Frat 1977; Emory O Jackson Journalism Awd 1978 & 1996; Distinguished Research Awd NAFEO 1980; Distinguished Faculty Awd Benedict Coll 1980; Distinguished Serv Awd Columbia Urban League 1981; Distinguished Alumni Awd Boston Univ 1981; Distinguished Alumni Awd SC State Coll 1981; Par Excellence Awd in Educ Operation PUSH 1982; Outstanding Citizen Awd, Cleveland, OH, 1984; Kappa Alpha Psi of SC Outstanding Black Woman Awd 1987; Jacob Javits Fellowship Bd, Presidential Appointment, 1993; Governor's Awd, Outstanding Achievement, 1995; contributed papers to Boston Univ (Mugar Memorial Library), 1989; exec producer, "The Struggle Continues," black history teleconf on PBS, 1986-. **MEMBERSHIPS** Bd dir Natl Council of Teachers of English 1958-80; co-founder & sec ABC Devel Corp 1972; chmn Conf on Coll Composition & Comm 1975-76; exec comm ADE Modern Language Assn 1976-79; commr SC Educational TV 1980-95; mem Public Broadcasting System Adv Bd 1981-83; Francis Burns United Methodist Ch; bd chm, Columbia Urban League Bd, 1981-82; Natl Council of Negro Women; YWCA; life mem NAACP; The Moles; coord, Coalition for Concerns of Blacks in Post Secondary Educ in SC; Alpha Kappa Alpha Sor; Order of Eastern Star; Chmn SC Intl Women's Yr Commission; founder VICOS Women's League for Comm Action; TISAWS; The Girl Friends, Inc; Civil Rights Comm Adv Bd 1985-; natl publicity chair, The Moles, 1988-92; bd of educ, S Carolina United Methodist Church 1988-96; board mem, board of visitors, Claflin Coll. **SELECTED PUBLICATIONS** Author of 18 books, numerous articles. **CONTACT ADDRESS** PO Box 3097, Columbia, SC 29230.

DAVIS, MARIE
PERSONAL Born St. Catherine's, ON, Canada **DISCIPLINE** ENGLISH **EDUCATION** McMaster Univ, MA, 85. **CAREER** Lectr, Univ Western Ont, 91-96; asst ed, 90-92, Assoc Ed, Can Children's Lit, 92-. **HONORS AND AWARDS** Rotary Youth Leadership Awd, 81; Pan-Hellenic Coun Tchr Awd, Univ Western Ont, 93-94. **MEMBERSHIPS** ACCUTE; Children's Lit Asn; Can Soc Eighteenth-Century Studs. **SELECTED PUBLICATIONS** Auth, Walking on Revolving Walls: Coming of Age in Calgary, 90; auth, Susan Musgrave: An Interview with Paul Yee in CCL, 82, 96; auth, Parable or Parody: Tom King's Coyote Columbus Story in CCL, 83, 96. **CONTACT ADDRESS** Dept of English, Univ of Guelph, Guelph, ON, Canada N1G 2W1. **EMAIL** mdavis@bosshog.arts.uwo.ca

DAVIS, NATHAN T.
PERSONAL Born 02/15/1937, Kansas City, KS, m **DISCIPLINE** ETHNOMUSICOLOGY **EDUCATION** Univ KS, BME 1960; Wesleyan U, CT, PhD Ethnomusicology. **CAREER** Club St Germain, Paris, prof debut with Kenny Clark 63; Donald Byrd, Blue Note Club Paris, 63; Chat Que Peche, Eric Dolphy, Paris, 64; toured Europe with Art Blakly & New Jazz Messengers, 65; Europe & Amer, recorded several albums as leader; total 10 LP's as leader; Belgium Radio-TV, staff composer. **HONORS AND AWARDS** Honorary Doctorate of Humane Letters, Florida Memorial College. **MEMBERSHIPS** Mem SACEM, Soc of Composers, Paris, France; co-chmn ed com Inst of Black Am Music; mem Afro-Am Bi-Cen Hall of Fame; est & created PhD degree prog in Ethnomusicology, Univ Pittsburgh; created Jazz Program at Univ Pittsburgh; created Jazz Program Paris-Am Acad Paris. **CONTACT ADDRESS** Music Dept, Univ of Pittsburgh, 4337 Fifth Ave, Pittsburgh, PA 15260. **EMAIL** ndavis+@pitt.edu

DAVIS, PETER
DISCIPLINE MUSIC **EDUCATION** Univ Southern CA, PhD. **CAREER** Assoc prof, Univ IL Urbana Champaign. **RESEARCH** Theatre hist; Am theatre; censorship; dramaturgy. **SELECTED PUBLICATIONS** Auth, pubs on hist of Am theatre; class theatre hist; acting and directing. **CONTACT ADDRESS** Dept of Music, Univ of Illinois, Urbana-Champaign, E Gregory Drive, PO Box 52, Champaign, IL 61820. **EMAIL** padavis@staff.uiuc.edu

DAVIS, PHOEBE STEIN
PERSONAL Born 02/26/1967, Washington, DC, m, 1997 **DISCIPLINE** LITERATURE **EDUCATION** Univ Mich, BA; Loyola Univ, MA, 93; PhD, 98. **CAREER** Adj prof, Loyola Univ, 91-00; adj prof, DePaul Univ, 99-00; community coord, Ill Humanities Council, 00-. **HONORS AND AWARDS** Arthur J. Schmitt Fel, Loyola Univ, 96-97; Grad Asstshp, Loyola Univ, 91-94, 95-96; Teaching Fel, Loyola Univ, 94-95; Stanley Clayes Member, Loyola Univ, 93. **MEMBERSHIPS** MLS; MSA. **RESEARCH** American modernism; women writers; writing and war. **SELECTED PUBLICATIONS** Auth, "'Even Cake Gets to Have Another Meaning': History, Narrative, and 'Daily Living' in Gertrude Stein's World War II Writings," Modern Fiction Studies (98): 568-607; auth, "Subjectivity and the Aesthetics of National Identity in Gertrude Stein's The Autobiography of Alice B. Toklas," Twenty Century Lit (99): 18-45. **CONTACT ADDRESS** 1435 W Elmdale Ave, Apt 1S, Chicago, IL 60660-2446. **EMAIL** psd@prairie.org

DAVIS, ROBERT LEIGH
DISCIPLINE ENGLISH AND EDUCATION **EDUCATION** Stanford Univ, BA, 78; MA, 81; Univ Calif Berkeley, PhD, 92. **CAREER** Eng tchr, Serra High Sch, San Mateo, Calif, 80-85; instr, Golden Gate Univ, San Francisco, Calif, 85-92; grad student instr, Univ Calif Berkeley, 85-92; asst prof eng, Wittenburg Univ, 92-. **HONORS AND AWARDS** BA with distinction, Stanford Univ, 78; fel, NEH Summer Sem for Secondary Sch Tchrs, Co Col, 84; Tchr of the Year, Serra High Sch, San Mateo, Calif, 85; Benjamin Putnam Kurtz Graduate Essay Prize, Univ Calif Berkeley, 89; highest distinction, comprehensive oral exam, Univ Calif Berkeley, 89; Omicron Delta Kappa Excellence in Tchr, Wittenburg Univ, 96; Southwest Oh Coun of Higher Educ Facult Excellence, 97. **SELECTED PUBLICATIONS** Auth, Whitman and the Romance of Medicine, Berkeley and Los Angeles, Univ Calif Press, 97; Articles, The Lunar Light of Student Writing: Portfolios and Literary Theory, Situating Portfolios: Four Perspectives, ed Kathleen Blake Yancy and Irwin Weiser, Provo, Ut State Univ Press, 97; Review Essay: Richard Selzer's Raising the Dead, Lit and Med, 13:2, fall, 94; America, Brought to Hospital: The Romance of Medicine and Democracy in Whitman's Civil War, The Wordsworth Cir, 24:2, winter, 94; Deconstruction and the Prophets of Literary Decline, The Chicago Tribune, Op-Ed, 29 March 94; The Art of the Suture: Richard Selzer and Medical Narrative, Lit and Med, 12:2, fall, 93; Whitman's Tympanum: A Reading of Drum-Taps, The Amer Transcendental Quart, 6:3, fall, 92; Medical Representation in Walt Whitman and William Carlos Williams, The Walt Whitman Quart Rev, 6:3, winter, 89; That Two-Handed Engine and the Consolation of Lycidas, Milton Quart, 20:2, May, 86. **CONTACT ADDRESS** Wittenberg Univ, 3388 Petre Rd., Springfield, OH 45502.

DAVIS, RON
DISCIPLINE ENGLISH **EDUCATION** Mercer Univ, BA; Univ NC Chapel Hill, PhD, 75. **CAREER** Fac, Plattsburgh State Univ of NY. **RESEARCH** 19th century Eng lit; jour; the Bible. **SELECTED PUBLICATIONS** Auth, bk on American playwright Augustus Thomas; publ(s) about journalism. **CONTACT ADDRESS** SUNY, Col at Plattsburgh, 101 Broad St, Plattsburgh, NY 12901-2681.

DAVIS, SUSAN
PERSONAL Born 10/08/1953, Denver, CO **DISCIPLINE** COMMUNICATIONS **EDUCATION** Univ Pa, PhD, 83. **CAREER** Prpf, Univ Calif, San Diego. **HONORS AND AWARDS** Gusseuheum, 1991-92. **RESEARCH** Processes of cult product and folklore; history of culture spectacle; toursim, consumer culture; public presentation of history. **SELECTED PUBLICATIONS** Auth, "'Set Your Mood to Patriotic': History as Televised Special Event," Radical His Rev, 88; Parades and Power: Street Theatre in Nineteenth-Century Philadelphia, Univ Calif, 88; Spectacular Nature University of California, 97. **CONTACT ADDRESS** Dept of Commun 0503, Univ of California, San Diego, 9500 Gilman Dr, La Jolla, CA 92093. **EMAIL** sgdavis@weber.ucsd.edu

DAVIS, TERRY
DISCIPLINE ENGLISH **CAREER** E Carolina Univ, 76-80; Univ Idaho, 81; E Washington Univ, 81-82; Gonzaga Univ, 84-86; Shadle Park High School, 85-86; Mankato State Univ, 86-. **HONORS AND AWARDS** Edwin M Hopkins English Journal Awd, 96; Best Books for Young Adults, 95, 93, 80; Am Library Asn, 95; Books for the Teen Age, NY Public Library, 94. **SELECTED PUBLICATIONS** Auth, "On the Question of Integrating Young Adult Literature into the Mainstream," The ALAN Review, 97; auth, "A Healing Vision," English Journal, 94; auth, "In the Valley of Elephants," in On the Edge, Simon & Schuster, 00; auth, "Unaccompanied Minor," Northfield Magazine, 90; auth, If Rock and Roll Were a Machine, Delacorte Press, 93; auth, Mysterious Ways, Viking Press, 84; auth, Vision Quest, Viking Press, 70; auth, The Silk Ball, Delacorte Press; auth, Playing Ball adapted from the novel The Man Who Wanted to Pay Center Field for the New York Yankees, Redwood Productions, 84; auth, Presenting Chris Crutcher, Simon & Schuster, 97. **CONTACT ADDRESS** Dept English, Mankato State Univ, Mankato, MN 56002-8400.

DAVIS, THADIOUS
DISCIPLINE 20TH CENTURY AMERICAN LITERATURE, AFRICAN-AMERICAN LITERATURE **EDUCATION** Boston Univ, PHD. **CAREER** Gertrude Conaway Vanderbilt Prof Eng, Vanderbilt Univ. **RESEARCH** Faulkner, Langston Hughes, Jessie Fauset, Carson McCullers. **SELECTED PUBLICATIONS** Auth, William Faulkner's "Negro" : Art and the Southern Context, 82; Nella Larsen, Novelist of the Harlem Renaissance: A Woman's Life Unveiled, 94; ed, Satire or Evasion: Black Perspectives on Huckleberry Finn, 92. **CONTACT ADDRESS** Vanderbilt Univ, Nashville, TN 37203-1727.

DAVIS, THOMAS M.
PERSONAL Born 07/20/1930, Ashland Kans **DISCIPLINE** ENGLISH **EDUCATION** Kansas State Univ, BS, 57, MS, 59; Univ Missouri, PhD, 68. **CAREER** Prof & PROF EMER, ENG, KENT STATE UNIV **MEMBERSHIPS** Am Antiquarian Soc **SELECTED PUBLICATIONS** Ed, 14 by Emily Dickinson, 64; co-ed, College Reading and College Writing, 66 & 70; Edward Taylor's "Church Records" and Related Sermons, 81; Edward Taylor vs. Solomon Stoddard: The Nature of the Lord's Supper,81; ed, Edward Taylor's "Harmony of the Gospels," 82; auth, A Reading of Edward Taylor, Associated Univ Press, Univ of Delaware Press, 92. **CONTACT ADDRESS** Dept of English, Kent State Univ, Kent, OH 44242. **EMAIL** tdavid4@kent.edu

DAVIS, TODD FLEMING
PERSONAL Born 03/29/1965, Elkhart, IN, m, 1988, 2 children **DISCIPLINE** LITERATURE, CREATIVE WRITING **EDUCATION** Grace Col, BA, 87; N Ill Univ, MA, 91; PhD, 95. **CAREER** Instr, N Ill Univ, 89-95; asst prof, SUNY Jeff Comm Col, 95-96; asst prof to assoc prof, Goshen Col, 96-. **HONORS AND AWARDS** Goshen Col Fac Res Grants, 97, 98, 99, 00, 01; Midwest Poetry Fest Hon Men; N Ill Univ Distinguished Compl Awd; Jennifer M. Giannasi Awd; Radix Poetry Contest, Hon Men; Who's Who Among Students; Outstanding Prospective Teacher, Dept English Awd, Dean Study Awd, Grace Col. **MEMBERSHIPS** MLA; NCTE; CLA; SSML; Sigma Tau Delta. **RESEARCH** Intersection of postmodernism and ethical criticism in contemporary American fiction. **SELECTED PUBLICATIONS** Auth, "The Narrator's Dilemma in 'Bartleby the Scrivener': The Excellently Illustrated Restatement of a Problem," Study of Short Fiction 34 (97): 183-92; co-auth, "Shepherding the Weak: The Ethics of Redemption

in Quentin Tarantino's Pulp Fiction," Lit Film Quart 26 (98): 60-66; co-ed, "Lit and Ethical Criticism," Style 32 (98):181-380; auth, rpt in Contemporary Literary Criticism, ed. Jeffrey W. Hunter (Detroit: Gale Res, 00): 379-83; co-auth, "'Haunted by Waters': Narrative Reconciliation in Norman MacLean's A River Runs through It," Study in Contemporary Fiction 42 (01): 192-204; co-auth, Formalism and Reader-Response Theory, St. Martin's Pr (US)/Macmillan Pr (UK), (forthcoming); co-ed, The Critical Response to John Irving , Greenwood Pr, (forthcoming); co-auth, "'O my brothers': Reading the Anti-Ethics of the Pseudo-Family in Anthony Burgess's A Clockwork Orange," Col Lit (forthcoming); co-auth, "In Defense of an Ethical Criticism," Penn English (forthcoming); co-ed, Mapping the Ethical Turn: A Reader in Ethics, Culture, and Literary Theory, UP Vir, (forthcoming). **CONTACT ADDRESS** English Dept, Goshen Col, 1218 Wilson Ave, Goshen, IN 46526. **EMAIL** toddfd@goshen.edu

DAVIS, WENDELL EUGENE
PERSONAL Born 09/30/1934, Toledo, OH, m, 1962 **DISCIPLINE** ENGLISH LITERATURE **EDUCATION** Bowling Green State Univ, BA, 56, MA, 58; Western Reserve Univ, PhD, 62. **CAREER** Asst prof English, Thiel Col, 61-63; asst prof, 63-74, Assoc Prof English, Purdue Univ, West Lafayette, Mem res & bibliog comt, conf English lit in transition, MLA, 66-69; Fulbright prof, Humboldt Univ, Freiburg, Ger, 69-70. **MEMBERSHIPS** Midwest Mod Lang Asn; MLA. **RESEARCH** The English novel; English literature 1880-1920; Victorian literature. **SELECTED PUBLICATIONS** Auth, Neglected Novelist of the 1890s, Batson,Henrietta,M--An Essay and Annotated Secondary Bibliography, Eng Lit in Transition 1880-1920, Vol 0040, 97; Hardy--The Margin of the Unexpressed, Eng Lit in Transition 1880-1920, Vol 0037, 94; Critical Essays on Hardy Poetry, Eng Lit in Transition 1880-1920, Vol 0039, 96; The Structures of Justice in the Secret Sharer, Conradiana, Vol 0027, 95; Letters of Hardy,Emma And Hardy,Florence, Eng Lit in Transition 1880-1920, Vol 0040, 97; Testamentary Acts--Browning, Tennyson, James, Hardy, Eng Lit in Transition 1880-1920, Vol 0036, 93; Thomas Hardy--Man of Wessex, Eng Lit in Transition 1880-1920, Vol 0038, 95. **CONTACT ADDRESS** Dept of English, Purdue Univ, West Lafayette, West Lafayette, IN 47906.

DAVIS, WILLIAM V.
PERSONAL Born 05/26/1940, Canton, OH, m, 1971, 1 child **DISCIPLINE** ENGLISH, RELIGION **EDUCATION** Ohio Univ, AB, 62, MA, 65, PhD(English), 67; Pittsburgh Theol Sem, MDiv, 65. **CAREER** Teaching Fel, Ohio Univ, 65-67, Asst prof, 67-68; Asst Prof, Central Connecticut State Univ, 68-72; Asst prof, Univ of Ill, 72-77; Assoc prof, Baylor Univ, 78-79; Guest prof, Univ of Vienna, 79-80; Vis Scholar/Guest prof, Univ of Wales, Swansea, 83; Writer-in-Residence, Univ of Montana, 83; Guest prof, Univ of Copenhagen, 84; Guest prof, Univ of Vienna, 89-90; Adj MFA Fac, Southwest Tex State Univ, 90-98; Adj Mem of the Grad Fac, Tex Christian Univ, 92-96; Consult to the Creative Writing Prog, Ohio Univ, 92-98; Guest prof, Univ of Vienna, 97; Prof of English and Writer-in-Residence, Baylor Univ, 79-. **HONORS AND AWARDS** Scholar in Poetry, Bread Loaf Writers' Conf, 70; Grad Fac Fel in Creative Writing, Univ of Ill, 74; Lilly Found Grant, 79-80; Yale Series of Younger Poets Awd for One Way to Reconstruct the Scene, 79; Winner of the Calliope Press Chapbook Prize. **MEMBERSHIPS** MLA; Poetry Soc Am; Assoc Writing Prog; Acad of Am Poets; IAUPE; PEN; Phi Kappa Phi; Tau Kappa Alpha; Tex Asn of Creative Writing Teachers; Tex Inst of Letters. **RESEARCH** Twentieth century English and American literature; creative writing; contemporary American poetry. **SELECTED PUBLICATIONS** Ed, George Whitefield's Journals, 1737-1741, ed, Scholar's Facsimiles & Reprints, 69; contrib ed, Theodore Roethke: A Bibliography, Kent State Univ Press, 73; auth, One Way to Reconstruct the Scene, Yale Univ Press, 80; auth, The Dark Hours, Calliope Press, 84; auth, Understanding Robert Bly, Univ of South Carolina Press, 88; auth, Winter Light, Univ of North Tex Press, 90. **CONTACT ADDRESS** Dept of English, Baylor Univ, Waco, Waco, TX 76798. **EMAIL** William_Davis@baylor.edu

DAVISON, CAROL MARGARET
PERSONAL Born 05/19/1963, Broxburn, Scotland, s **DISCIPLINE** ENGLISH LITERATURE **EDUCATION** Concordia Univ, BA, 86; York Univ, MA, 88; McGill Univ, PhD, 97. **CAREER** Lectr, Concordia Univ, 91-98; lectr, McGill Univ, 98-99; asst prof, Univ of Toronto, 99-00; asst prof, Univ of Windsor, 00-. **HONORS AND AWARDS** SSHRC Fel, 90-93, 00; Lord Ruthven Assembly Awd, 97. **MEMBERSHIPS** MLA, PAMLA, Int Gothic Assoc. **RESEARCH** Various Gothic-related literatures - American Gothic, Scottish Gothic, Victorian Gothic, Female Gothic, African-American Literature. **SELECTED PUBLICATIONS** Auth, "Love 'em and Lynch 'em: The Castration Motif in Gayl Jones's 'Eva's Man,'" African Am Rev 29, (95): 393-410; ed, Bram Stoker's Dracula: Sucking Through the Century, 1897 - 1997, Dundurn Pr, (Oxford/Toronto), 97; auth, "Margaret Atwood," Gothic Writers: A Critical and Bibliographical Guide, eds Douglass H Thomson, Jack G Volker and Frederick S Frank, (Westport, CT/London: Greenwood Pr, 01): 66-80. **CONTACT ADDRESS** Eng Lit & Creative Writing, Univ of Windsor, 401 Sunset, Windsor, ON, Canada N9B 3P4. **EMAIL** cdavison@uwindsor.ca

DAVISON, NANCY R.
DISCIPLINE AMERICAN CULTURE **EDUCATION** Smith, BA, 66; Univ Mich, MA, 73, PhD, 80. **CAREER** ARTIST, PRINTMAKER & GALLERY OWNER **MEMBERSHIPS** Am Antiquarian Soc **SELECTED PUBLICATIONS** Author, American Sheet Music Illustration: Reflections of the Nineteenth-Century, Clements Library Exhibition, 73; auth, "Andrew Jackson in Cartoon and Caricature," American Printmaking Before 1876: Fact, Fiction, and Fantasy, Lib Congress, 75; auth, "Bickham's Musical Entertainer and Other Curiosities," in Eighteenth-Century Prints in Colonial America: To Educate and Decorate, Colonial Williamsburg Found, 79; auth, E. W. Clay and the American Caricature Business, in Prints and Printmakers of New York State, 1825-1940, Syracuse Univ Press, 86; York Beach Activity Book, Blue Stocking, 96. **CONTACT ADDRESS** PO Box 1257, York Beach, ME 03910.

DAVISON, NEIL
PERSONAL Born 07/12/1960, Takoma Park, MD, m, 1991, 1 child **DISCIPLINE** MODERNIST LITERATURE **EDUCATION** Univ Md, BA, 82; Columbia Univ, MFA, 84; Univ Md, PhD, 93. **CAREER** Engl, Oregon St Univ. **MEMBERSHIPS** Modern Lang Asn, Int ; Jame Joyce Found, Asn for Jewish Studies. **RESEARCH** James Joyce; Irish Renaissance; Jewish Cultural Studies; British Modernism, Modernism, Postmodernism. **SELECTED PUBLICATIONS** Auth, Joyce's Matriculation Examination, James Joyce Quart, 93; Joyce's Homosocial Reckoning: Italo Svevo, Aesthetics and A Portrait of the Artist as a Young Man, Mod Lang Studies, 94; Inside the Sho'ah: Narrative, Documentation, and Schwarz-Bart's The Last of the Just, Clio, 95; James Joyce, Ulysses. And the Construction of Jewish Identity; Culture, Biography and The Jew in Modernist Europe. Cambridge Univ Press, 96, Paperback edition, Cambridge 98; auth, "Cyclops, Sinn Fein, and The Jew," Journal of Modern Lit; Representations of Irishness in the Untilled Field, Textual Practice; "We are not a doctor for the body: Catholicism, the Female Grotesque, and Flann O'Brien's The Hard Life," Literature and Psychology; Paperback edition of James Joyce, Ulysses, and the Construction of Jewish Identity, Cambridge UP, 98. **CONTACT ADDRESS** Oregon State Univ, Corvallis, OR 97331-4501. **EMAIL** ndavison@orst.edu

DAVISSON, MARY H. T.
PERSONAL Born 12/05/1952, Baltimore, MD, m, 1980, 3 children **DISCIPLINE** CLASSICS **EDUCATION** Brown Univ, AB, 74, MA, 74; Univ CA, Berkeley, PhD (Classics), 79. **CAREER** Asst prof, Univ VA, 81-83; adjunct asst prof, Loyola Col in Maryland, 84-. **HONORS AND AWARDS** Phi Beta Kappa; Sather Res assistantship, 75-76. **MEMBERSHIPS** Am Philol Asn; Classical Asn of the Middle West and South; Classical Asn of the Atlantic States; Am Classical League; Maryland Junior Classical League. **RESEARCH** Ovid; Virgil; pedagogy. **SELECTED PUBLICATIONS** Auth, Sed sum quam medico notior ipse mihi: Ovid's Use of Some Conventions in the Exile Epistles, Clasical Antiquity 2, 83; Magna Tibi Imposita Est Nostris Persona Libellis: Playwright and Actor in Ovid's Epistulae ex Ponto 3-1, Classical J 79, 84; Parents and Children in Ovid's Poems from Exile, Classical World 78, 84; Tristia 5-13 and Ovid's Use of Epistolary Form and Content, Classical J 80, 85; Quid moror exemplis?: Mythological Exempla in Ovid, Phoenix 47, 93; The Treatment of Festering Sores in Virgil, Classical World 86, 93; Mythological Exempla in Ovid's Remedia Amoris, Phoenix 50, 96; The Observers of Daedalus in Ovid, Classical World 90, 97. **CONTACT ADDRESS** Classics Dept, Loyola Col, 4501 N Charles St, Baltimore, MD 21210. **EMAIL** mdavisson@loyola.edu

DAWSON, ANTHONY BLANCHARD
PERSONAL Born Toronto, ON, Canada **DISCIPLINE** ENGLISH LITERATURE, DRAMA **EDUCATION** Concordia Univ, BA, 63; Harvard Univ, MA, 65, PhD(English), 69. **CAREER** Lectr English, Harvard Univ, 69-70; asst prof, 70-79, Assoc Prof English, Univ BC, 70-. **MEMBERSHIPS** Shakespeare Asn Am, Asn Can Univ Teachers English. **RESEARCH** Shakespeare, Renaissance literature, Canadian literature. **SELECTED PUBLICATIONS** Auth, Indirections: Shakespeare and the Art of Illusion; auth, Watching Shakespeare: A Playgoers' Guide; auth, Hamlet (Shakespeare in Performance), 98; auth, The Culture of Playgoing in Shakespeare's England: A Collaborative Debate, 01. **CONTACT ADDRESS** Dept of English, Univ of British Columbia, 397-1873 E Mall, Vancouver, BC, Canada V6T 1Z1. **EMAIL** dawson@interchange.ubc.ca

DAWSON, CARL
PERSONAL Born 05/02/1938, Leeds, England, m, 1995, 2 children **DISCIPLINE** ENGLISH **EDUCATION** Occidental Col, AB, 59; Columbia Univ, MA, 60; PhD, 66. **CAREER** Instr, Dartmouth Col, 64-66; asst prof, Univ Calif, Berkeley, 66-70; assoc prof, UNH, 70-76, prof, 76-89, chair, 81-87; prof, Univ of Del, 89-, chair, 89-94. **HONORS AND AWARDS** MA High Honors, Columbia Univ, 60; Woodrow Wilson Fel, 59-60; President's Fel, 60-62, 63-64; Dankstipendium, Univ Munich, 61-62; Fulbright Prof, Univ Berlin, 67-68; Univ Calif, Berkeley, Humanities Inst Awd, 69-70; John Simon Guggenheim Fel, 73-74; Am Acad of Learned Soc Fel, 74; NEH Sr Awd, 81-82. **RESEARCH** Nineteenth-century British America. **SELECTED PUBLICATIONS** Co-ed with John Pfordresher, Matthew Arnold: The Critical Heritage, Prose Writings, Routledge & Kegan Paul (79); auth, Victorian Noon: English Literature in 1850, Johns Hopkins Univ Press (79); auth, Prophets of Past Toime: Seven British Autobiographers, 1880-1914, Johns Hopkins Univ Press (88); auth, November 1948, Univ Press of Va (90); auth, Lafcadio Hearn and the Vision of Japan, Johns Hopkins Univ Press (92); auth, Living Backwards: a Transatlantic Memoir, Univ Press Va (95); auth, "The Ambassadors: Hearn and Lowell in Japan," Shoin Lit Rev (95); auth, "Western Critic in an Eastern World," Centennial Essays on Lafcadio Hearn, Hearn Soc, Matsue, Japan (96). **CONTACT ADDRESS** Dept English, Univ of Delaware, 42 Amstel Ave, Newark, DE 19716-2799.

DAWSON, WILLIAM
DISCIPLINE BRITISH ROMANTICISM **EDUCATION** Univ Mo, PhD, 84. **CAREER** Dir Undergrad Stud & Acad Adv. **HONORS AND AWARDS** Blue Chalk Award, 93; Execellence in Advising Award, 00. **RESEARCH** British romanticism. **SELECTED PUBLICATIONS** Publ on, British Romanticism, Shakespeare, Washington Irving & William Faulkner. **CONTACT ADDRESS** Dept of English, Univ of Missouri, Columbia, 107D Tate Hall, Columbia, MO 65211. **EMAIL** DawsonW@missouri.edu

DAY, MICHAEL
DISCIPLINE RHETORIC **EDUCATION** Dartmouth Col, BA, 78; Univ Wyo, MA, 82; Univ Calif, Berkeley, PhD, 96. **CAREER** Exchange lectr, Osaka Univ, 82-83; lectr, Mukogawa Women's Univ, 83-85; vis lectr, Kobe Univ, 85-86; Grad Student instr to res asst, Univ Calif, Berkeley, 86-92; asst prof, S Dak Sch of Mines and Technol, 92-97, assoc prof, 97-99; asst prof, Northern Ill Univ , 99-. **HONORS AND AWARDS** Acad of Am Poets, Univ of Wyo, 81; Phi Kappa Phi, 82; Outstanding Grad Instr Awd, Univ Calif, Berkeley, 90; Innovative Teaching Awd, Honorable Mention, SDak Sch of Mines and Technol, 94; Who's Who in the Midwest, 97-98. **MEMBERSHIPS** S Dak Coun of Teachers of English, Modern Lang Asn of Am, Allliance for Computers and Writing, Nat Coun of Teachers off English, Commun Inst for Online Scholarship, ACW-L. **RESEARCH** Computers, Internet and the teaching of writing; rhetoric and composition, composition pedagogy, rhetoric of computer mediated communication, intercultural communication, comparative rhetoric, oral tradition and folklore. **SELECTED PUBLICATIONS** Auth, A Place for Yourself, Laramie, Wyo: Jelm Mountain Press (82); auth, Managing in America: An Intercultural Communication Training Manual for Japanese Businessmen, Osaka, Japan: Nippon Information and Commun Co (March 90); auth, "The On Line Renaissance: A New Epistolary Culture," Necessary Conversations, Margit Watts, ed, (forthcoming); auth, "A Meshing of Minds: The Future of Online Research for Print and Electronic Publication," in New Worlds, New Words: Exploring Pathways for Writing about and in Electronic Environments, John F. Barber and Dene Grigar, eds, Cresskill, NJ: Hampton Press (in press); auth, "A Tribute to Dr. Stephen Marcus, 1945-1999," ed, Assembly on Computers in English J, Vol 3 , No 1 (April 2000); auth, "Teachers at the Crossroads: Evaluating Teaching in New Electronic Environments," Computers and Composition, Vol 17, No 1 (2000); co-ed, The Online Writing Classroom, Cresskill, NJ: Hampton Press (2000). **CONTACT ADDRESS** Dept English, No Illinois Univ, 1425 W Lincoln Highway, Dekalb, IL 60115-2828.

DE ALMEIDA, HERMIONE
DISCIPLINE ENGLISH **EDUCATION** Vassar Col, AB, 72; Columbia Univ, MA, 73; PhD, 78. **CAREER** From asst prof to prof, Univ Miami, 79-91; prof, Univ of Tulsa, 91-. **HONORS AND AWARDS** Am Council of Learned Scholars, 81; Nat Humanities Ctr, 82-83; NEH, 88; Woodrow Wilson Int Ctr for Scholars, 88-89; **MEMBERSHIPS** MLA, Keats-Shelley Asn, Nat Asn of Scholars and Critics, Int Asn of Univ Prof of English. **RESEARCH** English and European romanticism, modern and contemporary British literature, history of the novel, history of medicine, romantic science, post-colonial literature and art. **SELECTED PUBLICATIONS** Auth, Byron & Joyce Through Homer: 'Don Juan' & 'Ulysses', Columbia Univ Press & Macmillan, 81; auth, Romantic Medicine & John Keats, Oxford Univ Press, 91. **CONTACT ADDRESS** Dept English, Univ of Tulsa, 600 S College Ave, Tulsa, OK 74104-3126.

DE GRAVE, KATHLEEN R.
PERSONAL Born 10/20/1950, Green Bay, WI, m, 1978, 3 children **DISCIPLINE** ENGLISH LITERATURE **EDUCATION** University Wis Green Bay, BA; Univ Ark, MA; Univ Wis Madison, PhD. **CAREER** Assoc prof. **MEMBERSHIPS** MLA; NCTE; AWP **RESEARCH** American literature, 19th century women writers, Native American Literature. **SELECTED PUBLICATIONS** Publ, Swindler, Spy, Rebel: The Confidence Woman in Nineteenth-Century America, 95; short stories, reviews, and articles on women's writing; auth, "Company Woman, 95." **CONTACT ADDRESS** Dept of Eng, Pittsburg State Univ, 1701 S Broadway St, Pittsburg, KS 66762. **EMAIL** kdegrave@pittstate.edu

DE GRAZIA, EDWARD
DISCIPLINE INTERNATIONAL TRANSACTIONS, COMMUNICATIONS LAW **EDUCATION** Univ Chicago, BA, 48; JD 51. **CAREER** Prof; **HONORS AND AWARDS** Dir, Georgetown Univ Prog Pretrial Diversion Accused Offenders to Community Mental Health Treatment Prog; Asso fel, Inst Policy Studies. **MEMBERSHIPS** Office Dir Gen UNESCO, 56-59; U.S. Dept State; U.S. Agency Int Devel; PEN Am Ctr. **RESEARCH** International transations; community law; first admenment legislation. **SELECTED PUBLICATIONS** Coath, Censorship Landmarks and Banned Films: Movies, Censors; First Amendment; auth, Girls Lean Back Everywhere: The Law of Obscenity and the Assault on Genius, Random House, 92. **CONTACT ADDRESS** Yeshiva Univ, 55 Fifth Ave, New York, NY 10003-4301.

DE JONGH, JAMES LAURENCE
PERSONAL Born 09/23/1942, St Thomas, Virgin Islands of the United States, s **DISCIPLINE** ENGLISH **EDUCATION** Williams College, BA 1964; Yale Univ, MA 1967; New York Univ, PhD 1983. **CAREER** Rutgers Univ Newark, instructor 1969-70; The City Coll of the City Univ of New York (CUNY), prof 1970-; CUNY Inst for Research on the African Diapora in the Americas and the Caribean (IRADAC), interim dir, 97-. **HONORS AND AWARDS** Fellow Center for Black Studies Univ of CA Santa Barbara 1981; Outstanding Achievement Awd The Black Action Council of the City Coll of New York 1982; Audelco Recognition Awd Outstanding Musical Creator 1984; Honorary Fellow Brookdale Ctr on Aging of Hunger Coll 1985; Natl Endowment for the Humanities Fellowship for College Teachers 1986; major plays and publications "Hail Hail the Gangs!" w/Carles Cleveland produced by NY Theatre Ensemble Inc 1976; "City Cool, A Ritual of Belonging," w/Carles Cleveland Random House 1978; "Do Lord Remember Me" Off-Broadway Premier Oct 10, 1982 produced by Wynn Handman The Amer Place Theater; "Play to Win, Jackie Robinson" w/ Carles Cleveland Natl school tour 1984-86. **MEMBERSHIPS** Mem The Dramatists Guild, Writers Guild of Amer East, Modern Language Assoc, Harlem Writers Guild, Zeta Psi Frat. **SELECTED PUBLICATIONS** Auth, Vicious Modernism: Black Harlem and the Literary Imagination, Cambridge Univ Press, 1990. **CONTACT ADDRESS** English Department, City Col, CUNY, IRADAC, Y-Bldg 307, New York, NY 10031.

DE LORME, DENISE
PERSONAL Born 05/19/1968, Alexandria, VA, m, 1999 **DISCIPLINE** ADVERTISING **EDUCATION** Univ Ga, ABJ, 89; MA, 91; PhD, 95. **CAREER** Instr to asst prof, Univ of Ga, 93-. **HONORS AND AWARDS** Alpha Delta Sigma; Kappa Tau Alpha; Ga Merit Scholar; Phi Kappa Phi; Outstanding Young Woman of Am, 97; Grant Univ of Central Fla, 97-98; Outstanding Res Paper Awd, Asn for Educ in Jour and Mass Commun, 98; Res Grant, Fla Fish and Wildlife Conserv Comm. **MEMBERSHIPS** Am Acad of Advertising; Assoc for Consumer Res; Am Marketing Assoc; Assoc for Educ in Jour and Mass Commun. **RESEARCH** Qualitative Research Methods, Consumer Behavior, Brand Placement in Motion Pictures. **SELECTED PUBLICATIONS** Coauth, "Toward an Advertising Research Code of Ethics", Proceedings of the 1996 Conf of the Am Acad of Advertising, ed Gary Wilcox, (Austin, TX, 96): 149-155; coauth, "Beyond the World of Packaged Goods: Assessing the Relevance of Integrated Marketing Communications for Retail and Consumer Service Marketing", J of Marketing Commun 2.3 (96): 173-190; coauth, "Top Level Agency Creatives Look at Advertising Creativity Then and Now", J of Advertising 27.2 (98): 1-15; auth, "Consumers' Experiences and Interpretations of Brands in Pop Culture Contexts", Proceedings of the 1998 Conf of the Am Acad of Advertising, ed Darrel D Muehling, (Pulman, WA, 98): 216-222; coauth, "Moviegoers' Experiences and Interpretations of Brands in Films Revisited", J of Advertising 28.2 (99): 71-95; coauth, "A Cross-Cultural Comparison of Consumers' Perceptions and Evaluations of Brand Placement in Motion Pictures", Proceedings of the 2000 Am Marketing Assoc Winter Educ Conf (00): 27-34; auth, "Potential Ethical Issues Associated with Qualitative Research Conducted Face-to-Face and in Cyberspace", Advertising Res at the Am Marketing Assoc, ed George M. Zinkhan, (forthcoming). **CONTACT ADDRESS** Sch of Commun, Univ of Central Florida, PO Box 161344, Orlando, FL 32816-1344. **EMAIL** ddelorme@pegasus.cc.ucf.edu

DE MOTT, ROBERT J.
PERSONAL Born 11/22/1943, New Cannan, CT, m, 1991, 1 child **DISCIPLINE** LITERATURE **EDUCATION** Assumption Col, BA, 65; John Carroll Univ, MA, 67; Kent State Univ, PhD, 69. **CAREER** From Asst Prof to Edwin and Ruth Kennedy Distinguished Prof, Ohio Univ, 69-; Vis Prof, Steinbeck Res Center, San Jose State Univ, 84-85. **HONORS AND AWARDS** Outstanding Grad Prof, Ohio Univ, 75; Univ Prof Undergraduate Teaching Awd, Ohio Univ, 78; Outstanding Teacher Awd, Col of A&S, 96; Jeanette G. Graseeli Fac Awd in Humanities, Col of A&S, 98; Nancy Dasher Book Awd, Col English Asn, 98; Hon Tutorial Col Outstanding Tutor, 99. **MEMBERSHIPS** Am Lit Asn, Asn of Lit Critics and Scholars, Asoc Writer's Prog. **RESEARCH** 19th and 20th Century American Literature, John Steinbeck, Contemporary American Poetry, American Nature Writing. **SELECTED PUBLICATIONS** Co-ed, Artful Thunder: Versions of the Romantic Tradition in American Literature in Honor of Howard P. Vincent, Kent State Univ Press (Kent, Ohio), 75; auth, Steinbeck's Reading: A Catalogue of Books Owned and Borrowed, Garland Press (NY), 84; ed, Working Days: The Journals of the 'The Grapes of Wrath', 1938-1941, The Viking Press (NY), 89; co-ed, John Steinbeck: Novels and Stories 1932-1937, The Libr of Am (NY), 94; co-ed, After 'The Grapes of Wrath': Essays on John Steinbeck in Honor of Tetsumaro Hayashi, Ohio Univ Press (Athens), 95; auth, "News of Loss," in Men and Women/ Women and Man: Chapbook Collection (Huron, OH: Bottom Dog Press, 95); co-ed, John Steinbeck: 'The Grapes of Wrath' and Other Writings 1936-1941, The Libr of Am (NY), 96; auth, Steinbeck's Typewriter: Essays on His Art, Whitston Publ Co (Troy, NY), 96; auth, Dave Smith: A Literary Archive, Ohio Univ Libr (Athens), 00. **CONTACT ADDRESS** Dept English, Ohio Univ, Ellis Hall, Athens, OH 45701-2942. **EMAIL** demott@oak.cats.ohiou.edu

DE ORTEGO Y GASCA, FELIPE
PERSONAL Born Blue Island, IL **DISCIPLINE** COMMUNICATION STUDIES **EDUCATION** Univ Tex, BA, 59, MA, 66; Univ NMex, PhD, 71. **CAREER** Prof to dist prof emer, Sul Ross State Univ, 93-. **HONORS AND AWARDS** Distinguished Fac Awd, 97. **MEMBERSHIPS** Am Libr Asn; Tex Libr Asn; Nat Asn Bilingual Edu; Am Asn Higher Edu. **SELECTED PUBLICATIONS** Auth, pubs on British and American writers. **CONTACT ADDRESS** Sul Ross State Univ, PO Box C-114, Alpine, TX 79832. **EMAIL** fortego@sulross.edu

DE SANTIS, CHRISTOPHER
PERSONAL Born 12/29/1966, Longmont, CO, s **DISCIPLINE** AMERICAN AND AFRICAN-AMERICAN LITERATURE **EDUCATION** Lewis and Clark Col, BA, 89; Univ Wis-Madison, MA, 90; Univ Kans, PhD, 97. **CAREER** Asst prof, Westfield St Col, 97-99; asst prof, Ill State Univ, 99-. **RESEARCH** Interdisciplinary study of the cultural myths engendered by social transformations of the post-Civil War era. **SELECTED PUBLICATIONS** Ed, Langston Hughes and the Chicago Defender, Univ Ill Press, 95; bk rev(s), African Am Rev, The Langston Hughes Rev, The Southern Quart; published essays and reviews in African Am Rev, Col Lang Assoc Jrnl, Am Stud, Southern Qtly, Langston Hughes Rev, Oxford Companion to African Am Lit, Jrnl of Am Culture. **CONTACT ADDRESS** Dept of Engl, Illinois State Univ, Normal, IL 61790. **EMAIL** ccdesan@ilstu.edu

DE TORO, FERNANDO
DISCIPLINE ENGLISH LITERATURE **EDUCATION** Univ Carleton, BA; MA; Univ Montreal, PhD. **CAREER** Prof **RESEARCH** Colonial and post colonial literature; history of Latin American theatre; modern and post-modern fiction; architecture; theatre; philosophy; politics; post colonial theory; feminism; Latin American literature; literary theory; and structuralism and semiotics. **SELECTED PUBLICATIONS** Auth, pubs on colonial and post colonial poetry, fiction, feminism and literary theory. **CONTACT ADDRESS** Dept of English, Univ of Manitoba, Winnipeg, MB, Canada R3T 2N2. **EMAIL** fdetoro@ms.umanitoba.ca

DE VEAUX, ALEXIS
PERSONAL Born 09/24/1948, New York, NY **DISCIPLINE** LITERATURE **EDUCATION** Empire State College, BA, 1976; SUNY at Buffalo, MA, 1989, PhD, 1992. **CAREER** New Haven Board of Education, master artist, 74-75; Sarah Lawrence College, adjunct lecturer, 79-80; Norwich University, assoc faculty, 84-85; Wabash College, Owen Dutson visiting scholar, 86-87; Essence Magazine, editor-at-large, 78-90; SUNY at Buffalo, visiting assistant professor, 91-92, Asst Prof, 92-. **HONORS AND AWARDS** Drew Child Development Corp., Lorraine Hansberry Awd, 1991; American Library Association, Coretta Scott King Awd, 1981, 1988; MADRE, Humanitarian Awd, 1984; Medgar Evers College, Fannie Lou Hamer Awd, 1984; Lincoln University, Unity in Media Awd, 1982, 1983; Brooklyn Museum, Art Books for Children Awd, 1974, 1975; numerous others. **MEMBERSHIPS** Organization of Women Writers of Africa, Inc (OWWA). **SELECTED PUBLICATIONS** Author: An Enchanted Hair Tale, 1987, Don't Explain: A Song of Billie Holiday, 1980, Na-Ni, 1973, (all Harper & Row); Blue Heat, Poems, Diva Publishing, 1985; Spirits In The Street, Doubleday, 1973; writer: "Walking into Freedom with Nelson and Winnie Mandela," June 1990, "Forty Fine: A Writer Reflects on Turning Forty," Jan 1990, "Alice Walker: Rebel With A Cause," Sept 1989, (all Essence Magazine); numerous other poems, short stories and plays. **CONTACT ADDRESS** Dept Amer Studies, SUNY, Buffalo, 1010 Clemens Hall, Buffalo, NY 14260.

DE VILLERS, JEAN-PIERRE
PERSONAL m **DISCIPLINE** MODERN LITERATURE **EDUCATION** Univ Colorado, PhD. **CAREER** Prof, Univ Windsor; Fulbright Scholar, Wesleyan Univ & Univ Colo at Boulder, 61-68; taught at, Univ Colo; Univ Notre Dame; US Air Force Lang Sch at Sacramento & Univ Calif. **HONORS AND AWARDS** Fulbright Scholar from 1961 to 1968 at Wesleyan Univ, Middletown, Conn; Univ of Colo at Boulder; founder and ed, stud on futurism and the avant-garde. **RESEARCH** Futurist participation in the genesis of the Avant-Garde. **SELECTED PUBLICATIONS** Auth, Les drames de Roger Vitrac et le theatre d'avant-garde,Ann Arbor: Univ Microfilms, 67; Futurism And the Arts - Le Futurisme et les Arts - II e le Arti, Toronto and Buffalo: U of Toronto P, 75; FT Marinetti et le Premier Manifeste du Futurisme, U of Ottawa P, 86; Futurist Manifestoes / Manifestes Futuristes, U of Ottawa P, 98; Guns of Babylon Docudrama-novel, Toronto: Lugus Publ, 93; Le cas d'un marginal de genie: Alfred Jarry, Exile, Marginaux et parias dans les litteratures francophones, Toronto: Editions du Gref, 94; Con Marinetti e Boccioni a Dosso Casina, Simultaneita, Roma, Vol I, 97; Duchamp-Picabia et le Cubo-Futurisme. Penetration de l'Art Moderne aux Etats-Unis, Ligeia - Dossiers sur l'art, Paris, Centre National de la Recherche Scientifique, Oct 97-Juin 98; contrib, Dada in America, Edizioni De Luca, Roma: Dada, l'arte della negazione, 94; rev, Balla in Canada, Futurismo Oggi, 87 & Boccioni: Une retrospective, Ligeia - Dossiers sur l'Art, Paris: Centre National de la Recherche Scientifique, Oct 88-Mar 89. **CONTACT ADDRESS** Dept of French Language and Literature, Univ of Windsor, 401 Sunset Ave, Windsor, ON, Canada N9B 3P4. **EMAIL** deville@uwindsor.ca

DE YOUNG, JAMES
PERSONAL Born 02/13/1938, Milwaukee, WI, m, 1959, 2 children **DISCIPLINE** THEATRE ARTS **EDUCATION** Beloit Col, BA, 59; Bowling Green State Univ, MA, 60; Univ Minn, PhD, 74. **CAREER** Instr, Hope Col, 60-62; prof, Monmouth Col, 63-. **HONORS AND AWARDS** Sears-Roebuck Teaching Awd; NEA Fel, 84, 93; Fac Admin, ACM London Arts Prog, 72, 86. **MEMBERSHIPS** AAUP; Assoc for Theatre in Higher Educ. **RESEARCH** British Drama, Theatre History. **SELECTED PUBLICATIONS** Auth, London Theatre Walks, Applause Books, 98. **CONTACT ADDRESS** Dept Theatre Arts, Monmouth Col, 700 E Broadway, Monmouth, IL 61462-1963. **EMAIL** jim@monm.edu

DEAGON, ANN FLEMING
PERSONAL Born 01/19/1930, Birmingham, AL, w, 1951, 2 children **DISCIPLINE** CLASSICS, CREATIVE WRITING **EDUCATION** Birmingham-Southern Col, BA, 50; Univ NC, MA, 51, PhD(Latin), 54. **CAREER** Asst prof classics, Furman Univ, 54-56; from asst prof to assoc prof, 56-75, prof Classics, Guilford Col, 75-92; Nat Endowment for Arts literary fel, 82. **MEMBERSHIPS** Am Philol Asn; Class Asn Midwest & S; Poetry Soc Am; Archaeological Inst Am. **SELECTED PUBLICATIONS** Auth, Poetics South, Blair, 74; Carbon 14, Univ Mass, 74; Indian Summer, Unicorn Press, 75; Women and Children First, Iron Mountain, 76; There is No Balm in Birmingham, Godine, 78; The Flood Story, Winthrop Col, 81; Habitats, Green River Press, 82; auth, The Diver's Tomb, St martins, 84; auth, The Polo Poems, Nebraska, 90. **CONTACT ADDRESS** 802 Woodbrook Dr, Greensboro, NC 27410. **EMAIL** anndeagon@worldnet.att.net

DEAKINS, ROGER LEE
PERSONAL Born 12/04/1933, Decatur, IL, m, 1967, 3 children **DISCIPLINE** ENGLISH LITERATURE **EDUCATION** Univ Ill, BA, 56; Harvard Univ, MA, 58, PhD(English), 65. **CAREER** Instr English, Beloit Col, 61-65 & City Col New York, 65-68; asst prof, 68-72, Assoc Prof English, NY Univ, 72- Am Coun Learned Soc fel, 72-73. **MEMBERSHIPS** Renaissance Soc Am; MLA. **RESEARCH** Renaissance literature; philosophy; history. **SELECTED PUBLICATIONS** Ed, Il Moro: Ellis Heywood's Dialogue in Memory of Thomas More, Harvard Univ, 72. **CONTACT ADDRESS** Dept of English, New York Univ, 19 University Pl, New York, NY 10003-4556.

DEAN, DENNIS RICHARD
PERSONAL Born 05/29/1938, Belvidere, IL, m, 1968 **DISCIPLINE** ENGLISH, HISTORY OF SCIENCE **EDUCATION** Stanford Univ, AB, 60, AM, 62; Univ Wis-Madison, PhD(English), 68. **CAREER** Instr English, Kenosha Ctr, Univ Wis, 67-68; asst prof, 68-73, assoc prof English, 73-82, Prof English & Humanities, Univ Wis-Parkside, 82-, Fulbright award, Korea, 77; NSF grant, New Zealand, 82. **MEMBERSHIPS** AAUP; Hist Sci Soc; Keats-Shelley Asn. **RESEARCH** Literature and science; British romantics; history of science, especially geology. **SELECTED PUBLICATIONS** Auth, The San-Francisco Earthquake of 1906, Annals of Sci, Vol 0050, 93. **CONTACT ADDRESS** Humanities Div, Univ of Wisconsin, Parkside, Kenosha, WI 53140.

DEAN, JAMES S.
DISCIPLINE ENGLISH **EDUCATION** Birmingham Univ, PhD. **CAREER** Prof; taught in, NAm, SAm & Europe; done, oceanographic study, Mediter. **SELECTED PUBLICATIONS** Auth, The Art of Double Bass Playing, 73; Robert Greene: A Reference Guide, 84; Sailing A Square-Rigger, 95. **CONTACT ADDRESS** Dept of Eng, Univ of Wisconsin, Parkside, 900 Wood Rd, 272 Commun, PO Box 2000, Kenosha, WI 53141-2000. **EMAIL** dean@uwp.edu

DEAN, JOAN FITZPATRICK
PERSONAL Born 12/24/1949, Dunkirk, NY **DISCIPLINE** ENGLISH **EDUCATION** Canisius Col, AB, 70; Purdue Univ, MA, 72, PhD(English), 75. **CAREER** Asst English, Purdue Univ, 70-74, grad instr, 74-75; asst prof, 75-81, Assoc Prof En-

glish, Univ MO, Kansas City, 81-. **MEMBERSHIPS** MLA. **RESEARCH** Contemporary drama; contemporary film; Renaissance literature. **SELECTED PUBLICATIONS** Auth, Shaffer's recurrent character type, Mod Drama, 9/78; Between 2001 and Star Wars, J Popular Film 78; Tom Stoppard: Comedy as a moral matrix, Univ Mo Press, 81; Joe Orton and the redefinition of farce, Theatre J, 78. **CONTACT ADDRESS** Dept of English, Univ of Missouri, Kansas City, 5100 Rockhill Rd, Kansas City, MO 64110-2499.

DEAN, MARGARET J.
PERSONAL Born 04/19/1950, Logansport, IN, m, 1973, 2 children **DISCIPLINE** ENGLISH, LITERATURE **EDUCATION** Radcliffe Col, AB, 72; Univ Colo Boulder, MA, 85; Univ Ky, PhD, 98. **CAREER** Teacher, Salem Class HS, 73-76; teacher, Evergreen Jr HS, 85; cen dir to assoc prof, Eastern Ky Univ, 86-. **HONORS AND AWARDS** NEH Milton Inst; NEH English Reformation Seminar; Travel Grant, Univ Ky; EKU Res Grant. **MEMBERSHIPS** MLA; KPA; SCSA; ENCEWW. **RESEARCH** John Milton; Edmund Spenser; John Foxe; Harriet Beecher Stowe. **SELECTED PUBLICATIONS** Auth, Marriage as Unreliable Narrative In Paradise Lost, UMI, 98; auth, "Moments with John Shawcross," Ky Philol Rev (98); co-auth, "Packaging Women's Narratives in Early America: Presenting Mary White Rowlandson and Harriet Jacobs," Ky Philol Rev (98). **CONTACT ADDRESS** English Dept, Eastern Kentucky Univ, 521 Lancaster Ave, 467 Case Annex, Richmond, KY 40475-3102. **EMAIL** margaret.dean@acs.eku.edu

DEAN, MISAO A.
DISCIPLINE CANADIAN LITERATURE **EDUCATION** Carleton Univ, BA, MA; Queen's Univ, PhD. **CAREER** Assoc prof **RESEARCH** Canadian novel writing by women; gender stud; pop culture in Canada. **SELECTED PUBLICATIONS** Auth, A Different Point of View: Sara Jeannette Duncan, McGill-Queen's Press, 91; Practising Femininity: Domestic Realism and Gender in Early Canadian Fiction, Univ Toronto, 98. **CONTACT ADDRESS** Dept of English, Univ of Victoria, PO Box 3070, Victoria, BC, Canada V8W 3W1. **EMAIL** mdean@uvic.ca

DEAN, SUSAN DAY
PERSONAL Born 02/05/1937, Richmond, VA, d, 2 children **DISCIPLINE** ENGLISH LITERATURE, AMERICAN LITERATURE **EDUCATION** Sweet Briar Col, BA, 58; Bryn Mawr Col, MA, 68, PhD, 75. **CAREER** Librn, New York Pub Libr, 61-66; Prof Emeritus, American Literature, Bryn Mawr Col, 76-00. **MEMBERSHIPS** MLA; Northeast Mod Lang Asn; Thomas Hardy Soc Am; Soc Values Higher Educ. **RESEARCH** Walt Whitman and the American long poem; American Romanticism; Thomas Hardy; Native American literature. **SELECTED PUBLICATIONS** Auth, Hardy's Poetic Vision in The Dynasts: The Diorama of A Dream, Princeton Univ, 77; ed, From Hardy to Max Gate: Ten Unpublished Hardy Letters, Bryn Mawr Col, 79. **CONTACT ADDRESS** Dept of English, Bryn Mawr Col, 101 N Merion Ave, Bryn Mawr, PA 19010-2899. **EMAIL** sdean@brynmawr.edu

DEAN, TIM
PERSONAL Born 12/27/1964, Coventry, England **DISCIPLINE** ENGLISH **EDUCATION** Univ E Anglia, BA, 88; Johns Hopkins Univ, MA, 92; PhD, 94. **CAREER** Asst prof, Univ Wash, 94-97; from asst prof to assoc prof, Univ Ill Urbana-Champaign, 97-. **HONORS AND AWARDS** Residential Fel, Stanford Humanities Ctr, 97-98. **RESEARCH** Poetry & Poetics, Anglophone Modernism, Queer Theory, Psychoanalytic Theory. **SELECTED PUBLICATIONS** Auth, Gary Snyder and the American Unconscious, Macmillan, 91; auth, Beyond Sexuality, Univ Chicago Press, 00. **CONTACT ADDRESS** Dept English, Univ of Illinois, Urbana-Champaign, 608 S Wright St, Urbana, IL 61801-3613. **EMAIL** dean@uiuc.edu

DEARIN, RAY DEAN
PERSONAL Born 12/17/1941, Paragould, AK, m, 1964, 2 children **DISCIPLINE** SPEECH **EDUCATION** Harding Col, BA, 63; Univ Ill, Champaign, MA, 65, PhD, 70. **CAREER** From instr to assoc prof, 65-77, Prof Speech, IA State Univ, 77-; Consult ed, Cent States Speech J, 73-74. **MEMBERSHIPS** Cent States Commun Asn; Nat Commun Asn. **RESEARCH** Rhetoric; public address. **SELECTED PUBLICATIONS** Auth, Aristotle on Psychology and Rhetoric, Cent States Speech J, 11/66; The Philosophical Basis of Chaim Perelman's Theory of Rhetoric, Quart J Speech, 10/69; Justice in Ethics, Politics and Rhetoric, IA J Speech, fall 69; auth, The Fourth Stasis in Greek Rhetoric, In: Rhetoric and Communication, Univ IL, 76; Public address history as part of the speech communication discipline, Commun Educ, 9/80; The New Rhetoric of Chaim Perelman, 89; auth, The American Dream as Depicted in Robert J. Dole's 1996 Presidential Nominatioan Acceptance Speech," Presidential Studeis Quarterly, 97. **CONTACT ADDRESS** Program in Speech Communication, Iowa State Univ of Science and Tech, Ames, IA 50011-2204. **EMAIL** rdearin@iastate.edu

DEBLY, PATRICIA
PERSONAL Born, Canada **DISCIPLINE** MUSICOLOGY **EDUCATION** Univ Victoria, MA; PhD. **CAREER** Assoc prof, Brock Univ, 90-. **RESEARCH** Eighteenth century Italian opera. **CONTACT ADDRESS** Dept of Music, Brock Univ, 500 Glenridge Ave, Thistle Complex, West, Rm 137B, Saint Catharines, ON, Canada L2S 3A1. **EMAIL** pdebly@spartan.ac.BrockU.CA

DEBO, ANNETTE R.
DISCIPLINE ENGLISH **EDUCATION** Va Tech, BS, 86; MA, 90; Univ Md Col Pk, PhD, 98. **CAREER** Vis asst prof, Am Univ, 98-99; lectr, Univ Md Col Pk, 99; asst prof, Western Carolina Univ, 01-. **HONORS AND AWARDS** Carl Bode Prize, 99; CAAR Grant, 98; Phi Beta Kappa; QCB Res/Travel Grant, 97; Outstanding Teacher Award nomination, 97; Outstanding Teacher Recognition Cert, 90. **MEMBERSHIPS** MLA; ASA; MSA; CLA; H. D. Soc; AALCS; EDEC. **RESEARCH** 19th and 20th century American literature; African American literature; women's literature; critical literature. **SELECTED PUBLICATIONS** Contrb, "Margaret Walker," in Contemporary African American Novelists: A Bio-Bibliographical Critical Sourcebook, ed. Emmanuel S. Nelson (NYork: Greenwood, 99): 469-474; auth, "Dickinson Manuscripts in the Undergraduate Classroom," Col Lit 27 (00): 131-144; auth, "Interracial Modernism in Avant-Garde Film: Paul Robeson and H. D. in the 1930 Borderline," Quart Rev Film Video 18 (01); auth, "Power, Destiny and Individual Choice: Gloria Naylor's Naturalism," CLA J (forthcoming). **CONTACT ADDRESS** English Dept, Western Carolina Univ, 307 Coulter, Cullowhee, NC 28723. **EMAIL** adebo@rock-creek.com

DEBOO, EDWARD L.
PERSONAL Born 05/07/1967, Chicago, IL **DISCIPLINE** CLASSICS **EDUCATION** Knox Col, BA, 91; Brown Univ, MA; PhD, 01. **CAREER** Instr, Univ RI, 94-95, 01-. **HONORS AND AWARDS** Fel, Brown Univ Grad Res, 96-97; Fel, Javits Found, 91-95; Fel, Ford Found, 90; Phi Beta Kappa, 91. **MEMBERSHIPS** Am Philol Asn. **RESEARCH** Classical rhetoric and literary theory; Greco-Roman philosophic literature; Greek and Latin poetry; Roman comedy; Early Christianity. **SELECTED PUBLICATIONS** Auth, "Phrynichus Fragment 27K-A: A pun," Class Quart, 98. **CONTACT ADDRESS** Dept Classics, Univ of Rhode Island, 83 John St, Providence, RI 02903-1803. **EMAIL** Edward_DeBoo@Brown.edu

DECATUR, LOUIS AUBREY
PERSONAL Born 04/27/1931, Washington, DC, m, 1965, 2 children **DISCIPLINE** RENAISSANCE LITERATURE **EDUCATION** Univ Md, College Park, BA, 54, MA, 63, PhD, 70. **CAREER** Lectr English, Univ Md, Europ Div, 63-65; instr, Univ Md, College Park, 65-68; asst prof, US Naval Acad, 68-70; asst prof, 70-80, assoc prof Eng, Ursinus Col, 80-. **HONORS AND AWARDS** Christian & Mary Lindback Awd for Outstanding Teaching, 78. **MEMBERSHIPS** MLA; AAUP; Renaissance Soc Am. **RESEARCH** Renaissance prose fiction; folklore, prose; Renaissance drama. **SELECTED PUBLICATIONS** Art, West German Shakespeare as Seen by a Teacher Abroad, Shakespeare Quarterly, 82; art, The New Japanese Hamlet, Shakespeare Yearbook IX, 98. **CONTACT ADDRESS** Dept of English, Ursinus Col, PO Box 1000, Collegeville, PA 19426-1000. **EMAIL** ldecatur@ursinus.edu

DECKER, PHILIP H.
PERSONAL Born 04/19/1932, Lakewood, OH, m, 1955, 2 children **DISCIPLINE** SPEECH & DRAMA **EDUCATION** Knox Col, BA, 54; Northwestern Univ, MA, 55, PhD(theatre), 66. **CAREER** From asst prof to assoc prof, 57-71, chemn dept, 66-73, prof speech & theatre arts, MacMurray Col, 71-84-, chemn dept, 76-84; prof of English & Drama, 84-97, chair, dept English & Drama, 88-91, 94-97, prof emer, MacMurray Col, 97-, development officer, 97-. **HONORS AND AWARDS** Northwestern Univ fel, 54-55, 60-61; ISTA Pres Awd for Outstanding Service, 85; MacMurray Col Wilkins Awd for Excellence in Teaching, 86, 91; IL Col Citation in the Arts for distinguished contributions to the Fine Arts, 91; IL State Hist Soc Cert of Excellence for A Window on the Past, 91; Phi Beta Kappa, 94; Dept Honors, 94; listed in: Outstanding Educators of America, 90; Personalities in the Midwest. **MEMBERSHIPS** Speech Commun Asn; Am Educ Theatre Asn; Cent States Speech Asn. **RESEARCH** Dramatic literature, especially 20th century English, American and Elizabethan; theatre history; aesthetics of performance. **SELECTED PUBLICATIONS** Coauth, An Annotated Bibliography of Sources for Period Patterns, Educ Theatre J, 3/62; A Window on the Past: Residences of Jacksonville, IL, Their History and Design, 90. **CONTACT ADDRESS** Dept Theatre Arts, MacMurray Col, 477 E College Ave, Jacksonville, IL 62650-2510. **EMAIL** pdecker@mac.edu

DECKER, WILLIAM
DISCIPLINE 19TH CENTURY AMERICAN LITERATURE **EDUCATION** Iowa, PhD, 84. **CAREER** Engl, Okla St Univ. **RESEARCH** Poetry of Whitman, Dickinson and their contemporaries. **SELECTED PUBLICATIONS** Auth, The Literary Vocation Of Henry Adams, Univ N Carolina Press, 90; Epistolary Practices: Letter Writing In America Before The Era Of Telecommunications, Univ N Carolina Press, 98. **CONTACT ADDRESS** Oklahoma State Univ, Stillwater, 101 Whitehurst Hall, Stillwater, OK 74078.

DEE, JULIET L.
DISCIPLINE COMMUNICATION **EDUCATION** Princeton Univ, AB, 74; Northwestern Univ, MA, 75; Temple Univ, PhD, 81. **CAREER** Asst prof, Rugers Univ, 80-82; vis asst prof, Univ Calif, 82-84; asst prof, 84-92; assoc prof, 92-; dir, Legal Stud prog, 96-. **HONORS AND AWARDS** Awd, Del Hum Forum, 86; grant, 86; ch, fac senate comm on cult act and pub events, 94-95, 97-. **RESEARCH** Communications and law. **SELECTED PUBLICATIONS** Co-auth, Mass Communs Law in a Nutshell, West, 88; To Avoid Charges of Indecency, Please Hang Up Now: An Analysis of Legislation and Litigation Involving Dial-a-Porn, Commun and the Law, 94; Reconciling the Preferences of Environmental Activists and Corporate Policymakers, Jour of Pub Rel Res, 96; News Coverage of Abortion between Roe and Webster: Public Opinion and Real-World Events, Commun Res Rpt, 97; auth, Subliminal Lyrics in Heavy Metal Music: More Litigation, Anyone?, Commun and the Law, 94; Little Red Riding Hood, Justice Rehnquist and the NEA, Free Speech Yrbk, 95; Twins Separated at Birth: The Strange Cases of Michael Levin and Leonard Jeffries, The Howard Jour Commun, 95; Identifying a Victim when the Criminal is at Large: Is It Negligent or Newsworthy?, Commun and the Law, 96; When Classified Ads Lead to Murder: Hitmen, Soldier of Fortune, and the Question of Commercial Speech, Commun and the Law, 96. **CONTACT ADDRESS** Dept of Commun, Univ of Delaware, 162 Ctr Mall, Newark, DE 19716.

DEENA, SEODIAL
PERSONAL Born 08/22/1956, Guyana, m, 1982, 4 children **DISCIPLINE** ENGLISH **EDUCATION** Univ Guyana, BA, 86; Chicago State Univ, MA, 90; Ind Univ Penn, PhD, 96. **CAREER** Instr, Lodge Community High School, 79-86; Instr, Richard Ishmael High School, 86; Instr, United Pentecostal School, 89; Lecturer, Cyril Potter Col of Educ, 87-88; Lecturer, Daley Col, 90; Lecturer, Chicago State Univ, 90-91; Teaching Assoc, Ind Univ of Pa, 92-94; Asst Prof to Assoc Prof, 97-. **HONORS AND AWARDS** Teaching Assoc, Ind Univ of Penn, 92-94; Scholarship, Chicago State Univ, 90; Joyce Adler Literature Prize, Univ Guyana, 86; Lillian Dewar Awd, Univ Guyana, 85; Kappa Delta Pi, 92. **MEMBERSHIPS** Asn for Caribbean Studies, British Commonwealth an d Postcolonial Studies Asn, Col Lang Asn, Indian Soc for commonwealth Studies, Intl conf on Caribbean Literature, Reg and Nat Studies Asn, Mod Lang Asn, Philol Asn of the Carolinas, Kappa Delta Pi. **RESEARCH** Postcolonial, Caribbean, Multicultural, African American, World African, Indian, and biblical literatures; cultural, Post-Marxist, Postcolonial, and feminist Criticism. **SELECTED PUBLICATIONS** Auth, Decolonization of colonial and Canonical Marginalization in the Works of Writers of color, Peter Lang Pub, forthcoming; auth, "Colonization and Canonization: class Marginalization Through Education,": Journal of Caribbean Studies, (00): 229-242; auth, "The Caribbean: colonial and Postcolonial Representations of the Land and the Peoples' Relationships to Their Environment," in Environment and Literature: an International Sourcebook, Fitzroy Dearborn Pub, 98; auth, "Racism and Cultural Imperialism in Conrad's Heart of Darkness," UFAHAMU: Journal of the African Activist Asn, (97): 130-155; auth, "Progression from single-dimensional Incompetence to Multi-dimensional Competence in Wright's Native son and gains' Of Love and dust and A Lesson Before Dying," in working with Students: Proceedings: The 1998 conference of the English Association of the Pennsylvania state Universities, (99): 320-326; auth, "colonization and Canonization: class Marginalization through Education," Seventh International Literature of Region and Nation conference Abstract, (98): 16-17; auth, "an Overview of the Socio-Economic and Political Problems Facing Third World Writers," Univ New Brunswick in Saint John, (98): 341-361; auth, "Derek Walcott," Issues and Identities in Literature, Salem Press, (97): 93-94; auth, "Another Life," issues and Identities in Literature, Salem Press, (97): 962-963; auth, "Language Implications Facing Caribbean Writers," Association of Caribbean Studies 1996 Abstracts, (96): 15. **CONTACT ADDRESS** Dept English, East Carolina Univ, 1000 E 5th st, Greenville, NC 27858-2502. **EMAIL** deenas@mail.ecu.edu

DEERING, RONALD F.
PERSONAL Born 10/06/1929, Ford County, IL, m, 1966, 2 children **DISCIPLINE** HISTORY; NEW TESTAMENT; LIBRARY SCIENCE **EDUCATION** Georgetown Col, BA, 51; MDiv, 55, PhD, 61, Southern Baptist Theological Seminary; Columbia Univ, MSLS, 67. **CAREER** Instr, 58-61, Research Librarian, 61-67; Assoc Librarian, 67-71, Seminary Librarian, 71-95, Assoc VP for Academic Resources, Southern Baptist Theological Seminary. **HONORS AND AWARDS** Lilly Endowment Scholarship in Theological Librarianship **MEMBERSHIPS** Amer Theological Library Assoc; Amer Library Assoc; Kentucky Library Assoc; Soc of Biblical Lit; Southeastern Library Assoc; Church and Synagogue Library Assoc. **RESEARCH** Theological librarianship **CONTACT ADDRESS** So Baptist Theol Sem, 2825 Lexington Rd., Louisville, KY 40280. **EMAIL** rdeering@compuserve.com

DEESE, HELEN R.
DISCIPLINE ENGLISH **EDUCATION** David Lipscomb Coll, BA, 65; Univ Tenn, MA, 67; George Peabody Coll, PhD, 73. **CAREER** Prof, eng, Tenn Tech Univ. **MEMBERSHIPS** Am Antiquarian Soc **SELECTED PUBLICATIONS** Ed & intro, Jones Very: The Complete Poems, 93. **CONTACT ADDRESS** Dept of Eng, Tennessee Tech Univ, Cookeville, TN 38505. **EMAIL** HDeese@tntech.edu

DEETZ, STANLEY A.
PERSONAL Born 03/20/1948, Garrett, IN, s, 3 children **DISCIPLINE** COMMUNCATION STUDIES **EDUCATION** Manchester Col, BS, 70; Univ Ohio, MA, 72, PhD, 73. **CAREER** Asst Prof, Bridgewater State Col, 73-77; Assoc Prof So. Ill Univ, Carbondale, 77-84; Prof Rutgers Univ, 84-97; Prof U Colo, 97-. **HONORS AND AWARDS** Outstanding Res Bk Awd, 94; Fel, Int Comm Assoc; Pres, Int Comm Assoc. **MEMBERSHIPS** Int Comm Assoc; National Comm Assoc. **RESEARCH** Organizational communication. **SELECTED PUBLICATIONS** Auth, Describing differences in approaches to organizational science: Rethinking Burrell and Morgan and their legacy, 96; Transforming communication, transforming business: Building responsive and responsible workplaces, Hampton, 95; Democracy in an age of corporate colonization: Developments in communication and the politics of everyday life, Univ NY, 92; auth, "Leading Organizations through Transition: Communication and Cultural Change," Thousand Oaks, CA: Sage; auth, "Doing Critical Management Research," London: Sage. **CONTACT ADDRESS** Dept of Communication, Univ of Colorado, Boulder, Boulder, CO 80309. **EMAIL** Stanley.Deetz@Colorado.edu

DEFORD, RUTH
PERSONAL Born 12/08/1946, Lawrence, KS, m, 1977, 2 children **DISCIPLINE** MUSIC HISTORY AND LITERATURE **EDUCATION** Harvard Univ, PhD. **CAREER** Prof. **RESEARCH** Music of the Renaissance. **SELECTED PUBLICATIONS** Ed vol(s) mus by, Giovanni Ferretti & Orazio Vecchi; contribur, The New Grove Dictionary of Mus and Musicians & Die Musik in Geschichte und Gegenwart; articles in, Studi musicali, Acta musicol, Mus disciplina, Early Mus Hist & J Musicol; auth, Early Music. **CONTACT ADDRESS** Dept of Music, Hunter Col, CUNY, 695 Park Ave, New York, NY 10021. **EMAIL** rdeford@shiva.hunter.cuny.edu

DEFOREST, MARY MARGOLIES
PERSONAL Born 09/11/1946, Washington, DC, s **DISCIPLINE** CLASSICS **EDUCATION** Holyoke Col, BA, 67; Univ Chicago, MA, 70; Univ Colo Boulder, PhD, 81. **CAREER** Teaching asst, Univ Colo Boulder, 76-81; asst prof, Creighton Col, 81-81; asst prof, Hamilton Col, 82-89; vis asst prof, Univ Iowa, 89-90; lectr, Wayne State Univ, 90-91; vis asst prof, Creighton Univ, 91; lectr, Wayne State Univ, 92; vis asst prof, Univ Colo Boulder, 92-96; vis asst prof, Metropolitan State Col, 96-97; instr, Univ Colo Denver, 00-. **HONORS AND AWARDS** Feminist Essay Prize, Rocky Mountain, MLA, 93; Summer Res Grant, Hamilton Col, 88; Cornelia Coulter Award, Holyoke Col, 67. **MEMBERSHIPS** RMMLA; ACLA. **RESEARCH** Classical literature and the classical tradition. **SELECTED PUBLICATIONS** Auth, "Mary Poppins and the Great Mother," Class and Mod Lit, (91): 139-154; auth, "Eighteenth-Century Women and the Languages of Power," Class and Mod Lit, (92): 191-207; ed, Women's Power, Man's Game: Essays in Honor of Joy King, Wauconda, 93; auth, "Clytemnestra's Breast and the Evil Eye," in Women's Power, Man's Game: Essays in Honor of Joy King, Wauconda, 93; auth, "Female Choruses in Greek Tragedy," Didaskalia, 98. **CONTACT ADDRESS** Dept Class, Univ of Colorado, Denver, 1220 Marion St, Denver, CO 80218. **EMAIL** crypto@ecentral.com

DEKOVEN, MARIANNE
DISCIPLINE ENGLISH LANGUAGE AND LITERATURE **EDUCATION** Radcliffe Univ, BA; Stanford, PhD. **CAREER** Prof. **RESEARCH** Feminist theory and criticism; modernism and postmodernism; cultural history. **SELECTED PUBLICATIONS** Auth, A Different Language: Gertrude Stein's Experimental Writing; auth, Rich and Strange: Gender, History, Modernism. **CONTACT ADDRESS** Dept of English, Rutgers, The State Univ of New Jersey, New Brunswick, 510 George St, Murray Hall, New Brunswick, NJ 08901-1167. **EMAIL** dekoven@rci.rutgers.edu

DELAHOYDE, MICHAEL
PERSONAL Born 07/03/1960, Poughkeepsie, NY, s **DISCIPLINE** ENGLISH **EDUCATION** Vassar Col, BA eng, 83, BA mus, 83; Univ Mich, MA, 85; PhD, 89. **CAREER** Instr, Wash State Univ, 92-. **HONORS AND AWARDS** Dist Train Awd, WSU, 96. **MEMBERSHIPS** Rocky Mtn MLA; MAA; NCS; PCA. **RESEARCH** Chaucer; popular culture; film. **SELECTED PUBLICATIONS** Auth, "Creating Meat Eaters: The Child as Advertising Target," J Pop Cult 28 (94): 159-174; auth, "Medieval Dragons and Dinosaur Films," Pop Cult rev 9 (98): 17-30; auth, " 'Heryng Th'Effect' of The Names in Troilus and Criseyde," Chaucer Rev (forthcoming). **CONTACT ADDRESS** Dept English, Washington State Univ, PO Box 645020, Pullman, WA 99164-5020. **EMAIL** delahoyd@wsu.edu

DELAHUNTY, GERALD
DISCIPLINE ENGLISH LITERATURE **EDUCATION** Univ Dublin, BA, MA; Univ Ca, PhD. **CAREER** Assoc prof. **SELECTED PUBLICATIONS** Auth, pubs on syntactic theory; sociolinguistics; functional grammar; Irish archaeology; co-auth, Communication Language and Grammar, McGraw Hill, 94. **CONTACT ADDRESS** Dept of English, Colorado State Univ, Fort Collins, CO 80523-1773. **EMAIL** gerald.delahunty@colostate.edu

DELANEY, PAUL
PERSONAL Born 08/25/1948, Lexington, KY, m, 1968, 2 children **DISCIPLINE** ENGLISH **EDUCATION** Emory University, PhD, 72. **CAREER** Prof, 72-. **HONORS AND AWARDS** Danforth fel, Emory Univ, 69-72; fac res award, 92. **MEMBERSHIPS** Mem, Nat CCL Bd Dir, 93-96. **RESEARCH** Modern drama; modern poetry; Shakespeare; 19th & 20th cent Am lit; 20th cent Irish lit. **SELECTED PUBLICATIONS** Auth, Tom Stoppard: The Moral Vision of the Major Plays, London: Macmillan Press, New York: St. Martin's Press, 90; Structure and Anarchy in Tom Stoppard, PMLA 106, 91; Tom Stoppard: Craft and Craftiness, PMLA 107, 92; auth, Tom Stoppard in Conversation, Univ Mich Press, 94; auth, Hearing the Other: Voices in U.A. Fanthorpe's Poetry, Christianity and Literature, 46, 97; auth, Brian Friel in Conversation, Univ Mich Press, 00; auth, The Hospital Poetry of U.A. Fanthorpe's in Teaching Ltierature and Medicine New York: Modern Language Association, 00. **CONTACT ADDRESS** Dept of Eng, Westmont Col, 955 La Paz Rd, Santa Barbara, CA 93108-1099. **EMAIL** delaney@westmont.edu

DELANO, STERLING F.
PERSONAL Born 12/28/1942, New Rochelle, NY, m, 1967, 2 children **DISCIPLINE** ENGLISH **EDUCATION** Villanova Univ, BS, 65; Northeastern Univ, MA, 67; Southern Ill Univ, PhD, 74. **CAREER** From Asst Prof to Prof, Villanova Univ, 74-. **HONORS AND AWARDS** NEH Travel Fel, 86, 88; Phi Kappa Phi, 92-93; Fac Summer Fel, Villanova Univ, 85, 95; Lindback Awd for Distinguished Teaching, 96; NEH Fel, 97-98. **MEMBERSHIPS** Thoreau Soc, Emerson Soc, Margaret Fuller Soc, Hawthorne Soc, AAUP. **RESEARCH** New England transcendentalism, 19th Century utopian communities, Brook Farm, Concord writers. **SELECTED PUBLICATIONS** Auth, The Harbinger and New England Transcendentalism: A Portrait of Associationism in America, Fairleigh Dickinson UP (Rutherford, NJ), 83; coauth, "Academic Freedom and Tenure: Wesley College (Delaware)," Academe (92): 24-36; auth, "Brook Farm (1841-47)," Encycl of Transcendentalism (Westport, CT: Greenwood Pr, 96); auth, "George P Bradford's Letters to Ralph Waldo Emerson from Brook Farm," Resources for Am Lit Study 25 (99): 26-45; auth, "The Harbinger (1845-49)," The Am Renaissance, vol 1: Dict of Lit Biog, rev, Gale Res (forthcoming); auth, "Brook Farm," The Am Renaissance, vol 1: Dict of Lit Biog, rev, Gale Res (forthcoming). **CONTACT ADDRESS** Dept English, Villanova Univ, 800 E Lancaster Ave, Villanova, PA 19085-1603. **EMAIL** sterling.delano@villanova.edu

DELANY, PAUL
PERSONAL Born 07/18/1937, Purley, England **DISCIPLINE** ENGLISH **EDUCATION** McGill Univ, BComm, 57; Stanford Univ, AM, 58; Univ Calif Berkeley, MA, 61, PhD, 65. **CAREER** Econ, Int Labour Off Geneva, 58-59; instr, Columbia Univ, 64-66; asst to assoc prof, 66-77, prof Eng, Simon Fraser Univ, 77-; exch prof, Univ Waterloo, 85-86. **HONORS AND AWARDS** Guggenheim fel, 73; Killam res fel, 92-93; vis fel, Corpus Christi Col, Cambridge, 95-96; fel, Royal Soc Lit; fel, Royal Soc Can. **MEMBERSHIPS** MLA; ACUTE; DH Lawrence Soc Am. **RESEARCH** Modern British Literature and Cultural Studies; Literary Theory; Computers and the Humanities; Renaissance and Seventeenth Century British Literature. **SELECTED PUBLICATIONS** Co-ed, Hypermedia and Literary Studies, Cambridge: the MIT Press, (91): 352; co-ed, The Digital Word: Text-based Computing in the Humanities, Cambridge: the MIT Press, 93; ed, In the Year of Jubilee, (94): 399; auth, "Vancouver as a Postmodern City," in Vancouver: Repesenting the Postmodern City, ed. P. Delany, (94): 1-24; co-ed, "Giving Yourself Awar: Lawrence's Letters in Context," in Editing D. H. Lawrence: New Versions of a Modern Author, eds. Dennis Jackson and Charles L. Ross, (95): 173-187; auth, "The Discourse of Computer-Supported Media: Reading and Writing on Usenet," in The Yearbook of English Studies, vol. 25, (95): 213-224; co-ed, "A Would-be-dirty Mind: D.H. Lawrence as an Enemy of Joyce," in Joyce in the Hibernian Metropolis: Essays, eds. Morris Beja and David Norris, (Columbus: Ohio State Univ Press, 96): 76-82; co-ed, "A Secret Riches: Universal and Particular Feminism in The Rainbow," in D.H. Lawrence: The Cosmic Adventure, eds. L. Gamache and I. MacNiven, (Ottawa: Borealis Press, 96): 106-122; auth, "Gissing in Prison," The Gissing Journal 32, no. 4, (96): 11-13; auth, "Tailors of Malt, Hot, All Round: Homosocial Consumption in Dubliners," Studies in Short Fiction, vol. 32, no. 3, (95): 381-393. **CONTACT ADDRESS** Dept of English, Simon Fraser Univ, 8888 Univ Dr, Burnaby, BC, Canada V5A 1S6. **EMAIL** delany@sfu.ca

DELANY, SHEILA
PERSONAL Born New Haven, CT **DISCIPLINE** ENGLISH **EDUCATION** Wellesley Col, BA, 61; Univ Calif Berkley, MA, 63; Columbia Univ, PhD, 67. **CAREER** Queen's Col, City Univ NY, 67-69; prof, Simon Fraser Univ, 70-. **HONORS AND AWARDS** Woodrow Wilson fel, 61-62; Fiction Awd, Berkley, 63; Killam Res fel, 93-95. **MEMBERSHIPS** MLA; Medieval Academy Am; New Chaucer Soc; Can Col Univ Tchrs Eng; Hagiography Soc; Soc of Canadian Medievalists. **SELECTED PUBLICATIONS** Auth, Counter-Tradition, The Literature of Dissent and Alternatives, Basic Books, 70; auth, Chauncer's House of Fame, The Poetics of Skeptical Fideism, Univ of Chicago Press, 72; auth, Writing Women, Women Writers and Women in Literature, Medieval to Modern, Schocken, 83; auth, Medieval Literary Politics, Shapes of Ideology, Manchester Univ Press and St. Martin's Press, 90; auth, Telling Hours and other journal stories, Vancouver; New Star, 91; auth, A Legend of Holy Women, Univ of Notre Dame Press, 92; auth, The Naked Text, Chaucer's Legend of Good Women, Univ of Calif Press, 94; auth, Impolitic Bodies, Poetry, Saints and Society in Fifteenth Century England, Oxford Univ Press, 98; auth, Turn it and turn it again: Medieval Jewish studies and literary theory, Exemplaria 12, 00; auth, Chaucer and the Jews: Sources, contexts, meanings. **CONTACT ADDRESS** Dept of English, Simon Fraser Univ, Burnaby, BC, Canada V5A 1S6. **EMAIL** sdelany@sfu.ca

DELASANTA, RODNEY
PERSONAL Born 11/06/1932, Winchendon, MA, m, 1953, 4 children **DISCIPLINE** ENGLISH LITERATURE **EDUCATION** Providence Col, AB, 53; Brown Univ, AM, 55, PhD, 62. **CAREER** Teaching asst, Brown Univ, 55-57, instr English, 57-61; from asst prof to assoc prof, 61-70 Prof English Literature, Providence Col, 70-; Vis prof English literature, Univ Fribourg, 68-70; Univ Neuchatel, 69-70; Vis prof, Brown Univ, 83. **HONORS AND AWARDS** Sears Roebuck Prize, Distinguished Teaching, 91. **MEMBERSHIPS** MLA; Medieval Acad Am; New Chaucer Soc. **RESEARCH** English medieval and Renaissance literature. **SELECTED PUBLICATIONS** Auth, The Epic Voice, Mouton, 67; Christian affirmation in the Book of the Duchess, PMLA, 1/69; The theme of judgment in the Canterbury Tales, Mod Lang Quart, 9/70; And of great reverence: Chaucer's Man of Law, Chaucer Rev, spring 71; Sacrament and sacrifice in the Pardoner's Tale, Ann Mediaevale, 73; Penance and poetry in the Canterbury Tales, PMLA, 3/78; Alisoun and the saved harlots: A Cozening of our expectations, Chaucer Rev, spring 78; Chaucer and the problem of universals, Medievalia, 82; Chaucer and Strode, Chaucer Rev, 91; Nominalism and typology in Chaucer, in Typology and English Medieval Literature, AMS Press, 92; co-auth, Chaucer's Orygnes Upon the Maudeleyne: A Translation, Chaucer Rev, 96; Nominalism and the Clerk's Tale Revisited, Chaucer Rev, 97. **CONTACT ADDRESS** Dept of English, Providence Col, 549 River Ave, Providence, RI 02918-0002. **EMAIL** delasant@providence.edu

DELAURA, DAVID JOSEPH
PERSONAL Born 11/19/1930, Worcester, MA, m, 1961, 3 children **DISCIPLINE** ENGLISH LITERATURE **EDUCATION** Boston Col, AB, 55, AM, 58; Univ Wis, PhD, 60 **CAREER** From instr to prof English, Univ Tex, Austin, 60-74; Avalon Found Prof Humanities & Prof English, Univ PA, 74-99, Guggenheim Found fel, 67-68; Nat Endowment for Humanities fel, 78-79. **HONORS AND AWARDS** First William Riley Parker Prize of the Mod Lang Asn, Outstanding Article, PMLA, 64. **MEMBERSHIPS** MLA **RESEARCH** Nineteeth and 20th century English literature. **SELECTED PUBLICATIONS** Auth, Arnold and Carlyle, PMLA, 3/64; The place of the classics in T S Eliot's Christian humanism, In: Hereditas: Seven Essays on the Modern Experience of the Classical, Univ Tex, 64; The ache of modernism in Hardy's later novels, ELH, 9/67; Hebrew and Hellene in Victorian England: Newman, Arnold, and Pater, Univ Tex, 69; ed, Victorian prose: a guide to research, MLA, 73; The context of Browning's painter poems: Asthetics, polemics and historics, PMLA, 5/80; Arnold and Goethe: The one on the intellectual throne, In: Victorian Literature and Society, Ohio State Univ, 84; Ruskin, Arnold and Browning's Grammarian: Crowded with culture, In: Victorian Perspectives, Macmillan, 89. **CONTACT ADDRESS** Dept of English, Univ of Pennsylvania, 3340 Walnut St, Philadelphia, PA 19104-6273. **EMAIL** ddelaura@sprynet.com

DELBANCO, ANDREW
PERSONAL Born 02/20/1952, White Plains, NY, m, 1973, 2 children **DISCIPLINE** AMERICAN LITERATURE **EDUCATION** Harvard Univ, AB, 73; AM 76; PhD, 80. **CAREER** Julian Clarence Levi prof, 95-. **HONORS AND AWARDS** Grants, Guggenheim found; NEH, NH Ctr; NYPL Center for scholars, Lionel Trilling award. **SELECTED PUBLICATIONS** Auth, William Ellery Channing, 81; coed, The Puritans in America, 85; auth, The Puritan Ordeal, 89; ed, The Portable Abraham Lincoln, 92; The Death of Satan: How Americans Have Lost the Sense of Evil, Farrar, Straus, and Giroux, 95; Required Reading: Why Our American Classics Matter Now, 97; auth, The Real American Dream, Harvard, 99; contrib, The New Repulic & New York Review of Books. **CONTACT ADDRESS** Dept of Eng, Columbia Univ, 2960 Broadway, New York, NY 10027-6902.

DELL, CHAD E.
PERSONAL Born 10/25/1956, Boston, MA **DISCIPLINE** COMMUNICATION ARTS **EDUCATION** Univ of Wis at Madison, BA, 87, MA, 91, PhD, 97. **CAREER** Asst prof, Dept of Commun, Monmouth Univ, 96-. **HONORS AND AWARDS** Award for Outstanding Teaching by a Grad Student, 92-93. **MEMBERSHIPS** Am Studies Asn; Asn for Ed in Journalism and Mass Commun; Int Commun Asn; Nat Commun Asn; NJ Commun Asn; Soc for Cinema Studies; Union for Democratic Commun. **RESEARCH** Media audiences and fandom **SELECTED PUBLICATIONS** Auth, Lookit That Hunk of Man!: Subversive Pleasures, Female Fandom and Professional Wrestling, Theorizing Fandom: Fans, Subculture and Identity, Hampton, 98; coauth, Big Differences on the Small Screen: Race, Class, Gender, Feminine Beauty and the Characters at Frank's Place, Women Making Meaning: New Feminist Directions in Commun, Routledge, 92. **CONTACT ADDRESS** Communication Dept, Monmouth Univ, 400 Cedar Ave, West Long Branch, NJ 07764-1898. **EMAIL** cdell@mondec.monmouth.edu

DELL' ANTONIO, ANDREW
PERSONAL Born 06/08/1963, Naples, Italy **DISCIPLINE** MUSIC HISTORY **EDUCATION** Univ CA at Berkeley, PhD. **CAREER** Asst prof, Univ of TX at Austin. **HONORS AND AWARDS** Int prize for Musicol scholar. **MEMBERSHIPS** AMS, SSCM, RSA. **RESEARCH** Musical historiography; feminist/queer theory; cultural studies. **SELECTED PUBLICATIONS** Auth, doctoral dissertation on the early sonata, Libreria Musicale Italiana; publ, in Cambridge Opera J, Notes, repercussions & Il saggiatore musicale; contrib to New Grove & Die Musik in Geschichte und Gegenwart; co-ed, archive of dissertation abstracts in Musicol on the WWW. **CONTACT ADDRESS** School of Music, Univ of Texas, Austin, Austin, TX 78712. **EMAIL** dellantonio@mail.utexas.edu

DELLEPIANE, ANGELA B.
PERSONAL Born 05/13/1926, Rio Cuarto, Argentina, m, 1962 **DISCIPLINE** SPANISH AMERICAN LITERATURE **EDUCATION** Univ Buenos Aires, MA, 48, PhD, 52. **CAREER** Prof Latin, Teacher's Col, Buenos Aires, 48-57; asst prof Span lit, Fordham Univ, 61-63; from asst prof to assoc prof philol, phonetics & Span lit, 63-72, Prof Span Am Lit, City Col New York, 73-; Prof emer, Prof Span Am Lit, Grad Ctr, City Univ New York, 69-. **HONORS AND AWARDS** Consult & panelist, Fel Div, Nat Endowment for Humanities, 77-79; vis prof, Univ Ky, 78. **MEMBERSHIPS** Int Inst Ibero-Am Lit; Asn Int de Hispanistas; Am Asn Teachers Span & Port; Latin Am Studies Asn. **RESEARCH** Spanish American narrative; Gauchesca literature; structural stylistics. **SELECTED PUBLICATIONS** Auth, A Tribute to Earle, Peter,G., Hisp Rev, Vol 0061, 93. **CONTACT ADDRESS** Span Doctoral Frog Grad Ctr, Graduate Sch and Univ Ctr, CUNY, 33 W 42nd St, New York, NY 10016-4309.

DELLER, DAVID C.
PERSONAL Born 09/20/1956, Tulsa, OK, s **DISCIPLINE** ENGLISH **EDUCATION** Stanford Univ, BA, 79; San Francisco State Univ, MA, 86; Calif State Univ Los Angeles, MA, 93; Univ Ark, PhD, 99. **CAREER** Instr, ALC, Rabbat, Morocco, 90-91; instr, Los Angeles Comm Col, 91-94; grad instr, Univ Ark, 94-99; instr, Tulsa Comm Col, 99-00; lectr, Sultan Qzboos Univ, Oman, 00-. **HONORS AND AWARDS** Vance Randolph and Mary Celesha Parler Randolph Fel, 96. **MEMBERSHIPS** MLA. **RESEARCH** American folk and popular music; American drama; world literature; American film. **SELECTED PUBLICATIONS** Auth, "E. M. Bartlett and the Hartford Music Company: Gospel Music," Ark Hist Quart; auth, "Living Tradition: The Jeffress Music Company," Midwestern Folk Quart; auth, "Albert Brumley: Songbook Gospel Superstar," Country Music. **CONTACT ADDRESS** 2004 E 13th St, Tulsa, OK 74104-4402. **EMAIL** dcdeller@hotmail.com

DELOMBARD, JEANINE
DISCIPLINE EARLY AMERICAN LITERATURE **EDUCATION** Vassar Col, BA, 89; Yale Univ, MA, 91; Univ Pa, MA, 92; PhD, 98. **CAREER** Vis lectr, Univ of Pa, 97-98; asst prof, Univ of Puget Sound, 98-. **HONORS AND AWARDS** Phi Beta Kappa, 89; Margaret C. Peabody Fel, 89; Title VI Foreign Lang Fel, Yale, 89-90, 90-91; William Penn Fel, 92-96; Mellon Found Fel, 96-97; Charles Meredith Journalism Fel, 96, 97; Wyatt Humanties Fel, 98; Fac Res Fel, Univ of Puget Sound, 99; Res Fel, Libr Co of Philadelphia, 99. **MEMBERSHIPS** MLA; Am Studies Assoc; Harriet Beecher Stowe Soc; Phi Beta Kappa Soc; Delta of Wash. **RESEARCH** Auth, "Sisters, Servants or Saviors? African-American Baptist Women Missionaries in Liberia in the 1920s", Int J of Afr Hist Studies 23.2 (91): 323-47; auth, "Mzee's New Clothes: Neo-Colonial Detention as a Spectacle of Invisibility", Ngugi wa Thiong'o: Texts and Contexts, ed Charles Cantalupo, Africa World Pr, (Trenton, 95): 49-60; auth, "Feminism", To Be Real: Telling the Truth and Changing the Face of Feminism, ed Rebecca Walker, Anchor-Doubleday, (NY, 95): 21-33; auth, "Who Cares? Lesbian Caregivers", Dyke Life: From Growing Up to Growing Old - A Celebration of the Lesbian Experience, ed Karla Jay, HarperCollins, (NY, 95): 344-361; auth, "Postcolonial East African Literature: Towards a Literature of the People, for the People and by the People", English Postcoloniality: Literature from Around the World, eds Gita Rajan and Radhika Mohanram, Greenwood Pr, (Westport, 96): 63-76; auth, "Charles Ball", "Broteer Venture (Venture Smith)", "Aaron Douglas", American National Biography, ed John A Garraty, Oxford Univ Pr, 98; auth, "Getting (The) Man Off (Our) Eyeball: White Critical Discourse and African-American Literature", Minn Rev 52.3 (99); auth, "Representing the Slave: White Advocacy and Black Testimony in Harriet Beecher Stowe's Dred", Am Quarterly (forthcoming); auth, "Of Eyeballs, Transparent and Burst: Witnessing Southern Violence in Frederick Douglass' 1845 Narrative, Am Lit (forthcoming). **CONTACT ADDRESS** Dept English, Univ of Puget Sound, 1500 N Warner St, Tacoma, WA 98416-0001. **EMAIL** jdelombard@ups.edu

DELOUGHREY, ELIZABETH M.
DISCIPLINE ENGLISH **EDUCATION** Boston Col, BA, 89; York Univ, MA, 92; Univ Waikato, DPhil Cert, 98; Univ Md, PhD, 99. **CAREER** Asst prof, Cornell Univ, 99-. **HONORS AND AWARDS** Fulbright Fel, 97-98; Cornell Soc of Fel, 01. **MEMBERSHIPS** MLA. **RESEARCH** Postcolonial, Pacific and Caribbean literature **SELECTED PUBLICATIONS** Auth, "The Spiral Temporalities of Patricia Grace's Potiki," Ariel, (98); auth, "Tidalectics: Charting Caribbean Peoples of the Sea," SPAN: Jour of the S Pac Assoc, (98); auth, "Gendering the Voyage: Trespassing the (Black) Atlantic and Caribbean," Thamyris, (98); auth, "Towards a Post-Native Aiga: Albert Wendt's Black Rainbow," Indigeneity: Construction and Re/Presentations, (99); auth, "The Caribbean Sea as a Regionalist Metaphor," Jour of Caribbean Lit, (01); auth, "White Fathers, Brown Daughters," Literature and Racial Ambiguity: Rodpi Perspectives on Mod Lit, (01); auth, "The litany of islands, The Rosary of archipelagoes," Ariel, (01). **CONTACT ADDRESS** Dept English, Cornell Univ, Ithaca, NY 14850. **EMAIL** emd23@cornell.edu

DEMARIA, ROBERT, JR.
PERSONAL Born 11/30/1948, New York, NY, m, 1977, 2 children **DISCIPLINE** ENGLISH **EDUCATION** Amherst College, BA, 70; Rutgers Univ, PhD, 75. **CAREER** Asst, Assoc, Prof, Henry Noble MacCracken Prof, 75-, Vassar College. **HONORS AND AWARDS** Guggenheim Fel; CASBS Fel. **MEMBERSHIPS** MLA; ALSC; ASECS; Samuel Johnson Soc.; Editorial Board, The age of Johnson; Yale edition of the works of Samuel Johnson, Johnsonian News Letter. **RESEARCH** 18th Cent British Literature; History of English. **SELECTED PUBLICATIONS** Auth, British Literature: A Critical Reader, Oxford, Blackwell, 99; auth, Samuel Johnson and the Life of Reading, Baltimore, JHU Press, 97; British Literature 1640-1789: An Anthology, Oxford, Blackwell, 96; auth, The Life of Samuel Johnson, Oxford, Blackwell, 93; auth, Johnson's Dictionary and the Language of Leaining, Chapel Hill and Oxford: Univ of NC and the Clarendon Press, 86; Johnson's Dictionary and Dictionary Johnson, Yearbook of Eng Studies, 98; auth, Gulliver's Travels, London: Penguin Books , 01; auth, British Literatture 1640-1789: An Anthology, Oxford, Blackwell, 2nd ed, 01. **CONTACT ADDRESS** Vassar Col, Box 140, Poughkeepsie, NY 12604. **EMAIL** demaria@vassar.edu

DEMARR, MARY JEAN
PERSONAL Born 09/20/1932, Champaign, IL **DISCIPLINE** ENGLISH, WOMEN'S STUDIES **EDUCATION** Lawrence Col, BA, 54; Univ Ill, Urbana, AM, 57, PhD(English), 63. **CAREER** Asst prof English, Willamette Univ, 64-65; from asst prof to assoc prof, 65-75, prof english and Women's studies, Ind State Univ, Terre Haute, 75-95, prof emeritus, 95-. **HONORS AND AWARDS** Phi Beta Kappa; Phi Kappa Phi; George N. Dove Award for "Outstanding Contribution to the Serious Study of Mystery and Crime Fiction," 95; MidAmerica Award for "Distinguished Contributions to the Study of Midwestern Literature," 00. **MEMBERSHIPS** MLA; Mod Humanities Res Asn; NCTE; AAUP; Popular Cult Asn. **RESEARCH** American literature; women's studies. **SELECTED PUBLICATIONS** Contributor and ed; Annual Bibliography of English Language and Literature, Modern Humanities Research Asn (Leeds, England), 66-69, 70-73; 74-92; coauth, The Adolescent in the American Novel Since 1960, Frederick Ungar Publishing Co (NYork), 86; auth, "Chopin,Kate Reconsidered--Beyond the Bayou," Jour Pop Cult (94); auth, "The Darkness of the Women': Two Short Stories by Ruth Suckow," MidAmerica XXI (94): 112-121; ed, In the Beginning: First Novels in Mystery Series, Popular Press (Bowling Green, OH), 95; auth, "Clifford D. Simak's Use of the Midwest in Science Fiction," MidAmerica XXII (95): 108-121; auth, Colleen McCullough: A Critical Companion, Greenwood Press (Westport, CT), 96; auth, "True-Crime Books: Socio/Psycho-Babble or Socially Redeeming Voyeurism?" Clues (96): 1-18; auth, Barbara Kingsolver: A Critical Companion, Greenwood Press (Westport, CT), 99; auth, "Dana Stabenow's Alaska Mysteries," Diversity and Detective Fiction, ed. Kathleen Gregory Klein (Bowling Green, OH, Popular Press, 99), 115-129. **CONTACT ADDRESS** Dept of English, Indiana State Univ, Terre Haute, IN 47809. **EMAIL** mjd594@msn.com

DEMASTES, WILLIAM
DISCIPLINE MODERN DRAMA, AMERICAN LITERATURE, SHAKESPEARE **EDUCATION** Wis, PhD, 86. **CAREER** Prof, La State Univ; dir, MA in Hum prog, 96-, dir, grad stud, 92-94, dir, LSU in London, 95, ser ed, Mod Dramatists Res and Prod Sourcebooks. **RESEARCH** Modern dramatists. **SELECTED PUBLICATIONS** Auth, The Future of Avant-Garde Drama and Criticism: The Case of Sam Shepard, J of Dramatic Theory and Criticism, 90; Of Sciences and the Arts: From Influence to Interplay Between Natural Philosophy and Drama, Stud in the Lit Imagination, 91; Clifford Odets, 91; 'We Gotta Hang Together': Horovitz and the National Cycles of Violence, Israel Horovitz, 94; Re-Inspecting the Crack in the Chimney: Chaos Theory From Ibsen to Stoppard, New Theatre Quart, 94; Jessie and Thelma Revisited: Marsha Norman's Conceptual Challenge in 'night, Mother, Mod Drama, 94; Arthur Miller's Use and Modification of the American Realist/Naturalist Tradition, in Approaches to Teaching Arthur Miller's Death of a Salesman, 95; Theatre of Chaos, 97; ed, American Playwrights, 1880-1945, 94; British Playwrights, 1956-1995, 96; Realism and the American Dramatic Tradition, 96; coed, British Playwrights, 1880-1956, 96; Irish Playwrights, 1880-1995, 97. **CONTACT ADDRESS** Dept of Eng, Louisiana State Univ and A&M Col, 244 Hodges Hall, Baton Rouge, LA 70803.

DEMING, ROBERT HOWARD
PERSONAL Born 10/12/1937, Hartford, CT, m, 1962, 3 children **DISCIPLINE** ENGLISH **EDUCATION** Union Col, BA, 59; Univ KS, MA, 61, Univ Wis, PhD, 65. **CAREER** Asst prof Eng, Miami Univ, 65-70; assoc prof, 70-72, prof eng, State Univ NY Col Fredonia, 72, ch person, 75-81, 97-00; Prof Emeritus, 01. **RESEARCH** Film study; non-fiction film; cult studies; feminism; TV studies. **SELECTED PUBLICATIONS** Auth, A Bibliography of James Joyce Studies, Univ Kans Libr, 64, 65, rev ed, 77; ed, Joyce: The Critical Heritage, Routledge & Kegan Paul, 70; auth, Ceremony and Art: Robert Herrick's Poetry, Mouton, Hague, 74; Love and knowledge in the Renaissance lyric, Tex Studies Lang & Lit, 74. **CONTACT ADDRESS** Dept of English, SUNY, Col at Fredonia, 1 Suny at Fredonia, Fredonia, NY 14063. **EMAIL** deming@fredonia.edu

DENDINGER, LLOYD N.
PERSONAL Born 07/28/1929, New Orleans, LA, m, 1951, 3 children **DISCIPLINE** ENGLISH **EDUCATION** Tulane Univ, BA, 53; Vanderbilt Univ, MA, 61; La State Univ, PhD(-English), 66. **CAREER** Instr English, Nicholls State Col, 61-64 & La State Univ, 64-66; from asst prof to assoc prof, 66-76, prof English & chmn dept, Univ S Ala, 76-85. **HONORS AND AWARDS** NEH Scholar, Princeton, Summer 76; Univ S Ala Alum Assn Prof of the Year. **MEMBERSHIPS** MLA; S Atlantic Mod Lang Asn. **SELECTED PUBLICATIONS** Auth, The Irrational Appeal of Frost's Dark Deep Woods, Southern Rev, Fall 66; Crane's Inverted Use of Images of The Rime of the Ancient Mariner, Studies Short Fiction, Winter 68; Robert Frost: The Popular and Central Poetic Images, Am Quart, Winter 69; Robert Frost in Birmingham, Ball State Forum X1V, Summer 73; The Ghoul-Haunted Woodland of Robert Frost, S Atlantic Bull, 11/73; Emerson's Influence on Frost Through William Dean Howells, In: Frost: Centennial Essays, Univ Press of Miss, 74; ed, E E Cummings: The Critical Reception, Burt Franklin, 81. **CONTACT ADDRESS** Dept of English, Univ of So Alabama, 307 University Bvd N, Mobile, AL 36688-3053. **EMAIL** ldending@jaguarl.usouthal.edu

DENEEF, LEIGH A.
DISCIPLINE ENGLISH LITERATURE **EDUCATION** PA State Univ, PhD, 69. **CAREER** Assoc prof, Duke Univ. **RESEARCH** Psychoanalytical approaches to lit. **SELECTED PUBLICATIONS** Auth, This Poetick Liturgie: Robert Herrick's Ceremonial Mode, Duke, 74; Spenser and the Motives of Metaphor, Duke, 82; Traherne in Dialogue: Heidegger, Lacan, and Derrida, Duke, 88. **CONTACT ADDRESS** Eng Dept, Duke Univ, 127 Allen Bldg, Durham, NC 27708. **EMAIL** idn@acpub.duke.edu

DENNISON, CORLEY F.
PERSONAL Born 12/06/1953, Sutton, WV, m, 1978, 3 children **DISCIPLINE** JOURNALISM **EDUCATION** James Madison Univ, Ba, 76; Northwest Mo State Univ, MA, 85; West Va Univ, EdD, 92. **CAREER** Commercial broadcasting, 76-80; KXCV, Northwest Mo State Univ, 80-85; prof, Marshall Univ, 85-. **HONORS AND AWARDS** Presidential Service Awd, 99. **MEMBERSHIPS** BEA, Popular culture Asn, Asn of Deans and Directors of Univ Col. **RESEARCH** Radio history, Digital broadcasting. **SELECTED PUBLICATIONS** co-auth, "A History of Mass of Mass Media," Journal of Radio Studies. **CONTACT ADDRESS** Dept Journalism, Marshall Univ, 400 Hal Greer Blvd, Huntington, WV 25755-0001. **EMAIL** dennisoc@marshall.edu

DENNISTON, DOROTHY L.
PERSONAL Born 08/10/1944, Springfield, MA, d **DISCIPLINE** ENGLISH **EDUCATION** Northeastern Univ, BA 1967; Simmons College, MA 1975; Brown Univ, PhD 1983. **CAREER** Secondary Schools, teacher of English, 67-71; Simmons Coll, asst to dir of admiss, 71-72, instr of English, 72-74, assoc dean, 74-76, 79-80; Univ of TN, asst prof of English, 83-86; Brown Univ, vstg prof English, 87-88, asst prof, 88-94, assoc prof, 94-. **HONORS AND AWARDS** Omega Psi Phi

Fraternity Scholarship Boston Chptr 1962; J Rosen Scholarship Awd Boston Chptr NE Univ 1965; Fellow Natl Fellowship Fund 1976-79; Brown University, Dorothy Danforth Compton Fellowship, 1981-82, Howard Post-doctoral Fellowship, 1986-87, Wriston Fellowship for Excellence in Teaching, 1990; University of TN, Faculty Rsch Awd, 1985, Faculty Rsch Awd Dept of English, 1984; Ford Foundation, Summer Seminar for Coll Professors, Fellow, 1993. **MEMBERSHIPS** Nat Assoc Foreign Student Affairs, 1972; Assoc for Study of Negro Life & History, 1972-; Modern Lang Assn, 1975-; Alpha Kappa Alpha Sorority, 1963-67; adv com for scholars-internship prog Martin L King Jr Cntr for Social Change, 1976-; Natl Assoc of Interdisciplinary Ethnic Studies 1977-; standing comm on black studies Coll Lang Assoc 1983-86; SE Lang Assoc, 1984-86; Langston Hughes Center for the Arts, 1988-; NE Lang Association 1991-; college bd, English Composition Test Committee 1984-87; Coll Language Assn, 1984-. **SELECTED PUBLICATIONS** Auth, The Fiction of Paule Marshall: History, Culture & Gender, Univ Tenn Press, 1995; "Paule Marshall," American Women Writers from Colonial Times to Present, 1980, updated 1992; assoc ed, Langston Hughes Review; assoc ed, Abafazi: The Simmons College Review of Women of African Descent; "Paule Marshall," Black Women in America: An Historical Encyclopedia, 1992; Early Short Fiction by Paule Marshall, Short Story Criticism, 1990; Faulkner's Image of Blacks in Go Down Moses, Phylon, March, 1983. **CONTACT ADDRESS** Brown Univ, Box 1852, Providence, RI 02912.

DENNISTON, ELLIOTT AVERETT
PERSONAL Born 06/08/1940, Philadelphia, PA, m, 1966, 2 children **DISCIPLINE** ENGLISH **EDUCATION** Princeton Univ, BA, 62; Univ Mich, Ann Arbor, MA, 67, PhD, 70. **CAREER** Asst prof English Ky Wesleyan Col, 70-74; Prof English, MO Southern State Col, 74-, Ed, Green River Rev, 73-75. **RESEARCH** Ben Jonson; English Renaissance drama; British drama. **CONTACT ADDRESS** Dept of English, Missouri So State Col, 3950 Newman Rd, Joplin, MO 64801-1512.

DENT, GINA
DISCIPLINE AFRICAN DIASPORIC LITERATURE **EDUCATION** Univ Calif, BA, 89; Columbia, PhD, 97. **CAREER** English and Lit, Columbia Univ **SELECTED PUBLICATIONS** Ed, Black Popular Culture, 92. **CONTACT ADDRESS** Columbia Univ, 2960 Broadway, New York, NY 10027-6902.

DEPAS-ORANGE, ANN
PERSONAL Born 09/29/1949, Tuskegee, AL, m, 1971, 1 child **DISCIPLINE** ENGLISH **EDUCATION** Tuskegee Inst, BA, 71; M Ed, 77; Auburn Univ EdD, 99. **CAREER** Instr, S Vocational Col, 77-79; instru, Tuskegee Univ, 82-89; asst prof, Auburn Univ Montgomery, 90-. **HONORS AND AWARDS** Bush Found Fac Develop Awd, 79-80; Scholar, Ala Pub Libr Ser, Nat Issues Forums, 90-92, 93-94; Outstanding Graduate Awd, Auburn Univ, 99. **MEMBERSHIPS** Nat Coun of Col Teachers of English; Nat Col Learning Center Assoc; Assembly on Expanded Perspectives for Learning; Assoc for Bus Commun. **RESEARCH** Renaissance Poets, Male/Female Dialogue Poems in the Age of Shakespeare, Studies in Composition, Business/ Technical Writing. **SELECTED PUBLICATIONS** Auth, "The Communication Square: Audience, Purpose, Message" and "Personal Writings", Sunsource VI, (Auburn: Sun Belt Writing Project, 86): 145-149, 75-81; auth, "Notes on Thomas Hassall's Funeral Sermon on Martha Moulsworth", The Muses Females Are - Martha Moulsworth and Other Women Writers of the English Renaissance, (CT: Locust Hill Pr, 95); 243-261; auth, "Preface", Moulsworth's Life and Times", and "Notes and Commentary", in The Birthday of My Self: Martha Moulsworth, Renaissance Poet, Critical Matrix: the Princeton Jof Women, Gender and Culture (96): 2-10, 15-18; coed, The Birthday of My Self: Martha Moulsworth, Renaissance Poet, Critical Matrix: The Princeton Jof Women, Gender and Culture, (Princeton, NJ), 96. **CONTACT ADDRESS** Dept English and Philos, Auburn Univ, Montgomery, PO Box 244023, Montgomery, AL 36124-4023. **EMAIL** adepas-orange@mickey.aum.edu

DEPORTE, MICHAEL V.
PERSONAL Born 04/24/1939, Albany, NY, m, 1992, 2 children **DISCIPLINE** ENGLISH **EDUCATION** Univ Minn, BA, 60; Stanford Univ, MA, 64; PhD, 66. **CAREER** Instructor to Asst Prof, Univ Chicago, 65-66; Visiting Asst Prof, Stanford Univ, 72; Asst Prof to Prof, Univ NHamp, 72-. **HONORS AND AWARDS** Woodrow Wilson Fel, 60; Stanford Dissertation Fel, 63; Stanford Travel Grant, 63; Res Grant, Univ Chicago, 68; Lindberg Awd, Univ NH, 86. **MEMBERSHIPS** Mod Lang Asn, Am Soc for Eighteenth-Century Studies, Eighteenth-Century Ireland Soc, Friends of the Ehrenpreis Center for Swift Studies. **RESEARCH** Restoration and eighteenth-century literature; Psychology and literature; James Joyce; The European novel. **SELECTED PUBLICATIONS** Auth, "Introduction to 'Philip Harth's Iswift and Anglican Rationalism: A Retrospective and Evaluation'," Swift Studies, 99; auth, "Contemplating Collins: Freethinking in Swift," in The Third Munster Symposium Papers, Wilhelm Fink Verlag, 98; auth, "Vium Daemonum: Swift and the Grape," Swift Studies, 97; auth, "Novelizing the Travels: Simon Moore's Gulliver," Swift Studies, 97; auth, "Swift, God, and Power," in Walking Naboth's Vineyard, Notre Dame Univ Press, 95; co-ed, Approaches to Teaching Gulliver's Travels, Mod Lang Asn of Am 88; ed, Marius D'Assigny, The Art of Memory, AMS Press, 85; ed, James Carkesse, Lucida Intervalla, Augustan Reprint Soc, 79; ed, Thomas Tryon, A Discourse on Madness, Augustan Reprint Soc, 72; ed, Henry More, Enthusiasmus Triumphatus, Augustan Reprint Soc, 66; auth, Nightmares and Hobbyhorses: Swift, Sterne, and Augustan Ideas of Madness, Huntington Library, 74. **CONTACT ADDRESS** Dept English, Univ of New Hampshire, Durham, Durham, NH 03824. **EMAIL** mdeporte@christa.unh.edu

DEPROSPO, RICHARD CHRIS
PERSONAL Born 02/06/1949, Glen Cove, NY **DISCIPLINE** AMERICAN LITERATURE **EDUCATION** Yale Univ, BA, 71; Univ Va, PhD(Am lit), 77. **CAREER** Asst Prof English, Washington Col, 75-. **MEMBERSHIPS** MLA. **RESEARCH** Eighteenth-and 19th-century American literature. **SELECTED PUBLICATIONS** Auth, Nature and Spirit in the Writings of Jonathan Edwards, Univ Va Libr, 77; The New Simple Idea of Edwards' personal narrative, Early Am Lit, 79. **CONTACT ADDRESS** Washington Col, 300 Washington Ave, Chestertown, MD 21620-1197.

DERESIEWICZ, WILLIAM
PERSONAL Born 01/13/1964, Englewood, NJ, m **DISCIPLINE** ENGLISH LITERATURE **EDUCATION** Columbia Univ, BA, 85, MS, 87, MA, 90, MPhil, 93, PhD, 98. **CAREER** Asst prof, 98-, Yale Univ. **RESEARCH** 19th & early 20th century Brit fict. **CONTACT ADDRESS** 15 N Bank St, New Haven, CT 06511. **EMAIL** wd38@pantheon.yale.edu

DERITTER, JONES
DISCIPLINE ENGLISH **EDUCATION** Oberlin Col, AB, 77; Univ VA, MA, 80, PhD, 88. **CAREER** Asst to assoc prof, Univ Scranton, 90-; vis asst prof, Skidmore Col, 89-90 & New Col, Univ S FL, 88-89; grad instr to instr, Univ VA, 81-88. **MEMBERSHIPS** MLA; Am Soc 18th-century Stud; Gp Early Mod Cult Stud. **RESEARCH** A collective biog of sev early mod women Pocahontas, Mary Jemison and Frances Slocum; who moved across the cult divide between Anglo-Am and native Am soc. **SELECTED PUBLICATIONS** Auth, Wonder not, princely Gloster, at the notice this paper brings you': Women, Writing, and Politics in Rowe's Jane Shore, Comp Drama 37, 97; Blaming the Audience, Blaming the Gods: Unwitting Incest in Three Eighteenth-century English Novels, Illicit Sex: Identity Politics in Early Modern Culture Athens, Univ GA Press, 96; The Embodiment of Characters: The Representation of Physical Experience on Stage and In Print, Univ Pa Press, 94; Not the Person she conceived me': The Public Identities of Charlotte Charke, Genders 19, 94; How Came This Muff Here: A Note on Tom Jones, Eng Lang Notes 26, 89 & A Cult of Dependence: The Social Context of The London Merchant, Comp Drama 21, 88. **CONTACT ADDRESS** Dept of Eng, Univ of Scranton, Scranton, PA 18510.

DERNOVSEK, VERA
PERSONAL Born 06/05/1946, Karlovy Vary, Czechoslovakia, m, 1965, 1 child **DISCIPLINE** LITERATURE **EDUCATION** McMaster Univ, BA, 92; MA, 94; Rice Univ, PhD, 00. **CAREER** Instr, Univ Haute Bretagne, 96-97; instr, asst teach, Rice Univ, 97-99; adj prof, Tomball Col, 01-. **HONORS AND AWARDS** Bull Ferguson Awd; Edwin Marwin Dalley Memo Scholar. **MEMBERSHIPS** MLA, ACLA, ASECS. **RESEARCH** 18th-century France literature and art; postmodernism philosophy, literature and art. **SELECTED PUBLICATIONS** Auth, "La Morale en Peinture," in Bourgeois and Feminist Discourses in the Paintings of Jean-Baptiste Greuze (UMI, 00). **CONTACT ADDRESS** Humanities Div, Tomball Col, 30555 Tomball Pkwy, Tomball, TX 77375-4036.

DEROSA, ROBIN
PERSONAL Born 01/16/1972 **DISCIPLINE** ENGLISH **EDUCATION** Brown Univ, BA, 94; Tufts Univ, MA, 97; PhD, 02. **CAREER** Lectr, Tufts Univ, 96-00; lectr Plymouth State Col, 00-. **HONORS AND AWARDS** Tufts Univ Fel, 97-00, 01. **MEMBERSHIPS** MLA, NEMLA. **RESEARCH** Cultural Studies, Performance Theory, Early American Literature, Queer Theory, Women's Studies. **SELECTED PUBLICATIONS** Auth, "To Save the Life of the Novel: Sadomasochism and Representation in Wuthering Heights," Rocky Mt Rev of Lang and Lit, (98); auth, "What Have I On A Petticoat?: The Convent of Pleasure and the Reality of Performance," In-Between, (01); auth, "Reinscription and Revolution: Parody in the Narrative of Olaudah Equiano," Conn Rev, (01); auth, "A Criticism of Contradiction: Anna Leticia Barbauld and the 'Problem' of Nineteenth Century Women's Writing," Women as Sistes of Culture, (Ashgate Pr, forthcoming). **CONTACT ADDRESS** Plymouth State Col of the Univ System of New Hampshire, MSC 40, Plymouth, NH 03264. **EMAIL** rderosa@mail.plymouth.edu

DERRICK, CLARENCE
PERSONAL Born 04/08/1912, New Britain, CT, m, 1945, 2 children **DISCIPLINE** ENGLISH **EDUCATION** Trinity Col, Conn, AB, 35; Western Reserve Univ, MA, 38; Univ Chicago, PhD (educ), 53. **CAREER** Teacher, Avon Sch, Conn, 35-41 and Univ Sch, Shaker Heights, Ohio, 41-47; asst dir dept exam, Bd of Educ, Chicago, 48-49; supvr humanities sect, Test Develop, Educ Testing Serv, Princeton, NJ, 49-53; assoc prof, 53-59, chmn dept humanities, 62-75, Prof Humanities, Univ Fla, 59-. **RESEARCH** Evaluation; general education. **SELECTED PUBLICATIONS** Auth, Race and Touch of Evil, Sight Sound, Vol 6, 96. **CONTACT ADDRESS** Dept of Humanities, Univ of Florida, Gainesville, FL 32601.

DERRY, JAMES
DISCIPLINE COMMUNICATION STUDIES **EDUCATION** Univ ND, BA; Univ Wis, MA; Purdue Univ, PhD. **CAREER** Assoc prof, USU **MEMBERSHIPS** Int Sociol Asn; Nat Asn Higher Edu. **SELECTED PUBLICATIONS** Auth, pubs on assessment of education and training. **CONTACT ADDRESS** Dept of Communication, Utah State Univ, 3580 S Highway 91, Logan, UT 84321. **EMAIL** jderry@cc.usu.edu

DERRYBERRY, BOB R.
PERSONAL Born 07/19/1937, Wardville, OK, m, 1958, 2 children **DISCIPLINE** SPEECH COMMUNICATION **EDUCATION** East Central State Univ Okla, BA, 60; East Central State Univ, MT, 62; Univ Ark, MA, 66; Univ Mo, PhD, 73 **CAREER** Instr, Southwest Baptist Col, 61-69; instr, Univ Mo, 69-70; assoc prof, Southwest Baptist Univ, 70-78; prof & chair, Ouachita Baptist Univ, 78-81; senior prof, dept chair, dir Forensics, Southwest Baptist Univ, 81- **HONORS AND AWARDS** Mo Gov Awd Excellence in Teaching, 92, 97; Ed Board, Southern Jrn Forensics, 97-98; Keynote Address Presenter, Pi Kappa Delta Ntl Convention Develop Conf, 93; Loren Reid Serv Awd, 92; E.R. Nichols Awd Outstanding Forensics Educator, Pi Kappa Delta, 90 **MEMBERSHIPS** Speech & Theatre Assoc Missouri President, 90; Pi Kappa Delta Ntl Forensic Fraternity; **SELECTED PUBLICATIONS** Auth, "Linking department and forensics directing in the small college," Speech Communication Assoc Annual Meeting, ERIC, 96; auth, "Future considerations for multidimensional forensic programs," Speech Theatre Assoc Mo Jrnl, 96; auth, "Understanding and utilizing academic freedom in the religious affiliated university," Speech Communication Assoc Annual Meeting, ERIC, 95 **CONTACT ADDRESS** 341 S Chicago Place, Bolivar, MO 65613.

DESAI, GAURAV GAJANAN
DISCIPLINE AFRICAN AND DIASPORA STUDIES, POSTCOLONIAL LITERATURE **EDUCATION** Northwestern Univ, BA, 88; Duke Univ, PhD, 97. **CAREER** Engl, Tulane Univ. **SELECTED PUBLICATIONS** Auth, Theater as Praxis: Discursive Strategies in African Popular Theater, African Stud Rev 33, 90; The Invention of Invention, Cult Critique 24, 93; English as an African Language, Eng Today 9, 93; Out in Africa, Genders 25, 97. **CONTACT ADDRESS** Dept of Eng, Tulane Univ, 6823 St Charles Ave, New Orleans, LA 70118. **EMAIL** gaurav@mailhost.tcs.tulane.edu

DESALVO, LOUISE ANITA
PERSONAL Born 09/27/1942, Jersey City, NJ, m, 1963, 2 children **DISCIPLINE** MODERN LITERATURE, MEMOIR **EDUCATION** Douglass Col, BA, 63; New York Univ, MA, 72, PhD(English educ), 77. **CAREER** Teacher English, Wood-Ridge High Sch, NJ, 63-67; coordr, English educ, Fairleigh Dickinson Univ, Teaneck, 77-82; Prof english, Hunter Col, City Univ New York, 82-, Contrib ed, Media & Methods Mag, 80-81. **HONORS AND AWARDS** Feature Article Awd, Educ Press Asn Am, 80; Scholarly Ed Awd, MLA, 80; Gaytalese Awd, 97. **MEMBERSHIPS** Virginia Woolf Soc (treas, 79-82); MLA; NCTE; Bronte Soc. **RESEARCH** Virginia Woolf; Women's fiction; memoir. **SELECTED PUBLICATIONS** auth, Virginia Woolf's First Voyage: A Novel in the Making, Rowman & Littlefield & Macmillan, London, 80;ed, Virginia Woolf: Melymbrosia, NY Publ Libr, 82; ed, The Letters of Vita Sackville-West to Virginia Woolf, Morrow, 85; ed, Territories of the Voice, Beacon, 89; auth, Nathaniel Hawthorne, Harvester, Humanities, 87; auth, Virginia Woolf: The Impact of Childhood Sexual Abuse on her Life and Work, Beacon, 89, Women's Press, 89; ed, Between Women, Routledge, 93; auth, Conceived with Malice, Literature as Revenge, Dutton, 94; auth, Vertigo: A Memoir, Dutton, 96; auth, Breathless, Beacon, 97; auth, Writing as a Way of Healing, Harper San Francisco, 99; auth, Adultery, Beacon, 99. **CONTACT ADDRESS** Hunter Col, CUNY, 695 Park Ave, New York, NY 10021. **EMAIL** lad1942@aol.com

DESHONG, SCOTT
PERSONAL Born 09/05/1957, Kalamazoo, MI, m, 1996 **DISCIPLINE** ENGLISH **EDUCATION** Western Mich Univ, BA, 86, MA, 88; Univ Iowa, PhD, 94. **CAREER** Vis fac, Conn Col, 96-; asst prof, Quinebaug Valley Community Col, 97-. **HONORS AND AWARDS** Sherman Paul/Prairie Lights Diss Scholarship, Univ Iowa, 94; Postdoctoral fel, Ctr for the Study of Theory & Criticism, Univ Western Ont, 94; School of Criticism & Theory, Dartmouth Col, 94. **MEMBERSHIPS** Modern Lang Asn, Northeast MLA, Soc for Critical Exchange, Int Asn for Philos and Lit. **RESEARCH** 20th-century American literature, Afro-American literature, critical theory. **SELECTED PUBLICATIONS** Auth,"Protagonism in 'The Reef': Edith Wharton's

Novelistic Discourse," Edith Wharton Rev, 8.2 (fall 91): 19-23; rev, of The Institution of Theory by Murray Krieger, Yearbk of Comp and Gen Lit, 42 (94): 158-60; auth, "Toward an Ethics of Reading Faulkner's 'Sanctuary'," The J of Narrative Tech, 25.3 (fall 95): 238-57; auth, "Sylvia Plath, Emmanuel Levinas, and the Aesthetics of Pathos," Postmodern Culture, 8.3 (May 98), http://www.iath.virginia.edu.pmc. **CONTACT ADDRESS** Dept English, Quinebaug Valley Comm-Tech Col, 742 Upper Maple St, Danielson, CT 06239-1436. **EMAIL** spedes@conncoll.edu

DESJARDINS, MARY
DISCIPLINE FILM STUDIES **EDUCATION** Univ S CA, PhD. **CAREER** Fac, Univ CA Santa Barbara; fac, Univ Tex Austin; Asst prof, Dartmouth Col. **RESEARCH** Film and television stardom; feminist theory; gender and media; feminist filmmaking; melodrama. **SELECTED PUBLICATIONS** Auth, articles in Film Quart, The Velvet Light Trap, Quart Rev Film and Video, The Spectator, On Film, and Montage; book chapters in Questioning the Media, Fires Were Started: British Cinema and Thatcherism, and Television and Cultural History; entries in The Encyclopedia of TV. **CONTACT ADDRESS** Dartmouth Col, 3529 N Main St, #207, Hanover, NH 03755. **EMAIL** Mary.Desjardins@Dartmouth.edu

DESMIDT, BEN
PERSONAL Born 08/04/1973, Madison, WI **DISCIPLINE** CLASSICS **EDUCATION** Univ Chicago, BA, 95; Columbia Univ, MA; MPhil, 01 **CAREER** Teaching Asst to Preceptor, Columbia Univ, 96-. **HONORS AND AWARDS** Pres Fel, Columbia Univ, 95-00. **MEMBERSHIPS** Am Philol Asn. **RESEARCH** Roman moral philosophy and philosophical rhetoric. **CONTACT ADDRESS** Dept Class, Columbia Univ, 617 Hamilton Hall, New York, NY 10011. **EMAIL** dbd5@columbia.edu

DESMOND, JOHN F.
DISCIPLINE AMERICAN LITERATURE, SOUTHERN LITERATURE, MODERN IRISH LITERATURE **EDUCATION** Univ Detroit, PhD, 60; Univ Okla, MA; PhD, 71. **CAREER** Instr, Ohio Univ; exec comm, Soc Stud S Lit; prof-. **HONORS AND AWARDS** Founder, pres, The Walker Percy Soc; ed bd, Bd of Adv for the Flannery O'Connor Soc; ed bd, Lit and Belief. **RESEARCH** Modern South, modern Irish poetry, and ethical and religious themes in 20th century writers. **SELECTED PUBLICATIONS** Ed, contribu, A Still Moment: Essays on the Art of Eudora Welty, auth, Risen Sons: Flannery's O'Connor's Vision of History, 87; At the Crossroads: Ethical and Religious Themes in the Writings of Walker Percy, 97. **CONTACT ADDRESS** Dept of Eng, Whitman Col, 345 Boyer Ave, Walla Walla, WA 99362-2038. **EMAIL** desmond@whitman.edu

DESSEN, ALAN CHARLES
PERSONAL Born 11/16/1935, Baltimore, MD, m, 1963, 2 children **DISCIPLINE** ENGLISH **EDUCATION** Harvard Univ, BA, 57; Johns Hopkins Univ, MA, 61, PhD (English), 63. **CAREER** From instr to assoc prof English, Univ Wis-Madison, 63-69; assoc prof, Northwestern Univ, 69-73;from prof English to Peter G. Phialas Prof, Univ NC, Chapel Hill, 73-; dir, Acter, 94-. **HONORS AND AWARDS** Sr res fel, Nat Endowment for the Humanities, Folger Shakespeare Libr, 77-78, 91; fel, Nat Humanities Center, 00-01. **MEMBERSHIPS** MLA; Shakespeare Asn Am. **RESEARCH** Shakespeare; Elizabethan-Jacobean drama and dramatic history. **SELECTED PUBLICATIONS** Auth, Jonson's Moral Comedy, Northwestern Univ Pr, 71; auth, Elizabethan Drama and the Viewer's Eye, Univ North Carolina Pr, 77; auth, Elizabethan Stage Conventions and Modern Interpreters, Cambridge Univ Pr, 84, 86; auth, Shakespeare and the Late Moral Plays, Univ Nebr Pr, 86; auth, Titus Andronicus: Shakespeare in Performance, Manchester Univ Pr, 89, 92; auth, Recovering Shakespeare's Theatrical Vocabulary, Cambridge Univ Pr, 95; coauth, A Dictionary of Stage Directions in English Drama, 1580-1642, Cambridge Univ Pr, 99. **CONTACT ADDRESS** Dept of English, Univ of No Carolina, Chapel Hill, CB #3520, Chapel Hill, NC 27599-3520. **EMAIL** acdessen@email.unc.edu

DESSEN, CYNTHIA SHELDON
PERSONAL Born 05/14/1938, New York, NY, m, 1963, 2 children **DISCIPLINE** ROMAN LITERATURE **EDUCATION** Oberlin Col, BA, 60; Johns Hopkins Univ, MA, 62, PhD (classics), 64. **CAREER** Asst prof classics, Univ Wis, 68-69, Northwestern Univ, 70-73; Asst Prof Classics, Univ NC, Chapel Hill, 74-. **MEMBERSHIPS** Am Philol Asn. **RESEARCH** Latin literature; Roman satire; classics and English literature. **SELECTED PUBLICATIONS** Auth, The Figure of The Eunuch in Terence Eunuchus, Helios, Vol 22, 95. **CONTACT ADDRESS** Dept of Classics, Univ of No Carolina, Chapel Hill, Chapel Hill, NC 27514.

DESSNER, LAWRENCE JAY
PERSONAL Born 03/29/1934, New York, NY, m, 1961, 2 children **DISCIPLINE** ENGLISH LITERATURE **EDUCATION** Yale Univ, BA, 55; NYork Univ, BA, 67, PhD (English), 69. **CAREER** From asst prof to assoc prof, 69-77, Prof English, Univ Toledo, 77-; Prof Emeritus, 99. **MEMBERSHIPS** MLA. **RESEARCH** British Victorian literature; popular culture. **SELECTED PUBLICATIONS** Auth, "Class, Gender, and Sexuality in Gene Stratton-Porter's Freckles," Papers on Language and Literature 36:2 (00): 139-57; auth, "Malamud's Echoes of Hawthorne's 'Young Goodman Brown,'" Notes on Contemporary Literature 29:2 (99): 6-8; auth, "I rise with circustances': Making it in Dickens's Martin Chuzzelwit," Dickens Quarterly 14:3 (97): 146-53; auth, "Arthur Havisham or Mr. Arthur?" The Dickensian 91:2 (95): 123-25; auth, Arthur Havisham or Mr Arthur, Dickensian, Vol 91, 95; auth, "Gender and Structure in John Cheever's ' The Country Husband,'" Studies in Short Fiction 31:1 (94):57-68; auth, "Space, Time, and Coincidence in Hardy, "Studies in the Novel, 24:2 (92): 154-72; auth, "The Autobiographical Matrix of Trollope's The Bertrams," Nineteenth-Century Literature, 45:1 (90):26-58; auth, "A Possible Source for Dickens's Lammles," The Dickensian, 85:2 (89): 105-107; auth, How to Write a Poem, New York: New York University Press, 79; auth, The homely web of truth: A Study of Charlotte Bronte's Novels, The Hague: Mouton, 75. **CONTACT ADDRESS** Dept of English, Univ of Toledo, 2718 Barrington Dr., Toledo, OH 43606. **EMAIL** ldessne@uoft02.utoledo.edu

DETENBER, BENJAMIN H.
DISCIPLINE COMMUNICATION **EDUCATION** Stanford Univ, AB, 83; PhD, 95. **CAREER** Consult, producer/dir, Stanford Instructional TV Network, 89-92; TV producer/dir, SITN, 83-89; tchg asst, Stanford Univ, 91-94; lectr, Stanford Univ, 94-95; asst prof, 95-. **MEMBERSHIPS** Mem, Broadcast Educators Assn; Intl Commun Assn. **RESEARCH** Social and individual level effects of media. **SELECTED PUBLICATIONS** Co-auth, A Bio-informational Theory of Emotion: Motion and Image Size Effects on Viewers, Jour Commun, 96; The Effects of Picture Motion on Affective Judgments and Psychophysiological Responses, Info Sys Div Intl Commun Assn, Montreal, Canada, 97. **CONTACT ADDRESS** Dept of Commun, Univ of Delaware, 222 S Chapel St, Newark, DE 19716-5600.

DETMER, HELLENA R.
PERSONAL Born 12/09/1950, Huntington, IN, m, 1989, 5 children **DISCIPLINE** CLASSICS **EDUCATION** IN Univ, BA, 72; Univ MI, PhD, 76. **CAREER** Act ch, 82-89;co-supvr, Elem Latin prog, 89; ch, 93-. **HONORS AND AWARDS** Mellon fel, Duke Univ, 78-79; May Brodbeck Awd, 83; Faculty Scholar 85-87; pres-elect, CAMWS, 95-96; vp, camws, 88-91; ch, camws col awards comm for transl, 90-92; ch, tchg award comm camws, 94-96; exec comm, camws, 94-98; pres, camws, 96-97. **SELECTED PUBLICATIONS** Auth, Horace: A Study in Structure, Hildesheim, 83; A Workbook to Ayers' English Words From Latin And Greek Elements, Tucson 86; Love by the Numbers: Form and Meaning in the Poetry of Catullus, NY, 97; co-ed, Syllecta Classica 1, 89; Syllecta Classica 2, 90; Syllecta Classica 3, 92; Syllecta Classica 4, 93; Syllecta Classica 5, 94; Syllecta Classica 6, 96; The First and Last of Catullus, Syllecta Classica 5, 94; rev(s), Murgatroyd's Tibullus Elegies II, Class Outlook 74, 96; Catullus: Advanced Placement Edition, Class Outlook 75, 97; Thompson's Catullus Rel Stud Rev, 97. **CONTACT ADDRESS** Dept of Class, Univ of Iowa, 202 Schaeffer Hall, Iowa City, IA 52242. **EMAIL** helena-dettmer@uiowa.edu

DETMER-GROEBEL, EMILY
PERSONAL Born 04/08/1961, Hamilton, OH, m, 2000 **DISCIPLINE** ENGLISH **EDUCATION** Wright State Univ, BA, 83; Miami Univ, MA, 85; MA, 92; PhD, 97. **CAREER** TA, Miami Univ, 92-98; asst prof, Millikin Univ, 98-. **HONORS AND AWARDS** William A. Ringler, Jr. Fel, Huntington Libr; Diss Fel, Miami Univ. **MEMBERSHIPS** MLA; Studies of Early Modern Women; Shakespeare Assoc. **RESEARCH** Gender, violence and the law in Early Modern English Drama. **SELECTED PUBLICATIONS** Auth, "Civilizing Subordination: Domestic Violence and The Taming of the Shrew, Shakespeare Quart 48, (97): 273-94; auth, "In Need of Lavinia's Voice: Titus Andronicus and the Telling of Rape, Shakespeare Studies (forthcoming). **CONTACT ADDRESS** Dept English, Millikin Univ, 1184 W Main St, Decatur, IL 62522-2039. **EMAIL** edetmer@mail.milliken.edu

DETTMAR, KEVIN
DISCIPLINE ENGLISH LITERATURE **EDUCATION** Univ Calif, PhD, 90. **CAREER** Dept Eng, Clemson Univ **RESEARCH** 20th Century British and American Literature. **SELECTED PUBLICATIONS** Auth, The Rise and Fall of ono Vox and the Spiders from Dublin; Or, the Musical Logic of Late Capitalism, SAQ, 97); The Illicit Joyce of Postmodernism: Reading Against the Grain, Univ Wis, 96; Ulysses and the Preemptive Power of Plot, Pedagogy, Praxis, Ulysses: Using Joyce's Text to Transform the Classroom, Univ Mich, 95; Joyce/Irishbess Modernism, Bucknell Rev, 94; The Joyce That Beckett Built, James Joyce Quart; To Pirate The Pirate: Kathy Acker and the Politics of (post) Modernist Appropriation in Perspectives on Plagiarism and Intellectual Property in a Postmodern World, SUNY P; Alternative Rock Cello and the Importance of Being Earnest, Rocking Theory/Theorizing Rock: Literary Theory Meets Rock and Roll; H.G. Wells, British Short Fiction 1880-14: The Romantic Tradition, Dic Lit Biog, 96; James Joyce in British Short Fiction Writers 1914-1945, Dic Lit Biog. **CONTACT ADDRESS** Clemson Univ, 305 Strode, Clemson, SC 29634. **EMAIL** dkevin@clemson.edu

DEVEAUX, SCOTT
PERSONAL Born 11/11/1954, Red Bank, NJ, m, 1981, 2 children **DISCIPLINE** MUSIC **EDUCATION** Princeton Univ, AB, 76; Univ Calif-Berkeley, MA, PhD 85. **CAREER** Vis asst prof, Humboldt State Univ, 81-82; Assoc prof, Univ Va, 83-. **HONORS AND AWARDS** Irving Lowens Award, 91; Am Book Award, for The Birth of Bebop, 98; Assoc for Recorded Sound Coll Award for Excellence, for The Birth of Bebop, 98; Otto Kinkeldey Award; US-IASPM Book Award; Fulbright Distinguished ch, Center for Am Studies, 01-02. **MEMBERSHIPS** Am Musicol Soc; Sonneck Soc Am Mus; Soc Ethnomusicol. **RESEARCH** Jazz, Am music and culture, African-American music, popular music, 20th-century music, traditional music of West Africa. **SELECTED PUBLICATIONS** Bebop and the Recording Industry: The 1942 AFM Recording Ban Reconsidered, Jour Am Musicol Soc, 41, Spring 88, 126-165; Constructing the Jazz Tradition: Jazz Historiography, Black Am Lit Forum, 25, Fall 91, 525-560; Coed, The Music of James Scott, Smithsonian Inst Press, 92; Black, Brown and Beige and the Critics, Black Mus Res Jour, 13, Fall 93, 125-146; Jazz in America: Who's Listening?, NEA Res Div Rep #31, Seven Locks Press, 95; What Did We Do to Be So Black and Blue? Mus Quart 80, Fall 96, 392-430; The Birth of Bebop: A Social and Musical History, Univ Calif Press, 97; auth, "Nice Work if You Can Get It: Thelonious Monk and Popular Song," Black Music Research Journal 19:2, 99. **CONTACT ADDRESS** Dept of Music, Univ of Virginia, PO Box 400176, Charlottesville, VA 22906-4176. **EMAIL** deveaux@virginia.edu

DEVENYI, JUTKA
DISCIPLINE THEATER HISTORY **EDUCATION** Eotvos Lorand Univ Liberal Arts, MA; Univ CA Santa Barbara, PhD, 92. **CAREER** Asst prof, Cornell Univ; fac Actors Studio, Eugene Lang Col, present. **RESEARCH** Dramatic theory; contemp French and Eastern Europ drama. **SELECTED PUBLICATIONS** Auth, Metonymy and Drama: Essays on Language and Dramatic Strategy, Bucknell UP, 96; articles on contemp Hungarian and 19th century Ger drama. **CONTACT ADDRESS** Eugene Lang Col, New Sch for Social Research, 66 West 12th St, New York, NY 10011.

DEVIN, LEE
PERSONAL Born 04/28/1938, Glendale, CA, m, 1958, 2 children **DISCIPLINE** DRAMA **EDUCATION** San Jose State Col, AB, 58; Ind Univ, MA, 61, PhD(speech & drama), 67. **CAREER** Lectr speech & drama, Ind Univ Exten, 60-62; instr & tech dir, Univ Va, 62-66; from instr to asst prof drama, Vassar Col, 66-71; assoc prof, 71-80, prof English, Swarthmore Col, 80-, Dir Theatre, 71-, Vis artist, Ball State Univ, 64; guest dir, High Tor Opera Co, fall 67; NEA fel grant, 74, Librettist's grants, 73, 74 & 76; artist in residence, People Light & Theatre Co, 77-. **HONORS AND AWARDS** NEA Librettist's grants, 73, 74, 76; Mellon Fel 73, 77; Lang Fel, 90. **MEMBERSHIPS** Actors Equity Asn; Am Theatre Asn; Lit Mgrs and Dramaturgs of the Americas. **RESEARCH** Acting; dramaturgy. **SELECTED PUBLICATIONS** Auth, Ballad for Wanton Boy, 72 & Elegy for Irish Jack, 73, Earplay; Vox populous, St Paul Chamber Orchestra, 73; Where The Time Comes, 79, Frankenstein, 82, Earplay, St Carmen of the Main, Guelph Festival and G Shirmer, 87. **CONTACT ADDRESS** Theatre, Swarthmore Col, 500 College Ave, Swarthmore, PA 19081-1397. **EMAIL** ldevin1@email.msn.com

DEVITT, AMY J.
PERSONAL Born 02/14/1955, Fort Collins, CO, m, 1991 **DISCIPLINE** ENGLISH **EDUCATION** Trinity Univ, BA, 77; Univ Kans, MA, 79; Univ Mich, PhD, 82. **CAREER** Asst prof, Univ Tulsa, 82-85; assoc dir, assoc prof, dir, 85-, Univ Kans. **HONORS AND AWARDS** Phi Beta Kappa; Rackham Fel; CLAS Grad Mentor Award; Kemper Tchg Fel. **MEMBERSHIPS** NCTE; MLA; ADS; CCCC. **RESEARCH** Genre theory; composition and rhetoric; English language; standardization. **SELECTED PUBLICATIONS** Auth, Standardizing Written English: Diffusion in the Case of Scotland, 1520-1659, 89; auth, art, Genre as Textual Variable: Some Historical Evidence from Scots and American English, 89; auth, art, Intertexuality in Tax Accounting: Generic, Referential, and Functional, 91; auth, art, Generalizing About Genre: New Conceptions of an Old Concept, 93; auth, art, Genre as Language Standard, 97; auth, "Integrating Literary and Rhetorical Theories of Genre," 00. **CONTACT ADDRESS** Dept of English, Univ of Kansas, Lawrence, Lawrence, KS 66045. **EMAIL** devitt@ukans.edu

DEVLIN, ALBERT J.
DISCIPLINE ENGLISH **EDUCATION** Univ Kans, PhD, 70. **CAREER** Prof; ed bd(s), Miss Quart & Tennessee Williams Lit J. **HONORS AND AWARDS** Eudora Welty Soc Award for Distinguished Achievement; NEH Fel, 97. **RESEARCH** Southern American literature and drama. **SELECTED PUBLICATIONS** Auth, Eudora Welty's Chronicle, UP Miss, 83; ed, Conversations with Tennessee Williams, UP Miss, 86; ed, Eudora Welty: A Life in Literature, UP Miss; co-ed, The Selected Letters of Tennessee Williams; acad adv, PBS documentary, Tennessee Williams: Orpheus of the American Stage, Amer Masters Ser, 94. **CONTACT ADDRESS** Dept of English, Univ of Missouri, Columbia, 218 Tate Hall, Columbia, MO 65211. **EMAIL** DevlinA@missouri.edu

DEVLIN, JAMES E.
PERSONAL Born 05/06/1938, Boston, MA, m, 2 children **DISCIPLINE** ENGLISH **EDUCATION** Harvard; SUNY Binghamton; Boston College. **CAREER** Fac, SUNY Col at Oneonta. **HONORS AND AWARDS** Fulbright Germany, Dir of James Fenimore Cooper Seminar; ed, satire newsletter; chr, prog comm, suny col oneonta. **RESEARCH** Am lit; crime fiction. **SELECTED PUBLICATIONS** Auth, articles in Am lit from the Transcendentalist period to the present; auth, Elmore Leonard, Twayne, 99. **CONTACT ADDRESS** SUNY, Col at Oneonta, 321 Netzer Admin Bldg, Oneonta, NY 13820. **EMAIL** diver@oneonta.edu

DEVLIN, KIMBERLY J.
DISCIPLINE AMERICAN LITERATURE **EDUCATION** Bryn Mawr Univ, BA; Univ Mich, PhD. **CAREER** Prof, Art Hist, Univ Calif, Riverside. **RESEARCH** James Joyce, feminist and psychoanalytic theory. **SELECTED PUBLICATIONS** Auth, Wandering and Return in "Finnegans Wake," Princeton Univ Press, 91; "'See Ourselves As Others See Us': Joyce's Look at the Eye of the Other," PMLA, 89; "Pretending in 'Penelope': Masquerade, Mimicry, and Molly Bloom," Novel, 91; "Castration and its Discontents: A Lacanian Approach to Ulysses," spec issue of James Joyce Quart on Joyce and Lacan, 91; "The Eye and the Gaze in Heart of Darkness: A Symptomological Reading," Mod Fiction Stud, 94; Bloom and the Police, Novel, 95. **CONTACT ADDRESS** Dept of Eng, Univ of California, Riverside, 1156 Hinderaker Hall, Riverside, CA 92521-0209.

DEWS, CARLOS L.
PERSONAL Born 09/24/1963, Nacogdoches, TX, s **DISCIPLINE** ENGLISH, AMERICAN LITERATURE **EDUCATION** Univ Tex, BA, 87; Univ Minn, MA, 92; PhD, 94. **CAREER** Asst prof to assoc prof, Univ of W Fla, 94-; chair, 00-. **HONORS AND AWARDS** Grant, Univ of W Fla, 96, 98, 99, 00; John C Pace Awd, 96; Teaching Incentive Prog Awd, Univ of W Fla, 98-99. **MEMBERSHIPS** MLA; United Fac of Fla; NCTE; Eudora Welty Soc; Flannery O'Connor Soc; Am Cult Assoc; Toni Morrison Soc; Am Lit Assoc; W Fla Literary Federation; Carson McCullers Soc. **SELECTED PUBLICATIONS** Coed, This Fine Place So Far From Home: Voices of Academics from the Working Class, Temple UP, (Philadelphia), 95; auth, "Mentions of Richard Wright in Carson McCuller's Unfinished Autobiography Illumination and Night Glare", Richard Wright Newsletter, (95): 3-4; auth, "Resisting Henry Ford in the Degree Factory", Communitas X, (97): 117-25; coauth, "Anti-Intellectualism, Homophobia and the Working Class Gay/Lesbian Academic", Radical Teacher 53, (98): 8-12; auth, "Carson McCullers", Am Nat Biography, Oxford UP, (NY), 99; ed, "Illumination and Night Glare: The Unfinished Autobiography of Carson McCullers", Univ ofwis Pr, (Madison), 99; coed, Out in the South, Temple UP, (Philadelphia), (forthcoming); ed, "Why I Cannot Read Faulkner: Reading and Resisting Southern Masculinty", Faulkner J (forthcoming); auth, "The Necessary Lie: Exaggeration in the Life and Work of Carson McCullers", Reflections on Carson McCullers, ed Keith Byerman, Univ of Ga Pr, (Athens), (forthcoming); ed, Selected Works of Carson McCullers, Libr of Am, (NY), (forthcoming). **CONTACT ADDRESS** Dept English and Lang, Univ of West Florida, 11000 University Pky, Pensacola, FL 32514-5732. **EMAIL** cdews@uwf.edu

DEZEEUW, ANNE MARIE
PERSONAL Born 02/18/1947, Minneapolis, MN, m, 1984, 1 child **DISCIPLINE** MUSIC THEORY **EDUCATION** BM, Mich State Univ, 68; MA, Univ TX, Austin, 71, PhD, 83. **CAREER** Lectr, 74-77, Inst, 77-83, Asst Prof 83-84, Univ NY, Stony Brook; Asst Prof 85-91, Assoc Prof, 91-98, Prof, 98-, Univ Louisville. **HONORS AND AWARDS** Univ of Louisville Distinguished Teaching Prof, 00. **MEMBERSHIPS** Soc Music Theory; Music Theory Soc NY State; Music Theory Midwest, Sec 91-94, Pres, 97-99. **RESEARCH** Tonal theory; music of the early 20th century; theory pedagogy; contemporary music. **SELECTED PUBLICATIONS** Auth, Teaching Score Analysis: A Guided Study of the Third Movement (Meunuetts) of Beethoven's String Trio in E-Flat Major, Op 3, in Teachers Guide to the Advanced Placemnt (AP) Course in Music, ed Marie Lerner-Sexton, 99; with Rebecca Jemian: An Interview with John Adams, Perspectives of New Music, Vol 34, No 2, 96; Review of Nightingale version 1,4 music notation software, Notes 95; Some Notes on Teaching Score Analysis, in Teacher's Guide to the Advanced Placement Course in Music Theory, ed. Kathlyn J Fujikawa, NY: College Entrance Examination Board, 93; auth, A Numerical Metaphor in a Schoenberg Song, Op 15, Journal of Musicology, Vol 11, 93; Overall Structure and Design in a Variation Form, Journal of Music Theory Pedagogy 1, 87; With Roger E Foltz: Sight Singing: Melodic Structures in Functional Tonality, Austin, TX: Sterling Swift Publishing Co, 78; Teaching College Music Theory Classes that Include Blind Students, College Music Symposium 17 no 2, 77; auth, Sight Singing and Related Skills, with Roger E Foltz, Austin, TX: Univ Stores, Inc. 73. **CONTACT ADDRESS** School Music, Univ of Louisville, Louisville, KY 40292. **EMAIL** amdeze01@athena.louisville.edu

DHARWADKER, APARNA
PERSONAL Born 06/14/1955, Jaipur, India, m, 1976, 2 children **DISCIPLINE** LITERARY AND CULTURAL STUDIES **EDUCATION** Univ Rajasthan, BA, 75; Delhi Univ, MA, 77; Pa State Univ, PhD, 90. **CAREER** Instr, Univ of Il Chicago, 87-89; instr, Univ of Ga Athens, 89-91; asst to assoc prof, Univ of Okla, 91-. **HONORS AND AWARDS** Folger Fel, 84; Newberry Libr Fel, 87; Okla Found for Humanities Grant, 93; AIIS Res Fel, 98; NEH Res Fel, 98. **MEMBERSHIPS** MLA; Am Soc for Theatre Res; Am Soc for Eighteen-Century Studies. **RESEARCH** Postcolonial studies, comparative modern drama and theatre, restoration and 18th century British literature. **CONTACT ADDRESS** Dept English, Univ of Oklahoma, 900 Asp Ave, Norman, OK 73019-4050. **EMAIL** adhar@ou.edu

DI PARDO, ANNE
PERSONAL Born 06/14/1953, Eugene, OR, m, 1974, 1 child **DISCIPLINE** ENGLISH, EDUCATION **EDUCATION** Calif State Univ, BA, 75; Univ Calif at Los Angeles, MA, 76; Univ Calif at Berkeley, EdD, 91. **CAREER** Assoc prof, Univ of Iowa, 91-. **HONORS AND AWARDS** Post0doctoral fel, Nat Acad of Educ; NCTE Promising Researcher Awd; NWCA Outstanding Scholar Awd. **MEMBERSHIPS** NCTE, AERA, NCRLL. **RESEARCH** Literacy Practices, Issues in Teachers' Professional Lives. **SELECTED PUBLICATIONS** Auth, A Kind of Passport: A Basic Writing Adjunct Program and the Challenge of Student Diversity, NCTE, 93; auth, Teaching n Common: Challenges to Joint Work in Classrooms and Schools, Teachers Col Press, 99. **CONTACT ADDRESS** Dept English, Univ Iowa, N246 Lindquist Ctr, Iowa City, IA 52242. **EMAIL** anne-dipardo@uiowa.edu

DIAL-DRIVER, EMILY
PERSONAL Born Granite, OK, m, 2 children **DISCIPLINE** ENGLISH **EDUCATION** Okla State Univ, BS, 68; MA, 71; EdD, 91. **CAREER** Rogers State Univ, 71-. **HONORS AND AWARDS** Phi Kappa Phi; Omicron Nu; Delta Kappa Gamma; Thunderbird Libr Patron of the Year, 91; Who's Who Among Am Teachers, 94, 98; Directory of Am Philos, 95-; TIPS Master Teacher, 87; Fac Member of the Year, 96; Nat Inst for Staff and Organizational Develop Excellence Awd, 98; Pixley Excellence In Teaching Awd, 98; Okla Leadership Acad Outstanding Prof, 99-00. **MEMBERSHIPS** NCTE; AAUP; Soc for Col and Univ Planning; Okla Educ Assoc; NEA; MLA; Assoc for Supervision and Curriculum Develop. **RESEARCH** Writing curriculum, distance curriculum. **SELECTED PUBLICATIONS** Auth, Moment by Moment, KXON, 88; auth, "Multiple Learning Opportunities: Inception and Innovation", Community Col Rev 16.3 (88): 38-41; auth, "Building Bridges", Community Col Rev 21.1 (93): 26-30; auth, "A Place for the Personal: Using Anecdotes to Illustrate Principles", GIFTS, (April 95); auth, "Mommies: An Essay on Student Success", TYCA Newsletter 23.1 (95): 14-15; auth, "The Accidental Leader", Executive Educ 18.1 (96): 32; auth, A Guide to College Writing, McGraw Hill, (Claremore), 96; auth, "distant bonds", Cooweescoowee: A J of Arts and Letters, 96; auth, "Welcome John Lucas", Okla English J 11.3 (97): 22; auth, "Mirror Images", Writers & Projects, (99): 8. **CONTACT ADDRESS** Dept Commun and Fine Arts, Rogers State Col, 1701 W Will Rogers Blvd, Claremore, OK 74017-3259. **EMAIL** edial-driver@rsu.edu

DIAMOND, ELIN
DISCIPLINE FEMINIST THEORY AND FEMINIST THEATER, AMERICAN DRAMA, EARLY MODERN DRAMA **EDUCATION** Brandeis, BA; Univ Calif, Davis, MA, PhD. **CAREER** Prof Eng, Rutgers, The State Univ NJ, Univ Col-Camden. **RESEARCH** Drama and performance; dramatic theory; critical theory. **SELECTED PUBLICATIONS** Auth, Unmaking Mimesis: Essays on Feminism and Theater; Performance and Cultural Politics; ed, Printer's Comic Play. **CONTACT ADDRESS** Dept of Lit in Eng, Rutgers, The State Univ of New Jersey, New Brunswick, Murray Hall 205B, New Brunswick, NJ 08903. **EMAIL** ediamond@rci.rutgers.edu

DIAZ, ROBERTO IGNACIO
DISCIPLINE SPANISH AMERICAN LITERATURE **EDUCATION** Harvard Univ, PhD. **CAREER** Asst prof, Univ Southern Calif. **RESEARCH** Literary-historical study of Spanish American writing in English and French. **SELECTED PUBLICATIONS** Publ on, 19th and 20th century Spanish American literature. **CONTACT ADDRESS** Dept of Spanish and Portuguese, Univ of So California, University Park Campus, Los Angeles, CA 90089. **EMAIL** rdiaz@bcf.usc.edu

DICENZO, MARIA
DISCIPLINE 20TH-CENTURY BRITISH LITERATURE; THEATRE **EDUCATION** McMaster, BA; Queen's, MA; McMaster, PhD. **CAREER** Asst prof. **RESEARCH** 20th century British lit and theatre, political/feminist theatre, suffrage periodicals, the politics of arts funding. **SELECTED PUBLICATIONS** Auth,: The Politics of Alternative Theatre: The Case of 7:84 (Scotland), Cambridge Univ Press, 96; The Charabanc Theatre Company: Placing Women Centre-Stage in Northern Ireland; The Company of Sirens: Feminist Theatre for Social Change; Battle Fatigue: Notes from the Funding Front; auth, "Negotiating Audiences: Confronting Social Issues in Theatre for Young Audiences," Canadian Children's Literature 85, 23, (97): 7-19. **CONTACT ADDRESS** Dept of English, Wilfrid Laurier Univ, 75 University Ave W, Waterloo, ON, Canada N2L 3C5. **EMAIL** mdicenzo@wlu.ca

DICK, BERNARD F.
PERSONAL Born 11/25/1935, Scranton, PA, m, 1965 **DISCIPLINE** ENGLISH **EDUCATION** Univ Scranton, BA, 57; Fordham Univ, MA, 60; PhD, 62. **CAREER** Asst Prof to Prof, Fairleigh Dickinson Univ, 73-. **HONORS AND AWARDS** Univ Awd, Fairleigh Dickinson Univ, 91; Outstanding Scholar Book of the Year, Univ Ky, 95. **RESEARCH** Film history. **SELECTED PUBLICATIONS** Auth, Columbia Pictures: Portrait of a Studio, UP of Ky (Lexington, KY), 91; auth, The Merchant Prince of Poverty Row: Harry Cohn of Columbia Pictures, UP of KY (Lexington, KY), 93; auth, Billy Wilder, updated edition, DaCapo (New York), 96; auth, The Star-Spangled Screen: The American World War II Film, UP of Ky (Lexington, KY), 96; auth, City of Dreams: The Making and Remaking of Universal Pictures, UP of Ky (Lexington, KY), 97; auth, Anatomy of Film, 3rd ed, St Martin's Pr (New York), 98. **CONTACT ADDRESS** Dept English, Fairleigh Dickinson Univ, Teaneck-Hackensack, 1000 River Rd, Teaneck, NY 07666-1914.

DICK, DONALD
PERSONAL Born 06/21/1932, Lincoln, NE, m, 1955, 3 children **DISCIPLINE** SPEECH **EDUCATION** Union Col, NE, BA, 55; Univ NE, MA, 57; Mich State Univ, PhD, 65. **CAREER** From instr to assoc prof speech, La Sierra Col, 57-67; assoc prof, Loma Linda Univ, 67-68; prof speech & head, dept commun, 68-81, prof Commun, Southern Missionary Col, 81-82; Southern Col of Seventh-Day Adventists, 82-96; Southern Adventist Univ, 96-97, retired 9/30/97, Adjunct Prof Eneritus, Southern Adventist Univ, 97, Pres, Adventist Radio Network, 65-74, mem bd dir, 74-81; secy-treas adv bd, Faith For Today, 71-74, producer, 75-76. **MEMBERSHIPS** Speech Commun Asn; Broadcast Educ Asn. **RESEARCH** Broadcasting audience research; religious radio broadcasting. **SELECTED PUBLICATIONS** Auth, Religious broadcasting: 1920-1965, A bibliography, J Broadcasting, fall 65, spring 66 & summer 66. **CONTACT ADDRESS** PO Box 370, Collegedale, TN 37315-0370. **EMAIL** donandjoyce@mindspring.com

DICK, ROBERT C.
DISCIPLINE COMMUNICATION STUDIES **EDUCATION** Emporia State Univ, BA, 60; Univ NMex, MA, 61; Stanford Univ, PhD, 69. **CAREER** Prof. **MEMBERSHIPS** World Commun Asn. **SELECTED PUBLICATIONS** Auth, pubs on the argumentation process; black intellectual and social history. **CONTACT ADDRESS** Dept of Communication, Indiana Univ-Purdue Univ, Indianapolis, 425 Univ Blvd, Indianapolis, IN 46202. **EMAIL** rdick@iupui.edu

DICK, SUSAN M.
PERSONAL Born 11/06/1940, Battle Creek, MI **DISCIPLINE** ENGLISH **EDUCATION** Western Mich Univ, BA, 63; Northwestern Univ, MA, 64, PhD, 67. **CAREER** PROF ENGLISH, QUEEN'S UNIV, 67- **HONORS AND AWARDS** Fel, Royal Soc Can, 89 **RESEARCH** Virginia Woolf. **SELECTED PUBLICATIONS** Auth, Virginia Woolf, 89; ed, Confessions of a Young Man (George Moore), 72; ed, To the Lighthouse: The Original Holograph Draft (Virginia Woolf), 82; The Complete Shorter Fiction of Virginia Woolf, 85, 2nd enl ed, 89; co-ed, Omnium Gatherum: Essays for Richard Ellman, 89; To the Lighthouse (Virginia Woolf), 92. **CONTACT ADDRESS** English Dept, Queen's Univ at Kingston, Kingston, ON, Canada K7L 3N6. **EMAIL** dick@post.queensu.ca

DICKERSON, GREGORY WEIMER
PERSONAL Born 03/08/1937, Hanover, NH, m, 1967, 2 children **DISCIPLINE** CLASSICAL LANGUAGES & LITERATURE **EDUCATION** Harvard Univ, AB, 59; Princeton Univ, MA, 65, PhD, 72. **CAREER** Teaching fel classics, Phillips Acad, Andover, Mass, 59-60; secy, Am Sch Class Studies, Athens, 63-64; instr, Gilman Sch, Baltimore, 64-66; instr classics, 67-70, asst prof Greek, 70-76, assoc prof Greek, Bryn Mawr Col, 76-. **MEMBERSHIPS** Am Phil Asn. **RESEARCH** Greek drama. **SELECTED PUBLICATIONS** Auth, Aristophanes' Ranae 862: A note on the anatomy of Euripidean Tragedy, Harvard Studies Class Philol, 74; coauth, Sophocles' Women of Trachis, Oxford Univ, 78. **CONTACT ADDRESS** Dept of Greek, Bryn Mawr Col, 101 N Merion Ave, Bryn Mawr, PA 19010-2899. **EMAIL** gdickers@brynmawr.edu

DICKEY, JAMES
PERSONAL Born 02/02/1923, Atlanta, GA, 3 children **DISCIPLINE** ENGLISH **EDUCATION** Vanderbilt Univ, BA, 49, MA, 50. **CAREER** Instr English and creative writing, Rice Univ, 50, 52-54 and Univ Fla, 55-56; copywriter to creative dir var adv agencies, NY and Atlanta, 56-62; writer-in-residence, Reed Col, 63-64, San Fernando Valley State Col, 64-66 and Univ Wis-Madison, 66; consult poetry, Libr Cong, Washington, DC, 66-68; writer-in-residence, Wash Univ, 68; Franklin distinguished prof English, Ga Inst Technol, 68; Poet-in-Residence and Prof English, Univ SC, 69-, Guggenheim fel, 62-63; Nat Inst Arts and Lett grant, 67. **HONORS AND AWARDS** Nat

Bk Awd for Poetry, 66; Levinson Prize, 81. **MEMBERSHIPS** Am Acad Arts and Sci; Nat Inst Arts and Lett. **SELECTED PUBLICATIONS** Auth, The Cancer Match, Lit Med, Vol 13, 94; Treadwell, Sophie Versus Barrymore, John, Playwrights, Plagiarism and Power in the Broadway Theater of the 1920s, Theatre Hist Stud, Vol 15, 95; Saar the Yellow Boat, Theatre J, Vol 46, 94; Contemporary Poets, Dramatists, Essayists, and Novelists of the South--A Biobibliographical Sourcebook, Essays Theatre Etudes Theatrales, Vol 14, 95; American Playwrights, 1880-1945A Research and Production Sourcebook, Essays Theatre Etudes Theatrales, Vol 14, 95; Diabetes, Lit Med, Vol 13, 94. **CONTACT ADDRESS** 4620 Lelia's Ct, Columbia, SC 29206.

DICKINSON, LOREN
PERSONAL Born 09/01/1932, Bemidji, MN, m, 1957, 2 children **DISCIPLINE** SPEECH **EDUCATION** Union Col, BA, 57; Univ Nebr, MA, 60; Univ Denver, PhD(speech), 68. **CAREER** Instr speech & dir pub rels, Columbia Union Col, 58-62; Prof Speech, Walla Walla Col, 62- **MEMBERSHIPS** Nat Speech Commun Asn. **CONTACT ADDRESS** Dept of Speech, Walla Walla Col, 204 S College Ave, College Place, WA 99324-1198.

DICKISON, SHEILA KATHRYN
PERSONAL Born 11/14/1942, Walkerton, ON, Canada **DISCIPLINE** CLASSICS, ANCIENT HISTORY **EDUCATION** Univ Toronto, BA, 64; Bryn Mawr Col, MA, 66, PhD (Latin and Greek), 72. **CAREER** From instr to asst prof Greek, Latin and ancient hist, Wellesley Col, 69-76; actg chmn classics, 77-78, Assoc Prof Classics, Univ Fla, 76-. **MEMBERSHIPS** Archaeol Inst Am; Am Class League. **RESEARCH** Roman historiography; ancient social history **SELECTED PUBLICATIONS** Auth, The Reasonable Approach to Beginning Greek and Latin, Class J, Vol 87, 92. **CONTACT ADDRESS** ASB-3C, Univ of Florida, 3c Arts and Sciences, Gainesville, FL 32611-9500.

DICKS, VIVIAN I.
DISCIPLINE COMMUNICATION **EDUCATION** Wayne State Univ, BA; Ohio State Univ, MA, PhD; Detroit Col Law, JD. **CAREER** Prof, dept ch; Univ Detroit Mercy, 79-. **CONTACT ADDRESS** Dept of Commun Studies, Univ of Detroit Mercy, 4001 W McNichols Rd, PO Box 19900, Detroit, MI 48219-0900. **EMAIL** dicksvi@udmercy.edu

DICKSON, DONALD R.
PERSONAL Born 08/19/1951, Biloxi, MS, m, 1 child **DISCIPLINE** LITERATURE **EDUCATION** Univ of Conn, BA, 73; Univ of Ill, AM, 76; PhD, 81. **CAREER** Gastprof, Ins fur Anglistik u Am, Univ Erlangen-Nurnberg, 92-93; from asst prof to prof, Tex A & M Univ, 81-; ed, Seventeenth Century News, 96-. **HONORS AND AWARDS** Phi Kappa Phi; Fel, Unof of Ill, 80; Fel, NEH Summer Inst, 83; Res Fel & European Fel, Alexander von Humboldt Found, 83; Phi Beta Delta, Nat Honor Soc for Int Scholars, 94; Teacher/Scholars Awd, Univ Honors Program, Tex A & M Univ, 98; Fel, Am Council on Educ, 00-01. **MEMBERSHIPS** MLA, S Cent MLA, Renaissance Soc of Am, S Cent Renaissance Conf, John Donne Soc, Milton Soc of Am, Alexander von Humboldt Asn, Alexander von Humboldt Asn of Am, Usk Valley Vaughan Asn, Phi Kappa Phi Honorary, Int Asn of Univ Prof of English. **RESEARCH** Religion and literature, hermeticism, utopianism. **SELECTED PUBLICATIONS** Auth, "Johannes Saubert, Johann Valentin Andreae and the Unio Christiana," Ger Life & Letters 49 (96): 18-31; auth, "Johann Valentin Andreae's Utopian Brotherhoods," Renaissance Quart 49 (96): 860-902; auth, "The Alchemistical Wife: The Identity of Thomas Vaughan's 'Rebecca,'" The Seventeenth Century 13 (98): 34-46; auth, "The Hunt for Red Elixir: An Early Collaboration Between Fellows of the Royal Society," Endeavour 22 (98): 69-72; auth, The Valiorum Edition of the Poetry of John Donne: The Anniversaries, Epicedes and Obsequies, Ind Univ Press (Bloomington), 95; auth, The Tessera of Antilia: Utopian Brotherhoods & Secret Societies in the Early Seventeenth Century, Brill's Studies in Intellectual History series 88 (Leiden, New York, and Koln: E.J. Brill, 98). **CONTACT ADDRESS** Dept English, Texas A&M Univ, Col Station, College Station, TX 77843. **EMAIL** d-dickson@tamu.edu

DICKSON, JOHN H.
DISCIPLINE CONDUCTING **EDUCATION** Dallas Baptist Col, BA; Baylor Univ, MM; Univ Tex, DMA; addn stud, Cambridge Univ. **CAREER** Instr, Univ Tex; Baylor Univ; assoc dean, Dr Stud, prof, S Baptist Theol Sem, 85- ; Director of Choral Activities, Texas Tech Univ, 00. **RESEARCH** Sch Church Mus and Worship. **SELECTED PUBLICATIONS** Pub(s), The Choral Jour **CONTACT ADDRESS** School of Music, Texas Tech Univ, 42033, Lubbock, TX 79409-2033. **EMAIL** MPROFJHD@AOL.COM

DICKSON-CARR, DARRYL
PERSONAL Born 11/28/1968, Los Angeles, CA, m, 1994, 1 child **DISCIPLINE** ENGLISH **EDUCATION** Univ Calif Santa Barbara, BA, 90; MA, 93; PhD, 95. **CAREER** TA and res asst, Univ of Calif Santa Barbara, 91-95; asst prof, Fla State Univ, 95-. **HONORS AND AWARDS** President's Fel, Univ Calif, 91-92; Grants, Fla State Univ, 97, 98, 99. **MEMBERSHIPS** MLA; NE MLA; Pacific Ancient and MLA; Col Lang Assoc; Popular Cult Assoc; Am Cult Assoc. **RESEARCH** African-American Literature, American Literature, Satire, African American Satire, Literary Theory. **SELECTED PUBLICATIONS** Auth, "The Emptiness of his Character: A Critique of Shelby Steele", Thresholds: Viewing Culture 5, (91): 106-14; auth, "Annotated Bibliography", Mapping Multiculturalism, eds Avery Gordon and Christopher Newfield, Univ of Minn Pr, (96): 445-69; auth, "Signs of Adolescence: Problems of Group Identity in Wallace Thurman's Infants of the Spring", Studies in Contemp Satire 20, (96): 145-159; auth, "African American Literature", Encycl of Am Lit, ed Steven Serafin, Continuum, (NY, 98): 15-22; auth, "William Melvin Kelley", Encycl of Am Lit, ed Steven Serafin, Continuum, (NY, 98): 610-11; auth, "James Weldon Johnson", Encycl of Am Lit, ed Steven Serafin, Continuum, (NY, 98): 598-99; auth, "The Next Round: The Novels of Ishmael Reed in the 1980s and 1990s", Critical Response to Ismael Reed, ed Bruce Dick, Greenwood, (Westport, 99): 214-28; auth, "Taking the Offensive: The Quest for New Politics in Contemporary Black Satire", Can Rev of Am Studies (forthcoming); auth, "Now You Shall See How a Slave Was Made a Man: Gendering Frederick Douglass's Struggles with Christianity", The Puritan Origins of American Sex, eds Tracy Fessenden, Nicholas Radel and Magdalena Zaborowska, Routledge, (forthcoming); auth, "Why Am I Called Upon to Speak Here To-day?: The Role of the Jeremiad in African American Political Rhetoric from Frederick Douglass to Malcolm X", Nineteenth Century Prose, (forthcoming). **CONTACT ADDRESS** Dept English, Florida State Univ, PO Box 3061580, Tallahassee, FL 32306-1580. **EMAIL** dbcarr@english.fsu.edu

DICKSTEIN, MORRIS
PERSONAL Born 02/23/1940, New York, NY, m, 1965, 2 children **DISCIPLINE** ENGLISH & COMPARATIVE LITERATURE **EDUCATION** Columbia Univ, AB, 61; Yale Univ, MA, 63, PhD, 67. **CAREER** From instr to asst prof Eng & comp lit, Columbia Univ, 66-71; from Assoc Prof to Prof, 71-94, Distinguished Prof Eng, Queens Col, NY, 94-; vis prof Am studies, Univ Paris, 80-81; dir, Ctr for the Hum, CUNY Grad Sch, 93-. **HONORS AND AWARDS** Soc Relig Higher Educ fel, 69-70; Chamberlain fel, Columbia Univ, 69-70; Guggenheim fel, 73-74; Am Coun Learned Socs fel, 77; Rockefeller Found Hum fel, 81-82; NEH Fel, 86-87; Mellon Fel, Nat Hum Ctr, 9-90. **MEMBERSHIPS** MLA; PEN Club; Nat Book Critics Circle (bd mem 83-89); Nat Soc Film Critics. **RESEARCH** Eng and Europ romanticism; mod lit and criticism; film and lit; Am cult hist. **SELECTED PUBLICATIONS** Auth, Allen Ginsberg and the 60's, Commentary, 1/70; Keats and His Poetry: A Study in Development, Univ Chicago, 71; The Black aesthetic in white America, Partisan Rev, winter 71-72; Coleridge, Wordsworth, and the conversation poems, Centennial Rev, fall 72; Fiction hot and kool: Dilemmas of the experimental writer, Tri Quart, 75; Seeds of the sixties: The growth of Freudian radicalism, Partisan Rev, 76; Gates of Eden: American Culture in the Sixties, Basic Bks, 77; co-ed, Great Film Directors: A Critical Anthology, Oxford Univ, 78; auth, Double Agent: The Critic and Society, Oxford Univ, 92; ed, The Revival of Pragmatism: New Essays on Social Thought, Law, and Culture, Duke Univ, 98; coauth, Cambridge History of American Literature, Vol 8, Cambridge Univ, 99. **CONTACT ADDRESS** Center for the Hum, Queens Col, CUNY, 65-30 Kissena Blvd, Flushing, NY 11367. **EMAIL** mdickste@gc.cuny.edu

DIEDRICK, JAMES K.
PERSONAL Born 04/23/1951, Renton, WA, m, 1997, 2 children **DISCIPLINE** ENGLISH **EDUCATION** West Wash Univ, BA, 73; Univ Wash, PhD, 78. **CAREER** Teach fel, Univ Wash, 73-78; asst prof, Chap Univ, 78-80; prof, Albion Col, 80-. **HONORS AND AWARDS** Brit Acad Fel, 01-02; Newberry Lib Fel, 00-01; NEH, 97; Helm Fel , Lilly Lib, 96; Newberry Lib Fel, 87; Howard L. McGregor Prof of Hum, Albion Col ; Phi Beta Kappa Scholar of Yr, Albion Col, 97-98. **MEMBERSHIPS** MLA; MVSA. **RESEARCH** Victorian literature and culture; the British novel. **SELECTED PUBLICATIONS** Auth, Understanding Martin Amis (Univ SC Press, 95); auth, "The Grotesque Body: Physiology in The Mill on the Floss," Mosaic (88); auth, "The Sublimation of Carnival in Ruskin's Theory of the Grotesque," Vict NL (88); auth, "Dickens's Alter-Ego in Bleak House: The Importance of Lawrence Boythorn," Dickens Qtly (78); auth, "Jane Eyre and A Vindication of the Rights of Woman," Appr to Teach Jane Eyre (93); auth, "The Polyphonic Novel," Encycl Contemp Lit Theory (93); auth, "Charles Dickens," Dict Lit Bio (87); auth, "Dialogical History in Ivanhoe," Scott in Carnival (93); auth, "Mathilde Blind," Dict Lit Bio (98); auth, "Edith Simcox," Dict Lit Bio (98). **CONTACT ADDRESS** Eng Dept, Albion Col, 316 Vulgamore Hall, Albion, MI 49224. **EMAIL** jdiedrick@albion.edu

DIEHL, HUSTON
PERSONAL Born 10/01/1948, Greenville, PA **DISCIPLINE** ENGLISH, ICONOGRAPHY **EDUCATION** Colo Col, BA, 70; Duke Univ, MA, 71, PhD, 75. **CAREER** ASsst prof English, State Univ NY Genesco, 75-79; asst prof, 79-82, Assoc Prof English, Univ Okla, 82-, prof, Univ Iowa. **HONORS AND AWARDS** Nat Endowment Humanities fel in residence, Univ Chicago, 78-79. **MEMBERSHIPS** Renaissance Soc Am; MLA. **RESEARCH** Tudor and Stuart drama; sixteenth and seventeenth century literature; Renaissance iconography. **SELECTED PUBLICATIONS** Auth, Bewhored Images and Imagined Whores--Iconophobia and Gynophobia in Stuart Love Tragedies, Eng Lit Renaissance, Vol 26, 96, auth, Staging Reform, Reforming the Stage: Protestantism and Popular Theater in Early Modern England, Cornell UP, 97. **CONTACT ADDRESS** Dept of English, Univ of Iowa, 308 EPB, Iowa City, IA 52242. **EMAIL** huston-diehl@uiowa.edu

DIETRICH, BRYAN
PERSONAL Born 12/30/1965, Oklahoma City, OK, d **DISCIPLINE** ENGLISH **EDUCATION** Univ Sci and Arts Okla, Chickaska, Okla, BA, 86; Univ Southern Calif, MPW, 88; Univ N Tex, Denton, PhD, 94. **CAREER** Teaching Fel, Univ of N Tex, 91-94; Instr, Hesston Col, 94-95; Chair, Dept English, Newman Univ, 95-00. **HONORS AND AWARDS** Mary Patchell Fel, 92; Teacher of the Year Awd, Newman Univ, 96; Writers at Work Fel in Poetry, 96; Eve of St. Agnes Awd in Poetry, 98; Who's Who im Am, 00-01. **MEMBERSHIPS** Acad of Am Poets, Assoc Writing Prog, MLA, Semiotic Soc of Am, Int Asn for the Fantastic in Arts, The Milton Center. **RESEARCH** Creative Writing, 20th Century Poetry, Poetics, Semiotics, Gynocritics. **SELECTED PUBLICATIONS** Auth, "The Ghost of the Corpus Callosum: Doppleganger as Mind in Poe's 'William Wilson'," in Semiotics 1992 (Lanham: Univ Press of Am, 93), 279-287; auth, "The Truths Kiss: Intimations of Ofermod in Robert Penn Warren's 'Chief Joseph of the Nez Perce' and 'The Battle of Maldon'," The Distillery 1.1 (94); auth, "The Semiotic Monster: Frankestein and the Evolution of Sign," in Semiotics 1994, ed. C.W. Spinks and John Deely (NY: Peter Lang, 95), 87-89; coauth, "Archetype, Instinct and the Tree of Human Dream: Toward a Unification of Current Reader-Response and Evolutionary Brain Theories," in Semiotics 1993, ed. Robert S. Corrington and John Deely (NY: Peter Lang, 95), 3-16; auth, "The Age of Baum: Toward a Semiosic Understanding of Child's-Tale-Turned-Nuclear-Parable," in Semiotics 1993, ed. Robert S. Corrington and John Deely (NY: Peter Lang, 95), 123-132; auth, "The Stories of Raymond Carver: A Critical Study," book rev, Am Lit (Mar 96); auth, "Bodies at Rest, In Motion: Gynocritical Cosmography and the Semiosis of the Sublime in Postmodern American Poetry," in Semiotics 1995, ed. C.W. Spinks and John Deely (NY: Peter Lang, 96), 343-353; auth, "Atlantis," Chelsea 66 (99); auth, "A Sensible Longing," Nimrod 43-1 (99); auth, "The Magician," seven sonnets, Paris Rev 42-154 (00). **CONTACT ADDRESS** Dept Humanities and Soc Sci, Newman Univ, 3100 McCormick St, Wichita, KS 67213-2008. **EMAIL** dietrichb@newmanu.edu

DIETRICH, WILFRED O.
PERSONAL Born 05/22/1924, Burton, TX, m, 1969 **DISCIPLINE** ENGLISH, HISTORY **EDUCATION** Blinn Col, AA, 43; Sam Houston State Univ, BA, 46, MA, 48; East Tex State Univ (now Tex A & M Commerce), Doctor Education and English, 78. **CAREER** Public school teacher, Burton Independent Sch District, 43-58; instr and chemn of the Div of Humanities, Blinn Col, 58-. **HONORS AND AWARDS** Several fels during the summers; distinguished teacher Awd several times from public schools; many teaching Awds from Blinn Col. **MEMBERSHIPS** Tex Jr Col Asn, Tex Coun of English, Nat Coun of English, Am Folk Soc, Tex Hist Soc, many others. **RESEARCH** History--country, regional, families, special groups that have made an impact on the heritage of Washington County and the State of Texas, for example, several Indian tribes, Old Three Hundred, family history and the like. **SELECTED PUBLICATIONS** Auth, The Blazing Story of Washington County; auth, revision of The Blazing Story of Washington County; auth, History of the Brenham Manifest; auth, Work of Junior College Registrars. **CONTACT ADDRESS** Dept Humanities, Blinn Col, 902 College Ave, Brenham, TX 77833-4049.

DIGAETANI, JOHN LOUIS
PERSONAL Born 06/23/1943, Chicago, IL, d **DISCIPLINE** ENGLISH **EDUCATION** Univ Ill, BA, 65; North Ill Univ, MA, 67; Univ Wisc, PhD, 73. **CAREER** Instr, Providence Col, 67-69; instr, Univ New Orleans, 73-76; guest assoc prof, Harvard Univ, 81-82; prof, Hofsta Univ, 78-. **MEMBERSHIPS** MLA; Pirandello Soc Am. **RESEARCH** Literature; opera. **SELECTED PUBLICATIONS** Ed, The Handbook of Executive Communications, Dow Jones-Irwin, 86; auth, An Invitation to the Opera, Facts On File, 86, ppbk ed, Anchor/Doubleday, 91; auth, Puccini the Thinker, Peter Lang Press, 87; ed, A Companion to Pirandello Studies, Greenwood Press, 91; auth, Search for a Postmodern Theater: Interviews with Contemporary Playwrights, Greenwood Press, 92; ed, Opera and the Golden West, Fairleigh Dickinson Univ Press, 94; ed, Money: Lure, Lore, and Literature, Greenwood Press, 94; auth, Carlo Gozzi: A Life in 18th Century Venetian Theater, an Afterlife in Opera, McFarland and Co, 99. **CONTACT ADDRESS** Dept English, Hofstra Univ, 223 Calkins Hall, Hempstead, NY 11550. **EMAIL** jdigaetani@aol.com

DIGBY, JOAN
DISCIPLINE EIGHTEENTH CENTURY BRITISH LITERATURE, ART AND LITERATURE **EDUCATION** NYork Univ, PhD. **CAREER** Prof, dir, honors prog, Long Island Univ, C.W. Post Campus. **SELECTED PUBLICATIONS** Auth, Philosophy in the Kitchen; or, Problems in Eighteenth-Century

Culinary Aesthetics; Reading Goya's Dispartes; A Sound of Feathers; coauth, The Collage Handbook; coed, Permutations, Food for Thought; Inspired by Drink. **CONTACT ADDRESS** Long Island Univ, C.W. Post, Brookville, NY 11548-1300.

DIJKSTRA, BRAM
PERSONAL Born 07/05/1938, Tandjung Pandan, Indonesia, m, 1964 **DISCIPLINE** AMERICAN & COMPARATIVE LITERATURE **EDUCATION** Ohio State Univ, BA, 61, MA, 62; Univ Calif, Berkeley, PhD, 67. **CAREER** From actg instr to asst prof, 66-73, assoc prof, 73-85, prof Am & comp lit, Univ Calif, San Diego, 85-. **RESEARCH** Visual arts and literature; sociology of literature; literature and ideology. **SELECTED PUBLICATIONS** Auth, Faces in Skin, Oyez, 65; The Hieroglyphics of a New Speech; Cubism, Stieglitz and the early Poetry of William Carlos Williams, Princeton, 69; contribr, Encounters: Essays in Literature and the Visual Arts, Studio Vista, London, 71; Un Reve Americain: Norman Mailer et l'esthetique de la domination, Temps Mod, Paris 4/72; The androgyne in nineteenth-century art and literature, Comp Lit, winter 74; Painting and ideology: Picasso and Guernica, Praxis, 76; ed, William Carlos Williams on Art and Artists, New Directions, 78; Nicht-repressive rhythmische Strukturen in einigen Formen afro-amerikanischer und westindischer Musik, Die Zeichen, Fischer Verlag, Frankfurt, 81; auth Idols of Perversity: Fantasies of Feminine Evil in Fin-de-siecle Culture. Oxford Univ, 86; Defoe and Economics: The Fortunes of ROXANA in the History of Interpretation, MacMillan, 87; The High Cost of Parasols: Images of Women in Impressionist Art, California Light, Chronicle Books, 90; America and Georgia O'Keefe, Georgia O'Keefe, The New York Years, A A Knopf, 91; Early Modernism in Southern California: Provincialism or Eccentricity Modernist Art 1900-1950, Univ Calif, 96; Evil Sisters: The Threat of Female Sexuality and the Cult of Manhood, A A Knopf, 96; Georgia O'Keefe and the Eros of Place, Princeton Univ, 98. **CONTACT ADDRESS** Dept Lit, Univ of California, San Diego, 9500 Gilman Dr., La Jolla, CA 92093-5003.

DIK, HELMA
DISCIPLINE CLASSICS **EDUCATION** Univ Amsterdam, PhD, 95. **CAREER** Asst prof, Univ Chicago. **HONORS AND AWARDS** Junior Fel; Fel Lexikon des fruhgriechischen Epos; Graduate fel. **SELECTED PUBLICATIONS** Auth, 'Senex: een case-study uit de oudheid', Pentecostalia, 92; auth, 'Gekloofde zinnen langs de lijn', ICG, 94; auth, 'Vrij maar niet willekeurig: Pragmatische aspecten van constituentvolgorde in twee fragmenten uit Herodotus', Lampas, 94; auth, 'Ancient Greek warfare--a case study in constituent ordering, Mouton de Gruyter, 94; auth, Word Order in Ancient Greek. A Pragmatic Account of Word Order Variation in Herodotus, Gieben, 95. **CONTACT ADDRESS** Univ of Chicago, 5801 S Ellis, Chicago, IL 60637.

DILGEN, REGINA M.
PERSONAL Born 02/09/1954, Brooklyn, NY, m, 1988, 2 children **DISCIPLINE** ENGLISH **EDUCATION** Univ Fla, BA, 76; Fla Atlantic Univ, MA, 85; Univ S Fla, MA, 90. **CAREER** Assoc prof, Palm Beach Community Col. **MEMBERSHIPS** MLA, Nat Coun of Teachers of English, Fla Coun of Teachers of English, Fla Col English Asn. **RESEARCH** American Literature, Women's Literature. **CONTACT ADDRESS** Dept Commun, Palm Beach Comm Col, 42000 Congress Ave, Lake Worth, FL 33461. **EMAIL** dilgenr@pbcc.cc.fl.us

DILLARD, J. L.
PERSONAL Born 06/26/1924, Grand Salone, TX, w, 1985, 1 child **DISCIPLINE** ENGLISH **EDUCATION** SMU, BA, 49; MA, 51; Univ of Tex, PhD, 56. **CAREER** Unive of Puerto Rico and Institute of Caribbean Studies, 61-63, 64-66; Fer kauf Graduate School of Yeshivau, NYC, 68-71, 73-74; Prof of English, Northwestern State Univ, Natchitoches, LA, 75-89. **HONORS AND AWARDS** BA, With Highest Honors; Alumnus Phi Beta Kappa Research Associateship; Dept of Germanic Lgs, UT Austin; Travel and Research Grant, Institute of Caribbean Studies, Univ of Puerto Rico, 61. **MEMBERSHIPS** Society for Pidgin and Creole Linguistics; Linguistic Society of America; American Name Society. **RESEARCH** Social Dialects; History of Amer Vernacular English. **SELECTED PUBLICATIONS** Auth, "Black English, Its History and Usage in the United States," Random House, 72; auth, "A History of American English," Longman, 92. **CONTACT ADDRESS** Dept Humanities & Fine Arts, Shawnee State Univ, 940 2nd St, Portsmouth, OH 45662-4303. **EMAIL** mdillard@shawnee.edu

DILLER, CHRISTOPHER G.
PERSONAL Born 02/23/1964, Cleveland, OH, m, 1991, 2 children **DISCIPLINE** ENGLISH **EDUCATION** Miami Univ Ohio, BA, 87; Northwestern Univ, MA, 89; Univ Ut, PhD, 99. **CAREER** Asst prof, Berry Col, 99-. **HONORS AND AWARDS** Res Fel, Univ Ut, 97-98; Tanner Res Fel, Univ Ut, 96-97. **MEMBERSHIPS** MLA; MMLA; SCE; ISHR. **RESEARCH** History of rhetoric; elocution and aesthetics; 19th century American literature and culture; composition studies. **SELECTED PUBLICATIONS** Auth, "The Rhetoric of Reason: Writing and the Attractions of Argument," Rhetoric Soc Quart (98); auth, "The Art of Rhetoric: Aesthetics and Rhetoric in the American Renaissance," Rhetoric Soc Quart (98); auth, "Reality by Design: The Rhetoric and Technology of Authenticity in Education," Rhetoric Soc Quart (99); auth, "The Cultivation of Mind and Body in Nineteenth-Century American Delsartism," Rhetoric Soc Quart (00); auth, "'Fiction in Color:' Domesticity, Aestheticism, and the Visual Arts in the Criticism and Fiction of William Dean Howells," Nineteenth Century Lit (00); auth, "Infusing Disciplinary Rhetoric into Liberal Education: A Cautionary Tale," Rhetoric Rev (01); auth, "The Employment of English: Theory, Jobs, and the Future of Literary Studies," MMLA (01). **CONTACT ADDRESS** English Dept, Berry Col, PO Box 350, Mount Berry, GA 30149. **EMAIL** cdiller@berry.edu

DILLINGHAM, WILLIAM B.
PERSONAL Born 03/07/1930, Atlanta, GA, m, 1952, 3 children **DISCIPLINE** AMERICAN LITERATURE **EDUCATION** Emory Univ, AB, 55, AM, 56; Univ Pa, PhD, 61. **CAREER** From asst to assoc prof, 55-68, chmn, dept English, 79-82, Prof English, Emory Univ, 68-, Fulbright lectr, Univ Oslo, 64-65, Nat Endowment for Humanities res fel, 78-79; Guggenheim fel, 82-83. **MEMBERSHIPS** MLA; SAtlantic Mod Lang Asn; Melville Soc. **RESEARCH** Nineteenth century American literature. **SELECTED PUBLICATIONS** Auth, Dreaming Revolution, Transgression in the Development of American Romance, Am Lit, Vol 66, 94; The Civil War World of Melville, Herman, Sewanee Rev, Vol 103, 95p; Melville, Herman Malcolm Letter--Mans Final Lore, Rsrcs Am Lit Stud, Vol 22, 96; The Pluralistic Philosophy of Crane, Stephen, Am Lit, Vol 66, 94. **CONTACT ADDRESS** Dept of English, Emory Univ, Atlanta, GA 30322.

DILLMAN, RICHARD H.
PERSONAL Born 12/16/1942, Washington, DC, m, 1966, 2 children **DISCIPLINE** ENGLISH **EDUCATION** Univ Conn, BA, 65; Southern Conn St Univ, MA, 72; Univ Ore, MA, 75; DA, 76; PhD, 78. **CAREER** From Asst Prof to Prof, St Cloud St Univ, 78-. **HONORS AND AWARDS** Teaching Fel, Univ Ore, 75-78; Outstanding Contribution Awd, St Cloud St Univ, 89; NEH Summer Fel, 84; Can Embassy Enrichment Grant, 89; Grants, Minn St Univ. **MEMBERSHIPS** MEA, Thoreau Soc, ASLGS, ASLE, MCTE, ASCS. **RESEARCH** American literature, American transcendentalism, works of Henry David Thoreau. **SELECTED PUBLICATIONS** Ed, The Essays of Henry David Thoreau, 92; auth, "The Long Shadow of Thoreau: The Thoreauvian Tradition in Twentieth-Century American Nonfiction," in Essays on Henry David Thoreau: Rhetoric, Style and Audience (W Cornwall, CT: Locust Hill Pr, 93); coauth, Essays on Henry David Thoreau: Rhetoric, Style and Audience, Locust Hill Pr (W Cornwall, CT), 93; auth, "Reader Response to Walden: A Study of Undergraduate Reading Patterns," Teaching Thoreau's Walden and Other Works, MLA (96): 70-77; auth, "Fishing with a Heron on the Gooseberry River," Bird Watcher's Dig (99): 67-72; auth, The Major Essays of Henry David Thoreau, Whitston Publ, forthcoming. **CONTACT ADDRESS** Dept English, St. Cloud State Univ, 720 4th Ave S, Saint Cloud, MN 56301-4442. **EMAIL** rdillman@stcloudstate.edu

DILLON, BERT
PERSONAL Born 06/23/1937, Cherokee, OK, m, 1966 **DISCIPLINE** ENGLISH **EDUCATION** Univ Colo, BA, 60; Columbia Univ, MA, 63; Duke Univ, PhD (English), 72. **CAREER** From instr to asst prof, 65-74, Assoc Prof English, Univ SC, 75-. **MEMBERSHIPS** MLA; Mediaeval Acad Am. **RESEARCH** Chaucer; Middle English literature; Malory. **SELECTED PUBLICATIONS** Auth, My Brothers Voice, Virg Quart Rev, Vol 73, 97; Never Having Had You, I Cannot Let You Go, Olds, Sharon Poems of a Father Daughter Relationship, Lit Rev, Vol 37, 93. **CONTACT ADDRESS** Dept of English, Univ of So Carolina, Columbia, Columbia, SC 29205.

DILTS, MERVIN R.
PERSONAL Born 02/26/1938, Flemington, NJ **DISCIPLINE** CLASSICS **EDUCATION** Gettysburg Col, BA, 60; Ind Univ, MA, 61, PhD (classics), 64. **CAREER** Asst prof classics, Knox Col, 64-65 and Univ Ill, Urbana, 65-69; assoc prof, 69-79, Prof Classics, NY Univ, 79-, Am Philol Soc grant, 71; Am Coun Learned Soc grant-in-aid, 77. **MEMBERSHIPS** Am Philol Asn; Class Asn Atlantic States; Soc Textual Scholarship. **RESEARCH** Greek textual criticism; Greek codicology. **SELECTED PUBLICATIONS** Auth, Hiatus in the Orations of Aeschines, Am J Philol, Vol 115, 94. **CONTACT ADDRESS** Dept of Classics, New York Univ, 25 Waverly Pl, New York, NY 10003-6701.

DILWORTH, THOMAS
PERSONAL Born 03/31/1945, Detroit, MI **DISCIPLINE** ENGLISH **EDUCATION** St Michael's Col, BA, 69; Univ Toronto, MA, 71, PhD, 77. **CAREER** Lectr, St John Fisher Col (NY), 70-72; asst to assoc prof, 77-86, ch comp lit prog, 79-96, PROF ENGLISH, UNIV WINDSOR, 86-. **HONORS AND AWARDS** Woodrow Wilson fel, 69; SSHRC res grants, 86-89, 89-94; Killam fel, 92-94. **SELECTED PUBLICATIONS** Auth, The Liturgical Parenthesis of David Jones, 79; auth, The Shape of Meaning in the Poetry of David Jones, 88; coauth, The Talented Intruder: Wyndham Lewis in Canada 1939-45, 92; ed, Inner Necessities: The Letters of David Jones to Desmond Chute, 84. **CONTACT ADDRESS** Dept of English, Univ of Windsor, 2127 Chrysler Hall N, Windsor, ON, Canada N9B 3P4. **EMAIL** dilworth@uwindsor.ca

DIMAIO, MICHAEL
PERSONAL Born 06/05/1949, Providence, RI, d, 1980, 2 children **DISCIPLINE** CLASSICS **EDUCATION** Johns Hopkins Univ, BA, 70; Univ Mo, MA, 73, PhD, 77; Univ of RI, M.L.S., 80. **CAREER** Grad Teaching Asst, Univ of Mo-Columbia, 73; Instr, Dundee, Ill, 74-76; Substitute Teacher, Geneva Sch District, 77-78; Instr, St. Johns Country Day Sch, 78-79; Grad Asst, Univ of RI, 80; Instr, Nash Library, Gannon Univ, 80-83; Asst prof, Salve Regina Col, 83-87; Asst prof, Salve Regina Col, 87-88; Asst prof, Salve Regina Col, 88-90; Assoc prof, Salve Regina Univ, 90-97; Prof, Salve Regina Univ, 97-. **HONORS AND AWARDS** Dept & general honors, Johns Hopkins Univ; NDEA Title IV grant, MU; chemn, De Imperatonibus Romains, 96-97. **MEMBERSHIPS** APA; Asn of Ancient Hist. **RESEARCH** Roman history; Byzantine literature. **SELECTED PUBLICATIONS** Auth, "Zonaras, Julian, and Philostorgios on the Death of Constantine I," GOTR 26 (81): 118-124; auth, "Infaustis Ductoribus Praeviis: The Antiochene Connection, Part II," Byzantion 51 (81): 501-511; auth, The Early Church and State, Fortress Press, 82; auth, "History and Myth in Zonaras Epitome Historiarum," Byzantine Studies/Etudes byzantines, 10 (83): 230-255; auth, "Smoke in the Wind: Zonaras Use of Philostorgius in his Account of the Late Neo-Flavian Emperors, Byzantion 58 (88): 230-255; auth, "Ambiguitas Constantiniana: The Caeleste Signum Dei of Constantine the Great," Byzantia, 58 (88): 334-360; auth, "The Emperor Julian's Edicts of Religious Toleration," Ancient World, 20 (89): 99-110; auth, "The Proelium Cibalense et Proelium Campi Ardiensis: The First Civil War of Constantine I and Licinius I," Ancient World 21, (90): 67-91; auth, "Per Vim, Per Caedem, Per Bellum: A Study of Murder and Ecclesiastical Politics in the Year 337 A.D.," Byzantion 72 (92): 158-211; auth, "Imago Veritatis aut Verba in Speculo: Athanasius, the Meletians, and Linguistic Frontiers in Fourth Century Egypt," in Shifting Frontiers in Late Antiquity, ed. Ralph W. Mathisen and Hagith S. Sivan, (Aldershot, 96), 271-278. **CONTACT ADDRESS** 226 Davis St., Fall River, MA 02720. **EMAIL** mdimaio@atsids.net

DIMMITT, JEAN POLLARD
PERSONAL Born 11/22/1941, Richmond, VA, m, 1991, 2 children **DISCIPLINE** ENGLISH **EDUCATION** Longwood Col, BA, 63; Univ of Va, MA, 66; Univ of Kans, PhD, 88. **CAREER** Asst prof of education, Kans Wesleyan Univ, 88-90; Asst Prof of English to Assoc Prof of English, Washburn Univ, 90-. **MEMBERSHIPS** Nat Coun of Teachers of English; Kans Asn of Teachers of English; Confr on Col Composition and Commun. **RESEARCH** English pedagogy; composition; young adult Lit. **SELECTED PUBLICATIONS** Auth, Leaving Cold sassy: A Writer's Valediction, Kans English, 98; Cooperating Teachers: A guide and a Plea, Kans English, 96; More on Model Writers in Adolescent Lit, The ALAN Rev, 93; coauth, Energizing Social Studies Through Writing: A Handbook for Middle and High School Teachers, GSP Inc., 93; Integrating Writing and Social Studies: Alternatives to the Formal Research Paper, Soc Ed, 92. **CONTACT ADDRESS** Washburn Univ of Topeka, 1700 College Ave, Topeka, KS 66621. **EMAIL** zzdimm@washburn.edu

DIMOCK, WAI CHEE
PERSONAL Born 10/29/1953, Macau, d **DISCIPLINE** AMERICAN LITERATURE **EDUCATION** Harvard Univ, BA, 76; Yale Univ, PhD, 82. **CAREER** Asst to assoc prof, rutgers Univ, 82-90; assoc prof, Univ Calif San Diego, 90-92; assoc prof, Brandeis Univ, 92-97; prof, Yale Univ, 97-. **HONORS AND AWARDS** ACLS Fel; Dactyl Awd for Lit Theory; Hon Mention, James Russell Lowell Prize, MLA. **MEMBERSHIPS** MLA, ACLA, Lit and Sci Soc. **RESEARCH** American Literature, Law and Literature, World Literature. **SELECTED PUBLICATIONS** Auth, Empire for Liberty: Melville and the Poetics of Individualism, Princeton Univ Pr, 89; auth, "Feminism, New Historicism, and the Reade,r, Am Lit, (91); coed, Rethinking Class, Columbia Univ Pr, 94; auth, Residues of Justice: Literature, Law, Philosophy, Univ Calif Pr, 96; auth, "A Theory of Resonance,, PMLA, (97); auth, "Literature for the Planet," PMLA, (01); auth, "Deep Time: American Literature and World History," Am Lit Hist, (01). **CONTACT ADDRESS** Dept English, Yale Univ, New Haven, CT 06520. **EMAIL** wai.chee.dimock@yale.edu

DIONISOPOULOS, GEORGE N.
DISCIPLINE COMMUNICATIONS **EDUCATION** San Diego State Univ, BA, 76, MA, 80; Purdue Univ, PhD, 84. **CAREER** Grad tchg asst, , 77-79; instr, San Diego Miramar Col, 80-81; grad tchg asst, Purdue Univ, 81-82; asst prof, Stae Univ NJ, 84-85; asst prof, 85-91; assoc prof, 91-. **HONORS AND AWARDS** Student choice award, San Diego Miramar Col, 80-81; David Ross fel, Purdue Univ, 82-83; scholar and creative activity award, CA State Univ Res, 89; aff action fac develop prog award, 89; Meritorious perf and prof promise awards, 87, 90; B Aubrey Fisher award, outstanding article yr, W Jour Commun, 92; cert of appreciation, San Diego AIDS Network for Edu, 93; assoc ed, w jour of speech commun, 89-94; ch, w jour of speech commun, rhetoric and pub address interest gp, 89-90; ch, col curriculum comm, 93-; assoc ed, w jour of speech commun, 94-. **MEMBERSHIPS** Mem, Speech Commun Assn; W States Commun Assn. **SELECTED PUBLICATIONS** Coauth, Enthymematic Solutions to the Lockshin Defection Story: A Case Study in the Repair of a Problematic Narrative, Com-

mun Stud 41, 90; The Meaning of Vietnam: Political Rhetoric as Revisionist Cultural History, Quart Jour of Speech 78, 92; Martin Luther King, The American Dream and Vietnam: A Collision of Rhetorical Trajectories, W Jour Commun 56, 92; Crisis at Little Rock: Eisenhower, History, and Mediated Political Realities, Eisenhower's War of Words: Rhetoric and Leadership Mich State UP, 94. **CONTACT ADDRESS** Dept of Commun, San Diego State Univ, 5500 Campanile Dr, San Diego, CA 92182. **EMAIL** dionisop@mail.sdsu.edu

DIPASQUALE, THERESA M.
PERSONAL Born 06/15/1962, Greensburg, PA, m, 1999 **DISCIPLINE** LYRIC POETRY, THE LITERATURE CULTURE AND RELIGION OF THE ENGLISH RENAISSANCE **EDUCATION** Univ Notre Dame, BA, 83; Univ Va, MA, 83; PhD, 89. **CAREER** Asst Prof, Carleton Col; Fla Intl Univ; asst prof 92-96; Assoc Prof, 97-98; Asst Prof, Whitman Col, 98-. **MEMBERSHIPS** Phi Beta Kappa, MLA, John Donne Society. **RESEARCH** English Renaissance culture and religion; cross cultural reception of shakespeare. **SELECTED PUBLICATIONS** Auth, Heavens Last Best Gift, Eve and Wisdom in Paradise Lost, Mod Philol, 97; auth, Literature and Sacrament: The Sacred and the Secular in John Donne, Dequesne, Univ Press, 99. **CONTACT ADDRESS** Dept of Eng, Whitman Col, 345 Boyer Ave, Walla Walla, WA 99362-2038. **EMAIL** dipasqtm@whitman.edu

DIRCKS, PHYLLIS T.
PERSONAL Born 01/08/1935, New York, NY, m, 1963, 6 children **DISCIPLINE** ENGLISH **EDUCATION** St. John's Univ, BA, 57; Brown Univ, MA, 60; NY Univ, PhD, 67. **CAREER** Instr, Col of New Rochelle, 58-61; instr, St John's Univ, 61-63; instr to prof, Long Island Univ, 63-. **HONORS AND AWARDS** Woodrow Wilson Fel, 57; Danforth Found Grant, 65-67; Am Coun of Learned Soc Fel, 72-73; Danforth Found Assoc, 86-92; NEH Seminar 93, NEH Fel, 94; Long Island Univ Trustees Awd for Scholarship, 95; Long Island Univ Newton Awd for Distinguished Teaching 99. **MEMBERSHIPS** MLA; Am Soc for Eighteenth Century Studies; Soc for Theatre Res, Am Soc for Theatre Res; Theatre Libr Assoc. **RESEARCH** 18th Century English Literature, 18th Century English Drama and Theatre, 20th Century American Drama and Theatre. **SELECTED PUBLICATIONS** Auth, David Garrick, G.K. Hall, 85; auth, Two Burlettas of Kane O'Hara, Garland Pr, 87; auth, "Rich's Eclectic Comic Genius in the Necromancer", Theatre Notebook, Summer 95; auth, "David Garrick, George III, and the Politics of Revision", Philog Quarterly, Summer 97; auth, The Eighteenth-Century English Burletta, Univ of Victoria Pr, 99. **CONTACT ADDRESS** Dept English, Long Island Univ, C.W. Post, 720 Northern Blvd, Greenvale, NY 11548-1319. **EMAIL** dircks@liu.edu

DIRCKS, RICHARD J.
PERSONAL Born 05/22/1926, New York, NY, m, 1963, 6 children **DISCIPLINE** ENGLISH **EDUCATION** Fordham Coll, BA, 49; Fordham Univ, MA, 50; PhD, 61. **CAREER** Asst prof, Seaton Hall Univ, 50-56; asst prof, prof, St Johns Univ, 56-; chair, 64-67; assoc dean, 73-75; dir Human Res Cen, 75-77; inst, Fordham Univ Sch, 63-69. **HONORS AND AWARDS** Medal Outstanding Fac Achiev, ST Johns; Res Merit Awd, 89, 91, St Johns; Asn Danforth Found, 78-86; Shell Res Gnt, 67. **MEMBERSHIPS** MLAA; Am Soc 18th Cen Stud; Am Soc Theater Res. **RESEARCH** 18th Cent studies, especially novel and drama of England, critical theory. **SELECTED PUBLICATIONS** Coauth, Functional English, Republic (NY), 59; auth, Richard Cumberland, Twayne (Boston), 76; auth, Henery Fielding, Twayne (Boston), 83; ed, The Letters of Richard Cumberland, AMS Press (NY), 88; ed, The Unpublished Plays of Richard Cumberland, AMS Press (NY), vol 1, 91, vol 2, 92; ed, The Memoirs of Richard Cumberland, AMS Press (NY), 00. **CONTACT ADDRESS** Dept Eng, St. John's Univ, 8150 Utopia Pkwy, Jamaica, NY 11439-0001. **EMAIL** rjdircks@erols.com

DIRST, MATTHEW
PERSONAL Born 09/06/1961, Aurora, IL **DISCIPLINE** MUSICOLOGY, ORGAN, HARPSICHORD **EDUCATION** Univ Ill, BM, 83; Southern Methodist Univ, MM, 85; Stanford Univ, PhD, 96. **CAREER** Lect Harpsichord, Stanford Univ, 94-96; Lect in Mus Hist, San Jose State Univ, 95-96; Asst Prof Music, University of Houston, 96- . **HONORS AND AWARDS** Fulbright Scholar, France, 85-87; Am Guild of Organists Young Artist Compet, 90; 2nd Prize, Warsaw Int Harpsichord Comp, 93. **MEMBERSHIPS** Am Musicol Soc; Am Guild of Organists; Am Organ Inst. **RESEARCH** Bach, Bach reception, Baroque Performance Practice. **SELECTED PUBLICATIONS** Bach's French Overtures and the Politics of Overdotting, Early Mus, Feb 97. **CONTACT ADDRESS** Moores School of Music, Univ of Houston, Houston, TX 77204-4201. **EMAIL** mdirst@uh.edu

DISCENZA, NICOLE GUENTHER
PERSONAL Born Detroit, MI **DISCIPLINE** ENGLISH **EDUCATION** Univ Mich, BA, 91; Univ Notre Dame, Master Medieval Studies, 93; PhD, 96. **CAREER** From adj asst prof to asst prof & dir of undergrad studies in the Medieval Inst, Univ of Notre Dame, 96-98; asst prof, Hillsdale Col, 98-. **HONORS AND AWARDS** Golden Key Nat Hon Soc, Univ of Mich, 90; Phi Beta Kappa, Univ of Mich, 90; Mellon Fel, 91-95; Mellon Dissertation Year Fel, 95-96; Summer Leave Grant, Hillsdale Col, 00. **MEMBERSHIPS** Int Soc of Anglo-Saxonists, Modern Lang Asn, Medieval Acad, Medieval Asn of the Midwest. **RESEARCH** Alfred the Great: his texts and his program of translation. **SELECTED PUBLICATIONS** Auth, "Dialectical Structure in Chretien de Troyes's 'Cliges,'" Romance Lang 8 (96): 21-25; auth, "Power, Skill and Virtue in the Old English 'Boethius,'" Anglo-Saxon England 26 (97): 81-108; auth, "'Wise wealhstodas': The prologue to Sirach as a Model for Alfred's Preface to the 'Pastoral Care,'" J of English and Germanic Philol 97 (98): 488-499; auth, "Alfredian Texts," in Blackwell Encycl of Anglo-Saxon England, ed. Michael Lapidge (Oxford: Blackwell, 99), 29-30; auth, "The Influence of Gregory the Great on the Alfredian Social Imaginary," in Gregory the Great and the Germanic World, ed. Rolf H. Bremmer (Leuven: Peeters, in press); auth, King Alfred: A Bibliography, with Special Attention to Literature," in Basic Readings in Old English Prose, ed. Paul E. Szarmach (New York: Garland, in press). **CONTACT ADDRESS** Dept English, Hillsdale Col, 33 E College St, Hillsdale, MI 49242-1205. **EMAIL** nicole.discenza@hillsdale.edu

DITSKY, JOHN M.
DISCIPLINE ENGLISH LANGUAGE; LITERATURE **EDUCATION** Detroit, PhB, MA; NY Univ, PhD, 67. **CAREER** Prof **SELECTED PUBLICATIONS** Auth, essays on East of Eden; John Steinbeck: Life, Work and Criticism; The Onstage Christ; The Grapes of Wrath; Friend & Lover; poetry ed, The Windsor Rev. **CONTACT ADDRESS** Dept of English Language and Literature, Univ of Windsor, 401 Sunset Ave, Windsor, ON, Canada N9B 3P4. **EMAIL** ditsky@uwindsor.ca

DIXON, KATHLEEN
PERSONAL Born 01/23/1955, Richland, WA **DISCIPLINE** ENGLISH **EDUCATION** Univ Mich, PhD, 91 **CAREER** Asst prof, E Ore St Col, 84-85; asst prof, Ohio St Univ, 89-91; asst prof, Univ N Dak, 91-96; assoc prof, Univ N Dak, 96- **MEMBERSHIPS** Modern Lang Assoc; Ntl Council Teachers of English; **RESEARCH** Ntl Women's Studies Assoc; Rhetoric; Culture Studies **SELECTED PUBLICATIONS** Outbursts in Academe: Multicuturalism and Other Conflicts, Heinemann/Boynton/Cook, 98; Making Relationships: Gender in the Forming of Academic Community, Lang Publ, 97 **CONTACT ADDRESS** Univ of No Dakota, Box 7209, Grand Forks, ND 58202. **EMAIL** dixon@badlands.nodak.edu

DIXON, LYNDA D.
PERSONAL Born 11/01/1944, Enid, OK, m, 1999, 2 children **DISCIPLINE** COMMUNICATION **EDUCATION** Southwest Mo State Univ, BS, 66, MA, 69; Univ of Ok, PhD, 90. **CAREER** Vis lectr/asst prof, Univ of Ok, 88-91; asst prof, Univ of New Mex, 91-92; asst prof/vis prof, Indiana Univ South Bend, 91-96; Assoc prof, Grad coord, Bowling Green State Univ, 96-; Fac Assoc Graduate Col, BGSU. **HONORS AND AWARDS** Alumni Fel, Bowling Green State Univ, 97; doctoral minority fel, Ok State Regents for Higher Ed, 87-88; Top Paper, Intercultural ICA, 96, NCA, 98. **MEMBERSHIPS** Nat Commun Asn; Central States Commun Asn; Ohio State Commun Asn; Int Commun Asn; Int Asn of Intercultural Studies; Cherokee Nation of Oklahoma. **RESEARCH** Health communication; intercultural communication; organizational communication; Native Americans in Society. **SELECTED PUBLICATIONS** Coauth," Icons of Bureaucratic Therapy: An application of Eco's Semiotic Methodology in an Intercultural Health Care Setting," Intercultural Commun Studies, 99; auth, "I Can Walk Both Ways: Identity Integration of American Indians in Oklahoma," Human Commun Res, 98; auth, Signs in the Organization: Architectural Changes as Organizational Rhetoric in a Public Health Facility, Commun and Identity Across Cultures: Int and Intercultural Commun Annual NCA 23, Sage, 98; "Patterns of Communication and Interethnic Integration: A Study of American Indians in Oklahoma," Canadian J of Native Ed, 98; auth, The Cultural Deprivation of an Oklahoma Chrokee Family, Commun and Identity Across Cultures: Int and Intercultural Commun Annual NCA 22, Sage, 97; auth, The Dilemma of Oklahoma Indian Women Elders: Women's Traditional Roles and Sociocultural Roles, Cross-cultural Aging in the U.S., Erlbaum, 97; auth, The Language Culture of Rap Music, Language, Rhythm, and Sound, Univ of Pittsburgh Press, 97; auth, Strategic Communication in Business and the Professions, Houghton Mifflin, 97; coauth, "Intercultural communication: Trends, problems, and prospects," Intercultural Communication Studies, 00; coauth, The cultural perspective of a publlic health facility for Oklahoma American Indians: Architectural changes as organizational rhetoric, Rhetoric in intercultural contexts: International and intercultural communication annual NCA 22, 00. **CONTACT ADDRESS** Dept of Interpersonal Commun, Bowling Green State Univ, 313 West Hall, Bowling Green, OH 43403. **EMAIL** lyndad@bgnet.bgsu.edu

DIXON, MIMI S.
PERSONAL m, 4 children **DISCIPLINE** ENGLISH **EDUCATION** Sarah Lawrence Col, AB, Chicago, MA, PhD. **CAREER** Prof, 80-; dept chair. **RESEARCH** Writing programs, composition theory and teaching. **SELECTED PUBLICATIONS** Auth, Tragicomic Recognitions: From Medieval Liturgy to Shakespearean Romance; Seeing and Saying in The Winter Tale; Thys Body of Mary: Femynyte and Inward Mythe, The Digby Mary Magdalene; Not Know me Yet?: Looking at Cleopatra, Three Renaissance Tragedies. **CONTACT ADDRESS** Wittenberg Univ, Springfield, OH 45501-0720.

DIXON, NANCY J.
PERSONAL Born 05/06/1955, Karachi, Pakistan, s **DISCIPLINE** LITERATURE **EDUCATION** Univ New Orleans, BA, 88; MA, 91; La State Univ, PhD, 95. **CAREER** Instr, Univ New Orleans, 95-. **HONORS AND AWARDS** LEH, 99; 00. **MEMBERSHIPS** MLA. **RESEARCH** Southern women writers; 19th and 20th-century American literature. **SELECTED PUBLICATIONS** Auth, Fortune and Misery: Sallie Rhett Roman of New Orleans: A Biographical Portrait and Selected Fiction, 1891-1920, La State UP, 99; auth, Sallie Rhett Roman of the New Orleans Times Democrat: Race, Women and Southern Aristocracy in the Novellas 'Tonie' and 'Folette of Timbalier Island, Greenwood Pub, 01. **CONTACT ADDRESS** 3216 Saint Philip St, New Orleans, LA 70119-3925. **EMAIL** ndixon@uno.edu

DIXON, WHEELER WINSTON
PERSONAL Born 03/12/1950, New Brunswick, NJ, m, 1986 **DISCIPLINE** ENGLISH **EDUCATION** Livingston Col, AB, 72; Rutgers Univ, MA, MPhil, 80; PhD, 82. **CAREER** Inst, Livingston Col, 69-72; inst, Rutgers Univ, 74-84; lectr, New Sch for Social Res, 83; asst prof, Univ Neb, 84-88; assoc prof, chemn, Film Stud Prog, Univ Neb, 88-92; guest lectr and progrmr, Natl Film Theatre of the Brit Film Inst and Mus of the Moving Image, 91; guest progrmr, Natl Film Theatre of the Brit Film Inst, 92; Chemn, Film Stud Minor, prof, Univ Neb, 92-98; guest lectr, New Sch for Social Res, 97; guest lectr, Univ Amsterdam, 99; chemn, Film Stud Major, prof, Univ Neb, 99- . **HONORS AND AWARDS** Col of Arts & Sci Awd for Distinguished Teaching, 93; Recognition Awd for Contributions to Students, 90-91, 91-92, 93-94, 94-95, 95-96, 96-97. **MEMBERSHIPS** Southwest Popular Culture Assn; Univ Film & Video Assn, Soc for Cinema Studies; Modern Lang Assn; Amer Assn of Univ Profs. **RESEARCH** Film studies. **SELECTED PUBLICATIONS** Auth, The Early Film Criticism of Francois Truffaut, Ind Univ Pr, 93; auth, Re-Viewing British Cinema 1900-1992: Essays and Interviews, SUNY Pr, 94; auth, It Looks at You: The Returned Gaze in Cinema, SUNY Pr, 95; auth The Films of Jean-Luc Godard, SUNY Pr, 97; auth, The Exploding Eye: A Re-Visionary History of 1960s American Experimental Cinema, SUNY pr, 97; auth, The Transparency of Spectacle, SUNY Pr, 98; auth, Disaster and Memory: Celebrity Culture and the Crisis of Hollywood Cinema, Columbia Univ Pr, 99; auth, Film Genre 2000: New Critical Essays, SUNY Pr, 00; auth, The Second Centruy of Cinema: The Past and Future of the Moving Image, SUNY Pr, 00; auth, Collected Interviews: Voices from 20th Century Cinema, So Ill Univ Pr, forthcoming. **CONTACT ADDRESS** Dept of English, Univ of Nebraska, Lincoln, 202 Andrews Hall, Lincoln, NE 68588-0333. **EMAIL** wdixon@unlserv.unl.edu

DJOS, MATTS G.
PERSONAL Born 11/18/1937, Seattle, WA, m, 1961, 3 children **DISCIPLINE** ENGLISH **EDUCATION** Univ Washington, BA, 61; Univ Idaho, MA, 68; Tex A & M Univ, PhD, 75. **CAREER** Prof, Mesa State Col, **HONORS AND AWARDS** Fel, Tex A & M Univ, 69-70. **MEMBERSHIPS** PCA/ACA, ALA, John Donne Soc. **RESEARCH** Literature of Addiction. **SELECTED PUBLICATIONS** Auth, "Trailer Sailing: Cars and Driving," Sail, (00): 52-60; auth, "doubling Back: Two Landlocked Coloradans Return to the Southern California Coast for a Second Look," 48 North, (00): 54-59; auth, "Marriage, Impotence, and Objectification in Berryman and Lowell," Dionysos; auth, "John Berryman's Testimony of alcoholism: Through the Looking glass of Poetry and the Henry Persona," The Languages of Addiction, St Martin's Press, 99; auth, "John Berryman's 'Phase Four' and His Precarious Attempt to Find a compromise Between Drunkenness, Sobriety, and the A.A. Twelve Step Program," Dionysus: Journal of Literature and Addiction, 99; auth, "Recreation for Aging Athletes," chronicle of Higher Education, 98; "Alcoholism in Literature," Issues and Identities in Literature, Salem Press, 97; auth, "Twelve-step Programs in Literature," Issues and Identities in Literature, Salem Press, 97; auth, "alcoholism in Ernest Hemingway's The Sun also Rises: A wine and Roses Perspective of the Lost Generation," Hemingway Review, (95): 64-78; auth, "analysis and explication, Bjornstjerne Bjornson's The fisher Maiden. Masterplots: Twentieth Anniversary Revised 2nnd ed, Salem Press, 97; auth, "Analysis and explication: To Earthward. A Poem by Robert Frost, Salem Press; 92 **CONTACT ADDRESS** Dept Lang & Lit, Mesa State Col, PO Box 2647, Grand Junction, CO 81502-2647. **EMAIL** djos@mesastate.edu

DJWA, SANDRA A.
PERSONAL Born St. John's, NF, Canada **DISCIPLINE** ENGLISH **EDUCATION** Memorial Univ, tchr A level, 56; Univ British Columbia, BEd, 64, PhD, 68. **CAREER** Prof Eng, Simon Fraser Univ, 68-73; assoc prof, Simon Fraser Univ, 73-80; ch, Eng, Simon Fraser Univ, 86-94, bd govs, 90-96; prof, Simon Fraser Univ, 81-99. **HONORS AND AWARDS** Sr. Kil-

lam Res Fel, 81-83; Fel, Royal Soc of Canada, 94; Trimark Women's Mentor Awd, 99. **MEMBERSHIPS** Asn Can & Quebec Lits; Can Asn Chs Eng; Asn Can Tchrs Eng; Royal Soc Can. **SELECTED PUBLICATIONS** Auth, "F.R. Scott," Canadian Writers and Their Works, Toronto: ECW Press, (90): 173-227; auth, "No Other Way: Sinclair Ross's Stories and Novels," Sinclair Ross's As For Me and My House: Five Decades of Criticism, Toronto: Unvi of Toronto Press, 91; auth, Giving Canada a Literary History: A Memoir by Carl F. Klinck, Ottawa/London: Carleton Univ Press for Univ of Western Ontario, 91; auth, "Who Is This Man Smith?: Second and Third Thoughts on Canadian Modernism," Toronto: Oxford Univ Press, (92): 204-15; auth, "Forays in the Bush Garden: Northrop Frye and Canadian Poetry," The Lagacy of Northrop Frye, Toronto: Univ of Toronto Press, (94): 130-45; auth, "Getting Down to the Primal: The Apprenticeship of Margaret Atwood," Toronto: Anansi, (95): 13-46; auth, "P.K. Page: A Bbiographical Interview," P.K. Page: A Special Issue, The Malahat Review, 117, (96): 33-54; auth, "Alfred Earle Birney 1904-1995," Proceedings of the Royal Society of Canada 6:7, (96): 130-32; auth, "Pratt's Modernism, or Digging into the Strata," Boulder Flights: Essays on the Canadian Long Poem, eds. Frank Tierney and Angela Robbeson, (Ottawa: Univ of Ottawa Press, 98): 65-80; co-ed, Selected Poems of E.J. Pratt, with an Introduction by Sandra Djwa, Toronto: Univ of Toronto Press, 99. **CONTACT ADDRESS** Dept of English, Simon Fraser Univ, 8888 Univ Dr, Burnaby, BC, Canada V5A 1S6. **EMAIL** djwa@sfu.ca

DOAK, ROBERT
PERSONAL 1 child **DISCIPLINE** ENGLISH LITERATURE **EDUCATION** Ark State Univ, BA; Univ Ark, MA, PhD. **CAREER** Prof. **HONORS AND AWARDS** Pres, Newsletter Pop Cult in the S. **RESEARCH** Popular literature and film. **SELECTED PUBLICATIONS** Ed, Newsletter of the Pop Cult in the South. **CONTACT ADDRESS** Dept of Eng, Wingate Univ, Campus Box 3059, Wingate, NC 28174. **EMAIL** robdoak@wingate.edu

DOAN, JAMES E.
PERSONAL Born 04/11/1953, Palo Alto, CA **DISCIPLINE** FOLKLORE, CELTIC STUDIES, MEDIEVAL LITERATURE **EDUCATION** Univ Calif, BA, 75; MA, 77; Harvard Univ, MA, 78; PhD, 81. **CAREER** Assoc prof, dean, Chamberlayne Jr. Col, 81-88; prof, Nova Southeastern Univ, 88-. **HONORS AND AWARDS** NEH, 84; British Coun, 93, 96; Nova Southeastern Univ Fac Awd, 01. **MEMBERSHIPS** MLA, Am Conf for Irish Studies, Int Assoc for the Study of Irish Lit. **RESEARCH** Folklore, Celtic Studies, Medieval Literature, Irish-American Studies. **SELECTED PUBLICATIONS** Auth, The Romance of Cearbhall and Fearbhlaidh, Dolmen Pr, 85; auth, Women and Goddesses in Early Celtic History, Myth and Legend, Northeastern Univ, 87; auth, Cearbhall O Dalaigh: An Irish Poet in Romance and Oral Tradition, Garland Pr, 90; auth, Early Celtic, Irish and Mediterranean Connections, Tema, Cagliari, Italy, 96; auth, The Otherworld Journey: A Celtic and Universal Theme, Princess Grace Libr, Monaco, 98; auth, "How the Irish and Scots Became Indians: Colonial Traders and Agents and the Southeastern Tribes," New Hibernia Rev, (99); auth, "The Voyage of St Brendan: Otherworld Tale, Christian Apologia or Medieval Travelog?" ABEI Jour, (00); auth, "Revisiting the Blasket Island Memoirs," Irish Studies Rev, (00); coauth, "Reverine Crossings: Gender, Identity and the Reconstruction of National Mythic Narrative in the Crying Game," Cult Studies, (01). **CONTACT ADDRESS** Dept Lib Arts, Nova Southeastern Univ, Fort Lauderdale, 3301 College Ave, Ft Lauderdale, FL 33314. **EMAIL** doan@nova.edu

DOAN, LAURA L.
PERSONAL Born 07/16/1951, San Diego, CA **DISCIPLINE** ENGLISH, WOMEN'S STUDIES **EDUCATION** Univ San Diego, BA, 73; San Francisco State Univ, MA, 75; Univ Chicago, PhD, 83. **CAREER** Asst prof, Stetson Univ, 83-89; prof, SUNY Geneseo, 89-. **HONORS AND AWARDS** NEH Fel, 97-98; Robert W MacVittie Supported Prof, 99-02. **MEMBERSHIPS** MLA, N Am Conf on Brit Studies. **RESEARCH** Lesbian and Gay Studies, History of Sexuality, Modern/Contemporary British Literature and Culture. **SELECTED PUBLICATIONS** Ed, Old Maids to Radical Spinsters: Unmarried Women in the Twentieth-Century Novel, Univ of Ill Pr, 91; ed, The Lesbian Postmodern, Columbia Univ Pr, 94; coed, Sexology in Culture: Labelling Bodies and Desires, Univ Chicago Pr, 98; coed, Sexology Uncensored: The Documents of Sexual Science, Univ Chicago Pr, 98; coed, Palatable Poison: Critical Perspectives on the Well of Loneliness, Columbia Univ Pr, 01; auth, Fashioning Sapphism: The Origins of a Modern English Lesbian Culture, Columbia Univ Pr, 01. **CONTACT ADDRESS** Dept English, SUNY, Col at Geneseo, Geneseo, NY 14454. **EMAIL** doan@geneseo.edu

DOANE, ALGER NICOLAUS
PERSONAL Born 08/16/1938, Fairfield, CA, m, 1979, 4 children **DISCIPLINE** ENGLISH & MEDIEVAL EUROPEAN LITERATURE **EDUCATION** Univ CA, Berkeley, BA, 61, MA, 63; Univ Toronto, PhD, 71. **CAREER** Lectr Eng, Victoria Univ Wellington, 65-71; asst prof, 71-77, assoc prof, 77-89, prof eng, Univ WI-Madison, 90, Am Coun Learned Soc fel, 73-74. **HONORS AND AWARDS** NEH summer stipend, 76; NEH proj grant, 94, 97, 00. **MEMBERSHIPS** Mediaeval Acad Am; ISAS. **RESEARCH** Old Eng poetry. **SELECTED PUBLICATIONS** Auth, Anglo Saxon Manuscripts, Orality and Texuality, 74; ed, Genesis A: A New Edition, Univ Wis, 78; The Saxon Genesis 991, 91; co-auth (with C P Pasternack) Vox Intexta: Orality and Texuality in the Middle Ages, 91; co-ed, Anglo-Saxon Manuscripts in Microfiche Facsimile. **CONTACT ADDRESS** Dept of Eng, Univ of Wisconsin, Madison, 600 North Park St, Madison, WI 53706-1403. **EMAIL** andoane@facstaff.wisc.edu

DOBSON, FRANK
PERSONAL Born 07/03/1952, Buffalo, NY, m, 1991, 3 children **DISCIPLINE** ENGLISH **EDUCATION** SUNY, BA; UNLV, MA, 75; Bowling Green SU, PhD, 85. **CAREER** Assoc prof, Ind Univ, 91-94; from asst prof to assoc prof, Wright State Univ, 94-. **HONORS AND AWARDS** Ford Found Fel, 92; Zora Neale Hurston/Bessie Head Fiction Awd, 94; Master Artists Awd, 96. **MEMBERSHIPS** AWP **RESEARCH** Fiction writing, African American literature and culture. **SELECTED PUBLICATIONS** Auth, The Race is not Given. **CONTACT ADDRESS** Dept English, Wright State Univ, Dayton, 3640 Colonel Glenn Hwy, Dayton, OH 45435-0001.

DOBSON, JEANNIE S.
PERSONAL Born Birmingham, AL, m, 2 children **DISCIPLINE** ENGLISH **EDUCATION** Queens Col, BA; Fairleigh-Dickinson Univ, MAT. **CAREER** Instructor and Writing Center Dir, Greenville Tech Col, 84-. **HONORS AND AWARDS** Thomas Brockman Scholarship, Oxford Univ. **MEMBERSHIPS** SE Writing Center Asn; Two-Year Col Teachers of Eng, SE; Eng Speaking Union. **RESEARCH** Legends and Folklore of Oconee County, SC. **CONTACT ADDRESS** Dept Eng, Greenville Tech Col, PO Box 5616, Greenville, SC 29606-5616.

DOBSON, JOANE
PERSONAL Born 03/27/1945, New York, NY, m, 1963, 3 children **DISCIPLINE** ENGLISH **EDUCATION** Kings Col, BA, 63; SUNY Albany, MA, 77; Univ Mass, PhD, 85. **CAREER** Vis asst prof, Amherst Col, 85-86; vis asst prof, Tufts Univ, 86-87; asst to assoc prof, Fordham Univ, 87-. **HONORS AND AWARDS** NEH Grants, 90-91; Agatha Awd Nomination, 97. **MEMBERSHIPS** MLA; Am Lit Soc; Mystery Writers of Am; Sisters in Crime. **RESEARCH** Nineteenth-century women's literature and history; mystery fiction. **SELECTED PUBLICATIONS** Auth, "The Hidden Hand: Subversion of Cultural Ideology in Three Mid-Nineteenth-Century American Women's Novels", Am Quarterly 38.2, (86): 223-242; auth, "Dickinson and Strategies of Reticence: The Women Writer in Nineteenth-Century America, Ind Univ Pr, 89; auth, "The American Renaissance Re-envisioned", The (Other) American Traditions, ed Joyce Warren, Rutgers Univ Pr, (93): 164-182; auth, "Sex, Wit and Sentiment: Frances Osgood and the Poetry of Love", Am Lit 65.4, (93); 631-48; auth, "Reclaiming Sentimental Literature", Am Lit 69.2 (97): 263-288; auth, Quieter Than Sleep, Doubleday, (NY), 97; auth, The Northbury Papers, Doubleday, (NY), 98; auth, The Raven and the Nightingale, Doubleday, (NY), 99; auth, Cold and Pure and Very Dead, Doubleday, (NY), (forthcoming). **CONTACT ADDRESS** Dept English, Fordham Univ, 441 E Fordham Rd, Bronx, NY 10458-5149. **EMAIL** dedcons@aol.com

DOBSON, JOANNE
DISCIPLINE 19TH-CENTURY AMERICAN LITERATURE **EDUCATION** Univ MA/Amherst, PhD. **CAREER** Assoc prof, Fordham Univ. **RESEARCH** Emily Dickinson, the canon. **SELECTED PUBLICATIONS** Auth, Sex, Wit and Sentiment: Frances Osgood and the Poetry of Love, Amer Lit 65, 93; The American Renaissance Reenvisioned, American Traditions: Nineteenth Century Women Writers, Rutgers UP, 93. **CONTACT ADDRESS** Dept of Eng Lang and Lit, Fordham Univ, 113 W 60th St, New York, NY 10023.

DODD, WAYNE DONALD
PERSONAL Born 09/23/1930, Clarita, OK, m, 1958, 2 children **DISCIPLINE** ENGLISH **EDUCATION** Univ Okla, BA, 55, MA, 57, PhD(English), 63. **CAREER** Teaching asst English, Univ Okla, 55-59; from instr to prof English, 60-73, Univ Colo; Prof to Distinguished Prof English, Ohio Univ, 73-; Ed, Abstr English Studies, 62-65; Am Coun Learned Soc study fel, 64-65; ed, Ohio Rev, 71-; lit adv, Ohio Arts Coun, 75-. **HONORS AND AWARDS** NEA Fel in Poetry; Fel, Rockefeller Found, Italy; Individual Artist Fel, Ohio Arts Coun; Krout Awd for Lifetime Contributions to Poetry; CCLM Awd for Distinguished Editing. **RESEARCH** Contemporary poetry. **SELECTED PUBLICATIONS** Auth, The Names You Gave It, LSU Press, 80; General Mule Poems, 81; Sometimes Music Rises, Univ Ga Press, 85; Echoes of the Unspoken, Univ Ga Press, 90; Of Desire & Disorder, Carnegie Mellon Univ Press, 94; Toward the End of the Century, Univ Iowa Press, 95; The Blue Salvages, Carnegie Mellon Univ Press, 98. **CONTACT ADDRESS** Ohio Univ, 343 Scott Quad, Athens, OH 45701-2979. **EMAIL** doddw@ohiou.edu

DODGE, ROBERT KENDALL
PERSONAL Born 03/29/1941, Cortland, NY, m, 1963, 2 children **DISCIPLINE** ENGLISH **EDUCATION** Rice Univ, BA, 63; Univ Tex, Austin, MA, 64, PhD(English), 67. **CAREER** Asst prof English, Wis State Univ, Stevens Point, 67-70; asst prof, 70-76, assoc prof to prof English, Univ Nev, Las Vegas, 76-. **RESEARCH** Literature of the American Indian; Herman Melville; Early American Almanacs. **SELECTED PUBLICATIONS** Auth, Didactic Humor in the Almanacs of Early America, J Popular Cult, winter 71; co-ed, Voices from Wah' Kontah, An Anthology of Native American Poetry, Int Publ, 74; coed, New and Old Voices from Wah' Kon-tah, Int Publ, 84; ed, Early American Almanac Humor, The Popular Press, Bowling Green State Univ, 87; coauth, A Tale Type and Motif Index of Early U.S. Almanac Narrative, Greenwood Press, 92; auth, A Topical Index of Early U.S. Almanacs, 1776-1800, Greenwood Press, 97. **CONTACT ADDRESS** Dept of English, Univ of Nevada, Las Vegas, PO Box 455011, Las Vegas, NV 89154-5011. **EMAIL** dodge@nevada.edu

DODGE, TIMOTHY
PERSONAL Born 04/15/1957, Boston, MA **DISCIPLINE** LIBRARY SCIENCE & HISTORY **EDUCATION** Swarthmore Col, BA, 79; Columbia Univ, MLS, 80; Univ NH, MA, 82 PhD, 92. **CAREER** Librn, Univ NH, 82-84, 87-92; librn, Barry Univ, 84-87; librn, Auburn Univ, 92-. **HONORS AND AWARDS** Prof Achievement Awd, 86-87, Barry Univ. **MEMBERSHIPS** Am Libr Asn; Ala Libr Asn; Asn Col & Res Librs; Ala Asn Col & Res Librs; Psi Gamma Mu; Phi Alpha Theta; Org Am Hist; NH Hist Society. **RESEARCH** Modern American history; library science. **SELECTED PUBLICATIONS** Auth, art, From Spirituals to Gospel Rap: Gospel Music Periodicals, 94; auth, art, Crime and Punishment in New Hampshire, 1812-1914, 95; auth, Poor Relief in Durham, Lee, and Madbury, New Hampshire, 1732-1891, 95; auth, art, US Department of Commerce CD-ROM Serial Databases, 96; auth art, Criminal Justice Web Sites, 98. **CONTACT ADDRESS** 1772 Lee Rd 88, Waverly, AL 36879. **EMAIL** dodgeti@auburn.edu

DODSON, DANITA JOAN
PERSONAL Born 02/16/1964, Morristown, IN, s **DISCIPLINE** ENGLISH **EDUCATION** Lincoln Memorial Univ, BA, 85; E Tenn State Univ, MA, 86; Univ S Miss, PhD, 94. **CAREER** Teacher and dept chair, Hancock County High Sch, 86-95, 96-; adj prof, Walters State Col, 86-91, 96-; prof and dept chair, Univ Mobile Latin Am Campus, Nicaragua, 95-96. **HONORS AND AWARDS** Distinguished Fac Award, Walters State Col, 00; Fel, NEH, 97; Who's Who in Am, 02. **MEMBERSHIPS** MLA; Nat Coun of Teachers of English; Nat Educ Asn; Soc for Utopian Studies; Delta Kappa Gamma; Intl Women's Educ Soc; Nat Women's Studies Asn. **RESEARCH** 20th Century literature; Utopian/Dystopian literature; Women's studies; Postcolonial literature. **SELECTED PUBLICATIONS** Auth, "The Cycle of Utopia in Buchi Emecheta's Rape of Shavi," Obsidian II: Black Literature in Review, (96): 3-20; auth, "An Interview with Margaret Atwood," Critique, (97): 96-104; auth, "We Lived in the Blank White Spaces: Emancipating Enslaved Voices in Margaret Atwood's 'The Handmaid's Tale," Utopian Studies, 997): 66-86. **CONTACT ADDRESS** Dept English, Walters State Col, R.R. 3, PO Box 416, Sneedville, TN 37869-9536. **EMAIL** danita@naxs.net

DOENGES, NORMAN ARTHUR
PERSONAL Born 08/23/1926, Ft Wayne, IN, m, 1952, 3 children **DISCIPLINE** ANCIENT HISTORY, CLASSICS **EDUCATION** Yale Univ, BA, 47; Oxford Univ, BA, 49; Princeton Univ, MA, 51, PhD (classics), 54; American School Classical Studies, 51-52. **CAREER** Instr classics, Princeton Univ, 49-50 and 52-53; from instr to assoc prof, 55-65, chmn dept classics, 59-63, 67-71 and 78-79, chmn div humanities, 63-67, assoc dean fac, 64-66, prof-in-chg, Intercol Ctr Class Studies, Rome, Italy, 66-67, Prof Classics, Dartmouth Col, 65-, Mem managing comt, Am Sch Class Studies; mem adv coun, Am Acad in Rome; Field Dir Excavation of the Roman colony of Pollentia, Mallorca, Spain, 84-97. **HONORS AND AWARDS** Woodrow Wilson Fellow, 50-51; Fulbright Fellow, 51-52. **MEMBERSHIPS** Soc Prom Hellenic Studies; Am Philol Asn; Class Asn Can; Class Asn New Eng(secy-treas, 63-68); Asn of Ancient Historians. **RESEARCH** Greek and Roman history; Greek pseudonymic letters. **SELECTED PUBLICATIONS** Auth, The Letters of Themistokles, New York: Arno Press, 81; auth, A. Arribas y N. Doenges, Piezas Singulares de una Estancia del Area Commercial del Foro de Pollentia, Travalhos de Antropologia e Etnologia 35, 95, 397-412; auth, Ostracism and the Boulai of Kleisthenes, Hist Zeitschrift Alte Geschichte, Vol 45, 96; The Campaign and Battle of Marathon, Historia 47 (1998)1-17. **CONTACT ADDRESS** Dept of Classics, Dartmouth Col, Hanover, NH 03755. **EMAIL** doenges@dartmouth.edu

DOERFEL, MARYA L.
DISCIPLINE COMMUNICATION **EDUCATION** SUNY, Buffalo, PhD, 96. **CAREER** Asst prof, Univ NC, Charlotte. **RESEARCH** The impact of soc networks and competition on relationships, both inside and among organizations. **CONTACT ADDRESS** Dept of Commun, Univ of No Carolina, Charlotte, 9201 Univ City Blvd, Charlotte, NC 28223-0001.

DOERKSEN, DANIEL WILLIAM
PERSONAL Born 11/27/1931, Winnipeg, MB, Canada, m, 1959, 3 children **DISCIPLINE** ENGLISH **EDUCATION** Univ Man, BA, 57; BEd, 62; Univ Wis, Madison, MA, 66; PhD, 73. **CAREER** Teacher English, Man Schs, 57-65; from asst prof to full prof English, 68-97, Hon Res Prof, 98-, Univ NBruns. **HONORS AND AWARDS** Woodrow Wilson Fel, 65; Special Wilson Fel, Univ Wis, 66; Can Council Doctoral Fel, 67; Can Council Res Grant, 75; Soc Sci and Humanities Res Council of Can Res Grant, 82. **MEMBERSHIPS** MLA; Can Soc for Renaissance Studies; Milton Soc; John Donne Soc. **RESEARCH** Literature of the English Renaissance; John Donne (especially Sermons and Devotions), Herbert, Milton, Spenser; religious and historical backgrounds. **SELECTED PUBLICATIONS** Auth, "'All the Good is God's': Predestination in Spenser's 'Faerie Queene,' Book I," Christianity and Lit 32 (83): 11-18; auth, "Recharting the 'Via Media' of Spenser and Herbert," Renaissance and Reformation 8 (84): 214-225; auth, "'Too Good for Those Times': Politics and the Publication of George Herbert's 'The Country Parson,'" Seventeenth-Century News 49 (91): 10-13; auth, "The Laudian Interpretation of George Herbert," Lit and Hist 3 (94): 36-54; auth, "Preaching Pastor versus Custodian of Order: Donne, Andrewes, and the Jacobean Church," Philol Quart 73 (94): 417-429; auth, "Milton and the Jacobean Church of England," Early Mod Lit Studies 1 (95): 5.1-23; auth "'Saint Pauls Puritan': John Donne's 'Puritan' Imagination in the 'Sermons,'" in John Donne's Religious Imagination: Essays in Honor of John T. Shawcross, ed. Raymond-Jean Frontain and Frances Malpezzi (AR: Univ Central Ark Press, 95); auth, "'Let There be Peace': Eve as Peacemaker in 'Paradise Lost, Book X,'" Milton Quart 31 (97): 124-130; auth, Conforming to the Word: Herbert, Donne, and the English Church before Laud, Bucknell Univ Press, 97; auth, "Polemist or Pastor? Donne and Moderate Calvinist Conformity," in John Donne and the Protestant Reformation, ed. Mary Papazian (forthcoming). **CONTACT ADDRESS** Dept of English, Univ of New Brunswick, Fredericton, PO Box 4400, Fredericton, NB, Canada E3B 5A3. **EMAIL** dwd@unb.ca

DOHERTY, KAREN A.
DISCIPLINE COMMUNICATION SCIENCES AND DISORDERS **EDUCATION** Univ Wis Madison, PhD, 94. **CAREER** Asst prof CCC-A, Syracuse Univ. **RESEARCH** Speech perception in the hearing-impaired; psychoacoustics and amplification. **SELECTED PUBLICATIONS** Coauth, Spectral Weights for Overall Discrimination in Listeners with Sensorineural Hearing Loss, Jour Acoustical Soc Am, 96; Psychometric Functions for the Discrimination of Spectral Variance, Jour Acoustical Soc Am, 96; Use of a Correlational Method to Estimate a Listener's Weighting Function for Speech, Jour Acoustical Soc Am, 96. **CONTACT ADDRESS** Syracuse Univ, Syracuse, NY 13244.

DOLAN, FRANCES E.
PERSONAL Born Chicago, IL **DISCIPLINE** ENGLISH **EDUCATION** Univ Chicago, PhD, 88. **CAREER** Asst prof, eng, 89-95, assoc prof, eng, Affil Women's Studies and Hist, 95-99, Miami Univ; prof, 99-. **HONORS AND AWARDS** Monticello Found fel, Newberry Libr, 91; NEH/Folger Libr fel, 96; Soc for the Study of Early Mod Women, Best Article, 96; NEH/Newberry Library Fel, 99-00. **MEMBERSHIPS** Mod Lang Asn; Shakespeare Asn of Amer. **RESEARCH** Early modern women; Law; Popular culture; Violence. **SELECTED PUBLICATIONS** Ed, The Taming of the Shrew: Texts and Contexts, Boston, Bedford Books, 96; article, Reading, Writing, and Other Crimes, Feminist Readings of Early Modern Culture: Emerging Subjects, Cambridge Univ Press, 96; article, Ridiculous Fictions: Making Distinctions in the Discourses of Witchcraft, Differences: A Journal of Feminist Cultural Studies, 7.2, 82-110, 95; auth, Dangerous Familiars: Representations of Domestic Crime in England, 1550-1700, Ithaca, Cornell Univ Press, 94; ed, Renaissance Drama, Renaissance Drama and the Law, 94; article, Gentlemen, I Have One Thing More to Say, Women on Scaffolds in England, 1563-1680, Mod Philol, 92.2, 157-78, 94; article, Taking the Pencil Out of God's Hand: Art, Nature, and the Face-Painting Debate in Early Modern England, Publ of the Mod Lang Asn, 108, 2, (93): 224-39; article, The Subordinate's Plot: Petty Treason and the Forms of Domestic Rebellion, Shakespeare Quart, 43.3, 317-40, 92; article, Home-rebels and House-traitors: Murderous Wives in Early Modern England, Yale Jour of Law and the Humanities, 4.1, 1-31, Winter, 92; auth, Whores of Babylon: Catholicism, Gender, and Seventeenth-Century Print Culture, Cornell, 99. **CONTACT ADDRESS** Dept. of English, Miami Univ, Oxford, OH 45056. **EMAIL** dolanfe@aol.com

DOLAN, MARC
PERSONAL Born 10/08/1961, Jersey City, NJ, m, 1990 **DISCIPLINE** ENGLISH **EDUCATION** Harvard Univ, AB, 83; PhD, 88. **CAREER** Lecturer, Harvard Univ, 88-91; Asst Prof to Assoc Prof, John Jay Col, 92-. **RESEARCH** 19th and 20th Century American Literature and Culture; Cultural Studies; Ethnic Studies; New York City in Literature. **CONTACT ADDRESS** Dept Eng, John Jay Col of Criminal Justice, CUNY, 445 W 59th St, New York, NY 10019-1104. **EMAIL** mdolan@gc.cuny.edu

DOLIS, JOHN
PERSONAL Born 04/25/1945, St Louis, MO, d **DISCIPLINE** ENGLISH **EDUCATION** St Louis Univ, BA, 67; Loyola Univ Chicago, MA, 69; PhD, 78. **CAREER** Teaching asst, Loyola Univ of Chicago, 67-69; instr, Notre Dame High Sch, 69-70; instr, Columbia Col, 70-71; from teaching asst to lectr, Loyola Univ of Chicago, 70-80; instr, Northeastern Ill Univ, 78-80; Fulbright lectr, Univ Turin, 80-81; instr, Univ Kans, 81-85; sr Fulbright lectr, Univ Bucharest, 89-90; from asst prof to prof, Pa State Univ at Scranton, 85-; vis prof, Bilkent Univ, 95-96. **HONORS AND AWARDS** President's Medallion, Loyola Univ of Chicago, 72; NEH Fel, 79, 88, & 89; Fulbright Fel, 80; CIES Scholar, Univ Pittsburgh, 89; Res Development Grant, Pa State Univ, 91 & 92; Pharmakon Res Int Awd for Excellence in Scholarly Activities, Pa State Univ, 91. **MEMBERSHIPS** Am Culture Asn, Am Lit Asn, Am Philos Asn, Asn for Applied Psychoanalysis, Ctr for Psychoanalytic Studies, Fulbright Asn, Int Asn for the Fantastic in the Arts, Int Asn for Philos and Lit, Int Husserl and Phenomenological Res Soc, Int Imagery Asn, Int Soc for Phenomenology and the Human Sciences, Int Soc for Phenomenology and Lit, Mark Twain Circle, MLA, Nathaniel Hawthorne Soc, Nat Soc Sci Asn, Northeast MLA, Northeast Popular Culture Asn, Soc for the Advancement of Am Philos, Soc for Phenomenology and Existential Philos, Soc for Philos and Psychiat, Soc for Romanian Studies, Thoreau Soc. **RESEARCH** Phenomenology, Psychoanalysis, Deconstruction. **SELECTED PUBLICATIONS** Auth, "Twain's Innocents Abroad: Textuality of the Socius," Soc Sci Perspectives J 6 (94): 1-7; auth, "The Mechanical Eye: Photograph and Subject Space," Soc Sci Perspectives J 6 (92): 72-78; auth, The Style of Hawthorne's Gaze: Regarding Subjectivity, Univ of Ala Press (Tuscaloosa, AL), 93; auth, Blank Space, Runaway Spoon Press (Port Charlotte, FL), 93 & 99; auth, "Twain's (Dis)figuration of Travel: Humoring the (B)east," Studies in the Humanities 24 (97): 52-64; auth, "Thoreau and Subjectivity: Nature, Technology, Technique," Nat Soc Sci Perspectives J 10 (97): 1-7; auth, "Calvino's Cosmicomics: Original Si(g)n," Extrapolation 39 (98): 57-67; auth, "Hawthorne's Circe: Turning Water to (S)wine," Nathaniel Hawthorne Rev 24 (98): 36-45; auth, Time Flies: Butterflies, Runaway Spoon Press (Port Charlotte, FL), 99. **CONTACT ADDRESS** Dept English, Pennsylvania State Univ, Worthington Scranton, 120 Ridgeview Dr, Dunmore, PA 18512-1602. **EMAIL** jjd3@psu.edu

DOLLENMAYER, DAVID BRISTOL
PERSONAL Born 04/05/1945, TN, m **DISCIPLINE** LINGUISTICS, LITERATURE **EDUCATION** Princeton Univ, BA, 67; PhD, 77. **CAREER** Instr, Middlebury Col, 75-76; instr, Smith Col, 76-78; asst prof, MIT, 78-88; prof, Worcester Poly Inst, 88-. **HONORS AND AWARDS** Fulbright-Hays Fel, 67-68; Woodrow Wilson Fel, 71-72. **MEMBERSHIPS** MLA; AATG. **RESEARCH** 20th-century German literature. **SELECTED PUBLICATIONS** Auth, The Berlin Novels of Alfred Dobun, 88; auth, Neve Horizonte, 99, 5th ed. **CONTACT ADDRESS** Dept Humanities and Arts, Worcester Polytech Inst, 100 Institute Rd, Worcester, MA 01609-2247. **EMAIL** dbd@wpi.edu

DOLOFF, STEVEN
PERSONAL Born New York, NY **DISCIPLINE** ENGLISH **EDUCATION** SUNY, BA; CUNY, PhD, 95. **CAREER** Asst Prof to Assoc Prof, Pratt Inst, 91-. **MEMBERSHIPS** MLA, Shakespeare Asn of Am. **RESEARCH** Renaissance Studies, Shakespeare, James Joyce. **CONTACT ADDRESS** Dept Humanities & English, Pratt Inst, 200 Willoughby Ave, Brooklyn, NY 11205-3817.

DOLSKAYA-ACKERLY, OLGA
PERSONAL 1 child **DISCIPLINE** MUSIC HISTORY **EDUCATION** Manhattan Sch Mus, Master of Mus; Univ Kans, MS, PhD. **CAREER** Assoc prof, Univ Mo, Kansas City. **RESEARCH** The Moscow Baroque. **SELECTED PUBLICATIONS** Her publications include transcriptions of seventeenth-century Russian choral works in Monuments of Russian Sacred Music, a facsimile edition of a 17th-century collection of polyphonic songs in Russia, and articles on various aspects of Russian music. **CONTACT ADDRESS** The Conservatory of Music, Univ of Missouri, Kansas City, Kansas City, MO 64110-2499. **EMAIL** admit@umkc.edu

DOMBROWSKI, PAUL M.
PERSONAL Born 12/22/1948, Pittsburgh, PA, m, 2 children **DISCIPLINE** ENGLISH **EDUCATION** Ind Univ, AB, 70; Penn State Univ, MEd, 84; MA, 87; Rensselaer Polytechnic Inst, PhD, 90. **CAREER** Asst Prof, Ohio Univ, 86-90; Visiting Asst Prof to Assoc Prof, Univ Cent Fla, 86-. **HONORS AND AWARDS** Chair, Ethics Committee Asn of Teachers of Tech Writing. **MEMBERSHIPS** Asn of Teachers of Tech Writing; Soc for Tech Comm; Coun of Programs in Tech and Sci Comm; IEEE; Mod Lang Asn; Nat Coun of Teachers of Eng. **RESEARCH** Technical Writing and Communication; Rhetoric; Language in relation to specialized knowledge. **SELECTED PUBLICATIONS** Auth, "The Lessons of the Challenger Investigations," IEEE Transactions of Professional Communication, (91): 211-217; auth, "Challenger and the Social Contingency of Meaning," Technical Communication Quarterly, (92): 73-86; auth, "Challenger Through the Eyes of Feyerabend," Journal of Technical Writing and Communication, (94): 7-18; ed, Humanistic Aspects of Technical Communication, Baywood, 94; auth, "Post-modernism as the Resurgence of Humanism in Technical Communication Studies," Technical Communication Quarterly, (95): 165-185; auth, "Can Ethics Be Technologized?", IEEE Transactions on Professional Communication, (95): 146-150; auth, "Ethics in Technical Communication: The First Quarter Century," Journal of Technical Writing and Communication, (00): 7-23; auth, Ethics in Technical Communication, Allyn & Bacon, 00. **CONTACT ADDRESS** Dept Eng, Univ of Central Florida, PO Box 161346, Orlando, FL 32816-1346. **EMAIL** pdombrow@pegasus.cc.ucf.edu

DOMINGO-FORASTE, DOUGLAS
PERSONAL Born 05/04/1954, Los Angeles, CA, m, 1999, 2 children **DISCIPLINE** COMPARATIVE LITERATURE, CLASSIC STUDIES **EDUCATION** Univ Calif Davis, AB, 76; Univ Calif Santa Barb, MA, 81; PhD, 88. **CAREER** Res, Univ Calif Irvine, assoc prof, ICCS, Rome, 99-00; 86-90; lectr, asst prof, assoc prof, prof, Calif State Long Beach, 88-. **HONORS AND AWARDS** CSULB Col Lib Arts, Most Val Prof, 96, 98. **MEMBERSHIPS** ANS; AIA; APA; CCA; BSC. **RESEARCH** Greek numismatics; Greek law; Menander. **SELECTED PUBLICATIONS** Trans, "Life of Sts. David, Symeon, and George of Lesbos," in Byzantine Defenders of Images, ed. A. M. Talbot (DC: Dumbarton Oaks, 98): 143-241; ed, Claudius Aelianus Epistulae et Fragmenta, Bibliotheca Teubneriana (Leipzig: Teubner, 94); ed, Lysias On the Murder of Eratosthenes (Amherst, Mass: CANE, 94); auth, "Walcott's Other: Philoctete and Philoctetes," Genre 16 (95): 84-93; auth, "The Dual Number," Athen NL (95): 18-20; auth, "The Fourth Century Mint of Anaktorion" in La Monetazione corinzia in Occidente: Atti del IX Convegno del Centro Internazionale di Studi Numismatici, eds. A. Stazio, M. Taliercio Mensitieri, R. Vitale (Rome, 93): 43-59; auth, "Piety in Menander, " Laetaberis 7 (89): 1-8; auth, "The Fourth Century Mint at Anaktorion, " Am J Arch 88 (84): 242-243. **CONTACT ADDRESS** Dept of Comp Lit and Classics, California State Univ, Long Beach, 1250 Bellflower Rd, Long Beach, CA 90840-2404. **EMAIL** dforaste@csulb.edu

DOMINIK, JANE
PERSONAL Born 09/18/1957, Madison, WI, s **DISCIPLINE** ENGLISH **EDUCATION** Univ of the Pacific, BA, 80; Univ Chicago, AM, 81; Rutgers Univ, MFA, 84. **CAREER** Ed Asst, St Marten's Press, 85-86; Ed Services Spec, Ginn Press, 86-87; Teacher, Tabor Acad, 87-90; Instr, San Joaquin Delta Col, 90-. **HONORS AND AWARDS** New Educator's Awd, Calif Teachers Asn, 93. **MEMBERSHIPS** Arthur Miller Soc. **RESEARCH** Arthur Miller, Dramatic literature, Pedagogy. **SELECTED PUBLICATIONS** Auth, "A View from 'Death of a Salesman'" in The Salesman Has a Birthday. Essays Celebrating the fiftieth Anniversary of Death of a Salesman. **CONTACT ADDRESS** Dept Comm Skills, San Joaquin Delta Col, 5151 Pacific Ave, Stockton, CA 95207-6304.

DOMVILLE, ERIC W.
PERSONAL Born 04/27/1929, Liverpool, England **DISCIPLINE** ENGLISH **EDUCATION** Univ London, BA, 61, PhD, 65. **CAREER** Lectr to prof, 64-94, prof emer, Trinity Col, Univ Toronto, 94-. **SELECTED PUBLICATIONS** Ed, A Concordance to the Plays of W.B. Yeats, 2 vols, 72; ed, Editing British and American Literature 1880-1920, 76; co-ed, The Collected letters of W.B. Yeats, vol 1, 86. **CONTACT ADDRESS** Trinity Col, English Dept, Univ of Toronto, Toronto, ON, Canada M5S 1H8.

DONAHUE, JOHN F.
DISCIPLINE CLASSICAL STUDIES **EDUCATION** Col Holy Cross, AB, 80; Univ NC at Chapel Hill, MA, 90, PhD, 96. **CAREER** Adj instr; Col William and Mary, 97; adj asst prof, Williamsburg, Va; tchg asst, Med Word Formation and Entymology, 94 & Latin, 91-93, Univ NC at Chapel Hill; Fay Sch, 86-88; UNC res ast, L'Annee Philiologique, 89-91, 94; Latin tutor, 91-93; fact checker, Amer Nat Biog, Oxford UP, 95-. **HONORS AND AWARDS** UNC Grad Sch Dissertation fel, 95; UNC Grad Sch Dept Class Travel Awd(s), 94 & Kappa Delta Pi Honor Soc, Colombia Univ, 84. **MEMBERSHIPS** Amer Philol Asn; Asn Int d'Epigraphie Grecque et Latine; Class Asn Mid W and S. **RESEARCH** Roman social history; Ancient dining; Latin inscriptions. **SELECTED PUBLICATIONS** Auth, Feasts and Females: Sex Roles, Public Recognition and Community Banquets in the Western Roman Empire, Class Asn Mid W and S, Nashville, 96; Public Banqueting in the Roman Empire: Issues for Consideration, Class Asn Mid W and S, Southern Section, Chapel Hill, 94 & Distributions of Bread During the Later Roman Empire: Some Chronological Problems, Class Asn Mid W and S, Atlanta, 94. **CONTACT ADDRESS** Dept of Classical Studies, Col of William and Mary, Morton Hall, PO Box 8795, Williamsburg, VA 23187-8795. **EMAIL** jfdona@facstaff.wm.edu

DONAHUE, THOMAS JOHN
PERSONAL Born 01/09/1943, Philadelphia, PA, 2 children **DISCIPLINE** FRENCH LITERATURE, THEATRE **EDUCATION** Univ Pa, AM, 67 PhD, 73. **CAREER** Asst prof, 65-80, Assoc Prof, 80-91, prof, 91-, St Joseph's Univ. **HONORS AND AWARDS** Scholarship of the Alliance Francaise de

Philadelphie, 64-65; fel Camargo Found, 78; Awd for Tchg, Awd for Scholarship, St Joseph's Univ. **MEMBERSHIPS** Am Asn of Tchrs of French; Alliance Francaise de Philadelphie. **RESEARCH** Auth, 20th-Century French theater; French theater history; theater semiotics. **SELECTED PUBLICATIONS** The Theater of Fernando Arrabal, New York Univ Press, 80; auth, Structures of Meaning: A Semiotic Approach to the Play Text, Fairleigh Dickinson. **CONTACT ADDRESS** Dept of French, Saint Joseph's Univ, 5600 City Ave, Philadelphia, PA 19131-1376. **EMAIL** tdonahue@sju.edu

DONAKOWSKI, CONRAD L.
PERSONAL Born 03/13/1936, Detroit, MI, m, 1961, 2 children **DISCIPLINE** RELIGION, HISTORY, MUSIC **EDUCATION** Xavier Univ, BA, 58, MA, 59; Columbia Univ, PhD, 69. **CAREER** Instr humanities, Mich State Univ, 66-69; coordr, James Madison Col, Mich State Univ, 67-72; from asst to assoc prof humanities, 69-78, prof, 78-81, prof music hist, Mich State Univ, 81-, asst dean arts & lett, 79-, Am Coun Learned Soc grant, 73. **HONORS AND AWARDS** American Revolutionary Bicentennial Article Prize, Ohio Hist Comt, 76; Rockefeller Found grants, 76 & 77; DAAD, 88, 95. **MEMBERSHIPS** AHA; Am Soc Eighteenth Century Studies; Am Soc Church Hist; Soc Fr Hist Studies. **RESEARCH** Romanticism; enlightenment; popular culture; ritual and liturgy; music. **SELECTED PUBLICATIONS** Auth, A Muse for the Masses: Ritual and Music in an Age of Democratic Revolution, Univ Chicago, 77. **CONTACT ADDRESS** School of Music, Michigan State Univ, East Lansing, MI 48824-1043. **EMAIL** donakows@msu.edu

DONALDSON, JEFFERY
DISCIPLINE ENGLISH LITERATURE **EDUCATION** Univ Toronto, BA, MA, PhD. **RESEARCH** Mod and contemp Amer and Brit poetry; W.H. Auden, poetry and poetics; criticism of Northrop Frye. **SELECTED PUBLICATIONS** Auth, Mark Strand. American Writer's Supplement IV, Scribner, 96; auth, Waterglass, 99; auth, Once Out of Nature, 91. **CONTACT ADDRESS** English Dept, McMaster Univ, 1280 Main St W, Hamilton, ON, Canada L8S 4L9. **EMAIL** jdonalds@mcmaster.ca

DONALDSON, PETER SAMUEL
PERSONAL Born 11/21/1942, New York, NY, m, 1965, 3 children **DISCIPLINE** ENGLISH **EDUCATION** Columbia Univ, AB, 64; PhD, 74; Cambridge Univ, BA, 66; MA, 70. **CAREER** Lectr, City Col NYork, 67-69; from instr to asst prof, 69-78, assoc prof, 78-88, prof, 88-, Ann Fetter Friedlaender prof hum, 93-98, dept hd, Lit, Mass Inst Technol, 89- ; dir, Shakespeare Elect Arch, 92- . **HONORS AND AWARDS** Old Dom fel lit, Mass Inst Technol, 73; NEH Fel, 75; Fel, Royal Hist Soc, (UK), 79-; Am Counc Learned Soc Fel, 82. **MEMBERSHIPS** MLA; SAA. **RESEARCH** Renaissance thought and letters: Machiavellian political tradition; Shakespeare in film and digital media. **SELECTED PUBLICATIONS** Transl & ed, A Machiavellian Treatise by Stephen Gardiner, Cambridge Univ Pr, 76; auth, Machiavelli and Mystery of State, Cambridge Univ Press, 88; auth, Shakespearean Films/Shakespearean Directors, Urwin Hyman, 90. **CONTACT ADDRESS** Massachusetts Inst of Tech, 77 Massachusetts Ave, Cambridge, MA 02139-4307. **EMAIL** psdlit@mit.edu

DONALDSON, SANDRA
PERSONAL Born 08/29/1943, Buffalo, NY, m, 1989 **DISCIPLINE** ENGLISH **EDUCATION** State Univ NY at Buffalo, BA, 68; Univ Conn, MA, 70; PhD, 77. **CAREER** from part-time instr to asst prof, Eastern Conn State Col, 70-77; from asst prof to prof, Univ NDak, 77-; dir of Women Studies Prog, Univ NDak, 82-85 & 96-; assoc ed, Victorian Lit and Culture, 91-. **HONORS AND AWARDS** Libr Fel, Armstrong Browning Libr at Baylor Univ, 89 & 95; Newberry Libr Fel, 90; Mellon Fel, Univ Tex Harry Ransom Humanities Res Ctr, 95; Fel, Biblio Soc of Am, 96; Fac Achievement Awd, Univ NDak, 00. **MEMBERSHIPS** MLA, Am Asn of Univ Professors, Am Federation of Teachers, Int Virginia Woolf Soc, Browning Soc, Midwest Victorian Studies Asn, Nat Women's Studies Asn. **RESEARCH** Works and the Life of Elizabeth Barrett Browning, Women Studies, Bibliography. **SELECTED PUBLICATIONS** Auth, "'For Nothing was Simply One Thing': The Reception of Elizabeth Barrett Browning's 'A Curse For a Nation," Studies in Browning and His Circle 20 (97): 137-144; auth, "Editor's Introduction," in Critical Essays on Elizabeth Barrett Browning (NY: G. K. Hall, 99), 1-14; auth, "Elizabeth Barrett's Two Sonnets to George Sand," in Critical Essays on Elizabeth Barrett Browning (NY: G. K. Hall, 99), 38-41; auth, "Elizabeth Barrett Browning," in Cambridge Bibliography of English Literature (Cambridge Univ Press, forthcoming). **CONTACT ADDRESS** Dept English, Univ of No Dakota, PO Box 7209, Grand Forks, ND 58202-7209.

DONALDSON, SCOTT
PERSONAL Born 11/11/1928, Minneapolis, MN **DISCIPLINE** AMERICAN LITERATURE, AMERICAN STUDIES **EDUCATION** Yale Univ, Ba, 51; Univ Minn, MA, 52, PhD (Am studies), 66. **CAREER** Reporter, Minneapolis Star, 55-57; ed and publ, Bloomington Sun, 58-63; from asst prof to assoc prof English, 66-74, Prof English, Col William and Mary, 74-, Fulbright lectr, Turku Univ, 70-71; vis prof, Univ Leeds, 72-73; Fulbright lectr, Univ Milan, 79. **MEMBERSHIPS** MLA; Am Studies Asn; Fulbright Alumni Asn; Int PEN; Auths Guild. **RESEARCH** Fitzgerald and Hemingway; American poetry; modern American fiction. **CONTACT ADDRESS** Dept of English, Col of William and Mary, Williamsburg, VA 23185. **EMAIL** scottd@amug.org

DONALDSON-EVANS, MARY P.
PERSONAL Born 01/15/1943, Duluth, MN, m, 1968, 2 children **DISCIPLINE** LITERATURE **EDUCATION** Marquette Univ, BA, 65; Univ Wisconsin-Milwaukee, MA, 68; Univ Pa, PhD, 75. **CAREER** Prof, 91; Univ of Delaware, 69-. **HONORS AND AWARDS** Excellence-in-Teaching Awd, 83; NEH Grant for College Teachers, 93-94; Outstanding Teacher in The College of A & S, Univ of Delaware, 95; Chevalier, Palmes Academiques, 89. **MEMBERSHIPS** AAUP, MLA, AATF. **RESEARCH** 19th Century French Literature. **SELECTED PUBLICATIONS** Auth, A Woman's Revenge: The Chronology of Dispossession in Maupassant's Fiction., French Forum Monographs, 86; auth, Medical Examinations: Dissecting the Doctor in French Narrative Prose (Press Uniiv of Nebraska), 1857-1894; co-ed, Modernity and Revolution in Late Nineteenth-Century France, co-edited with Barbara Cooper, Univ of Delaware, 92; co-ed, Autobiography, Historiography and Rhetoric, co-edited with Lucienne Frappier-Mazur and Gerald Prince, Rodopi, 94; co-ed, Kaleidoscope: Essays in Nineteenth-Century French Literature in honor of Thomas H. Goetz, co-edited with Graham Falconer(Toronto: Centre d'Etudes romantiques J. Sable, 96); co-ed, Moving Forward, Holding Fast: The Dynamics of Nineteenth-Century French Culture, co-edited with Barbara Cooper (Amsterdam: Rodopi, 1997). **CONTACT ADDRESS** Dept Foreign Language, Univ of Delaware, 18 Amstel Ave, Rm 325, Newark, DE 19716-2599. **EMAIL** maryde@udel.edu

DONATELLI, JOSEPH M. P.
DISCIPLINE ENGLISH LITERATURE **EDUCATION** State Univ NY Binghamton, BA; Univ NMex, MA; Univ Toronto, PhD. **CAREER** Assoc prof **RESEARCH** Fourteenth and fifteenth century narrative poetry; Anglo-Latin literature; reception of medieval texts in eighteenth century fiction. **SELECTED PUBLICATIONS** Auth, pubs on textual studies, media and communications theory, popular culture, and the effects of digital technology on literary forms. **CONTACT ADDRESS** Dept of English, Univ of Manitoba, Winnipeg, MB, Canada R3T 2N2.

DONAVIN, GEORGIANA
DISCIPLINE ENGLISH LITERATURE **EDUCATION** Ca State Univ, BA, 83, MA, 85; Univ Oregon, PhD, 92. **CAREER** Tchg asst, 84-85; instr, Ca State Univ, 86; grad tchg fel, Univ Oregon, 87-92; asst prof, 92-97; assoc prof, Westminster Col, 97-. **HONORS AND AWARDS** Manford A. Shaw Publ Prize. **SELECTED PUBLICATIONS** Auth, De sermone sermonem fecimus: Alexander of Ashby's De artificioso modo predicandi, 97; Locating a Public Forum for the Personal Letter in Malory's Morte Darthur, 96; The Medieval Rhetoric of Identification: A Burkean Reconception, 96. **CONTACT ADDRESS** Westminster Col of Salt Lake City, 1840 S 1300 E, Salt Lake City, UT 84105. **EMAIL** g-donavi@wcslc.edu

DONAWERTH, JANE L.
DISCIPLINE ENGLISH, LITERATURE **EDUCATION** Miami Univ, BA, 69; Univ Wis Madison, MA, 70; PhD, 75. **CAREER** Lectr to prof, Univ Md, 74-. **HONORS AND AWARDS** NEH Fel; NEH Grant; Univ Md Distinguished Scholar and Teacher; SSEMW Founders Award; Phi Beta Kappa Pres. **MEMBERSHIPS** MLA; CCCC; SCS; SFRA. **RESEARCH** Shakespeare; early modern women writers; history of rhetoric; science fiction by women. **SELECTED PUBLICATIONS** Auth, Shakespeare and the Sixteenth-Century Study of Language, Univ Ill Pr, 87; co-ed, Utopian and Science Fiction by Women: Worlds of Difference, Syracuse Univ Pr, 94; auth, Daughters of Frankenstein: Women Writing Science Fiction, Syracuse Univ Pr, 97; auth, "Conversation and the Boundaries of Public Discourse in Rhetorical Theory by Renaissance Women," Rhetorica (98): 1-17; co-ed, Women Writing and the Reproduction of Culture in Tudor and Stuart Britain, Syracuse Univ Pr, 00; co-ed, "Attending to Early Modern Women," Crossing Boundaries (00); ed, Rhetorical Theory by Women Before 1900: An Anthology, Rowan/Littlefield, 02; co-ed, transl, Selected Rhetorical Writings by Madeleine de Scud¤ry Univ Chicago Pr (forthcoming). **CONTACT ADDRESS** English Dept, Univ of Maryland, Col Park, College Park, MD 20742-0001. **EMAIL** jd32@umail.umd.edu

DONLAN, WALTER
PERSONAL Born 07/30/1934, Boston, MA **DISCIPLINE** CLASSICS **EDUCATION** Harvard Col, BA, 56; Northwestern Univ, PhD, 68. **CAREER** Asst prof to prof, classics, Penn St Univ, 67-86; prof classics, Univ of Calif, Irvine, 86- . **HONORS AND AWARDS** Pres, Class Asn of the Atlantic states, 79-80. **MEMBERSHIPS** Am Philol Asn; Archaeol Inst of Am; Asn of Ancient Hist; Calif Class Asn. **RESEARCH** Early Greek literature, Greek social history. **SELECTED PUBLICATIONS** Auth, Duelling with Gifts in the Illiad: As the Audience Saw It, in Colby Q, 93; coauth, The Village Community of Ancient Greece: Neolithic, Bronze and Dark Ages, in Studi Micenei ed Egeo-Anatolici, 93; auth, Chief and Followers in Pre-State Greece, in From Political Economy to Anthropology: Situating Economic Life in Past Societies, Black Rose, 94; auth, The Homeric Economy, in A New Companion to Homeric Studies, Brill, 97; auth, The Relations of Power in the Pre-State and Early State Politics, in The Development of the Polis in Archaic Greece, Routledge, 97; auth, Political Reciprocity in Dark Age Greece: Odysseus and his Hetairoi, in Reciprocity in Ancient Greece, Oxford,, 97; coauth, Ancient Greece: A Political, Social, and Cultural History, Oxford, 99; auth, The Aristocratic Ideal and Selected Papers, Bulchazy-Carducci, 99. **CONTACT ADDRESS** Dept of Classics, Univ of California, Irvine, 120 Humanities Office Bldg 2, Irvine, CA 92697. **EMAIL** wdonlan@uci.edu

DONOVAN, JOSEPHINE
PERSONAL Born 03/10/1941, Manila, Philippines **DISCIPLINE** LITERATURE **EDUCATION** Bryn Mawr Col, BA, 62; Univ Wisc, Madison, MA, 67, PhD, 71. **CAREER** Prof, Univ Maine, Orono, 87- . **RESEARCH** Critical theory; women's literature (early modern, American). **SELECTED PUBLICATIONS** Auth, Sarah Orne Jewett, Ungar, 80; auth, New England Local Color Literature: A Women's Tradition, Ungar, 83; auth, After the Fall: The Demeter-Persephone Myth in Cather, Wharton and Glasgow, Penn State Univ, 89; ed., Feminist Theoretical Explorations with Carol J. Adams, Duke University Press, 95; ed., Beyond Animal Rights: A Feminist Caring Ethic for the Treatment of Animals with Carol J. Adams, Continuum, 96; ed., P.O.W. in the Pacific: Memoirs of an American Doctor in World War II by William N. Donovan, Scholarly Resources, 98; auth, Gnosticism in Modern Literature: A Study of Selected Works of Camus, Sartre, Hesse, and Kafka, Garland, 90; auth, Uncle Tom's Cabin: Evil, Affliction, and Redemptive Love, Twayne, 91; auth, Feminist Theory: The Intellectual Traditions of Amer Feminism, third ed, Continuum, 00; auth, Women and the Rise of the Novel, 1405-1726, St. Martin's, 99. **CONTACT ADDRESS** Univ of Maine, 294 Dennett St., Partsmouth, HH 03801. **EMAIL** josephine.donovan@umit.maine.edu

DONOVAN, MAUREEN H.
PERSONAL Born 12/13/1948, Boston, MA, m, 1978, 1 child **DISCIPLINE** LIBRARY SCIENCE **EDUCATION** Manhattanville Col, BA, 70; Columbia Univ, MA, 73, MS, 74. **CAREER** Librn, Princeton Univ, 74-78; Librn, Ohio State Univ, 78-. **MEMBERSHIPS** Council East Asian Librys; Asn Asian Stud. **RESEARCH** Digital library; Japanese studies librarianship. **SELECTED PUBLICATIONS** Auth, art, East Asian Libraries Cooperative World Wide Web: An Experiment in Collaboration to Build Interdependence, 96. **CONTACT ADDRESS** Main Library, The Ohio State Univ, 1858 Neil Ave Mall, Columbus, OH 43210. **EMAIL** donovan.1@osu.edu

DOOB, PENELOPE
PERSONAL Born Hanover, NH **DISCIPLINE** ENGLISH **EDUCATION** Harvard Univ, BA, 64; Stanford Univ, MA, 67, PhD, 69. **CAREER** Asst prof, 74-84, assoc prin, 81-85, prof Eng & Multidisciplinary Studs,York Univ, 85-; academic dir, Centre for the Support of Teaching. **HONORS AND AWARDS** Guggenheim Fel, 74; Kent Fel, Danforth Found, 66-69; Woodrow Wilson Fel, 65-69; Medical Res Fel, Nat Sci Found, 64, 65. **MEMBERSHIPS** Actors' Fund of Can; Soc Tchg & Learning in Higher Educ; Sr Women Acad Admins Can; Am Asn Higher Educ; World Dance Alliance; Soc Dance Hist Scholars; MLA. **SELECTED PUBLICATIONS** Auth, Nebuchadnezzar's Children: Conventions of Madness in Middle English Literature, 74; auth, The Idea of the Labyrinth from Classical Antiquity through the Middle Ages, 90; coauth, Karen Kain: Movement Never Lies, 94. **CONTACT ADDRESS** Dept of English, York Univ, North York, ON, Canada M3J 1P3. **EMAIL** prdoob@yorku.ca

DOODY, MARGARET A.
PERSONAL Born St John, NE, s, 1939 **DISCIPLINE** RESTORATION AND 18TH-CENTURY BRITISH LITERATURE, THE NOVEL **EDUCATION** Dalhousie Univ, BA, 60; Oxford Univ, BA, 62; MA, 67; DPhil, 68. **CAREER** Instr, 62-64; asst prof, Univ Victoria, Can, 68-69; lectr, Univ Col Swansea, UK, 69-70.; vis assoc prof, 76-77, assoc prof, UCLA, Berkeley, 77-80; prof, Princeton Univ, 80-89; vis prof, Columbia Univ, 81, 87; vis prof, Stanford Univ, 83; Andrew W Mellon Prof Hum and Eng, 89-; dir, comp lit prog, Vanderbilt Univ, 92-; Prof, Univ of Notre Dame, 00-. **HONORS AND AWARDS** Atlantic Provinces scholar, 56-60; Commonwealth fel, 60-62; Can Coun grad fel, 64-65; Imperial Oil fel, 65-68; Can Coun postdoctoral res and travel grant, 69; John Simon Guggenheim Mem Found fel, 78; Ford Found Women's Stud grant, 85; Hon LLD, Dalhousie Univ, 85; Rose Mary Crawshay Prize, Brit Acad, 86; ACLS grant, 88; vis fel, Univ Otago, NZ, 93. **RESEARCH** Hymns; Venice; Apuleius. **SELECTED PUBLICATIONS** Ed, Frances Burney's Evelina or The History of a Young Lady's Entrance into the World, Penguin Bks, 94; co-ed, Hester Lynch Thrale Piozzi. The Two Fountains. A Fairy Tale in Three Acts, Johnsoniana, 94; coauth, A Portrait of Jane Austen, Henry Rice, 95; auth, The True Story of the Novel, Rutgers Univ Press, 96. **CONTACT ADDRESS** English Dept, Univ of Notre Dame, Notre Dame, IN 46556. **EMAIL** marjaret.doody@md.edu

DOOLEY, ALLAN C.
PERSONAL Born 07/27/1943, Chicago Heights, IL, m, 1987, 1 child **DISCIPLINE** LITERATURE **EDUCATION** Wabash Col, AB, 65; Northwestern Univ, MA, 66; PhD, 70. **CAREER** From asst prof to prof, Kent State Univ, 69-. **HONORS AND AWARDS** Woodrow Wilson Fel; Bibliog Soc Fel; Kent State Univ Res Awds. **MEMBERSHIPS** Inst for Bibliog and Editing at Kent State Univ, Editorial Board of The Complete Works of Robert Browning. **RESEARCH** Victorian Literature, Printing History, Textual Editing. **SELECTED PUBLICATIONS** Auth, Author and Printer in Victorian England, Univ of Va, 92; ed, The Complete Works of Robert Browning Vols 5, 6, & 10, Ohio Univ Press, 81, 96, & 99. **CONTACT ADDRESS** Dept English, Kent State Univ, PO Box 5190, Kent, OH 44242-0001. **EMAIL** adooley@kent.edu

DOOLEY, DEBORAH
PERSONAL Born 05/12/1953, Rochester, NY, m, 1995 **DISCIPLINE** ENGLISH **EDUCATION** Nazareth Col, BA, 75; Univ Rochester, MS, 90; Univ Rochester, PhD. **CAREER** From Adj Asst Prof to Prof, Nazareth Col, 80-. **HONORS AND AWARDS** Charles Mills Awd for Excellence in Writing, 75; Fel Grants, Univ Rochester, 75-78; Outstanding Young Women in Am Awd, 86; Who's Who in the E, 94; Who's Who Among Am Women, 95. **MEMBERSHIPS** AAUP, MLA, AAUW, NWSA, NCTE. **RESEARCH** Redesign of writing, communication and information design, reading writing and study skills. **SELECTED PUBLICATIONS** Rev, "Bitter Milk: Women and Teaching" by Madeleine Grumet, Harvard Educ Rev (90); rev, "Ancient Cultures of Conceit: British University Fiction in the Post-War Years" by Ian Carter, J of Higher Educ (91); auth, Plain and Ordinary Things: Reading Women in the Writing Classroom, NY St UP (Albany, NY), 95; auth, "Intimacy, Knowledge and Feminist Pedagogy in the Computer Assisted Classroom," Col English Asn, 96; auth, "Exile's Return: Family Systems Theory in Alice Walker's 'The Temple of My Familiar'," Col English Asn, 98; auth, "Jamaica Kincaid and the Legacy of the Garden in 20th-Century Literature by Women," Col English Asn, 99. **CONTACT ADDRESS** Dept English, Nazareth Col of Rochester, 4245 East Ave, Rochester, NY 14618-3703. **EMAIL** dadooley@naz.edu

DOOLEY, PATRICIA
DISCIPLINE MASS COMMUNICATION, AND MEDIA ETHICS AND LAW **EDUCATION** Univ Minn, MA, PhD. **CAREER** Writer, Minn Hist Soc; asst prof, Univ Maine; dir, Kans Scholastic Press Assn District Four; asst prof. **RESEARCH** History of mass communication; media ethics and law. **SELECTED PUBLICATIONS** Auth, book on the history of journalism as an occupational group. **CONTACT ADDRESS** Dept of Commun, Wichita State Univ, 1845 Fairmont, Wichita, KS 67260-0062. **EMAIL** dooley@elliott.es.twsu.edu

DOPP, JAMES A.
DISCIPLINE CANADIAN LITERATURE **EDUCATION** Univ Laurier, BA; Univ Victoria, MA; Univ York, PhD. **CAREER** Asst prof, Univ of Victoria. **RESEARCH** Contemporary Canadian poetry and fiction; critical theory; popular culture. **SELECTED PUBLICATIONS** Auth, On the Other Hand, 96; auth, Prospects Unknown: A Mystery with a Difference, 00. **CONTACT ADDRESS** Dept of English, Univ of Victoria, PO Box 3070 STN CSC, Victoria, BC, Canada V8W 3W1.

DORAN, MADELEINE
PERSONAL Born 08/12/1905, Salt Lake City, UT **DISCIPLINE** ENGLISH **EDUCATION** Stanford Univ, AB, 27, PhD, 30; Univ Iowa, AM, 28. **CAREER** Instr English lit, Wellesley Col, 30-33; from instr to prof English, 35-67, Ruth C Wallerstein prof English lit, 67-75, Emer Prof English, Univ Wis-Madison, 75-, Am Coun Learned Soc fel, 33-34; Am Asn Univ Women fel, 46-47; Calkins vis prof, Wellesley Col, 57; vis prof, Stanford Univ, 60; Huntington Libr grant, 60 and 64; Folger Shakespeare Libr fel, 64; Guggenheim fel, 67-68; mem, Inst Res in Humanities, Univ Wis, 70-75. **HONORS AND AWARDS** LittD, Wheaton Col, Mass, 63, Carthage Col, 75 and Regis Col, 77. **MEMBERSHIPS** MLA; Renaissance Soc Am; Shakespeare Asn Am (pres, 74); Am Acad Arts and Sci. **RESEARCH** Shakespeare; Elizabethan drama; Renaissance literature. **SELECTED PUBLICATIONS** Auth, Orr Piano Trios Nos.1-3, Tempo, Vol 201, 97; Vw9 and the St. Matthew Passion, Tempo, Vol 201, 97. **CONTACT ADDRESS** 4238 Wanda Pl, Madison, WI 53711.

DORE, FLORENCE W.
PERSONAL Born 09/24/1965, Nashville, TN **DISCIPLINE** LITERATURE, AMERICAN LITERATURE **EDUCATION** Wesleyan Univ, BA, 87; Brandis Univ, MA, 91; Univ Calif Berkeley, PhD, 99. **CAREER** Asst prof, Kent State Univ, 99-; fac fel, NYU, 00-. **HONORS AND AWARDS** NEH, 01; Univ Calif Berkeley Fel; Dist Teach Awd, 98; Dean's Dis fel, 97-98; Vice-Chanc Res Grnt, 97; Mellon Fel, 94, 96-7; Phi Beta Kappa. **MEMBERSHIPS** MLA. **RESEARCH** 19-20th-century American literature and culture; Faulkner; gender and feminist theory; popular culture. **SELECTED PUBLICATIONS** Auth, "Free Speech and Exposure: Obscenity, the Phallus, and William Faulkner's Sanctuary," Narr 9 (01). **CONTACT ADDRESS** Draper Prog, New York Univ, 14 University Place, New York, NY 10003. **EMAIL** fd23@nyu.edu

DORGAN, HOWARD
PERSONAL Born 07/05/1932, Ruston, LA, m, 1961, 2 children **DISCIPLINE** COMMUNICATION AND APPLACHIAN ETHNOGRAPHY **EDUCATION** Univ Tex, El Paso, BA, 53; Univ Tex, Austin, MFA, 57; La State Univ, PhD, 71. **CAREER** Asst prof speech, lamar Univ, 66-69; assoc prof commun, 71-77, prof commun, 77-98, prof emeritus commun, 98-, Appalachian State Univ; ed, Southern Commun Jour, 81-84; exec sec, Southern Commun Asn, 85-90; pres, Southern Commun Asn, 91-92; pres, Appalachian Studies Asn, 95-96. **HONORS AND AWARDS** Trustees Award for Excellence in Teaching, 75; Outstanding Fac Award, 93; Thomas Wolfe Literary Award, 93; Southern Commun Outstanding Service Award, 95; Appalachian Consortium Distinguished Service Award, 98; Appalachian Studies Distinguished Service Award, 00. **MEMBERSHIPS** Southern Commun Asn; Appalachian Consortium; Appalachian Studies Asn. **RESEARCH** Southern rhetoric and public address; Appalachian religious traditions. **SELECTED PUBLICATIONS** Coed, The Oratory of Southern Demagogues, LSU Press, 82; coed, A New Diversity in Contemporary Southern Rhetoric, LSU Press, 87; auth, Giving Glory to God in Appalachia, Univ of Tenn Press, 87; auth, The Old Regular Baptists of Central Appalachia, Univ of Tenn Press, 89; auth, Airwarves of Zion, Univ Tenn Press, 93; Auth, In the Hands of a Happy God, Univ of Tenn Press, 97. **CONTACT ADDRESS** Dept of Commun, Appalachian State Univ, Boone, NC 28608. **EMAIL** dorganch@appstate.edu

DORLAND, MICHAEL
DISCIPLINE COMMUNICATIONS **EDUCATION** McGill Univ; Univ London; Concordia Univ, PhD. **CAREER** Vis scholar, Duke Univ; assoc prof, Carleton Univ. **HONORS AND AWARDS** Res, Univ du Quebec a Montreal. **RESEARCH** History of the Canadian public sphere. **SELECTED PUBLICATIONS** Ed, Canada's Cultural Industries: Policies, Problems and Prospects, 96; auth, So Close To The State/s: The Emergence of Canadian Feature Film Policy, 98. **CONTACT ADDRESS** Dept of Commun, Carleton Univ, 1125 Colonel By Dr, Ottawa, ON, Canada K1S 5B6. **EMAIL** michael_dorland@carleton.ca

DORNAN, CHRISTOPHER
DISCIPLINE COMMUNICATIONS **EDUCATION** Bachelor of Journalism from Carleton University, an M.A. in the History and Philosophy of Science from the University of Cambridge and a Ph.D. in Communication from McGill University **CAREER** Instr,Cornell Univ; dir; prof, 87. **HONORS AND AWARDS** Reporter, Edmonton Jour; sci writer, Globe and Mail; ed, edit writer, Ottawa Citizen; contributor, CBC Radio's Prime Time. **RESEARCH** News media as cultural form. **SELECTED PUBLICATIONS** Auth, Newspaper Publishing, The Cult Industries in Can, James Lorimer Publ, 96; Television Coverage: A History of the Election in 65 Seconds, The Can Gen Election of 1997, Dundurn Press, 97. **CONTACT ADDRESS** Dept of Commun, Carleton Univ, 1125 Colonel By Dr, 344 St. Patricks, Ottawa, ON, Canada K1S 5B6. **EMAIL** chris_dornan@carleton.ca

DORNAN, READE W.
PERSONAL Born 12/07/1940, Denver, CO, m, 1964, 2 children **DISCIPLINE** ENGLISH EDUCATION **EDUCATION** Univ Colo, BA, 63; Mich State Univ, MA, 80; PhD, 88. **CAREER** Teacher, Hinckley High School, 63-65, Fleur du Lac School, 65-66, Garden School, Malaysia, 72-74; adj asst prof, Univ Mich, 85-95; vis prof, Purdue Univ, 95-96; lectr, 96-98, tchg asst, 78-85, Mich State Univ; asst prof, Cent Mich Univ, 98- . **HONORS AND AWARDS** Phi Beta Kappa; SLATE Rep Nat Coun Teachers English. **MEMBERSHIPS** Ctr Exten Lang & Thinking; Ger Soc Contemp Theatre & Drama English; Int Reading Asn; Mod Lang Asn & Midwest Mod Lang Asn; Nat Coun Teachers English and Mich Coun TE; Soc Values Higher Educ. **RESEARCH** Literacy, Drama in education, Whole language for secondary students, young adult literature. **SELECTED PUBLICATIONS** Auth, "Women Playwrights Since 1975", Oxford Companion to Women's Writing in the US, Oxford Univ Press, 95; auth Arnold Wesker Revisited. NY: Twayne, Simon & Schuster, 95; auth, "Omaha Magic Theatre: Not Corn, But Babes Unchained." Contemp Drama in English, Spring, 97; auth "Looking for Commonalties: The Pragmatist's Approach to Our Differences." J of Midwest Mod Lang Asn, Spring, 97; co-auth, Multiple Voices, Multiple Texts: Reading in the Secondary Content Areas, Heinemann Boynton/Cook, 97; ed, Arnold Wesker: A Casebook, NY: Garland, 98. **CONTACT ADDRESS** Dept English, Central Michigan Univ, 206 Anspach Hall, Mount Pleasant, MI 48859-0001. **EMAIL** reade.dornan@cmich.edu

DORNSIFE, ROB
DISCIPLINE ENGLISH **EDUCATION** Penn State Univ, MA; Lehigh, PhD. **CAREER** Dir, Grad Study & Writing Ctr. **HONORS AND AWARDS** Robert F Kennedy Stud Awd for Excellence Tchg, Creighton Univ, 96; Greek Awds banquet, 97 & 98; Outstanding Young Alumni Awd, Shippensburg Univ, 94; 1st Annual Creighton Univ Greek Commun Awd; Alpha Sigma Nu & Omicron Delta Kappa, 97. **SELECTED PUBLICATIONS** Publ in, J Adv Compos, Comput-Assisted Compos J, Writing Lab Newsl, NEJ, KE, MEJ, Nat Tchg and Lrng Forum, Tchg Prof. **CONTACT ADDRESS** Dept of Eng, Creighton Univ, 2500 CA Plaza, CA 306D, Omaha, NE 68178. **EMAIL** robert@creighton.edu

DORSEY, JAMES
DISCIPLINE ASIAN AND MIDDLE EASTERN LANGUAGES AND LITERATURES **EDUCATION** Colgate Univ, BA, 83; IN Univ, MA, 92; Univ WA, PhD, 97. **CAREER** Asst prof, Dartmouth Col; lecturer and teaching asst, 90-96; dir, 97; Darthmouth Japan Foreign Study prog, 98-99. **HONORS AND AWARDS** Soc Sci Res Coun/Japan Soc for the Promotion for Sci res grant, 00-01. **RESEARCH** Mod Japanese lit, criticism, and intellectual hist; class Japanese drama and lit theory. **SELECTED PUBLICATIONS** Transl, Japanese fiction; transl "The Unsinkable Molly Brown, " by Kageyama Tamio. In New Japanese Voices: The Best Contemporary Fiction, Atlantic Monthly Pr, 91; auth, "Escaping the Impasse in the Discourse on National Identity: Hagiwara Sakutaro, Sakaguchi Ango, and Nishitani Keiji," In New Historicism and Japanese Library Studies: Proceedings of the Midwest Association for Japanese Literary Studies, 98. **CONTACT ADDRESS** Dept of Asian an Middle Eastern Lang and Lit, Dartmouth Col, 6191 Bartlett Hall, Hanover, NH 03755. **EMAIL** james.dorsey@dartmouth.edu

DORSEY, LEROY
DISCIPLINE POLITICAL COMMUNICATION, PRESIDENTIAL RHETORIC **EDUCATION** Ind Univ, PhD. **CAREER** Asst prof, Texas A&M Univ. **HONORS AND AWARDS** Aubrey Fisher Awd, 95. **SELECTED PUBLICATIONS** Publ in, Quart J Speech; Presidential Stud Quart & Southern Commun J; contribur, African American Orators. **CONTACT ADDRESS** Dept of Speech Communication, Texas A&M Univ, Col Station, College Station, TX 77843-4234.

DORSEY, PETER
DISCIPLINE AMERICAN AUTOBIOGRAPHY, AFRICAN AMERICAN LITERATURE **EDUCATION** Univ Pa, PhD. **CAREER** Dept Eng, Mt Saint Mary's Col **SELECTED PUBLICATIONS** Auth, Sacred Estrangement: The Rhetoric of Conversion in Modern American Autobiography. **CONTACT ADDRESS** Dept of English, Mount Saint Mary's Col and Sem, 16300 Old Emmitsburg Rd, Emmitsburg, MD 21727-7799. **EMAIL** dorsey@msmary.edu

DORSEY, SCOTT W.
PERSONAL Born 02/01/1961, Lincoln, Nebr, m, 1987 **DISCIPLINE** MUSIC **EDUCATION** Nebr Wesleyan Univ, BA; Calif State Univ, MA; Univ Iowa, PhD. **CAREER** Dir, Choral Act at Mt Union Col; past fac, Mont State Univ-Billings; Univ Northern Iowa, Cedar Falls; William Penn Col, Oskaloosa, Iowa & Vennard Col, Univ Park, Iowa; mus dir & conductor, Alliance Symphony Orchestra; commercial pilot and flight instructor. **HONORS AND AWARDS** Amer Choral Directors Asn awd; appeared at, Amer Theatre Festival & before Cong US. **MEMBERSHIPS** Nat chem, Amer Choral Directors Association's Comt on Youth and Stud Act. **SELECTED PUBLICATIONS** Auth, The Choral Journal: An Index to Volumes 19-32, Amer Choral Directors Asn, 92; coauth, Up Front! Becoming the Compete Choral Conductor, EC Schirmer, Boston, 93; regular contribur, ACDA's Choral J; ed, Stud Times. **CONTACT ADDRESS** Dept of Music, Mount Union Col, 1972 Clark Ave, Alliance, OH 44601. **EMAIL** dorseysw@muc.edu

DORSINVILLE, MAX
PERSONAL Born 01/30/1943, Port-au-Prince, Haiti, m, 1964, 1 child **DISCIPLINE** ENGLISH, COMPARATIVE LITERATURE **EDUCATION** Univ Sherbrooke, BA, 66, MA, 68; City Univ New York, PhD (comp lit), 72. **CAREER** Lectr, 70-72, asst prof, 72-75, dir, Ctr for French-Can Studies, 75-80, Assoc Prof English, McGill Univ, 75-, Can Coun fel, 77-78. **HONORS AND AWARDS** Canada Coun leave fel, Humanities Research Council and Multiculturalism Directoraate publication grants, McGill Graduaate Fac interntional travel and res grants. **MEMBERSHIPS** Can Comp Lit Asn (treas, 75-77); Asn Can Univ Teachers English. **RESEARCH** 20th century lit (Canadian, Am, Caribbean), Modernism, fiction, Derek Waalcott's poetry. **SELECTED PUBLICATIONS** Auth, Caliban without Prospero: Essay on Quebec and Black Literature, 74; auth, Le Pays natal: Essais sur les litteratures du Tiers-Monde et du Quebec, 83; auth, Solidarites: Tiers-Monde et litterature comparee, 88; auth, "Remembering Rogeer Dorsinvill," Res in African Literatures 25, (94), 171-175; auth, James Wait, novel, 95; auth, Ronald Sutherland, in The Oxford Companion to Canadian Literature, 2nd ed, 97; auth, Erzulie Loves Shango, novel, 98; auth, "The Heat of Home: Metaphors of Incorporation in Derek Walcott's Poetry," Anglistica 3:1, 99; auth, The Rule of Francois ("Papa Doc") Duvalier Realism and Magic Realism in Haiti, 00. **CONTACT ADDRESS** Dept of English, McGill Univ, 853 Sherbrooke W, Montreal, QC, Canada H3A 2T6. **EMAIL** mdorsi@po-box.mcgill.ca

DORWICK, KEITH
PERSONAL Born 10/18/1957, Chicago, IL **DISCIPLINE** ENGLISH **EDUCATION** DePaul Univ, BA, 89; Univ Ill, MA, 91; PhD, 98. **CAREER** TA, instr media planner, Univ of Il, 89-00; asst prof, Univ of La, 00-. **HONORS AND AWARDS** Univ of Ill Awd, 98; Ill Board of Higher Educ, 98; Univ of La, Grant, 00, 01. **MEMBERSHIPS** MLA, NCTE. **RESEARCH** Computers and Writing, Hypertext and Hypermedia, Pedagogy, Sexuality and Spirituality. **SELECTED PUBLICATIONS** Auth, "Syllabus for a literature course focusing on lesbian and gay writings," Lesbian and Gay Studies Newsletter 23.2, (95); auth, "The Last Bastion: Student Self-Determination and the Making of A Syllabus," Teaching the Community Col Jour, (96); auth, "Rethinking the Academy: Problems and Possibilities of Teaching, Scholarship, Authority, and Power in Electronic Environments," Kairos 1.3, (96); coauth, "If They Build It, They Will Come," Proceedings of ACM SIGUCCS XXIV, (96); auth, "Saving Their Own Selves: Female-to-Male Cross-Dressing as a Means of Survival for Married Women in Two English Plays," Gender Blending, ed Bonnie Bullough, Vern L Bullough, James Elias, (97); coauth, "Looking Elsewhere: Career Options Other than the Tenure Track Teaching Position for M.A.s and PhDs in English: An Annotated MOO Conversation," Computers and Comp Jour, 17.1 (00): 69-96; ed, "Tenure2000: Issues of Employment In and Out of the Computers and Writing Community," Computers and Comp Jour, (00); auth, "Believing Impossible Things about Our Work Life: A Review of Michael Beruge's the Employment of English: Theory, Jobs, and the Future of Literature Studies," Computers and Comp Jour, (01); auth, "Weeping Stones, Living Trees: Creating and Archiving Electronic Texts in Student and Scholarly Writing," Texts and Tech: Reading and Writing in a Tech World, forthcoming. **CONTACT ADDRESS** Univ of Louisiana, Lafayette, PO Box 44691, Lafayette, LA 70504-4691. **EMAIL** kdorwick@louisiana.edu

DOSKOW, MINNA
PERSONAL Born 02/12/1937, New York City, NY, m, 1956, 2 children **DISCIPLINE** ENGLISH **EDUCATION** Univ Md, PhD. **CAREER** Dean, Lib Arts, Univ Baltimore; dean, Lib Arts & Sciences, lecturer, Rowan Univ; prof, English Dept, Rowan Univ. **HONORS AND AWARDS** Post-doctoral fel, Princeton Univ, 91-92; Japan Studies Institute fel, 94; Asian Studies Development Program fel, 98, 99. **RESEARCH** Japanese literature; Women's Lit. **SELECTED PUBLICATIONS** Auth, William Blake's 'Jerusalem:' Structure and Meaning in Poetry and Picture, Fairleigh Dickinson UP (New Jersey), Associated UP (London), 82; coauth, "Honors Teaching: Intersections of the Real and the Ideal," Forum for Honors 16.1 (fall 85): 25-30; auth, "William Blake and the Wheels of Compulsion," in History and Myth: Essays on English Romantic Lit, ed. Stephen C. Behrendt (Detroit, Mich: Wayne State Univ Pr, 90), 53-72; auth, "'Herland:' Utopia in a Different Voice," in Politics, Gender, and the Arts, ed. Ronald Dotterer and Susan Bowers (Selinsgrove: Susquehanna Univ Pr, London and Toronto: Asociated Univ Pr, 90) 52-63; auth, "Charlotte Perkins Gilman: The Female Face of Social Darwinism," Weber Studies, 14.3 (fall 97): 9-22; auth, Charlotte Perkins Gilman's Utopian Novels, Fairleigh Dickinson Univ Pr (Madison, N.J.), Associated Univ Pr (London), 99. **CONTACT ADDRESS** Rowan Univ, Glassboro, NJ 08028-1701. **EMAIL** doskow@rowan.edu

DOTY, GRESDNA ANN
PERSONAL Born 02/22/1931, Oelwein, IA, m, 1980 **DISCIPLINE** THEATRE **EDUCATION** Iowa State Teachers Col, BA, 53; Univ Fla, MA, 57; Ind Univ, PhD (theatre), 67. **CAREER** From instr to asst prof speech & theatre, Southwest Tex State Col, 57-65; asst prof, 67-72, assoc prof, 72-79, prof Theatre, La State Univ, Baton Rouge, 79-96, alumni prof Theatre, 84-96, alumni prof emer, La State Univ, 96-; Nat comt chmn, Am Col Theatre Festival, 76-79; Research grantee Nat Endowment Humanities, 81; Exxon Edn Found, 81. **MEMBERSHIPS** Am Soc Theatre Res, member exec comm, 88-91, vice-pres, 94-97; Speech Commun Asn; Am Theatre Asn; col of Fellows of Am Theatre. **RESEARCH** Theatre history. **SELECTED PUBLICATIONS** Auth, Anne Brunton in Bath and London, Theatre Surv, 5/67; Anne Merry and the Beginning of Stardom in the United States, Quart J Speech, 68; The Career of Anne Brunton Merry in the American Theatre, La State Univ, 71; coauth, Theatre Festivals: Practical Education for Actors, Directors and Designers, The Speech Teacher, 73; Contemporary Speech: A Comprehensive Approach to Communication, Nat Bk Co, 76; Southern Theatre History: A Bibliography of Theses and Dissertations, Southern Speech Commun J, 77; An interview with Geral Freedman, Lit in Performance, 80; Anne Brunton Merry: First Star, In: Women in American Theatre, Crown, 81; co-auth, Inside the Royal Court Theatre, 1956-81: Artists-Talk, LA State Univ, 90; . **CONTACT ADDRESS** Dept of Theatre, Louisiana State Univ, Baton Rouge, LA 70803-2504.

DOUDNA, MARTIN KIRK
PERSONAL Born 06/04/1930, Louisville, KY, m, 1962, 3 children **DISCIPLINE** ENGLISH LITERATURE, AMERICAN CULTURE **EDUCATION** Oberlin Col, AB, 52; Univ Louisville, MA, 59; Univ Mich, PhD (Am cult), 71. **CAREER** Asst prof English, Mackinac Col, 66-69; assoc prof, 71-78, Prof English, Univ Hawaii, Hilo, 78-. **MEMBERSHIPS** MLA; Thoreau Soc; Thoreau Lyceum. **RESEARCH** Nineteenth century American literature; American liberalism and radicalism; American magazine journalism. **SELECTED PUBLICATIONS** Auth, Nay Lady Sit, The Dramatic and Human Dimensions of Comus, Anq A Quart J Short Articles Notes Revs, Vol 8, 95. **CONTACT ADDRESS** Humanities Div, Univ of Hawaii, Hilo, Hilo, HI 96720.

DOUGHERTY, JAMES P.
DISCIPLINE 19TH-CENTURY AMERICAN LITERATURE **EDUCATION** Univ Pa, PhD. **CAREER** Instr, Univ Notre Dame; coed, Relig and Lit. **RESEARCH** Connections between religion and literature, Am Romanticism. **SELECTED PUBLICATIONS** Auth, The Fivesquare City; Walt Whitman and the Citizen's Eye. **CONTACT ADDRESS** Dept of English, Univ of Notre Dame, 356 O'Shaughnessy Hall, Notre Dame, IN 46556. **EMAIL** james.p.dougherty.1@nd.edu

DOUGLAS, ANN
DISCIPLINE TWENTIETH-CENTURY AMERICAN LITERATURE **EDUCATION** Harvard Univ, BA, 64, PhD, 70; Oxford Univ, BPhil, 66. **CAREER** Instr, Princeton Univ, 70-74; prof. **HONORS AND AWARDS** Bicentennial preceptorship, Princeton Univ, 74; fel, Nat Hum Ctr, 78-79; fel, NEH, Guggenheim, 93-94; Alfred Beveridge award, Amer Hist Assn; Lionel Trilling award, Columbia Univ; Merle Curti intellectual hist award, Org Amer Historians. **SELECTED PUBLICATIONS** Auth, The Feminization of American Culture, 77; Terrible Honesty: Mongrel Manhattan in the 1920's, Farrar, Straus, 95; Little Women, Uncle Tom's Cabin, and Charlotte Temple, Penguin editions, and Word Virus, a William Burroughs anthology, 98. **CONTACT ADDRESS** Dept of Eng, Columbia Col, New York, 2960 Broadway, New York, NY 10027-6902.

DOUGLAS, GEORGE HALSEY
PERSONAL Born 01/09/1934, East Orange, NJ, m, 1961, 1 child **DISCIPLINE** AMERICAN LITERATURE & STUDIES **EDUCATION** Lafayette Col, AB, 56; Columbia Univ, MA, 66; Univ Ill, PhD(philos), 68. **CAREER** From instr to prof, 66-88, prof English, Univ Ill, Urbana, 88-. **MEMBERSHIPS** MLA; Am Soc Aesthet; Am Studies Asn; Popular Cult Asn. **RESEARCH** American culture and social history. **SELECTED PUBLICATIONS** Auth, H L Mencken: Critic of American Life, Archon, 78; Rail city: Chicago and the Railroad, Howell-North Bks, 82; auth, Edmund Urban's America, Ky, 83; auth, Women of the Twenties, Saybrook, 86; auth, The Early Days of Radio Broadcasting, McFarland, 87; All Aboard: The Railroad in American Life, Paragon House, 92; Education Without Impact, Birch Lane Press, 92; Skyscraper Odyssey, McFarland, 96; Postwar America, Krieger Publishing, 98; auth, The Golden Age of the Newspaper, Greenwood, 99. **CONTACT ADDRESS** Dept of English, Univ of Illinois, Urbana-Champaign, 608 S Wright St, Urbana, IL 61801-3613. **EMAIL** ghdougla@vivc.edu

DOUGLAS, JANE YELLOWLEES
PERSONAL Born 06/25/1962, Detroit, MI, m, 1994 **DISCIPLINE** ENGLISH, NEW MEDIA **EDUCATION** Univ Mich, BA, 82; MA, 83; NY Univ, PhD, 92. **CAREER** Res Fel, Brunel Univ, 92-93; asst prof, CUNY, Lehman Col, 93-96; asst to assoc prof, Univ of Fla, 96-. **HONORS AND AWARDS** Phi Beta Kappa, 63; Hopwood Writing Awd, Univ Mich, 84; Finalist, Ellen Nold Awd, 97. **MEMBERSHIPS** MLA, Post Modern Cult Media Ecology, Electronic Lit Org. **RESEARCH** Adoption of innovations, narrative, interactive narratives, new media, schema theory, cognitive psychology and writing. **SELECTED PUBLICATIONS** Auth, "Wandering through the Labyrinth: Encountering Interactive Fiction," Computers and Composition 6.3 (89): 93-105; auth, "Social Impacts of Computing: The Framing of Hypetext--Revolutionary for Whom?" Soc Sci Computer Rev 11.4 (93): 417-429; auth, "Dipping into Possible, Plausible Worlds: the Experience of Interactivity from Virtual Reality to Interactive Fiction," TDR, the Drama Review: The Journal of Performance Studies 37.4 (93): 18-37; auth, "Tell Me When to Stop: Closure and Indeterminacy in Interactive Narratives," Hyper/Text/Theory, ed George Landow (Baltimore: Johns Hopkins Univ Pr, 94): 159-188; auth, "Sorry, We Ran Out of Space, So It's Just a Guy Thing: Virtual Intimacy and the Male Gaze Cubed," Leonardo: Jour of the Int Soc for Art, Sci and Tech 29.3, (96): 205-215; auth, "Will the Most Reflexive Relativist Please Stand Up? Hypertext, Argument, and Relativism," Page to Screen: Taking Literacy into the Electronic Age, ed Ilana Snyder, (Sydney: Allen & Unwin, NY: Routledge, 97): 144-162; auth, "Have I Said Nothing," Post Mod Am Fiction: A Norton Anthology, eds Paula Geyh, Fred G. Lebron and Andrew Levy, (NY: WW Norton, 97): 573-576; auth, "The Three Paradoxes of Hypertext: How Theories of Textuality Shape Interface Design," The Emerging CyberCulture: Literacy, Paradigm, and Paradox, eds Stephanie B Gibson and Ollie Oviedo, (Cresskill, NJ: Hampton Pr, 00); auth, the End of Books - Or Books without End? Reading Interactive Narratives, Univ of Mich Pr, (Ann Arbor, MI), 00; auth, "Here Even When You're Not: Teaching in an Internet Degree Program," Silicon Literacies, ed Ilana Snyder, (NY, Sydney: Routledge) in press. **CONTACT ADDRESS** PO Box 1086, Fairfield, FL 32634-1086. **EMAIL** jdouglas@new.ufl.edu

DOUGLAS, MARCIA B.
PERSONAL Born Watford, England **DISCIPLINE** CREATIVE WRITING, LITERATURE **EDUCATION** Oakwood Col, BA, 90; Ohio State Univ, MFA, 93; State Univ NY, PhD, 97. **CAREER** Asst prof, NC State Univ, 98-. **SELECTED PUBLICATIONS** Auth, Madam Fate, Soho Press, 99; auth, Electricity Comes to Cocoa Bottom, Peepal Tree Press, 99. **CONTACT ADDRESS** Dept English, No Carolina State Univ, PO Box 8105, Raleigh, NC 27695-0001. **EMAIL** mdouglas@unity.ncsu.edu

DOUGLAS, PAUL H.
PERSONAL Born 02/24/1940, Hartford, CT, m, 1968, 2 children **DISCIPLINE** ENGLISH **EDUCATION** Univ CT, BA, 62; Univ Ore, MA, 64; George Washington Univ, PhD, 72. **CAREER** Instructor, W Mich Univ, 64-67; Prof, Towson Univ, 69-. **HONORS AND AWARDS** Phi Beta Kappa; Fulbright Sen Lecturer, Turkey, 76-77. **MEMBERSHIPS** Am Studies Asn; Am Folklore Soc. **CONTACT ADDRESS** Dept Eng, Towson State Univ, 8000 York Rd, Baltimore, MD 21252-0001. **EMAIL** pdouglas@towson.edu

DOUGLASS, PAUL
PERSONAL Born 06/01/1951, Oakland, CA, m, 1973, 2 children **DISCIPLINE** ENGLISH **EDUCATION** Amherst Col, BA, 73; Claremont Grad Sch, MA, 76; UCLA, PhD, 81. **CAREER** Lectr, UCLA, 81-84; asst to assoc prof, Mercer Univ, 84-90; prof, chair, San Jose State Univ, 90-. **HONORS AND AWARDS** NEH Grant; ACLS Award; Nat Teacher Center Award. **MEMBERSHIPS** MLA, Pacific Ancient and Mod Lang Asn; Int Byron Soc. **RESEARCH** Modernism, Critical Theory, Byron Studies. **SELECTED PUBLICATIONS** Auth, Bergson, Elliot, and American Literature, Univ Pr of Ky, 86; ed, Cradle of the Copperheads, a novel by Jesse Stuart, McGraw-Hill, 88; coed, A Selection of Hebrew Melodies, Ancient and Modern, by Isaac Nathan and Lord Byron, Univ Ala Pr, 88; coed, The Crisis in Modernism: Bergson and the Vitalist Controversy, Cambridge Univ Pr, 92. **CONTACT ADDRESS** Dept English, San Jose State Univ, San Jose, CA 95192-0090. **EMAIL** pdouglass@email.sjsu.edu

DOUGLASS, THOMAS E.
PERSONAL Born 08/20/1951, Baltimore, MD, m, 1972, 2 children **DISCIPLINE** ENGLISH **EDUCATION** Davis & Elkin Col, BA, 73; Ind Univ, MLS, 74; Univ NCar, MA, 89; PhD, 95. **CAREER** Visiting Asst Prof, E Carolina Univ, 92-. **MEMBERSHIPS** SAMLA. **RESEARCH** Applachian literature; Visual Arts and literature. **SELECTED PUBLICATIONS** Auth, A Room Forever: The life and work of Breere D J Pancake, Univ Tenn Press, 98. **CONTACT ADDRESS** Dept Eng, East Carolina Univ, 1000 E 5th St, Greenville, NC 27858-2502. **EMAIL** doublasst@mail.ecu.edu

DOVE, LINDA L.
PERSONAL Born 09/18/1966, Berkeley, CA, d **DISCIPLINE** ENGLISH LITERATURE **EDUCATION** Mt Holyoke Col, AB, 88; Univ Md, MA, 91; PhD, 97. **CAREER** Teaching Asst, Univ Md, 89-95; Lectr, Univ Md, 96-97; Asst Prof, Hope Col, 97-. **HONORS AND AWARDS** Mary Lyon Scholar Awd, 88; Ruth Elsbeth Raymond Prize, 88; Alice L Geyer Awd, 97; Fac Develop Grants, Hope Col, 98, 99, 00. **MEMBERSHIPS** Soc for the Study of Early Mod Women, MLA. **RESEARCH** Early modern English poetry, women writers, race in the Renaissance. **SELECTED PUBLICATIONS** Co-ed, "An Annotated Bibliography of the History of Non-Western Rhetorical Theory Before 1900," Rhetoric Soc Quart, 24 (94): 167-180; auth, "Composing (To) A Man of Letters: Lady Anne Southwell's Acrostic to Francis Quarles," ANQ: A Quart J of Short Articles, Notes and Rev, 11 (98): 12-17; co-ed, "Mary Wroth and the Politics of the Household in 'Pamphilia to Amphilanthus'," in Women, Writing and the Reproduction of Cult in Tudor and Stuart Brit (Syracuse UP, 00), 141-156; co-ed, Women, Writing and the Reproduction of Culture in Tudor and Stuart Britain, Syracuse UP, 00. **CONTACT ADDRESS** Dept English, Hope Col, 137 E 12th St, Holland, MI 49423-3607.

DOWDEY, DIANE
DISCIPLINE NINETEENTH-CENTURY LITERATURE **EDUCATION** TX Christian Univ, BA, 76; Univ MS, MA, 77; Univ Wis, PhD, 84. **CAREER** EngDept, Sam Houston State Univ **HONORS AND AWARDS** Delta Kappa Gamma Soc Int; Who's Who in Am Educ; Outstanding Young Women Am; Who's Who Am Women; Domestic Travel Fel Univ WI; Master's Fel Univ MS; Phi Beta Kappa, Sigma Tau Delta. **MEMBERSHIPS** S Central Mod Lang Asn, Nat Coun Tchrs Engl, Conf Col Compos & Comm, TX Coun Tchrs Engl, Conf Col Tchrs Eng, Nat Asn Develop Educs. **SELECTED PUBLICATIONS** Auth, The Researching Reader: Source-Based Writings Across the Disciplines, Holt, Rinehart, & Winston, 90; Instructor's Manual, Holt, Rinehart, & Winston, 91; I Do Not Want to Leave Alone, Pawn Rev, 76; Song for a Widow, Descant, 79-80; Bridging the Gap: Science for a Popular Audience, IA State Univ, 85; Rhetorical Techniques Audience Adaptation in Popular Science Writing, Jour Technical Writing in Popular Sci Writing, 87; Stephen Jay Gould: 'This View Science,' Markham Rev, 87; Society Mind by Marvin Minsky, Masterplots II: Nonfiction Series, Salem Press, 89; Citation and Documentation

Across the Curriculum, Southern IL Univ Press, 92. **CONTACT ADDRESS** Dept of English, Sam Houston State Univ, Huntsville, TX 77341.

DOWELL, PETER W.
DISCIPLINE ENGLISH LANGUAGE AND LITERATURE **EDUCATION** Univ Minn, PhD, 65. **CAREER** Assoc prof/sr assoc dean Emory Col. **RESEARCH** 20th century American literature; American poetry and poetics; American studies. **SELECTED PUBLICATIONS** Ed, "Ich Kuss Die Hand:" The Letters of H L Mencken to Gretchen Hood. **CONTACT ADDRESS** English Dept, Emory Univ, 1380 Oxford Rd NE, Atlanta, GA 30322-1950.

DOWELL, RICHARD WALKER
PERSONAL Born 11/26/1931, Bloomington, IN, m, 1957, 4 children **DISCIPLINE** ENGLISH, AMERICAN LITERATURE **EDUCATION** Ind State Univ, BS, 57; Univ Colo, MA, 60; Ind Univ, PhD (English), 68. **CAREER** Instr English, Univ Colo, 57-60; from instr to assoc prof, 63-74, Prof English, Ind State Univ, Terre Haute, 74-, Ed, Dreiser Newsletter, 69-89, Retired, 93. **HONORS AND AWARDS** Sigma Tau Delta Teacher of the Year, 71. **RESEARCH** American literature 1875-1925; Theodore Dreiser. **SELECTED PUBLICATIONS** Ed, Mesdore Dreisers An Amatuer Laborer, U Penn Press, 83; co-auth, Meodore Dreiser: A Primary Bibliograpy and Reference Guide, G.K. Hall, 91; auth, Mechanism and Mysticism, The Influence of Science on the Thought and Wok of Dreiser, Theodore, Am Lit, Vol 66, 94. **CONTACT ADDRESS** Dept of English, Indiana State Univ, Terre Haute, IN 47809.

DOWLING, WILLIAM C.
PERSONAL Born 04/05/1944, Warner, NH **DISCIPLINE** ENGLISH AND AMERICAN LITERATURE **EDUCATION** Dartmouth Univ, BA, 66; Harvard Univ, MA, 68; PhD, 74. **CAREER** Assoc to prof of English, Rutgers Univ, 88-92. **HONORS AND AWARDS** Woodrow Wilson Fel, 66; Fel, NEH Ctr, 79-80; NEH Fel, 80; Fel, Institute for Advanced Studies in the Humanities, Univ of Edinburgh, 82-85; Guggenheim Fel, 83-84; Howard Fuond Fel, 86-88; Richard Beale Davis Prize, 93. **MEMBERSHIPS** SHEAR; Henry Sweet Soc; ALSC. **RESEARCH** 18th-Century English literature; American literature of the Revolution and early republic; semantic theory and philosophy of language. **SELECTED PUBLICATIONS** Auth, The Critic's Hornbook, The Boswellian Hero, Language and Logos in Boswell's Life of Johnson, Jameson/Althusser/ Marx, Poetry and Ideology in Revolutionary Connecticut, The Epistolary Moment: the Poetics of the Eighteenth-Century Verse Epistle, Literary Federalism in the Age of Jefferson; The Senses of the Text: Intensional Semantics and Literary Theory. **CONTACT ADDRESS** Dept of English, Rutgers, The State Univ of New Jersey, New Brunswick, 510 George St, Murray Hall, New Brunswick, NJ 08901-1167. **EMAIL** wcdowling@aol.com

DOWNES, DAVID ANTHONY
PERSONAL Born 08/17/1927, Victor, CO, m, 1949, 3 children **DISCIPLINE** ENGLISH **EDUCATION** Regis Col, BA, 49; Marquette Univ, MA, 50; Univ Wash, PhD (English), 55. **CAREER** Instr English, Gonzaga Univ, 50-53; from asst prof to assoc prof, Seattle Univ, 53-64, prof and chmn dept, 64-67; coordr humanities prog, 73-77, Prof English, Calif State Univ, Chico, 68-, Seattle Univ res grants, 61-63; dean humanities, Calif State Univ, Chico, 68-72, res grant, 70, dean educ develop, 72-73, ed, Univ J, 74-77, dir English dept grad progs 77-79, chair, Dept English, 79-; Lilly grant for Stanford Sem Lit and Art, 82. **MEMBERSHIPS** MLA. **RESEARCH** The genius of John Ruskin; criticism; western novel. **SELECTED PUBLICATIONS** Auth, The Hopkins enigma, Thought, 60; Gerard Manley Hopkins: A Study of his Ignatian Spirit, 60 & Victorian Portraits: Hopkins and Pater, 65, Twayne; Hopkins and Aquinas, Victorian Poetry, 65; Studies in structure, Renascence, 66; The Temper of Victorian Belief: Studies in the Religious Novels of Pater, Kingsley and Newman, Twayne, 72; Beatific landscapes in Hopkins, (parts 1 & 2), Hopkins Quart, 74-75; Ruskin's Landscape of Beatitude, Univ Microfilms Int, 80. **CONTACT ADDRESS** Dept of English, California State Univ, Chico, Chico, CA 95926.

DOWNEY, JAMES
PERSONAL Born 04/20/1939, Winterton, NF, Canada **DISCIPLINE** ENGLISH **EDUCATION** Memorial Univ Nfld, BA, 62, BEd 63, MA, 64, DLitt(hon), 91; Univ London, PhD, 1966; DHL(hon), Univ Maine, 87; LLD(hon), Univ NB, 91. **CAREER** Ch, dept Eng, 72-75, dean arts, 75-78, vice pres acad, Carleton Univ, 78-80; pres, Univ NB, 80-90; PRES, UNIV WATERLOO, 93-. **HONORS AND AWARDS** Fel, Univ Georgia, 85; off, Order Can, 97. **SELECTED PUBLICATIONS** Auth, The Eighteenth Century Pulpit, 69; co-ed, Fearful Joy, 74. **CONTACT ADDRESS** Univ of Waterloo, Waterloo, ON, Canada N2L 3G1. **EMAIL** jdowney@nh4.adm.uwaterloo.ca

DOWNING, DAVID
PERSONAL Born 05/03/1947, Newton, MA, m, 1974, 2 children **DISCIPLINE** ENGLISH **EDUCATION** Beloit Coll, BA, 70; San Francisco State Univ, MA, 74; SUNY/Buffalo, PhD, 80. **CAREER** Asst, assoc, prof, 79-88, Eastern IL Univ; Prof, 88-, Indiana Univ of PA **HONORS AND AWARDS** Innovative Excellence in Teaching, Learning and technology Awd, 98; Teaching Excellence Awd for Outstanding Teaching: Innovative Practice, 93; Soc for Critical Exchange Grant for the Symposium, Problemss of Affirmation in Cultural Theory, 91; Soc for Critical exchange Grant for the conference, The Role of Theory in the Undergraduate Literature Classroom, 90. **MEMBERSHIPS** Soc for Critical Exchange, member, board of directors; The GRIP Project, member, Steering committee; Alternative Educational Environments, assoc dir; MLA, Midwest MLA; Soc for the Advancement of Amer Phil; Natl Council of Teachers of Eng. **SELECTED PUBLICATIONS** Auth, Image and Ideology in Modern/Postmodern Discourse, 91; Practicing Theory in Introductory College Literature Courses, 91; Founding ed Work and Days, 84; Changing Classroom Practices: Resources for Literary and Cultural Studies, 94; The TicToc Project: Teaching in Cyberspace Through On-Line Courses, Spring/ Fall 97; co auth, Coming to Terms with Terms in Academic Cyberculture, The Emerging Cyberculture: Literacy, Paradigm, and Paradox, forthcoming. **CONTACT ADDRESS** 1252 Malvern Ave., Pittsburgh, PA 15217. **EMAIL** downing@grove.iup.edu

DOXEY, WILLIAM S.
PERSONAL Born 01/20/1935, Coral Gables, FL, m, 1999, 5 children **DISCIPLINE** ENGLISH **EDUCATION** Fla State Univ, BA, 61; MA, 65; Univ NC, Chapel Hill, PhD, 70. **CAREER** Prof, State Univ of W Ga, 68-. **MEMBERSHIPS** Westar, MENSA, ACLU. **RESEARCH** Neurolinguistics; metaphor; sci-fi; creative writing; modern and postmodern literature. **SELECTED PUBLICATIONS** Ed/pub, Notes on Contemporary Literature; auth, Cousins to Kudzu; auth; Dead Wrong; auth, Bye-bye; auth, Lonesome Blues; auth, Countdown; auth, ESPionage; auth, The Star Poem. **CONTACT ADDRESS** Dept of English, State Univ of West Georgia, Carrollton, GA 30118. **EMAIL** bdoxey@westga.edu

DOYLE, CHARLES CLAY
PERSONAL Born 07/20/1943, Marlin, TX **DISCIPLINE** ENGLISH, FOLKLORE **EDUCATION** Univ Tex, Austin, BA, 64, PhD (English), 69. **CAREER** Asst prof, Univ Southern Calif, 69-74; asst prof, 74-79, Assoc Prof English, Univ GA, 79-. **MEMBERSHIPS** MLA; Am Folklore Soc; Am Dialect Soc; Amici Thomae More; Male-dicta: Int Res Ctr Verbal Aggression. **RESEARCH** Renaissance literature; European and American folklore; the English language. **SELECTED PUBLICATIONS** Auth, More Epigrams in the 16th Century and 17th Century 94p; Bourbon Nugae and More Epigrammata, Moreana, Vol 32, 95; The Long Story of the Short End of the Stick , Am Speech, Vol 69, 94; Another Elliptic with aand an Elliptic to, Am Speech, Vol 72, 97; Duck Butter Redux , Am Speech, Vol 72, 97; The Proverbial Hole in the Ground, Anq A Quart J Short Articles Notes Revs, Vol 8, 95; He That Will Swear Will Lie, Chaucer Rev, Vol 32, 97. **CONTACT ADDRESS** Dept of English, Univ of Georgia, 0 Georgia University, Athens, GA 30602-0001. **EMAIL** cdoyle@arches.uga.edu

DOYLE, ESTHER M.
PERSONAL Born 03/21/1910, Boston, MA **DISCIPLINE** ENGLISH, SPEECH **EDUCATION** Emerson Col, BLI, 35; Boston Univ, MA, 40; Northwestern Univ, PhD, 64. **CAREER** Tchr elem schs, Mass 29-37; oral English supvr & teacher, high schs, NY, 37-44; hosp recreation worker, Mil Welfare Serv, Am Red Cross, 44-45; from instr to prof English, 45-71, chmn dept, 67-75, Dana prof, 71-75, emer prof eng, 75-, Juniata Col; lectr, 60-61, Bethany Bible Sem; partic, Nat Humanities Series Progs, 69-73; vis prof, 71, Univ Ariz. **MEMBERSHIPS** Speech Commun Assn; AAUP. **RESEARCH** Verse drama. **SELECTED PUBLICATIONS** Co-ed, Studies in Interpretation, Vol I, 72 & Vol II, Amsterdam, 77. **CONTACT ADDRESS** Dept of English, Juniata Col, Huntingdon, PA 16652.

DOYLE, JACQUELINE
PERSONAL Born 12/11/1951, Jersey City, NJ, m, 1987, 1 child **DISCIPLINE** ENGLISH **EDUCATION** Brown Univ, BA, 74; Cornell Univ, MA, 83; PhD, 86. **CAREER** From asst prof to assoc prof, Calif State Univ at Fresno, 86-94; from assoc prof to prof, Calif State Univ at Hayward, 94-. **HONORS AND AWARDS** Incentive Grant, Am Asn of Univ Women, 77-78; Andrew Dickson White Fel, Cornell Univ, 77-78, 78-79, & 81-82; Graduate Res Fel, Cornell Univ, 84, 85, & 86; Guilford Essay Prize, Cornell Univ, 87; Res Awd, Calif State Univ, 87-88; Meritorious Performance and Professional Promise Awds, 87 & 88; Affirmative Action Fac Development Grants, Calif State Univ, 88-89, 89-90, 95-96, & 96-97; Summer Stipends, Res, Scholar, and Creative Activity Awds, Calif State Univ, 89 & 90; Sabbatical Leave Awd, Calif State Univ, 91-92; Katherine Newman Awd, 95; Performance Salary Step Increase Awds, Calif State Univ, 96 & 97; Fac Summer Stipends for Course Development, Calif State Univ, 97; Fac Merit Increas, 99. **MEMBERSHIPS** Soc for the Study of Multi-Ethnic Literature of the United States, MLA, Am Lit Asn, Poe Studies Asn. **RESEARCH** Contemporary American women's literature, ethnic American literature, Nineteenth- and Twentieth-Century American literature. **SELECTED PUBLICATIONS** Auth, "Haunting the Borderlands: La Llorona in Sandra Cisneros' 'Woman Hollering Creek,'" Frontiers: A J of Women Studies vol 16, no 1 (96): 53-70; auth, "Assumptions of the Virgin and Recent Chicana Literature," Women's Studies: An Interdisciplinary J vol 26 (97): 171-201; auth, "'A Love Letter to My Motherland': Maternal Discourses in Jessica Hagedorn's Dogeaters," Hitting Critical Mass: A J of Asian Am Cultural Criticism vol 4, no 2 (summer 97):1-25; auth, "Developing Negatives: Jamaica Kincaid's Lucy," Literature of Immigration, Greenwood Press (Westport, CT), 99; auth, "'These Dark Woods Yet Again': Rewriting Redemption in Lee Smith's Saving Grace," Critique: Studies in Contemporary Fiction vol 41, no 3 (spring, 2000): 273-289. **CONTACT ADDRESS** Dept English, California State Univ, Hayward, 25800 Carlos Bee Blvd, Hayward, CA 94542-3001. **EMAIL** jdoyle@csuhayward.edu

DOYLE, JAMES
DISCIPLINE BIOGRAPHY AS A LITERARY GENRE **EDUCATION** Laurentian, BA; Toronto, MA; British Columbia, PhD. **CAREER** Prof emer, Wilfrid Laurier Univ. **SELECTED PUBLICATIONS** Auth,: North of America: Images of Canada in the Literature of the United States, 1775-1900, ECW Press, 83; Stephen Leacock: The Sage of Orillia , ECW Press, 92; The Fin de Si?cle Spirit: Walter Blackburn Harte and the American/ Canadian Literary Milieu of the 1890s, ECW Press, 95; Margaret Fairley and the Canadian Literary Tradition; Red Letters: Notes Toward a Literary History of Canadian Communism. **CONTACT ADDRESS** Dept of English, Wilfrid Laurier Univ, 75 University Ave W, Waterloo, ON, Canada N2L 3C5. **EMAIL** jdoyle@mach1.wlu.ca

DOYLE, PAUL A.
PERSONAL Born 12/06/1925, Carbondale, PA, m, 1970, 3 children **DISCIPLINE** ENGLISH **EDUCATION** Univ Scranton, BA, 46; Fordham Univ, MA, 48; PhD, 55. **CAREER** Instr to Asst Prof, Fordham Univ, 48-60; Asst Prof to Assoc Prof, St John's Univ, 60-62; Assoc Prof to Prof, Nassau Community Col, 62-. **HONORS AND AWARDS** Chancellor's Awd, SUNY, 81. **MEMBERSHIPS** Am Asn of School Admin. **RESEARCH** Twentieth Century English, Irish and American novelists and Short Story Writers. **SELECTED PUBLICATIONS** Auth, Sean O'Faolain: A Critical Study, Twayne Pub, 68; auth, Evelyn Waugh: A Critical Essay, Eerdmans, 69; auth, Liam O'Flaherty, Twayne Pub, 71; auth, Liam O'Flaherty: An Annotated bibliography, Whitston Pub, 72; co-auth, Early American Trains, Greenberg-Kalmbach, 93; contrib, Contemporary Novelists, 6th ed, St James Press, 96; contrib, Contemporary Popular Writers, St James Press, 97; contrib, Reference guide to short Fiction 2nd ed, St James Press, 99; contrib, American National Biography, Oxfod, 99. **CONTACT ADDRESS** Dept English, Nassau Comm Col, 1 Educ Dr, Garden City, NY 11530-6719.

DOYNO, VICTOR
PERSONAL Born 07/12/1937, Chicago, IL, m, 1959, 3 children **DISCIPLINE** ENGLISH, LITERATURE **EDUCATION** Miami Univ Ohio, BA, 59; Harvard, MA, 60; Ind Univ, PhD, 66. **CAREER** Instr, Princeton, 65-66; From Asst to Full Prof, SUNY at Buffalo. **MEMBERSHIPS** Mark Twain Circle, ALA, MLA. **RESEARCH** Mark Twain, F.S. Fitzgerald, Chaucer. **SELECTED PUBLICATIONS** Auth, Writing Heuk Finn, 91; auth, Heuk, Random House, 96. **CONTACT ADDRESS** Dept English, SUNY, Buffalo, Clemens Hall, PO Box 604610, Buffalo, NY 14260-0001.

DRAGGA, SAM A.
DISCIPLINE TECHNICAL COMMUNICATION **EDUCATION** Univ OH, PhD, 82. **CAREER** Prof, TX Tech Univ; ser ed, Allyn & Bacon Ser in Tech Commun. **MEMBERSHIPS** Vice-pres, Asn of Tchr of Tech Writing. **SELECTED PUBLICATIONS** Coauth, Ed: The Design of Rhetoric, Baywood, 89; A Writer's Repertoire, HarperCollins, 95; A Reader's Repertoire, HarperCollins, 96; ed, Technical Writing: Student Samples and Teacher Responses, ATTW, 92. **CONTACT ADDRESS** Texas Tech Univ, Lubbock, TX 79409-5015. **EMAIL** ditsd@ttacs.ttu.edu

DRAINE, BETSY
PERSONAL Born 08/21/1945, Boston, MA, m, 1981 **DISCIPLINE** BRITISH AND AMERICAN LITERATURE **EDUCATION** Mt Holyoke Col, AB, 67; Temple Univ, MA, 72, PhD (English), 77. **CAREER** Instr, 76-77, asst prof, 77-82, Assoc Prof English Lit, Univ Wis-Madison, 82-, Bk rev ed, Contemp Lit, 78-81, assoc ed, 79-; consult, Feminist Studies, 78-82. **HONORS AND AWARDS** Mark H Ingraham Prize, Univ Wis Press, 82. **MEMBERSHIPS** MLA; Doris Lessing Soc. **RESEARCH** British and American novel, 20th century; women novelists; literary theory. **SELECTED PUBLICATIONS** Auth, Changing frames: Doris Lessing's Memoirs of a Survivor, Studies in the Novel, spring 79; Interview with Angus Wilson, Contemp Lit, winter 80; Nostalgia and irony: The postmodern order of The Golden Notebook, Mod Fiction Studies, spring 80; Writing deconstruction, and other unnatural acts, Boundary 2, spring-fall 81; Substance Under Pressure: The Novels of Doris Lessing, Univ Wis Press (in prep). **CONTACT ADDRESS** 1446 Rutledge St, Madison, WI 53703.

DRAKE, BARBARA
PERSONAL Born 04/13/1939, Abilene, KS, m, 1986, 8 children **DISCIPLINE** LITERATURE, CREATIVE WRITING **EDUCATION** Univ Ore, BA, 61; MFA, 66. **CAREER** TA, Univ of Ore, 61-62, 64-66; asst prof, Mich State Univ, 74-83; asst prof to prof, Linfield Col, 83-. **HONORS AND AWARDS** NEA Awd, 66; NEA Fel, 86; Northwest Area Found Grant 85; Edith Green Distinguished Professor Awd, Linfield Col, 93. **MEMBERSHIPS** PEN, Ore Counc for Teachers of English. **RESEARCH** American poetry, Irish literature, women writers. **SELECTED PUBLICATIONS** Auth, Love At The Egyptian Theatre, Red Cedar Pr, Mich State Univ, 78; auth, Life In A Gothic Novel, White Ewe Pr, (Baltimore, MD), 81; auth, What We Say to Strangers, Breitenbush Pub, 86; auth, Bees in Wet Weather, Canoe Pr, 92; auth, Writing Poetry, Harcourt Brace, 94; auth, Space Before A, 26 Books Pub, 96. **CONTACT ADDRESS** Dept English, Linfield Col, 900 SE Baker St, McMinnville, OR 97128-6808. **EMAIL** bdrake@linfield.edu

DRAKE, HAROLD A.
PERSONAL Born 07/24/1942, Cincinnati, IL, m, 1969, 1 child **DISCIPLINE** HISTORY, CLASSICS **EDUCATION** Univ S Calif, AM, 63; Univ Wis, MA, 66; MA, 69; PhD, 70. **CAREER** Teach asst, Univ Wis, 62-65; lectr, asst prof, assoc prof, prof, UCSB, 70-. **HONORS AND AWARDS** NEH Fel, Inst Adv Stud, 73-74; Sr Fel, Annenburg Res Inst, 91-92; Asn Stud Out Teach Awd, 73-74; Plous Memo Awd, Out Asst Prof, 76; Mortar Bd Prof of Yr, 86-87; Alumni Dist Teach Awd, 95-96. **MEMBERSHIPS** Phi Beta Kappa; APA; AIA; SPRS; AAH; NAPS; BSA; ASCH; SBL. **RESEARCH** Late Roman empire; early Christianity; late antiquity; ancient histiography. **SELECTED PUBLICATIONS** Auth, In Praise of Constantine, Univ Calif Press, 76; co-auth, Eudoxia and the Holy Sepulchre, Cisalpino Golliardica (Milan), 81; auth, "Eusebius on the True Cross," Eccle Hist (85); auth, "Lambs Into Lions," Past and Pres (96); auth, Constantine and the Bishops, John Hopkins Press, 00. **CONTACT ADDRESS** Hist Dept, Univ of California, Santa Barbara, Santa Barbara, CA 93106-9410. **EMAIL** drake@humanities.ucsb.edu

DRAKE, ROBERT Y., JR.
PERSONAL Born 10/20/1930, Ripley, TN, s **DISCIPLINE** ENGLISH **EDUCATION** Vanderbilt Univ, BA, 52, MA, 53; Yale Univ, MA, 54, PhD, 55. **CAREER** Instr, Univ of Mich, 55-58; instr, Northwestern Univ, 58-69; asst prof, Univ of Tex, Austin, 61-65; assoc prof, 73-95, prof, 73-, Lindsay Young Prof, Univ Tenn, 98-. **HONORS AND AWARDS** Visiting Prof, Hendrix Col, Conway, Ark. **MEMBERSHIPS** Phi Beta Kappa; MLA; SAMLA; SSSL; CEA. **RESEARCH** Southern literature; shape and form of fiction. **SELECTED PUBLICATIONS** Auth, Amazing Grace, 65; The Single Heart, 71; The Burning Bush, 75; Survivors and Others, 87; My Sweetheart's House, 93; What Will You Do for an Encore?, 96; The Home Place: A Momory and a Celebration, 80 & 98. **CONTACT ADDRESS** English Dept, Univ of Tennessee, Knoxville, Knoxville, TN 37916.

DRAMIN, EDWARD
PERSONAL Born Long Meadow, MA, s **DISCIPLINE** ENGLISH **EDUCATION** Amhurst Col, BA; Columbia Univ, MA; PhD. **CAREER** Ohio State Univ; prof, Iona Coll. **HONORS AND AWARDS** Fac Fel, Iona Coll, 78, 83, 85-86, 88, 98-99. **MEMBERSHIPS** MLA: NHS; NVSA; NASW. **RESEARCH** Colonial early American architecture; marches, songs and leaders of American Civil War; romanticism in literature and classical music. **SELECTED PUBLICATIONS** Auth, "Amid the Jagged Shadows: The Gothic Tradition and the Debilitating Power of Anxiety in Coleridge's Chistobel," The Wordsworth Circle (83); auth, "Romanticism in the Victorian Period," in Victoria Britain, ed. Sally Mitchell (Garland Press, 88); auth, Light in a Dark Place: Romanticism in the Victorian Social-political Novel, Univ Press Am, 88; auth, "Work of Noble Note: Tennyson's 'Ulysses,' Victorian Ideals of Heroism and Narcissistic Personality," Victorian Lit and Culture, 94; auth, "George Eliot's Silas Marner in the Context of the 19th-Century," in Silas Marner, ed. Harold Bloom (Chelsea House, 94); auth, "When Great Hitting Wasn't Enough: The 1950 Boston Red Sox," in The National Pastime, Soc Am Baseball Res (94); auth, " 'A New Unfolding of Life'" Romanticism in the Late Novels of George Eliot," in Victorian Lit and Culture (Cambridge Univ Press, 98). **CONTACT ADDRESS** Dept English, Iona Col, 1273 North Ave, New Rochelle, NY 10804.

DRANE, JAMES FRANCIS
PERSONAL Born 04/06/1930, Chester, PA, s **DISCIPLINE** LIBRARY **EDUCATION** Little Rock Col, AB, 51; Pontif Gregorian Univ, Rome, BD, 53; Middlebury Col, MA, 61; Univ Madrid, PhD(philos), 64. **CAREER** Asst philos, St John's Sem, Ark, 56-67; assoc prof relig studies, Webster Col, 67-69; prof Philos, Edinboro State Col, 69-, Assoc, Danforth Found, 73-; interdisciplinary fel psychiat, Menn Sch Psychiat, 76-77; res scholar, Kennedy Inst Bioethics, Georgetown Univ, 81 & Univ Tenn, Memphis, Med Complex, 82. **HONORS AND AWARDS** Distinguished Teaching Chair Pa, Pa Dept Educ, 76. **MEMBERSHIPS** Cath Philos Asn; Am Philos Asn; Soc Phenomenol & Existential Philos; Soc Sci Studies Relig; Soc Christian Ethics. **RESEARCH** Philosophy of man; medical ethics; ethics and psychiatry. **SELECTED PUBLICATIONS** Auth, Las Bases de la Tolerancia (2 vols), Univ Madrid, 64; Pilgrimage to Utopia, 65 & Authority and Institution, 69, Bruce; La Rusia Actual, Ed Juventud, 67; A New America Reformation, Littlefield & Adams, 74; Natural Law and Politics, J Value Inquiry, 74; The Possibility of God, Littlefield & Adams, 76; Religion and Ethics, Paulist Press, 77; auth, Your Emotional Life, Thomas Moore, 84; auth, Becoming A Good Doctor, Sheed & Ward, 89; auth, Making Life and Death Decisions for Others: Applying the Quality of Life Concept, Quinnipiac Col, 91; auth, Como Ser Un Buen Medico, San Pablo, 93; auth, Clinical Bioethics: Theory and Practice in Medical-Ethical Decision Making, Sheed & Ward, 94; auth, Caring to the End, Lake Area Health Education Center, 97; auth, El Ciudado Del Enfermo Terminal Organization Pan Americana de la Salud, (Washington, DC), 99. **CONTACT ADDRESS** Dept of Philos, Edinboro Univ of Pennsylvania, Edinboro, PA 16444.

DRAPER, DAVID E.
PERSONAL Born 01/29/1943, Greenville, MS, s **DISCIPLINE** MUSIC **EDUCATION** Col-Conservatory Music, Univ Cincinnati, BM, 65; MM, 67; Tulane Univ, PhD, 73. **CAREER** Asst prof, Calif State Col, 73-76; asst prof, Univ Calif at Los Angeles, 76-84; prof, Delgado Community Col City Park, 84-. **HONORS AND AWARDS** Pi Kappa Lambda; Phi Mu Alpha; listed in Int Who's Who in Music; listed in Who's Who in Am Music, listed in Who's Who in Am Teachers; Trustee, Am Folklife Ctr of the Libr of Congress, 76-86. **MEMBERSHIPS** Soc for Ethnomusicology, Am Guild of Organists, Organ Hist Soc. **RESEARCH** American Indian Music and Culture, Afro-American Music and Culture. **SELECTED PUBLICATIONS** Auth, "The Musical Occasion: The contexts of Musical Performance among the Mardi Gras Indians," in Proceeding of a Symposium on Form and Performance, eds Herndon and Brunyate (TX: Col of Fine Arts, 76); auth, "Occasions for the Performance of Native Choctaw music," Selected Reports in Ethnomusicology 3.2 (80): 147-173; auth, "Abba Isht Tuluwa: The Christian Hymns of the Mississippi Choctaw," Am Indian Culture and Res J 6.1 (92): 43-61; auth, "Breath in Music: Concept and Practice Among the Choctaw Indians," Selected Reports in Ethnomusicology 4.1 (83): 285-300; auth, "The Ritual Music of the Choctaw Stickball Game," La Folklore Miscellany 5.4 (84): 11-22; auth, "Sensitivity vs Objectivity: An Indian Researcher's Dilemma," in Sharing a Heritage, ed. Charlotte Heth (CA: Am Indian Studies Ctr, 84); auth, "Forward," in Southeastern Catalogue, American Indian Series, Federal Cylinder Projects, Am Folklife Ctr, the Libr of Congress, 85; auth, "Choctaw Music," in The New Grove Dictionary of American Music (1986), 429. **CONTACT ADDRESS** Dept Humanities & Fine Arts, Delgado Comm Col, 615 City Park Ave, New Orleans, LA 70119.

DREHER, DIANE ELIZABETH
PERSONAL Born 05/06/1946, Louisville, KY, m, 1997 **DISCIPLINE** ENGLISH **EDUCATION** Univ Calif, Riverside, BA, 68; Univ Calif, Los Angeles, MA, 70, PhD, 73. **CAREER** Tchg asst, Univ Calif, Los Angeles, 69-71; from asst to assoc prof English, 74-92, prof English, 92- , chemn Dept of English, 92-97, Santa Clara Univ. **HONORS AND AWARDS** Phi Beta Kappa, 68; Danforth Assoc, 81; Outstanding Young Woman of Am, 78, 82; Graves Awd in the Hum, 82; Sisterhood is Powerful Awd, Santa Clara Univ, Women's Stud Prog, 96. **MEMBERSHIPS** MLA; Nat Writers' Union; AAUP. **RESEARCH** Early modern literature; feminist studies; autobiography; creative nonfiction. **SELECTED PUBLICATIONS** Auth, The Fourfold Pilgrimage: The Four Estates in Seventeenth-Century Literature, Univ Press of Am, 82; auth, Domination and Defiance: Fathers and Daughters in Shakespeare, Kentucky, 86; auth, The Tao of Inner Peace, HarperCollins, 91; auth, The Tao of Personal Leadership, HarperCollins, 96; auth, The Tao of Womanhood, Morrow, 98; auth, "The Tao of Inner Peace," Penguin Putnam, 00; auth, "Inner Gardening," Morrow, 01. **CONTACT ADDRESS** Dept of English, Santa Clara Univ, 500 El Camino Real, Santa Clara, CA 95053. **EMAIL** ddreher@scu.edu

DREKONJA, OTMAR MAXIMILIAN
PERSONAL Born 11/30/1934, Austria, m, 1961, 3 children **DISCIPLINE** LITERATURE **EDUCATION** Univ Salzburg/Austria, PhD, 71. **CAREER** TA, 62-63, Kent St Univ; SW at Memphis, Rhodes Col, 63-64; res asst, 64-67, Univ Innsbruck/Austria; St John's Univ, 67-00; CUNY Richmond Col, 72-; Prof Emer, St John's Univ, 00. **HONORS AND AWARDS** Teacher of the Year Awd, St John's Univ, 91; Burlington Northern Awd, 91; Fulbright fel, Kent State Univ, 62; pres, AATG, 88-92. **RESEARCH** Austrian lit; Central Europe, GDR tradition, exile lit. **CONTACT ADDRESS** St. John's Univ, Collegeville, MN 56321. **EMAIL** odrekonja@sbsju.edu

DREW, SHIRLEY K.
PERSONAL Born 11/28/1956, m, 1998 **DISCIPLINE** INTERPERSONAL & PUBLIC COMMUNICATION **EDUCATION** Bowling Green State Univ, BA, MA, PhD. **CAREER** Assoc prof. **MEMBERSHIPS** Nat Commun Assoc; Central States Commun Assoc; Phi Kappa Phi. **RESEARCH** Relationship disengagement; Interpersonal, Group & Organizational Communication; Ethnography & Communication. **SELECTED PUBLICATIONS** Publ, health communication, personal narratives; auth, Group communication; Orgn Personal Narratives. **CONTACT ADDRESS** Dept of Commun, Pittsburg State Univ, 1701 S Broadway St, Pittsburg, KS 66762.

DREWRY, CECELIA HODGES
PERSONAL Born New York, NY, m **DISCIPLINE** ENGLISH **EDUCATION** Hunter Coll, AB 1945; Columbia U, AM 1948; Shakespeare Univ of Birmingham, England, Cert 1949; Northwestern U, PhD 1967; Univ of Ghana, Cert 1969. **CAREER** Princeton Univ, asst dean, asst prof; Haverford Coll, visiting prof of english 77; Teachers Coll Columbia Univ, visiting instructor 68; African & Afro-Amer Studies Prog, chairperson 69-70; Rutgers Univ, assoc prof 62-70; High School of Performing Arts NY, teacher 52-59; Talladega Coll, instrutor 45-47; Penthouse Dance & Drama Theatre NY, dir of speech 48-52; Princeton High School, teacher 59-61; various theatre appearances. **HONORS AND AWARDS** Awd for excellence in oral interpretation of literature Northwestern Univ Sch of Speech; Alpha Psi Omega Hon Soc; Danforth Assn; Honoree Phi Delta Kappa. **MEMBERSHIPS** Mem AAVP; AAUW, MLA, SCA; trustee Cedar Crest Coll PA; mem Carnegie Found for Advmt of Tching; NAACP; Nat Council of Negro Women; Princeton Assn of Hum Rights. **CONTACT ADDRESS** Princeton Univ, 408 W College, Princeton, NJ 08540.

DRIVER, MARTHA WESTCOTT
PERSONAL Born 10/24/1952, New York, NY, m, 1982 **DISCIPLINE** MEDIEVAL AND RENAISSANCE LITERATURE **EDUCATION** Vassar Col, AB, 74; Univ Pa, MA, 75; PhD, 80. **CAREER** Asst, Inst Medieval Studies Paleography, 76; lectr English, Univ Pa, 77-79 and Vassar Col, 80-81; asst prof to prof english, Pace Univ, 81-, Reader, Pierpont Morgan Libr, 79-; writer, Publ Weekly, 82-. **HONORS AND AWARDS** Mem, Inst Res Hist, 81-; intern, Nat Endowment Humanities, 82. **MEMBERSHIPS** MLA; New Chaucer Soc; Midwest Mod Lang Asn. **RESEARCH** Manuscripts and early printed editions, particularly of Chaucer's works; medieval and Renaissance book illustration; paleography and early printing. **SELECTED PUBLICATIONS** Auth, A Directory of London Stationers and Book Artisans, 1300-1500, Speculum, J Medieval Stud, Vol 67, 92; The Pilgrimage of Prayer--The Texts and Iconography of the Exercitium Super Pater Noster, Speculum J Medieval Stud, Vol 67, 92; The Pilgrimage of Prayer--The Texts and Iconography of the Exercitium Super Pater Noster, Speculum J Medieval Stud, Vol 67, 92; A Directory of London Stationers and Book Artisans, 1300-1500, Speculum J Medieval Stud, Vol 67, 92. **CONTACT ADDRESS** Dept of English, Pace Univ, New York, 1 Pace Plaza, New York, NY 10038.

DRIVER, TOM FAW
PERSONAL Born 05/31/1925, Johnson City, TN, m, 1952, 3 children **DISCIPLINE** THEOLOGY, LITERATURE **EDUCATION** Duke Univ, AB, 50; Union Theol Sem, NYork, MDiv, 53; Columbia Univ, PhD, 57. **CAREER** Instr drama, 56-58, from asst prof to assoc prof theol, 58- 67, prof theol & lit, 67-73, Paul J Tillich Prof Theol & Cult, 73-93, emeritus, 93-, Union Theol Sem; Kent fel, 53-56; Mars lectr, Northwestern Univ, 61; Earl lect, Pac Sch Relig, 62; vis assoc prof, Columbia Univ, 64-65; vis prof, Univ Otago, NZ, 76, Vassar Col, 78 & Montclair State Col, 81. **HONORS AND AWARDS** Guggenheim fel, 62; ODK, 49; Phi Beta Kappa, 49; dlitt, dennison univ, 70. **MEMBERSHIPS** Soc Values Higher Educ; Am Acad Relig; New Haven Theol Discussion Gp; Witness for Peace; United Methodist Church; Presbyterian Church USA; United Church of Christ. **RESEARCH** Classical and modern drama; contemporary theology; ritual studies. **SELECTED PUBLICATIONS** Auth, The Sense of History in Greek and Shakespearean Drama, Columbia Univ, 60; co-ed, Poems of Belief and Doubt, Macmillan, 64; auth, The Shakespearian Clock, Shakespeare Quart, fall 64; Jean Genet, Columbia Univ, 66; History of the Modern Theatre, Delta, 71; The Twilight of Drama: From Ego to Myth, In: Humanities, Religion and the Arts, 72; Patterns of Grace: Human Experience as Word of God, Harper & Row, 77; Christ in a Changing World, Crossroad, 81; auth, The Magic of Ritual, Harper San Francisco, 91; auth, Liberating Rites: Understanding the Transformative Power of Ritual, Westview, 97. **CONTACT ADDRESS** 501 W 123rd St, #14G, New York, NY 10027. **EMAIL** tfd3@columbia.edu

DROUT, MICHAEL D. C.
PERSONAL Born 05/03/1968, Neptune, NJ, m, 1994 **DISCIPLINE** ENGLISH **EDUCATION** Carnegie Mellon Univ, BA, 90; Stanford Univ, MA, 91; Univ of Mo-Columbia, MA, 93; Loyola Univ, PhD, 97. **CAREER** Asst Prof of English, Wheaton Col, 97-. **HONORS AND AWARDS** Alpha Sigma Nu nat Jesuit honor soc; Arthur G. Schmitt fel. **MEMBERSHIPS** Int Soc of Anglo-Saxonists; MLA; Medieval Acad. **RESEARCH** Anglo-Saxon and medieval Lit; linguistics; J.R.R. Tolkien; fantasy and science fiction. **SELECTED PUBLICATIONS** Auth, Hoisting the Arm of Defiance: Beowulfian Elements in ken Kesey's Sometimes a Great Notion, Western Am Lit, 93; The Influence of J.R.R. Tolkien's Masculinist Medievalism, Medieval Feminist Newsletter, 96; Reading the Signs of Light: Anglo-Saxonism, Education and obedience in Susan Cooper's The Dark is Rising, The Lion and the Unicorn, 97; The Fortunes of Men 4a: Reasons for Adopting a Very Old Emendation, Modern Philol, 98. **CONTACT ADDRESS** Wheaton Col, Massachusetts, Norton, MA 02766. **EMAIL** mdrout@wheatonma.edu

DRUESEDOW, JOHN E.
PERSONAL Born 05/01/1939, Cambridge, OH, m, 1972, 2 children **DISCIPLINE** MUSIC **EDUCATION** IN Univ, PhD. **CAREER** Music libr dir. **HONORS AND AWARDS** Phi Beta Kappa. **MEMBERSHIPS** AMS, MLA. **RESEARCH** Music bibliog; 19th century Am music; Span Baroque; contemp Latin Am music. **SELECTED PUBLICATIONS** Auth, publ(s) on music libr res for undergraduates. **CONTACT ADDRESS** Dept of Music, Duke Univ, Mary Duke Biddle Music Bldg, Box 90661, Durham, NC 27708-0661. **EMAIL** john.druesedow@duke.edu

DRUMMOND, RICHARD HENRY
PERSONAL Born 12/14/1916, San Francisco, CA, m, 1943, 3 children **DISCIPLINE** CLASSICS **EDUCATION** UCLA, BA, 38, MA, 39; Univ Wisc, PhD, 41; Luth Theol Sem, BD, 44. **CAREER** Pastor, The Japanese Church of Christ, San Fran, 47-49; fraternal worker in Japan, 49-62; prof Christian Stud & Class Lang, 58-62, vis prof, 68-69, 76-78, & 86-87, Meiji Gakuin Univ, Tokyo; prof Ecumenical Mission & Hist of Relig, 62-85, Florence Livergood Warren Prof Comp Relig, 84-87, Prof Ecumenical Mission & Hist of Relig Emer, 87- , Univ Dubuque Theol Sem; vis prof, Atlantic Univ, 87-89 & Old Dominion Univ, 89. **HONORS AND AWARDS** Phi Beta Kappa, 38; Outstanding Educ Am, 72 & 74; Univ fel, Univ Dubuque, 91. **SELECTED PUBLICATIONS** Auth, Missiological Lessons-From Events New and Old, Missiology, 94; A New History of Japanese Theology, Mission Studies, 94; A Broader Vision, Stud in Interreligious Dialogue, 96; A Boarder Vision: Perspectives on the Buddha and the Christ, ARE Press, 95. **CONTACT ADDRESS** Univ of Dubuque, 2000 University Ave, Dubuque, IA 52001.

DRYDEN, EDGAR A.
PERSONAL Born 06/28/1937, Salisbury, MD, m, 1959, 3 children **DISCIPLINE** AMERICAN LITERATURE **EDUCATION** Wash Col, BA, 59; Univ RI, MA, 61; Johns Hopkins Univ, PhD(Am lit), 65. **CAREER** Asst prof English, Johns Hopkins Univ, 65-57; asst prof English, State Univ NY, Buffalo, 67-68, assoc prof, 68-78, assoc provost fac arts & lett, 72-78; prof English & Dept Head, Univ Az, 78-86, Guggenheim fel, 82-83. **MEMBERSHIPS** MLA. **RESEARCH** American literature; the novel. **SELECTED PUBLICATIONS** Auth, Melville's Thematics of Form, Johns Hopkins Univ, 68; Hawthorne's Castle in the Air: Form and Theme in The House of the Seven Gables, ELH, 6/71; History and Progress: Some Implications of Form in Cooper's Littlepage Novels, Nineteenth-Century Fiction, 6/71; Nathaniel Hawthorne: The Poetics of Enchantment, Cornell, 77; The entangled text: Melville's Pierre and the Problem of Reading, Boundary, spring 79; The Image of the Mirror: The Double Economy of James' Portrait, Genre, spring 80; The Form of American Romance, John Hopkins, 87; Editor, Arizona Quarterly, 88-. **CONTACT ADDRESS** Dept of English, Univ of Arizona, 1 University of Az, Tucson, AZ 85721-0001. **EMAIL** edryden@u.arizona.edu

DRYDEN, M.
PERSONAL Born 01/11/1946, San Antonio, TX, d, 1 child **DISCIPLINE** ENGLISH, ENGLISH LITERATURE **EDUCATION** Univ Tex-Austin, BA, 80; MA, 92. **CAREER** Instr, Austin Commun Col; refugee ESL coordinator, 97- . **HONORS AND AWARDS** Phi Zeta Kappa teaching excellence, 93. **MEMBERSHIPS** TESOL **RESEARCH** Adult education ESL; refugee ESL. **SELECTED PUBLICATIONS** Auth, Teaching Language Teachers to be More Collaborative: The Second Language Learner Course at the University of Texas at Austin, MLA J, 97. **CONTACT ADDRESS** Dept of Adult Educ, Austin Comm Col, Austin, TX 78741. **EMAIL** mdryden@mail.utexas.edu

DU PLESSIS, ERIC
PERSONAL Born 09/19/1950, Albertville, France, d, 5 children **DISCIPLINE** LITERATURE **EDUCATION** Va Commonwealth Univ, BA, 74; Univ Richmond, MA, 75; Univ Va, PhD, 79. **CAREER** Asst Prof, Tex A&M Univ, 79-86; Assoc Prof, Radford Univ, 87-93; Prof, Radford Univ, 94-. **RESEARCH** French literature, world literature, dynamics of literary translation. **SELECTED PUBLICATIONS** Auth, "The Evolving Role of French Nuclear Weapons in Europe," European Studies J, 12 (95): 1-15; ed, The Last Fay, by Honore de Balzac, Edwin Mellen Pr (Lewiston, NY), 96; auth, "Les Traductions Francaises de 'MacBeth' en Alexandrins," ALFA: Actes de Langue Francaise et de Linguistique, 10 (97): 221-232; auth, "'He Has No Children': Translators as Interpreters in the French Versions of 'Macbeth'," Revue de Litterature Comparee, 72 (98): 369-372. **CONTACT ADDRESS** Dept Lit, Radford Univ, PO Box 6937, Radford, VA 24142-6937. **EMAIL** ehduples@runet.edu

DUBAN, JAMES
PERSONAL Born 03/14/1951, Paris, France **DISCIPLINE** AMERICAN LITERATURE **EDUCATION** Univ Mass, Amherst, BA, 72; Cornell Univ, MA, 75, PhD (Am lit), 76. **CAREER** Lectr English and Am lit, Cornell Univ, 76-77; Asst Prof American Lit, Univ Tex, Austin, 77-, Am Coun Learned Soc grant, 78. **MEMBERSHIPS** MLA; Nathaniel Hawthorne Soc; Herman Melville Soc. **RESEARCH** Nineteenth-century American literature. **SELECTED PUBLICATIONS** Auth, The sceptical context of Hawthorne's Mr Higginbotham's Catastrophe, Am Lit, 11/76; Hawthorne's debt to Edmund Spenser and Charles Chauncy in The Gentle Boy, Nathaniel Hawthorne J, 76; The Spenserian maze of Melville's Pierre, ESQ: J Am Renaissance, 10-12/77; The translation of Pierre Bayle's An Historical and Critical Dict owned by Melville, Papers Bibliog Soc Am, 7-9/77; The triumph of infidelity in Hawthorne's The Story Teller, SAF, spring 79; Satiric precedent for Melville's The Two Temples, Am Transcendantal Quart, spring 79; Melville's use of Irving's Knickerbocker History in White-Jacket, MSex, 5/81; A pantomime of action: Starbuck and American Whig dissidence, New England Quart, 5/82. **CONTACT ADDRESS** Dept of English, Univ of Texas, Austin, Austin, TX 78712.

DUBEY, MADHU
DISCIPLINE ENGLISH **EDUCATION** Ill Univ, PhD. **CAREER** Prof, Northwestern Univ. **RESEARCH** African American literature; women's fiction; feminist theory. **SELECTED PUBLICATIONS** Auth, Black Women Novelists and the National Aesthetic, 94; Carlene Polite, Black Women in the US, 93; essays on, African-Am culture. **CONTACT ADDRESS** Dept of English, Northwestern Univ, 1801 Hinman, Evanston, IL 60208. **EMAIL** madhu_dubey@brown.edu

DUBINO, JEANNE
PERSONAL Born 05/07/1959, MD **DISCIPLINE** ENGLISH **EDUCATION** Boston Col, BA, 81; Univ Delaware, MA, 87; Univ Mass, PhD, 92. **CAREER** Instr, Univ Delaware, 82-83; instr, Univ Mass, 84-92; adj asst prof, Westfield State Col, 92; asst prof, Plymouth State Col, 93; vis asst prof, Bilkent Univ, 97-99; asst prof, Plymouth State Col, 93-97; assoc prof, 99-. **HONORS AND AWARDS** Who's Who in Am Teach, Turkey; NEH alt; Fac Grant, PSC; Phi Kappa Phi. **MEMBERSHIPS** VWS; PCA; MLA; NWSA; NPCA; NMLA; NHHC. **RESEARCH** Postcolonial literature; Virginia Woolf; Popular culture; gender studies and feminist theory; Orientalism. **SELECTED PUBLICATIONS** Co-ed, Virginia Woolf and the Essay, St. Martin's Press (NY), 97; auth, "Virginia Woolf: From Book Reviewer to Literary Critic, 1904-1918." Virginia Woolf and the Essay, St. Martin's (NY), 97: 25-40; auth, "Wayne's World: Postmodern or Nostalgic?" Pop Cul Rev 6 (95): 145-53; auth, "The influence of something upon somebody: Reflections on the Seventh Annual Conference on Virginia Woolf," Virginia Woolf and Her Influences: Selected Papers from the Seventh Annual Conference on Virginia Woolf, eds. Laura Davis, Jeanette McVicker (NY: Pace Univ Press, 98); rev of, Turkish Reflections, by Mary Lee Settle, J Am Stud Turkey, forthcoming; rev of, Images of Turkey in Western Literature, by Kamil Aydin, J Am Stud Turkey, forthcoming. **CONTACT ADDRESS** Dept English, Plymouth State Col of the Univ System of New Hampshire, 36 High St, Plymouth, NH 03264.

DUBROVSKY, GERTRUDE
PERSONAL Born 03/10/1926, New York, NY, d, 3 children **DISCIPLINE** ENGLISH LITERATURE **EDUCATION** Georgian Court Col, AB, 56; Rutgers Univ, MA, 59; Columbia Univ, EdD, 73. **CAREER** Yiddish instr, Princeton Univ Ctr for Jewish Life, 75-95; res, YIVO Inst for Jewish Res and Carnegie Found for Advan of Tchg; YIVO, 74-80, and CFAT, 84-86, independent scholar; social historian, 74- ; pres, DOCUMENTARY III, 84- . **HONORS AND AWARDS** Oxford Ctr for Jewish Stud fel, 94; NEH grant 76-78. **MEMBERSHIPS** Natl Coalition of Indep Scholars; Princeton Res Forum; Am Jewish Hist Soc; NJ Hist Soc. **RESEARCH** American Jewish experience; Kindertransport, Holocaust history. **SELECTED PUBLICATIONS** Auth, The Farmingdale Collection, YIVO Inst, 77; auth, The Land Was Theirs, Univ Alabama Pr, 92; auth numerous articles and book reviews. **CONTACT ADDRESS** 244 Hawthorne Ave., Princeton, NJ 08540. **EMAIL** gdubrovsky@aol.com

DUCHARME, ROBERT
DISCIPLINE ENGLISH **EDUCATION** NYork Univ; Univ Notre Dame, PhD. **CAREER** Dept ch. **HONORS AND AWARDS** Develop crs(es) in, Japanese Lit and Cult & Latin Amer fiction. **SELECTED PUBLICATIONS** Publ bk on, novels of Bernard Malamud & study of Joseph Conrad's Lord Jim. **CONTACT ADDRESS** Dept of English, Mount Saint Mary's Col and Sem, 16300 Old Emmitsburg Rd, Emmitsburg, MD 21727-7799.

DUCHOVNAY, GERALD
PERSONAL Born 12/06/1944, Philadelphia, PA, 2 children **DISCIPLINE** FILM, ENGLISH **EDUCATION** Univ Pa, BA, 66; Ind Univ, MA, 66; PhD, 71. **CAREER** Asst prof to prof, Jacksonville Univ, 71-90; prof, dept head, Tex A and M Univ, 90-. **HONORS AND AWARDS** Fel, Mod Media Inst, 80; NEH Fel, 78, 83; Dana Fel, 88-89; Honors Prof of Year, 99; Texas A and M Univ, Prof Achievement Awd, 01. **MEMBERSHIPS** MLA, S Central MLA, Soc for Cinema Studies, Univ Film and Video Assoc, NCTE, Conf of Col Teachers of English. **RESEARCH** American Film, Film History, Film and Culture. **SELECTED PUBLICATIONS** Auth, Humphrey Bogart, Greenwood Pr, 99. **CONTACT ADDRESS** Dept Lit and Lang, Texas A&M Univ, Commerce, Commerce, TX 75429. **EMAIL** gerald_duchovnay@tamu-commerce.edu

DUCKWORTH, ALISTAIR MCKAY
PERSONAL Born 08/04/1936, Balmullo, Scotland, m, 1964, 2 children **DISCIPLINE** ENGLISH **EDUCATION** Univ Edinburgh, MA, 58; Johns Hopkins Univ, MA, 64, PhD (English), 67. **CAREER** Instr English, Johns Hopkins Univ, 63-67; asst prof, Univ Va, 67-73; assoc prof, 73-80, Prof English, Univ Fla, 80-, Sesquicentennial assoc, Ctr Advan Studies, Univ Va, 71-72; vis prof prog in mod lit, State Univ NY, Buffalo, summer 74; Guggenheim Mem Found fel, 77-78; patron, Jane Austin Soc NAm, 79-; T. Walter Herbert Commemorative Term Prof, Univ of Fla, 98. **HONORS AND AWARDS** Presidential Scholar, Univ Fla, Gainesville, 76-77; John Simon Guggenheim Fel, 77-78; Vis fel, Magdalen Col, Oxford, 88; Hon Mem of SCR, 89; Outstanding Undergraduate Teaching Awd, CLAS, Univ of Fla, 90, Univ Awd for Outstanding Teaching, 90, Teaching Incentive Prog Awd, 93, 98, Teacher of the Year Awd, 98; Nominations for SAMLA Teacher of the Year Awd, 91, 92; Dir, NEH Sem, 92. **MEMBERSHIPS** MLA; SAtlantic Mod Lang Asn; Am Soc 18th Century Studies; Asn Scottish Lit Studies. **RESEARCH** English novel; literature and landscape. **SELECTED PUBLICATIONS** Auth, The Improvement of the Estate: A Study of Jane Austen's Novels, Baltimore: Johns Hopkins UP, 71, Second Printing, 74; auth, Landscape in the Gardens and the Literature of Eighteenth-Century England, Los Angeles: William Andrews Clark Memorial Library, 81; auth, "Garden, Houses, and the Rhetoric of Description in the English Novel," The Fashioning and Functioning of the Country House, ed. G. Jackson-Stops, Wash.: Nat. Gall, (89): 395-413; auth, "Literature and Landscape," Encyclopedia of Literature and Criticism, ed. Martin Coyle et al, London: Routledge, (90): 1015-1028; auth, "Jane Austen and The Construction of a Progressive Author," College English 53.1 (91): 77-90; auth, Howards End: E.M. Forster's House of Fiction, New York: Twayne, 92; auth, "Karl Shapiro's University and the Ideology of Place," in Seriously Meeting Karl Shapiro, ed. Sue Walker, Mobile: Negative Capability Press (93): 10-27; auth, The Improvement of the Estate: A Study of Jane Austen's Novels, With a new preface by the Author, Baltimore: Johns Hopkins UP, 94; auth, Howards End: A Casebook in Contemporary Criticism, Boston: Bedford Books, 97; auth, "Emma, dir. Douglas McGrath," "Emma, dir Diarmud Lawrence," ECF 10.1 (97): 110-117; **CONTACT ADDRESS** Dept of English, Univ of Florida, Gainesville, FL 32601.

DUCLOW, DONALD F.
PERSONAL Born 01/11/1946, Chicago, IL, m, 1970 **DISCIPLINE** ENGLISH, PHILSOSOPHY, MEDIEVAL STUDIES **EDUCATION** DePaul Univ, BA, English, philosophy, 68, MA, philosophy, 69; Bryn Mawr Coll, MA, medieval studies, 72, PhD, philosophy, 74, Divinity School, Unv. Of Chicago, 98. **CAREER** Visiting prof, philosophy, Fordham Univ, 78; asst prof of philosophy, 74-79, assoc prof of philosophy, 79-89, prof of philosophy, 89-, Gwynedd-Mercy Coll. **HONORS AND AWARDS** Mellon Fellow in the Humanities, Univ Pa, 80-81; NEH summer seminars, 87, 93; Senior Fellow, Institute for the Advanced Study of Religion, Divinity School, University of Chicago, Spring, 98; Inst for the Advan Study of Relig Sen Fel. **MEMBERSHIPS** Amer Acad Religion; Medieval Acad Am; sec, Amer Cusanus Soc; Amer Assn Univ Profs; pres, Gwynedd-Mercy Coll Chap, 96-97; Exec Committee, Pennsylvania AAUP, 00. **RESEARCH** Medieval philosophy and religion. **SELECTED PUBLICATIONS** Auth, "Divine Nothingness and Self-Creation in John Scotus Eriugena," The Journ of Religion, vol 57, 77; "'My Suffering Is God': Meister Eckhart's Book of Divine Consolation," Theological Studies, vol 44, 83, reprinted in Classical and Medieval Literature Criticism, 93; "Into the Whirlwind of Suffering: Resistance and Transformation," Second Opinion, Nov 88; "Nicholas of Cusa," in Medieval Philosophers, vol 15, Dictionary of Literary Biography, 92; "Isaiah Meets the Seraph: Breaking Ranks in Dionysius and Eriugena?" in Eriugena: East and West, 94. **CONTACT ADDRESS** Gwynedd-Mercy Col, Gwynedd Valley, PA 19437-0901. **EMAIL** duclow.d@gmc.edu

DUDGEON, RALPH T.
PERSONAL Born 11/08/1948, McKeesort, PA, m, 1973, 2 children **DISCIPLINE** MUSICOLOGY **EDUCATION** San Diego State Univ, BA, 70, MA, 72; Univ Calif, San Diego, PhD, 80. **CAREER** Music tchr, San Dieguito High Sch, 71-74; applied trumpet instr, Point Loma Col, 76; ensemble dir, Mira Costa Col, 76; dept chmn, Torrey Pines High Sch, 74-81; asst prof, Univ Tex, Dallas, 81-85; assoc prof, 85-93, prof, 94- , chemn, 97-00, State Univ New York; acting dir, cur, Streitwieser Found Trumpet Museum, 93-94; music res, consult, Musica Kremsmunster, Instrumentenmuseum, 96-; ensemble dir, Syracuse Univ, 98-99. **HONORS AND AWARDS** Res Grant, Univ Calif, 79, 80; Org Res Grant, 84; Who's Who in Am Music, 85;Who's Who East,85; Pa Arts Council Grant 87; Fac Res Grant, State Univ New York, 91; Men Achievement, 93; Hon Life Membership, Tri-M Music Honor Soc,93; Crystal Trust Grant, Admin Streitwieser Found, 93-94; Mus Assesment Prog Grant, Am Asn Mus, 94. **MEMBERSHIPS** Am Fed Musicians; Am Musical Instrument Soc; Am Musicological Soc; Hist Brass Soc; Int Trumpet Guild; Nat Asn Col Wind Percussion instrs, New York State Sch Music Asn; Sonneck Soc; Streitwieser Found Trumpet Mus. **RESEARCH** Musical instruments of the 19th century & period instrument performance. **SELECTED PUBLICATIONS** Auth, art, An Interview with

Edna White Chandler, 90; auth, art, Nineteenth-Century Keyed Bugle Performers: A Checklist, 92; auth, The Keyed Bugle, 93; auth, art, A Conversation with John Wallace and Trevor Herbert, 96; auth, art, The Legacy of Walter M. Smith, 98. **CONTACT ADDRESS** 5745 US Rte 11, Homer, NY 13077. **EMAIL** dudgeonr@cortland.edu

DUDLEY, EDWARD J.
PERSONAL Born 07/18/1926, St. Paul, MN, m, 1959, 2 children **DISCIPLINE** SPANISH, ENGLISH **EDUCATION** Univ MN, Minneapolis, BA, 49, MA, 51, PhD, 63. **CAREER** Tchr, Am Sch, Managua, Nicaragua, 54-55; instr Span, St John's Univ, MN, 56-60; asst prof, UCLA, 63-70; chmn & prof Hisp lang & lit & dir comp lit prog, Univ Pittsburgh, 70-74; chmn dept Span, Ital & Port, 74-77, chmn dept French & Dept Ger & Slavic, 76-77, Prof Span & Comp Lit, State Univ NY Buffalo, 74-, Chmn Dept Mod Lang & Lit, 77-, Consult, Nat Bd Consult, Nat Endowment for Hum, 76. **MEMBERSHIPS** MLA; Mediaeval Acad Am; Asn Int Hispanistas; Cervantes Soc Am; Conrad Soc Am. **RESEARCH** Cervantes; early prose fiction; comp lit. **SELECTED PUBLICATIONS** Auth, Three patterns of imagery in Conrad's Heart of Darkness, Rev des Langues Vivantes, 65; coauth, El cuento, Holt, 66; auth, Court and country: The fusion of two images of love in Juan Rodriguez's El siervo libre de amor, PMLA, 67; Don Quixote as magus: The rhetoric of interpolation, Bull Hisp Studies, 72; co-ed, The Wild Man Within: An Image in Western Thought from the Renaissance to Romanticism, Univ Pittsburgh, 72; co-ed, 2nd ed, El cuento, Holt, 84; co-ed, American Attitudes toward Foreign Languages and Foreign Cultures, Bouvier, Bonn, 83; auth, The Endless Text: Don Quijote and The Hermeneutics of Romance, SUNY Press, 97; various other articles and essays on Cervantes. **CONTACT ADDRESS** Dept of Mod Lang & Lit, SUNY, Buffalo, PO Box 604620, Buffalo, NY 14260-4620. **EMAIL** edudley@acsu.buffalo.edu

DUDT, CHARMAZEL
PERSONAL Born 08/30/1940, Allahabad, India **DISCIPLINE** ENGLISH LITERATURE **EDUCATION** Allahabad Univ, India, BA, 59, MA, 61; Tex Tech Univ, PhD(English), 71. **CAREER** Lectr English, St John's Col, Agra, India, 62-63, Isabella Thoburn Col, Lucknow, India, 63-64; asst prof, 70-78, assoc prof, 78-84, Prof English, WTex State Univ, 84-, Chair, Shakespeare Studies, 95-. **MEMBERSHIPS** MLA; Conf Christianity & Lit; Asn Asian Studies; SCent Renaissance Soc **RESEARCH** Shakespeare; nineteenth century British literature; Asian studies. **SELECTED PUBLICATIONS** Auth, Of that time, of that place: Shakespeare's Illyria, Conf Col Teachers English, 5/75. **CONTACT ADDRESS** Dept of English, West Texas A&M Univ, 2501 4th Ave, Canyon, TX 79016-0001. **EMAIL** cdudt@wtamu.edu

DUERDEN, RICHARD Y.
PERSONAL Born 07/09/1955, Salt Lake City, UT, m, 1977, 4 children **DISCIPLINE** ENGLISH LITERATURE **EDUCATION** Brigham Young Univ, BA, 79; MA, 81; Univ Chicago, PhD, 89. **CAREER** From asst prof to assoc prof, Brigham Young Univ, 89-; dir grad studies, Brigham Young Univ, 97-. **HONORS AND AWARDS** Charlotte W. Newcombe Fel, Woodrow Wilson Nat Fel Found, 88-89; NEH Inst, Claremont Grad Sch, 96. **MEMBERSHIPS** Tyndale Soc. **RESEARCH** Sixteenth-Century English Literature, Religion, Politics. **SELECTED PUBLICATIONS** Auth, "John Field," in Dictionary of Literary Biography Vol 167: Sixteenth-Century Nondramatic Prose, ed. David A. Richardson (MI: Gale, 96), 53-60; auth, "Miles Coverdale," in Dictionary of Literary Biography Vol 167: Sixteenth-Century Nondramatic Prose, ed. David A. Richardson (MI: Gale, 96), 27-36; auth, "The Temporal and Spiritual Kingdoms: Tyndale's Doctrine and its Practice," Reformation 1 (96): 118-128; auth, "Equivalence or Power? Authority and Reformation Bible Translation," in The Bible as Book: The Reformation, eds. Kimberly Van Campen and Orlaith O'Sullivan (London: British Libr and Oak Knoll Press, 00), 9-23; auth, "Crossings: Class, Gender, Chiasmus, and the Cross in Aemilia Lanyer's Salve Deus Rex Judaeorum," Metaphysical Poetry and Belief (00); co-ed, "The Tradition of Metaphysical Poetry and Belief," Lit and Belief (00). **CONTACT ADDRESS** Dept English, Brigham Young Univ, 3146 Jkhb, Provo, UT 84602-6280. **EMAIL** richard_duerden@byu.edu

DUFFY, ANDREW E.
PERSONAL Born 11/30/1960, Roscommon, Ireland, m, 1988, 1 child **DISCIPLINE** ENGLISH **EDUCATION** Nat Univ of Ireland, BEd, Rutgers Univ, MA, 83; Harvard Univ, PhD, 90. **CAREER** Asst Prof, Reed Col, 90-91; Asst Prof, Wesleyan Univ, 91-93; Asst to Assoc Prof, Univ Calif, 93-. **HONORS AND AWARDS** Fel, Univ Calif, 00; Fel, Wesleyan Univ, 93; Whiting Fel, Harvard Univ, 89. **MEMBERSHIPS** Intl James Joyce Foundation; Am Committee on Irish Studies; Mod Lang Asn. **RESEARCH** Modernist and Post-modernist Literature and cultural studies; Post-colonial Studies; Joyce; Theories of Space. **SELECTED PUBLICATIONS** Auth, The Subaltern Ulysses, Univ of Minn Press, 94; auth, Essays in Engendering Joyce, 99; auth, Marketing Modernisms. **CONTACT ADDRESS** Dept English, Univ of California, Santa Barbara, 552 Univ Rd, Santa Barbara, CA 93106-0002. **EMAIL** duffy@humanitas.ucsb.edu

DUFFY, BERNARD K.
PERSONAL Born 04/27/1948, Bremen, Germany, m, 1976, 1 child **DISCIPLINE** COMMUNICATION **EDUCATION** San Jose State Col, BA, 70; MA, 71; Univ Pittsburgh, PhD, 76. **CAREER** Instr, William Paterson Col, 73-74; asst prof & asst to the Pres, Hiram Col, 76-79; from asst prof to prof, Clemson Univ, 79-88; prof, Calif Polytech State Univ, 88-; dept of speech commun chemn, Calif Polytech State Univ, 88-91. **HONORS AND AWARDS** Grad Fel, Univ Pittsburgh; Phi Kappa Phi; NEH grant (twice). **MEMBERSHIPS** Nat Commun Asn. **RESEARCH** Contemporary Rhetorical Theory, History and Criticism of American Public Address. **SELECTED PUBLICATIONS** Co-ed, American Orators Before 1900: Critical Studies and Sources, Greenwood Press (New York), 87; co-ed, American Orators Twentieth Century: Critical Studies and Sources, Greenwood Press (New York), 87; coauth, The Politics of Rhetoric: Richard Weaver and the Conservative Tradition, Greenwood Press (Westport, CT), 93; coauth, Douglas MacArthur: Warrior and Wordsmith, Greenwood Press (Westport, CT), 97; coauth, Health Communication Research: A Guide to Developments and Directions, Greenwood Press, 98. **CONTACT ADDRESS** Dept Speech Commun, California Polytech State Univ, San Luis Obispo, 1 Grand Ave, San Luis Obispo, CA 93407-9000. **EMAIL** bduffy@calpoly.edu

DUFFY, DENNIS
PERSONAL Born 10/08/1938, Louisville, KY **DISCIPLINE** ENGLISH **EDUCATION** Georgetown Univ Wash, 56-60; Univ Toronto, MA, 62, PhD, 64. **CAREER** Prin, Innis Col, 79-84, PROF ENGLISH, UNIV TORONTO; lectr, Shastri Indo-Can Inst, 82; lectr, Indian Asn Can Stud, 92-93; Fulbright fel, 93; Craig Dobbin Prof Can Stud, Univ Col, Dublin, 95-97. **RESEARCH** Canadian literature; John Richardson. **SELECTED PUBLICATIONS** Auth, Marshall McLuhan, 68; auth, Gardens, Covenants, Exiles: Loyalism in the Literature of Upper Canada, 82; auth, John Richardson and His Works, 83; auth, Sounding the Iceberg, 86; auth, Introducing John Richardson's 'Wacousta', 93; auth, A World Under Sentence: John Richardson and the Interior, 95. **CONTACT ADDRESS** Innis Col, Univ of Toronto, Toronto, ON, Canada M5S 1J5. **EMAIL** d.duffy@utoronto.ca

DUFRESNE, JOHN
PERSONAL Born 01/30/1948, Worcester, MA, m, 1985, 1 child **DISCIPLINE** CREATIVE WRITING **EDUCATION** Worcester State Col, BA, 70; Univ Ark, MFA, 84; Worcester State Col, Doctor Lit, 99. **CAREER** Soc worker, Community Action Coun, 70-73; prog dir & drug abuse counselor, Crisis Ctr, Inc., 73-77; freelance writer, 78-79; admin supvr, U.S. Census Bureau, 80; grad asst, Univ Ark, 82-84; vis writer, Ark Public Schs, 84; instr, Northeast La Univ, 84-87; grad asst, State Univ NYork at Binghamton, 87-88; instr, Worcester State Col, 87-88; instr, Augusta Col, 88-89; from asst prof to prof, Fla Int Univ, 89-. **MEMBERSHIPS** Nat Coun of Teachers of English, Authors' Guild, United Fac of Fla, Associated Writing Programs, MLA, Augusta Authors' Club, Book Group of S Fla, Nat Writers Asn (S Fla Chapter). **SELECTED PUBLICATIONS** Auth, Louisiana power & Light, W. W. Norton & Co., 94; auth, Lethe, Cupid, Time, and Love, LeBow, 94; auth, Well Enough Alone: Two Stories and Thirteen poems, LeBow, 96; auth, Love Warps the Mind a Little, W. W. Norton & Co., 97; auth, "Smiling Mighty Jesus," Tropic--Miami Herald (June 97): 14-18; contribur, Naked Came the Manatee, Putnam, 97; co-ed, Having a Wonderful Time: An Anthology of South Florida Writers, Simon & Schuster, 97; auth, I Will Eat a Piece of the Roof and You Can Eat the Window, Midnight Paper Sales, 99; auth, "Eugenics," Channel (May 99): 76-78. **CONTACT ADDRESS** Dept English, Florida Intl Univ, 3000 NE 145th St, North Miami, FL 33181-3612.

DUGAW, DIANNE M.
PERSONAL Born 08/24/1948, Seattle, WA **DISCIPLINE** ENGLISH, FOLKLORE **EDUCATION** Univ Portland, BA, 72; Univ Colo, MMus, 74; Univ Calif at Los Angeles, PhD, 82. **CAREER** Vis lectr, Univ Calif, 82-85; asst prof, Univ Colo, 85-90; from assoc prof to prof, Univ Ore, 91-. **MEMBERSHIPS** Am Soc for Eighteenth-Century Studies, MLA, Am Folklore soc, Calif Folklore Soc, Northwest Soc for Eighteenth-Century Studies. **RESEARCH** British and American Folklore and Popular Culture (especially folk songs), Seventeenth- and Eighteenth-Century British Literature and Culture. **SELECTED PUBLICATIONS** Auth, Warrior Women and Popular Balladry, 1650-1850, Cambridge Univ Press, 89 & 96; ed, The Anglo-American Ballad, Garland Press, 95; auth, "Deep Play": John Gay and the Invention of Modernity, Univ Del Press, 00. **CONTACT ADDRESS** Dept English, Univ of Oregon, 1286 Univ Ore, Eugene, OR 97403.

DUIN, ANN HILL
DISCIPLINE RHETORIC STUDIES **EDUCATION** Univ Minn, MA, PhD. **CAREER** Assoc prof **RESEARCH** Collaboration via emerging technologies; cognitive processes and computers; distance learning; virtual learning environments. **SELECTED PUBLICATIONS** Auth, Techniques for Evaluating the Usability of Documents; Computer-Supported Collaborative Work: The Workplace and the Writing Classroom. **CONTACT ADDRESS** Rhetoric Dept, Univ of Minnesota, Twin Cities, 64 Classroom Office Bldg, 1994 Buford Ave, Saint Paul, MN 55108. **EMAIL** ahduin@maroon.tc.umn.edu

DUNAWAY, DAVID K.
PERSONAL Born 10/03/1948, New York, NY **DISCIPLINE** ENGLISH, AMERICAN AND MEDIA STUDIES **EDUCATION** Univ of Wis, BA, 70; Univ of Calif, Berkeley, MAT, 72; PhD, 81. **CAREER** Instr, Los Medanos Col, 76-77; asst prof to assoc prof, Univ of NMex, 81-. **HONORS AND AWARDS** NEH Grant, 92, 99-00; Fabriel Awd, U.S. Cath Broadcasting Assoc, 96; Silver Reel, Nat Fed of Community Broadcasters, 96; Fulbright Lecturer, Colombia, 97; World Gold Medal, Int Radio Programming, 99; Crystal Awd of Excellence, Communicator Awds, 99; Wertheim Distinguished Lecturer, Univ NMex, 00. **MEMBERSHIPS** Broadcast Educator's Assoc; Nat Writers Union; Int Assoc of Media and Commun Res; Am Folklore Soc; Authors Guild. **RESEARCH** Media Studies / Communication, Biography, Southwest Writers and Literature, Oral History, and Folklore. **SELECTED PUBLICATIONS** Coauth, Oral History: An Interdisciplinary Anthology, with W.K. Baum, Amer Asn for State and Local Hist, Nashville, 84, Sage, 96; How Can I Keep From Singing: Peter Seeger, McGraw Hill, 81, 82, Harrap, London, 85, Shakai Shiso Sha, Tokyo, 85, Jucar, Barcelona, 88; World's Non-Physical Heritage: A Typology, UNESCO, Paris, 84; Radio Management and University Neglect, Col Broadcasting, Dec. 92; articles, Radio and Biography, Biog, Winter, 97; Communications Bill Tunes Out Public, Albuquerque Jour, 8 Feb, 96; Broadcasting History, Proceedings of IX International Oral History Conference Goreborg, Sweden, 96; coauth, Writing the Southwest, Plume Books (Penguin), 95; auth, Aldoux Huxley Recollected, Carrol & Graf, 95; auth, "Broadcasting Biography", biography, Winter 97; auth, "Political-Protest Music", J of Am Folklore 8, Winter 97; auth, "Elections in Colombia", Albuquerque J, Nov 14, 97; auth, "Colombia's Struggle for Peace", Albuquerque J, June 26, 99; auth, "Colombia's March for Peace", San Francisco Chronicle, July 12, 99. **CONTACT ADDRESS** Dept English, Univ of New Mexico, Albuquerque, 1 University Campus, Albuquerque, NM 87131-0001. **EMAIL** dunaway@unm.edu

DUNBAR, MARY JUDITH
PERSONAL Born 02/03/1940, Gary, IN **DISCIPLINE** ENGLISH LITERATURE **EDUCATION** Univ Redlands, BA, 61; Stanford Univ, MA, 67; PhD, 77. **CAREER** Lecturer, Univ London, 70-78; visiting Asst Prof, Claremont McKenna Col, 77-78; Assoc Prof to Asst Prof, Santa Clara Univ, 78-. **HONORS AND AWARDS** Fulbright Scholarship, Univ Bristol, 61-62; Woodrow Wilson Fel, Stanford Univ, 62-63; Fel, Stanford Univ, 64-65; Leverhulme Fel, Univ London, 66-67; Res Grant, Santa Clara Univ; NEH Grant, 82, 85, 92; Phi Beta Kappa. **MEMBERSHIPS** Shakespeare Asn of Am, Intl Shakespeare Asn. **RESEARCH** Shakespeare; Modern and contemporary literature, especially women poets. **SELECTED PUBLICATIONS** Auth, The Winter's Tale Shakespeare in Performance, Manchester Univ Press, forthcoming; auth, "Critical Acts: Performance as Interpretation," Approaches to Hamlet, Mod Lang Asn, 00; auth, "Richard III," Theater Journal, (98): 240-242; auth, "Denise Levertov: 'The Sense of Pilgrimage'," America, (98): 22-25; auth, "Excellence in the Service of Justice and Compassion," in The Future of Prophetic Christianity: Essays in Honor of Robert McAfee Brown, Orbis Books, 93; auth, "Richard II and Twelfth Night at Santa Cruz," Shakespeare Quarterly, (87): 220-225; auth, "Hamlet and As You Like It at Santa Cruz," Shakespeare Quarterly, (86): 241-245; auth, "Henry IV and The Tempest at Santa Cruz," Shakespeare Quarterly, (84): 475-479; auth, Shakespeare/Santa Cruz," Shakespeare Quarterly, (84): 107-112; ed, In Celebration: Anemos, Matrix Press, 83; auth, "To the judgment of your eye" Iconography and the Theatrical Art of Pericles," Shakespeare, Man of the theatre, Assoc Univ Press, 83. **CONTACT ADDRESS** Dept English, Santa Clara Univ, 500 El Camino Real, Santa Clara, CA 95053-0001. **EMAIL** jdunbar@scu.edu

DUNCAN, BONNIE I.
PERSONAL Born 06/07/1943, Pittsburgh, PA **DISCIPLINE** ENGLISH **EDUCATION** Columbus Col, BA, 81; Univ Iowa, MA, 85; PhD, 88. **CAREER** Assoc pro, 96-97; asst prof, 91-96, Millersville Univ; asst prof & ch, Upper Iowa Univ, 89-91. **HONORS AND AWARDS** NEH Summer Inst, Northwestern Univ, 95 & Stanford Univ, 91. **MEMBERSHIPS** Mem, Engl Inst, Harvard Univ, 95; SSHE Fac Prof Develop Symp, 92; Fac Develop Coun of the State Syst Higher Educ Workshop, 92. **RESEARCH** Medieval Literature; Medieval Women's Studies; Linguistics. **SELECTED PUBLICATIONS** Ed, The Political and Satirical Poems of Harley 2253: A Diplomatic Edition, Univ Pa Press, 96; ed, Resoundings, 1995-. **CONTACT ADDRESS** Dept of English, Millersville Univ of Pennsylvania, PO Box 1002, Millersville, PA 17551-0302. **EMAIL** bduncan@millersville.edu

DUNCAN, CHARLES
DISCIPLINE ENGLISH LITERATURE **EDUCATION** Emory Univ, PhD. **CAREER** Sr prof Eng; coord, DAH prog. **HONORS AND AWARDS** Proj dir, NEH Focus grant, 97. **RESEARCH** Popular culture and global literature. **SELECTED PUBLICATIONS** Ed, Global Literature, One World, Many Voices. **CONTACT ADDRESS** Clark Atlanta Univ, 223 James P Brawley Dr, SW, Atlanta, GA 30314.

DUNCAN, JEFFREY LIGHT
PERSONAL Born 01/26/1939, Tulsa, OK, m, 1969, 2 children **DISCIPLINE** AMERICAN LITERATURE **EDUCATION** Calif State Univ, Long Beach, AB, 61; Univ Va, MA, 62, PhD (Am lit), 65. **CAREER** Asst prof Am lit, Washington Univ, 65-69; temp lectr Am civilization, Univ Leeds, Eng, 70-71; assoc prof Am lit, 71-78, prof Am lit, 78-79, Prof English Lang and Lit, Eastern Mich Univ, 79-, Bruern fel, Univ Leeds, Eng, 69-70; Nat Endowment for Arts fel, 78-79. **MEMBERSHIPS** Midwest Mod Lang Asn; MLA. **RESEARCH** American literature; language theory. **SELECTED PUBLICATIONS** Auth, Sutro Baths, Smithsonian, Vol 24, 93. **CONTACT ADDRESS** Dept of English, Eastern Michigan Univ, 612 Pray Harrold, Ypsilanti, MI 48197-2201.

DUNCAN, KIRBY LUTHER
PERSONAL Born 12/02/1936, Deport, TX, m, 1966 **DISCIPLINE** ENGLISH **EDUCATION** Arlington State Col, BA, 63; Tex Technol Col, MA, 64; Univ SC, PhD (English),. **CAREER** Instr English, Univ SC, 66-67; asst prof, 67-72, assoc prof, 72-80, Prof English, Stephen F Austin State Univ, 80-. **MEMBERSHIPS** MLA; NCTE; Am Studies Asn. **RESEARCH** Novels of Henry James; Pamela Hansford Johnson; teaching college composition. **SELECTED PUBLICATIONS** Auth, Lies, Damned Lies, and Statistics--Psychological Syndrome Evidence in the Courtroom After Daubert, Indiana Law Journal, Vol 71,96. **CONTACT ADDRESS** Dept of English and Philos, Stephen F. Austin State Univ, Nacogdoches, TX 75962.

DUNLAP, ISAAC H.
PERSONAL Born Chapel Hill, NC **DISCIPLINE** LIBRARY AND INFORMATION STUDIES **EDUCATION** Univ of NC, MLIS, 96 **CAREER** Asst Prof, 97-, Wstrn IL Univ **HONORS AND AWARDS** Beta Phi MU, 97 **MEMBERSHIPS** ALA, ACRL, ILA, IACRL **RESEARCH** Medieval Scholarship **SELECTED PUBLICATIONS** Auth, Gerard of Cremona: A manuscript Location Guide and Annotated Bibliography, Bulletin of Bibliography, 53:4, 96 **CONTACT ADDRESS** Macomb, IL 61455-1239. **EMAIL** ih-dunlap@win.edu

DUNLAP, KAREN F. BROWN
PERSONAL Born 07/13/1951, Nashville, TN, m, 1997, 4 children **DISCIPLINE** JOURNALISM **EDUCATION** Michigan State University, East Lansing, MI, BA, 1971; Tennessee State University, Nashville, TN, MS, 1976; University of Tennessee, Knoxville, TN, PhD, 1982. **CAREER** Nashville Banner, Nashville, TN, staff writer, 69, 71, 83-85 (summers); Macon News, Macon, GA, staff writer, 72-73; Tennessee State University, Nashville, TN, assistant professor, 76-85; University of South Florida, Tampa, FL, assistant professor, 85-; The Poynter Institute, St Petersburg, FL, associate professor, 89-93; The Poynter Institute, St. Petersburg, FL, dean of fac, 94-. **HONORS AND AWARDS** McKnight Fellow, Florida Endowment Fund, 1986-87; Karl A. & Madira Bickel Fellow, Bickel Foundation, 1979-80; Pulitzer Jurist, 00 & 01. **MEMBERSHIPS** Society of Professional Journalists, 1980-; Delta Sigma Theta Sorority, 1982-; National Association of Black Journalists, 1985-; Association of Educators in Journalism and Mass Communications, 1981-. **SELECTED PUBLICATIONS** Auth, The Effective Editor, 00. **CONTACT ADDRESS** Poynter Inst for Media Studies, 801 3rd St, S, Saint Petersburg, FL 33701. **EMAIL** kdunlap@poynter.org

DUNN, CHARLES W.
PERSONAL Born 11/30/1915, Arburhnott, Scotland, m, 1974, 3 children **DISCIPLINE** ENGLISH **EDUCATION** McMaster Univ, BA, 38; Harvard Univ, AM, 39; PhD, 48. **CAREER** Instr, Stephens Col, 41-42; instr, Cornell Univ, 43-46; instr, asst prof, Univ Col, 46-56; prof, New York Univ, 56-63; prof, emer, Harvard Univ, 63-. **HONORS AND AWARDS** Dexter Fel, Harvard Univ, 41; Rockefeller Fel, 42; Nuffield Fel, 54-55; LL.D, St Fran Xav Univ. **MEMBERSHIPS** MLA; MAA; AAAS. **RESEARCH** Celtic literature; Scottish folklore. **SELECTED PUBLICATIONS** Auth, The Foundling and the Werewolf, Univ Tor Press, 60; auth, Highland Settler, Univ Tor Press, 53; co-auth, The Role of the Poet in Early Societies, D.S. Brewer (Cambridge, MA), 89; co-ed, Middle English Literature (Harcourt Brace: Garland, 73, 90); ed, "Chaucer," in Major British Writers (Harcourt Brace: Garland, 54); auth, "Celtic Versification," in Major Language Types (NYU Press, 72). **CONTACT ADDRESS** 25 Longfellow Rd, Cambridge, MA 02138. **EMAIL** cwdunn@mediaone.net

DUNN, E. CATHERINE
PERSONAL Born 07/30/1916, Baltimore, MD, s **DISCIPLINE** ENGLISH, LITERATURE **EDUCATION** Col Notre Dame, AB, 38; Cath Univ America, MA, 40; PhD, 47. **CAREER** Lectr, Notre Dame Col, 45-47; lectr to undergrad advisor to prof to emer, Catholic Univ America, 47-. **HONORS AND AWARDS** Chmn Dept Eng, Cath Univ Am, 69-78; Outstanding Educat Am Cit, 73; Pres, S Atlantic Asn Dept Eng, 72-73. **MEMBERSHIPS** AAUP; CRS; MLA. **RESEARCH** Retired as Prof Emerita. **SELECTED PUBLICATIONS** Auth, The Gallican Saint's Life and the Late Roman Dramatic Tradition, Catholic UP (Washington, DC), 89; co-ed, Pioneering Women at the Catholic University of America, Intl Graphics (Hattsville; MD), 88; auth, "The Medieval 'Cycle ' as History Play: An Approach to the Wakefield Plays," Renaissance Studies 7 (59): 76-89; auth, "The Origin of the Saints' Plays: The Question Reopened," in Medieval Drama Collection of Festival Papers, ed. Williana Selz (SD: Dakota Pr, 68): 46-54; auth, "The Saint's Leveni as History and as Poetry," Am Benedict Rev 27 (76): 359-78; auth, "The Farced Epistle as Dramatic Form in the Twelfth Century Renaissance," Comparative Drama 29 (95) : 863-31; auth, "The 'New Criticism' After Fifty Years: A Memoir," Mod Age 41 (99): 328-36 . **CONTACT ADDRESS** 8800 Walther Blvd, Apt 3311, Parkville, MD 21234-9001.

DUNN, FRANCIS M.
PERSONAL Born 10/15/1955, Aberdeen, Scotland, m, 1986, 2 children **DISCIPLINE** CLASSICAL LITERATURE, GREEK DRAMA **EDUCATION** Yale Univ, BA, 76; MA, 80; PhD, 85. **CAREER** Vis instr, NC State Univ, 85-86; asst prof, Northwestern Univ, 86-93; asst to assoc prof, Univ of Calif Santa Barbara, 93-. **HONORS AND AWARDS** Fel, NEH; Fel, ACLS; Regents Jr Fel, Univ of Calif; Grant, Ill Humanities Coun. **MEMBERSHIPS** Am Philol Assoc, Classical Assoc of the Middle W and S. **RESEARCH** Time and Narrative in Athens, A Commentary on Sophocles' Electra. **SELECTED PUBLICATIONS** Coed, Beginnings in Classical Literature, Cambridge, 92; auth, "Beginning at the End in Euripides' Trojan Women," Rheinisches Museum 136, (93): 22-36; auth, Tragedy's End: Closure and Innovation in Euripidean Drama, Oxford, 96; auth, Sophocles' Electra in Performance, Stuttgart, 96; coed, Classical Closure, Princeton, 97; auth, "Tampering with the Calendar," Zeitschrift fur Papyrologie und Epigrafik 123, (98): 213-231; auth, "Euripidean Aetrologies," Classical Bull 76, (00): 3-27. **CONTACT ADDRESS** Dept Classics, Univ of California, Santa Barbara, Santa Barbara, CA 93106. **EMAIL** fdunn@humanitas.ucsb.edu

DUNN, RICHARD JOHN
PERSONAL Born 06/08/1938, Pittsburgh, PA, m, 1961, 3 children **DISCIPLINE** NINETEENTH CENTURY ENGLISH **EDUCATION** Allegheny Col, BA, 60; Western Reserve Univ, MA, 61, PhD (English), 64. **CAREER** Lectr English, Univ Colo, Colo Springs, 66-67; instr, US Air Force Acad Prep Sch, 64-67; asst prof, US Air Force Acad, 65-67; asst prof, 67-71, assoc prof, 71-81, assoc chmn dept, 76-80, dean, summer, 80-82, Prof English, Univ Wash, 81-, Chmn Dept, 82-92, Assoc bibliogr, MLA Bibliog, 70-75; divisional dean humanities, 92-97. **MEMBERSHIPS** MLA; Philol Asn Pac Coast; Dickens Soc; Dickens Fel. **RESEARCH** English novel; Victorian literature. **SELECTED PUBLICATIONS** Auth, Inverse sublimity: Carlyle's theory of humor, Univ Toronto Quart, 70; David Copperfield's Carylean Retailoring, Dickens the Craftsman, 70; ed, Norton Critical Edition of Jane Eyre, Norton, 71, 87, 00; auth, Narrative distance in Frankenstein, Studies in the Novel, 74; ed, The English Novel: A Checklist of 20th Century Criticism, Swallow Press, 76; auth, Far, far better things: Dicken's later endings, Dickens Studies Annual, 78; Vision and revision: In Memoriam XCV, Victorian Poetry, 80; ed, David Copperfield: An Annotated Bibliography, Garland, 81; ed, Approaches to Teaching David Copperfield, MLA, 84; auth, Oliver Twist: Whole Heart and Soul, Twayne, 93; ed, Norton Critical Edition of Wuthering Heights, 90. **CONTACT ADDRESS** Dept of English, Univ of Washington, Seattle, WA 98195. **EMAIL** dickd@u.washington.edu

DUNN, ROBERT P.
PERSONAL Born 11/18/1941, Rockford, IL, m, 1963, 2 children **DISCIPLINE** ENGLISH **EDUCATION** Pacific Union Col, BA, 63; Univ Wis, Madison, MA, 66, PhD, 70; Sch Theol, Claremont, RelM, 77. **CAREER** Prof, 80-, Chemn, 77-81, 87-90, 95-99, assoc dean, 90-94, La Sierra Univ. **MEMBERSHIPS** Modern Lang Asn; Shakespeare Asn Am; Conference on Christianity and Lit. **RESEARCH** English renaissance; religion & literature. **CONTACT ADDRESS** Dept of English, La Sierra Univ, 4700 Pierce St, Riverside, CA 92515-8247. **EMAIL** rdunn@lasierra.edu

DUNNE, JOSEPH FALLON
PERSONAL Born 12/12/1941, St. Louis, MO, m, 1964, 5 children **DISCIPLINE** ENGLISH, COMMUNICATIONS **EDUCATION** St Benedict's Col, AB, 63; Univ Kans, MA, 67; St Louis Univ, MA, 75. **CAREER** Prof English, St Louis Community Col, Meremec, 64-. **HONORS AND AWARDS** Fac Lect Awd, 96; Gov Awd for Excellence in Teaching, 96. **MEMBERSHIPS** Soc Tech Commun. **CONTACT ADDRESS** Dept of English, St. Louis Comm Col, Meramec, 11333 Big Bend Rd, Saint Louis, MO 63122-5799. **EMAIL** jdunne@stlcc.cc.mo.us

DUPLESSIS, RACHEL BLAU
PERSONAL Born 12/14/1941, Brooklyn, NY, m **DISCIPLINE** ENGLISH **EDUCATION** Barnard Col, BA, 63; Columbia Univ, PhD, 70. **CAREER** Asst Prof, Trenton St Col, 72-73; Lectr, Rutgers Univ, 73-74; From Asst Prof to Prof, Temple Univ, 74-. **HONORS AND AWARDS** Fulbright Fel, The Netherlands, 85; NEH Fel, 88; Serv Awd for Poetry, 93; Fac Awd, Temple Univ, 98-99. **MEMBERSHIPS** MLA. **RESEARCH** Modern and contemporary poetry, feminist theory, creative writing. **SELECTED PUBLICATIONS** Auth, Drafts 15-XXX, The Fold, Potes and Poets Pr (Elmwood, CT), 97; auth, Renga: Draft 32, BeautifulSwimmer Pr (Philadelphia, PA), 98; co-ed, The Feminist Memoir Project: Voices of Women's LIberation, Crown Publ Pr (NY), 98; coauth, The Objectivist Nexus: Cultural Poetics, Univ Ala Pr (Tuscaloosa, AL), 99; auth, Drafts 1-38, Toll, Wesleyan UP (Middletown, CT), forthcoming; auth, Genders, Races and Religious Cultures in Modern American Poetry 1908-1934, Cambridge UP (Cambridge), forthcoming. **CONTACT ADDRESS** Dept English, Temple Univ, 1114 W Berks St, Philadelphia, PA 19122-6007. **EMAIL** rduplessis@vm.temple.edu

DUPRIEST, TRAVIS TALMADGE, JR.
PERSONAL Born 08/15/1944, Richmond, VA, m, 2000, 2 children **DISCIPLINE** ENGLISH LITERATURE; LITERATURE; SPIRITUALITY; AND CREATIVE NON-FICTION **EDUCATION** Richmond Univ, BA; Harvard Divinity Sch, MTS; Univ Ky, PhD. **CAREER** English, Carthage Col. **HONORS AND AWARDS** Grants: Nat Endowment Hum; Univ Chicago Midwest Fac Seminar; danforth fel, pres nat huguenot soc; fel huguenot, fel ctr renaissance & reformation studies; vis/occas fel univ chicago, cambridge univ. **MEMBERSHIPS** MLA; Conference Christianity & Literature; former dir Honors Prog Carthage. **SELECTED PUBLICATIONS** Auth, Noon at Smyrna; Summer Storm; Soapstone Wall; auth, Jeremy Taylor's Discourse on Friendship, Scholars Facsimiles; Katherine Philips' Poems, scholars Facsimiles. **CONTACT ADDRESS** Carthage Col, 2001 Alford Dr., Kenosha, WI 53140. **EMAIL** dekoven.center@juno.com

DURER, CHRISTOPHER
PERSONAL Born 09/15/1928, Warsaw, Poland, m, 1967, 1 child **DISCIPLINE** ENGLISH, COMPARATIVE LITERATURE **EDUCATION** Chicago Teachers Col, BEd, 61; Univ Calif, Berkeley, MA, 63, PhD (comp lit), 69. **CAREER** Instr humanities, Univ Mo, Rolla, 63-64; instr comp lit, San Francisco State Col, 65-67, Univ Calif, Berkeley, 68-69; asst prof English, 69-73, Assoc Prof English and Mod Lang, Univ Wyo, 73-. **MEMBERSHIPS** MLA; Am Comp Lit Asn; Int Comp Lit Asn; Am Soc 18th Century Studies. **RESEARCH** Comparative theory and history; English 18th century literature; 20th century drama. **SELECTED PUBLICATIONS** Auth, Musical Metamorphoses--Forms and History of Arrangement, Musik und Kirche, Vol 63, 93; The International Glen Gould Festival in Groningen , Musica, Vol 47, 93; Report on the 17th Edition of the Tage Alter Musik Held in Herne, December 1992, Musica, Vol 47, 93; Kagel Die Erschopfung Der Welt, Musica, Vol 48, 94; Freyer Distanzen, Musica, Vol 48, 94; 100 Years of Opera in Essen 1893-1993, Musica, Vol 47, 93; Fortner in Seinem Garten Liebt Don Perlimplin Belisa, Musica, Vol 48, 94; Geister Der ModerneReport on a Recent Concert Series in Recklinghausen March 7-14, 1993, Musica, Vol 47, 93; Hummel Gorbatschow, Musica, Vol 48, 94; Freyer Flugel Schlage, Musica, Vol 48, 94. **CONTACT ADDRESS** Dept of English, Univ of Wyoming, Laramie, WY 82070.

DUSSINGER, JOHN ANDREW
PERSONAL Born 11/18/1935, Reading, PA, m, 1959, 2 children **DISCIPLINE** ENGLISH **EDUCATION** Lehigh Univ, AB, 58; Oxford Univ, IIE, 59; Princeton Univ, MA, 61, PhD (English), 64. **CAREER** Instr English, Douglass Col, 62-65; asst prof, 65-68, Assoc Prof English, Univ Ill, Urbana-Champaign, 68-, Lectr English lit, Aarhus Univ, 70-72. **MEMBERSHIPS** MLA; Johnson Soc Midwest (pres, 68-69); Am Soc 18th Century Studies. **RESEARCH** Eighteenth century prose; the novel; history of ideas. **SELECTED PUBLICATIONS** Auth, Conscience and the pattern of Christian perfection in Clarissa, PMLA, 66; What Pamela knew: An interpretation, J Eng Ger Philol, 70; Style and intention in Johnson's Life in Savage, ELH, 70; The Discourse of the Mind in 18th Century Fiction, Mouton, 74; David Humme, Denial of Personal Identity, Al, 80; Shaftesbury's answer to Locke, J Hist Ideas, 80; auth, In the Pride of the Moment: Encounters in Jane Austen's World. **CONTACT ADDRESS** Univ of Illinois, Urbana-Champaign, 317d English Bldg, mc 718, 608 S Wright, Urbana, IL 61801. **EMAIL** dussinge@staff.uiuc.edu

DUST, PATRICK
DISCIPLINE TWENTIETH-CENTURY SPANISH LITERATURE **EDUCATION** Univ Chicago, PhD. **CAREER** Literature, Carleton Univ. **MEMBERSHIPS** Auth, Ortega y Gasset and the Question of Modernity. **CONTACT ADDRESS** Carleton Col, 100 S College St., Northfield, MN 55057-4016.

DUTTON, WILLIAM H.
PERSONAL Born 08/23/1947, St Joseph, MO, m, 1981, 2 children **DISCIPLINE** COMMUNICATION AND POLICY, PLANNING & DEVELOPMENT **EDUCATION** Univ Mo, BA; SUNY, Buffalo, MA, PhD. **CAREER** Prof; USC, 80-; vis prof, Brunel Univ, 86-87; Nat dir, UK's Prog on Information & Commun Technol, 93-95; taught & conducted res, Univ S Fl, San Diego State Univ, & Univ CA at Irvine; Academic VP, Academic Senate, 90-00; Pres of the Faculty, Univ Southern CA, 00-01. **HONORS AND AWARDS** Fulbright Scholar, 86-87. **MEMBERSHIPS** Social Aspects of Technology. **SELECTED PUBLICATIONS** Auth, Society on the Line: Information Politics in the Digital Age, Oxford UP; coauth, The Management

of Information Systems, Columbia UP, 81; Computers and Politics, Columbia UP, 82; Modeling as Negotiating, Ablex, 85 & The Social Shaping of Information Superhighways, Campus Verlay/St Marten's Press, 97; ed, Information and Communication Technologies- Visions and Realities, Oxford UP; co ed, Wired Cities, GK Hall, 85. **CONTACT ADDRESS** Annenberg School for Commun, Univ of So California, University Park Campus, Los Angeles, CA 90089. **EMAIL** wdutton@bcf.usc.edu

DUYFHUIZEN, BERNARD
PERSONAL Born 01/28/1953, Brooklyn, NY, m, 1978, 1 child **DISCIPLINE** ENGLISH LITERATURE **EDUCATION** Univ Tulsa, PhD, 83. **CAREER** Fac, 83-; to prof; chr, 92-98, to assoc dean, 99-. **HONORS AND AWARDS** Ed, Jour Pynchon Notes. **RESEARCH** Narrative literature; literary criticism; the reader and Thomas Pynchon's Gravity's Rainbow. **SELECTED PUBLICATIONS** Auth, Narratives of Transmission, Fairleigh Dickinson UP, 92; articles on critical theory, especially in the areas of feminism and narratology. **CONTACT ADDRESS** Dept of English, Univ of Wisconsin, Eau Claire, College of Arts and Sciences, PO Box 4004, Eau Claire, WI 54702-4004. **EMAIL** pnotesbd@uwec.edu

DYBEK, STUART
PERSONAL Born 04/10/1942, Chicago, IL, m, 2 children **DISCIPLINE** ENGLISH **EDUCATION** Loyola Univ, BA, 65; MA, 67; Univ Iowa, MFA, 70. **CAREER** Vis prof, Univ Iowa; vis prof, Univ Calif Irvine; vis prof, Princeton Univ; prof, Western Mich Univ. **HONORS AND AWARDS** Whiting Writer's Awd; Lannan Awd; Fiction Awd, Acad of Arts & Letters; Guggenheim Fel; NEA (twice). **MEMBERSHIPS** PEN, AAUP, AWP. **CONTACT ADDRESS** Dept English, Western Michigan Univ, 1201 Oliver St, Kalamazoo, MI 49008-3804.

DYC, GLORIA
PERSONAL Born 04/15/1950, Detroit, MI, s, 1 child **DISCIPLINE** ENGLISH **EDUCATION** Monteith Col, WSU, BA, 73; Wayne State Univ, MA, 76; Univ of Mich, PhD, 90. **CAREER** Instr, Sinte Gleska Col, Rosebud, SD, 82-88; Assoc Prof, Chair of Arts and Letters, Univ of NMex Gallup, 88-00. **HONORS AND AWARDS** Phi Beta Kappa; Hopwood Awds for Fiction, Univ of Mich. **MEMBERSHIPS** RMMLA, NCTE, NANAS. **RESEARCH** Literacy in Native American Communities, Multicultural Literature of the Southwest. **SELECTED PUBLICATIONS** Auth, articles in Am Indian Culture and Res J; auth, articles in Navajo J of Educ. **CONTACT ADDRESS** Dept Humanities, Univ of New Mexico, Gallup, 200 College Rd, HC 32 Box 1, Gallup, NM 87301-5603. **EMAIL** gdyc@unm.edu

DYCK, ANDREW R.
PERSONAL Born 05/24/1947, Chicago, IL, m, 1978 **DISCIPLINE** CLASSICS **EDUCATION** Univ of Wis, BA; Univ of Chicago, PhD. **CAREER** Lect, Univ of Alberta, 75-76; Vis Asst Prof, UCLA, 76-77; Asst Prof, Univ MN, 78-79; Asst Prof, Prof, UCLA, 79-. **HONORS AND AWARDS** Fel, Alexander VonHumboldt-Stiftung, 81-82; Fel, Nat Endowment for Humanities, 91-92; Mem, Ints for Adv Stud, 91-92; Vis Fel, All Souls Col Oxford, 98; Vis Fel and Life Member, Clare Hall, Cambridge, 99. **MEMBERSHIPS** APA; Calif Class Asn; US Nat Com on Byzantine Studies **RESEARCH** Cicero's Philosophical Essays **SELECTED PUBLICATIONS** Epimerismi Homerici, Berlin-NY, 83-95; The Essays on Euripides and George of Pisidia and on Heliodorus and Achilles Tatius, ed Michael Psellus, Vienna, 86; A Commentary on Cicero, De Officiis, AA, 96; Schliemann on the Excavation of Troy: Three Unpublished Letters, Greek, Roman and Byzantine Stud, 90; Cicero the Dramaturge, Qvi Miscvit Vtile Dvlci: Festschrift Essays for Paul Lachlan MacKendrick, 98; Narrative Obfuscation, Philosophical Topoi, and Tragic Patterning in Cicero's Pro Milone, Harvard Stud in Class Philo, 98. **CONTACT ADDRESS** 405 Hilgard Ave, Los Angeles, CA 90095-1417.

DYER, JOYCE
PERSONAL Born 07/20/1947, OH, m, 1969, 1 child **DISCIPLINE** ENGLISH **EDUCATION** Wittenberg Univ, BA, 69; Kent State Univ, PhD, eng, 77. **CAREER** Lake Forest Col, instr, 78-79; Western Res Acad, teacher, 79-90; Hiram Col, dir writing, assoc prof eng, 91-00. **HONORS AND AWARDS** NEH fels, 87, 88, 90; writer residencies at Wittenberg U, 98; Hinden Settlement School, 99; Radford U, 00; OH Arts Counc, 97; Appalachian Stud Awd, 97; Michael Starr Awd, 96. **MEMBERSHIPS** MLA; AWP; Appala Stud Asn. **RESEARCH** Nonfiction; memoir; Appala studies; contemp fiction; Am lit; southern letters. **SELECTED PUBLICATIONS** The Awakening: A Novel of Beginnings, Twayne/Macmillian, 93; In a Tangled Wood: An Alzheimer's Journey, SO Meth Press, 96; Bloodroot: Reflections on Place by Appalachian Women Writers, Univ Press KY, 98. Hundreds of essays. **CONTACT ADDRESS** 30 Church St, Hudson, OH 44236-3007. **EMAIL** dyerja@hiram.edu

DYER, KLAY
DISCIPLINE ENGLISH **EDUCATION** Univ Ottawa, PhD, 98. **CAREER** Asst prof., Brock Univ, 98- **RESEARCH** Influence of Cervantine thought and Don Quixote on the North American imagination; 19th Century Canadian & American Literature and Culture. **SELECTED PUBLICATIONS** Auth, Labyrinths, Windmills, Wonders: Exploring the Frontiers of the Digital Library, 99; auth, George Bowering, Contemporary Novelists, St James Press, 00, 118-20; auth, Guy Vanderhaeghe, Contemporary Novelists, St. James Press, 00, 158-9; Ed, Joseph Howe, Peter McArthur, The Week, Encyc of the Essay, Fitzroy Dearborn, 96; Alice Munro, Encyc Pop Fiction, Beacham, 96; The Albanian Virgin; The Beggar Maid: Stories of Flo and Rose, About the Author, Lives of Girls and men; Jack McClelland, McClelland and Stewart, Oxford Companion to Can Lit, Oxford UP, 97; co-auth, Biographies and Memoirs in English, Oxford Companion to Can Lit, Oxford UP, 97; Canadian Women's History Bibliography, Can Inst for Hist Microreproductions, 97; rev(s), E.K. Brown: A Study in Conflict, by Laura Smyth Groening, Jour Can Poetry 10, 95; Touch Monkeys: Nonsense Strategies for Reading Twentieth-Century Poetry, by Marnie Parsons, Jour Can Poetry 11, 96; Rev of Voice, by Marie Elise St. George and Anne Szumigalski, Jour of Can Poetry 12, 97. **CONTACT ADDRESS** Dept of Eng Lang and Lit, Brock Univ, 500 Glenridge Ave, Saint Catharines, ON, Canada L2S 3A1. **EMAIL** kdyer@spartan.ac.brocku.ca

DYER, SAM COAD
DISCIPLINE PUBLIC RELATIONS **EDUCATION** Univ TN, PhD, 91. **CAREER** Southwest Tex State Univ **SELECTED PUBLICATIONS** Areas: sale of electric corporations in New Zealand, the use of public opinion polls in news copy in Australia, and environmental monitoring strategies for public relations firms analysing media coverage of their clients. **CONTACT ADDRESS** Southwest Missouri State Univ, Springfield, 901 S. National, Ste. 50, Springfield, MO 65804-0094.

DYKEMAN, THERESE B.
PERSONAL Born 04/11/1936, Anamosa, IA, d, 3 children **DISCIPLINE** RHETORIC **EDUCATION** Creighton Univ, BS; Loyola Univ, MA; Union Inst, PhD. **CAREER** Rhetoric and lit, Univ Bridgeport, 81-90; adj prof rhetoric and lit, Univ Conn, Stamford, 82; adj prof, Fairfield Univ, 85- ; adj prof, Sacred Heart Univ, 94- . **HONORS AND AWARDS** Distinguished Service Awd, Marycrest Int Univ, Iowa, 93. **MEMBERSHIPS** Danforth Assoc of New England; Ctr for Independent Stud, New Haven; Nat Coalition of Independent Scholars; Soc for the Stud of Women Philosophers; Rhetoric Soc of Am. **RESEARCH** Philosophy by women or women philosophers; rhetorical theory. **SELECTED PUBLICATIONS** Auth, American Women Philosophers 1650-1930: Six Exemplary Thinkers, Mellen, 93; auth, The Infant Famished: Mary Moody Emerson, A Review, Transactions of the C.S. Peirce Society, 98; auth, The Neglected Canon: Nine Women Philosophers First to the Twentieth Century, Kluwer, 99; auth, The American Aesthetics of Ednah Dow Cheney, in Tougas, ed, Hearing Women Philosophers, 00. **CONTACT ADDRESS** 47 Woods End Rd, Fairfield, CT 06430. **EMAIL** TDykeman@fairl.Fairfield.edu

DYSON, STEVEN L.
DISCIPLINE CLASSICS **EDUCATION** Brown Univ, BA; Yale Univ, PhD, 63. **CAREER** Mellon prof, Intercollegiate Ctr Class Studies; Charles Eliot Norton Lectureship, Archaeolog Inst Am, 93-94; chr class dept, SUNY Buffalo, present. **HONORS AND AWARDS** Fellow, Am Coun Learned Soc; fellow, NEH; pres, archaeolog inst am. **RESEARCH** Romanization of Sardinia; urban develop and soc hist of ancient Rome; the hist of Class archaeol. **SELECTED PUBLICATIONS** Auth, The Roman Villas of Buccino, 83; The Creation of the Roman Frontier, 85; Community and Society in Roman Italy, 92. **CONTACT ADDRESS** Dept Classics, SUNY, Buffalo, 712 Clemens Hall, Buffalo, NY 14260.

E

EADIE, WILLIAM F.
PERSONAL Born 09/22/1946, Evanston, IL, s **DISCIPLINE** COMMUNICATION **EDUCATION** Univ Calif Los Angeles, AB, 68, MA, 71; Purdue Univ, PhD, 74. **CAREER** Asst prof, Oh Univ, 74-79; prof & chemn, Calif State Univ, 79-93; assoc dir, Nat Comm Asn, 93-. **HONORS AND AWARDS** Ed, Jour of Applied Commun Res, 91-93; pres, Western States Commun Asn, 93-94; Phi Kappa Phi, Golden Key, Golden Anniversary award, Nat Commun Asn, 81. **MEMBERSHIPS** Nat Commun Asn; Intl Commun Asn; Western States Commun Asn. **RESEARCH** Applied Communication; Individual differences in communication. **SELECTED PUBLICATIONS** Auth, Hearing what we ought to hear, Vital Speeches, 89; auth, Being applied: Communication research comes of age, Jour of Applied Commun Res, 90; coauth, Communication research: Making a difference in the real world, Jour of Commun, 93; auth, On having an agenda, Jour of Applied Commun Res, 22, 94; auth, Making a difference: The status and challenges of applied communication research, Applied communication in the 21st century: Report of the Tampa conference on applied communication, Lawrence Erlbaum Assoc, 95; Rev, Conditions of Liberty: Civil Society and its Rivals, Jour of Applied Commun Res, 96; auth, The Language of Coinflict and Resolution, Sage Pub, 01. **CONTACT ADDRESS** National Communication Association, 5105 Backlick Rd, Annandale, VA 22003-6005. **EMAIL** weadie@natcom.org

EAKIN, PAUL JOHN
PERSONAL Born 03/08/1938, Cleveland, OH, M, 1964, 4 children **DISCIPLINE** ENGLISH **EDUCATION** Harvard Univ, AB, 59, AM, 61, PhD, 66. **CAREER** Asst prof, Indiana Univ, 66-72, assoc prof, 72-79, prof, 79-99, Ruth N. Halls Prof of English, 99-; Sr Fulbright Lectr, Univ Paris XII, 72-73, 91, and Univ Athens, 78-79. **MEMBERSHIPS** Modern Lang Asn of Am, Am Asn of Univ Profs. **SELECTED PUBLICATIONS** Auth, The New England Girl: Cultural Ideals in Hawthorne, Stowe, Howells, and James, Univ Ga Press (77); auth, Fictions in Autobiography: Studies in the Art of Self-Invention, Princeton Univ Press (85); ed and auth of intro, "Philippe Lejeune," On Autobiography, Univ Minn Press (87); ed and auth of intro, American Autobiography: Retrospect and Prospect, Univ Wisc Press (91); auth, Touching the World: reference in Autobiography, Princeton Univ Press (92); auth, How Our Lives Become Stories: Making Selves, Cornell Univ Press (99). **CONTACT ADDRESS** Dept English, Indiana Univ, Bloomington, 1020 E Kirkwood Ave, Bloomington, IN 47405-7103.

EARLY, GERALD
PERSONAL Born 04/21/1952, Philadelphia, PA, m, 1982 **DISCIPLINE** ENGLISH, AFRICAN-AMERICAN STUDIES **EDUCATION** University of Pennsylvania, Philadelphia, PA, BA, 1974; Cornell University, Ithaca, NYork, MA, 1982, PhD, 1982. **CAREER** Washington University, St Louis, MO, professor of English & African & Afro-American studies, 82; Randolph Macon College for Women, Lynchburg, VA, writer in residence, 90. **HONORS AND AWARDS** Whiting Foundation Writer's Awd, Whiting Foundation, 1988; CCLM/General Electric Foundation Awd for Younger Writers, 1988; The Passing of Jazz's Old Guard, published in Best American Essays, 1986; University of Kansas Minority Postdoctoral Fellowship, 1985-87. **SELECTED PUBLICATIONS** Daughters: On Family and Fatherhood, Addison-Wesley, 1994. **CONTACT ADDRESS** Professor, African and Afro-American Studies, Washington Univ, One Brookings Dr, Box 1109, Saint Louis, MO 63130-4899.

EARNEST, ROBERT S.
PERSONAL Born 05/16/1959, Winfield, AL, m, 1983, 2 children **DISCIPLINE** COMMUNICATIONS **EDUCATION** Univ N Ala, BA, 82; Univ Miami, MFA, 86; Univ Colo, PhD, 95. **CAREER** Asst Prof, Palm Beach Atlantic Col, 92-96; Asst Prof, Univ Montevallo, 96-97; Asst Prof, St Univ W Ga, 97-. **HONORS AND AWARDS** Grad Studies Awd, Univ N Ala, 83; Fels, Univ Colo, 89-93; Dean's Grants, Univ Colo, 92, 93; Fac Develop Grant, Univ Sys of Ga, 98; Fac Develop Grant, Univ W Ga, 98. **MEMBERSHIPS** AEA, SAG, ATHE, GTC, STC. **RESEARCH** German theater, postmodernism, acting. **SELECTED PUBLICATIONS** Auth, "'An Enemy of the People' and Current Environmental Issues," Ibsen News and Comment, vol 12 (91); auth, "The Image of Caesar - Production Approaches to 'Julius Caesar'," On-Stage Studies (92): auth, "Summer 1998 at the Royal National Theatre," Western European Stages (98); auth, "Summer 1998 at Schauspiel Leipzig," Western European Stages (99); auth, The State Acting Academy of East Berlin: Max Reinhardt's Schauspielschule to The Hochschule fur Schauspielkunst 'Ernst Busch' Berlin," Edwin Mellen Pr (New York), 99. **CONTACT ADDRESS** Dept Commun, State Univ of West Georgia, 1601 Maple St, Carrollton, GA 30117-4116.

EARNEST, STEVE
DISCIPLINE THEATER **EDUCATION** Univ N Ala, BA, 82; Univ Miami, MFA, 86; Univ Colo, PhD, 95. **CAREER** Asst prof. **HONORS AND AWARDS** Graduate Studies Awd, Univ of North Alabama, 83; Doctoral Fels, Univ of Colorado, 89-93; Dean's Grant, Univ of Colorado, 92; Dean's Grant Univ of Colorado, 93; Fac Development Grant, Univ System of Georgia, 98; Fac Development Grant, Univ of West Georgia, 99. **MEMBERSHIPS** Actors' Equity Asn; Asn Theatre Higher Edu. **SELECTED PUBLICATIONS** Auth, "Julius Caesar" Colorado Shakespeare Festival Souvenir Program, 91; auth, "An Enemy of the People and Current Environmental Issues," Ibsen News and Comment, vol 12, 91; auth, "The Image of Caesar - Production Approaches to Julius Caesar," On-Stage Studies, 92; auth, "Summer 1998 at the Royal National Theatre," Western European Stages, 98; auth, "Summer 1999 at Schauspiel Leipzig," Western European Stages, 99; auth, The State Acting Academy of East Berlin; Max Reinhardt's Schauspoelschule to The Hochschule fur Schuspielkunst 'Ernst Busch' Berlin: Lewiston, N.Y.: The Edwin Mellen Pr, 99; auth, "The Hochschule fur Schauspielkunst 'Ernst Busch' Berlin: Theatre Training in Post-GDR Berlin," Performer Training: Developments Across Cultures, Gordon & Breach Publishing Co, U.K., 00. **CONTACT ADDRESS** Dept of Theatre Arts, California State Univ, San Bernardino, 5500 Univ Parkway, San Bernardino, CA 92407. **EMAIL** searnest@westga.edu

EATON, CHARLES EDWARD
PERSONAL Born 06/25/1916, Winston-Salem, NC, m, 1950 **DISCIPLINE** ENGLISH **EDUCATION** Univ NC, AB, 36; Harvard Univ, MA, 40. **CAREER** Instr English, Univ Mo, 40-42; vconsul, Am Embassy, Brazil, 42-46; Asst Prof English, Univ NC, 46-51; Res and Writing, 51-, Lectr, NC Poetry Circuit, 63. **HONORS AND AWARDS** Ridgely Torrence Awd, 51; Golden Rose, New England Poetry Club, 72; Alice Fay Di Castagnoba Awd, Poetry Soc Am, 74; Arvon Found Int Poetry Competition Awd, London, 81. **MEMBERSHIPS** American literature. **SELECTED PUBLICATIONS** Auth, Petrified Forest, Centennial Rev, Vol 38, 94; La Vie En Rose, Ariel Rev Int Eng Lit, Vol 27, 96; The Truss, Centennial Rev, Vol 37, 93; The Winged Eye, Ariel Rev Int English Lit, Vol 24, 93; The Liaison, Sewanee Rev, Vol 104, 96; Metronome, Sewanee Rev, Vol 104, 96; Epitaphs, Ariel Rev Int Eng Lit, Vol 25, 94; The Gold Tooth, Centennial Rev, Vol 38, 94; Red Carpet Treatment, Col Eng, Vol 56, 94;Tapeworm, Centennial Rev, Vol 41, 97. **CONTACT ADDRESS** 808 Greenwood Rd, Chapel Hill, NC 27514.

EATON, RICHARD B.
DISCIPLINE ENGLISH **EDUCATION** Univ Richmond, BA, 53; Univ NC Chapel Hill, MA, 55; PhD, 67. **CAREER** Instr, Winthrop Univ, 55-56; instr, Wake Forest, 60-64; asst prof, Univ of Richmond, 65-67; prof W Va Univ, 67-99. **HONORS AND AWARDS** Chi Beta Kappa. **MEMBERSHIPS** MLA; NEMLA; ACIS; Eugene O'Neill Soc. **RESEARCH** Eugene O'Neill. **SELECTED PUBLICATIONS** Auth, Eugene O'Neill in Court; auth, Eugene O'Neill: An Annotated Bibliography, 1973-2000. **CONTACT ADDRESS** Dept English, West Virginia Univ, Morgantown, PO Box 6296, Morgantown, WV 26506-6296. **EMAIL** reaton@wvu.edu

EAVES, MORRIS
PERSONAL Born 05/12/1944, m, 1963, 2 children **DISCIPLINE** ENGLISH **EDUCATION** Long Island U, BA, 66; Tulane U, PhD, 72. **CAREER** Asst prof, U of New Mexico, 70-74; assoc prof, U of New Mexico, 74-82; vis assoc prof, Tulane U, 79-80; prof, U of New Mexico, 82-85; Presidential prof, U of New Mexico, 85-86. **HONORS AND AWARDS** William Riley Parker Prize, 77-78; National Humanities Ctr Fel, 84-85; Presidential Prof of Eng, U of New Mexico, 85-86; Getty Grant Program publication grant for The Counter-Arts Conspiracy, 92; Assoc Fel, Institute for Advanced Technology in the Humanities, U of Va, 94-; Getty Grant Program grant to the Institute of Advanced Technology in the Humanities, U of Va in support of the William Blake Archive, 95-98; proj dir, the blake arch, an online, hypermedia ed of william blake's illuminated bk(s), **RESEARCH** Lit and the visual arts; cult contexts of Brit Romanticism; editorial theory and practice; hist of technol and commerce; institutionalization of the arts; organized work. **SELECTED PUBLICATIONS** Auth, "The Title-Page of The Book of Urizen," in Willliam Blake: Essays in Honour of Sir Geoffrey Keynes, ed. Morton D. Paley and Michael Phillips, (Oxford: Clarendon Press, 73): 225-30; auth, "Lamb, Charles [and John Milton]," in The Milton Encyclopedia, ed. William B. Hunter et al., (Lewisburg, Pa, and London: Bucknell U Press and Assoc U Press, 79): 198-203; auth, "Teaching Blake's Relief Etching," in Sparks of Fire: Blake in a New Age, ed. James Bogan and Fred Goss, (Richmond, CA: North Atlantic Books, 82): 127-40; ed, Romantic Texts, Romantic Times: Homage to David V. Erdman, Studies in Romanticism, 82; auth, William Blake's Theory of Art, Princeton, NJ: Princeton UP, 82; ed, Romanticism and Contemporary Criticism, Ithaca, NY: Cornell UP, 86; auth, "Blake and the Artistic Machine," in Essential Articles for the Study of Blake, 1970-1984, ed. Nelson Hilton, (Hamden, CT: Shoestring Press, (86): 175-209; ed, A Blake Dictionary, NH: U Press of New England, 88; auth, The Counter Arts Conspiracy: Art and Industry in the Age of Blake, Ithaca, NY: Cornell UP, 92; ed, William Blake: The Early Illuminated Books, London: William Blake Trust/Tate Gallery and Princeton: Princeton U Press, 93. **CONTACT ADDRESS** Dept of Eng, Univ of Rochester, Rochester, NY 14627. **EMAIL** meav@mail.rochester.edu

EBBITT, WILMA ROBB
PERSONAL Born 06/29/1918, Can, m, 1942 **DISCIPLINE** ENGLISH **EDUCATION** Univ Sask, BA, 38, MA, 40; Brown Univ, PhD (English), 43. **CAREER** Instr English, Brown Univ, 43-45; from instr to prof, Univ Chicago, 45-68; lectr, Univ Colo, 68-69; vis prof, Univ Tex, Austin, 73-74; Prof English, PA State Univ, 74-. **MEMBERSHIPS** NCTE; MLA. **RESEARCH** American literature; rhetorical theory; editing. **SELECTED PUBLICATIONS** Auth, Vital Signs--Essays on American Literature and Criticism, Sewanee Rev, Vol 105, 97; Forms of Uncertainty--Essays in Historical Criticism, Sewanee Rev, Vol 101, 93; American Trajectories--Authors And Readings, 1790-1970, Sewanee Rev, Vol 104, 96; The Problem of American Realism--Studies in the Cultural History of a Literary Idea, Sewanee Rev, Vol 102, 94. **CONTACT ADDRESS** Dept of English, Pennsylvania State Univ, Univ Park, University Park, PA 16802.

EBERHART, RICHARD
PERSONAL Born 04/05/1904, Austin, MN, m, 1941, 2 children **DISCIPLINE** ENGLISH **EDUCATION** Dartmouth Col, AB, 26; Cambridge Univ, BA, 29, MA, 33. **CAREER** Tutor to son of King of Siam, 31; master English, St Mark's Sch, 33-41; poet in residence, Univ Wash, 52-53; prof, Univ Conn, 53-54; vis prof and poet in residence, Wheaton Col, 54-55; Gauss lectr and resident fel, Princeton Univ, 55-56; prof, 56-68, class of 25 prof, 68-70, Emer Prof English, Dartmouth Col, 70-, Poet in Residence, 56-, Asst mgr, Butcher Polish Co, 46-52, vpres, 52-58, dir, 58-; founder and pres, Poet's Theatre, Inc, Cambridge, Mass, 50; dir, YADDO, Saratoga Springs, NY, 55-; consult poetry, Libr Cong, 59-61, hon consult Am lett, 63-66, 66-69; mem adv comt, John F Kennedy Mem Ctr, Washington, DC, 59-; Elliston lectr, Univ Cincinnati, 61; lectr, Washington and Lee Univ, Trinity Col, Swarthmore Col and Col William and Mary, 63; Robert Frost mem lect, San Francisco Pub Libr, 64 and Wallace Stevens Prog, Univ Conn, 65; vis prof poetry, Univ Wash, 72 and Univ Fla, 74; adj prof, Columbia Univ, spring 75. **HONORS AND AWARDS** Shelley Awd, Poetry Soc Am, 51; Harriet Monroe Mem Awd, Univ Chicago, 55; Bollingen Prize, Yale Univ, 62; Pulitzer Prize, 66; Nat Bk Awd, 77; president's Medallion, Univ Fla, 77; dlitt, skidmore col, 66, col wooster, 69 and colgate univ, 74; dhl, franklin pierce col, 78. **MEMBERSHIPS** Fel Acad Am Poets; Poetry Soc Am; MLA; Am Inst Arts and Lett; Nat Acad Arts and Sci. **SELECTED PUBLICATIONS** Auth, A Dream, New England Rev Middlebury Series, Vol 15, 93. **CONTACT ADDRESS** Dept of English, Dartmouth Col, Hanover, NH 03755.

EBERLE, GARY M.
PERSONAL Born 06/07/1951, Toledo, OH, m, 1976, 1 child **DISCIPLINE** LITERATURE **EDUCATION** Univ Detroit, BA, 73; MA, 76, ABD, 78. **CAREER** Director to assoc prof, Aquinas Col, 85-. **HONORS AND AWARDS** PrePress Awd for Fiction, 92; Suburban Newspapers of Am Ed Awd, 93; Best Adult Novel, Soc of Midland Authoris, 96; NY Publ Libr, Best Books for Young People Awd, 97. **MEMBERSHIPS** MLA, CG Jung Soc of Western Mich, Soc of Midland Authors. **RESEARCH** Cross-disciplinary studies as they relate to spirituality in the contemporary world. **SELECTED PUBLICATIONS** Auth, The Geography of Nowhere: Finding One's Self in the Postmodern World, Sheed and Ward, Inc, 94; auth, Angel Strings, Coffee House Pr, 95; auth, "The Aytenbite of Inwit," Parabola Magazine, (97); auth, A City of Rain, short stories, Xlibris, 01. **CONTACT ADDRESS** Aquinas Col, Michigan, 1607 Robinson Rd SE, Grand Rapids, MI 49506. **EMAIL** eberlgar@aquinas.edu

EBERWEIN, JANE DONAHUE
PERSONAL Born 09/13/1943, Boston, MA, m, 1971 **DISCIPLINE** AMERICAN LITERATURE AND STUDIES **EDUCATION** Emmanuel Col, AB, 65; Brown Univ, PhD (Am civilization), 69. **CAREER** Asst prof, 69-75, assoc prof, 75-84, prof, English, Oakland Univ, 84-. **MEMBERSHIPS** MLA; Col English Asn; Am Studies Asn; Emily Dickinson Int Soc; Soc for the Study of Am Women Writers; Soc of Early Americanists. **RESEARCH** Colonial American literature; American poetry; Emily Dickinson. **SELECTED PUBLICATIONS** Auth, Early American Poetry: Bradstreet, Taylor, Dwight, Freneau, and Bryant, Madison, Univ Wisc Pr, 78; auth, Dickinson: Strategies of Limitation, Univ Mass Pr (Amherst), 85; auth, "Graphicer for Grace: Emily Dickinson's Calvinist Language," Studies in Puritan American Sprituality 1 (90): 170-201; auth, "Introducing a Religious Poet: The 1890 Poems of Emily Dickinson," Christianity and Literature 39 (90): 241-260; auth, "Civil War and Bradstreet's Monarchies," Early American Literature 26 (91): 119-44; auth, "Harvardine quil: Benjamin Tompson's Poems on King Philip's War," Early American Literature 28 (93): 1-20; auth, An Emily Dickinson Encyclopedia, Greenwood Press (Westport, CT), 98; "Emily Dickinson" entry American National Biography New York: Oxford Univ Press (99): 563-66; auth, "Dickinson's Local, Global, and Cosmic Perspectives," Emily Dickinson Handbook, ed. Gudrun Grabher, Roland Hagenbuchle, and Cristanne Miller, University of Massachusetts Press, (98): 27-43; auth, "Art, natures Ape: The Challenge to the Puritan Poet," Poetics in the Poem: Critical Essays on American Self-Reflexive Poetry, ed. Dorothy Z. Baker, New York: Peter Lang (97): 24-25; **CONTACT ADDRESS** Dept of English, Oakland Univ, Rochester, MI 48309-4401. **EMAIL** jeberwei@oakland.edu

EBLE, CONNIE C.
PERSONAL Born 11/20/1942, New Orleans, LA **DISCIPLINE** LINGUISTICS, ENGLISH **EDUCATION** St Mary's Dominican Col, BA, 64; Univ NCar, MA, 67; PhD, 70. **CAREER** Instr, Univ Ky, 68-71; prof, Univ NCar, 71-. **HONORS AND AWARDS** ACLS Fel, 75; CNDCT Fel, Brazil, 94; IBM Fel, 67; NDEA Fel, 64-67. **MEMBERSHIPS** ADS; SAMLA; LACUS; SCL; LSA; MLA; DSNA; AAUP. **RESEARCH** American slang; college slang; English's of Louisiana; history of American English. **SELECTED PUBLICATIONS** Auth, College Slang 101, Spectacle Lane Pr, 89; auth, "Prolegomenon to the Study of Cajun English," Secol Rev 17 (93): 164-177; ed, American Speech, Duke Univ Pr, 95-; auth, Slang and Sociability: In Group Language Among College Students, Univ NCar Pr, 96. **CONTACT ADDRESS** Ling Dept, Univ of No Carolina, Chapel Hill, PO Box CB3520, Chapel Hill, NC 27599-3520. **EMAIL** cceble@email.unc.edu

EBY, CARL P.
PERSONAL Born 09/23/1964, Pleasanton, CA, m, 1988 **DISCIPLINE** ENGLISH **EDUCATION** Univ Calif, Davis, BA, 87; MA, 91; PhD, 95. **CAREER** Instr and lectr, Univ Calif, Davis, 89-96; lectr, Mich State Univ, 96-98; asst prof, Univ SC, Beaufort, 98-. **HONORS AND AWARDS** Hemingway Found and Soc Fel, 94; John F. Kennedy Library Found, Hemingway Res Grant, 96; Robert J. Stoller Found Awd for Postdoctoral Psychoanalytically Informed Res in the Bio-Behav Scis, Soc Scis, and Humanities, 96. **MEMBERSHIPS** MLA, Hemingway Soc, Am Studies Asn. **RESEARCH** American literature, modernism, psychoanalysis, gender studies. **SELECTED PUBLICATIONS** Auth, " 'Come Back to the Beach Ag'in, David Honey!': Hemingway' Fetishization of Race in the Garden of Eden Manuscripts," The Hemingway Rev, 14.2 (95): 97-117, reprinted in Ernest Hemingway: Seven Decades of Criticism, ed Linda Wagner-Martin, East Lansing: Mich State Univ Press (98): 329-348; auth, "'The Ogre' and the 'Beautiful Thing': Voyeurism, Exhibitionism, and the Image of Woman in the Poetry of William Carlos Williams," The Williams Carlos Williams Rev, 22.2 (96): 29-45; auth, auth, "Rabbit Stew and Blowing Dorothy's Bridges: Love, Aggression, a and Fetishism in For Whom the Bell Tolls," Twentieth Century Lit, 44.2 (98): 204-218; auth, "Ernest Hemingway and the Mirror of Manhood: Fetishism, Transvestism, Homeovestism, and Perverse Meconnaissance," Ariz Quart, 54.3 (98): 27-068; auth, Hemingway's Fetishism: Psychoanalysis and the Mirror of Manhood, Series: Psychoanalysis and Culture, gen ed, Henry Sussman, Albany: State Univ of New York Press (Dec 98); auth, "A Farewell to Arm: Amputation, Castration, and Masculinity in To Have and Have Not," in One Man Alone: Hemingway and To Have and Have Not, Ed, Toni D. Knott, New York: Univ Press of Am (99): 155-172; auth of rev, "Hemingway's Truth and Tribal Politics," in "First Perspectives on True At First Light," The Hemingway Rev, 19.1 (99): 24-27; rev, Reading Desire: In Pursuit of Ernest Hemingway, by Debre Ann Moddelmog, Am Lit (forthcoming). **CONTACT ADDRESS** Dept English, Univ of So Carolina, Beaufort, 801 Carteret St, Beaufort, SC 29902-4601. **EMAIL** carlpeby@gwm.sc.edu

EBY, CECIL DEGROTTE
PERSONAL Born 08/01/1927, Charles Town, WV, m, 1956, 2 children **DISCIPLINE** AMERICAN LITERATURE AND STUDIES **EDUCATION** Shepherd Col, BA, 50; Northwestern Univ, MA, 51; Univ Pa, PhD, 58. **CAREER** From instr to asst prof English, High Point Col, 55-57; from asst prof to assoc prof, Madison Col, Va, 57-60; from asst prof to assoc prof, Washington and Lee Univ, 60-65; assoc prof, 65-68, Prof English, Univ Mich, Ann Arbor, 68-, chmn, Dept English, Univ Miss, 75-76. **HONORS AND AWARDS** Fulbright lectr Am lit, Lit Univ Salamanca, 62-63; Fulbright lectr Am studies, Univ Valencia, 67-68; Rackham res grants, 67, 71 and 77. **RESEARCH** Literature of the First World War; Spanish Civil War in literature; midwestern literature. **SELECTED PUBLICATIONS** Auth, Popular Fiction in England, 1914-1918, Eng Lit Transition 1880-1920, Vol 36, 93; Hemingway the Short Happy Life of Francis Macomber, Explicator, Vol 51, 92; Fitzgerald Babylon Revisited, Explicator, Vol 53, 95. **CONTACT ADDRESS** Dept of English, Univ of Michigan, Ann Arbor, Ann Arbor, MI 48104. **EMAIL** cdeby@umich.edu

ECHERUO, MICHAEL
PERSONAL Born 03/14/1937, Umunumo, Nigeria, m, 1968, 5 children **DISCIPLINE** ENGLISH LITERATURE **EDUCATION** Univ London, BA, 60; Cornell Univ, MA, 63; Cornell Univ, PhD, 65 **CAREER** Prof English, Univ Nigeria, Univ Ibadan, Indiana Univ, Syracuse Univ, 73-; dean Grad School, Univ Ibadan, 78-80; President, IMO State Univ, 81-88; William Safire prof Modern Letters, Syracuse Univ, 90- **HONORS AND AWARDS** Phi Beta Kappa; Phi Kappa Phi, 65; Hon D. Litt, Lincoln Univ, 91; Hon LL. D, Abia State Univ, 97 **MEMBERSHIPS** Modern Lang Assoc Amer; African Studies Assoc; African Lit Assoc **RESEARCH** Shakespeare; African lit & theory. **SELECTED PUBLICATIONS** Comprehensive Dictionary of the Igbo Language, 98; Mortality and Other Poems, 95; The Tempest, Longman, 80 **CONTACT ADDRESS** English Dept, Syracuse Univ, 425 HL, Syracuse, NY 13244. **EMAIL** mecheruo@syr.edu

ECKERSLEY, L. LYNNETTE
PERSONAL Born 09/30/1967, Scranton, OH, p, 1993, 2 children **DISCIPLINE** ENGLISH, LITERATURE **EDUCATION** Lehigh Univ, BA, 89; MA, 91; Claremont Grad Univ, PhD, 98. **CAREER** Teaching Fel, Lehigh Univ, 89-91; res asst, Claremont Grad Univ, 91-93; adj prof, Pasadena Cty Col, 93-95; fac adv to lectr, Bryn Mawr Col, 95-99; asst prof, Bates Col, 99-00. **HONORS AND AWARDS** Master's Fel, Lehigh Univ, 89-91. **MEMBERSHIPS** MLA; ABS; ASECS; ISECS. **RESEARCH** Gay and lesbian studies; eighteenth-century literature; women's studies. **SELECTED PUBLICATIONS** Auth "Gender Theory," in Reader's Guide to Lesbian and Gay Studies, ed. Timothy F. Murphy (Chicago: Fitzroy Dearborn, 99); auth, "The Role of Evelina's 'Worthiest Object' in Frances Burney's Resistance to Eighteenth-Century Gender Ideology," Eighteenth-Century Novel (01; rev, The Cambridge Companion to English Restoration Theatre, ed. Deborah Payne Fisk (Cambridge: Cambridge UP, 00); auth, "James Townley- A Biography," in The New Dictionary of National Biography, ed. H.C.G. Matthew (Ox-

ford: Oxford UP, 01); auth, The Scriblerian, (forthcoming). **CONTACT ADDRESS** 5 Gloucester Hill Rd, New Gloucester, ME 04260-3853. **EMAIL** eckray@aol.com

ECKHARDT, CAROLINE DAVIS
PERSONAL Born 02/27/1942, New York, NY, m, 1964, 4 children **DISCIPLINE** ENGLISH AND COMPARATIVE LITERATURE **EDUCATION** Drew Univ, BA, 63; Ind Univ, Bloomington, MA, 65; Univ Mich, Ann Arbor, PhD (comp lit), 71. **CAREER** Asst prof, 71-76, Assoc Prof English and Comp Lit, PA State Univ, 76-, Dir Comp Lit Prog, 77-, Co-ed, JGE (jour), 74-; fel palaeography, Univ Pa Medieval Inst, 76. **MEMBERSHIPS** MLA; Mediaeval Acad Am; Int Arthurian Soc; Am Comp Lit Asn; Conf Ed Learned Jours. **RESEARCH** Medieval romance; medieval lyric; Chaucer. **SELECTED PUBLICATIONS** Auth, The Meaning of Ermonie in Sir Tristrem, Stud Philol, Vol 93, 96; The Historia Regum Britannie of Geoffrey of Monmouth, Vol 4--Dissemination and Reception in the Later Middle Ages, Speculum J Medieval Stud, Vol 69, 94; Comparative Poetics--An Intercultural Essay on Theories of Literature, World Lit Today, Vol 67, 93; The Meaning of Ermonie in Sir Tristrem, Stud in Philol, Vol 93, 96; The Historia Regum Britannie of Geoffrey of Monmouth, Vol 4--Dissemination and Reception in The Later Middle Ages, Speculum J Medieval Stud, Vol 69, 94. **CONTACT ADDRESS** Dept of English, Pennsylvania State Univ, Univ Park, 434n Burrowes Bldg, University Park, PA 16802-6204.

EDDINGS, DENNIS WAYNE
PERSONAL Born 06/07/1938, Everett, WA, m, 1960, 2 children **DISCIPLINE** AMERICAN AND BRITISH LITERATURE **EDUCATION** Univ Wash, BA, 66, MA, 68; Univ Ore, PhD (English), 73. **CAREER** Instr, 68-71, asst prof, 71-75, Assoc Prof Humanities, Western Ore State Col, 75-82; Prof Humanities, Western Ore Univ, 82-. **MEMBERSHIPS** MLA; Poe Studies Asn; Am Humor Studies Asn; Mach Twins Circle. **RESEARCH** Edgar Allan Poe; Mark Twain. **SELECTED PUBLICATIONS** Auth, Theme and Parody in The Raven," Poe and His Times, The Edgar Allan Poe Soc, 90; auth, "The Frogund The Raven Redux: A Response to John Bryant," Studies in American Humor, New Series, 3.2, 95; auth, Horse Sense in Rongling It," Studies in American Humor, New Series 3.4, 97; auth, The Emergence of Sut Lovingood: An Essay Review, Essays in Arts and Sciences 26, 97; auth, From Innocence to Death: An Approach to Teaching Twain, Mark Twain in The Classroom, Duke; auth, Lew Wallace, The Dictionary of Literary Biography, 19th Century Authors, Gale; ed, The Naiad Voice: Poe as Satiric Hoaxer; A Suggestion on the Unity of Poe's Fiction in The Naiad Voice (in press); **CONTACT ADDRESS** 4560 18th Place S, Salem, OR 97302. **EMAIL** eddingd@woo.edu

EDE, LISA
PERSONAL Born 09/09/1947, Findlay, OH, m, 1974 **DISCIPLINE** RHETORIC, COMPOSITION HISTORY **EDUCATION** Ohio State Univ, BS, 69; Univ Wisc, MA, 70; Ohio State Univ, PhD, 75 **CAREER** Engl, Oregon St Univ. **HONORS AND AWARDS** CCCC Braddock Awd, 85; MLA Shaughnessy Awd, 85; National Writing Center Awd for Outstanding Scholarshp, 90; OSU College of Liberal Arts Excellence Awd, 93; OSU Alumni Association Distinguished Prof Awd 96. **SELECTED PUBLICATIONS** Auth, Edider, On Writing Research: CCCC Braddock Award Essays, 99; auth, Work in Progress: A Guide to Academic Writing & Revising, 5th ed., 00. **CONTACT ADDRESS** Oregon State Univ, Corvallis, OR 97331-4501. **EMAIL** lede@orst.edu

EDELSTEIN, ARTHUR
PERSONAL Born New York, NY **DISCIPLINE** AMERICAN LITERATURE, AMERICAN STUDIES **EDUCATION** Brooklyn Col, BA, 56; Stanford Univ, MA, 63, PhD (English), 77. **CAREER** Lectr English, Hunter Col, City Univ NY, 63-66; asst prof English and Am studies, Brandeis Univ, 66-76; assoc prof English, Col William and Mary, 77-78; Adj Prof English, Brandeis Univ, 79-, Dir writing prog, Brandeis Univ, 71-74; Nat Endowment for Humanities fel Am social hist, 73-74; mem adv comt to bd trustees humanities, Suffolk Univ, Boston, 78-79; vis prof English, Wellesley Col, fall, 81; Consult, Mass Found Humanities and Public Policy, 80-. **MEMBERSHIPS** MLA. **RESEARCH** American realist fiction; American working class history; contemporary world literature. **SELECTED PUBLICATIONS** Auth, Weber, Max and the Jewish Question--A Study of the Social Outlook of His Sociology, Am Hist Rev, Vol 99, 94. **CONTACT ADDRESS** 2 Dale St, Wellesley, MA 02181.

EDEN, KATHY
DISCIPLINE HISTORY OF RHETORICAL AND POETIC THEORY IN ANTIQUITY **EDUCATION** Smith, BA, 74; Stanford, PhD, 80. **CAREER** English and Lit, Columbia Univ **SELECTED PUBLICATIONS** Auth, Poetic and Legal Fiction in The Aristotelian Tradition, Princeton, 86; Hermeneutics and the Rhetorical Tradition: Chapters in the Ancient Legacy and its Humanist Reception, New Haven, 97. **CONTACT ADDRESS** Columbia Univ, 2960 Broadway, New York, NY 10027-6902.

EDEN, MELISSA
PERSONAL Born 11/07/1960, Burlington, VT, m, 1991, 2 children **DISCIPLINE** 18TH AND 19TH CENTURY LITERATURE, WOMEN'S LITERATURE **EDUCATION** Middlebury Col, AB; Univ VA, MA, PhD. **CAREER** Asst prof, Hanover Col, 97. **HONORS AND AWARDS** Phi Beta Kappa, 82. **MEMBERSHIPS** Nineteenth Century Studies Assoc. **SELECTED PUBLICATIONS** Auth, Studies in Afro-Am Lit: An Annual Annotated Bibliography, 1986, Callaloo 10, 86. **CONTACT ADDRESS** Hanover Col, Hanover, IN 47243. **EMAIL** edenm@hanover.edu

EDER, DORIS LEONORA
PERSONAL Born 05/12/1936, Teplitz, Czechoslovakia, m, 1961 **DISCIPLINE** MODERN AND CONTEMPORARY LITERATURE **EDUCATION** Barnard Col, BA, 61; Hunter Col, MA, 65, PhD (English and comp lit), 68. **CAREER** From instr to asst prof English, Ohio State Univ, 66-70; from asst prof to assoc prof, Univ Rochester, 70-77; dean fac, Schenectady County Community Col, 77-78; dean prog develop and grad studies, Keene State Col, 78-82; Dean, Sch Arts and Sci, Univ New Haven, 82-. **MEMBERSHIPS** MLA; AAUP; Am Asn Higher Educ; Am Asn Univ Women. **SELECTED PUBLICATIONS** Auth, In Pursuit of the Phd, Virg Quart Rev, Vol 69, 93. **CONTACT ADDRESS** Sch of Arts and Sci, Univ of New Haven, New Haven, CT 06516.

EDGERTON, GARY R.
PERSONAL Born 07/21/1952, Pittsfield, MA, m, 1983, 2 children **DISCIPLINE** COMMUNICATION ; THEATRE ARTS **EDUCATION** Univ of London, BA, 74; Univ of Mass, MA, 79, PhD, 81. **CAREER** From tchg asst to assoc, Univ of Mass, 76-80; from instr to asst prof, Bowling Green State Univ, 80-85; from assoc prof and ch to prof and ch, Goucher Col, 85-94; vis prof, Univ of Exeter, 90-91; prof and ch, Old Dominion Univ, 94- . **HONORS AND AWARDS** Outstanding Tchr in Commun, 82-83; Goucher Col Distinguished Tchg Awd in the Hum, 89; Phi Kappa Phi Nat Hon Soc for Special Distinction in Scholar and Tchg, 96. **MEMBERSHIPS** Am Culture Asn; Asn for Commun Admin; Asn for Educ in Journalism and Mass Commun; Broadcast Educ Asn; Internat Commun Asn; Internat Asn for Media and Hist; Nat Commun Asn; Popular Culture Asn; Univ Film and Video Asn; Soc for Cinema Studies. **RESEARCH** Media History; Critical Analysis of Television; Film Theory and Criticism, and Theories and Issues in Cultural Studies; Qualitative Methods; The Documentary Tradition; Electronic Journalism; Mass Media and the Political Process; Mass Media and Social Impact; Making Sense of Popular Culture, and Art, Media, and Postmodernist Culture. **SELECTED PUBLICATIONS** Coauth, Redesigning Pocahontas: Disney, the White Man's Indian, and the Marketing of Dreams, Jour of Popular Film and Television 24.2, 96; In the Eye of the Beholder: Critical Perspectives in Popular Film and Television, 97; auth, Ken Burn's America: Style, Authorship, and Cultural Memory, Jour of Popular Film and Television 21.2, 93; Revisiting the Recordings of Wars Past: Remembering the Documentary Trilogy of John Huston, Reflections in a Male Eye: John Huston and the American Experience, ed G. Studlar and D. Desser, 93; A Breed Apart: Hollywood, Racial Stereotyping, and the Promise of Revisionism in The Last of the Mohicans, Jour of Am Culture 17.2, 94; Ken Burns -- A Conversation with Public Television's Resident Historian, Jour of Am Culture 18.1, 95; Quelling the Oxygen of Publicity: British Broadcasting and the Troubles During the Thatcher Years, Jour of Popular Culture 30.1, 96; Digital Color Imaging and the Colorization Controversy: Culture, Technology, and the Popular as Lightning Rod, Technohistory: Using the History of American Technology in Interdisciplinary Research, ed C. Hables Gray, 96; Ken Burn's The Civil War: Public Television, Popular History, and the Academy, An American Mosaic: Rethinking American Culture Studies, ed M. Fishwick, 97; guest ed, Spec Issue on Ethical Issues in Popular Film and Television, Jour of Popular Film and Television 21.3, 93; Spec Issue on Television as Historian, Film & Hist: An Interdisciplinary Jour of Film and Television Studies 29.1-4, forthcoming. **CONTACT ADDRESS** Dept of Communication and Theatre Arts, Old Dominion Univ, 4100 Powhatan Ave, Norfolk, VA 23529-0087. **EMAIL** Gedgerto@ODU.EDU

EDGEWORTH, ROBERT J.
PERSONAL Born 01/02/1947, Chicago, IL, m, 2000, 2 children **DISCIPLINE** CLASSICS **EDUCATION** Loyola Univ, AB, 67; Univ Mich, MA, 68; PhD, 74. **CAREER** Lecturing Fel, Australian Nat Univ, 74-80; Lecturer, San Diego State Univ, 81; Asst Prof to Prof, La State Univ, 81-. **MEMBERSHIPS** Am Philol Asn, Classical Asn of the Middle West and South, La Classical Asn, Vergilian Soc. **RESEARCH** The Epic; Ancient color terminology. **SELECTED PUBLICATIONS** Auth, the colors of the Aeneid, Peter Lang, 92. **CONTACT ADDRESS** Dept For Lang, La State Univ, Baton Rouge, LA 70803-0104.

EDMISTON, WILLIAM F.
PERSONAL Born 08/30/1948, Lock Haven, PA **DISCIPLINE** LITERATURE, CLASSICS **EDUCATION** Penn State Univ, BA, 70; Ind Univ, MA, 72; PhD, 78. **CAREER** Asst prof to assoc prof to prof to dept chmn, Univ SCar, 79-. **HONORS AND AWARDS** Mortar Bd Excellence in Teaching Awd. **MEMBERSHIPS** AATF; ASECS; MLA. **RESEARCH** 18th-century French fiction; gender and sexuality. **SELECTED PUBLICATIONS** Auth, "Sacrifice and Innocence in La Religieuse," Diderot Studies 19 (78): 67-84; auth, "Narrative Voice and Cognitive Privilege in Diderot's La Religieuse," Fr For 10 (85): 133-144; auth, Diderot and the Family: a Conflict of Nature and Law, Anma Libri, 85; auth, "Focalization and the First-Person Narrator: A Revision of the Theory," Poet Today 10 (89): 729-744; auth, "Nature, Sodomy, and Semantics in Sade's La Philosophie Dans le Boudoir," Studies in Eighteenth-Century Cult 24 (95): 121-36; auth, Hindsight and Insight: Focalization in Four Eighteenth-Century French Novels, Penn State UP, 91; co-auth, La France Contemporaine: A Third-year Textbook on Contemporary French Civilization, Accompanied by an Instructor's Manual, Harcourt Brace Col Pub, 93, 2nd ed, 97; auth, "Shifting Ground: Sade, Same-Sex Desire, and the One-, Two- and Three-Sex Models," in Illicit Sex: Identity Politics in Early Modern Culture, eds. Thomas DiPiero, Pat Gill (Athens and London: Univ Ga Pr, 97): 143-60; auth, "Making Connections: Sexuality as Satire in Voltaire's Philosophical Tales," in Voltaire et Ses Combats, eds. Ulla Kolving, Christiane Mervaud (Oxford: Voltaire Found, 97): 189-97; auth, "Plots, Patterns, and Challenges to Gender Ideology in Gomez and Sade," Fr Rev 73 (00): 463-74. **CONTACT ADDRESS** Foreign Lang Dept, Univ of So Carolina, Columbia, Welsh Bldg Fr, Columbia, SC 29208-0001. **EMAIL** edmistonw@sc.edu

EDMUNDS, LOWELL
PERSONAL Born 10/11/1938, Franklin, NH, m, 1966, 2 children **DISCIPLINE** CLASSICS **EDUCATION** Harvard, PhD, 70. **CAREER** Teaching asst, Classics, Berkeley, 63-64; teaching fel, Classics, Harvard, 67-69; teaching fel, Harvard summer school, 68, 69; instr Classics, Wheaton Col, 69-70; tutor, St John's Col, Santa Fe, NM, summers 70, 71; asst prof Classics, Harvard, 70-75; asst prof Classics, Harvard Univ Extension, 72-73; assoc prof Classics, Harvard, 75-78; assoc prof Classics, Harvard Univ Exrension, 76-80; assoc prof Classics, Boston Col, 78-83; ed, Comparative Civilizations Bul, 79-82; chmn, Dept Classical Studies, Boston Col, 83; prof Classics and chmn, Johns Hopkins Univ, 83-88; member, fac ed bd, Johns Hopkins Univ Press, 83-86; member ed bd, Am J of Philol, 83-87; member, subcommittee on the Thesaurus Linguae Graecae of the Res Comm of the Am Philol Asn, 86-; chmn, Ed Adv Comm, Perseus: A New Curriculum on Ancient Greek Civilization, Harvard based, 86-92; first vice pres, Baltimore Soc of the Archaeological Inst of Am, 87-88; member, ed bd, Lexis (Univ Venice), 87-; co-dir, Coppin-Hopkins Prog in the Baltimore City Schools, 87-89; prof Classics, Rutgers Univ, 88-, dir, graduate prog in Classics, 88-90, chair, 90-96, acting dir, graduate prog in Classics, 94-96; professore a contratto, Universita degli Studi di Venezia, April 90; prof a contratto, Universita degli Studi di Trento, Nov 93; vis prof, Princeton Univ, spring 95; asst ed, Classical World, 97-00. **HONORS AND AWARDS** Pushcart Prize for "Choosing Your Names," 93-94. **MEMBERSHIPS** Am Philol Asn; Int Soc for Folk Narrative Res. **RESEARCH** Greek lit; Greek mythology; Roman lit. **SELECTED PUBLICATIONS** Auth, Choosing Your Names, Raritan 11 3, winter 92, under pseudonym, Kothar wa-Khasis, reprinted in The 1993-1994 Pushcart Prize XVIII: Best of the Small Presses; Intertextuality Today, Lexis 13, 95; Theatrical Space and Historical Place in Sophocles' Oedipus at Colonus, Rowman and Littlefield, 96; Poet, Public, and Performance: Essays in Ancient Greek Literature and Literary History, ed with Robert Wallace, The Johns Hopkins Univ Press, 97; Myth in Homer, in New Companion to Homer, ed by Barry Powell and Ian Morris, Brill, April 97; The Silver Bullet: The Martini in American Civilization, Contributions in Am Studies 52, Greenwood Press, 81, 2nd ed, titled Martini Straight Up: The Classic American Cocktail, Johns Hopkins Univ Press, 98. **CONTACT ADDRESS** 440 Grant Ave, Highland Park, NJ 08904. **EMAIL** edmunds@rci.rutgers.edu

EDWARDS, ANTHONY S. G.
PERSONAL Born 07/04/1942, Scarborough, England, m, 1975, 2 children **DISCIPLINE** MEDIEVAL; EARLY RENAISSANCE LITERATURE **EDUCATION** Univ Reading, BA; Univ McMaster, MA; Univ London, PhD. **CAREER** Vis prof, Univ Washington, 88; prof., Univ of Victoria. **HONORS AND AWARDS** Can Coun Leave fel, 76-77; Leave fel, SSHRCC, 83-84; Guggenheim fel, 88-89. **MEMBERSHIPS** Mem, Chaucer Variorum; Yale Edition of the Works of St. Thomas More. **RESEARCH** Bibliography and textual criticism. **SELECTED PUBLICATIONS** Auth, John Skelton: the Critical Heritage, Routledge, 81; auth, Stephen Hawes, Twayne, 83; coauth, An Index of Printed Middle English Prose, Garland, 85; contrib, Chaucerian Religious Tales, ed C.D. Benson and E. Robertson, Cambridge 90; contib, Medieval Lietrature: Text and Interpretation, ed T.W. Machon, Binghamton, 91; contrib, The Transmission of Late Medieval Religious Texts in Late Medieval England, ed A.J. Minnis, Cambridge, 94; contib, readings in Middle English Romance, ed C. Meale , Cambridge, 94. **CONTACT ADDRESS** Dept of English, Univ of Victoria, PO Box 3070, Victoria, BC, Canada V8W 3W1.

EDWARDS, BRENT HAYES
PERSONAL Born 01/24/1968, IL, m, 1998 **DISCIPLINE** ENGLISH **EDUCATION** Yale Univ, BA, 90; Columbia Univ, MA, 92; PhD, 97. **CAREER** Asst Prof, Rutger Univ, 97-. **HONORS AND AWARDS** Phi Beta Kappa. **MEMBERSHIPS** MLA, ASA. **RESEARCH** 20th-Century American literature, African-American literature, Francophone African and Caribbean literature. **SELECTED PUBLICATIONS** Auth, "Ear Work, Cock Drill," Hambone 12 (95): 253-261; Auth, "The Race for Space: Sun Ra's Poetry," Hambone 14 (99): 177-200; auth "The Ethics of Surrealism," Transition 78 (99): 84-135; auth, "Abecedarium (Selections)," Callaloo 22.4 (00): 775-783; ed, "An Interview with Brent Hayes Edwards," by Charles Rowell, Callaloo 22.4 (00): 784-797; auth, "Middle Ear Recitation," Callaloo 22.4 (00): 771-774; auth, "Three Ways to Translate the Harlem Renaissance," in The Harlem Renaissance: Temples for Tomorrow (Bloomington: Ind Univ Pr, 00); auth, Rethinking Black Marxism, Duke Univ Pr (Bloomington, IN), 00; auth, The Practice of Diaspora: Black Internationalism in Translation, Harvard Univ Pr (Cambridge). **CONTACT ADDRESS** Dept English, Rutgers, The State Univ of New Jersey, New Brunswick, 510 George St, Murray Hall, New Brunswick, NJ 08901. **EMAIL** bedwards@rci.rutgers.edu

EDWARDS, CLARK
DISCIPLINE COMMUNICATION STUDIES **EDUCATION** Southern IL Univ, BS, 66; Univ MO, MA, 71; Univ NM, PhD, 89. **CAREER** Assoc prof commun, Duquesne Univ. **SELECTED PUBLICATIONS** Auth, articles in Presidential Studies Quarterly; Polit Sci; Polit; Jour Mediated Commun; News Comput Jour; publ(s) on broadcast news writing and style. **CONTACT ADDRESS** Dept of Commun, Duquesne Univ, Forbes Ave, PO Box 600, Pittsburgh, PA 15282.

EDWARDS, CLIFFORD DUANE
PERSONAL Born 01/20/1934, Atwood, KS, m, 1954, 3 children **DISCIPLINE** ENGLISH **EDUCATION** Ft Hays Kans State Col, AB, 58; Univ Mich, MA, 59, EdD, 63. **CAREER** Lectr English, Univ Mich, 63; from asst prof to assoc prof, Ft Hays Kans State Col, 63-69; prof & head, Dept English, Univ Wis-Platteville, 69-74; prof Eng & dir compos, Ft Hays State Univ, 74-83; Danforth assoc, 66-78; dir, NDEA Inst English, 68; English Inst Educ Prof Develop grant, US Off Educ, 69, chmn Eng, Ft. Hays State Univ, 83-. **MEMBERSHIPS** NCTE. **RESEARCH** American literature; literary criticism; composition. **SELECTED PUBLICATIONS** Auth, Arnold and Pater discuss Dylan Thomas: A conversation in limbo, LIT, 59; art, Existential absurdity on the campus, Christianity Today, 5/67; auth, Conrad Richter's Ohio Trilogy, Mouton, 70; art, Left brain and the teaching of writing, Improving Instr, 9/77. **CONTACT ADDRESS** Dept of English, Fort Hays State Univ, 600 Park St, Hays, KS 67601-4009.

EDWARDS, DON R.
PERSONAL Born 05/26/1955, Lafayette, IN **DISCIPLINE** CLASSICS **EDUCATION** St. John's Col, BA, 78; Johns Hopkins, MS, 96; Brown Univ, PhD, 84. **CAREER** Author **RESEARCH** Philosophy **CONTACT ADDRESS** 218 East Del Ray Ave, Alexandria, VA 22301.

EDWARDS, EMILY D.
DISCIPLINE BROADCASTING, CINEMA **EDUCATION** Florence State Univ, BA, 74; Univ London, Postbaccalaureate stud, 74; Univ TN, Knoxville, MA, 77, PhD, 84. **CAREER** Grad tchg asst, 74-77, 81-82, PR mgr, dept Speech and Theatre, 79-81, instr, Univ TN, Knoxville, 80-81; dir Broadcast Sequence, dept Commun Stud, Univ AL, Birmingham, 83-87; asst prof, 87-, dir Graduate Stud, Univ NC, Greensboro, 92-95; nat adv bd, Birmingham Int Educ Film Festival, 87-; assoc ed, Southern Speech Commun J, 88-89. **HONORS AND AWARDS** Alpha Gamda Delta; Sigma Tau Delta; acad award, dept Art, 74; acad award, dept Speech and Drama, 74; Bickel Scholar, 83; Prog Dir Awd, BIEFF, 86-87; Spec Achievement Awd, Smokey Mt Film Festival, 92; New Works Proj Scriptwriting Awd, Charolotte Theatre, 94; Bronze Apple Awd, Nat Educ Media Network, 97. **MEMBERSHIPS** Univ Film and Video Asn; Asn for Edu in Jour and Mass Commun; Broadcast Edu Asn; Int Commun Asn; ITVA Int TV Asn Society of Prof Journalists; Sigma Delta Chi; Southern Sociol Asn; Speech Commun Asn; Southern Speech Commun Asn. **SELECTED PUBLICATIONS** Auth, No more slack jaws before the tube: a case for tech literacy, Speech Asn Minn J, 15, 1-13, 88; Ecstasy of Horrible Expectation: Correlations between Sensation-seeking and interest in horror movies, in, B. Austin, ed, Current Research In Film, Vol 5, Ablex Press, 91; Love Stinks: The Mean World of Love and Sex in Popular Music of the1980s, in, J. Epstein, ed, Teenagers and Their Music, Garland Press, 94; coauth, Mass Media Images in Popular Music, Popular Mus and Soc, 9, 4, 84; Children's construction of fantasy stories, Sex Roles, 18, 88; Life's Soundtracks: Correlations Between Music Subcultures and Listener Belief Systems, Southern Speech Commun J, 89; The Incubus in Experience, Folklore and Film, Southern Folklore, 52, 96. **CONTACT ADDRESS** Univ of No Carolina, Greensboro, Greensboro, NC 27412-5001.

EDWARDS, GRACE TONEY
DISCIPLINE APPALACHIAN LITERATURE & FOLKLORE, AMERICAN LITERATURE, COMPOSITION **EDUCATION** Appalachian State Univ, BS, MA; Univ VA, PhD. **CAREER** Prof, dir, Appalachian Reg Stud Ctr, ch, Appalachian Stud prog, Radford Univ. **SELECTED PUBLICATIONS** Auth, Emma Belle Miles: Feminist Crusader in Appalachia, in the anthology Appalachia Inside Out; Our Mother's Voices: Narratives of Generational Transformation, in the J of Appalachian Stud. **CONTACT ADDRESS** Radford Univ, Radford, VA 24142. **EMAIL** gedwards@runet.edu

EDWARDS, JANIS
DISCIPLINE MEDIA CRITICISM **EDUCATION** PhD. **CAREER** Asst prof, Univ Albany, SUNY; asst prof, Western Ill Univ, 00-. **SELECTED PUBLICATIONS** Auth, Womanhouse: Making the Personal Story Political in Visual Form, Women & Lang, 96; Coauth, The Visual Ideograph: The Iwo Jima Image in Editorial Cartoons, Quart Jour Speech, 97; Political Cartoons in the 1988 Presidential Campaign: Image, Metaphor, and narrative, Garland Press, 97. **CONTACT ADDRESS** Dept of Commun, Western Illinois Univ, 304c Mem Hall, Macomb, IL 61455-1390.

EDWARDS, LEE R.
PERSONAL Born 04/30/1942, Brooklyn, NY, d, 1964, 1 child **DISCIPLINE** ENGLISH LITERATURE **EDUCATION** Swarthmore Col, BA, 62; Univ CA, Berkeley, MA, 65; Univ CA, San Diego, PhD, 69. **CAREER** Asst prof, 67-75, assoc prof, 75-80, prof eng & Am lit, Univ MA, Amherst, 80, Ed, Mass Rev, 74-80; Nat Endowment for Humanities independent study & res fel, 78; Dean, col umanities and Fine Arts, 91. **HONORS AND AWARDS** Phi Beta Kappa; Council of col of arts and sci. **MEMBERSHIPS** MLA; Women's Caucus Mod Lang Asn. **RESEARCH** Mod fiction; women's studies. **SELECTED PUBLICATIONS** Contribr, Twentieth Century Interpretations of Moll Flanders, Prentice-Hall, 70; ed, Charles Brockden Brown's Alcuin, Grossman, 71; co-ed, Woman: An Issue, Little, 72; auth, Women, Energy and Middlemarch, Mass Rev, winter-spring 72; American Voices, American Women, Avon, 73; co-ed, An Authority of Experience: Essays in Feminist Criticism, Univ Mass, 77;Psyche as Hero: Female Heroism and Fictional Form, Wesleyan Univ Press, 84. **CONTACT ADDRESS** Dean's Office CHFA South Col, Univ of Massachusetts, Amherst, Amherst, MA 01003-0002. **EMAIL** lee.edwards@cas.umass.edu

EDWARDS, MARY LOUISE
PERSONAL Born 01/25/1946, Portland, ME, m, 1981, 1 child **DISCIPLINE** COMMUNICATION SCIENCES AND DISORDERS **EDUCATION** Stanford Univ, 79. **CAREER** Prof, Syracuse Univ. **HONORS AND AWARDS** Am Speech-Lang-Hearing Asn; Linguistic Soc of Am. **RESEARCH** The nature, develop and remediation of disordered phonology in children; clinical applications of phonological theory; long-range outcomes for phonologically disordered preschoolers; stuttering and disorded phonology. **SELECTED PUBLICATIONS** Auth, "Children's phonology disorders: Pathways and Patterns," Phonological process analysis, in eds, E.J. Williams and J. Langsam Rockville, MD: American Speech-Lang-Hearing Asn, (94); auth, Phonogroup: A Practical Guide for Enhancing Phonological Remediation, Thinking Publications, (Eau Claire, WI), 94; auth, "Stuttering: Proceedings of the First World Congress on Fluency Disorders," Childhood stuttering and disordered phonology, in C.W. Starkweather and H.F.M. Peters, Nijmegen, Nederland: Univ Press, (95); auth, "Human communication and its disorders, vol. IV, Development phonology, in H. Wintz, ed, Timonium, MD: York Press (95); auth, "Proceedings of the UBC International Conference on Phonological Acquision, Word position effects in the product of fricatives, in Bernhardt, J. Gilbert, & D. Ingram eds, Somerville, MA: Cascadilla Press, (96); auth, Perspectives in applied phonology, Aspen Publishers, Inc (Gaithersburg, MD), 97; auth, "Perspectives in applied phonology, Historical Overview of Clincal Phonology, Aspen Publishers, Inc. (Gaithersburg, MD), 97; auth, Stuttering and related disorders of fluency, Treating children who exhibit co-occurring stuttering and disordered phonology, in R. Curlee, Thieme Medical Publishers, Inc. (New York), 99; auth, Concise Encyclopedia of Educational Linguistics, Phonology in language acquisition, in B. Spolsky, 99. **CONTACT ADDRESS** Syracuse Univ, Syracuse, NY 13244-2280. **EMAIL** mledward@syr.edu

EDWARDS, MARY-JANE
DISCIPLINE ENGLISH **EDUCATION** Univ Toronto, BA, 60, PhD, 69; Queen's Univ, MA, 63. **CAREER** Lectr, Acadia Univ, 61-63; instr, Univ BC, 66-69; asst prof, 70-73, assoc prof, 73-82, Prof, Carleton Univ, 82-. **MEMBERSHIPS** Bibliog Soc Can; Shastri Indo-Can Inst. **SELECTED PUBLICATIONS** Auth, The Evolution of Canadian Literature in Engish: Beginnings to 1867, 73; auth, The Evolution of Canadian Literature in English : 1867-1914, 73; auth, Canadian Literature in the 70's, 80. **CONTACT ADDRESS** Dept of English, Carleton Univ, 1125 Colonel By Dr, 1812 Dunton Tower, Ottawa, ON, Canada K1S 5B6. **EMAIL** mary_jane_edwards@carleton.ca

EGAN, JAMES
PERSONAL Born 10/09/1945, Cleveland, OH, m **DISCIPLINE** ENGLISH **EDUCATION** St Joseph's Col, BA, 67; Univ Notre Dame, MA, 69; PhD, 71. **CAREER** From Asst Prof to Prof, Univ Akron, 71-. **HONORS AND AWARDS** Woodrow Wilson Fel, 70-71; Grants-in-Aid, Newberry Libr, 72, 77; Res Grant-in-Aid APS, 76; Fac Summer Res Fel, Univ Akron, 77. **MEMBERSHIPS** Milton Soc. **RESEARCH** John Milton, Andrew Marvell, Renaissance prose, fantasy and science fiction, Gothic literature, satire. **SELECTED PUBLICATIONS** Auth, "'Romance of a Darksome Type': Versions of the Fantastic in the Novels of Joyce Carol Oates," Studies of Weird Fiction 7 (90): 12-21; auth, "Proto-Fictive Structures in Joseph Hall's 'Contemplations'," WEVSARA: Selected Papers of the Shakespeare and Renaissance Asn of WVa 16 (93): 15-32; auth, "Creator-Critic: Aesthetic Subtexts in Milton's Antiprelatical and Regicide Pamphlets," Milton Studies 30 (93): 45-66; auth, "The Rhetoric of Animadversion in Andrew Marvell's Pamphlets," WEVSARA: Selected Papers of the Shakespeare and Renaissance Asn of WVa 17 (94): 10-27; auth, "Andrew Marvell Refashions the Marprelate Tradition: An Aesthetic Reading of 'The Rehearsal Transpos'd'," Prose Studies 18 (95): 135-158; auth, "Milton's Aesthetic of Plainness 1659-1673," The Seventeenth Century 12 (97): 57-83; auth, "Poetical Historiography: Milton's 'History of Britain' as a Literary Text," WEVSARA: Selected Papers of the Shakespeare and Renaissance Asn of WVa 21 (98): 1-20. **CONTACT ADDRESS** Dept English, Univ of Akron, 302 Buchtel Mall, Akron, OH 44325-0001. **EMAIL** ejames@uakron.edu

EGAN, MARY JOAN
PERSONAL Born 06/23/1932, Tuscaloosa, AL, m, 1974 **DISCIPLINE** ENGLISH LITERATURE, IRISH STUDIES **EDUCATION** Univ Ala, BA, 52; Cath Univ Am, MA, 58, PhD (English and philos), 69. **CAREER** Instr English, Univ Md, 66-69; asst prof, Centenary Col La, 69-72; asst prof, 72-80, Assoc Prof English, Slippery Rock State Col, 80-, Instr English, Wiley Col, 69-70. **MEMBERSHIPS** Wallace Stevens Soc; Irish Am Cult Inst. **RESEARCH** Modern poetry; myth and archetype. **SELECTED PUBLICATIONS** Auth, Stevens, Wallace Homunculus et la Belle Etoile--An Echo of Goethe Faust, Eng Lang Notes, Vol 31, 93. **CONTACT ADDRESS** Dept of English, Slippery Rock Univ of Pennsylvania, Slippery Rock, PA 16057.

EGAN, RORY BERNARD
PERSONAL Born 02/06/1942, Sutton West, ON, Canada, m, 1970 **DISCIPLINE** CLASSICS **EDUCATION** Assumption Univ, Windsor, BA, 63; Univ Western Ont, MA, 65; Univ Southern Calif, PhD (classics), 71. **CAREER** Asst prof classics, Univ Southern Calif, 70-77; Assoc Prof Classics and Dept Head, Univ Man, 77-. **MEMBERSHIPS** Am Class League; Am Inst Archaeol; Am Philol Asn; Class Asn Can; Philol Asn Pac Coast. **RESEARCH** Classical mythology; Greek literature; Greek language. **SELECTED PUBLICATIONS** Auth, Stesichorus and Helen, Dallan and Columba, Class World, Vol 87, 93; Corydon Winning Words in Eclogue 7, Phoenix J Class Assn Can, Vol 50, 96. **CONTACT ADDRESS** Dept of Classics, Univ of Manitoba, Winnipeg, MB, Canada R3T 2N2. **EMAIL** regan@ms.umanitoba.ca

EGGERT, KATHERINE
DISCIPLINE ENGLISH LITERATURE **EDUCATION** Rice Univ, BA, 84; Univ Calif at Berkeley, MA, 86; PhD, 91. **CAREER** Asst prof to assoc prof, Univ of Colo at Boulder, 91-. **HONORS AND AWARDS** Mellon Fel; NEH Fel. **MEMBERSHIPS** MLA, Renaissance Soc of Am, Spense Soc, Shakespeare Asn, Soc for the Study of Early Modern Women. **RESEARCH** 16th- and 17th-century English literature, cultural studies, feminist studies. **SELECTED PUBLICATIONS** Auth, Showing Like a Queen: Female Authority and Literary Experiment in Spense, Shakespeare, and Milton, Univ of Pa Press, 00. **CONTACT ADDRESS** Dept English, Univ of Colorado, Boulder, PO Box 226, Boulder, CO 80309-0226. **EMAIL** katherine.eggert@colorado.edu

EGGINTON, WILLIAM
PERSONAL Born 03/24/1969, Syracuse, NY, m, 1999 **DISCIPLINE** ENGLISH, COMPOSITION, LITERATURE, SPANISH **EDUCATION** Dartmouth Univ, AB, 91; Univ Minn, MA, 94; Stanford Univ, AM, 96; PhD, 99. **CAREER** Asst prof, SUNY Buffalo, 99-. **HONORS AND AWARDS** Stanford Hum Cent Fel, 96-97; Bradley Rubidge Mem Dis Prize, Stan Univ. **MEMBERSHIPS** MLA; SLS; IAPL. **RESEARCH** European literary history; continental philosophy; psychoanalysis. **SELECTED PUBLICATIONS** Auth, "Gracidn and the Emergence of the Modern Subject," Hisp Issue (97); auth, "On Relativism, Rights and Differends, or, Ethics and the American Holocaust," Qui Parle (95); auth, "A Wrinkle in Historical Time," Substance (96); auth, "An Epistemology of the Stage: Subjectivity and Theatricality in Early Modern Spain," New Lit Hist (96); auth, "From the End of History to the Death of Man," Annalecta Husserlina (96); auth, "On Dante, Hyper spheres, and the Curvature of the Medieval Cosmos," J Hist Ideas (99); auth, "Psychoanalysis and the Comedia: Skepticism and the Paternal Function in La vida es sueno," Bullit Comediantes (00); auth, Borges: The Passion of an Endless Quote, SUNY P, forthcoming; auth, How the World Became a Stage, SUNY, forthcom-

ing; auth, The Pragmatic Turn in Philosophy, SUNY P, forthcoming. **CONTACT ADDRESS** Eng Dept., SUNY, Buffalo, 910 Clemens, Buffalo, NY 14260-4620. **EMAIL** egginton@ascu.buffalo.edu

EHRET, TERRY
PERSONAL Born 11/12/1955, San Francisco, CA, m, 1979, 3 children **DISCIPLINE** ENGLISH **EDUCATION** Stanford Univ, BA, 77; Chapman Col, Credential, 80; San Francisco State Univ, MA, 84. **CAREER** Eng Dept Chair/Art History instr, Notre Dame High School, 84-90; English instr, Santa Rosa Junior Col 91-; English and Creative Writing Lecturer, Sonoma State Univ, 93-; Creative Writing Lecturer, San Francisco State Univ, 96-. **HONORS AND AWARDS** National Poetry Series, 92; California Commonwealth Book Awd for Poetry. 93; Pablo Neruda Poetry Prize, 95; SRJC Fac Recognition Awd, 92; Poets and Writers Writers-on-site Residency, 97; Notre Dame High School Woman of Vision Awd, 95. **MEMBERSHIPS** AFA (All Faculty Assoc at SRJC); Academy of Amer Poets; Associated Writing Programs; Calif Poets in the Sch. **RESEARCH** Pre-Homeric Troy; Matristic Cultures of Anatolia and Old Europe; Modernist movements in Literature and Visual Arts Pablo Picasso. **SELECTED PUBLICATIONS** Auth, "Suspensions," with Susan Herron Sibbet and Steve Gilmartin, White Mountain Press, 90; auth, "Lost Body," National Poetry Series Winner, Copper Canyon Press, 93; auth, "Travel/How We Go on Living," Protean Press, 95; auth, "The Thought she might Picasso Portraits.' Nimrod Awards issue, 95. **CONTACT ADDRESS** Dept English, Santa Rosa Junior Col, 1501 Mendocino Ave, Santa Rosa, CA 95401-4332. **EMAIL** tehret99@msn.com

EHRSTINE, JOHN
DISCIPLINE LITERATURE **EDUCATION** Wayne State Univ, PhD. **CAREER** Prof, Washington State Univ. **RESEARCH** Literary criticism, Old English, British romantic, and modern literature **SELECTED PUBLICATIONS** Auth, William Blake's Poetical Sketches, 67 & The Metaphysics of Byron: A Reading of the Plays, 75; co-ed, The HBJ Reader, 87. **CONTACT ADDRESS** Dept of English, Washington State Univ, 1 SE Stadium Way, PO Box 645020, Pullman, WA 99164-5020. **EMAIL** ehrstine@mail.wsu.edu

EICHELMAN, SARAH M.
PERSONAL Born 01/23/1952, m, 2 children **DISCIPLINE** ENGLISH **EDUCATION** Univ Tenn, BS, 73; MA, 75, Post Grad, 88. **CAREER** Instr, Univ tenn, 75; Instr to Assoc Prof, Walters State Community Col, 76-. **HONORS AND AWARDS** Who's Who of Contemp Achievement; 2000 Notable Am Women; The World's Who's Who of Women; Who's Who of Young Am Prof; Who's Who in Am Educ; Who's Who in Southwest; Dict of Int Biog; Who's Who of Emerging Leaders in Am; Nat Peacemaker Awd, Walters State Community Col, Col Media, 91; President's Meritorious Achievement Leadership Awd, Walters State Community Col, 99. **MEMBERSHIPS** Col Media Advisors/Col Press Asn, Community Col Humanities Asn, Southeastern Conf of English Teachers in the 2-Years Col, South Atlantic MLA, Soc for Col Jour, Tenn Col Eng Asn, Tenn Philol Asn, W Tenn Alumni Asn, Phi Kappa Phi, Alpha Delta Pi, Am Cancer Soc, 87-; Rose Center Cultural Soc, 88-; Am Heart Asn, 92-; March of Dimes, 93-. **RESEARCH** World Literature, Composition Rhetoric and Argumentation. **SELECTED PUBLICATIONS** Ed, Lit Magazine Gallery, 86-; Tag Maga, 85-. **CONTACT ADDRESS** Dept Humanities, Walters State Comm Col, 500 S Davy Crockett Pky, Morristown, TN 37813-1908. **EMAIL** Sarah.Eichelman@wscc.cc.tn.us

EICHENLAUB, CONSTANCE
PERSONAL Born 01/08/1954, Chicago, IL, m, 1985, 1 child **DISCIPLINE** ENGLISH, COMPARATIVE LITERATURE **EDUCATION** Duquesne Univ, BA, 84; MS, 85; Univ Wash, MA, 87; PhD, 98. **CAREER** Adj fac, Antioch Univ, 95, 98-99; lectr, Univ Wash, 98-00; adj fac, Trinity Luth Col, 00-01; fac, Cornish Col, 99-. **HONORS AND AWARDS** David C Fowler Trav Awds; Cornish Col Fac Dev Fund; Beinecke Fel, 01-02. **MEMBERSHIPS** CAAS; APA; ISSEI; MLA; ACLA. **RESEARCH** The life and work of Marguerite Young, American author (1908-1995). **SELECTED PUBLICATIONS** Auth, "Overview essay of the life and work of Marguerite Young," Rev Contemp Fict (00): 121-148; auth, "Aristotelian katharsis as Ethical Conversion in Plotinian Aesthetics," in Dionysius XVII (99): 57-82; auth, "Anamnesis and the Unconscious: Ancient Concepts of Memory in Plato, Aristotle and Plotinus," Pro Fifth ISSEI Conf (98); auth, "Rediscovery of Anima - American Culture in Search of Soul," Euro Legacy: Toward New Paradigms 2 (97): 668-674; auth, "Transformative Aisthesis," in Western Esoteric Traditions, SUNY Press, forthcoming. **CONTACT ADDRESS** Eng Dept, Univ of Washington, 321 W Garfield, Seattle, WA 98119. **EMAIL** connieei@u.washington.edu

EIDENMULLER, MICHAEL
PERSONAL Born 12/14/1960, San Francisco, CA, s **DISCIPLINE** SPEECH COMMUNICATION **EDUCATION** Calif State Univ, Long Beach, BA, 86; Florida State Univ, MA, 94; Louisiana State Univ, PhD, 98. **CAREER** Asst Prof, Northwestern State Univ, 97-00; Asst Prof, Univ of Texas, 00- . **MEMBERSHIPS** National Communication Assoc; Religious Communication Assoc; Southern States Communication Assoc; Society for the Scentific Study of Religion. **RESEARCH** Evangelicalism & Its Rhetoric; Popular Music & Communication. **SELECTED PUBLICATIONS** Auth, "Contemporary religious music preference and audience orientation: Do the lyrics really matter?," Eidenmuller, M.E., The Journal of Communication and Religion, 96, 37-46; auth, " Promise Keepers and the rhetoric of recruitment: The context, the persona, and the spectacle," Emidenmuller, M.E., In D. Claussen (Ed.), The Promise Keeper: Essays on Masculinity and Christianity. Jefferson, NC: McFarland & Company, Inc; rev, "Homiletic," (Review of the book Folly of God: The rise of Christian preaching); rev, Rhetoric & Public Affairs, Eidenmuller, M.E. (Review of the book Temporality, eternity, and wisdom: The rhetoric of Augustine's confessions). Auth, "Communication and attribution: The effects of music on intimate couples' verbal and nonverbal conflict-resolution behaviors," In V. Manusov & J.H. Harvey (Eds.) Attribution, communication behavior, and close relationships," Cambridge: Cambridge Univ Press. **CONTACT ADDRESS** Dept of Communciation, Univ of Texas, Tyler, Tyler, TX 75799. **EMAIL** eiden@mail.uttyl.edu

EIGNER, EDWIN MOSS
PERSONAL Born 04/03/1931, Boston, MA, m, 1956, 2 children **DISCIPLINE** ENGLISH AND AMERICAN LITERATURE **EDUCATION** Cornell Univ, BA, 53; State Univ Iowa, MFA, 55; PhD, 63. **CAREER** Instr English, Univ Md Overseas Prog, 56-57; instr, Northwestern Univ, 60-63; from asst prof to assoc prof, Univ Kans, 63-70; chmn dept English, 72-75, dir, Study Ctr for UK and Ireland, 75-77, Prof English, Univ Calif, Riverside, 70-, Fulbright-Hays grant and Fulbright lectr, Univ Erlangen, Ger, 67-68; Nat Endowment for Humanities younger scholar fel, 69. **HONORS AND AWARDS** Guggenheim Fel, 85-86; NEH Scholar, 89-90. **MEMBERSHIPS** MLA. **RESEARCH** History of prose fiction. **SELECTED PUBLICATIONS** Auth, Robert Louis Stevenson and Romantic Tradition, 66; auth, The Metaphysical Novel in England and America, 78; auth, The Dickens Pantomime, 89. **CONTACT ADDRESS** 3916 Riviera Dr, # 508, San Diego, CA 92109. **EMAIL** eeigner@popmail.ucsd.edu

EISENSTEIN, PAUL S.
PERSONAL Born 06/28/1967, Columbus, OH, m, 1997, 1 child **DISCIPLINE** ENGLISH **EDUCATION** Ohio State Univ, BA, 89; MA, 91; PhD, 96. **CAREER** TA, Ohio State Univ, 90-96; vis asst prof to asst prof, Otterbein Col, 96-. **HONORS AND AWARDS** Presidential Fel, Ohio State Univ, 95. **MEMBERSHIPS** MLA, Midwest MLA, Asn for the Psychoanalysis of Culture and Soc, Soc for the Philos Study of Genocide and the Holocaust. **RESEARCH** The Literature of the Holocaust and Contemporary Critical Theory, The Novel since 1945, Psychoanalysis, Film. **SELECTED PUBLICATIONS** Auth, "Leverkuhn as Witness: The Holocaust in Thomas Mann's Doktor Faustus," German Quart, (97); auth, "Universalizing the Jew: The Absolute as Antidote for Paranoia," Jour for the Psychoanalysis of Cult and Soc, (98); coauth, "Working-Through Professional Fantasy: Changing the Myths We Live By," Jour of the Midwest MLA, (98); auth, "Holocaust Memory and Hegel," Holocaust and Memory, (99). **CONTACT ADDRESS** Otterbein Col, Towers Fac Bldg, Westerville, OH 43081. **EMAIL** peisenstein @otterbein.edu

EISNER, SIGMUND
PERSONAL Born 12/09/1920, Red Bank, NJ, m, 1949, 6 children **DISCIPLINE** ENGLISH **EDUCATION** Univ Calif, Berkeley, BA, 47, MA, 49; Columbia Univ, PhD, 55. **CAREER** From instr to asst prof English, Ore State Col, 54-58; from asst prof to assoc prof, Dominican Col San Rafael, 60-66; assoc prof, 66-67, Prof English to Prof Emer, Univ Ariz, 67-. **HONORS AND AWARDS** Fulbright award, Ireland, 58-59. **MEMBERSHIPS** MLA; Int Arthurian Soc; Mediaeval Acad Am; NCTE. **RESEARCH** Arthurian period and Chaucer. **CONTACT ADDRESS** Dept of English, Univ of Arizona, 469 Modern Lang Bldg, PO Box 210067, Tucson, AZ 85721.

EISS, HARRY EDWIN
PERSONAL Born 05/17/1950, Minneapolis, MN, m, 5 children **DISCIPLINE** ENGLISH **EDUCATION** Univ of Minn, BA, 75; Mankato State Univ, MS, 76; Univ of NDak, PhD, 82. **CAREER** NEH Inst, 89-90; NEH Tchr Scholar Prog, 90-91; Northern Mont Col, 82-87; prof, Eastern Mich Univ, 87- . **HONORS AND AWARDS** MCH Grant for Children's Lit Conf, 82-82; Merit Awd to Outstanding Fac, NMC, 83-84; 86-87; Res Grant, NMC, 85; Fac Ctr for Instructional Effectiveness Grant for Tchg Innovations, EMU, 88; Spec Serv Awd, Sigma Tau Delta, 93. **MEMBERSHIPS** Chdn. Area Popular Cult Asn; Mich Col Engl Asn; Soc of Children's Book Writers; Int Res Soc of Children's Lit; MLA; Nat Coun of Tchrs of Eng. **RESEARCH** Mythology; Children's and Young Adult Lit. **SELECTED PUBLICATIONS** Auth, Dictionary of Language Games, Puzzles and Amusements, 86; Dictionary of Mathematical Games, Puzzles and Amusements, 88; Literature for Youth On War and Peace, 89; Images of the Child: Past, Present, Future, 94. **CONTACT ADDRESS** Dept of English, Eastern Michigan Univ, Ypsilanti, MI 48197. **EMAIL** harry@kennon.com

ELDER, ARLENE ADAMS
PERSONAL Born 05/11/1940, Los Angeles, CA, 1 child **DISCIPLINE** AFRICAN, ETHNIC AMERICAN, & AUSTRALIAN-ABORIGINAL LITERATURE **EDUCATION** Immaculate Heart Col, AB, 61; Univ Denver, MA, 62; Univ Chicago, PhD(English), 70. **CAREER** Instr English, Emmanuel Col, 62-65; lectr, 70-71, asst prof, 71-76, assoc prof, 76-90, prof English & comp lit, Univ Cincinnati, 91-; vis Fulbright lectr lit, Univ Nairobi, Kenya, 76-77. **MEMBERSHIPS** MLA, member exec coun, division of African lit, 95-2000; MELUS Soc Study Multi-Ethnic Lit US; AAUP; member, exec coun, African Lit Asn, 94-2000; member of the Delegate Assembly 00-02; African Studies Cert Prog. **RESEARCH** African lit; ethnic Americans; Australian-Aboriginal lit.; orature int literature. **SELECTED PUBLICATIONS** Auth, The Hindered Hand: Cultural Implications of Early African-American Fiction, Greenwood, 79; and many essays on African, African-Am, and women's literature. **CONTACT ADDRESS** Dept of English, Univ of Cincinnati, PO Box 210069, Cincinnati, OH 45221-0069. **EMAIL** elder2@fuse.net

ELDER, JOHN
PERSONAL Born 03/22/1947, Louisville, KY, m, 1970, 3 children **DISCIPLINE** ENGLISH **EDUCATION** Pomona Coll, BA 69; Yale univ PhD 73. **CAREER** Middlebury Col, Stewart Prof eng environ studies 73. **HONORS AND AWARDS** Danforth Fellow; NEH Fellow; Fulbright Fellow. **MEMBERSHIPS** Assn Study Lit Environ. **RESEARCH** Environmental Literature. **SELECTED PUBLICATIONS** Imagining the Earth: Poetry and the Vision of Nature, Urbana, Chicago, Univ of IL Press, 85, exp 2d ed, Univ GA Press 96; Following the Brush, Boston, Beacon Press, 93, Jap trans, Bunjinsha, 98; The Family of Earth and Sky:Indigenous Tales of Nature from Around the World, Boston, co ed Hertha Wong, Beacon Press, 94; American Nature Writers, NY Chas Scribner's Sons, 96; Reading the Mountains of Home, Cambridge, Harvard Univ Press, 98. **CONTACT ADDRESS** Dept of Eng, Middlebury Col, Middlebury, VT 05753. **EMAIL** elder@middlebury.edu

ELDRED, KATHERINE O.
DISCIPLINE CLASSICS **EDUCATION** Brown Univ, BA, 89; Princeton Univ, MA, 93, PhD, 97. **CAREER** Prof, Northwestern Univ; Mellon postdoctoral fel, 97-99. **RESEARCH** Latin poetry; Roman violence; Roman cultural studies. **SELECTED PUBLICATIONS** Auth, Off With Her Head! Reading Lucan's Medusa, Bristol Univ Dept Class and Ancient Hist, 98; Telemachus Strings the Bow, in Aspects of the Hero: A Colloquium on Violence, Gender, and Self-Definition in Homer, Northwestern Univ, 98; Face/Off: Lucan's Medusa and the Gaze of Tyranny, Northwestern Univ, 98; Lucan's Medusa: Resisting Civil War, Am Philol Asn,97; All for One: the Sacrifice of Vulteius, Am Philol Asn, 96. **CONTACT ADDRESS** Dept of Classics, Northwestern Univ, 1801 Hinman, Kresge 17, Evanston, IL 60208. **EMAIL** koeldred@nwu.edu

ELFE, WOLFGANG DIETER
PERSONAL Born 12/02/1939, Berlin, Germany, m, 1964, 2 children **DISCIPLINE** MODERN GERMAN LITERATURE **EDUCATION** Philipps-Univ, Marburg, WGer, BA, 64; Univ Mass, MA, 66, PhD (Ger), 70. **CAREER** Instr, Williams Col, 66-68; from instr to asst prof, State Univ NY Albany, 68-73; asst prof, 73-76, Assoc Prof Ger, Univ SC, 76-, Dir, State Univ NY-Prog in Wuzburg, WGer, 72-73. **MEMBERSHIPS** MLA; SAtlantic Mod Lang Asn; Am Asn Teachers Ger; Soc Exile Lit (exec secy, 78-). **RESEARCH** German exile literature; German expressionism; literature of East Germany. **SELECTED PUBLICATIONS** **CONTACT ADDRESS** Univ of So Carolina, Columbia, Columbia, SC 29210.

ELIA, RICHARD LEONARD
PERSONAL Born 06/30/1941, Boston, MA, m, 1969 **DISCIPLINE** ENGLISH LITERATURE **EDUCATION** Providence Col, AB, 64; Northeastern Univ, AM, 65; Univ Mass, PhD(English), 73. **CAREER** Instr English, Northeastern Univ, 64-69; Assoc Prof English, Salem State Col, 69-, Publ & ed, The Quart Rev of Wines, 81-. **MEMBERSHIPS** MLA; Col English Asn; Victorian Periodical Soc; Victorian Soc Am; Browning Soc, Boston **RESEARCH** Newspapers of victorian age; 19th century English; American painting. **SELECTED PUBLICATIONS** Auth, Platonic irony in Sidney's Apology, 72 & Three symbols in Snows of Kilimanjaro, 73, Rev del Lang Vivantes; T B Macaulay & W M Praed, 75 & W M Praed & B Disraeli, 76, Notes & Queries; Disraeli & Marylbone, Disraeli Newsletter, 77; Edward Clark Cabot: Watercolorist, Mag Antiques, 78; Some leaders of the Morning Post, Victorian Periodicals Newsletter, 78; Marshall Johnson, Jr, Marine Artist, Mag Antiques, 11/81. **CONTACT ADDRESS** Dept of English, Salem State Col, 352 Lafayette St, Salem, MA 01970-5353. **EMAIL** qrwiuc@qrw.com

ELKIN, ROBERT TERRELL
PERSONAL Born 05/12/1963, Doylestown, PA, s **DISCIPLINE** ENGLISH **EDUCATION** SUNY Stony Brook, BA, 93; PhD, 99. **CAREER** Adj asst prof, St John's Univ, 00-; adj asst prof, Dowling Col, 01-. **HONORS AND AWARDS** Post-Doc Lectrshp, SUNY, 99-00. **MEMBERSHIPS** MLA; Phi

Beta Kappa. **RESEARCH** American literature; H. P. Lovecraft; Philip K. Dick; gnosticism in literature; Shakespeare; narrative theory. **SELECTED PUBLICATIONS** Auth, Double Indemnity as Anti-Plague: Desire-laden Narrative, Memic Structure, and Narratological Shifting in James M. Cain's 'Double Indemnity,' Univ Mich Pr, 99; auth, "Locating the Kalem Klub: H. P. Lovecraft and the Amateur Aesthetic," (forthcoming). **CONTACT ADDRESS** 27 Brookhaven Dr, Sound Beach, NY 11789-1214. **EMAIL** rictusaporia@yahoo.com

ELKIN, SAUL
PERSONAL Born 04/08/1932, New York, NY, m, 1982 **DISCIPLINE** THEATRE **EDUCATION** Columbia Univ, BA, 53; MFA, 63; Carnegie Mellon, PhD, 69. **CAREER** Asst Prof, Castleton State Col, 60-69; Assoc Prof to Distinguished Service Prof, SUNY, 69-. **HONORS AND AWARDS** Distinguished Teaching Awd, SUNY, 75; Artist of the Year, NY State Arts Coun, 98 **MEMBERSHIPS** Actors Equity Asn. **RESEARCH** Shakespeare; Brecht; Play Direction. **CONTACT ADDRESS** Dept Theatre & Dance, SUNY, Buffalo, PO Box 605030, Buffalo, NY 14260-0001. **EMAIL** elkin@qcsu.buffalo.edu

ELKINS, MICHAEL R.
PERSONAL Born 02/03/1959, Knoxville, TN, s **DISCIPLINE** SPEECH COMMUNICATION **EDUCATION** Univ of Tenn-Knoxville, BS, 8/82, MA, 12/85; South Ill Univ-Carbondale, PhD, Speech Communication, 8/97. **CAREER** Teaching asst, Univ of Tenn-Knoxville, 83-85; lecturer, Tex A&M Univ, 86-89; course/coord/visiting instr/lecturer, Texas A&I Univ, 89-92; instructor, 97-, asst prof & ch, 97-, Tex A&M Univ, 95-97. **HONORS AND AWARDS** South Ill Univ Dept of Speech Commun Thomas J Pace, Jr, Outstanding Teacher Awd, 95; College of Arts and Sci Teaching Awd, Texas A & M Univ -- Kingsville, 00; ch, dept of commun & theatre arts, tex a&m univ kingsville, 97. **MEMBERSHIPS** Nat Commun Assoc; Cent Speech Commun Assoc; Southern States Commun Assoc; Tex Speech Commun Assoc; Int Soc for Gen Semantics; Pac & Asian Commun Assoc; Commun Educ Assoc; Am Assoc of Univ Women; Phi Kappa Phi; Golden Key; Kappa Delta Pi; Phi Delta Kappa; Pi Kappa Delta; Gamma Beta Pi; Alpha Zeta. **RESEARCH** Communication. **SELECTED PUBLICATIONS** Auth, Communication apprehension, teacher preparation, and at-risk students: Revealing South Texas secondary school teacher perceptions, Tex Speech Commun J, vol 20, 3-10, 95; auth, I will fear no audience: General semantics to the rescue, J of the Ill Speech & Theatre Assoc, vol 47, 41-43, 96; co-auth, Perceptions of cultural differences from international faculty in selected colleges and universities in South Texas, Tex Speech Commun J, vol 21, 3-12, 97; co-auth, The Texas Speech Commun J: A twenty year retrospective, Tex Speech Commun J, vol 23, 73-77, 98; Cultural issues in the workplace, J of the Ill Speech & Theatre Assoc. **CONTACT ADDRESS** Dept of Commun & Theatre Arts, Texas A&M Univ, Kingsville, MSC Box 178, Kingsville, TX 78363. **EMAIL** kfmre00@tamuk.edu

ELLEDGE, PAUL
DISCIPLINE BRITISH ROMANTICISM, AUTOBIOGRAPHY **EDUCATION** Tulane Univ, PhD. **CAREER** Prof of English and Assoc Dean, Col of Arts & Scis, Vanderbilt Univ. **RESEARCH** British Romanticism. **SELECTED PUBLICATIONS** Essays published in ELH, Texas Stud in Lang and Lit; Essays on Criticism on Childe Harold's Pilgrimage; auth, Lord Byrone and Harrow School, Johns Hopkins Univ Press, 00. **CONTACT ADDRESS** Vanderbilt Univ, Nashville, TN 37235.

ELLER, JONATHAN R.
PERSONAL Born 01/13/1952, Washington, DC1, m, 1973, 1 child **DISCIPLINE** ENGLISH LITERATURE **EDUCATION** B.S., United States Air Force Academy; Univ Md, BA; Ind Univ, MA, PhD. **CAREER** Prof **MEMBERSHIPS** Bibliographical Society of America; Society for Textual Scholarship; Association for Documentary Editing. **SELECTED PUBLICATIONS** Auth, pubs on contemporary American authors. **CONTACT ADDRESS** Peirce Edition Project, Indiana Univ-Purdue Univ, Indianapolis, 425 Univ Blvd, Indianapolis, IN 46202. **EMAIL** jeller@iupui.edu

ELLERBY, JANET MASON
PERSONAL Born Altadena, CA, m, 1997, 3 children **DISCIPLINE** AMERICAN LITERATURE **EDUCATION** Univ Ore, BS; Calif State Univ, Northridge, MA; Univ Wash, PhD. **CAREER** Assoc prof, Univ NC, Wilmington. **RESEARCH** Contemporary fiction by and about women. **SELECTED PUBLICATIONS** Her publishing has, for the most part, involved theoretical analysis of 20th century literature, theory, and pedagogy with gender as an overarching theme. **CONTACT ADDRESS** Univ of No Carolina, Wilmington, 130 Morton Hall, Wilmington, NC 28403-3297. **EMAIL** ellerbyj@uncwil.edu

ELLIOTT, CLARK ALBERT
PERSONAL Born 01/22/1941, Ware, MA, m, 1965, 2 children **DISCIPLINE** ARCHIVES, BIBLIOGRAPHY, HISTORY OF SCIENCE **EDUCATION** Marietta Col, AB, 63; Western Reserve Univ, MSLS, 65; Case Western Reserve Univ, MA, 68, PhD(libr & info sci), 70. **CAREER** Archivist, Case Inst Technol, 64-66; asst prof libr sci, Sch of Libr Sci, Simmons Col, 69-71; assoc cur, Harvard Univ archives, 71-97; Librn, Burndy Libr, Dibner Inst for the Hist of Sci and Technol, 97-00. **MEMBERSHIPS** Soc Am Archivists; New England Archivists; Hist Sci Soc; Forum for the Hist of Sci in Am, chm, 97-99. **RESEARCH** History of science in America, especially scientific careers, and institutions; documentation and historiography in history of science. **SELECTED PUBLICATIONS** Auth, The Royal Society Catalogue as an Index to Nineteenth Century American Science, J of Am Soc for Info Sci, 11-12/70; Sources for the History of Science in the Harvard University Archives, Havard Libr Bull, 1/74; Experimental Data as a Source for the History of Science, Am Archivist, 1/74; A Descriptive Guide to the Harvard University Archives, Harvard Univ Libr, 74; The American scientist in Antebellum Society: A Quantitative View, Social Studies of Sci, 1/75; Biographical Dict of American Science: The Seventeenth Through the Nineteenth Centuries, Greenwood Press, 79; Citation patterns and Documentation for the History of Science: Some Methodological Considerations, Am Archivist, Spring 81; Models of the American scientist: A look at Collective Biography, Isis, 3/82; auth, Biographical Index to American Science: The Seventeenth Century to 1920, Greenwood, 90; co-ed, Science at Harvard University: Historical Perspectives, Lehigh, 92; auth, History of Science in the United States: A Chronology and Research Guide, Garland, 96; coed, Commemorative Practices in Science: Historical Perspectives on the Politics of Collective Memory, Univ of Chicago Press, 99. **CONTACT ADDRESS** 105 Beech St No. 2, Belmont, MA 02478. **EMAIL** claelliott@earthlink.net

ELLIOTT, DORICE W.
PERSONAL Born 01/19/1951, Boone, IA, m, 1975, 3 children **DISCIPLINE** ENGLISH **EDUCATION** Brigham Young Univ, BA, 73; Univ Utah, MA, 86; Johns Hopkins Univ, MA, 89; PhD, 94. **CAREER** Teacher, Utah, 73-76; teacher, NY, 76-80; adj instr, Brigham Young Univ, 85-87; GTA to adj instr, Johns Hopkins Univ,88-95; adj instr, York Col, 95-96; asst prof, Univ of Kans, 96-01. **HONORS AND AWARDS** Nat Meric Scholar, 69; US Pres Scholar, 69; Phi Kappa Phi, 72, 85; Johns Hopkins Fel, 87-91; Ballman Fund Fel, 91; Ford Found Fel, 91, 92; Dean's Teaching Fel, 92; Folger Inst, 90-93; Univ of Kans Res Grant, 97, 98, 00. **MEMBERSHIPS** MLA, Brit Womens Writers Assoc, Australasian Victorian Studies Assoc. **RESEARCH** Victorian literature, women's philanthropy, Australian convict narratives, factory novels, literature and mental science. **SELECTED PUBLICATIONS** Auth, "Hearing the Darkness: The Narrative Chain in Conrad's Heart of Darkness," Eng Lit in Transition, (85); auth, "The Marriage of Classes in Gaskell's 'North and South,'" Nineteenth-Century Lit, (94); auth, "Sarah Scott's Millennium Hall and Female Philanthropy," Studies in Eng Lit, 1500-1900, (95); auth, "The Care of the Poor is Her Profession: Hannah More and Women's Philanthropic Work," Nineteenth-Century Contexts, (95); auth, "The Victorian Novel of Social Criticism" and "Servants and Hands: Conflicting Class Loyalties in Victorian Factory Novels," Encyl of the Novel, Fitzroy-Deanborn Pr, (98); auth, "Ways of Teaching about Free Indirect Discourse in Emma," MLA Approach to Teaching Jane Austen's Emma, forthcoming; auth, The Angel Out of the House: Philanthropy and Gender in Nineteenth-Century England, Univ Pr of Va, forthcoming. **CONTACT ADDRESS** English Dept, Univ of Kansas, Lawrence, 3031 Oxford Cir, Lawrence, KS 66049. **EMAIL** delliott@ukans.edu

ELLIOTT, EMORY B.
PERSONAL Born 10/30/1942, Baltimore, MD, m, 1966, 5 children **DISCIPLINE** ENGLISH **EDUCATION** Loyola Col, AB, 64; Bowling Green State Univ, MA, 66; Univ of Ill Urbana, PhD, 72. **CAREER** Intr, US Milit Acad West Point, 67-69; asst prof to prof, Princeton Univ, 72-89; prof, pres chair, distinguished prof, Univ of Calif, 81-. **HONORS AND AWARDS** Woodrow Wilson Fel, 71-72; ACLS Fel, 73; Guggenheim Fel, 76-77; NEH, 79-80, 86-87; Prof, Salzburg Sem, 85, 94, 98; Am Book Awd, 88; Distinguished Teaching Awd, Univ Calif Riverside, 93; Rosemary Schraer Humanitarian Awd, 97; Ford Found Grant, 98-99. **MEMBERSHIPS** MLA; ASA; IAUPE; MELUS. **RESEARCH** American Literature. **SELECTED PUBLICATIONS** Auth, Power and the Pulpit in Puritan New England, Princeton Univ Pr, 75; auth, Revolutionary Writers: Literature and Authority in the New Republic, 1725-1810, Oxford Univ Pr, 82; ed, The American Novel, Cambridge Univ Pr, 85-; ed, Pen Studies in Contemporary American Fiction, Univ of Pen Pr, 87-; ed, Am Literature: A Prentice Hall Anthology, 91; coed, Readers' Guide to English and American Literature, Bowker, 94; coauth, "The Cultural Roots of the American Short Story", Encyclopedia of Storytelling, Bowker, (NY), 97; auth, "Saints and Strangers: America's Chiliastic Dualism and the Emergence of Racialism", The Unfolding of America's National Identity, ed Roland Hagenbuchle, 98; auth, "Race and Writing in Mark Twain and Toni Morrison: The More Things Change..", Ends and Beginnings: End-of-the-Century Crises, ed Manual Broncano, Univ of Madrid Pr, 98; auth, "American Studies and Cultural Studies, 1999", John of Kennedy Inst, Free Univ of Berlin, 99. **CONTACT ADDRESS** Dept English, Univ of California, Riverside, 900 University Ave, Riverside, CA 92521-0001. **EMAIL** emory.elliott@ucr.edu

ELLIOTT, GARY D.
PERSONAL Born 10/10/1940, Chickasha, OK, m, 1963, 2 children **DISCIPLINE** LITERATURE **EDUCATION** Harding Univ, BA, 62; Univ N Tex, MA, 68; Kans State Univ, PhD, 73. **CAREER** Sen Dev Off, Pepperdine Univ, 91-93; vp, 93-97, prof, 67-81, 97-, chamn, 73-81, Harding Univ; dean, 82-86, pres, Columbia Christian Col, 86-91. **HONORS AND AWARDS** Dist Tchg Awd; Outstanding Alumnus Awd; NEH Summer Grant. **MEMBERSHIPS** Conference on Christianity & Literature; Asn Literary Scholars & Critics. **RESEARCH** Ernest Hemingway; William Dean Howells. **CONTACT ADDRESS** Harding Univ, Box 10847, Searcy, AR 72149. **EMAIL** gelliott@harding.edu

ELLIOTT, MICHAEL
DISCIPLINE ENGLISH LANGUAGE AND LITERATURE **EDUCATION** Amherst Col, BA, 92; Columbia Univ, PhD, 98. **CAREER** Asst prof **RESEARCH** 19th and 20th century American literature, Native American literature, and cultural studies; ties between literature and social science in the history of ideas about "race" and "culture" in the United States. **SELECTED PUBLICATIONS** Auth, pubs about Native American literature in arts/revs for Am Quart, Early Am Lit, Studies Am Indian Lits, and Biography. **CONTACT ADDRESS** English Dept, Emory Univ, 1380 Oxford Rd NE, Atlanta, GA 30322-1950. **EMAIL** mellio2@emory.edu

ELLIOTT, THOMAS G.
PERSONAL Born 09/12/1938, Toronto, ON, Canada, m, 1983, 1 child **DISCIPLINE** CLASSICS **EDUCATION** Harvard, PhD, 71 **CAREER** Inst Class Lang, 64-67, Trinity Col; asst assoc Prof, 67-98, Univ of Toronto. **RESEARCH** Constantine, Athanasius. **SELECTED PUBLICATIONS** Auth, Ammianus Marcellinus and Fourth-Century History, Toronto, 83; auth, "Constantine's Conversion: Do we really need it?" Phoenix 41, (87): 420-438; auth, "The Language of Constantine's Propaganda" TAPA 120, (90): 359-363; auth, "Eusebian frauds in the Vita Constantini," Phoenix 45, (91): 162-171; auth, "Constantine's Preparation for the Council of Nicaea", Journal of Religious Hist 17, (92): 127-37; auth, "Constantine's Explanation of His Career," Byzantion 62, (92): 212-234. **CONTACT ADDRESS** Dept of Classics, Erindale Col, 97 St. George St, Toronto, ON, Canada M5S 2E8. **EMAIL** telliott@credit.erin.utoronto.ca

ELLIS, CAROLYN SUE
PERSONAL Born 10/13/1950, Luray, VA, m, 1995 **DISCIPLINE** SOCIOLOGY, COMMUNICATION **EDUCATION** The Col Wiilliam & Mary, BA, 73; State Univ NYork, Stony Brook, MA, 77; PhD, 81. **CAREER** Asst prof, Univ South Fla, 81-85, assoc prof, 85-94, Co-Dir for Inst for Interpretive Human Studies, Col of Arts and Scis, 90-, joint appt, Special Educ, assoc mem, Inst on Aging, Courtesy appt, Gerontology, 96-, prof, Dept of Sociol, 94-, prof, Dept of Commun, 96-. **HONORS AND AWARDS** Nominated for Cooley Awd, Soc for the Study of Symbolic Interaction, 95; Provost's Salary Awd for Outstanding Career Performance, 95; the USF Grad Student Commun Asn Outstanding Fac Recognition Awd, 97-98; Dow Vis Scholar, Saginaw Valley State Univ, spring 99; Teaching Incentive Prog Awd, USF, 98; Univ Teaching Awd, USF, 99; Merit Pay Awd, USF, 99; HUB Awd, Outstanding fac Awd, selected by USF Commun graduating MA students, 98-99; Feminist Mentor Awd, given by Soc for the Study of Symbolic Interaction, 2000. **MEMBERSHIPS** Am Sociol Asn, Int Soc for Res on Emotions, Soc for the Study of Symbolic Interaction, Midwest Sociol Soc, Nat Commun Asn, Int Soc for the Study of Interpersonal Relationships. **RESEARCH** Qualitative methods, ethnography, emotions, health and illness, interpersonal relationships, race and emotions, narrative inquiry, interpretive social science, death and dying, writing lives. **SELECTED PUBLICATIONS** Auth, Fisher Folk: Two Communities on Chesapeake Bay, Lexington, Ky: The Univ Press of Ky (86); auth, Final Negotiations: A Story of Love, Loss, and Chronic Illness, Philadelphia: Temple Univ Press (95); co-ed with A. Bochner, Composing Ethnography: Alternative Forms of Qualitative Writing, AltaMira Press (96); co-ed with A. Bochner, Taking Ethnography into the Twenty-First Century, special issue of J of Contemporary Ethnography, Vol 25, No 1 (April 96): 1-168; auth, "What Counts as Scholarship in Communication? An Autoethnographic Response," Am Commun J (online), Vol 1, Issue 2 (Feb 14, 98); coauth with A. Bochner, "Bringing Emotional and Personal Narrative into Medical Social Science," Health, Vol 3, No 3 (99): 229-237; coauth with A. Bochner, "Which Way to Turn?," J of Contemporary Ethnography, Vol 28, No 5 (99): 485-499; auth, "He(art)ful Autoethnography," Qualitative Health Res, Vol 9, No 5 (99): 653-667; auth, "Creating Criteria: An Ethnographic Short Story," Qualitative Inquiry, Vol 6, No 2 (in press); auth, Doing Autoethnography: A Methodological Novel, Walnut Creek, Calif: AltaMira Press (forthcoming). **CONTACT ADDRESS** Dept of Commun, Univ of So Florida, 4202 E Fowler Ave, CIS 1040, Tampa, FL 33620-7800. **EMAIL** cellis@chumal.cas.usf.edu

ELLIS, DONALD
PERSONAL Born 09/10/1947, Burbank, CA, m, 1987, 2 children **DISCIPLINE** COMMUNICATION **EDUCATION** Univ Utah, PhD **CAREER** Asst prof, Purdue Univ, 76-80; assoc prof, Michigan State, 80-83; prof, Univ Hartford, 83-present **MEMBERSHIPS** Natl Communication Assoc; Assoc for Applied Linguistics; Intl Communication Assoc **RESEARCH**

Language and social interaction; communication theory **SELECTED PUBLICATIONS** Auth, Fixing Communicative Meanning: A Coherentist Theory, Communication Research, 95; Coherence Patterns in Alzheimer's Discourse, Communication Research, 96; Research on Social Interaction and the Micro-Macro Issue, Research on Language and Social Interaction, in press; Language and Civility: The Semantics of Anger, Conflict and Communication, in press. **CONTACT ADDRESS** Dept of Communication, Univ of Hartford, West Hartford, CT 06117. **EMAIL** dellis@mail.hartford.edu

ELLIS, KATHERINE
DISCIPLINE THE GOTHIC NOVEL, WOMEN WRITERS, ROMANCE AS A GENRE, CREATIVE WRITING **EDUCATION** Columbia Univ, BA, MA, PhD, 72. **CAREER** Instr, Rutgers, State Univ NJ, Livingston. **RESEARCH** Genre theory as it applies to the Gothic, to "romance" and to first-person writing. **SELECTED PUBLICATIONS** Auth, The Contested Castle: Gothic Novels and the Subversion of Domestic Ideology. **CONTACT ADDRESS** Dept of Eng, Rutgers, The State Univ of New Jersey, Livingston Col, 36 Union St., Piscataway, NJ 29232. **EMAIL** katelis@rci.rutgers.edu

ELLIS, LAURA
PERSONAL Born 12/11/1963, Albert Lea, MN, s **DISCIPLINE** MUSIC **EDUCATION** Luther Col, BA, 86; Univ Kansas, MM, 88, DMA, 91. **CAREER** Asst prof, 91-96, Univ Ozarks; chmn, Music dept, 97-, assoc prof, 96-, McMurry Univ. **RESEARCH** French organ music **CONTACT ADDRESS** 698 McMurry Station, Abilene, TX 79697. **EMAIL** ellis@mcmurryadm.mcm.edu

ELLISON, JEROME
PERSONAL Born 10/28/1907, Maywood, IL, m, 1934, 2 children **DISCIPLINE** ENGLISH **EDUCATION** Univ Mich, Ab, 30; Southern Conn State Col, MA, 64. **CAREER** Asst ed, Life Mag, 32-33; assoc ed, Reader's Digest, 35-42; ed-in-chief, Liberty Mag, 42-43; managing ed, Collier's Mag, 43-44; ed dir, bur overseas publ, Off War Info, 44-45; instr, night sch, NY Univ, 45; founder and publ, Mag of the Year, 45-47; writer, 47-55; assoc prof jour, Ind Univ, 55-60; writer, 60-64; from assoc prof to prof English and Humanities, Univ New Haven, 64-74; PRES and Founder, Phenix Soc, Inc, 73-, Ed and publ, Best Articles and Stories Mag, 57-61; lectr, Div Continuing Educ, Univ Conn, 61-62. **RESEARCH** Literary criticism; contemporary fiction; literature of social protest. **SELECTED PUBLICATIONS** Auth, The Supplement of Reading, Wordsworth Cir, Vol 23, 92; Gorchakova, Galina, Tchaikovsky and Verdi Arias, Opera, Vol 47, 96; Feeling Strange, Anq A Quart J Short Articles Notes Rev, Vol 6, 93; A Short History of Liberal Guilt, Critical Inquiry, Vol 22, 96; From Reconstruction to Integration, Britain and Europe Since 1945, Albion, Vol 26, 94; Catos Tears, Elh Eng Lit Hist, Vol 63, 96; Race and Sensibility in the Early Republic, Am Lit, Vol 65, 93; Paleoenvironmental Evidence for Human Colonization of Remote Oceanic Islands, Antiq, Vol 68, 94. **CONTACT ADDRESS** 43 Wallingford Rd, Cheshire, CT 06410.

ELLISON, ROBERT
DISCIPLINE ENGLISH **EDUCATION** Univ Tex at Austin, BA, 88; Univ N Tex, MA, 91; PhD, 95. **CAREER** Asst prof, E Tex Baptist Univ, 95-; chemn of dept of english, E Tex Baptist Univ, 98-. **MEMBERSHIPS** Confr on Christianity and Lit, Relig Speech Asn. **RESEARCH** Victorian Literature, Christianity and Literature. **SELECTED PUBLICATIONS** Auth, The Victorian Pulpit: Spoken and Written Sermons in Nineteenth-Century Britain, Susquehanna Univ Press, 98. **CONTACT ADDRESS** Dept English, East Texas Baptist Univ, 1209 N Grove St, Marshall, TX 7560-1423. **EMAIL** rellison@etbu.edu

ELLSWORTH, JAMES DENNIS
PERSONAL Born 10/25/1939, Los Angeles, CA **DISCIPLINE** CLASSICS **EDUCATION** Univ Calif, Berkeley, BA, 62, PhD(classics), 71. **CAREER** From instr to asst prof classics, Univ Conn, 67-73; asst prof, Southern Ill Univ, Carbondale, 73-74; asst prof, 74-79, assoc prof, 79-86, prof classics, Univ Hawaii, 86-. **HONORS AND AWARDS** Dean's Awd for Excellence in Teaching, Univ Hawaii **MEMBERSHIPS** Am Philol Asn. **RESEARCH** Greek mythology; Greek pedagogy; Classical Philology. **SELECTED PUBLICATIONS** Auth, Ovid's Iliad (Met 12.1-13.622), Prudentia, 80; Ovid's Odyssey (Met 13.623-14.608), Mnemosyne, 88; Ovid's Aeneid Reconsidered (Met 13.623-14.608), Vergilius, 86; Reading Ancient Greek: A Reasonable Approach (2nd ed), McGraw-Hill, 97; Reading Ancient Greek: The Second Year (2nd ed), McGraw-Hill, 98. **CONTACT ADDRESS** Dept Europ Lang & Lit, Univ of Hawaii, Manoa, 1890 E West Rd, Honolulu, HI 96822-2318. **EMAIL** ellswort@hawaii.edu

ELLSWORTH, OLIVER B.
PERSONAL Born 04/22/1940, Oakland, CA, s **DISCIPLINE** MUSICOLOGY **EDUCATION** Univ Calif, Berkeley, BA, 61; MA, 63; PhD, 69. **CAREER** Part-time instr, Univ Calif, 67-68; instr, Univ Colo, 69-70; asst prof, Univ Colo, 70-77; assoc prof, Univ Colo, 77-94; prof, Univ Colo, 94-. **MEMBERSHIPS** Am Musicology Soc. **RESEARCH** Translations and editions of late Medieval music theory treatises. **SELECTED PUBLICATIONS** Auth, The Berkeley Manuscript: University of California Music Library, Univ Nebraska Press, 84; auth, The Theory of Johannes Ciconia and the Revision of the Medieval Curriculum, The Influence of the Classical World on Medieval Literature, Architecture, Music and Culture: A Collection of Interdisciplinary Studies, Edwin Mellen Press, 92. **CONTACT ADDRESS** College of Music, Univ of Colorado, Boulder, Campus Box 301, Boulder, CO 80309-0301. **EMAIL** ellswort@spot.colorado.edu

ELLSWORTH, RALPH E.
DISCIPLINE LIBRARY SCIENCE **EDUCATION** Oberlin Univ, AB, 74; W Reserve Univ, BS, 31; Univ Chicago, PhD, 37. **MEMBERSHIPS** Amer Libr Assoc **RESEARCH** Student reading behavior **SELECTED PUBLICATIONS** 6 books; 21 jour articles **CONTACT ADDRESS** 1072 N 22nd St., Laramie, WY 82072-5303.

ELSBREE, LANGDON
PERSONAL Born 06/23/1929, Trenton, NJ, m, 1952, 1 child **DISCIPLINE** ENGLISH **EDUCATION** Earlham Col, BA, 52; Cornell Univ, MA, 54; Claremont Grad Sch, PhD (English), 63. **CAREER** Instr English, Miami Univ, 54-57, Harvey Mudd Col, 58-59 and humanities, Scripps Col, 59-60; from instr to assoc prof, 60-71, Prof English, Claremont McKenna Col, 71-94, Hays-Fulbright lectr Am lit, Cairo, 66-67; lectr grad English prog, Calif State Univ, Los Angeles, 68-70; vis prof, Carleton Col, 89. **MEMBERSHIPS** MLA; Thomas Hardy Soc; Science Fiction Res Asn. **RESEARCH** Science fiction; the sacred and profane in the fiction and poetry of Thomas Hardy and D H Lawrence; ritual passages and narrative structures. **SELECTED PUBLICATIONS** Auth, "Jane Austen and the Dance of Fidelity and Complaisance," Nineteenth Century Lit (60); auth, "D.H. Lawrence, Homo ldens, and the Dance," D.H. Lawrence Rev (68); auth, "Huck Finn on the Nile," S Atlantic Quarterly (70); auth, "The Purest and Most Perfect Form of Play: Some Novelists and the Dance," Criticism (72); auth, The Rituals of Life: Patterns in Narratives, Kennikat Press, 82; auth, Ritual Passages and Narrative Structures, Peter Lang Publishers, 91; auth, "The Language of Extremity: The Four Elements in Golding's The Inheritors," Extrapolation (99); coauth, Heath Handbook, 6 editions. **CONTACT ADDRESS** Dept of English, Claremont McKenna Col, Claremont, CA 91711. **EMAIL** lelsbree@earthlink.net

ELTON, WILLIAM R.
PERSONAL Born 08/15/1921, New York, NY, d, 1970 **DISCIPLINE** ENGLISH LITERATURE **EDUCATION** Brooklyn Col, AB, 41; Univ Cincinnati, AM, 42; Oh State Univ, PhD, 57. **CAREER** Asst, Ohio State Univ, 42-45, instr, 45-46; instr, Brown Univ, 46-50; instr, NY Univ, 50-51; vis asst prof English, Univ Conn, 52-53; asst prof, Ohio State Univ, 53-55; from asst prof to prof, Univ Calif, Riverside, 55-69; vis prof, Columbia Univ, summer, 69; Prof English Lit, Grad Sch, City Univ NYork, 69-, Huntington Libr grants, 59-62 and 76, sem, 63; Folger Shakespeare Libr grants, 59, 70 and 71; Am Coun Learned Soc grants, 60-61; Am Philos Soc grant, 61; Fulbright lectr, India, 61-62; prof, City Col, New York, 63-64; ed, Shakespearean Res and Opportunities, Univ Calif, 65-69; adv ed, Shakespeare Studies, 65-; Folger Shakespeare Libr sr fel, 75-76; Nat Endowment for Humanities fel, Huntington Libr, 76 and Folger Libr, 77; mem exec comt, Shakespeare Div, MLA, 78, NEH, 78; Mem, Univ Sem in Renaissance, Columbia Univ, 70-, Acad Coun, New Shakespeare Globe Theater Ctr, South Bank, London, 81. **MEMBERSHIPS** PEN Club; Malone Soc; Renaissance Soc Am; Shakespeare Asn Am; MLA. **RESEARCH** Shakespeare and Renaissance drama; Renaissance intellectual history, especially philosophy and theology; modern poetry. **SELECTED PUBLICATIONS** Rev, 'King Lear' and the Gods, (San Marino CA, Hungington Library), ed. Univ Press of Kentucky, 88; auth, Home From India, Partisan Rev, Vol 64, 97; Aristotle Nicomachean Ethics and Shakespeare Troilus And Cressida, J Hist Ideas, Vol 58, 97; coed, Shakespearean International Yearbook, 99-; auth, Shakespeare's 'Troilus and Cressida' and the Inns of Court Revels, London: Ashgate, 00. **CONTACT ADDRESS** PhD Prog English, Graduate Sch and Univ Ctr, CUNY, 33 W 42nd St, New York, NY 10036.

ELWOOD, WILLIAM N.
PERSONAL Born 09/21/1962, East Orange, NJ, d **DISCIPLINE** HUMAN COMMUNICATION **EDUCATION** Purdue Univ, PhD, 92. **CAREER** Asst prof, Dept Commun, Auburn Univ, 92-94; res assoc, Affiliated Systems Corp, 94-96; adj asst prof, Sch of Public Health, Univ Tex; 96-, sr res scientist, Behavioral Research Group, 96-00; res asst prof, Univ Miami Sch of Medicine, 00-. **HONORS AND AWARDS** Best Book, Nat Commun Asn, 96. **MEMBERSHIPS** Int AIDS Soc; Am Public Health Asn; Nat Commun Asn. **RESEARCH** Drug abuse; HIV prevention; communication rules. **SELECTED PUBLICATIONS** Auth, Rhetoric in the War on Drugs: The Triumphs and Tragedies of Public Relations, Praeger Publ, 94; ed, Public Relations Inquiry as Rhetorical Criticism: Case Studies of Corporate Discourse and Social Influence, Praeger Series in Political Communication, Best Book Award, 95; auth, Power in the Blood: A Handbook on AIDS, Politics, and Communication, Lawrence Erlbaum Assoc, 98; assoc Amer ed, AIDS Care: Psychological and Socio-medical Aspects of AIDS/HIV, 97-00; author of numerous articles. **CONTACT ADDRESS** 1630-4 Flagg Court, Key West, FL 33040-4472. **EMAIL** wnelwood@earthlink.net

ELWOOD, WILLIAM R.
PERSONAL Born 07/25/1935, Smith Center, KS, m, 4 children **DISCIPLINE** THEATRE, DRAMA **EDUCATION** Western Wash Univ, BA, 57; Univ Iowa, MA, 61; Univ Ore, PhD, 66. **CAREER** Prof, Univ of Wis Madison, 67-88; Chair of Theatre Dept, Univ of Wis Madison, 78-88; Dean of Grad Studies, Emerson Col, Boston, Mass, 88-94; Adj Fac, Boston Col, 95-99; Chair Theatre Dept, SCSU, 00-. **HONORS AND AWARDS** Fulbright Hayes Fel, Freie Universitat, Berlin, 66-67; Fulbright Hayes Fel, Maximilian Universitatm Munich, 75-76. **MEMBERSHIPS** ATHE, Comp Drama Conf. **RESEARCH** German Theatre and Drama. **SELECTED PUBLICATIONS** Auth, "Incoherence as Meaning: From the Real to the Expensive," Comp Drama Papers VIII (88): 1-25; auth, "Schiller and Tamayo: the Influential Essay," Comp Drama Papers IX (89): 35-46; auth, "Expressionism and Deconstructionism: A Critical Comparison," Comp Drama Papers X (90): 19-25; auth, "'Mankind' and 'Sun': German-American Expressionism," Comp Drama Papers XI (91): 9-13; auth, "Hasencelever's 'Sinnengluck und Seelenfrieden' as Metaphor for Suicide," Comp Drama Papers XII (92): 15-21; auth, "Eugene O'Neill's 'Dynamo' and the Expressionist Canon," in Eugene O'Neill in China, ed. Haiping Liu and Lowell Swortzell (Westport, CT: Greenwood Press, 92), 129-137; auth, "Adreinne Kennedy Though the Lens of German Expressionism," in Intersecting Boundaries, The Theatre of Adrienne Kennedy, ed. Paul K. Bryant-Jackson and Lois More Overbeck (Minneapolis: Univ of Minn Press, 92), 129-137; auth, "Darkness Visible; Peter Turrini and the Scripted Life," Comp Drama Conf Papers XIV (93): 27-33; auth, "Werner Kraub and the Third Reich," in Theatre in the Third Reich, the Prewar Tears, ed. Glen W. Gadberry (Westport, CT: Greenwood Press, 95), 91-103; auth, "Fernando Krapp Wrote Me This Letter: The Moral Force Examined," Text & Presentation 20 (99): 79-86. **CONTACT ADDRESS** Theatre Dept, So Connecticut State Univ, 501 Crescent St, New Haven, CT 06515-1330. **EMAIL** elwood@scsu.ctstateu.edu

ELY, ROBERT EUGENE
PERSONAL Born 08/18/1949, Fort Wayne, IN, m, 1973, 1 child **DISCIPLINE** ENGLISH **EDUCATION** Manchester Col, BA, 71, MA, 75; Purdue Univ, PhD studies, 75-77; Ind Univ, JD, 85. **CAREER** Journalist & publications ed, Lincoln Nat Corp, 71-73; Instr to Prof of English & Humanities, 77-81 & 84-, VP for Academic Affairs, Ala State Univ, 84-85; Attorney in Private Practice, 85-. **HONORS AND AWARDS** Listed in Who's Who Among America's Teachers & Marquis' Who's Who in Am Law; Shaw-Montgomery Prize for Poetry, 85; Mobil Foundation Fel for Islamic Studies in Turkey, Mideastern Technical University, Ankara, 99; Henry Luce Foundation Fel for Southeastern Asian Studies, East - West Center, Univ of Hawaii, 00; Council 1 for International Educational Exchange Seminar: Spain Past and Present, Univ of Leon, 00; Marquis' Who's Who in America, 01. **MEMBERSHIPS** Montgomery County Bar Asn; Ala State Bar; Ala Writers' Forum; Phi Eta Sigma; Lower Audubon Brook Soc. **RESEARCH** Aesthetics; modern poetry and drama; law, Lit, and society; phenomenology. **SELECTED PUBLICATIONS** Auth, The Wordy Shapes of Women in the Poetry of Dylan Thomas, English Studies Collections Series, Esco, 76; A Grammar of Narrative for Synge's Riders to the Sea, Standpoints: Essays in Honor of Charles Klingler, Manchester CP, 95; Mose T's Slapout Family Album, Black Belt, 96; coauth, The Humanities: A Cross-cultural Approach, 79. **CONTACT ADDRESS** Dept of Humanities, Alabama State Univ, TH 106, PO Box 271, Montgomery, AL 36101-0271. **EMAIL** relylaw@juno.com

EMANUEL, JAMES ANDREW
PERSONAL Born 06/15/1921, Alliance, NE, d, 1950 **DISCIPLINE** ENGLISH **EDUCATION** Howard Univ, Washington DC, AB, 1950; Northwestern Univ, MA, 1953; Columbia Univ, PhD, 1962. **CAREER** US War Dept, Office of Inspector General, Washington DC, confidential secretary to asst inspector general of the Army, 42-44; Army and Air Force Induction Station, Chicago IL, chief of pre-induction section (as civilian), 50-53; YWCA Business School, New York City, teacher of English and commercial subjects, 54-56; City Coll of the City Univ of NY, instructor, 57-62, asst prof, 62-70, assoc prof, 70-73, Prof of English, 73--. **HONORS AND AWARDS** John Hay Whitney Found Opportunity fellowship, 1952-54; Eugene F. Saxon Memorial Trust fellowship, 1964-65. **MEMBERSHIPS** Mem, Fulbright Alumni Assn. **SELECTED PUBLICATIONS** Author of Langston Hughes (essays), Twayne, 1967; author of The Treehouse and Other Poems, Broadside Press, 1968; author ofA Chisel in the Dark: Poems, Selected and New, Lotus Press, 1980; author of A Poet's Mind, Regents Publishing, 1983; author of The Broken Bowl: New and Uncollected Poems, Lotus Press, 1983; works have been published in many anthologies and periodicals. **CONTACT ADDRESS** Dept of English, City Col, CUNY, Convent Ave at 138th St, New York, NY 10031.

EMBLETON, SHEILA
PERSONAL Born Ottawa, ON, Canada **DISCIPLINE** LANGUAGE, LITERATURE, LINGUISTICS **EDUCATION** Univ Toronto, BS, 75, MS, 76, PhD, 81. **CAREER** Lectr, 80-81, asst prof, Grad Prog Interdisciplinary Studs, 83-84, asst prof, 82-84, Assoc Prof Langs, Lit & Ling, York Univ 84-, assoc dean, Fac Arts, 94-97. **HONORS AND AWARDS** Queen Elizabeth II Scholar, 79-80; Gov Gen Gold Medal, 75; Dr. Harold C. Parsons Scholar, 72-73; Archibald Young Scholar, 73-74. **MEMBERSHIPS** Can Soc Stud Names; Finno-Ugic Stud Asn; Int Soc Hist Ling Asn; Ling Soc Am; Int Coun Onomastic Sci; Can Friends Finland. **RESEARCH** Historical linguistics and language change, sociolinguistics, dialectology, onomastics, finnish literature, and women and language. **SELECTED PUBLICATIONS** Auth, Statistics in Historical Linguistics, 86; ed, the Fourteenth LACUS Forum, 88; co-ed, Indo-European and the Indo-Eurpeans, 92/93; ed, Twenty-Fourth LACUS Forum, 98; co-ed, The Emergence of the Modern language Sciences: Studies on the Transition form Historical-Comparative to Structural Linguistics, 99 **CONTACT ADDRESS** Dept of English, York Univ, 208 Stong College, 4700 Keele St, Toronto, ON, Canada M3J 1P3. **EMAIL** embleton@yorku.ca

EMERSON, EVERETT
PERSONAL Born Malden, MA **DISCIPLINE** LITERATURE **EDUCATION** Harvard Univ, AB, 48; Duke Univ, MA, 49; La State Univ, PhD, 55. **CAREER** Asst prof, Lehigh Univ, 55-60; assoc prof, Ecker D Col, 60-65; prof, Univ Mass, 65-83; distinguished prof to emer, Univ NCar Chapel Hill, 93-. **HONORS AND AWARDS** Folger Shakespeare Lib Fel, 71-72; APS Grant, 72; NEH, 82; BSA Grant, 88. **MEMBERSHIPS** MLA. **RESEARCH** St John de Creve Coeur. **SELECTED PUBLICATIONS** Auth, English Puritanism from John Cooper to John Milton, Duke UP, 68; auth, Letters from New England, 1629-1638, 76; auth, John Cotton, Twayne (NYork), 90; auth, Captain John Smith, Twayne, 93; auth, Mark Twain: A Literary Life, 00. **CONTACT ADDRESS** 130 Lake Ellen Dr, Chapel Hill, NC 27514-1937. **EMAIL** e-emerson@mindspring.com

EMERY, SARAH W.
PERSONAL Born 08/08/1911, Pleasant City, OH, w, 1948, 2 children **DISCIPLINE** PHILOSOPHY, ENGLISH **EDUCATION** Emory Univ, AB, 33; Ohio State Univ, MA, 38; PhD, 42. **CAREER** Tchg asst, Ohio State Univ, 38-42; tchg asst, Univ Ill, 42-43; instr, Packer Collegiate Inst, 43-46; instr, Syracuse Univ, 46-47; asst prof, Hollins Coll, 47-48; asst prof, Duke Univ, 51-52. **MEMBERSHIPS** Am Philos Asn; Phi Beta Kappa, The Poetry Soc of Tex. **SELECTED PUBLICATIONS** Auth, Blood on the Old Well, 63; auth (pseudonym, J.A. Cheadle), A Donkey's Life, A Story for Children, 79; They Walked into the Rose Garden and Other Poems, 92; Plato's Euthyphro, Apology and Crito, Arranged for Dramatic Presentation from the Jowett Translation with Chornses, 96; auth, J.F.K. and Other Poems, 99. **CONTACT ADDRESS** Box 683, Denton, TX 76202-0683.

EMMA, RONALD DAVID
PERSONAL Born 07/21/1920, London, England, m, 1948, 1 child **DISCIPLINE** ENGLISH, PHILOLOGY **EDUCATION** City Col New York, BBA, 41; Duke Univ, MA, 51, PhD, 60. **CAREER** Instr English, Col William & Mary, 54-60; asst prof, Cent Mich Univ, 60-61; from asst prof to assoc prof, Southern Conn State Col, 61-66; prof English, Windham Col, 66-78, chmn dept English, 66-70, chmn div humanitites, 66-74; Asst Prof Acct, Albertus Magnus Col, 81-, Asst, Duke Univ, 52-53; Col William & Mary res grants-in-aid, 58 & 59; vis lectr English, Univ Mass, 76-77; consult ed, English Literary Renaissance. **MEMBERSHIPS** MLA; Milton Soc Am; Yeats Soc; Int Asn Philos & Lit; Am Acct Asn. **RESEARCH** Grammar and style in Milton; Milton and 17th century poetry; contemporary Irish poetry. **SELECTED PUBLICATIONS** Auth, Milton's Grammar, Mouton The Hague, 63; co-ed, Language and Style in Milton, Ungar, 67 & Seventeenth-Century English Poetry, Lippincott, 69; The exordium and Paradise Lost, S Atlantic Quart, autumn 72; Milton's grammar, In: Milton Encyclopedia, Vol II; Poetry (a variety), in var Jours, US & Abroad. **CONTACT ADDRESS** 61 Elizabeth St, West Haven, CT 06516.

EMMERSON, RICHARD K.
PERSONAL Born 05/11/1948, Mexico, m, 1976, 2 children **DISCIPLINE** ENGLISH AND MEDIEVAL STUDIES **EDUCATION** Columbia Union Col, BA, 70; Andrews Univ, MA, 71; Stanford Univ, PhD, 77. **CAREER** From Asst to Full Prof, Walla Walla Col, 75-86; Prog Officer, Summer Sem for Col Teachers, Nat Endowment for the Humanities, 83-85; Deputy Dir, Div of Fel and Sem, Nat Endowment for the Humanities, 87-90; Prof Lectr, Georgetown Univ, 87-90; Prof, Chair Dept of English, Western Wash Univ, 90-99; Exec Dit, Medieval Acad of Am, 99-. **HONORS AND AWARDS** Woodrow Wilson Fel, 70; Nat Endowment for the Humanities Fel, 78-79, 96-97. **MEMBERSHIPS** Medieval Acad of Am, Medieval and Renaissance Drama Soc, MLA, New Chaucer Soc. **RESEARCH** Medieval Apocalypticism, Medieval Drama and Visionary Poetry, Illustrated Manuscripts, 13th-15th centuries. **SELECTED PUBLICATIONS** Auth, Antichrist in the Middle Ages: A Study of Medieval Apocalypticism, Art, and Literature, (Seattle), 81; auth, Approaches to Teaching Medieval English Drama, (NY), 90; coauth, The Apocalyptic Imagination in Medieval Literature, (Philadelphia), 92; co-ed, The Apocalypse in the Middle Ages, (Ihaca, NY), 92; co-transl, co-ed, Antichrist and Doomsday: The Middle French 'Jour du Judgement', (Asheville, NC), 98. **CONTACT ADDRESS** Medieval Acad Of Am, 1430 Massachusetts Ave, Cambridge, MA 02138. **EMAIL** rke@medievalacademy.org

EMMITT, HELEN
DISCIPLINE ENGLISH **EDUCATION** Univ Calif, Berkeley, PhD **RESEARCH** Women's Studies and Irish literature. **SELECTED PUBLICATIONS** Articles on, Pound, Eliot, Kate Chopin, & Woolf. **CONTACT ADDRESS** Dept of English and Fine Arts, Virginia Military Inst, Lexington, VA 24450. **EMAIL** emmitthv@mail.vmi.edu

ENDO, PAUL
DISCIPLINE ENGLISH **EDUCATION** Simon Fraser Univ, BA, 86; Univ Toronto, MA, 87; PhD, 93. **CAREER** Instr, Univ BC, 97-. **RESEARCH** English romanticism; Modernist poetry; Freud; Literary theory. **SELECTED PUBLICATIONS** Auth, "Mont Blanc, Silence, and the Sublime," English Studies in Canada, 95; auth, "Stevens and the Two Sublimes," Wallace Stevens Journal, 95; auth, "The Cenci: Recognizing the Shelleyan Sublime," Tex Studies in Lit and Lang, 96; auth, "Freud's Psychoanalysis: Interpretation and Property," Am Imago, 98; auth, "Seeing Romantically in Lamia, ELH, 99. **CONTACT ADDRESS** Dept English, Univ of British Columbia, 397-1873 E Mall, Vancouver, BC, Canada V6T 1Z1. **EMAIL** paulendo@interchange.ubc.ca

ENG, DAVID L.
DISCIPLINE ASIAN AMERICAN LITERATURE **EDUCATION** Columbia, AB, 90; Berkeley, MA, 92, PhD, 95. **CAREER** English and Comparative Lit, Columbia Univ **HONORS AND AWARDS** Mellon Found grant; Pres Postdoctoral Fel; Lambda Literary Award. **SELECTED PUBLICATIONS** Coed, Queer in Asian America, Temple University Press, 98, auth, Racial Castration: Managing Masculinity in Asian America, Duke Univ Pr, 01. **CONTACT ADDRESS** Columbia Univ, 1150 Amsterdam Ave, New York, NY 10027-6902.

ENGBERG, NORMA J.
DISCIPLINE MEDIEVAL LITERATURE, OLD ENGLISH, LATIN **EDUCATION** George Washington Univ, BA, 61; Univ Fla, MA, 63; Univ Pa, Philadelphia, PhD, 69. **CAREER** Instr, George Washington Univ, 64-67; asst prof, Calif State Col, 68; asst prof, 69-75, assoc prof, 75-, dir, grad stud, 76-83, pres, past pres, Phi Kappa Phi, 79-81, ch, grad coun, Univ Nev, Las Vegas, 81-83. **MEMBERSHIPS** UNLV corp rep, Am Assn Univ Women, 82-84. **RESEARCH** Translations from Latin. **SELECTED PUBLICATIONS** Auth, Exposing Readers of Beowulf-in-Translation to the Original Poem's Phonology, Morphology, and Syntax, Old Eng Newsl; vol15, no 2, 82; Mod-Maegen Balance in Elene, The Battle of Maldon and The Wanderer, Neuphilologische Mitteilungen, vol 85, no 2, 84; PE100-408 Anglo Saxon Language, PE1075-1400 History, and PR1490-1799 Anglo-Saxon Literature, in 3rd ed of Books for College Libraries, Virginia Clark, ed, Am Libr Asn, 88. **CONTACT ADDRESS** Dept of Eng, Univ of Nevada, Las Vegas, 4505 Maryland Pky, PO Box 455011, Las Vegas, NV 89154-5011. **EMAIL** adamsc@nevada.edu

ENGEL, DAVID M.
PERSONAL Born 12/11/1964, Charleston, WV, m, 1998 **DISCIPLINE** CLASSICS **EDUCATION** Univ Calif Berkeley, PhD **CAREER** Pa St Univ **MEMBERSHIPS** Amer Philolog Assoc; Amer Philos Assoc, Amer Inst of Archaeol. **RESEARCH** Ancient Greek' ancient philos; mind; lang; ethics. **CONTACT ADDRESS** Pennsylvania State Univ, Univ Park, 108 Weaver Bldg, University Park, PA 16802. **EMAIL** dme8@psu.edu

ENGEL, KIRSTEN H.
PERSONAL Born 11/28/1961, Chicago, IL, m, 1997 **DISCIPLINE** ENGLISH **EDUCATION** Brown Univ, BA, 83; Northwestern Sch of Law, JD, 86. **CAREER** Assoc Prof, 92-, Tulane Law Sch; staff att, 90-92, Sierra Club Legal Def Fund DC; staff att, 87-90, US EPA Gen Coun DC; clerk, 86-87, Judge MH Bright US CT Appeals. **RESEARCH** Environmental Law; Intl Envtl Law; Federalism; Environ Justice; Utility Restructuring; The Environment. **SELECTED PUBLICATIONS** Coauth, An Empirical Palliative for Theoretical hubris in the Race-to-the-Bottom Debate Over State Environmental Standard-Setting, Cornell J L, and Pub Policy, 98; auth, Brownfields Initiatives and the Requirements of Markets Based Rights Based and Pragmatic Conceptions of Environmental Justice, J Ntl Res, and Envtl L, 98; State Environmental Standard-Setting: Is There A Race and Is It to the Bottom?, Hastings L J 97; rev, Intl Mgmt of Hazardous Waste: The Basel Convention and Related Legal Rules, Intl Envtl L, 96; auth, Reconsidering the Ntl Market in Solid Waste: Trade-offs In Equity Efficiency Envtl Protection and State Autonomy, N C L Rev, 95; coauth, Intl Envtl Law Anthology, Anderson, 96. **CONTACT ADDRESS** Law School, Tulane Univ, 6329 Freret St, New Orleans, LA 70118. **EMAIL** Kengel@law.tulane.edu

ENGEL, LEONARD W.
PERSONAL Born 11/11/1936, Philadelphia, PA, m, 1988, 6 children **DISCIPLINE** ENGLISH, AMERICAN LITERATURE **EDUCATION** Rutgers Univ, BA, 58; Fordham Univ, MA, 61; PhD, 77. **CAREER** English fac, Quinnipiac Col, 64-, prof, 79-, grad lit courses in MAT prog, 92-, acting chair of English, 96-97. **HONORS AND AWARDS** Yearly grant-in-aid, Quinnipiac Col, 90-98; NEH summer inst, 96; ed bd, Isle: Interdisciplinary Studies in Literature and Environment, 96; vis fac fel, Yale Univ, 98-99. **MEMBERSHIPS** Asn for the Study of Lit and the Environment, Northeast Popular Culture Asn, Southwest/Tex Popular Culture Asn, Western Lit Asn. **SELECTED PUBLICATIONS** Ed, The Big Empty: Essays on the Land as Narrative, Albequerque: Univ of NMex Press (April 94), coauth of the intro with John Gourlie and auth of Chapter 12, "Freedom, Entrapment, and Playing the 'String out to the End': Imagery of Space and Enclosure in Sam Peckinpah's The Wild Bunch"; auth, "Rewriting Western Myths in Clint Eastwood's New 'Old Western'," in WAL, XXIX, 3 (fall 94): 261-69; auth, "Mythic Space and Monument Valley: Another Look at John Ford's Stagecoach," in Lit/Film Quart, 22, 3 (94): 174-181; rev of Place and Function: The Function of Landscape in Native American Fiction, by Robert Nelson, WAL, 30, 1 (spring 95); auth, "John Ford," "Sam Peckinpah," and "Stagecoach," in Popular Culture Encyclopedia (fall 99). **CONTACT ADDRESS** Dept English, Quinnipiac Col, 275 Mt Carmel Ave, Hamden, CT 06518-1961.

ENGELBERG, EDWARD
PERSONAL Born 01/21/1929, Germany, m, 1950, 3 children **DISCIPLINE** COMPARATIVE LITERATURE AND ENGLISH **EDUCATION** Brooklyn Col, BA, 51; Univ Ore, MA, 52; Univ Wis, PhD, 57; Fulbright Research Scholar, St. Catharine's College, Cambridge, 55-57. **CAREER** From instr to assoc prof English, Univ Mich, 57-65; assoc prof, 65-67, chmn, Comp Lit Prog, 65-72, chmn, Dept Romance and Comp Lit, 71-75, chmn, Joint Prog Lit Studies, 71-75, Prof Comp Lit, Brandeis Univ, 67-, Nat Endowment for Humanities sr fel, 75; fac rep, Bd Trustees, Brandeis Univ, 76-78, mem, Acad Planning Comt, 75-78; mem, exec comt, Eastern Comp Lit Conf. **HONORS AND AWARDS** Phi Beta Kappa, Brooklyn College; Honorary Alumnus Awd, Brooklyn College, 94. **MEMBERSHIPS** MLA; Am Comp Lit Asn; AAUP. **RESEARCH** Romanticism and literary history; modern poetry; English-German relations. **SELECTED PUBLICATIONS** Auth, "The Vast Design: Pattern in W. B. Yeats's Aesthetic," 64; (Second Edition, revised and enlarged, 88; auth, "The Unknown Distance: From Consciousness to Conscience, Goethe to Camus," 72; auth, "The Symbolist Poem: The Development of the English Tradition," 67; auth, "Elegiac Fictions: The Motif of the Unlived Life," 89. **CONTACT ADDRESS** Dept of Romance and Lit Comp, Brandeis Univ, Waltham, MA 02154. **EMAIL** engelberg@brandeis.edu

ENGELS, DONALD W.
PERSONAL Born 05/15/1946, Rockville Centre, NY, s **DISCIPLINE** HISTORY, CLASSICS **EDUCATION** Univ of Fla, Ba, 69; Univ of Tex, MA, 72; Univ of Pa, PhD, 76. **CAREER** Instr for Greek & Roman Hist, Univ of Pa, 77; vis asst prof in Hist & Classics, Brandeis Univ, 77-78; asst prof of Hist & Greek & Latin, Wellesley Col, 78-85; from asst prof to prof, Univ Ark, 83-; vis asst prof o fhist & classics, Univ of Chicago, 83; vis asst prof, Boston Col, 85-86. **HONORS AND AWARDS** Tchg fel for Greek and Roman Hist, Univ of Pa, 75-76; Ford Found Archaeol Traineeship, 70; res & tchg fels, Univ of Pa, 73-76; Am Philos Soc Grant, 79; travel grant, Wellesley Col, 79; NEH summer stipend, Brown Univ, 81; res fel, Wolfson Col, Cambridge Univ, 00-01. **MEMBERSHIPS** Am Philol Asn; Asn of Ancient Historians; Friends of Ancient Hist; Soc for Ancient Medicine; Historical Soc. **RESEARCH** Greek and Roman history. **SELECTED PUBLICATIONS** Auth, Alexander the Greant the Logistics of the Macedonian Army, Univ Calif Pr, 78; auth, Roman Corinth: An Alternative Model for the Classical City, Univ of Chicago Press, 90; Classical Cats: The Rise and Fall of the Sacred Cat, Routledge, 99; Ptolemy I, World Book Encycl, 81; The Use of Historical Demography in Ancient History, Classical Quart, 84; The Length of Eratosthenes' Stade, Am J of Philol, 85; The Classical City Reconsidered, The Eye Expanded, Berkeley, 98. **CONTACT ADDRESS** Dept of Hist, Univ of Arkansas, Fayetteville, Fayetteville, AR 72701. **EMAIL** dengles@comp.uark.edu

ENGESTROM, YRJO
DISCIPLINE COMMUNICATIONS **EDUCATION** Univ Helsinki, Finland, PhD, 87. **CAREER** Prof, Commun, Univ Calif, San Diego. **RESEARCH** Teams and networks in a variety of work settings and cultures. **SELECTED PUBLICATIONS** Auth, Learning, Working and Imagining: Twelve Studies in Activity Theory, Orienta-Konsultit, 90; Training for Change: New Approach to Learning and Teaching in Working Life, Intl Labour Office, 94. **CONTACT ADDRESS** Dept of Commun, Univ of California, San Diego, 9500 Gilman Dr, La Jolla, CA 92093. **EMAIL** yengestr@weber.ucsd.edu

ENGLAND, ANTHONY BERTRAM
PERSONAL Born 07/29/1939, m, 1964, 2 children **DISCIPLINE** ENGLISH LITERATURE **EDUCATION** Univ Man-

chester, BA, 61, MA, 63; Yale Univ, PhD (English), 69. **CAREER** Asst lectr English, Univ Manchester, 63-64; instr, Univ BC, 64-66; asst prof, 69-76, Assoc Prof English, Univ Victoria, BC, 76-. **RESEARCH** Swift's poetry; Byron and the 18th century; early 18th century burlesque poetry. **SELECTED PUBLICATIONS** Auth, Byron and the Emergence of Japhet in Heaven and Earth, Eng Stud Can, Vol 21, 95. **CONTACT ADDRESS** Dept of English, Univ of Victoria, Victoria, BC, Canada V8W 2Y2.

ENGLAND, MICHAEL TIMOTHY
PERSONAL m, 2 children **DISCIPLINE** MASS COMMUNICATION **EDUCATION** Western KY Univ, BA, 78; IN Univ, MA, 82; Univ TN, PhD, 94. **CAREER** Vis Lect/Assoc Instr, IN Univ, 79-82; asst prof, Western KY Univ, 86-90, instr/grad tchg asst, Univ TN, 90-93; asst prof, Southwest TX State Univ, 93-00; assoc prof, Southwest TX State Univ, 00-. **HONORS AND AWARDS** Nat Asn Television Prog Execs fel; Nat Alumni Asn Grad fel; Public Radio News Dirs Asn Awd; Am Heart Asn award; KY Educ Asn award. **MEMBERSHIPS** Asn Educ Journalism & Mass Comm, Broadcast Educ Asn; Tex Asn Broadcast Educators, Radio Television News Dirs Asn; Nat Asn Col Broadcasters. **SELECTED PUBLICATIONS** Auth, Your Hit Parade and Gospel Music Formats, Greenwood Publ, 98; Rev, Pioneer of Television, Mass Comm Quart, 95; High-Definition Television: A Global Perspective, Int Comm Res. **CONTACT ADDRESS** Southwest Texas State Univ, 601 University Dr, San Marcos, TX 78666-4604. **EMAIL** me04@swt.edu

ENGLISH, DAYLANNE K.
DISCIPLINE AFRICAN AMERICAN LITERATURE **EDUCATION** Oberlin Col, BA, 84; Univ Va, MA, 92; PhD, 96. **CAREER** Instr, Univ Va, 92-95; vis asst prof, Brown Univ, 96-98; lectr, Brandeis Univ, 99; asst prof, Bowie State Univ, 99-. **HONORS AND AWARDS** Oberlin Alumni Grad Fel, 94-95; Thomas J Griffis Prize, 94, 95; NEH Grant, 95-96; Foerster Prize, 00. **MEMBERSHIPS** AAUP, MLA, Nat Women's Studies Assoc, Am Studies Assoc. **RESEARCH** African American Literature, Modern American Literature, The Harlem Renaissance, Caribbean Literature, African Women's Novels. **SELECTED PUBLICATIONS** Auth, "Gertrude Stein and the Politics of Literary-Medical Experimentation," Lit and Med, (97); auth, "Somebody Else's Foremother: David Haynes and Zora Neal Hurston," African Am Rev, (99); auth, "Selecting the Harlem Renaissance," Critical Inquiry, (00); auth, "W.E.B. Du Bois's Family Crisis," Am Lit, (00). **CONTACT ADDRESS** Bowie State Univ, 14000 Jericho Park Rd, MLK 253, Bowie, MD 20715. **EMAIL** dke4b@aol.com

ENNS, LEONARD
DISCIPLINE MUSIC **EDUCATION** Northwestern Univ, MA, 75; PhD, 82. **CAREER** Prof of Music; ch, UW Music Dept. **RESEARCH** Canadian music; music theory. **SELECTED PUBLICATIONS** Auth, The Composer as Preacher, Can Mennonite Bible Col. **CONTACT ADDRESS** Dept of Music, Univ of Waterloo, Conrad Grebel Col, 200 Westmount Rd, Waterloo, ON, Canada N2L 3G6. **EMAIL** ljenns@uwaterloo.ca

ENSOR, ALLISON R.
PERSONAL Born 10/03/1935, Cookeville, TN, m, 1958, 2 children **DISCIPLINE** ENGLISH **EDUCATION** Tenn Tech, BA, 57; Univ Tenn, MA, 59; Ind Univ, PhD, 65. **CAREER** From Asst Prof to Prof, Univ of Tenn, 65-. **HONORS AND AWARDS** Advising Excellence Awd, 96. **MEMBERSHIPS** MLA, S Atlantic MLA, Soc for Study of Southern Lit, Mark Twain Soc of Am, Kent-Tenn Am Studies Asn, Tenn Philol Asn. **RESEARCH** 19th Century American Literature, Southern Literature, Mark Twain. **SELECTED PUBLICATIONS** Auth, Mark Twain & the Bible, Kent, 69; ed, A Connecticut Yankee in King Arthur's Court, by Mark Twain, Norton Critical Ed, Norton, 82; auth, "'Norman Rockwell Sentimentality': The Rockwell Illustrations for 'Tom Sawyer' and 'Huckleberry Finn'," in The Mythologizing of Mark Twain (Ala, 84); auth, "The Illustrating of 'Huckleberry Finn-A Centennial Perspective'," in One Hundred Years of Huckleberry Finn (Mo, 85); auth, "Mary Noailles Murfree," in Fifty Southern Writers Before 1900 (Greenwood, 87); auth, "Music," "Tennessee Land," and other entries, in The Mark Twain Encyclopedia (Garland, 93); auth, "Literature," and other entries, in Tennessee Encyclopedia of History and Culture (Rutledge Hill, 98). **CONTACT ADDRESS** Dept English, Univ of Tennessee, Knoxville, Knoxville, TN 37996-0430. **EMAIL** aensor@utk.edu

ENTERLINE, LYNN
DISCIPLINE GENDER STUDIES, CLASSICAL, MEDIEVAL, AND EARLY MODERN LITERATURE **EDUCATION** Cornell, PhD. **CAREER** Instr, Vanderbilt Univ. **RESEARCH** Theories of rhetoric, language, and poetics from the classical period through the 17th century; contemporary intersections between feminist, queer, materialist and psychoanalytic critiques of literature and culture. **SELECTED PUBLICATIONS** Auth, The Tears of Narcissus: Melancholia and Masculinity in Early Modern Writing; The Rhetoric of the Body in Renaissance Ovidian Poetry. **CONTACT ADDRESS** Vanderbilt Univ, Nashville, TN 37203-1727.

ENTZMINGER, ROBERT L.
PERSONAL Born 02/25/1948, Charleston, WV, m, 1972, 2 children **DISCIPLINE** ENGLISH **EDUCATION** Wash & Lee Univ, BA, 70; Rice Univ, PhD, 75. **CAREER** Instr, 75-76, Rice Univ; asst prof, 76-82, assoc prof, 82-87, Virginia Tech; TK Young Prof Eng, chmn eng dept, 87-00, Rhodes Col. **HONORS AND AWARDS** Phi Beta Kappa, 70; Omicron Delta Kappa, 70; Certificate of Teaching Excellence, Virginia Tech, 81; Fel for College Teachers, NEH, 80, 94-95; SCMLA New Historical Studies Conference Paper Awd, 96. **MEMBERSHIPS** Phi Beta Kappa, Omicron Delta Kappa, Modern Lang Asn, Milton Soc of America. **RESEARCH** 17th century British lit; Milton; Ben Jonson. **SELECTED PUBLICATIONS** Auth, "Courtesy: The Cultural Imperative," Philological Quarterly 53, (74): 389-400; auth, "The Pattern of Time in the Parlement of Foules," The Journal of Medieval and Renaissance Studies 5, (75): 1-11; auth, "Epistemology and the Tutelary Word in Paradise Lost," Milton Studies X, (77): 93-109; auth, "Michael's Options and Milton's Poetry: Paradise Lost XI and XII," English Literary Renaissance 8, (78): 197-211; auth, "The Epiphanies in Milton's Nativity Ode," Renaissance Papers, (81): 21-31; auth, "Samson Agonistes and the Recovery of Metaphor," SEL 22, (82): 137-156; auth, Divine Word: Milton and the Redemption of Language, Duquesne Univ Press, 85; auth, "George and the Augustinian Rhetoric of Example," George Herbert Journal, 13. 1-2, (89/90): 37-47; auth, "The Politics of Love: Tasso's Aminta and Milton's Comus," Milton in Italy: Contexts, Images, Contradictions, Binghamton, NY, (91): 463-476; auth, " Jonson, the Myth of Sidney, and Nostalgia for Elizabeth," Reinventing the Middle Ages and the Renaissance: Constructions of the Medieval and Early Modern Periods, Brepols, (98): 89-106. **CONTACT ADDRESS** Dept of English, Rhodes Col, 2000 North Parkway, Memphis, TN 38112. **EMAIL** entzminger@rhodes.edu

EPPERLY, ELIZABETH ROLLINS
PERSONAL Born 04/23/1951, Martinsville, VA **DISCIPLINE** ENGLISH LITERATURE **EDUCATION** Univ PEI, BA, 73; Dalhousie Univ, MA, 74; Univ London, PhD (English novel), 78. **CAREER** Lectr, 76-77; Asst Prof English, Univ Pel, 77-. **MEMBERSHIPS** Asn Can Univ Teachers English, Can Coun Teachers English. **RESEARCH** The importance of literary allusion in the novel, the works of Anthony Trollope, and the works of L M Montgomery. **SELECTED PUBLICATIONS** Auth, Patterns of Repetition in Trollope; auth, Anthony Trolloope's Notes on the Old Drama (E L S Monograph Series, No 42), 88. **CONTACT ADDRESS** Dept of English, Univ of Prince Edward Island, 550 Univ Ave, Charlottetown, PE, Canada C1A 4P3. **EMAIL** eepperly@upei.ca

EPPLE, JUAN ARMANDO
PERSONAL Born 04/26/1946, Osorno, Chile, m, 1967, 1 child **DISCIPLINE** SPANISH AMERICAN LITERATURE **EDUCATION** Austral Univ Chile, BA, 71; Harvard Univ, MA, 77, PhD (romance lang), 80. **CAREER** Asst prof lit theory, Austral Univ Chile, 72-74; instr Span, Ohio State Univ, 79-80; Asst Prof Romance Lang, Univ Ore, 80-. **MEMBERSHIPS** MLA; Inst Internac Lit Iberoamericana; Midwest Mod Lang Asn; Pac Coast Coun Latin Am Studies. **RESEARCH** Chicano literature; Latin American literary historiography. **SELECTED PUBLICATIONS CONTACT ADDRESS** Dept Romance Lang, Univ of Oregon, Eugene, OR 94703.

EPSTEIN, BONNIE W.
PERSONAL Born 11/01/1950, Somerville, NJ, m, 1982, 1 child **DISCIPLINE** ENGLISH, LITERATURE **EDUCATION** Plymouth State Col, BA, 72; MEd, 77; Union Inst, PhD, 93. **CAREER** Asst Dean of Col, Plymouth State Col, 88-94; Asst Prof, Plymouth State Col, 94-. **HONORS AND AWARDS** Phi Kappa Phi; Who's Who Among Am Teachers; Who's Who of Am Women. **MEMBERSHIPS** MLA, NCTE, CEA, Western Lit Asn, Thomas Hardy Soc. **RESEARCH** Thomas Hardy, 19th century women writers, Western American Literature, Oregon Trail. **SELECTED PUBLICATIONS** Auth, "Teaching Freshman Composition: Getting Started," PSC Writing Across the Curric J 1 (89); auth, "Making It Real: Teaching Gothic Fiction to a Diverse Student Audience," PSC Writing Across the Curric J 7 (96); auth, "Foreword," PSC Writing Across the Curric J 8 (97); auth, "Syllabus and Course Statement," in Western Lit Syllabus Collection, ed. D. Quantic (Western Lit Asn, 97); auth, "Writing Makes It Real: Conveying the Essentials of Gothic Fiction to a Varied Student Audience," Statement: J of Colo Lang Arts Soc 34-1 (Fall 97): 42-43; auth, "Bringing the Westward Experience to East Coast Students," Statement: J of Colo Lang Arts Soc 34-3 (Summer 98): 26-28. **CONTACT ADDRESS** Dept English, Plymouth State Col of the Univ System of New Hampshire, 17 High St, Plymouth, NH 03264. **EMAIL** bonniee@mail.plymouth.edu

EPSTEIN, EDMUND LLOYD
PERSONAL Born 10/15/1931, New York, NY, m, 1965, 3 children **DISCIPLINE** ENGLISH, LINGUISTICS **EDUCATION** Queens Col, NYork, BA, 51; Yale Univ, MA, 53; Columbia Univ, PhD(English), 67. **CAREER** Ed dict, various publ, 53-55; instr English, Univ Buffalo, 55-57; ed trade-and-text-bks, G P Putnam's Sons, 57-63 & Farrar, Straus & Giroux, 63-65; from assoc prof to prof English, Southern Ill Univ, Carbondale, 65-74; prof English, Queens Col City Univ New York 74-; The Graduate Center CUNY; Ed-in-chief, James Joyce Rev, 57-61; consult, James Joyce Quart, 63-; ed-in-chief, Lang & Style, 68-; vis scholar, Univ Col, Univ London, 71-72; prof English,Grad Ctr., City Univ New York, 81-; exchange prof, Univ Paris, 82, 95. **HONORS AND AWARDS** Excellence in Teaching Awd, Standard Oil Found, Ind, 71, nominated Distinguished Prof of English, 97; nominated for Awd for Excellence in Teaching, 97. **MEMBERSHIPS** MLA; Ling Soc Am; Mediaeval Acad Am. **RESEARCH** Modern British literature; linguistics, the analysis of style, structural semantics, the analysis of meaning. **SELECTED PUBLICATIONS** Coauth, Linguistics and English prosody, Studies Ling, 58; Interpretation of Finnegans Wake, James Joyce Quart, summer 66; auth, The Ordeal of Stephen Dedalus: Conflict of the Generations in James Joyce's A Portrait of the Art as a Young Man, Southern Ill Univ, 71; Language and Style, Methuen, London, 78; auth Women's Language and Style: Studies in Contemporary Language #1, Queens Col, 78; auth A Starchamber Quiry: a Joyce Centennial Publication, 1882-1982, Methuen, London, 82; auth Joyce Centenary Essays, Southern Ill Univ, 1983; auth Mythic Worlds, Modern Worlds: the Writings of Joseph Campbell on James Joyce, Harper-Collins, 93; auth The Language of African Literature, Africa World Press, 98. **CONTACT ADDRESS** Dept of English, Queens Col, CUNY, 6530 Kissena Blvd, Flushing, NY 11367-1597. **EMAIL** bloom1866@aol.com

EPSTEIN, LESLIE
PERSONAL Born 05/04/1938, Los Angeles, CA, m, 1969, 3 children **DISCIPLINE** CREATIVE WRITING **EDUCATION** Yale Univ, BA, 60; UCLA, MA, 62; Yale Drama School, DFA, 67. **CAREER** Instr to prof, Queens Col, 65-78; prof, Boston Univ, 78-. **HONORS AND AWARDS** Rhodes Scholarship; Guggenheim Fel; Fulbright Fel; Rockefeller Fel; NEA Grants. **MEMBERSHIPS** Authors Guild, PEN, Am Assoc of Rhodes Scholars. **SELECTED PUBLICATIONS** Auth, P.D. Kimeraku, Little Brown, 75; auth, Steinway Quintet, Little Brown, 76; auth, King of the Jews, McCann, 79; auth, Regina, Putnam 83; auth, Goldkorn Tales, Dutton, 85; auth, Pinto and Sons, Houghton Mifflin, 89; auth, Pandaemonium, Norton, 97; auth, Ice Fire Water: A Leib Goldkorn Cocktail, Norton, 99 **CONTACT ADDRESS** Dept English, Boston Univ, 23 Parkman St, Brookline, MA 02446. **EMAIL** leslieep@bu.edu

EPSTEIN, WILLIAM HENRY
PERSONAL Born 10/31/1944, Easton, PA, m, 1968 **DISCIPLINE** ENGLISH LITERATURE, LITERARY THEORY **EDUCATION** Dartmouth Col, BA, 66; Columbia Univ, MA, 67, PhD (English, comp lit), 72. **CAREER** Asst prof, 70-76, Assoc Prof English Lit, Purdue Univ, West Lafayette, 76-. **MEMBERSHIPS** MLA; Am Soc 18th Century Studies; Johnson Soc Cent Region. **RESEARCH** Eighteenth century British literature; biography; the novel. **SELECTED PUBLICATIONS** Auth, John Cleland: Images of a Life, Columbia Univ, 74. **CONTACT ADDRESS** Dept of English, Purdue Univ, West Lafayette, Lafayette, IN 47907.

ERDENER, YILDIRAY
DISCIPLINE FOLKLORE, ETHNOMUSICOLOGY **EDUCATION** Indiana Univ, MA; PhD, 87. **CAREER** Instr, Defense Lang Inst Monterey Calif, 85-86; Instr, Univ of Calif Berkeley, 86-87; Res, Scholar in Residence, "Shifting Gears, the meaning of work,", 88-91; Asst Prof, Univ of tex at Austin, 93-. **HONORS AND AWARDS** Fulbright-Hays Doctoral Dissertation Abroad; Inst of Turkish Studies; Nat Endowment for the Humanities. **MEMBERSHIPS** Am Folklore Soc, Soc of Asian Music. **RESEARCH** Minstrel tradition of Turkey and Central Asia, Shamanism in Siberia and Central Asia, Middle Eastern Music. **SELECTED PUBLICATIONS** Auth, Muzik Formlari (The Forms of Music), 76; auth, "Turkish Minstrels in Song Duel ," Int Folklore Rev (93): auth, The Song Contests of Turkish Minstrels, Garland Publ, 95. **CONTACT ADDRESS** Dept of Middle Eastern Lang and Cultures, Univ of Texas, Austin, Austin, TX 78712-1013. **EMAIL** y.erdener@mail.utexas.edu

ERDMAN, HARLEY M.
DISCIPLINE THEATRE STUDIES **EDUCATION** Univ Tex Austin, MA, PhD. **CAREER** Assoc prof. **SELECTED PUBLICATIONS** Auth, Staging the Jew, Rutgers Univ, 97. **CONTACT ADDRESS** Theatre Dept, Univ of Massachusetts, Amherst, 720 Massachusetts Ave, Amherst, MA 01003. **EMAIL** harley@theater.umass.edu

ERICKSON, DARLENE E. WILLIAMS
PERSONAL Born 11/05/1941, Bay City, MI, m, 1962, 2 children **DISCIPLINE** ENGLISH **EDUCATION** BA, Aquines Col, 63; MA, Western MI Univ, 70; PhD, Miami Univ, 89. **CAREER** Chair/Assoc Prof Ohio Dominican Col, 89-98. **HONORS AND AWARDS** Conley Awd; Outstanding Tchg, 91; PhD awarded with Distinction in all areas, 89; Phi Kappa Phi. **MEMBERSHIPS** MLA; MMLA; AAHE; ISCLT. **RESEARCH** Marianne Moore; Women in Lit; Contemporary Novals; Usin Tech in the Univ Classrooms. **SELECTED PUBLICATIONS** Illusion is More Precise than Precision: Poetry of Marianne Moore, Univ Alabama Press, 92; With Skill, Endurance and Generosity of Heart: Frank McCourt's Angela's

Ashes, 98; ed of The Dolphin ed by Kari-Heinz Westarp and Michael Boss, Aarhus Univ Press, title of Ireland: Towards New Identities, Low Countries of the Mind: Richard Powers's Galatea 2,2, 98; Co-presented with Dr Larry Cepek, Educom Conference in Milwaukee WI, Using Technology to Enhance Teaching and Learning, 98. **CONTACT ADDRESS** Ohio Dominican Col, 1216 Sunbury Rd, room 223 E, Columbus, OH 43219. **EMAIL** ericksoa@ODC.EDU

ERICKSON, GREGORY T.
PERSONAL Born 10/19/1962, Moorhead, MN, s **DISCIPLINE** MUSIC, ENGLISH **EDUCATION** Univ Minn, BM, 94; Hunter Col, MA, 96. **CAREER** Instr and writing fel, Medgar Evers Col, 96-01; div dir, Brooklyn Conservatory of Music, 01-. **MEMBERSHIPS** MLA; Am Acad of Relig; Am Musicol Soc. **RESEARCH** Modernist literature and music; Postmodern literary theory, musicology, theology; American popular culture and popular religion. **SELECTED PUBLICATIONS** Auth, "Closing the Circle: Explorations in the Language of Music Criticism," Encultaration, 99; auth, "Sometimes you need a story: American Christianity, Vampires and Buffy," in Fighting the Forces: Essays on the Meaning of Buffy the Vampire Slayer, Rouman and Littlefield, 01; auth, "Jesus is Standing at the Home Plate: Baseball and American Religion," in The Cooperstown Symposium on Baseball and American Culture, McFarland, 01; auth, "The Golden Bowl, A/Theology, and Nothing," in Henry James Rev, 01. **CONTACT ADDRESS** Class Music Div, Brooklyn Conservatory of Music, 84 Cambridge Pl, Brooklyn, NY 11238-2402. **EMAIL** gregterickson@aol.com

ERICKSON, NANCY LOU
PERSONAL Born 07/14/1941, Berea, OH, m, 1964, 2 children **DISCIPLINE** HISTORY, ENGLISH **EDUCATION** Kent State Univ, BS, 61; Univ IL, Urbana, AM, 64; Univ NC, Chapel Hill, PhD(hist), 70. **CAREER** Teacher hist, Champaign Sr High Sch, IL, 63-64; teacher, Maine Twp High Sch West, Des Plaines, IL, 64-66; assoc prof to prof hist, Erskine Col, 74-, dir of institutional res, 88-; Lilly Scholar Hist, Duke Univ, 76-77; pres acad affairs & prof hist, Iowa Wesleyan Col, 99- . **HONORS AND AWARDS** Excellence in Teaching Awd, 78; Renaissance Person of the Year, 92. **MEMBERSHIPS** Am Hist Asn; Orgn Am Historians; Coun Faith & Hist. **RESEARCH** Comparative cultures; United States-Soviet Union; national character; 17th century America. **CONTACT ADDRESS** Iowa Wesleyan Col, 601 N Main, Mount Pleasant, IA 52641. **EMAIL** nericksn@iwc.edu

ERICKSON, RAYMOND FREDERICK
PERSONAL Born 08/02/1941, Minneapolis, MN, m, 1982 **DISCIPLINE** MUSICOLOGY **EDUCATION** Whittier Col, BA, 63; Yale Univ, PhD(hist of music), 70. **CAREER** Actg instr music, Yale Univ, 68-70; res fel, IBM Syst Res Inst, 70-71; asst prof, 71-74, assoc prof, 74-81, prof music, 82-, dean of arts & humanities, 93-, Queens Col, NY; doctoral fac, music, CUNY Grad School, 76-; assoc fel, Pierson Col, Yale Univ, 71-; prin investr grant, 73-74; dir, 13 NEH Summer Insts, Aston Magna Acad, 78-; chemn & founding dir, Aaron Copland Sch of Music, 78-81; adj prof, Sch Advan Technol, SUNY Binghamton, 82-. **HONORS AND AWARDS** Phi Beta Kappa, Omicron Delta Kappa, Pi Delta Phi; Res Fel, IBM Systems Res Inst, 70-71; Alexander von Humboldt Found, 77-78, 84-85; NEH Res Fel, 73-74. **MEMBERSHIPS** Am Musicol Soc; Int Schubert Institute; Board of Dir, VP, 97-99, Pres 99-01, Alexander von Humboldt Asn of Am; Am Bach Soc, Early Music America. **RESEARCH** European and American cultural history, 17th and 18th centuries; medieval polyphony; computer applications in musicology; historical performance practice; improvisation. **SELECTED PUBLICATIONS** Auth, Music analysis and the computer, 68 & A general purpose system for computer-aided music research, 69, J Music Theory; The DARMS Project: A status report, Computers & Humanities, 75; DARMS: A Reference Manual, private publ; Musicomp '76 and the state of DARMS, Col Music Soc Symp; J S Bach, The Six Brandenbury Concertos (rec), Smithsonian Collection of Rec, 77; Musica enchiriadis and Scolica enchiriadis, Yale Univ Press, 95; ed, Schubert's Vienna, Yale Univ Press, 97. **CONTACT ADDRESS** Dean of Arts and Humanities, Queens Col, CUNY, 6530 Kissena Blvd, Flushing, NY 11367-1597. **EMAIL** raymond_erickson@qc.edu

ERICKSON, ROBERT A.
PERSONAL m, 1966, 3 children **DISCIPLINE** ENGLISH LITERATURE **EDUCATION** Boston Univ, AB, 62; Yale Univ, MA, 64; PhD, 66. **CAREER** Asst instr Engl, Yale Univ, 65; prof, Univ Calif-Santa Barbara, 66- . **HONORS AND AWARDS** Woodrow Wilson fel, 62-62; Fulbright fel, 65-66; Who's Who Among Am Tchrs, 96-97; Fulbright Sr fel, 99-00. **MEMBERSHIPS** MLA, ASECS **RESEARCH** Early modern English literature & culture (1600-1750), Milton & epic, Representatives of the heart, the body, and sexuality. **SELECTED PUBLICATIONS** Co-ed, The History of John Bull, Clarendon Press Oxford, 76; auth, Mother Midnight: Birth, Sex, and Fate in Eighteenth Century Fiction, AMS Press, 86; auth The Language of the Heart, 1600-1750, Univ Penn Press, 97; auth "Lady Fulbank and the Poet's Drean ub Gehn's The Lucky Change", in Broken Boundaries, Univ Press Kent, 96. **CONTACT ADDRESS** Dept English, Univ of California, Santa Barbara, S Hall 2706, Santa Barbara, CA 93106-0002. **EMAIL** erickson@humanities.vcsb.edu

ERICSON, ROBERT EDWARD
PERSONAL Born 07/19/1926, Poplar, MT, m, 1952, 3 children **DISCIPLINE** THEATRE HISTORY AND THEORY **EDUCATION** Pac Univ, BS, 51; Ind Univ, MA, 54; Univ Ore, PhD, 70. **CAREER** Grad asst theatre, Ind Univ, 53-54; asst prof, Radford Col, 54-55; instr, Columbia Basin Jr Col, 55-56; asst prof, Pac Univ, 56-60; grad asst, Univ Ore, 60-63; asst prof, Ore Col Educ, 63-64; dir univ theatre, Univ Nev, 64-70; Assoc Prof Theatre Arts, Boise State Col, 70-, Chmn Dept, 71-. **MEMBERSHIPS** Am Theatre Asn; Rocky Mountain Theatre Conf. **RESEARCH** American theatre history; cinema theory and history; classical theatre. **SELECTED PUBLICATIONS** Auth, Russia and The Nis in the World Economy--East West Investment, Financing and Trade, Slavic Rev, Vol 54, 95. **CONTACT ADDRESS** 2505 Sunrise Rim, Boise, ID 83705.

ERISMAN, FRED RAYMOND
PERSONAL Born 08/30/1937, Longview, TX, m, 1961, 1 child **DISCIPLINE** AMERICAN STUDIES & LITERATURE **EDUCATION** Rice Inst, BA, 58; Duke Univ, MA, 60; Univ Minn, Minneapolis, PhD(Am studies), 66. **CAREER** From instr to assoc prof, 65-77, actg dean, Col Arts & Sci, 70-71 & 72-73, dir honors prog, 72-74, prof English, Tex Christian Univ, 77-, Co-ed, The French-American Rev J, 76-; book rev ed, Soc Sci J, 78-82; publ ed & mem exec bd, Int Res Soc Children's Lit, 81-83; Hess fel, Univ Minn, 81; Kinnucan Arms Chair fel, Buffalo Bill Hist Ctr, 82; chrmn, dept English; Chm, Dept English, 83-89, 95-98; Lorraine Sherley Prof of Literature, Emeritus, 00. **HONORS AND AWARDS** Lorraine Sherley Prof of Literature, 86; Phi Beta Kappa, 88. **MEMBERSHIPS** Am Studies Asn; MLA; Orgn Am Historians; Western Lit Asn; Popular Cult Asn. **RESEARCH** American popular literature; detective and suspense fiction; Science Fiction. **SELECTED PUBLICATIONS** Auth, The environmental crisis and present-day romanticism, Rocky Mountain Soc Sci J, 73; The romantic regionalism of Harper Lee, Ala Rev, 73; Frederic Remington, Western Writers Ser, Boise State Univ, 75; Prolegomena to a theory of American life, Southern Quart, 76; Romantic reality in the spy stories of Len Deighton, Armchair Detective, 77; Jack Schaefer: The writer as ecologist, Western Am Lit, 78; Western regional writers and the uses of place, J of the West, 80; co-ed (with Richard W Etulain), Fifty Western Writers, Greenwood Press, 82; Barnboken i USA, 86; contribur, A Literary History of the American West, 87; Laura Ingalls Wilder, Western Writers Ser, 94; auth, The Technological Utopias of Thorstein Veblen and Nevil Shute, Weber Studeis, 94; auth, Robert A. Heinlein's Primers of Politics, Extrapolation, 97; Updating the Literary West; 97; auth, McCrumb's Comic Critiques of SF Fandom, Extrapolation, 99; auth, Thoreau, Alcott, and the Mythic West, Western Am Lit, 99; Reading A.B. Guthrie's THE BIG SKY, Western Writers Ser, 00. **CONTACT ADDRESS** Dept of English, Texas Christian Univ, Box 297270, Fort Worth, TX 76129-0002. **EMAIL** ferisman@swbell.net

ERLER, MARY C.
PERSONAL Born 11/15/1937, Tiffin, OH, m, 1962, 2 children **DISCIPLINE** ENGLISH LITERATURE **EDUCATION** St Mary's Col, BA, 59; Univ Chicago, MA, 63; PhD, 81. **CAREER** Instructor to Prof, Fordham Univ, 80-. **HONORS AND AWARDS** Who's Who of Am Women; Best Teacher, New York, 90. **MEMBERSHIPS** MLA; Medieval Acad of Am; Renaissance Soc of Am; Early Book Soc. **RESEARCH** Early English printing; 15th and 16th Centruy womens' book ownership. **SELECTED PUBLICATIONS** Co-ed, Women and Power in the Middle Ages, Univ GA Press, 88; co-ed, Poems of Cupid, God of Love, Leiden, 91; auth, Robert Copland: Poems, Univ Toronto Press, 93; auth, "Devotional Literature," in Cambridge History of the Book in Britain Vol III, 1400-1557, Cambridge Univ Press, 99. **CONTACT ADDRESS** Dept Eng, Fordham Univ, 441 E Fordham Rd, Bronx, NY 10458-5149.

ERLICH, RICHARD D.
PERSONAL Born 02/07/1943, Terre Haute, IN, s **DISCIPLINE** ENGLISH **EDUCATION** Univ of Ill, Urbana, BA, 65; PhD, 71; Cornell Univ, MA, 66. **CAREER** Univ of Ill Urbana, 68-70; Miami Univ 71-. **HONORS AND AWARDS** Woodrow Wilson Grad Fel; Danforth Grad Fel; Merit Instr, Univ of IL Urbana. **MEMBERSHIPS** Sci Fiction Res Assoc; AAUP; Soc for Utopian Studies; Int Assoc for the Fantastic in the Arts. **RESEARCH** Science Fiction, Film, Shakespeare. **SELECTED PUBLICATIONS** Coauth, "Environmental Concerns in Arthur C. Clarke's The City and the Stars", in Aspects of Fantasy: Selected Essays from the Second Int Conf on the Fantastic, ed William Coyle, Greenwood Pr, (86): 203-11; auth, "That Old White-Bearded Satan (or Sympathy for the Deveil): Outsiders Inside Some Fictive Worlds", W Va Philog Papers 32 (86): 1-11; coauth, "Beyond Topeka and Thunderdome: Variations on the Comic-Romance Pattern in Recent SF Film", Sci-Fiction Studies 14 (87): 316-25; auth, "Ursula K. LeGuin and Arthur C. Clarke on Immanence, Transcendence, and Massacres", Extrapolation 28 (87): 105-29; coauth, "A Prefilmic, Post-PostStructuralist Prostruction of Alien/Aliens 3: Heinleinian/Stallonian Vs Wimpoid Approaches", Australian Sci Fiction Rev 2.6 (87): 3-5; coauth, "For Our Balls Were Sheathed in Inertron: Textual Variations in "The Seminal Buck Rogers Story"", Extrapolation 29.4 (88): 303-18; ed, Clockworks: A Multimedia Bibliography of Works Useful for the Study of the Human/Machine Interface in SF, Greenwood (Westport, CT), 93; auth, "From Shakespeare to Le Guin: Authors as Auteurs", Extrapolation (99): 342-51; auth, Coyote's Song: The Teaching Stories of Ursula K. Le Guin, Sci Fiction Res Assoc (forthcoming); auth, "The Forever War (1972-75, 1975/76, 1997) and Forever Peace (1997): Haldeman's Variations on a Theme by Haldeman", in Flashes of the Fantastic, ed David Ketterer, Greenwood (Westport, CT) (forthcoming). **CONTACT ADDRESS** Dept English, Miami Univ, Oxford, OH 45056-3414. **EMAIL** erlichrd@muohio.edu

ERLMANN, VEIT
DISCIPLINE MUSIC HISTORY **EDUCATION** Berlin; Cologne, PhD, 78. **CAREER** Prof & Endowed ch; past fac, Univ Natal, Univ Chicago, Unive Witwatersrand in Johannesburg & Free Univ Berlin. **RESEARCH** Music and globalizatio; music, and the politics of broadcasting in Cameroon; critical issues concerning the role of music in late modernity. **SELECTED PUBLICATIONS** Auth, African Stars, Studies in Black South African Performance and Nightsong, Univ Chicago Press, Performance, Power and Practice in South Africa, Univ Chicago Press. **CONTACT ADDRESS** School of Music, Univ of Texas, Austin, 2613 Wichita St, Austin, TX 78705.

ERVIN, HAZEL A.
DISCIPLINE ENGLISH, LITERATURE **EDUCATION** Guilford Col, AB, 80; N.C. A&T State Univ, MA, 85; Howard Univ, PhD, 93. **CAREER** Asst prof English, Shaw Univ,85-96; Chemn, Shaw Univ, 93-96; Assoc Prof, Morehouse Col, 96-. **HONORS AND AWARDS** UNCF/Mellon fellow; John Lennon Grant for Summer Enrichment; Who's Who Among African Am; World Who's Who of Women; Nat Consortium Educ Access Fellow. **MEMBERSHIPS** MLA; CLA; MELUS; The Langston Hughes Society. **RESEARCH** Ann Petry and literary criticism. **SELECTED PUBLICATIONS** Auth, Ann Petry: A Bio-Bibliography, 93; Auth, Tituba of Salem Village; Auth, Adieu, Harlem's Adopted Daughter Ann Petry, 97; Auth, African American Literary Criticism 1773 to 2000, 99; Auth, Race and Desire as New Paridigm in New Biography of Jean Toomer, 98; Auth, Stephen E. Henderson: In Memoriam, CIA Journ Vol 6, jun 97; Auth, Ann Petry, A Crtitcal Collection, (forthcoming). **CONTACT ADDRESS** Dept of English, Morehouse Col, 830 Westview Dr SW, Atlanta, GA 30314. **EMAIL** hervin@morehouse.edu

ERWIN, D. TIMOTHY
PERSONAL Born Balitmore, MD, m, 1 child **DISCIPLINE** 18TH CENTURY LITERATURE **EDUCATION** Marquette Univ, AB; Univ Chicago, MA, PhD, 84. **CAREER** Ch, adv, guest ed, Chicago Rev, 75-81; resident hd, univ housing, Univ Chicago, 76-81; instr, Univ San Diego, 81-84; asst prof, Rutgers Univ, 85-90; prof, ch, Multidisciplinary stud prog, Univ Nev, Las Vegas; ed, Stud in 18th-Century Cult, Johns Hopkins Univ Press. **HONORS AND AWARDS** Ellison Fund scholar, Univ Chicago, 75-76; Fels Awd, Coord Coun of Lit Mag, 76; Chicago Rev, Best Ill Mag, Ill Arts Coun, 76; ed grantee, Nat Endowment for the Arts, 78; grant, Am Soc for 18th-Century Stud/Clark Libr, 85; NEH summer inst, Hobart and William Smith Col, 87; NEH summer sem UCSB, 93; short-term fel, Clark Libr, UCLA, 96; NEH fel, Aston Magna Acad, Yale Univ, 97; short-term fel, Yale Ctr for Brit Art, 98. **MEMBERSHIPS** MLA; ASECS. **RESEARCH** Literary Pictorialism. **SELECTED PUBLICATIONS** Auth, The Extraordinary Language of Robert Pinsky, Halcyon /94: J of the Hum 16, 94; Alexander Pope and the Disappearance of the Beautiful, in So Rich a Tapestry: The Sister Arts and Cultural Studies, eds, Kate Greenspan and Ann Hurley, 13ucknell UP, 95; A Memoir, Chicago Rev: Fifty Years: A Retrospective Issue 42, 96; six articles, in Hanoverian Britain: An Encyclopedia, Garland, 97; coauth, Restoration and Eighteenth-Century Literature, The Reader's Adviser, 14th ed, Bowker, 94. **CONTACT ADDRESS** Dept of Eng, Univ of Nevada, Las Vegas, 4505 Maryland Pky, PO Box 455011, Las Vegas, NV 89154-5011. **EMAIL** timothy@nevada.edu

ERWIN, JOANNE
DISCIPLINE STRINGED INSTRUMENTS **EDUCATION** Univ Ill, BM, MM; Univ N Tex, PhD. **CAREER** Asst prof; act dir, Mus Edu Div, Oberlin Col, 96; pres. **HONORS AND AWARDS** Dir, Oberlin Coll String Preparatory Prog; dir Suzuki Sch for violin and cello; founder, conductor, Symphonetta of the Northern Ohio Youth Orchestra. **MEMBERSHIPS** Pres, Ohio String Tchr(s) Assn. **SELECTED PUBLICATIONS** Contribu, Am String Tchr Jour, Suzuki Jour, Tchg Mus. **CONTACT ADDRESS** Coun of Mus, Oberlin Col, Oberlin, OH 44074. **EMAIL** joanne.erwin@oberlin.edu

ESKEW, HARRY LEE
PERSONAL Born 07/02/1936, Spartanburg, SC, m, 1965, 2 children **DISCIPLINE** HYMNOLOGY, AMERICAN MUSIC HISTORY **EDUCATION** Furman Univ, BA, 58; New Orleans Baptist Theol Sem, MSM, 60; Tulane Univ, PhD(musicol), 66; La State Univ, MLIS, 95. **CAREER** Assoc prof, 65-75, Prof

Music Hist & Hymnol, New Orleans Baptist Theol Sem, 75-, Music Librarian, 89-; Am Asn Theol Schs fel, Univ Erlangen, 70-71; mem Baptist hymnal rev comt, Southern Baptist Sunday Sch Bd, 73-75, 89-91; ed, The Hymn Quart, Hymn Soc Am, 76-83. **MEMBERSHIPS** The Hymn Soc in the U.S. and Canada; Southern Baptist Hist Soc; Southern Baptist Church Music Conf; Music Libr Asn. **RESEARCH** Church music; American folk and popular hymnody. **SELECTED PUBLICATIONS** Auth, American Folk Hymnody, Bull Hymn Soc Gt Brit & Ireland, 71; Music in the Baptist Tradition, Rev & Expositor, 72; A Cultural Understanding of Hymnody, Hymn, 72; Hymnody Kit, Part II, Convention Press, 75; coauth (with Hugh T McElrath), Sing With Understanding: An Introduction to Christian Hymnology, rev ed, Church Street Press, 95; Gospel Hymnody, Shape-note Hymnody In: The New Grove Dictionary of Music and Musicians, Macmillan, 80; coauth, Singing Baptists, Church Street Press, 94. **CONTACT ADDRESS** New Orleans Baptist Theol Sem, 3939 Gentilly Blvd., New Orleans, LA 70126-4858. **EMAIL** Heskew@nobts.edu

ESPOSITO, STEVEN
PERSONAL Born 07/15/1959, Cincinnati, OH, m, 1991, 4 children **DISCIPLINE** COMMUNICATION **EDUCATION** Miami Univ, BS, 81; Univ Cincinnati, MA, 93; Wayne State Univ, PhD, 96. **CAREER** Broadcast Journalist; Asst Prof to assoc prof and Dir of Univ TV, Capital Univ. **HONORS AND AWARDS** Production, Aesthetics and Criticism Competitive Paper, Broadcast Ed Asn, 97. **MEMBERSHIPS** Broadcast Educ Asn; Nat Commun Asn; Asn Educ in Jour and Mass Commun. **RESEARCH** Media criticism. **SELECTED PUBLICATIONS** Auth, Cohesion & Adaptability in the non-custodial father/child relationship: The effects of interaction quality, Jour Divorce & Remarriage, 23, 95; auth, Presumed innocent?: A comparative analysis of network news', prime time newsmagazines', and tabloid tv's pretrial coverage of the O.J. Simpson criminal case, Commun and the Law, 18, 96; auth, Source Utilization in Legal Jounalism: Network TV news coverage of the Timothy McVeigh Oklahoma City Bombing Trial, Commun and the Law, 20, 98. **CONTACT ADDRESS** Capital Univ, 2199 E Main St, Bexley, OH 43209. **EMAIL** sesposit@capital.edu

ESSICK, ROBERT N.
DISCIPLINE BRITISH ROMANTIC LITERATURE AND ART **EDUCATION** UCLA, BA; Univ Calif-San Diego, PhD. **CAREER** Fac res lectr, 90-91; prof, English, Univ Calif, Riverside. **HONORS AND AWARDS** Outstanding Acad bk, Choice, 80-81; outstanding bk, Chioce, 91-92; fel(s), NEH; Amer Coun of Learned Soc; Guggenheim; on-line fel, inst adv tech in the hum, univ va. **MEMBERSHIPS** Mem, Bd of Overseers Huntington Lib; ed bd, Stud Eng Lit. **RESEARCH** William Blake, Blake electronic archive. **SELECTED PUBLICATIONS** Auth, William Blake, Printmaker, Princeton Univ Press, 80; William Blake and the Language of Adam, Oxford Univ Press, 89; William Blake's Commercial Book Illustrations, Oxford Univ Press, 91; William Blake at the Huntington, 94; **CONTACT ADDRESS** Dept of Eng, Univ of California, Riverside, Riverside, CA 92521-0209. **EMAIL** robert.essick@ucr.edu

ESTERHAMMER, ANGELA
DISCIPLINE ENGLISH LITERATURE **EDUCATION** Univ Toronto, BA; Princeton Univ, PhD. **CAREER** Prof, Univ of Western Ontario. **HONORS AND AWARDS** Toronoto Arts Awds Found Protege Awd, 88; John Charles Polanyi Prize in Lit, 90; Alexander von Humboldt Found Res Fel, 96-97. **RESEARCH** Romantic literature and theory; philosophy of language; speech-act theory; performativity. **SELECTED PUBLICATIONS** Auth, Creating States: Studies in the Performative Language of John Milton and William Blake, Toronto, 94; transl, Two Stories of Prague, by R.M. Rilke, (94); co-ed, 1798 and Its Implications, European Romantic Review, 99. **CONTACT ADDRESS** English Dept, Univ of Western Ontario, University College, London, ON, Canada NGA3K7. **EMAIL** angelae@julian.uwo.ca

EUBA, FEMI
PERSONAL Born 04/02/1942, Lagos, Nigeria, m **DISCIPLINE** THEATER, ENGLISH **EDUCATION** Rose Bruford Coll, RBTC, 65; Yale Sch, MFA; 73; Yale Univ, MA, 82; Univ Ife, PhD. **CAREER** Res art, Ethel Walker Sch, 73-75; lectr, Univ Ibad, 75-76; lectr, Univ Ife, 76-80; teach asst, Yale Univ, 80-82; sr lectr, Univ Ife, 82-86; vis prof, Coll William and Mary, 86-88; res art, 88-91; assoc prof, 91-96; prof, 96-; La St Univ. **HONORS AND AWARDS** Alum Fac Awd; Phi Kappa Phi; KC/ACTF Awd; ANAL Awd; Yale Fel; Ife Fel. **MEMBERSHIPS** BTN' MLA; ALA; ATHE; SWTC; BAE. **RESEARCH** Comparative Black Drama and Theater; Ritual Process; Creative process in playwriting. **SELECTED PUBLICATIONS** Auth, The Gulf: a full length play, Longman (Lagos, Nigeria), 91; auth, Archetypes, Imprecators and Victims of Fate: Origins and Developments of Satire in Black Drama, Greenwood Press (Westport, CT), 89; auth, "The Theatre of Edouard Glissant: Resolving the Problems of Monsieur Toussaint LSU Theatre," J&D Editions (Pau, France), 92; auth, "Crocodiles," a one-act play, in Quart J Ideol (95); auth, "Soyirika's Satiric Development and Maturity," in Mapping Intersections, ed. Arme V Adams et al. (NJ: Africa World Press, Inc., 98):174-187; auth, "Wole Soyinka" Postcolonial African Writers: A Dio-Biblio graphical Sourcebook, ed. Pushpa Parekh et al (Westport, CT: Greenwood Press, 1998), 438-454. **CONTACT ADDRESS** Dept English, Louisiana State Univ, Baton Rouge, LA 70803-0104. **EMAIL** theuba@lsu.edu

EUBANKS, RACHEL AMELIA
PERSONAL Born San Jose, CA, d **DISCIPLINE** MUSIC COMPOSITION, THEORY **EDUCATION** Univ of CA Berkeley, BA 1945; Columbia Univ NYork, MA 1947; Pacific Western Univ, DMA 1980; Fontabl, France, Eastman Schl of Music, UCLA, USC, additional studies. **CAREER** Wilberforce Univ, chmn Music Dept 49-50; Albany State Coll, hd of Music Dept 47; Eubanks Conser of Music, pres, founder, 51. **HONORS AND AWARDS** Mosenthal flwhp Columbia Univ 1946; Musicianship: Vols I II and Tapes, Symphonic Requiem, Oratorio, Trio, & others; Alpha Mu Honor Society, Univ of CA Berkley 1946; Composition Awd, Natl Assn Negro Musicians 1948; Symphonic Requiem, Korean Philharmonic, Los Angeles 1982; three songs, Res Musica, Baltimore 1985; Interlude #5, National Women's Music Festival, Bloomington, Indiana, 1988. **MEMBERSHIPS** Afro-American Museum; Crenshaw Chamber of Commerce; Natl Guild of Piano Teachers; Intl Congress on Women in Music; Musicians Union, Local 47; Music Teacher's Natl Assn; Natl Assn of Negro Musicians; Ethnomusicology Society; American Musicological Society. **RESEARCH** Ethnomusicology. **SELECTED PUBLICATIONS** Sonata for Piano, premiered by Helen Walker-Hill, Sonneck Society, 93; Five Interludes for Piano, Vivace Press, 95; The First & Fifth Interludes on CD, Leonarda Records; auth, Hon Do Ban, Hildegard Publ Company, 00; auth, Nocturne, Vivace Pr, 00. **CONTACT ADDRESS** Eubanks Conservatory of Music, 4928 Crenshaw, Los Angeles, CA 90043.

EVANS, ADELINE
PERSONAL Born Eunice, LA, m, 2 children **DISCIPLINE** SPEECH COMMUNICATION **EDUCATION** Grambling State Univ, BS, 60; La State Univ, MA, 64; La Tech Univ, ASHA in SP, 68; Fla State Univ, PhD, 80. **CAREER** Instr to asst prof, Grambling State Univ, 60-76; asst prof to assoc prof, Fla A&M Univ, 76-88; prof, 88-. **HONORS AND AWARDS** AACC Scholar Cert; Scholar of the Year; Teach of Year; Outstand Ser Awd; Gold Medal Awd; PEP Awd; Dist Teach Awd. **MEMBERSHIPS** NCA; AACCD; ASLHA; FCA; Delta Sigma Theta; NAACP. **RESEARCH** Teaching pedagogy; oratorical contests; historical perspectives; black dialect. **SELECTED PUBLICATIONS** Auth, Speech Up: Issues and Opinions, McGraw Hill, 99; auth, Speech and Language Control, McGraw Hill, 99; auth, "Increasing Self-Confidence in the Classroom," Nat Hon Report Mag (99); auth, "Speech Across the Curriculum," Fla Comm J (98); auth, "Mentoring Students," Nat Hon Report Mag (98). **CONTACT ADDRESS** Sch Gen Studies, Florida A&M Univ, 1500 Wahnish Way, Tallahassee, FL 32307-3100.

EVANS, DALE WILT
PERSONAL Born 09/27/1939, Philadelphia, PA **DISCIPLINE** PHILOSOPHY, CLASSICS **EDUCATION** Pa State Univ, BA, 65, MA, 66, PhD (Philos), 73. **CAREER** Instr philos, Univ Wyo, 69-72; programmer, Sperry Univac, 74-75; ASST PROF PHILOS, PA STATE UNIV, 75-, Fulbright fel, 70-71. **MEMBERSHIPS** Am Philos Soc. **RESEARCH** Contemporary philosophy; contemporary man. **SELECTED PUBLICATIONS** Auth, Prisoners of objective thinking, 81 & The heterogeneous symmetry of nature, 82, Contemp Philos. **CONTACT ADDRESS** Dept of Philos, Pennsylvania State Univ, DuBois, Du Bois, PA 15801.

EVANS, DAVID ALLAN
PERSONAL Born 04/11/1940, Sioux City, IA, m, 1958, 3 children **DISCIPLINE** ENGLISH **EDUCATION** Morningside Col, BA, 62; Univ of Iowa, MA, 64; Univ of Ark, MFA, 76. **CAREER** Asst prof, Adams State Univ, 66-68; prof & writer in residence, Sdak State Univ, 68-; Prof English, South Dakota State Univ, 78-; Writer in Residence, 96-. **HONORS AND AWARDS** Nat Endowment for the Arts artist's award; Bush Artist Found, artist's award; South Dakota Arts Counc, artist's award; Poetry Soc of Am; Human Behavior and Evolution Soc. **MEMBERSHIPS** Poetry Soc of Am, ASCAP, HBES. **RESEARCH** Contemporary American and British poetry; evolutionary psychology and literature. **SELECTED PUBLICATIONS** Ed, What the Tallgrass Says, Augustana Col (Sioux Falls, SD), 81; auth, "Almost a Rememberence," in A Book of Re-readings (Best Cellar Press, 78); auth, "Poetry, Science, and Survival," Seems (81); auth, "Poetry and Sport," Aethlon (87); auth, "From the Pole Vaulter's Bluff," in Imagining Home: Writings from the Midwest (Univ of Ninn Press, 95); auth, "Trailing Buddy," Sport Literate (97); auth, preface to, "Skeletons of the Prairie," Codington County Hist Soc, 00. **CONTACT ADDRESS** Dept English, So Dakota State Univ, 1 Sd State Univ, CB 504, Brookings, SD 57007-0001. **EMAIL** evans@brookings.net

EVANS, DAVID HUHN
PERSONAL Born 01/22/1944, Boston, MA, m, 1990, 2 children **DISCIPLINE** MUSIC **EDUCATION** AB, Harvard, 65; MA, 67; PhD, 76; Univ of CA, Los Angeles. **CAREER** Prof of Music, Dir of Reg Studies, Ethnomusicology, Univ of Memphis, Tchg Asst Classics, 65-68; Tchg Asst, Folklore and Mythology, Univ of CA, Los Angeles 66-69; Lecturer in Anthro, CA State Univ, Fullerton, 69-72; Lecturer in Folklore and Hist, Univ of CA, 72-; Asst Prof Anthro, 72-76, Assoc Prof Anthro, 76-78, Univ of CA, Fullerton; Assoc Prof of Music, Memphis State Univ, 78-81. **HONORS AND AWARDS** Commencement Latin Oration; Harvard Coll, 65; Faculty Res Grant, CA State Univ, Fullerton Found, 71, 72, 78; Seed Grant to Facilitate Learning, Memphis State Univ, 78; Chicago Folklore Prize, 81-82; Univ Distinguished Res Awd, Memphis State Univ, 87; Grant, Partners of the Americas for recording Venezuelan traditional music, 89, 90; Grant, Tennessee Hum Council, 98; Dean's Creative Achievement Awd, 99. **RESEARCH** Afro Amer Folk music, **SELECTED PUBLICATIONS** Spec Ed, New Perspectives on the Blues, American Music 14 No4, 393-526, 96; ed, Shane K. Bernard, Swamp Pop: Cajun and Creole Rhythm and Blues, 96; Charles Wolfe, In Close Harmony: The Story of the Louvin Brothers, 97; Guido van Rijin, Roosevelt's Blues: African-American Blues and Gospel Songs on FDR, 97; Kenneth M. Johnson, The Johnson Family Singers: We Sang for Our Supper, 97; Sebastian Danchin, Blues Boy: The Life and Music of B.B. King, 98; ed, "Gerhard Kubik, Africa and the Blues," 99; Blues, in Garland Encyclopedia of World Music Vol3: The United States and Canada NY Garland (in press); Beale Street, Helena, Memphis, and Mississippi Valley, in Encyclopedia of Popular Music of the World, editors Mick Gidley, David Horn, Paul Oliver and John Shepherd London Cassell (in press). **CONTACT ADDRESS** Dept of Music, Univ of Memphis, Memphis, TN 38152. **EMAIL** dhevans@cc.memphis.edu

EVANS, DEANNA G.
PERSONAL Born 02/01/1943, Bastrop, TX, d, 3 children **DISCIPLINE** ENGLISH **EDUCATION** Univ Penn, BA, 63; Univ Tex-Austin, MA, 66; Case W Reserve, PhD, 71. **CAREER** Adj fac, Cleveland State Univ, 76-83; prof, Bemidji State Univ, 83-. **HONORS AND AWARDS** NEH, Stanford Univ, 84; NEH, SUNY, 85; NEH, Rice Univ, 97. **MEMBERSHIPS** MLA, MMLA, Medieval Asn Midwest, Medieval Acad Am, New Chaucer Soc, Asn Scottish Lit Student. **RESEARCH** Chaucer, Middle Scots literature, Medieval women. **SELECTED PUBLICATIONS** Auth, "Teaching Baker's 'Classrood Edition' of Wulf and Eadwacer," Old English Newsletter, (90); auth, "Bakhtin's Literary Carnivalesque and Dunbar's Fasternis Evin in Hell," Stud in Scottish Lit, 26, pp 354-65, (91); auth, "Donald Owre and ernard Stewart: Responding to a Villain and a Hero in Dunbar's Poetry," Proceedings of the Medieval Asn of MidW, 1, pp 117-130, (91); auth, "Using Student Dramatic Performance to Introduce Medieval Women Writers to the General Public," Medieval Feminist Newsletter, 25, pp 37-40, (98); auth, "Scott's Redgauntlet and the Late Medieval Romance of Friendship, Eger and Grime," Stud in Scottish Lit, 31 pp 31-45, (99). **CONTACT ADDRESS** Dept Engish, Bemidji State Univ, 1500 Birchmont Dr NE, Bemidji, MN 56601-2699. **EMAIL** devan@vaxl.bemidji.msus.edu

EVANS, GWYNNE BLAKEMORE
PERSONAL Born 03/31/1912, Columbus, OH, m, 1943, 2 children **DISCIPLINE** ENGLISH **EDUCATION** Ohio State Univ, AB, 34; Univ Cincinnati, AM, 36; Harvard Univ, PhD, 40. **CAREER** Asst & tutor, Brooklyn Col, 40-41; instr Univ Wis, 41-42, 45-56, asst prof, 46-47; from asst prof to prof English, Univ Ill, Urbana, 47-67; prof English, 67-75, Cabot Prof English Lit, Harvard Univ, 75-, Dexter traveling fel, Harvard Univ, 40 & Guggenheim Mem Found, 48-49; ed, J English & Ger Philol, 55-63. **MEMBERSHIPS** Am Acad Arts Scis, 88-. **RESEARCH** Elizabethan drama; Shakespeare; 17th century prompt materials. **SELECTED PUBLICATIONS** Auth, Plays and Poems of William Cartwright, Univ Wis; Shakespearean Promptbooks of the 17th Century, Vols I-VIII, Univ Va; ed, Supp, In: Variorum I Henry IV, Shakespeare Asn Am; textual ed, Complete Works of Shakespeare, Houghton, 74, gen and text ed, second ed, 97; ed, New Cambridge Shakespeare's Romeo and Juliet, 84; ed, Elizabethan-Jacobean Drma, A New Mermaid Background Book, 88; ed, New Cambridge Shakespeare's Sonnets, 96. **CONTACT ADDRESS** Barker Center, Harvard Univ, Cambridge, MA 02138.

EVANS, JAMES A. S.
PERSONAL Born 03/24/1931, Galt, ON, Canada **DISCIPLINE** CLASSICS **EDUCATION** Univ Toronto, BA, 52; Yale Univ, MA, 53, PhD, 57. **CAREER** Prof, Univ Western Ont, 55-60; vis lectr, Victoria Col, 60-61; vis asst prof, Univ Texas Austin, 61-62; fac mem hist, McMaster Univ, 62-72; prof, 72-96, dept head, 86-93, PROF EMER CLASSICS, UNIV BC, 96-; Gertrude Smith prof, Am Sch Class Stud (Athens), 91; non-resident fac mem, Cecil Green Col, 93-94; vis prof, Univ Wash, 97; Whitehead prof, Am Sch Class Stud (Athens), 98-99. **HONORS AND AWARDS** Fel, Royal Soc Can, 92. **MEMBERSHIPS** Mng comt, Am Sch Class Stud (Athens); Class Asn Can (pres 82-84); Asn Ancient Hist (secy treas 79-82). **SELECTED PUBLICATIONS** Auth, Social and Economic History of an Egyptian Temple in Greco-Roman Egypt, 61; auth, Procopius, 72; auth, Herodotus, 82; auth, Herodotus, Explorer of the Past: Three Essays, 91; auth, The Age of Justinian: The Circumstances of Imperial Power, 96; ed, Waterloo Rev, 57-60; ed, Vergilius, 63-73; ed Polis and Imperium: Studies in Honour

of Edward Togo Salmon, 74; co-ed, Studies in Medieval and Renaissance History, 77-96;. **CONTACT ADDRESS** Classics Dept, Univ of British Columbia, Buch C625, Vancouver, BC, Canada V6T 1Z1. **EMAIL** jaevans@interchange.ubc.ca

EVANS, JAMES EDWARD
PERSONAL Born 09/25/1946, Savannah, GA, m, 1969, 3 children **DISCIPLINE** ENGLISH LITERATURE **EDUCATION** Univ NC, Chapel Hill, BA, 67; Univ Pa, MA, 68, PhD, 71. **CAREER** Asst prof, 71-76, assoc prof Eng, 76-88, dir, grad studies Eng, 81-88, prof, 88, dept head, 90-99, Univ NC, Greensboro. **HONORS AND AWARDS** Phi Beta Kappa **MEMBERSHIPS** MLA; Am Soc 18th Century Studies; S Atlantic Mod Lang Assn. **RESEARCH** Early English periodicals; 18th century English novel; comedy. **SELECTED PUBLICATIONS** Art, Resisting a Private Tyranny in Two Humane Comedies, Broken Boundaries: Women & Feminism in Restoration Drama, University Press of Kentucky, 96; ed, John Gay and Oliver Goldsmith, Encyclopedia of British Humorists, S. Gale, Garland, 96. **CONTACT ADDRESS** Dept of English, Univ of No Carolina, Greensboro, 1000 Spring Garden, Greensboro, NC 27412-0001. **EMAIL** evansj@fagan.uncg.edu

EVANS, JAMES L.
PERSONAL Born 08/231/1927, Paris, MO, w, 1973 **DISCIPLINE** ENGLISH, SOCIOLOGY **EDUCATION** Cen Mo State Col, BA, BS, 50; Univ Colo, MA, 55; Univ Tex Austin, MA, 64; PhD, 67. **CAREER** U.S. Army Med Corp, 51-53; teacher, pub sch, 55-60; teacher, Laredo Jr Col, 61-64; teacher asst to asst prof to assoc prof to prof to emer, Univ Tex, 65-. **HONORS AND AWARDS** Alum Asn Master Prof, 98; Who's Who Am Teachers, 96; Emeritus, 97. **MEMBERSHIPS** MLA; TKS; WCPM; Ellen Glasgow Soc; HCHS. **RESEARCH** Beadle Dime novels of 1800s; literature and history of American West; sources of place names; Willa Cather; travel and travel literature of Europe. **SELECTED PUBLICATIONS** Auth of 12 articles on Beadle Dime Novels, Round-Univ Pr (87-98); auth, "Ethnic Tensions in the Lower Rio Grande Valley to 1860," in American Folklore (Utah Pr, 76); auth, "Teaching My Antonia to Non-English Majors from Spanish to-Speaking Homes," in Approaches to Teaching My Antonia (MLA, 89). **CONTACT ADDRESS** PO Box 672, McAllen, TX 78505-0672.

EVANS, JOAN
DISCIPLINE MUSIC HISTORY **EDUCATION** Boston Univ, PhD. **CAREER** Teacher, Wash State Univ and York Univ. **RESEARCH** Musical life in Germany during the first half of the 20th century, particularly the reception of modernist music during the Nazi era. **SELECTED PUBLICATIONS** Auth, Hans Rosbaud: A Bio-Bibliography. **CONTACT ADDRESS** Dept of Music, Wilfrid Laurier Univ, 75 University Ave W, Waterloo, ON, Canada N2L 3C5. **EMAIL** jevans@wlu.ca

EVANS, JOHN MARTIN
PERSONAL Born 02/02/1935, Cardiff, England, m, 1963, 2 children **DISCIPLINE** ENGLISH LITERATURE **EDUCATION** Oxford Univ, BA, 58, MA and DPhil(English), 63. **CAREER** From asst prof to assoc prof, 63-75, assoc dean humanities and sci, 77-81, Prof English, Stanford Univ, 75-, Harmsworth scholar, Oxford Univ, 61-63. **HONORS AND AWARDS** NEH fel; ACLS fel. **MEMBERSHIPS** Renaissance Soc Am; Milton Soc. **RESEARCH** Renaissance English, Milton; travel literature; history of ideas. **SELECTED PUBLICATIONS** Auth, The Road from Horton, Victoria Univ, 83; auth, Moral Fiction in Milton and Spencer, Review of Eng Stud, Vol 48, 97; A Poem of Absences, Milton Quart, Vol 27, 93; The Humanism of Milton Paradise Lost, Rev Eng Stud, Vol 46, 95; auth, Milton's Imperial Epiu, Cornel Univ, 96; Heirs of Fame--Milton and Writers of the English Renaissance, Rev Eng Stud, Vol 48, 97; auth, The Metonic Moment, Kentucky Univ, 98. **CONTACT ADDRESS** Dept of English, Stanford Univ, Stanford, CA 94305-1926. **EMAIL** evans@stanford.edu

EVANS, LAWRENCE
DISCIPLINE ENGLISH **EDUCATION** Harvard Univ, PhD. **CAREER** Prof, Northwestern Univ. **RESEARCH** Victorian and 20th century fiction. **SELECTED PUBLICATIONS** Ed, The Letters of Walter Pater, 70. **CONTACT ADDRESS** Dept of English, Northwestern Univ, 1801 Hinman, Evanston, IL 60208.

EVANS, MEI MEI
PERSONAL Born 08/18/1953, Philadelphia, PA, 1 child **DISCIPLINE** ENGLISH **EDUCATION** Hampshire Col, BA, 75; Vt Col, MFA, 84; Univ Wash, PhD, 99. **CAREER** Asst prof, Univ Alaska Anchorage, 94-95; asst prof, Alaska Pac Univ, 00-. **HONORS AND AWARDS** Barbara Himmelman Awd, Univ Wash, 95. **MEMBERSHIPS** Asn for the Study of Lit and the Environ. **RESEARCH** The social construction of 'nature'; Environmental justice; Alaska as 'last frontier'. **SELECTED PUBLICATIONS** Co-ed, Environmental Justice Politics, Poetics, and Pedagogy, Univ Ariz Press, (forthcoming). **CONTACT ADDRESS** Dept Liberal Studies, Alaska Pacific Univ, 4101 University Dr, Anchorage, AK 99508. **EMAIL** m2evans@alaskapacific.edu

EVANS, ROBERT C.
PERSONAL Born 03/01/1955, Braddock, PA, m, 1978 **DISCIPLINE** ENGLISH **EDUCATION** Univ Pittsburgh, BA, 77; Princeton Univ, PhD, 84. **CAREER** Instructor to Prof, Auburn Univ, 82-. **HONORS AND AWARDS** Richard M. Weaver Fel, 79; Fel, Princeton Univ, 80; Whiting Fel, 82; G.E. Bentley Prize, 82; Res Fel, Newberry Library, 84; Res Fel, Am Coun of Learned Soc, 85; Res Grant, Auburn Univ, 86; Res Fel, Folger Shakespeare Library, 86; Mellon Fel, 86; Res Fel, Huntington Library; Res Grant, Auburn Univ, 87; NEH Travel Grant, 88; Res Grant, Am Philos Soc, 88; Res Grant, Auburn Univ, 88; Res Fel, Univ CA, 89;p Res Fel, Folger Shakespeare Library, 89; CASE Prof of the Year, AL, 89; Raculty Excellence Awd, Auburn Univ, 89; Res Grant, Auburn Univ, 90-92; NEH Summer Stipend, 92; Phi Kappa Phi; Who's Who Among Col Teachers; Special Awd, AUM, 98. **SELECTED PUBLICATIONS** Auth, Jonson and the Contexts of His Time, Bucknell Univ Press, 94; co-auth, My Name Was Martha: A Renaissance Woman's Autobiographical Poem, Locust Hill Press, 93; auth, Habits of Mind: Evidence and Impact of Ben Jonson's Reading, Bucknell Univ Press, 95; co-auth, The Muses Females Are: Martha Moulsworth and Other Women Writers of the English Renaissance, Locust Hill Press, 95; co-auth, "The Birthday of My Self: Martha Moulsworth, Renaissance Poet," Princeton Journal of Women, Gender, and Culture, 96; co-auth, Short Fiction: A Critical Companion, Locust Hill Press, 97; co-auth, Frank O'Connor: New Perspectives, Locust Hill Press, 98; co-auth, Ben Jonson's Major Plays: Summaries of Modern Monographs, Locust Hill Press, 00; co-auth, Brian Friel: New Perspectives, Locust Hill Press, 01. **CONTACT ADDRESS** Dept Eng & Philos, Auburn Univ, PO Box 244023, Montgomery, AL 36124-4023. **EMAIL** litpage@aol.com

EVANS, ROBLEY JO
PERSONAL Born 11/28/1933, Portland, OR, 1 child **DISCIPLINE** ENGLISH **EDUCATION** Reed Col, BA, 56; Univ Wash, MA, 61, PhD (English), 68. **CAREER** From instr to assoc prof, 64-78, Prof English, Conn Col, 78-, Fulbright scholar, France, 56-57. **RESEARCH** Romantic poets; Victorian poets and critics; American Indian literature. **SELECTED PUBLICATIONS** Auth, J R R Tolkien, Warner Paperback Libr, 72. **CONTACT ADDRESS** Dept of English, Connecticut Col, 270 Mohegan Ave, New London, CT 06320-4125.

EVANS-GRUBBS, JUDITH
PERSONAL Born 11/30/1956, Atlanta, GA, m, 1979, 1 child **DISCIPLINE** CLASSICS **EDUCATION** Emory Univ, BA, 78; Amer School of Classical Studies, 78-79; Stanford Univ, PhD, 87. **CAREER** Prof, 00-; Assoc prof Classical Studies, Sweet Briar Col, 93-98; asst prof Classical Studies, Sweet Briar Col, 87-93; Tchg Fel, Stanford Univ, 83-84, 85-87; lctr, Intercollegiate Center for Classical Studies, 84-85. **HONORS AND AWARDS** Nat Endowment for Humanities Fel for Col Tchrs, 97-98; NEH Summer Sem for Col Tchrs, Amer Acad Rome, 95; Jessie Ball Dupont Fel, Nat Humanities Center, 93-94; Nat Endowment Humanities Summer Stipend, 88; Mednick Grant, Va Found Independent Cols, 88. **MEMBERSHIPS** Am Philoi Asn; Am Soc Greek & Latin Epigraphy; Am Soc Papyrologists; Asn Ancient Historians; Classical Asn Middle West & South; Classical Asn Va; N Amer Patristics Soc; Women's Classical Caucus. **RESEARCH** Marriage and Family in Ancient Roman Society; Roman Imperial Law; Slavery in Ancient Rome; Women and Gender in Antiquity. **SELECTED PUBLICATIONS** Auth, 'Pagan' and 'Christian' Marriage: the State of the Question, Jour Early Christian Studies, 94; auth, Law and Family in Late Antiquity: the Emperor Constantine's Marriage Legislation, Oxford Univ Pr, 95; auth, articles on "Marriage," "Divorce," and Concubinage" in Guide to Late Antiquity, ed. G. Bowersock, P. Brown, and O. Grabar; auth, "The Slave who Avenged her Master's Death," Ancient History Bulletin (00). **CONTACT ADDRESS** Dept of Classical Studies, Sweet Briar Col, Sweet Briar, VA 24595. **EMAIL** evansgrubbs@sbc.edu

EVELEV, JOHN
DISCIPLINE ENGLISH **EDUCATION** Bowdoin Col, BA, 87; Duke Univ, MA, 90, PhD, 95. **CAREER** VIS ASST PROF, ENG, UNIV TENN **MEMBERSHIPS** Am Antiquarian Soc **RESEARCH** Herman Melville **SELECTED PUBLICATIONS** Auth, "Made in the Marquesas: Typee, Tattooing and Melville's Critique of the Literary Marketplace," Ariz Quart 48:4, 92; auth, "The Contrast: The Problem of Theatricality and Political and Social Crisis in Postrevolutionary America," Early Am Lit 31:1, 96. **CONTACT ADDRESS** Dept of Eng, Univ of Tennessee, Knoxville, 301 McClung Tower, Knoxville, TN 37996.

EVENSON, BRIAN
DISCIPLINE ENGLISH **EDUCATION** Brigham Young Univ, BA, 89; Univ Wash, MA, 90; PhD, 93. **CAREER** Asst Prof, Brigham Young Univ, 94-96; Asst prof, Oklahoma State Univ, 95-99; Asst prof, Univ Denver, 99-. **HONORS AND AWARDS** O Henry Awd, 98; Res grant, Oklahoma Foundation for the Humanities, 97; Lilly Library Helm Fel, 95. **MEMBERSHIPS** MLA, Cormac McCarthy Soc. **RESEARCH** Narratology; Gilles Deleuze; Samuel Beckett; Cormac McCarthy; 18th Century Novel; 20th Century Novel. **SELECTED PUBLICATIONS** Auth, Understanding Robert Cooter, Univ SC Press, forthcoming; auth, Altmann's Tongue, New York, 94; auth, Father of Lies, New York, 98. **CONTACT ADDRESS** Dept English, Univ of Denver, 2140 S Race St, Denver, CO 80210-4639. **EMAIL** bevenson@du.edu

EVETT, DAVID HAL
PERSONAL Born 06/17/1936, Denver, CO, m, 1960, 3 children **DISCIPLINE** ENGLISH **EDUCATION** Univ South, BA, 58; Harvard Univ, AM, 62, PhD(English), 65. **CAREER** Asst prof English, Univ Wis, Madison, 65-70; Prof English, Cleveland State Univ, 70-, Am Philos Soc grant-in-aid, 68-69. **HONORS AND AWARDS** British Cnl Prz in the Human **MEMBERSHIPS** MLA; Shakespeare Asn of Am; Renaissance Soc Am. **RESEARCH** Visual imagery; Shakespeare. **SELECTED PUBLICATIONS** Auth, Paradise's Other map: Marvell's Upon Appleton House and the Topos of the Locus Amoenus, Pub Mod Lang Asn Am, 5/70; Travail of a Department, In: Academic Supermarkets, Jossey-Bass, 71; Types of King David in Shakespeare's Lancastrian Tetralogy, Shakespeare Studies, 10/81; Mammon's Grotto: Renaissance Grotesque Decor and Some Features of Spenser's Faerie Queene, English Lit Renaissance; auth, Literature and the Visual Arts in Tudor England, Univ of Ga, 91. **CONTACT ADDRESS** Dept of English, Cleveland State Univ, 1983 E 24th St, Cleveland, OH 44115-2440. **EMAIL** d.evett@csuohio.edu

EWALD, HELEN ROTHSCHILD
PERSONAL Born 04/30/1947, Berwyn, IL, m, 1976, 2 children **DISCIPLINE** RHETORICAL THEORY, COMPOSITION **EDUCATION** Valparaiso Univ, BA, 69; Univ Ariz, MA, 71; Ind Univ, PhD (drama and Renaissance lit), 77. **CAREER** Grad asst compos, Univ Ariz, 69-71; instr English and Am lit, Valparaiso Univ, 71-73; instr compos and Shakespeare, Ind Univ, 74-76; asst prof compos and lit, Washburn Univ, Topeka, 77-80; Full Prof-Rhetoric and Professional Communication, Compos, Iowa State Univ, 80-. **MEMBERSHIPS** CCC, NCTE; Am Soc Theater Res. **RESEARCH** Rhetorical theory, specifically feminist theory and composition; alternative pedagogy. **SELECTED PUBLICATIONS** Auth, Exploring Agency in Classroom Discourse or, Should David Have Told his Story, Coll Compos Comm, Vol 45, 94; Waiting for Answerability--Bakhtin and Composition Studies, Coll Compos Comm, Vol 44, 93; auth, Business Communication, 1997; auth, Mutuality: Alternative Pedagogies, in Rhetoric and Composition Classroom, 00. **CONTACT ADDRESS** 203 Ross, Ames, IA 50011-1201. **EMAIL** hewald@iastate.edu

EWALD, OWEN M.
PERSONAL Born 11/18/1969, Washington, DC, m, 1995, 2 children **DISCIPLINE** CLASSICS **EDUCATION** Yale Univ, BA, 92; Univ Wash, PhD, 99. **CAREER** Instr, Univ Wash, 92-01; Asst Prof, Seattle Pac Univ, 01-. **HONORS AND AWARDS** Simpson Humanities Fel, 98-99. **MEMBERSHIPS** Am Philol Asn; Class Asn of the Pac NW. **RESEARCH** Roman Historiography; Greco-Roman Mythology; Ancient comedy; Ancient Jobs. **SELECTED PUBLICATIONS** Auth, "Virgilian End Rhymes: Geo 1.393-423," Harvard Studies in Class Philol, (90): 311-313. **CONTACT ADDRESS** Dept Class, Seattle Pacific Univ, 3307 3rd Ave W, Seattle, WA 98119. **EMAIL** ewald@spu.edu

EWELL, BARBARA CLAIRE
PERSONAL Born 03/10/1947, Baton Rouge, LA **DISCIPLINE** ENGLISH RENAISSANCE AND WOMEN'S LITERATURE **EDUCATION** Univ Dallas, BA, 69; Univ Notre Dame, PhD (English), 74. **CAREER** Asst prof English, Loyola Univ South, 74-75; instr, Newcomb Col, 75-76; asst prof, Univ Col, Tulane Univ, 76-79; Asst Prof English, Univ Miss, 79-, Lectr and instr, writing workshops, Mobil, Erns and Erns and Save the Children Conf, 77-79; consult, Allen Johnson and Assoc, 77-79; Prof of English, City College, Loyola Univ, 84-; Visiting prof, Fordham Univ, 94. **HONORS AND AWARDS** National Endowment for the Humanities, dir, summer seminar, 88; Louisana Endowment for the Humanities, 92; Fulbright Comission/CIES, Sr. Lecture Awd, Universidad Catolica, Santiago Chile, fall 92; NEH Faculty Focus Group, picturing America, Loyola Univ, 99; Monticello Col Found fel, Newberry libr, 82-83. **MEMBERSHIPS** MLA, Women's Caucus; SCent Mod Lang Asn; Nat Women's Studies Asn; NCTE; SCent Renaissance Asn. **RESEARCH** Michael Drayton and related poets; Kate Chopin in the context of 19th century popular fiction; women writers of the English Renaissance. **SELECTED PUBLICATIONS** Auth, Kate Chopin, Ungar (New York), 86; co-ed, New Orleans Review: Special Issue on Louisiana Women Writers, 15:1 (Spring 88); auth, "Kate Chopin and the Dream of Female Selfhood," in Beyond the Bayou: Essays on Kate Chopin (Louisiana State UP, Baton Rouge, 92), 157-65; ed, Louisiana Women Writers: New Critical Essay and a Comprehensive Bibliography, LSU Press (Baton Rouge), 92; auth, "Telling Stories, Teaching Narrative: A Progressive Writing Assignment," Teaching Faulkner 5 (Spring 94):1-2; auth, "Making Places: Kate Chopin and the Art of Fiction," Louisiana Literature 11 (Spring 94):157-71; co-auth, "Creating Conversations: A Model for Interdisciplinary Team-Teaching," College Teaching 48.4 (Fall 95):127-131; ed, Performance for a Lifetime: A Festschrift Honoring Dorothy Brown: Essays on Women, Religion, and the Renaissance, Loyola (New Orleans),

97; co-auth, "Taking on the World: Women and the Fulbright Program," National Women's Studies Journal (Spring 98); Guest ed, Ocentennial of The Awakening Special Issue, The Southern Quarterly (spring 99). **CONTACT ADDRESS** Dept of English, Loyola Univ, New Orleans, 6363 St. Charles Ave., New Orleans, LA 70118. **EMAIL** bewell@loyno.edu

EYLER, AUDREY S.
PERSONAL Born 03/16/1943, NY, m, 1966 **DISCIPLINE** ENGLISH **EDUCATION** Houghton Col, BA, 64; Alfred Univ, MA, 67; Univ Minn, PhD, 78. **CAREER** Milton Col, 66-81; Pacific Lutheran Univ, 81-. **MEMBERSHIPS** Anglican Conf for Irish Studies. **RESEARCH** Irish Literature - 20th Century Fiction and Drama. **SELECTED PUBLICATIONS** Auth, "The Uses of the Past," Essays on Irish Culture, ed Robert Carrall; auth, Celtic, Christian, Socialist: The Novels of Anthony C. West, 93. **CONTACT ADDRESS** Dept English, Pacific Lutheran Univ, Tacoma, WA 98447-0001.

EYSTER, KEVIN IRENIES
PERSONAL Born 09/11/1955, Mansfield, OH, m, 1990, 2 children **DISCIPLINE** ENGLISH, COMMUNICATION ARTS **EDUCATION** Ohio State Univ, BA, 79; MA, 84; E Mich Univ, MA, 98; Univ Ky, PhD, 91. **CAREER** Adj instr, Univ Mich Dearborn, 90-94; adj instr to asst prof to assoc prof, Madonna Univ, 91-. **HONORS AND AWARDS** NEH, Distinguished Prof, Madonna Univ, 01-03; Fac Excellence Awd, 94; Distinguished Teaching Awd, Univ Ky, 87. **MEMBERSHIPS** AFS; MCEA; MMLA; MLA; NCTE. **RESEARCH** American literature; portfolios and writing; American folklore; composition studies. **SELECTED PUBLICATIONS** Auth, "The Personal Narrative in Fiction: Faulkner's The Reivers," West Folklore 51 (92): 11-21; auth, "'My Name's Not Hugo, You Fool, I'm Jack!': An Analysis of Gurvey Norman's Ancient Creek," J Ky Study 12 (95): 119-27; auth, "Portfolios in the Literature Classroom: Pedagogical and Assessment Tool," Mich Col English Asn J 1 (95): 56-66. **CONTACT ADDRESS** English Dept, Madonna Univ, 36600 Schoolcraft Rd, Livonia, MI 48150. **EMAIL** eyster@smtp.munet.edu

F

FAAS, EKBERT
PERSONAL Born 05/07/1938, Berlin, Germany **DISCIPLINE** LITERATURE **EDUCATION** Univ Munich, Drphil; Univ Wurzburg, Drhabil. **CAREER** FAC MEM, YORK UNIVERSITY. **SELECTED PUBLICATIONS** Auth, Towards a New American Poetics, 78; auth, Ted Hughes, 80; auth, Young Robert Duncan, 83; auth, Tragedy and After: Euripides, Shakespeare, Goethe, 84; auth, Shakespeare's Poetics, 86; auth, Retreat into the Mind: Victorian Poetry and the Rise of Psychiatry, 88; auth, Woyzeck's Head, 91. **CONTACT ADDRESS** York Univ, 4700 Keele St, North York, ON, Canada M3J 1P3. **EMAIL** efmt@yorku.ca

FABER, J. ARTHUR
DISCIPLINE MEDIEVAL AND RENAISSANCE LITERATURE **EDUCATION** Calvin, AB, Bowling Green, MA; Univ Mass, PhD. **CAREER** Prof; **RESEARCH** Interplay of language and thought, comparative linguistics, English language and style. **SELECTED PUBLICATIONS** Areas: poetry, literary criticism. **CONTACT ADDRESS** Wittenberg Univ, Springfield, OH 45501-0720. **EMAIL** jafaber@wittenberg.edu

FABER, RONALD
PERSONAL Born 01/27/1948, Newark, NJ, m, 0 child **DISCIPLINE** MASS COMMUNICATION STUDIES **EDUCATION** Univ Pa, MS; Univ Wis Madison, PhD. **CAREER** Prof. **HONORS AND AWARDS** Ed, Journal of Advertising **RESEARCH** Compulsive buying; third-person effects; advertising effects. **SELECTED PUBLICATIONS** Auth, Two Forms of Compulsive Compunction: Comorbidity Between Compulsive Buying and Binge Eating, J Consumer Res, 95; auth, The Future of Advertising After the Millennium, Marketing Rev, 96; auth, "Susceptibility and Severity: Perceptual Dimensions Underlying the Third-Person Effect, "Communication Research (99): 240-267; auth, "A Programmatic Investigation into Compulsive Buying," in I Shop, Therefore I Am: Compulsive Buying and the Search for Self, ed. A.L. Benson (Northvale, NJ, Aronson Press, 00), 27-53; auth, "The Urge to Buy: A Uses and Gratifications Perspective on Compulsive Buying," in The Why of Consumption, ed. S. Ratneshwar, D.G. Mick, and C. Huffman (London, Routledge, 01). **CONTACT ADDRESS** Mass Commun Dept, Univ of Minnesota, Twin Cities, 206 Church St SE, 111 Murphy Hall, Minneapolis, MN 55455. **EMAIL** faber001@maroon.tc.umn.edu

FABRICANT, CAROLE
PERSONAL Born Brooklyn, NY **DISCIPLINE** ENGLISH AND ANGLO-IRISH LITERATURE **EDUCATION** Bard Col, BA; Johns Hopkins Univ, PhD. **CAREER** Prof, Art Hist, Univ Calif, Riverside, Prof, English, VCR **HONORS AND AWARDS** James L. Clifford prize winner; Guggenheim Fellowship; Mellon Fellowship. **RESEARCH** Postcolonial studies, 18th century studies; Jonathan Swift; Irish Studies. **SELECTED PUBLICATIONS** Auth, Swift's Landscape, Johns Hopkins Univ Press, 82; reissued, Univ Notre Dame Press, 95; The Ideology of Augustan landscape design, Stud 18th-Century Cult; Gulliver's Travels, St Martin's Press series; Case Studies, Contemp Criticism, 95; The Shared Worlds of [Delariviere] Manley and Swift, Pope, Swift, and Women Writers, 96; Defining Self and Others: Pope and 18th-Century Gender Ideology, Criticism, 98; auth, Riding the Waves of Post Colonial Migrancy, Diaspora, 98; auth, Speaking for the Irish Nation: The Drapier, the Bishop, and the Problems of Colonial Representation, ELH, 99. **CONTACT ADDRESS** Dept of Eng, Univ of California, Riverside, Riverside, CA 92521-0323. **EMAIL** finaid@pop.ucr.edu

FACKLER, HERBERT VERN
PERSONAL Born 01/23/1942, Monroe, LA, m, 1964, 2 children **DISCIPLINE** ANGLOIRISH & MODERN LITERATURE **EDUCATION** Centenary Col, LA, BA, 64; NM Highlands Univ, MA, 65; Univ NC, Chapel Hill, PhD(English), 72. **CAREER** Teaching asst English, NMex Highlands Univ, 65; instr, Centenary Col, La, 65-68; asst prof, Northwestern State Univ, LA, 69-70; asst prof, Univ Tulsa, 70-71; asst prof English & dir creative writing, 71-76, assoc prof, 76-96, Prof, Univ Southwestern LA, 97-; NDEA fel, Univ NC, Chapel Hill, 72; dir, Deep South Writers Conf, 80, 8, 94. **HONORS AND AWARDS** Phi Kappa Phi; Phi Eta Sigma; Sigma Tau Delta; NDEA Fellow Univ NC, Chapel Hill, 68-69; USL Found Distinguished Prof, 81; Highlands Distinguished Alumnus, 91; Assoc Samuel P. Peters Int Lit Res Center, 92. **MEMBERSHIPS** Col English Asn (treas, 72-74); SCent Mod Lang Asn; Am Comt Irish Studies; MLA; Deep South Writers Conf (dir, 80 & 81); Popular Culture Asn. **RESEARCH** Nineteenth and twentieth century British and Am literature; AngloIrish lit; mystery and detective fiction. **SELECTED PUBLICATIONS** Auth, Series of studies of Deirdre works, Eire-Ireland, spring 72; Proust and Celine, Studies, by Mem SCent Mod Lang Asn, winter 73; The Dierdre legend in Anglo-Irish lit: A prolegomenon, Univ Southwestern La Res Ser, 74; That Tragic Queen: the Deirdre in Anglo-Irish Literature, Univ Salzburg, 79; ed, Modern Irish Novel, excluding Joyce, Univ Southwestern La Res Ser, 80; Reflections on a Slender Volume, in Lawrence Durrell: Comprehending the Whole, ed, Julian Raper, et al; Dialectic in the Corpus of Robert B. Parker's Spenser Novels, Clues, 94; Spenser's New England Conscience, Colby Quart, 98; novels: The Snow Pirates, The Last Long Pass, and Virginia Creeper, Dancing Jester Press, 99. **CONTACT ADDRESS** Dept of English, Univ of Southwestern Louisiana, Box 44691 USL, Lafayette, LA 70504-8401.

FADERMAN, LILLIAN
PERSONAL Born 07/18/1940, Bronx, NY, 1 child **DISCIPLINE** ENGLISH **EDUCATION** Univ Calif, Berkeley, BA, 62; Univ Calif, Los Angeles, MA, 64, PhD, 67. **CAREER** Chmn dept English, 71-72, dean, Sch Humanities, 72-73, asst vpres acad affairs, 73-76, prof English, Calif State Univ, Fresno, 67-. **HONORS AND AWARDS** Lambda Literary Awards, 91, 94, 99; ALA awards, 81, 91. **MEMBERSHIPS** MLA. **RESEARCH** Gay studies; American ethnic writing; women's studies. **SELECTED PUBLICATIONS** Auth, Odd Girls and Twilight Lovers: A History of Lesbian Life in Twentieth Century America, 91; ed, Chloe Plus Olivia: An Anthology of Lesbian Literature from the Seventeenth Century to the Present, 94; auth, I Begin My Life All Over: The Hmong and the American Immigrant Experience, 98; auth, To Believe in Women: What Lesbians Have Done for America - A History, 99. **CONTACT ADDRESS** Dept of English, California State Univ, Fresno, 5245 N Baker, Fresno, CA 93740-8001. **EMAIL** lillian_faderman@csufresno.edu

FAGLES, ROBERT
PERSONAL Born 09/11/1933, Philadelphia, PA, m, 1956, 2 children **DISCIPLINE** COMPARATIVE LITERATURE, ENGLISH **EDUCATION** Amherst Col, AB, 55; Yale Univ, MA, 56, PhD (English), 59. **CAREER** LTjg, United States Navy, 6th Fleet, 58-61; Instr English, Yale Univ, 59-60; from instr to asst prof, 60-65, assoc prof English and comp lit, 65-70, dir prog comp lit, 66-75, PROF COMPLIT, PRINCETON UNIV, 70-, chair of department, 75-94, Arthur W. Marks 19 prof of comp lit, vis prof, The Hebrew Univ, 74-75; vis prof, Comparative Lit, Yale Univ, 90; NY State Summer Writers Inst, Sem on Translation. **HONORS AND AWARDS** Calif Commonwealth Club Gold Medal for Non-fiction, 80; British Comparative Lit Asn, First Prize, Translation Competition, 91, British Comparative Lit Asn, Second Prize, Translations on a Jewish theme, 91; Coun for Advancement and Support of Education, Gold Medal for Looking for Kafka, 91; Landon Translation Award, The Acad of Am Poets, 91; Nat Bk Critics Circle award for nonfiction, Finalist, 95; PEN/Ralph Manheim Medal for Translation, 97; Truman Capote Prize for Literary Criticism, 97; Behrman Award, Princeton; Commander, Order of the Phoenix, Hellenic Republic. **MEMBERSHIPS** Am Acad of Arts and Letters; Am Acad of Arts and Sciences, Am Philosophical Soc. **RESEARCH** The epic tradition; Greek tragedy; Greek, Latin and English lyric poetry. **SELECTED PUBLICATIONS** Auth, Translations, Aeschylus Oresteia, Sophocles Three Theban Plays, Homer Iliad and Odyssey; auth, The Lies of Art: Max Beerbohm's Parody and Caricature, New York: Alfred A Knopf, 72, London: Victor Gollancz, 73; co-transl, The Dark Room and other Poems, by Enrique Lihn, New York: New Directions, 78, 2nd ed, 00; auth, Translating Neruda: The Way to Macchu Picchu, Stanford Univ Press, 80, paperback edition, 86; auth, Paul Celan: Poet, Survivor, Jew, Yale Univ Press, 95, paperback edition, 97, Nota Bene edition, 01, Verlag C.H. Beck, Munich, 97, pocketbook, 01; auth, Heights of Macchu Picchu/ Alturas de Macchu Picchu, Nevada, with photographs by Edward Ranney, Limited Editions Club, 98; coed, Jewish American Literature: A Norton Anthology, W.W. Norton, 00; ed and translator, Selected Poems and Prose of Paul Celan, W.W. Norton, 00; auth, Deathfugue/Todesfuge (Celan), Limited Editions Club, 01. **CONTACT ADDRESS** Dept of Comp Lit, Princeton Univ, Princeton, NJ 08540. **EMAIL** fagles@princeton.edu

FAGUNDO, ANA MARIA
PERSONAL Born 03/13/1938, Santa Cruz de Tenerife, Spain **DISCIPLINE** COMPARATIVE LITERATURE, SPANISH AND ENGLISH LITERATURE **EDUCATION** Univ Redlands, BA, 62; Univ Wash, MA, 64, PhD (comp lit), 67. **CAREER** Asst prof Span lit, 67-76, Assoc Prof Contemp Span Lit, Univ Calif, Riverside, 76-, Ed-in-Chief, Alaluz. **HONORS AND AWARDS** Carabela de Oro poetry prize. **MEMBERSHIPS** Am Asn Teachers Span and Port; Sociedad Colegial de Escritores. **RESEARCH** Contemporary Spanish poetry; contemporary American poetry. **SELECTED PUBLICATIONS** Auth, Cantico or a Tribute to Mother, Insula Revista De Letras Y Ciencias Humanas, Vol 48, 93. **CONTACT ADDRESS** Dept of Span, Univ of California, Riverside, Riverside, CA 92502. **EMAIL** ana.fagundo@ucr.edu

FAIGLEY, LESTER
PERSONAL Born Charleston, WV, m, 1969, 2 children **DISCIPLINE** ENGLISH; RHETORIC **EDUCATION** Univ Wash, PhD, 76. **CAREER** Prof English, Univ Tex at Austin, 79-; Dir, Div of Rhet & Composition. **HONORS AND AWARDS** MLA Mina P Shaughnessy Prize, 92; Conf of Col Composition & Commun Outstanding Book Awd, 94. **MEMBERSHIPS** Conf of Col Composition & Commun; Modern Language Asn; Rhet Soc of Am. **RESEARCH** Rhetorical theory; impacts of technology on writing; visual rhetoric. **SELECTED PUBLICATIONS** Auth, Fragments of Rationality: Postmodernity and the Subject of Composition, Univ Pittsburgh Press, 92; co-auth, Discursive Strategies for Social Change: An Alternative Rhetoric of Argument, Rhet Rev, 14, 142-72; 95; auth, Literacy After the Revolution, Col Composition & Commun, 48, 30-43, 97; auth, "Material Literacy and Visual Design" Rhetorical Bodies: Toward a Materrial Rhetoric, Univ Wisconsin Press, (99): 171-201; co-auth, God Reasons, Allyn & Bacon, 00; auth, The Longman Guide tot the Web, Longman, 00 . **CONTACT ADDRESS** Div of Rhet & Composition, Univ of Texas, Austin, Austin, TX 78712-1122. **EMAIL** faigley@uts.cc.utexas.edu

FAIRBANKS, CAROL
PERSONAL 3 children **DISCIPLINE** ENGLISH LITERATURE **EDUCATION** Univ Mich, BA; Univ Wis Eau Claire, MA; Univ Minn, PhD. **CAREER** Fac. **RESEARCH** Japanese women fiction writers in translation. **SELECTED PUBLICATIONS** Auth, seven books: two on African-American writers, two on women in literature, and three on American and Canadian farm women in literature. **CONTACT ADDRESS** Dept of English, Univ of Wisconsin, Eau Claire, Hibbard Hall 359, PO Box 4004, Eau Claire, WI 54702-4004. **EMAIL** fairbacf@uwec.edu

FAIRCHILD, BERTRAM H.
PERSONAL Born 10/17/1942, Houston, TX, s, 2 children **DISCIPLINE** ENGLISH LITERATURE **EDUCATION** Univ Kans, BA, 64; MA, 68; Univ Tulsa, PhD, 75. **CAREER** Instr, Univ of Nebr, 68-70; instr, SW Tex State Univ, 73-76; asst to assoc prof, Tex Woman's Univ, 76-83; prof, Calif State Univ, 83-00. **HONORS AND AWARDS** Award, NEA; Guggenheim Fel; Rockefeller Grant. **MEMBERSHIPS** Assoc of Lit Scholars and Critics. **RESEARCH** William Blake, British Romantics. **SELECTED PUBLICATIONS** Auth, Such Holy Song: Music As Idea, Form and Image in the Poetry of William Blake, Kent State Univ Pr, (Kent, OH), 80. **CONTACT ADDRESS** Dept English, California State Univ, San Bernardino, San Bernardino, CA 91711. **EMAIL** bhfairchil@aol.com

FAIRLEY, IRENE R.
PERSONAL Born 01/02/1940, Brooklyn, NY, 2 children **DISCIPLINE** LINGUISTICS, ENGLISH **EDUCATION** Queens Col, NYork, AB, 60; Harvard Univ, MA, 61, PhD (ling), 71. **CAREER** From instr to asst prof English, C W Post Col, Long Island Univ, 68-73; from asst prof English and ling to prof, Northeastern Univ, 73-. **HONORS AND AWARDS** Am Coun Learned Soc grant-in-aid, 77-78; Guggenheim fel, 79-80. **MEMBERSHIPS** Ling Soc Am; MLA; Semiotic Soc Am; Millay Colony for Arts. **RESEARCH** Linguistic approaches to literature, stylistics, poetics. **SELECTED PUBLICATIONS** Auth, Millay, Edna, Stvincent Gendered Language and Form, Sonnets from an Ungrafted Tree, Style, Vol 29, 95. **CONTACT ADDRESS** 34 Winn St, Belmont, MA 02478. **EMAIL** irfairley@nev.edu

FAJARDO, SALVADOR J.
PERSONAL Born 01/06/1940, Zaragoza, Spain, m, 1970, 4 children **DISCIPLINE** SPANISH, LITERATURE **EDUCATION** Col Stemisles, BA, 58; Univ Montreal, MA, 62; Univ Chicago, PhD, 68. **CAREER** Asst prof, N Ill Univ, 65-66; asst prof, Univ Fla, 66-67; asst prof, Univ SCar, 67-68; asst prof, Univ West Ont, 70-71; asst prof, Neth Hawthorn Col, 72-75; asst prof, New Eng Col, 75-78; assoc prof to prof to dept chmn, Wesleyan Univ, 78-90; prof to dept chmn, SUNY Binghamton, 90-. **HONORS AND AWARDS** Woodrow Wilson Fel, 63; Univ Chicago Humanities Fel, 64; NEH, 92, 94, 95, 98, 00. **MEMBERSHIPS** MLA; AATSD; SSSAS; Cervantes Soc. **RESEARCH** Contemporary Spanish poetry; Cervantes. **SELECTED PUBLICATIONS** Auth, Claude Simon; auth, Luis Cernude; auth, Multiple Species; auth, The Poetry of Rafael Alseih; auth, The Word and the Mirror; ed, Essays on the Poetry of Luis Cernude; co-ed, At Home and Beyond: New essays on Spanish Poets of the Twenties; co-ed, After the War: essays on Recent Spanish Poetry; co-ed, Don Quixote. **CONTACT ADDRESS** Span Studies Dept, SUNY, Binghamton, PO Box 6000, Binghamton, NY 13902-6000. **EMAIL** farardo@binghamton.edu

FALK, THOMAS HEINRICH
PERSONAL Born 09/25/1935, Frankfurt, Germany, m, 1967, 2 children **DISCIPLINE** CONTEMPORARY LITERATURE **EDUCATION** Wagner Col, BA, 58; Univ S Calif, AM, 63, PhD, 70. **CAREER** Instr, 65-70, asst prof, 70-79, assoc prof to assoc prof emeritus, dept linguistics & languages-German, Mich State Univ, 79-. **MEMBERSHIPS** Am Asn Tchr Ger. **RESEARCH** Contemporary Literature. **SELECTED PUBLICATIONS** auth Elias Canetti: A Critical Study, 93. **CONTACT ADDRESS** Thomas Heinrich Falk, 8939 Caminito Verano, La Jolla, CA 92037-1606. **EMAIL** thfalk@san.rr.com

FALLER, GREG
PERSONAL Born 09/18/1954, Camden, NJ, m, 1979, 1 child **DISCIPLINE** FILM, DIGITAL MEDIA, CULTURAL STUDIES **EDUCATION** Northwestern Univ, PhD, 87. **CAREER** Prof, Towson univ; coord, Student Media Atts Festival & Annual Fall Film Series. **MEMBERSHIPS** Coordr, TU Film & Video Soc; SCS; UFVA; L/FA. **SELECTED PUBLICATIONS** Essayist & advisor, The International Dictionary of Films & Filmakers, St James Pr. **CONTACT ADDRESS** Dept of Electronic Media & Film, Towson State Univ, 8000 York Rd, Towson, MD 21252. **EMAIL** gfaller@towson.edu

FALLER, LINCOLN B.
PERSONAL Born 01/26/1943, Huntington, NY, m, 1964, 1 child **DISCIPLINE** ENGLISH **EDUCATION** Oberlin Col, AB, 64; Univ Chicago, AM, 65; PhD, 71. **CAREER** Lectr, Roosevelt Univ, 66-67; lectr to prof, assoc dean, 95-98, chmn 98-02, Univ Mich, 68-. **HONORS AND AWARDS** NEH, 72, 73-74; Fulbright Fel, 86-87; Sr Fel, Mich Soc Fel, 99-03; Excel Edu Awd Col LS and A, Univ Mich, 91, 92, 93, 94, 95; Fac Recog Awd, Univ Mich, 95; APS Res Grnt, 76; Res Grnts, Rackham Sch Grad Stud, Univ Mich, 72, 73, 75, 91. **MEMBERSHIPS** MLA; ASECS; ASA; EMCS; NCTE. **RESEARCH** Native American literature, eighteenth-century English literature, rise of modern novel, criminal biography, travel narratives, Cheyenne historiography and ethnography, the Southwest, the Santa Fe trail, literature and culture, history and culture. **SELECTED PUBLICATIONS** Auth, Between Jest and Earnest: The Comedy of Sir John Vanbrugh, Mod Philo (74); auth, In Contrast to Defoe: The Rev. Paul Lorrain, Historian of Crime, Hunt Lib Qtly (76); auth, The Myth of Captain James Hind: A Type of Primitive Fiction before Defoe, Bull NY Pub Lib (76); auth, Turned to Account: The Forms and Functions of Criminal Biography in Late Seventeenth and Early Eighteenth Century England, Cambridge UP, 87; auth, The Popularity of Addison's "Cato," and Lillo's "The London Merchant," 1700-76, Garland, 88; auth, "King William, K.J. and James Whitney: The Several Lifes and Affiliations of a Jacobite Robber," Eighteenth-Cen Life (88); auth, "Criminal Opportunities in the Eighteenth Century: The "Ready Made" Contexts of the Popular Literature of Crime, Comp Lit Stud (87); auth, Crime and Defoe: A New Kind of Writing, Cambridge UP, 93; auth, Making Medicine Against "White Man's Side of Story": George Bent's Letters to George Hyde, Am Ind Qtly (00); auth, "Captain Misson's Failed Utopia, Crusoe's Failed Colony: Race and Identity in New, Not Quite Imaginable Worlds" Eighteenth-century Theo Interp (01). **CONTACT ADDRESS** Eng Dept, Univ of Michigan, Ann Arbor, 3187 Angell Hall, Ann Arbor, MI 49109. **EMAIL** faller@umich.edu

FALLON, JEAN
DISCIPLINE 16TH CENTURY FRENCH LITERATURE, 19TH CENTURY POETRY **EDUCATION** Univ VA, PhD. **CAREER** Instr, Hollins Col, 90. **RESEARCH** French lyric poets of the 16th century. **SELECTED PUBLICATIONS** Auth, Voice and Vision in Ronsard's Les Sonnets pour Helene. **CONTACT ADDRESS** PO Box 9576, Roanoke, VA 24020.

FALLON, RICHARD GORDON
PERSONAL Born 09/17/1923, New York, NY, m, 1946, 2 children **DISCIPLINE** SPEECH & DRAMA **EDUCATION** Columbia Univ, BA, 48, MA, 51. **CAREER** Asst prof speech & theatre & dir theater, Hartwick Col, 48-51, Md State Teachers Col, 51-54; gen dir, Little Theater, Jacksonville, Fla, 54-56; asst prof speech & theater, 57-60, assoc prof theater, 60-65, dean sch theatre, 73-82, Prof Speech & Theater & Dir Theater, Fla State Univ, 65-, Emer Dean & Dir Prof Progs, 82-, Gen dir, Asolo Theater Festival, 62; mem, Princeton Conf Theater Res, 66; chmn Theater Res Coun Am, 66-68; theater consult, New England Cols, 67; dir grant, Cult Enrichment Through Live Theatre, 67-69; dir, Burt Reynolds Inst Theatre Training. **HONORS AND AWARDS** Nat Conf Christians & Jews Gold Medal Awd, 62; E Harris Harbison Awd for Gifted Teaching, 71. **MEMBERSHIPS** Am Nat Theatre & Acad; Am Theatre Asn (pres-elect, 81-82, pres, 82-83); Speech Commun Asn; Nat Theatre Conf; Univ Resident Theatre Asn **RESEARCH** Development of cultural enrichment through live theatre in high schools of Florida; development of Eddie Dowling University Theatre Foundation for new playwrights; quantitative research in theater audiences in Miami, Florida. **SELECTED PUBLICATIONS** Assoc-ed, Works in progress, Theatre Documentation, 67. **CONTACT ADDRESS** Office of the Dean, Florida State Univ, 600 W College Ave, Tallahassee, FL 32306-1096. **EMAIL** rfallon23@cs.com

FALLON, ROBERT THOMAS
PERSONAL Born 06/06/1927, New York, NY, d, 2 children **DISCIPLINE** ENGLISH AND COMPARATIVE LITERATURE **EDUCATION** US Mil Acad, BS, 49; Canisius Col, MA, 60; Columbia Univ, PhD, 65. **CAREER** Asst prof English, US Mil Acad, 61-64; chmn dept mil sci, 69-70, asst to the pres, 70-71, assoc prof, 70-79, prof English, 79-95, prof Emer, 95-, Lasalle Col. **HONORS AND AWARDS** James Holly Hanford Awd, 94, NEH fel, 90-91; Outstanding Acad Book, Choice, 96. **MEMBERSHIPS** Milton Soc Am (treas, 77-86, vpres, 87, & pres, 88); MLA; John Donne Soc; ALSC. **RESEARCH** John Milton--military and political imagery; English history -- The Interregnum; contrib ed, The Variorum Edition of the Poetry of John Donne. **SELECTED PUBLICATIONS** Auth, John Milton and the honorable artillery company, Milton Quart, 5/75; Filling the gaps: New perspectives on Mr Secretary Milton, Milton Studies XII, 78; Miltonic documents in the public records office, London, Studies Bibliog, 78; Milton's defenseless doors: The limits of irony, Milton Quart, 12/79; Milton in the anarchy, 1659-1660: A question of consistency, Studies English Lit, winter 81; Milton's Epics and the Spanish War: Toward a Poetics of Experience, In: Milton Studies XV, Univ Pittsburgh Press, 82; Captain or Colonel: The Soldier in Miltons Life and Art, Univ Missouri Press, 84; Milton in Government, Penn State Univ Press, 93; Divided Empire: Miltons Political Imagery, Penn State Univ Press, 95; Shakespeare: A Theater goer's Guide, Ivan R. Dee, Pub, 00. **CONTACT ADDRESS** River Rd, Lumberville, PA 18933. **EMAIL** fallon@lasalle.edu

FALLON, STEPHEN
PERSONAL Born Washington, DC, w, 3 children **DISCIPLINE** LITERATURE **EDUCATION** Univ Va, PhD. **CAREER** Instr, Univ Notre Dame. **HONORS AND AWARDS** 2 NEH fel; Hanford Book Awd; Phi Beta Kappa. **RESEARCH** Philosophical and theological contexts of early modern poetry and prose. **SELECTED PUBLICATIONS** Auth, "'To Act of Not': Milton's Conception of Divine Freedom," J of the Hist of Ideas 49 (88): 425-49; auth, "The Metaphusics of Milton's Divorce Tracts," in Politics Poetics, and Hermeneutics in Milton's Prose, ed David Loewentstein & James Grantham Turner (Cambridge: Cambridge Univ Pr, 90), 69-83; auth, "Hunting the Fox: Equivocation and Authorial Duplicity in 'The Prince'," PMLA 107 (92): 1181-95; auth, "Intention and its Limits in 'Paradise Lost': The Case of Bellerophon," in Literary Milton: Text, Pretext, Context, ed Diana Trevino Benet & Michael Lieb (Pittsburgh: Duquesne Univ Pr, 94): 161-79, 246-49; auth, "'Elect above the Rest': Self-Representation and Theology in Milton," in Milton and Heresy, Ed John Rumrich & Stephen Dobranski (Caambridge: Cambridge Univ Pr, 98), 93-116; auth, "Milton's Arminianism and the Authorship of 'De Doctrina Christiana'," Tex Studies in Lits & Lang 41 (99): 103-27; auth, "'The Spur of Self-Concernment': Milton in his Divorce Tracts," in John Milton: The Writer in his Works (spec vol of Milton Studies 38), ed Albert C. Labiola & Michael Lieb (Pittsburgh: Univ of Pitts Pr, 00), 220-42; auth, "'Paradise Lost' in Intellectual History," in Blackwell's Milton Companion, ed Thomas N. Corns (London: Blackwells), forthcoming. **CONTACT ADDRESS** Univ of Notre Dame, Notre Dame, IN 46556. **EMAIL** fallon.1@nd.edu

FANG, IRVING E.
PERSONAL Born 05/04/1929, New York, NY, d, 2 children **DISCIPLINE** COMMUNICATION **EDUCATION** UCLA, PhD, 66. **CAREER** Eight years as a newspaper reporter & editor; one year with Reuters, London; eight years with ABC-TV News as news writer then as asst mgr of political unit; Prof, School of Journalism, Univ Minn, 69-; Vist Prof, Nanyang Tech Univ Singapore. **HONORS AND AWARDS** Mitchell Charnley Awd, 84; Distinguished Broadcast J Ed, Asn for Ed in Journalism and Mass Commun, 90; Fulbright Prof, Univ of the Philippines, 96-97. **RESEARCH** Broadcast journalism; history of media technology. **SELECTED PUBLICATIONS** Auth, A History of Mass Communication: Six Information Revolutions, Focal Press, 97; Television News, Radio News, Rada Press, 85; Those Radio Commentators, Iowa State Univ Press, 77. **CONTACT ADDRESS** School of Journalism and Mass Commun, Univ of Minnesota, Twin Cities, Minneapolis, MN 55455. **EMAIL** fangx001@tc.umn.edu

FANNING, CHARLES F.
DISCIPLINE ENGLISH **EDUCATION** Harvard Univ, BA, 64; MAT, 66; Univ Penn, MA, 68, PhD, 72. **CAREER** Assoc, prof, Eng, Bridgewater State Univ; current, PROF, ENG & HIST & DIR IRISH STUD, SO ILL UNIV CARBONDALE. **HONORS AND AWARDS** T.J. Turner Awd of Org of Am Historians, 79; Am Book Awd, 89; Am Conf for Irish Stud Book Prize for Lit Criticism, 91. **MEMBERSHIPS** Am Conference for Irish Studies. **SELECTED PUBLICATIONS** Auth, Finley Peter Dunne and Mr. Dooley: The Chicago Years, 78; auth, Mr. Dooley and the Chicago Irish: An Anthology, 76, 87; ed, The Exiles of Erin: Nineteenth-Century Irish-American Fiction, Dufour Editions, 87 & 97; auth, The Irish Voice in America: Irish-American Fiction from the 1760s to the 1980s, 90, 99. **CONTACT ADDRESS** Dept of English, So Illinois Univ, Carbondale, Mailcode 4503, Carbondale, IL 62901. **EMAIL** celtic42@siu.edu

FANT, GENE C., JR.
PERSONAL Born 06/30/1963, Laurel, MS, m, 1989, 2 children **DISCIPLINE** ENGLISH, EDUCATION **EDUCATION** James Madison Univ, BS, 84-; Old Dominion Univ, MA, 87; New Orleans Baptist Theolog Sem, Mdiv, 91; Univ Southern Miss, MED, 95, PhD, 95. **CAREER** Asst dir, Univ Southern Miss, 94-95; asst prof, dir, Miss Col, 95-; assoc prof, ch, Dept of Eng, Miss Col, 99-. **HONORS AND AWARDS** Dave-Maher Prize, 94; Linwood Orange Award & Fel, 94; Who's Who in the World, 99; doctoral fel, usm. **MEMBERSHIPS** MLA; SCMLA; Conf on Christianity and Lit; Miss Philol Asn; Int Arthurian Society. **RESEARCH** Medieval/Renaissance English literature; Bible as literature; popular culture. **SELECTED PUBLICATIONS** Auth, Petrarchan Hagiography, Gender, and Subjectivity in Mary Wroth's Pamphilia to Amphilanthus, 95; auth, art, Pun's on the Name of the Beloved in Wroth's Pamphilia to Amphilanthus, 96; auth, art, Peachwood Remembered: The Photography of Marian Stark Gaines, 97; auth, art, John Stewart Bryan, Eugene S. Pulliam, Theodore Lothrop Stoddard, 98; coauth, Expectant Moments, 99. **CONTACT ADDRESS** Mississippi Col, Clinton, PO Box 4022, Clinton, MS 39058. **EMAIL** fant@mc.edu

FANT, J. CLAYTON
DISCIPLINE CLASSICAL STUDIES **EDUCATION** Williams Coll, BA, 69; Univ of Mich, PhD, 76. **CAREER** Asst Prof, 76-79, Wellesley Coll; Instr, 79-81, St Stephen's School Rome; vis Asst Prof, 81-83, Univ of Mich; Asst Prof, Assoc Prof, 84-, Univ of Akron. **HONORS AND AWARDS** Amer Acad Rome Fel. **MEMBERSHIPS** AIA, APA, ASMOSIA, Vergilian Society. **RESEARCH** Roman Archaeology **SELECTED PUBLICATIONS** Auth, Cavum Antrum Phrygiae, The Organization and Operations of the Roman Imperial Marble Quarries at Docimium, BAR Intl Series, 89; Ancient Marble Quarrying and Trade, BAR Intl Series, 88; Ideology Gift and Trade, A Distribution Model for the Roman Imperial Marbles, in: The Inscribed Economy, Production and Distribution in the Roman Empire in the Light of Instrumentum Domesticum, ed W V Harris & S Panciera, JRA, 93; The Imperial Marble Yard at Portus, in: Ancient Stones, Quarrying Trade and Provenance. Interdisciplinary Studies on Stones and Stone Technology in Europe and Near East from the Prehistoric to the Early Christian Period, ed, M Waelkens, N Herz & L Moens, 92. **CONTACT ADDRESS** Dept of Classics, Univ of Akron, 326 Olin, Akron, OH 44325-1910. **EMAIL** cfant@uakron.edu

FANTHAM, ELAINE
PERSONAL Born 05/25/1933, Liverpool, England, w, 1958, 2 children **DISCIPLINE** CLASSICS **EDUCATION** Oxford Univ, MA, B.Litt, 57; Liverpool Univ, PhD, 62. **CAREER** Vis prof, 66-68, Indiana Univ; from asst to full Prof of Classics, 68-86, Univ Toronto; Giger Prof of Latin, Princeton Univ, 86-99. **HONORS AND AWARDS** Former vpres, Res Div, APA; trustee, Am Acad in Rome. **MEMBERSHIPS** Am Philol Asn; Class Asn of Canada; Int Soc for the Hist of Rhetoric. **RESEARCH** Latin epic; rhetoric; Roman social history; women's history. **SELECTED PUBLICATIONS** Auth, A Commentary on Lucan De Bello Civili Book 2, Cambridge, 92; co-auth, Women in the Classical World: Image and Text, Oxford, 94; auth, Roman Literary Culture: from Cicero to Apuleius, Johns Hopkins, 96; transl, The Hidden Author by Gian Biagio Conte, Berkeley, 96; ed. and commentator , Ovid: Fasti Book IV, Cambridge, 96; auth, Envy and Fear the Begetters of Hate: Statius Thebaid and the Genesis of Hatred, in, Gill, ed, The Passions in Latin Literature and Thought, Cambridge, 97; auth, Occasions and Contexts of Roman Public Oratory, in Dominik, ed, Roman Eloquence, London, 97; auth, Propertius' Old New Rome, in Habinek, ed, The Roman Cultural Revolution, Cambridge, 97; auth, Allecto's First Victim, in, Vergil's Aeneid in Its Political Context, Duckworth, 98; auth, "Fighting Words; Turnus at bay in the Latin council," Am Journal of Philology, 99. **CONTACT ADDRESS** 28 1/2 Wiggins St, Princeton, NJ 08540. **EMAIL** fantham@ariel.princeton.edu

FARAONE, CHRISTOPHER
DISCIPLINE CLASSICS **EDUCATION** Stanford Univ, PhD, 88. **CAREER** Asst prof, Va Polytech Inst & State Univ, 88-91; Asst prof, Univ Chicago, 91-93; Assoc prof, Univ Chicago, 93-. **HONORS AND AWARDS** John Simon Guggenheim Memorial Foundation Fel; Nat Endowment Hum; Jr Fel; ACLS Grant; NEH Summer Stipend; State Coun Higher Educ Va (SCHEV) Grant; Phi Beta Kappa Sch; Whiting Dissertation Fel; Stanford Grad Fel. **MEMBERSHIPS** Am Philol Asn; Clas Asn Midwest & South; Int Plutarch Soc; Soc Ancient Med; Soc Biblical Lit; Women's Clas Caucus. **SELECTED PUBLICATIONS** Auth, Talismans and Trojan Horses: Guardian Statues in Ancient Greek Myth and Ritual, Oxford Univ Press, 92, 96; auth, Ancient Greek Love Magic, Harvard Univ Press, 98; Co-ed, Magika Hiera: Ancient Greek Magic and Religion, Oxford Univ Press, 91; co-ed, Masks of Dionysus, Cornell Univ Press, 93. **CONTACT ADDRESS** Univ of Chicago, 5801 S Ellis, Chicago, IL 60637.

FARBER, CAROLE
DISCIPLINE COMMUNICATION STUDIES **EDUCATION** Univ British Columbia, BA; PhD. **RESEARCH** Feminist theory and pedagogy; social organization of anthropological knowledge; cultural studies; cultural performances. **SELECTED PUBLICATIONS** Auth, Subject Matters: Critical Essays in Feminist Teaching, Curriculum and Ethnography. **CONTACT ADDRESS** Dept of Communication, Univ of Western Ontario, London, ON, Canada N6A 5B8. **EMAIL** farber@uwo.ca

FARBER, GERALD HOWARD
PERSONAL Born 03/21/1935, El Paso, TX, m, 1967, 4 children **DISCIPLINE** COMPARATIVE LITERATURE, ENGLISH & AMERICAN LITERATURE **EDUCATION** Univ CA, Los Angeles, BA, 58; CA State Univ, Los Angeles, MA, 62; Occidental Col, PhD, 70. **CAREER** Lectr English, 62-65, asst prof, CA State Univ, Los Angeles, 66-68; from lectr to asst prof, 68-74, assoc prof, 74-81, Prof Comp Lit, San Diego State Univ, 81-; Maitre assistant associe, 74 & maitre de conferences associe, 77, Univ Paris VII. **HONORS AND AWARDS** Outstanding Fac Awd, SDSU, 93. **RESEARCH** Aesthetics; the teaching of literature; comedy; eighteenth-century European lit; Marcel Proust. **SELECTED PUBLICATIONS** Auth, The Student as Nigger, 70 & The University of Tomorrowland, 72, Simon & Schuster; A Field Guide to the Aesthetic Experience, Foreworks Press, 82; The Third Circle: On Education and Distance Learning, Sociological Perspectives, vol 41, no 4, 98; auth, Scott Moncrieff's Way: Proust in Translation, Proust Said That, no 6, March 97; Aesthetic Resonance: Beyond the Sign in Literature, Reader: Essays in Reader-Oriented Theory, Criticism, and Pedagogy, no 32, fall, 94; Golden Grove Unweaving (and not a moment too soon), Fiction International, no 27, 94; Learning How To Teach: A Progress Report, College English, vol 52, no 2, Feb 90. **CONTACT ADDRESS** Dept of English and Comp Lit, San Diego State Univ, San Diego, CA 92182-8140. **EMAIL** jfarber@mail.sdsu.edu

FARBER, JAY JOEL
PERSONAL Born 11/06/1932, Philadelphia, PA, m, 1952, 2 children **DISCIPLINE** CLASSICAL LANGUAGES AND LITERATURES **EDUCATION** Univ Chicago, BA, 52, MA, 54; Yale Univ, PhD (Greek and ancient hist), 59. **CAREER** Instr classics, Univ Chicago, 57-60; asst prof, Rutgers Univ, 60-63; assoc prof, 63-70, chmn dept, 63-79, Prof Classics, Franklin and Marshall Col, 70-95, Rutgers Univ Res Coun grants, 61 and 62; vis res assoc, Ctr Int Studies, Princeton Univ, 62-63; examnr, comt advan placement classics, Col Entrance Exam Bd, 71-74; Shirley Watkins Seinman Prof of Classics Emer, 95-. **MEMBERSHIPS** Am Philol Asn; Am Soc Papyrologists; Class Asn Atlantic States. **RESEARCH** Greek myth; Greek tragedy; Greek political theory. **SELECTED PUBLICATIONS** Auth, "Family Financial Disputes in the Patermouth's Archive," Bul Am Soc Papyrologists, Vol 27, 90. **CONTACT ADDRESS** Dept of Classics, Franklin and Marshall Col, 1415 Hillcrest Rd, Lancaster, PA 17603. **EMAIL** farberjoel@aol.com

FARBER, JIMMIE D.
PERSONAL Born 07/25/1927, Lyons, NE, m, 1947, 2 children **DISCIPLINE** ENGLISH **EDUCATION** Midwestern Univ, BA, 68; MA, 70; Texas Tech Univ, EdD, 79. **CAREER** Teaching asst, Midwestern Univ, 68-70; instr, Lamar Univ, 70-72; instr & English Dept Chemn, Vernon Regional Jr Col, 72-. **HONORS AND AWARDS** Alpha Chi; Phi Kapp Phi; listed in Who's Who in the Southwest; listed in Who's Who Among Teachers. **MEMBERSHIPS** Nat Coun Teachers of English, Tex Commun Col Teachers Asn. **RESEARCH** Developmental English--Bring the under prepared student up to speed. **CONTACT ADDRESS** Dept Commun Arts & Sci, Vernon Regional Junior Col, 4400 College Dr, Vernon, TX 76384-4005. **EMAIL** jfarber@vrjc.cc.tx.us

FARNHAM, ANTHONY EDWARD
PERSONAL Born 07/02/1930, Oakland, CA, m, 1957, 2 children **DISCIPLINE** ENGLISH, PHILOLOGY **EDUCATION** Univ Calif, Berkeley, AB, 51; Harvard Univ, MA, 57, PhD(English), 64. **CAREER** From instr to assoc prof, 61-72, Prof English, Mt Holyoke Col 72-, Vis asst prof, Amherst Col, 64-65; lectr, Smith Col, 65-66; vis asst prof, Univ Calif, Berkeley, 66-67; Prof, Emeritus, 99-. **MEMBERSHIPS** Mediaeval Acad Am; MLA; Am Cath Hist Asn; Asn Literary Scholars & Critics; Dante Soc Am; New Chaucer Soc; Phi Beta Kappa **RESEARCH** Old and Middle English language and literature; history of the English language. **SELECTED PUBLICATIONS** Ed, A Sourcebook in the History of English, Holt, Rinehart & Winston, 69; auth, Statement and Search in the Confessio Amantis, Mediaevalia, 93. **CONTACT ADDRESS** Dept of English, Mount Holyoke Col, 50 College St, South Hadley, MA 01075-1461. **EMAIL** afarnham@mtholyoke.edu

FARR, JUDITH BANZER
PERSONAL Born 03/13/1937, New York, NY, m, 1962, 1 child **DISCIPLINE** ENGLISH & AMERICAN LITERATURE, AMERICAN PAINTING & LITERATURE **EDUCATION** Marymount Manhattan Col, BA, 57; Yale Univ, MA, 59, PhD(English & Am lit), 65. **CAREER** Instr English, Vassar Col, 61-63; asst prof, St Mary's Col, CA, 64-68; from asst prof to assoc prof, State Univ NY Col New Paltz, 68-76; vis assoc prof, assoc prof, 77-88, PROF ENGLISH, GEORGETOWN UNIV, 89-99, prof emerita, 99-; State Univ NY res award fel, 72; grant-in-aid, Am coun Learned Soc, 74, 83, 86; Am Philos Soc Award, 86; Georgetown Univ Center for German Studies award, 93. **HONORS AND AWARDS** Alumnae Awd for Achievement in Arts and Letts, Marymount-Manhattan Col, 76; Honorary LL D, Marymount Manhattan Col, 92. **MEMBERSHIPS** Cosmos Club. **RESEARCH** 19th century Am lit & painting; modern poetry & fiction; Brit fiction. **SELECTED PUBLICATIONS** Auth, The Passion of Emily Dickinson, Harvard Univ Press, 92; I Never Came to You in White: A Novel, Houghton Mifflin, 96; The Life and Art of Elinor Wylie, LA State Univ Press, 83; poems, fiction, & essays in professional & commercial publications; ed, Twentieth Century Interpretations of Sons and Lovers, Prentice-Hall, 69; Emily Dickinson: New Century Views, Simon & Schuster, 95. **CONTACT ADDRESS** 5064 Lowell St NW, Washington, DC 20016. **EMAIL** jgfarr@dellnet.com

FARR, MARIE T.
PERSONAL Born 12/16/1940, Chicago, IL **DISCIPLINE** ENGLISH **EDUCATION** Loyola Univ, BS, 62; Purdue Univ, MA, 65; Univ Washington, PhD, 78. **CAREER** Instr, Seattle Univ, 66-68; Instr to Prof and Assoc Chair, East Carolina Univ, 72-. **HONORS AND AWARDS** English Dept Awd, 97; NC Humanities Council Grant, 94; Honorable Mention, Kathleen Gregory Klein Awd, 92; Marie T Farr Fund, 91; Grant, NC Humanities Council, 88; Awd for Teaching Excellence, Robert L Jones Alumni Asn, 77-78. **MEMBERSHIPS** Mod Lang Asn, Women's Caucus of the Mod Lang Asn, South Atlantic Mod Lang Asn, Nat Women's Studies Asn, SE Women's Studies Asn, Am Asn of Univ Women, Nat Org for Women, League of Women Voters. **RESEARCH** Twentieth century British and American fiction and drama; Women's literature and women's Studies; Feminist pedagogy. **SELECTED PUBLICATIONS** Auth, "Anna Katharine Green," American Women Prose Writers: 1870-1920, forthcoming; auth, "Everything I didn't Want to Know I Learned in Lit class: Sex, Sexual Orientation, and Student Identity," International Journal of Sexuality and Gender Studies, 00; auth, "Home is Where the Heart Is--Or Is It? Three Women and Charlotte Perkins Gilman's Theory of the Home," in Charlotte Perkins Gilman: Optimist Reformer, Univ Iowa Press, 99; auth, "Inglis Fletcher," American National Biography, Oxford Univ Press, 98; auth, "Revisiting a Classic Feminist Technotopia: Marge Piercy's Woman on the Edge of Time," Women and Environments International, (98): 16-17; auth, "Freedom and Control: Automobiles in American Women's fiction of the 70s and 80s," Journal of Popular Culture, (95): 157-169. **CONTACT ADDRESS** Dept English, East Carolina Univ, 1000 E 5th St, Greenville, NC 27858.

FARRAR, RONALD
PERSONAL Born 07/03/1935, Fordyce, AR, m, 1961, 2 children **DISCIPLINE** JOURNALISM AND MASS COMMUNICATIONS **EDUCATION** Univ AR, BS; Univ IA, MA; Univ MO, PhD. **CAREER** Reynolds-Faunt Memorial prof, Jour & interim dean, Grad Stud & Res; worked as reporter, ed, mgr, newspapers in AR & IA; past dir, jour prog, Southern Methodist Univ, Univ MS & Univ KY. **HONORS AND AWARDS** Nat Res Awd, Soc of Prof Journalists. **RESEARCH** Media law; press hist; reporting; community journalism. **CONTACT ADDRESS** Col of Journalism & Mass Commun, Univ of So Carolina, Columbia, Carolina Coliseum rm 2044, Columbia, SC 29208. **EMAIL** Ron_Farrar@USC.jour.sc.edu

FARRED, GRANT
DISCIPLINE ENGLISH **EDUCATION** Univ Western Cape, South Africa, BA, 87 & 88; Columbia Univ, MA, 90; Princeton Univ, PhD, 96. **CAREER** Vis asst prof. **RESEARCH** South African literature and politics; contemporary African-American film, with a special focus on postcolonialism; cultural studies and the construction of intellectuals. **SELECTED PUBLICATIONS** Auth, What's My Name:Vernacular and Organic Intellectuals; First Stop Port-au-Prince:Mapping Postcolonial Africa Through Tousssaint L'Ouverture and his Black Jacobins; It's an X-Thing:The Culture of Black Nationalism in Contemporary South Africa; The Intellectual As Outsider; Take Back The Mike:Producing a Language for Date Rape. **CONTACT ADDRESS** Program in Literature, Duke Univ, Art Museum Building, Durham, NC 27707. **EMAIL** gfarred@williams.edu

FARRELL, JOHN C.
PERSONAL Born 01/12/1957, Providence, RI, s **DISCIPLINE** ENGLISH & AMERICAN LITERATURE **EDUCATION** Brown Univ, AB, 79; Harvard Univ, MA, 81; PhD, 88. **CAREER** Lectr english & am hist, Harvard Univ, 88-90; asst to assoc prof dept lit, Claremont McKenna Col, 90- . **RESEARCH** Critical theory, History of ideas, History of literary criticism, Critique of Psychoanalysis. **SELECTED PUBLICATIONS** Auth, Freud's Paranoid Quest, NY Univ Press, (96). **CONTACT ADDRESS** Dept Lit, Claremont McKenna Col, 850 Columbia Ave, Claremont, CA 91711-5903. **EMAIL** jfarrell@mckenna.edu

FARRELL, JOHN P.
PERSONAL Born 11/19/1939, Brooklyn, NY, m, 2 children **DISCIPLINE** ENGLISH **EDUCATION** Fordham Univ, BS, 61; Ind Univ, PhD, 67. **CAREER** From asst prof to assoc prof, Univ of Ks, 66-73; prof, Univ of Tex at Austin, 74-. **HONORS AND AWARDS** NEH Fel, 73; Outstanding Teacher Awd, Univ of Tex, 77; ACLS Fel, 80; Friar Centennial Teaching Awd Nominee, 88. **MEMBERSHIPS** Asn of Lit Scholars & Critics, Tex Fac Asn. **RESEARCH** Victorian literature, modern poetry, dialogics. **SELECTED PUBLICATIONS** Auth, "The Beautiful Changes in Richard Wilbur's Poetry," Contemp Lit 12 (71): 74-87; auth, "Homeward Bound: Arnold's Late Criticism," Victorian Studies 17 (73): 187-206; auth, Revolution as Tragedy: The Dilemma of the Moderate from Scott to Arnold, Cornell Univ Press, 80; auth, "The Partners' Tale: Dickens and Our Mutual Friend," ELH 66 (99): 759-799. **CONTACT ADDRESS** Dept English, Univ of Texas, Austin, B5000, Austin, TX 78712. **EMAIL** jackfar@mail.utexas.edu

FARROKH, FARIDOUN
PERSONAL Born 05/27/1936, Mashad, Iran, m, 1979, 1 child **DISCIPLINE** ENGLISH **EDUCATION** Mashad Univ, BA, 61; Univ Kans, MA, 68; Middle Tenn State Univ, DA, 77. **CAREER** Chair, Ferdowsi Univ, 77-80; chair, Laredo State Univ, 91-94; prof, assoc vpres, Texas A&M Int Univ, 96, 99-. **HONORS AND AWARDS** Grant, London Univ, 72; Fel, Middle Tenn State Univ, 74-77; Grant, Oxford Univ, 78; Sr Fel, Tex Higher Educ Coordinating Board, 99-00; Dow Vis Scholar, Saginaw Valley State Univ, 00. **MEMBERSHIPS** MLA, MESA, NCTE, AAUP. **RESEARCH** English Literature, Contemporary Iranian Fiction. **SELECTED PUBLICATIONS** Auth, "The Vanity of Human Wishes: Samuel Johnson and the Discovery of the Poetic Self," Word & World of Discovery, (44); auth, "Parvin E'tesami and Lady Mary Wortley Montagu: Contrasts in Unison," Once a Dew Drop: Essays on the Poetry of Parvin E'tesami," (94); transl, My Little Friend, (Lit Rev, Fall 96). **CONTACT ADDRESS** Dept English, Texas A&M Intl Univ, 5201 University Blvd, Laredo, TX 78041-1920. **EMAIL** ffarrokh@tamiu.edu

FARROW, ANTHONY
DISCIPLINE ENGLISH **EDUCATION** Cornell Univ, MA, 70; PhD, 72. **CAREER** Prof, St Bonaventure Univ, 72-; Chair English Dept, St Bonaventure Univ, 97-. **MEMBERSHIPS** ACIS, ALA. **RESEARCH** Twentieth Century British Literature. **SELECTED PUBLICATIONS** Auth, Diarmuid and Grania, 75; auth, George Moore, 78; auth, Early Beckett, 91. **CONTACT ADDRESS** Dept English, St. Bonaventure Univ, Saint Bonaventure, NY 14778-2400.

FARROW, J. G.
PERSONAL Born 09/19/1948, England **DISCIPLINE** CLASSICS **EDUCATION** Oxford, Master of Letters, 79 **CAREER** Head class, relig stud, Haberdashers' Monmouth, Wales, 80-86; ADJ PROF CLASS, WAYNE STATE UNIV, 88-; PROF HUM, MACOMB COMMUNITY COL, 89-. **CONTACT ADDRESS** Dept of Classics, Wayne State Univ, Manoogian Hall 430, Detroit, MI 48101. **EMAIL** farrowj@exchange.macomb.cc.mi.us

FARWELL, TRICIA M.
DISCIPLINE ENGLISH **EDUCATION** Ariz State Univ, BA, 94; MMC, 98; MA, 98. **CAREER** Grad asst to fac assoc, Ariz State Univ. **HONORS AND AWARDS** Golden Key Nat Honor Soc, Ariz State Univ, 90; Phi Eta Sigma, 90; Who's Who Among Students in Am Univ, 92-93; Phi Kappa Phi, 00. **MEMBERSHIPS** Edith Wharton Soc, Edith Wharton Restoration. **RESEARCH** American Literature 1890-1940, Desktop Publishing, Public Relations, Web Design, Edith Wharton. **SELECTED PUBLICATIONS** Coauth, "Sex on the Soaps: An Analysis of Intimacy," Mediated Messages and African-American Culture, ed V.T. Berry and C.L. Manning-Miller, Sage Publ, Thousand Oaks, CA, (96); coauth, "Sex on the Soaps: An Analysis of Black, White, and Interracial Intimacy," Facing Difference: Race, Gender and Mass Media, ed S. Biagi and M. Kern-Foxwoth, Pine Forge Pr, (CA: Thousand Oaks, CA), 97. **CONTACT ADDRESS** Cronkite Sch of Jour and Telecommunication, PO Box 14687, Scottsdale, AZ 85267-4687. **EMAIL** tfarwell@asu.edu

FAST, ROBIN RILEY
PERSONAL Born Juneau, AK **DISCIPLINE** ENGLISH **EDUCATION** Hunter Col, 74; Univ Minn, PhD, 79. **CAREER** Assoc prof, Univ Akron, 80-89; Univ Barcelona, Fulbright Lecturer, 82-83; assoc prof, Emerson Col, 89-. **HONORS AND AWARDS** Univ Barcelona, Fulbright Lecturer, 82-83. **MEMBERSHIPS** MLA, ASA, ASAIL, NWSA, MELUS, Women's Caucus in the Modern Langs. **RESEARCH** Poetry, American Indian literature, 19th-century US literature, US women writers. **SELECTED PUBLICATIONS** Auth, The Heart as a Drum: Continuance and Resistance in American Indian Poetry, Univ Mich (99); coed with Christine Mack Gordon, "Approaches to Teaching Dickinson's Poetry," MLA (89-); essays on contemporary Am Indian poetry and poets, Mary Oliver, Emily Dickinson, Elizabeth Bishop, and others in Contemporary Lit, Am Indian Culture & Res J, Am Quart, ESQ, Ky Rev, and others. **CONTACT ADDRESS** Dept Writing, Lit, and Pub, Emerson Col, 100 Beacon St, Boston, MA 02116-1501.

FAULCON, CLARENCE AUGUSTUS, II
PERSONAL Born 08/08/1928, Philadelphia, PA, m **DISCIPLINE** MUSICOLOGY **EDUCATION** Lincoln U, 1946-48; Univ PA, BMus Ed 1950; Univ PA, MMus Ed 1952; Philadelphia Conservatory of Music, MusD in Musicolgy 1962-. **CAREER** Chairperson Sulzberger Jr Hi (Phila), music teacher, chairperson 51-63; Cazenovia Coll (Cazenovia, NY), asst prof, chairperson 63-68; Morgan State Univ (Balt), prof, chairperson 68-79; Morgan State Univ, prof 79-. **HONORS AND AWARDS** Morgan State Univ Promethan Soc Faculty Awd, 1983; Intl Biographical Cong Medal of Cong, Budapest, Hungary, 1985; Afro Amer Music in Health Promotion Disease Prevention and Therapy, Montreal, Canada, Conf Natl Medical Assn 1984; recital accompanist & artist accompanist in various countries, 1982-88; accompanist, voice concert, and conducted plenary session interviews of eight delegates, International Biographical Centre Congress on Arts and Communications, Nairobi, Kenya, 1990; received IBC Silver Medal struck at the mint of the Queen of England. **MEMBERSHIPS** Delegate, Intl Biographical Centre Arts & Communication Congresses, 1981-. **CONTACT ADDRESS** Music, Morgan State Univ, Baltimore, MD 21239.

FAULKENBERG, MARILYN
PERSONAL Born 12/21/1943, Mayville, WI, m, 1985 **DISCIPLINE** LITERATURE **EDUCATION** Marian Col, BA; Univ Minn, MA, 74; PhD, 77. **CAREER** Instr, Univ Minn, 76-77; From Instr to Prof, Marian Col, 73-83; Prof, Menlo Col, 86-. **HONORS AND AWARDS** NEH Fel, Yale Univ, 80; Teaching Awds, Menlo Col, 92, 93; Fels, Oxford Univ, 95, 98. **MEMBERSHIPS** Asn of Lit Scholars & Critics. **RESEARCH** Biography of Frederick W Robertson. **SELECTED PUBLICATIONS** Auth, "Casing the News," J of the Asn of Bus Communicators (88); auth, "The Reader as Protagonist in Kierkegaard's Literary Labyrinth," Nineteenth-Century Lit Criticism, vol 34 (92); auth, Church, City and Labyrinth in Bronte, Dickens, Hardy and Butor, Peter Lang Publ (New York, NY), 93; auth, "The Cleric and the Lady," Faith and Freedom, Oxford UP (99); auth, Frederick W Robertson: A Voice that Shaped Victorian Society, forthcoming. **CONTACT ADDRESS** Dept Humanities, Menlo Col, 1000 El Camino Real, Atherton, CA 94027-4300. **EMAIL** mfaulken@menlo.edu

FAULKNER, THOMAS CORWIN
PERSONAL Born 01/02/1941, Celina, OH, m, 1977 **DISCIPLINE** ENGLISH LITERATURE **EDUCATION** Hope Col, BA, 62; Miami Univ, MA, 64; Univ Wis, Madison, PhD(English), 72. **CAREER** Instr English, Wis State Univ, Whitewater, 64-67; lectr, Loyola Col, Montreal, 67-71; asst prof, 71-76, assoc prof, 76-81, prof English, Wash State Univ, 81-, dir, Humanities Res Ctr, Washington State Univ, 80-. **HONORS AND AWARDS** W K Kellogg Nat fel, 81-84. **MEMBERSHIPS** Am Soc Eighteenth-Century Studies. **RESEARCH** Iconography and literature; eighteenth-century English literature; bibliography and textual editing. **SELECTED PUBLICATIONS** Auth, Halifax's The Character of a Trimmer and L'Estrange's Attack on Trimmers in the Observator, Huntington Libr Quart, 73; Letters of George Crabbe and Francis Fulford, Rev English Studies, 75; George Crabbe: Murray's 1834 edition of the life and poems, Studies Bibliog, 78; coauth, The Classical and Mythographic Sources of Pope's Dulness, Huntington Libr Quart, 80; auth, Computer Applications for an edition of Robert Burton's The Anatomy of Melancholy: A System for Scholarly Publishing, Comput & the Humanities, 81; ed, The Letters and Journals of George Crabbe, Oxford, Clarendon, 85; ed, Robert Burton, The Anatomy of Melancholy, 3 vols, Oxford, Clarendon, 89-94. **CONTACT ADDRESS** Dept of English, Washington State Univ, PO Box 645020, Pullman, WA 99164-5020. **EMAIL** fau@wsu.edu

FAVOR, J. MARTIN
DISCIPLINE ENGLISH LITERATURE **EDUCATION** Univ MI Ann Arbor, PhD, 93. **CAREER** Assoc prof of English and African & African, Am Studies, Dartmouth Col. **RESEARCH** English and African literature; African American Studies. **SELECTED PUBLICATIONS** Auth, Ain't Nothin Like the Real Thing, Baby: Trey Ellis' Search for New Black Voices; Callaloo, 93; Inventions of Africa: A Selective Bibliography in Ann Arbor: Center for Afro-American and African Studies, Univ MI, 92; auth, Authentic Blackness: The Folk in the New Negro Renaissance, Duke Univ Press, 99. **CONTACT ADDRESS** Dept of English, Dartmouth Col, 6032 Sanborn House, Hanover, NH 03755. **EMAIL** J.Martin.Favor@dartmouth.edu

FAWZIA, MUSTAFA
DISCIPLINE POST-COLONIAL LITERATURES **EDUCATION** IN Univ, PhD. **CAREER** Assoc prof, Fordham Univ. **RESEARCH** Cult studies, contemp critical theory. **SELECTED PUBLICATIONS** Auth, V.S. Naipaul, Cambridge UP, 95. **CONTACT ADDRESS** Dept of Eng Lang and Lit, Fordham Univ, 113 W 60th St, New York, NY 10023.

FAYMONVILLE, CARMEN
PERSONAL Born 02/02/1965, Stolberg, Germany, s **DISCIPLINE** ENGLISH **EDUCATION** Ripon Col, BA, 88; Univ Cologne, MA, 90; Loyola Univ, PhD, 00. **CAREER** Asst Prof, Univ Wisc, 98-. **HONORS AND AWARDS** Dean's Fund Fac Development grant; Harold Saenger Writing fund, Univ Wisc; Dissertation Fel, Loyola Univ, 97; Teaching Fel, Loyola Univ, 96; Teaching Assistantship, Loyola Univ, 95; Clayes Awd, Loyola Univ, 94; Teaching Asst Fel, Ill State Univ, 93; Teaching Fel, Ripon Col, 88; Res Grant, Bundesverwaltungsamt, 89; English Dept Honors, Ripon Col, 88; Dan's List, Ripon Col, 88; Scholarship, Bonn Univ, 87. **MEMBERSHIPS** MLA, MMLA, MELUS, Am Studies Asn. **RESEARCH** Post-colonial Literature; World Literature; Women's Studies; Ethnic Literatures of the Americas; Literary Theory; European Literature; American Literature. **SELECTED PUBLICATIONS** Auth, "The Love of Cramps," Moon Days, Columbia, 99; auth, "Motherland versus Daughterland in Judith Ortiz Cofer's The Line of the Sun," Carving Out a Niche: Immigrant Writing, Greenwood Press, 99; auth, "Against the Paradigm of the Native Writer: Non-Native Strategies in the Teaching of Writing," in In Our Own Voice: Graduate Students Teach Writing, forthcoming; auth, "Still the Frontier: The American West and Immigrant Women's Narratives," The Image of the American West, UP of Southern Colo, 96; auth, "Waste Not, Want Not, Even Redundant Women have Their Uses," Imperial Objects: Victorian Women and the Unauthorized Emigration Experience, 98; auth, "Kenneth Rexroth," Dictionary of Literary Biography: Twentieth Century American Western Writers, 99; auth, "Matt Braun," Dictionary of Literary Biography: Twentieth Century American Western Writers, Gale, 99; auth, "Black Germans and Transnational Identification,"; Black Voices Against Social Exclusion, Berghahn Books, in press, auth, "Adult Undergraduates, Nontraditional Teachers and Reciprocal Resistance," Nebraska English Journal, (97): 19-33. **CONTACT ADDRESS** Dept Humanities, Univ of Wisconsin, Platteville, 1 Univ Plaza, Platteville, WI 53818-3001. **EMAIL** faymonvc@uwplatt.edu

FEARN-BANKS, KATHLEEN
PERSONAL Born 11/21/1941, Chattanooga, TN, d **DISCIPLINE** COMMUNICATIONS **EDUCATION** Wayne State Univ, BA, Journalism, 1964; UCLA, MS, Journalism, 1965; University of Southern California, Los Angeles, CA, ABD for PhD, 1978-81. **CAREER** NBC Publicity Dept, mgr, media relations, 69-90; KNXT-TV News LA, newswriter, producer, 68-69; Los Angeles Ctn Coll, instructor, Journalism, English, Creative Writing, 65-; Los Angeles Times, Feature Writer, 68; Univ of Wash, Seattle, WA, asst prof, 90-; freelance motion picture publicist, currently. **HONORS AND AWARDS** CA Sun Magazine writers Awd, UCLA 1965; Will Rogers Fellowship, UCLA, 1964-65. **MEMBERSHIPS** Member, Public Relations Society of America 1989-; mem, Writers Guild Amer; mem, Publicists Guild; member, Acad of TV & Sciences; bd of dir, vice pres, Neighbors of Watts; mem, Delta Sigma Theta Sorority, chapter vp; member, Association for Education in Journalism & Mass Comm, 1990-. **SELECTED PUBLICATIONS** Numerous freelance magazine & journal articles; 3 Textbooks, The Story of Western Man, co-authored w/David Burleigh; Woman of the Year, Los Angeles Sentinel (newspaper) 1986; Author: Crisis Communications; A Case Book Approach; Teacher of the Year, School of Communications, University of Washington, 1993, 1995. **CONTACT ADDRESS** Univ of Washington, DS-40, Seattle, WA 98101.

FEARNOW, MARK
PERSONAL Born 01/24/1958, Wabash, IN, s **DISCIPLINE** THEATRE AND DRAMA **EDUCATION** Indiana Univ, PhD, 90. **CAREER** Lehigh Univ, 90-91; Penn State Univ, 91-98; Hanover College, 00. **MEMBERSHIPS** Amer Soc Theatre Res; Asn Theatre in Higher Educ; Lit Mgr and Drama of the Amer. **RESEARCH** Twentieth century Amer theatre; riots as theatre. **SELECTED PUBLICATIONS** The American Stage and the Great Depression, Cambridge, 97; Clare Booth Luce, Greenwood, 95. **CONTACT ADDRESS** Hanover Col, Hanover College, Hanover, IN 47243. **EMAIL** fearnow@hanover.edu

FEARS, J. RUFUS
PERSONAL Born 03/07/1945, Atlanta, GA, m, 1966, 2 children **DISCIPLINE** CLASSICS; HISTORY **EDUCATION** Emory Univ, BA, 66; Harvard Univ, MA, 67, PhD, 71. **CAREER** Asst Prof Classical Lang, Tulane Univ, 71-72; from Asst Prof to Prof Hist, Ind Univ, 72-86; Prof Classics and Dept Chair, Boston Univ, 86-90; Prof Classics, 90-92, G.T. and Libby Blankenship Prof Classics, Univ Okla, 92-, Dean Col Arts & Sci, 90-92. **HONORS AND AWARDS** Woodrow Wilson Fel, 66-67; Danforth Fel, 66-71; Harvard Prize Fel, 66-71; Sheldon Traveling Fel, 69-71; Fel of the Am Acad in Rome, 69-71; Howard Found Fel, 77-78; Guggenheim Fel, 76-77; Alexander von Humboldt Fel, 77-78, 80-81; Distinguished Fac Res Lectr, Ind Univ, 80; NEH Fel, 86; Woodrow Wilson Ctr Fel, 86; ACLS Fel, 86; Nat Humanities Ctr Fel, 86; Wash Univ Ctr Hist Freedom Fel, 89-90; Judah P. Benjamin Nat Merit Awd, 96; 15 awards for outstanding teaching, 76-00; Univ of Okla Prof of Year, 96, 99. **MEMBERSHIPS** Phi Beta Kappa; Golden Key Nat Honor Soc; Am Philol Asn; Archaeol Inst Am; Classical Asn Middle West and South; Vergilian Soc; Soc for Classical Tradition. **RESEARCH** Ancient history; history of freedom. **SELECTED PUBLICATIONS** Auth, Atlantis and the Myth of the Minoan Thalassocracy, Atlantis: Fact of Fiction, 78; Princeps A Diis Electus, 77; The Cult of Jupiter and Roman Imperial Ideology, 81; The Theology of Victory at Rome, 81; The Cult of Virtues and Roman Imperial Ideology, 81; Roman Liberty, 80; Gottesgnadentum, Reallexikon fur Antike und Christentum XI, 81; Herrscherkult, Reallexikon fur Antike und Christentum XIV, 88; Selected Writings of Lord Acton (3 vols), 85-88; Michael Rostovtzeff, Classical Scholarship: A Biographical Encyclopedia, 90; Antiquity: The Model of Rome, An Uncertain Legacy: Essays in Pursuit of Liberty, 97; Natural Law: The Legacy of Greece and Rome, Common Truths, 00; The Lessons of Rome for Our Own Day, Preparing America's Foreign Policy for the 21st Century, 99. **CONTACT ADDRESS** Dept of Classics, Univ of Oklahoma, Norman, OK 73019. **EMAIL** jrfears@ou.edu

FEDDER, NORMAN JOSEPH
PERSONAL Born 01/26/1934, New York, NY, m, 1955, 2 children **DISCIPLINE** PLAYWRITING, DRAMA THERAPY **EDUCATION** Brooklyn Col, BA, 55; Columbia Univ, MA, 56; NYork Univ, PhD, 62. **CAREER** Asst prof English, Trenton State Col, 60-61; assoc prof English & speech, Ind State Col, Pa, 61-64; assoc prof English, Fla Atlantic Univ, 64-67; assoc prof drama, Univ Ariz, 67-70; assoc prof, 70-80, prof speech & theatre, chmn, Relig and Theatre Prog, Am Theatre Asn, 75-80; pres, Kans Asn Relig Communities and the Arts, 76-77; mem, Theatre Adv Bd, Kans Arts Comn, 76-81; Kansas State Univ, 80-89, Distinguished prof, 89-99, Registered Drama Therapist/Board Certified Trainer, 89-, dir, Israel Theatre Program, 95 Distinguished Prof. Emeritus, 99-. **HONORS AND AWARDS** Kans Bicentennial Comn, 75-76; Nat Found Jewish Culture, 77-78 Res; Outstanding Teacher Awd, 88; Kansas Theatre Hall of Fame, 90. **MEMBERSHIPS** Assoc for Theatre in Higher Education, National Assoc for Drama Therapy (Board of Directors), Jewish Theatre Asn. **RESEARCH** Jewish Theatre; playwriting; creative dramatics, drama therapy. **SELECTED PUBLICATIONS** Auth, We Can Make Our Lives Sublime, produced by CBS TV, 70; The Planter May Weep, produced by Univ Judaism, 70; Some Events Connected with the Early History of Arizona, produced by Ariz Pioneers Hist Soc, Kans State Univ & Sacramento State Col, 70; Earp!, produced by Kans State Hist Theatre, 71, Manhattan Civic Theatre, 78; Tennessee Williams' Dramatic Technique, In: Tennessee Williams: A tribute, Univ Miss, 77, reprinted, 80; The Betrayal, Baker's Plays, Boston, 78; A Jew in Kansas, produced by National Jewish Theatre Festival, New York, 80; The Buck Stops Here!, produced by AMAS Repertory Theatre, New York, 83; Out of the Depths, produced by Univ of Tx--El Paso, 98. **CONTACT ADDRESS** Dept of Speech, Communication, Theatre and Dance, Kansas State Univ, 129 Nichols Hall, Manhattan, KS 66506-2301. **EMAIL** fedder@ksu.edu

FEDERMAN, RAYMOND
PERSONAL Born 05/15/1928, Paris, France, m, 1960, 1 child **DISCIPLINE** ENGLISH, COMPARATIVE LITERATURE **EDUCATION** Columbia Univ, BS, 57; Univ Calif, MA, 59, PhD, 63. **CAREER** Tchg asst French, Univ CA, Los Angeles, 57-59; lectr, Univ CA, Santa Barbara, 59-62, asst prof, 62-64; from Assoc Prof to Prof French, 64-68, Prof English & Comp Lit, 73-90, Distinguished Prof Eng and Comp Lit, State Univ NY-Buffalo, 90-, Melodia E. Jones Ch of Lit, 94-; mem bd consult, Coord Coun Lit Mags, 73-76. **HONORS AND AWARDS** Guggenheim fel, 66-67; Frances Steloff Fiction Prize, 71; Panache Exp Fiction Prize, 72; Fulbright Fel, Israel, 82-83; NEH Fel/Fiction, 86; Am Bk Awd, 86; DAAD Fel, Berlin, 89-90. **MEMBERSHIPS** PEN Am; MLA; Am Comp Lit Asn; Am Asn Tchr(s) Fr. **RESEARCH** Twentieth century French lit; contemp fiction; creative writing. **SELECTED PUBLICATIONS** Auth, Double or nothing (novel), 71 & ed, Surfiction (essays on modern fiction), 75, Swallow; auth, Amer Eldorado (novel), Ed Stock, 74; Take it or leave it (novel), Fiction Collective, 76; Me too (poems), Westcoast Rev, 76; co-ed, Cahier de L'herne: Samuel Beckett, Eds L'Herne Paris-France, 77; auth, Imagination as plagiarism, New Lit Hist, 77; The voice in the closet (fiction), Tri-Quart, 77; The Two Fold Vilration (novel), Ind Univ Press, 82; Smiles on Washington Square, 85; To Whom it May Concern, 90; CRITIFICTION, 94; La Fourrure de oya Tante Rachel, 96. **CONTACT ADDRESS** Dept of Eng, SUNY, Buffalo, PO Box 604610, Buffalo, NY 14260-4610. **EMAIL** moinous@aol.com

FEENEY, JOSEPH JOHN
PERSONAL Born 10/08/1934, Philadelphia, PA, s **DISCIPLINE** AMERICAN & MODERN BRITISH LITERATURE

EDUCATION Fordham Univ, AB, 58, MA, 61; Woodstock Col, STB, 64, STL, 66; Univ Pa, PhD, 71. **CAREER** Teacher English & math, St Joseph's Prep Sch, 59-60; teacher English & Latin, Loyola High Sch, Md, 60-62; from lectr to assoc prof, 69-83, prof Eng, St Joseph's Univ, PA, 83-, Trustee, St Joseph's Prep Sch, 76-82, Fordham Univ, 94-, Loyola Sch (NYC), 97-; vis prof Georgetown Univ, 86-87; vis prof, Santa Clara Univ, 98; co-ed, The Hopkins Quarterly, 94-. **HONORS AND AWARDS** Lindback Awd for Distinguished Teaching, 83; Alpha Sigma Nu, 88; Tengelmann Awd for Research and Teaching, 99. **MEMBERSHIPS** MLA; Northeast Mod Lang Assn; AAUP; Int Hopkins Assn; Christianity and Lit Assoc; Council of Editors of Learned Jrnls. **RESEARCH** American novel; G M Hopkins; contemp British and Irish drama. **SELECTED PUBLICATIONS** Art, His Father's Son: Common Traits in the Writing of Manley Hopkins and Gerard Manley Hopkins, Gerard Manley Hopkins and Critical Discourse, AMS Press, 93; auth, Hopkins: A Religious and a Secular Poet, Studies, Dublin, 95; auth, My dearest Father: Some unpublished letters of Gerard Manley Hopkins, TLS: The Times Literary Supplement, 95; auth, The Bischoff Collection at Gonzaga University: A Preliminary Account, The Hopkins Quarterly, 96; auth, I Do Otherwise: Hopkins' Patterns of Creativity, Studies, Dublin, 97; auth, Martin McDonagh: Dramatist of the West, Studies, Dublin, 98; auth, "At St. Beuno's: Newly discovered work by Gerard Manley Hopkins, TLS: The Times Literary Supplement, 99; auth, "A new-found poem by Gerard Manley Hopkins," The Month, London (99). **CONTACT ADDRESS** Dept of English, Saint Joseph's Univ, 5600 City Ave, Philadelphia, PA 19131-1376. **EMAIL** jfeeney@sju.edu

FEIN, RICHARD J.
PERSONAL Born 12/05/1929, Brooklyn, NY, m, 1955, 2 children **DISCIPLINE** ENGLISH **EDUCATION** Brooklyn Col, BA, 53, MA, 55; NYork Univ, PhD, 60. **CAREER** Teaching fel, NY Univ, 56-57; lectr English, Hunter Col, 58-60; instr, Fairleigh Dickinson Univ, 60-61; asst prof, Univ PR, 61-63; from asst prof to assoc prof, 63-77, PROF ENGLISH, STATE UNIV NY COL NEW PALTZ, 77-, Fulbright lectr Am lit, Univ Madras, India, 71-72. **HONORS AND AWARDS** Founders' Day Distinguished Scholar Awd, NY Univ, 61. **MEMBERSHIPS** MLA. **RESEARCH** Am Lit; modern Jewish literature. **SELECTED PUBLICATIONS** Auth, Glatshteyn, Yankev Critical Motive , Yiddish, Vol 9,94. **CONTACT ADDRESS** Dept of English, SUNY, New Paltz, New Paltz, NY 12561.

FEINBERG, LEONARD
PERSONAL Born 08/26/1914, Vitebsk, Russia, m, 1938, 1 child **DISCIPLINE** ENGLISH **EDUCATION** Univ Ill, PhD (English), 46. **CAREER** Instr English, Univ Ill, 38-43; from asst prof to assoc prof, 46-57, prof, Iowa State Univ, 57-73, Dist prof to Dist prof emer, 73-; Lectr Am lit, Univ Ceylon, 57-58. **MEMBERSHIPS** Satire. **RESEARCH** Humor of the world. **SELECTED PUBLICATIONS** Auth, The Satirist, 63 & Introduction to Satire, 67, Iowa State Univ; Satire: recent definitions, Genre, 1/68; Asian Laughter, John Weatherhill, Tokyo, 71; Satire: In the Orient and in the West, Costerus, Amsterdam, 72; The Secret of Humor, Rodopi, Amsterdam, 78. **CONTACT ADDRESS** Dept of English, Iowa State Univ, Ames, IA 50011.

FEINMAN, PAUL I.
PERSONAL Born 07/06/1939, Brooklyn, NY, m, 1968, 2 children **DISCIPLINE** COMMUNICATIONS **EDUCATION** Bradley Univ, BS, 78; Univ Ill, MA, 80. **CAREER** Prog Dir, Ill State Univ, 80-81; Prog Dir, Butler Univ, 81-82; Adj Prof, Marion Col, 84-92; Adj Prof, Univ Indianapolis, 91-. **HONORS AND AWARDS** Dean's List, Bradley Univ. **RESEARCH** Theatre; Music; Entertainment. **SELECTED PUBLICATIONS** Auth, Popular Indiana, forthcoming. **CONTACT ADDRESS** Dept Comm, Univ of Indianapolis, 1400 E Hanna Ave, Indianapolis, IN 46227-3630. **EMAIL** pif60@yahoo.com

FEINSTEIN, HERBERT CHARLES VERSCHLEISSER
PERSONAL Born 05/28/1927, New York, NY **DISCIPLINE** ENGLISH, MASS MEDIA OF COMMUNICATIONS **EDUCATION** Columbia Univ, AB, 48; Harvard Univ, JD, 51; Univ Calif, Berkeley, MA, 59, PhD, 68. **CAREER** Lawyer, Admiralty law off, Harry Kisloff, Boston, 51-53; mem res coun, Fund for Repub, Harvard Law Sch, 53-54; corp lawyer & adminr, Music Corp Am, Universal Studios, Calif, 55-56; lectr speech, Univ Calif, Berkeley, 57-59; asst prof English & jour, 59-66, assoc prof English, 66-72, Prof English, San Francisco State Univ, 72-; Admitted to law practice, Bar of Mass, 51 & Calif, 55; mem, Fed Int Presse Cinematographique, 67-; Am Coun Learned Soc fel, 69-70, grant-in-aid, 72; Huntington Libr & Art Gallery fel, 73, film consult, 73-; lectr & tutor, Nat Film Sch, Eng, 74. **MEMBERSHIPS** MLA; Am Judicature Soc; Am Bar Asn; Am Studies Asn. **RESEARCH** Clemens scholarship; mass media communications, especially films; relationship between literature and the law. **SELECTED PUBLICATIONS** Auth, Two pair of gloves: Mark Twain and Henry James, Am Imago, winter 60; Mark Twain and the pirates, Harvard Law Sch Bull, 4/62; 3 in search of cinema, Columbia Univ Forum, summer 65. **CONTACT ADDRESS** Dept of English, San Francisco State Univ, 1600 Holloway Ave, San Francisco, CA 94132-1740.

FEINSTEIN, SANDY
PERSONAL Born 01/22/1952, White Plains, NY **DISCIPLINE** ENGLISH **EDUCATION** Pomona Col, BA, 74; Ind Univ, MA, 77; PhD, 84. **CAREER** Instr, Univ South, 80-82; lectr, UCLA, 82-84; asst prof to assoc prof, SW Col, 84-99; vis assoc prof, Am Univ, 92-293; hon coord, Penn State Univ Berks Lehigh, 99-. **HONORS AND AWARDS** Fulbright Awd, Denmark, 89-90; Fulbright Awd, Syria, 98-99; NEH, 85-96; Ore Humanities Sum Res Fel 97; Teaching Awd, 88, 89. **MEMBERSHIPS** PMLA; PCMLA; IAS; NCS. **RESEARCH** Medieval; renaissance. **SELECTED PUBLICATIONS** Auth, "About That Horse," Chaucer Rev 26 (91): 99-106; auth, "Dunne's Elegy 19: The Bush Between a Pair of Bodies," Studies English Lit 34 (94): 61-78; auth, "Hypertextuality and Chaucer or Reordering the Canterbury Tales and Other Reader Prerogatives," Read Write Text 3 (96): 135-148; auth, "Crossbows, Lutes and Coitus, or What Does Editing Lady McBeth Mean?" Exemp 9 (97): 165-187; auth, "Losing Your Head in Chretion's Knight of the Court," Arthurian 9 (99); auth, "Teehee and Teaching Chaucer Cross Culturally in Kansas, Denmark and Bulgaria," Studies Medieval Renaissance Teaching 7 (99): 31-42. **CONTACT ADDRESS** English Dept, Pennsylvania State Univ, Berks, Tulpehocken Rd, Reading, PA 19610.

FELDER, MIRA B.
PERSONAL Born 05/05/1938, Poland, m, 1959, 3 children **DISCIPLINE** LINGUISTICS, ENGLISH **EDUCATION** Brooklyn Col, BA; Temple Univ, MA. **CAREER** Asst prof, Touro Col, New York, NY, 78-, E. S. L. Divisional Officer, 78-, assoc dean, 91-. **SELECTED PUBLICATIONS** Coauth, Light and Lively, 2nd ed, Addison Wesley Longman (97); coauth, Laugh and Learn, 2nd ed, Addison Wesley Longman (97). **CONTACT ADDRESS** Dept Lang & Lit, Touro Col, New York, 27 W 23rd St #33, New York, NY 10010-4202.

FELDMAN, IRVING
PERSONAL Born 09/22/1928, Brooklyn, NY, m, 1955, 1 child **DISCIPLINE** ENGLISH LITERATURE **EDUCATION** City Col NYork, BS, 50; Columbia Univ, MA, 53. **CAREER** Instr English & Humanities, Univ PR, 54-56; asst prof English, Kenyon Col, 58-64; assoc prof, 64-68, prof English, State Univ NY, Buffalo, 68-, Fulbright scholar, 56; Ingram Merrill Found grant, 63; Guggenheim fel, 73-74; Creative Artists Pub Serv grant, 80. **HONORS AND AWARDS** Kovner Mem Awd, Jewish Bk Counc Am, 62; Nat Inst Arts & Lett Awd, 73; The Poetry of Irving Feldman: Nine Essays, Bucknell Univ Press, 92. **SELECTED PUBLICATIONS** Auth, Works and days, and other poems, Atlantic Monthly, 61; The Pripet Marshes, and other poems, Viking, 65; Magic Papers and other poems, Harper, 70; Lost Originals (poems), Holt, 72; Leaping Clear and other poems, Viking, 76; New and Selected Poems, Viking, 79; All of Us Here, Press of Appletree Alley, Lewisburg PA, 91 (reprint); The Life and Letters, Univ of Chicago, 94; auth, Beautiful False Things, Grove, 00. **CONTACT ADDRESS** Dept of English, SUNY, Buffalo, PO Box 604610, Buffalo, NY 14260-4610. **EMAIL** feldman@acsu.buffalo.edu

FELDMAN, JESSICA R.
PERSONAL Born Oak Ridge, TN, m, 2 children **DISCIPLINE** LITERATURE **EDUCATION** Stanford Univ, BA, 71; Univ Calif Berkeley, PhD, 78. **CAREER** Asst prof to assoc prof, Univ Va, 91-. **HONORS AND AWARDS** Phi Beta Kappa Book Awd; Regents Fel; Phi Beta Kappa. **MEMBERSHIPS** MLA; MSA. **RESEARCH** American, British French literature. **SELECTED PUBLICATIONS** Auth, Gender on the Divide: The Dandy in Modernist Literature, Cornell Univ Pr, 93. **CONTACT ADDRESS** 1698 Rugby Ave, Charlottesville, VA 22903-5141. **EMAIL** jrfzj@virginia.edu

FELDMAN, LOUIS H.
PERSONAL Born 10/29/1926, Hartford, CT, m, 1966, 3 children **DISCIPLINE** CLASSICAL STUDIES **EDUCATION** Trinity Col, BA, 46; Trinity Col, MA, 47; Harvard Univ, PhD, 51. **CAREER** Instr, Harvard Sem Found, 51-52; Instr, Trinity Col, 52-53; Instr, Hobart and William Smith Cols, 53-55; Instr, Yeshiva and Stern Cols, 55-56; Asst Prof, Yeshiva Col, 55-61; Assoc Prof, Yeshiva Col, 61-66; Prof, Yeshiva Univ, 66-. **HONORS AND AWARDS** Guggenheim Found Fel; Senior Fel, Am Coun of Learned Soc; Awd for Excellence, Am Philol Asn, 81; Judaica Ref Book Awd, Asn of Jewish Libr, 85; Fel, Annenberg Acad for Jewish Res, 93; Fel, Inst for Advancaed Study, Princeton, 94. **MEMBERSHIPS** Am Acad for Jewish Res, Assoc for Jewish Studies, Am Philol Asn, Soc of Bibl Lit. **RESEARCH** Hellenistic Judaism, especially Josephus. **SELECTED PUBLICATIONS** Auth, Scholarship on Philo and Josephus (1937-1962), Yeshiva Univ Pr (New York, NY), 63; auth, Josephus and Modern Scholarship (1937-1980), de Gruyter (Berlin, Germany), 84; ed, Josephan Studies (Japanese), 4 vols, Yamamoto Shoten (Tokyo, Japan), 85-86; auth, Josephus: A Supplementary Bibliography, Garland (New York, NY), 86; ed, Josephus, Judaism and Christianity, Wayne st Univ Pr (Detroit, MI), 87; ed, Josephus, The Bible and History, Wayne St Univ Pr (Detroit, MI), 89; auth, Jew and Gentile in the Ancient World: Attitudes and Interactions from Alexander to Justinian, Princeton Univ Pr, 93; auth, Studies in Hellenistic Judaism, Brill (Leiden), 96; coauth, Jewish Life and Thought Among Greeks and Romans: Primary Readings, Fortress Pr (Minneapolis, MN), 96; ed, Josephus' Contra Apionem: Studies in its Character and Context with a Latin Concordance to the Portion Missin in Greek, Brill (Leiden), 96; auth, Studies in Josephus' Rewritten Bible (Leiden: Brill) 96; auth Josephus's Interpretation of the Bible, (Berkeley: Univ Ca Pr) 98; auth, Flavius Josephus, Judean Antiquities 1-4: Translation and Commentary, (Leiden: Brill) 00. **CONTACT ADDRESS** Dept Humanities, Yeshiva Univ, 500 W 185th St, New York, NY 10033-3201. **EMAIL** lfeldman@ymail.yu.edu

FELDMAN, PAULA R.
PERSONAL Born 07/04/1948, Washington, DC **DISCIPLINE** BRITISH LITERARY HISTORY, ENGLISH ROMANTICISM **EDUCATION** Bucknell Univ, BA, 70; Northwestern Univ, MA, 71, PhD (English), 74. **CAREER** Asst prof, 74-79, ASSOC PROF ENGLISH, UNIV SC, 79-. **MEMBERSHIPS** MLA; Byron Soc; Asn Documentary Editing; Keats Shelley Asn Am. **RESEARCH** English romanticism; biography. **SELECTED PUBLICATIONS** Auth, Hemans, Felicia and the Mythologizing of Blake Death, Blake Illustrated Quart, Vol 27, 94; The Poet and the Profits, Keats Shelley J, Vol 46, 97. **CONTACT ADDRESS** Dept of English, Univ of So Carolina, Columbia, Columbia, SC 29208.

FELGAR, ROBERT
DISCIPLINE ENGLISH **EDUCATION** Occidental Col, BA, 66; Duke Univ, MA, 68; PhD, 70. **CAREER** Asst prof, Va Wesleyan Col, 69-70; head, Jacksonville State Univ, 71-. **MEMBERSHIPS** MLA, NCTE, Richard Wright Circle. **RESEARCH** Richard Wright. **SELECTED PUBLICATIONS** Auth, Richard Wright, Twayne, 80; auth, "Native Son and Its Readers," Approaches to Teaching Native Son, MLA, (97); auth, Understanding Richard Wright's Black Boy, Greenwood Pr, 98; auth, Student Companion to Richard Wright, Greenwood Pr, 00. **CONTACT ADDRESS** Dept English, Jacksonville State Univ, PO Box 640, Jacksonville, AL 36265. **EMAIL** bfelgar@jsucc.jsu.edu

FELLUGA, DINO F.
PERSONAL Born 08/07/1966, London, ON, Canada, m **DISCIPLINE** ENGLISH **EDUCATION** Huron Col, Univ W Ont, BA, 89; Queen's Univ, MA, 90; Univ Calif, PhD, 95. **CAREER** Asst prof, Perdue Univ, 97-. **HONORS AND AWARDS** Postdoctoral Fel, Inst of Humanities, Univ Calgary, 94-95; Postdoctoral Fel, Hum Res Con, Stanford Univ, 95-97. **MEMBERSHIPS** MLA, NASSR, ACR, ACCUTE. **RESEARCH** 14th Centruy Literature, Critical Theory. **SELECTED PUBLICATIONS** Auth, "The Critic's New Clothes: Sartor Resartus as 'Cold Carnival'," Criticism 37 (95): 593-599; auth, "Tennyson's Edylls, Pure Poetry and the Market," SEL 37 (97): 783-803; auth, "'With a Most Voiceless Thought': Byron and the Radicalism of Textual Culture," European Romantic Review 8(00): 148-165. **CONTACT ADDRESS** Dept English, Purdue Univ, West Lafayette, West Lafayette, IN 47907. **EMAIL** felluga@omni.cc.purdue.edu

FELSKI, RITA
DISCIPLINE ENGLISH **EDUCATION** Cambridge Univ, BA, 79; Monash Univ, MA82; PhD, 87. **CAREER** Lectr, Murdoch Univ, 87-93; prof, Univ Va, 94-. **HONORS AND AWARDS** Soc Humanities, Cornell Univ, 89-90; Commonwealth Cen, Univ Va, 91; Austral Res Grant, 93; Inst Humanities Sci, Vienna, 00; William Riley Parker Prize, 00. **RESEARCH** Feminist theory; modernity and postmodernity; cultural studies. **SELECTED PUBLICATIONS** Auth, Beyond Feminist Aesthetics, Harvard Univ Pr, 89; auth, The Gender of Modernity; Harvard Univ Pr, 95; auth, Doing Time: Feminist Theory and Postmodern Culture, NYork Univ Pr, 00. **CONTACT ADDRESS** English Dept, Univ of Virginia, Charlottesville, VA 22903. **EMAIL** rf6d@virginia.edu

FELSTINER, JOHN
PERSONAL Born 07/05/1936, Mt. Vernon, NY, m, 1966, 2 children **DISCIPLINE** LITERARY TRANSLATION, MODERN POETRY; JEWISH LITERATURE **EDUCATION** Harvard Col, AB, 58--Magna Cum Laude and Class Odist, PhD, 65. **RESEARCH** Poetry; Art; Music from The Holocaust; Poetry and the Environment. **SELECTED PUBLICATIONS** Auth, Celan, Paul--Holograms of Darkness, Compar Lit, Vol 45, 93; Translation as Reversion--Celan, Paul Jerusalem Poems, Judaism, Vol 43, 94. **CONTACT ADDRESS** Dept of English, Stanford Univ, 660 Salvatierra St, Stanford, CA 94305-2087. **EMAIL** felstiner@stanford.edu

FELTES, NORMAN NICHOLAS
PERSONAL Born 03/20/1932, Chicago, IL, m, 1959, 3 children **DISCIPLINE** ENGLISH **EDUCATION** Univ Notre Dame, AB, 53; Univ Col, Dublin, MA, 57; Oxford Univ, BLitt, 59. **CAREER** Lectr English, Univ Col, Dublin, 60; asst prof, Loyola Col, Que, 60-63; asst prof, Kenyon Col, 63-65; asst prof, Emory Univ, 65-69; ASSOC PROF ENGLISH, YORK UNIV, 69-. **MEMBERSHIPS** MLA; Can Asn Univ Teachers; Asn Can Univ Teachers English. **RESEARCH** Victorian prose; Victorian fiction and social history; Marxist history criticism. **SELECTED PUBLICATIONS** Auth, Voyageuse, Gender and Gaze in the Canoe Paintings of Hopkins, Frances, Anne, Ariel

Rev Int Eng Lit, Vol 24, 93; Visions of the People, Industrial England and the Question of Class, 1840-1914, Victorian Stud, Vol 35, 92. **CONTACT ADDRESS** Dept of English, York Univ, Downsview, ON, Canada M3J 1P3.

FELTON, SHARON
DISCIPLINE ENGLISH, MODERN BRITISH AND AMERICAN LITERATURE, TECHNICAL WRITING **EDUCATION** Austin Peay State Univ, BS, 83; Purdue Univ, MA, 85; PhD, 90. **CAREER** Purdue Univ, West Lafayette, IN, 83-90; Univ of Conn, Waterbury, CT, 90-92; Univ of Ottawa, Ottawa, ON, and McGill Univ, Montreal, PQ, 92-93; Austin Peay State Univ, Clarksville, TN, 95-96; Belmont Univ, Nashville, TN, 96-99. **RESEARCH** Modern and contemporary American literature; Modern and Contemporary British literature; Philosophy, especially existentialism; Women's Studies; Literature of the American South. **SELECTED PUBLICATIONS** Auth, 4 entries in The Robert Frost Encycl, Westport: Greenwood, 98; auth, "Portraits of the Artists as Young Defiers: James Joyce and Muriel Spark," Tenn Philol J 33 (96); auth, "Joan Didion: A Writer of Scope and Substance," Hollins Critic 26.4 (89); auth, "The Lie and the Liar: A Linguistic and Literary Analysis," Conn Rev 13 (91); ed, The Critical Response to Joan Didion, Greenwood Press (Westport, CT), 94; co-ed, The Critical Response to Gloria Naylor, Greenwood Press (Westport, CT), 97; bk rev in, Stud in Short Fiction, Miss Quart & Mod Fiction Stud; essays in Criticism, Amer Lit, Thalia & Stud in the Humanities. **CONTACT ADDRESS** Belmont Univ, 1900 Belmont Blvd., Nashville, TN 37212-3757. **EMAIL** feltons@mail.belmont.edu

FENG-CHECKETT, GAYLE
PERSONAL Born 12/08/1952, Los Angeles, CA, m, 1994, 3 children **DISCIPLINE** ENGLISH, ESL **EDUCATION** Univ Redlands, BA, 74; Univ N Dak, MA, 76. **CAREER** Instr, Concordia Col, 78-80; instr, St Louis Community Col, 86-93; prof, St Charles County Community Col, 93-. **HONORS AND AWARDS** Golden Apple Awd, St Peters Chamber of Commerce. **MEMBERSHIPS** TESOL; MCCA; NCTE; TYCA; CWA; M/MLA. **RESEARCH** Teaching English as a second language, teaching/learning for developmental writers, critical thinking. **SELECTED PUBLICATIONS** Coauth, "The Write Start: Sentence to Paragraph", The Write Start: Paragraph to Essay" in Develop Writing Textb Series, Addison Wesley Longman. **CONTACT ADDRESS** Dept English, Saint Charles County Comm Col, PO Box 76975, Saint Peters, MO 63376-0092. **EMAIL** gfeng@chuck.stchas.edu

FENNELL, FRANCIS L.
PERSONAL Born 05/08/1942, Pawtucket, R.I., m, 1963, 3 children **DISCIPLINE** ENGLISH **EDUCATION** Univ Rochester, BA, 64; Northwestern Univ, MA, 65, PhD, 68. **CAREER** Prof. **RESEARCH** Victorian literature; rhetoric and composition; pedagogy. **SELECTED PUBLICATIONS** Auth, The Fine Delight: Centenary Essays ono Gerard Manley Hopkins, (Chicago: Loyola UP, 89); auth, Rereading Hopkins: Selected New Essays, Univ Victoria Pres, Can, 96; Ladies Loaf Givers: Food, Women, and Society in the Novels of Charlotte Bronte and George Eliot, in Keeping the Victorian House, Garland, 95; auth, Collegiate English Handbook, 4th edition, (San Diego: Collegiate P, 98). **CONTACT ADDRESS** Dept of English, Loyola Univ, Chicago, 6525 N. Sheridan Rd., Chicago, IL 60626. **EMAIL** ffennel@wpo.it.luc.edu

FENNELLY, LAURENCE W.
PERSONAL Born 05/03/1943, Nassawadox, VA, m, 1984, 4 children **DISCIPLINE** COMMUNICATION, TECHNOLOGY **EDUCATION** Col Will Mary, AB, 65; Fla State Univ, MA, 70; PhD, 73. **CAREER** Dept chmn, Macon State Col, 73-. **HONORS AND AWARDS** Fla State Univ Fel, 72; SRPI, Wilton C. Scott Awd, 92. **MEMBERSHIPS** CMA; MLA; SAMLA; NAAA; SPJ. **RESEARCH** Effects of information on contemporary culture. **SELECTED PUBLICATIONS** Columnist for the Macon Telegraph, 79-. **CONTACT ADDRESS** Learning Support Dept, Macon Col, Macon, GA 31206. **EMAIL** lfennell@mail.maconstate.edu

FEOLA, MARYANN
DISCIPLINE ENGLISH **EDUCATION** City Univ, NY, PhD, 90. **CAREER** asst chair, assoc prof, 80-; coord PSLS, 99-, Col Staten Island. **HONORS AND AWARDS** Mellon Fel; Predoc Res Awd. **MEMBERSHIPS** MLA; FHS; MSA; NACBS. **RESEARCH** 16th and 17th century English poets and politicians; pedagogy. **SELECTED PUBLICATIONS** Auth, George Bishop: Seventeenth Century Soldier Turned Quaker, Ebor Press (York: England), 97. **CONTACT ADDRESS** Dept English, Col of Staten Island, CUNY, 2800 Victory Blvd, Staten Island, NY 10314-6609.

FERGENSON, LARAINE R.
PERSONAL Born 10/25/1944, Newark, NJ, m, 1967, 3 children **DISCIPLINE** ENGLISH **EDUCATION** Smith Col, AB, Columbia Univ, MA, 67; PhD, 71. **CAREER** Bronx Comm Col, 70-; Co-dir Honors Program, BCC, CUNY. **MEMBERSHIPS** ADL; AI; CEA; CUA; Friends of the Wordsworth Trust; Margaret Full Soc; MLA; NCTE; NOW; NRDC; Phi Beta Kappa; Sierra Club; The Thoreau Soc. **SELECTED PUBLICATIONS** Coauth, All in One: Basic Writing Text, Workbook, and Reader, Prentice-Hall, 80, 86, 92, 99; auth, Writing With Style: Rhetoric, Reader, Handbook, Holt, Rinehart and Winston, 89; auth, "Teaching The Diary of Anne Frank," Martyrdom and Resistance [Pub Intl Soc Yad Vashem]; 99: 11-15; auth, "Teaching Thoreau's 'Civil Disobedience' (or Is It 'Resistance to Civil Government?') to Composition Students," in Approaches to Teaching Thoreau, ed. Richard Schneider (NY: MLA, 96): 155-161; auth, "George Orwell's Animal Farm: A Modern Beast Fable," Bestia 2 (90): 109-118; auth, "Margaret Fuller as a Teacher in Providence: The School Journal of Ann Brown." Stud Am Renaissance (91): 59-118; auth, Politics and the English Instructor: Using Political Literature to Teach Composition, ERIC, 92; auth, "A Comment on George Orwell." College English 54 (92): 606-608; auth, "A Danish Appreciation of Thoreau: Jacob Paludan's Foreword to Livet i Skovene [Life in the Woods: Walden]." Thoreau Soc Bull 205 (93): 1-3; auth, "Headnote on Susanna Haswell Rowson and intro to selection from, Charlotte, a Tale of Truth, in The Heath Anthology of American Literature (Boston: D.C. Heath, 90), 2nd ed 93; auth, "The Politics of Fear on a CUNY Campus." Midstream 40 (94): 25-28; auth, "Group Defamation: From Language to Thought to Action." in Group Defamation and Freedom of Speech: The Relationship Between Language and Violence, eds. Eric and Monroe Freedman (Westport, CT.: Greenwood Press, 95). **CONTACT ADDRESS** Dept English, Bronx Comm Col, CUNY, 2155 University Ave, Bronx, NY 10453-2804. **EMAIL** lfergens@bellatlantic.net

FERGUSON, MARGARET WILLIAMS
PERSONAL Born 12/28/1948, Columbus, OH **DISCIPLINE** ENGLISH LITERATURE, COMPARATIVE LITERATURE **EDUCATION** Cornell Univ, BA, 69; Yale Univ, MPhil, 72, PhD (comp lit), 74. **CAREER** ASST PROF ENGLISH, YALE UNIV, 74-, Morse fel, Yale Univ, 77-78. **MEMBERSHIPS** MLA; Shakespeare Asn Am. **RESEARCH** Renaissance literature; literary theory. **SELECTED PUBLICATIONS** Auth, Dangerous Familiars--Representations of Domestic Crime in England, 1550-1700, Mod Philol, Vol 94, 96. **CONTACT ADDRESS** Dept English, Univ of California, Davis, 1 Shields Ave, Davis, CA 95616-5271.

FERGUSON, OLIVER WATKINS
PERSONAL Born 06/07/1924, Nashville, TN, m, 1949, 2 children **DISCIPLINE** ENGLISH **EDUCATION** Vanderbilt Univ, BA, 47, MA, 48; Univ Ill, PhD (English), 54. **CAREER** Instr English, Univ Ark, 48-50; asst prof Ohio State Univ, 54-57; from asst prof to assoc prof, 57-67, chmn dept, 67-73, PROF ENGLISH, DUKE UNIV, 67-, Guggenheim fel, 63-64; assoc ed, S Atlantic Quarterly, 61-72, ed, 72-; prof emer, Duke, 93-. **RESEARCH** Eighteenth century English literature. **SELECTED PUBLICATIONS** Auth, Swift and Ireland; ed, S Atlantic Quarterly, 77-87. **CONTACT ADDRESS** 1212 Arnette Ave, Durham, NC 27707. **EMAIL** ferguson@pub.Duke.edu

FERGUSON, ROBERT A.
DISCIPLINE AMERICAN LITERATURE **EDUCATION** Harvard Col, AB, 64; Harvard Law Sch, JD, 68; Harvard Univ, PhD, 74. **CAREER** Instr, Stanford, Harvard Univ; Andrew W Mellon prof, Univ Chicago; George Edward Woodberry prof-. **HONORS AND AWARDS** NEH fel; Nati Hum Ctr; Guggenheim found; Willard Hurst award, Law and Soc Assn. **RESEARCH** Courtroom trial as a central ceremony in American life. **SELECTED PUBLICATIONS** Auth, Law and Letters, Amer Cult, 84; The American Enlightenment, 1750-1829, 94. **CONTACT ADDRESS** Dept of Eng, Columbia Col, New York, 2960 Broadway, New York, NY 10027-6902.

FERGUSON, SHERILYN
DISCIPLINE COMMUNICATION **EDUCATION** BS, MA, PhD. **CAREER** Prof, Univ Northern CO. **MEMBERSHIPS** Speech Commun Asn; Western Speech Commun Asn; Am Asn of Marriage and Family therapists. **RESEARCH** Single parent families; organizational restructuring. **SELECTED PUBLICATIONS** Coauth, Children's Expectations of their single parents dating bahaviors: A premliminary investigation of emergent themes revelant to single parent dating, J of Appl Commun Res 23, 95. **CONTACT ADDRESS** Univ of No Colorado, Greeley, CO 80639.

FERGUSON, SUZANNE
PERSONAL Born E Stroudsburg, PA, w, 1960, 1 child **DISCIPLINE** MODERN AMERICAN AND ENGLISH LITERATURE **EDUCATION** Converse Col, BA; Vanderbilt Univ, MA; Stanford Univ, PhD. **CAREER** English, Case Western Reserve Univ; English, Univ CA, 66-71; Ohio State Univ, 71-83; Wayne State Univ, 83-89; Case Western Reserve Univ, 89-00. **HONORS AND AWARDS** Samuel B and Virginia C Knight Prof of Humanities, 98-00; Emerita, 00-; Who's Who in America, 94-; chair, engl dept. **MEMBERSHIPS** Modern Language Asn of Am, Society for the Study of the Short Story, Asn for the Study of American Indian Lit, American Lit Asn. **SELECTED PUBLICATIONS** Auth or ed, The Poetry of Randall Jarrell; Literature and the Visual Arts in Contemporary Society; Critical Essays on Randall Jarrell; auth, "Essays on the Theory and History of the Short Story". **CONTACT ADDRESS** Case Western Reserve Univ, 10900 Euclid Ave, Cleveland, OH 44106-7117. **EMAIL** scf@po.cwru.edu

FERNANDES, JAMES
PERSONAL Born 01/18/1947, Lihue, HI, m, 1988, 3 children **DISCIPLINE** SPEECH COMMUNICATION **EDUCATION** Univ Michigan, PhD, 80. **CAREER** Prof, commun, 75-, dir univ outreach, 95-96, acting dean, College for Continuing Educ, 96, Gallaudet Univ; adj prof, Univ Hawaii, 87-95; dir, Gallaudet Univ Pacific Reg Ctr, Univ Hawaii, 87-95. **HONORS AND AWARDS** Phi Beta Kappa, 69; pres award, Gallaudet Univ, 86; Nat Assoc of the Deaf, Golden Hand Awd, 95. **MEMBERSHIPS** Nat Assoc of the Deaf; Nat Commun Assoc; ADARA; International Communication Assocation. **RESEARCH** Deaf American public address; communication pedagogy with deaf students. **SELECTED PUBLICATIONS** Coauth, Guide to Better Hearing: A Resource Manual, City of Honolulu/GTE, 94; coauth, Signs of Eloquence: Selections from Deaf American Public Address, in, Readings in the Language, Culture, History, and Arts of Deaf People: Selected Papers from the Deaf Way Conference, Gallaudet, 94; auth, Communication Cops and Language Police, in Garretson, ed, Deafness: Life and Culture II, National Association of the Deaf, 95; auth, Partners in Education, Gallaudet Today, 96; auth, Creative Problem Solving--From Top to Bottom, Speech Commun Tchr, 98, auth, Signs of Eloquence: Foundations of Deaf American Public Address (1st author with Jane Kelleher Fernandes), San Diego: Dawn Sign Press; auth, "Creative Problem Solving-From Top to Bottom," Selections form the Speech Communication Teacher, 69-99, ed S Lucas, McGraw-Hill, 99. **CONTACT ADDRESS** Dept of Communication Arts, Gallaudet Univ, 800 Florida Ave NE, Washington, DC 20002. **EMAIL** james.fernandes@gallaudet.edu

FERNANDEZ, RAMONA E.
PERSONAL Born 11/26/1947, Elizabeth, NJ, s **DISCIPLINE** ENGLISH, LITERATURE **EDUCATION** SUNY, Old Westbury, BA, 70; Univ Ariz, MA, 73; Univ Calif, Santa Cruz, PhD, 95. **CAREER** Teaching Asst, Univ Calif, 88-92; Prof, Sacramento City Col, 75-97; Asst Prof, Mich St Univ, 98-. **HONORS AND AWARDS** NEH Fel, Univ Calif, 74; NEH Fel, Univ S Calif, 78; Fel, Cent Calif Writing Proj, 89; Fel, Ford Found, 89-94; NEH Fel, Univ Hawaii, 97. **MEMBERSHIPS** ASA, MLA, PCA. **RESEARCH** Race and gender, literacy, literature of women of color, museums, theme parks, narrative theory, feminist theory, science fiction. **SELECTED PUBLICATIONS** Auth, "Pachuco Mickey," in From Mouse to Mermaid: The Polit of Film, Gender and Cult (Bloomington, IN: Ind Univ Pr, 95); rev, Cannibals by Frank Lestringant, J of World Hist (forthcoming); auth, Imagining Literacy: Race, Gender, Culture and Knowledge in American Literatures, Theme Parks and Museums, Tex UP, forthcoming. **CONTACT ADDRESS** Dept English Lit, Michigan State Univ, 235 Bessey Hall, East Lansing, MI 48824-1033. **EMAIL** fernan47@msu.edu

FERNS, JOHN
DISCIPLINE ENGLISH LITERATURE **EDUCATION** Oxford Univ, MA; Univ Western Ontario, MA, PhD. **RESEARCH** Victorian, Canadian and modern British poetry; literary criticism. **SELECTED PUBLICATIONS** Auth, A.J.M Smith, 79; auth, The Poetry of L.M. Montgomery, 87; auth, Lytton Strachey, 88. **CONTACT ADDRESS** English Dept, McMaster Univ, 1280 Main St W, Hamilton, ON, Canada L8S 4L9. **EMAIL** fernshj@mcmaster.ca

FERRARI, RITA
DISCIPLINE ENGLISH **EDUCATION** SUNY, Buffalo, PhD. **CAREER** Eng Dept, St. Edward's Univ; assoc prof, St. Louis Univ, 97--. **SELECTED PUBLICATIONS** Auth, Innocence, Power, and the Novels of John Hawkes, Univ Pa Press, 96; The Innocent Imagination in John Hawkes' Whistlejacket and Virginie: Her Two Lives, Ariz Quart, 90; Masking, Revelation, and Fiction in Katherine Anne Porter's 'Flowering Judas' and 'Pale Horse, Pale Rider', Jour Short Story Eng, 95. **CONTACT ADDRESS** Verhaegen Hall, Saint Louis Univ, 3634 Lindell Blvd., Ste. 117, Saint Louis, MO 63108.

FERRARO, THOMAS J.
DISCIPLINE ENGLISH LITERATURE **EDUCATION** Yale Univ, PhD, 88. **CAREER** Prof, Duke Univ. **SELECTED PUBLICATIONS** Auth, Ethnic Passages: Literary Immigrants in 20th-Century America, Chicago, 93; Ethnicity and the Literary Marketplace in the Columbia History of American Novel, Columbia, 91; ed, Catholic Lives Contemporary America, Duke, 97. **CONTACT ADDRESS** Dept English, Duke Univ, 310 Allen Bldg., Box 90015, Durham, NC 27708. **EMAIL** feraro@acpub.duke.edu

FERRE, JOHN P.
PERSONAL Born 10/29/1956, Charlottesville, VA, m, 1985, 2 children **DISCIPLINE** COMMUNICATIONS **EDUCATION** Mars Hill Coll, BA, Relig, 77; Purdue Univ, MA, Commun, 78; Univ Chicago, MA, Divinity, 82; Univ Ill-Urbana Champaign, PhD, Commun, 86. **CAREER** Vis instr, Eng, Philos, Purdue Univ Calumet, 79-80; asst prof, Commun, Univ Louisville, 85-90, assoc prof, Commun, Univ Louisville, 90-98; PROF, COMMUN, UNIV LOUISVILLE, 98-. **HONORS AND AWARDS** Krieghbaum Uner-40 Awd of Outstanding Achievement in Research, Teaching, and Public Service, Asn for Education in Journalism and Mass Communication. **MEM-**

BERSHIPS Am Jour Hist Asn; Asn Educ Jour & Mass Commun; Soc Profess Jou **RESEARCH** Ethical, religious, & historical dimensions of mass media in US **SELECTED PUBLICATIONS** coauth, Good News: Social Ethics and the Press, Oxford Univ Press, 93; coauth, "Charles E. Coughlin," Historical Dictionary of American Radio, Greenwood, 98; auth, "Suicide," Censorship, Salem Press, 97; "Foremost in Service, Best in Entertainment," Television in America: Local Station History from Across the Nation, Iowa State Univ Press, 97; "Should Churches Boycott?" The Banner, 96; "Western Recorder," Popular Religious Magazines, Greenwood, 95. **CONTACT ADDRESS** Dept Commun, Univ of Louisville, Louisville, KY 40292. **EMAIL** ferre@louisville.edu

FERREIRA, DEBORA R. S.
PERSONAL Born 07/29/1964, Recife, PE, Brazil, m, 1987, 2 children **DISCIPLINE** CLASSICS **EDUCATION** Univ Fed de Pern, BA, 89; Univ Ga, MA, 94; PhD, 99. **CAREER** Res asst, Univ Fed de Pern, 88-92; teaching asst to instr, Univ Ga, 92-. **HONORS AND AWARDS** Grad Sch Asstshp, 99; Outstanding Teaching Awd, 94; Merit Awd, 94-95; Hon Soc Phi Kappa Phi; Hon Soc Phi Lambda Beta; Res Asstshp, 88-91. **MEMBERSHIPS** AATSP; BSA; MLA; SAMLA; ALFH. **RESEARCH** Latin American novel; post-colonial studies, negotiating power; feminist theory, gender relations; literary and cultural relations in the Lusephone world; production of teaching media. **SELECTED PUBLICATIONS** Auth, "O Imaginario Nacionalistico na Obra Clarice Lispector," Romance Lang Ann (98): 472-73; auth, "Carolina Maria de Jesus and Clarice Lispector: Constructing Brazil and Brasileiras," Torre de Papel. **CONTACT ADDRESS** Dept Romance Lang, Univ of Georgia, Gilbert Hall, Athens, GA 30602-1815. **EMAIL** ferreira@arches.uga.edu

FETTERLEY, JUDITH
PERSONAL Born 11/28/1938, New York, NY **DISCIPLINE** AMERICAN LITERATURE, WOMEN'S STUDIES **EDUCATION** Swarthmore Col, BA, 60; Ind Univ, MA, 66, PhD (English), 69. **CAREER** Asst prof English, Univ Pa, 67-73; asst prof, 73-78, ASSOC PROF ENGLISH, STATE UNIV NY, ALBANY, 78-. **MEMBERSHIPS** Nat Women's Studies Asn; MLA. **RESEARCH** Nineteenth century Am Lit; American women writers; Mark Twain. **SELECTED PUBLICATIONS** Auth, The sanctioned rebel, Studies Novel, fall 71; Disenchantment: Tom Sawyer in Huckleberry Finn, PMLA, 72; Yankee Showman and reformer: The character of Mark Twain's Hank Morgan, Tex Studies Lang & Lit, 73; Beauty as the beast: Fantasy and fear in I, The Jury, J Popular Cult, 75; Growing up female in The Old Order, Kate Chopin Newslett, 76; The temptation to be a beautiful object: Double standard and double bind in The House of Mirth, Studies Am Fiction, 77; The Resisting Reader: A Feminist Analysis of American Fiction, Ind Univ, 78. **CONTACT ADDRESS** Dept of English, SUNY, Albany, Albany, NY 12222.

FEWER, COLIN D.
PERSONAL Born 08/26/1969, Montreal, PQ, Canada **DISCIPLINE** ENGLISH, PHILOSOPHY **EDUCATION** Univ Manitoba, BA, 91; Penn State Univ, MA, 94; PhD, 01. **CAREER** Lectr, Penn State Univ, 99-00; asst prof, Purdue Univ Calumet, 00-. **MEMBERSHIPS** MLA; MAA. **RESEARCH** Chaucer; 15th-century English literature. **SELECTED PUBLICATIONS** Auth, "The 'fygure' of the Market: The N-Town Cycle and East Anglian Lay Piety," Philo Qtly (98). **CONTACT ADDRESS** Eng Dept, Purdue Univ, Calumet, 2200 169th Street, Hammond, IN 46323-2094. **EMAIL** fewer@calumet.edu

FIEDLER, LESLIE AARON
PERSONAL Born 03/08/1917, Newark, NJ, m, 1973, 8 children **DISCIPLINE** ENGLISH LITERATURE **EDUCATION** NYork Univ, AB, 38; Univ Wis, AM, 39, PhD, 41. **CAREER** Asst English, Univ Wis, 40-41; instr, Univ Mont, 41-43; Rockefeller fel humanities, Harvard Univ, 46-67; from asst prof English to prof, Univ Mont, 47-65 & chmn dept, 54-56; prof English, State Univ NY, Buffalo, 64-, Fulbright fel & lectr, Univs Rome & Bologna, Italy, 52-54; jr fel, Sch Let, Ind Univ, 53-; resident fel creative writing & Gauss lectr, Princeton Univ, 56-67; Kenyon Rev fel criticism, 56-67; Am Coun Learned Soc grants-in-aid, 60-61; Fulbright fel, Univ Athens, Greece, 61-62; assoc ed, Ramparts; English adv, St Martin's Press; lit ed, The Running Man; vis prof Am Studies, Univ Sussex, Eng, 68; assoc fel, Calhoun Co, Yale Univ, 70-; vis prof, Univ Vincennes, Paris, 71-72; Samuel Clemens Prof of English, State Univ NY, Buffalo, 72- **HONORS AND AWARDS** Mod Lang Asn Hubbell Medal for Lifetime Contribution to the Study of American Literature; elected to Am Acad and Inst of Arts and Letters; Nat Book Critics Circle Awd for Lifetime Contribution to American Arts and Letters. **RESEARCH** The novel; 19th and 20th century American and British literature; humanities. **SELECTED PUBLICATIONS** Auth, The Second Stone; Love and Death in the American Novel, 66, Nude Croquet and Other Stories, 69, The Stranger in Shakespeare, 72 & The Messengers Will Come No More, 74, Stein & Day; Freaks: Myths and Images of the Secret Self, Simon & Schuster, 78; Tyranny of the Normal, 96; The New Fiedler Reader, 99. **CONTACT ADDRESS** Dept of English, SUNY, Buffalo, PO Box 604610, Buffalo, NY 14260-4610. **EMAIL** fiedler@acsu.buffalo.edu

FIELD, MICHAEL J.
PERSONAL Born 05/01/1943, New York, NY, m, 1964 **DISCIPLINE** ENGLISH **EDUCATION** SUNY Stony Brook, BA, 64; Cornell Univ, MA, 65; PhD, 70. **CAREER** Asst prof, Temple Univ, 68-72; asst prof to assoc prof to prof, Bemidji Univ, 72-99; provost, Shawnee State Univ, 99-. **HONORS AND AWARDS** Cornell Grad Fel, 64; NDEA Fel, 65; NEH Fel, 79. **MEMBERSHIPS** AIS; SVHE; MLA. **RESEARCH** Assessment of student outcomes; strategic planning. **SELECTED PUBLICATIONS** Co-auth, Evaluation in General Education," Perspectives 16 (86); co-auth, "Assessment of Interdisciplinary Programs," Europ J Educ 27 (92); co-auth, "Assessing Interdisciplinary Learning," Interdisciplinary Studies Today (94). **CONTACT ADDRESS** English Dept, Shawnee State Univ, 940 2nd St, Portsmouth, OH 45662-4303. **EMAIL** mfield@shawnee.edu

FIELDS, BEVERLY
PERSONAL Born 12/07/1917, Chicago, IL, m, 1940, 2 children **DISCIPLINE** ENGLISH **EDUCATION** Northwestern Univ, BA, 39, MA, 58, PhD (English romantic lit), 65. **CAREER** Instr English, Lake Forest Col, 61-62 and Northwestern Univ, 62-65; asst prof, 65-69, assoc prof to assoc prof emer, Univ Ill, Chicago, 69-. **MEMBERSHIPS** MLA. **RESEARCH** English romantic literature; English and American contemporary literature; literary criticism. **CONTACT ADDRESS** Dept of English, Univ of Illinois, Chicago, 601 S Morgan St, M/C 162, Chicago, IL 60607-7120.

FIELDS, DARIN E.
PERSONAL m, 1987, 2 children **DISCIPLINE** AMERICAN LITERATURE **EDUCATION** Univ Ariz, BA, 86; Univ Delaware, MA, 89; PhD, 92. **CAREER** Asst prof, Univ Delaware, 92-93; ch, grad stud comm, 97-98; asst prof, 93-; assoc prof, 93-, dept chair, 99-, Wilkes Univ. **HONORS AND AWARDS** Alsie Schulman and Edmund Schulman Mem scholar, Univ Ariz, 86; tchg asstship, Univ Del, 87-89; res asstship, Univ Del, 89-91; Mellon res fel, Va Hist Soc, 91; fel, Univ Del, 91-92; outstanding fac award, 94, Wilkes Univ. **MEMBERSHIPS** Mem, Amer Lit Assn; Amer Soc Eighteenth Century Stud; Assn Doc Ed; Mod Lang Assn; Soc Eighteenth Century Amer Stud; Soc Stud S Lit; Va Hist Soc. **RESEARCH** Early American Literature; 18th Century British Literature; Travel Literature. **SELECTED PUBLICATIONS** Auth, Some Current Publications, Restoration: Studies in English Literary Culture, 93; George Alsop's Indentured Servant, A Character of the Province of Maryland, Md Hist Mag, 90; Two Spheres of Action and Suffering: Empire and Decadence in Little Dorrit, Dickens Quart, 90; auth, "George Alsop," biographical entry in American National Biography, Oxford Univ Press (New York), 99; auth, "Touring Colonial America," review essay, Documentary Editing 20.4 (98): 95-97. **CONTACT ADDRESS** Dept of Humanities, Wilkes Univ, 170 S Franklin St, Wilkes-Barre, PA 18766. **EMAIL** dfields@wilkes.edu

FIELDS, POLLY STEVENS
PERSONAL Born, TN **DISCIPLINE** ENGLISH **EDUCATION** Vanderbilt Univ, BA, 78; Univ Miss, MA, 89; La State Univ, PhD, 92. **CAREER** Sr fac, Univ Prep Sch Nash, 78-85; sr fac, Miami Val Prep Sch, 85-87; instr, Univ Miss, 87-89; res fel, asstshps, La State Univ, 89-92; instr, Univ Ala, 93-95; asst prof to assoc prof, Lake Sup State Univ, 95-. **HONORS AND AWARDS** UCLA-Clark Post-Doct Fel, 97-98, 00-01; Fac Awd Teaching Excellence, 98; Capstone Found Fac 96-98; LSU Distinguished Awd, 92-93; LSU Res Fel, 90, 91, 91-92. **MEMBERSHIPS** ASECS; Aphra Behn Soc; ALSC; BAWW; CSECS; GEMS; Ireland Soc; John Donne Soc; MRTS; MAAL; Milton Soc; MLA; NCTE; RMMLA; SCS; Shakespeare Soc; SBAWW; SAMLA; SECS; Voltaire Soc. **RESEARCH** Early modern Anglican sermons; early modern women dramatists; Chippewa-Ojibwa pictographs; Native-American women writers; post-colonial. **SELECTED PUBLICATIONS** Auth, "'And They Laid Poor Jesse in His Grave': A Study of Four James Ballads, " Festschrift in Honor of Dr. George Boswell, Jackson: Miss Folklore Soc (90); auth, "'Manly Vigor and Woman's Wit': Engendering Dialogue in the Dramas of Eliza Haywood.," in Compendious Conversations: The Methods of Dialogue in the Early Enlightenment, ed. K. C. Cope (NYork: Lang, 93): 257-266; auth, "An Annotated Bibliography of the Works of Mary Davys," in Eighteenth-Century Anglo-American Women Novelists, eds. Doreen Alvarez-Saar, Mary Anne Schofield (NYork: G K Hall, 98): 118-131; auth, "George Lillo and the Victims of Economic Theory, " Study Lit Imagine 32 (00): 77-88; auth, "Charlotte Charke and the Liminality of Bi-Gendering: A Study of the Canonical Works," in A Pilgrimage for Love: New Essays in Early Modern Literature, ed. Sigrid King (Tempe, AZ: Ariz Cen Medieval Renai Txt Studies 00): 221-239; auth, "Elizabeth Sophia Tomlins," in New Dictionary of National Biography (England: Oxford Univ Pr, forthcoming); auth, "Eliza K. Mathews, " in New Dictionary of National Biography (England: Oxford Univ Pr, forthcoming); auth, "Samson Occom And/In the Missionary's] Position: Consideration of the Post Colonial Preacher," Wordsworth Cir (01). **CONTACT ADDRESS** English Dept, Lake Superior State Univ, 650 W Easterday Ave, Sault Ste. Marie, MI 49783. **EMAIL** pfields@gw.lssu.edu

FIFER, ELIZABETH
PERSONAL Born 08/05/1944, Pittsburgh, PA, m, 1970, 1 child **DISCIPLINE** COMPARATIVE LITERATURE, ENGLISH **EDUCATION** Univ MI, Ann Arbor, BA, 65, MA, 66, PhD, 69. **CAREER** Lectr hum, Res Col, Univ MI, 69-72; asst prof, 73-80, Assoc Prof Eng, Lehigh Univ, 80-, prof eng, Lehigh Univ. **HONORS AND AWARDS** Stabler Awd for Excellence in Teaching, 99. **MEMBERSHIPS** MLA; Asn Theater Res. **RESEARCH** Gertrude Stein; Contemp lit; Contemp drama; Contemp fiction (U S & World). **SELECTED PUBLICATIONS** Auth, The Confessions of Italo Sveno, Contemp Lit, 73: Sex-stereo Typing in Geography & Plays, Univ Mich Papers Women's Studies, 75; Tragedy into Melodrama, Lex et Scientia, 77; The Interior Theater of Gertrude Stein, Signs, 78; Rescued Readings: Reconstruction of Gertrude Stein's Difficult Texts, Wayne State Univ, 92; auth, 'Black is Black' The Other in Jewish Thought and Hist, 95. **CONTACT ADDRESS** Dept of Eng, Lehigh Univ, 35 Sayre Dr, Bethlehem, PA 18015-3076. **EMAIL** EF00@lehigh.edu

FIGG, KRISTEN MOSSLER
PERSONAL Born 06/23/1952, Akron, OH, m, 2 children **DISCIPLINE** ENGLISH **EDUCATION** Univ Akron, BA, 72; MA, 74; MA, 82; Kent State Univ, PhD, 88. **CAREER** Asst prof to prof, Kent State Univ Salem, 89-. **MEMBERSHIPS** Medieval Acad of Am, Medieval Assoc of Midwest, Early Book Soc, MLA, NCTE, Conf on Col Comp and Commun. **SELECTED PUBLICATIONS** Auth, "Jean Froissart's 'Lay de la Mort La Royne D'Engleterre,'" Allegorica 14 (93): 61-76; auth, "Critiquing Courtly Convention: Jean Froissart's Playful Lyric Persona," Fr Studies 48, (94): 129-42; auth, The Short Lyric Poems of Jean Froissart: Fixed Forms and the Expression of the Courtly Ideal, Garland Studies in Medieval Lit 10, (NY), 94; coed, Trade, Travel, and Exploration in the Middle Ages: An Encyclopedia, Garland Publ, (NY), 00; coauth, The Princess with the Golden Hair: Letters of Elizabeth Waugh to Edmond Wilson: 1933-1942, Fairleigh Dickinson Univ Pr, 00; ed and transl, Jean Froissart: An Anthology of Narrative and Lyric Poetry, Routledge, (NY), 01; auth, "Froissart's 'Debate of the Horse and the Greyhound': Companion Animals and Signs of Social Status in the Fourteenth Century," Marvels, Monsters, and Miracles: Studies in the Medieval and Early Modern Imagination, eds David A Sprunger and Timothy S Jones, Medieval Inst Publ, (Kalamazoo, MI: 01). **CONTACT ADDRESS** Dept English, Kent State Univ, Salem, 2491 Sr 45 South, Salem, OH 44460. **EMAIL** figg@salem.kent.edu

FILEMYR, ANN
DISCIPLINE JOURNALISM, COMMUNICATIONS AND ENVIRONMENTAL STUDIES **EDUCATION** Thomas Jefferson Col, BA; Univ Wis, Milwaukee, MA; Un Inst, PhD. **CAREER** Assoc prof, Antioch Col; assoc dean of fac, Antioch Col. **HONORS AND AWARDS** Fel, Environ Journalism Inst, MSU; Fel, Antioch Writers Workshop; Fel Pew Ctr for Civic Journalism. **MEMBERSHIPS** AWP; Soc for Environ Journalists. **RESEARCH** Gender; race; class and environmental justice; ecofeminism; ecopoetry; nature writing. **SELECTED PUBLICATIONS** Auth, Loving Across the Boundary, in Skin Deep: Black Women and White Women Write About Race, Doubleday, 95; Media and Journalism, in Greening the College Curriculum: A Guide to Environmental Teaching in the Liberal Arts, Island Press, 95; auth, Skin on Skin, Starfire Press, 00. **CONTACT ADDRESS** Antioch Col, Yellow Springs, OH 45387. **EMAIL** afilemyr@antioch-college.edu

FILER, MALVA ESTHER
PERSONAL Born 02/25/1933, Argentina, m, 1964, 2 children **DISCIPLINE** SPANISH AMERICAN LITERATURE **EDUCATION** Univ Buenos Aires, BA, 58; Columbia Univ, PhD(philos), 66. **CAREER** Lectr Span, 63-66, instr, 66-68, asst prof, 69-72, Assoc Prof Span, Brooklyn Col, 73- **MEMBERSHIPS** MLA; Inst Int Lit Iberoam; Assoc Int de Hispanistas **RESEARCH** Contemporary Spanish American literature. **SELECTED PUBLICATIONS** Coauth, Voces de Hispanoamerica: Antologia literia, 88, 96; auth, Salvador Elizondo and Servero Sarduy: Two Borgesian Writers, Borges and his Successors, Univ of MO, 90; auth, Los perros del paraiso y la nueva novela historica, En este aire y Iuz de America: Homenaje a Alfredo A. Roggiano, Inst Unt de Lit Iberoam, 90; auth, La vision de America en la obra de Abel Posse, La novel argentina de los aflos 80; Vervuert Verlag, 91; auth, Cesar Aira y su aprcrifa historia de los caciques cura, VII Congreso Nacional de Literatura Argentina, Univ Nacional de Tueuman, 93; auth, Los nuevos narradores de la Conquista, Reflejos, Vol 1, No 2, 93; auth, Maluco: re-escritura de los relatos de la expedicion de Mafallanes, Actas Irvine, 92; auth, La historia apocrifa en las novelas de los postmodernistas rioplatenses, Alba de America, 12:22-23, 94; auth, Hispanoamerica en la obra de Jose Maria Merino, Actas XXIX Congreso del Instituto Internacionnal del Literatura Iberoamericana, Univ Barcelona, 94. **CONTACT ADDRESS** Dept of Mod Lang, Brooklyn Col, CUNY, 2900 Bedford Ave, Brooklyn, NY 11210. **EMAIL** mfiler@brooklyn.cuny.edu

FILIPOWICZ, HALINA
DISCIPLINE ENGLISH & AMERICAN LITERATURE **EDUCATION** Warsaw Univ, MA 69; Univ KS, PhD, 79. **CA-**

REER Prof Dept Slavic Lang & Lit, Univ Wisc, 97-; assoc prof Dept Slavic Lang & Lit, Univ Wisc, 89-97; asst prof Dept Slavic Lang & Lit, Univ Wisc, 82-89 **HONORS AND AWARDS** Univ Wisc Vilas Assoc Fel, 96-98; Ntl Endowment Humanities Fel, 92-93; Non-Tenured Fac Fel at Bunting Ist, Radcliffe Col, 85, 86; Univ Wisc Grad School Summer Res Grants, 87, 89, 90, 94; Univ Wisc Fac Recognition Awd, 83; Intl Res & Exchanges Board Travel Grant, 83, 91, 93; Summer Stipend for Independent Res, Ntl Endowment Humanities, 82; Amer Council Learned Soc Fel, 81-82, 88-89; Oswald Prentiss Backus III Awd, Univ KS, 81; Grad School Dissertation Fel, Univ KS, 78-79. **MEMBERSHIPS** Modern Lang Assoc; Amer Assoc of Tchrs of Slavic & East European Lang; Amer Assoc for Advancement of Slavic Studies. **RESEARCH** Polish Theatre & Drama; Polish Literature; Performance Studies; Gender Studies; Colonial/Postcolonial Cultural Studies; Critical Theory. **SELECTED PUBLICATIONS** Auth, A Laboratory of Impure Forms: The Plays of Tadeusz Rozewicz, New York: Greenwood Press, 91; auth, "The Daughters of Emilia Plater," in Pamela Chester and Sibelan Forrester, eds, Engendering Slavic Literatures, Bloomington: Indiana Univ Pr, 96; auth, "Textualizing Trauma: Velesa to Kosciuszko in Polish Theatre of the 1980s, " Theatre Journal 48 (96): 443-60; auth, "Where is Gurutowski?" in Richard Schechner and Lisa Wolford, eds, Grotowski Sourcebook, New York: Routledge, 97; auth, "Polska litratura emigracyjna' - proba teorii," Trans, Krzysztf, Teksty Drugie 3-4 (98): 43-62; auth, "Performing Bodies, Performing Mickiewicz: Drama as Problem in Performance Studies," Slavic and East European Journal 43 (99): 1-18; auth, "Hera's Glass Eyes; A Counterreading of Zbigniew Herbert's Plays," The Other Herbert, ed, Bozena Shallcross, Spec. issue of Indiana Slavic Studies, 99; coed, The Great Tradition: Dramatic and Musical Theater in Austria and Central Europe, ed, Michael Cherlin, Halina Filipowicz, and Richard L. Rudolf, (forthcoming). **CONTACT ADDRESS** Dept of Slavic Languages & Literature, Univ of Wisconsin, Madison, 1432 Van Hise Hall, 1220 Linden Dr., Madison, WI 53706. **EMAIL** hfilipow@facstaff.wisc.edu

FINDLAY, LEONARD MURRAY
PERSONAL Born 12/14/1944, Aberdeen, Scotland, m, 1968, 2 children **DISCIPLINE** ENGLISH **EDUCATION** Univ Aberdeen, MA, 67; Univ Oxford, DPhil, 72. **CAREER** Lectr English, City Birmingham Polytech, 70-72; Asst Prof English, Univ Sask, 72-. **MEMBERSHIPS** MLA, Asn Can Univ Teachers English, Victorian Studies Asn Western Can. **RESEARCH** Nineteenth Century Poetry and Prose, Literary Theory and Criticism, The Interrelationship of the Arts. **SELECTED PUBLICATIONS** Auth, "Valuing Culture, Interdisciplining the Economic"; auth, "Interdisciplining Canada: Cause Breaking Up Is Hard To Do." **CONTACT ADDRESS** Dept of English, Univ of Saskatchewan, 320 Arts Tower, 9 Campus Dr, Saskatoon, SK, Canada S7H 5A5. **EMAIL** findlay@sask.usask.ca

FINDLAY, ROBERT
PERSONAL Born 08/16/1932, Joliet, IL **DISCIPLINE** THEATRE AND DRAMA **EDUCATION** Ill State Univ, BS, 57; Ohio Univ, MFA, 59; Univ Iowa, PhD (theatre), 64. **CAREER** Instr speech and drama, Allegheny Col, 59-60; from instr to asst prof, Bowling Green State Univ, 63-67; from asst prof to assoc prof, 67-73, PROF THEATRE and DRAMA, UNIV KANS, 73-, Nat Endowment for Humanities grants, 78 and 80; Kosciuszko Found grant, 80-81. **HONORS AND AWARDS** Amicus Poloniae badge, Poland mag, 76. **MEMBERSHIPS** Am Soc Theatre Res; Am Theatre Asn; Polish Inst Arts and Sci. **RESEARCH** Modern and contemporary theatre and drama. **SELECTED PUBLICATIONS** Auth, A confrontation in waiting: Godot and the Wakefield play, Renascence, 69; The Emperor Jones: O'Neill as scene designer, Players, 69; coauth, Century of Innovation: A History of European and American Theatre and Drama Since 1870, Prentice-Hall, 73; The Other Theatre of Wroclaw: Henryk Tomaszewski and the Pantomima, Educ Theatre J, 75; Czarny Teatr w USA (Black Theatre in the USA), 77 & Czarny Dramat w USA (Black Drama in the USA), Dialog, Warsaw, Poland, 77; Grotowski's Cultural Explorations Bordering on Art, Especially Theatre, Theatre J, 80; Grotowski's l'homme pur: Towards De-Mystification, Theatre Perspectives, 82. **CONTACT ADDRESS** Dept of Speech and Drama, Univ of Kansas, Lawrence, Lawrence, KS 66045-0001.

FINDON, JOANNE
PERSONAL Born 01/28/1957, Surrey, BC, Canada **DISCIPLINE** WRITING **EDUCATION** Univ BC, BA, 82; Univ Toronto, MA, 87, PhD, 94. **CAREER** Instr lit, dept Celtic stud, St Michael's Col, 86-89; instr, Univ Guelph, 94; instr, Univ Toronto & York Univ, 95-96. **HONORS AND AWARDS** IODE Awd; York Univ res grant, 96-97. **MEMBERSHIPS** Ed Asn Can; Celtic Stud Asn N Am; Can Asn Irish Stud; Can Soc Medievalists. **SELECTED PUBLICATIONS** Auth, The Importance of Being Bracknell in The Blue Jean Collection, 92; auth, The Dream of Aengus, 94; auth, On the Road in Takes, 96; auth, Auld Lang Syne, 97; auth, A Woman's Words: Emer and Female Speech in the Ulster Cycle, 97. **CONTACT ADDRESS** 5886-128 St, Surrey, BC, Canada V3X 1T3.

FINE, AFRICA R.
PERSONAL Born 06/01/1972, Milwaukee, WI, m, 1998 **DISCIPLINE** ENGLISH COMPOSITION **EDUCATION** Duke Univ, BA, 93; Fla Atlantic Univ, MA, 01. **CAREER** Asst prog coord, Cities in Schs, 94-95; staff writer, Palm Beach Post, 95-98; copywriter, First Marketing, 98-01; instr, Fla Atlantic Univ, 01-. **MEMBERSHIPS** MLA; Sigma Tau Delta. **RESEARCH** Creative writing (prose); African American literature; rhetoric and composition. **SELECTED PUBLICATIONS** Auth, "Riding the Number 12," Anthology Lit Mag (96); auth, "In March I Always Think of You," Coastlines Lit Mag (00); auth, "Katrina," Five Star (01); auth, Second Orality in Their Eyes Were Watching God and The Color Purple, Fla Atlantic Univ, 01. **CONTACT ADDRESS** PO Box 243014, Boynton Beach, FL 33424. **EMAIL** arfine@bellsouth.net

FINE, ELIZABETH C.
PERSONAL Born 12/20/1948, Cincinnati, OH, m, 1977, 1 child **DISCIPLINE** PERFORMANCE STUDIES, FOLKLORE **EDUCATION** Univ Tex, Austin, BS, 71, PhD (commun), 78; Univ Calif, Berkeley, MA, 73. **CAREER** Lect and asst prof, Univ Il, Urbana 77-79; asst and assoc prof Virginia Tech , 79-; dir, Humanities Progms, Center for Interdisciplinary Studies, Virginia Tech, 99-, asst and assoc prof, Virginia Interdiciplinary Studies, Virginia Tech, 99-. **HONORS AND AWARDS** Woodrow Wilson Fel, 71; Oustanding Dissertation Awd, Univ of Texas at Austin, 78-79; The Lilla A Heston Awd for Outstanding Scholarship in Interpretation and Performance Studies, presented by the Speech Communn Asn, 93; Third Place, Chicago Folklore Prize 85; Choice's Outstanding Academic Book of 85. **MEMBERSHIPS** Nat Commun Assoc, Am Folklore Soc **RESEARCH** Performance Studies, Appalachian Studies, African American Folklore. **SELECTED PUBLICATIONS** Auth, The Folklore Text: From Performance to Print, Bloomington: Indiana Univ Press, 84,94; auth, Fine Elizabeth and Speer, Jean Haskell, eds Performance, Culture and Identity, NY: Prager, 92; auth, " Lazy Jack": Coding and Contexualizing Resistance in Appalachia and the South: Place, Gender, Pedagogy, Vol 11, (3), 99: 112-137; auth, Leading Proteus Captive." Teaching Oral Traditions, MLA, 98, 59-71. **CONTACT ADDRESS** Dept of Commun Studies, Virginia Polytech Inst and State Univ, Blacksburg, VA 24060. **EMAIL** bfine@vt.edu

FINE, LAURA
PERSONAL Born Washington, DC **DISCIPLINE** ENGLISH LITERATURE **EDUCATION** Univ Calif Davis, PhD. **CAREER** Asst prof, Dept Eng, Clark Atlanta Univ. **RESEARCH** Autobiography; 20th century American and 20th century British literature; Southern literature. **SELECTED PUBLICATIONS** Auth, articles published in Biography, Southern Quart and Southern Lit Quart **CONTACT ADDRESS** Clark Atlanta Univ, 223 James P Brawley Dr, SW, Atlanta, GA 30314. **EMAIL** lfines@aol.com

FINE, MARLENE G.
PERSONAL Born 01/07/1949, NJ, s, 2 children **DISCIPLINE** COMMUNICATION **EDUCATION** Univ Mass, BA, 70; Univ Minn, MA, 72; Univ Mass, PhD, 80; MBA, 84. **CAREER** Dean Grad Studies, Emerson Col, 95-; Chair, Dept Marketing & Communication, Univ Mass, 93-95; assoc prof, Univ Mass, 91-95; asst prof, Univ Mass, 85-91; dir, Bus Admin Program, Univ Mass, 85-89; financial analyst, Small Bus Development Center, Univ Mass, 83; dir, Master's in Communications Management, Simmons Coll, 99-; Dean Grad Studies, Emerson Col, 95-99. **HONORS AND AWARDS** Who's Who in Media & Communication, 96; Dictionary of Intl Biog, 95; Intl Who's Who Prof Bus Women, 94; World Who's Who of Women, 94; Who's Who of Amer Women, 94; Who Who in the East, 92; Univ Mass Prof of Year, 89; Beta Gamma Sigma, 84; Shaeffer Eaton Awd for Academic Excellence, Univ Mass, 84; Pi Kappa Delta, 73; Delta Sigma Rho--Tau Kappa Alpha, 68. **MEMBERSHIPS** National Communication Assoc, Academy of Mgt; Assoc for Business Communication Correction. **RESEARCH** Organizational Communication; Cultural Diversity in Organizations **SELECTED PUBLICATIONS** Auth, Cultural diversity in the workplace: Organizational challenges and opportunities, Quorum, 95; Cultural diversity: The state of the field, Jour Bus Commun, 96; New voices in the workplace: Research directions in mulitcultural communication, Jour Bus Commun, 91; Epistemological and methodological commitments of a feminist perspective, Women and Lang, 91; Building Successful Multicultural Organizations: Challenges and Opportunities, Quorum, 95. **CONTACT ADDRESS** Master's in Community Management, Simmons Col, 300 The Fenway, Boston, MA 02115. **EMAIL** fine@simmons.edu

FINK, EDWARD L.
DISCIPLINE COMMUNICATIONS **EDUCATION** Univ Wis-Madison, PhD, 75. **CAREER** Prof and chair, dept of comm, Univ MD. **RESEARCH** Cognitive processes involved in persuasion. **SELECTED PUBLICATIONS** Co-auth, Cybernetics of Attitudes and Decisions, Dynamic Patterns, Commun Processes, Sage Publ, 96. **CONTACT ADDRESS** Dept of Commun, Univ of Maryland, Col Park, 2130A Skinner Bldg., College Park, MD 20742-7635. **EMAIL** elf@deans.umd.edu

FINK, ROBERT J.
PERSONAL Born 02/17/1931, Rochester, NY, m, 1974, 1 child **DISCIPLINE** FRENCH RENAISSANCE, CINEMA **EDUCATION** Univ Toronto, BA, 54, MA, 58; Univ Chicago, PhD (Romance lang), 71. **CAREER** From instr to asst prof French, St Michael's Col, Univ Toronto, 65-73; arts officer, Can Coun, 73-77; assoc prof, St Francis Xavier Univ, 78-80; assoc prof, Mt Allison Univ, 80-81; Prof French, Acadia Univ, 81-. **MEMBERSHIPS** MLA; Renaissance Soc Am; Can Soc Renaissance Studies. **RESEARCH** French Renaissance humanism; French-Canadian novel and cinema. **SELECTED PUBLICATIONS** Auth, The National Wildlife Refuges--Theory, Practice, and Prospect, Harvard Environmental Law Rev, Vol 18, 94. **CONTACT ADDRESS** Dept of Mod Lang, Acadia Univ, Wolfville, NS, Canada B0P 1Z1.

FINK, THOMAS A.
PERSONAL Born 03/25/1954, New York, NY, m, 1988, 2 children **DISCIPLINE** ENGLISH **EDUCATION** Columbia Univ, MA, 77; M Phil, &9; PhD, 81. **CAREER** Prof, La Guardia Com Col, 81-. **RESEARCH** Twentieth century literature and literary theory. **SELECTED PUBLICATIONS** Auth, The Poetry of David Shapiro, Fair Dick Univ Press (Rutherford, NJ), 93; auth, Surprise Visit, Domes Press (NY), 93; co-ed Literature Around the Globe, Kendall/Hunt Pub (Dubuque, IA), 94; auth, Gossip, Amar Press (Medford, NY), 00; auth, Different Sense of Power: Problems of Community in Late Twentieth Century U.S. Poetry, Fair Dick Univ Press (Rutherford, NJ), 00; auth, "Tracing David Shapiro's 'The Seasons," Contem Lit 37 (96): 416-38; auth, "John Ashbery's Wakefulness," Confront 66 (98): 319-21; auth, "Visibility and History in the Poetry of Martin Espada," Am Rev 25 (99): 202-221; auth, "David Shapiro," in Contemp Jew Am Authors: A Bio-Critical Sourcebook, ed. Joel Shatzky, Michael Taub (Westport, Ct: Greenwood, 99): 542-8; auth, "Between/After Language Poetry and the New York School" in The World in Time and Space: Towards a History of Innovative American Poetry, 1970-2000, ed. Edward Foster, Joseph Donahue (Jersey City, NJ: Talisman, 00); auth, "The Figure of Jesse Jackson in Contemporary African-American Poetry," Comm Rev (forthcoming). **CONTACT ADDRESS** Dept English, LaGuardia Comm Col, 3110 Thomson Ave, Long Island, NY 11101-3007. **EMAIL** mamtaf@juno.com

FINKE, L. A.
PERSONAL Born 03/07/1952, Dayton, OH, m, 1983, 2 children **DISCIPLINE** ENGLISH **EDUCATION** Univ Pa, PhD, 80 **CAREER** Inst, Univ Okla, 80-83; assoc prof, Lewis & Clark Coll, 84- 92; Prof Women's & Gender Stud, Kenyon Coll, 92-. **MEMBERSHIPS** MLA; NWSA; Soc Medieval Fem Scholarship. **RESEARCH** Middle ages; literary theory; feminist theory. **SELECTED PUBLICATIONS** various **CONTACT ADDRESS** Women's & Gender Studies, Kenyon Col, Gambier, OH 43022. **EMAIL** finkel@kenyon.edu

FINKELPEARL, PHILIP J.
PERSONAL Born 06/09/1925, Pittsburgh, PA, m, 1948, 2 children **DISCIPLINE** ENGLISH **EDUCATION** Princeton Univ, AB, 48; Harvard Univ, AM, 49, PhD (English), 54. **CAREER** From instr to asst prof English, Brandeis Univ, 52-57; from asst prof to assoc prof, Vassar Col, 62-70; assoc prof, Lehman Col, 70-71; assoc prof, Univ Mass, Boston, 71-72, prof English, 72-82; PROF ENGLISH, WELLESLEY COL, 82-, Guggenheim fel, 71-72. **RESEARCH** Elizabethan drama and poetry. **SELECTED PUBLICATIONS** Auth, John Marston of the Middle Temple: an Elizabethan Dramatist in his Social Setting, Harvard Univ Pr, 69; auth, Court and Country Politics in the Plays of Beaumont and Fletcher, Princeton Univ Pr, 90; auth, The Authorship of the Anonymous Coleorton Masque of 1618, Notes Queries, Vol 40, 93; The Fairies Farewell--The Masque at Coleorton 1618, Rev Eng Stud, Vol 46, 95. **CONTACT ADDRESS** Shaker Village, Harvard, MA 01451. **EMAIL** pfinkelpearl@msn.com

FINKELSTEIN, NORMAN MARK
PERSONAL Born 05/30/1954, New York, NY **DISCIPLINE** CONTEMPORARY AMERICAN POETRY **EDUCATION** State Univ NYork Binghamton, BA, 75; Emory Univ, PhD(English), 80. **CAREER** Prof English, dept chemn, Xavier Univ, 80-. **MEMBERSHIPS** MLA. **RESEARCH** 20th-Century Am Poetry; Jewish Lieterature; literary theory. **SELECTED PUBLICATIONS** The Utopian Moment In Contemporary American Poetry, Bucknell, 88, 93; The Ritual of New Creation: Jewish Tradition and Contemporary Literature, SUNY, 92; Restlesss Messengers, Georgia, Track, 92; auth, Literary Criticism: The Utopian Moment, The Ritual of New Creation, Not the One of Them In Place; auth, "The Master of Turning: Walter Benjamin, Gershom Scholem, Harold Bloom, and the Writing of a Jewish Life," People of the Book: Thirty Scholars Reflect On Their Jewish Identity, Univ of Wis Press, (96): 415-26; auth, "The Messianic Ethnography of Jerome Rothenberg's Poland/1931," Contemporary Literature 39.3, (98): 356-79; auth, "Looking for the Way: The Poetry of Harvey Shapiro," Religion and Literature 30.3, (98): 97-120; auth, "Tradition and Modernity, Judaism and Objectivism: The Poetry of Charles Reznikoff," The Objectivist Nexus, Univ of Alabama Press, (99): 191-209; auth, Track, Spuyten Duyvil, 99; auth, "Acher," Jewish

American Poetry: Reflections, Poems, and Commentary, Brandeis Univ Press/Univ Press of New England, (00): 65-69; auth, Not one of Them In Place: Modern Poetry and Jewish American Identity, SUNY, 01. **CONTACT ADDRESS** Dept of English, Xavier Univ, Ohio, 3800 Victory Pky, Cincinnati, OH 45207-4446. **EMAIL** finkelst@xavier.xu.edu

FINLAYSON, JOHN
DISCIPLINE ENGLISH LITERATURE **EDUCATION** Cambridge Univ, PhD. **CAREER** Dept Eng, Queen's Univ **RESEARCH** Medieval romance and allegory; Chaucer; editing medieval texts; historical contextualization. **SELECTED PUBLICATIONS** Auth, pubs on Arthurian romance, Chaucer, Pearl, Sir Gawain, Caxton, Petrarch, and Boccaccio; ed, Morte Arthure. **CONTACT ADDRESS** English Dept, Queen's Univ at Kingston, Kingston, ON, Canada K7L 3N6. **EMAIL** jf@qsilver.queensu.ca

FINN, MARGARET R.
PERSONAL Born 08/03/1916, Jersey City, NJ **DISCIPLINE** CLASSICS **EDUCATION** Col St Elizabeth, AB, 37; Fordham Univ, MA, 42, PhD, 50. **CAREER** Instr Latin, Col St Elizabeth, 37-38; teacher, St Michael's High Sch, Jersey City, NJ, 38-43; teacher Latin and math, pub high schs, Jersey City, 43-50; asst to prin, Ferris High Sch, 50-62, from vprin to prin, 62-72; coordr non-pub secular educ prog, 72-73, actg dir, 72-80, Dir Adult Educ, Jersey City Bd Educ, 80-, Instr Latin, Seton Hall Univ, 51-54; adj asst prof, Fordham Univ, 55-69. **HONORS AND AWARDS** Women of Achievement, Jersey J, 69. **MEMBERSHIPS** Am Class League; Am Philol Asn. **RESEARCH** History of Latin paleography; medieval Latin literature. **SELECTED PUBLICATIONS CONTACT ADDRESS** 144 Erie St, Jersey City, NJ 07302.

FINNEGAN, ROBERT EMMETT
DISCIPLINE ENGLISH LITERATURE **EDUCATION** St. Peter's Univ, MA; Univ Notre Dame, PhD. **CAREER** Prof **HONORS AND AWARDS** Life member of Clare Hall, Cambridge. **RESEARCH** Special interest in the study of Old and Middle Eng lit. **SELECTED PUBLICATIONS** Auth, pubs on old and middle English literature. **CONTACT ADDRESS** Dept of English, Univ of Manitoba, Winnipeg, MB, Canada R3T 2N2. **EMAIL** finnegn@cc.umanitoba.ca

FINNERAN, RICHARD JOHN
PERSONAL Born 12/19/1943, New York, NY, m, 1976 **DISCIPLINE** ENGLISH AND AM LIT **EDUCATION** NYork Univ, BA, 64; Univ NC, Chapel Hill, PhD, 68. **CAREER** Instr English, Univ Fla, 67-68; instr, NY Univ, 68-70; from asst prof to assoc prof, 70-77, PROF ENGLISH, NEWCOMB COL, TULANE UNIV, 77-, Lectr, Yeats Int Summer Sch, Sligo, Ireland, 72 and 76; Am Coun Learned Soc grants-in-aid, 73-74 and 77; Nat Endowment for Humanities summer grant, 75; Am Philos Soc res grants, 76 and 80; Huntington Libr fel, 78. **MEMBERSHIPS** MLA; Int Asn Studies Anglo-Irish Lit; Southern Atlantic Mod Lang Asn; Am Comt Irish Studies. **RESEARCH** Anglo-Irish literature, especially W B Yeats. **CONTACT ADDRESS** Dept of English, Univ of Tennessee, Knoxville, Knoxville, TN 37996-0430. **EMAIL** finneran@utk.edu

FINSON, JON WILLIAM
PERSONAL Born 11/04/1950, Chicago, IL **DISCIPLINE** MUSICOLOGY **EDUCATION** Univ Colo, Boulder, BM, 73; Univ Wis-Madison, MA, 75; Univ Chicago, PhD (musicol), 80. **CAREER** Asst Prof Music, Univ NC, Chapel Hill, 78-, Dir, Int Mendelssohn-Schumann Conf, 81-82. **MEMBERSHIPS** Am Musicol Soc. **RESEARCH** German music of the 19th century; American popular music. **SELECTED PUBLICATIONS** Auth, The violone in Bach's Brandenburg Concerti, Galpin Soc J, 76; Music & Medium: Two versions of Manilow's Could it be Magic, 79 & Nineteenth-century music: A review of The New Grove Dict, 82, Musical Quart; Schumann's C Minor Symphony, J Musicol, 82; Schumann and popularity: The overture, scherzo and finale, Musical Quart, 83. **CONTACT ADDRESS** Dept of Music, Univ of No Carolina, Chapel Hill, Chapel Hill, NC 27514.

FIORDO, RICHARD A.
PERSONAL Born 11/02/1945, Chicago, IL, d, 1 child **DISCIPLINE** ENGLISH, SPEECH, COMMUNICATION **EDUCATION** Northern Ill, BA, 67; San Francisco State Univ, MA, 70; Univ Ill, PhD, 74 **CAREER** Instr, E Stroudsberg State Univ, 75; assoc prof, Univ Calgary, 75-95; assoc prof, Eureka Col, 95-97; prof, Univ N Dak, 97- **HONORS AND AWARDS** Distinguished Service **MEMBERSHIPS** Ntl Communication Assoc; Assoc Education in Jour & Mass Communication **RESEARCH** Communications assessment; theories of meaning; intercultural communication. **SELECTED PUBLICATIONS** "Truth and Justice in Mass Media Reporting and Commentary: More Than One Master in American Adversarial Contests," Proceedings of the International Society for the Study of Argumentation, 98 **CONTACT ADDRESS** School of Communication, Univ of No Dakota, PO Box 7169, Grand Forks, ND 58202. **EMAIL** rfiordo@gpc.peachnet.edu

FIORE, PETER AMADEUS
PERSONAL Born 09/08/1927, Glens Falls, NY **DISCIPLINE** ENGLISH **EDUCATION** Siena Col, BA, 49; Cath Univ Am, MA, 55; London Univ, PhD, 61. **CAREER** From instr to prof, 56-75, chmn dept, 62-67, chmn div arts, 67-71, chmn Eng dept, 75-, Siena Col. **MEMBERSHIPS** MLA; Milton Soc Am; NCTE. **RESEARCH** Milton. **SELECTED PUBLICATIONS** Auth, Th'upright Heart and Pure, Duquesne Univ, 67; art, Freedom, Liability, and The State of Perfection in Paradise Lost, Milton Quart, 71; auth, Just So Much Honor, Pa State Univ, 72; auth, Milton and Kubrick: Eden's Apple Or Clockwork Orange, CEA Critic, 73; art, Account mee Man: The Incarnation in Paradise Lost, Huntington Lib Quart, 75; art, Eight Arts on Milton & the Church Fathers, Milton Encycl, 78; auth, Milton and Augustine, Pa St Univ, 81. **CONTACT ADDRESS** Dept of English, Siena Col, Loudonville, NY 12211. **EMAIL** fiore@siena.edu

FIRCHOW, PETER EDGERLY
PERSONAL Born 12/16/1937, Needham, MA, 1 child **DISCIPLINE** ENGLISH & COMPARATIVE LITERATURE **EDUCATION** Harvard Univ, BA, 59, MA, 61; Univ Wis, PhD, 65. **CAREER** Asst prof English, Univ Mich, 65-67; from asst prof to assoc prof, 67-73, chmn comp lit prog, 72-78, Prof English & Comp Lit, Univ Minn, Minneapolis, 73-; Fel, Inst Advan Studies in Humanities, Univ Edinburgh, Scotland, 77; Distinguished vis prof, Chong King Univ, Taiwan, 82-83; vis prof, Jipin Univ, PRC, 87; vis prof, Univ Munidu, 88-89; vis prof, Univ Graz, 90; Fulbright vis prof, Univ Bonn, 95-96. **HONORS AND AWARDS** Fulbright Vis Prof, Natl Univ of Costa Rica, 00. **MEMBERSHIPS** Midwest Mod Lang Asn; Am Comp Lit Asn; Asn of Literary Scholars & Critics; Aldous Huxley Literary Soc. **RESEARCH** Modern literature, English, European and American. **SELECTED PUBLICATIONS** Auth, Aldous Huxley: Satirist and Novelist, Univ Minn Press, 72; auth, "Margaret Drabble's The Millstone: Rosamund's Complaint," in Old Lines, New Forces, Fairleigh Dickinson Univ, 76; ed & co-transl, East German Short Stories: An Introductory Anthology, Twayne, 79; auth, Hilda Doolittle, in American Writers, Supplement I, Scribner's, 79; auth, "Germany and Germanic Mythology," in E M Forster's Howards End, Comp Lit, winter 81; auth, Lewis Mumford, in American Writers, Supplement II, Scribner's, 81; auth, The End of Utopia: A Study of Brave New World, Buckwell Univ Press, 84; auth, The Death of the German Cousin, Buckwell Univ Press, 86; co-ed & transl, Alois Brandstetter, The Abbey, Ariadne Press, 98; auth, Envisioning Africa: Racism and Imperialism in Conrad's 'Heart of Darkness', Univ of Ky Pr, 00. **CONTACT ADDRESS** Dept of English, Univ of Minnesota, Twin Cities, 207 Church St SE, Minneapolis, MN 55455-0156. **EMAIL** firch002@tc.umn.edu

FISCELLA, JOAN B.
PERSONAL Born 12/24/1939, Chicago, IL **DISCIPLINE** PHILOSOPHY; LIBRARY SCIENCE **EDUCATION** St. Mary's Col, S Bend, Ind, BA, 63; Univ Notre Dame, PhD, 77; Univ Mich, AMLS, 83. **CAREER** Asst prof, Mary Manse Col, Toledo, Oh, 73-75; vis asst prof, Univ Il, 80-81; asst prof, Wayne St Univ, Detroit, Mich, 75-82; head, Auraria Library, 84-86, 88-90; dept head, Univ Houston Libr, 87; bibliographer, asst prof to assoc prof, Univ Il Chicago, 90- . **HONORS AND AWARDS** Beta Phi Mu, Libr Sci Honor Soc, 83 **MEMBERSHIPS** Amer Libr Assoc; Amer Soc Infor Sci; Assoc Integ Studies. **RESEARCH** Characteristics of interdisciplinary lit & its implications for scholarly commun **SELECTED PUBLICATIONS** Coauth, Independent Office Collections and the Evolving Role of Academic Librarians, Libr Resources & Tech Svc, 94; An Approach to Assessing Faculty Use of Locally Loaded Databases, Col & Res Libr, 95; Collection Development, in Managing Business Collections in Libraries, Greenwood Press, 96; auth, Bibliography as an Interdisciplinary Service, Libr Trends, 96; Interdisciplinary Education: A Guide to Resources, New York, The Col Bd, 99. **CONTACT ADDRESS** Collections Develop Dept, Univ of Illinois, Chicago, PO Box 8198 M/C 234, Chicago, IL 60680. **EMAIL** jbf@uic.edu

FISCHER, JOHN IRWIN
PERSONAL Born 05/26/1940, Chicago, IL, m, 1976, 1 child **DISCIPLINE** ENGLISH **EDUCATION** Ohio St Univ, BA, 62; Univ Florida, PhD, 68. **CAREER** Asst prof to prof, La State Univ, 68-; chmn, La State Univ, 92-95; dir Grad Stud, La State Univ, 98- . **HONORS AND AWARDS** NEH sr fel, 83; Phi Beta Kappa; Woodrow Wilson fel; NDEA fel; Univ Fla fel; Alumni Asn Fac Excellence Award, 98. **MEMBERSHIPS** Mem, Phi Kappa Phi. **RESEARCH** Restoration and eighteenth Century English Literature; textual scholarship. **SELECTED PUBLICATIONS** Auth, On Swift's Poetry, 78; coed, Contemporary Studies of Swift's Poetry, 81; auth, "The Government's Response to An Epistle to a Lady," Philological Quarterly (86); auth, "Dividing to Conquer: The Achievement of Irvin Ehrenpreis's Swift: The Man, His Works, and the Age," The 18th Century: Theory and Interpretation (86); coed, Swift and His Contexts, 89; auth, "Swift's Early Odes, Dan Jackson's Nose, and 'The Character of Sir Robert Walpole,'" Reading Swift (93); coauth, "The Full Text of Swift's On Poetry: A Rhapsody," Swift Stud (94); auth, "Swift Waiting Poetry: The Example of 'The Grand Question Debated,'" Swift: The Enigmatic Dean (98). **CONTACT ADDRESS** Dept of Eng, Louisiana State Univ and A&M Col, 2100 Allen Hall, Baton Rouge, LA 70803. **EMAIL** jfische@unix1.sncc.lsu.edu

FISCHER, KATHERINE
PERSONAL Born Milwaukee, WI, m, 1973, 5 children **DISCIPLINE** CREATIVE WRITING **EDUCATION** Clarke Col, BA, 73; Loras Col, MA, 85; Goddard Col, MFA, 98. **CAREER** Instr, Writing Center Dir, 89-98, asst prof of English, Clarke Col, 98-2000. **HONORS AND AWARDS** Who's Who Among Am Women, 98; Who's Who in Am, 99; Best Writer, Young Rhetoricians, 99; Excellence in Teaching Honor Roll, Nat Coun of Teachers of English, 99; Outstanding People of the Twentieth Century, Int Biographical Ctr, Cambridge, England, 2000; Meneve Dunham Awd for Excellence in Teaching, 2000; Am Scholars Directory, 2000; Who's Who Among Teachers, 2000. **MEMBERSHIPS** Nat Coun Teachers of English, Assoc Writing Progs, Nat Writing Center Asn, Humanities Iowa, Iowa Arts. **SELECTED PUBLICATIONS** Auth, "The Next Hill (poem)," in Wise Woman (winter 96); auth, "Effigy Mounds (poem)," Lyrical Iowa (96); auth, "Birth Day (poem)," Lyrical Iowa (97); auth, "RiverRise (poem)," Lyrical Iowa (98); auth, "Re-radicalizing Whitman in a Post Reganomic Era," essay in The Cream City Rev (summer 98); auth, "Alewives," in Weaving A Virtual Web: Practical Approaches to New Information Technologies, Sibylle Gruber, ed, NCTE (99); auth, "WAC and the Writing Center," in Comp Tales, ed by Richard H. Haswell and Min-Zhan Lu, Longman Press (99); auth, "The Clarke Writing Lab," Julian's J (April 2000); auth, "RiverRising," essay in Heartlands, An Anthology of Midwestern Voices, Nancy Durham, ed, Firelands (2000); auth, "Wingdams: Piloting New Channels in Writing About Literature," in Learning Literature in an Era of Change, Hickey, Reiss, eds, Stylus (2000); coauth, "Filler Up, Pass the Band-Aids, Praise the Lord, and Center The Margins: Metaphors and Politics in Writing Centers," in Cross Currents: Writing Centers in the Millenium, Boynton Cook (forthcoming Sept 2000). **CONTACT ADDRESS** Dept English, Clarke Col, 1550 Clarke Dr, Dubuque, IA 52001-3117. **EMAIL** kfischer@clarke.edu

FISCHER, MICHAEL
DISCIPLINE LITERARY CRITICISM AND ENGLISH ROMANTICISM **EDUCATION** Northwestern Univ, PhD, 75. **CAREER** Instr, Univ NMex, 75-. **SELECTED PUBLICATIONS** Auth, Stanley Cavell and Literary Skepticism, 89. **CONTACT ADDRESS** Univ of New Mexico, Albuquerque, Albuquerque, NM 87131. **EMAIL** mfischer@unm.edu

FISH, CHERYL
PERSONAL Born 03/12/1959, Bronx, NY, s, 1 child **DISCIPLINE** ENGLISH **EDUCATION** Mich State Univ, BA; Brooklyn Col, MA; CUNY, PhD, 96. **CAREER** Grad Fel and Adj Lectr, Brooklyn Col, 85-88; Adj Lectr, Rutgers Univ, 87-88; Grad Fel and Adj Lectr, Hunter Col, 88-93; Instr, Nassau Community Col, 93-96; Asst Prof, Bor Manhattan Community Col (CUNY), 97-. **HONORS AND AWARDS** Andrew W Mellon Res Fel, 93-94; Summer Stipend, CUNY, 98; Fac Grant, CUNY, 98-99; Fac Fel, Rutgers Univ, 98-99. **MEMBERSHIPS** Women's Studies Proj, MLA. **RESEARCH** American literature, Nineteenth and Twentieth-Century literature, African-American literature, ethnic studies, Early American literature, women's studies, race and class, gender and science, creative writing, poetry, fiction, creative non-fiction, composition and writing, journalism, computers in the classroom, science writing, business writing. **SELECTED PUBLICATIONS** Auth, Wing Span, Mellen Poetry Pr (Lewiston, NY), 92; auth, "Voices of Restless (Dis)Continuity: The Significance of Travel for Black Women in the Ante-Bellum Americas," Women's Studies, An Interdisciplinary J, vol 26, no 5 (97): 475-495; auth, "'Unconnected Intelligence' and the Public Intellectual: Margaret Fuller's Letters and Critical Writing," in Margaret Fuller's Cult Critique: Her Age and Legacy (New York: Peter Lang Publ, 00), 153-165; auth, "Journeys and Warnings: Nancy Prince's Travels as Cautionary Tales for African-American Readers," Women Travelers and the Margins of Caribbean Discourse, St Martin's Pr (forthcoming). **CONTACT ADDRESS** Dept English, Borough of Manhattan Comm Col, CUNY, 199 Chambers St, New York, NY 10007-1044.

FISH, STANLEY E.
PERSONAL Born 04/19/1938, Providence, RI, 1 child **DISCIPLINE** ENGLISH, LAW **EDUCATION** Univ of Pa, BA, 59; Yale Univ, MA, 60; PhD, 62. **CAREER** Chair, Johns Hopkins Univ, 83-84; chair, prof, Duke Univ, 86-98; dean, Yale Univ, 99-. **HONORS AND AWARDS** Guggenheim Fel, 69-70; PEN/Spielvogel-Diamonstein Awd, 94; Honored Scholar, Milton Soc of Am; Hanford Book Awd, 98. **RESEARCH** Milton, First Amendment Issues, Affirmative Action, Holocaust Denial. **SELECTED PUBLICATIONS** Auth, Surprised by Sin: The Reader in Paradise Lost, MacMillan, 69; auth, Self-Consuming Artifacts: The Experience of Seventeenth Century Literature, Berkeley, 72; auth, Is There a Text in This Class? The Authority of Interpretive Communities, Harvard, 80; auth, Doing What comes Naturally: Change, Rhetoric, and the Practice of Theory in Literary and Legal Studies, Duke, 89; auth, There's No Such Thing as Free Speech, and It's A Good Thing Too, Oxford, 94; auth, Professional Correctness: Literary Studies and Political

Change, Oxford, 95; auth, the Trouble with Principle, Harvard, 99; auth, How Milton Works, Harvard, 01. **CONTACT ADDRESS** Col of Lib Arts and Sci, Univ of Illinois, Chicago, 601 S Morgan St, Rm 425 UH, Chicago, IL 60607. **EMAIL** sfish@uic.edu

FISH, THOMAS EDWARD
DISCIPLINE ENGLISH **EDUCATION** Iowa State Univ, BA, 74; Univ Kans, MA, 76; MPhil, 79; PhD, 81. **CAREER** Adj asst prof, Iowa State Univ, 81-84; asst prof to prof, Cumberland Col, 84-. **HONORS AND AWARDS** Phi Beta Kappa; Phi Kappa Phi; Sigma Tau Delta; Honored Prof for Excellence in Teaching, Cumberland Col, 90; Lilly Grant, 90; Tech Grant, Cumberland Col, 98; Grant, APA, 99; Cutting Edge Awd, APA, 99; Teaching with Tech Advocate, ACA, 00-01. **MEMBERSHIPS** MLA, SAMLA, NCTE, Browning Inst, Popular Cult Assoc. **RESEARCH** Romantic poets, Victorian Culture, Contemporary Critical Theory, Teaching with Technology. **SELECTED PUBLICATIONS** Auth, "Browning and Mr. Sludge: The Visata and the Impasse of Character," Studies in Browning and His Circle 11.2, (83): 61-76; auth, "Action in Character: The Epiphanies of Pippa Passes," Studies in Eng Lit 25, (85): 845-64; auth, "Questing for 'the Base of Being': The Role of Epiphany in Prince Hohenstiel-Schwangau," Victorian Poetry 25, (87): 27-43; auth, "Be Whole and Sole Yourself: The Quest for Selfhood in bishop Blougram's Apology," S Atlantic Rev 56.1, (91): 17-34; ed, Institutional Self-Study, SACS, 94. **CONTACT ADDRESS** 260 Brush Arbor Rd, Williamsburg, KY 40769-1717. **EMAIL** tfish@cc.cumber.edu

FISHBURN, KATHERINE RICHARDS
DISCIPLINE BRITISH & AMERICAN LITERATURE **EDUCATION** Western MD Col, BA, 66; MI State Univ, MA, 71, PhD(English), 73. **CAREER** Team teacher English, Gov Thomas Johnson High Sch, 67-69; grad asst, 69-71, instr, 71-73, asst prof English, 73-85, prof English, MI State Univ, 86-; acad admin intern, MI State Univ, 78-79. **MEMBERSHIPS** MLA; Popular Cult Asn; Doris Lessing Soc. **RESEARCH** Contemporary literature; women's literature; Black literature; cultural criticism. **SELECTED PUBLICATIONS** Auth, Richard Wright's Hero: The Faces of a Rebel-Victim, Scarecrow, 77; Women in Popular Culture, In: A Handbook of American Popular Culture, Greenwood Press, 82; The Unexpected Universe of Doris Lessing: A Study in Narrative Technique, Greenwood Press, 85; Doris Lessing: Life, Work, and Criticism, York Press, 87; Reading Buchi Emecheta: Cross-Cultural Conversations, Greenwood Press, 95; The Problem of Embodiment in Early African American Narrative, Greenwood press, 97; The Dead Are So Disappointing, MI State Univ Press, forthcoming. **CONTACT ADDRESS** Dept English, Michigan State Univ, 201 Morrill Hall, East Lansing, MI 48824-1036. **EMAIL** fishbur1@pilot.msu.edu

FISHER, BENJAMIN
PERSONAL Born 07/21/1940, Orwigsburg, PA, m, 1989, 1 child **DISCIPLINE** ENGLISH **EDUCATION** Ursinus Col, BA, 62; Duke Univ, MA, 63; Duke Univ, PhD, 69. **CAREER** From Instr to Asst Prof, Univ Pa, 67-73; Assoc Prof, Hahnemann Univ, 76-79; From Assoc Prof to Prof, Univ Miss, 84-. **HONORS AND AWARDS** Phi Beta Kappa, Duke Univ, 88. **MEMBERSHIPS** MLA, ALA, PSA, Edgar Allan Poe Soc, Frank Norris Soc, Simms Soc, Tennyson Soc, 1890s Soc, Int Gothic Asn, Housman Soc, Am Humor Studies Asn. **RESEARCH** 19th-Century American and British studies, gothicism, 1890s, Housman. **SELECTED PUBLICATIONS** Auth, The Very Spirit of Cordiality, 78; auth, Poe at Work, 78; auth, Frederick Irving Anderson, 88; auth, The Gothic's Gothic, 88. **CONTACT ADDRESS** Dept English, Univ of Mississippi, PO Box 941, Oxford, MS 38655. **EMAIL** bfisher@olemiss.edu

FISHER, EDITH MAUREEN
PERSONAL Born 07/29/1944, Houston, TX, s **DISCIPLINE** LIBRARY SCIENCE **EDUCATION** University of Illinois, Urbana IL, MLS, 1972; Queens College CUNY, Certificate of Ethnicity and Librarianship, 1975; University of Pittsburgh, PhD 1991. **CAREER** University of California, San Diego, La Jolla CA, Central University Library, 72-90, Contemporary Black Arts Program, adjunct lecturer, 81-90; University of California, Los Angeles, School of Library and Information Science, lecturer, 89; Evaluation and Training Institute, Los Angeles, CA, consultant/technical advisor, 91; Tenge Enterprises, Encinitas, CA, president, currently. **HONORS AND AWARDS** Carnegie fellowship, 1971; PhD fellowship, 1987; Provost fellowship, Univ of CA, San Diego, 1987; Provost fellowship, Univ of Pittsburgh, 1988; Black Caucus of the American Library Association President's Awd, 1990. **MEMBERSHIPS** Carlson Learning. **SELECTED PUBLICATIONS** Author of numerous publications. **CONTACT ADDRESS** President, Tenge Enterprises, 204 N El Camino Real, Encinitas, CA 92024.

FISHER, JAMES
PERSONAL Born 11/08/1950, Long Branch, NJ, m, 1977, 2 children **DISCIPLINE** THEATER **EDUCATION** Monmouth Col, NJ, BA, 73; Univ NC Greensboro, MFA, 76. **CAREER** Prof, Wabash Col, Crawfordsville, IN, 78-. **HONORS AND AWARDS** Wabash Relig Center Summer grant, 98; theater person of the year, in, 97. **MEMBERSHIPS** Int Fedn of Theatre Res; S Theatre Conf; In Theatre Assoc; Theatre Libr Assoc; Soc for Theatre Res; Assoc for Theatre in Higher Educ; Assoc for Recorded Sound. **SELECTED PUBLICATIONS** Publ, The Theater of Yesterday and Tomorrow: Commedia Dell'arte on the Modern Stage, Mellen, 92, 98; auth, Al Jolson, Greenwood, 94; auth, Spencer Tracy, Greenwood, 94;auth, Eddie Cantor, Greenwood, 97; ed, The Puppetry Yearbook, three volumes. **CONTACT ADDRESS** Theatre Dept, Wabash Col, Crawfordsville, IN 47933. **EMAIL** fisherj@wabash.edu

FISHER, JAMES RANDOLPH
PERSONAL Born 11/05/1906, Norfolk, VA **DISCIPLINE** ENGLISH LANGUAGE AND LITERATURE **EDUCATION** Howard Univ, AB, 31, AM, 33. **CAREER** Chmn dept lang and lit, Rust Col, 35-38; Allen Univ, 40-43; sophomore English, Tenn State Col, 45-47; prof, 47-72, chmn sophomore English, 48-74, chmn dept lang and lit, prof, 72-74, EMER PROF ENGLISH, SAVANNAH STATE COL, 74-. **MEMBERSHIPS** MLA; Mod Humanities Res Asn; Int Asn Univ Prof English; Col English Asn; Milton Soc Am. **SELECTED PUBLICATIONS** Auth, British Physicians, Medical Science, and the Cattle Plague, 1865-66, Bulletin of the History of Medicine, Vol 67, 93; Not Quite a Profession--The Aspirations of Veterinary Surgeons in England in the Mid 19th Century, Hist Rsch, Vol 66, 93. **CONTACT ADDRESS** Dept of English, Savannah State Univ, Box 20434, Savannah, GA 31404.

FISHER, JOHN C.
PERSONAL Born 11/27/1927, Mendon, NY, m, 1956, 2 children **DISCIPLINE** LINGUISTICS, LITERATURE **EDUCATION** Champlain Col, BA, 53; Univ Mich, AM, 54, EdD(English lang and lit), 62. **CAREER** From instr to assoc prof, 57-62, dir summer instr, 62-68, chmn dept, 72-74, Prof English, State Univ NY Col, Oswego, 63-, Vis lectr, English Lang Inst, Univ Mich, 57-61; instr, State Univ NY, Ford Found Indonesia Proj, 62-63; Fulbright lectr, Univ Rome, 63-64; dir, NEA Inst English, 65; coordr, BA Ling Prog, State Univ NY Col, Oswego, 66-73; exec secy, NY State English Coun, 68-70, fel, 70; vis prof, ling, Univ Hawaii, Hilo, 70; vis prof, English, Inter-Am Univ PR, 70. **MEMBERSHIPS** MLA; NCTE. **RESEARCH** Nineteenth century British literature; linguistics, especially in literary criticism; English as a foreign language. **SELECTED PUBLICATIONS** Auth, Reinventing a Livelihood--How United States Labor Laws, Labor Management Cooperation Initiatives, and Privatization Influence Public Sector Labor Markets, Harvard J Legislation, Vol 34, 97. **CONTACT ADDRESS** Perry Hill RD 3, Oswego, NY 13126.

FISHER, JOHN HURT
PERSONAL Born 10/26/1919, Lexington, KY, m, 1942, 3 children **DISCIPLINE** ENGLISH **EDUCATION** Maryville Col, AB, 40; Univ Pa, AM, 42, PhD, 45. **CAREER** From asst to instr, Univ Pa, 42-45; instr, Washington Sq Col, NY Univ, 45-48, asst prof English, 48-55; from assoc prof to prof, Duke Univ, 55-60; prof, Ind Univ, 60-62 and NY Univ, 62-72; head dept, 76-78, JOHN C HODGES PROF ENGLISH, UNIV TENN, KNOXVILLE, 72-, Asst secy, MLA, 49-51, exec secy, 63-71; consult, US Off Educ, 62-65; ed, PMLA, 63-71; mem, US Comn, UNESCO, 63-69; chmn, Am Coun Learned Soc Conf Secys, 65-68; mem exec comt, Int Fed Mod Lang and Lit, 67-71, Am vpres, 72-78; trustee, Woodrow Wilson Nat Fel Found, 72-75; dir, Maryville Col, 72-75; Nat Endowment on Humanities sr fel, 75-76, consult, 76-; dir, New Chaucer Soc, 81-. **HONORS AND AWARDS** LittD, Middlebury Col, 70; LHD, Loyola Univ Chicago, 70. **MEMBERSHIPS** MLA (treas, 52-55, pres, 74); Mediaeval Acad Am; NCTE; New Chaucer Soc (pres, 82-). **RESEARCH** Medieval literature and the English language. **SELECTED PUBLICATIONS** Auth, England the Nation, Medium Aevum, Vol 66, 97; The New Humanism and Chaucer, Geoffrey, Soundings, Vol 80, 97; An Ars Legendi for Chaucer Canterbury Tales--A Reconstructive Reading, J Eng Ger Philol, Vol 92, 93; Textual Criticism and Middle English Texts, J Eng Ger Philol, Vol 95, 96; The Manuscripts of the Canterbury Tales, J Eng Ger Philol, Vol 92, 93; Early Chaucer Manuscripts, PMLA Publications of the Modern Language Association of America, Vol 108, 93; Textual Criticism and Middle English Texts, J Eng Ger Philol, Vol 95, 96. **CONTACT ADDRESS** Dept of English, Univ of Tennessee, Knoxville, Knoxville, TN 37916.

FISHER, JUDITH LAW
PERSONAL Born 08/31/1952, Montclair, NJ, m, 1982 **DISCIPLINE** VICTORIAN LITERATURE, THEORY OF WRITING **EDUCATION** Oberlin Col, AB, 74; Univ Tenn, MA, 75; Univ Ill, PhD (English), 80. **CAREER** Teaching asst English comp, Univ Tenn, 74-75, English, Univ Ill, 75-80; staff asst pub rel, Continuing Educ, Univ Ill, 76-79; fel English, Univ Kans, 80-82; LECTR ENGLISH, UNIV TEX AT SAN ANTONIO, 82-, Ed, Res Press, Champaign, Ill, 80. **MEMBERSHIPS** Mod Lang Asn. **RESEARCH** William Makepeace Thackeray; Victorian art history; history of the novel. **SELECTED PUBLICATIONS** Auth, Review of Texas studies in the novel: William Makepeace Thackeray, Thackeray Newsletter, 11/81; Thackeray and the visual arts, Victorian Studies, fall 82; ed, The Art Criticism of William Makepeace Thackeray, Works, Univ Tenn/Dawson Press (in prep); auth, Trouble in paradise: The twentieth century utopian ideal, Extrapolation (in prep). **CONTACT ADDRESS** Div English Classics and Philos, Univ of Texas, San Antonio, San Antonio, TX 78285.

FISHER, LEONA W.
PERSONAL Born 08/22/1944, CA **DISCIPLINE** ENGLISH LITERATURE, WOMEN'S STUDIES **EDUCATION** Stanford Univ, BA; Univ Santa Barbara Ca, MA, PhD. **CAREER** Prof. **HONORS AND AWARDS** CHLA 1st runner-up, Best Critical Article, 90; Res grant, 94; CASE, Silver Medal, 85; Bronze Medal, 86; Bibliog Soc of Am, 00. **MEMBERSHIPS** MLA, Children's Lit Assoc, Nineteenth-Century Studies Assoc. **RESEARCH** Children's Literature, Victorian literature, women writers, nonfiction prose, 19th century drama, feminist theory. **SELECTED PUBLICATIONS** Auth, "Mystical Fantasy for Children: Silence and Community," 90; Lemn, Dickens, and 'Mr. Nightingale's Diary': A Victorian Farce, 88; "Mark Lemon's Three Farces on the 'Woman Question'," 88; "The Challenge of Women's Studies: Questions for a Transformed Future at Georgetown," 90. **CONTACT ADDRESS** English Dept, Georgetown Univ, PO Box 571131, Washington, DC 20057-1131. **EMAIL** fisherl@georgetown.edu

FISHER, NANCY
PERSONAL Born 05/10/1934, New Bern, NC, m, 1956, 2 children **DISCIPLINE** ENGLISH **EDUCATION** WCNUC, BA, 56; FSU, MA, 59; UTK, PhD, 69. **CAREER** Coppin State Col, 69-70; Knoxville Col, 70-71; Roane State Community Col, 71-91; Tenn Wesleyan Col, 91- . **HONORS AND AWARDS** Fel FSU **MEMBERSHIPS** MLA; SAMLA; NCTE. **RESEARCH** America literature, Poetry, Women's studies, Writing across the curriculum. **SELECTED PUBLICATIONS** Auth, Witnessing, 89; auth, Vision at Delphi, 95. **CONTACT ADDRESS** Dept English, Tennessee Wesleyan Col, 149 County Rd 253, Athens, TN 37303. **EMAIL** Lnmfisher@usit.net>

FISHER, PHILIP
PERSONAL Born 10/11/1941, Pittsburgh, PA, d, 1 child **DISCIPLINE** ENGLISH & AMERICAN LITERATURE **EDUCATION** Univ Pittsburgh, AB, 63; Harvard Univ, AM, 66, PhD(English), 70. **CAREER** Asst prof English, Univ Va, 70-72; from Asst Prof to Assoc Prof, Brandeis Univ, 73-87; Prof English, 88-, Reid Prof English, Harvard Univ, 95-, Chair, Dept English, 90-93; Andrew Mellow asst prof, Harvard Univ, 76-77; vis scholar, Mass Inst Technol, 77-81; vis prof, Harvard Univ, summer 77; vis prof Frei Univ, Berlin, 81; mem, Cambridge Humanities Sem, 77-. **HONORS AND AWARDS** Fel, Inst Advanced Study, Berlin, 87-88; Guggenheim Fel, 96-97; Sr Fel, Getty Inst, 98-99. **MEMBERSHIPS** MLA. **RESEARCH** The novel; the city; theory of art objects. **SELECTED PUBLICATIONS** Contribr, Uses of Literature, 73 & The Worlds of Victorian Fiction, 75, Harvard Univ Press; auth, The future's past, New Lit Hist, 75; Hand-made space, Arts Mag, 77; Looking around to see who I am: Dreiser's territory of the self, J English Lit Hist, 78; Making Up Society, Univ Pittsburgh Press, 81; contribr, American Realism: New Essays, Johns Hopkins Univ Press, 82; Pins, a table, works of art, Representations, 82; Hard Facts, Oxford Univ, 87; Making and Effacing Art, Oxford Univ Press, 91; The New American Studies, Univ Calif Press, 91; Wonder, the Rainbow and the Aesthetics of Rare Experiences, Harvard Univ Press, 98; Still the New World: American Literature in a Culture of Creative Destruction, Harvard Univ Press, 99. **CONTACT ADDRESS** Dept English, Harvard Univ, Barker Center, Cambridge, MA 02138-3800.

FISHER, WALTER R.
PERSONAL Born 01/01/1931, Honolulu, HI, m, 3 children **DISCIPLINE** COMMUNICATION **EDUCATION** Univ IA, PhD. **CAREER** Prof, Sch Commun; ed, Quart J Speech & Western J Commun. **HONORS AND AWARDS** National Commun Asn Distinguished Scholar Awd; Distinguished Service Awd; Western States Communication Assoc; James A. Winans-Herbert A. Wichens Awd for Distinguished Scholarship; National Communication Asn. **MEMBERSHIPS** National Commun Asn; Western Speech Commun Asn; The Rhetoric Society of Am. **RESEARCH** Rhetorical theory and criticism; politic commun & argumentation; addressing in particular problems in reason and ethics. **SELECTED PUBLICATIONS** Co-ed, Rethinking Knowledqe: Reflections Across the Disciplines, SUNY Press, 95 & Human Communication as Narration: Toward a Philosophy of Reason, Value, and Action, Univ SC-Press, 89. **CONTACT ADDRESS** Annenberg School for Commun, Univ of So California, University Park Campus, Los Angeles, CA 90089. **EMAIL** wfisher@usc.edu

FISHERKELLER, JOELLEN
DISCIPLINE EDUCATION & COMMUNICATION **EDUCATION** Univ CA, Berkeley, PhD, 95. **CAREER** Asst prof, New York Univ, 95-. **RESEARCH** Young people; media cultures; media education. **SELECTED PUBLICATIONS** Auth, The Hidden Persistence of Immigrant Drop Outs: Distortions, Blank Spots and Blind Spots in Research on Schooling Careers, with Donald A Hansen and Vicky Johnson, Int J of Educational; Research, Pergamon Press, vol 23, no 1, 95; Representing Student's Thinking About Nutrient Cycles in Ecosystems, Bidimensional Coding of a Complex Topic, with Kathleen Hogan, J of Research in Science Teaching, vol 33, no 9, 96; Review of

Children and the Movies: Media Influence and the Payne Fund Controversy, by Garth S Jowett, Ian C Jarvie, and Kathryn H Fuller, Cambridge Univ Press, 96, J of Commun, autumn 97; Review of Writing Superheroes: Contemporary Childhood, Popular Culture, and Classroom Literacy, by Anne Haas Dyson, Teachers Col Press, 97, Anthropology and Education Quart, 97; Learning from Young Adolescent TV Viewers, NJ J of Commun, fall 97; Everyday Learning About Identities Among Young Adolescents in TV Culture, Anthropology and Ed Quart, vol 28, no 4, winter 97; Learning About Power and Success: Young Adolescents Interpret TV Culture, The Commun Rev, March 98. **CONTACT ADDRESS** Dept of Culture and Commun, New York Univ, 239 Greene St, Rm 735, New York, NY 10003-6674. **EMAIL** jf4@is2.nyu.edu

FISHMAN, JERRY
PERSONAL Born 10/31/1933, Brooklyn, NY, m, 1961, 2 children **DISCIPLINE** ENGLISH **EDUCATION** New England Col, BS, 56; Univ Calif Berkeley, MA, 65. **CAREER** Instr, Sacramento City Col, 65-95; teacher, Sierra Col, 97-. **HONORS AND AWARDS** Honorary mem, Multi-Cultural Educ Hall of Fame, 96. **MEMBERSHIPS** CTA. **CONTACT ADDRESS** Liberal Arts Div, Sierra Col, 5000 Rocklin Rd, Rocklin, CA 95677-3337. **EMAIL** fishy777@lanset.com

FISHWICK, DUNCAN
PERSONAL Born 05/12/1929, Adlington, England **DISCIPLINE** CLASSICS **EDUCATION** Manchester Univ, BA, 50; Oxford Univ, BA, 53, MA, 56. **CAREER** Lectr, McGill Univ, 56-57; asst prof, Univ Toronto, 57-64; assoc prof, St Francis Xavier Univ, 74-71; assoc prof to prof classics, 71-86, univ prof, 86-94, ch classics, 87-92, Univ Prof Emer, Univ Alberta, 94-. **HONORS AND AWARDS** Univ Alta Res Prize, 85; McCalla Res Prof, 85-86. **SELECTED PUBLICATIONS** Auth, Studies in Roman Imperial History, 76; auth, The Imperial Cult in the Latin West, vol I, 87, vol II, 91/92; coauth, The Foundations of the West, 64. **CONTACT ADDRESS** Dept of Hist and Classics, Univ of Alberta, Edmonton, AB, Canada T6G 2F6.

FISK, DEBORAH PAYNE
PERSONAL Born 07/17/1952, Los Angeles, CA, m, 1999, 1 child **DISCIPLINE** SEVENTEENTH- AND EIGHTEENTH-CENTURY STUDIES, THEATER HISTORY **EDUCATION** PhD, UCLA. **CAREER** Assoc prof, Depts of Literature and Performing Arts. **HONORS AND AWARDS** Distinguished Tchg Awd, Am Univ, 92; Huntington Lib Fel, 98; William Andrew Clark Mem Lib Fel, 99; Folger Shakespeare Lib/NEH Fel, 00-01. **MEMBERSHIPS** Am Soc for Eighteenth-Cent Stud; British Soc for Eighteenth-Cent Stud; Aphra Behn Soc; Am Soc for Theatre Res. **RESEARCH** Seventeenth- and eighteenth-century studies **SELECTED PUBLICATIONS** Co-ed, Cult Readings Restoration & Eighteenth-Century Eng Theatre, 95; ed, The Cambridge Companion to Restoration Theater, 00; ed, Four Libertine Plays, 01. **CONTACT ADDRESS** Dept of Literature, American Univ, 4400 Massachusetts Ave, Washington, DC 20016-8047. **EMAIL** paynefisk@earthlink.net

FITCH, J. G.
DISCIPLINE GREEK; ROMAN DRAMA **EDUCATION** Cornell Univ, BA, 63, Cert Edu, 66, MA, 67, PhD, 74. **CAREER** Prof, 73-; ch, Univ of Victoria. **HONORS AND AWARDS** Pres, Class Asn of Vancouver Island, 82-83; coun mem, Class Asn of Can, 84-86; prog ch, Class Asn of Can, 90. **MEMBERSHIPS** Mem, Am Philol Assn; Soc for Lit and Sci. **RESEARCH** Senecan tragedy; didactic poetry. **SELECTED PUBLICATIONS** Auth, "Sense-Pauses and Relative Dating in Seneca, Sophocles and Shakespeare," Am Journal of Philosophy 102, (81): 289-307; coauth, "Theory and Contet of the Didactic Poem," Florilegium 5, (83): 1-43; auth, Seneca's Hercules Furens, Cornell: Cornell Univ Press, 87; auth, Seneca's Anapaests, Scholars Press, 88. **CONTACT ADDRESS** Dept of Greek and Roman Studies, Univ of Victoria, PO Box 1700 STN CSC, Victoria, BC, Canada V8W 2Y2. **EMAIL** fitch@uvvm.uvic.ca

FITCH, NOEL FILEY
PERSONAL Born 12/24/1937, New Haven, CT, m, 1987, 1 child **DISCIPLINE** LITERATURE **EDUCATION** Northwest Nazarene Col, BA, 59; Wash State Univ, MA, 66; PhD. **CAREER** Instr, Wash State Univ, 67-68; asst prof, Eastern Naz Col, 66-71; assoc prof to prof, Point Loria Col, 71-87; Chair, 82-85; lectr, Univ of S Calif 86-, vis prof, Univ of Paris, 87-. **HONORS AND AWARDS** NEH Fel; Am Philos Soc Grant. **MEMBERSHIPS** PEN; Authors Guild. **RESEARCH** Expatriate Literary Paris. **SELECTED PUBLICATIONS** Auth, Sylvia Bench and the Lost Generation, Norton; auth, Walks in Hemingway's Paris, St. Martins; auth, Literary Cafes of Paris, Black Belt; Anais: The Erotic Life of Anais Nin, Little Brown; auth, Appetite for Life: The Biography of Julia Child, Doubleday. **CONTACT ADDRESS** Dept Prof Writing, Univ of So California, 3470 Watts Way, Los Angeles, CA 90089-0037. **EMAIL** noelriley@aol.com

FITCH, RAYMOND E.
PERSONAL Born 01/23/1930, Boston, MA, m, 1952, 1 child **DISCIPLINE** NINETEENTH CENTURY LITERATURE, CRITISISM **EDUCATION** Harvard Univ, AB, 52; Univ MI, AM, 55; Univ PA, PhD, 65. **CAREER** Asst prof Eng, Pa Mil Col, 57-60; asst prof, SCT State Col, 61-66; assoc prof, 66-77, prof eng, OH Univ, 77, chmn grad prog, 78, emeritus prof 98. **MEMBERSHIPS** MLA. **RESEARCH** Lit and myth; works of Ruskin; critical theory. **SELECTED PUBLICATIONS** Ed, Dramatic romances and lyrics, : Complete Works of Robert Browning, OH Univ, 73; Literary Theory in the English Classroom, SCTE/NCTE, 81; The Poison Sky: Myth and Apocalypse in Ruskin, OH Univ, 82; Ed, Breaking With Burr: Harmon Blenner Hassett's Journal, 1801, Oh Univ, 1986. **CONTACT ADDRESS** Dept of Eng, Ohio Univ, Athens, OH 45701-2979. **EMAIL** nemo32@hotmail.com

FITTER, CHRIS
PERSONAL Born 01/01/1955, England, m, 1994 **DISCIPLINE** SHAKESPEARE, 17TH CENTURY LITERATURE AND POLITICS, MARXIST AND NEW HISTORICISM **EDUCATION** Oxford Univ, PhD. **CAREER** Assoc prof, Rutgers, State Univ NJ, Camden Col of Arts and Sci. **RESEARCH** Shakespeare. **SELECTED PUBLICATIONS** Auth, Paradise Lost and the Tradition of Exile Consolation, Milton Stud, 84; The Landscape of Henry Vaughan, Essays in Criticism; Henry V, Ideology, and the Mekong Agincourt, Shakespeare Left and Right, Routledge, 91; Poetry, Space, Landscape, Cambridge Univ Press, 95; W. J. Cash and the Southerner as Superman: Philosophic Influences on The Mind of the South, Southern Lit J, 95; auth, 'The Poetic Nocturne: from Ancient Motif to Renaissance Genre,' in Early Modern Literary Studies 3.2, 97; auth, 'Landscape': essay in 'The Encyclopedia of Aesthetics,', Oxford Univ Press, 98; auth, 'From the Dream to the Womb: Visionary Impulse and Political Amvicalence,' in Journal X', Univ of Mississippi, 98; auth, ' The Slain Deer and Political Imperium in "As You Like It," and Marvell's "Nymph Complaining for the Death of her Fawn," in Journal of English and Germanic Philology', 99. **CONTACT ADDRESS** Dept of Eng, Rutgers, The State Univ of New Jersey, Camden, 311 North 5th St, Camden, NJ 08102. **EMAIL** fitter@camden.rutgers.edu

FITZPATRICK, CAROLYN H.
PERSONAL Born 02/03/1952, New Orleans, LA, m, 1981, 1 child **DISCIPLINE** WRITING **EDUCATION** Univ N Carolina, BA, 73; SUNY, MA, 74. **CAREER** Adj instr, Kingsbor Comm Col, 74-75; adj instr, Rio Hondo Comm Col, 75-76; adj instr, C. W. Post Col, 77-78; comm skill spec, Bloomfield Col, 78-80; asst prof, Cumber Cnty Col, 80-81; adj prof, instr, dir, Univ Maryland, 83-. **HONORS AND AWARDS** Who's Who in Am Edu, 93, 94; Who's Who in the East, 93; Intl Who's Who of Women, 94; Who's Who in Am, 94. **MEMBERSHIPS** MLA, NCTE, Mencken Soc. **RESEARCH** Composition and rhetoric. **SELECTED PUBLICATIONS** Co-auth, Reading Thresholds, Houghton Mifflin, 93, 2nd ed, 99; co-auth, Reading Passages, D. C. Heath and Co, 97; co-auth, Reading Pathways, D. C. Heath and Co, 91, 2nd ed, 95; co-auth, The Complete Paragraph Workout Book, D. C. Heath and Co, 89, 2nd ed, 93; co-auth, The Complete Writer's Workout Book, D. C. Heath and Co, 88; co-auth, The Complete Sentence Workout Book, Allyn and Bacon, 85, D. C. Heath and Co. pub 2nd ed, 88, 3rd ed, 94, 4th ed, 00. **CONTACT ADDRESS** English, Univ of Maryland, Baltimore, 1000 Hilltop Circle, Baltimore, MD 21250. **EMAIL** cfitzpat@umbc.edu

FITZPATRICK, VINCENT D.
PERSONAL Born 06/18/1950, Baltimore, MD, m, 1981, 1 child **DISCIPLINE** ENGLISH **EDUCATION** Univ Va, BA, 72; SUNY Stony Brook, MA, 74; PhD, 79. **CAREER** Asst curator to curator, HL Mencken Collection, Enoch Pratt Free Libr, 80-. **HONORS AND AWARDS** Phi Beta Kappa, 72. **MEMBERSHIPS** MLA, Mencken Soc. **RESEARCH** American Literature, Biography. **SELECTED PUBLICATIONS** Auth, HLM, The Mencken Bibliography: A Second Ten-Year Supplement, 1972-1981, Enoch Pratt Free Libr, 86; auth, HL Mencken, Continuum, (NY), 89; coauth, The Complete Sentence Workout Book, DC Heath, (Lexington, MA), 91; coed, Thirty-Five Years of Newspaper Work: A Memoir by HL Menckem, Johns Hopkins Univ Pr, (Baltimore), 94; auth, Gerald W Johnson: From Southern Liberal to National Conscience, La State Univ Pr, (Baton Rouge, LA), 02. **CONTACT ADDRESS** Humanities Dept, Enoch Pratt Free Libr, 404 Cathedral St, Baltimore, MD 21201.

FITZSIMMONS, THOMAS
PERSONAL Born 10/21/1926, Lowell, MA, m, 1955, 2 children **DISCIPLINE** ENGLISH **EDUCATION** Stanford Univ, BA, 51; Sorbonne and Inst Sci Polit, cert Fr lit, philos and int affairs, 49 and 50; Columbia Univ, MA, 52. **CAREER** From staff writer to assoc ed, New Repub Mag, 52-55; dir res anthrop and publications, Human Relat Area Files, 55-59; from asst prof to assoc prof, 59-65, PROF ENGLISH, OAKLAND UNIV, 65-, Spec consult, Hist Div Dept of Defense, 52; res assoc, Yale Univ, 56-59; Fulbright prof, Tokyo Univ Educ and Tsuda-Juku Women's Col, Japan, 62-64; vis prof, Univ Bucharest, 67-68; prof, Tokyo Univ Educ and vis poet, Japan women's Univ and Keio Univ, Japan, 73-75. **HONORS AND AWARDS** Nat Found for Arts poetry grant, 67, world wide poetry reading tour, USIS, 75-76. **MEMBERSHIPS** PEN Club. **RESEARCH** Poetry; cultural anthropology; Asian poetry. **SELECTED PUBLICATIONS** Auth, Writing in the Margins--The Theatrical Voice of Women, Overland, Vol 136, 94. **CONTACT ADDRESS** Dept of English, Oakland Univ, Rochester, MI 48063.

FIX, STEPHEN
DISCIPLINE ENGLISH **EDUCATION** Boston Col, BA, 74; Cornell Univ, PhD, 80. **CAREER** Prof. **RESEARCH** 18th-century British literature. **SELECTED PUBLICATIONS** Auth, Distant Genius: Johnson and the Art of Milton's Life; Johnson and the Duty of Reading Paradise Lost; The Contexts and Motives of Johnson's Life of Milton; Teaching Johnson's Critical Writing; Prayer, Poetry and Paradise Lost, Editing Johnson's Life of Milton, Yale Edition of the Works of Samuel Johnson. **CONTACT ADDRESS** Dept of English, Williams Col, Stetson C-12, Williamstown, MA 01267. **EMAIL** sfix@williams.edu

FJELDE, ROLF GERHARD
PERSONAL Born 03/15/1926, Brooklyn, NY, m, 1964, 3 children **DISCIPLINE** MODERN DRAMA **EDUCATION** Yale Univ, BA, 46; Columbia Univ, MA, 47; Univ Copenhagen, 53; Univ Heidelberg, 53; Univ Oslo, 65. **CAREER** From instr to assoc prof, 54-69, PROF ENGLISH & DRAMA, PRATT INST, 69-, Am-Scand Found fel, Univ Copenhagen, 52-53; Yaddo Found fel, 52, 54; playwright-in-residence, Eugene O'Neill Mem Theatre Ctr; Nat Transl Ctr, Ford Found fel, 67-68; lectr drama, Juilliard Sch, 73-83; ed, Ibsen News & Comment, 79-. **MEMBERSHIPS** Dramatists Guild; Auth League Am; Am Theatre Asn; Soc Advan Scand Studies; Ibsen Soc Am (pres, 79-). **RESEARCH** Henrik Ibsen; classic and modern drama; contemporary poetry and film. **SELECTED PUBLICATIONS** Auth, The image word, Ablib, 62; transl & ed, Peer Gynt, 64 & 80, Ibsen: Four major plays, Vol, 65 & Vol II, 70, New Am Libr; ed, Ibsen: A collection of critical essays, Prentice-Hall, 65; auth, Peer Gynt, naturalism and the dissolving self, Drama Rev, 69; The dimensions of Ibsen's dramatic world, Universitetsforlaget, 71; Ibsen: The complete major prose plays, New Am Libr/Farrar Straus & Giroux, 78. **CONTACT ADDRESS** Dept of English & Humanities, Pratt Inst, 200 Willoughby Ave, Brooklyn, NY 11205-3899.

FLACHMANN, MICHAEL C.
PERSONAL Born 11/03/1942, St. Louis, MO, m, 1969, 2 children **DISCIPLINE** ENGLISH **EDUCATION** Univ of the South, BA, 64; Univ Va, MA, 65; Univ Chicago, PhD, 72. **CAREER** Instr, Southern Ill Univ, 65-68; Asst Prof to Assoc Prof, 72-81, Prof English, Calif State Univ, 81-, Dir Honors Prog, 81-, Company Dramaturg Utah Shakespearean Festival, 85-. **HONORS AND AWARDS** Phi Beta Kappa; Philip Frances DuPont Schol, Univ Va, 65; William Raney Harper Doctoral Fel, Univ Chicago, 68; Outstanding Prof Awd, Calif State Univ-Bakersfield, 92; Calif State Univ System-Wide Outstanding Prof Awd, 93; U.S. Prof of the Year, Carnegie Found & Coun for the Advancement and Support of Educ, 95; CSU Wang family execellence award in teaching, 99. **MEMBERSHIPS** Mod Lang Asn; Shakespeare Asn Am; Bibliographical Soc. **RESEARCH** Shakespeare, Renaissance literature; dramaturgy. **SELECTED PUBLICATIONS** Auth, Ben Jonson and the Alchemy of Satire, Studies English Lit, 77; coauth, Shakespeare's Lovers: A Text for Performance and Analysis, Southern Ill Press, 82; auth, Epicoene: A Comic Hell for a Comic Sinner, Medieval & Renaissance Drama in England I, 84; Teaching Shakespeare Through Parallel Scenes, Shakespeare Quart, 85; coauth, Shakespeare's Women: A Playscript for Performance and Analysis, Southern Ill Press, 86; auth, All Corners of the World: Spatial and Moral Geography in Cymbeline, On-Stage Studies XII, 89; The First English Epistolary Novel: The Image of Idleness (1555), Studies Philol, 90; Fitted for Death: Measure for Measure and the Contemplatio Mortis, English Lit Renaissance, 92; The Merchant of Ashland, On-Stage Studies, 92; Changing the W's in Shakespeare's Plays, Teaching Shakespeare Today, NCTE Press, 93; William Baldwin, Dictionary of Renaissance Biographies, 97; Suit the Action to the Word: Teaching Minds and Bodies in the English Classroom, Inspiring Teaching: Carnegie Professors of the Year Speak, Anker Press, 97; ed, Teaching Exellence: A Collection of Essays on College Education Written by Recipients of the California State University Trustees' Outstanding Professor Award, The Calif State Univ Inst Press, 98; coauth, The Prose Reader: Essays for Thinking, Reading, and Writing, Prentice Hall, 87, 90, 93, 96, 99; author of numerous other articles and publications. **CONTACT ADDRESS** English Dept, California State Univ, Bakersfield, 9001 Stockdale Hwy., Bakersfield, CA 93311-1099. **EMAIL** mflachmann@csub.edu

FLAHIVE, DOUG
DISCIPLINE ENGLISH LITERATURE **EDUCATION** Southern Ill Univ, BA, MA, PhD. **CAREER** Assoc prof. **SELECTED PUBLICATIONS** Auth, pubs on second language discourse processing; language testing; first and second language acquisition. **CONTACT ADDRESS** Dept of English, Colorado State Univ, Fort Collins, CO 80523. **EMAIL** dflahive@vines.colostate.edu

FLANNAGAN, ROY C.
PERSONAL Born 12/02/1938, Richmond, VA, m, 5 children **DISCIPLINE** ENGLISH **EDUCATION** Wash & Lee Univ, BA, 60; Univ Va, MA, 61, PhD, 66. **CAREER** Asst prof English, Va Mil Inst, 65-66; assoc prof, 66-82, prof, Oh Univ, 82; Ed, Milton Quart, 70-; Pres, Coun Eds Learned Journals, 98. **HONORS AND AWARDS** OH Univ Baker Awd, 67; Folger Shakespeare Libr fel, 67; Fulbright Travel grant, 70; Who's Who, 00. **MEMBERSHIPS** MLA; Milton Soc Am (pres 90); Renaissance Soc Am. **RESEARCH** Milton; Renaissance Italian and Eng lit; ecology. **SELECTED PUBLICATIONS** Auth, Riverside Milton, Houghton Mifflin, 98. **CONTACT ADDRESS** Dept of English, Univ of So Carolina, Beaufort, 801 Carteret St, Beaufort, SC 29902. **EMAIL** roy@gpw.sc.edu

FLECK, GEORGE
PERSONAL Born 03/06/1930, Bronx, NY, m, 1985, 4 children **DISCIPLINE** DRAMA, SPEECH **EDUCATION** Fairleigh Dickinson Univ, BS, 57; York Univ, MBA, 58; Fairleigh Dickinson Univ, EdD, 74. **CAREER** Instr, Upsala Col, 60-61; Asst Prof, New York Inst for Tech, 76-77; Asst Prof, Williams Patterson Col, 77-78; Adj Prof, New York Univ, 78-80; Adj Prof, Fairleigh Dickinson Univ, 78-81; Dir, Corporate and Cable Commun, Bor of Manhattan Community Col, 81-95; ch, Dept Speech Commun, Bor of Manhattan Community Col, 95-; Adj Prof, Bergen, Bergen Community Col, 96-. **HONORS AND AWARDS** Bronze Medal, New York Film and Video Festival, 85; CUNY Chancellor's Reception, 92. **RESEARCH** Media. **SELECTED PUBLICATIONS** Thirty minute TV documentary, Air Safety, FAA, 88; three minute music video, Dressing in America, US Navy, 89; Ser of five, thirty minute "Good Morning, Roche" corporate news shows, 90. **CONTACT ADDRESS** Dept, Drama & Speech, Borough of Manhattan Comm Col, CUNY, 199 Chambers St, New York, NY 10007-1044. **EMAIL** gwfleck@yahoo.com

FLECK, RICHARD F.
PERSONAL Born 08/24/1937, Philadelphia, PA, m, 1963, 3 children **DISCIPLINE** ENGLISH **EDUCATION** Rutgers Univ, BA, 59; Colo State Univ, MA, 62; Univ N Mex, PhD, 70. **CAREER** Instr, North Adams State Col, 63-65; prof, Univ Wyo, 65-90; dir, Teikyo Loretto Heights Univ, 90-93; dean, Commun Col, Denver, 93-. **HONORS AND AWARDS** Colo Arts Counc Awd, 95; Who's Who West; Who's Who in Am. **MEMBERSHIPS** Nat Asn Col Admin; Sierra Club. **RESEARCH** Native American literature; natural history essay. **SELECTED PUBLICATIONS** Auth, Critical Perspectives on Native American Fiction, 93; auth, art, The World of N. Scott Momaday, 95; auth, John Muir's Mountaineering Essays, 97; auth, John Burroughs' Deep Woods, 98; ed, Colorado River Reader, 00. **CONTACT ADDRESS** Center for Language, Arts and Behavioral Sciences, Comm Col of Denver, Box 173363, Denver, CO 80217. **EMAIL** cd_richard@cccs.cccoes.edu

FLEISCHER, GEORGETTE
PERSONAL Born 07/31/1957, New York, NY **DISCIPLINE** ENGLISH, COMPARATIVE LITERATURE **EDUCATION** Univ Mich, BA, 79; Columbia Univ, MFA, 94; MA, 95; MPhil, 98; PhD, 01. **CAREER** Teaching fel, Brooklyn Col, CUNY, 91-92; TA, preceptor, Columbia Univ, 95-01; assoc prof, Barnard Col, 00-01. **HONORS AND AWARDS** Fel, Univ of Mich, 75-79; Louise B. Goodman Awd, 92; Fel, Columbia Univ, 92-93, 95-01; Edward F. Albee Found Fel, 94; Miron Christo-Levaunu Awd, 95. **MEMBERSHIPS** MLA, ACLA, Virginia Woolf Soc, Samuel Beckett Soc. **RESEARCH** Genre Departures: Women Writers and the Crisis of Representing National Socialism and World War II. **SELECTED PUBLICATIONS** Auth, "Light on Nightwood," Nation, (95); auth, "Hitler Was Their Boy," Nation, (96); auth, "Under the Sign of Wittgenstein: Postmodernist Poetics Explained," Contemp Lit, (97); auth, "Djuna Barnes and T.S. Eliot: The Politics and Poetics of Nightwood," Studies in the Novel, (98) auth, "Ingeborg Bachmann's Malina (1971): Wittgensteinian Poetics Out of the Austrian National Socialist Past," how2, (90); rev, "Her Own Lambs and Falcons" of Selected Letters of Rebecca West, Nation, (00); auth, "(Judith) Butler: Is It All Greek?" Nation, (00). **CONTACT ADDRESS** Barnard Col, 19 Cleveland Pl, #4A, New York, NY 10012. **EMAIL** gf24@columbia.edu

FLEISHMAN, AVROM
PERSONAL Born 07/27/1933, New York, NY, m, 1960, 2 children **DISCIPLINE** ENGLISH **EDUCATION** Columbia Univ, BA, 54; Johns Hopkins Univ, MA, 56, PhD (English), 63. **CAREER** Instr English, Columbia Univ, 58-59; instr Hofstra Univ, 60-63; asst prof, Univ Minn, 63-66; asst prof, Mich State Univ, 66-67; assoc prof, 68-70, PROF ENGLISH, JOHNS HOPKINS UNIV, 70-99, Belgian-Am Educ Found fel, 59-60; Guggenheim fel, 67-68; Explicator Lit Found Award, 75-76; sem dir, Nat Endowment for Humanities, 75 and 81. **RESEARCH** Modern and Victorian literature. **SELECTED PUBLICATIONS** Auth, Conrad's Politics, 67; auth, A Reading of Mansfield Park, 67; auth, The English Historical Novel, 71; auth, Virginia Woolf, 75; auth, Fiction and the Ways of Knowing, 78; auth, Figures of Autobiography, 83; auth, Narrated Films, 92; auth, The Condition of English, 98; auth, New Class Culture, 00. **CONTACT ADDRESS** Dept of English, 1123 Bellemore Rd, Baltimore, MD 21210. **EMAIL** avrom.fleishman@mciworld.com

FLEISSNER, ROBERT F.
PERSONAL Born 10/17/1932, Auburn, NY, d **DISCIPLINE** ENGLISH **EDUCATION** Cath Univ Am, BA, 57, MA, 58; Univ NC, 59-60; OH State Univ, 60-61; NYork Univ, PhD, 64. **CAREER** Instr English, speech & drama, Spring Hill Col, 58-59; asst instr English, OH State Univ, 60-61; lectr English & World Lit, Bernard Baruch Sch, City Col NY, 62-64; asst prof English & chemn dept, Dominican Col, NY, 64-66; vis instr, Univ NM, 66-67; asst to assoc prof English, Cent State Univ, 67-; Dir, OH Shakespeare Conf, 77, co-dir, 96. **MEMBERSHIPS** MLA; Frost Soc; Shakespeare Asn Am; Col Lang Asn; T S Eliot Soc. **RESEARCH** Renaissance, Romantic, and Victorian periods; Robert Frost; T S Eliot. **SELECTED PUBLICATIONS** Auth, Dickens and Shakespeare, NY: Haskell House, 69; Frost on Frost .. at Midnight, Studies Humanities, 76; A Table of Greene Felds', Grasse-Greene/table, and Balladry, Shak Jahrbuch, East, 76; Herberts Aethiopesa and the Dark Lady, CLA J, 76; Stopping yet Again by Frost's Woods, Res Studies, 77; Nons sans Droict: Law and Heraldry, in Julius Caesar, Hartford Studies Lit, 77; The Malleable Knight and the Unfettered Friar: The Merry Wives of Windsor and Boccaccio, Shakespeare Studies XI, 78; Ruelle, In: Robert Frost: Studies of the Poetry, 80; Resolved to Love: The 1592 Edition of Henry Constable's Diana Critically Considered, Univ Salzburg Press, 80; The Prince and the Professor, Heidelberg: Carl Winter U P, 86; Ascending the Prufrockian Stair, NY: Peter Lang, 88; A Rose by Another Name, West Cornwall: Locust Hill Press, 89; Shakespeare and the Matter of the Crux, Lewiston: Mellon, 91; T S Eliot and the Heritage of Africa, NY: Peter Lang, 92; Frost's Road Taken, NY: Peter Lang, 96. **CONTACT ADDRESS** Dept of Humanities, Central State Univ, Wilberforce, OH 45384-9999. **EMAIL** rfleissner@csu.ces.edu

FLEMING, BRUCE E.
PERSONAL Born 07/25/1959, Md, m, 2000 **DISCIPLINE** ENGLISH **EDUCATION** Haverford Col, BA, 74; Univ Chicago, MA, 78; Vanderbilt Univ, PhD, 82. **CAREER** Lecturer, Univ Freeburg W Germany,; Asst prof to prof, US Naval Academy, 87-. **HONORS AND AWARDS** O'Henry Awd, 90; Book Awd, Northeast Mod Lang Asn, 91. **MEMBERSHIPS** MLA. **RESEARCH** Modernism, Theory. **SELECTED PUBLICATIONS** Auth, An Essay in Post-Romantic Literary Theory: Art, Artifact and the Innocent Eye, Lewiston, New York, 91; auth, Caging the Lion: Cross-Cultural Fictions, New York, 93; auth, Modernism and its Discontents: Philosophical Problems of Twentieth-Century Literary Theory, New York, 95; auth, Structure and Chaos in Modernist Works, New York, 95; auth, Twilley, a novel, New York, 97; auth, Sex, Art, and Audience; Dance Essays, New York, 00. **CONTACT ADDRESS** Dept English, United States Naval Acad, 107 Maryland Ave, Annapolis, MD 21402-1316. **EMAIL** fleming@nadu.navy.mil

FLEMING, DEBORAH
DISCIPLINE ENGLISH **EDUCATION** Ohio State Univ, BA, 72; MA, 76; PhD, 85. **CAREER** Assoc prof, Ashland Univ, 93-. **HONORS AND AWARDS** Vandewater Poetry Awd. **MEMBERSHIPS** Asn for Study of Lit and Environment, Robinson Jeffers Asn. **RESEARCH** Modern poetry, Anglo-Irish Literature, Environmentalist Literature. **SELECTED PUBLICATIONS** Auth, 'A Man Who Does Not Exist': The Irish Peasant in W. B. Yeats and J. M. Synge, Univ Mich Press, 95. **CONTACT ADDRESS** Dept English, Ashland Univ, 401 College Ave, Asland, OH 44805-3702. **EMAIL** dfleming@ashland.edu

FLEMING, JOHN
PERSONAL Born 12/08/1964, Detroit, MI, m, 1996, 1 child **DISCIPLINE** ENGLISH **EDUCATION** Univ Va, BA; Univ S Miss, MA; Univ Southwestern La, PhD. **CAREER** Univ of NC at Wilmington, vis asst prof, 96-97; Saint Mary's Col of Calif, asst prof, 97-. **SELECTED PUBLICATIONS** Auth, The Legend of the Barefoot Mailman, Faber & Faber, 96. **CONTACT ADDRESS** Dept English, Saint Mary's Col, California, 1928 Saint Mary's Road, Moraga, CA 94556-2715. **EMAIL** drgigantor@cs.com

FLEMING, ROBERT
DISCIPLINE AMERICAN LITERATURE **EDUCATION** Univ Ill, PhD, 67. **CAREER** Instr, Univ NMex, 67-; ed, Am Lit Realism, 86-. **RESEARCH** African American literature. **SELECTED PUBLICATIONS** Auth, The Face in the Mirror: Hemingway's Writers, Univ Ala Press, 94. **CONTACT ADDRESS** Univ of New Mexico, Albuquerque, Albuquerque, NM 87131. **EMAIL** bfleming@unm.edu

FLETCHER, ALAN D.
DISCIPLINE ADVERTISING **EDUCATION** Univ Ill, PhD, 69. **CAREER** Prof, La State Univ; contributing ed, J of Advert, rev bd, J of Current Issues and Res in Advert; referee, Jour Quart, J Educr; steering comt, Freedom Forum Sem for New Prof of Advert; acad host, Very Important Prof sem, Promotional Products Asn Int. **MEMBERSHIPS** Am Acad of Advert; Acad Div of the Am Advert Fedn; Advert Div of the Asn for Educ in Journ and Mass Commun. **SELECTED PUBLICATIONS** Auth, Target Marketing Through the Yellow Pages, Yellow Pages Publ Asn, 91; auth, Lessons in Promotional Products Marketing, Promotional Products Asn Int, 94; coauth, Fundamentals of Advertising Research, 4th ed Wadsworth, 91; auth, "Yellow Pages: The Medium No One Thinks About," in Mass Communication in the Information Age (Northport, AL, Vision Press, 96), 243; auth, "Advertising Specialties: Important Ingredient in the Promotional Communications Mix, in "Mass Communicaiton in the Information Age (Northport, AL, Vision Press, 96), 248; coauth, "Manship School of Mass Communication Assesses the Intership Experience," Assessment Outcomes 1.4 (Baton Rouge, Louisiana State Univ, 97); coauth, "Who are Today's Buyers? (And What do They Really Want?)," Promotional Products Business (99): 70-84. **CONTACT ADDRESS** The Manship Sch of Mass Commun, Louisiana State Univ and A&M Col, Baton Rouge, LA 70803. **EMAIL** adfletcher@aol.com

FLETCHER, ANGUS S.
PERSONAL Born 06/23/1930, New York, NY **DISCIPLINE** ENGLISH LITERATURE **EDUCATION** Yale Univ, BA, 50, MA, 52; Univ Grenoble, France, dipl, 51; Harvard Univ, PhD, 58. **CAREER** Instr English lit, Cornell Univ, 58-62; from asst prof to assoc prof, Columbia Col, Columbia Univ, 62-68; prof, State Univ NY Buffalo, 68-74; DISTINGUISHED PROF ENGLISH & COMP LIT, LEHMAN COL & GRAD CTR, CITY UNIV NEW YORK, 74-, Vis prof English & comp lit, Univ Calif, Los Angeles, 73-74; Dreyfuss vis prof humanities, Calif Inst Technol, 77-78. **MEMBERSHIPS** Renaissance Soc Am; English Inst. **RESEARCH** History of opera and mixed media; Renaissance studies; theory of literature. **SELECTED PUBLICATIONS** Auth, Allegory: Theory of a Symbolic Mode, 64 & The Transcendental Masque: An Essay on Milton's Comus, 71, Cornell Univ; The Prophetic Moment: An Essay on Spenser, Univ Chicago, 71; Positive negation: Threshold, sequence and personfication in Coleridge, English Inst, 72; I Richards and the Art of Critical Balance, Oxford Univ, 73; Allegory, Dictionary of the History of Ideas, Scribner, 73; On two words in the libretto of the Magic Flute, Ga Rev, spring 75; ed, The Literature of Fact: English Institute Essays, Columbia Univ, 76; Colors of the Mind, Harvard Univ, 91. **CONTACT ADDRESS** 20 W 64th St, New York, NY 10023.

FLETCHER, JUDITH
DISCIPLINE GREEK DRAMA **EDUCATION** Western, BA, MA; Bryn Mawr, PhD. **CAREER** Asst prof. **RESEARCH** Greek Drama (Aeschylus and Euripides); Women in the Ancient World; Gender and narrative in the tragic chorus. **SELECTED PUBLICATIONS** Auth, "Exchanging glances: Vision and representation in Aeschylus Agamemnon," Helios, vol. 26, no. 1, (99): 11-34; auth, "An Odyssey Rewoven: A.S. Byatt's Angels and Insects" Classical and Modern Literature, vol. 19, (99); auth, "Choral Voice and Narrative in the First Stasimon of the Agamemnon," (forthcoming); auth, "Exchanging glances: Vision and representation in Aeschylus Agamemnon," Helios, v. 26, no. 1, (99): 11-34; auth, "An Odyssey Rewoven: A.S. Byatt's Angels and Insects," Classical and Modern Literature, v. 19, (forthcoming, 99); auth, "Aeschylus Cassandra: The Woman Who Knew Too Much"; auth, "Vision and Representation in Aeschylus Agamemnon". **CONTACT ADDRESS** Dept of Classics, Wilfrid Laurier Univ, 75 University Ave W, Waterloo, ON, Canada N2L 3C5. **EMAIL** jfletche@mach1.wlu.ca

FLETCHER, LUANN MCCRACKEN
DISCIPLINE EIGHTEENTH CENTURY BRITISH LITERATURE **EDUCATION** Lehigh Univ, BA, MA; UCLA, PhD. **CAREER** English Lit, Cedar Crest Col. **SELECTED PUBLICATIONS** Areas: Charlotte Bronte, Charles Dickens, and Virginia Woolf. **CONTACT ADDRESS** Cedar Crest Col, 100 College Drive, Allentown, PA 18104.

FLETCHER, MARIE
PERSONAL Born 10/11/1913, New Verda, LA **DISCIPLINE** ENGLISH **EDUCATION** La State Normal Col, AB, 38; La State Univ, MA, 44, PhD, 63. **CAREER** Instr, High Schs, La, 32-48; from instr to assoc prof English, Nicholls State Col, 48-63; from assoc prof to prof, Northwestern State Col, La, 63-67; chmn dept, 73-77, PROF ENGLISH, NICHOLLS STATE UNIV, 77-. **HONORS AND AWARDS** Distinguished Service Awd, La Coun Teachers Eng, 75. **MEMBERSHIPS** S Cent Mod Lang Asn. **RESEARCH** Am Lit. **SELECTED PUBLICATIONS** Auth, Franklin's General magazine: An image of the Colonial mind, McNeese Rev, 66; The southern woman in the fiction of Kate Chopin, La Hist, spring 66; The fate of women in a changing South: A persistent theme in the fiction of Caroline Gordon, Miss Quart, winter 68. **CONTACT ADDRESS** Dept of English, Nicholls State Univ, Thibodaux, LA 70301.

FLETCHER, WINONA LEE
PERSONAL Born 11/25/1926, Hamlet, NC, m, 1952, 1 child **DISCIPLINE** SPEECH AND DRAMA **EDUCATION** J C Smith Univ, AB 47; State Univ, Iowa, MA, 51; Ind Univ, PhD (speech and theatre), 68. **CAREER** Instr English, Delwatt's Radio and Electronics Inst, 47-50; from instr to assoc prof English, Speech and Theatre, Ky State Univ, 51-68, dir theatre, 66-78, prof, 68-78; PROF DRAMA, THEATRE and AFRO-AM STUDIES, IND UNIV, 78-, ASSOC DEAN, COL ARTS and SCI, 81-, Consult, Ind Univ Bloomington, 70-71, vis assoc prof Afro-Am studies and theatre, 71-73; comnr, Ky Arts Comn, 76-

80; mem task force, Comn on Blacks, Kennedy Ctr, 77-; coordr, Am Coun Teacher Fr and Black Col Proj, John F Kennedy Ctr, 81-. **MEMBERSHIPS** Fel Am Theatre Asn; Nat Asn Dramatic and Speech Arts (exec secy, 58-62); Speech Commun Asn; AAUP; Southeastern Theatre Conf. **RESEARCH** American theatre; Black drama and theatre; drama and theatre of the Federal Theatre Project. **SELECTED PUBLICATIONS** Auth, Sorrow is the Only Faithful one, The Life of Dodson, Owen, Theatre J, Vol 46, 94. **CONTACT ADDRESS** Dept of Afro-Am Studies, Indiana Univ, Bloomington, 1021 E Third St, Memorial Hall M37, Bloomington, IN 47405.

FLIBBERT, JOSEPH THOMAS
PERSONAL Born 07/24/1938, Worcester, MA, m, 1963, 3 children **DISCIPLINE** AMERICAN LITERATURE **EDUCATION** Assumption Col, AB, 60; Boston Col, MA, 63; Univ IL, Urbana, PhD, 70. **CAREER** Instr Eng, Al-Hikma Univ, Bagdad, 61-62; instr French, Worcester Acad, MA, 62-63; asst prof Eng, Merrimack Col, 63-67; tchg asst, Univ IL, Urbana, 67-69; ch person dept, 74-77, dir advising & coun ctr, 77-78, assoc prof, 70-78, prof eng, Salem State Col, 70, Sr Fulbright-Hays scholar, 79. **MEMBERSHIPS** MLA; NEA; Melville Soc; Nathaniel Hawthorne Soc. **RESEARCH** Am lit, 1820-1860; Herman Melville; lit of the sea; Nathaniel Hawthorne. **SELECTED PUBLICATIONS** Auth, Hawthorne, Salem, and the Sea, Sextant, 94; Fragments From the Writings of a Solitary Man: Defeat and Death in Hawthorne's Shorter Works, Forum, 4/95; That Look Beneath: Hawthorne's Portrait of Benevolence in the House of the Seven Gables, In: Critical Essays on Hawthorne's House of the Seven Gables, G.K. Hall, 95; Poetry in the Mainstream, In: America and the Sea: A Literary History, Univ Ga, 95; The American Scholar: 1997, Values Realization J, 97. **CONTACT ADDRESS** Dept of Eng, Salem State Col, 352 Lafayette St, Salem, MA 01970-5353. **EMAIL** jflibber@salem.mass.edu

FLICK, ROBERT GENE
PERSONAL Born 10/18/1930, Oblong, IL, m, 1951, 4 children **DISCIPLINE** ENGLISH, LITERATURE **EDUCATION** Eastern Ill State Col, BSEd, 52; Univ Fla, MA, 54, PhD, 67. **CAREER** Tchr high sch, IL, 54-56; from instr to assoc prof Eng, Jacksonville Univ, 56-68; assoc prof & actg chmn hum, 68-69, chmn, Dept Hum, Philos & Relig, 69-79, prof hum, Univ Central Fla, 69-98, prof emer, 98-; Tchr, State Univ System Study Center, Florence, Italy, 76, 81 & 85. **HONORS AND AWARDS** NEH Summer Seminar Grant, Univ MN, 80; Omicron Delta Kappa (hon mem 11/88); Phi Kappa Phi (hon mem 4/92); Excellence in Tchg Awd, Col Arts and Sci, Founders Day, 4/26/90. **MEMBERSHIPS** AAUP, 57-77; SAtlantic Mod Lang Asn, 57-; Southern Hum Conf; FL Col Eng Asc, 64. **RESEARCH** Creative writing; Emily Dickinson and nineteenth century Am lit; Greek art and cult. **SELECTED PUBLICATIONS** Emily Dickinson: Mystic and Skeptic, Univ Microfilms, 67; Humanities Colloquium at SAMLA, In: Humanties in the South, Fall 72; Prospects for the Humanist in Public Policy Debate, Humanews, 77-78. **CONTACT ADDRESS** 1028 Golfside Dr, Winter Park, FL 32792-5128. **EMAIL** rflick@pegasus.cc.ucf.edu

FLIEGELMAN, JAY
DISCIPLINE ENGLISH **EDUCATION** Ohio Wesleyan, BA, 71; Stanford Univ, PhD, 77. **CAREER** PROF, ENG, STANFORD UNIV **HONORS AND AWARDS** Mellon Distinguished Scholar-in-Res, 98-99. **MEMBERSHIPS** Am Antiquarian Soc **RESEARCH** Am Lib Bks, 1650-1860. **SELECTED PUBLICATIONS** Auth, Declaring Independence: Jefferson, Natural Language, and the Culture of Performance, Stanford Univ Press, 93; auth, Prodigals and Pilgrims: The American Revolution Against Patriarchical Authority, 1750-1800, Cambridge Univ Press, 82. **CONTACT ADDRESS** Dept of Eng, Stanford Univ, Stanford, CA 94305.

FLINT, ALLEN DENIS
PERSONAL Born 11/15/1929, Park River, ND, m, 1953, 5 children **DISCIPLINE** ENGLISH, AMERICAN STUDIES **EDUCATION** Univ Minn, BA, 55, MA, 56, PhD(Am studies), 65. **CAREER** Col Counsel & freshman adv, Col Lib Arts, Univ Minn, 56-58, scholastic comt rep, 58-59, sr scholastic comt rep, 59-62, instr & counsel, 62-64, asst dir, corres studies dept, 64-65, actg dir, 65-66; from asst prof to assoc prof English, Western Ill Univ, 66-70; chmn dept, 71-75, PROF ENGLISH, UNIV MAINE, FARMINGTON, 70-, Fulbright lectr, Romania, CIES, 75-76. **MEMBERSHIPS** MLA; Am Studies Asn. **RESEARCH** American renaissance; Black literature; contemporary literature. **SELECTED PUBLICATIONS** Auth, Hawthorne and the slavery crisis, New Eng Quart, 68; Essentially a daydream: Hawthorne's Blithedale, Hawthorne J, 72; The saving grace of marriage in Hawthorne's fiction, Emerson Soc Quart, 73. **CONTACT ADDRESS** Dept of English, Univ of Maine, Farmington, ME 04938.

FLIPPEN, CHARLES
DISCIPLINE COMMUNICATION **EDUCATION** Univ NC, PhD, 68. **CAREER** Instr, Towson Univ. **RESEARCH** Audience analysis of popular cult. **SELECTED PUBLICATIONS** Auth, Liberating the Media: The New Journalism. **CONTACT ADDRESS** Towson State Univ, Towson, MD 21252-0001. **EMAIL** cflippen@towson.edu

FLITTERMAN-LEWIS, SANDY
DISCIPLINE LITERATURES IN ENGLISH **EDUCATION** Berkeley, BA, MA, PhD. **CAREER** Assoc prof Eng, Rutgers, The State Univ NJ, Univ Col-Camden. **SELECTED PUBLICATIONS** Auth, To Desire Differently: Feminism and the French Cinema. **CONTACT ADDRESS** Dept of Lit in Eng, Rutgers, The State Univ of New Jersey, New Brunswick, Murray Hall 045, New Brunswick, NJ 08903. **EMAIL** sweetsod@aol.com

FLORA, JOSEPH M.
PERSONAL Born 02/09/1934, Toledo, OH, m, 1959, 4 children **DISCIPLINE** ENGLISH **EDUCATION** Univ of Mich, BA, 56; MA, 57; PhD, 62. **CAREER** Instr, Univ of Mich, 61-62; From Instr to Prof, Univ NC, 62-; Chair of English Dept, Univ NC, 80-91; Vis Prof, Univ of NMex, 76, 96. **HONORS AND AWARDS** Phi Eta Sigma; Phi Beta Kappa; Mayflower Awd. **MEMBERSHIPS** MLA, S Atl MLA, Western Lit Asn, Soc for Study of Southern Lit, Hemingway Soc, Thomas Wolfe Soc. **RESEARCH** Ernest Hemingway, Southern Literature, Western American Literature, Modern Fiction. **SELECTED PUBLICATIONS** Auth, Vardis Fisher, 62; auth, William Ernest Henley, 70; auth, Frederic Manfred, 74; auth, Hemingway's Nick Adams, 82; auth, Ernest Hemingway: A Study of the Short Fiction, 89. **CONTACT ADDRESS** Dept English, Univ of No Carolina, Chapel Hill, Greenlaw Hall, CB 3520, Chapel Hill, NC 27599-3520. **EMAIL** jflora@email.unc.edu

FLORES, CAROL A.
PERSONAL Born Lockport, NY, m, 1968 **DISCIPLINE** ARCHITECTURE, HISTORY, THEORY & CRITICISM **EDUCATION** Univ NYork Albany, BA, 66; Ga Inst of Tech, MS, 90; Ga Inst of Tech, PhD, archit, 96. **CAREER** Teacher, LaSalle Sch for Boys, 66-71; asst to pres, Environment/One Corp, 71; svc adv, N Eng Telephone, 72-76; chief svc adv, Southern Bell, 76-77; mgr, Southern Bell, 78-79; district mgr, Southern Bell, 80-82; operations mgr, Bell South Svc, 83-85; owner and commercial and residential designer, Design Options, 86-90; grad teaching asst, Col of Archit, Ga Inst of Tech, 89; doctoral fel, Col of Archit, Ga Inst of Tech, 90-94; asst prof, Col of Archit and Planning, Ball State Univ, 96-; Assoc prof, College of Archit & Planning, Ball State Univ, 00. **HONORS AND AWARDS** Outstanding rating, Mgt Assessment Prog, Southern Bell, 78; Outstanding Mgt Candidate, Southern Bell, 80; Individual Incentive award, BellSouth Svc, 84; Fel, Colonial Williamsburg Found, Antiques forum, 93; Ga Tech Alumni Asn Student Leadership travel award for Rome study, 93; Scholar, Nineteenth Century Studies Prog in London, Victorian Soc, 94; GTA teaching excellence award, col of archit, Ga Inst of Tech, 94; CETL/AMOCO Found GTA teaching excellence award, 94; pres fel, col of archit, Ga Inst of Tech, 90-94; doctoral fel, col of archit, Ga Inst of Tech, 91-94; Best Article Awd, Southeast Chap, Soc of Archit Hist, 95; Outstanding Student in Archit, Ga Inst of Tech, dec, 96; Doctoral prog achievement award, Ga Inst of Tech, may, 97; Dept of Archit res award, 99; new faculty grant, 99. **MEMBERSHIPS** Soc of Archit Hist; Southeast Chap, Soc of Archit Hist; Vernacular Archit Forum; Soc for Am City and Regional Planning Hist; Asn of Coll Sch of Archit; Nineteenth-Century Studies Asn; Victorian Soc; Soc for Emblem Studies; Decorative Arts Soc; Intl Soc for Amer City and Regional Planning Hist; Wallpaper Hist Soc. **RESEARCH** 19th-Century British architecture, theory, and decorative arts; Architecture, theory and decorative arts of Owen Jones 1809-1874; Public housing; Inscriptions and Symbolism in architecture. **SELECTED PUBLICATIONS** Auth, Owen Jones, Architect, Ga Inst of Tech, 96; contr, The Grammar of Ornament, Professional Artists' Edition, Pasadena, Direct Imagination Inc, 96; auth, US public housing in the 1930s: the first projects in Atlanta, Georgia, Planning Perspectives, 9, 405-430, 94; coauth, " Sixty and Out: Termwood Houes Transformed by Enemies and Friends," Journal of Urban History, Vol 26, no 3, 00. **CONTACT ADDRESS** Col of Architecture and Planning, Ball State Univ, Muncie, IN 47306-0305. **EMAIL** cflores@gw.bsu.edu

FLORY, MARLEEN BOUDREAU
PERSONAL Born 01/02/1944, CT, m, 1970 **DISCIPLINE** CLASSICS **EDUCATION** Mount Holyoke Col, BA, 65; Yale Univ, PhD, 75. **CAREER** Inst, Asst Acad Dean, 70-73, Asst Prof, 70-77, Classics, Mount Holyoke Coll, Classics; Res Fel, 74-75, Sr Assoc Member, 82-83 and 91-92, Amer School of Classical Stud, Athens; Asst Prof, Assoc Prof to Prof, Classic, 78-, Gustavus Alodolophus Coll, Asst Prof, 77-78, Salem Coll, Classics; Andrew W. Mellon Fellow, 85-86, Amer Acad in Rome. **HONORS AND AWARDS** Phi Beta Kappa; Fellow of the Amer Acad. **MEMBERSHIPS** Chair, Classical Association of the Midwest and South; Member of Ed Bd, Consult Evaluator; Executive Bd. **RESEARCH** Roman Society History. **SELECTED PUBLICATIONS** Auth, Octavian's Felicitas, Rheinisches Museum fur Philology, 107, pp 89-112, 94; Deification of Roman Women, Ancient History Bulletin, 95; The Meaning of the Name Augusta in the Julio-Claudian Period, Amer J of Ancient Hist, 97; The Integration of Women in the Roman Triumph, forthcoming in Historia, 98; Review, The Late Roman Army, by P Southern & KR Dixon, in: Religious Studies Review, 98, Atia and Julia and late Republic Political propaganda, CAMWS, 98. **CONTACT ADDRESS** Dept of Classics, Gustavus Adolphus Col, 800 W College Ave, Saint Peter, MN 56082-1498. **EMAIL** mflory@gustavus.edu

FLORY, STEWART GILMAN
PERSONAL Born 10/28/1941, New York, NY, m, 1970 **DISCIPLINE** CLASSICAL LANGUAGES & LITERATURES **EDUCATION** Yale Univ, BA, 64, MA, 67, MPhil, 68, PhD(-classics), 69. **CAREER** Asst prof classics, Amherst Col, 69-77; Chmn Dept Classics, Gustavus Adolphus Col, 79-, Am Sch Class Studies fel, Athens, 74-75 & sr assoc, 82-83; Nat Endowment for Humanities fel, Rome, summer, 80 & foreign col teachers, 82-83. **MEMBERSHIPS** Am Philol Asn; Archaeol Inst Am. **RESEARCH** Herodotus; Homer; Plato. **SELECTED PUBLICATIONS** Auth, The Personality of Herodotus, Arion, 69; Laughter, tears and wisdom in Herodotus, Am J Philol, 78; Medea's right hand, Tapa, 78; Who read Herodotus' histories, Am J Philol, Vol 101. **CONTACT ADDRESS** 800 W College Ave, Saint Peter, MN 56082-1498. **EMAIL** sflory@gac.edu

FLORY, WENDY STALLARD
PERSONAL Born 11/14/1943, Fulmer, England, m, 1966, 2 children **DISCIPLINE** ENGLISH, AMERICAN LITERATURE **EDUCATION** Univ of London, Bedford Col, BA Hons English, 65; Univ of Texas at Austin, PhD(English), 70. **CAREER** asst prof, English, Rutgers Univ, Doulgas Col 70-79; vis asst prof, English, Univ of Pa, 80-82; asst prof, English, Univ of Pa, 82-89; assoc prof, English, Purdue Univ, 89-90; Prof English Purdue Univ, 90-. **HONORS AND AWARDS** Nat Endowment for the Humanities Fel, 82-83; Am Asn of Univ Women Fel, 79-80; Fulbright Grant, 65. **MEMBERSHIPS** MLA; Melville Soc. **RESEARCH** Poetry; American romance; literary symbolizing; Holocaust documents; psychology of persecutors. **SELECTED PUBLICATIONS** auth, The American Ezra Pound, Yale Univ Pr, 89; auth, Ezra Pound and The Cantos: A Record of Struggle, Yale Univ Pr, 80; auth, "A new Century-A New Symbol Criticism: Pierre and an A-Freudian Approach to Melville's Symbolizing," Melville Soc Extracts, 96; auth, "Maurice Sendak's Pierre Pictures," Melville Soc Extracts, 97; auth, "On Goldhagen's Refusal to Address the Psychological Dynamics of Holocaust Murder," Shofar: An Intedisciplinary Jour of Jewish Studies, 97; auth, "Pound and Antisemitism," The Cambridge Comparison to Exra Pound, Camb Univ Pr, 99; auth "The Symbolizing Mind: Psychological Criticism Reconceived and the Romance Rediscovered." **CONTACT ADDRESS** Dept of English, Purdue Univ, West Lafayette, 711 Hillcrest Rd, West Lafayette, IN 47906. **EMAIL** wflory@sla.purdue.edu

FLOWER, DEAN SCOTT
PERSONAL Born 08/17/1938, Milwaukee, WI, 4 children **DISCIPLINE** ENGLISH **EDUCATION** Univ Mich, AB, 60; Stanford Univ, PhD(English), 66. **CAREER** Asst prof English, Univ Southern Calif, 64-69; assoc prof English, 69-85, PROF ENGLISH, 85-, chair English dept, 85-88, SMITH COL; Consult, Orff-Schulwerk Prof creativity & participation music educ, 65-67; advisory ed, The Hudson Review, 82-; chair, Advanced Placement Test Dev Com, 95-. **HONORS AND AWARDS** NEH award, 85, 87; NEH summer stipend, 89. **MEMBERSHIPS** MLA, SLE. **RESEARCH** American literature; contemporary prose fiction. **SELECTED PUBLICATIONS** Ed, The Great Short Works of Henry James, Harper, 66; Eight Short Novels, 67 & Counterparts: Classic and Contemporary American Stories, 71, Fawcett; auth, Henry James in Northampton: Visions and Revisions, Neilson Libr, 71; ed, Henry David Thoreau: Essays, Journals and Poems, Fawcett, 75; coauth, A Catalogue of American Paintings, Water Colors and Drawings, George Walter Vincent Smith Art Mus, 76. **CONTACT ADDRESS** Dept of English, Smith Col, Northampton, MA 01063. **EMAIL** dflower@sophia.smith.edu

FLOWER, LINDA S.
PERSONAL Born 03/03/1944 **DISCIPLINE** ENGLISH, WRITING **EDUCATION** Simpson Col, BA, 65; McGill Univ, BA, 64; Rutgers Univ, PhD, 72. **CAREER** Tchg asst Eng, Rutgers Univ, 70-71; lectr Eng, Univ Pittsburgh, 72-73; asst prof, 73-74, dir bus & prof commun, 74-80, prof eng, Carnegie-Mellon Univ, 80-, Dir, Center for Univ Outreach, 96-, Series ed, Res in Writing Series, Guilford Press; grants, Nat Inst Educ, 78-84. **MEMBERSHIPS** Conf Col Compos & Commun; Nat Coun Tchr(s) Eng; Am Educ Res Asn. **RESEARCH** Cognitive processes in writing--studying the thinking in writing--studying the thinking processes, the skills and strategies that distinguish experts and novices; tchg problem-solving strategies for writers. **SELECTED PUBLICATIONS** Coauth (with J R Hayes), Problem-solving strategies and the writing process, Col English, Vol 39, 449-461; auth, Writer-based prose: A cognitive basis for problems in writing, Col English, Vol 41, 19-37; coauth (with J R Hayes), The cognition of discovery: Defining a rhetorical problem, Col Compos & Commun, Vol 31, 21-32; auth, Problem-solving strategies for writing in college and community, Harcourt Brace Col Publ, 98; coauth (with J R Hayes), A cognitive process theory of writing, Col Compos & Commun, Vol 32, 365-387; coauth (with W C Peck, L Higgins), Community Literacy, Col Compos & Commun Vol 46, 199-222; auth Negotiating meaning of difference, Written Commun, Vol 13, 44-92; auth, The Construction of Negotiated Meaning: A Social Cognitive Theory of Writing, Univ Southern IL Press, 94. **CONTACT ADDRESS** Dept of Eng, Carnegie Mellon Univ, 5000 Forbes Ave, Pittsburgh, PA 15213-3890. **EMAIL** lf54@andrew.cmu.edu

FLOWERS, BETTY SUE
PERSONAL Born 02/02/1947, Waco, TX, m, 1967 **DISCIPLINE** ENGLISH LITERATURE, CREATIVE WRITING **EDUCATION** Univ Tex, BA, 69, MA, 70; Univ London, PhD (English), 73. **CAREER** Teaching asst English, Univ Tex, 68-70; lectr drama and English, Beaver Col, London, 71-72; asst prof, 73-79, ASSOC PROF ENGLISH, UNIV TEX, 79-, ASSOC DEAN GRAD SCH, 79-, Mellon Found fel, 76. **MEMBERSHIPS** AAUP; MLA; Am Asn Advan Humanities. **RESEARCH** Nineteenth and 20th century poetry; psychological approaches to literature; women's studies. **SELECTED PUBLICATIONS** Auth, Barthelme's Snow White: The reader-patient relationship, Critique, 75; coauth, Walking Over the Land, Fiction and Poetry by Texas Women, Tex Ctr for Writers, 75; Browning and the Modern Tradition, Macmillan, London, 76; auth, Proprieties (poems), Thicket, 76; Transport in French translation, Poetes Americains D'Aujourd hui, Cahiers Renaud Barrault, 77; How to make fiction out of your friends, Tex Quart, 21: 25-34; Madman, architect, carpenter, judge: Roles and the writing process, Proc Conf Col Teachers English, 9/79 & Lang Arts, 10/81; The I in Adrienne Rich: Individuation and the androgyne archetype, In: Theory and Practice of Feminist Literary Criticism, Bilingual Press, 82. **CONTACT ADDRESS** Dept of English, Univ of Texas, Austin, 0 Univ of Texas, Austin, TX 78712-1026.

FLOYD, EDWIN DOUGLAS
PERSONAL Born 05/19/1938, Prescott, AZ, m, 1967, 4 children **DISCIPLINE** CLASSICS **EDUCATION** Yale Univ, BA, 58; Princeton Univ, MA, 60, PhD (classics), 65. **CAREER** Instr ancient lang, Col William and Mary, 62-66; asst prof, 66-72, Assoc Prof Classics, Univ Pittsburgh, 72-. **MEMBERSHIPS** Am Philol Asn; Archaeol Inst Am; Ling Soc Am; Am Oriental Soc. **RESEARCH** Greek poetry; Greek historical linguistics; Sanskrit poetry. **SELECTED PUBLICATIONS** Auth, Homeric Epios Friendly and Vedic Api Friend, Glotta Zeitschrift Griechische Lateinische Sprache, Vol 71, 93; Bacchylides 18.31 and Indo European Poetics, J Indo Europ Stud, Vol 20, 92; Homer Iliad, Book 1, Line 191, Explicator, Vol 53, 95. **CONTACT ADDRESS** Dept of Classics, Univ of Pittsburgh, 1518 Cathedral of Learning, Pittsburgh, PA 15260-0001. **EMAIL** edfloyd@pitt.edu

FLOYD, SAMUEL A., JR.
PERSONAL Born 02/01/1937, Tallahassee, FL, m, 1956, 3 children **DISCIPLINE** MUSIC EDUCATION **EDUCATION** Florida A&M Univ, BS, 57; Southern Ill Univ, MME, 65, PhD, 69. **CAREER** Instr, Fla A&M Univ, 62-64; Instructor, Dept of Music, Florida A&M University, Asst Dir of Bands, Florida A&M University, 62-64; Instructor, Assoc Prof, Southern Ill Univ Carbondale, 64-78; instr/assoc prof, Music, South Ill Univ, Carbondale, 65-78; dir, Inst Res Black Am Music, Fisk Univ, 78-83; Dir, Center Black Music Res, Columbia Coll, 83-. **MEMBERSHIPS** Coll Music Soc; A, Musicol Soc; Sonneck Soc Am Music; Am Musicological Society; Coll Music Society; Council Member, 78-80; College Music Society; Pi Kappa Lambda; Soc for Am Music. **RESEARCH** Music in Black Diaspora. **SELECTED PUBLICATIONS** "Eileen Jackson-Southern: Quiet Revolutionary," New Perspectives on Music: Essays in Honor of Eileen Southern, Harmonie Park Press, 92; "Troping the Blues: From Spirituals to the Concert Hall," Black Music Res Jour, 93; The Power of Black Music, Oxford Univ Press, 95; auth, "The Power of Black Music," New York: Oxford University Press, 95; ed. International Dictionary of Black Composers, 2 vols, Chicago: Fitzroy Dearborn Publishers, 99; auth, "Troping the Blues: From Spirituals to the Concert Hall," Black Music Research Journal 13, no. 1, Spring 93: 31-50; auth, "Black Music in the Circum-Caribbean," American Music 17, no. 1, Spring 99, pp. 1-37. **CONTACT ADDRESS** Center Black Music Res, Columbia Col, Illinois, 600 S Mich Ave, Chicago, IL 60605. **EMAIL** sfloyd@popmail.colum.edu

FLYNN, DAVID
PERSONAL Born 04/04/1948, Jackson, TN, d, 1 child **DISCIPLINE** ENGLISH, JOURNALISM **EDUCATION** Univ Missouri, BA, BJ, 71; Univ Denver, MA, 72; Boston Univ, MA, 80; Univ Nebraska, PhD 84. **CAREER** Instr, Tennessee State Univ, 78-79; vis lect, Boston Univ, 80-81; temp asst prof, Tennessee State Univ, 88-89; temp asst prof, Univ Hawaii, 89-91; asst prof, Tokai Univ, Honolulu, 92-93; assoc prof, Volunteer State Univ, 93-. **HONORS AND AWARDS** Write Resid, Millay Col Arts, NY, 87; Tyrone Guthrie Cen, IRE, 90; Israeli Cen, 91; Wurlitzer Found, 93; , 97, 98; Japan Exch Teach Prog, 87. **MEMBERSHIPS** Poets and Writers. **RESEARCH** Writing of Poetry; fiction; creative non-fiction; journalism. **SELECTED PUBLICATIONS** Auth, "A House," Jones Av (Canada), 97; auth, "A Staircase," Braquemard (England), 97; auth, "Night of No Result," Heist (Australia), 98; auth, "Ardor," Splizz (Wales), 98; auth, "I Ate a Cobra," Vigil (England), 98; auth, "Feeling for the Edge," Jones Av (Canada), 98; auth, "Furin," Seam (England), 98; auth, "For Brenda," "Fixing the Bed," "Objects," "The Break-Up," "Lovers Waiting," "Horseback," "Short Wave," "Winding Down,' and "Wrestling with My Lover," Peer Poetry Review (England), 99; auth, "You Changed Your Name," Jones AV. (Canada), 99, auth, "Magdalene Kneeling in the Mountains," The Penwood Review (U.S.), 00; auth, "The Maktesh," The Seed of Thoughts, Poetry Now (England), 00; auth, "Darkwood," Paris Transcontinental (France), 97; auth, "Bomb," Barbaric Yawp (U.S.), 98; auth, "Cowoids," Barbaric Yawp (U.S.), 98; auth, "The Rooming House," Breakfast All Day (France), 98; auth, "In the grid," and "Bed Like a Mountain" Heist (Australia), 99; auth, "Bemis Hoods," Breakfast All Day (France), 99; auth, "Spiritual Dyslexia," Heist (Australia), 99; auth, Barbers in Japan are Different, Japanophile (US), 97. **CONTACT ADDRESS** Dept Humanities, Volunteer State Comm Col, 1480 Nashville Pike, Gallatin, TN 37066-3148. **EMAIL** dflynn@vscc.cc.tn.us

FOGEL, DANIEL MARK
DISCIPLINE MODERN NOVEL, 19TH AND 20TH CENTURY ENGLISH AND AMERICAN LITERATURE, CREATI **EDUCATION** Cornell, PhD, 76. **CAREER** Prof, La State Univ; Ed Henry James Rev, 79-95; PMLA, adv comt, 86-90; Prof, Exec Vice-Chancellor and Provost; exec comt, Div on Late 19th and Early 20th-Century Am Lit, MLA, 89-92. **HONORS AND AWARDS** LSU Alumni Asn Distinguished Fac Awd, 88; founder, henry james rev. **RESEARCH** Henry James; James Joyce; Virginia Woolf; Modern Poetry. **SELECTED PUBLICATIONS** Auth, Covert Relations: James Joyce, Virginia Woolf, and Henry James, 90; Daisy Miller: A Dark Comedy of Manners, 90; Schindler's List in Novel and Film: Exponential Conversion, the Hist J of Film, Radio, and TV 14, 94; The Editor as Teacher and Learner, the Henry James Rev 17, 96; ed, A Companion to Henry James Studies, 93. **CONTACT ADDRESS** Dept of Eng, Louisiana State Univ, 146 Thomas Boyd Hall, Baton Rouge, LA 70803. **EMAIL** evcp@lsu.edu

FOGEL, JERISE
PERSONAL Born 11/30/1964 **DISCIPLINE** CLASSICS **EDUCATION** Smith Col, AB, 85; Columbia Univ, MA, 87, MPhil, 90, PhD, 94. **CAREER** Vis asst prof, Smith Col, 90; asst prof, Univ Il Urbana-Champaign, 94-97; asst prof, Gettysburg Col, Pa, 97-98; asst prof, Mich St Univ, 98- . **HONORS AND AWARDS** Mellon Fel, 86-91 **MEMBERSHIPS** Amer Philol Assoc; Archaeol Inst of Amer; AAUW; AAUP; Int Soc for Hist of Rhetoric; Lesbian/Gay/Bisexual Classical Caucus. **RESEARCH** Greek & Roman rhetoric; oratory; political theory. **SELECTED PUBLICATIONS** Auth, Order for Payment to a Banker, Business Letter, Columbia Papyri, 97; Clientela System, Papian-Poppacan Law(Lex Papia-Poppaea, Pax romana, Roman Republic, of The Historical Encyclopedia of world Slavery, 97; Formalized speech in twentieth-century Madagascar and the Late Republic, in Retorica, Politica e Ideologia: Desde la Antiguedad hasta nuestros dias, Salamanca, Spain, 98; Cicero, On Friendship, translation, Copley Publ Co, forthcoming. **CONTACT ADDRESS** Dept of Romance & Classical Lang, Michigan State Univ, East Lansing, MI 48824. **EMAIL** fogell@ux1.cso.uiuc.edu

FOGEL, STAN
DISCIPLINE ENGLISH LITERATURE **EDUCATION** Carleton Univ, BA, 68; Univ British Columbia, MA, 70; Purdue Univ, PhD, 73. **CAREER** Ch, St. Jerome's Univ; member of Senate, Univ of Waterloo; member, Univ of Waterloo; prof, St. Jerome's Univ; vis prof, Instituto Superior de Arte, 93, 95, 97. **RESEARCH** Contemporary literature; critical theory. **SELECTED PUBLICATIONS** Auth, A Tale of Two Countries; auth, Gringo Star; auth, The Postmodern University: Essays on Deconstruction of the Humanities; auth, Understanding John Barth; auth, "Decolonizing CanLit"; auth, Entries for: The Encyclopedia of Jewish-American History and Culture; auth, "I See England, I See France, Robert Kroetsch's Alibi"; auth, "And all the little typtopies," Notes on Language Theory in the Contemporary Experiment Novel," auth, "American Graffiti: Gass's In the Heart of the Heart of the Country". **CONTACT ADDRESS** Dept of English, St. Jerome's Univ, Waterloo, ON, Canada N2L 3G3.

FOLEY, BARBARA
PERSONAL Born 03/29/1948, New York, NY, m, 1972, 2 children **DISCIPLINE** ENGLISH **EDUCATION** Radcliffe Col, BA, 69; Univ Chicago, MA, 71, PhD, 76. **CAREER** Asst prof, Eng, 76-79, Univ Wisc; asst prof, Eng & Amer stud, 80-87, Northwestern Univ; assoc prof, 87-95, tenured, 90, prof, 95-, Rutgers Univ. **HONORS AND AWARDS** Phi Beta Kappa; NH grants. **MEMBERSHIPS** MLA; AAUP. **RESEARCH** Amer Lit, African-Amer Lit; Marxist criticism, theory of the novel; politics & lit. **SELECTED PUBLICATIONS** Auth, Telling the Truth: The Theory and Practice of Documentary Fiction, Cornell UP, 86; auth, Radical Representations: Politics and form in US Proletarian Fiction 1929-1941, Duke UP, 93; art, Generic and Doctrinal Politics in the Proletarian Bildungsroman, Understanding Narrative, Ohio SUP, 94; art, Tillie Olsen, Companion to Amer Thought, Basil Blackwell, 95; art, Wayne Booth and the Politics of Ethics, Rhetoric & Pluralism: Legacies of Wayne Booth, Ohio SUP, 95; art, Jean Toomer's Sparta, Amer Lit 67, 95; art, Introduction to Myra Page, Moscow Yankee, Univ Ill Press, 96; art, Jean Toomer's Washington and the Politics of Class: From 'Blue Veins' to Seventh-Street Rebels, Modern Fiction Stud 42, 96; art, The Federal Writers Project, Encycl African-Amer Hist & Cult, Macmillan, 97; art, The Rhetoric of Anticommunism in Ralph Ellison's Invisible Man. Col Eng 59, 97; art, Interview with Barbara Foley, Conducted by Ron Strickland, Mediations 21, 98; art, Roads Taken and Not Taken: Anticommunism, Post-Marxism, an African American Literature, Cult Logic, 98; art, From Astor Place to Wall Street: Historicizing Melville's 'Bartleby', The Other Romance: Essays in Honor of James E. Miller, Jr, Univ Chicago Press 98; art, U.S. Proletarian Literature, SAMAR, 98; art, In The Land of Cotton; Economics and Violence in Jean Toomer's Cane, African Amer Rev 32, 98; art, Ralph Ellison as Proletarian Journalist, Sci & Soc, 99. **CONTACT ADDRESS** English Dept, Rutgers, The State Univ of New Jersey, Newark, 360 Kings Blvd, Newark, NJ 07102. **EMAIL** bfoley@andromeda.rutgers.edu

FOLEY, MARY KATHLEEN
DISCIPLINE ASIAN THEATER **EDUCATION** Rosemont Col, BA, 69; Univ Bochum, W Germany, Fulbright cert, 70; Univ Mass, Amherst, MA, 75; Univ Hawaii, PhD, 79. **CAREER** Asst to assoc PROF, UNIV CALIF, 80-, PROVOST PORTER COL, 89-, UNIV CALIF, SANTA CRUZ. **HONORS AND AWARDS** Fulbright Schlarship, NEH, NEA, Asian Cultural Council Grants, Chandra Bhandar, Endow Chair. **MEMBERSHIPS** Asn fro Asian Performance, Asn of Asian Studies, Assoc for Theatre in Higher Education, Puppeteers of America, UNIMA. **RESEARCH** Performance of South and Southeast Asia, Puppetry and Perfoming Objects. **SELECTED PUBLICATIONS** Auth, Local Manifestations and Corss-Cultural Implications: Essays on Southeast Asian Performing Arts, Berkeley, 92. **CONTACT ADDRESS** Porter Col, Univ of California, Santa Cruz, 301 Heller Dr, Santa Cruz, CA 95064. **EMAIL** kfoley@cats.ucsc.edu

FOLKENFLIK, ROBERT
PERSONAL Born 05/23/1939, Newark, NJ, m, 1965, 2 children **DISCIPLINE** ENGLISH **EDUCATION** Rutgers Univ, BA, 61; Univ Minn, MA, 66; Cornell Univ, PhD (English), 68. **CAREER** From instr to asst prof English, Univ Rochester, 67-75, dir freshman English, 71-73; ASSOC PROF ENGLISH, UNIV CALIF, IRVINE, 75-, Asst ed, Studies in Burke and His Time, 72-74; Nat Endowment for Humanities younger humanist fel. **MEMBERSHIPS** MLA; Am Soc Eighteenth Century Studies; Western Soc Eighteenth Century Studies (vpres, 78-79). **RESEARCH** Eighteenth-century literature; the novel; biography. **SELECTED PUBLICATIONS** Auth, Rasselas and the Closed Field, Huntington Lib Quart, Vol 57, 94. **CONTACT ADDRESS** Dept of English and Comp Lit, Univ of California, Irvine, Irvine, CA 92664.

FOLKS, JEFFREY J.
PERSONAL Born 10/16/1948, Tulsa, OK, 1 child **DISCIPLINE** AMERICAN AND SOUTHERN LITERATURE **EDUCATION** Reed Col, BA, 69; Ind Univ, MA, 72, PhD (English), 77. **CAREER** Assoc instr, Ind Univ, 70-72; instr, 76-79, asst prof, 79-82, ASSOC PROF ENGLISH, TENN WESLEYAN COL, 82-, Nat Endowment for Humanities summer sem, 79 and 82. **MEMBERSHIPS** MLA; Soc Study Southern Lit; Conf Christianity and Lit. **RESEARCH** American fiction. **SELECTED PUBLICATIONS** Auth, Faulkner's The Rosary and Florence Barclay, Studies in Short Fiction, fall 81; William Faulkner and the silent film, Southern Quart, spring 81; Honor in Faulkner's short fiction, Southern Rev, summer 82. **CONTACT ADDRESS** English Dept, Tennessee Wesleyan Col, Athens, TN 37303.

FOLSOM, LOWELL EDWIN
PERSONAL Born 09/30/1947, Pittsburgh, PA, m, 1969, 1 child **DISCIPLINE** ENGLISH, AMERICAN STUDIES **EDUCATION** Ohio Wesleyan Univ, BA, 69; Univ Rochester, MA, 72, PhD(English), 76. **CAREER** Instr humanities, Eastman Sch Music, 74-75; vis asst prof English, State Univ NY, Geneseo, 75-76; asst prof, 76-81, assoc prof , 81-87, prof English & Am Studies, Univ Iowa, 87-; ed, Walt Whitman Qtly Rev, 83-, co-dir, Walt Whitman Hypertext Archive, 97-. **HONORS AND AWARDS** Director, NEH Summer Seminar, 84; Collaborative Research Awd, NEH, 91-94; Univ Rochester Distinguished Scholar Medal, 95; Iowa Regents Awd for Faculty Excellence, 96; Fullbright Senior Professorship, Germany, 96; F. Wendell Miller Distinguished Professorship, 97-. **MEMBERSHIPS** MLA; Midwest MLA; Am Lit Asn, Whitman Studies Asn. **RESEARCH** American poetry and culture; Walt Whitman; contemporary American literature. **SELECTED PUBLICATIONS** Ed, Walt Whitman: The Measure of His Song, Holy Cow! Press, 81, second ed, 98, Choice Best Academic Book, 82; Regions of Memory: Uncollected Prose of W.S. Merwin, Univ of Il Press, 87; W.S. Merwin: Essays on the Poetry, Univ of Il Press, 87; Walt Whitman: The Centennial Essays, Univ of Iowa Press, 94, Walt Whitman and the World, Univ of Iowa Press, 95; Major Authors: Walt Whitman, CD-ROM, Primary Source Media, 97, Choice Best Academic Book, 98; Auth, Walt Whitman's Native Representations, Cambridge UP, 94, Choice Best Academic Book, 95. **CONTACT ADDRESS** Dept of English, Univ of Iowa, 308 English Phil Bld, Iowa City, IA 52242-1492. **EMAIL** ed-folsom@uiowa.edu

FOLSOM, MARCIA M.
PERSONAL Born 12/18/1940, Evanston, IL, w, 1967, 2 children **DISCIPLINE** ENGLISH **EDUCATION** Wellesley Col, BA, 62; Univ Calif, Berleley, MA, 64, PhD, 77. **CAREER** Lect, Radcliffe sems, 87-95; prof, Wheelock Col, Boston, 86-2000, chair, 86-93, vice pres Academic Affairs, 93-97. **HON-**

ORS AND AWARDS General Honors, English, Wellesley Col, 62; Whiting Found, Travel grant, 97; Edward H. Ladd Awd for Academic Excellence and Service, Wheelock Col, 97; proj dir, NEH fac develop grant, 94-95; fac mem, Teachers as Scholars, Harvard, 97-2000; coord, JASNA Conf, 2000. **MEMBERSHIPS** MLA, JASNA, WCMLA. **RESEARCH** Austen's novels, Austen's Reading of Shakespeare, scholarship of teaching. **SELECTED PUBLICATIONS** Auth, Approaches to Teaching Austen's Pride and Prejudice, MLA Press (93). **CONTACT ADDRESS** Dept Arts & Sci, Wheelock Col, 200 Riverway, Boston, MA 02215-4104. **EMAIL** mfolsom@wheelock.edu

FONESCA, TEREZINHA

PERSONAL Born 08/11/1939, Brazil, m, 1970 **DISCIPLINE** ENGLISH **EDUCATION** NY Univ, PhD, 88. **CAREER** Adj Instr, SUNY Purchase and Manhattanville Col; Assoc Prof, Queensborough Community Col, 90-. **HONORS AND AWARDS** Fulbright Scholar, Ind Univ, 65. **MEMBERSHIPS** MLA. **RESEARCH** Renaissance Studies, Love and Sexuality in Literature. **SELECTED PUBLICATIONS** Coauth, Pathway to College Writing, CAT Publ Co (Redding, CA), 99; Auth, Instructor's Manual to Literature Across Cultures, 3rd ed; coauth, Literature Across Cultures, Allyn & Bacon (Boston), 00. **CONTACT ADDRESS** Dept English, Queensborough Comm Col, CUNY, 22205 56th Ave, Oakland Gardens, NY 11364-1432.

FONG, BOBBY

PERSONAL Born 01/28/1950, Oakland, CA, m, 1974, 2 children **DISCIPLINE** ENGLISH LITERATURE **EDUCATION** Harvard Univ, BA, 73; UCLA, PhD, 78. **CAREER** Assoc prof, Berea Col, 78-89; prof and dean, Hope Col, 89-95; prof and dean, Hamilton Col, 95-01; prof, pres, Butler Univ, 01-. **HONORS AND AWARDS** Phi Beta Kappa, 73; Phi Kappa Phi, 81; NEH Summer Fel, 82; Nat Fel, Asn of Am Col, 86-87. **MEMBERSHIPS** MLA, NCTE, AACU, Soc for Values in Higher Educ. **RESEARCH** Oscar Wilde, 19th and 20th Century English and American Literature, Higher Education, Religion, Baseball. **SELECTED PUBLICATIONS** Auth, "Commonplaces About Teaching: Second Thoughts," Change Mag, (87); auth, "Maxine Hong Kinston's Autobiographical Strategy in 'The Woman Warrior,'" Biography, (89); auth, "Wilde's 'Harlot's House,'" Explicator, (90); auth, "Local Canons: Professing Literature at the Small College," Contemporary Critical Theory and the Teaching of Literature, ed Charles Moran and Elizabeth Penfield, (90); auth, "The Magic Cocktail: the Enduring Appeal of the 'Field of Dreams,'" Aethlon, (93); auth, "A View From the Inside: Reflections of a Christian Multiculturalist," Christian Scholar's Rev, (96); ed, Christianity and culture in the Crossfire, William B Eerdman's, (97); ed, The Oxford English Text Edition of the Complete Works of Oscar Wilde, vol one, Poems and Poems in Prose, (00); auth, "Toto, I Think We're Still in Kansas: Supporting and Mentoring Minority Faculty and Administrators," Liberal Educ, (00); auth, "Teaching Professions Liberally," Peer Review, (01). **CONTACT ADDRESS** Butler Univ, 4600 Sunset Ave, Indianapolis, IN 46208. **EMAIL** bfong@butler.edu

FONTANA, ERNEST L.

PERSONAL Born 02/20/1941, Cleveland, OH, m, 2 children **DISCIPLINE** ENGLISH **EDUCATION** John Carroll Univ, BS, 62; Notre Dame, MA, 63; PhD, 69. **CAREER** Asst Prof to Prof and Dept Char, Xavier Univ, 66-. **HONORS AND AWARDS** Fel, NEH, 79, 83; Bishop Fenwick Awd, 84. **MEMBERSHIPS** MLA, William Morris Soc. **RESEARCH** The Pre-Raphaelites, Hopkins, Conrad, Dante. **CONTACT ADDRESS** Dept English, Xavier Univ, Ohio, 3800 Victoy Pkwy, Cincinnati, OH 45207-1035. **EMAIL** fontana@xavier.xu.edu

FONTENOT, CHESTER J.

PERSONAL Born Los Angeles, CA, m, 3 children **DISCIPLINE** AMERICAN & AFRO-AMERICAN LITERATURE **EDUCATION** Whittier Col, BA, 72; Univ Calif, Irvine, PhD, 75. **CAREER** Asst prof, Univ Nebr-Lincoln, 75-77 & Cornell Univ, 77-79; assoc prof Lit, Univ Ill, Urbana-Champaign, 79-, vis scholar, Colgate Univ, Fall, 78, State Univ NY Binghamton, Spring, 78; vis artist, Purdue Univ, 80; reviewer & panelist, Nat Endowment for the Humanities, 81-, NSF, 82-; Griffith Dept Ch and Prof Englsit, Mercer Univ. **HONORS AND AWARDS** Incomplete List of Teachers Rated Excellent By Their Students, The Univ Ill at Urbana-Champaign; Phi Beta Sigma Distinguished Faculty Awd for Outstanding Teaching, The Univ Ill, Urbana-Champaign. **MEMBERSHIPS** MLA; Midwest Mod Lang Asn; Asn Study Afro-Am Life & Hist; Asn Study Multi-Ethnic Lit in the US; Col Lang Asn. **RESEARCH** Afro-American literature and culture; contemporary American literature; literary criticism and theory with emphasis on myth and symbolism. **SELECTED PUBLICATIONS** Ed, Writing About Black Literature, Nebr Curric Develop Ctr, 76; auth, Black fiction: From tragedy to romance, Cornell Rev, Spring 78; Ishmael Reed and the politics of Aesthetics, Black Am Lit Forum, Spring 78; Black fiction: Apollo or Dionysus, Twentieth Century Lit, Fall 78; Frantz Fanon and the Devourers, J of Black Studies, 9/78; Frantz Fanon: Language as the God Gone Astray in the flesh, Univ Nebr Studies, 79; Angelic dance or tug of war: The humanistic implications of cultural formalism, Black Am Lit and Humanism, 81; Mythic patterns in River Niger and Ceremonies in Dark Old Men, Melus, 81. **CONTACT ADDRESS** Dept of English, Mercer Univ, Macon, 1400 Coleman Ave, Macon, GA 31207. **EMAIL** fontenot_cj@mercer.edu

FONTES, MANUEL D.

PERSONAL Born 07/02/1945, Azores, Portugal, m, 1974, 3 children **DISCIPLINE** CLASSICS, LANGUAGE **EDUCATION** Modesto Jr Col, AB, 64; Stanislaus State Col, BA, 69; Univ Calif Berkeley, MA, 72; Univ Calif Las Angeles, PhD, 75. **CAREER** Lectr, Stanford Univ, 72, 73; asst prof to assoc prof to prof, Kent State Univ, 75-. **HONORS AND AWARDS** NEH Fel, 78, 80-81; Guggenheim Fel 84-85; Distinguished Scholar Award, 97. **MEMBERSHIPS** AATSP; CSA; AIL; MLA; SRBHP; SCSM. **RESEARCH** Medieval and renaissance Spanish and Portuguese literature; relations between folklore and literature; the role of conversos in Spanish literature; crypto-Judaism in Portugal and Spain. **SELECTED PUBLICATIONS** Ed, Romanceiro Portuguese do Canada, Acta Univ, 79; ed, Romanceiro Portuguese dos Estados Unidos, 1: Nova Inglaterra; 2: California, Acta Univ, 80; ed, Romanceiro da Ilha de Sao Jorge, Acta Univ, 83; auth, "The Ballad of 'Floresvento' and Its Epic Antecedents," Ky Romance Quart 32 (85): 309-319; co-ed, Romanceiro da Provincia de Trds-os-Montes, Acta Univ, 87; auth, "Four Portuguese Crypto-Jewish Prayers and Their Inquisitorial Counterparts," Mediterranean Lang Rev 6-7 (90): 67-104; auth, "The Holy Trinity in 'La Lozana Andaluza," Hisp Rev 62 (90): 249-266; auth, "Celestina as an Antithesis of the Virgin Mary," J Hisp Philol 14 (90): 7-41; auth, Portuguese and Brazil Bibliographic Index, Hisp Sem Medieval Studies, 97; auth, Folklore and Literature: Studies in the Portuguese, Brazilian, Sephardic, and Hispanic Oral Traditions, SUNY Pr, 00. **CONTACT ADDRESS** Dept Class, Kent State Univ, Kent, OH 44242. **EMAIL** mfontes@neo.rr.com

FONTIJN-HARRIS, CLAIRE

PERSONAL Born 03/23/1960, Montreal, PQ, Canada, m, 2000 **DISCIPLINE** MUSIC, FRENCH, BAROQUE FLUTE, MUSICOLOGY **EDUCATION** Oberlin Col, BA, 82; Royal Conserv of the Hague, cert, 85; Duke Univ, MA, 89, PhD 94. **CAREER** Asst Prof Music, Dir Collegium Musicum, 94-, Wellesley Col. **HONORS AND AWARDS** Prize winner, Case Western Res Univ Baroque Mus Comp, 89; Gladys Krieble Delmas Grant, Venice, 94 and 00; Woodrow Wilson Nat Fellow Found Women's Stud Awd, 92, Am Musicol Soc Publ Subvention, 00. **MEMBERSHIPS** Am Musicol Soc; Soc 17th Cent Mus; Int Assoc of Women in Mus; Heinrich Schuetz Soc. **RESEARCH** Baroque Music; Baroque Flute; Women in Music; Women in Baroque Music. **SELECTED PUBLICATIONS** Bembo, Antonia, entry in The Norton/Grove Dict of Women Composers, London, Macmillan, 94; Quantz's 'unegal': implications for the performance of 18th-century music, Early Mus, Feb 95, 55-62; In Honour of the Duchess of Burgundy: Antonia Bembo's Compositions for Marie-Adelaide of Savoy, Cahiers de l'IRHMES, 3, 95, 45-89; Antonia Bembo, in Women Composers: Music Through the Ages, New York, G.K. Hall, 96, 201-16. **CONTACT ADDRESS** Wellesley Col, 106 Central St., Dept. of M, Wellesley, MA 02481. **EMAIL** cfontijn@wellesley.edu

FOOTE, BUD

PERSONAL Born 08/19/1930, Laconia, NH, m, 6 children **DISCIPLINE** MODERN LITERATURE, FOLKLORE & SCIENCE FICTION **EDUCATION** Princeton Univ, AB, 52; Univ Conn, MA, 58. **CAREER** Instr English, Univ Conn, 53-56; instr, Arnold Sch, Pembroke, Mass, 56-57; from instr to asst prof, 57-69, assoc prof, 69-85, Prof English, GA Inst Technol, 85-, NEH proj staff, 71-72, 72-73, dir, 73, 74. **MEMBERSHIPS** S Atlantic Mod Lang Asn; MLA; Science Fiction Res Asn. **RESEARCH** American humor; science fiction. **SELECTED PUBLICATIONS** Auth, Richard Condon & David Karp, in Contemporary Novelists, St Martin, 72; The Connecticut Yankee in the Twentieth Century: Travel to the Past in Science Fiction, Greenwood Press, 91. **CONTACT ADDRESS** School of Lit, Commun & Culture, Georgia Inst of Tech, 225 North Ave NW, Atlanta, GA 30332-0002.

FORBES, JOYCE

PERSONAL Born Trinidad, West Indies **DISCIPLINE** ENGLISH **EDUCATION** Howard Univ, BA, 61; Queen's Univ, MA, 64; Univ West Indies, PhD, 77. **CAREER** Chair, Dept English, Lakehead Univ, 89-92. **HONORS AND AWARDS** Can Commonwealth Schol, 61-63; 3M Can Tchr Fel Outstanding Contrib Univ Tchr, 88. **MEMBERSHIPS** Can Asn Univ Tchrs; Ont Confed Univ Fac Adminr; Can Res Inst Advan Women; Caribbean African Asn. **SELECTED PUBLICATIONS** Auth, The Tears of Things in Arts & Lit Rev, 72; auth, Wilson Harris's Guyana Quartet: The Outsider as Character and Symbol, 86; auth, William Golding as Essayist in British Essays 1880-1960 in Dictionary of Lit Biog, 90. **CONTACT ADDRESS** Dept of English, Lakehead Univ, Thunder Bay, ON, Canada P7B 5E1. **EMAIL** jforbes@flash.lakehead.ca

FORD, ANDREW

PERSONAL Born New York, NY, m, 2 children **DISCIPLINE** CLASSICS **EDUCATION** Cornell Univ, BA, 74; Yale Univ, PhD, 81. **CAREER** Instr, Smith Col, 80-85; fel, Cornell Univ, 85-87; asst/assoc prof, Princeton Univ, 87-; Prof. **HONORS AND AWARDS** NEH fel. **MEMBERSHIPS** Am Philol Asn. **RESEARCH** Classics. **SELECTED PUBLICATIONS** Auth, Aomen: the poetry of the past. **CONTACT ADDRESS** 75 Dryads Green, Northampton, MA 01060. **EMAIL** aford@princeton.edu

FORD, JAMES ERIC

PERSONAL Born 11/04/1943, Los Angeles, CA, m, 1973, 6 children **DISCIPLINE** ENGLISH LANGUAGE & LITERATURE **EDUCATION** Brigham Young Univ, BA, 68; San Francisco State Univ, MA, 71; Univ Chicago, PhD(English), 81. **CAREER** Asst prof to assoc prof, Brigham Young Univ, 76-81; asst prof English, Univ Nebr - Lincoln, 81-. **MEMBERSHIPS** MLA; Am Philol Asn. **RESEARCH** History and theory of criticism; literary criticism; research methods. **SELECTED PUBLICATIONS** Auth, On thinking about Aristotle's Thought, Critical Inquiry, spring 78; The Rebirth of Greek Tragedy and the Decline of the Humanities, Ga Rev, fall 80; A Generalized Model for Research Paper Instruction, Lit Res Newsletter, winter-spring 81; Barnardine's Nominal Nature in Measure for Measure, Papers on Lang & Lit, winter 82; ed, Teaching the Research Paper, Scarecrow Press; ed, The Foundations of Critical Plurlism, Critical Inquiry (spec ed) 96. **CONTACT ADDRESS** Dept English, Univ of Nebraska, Lincoln, Lincoln, NE 68588-0333. **EMAIL** jford@unl.edu

FORD, THOMAS WELLBORN

PERSONAL Born 12/23/1924, Houston, TX, m, 1953, 2 children **DISCIPLINE** AMERICAN LITERATURE **EDUCATION** Rice Univ, BA, 50; Univ Tex, MA, 51, PhD, 59. **CAREER** Instr, Kinkaid Prep Sch, Houston, Tex, 53-55; spec instr Eng, Univ Tex, 58-59; spec instr, Univ SC, 59-61; asst prof, 61-66; assoc prof, 66-71, PROF ENGLISH, UNIV HOUSTON, 71-. **MEMBERSHIPS** MLA; Am Studies Asn; Col English Asn; Western Lit Asn. **RESEARCH** Western Am Lit; nineteenth century and contemporary Am Lit. **SELECTED PUBLICATIONS** Auth, Emily Dickinson and the Civil War, Univ Rev, 65; Heaven Beguiles the Tired: Death in the Poetry of Emily Dickinson, Univ Ala, 66; The American rhythm: Mary Austin's poetic principle, Western Am Lit, 70; Thoreau's cosmic mosquito and Dickinson's terrestrial fly, New England Quart, 75; Whitman's Excelsior: The poem as microcosm, Tex Studies Lit & Lang, 76; A B Guthrie, Jr: A sense of place, NDak Quart, 80; Indian summer and blackberry winter: Emily Dickinson and Robert Penn Warren, Southern Rev, 81; A B Guthrie, Jr, Twayne Publ, 81. **CONTACT ADDRESS** Dept of English, Univ of Houston, Houston, TX 77004.

FOREMAN, GEORGE

DISCIPLINE MUSIC HISTORY **EDUCATION** Univ NMex, BA and MA; Univ Kan, PhD. **CAREER** Dir Bowlus Fine Arts Ctr, Iola Kan, 75; fac, Centre Col, 83-; manage dir, Jane Morton Norton Ctr Arts, present; assoc prof, Hum, present. **HONORS AND AWARDS** Bruce Montgomery Leadership award, 96; formed and directs the advocate brass band, fdr, gt am brass band festival, 90, danville. **RESEARCH** C. L. Barnhouse; American band history. **SELECTED PUBLICATIONS** Auth, pubs and articles on music history. **CONTACT ADDRESS** Centre Col, 600 W Walnut St, Danville, KY 40422. **EMAIL** foreman@centre.edu

FORKER, CHARLES RUSH

PERSONAL Born 03/11/1927, Pittsburgh, PA **DISCIPLINE** ENGLISH LITERATURE **EDUCATION** Bowdoin Col, AB, 51; Merton Col, Oxford, BA, 53, MA, 55; Harvard Univ, PhD, 57. **CAREER** Instr English, Univ Wis, 57-59; asst prof 59-63; assoc prof, 63-68, PROF ENGLISH LIT, IND UNIV, BLOOMINGTON, 68-; Fulbright Fellow, 51-53; Folger Shakespeare Libr fel, 68; Am Coun Learned Soc grant, 65-66; vis prof, Univ Mich, Ann Arbor, 68-69; Huntington Libr fel, 69; mem ed bd, Hamlet Studies and English Medieval and Renaissance Drama; auth, "Visiting Prof, Dormouth College, 82-83; Visiting Prof, Concordia Univ, Montreal, Quebec, 89; Pres., Guild of Scholars of the Episcopal Church, 93-99. **MEMBERSHIPS** MLA; Shakespeare Asn Am; Int Shakespeare Soc; Renaissance Soc Am; Malone Soc; Marlowe Society; Phi Beta Kappa. **RESEARCH** Shakespeare studies; Elizabethan drama. **SELECTED PUBLICATIONS** Auth, "Shirley's The Cordinal," ed., 64; auth, "Henry V: An Annotated Bibliography," (with J. Condido), 83; auth, "Skull Beneath the Skin: The Achievement of John Webster," 86; auth, "Fancy's Images: Contexts, Settings, and Perspectives in Shakepeare and His Contemporaries," 90; auth, "Marlowe's Edward II," ED. 94, Shakespeare: The Critical Tradition, Richard II, 98. **CONTACT ADDRESS** Dept of English, Indiana Univ, Bloomington, Bloomington, IN 47401. **EMAIL** forker@indiana.edu

FORMAN, ROBERT

PERSONAL Born 11/01/1946, New York, NY **DISCIPLINE** ENGLISH **EDUCATION** NYU, PhD, 73. **CAREER** Prof, St Johns Univ, 83-. **HONORS AND AWARDS** Faculty Outstanding Achiev Medal, 85; Prof of the Year, Eng Honor Soc, 98-99. **RESEARCH** Epic; aesthetics. **SELECTED PUBLICATIONS** Auth, Augustine and the Making of a Christian Literature, 95. **CONTACT ADDRESS** Dept English, St. John's Univ, 8000 Utopia Pkwy, Jamaica, NY 11439.

FORMAN, SANDRA
PERSONAL Born 07/09/1944, Charlotte, NC, 3 children **DISCIPLINE** THEATRE ARTS **EDUCATION** Univ NC at Greensboro, BA, 66; MFA, 71. **CAREER** Instr, Guilford Col, 69-72; from asst to assoc prof, Univ NC at Greensboro, 77-89; prof, Northern Ky Univ, 90-. **HONORS AND AWARDS** Fel, the Kennedy Ctr/American Col Theatre Festival; Ford Found Curriculum Development Project, Duke Univ. **MEMBERSHIPS** Southeastern Theatre Confr, Voice and Speech Trainers Asn, Int Hemingway Soc, Delta Kappa Gamma, Nat Commun Asn. **RESEARCH** Presentational Performance in Reader's Theatre, Chamber Theatre, Federico Garcia Lorca and Spanish Theatre, Short Fiction of Ernest Hemingway in Performance. **SELECTED PUBLICATIONS** Auth, Your Voice and Articulation, Prentice-Hall; auth, Public Speaking: Today and Tomorrow, Prentice-Hall; auth, Only Mystery: Federico Garcia Lorca's Poetry in Word and Image, Univ Press of Fla. **CONTACT ADDRESS** Dept Theatre, No Kentucky Univ, Newport, KY 41099-1007. **EMAIL** forman@nku.edu

FORNARA, CHARLES WILLIAM
PERSONAL Born 11/19/1935, New York, NY **DISCIPLINE** CLASSICS **EDUCATION** Columbia Col, AB 56; Univ Chicago, AM, 58; Univ Calif, Los Angeles, PhD, 61. **CAREER** Instr classics, Ohio State Univ, 61-63; from asst prof to prof, 63-77, Prof Class and Hist, Brown Univ, 77-. **MEMBERSHIPS** Am Philol Asn; Am Hist Asn; Am Asn Ancient Hists; Soc Promotion of Hellenic Studies. **RESEARCH** Greek history; epigraphy and historiography; late antiquity. **SELECTED PUBLICATIONS** Auth, Diodorus Siculus and the 1st Century, Classic Philol, Vol 87, 92; Studies in Ammianus Marcellinus .2. Ammianus Knowledge and Use of Greek and Latin Literature, Hist Zeitschrift Alte Geschichte, Vol 41, 92; Studies in Ammianus Marcellinus .2. Ammianus Knowledge and Use of Greek And Latin Literature, Historia Zeitschrift Alte Geschichte, Vol 41, 92. **CONTACT ADDRESS** Dept of Classics, Brown Univ, 1 Prospect St, Providence, RI 02912-9127.

FORSYTH, PHYLLIS
PERSONAL Born Boston, MA, m, 1969 **DISCIPLINE** CLASSICAL STUDIES, HISTORY, FINE ART **EDUCATION** Mount Holyoke Col, BA, 66; Univ Toronto, MA, 67, PhD, 72. **CAREER** Tchr Fel, Univ Toronto, 67-69; prof, Univ Waterloo, 69-, founding ch, dept class studs, 79-88, acting ch 94-. **HONORS AND AWARDS** Distinguished Tchr Awd. **MEMBERSHIPS** Ont Class Asn; Can Fedn Hum; Archeol Inst Am; Can Mediter Inst. **RESEARCH** The Aegean Bronze Age; Thera in the Bronze Age; Minoan Civilization; Cycladic Civilization; Volcanic Eruptions in Antiquity; Natural Caatastrophes in the Ancient World; The Myth of Atlantis; Catullus. **SELECTED PUBLICATIONS** Auth, Atlantis: The Making of Myth, 80; ed, Labyrinth: A Classical Magazine for Secondary Schs, 73-84, 88-94; auth, Thera in the Bronze Age, Peter Lang Publ, 97. **CONTACT ADDRESS** Dept of Classical Studies, Univ of Waterloo, 200 University Ave W, Waterloo, ON, Canada N2L 3G1. **EMAIL** forsyth@watarts.uwaterloo.ca

FORT, KEITH
DISCIPLINE ENGLISH LITERATURE **EDUCATION** Univ of South, BA; Univ Minn, MA, PhD. **CAREER** Prof. **SELECTED PUBLICATIONS** Auth, The Psychopathology of the Everyday Language of Literary Studies, 79; Form, Authority, and the Critical Essay, 71. **CONTACT ADDRESS** English Dept, Georgetown Univ, 37th and O St, Washington, DC 20057.

FORTE, ALLEN
PERSONAL Born 12/23/1926, Portland, OR, m, 1998 **DISCIPLINE** THEORY OF MUSIC **EDUCATION** Columbia Univ, BA, 50, MA, 52. **CAREER** Instr music, Columbia Teachers Col, 54-59; instr music theory, Mannes Col Music, 57-59; from instr to assoc prof, Yale Univ, 59-64; prof music, Mass Inst Technol, 67-68; Prof Music, Yale Univ, 68-, Battell Prof Teory of Music, 91-; Dir Grad Studies Music, 70-77; Ed, J Music Theory, 60-67; Gen Ed Composers of the 20th c Yale Univ Press, 80-. **HONORS AND AWARDS** MA, Yale Univ, 68 MUS DOC, Eastman School of Music 78; Pres, Society for Music Theory, 77-82; Fellow, American Academy of Arts and Sciences 95; Lifetime Member, Society for Music Theory, 95; Festschrift: Music Theory in Concept and Practice, 97; Wallace Berry Book Publ Awd, 97; ma, yale univ, 68. **MEMBERSHIPS** Soc for mus Theory, Am Musicol Soc. **RESEARCH** Theory of tonal music; Scenkerian analysis; 18th and 19th century music theory; early 20th cavant-garde music; formal music theory; American popular song 1920-50. **SELECTED PUBLICATIONS** Auth, "Tonal Harmony in Concept and Practice," 62; auth, "The Structure of Atonal Music," 73; auth, "The American Popular Ballard of the Golden Era, 95; auth, "The Atonal Music of Anton Webern," 98; auth, "The Structural Origin of Exact Tempi in the Brahms-Haydn Variations," Music Review May 57; auth, "Aspects of Rhythm in Webern's Atonal Music, Music Theory Spectrum, vol 2," 80; auth, "Middleground Motives in the Adagietto of Mahler's Fifth Symphony," 19th Century Music, vol. viii, 84; auth, "New Approaches to the Linear Analysis of Music," Jnl of Mus Teory vol 36, 92; auth, "The Golden Thread: Octatonic, Jnl of Mus Theory," Music Analysis vol 10 91; auth, "Concepts of Linearity in Schoenberg's Atonal Music, Jnl of Mus Theory vol 36, 92; auth, "The Golden Thread: Octatonic Music in Webern's Early Songs," Bailey ed, Webern Studies, 96; auth, "Reflections upon the Gershwin-Berg Connection," The Musical Quarterly, vol 83, 99. **CONTACT ADDRESS** Dept of Music, Yale Univ, P O Box 208310, New Haven, CT 06520. **EMAIL** allen.forte@yale.edu

FORTENBAUGH, WILLIAM WALL
PERSONAL Born 07/10/1936, Philadelphia, PA, m, 1959, 3 children **DISCIPLINE** CLASSICS **EDUCATION** Princeton Univ, BA, 58; Oxford Univ, BA, 61; Univ PA, PhD(classics), 64. **CAREER** From instr to asst prof, 64-68, assoc prof, 68-80, prof I, classics, 79-91, prof II, Rutgers Univ, 91-; Ctr Hellenic Studies jr fel, 67-68; Am Coun Learned Soc study fel & hon res fel, Univ Col, London, 72-73; Alexander von Humboldt-Stiftung res fel, Univ Heidelberg, 76-77; vis prof, Univ WA, spring 87; res fel, Netherlands Inst for advanced study, 90-91; Alexander von Humboldt-Stiftung, res fel, Univ Saarbrucken, 92; Study fel, Bogliasco Found, 99. **HONORS AND AWARDS** Phi Beta Kappa, 58; NEH, summer stipend, 67, project grants, 80-83, 84-85, 88. **MEMBERSHIPS** Am Philol Asn; Soc for Ancient Greek Philos (pres, 76-77, prog comm, 82-98). **RESEARCH** Ancient philosophy. **SELECTED PUBLICATIONS** Auth, Nicomachean Ethics 1096 b26-29, Phronesis, 66; Recent Scholarship on Aristotle's Psychology, Class World, 67; Aristotle on Emotion, Duckworth, London, NY: Barnes & Noble, 74; Quellen zur Ethik Theophrasts, Amsterdam: B R Gruener Verlag, 84; Theophrastus of Eresus: Sources for His Life, Writings, Thought & Influence, 2 vols, ed and trans with P Hughby, R Sharples, & D Gutas, Leiden: E J Brill, 92, reprinted with corrections, 93. **CONTACT ADDRESS** Dept Classics, Rutgers, The State Univ of New Jersey, New Brunswick, PO Box 270, New Brunswick, NJ 08903-0270. **EMAIL** fortenb@rci.rutgers.edu

FORTIER, JAN MARIE
PERSONAL Born 05/05/1946, Los Angeles, CA, m **DISCIPLINE** ENGLISH **EDUCATION** Univ Ore, MLS, 73; Temple Univ, PhD, 87. **CAREER** Instr, librn, Marylhurst Univ, 90-. **MEMBERSHIPS** ALA; ACRL; Asn Lit Scholar Critics. **RESEARCH** Literature of home. **CONTACT ADDRESS** 3112 SE Morrison St, Portland, OR 97214-3045. **EMAIL** jfortier@marylhurst.edu

FOSHAY, TOBY
DISCIPLINE ENGLISH LITERATURE **EDUCATION** Acadia Univ, BA, MA; Dalhousie Univ, PhD. **CAREER** Assoc prof, Univ of Victoria. **HONORS AND AWARDS** Post-dr fel(s), Calgary Inst for the Hum, 87-88; SSHRCC, 89-90; Clare Hall, Cambridge Univ, 98. **RESEARCH** Literary theory; cultural theory. **SELECTED PUBLICATIONS** Ed, Derida and Negative Theology, SUNY, 91; auth, Wyndham Lewis and the Avant-Garde: The Politics of the Intellect, McGill-Queen's, 92; contrib, Shadow of Spirit: Postmodernism and Religion, Routledge, 92; contrib, Isak Dinesen: A Reassessment of Her Work for the 1990's, Carleton Univ Press, 93; contrib, Negation, Critical Theory, and Postmodern Textuality, Kluwer, 94. **CONTACT ADDRESS** Dept of English, Univ of Victoria, PO Box 3070, Victoria, BC, Canada V8W 3W1. **EMAIL** tfoshay@uvic.ca

FOSTER, DAVID
DISCIPLINE LITERATURE, ENGLISH LITERATURE **EDUCATION** Univ Wis, PhD. **CAREER** Prof, Drake Univ. **HONORS AND AWARDS** Fulbright Senior Scholar, Univ of Muenster, Germany, 97-98. **MEMBERSHIPS** Nat coun of Teachers of english, Conf on Col Compositon and Communication, Assoc of Advanced Compsition, Assoc of Genreral and Liberal Studies. **RESEARCH** Academic litereacy development, writing, nonfiction. **SELECTED PUBLICATIONS** Auth, publ(s) on postmodernist rhet and aesthet; critiques of pedagog theory and practice; auth, A Primer for Writing Teachers: Theories, Issues, Problems, 2nd ed., revised, Heinemann Boynton/Cook, 92; auth, "In Every Drop of Dew: Imagination and the Rhetoric of Religious Assent on the English Enlightenment," Rhetorica: A J of te Hist of Rhetoric 12, (94), 293-325; auth, "Readings in the Writing Classroom," JAC: A J of Compostion Theory 17.3, (97), 325-342; auth, "The Challenge of Contingency: Process and the Turn to the Social," Post Process Theory: Beyond the Writing Process pardigm, Thomas Kent, Southern ILL Univ Press, (99); auth, "Community and Cohesion in the Writing/Reading Classroom," JAC: A J of Composition Theory 17.3, (97), 325-342; auth, "Oscar Wilde, De Profundis, and the Rhetoric of Agency," Papers in Language and Lit, vol 35, (01), 1-25; auth, "Destructive Innocence: an Essay on Race," Genre By exalmple: Writhing What We Teach, ed, David Starkey, Portsmouth, NH: Heinemann, (01), 18-28. **CONTACT ADDRESS** English Dept, Drake Univ, Des Moines, IA 50311. **EMAIL** david.foster@drake.edu

FOSTER, DONALD W.
PERSONAL Born 06/22/1950, Chicago, IL, m, 1974, 2 children **DISCIPLINE** ENGLISH **EDUCATION** Wheaton Col, BA, 72; UC Santa Barbara, PhD, 85. **CAREER** Vis lectr, 85-86, UCSB; asst prof, 86-90, assoc prof, 90-, Vassar Col. **HONORS AND AWARDS** MLA, William Riley Parker Prize, 87; Delaware Shakespeare Prize, 87; Appointed to Jean Webster Chair, Vassar Col, 91. **MEMBERSHIPS** SAA; MLA; Malone Soc. **RESEARCH** Shakespeare; renaissance lit; forensic linguistics. **SELECTED PUBLICATIONS** Auth, Elegy by W S: A Study in Attribution, Assoc Univ Press, 89; auth, Resurrecting the Author: Elizabeth Tanfield Cary, Privileging Gender in Early Modern Britain, 16th Century Stud, 93; auth, Against the Perjured Falsehood Of Your Tongues: Frances Howard on the Course of Love, Eng Lit Renaissance 24.1, 94; auth, Shaxicon Update, SNL 45.2, 95; auth, Primary culprit, NY, 96; ed, A Funeral Elegy, PMLA 111.5, Shakespeare Stud, 97; auth, A Funeral Elegy: William Shakespeare's Best Speaking Witnesses, PMLA 11.5, Shakespeare Stud, 97; auth, Ward Elliot and Ron Valenza And Then There Were None: A Response, Computers and the Humanities 30, 96; ed & intro, William Shakespeare A Funeral Elegy, The Norton Shakespeare, Norton, 97; ed & intro, Elegie Funebre par William Shakespeare, Editions Stock, 96; auth, Shaxicon and Shakespeare's Acting Career, SNL 46.3, 96; auth, The Webbing of Romeo and Juliet, Critical Essays on Shakespeare's Romeo and Juliet, Hall, 97; auth, A Romance of Electronic Scholarship, part 1: The Words, EMLS, 98. **CONTACT ADDRESS** Vassar Col, PO Box 388, Poughkeepsie, NY 12601. **EMAIL** foster@vassar.edu

FOSTER, DUDLEY E.
PERSONAL Born 10/05/1935, Orange, NJ, s **DISCIPLINE** MUSIC **EDUCATION** Univ Calif at Los Angeles, AB, 57; MA, 58; Fel Trinity Col London Trinity Col Music, 60. **CAREER** Lectr, Immaculate Heart Col, 60-63; lectr, Calif State Univ, 67-71; From asst prof to prof, Los Angeles Musician Col, 75-. **HONORS AND AWARDS** Distinguished Teaching Awd, Lost Angeles Mission Col, 94. **MEMBERSHIPS** Medieval Acad of Am, Nat Asn of Scholars. **RESEARCH** Music of the Middle Ages, French Romantic Organ Music. **SELECTED PUBLICATIONS** Auth, Passacaglia for Brast Instruments; auth, Introduction, Arioso, and Fugue for Cello and Piano. **CONTACT ADDRESS** Dept Arts & Letters, Los Angeles Mission Col, 13356 Eldridge Ave, Sylmar, CA 91342-3200.

FOSTER, EDWARD E.
PERSONAL Born 11/19/1939, West New York, NJ, m, 1966 **DISCIPLINE** ENGLISH **EDUCATION** St Peter's Col, NJ, AB, 61; Univ Rochester, PhD, 65. **CAREER** From instr to assoc prof English, Grinnell Col, 64-73; prof & dean, Col Arts & Sci, Univ San Diego, 73-76; chmn dept humanities, St Mary's Col, Md, 76-79; Prof & Dean Fac, Whitman Col, WA, 79-. **MEMBERSHIPS** MLA; Medieval Acad Am. **RESEARCH** Middle English narrative; Restoration and 18th century political and religious poetry; literary taxonomy. **SELECTED PUBLICATIONS** Coauth, A Modern Lexicon of Literary Terms, Scott, 68; Humor in The Knight's Tale, Chaucer Rev, 68; Allegorical consolation in The Book of the Duchess, Ball State Univ Forum, 70; The text of William of Palerne, Neuphilol Mitt, 73. **CONTACT ADDRESS** Whitman Col, 345 Boyer Ave, Walla Walla, WA 99362-2083. **EMAIL** fosteree@whitman.edu

FOSTER, EDWARD H.
PERSONAL Born 12/17/1942, Northampton, MS, d, 2 children **DISCIPLINE** AMERICAN LITERATURE, CONTEMPORARY LITERATURE **EDUCATION** Columbia Univ, BA, 65; MA, 66; PhD, 70. **CAREER** Vis prof, Hacettepe Univ, 78-79; vis prof, Univ Istanbul, 85-86; ed, Talisman, 88-; vis prof, Drew Univ, 90, 92, 94, 96; ed, Multicultural Rev, 91-95; pres, Talisman House 93-; ed, Jensen/Daniels, 98-; prof, Stevens Inst Tech, 85-. **HONORS AND AWARDS** Choice Awd; NEH; Fulbright Fel; NEA Fel; USIA; Greve Found; Fund for Poetry. **MEMBERSHIPS** PEN; MLA. **RESEARCH** Contemporary literature; 19th century American literature. **SELECTED PUBLICATIONS** Auth, Jack Spicer, 91; auth, William Saroyan: A Study of The Short Fiction, 91; auth, Understanding the Beats, 92; auth, Understanding the Black Mountain Poets, 95; auth, Answerable to None: Berrigan, Bronk, and the American Real, 99; auth, The Space Between Her Bed and Clock, 93; auth, The Understanding, 94; auth, All Acts Are Simply Acts, 95; auth, The Boy in the Key of E, 98; co-ed, The New Freedoms, 94; co-ed, Primary Trouble: An Anthology of Contemporary Poetry, 96; ed, Stuart Merril: Selected Works, 99; ed, Decadents, Symbolists, and Aesthetes in America: An Anthology, 00. **CONTACT ADDRESS** Dept Humanities, Stevens Inst of Tech, 1 Castle Point Terrace, Hoboken, NJ 07030-5906. **EMAIL** talismaned@aol.com

FOSTER, FRANCES SMITH
PERSONAL Born 02/08/1944, Dayton, OH, m **DISCIPLINE** AFRICAN-AMERICAN LITERATURE **EDUCATION** Miami Univ, BS, 1964; Univ of South CA, MA, 1971; Univ of CA, PhD, 1976. **CAREER** Cincinnati Public Schools, teacher, 64-66; Detroit Public Schools, teacher, 66-68; San Fernando Valley State Coll, instructor, 70-71; San Diego State Univ, asst dean, 76-79, prof, beginning 71; Univ of Calif, San Diego, prof, currently. **HONORS AND AWARDS** Ford Found Fellowship; San Diego Fellowship; Gen Motors Scholar; SDSU Outstanding Faculty Awd; numerous articles and reviews on Afro-Amer literature. **MEMBERSHIPS** Humanities Adv Council; KPBS; San Diego State Univ, Career Plan & Placemt Ctr, Adv Comm; NAACP, Coll Lang Assn; Modern Lang Assn; Philological

Assn of the Pac Coast; West Coast Women's Historical Assn; NEH Rsch Fellowship; CSU Faculty Rsch Fellowship; Phi Beta Kappa; Phi Kappa Pi; Althenoi Phi Kappa Delta; Alpha Kappa Alpha; Children's Literature Assoc; MELUS. **SELECTED PUBLICATIONS** Auth, "Changing Concepts of the Black Woman," "Charles Wright, Black Black Humorist," "The Black & White Masks of Franz Fanon & Ralph Ellison," "Witnessing Slavery, The Develop of the Ante-Bellum Slave Narrative," Greenwood Press, 1979; "Voices Unheard Stories Untold, Teaching Women's Literature from a Regional Perspective;" **CONTACT ADDRESS** Univ of California, San Diego, 9500 Gilman Dr, La Jolla, CA 92093. **EMAIL** ffoster@emory.edu

FOSTER, JOHN BURT
PERSONAL Born 12/19/1945, Chicago, IL, m, 1970, 1 child **DISCIPLINE** ENGLISH **EDUCATION** Harvard, BA, 67; Yale, PhD, 74. **CAREER** Asst prof, Stanford Univ, 72-81; assoc prof to prof, George Mason Univ, 83-. **HONORS AND AWARDS** Phi Beta Kappa, 67, Acad Exchange Fel, Univ of Koustanz, Germany, 71-72; ACLS Grant, 81-82; NEH Fel, 87, 97; Mellon Fac Fel, Harvard, 82-83. **MEMBERSHIPS** MLA; Am Comp Lit Assoc; S Comp Lit Assoc; Int Vladimir Nabokov Soc; Int Assoc for Philos and Lit. **RESEARCH** Modern fiction, comparative literature. **SELECTED PUBLICATIONS** Auth, Heirs to Dionysus: A Nietzschean Current in Literary Modernism, Princeton UP, 81; auth, Dostoevsky versus Nietzsche in the Work of Andrey Bely and Thomas Mann, Mosaic, 91; auth, Nabokov's Art of Memory and European Modernism, Princeton UP, 93; auth, "Cultural Multiplicity in Two Modern Autobiographies: Friedlander's 'When Memory Comes" and Dinesen's 'Out of Africa'", S Human Rev, 95; auth, "Magical Realism, Compensatory Vision, and Felt History: Classical Realism Transformed in The White Hotel, Magical Realism: Theory, History, Community, 95; auth, "Working with Nietzsche, Nabokov, and Tolstoy: Cultural Variables in the Literary Reception of Philosophy", REAL: The Yearbook for Res in English and Am Lit, 97; auth, "Why is Tadzio Polish? Kultur and Cultural Multiplicity in Death in Venice", Thomas Mann's Death in Venice: A Case Study in Contemporary Criticism, 98; auth, Poshlust, Culture Criticism, Adorno, and Malraux, Nabokov and His Fiction: New Perspectives, 99; auth, "Zarathustrian Millennialism Before the Millenium: From Bely to Years to Malraux", Why Nietzsche Still? Reflections on Drama, Culture, Politics, 00. **CONTACT ADDRESS** Dept English, George Mason Univ, Fairfax, 4400 University Dr, Fairfax, VA 22030-4422. **EMAIL** jfoster@gmu.edu

FOSTER, VERNA A.
DISCIPLINE ENGLISH **EDUCATION** Univ London, BA, 67, MPhil, 70, PhD, 77. **CAREER** Assoc prof; Book Review Editor, Text and Presentation Journal of the Comparative Drama Conference. **RESEARCH** Modern drama; Shakespeare; Renaissance drama; History and theory of drama; Comparative drama. **SELECTED PUBLICATIONS** Auth, Buckets o' Beckett in Chicago 1996, J Beckett Stud 5, 96; Sex, Power, and Pedagogy in Mamet's Oleanna and Ionesco's The Lesson, Am Drama 5, 95; Ibsen's Tragicomedy: The Wild Duck, Modern Drama 38, 95; A sad tale's best for winter: Storytelling and Tragicomedy in the Late Plays of Shakespeare and Beckett, in Past Crimson Past Woe: The Shakespeare-Beckett Connection, Garland Publ, Inc, 93; Sex Averted or Converted: Sexuality and Tragicomic Genre in the Plays of Fletcher, Stud in Engl Lit 32, 92; "Desire, Death, and Laughter: Tragicomic Dramaturgy in A Streetcar Named Desire," American Drama 9, (99); "Convicts, Characters, and Conventions of Acting in Timberlake Wertenbaker's Our Country's Good," Connotations 8, 99. **CONTACT ADDRESS** Dept of English, Loyola Univ, Chicago, 6525 N. Sheridan Rd., Chicago, IL 60626. **EMAIL** vfoster@wpo.it.luc.edu

FOULKE, ROBERT DANA
PERSONAL Born 04/25/1930, Minneapolis, MN, m, 1953, 3 children **DISCIPLINE** ENGLISH LITERATURE **EDUCATION** Princeton Univ, AB, 52; Univ Minn, MA, 57, PhD(English), 61. **CAREER** Teaching asst English, Univ Minn, 54-56, instr, 56-58, 60-61; from asst prof to assoc prof, Trinity Col, Conn, 61-70; prof English, 70-92 & chmn dept, 70-80, Skidmore Col; Vis prof lit criticism, NDEA Inst, Univ Minn, 65; vis prof stylistics, NDEA Inst, Macalester Col, 67; Nat Endowment Humanities Asian studies fel, 77-78. **HONORS AND AWARDS** Fulbright fel, 59-60; Asian Stud fel, Cambridge Univ, 76-77; Skidmore Col Fac Res Grant, 82-83, 85-86, 86-87, 89-90; Odysssey project grant, 86; vis fel, Princeton Univ, 88; Life mem, Claare Hall, 90-91; Alexander D Victor Fel, John Carter Brown Library , Brown Univ, 93. **MEMBERSHIPS** Mel **RESEARCH** Joseph Conrad; 19th and 20th century novel; theory of the novel; literary criticism; sea literature; maritime history. **SELECTED PUBLICATIONS** Coauth, An Anatomy of Literature, Harcourt Brace Tovanovich, 72; auth, " The Literature of Voyaging," Life in the Dying World of Sail", and " The Elegiac Structue of The Mirror of Sea, The Literature and Love of the Sea, Rodop, 86; auth " From the Center to the Dangerous Hemisphere: Heart of Darkness and Typhoon, Convedis Literary Career, Vol 1, East European Monograhs, 92; auth, Conrad and the British Merchant Service: A Case History in Maritime History and Literary Interpretation, Bermuda J of Archaeol and maritime Hist, 93; coauth, Hong Kong Dragon Boas Festival and International Races, Sea History, 96; guest ed, special ed, James Fenimore Cooper: The Birth of American Maritime Experience; Am Neptune, 97; auth, The Sea Voyage Narrative, Twayne, 97; contribur, Gidmark, ed, An Encyclopedia of American Literature of the Sea and the Great Lakes, Greenwood, forthcoming; auth, Appointed Literary Advisor for the Oxford Encyclopedia of Maritime History, forthcoming. **CONTACT ADDRESS** 25 Dark Bay Ln, Lake George, NY 12845.

FOURNIER, LUCIEN
DISCIPLINE VICTORIAN LITERATURE **EDUCATION** Univ Notre Dame, PhD. **CAREER** Assoc Prof, St. Louis Univ. **SELECTED PUBLICATIONS** Auth, The Tragic Hero in a Naturalistic World, Notre Dame Juggler 64; "Introduction" to Charles Dickens and the Seven Deadly Sins, Interstate Press, 79. **CONTACT ADDRESS** Dept of English, Saint Louis Univ, 221 N. Grand Blvd, Saint Louis, MO 63103.

FOWLER, DOREEN
PERSONAL Born 01/14/1948, Brooklyn, NY, m, 1972, 1 child **DISCIPLINE** ENGLISH **EDUCATION** Manhattanville Col, BA, 69; Brown Univ, PhD, 74. **CAREER** Asst, 70-72, Brown Univ; instr to asst prof, 74-76, Memphis St Univ; instr to assoc prof to prof, 79-97, Univ Miss; vis assoc prof, 85-86, Univ Calif Santa Barbara; vis prof to assoc prof, 94-, Univ Kan. **HONORS AND AWARDS** Grad fel, Brown Univ, 69-70, 73-74; teaching assistantship, Brown Univ, 70-71, 71-72; summer Stipend, Univ Ms, 84, 88, 90; faculty res grant, Univ Ms, 85, 87, 89. **MEMBERSHIPS** MLA; Amer Lit Assoc; Soc for Study of S Lit; Walker Percy Soc; Faulkner Soc; Eudora Welty Soc; Toni Morrison Soc; Richard Wright Soc; Carson McCullers Soc; Flannery O'Connor Soc. **RESEARCH** Lit of Amer South **SELECTED PUBLICATIONS** Auth, The Nameless Women of Go Down, Moses, Women's Stud, 93; art, I am dying: Faulkner's Hightower and the Oedipal Moment, Faulkner J 93, 94, 95; art, You Can't Beat a Woman: The Preoedipal Mother in Light in August, Faulkner J, 95, 96; art, Deconstructing Racial Difference: Flannery O'Connor's The Artificial Nigger, Flannery O'Connor Bull, 95-96; auth, Faulkner: The Return of the Repressed, Univ Press Va, 97. **CONTACT ADDRESS** Dept of English, Univ of Kansas, Lawrence, Lawrence, KS 66045. **EMAIL** dfowler@eagle.cc.ukans.edu

FOWLER, VIRGINIA C.
PERSONAL Born 03/29/1948, Lexington, KY, s **DISCIPLINE** ENGLISH **EDUCATION** Univ of Ky, BA, 69; Univ of Pittsburgh, MA, 71, PhD, 76. **CAREER** From asst prof to prof, Va Tech, 77- . **HONORS AND AWARDS** Phi Beta Kappa; Woodrow Wilson fel; NDEA fel; Sigma Tau Delta. **RESEARCH** African-Am lit, espec women's fiction. **SELECTED PUBLICATIONS** Auth, Henry James's American Girl: The Embroidery on the Canvas, 84; Nikki Giovanni, 92; Conversations With Nikki Giovanni, 92; Gloria Naylor: In Search of Sanctuary, 96. **CONTACT ADDRESS** Dept of English, Virginia Polytech Inst and State Univ, Blacksburg, VA 24061-0112. **EMAIL** vfowler@vt.edu

FOX, ALICE
PERSONAL Born 07/29/1928, Trenton, NJ, 2 children **DISCIPLINE** SIXTEENTH AND SEVENTEENTH CENTURY ENGLISH **EDUCATION** Univ Mo, AB, 50; Univ Tenn, MA, 57; Mich State Univ, PhD (English), 65. **CAREER** Instr English, Wash State Univ, 59-60; from instr to prof, Western Col, 61-74, chmn dept, 68-70; assoc prof, 74-80, PROF ENGLISH, MIAMI UNIV, 80-, Screening comt for Fulbrights to the UK, Inst Int Educ, 77-. **HONORS AND AWARDS** Outstanding Univ Woman, Miami Univ, 78. **MEMBERSHIPS** MLA; Shakespeare Asn Am; Spenser soc. **RESEARCH** Spenser; Shakespeare; seventeenth century English literature; Renaissance lyric, Virginia Woolf. **SELECTED PUBLICATIONS** Auth, Social Change in the Age of Enlightenment--Edinburgh, 1660-1760, Economic Hist Rev, Vol 48, 95; The Art of Rulership--A Study of Ancient Chinese Political Thought, J Chinese Philos, Vol 22, 95; Political Protest and Prophecy Under Henry VIII, Albion, Vol 24, 92; More, Thomas--The Search for the Inner Man, J Mod Hist, Vol 65, 93; Reflex and Reflectivity, Wuwei in the Zhuangzi, Asian Philos, Vol 6, 96; In the Mirror of Memory--Reflections on Mindfulness and Remembrance in Indian and Tibetan Buddhism, Philos East W, Vol 47, 97; Cranmer, Thomas--A Life, J Ecclesiastical Hist, Vol 48, 97; Rethinking Social History, English Society, 1570-1920, and its Interpretation, Economic Hist Rev, Vol 48, 95; The Local Origins of Modern Society--Gloucestershire, 1500-1800, Economic Hist Rev, Vol 49, 96; Popular Culture in England, C. 1500-1850, Hist, Vol 82, 97; Rumor, News and Popular Political Opinion in Elizabethan and Early Stuart England, Hist J, Vol 40, 97; Interpreting More, Thomas Utopia, J Mod Hist, Vol 65, 93; The Body, Self Cultivation, and Ki Energy, Asian Philos, Vol 6, 96. **CONTACT ADDRESS** Dept of English, Miami Univ, Oxford, OH 45056.

FOX, HUGH B.
PERSONAL Born 02/12/1932, Chicago, IL, m, 1988, 6 children **DISCIPLINE** ENGLISH AMERICAN LITERATURE **EDUCATION** Loyola Univ, Chica, BS, hum, 55, MA, 56; Univ IL, PhD, 58. **CAREER** Mich State Univ, prof, dept Am thought and lang, 68-99; Loyola Univ, Los Angeles, prof, eng, 58-68; Univ Sonora, Mexico, prof Am studies, 61. **HONORS AND AWARDS** John Carter Brown Lib fel, 58. **MEMBERSHIPS** COSMEP, founder, Bd mem, IAIP, 68-80. **RESEARCH** Contemp Am poetry; pre-Columbian trans oceanic contacts between new and old worlds in ancient times. **SELECTED PUBLICATIONS** The Gods of the Cataclysm, 76; First Fire: Central and South American Indian Poetry, 78; The Mythological Foundations of the Epic Genre: The Solar Voyage as the Hero's Journey, 96; Stairway to the sun, 96. **CONTACT ADDRESS** 815 Seymour, Lansing, MI 48906. **EMAIL** hughfox@excite.com

FOX, PAMELA
DISCIPLINE ENGLISH LITERATURE **EDUCATION** Univ Ill, BA, MA; Univ Wash, PhD. **CAREER** Eng Dept, Georgetown Univ **RESEARCH** Cultural studies; feminist theory; working class writing and culture; British social novel; popular culture; 20th century writing by women. **SELECTED PUBLICATIONS** Auth, Recasting the 'Politics of Truth': Thoughts on Class, Gender, and the Role of Intellectuals, 93; Ethel Carnie Holdsworth's 'Revolt of the Gentle': Romance and the Politics of Resistance in Working-Class Women's Writing, 93; De/Refusing the Reproduction-Resistance Circuit of Cultural Studies: A Methodology for Reading Working-Class Narrative, 94; Class Fictions: Shame and Resistance in the British Working-Class Novel, 94; auth, Recycled Trash: Gender & Anthenticity in Country Music Autobiography, 98. **CONTACT ADDRESS** English Dept, Georgetown Univ, 37th and O St, Washington, DC 20057. **EMAIL** foxp@georgetown.edu

FOX, ROBERT CHARLES
PERSONAL Born 04/17/1920, Portland, OR **DISCIPLINE** ENGLISH **EDUCATION** Univ Portland, BA, 42; Columbia Univ, MA, 47, PhD (Eng), 56. **CAREER** Instr Eng, Wayne Univ, 47-49; lectr and instr, Rutgers Univ, 50-55; from instr to assoc prof, 55-68, PROF ENGLISH, ST FRANCIS COL, NY, 68-, CHMN DEPT, 73-. **MEMBERSHIPS** MLA; Milton Soc Am; NCTE; Renaissance Soc Am. **RESEARCH** English literature of the seventeenth century; Milton; Chaucer. **SELECTED PUBLICATIONS** Auth, Experiment Perilous--45 Years as a Participant Observer of Patient Oriented Clinical Research, Perspectives in Biology and Medicine, Vol 39, 96; Parsons, Talcott, My Teacher, Am Scholar, Vol 66, 97; Les Roses Mademoiselle, The Universe of Ghelderode, Michel, De, Am Scholar, Vol 63, 94. **CONTACT ADDRESS** 175 Adams St Apt 6F, Brooklyn, NY 11201.

FOX, STEPHEN D.
PERSONAL Born 08/10/1943, Roanoke, VA **DISCIPLINE** ENGLISH **EDUCATION** Duke Univ, BA, 65; Emory Univ, MA; PhD, 70. **CAREER** Asst prof, Univ Cincinnati, 70-77; instr, Univ Okla, 77-79; instr, Univ New Orleans, 79-83; prof, Gallaudet Univ, 83-. **HONORS AND AWARDS** Emory Univ Fel, 66-68; Univ Cincinnati Fel, 75; Outstanding Teacher, 77; NEH 83, 00; Fallaudet Grant, 99, 00. **MEMBERSHIPS** MLA, Asn Lit Scholars and Critics, Am Comp Lit Asn, Int Comp Lit Asn, Southern Comp Lit Asn, Japan Studies Asn, Disability Studies Asn. **RESEARCH** Classical and modern comparative literature. **SELECTED PUBLICATIONS** Auth, "The Fish Pond as Symbolic Center in Between the Acts," Mod Fiction Studies, (72); auth, "Hemingway's The Doctor and the Doctor's Wife," Ariz Quart, (73); auth, "An Unwritten Novel and a Hidden Protagonist," Virginia Woolf Quart, (80); auth, "The Use of Metacognitive Techniques in a College Literature Course," Am Annals of the Deaf, (94); auth, "Edwin Morgan: Poetry in the Closet," Jour of Evolutionary Psych, (01); auth, "Edwin Morgan and the Two Cultures," Studies in Scottish Lit, (01). **CONTACT ADDRESS** Dept English, Gallaudet Univ, 800 Florida Ave NE, Washington, DC 20002. **EMAIL** stephen.fox@gallaudet.edu

FRADENBURG, L. O. ARANYE
DISCIPLINE MEDIEVAL ENGLISH AND SCOTTISH LITERATURE **EDUCATION** Univ Va, Phd, 82. **CAREER** Prof, Eng, Univ Calif, Santa Barbara. **RESEARCH** Crit theory; Gender and sexualities. **SELECTED PUBLICATIONS** Auth, City, Marriage, Tournament: Arts of Rule in Late Medieval Scotland, Univ Wis Press, 91; ed, Women of Sovereignty, Univ Edinburgh Press, 92; pub(s), articles on Chaucer, Dunbar, Henryson, and on psychoanalysis and medieval studies; co-ed, Premodern Sexualities, Routledge, 96; auth, Sacrifice Your Love: Psychoanalysis, Historicism, Chaucer, Univ Minn Press (forthcoming). **CONTACT ADDRESS** Dept of Eng, Univ of California, Santa Barbara, Santa Barbara, CA 93106-7150. **EMAIL** lfraden@humanitas.ucsb.edu

FRAISTAT, NEIL R.
PERSONAL Born 04/19/1952, Bronx, NY, s, 2 children **DISCIPLINE** ENGLISH **EDUCATION** Univ Conn, BA, 74; Univ Pa, MA, 76; PhD, 79. **CAREER** Asst Prof to Full Prof, Univ Md, 79-. **HONORS AND AWARDS** Fredson Bowers Memorial Prize, Soc for Textual Scholarship, 94; Fel Univ Teachers; NEH, 90; Fel, Am Coun Learned Soc; Fel, Huntington Libr, 81, Who's Who in Am. **SELECTED PUBLICATIONS** Auth, The Poem and the Book, 85; ed, Poems in Their Place, 86; auth, The 'Prometheus Unbound' Notebooks, 91; auth, The Complete Poetry of Percy Bysshe Shelley, 99. **CONTACT ADDRESS** Dept English, Univ of Maryland, Col Park, 3101 Susquehanna Hall, College Park, MD 20742-8800. **EMAIL** nf5@umail.umd.edu

FRALEIGH, DOUGLAS
DISCIPLINE COMMUNICATION, ARGUMENTATION, FREEDOM OF SPEECH **EDUCATION** Univ CA, Berkeley, JD. **CAREER** Instr, dir, Forensics, CA State Univ. **MEMBERSHIPS** Pres, WSCA Freedom of Speech Interest Gp; exec coun, CEDA. **SELECTED PUBLICATIONS** Coauth, Freedom of Speech in the Marketplace of Ideas, St Martin's Press, 97. **CONTACT ADDRESS** California State Univ, Fresno, Fresno, CA 93740.

FRANCESE, JOSEPH
PERSONAL Born 09/05/1955, Westerly, RI, m, 1979, 2 children **DISCIPLINE** ITALIAN LITERATURE, AMERICAN LITERATURE **EDUCATION** Univ RI, BA, 77; Univ Rome, LL, 81; Univ Ct, PhD, 90. **CAREER** From Asst Prof to Prof, Mich St Univ, 90-. **HONORS AND AWARDS** NEH Summer Fel, Mich St Univ, 94; Global Competence Grant, Mich St Univ, 95; Int Activities Res Grant, Midwest Univs Consortium, 95, 97. **MEMBERSHIPS** MLA, ACLA, AATI, AAIS, IGS. **RESEARCH** 16th and 20th Century Italian literature, contemporary American literature. **SELECTED PUBLICATIONS** Auth, Il realismo impopolare de Pier Paolo Pasolini, Bastogi Editrice Ital (Foggia), 91; auth, Narrating Postmodern Time and Space, St Univ NY Pr (Albany, NY), 97; auth, Cultura e politica negli anni Cinquanta. Salinari Pasolini Calvino, Lithos Editrice (Rome, Italy), 00; ed, "The Critic and His Craft: Essays in Memory of Glauco Cambon, Bordighera Pr (00). **CONTACT ADDRESS** Dept Lang, Michigan State Univ, East Lansing, MI 48824-1112.

FRANCO, JEAN
PERSONAL Born 03/31/1924, Dukinfield, England **DISCIPLINE** LITERATURE **EDUCATION** Univ Manchester, BA, 44, MA, 46; Univ London, BA, 60, PhD (Span), 64. **CAREER** Lectr Span, Queen Mary Col, Univ London, 60-64, reader, King's Col, 64-68; prof lit, Univ Essex, 68-72; Prof Span and Comp Lit, Standard Univ, 72-, Guggenheim fel, 76-77. **MEMBERSHIPS** MLA; Latin Am Studies Asn. **RESEARCH** Latin Am Lit and society; poetry; social theories of literature. **SELECTED PUBLICATIONS CONTACT ADDRESS** Dept of Span and Port, Stanford Univ, Stanford, CA 94305.

FRANCOZ, MARION
PERSONAL Born 03/20/1944, London, England, m, 1970, 1 child **DISCIPLINE** ENGLISH **EDUCATION** Sonoma State Univ, BA, 72; Sonoma State Univ, MA, 73; San Francisco State Univ, MA, 80; Univ Calif, MA, 95. **CAREER** Prof, Napa Valley Col, 73. **HONORS AND AWARDS** Fellow of the Bay Area Writing Project. **MEMBERSHIPS** NCTE; MLA; NCA (National Communication Assoc). **RESEARCH** The Connections between sneaking, writing, and memory; Joseph Conrad's short fiction; The connection betwwwn habit and . **SELECTED PUBLICATIONS** Auth, "Habit as Memory Incarnate," College English, Seno, 99; auth, "The Interview as a Model of Collaboration," Teaching English in the Two/year College, oct 86; auth, "Holography: A New Kind of Perception, New Orleans Review, Winter 81; auth, "Writing as Inquiry," College English, Nov 79. **CONTACT ADDRESS** Dept Fine & Performing Arts, Napa Valley Col, 2277 Napa Vallejo Highway, Napa, CA 94558-6236. **EMAIL** mjfrancoz@yahoo.com

FRANK, DAVID A.
PERSONAL Born 03/23/1955, Topeka, KS, m, 1988, 2 children **DISCIPLINE** RHETORIC **EDUCATION** Western Washington Univ, BA, 78, MA, 79; Univ Oregon, PhD, 83. **CAREER** Grad asst, Western Washington Univ, 79-80; grad tchg fel,Univ Ore, 79-81, instr, 81, asst prof, 82, assoc prof, 88-. **HONORS AND AWARDS** Grad tchg fel awd for outstanding tchg, 91. **MEMBERSHIPS** Natl Commun Asn; Rhetoric Soc of Am. **RESEARCH** Israeli-Palestinian rhetoric; rhetorical theory and the new Rhetoric Project. **SELECTED PUBLICATIONS** Coauth, Lincoln-Douglas Debate, Natl Textbook, 93; auth, Debate as Rhetorical Scholarship, in CEDA 1991: 20th Anniversary Conference Proceedings, 93; auth, On the Study of Ancient Chinese Rhetoric, in Western J of Commun, 93; auth, Creative Speaking, Natl Textbook, 94; coauth, NonPolicy Debate, Gorsuch Scarisbrick, 94; auth, My Enemy's Enemy is My Friend: Palestinian Rhetoric and the Gulf Crisis, in Commun Stud, 95; auth, Diversity and the Public Space: A Response to Stepp, in Argumentation and Advocacy, 97; auth, The New Rhetoric, Judaism, and Post-Enlightenment Thought: The Cultural Origins of Perelmanian Philosophy, in Q J of Speech, 97; auth, A New Forensics for a New Millennium, in The Forensics, 97; auth, Dialectical Rapprochement in the New Rhetoric, in Argumentation and Advocacy, 98. **CONTACT ADDRESS** Robert D Clark Honors Col, Univ of Oregon, Eugene, OR 97403. **EMAIL** dfrank@oregon.uoregon.edu

FRANK, JOSEPH
PERSONAL Born 12/20/1916, Chicago, IL, m, 1946, 3 children **DISCIPLINE** ENGLISH **EDUCATION** Harvard Univ, BA, 39, MA, 47, PhD (English), 53. **CAREER** From instr to prof English, Univ Rochester, 48-67; prof and chmn dept, Univ NMex, 67-69; head dept, 69-75, PROF ENGLISH, UNIV MASS, AMHERST, 69-, Huntington fel, 55-56; Guggenheim fels, 58-59, 61; Folger Shakespeare libr fel, 61-62; assoc ed, Seventeenth Century News, 61-69; consult, Univ Fla, City Col New York, Roger Williams, Ft Lewis and Mass Community Cols, 68-72; vis prof, Univ Kent, 76-77. **MEMBERSHIPS** MLA; Asn Depts English (pres, 69). **RESEARCH** Pedagogy; modern drama; seventeenth century literature. **SELECTED PUBLICATIONS** Auth, The Levellers, 55 & Beginnings of the English Newspaper, 61, Harvard Univ, Literature from the Bible, 63 & Modern Essays in English, 66, Little; Hobbled Pegasus, Univ NMex, 68; ed, You, Harcourt, 72; The Doomed Astronaut, Winthrop, 72; Milton Without Footnotes, Harper, 75. **CONTACT ADDRESS** Dept of English, Univ of Massachusetts, Amherst, Amherst, MA 01002.

FRANK, MORTIMER HENRY
PERSONAL Born 01/14/1933, New York, NY, m, 1961, 1 child **DISCIPLINE** ENGLISH, MUSICOLOGY **EDUCATION** New York Univ, AB, 54, MA, 58, PhD (English), 68. **CAREER** Instr English, New York Univ, 62-65; from instr to assoc prof, 65-74, PROF ENGLISH, BRONX COMMUNITY COL, 74-, Fac res fel, State Univ NY, 73 and 74; producer, Rare Recordings, broadcast by WFUY, 75-; music ed, 17th Century News, 78- and Class Record, Chron Higher Educ, 78-80; cur, Toscanini Collection, Wave Hill, 81-. **MEMBERSHIPS** MLA; Northeast Mod Lang Asn. **RESEARCH** Am Lit; 17th century poetry; relationship between poetry and music. **SELECTED PUBLICATIONS** Auth, Mencken on music, Carnegie Hall Mag, 1/66; In praise of Huneker, Univ Windsor Rev, fall 73; ed, Huneker on Music, John Colet, 74; auth, Karayan's third Beethoven cycle: A legacy for future generations, Fanfare, 3/78; George Hebert's Deniall: Poetry as pure music, Sci, Technol & the Humanities, fall 78; John Milton's Knowledge of Music: Some Speculations, Univ Wis, 79; Ezra Pound's Musical Excursions, Univ Windsor Rev, 80; Leonard Blinsten's Beethoven cycle: A triumph of talent, torte, and technology, 5/81 & A retrospective, 9/81, Fanfare; articles in 17th Century News & Listen: Music monthly. **CONTACT ADDRESS** Dept of English, Bronx Comm Col, CUNY, 181st St and University Ave, Bronx, NY 10453.

FRANK, ROBERT
DISCIPLINE ENGLISH ROMANTICS **EDUCATION** St. John's Univ, BA, 62; Univ Minn, MA, 68, PhD, 69. **CAREER** Engl, Oregon St Univ. **RESEARCH** Greek myth; poetry, nw lit. **SELECTED PUBLICATIONS** Auth, Don't Call Me Gentle Charles: A Reading of Lamb's Essays of Elia. Corvallis: Ore State Univ Press, 76; The Pacific Northewst: A Region in Myth and Reality. Ore State Univ Press, 83; The Grains or Passages in the Life of Ruth Rover, with Occasional Pictures of Oregon, Natural and Moral, Ore State Univ Press, 86; The Line in Postmodern Poetry, Univ Ill Press, 88; ed, Northwest Reprint Series, Oregon State Univ Press; ed, Northwest Readers Series, Oregon State Univ Press. **CONTACT ADDRESS** Oregon State Univ, Corvallis, OR 97331-4501. **EMAIL** rfrank@orst.edu

FRANK, ROBERTA
DISCIPLINE ENGLISH **EDUCATION** New York Univ, BA, 62, Harvard Univ MA, 64, PhD, 68. **CAREER** Asst prof, 68-73, assoc prof, 73-78, Prof English & Ctr Medieval Studs, Univ Toronto, 78-. **HONORS AND AWARDS** Bowdoin Prize Hum, Harvard Univ, 68; Elliott Prize, Medieval Acad Am, 72. **MEMBERSHIPS** Fel, Royal Soc Can; Asn Advan Scand Studs Can; Medieval Acad Am; Int Saga Soc; MLA. **SELECTED PUBLICATIONS** Auth, Old Norse Court Poetry: The Drv. of Toronto, 78; auth, Old Norse Memorial Eulogies and the Ending of Beowulf, in ACTA, 79; auth, Did Anglo-Saxon Audiences Have a Skaldic Tooth?, in Scand Studs, 87; auth, On a Changing Field: Medieval Studies in the New World, in S African J Medieval and Renaissance Studs, 94. **CONTACT ADDRESS** Dept of English & Ctr Medieval Studies, Univ of Toronto, Toronto, ON, Canada M5S 1A1. **EMAIL** rfrank@chass.utoronto.ca

FRANKLIN, BENJAMIN
PERSONAL Born 09/10/1939, Gallipolis, OH, m, 1962, 2 children **DISCIPLINE** AMERICAN LITERATURE **EDUCATION** Ohio State Univ, BA and BS, 65; Ohio Univ, MA, 66, PhD (English), 69. **CAREER** Asst prof English, Univ Mich, Ann Arbor, 69-76; assoc prof, 76-81, PROF ENGLISH, UNIV SC, 81-, Fulbright lectr, Univ Athens, Greece, 82-84; ed, Camden House, Inc; vis prof, Univ of Helsinki, Finland, 95. **HONORS AND AWARDS** Louis I Bredvold Award, Univ Mich, 75. **SELECTED PUBLICATIONS** Auth, Brown, Goodman and the Puritan Catechism, Esq J Am Renaissance, Vol 40, 94; auth, Advertisements for Herself--The Anais Nin Press, Papers Bibliog Soc Am, Vol 91, 97; auth, "Identity of L.H., Amender of John Cotton's Milk for Babes," Resources for American Literary Study, vol 25 (99): 159-173; auth, "Adventures in the Skins Trade, or The Enigma of White Stains," Bulletin of the Bibliographical Society of Australia and New Zealand, vol 24 (00): 106-15; auth, "Noli Me Tangere: The Structure of Anais Nin's Under a Glass Bell Studies in Short Fiction, vol 34 (97): 459-79; auth, "The Selling of A Spy in The House of Love," in Anais Nin" Literary Perspectives, ed. Suzanne Nalbantian (London: Macmillan, New York: St. Martin's, 97), 254-77. **CONTACT ADDRESS** Dept of English, Univ of So Carolina, Columbia, Columbia, SC 29208.

FRANKLIN, H. BRUCE
PERSONAL Born 02/28/1934, Brooklyn, NY, m, 1956, 3 children **DISCIPLINE** ENGLISH & AMERICAN STUDIES **EDUCATION** Amherst Col, BA, 55; Stanford Univ, PhD, 61. **CAREER** Asst prof English & Am lit, Stanford Univ, 61-64; asst prof English, Johns Hopkins Univ, 64-65; assoc prof, Stanford Univ, 65-72; vis fel, Ctr for Humanities, Wesleyan Univ, 74; prof English & Am stud, Rutgers Univ, Newark, 75-. **HONORS AND AWARDS** Alexander Cappon Prize, 78; Eaton Awd, 81; bd adv eds, ser wkg papers hist sys, nat, and peoples, 98- ; adv bd, viet nam gen, 94-; script consult, sugarloaf films, 93; pres, melville soc, 93. **MEMBERSHIPS** MLA; ASA. **RESEARCH** Literature and society; American literature; science fiction; Vietnam War. **SELECTED PUBLICATIONS** Auth, The Wake of the Gods: Melvilles Mythology, Stanford Univ, 63; Back Where You Came From: A Life in the Death of the Empire, Harper, 75; The Victim as Criminal and Artist: Literature from the American Prison, 78 & Robert A Heinlein: America as Science Fiction, Oxford Univ, 80; Prison Literature in America, Lawrence Hill, 82; ed, Countdown to Midnight, New Am Libr, 84; co-ed, Vietnam and America, Grove/Atlantic, 85,95; auth, War Stars: The Superweapon and the American Imagination, Oxford Univ, 90; ed, The Vietnam War in American Stories, Songs, and Poems, Bedford Books, 96; ed, Prison Writing in 20th Century America, Penguin, 98; auth, Vietnam and Other American Fantasies, Vair Mass, 00. **CONTACT ADDRESS** Dept of English, Rutgers, The State Univ of New Jersey, Newark, 180 University Ave, Newark, NJ 07102-1897. **EMAIL** hbf@andromeda.rutgers.edu

FRANKLIN, JAMES L.
PERSONAL Born 07/19/1947, Dayton, OH, s **DISCIPLINE** CLASSICS **EDUCATION** Denison Univ, BA, 69; Queen's Univ, MA, 70; Duke Univ, PhD, 75. **CAREER** Asst Prof, Columbia Univ, 75-76; Asst Prof, Wellesley Col, 76-77; Vis Asst Prof, Univ Mich, 77-80; From Asst Prof to Prof, Ind Univ, 81-. **HONORS AND AWARDS** Phi Beta Kappa, 69; Fel, Am Acad of Rome, 73-75; ACLS Grand-in-Aid, 76; NEH Category B Fel, 80-81; Amoco Found Distinguished Teaching Awd, 87. **MEMBERSHIPS** APA, Am Soc of Greek and Latin Epigraphy, Archaeol Inst of Am, Asn Int d'Epigraphie Grecque et Latine, Class Asn of the Middle East and S. **RESEARCH** Pompeian studies, Roman archaeology, Latin literature. **SELECTED PUBLICATIONS** Auth, Games and a Lupanar: Prosopography of a Neighborhood in Ancient Pompeii," Class J 81 (86): 319-328; auth, "Pantomimists at Pompeii: Actius Anicetus and his Troupe," Am J of Philol 108 (87): 95-107; auth, "Literacy and the Parietal Inscriptions of Ancient Pompeii," J of Roman Archaeol (91): 77-98; auth, "Cn. Alleius Nigidius Maius and the Amphitheatre: Munera and a Distinguished Career at Ancient Pompeii," Historia 46 (97): 434-447; auth, Pompeis Difficile Est: Studies in the Political Life of Imperial Pompeii, Ann Arbor, 99; auth, "Aulus Vettius Caprasius Felix of Ancient Pompeii," Qui Miscuit Utile cum Dulci, (98), 165-175. **CONTACT ADDRESS** Dept Classical Studies, Indiana Univ, Bloomington, 1020 E Kirkwood Ave, Bloomington, IN 47405-7103. **EMAIL** franklin@indiana.edu

FRANKLIN, PHYLLIS
PERSONAL Born New York, NY **DISCIPLINE** AMERICAN REALISM **EDUCATION** Vassar Col, AB, 54; Univ Miami, MA, 65, PhD (English), 69. **CAREER** Teaching asst English, Univ Miami, 65, asst prof, 69-76, assoc prof, 76-81; Dir English Progs and Asn, Dept English, Mod Lang Asn, 81-85, Executive Dir, Mod Lang Asn, 85-; Nat Endowment for Humanities summer stipend. **HONORS AND AWARDS** Florence Howe Awd for feminist criticism, Women's Caucus Mod Lang, 74. **MEMBERSHIPS** MLA; Women's Caucus Mod Lang (vpres, 76-78); Women's Studies Asn. **RESEARCH** American literary realism, Robert Herrick; women's studies; history of English studies in American higher education. **SELECTED PUBLICATIONS** Auth, A History of Western Musical Aesthetics, Mus Times, Vol 134, 93; Schumann Manfred, Mus Times, Vol 135, 94; Blake Violin Concerto, Mus Times, Vol 134, 93; Undertones of Insurrection--Music, Politics and the Social Sphere in the Modern German Narrative, Mus Times, Vol 135, 94; A Mass for the Masses--Proceedings o te Mahler Eight Symposium, Amsterdam 1988, Mus Letters, Vol 75, 94; Schreker, Franz, 1878-1934--A Cultural Biography, Opera, Vol 44, 93; A History of Music Aesthetics, Mus Times, Vol 134, 93; Contemplating Music--Source Readings in the Aesthetics of Music, Vol 3, Essence, Mus Times, Vol 134, 93; Mendelssohn Die Hochzeit des Camacho, Mus Times, Vol 135, 94; Hoffmann, Eta Undine, Mus Times, Vol 135, 94; Mahler Sixth Symphony--A Study in Musical Semiotics, Mus Letters, Vol 78, 97; Musicology and Difference--Gender and Sexuality in Music Scholarship, Mus Letters, Vol 76, 95; Mahler--A Musical Physiognomy, Mus Times, Vol 134, 93; The Music of Pfitzner, Hans, Mus Letters, Vol 74, 93; Report of the Executive Director, PMLA Publications of the Mod Lan Assoc Am, Vol 110, 95; Fragment or Completion--Proceedings of the Mahler Tenth Symposium, Utrecht, 1986, Mus Letters, Vol 75, 94; Schmidt, Franz 1874-1939--A Discussion of his Style with Special Reference to the 4 Symphonies and Das Buch Mit Sieben Siegeln, Mus Letters, Vol 74, 93; Adorno Aesthetics of Music, Mus Times, Vol 135, 94; Strauss, Richard and his World, Mus Times, Vol 134, 93; Report of the Executive Director, PMLA Pubs Mod Lan Assoc Am, Vol 112, 97; Strauss, Richard--New

Perspectives on the Composer and his Work, Mus Times, Vol 134, 93; Report of the Executive Director, PMLA Pubs Mod Lan Asso Am, Vol 111, 96; Light in Battle with Darkness, Mus Letters, Vol 74, 93; Ullmann Piano Concerto, Variations Op.5, Second Symphony, Mus Times, Vol 134, 93; Mason Playing Away, Mus Times, Vol 135, 94; Schumann Genoveva, Mus Times, Vol 135, 94; Strauss Also Sprach Zarathustra, Mus Times, Vol 134, 93. **CONTACT ADDRESS** Modern Language Association, 26 Broadway, 3rd Floor, New York, NY 10004-1789.

FRANKLIN, RALPH WILLIAM
PERSONAL Born 08/20/1937, Ojus, FL **DISCIPLINE** ENGLISH, BIBLIOGRAPHY **EDUCATION** Univ Puget Sound, BA, 59; Northwestern Univ, MA, 60, PhD (Am lit), 65; Univ Chicago, MA, 68. **CAREER** Asst prof English, Univ Wis, 64-66; asst prof and cur Abernethy Libr, Middlebury Col, 68-70; asst chief tech serv and develop, Wash State Libr, 70-71; asst prof and dean students, Grad Libr Sch, Univ Chicago, 71-74; bibliog syst consult, Wash State Libr, 74-76; from assoc prof to prof and dir libr, Whitworth Col, 77-82; LIBRN, BEINECKE RARE BK and MANUSCRIPT LIBR, YALE UNIV, 82-, Consult, Wash State Libr, 71-74; Nat Endowment for Humanities grant, 78; Guggenheim fel, 80-81. **MEMBERSHIPS** Asn Col and Res Libr; Am Libr Asn; Bibliog Soc Am. **RESEARCH** Emily Dickinson; bibliography and textual criticism. **SELECTED PUBLICATIONS** Auth, Housman's Shropshire, Mod Lang Quart, 63; The Editing of Emily Dickinson, Univ Wis, 67; The narrative management of As I Lay Dying, Mod Fiction Studies, 67; Conjectures on rarity, Libr Quart, 74; Two Emily Dickinson manuscripts, Papers Bibliog Soc Am, 75; Three additional Dickinson manuscripts, Am Lit, 78; The Manuscript Books of Emily Dickenson, Belknap/Harvard Univ, 81; The Emily Dickenson fascicles, Studies in Bibliog, 82. **CONTACT ADDRESS** Beinecke Rare Bk and Manuscript Libr, Yale Sta, PO Box 1603A, New Haven, CT 06520.

FRANKLIN, ROSEMARY F.
PERSONAL Born 04/15/1941, Birmingham, AL, m, 1975 **DISCIPLINE** ENGLISH **EDUCATION** Birmingham Southern Col, AB, 63; Wake Forest Univ, MA, 64; Emory Univ, PhD, 68. **CAREER** Asst Prof, Ga State Univ, 67-83; Asst to Assoc Prof, Univ of GA, 83-. **HONORS AND AWARDS** Phi Beta Kappa; Sandy Beaver Assoc Prof of English; Humanities Center Fel. **MEMBERSHIPS** MLA; South Atlantic MLA; Hawthorne Soc; Melville Soc; Soc for the Study of Southern Lit. **RESEARCH** Am Lit; Lit by Am women writers. **SELECTED PUBLICATIONS** Auth, Edna as Psyche: The Self and the Unconscious, Approaches to Tchg Chopin's The Awakening, MLA, 88; An Index to Henry James's Prefaces to the New York Edition, Univ of Va Bibliographical Soc, 66; The Awakening and the Failure of Psyche, Am Lit, 84; The Minister's Black Veil: A Parable, Am Transcendental Quart, 85; Poe and Chopin's Awakening, Miss Quart, 94; Oates's Romantic Love Stories and Kristeva, South Atlantic Rev, 98. **CONTACT ADDRESS** Dept of English, Univ of Georgia, Park Hall, Athens, GA 30602. **EMAIL** franklin@arches.uga.edu

FRANKLIN, WAYNE S.
PERSONAL Born 07/28/1945 **DISCIPLINE** AMERICAN LITERATURE **EDUCATION** Union Col, BA, 67; Pittsburgh, MA, 68, PhD, 72. **CAREER** Davis dist prof, Am Lit, Northwestern Univ. **MEMBERSHIPS** Am Antiquarian Soc. **RESEARCH** James Fenimore Cooper. **SELECTED PUBLICATIONS** Auth, Discoverers, Explorers, Settlers, Univ Chicago Press, 79; auth, The New World of James Fenimore Cooper, Univ Chicago Press, 82; auth, A Rural Carpenter's World, Univ Iowa Press, 90; co-ed, Mapping American Culture, Univ Iowa Press, 92; auth, American Voices, American Lives: A Documentary Reader, WW Norton, 97. **CONTACT ADDRESS** Northeastern Univ, 406 Holmes Hall, Boston, MA 02115. **EMAIL** w.s.franklin@worldnet.att.net

FRANSON, J. KARL
PERSONAL Born 11/18/1941, Coalville, UT, m, 1965, 8 children **DISCIPLINE** ENGLISH LITERATURE **EDUCATION** Brigham Young Univ, BA, 66, MA, 69; Univ Ill, Urbana, PhD (English), 72. **CAREER** Asst prof English, Ark State Univ, 72-75; asst prof, 75-77, assoc prof, 77-82; Prof English, Univ Maine Farmington, 82-. **HONORS AND AWARDS** Distinguished scholar, Univ of Maine Farmington, 88; Arkansas State Univ, Fac Res Com.; Univ of Maine Farmington, Experimental Studies Council (5 grants); Teaching Effectiveness Comt; Ctr for Human Development: Service-Learning Comt. **RESEARCH** Renaissance; Romantics. **SELECTED PUBLICATIONS** Auth, Christ on the Pinnacle, Milton Quarterly 10: 48-53; auth, Serpent-Driving Females in Blake's, Comus 4 Blake: An Illustrated Quarterly, 12: 164-77; By His Own Independent Power, Milton Quarterly 14: 55-60; auth, The Fatal Voyage of Edward King, Milton Studies 25: 46-67; auth, Numbers in Shakespeare's Dedications to Venus and Adonis and The Rape of Lucrece, Notes and Queries ns 38: 51-54; auth, From Vanity Fair to Emerald City: Baum's Debt to Bunyan, Children's Literature 23: 91-114; auth, Too soon marr'd: Juliet's Age as Symbol in Romeo and Juliet, Papers on Language & Literature 32: 244-62; auth, His volant touch: Milton and the Golden Section, Milton Studies 34: 117-35; ed, Milton Reconsidered, Univ of Salzburg Press, 76; coauth, Structure and Meaning: An Introduction to Literature, Houghton Mifflin, 1976, 2nd ed. Rev., 82. **CONTACT ADDRESS** Dept of Humanities, Univ of Maine, Farmington, Farmington, ME 04938. **EMAIL** franson@maine.edu

FRANTZ, DAVID OSWIN
PERSONAL Born 08/16/1942, Lancaster, PA, m, 1970, 2 children **DISCIPLINE** RENAISSANCE LITERATURE **EDUCATION** Princeton Univ, BA, 64; Univ Mich, MA, 65; Univ Pa, PhD, 68. **CAREER** Asst prof, 68-75, assoc prof to prof Eng, Ohio State Univ, 75-. **HONORS AND AWARDS** Phi Beta Kappa **MEMBERSHIPS** Renaissance Soc Am; MLA; Mediaeval Acad Am; Dict Soc N Am. **RESEARCH** Renaissance. **SELECTED PUBLICATIONS** Auth, The Union of Florine and Marinelll: The Triumph of Hearing, Spenser Studies, 86; auth, Festum Voluptatis: A Study of RennaissanceErotica, OSU Press, 89; art, Negotiating Florio's A Worlde of Words, Dictionaires 18, 97; auth, Florio's Worlde of Wordes: A Bridge Between Cultures, Jtaliana, 99 . **CONTACT ADDRESS** Dept of English, Ohio State Univ, Columbus, 164 W 17th Ave, Columbus, OH 43210-1326. **EMAIL** frantz.1@osu.edu

FRANTZEN, ALLEN J.
DISCIPLINE ENGLISH **EDUCATION** Loras Col, BA, 69; Univ Va, MA, 73, PhD, 76. **CAREER** Prof; dir, Loyola Literacy Center; co-ch, Medieval Stud Comt; exec secy, Ill Medieval Asn. **HONORS AND AWARDS** Guggenheim Fel, 94; Nat Endowment for Hum Fel, 90-91; Rockefeller Found Fel, 00. **MEMBERSHIPS** MLA; Medieval Academy of Am; International Soc of Anglo-Saxonists. **RESEARCH** Old and Middle English lit; literary hist; hist of sexuality; gay and lesbian Stud; literary theory and criticism; textual criticism; First World War. **SELECTED PUBLICATIONS** Auth, Desire for Origins: New Language, Old English, and Teaching the Tradition, Rutgers UP, 90; The Disclosure of Sodomy in the Middle English Cleanness, PMLA 111, 96; Co-ed, Anglo-Saxonism and the Construction of Soc Identity, UP Fla, 97; auth, Before the Closet: Same-Sex Love from "Beowulf" to "Angels in America", U of Chicago Press, 98. **CONTACT ADDRESS** Dept of English, Loyola Univ, Chicago, 6525 N. Sheridan Rd., Chicago, IL 60626. **EMAIL** afrantz@luc.edu

FRAZER, JUNE
DISCIPLINE NINETEENTH AND TWENTIETH CENTURY BRITISH LITERATURE **EDUCATION** Stetson Univ , BA, 56; Univ N C Chapel Hill, MA, 58; PhD, 64. **CAREER** Prof, Western Ill Univ. **RESEARCH** Women's Literature, and Literary Criticism. **SELECTED PUBLICATIONS** . **CONTACT ADDRESS** Western Illinois Univ, 1 University Circle, Macomb, IL 61455.

FRAZER, TIMOTHY C.
PERSONAL Born 07/11/1941, Sterling, IL, m, 1970, 4 children **DISCIPLINE** ENGLISH LANGUAGE, LINGUISTICS **EDUCATION** Univ Chicago, MA, 61, PhD, 73; Western IL Univ, BS, 67. **CAREER** Asst prof to prof, Western IL Univ, 72-. **HONORS AND AWARDS** NEH Summer Fel, 83, 87. **MEMBERSHIPS** Ling Soc of Am; Am Dialect Soc; Am Names Soc. **RESEARCH** American Dialects, Spanish in the USA. **SELECTED PUBLICATIONS** Auth, "South Midland Pronunciation in the North Central States", Dialect and Language Variation, ed Harold B Allen and Michael D Linn, Acad Pr, (London, 86): 142-150; auth, "Microdialectology" Am Speech 61.3 (86): 307-17; auth, "Attitudes Toward Regional Pronunciation", J of English Ling 20, (87): 89-100; auth, Midland Illinois Dialect Patterns, Univ of Ala Pr, (Tuscaloosa), 87; auth, "More on the Semantics of A-Prefixing", Am Speech 65.1 (90): 89-93; auth, "The Language of Yankee Cultural Imperialism", Heartland English, (93): 59-66; auth, "Problems in Midwest English, Heartland English, (93): 1-19; ed, Heartland English, Univ of Ala Pr, 93; auth, "Perception and Gender in Virginia Speech: the Case of /aw/", Am Speech 69.2 (94): 145-154; auth, "The Dialects of the Middle West", Focus on the USA, ed Edgar Schneider, John Benjamins, (Amsterdam, 96): 81-102. **CONTACT ADDRESS** Dept English and Jour, Western Illinois Univ, 1 University Circle, Macomb, IL 61455-1367. **EMAIL** mftcf@wiu.edu

FRAZIER, LETA J.
PERSONAL Born, IL, m, 1958, 2 children **DISCIPLINE** COMMUNICATION **EDUCATION** Tn Temple Col, BA, 59; Univ Tn, MAT, 61; Univ Mn, MA, 80, PhD, 88. **CAREER** Instr, 74-78, Crown Col; instr, 78-82, Normandale Commun Col; chair, prof, 83-, Bethel Col. **HONORS AND AWARDS** Phi Kappa Phi; faculty develop coordinator, dir, grad program, bethel col; consultant in org commun. **MEMBERSHIPS** Nat Commun Assoc; Assoc for Supervision & Curric Devel. **RESEARCH** Family commun; cross cultural & gender; curric develop. **CONTACT ADDRESS** Bethel Dr, PO Box 13-3900, Saint Paul, MN 55112. **EMAIL** fralet@bethel.edu

FREDEMAN, WILLIAM E.
PERSONAL Born 07/19/1928, Pine Bluff, AR **DISCIPLINE** ENGLISH **EDUCATION** Hendrix Col (Ark), BA, 48; Univ Okla, MA, 50, PhD, 56. **CAREER** High sch tchr, Okla, 48-53; instr to prof, 56-90, PROF EMER ENGLISH, UNIV BRITISH COLUMBIA, 91-; SW Brooks vis lectr, Univ Queensland, 78. **HONORS AND AWARDS** SSHRCC res grants, 74-80, 83-88; Can Coun/SSHRCC leave fel, 59-60, 70-71, 78-79, 83-84; Guggenheim fel, 65-66, 71-72; Killam sr res fel, 70-71, 78-79, 83-84; UBC Isaak Walton Killam res prize, 88. **MEMBERSHIPS** MLA; Bibliog Soc (London); Int Asn Univ Profs Eng. **SELECTED PUBLICATIONS** Auth, A Pre-Raphaelite Gazette: A Bibliocritical Study, 65; auth, A Pre-Raphaelite Gazette: The Letters of Arthur Hughes, 67; auth, Prelude to the Last Decade: Dante Gabriel Rossetti in the Summer of 1872, 71; auth, The Letters of Pictor Ignotus: William Bell Scott's Correspondence with Alice Boyd 1859-1884, 76; ed, The P.R.B. Journal, 75; ed, Victorian Poetry, 75, 82, 87; ed, A Rossetti Cabinet, 91; co-ed, Dictionary of Literary Biography, 4 vols, 83-85. **CONTACT ADDRESS** 35269 McKee Place, Abbotsford, BC, Canada V3G 1A7.

FREDERICKSON, RONALD Q.
DISCIPLINE THEATRE ARTS **EDUCATION** Univ Utah, MA, PhD. **CAREER** Prof, 72-. **HONORS AND AWARDS** Inducted into the Kansas Theatre Hall of Fame by the Asn of Kans Theatre. **MEMBERSHIPS** Asn Kans Theatre. **SELECTED PUBLICATIONS** Auth, pubs on directing and acting. **CONTACT ADDRESS** Div of Communcation and Theatre Arts, Emporia State Univ, Emporia, KS 66801-5087. **EMAIL** frederir@esumail.emporia.edu

FREDMAN, STEPHEN ALBERT
PERSONAL Born 05/20/1948, San Diego, CA, m, 1 child **DISCIPLINE** AMERICAN LITERATURE **EDUCATION** Calif Inst Arts, BFA, 71; Calif State Col, MA(English), 75; Stanford Univ, PhD(mod thought & lit), 80. **CAREER** Teaching asst English, Stanford Univ, 78-80; asst prof Am lit to prof, 80-; Joseph Morahan Dir of the Arts and Letters Core Course, 99-. **HONORS AND AWARDS** Nat Endowment for the Humanities Summer Stipend, 82 & 95; Lilly Fac Open Fel, 91-92; res fel, Recent Recipients of the PHD, ACLS, 82; Stanford fel, 77-80; res fel, Am Coun Learned Soc, 82. **MEMBERSHIPS** MLA; Modernist Studies Asn; Ed Board, Sagetrieb; Ed Board, William Carlos Williams Rev. **RESEARCH** Contemporary American poetry; Judaism & Modernism; the question of tradition in American poetry; poetry and performance; prose poetry; translation theory; the impact of Indic thought upon American literature. **SELECTED PUBLICATIONS** Auth, The Grounding of American Poetry: Charles Olson and the Emersonian Tradition, Cambridge Studies in American Literature and Culture; Cambridge Univ Press, 93; First Annotations to Edward Dorn's Gunslinger, Stephen Fredman and Grant Jenkins, Sagetrieb 15.3, 96; How to Get Out of the Room That Is the Book?: Paul Auster and the Consequences of Confinement, Postemodern Culture, 6.3, 5/96; Review of Lawrence Rainey and Robert von Hallberg, Sagetrieb 13.3, 96; Review of Barbara Einzig, Distance Without Distance, Talisman 14, fall 95; Review of Michael Davidson, The San Francisco Renaissance, Resources for Am Lit Study, 21.1, 95; auth, "'And All Now Is War': Charles Olson, George Oppen, and the Problem of Literary Generations," The Objectivist Nexus, eds. Rachel Blau Du Plessis and Peter Quartermain, Univ Ala Pr, 99; auth, A Menorah for Athena: Charles Reznikoff and the Jewish Dilemmas of Objectivist Poetry, Univ Chicago Pr (forthcoming). **CONTACT ADDRESS** Dept of English, Univ of Notre Dame, 356 O'Shaughnessy Hall, Notre Dame, IN 46556. **EMAIL** fredman.1@nd.edu

FREDRICKSMEYER, ERNST A.
PERSONAL Born 01/14/1930, Bismarck, ND, m, 1957, 3 children **DISCIPLINE** CLASSICS **EDUCATION** Lakeland Col, BA, 52; Univ Wis, MA, 53, PhD, 58. **CAREER** Instr, Cornell Col, 58-59; instr, Dartmouth Col, 59-60; instr, Bryn Mawr Col, 60-61; asst prof, Univ Wash, 61-66; assoc prof, Univ Colo, 66-71; vis prof, Univ Ore, 71; vis prof, Univ Wis, 78-79; prof, Univ Colo, 71-98. **HONORS AND AWARDS** Tchg Excellence Awd, Univ Colo, 87. **MEMBERSHIPS** Am Philos Asn; Class Asn Middle W & S; Am Archeol Inst; Nat Asn Scholars. **RESEARCH** Golden Age Latin poetry; fourth century Greek history. **CONTACT ADDRESS** Dept of Classics, CB 348, Boulder, CO 80309-0248.

FREDRICKSON, ROBERT STEWART
PERSONAL Born 06/16/1940, Minneapolis, MN, m, 1964, 2 children **DISCIPLINE** ENGLISH AND AM LIT **EDUCATION** DePauw Univ, BA, 61; Univ Minn, MA, 64; Univ NC, Chapel Hill, PhD (English), 70. **CAREER** Instr English, Univ NC, Charlotte, 64-66; instr, Univ NC, Chapel Hill 66-69; asst prof, 69-78, ASSOC PROF ENGLISH, GETTYSBURG COL, 78-. **MEMBERSHIPS** MLA. **RESEARCH** Psychology and literature; 19th century realism. **SELECTED PUBLICATIONS** Auth, Stone, Robert Decadent Leftists, Papers on Lan Lit, Vol 32, 96. **CONTACT ADDRESS** Dept of English, Gettysburg Col, 300 N Washington St, Gettysburg, PA 17325-1483.

FREE, KATHERINE B.
DISCIPLINE THEATRE HISTORY **EDUCATION** Marymount Col, BA; Univ Calif, Los Angeles, MA, PhD. **CAREER** Prof; consult & actress, theatre LA. **MEMBERSHIPS** Amer

Soc Theatre Res, ASTR; Int Fedn for the Theatre Res, IFTR; Amer Edu Theatre Assoc, ATHE. **RESEARCH** Ancient Greek theatre & the folk theatre of India. **SELECTED PUBLICATIONS** Articles in, Theatre Res Int, Theatre J, & UCLA J of Dance Ethnol. **CONTACT ADDRESS** Dept of Theatre, Loyola Marymount Univ, 7900 Loyola Blvd, Los Angeles, CA 90045.

FREE, WILLIAM JOSEPH
PERSONAL Born 03/18/1933, Chattanooga, TN, m, 1971 **DISCIPLINE** ENGLISH **EDUCATION** Univ Chatanooga, AB, 57; Univ NC, MA, 59, PhD, 62. **CAREER** From instr to asst prof, 62-68, ASSOC PROF ENGLISH, UNIV GA, 68-. **MEMBERSHIPS** SAtlantic Mod Lang Asn; Am Soc Aesthetics; Am Theatre Asn. **RESEARCH** Literary criticism; contemporary drama; literature and film. **SELECTED PUBLICATIONS** Auth, The Columbian Magazine and American Literary Nationalism, Mouton, 68; Aesthetic and moral value in Bonnie and Clyde, Quart J Speech, 69; William Cullen Bryant on nationalism, originality and imitation, Studies Philol, 69; Fellini's I Clowns and the Grotesque, J Mod Lit, 73; The ironic anger of David Storey, Mod Drama, 74; Structuralism, Literature and Tacit Knowledge, J Aesthetic Educ, 74; Williams in the Seventies, In: Tennessee Williams: A Tribute, Univ Miss, 77; Robert Bolt and the Marxist view of history, Mosaic, 81; Beckett's Plays and the photographic vision, Ga Rev, 80. **CONTACT ADDRESS** Dept of English, Univ of Georgia, Athens, GA 30601.

FREEDMAN, CARL H.
PERSONAL Born 04/13/1951, Durham, NC, d, 1 child **DISCIPLINE** ENGLISH **EDUCATION** Univ of NC Chapel Hill, BA, 73; Oxford Univ, BA, 75; Yale Univ, PhD, 83. **CAREER** Asst prof to assoc prof, La State Univ, 84-. **HONORS AND AWARDS** Mellon Fel, Wesleyan Univ, 83-84; Margaret Church Memorial Prize, 84; Res Grants, La State Univ, 85, 89, 92, 94; Pioneer Awd for Excellence in Scholar, Sci Fiction Res Assoc. **RESEARCH** Auth, "Beyond the Dialect of the Tribe: James Joyce, Hugh MacDiarmid, and World Language", Hugh MacDiarmid: Man and Poet, ed Nancy Gish, Edinburgh Univ Pr, (92): 253-273; auth, "Theory, the Canon and the Politics of Curricular Reform: A Response to Gerald Graff", Teaching the Conflicts: Gerald Graff, Curricular Reform, and the Culture Wars, ed William E. Cain, Garland (NY, 94): 566; auth, "How to Do things with Milton: A Study in the Politics of Literary Criticism", Critical Essays on John Milton, ed Christopher Kendrick, G.K. Hall, (NY, 85): 19-44; auth, "Science Fiction and the Question of the Canon", Science Fiction and Market Realities, eds Gary Westfahl, George Slusser and Eric Rabkin, Univ of Ga Pr, (Athens, 96): 117-127; auth, "Rhetorical Hermeneutics, Huckleberry Finn, and Some Problems with Pragmatism", Reconceptualizing American Literary/Cultural Studies, ed William E Cain, Garland (NY, 96): 111-121; auth, "The Case Against the Case Against Space -- And A Case for Science Fiction", Science Fiction Studies, (Mar 98): 143-152; auth, "Remembering the Future: Science and Positivism from Isaac Asimov to Gregory Benford, Extrapolation, (Summer 98): 128-138; auth, "Kubrick's 2001 and the Possibility of a Science-Fiction Cinema", Science-Fiction Studies, (July 98): 300-318; auth, "Science Fiction and Utopia: A Historico-Philosophical Overview", Cognition and Estrangement in Science Fiction and Utopian Literature, ed Patrick Parrinder, (forthcoming); auth, "Science Fiction and the Two Cultures: Reflections After the Snow-Leavis Controversy", Science Fiction at the Crossroads of the Two Cultures, eds Gary Westfahl and George Slusser, Univ of Ga Pr, (forthcoming). **CONTACT ADDRESS** Dept English, la State Univ Baton rouge, 0 La State Univ, Baton Rouge, LA 70803-0104. **EMAIL** cfreed2780@aol.com

FREEDMAN, DIANE P.
PERSONAL Born New York, NY, m, 1988, 1 child **DISCIPLINE** ENGLISH **EDUCATION** Cornell Univ, AB, 77; MAT, 78; Boston Univ, MA, 82; Univ Wash, PhD, 89. **CAREER** Lect, State Univ NY, Cortland, 79; exec asst, Cornell Univ, 82-84; asst prof, Skidmore Col, 89-92; asst prof, Univ New Hampton, 92-97; assoc prof, Univ New Hampton, 97-. **HONORS AND AWARDS** Regent Schl, Cornell, NY; Nat Letter Comm; ACA Awd; Susan Koppelman Awd, 93. **MEMBERSHIPS** MLA; ASLE; NCTE/CCU. **RESEARCH** US women's autobiography, poetry, memoirs; autobiographical scholarship; American lit, 19th and 20th century. **SELECTED PUBLICATIONS** Auth, An Alchemy of Genres: Cross-Genre Writing by American Feminist Poet-Critics, UP of Virginia (Charlottesville), 99; co-ed, The Intimate Critique: Autobiographical Literary Criticism, Duke UP (Durham), 93; ed, Millay at 100: A Critical Reappraisal, S Illinois Univ Press (Carbondale, IL), 95; coauth, Teaching Prose, Norton (New York), 84; co-ed, Personal Thoughts: The Autobiographical Nature of Reading, Writing and Research in the Disciplines, Duke UP, under review; auth, "Border Crossing as Method and Motif in Contemporary Feminist Writing; or, How Freud Helped Me Case the Joint." The Intimate Critique, 13-22; auth, "Using Personal Writing to Foster Student Learning," in Personal Voices in Teaching and Scholarship, eds. David Bleich, Deborah Holdstein (New York: MLA), forthcoming; auth, "A Whale of a Different Color--Melville and the Movies: The Great Whit Whale and Free Willy," ISLE (97), 87-95; auth, "Autobiographical Criticism," The Woman's Studies Encycl, eds. Cheris Kramarae, Dale Spender (New Brunswick, NJ, Rutgers UP, 99). **CONTACT ADDRESS** Dept English, Univ of New Hampshire, Durham, 125 Technology Dr, Durham, NC 03824-4724.

FREEDMAN, MORRIS
PERSONAL Born 10/06/1920, New York, NY, d, 2 children **DISCIPLINE** ENGLISH & COMPARATIVE LITERATURE **EDUCATION** City Col New York, BA, 41; Columbia Univ, MA, 50, PhD, 53. **CAREER** Lectr & instr English, City Col New York, 46-54; assoc ed, Commentary, 54-55; from asst prof to prof English, Univ NMex, 55-66; head dept, 67-72, prof English & Comp Lit, Univ Md, College Park, 66- **MEMBERSHIPS** MLA; NCTE; Milton Soc Am. **RESEARCH** Later seventeenth century; Milton; creative writing and contemporary drama, American studies. **SELECTED PUBLICATIONS** Auth, Dryden's Miniature Epic, J English & Ger Philol, 58; Milton and Dryden on Rhyme, Huntington Libr Quart, 61; ed, Essays in the Modern Drama, Heath, 64; auth, The Compact English Handbook, McKay, 65; Success and the American Dramatist, Am Theatre, 67; The Moral Impulse, Southern Ill Univ, 67; co-ed, Controversy in Literature, Scribner's, 68; auth, American Drama in Social Context, Southern Ill Univ, 71. **CONTACT ADDRESS** Dept of English, Univ of Maryland, Col Park, College Park, MD 20742. **EMAIL** mf18@umail.umd.edu

FREEDMAN-BAUM, ROSELYN L.
PERSONAL Born 01/03/1941, Charleston, WV, w, 1987 **DISCIPLINE** RHETORIC **EDUCATION** Morris Harvey Col, BA, 63; Oh Univ, MFA, 65; Univ Mich, PhD, 80. **CAREER** Vis prof, Am Col of Rome, fall 80; instr, asst prof, assoc prof, prof, Univ Charleston/Morris Harvey Col, 64-90 (retired); prof, St John Fisher Col, Rochester, NY, 88-. **HONORS AND AWARDS** Alpha Psi Omega, Gamma Theta Upsilon, Kappa Delta Pi, Sigma Tau Delta, Pi Kappa Delta, Delta Gamma Soc Int, Phi Delta Kappa; Special Awd, Contrib to Theatre Advancement, 63; Univ Mich Teaching Fel, 73-74; MHC Fac Fel, 73-74; Doctoral Honors Sem, Univ Mich, 78; Gertrude Roberts Grad Scholar for Diss Res, 79; Special Awd, Symposium on Greek Rhetoric in Honor of Everett Lee Hunt, Univ Pittsburgh, 81; nominated for Fulbright Lecture Awd to Nigeria, 83-84 (declined). **MEMBERSHIPS** NY State Speech Commun Asn, Speech Commun Asn, World Commun Asn, Am Film Inst, Am Forensics Asn, Am Asn of Univ Profs, Int Soc for the Hist of Rhetoric, Rhetoric Soc of Am, Mediaeval Acad of Am, Am Inst of Parliamentarians. **RESEARCH** Sixteenth-century English rhetoric; American and British public address and oratory. **SELECTED PUBLICATIONS** Auth, "A Bibliography of Sixteenth-Century English Rhetoric," Rhetoric Soc Quart (Spring 81); coauth, "1980s: Mass Communication in China," World Commun, 19:1(90): 77-82; ed, Directory of Outstanding Women Educators, Delta Kappa Gamma Soc Int, Alpha Phi State, WVa (87); auth, "Leonard Cox," in Encyclopedia of Rhetoric: Communication from Ancient Times to the Information Age, ed. Theresa Enos (NY: Garland Pub Co, 96), 153-154; auth, "Rhetorical Education and the English Reformation' (forthcoming); auth, Leonard Cox's "The Arte or Crafte of Rhetoric": A Critical edition (in process). **CONTACT ADDRESS** Dept Commun, St. John Fisher Col, 3690 E Ave, Rochester, NY 14618-3537. **EMAIL** baum@sjfc.edu

FREEMAN, BERNICE
PERSONAL Born 08/08/1909, La Grange, GA **DISCIPLINE** ENGLISH EDUCATION **EDUCATION** Tift Col, AB, 30; Univ NC, Chapel Hill, MA, 32; Columbia Univ, EdD(English educ), 52. **CAREER** Teacher high schs, Ga, 30-42; instr and critic, Demonstration High Sch, Ga Col, Milledgeville, 42-48, asst prof and prin, 48-51; co-dir, Ga Educ Ctr, 50-51; instructional supvr, Troup County Schs, Ga, 51-67; from assoc prof to prof educ, West Ga Col, 67-74, coordr, 69-73, chmn, Dept Sec Educ, 73-74; RETIRED., Mem high sch sect comt, NCTE, 52-54, mem bd dir elem sect, 66-69; mem, Publ and Constructive Studies Comt, Dept Rural Educ, NEA, 58-65, mem exec bd, 64-69, mem exec comt, 65-69. **MEMBERSHIPS** NCTE; NEA; MLA; SAtlantic Mod Lang Asn. **RESEARCH** The short story as a means of identifying a place; the Georgia short story. **SELECTED PUBLICATIONS** Auth, Precise Moments, Georg Rev, Vol 47, 93. **CONTACT ADDRESS** 305 Park Ave, La Grange, GA 30240.

FREEMAN, CHRISTOPHER EDWARD
PERSONAL Born 09/03/1965, Rome, GA, s **DISCIPLINE** ENGLISH **EDUCATION** Berry Col, BA, 87; Vanderbilt Univ, MA, 89; PhD, 93. **CAREER** Asst prof, St John's Univ, 95-. **HONORS AND AWARDS** Finalist, Lambda Literary Awd. **MEMBERSHIPS** MLA, MMLA. **RESEARCH** Biography/memoir, Paul Monette, Christopher Isherwood, Sexuality. **SELECTED PUBLICATIONS** Auth, The Isherwood Century: Essays on the Life and Work of Christopher Isherwood, Univ of Wisc, 00; auth, Conversations with Christopher Isherwood, Univ of Miss, 00. **CONTACT ADDRESS** Dept English, St. John's Univ, PO Box 2000, Collegeville, MN 56321-2000. **EMAIL** cfreeman@csbsju.edu

FREEMAN, DONALD C.
PERSONAL Born 03/19/1938, Boston, MA, m, 1970, 2 children **DISCIPLINE** ENGLISH, LITERATURE **EDUCATION** Middlebury Col, AB, 59; Brown Univ, AM, 61; Univ of Conn, PhD, 65. **CAREER** Asst prof, Univ of Calif Santa Barbara, 67-68; from asst prof to prof, Univ of Mass Amherst, 68-76; prof, Temple Univ, 76-81; dir, Shearman & Sterling NY, 81-84; dir, Baker & McKenzie, London, 84-87; prof, Univ of S Calif, 87-. **HONORS AND AWARDS** Nat Sci Found Postdoctoral Res Fel in Lings, Mass Inst of Technol, 67-68. **MEMBERSHIPS** MLA, Ling Soc of Am. **RESEARCH** Poetic language, meter, literary theory. **SELECTED PUBLICATIONS** Auth, Linguistics and Literary Style, Holt, Rinehart & Winston (New York, NY), 70; auth, Essays in Modern Stylistics, Methuen (London), 81. **CONTACT ADDRESS** Dept of English, Univ of So California, 3501 Trousdale Pkwy, Los Angeles, CA 90089-0091. **EMAIL** dfreeman@usc.edu

FREEMAN, JAMES A.
PERSONAL Born 03/27/1956, Montreal, QC, Canada, m, 1991, 1 child **DISCIPLINE** ENGLISH **EDUCATION** Shasta Col, AA, 76; Reed Col, BA, 81; Humboldt State Univ, MA, 81; MATW, 80; Columbia State Univ, PhD. **CAREER** Instr, Humboldt State Univ, 77-81; Asst Prof, Southern Oregon Univ, 81-82; Prof, Bucks County Col, 82-. **SELECTED PUBLICATIONS** Auth, Intent to Return, Charlotte Gusay Agency, forthcoming; auth, At The End of Halftime, Dry Crik Press, forthcoming; auth, Lady and Sierra's Storage Shed Summer, forthcoming; auth, Never the Same River Twice, Charles B McFadden Co, 96; auth, Death Threats, Northwoods press, 94; auth, Sins of the Father, Sins of the Son, Northwoods Press, 94; auth, Ishi's Journey from The Center to the Edge of the World, Naturegraph Publishers, 92; auth, Broken Things, Fixed Things, Conservatory of American Letters, 88; auth, Hidden Agenda, Northwoods Press, 87; auth, Glyphs of Tehama, Garall Press, 86; auth, Fever Dreams, Adams Press, 85. **CONTACT ADDRESS** Dept Lang & Lit, Bucks County Comm Col, 434 Swamp Rd, Newtown, PA 18940-9666.

FREEMAN, JOANNA MAE
PERSONAL Born 03/22/1929, Kansas City, MO, m, 1951, 2 children **DISCIPLINE** ENGLISH LITERATURE, TECHNICAL WRITING **EDUCATION** Southwest Mo State Univ, BS in Educ, 49; Univ Colo, MA 52; Univ Kans, PhD (English), 73. **CAREER** PROF ENGLISH, PITTSBURG STATE UNIV, 58-. **MEMBERSHIPS** MLA; NEA; NCTE; Soc Tech Commun. **RESEARCH** Samuel Butler; Bible as literature; advanced technical writing. **SELECTED PUBLICATIONS** Auth, Basic Technical and Business Writing, Iowa State Univ, 79; Technical Writing: Stimulus for English department growth in community colleges, 11th Int Inst Community Cols, 80; Biblical allusions that shape negative reactions to characters, In: The War of All Flesh, Albion, fall 80; Grants for religious activities and community projects, Heartland Harvest, 9/80; The technical writing consortium: Two-year, four-year, cooperation, 28th Int Conf Soc Tech Commun, 81; Samuel Butler's Influence on George Bernard Shaw, Albion, Winter 81; Samuel Butler's Search for Ethical Values, Eric, 81; Business and Professional Women of the Bible, Heartland Harvest, 5/81.

FREEMAN, JOHN
DISCIPLINE RENAISSANCE LITERATURE **EDUCATION** Mich State Univ, BA; Wayne State Univ, MA, PhD. **CAREER** Prof, 87-. **RESEARCH** Holographic potential in the Arnolfini Portrait. **SELECTED PUBLICATIONS** Pub(s) on, Thomas More's Utopia, Shakespeare's Hamlet, and Stoppard's Rosencrantz and Guildenstern Are Dead; contribu, ELH, Moreana, and Modern Language Rev. **CONTACT ADDRESS** Dept of Eng, Univ of Detroit Mercy, 4001 W McNichols Rd, PO BOX 19900, Detroit, MI 48219-0900. **EMAIL** FREEMAJC@udmercy.edu

FREEMAN, KATHRYN S.
DISCIPLINE ENGLISH **EDUCATION** Yale Univ, BA, 80, MA, 85, PhD, 90. **CAREER** Asst prof, Univ of Miami, 92-98; assoc prof, Univ of Miami, 98-. **CONTACT ADDRESS** Dept of English, Univ of Miami, PO Box 248145, Coral Gables, FL 33124-4632. **EMAIL** kfreeman@miami.edu

FREEMAN, MARGARET H.
PERSONAL Born 01/01/1940, Leicester, England, m, 1970 **DISCIPLINE** ENGLISH **EDUCATION** Univ Manchester, BA, 62; Univ Mass, MA, 70; PhD, 72. **CAREER** Asst Prof to Assoc Prof, SUNY, 75-89; Prof, Los Angeles Valley Col, 89-. **HONORS AND AWARDS** NEH Fel, Princeton Univ, 89. **MEMBERSHIPS** Mod Lang Asn, Am Lit Asn, Intl cognitive Linguistic Asn, Emily Dickinson Intl Soc. **RESEARCH** cognitive Linguistics approaches to literature (especially poetry) and translation. **SELECTED PUBLICATIONS** Auth, "Cognitive Poetics as an Adequate Theory of Literature," The Poetics of Cognition: studies in Mind, Language, Literature, and the Visual Arts; forthcoming; auth, "Poetry and the Scope of Metaphor: Toward a Cognitive Theory of Literature," Metonymy & Metaphor at the Crossroads; Mouton, 00; auth, "Tropes and Figures: Troping as Poetic Strategy," The Emily Dickinson Handbook, Univ Mass Press, 99; auth, "Metaphors of Mind: Analogical Mapping in Teaching Poetry," The Pedagogical Quarterly of Cognitive Linguistics, 98; auth, "Grounded Spaces: Deictic-Self Anaphors in the Poetry of Emily Dickinson," Language and Literature, (97): 7-28; auth, "Silence-Denote: The Intimacy of

Dickinson's Spaces," The Semantics of Silences, Heidelberg, 96; auth, "Metaphor Making Meaning: Dickinson's Conceptual Universe," Journal of Pragmatics, (95): 643-666. **CONTACT ADDRESS** Dept English, Los Angeles Valley Col, 5800 Fulton Ave, Valley Glen, CA 91401-4062. **EMAIL** freemamh@email.lavc.cc.ca.us

FREER, COBURN
PERSONAL Born 11/05/1939, New Orleans, LA, m, 1961, 2 children **DISCIPLINE** ENGLISH **EDUCATION** Lewis and Clark Col, BA, 60; Univ Wash, PhD (English), 68. **CAREER** Instr English, Univ Ariz, 65-67; from asst prof to assoc prof, Univ Mont, 67-76, prof, 76-80; PROF ENGLISH AND HEAD DEPT, UNIV GA, 80-, Fulbright lectr, Univ Oulu, 71-72; Nat Endowment for Humanities fel, 75. **HONORS AND AWARDS** Sr Fulbright-Hays Lectr; NEH Fel. **MEMBERSHIPS** MLA; Milton Soc Am; SAtlantic Mod Lang Asn; Southeast Renaissance Conf. **RESEARCH** Renaissance and seventeenth century lit; modern poetry. **SELECTED PUBLICATIONS** Auth, Music for A King, Johns Hopkins, 72; auth, The Poetics of Jacobean Drama, Johns Hopkins, 81; auth, Donne, John and Elizabethan Economic, Criticism Quart Lit Arts, Vol 38, 96. **CONTACT ADDRESS** Dept of English, Univ of Georgia, 312 Park Hall, Athens, GA 30602-6205. **EMAIL** cfreer@uga.edu

FREIBERT, LUCY MARIE
PERSONAL Born 10/19/1922, Louisville, KY **DISCIPLINE** AMERICAN LITERATURE **EDUCATION** Spalding Col, AB, 57; St Louis Univ, MA, 62; Univ Wis-Madison, PhD (English), 70. **CAREER** Teacher, St Cecilia Sch, Louisville, Ky, 47-52; teacher, Holy Name Sch, 52-57; teacher, Presentation Acad, 57-60; asst prof English, Spalding Col, 60-65; assoc prof, 69-71, prof english, Univ Louisville, 71-93; emerita prof, 93-. **HONORS AND AWARDS** Sarah Koppleman Awd for Hidden Hands, 86; Distinguished Teaching Prof, Univ of Louisville, 87; Trustees Awd, Univ of Louisville, 91; Woman of Distinction, Center for Women and Families, 93. **MEMBERSHIPS** MLA; Melville Soc; NWSA; NOW. **RESEARCH** Herman Melville; Am Lit; women's studies. **SELECTED PUBLICATIONS** Auth, The Artist as Picaro; auth, "The Revelation of Margaret Atwood," Canadian Lit, 83; auth, Hidden Hands: An Anthology of American Women Writers, 1790-1870, 85; auth, "Southern Song: An Interview with Margaret Walker," Frontiers, 87; auth, "Control and Creativity: The Politics of Risk in Atwood's The Handmaid's Tale," Critical Essays on Atwood, 88; auth, "Creative Women of Brook Farm," Women in Spiritual and Communitarian Societies in the U.S., 93. **CONTACT ADDRESS** Dept of English, Univ of Louisville, Louisville, KY 40292.

FREIER, MARY P.
DISCIPLINE ENGLISH **EDUCATION** Univ of IL, MS, 98, PhD, 84, AM, 79; Millikin Univ, BA, 77 **CAREER** Dir, 83-86, IN Univ E; prof, 86-97, Dakota St Univ; coord, 98-, Jacksonville St Univ; ref & instr librn, Carleton Col, 00-. **HONORS AND AWARDS** Summer Study Grant, NEH, 95 **MEMBERSHIPS** Am Libr Asn; Pop Cult Asn **RESEARCH** Infor anxiety **CONTACT ADDRESS** McKinley Gould Librn, Carleton Col, One Col St, Northfield, MN 55057. **EMAIL** mfreier@carleton.edu

FREIERT, WILLIAM K.
PERSONAL Born 04/26/1941, Baltimore, MD, m, 1970, 1 child **DISCIPLINE** CLASSICS **EDUCATION** St. Louis Univ, AB, 65, MA 66; Univ Minn, PhD, 72. **CAREER** Prof, Gustavus Adolphus Col, 72-; exchange prof, Kansai Gaidai Univ, 92. **HONORS AND AWARDS** Fulbright lectr. **MEMBERSHIPS** Am Philol Asn; Am Class League; Class Asn of Middle West and South; Int Soc for the Class Tradition. **RESEARCH** Classical studies. **SELECTED PUBLICATIONS** Auth, Paul T. Granlund: Spirit of Bronze, Shape of Freedom, 91; "Classical Myth in Post-War American Fiction" in The Class Tradition and the Am, 99; "Platonism in Saul Bellow's 'More Die of Heartbreak'" in J of Inquiry and Res, 93; "Bellow's 'Golden Ass': Greco-Roman Antecedents in 'More Die of Heartbreak'" in Saul Bellow J, 92. **CONTACT ADDRESS** 721 N Washington, Saint Peter, MN 56082-1847. **EMAIL** wfreiert@gac.edu

FREIMARCK, VINCENT
PERSONAL Born 06/11/1918, New York, NY **DISCIPLINE** ENGLISH **EDUCATION** NYork Univ, AB, 39; Columbia Univ, AM, 41; Cornell Univ, PhD, 50. **CAREER** Asst, NY Univ, 40, instr, 41-42; instr, Carnegie Inst Tech, 42-43; asst, Cornell Univ, 46-48; instr Eng, Wesleyan Univ, 48-52; from asst prof to assoc prof, 52-71, PROF ENGLISH, STATE UNIV NY BINGHAMTON, 71-. **MEMBERSHIPS** MLA. **RESEARCH** Am Lit of the eighteenth and nineteenth centuries; eighteenth century English criticism. **SELECTED PUBLICATIONS** Auth, The Bible and neo-classical views of style, J Eng & Ger Philol, 10/52; Rhetoric at Yale in 1807, Proc Am Philos Soc, 7/66; Introd & ed, Robert Lowth's Lectures on the Sacred Poetry of the Hebrews (2 vols, Georg Olms Verlag, Hildesheim, 69; co-ed, Race and the American Romantics, Schocken, 71, Japanese transl, Kenkyusha, 76; auth, Timothy Dwight's brief lives in Travels in New England and New York, Early Am Lit, spring 73. **CONTACT ADDRESS** Dept of English, SUNY, Binghamton, Binghamton, NY 13901.

FREIMUTH, VICKI S.
DISCIPLINE HEALTH COMMUNICATION **EDUCATION** FL State Univ, PhD. **CAREER** Prof, Univ MD. **RESEARCH** Public's search for and use of health information. **SELECTED PUBLICATIONS** Co-auth, College Students' Awareness and Interpretation of the AIDS Risk, Sci, Tech, and Human Values 12, 87; Searching for Health Information: The Cancer Information Service Experience, Univ Pa Press, 89. **CONTACT ADDRESS** Dept of Commun, Univ of Maryland, Col Park, 4229 Art-Sociology Building, College Park, MD 20742-1335.

FREIS, CATHERINE RUGGIERO
PERSONAL Born 10/18/1940, New York, NY, m, 1964, 2 children **DISCIPLINE** CLASSICAL STUDIES **EDUCATION** Brooklyn Col, CUNY, BA, 63; UC Berkeley, MA, 66; PhD, 80 **CAREER** From asst prof to prof & ch dept of classical studies, Millsaps Col, 75- . **HONORS AND AWARDS** Am Philol Soc Awd for Excel in the Tching of Classics; Millsaps Col Teaching Awd; Mississippi Humanities Coun Teach Awd. **MEMBERSHIPS** Am Philol Soc; Classical Assoc of Midwest & South **RESEARCH** Tragedy & East & South Asian Dance Drama **SELECTED PUBLICATIONS** Auth, "Intensive Latin and Greek Courses as adjuncts to the Humanities Core Curriculum", in Intensive and Innovative Methods of Teaching Latin and Greek, 81; auth, "The Ancient City", Arts Alliance, 87; rev, "The Roman Cookery of Apicius", Classical World, 89; ed, Introduction to Liberal Studies Reader, Copley Press, 95, 97; auth, "Kathakali and Greek Drama," Didaskalia, Ancient Theatre Today, 98; coauth, Ancient Greek Alive, Univ NCar Pr, 99. **CONTACT ADDRESS** Classical Studies Dept, Millsaps Col, Box 150223, Jackson, MS 39210. **EMAIL** freiscr@millsaps.edu

FRENCH, RICHARD FREDERIC
PERSONAL Born 06/23/1915, Randolph, MA **DISCIPLINE** MUSIC, RELIGION **EDUCATION** Harvard Univ, BS, 37, MA, 39. **CAREER** Mem Soc Fellows, Harvard Univ, 41-42, 46-47, asst prof music, 47-51; vpres, Assoc Music Publ, NY, 51-59; pres, NY Pro Musica, 58-70; prof sacred music, Union theol Sem, 66-73; Prof Music, Inst Music and Worship, Yale Univ, 73-, Trustee, Brooklyn Music Sch, 60-70 and Schola Musicae Liturgicae, NY, 73-; adj prof sacred music, Union theol Sem, 73-77. **MEMBERSHIPS** Am Musicol Soc. **RESEARCH** Music and liturgy; Russian; graduate educational curricula. **SELECTED PUBLICATIONS** Auth, Libraries, History, Diplomacy, and the Performing Arts--Essays in Honor of Smith, Carleton, Sprague, Notes, Vol 49, 93. **CONTACT ADDRESS** Sch of Music, Yale Univ, New Haven, CT 06520. **EMAIL** rfrench@pantheon.yale.com

FRENCH, ROBERTS WALKER
PERSONAL Born 07/16/1935, New York, NY, m, 1961, 2 children **DISCIPLINE** ENGLISH **EDUCATION** Dartmouth Col, BA, 56; Yale Univ, MA, 59; Brown Univ, PhD (English lit), 64. **CAREER** From asst prof to assoc prof, 64-77, PROF ENGLISH, UNIV MASS, AMHERST, 77-. **MEMBERSHIPS** MLA; Milton Soc Am. **RESEARCH** Modern poetry; Walt Whitman; Milton. **SELECTED PUBLICATIONS** Auth, Voice and Structure in Lyciday, Tex Studies Lit & Lang, 12: 15-25; Whitman in Crisis: A Reading of Scented Herbage of My Breast, 24: 29-32, Symbolic Values, In: The Dalliance of the Eagles, 24: 124-128 & Music for a Mad Scene: A Reading of To a Locomotive in Winter, 27: 32-39, Walt Whitman Rev; Reading the Bible: The Story of Adam and Eve, Col Lit, 9: 22-29. **CONTACT ADDRESS** Dept of English, Univ of Massachusetts, Amherst, Amherst, MA 01003.

FRENCH, WILLIAM WIRT
PERSONAL Born 06/26/1932, Beckley, WV, m, 3 children **DISCIPLINE** ENGLISH LITERATURE **EDUCATION** WVa Univ, BA, 54; Univ Pittsburgh, MA, 60, PhD, 67. **CAREER** Asst to dean, Col Arts & Sci, Univ Pittsburgh, 62-64; from instr to asst prof, 64-71, asst chmn dept, 68-72, assoc prof English, 71-86, prof English, 86-99, Emer prof, 99-, WVa Univ . **MEMBERSHIPS** MLA; Shakespeare Asn Am. **RESEARCH** Shakespeare; English Renaissance drama; American Drama. **SELECTED PUBLICATIONS** Auth, A Kind of Courage: King Lear at the Old Vic, London, 1940, Theatre Topics, 93; Murder Mystery Events: Playing, M yth-Making, and Smashing the Forth Wall, All At Once, Journal of Dramatic Theory & Criticism VIII:2, 94; auth, Maryat Lee's EcoTheater: A Theater for the Twenty-First Century, WVa Univ Press (Morgantown, WV), 98; auth, "The Reflective Hamlet: The Little Eyases Direst the Shenandoah Shakespeare Express," The Upstart Crow 17 (98): 69-90. **CONTACT ADDRESS** Dept English, West Virginia Univ, Morgantown, PO Box 6296, Morgantown, WV 26506-6296. **EMAIL** wfrench2@wvu.edu

FRENTZ, THOMAS S.
DISCIPLINE RHETORICAL STUDIES AND MASS MEDIA **EDUCATION** Univ Wisc, PhD. **CAREER** Comm Stu, Univ Ark **MEMBERSHIPS** Southern States Comm Asn. **SELECTED PUBLICATIONS** Articles, Quart Jour Speech; Critical Studies Mass Comm; Comm Monographs; Comm Quart; Western Jour Comm; Philosophy & Rhetoric; Southern Comm Jour. **CONTACT ADDRESS** Univ of Arkansas, Fayetteville, Fayetteville, AR 72701.

FRESCH, CHERYL
DISCIPLINE 16TH- AND 17TH-CENTURY ENGLISH LITERATURE **EDUCATION** Cornell Univ, PhD; 76. **CAREER** Instr, Univ NMex, 76-. **RESEARCH** Blake's and Milton's visualizations of the scene of expulsion from the garden. **SELECTED PUBLICATIONS** Auth, 'Whither thou goest': Paradise Lost XXII 610-623 and The Book of Ruth, Milton Stud XXXII, 95. **CONTACT ADDRESS** Dept of Lit, Univ of New Mexico, Albuquerque, Albuquerque, NM 87131. **EMAIL** chfresch@unm.edu

FRESE, DOLORES
DISCIPLINE MEDIEVAL LITERATURE **EDUCATION** Univ Iowa, PhD. **CAREER** Prof, Univ Notre Dame. **HONORS AND AWARDS** ACLS Fel. **RESEARCH** Figures of women in Old English and Middle English poetry. **SELECTED PUBLICATIONS** Auth, An Ars Legendi for the Canterbury Tales: Re-Constructive Reading; coed, Anglo-Saxon Poetry: Essays in Appreciation; coed, The Book and the Body. **CONTACT ADDRESS** Dept of English, Univ of Notre Dame, Notre Dame, IN 46556. **EMAIL** dolores.w.frese.1@nd.edu

FRIED, LEWIS FREDRICK
PERSONAL Born 01/29/1943, New York, NY **DISCIPLINE** AMERICAN LITERATURE **EDUCATION** Queens Col, NYork, BA, 64, MA, 66; Univ MA, PhD, 69. **CAREER** Asst ed fiction, Tower Publ, 66; copy-ed, Mass Rev, 66; asst prof Am lit, 69-76, assoc prof, 76-89, prof Am lit, Kent State Univ, 89-, Vis prof, Int Grad Ctr Hebrew & Judaica, World Union Jewish Studies, Israel, 73-74. **HONORS AND AWARDS** Fulbright prof, 89-90, 93-94; Rapoport Fel, Hebrew Union Col, 97; Marcus Fel, Hebrew Union Col, 98. **RESEARCH** Am lit naturalism; Am proletarian fiction; Am-Jewish lit. **SELECTED PUBLICATIONS** Auth, James T Farrell: Shadow and Act, Jahrbuch Amerikastudien, 72; The disinherited: The worker as writer, New Lett, fall 72; The Golden Brotherhood of McTeague, Zeitschrift Fur Anglistik und Amerikanistik, 73; co-ed, American Literary Naturalism, Carl Winter Universitatsverlag, 75; auth, The Magician of Lublin: I B Singer's Ironic Man of Faith, Yiddish, 76; Bernard Carr and his trials of the mind, Twentieth Century Lit, 76; coauth, Jacob A Riis: A Reference Guide, G K Hall, 77; Jacob A Riis and the Jews, Am Studies, 79; ed-in-chief, Handbook of American Jewish Literature, Greenwood Press, 88; Makers of the City, Univ Mass Press, 90. **CONTACT ADDRESS** Dept of Eng, Kent State Univ, PO Box 5190, Kent, OH 44242-0001. **EMAIL** dalamerica@aol.com

FRIEDENBERG, ROBERT VICTOR
PERSONAL Born 09/09/1943, Washington, DC, 2 children **DISCIPLINE** POLITICAL COMMUNICATION, RHETORICAL THEORY **EDUCATION** Towson State Col, BS, 65; Temple Univ, MA, 67, PhD(speech), 70. **CAREER** Asst prof 70-74, assoc prof, 74-80, prof speech communication, Miami Univ, 80-, Speech consult, Republican Nat Cont, 76. **HONORS AND AWARDS** Outstanding Young Teacher Awd, Cent States Speech Commun Asn, 74; pres, Relig Speech Assn, 90; variety of research grants from Shorenstein Cen of John F Kennedy School of Govern, Harvard Univ, Am Jewish Archives. **MEMBERSHIPS** Speech Commun Asn; Religious Speech Assn, Central States Speech Assn. **RESEARCH** Contemporary Political Communication; American Jewish Preaching; Political Debates. **SELECTED PUBLICATIONS** Auth, Communication Consultants in Political Campaigns: The Ballot Box Warriors, Hear O'Israel: The History of American Jewish Preaching 1642-1970; Rhetorical Studies of Political Debates: 1996; Rhetorical Studies of Political Debates: 1960-1992; Theodore Roosevelt and the Rhetoric of Militant Decency, with Judith S Trent, Political Campaign Communication: Principles and Practices. **CONTACT ADDRESS** Dept of Communication, Miami Univ, 1601 Peck Blvd, Hamilton, OH 45011-3399. **EMAIL** friederv@muohio.edu

FRIEDMAN, ALAN
PERSONAL Born 06/08/1939, Brooklyn, NY, m, 1985, 4 children **DISCIPLINE** ENGLISH **CAREER** Creator, director, and teacher, Brasenose coll, Oxford, 84-87; exchange prof, 00, Universite Paris, Sorbonne; 85, Universite, Paul Valery, Montpellier; chair, 87-89, UT faculty senate; exchange prof, 95, Univ Coll, Galway; Prof, Univ Tex, 76-. **HONORS AND AWARDS** Natl Endow for the Humanities Fell, 70-71; Fulbright research award, France, Dec-Jan 84-85; travel award, France, Spring 90; Parlin Fell, Plan II. **SELECTED PUBLICATIONS** Auth, Fictional Death and The Modernist Enterprise, Cambridge Univ Press, 95; auth, The Great War and Ritual, War and Literature, Stuttgart, 94; Standard English at the University of Texas, Situating College English, Greenwood, 96; Good Governance, Academe, July-Aug 96; Modernist Attitudes Toward Death, Death and the Quest for Meaning, 97; auth, Bechett in Black and Red, Kentucky Univ Pr, 99. **CONTACT ADDRESS** Dept of English, Univ of Texas, Austin, Austin, TX 78712. **EMAIL** friedman@uts.cc.utexas.edu

FRIEDMAN, BARTON ROBERT
PERSONAL Born 02/05/1935, Brooklyn, NY, m, 1958, 4 children **DISCIPLINE** MODERN LITERATURE **EDUCATION** Cornell Univ, BA, 56; Univ Conn, MA, 58; Cornell Univ, PhD(English), 64. **CAREER** Instr English, Bowdoin Col, 61-63;

asst prof, Univ wis, 63-68, assoc prof, 68-77, prof, 77-78; prof & chemn dept English, Cleveland State Univ, 78-, Assoc ed, Literary Monographs, 69-76 & Irish Renaissance Annual, 80-. **MEMBERSHIPS** MLA; Am Comt for Irish Studies. **RESEARCH** History and literary narrative; post-war American literature; the Irish literary revival. **SELECTED PUBLICATIONS** Auth, to tell the sun from the druid fires imagery of good and evil, In: The Ring and the Book, Studies in English Lit, 66; Years, Johnson and Ireland's heroic dead, Eire-Ireland, 72; Fabricating history: Narrative strategy, In: The Lord of the rings, Clio, 73; On Baile's strand to At the hawk's well: Staging the deeps of the mind, J Mod Lit, 75; Adventures in the Deeps of the Mind, Princeton Univ Press, 77; You Can't Tell the Players, Cleveland State Univ Poetry Ctr, 79; Fabricating history or John Banim refights the Boyne, Eire-Ireland, 82; Tolkien and David Jones: The great war and the war of the ring, Clio, 82; Fabricating History, Princeton Univ Press, 88; Dissolving Surfaces, Yeats Annual, 89; Yeatsian, Metaphysics, Yeats Annual, 91; Esoteric Yeatsism, Yeats Annual, 93. **CONTACT ADDRESS** Dept of English, Cleveland State Univ, 1983 E 24th St, Cleveland, OH 44115-2440. **EMAIL** sheilaf@stratos.net

FRIEDMAN, DONALD M.
PERSONAL Born 04/08/1929, New York, NY, m, 1959, 2 children **DISCIPLINE** ENGLISH **EDUCATION** Columbia Univ, BA, 49; Cambridge Univ, MA, 58; Harvard Univ, PhD, 60. **CAREER** Teaching fel, Harvard Univ, 56-60, instr English, 60-61; from asst prof to assoc prof, 61-73, PROF ENGLISH, UNIV CALIF, BERKELEY, 73-. **HONORS AND AWARDS** Guggenheim Fel, 74-76; Berkeley Distinguished teaching award; Berkeley citation; Phi Beta Kappa excellence in teaching award. **MEMBERSHIPS** MLA; Renaissance Soc Am; Milton Soc Am. **RESEARCH** Tudor poetry; seventeenth century poetry. **SELECTED PUBLICATIONS** Auth, Marvell's Pastoral Art. **CONTACT ADDRESS** Dept of English, Univ of California, Berkeley, Berkeley, CA 94720.

FRIEDMAN, JOHN BLOCK
PERSONAL Born 12/08/1934, Troy, NY, m, 1962, 2 children **DISCIPLINE** MEDIEVAL ENGLISH LITERATURE **EDUCATION** Reed Col, BA, 60; Johns Hopkins Univ, MA, 61; Mich State Univ, PhD (English), 65. **CAREER** Asst prof English, Conn Col, 65-68; from asst prof to assoc prof, Sir George Williams Univ, 68-71; PROF ENGLISH, UNIV ILL, URBANA, 71-, Res, Ctr Study Medieval Civilization, Poiters, France, 73; Inst Southeastern Medieval and Renaissance Studies fel, 75; assoc, Ctr Advanced Studies, Univ Ill, 75-76; Guggenheim Mem Found fel, 79-80. **MEMBERSHIPS** MLA; Mediaeval Acad Am; Philol Asn Pac Coast. **RESEARCH** Medieval literature and iconography; survival of the classics. **CONTACT ADDRESS** Dept of English, Univ of Illinois, Urbana-Champaign, Urbana, IL 61801. **EMAIL** johannes@raex.com

FRIEDMAN, MELVIN JACK
PERSONAL Born 03/07/1928, Brooklyn, NY, m, 1958, 2 children **DISCIPLINE** ENGLISH, COMPARATIVE LITERATURE **EDUCATION** Bard Col, AB, 49; Columbia Univ, AM, 52; Yale Univ, PhD (comp lit), 54. **CAREER** Assoc ed, French Studies, Yale Univ, 51-53; assoc prof comp lit, Univ Md, 62-66; PROF COMP LIT, UNIV WIS-MILWAUKEE, 66-, Vis sr fel, Univ EAnglia, 72; mem fel comt, Nat Endowment for Humanities, 73-74; Fulbright sr lectr, Univ Antwerp, 76. **MEMBERSHIPS** MLA; PEN. **RESEARCH** Twentieth century novel; 20th century literary criticism. **SELECTED PUBLICATIONS** Auth, 3 Views Of Modernism, Mississippi Quart, Vol 46, 93; Wandering and Home, Beckett Metaphysical Narrative, Contemporary Lit, Vol 36, 95; The Beckett Studies Reader, Contemporary Literature, Vol 36, 95; Beckett Dying Words, Contemporary Lit, Vol 36, 95; Nobodys Home, Speech, Self, and Place in American Fiction from Hawthorne to Delillo, Novel Forum Fiction, Vol 28, 95; Cabell, James, Branch and Richmond In Virginia, Am Lit, Vol 66, 94; Innovation in Beckett, Samuel Fiction, Contemporary Lit, Vol 36, 95; Accidents of Influence, Writing as a Woman and a Jew in America, Int Fiction Rev, Vol 20, 93. **CONTACT ADDRESS** Dept of Comp Lit, Univ of Wisconsin, Milwaukee, Milwaukee, WI 53201.

FRIEDMAN, MICHAEL D.
PERSONAL Born 02/09/1960, Kansas City, MO, m, 1987, 2 children **DISCIPLINE** ENGLISH **EDUCATION** Tulane Univ, BA, 82; Boston Univ, MA, 85, PhD, 90. **CAREER** Vis asst prof, St John's Univ, 90-91; from asst prof to assoc prof, Univ Scranton, 91-. **HONORS AND AWARDS** Grad fel, 84-85; Presidential Univ tchg fel, 85-89; tchg fel, Boston Univ, 86-90; Phi Beta Kappa & Engl Honor Soc, Tulane Univ; grad sch prize excellence tchg, Boston Univ, 89; Hum Found grant, 89; internal res grant, Univ Scranton, 91 & 92; stipend for Folger Shakespeare Libr Inst, Nat Endowment Hum, 96; tchg improvt grant, Univ Scranton, 97; Coop Endowment grant, Univ Scranton, 99. **MEMBERSHIPS** AAUP; MLA; Shakespeare Asn Am; Shakespeare and Renaissance Asn WV. **RESEARCH** Shakespeare; Renaissance lit; dramatic lit; film. **SELECTED PUBLICATIONS** Repr in, Gale Res Yearbook of Shakespearean Crit 16 (90); "'Hush'd on Purpose to Grace Harmony': Wives and Silence in Much Ado About Nothing," Theatre J 42 (90); "What is Harold Pinter's Middle Name?", Penn English 16 (92); auth, "'For Man is a Giddy Thing, and This is My Conclusion': Fashion and Much Ado About Nothing," Text Perf Quart 13 (93); rev, of Shakespearean Performance as Interpretation, by Herbert Coursen, Shakespeare Yearbk 4 (94); To be slow in words is a woman's only virtue': Silence and Satire in The Two Gentlemen of Verona, Selected Papers from the W Va Shakespeare and Renaissance Asn 17 (94); repr in, Two Gentlemen of Verona: Critical Essays, NY, Garland, 95; Wishing a more strict restraint': Feminist Performance and the Silence of Isabella, Selected Papers from the W Va Shakespeare and Renaissance Asn 19 (96); O, let him marry her': Matrimony and Recompense in Measure for Measure, Shakespeare Quart 46 (95); Male Bonds and Marriage in All's Well and Much Ado, Stud in Eng Lit 35 (95); Service is no heritage': Bertram and the Ideology of Procreation, Stud in Philol 92 (95); Wishing a more strict restraint': Feminist Performance and the Silence of Isabella, Selected Papers from the W Va Shakespeare and Renaissance Asn 19 (96); auth, Prostitution and the Feminist Appropriation of Measure for Measure on the Stage, Shakespeare Bull 15 (97); auth, "The Duke in Measure for Measure and the Virtue in 'What If?'" Shakespeare and the Classam 6 (98); auth, "Independence Day: The Am Henry V and the Myth of David," Lit/Film Quart 28 (00). **CONTACT ADDRESS** Dept of Eng, Univ of Scranton, Scranton, PA 18510. **EMAIL** friedmanm1@uofs.edu

FRIEDMAN, NORMAN
PERSONAL Born 04/10/1925, Boston, MA, m, 1945, 2 children **DISCIPLINE** ENGLISH, PSYCHOLGOY **EDUCATION** Harvard Univ, AB, 48, AM, 49, PhD (English), 52; Adelphi Univ, MSW, 78. **CAREER** From instr to assoc prof English, Univ Conn, 52-63; assoc prof to full prof english, Queens Col and Grad Center, CUNY, 63-88; Am Coun Learned Soc grants, 59 and 60; Fulbright lectr, Univs Nantes and Nice, 66-67; consult, PMLA. **HONORS AND AWARDS** Bowdoin Prize, 48; Northwest Rev Annual Poetry Prize, 63; Borestone Mountain Poetry Awds, 64, 67. **MEMBERSHIPS** MLA, NCTE, ALA, NASW. **RESEARCH** Literary criticism and critical theory; Victorian and modern literature; psychology and literature. **SELECTED PUBLICATIONS** Auth, E.E. Cummings: The Art of His Poetry, Baltimore: Johns Hopkins Press, London: Oxford University Press, 60; auth, Poetry: An Introduction to Its Form and Art, with Charles A. McLaughlin, New York: Harper, 61; auth, Logic, Rhetoric, and Style, with Charles A. McLaughlin, Boston: Little, Brown, 63; auth, E.E. Cummings: The Growth of a Writer, Carbondale: Southern Illinois University Press, 64; auth, E.E. Cummings: A Collection of Critical Essays, Englewood Cliffs, New Jersey: Prentice-Hall Spectrum Books, Twentieth Century Views, 72; auth, Form and Meaning in Fiction, Athens: University of Georgia Press, 75; auth, The Magic Badge: Poems 1953-1984, Austin, Texas: Slough Press, 84; auth, The Intrusions of Love, Poems, Lewiston, NY: Mellen Poetry Press, 92; auth, (Re)Valuing Cummings: Further Essays on the Poet, 1962-1993, Gainsville: University Press of Florida, 96. **CONTACT ADDRESS** 33-54 164 St, Flushing, NY 11358-1442. **EMAIL** nfriedman18@aol.com

FRIEDMAN, PHILIP ALLAN
PERSONAL Born 07/19/1927, Brooklyn, NY **DISCIPLINE** ENGLISH LITERATURE, AMERICAN PHILOSOPHY **EDUCATION** NYork Univ, BA, 48; Columbia Univ, MA, 49; Univ Heidelberg, cert ling and philol, 55. **CAREER** Reporter and bk reviewer, Jewish Examiner, 48-49; prof asst, Toby Press, New York, 50-51; asst ed, Random House, Inc, New York, 51-52; instr English compos and contemp lit, Wayne State Univ, 53-54, 55-58; from asst prof to assoc prof Am Lit and studies, Calif State Univ, Los Angeles, 59-77, prof, 77-80., Consult, State Dept Comt For Visitors, Mich, 53-54, 55-58; consult and mem bd, Jewish Community Libr, Jewish Fed Coun Greater Los Angeles, 72; consult drama, Henry Street Settlement Children's Theater, 77-; referee and consult history, Hist, 78-. **MEMBERSHIPS** AAUP. **RESEARCH** Am Lit and culture; philosophy of science. **SELECTED PUBLICATIONS** Auth, Slapping Back, Aba J, Vol 82, 96. **CONTACT ADDRESS** 100 N Detroit Los, Los Angeles, CA 90036.

FRIEDMAN, SIDNEY JOSEPH
PERSONAL Born 06/08/1939, Des Moines, IA, m, 1962, 2 children **DISCIPLINE** ENGLISH, DRAMA **EDUCATION** Princeton Univ, AB, 61; Univ IA, MA, 63, PhD, 66. **CAREER** Assoc prof Eng & drama, WA Univ, 66-81; assoc prof, 81-98, Prof Theatre Arts, Boston Univ, 98. **MEMBERSHIPS** Asn Theatre in High Educ. **RESEARCH** Acting; directing; dramatic criticism. **CONTACT ADDRESS** Sch of Theatre Arts, Boston Univ, 855 Commonwealth Ave, Boston, MA 02215-1303. **EMAIL** sidf@bu.edu

FRIEDMAN, STANLEY
PERSONAL Born 05/03/1933, New York, NY, m, 1967, 2 children **DISCIPLINE** VICTORIAN & ENGLISH RENAISSANCE LITERATURE **EDUCATION** Columbia Univ, AB, 54, AM, 55, PhD, 63. **CAREER** Instr English, Univ NE, 55-56; lectr, 61-63, instr, 63-66, asst prof, 67-79, assoc prof, 80-98, Assoc Prof Emeritus English, Queens Col, City Univ NY, 98-; co-ed, Dickens Studies Annual, 96-. **HONORS AND AWARDS** Danforth Asn (with wife), 70-85. **MEMBERSHIPS** Dickens Soc. **RESEARCH** Dickens; Shakespeare. **SELECTED PUBLICATIONS** Auth, The motif of reading in Our Mutual Friend, Nineteenth Century Fiction, 6/73; Dickens' Mid-Victorian theodicy: David Copperfield, Dickens Studies Annual, Vol 7, 78; The Complex Origins of Pip and Magwitch, Dickens Studies Annual, Vol 15, 86; Estella's Parentage and Pip's Persistence: the Outcome of Great Expectations, Studies in the Novel, winter 87; A Considerate Ghost: George Rouncewell in Bleak House, Dickens Studies Annual, Vol 17, 88; Sad Stephen and Troubled Louisa: Paired Protagonists in Hard Times, Dickens Quart, 6/90; Heep and Powell: Dickensian Revenge?, Dickensian, spring 94; Recent Dickens studies: 1992, Dickens Studies Annual, Vol 23, 94. **CONTACT ADDRESS** Dept of English, Queens Col, CUNY, 6530 Kissena Blvd, Flushing, NY 11367-1597.

FRIEDRICH, GUSTAV WILLIAM
PERSONAL Born 03/02/1941, Hastings, NE, m, 1962, 1 child **DISCIPLINE** COMMUNICATION **EDUCATION** Univ Minn, Minneapolis, BA, 64; Univ Kans, MA, 67, PhD(speech commun), 68. **CAREER** Teacher, St John's Lutheran Sch, Minn, 61-62; assoc prof commun, Purdue Univ, West Lafayette, 68-77; prof speech commun & chairperson dept, Univ Nebr-Lincoln, 77-81; prof Commun & Chemn dept, Univ Okla, 82-98; asst prof hist, 75-79; from assoc prof to prof, 79-87; Cameron Univ; prof and dean, School of Commun, Informarion and Library Studies, Rutgers Univ, 98-. **HONORS AND AWARDS** Phi Kappa Phi, 92; Regents' Awd for Superior Teching, 92; Henry Daniel Rinsland Memorial Awd for Excellence in Educational Res, 95; OSTCA Josh Lee Service Awd, 95; Kenneth E. Crook Fac Awd, Col of Liberal Studies, 98; Presidential Professorship, 98. **MEMBERSHIPS** Am Educ Res Asn; Cent States Speech Asn; Int Commun Asn; National Commun Asn; Am Psychol AsnSoc for Historians of the Early American Republic, Phi Alpha Theta Int Honor Soc in History. **RESEARCH** Classroom communication; interpersonal communication; experimental research methodology. **CONTACT ADDRESS** Dept of Communication, Univ of Oklahoma, 610 Elm Ave Rm 101, Norman, OK 73019-2081. **EMAIL** Fredrich@ou.edu

FRIEDRICH, PAUL
PERSONAL Born 10/22/1927, Cambridge, MA, m, 1996, 6 children **DISCIPLINE** LINGUISTICS, ANTHROPOLOGY, POETRY **EDUCATION** Harvard Univ, BA, 50, MA, 51; Yale Univ, PhD, 57. **CAREER** Res assoc, Russ Res Ctr, 49-50; asst prof anthrop, Harvard Univ, 57-58; asst prof jr ling, Deccan Col, India, 58-59; asst prof anthrop, Univ Pa, 59-62; assoc prof, 62-67, prof anthrop & ling, Univ Chicago, 67-; prof anthrop, ling & soc thought, 92. **MEMBERSHIPS** Ling See Am; Amer Anthro Assoc; Amer Acad Arts & Sci . **RESEARCH** Homeric Greek; Russian, Comp. Poetics. **SELECTED PUBLICATIONS** Auth, Russia and Eurasia, Encyclopedic 1 World, Cultures, 94; auth, Music in Russian Poetry, Lang, 98. **CONTACT ADDRESS** Dept of Anthrop, Univ of Chicago, 1126 E 59th St, Chicago, IL 60637-1539.

FRIEL, JAMES P.
PERSONAL Born Bronx, NY, m, 1976 **DISCIPLINE** PHILOSOPHY, LITERATURE **EDUCATION** Marist Col, BA, 56; Fordham Univ, MA, 65. **CAREER** Teacher English, Marist Bro Schs, 56-63 & Cent Sch Dist, Syosset, 63-68; prof philos, Marist Col & Col of Mt St Vincent, 68-69; Prof English & Philos, State Univ NY Farmingdale, 70-, Ed, Aitia Mag, 72-; State Univ NY grant, 73; Matchette Found grant & dir study group, 76-80; chmn two-yr teaching comt, Am Philos Asn, 77-82. **MEMBERSHIPS** Am Philos Asn; Nat Workshop Conf; Nat Info & Resource Ctr Teaching Philos. **RESEARCH** Metaphysics; humor; citizenship. **SELECTED PUBLICATIONS** Ed, Philosophy of Religion, State Univ NY, 73; auth, Citizen apprenticeship, Aitia Mag, 74-75; ed, Philosophy, Law, Modern Citizen, State Univ NY Farmingdale, 75; auth, Report on National Workship Conference, Aitia Mag, 76; Paying through the nose to lift those Sunday blues, Newday, 10/76; The mall the merrier, or is it?, NY Times, 11/76; ed, Nineteenth Century American Literature, State Univ NY, (in press). **CONTACT ADDRESS** SUNY, Col of Tech at Farmingdale, 1250 Melville Rd, Farmingdale, NY 11735-1389. **EMAIL** frieljp@suny.farmingdale.edu

FRIER, BRUCE W.
PERSONAL Born 08/31/1943, Chicago, IL, s **DISCIPLINE** HISTORY OF LAW, CLASSICAL STUDIES **EDUCATION** Trinity Col, BA, 64; Fel, Am Acad in Rome, 68; Princeton Univ, PhD, 70. **CAREER** Asst prof to prof, Univ Mich, 69-. **HONORS AND AWARDS** Fel, Am Coun of Learned Soc; Fel, NEH, 76-77; Goodwin Awd, Am Philol Asn, 83; Guggenheim Fel, 84-85; Fel, Clare Hall, 84-85; Fel, NEH, 92-93; Fel, Am Acad of Arts and Sci, 93-; LS and A Excellence in Res Awd, 96. **MEMBERSHIPS** Am Philol Asn; Am Soc for Legal Hist. **RESEARCH** Roman law and legal history; Roman social, economic, and demographic history; Hellenistic and Roman historiography, especially Polybius, Sallust, and Livy; Legal theory and the sociology of law; Classical and modern rhetoric. **SELECTED PUBLICATIONS** Co-auth, The Demography of Roman Egypt, Cambridge Univ Press, 94; co-auth, The Census Register P.Oxy 984: The Reverse of Pindar's Paeans, Univ Brussels, 97; auth, Libri Annales Pontificum Maximorum: The

Origins of the Annalistic Tradition, rev ed, Univ Mich Press, 99; co-auth, A Casebook on Roman Family Law, Scholars Press, (forthcoming); auth, Roman Law and the Social Sciences, Verlag, (forthcoming). **CONTACT ADDRESS** Sch of Law, Univ of Michigan, Ann Arbor, Univ Mich, Ann Arbor, MI 48109-1215. **EMAIL** bwfrier@umich.edu

FRIES, MAUREEN HOLMBERG
PERSONAL Born 07/14/1931, Buffalo, NY, d, 4 children **DISCIPLINE** ENGLISH LITERATURE **EDUCATION** D'Youville Col, AB, 52; Cornell Univ, MA, 53; State Univ NYork Buffalo, PhD, 69. **CAREER** Instr English, State Univ NY Buffalo, 64-69; asst prof to assoc prof, 69-77, prof Eng, State Univ NY Col Fredonia, 77-90. **HONORS AND AWARDS** NEH fel, 75-76; res awards, State Univ NY, 72, 73, 79 & 80; co-dir, Conversation in the Disciplines, 80; distinguished teach prof, 90; distinguished prof emerita, 97-, Chancellor's Awd for Excellence in Teaching, State Univ NY, 77. **MEMBERSHIPS** MLA; Int Arthurian Soc; Mediaeval Acad Am. **RESEARCH** Medieval English literature; Arthurian literature; women's studies. **SELECTED PUBLICATIONS** Co-ed, Approaches to Teaching the Arthurian Tradition, New York: Modern Language Association of America, 92; art, Sexuality and Women in the Old Irish Sagas, Celtic Connections, ACTA, Binghamton: SUNY Press, 93; Natural and art, Unnatural Childhoods in T.H. White's The Once and Future King, The Platte Valley Review, 93; art, How Many Roads to Camelot? The Married Knight in Malory's Morte Darthur,Culture and the King: The Social Implications of the Arthurian Legend, Essays in Honor of Professor Valerie M. LagorioAlbany: SUNY Press, 94; art, From the Lady to the Tramp: The Decline of Morgan le Fay in Medieval Romance, Arthuriana, 94; art, Geoffrey of Monmouth, The Dictionary of Literary Biography, Old and Middle English Literature, Detroit: Gale, 94; **CONTACT ADDRESS** Dept of English, SUNY, Col at Fredonia, Fredonia, NY 14063-1143.

FRIESEN, LAUREN
PERSONAL Born 01/05/1943, NE, m, 1970, 2 children **DISCIPLINE** THEATRE, RELIGION **EDUCATION** Bethel Col, BA, 67; Pac School Relig, MA, 81; Univ Berkeley, PhD, 85. **CAREER** Freelance writer, 70-75; educ dir, Wash Comm for Humanities, 76-98; prof, Goshen Col, 82-97; dir of playwriting, Univ of Mich, 97-. **HONORS AND AWARDS** Merit Awd for Excellence in Teaching, Mich, 99; Excellence in Univ Theater, 98; Outstanding Achievement in Univ Theatre, IA, 97. **MEMBERSHIPS** The Dramatists Guild, Asn for Theatre in Higher Educ. **RESEARCH** Playwriting, 20th Century Theatre. **SELECTED PUBLICATIONS** Ed, Best Student One-Acts, Dramatic Pub Co, 95; auth, Wildflowers, Aran Press, 99; auth, "Transcendence in Modern and Post Modern Plays, 99; auth, King David, Samuel French, Inc., 89. **CONTACT ADDRESS** Dept Drama & Theatre, Univ of Michigan, Flint, 303 E Kearsley St, Flint, MI 48502-1907. **EMAIL** lfriesen@flint.umich.edu

FRISCHER, BERNARD D.
PERSONAL Born 05/23/1949, Cleveland, OH, m, 1979 **DISCIPLINE** CLASSICAL STUDIES **EDUCATION** Wesleyan Univ, BA, 71; Univ Heidelberg, PhD, 75. **CAREER** Asst Prof to Full Prof and Dir, 76-. **HONORS AND AWARDS** Fel, Woodrow Wilson, 71; Mich Soc of Fel, 71-74; Fel, Am Acad in Rome, 74-76, 96; Fel, Am Coun of Learned Soc, 81-82, 96-97; Fel, Ctr for Adv Study in the Visual Arts, 97; Phi Beta Kappa, 70. **MEMBERSHIPS** Archaeol Inst of Am; Am Philol Asn; Renaissance Soc of Am. **RESEARCH** Virtual reality applied to cultural heritage; Roman archaeology and topography; Roman literature; Stylometrics; The reception of Antiquity. **SELECTED PUBLICATIONS** Auth, Shifting Paradigms. New Approaches to Horace's Ars Poetica, Am Philol Ans, 91; auth, "Rezeptionsgeschichte and Interpretation: The Quarrel of Antonio Riccoboni and Niccolo Cologno about the Structure of Horace's Ars Poetica," Zeitgenosse Horaz, 96; co-auth, "'Sentence' Length and Word-Type at 'Sentence' Beginning and End: Reliable Authorship Discriminators for Latin Prose? New Studies on the Authorship of the Historia Augusta," Res in Humanities Computing 96; co-auth, "Word-Order and Transference Between Latin and Greek: the Relative Position of the Accusative Director Object and the Governing Verb in Cassius Dio and Other Greek and Roman Prose Authors," Harvard Studies in Class Philol, 99; co-auth, "Virtual Reality and Ancient Rome: The UCLA Cultural VR Lab's Santa Maria Maggiore Project," Brit Archaeol Reports Intl Series, 00; co-auth, "Notes on the New Excavations at Horace's Villa near Licenza (Roma), Italy," in Memoirs of the American Academy in Rome, 01; co-auth, "From CVR to CVRO: The Past, Present, and Future of Cultural Virtual Reality," in British Archaeol Reports, 01; co-auth, Allan Ramsay and the Search for Horace's Villa, London, 01. **CONTACT ADDRESS** Dept Classics, Univ of California, Los Angeles, 405 Hilgard Ave, Los Angeles, CA 90095-1417. **EMAIL** frischer@ucla.edu

FRISCHKORN, CRAIG
PERSONAL Born 04/27/1963, San Gabriel, CA, m, 1990 **DISCIPLINE** ENGLISH **EDUCATION** SUNY, Buffalo, PhD, 2000. **CAREER** Asst prof, Jamestown Community Col, Jamestown, New York, 89-. **MEMBERSHIPS** MLA, NEMLA, Henry James Soc. **RESEARCH** Literature and film. **SELECTED PUBLICATIONS** Auth, "Jack Kerouac Comes Home to Lowell," Am Theatre (July/Aug 94): 72-73; auth, "Mark Twain's 'Edward Mills and George Benton: A Tale,' " The Explicator, 53:4 (summer 95): 214-15; auth, "Style in Advanced Composition: Active Students and Passive Voice," Teaching English in the Two-Year Col, 26:4 (May 99): 415-418; auth, "Rewriting Henry James's The Aspern Papers: A Study of Martin Gabel's The Lost Moment," Popular Culture Rev 10:2 (Aug 99): 21-32; auth, "The Shadow of Tsoai: Autobiographical Bear Power in N. Scott Momaday's The Ancient Child," J of Popular Culture, Vol 33.2 (fall 99): 23-29; auth, "Frank Lloyd's Berkeley Square: Readapting Henry James's The Sense of the Past," Lit/Film Quart, Vol 28.1 (Jan 2000). **CONTACT ADDRESS** Dept Humanities & Fine Arts, Jamestown Comm Col, PO Box 20, Jamestown, NY 14702-0020. **EMAIL** CraigFrischkorn@hotmail.com

FRITZ, DONALD WAYEN
PERSONAL Born 06/11/1933, Monroe, WI **DISCIPLINE** MEDIEVAL BRITISH LITERATURE **EDUCATION** Miami Univ, BA, 56, MA, 59; Stanford Univ, PhD(English), 68. **CAREER** Instr English, Southern Methodist Univ, 59-63, Stanford Univ, 67-68; prof english, Miami Univ, 68-; dir, Performing Arts Sci, 82-98. **HONORS AND AWARDS** Public Rel Mgr, Phi Kappa Phi, 97-00; Golden Key Nat Hon Soc, 94. **MEMBERSHIPS** MLA; Midwest Mod Lang Asn; S Atlantic Mod Lang Asn; Chaucer Soc; Board Memr: Cincinnati Chamber Music Society, 98-00; Cincinnati Opera, 98-; Campus Ministry Center; Coun on Minister, Oxford United Methodist Church. **RESEARCH** Chaucer; Anglo-Saxon poetry; 14th century British poetry of Chaucer. **SELECTED PUBLICATIONS** Auth, Caedmon: A traditional poet, Mediaeval Studies, 69; Caedmon: A monastic exeget, Am Benedictine Rev, 74; The prioress's avowal of ineptitude, Chaucer Rev, 74; Chronological impossibilities in Widsith, Ger Notes, 75; The origin and meaning of pattern in Kells, J Anal Psychol, 77; Perspectives on Creativity and the Unconscious, Oxford Univ, 79; The Pearl and the sacredness of number, Am Benedictine Rev, 80; The animus-ridden wife of Bath, J Anal Psychol, 80; Reflection in a Golden Eye: Chaucer's Narcissistic Pardon, Chaucer Rev, 84. **CONTACT ADDRESS** 4 Ives Woods Dr, Oxford, OH 45052. **EMAIL** fritzdw@muohio.edu

FRITZELL, PETER A.
PERSONAL Born 08/23/1940, Minneapolis, MN, m, 1962, 2 children **DISCIPLINE** ENGLISH, AMERICAN LITERATURE **EDUCATION** Univ NDak, BA, 62; Stan Univ, MA, 66; PhD, 66. **CAREER** Asst prof, Law Univ, 66-73; vis asst prof, Stan Univ, 68; vis schl, Dart Col, 72-73; assoc prof, Law Univ, 73-83; vis assoc prof, Stan Univ, 74, 77; dir, Law Univ, 77-78; ch, 73-77, 87-90; prof, 83-. **HONORS AND AWARDS** Phi Beta Kappa; NEH Fel, 72, 81; Danforth Assoc; Excell Teach, 88; Maxwell Anderson Awd in Arts and Letters, Univ ND, 99. **MEMBERSHIPS** MLA; FHS; ASLE; ISLE. **RESEARCH** Nature writing. **SELECTED PUBLICATIONS** Auth, "American Wetlands as Cultural Symbol," in Wetland Functions and Values: The State of Our Understanding, ed. Phillip Greeson et al, American Water Res Asn (79): 523-534; auth, "Walden and Paradox: Thoreau as Self-Conscious Ecologist," New Eng Rev 3 (80): 51-67; auth, "Changing Conceptions of the Great Lakes Forest: Jacque Cartier to Sigurd Olson," in The Great Lakes Forest: An Environmental and Social History, ed. Susan Flader (Minneapolis: Univ Minn Press, 83), 274- 294; auth, Nature Writing and America: Essays upon a Cultural Type, Iowa State Univ Press (Ames, IA), 90; auth, "Aldo Leopold," in American Nature Writers, ed. John Elder (NY: Scribner's, 96), 525-547. **CONTACT ADDRESS** Dept English, Lawrence Univ, PO Box 599, Appleton, WI 54912-0599. **EMAIL** fritzelp@lawrence.edu

FROEHLICH, CHARLES DONALD
PERSONAL Born 05/07/1927, Goose Creek, TX **DISCIPLINE** THEOLOGY, CLASSICS **EDUCATION** Concordia Sem, BA, 52, BD, 55, STM, 58; Univ Tex, Austin, MA, 52. **CAREER** Instr hist, Greek & Latin, St John's Col, Kans, 50-52; instr, New Testament & Greek, Concordia Sem, 55-57; instr, theol & Latin, Lutheran High Schs, St Louis, 57-62; assoc prof, 62-80, Prof Theol & Class Lang, Concordia Teachers Col, Ill, 80- **MEMBERSHIPS** Class Asn Midwest & S. **RESEARCH** New Testament; medieval Christianity; patristics. **SELECTED PUBLICATIONS** Auth, Logophiles of the world, unite!, Lutheran Educ, 11-12/73. **CONTACT ADDRESS** Dept of Theol, Concordia Univ, Illinois, 7400 Augusta St, River Forest, IL 60305-1402.

FROESE TIESSEN, HILDI
DISCIPLINE ENGLISH LITERATURE **EDUCATION** Univ Winnipeg, BA, 68; Univ Alberta, MA, 71, PhD, 81. **CAREER** Assoc prof **RESEARCH** Politics of art; literature of ethnic and religious minorities in Canada; Rudy Wiebe, Patrick Friesen and Di Brandt. **CONTACT ADDRESS** Dept of English, Univ of Waterloo, Conrad Grebel Col, 200 Westmount Rd, Waterloo, ON, Canada N2L 3G6. **EMAIL** htiessen@uwaterloo.ca

FROMM, GLORIA GLIKIN
PERSONAL Born 11/14/1931, Newark, NY **DISCIPLINE** ENGLISH **EDUCATION** NYork Univ, BA, 52, MA, 56, PhD (English), 61. **CAREER** Asst English, sch commerce, NY Univ, 57-59; instr, Brooklyn Col, 61-65, asst prof, 65-70; assoc prof, 70-78, PROF ENGLISH, UNIV ILL, CHICAGO CIRCLE, 78-, Am Coun Learned Soc grant, 67. **MEMBERSHIPS** MLA. **RESEARCH** Twentieth century novel, biography and autobiography. **SELECTED PUBLICATIONS** Auth, Richardson And Co , Library Chronicle Univ Texas Austin, Vol 23, 93; Women and Social Action in Victorian and Edwardian England, Eng Lit Transition 1880-1920, Vol 36, 93. **CONTACT ADDRESS** Dept of English, Univ of Illinois, Chicago, Box 4348, Chicago, IL 60680.

FROSCH, THOMAS RICHARD
PERSONAL Born New York, NY **DISCIPLINE** ENGLISH LITERATURE **EDUCATION** Wesleyan Univ, BA, 64; Yale Univ, MA, 66, PhD (English), 68. **CAREER** Asst prof English, NY Univ, 68-71; PROF ENGLISH, QUEENS COL, 71-. **SELECTED PUBLICATIONS CONTACT ADDRESS** Dept of English, Queens Col, CUNY, 6530 Kissena Blvd, Flushing, NY 11367-1597.

FROST, ELISABETH
DISCIPLINE MODERN AND CONTEMPORARY AMERICAN POETRY, CREATIVE WRITING **EDUCATION** Harvard-Radcliffe, AB; Stanford, MA; UCLA, PhD. **CAREER** Asst prof, Fordham Univ. **RESEARCH** Feminist theory, experimental writing. **SELECTED PUBLICATIONS** Auth, " The Didactic Comus: Henry Lawes and the Trial of Virtue," Comitatus: A Journal of Medieval and Renaissance Studies 22 (91), 87-103; auth, Revisions of Romanticism in 'Notes toward a Supreme Fiction,'" The Wallace Stevens Journal 15, (91), 37-54; auth " Fetishism and Parody in Stein's Tender Buttons." Sexual Artifice: Persons, Images, Politics,(Genders 19) NY U P (94): 64-93; auth, " Signifying on Stein: The Revisionist Poetics of Harryette Mullen and Leslie Scalapino," Postmodern Culture: An Electronic Journal of Interdisciplinary Criticism 5:3, (95); auth An Interview with Leslie Scalapino, Contemporary Literature 37:1, (96), 1-23; auth, Mina Loy's Mongrel Poetics, Mina Loy: Woman and Poet, Nat Poetry Found, (98), 149-179; auth, " Leslie Scalapino," The Dictionary of Literary Biography Vol 193: American Poets Since WWII, Sixth Series, Gale Research, (98), 318-328; auth, " 'Ruses of the lunatic Muse': Harryette Mullen and Lyric Hybridity," Women's Studies 27 (98), 465-481; auth, " Susan Howe, Modernism, and Antinomian Tradition," How2: A Journal of Innovative Writing by Women, 00; auth, "' Timeless-time or Hieroglyph': Self and Simulacrum in H D and Leslie Scalapino," H D and Poets After, Iowa City, U of Iowa, (00), 211-224. **CONTACT ADDRESS** Dept of Eng Lang and Lit, Fordham Univ, 113 W 60th St, New York, NY 10023.

FROST, LINDA ANNE
DISCIPLINE ENGLISH **EDUCATION** Bowling Green State Univ, BA, 85; SUNY at Stonybrook, PhD, 90. **CAREER** Asst prof, Eng, Penn State-Wilkes-Barre; asst prof to assoc prof, Univ Ala, Birmingham. **MEMBERSHIPS** Am Antiquarian Soc **SELECTED PUBLICATIONS** Auth, "'The Red Face of Man', The Penobscot Indian, and a Conflict of Interest in Thoreau's Maine Woods," ESQ 39, 93. **CONTACT ADDRESS** Dept of English, Univ of Alabama, Birmingham, HB 208, Birmingham, AL 35294-1260. **EMAIL** lfrost@uab.edu

FROULA, CHRISTINE
DISCIPLINE ENGLISH **EDUCATION** Chicago Univ, PhD. **CAREER** Guggenheim fel; Herman and Beulah Pearce Miller res prof, Northwestern Univ. **RESEARCH** Interdisciplinary modernism, 19th and 20th century literature. **CONTACT ADDRESS** Dept of English, Northwestern Univ, 1801 Hinman, Evanston, IL 60208.

FRUSHELL, RICHARD CLAYTON
PERSONAL Born 08/25/1935, Pittsburgh, PA, m, 1958, 5 children **DISCIPLINE** ENGLISH **EDUCATION** Duquesne Univ, PhD (English), 68. **CAREER** Teacher English, Oliver High Sch, Pittsburgh, Pa, 61-66; from asst prof to assoc prof, 68-71; PROF ENGLISH, IND STATE UNIV, TERRE HAUTE, 75-, Contribr, Annual Bibliog Eng Lang and Lit, Mod Humanities Res Asn, 71-75; fel, Lilly Libr, 77. **HONORS AND AWARDS** Caleb Mills Distinguished Teaching Awd, Ind State Univ, 74. **MEMBERSHIPS** Am Soc 18th Century Studies; MLA; Mod Humanities Res Asn; Spenser Soc; Poe Studies Asn. **RESEARCH** Restoration and eighteenth century English literature; Renaissance English literature; bibliography. **SELECTED PUBLICATIONS** Auth, Swift 6 August 1735 Letter to Delany, Mary, Pendarves, All Other Days I Eat My Chicken Alone Like A King, Philol Quart, Vol 74, 95. **CONTACT ADDRESS** Dept of Humanities and Fine Arts, Pennsylvania State Univ, McKeesport, 400 University Dr, McKeesport, PA 15131-7644.

FRY, CARROL LEE
PERSONAL Born 07/31/1932, New Hampton, MO, m, 1957 **DISCIPLINE** ENGLISH **EDUCATION** Northwest Mo State

Col, BS, 57; Univ Omaha, MA, 62; Univ Nebr, PhD (Eng), 70. **CAREER** Teacher hist and Eng, Maysville High Sch, Mo, 57-58; asst Eng, Univ Kans, 62-63; from instr to assoc prof, Mankato State Col, 63-72; ASSOC PROF and CHMN DEPT, NORTHWEST MO STATE UNIV, 72-, Ed consult, Houghton Mifflin Co, 71-; managing ed, Mo Eng Bull. **MEMBERSHIPS** AAUP; MLA; Midwest Mod Lng Asn. **RESEARCH** Eighteenth century English fiction; Jane Austen's novels; contemporary fiction. **SELECTED PUBLICATIONS** Auth, The Goddess Ascending--Feminist Neo Pagan Witchcraft in Bradley, Marion, Zimmer Novels, J Pop Cult, Vol 27, 93; Economic Issues in the Defense of Directors and Officers of Financial Institutions, Banking Law J, Vol 110, 93. **CONTACT ADDRESS** Dept of English, Northwest Missouri State Univ, Maryville, MO 64469.

FRY, DONALD K.
PERSONAL Born 03/31/1937, Raleigh, NC, m, 1965, 1 child **DISCIPLINE** JOURNALISM **EDUCATION** Duke Univ, AB, 59; Univ Calif Berkeley, MA, 64; PhD, 66. **CAREER** Asst prof, Univ of Va, 66-69; assoc prof to prof, SUNY, 69-86; assoc, Poyneter Inst, 84-93. **HONORS AND AWARDS** NEH; ACLS; Woodrow Wilson. **MEMBERSHIPS** MLA, Medieval Acad of Am. **RESEARCH** Benerable Bede, History of Printing Press, Johann Gutenberg. **SELECTED PUBLICATIONS** Auth, The Beowulf Poet, 68; auth, Beowulf and the Fight at Finnsbark, 69; auth, Finnsbark Episode and Fragment, 74; auth, Norse Sagas in Translation, 80; auth, Medieval Scandinavia, 93; auth, Believing the News, 86; auth, Best Newspaper writing, 85-90, 93; auth, Coaching Writers, 91. **CONTACT ADDRESS** 35 University Cir, Charlottesville, VA 22903-1801. **EMAIL** donaldfry@cs.com

FRY, KATHERINE G.
PERSONAL Born 11/03/1961, Hamilton, MT, m, 1990, 1 child **DISCIPLINE** COMMUNICATIONS **EDUCATION** Univ Minn, BA, 85; Temple Univ, MA, 89; PhD, 94 **CAREER** Ed, Univ of Minn, 86-87; Ed asst, Temple Univ, 88; teaching & res asst, Temple Univ, 88-92; asst dir, Inst of Culture and Commun, Temple Univ, 88-91; ed asst, Critical Studies in Mass Commun, 89-91; tutor, Univ Writing Ctr, Temple Univ, 91-92; inst, Drexel Univ, 92; inst, Ursinus Col, 90-93; inst, Long Island Univ-Brooklyn, 93; inst, Brooklyn Col, 93-94; assoc prof, Dept of Television & Radio, Brooklyn Col, CUNY, 94-. **MEMBERSHIPS** Nat Commun Assoc; Int Commun Assoc; NYork State Commun Assoc. **RESEARCH** Cultural studies of mass media; cultural geography; news; advertising. **SELECTED PUBLICATIONS** Auth, Regional Magazines and the Ideal White Reader: Constructing and Retaining Geography as Text, Elec J of Commun, 4 (94): 2-3; auth, Television and National Identity: The Case of Germany, ALMANAC, 96-97 ed; auth, essays in Encyclopedia of Television, Fitzroy Dearborn Publishers, 97; Myths of Nature and Place: Network Television News Coverage of the Great Flood of 1993, New Dimensions in Commun, 10 (97): 54-68; auth, "A Cultural Geography of Lake Wobegan," Howard J of Commun 9 (98): 303-321; auth, "Starbucks Coffee: Cultivating and Selling the Postmodern Brew," in Critical Studies in Media Commercialism (NY: Oxford Univ Press, 00). **CONTACT ADDRESS** 560 Dean St. #3R, Brooklyn, NY 11217-2113. **EMAIL** kfrbc@cunyvm.cuny.edu

FRYE, JOANNE S.
DISCIPLINE ENGLISH LITERATURE **EDUCATION** Bluffton, BA, 66; Ind Univ, PhD, 74. **CAREER** Prof. **SELECTED PUBLICATIONS** Auth, Living Stories, Telling Lives; Tillie Olson; articles reflecting a feminist approach to literary texts. **CONTACT ADDRESS** Dept of Eng, The Col of Wooster, Wooster, OH 44691.

FRYE, ROLAND MUSHAT
PERSONAL Born 07/03/1921, Birmingham, AL, m, 1947, 1 child **DISCIPLINE** ENGLISH **EDUCATION** Princeton Univ, AB, 43, PhD (English), 52. **CAREER** Instr English, Howard Col, 47-48; from asst prof to prof, Emory Univ, 52-61; res prof, Folger Shakespeare Libr, 62-65; FELIX E SCHELLING PROF ENGLISH, UNIV PA, 65-, Guggenheim res fel, 56-57 and 73-74; Stone lectr and vis lectr, Princeton theol Sem; Am Coun Learned Soc grant, 66, 71 and 78; Am Philos Soc grant, 68, 71 and 78; Nat Endowment Humanities res grant, 73-74; mem, Inst Advan Study, Princeton Univ, 73-74 and 79; fels, Nat Endowment for Humanities, Huntington Libr, 81 and Ctr Theol Inquiry, Princeton, 82. **HONORS AND AWARDS** John Frederick Lewis Prize, Am Philos Soc, 79; James Holly Hanford Awd, Milton Soc Am, 79; Am Philos Soc, Thomas Jefferson Medal, 97. **MEMBERSHIPS** MLA; Renaissance Soc Am; Milton Soc Am (pres, 77-78); Shakespeare Soc Am; Am Philos Soc (secy, 78-81). **RESEARCH** Literature; art; theology. **SELECTED PUBLICATIONS** Auth, Bentley, Gerald, Eades September 15,1901 July 25, 94, Proceedings Am Philos Soc, Vol 140, 96. **CONTACT ADDRESS** Dept of English, Univ of Pennsylvania, Philadelphia, PA 19174.

FRYER, JUDITH
PERSONAL Born 08/05/1939, Minneapolis, MN, 2 children **DISCIPLINE** AMERICAN LITERATURE, HISTORY **EDUCATION** Univ Minn, PhD (Am studies), 73. **CAREER** Instr women's studies, Am studies and Am lit, Univ Minn, 68-73; asst prof, 74-78, ASSOC PROF AM STUDIES, MIAMI UNIV, OXFORD, OHIO, 78-, DIR AM STUDIES PROG, 74-, Instr Am lit, Macalester Col, St Paul, 72; guest prof Am studies, Univ Tîbingen, West Ger, 76-77; res grants, Miami Univ, summers, 75, 79 and 82, Nat Endowment for the Humanities, summers 76 and 78, 79-80; Fulbright grant, 76; fel, Bunting Inst, Harvard Univ, 79-80. **MEMBERSHIPS** Am Studies Asn; Nat Trust for Hist Preservation; Hist Keyboard Soc. **RESEARCH** Women's studies; early music. **SELECTED PUBLICATIONS** Auth, Review of Developments in State Securities Regulation, Business Lawyer, Vol 49, 93. **CONTACT ADDRESS** American Studies Prog, Miami Univ, Oxford, OH 45056.

FRYKHOLM, AMY JOHNSON
PERSONAL Born 12/28/1931, Flint, MI, m, 1996 **DISCIPLINE** AMERICAN LITERATURE **EDUCATION** St Olaf Col, BA, 93; Duke Univ, PhD, 01. **CAREER** Instr, Duke Univ, 95-. **HONORS AND AWARDS** Charlotte Newcombe Dissertation Year Fel, 00-01. **MEMBERSHIPS** MLA; Am Studies Asn; Am Acad of Relig. **RESEARCH** American literature; American religion; Utopianism and apocalypticism; feminism. **SELECTED PUBLICATIONS** Auth, "Re-making Paradise: The Town of Celebration," in Riding on Faith: Essays on Religion, Culture, and the World of Disney, Oxford Univ Press, (forthcoming). **CONTACT ADDRESS** Dept Literature, Duke Univ, 1008 Mount Massive Dr, Leadville, CO 80461-3443. **EMAIL** amy.frykholm@duke.edu

FRYMIER, ANN BAINBRIDGE
PERSONAL Born 12/27/1963, MI, m, 1990, 1 child **DISCIPLINE** COMMUNICATION **EDUCATION** Western Mich Univ, NBS, 86; Univ NC, Chapel Hill, MPH, 88; West Va Univ, EdD, 92. **CAREER** Asst prof, 92-99, assoc prof, Grad Dir, Miami Univ, 99-. **HONORS AND AWARDS** Robert J. Kibler Awd for Outstanding Student Res, 91. **MEMBERSHIPS** Nat Commun Asn, Eastern Commun Asn, Western States Commun Asn, Central States Commun Asn, Int Commun Asn. **RESEARCH** Instructional communication, interpersonal communication. **SELECTED PUBLICATIONS** Coauth, " 'What's in it for me?': Increasing content relevance to enhance students' motivation," Commun Educ, 44 (95): 40-50; coauth, "Using student reports to measure immediacy: Is it a valid methodology?," Commun Res Reports, 12 (95): 85-93; coauth, "The development of a learner empowerment measure," Commun Educ, 45 (96): 181-199; coauth, "Does making content relevant make difference in learning?," Commun Res Reports, 15 (98): 121-129; coauth, "The relationship between student perceptions of instructor humor and students' reports of learning," Commun Educ, 48 (99): 48-62; coauth, "The revised learning indictors scale," Commun Studies, 50, (99): 1-12; coauth, "The teacher-student relationship as an interpersonal relationship," Commun Educ (in press). **CONTACT ADDRESS** Dept Commun, Miami Univ, 160 Bechelor, Oxford, OH 45056. **EMAIL** frymieab@muohio.edu

FU, HONGCHU
PERSONAL Born 01/12/1954, Shanghai, China, m, 1999 **DISCIPLINE** LITERATURE **EDUCATION** Univ Calif at Los Angeles, PhD, 95. **CAREER** Lectr, Smith Col, 95-. **HONORS AND AWARDS** A. Owen Aldridge Prize, 91. **MEMBERSHIPS** AAS, CLTA. **RESEARCH** Chinese Drama, Comparative Language Teaching. **SELECTED PUBLICATIONS** Auth, "Individual Ethics vs. Social Morality: A Comparative Study of Yu Rang Tun Tan and Meda," J of Asian Culture 15 (91-92); auth, "Deconstruction and Taoism: Comparisons Reconsidered," Comparative Lit Studies 29.3 (92); auth, "Historicity of Interpretation: Reflections on Xing in Chinese Poetry," Pacific Coast Philol 29.1 (94); auth, "The Cultural Fashioning of Filial Piety: A Reading of the Yuan Play Xiao Zhangtu (Little Zhang the Butcher)," J of Sung-Yuan Studies 29 (99); auth, "Internet, Multimedia and Chinese Language Teaching," the World of Chinese Lang 92 (99); auth, "Misogyny and Sympathy: Moral Ambivalence in Feng Menglong's Adaptation of the Tale of the White Serpent," Tamkang Rev 29.3 (99). **CONTACT ADDRESS** Dept E Asian Lang & Lit, Smith Col, 98 Green St, Northampton, MA 01063-1000. **EMAIL** hofu@smith.edu

FUCHS, JACOB
PERSONAL Born 12/02/1939, New York, NY, m, 1963, 3 children **DISCIPLINE** ENGLISH LITERATURE **EDUCATION** Univ Calif, Berkeley, BA, 61, MA, 64; Univ Calif, Irvine, PhD (comp lit), 72. **CAREER** PROF ENGLISH, CALIF STATE UNIV, HAYWARD, 71-. **MEMBERSHIPS** Philol Asn of Pac Coast; Am Soc 18th Century Studies. **RESEARCH** Neoclassicism. **SELECTED PUBLICATIONS** Auth, The Greek Gang At Troy, Classical W, Vol 87, 93; auth, Horace's latres and Epistles; auth, Reading Pope's Imitations of Horace; auth, Death of a Dad (mystery novel), articles, scholarly, short fiction. **CONTACT ADDRESS** California State Univ, Hayward, 25800 Carlos Bee Bvd, Hayward, CA 94542-3001.

FUKUYAMA, FRANCIS
PERSONAL Born 10/27/1952, Chicago, IL, m, 1986, 3 children **DISCIPLINE** CLASSICS **EDUCATION** Cornell Univ, BA, 74. **CAREER** Social sci, Rand Corp, 80-81, 83-89, 90-95; State Dept policy planning, 81-82, 89; George Mason Univ Inst of Public Policy, 95- . **HONORS AND AWARDS** Hon doctorate, Conn Col; Permio Capri; Los Angeles Times Critics Awd. **MEMBERSHIPS** Am Polit Sci Asn. **RESEARCH** Democracy, economic culture; social capital. **SELECTED PUBLICATIONS** Co-ed, The Soviet Union and the Third World: The Last Three Decades, Cornell, 87; auth, The End of History and the Last Man, Free Press, 92; auth, Trust: The Social Virtues and the Creation of Prosperity, Free Press, 95; auth, The Primacy of Culture, J of Democracy, 95; auth, Confucianism and Democracy, J of Democracy, 95; auth, Immigration, in Alexander, ed, The New Promise of American Life, Hudson Inst, 95; auth, Virtue and Prosperity, Natl Interest, 95; auth, On the Possibility of Writing a Universal History, in Melzer, ed, History and the Idea of Progress, Cornell, 95; auth, Social Capital and the Global Economy, For Aff, 95; auth, Trust Still Counts in a Virtual World, Forbes ASAP, 96; auth, The Illusion of Exceptionalism, J of Democracy, 97; auth, Is It All In the Genes? Commentary, 97; auth, Asian Values and the Asian Crisis, Commentary, 98; auth, Women and the Evolution of World Politics, For Aff, 98; auth, The great Disruption, Free Press, 99. **CONTACT ADDRESS** Esther Newberg International Creative Mgt, 40 West 57th St, New York, NY 10019. **EMAIL** ffukuyam@gmu.edu

FULK, JANET
DISCIPLINE COMMUNICATION **EDUCATION** OH State Univ, BA, 70, MBA, 77, PhD, 78. **CAREER** Assoc dir, Sch Commun, Univ Southern CA, 95-97 & asst, assoc & prof, 79-97; vis scholar, Stanford Univ, 97; res assoc, Univ Southern CA, 78-79; asst prof, Kent State Univ, 76-78 & vis lectr, Univ Aston Mgt Ctr, 78. **HONORS AND AWARDS** Best Res Article, OCIS Acad Mgt, 93; Int Commun Asn Top Paper Awd(s), 93, 91, 90 & 85; Speech Commun Asn Best Bk Awd, 90. **MEMBERSHIPS** Bd Gov, Acad Mgt, 90-93; Exec Comt, Orgn Behav Div, Acad Mgt, 88-90; div ch, Publ Sector Div, Acad Mgt, 81-82. **RESEARCH** Management and commun effectiveness in organizations and the interplay of organizational sys and commun technol. **SELECTED PUBLICATIONS** Auth, Social construct of commun tech, Acad Mgt Jl, 36, 93; coauth, Electronic Communication and Changing Organizational Forms, Orgn Sci, 95; A soc influence model of technol use, Orgn & commun technol, Newbury Park, Sage, 90; Cognitive elements in the soc construc of commun technol, Mgt Commun Quart, 94; Organizational colleagues, information richness, and electronic mail: A test of the soc influence model of technol use, Commun Res, 18, 91 & Emerging theories of commun in organizations, Yearly Rev J Mgt, 17, 91. **CONTACT ADDRESS** Annenberg School for Commun, Univ of So California, University Park Campus, Los Angeles, CA 90089.

FULKERSON, RAYMOND GERALD
PERSONAL Born 02/19/1941, Owensboro, KY, m, 1960, 3 children **DISCIPLINE** RHETORICAL CRITICISM, AMERICAN PUBLIC ADDRESS **EDUCATION** David Lipscomb Col, BA, 63; Univ IL, Champaign-Urbana, MA, 66, PhD(speech), 71. **CAREER** CHMN DEPT, COMMUN & LIT, FREED-HARDEMAN COL, 65-. **MEMBERSHIPS** Speech Commun Asn; Asn Study Afro-Am Life & Hist; Southern Speech Commun Asn; Int Soc Gen Semantics; Int Commun Asn. **RESEARCH** Rhetoric of the Abolition Movement; Theories and Methods of Rhetorical Criticism. **SELECTED PUBLICATIONS** Auth, Frederick Douglass and the Kansas-Nebraska Act: A Case Study in Agitational Versatility, Cent State Speech J, winter 72; Exile as Emergence: Frederick Douglass in Great Britain, 1845-1847, Quart J Speech, 2/74; textual ed, Frederick Douglass Papers, Yale Univ Press. **CONTACT ADDRESS** Dept of Commun, Freed-Hardeman Univ, 158 E Main St, Henderson, TN 38340-2306. **EMAIL** geraldf@aeneas.net

FULKERSON, RICHARD P.
PERSONAL Born 02/09/1942, Carterville, IL, m, 1963, 2 children **DISCIPLINE** ENGLISH **EDUCATION** SO Illinois Univ, BS 63; Ohio State Univ, PhD 70. **CAREER** Texas A&M Univ, prof 81-; East Texas State Univ, asst, assoc, prof 70-81. **HONORS AND AWARDS** Dist Fac Awd; Outstanding tchr. **MEMBERSHIPS** NCTE; CCCC; RSA; ATAC. **RESEARCH** Written argumentation; Teaching College writing; English as a Profession. **SELECTED PUBLICATIONS** Auth, Teaching the Argument in Writing, Urbana, NCTE, 96; Call Me Horatio: Negotiating Between Cognition and Affect in Composition, Col Comp Comm, 98; The English Doctoral Metacurriculum: An Issue of Ethics, eds, Sheryl Fontaine and Susan Hunter, Foregrounding Ethical Awareness in Eng Studies, Portsmouth NH, Boynton/Cook, 98; Transcending Our Conception of Argument in light of Feminist Critiques, Argumentation and Advocacy, 96; auth, "Transcending our Conception of Argument in Light of Feminist Critiques," Argumentation and Advocacy, 96. **CONTACT ADDRESS** Dept of Lit And Languages, Texas A&M Univ, Commerce, Commerce, TX 75428. **EMAIL** dick_fulkerson@tamu-commerce.edu

FULKERTH, ROBERT C.
PERSONAL Born 01/23/1944, Turlock, CA, m, 1990, 1 child **DISCIPLINE** COMPUTER SCIENCE, ENGLISH **EDUCATION** Calif State Univ, AB, 69; MA, 71; Univ Calif at Berkeley, EdD, 91. **CAREER** Dept of English, Golden Gate Univ at San Francisco, 91-93; assoc prof, Golden Gate Univ at San

Francisco, 93-;ed, Business, Educ and Tech J, Sch of Technol and Industry at Golden Gate Univ. **HONORS AND AWARDS** Golden Apple Awd. **MEMBERSHIPS** Asn of Internet Professionals, Asn for the Advancement of Computing in Educ. **RESEARCH** Online-distance approaches & pedagogy. **SELECTED PUBLICATIONS** Auth, "Teaching for Effectiveness in On-Line Courses," Proceedings for the Syllabus 97 Conference, Sonoma State Univ, 97; auth, "Teaching Business Writing Online: Toward Developing Student Learning and Responsibility in a Flexible Electronic Environment," Flexible Learning in Action: Case Studies in Higher Education, Kogan-Page, 97; auth, "Teaching Business Writing on the Internet: How an Electronic Conference Environment Can be Used in Place of Peer Editing Groups. Proceedings of the Ed-Media & Ed-Telecomm 98 10th World Conference vol 1," Asn for the Advancement of Computing in Educ (98): 360-368; auth, "Crossing the Bridge from Innovation to Market Share," Syllabus Magazine (98); auth, "Keys to the Culture: Factors in Successful DL Implementation. Proceedings, World Conference on Educational Multimedia, Hypermedia, and Telecommunications 99," Asn for the Advancement of Computing in Educ (99). **CONTACT ADDRESS** Dept English, Golden Gate Univ at San Francisco, 536 Mission St, San Francisco, CA 94105-2921. **EMAIL** bfulkerth@ggu.edu

FULLER, HOMER WOODROW
PERSONAL Born 08/14/1916, Dawn, MO, m, 1942, 2 children **DISCIPLINE** MODERN GERMAN LITERATURE **EDUCATION** Emory Univ, AB, 38; Univ Wis, Am, 40, PhD, 52. **CAREER** Teaching fel Ger, Univ NC, 40-41; instr, Emory Univ, 41-45; grad asst, Univ Wis, 45-47; assoc prof Ger lang, 47-73, Prof Ger, Univ Tenn, Knoxville, 73-, Fulbright res scholar, Vienna and Fund Advan Educ fel, 55-56. **MEMBERSHIPS** MLA; SAtlantic Mod Lang Asn. **RESEARCH** Nineteenth century German literature; the German novelle; Theodor Storm's easthetic theories. **SELECTED PUBLICATIONS** Auth, The Schooner Pilgrims Progress, A Voyage Around The World 1932-1934, Am Neptune, Vol 56, 96. **CONTACT ADDRESS** Dept of Ger and Slavic Lang, Univ of Tennessee, Knoxville, Knoxville, TN 37916.

FULLER, LAWRENCE BENEDICT
PERSONAL Born 07/27/1936, Orange, NJ, m, 1971, 2 children **DISCIPLINE** ENGLISH, HISTORY **EDUCATION** Dartmouth Col, AB, 58; Columbia Univ, MA, 63; Pennsylvania State Univ, MA, 83; Johns Hopkins Univ, PhD(Educ), 74. **CAREER** Prof English, Bloomsburg Univ, 71-00; Prof Emeritus, 00-. **HONORS AND AWARDS** Phi Betta Kappa; Phi Kappa Phi; Fulbright Scholar, Norway, 93-94; Czech Republic, 00-01. **MEMBERSHIPS** Hist Educ Soc; NCTE. **RESEARCH** History of education, media studies, literature for adolescents, methods of teaching secondary English. **SELECTED PUBLICATIONS** Auth, A sense of our own history, Independent Sch Bull, 12/71; Private secondary education: the search for a new model, 1880-1915, Foundational Studies, Spring 75; Research papers in English methods classes: introduction to varieties of opinion, English Educ, Summer 76; William M Sloane: A biographical study of turn of the century attitudes toward American education, Foundational Studies, Fall 78; Literature for adolescents: The early days, The ALAN Rev, Spring 79; Students' rights of expression: The decade since Tinker, English J, 12/79; Literature for adolescents: A historical perspective, English Educ, 2/80; Media Education: Where Have We Been? Where Are We Going?, English Education, February, 96. **CONTACT ADDRESS** Dept of English, Bloomsburg Univ of Pennsylvania, 400 E 2nd St, Bloomsburg, PA 17815-1399. **EMAIL** lfuller@planetx.bloomu.edu

FULLER, M. A.
DISCIPLINE CHINESE LITERATURE **EDUCATION** Yale, BA, 74, PhD, 82. **CAREER** Asst prof, Harvard, 84-90; asst prof, 92-93, assoc prof, Univ CA, Irvine, 93-. **RESEARCH** Classical Chinese poetry; literary theory. **SELECTED PUBLICATIONS** Auth, Road to East Slope: the Development of Su Shi's Poetic Voice, Stanford, 90; auth, An Introduction to Literary Chinese, Harvard, 99. **CONTACT ADDRESS** Univ of California, Irvine, Irvine, CA 92717. **EMAIL** mafuller@uci.edu

FULLER, MARSHALL TODD
PERSONAL Born 01/27/1965, Tacoma, WA **DISCIPLINE** ENGLISH **EDUCATION** Ind Univ, BA, 90; Wichita State Univ, MFA, 94; Okla State Univ, PhD, 99. **CAREER** Instr, N Okla Col, 99-00; vis asst prof, Drake Univ, 00-. **HONORS AND AWARDS** Phoenix Award Finalist, Okla State Univ, 99; Poets Prize, Acad of Am; Phi Kappa Phi. **MEMBERSHIPS** AWP; MLA. **RESEARCH** Native American literature and studies; Creative writing pedagogy. **SELECTED PUBLICATIONS** Auth, 60' 6" and Other Distances from Home: The (Baseball) Life of Mose Yellow Horse. **CONTACT ADDRESS** Dept English, Drake Univ, 1072 27th St, Des Moines, IA 50311-4137. **EMAIL** mtoddfuller@yahoo.com

FULLER, MARY J.
PERSONAL Born 01/25/1951, Windsor, NC, m, 1986, 1 child **DISCIPLINE** ENGLISH **EDUCATION** Appalacian State, BS, 73; MAT, 74; Fla State Univ, PhD, 79. **CAREER** From asst prof to assoc prof, Miami Univ, 79-; co-dir, Ohio Writing Project, 80-; dir, Col Composition, Miami Univ, 82-86 & 95-96; co-dir, Ohio Writing Project Teacher Researcher Network, 92-95. **HONORS AND AWARDS** Outstanding Educator, Miami Univ Col of Arts and Sci, 92-93. **MEMBERSHIPS** NCTE, CCCC. **RESEARCH** Language of Alternative Medicine. **SELECTED PUBLICATIONS** Co-ed, Literature: Options for Reading and Writing, Harper & Row, 85 & 89; co-ed, English Lang Art Bullet, 87-90; coauth, "Constructing Authority: Student Responses and Classroom Discourse," in Composition and Discourse Analysis, eds. Gayle Stygail and Ellen Barton (Hampton, in press). **CONTACT ADDRESS** Dept English, Miami Univ, 500 E High St, Oxford, OH 45056-1602. **EMAIL** fullermj@muohio.edu

FULLER, SARAH
PERSONAL Born 04/23/1939, Bangor, ME, m **DISCIPLINE** MUSIC **EDUCATION** Radcliffe Col, BA, 61; Univ Calif, Berkeley, MA, 63, PhD, 69. **CAREER** From asst to full prof, SUNY Stony Brook, 69- . **HONORS AND AWARDS** Magna cum laude, 61; Alfred Einstein Prize, Am Musicological Soc, 72; Pres Awd for Excellence in Tchg, 84. **MEMBERSHIPS** Am Musicological Soc; Col Music Soc; Soc for Music Theory. **RESEARCH** History of Western music; medieval and renaissance music, history and theory; history of European music theory. **SELECTED PUBLICATIONS** Auth, "A Phantom Treatise of the Fourteenth Century? The Ars Nova," The Journal of Musicology IV, (85-86); auth, "Modal Tenors and Tonal Orientation in Motets of Guillaume de Machaut;" Studies in Medieval Music Festschrift for Ernest Sanders, (90); ed, "Guillaume de Machaut: De toutes flours," Models of Music Analysis: Music before 1600," Mark Everist, (92); auth, Tendencies and Resolutions: The Directed Progression in Ars Nova Music, J of Music Theory, 92; auth, Defending the Dodecachordon: Ideological Currents in Glarean's Modal Theory, J of the Am Musicological Soc, 96; auth, Exploring Tonal Structure in French Polyphonic Song of the Fourteenth-Century, in Judd, ed, Tonal Structures in Early Music, Garland, 98. **CONTACT ADDRESS** Dept of Music, SUNY, Stony Brook, Stony Brook, NY 11794-5475. **EMAIL** sfuller@notes.cc.sunysb.edu

FULMER, CONSTANCE M.
DISCIPLINE ENGLISH **EDUCATION** Lipscomb Univ, AB, 58; Harding Univ, MA, 60; Univ Ala, MA, 62; Vanderbilt Univ, MAA, 65; PhD, 70. **CAREER** Instr to prof, Lipscomb Univ, Nashville, Tenn, 60-79; prof, Sever Col, Pepperdine Univ, 91-, chair, Div of Humanities and Teacher Educ, 98-. **MEMBERSHIPS** Modern Langs Asn, Women's Studies Asn. **SELECTED PUBLICATIONS** Auth, George Eliot: A Reference Guide, Boston: G. K. Hall (77); auth, "Edith Simcox: Feminist Critic and Reformer," Victorian Periodicals Rev, 31.1 (spring 98): 105-121; co-ed, A Monument to the Memory of George Eliot: Edith J. Simcox's Autobiography of a Shirtmaker, New York and London: Garland (98); auth, "A Nineteenth-Century 'Womanist' on Gender Issues: Edith Simcox in Her Autobiography of a Shirtmaker, Nineteenth-Century Prose, 26.2 (fall 99): 110-126. **CONTACT ADDRESS** Div Chair, Humanities and Teacher Education, Pepperdine Univ, Cultural Arts Center, 300, Malibu, CA 90263-3999. **EMAIL** cfulmer@pepperdine.edu

FULTON, DOVEANNA S.
PERSONAL Born 10/12/1967, Wayne, MI **DISCIPLINE** AFRICAN AMERICAN LITERATURE **EDUCATION** Wayne State Univ, BA, 91; Univ Mich, Trav Schl, 95-96; Univ Minn, PhD, 99. **CAREER** Adj fac, Law Tech Univ, 99; adj fac, Wayne St, 97-99; instr, Jimma Univ, 99-00; asst prof, Rochester Inst, 00-01; asst prof, Univ Memp, 01-. **HONORS AND AWARDS** Andrew Mellon Fel Human Stud, 94; C.I.C. Pre-Doct Fel, 95-98; Ford Found Hon Fel, 94; 99 Nom for Am Stud Asn Ralph Henry Gabriel Dis Prize, 99; Phi Beta Kappa; Golden Key Nat Hon Soc, 92. **MEMBERSHIPS** MLA, ASA, Soc for Values in Higher Edu. **RESEARCH** African American oral traditions in writing and cultural performance; African American women's lives and writings; slave narratives; 19th cen African American literature; black woman's labor issues; oral history. **SELECTED PUBLICATIONS** Auth, "Sisterhood Really Is Global," Monitor (99); auth biog ent, "Sylvia Dubois," and "Maria Stewart," in Hist Encycl of World Slavery (99-00); rev, Women in Chains: The Legacy of "Sylvia Dubois" and "Maria Stewart," J Am Women Writ (00); auth, "Speak Sister, Speak," J Am Women Writers (01). **CONTACT ADDRESS** Eng Dept, Univ of Memphis, Memphis, TN 38152. **EMAIL** dsfgsl@rit.edu

FULTON, GORDON D.
DISCIPLINE ENGLISH LITERATURE **EDUCATION** Univ Toronto, BA; Univ London, MA, PhD. **CAREER** Asst prof, Univ of Victoria. **RESEARCH** Restoration and 18th-century literature, literary stylistics. **SELECTED PUBLICATIONS** Ed, Benson and Greaves, Systemic Functional Approaches to Discourse, Ablex, 88; pub(s), articles in Lang and Lit, 93; Lumen, 94; Eighteenth-Century Life, 96; auth, "Styles of Meaning and Meanings of Style in Rricharrdson's "Clarrissa," (McGill-Queen's UniversityPress, 99). **CONTACT ADDRESS** Dept of English, Univ of Victoria, PO Box 3070, Victoria, BC, Canada V8W 3W1. **EMAIL** gdfulton@uvic.ca

FULTON, HENRY LEVAN
PERSONAL Born 04/16/1935, Pittsburgh, PA, m, 1974, 2 children **DISCIPLINE** ENGLISH LITERATURE **EDUCATION** Wesleyan Univ, BA, 57; Univ Mich, MA, 60, PhD (English), 67. **CAREER** Instr English, Univ Mich, 65-67; asst prof, 67-70, assoc prof, 70-78, PROF ENGLISH, CENT MICH UNIV, 78-. **MEMBERSHIPS** MLA; Johnson Soc Midwest; Scottish Church Hist Soc. **RESEARCH** Eighteenth century English culture; Scottish literature; Shakespeare. **SELECTED PUBLICATIONS** **CONTACT ADDRESS** Dept of English, Central Michigan Univ, Mount Pleasant, MI 48858.

FULTON, RICHARD DELBERT
PERSONAL Born 12/05/1945, Missoula, MT, m, 1976, 2 children **DISCIPLINE** VICTORIAN LITERATURE AND STUDIES **EDUCATION** Eastern Mont Col, BA, 67; Univ SDak, AM, 69; Wash State Univ, PhD (English), 75. **CAREER** Lectr English, Univ Col, Univ Md, 70-71; instr, 76-78, ASST PROF ENGLISH, WASH STATE UNIV, 78-, ASST DEAN GRAD SCH, 75-, Dean in residence, Coun Grad Sch in the US, 82-83. **MEMBERSHIPS** MLA; Conf Brit Studies; Philol Asn Pac Coast; Res Soc Victorian Periodicals. **RESEARCH** Victorian periodicals research and bibliography; history of the Spectator. **SELECTED PUBLICATIONS** Auth, Press, Politics and Society, A History of Jourism In Wales, Albion, Vol 26, 94; A Wider Range--Travel Writing by Women in Victorian England, J Pre Raphaelite Stud New Series, Vol 5, 96. **CONTACT ADDRESS** NW 605 Charlotte St, Pullman, WA 99163.

FULWEILER, HOWARD
PERSONAL Born 08/26/1932, m, 1953, 4 children **DISCIPLINE** ENGLISH **EDUCATION** Univ NC, PhD, 60. **CAREER** Prof; ed bd, Victorian Poetry & Explicator; prof emeritus, 00. **HONORS AND AWARDS** Purple Chalk awd, 92; Byler Distinguished Prof Awd. **SELECTED PUBLICATIONS** Auth, a study of Arnold and Hopkins, Letters from the Darkling Plain, Univ Miss Press, 72 & Here a Captive Heart Busted: The Sentimental Journey of Modern Literature, Fordham UP, 93. **CONTACT ADDRESS** Dept of English, Univ of Missouri, Columbia, 234 Tate Hall, Columbia, MO 65211. **EMAIL** fulweilerh@missouri.edu

FUMERTON, PATRICIA
DISCIPLINE SIXTEENTH- AND SEVENTEENTH-CENTURY CULTURE AND LITERATURE **EDUCATION** Stanford Univ, PhD, 81. **CAREER** Assoc Prof, Eng, Univ Calif, Santa Barbara. **RESEARCH** Renaissance popular cult; Mobility; Space. **SELECTED PUBLICATIONS** Auth, Cultural Aesthetics: Renaissance Literature and Practice of Social Ornament, Univ Chicago Press, 92; "Subdiscourse; Jonson Speaking Low," Eng Lit Renaissance, 95. **CONTACT ADDRESS** Dept of Eng, Univ of California, Santa Barbara, Santa Barbara, CA 93106-7150. **EMAIL** pfumer@humanitas.ucsb.edu

FUNSTON, JUDITH
DISCIPLINE ENGLISH **EDUCATION** Mich State Univ, BA, 72; MA, 76; PhD, 82. **CAREER** Specialist, Mich State Univ, 83-90; asst prof to prof, SUNY Col Potsdam, 90-. **HONORS AND AWARDS** Fac Folk Scholar, 69-71; Phi Beta Kappa, Tau Sigma, 72; Grad Council Fel, 80-81; Res Grant, Mich State Univ, 88, 90; Chancellors Awd for Excellence in Teaching, SUNY, 95; Sigma Tau Delta, 99. **RESEARCH** James, Wharton, 1880-1920 American literature and culture, women's writing. **SELECTED PUBLICATIONS** Auth, "A Note on Henry James's 'A Bundle of Letters'", Henry James Rev 10.3 (Fall 89):220; auth, "Macaws and Pekingnese: Vivienne de Watteville and Edith Wharton", Edith Wharton Rev 7.1 (90):13-14; auth, "Clocks and Mirrors, Dreams and Destinies: Edith Wharton's 'The Old Maid'", in Edith Wharton: New Critical Essays, ed Alfred Bendixen and Annette Zilversmith (NY: Garland, 92) 143-57; auth, "Travel Writing", in Oxford Companion to Women's Writing in the US, eds Cathy N. Davidson and Linda Wagner-Martin (Oxford Univ Pr, 94); auth, "An Early Backward Glance: Edith Wharton's Revision of 'A Tuscan Shrine'", Edith Wharton Rev 15.2 (Fall 99) 1,3-8; auth, "W.C. Falkner", Anne Moncure Crane", "Charles Scribner", "Arthur Hawley Scribner", "Jim Bishop", "James Clavell", "Louis Kronenberger", "Margaret Widdemer", "Jessica Savitch", "Edith Wharton", in Am Nat Biography, Oxford Univ Pr, 99; auth, "Katherine Fullerton Gerould", "Susan Glaspell", "Harriet Arnow", "Ellen Glasgow", "Will Rogers", "J.P. Marquand", "Carl Sandburg", Encycl of Am Lit, Continuum, 99. **CONTACT ADDRESS** Dept English, SUNY, Col at Potsdam, 44 Pierrepont Ave, Potsdam, NY 13676-2294. **EMAIL** funstoje@potsdam.edu

FUQUA, CHARLES
PERSONAL Born 10/05/1935, Paris, France, m, 1961, 3 children **DISCIPLINE** CLASSICS **EDUCATION** Princeton Univ, BA, 57; Cornell Univ, MA, 62, PhD(classics), 64. **CAREER** From instr to asst prof classics, Dartmouth Col, 64-66; chmn dept, 66-78, assoc prof, 66-72, Garfield Prof Ancient Lang, Williams Col, 72-, Mem adv coun, Am Acad Rome, 66- & exec comt, 71-74. **HONORS AND AWARDS** Phi Beta Kappa, 57; Phi Kappa Phi, 64. **MEMBERSHIPS** Am Philol Asn; Class Asn New Eng; Classical Asn Mass; Vergilian Soc.

RESEARCH Greek epic & drama; Latin lyric poetry. **SELECTED PUBLICATIONS** Auth, Possible implications of the ostracism of Hyperbolus, Trans Am Philol Asn, 65; Horace, Carmina 1.23-25, 1/68 & Aeschylus: Agamemnon 1446-47, 7/72, Class Philol; Studies in the use of myth in Sophocles' Philoctetes and the Orestes of Euripides, 76, The World of myth in Euripides Orestes, 78 & Heroism, Heracles, and the Trachiniae, 80, Traditio; Tyrtaeus and the cult of heroes, Greek, Roman & Byzantine Studies, 81; Hector, Sychaeus, and Deiphobus: Three mutilated figures in Aeneid, Class Philol, 1-6/82; auth, Proper Bevavior in the Odyssey, Ill Classical Stud, 46-58/91; auth, Moral Clusters in the Odyssey, Scholia, 56-68/93. **CONTACT ADDRESS** Dept of Classics, Williams Col, 880 Main St, Stetson Hall B25, Williamstown, MA 01267-2600. **EMAIL** cfuqua@williams.edu

FUREY, HESTER L.
PERSONAL Born 08/27/1963, Americus, GA, d, 2 children **DISCIPLINE** ENGLISH **EDUCATION** Valdosta State Col, BA, 85; Univ Ill Urbana, MA, 87; PhD, 92. **CAREER** Instr, Art Inst of Atlanta, 98-. **HONORS AND AWARDS** Teaching Fel, Univ Ill, 92-94; Newberry Libr Res Fel, 93; Henry J Kaiser Family Found Res Grant, 91; Fel, Univ Ill, 90. **MEMBERSHIPS** MLA; MMLA; SAMLA. **RESEARCH** American literary and labor history; Literature of social movements; Social theory; Modern poetry. **SELECTED PUBLICATIONS** Auth, "Poetry and the Rhetoric of Dissents in Turn-of-the-Century Chicago," Mod Fiction Studies, (92): 671-685; auth, "The Reception of Arturo Giovannitti's Poetry and 'The Trial of a New Society'," Left Hist, (94): 27-50; auth, "Cora Richmond," in The Historical Encyclopedia of Chicago Women, Ind Univ Press, (forthcoming); auth, "IWW Songs as Modernist Poetry," MMLA J, (forthcoming). **CONTACT ADDRESS** Art Inst of Atlanta, 2105 Harbor Lndg, Roswell, GA 30076-3107. **EMAIL** fureyhome@msn.com

FURIA, PHILIP GEORGE
PERSONAL Born 11/15/1943, Pittsburgh, PA, m, 1995, 3 children **DISCIPLINE** CREATIVE WRITING **EDUCATION** Oberlin Col, BA, 65; Univ Chicago, MA, 66; Univ Iowa, MFA & PhD, 70. **CAREER** Asst prof, 70-76, assoc prof English, 76-83, prof of English, 84, Chair, Univ Minn, 90-93, assoc Dean, Univ Minn, 94-95; Prof and Chair, Univ NC at Wilmington, 96-98; chair, Creative Writing, UNCW, 98-99; director of Film Studies, UNCW, 00-; Vis prof Am studies, Univ East Angia, 76-77; Fulbright prof, Univ Graz, AUT, 82. **HONORS AND AWARDS** Ford Found Fel, Univ Chicago, 65-66; Teaching Res Fel, Univ Iowa, 67-69; Sloan Doctoral Fel, Univ Iowa, 69-70; Fulbright Prof, Univ Graz Austria, 82-83; Distinguished Teaching Awd, Univ Minn, 89; Scholar of the Col, Univ Minn, 91-94. **MEMBERSHIPS** UFVA; AWP. **RESEARCH** American popular song, biography, musical film and theater; modern American poetry; literature and art. **SELECTED PUBLICATIONS** Auth, Is the Whited Monster Lowell's Quaker Graveyard Revisited, TX Studies in Lit & Lang, winter 76; coauth, Stevens' Fusky Alphabet, Publ Mod Lang Asn, 1/78; auth, Paterson's progress, Boundary 2, winter 81; auth, Pound's Cantos Declassified, PA State Press, 84; auth, The Poets of Tin Pan Alley: A History of America's Great Lyricists, Oxford Univ Press, 90; auth, Ira Gershwin: The Art of the Lyricist, Oxford Univ Press, 96; auth, Something to Sing About: A Centenary Celebration of America's Great Lyricists, in Am Scholar, summer 97; auth, Irving Berlin: A Life in Song, Schirmer/Simon & Schuster, 98. **CONTACT ADDRESS** Dept of Creative Writing, Univ of No Carolina, Wilmington, 601 South College Rd, 165 Morton Hall, Wilmington, NC 28403. **EMAIL** furiap@uncwil.edu

FURNESS, EDNA LUE
PERSONAL Born 01/26/1906, Knox Co, NE **DISCIPLINE** ENGLISH & SPANISH **EDUCATION** Univ CO, AB & BE, 28, MA, 39, EdD, 51. **CAREER** Teacher, High Schs, CO, 28-33 & WY, 33-39; instr Span, Pueblo Col, 42-45; instr English & mod lang, Casper Col, WY, 45-47; from asst prof to prof English & foreign lang educ, Univ WY, 47-61; prof English & Span, 61-72, Emer Prof Lang & Lit, WY State Univ 72-; Instr, Univ CO, 50-51; fac res grant, Univ WY, 57; Coe fel Am studies, Coe Found, 59; Delta Kappa Gamma res grant, 60-61; US Off Educ res grant, 66-67, humanities res grant, 71-72. **HONORS AND AWARDS** Haiku Awd, Washington Poets Asn, 80. **MEMBERSHIPS** NEA; Int Platform Asn; Nat Coun Teachers English. **RESEARCH** Comparative literature; translation; children's literature. **SELECTED PUBLICATIONS** Coauth, New Dimensions in the Teaching of English, Pruett, 67; auth, Trends in Literature on Teaching the Language Arts, contribr, Teaching of Listening, Scarecrow, 71, Linguistics in the Elementary School Classroom, Macmillan, 71 & Language Arts in the Elementary School, Lippincott, 72; auth, Mediterranean magic, 74 & Spelling is Serious Stuff, 78, Delta Kappa Gamma Bull; contribr, Educational Assessment of Learning Problems, 78; Assessment and Correction of Language Arts Difficulties, 80; Spelling for the Millions, 66; Guide to Better English Spelling, 91. **CONTACT ADDRESS** 725 S Alton Way Windsor Gardens-6B, Denver, CO 80231.

FURNISH, SHEARLE
PERSONAL Born 03/30/1953, Denver, CO, m, 1998 **DISCIPLINE** ENGLISH LITERATURE **EDUCATION** Transylvania Univ, AB, 75; Univ Ky, MA, 78; PhD, 84. **CAREER** Instr (part-time), Univ Ky, 81-84; vis asst prof, Univ NC at Asheville, 84-86; asst prof, Meredith Col, Raleigh, NC, 86-89; asst prof, West Tex State Univ, Canyon, 89-93; assoc prof, West Tex A & M Univ, 93-97, Dir of Freshman English, 96-, prof, 97-. **HONORS AND AWARDS** Who's Who in the Southwest (Marquis); Nat Merit Scholar, Transylvania Univ, 71-75; Delcamp Essay Awd, Transylvania Univ, 74; Nat Finalist, Honorable Mention, Danforth Fels, 79; Ellershaw Awd, Dept of English, Univ Ky, 79; Tex Col English Asn, Pres, 200-2001, Preselect, 99-2000, secretary, 98-99. **MEMBERSHIPS** Tex Col English Asn, Modern Lang Asn, Medieval Acad, Southeastern Medieval Asn, Panhandle-Plains Hist Soc, Asn of Lit Scholars and Critics, Conf of Col Teachers of English, New Chaucer Soc, Medieval and Renaissance Drama Soc, Tex Medieval Asn, Lib of Congress Assocs, South Central Modern Lang Asn, Am Asn of Univ Profs. **RESEARCH** Middle English literature and drama, composition and rhetoric, medieval devotional literature. **SELECTED PUBLICATIONS** Auth, "Metatheatre in the First Shepherds Play," Essays in Theatre 7 (May 89): 139-148; auth, "The Ordinatio of Huntington Library MS HM 149, an East Anglian Manuscript of Nicholas Love's Mirrour," Manuscripta 34 (90): 50-65; auth, "The Audience in the Text of the Wakefield Buffeting," Mediavalia: A J of Mediaeval Studies 14 (91 for 88): 231-51; auth, "The Modernity of The Erle of Tolous and the Decay of the Breton Lai," Medieval Perspectives 8 (93): 69-77; auth, "Nicholas Love, Carthusian: Writing as Apostlic Witness," Am Benedictine Rev, 45.1 (94): 22-32; auth, "The Chester Plays," Old and Middle English Literature, eds, Jeffrey Helterman and Jerome Mitchell, vol 146, of Dictionary of Literary Biography (94): 356-64; auth, "Loving Grading Writing," Col Lang Asn J 38 (95): 490-504; auth, "The Editorial Truncation of Nicholas Love's Mirrour in Huntington Library MS HM 149," Manuscripta (forthcoming); auth, "Play-within-the-Play in the Dramas of the Wakefield Master," Medieval Perspectives 14 (99): 61-68; auth, "The Breton Lai," in Companion to Old and Middle English Literature, eds, Bob and Laura Lambdin, Greenwood Press (forthcoming). **CONTACT ADDRESS** Dept English & Langs, West Texas A&M Univ, 2501 4th Ave, Canyon, TX 79016-0001. **EMAIL** sfurnish@mail.wtamu.edu

FURTWANGLER, ALBERT
PERSONAL Born 07/17/1942, Seattle, WA, m, 1968, 2 children **DISCIPLINE** ENGLISH LITERATURE **EDUCATION** Amherst Col, BA, 64; Cornell Univ, MA, 67, PhD (English), 68. **CAREER** Asst prof English and humanities, Univ Chicago, 68-71; asst prof English, 71-76, assoc prof English, 76-96, prof emer, Mt Allison Univ, 96- , Vis fel, Yale Univ, 77-78; vis prof, Linfield Col, 80-81. **RESEARCH** Rhetoric of American constitutional debates; 18th century periodicals. **SELECTED PUBLICATIONS** Auth, American silhouettes: Rhetorical Identities of the Founders, Yale Univ Pr (New Haven, CT), 87; auth, Answering Chief Seattle, Univ Wash Pr, 97; auth, Acts of Discoveries, Univ Ill Pr, 99. **CONTACT ADDRESS** 235 Oak way NE, Salem, OR, 97301.

FUSCO, RICHARD A.
PERSONAL Born 04/27/1952, Philadelphia, PA, s **DISCIPLINE** ENGLISH **EDUCATION** Univ Pa, BA, 73; MA, 74; Univ Miss, MA, 82; Duke Univ, PhD, 90. **CAREER** Teach asst, Univ Miss, 80-82; tutor, Duke Univ, 82-85; adj instr, Villanova Univ, 86-87; adj instr, St Joseph's Univ, 86-88; instr, 88-91; adj instr, Del Cnty Comm Col, 92-96; adj instr, St Joseph's Univ, 93-96; vis prof, 96-97; asst prof, 97-. **RESEARCH** American literature. **SELECTED PUBLICATIONS** Auth, Fin de millenaire: Poe 's Legacy for the Detective Story, Poe Society (Baltimore), 93; auth, "Entrapment, Flight and Death: A Recurring Motif in Dickens with Plot and Interpretive Consequences for Edwin Drood," Essays Art Sci 20 (91): 68-84; auth, Maupassant and the American Short Story: The Influence of Form at the Turn of the Century Penn State Univ Press, 94; auth, "John Reuben Thompson," in Dictionary of Literary Biography (Detroit: Gale, forthcoming); auth, rev, "Using Narrative Form to Teach Poe's Gothic Fiction," in Teaching Gothic Fiction, eds. Diane Long Hoeveler, Tamar Heller (NY: MLA, forthcoming); rev, "Pensive Jester: The Literary Career of W W Jacobs," by John D Cloy (Studies in Short Fiction, 98); rev, "Just what War Is: The Civil War Writings of De Forest and Pierce," by Michael W Schaefer, South Cen Rev 16 (99): 88-90; rev, "Cartesian Sonata and Other Novellas," by William H Gass,, America 181 (99): 28; rev, "Sherlock's Men: Masculinity, Conan Doyle, and Cultural History," by Joseph A Kestner, South Cen Rev (forthcoming). **CONTACT ADDRESS** Dept English, Saint Joseph's Univ, 5600 City Ave, Philadelphia, PA 19131-1308. **EMAIL** fusco@sju.edu

FUSSELL, EDWIN
PERSONAL Born 07/04/1922, Pasadena, CA, m, 1971 **DISCIPLINE** ENGLISH AND AM LIT **EDUCATION** Pomona Col, AB, 43; Harvard Univ, AM, 47, PhD, 49. **CAREER** Instr English, Univ Calif, Berkeley, 49-51; asst prof, Pomona Col, 51-55; asst prof, Claremont Grad Sch, 55-56, from assoc prof to prof English and Am lit, 56-67; PROF AM LIT, UNIV CALIF, SAN DIEGO, 67-, Fulbright univ lectr, Univ Florence and Pisa, 67-68. **MEMBERSHIPS** MLA. **SELECTED PUBLICATIONS** Auth, Edwin Arlington Robinson, Univ Calif, 54; Frontier: American literature and the American West, 65 & Lucifer in Harness: American Meter, Metaphor and Diction, 73, Princeton Univ; The purgatory poems, Little Sq Rev, 67. **CONTACT ADDRESS** Dept of Lit, Univ of California, San Diego, San Diego, CA 92093.

G

GABBIN, JOANNE VEAL
PERSONAL Born 02/02/1946, Baltimore, MD, m, 1967 **DISCIPLINE** ENGLISH **EDUCATION** Morgan State Univ, Baltimore MD, BA, 1967; Univ of Chicago, Chicago IL, MA, 1970, PhD, 1980. **CAREER** Catalyst for Youth Inc, Chicago IL, prog dir, instructor, 73-75; Lincoln Univ, University PA, asst prof of English, 77-82, assoc prof of English, 82-85; James Madison Univ, Harrisonburg VA, assoc prof of English, 85-86, dir, Honors Program, 86-, professor of English 1988-. **HONORS AND AWARDS** Outstanding Achievement Awd, Black Conf on Higher Educ, 1982; Distinguished Teaching Awd, The Christian R & Mary F Lindback Found, 1983; Creative Scholarship Awd, Coll Language Assn, 1986; Women of Color Awd, James Madison Uni, 1988; Honorary Mem, Golden Key Natl Honor Soc, 1988; Chairperson, Toni Morrison & The Supernatural, panel at the Middle Atlantic Writers Assn, 1988; Speaker, Creating a Masterpiece, Freshman Convocation James Madison Univ, 1988; Outstanding Faculty Awd, VA State Council of Higher Educ, 1993; George Kent Awd, Gwendolyn Brooks Ctr, Chicago State Univ, 1994. **MEMBERSHIPS** Langston Hughes Soc, Zora Neale Hurston Soc; Middle Atlantic Writer Assn Inc, the MAWA Journal; mem, Coll Language Assn; chair, Student Emergency Fund, First Baptist Church, 1989-; Board of the Virginia Foundation for the Humanities and Public Policy, chair. **SELECTED PUBLICATIONS** Sonia Sanchez: A Soft Reflection of Strength, Zora Neale Hurston Forum, 1987; A Laying on of Hands: Black Women Writers Exploring the Roots of their Folk & Cultural Tradition; Walk Together Children: Color and the Cultural Legacy of Sterling A Brown, 1988; Sterling A Brown: Building the Black Aesthetic Tradition, 1985 "A Laying on of Hands" Wild Women in the Whirlwind, Rutgers Univ Press, 1990, reprinted by Univ Press in VA, 1994. **CONTACT ADDRESS** Professor of English, Dir of the Honors Program, James Madison Univ, Hillcrest, Harrisonburg, VA 22807.

GAFFNEY, FLOYD
PERSONAL Born 06/11/1930, Cleveland, OH, m **DISCIPLINE** DRAMA **EDUCATION** Adelphi Univ, BA 1959, MA 1962; Carnegie Inst of Tech, PhD 1966. **CAREER** Gilpin Players Karamu House, actor 45-49; Pearl Primus African Dance Co, dancer 50-51; Jerome School of Dancing, teaching asst 60-62; Adelphi Univ, graduate teaching assistant of dance 61; Waltann School of Creative Arts, teacher of dance & drama 61; Clark Coll, asst prof, Speech 61-63; William Balls Amer Conservatory Theatre, guest artist 65; Univ of Pittsburgh, guest dance instructor 66; OH Univ, asst prof in theatre 66-69; FL A&M Univ, dir of fine arts project upward bound summer 68; Univ of CA Santa Barbara, assc prof drama 69-71, co-chmn of Black Studies dept. UC Santa Barbara. **HONORS AND AWARDS** Andrew Mellon Fellowship Drama 1964-65; OH Univ Bd Trustees Grant 1968; Fac Senate Grant Univ of CA Santa Barbara 1970; Ford Fnd Grant 1970; Faculty Sen Grant Univ of CA 1971-73; US Info Srv Cultural Exch Prof to Brazil 1972; Natl Humanities Fac 1974-75; grant Univ of CA Creative Arts Inst Grant 1974; Outstanding Educ of Amer Awd; special proj grant Natl Endowment for the Arts 1977; Fulbright Scholar to Brazil 1979; Instr Improvement Grant 1979-81, 1984; participant Intl Congress of Black Communication Univ of Nairobi Kenya 1981; moderator Realism To Ritual, Form & Style in Black Theatre ATA Black Theatre Prog Panel 1982; Black Achievement Awd forDrama Action Interprises Inc, 1984; Chancellor's Assocs, Merit Awd; Outstanding Community Serv, Univ of California, San Diego, 1983; Natl Endowment for the Arts; US-Japan Alliance Best Director of Drama, 1986; NAACP Creative Arts Awds, 1986; UCSD Faculty Senate Research, Japan, Summer, 1987, 1988; Oxford Univ, Oxford, English, Summer; Institute for Shipboard Educ, Semester at Sea, Professor, Spring, 1992; mem, the National Faculty, 1990-93, reappointed 1994; Honorary mem, Golden Key National Honor Society, 1990; UCSD Faculty Senate Research Grants; England Summer 1990, 1993, 1994, Netherlands/Belgium, 1996, Paris, 1995, 1998; UCSD Humanities Center Grant, Teatro Mascara Magica, 1998-. **MEMBERSHIPS** UCSD Black Fac & Staff Assn 1979-94; Intercampus Cultural Exch Comm 1979-81; Third Clge Fac Comm UCSD 1980-94; Performing Arts Sub-Comm 1972-74; Fac Mentor Prog UCSD 1982; Pres Chair Search Comm UCSD 1982; San Diego Div of Acad Senate UCSD; bd dir Free Southern Theatre 1963-65; Amer Soc for Theatre Research 1966-69; Natl Humanities Fac 1974-75, 1994-; bd dir Combined Arts & Educ Council of San Diego Cty 1982-84; Amer Theatre Assn Black Theatre Prog 1966; artistic dir Southern CA Black Repertory Theatre Inc San Diego 1980-83; Confederation for the Arts 1983-; Steering Comm State & Local Partnership of San Diego Cty 1982-; bd dir, Educ Cultural Complex Theatre, 1981-83; bd mem, Horton Plaza Theatre Fnd, 198384, 1995-; panel mem, Natl Research Council for Mi-

nority Fellowship, 1984-87; Phi Lambda Rho Frat, 1958; Theatre Assn, 1966-85; Amer Assn of Univ Prof; mem Education Committee, Escondido Center of the Performing Arts 1995; Commissioner, Horton Plaza Theatre Foundation 1996-. **SELECTED PUBLICATIONS** Contributing Editor: Theatre Forum Journal, 1992-; Editorial Advisory Board-Lenox Avenue: A Journal of Interartistic Inquire, 1994-96; Associate Artistic Director, Teatro Mascara Magica; A Common Ground Theatre, 1994. **CONTACT ADDRESS** Univ of California, San Diego, PO Box 0344, La Jolla, CA 92093. **EMAIL** fgaffney@ucsd.edu

GAGARIN, MICHAEL
PERSONAL Born 01/04/1942, New York City, NY, m, 1974, 2 children **DISCIPLINE** CLASSICS **EDUCATION** Stanford Univ, BA, 63; Harvard Univ, MA, 65; Yale Univ, PhD(classics), 68. **CAREER** From instr to asst prof classics, Yale Univ, 68-73; asst prof, 73-80, Assoc Prof Classics, Univ Tex, Austin, 80-86; prof classics, 86-; Jr fel, Ctr Hellenic Studies, Washington DC, 72-73; vis asst prof classics, Univ Calif, Berkeley, 76-77; Am Coun Learned Soc fel, 80-81. **HONORS AND AWARDS** NEH fellow 85-86 and 97-98. **MEMBERSHIPS** Am Philol Asn; Am Inst Archaeol; Soc Ancient Greek Philos. **RESEARCH** Greek literature; Greek law; Greek philosophy. **SELECTED PUBLICATIONS** Auth, Aeschylean Drama, Univ of CA Press, 76; auth, Drakon and Early Athenian Homicide Law, Yale Univ Press, 81; auth, Early Greek Law, Univ of CA Press, 86, paperback ed, 89; auth, The Murder of Herodes: A Study of Antiphon 5, Frankfurt, 89; ed, Symposion 1990. Akten der Gesellschaft fur griechische and hellenistische Rechtsgeschichte, vol. 8, Cologne, 92; co-auth, Early Greek Political Thought from Homer to the Sophists, Cambridge, 95; ed & comment, Antiphon, the speeches, Cambridge Greek and Latin Classics, Cambridge, 97; co-trans, Antiphon and Andocides, vol. 1 of Classical Greek Oratory, Austin, 98. **CONTACT ADDRESS** Classics Dept, Univ of Texas, Austin, Austin, TX 78712. **EMAIL** gagarin@mail.uTexas.edu

GAICHAS, LAWRENCE EDWARD
PERSONAL Born 03/30/1942, Chicago, IL, m, 1967, 2 children **DISCIPLINE** CLASSICS **EDUCATION** Xavier Univ, Ohio, HAB, 64; Ohio State Univ, MA, 68, PhD(classics), 72. **CAREER** Teaching asst classics, Ohio State Univ, 66-68; instr classics and English, Kalamazoo Col, 70-72; instr Columbus Pub Schs, 72-73; asst prof, 73-77, Assoc Prof Classics, 77-83, prof classics, 83-, Duquesne Univ, Chmn Dept, 78- Concurrent Pos: Circulation mgr, Class World, 78-. **MEMBERSHIPS** Am Philol Asn. **RESEARCH** Graeco-Roman historiography; Graeco-Roman epic; etymology. **SELECTED PUBLICATIONS** Auth, Latin Skills 1 and Latin Skills 2 for the IBM-PC and the PS/2, Version 1.0, Class World, Vol 0089, 1996. **CONTACT ADDRESS** Dept of Classics, Duquesne Univ, Pittsburgh, PA 15259. **EMAIL** gaichas@duq.edu

GAIDE, TANURE
PERSONAL Born 04/24/1948, Nigeria, m, 1976, 5 children **DISCIPLINE** LITERATURE, AFRICAN STUDIES **EDUCATION** Univ Ibadan, BA, 71; Syracuse Univ, MA, 79; PhD, 81. **CAREER** Lecturer, Univ Maiduguri Nigeria, 77-89; Visiting Prof, Whitman Col, 89-90; Asst Prof to Prof, Univ NCar, 90-. **HONORS AND AWARDS** Res Grant, UNC, 92-94, 95-96, 97, 99; Nigerian Authors' Poetry Awd, 94; All-Africa Okigbo Prize, 97; Fel, NEH, 00 **MEMBERSHIPS** African Studies Asn; African Lit Asn. **RESEARCH** African/Pan-African/Black Literatures; Non-western, World & Postcolonial literatures; Creative Writing/Poetry. **SELECTED PUBLICATIONS** Auth, The Blood of Peace, Oxford, 91; auth, "Orality in Recent West African Poetry," CLA Journal, (96): 302-319; auth, "African Literature and Its Context: Teaching Teachers of Chinua Achebe's Things Fall Apart," Women's Studies Quarterly, (97): 169-177; auth, Daydream of Ants, Malthouse, 97; auth, Delta Blues and Home Songs, Kraft books, 98; auth, Invoking the Warrior Spirit, Heinemann, 98; auth, Cannons for the Brave, Malthouse, 99; auth, Invoking the Warrior Spirit: New and Selected Poems, Africa World Press, 00. **CONTACT ADDRESS** Dept African Am Studies, Univ of No Carolina, Charlotte, 9201 University City Blvd, Charlotte, NC 28223-0001. **EMAIL** tojaide@email.unc.edu

GAINER, KIM
DISCIPLINE MEDIEVAL AND RENAISSANCE LITERATURE **EDUCATION** RI Col, BA; OH State Univ, MA, PhD. **CAREER** Prof, instr, Freshman Connections prog, Radford Univ. **RESEARCH** Censorship; adoption; archaeol. **SELECTED PUBLICATIONS** Auth, The Recalcitrance of Myth: The Conquest of the Americas in High School History Textbooks. **CONTACT ADDRESS** Radford Univ, Radford, VA 24142. **EMAIL** kgainer@runet.edu

GAINES, BARRY
DISCIPLINE SHAKESPEARE AND TEXTUAL CRITICISM **EDUCATION** Univ Wis, PhD; 70. **CAREER** Instr, 79-, dir, bachelor of univ stud prog, Univ NMex. **SELECTED PUBLICATIONS** Coed, Revels Edition of A Yorkshire Tragedy. **CONTACT ADDRESS** Univ of New Mexico, Albuquerque, Albuquerque, NM 87131. **EMAIL** bjgaines@unm.edu

GAINES, ELLIOT I.
PERSONAL Born 00/00/1950, d, 4 children **DISCIPLINE** MASS COMMUNICATION **EDUCATION** Ohio Univ, PhD 95, MA 94. **CAREER** Ashland Univ, prof, 4 years. **MEMBERSHIPS** NCA; SSA; PCA. **RESEARCH** Communication; culture and media. **SELECTED PUBLICATIONS** Auth, Communication for Osteopathic Manipulative Treatment: The Language of Lived Experience in OMT Pedagogy, Jour of Amer Osteopathic Assoc, 98; auth, "Building Community Through Stories about Real Eventsa: The Habitus of Broadcast Journalism"; auth, in Building Diverse Communities Through Research, eds Mark Orbe, Trevy McDonald, and T. Ford Ahmed, Hampton Press, 00. **CONTACT ADDRESS** Dept of Communications, Wright State Univ, Dayton, 3640 Colonel Glenn Hwy., Dayton, OH 45435. **EMAIL** egaines@ashland.edu

GAINES, JANE M.
DISCIPLINE ENGLISH LITERATURE **EDUCATION** Northwestern Univ, PhD, 82. **CAREER** Prof, Duke Univ. **SELECTED PUBLICATIONS** Auth, Contested Culture: The Image, the Voice, and the Law, Univ NC, 91; ed, Classical Hollywood Narratives: The Paradigm Wars, Duke, 92; co-ed, Fabrications: Costume and the Female Body, Routledge, 90; pubs on feminist film theory. **CONTACT ADDRESS** Eng Dept, Duke Univ, 104 Crowell Bldg, PO Box 90671, Durham, NC 27708. **EMAIL** jmgaines@duke.edu

GAINES, ROBERT N.
PERSONAL Born 01/15/1950, Sulphur, OK, m, 1993 **DISCIPLINE** PHILOSOPHY OF COMMUNICATIONS **EDUCATION** Univ Iowa, PhD, 82. **CAREER** Assoc prof; grad dir, Univ MD, 86-. **RESEARCH** Rhetorical theory in ancient times. **SELECTED PUBLICATIONS** Auth, Cicero's Response to the Philosophers in De oratore, Book 1, Rhetoric and Pedagogy: Its History, Philosophy, and Practice. Essays in Honor of James J. Murphy, Lawrence Erlbaum Assoc, Inc, 95; Knowledge and Discourse in Gorgias' On the Non-Existent or On Nature, Philos & Rhet 30, 97. **CONTACT ADDRESS** Dept of Commun, Univ of Maryland, Col Park, 4229 Art-Sociology Building, College Park, MD 20742-1335. **EMAIL** rg1@umail.umd.edu

GAJOWSKI, EVELYN J.
DISCIPLINE SHAKESPEARE, RENAISSANCE **EDUCATION** Cleveland State Univ, BA, 71; Case Western Reserve Univ, MA, 74, PhD, 87. **CAREER** Vis asst prof, Dept of Eng, Wittenberg Univ, 79-81; Lectr, Bd of Lit, Univ Calif, Santa Cruz, 88-91; asst prof, 91-94, asooc prof, Dept of Eng, Univ Nev, Las Vegas, 94-. **HONORS AND AWARDS** Grad Alumni Fund Awd, 87, Dean's Commendation for Acad Excellence, Case Western Reserve Univ, 87; Best Feminist Essay Awd, Rocky Mt MLA, 89; res grant, Univ Nev, Las Vegas, 92, 93, 94; Res grant, Univ Fac Travel Cmte, UNLV, 95; Fac Dev Leave, UNLV, 96-97; Res Grant, Univ Fac Travel Cmte, UNLV, 97; Res Grant, Res Resourves Cmte, Dept of Eng, UNLV, 97. **MEMBERSHIPS** VP, 94, Pres, 95, past Pres, 96, RMMLA; mem, Exec Bd, RMMLA, 94-96; mem, Bd of Trust, Arts Cound of Henderson, 97. **RESEARCH** Women in Shakespeare, Shakespeare, early modern English drama, early modern English women writers, gender theory. **SELECTED PUBLICATIONS** Auth, "The Female Perspective in Othello," in Othello: New Perspectives, ed. Virginia Mason Vaughan and Kent Cartwright (Fairleigh Dickinson Univ Press and Assoc Univ Press, 91); auth, The Art of Loving: Female Subjectivity and Male Discursive Traditions in Shakespeare's Tragedies, Univ Del Press and Assoc Univ Press, 92; auth, "Feminist Theory, Pedagogy, and Power," Connections 15 (99): 2-8; auth, "'Sigh no more, ladies, sigh no more': Genesis Deconstructed in Kenneth Branagh's 'Much Ado about Nothing,'" J of Theatre and Drama 7 (99); auth, "'Chloe Liked Olivia': Female Friendship, Chastity, and Power in Mary Wroth's 'Love's Victory,'" in Early Modern Women Writers, ed. Anne Russell (forthcoming); ed, Millennium Shakespeare: Essays in Honor of Robert Ornstein, forthcoming. **CONTACT ADDRESS** Dept of English, Univ of Nevada, Las Vegas, 4505 Maryland Pky, PO Box 455011, Las Vegas, NV 89154-5011. **EMAIL** shakespe@nevada.edu

GALCHINSKY, MICHAEL
PERSONAL Born 10/20/1965, Denver, CO, m, 1999, 1 child **DISCIPLINE** ENGLISH **EDUCATION** Northwestern Univ, BA, 87; Univ Calif, PhD, 94. **CAREER** Dept Eng, Georgia St Univ. **HONORS AND AWARDS** Postdoctoral Fellowship, Oxford Centre for Hebrew and Jewish Studies, 98. **RESEARCH** 19th-century Brit lit; novel; multiculturalism; Jewish cult stud & creative writing. **SELECTED PUBLICATIONS** Auth, The Origin of the Modern Jewish Woman Writer: Romance and Reform in Victorian England, Wayne State UP, 96. **CONTACT ADDRESS** Dept of English, Georgia State Univ, Atanta, GA 30303. **EMAIL** mgalchinsky@gsu.edu

GALE, RICHARD A.
DISCIPLINE THEATRE, INTERDISCIPLINARY ARTS **EDUCATION** San Jose State Univ, BA, 84; MA, 85; Univ Calif, MFA, 88; Univ Minn, PhD, 96. **CAREER** Asst prof, Bowling Green State Univ, 96-98; asst prof, Sonoma State Univ, 98-. **HONORS AND AWARDS** Carnegie Scholar, 00-01. **MEMBERSHIPS** Am Studies Assoc, Assoc for Theatre in Higher Educ, Dramatists Guild, Lit Managers and Dramaturgs of Am, Pedagogy and Theatre of the Oppressed, WHA. **RESEARCH** Playwriting, Theatre History, Theatre and the American West, Western History, Critical Pedagogy, Scholarship of Teaching and Learning. **SELECTED PUBLICATIONS** Auth, A Handbook for Teaching Assistants, Centre for Teaching Develop, USCD, 89; auth, "William Clerke's Marciano and Restoration Scotland," Restoration and Eighteenth-Century Theatre Res, (93); auth, "Archibald MacLaren's the Negro Slaves and the Scottish Response to British Colonialism," Theatre Survey, (94); auth, A Training Manual for Teachers, Program in Composition, Univ of Minn, 94-95. **CONTACT ADDRESS** Hutchins Sch of Lib Studies, Sonoma State Univ, Rohnert Park, CA 94928. **EMAIL** gale@sonoma.edu

GALEF, DAVID A.
PERSONAL Born 03/27/1959, New York, NY, m, 1992, 1 child **DISCIPLINE** ENGLISH **EDUCATION** Princeton Univ, BA, 81; Columbia Univ, MA, 83; PhD, 89. **CAREER** Teacher to Preceptor, Columbia Univ, 86-89; Head of workshop, Masters School, 90; Asst Prof to Assoc prof, Univ Miss, 90-. **HONORS AND AWARDS** Guest writer, New Walden Writers' Retreat, New Hebron, 99; Grant, Miss Arts Coun, 97-98; Writers Exchange Awd, Harvard Univ, 91; Henfield Foundation Grant, 81-82; Phi Beta Kappa. **MEMBERSHIPS** Nat Book Critics Circle, Acad of am Poets, Mad Lang Asn, Nat Coun of Teachers of English, S Central Mod Lang Asn. **RESEARCH** Modern British and American literature (including post-colonialism); British literature surveys; Literature humanities, (Western literary tradition); 17th Century poetry; Shakespeare; Creative writing; Composition. **SELECTED PUBLICATIONS** Auth, Flesh, Permanent Press, 95; ed, Second Thoughts: A Focus on Rereading, Wayne State Univ Press, 98; auth, The Supporting Cast: a Study of flat and Minor characters, Penn State Univ Press, 93; auth, Tracks, William Morrow, 96; auth, Turning Japanese, Permanent Press, 98; auth, "Malcolm Lowry," in British Writers, Charles Scribner's Sons, 96; auth, "Observations on Rereading," in Second Thoughts: A Focus on Rereading, Wayne State Univ Press, 98; auth, "Answers to a Rhetorical Question," Symploke, (95(: 77-85; auth, "Crossing Over: Authors Who Write both Children's and Adult's Fiction," Children's Literature Association Quarterly, (95): 29-35; auth, "Abigaboo," The MacGuffin, (98): 54; auth, "America," The Formalist, (97): 12; auth, "Bi-Cycle," Westview, (99): 27. **CONTACT ADDRESS** Dept English, Univ of Mississippi, General Delivery, University, MS 38677-9999. **EMAIL** dgalef@olemiss.edu

GALINSKY, KARL
PERSONAL Born 02/07/1942, Strassburg, m, 1986, 2 children **DISCIPLINE** CLASSICS **EDUCATION** Bowdoin, AB, 63; Princeton, PhD, 66. **CAREER** Instr, Princeton, 65-66; asst prof, 66-68; assoc prof, 68-72; dept chair, 74-90; Univ Tex Austin, Prof, 72-; Cailloux Centennial prof, 84-; Distinguished Teaching Prof., 99-. **HONORS AND AWARDS** Fellowships at NEH, ACLS, Guggenheim, Humboldt; Tchg Excellence at Univ Tex, Am Philol Asn. **MEMBERSHIPS** Am Philos Asn; Archaeol Inst of Am; Mommsen Gesellschaft. **RESEARCH** Roman Civilization, Augustan Age. **SELECTED PUBLICATIONS** Auth, Aeneas, Sicily, and Rome, 69; The Herakles Theme, 72; Perspectives of Roman Poetry, 74; Ovid's Metamorphoses, 75; Classical and Modern Interactions, 92; The Interpretation of Roman Poetry, 92; Augustan Culture, 96. **CONTACT ADDRESS** Dept of Classics, Univ of Texas, Austin, Austin, TX 78712-1181. **EMAIL** galinsky@utxvms.cc.utexas.edu

GALL, JOHN
PERSONAL Born 09/02/1955, Sewickley, PA, m, 1998 **DISCIPLINE** FILM STUDIES **EDUCATION** Duquesne Univ, Pittsburgh, Pa, BA, 78, MA, 83, PhD, 89. **CAREER** Asst prof, Slippery Rock Univ, 90-91; lectr, Cuyahoga Community Col, 91-92; asst prof, North Country Community Col, 92-96; dir of liberal arts and sciences, Community Col of Beaver County, 97-. **RESEARCH** Film, popular culture, genre studies. **SELECTED PUBLICATIONS** Rev of Prelude au Matin d'un Poete: Traditions Humanistes chez le Jeune Liton, ed Olivier Lutaud, Seventeenth-Century News, 43 (84): 57-8; auth, " 'O you panderly rascals': Plot and Characterization in 'The Merry Wives of Windsor'," Selected Papers from the West Va Shakespeare and Renaissance Asn, 9 (84): 1-7; auth, "'Paradise Lost, Suggested Readings," A Milton Encyclopedia, Lewisburg: Bucknell Univ Press (84); rev of The Mercurian Monarch: Magical Politics From Spenser to Pope, by Douglas Brooks-Davies, Seventeenth-Century News, 43 (85): 3-4; auth, "The Pregnant Death of Dorian Gray," The Victorian Newsletter, 82 (fall 92): 55-7. **CONTACT ADDRESS** Dept Arts & Scis, Comm Col of Beaver County, 1 Campus Dr, Monaca, PA 15061-2566. **EMAIL** john.gall@ccbc.cc.pa.us

GALLAGHER, VICTORIA J.
DISCIPLINE COMMUNICATION **EDUCATION** Mich State Univ, BA, 83; Northwestern Univ, MA, 89, PhD, 90. **CAREER** Teaching asst, Northwestern Univ, Evanston, Ill, 86-90; vis prof, Univ NC at Chapel Hill, spring 92; assoc prof, NC

State Univ, Raleigh, 90-. **HONORS AND AWARDS** Phi Beta Kappa, Northwestern Univ, 89; NC State Col of Humanities and Soc Scis Outstanding Advising Awd, 92; B. Aubrey Fisher J Article Awd, Runner Up, from the Western State Commun Asn, Feb 93; 1999 Best Paper Awd, Am Soc of Engineering Eds, June 99; Nominated for Bd of Governor's Awd for Excellence in Teaching, 98-99; nominated for NC State Col of Humanities and Soc Scis Outstanding Teacher Awd, 95, 96, 97, 99; Inductee into the NC State Univ Acad of Outstanding Teachers, 99; NC State Univ Col of Humanities and Soc Scis Outstanding Teacher Awd, 99; NC State Univ Outstanding Teacher Awd, 99; **MEMBERSHIPS** Nat Commun Asn, Southern States Commun Asn. **RESEARCH** Rhetorical analysis of civil rights discourse; civil rights related museums, monuments, and memorials; gender and communications; work teams; educational, organizational, and ethical issues in communication. **SELECTED PUBLICATIONS** Coauth with David Zarefsky, "From 'Conflict ' to 'Constitutional Question': Transformations in Early American Public Discourse," Quart J of Speech, 76:3 (Aug 90): 247-261; auth, "The Role of the TA in the Interactive Classroom," Preparing the Professoriate of Tomorrow to Teach: Selected Readings in TA Training, Dubuque, IA: Kendall-Hunt Pub Co (90); coauth with George N. Dionisopolous, Steven R. Goldzwig, and David Zarefsky, "Martin Luther King, the American Dream and Vietnam: A Collision of Rhetorical Trajectories," Western J of Commun, 56 (spring 92): 91-107; auth, "Ethical Considerations in College Admission Practices: A Proposal for Dialogic Involvement," in The J of Col Admissions, 13.7 (fall 92): 8-12; auth, "Remembering Together?: Rhetorical Integration and the Case of the Martin Luther King, Jr. Memorial," in The Southern Commun J, 60 (winter 95): 109-119; auth, "University Repositioning: A Review of Four Cases," in The J of Col Admission, 154 (winter 97): 12-17; coauth with Cynthia Haller, Tracey Weldon, and Richard Felder, "Dynamics of Peer Interactions in Cooperative Learning," in the Proceedings of the 1999 American Society of Engineering Educators Conference (June 99); auth, "Reconciliation and Amnesia in the Birmingham Civil Rights Institute," in Rhetoric and Public Affairs, 2 (summer 99): 303-320; coauth with Cynthia R. Haller, Tracey Weldon, and Richard Felder, "Cooperative Learning in Chemical Engineering Workgroups: Dynamics of Peer Teaching and Learning," in J of Engineering Ed (July 2000); coauth with Michael Carter and Carolyn Miller, "Integrated Approaches to Teaching Rhetoric: Unifying a Divided House," in The Realms of Rhetoric: A Multidisciplinary Inquiry into the Prospects for Rhetoric Education, SUNY Press (in press). **CONTACT ADDRESS** Dept Commun, No Carolina State Univ, PO Box 8104, Raleigh, NC 27695-0001.

GALLANT, CHRISTINE

PERSONAL Born Toledo, OH, 1 child **DISCIPLINE** ENGLISH **EDUCATION** Univ Minn, BA, 62, MA, 66, PhD, 77. **CAREER** Asst prof, Va Commonwealth Univ, 77-84; PROF ENGLISH, GA STATE UNIV, 84-. **HONORS AND AWARDS** NEH summer stipend, 81. **SELECTED PUBLICATIONS** Auth, Blake and the Assimilation of Chaos, Princeton, Princeton V P , 78; auth, Coleridge's Theory of Imagination, Today (ed), NY AMS Press, 89; auth, Shelly's Ambivalence, London, Macmillan and NY St Martins Press, 89; auth, Tabooed Tung: Marginality as Power, London Macmillan, and N Y, N Y V Press, 96. **CONTACT ADDRESS** Dept of English, Georgia State Univ, Atlanta, GA 30303. **EMAIL** engccg@panther.gsu.edu

GALLI, BARBARA E.

PERSONAL Born 12/01/1949, Montreal, PQ, Canada, d **DISCIPLINE** GERMANIC LANGUAGES; LITERATURE **EDUCATION** Carleton Univ Ottawa, BA 73; Univ Toronto, MA 76; McGill Univ, PhD 90. **CAREER** Univ Alabama, Aaron Aronov Ch, 97; assoc and lect, McGill Univ. **MEMBERSHIPS** AAR; AJS; ALA; MLA. **RESEARCH** Franz Rosenzweig; Jewish theology and literature. **SELECTED PUBLICATIONS** Auth, Franz Rosenzweig and Jehuda Halevi: Translating Translation Translators, McGill-Queen's Univ Press, 95; God Man and the World: Lectures and Essays, trans and ed, Syracuse Univ Press, 98; Franz Rosenzweig and the New Thinking, trans and ed, Afterward by Alan Udoff, SUP, 98; Orientation in the Modern World: Franz Rosenzweig's Writings in a Cultural Vein, trans and ed, SUP, forthcoming, March 99. **CONTACT ADDRESS** Fac of Religious Studies, McGill Univ, 3520 Univer, Montreal, Canada PQH3A2A7. **EMAIL** bgalli2@po-box.mcgill.ca

GALLO, LOUIS

PERSONAL Born New Orleans, LA **DISCIPLINE** CREATIVE WRITING AND MODERN AND CONTEMPORARY LITERATURE **EDUCATION** La State Univ, MA; Univ Mo, PhD. **CAREER** Prof, Radford Univ. **SELECTED PUBLICATIONS** His stories, poems, and essays have appeared in j(s) such as Glimmer Train, Greensboro Rev, Mo Rev, and New Orleans Rev. **CONTACT ADDRESS** Radford Univ, Radford, VA 24142. **EMAIL** lgallo@runet.edu

GALPERIN, WILLIAM

DISCIPLINE ENGLISH LANGUAGE AND LITERATURE **EDUCATION** Univ Chicago, BA; Brown Univ, MA, PhD. **CAREER** Prof. **RESEARCH** Late 18th-century and early 19th-century British poetry and fiction; literary and cultural theory; film studies. **SELECTED PUBLICATIONS** Auth, Revision and Authority in Wordsworth; auth, The Return of the Visible in British Romanticism. **CONTACT ADDRESS** Dept of English, Rutgers, The State Univ of New Jersey, New Brunswick, 510 George St, Murray Hall, New Brunswick, NJ 08901-1167. **EMAIL** whgl@ix.netcom.com

GAMBLE, JAMES D.

PERSONAL Born 03/19/1954, Birmingham, AL, m, 1998 **DISCIPLINE** ENGLISH **EDUCATION** Univ Ala, BA, 87; MFA, 91. **CAREER** Adj Instr, Univ Ala; Teaching Writer, Ala Writers' Forum, 99-. **MEMBERSHIPS** Ala Writers' Forum, Asn Writing Progs. **RESEARCH** Post World War II popular American culture. **SELECTED PUBLICATIONS** Auth, Letters from Suburbia: Poems 1978-1994, New Dawn Unlimited Pr, 00. **CONTACT ADDRESS** Dept English, Univ of Alabama, Birmingham, 1530 3rd Ave S, Birmingham, AL 35294-0001. **EMAIL** dannygamble@att.net

GANDAL, KEITH

DISCIPLINE AMERICAN LITERATURE AND CULTURE, FRESHMAN COMPOSITION, AND CREATIVE WRITING **EDUCATION** Univ Calif, Berkeley, MA, PhD. **CAREER** Dept Eng, Mt. Saint Mary's Col **RESEARCH** Lives and writings of modern literary rebels, Crane, Foucault; Bohemian writer Henry Miller; African-American folklorist Zora Neale Hurston. **SELECTED PUBLICATIONS** Publ on, Stephen Crane & Michel Foucault. **CONTACT ADDRESS** Dept of English, Mount Saint Mary's Col and Sem, 16300 Old Emmitsburg Rd, Emmitsburg, MD 21727-7799. **EMAIL** gandal@msmary.edu

GANESAN, INDIRA

DISCIPLINE WOMEN'S STUDIES, ENGLISH **EDUCATION** Vassar Col, 82; Univ Iowa, 84. **HONORS AND AWARDS** Phi Beta Kappa; Granta Finalist, 97; Fel, FAWC, Radcliffe Coll. **MEMBERSHIPS** MLA; AWD. **RESEARCH** Creative writing; women's studies; ethnic studies. **SELECTED PUBLICATIONS** Auth, The Journey, Alfred and Knopf, 90; auth, Inheritance, Alfred and Knopf, 98. **CONTACT ADDRESS** Dept Humanities, Long Island Univ, Southampton Col, 239 Montauk Hwy, Southampton, NY 11968-4100. **EMAIL** igaresan@southampton.livnet.edu

GANGOTENA, MARGARITA

DISCIPLINE COMMUNICATIONS **EDUCATION** Univ of Minn, BA, 72; MA, 74; PhD, 80. **CAREER** Instr, course dir, Univ Col and YMCA, Univ of Minn, 72; instr, curriculum developer, Foreign Studies Degree Prog, Univ of Minn, 76-78; prof, Commun, Politechnical Sch of Chimborazo, Riobamba, Ecuador, 81; instr, Citibank, N.A., Citicorp-Latin America, Puerto Rico, 82; prof, soc psych, Catholic Univ of Quito, 82; Courses for Middle Management on Commun Skills, CEFE, Quito, Ecuador, 86, 87; lectr, Chicano Studies Dept, Univ of Minn, spring, 88; asst prof, Univ of Houston-Downtown, 88-92; asst prof, Tex A&M Univ, 92-97; assoc fac, Col of Extended Learning, Cent Mich Univ, 93-; consult, Vet Sch, Tex A&M, 97-98; assoc fac, Blinn Col, 98-. **HONORS AND AWARDS** Tuition, Room and Board and Travel Scholar, Org of Am States, two year tuition scholar, Univ of Minn, 67-72; Room and Board scholar, Alpha Gamma Delta Soroity, Panhellenic Coun Scholar, Univ of Minn, 69; Order of Ski-U-Mah, Univ of Minn, 72; scholar and leadership award, Univ of Minn, 76; McNamara fel, 83; World Bank's Res fel, 83; res grant, Tex A&M Univ, 95; Phi Kappa; Mortar Bd; full scholar, Hamline Univ and Fulbright Comn. **MEMBERSHIPS** Speech Commun Asn of Am; Int Commun Asn; Soc for Intercultural Educ, Training, and Res; Int Asn for Cross-Cultural Psych; Latin American Psychol Asn; ANDE, Nat Asn of Execs of Ecuador. **SELECTED PUBLICATIONS** Auth, "The Rhetoric of la familia Among Mexican-Americans," in Our Voices: Essays in Culture, Ethnicity, and Communication. An Intercultural Anthology, ed. A. Gonzalez, M. Houston, and V. Chen (Los Angeles, CA: Toxbury Publishing, 92). **CONTACT ADDRESS** 3803 Sunnybrook Ln, Bryan, TX 77802.

GANIM, JOHN MICHAEL

PERSONAL Born 02/18/1945, Weehawken, NJ **DISCIPLINE** ENGLISH, LINGUISTICS **EDUCATION** Rutgers Univ, BA, 67; IN Univ, MA, 69, PhD, 74. **CAREER** From asst prof to assoc prof, 74-88, prof eng, Univ CA, Riverside, 88, ch Eng Dept, 96. **HONORS AND AWARDS** Jr Fac Awd, Ctr Medieval and Renaissance Studies, 77. **MEMBERSHIPS** MLA; Medieval Acad Am; Medieval Asn Pacific. **RESEARCH** Middle Eng lit; Chaucer; Old Eng lit. **SELECTED PUBLICATIONS** Auth, Disorientation, style and consciousness in Sir Gawain and the Green Knight, PMLA, 76; Tone and Time in Chaucer's Troilus, ELH, 76; Style and Consciousness in Middle English Narrative, Princeton Univ Press; Bakhtin, Chaucer, Carnival, Lent, Studies in the Age of Chaucer, 87; Chaucer, Boccaccio and the Problme of Popularity, In: Assays, Pittsburgh Univ Press, 87; Carnival Voices in the clerk's Envoy, Chaucer Rev, 87; Chaucer and the Noise of the People; Exemplaria, spring 90; Chaucerian Theatricality, Princeton Univ Press, 90; Forms of Talk in the Canterbury Tales, Poetica, 91; The Literary Uses of New History, In: The Idea of Medieval Literature: New Essays on Chaucer and Medieval Culture in Honor of Donald R Howard (James M Dean and Christian K Zacher, ed); Univ Del Press, 92; Chaucerian Ritual and Patriarchal Romance, Chaucer Yearbook, 92; Literary Anthropology at the Turn of the Centuries: E K Chambers' The Mediaeval Stage, Envoi, 93; The Devil's Writing Lesson, In: Oral Poetics in Middle English Poetry (Mark Amodio, ed), Garland, 94; Medieval Literature as Monster: The Grotesque Before and After Bakhtin, Exemplaria, 95; Recent Studies on Literature, Architecture, and Urbanism, MLQ, 9/95; The Myth of Medieval Romance, In: Medievalism and the Modernist Temper (R Howard Bloch and Stephen G Nichols, ed), Johns Hopkins Univ Press, 96; Double-Entry in the Shipman's Tale: Chaucer and Bookkeeping Before Pacioli, Chaucer Rev, 96; auth, "Urbanism, Experience and Rhetoric in Some Early Descriptions of London," in The Performance of Middle English Culture, ed James Paxon et al (D.S. Brewer, 98); auth, "Chaucer, Boccaccio, Confession and Subjectivity," in The Decameron and the Canterbury Tales, ed Brenda Schildgen and Leonard Koff (Farleigh Dickinson Press, 99); auth, "Native Studies: Orientalism and the Middle Ages," in The Postcolonial Middle Ages, ed Jeffrey Jerome Cohen (Garland, 00). **CONTACT ADDRESS** Dept of Eng, Univ of California, Riverside, 900 University Ave, Riverside, CA 92521-0001. **EMAIL** john.ganim@ucr.edu

GANS, BRUCE

DISCIPLINE ENGLISH **EDUCATION** Univ Wisc, BA, 73; Univ Iowa, MA, 75. **CAREER** Lectr, Lake Forest Col and Roosevelt Univ, 77-79; Washington col, 81-95; assoc prof, Wright Col, 95-. **HONORS AND AWARDS** NEA Fel, 74; Va Ctr for the Creative Arts Fel, 87; IL Arts Counc Fel, 91; Golden Apple Awd, Wright Col, 99; Phi theta Kappa, 99; Marjorie Kovler Found Grant, 00; Founder of Great Books Curriculum. **MEMBERSHIPS** Authors Guild; Assoc of Lit Critics and Scholars; Chicago Area Great Books Assoc; Core Text Assoc; Nat Assoc of Scholars; Nat Writers Union; Soc of Midland Auth. **SELECTED PUBLICATIONS** Auth, "Somebody Special", Mademoiselle Prize Stories 1951-1975, ed Ellen Stoianoff, M. Evans and Co, (NY); 76; coauth, The Other Generation Gap, Follett, (Chicago), 78; auth, "And Here In Chicago It's 78", Here's The Story: Fiction With Heart, ed Morty Sklar, Spirit That Moves Us Pr, (Iowa City), 85; auth, "What Does Ruthie Have To Do with It?", Amelia Mag 3.2 (86): 51-57; auth, "What Do You Want From Me?", Midland Rev 4 (88): 33-42; auth, "He Never Got The Message", Kingfisher 1.2 (88): 63-73; auth, "Jak Jest Shura", Kansas Quarterly 22.3 (91): 87-101; auth, "The Imago", Hawaii Rev 35 (92): 139-148; auth, "The Duel", Farmer's Market 10.1 (93): 65-90. **CONTACT ADDRESS** Dept English, Wilbur Wright Col N, 4300 N Narragansett Ave, Chicago, IL 60634-1591.

GANTAR, JURE

DISCIPLINE DRAMA **EDUCATION** Univ Ljubljana, BA, MA, Univ Toronto, PhD. **CAREER** Prof. **SELECTED PUBLICATIONS** Auth, Pred odprtimi vrati, (In Front of the Open Door), Pot v Rim, Aneks (The Passage to Rome. The Annexe), Zveza kulturnih organizacij Slovenije, 90; Atomska dramaturgija Vilija Ravnjaka, (Atomic Dramaturgy of Vili Ravnjak), Umetnost igre, Stirje eseji, (The Art of Playing. Four Essays), Ljubljana: Zveza kulturnih organizacij Slovenije, 91; Dramaturgija in smeh, (Dramaturgy and Laughter), Knjiznica Mestnega gledalisca ljubljanskega, 93; Creativity and Wit, Creativity and Discovery, Conf Proc, Cornerbrook: Memorial Univ Newfoundland, 94; Theatrical Laughter and the Concept of Cryptic Noise, Recherches semiotiques/Semiotic Inquiry, 94; Catching the Wind in a Net, The Shortcomings of Existing Methods for the Analysis of Performance, Mod Drama, 96; Postmodern Comedy: Tautology or Pleonasm?, Stud in the Hum, 97; Feydeau in razvoj motiva dvojckov, (Feydeau and the Development of the Motif of Twins), Gledaliski list Drame SNG Ljubljana, 97; rev(s), Review of Playtexts: Ludics in Contemporary Literature, by Warren Motte, Dalhousie Rev, 95; Review of Comedy: The Mastery of Discourse, by Susan Purdie, Dalhousie Rev, 94. **CONTACT ADDRESS** Dept of Theatre, Dalhousie Univ, Halifax, NS, Canada B3H 3J5. **EMAIL** jure.gantar@dal.ca

GANZ, ARTHUR F.

PERSONAL Born 05/15/1928, Milwaukee, WI, w **DISCIPLINE** ENGLISH **EDUCATION** Univ Wisc, BA, 49; Univ Tenn, MA, 50; Columbia Univ, PhD, 57. **CAREER** Adj instr, Columbia Univ, 55-57, 58-59; instr to asst prof, Rutgers Univ, 60-65; asst prof to prof, CUNY, 65-96; vis prof, Columbia Univ, 82-83; vis prof, Univ Paris, 83, 86. **MEMBERSHIPS** MLA. **RESEARCH** Modern drama; Opera libretti. **SELECTED PUBLICATIONS** Auth, Realms of the Self: Variations on a Theme in Modern Drama, NY Univ Press, 81; auth, George Bernard Shaw, Macmillan, 83; auth, "Don Giovannia Shavianized: Man and Superman as Mozartean Commentary," Opera Quart, (96): 21-28. **CONTACT ADDRESS** 14 Horatio St, Apt 15D, New York, NY 10014-1652. **EMAIL** arthuruth@aol.com

GANZEL, DEWEY ALVIN

PERSONAL Born 07/05/1927, Albion, NE, m, 1955, 3 children **DISCIPLINE** ENGLISH LANGUAGE & LITERATURE **EDUCATION** Univ Nebr, Bsc, 49, MA, 53; Univ Chicago, PhD, 58. **CAREER** Retired Prof, Eng, Oberlin Coll, 97. **RESEARCH** American fiction, Literary history. **SELECTED PUBLICATIONS** Mark Twain Abroad: The Cruise of the

Quaker City, Univ Chicago Press, 68; Fortune and Men's Eyes: The Career of John Payne Collier, Oxford Univ Press, 82. **CONTACT ADDRESS** Dept Eng, Oberlin Col, Oberlin, OH 44074. **EMAIL** dewey.ganzel@oberlin.edy

GARAY, MARY SUE
DISCIPLINE BUSINESS AND TECHNICAL COMMUNICATION, LITERACY **EDUCATION** Carnegie-Mellon Univ, PhD, 88. **CAREER** Asst prof, La State Univ; ch-Indust Outreach, Nat Coun of Tchr of Eng, 90-96; mem, Gov's Workforce Develop Comt, La, 93-95. **HONORS AND AWARDS** Excellence in Res Awd, Cont Educ, LSU-BR, 94; summer fac grant, LSU-BR, 96; La's Workforce Develop Inst, 96. **RESEARCH** Workplace literacy; data interpretation. **SELECTED PUBLICATIONS** Auth, Workplace Literacy in the 90's: Definitions, Descriptions, Opportunities, and Cautions, in Stud in Tech Commun, 92; Meeting Workplace Needs in an Introductory Business Writing Course, Assoc of Bus Commun Quart, 95. **CONTACT ADDRESS** Dept of Eng, Louisiana State Univ and A&M Col, 212A Allen Hall, Baton Rouge, LA 70803. **EMAIL** engara@unix1.sncc.lsu.edu

GARAY, RONALD
DISCIPLINE ELECTRONIC MEDIA HISTORY AND PUBLIC POLICY **EDUCATION** Ohio Univ, PhD, 80. **CAREER** Assoc dean, undergrad stud and admin, La State Univ. **RESEARCH** Electronic media history, law, and regulation. **SELECTED PUBLICATIONS** Auth, "Advocacy Groups," "Direct Broadcast Satellite," "Pay Cable," "Pay-Per-View," "U.S. Congress and Television," and "Watergate," in The Encyclopedia of Television, ed. Horace Newcomb (Chicago, Fitzroy Dearborn, 97); auth, "Code of Wartime Practices," "Office of Censorship," "Liberty Broadcasting System," "Huey Long," "Gordon McLendon," "Office of War Information," and "World War II and Radio," in Historical Dictionary of American Radio, ed. Donald Godfrey and Fritz Leigh (Westport, CT, Greenwood, 98); auth, "Radio Entertainment," in History of the Mass Media in the United States, An Encyclopedia (Chicago, Fitzroy Dearborn, 98); auth, "Army-McCarthy Hearings" and "Sig Mickelson," in Encyclopedia of Television News, ed. Michael D. Murray (Phoenix, Oryz Press, 99); auth, "Televising Presidential Impeachment: The U.S. Congress Sets the Stage," Historical Journal of Film, Radio, and Television 19 (99): 57-68. **CONTACT ADDRESS** The Manship Sch of Mass Commun, Louisiana State Univ and A&M Col, Baton Rouge, LA 70803. **EMAIL** rgaray@unix1.sncc.lsu.edu

GARCIA, HAZEL F. DICKEN
DISCIPLINE MASS COMMUNICATION STUDIES **EDUCATION** Univ Mich, MA; Univ Wis Madison, PhD. **CAREER** Prof **SELECTED PUBLICATIONS** Auth, To Western Woods, 91; Journalistic Standards in Nineteenth-Century America, 89; co-auth, Communication History, 80. **CONTACT ADDRESS** Mass Communication Dept, Univ of Minnesota, Twin Cities, 111 Murphy Hall, 206 Church St SE, Minneapolis, MN 55455. **EMAIL** dicke003@maroon.tc.umn.edu

GARCIA, WILLIAM BURRES
PERSONAL Born 07/16/1940, Dallas, TX **DISCIPLINE** MUSIC EDUCATION **EDUCATION** Prairie View A&M Univ, music courses 1958-61; N TX State Univ, BMus 1962, MMus Ed 1965; Univ of IA, PhD 1973; Howard Univ, NEH Fellow 1973-74; Carnegie-Mellon Univ, College Mgmt Prog 1984. **CAREER** Philander Smith Coll, instructor of music 1963-64; Langston Univ, asst prof of music 1965-69; Miles Coll, assoc prof of music 1974-77; Talladega Coll, acting academic vice pres 1982-83, prof of music 1977-, chmn of music dept 1977-, chmn of humanities div 1981-85; Selma Univ, acad dean 1986-. **HONORS AND AWARDS** Doctoral Fellowship Grants S Fellowships Fund Inc 1969-73; Ford Found Fellowship Grant for Dissertations in Ethnic Studies 1971-72; Outstanding Educators of Amer 1975; lecture, "John Wesley Work, Choral Composer" Ethnic Music Workshop Coll of Fine Arts 1974; lecture "John Wesley Work, Black Amer Composer" Afro-Amer Music Workshop Ctr for African & Afro-Amer Studies Atlanta Univ 1975; paper, "African Elements in Afro-Amer Music" Anniston Museum of Natl History AL 1982. **MEMBERSHIPS** Mem Phi Mu Alpha Sinfonia 1965; bd Div of Higher Educ Disciples of Christ 1978-81; bd Talladega Arts Council 1981-; life mem Amer Choral Dirs Assn; mem Amer Choral Found; mem Amer Musicological Soc; mem Coll Music Soc; mem Intl Heinrich Schutz Soc; mem Natl Assn of Teachers of Singing; mem Thomas Music Study Club of Natl Assn of Negro Musicians. **SELECTED PUBLICATIONS** "Church Music by Black Composers, A Bibliography of Choral Works" Black Perspective in Music 1974. **CONTACT ADDRESS** Academic Dean, Selma Univ, 1501 Lapsley St, Selma, AL 36701.

GARCIA-CASTANON, SANTIAGO
PERSONAL Born 09/23/1959, Aviles, Spain, m, 1997, 1 child **DISCIPLINE** LITERATURE **EDUCATION** Univ de Oviedo, BA, 82; Univ Ill at Urbana-Champaign, MA, 87; PhD, 92. **CAREER** Asst prof, Ill Wesleyan Univ, 90-92; asst prof, Univ Ga, 92-96; assoc prof, Univ de Oviedo, 96-98; assoc prof, Ga Col & State Univ, 98-. **HONORS AND AWARDS** Sarah H. Moss Fac Res Grant, Univ Ga, 94; Second Prize, "Ciudad De Miranda" Int Poetry Competition, 95; First Prize, Easter Poetry Competition, 96. **MEMBERSHIPS** MLA, South Atlantic MLA, For Lang Asn of Ga, The Cervantes Soc of Am, Asn for the Interdisciplinary Study of the Arts, Soc for Renaissance and the Baroque. **RESEARCH** Hispanic Poetry, Spanish Golden Age Literature (Sixteen- & Seventeen-Century), Spanish Lexicography, Spanish Poetry (Twentieth-Century). **SELECTED PUBLICATIONS** Auth, "Los Inicios de Bances Candamo como Dramaturgo: Varia Fortuna de una Olvidada Comedia," El Bollo 98 (94); auth, Tiempos Imperfectos, Aviles, 94; auth, Entre las Sombras, Miranda de Ebro, 96; auth, "Study and Critical Edition of Por su Rey y por su Dama," by Francisco Bances Candamo, Real Inst de Estudios Asturianos, 97; co-transl, "Teorias del Realismo Literario," by Dario Villanueva, State Univ of NY Press (Albany, NY), 97; auth, "Observaciones sobre el Discurso Poetico en el Siglo de Oro Espanol," in El Discurso Artistico en Oriente y Occidente: Semejanzas y Contrastes, eds. Jose Luis Carames, Carmen Escobedo, and Jorge Luis Bueno (Oviedo: Univ de Oviedo, 97), 447-463; auth, "Francisco Bances Candamo," Spanish Dramatists of the Golden Age, A Bio-Bibliographical Sourcebook, ed. Mary Parker (CT: Greenwood Press, 98), 28-38; auth, "La Presencia del Idear io de Saavedra Fajardo en Bances Candamo," Bullet of Comediantes 50.2 (98): 405-417. **CONTACT ADDRESS** Dept For Lang, Ga Col & State Univ, PO Box 490, Milledgeville, GA 31061-0490. **EMAIL** sgarcia@mail.gcsu.edu

GARCIA-GOMEZ, JORGE
PERSONAL Born 01/14/1937, Havana, Cuba, m, 1961, 3 children **DISCIPLINE** PHILOSOPHY, LITERATURE **EDUCATION** Univ Santo Tomas Villanueva, BA, 58; New Sch Social Res, MA, 65, PhD(Philos), 71. **CAREER** Asst prof Philos, Sacred Heart Univ, 66-69; assoc prof, 69-80, prof Philos, Southampton Col, Long Island Univ, 81-. **MEMBERSHIPS** Am Philos Asn; Am Cath Philos Asn; Am Asn Teachers Span & Port; AAUP. **RESEARCH** Metaphysics; phenomenology; aesthetics. **SELECTED PUBLICATIONS** Auth, A meditation of liberty, Abraxas, New York, fall 70; Ciudades, Ed Plenitud, Madrid, 74; ed & transl Aron Gurwitsch, El Campo de la Conciencia, Madrid, 78; Jose Ortega oy Gasset, Encyclopedia et Phenomenolozy, 97; A Bridge to Temporality, St Augustine's Confessions, Analecta Husser-liana, LII, 98 **CONTACT ADDRESS** Humanities Div Southampton Col, Long Island Univ, Southampton Col, 239 Montauk Hwy, Southampton, NY 11968-4198.

GARD, BETTY A.
PERSONAL Born 08/12/1938, Watseka, IL, m, 1958, 2 children **DISCIPLINE** ENGLISH, LIBRARY SCIENCE **EDUCATION** Univ Ill, BA, 65; Univ Vt, MA English, 72; Univ Minn, MA Libr Sci, 79. **CAREER** Head, Govt Documents, Chester Fritz Libr, 71-72; Ref Librn and Subject Bibliogr, Chester Fritz Libr, 72-75; Head, Ref and Res Serv, Univ of NDak, 75-. **HONORS AND AWARDS** Univ of Ndak Meritorious Serv Awd, 97; Ndak Libr Asn President's Awd, 97. **MEMBERSHIPS** Am Libr Asn, Ndak Libr Asn, Mountain Plains Libr Asn. **RESEARCH** D.H. Lawrence, Reference Librarianship, Fed Documents Librarianship. **SELECTED PUBLICATIONS** Auth, "Son of Man: Arthur Lawrence as a Missing Link in D.H. Lawrence Criticism," Studies in Humanities 7 (Fall 70); 13-20; coauth, "North Dakota's Joint Regional Depository of U.S. Government Publications," in Documents to the People (Am Libr Asn, 72); auth, "A Cheer for the Practical," The Ref Librn (fall/winter 81): 150; co-ed, "Reference Sources of 1982," "Reference Sources of 1983," Am Libr, 82, 84; auth, "Reference Collection Policy of Chester Fritz Library," and "Micro-computer Software and Equipment," in Reference and Online Services handbook Vol 1, ed. Bill Katz (NY: Neal Schuman, 86), 247-257 and 571-574; rev, of "Homophones and Homographs: An American Dictionary, in RO (Summer 86): 538. **CONTACT ADDRESS** Ref and Res Serv, Univ of No Dakota, PO Box 9000, Grand Forks, ND 58202.

GARDAPHE, FRED L.
PERSONAL Born 09/07/1952, Chicago, IL, m, 1982 **DISCIPLINE** ENGLISH; CULTURAL STUDIES **EDUCATION** Univ of Wis at Madison, 76; Univ of Chicago, AM, 82; Univ of Ill Chicago, PhD, 93. **CAREER** Prof of English and Ed Studies, Columbia Col, 80-98; Prof of Italian/American Studies, SUNY Srony Brook, 98-. **HONORS AND AWARDS** Fac Development Grant, Columbia Col, 86; Dept of English Awd, Univ of Chicago, 82; William F. Vilas Scholar, Univ of Wis, 75; Res fel, Immigration Hist Res Center, Minn, 86; Vis prof, Univ Sassari, Italy, 98; Road Scholar, Ill Humanities Counc, 96-98. **MEMBERSHIPS** Nat Book Critics Cr; MLA; Soc of Midland Authors; Midwast MLA; Soc for the Study of Multi-Ethnic Lit of the United States; Am Asn of Italian Studies; Nat Writers Union; Am Italian Hist Asn; Ill Ethnic Coalition. **RESEARCH** Italian/American culture; ethnic American cultures; immigration. **SELECTED PUBLICATIONS** Coauth, (Ex)tending or Escaping a Tradition: Don DeLillo and Italian/American Literature, Beyond the Margin, Farleigh Dickinson Univ Press, 98; (In)visibility: Cultural Representation in the Criticism of Frank Lentricchia, Differentia, 94; auth, Fascism and Italian/American Writers, Romance Languages Annual, Purdue Univ Press, 93; In Search of Italian/American Writers, Italian Am, 97; Here are the Italian/American Writers, Canadian J of Italian Studies, 96; Breaking and Entering: An Italian American's Literary Odyssey, Forkroads, 95, Beyond The Godfather, 97. **CONTACT ADDRESS** Dept of English/European Studies, SUNY, Stony Brook, Stony Brook, NY 11794-3359. **EMAIL** fgar@aol.com

GARDINER, JUDITH KEGAN
PERSONAL Born 12/17/1941, Chicago, IL, d, 2 children **DISCIPLINE** ENGLISH **EDUCATION** Radcliffe Col, AB, 62; Columbia Univ, MA, 64; PhD, 68. **CAREER** Asst prof, Fisk Univ, 68-69; asst prof to prof, Univ of Ill at Chicago, 69-; vis scholar, Stanford Univ Center for Res on Women, 83; res assoc, Newberry Libr, 86-87. **HONORS AND AWARDS** NEH Fel, 88; Individual Residency, Bellagio, Italy, Rockefeller Found, 96; Univ Ill at Chicago Teaching Excellence Awd, 98 & 99. **RESEARCH** Feminist theory; masculinity studies. **SELECTED PUBLICATIONS** Auth, Craftsmanship in Context: The Development of Ben Jonson's Poetry, Mouton, 75; auth, "On Female Indentity and Writing by Women," Critical Inquiry 8.2 (81): 347-361; auth, "Mind Mother: Psychoanalysis and Feminism," in Making a Difference: Feminist Literary Criticism, ed. Gayle Greene and Copp,lia Kahn (London: Methuen, 85), 113-145; auth, "The Marriage of Male Minds in Shakespeare's Sonnets," J of English and Ger Philol 84.3 (85): 328-347; auth, "Self Psychology as Feminist Theory," Signs 12.4 (87): 761-780; auth, "The First English Novel: Aphra Behn's Love Letters, The Canon, and Women's Tastes," Tulsa Studies in Women and Lit 8.2 (89): 201-222; auth, "Radical Optimism, Maternal Materialism, and Teaching Literature," in Changing Subjects: The Making of Feminist Literary Criticism, ed. Gayle Greene and Copp,lia Kahn (New York and London: Routledge, Chapman, Hall, 93), 83-94; auth, "Empathic Ways of Reading: Narcissism, Identity Politics, and Russ's Female Man," Feminist Studies 20.1 (94): 87-111; auth, "Feminism and the Future of Fathering," in Men Doing Feminism, ed. Tom Digby (New York: Routledge, 98), 255-273; ed, Masculinity Studies and Feminist Theories: New Directions, (forthcoming). **CONTACT ADDRESS** Dept English, Univ of Illinois, Chicago, 601 S Morgan, Chicago, IL 60607-7120. **EMAIL** gardiner@uic.edu

GARDNER, JOSEPH HOGUE
PERSONAL Born 09/15/1938, McDonough, GA, m, 1961, 2 children **DISCIPLINE** ENGLISH LITERATURE **EDUCATION** Harvard Univ, AB, 60; Univ Calif, Berkeley, MA, 63, PhD(English), 69. **CAREER** Actg instr English, Univ Calif, Berkeley, 65-66; from instr to asst prof, 66-71, ASSOC PROF ENGLISH, UNIV KY, 71-91; Prof, 91-. **MEMBERSHIPS** Dickens Fel; Dickens Soc; 1890's Soc; Nineteenth-Century Studies Assoc. **RESEARCH** Pre-Raphaelitism; aestheticism; decadence. **SELECTED PUBLICATIONS** Auth, "Rossetti as Wordsmith," Victoria Poetry, (82); auth, "Brightening the Domestic Corner," Studies-Popular Cult, (86); auth, "Dawson's Pastoral," Nineteenth-Century Lit, (93); auth, "On The Rear of Mr. Wilde," J of Pre-Raphaelite Studies, (00). **CONTACT ADDRESS** Dept of English, Univ of Kentucky, 500 S Limestone St, Lexington, KY 40506-0003. **EMAIL** jgardner@ukcc.uky.edu

GARGAN, WILLIAM M.
PERSONAL Born 04/18/1950, Brooklyn, NY, m, 1980, 2 children **DISCIPLINE** LIBRARY SCIENCE, ENGLISH **EDUCATION** SUNY, BA, 72; Columbia, MA, 73; MS, 76. **CAREER** Adj lectr, Kingsborough Community col, 73-74; libr, Brooklyn Public Libr, 74-79; prof, CUNY, 79-. **MEMBERSHIPS** Am Libr Assoc, Assoc of Col and Res Libr, MLA, James Joyce Soc, Ernest Hemingway Soc, LACUNY. **RESEARCH** Modern British and American literature, particularly the Beat Generation, Popular music and culture. **SELECTED PUBLICATIONS** Coauth, Find That Tune: An Index to Rock, Folk Rock, Disco and Soul in Collections, Neal-Schuman, 84; coauth, Find That Tune: An Index to Rock, Folk Rock, Disco and Soul in Collections, Vol 2, Neal-Schuman, 88; auth, "Film Section," Magazines for Libraries, ed Bill and Linda Katz, Neal Schuman, (89); auth, "Henry Miller," St James Guide to Literary Biography, ed Paul Schellinger, St James Pr, (91); auth, "Jack Kerouc," Bibliogr of Am Fiction, Ed Matthew Bruccoli, Facts on File, (91); auth, "Phil Ochs," "Katherine Anne Porter," "Margaret Anderson," "Jim Morrison," Dict of Am Biogr, Charles Scribner's Sons, (94); auth, "Charles Bukowski," "Herbert Huncke," "Frederick Exley," Scribner Encycl of Am Lives, Charles Scribner's Sons, (98); auth, "Jack Kerouac's The Town & The City: A Reconsideration," Beat Scene 36, (00): 9-12. **CONTACT ADDRESS** Libr, Brooklyn Col, CUNY, 423 Rugby Rd, Brooklyn, NY 11226. **EMAIL** wxgbc@cunyvm.cuny.edu

GARIEPY, MARGO R.
PERSONAL Born 12/14/1942, Evanston, IL **DISCIPLINE** ENGLISH, HISTORY **EDUCATION** N Ill Univ, BA, 66; MA, 71. **CAREER** Instructor, N Ill Univ, 69-72; Asst Prof, Kennedy-King Col, 72-87; Assoc Prof, Wright Col, 87-. **MEMBERSHIPS** AAUW; NCTE; TYCA; ALSC. **RESEARCH** Adult Learning Strategies; Great Books; Writing Across Curriculum. **CONTACT ADDRESS** Dept Eng, City Cols of Chicago, Wilbur Wright Col, 4300 N Narragansett Ave, Chicago, IL 60634-1591. **EMAIL** mgari17673@aol.com

GARLINGER, PATRICK P.
PERSONAL Born 04/08/1972, Fontana, CA **DISCIPLINE** SPANISH, LITERATURE **EDUCATION** Wash Univ, BA, 94; Emory Univ, PhD, 00. **CAREER** Asst prof, Univ Iowa, 00-. **MEMBERSHIPS** MLA. **RESEARCH** Twentieth-century Spanish literature; gay and lesbian studies; queer theory; feminist theory. **SELECTED PUBLICATIONS** Auth, "'Homoness' and the Fear of Femininity," Diacritics 29 (99): 57-71; auth, "Lost Lesbian Love Letters? Epistolary Erasure and Queer Readers in Martin Gaite's El Cuarto de Atras," Bulletin of Hisp Studies 76 (99): 513-33; auth, "Dragging Spain into the Post-Franco Era: Transvestism and National Identity in Eduardo Mendicutti's Una Mala Noche la Tiene Cualquiera," Rev Can de Estud Hisp 24 (00): 363-82. **CONTACT ADDRESS** Dept Mod Lang, Univ Iowa, 111 Phillips Hall, Iowa City, IA 52242. **EMAIL** patrick-garlinger@uiowa.edu

GARNER, RICHARD
PERSONAL Born 03/06/1953, Tahlequah, OK, s **DISCIPLINE** CLASSICAL LANGUAGE, CLASSICAL LITERATURE **EDUCATION** Princeton Univ, BA, 75; Harvard Univ, MA 76; Univ Chicago, MA, 80; PhD, 83. **CAREER** Asst prof to assoc prof, Yale Univ, 83-93; Olin prof, Yale Univ. 93-94; Dean, Honors Col, Adelphi, 94-. **HONORS AND AWARDS** Banchko Prize, Princeton, 75; Phi Beta Kappa; Fel, Harvard Univ, 80-83; Galler Prize, Univ of Chicago, 83; Sidonie Miskimin Clauss Prize, Yale Col, 86; Sarai Ribicoff Awd, Yale, 86; Heyman Prize, Yale, 86; Devane/Phi Beta Kappa Medal, Yale, 92; Fel, Olin Fac, 93-94; Loeb Lect, Harvard, 94. **SELECTED PUBLICATIONS** Auth, Law and Society in Classical Athens, St. Martin's, Croom Helm, 87; auth; "Death and Victory in Euripides 'Alcestis'", Classical Antiquity 7, (88): 58-71; auth, From Homer to Tragedy: The Art of Allusion in Greek Poetry, Routledge, 90; auth, "Mules, Mysteries, and Song in Pindar's Sixth Olympian", Classical Antiquity 11 (92): 45-67; auth, "Countless Deeds of Valor: Bacchylides 11", Classical Quarterly 42 (92): 523-25; auth, "Achilles in Locri: P.Oxy 3876, frr. 37-77", Zeitschrift fur Papyrologie und Epigraphik 96 (93): 153-65; auth, "Stesichorus' Althaia: P.Oxy. 3876", Zeitschrift fur Papyrologie und Epigraphik 100 (94): 25-37. **CONTACT ADDRESS** Dept Lang & Lit, Adelphi Univ, 1 South Ave, Garden City, NY 11530-4213. **EMAIL** garner@adelphi.edu

GARRATT, ROBERT FRANCIS
PERSONAL Born 12/27/1941, San Francisco, CA, m, 1970, 1 child **DISCIPLINE** ENGLISH LITERATURE, MODERN IRISH LITERATURE **EDUCATION** San Jose State Univ, BA, 64, MA, 69; Univ Ore, PhD(lit), 72. **CAREER** Asst prof English, Univ Puget Sound, 72-77; vis assoc prof, Pitzer Col, 77-78; ASSOC PROF ENGLISH, UNIV PUGET SOUND, 78-, Nat Endowment for Humanities grant, Johns Hopkins Univ, 75 and Yale Univ, 79; Nat Endowment for Humanities fel, 81-82. **MEMBERSHIPS** Am Soc Eighteenth Century Studies; Brit Studies Conf Northwest (secy, 76-77); Am Comt Irish Studies; Philol Asn Pac Coast. **RESEARCH** Twentieth century Irish Poetry; modern poetry; modern literature (18th--20th century). **SELECTED PUBLICATIONS** Auth, Browning's dramatic monologue: The strategy of the double mask, Victorian Poetry, summer 73; Austin Clarke in transition, Irish Univ Rev, spring 74; On John Berryman by J M Linebarger, Concerning Poetry, fall 75; Aware of my ancestor: Austin Clarke and the legacy of Swift, Eire-Ireland, summer 76; The poetry of Austin Clarke, Eire-Ireland, autumn 77; Patrick Kavanaugh and the killing of the Irish revival, Colby Libr Quart, fall 81; guest ed, special Irish poetry issue, Concerning Poetry, fall 81. **CONTACT ADDRESS** Dept of English, Univ of Puget Sound, 1500 N Warner St, Tacoma, WA 98416-0005.

GARRETT, JAMES M.
PERSONAL Born 08/23/1960, Anaheim, CA, m, 1985, 2 children **DISCIPLINE** ENGLISH **EDUCATION** UCLA, BA, 82; CSU Los Angeles, MA, 93; USC, PhD, 99. **CAREER** Lectr, CSU Los Angeles, 94-99; prof, Occidental Col, 00-. **MEMBERSHIPS** MLA, N Am Soc for the Study of Romanticism. **RESEARCH** 18th and 19th Century British literature, technology and language, canonicity, nationalism, postcolonial studies. **SELECTED PUBLICATIONS** Designer, Wordsworth Variorum Archive, online; 97-01; auth, "Surveying and Writing the Nation: Wordsworth's Black Comb and 1816 Commemorative Poems," REAL, (98); auth, "Writing Community: Bessie Head and the Politics of Narrative," Res in African Lit, (99); auth, "The Unaccountable 'Knot' of Wordsworth's 'Gipsies,' Studies in Eng Lit 1500-1900, (00). **CONTACT ADDRESS** Occidental Col, 1600 Campus Rd, Los Angeles, CA 91106. **EMAIL** jgarrett@oxy.edu

GARRETT, PETER
PERSONAL Born 11/16/1940, Cleveland, OH, m, 1961, 2 children **DISCIPLINE** ENGLISH LITERATURE **EDUCATION** Haverford Col, BA, 62; Yale Univ, MA, 63, PhD(English), 66. **CAREER** From instr to asst prof English, Princeton Univ, 66-75; assoc prof, 75-81, PROF ENGLISH, UNIV ILL, URBANA, 81-, Fel, Am Coun Learned Soc, 74-75 and 82-83. **MEMBERSHIPS** MLA. **RESEARCH** Victorian and modern fiction; narrative theory. **SELECTED PUBLICATIONS** Auth, Seeue and Symbol from George Eliot to James Joyce, 69; auth, The Victorian Multiplot Novel, 80. **CONTACT ADDRESS** Dept of English, Univ of Illinois, Urbana-Champaign, 608 S Wright St, Urbana, IL 61801-3613. **EMAIL** pgarrett@uiuc.edu

GARRIGAN, KRISTINE O.
DISCIPLINE ENGLISH **EDUCATION** Stanford Univ, BA, 60; Ohio State Univ, MA, 64; Univ Wisc-Madison, PhD, 71. **CAREER** Instr, Univ of Wisc, 68-78; vis asst prof, Denison Univ, 78-79; from asst prof to prof, DePaul Univ, 81-. **MEMBERSHIPS** MLA, Midwest Victorian Studies Asn, Res Soc for Victorian Periodicals, Historians of British Art, Asn of Historians of 19th Century Art, Virginia Woolf Soc, African Lit Asn. **RESEARCH** Victorian literature, art, architecture, John Ruskin. **SELECTED PUBLICATIONS** Auth, Ruskin on Architecture: His Thought and Influence, Univ of Wisc Press, 73; auth, Victorian Art Reproductions in Modern Sources: A Bibliography, Garland, 91; ed, Victorian Scandals, Ohio Univ Press, 92. **CONTACT ADDRESS** Dept English, DePaul Univ, 802 W Belden Ave, Chicago, IL 60614-3214. **EMAIL** kgarriga@wppost.depaul.edu

GARRISON, DANIEL H.
PERSONAL Born 12/24/1937, Hamilton, NY, m, 1992, 1 child **DISCIPLINE** CLASSICS **EDUCATION** Harvard Univ, BA, 59; Univ NC Chapel Hill, MA, 63; Univ Cal Berk, PhD, 68. **CAREER** Northwestern Univ, prof, 66-. **MEMBERSHIPS** APA; Classical Assoc Middle W & S; Soc Ancient Medicine; AAHM. **RESEARCH** Lyric poetry; Medical history. **SELECTED PUBLICATIONS** Coauth, "Vesalius on the Variability of the Human Skull: Book I Chapter V of De humani corporis fabrica," Clinical Anatomy 13, (00): 311-320; auth, Sexual Culture in Ancient Greece, Univ Oklahoma Press, 00; auth, Horace Epodes and Odes, A New Annotated Latin edition, Univ OK Press, 91, rev, Class Wld 92, Greece and Rome, 92, Classical Outlook, 93; coauth, "Andreas Vesalius on the Teeth: An Annotated translation from De humani corporis fabrica," Clinical Anatomy, 95; coauth, "Andreas Vesalius on the Larynx and Hyoid Bone", Medical History, 93; auth, The Locus Inamoenus: Another Part of the Forest, Arion II, 92; **CONTACT ADDRESS** Dept of Classics, Northwestern Univ, 1859 Sheridan Rd, Evanston, IL 60208. **EMAIL** d-garrison@northwestern.edu

GARRISON, JAMES DALE
PERSONAL Born 01/10/1943, Bremerton, WA, m, 1969, 2 children **DISCIPLINE** ENGLISH **EDUCATION** Princeton Univ, AB, 65; Univ Calif, Berkeley, MA, 67, PhD(English), 72. **CAREER** Asst prof, 73-79, from assoc prof English, Univ Tex, Austin, 79-93; Prof of English, 93-chmn English, 94. **MEMBERSHIPS** Am Soc Eighteenth-Century Studies. **RESEARCH** Restoration and eighteenth-century English literature; the Enlightenment. **SELECTED PUBLICATIONS** Auth, Dryden and the Tradition of Panegyric, Univ Calif, 75; Gibbon and the treacherous language of panegyrics, Eighteenth-Century Studies, 77; Lively and Laborious: Characterization in Gibbon's Metahistory, Modern Philol, 78; Dryden and the Birth of Hercules, Studies in Philol, 80; The Universe of Dryden's Fables, Studies in English Lit, 81; Pietas from Vergil to Dryden, Penn State Press, 92. **CONTACT ADDRESS** Dept of English, Univ of Texas, Austin, Austin, TX 78712-1026. **EMAIL** jdgar@mail.utexas.edu

GARSON, HELEN S.
PERSONAL Born, NY, m, 3 children **DISCIPLINE** LITERATURE **EDUCATION** George Wash Univ, BA; Univ Ga, MA; Univ Md, PhD. **CAREER** Instr, George Wash Univ; lectr, Univ Md; asst prof to assoc prof to prof to asst dean to assoc dean to grad coord, George Mason Univ. **HONORS AND AWARDS** George Mason Res Grant, Fac Res Grant, Found Grant; Grad Asstshp, Univ Md; Fel Univ Ga; Phi Kappa Phi; Pi Lambda Theta. **MEMBERSHIPS** MLA. **RESEARCH** Modern literature--fiction, popular culture, crime, mystery writing. **SELECTED PUBLICATIONS** Auth, Tom Clancy, Greenwood; auth, The Short Fiction of Truman Capote, Twayne/Macmillan; auth, Truman Capote, Ungar; auth, "Enter George Smiley," Modern Critical Views; auth, "Cold Comfort," in Realist of Distance; auth, "Pornography," in Oxford Companion to Mystery Writing (Oxford Univ Pr); auth, "Truman Capote," in Dict Lit Biog (Gale Group); auth, "Tom Clancy," in Dict Lit Biog (Gale Group); auth, "Truman Capote's Grass Harp," Southern Quart; auth, "Elizabeth LeMarchand," in Great Women of Mystery (Greenwood). **CONTACT ADDRESS** 130 Chevy Chase St, Apt 406, Gaithersburg, MD 20878. **EMAIL** hsgarson@juno.com

GARTON, CHARLES
PERSONAL Born 08/13/1926, Yorkshire, England, m, 1960, 2 children **DISCIPLINE** CLASSICS **EDUCATION** Cambridge Univ, BA, 49, MA, 53. **CAREER** Asst lectr classics, Univ Hull, 51-53; lectr, Univ Newcastle upon Tyne, 53-65; assoc prof, 65-72, actg chmn dept, 73-74, Prof Classics to Prof Emer, SUNY, Buffalo, 72-; Ed, Arethusa, 68-71, assoc ed, 74-. **MEMBERSHIPS** Class Asn England & Wales. **RESEARCH** Classical and comparative literature; theatre; educational history. **CONTACT ADDRESS** Dept of Classics, SUNY, Buffalo, 338 MFAC, Buffalo, NY 14261.

GARVEY, SHEILA HICKEY
PERSONAL Born 12/23/1949, Erie, PA, 2 children **DISCIPLINE** THEATER **EDUCATION** Emerson Col, BA, 71; Northwestern Univ, MA, 73; New York Univ, PhD, 75. **CAREER** Preceptor, English, NY Univ, 78-80; instr, theatre arts, Rutgers Univ, 80-81; asst prof, dramatic arts, Dickinson Col, 81-87; from assoc to full prof, 88- , app coord of theatre majors, 90, app coord of performance for Theatre Dept, 91, Southern Conn State Univ. **HONORS AND AWARDS** Dana Found grant, 87; AAUP/CSU res grants, 89, 90, 91, 95; John F. Kennedy Ctr for the Perf Arts, scholarship, 92; fac dev grants, 89, 90, 91, 92, 95, 97; summer curriculum grants, 91, 96, 98; bd dir, new england theatre conf, 92-95; chemn col div of new england theatre conf, 92-95; mem performance rev staff of new england theatre journal, 93- ; mem, conn critics circle, 97- . **MEMBERSHIPS** Board of Directors New England Theatre Conf; Eugene O'Neill Soc; AAUP. **RESEARCH** Eugene O'Neill in performance; contemporary trends in actor training; women in theater. **SELECTED PUBLICATIONS** Auth, Documentation of Long Wharf Theatre 1993-4 Theatrical Season, New England Theatre J, 94; auth, Anna Christie and The Fallen Woman Genre: A Performance Perspective, Eugene O'Neill Rev, 95; auth, Documentation of Long Wharf Theatre 1994-1995 Theatrical Season, Hartford Stage 1994-1995 Theatrical Season, New England Theatre J, 95; auth, Documentation of Long Wharf Theatre 1995-1996 Theatrical Season, Hartford Stage 1995-1996 Theatrical Season and the Goodspeed Opera House 1995 Theatrical Season, New England Theatre J, 96; auth, Hughie Directed by (and starring) Al Pacino, Eugene O'Neill Rev, 96; auth, Documentation of Long Wharf Theatre 1995-1996 Theatrical Season and the Goodspeed Opera House 1995 Theatrical Season, New England Theatre J, 97; auth, Documentation of Long Wharf Theatre 1996-1997 Theatrical Season, and the Goodspeed Opera House 1996 Theatrical Season, New England Theatre J, 98; auth, Documentation of Long Wharf Theatre 97-99. **CONTACT ADDRESS** Dept of Theatre, So Connecticut State Univ, 501 Crescent St, New Haven, CT 06515. **EMAIL** garvey@scsu.ctstateu.edu

GASIENICA-BYRCYN, ANNA ZOFIA
PERSONAL Born 04/25/1962, Zakopane, Poland, s **DISCIPLINE** CLASSICS, LITERATURE, LANGUAGE, SLAVIC, POLISH **EDUCATION** Univ Ill Chicago, MA, 89; PhD, 00. **CAREER** Teaching asst to vis lectr, Univ Ill, 84-90, 92-99, 00-. **HONORS AND AWARDS** Tracy Awd, Univ Ill, 93; ACLS Teaching Grant, 96, 97. **MEMBERSHIPS** PIASA; AATSEEL; MLA. **RESEARCH** Polish women's poetry, 20th-century; Marta Fox; Halina Powiatowska. **SELECTED PUBLICATIONS** Auth, "I'll Dance for You in Words," Lit 47 (01): 5-22; trans, intro, "Halina Powiatowska's Verbal Paintings," (Sarmat Rev, 1996): 363-370. **CONTACT ADDRESS** Dept Classics, Univ of Illinois, Chicago, 601 S Morgan St, MC 306, Chicago, IL 60607-7100. **EMAIL** anna-gb@uic.edu

GASKILL, GAYLE
PERSONAL Born 08/09/1945, MN, s **DISCIPLINE** ENGLISH **EDUCATION** Mankato State Univ, BS, 66; Univ Neb, MA, 86; Univ Minn, PhD, 86. **CAREER** Instr, Ind state Univ, 70-72; Instr, Fairleigh Dickinson Univ, 72-73; Teaching Assoc, Univ Minn, 73-79; Instr, Hamline Univ, 79-80; Instr, Clarke Col, 80-81; Instr, Normandale community Col, 86-87; Lecturer, Univ Minn, 81-93; Asst Prof to Prof, Col of St Catherine, 87-. **HONORS AND AWARDS** Teaching Awd, Col of St. Catherine, 92; NEH summer Inst, 93; HEH Summer Seminar, 90. **MEMBERSHIPS** Shakespeare Asn of am, Mod Lang Asn, John Donne soc, Midwest Mod Lang Asn, Sixteenth-Century Studies Asn. **RESEARCH** Shakespeare's sonnets and women readers; Shakespeare's comedies; John Donne's epithalamia. **SELECTED PUBLICATIONS** Auth, "Flodden Field, Battle of" and "Lady Jane Grey," Tudor England: An Encyclopedia, Garland Pub, forthcoming; auth, "To Present Moonshine: a Midsummer Night's Dream as a comic Reading of Political compliment," Shakespeare and Renaissance Association of West Virginia Selected papers, 00; auth, "Performance Theory and Research in the Undergraduate Shakespeare Survey," studies in Medieval and Renaissance Teaching, (00); 37-47; auth, "Madmen's Discourse: Reading (My love is as a fever, longing still] with Lady Mary Wroth," The Shakespeare Newsletter, (99): 69; auth, "Reading Shakespeare's sonnets in the contexts of His Plays," Shakespeare and the classroom, (95): 39-41; auth, "Partners of Greatness: The Love story in Macbeth," The Shakespeare Newsletter, (95): 57. **CONTACT ADDRESS** Dept English, Col of St. Catherine, 2004 Randolph Ave, Saint Paul, MN 55105-1750. **EMAIL** ggaskill@stkate.edu

GASQUE, THOMAS J.
PERSONAL Born 09/06/1937, Florence, SC, m, 1969, 1 child **DISCIPLINE** ENGLISH **EDUCATION** Wofford Col, AB, 59; Emory Univ, MA, 61; Univ Tenn, PhD, 70. **CAREER** Instr, Clemson Col, 61-62; instr, Columbia Col SCar, 62-63; TA, Univ Tenn Knoxville, 63-68; asst prof to prof, Univ SDak, 68-. **HONORS AND AWARDS** Fulbright Teaching and Res, 88-89; Fel, Inst for Southern Studies, 00; Harrington Lectr, 00. **MEMBERSHIPS** Am Name Soc, MLA, New Chaucer Soc, SDak Hist Soc, SCar Hist Soc, Can Soc for the Study of Names, Int Coun of Onomastic Sci, Am Dialect Soc, Coun of Geog Names Authorities. **RESEARCH** Onomastics, Lewis and

Clark, with focus on placenames. **SELECTED PUBLICATIONS** Auth, "Looking Back to Beaver and the Head: Male College Nicknames in the 1950s," NAMES 42.2, (94); 121-32; auth, "Lewis and Clark's Onomastic Assumptions," Midwestern Folklore 21.1/2 (95): 30-38; auth, "The Apostrophe in US Placenames," You Naje It: Perspectives on Onomastic Res, (Helsiniki, Finalnd, 97); ed, Silver Anniversary Anthology, SDak Humanities Coun, 97; auth, "Naming the Dakotas," Place Names in the Midwestern US, (Mellen, 00); auth, "Structure and Controversy: What Names Authorities ' Adjuticate," NAMES 48.3/4, (00): 199-206. **CONTACT ADDRESS** Dept English, Univ of So Dakota, Vermillion, 414 E Clark St, Vermillion, SD 57069. **EMAIL** tgasque@usd.edu

GASTIL, JOHN WEBSTER

PERSONAL Born 02/07/1967, San Diego, CA **DISCIPLINE** COMMUNICATIONS **EDUCATION** Swarthmore Col, BA, Polit Sci, 89; Univ Wis-Madison, PhD, Commun Arts, 94. **CAREER** Res mgr, Univ NMex, Inst Public Policy, 94-97; ASST PROF, UNIV WASH, SPEECH COMMUN, 98-. **RESEARCH** Public deliberation; small group decision making; political participation; public opinion **SELECTED PUBLICATIONS** Democracy in Small Groups: Participation, Decision Making, and Communication, New Soc Publ, 93; "Identifying Obstacles to Small Group Democracy," Small Group Research, 93; "A Meta-Analytic Review of the Productivity and Satisfaction of Democratic and Autocratic Leadership," Small Group Res, 94; " A Definition and Illustration of Democratic Leadership," Human Relations, 94; "Increasing Political Sophistication Through Public Deliberation," Political Communication, 98; auth, By popular demand: revitalizing representative democracy through deliberative elections, Berkeley, Ca: Univ of Cal, 00; auth, "The politcal belifs and orientations of people with disabilities," Soc Sci Quarterly, vol 81, (00), 588-603. **CONTACT ADDRESS** Dept Speech & Commun, Univ of Washington, PO Box 353415, Seattle, WA 98195. **EMAIL** jgastil@u.washington.edu

GASTON, EDWIN W., JR

PERSONAL Born 02/22/1925, Nacogdoches, TX, m, 1946, 3 children **DISCIPLINE** ENGLISH **EDUCATION** Stephen F Austin State Univ, BS, 47; MA, 51; Tex Tech Univ, PhD, 59. **CAREER** Newspaper editing and radio-tv broadcasting, Tex, 42-43, 47-60; asst prof to prof and dir, Stephen F Austin State Univ, 50-53, 55-64, 65-86; instr, Tex Tech Univ, 53-55; Fulbright lectr, Univ Helsinki, 64-65; dean and prof emeritus and vp, Stephen F Austin State Univ, 76-. **HONORS AND AWARDS** Distinguished Prof Award, Univ Helsinki, 65; Distinguished Prof Award, Stephen F Austin State Univ, 69, 70; Distinguished Alumnus Award, Tex Tech Univ, 85; distinguished Alumnus Award, Alpha Chi Nat Scholar Soc, 99. **MEMBERSHIPS** Alpha Chi; MLA; SW Am Lit Asn; Tex Folklore Soc; E Tex Hist Asn; W Am Lit Asn. **SELECTED PUBLICATIONS** Co-ed, Southwestern American Literature: A Bibliography, Swallow press, 80; auth, "Eugene Manlove Rhodes," in Fifty Western Writers, Greenwood Press, 82; auth, "Karle Wilson Baker," in The Handbook of Texas, Univ of Tex Press, 96. **CONTACT ADDRESS** Stephen F. Austin State Univ, 709 Bostwick St, Nacogdoches, TX 75961-2416.

GATES, BARBARA TIMM

PERSONAL Born 08/04/1936, Sheboygan, WI, d, 2 children **DISCIPLINE** ENGLISH LITERATURE, WOMEN'S STUDIES **EDUCATION** Northwestern Univ, BA, 58; Univ Del, MA, 61; Bryn Mawr Col, PhD(English), 71. **CAREER** Lectr English, Widener Col, 65-67; from asst prof to Alumni Distinguished prof, Univ Del, 71-. **HONORS AND AWARDS** Univ Del res grants, 72, 76, 79 and 81; Danforth assoc, 73-; Lindback Awd for Excellence in Teaching, Univ Del, 74; consult Excellence in Teaching and Distinguished Acad Serv, Dept Educ, Commonwealth Pa, 75-76; Am Philos Soc grant, 76; DIMER res grant, 77; Am Coun Learned Soc grant, 79; Nat Endowment for Humanities grant, 81; fel, Center for Advanced Study, Univ Deleware; E. Arthur Trabant Awd for Promoting Equity at the Univ Deleware, 92; CASE Prof of the Year, Carnegie Found, 95. **MEMBERSHIPS** MLA; AAUP; Dickens Soc; Northeastern Mod Lang Asn; Bronte Soc. **RESEARCH** Victorian literature; early romanticism. **SELECTED PUBLICATIONS** Auth, Victorian Suicide: Mad Crimes and Sad Historian, Princeton Univ Pr (Princeton), 88; ed, Critical Essays on Charlotte Bronte, G. K. Hall (Boston), 89; ed, J of Emily Shore, Univ Va Pr (Charlottsville), 91; co-ed, Natural Eloquence: Women Resinscribe Science, Univ Wisconisn Pr (Madison), 97; auth, Kindred Nature: Victorian and Edwardian Women Tell Nature's Story, Univ Chicago Pr (Chicago), 98; numerous scholarly articles, reviews, and presentations. **CONTACT ADDRESS** Dept of English, Univ of Delaware, Newark, DE 19711.

GATES, HENRY LOUIS, JR.

PERSONAL Born 09/16/1950, Keyser, WV, m, 1986 **DISCIPLINE** JOURNALISM **EDUCATION** Yale Univ, BA (summa cum laude), 1973; Clare Coll, Cambridge, England, MA, 1974, PhD, 1979. **CAREER** Time, London Bureau, London, England, staff correspondant, 73-75; Amer Cyanamid Co, Wayne, NJ, public relations representative, 75; Yale Univ, New Haven, CT, lecturer in English and Afro-American Studies, 76-79, asst prof of English and Afro-American Studies, 79-84, assoc prof of English and Afro-American Studies, 84-85; Cornell Univ, Ithaca, NY, prof of English, Comparative Literature, and Aricana Studies, 85-88, WEB Du Bois Prof of Literature, 88-90; Duke University, Durham, NC, John Spencer Bassett Professor of English and Literature, beginning 1990; Harvard Univ, WEB Du Bois prof of the Humanities, chair, African-American Studies, dir, WEB Du Bois Institute for African-American Research, dir, 91-. **HONORS AND AWARDS** Carnegie Found fellowship for Africa, 1970-71; Phelps fellowship, Yale Univ, 1970-71; Mellon fellowship, Yale Univ, 1973-75, 1983-; A Whitney Griswold fellowship, Yale Univ, 1980; Natl Endowment for the Humanities grants, 1980-84, 1981-82; Rockefeller Found fellowship, 1980-81; MacArthur Prize fellowship, MacArthur Found, 1981-86; Whitney Humanities Center fellowship, 1982-84; Afro-Amer Cultural Center Faculty Prize, 1983; Ford Found grant, 1984-85; Zora Neale Hurston Soc Awd for Creative Scholarship, 1986; Honorable Mention, John Hope Franklin Prize, Amer Studies Assn, 1988; Amer Book Awd, 1989; Anisfield Book Awd for Race Relations, 1989; Candle Awd, Morehouse Coll, 1989; Natl Medal of Arts, presented by President Clinton, 1998. **MEMBERSHIPS** Council on Foreign Relations; board of directors, Lincoln Center Theater and Whitney Museum; European Institute for Literary & Cultural Studies, board of directors, 1990-; American Council for Learned Societies, board of directors, 1990-; American Antiquarian Society; Union of Writers of the African Peoples; Association for Documentary Editing; African Roundtable; African Literature Association; Afro-American Academy; American Studies Association; Association for the Study of Afro-American Life and History; Caribbean Studies Association; College Language Association; Modern Language Association; The Stone Trust; Zora Neale Hurston Society; mem, Pulitzer Prize Board. **SELECTED PUBLICATIONS** Author, Figures in Black: Words, Signs, and the Racial Self, 1987, The Signifying Monkey: Towards a Theory Afro-Amer Literary Criticism, 1988; Loose Canons: Notes on the Culture Wars, 1991; author, Colored People: A Memoir, 1994; The Future of the Race, 1996; editor, Our Nig, 1983, Black Literature and Literary Theory, 1984, "Race," Writing, and Difference, 1986, The Classic Slave Narratives, 1987; series editor, The Schomburg Library of Nineteenth-Century Black Women Writers, 1988; co-compiler, Wole Soyinka: A Bibliography of Primary and Secondary Sources, 1986; Colored People: A Memoir, Knopf, 1994; editor, The Norton Anthology of African-American Literature, 1996; co-editor, Transition: An International Review; author, editor, and contributor of articles and reviews to periodicals, books, and journals; George Polk Award, 1993; Lilliam Smith Award, Southern Literature, 1994; Chicago Tribune Heartland Award, 1994; 22 Honorary Degrees; Distinguished Editorial Achievement, Critical Inquiry, 1996; Tikkun National Ethics Award, 1996; The Richard Ellman Lectures, Emory University, 1996; Alternative Press Award for Transition, An Intl Review, 1995; Thirteen Ways of Looking At A Black Man, Random House, 1997. **CONTACT ADDRESS** Chair, Afro-American Studies Dept, Harvard Univ, 12 Quincy St, Cambridge, MA 02138.

GATTA, JOHN J.

PERSONAL Born Schenectady, NY, m, 1970, 2 children **DISCIPLINE** ENGLISH **EDUCATION** Univ Notre Dame, BA, 68; Cornell Univ, PhD, 73. **CAREER** Vis Asst Prof, Univ MO, 73-74; asst prof to full prof, Univ Conn, 74-. **HONORS AND AWARDS** Woodrow Wilson Fel, 68; Phi Beta Kappa, 68; Scholarly Book of the Year Awd, 89; Choice outstanding Academic book, 98. **MEMBERSHIPS** MLA, Conf on Christianity and Lit. **RESEARCH** American Literature to 1900, Religion and literature. **SELECTED PUBLICATIONS** Auth, American Madonna: Images of the Divine Woman in Literary Culture, Oxford Univ Press, 97; auth, Gracious Laughter: The Meditative Wit of Edward Taylor, Univ MO Press, 89; auth, "The Anglican Aspect of Harriet Beecher Stowe." The New England Quarterly, (forthcoming): auth, "The Apocalyptic End of The Scarlet Letter," Texas Studies in Literature and Language, (90): 506-521; auth, "Peter Matthiessen," American Writers, Supplement, 00; auth, "Richard Wilbur's Poetry of Love," Renascence, (92): 3-15. **CONTACT ADDRESS** Dept English, Univ of Connecticut, Storrs, 337 Mansfield Road Unit U-25, Storrs, CT 06269-1025. **EMAIL** gatta2@uconnvm.uconn.edu

GAULL, MARILYN

PERSONAL Born 02/06/1938, Boston, MA, w, 1 child **DISCIPLINE** ENGLISH **EDUCATION** Univ Mass, BA, 58; Ind Univ, PhD(English), 64. **CAREER** Instr English, Col William and Mary, 63-64; lectr, Univ Mass, 64-66; asst prof, 67-72, assoc prof English, Temple Univ, 72-; Dir, Grasmere Summ Conf, 70; ed, The Wordsworth Circle, 70-; pres, Conf of Eds Learned J, 78-80; prof, NYU, 87- . **HONORS AND AWARDS** NEH Dist Schlr, 99. **MEMBERSHIPS** MLA; Keats-Shelley Asn; Wordsworth-Coleridge Asn; Soc for Textual Studies; NASSR; BARS; BWWA. **RESEARCH** Sociology of literature; romantic poetry; American studies; folklore & children's lit; bibliography. **SELECTED PUBLICATIONS** Auth, Love and order in King Lear, Educ Theatre J, 10/67 & In: Masterpeices of Western Literature, W C Brown, Vol I, 67; Language and identity in E E Cummings' The Enormous Room, Am Quart, 67; romantic humor, Mosaic, 76; Editors' News, Conf of Editors, 78-80; The Romantic Context, Norton, 88. **CONTACT ADDRESS** Dept of English, New York Univ, 19 Univ Pl, New York, NY 10003. **EMAIL** mg49@nyu.edu

GAUNT, KYRA D.

DISCIPLINE MUSIC **EDUCATION** Montgomery Community Col, AA; The Am Univ, BA; SUNY-Binghamton, MM; Univ of Mich, PhD. **CAREER** Grad Student Teaching Asst, SUNY-Binghamton, 87-88; Instr, Univ of Mich, 91-2; Guess Lectr, graduate student teaching asst, Univ of Mich, 92-3; instr, Univ of Mich, 93-4; instr, Univ of Mich, 94; Inst, Washtenaw Community Col, 95; Inst, Tufts Univ, 96; asst prof, Univ of VA, 96-. **HONORS AND AWARDS** Awd for Excellence in Teaching as a Graduate Student Teaching Asst, Univ of Mich, 93; Dean's Candidacy Fel, Univ of Mich, 94; Ford Travel Grant, Univ of Mich, 94; Dean's Dissertation Fel, Univ of Mich, 95; Summer Multicultural Teaching Postdoctoral Fel, Tufts Univ, 96; Fac Fel for Summer Res in the Humanities and Social Sciences, Univ of Virginia, 97; Univ-wide Distinguished dissertation award nominee, Univ of Mich, 97; Univ of Houston's Black Hist Workshop, 98. **MEMBERSHIPS** Soc for Ethnomusicology (SEM) & MACSEM; IASPM - International Asn for the Study of Polular Music, ASA - Am Studies Asn. **RESEARCH** African Am girls' musical games. Hip-hop performance and pedagogy. Music and the African diaspora. Gender, Race and the Body in Frrican Am Music. Body-musicking or oral-kinesic musical communication. Black musical styles (70-), Classical Voice Performance. African-Americans and Classical Music. Shirley Graham-DuBois (composer, author). Black vernacular dance. **SELECTED PUBLICATIONS** Auth, The Musical Games African-American Girls Play: Understanding Gender and the Black Vernacular in Popular Culture, Univ Pittsburgh, 97; African-American Women Between Hopscotch and Hip-Hop, Sage, 95; The Veneration of James Brown & George Clinton in Hip-Hop Music: Is It Live or it Re-Memory?, 95; auth, "Dancin' in the Street to a Black Girl's Beat: Music, Gender, and the 'Ins and Outs' of Double-Dutch," In Generations of Youth: Youth Cultures and History in Twentieth-Century Am, New York: New York Univ Press, 98. **CONTACT ADDRESS** Dept of Music, Univ of Virginia, Cabell Hall No 113, PO Box 400176, Charlottesville, VA 22904-4176. **EMAIL** kgaunt@virginia.edu

GAUNT, PHILIP

DISCIPLINE INTERNATIONAL MARKETING, PUBLIC RELATIONS, MEDIA CONSULTING **EDUCATION** Ind Univ, PhD. **CAREER** Vis prof, assoc dir, W Europ Ctr; prof, dir, Elliott Sch Commun; Interdisciplinary Commun Res Inst. **HONORS AND AWARDS** Accredited, Public Rel Soc of Am. **SELECTED PUBLICATIONS** Publ, 9 bk(s) in Linguistics and Mass Communication in both English and French. **CONTACT ADDRESS** Dept of Commun, Wichita State Univ, 1845 Fairmont, Wichita, KS 67260-0062. **EMAIL** gaunt@elliott.es.twsu.edu

GAVIN, ROSEMARIE JULIE

PERSONAL Born 01/26/1917, Tropico, CA **DISCIPLINE** EDUCATION, ENGLISH **EDUCATION** Univ Calif, Los Angeles, BEd, cum laude, 39; Cath Univ Am, MA, 52; Stanford Univ, PhD(educ), 55. **CAREER** Teacher, Notre Dame High Schs, Calif, 42-51; prof educ & English, Col Notre Dame, Calif, 51-, dir grad studies, 63-, Acad Dean, 68-83, dir teacher educ, 52-70 & evening div, 55-65; deleg, Int Chap of Sisters of Notre Dame de Namur, Rome, 68 & 69; mem bd trustees, Col Notre Dame, Calif & Asn Independent Calif Cols & Univs, 68-. **HONORS AND AWARDS** BEd cum laude. **MEMBERSHIPS** AAUP; Am Asn Higher Educ; Nat Soc Study Educ; Nat Cath Educ Asn. **RESEARCH** Individualized instruction; single campus plan. **SELECTED PUBLICATIONS** Auth, Training Teachers of Secondary School English in Catholic Colleges for Women, Cath Educ Rev, 2/56; Chief Influences Shaping the Poetic Imagery of Thomas Merton, Renascence, 57; Hopkins' The Candle Indoors, Explicator, 2/62. **CONTACT ADDRESS** Col of Notre Dame, 1500 Ralston Ave, Belmont, CA 94002-1997. **EMAIL** Sr.Gavin@cnd.edu

GAVRAN, JAMES HOLT

PERSONAL Born 09/12/1941, Columbus, OH, m, 1968, 3 children **DISCIPLINE** ENGLISH **EDUCATION** Col Wooster, BA, 63; Columbia Univ, MA, 65; Univ NC, PhD, 73. **CAREER** Asst Prof to Prof, Univ NC, 73-. **HONORS AND AWARDS** Finalist, Bank of Am Teaching Awd, 95. **MEMBERSHIPS** NASSR, ACR, CHLA. **RESEARCH** English Romantic writers, gender studies, ecocriticism. **SELECTED PUBLICATIONS** Auth, Romanticism and Children's Literature in Nineteenth Century England, Univ of GA Press, 91. **CONTACT ADDRESS** Dept English, Univ of No Carolina, Charlotte, 9201 University Cty Blvd, Charlotte, NC 28223-0001.

GAY, RICHARD R.

DISCIPLINE ENGLISH **EDUCATION** Univ Richmond, BA, 76, MA, 87; Univ NC, Greensboro, PhD, 91. **CAREER** From asst prof to asoc prof, Chowan Col, 91-97; tchr, Sussex County Public Sch(s), 90-91; tchg asst & campus-wide writing lab, Univ NC, Greensboro, 87-90; tchr, Prince George County Public Sch(s), Va, 87-88; tchr, Sussex County Public Sch(s), Va, 81-86; tchr, Cape Charles Public Sch(s), Va, 76-81; pres, Fac

Forum, 95-97; secy, Steering Comt & ed, Strategic Self-Stud Rep for Reaffirmation of Accreditation, COC/SACS, 95-97; mem, Steering Committee for NCATE accreditation, 95-97; mem, Coop Instnl Res Prog Comt, CIRP, 93-94; actv mem, Lit Club, 91-95. **HONORS AND AWARDS** Tenure, Chowan Col, 95, Sussex County Public Sch(s), 83 & Cape Charles Public Sch(s), 79; Sigma Tau Delta tchg excellence, Chowan Col, 97. **MEMBERSHIPS** MLA; MCTE; S Atlantic Mod Lang Asn; Popular Cul Asn S. **RESEARCH** Curriculum develop and effective-sch(s) research. **SELECTED PUBLICATIONS** Auth, Arthurian Tragedy in Faulkner's Absalom, Absalom, Notes on Mississippi Writers, 90. **CONTACT ADDRESS** Dept of Eng, Chowan Col, 320 E Vance St, Murfreesboro, NC 27855. **EMAIL** gayr@chowan.edu

GAYESKI, DIANE M.
DISCIPLINE COMMUNICATION STUDIES **EDUCATION** Univ Md, PhD. **CAREER** Assoc prof. **RESEARCH** Design and management of new technologies and practices. **SELECTED PUBLICATIONS** Auth, pubs on interactive media and the integration of internal and external communication, promotional strategies, and organizational learning. **CONTACT ADDRESS** Dept of Communication, Ithaca Col, 100 Job Hall, Ithaca, NY 14850.

GAYLORD, ALAN T.
DISCIPLINE ENGLISH LITERATURE **EDUCATION** Princeton Univ, PhD, 59. **CAREER** Henry Winkley Prof of Anglo-Saxon and Eng Lang and Lit. **RESEARCH** Eng and Medievil lit. **SELECTED PUBLICATIONS** Auth, Portrait of a Poet, in The Ellesmere Chaucer: Essays in Interpretation, Huntington Lib, 95; From Dorigen to the Vavasour: Reading Backwards in The Olde Daunce, Love, Friendship, Sex & Marriage in the Medieval World, SUNY Press, 91; Imagining Voices: Chaucer on Cassette, Studies in the Age of Chaucer, 90. **CONTACT ADDRESS** Dept of English, Dartmouth Col, 6032 Sanborn House, Hanover, NH 03755. **EMAIL** Alan.T. Gaylord@dartmouth.edu

GEARY, EDWARD ACORD
PERSONAL Born 12/10/1937, Price, UT, m, 1961, 6 children **DISCIPLINE** ENGLISH & AMERICAN LITERATURE & WESTERN REGIONAL STUDIES **EDUCATION** Brigham Young Univ, BA, 60, MA, 63; Stanford Univ, PhD, 71. **CAREER** Instr humanities, Col Eastern Utah, 63-64; asst prof, 68-75, assoc prof, 75-81, Prof English, Brigham Young Univ, 81-, Dir, Charles Redd Ctr for Western Studies, 97-. **HONORS AND AWARDS** Rosenblatt Awd, UT State Hist Soc, 85; Cert of Commendation, Am Asn for State and Local Hist, 94; Humanities Prize, Utah Academy of Sciences, Arts, and Letters, 94; P.A. Christensen Lectureship, 95. **MEMBERSHIPS** MLA. **RESEARCH** Western Am literature and hist, natural hist. **SELECTED PUBLICATIONS** Auth, An Ashy Halo: Woman as Symbol in Heart of Darkness, Studies Short Fiction, 76; The Need Beyond Reason and Other Essays, Brigham Young Univ, 76; Woman regionalists of Mormon country, Kate Chopin Newsletter, 76; Mormondom's lost generation: the novelists of the 1940s, Brigham Young Univ Studies, 77; The Europeans: a Centennial Essay, Henry James Rev, 82; Community Dramatics in Early Castle Valley, UT Hist Quart, 85; Women Regionalists of Mormon country, Regionalism and the Female Imagination, Hum Sci Press, 85; Goodbye to Poplarhaven, Univ UT, 85; T S Eliot and the fin de siecle, Rocky Mt Rev, 86; Undecidability in Joyce's The Sisters, Studies Short Fiction, 89; A visitable past: Virginia Sorensen's Sanpete, UT Hist Quart, 90; The proper edge of the sky: the high plateau country of UT, Univ UT, 92; History of Emery County, UT State Hist Soc, 96. **CONTACT ADDRESS** Charles Redd Ctr for Western Studies, Brigham Young Univ, Provo, UT 84602. **EMAIL** edward_geary@byu.edu

GEBHARD, ANN
PERSONAL Born 04/12/1930, Jersey City, NJ, m, 1958, 5 children **DISCIPLINE** ENGLISH **EDUCATION** Montclair Univ BA, 51; Middlebury Col, MA; Syracuse Univ, PhD. **CAREER** Asst to Assoc Prof, Syracuse Univ, 75-82; Prof, SUNY, 84-95 **HONORS AND AWARDS** Fulbright Teaching Scholar, Univ W Indies, Trinidad, 96; Danforth Fel, 72-74; Awd for Promising Res, Nat Coun of Teachers of English. **MEMBERSHIPS** Nat Coun of Teachers of English, Fulbright Asn, United Univ Prof **RESEARCH** Literacy Pedagogy. **SELECTED PUBLICATIONS** Auth, "The Emerging Self: Parallel Themes in Young Adult and Classic Novels of the Black Experience," English Journal, 93; auth, "Santha Rama Rau: Biography and Critical Commentary," in Indian Writers of the Diaspora, Greenwood Press, 91; auth, Teaching Writing across the curriculum: A guide for Simon and Schuster Handbook for Writers, Prentice-Hall, 89; auth, Writing Activities for Newspaper readers, New Readers press, 83; auth, "Teaching Writing in Reading and the content Areas," the Reading Journal, 83; auth, "the Composing Process: A New Model to Teaching Composition," in Written Composition: Process, Product and Program, New York State English Coun, 83; auth, 'Considerations of Form and Structure in the Modern Short Story," Wisc English Journal 81. **CONTACT ADDRESS** Dept English, SUNY, Col at Cortland, PO Box 2000, Cortland, NY 13045-0900. **EMAIL** gebharda@snycorva.cortland.edu

GEHERIN, DAVID J.
PERSONAL Born 06/05/1943, Auburn, NY, m, 1964, 3 children **DISCIPLINE** 20TH CENT BRITISH AND AMERICAN NOVEL **EDUCATION** Univ Toronto, BA, 64; Purdue Univ, MA, 67, PhD, 70. **CAREER** Eastern Mich Univ, Prof eng, 69-. **RESEARCH** Contemp fiction; mystery; detective fiction. **SELECTED PUBLICATIONS** Sons of Sam Spade, 80; John D MacDonald, 82; The American Private Eye: The Image In Fiction, 85; Elmore Leonard, 89. **CONTACT ADDRESS** Eastern Michigan Univ, Dept English, Ypsilanti, MI 48197. **EMAIL** eng_geherin@online.emich.edu

GEIST, JOSEPH E.
DISCIPLINE ENGLISH LANGUAGE AND LITERATURE **EDUCATION** Univ Kan, PhD. **CAREER** Prof and chr, Div English, For Langs, Comm-Theater Arts, and Art. **RESEARCH** American literature; contemporary theatre; and cinematic studies. **SELECTED PUBLICATIONS** Auth, articles on T.S. Eliot, the Liberal Arts, 20th Century Film and Drama. **CONTACT ADDRESS** Central Methodist Col, 411 Central Methodist Sq, Fayette, MO 65248.

GEIST, PATRICIA
DISCIPLINE ORGANIZATIONAL COMMUNICATION, HEALTH COMMUNICATION **EDUCATION** Purdue Univ, PhD, 85. **CAREER** Assoc prof, Fordham Univ. **RESEARCH** Negotiating ideology, control, and identity in organizations, predominantly in the health care professions. **SELECTED PUBLICATIONS** Co-auth, Negotiating the Crisis: DRGs and the Transformation of Hospitals, 92.; pub(s), Commun Monogr, Mgt Commun Quart, Health Commun, W Jour Commun, S States Speech Jour, Small Gp Behavior; Co-ed, Courage of Conviction: Womens Words, Women's Wisdom, 97. **CONTACT ADDRESS** Sch of Commun, San Diego State Univ, San Diego, CA 92182-4561. **EMAIL** pgeist@mail.sdsu.edu

GELDERMAN, CAROL W.
PERSONAL Born 12/02/1939, Detroit, MI, d, 3 children **DISCIPLINE** ENGLISH **EDUCATION** Manhattonville Col, BA; Northwestern Univ, MA; PhD, 72. **CAREER** Asst prof to prof, Univ of New Orleans, 72-. **HONORS AND AWARDS** Fels, NEH; Univ New Orleans Alumni Asn Achievement Awd. **MEMBERSHIPS** Cosmos Club; PEN Am Center. **RESEARCH** Biography, non-fiction writing. **SELECTED PUBLICATIONS** Auth, Henry Ford, The Wayward Capitalist, Dial Pr; auth, All the President's Words: The Bully Pulpit and the Creation of the Virtual Presidency, Walker and Co; auth, Mary McCarthy, A Life, St. Martin's Pr; auth, Louis Auchincloss, A Writer's Life, Crown. **CONTACT ADDRESS** Dept English, Univ of New Orleans, 2000 Lakeshore Dr, New Orleans, LA 70148-0001.

GELERNT, JULES
PERSONAL Born 07/13/1928, Berlin, Germany, m, 1958, 2 children **DISCIPLINE** ENGLISH & COMPARATIVE LITERATURE **EDUCATION** City Col New York, BA, 49; Columbia Univ, MA, 50, PhD(comp lit), 63. **CAREER** Instr English, Hofstra Univ, 56-63; from asst prof to assoc prof, 63-71, PROF ENGLISH & CHMN DEPT, BROOKLYN COL, 75-78; Professor Emerites, 96; Mem, Comt Comp & World Lit, NCTE, 67-. **MEMBERSHIPS** Dante Soc Am; Renaissance Soc Am. **RESEARCH** Renaissance and comparative literature. **SELECTED PUBLICATIONS** Auth, Review Notes on Dante's Divine Comedy, Monarch, 63; World of Many Loves: The Heptameron of Marguerite de Navarre, Univ NC, 66. **CONTACT ADDRESS** Dept English, Brooklyn Col, CUNY, 2901 Bedford Ave, Brooklyn, NY 11210-2813. **EMAIL** jrgelernt@worldnet.att.net

GELLER, LILA BELLE
PERSONAL Born 10/06/1932, Chicago, IL, w, 1952, 3 children **DISCIPLINE** ENGLISH LITERATURE **EDUCATION** UCLA, BA, 52, PhD, 69; San Fernando Valley State Col, MA, 65. **CAREER** Asst prof, 69-73, assoc prof, 73-78, prof eng, CA State Univ, Dominguez Hills, 78. **MEMBERSHIPS** MLA. **RESEARCH** Eng Renaissance lit; Spenser; Shakespeare. **SELECTED PUBLICATIONS** Auth, The Acidalian Vision: Spenser's Graces in Book VI of The Faerie Queene, Rev English Studies, 8/72; Spenser's Theory of Nobility in Book VI of The Faerie Queene, English Lit Renaissance, winter 75; Venus and the Three Graces: a Neoplatonic Paradigm for Book III of The Faerie Queene, J English & Ger Philol, 1-4/76; Cymbeline and the imagery of covenant theology, Studies English Lit, 80; Reading Renaissance Drama; A Process Approach, with catherine Gannon, NY: Peter Lang publ, 91; Widows Vows and Middletons More Dissemblers Besides Women, Medieval and Renaissance Drama in England, p287-308, 91. **CONTACT ADDRESS** Dept of Eng, California State Univ, Dominguez Hills, 1000 E Victoria, Carson, CA 90747-0005. **EMAIL** lgeller@dhvx20.csudh.edu

GELLRICH, JESSE M.
DISCIPLINE MEDIEVAL ENGLISH AND CONTINENTAL LITERATURE, HISTORY AND THEORY OF CRITICIS **EDUCATION** SUNY, Buffalo, PhD, 70. **CAREER** Prof, La State Univ; adv bd, Exemplaria, 87-. **HONORS AND AWARDS** Summer fac fel, Univ Calif, Irvine, 72, 73; pres grant, Univ Santa Clara, 80; ACLS fel, 86-87; John Nicholas Brown Prize, Medieval Acad of Am, 89; Manship fel, LSU, 90, 97; summer fac stipends, LSU, 94, 97; vis fel, Princeton Univ, 97. **RESEARCH** Medieval English and continental literature: orality and literacy in manuscript illumination, literature by women, and dream vision narrative in Latin, Old French, and Middle English. **SELECTED PUBLICATIONS** Auth, Deconstructing Allegory, Genre, 85; The Idea of the Book in the Middle Ages: Language Theory, Mythology, and Fiction, 85; Orality, Literacy and Crisis in the Later Middle Ages, Philol Quart, 88; Discourse and Dominion in the Fourteenth Century: Oral Contexts of Writing in Philosophy, Politics, and Poetry, 95; Figura, Allegory, and the Question of History, in Literary History and the Challenge of Philology: The Legacy of Erich Auerbach, 96. **CONTACT ADDRESS** Dept of Eng, Louisiana State Univ and A&M Col, 210A Allen Hall, Baton Rouge, LA 70803. **EMAIL** jgellri@unix1.sncc.lsu.edu

GELLRICH, MICHELLE
DISCIPLINE GREEK LITERATURE AND PHILOSOPHY, LITERARY THEORY, DRAMA **EDUCATION** Univ Calif, Berkeley, PhD, 82. **CAREER** Assoc prof, La State Univ. **HONORS AND AWARDS** Lily Found tchg grant, 84; ACLS fel, 86; LSU summer fac res stipend, 92; Alpha Lambda Delta, 96; Phi Beta Kappa. **RESEARCH** Greek literature and philosophy; classical rhetoric. **SELECTED PUBLICATIONS** Auth, Tragedy and Theory: The Problem of Conflict Since Aristotle, 88; auth, "Aristotle's Poetics and the Problem of Tragic Conflict," Ramus (94); auth, "Aristotle's Rhetoric: Theory, Truth, and Metarhetoric," Cabinet of the Muses (90); auth, "Socratic Magic: Enchantment, Irony, and Persuasion in Some Dialogues of Plato," Classical World (94); auth, "On Interpreting Greek Tragedy: History, Theory, and the New Philology," Tragedy, History, Theory (forthcoming). **CONTACT ADDRESS** Dept of Eng, Louisiana State Univ and A&M Col, 223E Allen Hall, Baton Rouge, LA 70803. **EMAIL** mgellri@lsu.edu

GEMMETT, ROBERT J.
PERSONAL Born 03/11/1936, Schenectady, NY, m, 1964, 4 children **DISCIPLINE** ENGLISH **EDUCATION** Siena Col, BA, 59; Univ Mass, MA, 62; Syracuse Univ, PhD, 67. **CAREER** Instr English, Clarkson Univ, 64-65; assoc prof, 65-70, chemn dept, 75-79, prof English, SUNY, Brockport, 70-, dean humanities, 79-82, dean letters & scies, 82-92, SUNY College, Buffalo, provst & VP, acad affairs, 92-97, prof 97-, SUNY College, Brockport, Res grants, SUNY, 67 & 68; assoc ed, English Record, 67-69; res grant, SUNY, 77. **HONORS AND AWARDS** Chancellor's Awd Excellence in Teaching, SUNY, 75. **RESEARCH** British 18th century studies and romantic period. **SELECTED PUBLICATIONS** Auth, The composition of William Beckford's Biographical Memoirs of Extraordinary Painters, Philol Quart, 1/68; ed, Biographical Memoirs of Extraordinary Painters, 69 & Dreams, Waking Thoughts and Incidents, 71, Fairleigh Dickinson Univ; Poets and Men of Letters, Mansell, London, 72; Vathek, The English Edition of 1786 and the French Editions of 1787, Scholars' Facsimiles, 72; auth, Beckford's Fonthill: The landscape as art, Gazette Beaux-Arts, 12/72; ed, The Episodes of Vathek, Fairleigh Dickinson Univ, 75; auth, William Beckford, Twayne, 77; The Consummate Collector, Michael Russell, 00. **CONTACT ADDRESS** Dept of English, SUNY, Col at Brockport, 350 New Campus Dr, Brockport, NY 14420-2914. **EMAIL** rgemmet@brockport.edu

GENCARELLI, THOMAS F.
PERSONAL Born 07/02/1959, Mount Vernon, NY, m, 1994, 1 child **DISCIPLINE** MEDIA STUDIES **EDUCATION** New York Univ, PhD, 93. **CAREER** Inst, Iona Col, 89-93; From Asst Prof to Assoc Prof, Montclair State Univ, 93-, Deputy chair. **HONORS AND AWARDS** Nat Honor Soc of Phi Kappa Phi. **MEMBERSHIPS** Int Communication Asn; Nat Communication Asn; Eastern Communication Asn, New Jersey Communication Asn; New York State Communication Asn; Media Ecology Asn. **RESEARCH** Popular music; popular culture; media theory and criticism; media and culture. **SELECTED PUBLICATIONS** Coauth, Archetypal Criticism, Communication Ed, 90; auth, Taste Groups in the Real World: Media and Interpretive Communities, New Dimensions in Communication: Proceedings of the 47th Annual New York State Speech Communication Asn, 90; auth, Trying to Learn How to Walk Like the Heroes: Bruce Springsteen, Popular Music, and the Hero/Celebrity, American Heroes in the Media Age, Hampton Press, 94; auth, V-Chip, TV Ratings Just Simplistic Solutions, Herald Statesman, 96; auth, Kidding Ourselves With Solutions to TV Violence, Star Ledger, 96; auth, Television and Violence: Updating the Argument for the Future, Nat Communication Asn Conf, NY, 98; auth, Radio Continues to Eat Itself: An Analysis of the Music Radio Business and its Relationship to Culture in the United States, Int Communication Asn Conf, IL, 96; guest ed, Special Issue: Media Education, The New Jersey Journal of Communication, 98; auth, "The Intellectual Roots of Media Ecology in the Work and Thought of Neil Postman," The New Jersey Journal of Commun, (00): 91-103; . **CONTACT ADDRESS** Dept of Broadcasting, Montclair State Univ, Upper Montclair, NJ 07043. **EMAIL** gencarellit@mail.montclair.edu

GENOVESE, EDGAR NICHOLAS
PERSONAL Born 09/18/1942, Baltimore, MD, m, 1969, 2 children **DISCIPLINE** CLASSICS **EDUCATION** Xavier Univ, Ohio, AB, 64; Ohio State Univ, PhD(classics), 70. **CAREER** From asst prof to assoc prof, 70-76, Prof Classics, San Diego State Univ, 76-, Chmn Dept Class & Humanities, 77-. **HONORS AND AWARDS** Phi Beta Kappa; Phi Kappa Phi. **MEMBERSHIPS** Amer Philol Assoc; Amer Assoc Univ Profs. **RESEARCH** Greek and Latin poetry; mythology. **SELECTED PUBLICATIONS** Auth, Propertius' tardus Amor, Class J, 1/73; Cicero and Sallust: Catiline's ruina, Class World, 74; Symbolism in the Passer poems, Maia, 74; Deaths in the Aeneid, Pac Coast Philol, 75; Case of the poor preposition, Class Outlook, 76; Serpent Leitmotif in the Metamorphoses, Latomus, 83; The Burnett Lectures: A Quarter Century, 93; Mythology: Texts and Contexts, 98. **CONTACT ADDRESS** Dept Class & Humanities, San Diego State Univ, 5500 Campanile Dr, San Diego, CA 92182-8143. **EMAIL** genovese@mail.sdsu.edu

GENTRY, MARSHALL BRUCE
PERSONAL Born 07/28/1953, Little Rock, AR, m, 1989, 3 children **DISCIPLINE** ENGLISH, AMERICAN LITERATURE **EDUCATION** Univ AR, Fayetteville, BA, 75; Univ Chicago, MA, 76; Univ TX at Austin, PhD, 84. **CAREER** Graduate student teaching positions, Univ TX at Austin, 76-83; vis asst instr, 83-84, vis asst prof, TX A&M Univ, 84-85; asst prof, 85-91, assoc prof, 81-98, prof English, Univ of Indianapolis, 98-, English chair, 97; ed, Literary Magazine The Flying Island. **HONORS AND AWARDS** Lilly Summer Stipend for Development of New Courses, 87; Phi Beta Kappa, 74; Phi Kappa Phi, 82. **MEMBERSHIPS** MLA; SCMLA; MMLA; SAMLA; NEMLA; Am Lit Asn; Flannery O'Connor Soc; Writers' Center of Indiana, etc. **RESEARCH** 20th century Am fiction, especially E L Doctorow, Philip Roth, Flannery O'Connor. **SELECTED PUBLICATIONS** Auth, Flannery O'Connor's Religion of the Grotesque, Univ Press MS, 86; coed, Conversations with Raymond Carver, Univ Press MS, 90; auth, Women's Voices in Stories by Raymond Carver, The OEA Critic, s6.1, 93; auth, Ventriloquists Conversations: The Struggle for Gender Dialogue in E.L. Doctrow and Philip Roth, Contemporary Literature, 34.3. 93; O'Connor's Legacy in Stories by Joyce Carol Oates and Paula Sharp, The Flannery O'Connor Bul 23, 94-95; Gender Dialogue and Ventriloquism in Julio Cortazar's Graffiti, The AR Rev 4, 95; Gender Dialogue in O'Connor, Flannery O'Connor: New Perspectives, ed Sura Rath and Mary Neff Shaw, Univ GA Press, 96; co-ed, The Practice and Theory of Ethics, Univ Indianapolis Press, 96; An Interview with Margaret Kingery, SD Rev 34.2, 96; auth, Ambition in the Poetry Boat: A Conversation with David Bottoms, conducted along with Alice Friman, The Southern Quart, 37.3-4, 99; ed, The Flying Island, 99; author of numerous other articles, book reviews, and other publications. **CONTACT ADDRESS** Dept of English, Univ of Indianapolis, 1400 E Hanna Ave, Indianapolis, IN 46227-3697. **EMAIL** bgentry@uindy.edu

GENTRY, THOMAS BLYTHE
PERSONAL Born 11/26/1922, Danville, KY, m, 1944, 2 children **DISCIPLINE** ENGLISH LITERATURE **EDUCATION** Centre Col, BA, 47; Univ KY, MA, 53, PhD, 62; VA Mil Inst, BA, 62. **CAREER** From instr to assoc prof, 48-66, Prof English, VA Mil Inst, 66-. **MEMBERSHIPS** Col English Asn. **CONTACT ADDRESS** Dept of English, Virginia Military Inst, Lexington, VA 24450.

GEORGALAS, ROBERT N.
PERSONAL Born 11/11/1951, New York, NY, m, 1981 **DISCIPLINE** ENGLISH **EDUCATION** Bronx Community Col, AA, 70; Lehman Col, BA, 72; City Col NY, MA, 74; Columbia Col, MFA, 97. **CAREER** Adj instr, Lehman Col, 74-77; adj assoc prof, Marymount Manhattan Col, 79-88; prof, Col of DuPage, 91-. **HONORS AND AWARDS** James R Friend Mem Awd, 89, 90; Ariz Authors Asn Awd, 94. **MEMBERSHIPS** MLA, NEA, NCTE. **RESEARCH** Film, Chaucer, Hemingway. **SELECTED PUBLICATIONS** Auth, "By the Sea," AU Rev, (89); auth, "Unscheduled Stops," Willow Rev, (89); auth, "Ice Age," Rambunctious Rev, (90); auth, "In the Cards," Sport Literate, (96); auth, "Thursday Tea," Urban Spaghetti, (98); auth, "A Little Fire in a Wild Place," Hair Trigger, (98); auth, "Trading Shots with Papa," Sport Literate, (98); auth, "Taking Off My Clothes," The Thing About Love Is, (99); auth, "The Dogs of Pompei," The Thing About Second Chances Is, (00); ed, The Thing About Second Chances Is, 00. **CONTACT ADDRESS** Col of DuPage, 360 E Randolph St, Apt 1407, Chicago, IL 60601. **EMAIL** georgala@cdnet.cod.edu

GEORGE, EDWARD
PERSONAL Born 12/10/1937, Buffalo, NY, m, 1968, 3 children **DISCIPLINE** CLASSICS **EDUCATION** Niagara Univ, BA, 59; Canisius Col, MEd, 62; Univ Wis, PhD, 66. **CAREER** Univ of Tex, 66-71; Tex Tex Univ, 71-, prof, 77-. **HONORS AND AWARDS** Acad Achievement Awd, Tex Tech Univ, 00. **MEMBERSHIPS** Am Philological Assoc; Classical Assoc of Middle West and S; AAUP; Renaissance Soc of Am; Int Assoc of Neo-Latin Studies. **RESEARCH** Greek and Latin Rhetoric, Renaissance Rhetoric, Jan Luis Vives, Greco-Roman Cultural Background to Hispanic New World Culture. **SELECTED PUBLICATIONS** Ed, Juan Luis Vives, Somnium et Vigilia in Somnium Scipionis, Attic Pr, 89; ed, Juan Luis Vives, Declamationes Sullanae: Part One, EJ Brill (Leiden, Netherlands), 89; auth, "Rhetoric in Vives", Opera Omnia Ioannis Lodovici Vivis, ed Antonio Mestre, Edicions Alfons el Magnanim, (Valencia, 92): 113-77; auth, "Justice and Discourse: New Light on Juan Luis Vives (1493-1540)", Recapturing the Renaissance: New Perspectives on Humanism, Dialogue and Texts, ed Diane S Wood and Paul Allen Miller, New Paradigm Pr, (96): 33-62; auth, "Persuading a Feminine Audience? Gratuitious Invective Apostrophe in Juan Luis Vives' On the Education of a Christian Woman", Scholia: Natal Studies in Classical Antiquity (96): 94-111; auth, "Latin and Spanish: Roman Culture and Hispanic America", Latin in the 21st Century, ed Richard A LaFleur, Scott Foresman-Addison Wesley (Reading, MA, 97): 227-236. **CONTACT ADDRESS** Dept Mod Lang and Lit, Texas Tech Univ, Lubbock, TX 79409-2071. **EMAIL** ed.george@ttu.edu

GEORGE, KEARNS
DISCIPLINE ENGLISH LANGUAGE AND LITERATURE **EDUCATION** Yale Univ, BA; Columbia Univ, MA; Boston Univ, PhD. **CAREER** Prof. **RESEARCH** Modernism; literature and philosophy; literary theory. **SELECTED PUBLICATIONS** Auth, Ezra Pound: The Cantos. **CONTACT ADDRESS** Dept of English, Rutgers, The State Univ of New Jersey, New Brunswick, 510 George St, Murray Hall, New Brunswick, NJ 08901-1167. **EMAIL** gwkearns@aol.com

GEORGE, LAURA J.
DISCIPLINE LITERARY CRITICISM **EDUCATION** PhD. **CAREER** E Mich Univ **SELECTED PUBLICATIONS** Auth, Fashionable Figures: Rhetoric and Costume in British Romanticisms. **CONTACT ADDRESS** Eastern Michigan Univ, Ypsilanti, MI 48197. **EMAIL** eng_George@online.emich.edu

GEORGE, LUVENIA A.
PERSONAL Born 02/26/1934, Chicago, IL, m, 1953, 2 children **DISCIPLINE** ETHNOMUSICOLOGY **EDUCATION** Howard University, BMEd, 1952; University of Maryland College Park, MEd, 1969; University of Maryland Baltimore County, PhD, 1995. **CAREER** District of Columbia Public Schools, music teacher, 54-92; Smithsonian Institution, research scholar, 93-94, coordinator DE youth proj, 94-. **HONORS AND AWARDS** African-American Museum, Hall of Fame Inductee, 1997. **MEMBERSHIPS** Sargent Presbyterian Church, organist, 1960-, elder, 1991-; District of Columbia Music Education Association, pres, 1970-72; District of Columbia Choral Directors Association, pres, 1978-80. **SELECTED PUBLICATIONS** Author: "Teaching the Music of Six Different Cultures," 2nd ed, 1987; Lucie Campbell in "We'll Understand It Better Bye & Bye," 1992; Duke Ellington: "Composer Beyond Category," 1993; "The Source of African-American Music," 1991. **CONTACT ADDRESS** CProgram in African-American Culture, Smithsonian Inst, 14th & Constitution Ave, NW, Washington, VT 20560. **EMAIL** lgeogal@hotmail.com

GEORGE, MICHAEL W.
PERSONAL Born 11/29/1967, Warren, OH **DISCIPLINE** ENGLISH **EDUCATION** Kent St, BA, 90; MA, 93; Mich State Univ, PhD, 00. **CAREER** Lectr, Purdue Univ, 99-00; asst prof, Ohio North Univ, 00-. **HONORS AND AWARDS** CARA Scholar for Latin, Univ Notre Dame. **MEMBERSHIPS** MAA, John Gower Soc, NCTE, MLA. **RESEARCH** Middle English literature; science fiction; educational technology; hypertext. **SELECTED PUBLICATIONS** Auth, "The York Play of Pilate Writings," Res Opp in Renais Drama (00); auth, "An Austere Age without Laughter," Misconceptions About the Mid Ages (98); auth, J. R. R. Tolkien, Dict of Lit Bio, forthcoming; auth, "Representation, Religion, and Sexuality," in Joseph's Troubles, Pageant, Intersections of Sexuality and the Divine in Medieval Literature: The Word Made Flesh, forthcoming. **CONTACT ADDRESS** Eng Dept., Ohio No Univ, Ada, OH 45810. **EMAIL** m-george@onu.edu

GEORGE, STEPHEN
PERSONAL Born 01/23/1965, Indianapolis, IN, m, 1990, 4 children **DISCIPLINE** ENGLISH **EDUCATION** BYU, BA, 91; MA, 92; Ball State Univ, PhD, 95. **CAREER** Asst prof, Ball State Univ, 92-96; asst prof, Boston Col, 96-98; secy of Fac Asn, Boston Col, 96-98; instr, Ricks Col, 98-; dir of Outlet Lit J, 98-. **MEMBERSHIPS** Steinbeck Soc. **RESEARCH** Literature and philosophy. **SELECTED PUBLICATIONS** Auth, "The Horror of Bigger Thomas: The Perception of Form Without Face in Richard Wright's Native Son," African-American Rev (97): 497-504; rev, "A New Study Guide to Steinbeck's Major Works," The Steinbeck Newsletter (94), 12-13; auth, "Tennyson's 'The Kraken,'" The Explicator (93): 25-27; auth, "The Disintegration of a Man: Moral Integrity in The Winter of Our Discontent," The Steinbeck Yearbook, Mellen Press, 90. **CONTACT ADDRESS** Dept English, Ricks Col, 525 S Center St, Rexburg, ID 83460-0001.

GERBER, DOUGLAS E.
PERSONAL Born 09/14/1933, North Bay, ON, Canada, m, 1986, 1 child **DISCIPLINE** CLASSICS **EDUCATION** Univ Western Ontario, BA, 55, MA, 56; Univ Toronto, PhD, 59. **CAREER** Lectr, Univ Toronto, 58-59; lectr, 59-60, asst prof, 60-64, assoc prof, 64-69, prof, 69- , dept ch, 69-97, Univ Western Ontario; prof emer. **HONORS AND AWARDS** William Sherwood Fox Ch of Classics, 77- ; Pres, Class Asn Canada, 88-90; ed, Transactions Amer Philol Asn, 74-82. **MEMBERSHIPS** Amer Philol Asn; Class Asn, Great Brit; Class Asn Canada; Class Asn Middle West and South. **RESEARCH** Greek Lyric Poetry. **SELECTED PUBLICATIONS** Ed and transl, Greek Iambic Poetry, LOEB, 99; ed and transl, Greek Elegiac Poetry, LOEB, 99; auth, "Pindar, Nemean Six: A Commentary," Harvard Studies in Classical Philology 99, (99): 33-91. **CONTACT ADDRESS** Dept of Classics, Univ of Western Ontario, London, ON, Canada N6A 3K7. **EMAIL** degerber@julian.uwo.ca

GERBER, SANFORD E.
PERSONAL Born 06/16/1933, Chicago, IL, m, 1986, 6 children **DISCIPLINE** COMMUNICATION DISORDERS **EDUCATION** Lake Forest Col, BA, 54; Univ Ill, MS, 56; Univ S Calif, PhD, 62. **CAREER** Speech clinician, E Whittier City School District, 56-58; Assoc Soc Scientist, System Development Co, 58-60; Speech and hearing Res, Hughes Aircraft Co, 60-65; Asst Prof to Emeritus Prof, Univ Calif, 65-; Visiting Prof, Eastern Washington Univ, 94-00; Adj Prof, Washington State Univ, 94-. **HONORS AND AWARDS** Fulbright Fel, Southampton Univ, 88; Corespondiente extranjero, Mex Soc of Phoniatry and Audiol, 95; Chairs' Excellence Awd, Eastern Washington Univ, 98; Sylvan E Stool Awd, Soc for Ear, Nose, and Throat Advances in Children, 98; Lake Forest Col Distinguished Service Citation, 94; Jean Tarneaud Lecturer, Costa Rica, 93. **MEMBERSHIPS** Am Speech-Lang-Hearing Asn, Am Acad of Audiol, Pan Am Soc of Audiol, Intl Soc of Audiol, Am Auditory Soc, Soc for Ear, Nose, and Throat Adv in Children, Am Acad of Otolaryngology- Head and Neck Surgery, Hearing Intl. **RESEARCH** Normal and abnormal communicative development; Early identification and intervention. **SELECTED PUBLICATIONS** Ed, The Handbook of Genetic Communicative Disorders, Academic Press, forthcoming; co-auth, Coprevalence of mental retardation and hearing impairment, forthcoming; auth, "Biennial meeting of the PanAmerican Society of Audiology," Hearing International, (99): 9; auth, Etiology and Prevention of Communicative Disorders, Singular Pub Group, 98; co-auth, Audiology and Auditory Dysfunction, Allyn & Bacon, 96; ed, The Handbook of Pediatric Audiology, Gallaudet Univ Press, 96; co-auth, "Recent changes in the etiology of hearing disorders: Perinatal drug exposures," Journal of the American Academy of Audiology, (95): 371-377. **CONTACT ADDRESS** Dept Comm, Eastern Washington Univ, Cheney, WA 99004-1619. **EMAIL** segerber@ewu.edu

GERHART, MARY
PERSONAL Born 03/04/1935, Stacyville, IA **DISCIPLINE** THEOLOGY, LITERATURE **EDUCATION** Col St Teresa, Minn, BA, 62; Univ Mo, MA, 68; Univ Chicago, MA, 70, PhD(relig, lit), 73. **CAREER** Asst prof, 72-80, Assoc Prof Relig Studies, Hobart & William Smith Cols, 80-, Ed Chair, Relig Studies Rev, 78-, Nat Endowment for Humanities grant, 76 & Fulbright grant, 82-83. **HONORS AND AWARDS** D J Bowden lectr, Ind Univ, 72; Ida Mae Wilson lectr, Vanderbilt Univ, 80. **MEMBERSHIPS** AAUP; Am Acad Relig; Cath Theol Soc Am. **RESEARCH** Hermeneutical theory; Religion and literature in science and religion. **SELECTED PUBLICATIONS** Auth, "The Question of Belief in Literary Criticism: An Introduction to the Hermeneutical Theory of Paul Ricoeur," Stuttgart: Akademischerr Verlag, Hans-Dieter Heinz, 79; auth, "Metaphoric Process: The Creation of Scientific and Religious Understanding," coauthored with Allan M. Russell, Texas Christian University Press, 84; auth, "Genre, Narrativity, and Theology," Semeia 43, 88, issue co-edited with James Williams; auth, "Morphologies of Faith: Essays in Religion and Culture in Honor of Nathan A. Scott, Jr., co-edited with Anthony C. Yu, Scholas Press, 90; auth, "Genre Choices: Gender Questions," University of Oklahoma Press, 92; auth, "Paul Ricoeur's Hermeneutical Theory as Resource for Theological Reflection," Thomist, 37, July, 77, pp. 496-527; auth, "Paul Ricoeur, La Metaphore vive," Religious Studies Review, 2, January, 76, pp. 23-30; auth, "Paul Ricoeur's Notion of Diagnostics:" Toward a Philosophy of the Human," The Journal of Religion, 56, april, 76, pp. 137-156; auth, "Generic Studies: Their Renewed Importance in Religious and Literary Interpretation," Journal of the American Academy of Religion, 45, September, 77, pp. 309-25; auth, "The Ironic ode of Religious Imagination in Heinrich Boll," CTSA Proceedings, 32, 77, pp. 178-94; auth, "The Extent and Limits of Metaphor," Philosophy Today, 21, Winter, 77, pp. 431-36; auth, "Imagination and History in Ricoeur's Interpretation Theory," Philosophy Today, 23, Spring, 79, pp. 51-68. **CONTACT ADDRESS** Dept of Relig Studies, Hobart & William Smith Cols, Scandling Center, Box 4040, Geneva, NY 14456-3382. **EMAIL** gerhart@hws.edu

GERLACH, JOHN CHARLES
PERSONAL Born 08/01/1941, Baltimore, MD, 2 children **DISCIPLINE** NINETEENTH CENTURY AMERICAN LITERATURE **EDUCATION** Kenyon Col, BA, 63; Columbia Univ, MFA, 65; Ariz State Univ, PhD, 69. **CAREER** Prof English, Cleveland State Univ, 68-, Asts Dean Col Arts & Sci, 79-85, Chmn, 90-94. **RESEARCH** Film; 19th century American fiction; fiction writing; Emily Dickinson; short story theory. **SE-**

LECTED PUBLICATIONS Auth, Messianic nationalism in the early works of Herman Melville, Ariz Quart, 4/72; James Fenimore Cooper and the kingdom of God, Ill Quart, 4/73; The Critical Index, Teachers Col, Columbia Univ, 74; Simpson Among Angels, NAm Rev, 80; Toward the End: Closure & Structure in the American Short Story, Univ Ala Press, 85; Reading Dickinson: Fascicle 39, Emily Dickinson J, 94. **CONTACT ADDRESS** Dept of English, Cleveland State Univ, 1983 E 24th St, Cleveland, OH 44115-2440. **EMAIL** j.gerlach@popmail.csuohio.edu

GERMAIN, EDWARD B.
PERSONAL Born 12/30/1937, Saginaw, MI, m, 1 child **DISCIPLINE** ENGLISH LANGUAGE; ENGLISH LITERATURE **EDUCATION** Univ Mich, PhD, 69. **CAREER** Instr, US Naval Reserve, 63-65; instr, Eastern Mich Univ, 64-66; teaching fel, Univ Mich Ann Arbor, 66-69; asst prof, eng, Pomona Col, 69-75; lectr, Wayne State Univ, 76; assoc prof, humanities, Nathaniel Hawthorne Col, 76-79; instr, eng, Rennes, France, 82-83; instr, eng, Phillips Acad, 79-. **HONORS AND AWARDS** Sabbatical grant, 97-98; Who's Who Among American Teachers, 96; appointment, sch yr abroad, France, 82-83; Keenan grant for writing, Phillips Acad, 82; sabbatical fel, Pomona Col, 75-76; fac res grant, Pomona Col, 70, 71, 75; Avery Hopwood award for creative writing, Univ Mich, 68; Phi Kappa Phi, 65. **MEMBERSHIPS** Intl James Joyce. **SELECTED PUBLICATIONS** Auth, The Annotated Sisters, teaching web site, http://www.andover.edu/english/joyce, 98; auth, Jane Kenyon, Ron Padgett, Lee Harwood, Robert Dana, Charles Henri Ford, Contemporary Poets of the English Language, St. James Press, London, revised, 96; ed, Surrealist Poetry in English, Penguin Books Ltd, London, 78; ed, Shadows of the Sun: the Diaries of Harry Crosby, Black Sparrow Press, Santa Barbara, Calif, 77; ed, Flag of Ecstasy: Selected Poems of Charles Henri Ford, Black Sparrow Press, 72. **CONTACT ADDRESS** PO Box 278, Dublin, NH 03444. **EMAIL** egermain@andover.edu

GERNES, SONIA
PERSONAL Born Winona, MN **DISCIPLINE** ENGLISH AND LITERATURE **EDUCATION** Col of St. Theresa, BA; Univ Wash Seattle, MA, PhD. **CAREER** Instr, Univ Notre Dame. **HONORS AND AWARDS** Sheedy Awd for Excellence in Tchg, 90; Lilly fel, 90-91; Fulbright sr lectr, 86-; Soc of Midland Authors Poetry Award; Notre Dame Faculty Award, 94; ALA Notable Book Award, Best Short Stories, 95, 98; Notre Dame Presidential Award, 96; NEA Creative Writing Fel, 99. **SELECTED PUBLICATIONS** Auth, The Mutes of Sleepy Eye, Inchbird Press, 81; auth, Brief Lives, University of Notre Dame Press, 81; auth, The Way to St. Ives, Charles Scribner's Sons, 82; auth, Women at Forty, University of Notre Dame Press, 88; auth, A Breeze Called the Fremantle Doctor, University of Notre Dame Press, 97. **CONTACT ADDRESS** Dept of English, Univ of Notre Dame, 210 Decio, Notre Dame, IN 46556. **EMAIL** sonia.g.gernes.1@nd.edu

GERNES, TODD STEVEN
DISCIPLINE ENGLISH **EDUCATION** Univ Mass at Amherst, BA, 84; MA, 86; Brown Univ, AM, 87, PhD, 92. **CAREER** Coord, Upp Level Writing, Univ Mich. **MEMBERSHIPS** Am Antiquarian Soc **SELECTED PUBLICATIONS** Auth, "Recasting the Culture of Ephemera: Young Women's Literary Culture in 19th Century America, PhD diss, 92; **CONTACT ADDRESS** Eng Comp Board, Univ of Michigan, Ann Arbor, 1111 Angell Hall, Ann Arbor, MI 48109-1003. **EMAIL** tsgernes@umich.edu

GERRY, THOMAS M. F.
PERSONAL Born 01/31/1948, Toronto, ON, Canada **DISCIPLINE** ENGLISH **EDUCATION** Univ Toronto, BA, 71, BEd, 75; York Univ, MA, 73; Univ Western Ont, PhD, 83. **CAREER** Sch tchr, Hastings Co, 75-78; asst prof, Trent Univ, 85-87; asst prof, Acadia Univ, 87-88; assoc prof Eng, Laurentian Univ, 88-. **HONORS AND AWARDS** Laurentian Univ res awards, 90, 92, 94. **MEMBERSHIPS** Asn Can Stud; Proj Ploughshares. **SELECTED PUBLICATIONS** Auth, "Violence and Narrative Metalepsis in Guy Vanderhaeghe's Fiction," Studies in Canadian Literature, 87; auth, "I Am Translated: Anna Jameson's Sketches and Winter Studies and Summer Rambles in Canada," Journal of Canadian Studies, 91; auth, "Green Yet Free of Seasons: Gwendolyn MacEwen and the Mystical Tradition of Canadian Poetry," Studies in Canadian Literature, 91; auth, "The Literary Crisis: The Nuclear Crisis," Twentieth-Century Literary Criticism 46, 93; auth, Contemporary Canadian and US Women of Letters, 93; auth, "The Lumiere Brothers: A Photographic Essay," Arachne: An Interdisciplinary Journal of Language and Literature, 95; auth, "Limelight on the Lumieres," Queens Quarterly, 96; auth, "Thomas Edison: The Wizard Lives," Queens Quarterly, 97; auth, "In Cases of Emergency: Margaret Laurence's Political Writing," Challenging Territory: The Writing of Margaret Laurence, 97. **CONTACT ADDRESS** Dept of English, Laurentian Univ, 935 Ramsey Lake Rd, Sudbury, ON, Canada P3E 2C6. **EMAIL** tgerry@nickel.laurentian.ca

GERSHON, ROBERT
DISCIPLINE EMERGING COMMUNICATION TECHNOLOGIES **EDUCATION** Princeton Univ, BA; Boston Univ PhD. **CAREER** Comm Stu, Castleton St Univ. **SELECTED PUBLICATIONS** Auth, Documentary Style Narration, 80, Video Grammar, Educational and Industrial Television, October, 81; Gershon, Robert, State Humanities Councils as Patrons of Film and Video Production 85. **CONTACT ADDRESS** Castleton State Col, Seminary Street, Castleton, VT 05735. **EMAIL** gershonr@sparrow.csc.vsc.edu

GERSTER, CAROLE
PERSONAL Born 07/24/1943, MN, m, 3 children **DISCIPLINE** ENGLISH LITERATURE, FILM **EDUCATION** Univ MN, MA, PhD. **CAREER** Prof, Univ of WI. **HONORS AND AWARDS** NEH Institutes, 96,00. **RESEARCH** Am film; lit and films by and about women and ethnic minorities; Brit women's novels; literary theory. **SELECTED PUBLICATIONS** Auth, pubs about women and ethnic minorities in film and Brit lit. **CONTACT ADDRESS** Eng Dept, Univ of Wisconsin, River Falls, 410 S 3rd St, River Falls, WI 54022-5001. **EMAIL** carole.j.jerster@uwrf.edu

GERTZMAN, JAY ALBERT
PERSONAL Born 05/10/1939, Philadelphia, PA **DISCIPLINE** ENGLISH **EDUCATION** Univ Pa, BS, 61; Columbia Univ, MA, 63; Univ Pa, PhD(English), 72. **CAREER** Teacher English, Olney High Sch, Philadelphia, 62-68; from asst prof to assoc prof, 68-77, PROF ENGLISH, MANSFIELD UNIV, 77-. **HONORS AND AWARDS** Nat Endowment Humanities summer sem, 76 & 80; Summer Res Fel, Andrew Mellon Found Fel, Harry Ransom Humanities Res Ctr, Univ Tex Austin, June-July 94. **MEMBERSHIPS** D.H. Lawrence Soc of N Am. **RESEARCH** Cavalier poetry; literary censorship; publishing history; D.H. Lawrence. **SELECTED PUBLICATIONS** Auth, Commitment and sacrifice in Heart of Darkness: Marlowe's response to Kurtz, Studies in Short Fiction, 72; Robert Herrick's Recreative Pastoral, Genre, 74; Literature of courtesy and the cavalier persona, Proc Patristic, Medieval and Renaissance Conf, 78; Changes of dedication in Brathwait's English gentleman, analytical and enumerative bibliography, 79; Hemingway's writer-narrator in the denunciation, Res Studies, 79; Fantasy, Fashion, and Affection: Editions of Robert Herrick's Poetry For the Common Reader, 1810-1968, The Popular Press, 86; A Descriptive Bibliography of Lady Chatterley's Lover, With Essays Toward a Publishing History of the Novel, Greenwood Press, 89; Esoterica and The Good of the Race: Mail Order Distribution of Erotica in the Nineteen-Thirties, Papers of the Bibliog Soc of Am, 9/92; Erotic Novel, Liberal Lawyer, and Censor-Moron: Sex for Its Own Sake and Some Literary Censorship Adjudications of the Nineteen-Thirties, The D.H. Lawrence Rev, Fall 92; Postal Service Guardians of Public Morals and Erotica Mail Order Dealers of the Thirties: A Study in Administrative Authority in the United States, Publ Hist, 37, 95; A Trap for Young Book-leggers: The First American Printings of Frank Harris' My Life, Volumes Three and Four (1927), Papers of the Bibliog Soc of Am, 9/95. **CONTACT ADDRESS** Dept of English, Mansfield Univ of Pennsylvania, Belknap Hall, Mansfield, PA 16933-1308. **EMAIL** jgertzma@earthlink.net

GESELL, GERALDINE C.
DISCIPLINE CLASSICAL STUDIES **EDUCATION** Vassar Col, BA, 53; Univ Okla, MA, 55; Univ NC, PhD, 72. **CAREER** Asst prof, 72-79, assoc prof, 79-85, prof, Univ Tenn, 85-. **MEMBERSHIPS** Advis Counc Am Acad Rome; Archaeol Inst Am; Class Asn Mid W and S; Tenn Class Asn. **SELECTED PUBLICATIONS** Auth, Town, Palace, and House Cult in Minoan Crete, 85. **CONTACT ADDRESS** Dept of Classics, Univ of Tennessee, Knoxville, Knoxville, TN 37996-0413. **EMAIL** ggesell@utk.edu

GEWANTER, DAVID
DISCIPLINE ENGLISH LITERATURE **EDUCATION** Univ Mich, BA; Univ Ca, MA, PhD. **CAREER** Assoc prof. **SELECTED PUBLICATIONS** Auth, In the Belly, Univ Chicago, 97. **CONTACT ADDRESS** English Dept, Georgetown Univ, 37th and O St, Washington, DC 20057.

GEYH, PAULA E.
PERSONAL Born 06/16/1958, OH, s **DISCIPLINE** LITERATURE, FILM, LITERARY THEORY **EDUCATION** Miami Univ, BA, 79; Univ Pa, AM, 90; PhD, 94. **CAREER** Lectr, Univ of Pa, 94-95; asst prof, Southern IL Univ, Carbondale, 95-; vis asst prof, Northwestern Univ, 97-98. **HONORS AND AWARDS** Fel, Univ of Pa, 86-89, 90-91, 92-93; Dean's Scholar Awd, Univ of Pa, 91; Mellon Fel, 91-92; ResGrant, Southern IL Univ, 96; Delta Zeta Outstanding Prof Awd, Northwestern Univ, 97; NEH Awd, 99; Fel, Southern IL Univ, 99. **MEMBERSHIPS** MLA; Am Comp Lit Assoc; Am Lit Assos; Am Studies Assoc; Modernist Studies Assoc. **RESEARCH** Postmodern fiction, film, literary theory and cultural studies, spatial theory. **SELECTED PUBLICATIONS** Auth, "Burning Down the House? Domestic Space and Feminine Subjectivity in Marilynne Robinson's Housekeeping", Contemp Lit 34.1, (Spring 93): 103-122; coed, Postmodern American Fiction: A Norton Anthology, W.W. Norton & Co, (NY), 98; auth, "Feminist Fiction and the Women's Liberation Movement, 1968-1977", Am Century: Art and Culture, 1900-2000, W.W. Norton & Company, 99; auth, "Barbara Kruger" and "Jenny Holzer", in Postmodernism: Key Figures, eds Hans Bertens and Joseph Natoli, Blackwell, (Oxford, UK) (forthcoming); auth, "The Short Fiction of Ha Jin", in Dictionary of Literary Biography: American Short Story Writers Since World War II (forthcoming); auth, "The Fortress and the Polis: From the Postmodern City to Cyberspace and Back", in New Technologies and Spatial Practices, ed Sally R. Munt, Continuum (London) (forthcoming). **CONTACT ADDRESS** Dept English, So Illinois Univ, Carbondale, Southern IL Union, Carbondale, IL 62901. **EMAIL** pgeyh@siu.edu

GHNASSIA, JILL DIX
DISCIPLINE ENGLISH LITERATURE **EDUCATION** Bucknell Univ, BA; Duke Univ, MA, PhD. **CAREER** Assoc prof, Hartford Univ. **RESEARCH** Humanities and literature; romanticism in the arts; interdisciplinary studies; discourse of the law. **SELECTED PUBLICATIONS** Auth, Metaphysical Rebellion in the Works of Emily Bronte (rev); pubs on Brontes, Percy Shelley, and Mary Wollstonecraft; co-auth, Epidemics and AIDS. **CONTACT ADDRESS** Univ of Hartford, 200 Bloomfield Ave, West Hartford, CT 06117.

GHOSE, ZULFIKAR AHMED
PERSONAL Born 03/13/1935, Sialkot, Pakistan, m, 1964 **DISCIPLINE** ENGLISH LITERATURE **EDUCATION** Keele Univ, BA, 59. **CAREER** Lectr, 69-73, assoc prof English, 74-82, PROF ENGLISH, UNIV TX, AUSTIN, 83-. **RESEARCH** Writing novels poetry and criticism. **SELECTED PUBLICATIONS** Auth, The Loss of India, Routledge & Kegan Paul, London, 64; The Murder of Aziz Khan, Macmillan, London, 67 & Day, 69; Jets from Orange, Macmillan, London, 67; The Incredible Brazilian, Macmillan, London, 72 & Holt, 72; The Beautiful Empire, Macmillan, London, 75; The Violent West, 72, Crump's Terms, 75 & A Different World, 78, Macmillan; Hamlet, Prufrock and Language, St Martin's, 78 & Macmillan, London, 78; Hulme's Investigations Into the Bogart Script, Curbstone Pub Co, Austin, 81; A New History of Torments, Hutchinson, London, 82 & Holt, 82; Don Bueno, Hutchinson, London, 83 & Holt, 83; A Memory of Asia, Curbstone Pub Co, Austin, 84; The Fiction of Reality, Macmillan, London, 83; Figures of Enchantment, Hutchinson, London, 86, and Harper & Row, 86; The Art of Creating Fiction, Macmillan, London, 91; Selected Poems, Oxford Univ Press, 91; The Triple Mirror of the Self, London, Bloomsbury, 92; Shakespeare's Mortal Knowledge, Macmillan (London), 93; auth, Veronica and the Gongora Passion, TSAR Publications (Toronto), 98. **CONTACT ADDRESS** Dept of English, Univ of Texas, Austin, 0 Univ TX, Austin, TX 78712-1026. **EMAIL** zulfji@mail.utexas.edu

GIANAKARIS, CONSTANTINE JOHN
PERSONAL Born 05/02/1934, Morenci, MI, m, 1957, 1 child **DISCIPLINE** ENGLISH **EDUCATION** Univ Mich, BA, 56, MA, 57; Univ Wis, PhD, 61. **CAREER** Asst to assoc dean Col Lett & Sci, Univ Wis, 58-60; from asst prof to assoc prof English, Ill State Univ, 61-66; assoc prof, 66-72, Western Mich Univ, prof English, 72-79, assoc dean, Col Arts & Sci, 79-82, prof English & Theatre, 89; Ill State Univ fac grant, 63-66; Westerm Mich fac res grant, 67-68; co-founder, co-ed, Comp Drama,66-91; jury panelist Nat Endowment for Humanities, 71-75. **HONORS AND AWARDS** Nat Endowment for Humanities Summer Awd 82; Teaching Excellence Awd, Western Mich Univ, 91. **MEMBERSHIPS** MLA; Renaissance Soc Am; NCent Renaissance Conf; Shakespeare Assn Am; Assn Higher Ed. **RESEARCH** Drama of Ben Jonson; modern British and American drama; Shakespeare. **SELECTED PUBLICATIONS** Auth, Rosencrantz and Guildenstern are dead: alterations in absurdism, Drama Surv, Fall 68; Identifying ethical values in Volpone, Huntington Libr Quart, 11/68; ed, Antony and Cleopatra, W C Brown, 69; auth, Plutarch, Twayne, 70; ed, Foundations of Drama, Houghton Mifflin, 75; auth, Mrozek's Tango and other savage comedies, In: Savage Comedy, Rodopi, 78; A playwright looks at Mozart: Peter Shaffer's Amadeus, Comp Drama, Spring 81; Peter Shaffer's treatment of Mozart in Amadeus, Opera News, 2/82; ed Peter Shaffer: A Casebook, Garland, 91; Peter Shaffer, Macmillan, UK & St Martin's SA, 92. **CONTACT ADDRESS** Dept of English, Western Michigan Univ, 1201 Oliver St, Kalamazoo, MI 49008-3805. **EMAIL** gianakaris@wmich.edu

GIANNETTI, LOUIS DANIEL
PERSONAL Born 04/01/1937, Natick, MA, d, 2 children **DISCIPLINE** CINEMA, DRAMA **EDUCATION** Boston Univ, BA, 59; Univ Iowa, MA, 61, PhD(English), 67. **CAREER** Grad teaching asst rhetoric & lit, Univ Iowa, 62-66; asst prof English, Emory Univ, 66-69; asst prof humanities, 70-73, assoc prof film & English, 73-75, prof film & English, Case Western Reserve Univ, 77-. **MEMBERSHIPS** Soc Cinema Studies; Am Film Inst; Univ Film Asn. **RESEARCH** Film form; ideology; film acting. **SELECTED PUBLICATIONS** Auth, Cinematic Metaphors, J Aesthet Educ, 72; The Gatsby Flap, Lit & Film Quart, 75; Godard and Others: Essays in Film Form, Fairleigh Dickinson Univ Press & Tantivy Press, London, 75; Amarcord: The Impure Art of Federico Fellini, Western Humanities Rev, spring

76; The Member of the Wedding, Lit & Film Quart, winter 76; Fred Zinnemann's High Noon, Film Criticism, winter 76-77; Masters of the American Cinema, Prentice-Hall, 81; Understanding Movies, Prentice-Hall, 72, 2nd ed, 76, 3rd ed, 82, 4th ed, 87, 5th ed, 90, 6th ed, 93, 7th ed, 96, 8th ed, 99; co-auth, Flashback: A Brief History of Film, with Scott Eyman, Prentice Hall, 86, 2nd ed, 91, 3rd ed, 96, 4th ed, 00; auth, Understanding Movies, 8th ed, 99; auth, Flashback, 4th ed, 00. **CONTACT ADDRESS** 23800 S Woodland Rd., Shaker Hts, OH 44122.

GIANNONE, RICHARD
PERSONAL Born 10/09/1934, Newark, NJ **DISCIPLINE** ENGLISH **EDUCATION** Cath Univ Am, AB, 56; Univ Mich, MA, 57; Univ Notre Dame, PhD(English), 64. **CAREER** Instr English, Univ Notre Dame, 58-60 & 61-62, asst prof, 64-67; assoc prof, 67-74, prof English, Fordham Univ, 74-, Vis scholar, Union Theol Sem, 75-76; Vis Scholar, Am Academy in Rome. **MEMBERSHIPS** MLA. **RESEARCH** American literature. **SELECTED PUBLICATIONS** Auth, One of ours: Willa Cather's suppressed Bitter Melody, SAtlantic Quart, winter 65; The quest motif in Thyrsis, Victorian Poetry, spring 65; Music in Willa Cather's Fiction, Univ Nebr, 68; The Shapes of Fiction, Holt, 71; John Keats: A Thematic Reader, Scott, 72; Vonnegut: A Preface to His Novels, Kennikat, 77; Flannery O'Connor and the Mystery of Love, Universtiy of Illinois Press, 89; auth, Flannery O'Connor, Hermit Novelist, Univ of Ill Press, 00. **CONTACT ADDRESS** Dept of English, Fordham Univ, 501 E Fordham Rd, Bronx, NY 10458-5191. **EMAIL** giannone@fordham.edu

GIARELLI, ANDREW
DISCIPLINE ENGLISH **EDUCATION** Yale Univ, BA, 75; State Univ NYork, PhD, 84. **CAREER** Adj asst prof, 96-. **HONORS AND AWARDS** Contrib ed, World Press Rev. **SELECTED PUBLICATIONS** Ed, publ, Edging West; contrib ed,World Press Rev. **CONTACT ADDRESS** Dept of Eng, Portland State Univ, PO Box 751, Portland, OR 97207-0751. **EMAIL** giarellia@pdx.edu

GIBALDI, JOSEPH
PERSONAL Born 08/20/1942, Brooklyn, NY, m, 1962, 2 children **DISCIPLINE** ENGLISH, COMPARATIVE LITERATURE **EDUCATION** City Col New York, BA, 65; MA, 67; NYork Univ, PhD(comp lit), 73. **CAREER** Instr English, Brooklyn Col, 71-73; asst prof comp lit, Univ Ga, 73-76; ASSOC DIR, BK PUBL AND RES PROG, MOD LANG ASN AM, 76-, Southeastern Inst Medieval and Renaissance Studies fel, 76; adj prof English, Fairleigh Dickinson Univ, 77-. **MEMBERSHIPS** MLA; Am Comp Lit Asn; Renaissance Soc; New Chaucer Soc. **RESEARCH** Medieval and Renaissance literature; interdisciplinary studies; professional subjects. **SELECTED PUBLICATIONS** Auth, Anatomy of the Novella; auth, Approaches to Teaching Chaucer's 'Cantebury Tales'; auth, Teaching Literature & Other Arts; auth, MLA Handbook for Writers of Research Papers. **CONTACT ADDRESS** New Sch for Social Research, 66 W 12th St, New York, NY 10011.

GIBBENS, E. BYRD
DISCIPLINE MODERN AMERICAN LITERATURE **EDUCATION** Univ NMex, PhD. **CAREER** English and Lit, Univ Ark. **SELECTED PUBLICATIONS** Auth, This Strange Country; "Strangers in the Arkansas Delta," The Arkansas Delta; "Beliefs and Customs," Folklore in Arkansas; Coauth, Far From Home. **CONTACT ADDRESS** Univ of Arkansas, Little Rock, 2801 S University Ave., Little Rock, AR 72204-1099. **EMAIL** bxgibbens@ualr.edu

GIBBONS, REGINALD
PERSONAL Born Houston, TX **DISCIPLINE** ENGLISH **EDUCATION** Stanford Univ, PhD. **CAREER** Prof, Northwestern Univ. **HONORS AND AWARDS** Carl Sandburg Awd, 92; Anisfield-Wolf Book Awd, 95; Balcones Poetry Prize, 98; Guggenheim fel; NEA Fel. **SELECTED PUBLICATIONS** Co-ed, Criticism in the University; ed, Triquarterly, 81-97; transl, Seleted Poems of Luis Cernuda; co-rransl, Guillen on Guillen: The Poetry and the Poet; transl, Euripides' Bakkhai; ed, The Poet's Work; auth, Five Pears or Peaches, Broken moon Pr, 91; auth, Sweetbitter, Penguin, 96; auth, Sparrow: New and Selected Poems, LSU, 97; auth, Homage to Longshot O'Leary, Holy Cow! Pr, 99. **CONTACT ADDRESS** Dept of English, Northwestern Univ, Univ Hall 215, 1897 Sheridan Rd, Evanston, IL 60208-2240. **EMAIL** rgibbons@nwu.edu

GIBSON, CLAUDE LOUIS
PERSONAL Born 11/27/1940, Okmulgee, OK, m, 1986, 3 children **DISCIPLINE** ENGLISH **EDUCATION** Univ Ark, Fayetteville, BA, 64, MA, 65, PhD, 76. **CAREER** Assoc Prof English, Tex A&M Univ, 76-, Dir Freshman English, 80-84, Dir Undergrad Studies, 94-; Managing ed, CEA Critic & CEA Forum, 77-80. **HONORS AND AWARDS** Distinguished Teaching Awd, 93; Inst for Educ Inquiry Assoc, 97; Mervin and Annette Peters Advising Awd, 99-00. **MEMBERSHIPS** Col English Asn; MLA; SCent Mod Lang Asn; NCTE. **RESEARCH** Modern British literature; 19th century; rhetoric and composition. **SELECTED PUBLICATIONS** Contribr, The historical study of style: an annotated bibliography, summer 77 & Author style, winter 78, Style; auth, The undergraduate English curriculum three years later, CEA Critic, 5/78; The CEA 1978 National Survey of the Teaching of College English, CEA Forum, 10/78. **CONTACT ADDRESS** Dept of English, Texas A&M Univ, Col Station, College Station, TX 77843-4227. **EMAIL** cgibson@tamu.edu

GIBSON, DIRK C.
PERSONAL Born 10/13/1953, Evergreen Park, IL, m, 1989, 3 children **DISCIPLINE** SPEECH COMMUNICATION **EDUCATION** S Ill Univ, BS, 77; Ind Univ, MA, 79; PhD, 83. **CAREER** Asst prof, Auburn Univ, 83-86; asst prof, Augusta Col, 86-90, assoc prof, Ga State Univ, 90-92; assoc prof, Ga S Univ, 92-96; assoc prof, Univ of NMex, 96-. **HONORS AND AWARDS** Award, Nat Commun Assoc, 99; Outstanding Young Men of Sci; Who's Who in Am Educ; Who's Who in SW and SE. **MEMBERSHIPS** Nat Commun Assoc, Int Commun Assoc, Int Acad of Bus Disciplines, Am Soc of Trial Consult, World Commun Assoc. **RESEARCH** Product recall processes and public relations, litigation public relations, Hispanic and cultural criticism, Japanese public relations, attorney and public relations, Ad and PR education. **SELECTED PUBLICATIONS** Auth, "Secrecy: the Communication Dilemma of CIA," Public Relations Rev, (85); auth, The Role of Communication in the Practice of Law, Univ Pr of Am, 90; auth, "Public Relations Considerations of Product Recall," Public Relations Rev, (90); "Hispanic Advertising: Problems and Banners," Bus Res Yearbook (98); auth, "Print Recall Guidelines for Product Recalls," Public Relations Quart, (98); auth, "A Critical Analysis of Green Communications: Advertising and Public Relations Strategy and Tactics," Bus Res Yearbook (98); auth, "Litigation Public Relations Problems and Issues," Public Relations Rev, (99); auth, "The Cyber-Revolution in Product Recall Public Relations," Public Relations Quart, (00). **CONTACT ADDRESS** Dept Commun, Univ of New Mexico, Albuquerque, 1 University Campus, Albuquerque, NM 87131-0001. **EMAIL** dirkegib@unm.edu

GIBSON, DONALD BERNARD
PERSONAL Born 07/02/1933, Kansas City, MO, m, 1963, 2 children **DISCIPLINE** ENGLISH **EDUCATION** Univ Kansas City, BA, 55, MA, 57; Brown Univ, PhD, 62. **CAREER** Instr English, Brown Univ, 60-61; from instr to asst prof English, Wayne State Univ, 61-66; from assoc prof to prof English, Univ Conn, 66-74; prof English, Rutgers Col, Rutgers Univ, 74-; Fulbright-Hayes Award, Krakow, Poland, 64-66; Nat Endowment for Humanities younger humanist fel, 70-71; vis prof English, Univ Iowa, 71. **MEMBERSHIPS** MLA; Col Lang Asn. **RESEARCH** Nineteenth century realism and naturalism; Black American writers. **SELECTED PUBLICATIONS** Ed, Five Black Writers: Essays on Wright, Ellison, Baldwin, Hughes and LeRoy Jones, New York Univ, 70; Twentieth Century Interpretations of Modern Black Poets, Prentice-Hall, 73; auth, The Politics of Literary Expression: A Study of Major Black Writers, Greenwood Press, 81; auth The Red Badge of Courage: Redefining the Hero. **CONTACT ADDRESS** Dept English, Rutgers, The State Univ of New Jersey, New Brunswick, PO Box 5454, New Brunswick, NJ 08903-0270. **EMAIL** dgibba@aol.com

GIBSON, MARGARET
PERSONAL Born 02/17/1944, Philadelphia, PA, m, 1975, 2 children **DISCIPLINE** ENGLISH **EDUCATION** Hollins Col, BA, 66; Univ Va, MA, 67. **CAREER** Va Commonwealth Univ, 68-70; George Mason Univ, 70-75; Conn Col, 76-77; Univ of Conn, 79-84; Philips Acad, 84-87; Univ of Pittsburgh, 89; Eastern Conn State Univ, 90-91; Univ of Conn, 92-. **HONORS AND AWARDS** Phi Beta Kappa; Woodrow Wilson Fel, 66; NEA Grant, 66, 85; Conn comm on the Arts Grant, 76, 88; Melville Cane Awd, 86-87; Nat Book Awd Finalist, 93; James Boatright Prize, 96; Res Found Grant, 97-98. **MEMBERSHIPS** AAUP; Acad of Am Poets, Poet Soc of Am. **RESEARCH** Poetry. **SELECTED PUBLICATIONS** Auth, Memories of the Future, The Daybooks of Tina Modotti, La State Univ Pr, 86; auth, Out in the Open, La State Univ Pr, 89; auth, "After Frost", Poetry in New England, ed Henry Lyman, 95; auth, "Atomic Ghost", Poets Respond to the Nuclear Age, ed John Bradley, Coffee House Pr, 95; auth, The Vigil, La State Univ Pr, 93; auth, Earth Elegy, New and Selected Poems, La State Univ Pr, 97; auth, "Core", Sewanee Theol Rev, Summer 97; auth, "Elegy in Soviet Georgia", Five Points II.2, (98): 85-89; auth, "Primary Reflections, After the Children's First Letters to God", Seneca Rev, Spring 98. **CONTACT ADDRESS** Dept English, Univ of Connecticut, Storrs, 337 Mansfield Rd, Unit U-25, Storrs, CT 06260-1025.

GIBSON, MELISSA K.
PERSONAL Born 09/18/1969, Erie, PA, s **DISCIPLINE** ORGANIZATIONAL COMMUNICATION **EDUCATION** Edinboro Univ, BA, 92; Ohio Univ, MA, 95, PhD, 97. **CAREER** Asst Prof, Western Mich Univ, 97-. **HONORS AND AWARDS** Res Fel, 96-97; Central States Commun Asn Outstanding New Teacher Awd, 98; Top Paper, Orgn Commun Div, Nat Commun Asn, 98. **MEMBERSHIPS** Nat Commun Asn; Central States Commun; Am Soc Training & Development; Int Commun Asn. **RESEARCH** Organizational communication; applied communication theory; training and development; nonprofit organizations. **CONTACT ADDRESS** Western Michigan Univ, 215 Sprau Tower, Kalamazoo, MI 49008. **EMAIL** melissa.gibson@wmich.edu

GIBSON, RICHARD J.
PERSONAL Born 08/13/1942, Barbourville, KY, s **DISCIPLINE** ENGLISH, THEATRE **EDUCATION** Stetson Univ, BA, 64; Univ NC, MA, 66; PhD, 72. **CAREER** Asst Prof, Ga State Univ, 70-75; Assoc Prof, Mercer Univ, 76-88; Prof, Jacksonville Univ, 89-. **HONORS AND AWARDS** Woodrow Wilson Fel. **MEMBERSHIPS** MLA, SAMLA, Renaissance Soc, NCTE. **RESEARCH** Shakespeare, theatre history. **SELECTED PUBLICATIONS** Auth, Speaking and Acting Shakespeare, forthcoming. **CONTACT ADDRESS** Dept Humanities, Jacksonville Univ, 2800 University Blvd N, Jacksonville, FL 32211. **EMAIL** dgibson@ju.edu

GIBSON, STEPHANIE
PERSONAL Born 10/26/1954, New York, NY **DISCIPLINE** COMMUNICATIONS **EDUCATION** NYork Univ, PhD. **CAREER** Assoc prof, Univ Baltimore. **MEMBERSHIPS** Media Ecology Assn. **SELECTED PUBLICATIONS** Ed, Communication and Cyberspace and The Emerging CyberCulture. **CONTACT ADDRESS** Commun Dept, Univ of Baltimore, 1420 N. Charles Street, Baltimore, MD 21201. **EMAIL** sgibson@ubmail.ubalt.edu

GIDMARK, JILL B.
PERSONAL Born 11/22/1947, Key West, FL, 2 children **DISCIPLINE** AMERICAN LITERATURE **EDUCATION** Hamline Univ, BA, 70; Univ ND, MA, 73; PhD, 78. **CAREER** Asst prof to prof, Univ Minn, 78-. **HONORS AND AWARDS** Ive D. Thomas Award, Col English Asn; Maxwell Anderson Award. **MEMBERSHIPS** Melville Soc; Col English Asn; Soc for the Study of Midwestern Literature. **RESEARCH** Literature of the sea; Herman Melville; Asian American literature; Contemporary American drama. **SELECTED PUBLICATIONS** Auth, Encyclopedia of American Literature of the Sea and Great Lakes, Greenwood Press, 01. **CONTACT ADDRESS** Dept English, Univ of Minnesota, Twin Cities, 140 Appleby Hall, Minneapolis, MN 55455.

GIFFORD, JAMES J.
PERSONAL Born 06/03/1946, Rome, NY **DISCIPLINE** AMERICAN LITERATURE, FILM **EDUCATION** Fordham Univ, AB, 68; Columbia Univ, MA, 70; Syracuse Univ, PhD, 94. **CAREER** Prof, 72-, Mohawk Valley Commun Col. **HONORS AND AWARDS** Doctoral Prize, Syracuse Univ, 95 **RESEARCH** Amer lit; nineteenth-twentieth centuries; gay Amer writing; film. **SELECTED PUBLICATIONS** Auth, Dayneford's Library: American Homosexual Writing 1900-1913, Univ Ma Press, 95. **CONTACT ADDRESS** Humanities Dept, Mohawk Valley Comm Col, 1101 Sherman Dr, Utica, NY 13501. **EMAIL** jgifford@mvcc.edu

GIGLIOTTI, GILBERT L.
PERSONAL Born 11/07/1961, Allentown, PA, m, 1988, 2 children **DISCIPLINE** ENGLISH **EDUCATION** Xavier Univ, HAB, 81, MA, 85; Cath Univ Am, PhD, 92. **CAREER** From asst prof to assoc prof & asst chm, dept English, Central Conn State Univ, 92-. **MEMBERSHIPS** Int Asn Neo-Latin Studies; Am Asn Neo-Latin Studies; Soc Early Am; NE Mod Lang Asn. **RESEARCH** American Neo-Latin Verse; Frank Sinatra; The Connecticut Wits; Cotton Mather. **SELECTED PUBLICATIONS** Auth, Voyage to Maryland: Relation itineris in Marylandiam, Neo-Latin News, 97; auth, Nail-Gnawing in a New World Landscape: From Allusion to Disillusion in John Beveridge's Epistolae familiares, Conn Rev, 96; auth, Off a Strange, Uncoasted Strand: Navigating the Ship of State Through Freneau's Hurricane, Class & Mod Lit, 95; auth, The Alexandrian Fracastoro: Structure and Meaning in the Myth of Syphilus, Renaissance & Reformation, 90. **CONTACT ADDRESS** Dept of English, Central Connecticut State Univ, 1615 Stanley St., New Britain, CT 06050. **EMAIL** Gigliotti@ccsu.edu

GIKANDI, SIMON E.
PERSONAL Born 09/30/1956, Kenya, m, 1993, 3 children **DISCIPLINE** ENGLISH **EDUCATION** Univ Nairobi, BA, 79; Univ Edinburgh, MLitt, 82; Northwestern Univ, PhD, 86. **CAREER** Asst prof, Univ Mass, 87-91; assoc prof to prof, Univ Mich Ann Arbor, 91-. **HONORS AND AWARDS** Guggenheim Fel; Fac Recognition Award; Am Coun of Learned Soc Award; Andrew Mellon Fel. **MEMBERSHIPS** MLA; African Studies Asn; African Lit Asn. **RESEARCH** Anglophone literature and cultural history; Literary and social theory; Modern novel; The Black Atlantic. **SELECTED PUBLICATIONS** Auth, Reading Chinua Achebe; auth, Writing in Limbo: Modernism and Caribbean Literature; auth, Maps of Englishness; auth, Ngugi wa Thiong'o. **CONTACT ADDRESS** Dept English, Univ of Michigan, Ann Arbor, 505 S State St, 3187 Angell Hall, Ann Arbor, MI 48109-1045. **EMAIL** gikandi@umich.edu

GILBERT, HARVEY R.
DISCIPLINE COMMUNICATION SCIENCES **EDUCATION** Univ Wis, PhD, 69. **CAREER** Prof , Univ Conn; dept ch. **RESEARCH** Normal and disordered voice, cleft palate and speech physiology. **SELECTED PUBLICATIONS** Coauth, Perceptions of Tonal Changes in Normal Laryngeal, Esophageal, and Artificial Laryngeal Male Cantonese Speakers, Folia Phoniatrica et Logopaedica, 64-70, 1998; Acoustic, Aerodynamic, Physiologic, and Perceptual Properties of Modal and Vocal Fry Registers. Acoustical Society of America, 2649-2658, 1998; Formant Frequency Development: 15-36 months, J Voice 3, 97; Formant Frequency and Bandwidth Development in Infants and Toddlers, Folia Phoniatrica et Logopaedica 49, 97; Some Aerodynamic Characteristics of Acute Laryngitic Voice, J Voice 3, 97; Vocal Fundamental Frequency Characteristics of Infant Hunger Cries: Birth to 12 months, Int J Pediatric Otorhinolaryngology 34, 96. **CONTACT ADDRESS** Dept of Communication Sci, Univ of Connecticut, Storrs, 850 Bolton Rd, Storrs, CT 06269-1085. **EMAIL** harveyg@uconnvm.uconn.edu

GILBERT, PAMELA K.
PERSONAL Born 01/16/1964, Los Angeles, CA **DISCIPLINE** ENGLISH **EDUCATION** Calif State Univ, BA, 83; MA, 88; Univ S Calif, PhD, 94. **CAREER** Instructor, Calif State Univ, 88-90; Asst Lecturer, Univ S Calif, 89-93; Lecturer, Calif State Univ, 90-93; Asst Prof, Univ Wisc, 93-98; Asst Prof to Assoc Prof, Univ Fla, 97-. **HONORS AND AWARDS** Networked Assoc Fel, Inst for Adv Techol in the Humanities; Fel, Ctr for 20th Cent Studies, 96-97; NEH Sem, Univ VA, 95; Middleton Dissertaion Fel, 92-93; Excellence in Teaching Awd, USC, 91. **SELECTED PUBLICATIONS** Auth, Disease, Desire and the Body in Victorian Women's Popular Novels, Cambridge Univ Press, 97; auth, "The Other Anne Finch: Lady Conway's Duelogue of Textual Selves," Essays in Arts and Sciences, (97): 15-26; auth, "Ingestion, Contagion, Seduction: Victorian Metaphors of Reading," LIT: Literature/Interpretation/Theory, (97): 83-104; auth, "meditations Upon Hypertext: A Rhetorethics for Cyborgs,; JAC: Journal of Composition Theory, (97): 23-38; auth, "A Sinful and Suffering Nation: Cholera and the Evolution of Medical and Religious Authority in Britain, 1832-1866," Nineteenth Century Prose, (98): 35-59; auth, "Ouida and the Other New Woman," in Victorian Woman Writers and the Woman Question, Cambridge Univ Press, 99; auth, M.E. Braddon and Victorian Realism: Joshua Haggard's Daughter," in Mary Elizabeth Braddon in Context, SUNY Press, 99; co-ed, Mary Elizabeth Braddon in Context, SUNY Press, 99; auth, "Scarcely to be Described: Urban Extremes as Real Spaces and Mythic Places in the London Cholera Epidemic of 1854," Nineteenth Century Studies, 00. **CONTACT ADDRESS** Dept Eng, Univ of Florida, PO Box 117310, Gainesville, FL 32611-7310. **EMAIL** pgilbert@english.ufl.edu

GILBERT, SANDRA MORTOLA
PERSONAL Born 12/27/1936, New York, NY, m, 1957, 3 children **DISCIPLINE** ENGLISH LITERATURE, WOMEN'S STUDIES **EDUCATION** Cornell Univ, BA, 57; NYork Univ, MA, 61; Columbia Univ, PhD, 68. **CAREER** Assoc prof and prof, Univ of Calif, Davis, 75-85; prof, Princeton Univ, 85-89; prof, Univ of Calif, Davis, 89. **HONORS AND AWARDS** Morrison Poetry Prize, Cornell Univ, 55; Guilford Essay Prize, Cornell Univ, 57; Van Rensselaer Poetry Prize, Columbia Univ, 64; Res Asst grant, CA State Hayward Found, 69-70; IN Univ Summer Fac Fel, 74; Univ CA Hum Inst, summer 76, 78; Finalist, Assoc Writing Prog Contest, 76-77; Univ CA Prog Develop Award, summer 79; Nominee, Nat Bk Critics' Circle Award, 80; Runner-up, Pulitzer Prize in Non-Fiction, 80; Eunice Tietjens Mem Prize, Poetry, 80; NEH Summer Seminar, Univ Calif Davis, summer 81; Univ CA Tchg Develop Award, summer 81; Gildersleeve Professorship, Barnard Col, Columbia Univ, fall 82; Joseph Warren Beach Lectr, Univ MN, May 84; Fac, School of Criticism & Theory, Northwestern Univ, Summer 84; USA Today, People Who Made a Difference, 85; Ms., Woman of the Year Award, 86; D. Litt., Wesleyan Univ, June 88; Paley Lectr, The Hebrew Univ, Jerusalem, 90; Charity Randall Award, Int Poetry Found, 1/90; Danz lectr, Univ WA Seattle, 92; Paterson Prize, 95; Union League Prize, 96; Fel, Am Acad Arts and Sci, 97. **MEMBERSHIPS** MLA. **RESEARCH** Nineteenth & 20th century Brit lit; mod poetry; feminist critical theory. **SELECTED PUBLICATIONS** Auth, Acts of Attention: The Poems of D.H. Lawrence, Cornell, 73; revised ed, Southern Illinois, 90; coauth, The Madwoman in the Attic: The Woman Writer and the Nineteenth-Century Literary Imagination, Yale, 79; auth, In the Fourth World: Poems, Alabama/AWP Poetry Series, 79; co-ed, Shakespeare's Sisters: feminist Essays on Women Poets, IU, 79; auth, The Summer Kitchen: Poems, Heyeck, 83; auth, Emily's Bread: Poems, Norton, 84; auth, Kate Chopin's The Awakening and Selected Stories, Penguin, 84; co-ed, The Norton Anthology of Literature by Women: The Tradition in English, Norton, 85; co-edd, A Guide to the Norton Anthology of Literature by Women, 85; co-ed, No Man's Land: The Place of the Woman Writer in the Twentieth Century, Vol. I, The War of the Words, Yale, 87. **CONTACT ADDRESS** Dept of Eng, Univ of California, Davis, Davis, CA 95616-5200. **EMAIL** sgilbert@ucdavis.edu

GILES, JAMES RICHARD
PERSONAL Born 10/26/1937, Bowie, TX, m, 1968, 1 child **DISCIPLINE** ENGLISH **EDUCATION** Tex Christian Univ, BA, 60, MA, 61; Univ Tex, PhD, 67. **CAREER** Instr English, 66, asst prof, 67-70, NTex State Univ; asst prof, 70-72, assoc prof, 72-80, prof Eng, Northern IL Univ, 80-. **MEMBERSHIPS** MLA. **RESEARCH** American literature; Black American literature; creative writing. **SELECTED PUBLICATIONS** Auth, Irwin Shaw: A Study of the Short Fiction, Twayne, 91; auth,The Naturalistic Inner-City novel in America, South Carolina, 95; auth, Understanding Hubert Selby, Jr., South Carolina, 98; auth, Violence in the Contemporary American Novel, South Carolina, 00. **CONTACT ADDRESS** Dept of English, No Illinois Univ, 1425 W Lincoln Hwy, De Kalb, IL 60115-2825.

GILINSKY, JOSHUA
PERSONAL Born 10/21/1959, New York, NY **DISCIPLINE** MUSIC THEORY **EDUCATION** Harvard Univ, BA, 81; Manhattan Sch Mus, 90. **CAREER** Asst Ed Dir, Opera Co Boston, 82; Tchg Fel Boston Univ, 84; Compos, Theory and Ear Training Fac, Manhattan Sch Mus Prep Div, 87-98. **HONORS AND AWARDS** Saul Braverman Awd for Outstanding Achievement in Mus Theory, Columbia Univ; Pres Fellow. **MEMBERSHIPS** Soc for Mus Theory; Am Musicol Soc. **RESEARCH** Methodological Construction; Orchestration **SELECTED PUBLICATIONS** Unity and Opposition in the Orchestration of Tchaikovsky's Romeo and Juliet Overture, 90. **CONTACT ADDRESS** Current Musicology, Columbia Univ, 2960 Broadway, Mail Code 1812, New York, NY 10027-7004. **EMAIL** jeg13@columbia.edu

GILL, ANN
DISCIPLINE COMMUNICATION STUDIES **EDUCATION** W State Univ, BA; Colo State Univ, MA; Univ Colo, JD; Univ Denver, PhD. **CAREER** Prof. **RESEARCH** Freedom of speech; law and policy of communication technologies; rhetorical theory. **SELECTED PUBLICATIONS** Auth, Rhetoric and Human Understanding; Public Policy and Public Concern: Freedom of Speech in the Workplace, Free Speech Yearbook, 90; In the Wake of 'Fraser' and 'Hazelwood', J Law Edu, 91; Renewed Concern for Free Speech on Campus, ACA Bul, 93; Revising Campus Speech Codes, Free Speech Yearbook, 93; The Oral Tradition of Gerry Spence in Pring v. Penthouse, SW Univ Law Rev, 98; co-auth, Help Wanted: An Inexperienced Job Seeker's Guide to Career Success. **CONTACT ADDRESS** Speech Communication Dept, Colorado State Univ, 202 Eddy Bldg, Fort Collins, CO 80523-1783. **EMAIL** agill@vines.colostate.edu

GILL, GLENDA E.
PERSONAL Born 06/26/1939, Clarksville, TN **DISCIPLINE** THEATRE HISTORY **EDUCATION** Ala A & M Col, BS, 60; Univ Wis at Madison, MA, 64; Univ Iowa, PhD, 81. **CAREER** Tuskegee Univ, 82-83; assoc prof, Winston-Salem State Univ, 84-90; prof, Mich Technol Univ, 90-. **HONORS AND AWARDS** NEH Summer Fel, Univ Iowa, 74; Rockefeller Fel, 76 & 77; NEH Summer Fel, Yale Univ, 85; NEH Summer Fel, Univ NC Chapel Hill, 89; Summer Fel, Nat Portrait Gallery, The Smithsonian Inst, 90; NEH Summer Fel, Duke Univ, 91. **MEMBERSHIPS** MLA, Am Soc for Theatre Res, The Eugene O'Neill Soc. **RESEARCH** The African American in the performing arts--especially in non-traditional roles. **SELECTED PUBLICATIONS** Auth, No Surrender! No Retreat! African American Pioneer Performers of Twentieth-Century American Theater, St Martin's Press, 00. **CONTACT ADDRESS** Dept Humanities, Michigan Tech Univ, 1400 Townsend Dr, Houghton, MI 49931-1200.

GILLAM, RONALD G.
PERSONAL Born 08/21/1955, Salina, KS, m, 1976, 2 children **DISCIPLINE** COMMUNICATIONS **EDUCATION** Colo State Univ, BS, 77; MS, 79; Ind Univ, PhD, 89. **CAREER** Asst Prof, Univ Mo, 88-92; Asst Prof, Univ Tex, 92-97; Assoc Prof, Univ Tex, 97-. **HONORS AND AWARDS** Ed Awd for the Article of Highest Merit in the Lang Section of the J of Speech, Lang and Hearing Res, 98; Innovational Instruct Technol Awd, Univ Tex, 99; Dean's Excellence Awd, Univ Tex, 99; Col of Commun Res Awd, Univ Tex, 93, 99. **MEMBERSHIPS** Am Speech-Lang-Hearing Asn, Int Asn of Phoniatrics and Logopedics, Am Psychol Soc. **RESEARCH** Specific language impairment, language assessment and intervention, literacy, discourse in school-age children. **SELECTED PUBLICATIONS** Coauth, "The Development of Abstract Language: Influences of Parent Talk During Book Sharing," J of Speech and Hearing Res, 40 (97): 1261-1271; coauth, "Evaluation of an Inservice Model to Teach Child Care Providers About Inclusion," J of Res in Childhood Educ, 12 (98): 130-142; coauth, Information Processing by School-Age Children with Specific Language Impairment: Evidence from a Modality Effect Paradigm," J of Speech, Lang and Hearing Res, 41 (98) 913-926; ed, Memory and Language Impairment in Children and Adults: New Perspectives, Aspen Publ (Gaithersburg, MD), 98; coauth, "Assessment in Communication Disorders: Some Observations on Current Issues," Lang Testing, 16 (99): 249-269; coauth, "Dynamic Assessment of Narrative and Expository Texts," Topics in Lang Disorders, 20 (99): 15-29; coauth, Communication Sciences and Disorders: From Science to Clinical Practice, Singular Pr (San Diego, CA), 00; coauth, Dynamic Assessment and Intervention: Improving Children's Narrative Abilities, Pro-Ed Pr (Austin, TX), forthcoming. **CONTACT ADDRESS** Dept Commun, Univ of Texas, Austin, Austin, TX 78712-1013.

GILLAN, JENIFFER
PERSONAL Born 09/01/1967, NJ, m, 1995 **DISCIPLINE** ENGLISH **CAREER** ASST PROF, ENG, BENTLEY COL, 95-. **HONORS AND AWARDS** Phi Beta Kappa, Bentley Col res, teach grants. **MEMBERSHIPS** MLA, MultiEthnic Lit Soc US; Am Lit Asn, Phi Beta Kappa, Alpha Sigma Nu. **RESEARCH** Am Lit; realism; Native Am Lit; Ethnic Am Lit. **SELECTED PUBLICATIONS** Co-ed, Growing Up Ethnic in America, Penguin, 99; co-ed, Identity Lessons, Penguin, 99; co-ed, Unsettling America, Penguin, 94; auth, Reservation Home Movies: Sherman Alexie's Poetry, Am Lit; auth, Hazards of Osage Fortunes: Gender and the Rhetoric of Compensation in Federal Policy and AMerican Indian Fiction, Az Q. **CONTACT ADDRESS** Dept of English, Bentley Col, Waltham, MA 02452.

GILLESPIE, DIANE F.
DISCIPLINE MODERN BRITISH LITERATURE **EDUCATION** Alberta, PhD. **CAREER** Prof, Washington State Univ. **SELECTED PUBLICATIONS** Auth, Julia Duckworth Stephen: Stories for Children, Essays for Adults, 87; The Sisters' Arts: The Writing and Painting of Virginia Woolf and Vanessa Bell, 88; The Multiple Muses of Virginia Woolf, 93; edition of Woolf's Roger Fry, 96 & edition of selected papers from 6th annual Virginia Woolf conf, 97. **CONTACT ADDRESS** Dept of English, Washington State Univ, 1 SE Stadium Way, PO Box 645020, Pullman, WA 99164-5020. **EMAIL** gillespi@mail.wsu.edu

GILLESPIE, MICHAEL PATRICK
PERSONAL Born 11/25/1946, Chicago, IL, m, 1977 **DISCIPLINE** ENGLISH **EDUCATION** Univ Ill, BS, 68; Univ Wis, MA, 76, PhD, 80. **CAREER** From asst prof to assoc prof, 80-92, prof, English, 92-, Marquette Univ; vis res schol, Humanities Res Ctr, Univ Tex, 81, 82. **HONORS AND AWARDS** Summer Fac Fel, Marquette Univ, 83, 86, 90, 92, 97; NEH Fel for Individual Study and Res, 84-85; Fel, William Andrews Clark Memorial Libr, 87; Fel, Coun for Int Studies, 94; recipient of numerous grants. **MEMBERSHIPS** MLA; James Joyce Found; Am Conf Irish Studies. **RESEARCH** 20th Century Irish and Irish-Am Lit. **SELECTED PUBLICATIONS** Auth, Library, UMI Res Press, 83; auth, A Catalogue of James Joyce's Trieste Library, Humanities Res Center, U on Tex, 86; auth, Reading the Book of Himself: Narrative Strategies in the Work of James Joyce, Ohio State UP, 89; auth, Oscar Wilde: Life, Work, and Criticism, York Press Ltd, 90; co-ed, Joycean Occassions: Essays from the Milwaukee James Joyce Conference, Univ Del Press, 91; auth, The Picture of Dorian Gray: "What the World Thinks Me", Twayne Publ, 95; coauth, James Joyce A to Z: The Essential Reference to His Life and Work, Facts on File, 95; auth, Oscar Wilde and the Poetics of Ambiguity, Univ Press Fla, 96; author of numerous articles and book reviews. **CONTACT ADDRESS** Dept English, Marquette Univ, PO Box 1881, Milwaukee, WI 53201-1881. **EMAIL** Michael.Gillespie@marquette.edu

GILLESPIE, PATTI P.
PERSONAL Born 01/26/1938, Bowling Green, KY, d **DISCIPLINE** THEATRE **EDUCATION** Wellesley Coll, 55-56; Univ Ky, BS, 58; Western Ky Univ, MA, spec ed, 62-64; Indiana Univ, PhD, 70. **CAREER** Prof, head, Dept Theatre, Univ South Carolina, 79-82; prof, chair, Dept Commun Arts & Theatre, prof, Dept Theatre, Univ Maryland, 89-; Fulbright Scholar, Dept English, Univ Botswana, 92-93. **HONORS AND AWARDS** ACT-NUCEA Natl Awd, 81; Omicron Delta Kappa, 83; Mitchell Distinguished Visiting Prof, Trinity Univ, 87; Goodman Scholar, Peace Coll, 90; Lilly Fel, Univ Maryland, 92-93. **MEMBERSHIPS** Natl Commun Assn, pres, 86, 87; Amer Soc Theatre Research; AAUP. **RESEARCH** Women in theatre and drama; theatre historiograph; American theatre. **SELECTED PUBLICATIONS** Coauth, Western Theatre: Revolution and Revival, 84; auth, "Aristotle and Arimneste ('Nicanor's Mother'): Theatre Studies and Feminism," in Feminist Critiques in Speech Communication, 93; auth, "Feminist Theory of Theatre: Revolution or Revival," in Theatre and Feminist Aesthetics, 95; coauth, The Enjoyment of Theatre, 4th ed, 96, 5th ed, in progress; auth, "The Dilemma of Wedlock: African Marriage in Plays and Life," The McNeese Review, vol 35, 97. **CONTACT ADDRESS** Dept of Theatre, Univ of Maryland, Col Park, College Park, MD 20742. **EMAIL** pg6@umail.umd.edu

GILLIAM, BRYAN
PERSONAL Born 04/23/1953, Lexington, KY, m, 1979, 2 children **DISCIPLINE** MUSICOLOGY **EDUCATION** Univ Cincinnati, Bmus, 75; Harvard, AM, 78; PhD, 84. **CAREER** Prof, Duke Univ. **HONORS AND AWARDS** NEH; DAAD; Mellon Teaching Awd. **MEMBERSHIPS** Am Musicol Soc; Int Richard-Strauss Soc. **RESEARCH** German opera (19th and 20th century); Richard Strauss; Kurt Weill; Anton Bruckner; Hollywood film music. **SELECTED PUBLICATIONS** Auth,

Richard Strauss's Elektra, Oxford, 91, 96; auth, Richard Strauss and His World, Princeton, 92; auth, Richard Strauss: New Perspectives, Duke, 92; auth, Music and Performance during the Weimar Republic, Cambridge, 94; auth, The Life of Richard Strauss, Cambridge, 99. **CONTACT ADDRESS** Dept of Music, Duke Univ, 73 Biddle Music Bldg, Durham, NC 27708. **EMAIL** bgilliam@acpub.duke.edu

GILLILAND, C. HERBERT
PERSONAL Born 12/04/1942, Alton, IL, m, 1979, 4 children **DISCIPLINE** ENGLISH **EDUCATION** Univ Fla, BA, 64, MA, 65, PhD, 76. **CAREER** Asst prof, Va Military Inst, 85-86; asst prof, US Naval Acad, 86-88, assoc prof, 88-89, prof, 99-. **HONORS AND AWARDS** NEH grant, 79; managing ed, 83-85, ed, The Arnoldian, 84-85; Fac consult, AP exams for Ed Testing Service, 96-. **MEMBERSHIPS** South Atlantic Modern Lang Asn, Renaissance Soc of Am. **RESEARCH** Naval literature, biography, Renaissance and 17th century literature. **SELECTED PUBLICATIONS** Transl, " Men and No," from the Catalan of Manuel de Pedrolo's "Homes i No," Modern Int Drama, Vol 10, No 1 (fall 76): 39-74; auth, "Limitary Patterns in 'Paradise Lost'," South Atlantic Modern Lang Asn, Atlanta (Nov 5, 76); auth, "William Bartram and the Romantics," Fla Col English Asn, Univ Fla, Gainsville (April 9, 77); auth, "King Lear III.ii.25-36: The Fool's Codpiece Song," in English Lang Notes, XXII No 2 (Dec 84): 16-19; ed with intro, Delilah, a novel by Marcus Goodrich, Annapolis: Naval Inst Press (85); auth, "Teaching the Renaissance: The Navy Way," Renaissance Soc of Am Renaissance News and Notes, Vol 8, No 2 (95): 2-3; auth, " 'Just Give Me the Facts': Influences of Individual Choice of Learning Strategy at a Military Academy," Teaching and Learning in the Next Century, ed Patricia Gandolfo, West Point (97); coauth with Robert Shenk, Admiral Dan Gallery: the Life and Wit of a Naval Original, Annapolis: Naval Inst Press (99); auth, "Cyrus Townsend Brady," "Edward Beach, Jr.," "Marcus Goodrich," "William P. Mack," "Hank Searles," and "Midshipman Literature," entries in An Encyclopedia of American Literature of the Sea and the Great Lakes, ed Jill Gidmark, et al, Greenwood Press (in press). **CONTACT ADDRESS** Dept English, United States Naval Acad, 107 Maryland Ave, Annapolis, MD 21402-1316. **EMAIL** gilliland@navy.nadn.mil

GILLILAND-SWETLAND, ANNE J.
PERSONAL Born 04/30/1959, Derry, Northern Ireland, m, 1990, 2 children **DISCIPLINE** ARCHIVAL SCIENCE **EDUCATION** Trinity Col, Univ Dublin, MA, 82; Univ Ill, Urbana-Champaign, cert of advan stud in libr and infor sci, 84; MS, 85; Univ Mich, PhD, 95. **CAREER** Archivist, Univ Cincinnati, 85-90; assoc archivist, Univ Mich, 91-92; adj lectr, Sch Libr Infor Sci, Univ Mich, 92-95; dir, Source LINK, Univ Mich Hist Ctr for Health Sci, 93-95; asst prof, Univ Calif, Los Angeles, Libr Infor Sci, 95- . **HONORS AND AWARDS** CFW Coker Awd, 98; Norton Awd, Midwest Arch Conf, 97; Mellon Found fel, 90, 95, 96; **MEMBERSHIPS** Midwest Arch Conf; Soc of Am Archivists; Asn Lib and Infor Sci Educators; Soc Calif Archivists. **SELECTED PUBLICATIONS** Auth, From Education to Application and Back: Archival Literature and an Electronic Records Curriculum, Am Archivist, 93; coauth, Uses of Electronic Communications to Document an Academic Community: A Research Report; Archivaria, 94; auth, Computer-based Communications and Archives: Documentary Opportunities Not to Be Missed, Archival Issues, 95; auth, Health Sciences Documentation and Networked Hypermedia: An Integrative Approach, Archivaria, 95; auth, Social Science Data Archives in the New World? Proceedings of For the Record Symposium, Royal Irish Academy and National Archives, 96; auth, Policy and Politics: A Case Study in the Management of Electronic Communications at the University of Michigan, Society of American Archivists, 96; auth, Defining Metadata, in, Introduction to Metadata: Pathways to Digital Information, Getty Information Institute, 98; auth, An Exploration of K-12 User Needs for Digital Primary Source Materials, Am Archivist, 98. **CONTACT ADDRESS** Graduate School of Education and Information Studi, Univ of California, Los Angeles, Los Angeles, CA 90095-1520. **EMAIL** swetland@ucla.edu

GILLINGHAM, BRYAN R.
PERSONAL Born 04/12/1944, Vancouver, BC, Canada **DISCIPLINE** MUSIC, HISTORY **EDUCATION** Univ BC, BA, 66, BMus, 68; Toronto Conserv, ARCT, 69; King's Col (UK), MMus, 71; Univ Wash, PhD, 76. **CAREER** Instr, Herdman Col & Memorial Univ, 70-72; lectr, Mt Allison Univ, 72-73; lectr, Univ Alta, 75-76; guest lectr, Univ Ottawa, 77-79; asst prof, 76-80, assoc ch, 80-84, ch, 84-91, prof music, Carleton Univ, 86-; dir, inst mediaeval music, 85-. **HONORS AND AWARDS** Scholarly Achievement Awds, Carleton Univ, 84, 88; Res Achievement Awd, 91. **RESEARCH** Medieval, renaissance and baroque music, early opera, and various aspects of music theory and analysis. **SELECTED PUBLICATIONS** Auth, The Polyphonic Sequences in Codex Wolfenbuttel, 82; auth, Saint-Martial Mehrstimmigkeit, 84; auth, Medieval Polyphonic Sequences, 85; auth, Modal Rhythm, 86; auth, Medieval Latin Song: An Anthology, 93; auth, Indices to the Notre-Dame Facsimiles, 94; auth, A Critical Study of Secular Medieval Latin Song, 95; co-ed, Beyond the Moon, 90. **CONTACT ADDRESS** School for Stud in Art and Cultural, Carleton Univ, 1125 Colonel By Dr, Ottawa, ON, Canada K1S 5B6. **EMAIL** bryan_gillingham@carleton.ca

GILLIS, CATHERINE L.
DISCIPLINE ENGLISH **EDUCATION** Univ Calif Riverside, BA, 95; MA, 97; ABD, 00. **CAREER** Instr, tutor, Chaffey Coll, 96-01; asst dir, Univ Calif, 99-01. **HONORS AND AWARDS** Kristine M. Scarano Mem Scholarship, 94; Phi Beta Kappa Awd, 95; Marshall Van Deusen Scholarship, 95; Outstanding TA Awd, 98-99. **MEMBERSHIPS** MLA, PAMLA. **RESEARCH** Shakespeare in Popular Culture, Mementos, relics, souvenirs and how they constitute aura (especially regarding Shakespeare). **SELECTED PUBLICATIONS** Auth, "History and Memory In Chaucer's Troilus and Criseyde," WVa Univ Philol Papers, (98); auth, "George Randolph Chester and Gustavus Dedman," Am Nat Biography, (98). **CONTACT ADDRESS** Univ of California, Riverside, University Ave, Riverside, CA 92521. **EMAIL** cathphone@hotmail.com

GILLIS, DANIEL J.
PERSONAL Born 09/25/1935, New Bedford, MA, s **DISCIPLINE** CLASSICS **EDUCATION** Harvard, AB, 57; Cornell Univ, MA, 59, PhD(classics), 63. **CAREER** Instr classics, Brown Univ, 59-60; asst prof, Univ Tex, 64-65 & Swathmore Col, 65-66; from ast prof to assoc prof, 66-76, Prof Classics, Haverford Col, 76-, Ger govt fel, Univ Munich, 63-64; Ford Found humanities res grant, 73. **MEMBERSHIPS** Am Philol Asn. **RESEARCH** Latin poetry; Roman history; Greek politics. **SELECTED PUBLICATIONS** Auth, Furtwangler Recalled, DeGraff, 66; Furtwangler and America, Manyland Bks, 70; Vita, Westworks, 79; Collaboration with the Persians, Steiner, 79; Measure of a Man, Iona Fdn, 82; Eros and Death in the Aeneid, Bretschneider, 82. **CONTACT ADDRESS** Dept of Classics, Haverford Col, 370 Lancaster Ave, Haverford, PA 19041-1392.

GILLMOR, ALAN
DISCIPLINE FRENCH MUSIC **EDUCATION** Univ Mich, MA, BM; Univ Toronto, PhD. **CAREER** Prof, Carleton Univ. **HONORS AND AWARDS** Distinguished tchg award, 82; Univ tchg award, 92; 3M tchg fel, 96. **RESEARCH** Life and works of the eccentric composer Erik Satie; contemporary experimental music, cultural identity as articulated through high-culture music. **SELECTED PUBLICATIONS** Auth, Erik Satie, Macmillan, 88; paperback ed, W.W. Norton, 92. **CONTACT ADDRESS** Carleton Univ, 1125 Colonel By Dr, Ottawa, ON, Canada K1S 5B6. **EMAIL** alan_gillmor@carleton.ca

GILLMOR, DONALD M.
DISCIPLINE MASS COMMUNICATION STUDIES **EDUCATION** Univ Minn, MA, PhD. **CAREER** Prof **SELECTED PUBLICATIONS** Auth, Power, Publicity and the Abuse of Libel Law, 92; co-auth, Mass Communication Law: Cases and Comment, 90; co-ed, Media Freedom and Accountability, 89. **CONTACT ADDRESS** Mass Communication Dept, Univ of Minnesota, Twin Cities, 111 Murphy Hall, 206 Church St SE, Minneapolis, MN 55455. **EMAIL** gillm001@maroon.tc.umn.edu

GILLON, ADAM
PERSONAL Born 07/17/1921, Kovel, Poland, m, 1946, 2 children **DISCIPLINE** ENGLISH AND COMPARATIVE LITERATURE **EDUCATION** Hebrew Univ, Jerusalem, MA, 48; Columbia Univ, PhD, 54. **CAREER** Lectr English, Sch Higher Studies, Jerusalem, 44-45; lectr English lang and lit, Hascalla Col, prin and teacher English, Montefiore Tech High Sch, Tel-Aviv, 49-50; instr English, Univ Kans, 56-57; assoc prof, Acadia Univ, 58-59, prof and head dept, 59-61; prof English and World Lit, 61-80, EMER PROF ENGLISH, STATE UNIV NY, NEW PALTZ, 80-; PROF ENGLISH LIT, UNIV HAIFA, ISRAEL, 81-, Can Res Coun grant-in-aid, 61; Polish ser ed, Twayne's World Auth Ser, 64-, Hebrew ser, 65-; State Univ NY Res Found res grants-in-aid, 65, 66, 68, 70 and 72-73; Alfred Jurzykowski Found award, 67; US Govt res grant, Israel, 68-69; Joseph Fels Found res grant, Israel, 68-69; ed, Joseph Conrad Today. **MEMBERSHIPS** Joseph Conrad Soc Am (pres, 75-82); MLA; Am Comp Lit Asn; NCTE; Int Comp Lit Asn. **RESEARCH** English, American, Polish, Russian and Hebrew literatures; creative writing of fiction, poetry and drama comparative and world literature. **SELECTED PUBLICATIONS** Auth, The 'Affair in Marseilles,' Another Polish Novel about Conrad, Conradiana, Vol 0025, 93. **CONTACT ADDRESS** Dept of English and World Lit, SUNY, New Paltz, New Paltz, NY 12561.

GILMAN, ERNEST B.
PERSONAL Born 04/20/1946, Denver, CO, m, 1968, 2 children **DISCIPLINE** ENGLISH LITERATURE **EDUCATION** Columbia Univ, BA, 68, MA, 71, PhD(English), 76. **CAREER** Asst prof English, Univ Va, 75-81; ASST PROF ENGLISH, NY UNIV, 81-. **MEMBERSHIPS** MLA. **RESEARCH** Renaissance literature and the visual arts. **SELECTED PUBLICATIONS CONTACT ADDRESS** Dept English, New York Univ, 19 University Pl, New York, NY 10003-4556.

GILMAN, OWEN W.
PERSONAL Born 04/02/1947, Farmington, ME, m, 1977, 2 children **DISCIPLINE** ENGLISH **EDUCATION** Univ NC, Chapel Hill, PhD eng 79, MA 73; Bowdoin Col, ME, AB eng 69. **CAREER** St Joseph's Univ, prof eng 79-, dept ch 97. **HONORS AND AWARDS** Linback Awd Excell in Tchg. **MEMBERSHIPS** MLA; SAMLA. **RESEARCH** Vietnam war lit; southern lit; native writing in Am. **SELECTED PUBLICATIONS** Vietnam and the Southern Imagination, Univ Press MS, 92; America Rediscovered; Critical essays on lit and films of the Vietnam War, with Lorrie Smith, Garland, 90; Barry Hannah, in: Contem Fic Writers of the South, Greenwood Press, 93. **CONTACT ADDRESS** Dept of Eng, Saint Joseph's Univ, 5600 City Av, Philadelphia, PA 19131. **EMAIL** mthrice@sju.edu

GILSON, JOAN
PERSONAL Born 08/20/1945, Kansas City, MO, m, 1965, 2 children **DISCIPLINE** HIGHER EDUCATION ADMINISTRATION, ENGLISH LANGUAGE, LITERATURE **EDUCATION** Univ Ark, BA, 65; Univ Missou, MA, 85; PhD, 94. **CAREER** Instr, Univ Missou, 82-95; adj assoc prof, John CCC, 95-. **HONORS AND AWARDS** Sosland Awd; Helen Kemper Doc Fel; Outstand Edu Diss; Leiberman Awd. **RESEARCH** Teaching of writing; organizational cultures. **SELECTED PUBLICATIONS** Auth, "The Service Learning Journal: A Resource Guide for Teachers," Am Asn Comm Coll (99); auth, From Weet to RW Jones: Letters from Home, 1861-1863 (93); auth, "An Overview of Student Development Theories: Their Relevance for Today's Student, " ERIC (91); auth, "Reconstructive Reflective Teaching: A Review of the Literature," ERIC (90); auth, "Values Education: Collaborative Efforts Between Academic Affairs and Student Services," ERIC (90); auth, "The Written English Proficiency Test at The University of Missouri-Kansas City," ERIC (91); coauth, "Collaborative Revision Groups and the Basic Writer," ERIC (88). **CONTACT ADDRESS** Dept Communications, Johnson County Comm Col, 12345 College Blvd, Shawnee-Mission, KS 66210-1283. **EMAIL** jgilson@jccc.net

GINDELE, KAREN C.
PERSONAL Born 11/08/1951, Scott City, KS, s **DISCIPLINE** ENGLISH **EDUCATION** Vassar Col, AB, 81; Brown Univ, PhD, 92. **CAREER** From Asst Prof to Assoc Prof, Ind Univ, 94-. **MEMBERSHIPS** MLA, Midwest Victorian Studies Asn, MMLA. **RESEARCH** Victorian fiction and culture, feminist theory, literary and cultural theory. **SELECTED PUBLICATIONS** Auth, "When Women Laugh Wildly and (Gentle) Men Roar: Victorian Embodiments of Laughter," in Look Who's Laughing: Gender and Comedy (Langhorne, PA: Gordon and Breach, 94), 139-160; auth, "The Web of Necessity: George Eliot's Theory of Ideology," in Tex Studies in Lit and Lang (99); auth, "Wonders Taken for Signs: Marian and Fosco in 'The Woman in White'," in Dickens Studies Annual (00); auth, "Desire and Deconstruction: Reclaiming Centers," in Dickens Studies Annual (00); **CONTACT ADDRESS** Dept English, Indiana Univ, South Bend, PO Box 7111, South Bend, IN 46634-7111. **EMAIL** kgindele@iusb.edu

GINGERY, GAIL ALVAH
PERSONAL Born 02/02/1928, Princeton, IL, m, 1954, 2 children **DISCIPLINE** VOCAL MUSIC **EDUCATION** Bob Jones Univ, BA, 51, MA, 53; Boston Univ, DMA, 65. **CAREER** Chairman, Div of Music, 56-81, Head, Dept of Voice, Bob Jones Univ, 76-98; regional governor, SE Region of Nat Asn of Teachers of Singing, 67-71; Minister of Music in several churches, incl 25 years at Faith Free Presbyterian Church, Greenville, SC. **HONORS AND AWARDS** Tenor soloist in numerous oratorio performances; tenor roles in Barber of Seville, Magic Flute, Don Pasquale, and in portions of La Traviata and La Boheme. **MEMBERSHIPS** Nat Asn of Teachers of Singing. **RESEARCH** 17th Century Italian Cantata: Dissertation: Solo Cantatas of Alessandro Stradella in MS; 32 E-11 of Fitzwilliam Museum, Cambridge. **CONTACT ADDRESS** 12 Sennet Dr., Greenville, SC 29609-5111. **EMAIL** ggingery@bju.edu

GINSBERG, ELAINE KANER
PERSONAL Born 02/29/1936, New York, NY, d, 3 children **DISCIPLINE** AMERICAN LITERATURE, WOMEN WRITERS **EDUCATION** Trinity Univ, BA, 57; Univ Okla, MA, 66, PhD(English), 71. **CAREER** Instr, Univ Okla, 67-68; asst prof, 68-75, assoc prof English, 75-84, chmn dept, 78-84; asst vp, W VA Univ, 84-89; fel, Am Antiquarian Soc, 76, 90; chair, Grad Studies Forum, SAtlantic Mod Lang Asn, 81-82; evaluator, Humanities Found of WVa, 81-; consultant Evaluator, North Cen Assn of Cols and Schools, 89. **MEMBERSHIPS** MLA; Am Studies Asn; pres Women's Caucus of Mod Lang Assn, 98. **RESEARCH** American fiction; British and American women writers; Colonial American literature. **SELECTED PUBLICATIONS** Auth, The female initiation theme in American literature, Studies in Am Fiction, 75; Style and identification in Common Sense, WVa Philol Papers, 77; contribr, American Literature, 1764-1789, Univ Wis Press, 77; American Women Writers: A Critical Reference Guide, Vols I, II & IV, Frederick Ungar Publ Co, 79-82; Toward the Second Decade, Greenwood Press, 81; co-ed, Virginia Woolf: Centennial Essays, Whitston Publ Co, Inc, 83; contrib Anti-Feminism in the Acedemy, Fuoutlege, 96; ed, Passing and the Fictions of Identity, Duke Univ Pr, 96. **CONTACT ADDRESS** Dept of English, West Virginia Univ, Morgantown, PO Box 6296, Morgantown, WV 26506-6296. **EMAIL** eginsber@wvu.edu

GINSBERG, LESLEY
DISCIPLINE ENGLISH **EDUCATION** Calif at Berkeley, BA, 87; Stanford Univ, PhD, 97. **MEMBERSHIPS** Am Antiquarian Soc **RESEARCH** Childhood & love in Am lit **CONTACT ADDRESS** 2035 Bowdoin St, Palo Alto, CA 94306-1211.

GIRAL, ANGELA
PERSONAL Born Madrid, Spain, 2 children **DISCIPLINE** LIBRARY SCIENCE **EDUCATION** Univ Mich, MSLS, 58. **CAREER** Ref libn, Biblioteca Central, Universidad Nacional Autonoma Mexico, 55-56; book scout, Princeton Univ in Brazil, 64-65; sr cataloger, 62-64, 65-67, libn, Urban And Environ Studies Library, Sch Archit Urban Planning, 67-75, Princeton Univ; upper school libn, Escola Americana, Rio de Janeiro, Brazil, 64-65; chief libn, Frances Loeb Library, Harvard Univ Grad Sch Design, 75-82; acting head, Sci and Eng Div, Columbia Univ Libraries, 90-91; acting asst vp human resources in info sci, 94-95, dir, 82-, Avery Archit Fine Arts Library, Columbia Univ. **HONORS AND AWARDS** Elected rep, Columbia Univ Senate, 98-01; principal invest, grant, Guastavino/Collins Archive Cataloguing and Preservation Project, Natl Endow Humanities, Getty Grant Prog, Gladys Kieble Delmas Found, 93-96; elected, Standing Comm Section Art Libraries Intl Fed. Library Assns Insts, 93. **MEMBERSHIPS** Intl Confed Archit Museums, 98-01, sec gen, 93-98; bd mem, Intl Coun Archit Museums, 91-; Athenaeum of Philadelphia on "Philadelphia Architects and Buildings Project," Steering Comm, 98; Columbia Univ Res Libraries Group Digital Image Access Project, 93-94; New York State Archit Records Needs Assessment Project, 92-93. **RESEARCH** Information science; technological advances in the study and research of art history and architecture. **SELECTED PUBLICATIONS** Auth, foreword to My Father Who Is on Earth, 94; coauth, "The Virtual Museum Comes to Campus: Two Perspectives on the Museum Educational Site Licensing Project," Art Libraries Journ, 96; auth, foreword, The Old World Builds the New: the Guastavino Company and the Technology of the Catalan Vault, 1885-1962, 96; auth, Avery's Choice: Five Centuries of Great Architectural Books, A Hundred Years of an Architectural Library, 97; ed, ICAM8 Proceedings, 98. **CONTACT ADDRESS** Avery Library, Columbia Univ, 1172 Amsterdam Ave, MC-0301, New York, NY 10027. **EMAIL** giral@columbia.edu

GIRGUS, SAM B.
DISCIPLINE FILM STUDIES, AMERICAN LITERATURE **EDUCATION** Univ NMex, PhD. **CAREER** Instr, Vanderbilt Univ. **SELECTED PUBLICATIONS** Auth, The Films of Woody Allen; Desire and the Political Unconscious; The New Covenant; The Law of the Heart; ed, The American Self. **CONTACT ADDRESS** Vanderbilt Univ, Nashville, TN 37235-1727. **EMAIL** sam.b.girgus@vanderbilt.edu

GIRON, ROBERT L.
PERSONAL Born 05/10/1952, Sidney, NE, s **DISCIPLINE** ENGLISH **EDUCATION** Univ Tex, BA, 73; Sout Ill Univ, MA, 75. **CAREER** Prof, Montgomery Col, 86-. **HONORS AND AWARDS** Nat Inst for Staff & Org Dev Excellence Awd, Austin, 97; Effective Team Awd, Montgomery Col, 94. **MEMBERSHIPS** AAUP, Nat Asn of English Teachers, Teachers of English to Speakers of Other Lang, Wash Indep Writers. **RESEARCH** Gender Studies, Linguistics, Creative writing. **SELECTED PUBLICATIONS** Auth, Songs for the Spirit, 00; auth, Metamorphosis of the Serpent God, 99; auth, Wrestling with Word, 99; auth, Recuerdes, 99; auth, Impressions Francaises, 98. **CONTACT ADDRESS** Dept English & Languages, Montgomery Col, Takoma Park, 7600 Takoma Ave, Takoma Park, MD 20912-4141. **EMAIL** robtx@erols.com

GISH, NANCY K.
PERSONAL Born 09/28/1942, Circleville, OH **DISCIPLINE** ENGLISH AND WOMAN'S STUDIES **EDUCATION** PhD, Eng, Univ Michigan, 73. **CAREER** Univ Southern Maine, Dir woman's Studies Prog, 95-, Prof, 85, Assoc Prof, 82-85, Asst Prof, 80-82; Dir Womans Studies, 87-89, Acting Dir Women's Studies Prog, Univ So ME, 85-86; Asst Prof, Univ Penn, 73-79; Coordin Rhetoric Inst, Univ Penn, 78-79; Lect, Univ Michigan, 72-73; Instr, Wayne State Univ, 66-72. **HONORS AND AWARDS** Russell Chair in Edu and Philos, 92-94; Schol to Sch of Criticism and Theory, 87; Univ southern ME Summer Faculty Fellowship, 84; Convocation Schol, 82-83; NEH Fellow, 79-80. **MEMBERSHIPS** MLA; ME Women's Studies Consortium. **RESEARCH** Mod and Contemp Poetry; Ident and Subjectivity; Scot Lit and Cult; Women's Poetry; Cross-cultural poetic Experimentation. **SELECTED PUBLICATIONS** Hugh MacDiarmid: Man and Poet, Nat Poet Found, Orono, Univ Edinburgh P, Edinburgh, 92; The Waste Land: A Poem of Memory and Desire, Twyane, Boston, 88; Hugh MacDiarmid: The Man and His Work, Macmillan, London, 84; Time in the Poetry of T S Elliot, Macmillan, London, 81. **CONTACT ADDRESS** 53 Lawn Ave, Portland, ME 04103. **EMAIL** ngish@usm.maine.edu

GISH, ROBERT F.
PERSONAL Born 04/01/1940, Albuquerque, NM, m, 1968, 3 children **DISCIPLINE** ENGLISH LITERATURE **EDUCATION** Univ New Mexico, PhD 72. **CAREER** Cal Poly, dir, prof, 91-00; Univ N Iowa, prof, 67-91. **HONORS AND AWARDS** Erna Fergusson Dist Alum Awd. **MEMBERSHIPS** PEN/WEST; Authors Guild; WALA; WWA. **RESEARCH** American Literature; ethnic literature; American West. **SELECTED PUBLICATIONS** Auth, Dreams of Quivira: Stories in Search of the Golden West, Clear Light Pub, 97; auth, Beautiful Swift Fox: Erna Fergusson and the Southwest, Texas A&M Univ Press, 96; auth, Bad Boys and Black Sheep: Fateful Tales from the West, Texas A&M Univ, 96; auth, Beyond Bounds: Cross Cultural Essays on Anglo American Indian and Chicano Literature, Univ New Mexico Press, 96; auth, Granada: Paul Horgan and the Southwest, Texas A&M Univ Press, 95; auth, When Coyote Howls: A Lavaland Fable, U of NM Press, 94; auth, First Horses: Stories of the New West, U of Nevada Press, 93; auth, William Carlos Williams: The Short Fiction, GK Hall 89. **CONTACT ADDRESS** PO Box 12562, Albuquerque, NM 87195. **EMAIL** bob@riobosque.com

GISSENDANNER, JOHN M.
PERSONAL Born 08/13/1939, d **DISCIPLINE** ENGLISH **EDUCATION** San Francisco State Univ, San Francisco, CA, BA, 1971, MA, 1972; Univ of California, San Diego, PhD, 1982. **CAREER** California State University, San Diego, CA, assistant professor, 72-75; Towson State University, Towson, MD, assistant professor, beginning 1975, associate professor, 91-98, prof, 98. **HONORS AND AWARDS** University Merit Awd, Towson State University, 1989; San Diego Fellowship Awd, University of California, San Diego, 1971-74; Ford Foundation Fellowship Awd, University of California, San Diego, 1973-74. **MEMBERSHIPS** American Association of University Professors, 1972-; National Association for the Advancement of Colored People, 1982-; Middle-Atlantic Writers' Association, 1978-; National Collegiate Honors Council, 1980-; Maryland Writers Council, 1980-. **CONTACT ADDRESS** English Dept, Towson State Univ, Towson, MD 21204.

GIULIANO, MICHAEL J.
DISCIPLINE COMMUNICATION **EDUCATION** Northwestern Univ, PhD, 93. **CAREER** Instr, Tenn Temple Univ, 81-84; asst prof, Trinity Col, 84-91; asst prof, Westmont Col, 91-. **RESEARCH** Film criticism; mass commun; commun ethics; televangelism. **SELECTED PUBLICATIONS** Auth, Reel History, Nixon, Audience Analysis in Debate; Prima Facie: A Guide to Value Debate; Smashing the Stone: When Christians Say Right Things in Wrong Ways. **CONTACT ADDRESS** Dept of Commun, Westmont Col, 955 La Paz Rd', Santa Barbara, CA 93108-1099.

GIVNER, JOAN
PERSONAL Born Manchester, England **DISCIPLINE** ENGLISH **EDUCATION** London Univ, BA, 58, PhD, 72; Univ St. Louis, MA, 63. **CAREER** High sch tchr, 59-61; lectr, Port Huron Jr Col, 61-65; lectr to assoc prof, 65-81, PROF ENGLISH, UNIV REGINA, 81-95. **HONORS AND AWARDS** Mary Ingraham Bunting Fel, Radcliffe Col, 79; Herbert M. Umbach Awd, 79; Awd Excellence Res, Univ Regina Alumni Asn, 92. **SELECTED PUBLICATIONS** Auth, Katherine Anne Porter: A Life, 82; auth, Tentacles of Unreason, 85; auth, Unfortunate Incidents, 88; auth, Scenes From Provincial Life, 91; auth, In the Garden of Henry James, 96. **CONTACT ADDRESS** English Dept, Univ of Regina, 3737 Wascana Pkwy Dr, Regina, SK, Canada S4S 0A2.

GLADISH, ROBERT WILLIS
PERSONAL Born 02/19/1931, Colchester, England, m, 1962, 4 children **DISCIPLINE** ENGLISH **EDUCATION** Univ Chicago, MA, 56, PhD(English), 64. **CAREER** Instr English, Tex A&M Univ, 56-58; from instr to assoc prof, Univ Ill, Chicago Circle, 60-71; head, Dept English, 71-77, dean, Col of Acad of The New Church, 77-; dean, Bryn Athyn Coll New Church 77-89; prof Emeritus, 96. **MEMBERSHIPS** MLA; AAUP. **RESEARCH** Nineteenth century English language and literature. **SELECTED PUBLICATIONS** Auth, Mrs Browning's contributions to the New York Independent, Bull NY Pub Libr, 1/67; Mrs Browning's A Curse for a Nation, Victorian Poetry, Autumn 69; Elizabeth Barrett and the Centurion, Baylor Browning Interests, 1/73. **CONTACT ADDRESS** Bryn Athyn Col, PO Box 717, Bryn Athyn, PA 19009-0717.

GLANCY, DIANE
PERSONAL Born 03/18/1941, Kansas City, MO, d, 2 children **DISCIPLINE** ENGLISH **EDUCATION** Univ Missouri, Columbia, BA, English lit, 64; Univ Iowa, writer's workshop, MFA, 88. **CAREER** Artist-in-residence, State Arts Coun Oklahoma, 80-86; assoc prof, English, Macalester Coll, 88-; Native American Inroads Mentor, The Loft, 97; Edelstein-Keller Minnesota Visiting Writer of Distinction, Univ Minn, 98. **HONORS AND AWARDS** Lannan Found Fellowship, Provincetown Art Center, MA, 95; Career Initiative Grant, The Loft, 96; Minnesota Humanities Commission Grant, 97; Playwriting Awd, prose, Wordcraft Circle of Native Writers, 97; Sundance Native Amer Screenwriting Fellowship, Univ Calif Los Angeles, 98. **MEMBERSHIPS** Poetry Soc Am; Associated Writing Programs; Modern Lang Assn. **RESEARCH** Writing; Native American critical thought. **SELECTED PUBLICATIONS** Auth, The Only Piece of Furniture in the House, 96; auth, The West Pole, 97; auth, Pushing the Bear, a Novel of the Trail of Tears, 98; auth, Flutie, 98; auth, The Cold-and-Hunger Dance, 98; auth, The Voice that Was in Travel, Univ of Okla Press (Norman, OK), 99; auth, Fuller Man, Moyer Bell (Wakefield, RI), 99; auth, The Closets of Heaven, Chax Press (Tucson), 99; auth, (Ado)ration, Chax Press (Tucson), 99; co-ed, Visit Teepee Town, Native Writing After the Detours, Coffee House Press (Minneapolis), 99; auth, The Relief of America, Tia Chucha Press (Chicago), 00. **CONTACT ADDRESS** 261 Brimhall, Saint Paul, MN 55105. **EMAIL** glancy@macalester.edu

GLANVILLE, PRISCILLA J.
PERSONAL Born 10/21/1969, Bar Harbor, ME, m, 2001 **DISCIPLINE** BRITISH LITERATURE **EDUCATION** Univ SFla Sarasota, BS, 96; Univ SFla Tampa, MA, 98; PhD, 01. **CAREER** Instr, Univ SFla, 96-. **HONORS AND AWARDS** Phi Kappa Phi Outstanding Graduate Student, 98; Provost's Award for Outstanding Teaching, 00. **MEMBERSHIPS** MLA, NEA, Tennyson Soc. **RESEARCH** British Literature 1500-1660 and 1780-1900, Active Collaborative Learning. **SELECTED PUBLICATIONS** Auth, "Moses Got the Blues: Langston Hughes in the Harlem Renaissance," Young Voices of the World, (Fukui, Japan: Fukui Univ Pr, 96); auth, "Caomposition's Most Comprehensive Web Sites," Text Tech: Jour of Computer Text Processing, (Ohio: Wright State Univ Pr, 97); auth, "Hunter Thompson," The Sixties in America, (Salem Pr, 99); auth, "John Turvil Adams," "John Wannuacon Quinney," "Samual Hopkins Adams," "John rollins Ridge," Encycl of Am War Lit, (NY: Greenwood Pr, 00); auth, Tennyson's Maud: Cultural, Critical, and Literary Contexts, (forthcoming). **EMAIL** pglanvil@chuma.cas.usf.edu

GLASER, HOLLIS F.
PERSONAL Born 12/08/1959, Champaign, IL, s **DISCIPLINE** COMMUNICATION **EDUCATION** Washington Univ, BA, 82; Univ Ill, PhD(Organizational Commun), 94. **CAREER** From asst prof to assoc prof, commun, Univ Nebr-Omaha, 94-. **MEMBERSHIPS** Nat Commun Asn. **RESEARCH** Sustainable food systems; democratic groups. **SELECTED PUBLICATIONS** Coauth, Bureaucatic Discourse and the Goddess: Toward an Ecofeminist Critique and Rearticulation, J Org Change & Management, 92; coauth, An Interdisciplinary Approach to Engendering Jewish Religious History, Shofar: An Interdisciplinary J Judaic Studies 5, 95; auth, Structure and Struggle in Egalitarian Groups: Dimensions of Power Relations, Small Group Res 27, 96; auth, Focusing the Students on Three Speech Topics, The Speech Communication Teacher: Ideas, Research, and Strategies for Learning 12, 98; auth, Organizing against Sexual Violence, in Sexual Aggression: Key Research and Activism, Charles C. Thomas (forthcoming); auth, A Multi-cultural Public Speaking Final Examination, The Speech Communication Teacher: Ideas, Research, and Strategies for Learning (forthcoming). **CONTACT ADDRESS** Dept Commun, Univ of Nebraska, Omaha, 6001 Dodge St., Omaha, NE 68182-0112. **EMAIL** Hollis@unomaha.edu

GLASSER, THEODORE L.
DISCIPLINE COMMUNICATIONS **EDUCATION** Univ IA, PhD, 79. **CAREER** Fac, Univ MN, 81-89; assoc dir Silha Ctr Study Media Ethics Law, Univ MN; Assoc prof, Stanford Univ, 90. **HONORS AND AWARDS** Hillier Krieghbaum Awd, Assoc Educ Jour Mass Comm, 87; sr Fulbright scholar, Israel, 92-93; vpres/ch mass commun div, int comm ass. **MEMBERSHIPS** Int Comm Ass; Assoc Ed Jour Mass Comm. **RESEARCH** Press practices and performance, with emphasis on questions of media responsibility and accountability. **SELECTED PUBLICATIONS** Auth, academic and professional publications, including Journalism & Mass Communication Quarterly, Journal of Communication, Journal of Broadcasting & Electronic Media, Critical Studies in Mass Communication, Policy Sciences, Communication and the Law, The Quill, and The Nieman Reports; co-ed, Public Opinion and the Communication of Consent, Guilford, 95. **CONTACT ADDRESS** Dept Commun, Stanford Univ, McClatchy Hall, Stanford, CA 94305.

GLASSMAN, STEVE
PERSONAL Born 09/04/1946, Hays, KS, s **DISCIPLINE** CREATIVE WRITING, ENGLISH **EDUCATION** Univ Southwest La, MA, 81; Vermont Col, MFA, 83. **CAREER** Lectr, Univ Tex at Austin; assoc prof, Embry Riddle Aeron Univ, 84-. **RESEARCH** Florida Studies, Creative Writing, Crime Fiction. **SELECTED PUBLICATIONS** Auth, Blood on the Moon: A Novel of Old Florida, Quality Publications, 90; auth, Zora in Florida, Univ Press of Fla, 91; ed, Crime Fiction and Film in the Sunshine State, Popular Press, 97. **CONTACT ADDRESS** Dept Humanities & Soc Sci, Embry-Riddle Aeronautical Univ, 600 S Clyde Morris Blvd, Daytona Beach, FL 32114-3966. **EMAIL** sglass8404@aol.com

GLAVAC, CYNTHIA
DISCIPLINE ENGLISH LITERATURE **EDUCATION** Bowling Green State Univ, PhD, 92. **CAREER** Assoc prof. **RESEARCH** Women's and world literature. **SELECTED PUBLICATIONS** Auth, In the Fullness of Life: A Biography of Dorothy Kazel, OSU. **CONTACT ADDRESS** Dept of English, Ursuline Col, 2550 Lander Road, Pepper Pike, OH 44124. **EMAIL** cglavac@ursuline.edu

GLAVIN, JOHN
DISCIPLINE ENGLISH LITERATURE **EDUCATION** Georgetown Univ, BA; Bryn Mawr Col, MA, PhD. **CAREER** Assoc prof. **RESEARCH** 19th century British literature by women; literary theory. **SELECTED PUBLICATIONS** Auth, Intimacies of Instruction, Univ New England, 95; Fay Weldon: Leader of the Frivolous Band, Univ New England; Pickwick on the wrong side of the door, Dickens Studies Annual, 93; Caught in the Act: or The Prosing of Juliet, Harvester, 91. **CONTACT ADDRESS** English Dept, Georgetown Univ, 37th and O St, Washington, DC 20057.

GLAZENER, NANCY K.
PERSONAL Born 12/10/1961, Amarillo, TX, m, 1984, 2 children **DISCIPLINE** ENGLISH **EDUCATION** Cornell Univ, BA, 83; Stanford Univ, PhD, 90. **CAREER** Asst to assoc prof, Univ of Pittsburgh, 90-. **MEMBERSHIPS** MLA, Am Studies Assoc, Soc for Critical Exchange, Soc for the Study of Narrative. **RESEARCH** 19th and 20th Century US Literature, ethics and literature, feminist approaches to literature. **SELECTED PUBLICATIONS** Auth, Reading for Realism: The History of a US Literary Institution, 1850-1910, Duke Univ Pr, 97. **CONTACT ADDRESS** Dept English, Univ of Pittsburgh, Pittsburgh, PA 15260. **EMAIL** glazener@pitt.edu

GLAZIER, LOSS PEQUENO
DISCIPLINE ENGLISH, LITERATURE **EDUCATION** Univ Calif Berkeley, BA, 75; MLIS, 85; MA, 86; SUNY Buffalo, PhD, 96. **CAREER** Curator, ALC, 86-88; bibliog to webmaster to assoc fac to adj assoc prof to fac to dir, SUNY Buffalo, 88-. **HONORS AND AWARDS** Digital Write in Residence, NYork Found for Arts, 00-01; SOS Grants, 99, 00; Elizabeth Agee Prize, 99; Harold Lancour Scholar, 98; Beta Phi Mu, ILISHS; Just Buffalo Lit Cen, Writer in Residence, 92. **RESEARCH** Digital literature. **SELECTED PUBLICATIONS** Auth, All's Normal Here: A Charles Bukowski Primer, Ruddy Dick Pr, 85; auth, Prayer Wheels of Bluewater: The Geographies, Opus 18, Ocean View Pr, 87; ed, "Concerning the Muse: A Convocation of L.A.," Poets, Am Lit Col (88); auth, Vowels and Single Vase (Walnut Creek: Entre Deux Cotes, 90); auth, Small Pr: An Annotated Guide, Greenwood Pub, 92; auth, The Parts, Meow Pr, 95; auth, Leaving Loss Glazier, Parisan Pr, 97; auth, White-Faced Bromeliads on 20 Hectares, Spontan Gen, 01; auth, Digital Poetics: The Making of E-Poetries, Univ Ala Pr, 01. **CONTACT ADDRESS** 1540 Hopkins Rd, Williamsville, NY 14221-1750. **EMAIL** glazier@acsu.buffalo.edu

GLAZIER, LYLE EDWARD
PERSONAL Born 05/08/1911, Leverett, MA, m, 1939, 3 children **DISCIPLINE** ENGLISH **EDUCATION** Middlebury Col, AB, 33; Bread Loaf Sch English, AM, 37; Harvard Univ, PhD, 50. **CAREER** Prin graded sch, Northfield, Mass, 34-35; instr & housemaster, Mt Hermon Sch, 35-37; instr English, Bates Col, 37-42 & Tufts Col, 42-44; teaching fel, Harvard Univ, 45-47; from asst prof to assoc prof English & chm Am studies, 52-63, prof English, 65-72, EMER PROF ENGLISH, STATE UNIV NY BUFFALO, 72- . **HONORS AND AWARDS** Am Coun Learned Soc fac fel, 51-52; Fulbright prof & chm, Dept Am Lit, Univ Istanbul, 61-63; Fulbright lectr, Hacettepe Univ, Ankara, 68-69, vis prof 70, 71; Fulbright prof Univ Madras, India, 70, 71; USIS vol expert in Am Lit, India, 71; vis prof, Sana'a Univ, Yemen Arab Repub, fall 80; IS, United States Info Service. **MEMBERSHIPS** MLA; Am Studies Asn. **RESEARCH** American fiction; poetry; Black literature. **SELECTED PUBLICATIONS** Auth, Orchard Park and Istanbul (poems), Big Mountain Press, Swallow, 65; You Too (poems), 69, The Dervishes (poems), 71 & VD (poems), 71, Istanbul Matbaasi; Decadence and Rebirth, Hacettepe Univ, 71; Stills from a Moving Picture, Paunch, (novel), 74; Two Continents (poems), Vt Coun Arts, 76; auth, Great Day Coming, Raaj Prakashan, 87; auth, Summer for Joey, (novel), 88; auth, Searching for Amy, (poem), Lanside Press, 00; auth, Papers Collected, Abernethy Collection, Middlebury Col, 00. **CONTACT ADDRESS** 608 Niles Rd, Bennington, VT 05201-8777.

GLEASON, MAUDE
DISCIPLINE CLASSICS **EDUCATION** BA, 75; Oxford Univ, MA, 77; Univ CA Berkeley, PhD, 90. **CAREER** Lctr, Stanford Univ. **RESEARCH** Relig and soc in Late Antiquity and the High Empire; rhetoric; gender. **SELECTED PUBLICATIONS** Auth, Festive Satire: Julian's Misopogon and the New Year at Antioch, JRS, 86; The Semiotics of Gender: Physiognomy and Self-Fashioning in Before Sexuality, 90; Making Men: Sophists and Self-Presentation in the Roman Empire, 95. **CONTACT ADDRESS** Stanford Univ, Bldg 20, Main Quad, Stanford, CA 94305.

GLEASON, PAUL W.
PERSONAL Born 09/14/1973, Milwaukee, WI, m, 1996 **DISCIPLINE** ENGLISH **EDUCATION** Univ Wis-Mad, BA, 95; Univ Tex-Austin, MA, 98; PhD, 00. **CAREER** Teach asst, Univ Tex, 96-97; mang ed, D. H. Lawrence Rev, 97-99; asst instr, Univ Tex, 99-00; pt asst prof, Southwest Univ, 01-. **MEMBERSHIPS** MLA; IJJF; Samuel Beckett Soc; Don DeLillo Soc; D.H. Lawrence Soc. **RESEARCH** Aesthetic philosophy and literature; contemporary historical novel; mythology and the twentieth-century novel; depictions of celebrity in the contemporary novel; the modernist novel; the postmodernist novel; James Joyce; D.H. Lawrence; Samuel Beckett; Salman Rushdie; Don DeLillo. **SELECTED PUBLICATIONS** Auth, "Dante, Joyce, Beckett and the Use of Memory in the Process of Literary Creation," Joyce Studies (99); auth, "A Note on Plato and Aaron's Rod," Lawr Rev 27 (97); rev, "The Novel in England, 1900-1950: History and Theory," by Robert L. Caserio, D.H. Lawr Rev 29 (00); auth, "Don DeLillo, T.S. Eliot, and the Redemption of America's Atomic Waste Land," in UnderWords (Univ Del Press, forthcoming). **CONTACT ADDRESS** Eng Dept., Southwestern Univ, Georgetown, TX 78627-0770. **EMAIL** gleasonpaul@earthlink.net

GLECKNER, ROBERT F.
PERSONAL Born 03/02/1925, Rahway, NJ, m, 1946, 2 children **DISCIPLINE** ENGLISH LITERATURE **EDUCATION** Johns Hopkins Univ, PhD, 54; William Col, BA, 48. **CAREER** English, Univ of Cincinnati, 52-54; Univ of Wisconsin, 54-57; Wayne State Univ, 57-62; Univ of Calif (Riverside), 62-78; Duke Univ, 78-. **HONORS AND AWARDS** Poetry Soc of Am Award for best Blake bk, 57; NEH Res Fel, 80-81; Keats-Shelley Soc Distinguished Scholar Award, 91. **MEMBERSHIPS** Byron Soc; Wordsworth-Coleridge Asn; Keats-Shelley Asn; Asn of Literary Scholars and Critics, et al. **RESEARCH** Romantics. **SELECTED PUBLICATIONS** Auth, The Piper and the Bard: William Blake, Wayne State Univ Press, 57; auth, Byron and the Ruins of Paradise, Johns Hopkins, 67; auth, Blakes Prelude: Poetical Sketches, Johns Hopkins, 82; auth, Blake and Spenser, Johns Hopkins, 85; co-ed, Critical Essays on Byron, GK Hall, 91; auth, Gray Agonistes: Thomas Gray and Masculine Friendship, Johns Hopkins, 96; coed, The Lessons of Romanticism, Duke Univ Press, 98. **CONTACT ADDRESS** Eng Dept, Duke Univ, Box 90015, Durham, NC 27708.

GLENN, GEORGE D.
DISCIPLINE THEATRE HISTORY **EDUCATION** Univ IL, PhD. **CAREER** Prof, ch, grad prog, dept Theater, dir, Iowa Regents London prog, Univ Northern IA, 91/92. **MEMBERSHIPS** Pres, Mid-Am Theatre Conf. **SELECTED PUBLICATIONS** Publ in a variety of areas from nautical drama to the use of firearms on stage. **CONTACT ADDRESS** Dept of Theatre, Univ of No Iowa, Cedar Falls, IA 50614.

GLENNY, SHARON
DISCIPLINE MUSIC HISTORY **EDUCATION** Western Conserv London, AMus; McMaster Univ, BMus; Ma; SUNY Buffalo, PhD. **CAREER** Adj lctr, 96, SUNY Binghamton. **RESEARCH** Music hist and theory; music criticism; Morton Feldman. **SELECTED PUBLICATIONS** Auth, Cyclic Form in Debussy's Nocturnes, Cahiers Debussy, 96. **CONTACT ADDRESS** Dept Music, SUNY, Binghamton, PO Box 6000, Binghamton, NY 13902-6000.

GLINERT, LEWIS
DISCIPLINE ASIAN AND MIDDLE EASTERN LANGUAGES AND LITERATURES **EDUCATION** Oxford Univ, BA; Univ London, PhD. **CAREER** Fac Schl Oriental and African Studies, Univ London; vis assoc prof Hebrew, Univ Chicago; asst prof Linguistics, Haifa and Bar-Ilan Univ; prof, Dartmouth Col. **HONORS AND AWARDS** Int Adv Bd, Israel Ctr Lang Policy. **MEMBERSHIPS** Int Advisory Bd to Israel Ctr for Lang Policy. **RESEARCH** Cult and linguistics of Israeli and Jewish soc in lang policy and in tech and safety discourse. **SELECTED PUBLICATIONS** Auth, The Grammar of Modern Hebrew; The Joys of Hebrew; Hebrew in Ashkenaz: A Language in Exile; Mamme Dear: A Turn-of the-Century Collection of Model Yiddish Letters; Product Safety Information and Language Policy in an Advanced Third World Economy; We Never Changed our Language: Attitudes of Hasidic Educators to Yiddish Language Acquisition; BBC documentaries: Tongue of Tongues: The Rebirth of Hebrew and Golem: The Making of a Modern Myth. **CONTACT ADDRESS** Dartmouth Col, 6161 Bartlett Hall, Hanover, NH 03755. **EMAIL** lewis.glinert@dartmouth.edu

GLISERMAN, MARTIN
DISCIPLINE LITERATURE AND PSYCHOLOGY, PSYCHOANALYSIS; THE BODY **EDUCATION** Colby, Center for Modern Psychoanalytic Studies, Psychoanalyst, BA; Ind, MA, PhD. **CAREER** Instr to Prof, Rutgers, State Univ NJ, Livingston; ed in ch, Am Imago; fac Ctr for Mod Psychoanalytic Stud. **MEMBERSHIPS** MLA, NAAP. **RESEARCH** Psychoanalysis; body studies. **SELECTED PUBLICATIONS** Auth, Psychoanalysis, Language, and the Body of the Text. **CONTACT ADDRESS** Dept of Eng, Rutgers, The State Univ of New Jersey, New Brunswick, 510 George St., New Brunswick, NJ 08901. **EMAIL** gliserma@rci.rutgers.edu

GLOVER, ALBERT G.
PERSONAL Born 11/19/1942, Boston, MA, d, 1962, 3 children **DISCIPLINE** ENGLISH **EDUCATION** McGill Univ, BA, 64; SUNY at Buffalo, PhD, 68. **CAREER** Asst to prof, St. Lawrence Univ, 68-78; prof, Anne & Frank P. Piskor, 83-. **MEMBERSHIPS** AAUP. **RESEARCH** 20th Century American Poetry. **SELECTED PUBLICATIONS** Ed, Charles Olson: Letters for Origin 1950-1956, London, 69; auth, ed Charles Olson: Letters for Origin 1950-1956 2nd ed, Paragon Press, 88; auth, Dylan Thomas in Print. A Bibliographical History, Univ Pittsburgh Press, 70; ed, River of Dreams. American Poetry from the St. Lawrence Valley, Glover Pub, 90; auth, "Evolution on Ezra Pound's Poetics of History and Charles Olson's 'Special View', " Paideuma, (95): 57-67. **CONTACT ADDRESS** Dept English, St. Lawrence Univ, 1 Romoda Dr, Canton, NY 13617-1423. **EMAIL** aglover@stlawu.edu

GLOWACKI, KEVIN T.
DISCIPLINE CLASSICAL STUDIES **EDUCATION** Loyola Univ, AB, 83, MA, 85; Bryn Mawr Col, MA, 87, PhD, 91. **CAREER** Asst prof, Indiana Univ-Bloom. **RESEARCH** Greek art and archaeology; Greek sculpture; topography & monuments of Athens; Aegean Bronze & Iron Ages; mythological representation in art. **SELECTED PUBLICATIONS** Auth, A New Fragment of the Erechtheion Frieze, Hesperia, 95; The Acropolis of Athens before 566 B.C, Univ Pa, 97. **CONTACT ADDRESS** Dept of Classical Studies, Indiana Univ, Bloomington, 547 Ballatine Hall, 1020 E Kirkwood Ave, Bloomington, IN 47405. **EMAIL** kglowack@indiana.edu

GLOWKA, ARTHUR WAYNE
PERSONAL Born 03/18/1952, Weimar, TX, m, 1992, 2 children **DISCIPLINE** MEDIEVAL LITERATURE, ENGLISH LINGUISTICS **EDUCATION** Univ Tex, BA, 73, MA, 75; Univ Del, PhD, 80. **CAREER** From asst prof to prof, Ga Col, 80-. **HONORS AND AWARDS** Fulbright-Hays, 89; Excellence in Res/Publ Award, Ga Col Found, 92; Post-Tenure Rev Fac Dev Award, Univ System of Ga, 99. **MEMBERSHIPS** S Atlantic Mod Lang Asn; New Chaucer Soc; Am Dialect Soc; Dictionary Soc of N Am. **RESEARCH** Prosody; history of the English language; neology; medieval literature. **SELECTED PUBLICATIONS** Auth, Yachtjacking, Boatnapping, or Getting Seajacked by Ship-jackers, Am Speech 62, 87; A Simplified Model of Language Variation and Change: A History of the Bot People, Glowka and Lance; A Guide to Chaucer's Meter, Univ Press of Am, 91; co-ed, Language Variation in North American English: Research and Teaching, MLA, 93; auth, The Poetics of Layamon's Brut, In: Text and Tradition in Layamon's Brut, Arthurian Studies 33, 94; Lawman and the Sabellian Heresy, Int J for the Semiotics of Law 8.24, 95; Layamon's Heathens and the Medieval Grapevine, In: Literacy and Orality in Early Middle English Literature, ScriptOralia 83, 96; coauth, Among the New Words, Am Speech 72, Fall and Winter 97. **CONTACT ADDRESS** Dept of English & Speech, Georgia Col, Milledgeville, GA 31061-0490. **EMAIL** wglowka@mail.gcsu.edu

GNAROWSKI, MICHAEL
PERSONAL Born 09/27/1934, Shanghai, China **DISCIPLINE** ENGLISH LITERATURE **EDUCATION** McGill Univ, BA, 56; Univ Montreal, MA, 60; Univ Ottawa, PhD, 67. **CAREER** Lectr English, Univ Sherbrooke, 61-62; asst prof, Lakehead Univ, 62-65; res assoc, Royal Comn Bilingualism & Biculturalism, 64-66; asst & assoc prof, Sir George Williams Univ, 66-72; vis prof, Univ Ottawa, 70-72; exch scholar & prof Can lit, Univ Leningrad, 77; exch scholar & prof Can lit, Univ Warsaw, 89; prof English, 72-96, adj res prof english, Carleton Univ, 96-; founding co-ed, YES: A Magazine of Poetry and Prose, 65-70; co-founder & mng partner, Tecumseh Press, 73-81; publ, 72-, vice pres 95- The Golden Dog Press. **SELECTED PUBLICATIONS** Auth, Postscript of St. James Street, 65; The Gentlemen Are also Lexicographers, 69; ed, The Rising Village of Oliver Goldsmith, 66; Three Early Poems From Lower Canada, 69; Joseph Quesnel: Selected Poems and Songs, 70; Archibald Lampman, 70; Selected Stories of Raymond Knister, 72; New Provinces, 76; Leonard Cohen: The Artist and His Critics, 76; Selected Poetry of Archibald Lampman, 90; co-ed, The Making of Modern Poetry in Canada, 67; introd & annotations, Memoirs of Montparnasse, 95; introd & notes, John Glassco: Selected Poems with Three Notes on the Poetic Process, 97; co-transl Quebec Is Killing Me, 95. **CONTACT ADDRESS** Dept of English, Carleton Univ, 1125 Colonel By Dr, 1910 Dunton Tower, Ottawa, ON, Canada K1S 5B6.

GOCHBERG, DONALD S.
PERSONAL Born 08/19/1933, Boston, MA, m, 1956, 4 children **DISCIPLINE** ENGLISH, LITERATURE **EDUCATION** Bates Col, AB, 55; Univ Md, MA, 60, PhD, 66. **CAREER** Instr English, Univ Md, 60-65; from Asst Prof to Assoc Prof, 65-77, Prof Humanities, 77-90, Prof English, Mich State Univ, 90-. **HONORS AND AWARDS** Distinguished Educator Awd, Mich State Univ, 73. **MEMBERSHIPS** AAUP. **RESEARCH** Seventeenth century English literature; Shakespeare; Milton; world literature and thought. **SELECTED PUBLICATIONS** Ed, The Twentieth Century, Harcourt Brace, 80; The Ancient World, Harcourt Brace, 88; gen ed, World Literature and Thought, 4 vols, Harcourt Brace, 97-. **CONTACT ADDRESS** Dept of English, Michigan State Univ, 201 Morrill Hall, East Lansing, MI 48824-1036. **EMAIL** gochberg@pilot.msu.edu

GODARD, BARBARA J.
PERSONAL Born 12/24/1941, Toronto, ON, Canada **DISCIPLINE** CANADIAN LITERATURE **EDUCATION** Univ Toronto, BA, 64; Univ Montreal, MA, 67; Univ Paris VIII Maitrise, 69; Univ Bordeaux, Doctorat 3e cycle, 71. **CAREER**

Lectr, Univ Montreal, 64-67; lectr, Univ Paris, 68-70; asst prof, 71-81, assoc prof Eng, York Univ, 81-. **HONORS AND AWARDS** Gabrielle Roy Prize, Asn Can & Que Lits 88; Award of Merit, Asn Can Stud, 95. **MEMBERSHIPS** MLA; PEN Int; Asn Can & Que Lits; Asn Can Univ Profs Eng; Can Comp Lit Asn; Asn Lit Transl; Can Semiotic Asn; Can Women's Stud Asn; Can Res Inst Advan Women. **RESEARCH** Semiotics and narratology, feminist theory, Canadian and Quebec literatures, and translation studies. **SELECTED PUBLICATIONS** Translation, History and Culture, 90; Studies on Canadian Literature, 90; Voix et images, 91; Traduction Terminologie et Redaction, 97; Theatre Research in Canada, 92; Questioni di teoria femminista, 93; English Studies in Canada, 92; RFR/DRF, 97; Gender and Narrativity, 97; Ghosts in the Machine and Women and Culture in Canada and Australia, 98. **CONTACT ADDRESS** Dept of English, Fac of Arts, York Univ, 4700 Keele St, North York, ON, Canada M3J 1P3. **EMAIL** bgodard@yorku.ca

GODDARD, NETTYE
PERSONAL Born 05/22/1923, Gadsden, AL, m, 1943, 2 children **DISCIPLINE** ENGLISH, LITERATURE **EDUCATION** Talladega Col, BA, 42; San Jose State Univ, MA, 73. **CAREER** Adj Prof, Evergreen Valley Community Col, 98-. **HONORS AND AWARDS** Phi Kappa Phi Hon Soc; Phi Kappa Phi Distinguished Serv Awd, 89; Distinguished Prof, San Jose State Univ, 91. **MEMBERSHIPS** Nat Coun of Teachers of English. **RESEARCH** Black linguistic tradition, black writers use of blues and jazz idioms in their imaginative literature, examining works of Hurston, Hughes, Ellison, Toomer, Murray, Walker, Morrison, Shange, Naylor, Mosley and Wilson. **SELECTED PUBLICATIONS** Auth, "Teaching Minority Culture," Am English Today, McGraw-Hill (70); auth, "Usage and Mechanics," Contemp English, Silver Burdett Co (72); auth, "'Betsey Brown' and 'Pocho'," Master Plots II: Juvenile and Young Adult Fiction, Salem Pr (91). **CONTACT ADDRESS** Dept Lang, Evergreen Valley Col, 3095 Yerba Buena Rd, San Jose, CA 95135-1513.

GODDU, TERESA
DISCIPLINE AMERICAN LITERATURE AND CULTURE **EDUCATION** Univ Pa, PhD. **CAREER** Instr, Vanderbilt Univ. **RESEARCH** American literature; American cultural study; African American literature. **SELECTED PUBLICATIONS** Auth, Gothic America, Columbia UP, 97. **CONTACT ADDRESS** Vanderbilt Univ, Nashville, TN 37203-1727.

GODFREY, AARON W.
PERSONAL Born 01/10/1929, New York, NY, m, 1981, 7 children **DISCIPLINE** CLASSICS **EDUCATION** Fordham Univ, BA, 58; Hunter Col, MA, 60. **CAREER** Asst Latin-Am rels, Grace Nat Bank, 52-60; instr lang, Newton Col Sacred Heart, 60-61, asst prof hist and class lang, 61-65; dir spec proj, 65-74, Dir Upware Bound Proj, State Univ NY Stony Brook, 66-, Lectr Classics, 67-, Consult, State Educ Dept NY, 67-73; Secy-Treas, Nat Coord Coun Educ Opportunity, 70-, ed, Review; consult, Esea Title I, New York Schs, 70-72. **MEMBERSHIPS** AHA; Medieval Acad Am; Liturgical Arts Soc; Class Asn Atlantic States; Asn Equality & Excellence Educ (secy, 77-). **RESEARCH** Ancient and medieval history; compensatory education; classical and medieval Latin. **SELECTED PUBLICATIONS** Auth, Catalogus-Translationum-Et-Commentariorum, Vol 7, Medieval and Renaissance Latin Translations and Commentaries, Class World, Vol 0087, 94; Theodoric in Italy, Class World, Vol 0088, 95; Suetonius 'De Grammaticis Et Rhetoribus,' Class World, Vol 0090, 97. **CONTACT ADDRESS** SUNY, Stony Brook, Stony Brook, NY 11794-3359.

GODFREY, MARY F.
DISCIPLINE MEDIEVAL SERMON LITERATURE, MEDIEVAL DRAMA, PSYCHOANALYTIC CRITICISM **EDUCATION** Princeton, PhD. **CAREER** Asst prof, Fordham Univ. **RESEARCH** Post-conquest literary cult in Engl. **SELECTED PUBLICATIONS** Auth, Beowulf and Judith: Thematizing Decapitation in Old English Poetry, Tex Stud Lit and Lang 35, 93; Sir Gawain and the Green Knight: The Severed Head and the Body Politic, Assays: Critical Approaches to Medieval and Renaissance Texts 8, 95. **CONTACT ADDRESS** Dept of Eng Lang and Lit, Fordham Univ, 113 W 60th St, New York, NY 10023.

GODSHALK, WILLIAM LEIGH
PERSONAL Born 07/12/1937, Pen Argyl, PA, m, 1967, 2 children **DISCIPLINE** ENGLISH LITERATURE **EDUCATION** Ursinus Col, BA, 59; Harvard Univ, MA, 60 PhD(English), 64. **CAREER** Instr English, Tufts Univ, 60-61; asst prof, Col William and Mary, 64-67; assoc prof, 67-73, PROF ENGLISH, UNIV CINCINNATI, 73-, Shakespeare consult, Widener Mem Collection, Harvard Col Libr, 63; fel coop prog in humanities, Duke Univ and Univ NC, Chapel Hill, 65-66; Taft Mem Fund grants, 68-71; assoc ed, Kalki, James Branch Cabell Soc, 72- **MEMBERSHIPS** MLA; Mod Humanities Res Asn; Renaissance Soc Am. **RESEARCH** English Renaissance literature; Shakespeare; modern fiction. **SELECTED PUBLICATIONS** Ed, Beyond Life: Dizain Des Demiurges, Johnson Reprint, 70; Voice of the People, Col & Univ, 72; auth, Measure for measure, Shakespeare Studies, 70; Patterning in Shakespearean Drama, 73 & The Marlovian World Picture, 74, Mouton; In Quest of Cabell, Revisionist, 75; Hamlet's dream of innocence, Shakespeare Studies, 76; Ben Johnson, In: The New Intellectuals, Univ Nebr, 77. **CONTACT ADDRESS** Dept of English, Univ of Cincinnati, Cincinnati, OH 45221.

GODWIN, JOSCELYN
PERSONAL Born 01/16/1945, Kelmscott, United Kingdom, m, 1979, 1 child **DISCIPLINE** MUSICOLOGY **EDUCATION** Magdalene Coll, BA, Musicol, 65, MusB, 66; Cornell Univ, PhD, 69. **CAREER** Instr, Music, Cleveland State Univ, 69-71; PROF, COLGATE UNIV, MUSIC, 71-. **MEMBERSHIPS** Am Musicol Soc **SELECTED PUBLICATIONS** Robert Fludd; Athanasius Kircher; Mystery Religions in the Ancient World; Harmonies of Heaven and Earth; Music and the Occult; The Mystery of the Seven Vowels; Arktos, the Polar Myth; The Theosophical Enlightenment; coauth, JFH von Dalberg. **CONTACT ADDRESS** Dept Music, Colgate Univ, Hamilton, NY 13346.

GOELLNICHT, DONALD
DISCIPLINE ENGLISH LITERATURE **EDUCATION** Queen's Univ, BA; McMaster Univ, MA, PhD. **RESEARCH** Asian American and Asian Canadian writing; North American minority writing; Romantic poetry and critical theory; contemporary critical theory. **SELECTED PUBLICATIONS** Auth, The Poet-Physician: Keats and Medical Science, 84. **CONTACT ADDRESS** English Dept, McMaster Univ, 1280 Main St W, Hamilton, ON, Canada L8S 4L9. **EMAIL** goellnic@atsmcmaster.ca

GOERING, ELIZABETH
DISCIPLINE COMMUNICATION STUDIES **EDUCATION** Bethel Col, BA, 79; Wichita State Univ, MA, 84; Purdue Univ, PhD, 91. **CAREER** Assoc prof. **SELECTED PUBLICATIONS** Auth, pubs on organizational communication, small group communication, the relationship between culture and communication, and communication and conflict. **CONTACT ADDRESS** Dept of Communication, Indiana Univ-Purdue Univ, Indianapolis, 425 Univ Blvd, Indianapolis, IN 46202. **EMAIL** bgoering@iupui.edu

GOERTZEN, CHRIS
DISCIPLINE MUSIC **EDUCATION** Univ IL, PhD. **CAREER** Prof ethnomusicol, Earlham Col. **RESEARCH** Music of Latin Am; music of Africa; music of Asia. **SELECTED PUBLICATIONS** Auth, Fiddling for Norway: Revival and Identity, Univ Chicago, 97; publ(s) on musics in oral tradition in America. **CONTACT ADDRESS** Music Dept, Earlham Col, Richmond, IN 47374-4095. **EMAIL** liffeyt@earlham.edu

GOFF, BARBARA E.
PERSONAL Born 01/23/1958, London, England, m, 1989, 1 child **DISCIPLINE** CLASSICS **EDUCATION** Berkeley, PhD, 85. **CAREER** Jr Res fel, Kings Col Cambridge, 86-90; Asst prof, 91-98, Assoc Prpf, Univ Texas-Austin, 98- . **MEMBERSHIPS** APA **RESEARCH** Greek tradegy; women in antiquity. **SELECTED PUBLICATIONS** Auth, Euripedes Ion, 88; The Tent, PCPS, 88; The shields of the Phoenissae, GRBS, 88; The Noose of Words: readings of desire, violence and language in Euripide's Hippolytos, Cambridge Univ Press, 90; The sign of the fall: the scars of Orestes and Odysseus, CA, 91; rev Synnove des Bouvrie, Women in Greek Tragedy, AJP, 92; rev, Ruth Padel, In and Out of the Mide, CPhil, 94; auth, Aithra at Eleusis, Helios, 95; The Women of Thebes, CJ, 95; The Figure of Antiquity in the Memoirs of Mme Roland: the classical, the revolutionary, and the feminine, CML, 96. **CONTACT ADDRESS** Classics Dept, Univ of Texas, Austin, Waggener Hall 123, Austin, TX 78712-1181.

GOFFMAN, ETHAN E.
PERSONAL Born 12/12/1961, Lafayette, IN, m, 2001 **DISCIPLINE** ENGLISH **EDUCATION** Earlham Col, BA, 83; Purdue Univ, MA, 86; Ind Univ, PhD, 97. **CAREER** TA, Purdue Univ, 84-86; adj prof, Jersey City State Col, 88-89; assoc instr, Ind Univ, 91-96; lectr, Purdue Univ, 97-01. **MEMBERSHIPS** MLA. **RESEARCH** Fiction Writing, Twentieth Century American Literature, African American Literature, Jewish American Literature, Ethnic Literature, Cultural Studies, English as A Second Language, Computers and Pedagogy. **SELECTED PUBLICATIONS** Auth, "Marianne Moore: Oddities and Eccentricities," Contact II, (88); auth, "Health Care: Some New Proposals," Dissent, (89); auth, "Frances Steloff, Past and Future," Contact II, (89); auth, "The Income Gap and Its Causes," Dissent, (90); auth, "Imag(in)ing Each Other: Blacks and Jews in Recent Literature," Shofar, (96); auth, "Between Guilt and Affluence: The Jewish Gaze and the Black Thief in Mr. Sammler's Planet," Contemp Lit, (97); auth, "Grace Paley's Faith: The Journey Homeward, the Journey Forward," MELUS, (00); auth, "Tangled Roots: History, Theory and African American Studies," Modern Fiction Studies, (00); auth, Imaging Each Other: Blacks and Jews in Contemporary American Literature, SUNY Pr, 00; auth, "Unresolved Conversations," Contemporary Lit, (01). **CONTACT ADDRESS** 1328 1/2 Ferry St, Layfayette, IN 47901. **EMAIL** goffmane@purdue.edu

GOGGIN, MAUREEN DALY
PERSONAL Born Boston, MA, m, 1985 **DISCIPLINE** ENGLISH **EDUCATION** Northeastern Univ, BS, 75; MA, 78; Carnegie Mellon Univ, PhD, 94. **CAREER** Adj prof, Bentley Col, 80-82; instr to assoc dir, Northeastern Univ, 79-87; instr, Bermuda Col, 87-88; instr, Wright State Univ, 88-89; teaching fel to instr, Carnegie Mellon Univ, 89-94; asst prof to assoc prof, Ariz State Univ, 94-. **HONORS AND AWARDS** Kappa Delta Pi; Anne Flecchia Eaton Mem Scholar, 74; Teaching Fel, Northeastern Univ, 76-78; Dean's Recognition for Outstanding Teaching, Carnegie Mellon Univ, 93; GSEA Outstanding Mentor for Rhetoric and Composition, Ariz State Univ, 95, 97, 98, 99, 00; PFF Mentor Cert, Ariz State Univ, 99; Top Prof Awd Manzanita Hall, 99; Student Affairs Recognition Awd, 99; PFF Mentor Certificate, 00. **MEMBERSHIPS** Conf on Col Composition and Comm; Nat Coun of Teachers of English; Rhetoric Soc of Am; Rhetoric Rev Asn of Am; Coun of Writing Prog Admin; MLA; Rocky Mountain MLA; S Central MLA; Asn for Adv Composition; Kappa Delta Pi. **RESEARCH** History of rhetoric and composition; Rhetoric in the late nineteenth century; The concomitant emergence of composition; Post WWII disciplinary formation of rhetoric and composition. **SELECTED PUBLICATIONS** Co-auth, "Some Issues in Dating the Birth of the New Rhetoric in Departments of English: A Contribution to a Developing Historiography," in Defining the New Rhetorics, (Sage, 93), 22-43; co-auth, "The Revival of Classical Rhetoric for Modern Composition Studies: A Survey," Rhetoric Soc Quart, (94): 11-26; auth, "Situation the Teaching and Learning of Argumentation within Historical Contexts," in competing and Consenting Voices, (Multilingual Matters Ltd, 95), 10-22; auth, "The Disciplinary Instability of Composition,' in Reconceiving Writing, Rethinking Writing Instruction, (Lawrence Erlbaum, 95), 27-48; auth, "Composing a Discipline: The Role of Scholarly Journals in the Emergence of Rhetoric and composition Since 1950," Rhetoric Rev, (97): 322-348; auth, "The Tangled Roots of Literature, Speech Communication, Linguistics, Rhetoric/Composition, and Creative Writing: Selected Bibliography on the History of English Studies," Rhetoric Soc Quart, (99): 63-88; co-auth, "EXTRA! EXTRA! Read all about it!: Constructions of Heterosexual Black Male Identities in the Personals," Social Identities, (99): 441-468; co-auth, "What is New about the 'New Abolitionists': Continuities and Discontinuities in the Great Debate," composition Studies, (00): 85-112; ed, Inventing a Discipline: Rhetoric Scholarship in Honor of Richard E. Young, Urbana, 00; auth, Authoring a Discipline: Scholarly Journals and the Post-World War II Emergence of Rhetoric and Composition, Lawrence Erlbaum, 00. **CONTACT ADDRESS** Dept English, Arizona State Univ, PO Box 0302, Tempe, AZ 85287-0302. **EMAIL** maureen.goggin@asu.edu

GOGWILT, CHRISTOPHER
PERSONAL Born 11/22/1961, Edinburgh, Scotland, m, 1985, 2 children **DISCIPLINE** ENGLISH **EDUCATION** Swarthmore Col, BA, 83; Princeton Univ, PhD, 88. **CAREER** Preceptor, Princeton Univ, 85-87; Asst Prof to Dir of Literary Studies Prog, Fordham Univ, 88-. **HONORS AND AWARDS** NEH Summer Stipend, 91; Fel, Fordham Univ, 91, 95, 00-01. **MEMBERSHIPS** MLA; Joseph Conrad Soc of Am. **RESEARCH** 19th and 20th Century Literary and Cultural Studies; Critical Theory; Comparative Literature. **SELECTED PUBLICATIONS** Auth, "Salome, Woman, and Modernity: Zig-zag Paths Through the Turn of the Century," New German Critique, (92): 182-192; auth, "True West: the changing idea of the West at the beginning of the 20th Century," in Enduring Western Civilization, (Westport, 95), 37-61; auth, The Invention of the West: Joseph Conrad and the Double-Mapping of Europe and Empire, Stanford Univ Press, 95; auth, "Pramoedya's Fiction and History: An Interview with Indonesian Novelist Pramoedya Ananta Toer," Yale Journal of Criticism, (96): 147-164; auth, "Broadcasting News from Nowhere: R.B. Cunninghame Graham and the Geography of Politics in the 1890s" in High and Low Moderns: Literature and Culture, 1889-1939, (Oxford Univ Press, 96), 235-254; auth, "Conrad's Alien Genealogies: Joseph Conrad's 'Karain: A Memory,' Pramoedya Ananta Toer, and Postcolonial American Perspectives," Western Humanities Review, (98): 96-109; auth, "The Geopolitical Image: Imperialism, Anarchism, and the Hypothesis of Culture in the Formation of Geopolitics," Modernism/Modernity, (98): 49-70; auth, The Fiction of Geopolitics: Afterimages of Culture from Wilkie Collins to Alfred Hitchcock, Stanford Univ Press, 00. **CONTACT ADDRESS** Dept Eng, Fordham Univ, 441 E Fordham Rd, Bronx, NY 10458-5149. **EMAIL** gogwilt@fordham.edu

GOINS, SCOTT
PERSONAL Born 05/02/1961, Cleveland, TN, s **DISCIPLINE** CLASSICS **EDUCATION** Univ Tenn, BA, 83; Fla State Univ, MA, 85, PhD, 88. **CAREER** Vis asst Prof, Classics, Univ of South, 88-89; asst prof, 89-95, assoc prof & asst dept head dept of languages, 95-, Mcneese State Univ, 89-; ed, McNeese Rev. **MEMBERSHIPS** Amer Philol Asn; Class Asn Midwst & S; La Class Asn; Class Asn Can. **RESEARCH** Virgil; Boethius; Fable; Greek drama. **SELECTED PUBLICATIONS** Auth, Penelope and Melantho: A Question of Jealousy in Odyssey 19?, Class Bull, 87;Horace, sermo 1.5.61, Latomus, 87; The Influence of Old Comedy on the Vita Aesopi, Class World, 89; Euripides Fr 863 Nauck, Rheinisches Museum fur Philologie, 89; The Heroism of Odysseus in Euripides, Cyclops

Eos, 91; Birds and Erotic Fantasies in Catullus and Goethe, Goethe Yearbook, 92; Two Aspects of Virgils Use of Labor in the Aeneid, Class Jour, 93; Pain and Authority in the Aeneid and Henry V, Class and Modern Lit, 95; The Date of Aeschylus Perseus Tetralogy, Rheinisches Museum fur Philol, 97; The Poetics in the Mythology Syllabus: Nothing to do with Dionysus, Class Bull, 97. **CONTACT ADDRESS** Dept of Languages, McNeese State Univ, Box 93465, Lake Charles, LA 70609-2655. **EMAIL** sgoins@mcneese.edu

GOIST, PARK DIXON
PERSONAL Born 09/07/1936, Seattle, WA, m, 1987, 1 child **DISCIPLINE** AMERICAN STUDIES, THEATRE **EDUCATION** Univ WA, BA, 58; Univ Rochester, PhD, 67. **CAREER** Instr hist, Colgate Univ, 63 & Kent State Univ, 63-64; from instr to asst prof, 66-71, assoc prof Am studies, Case Western Reserve Univ, 71, Nat Am Studies Fac, 77. **MEMBERSHIPS** Am Studies Asn; Gt Lakes Am Studies Asn. **RESEARCH** Am intellectual hist; Am urban and community studies; Am drama. **SELECTED PUBLICATIONS** Co-ed, The Urban Vision: Selected Interpretations of the Modern American Dity, Dorsey, 70; auth, City and community: the urban theory of Robert Park, Am Quart, spring 71; Seeing things whole: a consideration of Lewis Mumford, 11/72 & Patrick Geddes and the city, 1/74, J Am Inst Planners: Town, City and Community, 1890-1920's, Am Studies, spring 73; Community and self in the Midwest town: Dell's Moon-Calf, Mid America II, 75; From Main Street to State Street: Town, City and Community in America, Kennikat, 77; Oregon Trail Diary, Reserve, 4/81; auth, A Small Squall, Cleveland Play House, 94; auth, Partners, Harold Clorman Theatre, 96; auth, My Writer . My Actress, Hararo International Festival of the Arts (zimbabwe), 00. **CONTACT ADDRESS** Case Western Reserve Univ, 3021 Somerton Rd, Cleveland, OH 44118. **EMAIL** pdg8@aol.com

GOLD, BARBARA K.
PERSONAL Born 03/23/1945, Brooklyn, NY, m, 1986, 1 child **DISCIPLINE** CLASSICS **EDUCATION** Univ Michigan, BA, 66; Univ N Carolina, Chapel Hill, MA, 68, PhD, 75. **CAREER** Lectr, actg asst prof, Univ Calif, Irvine, 71-75; asst prof, Univ Richmond, 76-77; asst prof, Univ Va, 77-78; asst prof classics and comp lit, Univ Texas, 78-86; assoc prof classics, women's stud, Santa Clara Univ, 86-89; assoc prof to prof, 89- , Leonard C Ferguson Prof of Class, 94-97, Prof of Classics and Assoc Dean, 97- , Hamilton Col. **HONORS AND AWARDS** NDEA Fel, 67-68; Mellon Fel, 79; Univ Res Inst sum fel, 79, 81; Univ Res Inst res grant, 79-83, 80, 84; Thomas Terry Awd, 88-89; NEH summer stipend, 92. **MEMBERSHIPS** Am Class League; Am Philol Asn; Archaeol Inst Am; Calif Class Asn; Class Asn of the Atlantic States; Class Asn of the Empire State; Class Asn of the Middle West and South; Philol Asn of the Pacific Coast. **RESEARCH** Greek and Roman literature; Roman elegy, lyric and satire; Pindar; Greek tragedy; Plato; comparative literature; women in antiquity. **SELECTED PUBLICATIONS** Ed, Literary and Artistic Patronage in Ancient Rome, Univ Texas, 82; auth, Literary Patronage in Greece and Rome, Univ North Carolina, 87; co-ed, Sex and Gender in Medieval and Renaissance Texts: The Latin Tradition, SUNY, 97; co-ed, Vile Bodies: Roman Satire and Corporeal Discourse, special issue Arethusa, 98. **CONTACT ADDRESS** Dept of Classics, Hamilton Col, New York, Clinton, NY 13323. **EMAIL** bgold@hamilton.edu

GOLD, ELLEN REID
PERSONAL Born Kansas City, KS **DISCIPLINE** POLITICAL RHETORIC, TELEVISION CRITICISM **EDUCATION** Univ MO, BA, 60; Univ KS, MA, 65; Univ IL, PhD, 73. **CAREER** Asst dean, Col Lib Arts & Sci, KS Univ, 73-75; asst prof commun studies, 75-81, assoc prof commun studies, Univ KS, 81. **MEMBERSHIPS** Natl Commun Asn; Cent States Commun Asn. **RESEARCH** Presidential campaign rhetoric, Ronald Reagan, television criticism **SELECTED PUBLICATIONS** Auth, What debate reveals: An analysis of the Miller-Bennet Campaign, 1974, Kans Speech J, fall 76; coauth, Research and teaching about women and communication, SCA Women's Caucus Bibliog, 6/78; auth, Political apologia: The ritual of self-defense, Commun Monogr, 11/78; coauth (with Judith S Trent), Campaigning for President in New Hampshire: 1980, Exetasis, 4/1/80; auth, Recorded sound collections: New materials to explore the past, Centr States Speech J, summer 80; The Grimke Sisters and the emergence of the Woman's Rights Movement, Southern Speech Commun J, summer 81; Gladstone and the development of Stump oratory, Cent States Speech J, summer 82; Ronald Regan and the Oral Tradition, Commun Studies, 88. **CONTACT ADDRESS** Dept of Commun, Univ of Kansas, Lawrence, Lawrence, KS 66045-0001.

GOLD, JOEL JAY
PERSONAL Born 12/19/1931, Brooklyn, NY, m, 1956, 3 children **DISCIPLINE** ENGLISH **EDUCATION** Univ MO, AB, 55; IN Univ, PhD, 62. **CAREER** From instr to assoc prof, 62-74, prof eng, Univ KS, 72, Vis assoc prof Eng, Univ IL, Urbana-Champaign, 70-71; Am Coun Learned Soc grant, 70; Am Philos Soc grant, 70; Newberry Libr fel, 78; Bibliog soc of Am fel, 86. **HONORS AND AWARDS** Amoco Distinguished Tchg Awd, 80; Distinguished Alum Awd, Col Lib arts and Sci, univ MO, 98. **MEMBERSHIPS** MLA; AAUP; Am Soc Eighteenth-Century Studies. **RESEARCH** Humor **SELECTED PUBLICATIONS** Ed, A voyage to Abyssinia, In: Yale Edition of the Works of Samuel Johnson, Yale Univ, 85; auth, Johnson's translation of Lobo, PMLA, 3/65; In defense of single-speech Hamilton, Studies in Burke & Hist Time, winter 68-69; The return to Bath: Catherine Morland to Anne Elliot, Genre, fall 76; John Wilkes and the writings of Pensioner Johnson, Studies in Burke & His Time, spring 77; Mr Serjeant Glynn: Radical politics in the courtroom, Harvard Libr Bull, 5/81; auth, The Wayward Professor, univ Press Kansas, 89; The Battle of the Shorthand Books 1635-1800, publ hist, 84; Essays in The Chronicle of Higher Education, 82. **CONTACT ADDRESS** Dept of Eng, Univ of Kansas, Lawrence, Lawrence, KS 66045-0001. **EMAIL** jjg@kuhub.cc.ukans.edu

GOLD, JOSEPH
PERSONAL Born 06/30/1933, London, England **DISCIPLINE** ENGLISH **EDUCATION** Univ Birmingham (Eng), BA, 55; Univ Wisconsin, PhD, 59. **CAREER** Fac mem, Univ Man, 60-70; prof Eng, 70-94, ch, 70-73, PROF EMER, UNIV WATERLOO, 94-. **MEMBERSHIPS** Can Asn Am Stud (exec mem, 64-73); Asn Bibliotherapy Can. **SELECTED PUBLICATIONS** Auth, Faulkner: A Study in Humanism from Metaphor to Discourse, 66; auth, The Stature of Dickens: A Centenary Bibliography, 71; auth, Charles Dickens: Radical Moralist, 72; auth, Read For Your Life, 90; ed, King of Beasts and Other Stories, 67; ed, In the Name of Language, 75. **CONTACT ADDRESS** Box 1332, Haileybury, ON, Canada P0J 1K0.

GOLDBECK, JANNE
DISCIPLINE ENGLISH LITERATURE **EDUCATION** Univ Okla, PhD, 72. **CAREER** Prof. **RESEARCH** Medieval literature; gender studies; 1930s in American film and autobiography. **SELECTED PUBLICATIONS** Auth, All the Ways. **CONTACT ADDRESS** Dept of English and Philosophy, Idaho State Univ, Pocatello, ID 83209. **EMAIL** goldh@isu.edu

GOLDBERG, SANDER M.
DISCIPLINE CLASSICS **EDUCATION** Univ Rochester, 66-70, BA, 70; Univ Tex, 70-71; Ind Univ, MA, 74, PhD, 77; Univ Col London, 76-77. **CAREER** Vis asst prof, Ind Univ, 77-78; vis lectr, Univ Calif-Berkeley, 80-81; asst prof, Univ Colo, 81-85; asst prof, 85-87; assoc prof, 87-91; Prof, UCLA, 91-. **HONORS AND AWARDS** Phi Beta Kappa, 70; Woodrow Wilson fel, 70; NDEA Title IV fel, Univ Tex, 70-71; Ind Univ grad sch fel, 72-73, 76-77; Wheeler fel, Amer Sch Class Stud, Athens, 76; Fulbright-Hays scholar, 76-77; A.W. Mellon post-doc fel, Stanford Univ, 78-80; NEH fel, 84-85; President's res fel, Univ Calif, 89-90; ed, transactions of the amer philol assn, 91-95; ed bd, the class jour, 82-83; helios, 84-90; bryn mawr class rev, 96-; comparative drama, 96-; referee: amer jour philol; class antiquity; class jour; class philol; comparative drama; phoenix; transactions **SELECTED PUBLICATIONS** Auth, The Making of Menander's Comedy, Univ Calif Press, 80; Understanding Terence, Princeton Univ Press, 86; Epic in Republican Rome, Oxford Univ Press, 95; "Improvisation, Plot, and Plautus' Curculio," Plautus und die Tradition des Stegreifspiels, Tubingen, 95. **CONTACT ADDRESS** Dept of Classics, Univ of California, Los Angeles, PO Box 951436, Los Angeles, CA 90095-1436.

GOLDEN, ARTHUR
PERSONAL Born 08/22/1924, New York, NY, 1 child **DISCIPLINE** ENGLISH, AMERICAN LITERATURE **EDUCATION** NYork Univ, BA, 47, PhD(English & Am lit), 62; Columbia Univ, MA, 48. **CAREER** Instr English, NY Univ, 59-63; from instr to assoc prof, 63-72, PROF ENGLISH, CITY COL NEW YORK, 73-, gen fac comt res and publ grant, 67., Nat Endowment Humanities grant, 70-71. **MEMBERSHIPS** MLA; Bibliog Soc Am; PEN; Int Asn Univ Prof English. **RESEARCH** American literature, especially 19th century and Walt Whitman. **SELECTED PUBLICATIONS** Ed, New light on Leaves of Grass: Whitman's annotated copy of the 1860 edition, Bull New York Pub Libr, 5/65; Walt Whitman's Blue book: The 1860-61 Leaves of Grass containing his manuscript additions and revisions, Vol I, facsimile & Vol II, textual analysis, New York Pub Libr, 68; William Cullen Bryant, Oliver Wendell Holmes, Henry Wadsworth Longfellow, James Russell Lowell, John Greenleaf Whittier & Walt Whitman, In: The McGraw-Hall Encyclopedia of World Biography, 74; Walt Whitman: A collection of criticism, McGraw, 74; co-ed, Walt Whitman, Leaves of Grass: A Textual Variorum of the Printed Poems: 1855-1891, In: Collected Writings of Walt Whitman, NY Univ Press, 80. **CONTACT ADDRESS** Dept of English, City Col, CUNY, New York, NY 10031.

GOLDEN, BRUCE
PERSONAL Born 06/18/1933, Rochester, NY, m, 1969 **DISCIPLINE** ENGLISH AND COMPARATIVE LITERATURE **EDUCATION** Northwestern Univ, BS, 55; Columbia Univ, AM, 58, PhD(English & comp lit), 66. **CAREER** Mem acad fac humanities, Juilliard Sch Music, 62-65; from instr to assoc prof English, 65-77, PROF ENGLISH, CALIF STATE COL, SAN BERNARDINO, 77-, Nat Endowment Humanities younger humanist fel, 71-72. **MEMBERSHIPS** MLA; Renaissance Soc Am; Malon Soc. **RESEARCH** Renaissance dramatic literature; literature and the other arts; popular culture. **SELECTED PUBLICATIONS** Coauth, The Good Soldier: A tragedy of self-deception, Mod Fiction Studies, 63; auth, Calderon's tragedies of honor: Topos, emblem, and action in the popular theatre of the Siglo de oro, Renaissance Drama, 70; The Beach Boys: Southern California Pastoral, Newcastle/Borgo, 76. **CONTACT ADDRESS** Dept of English, California State Univ, San Bernardino, 5500 University Pky, San Bernardino, CA 92407-7500.

GOLDEN, LEON
PERSONAL Born 12/25/1930, Teasley City, NJ **DISCIPLINE** CLASSICS **EDUCATION** Univ Chicago, BA, 50, MA, 53, PhD, 58. **CAREER** Instr to asst prof, Col of William & Mary, 58-65; assoc prof to prof, Fl St Univ, 65- . **HONORS AND AWARDS** Phi Beta Kappa **MEMBERSHIPS** Amer Philol Assoc; Classical Assoc of Midwest & South; Amer Comparative Lit Assoc. **RESEARCH** Greek tragedy; Homer; classical literary criticism. **SELECTED PUBLICATIONS** Auth bibliogr, In Praise of Prometheus: Humanism and Rationalism in Aeschylean Thought, Chapel Hill, 66; The Clarification Theory of Catharsis, Hermes, 76; Comic Pleasure, Hermes, 87; Aristotle on Tragic and Comic Mimesis; 92; coauth bibliogr, Horace for Students of Literature: the Ars Poetica and its Tradition, 95. **CONTACT ADDRESS** Dept of Classics, Florida State Univ, Tallahassee, FL 32306. **EMAIL** lgolden@mallen.fsu.edu

GOLDEN, MARK
PERSONAL Born 06/08/1948, Winnipeg, MB, Canada, m, 1985, 2 children **DISCIPLINE** CLASSICS **EDUCATION** Univ Col, Toronto, BA, 70; Univ Toronto, PhD, 81. **CAREER** Lectr, asst prof, Univ British Columbia, 80-82; asst prof, prof, Univ Winnipeg, 82- . **HONORS AND AWARDS** Fel, Nat Hum Ctr. **MEMBERSHIPS** Class Asn of Can; APA; Asn of Ancient Hist; Soc for Socialist Stud. **RESEARCH** History of childhood; ancient family history; Greek sport. **SELECTED PUBLICATIONS** Co-ed, Inventing Ancient Culture: Historicism, Periodization and the Ancient World, Routledge, 97; auth, Sport and Society in Ancient Greece, Cambridge, 98. **CONTACT ADDRESS** Dept of Classics, Univ of Winnipeg, Winnipeg, MB, Canada R3B 2E9. **EMAIL** m.golden@uwinnipeg.ca

GOLDENBERG, MYRNA
PERSONAL Born 03/08/1937, Brooklyn, NY, m, 1957, 3 children **DISCIPLINE** ENGLISH **EDUCATION** City Col NY, BS; 57; Univ Ark, MA, 61; Univ Md, PhD, 87. **CAREER** Prof, Montgomery Col, 71-. **HONORS AND AWARDS** Kappa Delta Pi, 56; Phi Kappa Phi, 84; Lowenstein-Wiener Fel, 88; Outstanding Fac Awd, Montgomery Col, 90; Who's Who in the World, 96; William H Meardy Nat Outstanding Fac Awd, 96; Member, Goldner Holocaust Symp, 98. **SELECTED PUBLICATIONS** Auth, "Life with Annie: Writing Biography", Belles Lettres, (95): 38-39; auth, "Testimony, Narrative, and Nightmare: The Experience of Jewish Women in the Holocaust", Active Voices: Women and Jewish Culture, ed Maurie Sacks, Univ of IL Pr, (95): 94-106; auth, "Lessons Learned from Gentle Heroism: Women's Holocaust Narratives", Annals 548, (96): 78-93; coauth, "Faculty Development: A Consortial Model" and "Writing Everybody In", Womens Studies Quarterly 24, (96): auth, "From a World Beyond: Women in the Holocaust", Feminist Studies 22.3 (96): 667-687; auth, "Faye Moskowitz", Contemporary Jewish American Novelist: A Bio-Critical Sourcebook, eds Joel Shatsky and Michael Taub, Greenwood Pr, (Westport, CT), 97; auth, "Preface and Notes, Ana Novac", The Beautiful Days of My Youth, Holt, (NY), 97; auth, "Annie Nathan Meyer", Jewish Women in America: An Historical Encyclopedia Routledge, (NY), 98; auth, "Memoirs of Auschwitz Survivors: the Burden of Gender", Women in the Holocaust, eds Lenore Weitzman and Dalia Ofer, Yale Univ Pr, (New Haven), 98; auth, "Women's Voices in Holocaust Literary Memoirs", Shofar: An Interdisciplinary J of Jewish Studies 16.4 (98): 75-89. **CONTACT ADDRESS** Humanities Inst, Montgomery Col, Rockville, 51 Mannakee St, Rockville, MD 20850-1101. **EMAIL** mgoldenb@mc.cc.md.us

GOLDENBERG, ROBERT
PERSONAL Born 10/21/1942, Brooklyn, NY, m, 1986, 3 children **DISCIPLINE** ENGLISH LITERATURE **EDUCATION** Cornell Univ, BA, 63; Jewish Theol Seminary Am, MHL, 66; Brown Univ, PhD, 74. **CAREER** Eng Dept, SUNY Stony Brook **SELECTED PUBLICATIONS** Auth, Did the Amoraim See Christianity as Something New?, Sheffield Acad, 94; Patriarchat, Gruyter, 96; Eleazar ben Pedat; Shim'on ben Laqish; Talmud. **CONTACT ADDRESS** English Dept, SUNY, Stony Brook, Stony Brook, NY 11794.

GOLDENSOHN, BARRY
DISCIPLINE ENGLISH **CAREER** Goddard Col, 65-70; Vis Assoc Prof, Univ Iowa, 70-72; Goddard Col, 72-77; Assoc Prof to Prof and Dean, 77-82; Assoc Prof to Prof, Skidmore Col, 82-. **HONORS AND AWARDS** NEA Grant, Skidmore Col, 84-85; Awd for Poetry, NY Foundation for the Arts, 85; MacDowell Fel, 82-84, 89; NEH Summer Seminar, 80; NEH Seminar for Fac, Boston Univ, 77-78; Awd for Poetry, Vt Coun for the Arts, 77; Res Fel, Millay Colony, 89 **SELECTED PUBLICATIONS** Auth, Gulliver's Travels, Collier-Macmillan, 61, Introduction, bibliography; auth, Saint Venus Eve, Cummington Press, 72; auth, Uncarving the Block, Vermont Crossroads

Press, 78; auth, The Marrano, National Poetry Foundation, 88; auth, Dance Music, Cummington Press, 92; auth, East Long Pond, Cummington Press, 97; auth, Poems for Azania, forthcoming; auth, "David Mamet and Poetic Language in Drama," Agni, 99; auth, "Beautified is a vile phrase,: Parnassus, 91. **CONTACT ADDRESS** Dept English, Skidmore Col, 815 N Broadway, Saratoga Springs, NY 12866-1631.

GOLDFARB, NANCY D.
PERSONAL Born 07/22/1964, Cincinnati, OH, m, 2000 **DISCIPLINE** ENGISH **EDUCATION** Brandeis Univ, BA, 85; Univ Mich, MA, 89; PhD, 94. **CAREER** Vis Lecturer, Johannes Gutenberg Univ, 93-94; Adj Lecturer, Raymond Walters Col, 94-95; Asst Prof, Western Ky Univ, 95-. **HONORS AND AWARDS** Inst of Intl Educ Scholarship, 90; dissertation Fel, Univ Mich, 92; Junior Fac Res grant, Western Ky Univ, 96. **MEMBERSHIPS** MLA, ACLA, AAUP, AAUW, T.S.Eliot Soc. **RESEARCH** Modern European and American Poetry. **SELECTED PUBLICATIONS** AUTH, T.S. Eliot Society Bibliographer; auth, "Lewis Carroll's 'Jabberwocky'," The Explicator, (99): 86-89; rev, of "T.S. Eliot: Mystic, son and Lover," by Donald Childs, T.S. Eliot Soc Newsletter, (99): 4-5. **CONTACT ADDRESS** Dept English, Western Kentucky Univ, 1 Big Red Way St, Bowling Green, KY 42101-5730. **EMAIL** ngoldfarb@earthlink.net

GOLDGAR, BERTRAND ALVIN
PERSONAL Born 11/17/1927, Macon, GA, m, 1950, 2 children **DISCIPLINE** ENGLISH LITERATURE **EDUCATION** Vanderbilt Univ, BA, 48, MA, 49; Princeton Univ, MA, 57, PhD, 58. **CAREER** Instr English, Clemson Col, 48-50, asst prof, 51-52; from instr to assoc prof, 57-71, prof English, 71-80, JOHN N BERGSTROM PROF HUMANITIES, LAWRENCE UNIV, 80-, Nat Endowment for Humanities fel, 80-81. **MEMBERSHIPS** MLA; Am Soc 18th Century Studies. **RESEARCH** Eighteenth century English literature; Fielding's journalism. **SELECTED PUBLICATIONS** Auth, Walpole and the Wits, Lincoln, Nebr, 76; ed, Henry Fielding's 'Covent Garden Jour, Oxford, 88; auth, "The Champion and the Chapter on Hats in 'Jonathan Wild,'" Philol Quart, Vol 0072, 93; ed, Fielding's 'Miscellanies,' Vols II, III, Oxford, 93, 97. **CONTACT ADDRESS** Dept of English, Lawrence Univ, Appleton, WI 54912.

GOLDIN, MILTON
PERSONAL Born 01/08/1927, Cleveland, OH, m, 1950, 2 children **DISCIPLINE** MUSICOLOGY; PSYCHOLOGY **EDUCATION** New York Univ, BA, 53, MA, 55. **CAREER** Admin dir, Amer Choral Found, 55-61; assoc dir devel, Brookdale Hosp Ctr 63-66; fund raising campaign dir, Wash Sq. Col and Grad Sch, Arts and Sci, NYU, 66-67; VP Oram Assoc, Inc, 67-72, Exec VP, 72-75; fund raising counc, 75-78; pres, The Milton Goldin Co, 78-; mgr, Amor Artis Chorale and Orch, 61-78; contributing ed, periodicals, 96-. **HONORS AND AWARDS** ASCAP Deems Taylor award, 70; Phi Beta Kappa; Psi Chi; Mu Sigma **MEMBERSHIPS** National Coalition of Independent Scholars (NCIS) **RESEARCH** German economy 1917-1952; american philanthropy; environmental history. **SELECTED PUBLICATIONS** Auth, The Music Merchants, 69; auth, Why They Give, 76; PS, Goldhagen and the Holocaust, Jan 97; The Earth Times, The New York-New Jersey Follies, Mar 97; The Genocide Forum, Allianz's First Trial, Sept 97; History Today, Financing the SS, June 98; Gannett Newspapers, Tourism Isn't Going to Make Up for GM Loss, June 98. **CONTACT ADDRESS** 266 Crest Dr, Tarrytown, NY 10591-4328. **EMAIL** MiltonG525@aol.com

GOLDMAN, EDWARD A.
PERSONAL Born 03/25/1941, Toledo, OH, m, 1966, 2 children **DISCIPLINE** RABBINIC LITERATURE **EDUCATION** Harvard Col, BA, 63; Hebrew Union Col, MAHL, 69, PhD, 74. **CAREER** Prof of Rabbinics, Hebrew Union Col, 72-; Editor, Hebrew Union College Annual, 98-. **MEMBERSHIPS** Cent Conf of Am Rabbis; AAUP; Soc for Bibl Lit; Nat Asn of Prof of Hebrew; Jewish Law Asn; Asn for Jewish Stud. **RESEARCH** Midrash. **SELECTED PUBLICATIONS** Rev, Parables in Midrash: Narrative and Exegesis in Rabbinic Literatyre, by Stern, J of the Am Oriental Soc, 93; rev, Techniques and Assumptions in Jewish Exegesis before 70 CE by Brewer, J of the Am Oriental Soc, 94; rev, Introduction to the Talmud and Midrash by Strack, J of the Am Oriental Soc, 96; rev, The Bavli: An Introduction, and, The Bavli's Massive Miscellanies: The Problem of Agglutinative Discourse in the Talmud of Babylonia, by Neusner, in, Critical Rev of Books in Relig, 1994, 96; ed, Jewish Law Association Studies VIII: The Jerusalem 1994 Conference Volume, 96; auth, The Midrash and Healing, The Living Pulpit, 97; rev, Sukkah, Horayot, Shebuot, Temurah, Meilah and Tamic, South Florida Academic Commentary, by Neusner, in, Critical Rev of Books in Relig, 1996, 97; ed, Jewish Law Association Studies IV: The London 1996 Conference Volume, 97. **CONTACT ADDRESS** Hebrew Union Col-Jewish Inst of Religion, Ohio, 3101 Clifton Ave, Cincinnati, OH 45220. **EMAIL** Egoldman@huc.edu

GOLDSMITH, DAENA J.
PERSONAL Born Eugene, OR **DISCIPLINE** SPEECH COMMUNICATION **EDUCATION** Lewis and Clark Col, BS, 86; Univ Wash, MA, 88; PhD, 90. **CAREER** Asst prof, Univ Md, 90-93; asst prof, Univ Ill, Urbana, 93-99; assoc prof, 99-. **HONORS AND AWARDS** Rena J Ratle Awd; Phi Kappa Phi. **MEMBERSHIPS** NCA; ICA; INPR. **RESEARCH** Communication of social support in personal relationships; effects of different forms of supportive communication on relational satisfaction, identity, and coping. **SELECTED PUBLICATIONS** Coauth, "Helpful, supportive, and sensitive: Measuring the evaluation of enacted social support in personal relationships," J Soc Personal Relationships (forthcoming); coauth, "The impact of politeness and relationship on perceived quality of advice about a problem," Human Comm Res 26 (00): 234-263; auth, "Soliciting advice: The role of sequential placement in mitigating face threat," Comm Mono 67 (00): 1-19; auth, "Content-based resources for giving face-sensitive advice in troubles talk episodes," Res Lang Soc Interaction 32 (99): 303-336; coauth, "You just don't have the evidence: An analysis of claims and evidence, in Deborah Tannen's You Just Don't Understand," in Communication Year Book, ed. ME Roloff (Thousand Oaks, CA: Sage, 99); coauth, "How comforting messages work: Some mechanisms through which messages may alleviate emotional distress," in Handbook of Communication and Emotion: Research, Theory, Applications and Contexts, eds. PA Anderson, LK Guerrero (Orlando, FL: Academic Press, 97); coauth, "Sex differences in the provision of support," J Soc Personal Relationships 14 (97): 317-337; coauth, "The normative context of advice as social support," Human Comm Res 23 (97): 454-476; coauth, "Constituting relationships in talk: A taxonomy of speech events in social and personal relationships," Human Comm Res 23 (96): 87-114. **CONTACT ADDRESS** Dept Speech Communication, Univ of Illinois, Urbana-Champaign, 702 S Wright St, 244 Lincoln Hall, Urbana, IL 61801-3631. **EMAIL** goldsmit@uiuc.edu

GOLDSTEIN, R. JAMES
PERSONAL Born 09/19/1955, Hartford, CT, m, 1987 **DISCIPLINE** ENGLISH **EDUCATION** Univ Rochester, BA, 77; Univ Va, MA, 79; PhD, 87. **CAREER** For Lectr, Univ Salerno, 81-85; For Lectr, Aichi Univ, 87-88; Asst Prof, Ariz State Univ, 88-89; Asst Prof, Johns Hopkins Univ, 89-91; Asst Prof to Assoc Prof, Auburn Univ, 91-. **HONORS AND AWARDS** DuPont Fel, Univ Va, 78-79; NEH Summer Sem, 88, 92; NEH Summer Inst, 90, 94, 95. **MEMBERSHIPS** MLA; Medieval Acad of Am; New Chaucer Soc; Intl Asn for Medieval and Renaissance Scottish Lang and Lit; Dante Soc of Am; Soc for Medieval Feminist Scholar; Soc for the Study of Homosexuality in the Middle Ages; John Gower Soc; Asn of Am Univ Prof. **RESEARCH** Middle English Literature; Medieval Scottish Literature. **SELECTED PUBLICATIONS** Auth, The Matter of Scotland: Historical Narrative in Medieval Scotland, Univ Nebr Press, 93; auth, "Writing in Scotland, 1058-1560," in Cambridge History of Medieval Scottish Literature, Cambridge UP, 99; auth, "Chaucer, Suicide, and the Agencies of Memory: Troilus and the Death Drive," in Speaking Images, Pegasus press, 01; auth, "'Why calle ye hym crist, silpen Iewes called hym Iesus?': The Disavowal of Jewish Identification if Piers Plowman," Exemplaria, 01. **CONTACT ADDRESS** Dept English, Auburn Univ, 9030 Haley Center, Auburn, AL 36849. **EMAIL** goldsrj@auburn.edu

GOLDWEBER, DAVID E.
PERSONAL Born 06/19/1968, New York, NY **DISCIPLINE** ENGLISH **EDUCATION** Vassar Col, BA, 90; NY Univ, MA, 93; PhD, 98. **CAREER** Lectr, Audrey Cohen Col, 94-96; asst prof, Armstrong Univ, 97-; lectr, Merritt Col, 98-; lectr, Univ of San Francisco, 98-. **MEMBERSHIPS** MLA, Wordsworth-Coleridge Assoc. **RESEARCH** English Romantic Poetry, Harlem Renaissance, Surrealism, Utopian Literature, Science-Fiction and Fantasy. **SELECTED PUBLICATIONS** Auth, "Style and Structure of Blake's Bible," ELN, (95); auth, "Byron, Catholicism, and DJ XVII," Renascence, (97); auth, "Byron and Gifford," Keats-Shelley Rev, (98); auth, "Mr Punch, Dangerous Savior," Int Jour of Comic Art, (99); auth, "The Conversion of Claude McKay," Commonweal, (99); auth, Bounding Worlds, Caterpillar Pr, 00; auth, "Dreams and Stories in the Sandman," Int Jour of Comic Art, (01); auth, Countee Cullen and John Keats, PLL, forthcoming. **EMAIL** elroy1@mindspring.com

GOLDZWIG, STEVEN R.
PERSONAL Born 10/13/1950, San Antonio, TX, m, 1979, 2 children **DISCIPLINE** COMMUNICATION STUDIES **EDUCATION** Purdue Univ, PhD, 85. **CAREER** Asst prof, Univ of Southern Calif, 85-87; from asst prof to assoc prof, Marquette Univ, 87- . **HONORS AND AWARDS** Co-Recipient, M. Hochmut Nichols Awd for Outstanding Scholarship in Public Address, 95; Outstanding article of the year, 96. **MEMBERSHIPS** Nat Commun Asn; Central States Commun Asn. **RESEARCH** Polit commun; Legal commun; Contemp residency & civil rights. **SELECTED PUBLICATIONS** Auth, Multiculturalism, Rhetoric, and the 21st Century, Southern Commun Jour, 64, 98; coauth, Constructing a Postmodernist Ethic: The Feminist Quest for a New Politics, Differences that Make a Difference: Examining the Assumptions in Gender Reseach, ed H. Sterk and L. Turner, 94; Crisis at Little Rock: Eisenhower, History, and Mediated Political Realities, Eisenhower's War of Words: Rhetoric and Leadership, ed M.J. Medhurst, 94. Idealism and Pragmatism in American Foreign Policy Rhetoric: The Case of John F. Kennedy and Vietnam, Presidential Studies Quart, 24, 94; In a Perilous Hour: The Public Address of John F. Kennedy, 95; Legitimating Liberal Credentials for the Presidency: John F. Kennedy and The Strategy of Peace, Southern Commun Jour, 60, 95; A Relational Approach to Moral Decision-Making: The Majority Opinion in Planned Parenthood v. Casey, Quart Jour of Speech, 81, 95; Post-Assassination Newspaper Editorial Eulogies: Analysis and Assessment, Western Jour of Commun, 59, 95; Undue Burdens and Abortion Decision-Making: Justice Sandra Day O'Connor and Judicial Decision-Making, Women and Politics, 16 (3), 96; Women's Reality and the Untold Story: Designing Women and the Revisioning of the Thomas/Hill Hearings, Outsiders Looking In: A Communication Perspective on the Hill/Thomas Hearings, ed P. Siegel, 96. **CONTACT ADDRESS** Dept of Communication Studies, Marquette Univ, PO Box 1881, Milwaukee, WI 53201-1881. **EMAIL** goldzwigs@mu.edu

GOLIAN, LINDA MARIE
PERSONAL Born 03/27/1962, Woodbridge, NJ, m, 1988, 1 child **DISCIPLINE** LIBRARY **EDUCATION** Univ Miami, BA, 86; Florida St Univ, MA, 88; Fall Eds 96; Florida Atlantic Univ, EDD, 98. **CAREER** Volunteer, 94-96, Family Literacy Specialist; serials consul, 96-97, SIRS, FL; prog specialist, 94-96, Marriott Statford Court; adj instr, 94-, Univ S Florida; adj instr, 93-97, Florida Atlantic Univ; Florida Gulf Coast Univ Library-Librarian, 97; Florida Gulf Coast Univ Adjunct Prof, 99-. **MEMBERSHIPS** American Library ASSOC, 89. **RESEARCH** Mentoring, thinking style, learning styles, libr instruction, library admin. **CONTACT ADDRESS** Library, Florida Gulf Coast Univ Library, 10501 FGCU Blvd 5, Fort Myers, FL 33965. **EMAIL** lgolian@fgcu.edu

GOLLIN, RICHARD M.
DISCIPLINE ENGLISH **EDUCATION** Univ MN, PhD. **CAREER** Prof emer; taught at Univ MN & Colgate Univ. **HONORS AND AWARDS** Fulbright scholar, Oxford Univ; Fore fel; Wilson fel; NYSCA, ACLS, Rockefeller & NEH grants. **RESEARCH** Structure and meaning of narrative films. **SELECTED PUBLICATIONS** Coauth, A Viewer's Guide to Film Arts, Artifices, and Issues: AH Clough: A Descriptive Catalogue. **CONTACT ADDRESS** Dept of English, Univ of Rochester, 500 Wilson Blvd., RC Box 270451, Rochester, NY 14627-0451. **EMAIL** ffff@mail.rochester.edu

GOLLIN, RITA K.
PERSONAL Born 01/22/1928, New York, NY, m, 1950, 3 children **DISCIPLINE** ENGLISH LITERATURE **EDUCATION** Queens Col, NYork, BA, 49; Univ Minn, MA, 50, PhD, 61. **CAREER** Asst, Univ Minn, 49-53; lectr English, univ sch, Univ Rochester, 55-62 & 63-64, part-time instr, 60-62, part-time asst prof, 63-64, asst prof, 64-67; from asst prof to assoc prof, 67-75, Prof English, State Univ NY Col, Geneseo, 75-95, Distinguished Prof English, 95-, State Univ NY Res Found res grant, 68, 77, 80, 86, 87, 88, 91 & 98; fac exchange scholar, State Univ NY. **HONORS AND AWARDS** Phi Beta Kappa; AAUW fel; NEH fel, 84 & 88; Huntington Libr fel, 88; House of Seven Gables Hawthorne Awd, 84; UUP travel grant, 98. **MEMBERSHIPS** MLA; Northeast Mod Lang Asn (vpres, 77-78, pres, 78-79); Nathaniel Hawthorne Soc (pres, 79-82); ALA. **RESEARCH** Nineteenth century American fiction, especially Hawthorne and Melville; 20th century American fiction; writers and Shakers. **SELECTED PUBLICATIONS** Co-auth, Justice in an earlier treatment of the Billy Budd Theme, Am Lit, 57; co-auth, Exiles in India: An early Kipling variant, Notes and Queries, 65; Pierre's metamorphoses of Dante's Inferno, Am Lit, 68; Ed, A Little Journey in the World, 69 & Northwood: Or Life, North and South, 70, Johnson Reprint; The automobiles of The Great Gatsby, Studies in the Twentieth Century, 70; Modes of travel in Tender is the Night, Studies in the Twentieth Century, 71; contribr, Sarah Josepha Hale, Northwood, intro & bibliogr, Johnson, 72; auth, Dream-work in The Blithedale Romance, Emerson Soc Quart, 73; Little Souls Who Thirst for Fight in The Red Badge of Courage, Ariz Quart, 74; Understanding fathers in American Jewish fiction, Centennial Rev, 74; The forbidden fruit of Typee, Mod Lang Studies, 75; American Literature and An Introduction to Research and Bibliography in American Civilization, Everett Edwards, 75; auth, Painting and character in The Marble Faun, Emerson Soc Quart, 75; The Intelligence Offices of Hawthorne and Melville, Am Transcendental Quart, 75; The place of Walden in The Undiscovered Country, Thoreau Soc Bull, 76; The Quondam Sailor and Melville's Omoo, Am Lit, 76; Hawthorne on perception, lucubration , and reverie, Nathaniel Hawthorne J, 78; Hawthorne: The writer as dreamer, Studies in Am Renaissance, 78; Huckleberry Finn and The Time of the Evasion, Mod Lang Studies, 79; Nathaniel Hawthorne and the Truth of Dreams, La State Univ Press, 79; Nathaniel Hawthorne and the Truth of Dreams, La State Univ Press, 79; Arlin Turner, 1909-1980, Hawthorne Soc Newsletter, 80; Hester, Hetty, and the two Arthurs, Nathaniel Hawthorne J, 80; Getting a taste for pictures: Hawthorne at the Manchester Arts Exhibit, Nathaniel Hawthorne J, 80; Mathew Brady Photographs of Nathaniel Hawthorne, Studies in Am Renaissance, 82; Hawthorne's Golden Dora, Studies in Am Renaissance, 82; Louisa May Alcott's Hawthorne, Essex Inst Hist Collection, 82; co-ed, Hawthorne in Concord, Essex Inst Hist Collection Special Issue, 82; Malamud's Dubin and the Morality of Desire, PLL, 82; Standing on the Greensward: The Veiled

Correspondence of Nathaniel Hawthorne and Henry Wadsworth Longfellow, in Papers Presented at the Longfellow Commemorative Conference, April 1-3, 1982, Longfellow Nat Hist Park, 82; Portraits of Nathaniel Hawthorne: An Iconography, Northern Ill Univ Press, 83; Twentieth-Century American Fiction: Men and Women Writers, in Reconstructing American Literature, Feminist Press, 83; Hawthorne contemplates the Shakers: 1831-1851, Nathaniel Hawthorne Jour, 84; A Hawthornean in Japan, Hawthorne Soc Newsletter, 84; On atropine poisoning in The Scarlet Letter, New England J Medicine, 84; Some reminiscences of Japan, Jimyukadori, 85; Hawthorne and the anxiety of aesthetic response, Centennial Rev, 85; co-ed, Thoreau Inter Alia: Essays in Honor of Walter Harding, SUNY Geneseo, 85; Teaching Women in American Literature, in Towards Equitable Education for Women and Men, 86; Nathaniel Hawthorne, in American Literary Scholarship 1982, 1983, 1984, 1985, Duke Univ Press, 84, 85, 86, 87; Hawthorne on the Isles of Shoals, Nathaniel Hawthorne Rev, 87; Teaching Women, Geneseo Compass, Fac Forum, 4/87; Annie Field's Nathaniel Hawthorne: Grand as Ever, Postscript, 87; Legacy Profile: Annie Adams Fields (1834-1915), Legacy, 87; Again a Literary Man: Vocation and the Scarlet Letter, in Essays on the Scarlet Letter, G K Hall, 88; Subordinated Power: Mrs and Mr James T Fields, in Patrons and Protegees, Rutgers Univ Press, 88; Living in a world without Dickens, Huntington Libr Quart, 89; Pegasus in the Pound: The Editor, the author, their wives, and the Atlantic Monthly, Essex Inst Hist Collections, 89; First and last words on The Scarlet Letter, in From Cover to Cover: The Romances of Nathaniel Hawthorne, Essex Inst Hist Collection, 91; Nathaniel Hawthorne: The flesh and the spirit, or Gratifying Your Coarsest Animal Needs, Studies in the Novel, 91; co-auth, Prophetic Pictures: Hawthorne's Knowledge and Uses of the Visual Arts, Greenwood Press, 91; guest ed, Hawthorne in the Nineties, Studies in the Novel, special ed, 91; Ethan Brand's Homecomings, in New Essays on Hawthorne's Shorts Stories, Cambridge Univ Press, 93; Nathaniel Hawthorne, in Heath Anthology of American Literature, D C Heath, 90, 2nd ed, 93; Annie Adams Fields and Nathaniel Hawthorne, in American National Biography, Oxford Univ Press, forthcoming; Nathaniel Hawthorne and Annie Fields, in Scribbling Women: Engendering and Expanding the Hawthorne Tradition, Univ Mass Press; auth, Annie Adams Fields: Woman of Letters, Univ Mass Press, forthcoming; ed, The Scarlet Letter, for New Riverside Series, forthcoming. **CONTACT ADDRESS** Dept of English, SUNY, Col at Geneseo, 1 College Cir, Geneseo, NY 14454-1401. **EMAIL** gollin@geneseo.edu

GOLUMBIA, DAVID
PERSONAL Born 06/22/1963, Detroit, MI, m **DISCIPLINE** ENGLISH LANGUAGE AND LITERATURE **EDUCATION** Oberlin Col, BA, 95; Univ of Pennsylvania, PhD, 99. **CAREER** Independent scholar **MEMBERSHIPS** Modern Lang Assoc; Amer Phil Assoc; Linguistic Soc of Amer. **RESEARCH** Cultural studies; deconstruction; analytic philosophy (contemporary); linguistics (contemporary) as subjects for cultural studies; print and other media history; native languages and cultures. **SELECTED PUBLICATIONS** Auth, Toward an Ethics of Cultural Acts: The Jamesian Dialectic in Broken Wings, the Henry James Review, 94; Black and White World: Race, Ideology, and Utopia in Triton and Star Trek, Cultural Critique 32, 95-96; Resisting the World: Philip K. Dick, Cultural Studies, and Metaphysical Realism, Science Fiction Studies 23:1, 96; Hypercapital, Postmodern Culture 7:1, 96; Rethinking Philosophy in the Third Wave of Feminism, Hypatia: A Journal of Feminist Philosophy, 97; Quines Ambivalence, Cultural Critique 38, 97-98; Feminism and Mental Representation: Analytic Philosophy, Cultural Studies, and Narrow Content, Is Feminist Philsophy Philosophy?, 99; auth, Quine, Derrida, and the Question of Philos, The Philosophical Forum, 99; auth, Toward a Hist of 'Language': Ong and Derrida, Oxford Lit Rev, 00. **CONTACT ADDRESS** 502 West 122nd St., Apt 62, New York, NY 10027. **EMAIL** dgolumbi@sas.uenn.edu

GOMEZ, GILBERTO
PERSONAL Born 05/29/1957, Columbia, d, 1 child **DISCIPLINE** SPANISH AMERICAN LITERATURE **EDUCATION** Licenciatura en Edrcacion/Universidad del Quindio, Columbia; Washington Univ, St Louis, Mo, PhD. **CAREER** Assoc prof, Spanish, Wabash Col, 96-. **HONORS AND AWARDS** Fulbright scholar. **MEMBERSHIPS** MLA, Inst Int de Literatura Iberoamericana, Latin Am Studies Asn, Asn de Columbidinistos. **RESEARCH** Latin American narrative of the 19th and 20th centuries. **SELECTED PUBLICATIONS** Auth, Entre Maria y La Voragine: literatura columbiona Ginisecular 1886-1903, Bogota, Fondo Cultural Capetero (89). **CONTACT ADDRESS** Dept Modern Langs, Wabash Col, PO Box 352, Crawfordsville, IN 47933-0352. **EMAIL** gomezg@wabash.edu

GONTARSKI, S. E.
PERSONAL Born 02/27/1942, Brooklyn, NY, m, 1968, 1 child **DISCIPLINE** ENGLISH, IRISH, LITERATURE **EDUCATION** Long Island Univ, BA, 66; MA, 68; Ohio State Univ, PhD, 74. **CAREER** Asst prof to assoc prof, 74-84; vis assoc prof, Univ Calif Riverside, 82-83; assoc prof, Ga Inst Tech, 84-86; distinguished vis prof, Calif State Univ Long Beach, 87-88; prof, Fla State Univ, 88; distinguished vis prof, Univ Dublin, 94; Fulbright prof, Univ Col, 98-99; Sarah Herndon prof, distinguished res prof, Fla State Univ, 99-. **HONORS AND AWARDS** Distinguished Res Prof Awd, 00; TIP Awd, 99; Profess Excellence Awd, 99; Fla State Univ Awd, 91-92, 96-97; Rockefeller Found Grant, 01; Sr Fulbright Fel, 98-99; William Evans Vis Fel, Univ Otago, 94; NEH Fel, 93, 94. **MEMBERSHIPS** PEN; NBCC; MLA; Samuel Beckett Soc. **RESEARCH** 20th-century Irish studies, in British, US and European modernism, and in critical theory. **SELECTED PUBLICATIONS** Auth, Beckett's Happy Days': A Manuscript Study, Ohio State Univ Lib Pub, 77; co-ed, Samuel Beckett, Humanistic Perspectives, Ohio State UP, 83; auth, The Intent of Undoing in Samuel Beckett's Dramatic Texts, Ind UP, 85; ed, On Beckett: Essays and Criticism, Grove Pr, 86; auth, The Beckett Studies Reader, UP Fla, 93; ed, The Theatrical Notebooks of Samuel Beckett, Faber and Faber, 93 and Grove Pr, 93; ed, notes, Samuel Beckett. The Complete Short Prose, 1928-1989, Grove Pr, 96; ed and notes, The Theatrical Notebook of Samuel Beckett: The Shorter Plays, Vol. IV, Faber and Faber, 99 and Grove Pr, 99; auth, Modernism, Censorship, and the Politics of Puhlishing: The Grow Pr Legacy, Univ NCar, 00; ed, The Grove Pr Reader, 1951-2001, Grove Pr, 01. **CONTACT ADDRESS** English Dept, Florida State Univ, Tallahassee, FL 32306-1580. **EMAIL** sgontarski@english.fsu.edu

GONZALEZ, ALEXANDER G.
PERSONAL Born 05/29/1952, United Kingdom, m, 1998 **DISCIPLINE** ENGLISH **EDUCATION** Queens Col, CUNY, BA (magna cum laude), 76; Univ of Ore, MA, 78, PhD, 82. **CAREER** Half-time tutor of English Composition, 73-76, team-teacher, English Composition, Queens Col, 75-76; grad tchg fel, 77-80 & 81-82; dir, writing lab, 78-79, instr, Univ of Ore, 82-83; vis lectr, Univ of Calif at Santa Barbara, 80-81; asst prof of english, Ohio State Univ, 83-88; Asst Prof of English, 88-91, Assoc Prof of English, 91-94; Prof of English, SUNY Col at Cortland, 94-; distinguished scholar in residence, Pa State Univ, summer 91. **MEMBERSHIPS** MLA; South Atlantic MLA; Nat Coun of Teachers of English; Confr on Col Composition and Commun; James Joyce Found; Am Confr for Irish Studies; Irish-Am Cultural Inst; Int Asn for the Study of Irish Lit. **RESEARCH** Irish Lit. **SELECTED PUBLICATIONS** Auth, Darrell Figgis: A Study of His Novels, Moder Irish Lit Monographs Series, 92; Short Stories from the Irish Renaissance: An Anthology, Whitston, 93; Assessing the Achievement of J.M. Synge, Greenwood, 96; Peadar O'Donnell: A Reader's Guide, Dufour, 97; Modern Irish Writers A Bio-Critical Sourcebook, Greenwood, Aldwych Press, 97; Contemporary Irish Women Poets: Some Male Perspectives, 99; auth, Plays from the Irish Renaissance: An Anthology (forthcoming). **CONTACT ADDRESS** Dept of English, SUNY, Col at Cortland, Box 2000, Cortland, NY 13045. **EMAIL** gonzalez@cortland.edu

GONZALEZ, JOHN M.
PERSONAL Born 06/30/1966, Harlengey, TX, s **DISCIPLINE** US LITERATURE **EDUCATION** Princeton Univ, AB, 88; Stanford Univ, MA, 91; PhD, 98. **CAREER** Asst prof, Univ of Mich. **HONORS AND AWARDS** Award, Univ of Mich, 97; Travel Grant, Univ of Mich, 97; Fac Awd for Res, 97; YOHA Grant, 97; Awd, Univ of Mich, 98. **MEMBERSHIPS** MLA; Am Studies Assoc; Lat Am Studies Assoc; Nat Assoc for Chicana/o Studies; Western Lit Assoc. **RESEARCH** Post-Reconstruction Historical Romances, the Postcolonial condition, Narrative theory, literatures of the Americas. **SELECTED PUBLICATIONS** Auth, "Romancing Hegemony: Constructing Racialized Citizenship in Maria Amparo Ruiz de Burton's the Squatter and the Don", Recovering the U.S. Hispanic Literary Heritage, Vol 2, Arte Publico (Houston), 96; auth, "Interpreting California and the West", Western Am Lit 34.2 (99): 186-191; auth, "The Whiteness of Blushing: Racial Intelligibility in the Californio Borderlands", Maria Ampara Ruiz de Burton, eds Anne Goldman and Amelia Montes (forthcoming). **CONTACT ADDRESS** Dept English, Univ of Michigan, Ann Arbor, 505 S State St, Ann Arbor, MI 48109-1045. **EMAIL** jmgonzal@umich.edu

GOOCH, BRYAN N. S.
PERSONAL Born 12/31/1937, Vancouver, BC, Canada **DISCIPLINE** ENGLISH, MUSIC **EDUCATION** Royal Conserv Music (Toronto), ARCT, 57; Trinity Col Music, (London), LTCL, 59, FTCL, 61; Univ BC, BA, 59, MA, 62; Univ London, PhD, 68. **CAREER** Instr to assoc prof, 64-86, asst dean, 72-75, Prof English, Univ Victoria, 86-; fac mem, Victoria Conserv Music, 67-70; res fel, Craigdarroch Col, 68-69; Master, Lansdowne Col, 69-72; vis prof, Univ BC, 94-96; fac mem, Green Col, Univ BC, 95-99. **HONORS AND AWARDS** IODE Second World War mem post-grad schol, 62-64; Can Coun res grants, 73, 74, 75-78, leave fel, 76-77; SSHRCC grants, 78-80, 80-81, 82-88. **MEMBERSHIPS** Am Musicol Soc; Renaissance Soc Am; Shakespeare Asn Am; Can Asn Music Libr; life fel, Royal Commonwealth Soc. **SELECTED PUBLICATIONS** Coauth, Poetry os for People, Macmillan, 73; coauth, Musical Settings of Late Victorian and Modern British Literature: a Catalogue, Garland , 76; coauth, Musical Settings of Early and Mid-Victorian Literature: A Catalogue, 2 vol, Garland, 82; coauth, A Shakespeare Music Catalogue, 5 vols, Oxford, 91; coauth, The Emergenco of the Muse: Major Canadian Poest from Crawford to Pratt, Oxford Can, 93. **CONTACT ADDRESS** Dept of English, Univ of British Columbia, 397-1873 E Mall, BuTo, Vancouver, BC, Canada V6T1Z1.

GOOD, JACQUELYN FOX
DISCIPLINE ENGLISH LITERATURE **EDUCATION** Northwestern Univ, BA; Univ Chicago, MA; Univ Va, PhD. **CAREER** Asst prof, 89-. **RESEARCH** Shakespeare and the English Renaissance; American autobiography and fiction. **SELECTED PUBLICATIONS** Auth, pubs on Shakespeare, and fiction. **CONTACT ADDRESS** Dept of Humanities, Illinois Inst of Tech, 3301 S Dearborn, Chicago, IL 60616. **EMAIL** humfoxgood@minna.cns.iit.edu

GOODALL, HAROLD L.
PERSONAL Born 09/08/1952, Martinsburg, WV, m, 1989, 1 child **DISCIPLINE** COMMUNICATION **EDUCATION** Shepherd Col, BA, B Ed, 73; Univ NC Chapel Hill, MA, 74; Pa State Univ, PhD, 80. **CAREER** Instr, Clemson Univ, 74-77; asst to assoc prof, chair, Univ of Ala, 80-89; assoc prof, Univ of Utah, 89-91; prof, Clemson Univ, 91-95; prof, Head, Univ of NC Greensboro, 95-. **HONORS AND AWARDS** Outstanding Textb, Textbook and Acad Authors Asn, 94; Gerald M. Phillips Mentoring Awd, Am Commun Asn, 95; Vis Scholar, Ohio Univ, 98; Vis Scholar, Vis Scholar, Univ of Alaska Fairbanks, 99. **MEMBERSHIPS** Int Commun Assoc; Nat Commun Assoc; Am Commun Assoc; S States Commun Assoc; Soc for the Study of Symbolic Interaction. **RESEARCH** Ethnography, organizational communication, the social construction of identities and communities, Southern cultures. **SELECTED PUBLICATIONS** Auth, Casing a Promised Land: Expanded Edition, S IL Univ Pr, (Carbondale, IL), 94; auth, Divine Signs: Connecting spirit and Community, S IL Univ Pr, (Carbondale, IL), 96; auth, "Representation, Interpretation, and Performance: Opening the Text of Casing a Promised Land", Text and Performance Quart 17, (97): 109-122; coauth, "The Dispossessed", in Case Studies in Orgn Commun, Vol II, ed Beverly Davenport Sypher, (CA: Wadsworth, 97), 371-380; auth, "Transforming Communication Studies Through Ethnography", in Commun: View From the Helm for the Twenty-First Century, ed Judith Trent, (Allyn & Bacon, 97), 363-367; auth, Food Talk: A Man's Guide to Cooking and Communication with Women, Snowgoose Cover Pub, (Greensbobo, NC), 98; coauth, "The Death of Discourse in Our Own Chatroom: Sextext, Skillful discussion, and Virtual Communities", in Soudbite Cult: The Death of Discourse in a Wired World, ed David Slayden andRita K. Whillock, (CA: Sage, 99), 155-190; auth, "Casing the Academy for Community", Commun Theory 9, (99): 465-494; auth, Writing the New Ethnography, AltaMira/Rowman & Littlefield (Lanham, MD), 00; coauth, Organizational Communication: Balancing Creativity and Constraint, 3rd ed, St. Martin's Pr, (forthcoming). **CONTACT ADDRESS** Dept Commun, Univ of NC Greensboro, Greensboro, PO Box 26170, Greensboro, NC 27402-6170. **EMAIL** hlgoodal@uncg.edu

GOODBURN, AMY M.
PERSONAL Born 03/22/1966, Columbus, OH, m, 1997, 2 children **DISCIPLINE** COMPOSITION, LITERACY STUDIES **EDUCATION** Miami Univ, BA, 87; Ohio State Univ, MA, 90; MA, 91; PhD, 94. **CAREER** TA, Ohio State Univ, 89-94; asst to assoc prof, Univ of Nebr Lincoln, 94-. **HONORS AND AWARDS** UNL Layman Fund Awds, 94, 96; Col of Arts and Sci Distinguished Teaching Awd, 99; UNL Scholar In Teaching Awd, 99; Fac Dev Leave Awd, 01. **MEMBERSHIPS** NCTE, Conf on Col Comp and Commun, Writing Prog Adminr Assoc, Coalition of Women Scholars in Rhetoric and Comp. **RESEARCH** Critical and multicultural reading and writing pedagogies, ethnographic and teacher research, and community/school literacy practices. **SELECTED PUBLICATIONS** Coauth, "Collaboration, Critical Pedagogy, and Struggles Over Difference," Jour of Advan Comp 14.1, (94): 131-147; coauth, "Feminist Writing Program Administration: Resisting the Bureaucrat Within," Feminism and Composition: In Other Words, eds Susan Jarratt and Lynn Worsham, (NY: MLA, 97): 276-290; coauth, "Professionalizing TA Training: Commitment to Teaching or Rhetorical Response to Market Crisis?" Writing Program Admin 22, (98): 9-32; auth, "Processing the 'Critical' in Literacy Research: Issues of Authority, Ownership, and Representation," Eng Educ 30.2, (98): 121-145; auth, "It's a Question of Faith: Discourses of Fundamentalism and Critical Pedagogy in the Writing Classroom," JAC: A Jour of Comp Theory 18.2, (98): 333-353; auth, "Literacy Practices at the Genoa Industrial Indian School," Great Plains Quart 19, (99): 35-52; auth, "Racing (Eracing) Teacher/Researcher Authority in Writing About Race," Race, Rhetoric, and Composition, ed Keith Gilyard, (Portsmouth, NH: Boynton/Cook, 99): 66-86; coauth, "Composition Studies and Service Learning: Appealing to Communities?" Comp Studies 28, (00): 79-94; coauth, "The Ethics of Students' Community Writing as Public Text," Public Works, eds Emily J Isaacs and Phoebe Jackson, (Portsmouth, NH: Boyton/Cook, 01): 26-34; auth, "(Re)Presenting Our Practice: Documenting Teaching in Composition Studies," eds Amy Goodburn and Deborah Minter, (Portsmouth, NH: Boynton/Cook, forthcoming). **CONTACT ADDRESS** 2713 Sewell St, Lincoln, NE 68502-4143. **EMAIL** agoodburn1@unl.edu

GOODHEART, EUGENE
PERSONAL Born 06/26/1931, New York, NY **DISCIPLINE** ENGLISH LITERATURE **EDUCATION** Columbia Univ, BA, 53, PhD, 61; Univ Va, MA, 54. **CAREER** From instr to asst prof, 58-62, Bard Col; asst prof, 62-66, Univ Chicago;

assoc prof, 66-67, Mt Holyoke Col; from assoc to prof, 67-74, Mass Inst Technol; prof & chmn, 74-80, prof, 80-, Boston Univ; Edytha Macy Gross Prof of Hum, 83-, Brandeis Univ; Guggenheim Fel, 70-71; NEH panelist, 74, 81 & 82. **MEMBERSHIPS** MLA; AAUP. **RESEARCH** Ideology and literature. **SELECTED PUBLICATIONS** Auth, The Skeptic Disposition, Princeton Univ Press, 84; auth, Desire and Its Discontents, Columbia Univ Press, 87; auth, Pieces of Resistance, Cambridge Univ Press, 91; auth, The Reign of Ideology, Columbia Univ Press, 97; auth, Does Literary Studies Have a Future, Univ of Wisc Press, 99. **CONTACT ADDRESS** 25 Barnard Ave, Watertown, MA 02172.

GOODMAN, JENNIFER ROBIN
PERSONAL Born 01/19/1953, Urbana, IL, m, 1998 **DISCIPLINE** LITERATURE **EDUCATION** Radcliffe Col, AB, 74; Univ Toronto, AM, 75; Harvard Univ, AM, 77, PhD(English), 81. **CAREER** Lectr, English, Harvard Univ, 81-82; asst prof, 82-88, assoc prof, 88-97, prof, English, Tex A&M Univ, 97- . **MEMBERSHIPS** Medieval Acad Am; MLA; New Chaucer Soc. **RESEARCH** Medieval English literature; medieval studies; English and American literature. **SELECTED PUBLICATIONS** Auth, To display a clearly dramatic talent: The Theatre Historique of Alexandre Dumas, Harvard Libr Bull, 4/78; The captain's self-portrait: John Smith as chivalric biographer, Va Mag Hist & Biog, 1/81; auth, Malory and William Caxton's Prose Romances of 1485, 87; auth, The Legend of Arthur in British and American Literature 500-1985, 88; auth, British Drama before 1660, 91; auth, Chivalry and Exploration, 1298-1630, 98. **CONTACT ADDRESS** Dept of English, Texas A&M Univ, Col Station, 1 Texas A and M Univ, College Station, TX 77843-4227. **EMAIL** jennifer@nativecouncil.com

GOODMAN, MICHAEL B.
PERSONAL Born 07/10/1949, Dallas, TX, m, 1977, 2 children **DISCIPLINE** ENGLISH, COMMUNICATIONS **EDUCATION** Univ Texas, BA, 71; SUNY Stony, MA, 72; PhD, 79. **CAREER** Adj prof, New York Inst Tech, 76-82; asst prof, 79-81, adj asst prof, 82, SUNY; fac mem, Nat Fac, 84; asst prof, North East Univ, 82-86; vis prof, Univ Alas, 96; prof, Fairleigh Dickinson Univ, 90-. **HONORS AND AWARDS** Goldsmith Awd, IEEE; Dist Comm, STC. **MEMBERSHIPS** MLA; IEEE; STC; ABC. **RESEARCH** Corporate culture and change. **SELECTED PUBLICATIONS** Auth, Corporate Communication for Executives, SUNY Press (Albany), 98; auth, Working in a Global Environment: Understanding, Communicating, and Managing Transnationally, Inst Elec Electr Eng (NY), 95; auth, A Corporate Communication: Theory and Practice, SUNY Press (Albany), 94; auth, William S. Burroughs: A Research Guide, Garland Pub (NY), 90; auth, "Communication and Change: Effective Change Communication is Personal, Global, and Continuous," J Comm Man 2 (96): 115-133; auth, "Burroughs and Advertising: Fractured Language, Fractured Time, Fractured Image as the Universal Language," in Advertising and Culture,' Theoretical Perspectives, ed. Cross (Westport, CT: Praeger, 96): 85-91; auth, "Corporate and Organizational Communication," in Wiley Encyclopedia of Electrical and Electronics Engineering, ed. John Webster (NY: John Wiley & Sons, 99): 341-357; auth, "Corporate Communication: What Is It Now and into the 21st Century," Corp Comm J 5 (00); auth, Corporate Communication, forthcoming; coauth, "While You Were Looking the Other Way: Sixteen Forces That are Redefining Marketing and Advertising," forthcoming. **CONTACT ADDRESS** Dept English, Fairleigh Dickinson Univ, Florham-Madison, 285 Madison Ave, Madison, NJ 07940-1006. **EMAIL** goodman@alpha.fdu.edu

GOODMAN, SUSAN
PERSONAL Born 03/20/1951, Boston, MA, m **DISCIPLINE** AMERICAN LITERATURE **EDUCATION** Univ NHamp, BA, 72; MEd, 74; MA, 85; PhD, 88. **CAREER** Asst Prof to Assoc Prof, CSUF, 89-94; Asst Prof to Prof, Univ Del, 94-. **HONORS AND AWARDS** Project Development Awd, 97; Res Fel, VA Center for the Humanities, 94; Affirmative Action Grants, 92, 91, 89; Res Scholarship, 92. **MEMBERSHIPS** Mod Lang Asn; NE Mod Lang Asn; Am Lit Asn; Edith Wharton Soc; Ellen Glasgow Soc; Popular Culture Asn; Soc for the Study of S Lit. **RESEARCH** American literature and culture. **SELECTED PUBLICATIONS** Auth, Edith Wharton's Women: Friends and Rivals, Univ Press of N Eng, 90; auth, Edith Wharton's Inner Circle, Univ TX Press, 94; co-ed, Femmes de Conscience: Aspects du Feminisme Americain, 1848-1875, Sorbonne Univ Press, 94; auth, "Memory and Memoria in The Sheltered Life," Mississippi Quarterly, (96): 241-254; auth, "Ellen Glasgow: Calvinism and A Religious Odyssey," American Presbyterians: Journal of Presbyterian History, (96): 31-42; auth, "Edith Wharton at Yale," Edith Wharton Review, 96; auth, "The Fatherlode: Ellen Glasgow's Religious Inheritance," in The Calvinist Roots of the Modern Era, (Univ Press of N Eng, 97), 198-211; auth, Ellen Glasgow: A Biography, Johns Hopkins Univ, 98; auth, "Competing Histories: William Styron's The Confessions of Nat Turner and Sherley Ann Williams's Dessa Rose," in The World is our Home, Univ KY Press, 99; co-ed, Edith Wharton: A Forward Glance, Univ DE Press, 99; **CONTACT ADDRESS** Dept Eng, Univ of Delaware, Memorial Hall, Newark, DE 19716-2799. **EMAIL** sgoodman@odin.udel.edu

GOODNIGHT, G. THOMAS
PERSONAL Born 12/02/1948, Houston, TX, m, 1972, 3 children **DISCIPLINE** COMMUNICATION STUDIES; POLITICAL SCIENCE **EDUCATION** Univ of Houston, 71; Univ of Kansas, 77. **CAREER** Prof, Northwestern Univ, 75- ; dir of Forensics, 75-84; dir of grad studies, 83-86; 88-91. **HONORS AND AWARDS** Awd for outstanding scholar, Am Forensic Asn, 74, 80, 82; Charles Wohlbert Res Awd, SCA, 92; Outstanding Prof, Nat Speakers Asn, 94; Golden Monograph Awd, SCA, 95. ORG Nat Commun Asn. **RESEARCH** Public Culture; Rhet; Argumentation; Policy Controversy; Commun Theory & Practice. **SELECTED PUBLICATIONS** Auth, Toward a Social Theory of Argumentation, Argumentation and Advocacy, 89; The Rhetorical Tradition, Modern Communication, and the Rhetoric of Assent, The Rhetoric of Assent, eds Williams and Hazen, 90; Controversy, Proceedings of the 6th Annual Conference on Argumentation, ed D. Parson, 91; Habermas, the Public Sphere, and Controversy, World Jour of Pub Opinion Res, 4, 92; Rhetoric, Legitimation, and the End of the Cold War: Ronald Reagan at the Moscow Summit, 1988, Reagan and Public Discourse in America, eds M. Weiler and B. Pearce, 92; Legitimation Inferences: An Additional Component for the Toulmin Model, Informal Logic, 15, 93; A New Rhetoric for a New Dialectic, Argumentation: An Int Jour on Reasoning, 7, 93; The Park, The Firm, and the University, Quart Jour of Speech, 81, 95; Reagan, Vietnam and Central America: On Public Memory and the Politics of Fragmentation, Rhet and the Presidency, ed M. Medhurst, 96; Hans J. Morgenthau In Defense of the National Interest and the Recovery of the Rhetorical Tradition, The Rhet of Realism, eds Hariman and Beer, 96; coauth, Entanglements of Consumption, Cruelty, Privacy and Fashion, The Social Controversy over Fur, Quart Jour of Speech, fall issue, 94; Studies in the Public Sphere, Quart Jour of Speech, fall isssue, 97. **CONTACT ADDRESS** Dept of Communication Studies, Northwestern Univ, 1809 Chicago Ave, Evanston, IL 60201-4119. **EMAIL** GTQ@NWU.edu

GOODSON, ALFRED CLEMENT
PERSONAL Born 11/30/1946, Houston, TX, m, 1984, 1 child **DISCIPLINE** COMPARATIVE LITERATURE, ENGLISH **EDUCATION** Rice Univ, BA, 68; State Univ NYork Buffalo, PhD(comp lit), 73. **CAREER** Asst prof, 72-77, ASSOC PROF ENGLISH, MICH STATE UNIV, 77-, Alexander von Humboldt Stiftung res grant, Deutsches Seminar, Tubingen, 79; prof english, 88; dir, 91-. **RESEARCH** Romantic Lang Theory and Poetics; Critical History and Theory; Literature and Medicine. **SELECTED PUBLICATIONS** Auth, Verbal Imagination: Coleridge and the Language of Modern Criticism, Coxford, 88; auth, Frankenstein in the Age of Prozac: Artistic Creativity, Depression, Modern Medicine, Lit and Med, Vol 0015, 96; auth, Coleridge's Writing, on Language, Vol 3, MacMillan, 98. **CONTACT ADDRESS** 403 Kensington Rd, East Lansing, MI 48823. **EMAIL** goodson@pilot.msu.edu

GOODSON, CAROL F.
PERSONAL Born 03/28/1947, Detroit, MI **DISCIPLINE** LIBRARY SCIENCE **EDUCATION** State Univ New York, BA, 70, MLS, 72; State Univ Ga, MA, 96. **CAREER** From libr intern to Head of Access Services, 70-72, SUNY; from readers serv librn to branch head libr to commun sch dir, 73-77, St Louis Board of Education; ref librn, Ga Div Public Libr Serv, 81-84; Reference head, Mercer/Atlanta Univ, 85; librn, St Henry Sch, 85-86; libr dir, Aquinas Col, 89-90; asst dir, Clayton Country Libr Syst, 90-91, coordr, head Access Services, State Univ W Ga Libr, 91-. **HONORS AND AWARDS** Phi Kappa Phi; Beta Phi Mu; Sigma Tau Delta; Omicron Delta Kappa. **MEMBERSHIPS** Am Libr Asn; LAMA; ACRL; Ga Libr Asn. **RESEARCH** Personal performance evaluation; distance learning; library support; work of film director Woody Allen. **SELECTED PUBLICATIONS** Auth, The Complete Guide to Performance Standards for Library Personnel, 97; auth, art, I Have Seen the Future, and It Is Us, 97; auth, art, Access Services at the State Univ of West Georgia, 97; auth, art, Putting the Service Back in Library Service, 97; auth, art, I'm Going to be in OCLC, 97; auth, Providing Library Services For Distance Education Students, 01; auth, "Song as Subtext: the Virtual Reality of Lyrics in the Films of Woody Allen. **CONTACT ADDRESS** State Univ of West Georgia, Carrollton, GA 30118. **EMAIL** cgoodson@westga.edu

GOOSMAN, STUART
DISCIPLINE ETHNOMUSICOLOGY **EDUCATION** Univ WA, PhD. **CAREER** Asst prof; affil fac, Univ Ctr for African & African-Am Stud. **RESEARCH** African Diapora; jazz and popular music; politics and music. **SELECTED PUBLICATIONS** Publ on topics that range from, black group vocal harmony to George Clinton, rap & hip-hop, Juan Luis Guerra & Louis Moreua Gottschalk. **CONTACT ADDRESS** School of Music, Univ of Texas, Austin, 2613 Wichita St, Austin, TX 78705.

GOPALAN, LALITHA
DISCIPLINE ENGLISH LITERATURE **EDUCATION** Madras Christian Col, BA; Univ Rochester, MA, PhD. **CAREER** Assoc prof. **RESEARCH** Film theory and practice; national cinemas; history of anthropology; postcolonial theory; feminist film theory and practice; cultural studies; Marxist theory. **SELECTED PUBLICATIONS** Auth, Putting Asunder: Marriage of Maria Braun, Deep Focus, 89; Indian Cinema, Afterimage, 92; Coitus Interruptus & the Love Story in Indian Cinema, 96. **CONTACT ADDRESS** English Dept, Georgetown Univ, 37th and O St, Washington, DC 20057.

GOPEN, GEORGE D.
PERSONAL Born 06/14/1945, Cambridge, MA, m, 2000, 1 child **DISCIPLINE** ENGLISH LITERATURE **EDUCATION** Harvard Univ, JD, 72, PhD, 75. **CAREER** Rhetorical Prof. **RESEARCH** Rhetorical analysis of langs and lit. **SELECTED PUBLICATIONS** Auth, publ(s) on compos theory; rhet anal lit. **CONTACT ADDRESS** Eng Dept, Duke Univ, Durham, NC 27708. **EMAIL** ggopen@duke.edu

GORDON, ANDREW
PERSONAL Born 01/23/1945 **DISCIPLINE** LITERATURE AND PSYCHOLOGY **EDUCATION** Rutgers Univ, BA, 65; Univ Calif, MA, 67; PhD, 73. **CAREER** Tchg asst, Univ Calif, 68-70; Fulbright jr lectr, Univ Barcelona, Univ Valencia, Spain, 73-75; asst prof, 75-80; Fulbright jr lectr, Oporto, Portugal, 79; Fulbright sr lect, Univ Nis, Yugoslavia, 84-85; vis prof, Janus Pannonius Univ, Pecs, Hungary, 95; vis prof, Univ Alcala de Henares, Spain, 95; vis prof, Inst Superior de Psicologia Aplicada, Lisbon, Portugal, 95; vis prof, Ling Univ Nizhny Novgrorod, Russia, 97; assoc dir, IPSA, 85-93; dir, IPSA, 93-; ch, SAMLA, 84, 86; deleg assembly, MLA, 94-96; asst prof, 80-. **HONORS AND AWARDS** BA with high hon(s), Rutgers Univ, 65; Phi Beta Kappa, Rutgers, 65; NY State Regents tchg fel, 67-69; Fulbright jr lect, Spain, 73-75; Fulbright jr lect, Portugal, 79; Fulbright jr lect, Yugoslavia, 84-85; hum fac res award, 80; res award, 93. **SELECTED PUBLICATIONS** Auth, An American Dreamer: A Psychoanalytic Study of the Fiction of Norman Mailer, Fairleigh Dickinson Univ Press/ Assoc UP, 80; Smoking Dope with Thomas Pynchon: A Sixties Memoir, The Vineland Papers: Critical Takes on Pynchon's Novel, Dalkey Archv Press, 94; Cynthia Ozick's The Shawl and the Transitional Object, Lit and Psychol, 94; It's Not Such a Wonderful Life: The Neurotic George Bailey, The Amer Jour Psychoanalysis, 94; Shame in Saul Bellow's Something to Remember Me By, Saul Bellow Jour, 95; Close Encounters: Unidentified Flying Object Relations, The Psychoanalytic Rev, 95; Indiana Jones and the Temple of Doom: Bad Medicine, Foods of the Gods: Eating and the Eaten in Fantasy and Science Fiction, Ga Univ Press, 96; Herzog's Divorce Grief, Saul Bellow and the Struggle at the Center, AMS Press, 96; co-auth, Superior Intellect?: Sincere Fictions of the White Self, Jour Negro Edu, 95; The Beautiful American: Sincere Fictions of the White Messiah in the American Cinema, Lit and Psychoanalysis, Inst Superior de Psicologia Aplicada, 96; Les Mutines du Bounty: Malaise dans la civilisation, Gradiva: Revue Europeene d'Anthropolgie Litteraire 96; rev(s), Review of Science Fiction for Young Readers, Children's Lit, 96; Review of Family Plots: The De-Oedipalization of Popular Culture by Dana Heller, Yearbook of Comparative and General Literature, Ind Univ, 97. **CONTACT ADDRESS** Dept of Eng, Univ of Florida, Box 117310, Gainesville, FL 32611-7310. **EMAIL** agordon@ufl.edu

GORDON, LOIS G.
PERSONAL Born 11/13/1938, Englewood, NJ, m, 1961, 1 child **DISCIPLINE** ENGLISH & COMPARATIVE LITERATURE **EDUCATION** Univ MI, BA, 60; Univ Wis, MA, 62, PhD, 66. **CAREER** Lectr Eng, City Col NY, 64-66; asst prof, Univ MO, KS City, 66-68; from asst prof to assoc prof, 68-75, prof eng & comp lit, Fairleigh Dickinson Univ, 75-, vis prof, Rutgers Univ, 94, Asst ed, Lit & Psychol, 68-71. **HONORS AND AWARDS** Teaching Fel, 62-64; Univ of Wis: Tuition Scholarship; Dissertation Completion Fel, 66; Univ of Mo Res Grant, 67-68; Fairleigh Dickinson Univ Res Grant, 85-86, 89-90, 96-97; **MEMBERSHIPS** MLA; Pinter Soc; Beckett Soc; PEN; Acad of Am Poets; Int Bach Soc; Int League for Human Rights; Authors Guild; U.S. Nat Landmarks Commission. **RESEARCH** Twentieth century Eng and comp lit; postmoderism. **SELECTED PUBLICATIONS** Auth, Stratagems to Uncover Nakedness: The Dramas of Harold Pinter, Univ MO Press, 69; Donald Barthelme, G K Hall, 81; Robert Coover--The Universal Fictionmaking Process, Southern Ill Univ Press, 83; co-auth, American Chronicle: Six Decades in American Life, 1920-1979, Atheneum/Random House, 87; co-auth, American Chronicle: Seven Decades in American Life, 1920-1989, Random House, 80; Harold Pinter: A Caseboo, Garland Publ, 90; co-auth, The Columbia Chronicles of American Life, 1910-1992, Columbia Univ Press, 95; The World of Samuel Beckett, 1906-1946, Yale Univ Press, 96, reprint, 98; American Chronicle: Decade by Decade through the Twentieth Century, Yale Univ Press, 99. **CONTACT ADDRESS** Dept of Eng, Fairleigh Dickinson Univ, Teaneck-Hackensack, 1000 River Rd, Teaneck, NJ 07666-1996. **EMAIL** loisgord@aol.com

GORDON, RONALD D.
PERSONAL Born 02/21/1944, Los Angeles, CA, m, 1992, 3 children **DISCIPLINE** COMMUNICATION **EDUCATION** San Jose State Univ, BA, 66, MA, 68; Univ KS, PhD, 71. **CAREER** Calif State Univ-Humboldt; vis prof, Texas A&M Univ, Univ Hawaii-Manoa; full prof, Univ Hawaii-Hilo, 84-. **HONORS AND AWARDS** Pres, Pc & Asian Commun Asn, 98-01.

MEMBERSHIPS Nat Commun Asn. **RESEARCH** Human dialogue, Spiritual communication, Communication and culture, Mass media studies. **SELECTED PUBLICATIONS** Auth, "Multicultural Diversity and Human Communication Theory", Human Communication, Winter/Spring 99, 1-8; auth "Karl Jaspers: Existential Philosopher of Dialogical Communication", S Commun J, Winter/Spring 00, 105-118. **CONTACT ADDRESS** Dept Commun, Univ of Hawaii, Hilo, Hilo, HI 96720-4091. **EMAIL** rgordon@hawaii.edu

GORDON, WALTER MARTIN
PERSONAL Born 03/05/1928, San Francisco, CA **DISCIPLINE** ENGLISH, THEOLOGY **EDUCATION** Gonzaga Univ, MA, 53; Col St Albert de Louvain, STL, 60; Univ London, PhD(English), 66. **CAREER** Instr English, Univ Santa Clara, 55-56; asst prof, Loyola Univ, Calif, 67-71; asst prof, 72-79, ASSOC PROF ENGLISH, UNIV GA, 79-. **MEMBERSHIPS** Amici Thomae More; Renaissance Soc Am; SAtlantic Mod Lang Asn; MLA. **RESEARCH** Dramatic form in Thomas More's writings; More's writings on the Eucharist; seriocomic art of More and Erasmus. **SELECTED PUBLICATIONS** Auth, The Complete Works of More, Thomas, Vol 7--The 'Letter to Bugenhagen', the 'Supplication of Souls', the 'Letter Against Frith,' Moreana, Vol 0029, 92; Maiestas in More, Thomas Political-Thought, Moreana, Vol 0034, 97. **CONTACT ADDRESS** Dept of English, Univ of Georgia, 0 Georgia University, Athens, GA 30602-0001.

GORDON-SEIFERT, CATHERINE
PERSONAL Born 01/13/1954, Columbus, OH, m, 1986, 2 children **DISCIPLINE** HISTORY OF MUSIC **EDUCATION** Univ of MI, PhD, 94, MM, 83; IN Univ, MM, 80; Bowling Green St Univ, BM, 76 **CAREER** Facul, 96-98, Boston Conserv of Music; Asst Prof, 98-, Providence Col **HONORS AND AWARDS** Disting Svc Awd for Graduating Sr; alpha lambda delta **MEMBERSHIPS** Am Musicol Asn; Sonneck Soc **RESEARCH** Opera **CONTACT ADDRESS** Dept of Music, Providence Col, Providence, RI 02918. **EMAIL** cgordon@providence.edu

GORFAIN, PHYLLIS
PERSONAL Born 10/09/1943, Houston, TX, M, 1965 **DISCIPLINE** ENGLISH, FOLKLORE **EDUCATION** Butler Univ, BA, 65; Univ Calif, Berkeley, MA, 67, PhD(English), 73. **CAREER** ASSOC PROF ENGLISH, OBERLINE COL, 71-, Am Coun Learned Soc study fel, 75-76. **MEMBERSHIPS** MLA. **RESEARCH** Shakespeare; folklore and literature; African folklore. **SELECTED PUBLICATIONS** Coauth, Ambiguity and exchange the double dimension of Mbeere Riddles, J Am Folklore, 76; auth, Puzzle and artifice: The riddle as metapoetry in Pericles, Shakespeare Surv, 76; Riddles and reconciliation: The formal unity of All's Well That Ends Well, J Folklore Inst, 76; Riddles and the tragic structure of Macbeth, Miss Folklore Regist, 76; Toward a folkloristic approach to Shakespearean drama, Southern Folklore Quart, 77. **CONTACT ADDRESS** Dept of English, Oberlin Col, 135 W Lorain St, Oberlin, OH 44074-1076.

GORSEVSKI, ELLEN
PERSONAL Born 11/08/1965, WV, m, 1993 **DISCIPLINE** SPEECH COMMUNICATION **EDUCATION** Univ Colo, BA, 88; Ore State Univ, MA, 95; Pa State Univ, PhD, 99. **CAREER** Instr, Wash State Univ, 98-. **HONORS AND AWARDS** Mackenzie Mem Scholar, Univ of Colo, 85; Edwin Erle Sparks Fel, Pa State Univ, 96. **MEMBERSHIPS** Nat Commun Assoc. **RESEARCH** Non-violent Rhetoric, Rhetoric of Peace Makers, Human Rights. **SELECTED PUBLICATIONS** Auth, "A Peaceful Warrior Speaks: Kiro Gligorov at the United Nations", Macedonia Rev 27, (97); auth, "The Physical Side of Linguistic Violence", Peace Rev: A Transnational Quarterly, 10.4 (Dec 98); auth, "A Rhetorical Climate: The Power of Hope in Big Sky Country, J of Commun and Relig, (Sept 99); auth, "Nonviolent Theory on Communication: The Implications for Theorizing a Nonviolent Rhetoric", Peace and Change, (Oct 99); auth, "Peace, Nonviolence, and Speech Communication", Moscow-Pullman Daily News (Moscow, ID), 16-17 Jan 99. **CONTACT ADDRESS** Dept English, Washington State Univ, PO Box 645020, Pullman, WA 99164-5020. **EMAIL** elleng@mail.wsu.edu

GOSS, JAMES
PERSONAL Born 08/21/1939, San Pedro, CA, m, 1961, 3 children **DISCIPLINE** RELIGION & LITERATURE **EDUCATION** Univ Southern Calif, BA, 60; Southern Calif Sch Theol, MTh, 63; Claremont Grad Sch, PhD, 70. **CAREER** Assoc prof & campus minister, Cornell Col, 65-67; asst prof, 69-80, from prof to chemn, Relig Studies, Calif State Univ, Northridge, 80-; exec assoc to the pres, 98-; prof relig studies/ assoc to pres. **MEMBERSHIPS** Soc Bibl Lit; Am Acad Relig. **RESEARCH** Religion in literature; New Testament. **SELECTED PUBLICATIONS** Auth, Camus, God and process thought, Process Studies, summer 74; art, O'Connor's redeemed man: Christus et/vel Porcus?, Drew Gateway, winter-spring 74; art, The double action of mercy in The Artificial Nigger, Christianity & Lit, spring 74; art, Eschatology, autonomy, and individuation: The evocative power of the kingdom, Jour Am Acad of Relig, 81. **CONTACT ADDRESS** President's Office, 18111 Nordhoff St, Northridge, CA 91330-8200. **EMAIL** james.goss@csun.edu

GOSSETT, PHILIP
PERSONAL Born 09/27/1941, New York, NY, m, 1963, 2 children **DISCIPLINE** MUSICOLOGY **EDUCATION** Amherst Col, BA, 63; Princeton Univ, MFA, 65, PhD, 70. **CAREER** Asst instr, Princeton Univ, 64-65; From asst prof to assoc prof, 68-77, prof music, Univ Chicago, 77-84, Robert W. Reneker Distinguished Service Prof, Univ Chicago, 84-; Chmn, Dept Music, Univ Chicago, 78-84 & 89, Dean, Div hum, Univ Chicago, 89-99; Guggenheim fel, 71-72; Nat Endowment for Hum sr scholar, 82-83; general ed, The Works of Giuseppe Verdi; devettore, Edizoue critica delle opere di Gioachino Rossini; vis assoc prof, Columbia Univ, 75; Meadows Distinguished Vis Prof, Southern Methodist Univ, Fall 80; Professore Associato, Facolta di Musicologia, Universita degli Studi, Parma, Spring 83; Vis prof, Institut de Musicologie, Universite de Paris, France, Spring 88; Five-college vis prof, Amherst, Mount Holyoke, Smith; March 89; Gauss Seminars, Princeton Univ, Feb 91; Professore Associato, Istituto di Musicologia, Universita degli Studi, Roma, Fall 94; Ed board, Jour of Am Musicol Soc, 72-78; Ed board, Critical Inquiry, 74-; Ed board, Nineteenth-Century Music, 76-; Ed board, Cambridge Opera Jour, 87-; Ed board, Performance Practice Rev, 87-98. **HONORS AND AWARDS** Einstein Awd, Am Musicol Soc, 69; Quantrell Awd, excellence in undergraduate tchg, Univ Chicago, 74; Medaglia d'Oro, prima classe, Italian govt, serv to Italian cult, educ, and arts, 85; Deems Taylor, ASCAP, 86; Hon mem, Accademia Filarmonica di Bolobna, 92; Ryerson Lectr, Univ Chicago, 93; Grand Ufficiale dell'Ordine al Merito, Repub of Italy, 97; Order of Rio Branca, Repub of Brazil, 98; Cavaliere di Gran Croce, Repub of Italy, 98. **MEMBERSHIPS** Am Musicol Soc (coun, 72-74, 83-85, board dir, 74-76; mem prog comt and local arrangements, chmn for the Annual Meeting of the Soc, Chicago, 73; chmn, Campaign Comt for AMS 50, 84-86; vpres, 86-88; pres, 94-96); Chicago Symphony Orchestra, trustee, 91-; Court Theatre, board dir, 94-; Chicago Comt of the Chicago Coun on For Rel, 95-; Int Musicol Soc (Am rep in the Prog Comt for the Copenhagen Cong, 72); Am Inst of Verdi Studies (board of dir); Societa Italiana di Musicologia; Soc for Textual Scholarship (pres, 93-95); Am Acad of Arts and Sci (special nominating comt, 92-94; board of studies, 95). **RESEARCH** Nineteenth century Italian opera; music theory; Beethoven. **SELECTED PUBLICATIONS** Auth, Techniques of Unification in Early Cyclic Masses and Mass Pairs, JAMS, 66; Gli autografi rossiniani al Museo Teatrale alla Scala di Milano, Bollettino del Centro Rossiniano di Studi, 67; Le fonti autografe delle opere teatrali di Rossini, Nuova Rivista Musicale Italiana, 68; A Provisional Catalogue of the Works of Gioachino Rossini, In: Luigi Rognoni, Gioacchino Rossini, Edizioni RAI Radiotelevisione Italiana, 68, rev ed, Einaudi, Turin, 77; Rossini and Authenticity, The Musical Times, 68; Rossini in Naples: Some Major Works Recovered, Musical Quart, 68, in Italian, Bollettino del Centro Rossiniano di Studi, 71; A facsimile edition of the autograph score of La Cenerentola by Rossini, with an introduction, series Bibliotheca Musica Bononiensis, Arnaldo Forni, 69; Performing Editions: A Middle Ground, Opera Jour, 70; Rossini's Operas and their Printed Librettos, In: Report of the Tenth Congress of the IMS Ljubljana 1967, Ljubljana, 70; Gioachino Rossini and the conventions of Composition, Acta Musicologica, 70; The Operas of Rossini: Problems of Textual Criticism in Nineteenth-Century Opera, 2 vol, Princeton Univ, 70; Tancredi's Candeur virginale, The Musical Times, 71; Treatise on Harmony by Jean-Philippe Rameau, trans, intro and notes, Dover Publ, 71; La gazza ladra: Notes towards a Critical Edition, Bollettino del Centro Rossiniano di Studi, Anno, 72; Beethoven's Sixth Symphony: Sketches for the First Movement, JAMS, 74; Criteri per l'edizione critica di tutte le opere di Gioachino Rossini (with Bruno Cagli and Alberto Zedda), Bollettino del Centro Rossiniano di Studi, 74; The Mensural System and the Choralis Constantinus, In: Studies in Renaissance and Baroque Music in Honor of Arthur Mendel, Barenreiter Verlag, 74; Verdi, Ghislanzoni and Aida: The Uses of Convention, Critical Inquiry, 74; Editorial Norms for The Works of Giuseppe Verdi, Univ Chicago Press, 76-77; The Tragic Finale of Tancred, Fondazione Rossini, Pesaro, 77; Early Romantic Opera (Philip Gossett and Charles Rosen, ed), Garland Publ, 78-83; The Overtures of Rossini, 19th Century Music, 79; L'edizione critica delle opere di Verdi, In: Per un progetto Verdi, 80; Rossini e i suoi Peches de Vieillesse, Nuova Rivista Musicale Italiana, 80; Le Sinfonie di Rossini, Fondazione Rossini, Pesaro, 81; Frank Walker, The Man Verdi, Chicago, 82; The Four Versions of Marzelline's Aria: Beethoven as a Composer of Opera, Beethoven-Jahrbuch, 83; Gioachino Rossini, In: The New Grove: Masters of Italian Opera, London, 83; Critical Edition of Verdi's Macbeth, In: A Macbeth Sourcebook, W W Norton, 84; Facsimile of the 1857 Ricordi Catalogo (in ordine numerico) delle opere pubblicate (Agostino Zecca-Laterza, ed), Rome, 84, preface reprinted, Notes, 9/85; Tancredi by Gioachino Rossini, Opera Omnia di Gioachino Rossini, vol 10, Fondazione Rossini, Pesaro, 84; Italian Opera 1810-1840 (Philip Gossett, ed), 25 vol, Garland Publ, 84-92; Anna Bolena and the Maturity of Gaetano Donizetti, Oxford Univ Press, 85; L'edizione critica dell'opera lirica: lo specifico musicale, In: Per la tutela del lavoro musicologico, Milan, 86; Preface to Cent ans de mise en scene lyrique en France (by H. Robert Cohen and Marie-Odile Gigou), New York, 86; Music at the Theatre-Italien, In: Music in Paris in the Eighteen-Thirties, New York, 87; La fine dell'eta borbonica: 1838-1860, In: Il Teatro di San Carolo, Naples, 87; La composizione di Ernani, In: Ernani: ieri e oggi, Atti del convegno internazionale di studi, Modena, Teatro San Carlo, 12/84, Verdi X, 87, Engl trans, The Composition of Ernani, In: Analyzing Opera: Verdi and Wagner, Berkeley, 89; The Works of Giuseppe Verdi, In: Nuove prospettive nella ricerca verdiana, Parma/Milano, 87; Rossini's Ritornelli: A Composer and His Orchestral Soloists, In: Musiques-Signes-Images: Liber amicorum Francois Lesure, Geneva, 88; Omaggio a (liberazione da) Rossini, In: Messa per Rossini: La Storia, Il Testo, La Musica, Quaderni dell'Istituto di Studi Verdiani, 88; Carl Dahlhaus and the Ideal Type, 19th Century Music, 89; Becoming a Citizen: The Chorus in Risorgimento Opera, Cambridge Opera Jour, 90; Censorship and Self-Censorship: Problems in Editing the Operas of Giuseppe Verdi, In: Essays in Musicology: A Tribute to Alvin Johnson, Am Musicol Soc, 90; Audience Education, address, Chicago Symphony Orchestra Centennial Symposium, 6/92, The Aspen Inst Quart, 92; History and Works that Have No History: Reviving Rossini's Neapolitan Operas, In: Disciplining Music: Musicology and Its Canons (Katherine Bergeron and Philip V Bohlman, ed), Chicago, 92; I manoscritti musicali di Rossini, In: Rossini 1792-1992: Mostra Storico-Documentaria, Perugia, 92; Performers and Scholars, address, Am Acad Arts and Science, 11/91, Bull Am Acad of Arts and Sci, Boston, 92; The Rossini Thematic Catalog: When Does Bibliographical Access become Bibliographical Excess, In: Foundations in Music Bibliography, Part II, Music Reference Serv Quat, 93; New Sources for Stiffelio: A Preliminary Report, Cambridge Opera Jour, 93, reprinted Verdi's Middle Period, Chicago, 97; Translations and Adaptations of Operatic Texts, In: Palimpsest, Ann Arbor, 93; Facsimile edition of the autographe manuscript of Il Barbiere di Siviglia, with an introduction, Accademia di Santa Cecilia, Rome, 93; L'ocasione fa il ladro by Gioachino Rossini, Opera Omnia di Gioachino Rossini, vol 8, (Patricia Brauner, Giovanni Carli-Ballola, and Philip Gossett, ed), Fondazione Rossini, Pesaro, 94; Ermione by Gioachino Rossini, Opera Omnia di Gioachino Rossini, vol 27, (Patricia Brauner and Philip Gossett, ed), Fondazione Rossini, Pesaro, 95-; A New Romanza for Attila, In: Studi Verdiani, 95; Presidential Address: Knowing the Score: Italian Opera as Work and Play, In: Text: Transactions of the Society for Textual Scholarship, Ann Arbor, 95; The Repertory of the Teatro Carolino, In: Culture Musicali, 97; Auth, articles in: Enciclopedia di Musica Ricordi-Rizzoli, Grove's Dictionsary, and Penguin Opera Guide (with Patricia Brauner); Facsimile edition of the autograph manuscript of Don Pasquale with an introduction, Accademia di Santa Cecilia, Rome, 00; Performing Italian Opera, Univ Chicago Press; Thematic Catablogue of the Works of Rossini, Fondazione Rossini, Pesaro. **CONTACT ADDRESS** Dept of Music, Univ of Chicago, 1010 E 59th St, Chicago, IL 60637-1512. **EMAIL** phgs@midway.uchicago.edu

GOSSETT, SUZANNE
DISCIPLINE ENGLISH **EDUCATION** Smith Col, BA, 62; Princeton Univ, MA, 65, PhD, 68. **CAREER** Prof. **HONORS AND AWARDS** Special Award from the Soc for the Study of Early Modern Women, 00; Folger Sr Residential Fel, 00. **RESEARCH** Renaissance drama; feminist and gender Stud; editorial theory. **SELECTED PUBLICATIONS** Auth, Recent Stud in the English Masque, ELR 26, 96; auth, Why Should a Woman Edit a Man, Text, 96; coauth, Declarations of Independence: Women and Polit Power in Nineteenth-Century American Fiction, Rutgers UP, 90; auth, "Resistant Mothers and Hidden Children," Pilgrimage for Love: Essays on Early Modern Literature in Honor of Josephine A. Roberts, ed. Singrid King, Medieval and Renaissance Texts and Studie, (99): 191-207; auth, "Dramatic Achievements," The Cambridge Companion to English Literature 1500-1600, ed., Arthur F. Kinney, Cambridge Univ Press, (00): 153-177; co-ed, Lady Mary Wroth's Urania, Medieval and Renaissance Texts in English for RETS, 00; ed, Ben Jonson, Bartholomew Fair, Manchester and New York: Manchester Univ Press, 00. **CONTACT ADDRESS** Dept of English, Loyola Univ, Chicago, 6525 N. Sheridan Rd., Chicago, IL 60626. **EMAIL** sgosset@wpo.it.luc.edu

GOSSIN, PAMELA
PERSONAL Born 10/13/1956, Lincoln, NE, m, 4 children **DISCIPLINE** HISTORY OF SCIENCE & ENGL LIT **EDUCATION** Univ Wis, PhD, 89. **CAREER** Asst prof. **HONORS AND AWARDS** Howard Foundation Fellowship in History of Science; NEH Summer Stipend; Dudley Observatory Research Grant; Rockefeller Fellowship in Interdisciplinary Humanities. **RESEARCH** History of science and literature and science; women and science; scientific biography and autobiography; popularization of science; rhetoric of science; astronomy and literature. **SELECTED PUBLICATIONS** Auth, Literature and Science: An Encyclopedic Companion, Garland; Literature and Astronomy; Literature & Science, Guide Hist Lit, 94; auth, "An Encyclopedia of Literature & Science," Greenwood, forthcoming; auth, "Thomas Hardy's Novel Universe: Astronomy, Cosmology & the Cosmic Heroines of his Major & Minor Fichon, Ashgate, forthcoming; auth, "Literauture & The Modern Physical Sciences," in vol 5 of Cambridge History of Science, sem; ed., Mary Jo Nye; auth, "All Danae to the Stars: 19th C. Rpresentations of Women in the Cosmos," Victorian Studies, 96; auth, "Living Poetics, Enacting the Cosmos: Diane Ackerman's Popularization of Astronomy in the Planet: A Pastoral," Women's Stables. **CONTACT ADDRESS** Dept of Literary & Historical Studies, Univ of Texas, Dallas, Richardson, TX 75083-0688. **EMAIL** psgossin@utdallas.edu

GOSSY, MARY S.
DISCIPLINE FEMINIST THEORY AND GOLDEN AGE LITERATURE, PROSE NARRATIVE, PSYCHOANALYTIC, THEORY AND LITERATURE **EDUCATION** Bryn Mawr, BA, Harvard Univ, MA, PhD. **CAREER** Assoc prof, Rutgers, The State Univ NJ, Univ Col-Camden. **RESEARCH** Feminist theories and practices of representation, especially in lit. **SELECTED PUBLICATIONS** Auth, The Untold Story: Women and Theory in Golden Age Texts, 89; Freudian Slips: Woman, Writing, the Foreign Tongue, 95. **CONTACT ADDRESS** Dept of Span and Port, Rutgers, The State Univ of New Jersey, New Brunswick, New Brunswick, NJ 08903. **EMAIL** mgossy@rci.rutgers.edu

GOTTESMAN, LESLIE D.
PERSONAL Born 05/30/1945, Portland, OR, d, 2 children **DISCIPLINE** ENGLISH **EDUCATION** Columbia Univ, BA, 68; MA, 69; Univ San Francisco, EdD, 94. **CAREER** Assoc prof to prof, Golden Gate Univ, 89-. **HONORS AND AWARDS** Sears-Roebuck Found Teaching Excellence Awd, 90; Golden Gate Univ Outstanding Scholar Awd, 96-97, 97-98. **MEMBERSHIPS** MLA; African Studies Assoc; Assoc of Dept of English; Eritrean Studies Assoc. **RESEARCH** American Literature, Eritrean Studies, Hermeneutics and Critical Theory. **SELECTED PUBLICATIONS** Auth, To Fight and Learn: The Praxis and Promis of Literacy in Eritrea's Independence War, Red Sea Pr, 98. **CONTACT ADDRESS** Dept English, Golden Gate Univ San Francisco, 536 Mission St, San Francisco, CA 94105-2921. **EMAIL** lgottesman@ggu.edu

GOTTFRIED, ROY K.
DISCIPLINE MODERN LITERATURE, IRISH LITERATURE **EDUCATION** Yale Univ, PhD. **CAREER** Instr, Vanderbilt Univ. **SELECTED PUBLICATIONS** Auth, The Art of Joyce's Ulysses; Joyce's Iritis and the Irritated Text. **CONTACT ADDRESS** Vanderbilt Univ, Nashville, TN 37203-1727.

GOTTSCHALK, KATHERINE K.
PERSONAL Born 02/28/1941, Flint, MI, m, 1964, 2 children **DISCIPLINE** ENGLISH **EDUCATION** Univ Chicago, BA, 62; MA, 63; PhD, 70. **CAREER** Instr to asst prof, SUNY Cortland, 65-69; lectr to sr lectr, director, Cornell Univ, 77-. **HONORS AND AWARDS** Walter C Teagle Director, Cornell Univ; Clark Awd, Cornell Univ. **MEMBERSHIPS** MLA, NCTE, Writing Prog Admin, Am Assoc of Higher Educ. **RESEARCH** Composition and writing program administration. **SELECTED PUBLICATIONS** Auth, "Discoveries Concerning British Library MS Harley 6910," Mod Philol, (79); auth, "Classroom Activities" and "Writing in the Non-Writing Class," Teaching Prose: A Guide for Writing Instructors, (88); auth, "Paralyzed in the Present: Susan Fromberg Schaeffer's Mothers, or Daughters," Mother Puzzles: Daughters and Mothers in Contemporary American Literature, (89); auth, "Training TAs Across the Curriculum to Teach Writing: Embracing Diversity," Preparing the Professoriate of Tomorrow to Teach, (91); auth, "Isabel Huggan and Jane Urquhart: Feminine in This?" Canadian Women Writing Fiction, (93); auth, "The Writing Program in the University," ADE, (95); auth, "Uncommon Grounds: What Are the Primary Traits of a Writing Course?" Col Comp and Commun, (96); auth, "Putting-and Keeping-the Cornell Writing Program in Its Place: Writing in the Disciplines," Language and Learning Across the Disciplines, (97); auth, "Preparing Teachers of Writing Across the Curriculum at Cornell," Preparing College Teachers of Writing: Histories, Theories, Programs, and Practices, (01). **CONTACT ADDRESS** Cornell Univ, 159 Goldwin Smith Hall, Ithaca, NY 14853. **EMAIL** kkg1@cornell.edu

GOUGEON, LEN G.
DISCIPLINE ENGLISH **EDUCATION** St Mary's Univ, Halifax, BA; Univ MA, MA, PhD. **CAREER** Prof, Univ of Scranton. **MEMBERSHIPS** Am Lit Asn, Am Sec of the MLA, Thoreau Soc, Margaret Fuller Soc, The Ralph Waldo Emerson Society, 00-01. **RESEARCH** 19th-century Am Transcendentalists and Romantics; relationships of major writers and their works to the var reform movements of the time. **SELECTED PUBLICATIONS** Auth, Virtue's Hero: Emerson, Antislavery, and Reform, Ga, 90; co-ed, Emerson's Antislavery Writings, Yale, 95; articles in jour(s), New Eng Quart, Amer Lit, Am Transcendental Quart, S Atlantic Rev, Walt Whitman Quart Rev, Mod Lang Stud, Emerson Soc Papers, Thoreau Soc Bull, Stud in the Am Renaissance, Col Lang Asn J; rev(s) in, J the Early Rep, New Eng Quart, J Am Hist, 19th-Century Contexts, Resources for Am Lit Study, African Am Rev. **CONTACT ADDRESS** Dept of Eng, Univ of Scranton, Scranton, PA 18510. **EMAIL** GougeonL1@uofs.edu

GOULD, CHRISTOPHER
PERSONAL Born 10/07/1947, Pearl River, NY, m, 1982, 1 child **DISCIPLINE** ENGLISH **EDUCATION** Univ Va, BA, 69; Univ SC, MA, 75; PhD, 77. **CAREER** Instr, Francis Marion Col, 73-76; Instr, Southwest Mo State Univ, 76079; Asst Prof, Univ Ark, 7980; Asst prof, Southwestern Okla State Univ, 80-86; Assoc Prof to Prof and Dept Chair, Univ NC, 86-. **MEMBERSHIPS** Nat Coun Teachers of English **RESEARCH** Rhetoric and composition. **SELECTED PUBLICATIONS** Co-auth, South Carolina Imprints. 1731-1800: A Descriptive Bibliography, Clio, 85; co-auth, Writing, Reading, and Research. 2nd ed, Macmillan, 90; co-auth, Writing, Reading, and Research. 3rd ed, Macmillan, 94; co-auth, Writing, Reading, and Research. 4th ed, Macmillan, 97; co-auth, Writing, Reading, and Research. 5th ed, Macmillan, forthcoming; co-auth, Critical Issues in Contemporary Culture, Allyn, 97; auth, "Howard Johnson and the standardizing of Roadside Architecture," North American culture, (91): 5-20; auth, "Assessing Teaching Effectiveness in English: Procedures, Issues, Strategies," ADE Bulletin (92): 44-52; auth, "Fifty Years of Inspired Editorship for NCET,", NCETA Notes, (93): 3-5. **CONTACT ADDRESS** Dept English, Univ of No Carolina, Wilmington, 601 South Col Rd, Wilmington, NC 28403-3201. **EMAIL** gouldc@uncwil.edu

GOULDING, DANIEL J.
DISCIPLINE FILM STUDIES AND THEATER ARTS **EDUCATION** Marshall Univ, BA, 57; Ohio Univ, MA, 59; PhD, 64. **CAREER** Prof, 66-. **HONORS AND AWARDS** Close-up award, Yugoslav Film Inst. **RESEARCH** Dancing and cultural theory; film theory; hist; criticism. **SELECTED PUBLICATIONS** Auth, Liberated Cinema: The Yugoslav Experience, Ind Univ Press, 85; Five Filmmakers, Ind Univ Press, 94; ed, Post New Wave Cinema in the Soviet Union and Eastern Europe, Ind Univ Press 89; Occupation in 26 Pictures, 98. **CONTACT ADDRESS** Dept of Theatre and Dance, Oberlin Col, Oberlin, OH 44074. **EMAIL** daniel.goulding@oberlin.edu

GOUNARIDOU, KIKI
PERSONAL Born, Greece **DISCIPLINE** DRAMATIC ART **EDUCATION** Univ Calif, Davis, PhD, 92. **CAREER** Asst prof, Theatre and Performance Stud, Univ Pittsburgh, 92- . **HONORS AND AWARDS** Hewlett Int Res Awd; Chandler Awd for Acad Excellence; Best Dir Awd, Ithaca Int Theatre Festival. **MEMBERSHIPS** MLA; Int Fedn for Theatre Res; Am Soc for Theatre Res; Modern Greek Stud Asn. **RESEARCH** Theatre theory and performance studies; classical theatre; translation and translation theory. **SELECTED PUBLICATIONS** Coauth, Le Strasberg and Morris Carnovsky, Int Dictionary of Theatre, vol 3. Gale Res Int, London, England 95; Coauth, Euripides's Hecuba: A Trans, Mellen Press, 95; auth, "Intertext and the Regendering of Nietzsche's Superman in Kostis Palamas's Trisevyeni, " J of Modern Greek Studies 14, 96; auth, The Stranger of the House: Fin-de-Siecle speculations on Euripides's Alcestis, Millennium responses: displacing classical greek theatre, Univ studio press, 98; auth, The Quest for Identity in Tennessee williams's The Glass Menagerie, Text and Presentation, 98; coauth, Madame La Mort and Other Plays by Rachilde, John Hopkins Univ Press, 98; auth, Euripide's and Hecestis: Speculations, Speculations, and Stories of Love in the Athenian culture, Univ press Of Am, 98; coauth, The Fouquet Affair: The Politics of Patronage in theatre and Painting Under Louis XIV, Seventeenth-Century, News 57, 99; auth, Representations of Women in the films of Pnatelis Voulgaris: Akropole, thje Stone Years, and The Engagement of Anna, " J of Modern greek Studies 18, 00; auth, Horvath's don Juan: An Actor in Search of his soul , Maske Und Kothurn 42, 00. **CONTACT ADDRESS** Theatre, Smith Col, Northampton, MA 01063. **EMAIL** kgounari@email.smith.edu

GOURDINE, A. K. M.
DISCIPLINE AFRICAN-AMERICAN LITERATURE **EDUCATION** Mich State Univ, PhD, 94. **CAREER** Asst prof, La State Univ; ed bd, Calyx, 95. **HONORS AND AWARDS** Southern Regional Educational Board Fac Mentor of the Year, 97. **RESEARCH** African literature; African diaspora studies; women's studies; post- colonial studies. **SELECTED PUBLICATIONS** Auth, Rhetoric of Resistance, The Writing Instr, 91; Postmodern Ethnography and the Womanist Mission: Postcolonial Sensibilities in Possessing the Secret of Joy, African Am Rev, 96; coauth, Strategies for Educating African American Males: The Detroit Model, 93; auth, "hearing Reading and Being Read by Beloved," NWSA Journal (98); auth, "The Dynastical Drama of Lynching in Grimkes Rachel and Hansberry's Raisin in the Sun," Modern Drama (99); auth, "Slavery in the Diasporam Consciousness: Ama Ata Aidoo's Conversations," Emergining Perspectives on Ama Ata Aidoo (99). **CONTACT ADDRESS** Dept of Eng, Louisiana State Univ, 212 Allen Hall, Baton Rouge, LA 70803. **EMAIL** agourdi@lsu.edu

GOVAN, SANDRA YVONNE
PERSONAL Born 07/28/1948, Chicago, IL, s **DISCIPLINE** ENGLISH; AFRICAN AMERICAN STUDIES **EDUCATION** Valparaiso University, Valparaiso, IN, BA, 1970; Bowling Green University, Bowling Green, OH, MA, 1972; Emory University, Atlanta, GA, PhD, 1980. **CAREER** Luther College, Decorah, IA, instructor, 72-75; University of Kentucky, Lexington, KY, assistant professor, 80-83; University of North Carolina, Charlotte, NC, associate professor, 83-. **HONORS AND AWARDS** Schomburg Scholar in Residence, NEH, Schomburg Center for Research in Black Culture, 1990-91; Outstanding Alumni Awd, Valparaiso University, 1982; National Fellowship Fund Awd, Ford Foundation, 1976-80; Emory University Fellowship, 1975. **MEMBERSHIPS** Member, Association for the Study of African American Life and History; member, Modern Language Association, 1980-; member, College Language Association, 1975-; member, Langston Hughes Society; dir, Ronald E McNair Postbaccalaureate Achievement Program. **RESEARCH** African-American Literature; Science Fiction. **SELECTED PUBLICATIONS** Essays contributed to: Erotique Noire, Sexual Politics, Langston Hughes: The Man, His Art & His Continuing Influence, Notable Black American Woman VI & VII, Notable Black American Man, My Soul is a Witness: African American Women's Spiritly, Fatner Songs: testimonies by African American Sons and Daughter, Novello Anthology: 10 Years of Graf American Writing. **CONTACT ADDRESS** Professor of English, Univ of No Carolina, Charlotte, Charlotte, NC 28223. **EMAIL** sygovan@email.uncc.edu

GOWDY, ANNE R.
PERSONAL Born 11/22/1941, New Orleans, LA, m, 1965, 1 child **DISCIPLINE** ENGLISH **EDUCATION** Southeastern La Univ, BA, 63; La State Univ Baton Rouge, MA, 65; Univ Miss, PhD. 96. **CAREER** TA, La State Univ, 63-65; instr, Tallahassee Community Col, 67-68; instr, Univ of New Orleans, 65-66, 72-88; TA, Univ Miss, 91-92; assoc prof, Tenn Wesleyan Col, 96-. **HONORS AND AWARDS** Kappa Delta Pi; Phi Kappa Phi; Outstanding Young Women of Am, 65; Sigma Tau Delta, 90; Fel, Univ Miss, 90-91, 91-92; Univ Miss Grad School Achievement Awd, 91; Fulbright Fel, 01. **MEMBERSHIPS** S Central MLA, MLA, Poe Studies Assoc, Soc for the Study of Am Women Writers, Soc for the Study of Southern Lit, Am Lit Assoc, Res Soc for Am Periodicals. **RESEARCH** 19th Century American literature, women's writing, novels, regional and local color literature, humor. **SELECTED PUBLICATIONS** Auth, "Sherwood Bonner's Interview with Ralph Waldo Emerson," Am Renaissance Lit Report 9, (95): 49-59; auth, "The Illusory Angel: The Perfect Victorian Wife," Studies in English , (Univ Miss, 93-95): 11-24; auth, "After 'The Raven': 'The Radical Club' by 'An Atom," Poe Studies Assoc Newsletter 26, (98): 3-4; ed, A Sherwood Bonner Sampler, 1869-1884: What a Bright, Educated, Witty, Lively, Snappy Young Woman Can Say on a Variety of Topics, Univ Tenn Pr, (Knowville), 00; auth, "Sherwood Bonner (Katharine Sherwood Bonner McDowell)," Nineteenth Century Fiction Writers (99): 47-56; auth, "Alice Dunbar-Nelson," Hist of Southern Women's Lit, (La State Univ Pr, forthcoming). **CONTACT ADDRESS** Tennessee Wesleyan Col, PO Box 40, Athens, TN 47371. **EMAIL** gowdya@twcnet.edu

GRACE, DOMINICK M.
PERSONAL Born 05/24/1963, Peterborough, ON, Canada, m, 1993 **DISCIPLINE** ENGLISH LITERATURE **EDUCATION** Univ Toronto, BA, 85; Univ Western Ont, MA, 86; PhD, 91. **CAREER** Asst to assoc prof, Algona Univ Col, 92-. **HONORS AND AWARDS** SSHRCC, 89/90; OGS, 86/87, 87/88, 88/89. **MEMBERSHIPS** ACCUTE, MLA. **RESEARCH** SF, Fantasy, Children's Literature, Medieval Literature, Renaissance, Drama. **SELECTED PUBLICATIONS** Auth, "Ondaatje and Charlton Comics 'Billy the Kid, '" Can Lit 133, (92); auth, "Chaucer's Little Treatises," Florilegium 14, (95/96); auth, "Margaret Atwood's Northern Utopia: Nunavit and The Handmaid's Tale," Reflections on Northern Culture: Visions and Voices, (97); auth, "Romeo and the Apothecary," Early Theatre 1, (98); auth, "Valorizing the 'Normal': Phyllis Gotlieb's Sunburrst, Perspectives on the Can Fantastic, (98); auth, "Disease, Virtual Life, and Virtual Light," Foundation 81, (01). **CONTACT ADDRESS** Algoma Univ Col, 1520 Queen St E, Sault Ste. Marie, ON, Canada 061 2G4. **EMAIL** grace@auc.ca

GRACE, JOAN CARROLL
PERSONAL Born 03/06/1921, Brooklyn, NY, s **DISCIPLINE** ENGLISH **EDUCATION** Trinity Col, DC, AB, 43; Columbia Univ, MA, 51, PhD, 69. **CAREER** From asst to assoc to full prof, 68-91, prof emeritus, 91-, Eng, Fordham Univ. **MEMBERSHIPS** MLA. **RESEARCH** Shakespeare; Milton; modern British writers. **SELECTED PUBLICATIONS** Auth, Tragic Theory In The Critical Works Of Thomas Rymer, John Dennis and John Dryden, Fairleigh Dickinson Univ, 74. **CONTACT ADDRESS** 44 Morningside Dr, New York, NY 10025.

GRACE, NANCY
DISCIPLINE ENGLISH LITERATURE **EDUCATION** Otterbein, BA, 73; Ohio State Univ, MA, 81, PhD, 87. **CAREER** Assoc prof. **HONORS AND AWARDS** Dir, writing prog. **SELECTED PUBLICATIONS** Auth, The Feminized Male Character in Twentieth-Century Literature. **CONTACT ADDRESS** Dept of Eng, The Col of Wooster, Wooster, OH 44691.

GRACE, SHERRILL E.
DISCIPLINE ENGLISH **EDUCATION** Univ Western Ont, BA, 65; McGill Univ, MA, 70, PhD, 74. **CAREER** Asst prof, McGill Univ, 75-77; asst prof, 77-81, assoc prof, 81-87, Prof English, Univ British Columbia 91-. **HONORS AND AWARDS** F.E.L. Priestley Awd, 93; Killam Res Prize, 90; Killam Fac Res Fel, 90-91; Fel, Royal Soc Can. **MEMBERSHIPS** Asn Can Col Univ Tchrs Eng; Can Asn Am Studs; Asn Can Studs; Can Comp Lit Asn; Acad Women's Asn. **SELECTED PUBLICATIONS** Auth, Violent Duality: A Study of Margaret Atwood, 80; auth, The Voyage That Never Ends: Malcolm Lowry's Fiction, 82; auth, Regression and Apocalypse: Studies in North American Literary Expressionism, 89; auth, Sursum Corda: The Collected Letters of Malcolm Lowry, vol 1, 95, vol

2, 96. **CONTACT ADDRESS** Dept of English, Univ of British Columbia, Vancouver, BC, Canada V6T 1Z1. **EMAIL** grace@arts.ubc.ca

GRADDY, WILLIAM E.
DISCIPLINE LITERATURE OF THE AMERICAN RENAISSANCE **EDUCATION** Southern IL Univ, BA, MA, PhD. **CAREER** Lit, Trinity Int Univ **SELECTED PUBLICATIONS** Articles, Reformed Jour, New Oxford Rev, Emerson Soc Quart, Eerdman's Handbook Christianity Am. **CONTACT ADDRESS** Col of Arts and Sciences, Trinity Intl Univ, Col of Arts and Sciences, 2065 Half Day Road, Deerfield, IL 60015.

GRADIN, SHERRIE L.
DISCIPLINE ENGLISH, COMPOSITION THEORY **EDUCATION** Casper Col, AA, 81; Portland State Univ, BA, 84; MA, 86; Univ NH, PhD, 90. **CAREER** Dir wrtg; assoc prof. **HONORS AND AWARDS** Nat wrtg prog admin grant, 95; fac devel grant, 95, 96, 97; Comm-based Dev. Grnt, 96. **RESEARCH** Gender studies, feminist theory **SELECTED PUBLICATIONS** Auth, Romancing Rhetorics: Social-expressivist Perspectives on the Teaching of Writing, Boynton/Cook, 95; A Writing Teacher Asks Some Questions Concerning Discourse Forms and the Culturally Diverse Classroom, CEA Critic, 94; What's Gender Got to Do With It?, National Forum: The Phi Kappa Phi, Jour, 94. **CONTACT ADDRESS** Dept of Eng, Portland State Univ, PO Box 751, Portland, OR 97207-0751.

GRAFF, GERALD E.
PERSONAL Born 06/28/1937, Chicago, IL **DISCIPLINE** ENGLISH, EDUCATION **EDUCATION** Univ of Chicago, AB, 59; Stanford Univ, PhD, 63. **CAREER** Asst prof, Univ of NMex, Albuquerque, 63-66; from asst prof to prof, 66-90, chmn, English Dept, 77-83, Northwestern Univ; George M. Pullman Distinguished Service Prof of English and Educ, 90-99, dir, Master of Arts Prog in the Humanities, 96-99, Univ of Chicago; dean, Curric and Instr, Col of Lib Arts and Sci, prof, Dept of English, Univ of Ill at Chicago, 00-. **HONORS AND AWARDS** Am Bk Award, Before Columbus Found, 93. **RESEARCH** Problem of academic discourse for students, literary & cultural theory, history of education, pedagogy and curriculum. **SELECTED PUBLICATIONS** Auth, Poetic Statement and Critical Dogma, Northwestern Univ Press, 70; coed, W.B. Scott, Chicago Letter and Other Parodies, Ardis, 78; auth, Literature Against Itself: Literary Ideas in Modern Society, Univ of Chicago Press, 79; coed, Criticism in the University, Northwestern Univ Press, 85; coed, Scott, Parodies, Etc. and So Forth, Northwestern Univ Press, 85; auth, Professing Literature: An Institutional History, Univ of Chicago Press, 87; coed, The Origins of Literary Studies in America: A Documentary Anthology, Routledge, Chapman & Hall, 88; auth, Beyond the Culture Wars: How Teaching the Conflicts can Revitalize American Education, Norton, 92; auth, "Hiding It from the Kids," Col English 62 (99): 242-254; auth, "Scholars and Soundbites: The Myth of Academic Difficulty," PMLA 115 (00): 1041-1052. **CONTACT ADDRESS** Col of Liberal Arts and Sci, Univ of Ill at Chicago, 601 S Morgan St, 410 Univ Hall, Chicago, IL 60607-7104.

GRAHAM, A. JOHN
PERSONAL Born 03/09/1930, Lowestoft, England, m, 1963, 2 children **DISCIPLINE** CLASSICS **EDUCATION** Cambridge Univ, BA, 52, MA, 56, PhD, 57. **CAREER** Asst Lectr, Univ London, 55-57; Asst Lectr to Sr Lectr, Univ Manchester, 57-77; Prof Classical Studies, 77-95, Prof Emeritus, Univ Pa, 95-. **HONORS AND AWARDS** Cromer Greek Prize, British Acad, 56; Hare Prize, Univ Cambridge, 60; NEH Fel, 81-82. **MEMBERSHIPS** Soc Hellenic Studies; British Sch at Athens; Cambridge Philol Soc. **RESEARCH** Greek history; Greek colonization; Greek prose authors; ancient beekeeping. **SELECTED PUBLICATIONS** Auth, Colony and Mother City in Ancient Greece, 2nd ed, 83; Thucydides 7.13.2 and the Crews of Athenian Triremes, Transactions Am Philol Asn 122, 92; A Dedication from the Chersonese at Olympia, Nomodeiktes. Greek Studies in of Martin Ostwald, 93; The Odyssey, History and Women, The Distaff Side, 95; Themistocles' Speech before Salamis: the Interpretation of Herodotus 8.83.1, Classical Quart 46, 96; auth, "Thasos: the Topography of the Ancient City," Annual of the British School at Athens 95 (00); auth, Collected Papers on Greek Colonization, 01. **CONTACT ADDRESS** Classical Studies Dept, Univ of Pennsylvania, Logan Hall, Philadelphia, PA 19104-6304.

GRAHAM, DON B.
PERSONAL Born 01/30/1940, Lucas, TX, m, 1991 **DISCIPLINE** LITERATURE **EDUCATION** N Tex State Univ, BA, 62; MA, 64; Univ Tex, PhD, 71. **CAREER** Instr, SW Tex State Univ, 65-69; asst prof, Univ of Pa, 71-76; prof, Univ of Tex, 85-. **HONORS AND AWARDS** Austin Writers League for Best Non Fiction Book, 98; Spurs Teaching Awd, 01. **MEMBERSHIPS** PMLA. **RESEARCH** Southwestern American Literature and History, Australian Literature and Film, Film. **SELECTED PUBLICATIONS** Auth, The Fiction of Frank Norris: The Aesthetic Context, Univ Mo, 78; auth, "Cowboys and Cadillacs: How Hollywood Looks at Texas," Tex Monthly, (83): auth, No Name on the Bullet: A Biography of Audie Murphy, Viking, 89; auth, Giant Country: Essays on Texas, TCU, 98. **CONTACT ADDRESS** 8704 Mariscal Canyon Dr, Austin, TX 78759-7154. **EMAIL** dgbb@mail.utexas.edu

GRAHAM, JOYCE
PERSONAL Born Elliston, VA **DISCIPLINE** ENGLISH EDUCATION, ADOLESCENT LITERATURE **EDUCATION** Radford Univ, BS, MS; VA Tech, EdD. **CAREER** Prof, Radford Univ; adviser, Support for Learning, Educational Dept, Lowland, Scotland. **MEMBERSHIPS** Pres, VA Asn of Tchr of Eng. **SELECTED PUBLICATIONS** Contrib an essay to Writers for Young Adults, ed a column called "Global Issues" in the Eng J. **CONTACT ADDRESS** Educ Dept, Radford Univ, Council Offices, Shaw St, Lowland, Scotland L14 1HT. **EMAIL** j.graham@lowland.gov.uk

GRAHAM, KENNETH WAYNE
PERSONAL Born 03/26/1938, Winnipeg, MB, Canada, m, 1963, 2 children **DISCIPLINE** ENGLISH LITERATURE AND BIBLIOGRAPHY **EDUCATION** Royal Mil Col Can, BA, 61; Univ London, MPh, 67, PhD(English), 71. **CAREER** Lectr English, 66-70, asst prof, 70-77, ASSOC PROF ENGLISH, UNIV GUELPH, 77-. **MEMBERSHIPS** Asn Can Univ Teachers English; Can Soc 18th Century Studies; Am Soc 18th Century Studies; Can Fedn of Humanities. **RESEARCH** Bibliography; 18th century literature; Gothic novel; Restoration and 18th Century Literature; The Gothic; History of ideas; Romanticism and ideology. **SELECTED PUBLICATIONS** Auth, Man and Nature/L'Homme et la nature, AMS, 87; auth, Gothic Fictions: Prohibition/Trangression, AMS, 89; auth, "Vathek" and the Escape from Time, AMS, 90; auth, The Politics of Narrative, AMS, 90. **CONTACT ADDRESS** Dept of English, Univ of Guelph, Sch of Lits and Performance Studies in English, Guelph, ON, Canada N1G 2W1. **EMAIL** kwgraham@uoguelph.ca

GRAHAM, MARYEMMA
DISCIPLINE ENGLISH **EDUCATION** Univ N Carolina at Chapel Hill, BA; Northwestern Univ, MA, 69; Cornell Univ, MPS, 77, PhD, 77. **CAREER** Assoc Prof, Eng, Northeastern Univ; Prof, Univ KS. **HONORS AND AWARDS** W.E.B. Du Bois Fel, Howard Univ. **MEMBERSHIPS** Am Antiquarian Soc, Modern Lang Asn, Col Lang Asn, Am Studies Asn, Northeast Modern Lang Asn, Nat Coun Teachers of English, Nat Coun for Black Studies, Southern Conference on Afro-Am Studies, Soc for the Study of Southern Lit, Midwest Modern Lang Asn. **RESEARCH** Afro-Am authorship, 1746-1906, Richard Wright, Margaret Walker. **SELECTED PUBLICATIONS** Auth, Margaret Walker, An Intellectual Biography, Univ Pr of Virginia, 99. **CONTACT ADDRESS** Dept of English, Univ of Kansas, Lawrence, PO Box 6248, Lawrence, KS 66045-2107. **EMAIL** mgraham@ukans.edu

GRAHAM, PETER W.
PERSONAL Born 02/11/1951, Manchester, CT, m, 1973, 2 children **DISCIPLINE** ENGLISH **EDUCATION** Davidson, AB, 73; Duke, MA, 74, PhD, 77. **CAREER** Asst Prof, Va Polytech Inst & State Univ, 78-84; Assoc Prof, 84-90; Prof, 90-00, Clifford Cutchins Prof, 00-. **HONORS AND AWARDS** James B Duke Fellow, Duke Univ, 73-76; Eli Lilly Post-doctoral Fellow, Univ Fla, 77-78; Andrew Mellon Post-doctoral Fellow, Duke Univ, 80-81; Elma Dangerfield Prize for Byron Stud, 92. **MEMBERSHIPS** Int Byron Soc; Jane Austen Soc of North Am. **RESEARCH** 19th cent Brit lit & culture; med hu; Byron; Darwin. **SELECTED PUBLICATIONS** Auth, Byron's Bulldog, Ohio St, 84; auth, Don Juan and Regency England, Va, 90; co-auth, Fictive Ills: Literary Perspectives on Wounds and Diseases, Lit & Med, vol 9, Johns Hopkins Univ Press, 90; coauth, Articulating the Elephant Man: Joseph Merrick and His Interpreters, Johns Hopkins, 92; co-auth, Disorderly Eaters: Texts in Self-empowerment, Pa State, 92; co-auth, The Portable Darwin, Viking, 93; auth, Lord Byron, Twayne, 98. **CONTACT ADDRESS** Dept of English, Virginia Polytech Inst and State Univ, Blacksburg, VA 24061. **EMAIL** pegraham@vt.edu

GRAHAM, THEODORA RAPP
PERSONAL Born 02/05/1938, Kearny, NJ, m, 1989, 1 child **DISCIPLINE** ENGLISH LITERATURE **EDUCATION** Rutgers Univ, NCAS, AB, 59; Columbia Univ, MA, 64; Univ of PA, PhD(English), 74. **CAREER** Teacher English & French, NJ schs, 60-63; instr English, Moravian Col, Bethelehem, Pa, 63-65 & Pa State Univ, University Park, 65-69; instr English & sec educ, 70-74, asst prof humanities & English, 74-77, Assoc Prof Humanities & English, PA State Harrisburg, 77-99, Coordr Grad Prog Humanities, 75-82; founding ed, William Carlos Williams Rev, 74-83; reviewer-panelist, Nat Endowment for Humanities, 77-99. **HONORS AND AWARDS** Phi Beta Kappa; Provost's Awd for Teaching Excellence, 87; Penn State's Achieving Women Awd, 92; numerous Univ & campus research awards. **MEMBERSHIPS** MLA; Am Studies Asn; Academy of American Poets; Polish Institute of Arts and Sciences; Williams, Pound, Frost, Eliot, Stevens Societies; AAUW; CELJ, 77-83; Pres WCW Soc, 88-89. **RESEARCH** Modern American poetry; 20th century American fiction; contemporary fiction and drama. **SELECTED PUBLICATIONS** Contribr, Composition and the disadvantaged, In: English and the Disadvantaged, International, 67; Louise Bogan, Grace King, Josephine Miles & Harriet Monroe, In: American Women Writers, Ungar, 79-80, rev 83; William Carlos Williams, Dict American Biography, 81; Louise Bogan (81 & 98) and Anita Brookner (93 & 98), Encycl of World Lit in the 20th Century; contribr, Teaching the Divine Comedy in an Interdisciplinary Context, MLA, 82; auth, Her Heigh Compleynt: The Cress Letters of William Paterson, In: Ezra Pound and William Carlos Williams, Univ of Pa Press, 83; Myra's Emergence in Williams' A Dream of Love, Sagetrieb, 84; Williams, Flossie, and the Others: The Aesthetics of Sexuality, Contemp Lit, 87; guest ed WCWR, devoted to Marianne Moore and WCW, Spring 98; auth, A Place for the Genuine: A Tribute to Mary Ellen Solt, In: WCWR, 93; editorials and reviews. **CONTACT ADDRESS** Pennsylvania State Univ, Harrisburg, 328 Windcrest Rd, Harrisburg, PA 17112. **EMAIL** trg1@psu.edu

GRAMMER, JOHN M.
PERSONAL Born 05/02/1957, Midland, TX, m, 1991, 3 children **DISCIPLINE** ENGLISH **EDUCATION** Vanderbilt Univ, BA, 79; Univ Va, MA, 82, PhD, 91. **CAREER** Asst prof, Hollins Col, 91-92; asst prof, Univ of the South, 92-98, assoc prof, 98-. **HONORS AND AWARDS** C. Hugh Holman Awd, issued by the Soc for the Study of Southern Lit. **MEMBERSHIPS** Modern Lang Asn of North Am, Soc for the Study of Southern Lit. **RESEARCH** Southern literature, historical narrative. **SELECTED PUBLICATIONS** Auth, Pasoral and Politics in the Old South, LSU Press (96). **CONTACT ADDRESS** Dept English, Univ of the South, 735 University Ave, Sewanee, TN 37383-0001. **EMAIL** jgrammer@sewanee.edu

GRANDT, JURGEN E.
PERSONAL Born 09/22/1968, Glarus, Switzerland **DISCIPLINE** ENGLISH **EDUCATION** Univ Zurich, lic phil I, 93; Univ Ga, PhD, 00. **CAREER** Lehrbeauftragter, Kantonsschule Glarus, 92; lehrbeauftragter, Sekundarschule Schwanden, 94; lehrbeauftragter, Institut Montana, 94-95; TA, Univ of Ga, 95-00; teaching fellow, 00-. **HONORS AND AWARDS** Fel, Univ of Ga, 00-01. **MEMBERSHIPS** MLA, CLA, SAMLA, MAWA, EEAS, SANAS, Langston Hughes Soc. **RESEARCH** African American Literature, Jazz and Literature, Critical Theory, Southern Literature. **SELECTED PUBLICATIONS** Auth, "The Spirit that Produces Homes: Rooms of Enclosure in Jessie Redmon Fauset's Plum Bun," Langston Hughes Rev, forthcoming; auth, "Rewriting the Final Adjustment of Affairs: Culture, Race, and Politics in Alice Dunbay-Nelson's New Orleans," forthcoming. **CONTACT ADDRESS** English Dept, Univ of Georgia, 367 S Pope St, Athens, GA 30605. **EMAIL** jugrandt@arches.uga.edu

GRANOFSKY, RONALD
DISCIPLINE ENGLISH LITERATURE **EDUCATION** Trent Univ, BA; Canterbury Univ, MA; Queen's Univ, PhD. **RESEARCH** Mod Brit lit; the novel; Canadian fiction. **SELECTED PUBLICATIONS** Auth, Essays in Literature: Mosaic: Modern Language Studies: English Studies in Canada. **CONTACT ADDRESS** English Dept, McMaster Univ, 1280 Main St W, Hamilton, ON, Canada L8S 4L9. **EMAIL** granofsk@mcmaster.ca

GRANT, AUGUST E.
DISCIPLINE MASS COMMUNICATION TECHNOLOGY **EDUCATION** Univ FL, MA, JC; Univ Southern CA, PhD. **CAREER** Assoc prof & dir, Ctr Mass Commun Res; past fac, Univ TX at Austin; vis prof, USC, 96 & assoc prof, 97-; ed, Commun Technol Update. **RESEARCH** Convergence of commun forms through the application of new technol(s). **SELECTED PUBLICATIONS** Publ on, high-definition television, television audience behavior, television shopping serv, theories of new media & emerging commun technol(s). **CONTACT ADDRESS** Col of Journalism & Mass Commun, Univ of So Carolina, Columbia, Carolina Coliseum rm 3032A, Columbia, SC 29208. **EMAIL** augie@.sc.edu

GRANT, BARRY KEITH
PERSONAL Born New York, NY, m, 1947 **DISCIPLINE** FILM, POPULAR CULTURE **EDUCATION** State Univ NY Buffalo, BA, 69, PhD(English, Am lit & film), 75. **CAREER** Lectr, 75-76, asst prof, 76-81, ASSOC PROF FILM AND POPULAR CULT, BROCK UNIV, 81-, CHMN, DEPT FINE ARTS, 82-, Asst dir, Media Study, Buffalo, 74-75; film critic, CJQR-FM, St Catharines, Ont, 80-; reader, Post-Script: Essays in Film and the Humanities, 82-. **HONORS AND AWARDS** Recipient of the Brock Univ Distinguished Scholar Awd, 99. **MEMBERSHIPS** MLA; Popular Cult Asn; Film Studies Asn Can; Soc Educ Film and TV. **RESEARCH** American film; science fiction; popular music; film theroy; history; criticism; film and literature; genre studies; popular culture; cultural studies; Canadian cinema; documentary film; screen education. **SELECTED PUBLICATIONS** Auth, Film Study in the Undergraduate Curriculum ed. New York: Modern Language Association (Options for Teaching Series), 83; auth, "Purple Passages or Fiestas in Blue?: Notes Toward an Aesthetics of Jazz Vocalese." Popular Music and Society 18, no. 1 (94): 125-143; auth, The Dread of Difference: Gender and the Horror Film ed. Austin: University of Texas Press, 96; auth, Frederick Wiseman's "Near Death" London: Flicks Books, forthcoming 99; auth, The Films of Peter Jackson (Studies in New Zealand Culture Series), London: Nottingham Trent Univ, UK: Kakapo Books, forthcoming 99; auth, "'Sensuous Elaboration': Speculation and Spectacle in the Science Fiction Film." Alien Zone II: Cultural Theory and Contemporary Science Fiction Cinema,

ed. Annette Kuhn (London: Verso, forthcoming 1999); auth, "Two Rode Together: John Ford, Fenimore Cooper, and Generic Cycling." John Ford: A Reappraisal ed. Gaylyn Studlar and Matthew Bernstein (Washington: Smithsonian Institute, forthcoming 1999). **CONTACT ADDRESS** Communications, Popular Culture & Film, Brock Univ, 500 Glenridge Ave., Thistle Complex, room 146K, Saint Catharines, ON, Canada L2S 3A1. **EMAIL** bgrant@spartan.ac.BrockU.CA

GRANT, JOHN ERNEST
PERSONAL Born 08/28/1925, Newburyport, MA, m, 1974, 3 children **DISCIPLINE** ENGLISH **EDUCATION** Harvard Univ, AB, 51, AM, 54, PhD(English), 60. **CAREER** From instr to assoc prof English, Univ Conn, 56-65; PROF ENGLISH, UNIV IOWA, 65-92, Am Coun Learned Soc fel, 68-69; Am Philos Soc fel 72; vis prof English, Univ Alta, Alberta, 68, 73 and Emory Univ, 76; Nat Endowment Humanities fel, 77; Yale Ctr British Arts fel, 81, vis fel, Houghton Libr, 00-01. **MEMBERSHIPS** MLA; AAUP; Midwest Mod Lang Asn; Wordsworth-Coleridge Asn. **RESEARCH** The poetry and painting of William Blake: the imagery of apocalypse; literary archetypes. **SELECTED PUBLICATIONS** Ed, Discussions of William Blake, Heath, 60; co-ed, Blake's Visionary Forms Dramatic, Princeton Univ, 70; contribr, Vision in Vala, In Blake's Sublime Allegory, Univ Wis, 73; co-ed, Blake's Poetry and Designs, Norton, 79; William Blake's Designs for Edward Young's Night Thoughts, Oxford Univ, 80. **CONTACT ADDRESS** Dept of English, Univ of Iowa, Iowa City, IA 52242. **EMAIL** mary-grant@uiowa.edu

GRANT, JOHN NEILSON
PERSONAL Born 05/03/1940, Edinburgh, Scotland, m, 1962, 3 children **DISCIPLINE** CLASSICS **EDUCATION** Univ Edinburgh, MA, 62; Cambridge Univ, BA, 64; Univ of St Andrews, PhD(Latin), 70. **CAREER** Lectr classics, Univ Man, 65-67; asst prof, 67-72, assoc prof, 72-80, prof Classics, Univ Toronto, 80-, Chmn, 82-, Can Coun fel, 77-78. **MEMBERSHIPS** Class Asn Can; Am Philol Asn. **RESEARCH** Roman comedy; transmission of texts; republican Latin literature. **SELECTED PUBLICATIONS** Auth, Studies in the Textual Tradition of Terence, Toronto, 86; auth, 2 Syntactic Errors in Transcription, Seneca, 'Thyestes 33' and Lucan, 'BC 2.279,' Class Quart, Vol 0044, 94; Taide in 'Inferno 18' and Terence 'Eunuchus 937,' Quaderni D Italianistica, Vol 0015, 94. **CONTACT ADDRESS** Dept Class, Univ of Toronto, 97 St. George St, Toronto, ON, Canada M5S 2E8. **EMAIL** grant@chass.utoronto.ca

GRANT, JUDITH A. S.
PERSONAL Born 12/21/1941, Toronto, ON, Canada **DISCIPLINE** ENGLISH **EDUCATION** Univ Toronto, BA, 65, MA, 66, PhD, 74. **CAREER** Instr/lectr, Univ Toronto, 70-75; instr, Univ Toronto, Univ Guleph & Ryerson Polytech Inst, 75-80; asst prof, 80-82, adj prof Eng, Univ Guelph, 82-85; Writer, 82-. **MEMBERSHIPS** Victorian Stud Asn Ont 69-. **SELECTED PUBLICATIONS** Auth, Robertson Davies, 78; auth, Robertson Davies: Man of Myth, 94; ed, The Enthusiasms of Robertson Davies, 79, rev ed 90; ed, The Well-Tempered Critic: One Man's View of Theatre and Letters in Canada, 81. **CONTACT ADDRESS** 17 Admiral Rd, Toronto, ON, Canada M5R 2L4.

GRANT, PATRICK
DISCIPLINE ENGLISH LITERATURE **EDUCATION** Queen's Univ, Belfast, BA; Univ Sussex, PhD. **CAREER** Prof **HONORS AND AWARDS** Fel(s), Can Coun Leave; Killam Senior; Royal Soc Can. **RESEARCH** Renaissance and modern literature; literature and religion; literature and culture of modern Northern Ireland. **SELECTED PUBLICATIONS** Auth, The Transformation of Sin: Studies in Donne, Herbert, Vaughan and Traherne, Univ Mass Press, 74; Images and Ideas in Literature of the English Renaissance, Macmillan, 79); Six Modern Authors and Problems of Belief, Macmillan, 79; Literature of Mysticism in Western Tradition, Macmillan, 83; A Dazzling Darkness, An Anthology of Western Mysticism, Collins, 85; Literature and the Discovery of Method in the English Renaissance, Macmillan, 85; Reading the New Testament, Macmillan, 89; Literature and Personal Values, Macmillan, 92; Spiritual Discourse and the Meaning of Persons, Macmillan, 94; Personalism and the Politics of Culture, Macmillan, 96; auth, Breaking Enmities: Religion, Literature and Culture in Northern Ireland, 1967-97, Macmillan, 99. **CONTACT ADDRESS** Dept of English, Univ of Victoria, PO Box 3070, Victoria, BC, Canada V8W 3W1.

GRANT, RAYMOND JAMES SHEPHERD
PERSONAL Born 05/26/1942, Aberdeen, Scotland, m, 1973 **DISCIPLINE** LANGUAGE AND LITERATURE **EDUCATION** Univ Aberdeen, MA, 64; Cambridge Univ, PhD(English), 71. **CAREER** Asst prof, 67-74, assoc prof, 74-80, PROF ENGLISH, UNIV ALTA, 80-. **RESEARCH** Anglo-Saxon verse; homilies; texts transcribed in the 16th and 17th centuries. **SELECTED PUBLICATIONS** Auth, A Copied Tremulous Worcester Gloss at Corpus: Cambridge Manuscript-41 from Corpus-Christi-College Library Containing Bede 'Historia Ecclesiastica,' Neuphilologische Mitteilungen, Vol 0097, 96; The Pedlar-Poet and the Prince of Editors--Mcfarlan, James and Dickens, Charles, Dickensian, Vol 0093, 97. **CONTACT ADDRESS** Dept of English, Univ of Alberta, Edmonton, AB, Canada T6G 2E5. **EMAIL** raymond.grant@ualberta.ca

GRAS, VERNON W.
PERSONAL Born 02/11/1929, Oak Park, IL, m, 1959, 3 children **DISCIPLINE** ENGLISH **EDUCATION** Univ Chicago, BA, 52; PhD, 67. **CAREER** Chicago City Col, 63-67; Asst Prof, Temple Univ, 68-72; Assoc to Full Prof, George Mason Univ, 72-. **HONORS AND AWARDS** A.A. Stagg Awd for Scholarship & Athletics; NEH Summer Fel, 75. **MEMBERSHIPS** SAMLA, IAPL, ALSC **RESEARCH** Literary theory; Myth; Film; 20th Century British literature. **SELECTED PUBLICATIONS** ed, Peter Greenaway: Interviews, Univ Miss Press, 00; ed, The Passion of Dennis Potter: Changing Class, Religion, and Values 1965-1994, St Martin's Press, 99; ed, Selected Papers from the Synergos Seminars, 82; ed, European Literary Theory and Practice: From Existential Phenomenology to Structuralism, Dell Pub, 73; auth, "Dennis Potter's Legacy to His TV Viewers: Don't Remain Scripted," in English Literatures in Intercultural Contexts, Heidelberg, 00; auth, "Pondering the Anti-narrative Aesthetic of Peter Greenaway," in Interrogating Images, Northwestern Univ Press, 00; auth, "How Not to Get Lost in Literary Theory, Especially Cultural Studies," in Intercultural Encounters--Studies in English Literatures, Heidelberg, 99; auth, 'Dennis Potter's The Singing Detective: An Exemplum of Dialogical Ethics," in Why Literature Matters, Heidelberg, 96; auth, "Dramatizing the Failure to Jump the Culture/Nature Gap: The films of Peter Greenaway," New Literary History, 95; auth, "Cambridge Ritualist," in Johns Hopkins Guide to Literary Theory and Criticism, 94. **CONTACT ADDRESS** Dept English, George Mason Univ, Fairfax, 4400 Univ Dr, Fairfax, VA 22030-4422. **EMAIL** vgras@gmu.edu

GRASSIAN, ESTHER STAMPFER
PERSONAL Born 02/15/1946, Columbus, GA, d, 2 children **DISCIPLINE** LIBRARY SCIENCE **EDUCATION** Univ California, Los Angeles, BA,67, MLS, 69. **CAREER** Reference/Instruction librn, 69-95, electronic services coord, 95- 99, instructional services coord, 98- , Univ Calif Los Angeles Col Library. **HONORS AND AWARDS** Farband Awd, Best graduating student in Hebrew, UCLA, 67; NEH reviewer, 94- ; Librarian of the Year Awd, UCLA Librns Assoc, 95. **MEMBERSHIPS** ALA; ACRL; RUSA; LITA; CARL; Calif Clearinghouse on Libr Instruction. **RESEARCH** Information literacy; library instruction; critical thinking; Internet evaluation. **SELECTED PUBLICATIONS** Auth, Fear and Loathing on the Internet: Training the Trainers and Teaching the Users in change in reference and BI, Pierian Press, 96; auth, Thinking Critically About World Wide Web Resources, 95; auth, Appendix A: Thinking Critically About World Wide Web Resources, Greenwood, 97; auth, Librarian Teachers and the Virtual Library, in Laguardia, ed, Recreating the Academic Library, Neal-Schuman, 98; co-auth, Information Literacy Instruction: Theory and Technique, Neal-Schuman, forthcoming. **CONTACT ADDRESS** College Library, Univ of California, Los Angeles, PO Box 951450, Los Angeles, CA 90095-1450. **EMAIL** estherg@library.ucla.edu

GRAVEL, PIERRE
PERSONAL Born 03/13/1942, Montreal, PQ, Canada **DISCIPLINE** PHILOSOPHY, LITERATURE **EDUCATION** Univ Montreal, BPaed, 63; Univ Aix-Marseille, MA, 69, DPhil, 71. **CAREER** Asst lectr, Inst Am Univs and Univ Aix-Marseille, 68-71; prof, Col Maisonneuve, 71-73; asst prof, 73-78, ASSOC PROF PHILOS, UNIV MONTREAL, 78-, Consult philos, Rev Philos, 75-; mem, Comite de Lear, Rev Etudes Francaiscs, 78-; dir, Determinations, 82. **MEMBERSHIPS** Can Philos Asn. **RESEARCH** History of philosophy; aesthetics. **SELECTED PUBLICATIONS** Auth, 'Macbeth'--Shakespeare Depiction of the Workings of Power, Laval Theol et Philos, Vol 0051, 95. **CONTACT ADDRESS** 2910 Ed Montpetit, Montreal, QC, Canada H3C 3J7. **EMAIL** gravelpi@philo.umontreal.ca

GRAVER, LAWRENCE S.
PERSONAL Born 12/06/1931, New York, NY, m, 1960, 2 children **DISCIPLINE** ENGLISH **EDUCATION** City Col NY, BA, 53; Univ Calif at Berkeley, PhD, 61. **CAREER** From asst prof to prof, Williams Col, 64-97. **HONORS AND AWARDS** J. H. Roberts Professorship of English. **MEMBERSHIPS** MLA. **SELECTED PUBLICATIONS** Auth, Conrad's Short Fiction, Univ Calif Press, 69; auth, Carson McCullers, Univ Minn Press, 69; ed, Mastering the Film, Univ Tenn Press, 77; co-ed, Samuel Beckett: The Critical Heritage, Routledge and Kegan Paul, 79; auth, Samuel Beckett: Waiting for Godot, 89, 93, & 96; auth, An Obsession with Anne Frank: Meyer Levin and the Diary, Univ Calif Press, 95 & 97; asst ed, The Columbia Companion to the 20th Century American Short Story, Columbia Univ Press, forthcoming. **CONTACT ADDRESS** Dept English, Williams Col, 880 Main St, Williamstown, MA 01267-2600. **EMAIL** lgraver@williams.edu

GRAVER, SUZANNE
PERSONAL Born 08/17/1936, New York, NY, m, 1960, 2 children **DISCIPLINE** ENGLISH **EDUCATION** Queen's Col CUNY, BA, 57; Univ Calif Berkeley, MA, 60; Univ Mass Amherst, PhD, 76. **CAREER** John Hawley Roberts prof, English. **HONORS AND AWARDS** Queens College: Phi Beta Kappa, 56, Summa Cum Laude 57; Univ of California Fel, Los Angeles, 61-62; Univ of Massachusetts Fel, Amherst, 74-76; Nat Endowment for the Humanities Summer Stipend, 85; Am Council of Learned Societies Fel, 85-86; Robert B Partlow, Jr Prize, 87, Dickens Soc; Am Council of Learned Societies Fel, 89-90; Nat Humanities Center Fel, 89-90; Nat Endowment for the Humanities Fel, 95. **RESEARCH** Victorian literature and culture & gender studies; women's studies; theory of fiction. **SELECTED PUBLICATIONS** Auth, Incarnate History: The Feminisms of Middlemarch; Writing in a Womanly' Way and the Double Vision of Bleak House, George Eliot and Community: A Study in Social Theory and Fictional Form. **CONTACT ADDRESS** Dept of English, Williams Col, Stetson d 11, Williamstown, MA 01267. **EMAIL** sgraver@williams.edu

GRAVES, ROBERT
DISCIPLINE MUSIC **EDUCATION** Northwestern Univ, PhD. **CAREER** Assoc prof, Univ IL Urbana Champaign . **RESEARCH** Theatre hist; Renaissance theatre; mod theatre. **SELECTED PUBLICATIONS** Auth, publ on Elizabethan staging. **CONTACT ADDRESS** Dept of Music, Univ of Illinois, Urbana-Champaign, E Gregory Drive, PO Box 52, Champaign, IL 61820. **EMAIL** r-graves@staff.uiuc.edu

GRAVES, ROY NEIL
PERSONAL Born 02/02/1939, Medina, TN, d, 3 children **DISCIPLINE** ENGLISH **EDUCATION** Princeton Univ, BA, 61; Duke Univ, MA, 64; Univ Miss, DA, 77. **CAREER** Grad instr, Duke Univ, 64-65; asst prof, The Lynchburg Branch of the Univ of Va, 65-67; asst and assoc prof, coordr of Humanities and Soc Scis, Central Va Community Col, Lynchburg, 68-69; asst and assoc prof, The Univ of Tenn, Martin, 69-. **HONORS AND AWARDS** Bain-Swiggett Prize for poetry, Princeton, 60; Manners Prize for writing, Princeton, 61; NDEA fel, Duke, 61-64; 1st place for poetry, annual contest of The Miscellany: A Davidson Rev, 76; Carnegie fel, Ole Miss, 76-77; Cunningham Awd for teaching/scholarship, Univ Tenn, Martin, 77; 1st place, Mis-South Chapbook Competition, Ion Books, Memphis, 86; listings in: A Directory of Am Poets (79 ff), The Int Authors and Writers Who's Who, (86 ff), The Int Who's Who in Poetry (.and Poets' Encyclopedia, 82 ff), Men of Achievement, 14 ed, Cambridge, England (90), Personalities of Am (89), Personalities of the South (76 ff), Who's Who in the South and Southwest (78-79), Who's Who in U. S. Writers, Editors & Poets (86 ff), Who's Who in Writers, Editors & Poets: United States and Canada (89 ff). **MEMBERSHIPS** Tenn Philol Asn. **RESEARCH** Shakespeare's Sonnets; suppressed design and coterie composition elements, especially in early English literature but also in more recent cases. **SELECTED PUBLICATIONS** Auth, Medina and Other Poems, Jackson, TN: Old Hickory Press (76); poems in Homewords: A Book of Tennessee Writers, Univ Tenn Press (86, 96); auth, Somewhere on the Interstate, Memphis: Ion Books (87); poems in Always at Home Here: Poems and Insights from Six Tennessee Poets, ed Ernest Lee, McGraw-Hill (97, 98); journal articles in: The Upstart Crow: A Shakespeare Journal (79, 95, 97), The Explicator (95-97), TN Philol Bull (81, 82, 93, 95, 96, 97), Spenser Studies VII (87), Southeastern Am Studies Asn proceedings document (abstract 83), Phylon: The Atlanta Univ Rev of Race and Culture (79); numerous other articles in journals and magazines and essays in reference works. **CONTACT ADDRESS** Dept English, Univ of Tennessee, Martin, 554 University St, Martin, TN 38238-0001. **EMAIL** ngraves@utm.edu

GRAVLEE, JACK
DISCIPLINE COMMUNICATION STUDIES **EDUCATION** Howard Col, BA; La State Univ, MA, PhD. **CAREER** Prof. **RESEARCH** Public speaking; television criticism. **SELECTED PUBLICATIONS** Auth, Pamphlets and the American Revolution: Rhetoric, Politics, Literature and the Popular Press; Myths in the Rhetorical Context of 1983 British Electioneering, 86; Watts' Dissenting Rhetoric of Prayer, Quarterly J Speech, 73; Bishop Jonathan Shipley's Charge to His Clergy 1774-1782, Anglican Episcopal Hist, 96. **CONTACT ADDRESS** Speech Communication Dept, Colorado State Univ, Fort Collins, CO 80523. **EMAIL** jgravlee@vines.colostate.edu

GRAWE, PAUL H.
PERSONAL Born 08/13/1944, Chicago, IL, m, 1969, 4 children **DISCIPLINE** ENGLISH **EDUCATION** Carleton Col, BA, 66; Northwestern Univ, MA, 67, PhD, 73. **CAREER** Asst to full prof, Winona State Univ, 68-; assoc dir, External Studies, 73-74; proj dir, FIPSE Nat Model grant, 74-76; proj dir, various grants, 73-. **HONORS AND AWARDS** Univ fel, Northwestern Univ, 67-68; post-doctoral fel, Univ Minn, 79-80; Am.Lit.net and Brit.Lit.net, ed in chief. **MEMBERSHIPS** Int Soc of Humor Studies, Inst for Travesty, Comedy, and Humor Studies, **RESEARCH** Humor, comedy, dark comedy; literary criticism; American literature; technical writing; Shakespeare. **SELECTED PUBLICATIONS** Auth, A Key to Grant Success, Winona State Univ, Winona, MN (82); auth, Comedy in Space, Time, and the Imagination, Nelson-Hall, Chicago (83); ed, Humor Quotient Newsletter (94-); more than 50 other articles and papers. **CONTACT ADDRESS** Dept English, Winona State Univ, PO Box 5838, Winona, MN 55987-0838. **EMAIL** pgrawe@vax2.winona.msus.edu

GRAY, DONALD
PERSONAL Born 09/21/1927, Waukegan, IL, m, 1954, 2 children **DISCIPLINE** ENGLISH LITERATURE **EDUCATION**

Loyola Univ, Ill, PhB, 50; Univ Minn, MA, 51; Ohio State Univ, PhD, 56. **CAREER** From instr to assoc prof English, 56-68, chmn dept, 68-73, PROF ENGLISH, IND UNIV, BLOOMINGTON, 68-, ED, COL ENGLISH, 78-. **MEMBERSHIPS** MLA; NCTE. **RESEARCH** Nineteenth century British literature; literary theory. **SELECTED PUBLICATIONS** Auth, The uses of Victorian laughter, Victorian Studies, 67; ed, Alice in Wonderland, Norton, 72; coauth, Victorian Prose and Poetry, Macmillan, 76. **CONTACT ADDRESS** Dept of English, Indiana Univ, Bloomington, Bloomington, IN 47401.

GRAY, JEFFREY
PERSONAL Born Seattle, WA **DISCIPLINE** ENGLISH **EDUCATION** Univ WA, MA; Univ CA, Riverside, PhD. **CAREER** Asst prof; dir, Poetry-in-the-Round; participant. **HONORS AND AWARDS** NEH Summer Inst, San Juan, PR. **MEMBERSHIPS** Acad Am Poets; Nat Poetry Found; MELUS; MLA; Pac Ancient and Mod Lang Asn; Northeast MLA; Elizabeth Bishop Soc; Col Engl Asn. **RESEARCH** 20th c. Am poetry; music; ostcolonial stud. **SELECTED PUBLICATIONS** Auth, Una Sesion Musical con Carli Munoz, El Nuevo Dia 19, San Juan, PR, 97; It's Not Natural: Freud's Uncanny and O'Connor's Wise Blood, Southern Lit J 24 1, 96; Richard Hugo, Muriel Rukeyser, & Charles Reznikoff: three biographical essay for American National Biography, Oxford UP; Among the Amak, Ancient Love, & A Tunisian Story, Amer Poetry Rev 24 4, 95; John Ashbery's The Instruction Manual, Explicator 54, 96; Elizabeth Bishop's Brazil, January 1, 1502, Explicator 54, 95; Essence and the Mulatto Traveler: Europe as Embodiment in Nella Larsen's Quicksand, Novel: A Forum on Fiction 27 3, 94; Necessary Thought: Frank Bidart and the Post-Confessional, Contemp Lit 34 4, 93; ed, Memory and Imagination in Day by Day, The Critical Response to Robert Lowell; Steven Gould Axelrod, Greenwood Press, 97. **CONTACT ADDRESS** Dept of Eng, Seton Hall Univ, So Orange, 400 S Orange Ave, South Orange, NJ 07079. **EMAIL** grayjeff@shu.edu

GRAY, LAURA
DISCIPLINE MUSIC **EDUCATION** Univ Western Ontario, BM, 87; Univ British Columbia, MA, 89; Yale Univ, PhD, 97. **CAREER** Asst prof **RESEARCH** 19th and 20th century music, theory and aesthetics. **SELECTED PUBLICATIONS** Auth, pub(s) on Sibelius, and music in the 20th century. **CONTACT ADDRESS** Dept of Music, Univ of Waterloo, Conrad Grebel Col, 200 Westmount Rd, Waterloo, ON, Canada N2L 3G6. **EMAIL** ljgray@uwaterloo.ca

GRAYSON, JANET
PERSONAL Born 06/04/1934, Boston, MA, m, 1958, 4 children **DISCIPLINE** ENGLISH **EDUCATION** Brooklyn Col, BA, 58, MA, 62; Columbia Univ, PhD(English), 68. **CAREER** Lectr English, Brooklyn Col, 63-66; from asst prof to assoc prof, 66-75, PROF ENGLISH, KEENE STATE COL, 75-. **MEMBERSHIPS** Mediaeval Acad Am; Int Arthurian Soc. **RESEARCH** English and European medieval literature; Elizabethan literature; classical civilization. **SELECTED PUBLICATIONS** Auth, Structure and imagery in Ancrene Wisse, Univ New Eng, 74. **CONTACT ADDRESS** Keene State Col, Keene, NH 03431.

GRAYSON, NANCY JANE
PERSONAL Born 02/10/1934, Abilene, TX **DISCIPLINE** ENGLISH **EDUCATION** Tex Christian Univ, BA, 56; Univ Tex, Austin, MA, 58, PhD(English), 68. **CAREER** Instr English, Tex Christian Univ, 60-61; teaching asst, Univ Tex, Austin, 61-66, teaching assoc, Univ Tex, Austin, 66-68; asst prof, 68-72, assoc prof English, Southwest Tex State Univ, 72-83, prof, Southwest Tex State Univ, 83-, dir freshman English, 73-79, dept chair, 87-93, Assoc Dean Of Liberal Arts, 98-. **MEMBERSHIPS** Col Conf Teachers English; SCent Mod Lang Asn; Col English Asn; MLA; Col Conf Compos & Commun. **RESEARCH** English Romantics; childrens' classics on film. **CONTACT ADDRESS** Dept of English, Southwest Texas State Univ, 601 University Dr, San Marcos, TX 78666-4685. **EMAIL** NG01@swt.edu

GREAVES, GAIL-ANN
DISCIPLINE INTERCULTURAL COMMUNICATION AND RHETORIC **EDUCATION** Howard Univ, PhD. **CAREER** Asst prof and Dir of Forensics Prog, Long Island Univ, Brooklyn Campus. **HONORS AND AWARDS** Ten Years of Dedicated Service to Medgar Evers College and the Community; Outstanding Services to the Student Forensic, Academic Club Asoc at Brooklyn Col; Who's Who Int Students Certif of Merit; Awd of Merit; Outstanding Young Woman of Am. **MEMBERSHIPS** Nat Forensic Asoc; Nat Commun Asoc; Trinidad and Tobago Working Women Asoc; Caribbean Studies Asoc. **RESEARCH** Calypso music; popular rhetoric. **SELECTED PUBLICATIONS** Auth, The Evolution of Calypso and Carnival, Trinidad and Tobago Working Women's Asoc Scholar Award Luncheon J, 93; auth, The Rhetoric of the Calypso of Political Commentary from the Republic of Trinidad and Tobago: An African-Centered Historical-Critical Analysis, Howard J Commun, 95; auth, Call-Response in Selected Calypsoes of Political Commentary from the Republic of Trinidad and Tobago, J Black Studies, 98. **CONTACT ADDRESS** 390 52nd St., Brooklyn, NY 11203-4404. **EMAIL** gailann21@aol.com

GREBSTEIN, SHELDON NORMAN
PERSONAL Born 02/01/1928, Providence, RI, m, 1953, 2 children **DISCIPLINE** MODERN & AMERICAN LITERATURE **EDUCATION** Univ Southern Calif, BA, 49; Columbia Univ, MA, 50; Mich State Univ, PhD(English), 54. **CAREER** From instr to asst prof English, Univ Ky, 53-62; asst prof, Univ S Fla, 62-63; assoc prof, 63-68, dir grad English studies, 66-72, dean arts & sci, Harpur Col, 75-81; Prof English, State Univ NY, Binghamton, 68-81; Pres, 81-93, Prof Lit, SUNY Col Purchase, 93-95, Dir of Educ, Westchester Holocaust Cmn, 95- ; Fulbright-Hays lectr, Univ Rouen, France, 68-69. **RESEARCH** American and contemporary literature; Jewish-American literature; modern American fiction. **SELECTED PUBLICATIONS** Ed, Monkey Trial, Houghton, 60; auth, Sinclair Lewis, 62 & John O'Hara, 66, Twayne; ed, Perspectives in Contemporary Criticism, Harper, 68; Studies in For Whom the Bells Tolls, Merrill, 71; auth, Hemingway's Craft, Southern Ill Univ, 73. **CONTACT ADDRESS** Westchester Holocaust Cmn, 2900 Purchase St, Purchase, NY 10577. **EMAIL** whc@bestweb.net

GREELEY, ANDREW M.
PERSONAL Born 02/05/1928, Chicago, IL **DISCIPLINE** SOCIOLOGY, ENGLISH LITERATURE, RELIGION **EDUCATION** St Mary Lake Sem, STL, 54; Univ Chicago, MA, Soc, 61, PhD, 62. **CAREER** Sr stud dir, Nat Opinion Res Center, Univ Chicago, 62-68; prog dir, High Educ, univ Chicago, 68-70; lectr, Soc dept, Univ Chicago, 63-72; Prof, Soc, Univ Ariz, 78-; Prof, Soc Sci, Univ Chicago, 91-. **SELECTED PUBLICATIONS** Religion as Poetry, Trans Publ, 95; Sociology and Religion: A Collection of Readings, Harper Collins Coll Publ, 95; coauth, Common Ground, Pilgrim Press, 96; coauth, Forging a Common Future, Pilgrim Press, 1997; I Hope You're listening God, Crossroads Publ, 97. **CONTACT ADDRESS** Nat Opinion Res Center (NORC), Univ of Chicago, 1155 E 60th St, Chicago, IL 60637. **EMAIL** agreel@aol.com

GREELEY, JUNE-ANN T.
PERSONAL Born 03/21/1955, Brookline, MA, m, 1983, 1 child **DISCIPLINE** CLASSICS **EDUCATION** Conn Col, BA, 76; Univ Conn, MA, 82; Rutgers Univ, BA, 88; Fordham Univ, MA, 89; PhD, 00. **CAREER** Instr, Fordham Univ, 87-89; Instr, Univ Conn, 97; Instr, Fairfield Col Prep, 97-; Instr, Sacred Heart Univ, 95-. **MEMBERSHIPS** Am Philol Asn; Medieval Acad of Am; Dante Soc; Intl Center for Medieval Art; N Am Medieval Latin Asn; Vergilian Soc; Hagiography Soc; Class Asn of N Eng. **RESEARCH** Poetry of late antiquity; Early Christian poets; Medieval Latin literature; Medieval religion (mysticism); Sacred art/architecture; Classical tradition in (early) medieval literature; Gender studies (esp women in religious traditions); Sufism and medieval Islam. **CONTACT ADDRESS** 4 Merritt Lane, Westport, CT 06880. **EMAIL** june-ann@vocanda.com

GREEN, DOUGLASS MARSHALL
PERSONAL Born 07/22/1926, Rangoon, Burma, m, 1952, 3 children **DISCIPLINE** MUSIC HISTORY **EDUCATION** Univ Redlands, BMus, 49, MMus, 51; Boston Univ, PhD(compos musicol), 58. **CAREER** Sensei music and English, Nanko Gakuen, Sendai, Japan, 51-54; from asst to assoc prof music, St Joseph Col, Conn, 58-66; from asst to assoc prof, Univ Calif, Santa Barbara, 66-70; from assoc prof to prof, Eastman Sch of Music, Univ Rochester, 70-77; Prof Music, Univ Tex, Austin, 77-. **HONORS AND AWARDS** Am Soc Composers, Arrangers & Publ Deems Taylor award, 78. **MEMBERSHIPS** Am Musicol Soc; Soc Music Theory; Col Music Soc. **RESEARCH** Italian instrumental music of the 18th century; early 20th century music; musical analysis. **SELECTED PUBLICATIONS** Auth, Form in Tonal Music, 65; Harmony Through Counterpoint, New Century, 70; contribr, Progressive and conservative tendencies in violoncello concertos of Leonardo Leo, In: Studies in 18th Century Music, Allen & Unwin, London, 70; auth, Berg's De Profundis: The finale of the Lyric Suite, Int Alban Berg Soc Newsletter, 77; The Allegro Misterioso of Berg's Lyric Suite: Iso-and retro-rhythms, J Am Musicol Soc, fall 77. **CONTACT ADDRESS** Dept of Music, Univ of Texas, Austin, 0 Univ of Texas, Austin, TX 78712-1026.

GREEN, LAWRENCE DONALD
PERSONAL Born 07/14/1945, New York, NY **DISCIPLINE** RHETORIC, ENGLISH RENAISSANCE LITERATURE **EDUCATION** Univ Berkeley, BA, 69, MA, 71, PhD(rhet), 75. **CAREER** Lectr rhet, Univ Calif, Berkeley, 75-76; ASST PROF ENGLISH, UNIV SOUTHERN CALIF, 76-. **MEMBERSHIPS** MLA; Philol Asn Pac Coast; Shakespeare Soc; Rhet Soc Am; Nat Coun Teachers Educ. **RESEARCH** Elizabethan drama; Renaissance rhetoric and intellectual history; composition and language theory. **SELECTED PUBLICATIONS** Auth, Where's My Fool?- Some Consequences of the Omission of the Fool in Tate's Lear, Studies English Lit 1500-1900, spring 72. **CONTACT ADDRESS** Dept of English, Univ of So California, Los Angeles, CA 90007.

GREEN, LON C.
PERSONAL Born 07/27/1947, Salt Lake City, UT, m, 1993, 6 children **DISCIPLINE** RHETORIC, COMMUNICATION **EDUCATION** Univ of Nev, BA, 70; Utah State Univ, MS, 73; Kent State Univ, PhD, 83. **CAREER** Prof, ch, Dept of Speech & Theater, Lewis Univ, 77-85; prof, Ferris State Univ, 85- , head of dept of Hum, 85-93. **MEMBERSHIPS** AAHE; Nat Commun Asn; Am Soc for Sport Hist. **RESEARCH** Dispute resolution. **CONTACT ADDRESS** Dept of Humanities, Ferris State Univ, 820 Campus Dr, Big Rapids, MI 49307. **EMAIL** greenl@ferris.edu

GREEN, MARTIN
PERSONAL Born 11/13/1940, Brooklyn, NY, m, 1965 **DISCIPLINE** ENGLISH MEDIEVAL LITERATURE **EDUCATION** City Univ New York, BA, 61; Ind Univ, MA, 65, PhD(-English), 71. **CAREER** From instr to asst prof, 66-76, assoc prof English, Fairleigh Dickenson Univ, 76-83; prof English, 83; chmn English, 83-97; acting dean, Coll Arts & Sciences, 97-00; Asst and Provost for assessment, 00-; co-ed, Lit Rev, 76-. **MEMBERSHIPS** MLA; Medieval Acad Am; AAUP; Coord Coun Lit Mag. **RESEARCH** Old English poetry; myth and comparative literature; contemporary fiction; Literary & Popular magazines. **SELECTED PUBLICATIONS** Co-ed, The Other Sides of Reality, Boyd & Fraser, 72; auth, Man, time and apocalypse in the Wanderer, Seafarer, and Beowulf, J English Ger Philol, Fall 75; coauth, Vision and voice in the OE Christ III, Papers Lang & Lit, 76; auth, Old English Elegies: New Essays, FUD Press, 83; auth, The American Spectator: A Literary Newspaper and The Cultural Politics of the 1930's, Biblion, 98. **CONTACT ADDRESS** Dept of English, Fairleigh Dickinson Univ, Florham-Madison, 285 Madison Ave, Madison, NJ 07940-1099. **EMAIL** green@mailbox.fdu.edu

GREEN, PETER
PERSONAL Born 12/22/1924, London, England, m, 1975, 3 children **DISCIPLINE** CLASSICS **EDUCATION** Cambridge Univ, BA, 50; MA, 54; PhD, 54. **CAREER** Vis Prof, Univ Tex, 71-72; Vis Prof, Univ Calif, 76; Prof, Tulane Univ, 86; Prof, Univ Tex, 72-97; Vis Prof, Univ Iowa, 97-98; Adjunct Prof, Univ Iowa, 98-. **HONORS AND AWARDS** Heinemann Awd for Lit, 57; Grad Teaching Awd, Univ Tex, 84; NEH Sen Feel, 83-84. **MEMBERSHIPS** APA, CAMWS, Hellenic Assoc. (UK), ATA. **RESEARCH** Greek history, classical and Hellenistic, Latin satire and elegy, modern Greek and Anglo-American poetry. **SELECTED PUBLICATIONS** Auth, Alexander of Maredon, 356-323 B C: A Historical Biography, Rev Ed (London, UK), 74; auth, Alexander to Actium: The Historical Evolution of the Hellenistic Age, Rev Ed (Berkeley, CA), 93; auth, The Greco-Persian Wars (Berkeley, CA), 96; auth, Classical Beanings: Interpretive Ancient History and Culture (New York, NY), 98; auth, Juvenile: The Sixteen Satires, 3rd Rev Ed (New York, NY), 98. **CONTACT ADDRESS** Dept Class, Univ Iowa, 1268 Chamberlain Dr, Iowa City, IA 52240. **EMAIL** peter-green-1@uiowa.edu

GREEN, RICHARD F.
PERSONAL Born 08/19/1943, Oldham, United Kingdom, m, 2 children **DISCIPLINE** ENGLISH **EDUCATION** Oxford Univ, BA, 64; Univ Toronto, PhD, 75. **CAREER** Mt Allison Univ, 65-69; UBC, 74-76; Bishop's Univ, 78-82; Univ W Ont, 82-02; Ohio State Univ, 02-. **HONORS AND AWARDS** Guggenheim Fel, 89; Trustee, New Chaucer Soc, 90-96. **MEMBERSHIPS** Am Soc for Legal Hist; Medieval Acad of Am; MLA; New Chaucer Soc. **RESEARCH** Medieval literature and history; Literature and law. **SELECTED PUBLICATIONS** Auth, "John Ball's Letters: Literary History and Historical Literature," in Chaucer's England: Literature in Historical Context, (Univ Minn Press, 92), 176-200; auth, "The Pardoner's Pants (and Why They Matter)," Studies in the Age of Chaucer, (93): 131-145; auth, "The Ballad in the Middle Ages," in The Long Fifteenth Century: Essays for Douglas Gray, (Oxford Univ Press, 97), 163-184; auth, "Medieval Literature and Law," in The Cambridge History of Middle English Literature, (Cambridge Univ Press, 98), 407-431; auth, A Crisis of Truth: Literature and Law in Ricardian England, Univ Pa Press, 98. **CONTACT ADDRESS** Dept English, Univ W Ont, London, ON, Canada N6A 3K7. **EMAIL** rfgreen@uwo.ca

GREEN, SUZANNE DISHEROON
PERSONAL Born 11/27/1963, Dallas, TX, m, 1986, 2 children **DISCIPLINE** ENGLISH **EDUCATION** Southern Adventist Univ, BA, 85; Univ N Tex, MA, 94; PhD, 97. **CAREER** Instr, N Central Tex Col, 95-97; Teaching Fel, Univ N Tex, 93-97; Asst Prof, Northwestern State Univ, 97-. **MEMBERSHIPS** Mod Lang Asn, Soc for Study of Southern Literature, Am Literature Asn, South Central Mod Lang Asn. **RESEARCH** Women's writing, Southern writing and culture, Bibliography and research methods. **SELECTED PUBLICATIONS** Co-auth, At Fault, Univ Tenn Press; forthcoming; auth, Songs of the New South: Writing Contemporary Louisiana, Greenwood Press, forthcoming; auth, Proceedings of the 5th Kate Chopin International Conference, Northwestern State Univ Pres, forthcoming; auth, Kate Chopin: An Annotated Bibliography of Critical Works, Greenwood Press, 99; auth, "Jill McCorkle," in Contemporary American Women Novelists: A Bio-Bibliographical Sourcebook, Greenwood Press, forthcoming; auth, "Terri McMillan," in Contemporary American Women Novelists: A Bio-Bibliographical Sourcebook, Greenwood Press, forthcoming; auth, "Literature of the Louisiana Purchase," "Natchitoches," and "Louisiana," The Louisiana Purchase: An Encyclopedia, Santa Barbara, forthcoming; auth, "Creoles," in The Louisiana Purchase: An Encyclopedia, Santa

Barbara, forthcoming; auth, "How Edna Escaped: The LIFE IS A JOURNEY Conceptual Metaphor in The Awakening," The Poetics of Cognition: Studies in Cognitive Linguistics and the Verbal Arts, Cambridge Univ Press, forthcoming. **CONTACT ADDRESS** Dept Lang Arts, Northwestern State Univ of Louisiana, 350 Sam Sibley Rd, Natchitoches, LA 71497-0001. **EMAIL** green@alpha.nsula.edu

GREEN, WILLIAM
PERSONAL Born 07/10/1926, New York, NY, d, 1960, 2 children **DISCIPLINE** ENGLISH & DRAMA **EDUCATION** Queens Col, AB, 49; Columbia Univ, MA, 50; PhD, 59. **CAREER** Lectr English, Upsala Col, 53-56; tutor, 57-59, from instr to assoc prof, 59-72, prof English, Queens Col, NY, 72-, consult, col proficiency exam prog, NY State Educ Dept, 64-88; Andrew W Mellon Found fel, 82; Fulbright prof, Inst for Theatre Res, Univ of Vienna, Spring 83. **HONORS AND AWARDS** Phi Beta Kappa; PSC-CUNY Res Awd, 86-90; Andrew W. Mellon Found joint fel with prof Leo Hershkowitz, 83-84. **MEMBERSHIPS** Col English Asn; MLA; Malone Soc; Shakespeare Asn of Am; Theatre Library Asn; Am Soc for Theatre Res; Int Fedn for Theatre Res; Am Theatre Critics Asn. **RESEARCH** Shakespeare; Elizabethan drama; modern European and American drama. **SELECTED PUBLICATIONS** Co-ed, Elizabethan Drama: Eight Plays, Applause Thetre Book Pub, 90; auth, The Use of Legal Records in Reproducing Theatrical Performances, Records and Images of the Art of the Performer, 92; Robert Edmond Jones, John Barrymore e l'Amleto del 1922, La Scena di Amleto, Biblioteca Teatrale, 90; Caliban by the Yellow Sands: Percy MacKay's Adaptation of The Tempest, Maske und Kothurn, 89; Venice Hosts International Hamlet Conference, Shakespeare Bulletin 7, May/June 89; Three articles in The Encyclopedia of New York City, 95: auth, "Burlesque," The Encycl of NYork City (95); auth, "Minsky, Billy," The Encycl of NYork City (95); auth, "Weber and Fields," The Encycl of NYork City (95); coauth, "Gay Theatre," in The Cambridge Guide to Theatre, 2nd ed. Cambridge University Press, 95. **CONTACT ADDRESS** Dept of English, Queens Col, CUNY, 6530 Kissena Blvd, Flushing, NY 11367-1597.

GREENBERG, ALVIN D.
PERSONAL Born 05/10/1932, Cincinnati, OH, m, 1993, 3 children **DISCIPLINE** ENGLISH **EDUCATION** Univ Cincinnati, BA, 54, MA, 60; Univ Wash, PhD(English), 64. **CAREER** Instr, Univ Ky, 63-65; Asst prof, 65-68; Assoc prof, 68-72; Dept Chmn, 88-93; Prof, English Dept, MaCalester Col, 72-. **HONORS AND AWARDS** Witter Bynner Found for Poetry, 79; Associated Writing Progs Short Fiction Awd, 82; Stories in Best American Short Stories, 73 & 82; Nimrod/Pablo Neruda Prize in Poetry, 88; Loft-McKnight Poetry Awd, 91; Loft-McKnight Awd of Distinction in Poetry, 94; Fulbright lectr Am lit, Univ Kerala, 66-67; ed, Minn Rev, 67-71; Northwest Area Found Grant for opera, 75; Nat Endowment Arts fel, 72 & 92, artists fel, Bush Found, 76 & 81; Fel in Non-Fiction, 97; Jerome Found Travel & Res Grant, 98; Rockefeller/Bellagio Fel., 99; Ohioana Poetry Awd, 00. **RESEARCH** Literary criticism; 20th century literature; literature and psychology. **SELECTED PUBLICATIONS** Auth, Small Waves, El Corno Press, 65; Metaphysical Giraffe, New Rivers, 68; Going Nowhere, Simon & Schuster, 71; House of the Would-Be Gardener, New Rivers, 72; Dark Lands, Ithaca House, 73; Metaform, Univ Mass, 75; Invention of the West, Avon, 76; In/Direction, David R Godine, 78; Discovery of America & Other Tales, La State Univ, 80; And Yet, Juniper, 81; Delta q, Univ Mo, 83; Man in the Cardboard Mask, Coffee House, 85; Heavy Wings, Ohio Review, 88; Why We Live with Animals, Coffee House, 90; How the Dead Live, Graywolf, 98. **CONTACT ADDRESS** Dept of English, Macalester Col, 1304 N. 26th St., Boise, ID 83702. **EMAIL** alvindg@cs.com

GREENBERG, BRADLEY
PERSONAL m, 3 children **DISCIPLINE** JOURNALISM **EDUCATION** Bowling Green Univ, BS, 56; MS, 57, PhD, 61, Univ Wis **CAREER** Lectr, 60-61, research asst, 58-60, Univ WI; research assoc, 61-64, Stanford Univ; fel, 71-72, British Broadcasting Corp, senior fel, 78-79, 81, East-West Ctr, Communication Inst, research fel, 85-86, Independent Broadcasting Authority; Univ CA, fall 92; asst prof, 64-66, assoc prof, 66-71, chair of communication, 78-83, chair of telecommunication, 84-90, prof, 71, univ distinguished prof, 90, Michigan State Univ. **HONORS AND AWARDS** Univ of Wisc Chancellor's Awd for Distinguished Service in Journalism, 78; Journalism Hall of Fame Inductee, Bowling Green Univ, 80; Mich State Univ Distinguished Prof Awd, 90; MI State Univ Coll of Education Crystal Apple Awd, 96; MI Assn of Governing Boards Distinguished Faculty member, 97; Natl Assn of Broadcasters Lifetime Achievement Awd for Audience Research, 97; Intl Communication Assn, The B. Aubrey Fisher Mentorship Awd, 98. **MEMBERSHIPS** Assn for Education in Journalism; Intl Communication Assn; Intl Assoc for Mass Communication Research. **SELECTED PUBLICATIONS** Auth, Desert Storm and the Mass Media, 93; Media, Sex and the Adolescent, 93; coauth, US Minorities and News, Cultural Diversity and the US Media, 98; The Valence of Close Relationships and the Focus on Individual Attributes in Six Months of Television Talk Show Topics, in press; A Quantitative Content Analysis of the Television Talk Show, Talking up a Storm: The Social Impact of Daytime Talk Programs, in press; Disclosures and Privacy Issues on Television Talk Shows, Balancing Disclosure, Privacy, and Secrecy, in press. **CONTACT ADDRESS** Dept of Telecommunication, Michigan State Univ, 477 Communication Arts Bldg, East Lansing, MI 48824-1212. **EMAIL** bradg@pilot.msu

GREENBERG, ROBERT M.
PERSONAL Born 04/10/1943, Brooklyn, NY, m, 1965, 3 children **DISCIPLINE** ENGLISH, LITERATURE **EDUCATION** Columbia Col, BA, 64; CCNY, MA, 72; CUNY, PhD, 78. **CAREER** Grad fel, adj lectr, Queens Col, 72-78; vist asst prof, Frank Marsh Col, 78-79; vist asst prof, asst dean, act dean, vis assoc prof, Temple Univ, 79-. **MEMBERSHIPS** MLA; ASA. **RESEARCH** Post colonial literature; immigrant American literature; Caribbean literature. **SELECTED PUBLICATIONS** Auth, Complementarily, Freudianism, and Western Man, West Hum Rev (84); auth, "The Three-Day Chase: Multiplicity and Coherence in Moby-Dick," ESQ (83); auth, "Cetology: Center of Multiplicity and Discord in Moby-Dick," ESQ (81); auth, "Idealism and Realism in the Fiction of Claude McKay," in Twentieth Century Literary Criticism, ed. Laurie DiMauro (Detroit, MI: Gale Res, 91); auth, "Transgression in the Fiction of Philip Roth," Twentieth Cen Lit (97); auth, "Anger and the Alchemy of Literary Method in V. S. Naipaul's Political Fiction," Twentieth Cen Lit (00); auth, "The Big Picture: Race, Politics, and History in V. S. Naipaul's Caribbean Nonfiction," in Prospects: An Annual of American Cultural Studies (Cambridge UP, 00); auth, "Robert Hayden" in African American Writers (Charles Scribner's and Sons, 01); auth, "Splintered Worlds: Fragmentation and the Ideal of Diversity in the Work of Emerson, Melville, Whitman and Dickinson," (Northeastern Univ Press, 93). **CONTACT ADDRESS** Am Studies Program, Temple Univ, 1114 Berks St, Philadelphia, PA 191122-6090. **EMAIL** rgreen05@unix.temple.edu

GREENBURG, MARK LAWRENCE
PERSONAL Born 07/02/1948, Bronx, NY, m, 1972, 2 children **DISCIPLINE** ENGLISH **EDUCATION** Queens Col, CUNY, 71; Univ Mich, AM, 72, PhD, 78. **CAREER** Prof of Humanities, Drexel Univ, 91-, Dir, Univ Honors Prog, 95-, Dean of Undergrad Educ, 99-; ed bd, Synthesis Books and the biannual journal, 92-; ed bd, Soc for Lit and Sci-Univ Mich Press Book Series in Lit and Sci, 91-. **HONORS AND AWARDS** Vis NEH Fel, Princeton Univ, 81; nominated for James L. Clifford Prize, Am Soc for Eighteenth-Century Studies, 85; Christian R. and Mary F. Lindback Awd for distinguished Teaching, Drexel Univ, 86; Presidential Plaque, Soc for Lit and Sci, 92; Configurations, official j of the Soc for Lit and Sci, initiated under Greenberg's presidency, named Best New J--Sci/Technol/Med, by Prof and Scholarly Pub Div, Am Asn of Pubs, 95. **MEMBERSHIPS** Soc for Sci and Lit. **SELECTED PUBLICATIONS** Coauth, Approaches to Teaching Blake's Songs of Innocence and of Experience, Lang Studies, 20 (90); contributing co-ed, Literature and Technology, Bethlehem: Lehigh Univ Press, London and Toronto: Assoc Univ Presses (92); auth, "Disciplinary Antagonism: Its Antecedents and its Amerlioration," Decodings: The Newsletter of the Soc for Lit and Sci, 5 (95): 5-7; contrib ed, Speak Silence: Rhetoric and Culture in Blake's Poetical Sketches, London and Detroit: Wayne State Univ Press (96). **CONTACT ADDRESS** Honors Center, Drexel Univ, 5016 MacAlister Hall, Philadelphia, PA 19104. **EMAIL** Greenberg@drexel.edu

GREENE, DAVID LOUIS
PERSONAL Born 09/24/1944, Middletown, CT, m, 1974, 2 children **DISCIPLINE** ENGLISH LITERATURE **EDUCATION** Univ SFla, BA, 66; Univ Pa, MA, 67, PhD(English lit), 74. **CAREER** From asst prof to assoc prof English, 70-78, prof English, 78- , chemn dept, 72-92, chemn div humanities, 74-98, Piedmont Col. **MEMBERSHIPS** Am Antiquarian Soc; Am Soc of Genealogists. **RESEARCH** Restoration literature; children's literature; history of periodicals. **SELECTED PUBLICATIONS** Coauth, Introduction to L. Frank Baum's The Master Key, Hyperion Press, 74; auth, The concept of Oz, Children's Lit Ann, 74; auth, introd to William Godwin's Fables Ancient and Modern, 76 & Charles Lamb's The Adventures of Ulysses, Garland, 76; ed, L Frank Baum's The Purple Dragon & Other Fantasies, Fictioneer, 76; coauth, The Oz Scrapbook, Random, 77. **CONTACT ADDRESS** Dept of English, Piedmont Col, PO Box 10, Demorest, GA 30535-0010. **EMAIL** dgreene@piedmont.edu

GREENE, GAYLE JACOBA
PERSONAL Born 06/23/1943, San Francisco, CA **DISCIPLINE** ENGLISH LITERATURE **EDUCATION** Univ Calif, Berkeley, BA, 64, MA, 66; Columbia Univ, PhD, 74. **CAREER** Ed asst, Harper & Row Publ, 67-68; lectr English lit, Queens Col, 68-72 & Brooklyn Col, 72-74; from asst prof to assoc prof, 74-87, Prof English Lit, Scripps Col, 87-; Beatrice M. Bain Vis Fel, Univ Calif, Berkeley, 92-93; Vis Prof, Univ Wash, Seattle, Spring 93. **HONORS AND AWARDS** Graves award, Pomona Col, 77. **RESEARCH** Shakespeare; women's studies; health and environment. **SELECTED PUBLICATIONS** Co-ed, The Woman's Part: Feminist Criticism of Shakespeare, Univ Ill, 80; auth, Feminist and Marxist Criticism: An Argument for Alliances, Women's Studies; Shakespeare's Sense of Language in Othello, Etudes Anglaises, 81; co-ed, Making a Difference: Feminist Literary Criticism, Methuen, 85; auth, Changing the Story: Feminist Fiction and the Tradition, Ind univ Pressm 91; co-ed, Changing Subjects: The Making of Feminist Literary Criticism, Routledge, 93; auth, Doris Lessing: The Poetics of Change, Univ Mich Press, 94; The Woman Who Knew Too Much: Alice Stewart and the Secrets of Radiation, Temple Univ Press (forthcoming); author of numerous journal articles and reviews. **CONTACT ADDRESS** Scripps Col, 1030 Columbia Ave, Claremont, CA 91711-3948. **EMAIL** gaylegreene@earthlink.net

GREENE, GORDON K.
PERSONAL Born 12/27/1927, Cardston, AB, Canada **DISCIPLINE** MUSIC HISTORY **EDUCATION** Univ Alta, AMus, 52, BA, 54, BEd, 55, MA, 61; Ind Univ, PhD, 71. **CAREER** Lectr, Univ Alta, 55-63; fac mem, music hist dept, Univ Western Ont, 66-78; prof 78-93, dean music 79-89, PROF EMER MUSIC HISTORY, WILFRID LAURIER UNIV; vis prof, Univ Toronto, 93-96. **MEMBERSHIPS** Can Univ Music Soc; Am Musicol Soc; Int Musicol Soc. **RESEARCH** Medieval music. **SELECTED PUBLICATIONS** Auth, Polyphonic Music of the Fourteenth Century, 5 vols, 80-87; contribur, Grove's Dictionary of Music and Musicians; contribur, Dictionary of the Middle Ages. **CONTACT ADDRESS** Dept of Music History, Wilfrid Laurier Univ, Waterloo, ON, Canada N2L 3C5. **EMAIL** ggreene@wlu.ca

GREENE, JOHN
DISCIPLINE NINETEENTH-CENTURY FRENCH LITERATURE **EDUCATION** Univ Grenoble, PhD. **RESEARCH** Short fiction; novel and poetry; narrative technique. **SELECTED PUBLICATIONS** Auth, Structure et epistemologie dans Bouvard et Pecuchet, Flaubert et le Comble de l'art, SEDES, 1981; Le Sagittaire: symbolisme astrologique chez Barbey, Hommages a Jacques Petit, Les Belles Lettres, 85; co-ed, Barbey d'Aurevilly's Correspondance generale, 9 vols Les Belles Lettres, 81-89; Barbey d'Aurevilly, A Critical Bibliography of French Literature: The Nineteenth Century, Syracuse UP, 94. **CONTACT ADDRESS** Dept of French, Univ of Victoria, PO Box 3045 STN CSC, Victoria, BC, Canada V8W 3P4. **EMAIL** greenejc@uvvm.uvic.ca

GREENE, JOHN O.
PERSONAL Born 08/30/1954, Norfolk, VA, m, 1997 **DISCIPLINE** COMMUNICATION **EDUCATION** Purdue Univ, BA, 76; Pa State Univ, MA, 78; Univ of Wis, PhD, 83. **CAREER** Asst prof, Univ of Southern Calif, 83-85; asst prof, Purdue Univ, 85-88; assoc prof, Purdue Univ, 88-93; Prof, Purdue Univ, 93-. **HONORS AND AWARDS** Charles H. Woolbert Res Awd, Nat Commun Asn. **MEMBERSHIPS** Am Asn for the Advancement of Sci; Int Commun Asn; Nat Commun Asn; NY Acad of Sci. **RESEARCH** Communication theory; nonverbal communication; Interpersonal communication; Aging and communication; Cognitive processes and communication **SELECTED PUBLICATIONS** auth, "What sort of terms ought theories of human action incorporate?", Commun Studies, 94; auth, "Production of messages in pursuit of multiple social goals: Action assembly theory contributions to the study of cognitive encoding processes," Commun Yearbk, 95; auth, "Complexity effects on temporal characteristics of speech," Human Commun Res, 95; auth, "Adult acquisition of message-production skill," Commun Monogr, 97; ed, Message Production: Advances in Communication Theory, Lawrence Erlbaum, 97; auth, "The impact of individual differences on message-production skill acquisition," Commun Res, 98; auth, :The dawning of a new conception of the social actor," in Commun: Views from the helm for the Twenty-First Century, Allyn & Bacon, 98. **CONTACT ADDRESS** Dept of Commun, Purdue Univ, West Lafayette, 1366 Lib Arts & Educ Bldg 2114, West Lafayette, IN 47907-1366. **EMAIL** greene@vm.cc.purdue.edu

GREENE, MARTHA D.
PERSONAL Born 06/14/1965, Boone, NC, s **DISCIPLINE** ENGLISH, LITERATURE, RELIGION, THEATER **EDUCATION** Wake Forest Univ, BA, 87; MA, 93; Univ NCar Chapel Hill, MA, 96; PhD, 01. **CAREER** Counr, Wake Forest Univ, 87-89; rep, Appalachian State Univ, 89-90; hall dir, Salem Col, 92-93; asst dir to teaching fel, Univ NCar Chapel Hill, 95-01; Lilly fel/lectr, Valparaiso Univ, 01-03. **HONORS AND AWARDS** Lilly Found Fel, 01-03; PEW Found Mentoring Prog, 00-03; Teaching Fel, Univ NCar, 00-01; Rotary Ambassador Scholar, 91-92. **MEMBERSHIPS** MLA; SAMLA; Dorothy L. Sayers Soc; CCL. **RESEARCH** British modernism; drama; theology and literature. **SELECTED PUBLICATIONS** Auth, "H. D.'s Challenge to the Institution in 'The Flowering of the Rod,'" Theol 97 (94): 344-52; auth, "An Interview with Doris Betts," Carolina Quart 52 (00): 59-73; rev, "Literature in Christian Perspective," by Bridgit Nichols, Christianity/Lit 50 (01): 241-3; auth, "Dorothy L. Sayers's Anti-Romantic Comedies," Mod Drama (forthcoming). **CONTACT ADDRESS** Dept Humanities, Valparaiso Univ, Linwood House, Valparaiso, IN 463832. **EMAIL** Martha.Greene@valpo.edu

GREENE, ROLAND
PERSONAL Born 10/08/1957 **DISCIPLINE** ENGLISH **EDUCATION** Brown Univ, AB, 79; Princeton Univ, MA, 82;

PhD, 85. **CAREER** Lecturer, Princeton Univ, 83-84; Asst to Assoc Prof, Harvard Univ, 84-92; Prof, Univ Ore, 93-00; Prof, Stanford Univ, 01-. **HONORS AND AWARDS** ACLS Sen Fel, 92-93; Stanford Humanities Ctr Fel, 92-93; Danforth Grad Fel, 79-84. **MEMBERSHIPS** MLA. **RESEARCH** Early modern literatures of England, Europe, and the Americas; Transatlantic literature and society; Cultural semantics; Twentieth-century poetry and poetics; Latin American and Latino/a poetry, fiction, and criticism; Literary and cultural theory, especially lyric theory. **SELECTED PUBLICATIONS** Auth, Post-Petrarchism: Origins and Innovations of the Western Lyric Sequence, Princeton Univ Press, 91; co-ed, The Project of Prose in Early Modern Europe and the New World, Cambridge Univ Press, 97; auth, Unrequited Conquests: Love and Empire in the Colonial Americas, Univ Chicago Press, 99. **CONTACT ADDRESS** Dept Comp Lit, Stanford Univ, Stanford, CA 94305-2031.

GREENE, THOMAS R.
PERSONAL Born 10/17/1933, New York, NY, m, 1958, 2 children **DISCIPLINE** MEDIEVAL HISTORY, ENGLISH LITERATURE **EDUCATION** St Francis Col, NYork, BA, 58; NYork Univ, MA, 61, PhD(medieval hist), 67. **CAREER** Asst prof II Hist, Newark State Col, 63-64; instr, 64-66, Asst Prof II Hist, Villanova Univ, 66-. **MEMBERSHIPS** AHA. **RESEARCH** Twelfth century church history. **CONTACT ADDRESS** Dept of Hist, Villanova Univ, Villanova, PA 19385.

GREENFIELD, BRUCE R.
DISCIPLINE ENGLISH **EDUCATION** York, BA, 73; McGill, MA, 77; Columbia Univ, PhD, 85. **CAREER** Asst prof, Assoc Prof, Eng, Dalhousie Univ. **MEMBERSHIPS** Am Antiquarian Soc **SELECTED PUBLICATIONS** Auth, Narrating Discovery: The Romantic Explorer in American Literature, 1790-1855, Columbia Univ Press, 92; auth, "The Oral in the Written: The Irony of Representation in Louis Hennepin's Description de la Louisiane," Hist Reflections 21, 95. **CONTACT ADDRESS** Dept of Eng, Dalhousie Univ, Halifax, NS, Canada B3H 3J5. **EMAIL** bruce.greenfield@dal.ca

GREENFIELD, JOHN R.
PERSONAL Born 03/08/1947, Greenville, PA, m, 1989 **DISCIPLINE** LITERATURE **EDUCATION** Ind Univ, BA, 69; MA, 72; PhD, 80. **CAREER** Asst Prof, Stetson Univ, 81-84; From Asst Prof to Prof, McKendree Col, 84-. **HONORS AND AWARDS** Fel, Univ Kan, 80-81; NEH Summer Fel, Northwestern Univ, 85; NEH Summer Fel, Brown Univ, 89. **MEMBERSHIPS** MLA, NCTE, Keats-Shelley Asn of Am, Popular Cult Asn, Midwest Victorian Studies Asn, AAUP. **RESEARCH** Nineteenth-Century British literature, Romantic and Victorian, Arthur Morrison. **SELECTED PUBLICATIONS** Auth, "Arthur Morrison," Brit Short Fiction Writers, 1880-1914: The Realist Tradition, Gale Res (94); ed, The Dictionary of British Literary Characters: The Novel, Vol 2: 20th Century Novels, Facts-on-File (94); auth, "Ideology of Naturalism and Representation of Class in Arthur Morrison's 'A Child of the Jago'," Studies in the Lit Imagination, Gale Res (Detroit, MI), 96; auth, "Is Emma Clueless? Fantasies of Class and Gender from England to California," Topic 48: A J of the Lib Arts (98): 31-38; auth, "Transforming the Stereotype: Exotic Women in Shelley's 'Alastor' and 'The Witch of Atlas'," in The For Woman in Brit Lit: Exotics, Aliens and Outsiders, Greenwood Pr (99). **CONTACT ADDRESS** Dept Lit, McKendree Col, 701 College Rd, Lebanon, IL 62254.

GREENFIELD, SUSAN
DISCIPLINE ENGLISH LITERATURE **EDUCATION** PA Univ, PhD. **CAREER** Prof, Fordham Univ. **RESEARCH** Women writers, familial relationships. **SELECTED PUBLICATIONS** Auth, Fanny's Misreading and the Misreading of Fanny: Women, Literature and Inferiority in Mansfield Park, Tex Stud Lit and Lang 36, 94; Aborting the 'Mother Plot': Politics and Generation in Absalom and Achitophel, Eng Lit Hist 62, 95. **CONTACT ADDRESS** Dept of Eng Lang and Lit, Fordham Univ, 113 W 60th St, New York, NY 10023.

GREENSTEIN, MICHAEL
PERSONAL Born 06/27/1945, Toronto, ON, Canada **DISCIPLINE** ENGLISH **EDUCATION** SUNY Stony Brook, MA, 69; York Univ, PhD, 74. **CAREER** Asst-associe, Univ Bordeaux, 76-77; asst prof to assoc prof, 79-90, ADJ PROF ENGLISH, UNIV SHERBROOKE, 90-; vis lectr, Trent Univ, 85, 91; vis lectr, Univ Toronto Sch Cont Educ, 89-. **HONORS AND AWARDS** Toronto Jewish Cong Bk Awd, 90. **MEMBERSHIPS** MLA; ACUTE; PEN. **SELECTED PUBLICATIONS** Auth, Adele Wiseman and Her Works, 85; auth, Third Solitudes: Tradition and Discontinuity in Jewish-Canadian Literature, 89. **CONTACT ADDRESS** Dept of English, Univ of Sherbrooke, Ste. Foy, QC, Canada J1K 251.

GREENWOOD, TINA EVANS
PERSONAL Born 01/06/1964, Tucson, AZ, m, 1989 **DISCIPLINE** LIBRARY SCIENCE **EDUCATION** Univ Arizona, BA, 87, MALib, 93; Tulane Univ, MA, 90. **CAREER** Instr, 91, Career Blazers Learning Ctr; instr, 91-92, Portable Practical Ed Preparation; grad res asst, 92, Univ Arizona Schl of Lib Sci; prog asst, libr skills, 93, grad tchng asst, 93, Univ Arizona, Main Libr; ref/tech svcs libr, 93-94, Rend Lake Col Learning Res Ctr; ref libr/asst prof, 94-96, Western Ill Univ Libr; adj fac mem, 96, Univ Arizona Schl Info Res; libr instr coord/ ref libr, asst prof, 96-, John F. Reed Libr, Fort Lewis Col. **HONORS AND AWARDS** Beta Phi Mu library science honor society, member, 94-; Tulane Univ Departmental Fellowship, Latin American Studies, August 89-December 90; Phi Beta Kappa, member, 87-. **MEMBERSHIPS** Assoc of College and Research Libraries, fall 97-; Colorado Library Assoc, fall 97--; Computer Professionals for Social Responsibility, 95; GLOSAS (Global Systems and Simulations Association, USA, 95-; Am Library Assoc, 93-. **RESEARCH** Using the Internet & other technologies in education. **SELECTED PUBLICATIONS** Auth, The Cultural Revolution in Nicaraugua, Olas de LAGO, 4, Spring 92, pp. 20-38; auth, U.S. Government Infromation and the Nicaraguan Revolution 79-89: An Assessment of Bias, Journal of Government Information, 22 (3), June 95, pp. 237-252; auth, Greenwood, Tina Evans, et al. A Traveler's Guide to Exploring Planet Library or Coursepack for LIB 150, Information Literacy, 4th ed., 99; auth, Greenwood, Tina Evans, and Jeffrey Frisbie, Library Instruction That's Out of This World! Information Literacy at Fort Lewis College, Reference Services Review, 26 (3-4, 98, pp. 45-50; auth, A Travelers Guide to Exploring Planet Library--Information Literacy at Fort Lewis College, Colorado Libraries 24(4), winter 98, pp. 12-16; auth, Information Literacy (LIB 150) at Fort Lewis College: Innovative Approaches to Instruction in a Required Course, in Andrea Kross, ed., Making the Grade: Academic Libraries and Student Success, Chicago: American Library Assoc/Assoc of College and Research Libraries, forthcoming summer 00. **CONTACT ADDRESS** John F Reed Library, Fort Lewis Col, 1000 Rim Dr., Durango, CO 81301. **EMAIL** greenwood_t@fortlewis.edu

GREETHAM, DAVID CHARLES
PERSONAL Born 10/21/1941, Tilston, England, m, 1982, 2 children **DISCIPLINE** TEXTUAL CRITICISM AND BIBLIOGRAPHY **EDUCATION** Oxford Univ, BA, MA, 67; City Univ New York Grad Sch, PhD, 74. **CAREER** Head English Dept, Int Schule, Hamburg, Ger, 65-67; Prof English, City Univ New York, 67-, Doctoral Fac, 79-, Lectr, Brit Coun, WGer, 65-67; Andrew Mellon Found fel, City Univ New York Grad Ctr, 76-77; exec dir, Soc Textual Scholar, 81-; ed, text, AMS Press, 81-; dep exec off English, PhD Prog English, City Univ New York Grad Sch, 82-83. **MEMBERSHIPS** Medieval Acad Am; Asn Doc Ed; Renaissance English Text Soc; MLA. **RESEARCH** Interdisciplinary textual theory; paleography and codicology; editing of Middle English texts. **SELECTED PUBLICATIONS** Interdisciplinary textual theory; paleography and codicology; editing of Middle English texts. Renaissance Teaching, 10/77; On textual criticism, 79 & The properties of things: From patristic repository to Shakespeare's Encycl, 80, City Univ New York English Forum; The concept of nature in Bartholmaeus Anglicus, J Hist Ideas, 80; auth, Textual Scholarship: An Introduction, Garland, 92; auth, Theories of the Text, Clarendon Press, 95; auth, Scholarly Editing: A Guide to Research, ed, MLA, 95. **CONTACT ADDRESS** The Graduate Ctr, Graduate Sch and Univ Ctr, CUNY, 365 Fifth Ave, New York, NY 10016-4309. **EMAIL** dcgreetham@aol.com

GREGG, ROBERT C.
DISCIPLINE CLASSICS **EDUCATION** BA, 60; MDiv, 63; Univ PA, PhD, 74. **CAREER** Prof relig studies/class. **RESEARCH** Early Christianity , institutions, thought, ritual, Jews, Pagans, and Christians in Late Antiquity, asceticism in the late Roman and Early Christian periods, Comparative exegesis in Judaism, Christianity, and Islam. **SELECTED PUBLICATIONS** Auth, Jews, Pagans, and Christians in the Ancient Golan Heights, 96; coauth, Early Arianism, 81; ed, Arianism: Historical and Theological Assessments, 85. **CONTACT ADDRESS** Stanford Univ, Bldg 70, Main Quad, Stanford, CA 94305. **EMAIL** rgregg@stanford.edu

GREGORY, ELMER RICHARD
PERSONAL Born 09/25/1938, Baytown, TX, m, 1981, 1 child **DISCIPLINE** ENGLISH, COMPARATIVE LITERATURE **EDUCATION** Univ Tex, Austin, BA, 60; Rice Univ, MA, 61; Univ Ore, PhD(comp lit), 65. **CAREER** Asst prof English, Univ Ga, 65-67; from asst prof to assoc prof, 67-77, PROF ENGLISH, UNIV TOLEDO, 77-. **MEMBERSHIPS** Conf Christianity and Lit; Milton Soc Am; MLA. **RESEARCH** John Milton; 17th century British literature; detective stories. **SELECTED PUBLICATIONS** Auth, Milton and Tradition, Milton Stud, Vol 0029, 92; Moore, Marianne 'Poetry,' Explicator, Vol 0052, 93; Milton Protestant Sonnet Lady--Revisions in the Donna-Angelicata Tradition, Comp Lit Stud, Vol 0033, 96. **CONTACT ADDRESS** Dept of English, Univ of Toledo, Toledo, OH 43606.

GREGORY, JUSTINA
PERSONAL Born 09/24/1946, Brattleboro, VT, m, 2 children **DISCIPLINE** CLASSICS **EDUCATION** Smith Col, AB, 67; Harvard Univ, MA, 72; PhD, 74. **CAREER** Asst prof, Yale Univ, 74-75; asst prof to prof, Smith Col, 75-. **HONORS AND AWARDS** ACLS Fel; Fulbright Fel; Woodrow Wilson Fel. **MEMBERSHIPS** Am Philol Assoc, Women's Class Caucus, New England Class Assoc, Phi Beta Kappa. **RESEARCH** Greek tragedy, fifth-century intellectual history. **SELECTED PUBLICATIONS** Transl, Aesop's Fables, 75; auth, "Some Aspects of Seeing in the Bacchae," Greece and Rome 32.1 (85): 22-31; auth, Euripides and the Instruction of the Athenians, 91; auth, "The Encounter at the Crossroads in Sophocles' Oedipus Tyrannus," Jour of Hellenic Studies 115, (95): 141-6; auth, "Intertextuality and Genealogy in Hecuta," Am Jour of Philol 116, (95): 389-97; auth, Euripides' Hecuba: Introduction, Text and Commentary, 99; auth, "Comic Elements in Euripides," Ill Class Studies 24-25, (99-00). **CONTACT ADDRESS** Smith Col, Northampton, MA 01063-0001. **EMAIL** jgregory@smith.edu

GREGORY, MICHAEL J. P.
PERSONAL Born 04/07/1935, Great Crosby, England **DISCIPLINE** ENGLISH **EDUCATION** Balliol Col, Oxford, BA, 58, MA, 63; Leeds Univ, PGCE, 59. **CAREER** Master, Oratory Sch, 59-61; lectr, Royal Col Sci Tech, Glasgow, 61-62; lectr, Leeds Univ, 61-66; assoc prof to prof 66-94, ch Eng, 66-71, 73-74, dir dramatic arts prog, 67-80, coordr ling & lang stud, 83-94, PROF EMER & SR SCHOLAR, YORK UNIV, 94-. **SELECTED PUBLICATIONS** Auth, What Is Good English?, 69; auth, English Patterns, 72; auth, Before and Towards Communication Linguistics, 96; coauth, Linguistics and Style, 64; Language and Situation, 78; co-ed, Discourse and Meaning in Society, 95. **CONTACT ADDRESS** Dept of English, York Univ, 4700 Keele St, Toronto, ON, Canada M3J 1P3.

GREGORY, MICHAEL STRIETMANN
PERSONAL Born 10/06/1929, Oakland, CA, d, 1962, 3 children **DISCIPLINE** ENGLISH LITERATURE & CRITICISM **EDUCATION** Univ Calif, Berkeley, BA, 52, PhD, 69. **CAREER** Instr English, San Jose State Univ, 56-57; from instr to assoc prof, 59-71, prof English, San Francisco State Univ, 71-, Panel reviewer & site visitor humanities/gen ed curricula, Nat Endowment Humanities, 73-, proj dir planning grant, 73, mem, Nat Bd, Consults, 74, consult humanities and gen ed, 75-; panel reviewer ethical & value implications of sci & technol, NSF, 75- **MEMBERSHIPS** AAUP; MLA; AAAS; Am Anthrop Asn; Joseph Conrad Soc Am. **RESEARCH** History of ideas, with emphasis on development of paradigms in science and humanities; comparative value structure, with emphasis on value-inversions and technology transfer in modern China. **SELECTED PUBLICATIONS** Auth, On style, Aperture, 4/60; Sea-change (short story), San Francisco Rev, 6/60; Sisyphus in the classroom, Classroom J Conf Col Compos & Commun, 2/63; The Philosophy of light, Aperture, 2/64; Politics, Science and the Human Nature, J Calif Class Asn, 76; ed, Sociobiology and Human Nature, Jossey-Bass, 78; ed, Proceedings of the San Francisco State University Conference on Recombinant DNA, Blue Wind, 78; Science and Humanism, In: Beyond Two Cultures, Proc NEXA/CSUC Dissemination Conf, NEXA & San Francisco State Univ, 5/79; auth, The Science-Humanities Program at San Francisco State University, Leonardo, 80; auth, Science and Humanities: Toward a new World View, in Brock, ed, The Culture of Biomedicine, 84. **CONTACT ADDRESS** NEXA Prog Sch of Humanities, San Francisco State Univ, 1600 Holloway Ave, San Francisco, CA 94132-1740. **EMAIL** mgregory@concentric.net

GREINER, DONALD JAMES
PERSONAL Born 06/10/1940, Baltimore, MD, m, 1964, 2 children **DISCIPLINE** AMERICAN LITERATURE **EDUCATION** Wofford Col, BA, 62; Univ VA, MA, 63, PhD(Am lit), 67. **CAREER** Tchg asst Eng, Univ VA, 65-66; from asst prof to assoc prof Am lit, 67-74, prof am lit, Univ Sc, 74-; chair am lit, 87-. **HONORS AND AWARDS** Awd for Outstanding Tchg, 83; Awd for Distinguished Research, 84, Univ SC. **MEMBERSHIPS** MLA; S Atlantic Mod Lang Asn. **RESEARCH** Am lit; John Updike, John Hawkes, Robert Frost; contemp Am fiction. **SELECTED PUBLICATIONS** Co-ed, The notebook of Stephen Crane, Univ VA, 69; auth, Comic terror: The novels of John Hawkes, Memphis State Univ, 73; Robert Frost: The poet and his critics, Am Libr Asn, 74; ed. American Poets Since 1945, two vols., Gale Research, 80; The Other John Updike, OH UP, 81; John Updike's Novels, OH UP, 83; Adultery in the American Novel: Updike, James, Hawthorne, Univ SCP, 84; Understanding John Hawkes, Univ SCP, 85; Domestic Particulars: The Novels of Frederick Busch, Univ SCP, 87; Women Enter the Wilderness: Males Bonding and the American Novel of the 1980s, Univ SCP, 91; Women without Men: Female bonding and the American Novel in the 1980s, Univ SCP, 93; coed, The Vineland Papers: Essays on Pynchon's novel, Dalkey Archive Press, 94. **CONTACT ADDRESS** Dept of English, Univ of So Carolina, Columbia, Columbia, SC 29208. **EMAIL** greiner@sc.edu

GRELLA, GEORGE
DISCIPLINE AMERICAN LITERATURE, MODERN BRITISH LITERATURE, THE NOVEL, AND FILM **EDUCATION** Univ KS, PhD. **CAREER** Assoc prof; taught at, Bates Col & Univ KS. **HONORS AND AWARDS** NEH Younger Humanist awd & Nat Hum fac. **RESEARCH** 19th and 20th-century Am lit; 20th-century Eng lit; novel; film. **SELECTED PUBLICATIONS** Auth, hundreds rev(s), fiction, nonfiction &

film, articles on, detective fiction, gangster novels, baseball, film & on authors as Edgar Allan Poe, Sir Arthur Conan Doyle, Ian Flem ing, Georges Simenon, Ross Macdonald, Dashiell Hammett, John le Carr, Len Deighton, John Irving; adv and contrib ed, 20th-century Crime and Mystery Writers. **CONTACT ADDRESS** Dept of English, Univ of Rochester, 500 Wilson Blvd, RC Box 270451, Rochester, NY 14627-0451. **EMAIL** gjg5@mail.rochester.edu

GRENBERG, BRUCE L.

PERSONAL Born 04/14/1935, Rockford, IL, m, 1957, 1 child **DISCIPLINE** ENGLISH **EDUCATION** Beloit Col, BA, 57; Univ NC, Chapel Hill, MA, 58, PhD(English), 63. **CAREER** From instr to asst prof, 63-69, Can Coun res fel, 68-69; assoc prof english, Univ BC, 69-93; prof emer, Univ BC, 93-. **MEMBERSHIPS** MLA. **RESEARCH** American and English literature. **SELECTED PUBLICATIONS** Auth, Some Other World to Find: Quest and Negotiation in the Works of Herman Melville, Univ Ill Pr (Urbana, IL), 89. **CONTACT ADDRESS** 6225 Yew, Vancouver, BC, Canada V6M 3Z1.

GRENNEN, JOSEPH EDWARD

PERSONAL Born 09/03/1926, New York, NY, m, 1950, 6 children **DISCIPLINE** ENGLISH LITERATURE, MEDIEVAL SCIENCE **EDUCATION** Col Holy Cross, BS, 47; Fordham Univ, MA, 54, PhD, 60. **CAREER** Instr, High Sch, NY, 47-50; educ adv, Troop Info and Educ Div, US Army, Ger, 50-55; from asst prof to assoc prof, 56-76, chmn dept, 65-71, PROF ENGLISH, FORDHAM UNIV, 76-, Ed, Thought, 78-80. **MEMBERSHIPS** Mediaeval Acad Am; MLA; AAUP. **RESEARCH** Middle English literature; modern criticism; history of science. **SELECTED PUBLICATIONS** Auth, The Making of Works, Jones, David and the Medieval Drama, Renascence-Essays on Values in Lit, Vol 0045, 93. **CONTACT ADDRESS** Dept of English, Fordham Univ, New York, NY 10458.

GRIBBEN, ALAN

PERSONAL Born 11/21/1941, Parsons, KS, m, 1974, 2 children **DISCIPLINE** ENGLISH, PHILOSPHY **EDUCATION** Univ Kans, BA, 64; Univ Ore, MA, 66; Univ Calif, PhD, 74. **CAREER** Res Ed, Univ Calif, 67-74; From Asst Prof to Prof, Univ Tex, 74-91; Prof, Auburn Univ, 91-. **HONORS AND AWARDS** President's Assocs Teaching Excellence Awd, 83; Katherine Ross Richards Centennial Teaching Fel, 88-89; Phi Kappa Phi, 91; Henry Nash Smith Fel, Elmira Col, 97. **MEMBERSHIPS** Mark Twain Circle of Am. **RESEARCH** American literature, American humor, literary biography, library history, travel literature, history of academic administration. **SELECTED PUBLICATIONS** Auth, Mark Twain's Library: A Reconstruction, 2 vols, G K Hall and Co (Boston, MA), 80; ed, Mark Twain's Rybaiyat," Jenkins Publ Co (Austin, TX), 83; auth, "The Importance of Mark Twain," Am Quart 37 (New York: Oxford UP, 97), 24-49; co-ed, Overland with Mark Twain: James B Pond's Photographs and Journal of the North American Lecture Tour of 1895, Elmira Col Pr (Elmira, NY), 92. **CONTACT ADDRESS** Dept English & Philos, Auburn Univ, PO Box 244023, Montgomery, AL 36124-4023. **EMAIL** gribben@edla.aum.edu

GRIER, JAMES

DISCIPLINE MUSIC **EDUCATION** Univ Toronto, PhD, 85. **CAREER** Prof, Univ of Western Ontario. **HONORS AND AWARDS** Ed, De Musicae Cult. **RESEARCH** Medieval music; music and liturgy in Aquitaine 900-1200; textual criticism and editing music; popular music post-World War II. **SELECTED PUBLICATIONS** Auth, "The Stemma of the Aquitanian Versaria," Journal of the American Musicological Soc 41, (88): 250-88; auth, "Lachmann, Bedier and the Bipartite Stemma: Towards a Responsible Application of the Common-Error method, Revue d'Histoire des Textes 18, (88): 263-78; auth, "Some Codicological Observations on the Aquitanian Versaria, Musica Disciplina 4, (90): 5-56; auth, "Scribal Practices in the Aquitanian Versaria of the Twelfth Century: Towards a Typology of Error and Variant, Journal of the American Musicological Soc 45, (92): 373-427; auth, "A New Voice in the Monastery: Tropes and Versus from Eleventh and Twelfth-Century Aquitaine, Speculum 69, (94): 1023-69; auth, "Musical Sources and Stemmatic Filiation: A Tool for Editing Music," Journal of Musicology 13, (95): 73-102; auth, "Roger de Chabannes (d. 1025), Cantor of St. Martial, Limoges," Early Music History 14, (95): 53-119; auth, The Critical Editing of Music: History, Method, and Practice, Cambridge: Cambridge Univ Press, 96; auth, "Scriptio interrupta: Ademar de Chabannes and the Production of Paris, Bibliotheque Nationale de France, MS latin 909, Scriptorium 51, (97): 234-50. **CONTACT ADDRESS** Dept of Music, Univ of Western Ontario, London, ON, Canada N6A 5B8. **EMAIL** jgrier@julian.uwo.ca

GRIESINGER, EMILY

PERSONAL Born 02/07/1954, Ft Worth, TX, m, 1988 **DISCIPLINE** ENGLISH LITERATURE **EDUCATION** Baylor Univ, BA, 76; MA, 79; Vanderbilt Univ, PhD, 90. **CAREER** Teach fel, Baylor Univ, 77-79; teach fel, Vanderbilt Univ, 80-83; asst to exec dir, Claremont Grad Sch, 83-89; asst prof, Azusa Pac Univ, 90-99; assoc prof, 00-. **HONORS AND AWARDS** AZUSA Scholars Awd. **MEMBERSHIPS** MLA; AAR; SSCS; CCL; CS Lewis Found; Sigma Tau Delta; Alpha Chi; Alpha Lambda Delta; Kappa Delta Pi; Sigma Delta Pi; Nat Hon Soc; CHI'S. **RESEARCH** Religious themes in literature; hermeneutics of Christian autobiography and biography; the literature of Christian formation; medieval women writers; romanticism; women and literature; British novel; British survey; children's literature; young adult literature. **SELECTED PUBLICATIONS** Rev, Joann McNamara, Sisters in Arms: Catholic Nuns Through Two Millennia, Harvard UP, 96; Women's Studies: An Interdisciplinary J (98): 231-34; auth, "Your Daughters Shall Prophesy: The Charismatic Spirituality of Hildegard of Bingen," Christian Scholars Rev 29 (99): 25-47; auth, "A Hermeneutic Faith," Books and Culture (99): 37-38; auth, "Faith and Feminism in the Middle Ages: The Spirituality of Hildegard of Bingen," in Medieval Germany: Associations and Delineations, ed. Nancy van Deusen (Ottawa, Canada: Inst Medieval Music, 00). **CONTACT ADDRESS** Dept English, Azusa Pacific Univ, PO Box 7000, Azusa, CA 91702-7000. **EMAIL** egriesinger@apu.edu

GRIFFEL, L. MICHAEL

PERSONAL Born 11/12/1942, New York, NY, m, 1968, 1 child **DISCIPLINE** MUSIC HISTORY AND LITERATURE **EDUCATION** Columbia Univ, PhD. **CAREER** Hunter College, CUNY, Graduate Faculty; Juilliard School. **HONORS AND AWARDS** Performance Excellence Awd, Hunter College, 99; NEH Grant, 80. **MEMBERSHIPS** Mozart Society of America; Am Brahms Society; Am Bach Society; Am Schubert Institue; Am Beethoven Society (Vice Pres., New York Branch), Internationales franz Schubert Institut, International Musicological Society; College Music Society; Am Musicological Society. **RESEARCH** Schubert; Beethoven; Piano Music; Opera **SELECTED PUBLICATIONS** Publ on the symphonies in The Cambridge Companion to Schubert; auth, The Romantic and Post-Romantic Eras, in The Schirmer History of Music. **CONTACT ADDRESS** School of Arts and Sciences, Hunter Col, CUNY, 695 Park Ave, New York, NY 10021. **EMAIL** lgriffel@shiva.hunter.cuny.edu

GRIFFEN, CHARLES

PERSONAL Born 07/01/1953, St Louis, MO, m, 2 children **DISCIPLINE** SPEECH COMMUNICATION **EDUCATION** Northwestern Univ, BA, 75; Univ Mo, MA, 80; Univ Mo-Columbia, PhD, 83. **CAREER** Asst prof, Univ Missouri-Columbia, 83-84; asst prof, Kans State Univ, 84-90; assoc prof, 90-. **MEMBERSHIPS** NCA. **RESEARCH** History and criticism of American Public Address. **SELECTED PUBLICATIONS** Auth, "The Rhetoric of Form in Conversation Narratives," Quart J Speech (90); auth, "New Light on Eisenhower's Farewell Address," Pres Studies Quart (92); auth, "Movement as Motive: Self Definition Social Advocacy in Social Movement Autobiographies," W J Comm (00). **CONTACT ADDRESS** Dept Speech & Dramatic Arts, Kansas State Univ, 129 Nichols Hall, Manhattan, KS 66506-2300.

GRIFFIN, CINDY L.

PERSONAL Born 04/15/1957, CA, m, 1987, 1 child **DISCIPLINE** SPEECH COMMUNICATION **EDUCATION** Calif State Univ, Northridge, BS, 81; Univ Ore, MA, 87; Ind Univ, PhD, 92. **CAREER** Asst prof, Northern Ky Univ, Highland Heights, 92-93; asst prof, Speech Commun, Colo State Univ, Fort Collins, 93-98, assoc prof, 98-. **HONORS AND AWARDS** Robert Gunderson Awd, 92; Feminist Scholar Awd, 95; Karl Wallace Memorial Awd, 95. **MEMBERSHIPS** Nat Commun Asn, Western States Commun Asn, Org for Res on Women and Commun, Org for the Study of Women, Lang, and Soc. **RESEARCH** Feminist rhetorical theory; rhetorical theory; rhetorical criticism; gender; race; ethnicity; sexuality; public discourse; identity and rhetoric. **SELECTED PUBLICATIONS** Auth, "Rhetoricizing Alienation: Mary Wollstonecraft and the Rhetorical Construction of Women's Oppression," Quart J of Speech, 80 (94): 293-312; auth, "Teaching Rhetorical Criticism with 'Thelma and Louise'," Commun Educ, 44 (95): 165-176; coauth with Sonja K. Foss, "Beyond Persuasion: A Proposal for Invitational Rhetoric," Commun Monographs, 62 (96): 2-18; auth, "The Essentialist Roots of the Public Sphere: A Feminist Critique," Western J of Commun, 60 (96): 21-39; auth, "A Web of Reasons: Mary Wollstonecraft's 'A Vindication of the Rights of Woman' and the Re-Weaving of Form," Commun Studies, 47 (96): 272-288; coauth with Sonja K. Foss and Karen A,. Foss, "Transforming Rhetoric Through Feminist Reconstruction: A Response to the Gender-Diversity Perspective," Women's Studies in Commun, 20 (98): 117-136; coauth with Barbara M. Gayle, "Mary Ashton Rice Livermore's Relational Feminist discourse; A Rhetorically Successful Feminist Model, Women's Studies in Commun, 21 (98): 55-76; coauth with Karen A. Foss and Sonja K. Foss, Feminist Rhetorical Theories, Sage (99); auth, An Invitation to Speak Publicly, Wadsworth (forthcoming); auth, Evaluating Contemporary Rhetoric, Wadsworth (forthcoming). **CONTACT ADDRESS** Dept Speech Commun, Colorado State Univ, 215 Eddy Hall, Fort Collins, CO 80523. **EMAIL** cgriffin@vines.colostate.edu

GRIFFIN, CLAUDIUS WILLIAMS

PERSONAL Born 03/24/1935, Brooklyn, NY, m, 1969, 4 children **DISCIPLINE** ENGLISH COMPOSITION AND RHETORIC **EDUCATION** Univ Richmond, BS, 58, MA, 60; Ind Univ, PhD (English), 72. **CAREER** Teaching assoc English, Ind Univ, Bloomington, 62-66; asst prof, 69-75, dir spec serv summer prog, 72-78, ASSOC PROF ENGLISH, VA COMMONWEALTH UNIV, 75-86, 87-, DIR COMPOS AND RHET PROG, 70-, Va Commonwealth Univ grant, 78 and 80-82. **HONORS AND AWARDS** MLA excellence teaching award, 72; VCU Distinguished Teaching Award, 85. **MEMBERSHIPS** NCTE; SAtlantic Mod Lang Asn; Samla Teaching Award, 91. **RESEARCH** Composition and rhetoric, especially the teaching of composition in secondary schools and college; Shakespeare, especially pedogogy. **SELECTED PUBLICATIONS** Auth, "Responding to Student Writing," College Composition and Communication 33, (82): 296-301; ed, Teaching Writing in Many Disciplines, Josey -Bass (San Francisco), 82; auth, "Using Writing to Teach Our Disciplines: A New Way of Thinking," Improving College and University Teaching 31 (83); auth, "Programs for Writing Across the Curriculum: A Report," College Composition and Communication 36 (85): 398-403; auth, Writing: A Guide for Business Professionals, Harcourt, Brace, Jovanovich (San Diego, CA), 87; auth, "Teaching Shakespeare Through Videotapes," Shakespeare on Film Newsletter 13 (88): 5; auth, "Teaching Shakespeare on Video," English Journal 78.7, (89): 40-43; auth, "Writing Across the Curriculum Bibliography," in Writing Across the Curriculum Programs, eds. Toby Fulwiler and Art Young, (New York: Hinemann, 90); auth, "Subtext and Scopophilia: Dress and Undress in A Midsummer Night's Dream," Shakespeare in Performance Bulletin, (94): 43-4; auth, "Henry V's Decision: Interrogative Texts," Literature and Film Quarterly 25.2: 99-103; auth, "Teaching Shakespeare: A Report," Shakespeare and the Classroom 5 (97): 44-52; auth, Henry-V Decision: Shakespeare, Branagh, Kenneth--Interrogative Texts, Lit-Film Quart, Vol 0025, 97; auth, "Interrogative Paper Assignments," Shakespeare and the Classroom 6.1 (98): 38-40; auth, "Textual Studieds and Teaching Shakespeare," in Teaching Shakespeare into the Twenty-First Century, ed. Ronald E. Salomone and James E. Davis, Ohio U Press, (97): 104-111; auth, "Improving Students' Writing Strategies: Knowing Versus Doing," College Teaching 46.2 (98): 48-52; auth, "Students Reading Shakespeare," Shakespeare and the Classroom 7:2 (99): 35-39; auth, "Students Studying Shakespeare," The Upstart Crow 19 (99): 35-49; auth, "Reading and Teaching Shakespeare," Forthcoming in the International Shakespeare Yearbook. **CONTACT ADDRESS** Virginia Commonwealth Univ, Box 2005, Richmond, VA 23284-9004. **EMAIL** bgriffin@ocu.edu

GRIFFIN, DUSTIN

DISCIPLINE ENGLISH **EDUCATION** Williams Col, BA, 65; Oxford Univ, MA; Yale Univ, PhD, 69. **CAREER** Asst prof, Univ Calif, Berkeley, 69-76; assoc prof to prof, New York Univ, 76-. **HONORS AND AWARDS** Phi Beta Kappa; summa cum laude, Williams; Guggenheim Fel. **RESEARCH** Restoration and 18th-century English literature. **SELECTED PUBLICATIONS** Auth, Satires Against Man: The Poems of Rochester, Univ Calif (73); auth, Alexander Pope: The Poet in the Poems, Princeton (78); Regaining Paradise: Milton and the 18th Century, Cambridge (86); auth, Satire: A Critical Reintroduction, Kentucky (94); auth, Literary Patronnage in England, 1650-1800, Cambridge (96). **CONTACT ADDRESS** Dept English, New York Univ, 19 Univ Pl, New York, NY 10003-4556. **EMAIL** dustin.griffin@nyu.edu

GRIFFIN, EDWARD M.

PERSONAL Born 09/25/1937, Pittsburgh, PA, m, 1960, 3 children **DISCIPLINE** ENGLISH AND AMERICAN LITERATURE **EDUCATION** Univ San Francisco, BS, 59; Stanford Univ, MA & PhD(Am lit), 66. **CAREER** Asst prof English, 66-69, assoc prof, 69-79, dir grad studies, 72-75, prof English, 79- , chmn Prog Am Stud, 80-88, Univ Minn, Minneapolis; Vis assoc prof English, Stanford Univ, 71-72; Fulbright prof, Univ Salzburg, 83-84; vis prof English & Am Stud, Univ Amsterdam, 97; asst ed Am lit, 18th Century: A Current Bibliog, 71-80; ed bd, Early Am Lit, 77-80. **HONORS AND AWARDS** Danforth fel, 59-66; Univ Minn distinguished teacher, 88; Fulbright fel, 83-84; Univ San Francisco Edward J. Griffin Awd, 98; MidAm Am Stud Asn., Elizabeth Kolmer Awd, 99. **MEMBERSHIPS** MLA; Soc. Early Americanist; Am Studies Asn; MidAm Am Stud Asn. **RESEARCH** American poetry; early American literature; American studies. **SELECTED PUBLICATIONS** Auth, Jonathan Edwards, Univ Minn, 71; auth, Old Brick: Charles Chauncy of Boston, 1705-1787, Univ Minn, 80; auth, Patricia Hearst and Her Foremothers: The Captivity Fable in America, Centennial Rev, 92; auth, Something Else in Place of All That, Am Stud, 94; auth, William Alfred's Hogan's Goat: Power and Poetry in Brooklyn, Prospects, 94; co-ed, and contribur, The Telling Image, AMS Press, 96. **CONTACT ADDRESS** Dept of English, Univ of Minnesota, Twin Cities, 207 Church St SE, Minneapolis, MN 55455-1340. **EMAIL** griffin@tc.umn.edu

GRIFFIN, JOHN R.

DISCIPLINE BRITISH LITERATURE, INTRODUCTION TO LITERATURE, COMPOSITION **EDUCATION** Univ Ottawa, PhD, 63; Trinity, PhD, 72. **CAREER** Prof, Univ of Southern CO. **RESEARCH** Medieval and Victorian lit and hist; Engl 8th-19th centuries. **SELECTED PUBLICATIONS** Auth, A Commentary on the Cath Works of Cardinal Newman, 93; The Oxford Movement: A Revision, 2nd Ed, 84. **CONTACT ADDRESS** Dept of Eng, Univ of So Colorado, 2200 Bonforte Blvd, Pueblo, CO 81001-4901.

GRIFFIN, KATHLEEN
PERSONAL Born 10/05/1948, New York, NY, s **DISCIPLINE** ENGLISH **EDUCATION** Pace Univ, BA, 83; Southern Ill Univ, MA, 84. **CAREER** Adj prof, Pace Univ, 88-. **HONORS AND AWARDS** Charles Dyson Awd; Grad Fel Awd. **MEMBERSHIPS** ACAFAD. **RESEARCH** Modern poetry; college composition and rhetoric; Greek literature. **SELECTED PUBLICATIONS** Auth, Grave of an Amiable Child, Xilons Corp (Princeton), 98. **CONTACT ADDRESS** Dept English, Pace Univ, New York, 1 Pace Plaza, New York, NY 10038-1502. **EMAIL** kathleengriffin@gobi.com

GRIFFIN, LARRY D.
PERSONAL Born 10/12/1951, Vinita, OK, d, 1978, 1 child **DISCIPLINE** ENGLISH **EDUCATION** Univ of Oklahoma, PhD, 89; Northeastern St Univ, BA, 73. **CAREER** Prof of English and Dean of Arts and Sciences; Dyersburg state Community College Dyersburg, Tennessee, 90-97; Chair, Fine Arts and Communications Studies Division, Midland College, Midland, Texas, 81-89; Instructor of English, Midland College, Midland, Texas. **HONORS AND AWARDS** Leadership Dyer County, 98; Middle Tennessee State Univ Fall Creek Falls Leadership Conference, 98; Midland Reporter-Telegram Helping Hands Awd, 96; Northeastern State Univ Alumni Association Citation of Merit, 95; National Institute for Staff and Organization Development Teaching Excellence Awd, 91. **MEMBERSHIPS** College English Association (Board Member); Habitat for Humanity Construction Volunteer; Tennessee Quality (Baldridge) Award Examiner; National Endowment for the Humanities Grants Appraiser; Southern Association of Colleges and Schools (SACS) Accreditation Visitor (Humanities). **RESEARCH** Walt Whitman; Richard Ford; Poetry; Short Fiction; P.T. Barnum. **SELECTED PUBLICATIONS** Auth, "New Fires," Full Count, 82; auth, "The Blue Water Tower," Poetry Around, 84; auth, "Airspace," Slough, 89; auth, "A Gathing of Samphire and Other Stories," Poetry around, 90; auth, "Larry D. Griffin Gold," Pudding, 00. **CONTACT ADDRESS** Dept Arts & Sciences, Dyersburg State Comm Col, 1510 Lake Rd., 146 Dale F. Glover Bldg, Dyerburg, TN 38024-2450. **EMAIL** lgriffin@dscclan.dscc.cc.tn.us

GRIFFIN, MICHAEL S.
PERSONAL Born 02/09/1953, Minneapolis, MN **DISCIPLINE** COMMUNICATIONS **EDUCATION** Univ Pa, MA, PhD. **CAREER** Visiting Prof. **HONORS AND AWARDS** CBS Doctoral Fel, Annenenberg Scholars Program Postdoctoral Fel, Pres Ditinguished Monority Student Mentor, Future Faculty Grad Student Menbtor, Outstanding res and Teaching Merit Award, 95. **MEMBERSHIPS** Int commun Assoc; McBride Round Table; Int assoc for Mas Commun Res. **RESEARCH** Visual Commun, Media and Culture, Global media **SELECTED PUBLICATIONS** Auth, Looking at TV News: Strategies for Research, Commun, 92; auth, Gender Advertising in the U.S. and India: Exporting Cultural Stereotypes, 94; Auth, Picturing the Gulf War: Constructing an Image of the War in Time, Newsweek, and U.S. News and World Report, J Quarterly, 95; auth, "Between Art and Industry: Phoutgraphy and Middlebrow Culture," On The Art Worlds, Westview Press, 95; auth, "Picturing culture in Political Spots: 1992 Campaings in Israel and U.S., Political Commun vol 13, (96), 43-61; auth, "The great war Phoographs: Constuctiong Mythes of History and Photojournalism," Picturing the Hist and Photography, Univ of ILL Press, (99); auth, Internatioanl Media Monitoring, Hampton Press, 99; auth, "Camera as Witness, Image as Sign: The Study of Visual Communication in Communication research," Commun Yearbook vol 24, Sage Pub, 00. **CONTACT ADDRESS** Dept of Commun and Media Studies, Macalester Col, 1600 grand Ave, Saint Paul, MN 55105. **EMAIL** griffin@macalester.edu

GRIFFITH, LARRY D.
PERSONAL Born 06/29/1946, Thayer, MO, m, 1966, 4 children **DISCIPLINE** PERFORMING ARTS **EDUCATION** Harding Univ, BA, 69; Univ Mo, MA, 71; Vanderbilt Univ, PhD, 84. **CAREER** Tchr, 69-71; assoc instr, Univ Mo 71-72; asst prof, York Col, 73-77; prof, chemn, 77-, Lipscomb Univ. **HONORS AND AWARDS** Outstanding Young Men of Am; summer grants, lipscomb univ. **MEMBERSHIPS** NATS; ACDA; MENC; IFCM. **RESEARCH** Choral music **CONTACT ADDRESS** Lipscomb Univ, 3901 Granny White, Nashville, TN 37204. **EMAIL** larry.griffith@lipscomb.edu

GRIFFITH, MALCOLM A.
PERSONAL Born 08/27/1937, Lima, OH **DISCIPLINE** ENGLISH AND AMERICAN LITERATURE **EDUCATION** Oberlin Col, BA, 58; Ohio State Univ, MA, 62, PhD(English), 66. **CAREER** ASST PROF ENGLISH, UNIV WASH, 66-. **MEMBERSHIPS** MLA. **RESEARCH** American literature; fiction; aesthetics. **SELECTED PUBLICATIONS** Auth, A Deal for the Real-World, Humphreys, Josephine 'Dreams of Sleep' and the New Domestic Novel, Southern Lit J, Vol 0026, 93. **CONTACT ADDRESS** 4705 16th NE, Seattle, WA 98105.

GRIGSBY, BRYON L.
PERSONAL Born 09/24/1968, Newburgh, NY, m, 1996, 1 child **DISCIPLINE** ENGLISH LITERATURE **EDUCATION** Moravian Col, BA, 90; Wake Forest Univ, MA, 92; Loyola Univ Chicago, PhD, 00. **CAREER** Instr, Eastern Conn State Univ, 98-00; asst prof, Centenary Col, 00-. **MEMBERSHIPS** Medicus, MLA, NCTE, Del Valley Medieval Assoc, Renaissance Soc of Am. **RESEARCH** Medieval and Renaissance Medicine and Literature, Writing Centers. **SELECTED PUBLICATIONS** Auth, "The Social Position of the Surgeon in London, 1350-1450," Essays in Medieval Studies, (97); auth, "Acts of Bravery and Self-Discovery: The Teachings and Writing of Wally Lamb," Conn Rev, (00); auth, "Plague Medicine in Langland's PIERS PLOWMAN," MLA, (00); auth, "Selected Bibliography of Primary and Secondary Works in the History of Medicine," MLA, (00); auth, "Including Literacy in a Writing Center," Writing Lab Newsletter, (01); coed, Medieval Misconception, Online Reference Book, (01). **CONTACT ADDRESS** Centenary Col, 400 Jefferson St, Hackettstown, NJ 07840. **EMAIL** grigsbyb@centenarycollege.edu

GRIMES, KYLE
DISCIPLINE BRITISH ROMANTIC LITERATURE **EDUCATION** Univ IL, PhD, 90. **CAREER** Dept Eng, Univ Ala **SELECTED PUBLICATIONS** Articles, Keats-Shelley Jour, JEGP, Nineteenth-Century Studies **CONTACT ADDRESS** Univ of Alabama, Birmingham, 1400 University Blvd, Birmingham, AL 35294-1150. **EMAIL** kgrimes@uab.edu

GRIMSHAW, JAMES
PERSONAL Born 12/10/1940, Kingsville, TX, m, 1961, 2 children **DISCIPLINE** ENGLISH, PHILOSOPHY **EDUCATION** Tex Tech Univ, BA, 62; MA, 68; La State Univ, PhD, 72. **CAREER** Asst prof to prof, USAF Acad, 72-83; Head, E Tex State Univ, 83-90; prof, Tex A&M Univ, 90. **HONORS AND AWARDS** Flannery O'Connor Vis Prof, Ga Col, 77; Fac Senate Distinguished Fac Awd, E Tex State Univ, 88; Poet Magazine Editor's Choice Awd, 92; Tex Asn of Col Teachers Distinguished Fac Teaching Awd, 93; Honor Prof of the Yeard Awd, 93; Fac Senate Distinguished Fac Awd, 95; Regents Prof, 95; Tex A&m Univ System Regents Prof Serv Awd, 97. **MEMBERSHIPS** Soc for the Study of S Lit; Bibliog Soc of the Univ of Va; SCMLA; Col Teachers of English; Bibliog Soc of Am; Robert Penn Warren Circle; Am Lit Assoc; Assoc of Lit Scholars and Critics; Assoc of Teachers of Technical Writing. **RESEARCH** Southern Literature, Bibliography, Technical Writing, Moral Philosophy. **SELECTED PUBLICATIONS** Ed, Cleanth Brooks at the United States Air Force Academy, USAF Acad, 80; auth, The Flannery O'Connor Companion, Greenwood, (westport, CT), 81; auth, Robert Penn Warren: A Descriptive Bibliography, 1922-1979, Univ Pr of Va, 82; ed, Robert Pen Warren's Brother to Dragons: A Discussion, La State univ Pr, (Baton Rouge), 83; ed, Time's Glory: Original Essays on Robert Penn Warren, Univ of Central Ark Pr, 86; ed, The Paul Wells Barrus Lectures, 1983-1989, E Tex State Univ Pr, 90; ed, Robert Penn Warren/Cleanth Brooks: Friends of Their Youth, King Libr Pr, (Lexington), 93; ed, Cleanth Brooks and Robert Penn Warren: A Literary Correspondence, Univ of Mo Pr, (Columbia), 98; coed, Robert Penn Warren's All the Kings Men: Three Stage Versions, Univ of Ga Pr, (Athens), 00. **CONTACT ADDRESS** Dept Lang and Lit, Texas A&M Univ, Commerce, PO Box 3011, Commerce, TX 75429-3011. **EMAIL** james_grimshaw@tamu-commerce.edu

GRISWOLD, JEROME JOSEPH
PERSONAL Born Havre, MT **DISCIPLINE** CHILDREN'S & AMERICAN LITERATURE **EDUCATION** Seattle Univ, BA, 69; Univ Conn, MA, 73, PhD(English), 78. **CAREER** Asst prof & instr English, Northeastern Univ, 76-79; ed, Houghton Mifflin Publ Co, 79-80; prof English, San Diego State Univ, 80-. **MEMBERSHIPS** MLA; Children's Lit Asn; Wallace Stevens Soc. **RESEARCH** American children's literature; American popular culture; poetry of Wallace Stevens. **SELECTED PUBLICATIONS** The Children's Book of Randall Jarcel, Univ Ga Press, 88, Judacious Kids, Oxford Univ Press, 92; The Classic Am Children's Story, Penguin, 96. **CONTACT ADDRESS** Dept of English & Comp Lit, San Diego State Univ, 5500 Campanile Dr, San Diego, CA 92182-0002.

GRISWOLD, WENDY
DISCIPLINE ENGLISH **EDUCATION** Harvard Univ, PhD. **CAREER** Prof, Northwestern Univ. **RESEARCH** Sociology of literature. **SELECTED PUBLICATIONS** Auth, Renaissance Revivals: City Comedy and Revenge Tragedy in the London Theatre, 1576-1980; Cultures and Societies in a Changing World. **CONTACT ADDRESS** Dept of English, Northwestern Univ, 1801 Hinman, Evanston, IL 60208.

GROB, ALAN
PERSONAL Born 03/12/1932, New York, NY, m, 1958, 2 children **DISCIPLINE** ENGLISH LITERATURE **EDUCATION** Utica Col, BA, 62; Univ Wis, MA, 57, PhD, 61. **CAREER** From asst prof to assoc prof, 61-73, PROF ENGLISH, RICE UNIV, 73-, ASSOC OF HANSZEN COL, 76-. **MEMBERSHIPS** MLA. **RESEARCH** Romantic and Victorian poetry. **SELECTED PUBLICATIONS** Auth, Arnold the 'Scholar-Gipsy'--The Use and Abuse of History, Victorian Poetry, Vol 0034, 96. **CONTACT ADDRESS** Dept of English, Rice Univ, Houston, TX 77001.

GROCH, JOHN R.
DISCIPLINE COMPUTER-MEDIATED COMMUNICATION **EDUCATION** PhD **CAREER** Coordr, Commun Stud in Continuing Educ. **RESEARCH** Film; mass cult; postmodernism. **SELECTED PUBLICATIONS** Written on, popularity of The Wizard of Oz & comic authorship in the films of the Marx Brothers. **CONTACT ADDRESS** Commun Dept, Chatham Col, Woodland Rd., Pittsburgh, PA 15232.

GRODEN, MICHAEL
DISCIPLINE ENGLISH LITERATURE **EDUCATION** Univ Dartmouth, BA, 69; Princeton Univ, MA, 72; PhD, 75. **CAREER** Asst prof of Eng, Univ of Western Ontario, 77-78; assoc prof of Eng, Univ of Western Ontario, 78-83; prof of Eng, Univ of Western Ontario, 83-. **HONORS AND AWARDS** Magna cum laude, 69; Guggenheim Fel, 79-80. **MEMBERSHIPS** Modern Lang Asn of Am; Asn of Canadian Col and Univ Teachers of Eng; Asn for Literary Scholars and Critics; International Asn of Univ Professors of Eng; Soc for Textual Scholarship; Asn for Computers and the Humanities; Asn for Computing Machinery. **RESEARCH** Narrative theory; film theory; hypertext and the physical presentation of texts. **SELECTED PUBLICATIONS** Auth, "Ulysses," in progress, Princeton, NJ: Princeton Univ Press, 77; auth, The James Joyce Archive, 63 vols. New York and London: Garland Publishing, 77-79; auth, James Joyce's Manuscripts: An Index, New York and London: Garland Publishing, 80; auth, "Afterword," to James Joyce, Ulysses, London: The Bodley Head and New York: Vintage, (93): 647-57; auth, "Fiction Theory and Criticism: 3, Early Twentieth-Century British and American," in The Johns Hopkins Guide to Literary Theory and Criticism, eds. Michael Groden and Martin Kreiswirth, (Baltimore and London: Johns Hopkins Univ Press, 94): 261-68; co-ed, The Johns Hopkins Guide to Literary Theory and Critism, Baltimore and London: Johns Hopkins Univ Press, 94; coauth, "Post-Genetic Joyce," The Romanic Rev 86:33, (95): 501-12; auth, "Wandering in the Avant-texte: Joyce's Cyclops Copybook Revisited," in The Future of Modernism, ed. Hugh Witemeyer, (Ann Arbor: Univ of Michigan Press, 97): 181-99; auth, "Flying By the Net: James Joyce in Cyberspace (1) n Catalogue these [cyber]books," James Joyce Quarterly 35:1, (98): 129-47; auth, "Perplex in the Pennand in the Pixels: Reflections on The James Joyce Archive, Hans Walter Gabler's Ulysses, and James Joyce's Ulysses in Hypermedia," Journal of Modern Literature 22:2, (99): 225-44. **CONTACT ADDRESS** English Dept, Univ of Western Ontario, University College, London, ON, Canada NGA3K7. **EMAIL** mgroden@julian.uwo.ca

GROENING, LAURA S.
PERSONAL Born 08/29/1949, Winnipeg, MB, Canada **DISCIPLINE** ENGLISH **EDUCATION** Univ Man, BA, 72; Carleton Univ, MA, 79, PhD, 85. **CAREER** Asst prof, 90-94, Assoc Prof English, Concordia Univ, 94-. **HONORS AND AWARDS** Killam postdoctoral fel, 88-89; Can res fel, Dalhousie Univ, 89-90; QSPELL Awd, 94. **SELECTED PUBLICATIONS** Auth, E.K. Brown: A Study in Conflict, 93; auth, The Annotated Bibliography of Duncan Campbell Scott, 94. **CONTACT ADDRESS** Dept of English, Concordia Univ, Montreal, 1400 de Maisonneuve Blvd, Montreal, QC, Canada H3G 1M8.

GROGAN, CLAIRE
DISCIPLINE ENGLISH LITERATURE **EDUCATION** Trinity Col, BA; Univ Calgary, PhD. **CAREER** Engl, Bishop's Univ; vis asst prof, Univ Brit Colum, 99-. **SELECTED PUBLICATIONS** Auth, pubs on construct of female appetite in the 1790s and works by Jane Austen and Elizabeth Hamilton. **CONTACT ADDRESS** Dept of English, Univ of British Columbia, 2329 West Mall, 412 Buchanan Tower, Vancouver, BC, Canada V6T 1Z4. **EMAIL** grogan@interchange.ubc.ca

GROOME, MARGARET
DISCIPLINE ENGLISH LITERATURE **EDUCATION** McGill Univ, BA; MA; PhD. **CAREER** Asst prof, Univ of Manitoba. **RESEARCH** Shakespeare; critical theory; dramatic theory; feminist theory; modern British drama; voice and text; Chekhov. **SELECTED PUBLICATIONS** Auth, Canada's Shakespeare Myth Unmasked: Mass Culture Shakespeare at the Stratford Festival. **CONTACT ADDRESS** Dept of English, Univ of Manitoba, Winnipeg, MB, Canada R3T 2N2.

GROPPE, JOHN DANIEL
PERSONAL Born 04/23/1933, New York, NY, m, 1962, 3 children **DISCIPLINE** ENGLISH **EDUCATION** City Col New York, BSEduc, 54; Columbia Univ, MA, 60. **CAREER** Instr English, Villanova Univ, 57-58; teaching asst, Notre Dame Univ, 58-60; from Asst Prof to Assoc Prof, 62-97, prof English, St Joseph's Col, Ind, 97-, chmn dept, 80-. **HONORS AND AWARDS** Fel, Instr Ecumenical & Cult Res, St John's Univ, Minn, 69-70; Nat Endowment Humanities fel-in-residence, Sem Am Autobiography, Dartmouth Col, 75-76. **MEMBERSHIPS** NCTE; Conf Col Compos & Commun; AAUP; Rhet Soc Am; Conf Christianity & Lit. **RESEARCH** Autobiographical theory; stylistics; rhetorical theory; religion and literature. **SELECTED PUBLICATIONS** Auth, A Shred of Decency, Western Humanities Rev, spring 68; Ritualistic Language, S Atlantic Quart, winter 70; You Can't Always Look It Up, Thought, 12/71. **CONTACT ADDRESS** Dept of English, St. Joseph's Col, Alberta, PO Box 929, Rensselaer, IN 47978-0929. **EMAIL** johng@saintjoe.edu

GROSS, ALAN G.
PERSONAL Born 06/02/1936, New York, NY, m, 1978, 6 children **DISCIPLINE** ENGLISH **EDUCATION** Princeton Univ, PhD 62. **CAREER** Univ Minnesota, prof, 93-. **HONORS AND AWARDS** U of Pitts Cen Philo Fel; U of Minn Cen Philo Fel. **MEMBERSHIPS** MLA; NCA. **RESEARCH** Rhetorical theory and rhetoric of science. **SELECTED PUBLICATIONS** Auth, Rereading Aristotle's Rhetoric, coed, SO IL Press, 00; Rhetorical Hermeneutics: Invention and Interpretation in the Age of Science, coed, SUNY Press, 96; The Rhetoric of Science, 2nd ed, Cambridge, Harvard Univ Press, 96. **CONTACT ADDRESS** Dept of Rhetoric, Univ of Minnesota, Twin Cities, 2482 N Sheldon, Roseville, MN 55113. **EMAIL** grossalang@aol.com

GROSS, DANIEL D.
PERSONAL Born 02/02/1946, St. Paul, MN, m, 1991, 4 children **DISCIPLINE** COMMUNICATION, RHETORIC **EDUCATION** Bethel Col, BA, 68; Denver Theolog Sem, M.Div, 72; Univ Colo Denver, MA, 83; Univ Ore, PhD, 89. **CAREER** Ch and assoc prof Dept Communication & Theatre, Mont St Univ, 91-; asst prof Speech Communication, Tarleton St Univ, 90-91; Minister, Kimball & Dix Presbyterian Churches, Kimball & Dix, Nebraska, 87-90; teaching asst, Univ Ore, 86-87; intern, Clinical-Pastoral Education, Ft Logan Mental Health Center, 85-86; instr, Breckenridge Comm Col, 85-86; dir Educ, St James Presbyterian Church, Littleton, CO, 81-85; vis instr, Denver Sem, 75-80. **HONORS AND AWARDS** MSU-Billings tenured, 98; Fac Achievement Awd, 97; Cetificate of Recognition, 96; Outstanding Fac Awd, 95, 97; Cox Fel, 94; Merit Awd Tchg Excellence, 93; Winston & Helen Cox Fel Nominee, MSU Billings, 92-93; Tchg Fel, Univ Ore, 86-87; Denver Sem Tuition Scholar Awd, 68, 69. **MEMBERSHIPS** Ntl Communication Assoc, 90-; World Communication Assoc, 95-; Editorial Advisory Board Collgiate Pr, 95; Wadsworth Book Reviewers, 95; Conference of College Teachers of English, 94. **RESEARCH** Narrative Theory; Rhetorical Criticism; Communication and Law. **SELECTED PUBLICATIONS** Coauth, Oppression in Testing: An Examination of How Computer Adaptive Testing Alienates and Oppresses, Teaching in the Community Colleges Jour, 98; coauth, "Cybersex in the Wired Classroom: Facts, Issues, and Suggestions, Teaching in the Community Colleges Jour, 98; coauth, Language Boundaries and Discourse Stability: 'Tagging' as Form of Discourse Spanning International Borders, 97. **CONTACT ADDRESS** Dept of Communication and Theatre, Montana State Univ, Billings, MSU-B, 1500 N 30th St, Billings, MT 54101. **EMAIL** dgross@msubillings.edu

GROSS, DAVID STUART
PERSONAL Born 02/22/1942, Mineola, NY, m, 1971, 1 child **DISCIPLINE** ENGLISH, COMPARATIVE LITERATURE **EDUCATION** Wesleyan Univ, BA, 65; Univ Iowa, MA, 69, PhD(comp lit), 73. **CAREER** Asst prof English, Winona State Col, 71-73; assoc prof to prof, Univ of Okla, 73-. **MEMBERSHIPS** MLA; Soc Amis Flaubert. **RESEARCH** The novel; literature and society; Marxist theory. **CONTACT ADDRESS** Dept of English, Univ of Oklahoma, 760 Van Vleet Oval, Room 113, Norman, OK 73069. **EMAIL** david-gross@ou.edu

GROSS, KENNETH
PERSONAL Born 04/02/1954, New York, NY **DISCIPLINE** ENGLISH **EDUCATION** Yale Univ, PhD. **HONORS AND AWARDS** Mellon fel; Am Coun Learned Soc fel; Folger Shakespeare Libr fel & Guggenheim fel. **RESEARCH** Poetry, theater, literature, contemporary poetry, puppet theater, and visual arts. **SELECTED PUBLICATIONS** Auth, Spenserian Poetics: Idolatry, Iconoclasm, and Magic, The Dream of the Moving Statue; auth, Shakespeare's Noise. **CONTACT ADDRESS** Dept of Eng, Univ of Rochester, Rochester, NY 14627. **EMAIL** kgrs@troi.cc.rochester.edu

GROSSBERG, LAWRENCE
PERSONAL Born 12/03/1947, New York, NY, m, 1988, 1 child **DISCIPLINE** COMMUNICATION **EDUCATION** Univ Rochester, BA (philos, hist), 68; Univ IL, PhD (commun), 76. **CAREER** Asst prof, Purdue Univ, 75-76; asst, assoc, prof, Speech Commun, Communications Res, Criticism and Interpretive Theory, Univ IL, Champaign-Urbana, 76-94; Morris Davis distinguished prof of Commun Studies, Univ NC, Chapel Hill, 94-; Prof of Communication, Morris Davis, 00-. **HONORS AND AWARDS** Fisher Mentorship Award, Int Commun Asn, 95; Distinguished Scholar Award, Nat Commun Asn, 97; ICA fel, Int Commun Asn, 98. **RESEARCH** Cultural studies; popular music; philos of culture & commun; neo-conservatism. **SELECTED PUBLICATIONS** Ed, with James Hay and Ellan Wartella, The Audience and Its Landscape, Westview Press, 96; auth, Toward a Geneology of the State of Cultural Studies: The Discipline of Communication and the Reception of Cultural Studies in the United States, in Cary Nelson and Dilip Gaonkar, Disciplinary and Dissent in Cultural Studies, Routledge, 96; Cultural Studies, Modern Logics, and Theories of Globalization, in Angela McRobbie, ed, Back to Reality: The Social Experience of Cultural Studies, Manchester Univ Press, 97; Replacing Popular Culture, in The Clubcultures Reader: Readings in Popular Cultural Studies, ed, Steve Redhead with Derek Wynne and Justin O'Connor, Blackwells, 97; Doing Without Culture, or Cultural Studies in Helms' Country, in Judith S Trent, ed, Communication: Views from the Helm for the Twenty-First Century, Allyn & Bacon, 97; Con-figuring Space, in Unmapping The Earth: Catalog of the Kwang-ju Biennale 1997, Kwang-ju Biennale Press, 97; Dancing in Spite of Myself: Essays on Popular Culture, Duke Univ Press, 97; Bringing It All Back Home: Essays on Cultural Studies, Duke Univ Press, 97; with Ellen Wartella and Charles Whitney, MediaMaking, Sage, 98; The Cultural Studies' Crossroads Blues, European J of Cultural Studies 1, 98; numerous other books and articles, several publications forthcoming. **CONTACT ADDRESS** Dept of Commun Studies, Univ of No Carolina, Chapel Hill, CB 3285 Bingham Hall, Chapel Hill, NC 27599-3285. **EMAIL** docrock@email.unc.edu

GROSSKURTH, PHYLLIS M.
PERSONAL Born Toronto, ON, Canada **DISCIPLINE** ENGLISH **EDUCATION** Univ Toronto, BA, 46; Univ Ottawa, MA, 60; Univ London, PhD, 62. **CAREER** Lectr, Carleton Univ, 64-65; asst prof, 65-69, assoc prof, 69-72, Priof, Univ Toronto, 72-89. **HONORS AND AWARDS** Gov Gen Awd nonfiction, 65; Univ BC Awd Biog, 65; Hon Res Fel, Univ Kent, 91; Hon Fel, Univ Toronto, 92. **MEMBERSHIPS** Am Acad Psychoanalysis; PEN Int; Writer's Union Can. **SELECTED PUBLICATIONS** Auth, John Addington Symonds: A Biography, 64; auth, Gabrielle Roy, 69; auth, Melanie Klein: Her World and Her Work, 86; auth, Margaret Mead: A Life of Controversy, 89. **CONTACT ADDRESS** New College, Univ of Toronto, Toronto, ON, Canada M5A 2J6.

GROSSMAN, GEORGE S.
PERSONAL Born 05/31/1938, Czechoslovakia, m, 1960, 1 child **DISCIPLINE** LAW, LIBRARY SCIENCE **EDUCATION** Univ Chicago, BA, 60; Stanford Law School, LIB, 66; Brigham Young Univ, MSLS, 71. **CAREER** Tech Services Librarian, Univ of Pa, 66-68; prof of law and law librn, Univ of Ut, 68-73; prof of law and law librn, Univ of Minn, 73-79; prof of law and law librn, Northwestern Univ, 79-93. **MEMBERSHIPS** Am Asn of Law Libraries. **RESEARCH** Legal research, American legal history. **SELECTED PUBLICATIONS** Auth, Legal Research: Historical Foundations of the Electronic Age, Oxford, 94; auth, The Spirit of American Law, Westview, 99. **CONTACT ADDRESS** School of Law, Univ of California, Davis, 400 Mrak Dr, Davis, CA 95616. **EMAIL** gsgrossman@ucdavis.edu

GROSSMAN, JONATHAN H.
PERSONAL Born 04/17/1967, Oxford, Britain, 1 child **DISCIPLINE** ENGLISH LITERATURE **EDUCATION** Brown Univ, BA, 89; Univ Pa, PhD, 96. **CAREER** Asst prof, Univ Del, 97-. **HONORS AND AWARDS** Phi Beta Kappa. **RESEARCH** History of the English novel, Dickens, 19th Century British Literature. **SELECTED PUBLICATIONS** Auth, The Art of Alibi: English Law Courts and the Novel, Johns Hopkins, (forthcoming). **CONTACT ADDRESS** English Dept, Univ of Delaware, Newark, DE 19716-2537. **EMAIL** jgrossma@dept.english.upenn.edu

GROTH, JANET
DISCIPLINE ENGLISH **EDUCATION** Univ MN, BA; NYork Univ, MA and PhD, 82. **CAREER** Fac, Plattsburgh State Univ of NY . **HONORS AND AWARDS** Former editorial assistant for New Yorker magazine. **RESEARCH** Magazine and article writing; Am lit; Shakespeare. **SELECTED PUBLICATIONS** Auth, two bks about Edmund Wilson. **CONTACT ADDRESS** SUNY, Col at Plattsburgh, 101 Broad St, Plattsburgh, NY 12901-2681.

GROTON, ANNE H.
PERSONAL Born 04/08/1954, Oak Park, IL **DISCIPLINE** CLASSICAL STUDIES **EDUCATION** Wellesley Coll, AB, 76; Univ of Michigan, MA. 77, PhD 82. **CAREER** Asst Prof, Assoc Prof to Prof, 81-, St Olaf Coll. **HONORS AND AWARDS** Awd for Excellence in the Tchg of Class, Amer Philos Assoc. **MEMBERSHIPS** Amer Philos Assoc; Class Assoc Middle West and South; Class Assoc of Minnesota; Amer Soc Papyrologists; Vergilian Soc. **RESEARCH** Ancient Greek and Roman Drama, especially comedy. **SELECTED PUBLICATIONS** Auth, From Alpha to Omega: A Beginning Course in Classical Greek, Focus Publishing, 95. **CONTACT ADDRESS** Dept Classics, St. Olaf Col, 1520 St Olaf Ave, Northfield, MN 55057-1098. **EMAIL** groton@stolaf.edu

GROVE, JAMES PAUL
PERSONAL Born 10/22/1949, Minneapolis, MN, m, 1972, 1 child **DISCIPLINE** AMERICAN LITERATURE, BRITISH FICTION **EDUCATION** Univ Minn, BA, 71; Col St Thomas, MAT, 74; Southern Ill Univ, Carbondale, MA, 76, PhD(English), 80. **CAREER** Instr English, Mt Mercy Col, 80-, full prof and chair, English Dept. **HONORS AND AWARDS** NEH grants, 86, 89, 93; Fulbright Lecturer, Czech Republic, 89-90. **MEMBERSHIPS** MLA; NCTE. **RESEARCH** Place in Literature, Evil in Contemporary American Literature, Southern Literature, Midwest Literature. **SELECTED PUBLICATIONS** Auth, Stepping Away From the Snug Sofa: Melvilles Vision of Death in Moby-Dick, New England Quart, 6/79; The Neglected Dinner in James' The Wings of the Dove, Am Notes & Queries, 9/79; Pastoralism and Anti-Pastoralism in Peter Matthiessen's Far Tortuga, Critique, Winter, 79; Articles on American, Czech, and Latin American Literature in journals (The New England Quart, American Lit, Critique, Am Notes and Queries, Prarie Schooner, Review of Contemporary Fiction, Iowa Woman, Crab Orchard Review, High Plains Literary Review); and in books, The Best of American Literature: Mark Twain, The Last Quarter: Contemporary Southern Fiction, Magill's Literary Annual. **CONTACT ADDRESS** English Dept, Mount Mercy Col, 1330 Elmhurst Dr N E, Cedar Rapids, IA 52402-4797.

GROVE-WHITE, ELIZABETH M.
DISCIPLINE ENGLISH LITERATURE **EDUCATION** Trinity Col, Dublin, PhD. **CAREER** Assoc prof; dir, Wrtg Prog. **HONORS AND AWARDS** Peabody awd, 80; Hely-Hutchinson awd, 73; Found scholar, Trinity Col, Dublin, 70. **RESEARCH** Epistemic rhetoric; computer-mediated communication; transactional writing. **SELECTED PUBLICATIONS** Auth, Virginia Woolf's To the Lighthouse, Addison Longman, 80; articles and rev(s) in Globe and Mail, Amer Reporter, Hermathena, Hibernia, Brick. **CONTACT ADDRESS** Dept of English, Univ of Victoria, Clearihue Bldg, Rm C352, PO Box 3070, Victoria, BC, Canada V8W 3W1. **EMAIL** grovewhi@uvic.ca

GROVER, DORYS CROW
PERSONAL Born 09/23/1921, Pendleton, OR, s **DISCIPLINE** AMERICAN STUDIES, BRITISH LITERATURE **EDUCATION** Ore State Univ, BA, 51; Wash State Univ, PhD(Am studies), 69. **CAREER** Ed, The Pendleton Record, 59-69; news mgr., KUMA Radio, 59-64; news writer, KCRL-TV, Reno, NV, 70-71; asst instr English, Wash State Univ, 64-69; prof, Drake Univ, 71-72; prof, english, Tex A&M Univ, Commerce, 72-93, emerita prof, 93-; Fac res grants, 72-76 and 81-82. **HONORS AND AWARDS** Southwest Heritage Awd, 77; Distinguished prof award, 90; Nat Education Award, 92; Sandburg Award, 79; Fort Concho Cent. Poetry Award, 89; Poetry Awards, 78-79, 85, 87-90, 93; Short story awards, 75, 88-89, 92. **MEMBERSHIPS** MLA; Western Lit Asn; Soc for Study of Midwest Lit; Tex Folklore Soc; Sherwood Anderson Soc; Melville Soc; James Branch Cabell Soc. **RESEARCH** American novel and novelists; Colonial American literature; Western literature. **SELECTED PUBLICATIONS** Auth, A Solitary Voice: Collection of Critical Essays, 73; auth, Vardis Fisher: The Novelist as Poet, Revisionist Press, 73; auth, "The Antelope Sonnets," Tex Quarterly (74); auth, "Garland's Emily Dickinson - A Case of Mistaken Identity," Am Lit (74); auth, "W.H.D. Koerner & Emerson Hough: A Western Collaboration," Montana Magazine (79); auth, John Graves, Boise State Univ Press, 90; auth, The Valley of Tutuilla, and Other Lines, 97; **CONTACT ADDRESS** 71330 Tutuilla Road, Pendleton, OR 97801. **EMAIL** dg88@ucinet.com

GROVES, JEFFREY D.
DISCIPLINE ENGLISH **EDUCATION** LaVerne, BA, 81; Claremont Grad Sch, MA, 83, PhD, 87. **CAREER** Assoc Prof, Eng, Harvey Mudd Coll. **MEMBERSHIPS** Am Antiquarian Soc **SELECTED PUBLICATIONS** Auth, Ticknor-and-Fields-ism of all kinds: Thomas Starr King, Literary Promotion, and Canon Formation, New Eng Quart 68, 95; Judging Literary Books By Their Covers: House Styles, Ticknor and Fields, and Literary Promotion, in Reading Books: The Artifact as Text and Context, Univ Mass Press, 96. **CONTACT ADDRESS** Hum/Soc Sci, Harvey Mudd Col, Claremont, CA 91711.

GROW, LYNN
DISCIPLINE ENGLISH **EDUCATION** Univ S Calif, BA, 67; MA, 68, MA, 72; PhD, 71. **CAREER** Asst Prof, Wichita State Univ, 72-77; Lecturer, Univ Md, 77-81; Lecturer to Dept Head, Col of the Bahamas, 81-83; Instr to Sen Prof, Broward Community Col, 83-. **HONORS AND AWARDS** Res Grant, Wichita State Univ; Nomination for Regents' Awd for Excellence, Wichita State Univ; EIRS Commendation, Univ Md; Nominee, Prof of the year, Broward Community Col. **RESEARCH** Modern Philippine literature in English. **SELECTED PUBLICATIONS** Auth, The Prose Style of Samuel Taylor Coleridge, Romantic Reassessment Series, 76; auth, The epistolary Criticism of Manuel A Viray: In Memoriam, Giraffe Books, 98; auth, The Novels of Bienvenido N Santos, Giraffe Books, forthcoming; auth, "The Crafted Fact: Cornelio S. Reyes' Yesterday's Tomorrow," Philippine Studies, (94): 105-109; auth, "Ubi Sunt: Francisco Arcellana's Sacrament of Death," Pilipinas, (94): 73-80; auth, "Tita Lacambra-ayala: The Penetrating Eye," Saint Louis University research Journal, (94): 366-671; auth, "The Laughter of My Father: A Survival Kit," MELUS: The Journal of the Society for the Study of the Multi-Ethnic Literature of the United States, (95): 35-46; auth, "Gathering Grief: The Lonely Room of Isabelo T Crisostomi," Philippine Studies, (97): 281-286; auth, "And Quiet flows the Dawn," Philippine studies (97): 387-291; auth, "A Scattered Felicity," Philippine Studies, forthcoming; auth, "A Scattered Felicity: B-D," Philippine Studies, forthcoming; auth, "Paz Latorena: English Fiction's First Feminist," in Solidarity: Southeast Asian Current Affairs, Ideas and the Arts, forthcoming. **CONTACT ADDRESS** Dept English, Broward Comm Col, 3501 Davie Rd, Davie, FL 33314-1604.

GRUBER, LOREN C.
PERSONAL Born 09/17/1941, Carroll, IA, m, 1983, 3 children **DISCIPLINE** ENGLISH **EDUCATION** Simpson Col, BA, 63; Western Reserve Univ, MA, 64; Univ Denver, PhD, 72. **CAREER** Instr, Grove City Col, 64-66; instr to assoc prof, Simpson Col, 66-82; asst prof, Northwest Mo State Univ, 89-93; prof, Mo Valley Col, 93-. **HONORS AND AWARDS** Award of Excellence, ADDY Competition, 84; Tower Serv Awd, Northwest Mo State Univ, 92; Best Juvenile Short Story, Mo Writers Guild, 97, 98. **MEMBERSHIPS** Mo Writers Guild; Soc of Children's Book Writers and Illustrators; Medieval Acad of Am; Sigma Tau Delta; Soc for the Advan of Scandinavian Study. **RESEARCH** Old English, Middle English, Old Icelandic, Creative Writing for Children and Young Adults. **SELECTED PUBLICATIONS** Auth, "The Agnostic Anglo-Saxon Gnomes", Poetica 6.2 (76): 22-47; auth, "The Rites of Passage: Havamal, Stanzas 105", Scandinavian Studies 49, (77); auth, "Shaping the Portfolio Course: The Uses of Direct Assessment and the Portfolio as a Critical Thinking Tool", ERIC 5 (92): ED 345 275; auth, "Teaching Beowulf to Undergraduates: The Role of Translation", Proceedings of the Mo Philog Assoc 20, (95): 1-8; auth, Beowulf Earns His Name", Hodgepodge, 2.10 (96): 14-16; auth, "The Windigo Waits - and Watches", Hodgepodge, 3.13 (97): 6-10; auth, "Spoon Boy", Hodgepodge, 6.21 (00): 15-23; coed, Essays on Old, Middle, Modern English and Old Icelandic, Edwin Mellen, 00. **CONTACT ADDRESS** Div Arts and Humanities, Missouri Valley Col, PO Box 217, Marshall, MO 65340-0217. **EMAIL** lcgruber@cdsinet.net

GRUBER, WILLIAM
PERSONAL Born 09/26/1943, Hokendauqua, PA, m, 1968, 3 children **DISCIPLINE** ENGLISH **EDUCATION** Yale Univ, BA, 65; Univ of Idaho, MA, 74; Wash State Univ, PhD, 79. **CAREER** Asst prof, IL State Univ, 79-80; asst prof to prof, Emory Univ, 80-. **MEMBERSHIPS** MLA; SAMLA. **RESEARCH** Drama, Modern Drama, History of Drama. **SELECTED PUBLICATIONS** Auth, Comic Theaters: Studies in Performance and Audience Response, Georgia, 86; auth, Missing Persons: Character and Characterization on the Modern Stage, Georgia, 94. **CONTACT ADDRESS** Dept English, Emory Univ, 1364 Clifton Rd NE, Atlanta, GA 30322-1061. **EMAIL** wegrube@emory.edu

GRUBER-MILLER, JOHN C.
DISCIPLINE CLASSICS **EDUCATION** Ohio State Univ, MA, 79; Xavier Univ, PhD, 87. **CAREER** Vis Instr, Ohio Wesleyan Univ, 86-87; Asst Prof to Prof, Cornell Col, 87-. **HONORS AND AWARDS** Fulbright Fel, 89; Fel, NEH, 94, 96. **MEMBERSHIPS** Am Philol Asn; Am Class League; Class Asn of the Mid W and S; Comput Assisted Lang Inst Consortium; AMICI; Women's Class Caucus; Am Coun of Teachers of For Lang; Archaeol Inst of Am. **SELECTED PUBLICATIONS** Site Ed, Riley Collection of Roman Portrait Sculpture, http://vroma.org/~riley/; site ed, Let's Review Greek!, http://cornellcollege.edu/classical_studies/reviewgreek/; co-auth, "How Do You Say MOO in Latin? Assessing Student Learning and Motivation in Beginning Latin," CALICO J, 01; auth, When Dead Tongues Speak: Teaching Beginning Latin and Greek, Oxford Univ Press, 01. **CONTACT ADDRESS** Dept Class and Mod Lang, Cornell Col, 515 Third St NW, Mount Vernon, IA 52314. **EMAIL** jgruber-miller@cornellcollege.edu

GRUBGELD, ELIZABETH
DISCIPLINE MODERN BRITISH LITERATURE, IRISH LITERATURE **EDUCATION** Univ Iowa, PhD, 83. **CAREER** Engl, Okla St Univ. **HONORS AND AWARDS** Prize Literary and Cultural Criticism, 95. **RESEARCH** Elizabeth Bowen and John Montague. **SELECTED PUBLICATIONS** Auth, George Moore and the Autogenous Self: The Autobiography and Fiction, Syracuse Univ Press. **CONTACT ADDRESS** Oklahoma State Univ, Stillwater, 101 Whitehurst Hall, Stillwater, OK 74078.

GRUDIN, ROBERT
PERSONAL Born 03/04/1938, Newark, NJ, m, 1967, 2 children **DISCIPLINE** RENAISSANCE LITERATURE **EDUCATION** Harvard Univ, BA, 60; Univ Calif, Berkeley, Phd, 69. **CAREER** Asst prof, 71-78, assoc prof to prof emer, Univ Ore, 78-. **RESEARCH** Renaissance studies, creative writing, modern fiction, theory of creativity, philosophy of time. **SELECTED PUBLICATIONS** Auth, Mighty Opposites: Shakespeare and Renaissance Contrariety, Univ of Calif Press, 79; auth, Time and the Art of Living, Harper and Row, 82; auth, The Grace of Great Things: Creativity and Innovation, Ticknor and Fields, 90; auth, Book, A Novel, Random House, 92; auth, On Dialogue: An Essay in Free Thought, Houghton Mifflin, 96. **CONTACT ADDRESS** English Dept, Univ of Oregon, 1286 Univ of Ore, Eugene, OR 97403-1286. **EMAIL** rgrudin@yahoo.com

GRUNDY, ISOBEL
PERSONAL Born 05/23/1938, Weybridge, Surrey, England **DISCIPLINE** ENGLISH LITERATURE **EDUCATION** St Anne's Col, Oxford Univ, BA, 60; PhD, 71. **CAREER** Temp Lectr, St Anne's Col, 69-70; jr res fel, St Hugh's Col, 70-71; lectr, reader, Queen Mary Col, 71-85; vis assoc prof, Univ of Toronto, 75-76; vis assoc prof, Princeton Unv, 80; prof, Univ Albta, 90-. **HONORS AND AWARDS** J Gordin Kaplin Awd for Res, Univ Albta, 96; Fel, Royal Soc of Can, 97; Univ Cup, Univ Albta, 00. **MEMBERSHIPS** Can Soc for 18th Century Studies, Brit Soc for 18th Century Studies, Am Soc for 18th Century Studies, Johnsonians, Johnson Soc of London. **SELECTED PUBLICATIONS** Auth, Lady Mary Wortley Motagu: Coment of the Enlightenment, Clarendon (Oxford), 99. **CONTACT ADDRESS** Dept Humanities, Univ of Alberta, 3-5 Humanities Centre, Edmonton, AB, Canada T6G 2E5. **EMAIL** isobel.grundy@ualberta.ca

GRUNER, CHARLES R.
PERSONAL Born 11/06/1931, Pinckneyville, IL, m, 1958, 2 children **DISCIPLINE** SPEECH COMMUNICATION **EDUCATION** Southern Ill Univ, BS, 55, MA, 56; The Ohio State Univ, PhD, 63. **CAREER** Grad asst in Speech Dept, 55-56, res asst & res assoc, Southern Ill Univ, 63-64; teacher of speech, Webster Groves High School, 56-57; instr, 57-60, asst prof, St. Lawrence Univ, 60-64; asst prof, 64-66, assoc prof, Univ of Neb, 66-69; Ed, GA Speecj Commun J, 75-77, Assoc Prof, 69-74, Prof, Univ of GA, 74-. **HONORS AND AWARDS** Eagle Scout, 46-. **MEMBERSHIPS** Int Soc for General Semantics; Southern Speech Commun Asn; Ga Speech Asn; Am Inst of Parliamentarians; Workshop Libr on World Humor; Int Soc for Humor Studies. **SELECTED PUBLICATIONS** Auth, The Game of Humor: A Comprehensive Theory of Why We Laugh, Transaction Pub, 97; Parliamentary Procedure as the Major Part of a Course in Problem-Solving, Parliamentary J, 94; Appreciation and Understanding of Satire: Another Quasi-Experiment, Psychol Reports, 96; The Teachin/Research Symbiosis: A Two-Way Street, ERIC Clearinghouse on Reading, English, and Commun, 95; Satire as Persuasion, ERIC Document ED, microfische; coauth, Evaluative Responses to Jokes in Informative Speech With and Without Laughter by an Audience: A Partial Replication, Psychol Reports, 94; Semantic Differential Measurements of Connotations of Verbal Terms and Their Doublespeak Facsimiles in Sentence Context, Psychol Reports, 95. **CONTACT ADDRESS** Dept of Speech Communication, Univ of Georgia, Athens, GA 30602. **EMAIL** cgruner@uga

GRUNER, ELISABETH
DISCIPLINE ENGLISH **EDUCATION** Brown Univ, AB, 82; Univ Calif, 87; PhD, 92. **CAREER** Lecturer, Univ Calif, 92-93; Asst Prof to Assoc Prof, Univ Richmond, 93-. **HONORS AND AWARDS** A.A. Bennett Prize, Brown Univ, 82; UCLA Fel, 85-86; Mabel Wilson Richards Fel, 89-90, 87-88; Bradford A. Booth/Majl Ewing Fel, 89-90; Finalist, Mary Wollstonecraft Dissertation Awd, 92; UCAL Dissertation Awd, 92; PETE Summer Grant, Univ Richmond, 95-98; Summer Res Fel, Univ Richmond, 94, 97, 00; Jessie Ball DuPont Summer Sem, 97. **MEMBERSHIPS** Mod Lang Asn; Women's Caucus for the Mod Lang; Victorians Inst; 18th and 19th Century British Women Writers Asn. **RESEARCH** Nineteenth-Century British Literature; women and Literature; The Novel; Children's Literature; Feminist Theories. **SELECTED PUBLICATIONS** Auth, "Loving Difference: Sisters and Brothers from Frances Burney to Emily Bronte," in The significance of Sibling Relationship in Literature, (Bowling Green State Univ Popular Press, 93), 32-46; auth, "The Bullfinch and the Brother: Marriage and Family in Frances Burney's 'Camilla'," JEGP, (94): 18-34; auth, "Feminists Face the Job Market: Q & A (Questions & Anecdotes)," in Concerns, (94): 15-23; auth, "Family Secrets and the Mysteries of the 'The Moonstone'," Victorian Literature and Culture, (93): 127-145; auth, "Cinderella, Marie Antoinette, and Sara: Roles and role Models in 'A Little Princess," The Lion and the Unicorn, (98): 163-187; auth, "Plotting the Mother: Caroline Norton, Helen Huntingdon, and Isabel Vane," Tulsa Studies in Women's Literature, (97): 303-325; auth, "born and Made: Sisters, Brothers, and the Deceased Wife's sister Bill," SIGNS: Journal of Women in Culture and Society, (99): 423-447. **CONTACT ADDRESS** Dept Eng, Univ of Richmond, 28 Westhampton Way, Richmond, VA 23173. **EMAIL** egruner@richmond.edu

GRUPENHOFF, RICHARD
DISCIPLINE FILM PRODUCTION, FILM HISTORY, SCREENWRITING **EDUCATION** Xavier Univ BA; Purdue Univ, MA; Ohio State Univ, PhD. **CAREER** Instr, 75-, ch, dept Radio-TV-Film, Rowan Col of NJ. **SELECTED PUBLICATIONS** Auth, The Black Valentino: The Stage and Screen Career of Lorenzo Tucker. **CONTACT ADDRESS** Rowan Univ, Glassboro, NJ 08028-1701. **EMAIL** grupenhoff@rowan.edu

GRUSHOW, IRA
PERSONAL Born 04/11/1933, New York, NY, m, 1965, 2 children **DISCIPLINE** ENGLISH **EDUCATION** City Col New York, BA, 54; Yale Univ, MA, 57, PhD, 63. **CAREER** Instr English, Carnegie-Inst Technol, 60-62; from instr to asst prof, 62-68, chmn dept, 74-80, assoc prof, 68-84, prof, 84-90, Alumni Prof English Bellrd Lettres & Literature, Franklin & Marshall Col, 90-98, Prof Emer, 98-. **MEMBERSHIPS** MLA; Am Soc 18th Century Studies **RESEARCH** Satire; 18th century English literature; Travel literature; Sir Max Beerbohm **SELECTED PUBLICATIONS** Auth, The Imaginary Reminiscenses of Sir Max Beerbohm, Ohio Univ Press, 84. **CONTACT ADDRESS** Dept of English, Franklin and Marshall Col, PO Box 3003, Lancaster, PA 17604-3003. **EMAIL** i_grushow@acad.fandm.edu

GRUSIN, RICHARD A.
PERSONAL Born 09/29/1953, Chicago, IL, m, 2 children **DISCIPLINE** ENGLISH **EDUCATION** Univ Ill Urbana, BA, 76; Univ Calif Berkeley, PhD, 83. **CAREER** Asst prof, SAA, 86-91; assoc prof, SAA, 91-93; dir undergrad studies and assoc prof, SAA, 93-97; chair & assoc prof, sch of lit, comm & culture, Ga Inst of Tech, 97-. **HONORS AND AWARDS** Fel, NEH Inst on Image and Text in the Eighteenth Century, The John Hopkins Univ, summer, 88; fel, Sch of Criticism and Theory, summer, 85. **MEMBERSHIPS** Mod Lang Asn of Amer; South Atlantic Mod Lang Asn; Amer Studies Asn; Soc of Lit and Sci. **RESEARCH** New media studies; Ecocriticism; American cultural studies. **SELECTED PUBLICATIONS** Co-auth, Remediation: Understanding New Media, MIT Press, 98; auth, Transcendentalist Hermeneutics: Institutional Authority and the Higher Criticism of the Bible, Duke Univ Press, 91; co-auth, Remediation, Configurations, vol 4, no 3, 311-358, Fall, 96; article, Introduction, New Amer Studies in Sci and Tech: Essays in Cultural Historicism, Configurations, vol 3, no 3, 349-51, Fall, 95; article, Representing Yellowstone: Photography, Loss, and Fidelity to Nature, Configurations, vol 3, no 3, 415-36, Fall, 95; article, Theodore Parker, A Companion to American Thought, Blackwell, 516-17, 95; article, What Is an Electronic Author?, Configurations, vol 2, no 3, 469-83, Fall, 94. **CONTACT ADDRESS** Sch of Lit, Commun & Cult, Georgia Inst of Tech, 686 Cherry St, Atlanta, GA 30332-0165. **EMAIL** richard.grusin@lcc.gatech.edu

GUDDING, GABRIEL
PERSONAL Born 06/16/1966, MN, 1 child **DISCIPLINE** AMERICAN STUDIES, CREATIVE WRITING (POETRY) **EDUCATION** Evergreen Col, BA, 94; Purdue Univ, MA, 97. **CAREER** Grad stud, Purdue Univ, 95-97; Grad stud, Cornell Univ, 98-. **HONORS AND AWARDS** The Nation "Discovery" Awd, 98. **MEMBERSHIPS** Poetry Society of America **RESEARCH** American poetry; history of science **SELECTED PUBLICATIONS** The Phenotype/Genotype Distinction and The Disappearance of the Body, Journal of the History of Ideas, John Hopkins Univ Press, July 96; The Wallace Stevens Jour, I See Your Hammer in the Horologe of Time and I Raise You a Westclock, Spring 97; The Iowa Review, One Petition Lofted into the Ginkgos, Fall 97; The Nation, The Parenthesis Inserts Itself into the Transcripts of The Committee on Un-American Activities, May 18, 1998; River Styx, The Bosun, August 1998; The Beloit Poetry Journal, The Footnote Reconnoiters the Piedmont. **CONTACT ADDRESS** Cornell Univ, 250 Goldwin Smith, Ithaca, NY 14850. **EMAIL** gwg6@cornell.edu

GUENTHER, BARBARA J.
PERSONAL Born Port Huron, MI, s **DISCIPLINE** ENGLISH, COMMUNICATIONS **EDUCATION** Nazareth Col, BS, 61; Univ MI, MA, 64; Univ Wis, PhD, 74. **CAREER** Instr, Northwestern Univ; DePaul Univ; IN State Univ; Hillsdale Col; Univ N IA; Lake Forest Coll; assoc prof, Sch of Art Inst, 81. **HONORS AND AWARDS** Summer sem grant, NEH; travel res grants, Univ WI, Univ N IA; Fulbright award, 91, 98. **SELECTED PUBLICATIONS** Pub(s), Ariz Eng Bulletin; Handbk of Exec Commun; auth, Effective Writing for First-Year Students. **CONTACT ADDRESS** Dept of Lib Arts, Sch of the Art Inst of Chicago, 37 S Wabash Ave, Chicago, IL 60603.

GUENTNER, FRANCES J.
PERSONAL Born 03/10/1917, LaCrosse, WI **DISCIPLINE** MUSICOLOGY, CLASSICAL LANGUAGES **EDUCATION** St Louis Univ, AB, 39, MA, 42, Wash Univ, MA, 63. **CAREER** From instr to asst prof class lang, 49-64, assoc prof music, 64-70, chmn dept, 69-75; prof music, St Louis Univ, 70-, actg chmn dept, 80-, bk rev ed, Nat Asn Pastoral Musicians, 77-. **MEMBERSHIPS** Church Music Asn Am; Nat Asn Pastoral Musicians. **RESEARCH** Baroque music; music theory; synthesizer. **SELECTED PUBLICATIONS** Auth, A nineteenth-century chant revival, Sacred Music, summer 65; Alcestis in ancient drama and early opera, Class Bull, 11/66; Dulces exuviae in sixteenth century Music, Class J, 10-11/72; Medieval Treatise on Cistercian Chant, Am Inst Music, 74; Reassessing a recital heritage, Col Music Symp, fall 77. **CONTACT ADDRESS** Jesuit Hall, Saint Louis Univ, 3601 Lindell Blvd, Saint Louis, MO 63108-3393. **EMAIL** guentner@slu.edu

GUERIN, WILFRED LOUIS
PERSONAL Born 07/10/1929, New Orleans, LA, m, 1951, 6 children **DISCIPLINE** ENGLISH LITERATURE, CRITICISM **EDUCATION** Tulane Univ, BA, 51, MA, 53, PhD, 58. **CAREER** Instr, Holy Cross High Sch, New Orleans, 52-53; instr English, Centenary Col, 53-56, asst prof, 58-62; assoc prof, Univ Southwestern La, 62-63; prof, Centenary Col La, 63-74; prof English, La State Univ, Shreveport, 74-98, chair Dept English & For Langs, 78-85, vice-chancellor & provost, 85-91, dir Master's Prog, 93-98, coordr, Grad Studies, 94-98; fel, SEastern Inst Medieval and Renaissance Studies, Duke Univ, 66; fel, SEastern Inst Medieval and Renaissance Studies, NC Univ at Chapel Hill, 67; vis fac audit prog, Harvard Univ, 70. **HONORS AND AWARDS** Outstanding Teacher Awd, Centenary Col, 68; H. M. Cotton Fac Excellence Awd, La State Univ Found, 77; Phi Beta Kappa; Phi Sigma Iota; Kappa Delta Pi; Omicron Delta Kappa; Phi Kappa Phi; Sigma Tau Delta; Fac

Achievement Awd, LSUS, Spring 84; grant, La Comt for the Humanities, 84. **MEMBERSHIPS** MLA; SCent Mod Lang Asn; AAUP; SCent Renaissance Conf; Conf Christianity & Lit; SCentral Conf Christianity & Lit. **RESEARCH** Teilhard de Chardin; literary criticism; medieval and Renaissance literature. **SELECTED PUBLICATIONS** Auth, Christian Myth and Naturalistic Deity: The Great Gatsby, Renascence, 61; Irony and tension in Browning's Karshish, Victorian Poetry, 63; two chapters in Malory's Originality: A Critical Study of Le Morte Darthur, Johns Hopkins, 64; coauth, A Handbook of Critical Approaches to Literature, Harper & Row, 66 & 79, Oxford Univ Press, 92 & 99; auth, Death in the woods: Sherwood Anderson's Cold Pastoral, CEA Critic, 68; coauth, Mandala: Literature for Critical Analysis, Harper & Row, 70; auth, Browning's Cleon: A Teilhardian view, Victorian Poetry, 74; Dynamo, virgin and cyclotron: Henry Adams and Teilhard de Chardin on pilgrimage, Renascence, spring 76; coauth, L.I.T.: Literature and Interpretive Techniques, Harper & Row, 86; auth, Herbert's The Pulley, in Explicator 53.2, 95. **CONTACT ADDRESS** Dept of English, Louisiana State Univ, Shreveport, 1 University Pl, Shreveport, LA 71115-2301. **EMAIL** wguerin@pilot.lsus.edu

GUERINOT, JOSEPH VINCENT

PERSONAL Born 02/18/1928, Rochester, NY **DISCIPLINE** ENGLISH LITERATURE **EDUCATION** St Bernard's Sem, Ba, 49; Fordham Univ, MA, 53; Yale Univ, PhD, 62. **CAREER** Asst, Fordham Univ, 51-52; asst English, Lycee Jules Ferry, France, 54-55; from instr to asst prof, Bucknell Univ, 55-65; asst prof, Hunter Col, 65-67; assoc prof, 67-71, PROF ENGLISH, UNIV WIS, MILWAUKEE, 71-. **RESEARCH** Pope; mediaeval Latin literature; Henry James. **SELECTED PUBLICATIONS** Auth, Wake, William Gallican Correspondence and Related Documents, 1716-1731, Scriblerian and the Kit-Cats, Vol 0028, 95. **CONTACT ADDRESS** Dept of English, Univ of Wisconsin, Milwaukee, Milwaukee, WI 53201.

GUESS, CAROL A.

PERSONAL Born 01/03/1968, Bethesda, MD **DISCIPLINE** ENGLISH **EDUCATION** Columbia Univ, BA, 90; Indiana Univ, MA, 93, MFA, 94. **CAREER** Asst prof, Nebr Wesleyan Univ, 97-98; asst prof, Western Washington Univ, 98-. **RESEARCH** Creative writing, lesbian/gay studies, women's studies. **SELECTED PUBLICATIONS** Auth, Seeing Dell, Cleis Press (96); auth, Switch, Calyx Books (98). **CONTACT ADDRESS** Dept English, Western Washington Univ, M/S 9055, Bellingham, WA 98225. **EMAIL** guessc@cc.wwu.edu

GUETTI, JAMES L.

DISCIPLINE ENGLISH LANGUAGE AND LITERATURE **EDUCATION** Amherst Univ, BA; MA; Cornell, PhD. **CAREER** Prof. **RESEARCH** Philosophy of language; critical theory; modern literature. **SELECTED PUBLICATIONS** Auth, Wittgenstein and the Grammar of Literary Experience; auth, The Limits of Metaphor; Word-Magic. **CONTACT ADDRESS** Dept of English, Rutgers, The State Univ of New Jersey, New Brunswick, 510 George St, Murray Hall, New Brunswick, NJ 08901-1167.

GUIBBORY, ACHSAH

PERSONAL Born 06/30/1945, Norwalk, CT, m, 1972, 1 child **DISCIPLINE** ENGLISH **EDUCATION** Indiana Univ, BA, 66; Univ Calif, Los Angeles, MA, 67, PhD, 70. **CAREER** From asst prof to prof English & relig studies, Univ Ill, Urbana-Champaign, 70-; ed board, John Dorme J; managing ed, JEGP, 95-. **HONORS AND AWARDS** Univ Ill Campus Awd for Excellence Undergrad Teach, 79; William Prokasy College of LAS Awd for Excellence Teaching, 95; Luckman Awd, UIUC, Excellence in Undergrad Teach, 95. **MEMBERSHIPS** MLA; Milton Soc Am; John Donne Soc. **RESEARCH** Seventeenth-century English literature; views of history; religion. **SELECTED PUBLICATIONS** Auth, Dryden's views of history, Philol Quart, 73; Sir Thomas Browne's allusions to Janus, English Lang Notes, 75; Francis Bacon's view of history: The cycles of error and the progress of truth, J English & Ger Philol, 75; ed, The Ephesian Matron, Augustan Reprint Soc, 75; auth, The Poet as Myth-Maker: Ben Jonson's Poetry of Praise, Clio, 76; Sir Thomas Browne's Pseudodoxia Epidemica and the circle of Knowledge, Tex Studies Lang & Lit, 76; No lust theres like to poetry: Robert Herrick's passion for poetry, in Trust to Good Verses: Herrick Tercentenary Essays, 78; John Donne and memory as the art of salvation, HLQ, 80; A sense of the future: Projected audiences of Donne and Jonson, John Donne J, 83; The temple of Hesperides and Anglican Puritan controversy, in the Muses Commonweale: Poetry and Politics in the Earlier Seventeenth Century, 88; The Map of Time: Seventeenth Centruy English Literature and Ideas of Pattern in History, Univ Ill, 86; Imitation and orginality: Cowley and Bacon's vision of progress, SEL, 89; Oh let me not serve so: The politics of love in Donne's Elegies, ELH, 90; A rationall of old rites: Sir Thomas Browne's Urn Burial and the conflict over ceremony, YES, 91; Donne, the idea of woman and the experience of love, John Donne J, 90; Sexual politics political sex: Seventeenth Century love poetry, in Discoures of Desire: Sexuality in 17th Century Non-Dramatic Literature, 93; John Donne, in Cambridge Companion to English Poetry, Donne to Marvell, 94; Enlarging the units of the Religious Lyric: The case of Herrick's Hesperides, in New Perspectives on the Seventeenth-Century English Religious Lyric, 94; Charles's Prayer, idolatious imitation and true creation in Milton's Echonoulastes, in Of Poetry and Politics: New Essays on Milton and His World, 95; The Gospel according to Aemelia Lanyer: Women and the sacred in Aemelia Lanye's Salve Deis Rex Judaeouen, in Sacred and Profane: The Interplay of Secular and Devotional Literature 1500-1700, 95, rev ed in Aemelia Lanyer: Gender, Genre and the Canon, 98; Donne, Milton and holy sex, Milton Studies, 96; Fear of loving more: Death and the loss of sacremental love, in Donne's Desire of More: The Subject of Anne More Donne in His Poetry, 96; The Relique, The Song of Songs, and Donne's Songs and Sonets, John Donne J, 96; Ceremony and Community from Herbert to Milton: Literature, Religion, and Cultural Conflict in 17th Century England, 98. **CONTACT ADDRESS** Dept of English, Univ of Illinois, Urbana-Champaign, 608 S Wright St, Urbana, IL 61801-3613. **EMAIL** aguibbor@uiuc.edu

GUILDS, JOHN C.

DISCIPLINE AMERICAN LITERATURE **EDUCATION** Duke Univ, PhD. **CAREER** English and Lit, Univ Ark. **SELECTED PUBLICATIONS** Ed, "Long Years of Neglect": The Work and Reputation of William Gilmore Simms, 88; Auth, Simms: A Literary Life, Ark, 92; Guy Rivers: A Tale of Georgia, Univ Ark, 93; The Yemassee: A Romance of Carolina (1994), and Richard Hurdis: A Tale of Alabama, 95. **CONTACT ADDRESS** Univ of Arkansas, Fayetteville, Fayetteville, AR 72701.

GUILHAMET, LEON

PERSONAL Born 11/11/1937, New York, NY, m, 1995 **DISCIPLINE** ENGLISH **EDUCATION** Syracuse Univ, AB; Rutgers Univ, AM; Harvard Univ, PhD. **CAREER** Instr to asst prof, Yale Univ, 67-71; asst prof to Chair, CUNY City Col, 71-. **HONORS AND AWARDS** NEH Summer Grant; Eisner Fel. **MEMBERSHIPS** ASECS. **RESEARCH** 18th Century Novel, Satire, Poetry. **SELECTED PUBLICATIONS** Auth, The Sincere Ideal; auth, Satire and the Transformation of Genre. **CONTACT ADDRESS** Dept English, City Col, CUNY, 160 Convent Ave, New York, NY 10031-9101.

GUITAR, BARRY

DISCIPLINE COMMUNCATION SCIENCES **EDUCATION** Univ Wis, PhD, 74. **CAREER** Dept Comm, Vermont Univ **SELECTED PUBLICATIONS** Auth, Stuttering: An integrated approach to its nature and treatment, Williams & Wilkins, 98; coauth, Onset timing in selected labial muscles in stutterers and non stutterers, Jour Speech Hearing Res, 88; The tonic stretch reflexes in lip, tongue, and jaw muscles, Brain Res, 79; Stuttering therapy: The relation between attitude change and long-term outcome, Jour Speech Hearing Disorders, 78. **CONTACT ADDRESS** Dept of Communication Sciences, Univ of Vermont, 360 Waterman Bldg, Burlington, VT 05405. **EMAIL** bguitar@zoo.uvm.edu

GULLASON, THOMAS ARTHUR

PERSONAL Born 07/01/1924, Watertown, MA, m, 1955, 1 child **DISCIPLINE** ENGLISH **EDUCATION** Suffolk Univ, BA, 48; Univ Wis, MA, 49, PhD, 53. **CAREER** Asst prof English, Heidelberg Col, 52-53; instr, Wis State Col, 53-54; from instr to assoc prof, 54-64, PROF ENGLISH, UNIV RI, 64-, Mem ed comt, Studies Short Fiction, 65-; Emer, 86. **HONORS AND AWARDS** Speaker at Univ Rhode Island's Honors Day, 63. **MEMBERSHIPS** MLA. **RESEARCH** Modern American literature; realism and naturalism; the short story. **SELECTED PUBLICATIONS** Auth, American Stories, Vol 2, Fiction from the Atlantic-Monthly, Stud in Short Fiction, Vol 0030, 93; Lardner, Ring and the Other, Am Lit, Vol 0065, 93; Prize Stories 1992--The O-Henry-Awards, Stud in Short Fiction, Vol 0030, 93; The Best American Short-Stories 1992, Stud in Short Fiction, Vol 0030, 93; Contemporary New-England Stories, Stud in Short Fiction, Vol 0031, 94; Currentgarcia, Eugene--In-Memoriam, Stud in Short Fiction, Vol 0032, 95; Crane, Stephen and the 'New York Tribune'--A Case Reopened, Rsrcs for Am Lit Stud, Vol 0022, 96; auth, Stephen Crane's Literary Family: A Garland of Writings, Syracuse Univ Pr, 01. **CONTACT ADDRESS** 125 Linden Dr, Kingston, RI 02881-1729.

GUMBRECHT, HANS ULRICH

PERSONAL Born 06/15/1948, Wurzburg, Germany, m, 1989, 4 children **DISCIPLINE** LITERARY THEORY; ROMANCE LITERATURES **EDUCATION** Univ Konstanz, Germany, Phd, 74. **CAREER** Prof, Univ Bochum, 75-82; prof, Univ Siegen, 83-89; prof, Stanford Univ, 89-. **HONORS AND AWARDS** Albert Guerard Prof of Lit; Amer Acad of Arts & Sci; Walker Ames Prof, Univ Washington; Cuthbertson Awd, Stanford Univ, 00. **MEMBERSHIPS** MLA **RESEARCH** Medieval Culture; Contemporary Culture; Philosophical Aesthetics. **SELECTED PUBLICATIONS** Auth, On 1926. Living at the Edge of Time, Harvard Univ Press, 98; auth, Corpo eforma, Rio de Janeiro, 98; auth, A Modernizacao dos Sentidos, Sa Paulo, 98; auth, Per una epistemologia della presenza, Milano, 01. **CONTACT ADDRESS** Dept of Comparative Literature, Stanford Univ, Stanford, CA 94305. **EMAIL** sepp@stanford-jc.or.jp

GUNDY, JEFFREY G.

PERSONAL Born 08/07/1952, Bloomington, IL, m, 1973, 3 children **DISCIPLINE** ENGLISH, CREATIVE WRITING **EDUCATION** Goshen Col, BA, 75; Ind Univ, MA, 76; PhD, 83. **CAREER** Instr, Hesston Col, 80-84; prof, Bluffton Col, 84-. **HONORS AND AWARDS** C. Henry Smith Peace Lectrshp, 99, 89; Ohio Arts Coun 88, 91, 96, 99; White River Writer's Conf, 95. **MEMBERSHIPS** NCTE, MLA, Poets and Writers. **RESEARCH** Poetry; creative nonfiction; family history; landscape; depression; surrealism; Midwest. **SELECTED PUBLICATIONS** Auth, Surrendering to the Real Things, Pikestaff Press (88); auth, Inquiries, Bottom Dog Press (92); auth, Flatlands, U IL Press (95); auth, A Community of Memory, Bottom God Press (96); auth, Rhapsody with Dark Matter, Cleveland State U Poetry Center (00). **CONTACT ADDRESS** English Dept., Bluffton Col, 280 W College Ave, Bluffton, OH 45817. **EMAIL** gundyj@bluffton.edu

GUNN, GILES

PERSONAL Born 01/09/1938, Evanston, IL, m, 1983, 2 children **DISCIPLINE** AMERICAN LITERATURE, LITERARY THEORY, GLOBAL STUDIES **EDUCATION** Univ Chicago, PhD, 67. **CAREER** Prof, Eng, Global Studies, Univ Calif Santa Barbara. **HONORS AND AWARDS** John Simon Guggenheim fel, 77-78; Univ of California Pres Research fel, 80; Nat Endowment for the Humanities Summer Seminars, 79,87,85,88,99; Phi Beta Kappa, Nat Endowment for the Humanities fel,90. **RESEARCH** Lit and relig; Am lit; Lit theory and critic; Am cult and relig stud. **SELECTED PUBLICATIONS** Auth, F.O. Matthiessen: The Critical Achievement, Univ Wash Press, 75; The Interpretation of Otherness: Literature, Religion, and the American Imagination, Oxford Univ Press, 79; The Culture of Criticism and the Criticism of Culture, Oxford Univ Press, 87; Thinking Across the American Grain: Ideology, Intellect, and the New Pragmatism, Univ Chicago Press, 92; co-ed, Redrawing the Boundaries: The Transformation of English and American Literary Studies, Mod Lang Assn, 92; ed, Early American Writing, Penguin, 94. **CONTACT ADDRESS** Dept of Eng, Univ of California, Santa Barbara, Santa Barbara, CA 93106-7150. **EMAIL** ggunn@humanitas.ucsb.edu

GUNZERATH, DAVID

DISCIPLINE MEDIA HISTORY **EDUCATION** La Salle Col, PABS, 81; Temple Univ, IAMA, 84, Univ Iowa, Phd, 97. **CAREER** Hist, Old Dominion Univ; Nat Asn of Broadcasters. **HONORS AND AWARDS** Donald and Geraldine Hedberg Foundation Fel Awd; Broadcast Educ Asn (BEA) 1st place Paper winner for hist division, 97 **MEMBERSHIPS** Broadcast Educ Asn; NATPE Educ Div; Popular Cult Asn; Speech Comm Asn. **RESEARCH** Media Industries and Institutions; Media Law and Policy; Television Programming; Marketing and Management; New Technologies; TV Criticism. **SELECTED PUBLICATIONS** Auth, Encyclopedia of Television, Fitzroy Dearborn, 97. **CONTACT ADDRESS** Nat Asn of Broadcasters, 1771 N St NW, Washington, DC 20036. **EMAIL** dgunzerath@nab.org

GURAK, LAURA J.

DISCIPLINE RHETORIC STUDIES **EDUCATION** St Rose Col, BA, 89; Rensselaer Polytech Inst, MS, 90; PhD, 94. **CAREER** Assoc prof **HONORS AND AWARDS** Distinguished Tchg Awd, 97. **RESEARCH** Rhetoric of science and technology; rhetorical criticism; classical rhetorical theory; computer-mediated communication; social aspects of computing; intellectual property and electronic texts; technical and professional communication. **SELECTED PUBLICATIONS** Auth, Persuasion and Privacy in Cyberspace: The Online Protests over Lotus MarketPlace and the Clipper Chip, Yale, 97; Persuasion and Privacy (rev), Minn Daily's Arts. **CONTACT ADDRESS** Rhetoric Dept, Univ of Minnesota, Twin Cities, 64 Classroom Office Bldg, 1994 Buford Ave, Saint Paul, MN 55108. **EMAIL** gurakl@tc.umn.edu

GURALNICK, ELISSA SCHAGRIN

PERSONAL Born 03/04/1949, Philadelphia, PA, m, 1969, 2 children **DISCIPLINE** ENGLISH LITERATURE **EDUCATION** Univ Pa, AB & AM, 69; Yale Univ, MPhil, 71, PhD(English), 73. **CAREER** Asst prof, 73-79, assoc prof, 79-86, prof English, Univ Colo, Boulder, 86-. **HONORS AND AWARDS** Fellowship, Howard Foundation, 91-92. **MEMBERSHIPS** MLA. **RESEARCH** Modern and contemporary drama. **SELECTED PUBLICATIONS** Auth, Archimagical fireworks: The function of light imagery in Browning's Sordello, Victorian Poetry, 75; contribr, Improving student writing: A case history, Col English, 77; auth, Radical politics in Mary Wollstonecraft's A Vindication of The Rights of Woman, Studies in Burke and His Time, 77; The new segregation: A recent history of EOP at the University of Colorado, Boulder, Col English, 78; Contribr, Allusion and Meaning in A Woman of No Importance, Eire-Ireland, 78; auth, Rhetorical Strategy in Mary Wollstonecraft's A Vindication of the Rights of Woman, The Humanities Asn Review, 79; Radio Drama: The Stage of the Mind, Virginia Quart, 85; Artist Descending a Staircase: Stoppard Captures the Radio Station and Duchamp, PMLA 90; Sight Unseen: Beckett, Pinter, Stoppard, and Other Contemporary Dramatists on Radio, Athens: Ohio Univ Press, 96; co auth, The Weighty

Word Book, Court Wayne Press, 00; co auth, How Raven Found the Daylight, Univ Press of Colorado, 00. **CONTACT ADDRESS** Univ of Colorado, Boulder, Box 226, Boulder, CO 80309-0226. **EMAIL** elissa.guralnick@colorado.edu

GURUSWAMY, ROSEMARY
DISCIPLINE EARLY AMERICAN LITERATURE AND AFRICAN-AMERICAN LITERATURE **EDUCATION** Univ MD, MA; Kent State Univ, PhD. **CAREER** Prof, Radford Univ. **MEMBERSHIPS** Pres, Soc of Early Americanists. **RESEARCH** Anne Bradstreet's poetry. **SELECTED PUBLICATIONS** Publ var articles in Early Am Lit, New Eng Quart, and Stud in Puritan Am Spirituality. **CONTACT ADDRESS** Radford Univ, Radford, VA 24142. **EMAIL** rguruswa@runet.edu

GURVAL, ROBERT ALAN
PERSONAL Born 08/02/1958, Kingston, PA **DISCIPLINE** CLASSICS **EDUCATION** Brown Univ, BA, 80; Univ Calif Santa Barbara, MA, 82; Univ Calif Berkeley, PhD, 88. **CAREER** Lectr, 88-89; asst prof, Univ Ore, 89-90; asst prof, 90-96; ASSOC PROF, UCLA, 96-, chair, 00-. **HONORS AND AWARDS** Fel, Am Acad at Rome, 96-97; UCLA Honors Prog, Distinguished Teacher Awd, 00. **MEMBERSHIPS** APA; Am Numis Soc. **RESEARCH** Roman history; Latin literature; Roman coinage. **SELECTED PUBLICATIONS** Auth, Actium and Augustus, Mich, 96. **CONTACT ADDRESS** Dept of Classics, Univ of California, Los Angeles, Dodd 100, Los Angeles, CA 90095-1417. **EMAIL** gurval@humnet.ucla.edu

GUSHEE, LAWRENCE
DISCIPLINE MUSIC **EDUCATION** Yale Univ, PhD. **CAREER** Prof emer, 77-, Univ IL Urgana Champaign. **RESEARCH** Medieval music in Europ libr(s); early hist of jazz and related musics. **SELECTED PUBLICATIONS** Auth, Nineteenth-century Origins of Jazz, Black Music Res, 94. **CONTACT ADDRESS** Dept of Music, Univ of Illinois, Urbana-Champaign, E Gregory Dr, PO Box 52, Champaign, IL 61820. **EMAIL** lgushee@staff.uiuc.edu

GUSS, DONALD LEROY
PERSONAL Born 07/21/1929, New York, NY, m, 1960, 3 children **DISCIPLINE** ENGLISH LITERATURE **EDUCATION** City Col New York, BA, 50; Columbia Univ, MA, 52; Univ Wis, PhD, 61. **CAREER** Instr, Boston Col, 59-60; instr, Rutgers Univ, 60-63, res grant, 62-63; assoc prof, Wayne State Univ, 63-68; PROF ENGLISH AND CHMN DEPT, UNIV CALIF, SANTA BARBARA, 68-, Hungtington Libr grant, 63. **MEMBERSHIPS** MLA; Renaissance Soc Am; Am Asn Teachers Ital. **RESEARCH** Seventeenth century English; Renaissance Italian literature. **SELECTED PUBLICATIONS** Auth, The Power of Selfhood--Shakespeare 'Hamlet', Milton 'Samson,' Modern Lang Quart, Vol 0054, 93. **CONTACT ADDRESS** Dept of English, Univ of California, Santa Barbara, Santa Barbara, CA 93106.

GUSTAFSON, SANDRA
DISCIPLINE AMERICAN LITERATURE **EDUCATION** Univ Calif, Berkeley, PhD. **CAREER** Assoc prof, Univ Notre Dame. **HONORS AND AWARDS** Newcombe fel; Early Am Hist Asn fel, 94-96. **RESEARCH** Colonial to 19th-century American literature and culture, performance theory with emphasis on gender, ethnicity, and postcolonialism. **SELECTED PUBLICATIONS** Published an essay on Margaret Fuller and Jonathan Edwards. **CONTACT ADDRESS** Dept of English, Univ of Notre Dame, 277 Decio Fac Hall, Notre Dame, IN 46556. **EMAIL** sandra.m.gustafson.6@nd.edu

GUTHRIE, JAMES ROBERT
PERSONAL Born 05/05/1951, Ann Arbor, MI, m, 1980 **DISCIPLINE** AMERICAN LITERATURE **EDUCATION** Univ Mich, BA, 73; State Univ NYork Buffalo, MFA, 74, MA, 76, PhD(English), 79. **CAREER** ASST PROF ENGLISH, NORTH CENTRAL COL, 79-. **RESEARCH** Modern poetry; creative writing. **SELECTED PUBLICATIONS** Auth, Measuring the Sun, Dickinson, Emily Interpretation of her Optical Illness, Esq-J Am Renaissance, Vol 0041, 95; A Revolution in Locality, Astronomical Tropes in Dickinson, Emily Poetry, Midwest Quart-J Contemp Thought, Vol 0037, 96. **CONTACT ADDRESS** Dept of Eng, Wright State Univ, Dayton, Dayton, OH 45435.

GUTIERREZ, DONALD
PERSONAL Born 03/10/1932, Alameda, CA, m, 1953, 2 children **DISCIPLINE** MODERN BRITISH LITERATURE, NOVEL **EDUCATION** Univ Calif, Berkeley, BA, 56, MLS, 58; Univ Calif, Los Angeles, MA, 66, PhD(English), 68. **CAREER** Ref librn, Metrop Mus Art Libr, New York, 58-60; res and asst head librn, Tamiment Inst Libr, New York, 60-61; res librn, Grosset and Dunlap Bk Publ, 61-64; asst prof English, Univ Notre Dame, 68-75; asst prof, 75-79, ASSOC PROF ENGLISH, WESTERN NMEX UNIV, 80-. **MEMBERSHIPS** Rocky Mountain Mod Lang Asn; D H Lawrence Soc Am. **RESEARCH** D H Lawrence; Anthony Powell. **SELECTED PUBLICATIONS** Auth, World Outside the Window--The Selected Essays of Rexroth, Kenneth, Western Am Lit, Vol 0027, 92; An Autobiographical Novel, Western Am Lit, Vol 0027, 92; 'Flower Wreath Hill'--Later Poems, Western Am Lit, Vol 0027, 92; A Life of Rexroth, Kenneth, Lit Rev, Vol 0037, 93; Johnson, Spud and 'Laughing Horse,' D H Lawrence Rev, Vol 0025, 94; Rexroth 'Incartion,' Explicator, Vol 0053, 95. **CONTACT ADDRESS** Dept of English, Western New Mexico Univ, Silver City, NM 88061.

GUTIERREZ-JONES, CARL
PERSONAL Born 02/22/1960, Cheverly, MD, m, 1989, 2 children **DISCIPLINE** AMERICAN LITERATURE **EDUCATION** Stanford Univ, BA, 82; PhD, Cornell Univ, PhD, 91. **CAREER** Assoc prof, English Univ of Calif, Santa Barbara: acting dir, Center for Chicano Stuides. **HONORS AND AWARDS** Calif policy grant, 92-; Ford Foundation Post-Doctoral Fel, 93; Harold Plous Awd, UCSB, 94. **RESEARCH** Chicano stud; contemp fiction; Pan-American stud; multiculturalism. **SELECTED PUBLICATIONS** Auth, "Provisional Historicity: Reading Through Terra Nostra," Rev of Contemp Fiction, 88; "Legal Rhetoric and Cultural Critique: Notes Toward Guerilla Writing," Diacritics, 90; Rethinking the Borderlands: Between Chicano Narrative and Legal Discourse, Univ Calif Press, 95; auth, "Injury by Design," Cultural Critique 40, (98): 73-102; auth, " The New Western History: Theory and Trauma in the Work of Patricia Limerick," Arizona Quarterly 53:2, 97; auth, "Desiring B/orders," diatrics 25.1 (95): 99-112; auth, "Affirmative Action and Diversity: A Web Site for Reseach," (http://aad,english,ucsb,edu). **CONTACT ADDRESS** Dept of Eng, Univ of California, Santa Barbara, Santa Barbara, CA 93106-7150. **EMAIL** carlgj@humanitas.ucsb.edu

GUTIERREZ-VEGA, ZENAIDA
PERSONAL Born 06/23/1924, Union del Reyes, Cuba **DISCIPLINE** SPANISH, SPANISH AMERICAN LITERATURE **EDUCATION** Inst Sec Educ, Matanzas, Cuba, BA, 45; Univ Havana, PhD(Span lit), 50; Univ Madrid, PhD(Romance philol), 66. **CAREER** Prof Span & lit, Inst Sec Educ Velado, Havana, 52-62; prof, Univ Las Villas, Cuba, 59-62; asst prof Span & Span Am lit, Univ Mo, St Louis, 67-68; asst prof, State Univ NY Col Oswego, 68-72; Prof Span, Hunter Col, 72-; Mem, Ministry Educ, Cuba, 56-57; mem, Inst Hisp Cult, Madrid, 62-66. **HONORS AND AWARDS** Lit Prize, Inst Hisp Cult, Madrid, 66; Summa cum Laude, 66; fel, Inst de Cultura Hispanica, 62-67; PSC-CUNY grants, 84, 85, 87. **MEMBERSHIPS** MLA; Am Asn Teachers Span & Port. **RESEARCH** Hispanic American literature; poets, essayists, novelists of the twentieth century of Spain and Latin America. **SELECTED PUBLICATIONS** Auth, Jose Maria Chacon y Calvo, Hispanista Cubano, Ediciones Cultura Hispanica, 69; auth, Epistolario Alfonso Reyes-Jose Ma. Chacon, Fundacion Universitaria Espanola, 76; auth, Estudio Bibliografico de Jose Ma. Chacon, Fundacion Universitaria Espanola, 82; auth, Fernando Ortiz en sus Cartas a Jose Ma. Chacon, Fundacion Universitaria Espanola, 82; auth, Corresponsales Espanoles de Jose Ma. Chacon, Fundacion Universitaria Espanola, 86; auth, Carmen Conde: de Viva Voz, Senda Nueva de Ediciones, 92. **CONTACT ADDRESS** 220 E 63rd St, Apt 4L, New York, NY 10021.

GUTMAN, STANLEY T.
PERSONAL Born 12/24/1943, m, 2 children **DISCIPLINE** ENGLISH **EDUCATION** Hamilton Col, AB, 65; Duke Univ, PhD, 71. **CAREER** Prof English Chr Dept of English, Univ Vermont; Fulbright fel; Salzburg fel; vis speaker USIS. **MEMBERSHIPS** MLA. **RESEARCH** Modern poetry. **SELECTED PUBLICATIONS** Auth Mankind in Barbary: The Individual and Society in the Novels of Norman Mailer, Univ Press NE, 75; ed Technologies of the Self: A Seminar with Michel Foucault, Univ Mass Press, 88; As Others Read Us: International Perspectives on American Literature, Univ Mass Press, 91; coauth Outsider in the House, Verso, 97. **CONTACT ADDRESS** Dept of English, Univ of Vermont, PO Box 54030, Burlington, VT 05405-4030. **EMAIL** sgutman@zoo.uvm.edu

GUTTENBERG, BARNETT
PERSONAL Born 12/10/1937, Boston, MA, m, 1967, 1 child **DISCIPLINE** MODERN AMERICAN AND SOUTHERN LITERATURE **EDUCATION** Columbia Univ, BA, 59; Cornell Univ, MA, 66, PhD(English), 71. **CAREER** Asst prof Am lit, Vanderbilt Univ, 67-74; asst pref, 74-77, ASSOC PROF AM LIT, UNIV MIAMI, 77-. **MEMBERSHIPS** MLA. **RESEARCH** William Faulkner; Southern literature. **SELECTED PUBLICATIONS** Auth, Web of Being: The Novels of Robert Penn Warren, Vanderbilt Univ, 75; The Pattern of redemption in Dickey's Deliverance, Critique, 77; Sylvia Plath, myth, and The Hanging Man, Contemp Poetry, 78; Conrad's women, Conrad Newslett, 78; contribr, Sylvia Plath: A Reconsideration, Johns Hopkins (in press). **CONTACT ADDRESS** Univ of Miami, Coral Gables, FL 33124.

GUTTMAN, NAOMI E.
PERSONAL Born 07/10/1960, Montreal, PQ, Canada **DISCIPLINE** ENGLISH, CREATIVE WRITING **EDUCATION** Concordia Univ, BFA, 85; Warren Wilson Col, MFA, 88; Univ S Calif LA, PhD, 99. **CAREER** Asst Prof English, Hamilton Col, 96-. **HONORS AND AWARDS** Bliss Carman Awd Lyric Poetry, 89; QSPELL (A.M. Klein) Awd, 92; Canada Council Grant, 00. **RESEARCH** Poetry, feminist criticism, postcolonial literature, environmental literature. **SELECTED PUBLICATIONS** Auth, Reasons for Winter, 91. **CONTACT ADDRESS** Dept of English, Hamilton Col, New York, 198 College Hill Rd, Clinton, NY 13323.

GUTZWILLER, KATHRYN
PERSONAL Born 09/25/1948, Hinton, WV, m, 1971, 1 child **DISCIPLINE** CLASSICS **EDUCATION** Marshall Univ, BA, 70; Bryn Mawr Col, MA, 71; Univ of Wis Madison, PhD, 77. **CAREER** Asst to assoc prof, Case Western Reserve, 86-89; asst prof to prof, Univ of Cincinnati, 78-85, 89-. **HONORS AND AWARDS** Gildersleeve Prize, Am Jour of Philol, 92; McMicken Dean's Awd, 99; Charles J. Goodwin Awd of Merit, Am Philog Assoc, 01. **MEMBERSHIPS** Am Philol Assoc, Classical Assoc of Middle West and South, Ohio Classical Conf. **RESEARCH** Greek and Latin Poetry, Women in Antiquity and Gender Studies, Literary Theory. **SELECTED PUBLICATIONS** Auth, Studies in the Hellenistics Epyllion, 81; auth, "The Lorer and the Lena: Propertius 4.5," Ramus, (85); auth, "Women and Other Strangers: Feminist Perspectives in Classical Literature," (En)gendering Knowledge, (91); auth, Theocritus' Pastoral Analogirds: the Formation of a Genre, Madison, 91; auth, "Callimachus' Lock of Berenice," Am Jour of Philol, (92); auth, "The Evidence for Theocritein Poetry Books," Hellenistica Groningana 2, (96); auth, "The Poetics of Editing in Melenger's Garland," Transactions of Am Philol Assoc, (97); auth, Poetic Garlands: Hellenistic Epigrams in Context, Berkeley, 98; auth, "The Tragic Mask of Comedy: Metatheatricality in Menender," Classical Antiquity, (00). **CONTACT ADDRESS** Dept Classics, Univ of Cincinnati, Cincinnati, OH 45221-0226. **EMAIL** kathryn.gutzwiller@uc.edu

GUZMAN-MERCED, ROSA MARIA
PERSONAL Born 12/06/1954, Puerto Rico, m, 1974, 1 child **DISCIPLINE** BUSINESS COMMUNICATION, SPANISH **EDUCATION** Univ Puerto Rico, BA, 76; PhD, 96; Univ Paris, MA, 81. **CAREER** Head, CPN, 85-96; asst to assoc prof, Univ Puerto Rico, 96-. **HONORS AND AWARDS** Who's Who Among America's Teachers, 94, 96; Fel, AAUW, 95; Premio Luis Llorens Torres, 96. **MEMBERSHIPS** MLA, AAUW, AATSP, LASA. **RESEARCH** Autobiography, cultural studies, communication. **SELECTED PUBLICATIONS** Coauth, Historia y geografia de Puerto Rico, Serie Norma Estudios Sociales, (Colombia), 99; auth, Las narraciones autobiograficas puertoriquenas, Publicaciones Puertorrequenas, (San Juan), 00. **CONTACT ADDRESS** calle 7 F-21, Riberas del Rio, Bayamon, PR 00959. **EMAIL** miromi@coqui.net

H

HAAHR, JOAN GLUCKAUF
PERSONAL Born 01/18/1940, New York, NY, m, 1963, 3 children **DISCIPLINE** MEDIEVAL LITERATURE **EDUCATION** Univ Copenhagen, 61-62; Harpur Col (SUNY), BA 61; MA, 63, PhD, 70, Harvard Univ. **CAREER** Prof, Chr Dept English, Yeshiva Univ, 69-. **HONORS AND AWARDS** NEH Summer Seminar, 89; Danforth Fdn Fel, 78-84; NEH Summer Stipend, 70; Woodrow Wilson Fel, 62-63; Fulbright Grant, 61-62. **MEMBERSHIPS** AAUP, Yeshiva Univ (Chapter Pres); MLA; Medieval Acad; Harvard Grad School Alumni Assoc; Soc for Medieval Feminist Scholarship **RESEARCH** Medieval literature **SELECTED PUBLICATIONS** Auth; Criseyde's Inner Debate: The Dialectic of Enamorment in the Filostrato and the Troilus, Studies in Philology, 92; auth, Justifying Love: The Classical Recusatio in Medieval Love Literature, Desiring Discourse: The Literature of Love, Ovid Through Chaucer, 98; auth, The Princess and the Pea, The Red Shoes, The Snow Queen, The Steadfast Tin Soldier, Oxford Companion to Fairy Tales, 99. **CONTACT ADDRESS** Dept of English, Yeshiva Univ, 500 W 185 St, New York, NY 10033. **EMAIL** haahr@ymail.yu.edu

HAAPANEN, LAWRENCE W.
PERSONAL Born 04/24/1945, Seattle, WA, m, 1972, 2 children **DISCIPLINE** POLITCAL COMMUNICATION **EDUCATION** Univ Wash, BA, 67; Wash State Univ, MA, 72, PhD, 74. **CAREER** Instr/asst prof, Utah State Univ, 76-81; asst to assoc, Baker Univ, 81-87; assoc to full prof, Lewis-Clark State Col, 87-. **HONORS AND AWARDS** NEH Summer Fel, 80. **MEMBERSHIPS** Int Soc of Political Psychology. **RESEARCH** Political communication, propaganda. **SELECTED PUBLICATIONS** Auth, "The Missed Opportunity: The U-2 and Paris," in Eisenhower's War of Words, Mich State Univ Press (94); contribur, The Encyclopedia of Propaganda, M. E. Sharpe (98); contribur, The Sixties in America, Salem Press (99). **CONTACT ADDRESS** Div Fine & Performing Arts, Lewis-Clark State Col, 500 8th Ave, Lewiston, ID 83501-2691. **EMAIL** haapanen@lcsc.edu

HAAR, JAMES
PERSONAL Born 07/04/1929, St. Louis, MO **DISCIPLINE** HISTORY OF MUSIC **EDUCATION** Harvard Univ, BA, 50, PhD(music), 61; Univ NC, MA, 54. **CAREER** From instr to

asst prof music, Harvard Univ, 60-67; assoc prof, Univ Pa, 67-69; prof, NY Univ, 69-78; W R Kenan JR Prof Music, Univ NC, 78-, Villa I Tatti fel music, 65; Am Coun Learned Soc fel, 73. **MEMBERSHIPS** Am Musicol Soc (vpres, 72-74, pres, 76-78); Renaissance Soc Am. **RESEARCH** Italian Madrigal; history of theory; humanism and music. **SELECTED PUBLICATIONS** Ed, Chanson & Madrigal, 1480-1530, Harvard Univ, 64; auth, The Note Nere Madrigal, J Am Musicol Soc, 65; Pace non Troro: A study in literary and musical parody, Musica Disciplina, 66; Classicism & mannerism in 16th century music, Int Rev Music Aesthet & Sociol, 70; Pythagorean harmony of the Universe, In: Dictionary of the History of Ideas, 73; Some remarks on the Missa la sol fa re mi, Josouin des prez, 76; Chromaticism & false relations in 16th century music, J Am Musicol Soc, 77; co-ed, The Duos of Gero, Broude Bros, 78. **CONTACT ADDRESS** Dept of Music, Univ of No Carolina, Chapel Hill, Chapel Hill, NC 27514.

HAARBAUER, DON WARD
PERSONAL Born 09/17/1940, Charleroi, PA, m, 1964, 2 children **DISCIPLINE** THEATRE HISTORY **EDUCATION** Univ Ala, Tuscaloosa, BS, 62, MA, 65; Univ Wis, Madison PhD(theatre), 73. **CAREER** Asst prof speech & theatre, 68-73, asst dean sch humanities, 73-75, asst prof theatre, 73-77, chmn performing arts, 73-81, assoc prof, 77-80, prof theatre, Univ Ala, Birmingham, 80-, assoc dean sch arts & humanities, 81-, dir, Horn in the West, Boone, NC, 67-71. **MEMBERSHIPS** Southeastern Theatre Conf (admin vpres, 77-79, vpres, 79-80, pres, 80-81). **RESEARCH** Pre-twentieth century English theatre. **SELECTED PUBLICATIONS** Auth, The Birmingham theatres of Frank O'Brien, Southern Theatre, summer 77. **CONTACT ADDRESS** Univ of Alabama, Birmingham, 301 Humanities Bldg, Birmingham, AL 35294-1260. **EMAIL** whaar@uab.edu

HABA, JAMES
DISCIPLINE POETRY, FICTION, AND WORLD LITERATURE **EDUCATION** Reed Col, BA; Cornell Univ, PhD. **CAREER** Instr, Rowan Col NJ; poetry coordr, Geraldine R Dodge Found. **SELECTED PUBLICATIONS** Ed, The Language of Life, 95. **CONTACT ADDRESS** Rowan Univ, Glassboro, NJ 08028-1701.

HABIB, IMITIAZ
PERSONAL Born 07/11/1949, Dhaka, Bangladesh, m, 1978, 2 children **DISCIPLINE** ENGLISH **EDUCATION** Oxford Univ, BA, 73; MA, 75; Ind Univ, PhD, 84. **CAREER** Assoc prof, Dhaka Univ, 73-89; vis prof, Ind Univ, 89-90; lecturer, Univ Nev, 90-95; asst prof to assoc prof, Old Dominion Univ, 95-00 **MEMBERSHIPS** Shakespeare Asn of Am, S Atl Mod Lang Asn, Intl Shakespeare Asn. **RESEARCH** Shakespeare, English Renaissance, Mod Drama, Postcolonial literature and theory. **SELECTED PUBLICATIONS** Auth, Shakespeare and Race: Postcolonial Praxis in the Early Modern Period, Univ Press of Am, 00; auth, "Hel's Perfect Character or the Blackamoor Maid in Early Modern English Drama: The Postcolonial Cultural History of a Dramatic Type," Literature Interpretation Theory, 00; auth, "Sir Peter Negro, Othello and the Lost Blacks of Elizabethan England: Colonial Inscription and Postcolonial Excavation," Literature Interpretation Theory, (98): 15-30; auth, "Demotic Desire and Female Subjectivity in David Mamet: The Split Space of the Women of Edmond," (forthcoming); auth, Reading Black Women Characters in English Renaissance Literature," Renaissance Papers, (96): 67-80; auth, "Interrogating Cultures: Hybridity as Third Space in V.S. Naipaul's A House for Mr. Biswas, R.K. Narayan's The Guide and Salman Rushdie's Midnight's Children," Studies in the Humanities, (96): 28-52; auth, Shakespeare's Pluralistic Concepts of Character: A Study in Dramatic Anamorphism, 93; auth, Tennessee Williams: A Descriptive Bibiliography, Univ Press, 85. **CONTACT ADDRESS** Dept English, Old Dominion Univ, Norfolk, VA 23529. **EMAIL** ihabib@odu.edu

HABIB, M. A. RAFEY
DISCIPLINE LITERARY THEORY, MODERN BRITISH LITERATURE, NON-WESTERN LITERATURE **EDUCATION** Oxford Univ, PhD. **CAREER** Instr, dir, Writing prog, Rutgers, State Univ NJ, Camden Col of Arts and Sci. **RESEARCH** T. S. Eliot; history of Western literary criticism, Urdu poetry. **SELECTED PUBLICATIONS** Auth, The Dissident Voice: Poems of N.M. Rashed: Translated from the Urdu, Oxford, 91; Classical Marxism, The Johns Hopkins Guide to Literary Theory, Johns Hopkins Univ Press, 93; Karl Marx, Friedrich Engels, Materialism, Antonio Gramsci, Gyorgy Lukas, Edward Said, Islamic Studies, The Blackwell Dictionary of Cultural and Critical Theory, Blackwell, 96; Aesthetics and Justice in Plato's Republic, Law and Literature: Perspectives, Peter Lang, 96; Bergson Resartus and T.S. Eliot's Manuscript, J of the Hist of Ideas; Horace's Ars Poetica and the Deconstructive Leech, Brit J of Aesthet; The Prayers of Childhood: T. S. Eliot's Manuscript on Kant, J of the Hist of Ideas. **CONTACT ADDRESS** Rutgers, The State Univ of New Jersey, New Brunswick, Camden Col of Arts and Sci, New Brunswick, NJ 08903-2101. **EMAIL** mhabib@camden.rutgers.edu

HABICH, ROBERT D.
PERSONAL Born 04/12/1951, Bay Shore, NY, m, 2 children **DISCIPLINE** ENGLISH **EDUCATION** State Univ NY (SUNY), BA, 73; Colo State Univ, MA, 76; Pa State Univ, PhD, 82. **CAREER** Instr, Pa State Univ, 81-84; From Asst Prof to Prof, Ball State Univ, 84-. **HONORS AND AWARDS** NEH Summer Stipend, 86. **MEMBERSHIPS** MLA, Thoreau Soc. **RESEARCH** New England Transcendentalism, textual editing, literary biography. **SELECTED PUBLICATIONS** Auth, Emerson's Reluctant Foe: Andrews Norton and the Transcendental Controversy," New England Quart 65(92): 208-237; auth, "William Henry Channing" and "Andrews Norton," in Biog Dict of Transcendentalism (Westport, CT: Greenwood Pr, 96), 40, 186-187; auth, "Emerson's Lives: An Essay Review," New England Quart 69 (96): 631-639; auth, "George Washington Harris," in Antebellum Writers of NY and the South (00): forthcoming. **CONTACT ADDRESS** Dept English, Ball State Univ, 2000 W University Ave, Muncie, IN 47306-1022.

HACKMAN, MICHAEL
PERSONAL Born 04/06/1960, Queens, NY, m, 2 children **DISCIPLINE** COMMUNICATION **EDUCATION** Univ Colo, BA; Univ Denver, MA, PhD. **CAREER** Vis sr lectr, Univ Waikato, New Zealand; prof; ch-. **HONORS AND AWARDS** CU-Colo Springs outstanding tchr award, 95; Who's Who Among America's Teachers, 98. **MEMBERSHIPS** Nat Commun Assoc; Int Commun Assoc. **RESEARCH** Impact of gender and culture on leadership behavior. **SELECTED PUBLICATIONS** Co-auth, Leadership: A Commun Perspective; Creative Commun; pub(s), Commun Edu, Commun Quart, Distance Edu, Journal of Leadership Studies, Perceptual and Motor Skills, S Speech Commun Jour. **CONTACT ADDRESS** Dept of Commun, Univ of Colorado, Colorado Springs, PO Box 7150, Colorado Springs, CO 80933-7150. **EMAIL** mhackman@mail.uccs.edu

HACKMANN, WILLIAM KENT
PERSONAL Born 08/12/1937, Denver, CO, m, 1960, 2 children **DISCIPLINE** ENGLISH AND MODERN EUROPEAN HISTORY **EDUCATION** Yale Univ, BA, 59; Univ Mich, MA, 62, PhD(hist), 69. **CAREER** Chm, Univ of Iowa, 84-85, 93-94, sec of Fac Council, 95-. **MEMBERSHIPS** Conf Brit Studies; AHA; Selden Soc Brit Mus Soc; Am Soc Eighteenth-Century Studies. **RESEARCH** High politics in eighteenth-century England; for the period 1788-1833 studies the effort of the West India interest in the British House of Commons to block legislation. **CONTACT ADDRESS** Dept of Hist, Univ of Idaho, Administration Bldg 315, Moscow, ID 83844. **EMAIL** hackmann@uidaho.edu

HADAS, RACHEL
PERSONAL Born 11/08/1948, New York, NY, m, 1978, 1 child **DISCIPLINE** ENGLISH **EDUCATION** Radcliffe Col, BA, 69; Johns Hopkins Univ, MA, 77; Princeton Univ, PhD, 82. **CAREER** Prof, Rutgers, 81-. **HONORS AND AWARDS** Guggenheim Fel, 88-89; Ingram Merrill Foundation Grants, 77-78, 84-86; Literature award, Am Acad - Inst of Arts and Letters, 90. **SELECTED PUBLICATIONS** Auth, Living in Time, 90; auth, Unending dialogue: voices from an AIDS Poetry Workshop, 91; auth, Mirrors of Astonishment, 92; auth, Other Worlds than This, 94; auth, The Empty Bed, 95; auth, The double Legacy 95; auth, Halfway down the Hall: New and Selected Poems, 88; auth, Merrill, Cavafy, Poems, and Dreams, forthcoming; auth, Indelible, forthcoming; trans, "Oedipus the King" by Seneca, Johns Hopkins Univ Press, 94; trans, "Helen", by Euripides, Univ of Penn Press, 97. **CONTACT ADDRESS** Dept English, Rutgers, The State Univ of New Jersey, Newark, Hill Hall 520, Newark, NJ 07102-1803. **EMAIL** rhadas@andromeda.rutgers.edu

HAEGERT, JOHN
DISCIPLINE TWENTIETH CENTURY ENGLISH LITERATURE **EDUCATION** Univ Chicago, PhD. **CAREER** Vis assoc prof, Univ Paris IV-Sorbonne; prof. **SELECTED PUBLICATIONS** Auth, scholarly articles on twentieth century British and American literary figures; pub(s), S Rev, Contemp Lit, Mod Philol, Criticism. **CONTACT ADDRESS** Dept of Eng, Univ of Evansville, 1800 Lincoln Ave, Evansville, IN 47714. **EMAIL** jh52@evansville.edu.

HAGEMAN, ELIZABETH H.
PERSONAL Born 05/20/1941, Vancouver, BC, Canada **DISCIPLINE** ENGLISH LITERATURE **EDUCATION** Simmons Col, BS, 63; Columbia Univ, MA, 64; Univ NC, PhD, 71. **CAREER** Instr English, Colby Jr Col, 64-65 & Col William & Mary, 65-68; asst prof English, 71-77, assoc prof English, 77-87, prof English, 87-, Univ NH, 78-. **HONORS AND AWARDS** Fel frp, Folger Shakespeare Libr, Newberry Libr, Am Philos Soc, ACLS, NEH. **MEMBERSHIPS** Soc Study of Early Mod Women, Renaissance Soc Am, Shakepeare Asn Am, Mod Lang Asn, Renaissance Eng Text Soc. **RESEARCH** Recent studies in Renaissance literature, English Lit Renaissance **SELECTED PUBLICATIONS** Auth, Robert Herrick: A Reference Guide, G K Hall, 82; art early mod women writers, Katherine Philips, Richard Crashaw. **CONTACT ADDRESS** Dept English, Univ of New Hampshire, Durham, Durham, NH 03824. **EMAIL** ehageman@christa.unh.edu

HAGEN, PATRICIA
PERSONAL Born Colorado Springs, CO, m, 1985, 1 child **DISCIPLINE** ENGLISH **EDUCATION** Va Commonwealth Univ, BA, 74; Western Ill Univ, MA, 75; Univ Kans, PhD, 84. **CAREER** Grad Asst, Western Ill Univ, 74-75; Instr, Ill Central Col, 75-76; Grad Teaching Asst, Univ Kan, 76-78; Instr, Iowa State Univ, 78-84; Adj Asst Prof, Univ Kan, 84-87; Asst Prof, Univ Wis, 87-89; Asst Prof, Univ Minn, 89-90; Assoc Prof, Col of St Scholastica, 90-. **HONORS AND AWARDS** Phi Kappa Phi, 75; NEH Fel, Ireland, 93. **MEMBERSHIPS** ACIS, MMLA, IASIL. **RESEARCH** Irish literature poetry and drama, cross cultural elements in business communication. **SELECTED PUBLICATIONS** Auth, "Astrology, Schema and Lawrence's Poetic Method," D H Lawrence Rev, 22.1 (90): 23-37; auth, "Revision Revisited: Another Look at the 'French Lieutenant's Woman'," Col English, 53.4 (91): 439-451; auth, "We Were Never on the Scene of the Crime: Eavan Boland's Reclamation of History," Twentieth-Century Lit, 37.4 (91): 442-453; auth, Metaphor's Way of Knowing: The Poetry of D H Lawrence and the Church of Mechanism, Peter Lang Publ (New York, NY), 95; auth, "Gil's World," J of Popular Cult, 31.3 (97): 47-54; auth, "Teaching American Business Writing in Russia: Cross Cultures/Cross Purposes," J of Bus and Tech Commun, 12.1 (98): 109-126; auth, "Eavan Boland's Haunted Objects," A Vanishing Border: Feminist Remappings of Mod Anglo/Irish Lit (forthcoming). **CONTACT ADDRESS** Dept English, Col of St. Scholastica, 1200 Kenwood Ave, Duluth, MN 55811-4199. **EMAIL** phagen@css.edu

HAGER, ALAN
PERSONAL Born 02/18/1940, New York, NY, s, 2 children **DISCIPLINE** ENGLISH **EDUCATION** Harvard Col, MA, 62; Univ Calif, Berkeley, MA, 70; PhD, 78. **CAREER** Instr, Univ of Okla, 77-79; asst prof, Loyola Univ, 79-88; vis lectr, Univ of IL Chicago, 89-93; asst prof to prof, SUNY Cortland, 93-. **HONORS AND AWARDS** Outstanding Humanities Teacher, Loyola Univ, 86; Newberry Libr Fel, 89; Nominee Silver Circle Awd, Univ of IL, 92, 93; PDQWL Awd, SUNY Cortland, 93. **MEMBERSHIPS** Int Soc for Neoplatonic Studies, Mod Lang Assoc., Midwest Mod Lang Assoc., Milton Socs, Renaissance Soc of Am, Sixteenth-Century Studies Assoc., Fr Colonial Hist Soc. **RESEARCH** Prose creative writing, Renaissance literature, Shakespeare, Seventeenth-Century prose and poetry, British literature, modern drama and poetry. **SELECTED PUBLICATIONS** Auth, Shakespeare's Political Animal: Schema and Schemata in the Canon, Univ of Del Pr, (Newark), 90; auth, Dazzling Images: The Masks of Sir Philip Sidney, Univ of Del Pr, (Newark), 91; auth, "Castiglione's Bembo: Yoking Eros and Thanatos by Containment in Book four of il Cortegiano", Can J of Ital Studies 16, (93); 33-47; auth, "The Silent Order Conspiracy in Composition Instruction: A Drydenic Satirical Essay", Composition Chronicle 7.8, (94); 8-9; auth, "Copernicus", "John Skelton", Major Tudor Authors: A Bio-Critical Sourcebook, ed Alan Hager, Greenwood Pr, (Westport, 97); ed, Major Tudor Authors: A bio-Bibliographical Critical Sorucebook, Greenwood Pr, (Westport, CT), 97; auth, "Lear's Fool", Jesters and Clowns: A Bio-Critical Sourcebook, ed Vicki Janik, Greenwood Pr, (Westport, 98); auth, Understanding Romeo and Juliet: A Student Casebook to Issues, Sources, and Historic Documents, Lit in Context Series, Greenwood Pr, (Westport, CT), 99; auth, auth, Major Seventeenth Century British and American Authors: A Bio-Bibliographical Critical Sourcebook, Greenwood Pr, (Westport, CT), 00; auth, "Sir Philip Sidney", Encycl of the Renaissance, ed Michael JB Allen, Scribners, (NY, 00). **CONTACT ADDRESS** Dept English, SUNY, Col at Cortland, PO Box 2000, Cortland, NY 13045-0900. **EMAIL** hager@snycorva.cortland.edu

HAGGERTY, GEORGE E.
DISCIPLINE 18TH-CENTURY ENGLISH LITERATURE **EDUCATION** Holy Cross Col, BA; Univ Calif-Berkeley, PhD. **CAREER** Prof, Chm, Univ Calif Riverside. **HONORS AND AWARDS** Distinguished Tchg award, 87, UC Pres Res Fel, 99-00. **SELECTED PUBLICATIONS** Auth, Gothic Fiction/Gothic Form, Penn State, 89; Unnatural Affections: Women and Fiction in the Later 18th Century, Ind, 98; Men in Love; Masculinity and Sexuality in the 18th Century, Columbia, 98; co-ed, Professions of Desire: Lesbian and Gay Studies in Literature for the Modern Language Association, 95; edr, Encyclopedia of Gay Histories and Cultures, Garland Press. **CONTACT ADDRESS** Dept of Eng-40, Univ of California, Riverside, 1156 Hinderaker Hall, Riverside, CA 92521-0323. **EMAIL** haggerty@ucrac1.ucr.edu

HAHN, FRANCIS V. HICKSON
DISCIPLINE CLASSICS **EDUCATION** Univ NC, Chapel Hill, PhD, 86. **CAREER** Assoc Prof, Univ Calif, Santa Barbara. **RESEARCH** Religion of the Roman Republic. **SELECTED PUBLICATIONS** Auth, Roman Prayer Language: Livy and the Aeneid of Vergil, Teubner, 93; "Patruus: Paragon or Pervert? The Case of a Literary Split Personality," Syllecta Classica 4, 93; "Augustus Triumphator: Manipulation of the Triumphal Theme in the Political Program of Augustus," Latomus, 91; "Roman Religion," The Dictionary of Religion, Harper-Collins and Amer Acad of Rel, 95. **CONTACT ADDRESS** Dept of Classics, Univ of California, Santa Barbara, Santa Barbara, CA 93106-7150. **EMAIL** fhahn@humanitas.ucsb.edu

HAHN, H. GEORGE
PERSONAL Born 01/10/1942, Baltimore, MD, m, 1981, 1 child **DISCIPLINE** ENGLISH **EDUCATION** Mount St. Mary's Col, BA, 63; Univ of Md, MA, 66; Johns Hopkins Univ, MLA, 69; Univ of Md, PhD, 79. **CAREER** Grad Asst, Univ of Md, 63-66; Fel, Johns Hopkins Univ, 69; From Instr to Prof, Towson Univ, 65-87; Prof, Towson Univ, 87-; Dir Honors, College, 87-90; dir, Advanced Writing Courses, 98-; editor, "All Ahead Full," Navy League of The United States, 93-. **HONORS AND AWARDS** Mackie Prize for Editorship (Nat): Ed of All Ahead Full Navy League of the US, 98; Emmart Jour Awd for Writing about the Humanities, 84. **MEMBERSHIPS** E Central Am Asn for 18th Century Studies. **RESEARCH** Political and military history and literature. **SELECTED PUBLICATIONS** Auth, "Auburn in Goldsmith's 'Deserted Village'," Col Lang Asn J 22 (78); auth, Henry Fielding, Scarecrow (Metuchen, Nj, London), 79; auth, "Main Lines of Criticism of Fielding's 'Tom Jones'," Brit Studies Monitor 10.1 (80); auth, "Main Lines of Criticism of Fielding's 'Joseph Andrews'," (81); auth, "Twilight Reflections: The Hold of Victorian Baltimore on Lizette Woodworth reese and H.L. Mencken," The Souther Quart: A J of Arts in the S 22.4 (84); coauth, The Eighteenth-Century British Novel, Scarecrow (Metuchen, Nj, London),85; auth, The Country Myth: Political Motifs in the British Novel, Defoe to Smollett, Peter Lang (Frankfurt, London), 91; auth, "Tarsicius: A Hagiographical Allusions in Joyce's 'Araby'," Papers on Lang and Lit 27 (91); auth, "The Progress of Patriotism and Biography: The Battle of Trafalgar in Southey's 'Life of Nelson'," War, Lit and the Arts 9 (97); auth, The Patriot's Flame: War Poetry and Nationhood in England, 1793-1815, Peter Lang, forthcoming; auth, Charity Schools, Dissenting Academies, Hedge Schools, Univ of London, Hanoverian Britain: an Encyclopedia, 97; auth, Defoe, Fielding, Crabbe, Thomson, Cowper, Marryat, Cyclopedia of World Authors, 97; auth, Gray's Ode on Eton College, Masterplots II, 99. **CONTACT ADDRESS** Dept English, Towson State Univ, 8000 York Rd., English Dept, Baltimore, MD 21252-0001. **EMAIL** ghahn@Towson.edu

HAHN, LAURA K.
PERSONAL Born 08/25/1968, CA **DISCIPLINE** COMMUNICATION **EDUCATION** San Francisco State Univ, CA, BA (magna cum laude), 91, MA (Speech Commun), 94; OH State Univ, Columbus, PhD (Commun), 99. **CAREER** Grad teaching assoc, Dept of Speech and Comminiction Studies, San Francisco State Univ, CA, 92-94; undergrad adv, Dept of Commun and Journalism, OH State Univ, Columbus, 95; Project coord, Center for the Advanced Study of Telecommun, OH State Univ, Columbus, 96-97; Dir of the Basic Course, Dept of Commun and Journalism, OH State Univ, Columbus, 96-98, grad teaching assoc, 94-98; vis prof, Int Col of Beijing, China, spring 98; Lect, Dept of Commun, Humboldt State Univ, Arcata, CA, 98-. **HONORS AND AWARDS** Outstanding Scholastic Achievement, Golden Key Nat Honor Soc, 91; Outstanding Academic Achievement, San Francisco State Univ, 90-91; Prof Participation, OH State Univ, Columbus, 95, 96, 97. **SELECTED PUBLICATIONS** Auth, Status of the Animal Liberation Movement in the 1990's: The Rhetoric of Gandhi/Guerrilla, published through The 28th Annual CA State Univ Hayward Conf in Rhetorical Criticism, 93; Incorporating Theory and Practice: Student Involvement in a Social Movement, Speech Communication Teacher, 98. **CONTACT ADDRESS** Dept of Communication, Humboldt State Univ, Arcata, CA 95521. **EMAIL** lkh9@axe.humboldt.edu

HAHN, THOMAS GEORGE O'HARA
PERSONAL Born 04/26/1946, New York, NY, 2 children **DISCIPLINE** ENGLISH, LITERATURE **EDUCATION** Fordham Univ, AB, 68; Univ Calif Los Angeles, MA & PhD, 74. **CAREER** Asst prof, 73-80, assoc prof, 80-96, prof, Univ Rochester, 96, dir, Writing Prog, 76-81, dir, medieval sds ctr, 75-76, 83-84, 87-88, ch, cluster on pre-modern sds, 89-, dir grad sds Eng, 82-83, 96-97, , assoc, Susan B. Anthony Ctr for Women's Sds, 85-, gen ed, Chaucer Bibliographies, 84, gov brd, Robbins Lib, 87. **HONORS AND AWARDS** NEH Sum fel, ACLS fel, Vis mem, Wolfson Col, Cambridge; Ford Foun Tchg, PI, for NEH Prog Gra; E P Curtis Awd for Tchg Excel; Reach Teams Awd for Curricular Innov. **MEMBERSHIPS** Mediaeval Acad Am; MLA; New Chaucer Soc; Early English Text Soc; Index Mid English Prose. **RESEARCH** Old and Middle English language and literature; Medieval studies. **SELECTED PUBLICATIONS** Auth, Urian Oakes's Elegie and Puritan poetics, Am Lit, 73; General literary criticism--years work in Old English studies, Old English Newslett, 75 & 81; The audience in the medieval dramatic performance, Res Opportunities in Renaissance Drama, 77; I gentili e l'uom nasce a la riva de l'Indo, L'Alighierei, 77; The Indian tradition of the Middle Ages, Viator, 78; Primitivism and savagery in English discovery narratives of sixteenth century, J Medieval & Renaissance Studies, 78; ed, Me Letter of Alexander to Aristotle, Medieval Studies, 79; Upright Lives: Documents Concerning the Natural Virtue and Wisdom of the Indians, 81; coauth, Text and Context: Chaucer's Friar Tale; auth, Studies in the Age of Chaucer, 83; auth, Teaching the Resistant Woman: The Wife if Bath and the Academy, Exemplaria, 92; auth, The Performance of Gender in the Prioress, The Chaucer Yearbook, 92; auth, Traditional Religion, Social History, and Literary Study, Assays, 96; auth, Old Wives' Tales and Masculine Intuition, Retelling Stories, Lupack & Hahn, 97; auth, Early Middle English, Cambridge Hist of the Middle English Lit, Wallace, 98. **CONTACT ADDRESS** Dept of English, Univ of Rochester, 500 Joseph C Wilson Blvd, RC Box 270451, Rochester, NY 14627-0451. **EMAIL** thhn@mail.rochester.edu

HAI, AMBREEN
PERSONAL Born 10/22/1964, Karachi, Pakistan, m, 1996 **DISCIPLINE** ENGLISH, LITERATURE **EDUCATION** Wellesley Col, BA, 86; Yale Univ, MA, 89; PhD, 95. **CAREER** Asst prof, SUNY Albany, 94-96; asst prof, Smith Col, 96-. **HONORS AND AWARDS** NEH, 01-02; Jean Picker Fel, 98-99; Univ at Albany FRAP Grnt; 95-96; Andrew W. Mellon Found Yale Dis Fel , 93-94; Sterling Prize Fel, 89-90; Yale Univ Fel, 88-92; Alice Freeman Palmer Fel, 88-89; Nom for Yale Prize Teach Fel, 91; Oral Qual Exam passed with Distinct, 90; Phi Beta Kappa, 86; Grad Summa cum Laude, 86. **MEMBERSHIPS** MLA; SALA. **RESEARCH** Anglophone post colonial literature; literary theory; South Asian literature; 19-20th-century British literature; fiction. **SELECTED PUBLICATIONS** Auth, "On Truth and Lie in a Colonial Sense: Kipling's Tales of Tale-Telling," Eng Lit Hist (97); auth "Children of An Other Language: Kipling's Stories, Inter-racial Progeny, and Questions of Censorship," J Common Post Colon Lit (98); auth, "Marching in from the Peripheries': Rushdie's Feminized Artistry and Ambivalent Feminism," Crit Essays on Salman Rushdie (99); auth, "Border Work, Border Trouble: Postcolonial Feminism and the Ayah in Bapsi Sidhwa's Cracking India," Mod Fict Stud (00); auth, "Salman Rushdie" Encycl Americana (00); auth, "Sara Suleri" in South Asian Novelists in English: A Bio-Biographical Critical Sourcebook (01). **CONTACT ADDRESS** Eng Dept., Smith Col, Northampton, MA 01063. **EMAIL** ahai@smith.edu

HAIGHT, ROBERT C.
PERSONAL Born 08/19/1955, Detroit, MI, m, 1979, 2 children **DISCIPLINE** ENGLISH **EDUCATION** Western Mich, BA, 77; MFA, 86. **CAREER** Teacher, Kalamazoo Valley Community Col, 89-. **HONORS AND AWARDS** Creative Artist Awd, Arts Found of Mich; Fel, Vermont Studio Ctr. **MEMBERSHIPS** NCTE, Acad of Am Poets. **RESEARCH** Creative writing. **SELECTED PUBLICATIONS** Auth, Water Music; Poetry and essays in The Northern Rev, Oxford Mag, South Coast Poetry J, Contemporary Mich Poetry, etc. **CONTACT ADDRESS** Dept Commun Arts, Kalamazoo Valley Comm Col, PO Box 4070, Kalamazoo, MI 49003-4070. **EMAIL** Rhaight@kvcc.edu

HAINES, ANNETTE L.
DISCIPLINE LIBRARY SCIENCE **EDUCATION** Wayne State Univ, MS, 77. **CAREER** Ref Libr, Central Mich Univ, 97-. **MEMBERSHIPS** ALA; Michigan Library Assoc. **RESEARCH** Library and information science **CONTACT ADDRESS** Park Library, Central Michigan Univ, Mount Pleasant, MI 48859. **EMAIL** annette.haines@cmich.edu

HAINES, DOROTHY
PERSONAL Born Frankfurt, Germany, m, 1984 **DISCIPLINE** ENGLISH **EDUCATION** Bemidgi State Univ, BA, 88, MA, 92; Univ Toronto, Center Medieval Studies, MA, 93, PhD, 98. **CAREER** Asst prof of English, Shorter Col, 99-. **MEMBERSHIPS** Modern Lang Asn, Medieval Acad of Am, Int Soc of Anglo-Saxonists, Int Medieval Sermon Studies Soc. **RESEARCH** Old English language and literature, especially homiletic literature. **SELECTED PUBLICATIONS** Auth, "Unlocking Exodus II.516-532," J of English and Germanic Philol 98.4 (99): 481-98. **CONTACT ADDRESS** Dept Humanities, Shorter Col, Georgia, 315 Shorter Ave SW, Rome, GA 30165-4267. **EMAIL** dhaines@shorter.edu

HAINES, VICTOR YELVERTON
PERSONAL Born 03/21/1941, Toronto, ON, Canada, 3 children **DISCIPLINE** MEDIEVAL ENGLISH AND CANADIAN LITERATURE **EDUCATION** Queen's Univ, Kingston, BA Hons, 65; Carleton Univ, MA, 66; McGill Univ, PhD(English), 75. **CAREER** Prof English, Acadia Univ, 66-67 and Royal Mil Col, St Jean, 67-73; PROF ENGLISH, DAWSON COL, 74-. **MEMBERSHIPS** Int Arthurian Soc; MLA; Asn of Can Univ Teachers English; Mediaeval Acad Am. **RESEARCH** Doctrine of the felix culpa; mediaeval romance; Can poetry **SELECTED PUBLICATIONS** Auth, Rhetoric and Existence, Philos and Rhet, Vol 0029, 96; The Dragon in The Fog--Play and Artworlds, Can Rev of Comp Lit-Rev Can de Lit Comparee, Vol 0023, 96. **CONTACT ADDRESS** Dawson Col, 1001 Sherbrooke, Montreal, QC, Canada H2L 1L3. **EMAIL** vhaines@adm.usherb.ca

HAIR, DONALD S.
PERSONAL Born 11/24/1937, Strathroy, ON **DISCIPLINE** ENGLISH **EDUCATION** Univ W Ont, BA, 60; Univ Toronto, MA, 61; PhD, 64. **CAREER** Lectr 64-65, from asst prof to assoc prof, 65-73, assoc chmn dept, 67-73, PROF ENGLISH, UNIV WESTERN ONT, 73-, Can Coun leave fel, 73-74. **HONORS AND AWARDS** OCUFA Teaching Awd, 91; Raymond Klibansky Prize, 99-00. **MEMBERSHIPS** ACCUTE. **RESEARCH** Victorian poetry. **SELECTED PUBLICATIONS** Auth, Browning's Experiements with Genre, Univ of Toronto Pr, 72; auth, Domestic and Heroic in Tennyson's Poetry, Univ of Toronto Pr, 81; auth, Tennyson's Language, Univ of Toronto Pr, 91; Robert Browning's Language, Univ of Toronto Pr, 99. **CONTACT ADDRESS** Dept English, The Univ of Western Ontario, Univ Col, Rm 173, London, ON, Canada N6A 3K7. **EMAIL** dhair@uwo.ca

HAIRE, CAROL
PERSONAL Born 06/24/1949, Littlefield, TX, s **DISCIPLINE** SPEECH-LANGUAGE PATHOLOGY **EDUCATION** Tex Tech Univ, BA, 70; N Tex State Univ, MA, 71; Tex Tech Univ, PhD, 76. **CAREER** Teacher, Cooke Co Public Schs, 72; Teacher, Muleshoe Independent Sch Dist, 73-74; Instr, Tex Tech Univ, 74-76; Asst Prof, Howard Payne Univ, 76-77; Prof, Hardin-Simmons Univ, 77-. **HONORS AND AWARDS** Phi Kappa Phi; Fel, Am Col of Forensic Examrs; Outstanding Young Woman of the Year, 83-84; Pathfinder in Health Awd, YWCA, 93; Outstanding Woman of the Tex Midwest Awd, 98. **MEMBERSHIPS** Am Speech-Lang-Hearing Asn, Am Psychol Asn, AAUP. **RESEARCH** Forensic psycholinguistics, disability analysis, learning disabilities, dyslexia, dysgraphia, dyscalculia, speech and language development and disorders, intellectual and educational assessment. **SELECTED PUBLICATIONS** Auth, Clinic Handbook, Communicative Disorders Ctr, Howard Payne Univ Pr (Brownwood, TX), 76; auth, Early Childhood Language Development: Suggestions for Speech-Language Pathologists, Teachers and Parents, Big Country Speech and Hearing Asn (Abilene, TX), 78; auth, Is This Kid a Hopeless Behavior Problem or Could He Have a Learning Disability?" Cent Tex Foster Parents Asn (Brownwood, TX), 85; auth, "Learning to Learn: Educational Rehabilitation After Head Injury," Getting Ahead (87): 1,3. **CONTACT ADDRESS** Dept Speech, Lang Pathology, Hardin-Simmons Univ, Abilene, TX 79698. **EMAIL** chaire@hsutx.edu

HAKUTANI, YOSHINOBU
PERSONAL Born 03/27/1935, Osaka, Japan, m, 1967, 2 children **DISCIPLINE** AMERICAN LITERATURE, LINGUISTICS **EDUCATION** Hiroshima Univ, Japan, BA, 57; Univ Minn, Minneapolis, MA, 59; Pa State Univ, PhD(English), 65. **CAREER** Instr English, SDak State Univ, 59-61; asst prof, Calif State Univ, Northridge, 65-68; asst prof, 68-71, assoc prof, 71-80, Prof English, Kent State Univ, 80-, Res fel, Kent State Univ, 71-72. **HONORS AND AWARDS** Choice Awd, 88; Acad of Am Poets, 99, Nat Poetry Month. **MEMBERSHIPS** MLA; ALA; Dreiser Soc. **RESEARCH** Modern American Literature, African American Literature, Cross-Cultural Studies. **SELECTED PUBLICATIONS** Auth, Young Dreiser: A Critical Study, Assoc Univ Presses, 80; ed, Selected Magazine Articles of Theodore Dreiser: Life and Art in the American 1890s, Assoc Univ Presses, 85-87; ed, Selected English Writings of Yone Noguchi: An East-West Literary Assimilation, Assoc Univ Presses, 90-92; co-ed, The City in African-American Literature, Assoc Univ Presses, 95; ed, Postmodernity and Cross Culturalism, Fairleigh Dickinson UP, 01; ed, Modernity in East-West literary Criticism, Fairleigh Dickinson UP, 01; ed, Art, Music, and Literature, 1897-1902, by Theodore Dreiser, U of IL P, 01; ed, Theodore Dreiser and American Culture, U of Delaware P, 00. **CONTACT ADDRESS** Dept of English, Kent State Univ, PO Box 5190, Kent, OH 44242-0001. **EMAIL** yhakutan@kent.edu

HALABY, RAOUF J.
PERSONAL Born 11/22/1945, Jerusalem, Palestine, m, 1970, 2 children **DISCIPLINE** ENGLISH **EDUCATION** Ouachita Baptist Univ, Ar, BA, 68, MSE, 70; Texas A & M, EdD. **CAREER** Prof, chair, Ouachita Baptist Univ. **HONORS AND AWARDS** Who's Who, 71; Teacher of the Year, 79; Daughters of Amer Revolution Americanism Awd; Notable Amer. **MEMBERSHIPS** Sixteenth Century Soc; NCTE; SCMLA; MLA. **RESEARCH** Arkansas dialects; near eastern immigration to US; sixteenth century educators; Richard Mulcaster; William Baziotes & abstract expressionism. **SELECTED PUBLICATIONS** Auth, Sneaking Books Under the Bedclothes, Christian Sci Monitor, 90; art, Language of the Heart Communicates Best, Ar Gazette, 90; auth, Myth, Ritual and Folklore in Pietro Didonato's Christ in Concrete, Les Presses de L'Universite Laval, Quebec, Canada, 90; art, America's Magical Shores, Ar Gazette, 90; auth, On Tents and Tapestries, Ar Catholic, 92. **CONTACT ADDRESS** 123 Evonshire, Arkadelphia, AR 71923. **EMAIL** halabyr@alpha.obu.edu

HALASZ, ALEXANDRA W.
DISCIPLINE ENGLISH LITERATURE **EDUCATION** Johns Hopkins Univ, PhD, 91. **CAREER** Assoc prof, Dartmouth Col. **RESEARCH** Shakespearean drama and Renaissance lit. **SELECTED PUBLICATIONS** Auth, The Marketplace of Print: Pamphlets and the Public Sphere in Early Modern England, Cambridge UP, 97;'So beloved that men use his picture for their signs': Richard Tarlton and the Uses of Sixteenth-Century Celebrity, Shakespeare Studies, 95; Wyatt's David, Tex Studies Lit and Lang, 88, rptd in Rethinking the Henrician Era, Univ Il P, 93. **CONTACT ADDRESS** Dartmouth Col, 3529 N Main St, #207, Hanover, NH 03755.

HALE, DAVID GEORGE
PERSONAL Born 03/25/1938, Worcester, MA, m, 1964, 2 children **DISCIPLINE** ENGLISH **EDUCATION** Wesleyan Univ, BA, 60; Duke Univ, MA, 61, PhD(English), 65. **CAREER** Tutor English, Duke Univ, 61-64; asst prof, Univ Cincinnati, 64-67; from asst prof to assoc prof, 67-75, PROF ENGLISH, STATE UNIV NY COL BROCKPORT, 75-, Folger Shakespeare Libr fel, 70; Southeastern Inst Medieval and Renaissance Studies fel, 75; Nat Endowment for Humanities fel, 77 and 81; vis prof English, Loughborough Univ, 79-80. **MEMBERSHIPS** MLA; Mod Humanities Res Asn; Resnaissance Soc Am. **RESEARCH** Renaissance. **SELECTED PUBLICATIONS** Auth, "Interviews from the Brockport Writers Forum III: 90-94," Bulletin of Bibliography, 52: 95; auth, "Didn't perceive? Five Versions of the Mousetrap in Hamlet," Shakespeare Yearbook, 8: 97; auth, "Move than Magic in the Web: Plagiarism for the Shakespeare Class," Shakespeare and the Classroom, 6: 98. **CONTACT ADDRESS** 350 New Campus Dr, Brockport, NY 14420-2914. **EMAIL** dhale@brockport.edu

HALE, J. KEITH
PERSONAL Born Little Rock, AR **DISCIPLINE** ENGLISH **EDUCATION** Univ Central Ark, MA, 91; Purdue Univ, PhD, 94. **CAREER** Assoc prof, Univ Guam, 96-. **RESEARCH** Philippine literature in English, British literature. **SELECTED PUBLICATIONS** Auth, Cody; auth, In the Land of Alexander; auth, Friends and Apostles: The Correspondence of Rupert Brooke and James Stachey, 1905-1914, Yale Univ Press (98). **CONTACT ADDRESS** Dept English, Univ of Guam, 303 University Dr, Mangilao, Guam 96923-1800. **EMAIL** khale@netpci.com

HALE, JANE ALISON
PERSONAL Born 09/29/1948, Washington, DC, m, 1994, 2 children **DISCIPLINE** LITERATURE **EDUCATION** William & Mary, BA, 70, Univ Chicago, MST, 74; Stanford Univ, MA, 81, PhD, 84. **CAREER** Tchr, 70-72, Abeche, Chad, trainer, 72, St Thomas Virgin Isle, Peace Corps; tchr, 74-77, Pleasant Grove Union Elem Schl, NC; asst prof, 85-91, assoc prof, 91-, Brandeis Univ. **HONORS AND AWARDS** Who's Who in American Women; Fulbright Senior Scholar; Dana Faculty Fel; Phi Beta Kappa. **RESEARCH** Reading, writing, & tchng across cultures. **SELECTED PUBLICATIONS** Auth, The Lyric Encyclopedia of Raymond Quenedu, Univ of Mich, 89; auth, The Broken Window: Beckett's Dramatic Perspective, Purdue UP, 87. **CONTACT ADDRESS** Dept of Romance & Comp Lit, Brandeis Univ, MS 024, Waltham, MA 02454. **EMAIL** jhale@brandeis.edu

HALE, THOMAS ALBERT
PERSONAL Born 01/05/1942, Boston, MA, m, 1968, 1 child **DISCIPLINE** AFRICAN AND FRENCH LITERATURE **EDUCATION** Tufts Univ, BA, 64, MA, 68; Univ Rochester, PhD(French), 74. **CAREER** Agr co-op asst, Peace Corps, Union Nigerienne de Credit et de Cooperation, 64-66; admin asst, NDEA French Inst, Tufts Univ, 67; Assoc Prof French and Comp Lit, Pa State Univ, 73-, Co-ed, Cahiers Cesairiens, 74- and African Lit Asn Newsletter, 74-78; Fulbright sr lectr, Univ de Niamey, Niger, 80-81. **MEMBERSHIPS** MLA; African Lit Asn (secy-treas, 74-79, press, 81-82); Am Asn Teachers French; African Studies Asn; Am Comp Lit Asn. **RESEARCH** Caribbean literature; French literature outside France. **SELECTED PUBLICATIONS** Auth, Sur Une tempete d'Aime Cesaire, Etudes Lit, 4/73; Aime Cesaire: A bio-bibliography, Africana J, spring 74; From Afro-America to Afro-France: The literary triangle trade, French Rev, 5/76; Structural dynamics in a Third World classic: Aime Cesaire's Cahier d'un retour au pays natal, Yale French Studies, No 53, 76; co-ed, The Teaching of African Literature, Univ Tex Press, 77; auth, Les Ecrits d'Aime Cesaire: Bibliographie commentee, Univ Montreal Press, 78; co-ed, Artist and Audience: African Literature as a Shared Experience, Three Continents Press, 79; auth, From written literature to the oral tradition and back: Camara Laye, Babou Conde, and Le Maitre de la Parole: Kouma Lafolo Kouma, French Rev, 5/82. **CONTACT ADDRESS** French Dept, Pennsylvania State Univ, Univ Park, 434 N Burrowes Bldg, University Park, PA 16802-6204.

HALEWOOD, WILLIAM H.
PERSONAL Born 12/15/1929, Providence, RI, m, 1952, 3 children **DISCIPLINE** LITERATURE **EDUCATION** Univ Wichita, Ba, 53; Univ Minn, MA and PhD, 59. **CAREER** From asst prof to assoc prof lit, Reed Col, 59-67, chmn div lett and arts, 65-67; assoc prof, 67-72, PROF ENGLISH, UNIV COL, UNIV TORONTO, 72-, Am Coun Learned Socs fel, 63-64. **MEMBERSHIPS** MLA. **RESEARCH** Neoclassical aesthetics; early Protestant theology; 17th and 18th century English literature. **SELECTED PUBLICATIONS** Auth, Catching up with Bellamy, Edward, Univ Toronto Quart, Vol 0063, 94; The Predicament of the Westward Rider: Donne, John 'Good-Friday, 1613, Riding Westward,' Stud in Philol, Vol 0093, 96. **CONTACT ADDRESS** Dept of English, Univ of Toronto, Toronto, ON, Canada M5S 1A1.

HALIO, JAY L.
PERSONAL Born 07/24/1928, New York, NY, d, 2 children **DISCIPLINE** ENGLISH **EDUCATION** Syracuse Univ, BA, 50; Yale Univ, MA, 51, PhD, 56. **CAREER** Acting instr to assoc prof, Univ Calif, Davis, 55-68; prof, Univ Del, 68-, Assoc Provost for Instruction, 75-81, Dir, Humanities Semester, 78-90, Coordr, Comparative Lit Prog, 82-87, Dir, Center for Teaching Effectiveness, 86-87, acting dir, Jewish Studies Prog, spring 94. **HONORS AND AWARDS** Phi Beta Kappa, 49; Fulbright-Hays Sr Lectr, Univ Malaya, 66-67, Buenos Aires, Argentina, 74; Univ Del Summer Fac Res Fels, 69-71, 88, 92; H. Rodney Sharp Prof of Liberal Studies, Univ Del, spring 72; NEH Fel, Univ Ill, Nov 77; Proj Dir, "The Humanities Semester at the University Delaware," Develop grant, NEH, 78-81; Danforth Assoc, 81-86; Dir, NEH Summer Sem for School Teachers, grants in 85, 86, 87, 90, 91, 93; Folger Fel, spring 94; NEH Res grant, 95-97. **MEMBERSHIPS** MLA, Am Lit Asn, Asn of Lit Scholars and Critics, Shakespeare Asn of Am, **SELECTED PUBLICATIONS** Auth, "Romeo and Juliet": A Guide to the Play, Westport, CT: Greenwood Press (98); rev essay, "Writing on Shakespeare," Col Lit (98); rev, "The Akedah (the Binding of Isaac) in Shakespeare's Merchant of Venice," in Leslie Fiedler and American Culture, ed Steven G. Kellman and Irving Malin, Newark: Univ Del Press (99): 81-86; auth, "Arthur Miller's Broken Jews," in American Literary Dimensions, ed Halio and Ben Siegal, Newark: Univ Del Press (99); auth, Shakespeare's "King Henry VIII," Oxford: Oxford Univ Press (99); co-ed with Ben Siegal, American Literary Dimensions, Newark: Univ Del Press (99); co-ed with Ben Siegal, Comparative Literary Dimensions, Newark: Univ Del Press (2000); auth, Understanding the Merchant of Venice: A Casebook of Contexts, Greenwood Press (in press); auth, Philip Roth Special Issue, for Shofar (in press); auth, "Saul Bellow and Philip Roth Visit Jerusalem," in Saul Bellow J (forthcoming). **CONTACT ADDRESS** Dept English, Univ of Delaware, Newark, DE 19716. **EMAIL** jhalio@udel.edu

HALL, DENNIS R.
PERSONAL Born 10/24/1942, Columbus, OH, m, 1965, 3 children **DISCIPLINE** ENGLISH LITERATURE, RHETORIC, POPULAR CULTURE **EDUCATION** Univ Notre Dame, BA, 64; Ohio State Univ, MA, 66, PhD, 70. **CAREER** Instr, 70-76, assoc prof, 76-85, Prof, 85-, dir of composition, 91-96, Chair, Fac Senate & Member B of T, Univ of Louisville, 98-. **HONORS AND AWARDS** Univ Louisville Trustees Awd, 96; Arts & Sciences Superior Performances Awd, 97. **MEMBERSHIPS** Popular Culture Asn; Am Culture Asn; Popular Culture Asn/Am Culture Asn in the South. **RESEARCH** Popular culture. **SELECTED PUBLICATIONS** Ed, Studies in Popular Culture, 90-96; The Culture of the American South, 96; co-ed, Handbook of American Popular Culture, Greenwood, forthcoming; auth, The Triumph of Aesthetics, Eye on the Future: Popular Culture Scholar into the Twenty-First Century in Honor of Ray Browne, Popular Press, 94; No Laughing Matter: Values, Perception, and the Demise of AID jokes, J of Am Culture, 93; Lear's Vision of Modern Maturity: The Struggle for Modernity in the Context of Postmodernity, Pop Culture Rev, 93; ComPost: A Writing Program Newsletter and Its Rationale, WPA Writing Prog Admin, 93; Sm R. Watkins's Co. Aytch: A Literary Nonfiction, Ky Philol Rev, 93; Civil War Reenactors and the Postmodern Sense of History, J of Am Culture, 94; New Age Music: A Voice of Liminality in Postmodern Popular Culture, Popular Music and Soc, 94; Nicholson Baker's Vox: An Exercise in the Literature of Sensibility, Conn Rev, 95; Adertising as High Art, The Mid-Atlantic Almanack, 95; The Indeterminancy of the Question and Answer Format, Writing on the Edge, 95; 1996 Presidential [Kentucky Philological Association] Address: Why Jane Austen? Why Now?, Ky Philol Rev, 96; Spanish Fly Redivivus: Dietary Supplements as Sexual Stimulants, J of Popular Culture, 96; A Garden of One's Own: The Ritual Consolations of the Backyard Garden, J of Am Culture, 96. **CONTACT ADDRESS** Dept of English, Univ of Louisville, Louisville, KY 40292. **EMAIL** dennis.hall@louisville.edu

HALL, FREDERICK A.
PERSONAL Born 07/02/1944, Niagara-on-the-Lake, ON, Canada **DISCIPLINE** HISTORY OF MUSIC **EDUCATION** McGill Univ, BMus, 69; Univ Toronto, MA, 70; PhD 78. **CAREER** ASSOC PROF SCHOOL OF ART, DRAMA AND MUSIC, MCMASTER UNIV, 72-, chmn, 80-86, assoc dean, Hum, 88-96, acting dean, Hum, 96-97. **SELECTED PUBLICATIONS** Ed, Songs I to English Texts, 85; Songs IV to English Texts, 93; co-ed, Musical Canada: Words and Music Honouring Helmut Kallmann, 88; The Romantic Tradition, 92; contribur, Encyclopedia of Music in Canada; The Canadian Encyclopedia; Dictionary of Canadian Biography, vols XIII & XIV; Studies in Eighteenth Century Culture; Canadian Music: Issues of Hegemony and Identity. **CONTACT ADDRESS** Sch of Art, Drama & Music, McMaster Univ, 1280 Main St W, Hamilton, ON, Canada L8S 4M2. **EMAIL** hallfa@mcmaster.ca

HALL, JAMES R.
PERSONAL Born 03/17/1946, Rochester, NY, m, 1974, 2 children **DISCIPLINE** ENGISH **EDUCATION** St John Fisher Col, BA, 68; Univ Notre Dame, MA, 70; PhD, 73. **CAREER** Visiting Lec, Univ Ill, 73-74; Instructor, St Mary-of-the-Woods Col, 75; Asst Prof to Prof, Univ Miss, 78-. **HONORS AND AWARDS** Res Fel,Earhadt Foundation, 00; Res Fel, NEH, 93-94; Res Fel, Mellon Prog Harvard Univ; Res Fel, Am Coun of Learned Soc, 81-82. **MEMBERSHIPS** Intl Soc of Anglo-Saxonists; Medieval Acad of Am; SE Medieval Asn; S Atlantic Mod Lang Asn; Am Friends of the Bodleian Library. **RESEARCH** Old English Biblical Poetry; Beowulf; The History of Old English Studies. **SELECTED PUBLICATIONS** Auth, "William G. Medlicott (1816-1833): An American Book Collector and His Collection," Harvard Library Bulletin, (90): 13-46; auth, "The First Two Editions of Beowulf: Thorkelin's (1815) and Kemble's (1833)," in The Editing of Old English: Papers from the 1990 Manchester Conference, (Brewer Press, 94), 239-250; auth, "Old English Literature," in Scholarly Editing: A Guide to Research, (New York, 95), 149-183; auth, "Mid-Nineteenth-Century American Anglo-Saxonism: The Question of Language," in Anglo-Saxonism and the Construction of Social Identity, (Univ Press of FL, 97), 133-156; auth, "Nineteenth-Century America and the Study of the Anglo-Saxon Language: An Introduction," in The Preservation and Transmission of Anglo-Saxon Culture: Selected Papers from the 1991 Meeting of the International Society of Anglo-Saxonists, Kalamazoo, 97; auth, "F.J. Furnivall's Letter to the Royal Library, Copenhagen, Asking that the Thorkelin Transcripts of Beowulf Be Sent to London for the Use of Julius Zupitza," Notes and Queries, (98): 267-272. **CONTACT ADDRESS** Dept Eng, Univ of Mississippi, General Delivery, University, MS 38677-1848. **EMAIL** jrhall@olemiss.edu

HALL, JILL
PERSONAL Born 09/04/1946, Mobile, AL, m, 1968, 3 children **DISCIPLINE** COMMUNICATION **EDUCATION** Samford Univ, BA, 68; Univ Ky, MA, 70; PhD, 98. **CAREER** Assoc prof, Jefferson Community Col, 90-; mediator, Mediation Ctr of Ky, 92-94. **HONORS AND AWARDS** Dissertation Year Fel, Univ Ky, 96-97; Distinguished Educr, Jefferson Community Col, 98; The Applegate Scholar Awd, Ky Commun Asn, 98. **MEMBERSHIPS** Nat Commun Asn, Ky Commun Asn, Am Asn of Univ Women. **RESEARCH** Mediation, Interpersonal Communication. **SELECTED PUBLICATIONS** Auth, Mediation and Women at Risk: A Case for Transformation Communication, 98; auth, "Communicated Views of Conflict: How Students Describe the Social Interaction of Conflict," Ky J of Commun (98); auth, Interpersonal Communication Student Workbook, Jefferson Community Col Commun Dept, 99. **CONTACT ADDRESS** Dept Communication, Jefferson Community Col, 109 E Broadway, Louisville, KY 40202-2005. **EMAIL** jill.hall@kctcs.net

HALL, JOAN H.
PERSONAL Born 07/21/1946, Akron, OH, m, 1971, 1 child **DISCIPLINE** ENGLISH **EDUCATION** College of Idaho, BA, 68; Emory Univ, MA, 71, PhD, 76. **CAREER** Gen editor 75-, Assoc editor 79-, Dictionary of Amer Regional Eng, Univ Wisc-Madison. **HONORS AND AWARDS** Dist Alum Awd; Verbatim DNSA Awd. **MEMBERSHIPS** DSNA, pres 99-01; ADS. **RESEARCH** Lexicography; Amer English Dialects. **SELECTED PUBLICATIONS** Auth, Lags and Dare: A Case of Mutualism, in: Language Variety in the South Revisited, eds, Cynthia Bernstein, Thomas Nunnally, Robin Sabino, Tuscaloosa AL, U of AL Press, 97; Introduction to forum on Dialect Labeling in Dictionaries, Dictionaries, 97; coed, Dictionary of American Regional English, Cambridge MA, Belknap P of Harvard U Press, 85, 91, 96; rev, Heartland English, by Timothy C Frazer, J Eng Linguistics, 96; coed, Old English and New: Essays in Language and Literature in Honor of Frederick G Cassidy, NY, Garland, 92. **CONTACT ADDRESS** 600 N Park St, Madison, WI 53706. **EMAIL** jdhall@facstaff.wisc.edu

HALL, JOAN LORD
PERSONAL Born 03/07/1966, Hull, York, United Kingdom, m, 1977, 1 child **DISCIPLINE** ENGLISH LITERATURE, WRITING **EDUCATION** Univ Col, BA, 68; Girton Col, MLit, 73. **CAREER** Lectr, Univ Lancaster, 71-78; lectr to instr, Univ Colo at Boulder, 79-. **RESEARCH** Shakespeare and Renaissance Drama, Stylistics. **SELECTED PUBLICATIONS** Auth, The Dynamics of Role-Playing in Jacobean Tragedy, Macmillan, 91; auth, "Henry V:" A Guide to the Play, Greenwood Pr, 97; auth, "Othello:" A Guide to the Play, Greenwood Pr, 99. **CONTACT ADDRESS** Univ Writing Prog, Univ of Colorado, Boulder, PO Box 359, Boulder, CO 80309-0359. **EMAIL** cliffhall@juno.com

HALL, JONATHAN M.
DISCIPLINE CLASSICS **EDUCATION** Univ Oxford, BA, 88, MA, 91; Univ Cambridge, PhD, 93. **CAREER** Tchg fel, Marlboro Col, 88-89; Undergrad Supvr, Univ Cambridge, 89-96; Lectr, British Sch at Athens Summer Sch, 92-93; Res Fel, Downing Col, 93-96; Aff lectr, Univ Cambridge, 95-96; Asst prof, Univ Chicago, 96-. **HONORS AND AWARDS** Open Exhibition, Hertford Col, Univ of Oxford, 84; College Scholarship, Hertford Col, 87; Univ Prize for Fieldwork in Ancient Hist and Archaeology, Univ of Oxford, 87; British Academy Major State Studentship, Univ of Cambridge, 89-93; L.H. Jeffery Studentship in Archaic Greek Archaeology and Epigraphy, 91-92; Junior Fel, Center for Hellenic Studies, 98-99; Charles J. Goodwin Awd, 99. **RESEARCH** The social and cultural hist of archaic Greece, Greek history, hsitoriography, and archaeology. **SELECTED PUBLICATIONS** Auth, Ethnic identity in Greek antiquity, Cambridge, 97. **CONTACT ADDRESS** Dept of Classical Lang & Literature, Univ of Chicago, 1010 E 50th St, Chicago, IL 60637. **EMAIL** jhall@midway.uchicago.edu

HALL, KIM
DISCIPLINE ENGLISH LITERATURE **EDUCATION** Hood Col, BA; Univ Pa, PhD. **CAREER** Assoc prof. **HONORS AND AWARDS** Hood Scholar 1983; Mellon Fellowship in the Humanities, Woodrow Wilson Natl Fellowship Foundation; Folger Inst Fellowship, Washington DC 1986; Governor's Citation, Gov Harry Hughes MD 1986; Paul Robeson Awd, University of Pennsylvania, 1989; Folger Institute Fellowship, Folger Shakespeare Library, 1991; Mellon Dissertation Fellowship, Woodrow Wilson National Fellowship Foundation, 1988-89. **RESEARCH** Sixteenth and seventeenth century British literature and culture; theories of race and ethnicity; feminism; literature and visual arts; material culture; cultural studies. **SELECTED PUBLICATIONS** Auth, Things of Darkness: Economies of Race and Gender in Early Modern England, 96; pubs on Shakespeare, theater history, visual culture, women writers, black feminist theory, food and material culture, pedagogy, and multiculturalism. **CONTACT ADDRESS** English Dept, Georgetown Univ, 37th and O St, Washington, DC 20057.

HALL, LARRY JOE
PERSONAL Born 10/22/1937, Heavener, OK, m, 1959, 3 children **DISCIPLINE** AMERICAN LITERATURE & STUDIES **EDUCATION** Oklahoma City Univ, BA, 59; Garrett Theol Sem, MDiv, 62; NTex State Univ, MA, 70, PhD(Am Lit), 74. **CAREER** Asst prof, 74-81, from assoc prof to prof English, Okla Baptist Univ, 81-86. **HONORS AND AWARDS** Distinguished Teaching Awd, 88. **MEMBERSHIPS** MLA; Am Studies Asn; Midcontinent Am Studies Assn; Conf on Christianity and Lit. **RESEARCH** Myth criticism and the contemporary novel. **SELECTED PUBLICATIONS** Auth, "Three Consciousnesses in Wright Morris's Plains Song," Western American Literature 31.4, 97: 291-320; auth, "Slothrop's Progress: A Christian Ironist Reading of Gravity's Rainbow," Christianity and Literature 41.2, 92: 159-178. **CONTACT ADDRESS** Oklahoma Baptist Univ, 500 W University, Shawnee, OK 74801-2558. **EMAIL** joe_hall@mail.okbu.edu

HALL, N. JOHN
PERSONAL Born 01/01/1933, Orange, NJ, m, 1968, 1 child **DISCIPLINE** ENGLISH LITERATURE **EDUCATION** Seton Hall Univ, AB, 55, MA, 67; Cath Univ Am, STB, 59; New York Univ, PhD, 70. **CAREER** Lectr, Sch Continuing Educ, New York Univ, 67-70; from asst prof to assoc prof, 70-78, prof English, 78-, Bronx Commun Col; prof English, 80-, Grad Sch & Univ Ctr; lectr, New Sch Social Res, 70-74. **HONORS AND AWARDS** res award, City Univ New York, 71, 72; res award, City Univ New York Res Found, 71, 74, 76 & 77; Am Coun Learned Soc grant, 73, fel, 80; NEH fel, 74; Guggenheim fel, 77, 82. **RESEARCH** Nineteenth century English literature; Anthony Trollope; the novel; Max Beetbahm **SELECTED PUBLICATIONS** Ed, Anthony Trollope's The New Zealander, Clarendon, 72; auth, Salmagundi, Byron, Allegra, and the Trollope Family, Beta Phi Mu, 75; auth, Trollope and His Illustrators, Macmillan, 80; ed, The Trollope Critics, 81, Macmillan; auth, The Letters of Anthony Trollope, Stanford Univ; auth, Trollepe: A Biography, Clarendon Press, 91; auth, Max Beerbohm Caricatures, Yale, 97. **CONTACT ADDRESS** Dept of English, Bronx Comm Col, CUNY, 2155 University Ave, Bronx, NY 10453-2895. **EMAIL** njohnhall@earthlink.net

HALL, P. W.
PERSONAL m, 1 child **DISCIPLINE** ENGLISH, RELIGIOUS STUDIES **EDUCATION** Univ Ore, BS, 87; Northern Ariz Univ, MA, 99. **CAREER** Assoc fac, Coconino Community Col, 99-. **HONORS AND AWARDS** Nat Deans List; Outstanding Col Students of Am; Golden Key Nat Honor Soc; NAU Jr Scholar Awd. **MEMBERSHIPS** Asian Chamber of Commerce. **RESEARCH** Multicultural Issues, Gender and Race Issues. **SELECTED PUBLICATIONS** Articles in Asian American Encyclopedia, Mountain Living, Asian Week, Asian Sun News, Encyclopedia of Multiculturalism Supplement, and Brushstrokes. **CONTACT ADDRESS** Dept Liberal Arts, Coconino County Comm Col, PO Box 80000, Flagstaff, AZ 86003-8000. **EMAIL** hallpw@hotmail.com

HALL, TOM
PERSONAL Born 02/13/1955, Teaneck, NJ, m, 1986, 1 child **DISCIPLINE** MUSIC **EDUCATION** Univ Maryland, DMA, 96. **CAREER** Music Dir, Baltimore Choral Arts Soc, 82-; Dir Choral Activities, Goucher Col, 83-; Chorus Master, Baltimore Opera Company, 83-93; Music Dir, Concord Chorus, 79-82. **MEMBERSHIPS** Chorus Am; Am Choral Dir Asn; Am Symphony Orchestra League; Am Handel Soc; Am Musicol Soc. **RESEARCH** Handel; Bach; Haydn; Mozart. **SELECTED PUBLICATIONS** Voice Magazine; Hist Performance Magazine; Baltimore Sun; Choral Journal. **CONTACT ADDRESS** Baltimore Choral Arts Soc, 1316 Park Ave, Baltimore, MD 21217. **EMAIL** thall1@erols.com

HALL, WADE H.
PERSONAL Born 02/02/1934, Union Springs, AL **DISCIPLINE** ENGLISH **EDUCATION** Troy State Univ, BS, 53; Univ Ala, MA, 57; Univ Ill, PHD(English), 61. **CAREER** Instr English, Univ Ill, 57-61; asst prof, Univ Fla, 61-63; from assoc prof to prof, Ky Southern Col, 63-71; prof English, 71-96, prof emeritus, Bellarmine Col. **HONORS AND AWARDS** Ala Libr Asn Lit Awd, 67. **MEMBERSHIPS** MLA; Conf Christianity & Lit; S Atlantic Mod Lang Asn. **RESEARCH** Literature of the South; American humor; theology and literature. **SELECTED PUBLICATIONS** Auth, Reflections of the Civil War in Southern humor, 62 & The Smiling Phoenix: Southern Humor, 1865-1914, 65, Univ Fla; The mirror of humor, Ala Librn, 1/68; The lonely world of Carson McCullers, Twigs, summer 68; The Truth is Funny: Jesse Stuart's Humor, Ind Coun Teachers English, 70; The High Limb, Ky Poetry Press, 73; coed, This Place Kentucky, Courier-J, 75; contribr, Jesse Stuart: Essays on His Work, Univ Ky, 77; The Kentucky Book, Courier J, 79; auth, The Rest of the Dream, Univ Kentucky, 88; auth, Hell-Bent for Music, Univ Kentucky, 96; auth, Conecuh People, Black Belt Press, 98. **CONTACT ADDRESS** Dept of English, Bellarmine Col, 2000 Norris Pl, Louisville, KY 40205. **EMAIL** adeway@aol.com

HALLER, EVELYN
PERSONAL Born 03/07/1937, Chicago, IL, d, 2 children **DISCIPLINE** ENGLISH AND AMERICAN LITERATURE **EDUCATION** Barat Col of Sacred Heart, AB, 58; Emory Univ, MA, 59, PhD, 68. **CAREER** Lectr, Mission San Jose Campus, Col of the Holy Names, 63-67; asst prof, 68, lectr, 69, Creighton Univ; PROF, 83-, CHR ENGLISH, DOANE COL, 69-; AIFS London semester, 85, assoc fel Ctr for Great Plains Stud, 93, Univ v Nebraska; Newberry Libr fel, 84; NEH Summer, Princeton, 73, Brunnenburg, 94. **MEMBERSHIPS** Am Acad Relig; Mod Lang Asn; Nebraska Coun Hum, 76-80; Am Asn Univ Prof; AAUP Neb State Conf Pres; Assembly of State Conf treas. **RESEARCH** Modernism, especially Virginia Woolf, Willa Cather, and Exra Pound. **SELECTED PUBLICATIONS** Auth Isis Unveiled: Virginia Woolf Use of Egyptian Myth, Virginia Woolf: A Feminist Slant, Univ Nebraska Press, 83; Behind the Singer Tower: Willa Cather and Flaubert, Modern Fiction Studies, 90; Her Quill Drawn from the Firebird: Virginia Woolf and the Russian Dancers, The Multiple Muses of Virginia Woolf, Univ Missouri Press, 93; Octavia Wilberforce: A Portrain Unrealized, Women in the Milieu of Leonard and Virginia Woolf: Peace, Politics, and Education, Pace Univ Press, 98; "Willa Cather and Leon Bakst, Her Portratist Who Was Designer to Diaghiler," Willa Cather's New York, Fairleigh Dickinson Univ Press, 00. **CONTACT ADDRESS** Doane Col, 1014 Boswell, Crete, NE 68333. **EMAIL** ehaller@doane.edu

HALLETT, CHARLES A.
PERSONAL Born 07/19/1935, New Heaven, CT, m, 1958 **DISCIPLINE** ENGLISH **EDUCATION** The New Sch for Soc Res, NY City, BA, 61; Columbia Univ, NY City, MA, 63; Yale Univ, DFA, 67. **CAREER** Lectr, Brooklyn Col, 66-67; Vis Fel, Univ of Warwick, Coventry England, 78; Vis Prof, Loyola Univ, La, 94; form Asst Prof to Full Prof, Fordham Univ, 67-. **HONORS AND AWARDS** Fac Fel, Fordham Univ, 73-73, 78, 84, 92; NEH Fel, Symposium for Shakespeare Performance, Univ of Ill Urbana, 77; Grant-in-Aid, Am Coun of Learned Soc, 81. **RESEARCH** Mod utopianism. **SELECTED PUBLICATIONS** Auth, Middleton's Cynics, Jacobean Drama Ser, Univ of Salzburg (Salzburg), 75; coauth, The Revenger's Madness: A Study of Revenge Tragedy Motifs, Univ of Nebr (Lincoln), 80; auth, "Analyzing Action in Shakespeare's Plays: The Beat," Papers on Lang and Lit 19 (83): 124-144; auth, "Staging Shakespeare's Dramatic Questions: Intensifying techniques in Act Two of 'Ling Lear'm" Shakespeare Bul 9 (Summer 91): 5-12; coauth, Analyzing Shakespeare's Action: Scene vs. Sequence, Cambridge Univ Press (Cambridge), 91; auth, "Structure and Performance in 'Hamlet' 2.2," Shakespeare Bul 10 (Fall 92): 32-37; auth, "Is There 'Charity in Sin'?: Sexual Harassment in 'Measure for Measure'," Shakespeare Bul 11 (Fall 93): 23-26; auth, "'A Twitch Upon the Thread': Brideshead Revisited," (Vital Works Reconsidered #16) New Oxford Rec 61 (Nov 94): 19-22; auth, "Scene Versus Sequence: Distinguishing Action from Narrative in Shakespeare's Multipartite Scenes," Shakespeare Quart 46 (Summer 95): 183-195; auth, "'Metamorphosing' Proteus: Reversal Strategies in 'The Two Gentlemen of Verona'," in The Two Gentlemen of Verona: Critical Essays, ed. June Schlueter (NY: Garland Publ, 96), 153-177; auth, "Cynthia Lewis's 'Particular Saints: Shakespeare's Four Antonios'," Shakespeare Bul (98). **CONTACT ADDRESS** Dept English, Fordham Univ, 441 E Fordham Rd, Bronx, NY 10458-5149.

HALLIN, DANIEL C.
DISCIPLINE POLITICAL COMMUNICATION **EDUCATION** Univ Calif-Berkeley, PhD, 80. **CAREER** Prof, Dept Ch, Univ Calif, San Diego, 95-98. **HONORS AND AWARDS** Western Polit Sci Asn Diss Awd, 80; Woodrow Wilson Center for Scholars, Media Studies Proj Essay Contest, first prize, 90; Fel, Freedom Forum Media Studies Center, 91-92; Visiting Prof, Deutsche Forschungsgemeinschaft, 00. **MEMBERSHIPS** Int Commun Asn (board member); Latin Am Studies Asn. **RESEARCH** Comparative analysis of the news media's role in the public sphere. **SELECTED PUBLICATIONS** Auth, The Uncensored War: The Media and Vietnam, Oxford, 86; auth, We Keep America on Top of the World: Television Journalism and the Public Sphere, Routledge, 94. **CONTACT ADDRESS** Dept of Commun, Univ of California, San Diego, 9500 Gilman Dr, La Jolla, CA 92093. **EMAIL** dhallin@weber.ucsd.edu

HALLISSY, MARGARET
PERSONAL Born 07/28/1945, New York, NY, m, 1967, 3 children **DISCIPLINE** ENGLISH **EDUCATION** St John's Univ, BA, 66; Fordham Univ, MA, 71, PhD, 74. **CAREER** Adjunct lectr, Long Island Univ, C. W. Post Campus, 74-75, adjunct asst prof, 75-77, asst prof, 77-82, assoc prof, 82-87, prof, 87-, dir of Writing Center, 86-88, dir of the Office of Interdisciplinary Studies, 81-84, coord of the Life Experience Credit, 79-81; fac mem, Hutton House Lect Series, 92-; discussion leader, Hutton House Book Group, 98-; SCALE prog fac liaison with St Dominic's High Sch, Oyster Bay, NY, 98-. **HONORS AND AWARDS** Vis scholar in the humanities and participant in seminar "Medieval Culture: Love and Power in the Middle Ages," Humanities Seminars for Visiting Scholars sponsored by Andrew W. Mellon Found, New York Univ, fall 94; recipient of grants from Res Comt of Long Island Univ, 85-; Phi Eta Honor Soc, fac inductee, 86; Honors prog fac, 88-; Trustee Awd for Scholarly Achievement, Long Island Univ Bd of Trustees' highest recognition for fac res, given for "Venomous Women: Fear of the Female in Literature," 88; listed in Who's Who in the East, 23 ed, Marquis, 91-92; David Newton Awd for Excellence in Teaching, Long Island Univ Bd of Trustees' highest recognition for teaching, 97. **MEMBERSHIPS** Am Asn of Univ Women. **RESEARCH** Medieval literature, especially Chaucer; modern medievalia; contemporary Irish and Irish-American fiction. **SELECTED PUBLICATIONS** Auth, "Knight's and Canon's Yeoman's Tales," Essays in Arts and Scis, 10, no 1 (81): 31-40; auth, A Companion to Chaucer's Canterbury Tales, Greenwood Pub Group (95); auth, " 'No Innocent Work': Theology and Psychology in William Golding's The Spire," Christianity and Lit, 47, no 1 (autumn 97): 1-18; auth, "Writing a Building: Chaucer's Knowledge of the Construction Industry and the Language of the 'Knight's Tale'," Chaucer Rev, 32, no 3 (98): 239-259; auth, "The End of Literature: The Case of Geoffrey Chaucer," (forthcoming in Confrontations); auth, "Reading the Plans: The Architectural Drawings in Umberto Eco's The Name of the Rose," (forthcoming in Critique). **CONTACT ADDRESS** English Dept, Long Island Univ, C.W. Post, 720 Northern Blvd, Brookville, NY 11548-1300. **EMAIL** Profmarge@aol.com

HALLORAN, STEPHEN MICHAEL
PERSONAL Born 02/08/1939, Cohoes, NY, m, 1965, 2 children **DISCIPLINE** ENGLISH, SPEECH **EDUCATION** Holy Cross Col, BS, 60; Rensselaer Polytech Inst, PhD(commun & rhetoric), 73. **CAREER** English teacher, Hoosic Valley Cent Sch, 63-67; from instr to asst prof, 69-78, ASSOC PROF COMMUN, RENSSELAER POLYTECH INST, 78- **MEMBERSHIPS** NCTE; Coun Col Compos & Commun; Speech Commun Asn; Rhetoric Soc Am; Int Soc Hist of Rhetoric. **RESEARCH** Rhetorical criticism; theory of composition. **SELECTED PUBLICATIONS** Auth, Wittgensteinian grammar, Personalist, spring 70; The anti-aesthetics of Waiting for Godot, Centennial Rev, winter 72; Language and the absurd, Philol & Rhetoric, spring 73; On the end of rhetoric, classical and modern, Col English, 2/75; Tradition and theory in rhetoric, Quart J Speech, 10/76; contribr, Form and Genre: Shaping Rhetorical Action, Speech Commun Asn, 78; auth, Technical writing and the rhetoric of science, J Tech Writing & Commun, spring 78; On making choices, sartorial and rhetorical, Conf Col Compos & Commun (in press). **CONTACT ADDRESS** Dept of Lang, Rensselaer Polytech Inst, Troy, NY 12181.

HALLWAS, JOHN EDWARD
PERSONAL Born 05/24/1945, Waukegan, IL, m, 1966, 2 children **DISCIPLINE** AMERICAN AND BRITISH LITERATURE **EDUCATION** Western Ill Univ, BSEd, 67, MA, 68; Univ Fla, PhD(English), 72. **CAREER** Asst prof, 70-76, assoc prof, 76-81, prof english, Western Ill Univ, 81-, Dir regional collections, Western Ill Univ Libr; ed, Western Ill Regional Studies 79-91; columnist, Macomb J. 81-84. **HONORS AND AWARDS** Distinguished Prof Awd, WIU, 92; Mid America Awd, from the Society for the Study of Midwestern Literature, 94. **MEMBERSHIPS** Soc Study Midwestern Lit.; Illinois State Historical Society. **RESEARCH** Midwestern American Literature. **SELECTED PUBLICATIONS** Ed, The Poems of H: The Lost Poet of Lincoln's Springfield, Ellis Press, 82; auth, Western Illinois Heritage, 83; auth, Illinois Literature: The Nineteenth Century, 86; auth, Macomb: A Pictorial History, 90; auth, Spoon River Anthology: An Annotated Edition, 92; auth, The Bootlegger: A Seary of Small-Town America, 98, and others. **CONTACT ADDRESS** Dept of English, Western Illinois Univ, 1 University Cir, Macomb, IL 61455-1390.

HALPERIN, JOHN
PERSONAL Born 09/15/1941, Chicago, IL, s **DISCIPLINE** ENGLISH **EDUCATION** Bowdoin Col, AB, 63; Univ of NH, MA, 66; Johns Hopkins Univ, MA, 68; PhD, 69. **CAREER** Asst prof, Suny-Stony Brook, 69-72; assoc prof to prof, Univ of S Cal, 72-83; centennial prof, Vanderbilt Univ, 83-. **HONORS AND AWARDS** Guggenheim (2); Grad Teaching Awd, Vanderbilt Univ; Fel of the Royal Soc of Lit. **MEMBERSHIPS** MLA; PEN. **RESEARCH** English Novel **SELECTED PUBLICATIONS** Auth, Trollope and Politics, 77; auth, Gissing: A Life in Books, 82; auth, C.P. Snow: An Oval Biography, 83; auth, The Life of Jane Austen 84; auth, Jane Austen's Lovers (essays), 88; auth, Novelists in their Youth, 90; auth, Eminent Georgians, 95. **CONTACT ADDRESS** Dept English, Vanderbilt Univ, 2201 W End Ave, Nashville, TN 73235-0001.

HALPERIN, MIKE
PERSONAL Born 02/19/1940, New York, NY, m, 1966, 2 children **DISCIPLINE** ENGLISH **EDUCATION** Bard Col, BA, 60; Univ Iowa, MFA, 66; New Sch for Soc Res. **CAREER** Vis prof, Hertzen Univ; Fulbright, Moscow Ling Univ; vis prof, Univ of Ariz; vis prof, Simane Univ; prof, Central Wash Univ. **HONORS AND AWARDS** U.S. Awd, Int Poetry Forum, 76; Artist Trust Awd, Wash State, 99. **SELECTED PUBLICATIONS** Auth, Backroads, Univ of Pittsburgh Press; auth, A Place Made Fast, Copper Canyon Press; auth, The Measure of Islands, Wesleyan Univ Press; auth, Time as Distance, Western Mich Univ Press. **CONTACT ADDRESS** Dept English, Central Washington Univ, 400 E 8th Ave, Ellensburg, WA 98926-7502. **EMAIL** halperin@cwu.edu

HALPERN, MARTIN
PERSONAL Born 10/03/1929, New York, NY, m, 1985, 3 children **DISCIPLINE** DRAMA, MUSIC COMPOSITION **EDUCATION** Univ Rochester, BA, 50, MA 53; Harvard Univ, PhD, 59; Queens Col, MA, 97. **CAREER** From instr to asst prof English, Univ Calif, Berkeley, 59-64; asst prof, Univ Mass, 64-65; from asst prof to assoc prof, 65-77, chmn dept, 72-76, Schulman Prof Theater Arts, 77-94, prof emeritus, 94- , Brandeis Univ; theater panelist, Mass Coun Arts, 75-78. **HONORS AND AWARDS** Howard Found fel, 62-63; Fulbright travel grant, 62-63; Harold C Crain Awd Playwriting, San Jose State Univ, 78; Mass Artists Found fel, 82; 3 ASCAP awards. **MEMBERSHIPS** Dir, Long Island Composers Alliance, 97-. **RESEARCH** Dramatic literature, chiefly 19th and 20th century; playwriting; theory of poetry, chiefly metrics; music theory. **SELECTED PUBLICATIONS** Auth, Two Sides of an Island and Other Poems, Univ NC, 63; William Vaughn Moody, Twayne, 64; Keats and the Spirit That Laughest, Keat-Shelly J, winter 66; Verse in the theater, Mass Rev, winter 66; Aescylus, Atlantic Brief Lives; Selected Poems, Golden Quill, 76; Total Recall, In: Best Short Plays of 1978, Chilton, 78; What the babe said, Pioneer Drama Serv, 82. **CONTACT ADDRESS** 160 Henry St, Brooklyn, NY 11201. **EMAIL** marhalp@aol.com

HALPERN, SHELDON
PERSONAL Born 07/16/1932, New York, NY, m, 1957, 2 children **DISCIPLINE** ENGLISH LITERATURE **EDUCATION** City Col NYork, BA, 53; Columbia Univ, MA, 57, PhD(English), 63. **CAREER** Resident lectr English, Ind Univ, South Bend, 59-63; from asst prof to prof, Bowling Green State Univ, 63-78, vprovost, 74-78, vpres acad affairs, 78-80; VPRES COL PLANNING & RES, TRENTON STATE COL, 80-, Vis assoc prof, Tel-Aviv Univ, 68-69. **MEMBERSHIPS** MLA; Am Asn Higher Educ. **RESEARCH** English romantic literature. **SELECTED PUBLICATIONS** Auth, 'Eves Apple' (rev), NY Rev Bk, Vol 0044, 97; The 'Story of Junk' (rev), NY Rev Bk, Vol 0044, 97; The 'Kiss', NY Rev Bk, Vol 0044, 97. **CONTACT ADDRESS** Col Planning & Res, Trenton State Col, Trenton, NJ 08625.

HALPORN, JAMES W.
PERSONAL Born 01/14/1929, New York, NY, m, 1960, 2 children **DISCIPLINE** CLASSICAL STUDIES **EDUCATION** Columbia Univ, AB, 49; MA, 50; Cornell Univ, PhD, 53. **CAREER** Instr, Columbia Col, 54-58; Vis Lectr, Carleton Univ, 58-59; Vis Asst Prof, Univ Mo, 59-60; Prof to Prof Emeritus, Ind Univ, 60-; Vis Prof, Univ Calif Berkeley, 71-72; Prof, Ind Univ, 75-90; Assoc in the Class, Harvard Univ, 93-. **HONORS AND AWARDS** Fulbright Scholar, Univ Vienna, 53-54; Fel, Am Coun of Learned Soc, IBM, 65-66. **MEMBERSHIPS** Am Philol Asn; Class Asn of N Eng; Hagiography Soc. **RESEARCH** Late Latin literature; Latin palaeography; Early Saints' Lives. **SELECTED PUBLICATIONS** Auth, "Roman Comedy and Greek Models," in Theatre and Society in the Ancient World, *Univ Mich Press, 93), 191-213; co-auth, The Meters of Greek and Latin Poetry 2nd ed, Methuen and Bobbs Merrill, 94; auth, "Women and Classical Archaeology at the Turn of the Century: Abby Leach of Vassar College," in Assembling the Past: Studies in the Professionalization of Archaeology, (Univ N Mex Press, 00), 121-132; auth, "After the Schools: Grammar and Rhetoric in Cassiodorus," in Latin Grammar and Rhetoric: Classical Theory and Medieval Practice, (Continuum Press, forthcoming); auth, "Cassiodorus on the Soul and Institutiones, translation and commentary," in Translated Texts for Historians, (Liverpool Univ Press, forthcoming.) **CONTACT ADDRESS** 320B Harvard St, Cambridge, MA 02139-2002. **EMAIL** halporn@fas.harvard.edu

HAMALIAN, LEO
PERSONAL Born 01/13/1920, New York, NY, m, 1943, 3 children **DISCIPLINE** ENGLISH, COMPARATIVE LITERATURE **EDUCATION** Cornell Univ, BS, 42; Columbia Univ, MA, 47, PhD(English), 54. **CAREER** Instr English, New York Univ, 47-54; from instr to assoc prof, 54-67, PROF ENGLISH LIT, CITY COL NEW YORK, 67-, DIR, GRAD CREATIVE WRITING, 72-, Smith-Mundt grant, Syria, 62-64; Am Studies Sem fel, Columbia Univ, 68-; dean, Calif Inst of Arts, 70-72; mem, bd dir, Tuum Est Drug Rehabil Ctr, Venice, 71-; Fulbright lectr, Univ Tehran, 74-75 & Univ Hamburg, 80; ed, Ararat. **MEMBERSHIPS** MLA; NCTE; Am Studies Asn; English Union; PEN Club. **RESEARCH** T S Eliot; D H Lawrence; comparative continental literature. **SELECTED PUBLICATIONS** Auth, The secret career of Samuel Roth, J Popular Cult, summer 68; ed, In the Modern Idion, 73 & An Invitation to Semantics, 73, Crowell; auth, Hemingway as hunger artist, Lit Rev, winter 73; Amid bounty, longing, New York Times, 12/76; The figures in the window: Design in T S Eliot's The Family Reunion, Col Lit, 77-78; Sole: Stories of Women Alone, Dell Bks, 78; New Writing from the Middle East, New Am Libr, 78; Burn After Reading, 79 & As Others See Us: The Armenian Image in Literature, 80, Ararat Press; ed, In Search of Eden, New Am Libr, 80; ed & auth, Ladies on the Loose: Women Travellers of the 18th and 19th Centuries, Dodd, 81; auth, D H Lawrence in Italy, Tapinger, 82. **CONTACT ADDRESS** Dept of English, City Col, CUNY, New York, NY 10031.

HAMBLIN, ROBERT W.
DISCIPLINE ENGLISH LITERATURE **EDUCATION** NE Miss Community Col, AA, 58; Delta State Univ, BSE, 60; Univ MS, MA, 65, PhD, 76. **CAREER** Tchg asst, Univ MS, 64-65; mem, SE MO State Univ, 65-. **HONORS AND AWARDS** Governor's Awd, 77; SE Mo State Univ Alumni Asn Fac Merit Awd, 97; Halsell Prize, Miss Hist Soc,92. **RESEARCH** Am lit; merican Novel; Bible and lit; Faulkner studies; lit criticism; Poetry; southern lit; sport lit. **SELECTED PUBLICATIONS** Auth, publ(s) about Faulkner; sports; lit; poetry. **CONTACT ADDRESS** Eng Dept, Southeast Missouri State Univ, 1 University Plz, Cape Girardeau, MO 63701. **EMAIL** rhamblin@semovm.semo.edu

HAMEL, MARY
DISCIPLINE ANCIENT AND MEDIEVAL EUROPEAN LITERATURE, CHAUCER, AND THE ENGLISH LANGUAGE **EDUCATION** Pa State Univ, PhD. **CAREER** Dept Eng, Mt. Saint Mary's Col **SELECTED PUBLICATIONS** Publ, a bk and articles on, Middle Engl lit; assoc ed, scholarly jour Chaucer Rev. **CONTACT ADDRESS** Dept of English, Mount Saint Mary's Col and Sem, 16300 Old Emmitsburg Rd, Emmitsburg, MD 21727-7799. **EMAIL** hamel@msmary.edu

HAMILTON, ALBERT C.
PERSONAL Born 07/20/1921, Winnipeg, MB, Canada, m, 1950, 4 children **DISCIPLINE** ENGLISH **EDUCATION** Univ Man, BA, 45; Univ Toronto, MA, 48; Cambridge Univ, PhD, 53. **CAREER** Prof, Univ Wash, 52-68; fel, Huntington Libr, 59-60; PROF ENGLISH, QUEEN'S UNIV, 68-; fel, St John's Col, Cambridge, 74-75; fel, Hum Res Ctr, Canberra, 85; vis prof, Kumamoto Univ, 88. **MEMBERSHIPS** MLA; Renaissance Soc Am; Asn Can Univ Tchrs Eng; Spenser Soc Am. **RESEARCH** Renaissance literature; Shakespeare; Spenser. **SELECTED PUBLICATIONS** Auth, The Structure of Allegory in 'The Faerie Queene', 61; auth, The Early Shakespeare, 67; auth, Sir Philip Sidney: A Study of His Life and Works, 77; auth, Edmund Spenser's 'Faerie Queene', 77; auth, Northrop Frye: Anatomy of his Criticism, 90; gen ed, The Spenser Encyclopedia, 90; ed bd, English Literary Renaissance: Duquesne Studies in English. **CONTACT ADDRESS** Dept of English, Queen's Univ at Kingston, Kingston, ON, Canada K7L 3N6.

HAMILTON, CAROL VAN DER VEER
DISCIPLINE ENGLISH **EDUCATION** Univ Calif, PhD. **CAREER** Asst prof, Carnegie Mellon Univ. **MEMBERSHIPS** Modernist Studies Asn; MLA. **RESEARCH** Modernism; cultural politics. **SELECTED PUBLICATIONS** Auth, "Wagner as Anarchist, Anarchists as Wagnerians," Oxford Ger Studies 22 (93); auth, "Conrad's Natural Anarchists," The Conradian (95); auth, "American Writers and the Sacco-Vanzetti Case," Anarchis Studies 8 (00); auth, Dynamite: Anarchism, Modernism,a nd the Aesthetics of Explosion (Univ Ill Pr), forthcoming. **CONTACT ADDRESS** Carnegie Mellon Univ, 145 B Baker Hall, Pittsburgh, PA 15213.

HAMILTON, HARLAN
PERSONAL Born 11/29/1927, Medford, MA, s **DISCIPLINE** ENGLISH **EDUCATION** Univ Colo, BA, 55; Columbia Univ, MA, 65; Boston Univ, PhD, 74. **CAREER** Prof, NJers City Univ, 65-. **MEMBERSHIPS** U.S. Lighthouse soc; NY Film & Video Coun. **RESEARCH** Film; Lighthouses. **SELECTED PUBLICATIONS** Auth, Lights and Legends: A Guide to the Lighthouses of Long Island Sound, NY, Westcott Cove Pub, 57. **CONTACT ADDRESS** Dept Eng, New Jersey City Univ, 2039 Kennedy Blvd, Jersey City, NJ 07305-1527.

HAMILTON, JOHN MAXWELL
PERSONAL Born 03/28/1947, Evanston, IL, m, 1975, 1 child **DISCIPLINE** JOURNALISM **EDUCATION** Marquette Univ, BA, 69; Univ NH, 73; Boston Univ, MS, 74; Geo Washington Univ, PhD, 83. **CAREER** Reporter, Milwaukee J, 67-69; free-lance journalist, Washington DC, 73-75; for corresp, Lat Am, 76-78; spec asst/asst adm, Ag Int Dev, 78-81; staff assoc, House For Aff Subcomt Int Econ Policy, Trade, US Cong, 81-82; chief US For Policy Corresp Int Reporting Info Sys, Washing, 82-83; N Am Adv, Pub Aff, World Bank, 83-85; Dir Main St Am & Third World, Washington, 85-87; sen couns, World Bank, Washington, 83-85; dean, prof, Manship Sch Mass Commun, LA State Univ, 92-; commentator, Market Place, Public Radio. **HONORS AND AWARDS** Los Angeles Time Critic's Choice Awd; Frank Luther Mott-Kappa Tau Alpha Res Awd, 88; Ford Fdn, Carnegie Inst, US AID grants; Hopkins P Brazeale Prof, 98; Excellence in Journalism in Radio Commentary, Soc of Professional Journalists, 99; Pulitzer Prize Jury, 99, 00. **MEMBERSHIPS** Int Ctr Journalists; Asn for Educators in Journalism, Mass Commun; Soc Prof Journalists. **RESEARCH** Int aff **SELECTED PUBLICATIONS** Auth, Main Street America and the Third World, 86, 2d ed, 89; auth, Edgar Snow: A Biography, 88; auth, Entangling Alliances: How the Third World Shapes Our Lives, 90; co-auth, Hold the Press: The Inside Story on Newspapers, 96; auth, Casanova Was a Book Lover and Other Naked Truths and Provocative Curiosities about the Writing, Selling and Reading of Books, 00; various chapters in books, articles in prof journals inc Atlanta Constitution, Baltimore Sun, Bull Atomic Scientists, Boston Globe, Chicago Tribune, Christian Science Monitor, Columbia Journlism Rev, Jour Commerce, NY Times, The Nation. **CONTACT ADDRESS** Manship Sch Mass Commun, Louisiana State Univ and A&M Col, 221 Journalism Bldg, Baton Rouge, LA 70803. **EMAIL** jhamilt@lsu.edu

HAMILTON, MARK A.
PERSONAL Born 04/13/1958, Stanford, CT, m, 1 child **DISCIPLINE** COMMUNICATION **EDUCATION** San Jose State Univ, BA, 80; Mich State Univ, MA, 83; PhD 87. **CAREER** Univ Conn, assoc prof. **HONORS AND AWARDS** Univ of Conn res found grant, 89-90. **MEMBERSHIPS** ICA; NCA. **RESEARCH** Message processing, language, non-verbal communication. **SELECTED PUBLICATIONS** Coauth, "The elaboration likelihood model as a theory of attitude formation: A mathematical analysis," Commun Theory 3 (93): 50-65; coauth, "Extending an information processing model of language intensity effects," Commun Quart 41 (93): 231-246; coauth, "Testing an information processing account of message intensity effects," World Commun 23 (94): 1-14; coauth, "Dentist communication and patient utilization of dental services: Inhibited anxiety and enhanced competence effects," Health Commun 6 (94): 137-158; auth, "Verbal auditory hallucination and the invention of alter-ego mental constructs," in Reader on intrapersonal communication and social cognition, ed. J. Aitken and L.J. Shedletsky (VA: Speech Commun Asn, 95). **CONTACT ADDRESS** Dept of Communication Sciences, Univ of Connecticut, Storrs, Box U-85, Storrs, CT 06269-1085. **EMAIL** mhamil@uconnvm.uconn.edu

HAMILTON, PETER K.
DISCIPLINE PUBLIC RELATIONS, ORGANIZATIONAL COMMUNICATION **EDUCATION** Wis-Whitewater, BA; University Nebr, MA; Univ Okla, PhD. **CAREER** Prof, ch, 72-. **RESEARCH** Communications theory, quantitative methods. **SELECTED PUBLICATIONS** Publ, Trade Jour articles and bk chap(s). **CONTACT ADDRESS** Dept of Commun, Pittsburg State Univ, 1701 S Broadway St, Pittsburg, KS 66762.

HAMILTON, SHARON J.
PERSONAL Born 07/01/1944, Winnipeg, MB, Canada, d, 1 child **DISCIPLINE** ENGLISH **EDUCATION** Univ Winnipeg, BA, 69; Univ Manitoba, BEd, 69; MEd, 82; Univ London, PhD, 86. **CAREER** Asst prof, Univ of Manitoba, 87-91; assoc prof to prof, Ind Univ, 91-. **HONORS AND AWARDS** Res Coun Can Fel, 84, 85; IUPUI Fel, 88; Network for Excellence in Teaching Awd, 89; Honors Fac Fel, 92; Bryn Mawr Grant, 94; Pew Trust, UUPP Grant, 98, 99; Chancellor's Prof, 00. **MEMBERSHIPS** Sigma Theta Tau; Nat Counc of Teachers of English, Ind Teachers of Writing, Rocky Mtn MLA; Col Composition and Commun. **RESEARCH** Collaborative Learning, Electronic Institutional Portfolios as a way to document higher education accountability. **SELECTED PUBLICATIONS** Coauth, Sourcebook for Collaborative Learning in the Arts and Sciences, Ind Univ, 92; coed, Collaborative Learning in Higher Education: Underlying Processes and Effective Techniques, New Directions for Teaching and Learning, Jossey-Bass, 94; auth, My Name's Not Susie: A Life Transformed by Literacy, Heinemann, 95; auth, Collaborative Learning in the Arts, Sciences, and Professional Schools, IUPUI Center for Teaching and Learning, 97; auth, "Nancy's Promise", Narration as Knowledge, dc Joseph Trimmer, Heinemann, (97): 110-122; auth, "You Can Get by: A Cross-Cultural Odyssey in Search of Voice and Identity", The Personal Narrative: Writing Ourselves as Teachers and Scholars, ed, Gil Haroian-Guerin, Callendar Islands Pr, (99): 144-163; auth, "Anne Shirley and the Power of Literacy", L.M. Montgomery and Canadian Culture, eds Irene Gammel and Elizabeth Epperly, Univ of Toronto Pr, (99): 193-197; coauth, "Institutional Portfolios for Quality Assurance and Accreditation: The Urban Universities Portfolio Project", Higher Education 2000: What will be New? What will be Different?, Middle States Comm on Higher Educ (00): 99-112. **CONTACT ADDRESS** Dept English, Indiana Univ-Purdue Univ, Indianapolis, 815 W Michigan St, Indianapolis, IN 46202. **EMAIL** shamilto@iupui.edu

HAMLIN, WILLIAM
PERSONAL Born, MO, m, 2 children **DISCIPLINE** ENGLISH LITERATURE **EDUCATION** Univ Wash, PhD, 89. **CAREER** Prof. **RESEARCH** Early Modern travel literature and ethnography; Renaissance skepticism; Jacobean tragedy. **SELECTED PUBLICATIONS** Auth, The Image of America in Montaigne, Spenser, Shakespeare: Renaissance Ethnography

and Literary Reflection. **CONTACT ADDRESS** Dept of English and Philosophy, Idaho State Univ, Pocatello, ID 83209. **EMAIL** hamlwill@isu.edu

HAMMER, MITCHELL R.

PERSONAL Born 08/07/1951, Appleton, WI, m, 1980, 2 children **DISCIPLINE** COMMUNICATION **EDUCATION** St Norbert Coll, BA, 73; Ohio Univ, MA, 74; Univ Minn, PhD, 82. **CAREER** Instr, Southern W Va Community Coll, 74-75; tchg assoc, Univ Minn, 75-76; res assoc, Univ Minn, 76-77; evaluation res, Univ Minn, 77-78; asst prof, Univ Vis Milwaukee, 82-87; vis prof, Indiana Univ Kuala Lumpur Malaysia, 87-88; assoc prof, Am Univ Washington DC, 88-. **HONORS AND AWARDS** Top Three honors, Int Commun Asn, 77, 87; Top Four honors, Speech Commun Asn, 84; Top Four honors Acad of Mgt, 89; Sr Interculturalist Awd for Achievement, Soc of Intercultural Educ, Training and Res, 92; Top Three honors, Speech Commun Asn, 94; School of Int Service Awd for Outstanding Scholar, Res, and Other Professional Contributors, 97-98; Outstanding Book Awd, Int Asn of Conflict Mgt College Park Md, 98. **MEMBERSHIPS** Int Asn of Conflict Mgt; Int Commun Asn; Nat Commun Asn; Soc for Intercultural Educ, Training and Res; Int Acad of Intercultural Res. **RESEARCH** Negotiation dynamics involved in high intensity conflict situations; Discourse analysis of conflict escalation and de-escalation in hostage and crisis incidents; Patterns of cross-cultural adaptation; Effectiveness of international management training efforts. **SELECTED PUBLICATIONS** Auth, The Vietnam Experience, 91; numerous academic articles; coauth, Dynamic processes of crisis negotiation: Theory, research and practice, 97. **CONTACT ADDRESS** The School of International Service, American Univ, 4400 Massachusetts Ave NW, Washington, DC 20016. **EMAIL** Docmitch@msn.com

HAMMERBACK, JOHN C.

PERSONAL Born 10/06/1938, San Francisco, CA, m, 1965, 2 children **DISCIPLINE** COMMUNICATION **EDUCATION** San Francisco State univ, BA, 62; Univ of Okla, MA, 65; Ind Univ, PhD, 70. **CAREER** Prof, ch, asst VP, assoc Dean, Calif State Univ, 68-97; prof & dept head, NC State Univ, 97-99; prof chair, Calif State Univ, 99-. **HONORS AND AWARDS** Outstanding Fac Lecturer, 71; 1st nn Exceptional Merit Service Awd, 84; Who's Who in America, Who's Who in Educ outstanding scholarship award, intercultural communication Int. grp, Nat'l Commun Assoc, 95. **MEMBERSHIPS** Nat Commun Assoc; Western States Commun Assoc; Southern Commun Assoc; Rhet Soc of Am; Kenneth Burke Soc. **RESEARCH** Rhetorical criticism; discourse analysis; public communication. **SELECTED PUBLICATIONS** Auth, The Words of Cesar Chavez, Teacher of Truth, San Jose Studs, vol 20, 10-14, Spring 94; co-auth, Reies Tijerina, Leaders from the 1960s: A Biographical Sourcebook of American Activism, Praeger, 156-162, 94; co-auth, The Plan of Delano: Ethnic Heritage as Rhetorical Legacy, Quart J of Speech, vol 80, 53-70, 2/94; Jose Antonio's Rhetoric of Fascism, Southern Commun J, vol 59, 181-195, Spring 94; co-auth, Robert Parris Moses, African-American Orators, 261-269; co-auth, Leroy Eldridge Cleaver, African-American Orators: A Biocritical Sourcebook, Greenwood Press, 32-40, 96; co-auth, History and Culture as Rhetorical Constraint: Cesar Chavez' Letter from Delano in Doing Rhetorical History, Alabama Press, 98; co-auth, Te Rhetorical Laseer of Lesar Chavez, Texas A&M Univ Press, 98; co-auth, Your Tools Are Really the People: The Rhetoric of Robert Parris Moses, Commun Monographs, vol 65, 126-140, 6/97; auth, Future Research on Rhetoric and Intercultural Communication: Moving Forward from Starosta's Intersection, Int & Intercultural Commun Ann, 99; auth, Barry Gold Waters Rhetorical Legacy, Southern Univ, vol 64, 323-332, spring, 99; auth, The Community Organizing rhetoric of Robert Parris M&SRS, Howard S. of Common, vol 10, 1-17, Feb. 99. **CONTACT ADDRESS** Dept Speech Com, California State Univ, Hayward, PO Box 1677, Hayward, CA 94566-0167. **EMAIL** jhammerb@csnhayward.edu

HAMMILL, GRAHAM L.

DISCIPLINE LITERARY THEORY **EDUCATION** Duke Univ, PhD. **CAREER** Asst prof, Univ Notre Dame. **RESEARCH** Homosexuality and literature. **SELECTED PUBLICATIONS** Auth, Consum'd to Nought: Naming, Bodies, and Subjectivity in The Faerie Queene; Faustus's Fortunes: Commodification, Exchange, and the Form of Literary Subjectivity; Being and Knowledge: Lacan and the Institution of Psychoanalysis; The Epistemology of Expurgation: Bacon and The Masculine Birth of Time; Stepping to the Temple; auth, Sexuality and Form: Caravaggio, Marlowe, and Bacon. **CONTACT ADDRESS** Dept of English, Univ of Notre Dame, 356 O'Shaughnessy Hall, Notre Dame, IN 46556. **EMAIL** graham.l.hammill.1@nd.edu

HAMMOND, ALEXANDER

DISCIPLINE NINETEENTH- AND TWENTIETH-CENTURY AMERICAN LITERATURE AND CULTURE **EDUCATION** Northwestern Univ, PhD **CAREER** Assoc prof & dir, Washington State Univ. **RESEARCH** Poe's fiction in relation to the patterns of representation, figuration, and production in the literary marketplace. **CONTACT ADDRESS** Dept of English, Washington State Univ, 1 SE Stadium Way, PO Box 645020, Pullman, WA 99164-5020. **EMAIL** hammonda@wsu.edu

HAMMONS, PAMELA SUSANNE

PERSONAL Born 10/06/1969, Oak Ridge, TN, p **DISCIPLINE** ENGLISH LITERATURE **EDUCATION** Univ Va, BA, 91; Cornell Univ, MA, 94; PhD, 97. **HONORS AND AWARDS** Mellon Fel, 91. **MEMBERSHIPS** MLA, Renaissance Soc of Am, AAUP, Soc for the Study of Early Mod Women. **RESEARCH** Renaissance literature, Women's Studies, 17th Century Cultural History, Medieval Literature. **SELECTED PUBLICATIONS** Auth, "Despised Creatures: The Illusion of Maternal Self-Effacement in Seventeenth-Century Child Loss Poetry, ELH: English Literary History 66 (99): 25-49; auth, "Katherine Austen's Country House Innovations," SEL: Studies in English Lit 40.1, (00): 123-137; auth, "Widow, Prophet, and Poet: Lyrical Self-Figurations in Katherine Austen's 'Book M' (1664)," Write or Be Written: Early Modern Women Poets and Cultural Constraints, eds Ursula Appelt and Barbara Smith, (Aldershot, UK: Ashgate, 01): 3-27. **CONTACT ADDRESS** 3418 Bishop Park Dr, Apt 333, Winter Park, FL 32792-2837. **EMAIL** phammons@pegasus.cc.ucf.edu

HAMNER, ROBERT DANIEL

PERSONAL Born 01/16/1941, Tuscaloosa, AL, m, 1963, 2 children **DISCIPLINE** ENGLISH & AMERICAN LITERATURE **EDUCATION** Wayland Baptist Col, BA, 64; Univ Tex, Austin, MA, 66, PhD(English), 71. **CAREER** Instr English, Wayland Baptist Col, 68-70; asst prof, 71-74, assoc prof English, 74-78, PROF ENGLISH & HUMANITIES, HARDIN-SIMMOND UNIV, 78-96, Fulbright-Hays lectureship Am lit Univ Guyana, 75-76; Prof of English and Humanities, 96-. **HONORS AND AWARDS** Piper Prof **MEMBERSHIPS** MLA; SCent Mod Lang Asn; African Lit Asn; Caribbean Studies Asn; Joseph Conrad Soc Am. **RESEARCH** Twentieth century American and English novel and poetry; British Commonwealth literature; British West Indian literature. **SELECTED PUBLICATIONS** Auth, V.S. Naipaul. Twayne, 73; auth, V.S. Naipaul, A selected bibliography, J Commonwealth Lit 75l ed, contribr, Critical Perspectives on V.S. Naipail, Three Contenints, 77; auth, Mythological aspects of Derek Walcott's drama, Ariel, 77; auth, Derek Walcott, Twayne, 93; auth, Joseph Conrad: Third World Perspectives, Three Continents Press, 90; Epic of the Dispossessed, Missouri Press, 97; auth, "From Winslow Homer to Marcel Duchamp and the Fortuate Flaw in Walcott's Omcros, " Ariel, 99. **CONTACT ADDRESS** Dept of English, Hardin-Simmons Univ, Abilene, TX 79698-0002. **EMAIL** rdh@hsutx.edu

HAMPTON, BARBARA L.

DISCIPLINE ETHNOMUSICOLOGY **EDUCATION** Columbia Univ, PhD. **CAREER** Prof & dir, Grad Prog in Ethnomusicol. **MEMBERSHIPS** Served on, nat exec bd, Soc for Ethnomusicol. **SELECTED PUBLICATIONS** Contribur, Garland Encycl World Mus; JVC Anthology Mus and Dance in the Americas & Int Encycl of Dance; ed, Through African-Centered Prisms and Mus and Gender. **CONTACT ADDRESS** Dept of Music, Hunter Col, CUNY, 695 Park Ave, New York, NY 10021.

HANAN, PATRICK DEWES

PERSONAL Born 01/04/1927, New Zealand, m, 1951, 1 child **DISCIPLINE** CHINESE LITERATURE **EDUCATION** Univ NZ, BA, 48, MA, 49; Univ London, BA, 53, PhD, 60. **CAREER** Lectr Chinese, Sch Orient & African Studies, Univ London, 54-63; from assoc prof to prof, Stanford Univ, 63-68; prof Chinese lit, Harvard Univ, 68-89, Victor S. Thomas Prof of Chinese Lit, Harvard Univ, 89-98, Victor S Thomas Res Prof of Chinese Lit, Harvard Univ, 98-. **HONORS AND AWARDS** Guggenheim fel, 77; fel, Am Acad of Arts & Sci, 77-; Levenson Awd of Asn Asian Stud, 90; Concurrent Prof of Nanjimg Univ, 95-; Officer of New Zealand Order of Merit, 99-. **MEMBERSHIPS** Asn Asian Studies; **RESEARCH** Chinese literature. **SELECTED PUBLICATIONS** Auth, The Chinese Short Story, 73; auth, The Chinese Vernacular Story, 81; auth, The Invention of Li Yu, 88; transl, The Carnal Prayer Mat, 90; auth, A Tower for the Summer Heat, 92; transl, The Sea of Regret, 95; transl, The Money Demon, 99. **CONTACT ADDRESS** Dept of East Asian Lang, Harvard Univ, 2 Divinity Ave, Cambridge, MA 02138-2020. **EMAIL** hanan@fas.harvard.edu

HANCHER, CHARLES MICHAEL

PERSONAL Born 05/20/1941, Newark, NJ, m, 1971, 1 child **DISCIPLINE** ENGLISH **EDUCATION** Harvard Univ, AB, 63; Yale Univ, MA, 64, PhD(English), 67. **CAREER** Asst prof English, Johns Hopkins Univ, 67-72; asst prof, 72-73, assoc prof, 73-82, prof English, Univ Minn, Minneapolis, 82-, ed, Centrum, 73-77, coed, 79-83; dir grad studies, 83-88; assoc dean, 97-01. **HONORS AND AWARDS** National Endowment for Humanities fel, 77-78. **MEMBERSHIPS** MLA. **RESEARCH** Literary theory; pragmatics; Victorian literature. **SELECTED PUBLICATIONS** Auth, Performative Utterance, the Word of God, and the Death of the Author, Semeia, 88; auth, Judging Law and Literature, Univ Cincinnati Law Review, 90; Urgent Private Affairs': Millais's Peace Concluded, 1856, Burlington Mag, 91; Bailey and After: Illustrating Meaning, Word and Image, 92; The Law of Signatures, Law and Aesthetics, Lang, 92; Hunt's Awakening conscience, Journal of Pre-Raphaelite Studies, 95; The Century Dictionary: Illustrations, Dictionaries, 96; Tenniel's Allegorical Cartoons, The Telling Image: Explorations in the Emblem, AMS Press, 96; Gazing at The Imperial Dictionary, Book History, 98; auth, "From Street Ballad to Penny Magazine: 'March of Intellect in the Butchering Line,'" Nineteenth-Century Media and the Construction of Identities, 00. **CONTACT ADDRESS** Dept of English, Univ of Minnesota, Twin Cities, 207 Church St SE, 207 Lind Hall, Minneapolis, MN 55455-0156. **EMAIL** mh@umn.edu

HANCOCK, VIRGINIA

PERSONAL Born 02/13/1941, Phoenix, AZ **DISCIPLINE** MUSIC **EDUCATION** Reed Col, BA (chem), 62; Harvard Univ, AM (chem), 63; Univ Oregon, DMA (music hist), 77. **CAREER** Reed Col, prof (music), 91-. **MEMBERSHIPS** Am Musicol Soc, Am Brahms Soc **RESEARCH** Vocal music of Johannes Brahms **SELECTED PUBLICATIONS** Brahms: Volkslied/Kunstlied, in The Nineteenth-Century German Lied, ed Rufus Hallmark, Schirmer Books, 96; Brahms and Early Music: Evidence from His Library and His Choral Compositions, in Brahms Studies: Analytical and Hist Perspectives, ed George S. Bozarth, Oxford Univ Press, 90; Brahms's links with German Renaissance music: A discussion of selected choral works, in Brahms 2: Biographical, Documentary and Analytical Studies, ed Michael Musgrave, Cambridge Univ Press, 87; Brahms's performances of early choral music, 19th Century Music VIII/2, 84; Brahms's Choral Compositions and His Library of Early Music, UMI Res Press, 83; The growth of Brahms's interest in early choral music, and its effect on his own choral compositions, in Brahms: Biographical, Documentary and Analytical Studies, ed Robert Pascall, Cambridge Univ Press, 83; Sources of Brahms's manuscript copies of early music in the Archiv of the Gesellschaft der Musikfreunde in Wien, Fontes Artis Musicae 24, 77. **CONTACT ADDRESS** Music Dept, Reed Col, 3203 SE Woodstock Blvd, Portland, OR 97202. **EMAIL** virginia.hancock@reed.edu

HAND, SALLY NIXON

PERSONAL Born 06/24/1933, Augusta, GA, m, 1953, 3 children **DISCIPLINE** 18TH CENTURY ENGLISH LITERATURE, COMPOSITION, WOMEN'S STUDIES **EDUCATION** Univ Ga, BA, 54; Fla State Univ, MA, 57; NYork Univ, PhD, 73. **CAREER** Teaching asst English, Fla State Univ, 55-57; teacher, 64-76, chmn dept, 76-80, Prof English, William Paterson Univ, 80-. **HONORS AND AWARDS** Phi Beta Kappa; NEH. **MEMBERSHIPS** MLA. **RESEARCH** Samuel Johnson/Elizabeth Montague; Alex Pope's imitations of Horace; Shelley genealogy. **SELECTED PUBLICATIONS** Auth, When half gods to the god's arrive: feminine self sacrifice in the early fiction of Edith Wharton, Sociol & Arts Colloq Ser, William Paterson Col, 78; Timothy Shelley, merchant of Newark: the search for Shelley's American ancestor, Keats-Shelly J, spring 80. **CONTACT ADDRESS** William Paterson Col of New Jersey, 300 Pompton Rd, Wayne, NJ 07470-2103. **EMAIL** SallyHand1@aol.com

HANENKRAT, FRANK THOMAS

PERSONAL Born 05/24/1939, Appomattox, VA, m, 1966 **DISCIPLINE** AMERICAN LITERATURE **EDUCATION** Univ Richmond, BA, 61, MA, 67; Emory Univ, PhD(English), 71. **CAREER** Inst English, Va Commonwealth Univ, 65-67; teaching asst, Emory Univ, 69-70; instr, Univ Ga, 70-71; assoc prof, 74-79, chmn, Dept English, 80-82, PROF ENGLISH & JOUR, LYNCHBURG COL, 79-, DIR, JOUR PROG, 81-84. **MEMBERSHIPS** MLA; Auth Guild & Auth League Am. **RESEARCH** Nineteenth and 20th century American literature. **CONTACT ADDRESS** Dept of English, Lynchburg Col, Lynchburg, VA 24501. **EMAIL** hanenkrat@acavax.lynchburg.edu

HANEY, DAVID P.

PERSONAL Born 12/17/1952, Minneapolis, MN, m, 1991 **DISCIPLINE** ENGLISH **EDUCATION** Macalester Col, BA, 74; SUNY Buffalo, MA, 79; PhD, 80. **CAREER** Instr, Boston Col, 78-80; teacher, Nichols Sch Buffalo, 80-81; teacher and dean, Cambridge Sch, 83-88; vis asst prof, Swarthmore Col, 88-89; asst prof to prof, Auburn Univ, 89-. **HONORS AND AWARDS** Mortar Bd Outstanding Educator, 92; Panhellenic Coun Outstanding Prof, 97; Outstanding Grad Prog Off, 00. **MEMBERSHIPS** Phi Beta Kappa; MLA: SEMLA; Keats-Shelley Asn; Wordsworth-Coleridge Asn; Intl Asn for Philos and Lit; N Am Soc for the Study of Romanticism. **RESEARCH** Literature and ethics; Hermeneutics; Aesthetics; British Romanticism; Critical Theory; Literature and Philosophy. **SELECTED PUBLICATIONS** Auth, "Incarnation and the Autobiographical Exit: Wordsworth's the Prelude, Books IX-XIII (1805)," Studies in Romanticism, (90): 523-554; auth, William Wordsworth and the Hermeneutics of Incarnation, Penn State Univ Press, 93; auth, "Poetry as Super-Genre in Wordsworth: Presentation and Ethics," Europ Romantic Rev, (94): 73-89; auth, "Rents and openings in the ideal world" Eye and Ear in Wordsworth," Studies in Romanticism (97): 173-199; auth, "Aesthetics and Ethics in Gadamer, Levinas, and Romanticism: Problems of Phronesis and Techne," PMLA, (99): 32-45; auth, "Understanding and Ethics in Coleridge: Description, Evaluation, and Otherness," in The Ethics in Literature, (Macmillan, 99), 119-135; auth, The Challenge of Coleridge: Ethics and Interpretation in Romanticism and Modern Philosophy, Penn

State Univ Press, 01; auth, "Wordsworth and Levinas: Making a Habit of the Sublime," in Proximity: Levinas and the Eighteenth Century, (Tex Tech Univ Press, (forthcoming). **CONTACT ADDRESS** Dept English, Auburn Univ, 9030 Haley Center, Auburn, AL 36849-5203. **EMAIL** haneydp@auburn.edu

HANKE, ROBERT
DISCIPLINE COMMUNICATION **EDUCATION** The Annenbey School for Commun, Univ of Pa. **CAREER** Res Assoc, McLuhan Prog for Culture & Tech; instr, Ryerson Polytechnic Univ. **MEMBERSHIPS** Int Commun Asn; Canadian Commun Asn. **SELECTED PUBLICATIONS** Auth, Theorizing Masculinity with/in the Media, Commun Theory, 98; auth, The Mock-macho Situation Comedy: Vengeance Masculinity and its Reiterations, Western J of Commun, 98; auth, Yo Quiero Mi MTV! Making Music Television for Latin America, Mapping the Beat: Popular Music and Contemporary Theory, 98; auth, Difference and Identity in Northern Exposure, Critical Approaches to Television, Houghton-Mifflin, 98. **CONTACT ADDRESS** 67 Chester Ave, Toronto, ON, Canada M4K 2Z8. **EMAIL** bob@mcluhan.utoronto.ca

HANNAH, JAMES R.
PERSONAL Born 01/01/1951, Lufkin, TX, m, 1951, 2 children **DISCIPLINE** CREATIVE WRITING **EDUCATION** Stephen F. Austin, BS, 73, MA, 77; Univ Iowa, MFA, 80. **CAREER** Assoc prof English, Texas A & M Univ, 93- . **HONORS AND AWARDS** Nat Endowment for Arts Fel in Creative Writing; Dobie-Paisano fel; Texas Writing fel. **MEMBERSHIPS** Texas Inst Lett; Great War Soc. **RESEARCH** Great War literature, Fiction writing. **SELECTED PUBLICATIONS** Auth, Desperate Measures, SMU Press, (88); auth, Sign Languages: Stories, MO, (93); auth, Tobias Wolff: A Study of the Short Fiction, MacMillan, (96); auth, The Gret War Reader, A & M Univ Press, (00). **CONTACT ADDRESS** Dept English, Texas A&M Univ, Col Station, College Station, TX 77843-0001. **EMAIL** j-hannah@tamu.edu

HANNAY, MARGARET PATTERSON
PERSONAL Born 12/20/1944, Rochester, NH, m, 1965, 2 children **DISCIPLINE** ENGLISH LITERATURE **EDUCATION** Wheaton Col, BA, 66; Col St Rose, MA, 70; State Univ NYork, Albany, PhD(English), 76. **CAREER** Lectr, State Univ NY, Albany, 76-80; ASST PROF ENGLISH LIT, SIENA COL NY, 80-86, prof, 86-. **HONORS AND AWARDS** Josephine A. Roberts Ed Awd, for collected wrks of Mary Sidney Herbert, 98. **MEMBERSHIPS** MLA; Renaissance Eng Text Soc; Renaissance Soc of Am; Conf Christianity & Lit (vpres 80-84); Milton Soc Am. **RESEARCH** Women of the English renaissance; Sidneys. **SELECTED PUBLICATIONS** Ed, As Her Wimsey Took Her: Critical Essays on Dorothy L. Sayers, Kent State Univ, 79; auth, C.S. Lewis, Frederick Unger Pub, 81; ed, Silent but for the Word: Tudor Women as Patrons, Translators, and Writers of Religious Works, Kent State Univ, 85; auth, Philip's Phoenix: Mary Sidney, Countess of Pembroke, Oxford Univ, 90; co-ed, The Collected Works of Mary Sidney Hervert, Countess of Pembroke, Clarendon, 98. **CONTACT ADDRESS** Dept of English, Siena Col, 515 Loudonville Rd, Loudonville, NY 12211-1462. **EMAIL** hannay@siena.edu

HANNING, ROBERT W.
PERSONAL Born 04/21/1938, Brooklyn, NY, m, 1963, 2 children **DISCIPLINE** MEDIEVAL ENGLISH LITERATURE **EDUCATION** Columbia, BA, 58; Oxford, BA, 68; MA, 64; Columbia, PhD, 64. **CAREER** Prof, English & Comp Lit, Columbia Univ, 71- . **HONORS AND AWARDS** ACLS Fel; Guggenheim Fel; NEH Fel; Medieval Acad Am Fel. **MEMBERSHIPS** MLA; Medieval Acad Am; New Chaucer Soc. **RESEARCH** Med lit; hist & cult; 'race', ethnicity, & identity in Am 1880-present. **SELECTED PUBLICATIONS** Auth, The Vision & History in Early Britain, 66; auth, The Individual in Twelfth-Century Romance, 77; co-trans, The Lais of Marie de France; auth, "Toward a Lapsarian Poetic for the Canterbury Tales," Biennial Chaucer Lecture, Paris, 98. **CONTACT ADDRESS** Dept of English, Columbia Univ, 1150 Amsterdam Ave., 602 Philosophy Hall, New York, NY 10027-4927. **EMAIL** rwh2@columbia.edu

HANS, JAMES STUART
PERSONAL Born 05/06/1950, Elgin, IL, m, 1974, 1 child **DISCIPLINE** ENGLISH LITERATURE, PHILOSOPHY **EDUCATION** Southern IL Univ, Edwardsville, BA, 72, MA, 74; Washington Univ, St Louis, PhD(English), 78. **CAREER** Teaching asst English, Southern IL Univ, 72-74; asst prof, Kenyon Col, 78-82; asst to prof English, Wake Forest Univ, 82-; ed consult, Kenyon Rev, 79-82; dir, Kenyon & Exeter Prog, Exeter Univ, England, 80-81. **HONORS AND AWARDS** Listed in Outstanding Scholars of the 21st Century; Listed in Who's Who in the South and Southwest, 96-97; Listed in Men of Achievement, 97. **RESEARCH** Twentieth century lit; literary theory; contemporary philosophy. **SELECTED PUBLICATIONS** Auth, Gaston Bachelard and the Phenomenology of the Reading Consciousness, J Aesthetics & Art Criticism, spring 77; Hans-Georg Gadamer and Hermeneutic Phenomenology, Philos Today, spring 78; Derrida and Freeplay, Mod Lang Notes, 5/79; Presence and Absence in Modern Poetry, Criticism, fall 80; Hermeneutics, Play, Deconstruction, Philos Today, winter 80; The Play of the World, Univ MA Press, 81; Form and Measure in the Postmodern World, Kenyon Rev; Imitation and the Image of Man, John Benjaminis, 87; The Question of Value: Thinking Through Nietzsche, Heidegger and Freud, SIU Press, 89; The Value(s) of Literature, SUNY Press, 90; The Fate of Desire, SUNY Press, 90; The Origins of the Gods, SUNY Press, 91; Contextual Authority and Aesthetic Truth, SUNY Press, 92; The Mysteries of Attention, SUNY Press, 93; The Golden Mean, SUNY Press, 94; The Site of Our Lives: The Self and the Subject from Emerson to Foucault, SUNY Press, 95; auth, Named Wake Forest Professor of English, 99. **CONTACT ADDRESS** Dept English, Wake Forest Univ, PO Box 7387, Winston-Salem, NC 27109-7387. **EMAIL** hans@wfu.edu

HANSEN, BARBARA L.
PERSONAL Born 09/27/1935, Indianapolis, IN, s **DISCIPLINE** ENGLISH EDUCATION **EDUCATION** Ball State Univ, BS, 63; MA, 64; PhD, 71. **CAREER** Grad teaching asst to instr, Ball State Univ, 63-72; asst prof to prof, Univ of Cincinnati, 72-. **HONORS AND AWARDS** Venture Club National Awd for Outstanding Handicapped Student, 62; doctoral teaching fel, Ball State Univ, 67-68; Midwest Awd, President's Comt for the Handicapped, 72; Fac Achievement Awd, Univ of Cincinnati, 94; listed in The World Who's Who of Women, International Who's Who in Educ, and Who's Who Among America's Teachers. **SELECTED PUBLICATIONS** Coauth, Developing Sentence Skills, Prentice-Hall Inc., (Englewood Cliffs) 90; auth, "Commentary," Col Teaching (91); auth, "Is No an Outdated Word?," Children Today (91): 18-21; auth, "The Road Less Traveled," Careers & the Disabled (93); auth, Picking Up the Pieces: Healing Ourselves After Personal Loss, Taylor Pub Co. (Dallas, TX), 91 and Harper Collins Pub Co. (New York), 93; coauth, Simplified Sentence Skills, NTC/Contemporary Pub (Lincolnwood), 97; auth, The Strength Within: Cultivating Habist of Wholeness, Hope, and Joy, Hidden Spring/Paulist Press (Mahwah, NJ), 00. **CONTACT ADDRESS** Dept English, Univ of Cincinnati, 9555 Plainfield Rd, Cincinnati, OH 45236-1007.

HANSEN, BOB
DISCIPLINE THEATRE HISTORY, DRAMATIC LITERATURE **EDUCATION** Univ MN, BA; FL State Univ, MA; Univ MN, PhD. **CAREER** Instr, ch, dept Theatre, mng dir, Huron Playhouse, Bowling Green State Univ; instr, 86-, hd, dept, Broadcasting/Cinema and Theatre, Univ NC, Greensboro. **MEMBERSHIPS** NC Theatre Asn; USITT-Ohio; Am Theatre Asn; Southeastern Theatre Conf; Nat Asn Sch Theatre. **SELECTED PUBLICATIONS** Auth, Scenic and Costume Design for the Ballets Russes, UMI Res Press. **CONTACT ADDRESS** Univ of No Carolina, Greensboro, Greensboro, NC 27412-5001. **EMAIL** rchansen@dewey.uncg.edu

HANSEN, HELYNNE
PERSONAL Born 10/19/1951, Salt Lake City, UT, m, 1979, 2 children **DISCIPLINE** FRENCH, ENGLISH **EDUCATION** Univ Ut, BA; MA; PhD. **CAREER** Asst prof, Western State Col, 88-97; vis asst prof, Brigham Young Univ, 91-92. **MEMBERSHIPS** MLA, George Sand Asn, Rocky Mountain MLA, Women in French, Am Asn of Teachers of French. **RESEARCH** Nineteenth- and Twentieth-century Women Writers in French, Feminist Theory, French and Francophone Cinema and Film Theory, Napoleonic Era, Romanticism. **SELECTED PUBLICATIONS** Auth, Hortense Allart: The Woman and the Novelist. **CONTACT ADDRESS** Dept Commun Arts, Western State Col of Colorado, 600 N Adams St, Gunnison, CO 81231-7000. **EMAIL** hhansen@western.edu

HANSEN, WELLS S.
PERSONAL Born 12/08/1964, Southport Island, ME, s **DISCIPLINE** CLASSICAL LANGUAGE AND LITERATURE **EDUCATION** Boston Col, BA, 87; Univ Chicago, MA,88. **CAREER** Tchr, Mount Alvernia Acad, 87; lectr, Univ Chicago, 98-92; tchr, Princeton Day Sch, 93; tchr, Milton Acad, 93-. **HONORS AND AWARDS** Weiner Classics Medal, 87; Shorey Fel and Bobrinsky Fel, 90, 92; Klingenstein Sum Fel, 94; Fulbright Grant, 98; McKinlay Fel, 98. **MEMBERSHIPS** Am Philol Asn; Class Asn Mass; Pearl River Gibonian Soc. **RESEARCH** Latin literature, pedagogy of classical languages in secondary schools. **SELECTED PUBLICATIONS** "Catullus 75 and the Poetics of Separation," New Engl Classic J, 98. **CONTACT ADDRESS** Ware Hall, Suite 516, Milton, MA 02186. **EMAIL** wells_hansen@milton.edu

HANSEN, WILLIAM F.
PERSONAL Born 06/22/1941, Fresno, CA, m, 1994, 1 child **DISCIPLINE** CLASSICAL STUDIES, FOLKLORE **EDUCATION** Univ Calif, Berkeley, BA, 65, PhD, 70. **CAREER** From asst prof to prof, Class Stud & Folklore, Inst, Indiana Univ Bloomington, 70-; assoc dean fac, Indiana Univ Bloomington, 86-92; chmn, Class Stud, Indiana Univ Bloomington, 97-; co-dir, Program in Mythology Stud, 98-. **HONORS AND AWARDS** Phi Beta Kappa, 65; NEH Younger Hum Fel, 72-73; Am Coun Learned Soc fel, 77-78, 92. **MEMBERSHIPS** Am Philol Asn; Class Asn of the Middle West and South; Am Folklore Soc; Calif Folklore Soc; Hoosier Folklore Soc; Int Soc for Folk-Narrative Res; Int Soc for Contemp Legend Res. **RESEARCH** Mythology; folklore; early Greek epic; early fiction. **SELECTED PUBLICATIONS** Auth, The Theft of the Thunderweapon: A Greek Myth in Its International Context, Classica et Mediaevalia, 95; auth, Abraham and the Grateful Dead Man, in Bendix, ed, Folklore Interpreted: Essays in Honor of Alan Dundes, Garland, 95; auth, The Protagonist on the Pyre: Herodotean Legend and Modern Folktale, Fabula, 96; auth, Phlegon of Tralles' Book of Marvels, Univ Exeter, 96; auth, Homer and the Folktale, in Morris, ed, A New Companion to Homer, Brill, 97; auth, Idealization as a Process in Ancient Greek Story-Formation, Symbolae Osloenses, 97; auth, Mythology and Folktale Typology: Chronicle of a Failed Scholarly Revolution, J of Folklore Res, 97; ed, Anthology of Ancient Greek Popular Literature, Indiana, 98. **CONTACT ADDRESS** Classical Studies Dept, Indiana Univ, Bloomington, 1020 E Kirkwood Ave, Bloomington, IN 47405-7103. **EMAIL** hansen@indiana.edu

HANSON, COLAN T.
DISCIPLINE COMMUNICATIONS **EDUCATION** Wayne State Univ, PhD, 78. **CAREER** Educator for 25 years; Prof & Dept Chair Mass Commun, Minn State Univ Moorhead. **MEMBERSHIPS** NCA; PRSA; AAF. **RESEARCH** Public relations; advertising; persuasion. **CONTACT ADDRESS** Mass Communications Dept., Moorhead State Univ, 1104 7th Ave S, Moorhead, MN 56563. **EMAIL** hansonc@mnstate.edu

HANSON, ELIZABETH
DISCIPLINE ENGLISH LITERATURE **EDUCATION** Johns Hopkins Univ, PhD. **CAREER** Dept Eng, Queen's Univ **HONORS AND AWARDS** Alumni Tchg Awd, 97. **RESEARCH** Social and economic contexts of Renaissance drama; early modern cultural studies. **SELECTED PUBLICATIONS** Auth, Discovering the Subject in Renaissance England, Cambridge, 98; pubs on economics and Jacobean drama, Renaissance women's writing, Shakespeare and early modern bureaucracy, the Elizabethan use of interrogatory torture, and Milton's poetry. **CONTACT ADDRESS** English Dept, Queen's Univ at Kingston, Kingston, ON, Canada K7L 3N6. **EMAIL** hansone@qsilver.queensu.ca

HANSON, JOHN
DISCIPLINE MUSIC HISTORY **EDUCATION** Eastman Schl Music, BM; MA; PhD. **CAREER** Fac, Univ KS, Carroll Col, Eastman Sch Music; assoc prof, 77. **HONORS AND AWARDS** Founder/Pres, Music Theory Soc NY State. **MEMBERSHIPS** Music Theory Soc NY State. **SELECTED PUBLICATIONS** Auth, articles in Theory and Practice, Cole Music Symposium, and Jour Music Theory Pedag; Music Fundamentals Workbook. **CONTACT ADDRESS** Dept Music, SUNY, Binghamton, PO Box 6000, Binghamton, NY 13902-6000.

HAPGOOD, ROBERT
PERSONAL Born 12/11/1928, Lompoc, CA, m, 1950, 2 children **DISCIPLINE** ENGLISH **EDUCATION** Univ Calif Berkeley, BA, 50; MA, 51; PhD, 55. **CAREER** Instr, Univ Ind, 55-57; vis prof, Dijon Univ, 57-58; instr, Univ Calif Berk, 58-59; asst prof, Univ Calif Riverside, 59-65; assoc prof to prof to dept chmn to emer, Univ NHamp, 65-96-; exchg prof, Osaka Univ, 77-79; vis prof, Shoin Univ, 92. **HONORS AND AWARDS** Phi Beta Kappa; Renais Inst Fel; Mellon Postdoct Fel; English Inst Prize essay; SIMRS Fel; ACLS Fel; Univ NHamp Fac Fel; Folger Inst Fel; Lindberg Awd, Outstanding Sch Teacher; Distinguished Prof Awd; NEH Fel. **MEMBERSHIPS** ISA; MLA. **RESEARCH** Shakespeare; English and American drama; world drama; performance issues. **SELECTED PUBLICATIONS** Auth, "Shakespeare's Thematic Modes of Speech," Shake Surv 20 (67): 41-9; auth, "Shakespeare and the Included Spectator," in Reinterpretations of Elizabethan Drama (69): 117-36; auth, "Chimes at Midnight from Stage to Screen," Shake Surv 39 (87): 39-52; auth, Shakespeare the Theater-poet, Oxford UP, 88; auth, "The Rights of Playwrights," J Drama Theory Crit (92): 41-60; auth, "Kurosawa's Shakespeare Films," in Shakespeare and the Moving Image (Cambridge UP, 94): 234-49; auth, "Popularizing Shakespeare," in Shakespeare the Movie (Routledge, 97); auth, " A Playgoer's Journey," in Shakespeare and the Japanese Stage (Cambridge UP, 98): 243-54; ed, Hamlet, Shakespeare in Production, Cambridge UP, 99; auth, "Listening for the Playwright's Voice," in Teaching Shakespeare Through Performance, MLA (99): 145-54. **CONTACT ADDRESS** PO Box 451, Cape Neddick, ME 03902-0451. **EMAIL** hapgoodr@aol.com

HAPKE, LAURA
PERSONAL Born 01/04/1946, New York, NY, m **DISCIPLINE** ENGLISH; AMERICAN STUDIES **EDUCATION** Brandeis Univ, BA, 67; Univ of Chicago, MA, 69; City Univ of NYork, PhD, 74. **CAREER** Tchg fel, 72-74; adjunct instr, Queens Col, 78-81; instr, Nassau Comm Col, 78-81; from asst prof to prof Eng, Pace Univ, 81-91. **HONORS AND AWARDS** NEH awards, 80, 81; Choice Outstanding Acad Book Awd, 92. **MEMBERSHIPS** PMLA; ASA; NYLNA. **RESEARCH** Labor lit; Women's studies; American & Victorian lit and cult. **SELECTED PUBLICATIONS** Auth, Girls Who Went Wrong: Prostitutes in American Fiction, 1885-1917, Bowling Green Univ, 89; Tales of the Working Girl: Wage -

Earning Women in American Literature, 1890-1925, Twayne/ Macmillan, 92; The Ideology of the Salvation Army, The Eighteen Nineties: An Ecyclopedia of British Literature, Art and Culture, ed George Cevasco, Garland, 93; A Wealth of Possibilities: The Worker, the Text, and the Composition Classroom, Women's Studies Quarterly, 94; Homage to Daniel Horwitz, Liberating Memory: Working Class Intellectuals and Their Work, ed Janet Zandy, Rutgers Univ, 95; Daughters of the Great Depression: Women, Work, and Fiction in the American 1930s, Univ Georgia, 95. **CONTACT ADDRESS** Dept of English, Pace Univ, New York, Pace Plaza, New York, NY 10038-1502. **EMAIL** lhapke@tiac.net

HARBERT, EARL
PERSONAL Born 04/01/1934, Cleveland, OH **DISCIPLINE** ENGLISH, AMERICAN LITERATURE **EDUCATION** Hamilton Col, AB, 56; Johns Hopkins Univ, MA, 61; Univ Wis, PhD(English), 66. **CAREER** Instr English, George Washington Univ, 61-62; from asst prof to assoc prof, Tulane Univ, 65-77; PROF ENGLISH, NORTHEASTERN UNIV, 77- **MEMBERSHIPS** MLA; Northeast Mod Lang Asn. **RESEARCH** American literature; intellectual history. **SELECTED PUBLICATIONS** Auth, Washington Irving's Granada, In: Washington Irving Reconsidered, 69; co-ed, Fifteen American Authors before 1900 & auth, chap, In: Henry Adams, Univ Wis, 71; The Truth So Much Closer Home, NY Univ, 77; Henry Adams: A Reference Guide, 78 & Critical Essays on Henry Adams, 81, G K Hall & Co; American realists and naturalists, In: Dict of Literary Biographies, Gale Res Co, 82. **CONTACT ADDRESS** Dept of English, Northeastern Univ, Boston, MA 02115.

HARBIN, BILL J.
DISCIPLINE DRAMATIC LITERATURE **EDUCATION** Ind Univ, PhD. **CAREER** Prof, dir, grad stud, La State Univ. **RESEARCH** American and British theatre and drama; notable gays and lesbians in US theatre history. **SELECTED PUBLICATIONS** Coed, Inside the Royal Court, 1956-1981. **CONTACT ADDRESS** Dept of Theatre, Louisiana State Univ and A&M Col, Baton Rouge, LA 70803. **EMAIL** bjharb@aol.com

HARBIN, MICHAEL A.
PERSONAL Born 05/24/1947, Vincennes, IN, m, 1971, 3 children **DISCIPLINE** BIBLICAL STUDIES, OLD TESTAMENT AND SEMITIC STUDIES, ENGLISH LITERATURE **EDUCATION** US Naval acad, BS, 69; Calif State Univ, MA, 93; Dallas Theol Sem, ThM, 80, ThD, 88. **CAREER** Adj prof of Bible, Le Tourneau Univ, 90-93; adj prof English, El Centro Col, 90-93; assoc prof Biblical Stud (s), Taylor Univ, 93- . **HONORS AND AWARDS** Who's Who in Amer, 98, 00; Who's Who in Rel, 92-93; Who's Who in the Midwest, 95, 96; Phi Kappa Phi, 93. **MEMBERSHIPS** Soc Bibl Lit; Near East Archaeol soc; Inst Bibl res; Evangel Theol Soc. **RESEARCH** Old Testament History. **CONTACT ADDRESS** Dept of Biblical Studies, Taylor Univ, Upland, 236 W Reade Ave, Upland, IN 46989. **EMAIL** mcharbin@tayloru.edu

HARBISON, SHERRILL
PERSONAL Born 09/13/1943, Burlington, VT, m, 1966, 2 children **DISCIPLINE** ENGLISH **EDUCATION** Oberlin Col, BA, 65; Univ Mass Amherst, MA, PhD, 96. **CAREER** Vis lectr, Trintiy Col, 97-00; lectr, Smith Col, 01-. **HONORS AND AWARDS** Fulbright Grant, 88; Auroa Borealis Prize, 91, 95, 97; Norwegian Marshall Fund, 93; NEH Grant, 94. **MEMBERSHIPS** MLA, SASS, ALA, WCPMF. **RESEARCH** American and Scandinavian Literature. **SELECTED PUBLICATIONS** Auth, "Sigrid Undset and Willa Cather: A Friendship," Willa Cather Piorneer Mem Newsletter 2.3 (98): 53-59; ed and contributor, Gunnar's Daughter by Sigrid Undset, Penguin, 98; ed and contributor, The Song of the Lark by Willa Cather, Penguin 99; transl, Kristin Lavrausdatter, vols 2 and 3, by Sigrid Undset, Penguin 99, 00; auth, "Willa Cather and Sigrid Undset: the Correspondence in Oslo," Res for Am Lit Study 26.2, (00): 236-259; auth, "Cather, Freunstad, and Wagner," Willa Cather in New York, ed M Maguire Skaggs, (Assoc Univ Pr, 00): 53-59. **CONTACT ADDRESS** 70 Taylor St, Amherst, MA 01002-2135. **EMAIL** harbison@english.umass.edu

HARDEN, EDGAR FREDERICK
PERSONAL Born 02/10/1932, Scranton, PA **DISCIPLINE** ENGLISH **EDUCATION** Princeton Univ, AB, 53; Harvard Univ, AM, 58, PhD, 60. **CAREER** From instr to asst prof English, Oberlin Col, 60-66; from asst prof to assoc prof, 66-77, actg head dept, 68-69, PROF ENGLISH, SIMON FRASER UNIV, 77-, Can Coun grant, 67-68, 69-70 & res grant, 74-75; Am Philos Soc res grant, 77; Soc Sci Humanities Res Coun Can res grant, 81-82. **MEMBERSHIPS** MLA; Tennyson Soc; Browning Soc; William Morris Soc. **RESEARCH** Victorian literature--novel; poetry and prose; visual art; William M Thackeray. **SELECTED PUBLICATIONS** Auth, Thackeray's English Humourists and Four Georges, 85; auth, Vanity Fair: A Novel Without a Hero (Twayne's Masterworks Studies, No 157), 95; auth, Vanity Fair: A Novel Without a Hero (Twayne's Masterworks Studies, No 157), 95; auth, A Checklist of Contributions by William Makepeace Thackeray to Newspapers, Periodicals, Books, and Serial Part Issues, 1828-1864 (Els Monograph Series, 96; ed, Selected Letters of William Makepeace Thackeray, 96; auth, Thackeray the Writer: From Journalism to Vanity Fair, 98; ed, The Luck of Barry Lyndon: A Romance of the Last Century by Fitz-Boodle (Works of William Makepeace Thackeray), 99; auth, Thackeray the Writer: From Pendennis to Denis Duval, 00; ed, Annotations for the Selected Works of William Makepeace Thackeray: The Complete Novels, the Major Non-Fictional Prose, and Selected Shorter Pieces; auth, The Emergence of Thackeray's Serial Fiction: Strokes of the Great Clock; ed, The History of Henry Esmong (The Thackeray Edition Project 1), ed, The Letters and Private Papers of William Makepeace Thackeray (Garland Reference Library of the Humanities, Vol 946). **CONTACT ADDRESS** Dept of English, Simon Fraser Univ, 8888 Univ Dr, Burnaby, BC, Canada V5A 1S6.

HARDER, BERNHARD D.
DISCIPLINE ENGLISH LANGUAGE; LITERATURE **EDUCATION** BC, BA, MA; NC Univ, PhD, 70. **CAREER** Assoc prof. **RESEARCH** International and Aboriginal literatures. **SELECTED PUBLICATIONS** Co-ed, Oxford UP ed of On the Properties of Things: John Trevisa's Translation of Bartholomaeus Anglicus De Proprietatibus Rerum: A Critical Text, 3 vols; pub (s), relationships between lang and soc and on Medieval and int lit. **CONTACT ADDRESS** Dept of English Language and Literature, Univ of Windsor, 401 Sunset Ave, Windsor, ON, Canada N9B 3P4. **EMAIL** harder@uwindsor.ca

HARDER, HENRY LOUIS
PERSONAL Born 10/08/1936, Van Buren, AR, m, 1960, 5 children **DISCIPLINE** ENGLISH & AMERICAN LITERATURE **EDUCATION** Subiaco Col, BA, 58; Univ Ark, MA, 61; Univ Md, PhD, 70. **CAREER** Instr English, US Naval Acad, 65-69; asst prof, Anne Arundel Community Col, 69-70; asst prof, 70-73, assoc prof, 73-80, prof English, Mo Southern State Col, 80- **MEMBERSHIPS** MLA; AAUP; Mod Humanities Res Asn; Medieval Acad Am; Int Arthurian Soc. **RESEARCH** Middle English literature; Chaucer. **SELECTED PUBLICATIONS** Auth, Livy in Chaucer's and Gower's Lucrece Stories, Publ Mo Philol Asn, 77; Feasting in the Alliterative Morte Arthure, Chivalric Literature, Medieval Inst Publ, 80. **CONTACT ADDRESS** 3950 Newman Rd, Joplin, MO 64801-1512.

HARDER, SARAH
PERSONAL m **DISCIPLINE** ENGLISH LITERATURE **EDUCATION** Bowling Green State Univ, PhD. **CAREER** Fac, 68-. **HONORS AND AWARDS** Dir Women's Studies prog, Univ Wis Eau Claire, 84. **RESEARCH** Composition; drama; women in literature. **SELECTED PUBLICATIONS** Auth, published in journals such as Redbook and The American Woman. **CONTACT ADDRESS** Dept of English, Univ of Wisconsin, Eau Claire, Hibbard Hall 405, PO Box 4004, Eau Claire, WI 54702-4004. **EMAIL** harderss@uwec.edu

HARDIN, RICHARD F.
PERSONAL Born 11/09/1937, Los Angeles, CA, m, 1959, 6 children **DISCIPLINE** ENGLISH **EDUCATION** St. Mary's Univ, BA, 59; Univ of Tex Austin, MA, 64; PhD, 66. **CAREER** Asst Prof, Univ of Kansas, 66-70; Assoc Prof, Univ of Kansas, 70-76; Prof, Univ of Kansas, 76-; Chair, Univ of Kansas, 97-00. **HONORS AND AWARDS** Amer Philosophical Soc; Newberry Library; NEA Instituitonal; Marlow Society-Roma Gill. **MEMBERSHIPS** AAUP, Sixteenth Century Studies Conf; Amer Comp Lit Assoc; Southern Comp Lit Assoc, ALSC. **RESEARCH** Renaissance literature; Comparative literature. **SELECTED PUBLICATIONS** Auth, "Michael Drayton and the Passing of Elizabethan England," Lawrence: Univ Press of Kansas, 73; ed, "Survivals of Pastoral." Univ of Kansas Humanistic Studies, No. 52, Lawrence, 79; coauth, "Recent Studies in Myths and Literature, 70-90: An Annotated Bibliography, with Bernard Accardi, et al, New York, Westport CT, and London; Greenwood Press, 91; ed, "Poems on Events of the Day, 1582-1607," with Introduction, Notes, and Translation by John Ross, Delmar, NY: Scholars' Facsimiles and Reprints, 91; auth, "Civil Idolatry: Desacralizing and Monarchy in Spenser, Shakepeare, and Milton," Newark, DE: Univ of Delaware Press, 92; auth, "Love in a Green Shade: Idyllic Romances Ancient to Modern," Lincoln: Univ of Nebraska Press, 00. **CONTACT ADDRESS** Dept English, Univ of Kansas, Lawrence, Wescoe Hall, Lawrence, KS 66045-0001. **EMAIL** rhardin@ukans.edu

HARDT, JOHN S.
PERSONAL Born 12/27/1951, Atlanta, TX, m, 1983 **DISCIPLINE** ENGLISH **EDUCATION** Centenary Col La, BA, 74; Tex Tech Univ, MA, 76; Univ Mo Columbia, PhD, 83. **CAREER** Asst prof to prof, chair, assoc dean, Ferrum Col, 82-. **HONORS AND AWARDS** alpha Chi; Omicron Delta Kappa; Alpha Mu Gamma, 89; Fel, Univ Mo, 79-81; Jesse Ball duPont Found Fel, 92; Hurt Outstanding Faculty Achievement Award, Ferrum Col, 92. **MEMBERSHIPS** MLA, SAMLA, Col English Asn. **RESEARCH** 19th-Century American Literature, New Criticism. **SELECTED PUBLICATIONS** Auth, "And Faulkner Nodded: Calvin Coolidge in Sanctuary," Notes on Miss Writers, (79); coauth, "James Studies, 1978-79," Henry James Rev, (81); auth, "Doubts in the American Garden: Three Cases of Paradisal Skepticism," Studies in Short Fiction, (88). **CONTACT ADDRESS** Ferrum Col, PO Box 1000, Ferrum, VA 24088. **EMAIL** jhardt@ferrum.edu

HARDY, JOHN EDWARD
PERSONAL Born 04/03/1922, Baton Rouge, LA, m, 1942, 6 children **DISCIPLINE** ENGLISH & AMERICAN LITERATURE **EDUCATION** La State Univ, BA, 44; State Univ Iowa, MA, 46; Johns Hopkins Univ, PhD, 56. **CAREER** Instr English, Univ Detroit, 45-46, Yale Univ, 46-48 & Univ Okla, 48-52; instr writing, Johns Hopkins Univ, 52-54; from asst prof to prof English, 54-66, dir grad studies, Univ Notre Dame, 65-66; prof & head dept, Univ S Ala, 66-69; prof & chmn dept, Univ Mo-St Louis, 70-71; prof to prof emer, Univ Ill, Chicago, 72-; Fulbright prof Am lit, Am Inst, Univ Munich, 59-61; vis prof English, Univ Colo, 69-70. **HONORS AND AWARDS** Ford Found Fund Advan Educ fac studies fel, 52-53; Sewanee Rev fel poetry, 54. **MEMBERSHIPS** MLA. **RESEARCH** Poetry; literary criticism; modern fiction. **CONTACT ADDRESS** Dept of English, Univ of Illinois, Chicago, 601 S Morgan St, M/C 162, Chicago, IL 60607-7120.

HARIMAN, ROBERT
PERSONAL Born 06/17/1951, Grand Forks, ND, m, 1982, 2 children **DISCIPLINE** RHETORIC **EDUCATION** Macalester Col, BA, 73; Univ MN, MA, 75, PhD, 79. **CAREER** Asst prof, 79-85, assoc prof, 85-93, full prof, Drake Univ, 93-. **HONORS AND AWARDS** Case IA Professor of the Year; NCA Distinguished Scholarship Awd. **MEMBERSHIPS** Nat Comm Asn; Rhetorical Soc Am. **RESEARCH** Classical and contemporary rhetorical theolry; stylistic analysis; twentieth-century political discourse. **SELECTED PUBLICATIONS** Auth, Popular Trials: Rhetoric, Mass Media, and the Law, ed vol, Univ AL Press, 90, paperback ed, 93; Post-Realism: The Rhetorical Turn in International Relations, co-ed with Francis A Beer, MI State Univ Press, 96; Political Style: The Artistry of Power, Univ Chicago Press, 95. **CONTACT ADDRESS** Dept of Rhetoric and Communication Studies, Drake Univ, Des Moines, IA 50311-4505. **EMAIL** robert.hariman@drake.edu

HARK, INA RAE
PERSONAL Born 08/19/1949, Charleston, WV **DISCIPLINE** ENGLISH LITERATURE, FILM STUDIES **EDUCATION** Northwestern Univ, BA, 71; Univ Calif, Los Angeles, MA, 72, PhD(English), 75. **CAREER** Teaching asst, Univ Calif, Los Angeles, 72-74; asst prof, 75-80, ASSOC PROF ENGLISH, UNIV SC, 80-88, Am Coun Learned Socs grant-in-aid, 77; Prof, 88-; assoc dean, Col of Liberal Arts, 94-. **MEMBERSHIPS** MLA; Am Film Inst; Soc for Cinema Studies. **RESEARCH** Victorian literature; film; modern drama. **SELECTED PUBLICATIONS** Auth, The visual politics of The Adventures of Robin Hood, J Popular Film 76; Edward Lear: Eccentricity and Victorian Angst, Victorian Poetry, 78; Samuel Butler and the gospel of no gospel, In: Interspace and the Inward Sphere, Western Ill Univ, 78; Anti-Shavian satire in Heartbreak House, Dalhousie Rev, 78; Stop the World--I Want to Get Off: The vice as Everyman, Comp Drama, 78; Star Trek and Television's Moral Universe, Extrapolation, 79; Lady Cicely, I presume: Converting the heathen, shavian style, Shaw Annual, 81; Edward Lear, Twayne, 82; auth, "Keeping Your Amateur Standing: Audience Participation and Good Citizenship" in Hitchcock's Political Films, Cinema Journal 29, (90): 8-22; auth, "TheTheater Mani and the Girl in the Box Office: Gender in the Discourse of Motion Picture Theatre Management," Film History 6, (94): 178-87; ed, Screening the Male, Raitledge, 93; co-ed, The Road Movie Book, Routledge, 97. **CONTACT ADDRESS** Dept of English, Univ of So Carolina, Columbia, Welsh Bldg, Columbia, SC 29208. **EMAIL** hark@bellsouth.net

HARLAND, PAUL W.
PERSONAL Born Winnipeg, MB, Canada **DISCIPLINE** LITERATURE **EDUCATION** Univ Winnipeg, BA; Univ W Ontario, MA, PhD. **CAREER** Instr, Univ W Ontario; prof, Augustana Univ. **RESEARCH** Renaissance and twentieth century lit. **SELECTED PUBLICATIONS** Co-ed,Dianoia. **CONTACT ADDRESS** Dept of English, Augustana Univ Col, 4901-46th Ave, Camrose, AB, Canada T4V 2R3. **EMAIL** harlp@augustana.ab.ca

HARLEY, MARIA ANNA
PERSONAL Born 12/30/1957, Warsaw, Poland, m, 1987, 3 children **DISCIPLINE** MUSICOLOGY **EDUCATION** J Elsner State High Sch of Music, Warsaw, 79; Summer Courses for Young Composers 83-86; Ctr Acanthes Summer Course in New Music, 87; Univ Warsaw, MA Musicology, 86; F Chopin Acad of Music, MA, sound engineering, 87; McGill Univ, PhD, musicology, 94. **CAREER** Transl & libr, Int Soc Contemporary Music, Warsaw, 84-86; grad asst, McGill Univ, 88-90; instr, McGill Univ, 91-94; SSHRC postdoctoral res fel, McGill Univ, 94-96; Asst Prof, Sch of Music, Univ So Cal, 96-; Ed, Polish Music J, 98-; Gen Ed, Polish Music History Series, 98-. **HONORS AND AWARDS** M Kopernik St High Sch Gold Medal for Best Grad, 76; Rector's Awds for Outstanding Students, 76-79; Wilk Prize for Res in Polish Music, 95; First Prize Doctoral Dissertation, 98. **MEMBERSHIPS** Amer Musicology Soc; Canadian Univ Music Soc; Int Alliance for Women in Music; Int Musicological Soc; Int Soc for Contemporary Music; Mu Phi Epsilon; Sonneck Soc for Amer Mus; Polish Inst of Arts & Sciences in Amer; Polish Inst of Arts & Sciences in Canada; World Forum for Acoustic Ecology. **RESEARCH** 20th-century music; Music and/as culture. **SELECTED PUBLICATIONS**

auth, Technika komedii w 'Falstafie' Verdiego, Muzyka, 91; auth, Stowik I tajemnice nocy: o realizmie I symbolice spiewu slowika w muzyce, Polish Musicological Quart, 92; auth, From Point to Sphere: Spatial Organization of Sound in Contemporary Music (after 1950), Canadian Univ Music Rev, 94; auth, Birds in Concert: North-American Birdsong in Bartok's Piano Concerto No. 3, Tempo, Ju 94; auth, Musique, espace, et spatialisation: Entretien de Iannis Xenakis ave Maria Harley, Circuit, 94; auth, Spatial Sound Movement in the Instrumental Music of Iannis Xenakis, Interface, Aug 94; auth, 'To Be God with God': Catholic Composers and the Mystical Experience, Contemporary Music Rev, 95; auth, O (bez)uzytecznosci analizy dla potrzeb wykonawstwa muzyki dwudziestowiecznej (Xenakis, Bartok, Strawinski), Monochord, 95; auth, Notes on Music Ecology as a New Research Paradigm, Acoustic Ecology J, 95; auth, Natura Naturans, Natura Naturata and Bartok's Nature Music Idiom, Studia Musicologica Acad Sci Hungaricae, 95; auth, Notes on Polish Women Composers, Bulletin of the Polish Inst of Arts & Sci in Canada and the Polish Libr, 96; auth, Ritual und Klanglandschaft Zur Musik von R Murray Schafer, MusikTexte, 97; coauth, Triumphs of Modernity: Xenakis's Kraanerg at the National Arts Centre, Musicworks, 97; auth, Natura naturans, natura naturata a idiom 'muzyki natury' Bartoka, Polish Musicological Quart, 97; auth, An American in Space: Henry Brants' 'Spatial Music,' Amer Music, spring 97; auth, Polski sonoryzm I jego europejski kontekst, Dysonanse, 97; auth, Bacewicz, Picasso and the Making of Desire, J of Musicological Res, 97; auth, Into the City, Onto the Lake: Sit-Specific Music of Henry Brant and R Murray Schafer, Contemporary Mus Rev, 97; auth, Polish School as Sonorism and Its European Context, Crosscurrents and Counterpointes: Offerings in Honor of Bengt Hambraeus at 70, 98; auth, Maria Szymanowska's Vocal Music, Women Compsers, vol 4, 98; auth, Music of Sound and Light: Xenakis's Polytopes, Leonardo, 98; auth, About Life and Music: A Semi-Serious Conversation with Henryk Mikolaj Gorecki, Musical Quart, 98; auth, Gorecki and the Paradigm of the 'Maternal', Musical Quart, 98; auth, Music as Text, Musical Movement and Spatio-temporal Features of the Musical Work, Proceedings of the Int Kongress der Gesellschft fur Musikforschung 'Musik als Text,' 99; auth, At Home with Phenomenology: Roman Ingarden's Work of Music Revisited, Int J of Musicology, 98; auth, Technika ruchu dzwieku w muzyce instrumentalnej Xenakisa, Muzyka, 99; auth, Xenakis's World, Polish Musicological Quart, 99; auth, A Mystic in the Cathedral: Music, Image and Symbol in Andriessen's Hadewijch, Amer J of Semiotics, 98; auth, Canadian Identity, Deep Ecology and R Murray Schafer's The Princess of the Stars, Soundscape Yearbook, 98; auth, Sacred/Secular Constructs of National Identity: A Convoluted History Polish Anthems, auth, "After Chapin" ; ed, After Chopin: Essays on Polish Music, Friends of Polish Music at USC, 99; auth, Percussion, Poetry, and Color: The Music of Marta Ptanyinska, "Music Works", 99; auth, Spatiality of Sound and Stream Segregation in 20th-C instrumental Music, Organized sound 3 no 2, 98; auth, Dans La Nuit: The Themes of Night and Death in Lutoslawski's Oeuvre, Lutoslawski Studies, Oxford Univ, 00; auth, Bogurodzica Reborn: A Medieval Anthem in Contemporary Polish Music, The Yearning for the Middle Ages, 00. **CONTACT ADDRESS** Dept of Music, History & Lit, Univ of So California, Los Angeles, CA 91214-0851. **EMAIL** maharley@usc.edu

HARMON, DANIEL P.

PERSONAL Born 05/03/1938, Chicago, IL **DISCIPLINE** CLASSICS **EDUCATION** Northwestern Univ, MA, 65, PhD, 68. **CAREER** Asst prof, 67-75, assoc prof, 75-89, prof, 84- , chemn, Dept of Classics, 76-91, co-dir, 92-00 , Univ Washington Rome Ctr. **MEMBERSHIPS** APA; Archaeol Inst of Am; AAUP; Societe des Etudes Latines. **RESEARCH** Greek and Roman religion; Roman archaeology; classical linguistics. **SELECTED PUBLICATIONS** Auth, The Poet's Initiation and the Sacerdotal Imagery of Propertius 3.1-5, Stud in Latin Lit and Roman Hist, Coll Latomus, 79; auth, Religion in the Latin Elegists, in Haase, ed, Augstieg und Niedergang der Romischen Welt: Geschichte und Kultur Roms im Spiegel der Neuren Forschung, Walter de Gruyter, 85; auth, The Religious Significance of Games in the Roman Age, in Raschke, ed, The Archaeology of the Olympics, Univ Wisconsin, 87; auth, contribur, World Book Encyclopedia, 93; auth, Feriae, Der Neue Pauly, v.4, J.B. Metzger Verlag. **CONTACT ADDRESS** Dept of Classics, Univ of Washington, PO Box 353110, Seattle, WA 98195. **EMAIL** dph@u.washington.edu

HARMON, GARY L.

PERSONAL Born 08/16/1935, Aurora, NE, m, 1990, 3 children **DISCIPLINE** ENGLISH **HONORS AND AWARDS** Grad Res Grant, Ind Univ, 65-66; Fulbright Lectureship, Bahia Blanca, Buenos Aires, Arg, 83; TSI Res Grant, UNF, 88, 90; Leadership Awd, Popular Culture Asn in the S, 88; Teaching Incentive Performance (TIP) Awd, 96; Who's Who in Am, Who's Who in the World; Two Thousand Notable Americans; Men of Achievement; Dict of Int Biog; Contemporary Authors; Outstanding Educators of Am, Int Authors and Writers and Writer's Who's Who; The Nat Register of Promiment Americans. **MEMBERSHIPS** Am Cult Asn, Am Cult Asn of the S, MLA, S Atlantic MLA, Nat Coun for Teachers of English, Popular Cult Asn, Fla Col English Asn. **RESEARCH** American Literature and Culture, Film. **SELECTED PUBLICATIONS** Auth, "A Coming of Age for Literary Scholarship," in Scholar's Market: An International Dictionary of Periodicals Publishing Literay Scholarship (Ohio State Univ, Libr Publ, 74); auth, "William Inge: Dramatist of Middle America in the Fifties," in Contemporary Literary Scene (77); auth,"Joseph Heller: The Novelist as Social Critic," and "Conversations with Joseph Heller," in Contemp Literary Scene II (79); auth, "Tarzan and Columbo, Heroic Mediators," in Hero in Transition, ed. Ray B. Browne and Marshall F. Fishwick (The Popular Press, Bowling Green State Univ, 83); auth, "'Sophie's Choice': Pain That Refreshes," Spinnaker, 83; auth, "Reading Imaginary beings and Creatures Semiotically: The Talking Serpent, Medusa, Santa Claus, Vampires, and Others," Semiotics (89); auth, "From Fernandina to Picolata and Olustee," in The Book Lover's Guide to Fla, ed. Kevin McCarthy (Pineapple Press, 92); coauth, "Jung and Star Trek: the Coincidentia Appositorum and Images of the Shadow," J of Popular Cult 28-2 (95): 169-184; auth, "Ecofilm: Mythologies of Conservation and Ecology in Film," in Columbia Encyclopedia of Film and History, ed. Peter Rollins (ST. Martin's Press, forthcoming). **CONTACT ADDRESS** Dept of English, Univ of No Florida, 4567 Johns Bluff Rd, Jacksonville, FL 32224. **EMAIL** amepic@aol.com

HARNER, JAMES L.

PERSONAL Born 03/24/1946, Washington, IN, m, 1967, 1 child **DISCIPLINE** ENGLISH **EDUCATION** Ind State Univ, BS, 68; Univ Ill, MA, 70; PhD, 72. **CAREER** Asst Prof to Prof, Bowling Green state Univ, 71-88; Prof, Tex A & M Univ, 88-. **HONORS AND AWARDS** Besterman Medal, Library Asn, 97; choice Outstanding Acad Book, Literary Res Guide, 00; Choice Outstanding Acad book, Literary Res Guide, 91; Choice Outstanding Acad Book, English Renaissance Prose Fiction, 79. **MEMBERSHIPS** Mod Lang Asn, Shakespeare Asn of Am, Intl Shakespeare Asn, The Bibliographical Soc. **RESEARCH** Shakespeare; Bibliography. **SELECTED PUBLICATIONS** Auth, World Shakespeare Bibliography Online, Arden Shakespeare, 00; auth, On Compiling an Annotated bibliography, Mod Lang Asn, 00; auth, World Shakespeare Bibliography on CD-ROM 1980-1996, Cambridge Univ press, 99; auth, Literary Research Guide: A Guide to Reference sources for the Study of Literatures in English and Related Topics, Mod Lang Asn, 98; auth, World Shakespeare Bibliography on CD-ROM 1983-1995, Cambridge Univ Press, 98; auth, World Shakespeare Bibliography on CD-ROM 1987-1994, Cambridge Univ Press, 97; auth, World Shakespeare Bibliography on CD-ROM 1990-1993, Cambridge Univ Press, 96;auth, MLA Directory of Scholarly Presses in Language and Literature, Mod Lang Asn, 96. **CONTACT ADDRESS** Dept English, Texas A&M Univ, Corpus Christi, 1 Tex A & M Univ, College Station, TX 77843-0001. **EMAIL** j-harner@tamu.edu

HARPHAM, GEOFFREY GALT

DISCIPLINE ENGLISH LITERATURE **EDUCATION** Northwestern Univ, BA, 68; UCLA, PhD, 74. **CAREER** Prof, 86, Tulane Univ. **SELECTED PUBLICATIONS** Auth, On the Grotesque, Princeton, 82; The Ascetic Imperative in Culture and Criticism, Chicago, 87; Getting It Right: Language, Literature and Ethics, Chicago, 92; So..What Is Enlightenment, Critical Inquiry, 94; Ethics, Critical Terms for Literary Study, Chicago, 95; Of Rats and Men; Or, Reason In Our Time, Raritan, 95; One of Us: The Mastery of Joseph Conrad, Chicago, 96; Late Jameson, Salmagundi, 96; auth, Shadows of Ethics: criticism and the Just Soc, Duke, 99. **CONTACT ADDRESS** Dept of Eng, Tulane Univ, 6823 St Charles Ave, New Orleans, LA 70118. **EMAIL** harpham@mailhost.tcs.tulane.edu

HARPINE, WILLIAM

PERSONAL Born 09/15/1951, Washington, DC, m, 1977, 3 children **DISCIPLINE** COMMUNICATION **EDUCATION** Univ of Illinois, Phd, 82; Northern Illinois Univ, MA, 74; Coll of William & Mary, BA, 73. **CAREER** Prof, 97-; Assoc Prof, 87-97; Assist Prof, 82-87, Univ of Akron; Asst Prof, College of William and Mary, 79-82; Teaching Asst, Univ of Illinois, 76-79; Temporary Instructor, Iowa State Univ, 75-76; Graduate Asst, Northern Illinois Univ, 73-74. **MEMBERSHIPS** National Communication Assoc; Amer Society for the History of Rhetoric; Eastern Communication Assoc. **RESEARCH** 19th Century Political Oratory; Theology of Argumentation. **SELECTED PUBLICATIONS** Auth, "Stock Issues In Aristotle's Rhetoric," Journal of the American Forensic Association, 14, 77: 73-81; auth, "The Theoretical Bases of Stock Issues," The Forensic, 70, 84: 6-14; auth, "Can Rhetoric and Dialectic Serve the Purposes of Logic?" Philosophy and Rhetoric 18, 85: 96-112; auth, "The Argument of Extreme Variation Does Not Prove Field Dependence," Ohio Speech Journal, 27, 89: 48-55; auth, "The Appeal to Tradition: Cultural Evolution and Logical Soundness," Informal Logic, 15, 93: 109-119; auth, "Stock Issues and Theories of Ethnics," Southern Journal of Forensics, 1, 96: 166-182; auth, "Epideictic and Ethos in the Amarna Letters: The Withholding of Argument," Rhetoric Society Quarterly, 28, 98: 81-98. **CONTACT ADDRESS** School Communication, Univ of Akron, Akron, OH 44325-1003. **EMAIL** harpine@vakron.edu

HARPOLD, TERRY

DISCIPLINE LITERATURE, COMMUNICATION, AND CULTURE **EDUCATION** Univ Pa, PhD, 94. **CAREER** Asst prof, mem, Ctr for New Media Educ and Res, & Graphics, Visualization, & Usability Ctr, Ga Inst of Technol. **RESEARCH** Postmodern culture and literature. **SELECTED PUBLICATIONS** Publications include discussions of hypertextual narrative form and its graphical representations, the "inverted landscapes" of author J.G. Ballard, and the obscured political economies of cartographic depictions of the Internet. **CONTACT ADDRESS** Sch of Lit, Commun & Cult, Georgia Inst of Tech, Skiles Cla, Atlanta, GA 30332. **EMAIL** terry.harpold@lcc.gatech.edu

HARRIENGER, MYRNA J.

DISCIPLINE COMPOSITION AND RHETORIC **EDUCATION** Purdue Univ, PhD, 91. **CAREER** Asst prof, TX Tech Univ. **RESEARCH** Writing in old age; writing in illness; ethics and composition/rhetoric; ethics and pedagogy. **SELECTED PUBLICATIONS** Auth, Writing a Life: The Composing of Grace, in Feminist Principles and Women's Experience in Rhetoric and Composition, Univ Pittsburgh Press, 95; auth, "Composing an Ethics of Difference," in Ethics and the Teaching of Composition (forthcoming). **CONTACT ADDRESS** Dept of English, Texas Tech Univ, Lubbock, TX 79409-5015. **EMAIL** ditmh@ttacs.ttu.edu

HARRIES, ELIZABETH WANNING

PERSONAL Born 05/22/1938, East Orange, NJ, d, 3 children **DISCIPLINE** ENGLISH, COMPARATIVE LITERATURE **EDUCATION** Vassar Col, AB, 59; Yale Univ, MAT, 60; PhD, 73. **CAREER** Lectr, Yale Univ, 73-74; asst prof to prof, Smith Col, 74-. **HONORS AND AWARDS** Danforth Fel for Women, 67-73; Walker Cowen Mem Prize, Univ of Va, 93. **MEMBERSHIPS** MLA, ASECS, ACLA. **RESEARCH** European fairy tales, 18th century literature. **SELECTED PUBLICATIONS** Auth, The Unfinished Moment: Essays on the Fragment in the Later Eighteenth Century, Charlottesville: Univ Press of Va (94); auth, "Simulating Oralities: French Fairy Tales of the 1690's," Col Lit 23 (June 96): 100-115; auth, "Fairy Tales about Fairy Tales: Notes on Canon Formation," in Out of the Woods: The Origins of the Literary Fairy Tale in Italy and France, ed Nancy Canepa, Detroit: Wayne State Univ Press (97): 152-175; auth, " 'Out in Left Field': Charlotte Smith's Prefaces, Bourdieu's Categories, and the Public Sphere," Modern Lang Quart, 58 (97): 457-473; auth, "The Mirror Broken: Fairy Tales in Women's Autobiographies," Marvels and Tales (April 2000); auth, " 'Excited Ideas': Description, the Monstrous, and the Sublime," Recrueil d'essais sur l'estetique et l practique de l'ecriture fragmentaire, ed Rosa Maria Losito (forthcoming); auth, Twice Upon a Time: Re-Reading the History of the Fairy Tale (tentative title), Princeton Univ Press (forthcoming 2001). **CONTACT ADDRESS** Dept English, Smith Col, 98 Green St, Northhampton, MA 01063-1000. **EMAIL** eharries@sophia.smith.edu

HARRINGTON, E. MICHAEL

PERSONAL Born 02/02/1954, Cambridge, MA **DISCIPLINE** PERFORMING ARTS **EDUCATION** Univ Lowell, BM, 76; Univ Miami, MM, 78; Ohio State Univ, DMA, 85. **CAREER** Lectr, performed, taught master classes at Harvard Univ, Berklee Col Music, Eastman Sch Music, Emory Univ; prof, Belmont Univ. **HONORS AND AWARDS** Jemison Distinguished Prof Hum, 1995, Univ Ala; listed, Who's Who in the South, Who's Who Among Amer Teachers; Nashville Composer of the Year, 89. **MEMBERSHIPS** Board dir, Col Music Society Southern Chapter, Live Music in Am; ed board dir, Univ Ala Press. **RESEARCH** World music; copyright law; popular music. **SELECTED PUBLICATIONS** Articles publ, Col Music Symposium, Ex Tempore, Triad, Tenn Musician, Am Society Univ Composers Monograph Series, Ind Theory Review. **CONTACT ADDRESS** 2625 Link Dr, Franklin, TN 37064-4942. **EMAIL** harringtone@mail.belmont.edu

HARRINGTON, HENRY R.

PERSONAL Born 12/23/1943, Evanston, IL, m, 1968, 1 child **DISCIPLINE** ENGLISH LITERATURE & THEOLOGY **EDUCATION** Williams Col, AB, 66; Stanford Univ, MA, 68, PhD, 71. **CAREER** Asst prof, 71-80, ASSOC PROF ENGLISH, UNIV MONT, 80- **MEMBERSHIPS** MLA; AAUP; Am Acad Relig. **RESEARCH** Victorian literature; comtemporary theology and literature; novel. **SELECTED PUBLICATIONS CONTACT ADDRESS** Dept of English, Univ of Montana, Missoula, MT 59801.

HARRIS, CHARLES BURT

PERSONAL Born 11/02/1940, LaGrange, TX, m, 1968, 2 children **DISCIPLINE** AMERICAN LITERATURE **EDUCATION** Tex Lutheran Col, AB, 63; Southern Ill Univ, MA, 65, PhD(English), 70. **CAREER** Chairperson, Dept of English, Ill State Univ, 79-94; Univ Coun on Teacher Educ, Ill State Univ, 87-93; President's Task Force on Admin Efficiency, Ill State Univ, 90-91; Dir, Unit for Contemporary Lit, Ill State Univ, 94-; Col of Arts and Scis Ad Hoc Comt on Summer Sch, 95; Dept Fac Status Comt, 95-97, 99-01; mem bd of Trustees Presidential Search Comt, 98-99. **HONORS AND AWARDS** Col of Arts and Scis Lectr, Ill State Univ, Spring 80; One of sixty English educators from across the nation selected to participate in the three-week English Coalition Conf, Aspen Inst, July 87; Distinguished Alumnus Awd, Dept of English, Southern Ill Univ-

Carbondale, 89; Francis Andrew March Awd for Exceptional Serv to the Profession of English, Asn of Departments of English/Mod Lang Asn, 97 **MEMBERSHIPS** MLA; Midwest Mod Lang Asn; Asn Dept English; AAUP. **RESEARCH** Twentieth century American literature; the novel; recent American fiction. **SELECTED PUBLICATIONS** Auth, Contemporary American Novelist of the Absurd, New Haven: College and University P, 71; auth, Passionate Virtuosity: The Fiction of John Barth, Urbana: U of Ill P, 83; auth, Humor and the Recent American Novel, Paderborn, W. Germany: Paderborner Universitatsreden, 88; Guest Ed, Special issue on Independent Presses and Contemporary American Literature, Critique 37.3, Spring 96; auth, "Introduction," Leslie Fielder, Love and Death in the American Novel, Normal: Dalkey Archive P, (97): v-xii; auth, "The Dead Fathers: The Rejection of Modernist Distance in Carole Maso's The Art Lover," Review of Contemporary Fiction Fall (97): 157-174; auth, "The Downsizing of the American Mind: Academic Citizenship and the Current Crisis," ADE Bulletin 121 (98): 25-28; auth, "The Stereo View: Politics and the Role of the Reader in Richard Power's Gain," Review of Contemporary Fiction (98): 97-108; auth, "Blesses by Madness: Curtis White's Memories of My Father Watching TV," Review of Contemporary Fiction (98): 101-116; auth, "Renewing the Nexus: Strengthening Connections across the English and Foreign Language Programs," New York: MLA, (99): 17-48; **CONTACT ADDRESS** Dept of English, Illinois State Univ, Normal, IL 61761. **EMAIL** cbharri@ilstu.edu

HARRIS, CHARLES DAVID
PERSONAL Born 01/06/1939, Minneapolis, MN, d, 3 children **DISCIPLINE** MUSICOLOGY **EDUCATION** Northwestern Univ, BMus, 60, MMus, 61; Univ MI, PhD, 67. **CAREER** Asst prof, 65-71, assoc prof, 71-77, prof music, Drake Univ, 77, Fulbright res grant, Austrian-Am Educ Comn, Vienna, 71-72. **HONORS AND AWARDS** Ellis and Nelle Levitt Prof of Music Hist and Harpsichord, 89-; NEH grants, 89, 92 **MEMBERSHIPS** Am Musicol Soc. **RESEARCH** Baroque music hist and performance practice. **SELECTED PUBLICATIONS** Critical ed, A-R Editions, and The Broude Trust (Art of the Keyboard Series). **CONTACT ADDRESS** Fine Arts Center, Drake Univ, 2507 University Ave, Des Moines, IA 50311-4505. **EMAIL** david.harris@drake.edu

HARRIS, DANIEL A.
DISCIPLINE ENGLISH LANGUAGE AND LITERATURE **EDUCATION** Yale Univ, BA; MA; PhD. **CAREER** Prof. **RESEARCH** Jewish studies; Victorian poetry; modern and contemporary poetry; graduate student pedagogy. **SELECTED PUBLICATIONS** Auth, Yeats: Coole Park and Ballylee; auth, Inspirations Unbidden: the 'Terrible Sonnets' of Gerard Manley Hopkins. **CONTACT ADDRESS** Dept of English, Rutgers, The State Univ of New Jersey, New Brunswick, 510 George St, Murray Hall, New Brunswick, NJ 08901-1167. **EMAIL** dharris@aol.com

HARRIS, DUNCAN SEELY
PERSONAL Born 02/22/1944, Worland, WY, m, 1966, 2 children **DISCIPLINE** ENGLISH & AMERICAN LITERATURE **EDUCATION** Stanford Univ, BA, 65; Boston Univ, MA, 66; Brandeis Univ, PhD, 73. **CAREER** Instr English, Tougaloo Col, 69; from instr to asst prof, 70-77, assoc prof Eng, 77-, Univ Wyo; Danforth Found Assoc, 80-; dir, honor's prog, 93. **MEMBERSHIPS** MLA; Melville Soc; Shakespeare Assn. **RESEARCH** Nineteenth century American literature; Shakespeare; allegory. **SELECTED PUBLICATIONS** Auth, The End of Lear and a Shape for Shakespearean Tragedy, Shakespeare Studies, 76; art, Again for Cydnus: The Dramaturgical Resolution of Antony and Cleopatra, Studies in English Lit, 77; co-ed, Teaching Shakespeare, Princeton Univ, 77; coauth, The Other Side Of The Garden: An Interpretive Comparison of the Book of the Duchess and the Daphnaida, J Medieval and Renaissance Studies, 78; auth, Tombs, Guidebooks and Shakespearean Drama: Death in the Renaissance, Mosaic, 82. **CONTACT ADDRESS** Dept of English, Univ of Wyoming, Box 3353, Laramie, WY 82071. **EMAIL** dharris@uwyo.edu

HARRIS, ELIZABETH HALL
PERSONAL Born 11/27/1944, Ft. Worth, TX, m, 1995 **DISCIPLINE** CREATIVE WRITING (FICTION) & MODERN LITERATURE **EDUCATION** Carnegie-Mellon Univ, BS, 65; Stanford Univ, PhD(English), 76. **CAREER** Asst prof, 76-83, ASSOC PROF ENGLISH, UNIV TX, AUSTIN, 83-. **HONORS AND AWARDS** Honorable Mention, Best Short Stories of 1970 and Best Short Stories of 1985; New Stories from the South: The Year's Best, 86; The John Simmons Awd, 91; The Best of Wind, 199?. **SELECTED PUBLICATIONS** Auth, The Ant Generator (stories), IA, 91. **CONTACT ADDRESS** Dept of English, Univ of Texas, Austin, 0 Univ of TX, Austin, TX 78712-1026.

HARRIS, GIL W.
PERSONAL Born 12/09/1946, Lynchburg, VA, m **DISCIPLINE** COMMUNICATIONS **EDUCATION** Natl Acad of Broadcasting, 64-65; Winston-Salem Coll, AS 71; Shaw Univ, BA, 80; NC A&T St Univ, MS, 81-82; Pacific Western Univ, PhD, 86. **CAREER** WEAL/WQMG Radio Stations, oper dir, 72-79; Shaw Univ, dir of radio broadcasting, 79-81; Collegiate Telecommunications, system producer, sport dir, 81-84; SC St Univ, asst prof of broadcasting, 84-. **HONORS AND AWARDS** Citizen of the Week WGHP TV High Point NC, 77; Radio Announcer of the Year Dudley HS, 79; Outstanding Media Serv Triad Sickle Cell, 79; Outstanding Media Serv Mid-Eastern Athletic Conf, 83; Outstanding Media Serv Central Intercoll Athletic Assoc. **MEMBERSHIPS** Omega Psi Phi, Prince Hall Mason, NAACP. **CONTACT ADDRESS** Dept of Commun, So Carolina State Univ, PO Box 7656, Orangeburg, SC 29117. **EMAIL** gharris@scsu.edu

HARRIS, JANICE HUBBARD
PERSONAL Born 03/30/1943, Los Angeles, CA, m, 1966, 2 children **DISCIPLINE** BRITISH FICTION; WOMEN'S STUDIES; POST COLONIAL STUDIES **EDUCATION** Stanford Univ, AB, 65; Brown Univ, PhD, 73. **CAREER** Instr English, Tougaloo Col, 69-73; from asst prof English to prof, 75-, assoc dean arts sci, 83-84, dir univ honors prog, 82-86, dir women's studies, 95-99, Univ Wyo. **HONORS AND AWARDS** Danforth Teaching fel, 81. **MEMBERSHIPS** MLA; Nat Women's Studies Asn; Women's Caucus Mod Lang. **RESEARCH** Modern British fiction; women's studies; Post-Colonial Literatures. **SELECTED PUBLICATIONS** Auth, D H Lawrence and Kate Millett, Mass Rev, summer 74; Our mute, inglorious mothers, Midwest Quart, 4/75; Insight and experiment in D H Lawrence's early short fiction, Philol Quart, summer 76; Sexual antagonism in D H Lawrence's early leadership fiction, Mod Lang Studies, spring 77; The moulting of the plumed serpent, Mod Lang Quart, 3/79; Bushes, bears and the beast in the jungle, Studies in Short Fiction, spring 81; Gayl Jones' Corregidora, Frontiers, Vol 3; Feminist Representations of Wives and Work: An Almost Irreconcilable' Edwardian Debate, Women's Stud, 93; Challenging the Script of the Heterosexual Couple: Three Marriage Novels by May Sinclair, Papers on Lang & Lit, 93; Wifely Speech and Silence: Three Marriage Novels by H G Wells, Stud in Novel, 94; Edwardian Stories of Divorce, Rutgers Univ, 96. **CONTACT ADDRESS** Dept English, Univ of Wyoming, PO Box 3353, Laramie, WY 82071-3353. **EMAIL** jharris@vwyo.edu

HARRIS, JONATHAN GIL
PERSONAL Born 08/23/1963, Auckland, New Zealand **DISCIPLINE** ENGLISH LITERATURE **EDUCATION** Auckland Univ, BA, 83, MA, 86; Univ Sussex, PhD, 90. **CAREER** Assoc prof. **HONORS AND AWARDS** Folger Fel, 96; Fel, Cornell Soc for the Humanities, 95; Charles H. Dana Teaching Awd, 95. **MEMBERSHIPS** MLA; Shakespeare Soc of Am; Medieval and Renaissance Drama Soc; Shakespeare at Kalamazoo. **RESEARCH** Early modern English culture. **SELECTED PUBLICATIONS** Auth, Foreign Bodies and the Body Politic: Discourses of Social Pathology in Early Modern England, Cambridge, 98; Apples Beyond the Pale: The Irish Costermonger in the English Garden of Eden, Binghamton, 95; This is not a Pipe: Water Supply, Incontinent Sources, and the Leaky Body Politic, Cornell, 94; 'Narcissus in thy face': Roman Desire and the Difference it Fakes in Antony and Cleopatra, Cambridge, 94; auth, "The Canker of England's Commonwealth: Gerard de Malynes and the Origins of Economic Pathology," Textual Practice 13 (2) London, (99): 311-27; auth, Historicizing Greenblatt's Containment: The Cold War, Functionalism, and the Origins of Social Pathology, (Amsterdam and New York), 99; auth, Puck/Robin Goodfellow, (Westport, CT), 98. **CONTACT ADDRESS** English Dept, Ithaca Col, 953 Danby Rd, Muller 328, Ithaca, NY 14850. **EMAIL** harrisj@ithaca.edu

HARRIS, JOSEPH
DISCIPLINE FOLKLORE AND ENGLISH **EDUCATION** Univ Ga, BA; Univ Frankfurt; Cambridge Univ, England; Harvard Univ, AM, PhD. **CAREER** Prof. **RESEARCH** Tradition and language. **SELECTED PUBLICATIONS** Co-ed, Prosimetrum: Cross-Cultural Perspectives on Narrative in Prose and Verse, 97. **CONTACT ADDRESS** Dept of English, Harvard Univ, 8 Garden St, Cambridge, MA 02138. **EMAIL** harris@fas.harvard.edu

HARRIS, LAURILYN J.
DISCIPLINE THEATRE HISTORY AND DRAMATURGY **EDUCATION** Ind Univ, BA; Univ Iowa, MA, PhD. **CAREER** Prof & dir Grad Stud, Washington State Univ. **SELECTED PUBLICATIONS** Publ in, Theatre Res Int; Theatre Hist Stud; J Creative Behavior; Theatre J; Notable Women in the Amer Theatre; Theatre Annual; Theatre Southwest; Amer Theatre Companies; Stud in Amer Drama; Nineteenth Century Theatre Res; Confronting Tenn Williams' Streetcar Named Desire. **CONTACT ADDRESS** Dept of Music and Theater, Washington State Univ, Pullman, WA 99164-5300.

HARRIS, MARK
PERSONAL Born 11/19/1922, Mount Vernon, NY, m, 1946, 4 children **DISCIPLINE** ENGLISH **EDUCATION** Univ Minn, PhD, Am Studies, 56. **CAREER** Fac English, San Fransisco State Col, 54-68; vis prof, Brandeis, 63; Purdue Univ, 67-79; Calif Inst Arts, 70-73; Immaculate Heart Col, 73-74; Univ Southern Calif, 73-75; prof, Univ Pittsburgh, 75-80; Prof English, Ariz State Univ, 80-. **HONORS AND AWARDS** DHL, Ill Wesleyan Univ, 74; fulbright prof, univ hiroshima, 57-58; ford found fel, 60; nat inst arts & letters fel, 61; guggenheim mem found fel, 65, 74; nat endowment for arts, 66. **SELECTED PUBLICATIONS** Auth, Trumpet to the World, 46; City of Discontent, 52; The Southpaw, 53; Bang the Drum Slowly, 56; Something About A Soldier, 57; A Ticket for a Seamstitch, 57; Wake Up, Stupid, 59; The Goy, 70; Killing Everybody, Dial Press, 73; It Looked Like Forever, McGraw-Hill Co, 79; Short Work of It: Selected Writing..., Univ Pittsburgh Press, 79; Saul Bellow: Drumlin Woodchuck, Univ Ga Press, 80; The Heart of Boswell, McGraw-Hill Co, 82; Lying in Bed, 84; Speed, 90; The Tale Maker, 94. **CONTACT ADDRESS** English Dept, Arizona State Univ, Tempe, AZ 85281. **EMAIL** mark.harris@asu.edu

HARRIS, RANDY ALLEN
DISCIPLINE ENGLISH LITERATURE **EDUCATION** Univ Alberta, MS, 85; Dalhousie Univ, MA, 82; Queen's Univ, BA, 80; Rensselaer Polytech Inst, MS, 86; DPhil, 90. **CAREER** Teaching asst, Queen's Univ, 79-80; teaching asst, Univ of Alberta, 82-83; lectr, Dept of Eng, Grant MacEwan Commun Col, 84-85; lectr, Dept of Ling, Univ of Alberta, 90-91; assoc prof, Dept of Eng, Univ of Waterloo, 92-. **HONORS AND AWARDS** Rensselaer Scholar Fel, Rensselaer Polytech Inst, 85-86; Sir James Lougheed Awd of Distinction, Rensselaer Polytech Inst, 85-87; McKinney Writing Prizes, Rensselaer Polytech Inst, 86, 87; Beer Trust grant dissertation res, 87; Readers Digest Grants for Publ, 87, 88; The Jay Gould Awd for Excellence in Tech Writing, 88; SSHRC Doctoral Fel, Rensselaer Polytech Inst, 87-88; Izaak Walton Killam Mem Postdoctoral Fel, Univ of Alberta, 90-92; NYork Chapter STC Publ and Art Competition Awd of Merit, 93; SSHRC Res Grant, 93; Travel Grant, 98. **SELECTED PUBLICATIONS** Auth, The Chomskyan revolution 1: Science, syntax, and semantics, Perspectives Sci, 94; The Chomskyan revolution 2: Sturm und Drang, Perspectives Sci, 94; The linguistics wars, Oxford, 93; Acoustic dimensions of functor comprehension in Broca's aphasia, Univ Ind, 88; ed, Landmark essays in rhetoric of science: Case studies, Lawrence Erlbaum, 97; co-ed, Technical communication in Canada, Baywood, 94; coauth, "Technical Communication in Canada," in J of Tech Writing and Commun 24.3 (NY: Baywood Publ, 95); auth, "Carson and Bakhtin," in And no birds sang: Rhetorical analyses of Rachel Carson's Silent Spring, ed. Craig Waddell (Carbondale: Southern Ill Univ Press, 99); coauth, "Rhetoric of Science," Technostyle (99). **CONTACT ADDRESS** Dept of English, Univ of Waterloo, 200 University Ave W, Waterloo, ON, Canada N2L 3G1. **EMAIL** pwpmah@watarts.uwaterloo.ca

HARRIS, ROBERT ALLEN
PERSONAL Born 01/09/1938, Detroit, MI, m, 1963, 1 child **DISCIPLINE** CONDUCTING, COMPOSITION **EDUCATION** Wayne State Univ, BS 1960, MA 1962; Michigan State Univ, PhD 1971; post grad studies, Eastman School of Music, Aspen Music School. **CAREER** Detroit Public Schools, music teacher 1960-64; Wayne State Univ, asst prof 1964-70; MI State Univ, assoc prof, prof 1970-77; Northwestern Univ, School of Music, Prof, 77-; Church musician: currently Trinity United Methodist Church, Wilmette, IL. **HONORS AND AWARDS** Distinguished Alumni Awd Wayne State Univ 1983. **MEMBERSHIPS** Phi Mu Alpha Prof Music Frat; Pi Kappa Lambda Honor Music Soc; Phi Kappa Phi National Honor Soc; ASCAP; Am Choral Dirs Assoc. **RESEARCH** Choral music practice and performance; conducting pedagogy/performance. **SELECTED PUBLICATIONS** Publ, Composer: Oxford Univ Press, Boosey & Hawkes, Mark Foster Publ, Walton Music, Alliance Music, J.S. Paulch, Inc. articles: Western Journal of Black Studies; Black Studies: Theory, Method and Cultural Perspectives; Ars Nova Unisa Musica (South Africa); The Pretorian (South Africa). **CONTACT ADDRESS** Sch of Music, Northwestern Univ, 711 Elgin Rd, Evanston, IL 60208-1200. **EMAIL** robahar@northwestern.edu

HARRIS, SUSAN KUMIN
PERSONAL Born 08/29/1945, Baltimore, MD, m, 1968 **DISCIPLINE** AMERICAN LITERATURE & STUDIES **EDUCATION** Antioch Col, BA, 68; Stanford Univ, MA, 72; Cornell Univ, PhD(English), 77. **CAREER** ASSOC PROF ENGLISH, QUEENS COL, 77- **MEMBERSHIPS** MLA. **RESEARCH** Mark Twain studies; women's studies (American, 19th century); rhetoric. **SELECTED PUBLICATIONS** Auth, This peace, this deep contentment's images of temporal freedom in the writings of Mark Twain, Essays in Lit, fall 80; Narrative structure in Mark Twain's Joan of Arc, J Narrative Technique, winter 82; Mark Twain's Escape from Time: A Study of Patterns and Images, Univ Mo Press, 82; Mark Twain's good and bad women, Prospects (in prep). **CONTACT ADDRESS** Dept of English, Queens Col, CUNY, Flushing, NY 11367.

HARRIS, THOMAS E.
PERSONAL m **DISCIPLINE** COMMUNICATION **EDUCATION** George Washington Univ, BA, 66; Univ Maryland, MA, 67; Temple Univ, PhD, 81. **CAREER** Rutgers Univ; George Washington Univ; prof, Univ Evansville, 80-89; prof, Univ AL, 89-. **HONORS AND AWARDS** Outstand Fac, Univ AL, 96; Outstand Prof, Univ Evansville, 87. **MEMBERSHIPS** NCA; ABC. **RESEARCH** Organizational change; creativity; humor; leadership; impact of technology; communication; teams and groups. **SELECTED PUBLICATIONS** Auth, Ap-

plied Organizational Communication: Perspectives, Principles and Pragmatics, Lawrence Erbaum Assoc (Hillsdale, NJ), 93; auth, "Toward effective employee involvement: An analysis of parallel and self-managing teams," J Applied Business Res 9 (93): 25-33; auth, Analysis of the Clash over Issues Between Booker T Washington and WEB, DuBois (NY, Garland. 93); auth, "Diversity: Importance, ironies, and pathways," in Conflict and Diversity, eds. C D Brown, C C Snedeker, B Sykes (Cresskill, NJ: Hampton Press, 97): 16-34; auth, Small Group and Team Communication, Allyn and Bacon (Boston, MA), 99. **CONTACT ADDRESS** Dept Comm Studies, Univ of Alabama, Tuscaloosa, PO Box 870172, Tuscaloosa, AL 35487-0172. **EMAIL** tharris@ccom.ua.edu

HARRIS, TRUDIER

PERSONAL Born 02/27/1948, Mantua, AL, s **DISCIPLINE** ENGLISH **EDUCATION** Stillman Coll, Tuscaloosa AL, BA, 1969; Ohio State Univ, Columbus OH, MA, 1972, PhD, 1973. **CAREER** The Coll of William and Mary, Williamsburg VA, asst prof, 73-79; Univ of North Carolina, Chapel Hill NC, assoc prof, 79-85, prof, 85-88, J Carlyle Sitterson prof, 88-; Univ of Arkansas, Little Rock AR, William Grant Cooper Visiting Distinguished, prof, 87; Ohio State Univ, Columbus OH, visiting distinguished prof, 88. **HONORS AND AWARDS** NEH Fellowship for Coll Teachers, 1977-78; Carnegie Faculty Fellow, The Bunting Inst, 1981-83; Fellow, Natl Research Council/Ford Found, 1982-83; Creative Scholarship Awd, Coll Language Assn, 1987; Teaching Awd, South Atlantic Modern Language Assn, 1987; Rockefeller Fellowship, Bellagio, Italy, 1994; National Humanities Center Fellowship, 1996-97. **MEMBERSHIPS** Mem, The Modern Language Assn of Amer, 1973-, Amer Folklore Soc, 1973-, Coll Language Assn, 1974-South Atlantic Modern Language Assn, 1980-, The Langston Hughes Soc, 1982-, Zeta Phi Beta Sorority Inc. **SELECTED PUBLICATIONS** Auth, From Mammies To Militants: Domestics in Black American Literature, 82; Exorcising Blackness: Historical and Literary Lynching And Burning Rituals, 84; Black Women In The Fiction of James Baldwin, 85; Fiction and Folklore: The Novels of Toni Morrison, 91; The Power of the Porch: The Storyteller's Craft in Zora Neale Hurston, Gloria Naylor, and Randall Kenan, 96; ed, Afro-American Writers Before The Harlem Renaissance, 86; Afro-American Writers From The Harlem Renaissance to 1940, 87; Afro-American Writers From 1940 to 1955, 88; ed, Selected Works of Ida B Wells-Barnett, 91; Afro-American Fiction Writers After 1955 in the dictionary of Literary Biography Series, 84; Afro-American Writers After 1955: Dramatist and Prose Writers, 85; Afro-American Poets After 1955, 85; The Oxford Companion to Women's Writing in the United States, 94; The Oxford Companion to African American Literature 97; Call and Response The Riverside Anthology of the African American Literary Tradition, 97; The Literature of the American South: A Norton Anthology, 97; New Essays on Baldwin's Go Tell It On the Mountian, 96. **CONTACT ADDRESS** J Carlyle Sitterson Professor of English, Univ of No Carolina, Chapel Hill, CB# 3520 Greenlaw, Chapel Hill, NC 27599-3520.

HARRIS, VICTORIA

DISCIPLINE MUSIC **EDUCATION** Eastman Sch Mus, Rochester, BA, 61; Ohio State Univ, Columbus, MA, 63; Univ Iowa, MA, 68, PhD, 80. **CAREER** Dept Music, Mt Union Col **MEMBERSHIPS** Alliance Commun Concerts, bd dir; Amer Guild Organists, Akron; Mem-at-large, Canton; Amer Musicol Soc; Amer Mus Scholar Asn; Col Mus Soc; Hymn Soc Am; MENC-OMEA; Mus Teachers Nat Asn; Nat Guild of Piano Teachers: Nat Conf on Piano Pedagogy; Organ Hist Soc; Riemenschneider Bach Inst & Sigma Alpha Iota. **SELECTED PUBLICATIONS** Ed, First Lady of the Organ: Diane Bish, 95; rev, 85 Univ Kans Church Mus Inshtute, The Diapason, 86; concert rev, The Alliance Rev, 88-. **CONTACT ADDRESS** Dept of Music, Mount Union Col, 1972 Clark Ave, Alliance, OH 44601. **EMAIL** harrisvb@muc.edu

HARRIS, WILLIAM STYRON, JR.

PERSONAL Born 06/09/1936, Elizabeth City, NC, m, 1965, 1 child **DISCIPLINE** LITERATURE **EDUCATION** Wake Forest Univ, BA, 58; Duke Univ, AM, 63, PhD, 71 **CAREER** Inst, 68-69, Univ of VA; from asst prof to prof, E Tenn St Univ, 71-; grad dir, E Tenn St Univ, 79-82; chair, E Tenn St. Univ, 89-99. **HONORS AND AWARDS** Fulbright Asoc, 85-86 **MEMBERSHIPS** MLA, SAMLA, AAUP **RESEARCH** Charles Kingsley **SELECTED PUBLICATIONS** auth, Charles Kingsley: A Reference Guide, G.K. Hall, 81. **CONTACT ADDRESS** Dept of English, East Tennessee State Univ, PO Box 70683, Johnson CIty, TN 37614-0683. **EMAIL** harris@etsu.edu

HARRIS-WARRICK, REBECCA

PERSONAL m, 2 children **DISCIPLINE** MUSIC **EDUCATION** Brandeis Univ, BA, 71; Stanford Univ, DMA, 78. **CAREER** Assoc prof **HONORS AND AWARDS** Nat Endowment for the Humanities res fel, 85-86; Mellon Found grant, 89; NEH Summer fel, 91; Honorable Mention, De la Torre Bueno Prize, Dance Perspectives Found, 95. **MEMBERSHIPS** Coun mem, Amer Musicol Soc, 95-98; bd dir, Soc Dance Hist Scholars, 93-99; Soc for 17th-Century Music. **RESEARCH** French Baroque music and dance; J.-B. Lully; opera in France (17th-19th century); music editing. **SELECTED PUBLICATIONS** Auth, Magnificence in Motion: Stage Musicians in Lully's Ballets and Operas, Cambridge Opera J 6/3, 94; Interpreting Pendulum Markings for French Baroque Dances, Hist Performance 6/1, 93; Critical ed of G. Donizetti's opera, La Favorite, Milan: Casa Ricordi, 97; coauth, Musical Theatre at the Court of Louis XIV: Le Mariage de la Grosse Cathos, Cambridge: Cambridge UP, 94. **CONTACT ADDRESS** Dept of Music, Cornell Univ, 104 Lincoln Hall, Ithaca, NY 14853. **EMAIL** rh14@cornell.edu

HARRISON, ANTONY HOWARD

PERSONAL Born 10/09/1948, London, England, m, 1990, 1 child **DISCIPLINE** ENGLISH LITERATURE, NINETEENTH CENTURY POETRY **EDUCATION** Stanford Univ, AB, 70; MA, 71; Univ Chicago, PhD(English), 74. **CAREER** Asst prof, 74-80, assoc prof, 80-87, prof, English, NCar State Univ, 87- . **HONORS AND AWARDS** Fel, Nat Humanities Ctr, 81-82; NEH Fel, 92-98; NCSU Alum Outstanding Res Prof, 92. **MEMBERSHIPS** SAtlantic Mod Lang Asn; Victorians Inst; MLA. **RESEARCH** Victorian poetry; Victorian prose nonfiction; romantic poetry; literary theory; gender studies. **SELECTED PUBLICATIONS** Auth, Swinburne's Medievalism: A Study in Victorian Love Poetry, La State Univ Pr, 88; auth, Christina Rossetti in Context, Univ NCar Pr, 88; auth, Victorian Poets and Romantic Poems: Intertextuality and Ideology, Univ Pr Va, 90; co-ed, Gender and Discourse in Victorian Literature and Art, No Ill Univ Pr, 92; guest ed, Christina Rossetti: 1830-1894, in Victorian Poetry vol 32, nos. 3-4 (Winter 94); ed, The Letters of Christina Rossetti, Univ Pr of Va, vol 1, 97, vol 2, 98, vol 3, 00, vol 4, 02; auth, Victorian Poets and the Politics of Culture: Discourse and Ideology,Univ pr of Va, 98; co-ed, The Culture of Christina Rossetti, Ohio Univ Pr, 99; co-ed, The Blackwell Companion to Victorian Poetry, Blackwell, forthcoming, 02; ed, Christina Rossetti: Selected Writings, Brodview Pr, forthcoming 03. **CONTACT ADDRESS** Dept of English, No Carolina State Univ, Raleigh, NC 27650. **EMAIL** engahh@unity.ncsu.edu

HARRISON, CAROL LYNN

PERSONAL Born 11/15/1946, Buffalo, NY **DISCIPLINE** ENGLISH LITERATURE **EDUCATION** State Univ NYork, Buffalo, BA(psychol) & BA(English), 68, PhD, 70. **CAREER** From instr to asst prof English, 70-74, chmn dept commun, 72-74, assoc prof & actg dir, media-commun, 74-76, prog dir lib studies, 76-78, assoc prof, 76-82, actg dean prof studies, 79-80 prof humanities, Medaille Col, 82-, Danforth Found assoc, 78. **MEMBERSHIPS** MLA; NCTE. **RESEARCH** Freshman composition development; 17th century British literature; advanced writing skills development. **SELECTED PUBLICATIONS** Auth, Eagle's Grass, in Heirloom Collection, 73 & Waiting, in Golden Book Verse, 74, Golden Eagle Press. **CONTACT ADDRESS** Medaille Col, 18 Agassiz Circle, Buffalo, NY 14214-2695. **EMAIL** drcarole@buffnet.net

HARRISON, DAPHNE DUVAL

PERSONAL Born 03/14/1932, Orlando, FL, m **DISCIPLINE** MUSICOLOGY **EDUCATION** Talladega Coll, BMus 1953; Northwestern Univ, MMus 1961; Univ of Miami FL, EdD 1971. **CAREER** Marion & Broward Co FL, music tchr 53-66; Broward Co FL, TV instr 66-68; FL Atlantic Univ, asst prof educ 69-70; Hallandale Middle Sch FL, dean of girls 70-71; Benedict Coll, asso prof fine arts 71-72; Univ of MD Baltimore County, assoc prof, chairperson, prof, Africana studies dept 81-96, Center for the Study of Humanities, dir, 96-. **HONORS AND AWARDS** NEH Fellowship for University Professors, 1992-; NEH African Humanities Fellow UCLA 1979; Moton Ctr for Independent Studies Fellow Philadelphia 1976-77; So Fellowships Univ of Miami 1969-70; Theodore Presser Awd Talladega Coll 1951; Fulbright Fellow 1986; Outstanding Faculty of the Year, Black Student Union, UMBC 1988-89. **MEMBERSHIPS** Proj dir, summer inst African & African Amer History culture & literature, 1984-85; proj dir Racism Intervention Develop Proj UMBC 1975-77; social planner New Town Harbison SC 1971-72; consult FL Sch Desegregation Consult Ctr 1965-70; ch music dir St Andrews Ch Hollywood FL 1960-70; bd mem CTD FL Educators Assn 1965-67; bd mem FL State Tchrs Assn 1963-65; mem Natl Assn of Negro Business & Professional Women, Alpha Kappa Alpha, Assn for the Study of Afro-Amer Life & Hist; Co-chair Black Family Committee of African American Empowerment Project; Commissioner of the Maryland Commission on African-American History & Culture; Sonneck Society; Intl Assn for Study of Popular Music. **SELECTED PUBLICATIONS** Black Pearls: Blues Queens of the 1920's, Rutgers Univ Press 1988; The Classic Blues and Women Singers, Blackwell Press Guide to the Blues 1989. **CONTACT ADDRESS** Ctr Study of Humanities, Univ of Maryland, Baltimore County, 5401 Wilkens Ave, Baltimore, MD 21228.

HARRISON, GARY

DISCIPLINE BRITISH ROMANTICISM, WORLD LITERATURE, AND LITERARY THEORY **EDUCATION** Stanford Univ, PhD, 87. **CAREER** Instr, Univ NMex, 87-. **RESEARCH** The culture of the early 1790s; Wordsworth and Godwin. **SELECTED PUBLICATIONS** Auth, "Wordsworth's The Old Cumberland Beggar: The Economy of Charity in Late 18th-Century Britain," Criticism 30, (Winter 88): 23-42; auth, "Wordsworth's Leech Gatherer: Liminal Power and the Spirit of Independence," ELH 56 (Summer 89): 327-350; auth, "Leslie A. Marchand," Twentieth Century Literary Biographers, ed. Steven Serafin, Dictionary of Literary Biography, Detroit and London: Bruccoli, Clark, Layman, 91: 175-83; auth, "Spec(tac)ular Reversals: The Politics of the Sublime and Wordsworth's Transfiguration of the Rustic Poor," Criticism 34 (Fall 92): 563-590; auth, "William Godwin," Eighteenth-Century British Literary Biographers, ed. Steven Serafin, Dictionary of Literary Biography, Detroit: Bruccoli, Clark, Layman, 94: 78-94; auth, Wordsworth's Vagrant Muse, 94; coed, Western Literature in a World Context, 95; auth, "Ambitions Projects: Peasant and Poet in John Clare's The Wish and Helpstone," The John Clare Society Journal 17 (July 98): 41-58. **CONTACT ADDRESS** Dept of English, Univ of New Mexico, Albuquerque, Albuquerque, NM 87131. **EMAIL** garyh@unm.edu

HARRISON, KEITH

PERSONAL Born 06/18/1945, Vancouver, BC, Canada, m, 1965, 2 children **DISCIPLINE** ENGLISH, CREATIVE WRITING **EDUCATION** Univ Brit Colum, BA, 67; Univ Calif Berkeley, MA, 68; McGill Univ, PhD, 72. **CAREER** Instr, Dawson Col, 71-91; instr, Malaspina Univ Col, 91-. **HONORS AND AWARDS** Okanogan Short Story Awd; McConnel Grad Fel; Ethel Wilson Prize; BC2000 Book Awd; Hugh MacLennan Fiction Prize; QSpell Awd. **MEMBERSHIPS** MLA; Writer's Union Can; ACCUTE. **RESEARCH** Canadian literature; narrative theory; documentary film; romantic poetry; Shakespeare. **SELECTED PUBLICATIONS** Auth, "Montage in The Collected Works of Billy the Kid," JCP 3 (80): 32-38; auth, "Lowery's Allusions to Melville in Lunar Caustic," Can Lit 94 (82): 180-84; auth, "One Hundred Years of Solitude: The Only Mystery," Lit Psych 32 (86): 47-52; auth, "Patrick Lane: Barthesian Wrestler," Can Lit 141 (94): 75-83; auth, "Samuel Hearn, Matonabee, and the 'Esquimaux Girl': Cultural Subjects, Cultural Objects," Can Rev Comp Lit 22 (95): 647-657; auth, " McEwan's Black Dogs: (Anti) Gothic Narratives," Ann du Monde Anglo 4 (96): 125-132; auth, "Bakhtin's Novelization of Byron's Don Juan, or The Bildungsroman with a Loophole," Alpha 1 (96): 104-121; auth, "Imaging the Imagination: Films on Canadian Writers," J Can Studies 32 (97): 170-174; auth, Furry Creek, Oolichan Bks, 99; auth, "Telling the Untellable: Spiegelman's Maus," Rendezvous 34 (00): 59-73. **CONTACT ADDRESS** English Dept, Malaspina Univ Col, 900 5th St, Nanaimo, BC, Canada V9R 5S5. **EMAIL** kharriso@mars.ark.com

HARRISON, LELAND BRUCE

PERSONAL Born 06/16/1946, Scherectudy, NY, m **DISCIPLINE** LITERATURE AND COMPOSITION **EDUCATION** Hartwick Col , BA, 68; Rutgers Univ, PhD, 76. **CAREER** Tchg asst, Rutgers Col, 69-72; Asst prof, 72-86; Assoc prof, 86-91; prof, Western Ill Univ, 91-. **HONORS AND AWARDS** W Ill Univ Fac Excellence Awd, 91; actg chair, eng & journalism, 92; dir writing, 83-97. **MEMBERSHIPS** NCTE, CCCC, WPA. **RESEARCH** Computers and writing web rhetoric, Cyberpank literature. **SELECTED PUBLICATIONS** Auth, Discovery: Writing to Learn; Kendall-Hunt, 93; Connections: Reading and Writing, Kendall-Hunt, 92; Discovery: Writing to Learn. Kendall-Hunt, 90; Partners in the Process: Professionalism for Writing Instructors, ERIC, 91. **CONTACT ADDRESS** Western Illinois Univ, 1 University Circle, Macomb, IL 61455. **EMAIL** mfbhl@wiu.edu

HARRISON, RANDALL PAUL

PERSONAL Born 02/03/1929, Eau Claire, WI, w, 1983 **DISCIPLINE** COMMUNICATION **EDUCATION** Univ Wisc, BS, 50; Mich State Univ, PhD, 64. **CAREER** Prof, Mich State Univ, 64-73; adjunct prof Communications, 73-78, Clin Fac, Univ Cal San Fran, 78-, Fac Ctr Media & Independent Learning, Univ Cal Berkeley, 78-99; fel, Int Commun Asn; fel Am Asn Advan Sci; Helen Williams Award Excellence Col Independent Study, 95. **MEMBERSHIPS** Int Commum Asn **RESEARCH** Art; Non-verbal communication **SELECTED PUBLICATIONS** Beyond Words, Prentice Hall, 74; The Cartoon: Communication to the Quick, Saga, 80. **CONTACT ADDRESS** PO Box 22541, San Francisco, CA 94122. **EMAIL** harrisonrandyha@aol.com

HARRISON, W. DALE

DISCIPLINE JOURNALISM **EDUCATION** Fullerton Col, 85; Tenn State Univ, BS 90; Univ Tenn, MA, 91; Univ Ga, PhD, . **CAREER** Inst, Univ Ga, 94-96; Adjunc inst, Truell-McConell Coll, 96; John B. Ashcroft instruc, Wingate Univ; Asst. Prof- **HONORS AND AWARDS** Georgia Press Asn; Alpha Chi Honor Prof; Fac Mem Month; Wingate Univ Student Govt Asn; supvr, prof writing & editing internships; adv, jambar writers club; adv, frontiers newsl; adv, lifelines newsl; chair, acad senate charter & bylaws comt. **MEMBERSHIPS** Asn Educ Jour & Mass Comm; Col Media Advs; Tri-County Journalism Asn, Past: Ga Press Asn, Soc Collegiate Journalists, Tenn Press Asn. **SELECTED PUBLICATIONS** Articles, Rev Appeal; Knoxville Jour, Daily News Jour, Columbia Times. **CONTACT ADDRESS** Youngstown State Univ, One University Plaza, Youngstown, OH 44555. **EMAIL** wdharris@cc.ysu.edu

HARSH, CONSTANCE D.
DISCIPLINE 19TH CENTURY ENGLISH LITERATURE, WOMEN AND LITERATURE **EDUCATION** Univ PA, BA, MA, 82, PhD, 87. **CAREER** Instr, Bryn Mawr Col; assoc prof, Colgate Univ, 88-. **MEMBERSHIPS** MLA; RSVP. **RESEARCH** Victorian fiction, John Cowper Powys. **SELECTED PUBLICATIONS** Auth, Subversive Heroines: Feminist Resolutions of Social Crisis in the Condition-of-England Novel, Univ Mich Press, 94; Gissing's In the Year of Jubilee and the Epistemology of Resistance, SEL, 94; Thyrza: Romantic Love and Ideological Co-Conspiracy, Gissing Jour, 94); Gissing's The Unclassed and the Perils of Naturalism, ELH, 92; auth, "Reviewing New Women Fiction in the Daily Press," VPR 00; auth, "Eliza Lynn Linton as a New Women Novelist," Rebel of the Family, Broadview Press 01. **CONTACT ADDRESS** Dept of Eng, Colgate Univ, 13 Oak Drive, Hamilton, NY 13346. **EMAIL** charsh@mail.colgate.edu

HART, EDWARD LEROY
PERSONAL Born 12/28/1916, Bloomington, ID, m, 1944, 4 children **DISCIPLINE** ENGLISH LITERATURE **EDUCATION** Univ Utah, BS, 39; Oxford Univ, DPhil, 50; Univ Mich, AM, 41. **CAREER** Asst prof English, Univ Wash, 49-52; from asst prof to assoc prof, 52-59, prof to prof emer, Brigham Young Univ, 59-; vis prof, Univ Calif, Berkeley, 59-60; Fulbright-Hays lectr, 73-74; mem, Utah State Fine Arts Bd & chmn Lit Arts Comt, 77-. **HONORS AND AWARDS** Am Coun Learned Soc fel, 42; Charles Redd Awd in Humanities, Utah Acad, 76; Distinguished Fac Awd, Brigham Young Univ Col Humanities, 77. **MEMBERSHIPS** MLA; Rocky Mountain Mod Lang Asn; Am Soc 28th Century Studies. **RESEARCH** Some new sources of Johnson's Lives; contributions of John Nichols to Boswell's Life of Johnson; 18th century biographical works of John Nichols. **CONTACT ADDRESS** Dept of English, Brigham Young Univ, Provo, UT 84602. **EMAIL** elh4@email.byu.edu

HART, HENRY W.
PERSONAL Born 07/06/1954, Torrington, CT, m, 1991, 2 children **DISCIPLINE** ENGLISH **EDUCATION** Dartmouth Col, BA, 76; Oxford Univ, PhD, 83. **CAREER** Asst prof, The Citadel, 84-86; prof, Col of William and Mary, 86- **HONORS AND AWARDS** NEH Fel; Phi Beta Kappa Advan of Scholarship Awd. **RESEARCH** Modern Poetry and Fiction. **SELECTED PUBLICATIONS** Auth, The Poetry of Geoffrey Hill, S IL Univ Pr, (Carbondale, IL), 86; auth, Seamus Heaney: Poet of Contrary Progressions, Syracuse Univ Pr (Syracuse, NY), 91; auth, The Ghost Ship, Blue Moon Books, (NY), 90; auth, Robert Lowell and the Sublime, Syracuse Univ Pr, 95; auth, The Rooster Mask, Univ of IL Pr, 98; auth, The James Dickey Reader, Simon & Schuster, Touchstone, 99; auth, James Dickey: The Work as A Lie, St. Martin's Press, Picador, 00. **CONTACT ADDRESS** Dept English, Col of William and Mary, PO Box 8795, Williamsburg, VA 23187-8795. **EMAIL** hwhart@wm.edu

HART, JOHN AUGUSTINE
PERSONAL Born 12/06/1917, New Haven, CT, 1 child **DISCIPLINE** ENGLISH LITERATURE **EDUCATION** Yale Univ, AB, 40, AM, 42, PhD, 43. **CAREER** Instr English, Rensselaer Polytech Inst, 43-44; historian, Off Price Admin, Washington, DC, 44-46; from instr to asst prof English, 46-54, ASSOC PROF ENGLISH, CARNEGIE-MELLON UNIV, 54- **HONORS AND AWARDS** Golden Quill Awd **MEMBERSHIPS** MLA. **RESEARCH** Shakespeare; 18th century English literature; advanced placement program. **SELECTED PUBLICATIONS** Auth, Father-Daughter as Device in Shakespear's Romantic Comedies, Carnegie Series in English, 72; auth, Dramatic Structure in Shekespeare's Romantic Comedies, Carnegie Mellon Univ, 80; auth, As you like it, Shakespeare for Students, Gale Resm 92 **CONTACT ADDRESS** Dept of English, Carnegie Mellon Univ, 5000 Forbes Ave, Pittsburgh, PA 15213-3890. **EMAIL** jh46@andrew.cmu.edu

HART, JOY L.
PERSONAL Born 12/09/1959, Mt. Sterling, KY, s **DISCIPLINE** COMMUNICATION **EDUCATION** Univ Ky, PhD, 88. **CAREER** Asst prof, Univ Tulsa, 88-90; asst to Assoc Prof, Univ Louisville, 90-. **HONORS AND AWARDS** Gerald M. Phillips Mentoring Awd, Am Comm Assoc, 98; Article of the Yr Awd, Am Comm Asn, 98. **MEMBERSHIPS** South States Comm Asn, Nat Comm Asn, Am Comm Asn. **RESEARCH** Organizational and interpersonal communication. **SELECTED PUBLICATIONS** Co-auth, "When argument Fails: How Organizations deal with Incommensurabilities," in Proc of the Third Intl Conf on Argumentation, 95; co-auth, "The creation of, change in, and tension across narratives during organizational transformation: A longitudinal investigation," in Proc of the Third Ann Kentucky Conf on Narrative, 95; co-auth, "Detecting cultural knowledge in organization members' personal construct systems," in Jour of Constructivist Psych, 10, 97; co-auth, "Closings: Patient/provider communication about the end of life," in Patient Educ and Counseling, 98;co-auth, "Speaking for God: The functions of church leader storytelling in Southern Appalachia in the 1950s," in Am Comm Jour, 1, 98. **CONTACT ADDRESS** Dept of Communication, Univ of Louisville, Louisville, KY 40292. **EMAIL** joy.hart@louisville.edu

HART, RODERICK P.
PERSONAL Born 02/17/1945, Fall River, MA, m, 1966, 2 children **DISCIPLINE** COMMUNICATION **EDUCATION** Univ MA, BA 66; PA State Univ, MA 68, PhD 70. **CAREER** 83, Shivers Chair Comm Gvt, 79-, prof speech, Univ TX; 74-79, assoc prof, 70-74, asst prof, Purdue Univ. **HONORS AND AWARDS** Phi Kappa Phi Nat Schol of the Yr Awd; Diamond Ann Book Awd; Res Fell ICA; distg Schol Awd NCA; Winans-Wichelns Book Awd NCA; Adv Coun Res Awd; Chas H Woolbert Awd; Golden Ann Mono Awd; Phi Kappa Phi Nat Sch Hon; Woodrow Wilson Fell; NDEA Fell. **MEMBERSHIPS** NCA; ICA; APSA; Cen Stud Pres; RSA. **RESEARCH** Polit Commun; Rhetorical Studies. **SELECTED PUBLICATIONS** Software: Diction 5.0: The Text Analysis Program, Thousand Oaks, CA Sage, 97; Civic Hope: A Report on Citizenship, in preparation; Campaign Talk: Why Elections Are Good For Us, Princeton Press, 00; Seducing America: How Television Charms the Modern Voter, NY Oxford Univ Press, 94,98; The Search for Intimacy in American Politics, in: M Salvador P Sias, eds, The Pub Voice in a Democrat at Risk, NY Praeger, 98; Community by Negation: An Agenda for Rhetorical Inquiry, in: M Hogan, ed, Rhetoric and Comm, Columbia, Univ SC Press, 98. **CONTACT ADDRESS** Dept of Comm. Studies, Univ of Texas, Austin, Austin, TX 78712. **EMAIL** rodhart@mail.utexas.edu

HART, THOMAS JOEL
PERSONAL Born 06/01/1942, Grand Island, NE, s **DISCIPLINE** ENGLISH **EDUCATION** San Francisco State Univ, BA, 66; MA, 88. **CAREER** Instr, Merritt Coll; asst prof, Patten Col. **MEMBERSHIPS** NCTE, MLA. **RESEARCH** Humanities and language acquisition, reading and writing issues. **CONTACT ADDRESS** 2433 Coolidge Ave, Oakland, CA 94601-2630. **EMAIL** hartsong5@earthlink.net

HARTIGAN, KARELISA V.
PERSONAL Born 03/05/1943, Stillwater, OK, m, 1992, 5 children **DISCIPLINE** CLASSICS **EDUCATION** Col of Wooster, BA, 65; Univ Chicago, AM, 66, PhD, 70. **CAREER** Asst prof, St Olaf Col, 69-73; asst prof, 73-76, assoc prof, 76-90, Prof, Univ FL, 90-. **HONORS AND AWARDS** Various undergraduate awards, including Phi Beta Kappa; Woodrow Wilson fel, 65; Ford Found MA fel, 66; Univ Chicago fel, 66-68; Woodrow Wilson Dissertation fel, 68-69; numerous teaching awards, Univ FL; Amer Philos Assoc Nat Teaching Awd; Distinguished Alumni Prof, Univ FL; Classical Assoc of Middle West and South Ovatio Awd. **MEMBERSHIPS** Classical Assoc of Middle West and South, pres 92-93; Amer Philol Assoc; Modern Greek Studies Assoc. **RESEARCH** Greek drama; mythology; ancient cities; comparative lit. **SELECTED PUBLICATIONS** Auth, The Poets and the Cities, Anton Hain, 79; Ambiguity and Self Deception, Apollo & Artemis Plays of Euripides, Peter Lang, 91; Greek Drama on the American Stage, Greenwood, 95; Myths Behind Our Words, Forbes, 98; over 2 dozen articles on Greek drama, comparative lit, and myth in film; also slide sets with commentary: 4, with Pictures of Record. **CONTACT ADDRESS** Dept of Classics Dauer 3-C, Univ of Florida, Box 117435, Gainesville, FL 32611. **EMAIL** kvhrtgn@classics.ufl.edu

HARTLE, ANTHONY E.
PERSONAL Born 12/28/1942, Wichita, KS, m, 1964, 3 children **DISCIPLINE** PHILOSOPHY, LITERATURE **EDUCATION** US Mil Acad, BS, 64; Duke Univ, MA, 71; Univ of Texas, PhD, 82. **CAREER** Prof, Dep Head, English, USMA. **MEMBERSHIPS** Am Philos Asn, Joint Serv Conf on Prof Ethics. **RESEARCH** Moral philosophy; applied ethics **SELECTED PUBLICATIONS** Auth, Moral Issues in Military Decision Making; Dimensions of Ethical Thought. **CONTACT ADDRESS** Dept of English, United States Military Acad, West Point, NY 10996-1791. **EMAIL** ca5868@usma.edu

HARTMAN, C.
PERSONAL Born 11/26/1946, Phoenixville, PA, m, 1978, 1 child **DISCIPLINE** CHINESE LITERATURE **EDUCATION** Indian Univ, BA, 67; Indiana Univ, MA, 70; Indiana Univ, PhD, 75 **CAREER** Asst prof, Ntl Taiwan Univ, 77-79; asst prof, Univ Wis, 79-80; asst prof, St Univ NY Albany, 80-85; assoc prof, St Univ NY Albany, 85-93; prof, St Univ NY Albany, 93- **HONORS AND AWARDS** Assoc Asian Studies, Joseph Levenson Prize; National Endowment for the Humanities, Fellowship for College Teachers, 88-89; first place, best book in the humanities, State Univ of New York at Albany, 86 **MEMBERSHIPS** Assoc Asian Studies **RESEARCH** Literary Inquisitions during the Sung dynasty; Iconology and Meaning in the Chinese Literary Visual Arts; Traditional Chinese Literature, especially poetry. **SELECTED PUBLICATIONS** Auth, "LiuTsung-yuan", Twayne, (73); Han Yu and the T'ang Search for Unity, Princeton Univ Pr, 86; The Indiana Companion to Traditional Chinese Literature, Ind Univ Pr, 86; auth, ThePurloined Plum and the Heart of Iron: A Contribution to the History of Flowering Plum Imagery in the Sung and Yuan Dynasties," Journal of Sung-Yuan Studies, (95); auth, "Stomping Songs: Word and Image," Chinese Literature: Essays, Articles, Reviews, (95); "The Making of a Villian: Ch'in Kuei and Tao-hsueh," Harvard Jrnl Asiatic Studies, 98 **CONTACT ADDRESS** Dept E Asian Studies, SUNY, Albany, Humanities 210, Albany, NY 12222. **EMAIL** Hartman@albany.edu

HARTMAN, CHARLES O.
PERSONAL Born 08/01/1949, Iowa City, IA **DISCIPLINE** ENGLISH LITERATURE **EDUCATION** Harvard Univ, AB, 71, MA, 72; WA Univ, PhD, 76. **CAREER** Teaching asst, Washington Univ, 72-75; lectr, Northwestern Univ, 76-79; assoc prof, Conn Col, 90-91; visiting assoc porf, Conn Col, 84-90; prof, Conn Col, 91-. **HONORS AND AWARDS** Lloyd McKim Garrison Prize in Poetry, 70, 71; Dissertation Fel, Graduate Fel, 71-74; The Bess Hokin Prize, 76; NEH Fel, Univ of Calif at Irvine, 77; Teaching Awd, Northwestern Univ, 78; Illinois Arts Council Literary Awd, 78; NEA Fel in Poetry, 84; Andrews Prize in Narrative Poetry, Poet Lore, 86; Ingram Merrill Found Awd, 88; Fel, MacDowell Colony, 92; Fel, Hawthornden Castle International Retreat for Writers, 92; Grant from Conn Council on the Arts, 94. **RESEARCH** Poetry wirting, modern and contemporary poetry, prosody (metrics), music and poetry, computer arts. **SELECTED PUBLICATIONS** Auth, The Pigfoot Rebellion (poems), David R. Godine, 82; auth, Gravitaiton, Sea Pen Press, 82; auth, True North, Copper Beech, 90; auth, Jazz Text: Voice and Improvisation ni Poetry, Jazz, an dSong, Princeton Univ Press, 91; auth, Glass Enclosure, with Bryn Manly, 92; auth, English Metrics: Hypertext Tutorial and Reference, for Macintosh or DOS, 92; auth, Sentences, with Hugh Kenner, Sun & Moon Press, 95; auth, Glass Enclosure, Wesleyan Univ Press, 95; auth, Virtual Muse: Experiments in Computer Poetry, Wesleyan Univ Press, 96; auth, Free Verse: An Essay on Prosody, Princeton Univ Press, 81, Second edition, Nowthwestern Univ Press, 96. **CONTACT ADDRESS** English Dept, Connecticut Col, 15 Rogers Dr, Mystic, CT 06355. **EMAIL** cohar@conncoll.edu

HARTMAN, JAMES WALTER
PERSONAL Born 01/28/1939, Newark, OH **DISCIPLINE** ENGLISH LANGUAGE, LINGUISTICS **EDUCATION** OH Univ, BA, 61; Univ MI, MA, 62, PhD, 66. **CAREER** Instr Eng, Eastern IL Univ, 63-64; asst prof Eng & ling, OH Univ, 66-67; asst prof Eng lang, Univ WI-Madison, 67-70; Assoc Prof, 70-85, Prof Eng & Ling, Univ KS, 85-, Asst dir, Dict Am Regional Eng, 67-70; Assoc Ed, 70-; Assoc Ed, Am Speech, 72-97; Ed Publ, Am Dialect Soc, 76-85. **MEMBERSHIPS** Am Dialect Soc; NCTE. **RESEARCH** Dialectology; sociolinguistics; lexicography; Am Eng pronunciation. **SELECTED PUBLICATIONS** Auth, Phonological Variation in the United States, In: Dictionary of American Regional English, Vol I, 85; Some Possible Changes in the Pronunciation of Young Americans (maybe), Am Speech 59.3, 84; ed, Cambridge International Dictionary of English, Cambridge Univ Press, 96; co-ed, English Pronouns Dictionary, 15th, Cambridge Univ Press, 97; auth, Dictionary Pronunciations: Mine or Yours or Theirs, Am Speech Vol 75, No. 3, (00): 250-253. **CONTACT ADDRESS** Dept of Eng Wescoe Hall, Univ of Kansas, Lawrence, Lawrence, KS 66045-0001. **EMAIL** jwhartma@eagle.cc.ukans.edu

HARTOUNI, VALERIE
DISCIPLINE COMMUNICATIONS **EDUCATION** Univ Calif, Santa Cruz, PhD, 87. **CAREER** Asst Prof, Commun, Univ Calif, San Diego; assoc prof. **RESEARCH** Intersection of cultural and feminist studies. **SELECTED PUBLICATIONS** Auth, Cultural Conceptions: On Reproductive Technologies an dthe Remaking of Life, Univ of Minn Press, 97; auth, "Reflections on Abortion Politics and the Practices Called 'Person'", in Fetal Subjects, Feminist Positions, ed. Lynn M. Morgan and Meredith W. Michaels Univ of Penn Press, 99; auth, "A Study in Reproductive Technologies," in Revisioning Women, Health, and Healing, ed. Adele E. Clarke and Virginia L. Olesen Routledge, 99. **CONTACT ADDRESS** Dept of Commun, Univ of California, San Diego, 9500 Gilman Dr, La Jolla, CA 92093. **EMAIL** vhartoun@weber.ucsd.edu

HARTY, KEVIN JOHN
PERSONAL Born 07/20/1948, Brooklyn, NY, w **DISCIPLINE** ENGLISH LANGUAGE & LITERATURE **EDUCATION** Marquette Univ, AB, 70; Univ Pa, AM, 71, PhD(English), 74. **CAREER** Asst prof English, Centenary Col LA, 74-76; asst prof Eng, Temple Univ, 78-82; asst prof Eng & Commun, assoc prof, prof, Eng, co-ord of adjunct fac, co-ord of interns, La Salle Univ, 82-, consult in management comm, , Gino's, Fed Reserve Bank, First PA Bank, RCA Corp, Blue Cross/Blue Shield of PA, Fidelity Bank, First PA Bank, Brd of Pensions Presbyterian Church of Am, City of Philadelphia Dept of Health, Philadelphia Health Mgmt Corp, Philadelphia Inquirer and Daily News, 73-; CEA Critic, 74-76; mem of the adv committee to the Dictionary of the Middle Ages, 82-89; manuscript referee: Four Quarters 83-85; assoc ed, Arthuriana, the Journal of the North Am Br of the Int Arthurian Soc, 96-; Dramaturd, Films for the Humanities and Sciences, 98-. **HONORS AND AWARDS** Folger Shakespeare Library Fellow, 76; Am Philos Soc Grants-in-Aid, 76, 78; Lindback Awd for Outstanding Tchng, La Salle Univ, 92. **MEMBERSHIPS** Medieval Acad Am; MLA; Col English Asn; National Council of Tchrs of Eng, Int Courtly Lit Soc, Int Arthurain Soc. **RESEARCH** Mediaeval literature, modern literature, writing skills. **SELECTED PUBLICATIONS** Ed, Strategies for Business and Technical Writing, NY, Harcourt Brace Jovanovich, 80; co-auth, Writing for Business and Industry: Process and Product, NY: Mackmillan, 87; ed, Cinema Arthuriana: Essays on Arthurian Film, NY: Garland Publishing, 91; ed, The Chester Mystery Cycle, A Casebook, NY: Garland Publishing, 93; ed, King

Arthur on Film: New Essays on Arthurian Cinema, Jefferson, NC: McFarland & Co, 99; auth, The Reel Middle Ages: American, Western and Eastern, Middle Eastern and Asian Films About Medieval Europe, Jefferson, NC: McFarland & Co, 99. **CONTACT ADDRESS** Dept of English, La Salle Univ, 1900 W Olney Ave, Philadelphia, PA 19141-1199. **EMAIL** harty@lasalle.edu

HARVEY, ELIZABETH D.
DISCIPLINE ENGLISH LITERATURE **EDUCATION** Smith Univ, BA; Johns Hopkins Univ, MA; PhD. **CAREER** Assoc prof, Univ of Western Ontario. **RESEARCH** Gender theory; psychoanalytic theory; history and theory of medicine; Renaissance literature and culture. **SELECTED PUBLICATIONS** Co-ed, Soliciting Interpretation: Literary Theory & 17th-Century English Poetry, Chicago, 90; auth, Ventriloquized Voices: Feminist Theory and English Renaissance Texts, Routledge, 92; Women & Reason, Michigan, 92. **CONTACT ADDRESS** English Dept, Univ of Western Ontario, University College, London, ON, Canada NGA3K7. **EMAIL** eharvey@julian.uwo.ca

HARVEY, TAMARA
PERSONAL Born 03/14/1966, Pullman, WA, m, 2000 **DISCIPLINE** ENGLISH **EDUCATION** Harvard & Radcliffe Cols, AB, 88; Univ Wis at Madison, MA, 89; Univ Calif at Irvine, PhD, 98. **CAREER** Asst prof, Univ Southern Miss. **HONORS AND AWARDS** Humanities Associates Grad Student Teaching Awd; Univ Fel, Univ Wis at Madison, 88-91; Chancellor's Fel, Univ Calif at Irvine, 92-96. **MEMBERSHIPS** Soc of Early Americanists, MLA, Omohundra Inst of Early Am Hist & Culture. **RESEARCH** Early American Women, Feminist Theory, Critical Theory. **SELECTED PUBLICATIONS** auth, "'But what about the audience?/What about them?': Spectatorship and Cinematic Pleasure in Hal Hartley's Simple Men," Paroles Gelees 14.2 (96): 153-162; auth, "'Taken from her Mouth': Narrative Authority and the Conversion of Patience Boston," Narrative 6.3 (98): 256-270; auth, "'Now Sisters. . . impart your usefulness, and force': Anne Bradstreet's Feminist Functionalism in The Tenth Muse (1650)," Early Am Lit 35.1 (00): 5-28; auth, "This is not a test!: Assessing Students Assessing the University," ADE Bullet, (forthcoming); co-ed, George Washington and Conceptions of the late Eighteenth-Century American South, forthcoming. **CONTACT ADDRESS** Dept English, Univ of So Mississippi, 2805 Hardy St, Box 5037, Hattiesburg, MS 39406-5037. **EMAIL** tamara.harvey@usm.edu

HARWOOD, BRITTON JAMES
PERSONAL Born 07/12/1936, East Rutherford, NJ, m, 1985, 5 children **DISCIPLINE** MEDIEVAL LANGUAGE & LITERATURE **EDUCATION** Hamilton Col, BA, 59; Canisius Col, MS, 61; State Univ NYork, Buffalo, PhD, 70. **CAREER** Instr English & French, Lyndonville, Cent High Sch, NY, 59-61; from instr to asst prof, 64-74, assoc prof, 74-79, prof English, 79-, chemn dept, 82, Miami Univ. **HONORS AND AWARDS** NEH and Ford Found grants. **MEMBERSHIPS** Mediaeval Acad Am; English Inst; Early English Text Soc; Mod Lang Asc; Soc Crit Exchange. **RESEARCH** Fourteenth century English literature; theories of interpretation; theory of genre. **SELECTED PUBLICATIONS** Auth, Piers Plowman and the Problem of Belief, Toronto, 92; art, Chaucer on Speche: House of Fame, The Friar's Tale, and the Summoner's Tale, Chaucer Rev, 92; co-ed and contribur, Class, Gender, and Early English Literature: Intersections, Indiana, 94; auth, The Alliterative Morte Arthure As A Witness to Epic, Orality in the Middle English Period, Garland, 94. **CONTACT ADDRESS** Dept of English, Miami Univ, 500 E High St, Oxford, OH 45056-1602. **EMAIL** harwoobj@muohio.edu

HASHEM, MAHBOUB
PERSONAL Born 12/16/1946, Lebanon, m, 1989, 2 children **DISCIPLINE** COMMUNICATIONS **EDUCATION** Lebanese Univ, MA; Fla State Univ, MA; PhD. **CAREER** Ast Prof, Univ Toledo, 84-92; From Asst Prof to Assoc Prof, Ft Hays State Univ, 92-. **HONORS AND AWARDS** Book of the Year Awd, Nat Commun Asn; Top Prof Awd, Ft Hays State Univ, 95; Commun Club Awd, Ft Hays State Univ, 98. **MEMBERSHIPS** NCA, CSCA, PRSCA. **RESEARCH** Leadership and organizations, diversity and intercultural communication, political communication. **SELECTED PUBLICATIONS** Coverage of Arabs in Time and Newsweek; co-ed, The U S Media and the Middle East: Image and Perception, Greenwood Pr (Westport, CT), 95; auth, "The Power of Wastah in Lebanese Speech," in Our Voices: Essays in Culture, Ethnicity and Communication, (Los Angeles, CA: Roxbury Publ Co, 97), 99-104; auth, "The Role of Faculty in Teaching Leadership Studies," J of Leadership Studies, 4 (97): 89-100; auth, Fundamentals of Oral Communication: Theories and Practice, McGraw Hill (New York, NY), 97; auth, Human Diversity and Cross-Cultural Communication: A Global Approach, 2nd Ed, CEI Publ Co (Oklahoma City, OK), 00. **CONTACT ADDRESS** Dept Commun, Fort Hays State Univ, 600 Park St, Hays, KS 67601-4009. **EMAIL** mhashem@fhsu.edu

HASHIMOTO, I. Y.
DISCIPLINE LANGUAGE AND WRITING **EDUCATION** Stanford Univ, BA, 67; Univ Wis, MA, 69; Univ Mich, PhD, 78. **CAREER** Instr, Univ Mich; Idaho State Univ; prof, 83-. **HONORS AND AWARDS** Dir, Whitman Col Wrtg Ctr; exec comm, Conf Col Compos and Commun. **RESEARCH** Academic writing, modern non-fiction prose. **SELECTED PUBLICATIONS** Auth, Thirteen Weeks: A Guide to Tchg Col Writing. **CONTACT ADDRESS** Dept of Eng, Whitman Col, 345 Boyer Ave, Walla Walla, WA 99362-2038. **EMAIL** hashimiy@whitman.edu

HASKIN, DAYTON
PERSONAL Born 09/14/1946, Ann Arbor, MI, m, 1990, 3 children **DISCIPLINE** ENGLISH **EDUCATION** Univ of Detroit, BA, 68; Northwestern Univ, MA, 70; Univ of London, BD, 75; Yale Univ, PhD, 78. **CAREER** Instructor, John Carroll Univ, 70-72; from asst prof to prof English, Boston College, 78-. **HONORS AND AWARDS** John Donne Soc Awd for Dist Publ, 78-84; Hanford Awd, Milton Soc of Am, 95; John Simon Guggenheim Fel, 96-97. **MEMBERSHIPS** MLA; Milton Soc of Am; John Donne Soc. **RESEARCH** Seventeenth-Century English literature, Nineteenth-Century cultural history. **SELECTED PUBLICATIONS** Auth, "The Burden of Interpretation in The Pilgrim's Progress," Studies in Philol 79 (82): 256-78; auth, "New Historical Contexts for Appraising the Donne Revival from A.B. Grosart to Charles Eliot Norton," J of English Lit Hist 56 (89): 869-95; auth, "A History of Donne's Canonization' from Izaak Walton to Cleanth Brooks," J of English and Ger Philol 92 (93): 17-36; auth, "Tracing a Genealogy of 'Talent': The Descent of Matthew 25:14-30 into Contemporary Philanthropical Discourse," in Wealth in Western Thought: The Case For and Against Riches, ed. Paul G. Schervish, (CT: Praeger, 94), 65-102; auth, Milton's Burden of Interpretation, Univ of Pa Press, (Philadelphia, PA), 94; auth, "On Trying to Make the Record Speak More about Donne's Love Poems," in Donne's Desire of More: The Subject of Anne Donne in His Poetry, ed. M. Thomas Hester (DE: Univ of Del Press, 96), 39-65; auth, "When Performance Is at Odds with Narrative: The Designated Mourner as Wallace Shawn's Wager on John Donne," Narrative 8 (00): 182-209. **CONTACT ADDRESS** Dept English, Boston Col, Chestnut Hill, 140 Commonwealth Ave, Chestnut Hill, MA 02467-3800.

HASLAM, GERALD WILLIAM
PERSONAL Born 03/18/1937, Bakersfield, CA, m, 1961, 5 children **DISCIPLINE** AMERICAN LITERATURE, LINGUISTICS **EDUCATION** San Francisco State Col, AB, 63, MA, 65; Union Grad Sch, PhD, 80. **CAREER** Teaching asst English, Wash State Univ, 65-66; instr, San Francisco State Col, 66-67; from asst prof to assoc prof, 67-71, prof Eng, Sonoma State Univ, 71-, Gen Semantics Found res grant, 66; invitational scholar, Polish Acad Sci, Warsaw, 66; mem nat acad adv bd, Multi-Cult Inst, 67-; dir, Okie Studies Proj & Arch, Sonoma State Col, 76-; ed, Lit Hist Am West, Nat Endowment for Humanities, 79- **HONORS AND AWARDS** Honoable Mention (finalist) PEN USA West Nonfiction Award. **MEMBERSHIPS** Col Lang Asn; Western Am Lit Asn; Multi-Ethnic Lit of US. **RESEARCH** The West in Am lit; non-white Am writers; Am dialects. **SELECTED PUBLICATIONS** Auth, Hawk Flights: Visions of the West, Seven Buffaloes Press, 83; auth, Snapshots: Glimpses of the Other Californi, Devil Mountain Books, 85; auth, The Man Who Cultivated Fire and Other Stories, Capra Press, 87; auth, That Constant Coyote: California Stories, Univ of Nevada Press, 90; auth, The Great Central Valley: California's Heartland, Univ of Calif Press, 93; auth, The Other California: The Great Central Valley in Life and Letters, Univ of Nevada, 94; auth, Condor Dreams and Other Fictions, Univ of Nevada Press, 94; auth, The Great Tejon Club Jubilee, Devil Mountain Books, 95; auth, Workin' Man Blues: Country Music in California, Univ of Calif Press, 99; auth, Coming of Age in Califonia, Devil Mountain Books, 00. **CONTACT ADDRESS** Dept of English, Sonoma State Univ, Rohnert Park, CA 94928.

HASLER, ANTONY
DISCIPLINE MEDIEVAL LITERATURE **EDUCATION** Cambridge Univ, PhD. **CAREER** Eng Dept, Saint Louis Univ, asst prof. **RESEARCH** Chaucer; Medieval Literature; Late Medieval Early Modern British Literature; Drama. **SELECTED PUBLICATIONS** Auth, "William Dunbar: the Elusive Subject," in Brycht Lanternis: Essays on the Language and Literature of Medieval and Renaissance Scotland, ed. J. Derrick McClure and M.R.G. Spiller (Aberdeen Univ Press, 89), 194-208; auth, "The Three Perils of Woman and John Wilson's Lights and Shadows of Scottish Life," Studies in Hogg and His World 1 (90): 30-45; auth, "Hoccleve's Unregimented Body," Paragraph 13 (90): 164-183; auth, "Reading the Land: James Hogg and the Highlands," Studies in Hogg and His World 4 (93): 57-82; auth, An introduction to James Hogg, The Three Perils of Woman, Edinburgh Univ Press, 95; auth, "Romance and its Discontents in Eger and Grime," in The Spirit of Medieval English Popular Romance, ed. Ad Putter and Jane Gilbert (London, Longman Press, 00), 200-218; auth, "Skelton and Early Tudor Literary Relations," in John Skelton and Early Modern Culture: Essays Honouring Robert Kisman, ed. David R. Carlson, forthcoming. **CONTACT ADDRESS** Saint Louis Univ, 221 N. Grand Blivd., Saint Louis, MO 63103.

HASLETT, BETTY J.
DISCIPLINE SPEECH COMMUNICATION **EDUCATION** Univ Wis, MA, 68; Univ Minn, BA, 67; PhD, 71. **CAREER** Asst prof, 71-76; asoc prof, 76-86; prof, 87-; dept grad comm, 78-; ch, Univ Promotion & Tenure Comm, 92; dir, woman's stud prog, 96-. **HONORS AND AWARDS** Mortar Bd Awd for tchg excellence, 84; UDRF grant, 87; dean's grant, 92; reviewer, jour family rel(s), 91; commun monogr(s), 90, 92 - 95; jour broadcasting and electronic media, 92, 93; jour lang and soc psychol, 87, 92, 96; jour commun, 86; commun yrbk, 95; mayfield press, 95; assoc ed, commun monogr(s), 86, 88; human commun **MEMBERSHIPS** Mem, Intl Commun Assn; Speech Commun Assn, E Commun Assn. **SELECTED PUBLICATIONS** Auth, Commentary, Communication and Sex-Role Socialization, Garland Press, 93; Mary Anne Fitzpatrick, Women in Communication, Greenwood Press, 96; co-auth, Micro Inequities: Up Close and Personal, Subtle Discrimination: Principles and Practices, Sage, 97; **CONTACT ADDRESS** Dept of Commun, Univ of Delaware, 162 Ctr Mall, Newark, DE 19716.

HASSEL, JON
PERSONAL Born 01/28/1939, Fargo, ND, m, 1960, 1 child **DISCIPLINE** BALZAC AND THE ROMANTIC POETS **EDUCATION** Amherst Col, BA, 61, Brown Univ, MA, 64, PhD, 67. **CAREER** English and Lit, Univ Ark. **MEMBERSHIPS** The Romantic Movement bibliography team **SELECTED PUBLICATIONS** Area: middle-school language education. **CONTACT ADDRESS** Univ of Arkansas, Fayetteville, Fayetteville, AR 72701.

HASSEL, R. CHRIS, JR
DISCIPLINE LITERATURE **EDUCATION** Univ of Richmond, BA, 61; Univ of NC, MA, 62; Emory Univ, PhD, 68. **CAREER** Instr, Mercer Univ, 62-65; Teaching Fel, Emory Univ, 65-68; from asst prof to prof, Vanderbilt Univ, 68-. **HONORS AND AWARDS** Phi Beta Kappa, Omnicron Delta Kappa, Woodrow Wilson Fel, Emory Univ Fel, Folga Fel, ACLS, American Philos Soc Awds, Ellen Gregg Ingalls Awd for Excellence in Classroom Teaching. **MEMBERSHIPS** MLA, Am Shakespeare Asn, Int Shakespeare Asn. **RESEARCH** Shakespeare and Religion. **SELECTED PUBLICATIONS** Auth, "Hamlet's 'Too Too Solid Flesh'," The Sixteenth Century J 25 (94): 609-622; auth, "The Comedy of Errors in Context and in the Performance," The Upstart Crow 18 (97): 23-39; auth, "'Painted Women': Annunciation Motifs in Hamlet," Comparative Drama 32 (98): 23-39; auth, "Fluellen: Wars of Discipline and 'Disciplines of the Wars'," Lit and Tehol 12 (98): 350-362; auth, "Shakespeare's 'Removed Mysteries'," Connotations 7 (98): 355-367; auth, "Mouse and Mousetrap in Hamlet," Shakespeare Jahrbuch 135 (99): 77-92; auth, "'No boasting like a fool'? Herod and Macbeth," Studies in Philol (forthcoming). **CONTACT ADDRESS** Dept English, Vanderbilt Univ, 2201 West End Ave, PO Box 129-B, Nashville, TN 37235-0001. **EMAIL** r.chris.hassel@vanderbilt.edu

HASSELMAN, MARGARET
PERSONAL Born 10/15/1940, New York, NY, m, 1967, 2 children **DISCIPLINE** MUSIC **EDUCATION** Smith Col, BA, 62; Univ Calif Berkeley, MA, 64; PhD, 70. **CAREER** Adj asst prof, Va Polytech Inst, 81-; adj asst prof, Radford Univ, 90-00. **HONORS AND AWARDS** Phi Beta Kappa, 61; Fulbright Fel, 66; NEH Fel, 87. **MEMBERSHIPS** AMS; CMS; Int Machaut Soc. **RESEARCH** Medieval Music, (14th Century French, troubadour songs, tonal structures). **SELECTED PUBLICATIONS** Coauth, "More Hidden Polyphony in a Machaut Manuscript", Musica Disciplina XXVI (70): 7-10; coauth, "Mimesis and woodwind articulations in the fourteenth century", Studies in the Performance of Late Medieval Music, ed Stanley Boorman, Cambridge Univ Pr, (83): 101-107; auth, "Renaut de Bage: Le Bel Inconnu", Garland Libr of Medieval Lit 77, ed Karen Fresco, 92; auth, "Teaching Machaut's Remede de Fortune in the context of an undergraduate Humanities course", Studies in Medieval and Renaissance Teaching (forthcoming). **CONTACT ADDRESS** Humanities Prog, Virginia Polytech Inst and State Univ, 100 Virginia Tech, Blacksburg, VA 24061-0001. **EMAIL** mhasselm@vt.edu

HASSENCAHL, FRANCES J.
PERSONAL Born, MI, m, 1964, 1 child **DISCIPLINE** PUBLIC COMMUNICATION--RHETORIC **EDUCATION** Goshen Col, BA, Case-Western Reserve Univ, MA, Phd. **CAREER** Alfred Univ, Fac mem, 70-75; Old Dominion Univ, 76-. **RESEARCH** African-American Rhetoric, Public Speaking, Intercultural Communication. **SELECTED PUBLICATIONS** Auth, Jane Addams, chapter Woman Public Speakers: 1830-1925, Greenwood Press, 93. **CONTACT ADDRESS** Old Dominion Univ, 4100 Powhatan Ave, Norfolk, VA 23529. **EMAIL** FHassenc@odu.edu

HASSETT, CONSTANCE W.
DISCIPLINE ENGLISH LITERATURE **EDUCATION** Harvard Univ, PhD. **CAREER** Prof, Fordham Univ. **RESEARCH** Victorian women's auto-biographies, pre-Raphaelite poetry and painting. **SELECTED PUBLICATIONS** Auth, The Style of Evasion: William Morris's The Defense of Guenevere, and Other Poems, Victorian Poetry 29, 91; Esthetic Autonomy in

the Sister Arts: The Brotherly Project of Rossetti and Morris, Mosaic 25, 92. **CONTACT ADDRESS** Dept of Eng Lang and Lit, Fordham Univ, 113 W 60th St, New York, NY 10023. **EMAIL** hassett@fordham.edu

HASSLER, DONALD M.
PERSONAL Born 01/03/1937, Akron, OH, m, 1977, 4 children **DISCIPLINE** ENGLISH **EDUCATION** Columbia Univ, Phd, 67; MA, 60; Williams Col, BA, 59. **CAREER** Instr to Prof, Kent State, 65-; Instr, Univ of Montreal, 61-65; Writer, Crowell-Collier Encyclopedia, NYC, 61; Undergraduate Coordinator, 98-; Graduate Coordinator, 91-94; Undergraduate Coordinator, 87-91; Acting Dean, Honors Col, KSU, 79-80; Director, Experimental Programs, Honors Col, 73-83. **HONORS AND AWARDS** J. Lloyd Eaton Awd for best book of science fiction criticism in 91, April 93; Finalist, Distinguished Scholar Awd, KSU, 99; Summer Research Fel, 86; Summer Research Fel, 71; Univ Scholarship, Columbia, 61; Woodrow Wilson Fel, 59. **MEMBERSHIPS** MLA; Amer Society 18th Studies; Science Fiction Research Assoc. **RESEARCH** Science and Literature; Science Fiction. **SELECTED PUBLICATIONS** Auth, "Isaac Asimov," Mercer Island, WA: Starmont, 91, 129p; auth, "Death and the Serpent: Immortality in Science Fiction and Fantasy," edited with Carl B. Yoke, Westport, CT: Greenwood Press, 85, 236p.; auth, "Patterns of the Fantastic II, edited Mercer Island, WA: Starmont, 84, 91p.; auth, "Patterns of the Fantastic, edited Mercer Island, WA: Starmont, 83, 105p.; auth, "Comic Tones in Science Fiction: The Art of Compromise with Nature," Westport, CT: Greenwood, 82:143p; auth, "Hal Clement," Mercer Island, WA: Starmont, 82: 64p.; auth, "Erasmus Darwin," New York: Twayne, 74: 143p; auth, "The Comedian as the Letter D: Erasmus Darwin's Comic Materialism," The Hague: Martinus Nijhoff, 73: 99p, Reprinted by Kluwer Academic Publishers, Norwell MA: 98. **CONTACT ADDRESS** Dept English, Kent State Univ, PO Box 5190, Kent, OH 44242-0001. **EMAIL** extrap@kent.edu

HASTINGS, A. WALLER
PERSONAL Born 01/10/1952, St Catherine's, Canada, w, 1985, 2 children **DISCIPLINE** ENGLISH **EDUCATION** Brown Univ, AB, 74; DePaul Univ, MA, 83; Univ Wis at Madison, PhD, 86. **CAREER** Lectr, Univ Wis at Richland, 88; from asst prof to prof, Northern State Univ, 88-; Eng dept coord, Northern State Univ, 86-99. **HONORS AND AWARDS** Grad Fel, Univ Wis at Madison, 83-84; NEH Summer Sem, 89 & 92. **MEMBERSHIPS** Children's Lit Asn, MLA. **RESEARCH** Children's Literature, Historical Fiction, Genre in Children's Books, Disney Animation, Film Adaptations of Children's Books, L. Frank Baum & Oz. **SELECTED PUBLICATIONS** Auth, "Moral Simplification in Disney's 'The Little Mermaid,'" Lion & Unicorn, 93; auth, "Bambi and the Hunting Ethos," J of Popular Film & TV, 96. **CONTACT ADDRESS** Dept English & Lang, No State Univ, 1200 S Jay St, Aberdeen, SD 57401-7155. **EMAIL** hastingw@northern.edu

HATCH, JAMES V.
PERSONAL Born 10/25/1928, Oelwein, IA **DISCIPLINE** ENGLISH, THEATRE ARTS **EDUCATION** Northern Iowa State Univ, BA, 49; State Univ Iowa, MA, 55, PhD(theatre arts), 58. **CAREER** Asst prof theatre, Univ Calif, Los Angeles, 58-62; Fulbright lectr cinema, High Cinema Inst, Cairo, Egypt, 62-65; asst prof, 65-70, assoc prof, 71-76, PROF ENGLISH, CITY COL NEW YORK, 76-, US Dept State lectr theatre, India & Ceylon, 67-68; consult, Asian Theatre, JDR III Found, 69-70 & Drama Bk Specialist, New York, 70-73; res grant, City Col New York, 72-74; Nat Endowment Humanities grant, 73-74; exec secy, Hatch-Billops Collection, Inc 75-; guest prof English, Univ Hamburg, W Ger, 76; writing fel, MacDowell Colony, 76. **HONORS AND AWARDS** George Washington Honor Medal, Freedom Found, 58; Obie Awd, Village Voice, 62. **MEMBERSHIPS** Am Theatre Asn. **RESEARCH** Black theatre history; East Indian theatre; Asian and Middle East cinema. **SELECTED PUBLICATIONS CONTACT ADDRESS** Dept of English, City Col, CUNY, 160 Convent Ave, New York, NY 10031-9198.

HATCH, MARTIN
PERSONAL Born 12/17/1941, Philadelphia, PA **DISCIPLINE** MUSIC **EDUCATION** Cornell Univ, PhD. **CAREER** Assoc prof **HONORS AND AWARDS** Grant for study in Southeast Asia: Asian Cult Coun, NY, 87/88. **MEMBERSHIPS** Bd, treas, Soc Asian Music; Soc Ethnomusicol. **RESEARCH** Song in Southeast Asia; socio-cultural construction of music genres. **SELECTED PUBLICATIONS** Ed, Asian Music, jour, 85-96; Khmer Shadow Theater, 95. **CONTACT ADDRESS** Dept of Music, Cornell Univ, 104 Lincoln Hall, Ithaca, NY 14853. **EMAIL** mfh2@cornell.edu

HATCH, RONALD B.
PERSONAL Born 11/12/1939, Ft William, ON, Canada, m, 1963, 2 children **DISCIPLINE** ENGLISH LITERATURE **EDUCATION** Univ Brit Colum, BA; MA; Edinburgh Univ, PhD. **CAREER** Lectr, Batala Univ Christian Col, India, 64-66; asst prof to assoc prof, Univ of Brit Colum, 69-. **HONORS AND AWARDS** Award, Can Counc; Awd, SSHRC. **MEMBERSHIPS** Assoc of Can Col and Univ Teachers of Eng. **RESEARCH** 18th Century Canadian Literature. **SELECTED PUBLICATIONS** Auth, Crabbe's Arabesque: Social Drama in the Poetry of George Crabbe, McGill, Queen's; ed, Clayoquot and Dissent; cotransl, Fugitive Dreams: Poems by Sowol Kim; cotransl, Love's Silence and Other Poems by Yong-un Han. **CONTACT ADDRESS** Dept English, Univ of British Columbia, 397 - 1873 East Mall, BuTo, Vancouver, BC, Canada V6T 1Z1. **EMAIL** rbhatch@interchange.ubc.ca

HATHAWAY, RICHARD DEAN
PERSONAL Born 08/08/1927, Chillicothe, OH, m, 1978, 2 children **DISCIPLINE** AMERICAN LITERATURE **EDUCATION** Oberlin Col, AB, 49; Harvard Univ, AM, 52; Case Western Reserve Univ, PhD(Am studies), 64. **CAREER** Instr English, Maritime Col State Univ NY, 55 & Rensselaer Polytech Inst, 57-62; from asst prof to assoc prof, 62-70, PROF ENGLISH, STATE UNIV NY COL NEW PALTZ, 70-, Mem, Danforth assoc, 60-; assoc prof, Millsaps Col, 65-66. **MEMBERSHIPS** MLA. **RESEARCH** New England literature and culture. **SELECTED PUBLICATIONS** Auth, Sylvester Judd's New England, Penn State Univ Pr, 81; auth, "Wallace in Wonderland: Thirteen Ways of Looking at a Bantam," Southern Rev vol 23 (87); auth, Text: A Program About Literature, McGraw-Hill, 90. **CONTACT ADDRESS** 11 Crescent Ln, New Paltz, NY 12561. **EMAIL** hathawar@newpaltz.edu

HATLEN, BURTON NORVAL
PERSONAL Born 04/09/1936, Santa Barbara, CA, m, 1961, 2 children **DISCIPLINE** ENGLISH **EDUCATION** Univ Calif, Berkeley, BA, 58; Columbia Univ, MA, 59; Harvard Univ, MA, 61; Univ Calif, Davis, PhD(English), 71. **CAREER** Acting asst prof English, King Col, 61-62; instr, Univ Cincinnati, 62-65; asst prof, 67-73, assoc prof, 73-81, PROF ENGLISH, UNIV MAINE, ORONO, 81-. **MEMBERSHIPS** MLA. **RESEARCH** Renaissance and modern American poetry. **SELECTED PUBLICATIONS** Ed & coauth, George Oppen: Man and poet, Nat Poetry Found, 81. **CONTACT ADDRESS** Dept of English, Univ of Maine, Orono, ME 04473. **EMAIL** hatlen@maine.maine.edu

HATTMAN, JOHN
PERSONAL Born 08/22/1940, Pittsburgh, PA, s **DISCIPLINE** ENGLISH **EDUCATION** Wheeling Jesuit Univ, AB, 62; Univ Scranton, MA, 64; Carnegie-Mallon Univ, DA, 74. **CAREER** Instructor to Prof, W Liberty State Col, 64-. **HONORS AND AWARDS** Nat Merit Scholarship, 58; Prof of the Year, W Liberty State Col. **MEMBERSHIPS** FACDIS. **RESEARCH** Graham Greene; American Colonial New England. **CONTACT ADDRESS** Dept Humanities, West Liberty State Col, PO Box 295, West Liberty, WV 26074-0295.

HAUGRUD-REIFF, RAYCHEL A.
PERSONAL Born 01/09/1945, Pelican Rapids, MN, m, 4 children **DISCIPLINE** LITERATURE **EDUCATION** Concordia Col, BA, 67; Univ Ut, MA, 69; PhD, 71. **CAREER** From Lectr to Assoc Prof, Univ Wis, 90-. **HONORS AND AWARDS** NDEA Fel, Univ Ut, 67-70; Outstanding Young Woman of Am, 74; Who's Who of Women in Educ, 77; Fac Develop Grants, Univ Wis, 94-95; Who's Who Among Am Teachers, 98, 00. **MEMBERSHIPS** NCTE, AUWP. **RESEARCH** Literature, Chaucer, Ole E Rolvaag, Ralph Waldo Emerson, teaching activities. **SELECTED PUBLICATIONS** Auth, "Making Poems Come Alive," Statement: J of the Colo Lang Arts Soc of the Nat Coun of Teachers of English 34.1 (97): 8-9; auth, "My Christmas Story," Lutheran Women 11.10 (98): 32; auth, "Almost Like a Fairy Tale: The Ecstasy and the Agony of Norwegian Immigrants' Lives as Seen in O E Rolvaag's 'Giants in the Earth'," NDak Quart 65.4 (98): 58-79; auth, "Teaching an Appreciation of Poetry: Tennyson's 'The Lotos-Eaters'," The English Record 49.3 (99): 44-48; auth, "Helping Students Document Sources," Statement: The J of Colo Lang Arts Soc 36.1 (99): 58-59; auth, "Chaucer's 'The Pardoner's Tale,' 855-58," The Explicator 57.4 (99): 195-197; auth, "Fighting the Trolls on the Dakota Plains: The Ecstasy and Agony of Norwegian Immigrant Lives in O E Rolvaag's 'Giants in the Earth'." in The Immigrant Exper in Am Lit: Carving Out a Niche (Westport, CT: Greenwood Publ, 99), 31-44. **CONTACT ADDRESS** Dept Lang & Lit, Univ of Wisconsin, Superior, PO Box 2000, Superior, WI 54880-4500.

HAUSER, GERARD A.
PERSONAL Born 05/26/1943, Buffalo, NY, m, 1965, 2 children **DISCIPLINE** RHETORIC **EDUCATION** Canisius Col, BA, 65; Univ of Wis, Madison, MA, 66, PhD, 70. **CAREER** Asst prof, 69-73, assoc prof, 73-87, prof, 87-93, dir, Univ Scholars Prog, Pa State Univ, 87-93; PROF & CHEMN, COMMUN DEPT, UNIV OF COLO, BOULDER, 93-. **HONORS AND AWARDS** NY State Regents Scholar; NDEA Title IV Fel; CIC Traveling Fel; Phi Eta Sigma Scholastic Honorary; Liberal Arts Distinguished Teaching Awd; Inst for Arts & Humanistic Studies Res Fel; Eastern Commun Asn Scholar, Temple Univ Visiting Excellence Scholar; Phet Soc of Am Kneupper Awd for Best Article, 99; pres-elect, Rhet Soc Am, 00-01. **MEMBERSHIPS** Nat Commun Asn; Western States Commun Asn; Int Soc for the Hist of Rhetoric; Am Soc for the Hist of Rhetoric; Rhetoric Soc of Am; Nat Coun of Teachers of English; Conf on Col Composition & Commun. **RESEARCH** Rhetorical theory; rhetoric & the public sphere; critical theory. **SELECTED PUBLICATIONS** Auth, Vernacular Voices: The Rhetoric of Publics and Public Spheres, Univ of South Caroline Press, 99; Introduction to Rhetorical Theory, Harper & Row, 86, Waveland Press, 91; auth, Civil Society and the Principle of the Public Sphere, Philosophy and Rhetoric, 98; auth, "Aristotle on Epideictic: The Formation of Public Morality," Rhet Soc Q 999); auth, "Incongruous Bodies: Arguments for Personal Sufficiency and Public Insufficiency," Argumentation and Advocacy, 99; auth, Vernacular Dialogue and the Rhetoricality of Public Opinion, Commun Monographs, 98; auth, On Publics and Public Spheres, Commun Monographs, 97; Between Philosophy and Rhetoric: Interpositions within the Tradition, Philosophy and Rhetoric, 95; Constituting Publics and Reconstituting the Public Sphere: The Meese Commission Report on Pornography, in Warranting Assent: Case Studies in Argument Evaluation, SUNY, 95; coauth, Communication of Values, Handbook of Rhetorical and Commun Theory, 84; auth, The New Rhetoric and New Social Movements, Emerging Theories of Human Communication, SUNY, 97; ed, The Body as Source and Site of Argument, Argument and Advocacy, forthcoming; ed, Theory and Praxis, Philosophy and Rhetoric, 91. **CONTACT ADDRESS** Commun Dept, Univ of Colorado, Boulder, CB 270, Boulder, CO 80309-2070. **EMAIL** hauserg@spot.colorado.edu

HAVEN, RICHARD P.
PERSONAL Born 05/03/1949, New Castle, IN, m, 1975, 3 children **DISCIPLINE** COMMUNICATION **EDUCATION** Ball State Univ, BS 71, MA 73; Univ Wis Madison, PhD 80. **CAREER** Univ Wis Whitewater, 72-, rank to prof, Comm Dept ch, 93-98, asst to chancellor, 91-93, assoc Dean 98-. **MEMBERSHIPS** NCA; ACE; NAPAHE; CAA. **RESEARCH** Speech writing; Public speaking; Persuasion; Am Public Address. **SELECTED PUBLICATIONS** Auth, Working with a speech writer: Tips for Presidents and others in leadership roles, Ace Ntl Conf, 97, 98; Speech writing and Higher education: The role of the Presidential assistant, NAPAHE Ntl Conf with ACE, 95, 96, 98. **CONTACT ADDRESS** Dept of Communication, Univ of Wisconsin, Whitewater, CA 2029, Whitewater, WI 53190. **EMAIL** havend@mail.uww.edu

HAVERLY, THOMAS
PERSONAL Born 10/22/1953, Chicago, IL, 2 children **DISCIPLINE** RELIGION, LIBRARY STUDIES **EDUCATION** Olivet Nazarene Col, BA, 74; Nazarene Theol Sem, MDiv, 78; Edinburgh Univ, PhD, 83; Syracuse Univ, MLS, 93. **CAREER** Assoc Prof, Eastern Nazarene Col, 83-94; Assoc Librarian, Colgate Rochester Div School, 94-. **MEMBERSHIPS** SBL, ATLA. **RESEARCH** New Testament; Educational Technology and Media. **CONTACT ADDRESS** Ambrose Swasey Library, Colgate Rochester Divinity Sch/Bexley Hall/Crozer Theol Sem, 1100 Goodman St S, Rochester, NY 14620-2530. **EMAIL** thaverly@crds.edu

HAWES, WILLIAM K.
PERSONAL Born 03/06/1931, Grand Rapids, MI, d, 2 children **DISCIPLINE** TELEVISION, THEATER. **EDUCATION** Univ Mich, Ann Arbor, PhD, 60, MA, 56; Eastern Mich Univ, Ypsilanti, AB, 55. **CAREER** Univ Houston, Prof, 76-, assoc prof, 65-76, KUHF radio stn mgr 65-70, creator exec prod UH-TV, 67-; assoc prof, Univ NC, Chapel Hill, mgr WUNC, WTOP-TV, Washington, 64-65; Texas Christ Univ, Fort Worth, mgr found, KTCU, 60-64; asst prof, Eastern Mich Univ, 56-60; teach asst, Univ Mich, 56-57. **HONORS AND AWARDS** Eliz D Rockwell Fund, 96; UH NEH Granta, 80; Film Guest FRG, 81; UH London Prog, 84, 94; Avery Hopwood Awd, 57; J. William Fulbright Lecturer, Taiwan, 01. **MEMBERSHIPS** Am Film Inst; Museum of Fine Arts, Houston; KUHT Pub TV. **RESEARCH** Hist amer tv, drama cinema; pub tv; porn in film and TV. **SELECTED PUBLICATIONS** Auth, "Live Television Drama," 46-52, McFarland, 00; auth, "Public Television America's First Station," Sunstone, 96; auth, "Television Performing, Ante La Camara, Focal, 91, 93, Chinese edition, 99. **CONTACT ADDRESS** Univ of Houston, School of Communication, Houston, TX 77204-4072. **EMAIL** whawes@uh.edu

HAWKES, CAROL A.
PERSONAL Born New York, NY, s **DISCIPLINE** ENGLISH **EDUCATION** Barnard Col, BA, 43; Columbia Univ, MA, 44; PhD, 49. **CAREER** Prof and dept chair, Finch Col, 57-75; dean and vp, Hartwick Col, 75-80; pres, Endicott Col, 80-87; dean, W Conn State Univ, 87-. **HONORS AND AWARDS** Phi Beta Kappa. **MEMBERSHIPS** Phi Beta Kappa; Am Asn for Higher Educ; SCUP; CAEL; MLA; LAUPE **RESEARCH** State vs. Independent Higher Education; Education vs. Acculturation; Seta time vs. Learning Outcomes. **CONTACT ADDRESS** Dept English, Western Connecticut State Univ, 12 Silversmith Dr, Danbury, CT 06811-2602. **EMAIL** hawkesc@wcsu.edu

HAWKES, LORY
PERSONAL Born 01/04/1946, Fort Worth, TX, m, 1969, 4 children **DISCIPLINE** COMMUNICATIONS **EDUCATION** Univ Tex Arlington, BA; MA; Tex Christian Univ, PhD, 93. **CAREER** Prof, DeVry Inst of Technol, 84-; adj prof and teaching fel, Tex Christian Univ, 92-94. **HONORS AND AWARDS** Fel, Soc for Tech Comm, 98; Cultures Fair Lifetime Achieve-

ment Award, 98. **MEMBERSHIPS** Soc for Tech Comm; IEEE; ACM. **RESEARCH** Web Interfaces; Instructional Technology. **SELECTED PUBLICATIONS** Auth, Hyperspatial Travel into the Internet, Prentice Hall, 96; auth, Guide to the World Wide Web, Prentice Hall, 99; co-auth, Theory and Criticism of Virtual Texts: An Annotated Bibliography, Greenwood Press, 01. **CONTACT ADDRESS** Dept Comm, DeVry Inst of Tech, 3500 Meadowlark Ln, Colleyville, TX 76034-8664. **EMAIL** hawkes@mail.dal.devry.edu

HAWKINS, EMMA

PERSONAL Born, OK **DISCIPLINE** ENGLISH, RELIGION **EDUCATION** Okla Baptist Univ, BA, 68; SW Baptist Theol Sem, MDiv, 76; Univ N Tex, MA, 90, PhD, 95. **CAREER** Teacher, Univ of N Tex, 90-95; asst prof, Lamar Univ, 95-. **HONORS AND AWARDS** Mary Patchell Awd, Univ of N Tex, 93; Univ Writing Awd, Univ of N Tex, 93; Go the Extra Mile Awd, 97; James Sims Prize, SCCCL Conf, 00. **MEMBERSHIPS** SCMLA; TEMA; CCTE; SCCCL. **RESEARCH** Old English Literature and Language, Ancient, Classical, Medieval Mythology. **SELECTED PUBLICATIONS** Auth, "Hild und Guth, The War Maidens of Beowulf" in Geardagum 15 (94):55-75; auth, "Gender, Power and Language in 'The Dream of the Rood'", Women and Language 18.2 (95):33-36; auth, Topics for Writers in Media-Based, Entry-Level Composition Courses", English in Texas 27.3 (96):40-49; auth, "Chalk Figures and Scouring in Tolkien-land", Extrapolation (forthcoming); auth, "Chronicles" in Companion to Old and Middle English Literature, Greenwood Pr (forthcoming). **CONTACT ADDRESS** Dept English and Lang, Lamar Univ, Beaumont, PO Box 10023, Beaumont, TX 77710-0023.

HAWKINS, HUNT

PERSONAL Born 12/23/1943, Washington, DC, m, 1976, 2 children **DISCIPLINE** ENGLISH LITERATURE; AMERICAN LITERATURE **EDUCATION** Williams Col, BA, 65; Stanford Univ, MA, 69, PhD(English), 76. **CAREER** Teacher English, Kurasini Col, Tanzania, 66-67; instr, Tex Southern Univ, 68-70; teaching asst, Stanford Univ, 72-73; asst prof, Univ Minn, 77-78; from Asst Prof to Assoc Prof, 78-94, PROF ENGLISH, FLA STATE UNIV, 94-, chmn, 99. **MEMBERSHIPS** MLA; SAtlantic Mod Lang Asn., Pres, Joseph Conrad Society, 98-00 **RESEARCH** Joseph Conrad; Mark Twain; colonial fiction. **SELECTED PUBLICATIONS** Auth, Mark Twain's involvement with the Congo reform movement, New England Quart, 78; Conrad's critique of imperialism in Heart of Darkness, Publ Mod Lang Asn, 79; Women in Heart of Darkness, Joseph Conrad Today, 81; Conrad and Congolese exploitation, Conradiana, 81; Joseph Conrad, Roger Casement and the Congo reform movement, J Mod Lit, 81; The issue of racism in Heart of Darkness, Conradiana, 82; E M Forster's critique of imperialism in A Passage to India, SAtlantic Rev, 83; Similarities between Mark Twain and Joseph Conrad, Polish Rev, 84; Conrad and the psychology of colonialism, Conrad Revisited, 85; Aime Cesaire's Lesson about Decolonization, CLA J, 86; Things Fall Apart and the Literature of Empire, Teaching Approaches to Things Fall Apart, 91; Joyce as a Colonial Writer, CLA J, 92; Teaching Heart of Darkness, Conradiana, 92; Mark Twain's Anti-Imperialism, ALR, 93. **CONTACT ADDRESS** English Dept, Florida State Univ, 600 W College Ave, Tallahassee, FL 32306-1096. **EMAIL** hhawkins@english.fsu.edu

HAWKINS, KATE

DISCIPLINE SPEECH COMMUNICATION **EDUCATION** Univ Tex, PhD. **CAREER** Dir undergrad stud, Tex Tech Univ; assoc prof, asso dir, Elliot Sch Commun; Prof, Grad Coordr, Elliot Sch Commun. **HONORS AND AWARDS** Awds tchg excellence, Wichita state Univ. **MEMBERSHIPS** Nat commun Assoc; Southern States commun Assoc, Org for the Srudy of Commun, Language and Gender; Organization for Research on Women and Commun **SELECTED PUBLICATIONS** Auth, Analyzing the pure case: Women's narratives of academic life, Hawkins, K.W., 94; auth, Women's Studies in Communcation, Hawkins, K.W., 95; auth, "The effects of gender and communication content on emerged leadership in small, task-oriented groups," Small Group Res, (Sorenson, P.S., Hawkins, K.W., & Sorenson, R., 95), 234-249; auth, "Curricula comparison fo classes in listening," Journal of the Int Listening Assoc, (Hawkins, K.W. & Power, C.B. 99), 235-256; auth, "Gender, psychological type and conflict style preferecne," Management Commun Quarterly, (Wacker, K.g. & Hawkins, K.W., 95) , 115-126; auth, "Curricula comparison for classes in listening," Journal of the Int Listiening Assoc, (Hawkins, K.W. & Power, C.B., 99), 14-28; auth, gender differences in questions asked during small decision-making group discussions," Small group discussions res, (Hawkins, K.W. & Fillion, B. , 99), 235-256; auth, "Adolescents' perceptions of print cigarette advertising," Journal of Health Commun, (Hawkins, K.W. & Hane, A.C., 00), 83-96. **CONTACT ADDRESS** Dept of Commun, Wichita State Univ, 1845 Fairmont, Wichita, KS 67260-0062. **EMAIL** hawkins@elliott.es.twsu.edu

HAWKINSON, KENNETH S.

PERSONAL Born 06/14/1958, San Pedro, CA, s, 1 child **DISCIPLINE** COMMUNICATION **EDUCATION** Elgin Community Col, AA, 76; Western Ill Univ, BA, 78, MA, 79, PhD, 86. **CAREER** Grad asst, Western Ill Univ, 78-79; part-time instr, Univ of Md, 80; grad asst, Southern Ill Univ, 82-84; instr, Western Ill Univ, 84-85; lecturer, Southern Ill Univ, 85-86; Ecole Normale Superieur, Prof, 86-88. **HONORS AND AWARDS** Fulbright Scholar, 90-91; Faculty Excellence Awds, 92-93, 93-94, 94-95; Summer Stipend, 94; Phi Kappa Phi initiate, 95; Blue Key Fac Initiate, 95; Thompson professorship, 96-98. **MEMBERSHIPS** Nat Commun Assoc; Cent States Commun Assoc; Ill Speech & Theatre Assoc. **RESEARCH** Storytelling & oral tradition; African & Africam American folklore; Performance Studies; Rhetoric in fiction; literary criticism; creative writing. **SELECTED PUBLICATIONS** Auth, Two excercises on Diversity and gender, Speech Commun Teach, Fall 93; auth The Old Speech of the African Griot, Parabola, Spring, 94; auth, Performing Personal Narratives, Speech Commun Teach, Winter, 95; A New Individual Event: The Personal Narrative, J of the Ill Speech & Theatre Assoc, Spring 96; African Woman Grieves Dying Child, Eureka Lit Mag, Spring 98. **CONTACT ADDRESS** Dept of Commun, Western Illinois Univ, Western, IL 61455. **EMAIL** kenneth_hawkinson@ccmail.wiu.edu

HAWTHORNE, LUCIA SHELIA

PERSONAL Born Baltimore, MD, d **DISCIPLINE** SPEECH COMMUNICATION **EDUCATION** Morgan State Univ, BS Lang Arts 1964; Washington State Univ, MAT Speech 1965; PA State Univ, PhD Speech Comm 1971. **CAREER** Washington State Univ, teaching asst 64-65; Morgan State Univ, instructor 65-67; PA State Univ, teaching asst 67-69; Morgan State, asst prof 69-72, assoc prof 72-75, assoc dean of humanities 74-75, prof 75-, chmn dept of speech comm & theatre 72-75, 84-87. **HONORS AND AWARDS** Alpha Kappa Mu; Kappa Delta Pi; Lambda Iota Tau; Phi Alpha Theta; Promethean Kappa Tau; Alpha Psi Omega; Alpha Lambda Delta; Phi Eta Sigma; Danforth Assoc Danforth Found 1978-85; Academic Adminstrn Intern Amer Cncl on Educ 1974-75; Alumnus of the Year, Morgan State University, 1990-91; "Woman of The Year", Committee United to Save Sandtown, Inc, 1992. **MEMBERSHIPS** Chmn Commn on the Profession & Social Problems Speech Comm Assn 1972-75; mem Commn on Freedom of Speech Speech Comm Assn 1973-75; mem Bi-Lingual and Bi-Cultural Educ rep to TESOL for Speech Comm Assoc 1975-77; mem Speech Comm Assn, Eastern Comm Assn, MD Comm Assn, Assn of Comm Administrators; bd trustees Morgan Christian Ctr; life mem NAACP; Golden Heritage mem NAACP; Golden Life Member, Diamond Life Member, Delta Sigma Theta Sor Inc. **CONTACT ADDRESS** Dept of Speech Commun, Morgan State Univ, Baltimore, MD 21251.

HAWTHORNE, MARK D.

PERSONAL Born 12/09/1938, Berea, OH, m, 1960, 1 child **DISCIPLINE** ENGLISH **EDUCATION** Wake Forest Univ, BA, 60; Univ Fla, MA, 62, PhD(English), 64. **CAREER** Asst prof English, NC State Univ, 64-67; from asst prof to assoc prof, Jacksonville Univ, 68-74, chmn div humanities, 73-74; head dept, 74-81, PROF ENGLISH, JAMES MADISON UNIV, 74- **MEMBERSHIPS** MLA; S Atlantic Mod Lang Asn. **RESEARCH** Anglo-Irish literature; British romantic and Victorian poetry and prose fiction. **SELECTED PUBLICATIONS** Auth, A Hermaphrodite Sort of Deity--Sexuality, Gender, and Gender Blending in Thomas Pynchon, Studies Novel, Vol 0029, 97. **CONTACT ADDRESS** Dept of English, James Madison Univ, Harrisonburg, VA 22801.

HAY, FRED J.

PERSONAL Born 10/03/1953, Toccoa, GA, m, 1983, 1 child **DISCIPLINE** ANTHROPOLOGY; LIBRARY SCIENCE **EDUCATION** Rhodes Col, BA, 75; Univ Va, MA, 81; Fl St Univ, MLIS, 87; Univ Fl, PhD, 85. **CAREER** Asst prof, St Cloud St Univ, 85-86; librn, asst prof, Ks St Univ, 88-89; librn, Harvard Univ, 89-94; prof, librn, Appalachian St Univ, 94- . **HONORS AND AWARDS** Douglas W. Bryant Fel, 92-93; Brenda McCullum Mem Prize, Amer Folklore Soc, 97. **MEMBERSHIPS** Amer Anthrop Assoc; Appalachian Stud Assoc; Amer Libr Assoc; Assoc of Col & Res Libr; Assoc of Black Anthrop; Progressive Librn Guild. **RESEARCH** Appalachia, African-American cultures; Black music; soc sci bibliogr & documentation, southern US, Caribbean. **SELECTED PUBLICATIONS** Auth, Tozzer Library: How to Access the World's Largest Anthropology Bibliography, Cult Anthrop Methods Newsletter, 92; OCLC: An Essential Tool for Anthropological Documentation, Cult Anthrop Methods Newsletter, 93; The Significance of Caribbeanist Anthropology: A Bibliographic History, Ref Svc Rev, 95; coed, Documenting Cultural Diversity in the Resurgent American South: Collectors, Collecting and Collections; Assoc of Col & Res Libr; ed, auth, When Night Falls: Kric! Krac!, Libr Unlimited, 98; auth, "The Sacred/Profane Dialectic in Delta Blues as Exemplified in Excerpts from the Life and Lyrics of Sonny Bay Williamson," Phylon (87); auth, "Microethnography of a Haitian Boutique," Social and Economic Studies (90); auth, "The Subject Specialist in the Academic Library," Jrnl of Academic Librarianship (90); auth, African American Community Studies from North America, Garland, 91. **CONTACT ADDRESS** W. L. Evry Appalachian Col, Appalachian State Univ, Belk Library, Boone, NC 28608. **EMAIL** hayfj@appstate.edu

HAY, M. VICTORIA

PERSONAL Born 05/07/1945, Long Beach, CA, 1 child **DISCIPLINE** ENGLISH **EDUCATION** Univ Ariz, BA; Ariz State Univ, MA, 72; PhD, 79. **CAREER** Proprietor, Hay Writing & Editing; assoc editor, Ariz Highways and Phoenix magazines; sr lectr, Ariz State Univ, 93-. **HONORS AND AWARDS** NSF Grad Fel; Ford Found Fel. **MEMBERSHIPS** Author's Guild, Soc of Technical Communicators, MLA, Soc of Professional Journalists. **RESEARCH** Creative Nonfiction, Distance Learning. **SELECTED PUBLICATIONS** Auth, The Life of Robert Sidney, Earl of Leicester, 84; auth, The Essential Feature: Writing for Magazines and Newspapers, 90; coauth, Matte Magic, 93. **CONTACT ADDRESS** Dept Am Studies, Arizona State Univ, West, PO Box 37100, Glendale, AZ 85306. **EMAIL** victoria.hay@asu.edu

HAYES, ANN LOUISE

PERSONAL Born 05/13/1924, Los Angeles, CA, w **DISCIPLINE** ENGLISH **EDUCATION** Stanford Univ, BA, 48, MA, 50. **CAREER** From instr to assoc prof, 58-74, prof eng, Carnegie-Mellon Univ, 74-. **HONORS AND AWARDS** Irene Hardy poetry award, 43; Clarence Urmy Poetry, 43, 47, 50; Ina Coolbirth award, Univ CA, Stan, 43; 93 advan place award, mid states off, Philly. **RESEARCH** Advanced placement Eng programs: 17th and 20th century poetry. **SELECTED PUBLICATIONS** Auth, Essay on the sonnets in Starre of poets: discussions of Shakespeare, Carnegie Ser English, 66; coauth, Model for an Advanced Placement English course, ERIC, 68; auth, On reading Marianne Moore, Carnegie Ser English, 70; The dancer's step, Three Rivers Poetry J, 72; The Living and the Dead, Carnegie-Mellon Univ, 75; Witness: How All Occasions ..., Rook Press, 77; poems in Southern Rev, Am Scholar, Va Quart Rev & Three Rivers Poetry J; Progress Dancing, Robert L. Barth, 86; Circle of Earth, Robert L. Barth, 90. **CONTACT ADDRESS** Dept of Eng, Carnegie Mellon Univ, 5000 Forbes Ave, Pittsburgh, PA 15213-3890. **EMAIL** Ah13+@andrew.cmu.edu

HAYES, DOUGLAS W.

PERSONAL Born 10/17/1969, Hanna, AB, Canada **DISCIPLINE** LITERATURE **EDUCATION** Univ Albta, BA, 93; MA, 94; Univ Toronto, PhD, 00. **CAREER** Asst prof, Winona State Univ, 01-. **MEMBERSHIPS** MRDA; SIETM; SAA; MLA. **RESEARCH** Medieval and Tudor drama and intellectual culture. **SELECTED PUBLICATIONS** Auth, "Backbiter and the Rhetoric of Detraction," Comp Drama 34 (00): 53-78; rev, The Worlde and the Chylde, eds. C. Davidson, O. Happe, Medieval Online Rev (00). **CONTACT ADDRESS** English Dept, Winona State Univ, Minne Hall, Winona, MN 55987. **EMAIL** dhayes@vax2.winona.msus.edu

HAYES, KEVIN J.

PERSONAL Born 11/14/1959, Toledo, OH, s **DISCIPLINE** ENGLISH **EDUCATION** Univ Toledo, BA, 81; ME, 83; Univ Delaware, MA, 89; PhD, 91. **CAREER** From asst prof to prof, Univ of Cent Okla, 91-. **HONORS AND AWARDS** Mellon Fel, Va Hist Soc, 91; Fel, Libr Co of Philadelphia, 91; Distinguished Serv Awd, Asn for Doc Editing, 98; AAUP-UCO Distinguished Scholar Awd, 99; Va Libr Hist Awd, Libr of Va and the Va Ctr for the Book, 99. **MEMBERSHIPS** Am Lit Asn, Asn for Doc Editing, Cosmos Club, Stephen Crane Soc, MLA, Poe Studies Asn, Soc for Cinema Studies **RESEARCH** The history of the book, Edgar Allan Poe, Herman Melville, cinema. **SELECTED PUBLICATIONS** Auth, Captain John Smith: A Reference Guide, G.K. Hall (Boston, MA), 91; ed, The Critical Response to Herman Melville's Moby Dick, Greenwood (Westport, CT), 94; ed, Henry James: The Contemporary Reviews, Cambridge UP (New York, NY), 96; auth, A Colonial Women's Bookshelf, Univ of Tenn Press (Knoxville, TN), 96; auth, Folklore and Book Culture, Univ of Tenn Press (Knoxville, TN), 97; auth, The Library of William Byrd of Westover, Madison House (Madison), 97; auth, Melville's Folk Roots, Kent State UP (Kent, OH), 99; auth, The Library of John Montgomery, Colonial Governor of New York and New Jersey, Univ of Delaware Press (Newark), 00; auth, Poe and the Printed Word, Cambridge UP (New York, NY), 00. **CONTACT ADDRESS** Dept English, Univ of Central Oklahoma, 100 N Univ Dr, Edmond, OK 73034-5207. **EMAIL** khayes@aix1.ucok.edu

HAYES-SCOTT, FAIRY CESENA

DISCIPLINE ENGLISH **EDUCATION** Univ Mich, BA, 72, MA, 73, PhD, 83; intern, Nat Tech Inst for the Deaf, 79. **CAREER** ED, INT J TEACHERS OF ENG WRITING SKILLS, 95-; consult, Direct Success (prog for hearing-impaired) Det Pub Schs, Mich Rehab, 94, 95, 96; OWN/PUB, ROBBIE DEAN PRESS, 91-; PROF, MOTT COMMUNITY COL, 75-. **CONTACT ADDRESS** 2910 E Eisenhower, Ann Arbor, MI 48108. **EMAIL** FairyHa@aol.com

HAYLES, KATHERINE N.

PERSONAL Born 12/16/1943, St Louis, MO, m, 1994, 2 children **DISCIPLINE** ENGLISH **EDUCATION** Rochester Inst Technol, BS, 66; Calif Inst Technol, MS, 69; Mich State Univ, MA, 70; Univ Rochester, PhD, 77. **CAREER** Instr to asst prof, Dartmouth Col, 75-82; vis assoc, Calif Inst Technol, 79-80; asst prof, Univ Mo, 82085; vis assoc prof, Cal Tech, 88; assoc prof to prof, Univ Iowa, 85-92; prof, UCLA, 92-. **HONORS AND**

AWARDS NEH Seminar, 01; Rene Wellek Prize, Am Comparative Lit Asn, 98-99; Eaton Award, Princeton Univ, 00; Eby Award, UCLA, 99; Luckman Distinguished Teaching Award, UCLA, 99; NEH Fel, 99; Bellagio Res Fel, Rockefeller Found, 99; distinguished Scholar Award, Univ Rochester, 98; Medal of Honor, Univ Helsinki, 97; Distinguished Scholar Award, Intl Asn of Fantastic in the Arts, 97; Guggenheim Fel, 91-92; Fac Scholar Award, Univ Iowa, 86-89; Weldon Spring Res Grant, UMR, 83. **MEMBERSHIPS** MLA; Soc for Lit and Sci; Electronic Lit Org. **RESEARCH** Literature and Science of the Twentieth Century; Electronic Textuality; Modern and Postmodern American and British Fiction; Critical Theory; Science Fiction. **SELECTED PUBLICATIONS** Auth, Chaos Bound: Orderly Disorder in Contemporary Literature and Science, Cornell Univ Press, 90; ed, Chaos and Order: Complex Dynamics in Literature and Science, Univ Chicago Press, 91; co-ed, Technocriticism and Hypernarrative, 97; auth, "Schizoid Android: Cybernetics and the Mid-Sixties Novels of Philip K. Dick," J of the Fantastic in the Arts, (98): 22-45; auth, How We Became Posthuman: Virtual Bodies n Cybernetics, Literature and Informatics, Univ Chicago Press, 99; auth, "Simulated Narratives: What Virtual Creatures Can Teach Us," Critical Inquiry, (99): 1-26; auth, "The Illusion of Autonomy and the Fact of Recursivity: Virtual Ecologies, Entertainment, and Virtual Jest," New Literary Hist, (99): 675-697; auth, "The Invention of Copyright and the Birth of Monsters: Flickering Connectivities in Shelley Jackson's 'Patchwork Girl'," J of Postmodern Culture, 00; auth, "The Materiality of the Medium: Hypertext Narrative in Print and New Media," Narrative, 01; **CONTACT ADDRESS** Dept of English, Univ of California, Los Angeles, PO Box 90095-1530, Los Angeles, CA 90095-1530. **EMAIL** hayles@humnet.ucla.edu

HAYMAN, DAVID

PERSONAL Born 01/07/1927, New York, NY, m, 1951, 2 children **DISCIPLINE** ENGLISH **EDUCATION** New York Univ, BA, 48; Univ Paris, DUniv, 55. **CAREER** From instr to assoc prof English, Univ Tex, 55-65; prof comp lit, Univ Iowa, 65-73, chmn dept, 66-68; prof Am lit, Univ Paris VIII, 72-73; PROF COMP LIT & CHMN DEPT, UNIV WIS-MADISON, 73-, Guggenheim fel, 58-59; Nat Endowment for Humanities fel, 79-80; fel, Wis Humanities Res Inst, 79. **MEMBERSHIPS** MLA; Mod Humanities Res Asn, Gt Brit; Am Comp Lit Asn. **RESEARCH** Comparative literature; British modern literature; critical theory. **SELECTED PUBLICATIONS** Auth, The Tristan and Isolde theme in Finnegans wake: A study of the sources and evolution of a theme, Comp Lit Studies, 64; Louis-Ferdinand Celine, Columbis Univ, 65; Forms of folly in Joyce: A study of clowning in Ulysses, J English Lit Hist, 68; Au-dela de Bakhtine, Poetique, 73; co-ed, James Joyce's Ulysses, Critical Essays, Univ Calif, 74; auth, Writers in the wake of the Wake, TriQuart, 76; ed & co-ed, The James Joyce Archive (for Finnegans Wake), Garland, 78; Surface disturbances/grave disorders, TriQuart, 81; Ulysses: The Mechanics of Meaning, Univ Wis, 82. **CONTACT ADDRESS** Dept of Comp Lit, Univ of Wisconsin, Madison, 924 Van Hise Hall, Madison, WI 53706.

HAYNES, CYNTHIA

PERSONAL m, 1 child **DISCIPLINE** LITERATURE STUDIES **EDUCATION** Univ Tex, PhD, 94. **CAREER** Asst prof, Univ of Texas at Arlington. **RESEARCH** Rhetoric and composition; electronic pedagogy; critical theory; virtual rhetoric; Internet culture. **SELECTED PUBLICATIONS** Auth, Inside the Teaching Machine: Actual Feminism and (Virtual) Pedagogy, 96; co-ed, High Wired: On the Design, Use, and Theory of Educational MOOS, Univ Mich, 98; auth, Virtual Diffusion: Ethics, Techne, and Feminism at the End of the Cold Millennium, 99; coauth, MOOuniversty: A Student's Guide to Online Learning Environments, 00. **CONTACT ADDRESS** Dept of Literature, Univ of Texas, Dallas, School of Arts and Humanities, Richardson, TX 75083-0688. **EMAIL** cynthiah@utdallas.edu

HAYNES, HOLLY

PERSONAL Born 11/02/1965, TX **DISCIPLINE** CLASSICS **EDUCATION** Univ Washington, PhD 96. **CAREER** NY Univ, asst prof 95 to 98-. **MEMBERSHIPS** APA **RESEARCH** Critical Theory; Historiography **CONTACT ADDRESS** Dept of Classics, New York Univ, 25 Waverly Pl, 7th Fl, New York, NY 10003. **EMAIL** hh13@is5.nyu.edu

HAYNES, JONATHAN

PERSONAL Born 12/04/1952, Bethlehem, PA, m, 1998 **DISCIPLINE** LITERATURE **EDUCATION** McGill Univ, BA, 74; Yale Univ, MA, 74, PhD, 80. **CAREER** Vis asst prof, 80-82, Amer Univ, Cairo; vis asst prof, 82-83, Tufts Univ; asst prof, 83-85, Albion Col; fac mem, 85-94 Bennington Col; adj assoc prof, 95-96, Columbia Univ; assoc prof, 98-, Southampton Col. **HONORS AND AWARDS** Fulbright Sr Scholar grants, 91-93, 97; Residency, Rockefeller Found Bellagio Study and Conference Center, 95. **RESEARCH** African film & lit; renaissance lit. **SELECTED PUBLICATIONS** Auth, The Humanist as Traveller: George Sandy's "Relation of a Journey begun An. Dom. 1610," Rutherford, NJ: Farileigh Dickinson Univ. Press, 86; auth, The Social Relations of Jonson's Theater, New York and Cambridge: Cambridge Univ Press, 92; coauth, Cinema and Social Change in West Africa, Jos, Nigeria: Nigerian Film Corporation, 97; ed, Nigerian Video Films, Athens, OH: Ohio Univ Press, 00. **CONTACT ADDRESS** Humanities Div, Long Island Univ, Southampton Col, 239 Montauk Highway, Southampton, NY 11968. **EMAIL** jhaynes@suffolk.lib.ny.us

HAYS, PETER L.

PERSONAL Born 04/18/1938, Bremerhaven, Germany, m, 1963, 3 children **DISCIPLINE** ENGLISH **EDUCATION** Univ of Rochester, AB, 59; NY Univ, MA, 61; Ohio State Univ, PhD, 65. **CAREER** Instr, Ohio State Univ, 65-66; from asst prof to prof, Unif of Calif at Davis, 66-; coord of undergraduate studies, Univ of Calif at Davis, 73-74; chemn, Dept of English, Univ of Calif at Davis, 74-77; chemn, Dept of Ger, Univ of Calif at Davis, 97-98. **HONORS AND AWARDS** Fac Fel, Univ of Calif at Davis, 67; Danforth Found Fel, 76; Sr Fulbright Lectr, 77-78. **MEMBERSHIPS** MLA, Hemingway Soc, Faulkner Soc, Miller Soc, Wharton Soc. **RESEARCH** Twentieth-Century American Literature. **SELECTED PUBLICATIONS** Auth, Ernest Hemingway, 90; auth, A Concordance to Hemingway's 'In Our Time,' 90; auth, The Limping Hero, forthcoming. **CONTACT ADDRESS** Dept English, Univ of California, Davis, 1 Shields Av, Davis, CA 95616-5270. **EMAIL** plhays@ucdavis.edu

HAZEL, HARRY CHARLES

PERSONAL Born 05/28/1936, Seattle, WA, m, 1965, 6 children **DISCIPLINE** SPEECH COMMUNICATION **EDUCATION** Gonzaga Univ, AB, 60; Univ Wash, MA, 66; Wash State Univ, PhD(speech), 72. **CAREER** Instr speech, Yakima Valley Col, 66-70; asst prof speech, 71-76, dir summer sessions & continuing educ, 73-75, prof Commun Arts Dept, Gonzaga Univ, 76-, dean Sch Continuing Educ, 75-. **MEMBERSHIPS** Speech Commun Asn. **RESEARCH** Medieval communication theory and public address; American political campaigns; homiletics. **SELECTED PUBLICATIONS** Auth, The Bonaventuran Ars Concionandi, Western Speech, fall 72 & In: S Bonaventura 1274-1974, Vol II, Col St Bonaventure, Rome, 73; Harry Truman: Practical Persuader, Today's Speech, spring, 74; Images of War, Guilt, and Redemption in the First Crusade Speech of Urban II, Commun Quart, spring 78; Blending Speech, English and Logic, Commun, spring 81; The Art of Talking to Yourself and Others, Kansas City: Sheed and Ward, 87; Savonarola: The Disputatious Preacher, Journal of the Northwest Communication Asn, spring 87; The Power of Persuation, Kansas City: Sheed and Ward, 89; Power and Constraint in the Rhetoric of Catherine of Siena, Journal of the NW Comm Asn, spring 91; Public Speaking Handbook: A Liberal Arts Perspective, co-auth by John Caputo, Dubuque, Iowa: Kendall/Hunt, 94; Interpersonal Communication: Competency Through Critical Thinking, co-auth by John Caputo and Colleen McMahon, Boston: Allyn & Bacon, 94. **CONTACT ADDRESS** Dept Commun Arts, Gonzaga Univ, 502 E Boone Ave, Spokane, WA 99258-0001. **EMAIL** hazel@calvin.gonzaga.edu

HAZEN, JAMES F.

DISCIPLINE VICTORIAN AND MODERN BRITISH LITERATURE **EDUCATION** Princeton Univ AB, 57; Univ Wis, Madison, MS, 59, PhD, 63. **CAREER** Instr, Yale Univ, 63-66; asst prof, Univ Mo, St Louis, 66-71; assoc prof, 71-86, prof, 86-, actg dean, Grad Col, 72, chemn, dept Eng, 75-77, dir, grad stud Eng, 83-93, Univ Nev, Las Vegas; manuscript consult, Victorian Stud, Ind Univ, 70-80; assoc ed, 85-96, ed, Interim, 97-. **HONORS AND AWARDS** Fel, Silliman Col, Yale Univ, 64-69; Phi Kappa Phi, 80-;fac develop inst, Univ Nev, Las Vegas, NEH, 87, 88; William Morris Awd for Excellence in Tchg, Univ Nev, Las Vegas, 90; Grad Fac Mem of the Yr, 93-94. **MEMBERSHIPS** MLA, 65-; Directory of Am Scholars, 70-; Rocky Mt MLA, 71-; Philol Asn Pacific Coast, 71-; Who's Who in the West, 78-; International Who's Who in Education, 79-; Honor Society of Phi Kappa Phi, 80-; Acad Am Poets, 92-; Jane Austen Soc of N Am, 93-; NCTE, 95-. **RESEARCH** Victorian and modern British lit; Creative Writing-poetry. **SELECTED PUBLICATIONS** Auth, "Tess of the D'Urbervilles and Antigone," in English Literature in Transition, (71): 207-215; auth, "Angel's Hellenism in Tess of the D'Urbervilles," in College Literature, (77): 129-135; auth, "Morris Haystack: The Fate of Vision," in The Pre-Raphaelite Review, (77): 49-56; auth, "Hardy's War Poetry," in Four Decades of Poetry, (78): 76-93; auth, Graham Greene's America," in Essays in Graham Greene: An Annual Review, Vol. 1, (87): 1-24; auth, "John Henry Newman," in Victorian Prose Writers Before 1867, ed. William B. Thesing, vol. 55 of the Dictionary of Literary Biography, (Detroit: Gale Research, 87): 219-247; auth, "Bayard Taylor," in Encyclopedia of American Humorists, ed. Stephen Gale, (New York: Garland Publishing, 88): 425-27; auth, "Unitarianism," in Victorian Britain: An Encyclopedia, ed. Sally Mitchell, (New York: Garland Publishing, 89): 826-27; auth, "Newman on Toleration," in History and Humanities, ed. Francis X. Hartigan, (Reno: University of Nevada Press, 89): 253-269. **CONTACT ADDRESS** Dept of Eng, Univ of Nevada, Las Vegas, Las Vegas, NV 89154. **EMAIL** hazenj1@nevada.edu

HAZLETT, JOHN D.

PERSONAL Born 07/13/1949, IA, m, 1996, 1 child **DISCIPLINE** ENGLISH LITERATURE **EDUCATION** Coe Col, BA, 71; Univ Iowa, MA, 80; PhD, 84. **CAREER** Instr, Contra Costa Col, 83-85; Fulbright lectr, Complutense Univ of Madrid, 85-87; from asst prof to prof, Univ New Orleans, 86-; vis prof, Inst Tecnologico y de Estudios Superiores de Monterrey, 97-98; assoc dean for int studies, Univ of New Orleans Col of Liberal Arts, 99-. **HONORS AND AWARDS** Fulbright Fel, 85-. **MEMBERSHIPS** MLA, Autobiography Asn, Am Studies Asn. **RESEARCH** Travel Narrative, American Literature, Autobiography. **SELECTED PUBLICATIONS** Auth, "The Situation of American Autobiography: Generic Blurring in 'Contemporary' Historiography," Prose Studies: Hist, Theory, Criticism 13 (90): 261-277; auth, "The American Generational Autobiography: Malcolm Cowley and Michael Rossman," Prospects: An Annual J of Am Cultural Studies, ed. Jack Salzman (NY: Cambridge Univ Press, 91), 421-442; auth, "Generational Theory and Collective Autobiography," Am Lit Hist 4 (92): 77-96; rev, of "The Culture of Autobiography: Constructions of Self-Representation," ed by Robert Folkenflik, a/b: Auto/Biography Studies 9 (94): 277-285; rev, of "Versions of Deconversion: Autobiography and the Loss of Faith," by John D. Barbour, a/b: Auto/Biography Studies 11 (96): 139-143; rev, of "De/Colonizing the Subject: The Politics of Gender in Women's Autobiography," ed by Sidonie Smith and Julia Watson, a/b: Auto/Biography Studies 13 (98): 131-138. **CONTACT ADDRESS** Dept English, Univ of New Orleans, 2000 Lakeshore Dr, New Orleans, LA 70148-0001. **EMAIL** jhazlett@uno.edu

HEALEY, WILLIAM C.

PERSONAL Born 05/07/1935, Jefferson City, MO, m, 1957, 2 children **DISCIPLINE** COMMUNICATIVE DISORDERS, SPECIAL EDUCATION **EDUCATION** Univ Mo, PhD, 63. **CAREER** Ch, dept Spec Educ, Univ Nev, Las Vegas; Prof, Univ of Nevada. **HONORS AND AWARDS** Board of Regents Outstanding Faculty Member Awd; Families for Effective Autism Treatment "Outstanding Leadership and Service" Awd; Beam of Light Awd for Outstanding Service, Clark County School District; Outstanding Collaborator Awd, Gallaudet Univ, Honor Board Awd for Outstanding Lifelong Leadership, Arizona Assoc for the Gifted and Talented: President Jimmy Carter Appointee to the Commission on Mental Health; and Appointee by US Commissioner of Education, Dr. Ernest Boyer to Task Force on Basic Skills. **RESEARCH** Effective Treatments of Children with Disabilities; Basic Belief Systems of School Administrators. **SELECTED PUBLICATIONS** Auth, Monitoring and mainstreaming amplification units for the children: The need for standard practices, NSSHLA J, 18, 91; Inclusion in childhood services: Ethics and endocratic oughtness, in Hayes, L, Hayes, G, Moore, S, & Ghezzi, P, Ethics and Developmental Disabilities, Context Press, 94; What administrators want from special education teachers, CEC Today, 95; auth, Stages of Adjustment in Parents of Children with a Handicap, Journal of Defectology, Defectology Association of Yugoslavia, 98; auth, Early Intervention Programs for Children with Disabilities in Korea, International Journal of Disability, Development, and Education, 99. **CONTACT ADDRESS** Dept of Spec Educ, Univ of Nevada, Las Vegas, 4505 Maryland Pky, Las Vegas, NV 89154-3014. **EMAIL** healey@nevada.edu

HEARN, ROSEMARY

PERSONAL Born 05/01/1929, Indianapolis, IN, s **DISCIPLINE** ENGLISH **EDUCATION** Howard University, BA 1951; Indiana University, MA 1958, PhD 1973. **CAREER** Lincoln Univ, Jefferson City MO, English Prof, 58-, dir of honors program, 68-72, executive dean/acad affairs, 83-85, spec asst to pres for acad affairs, 85-87, Dean, College of Arts and Sciences, 89-, VP, Academic Affairs, 97-. **HONORS AND AWARDS** Outstanding teacher, Lincoln U, 1971; Development Proposals, Dept of HEW, district reader 1977-79; Phelps-Stokes (West Africa, 1975) NEH, grants received 1977-80; NEH, Division of Research Programs, proposal reviewer 1980-81; American Library Association, CHOICE, consultant-reviewer 1985-; Comm Serv Awd, Jefferson City United Way, 1987. **MEMBERSHIPS** Natl Assn of Teachers of English; College Language Assn; Delta Sigma Theta; Jefferson City United Way, secretary, board of directors 1983-; Missouri Community Betterment Awards Competition, judge 1983; Mo State Planning Committee, American Council on Education, Natl Identification Program, member 1983-; Planning Committee, Natl Association of State Land Grant Colleges and Universities, member 1985-; Mid-Missouri Associated Colleges & Universities, vice-chairperson executive committee mid-Missouri; mem Missouri Assn for Social Welfare; reviewer/consultant, Amer Assn of Univ Women; advisory panel, MO Council on Arts, 1987-; reviewer, Amer Library Assn; reviewer/consultant, US Dept of HEW, 1977-79; Commission, Urban Agenda, NASVLGC, 1992-; pres-elect, bd of dir, Council of Colleges of Arts and Sciences, 1997-. **CONTACT ADDRESS** Academic Affairs, Li coln Univ, Missouri, 820 Chestnut St, Jefferson City, 65102.

HEATH, WILLIAM

DISCIPLINE AMERICAN AND EUROPEAN TURE AND CREATIVE WRITING **EDUCA** Western Reserve, PhD. **CAREER** Adv, Lightc lit mag; Fulbright fel, Spain. **SELECTED P** Auth, The Children Bob Moses Led, 95; T **CONTACT ADDRESS** Dept of English,

Col and Sem, 16300 Old Emmitsburg Rd, Emmitsburg, MD 21727-7799. **EMAIL** heath@msmary.edu

HEATH, WILLIAM WEBSTER
PERSONAL Born 07/01/1929, Buffalo, NY, m, 2 children **DISCIPLINE** ENGLISH **EDUCATION** Amherst Col, BA, 51; Columbia Univ, MA, 52; Univ Wis, PhD(English), 56. **CAREER** Teaching asst , Univ Wis, 52-56; from instr to assoc prof, 56-69, PROF ENGLISH, AMHERST COL, 69-, Grants, Am Philos Soc, 67-68, 72 & Am Coun Learned Socs, 72. **MEMBERSHIPS** MLA; AAUP. **RESEARCH** Nineteenth century poetry; contemporary British literature; autobiography. **SELECTED PUBLICATIONS** Auth, Elizabeth Bowen: An Introduction to Her Novels, Univ Wis, 61; ed, Discussions of Jane Austen, Heath, 61; auth, Wordsworth and Coleridge, Clarendon, 71; Major British Poets of the Romantic Period, Macmillan, 71; The Literary Criticism of John Middleton Murry, PMLA. **CONTACT ADDRESS** Dept of English, Amherst Col, Amherst, MA 01002.

HEAVILIN, BARBARA A.
PERSONAL Born Birmingham, AL, m, 2 children **DISCIPLINE** LITERATURE **EDUCATION** Ind Wesleyan Univ, AB; Va Polytech Inst, MA; Ball State Univ, PhD. **CAREER** Engl, Taylor Univ. **HONORS AND AWARDS** Pruis Awd for Outstanding Work in Steinbeck. **MEMBERSHIPS** Midwest MLA; MLA; Ind Col Eng. **RESEARCH** Steinbeck; Women's studies; American, British, and world literatures. **SELECTED PUBLICATIONS** Auth, The Critical Response to John Steinbeck's The Grapes of Wrath, Greenwood, 00; auth, The Steinbeck Yearbook, vol 1, The Winter of our Discontent, Mellen Press, 00; articles and book reviews in South Dakota Review, Steinbeck Quarterly, and Kyusha American Literature. **CONTACT ADDRESS** Dept of Eng, Taylor Univ, Upland, 500 W Reade Ave., Reade Ctr , Upland, IN 46989-1001. **EMAIL** BRHEAVILI@tayloru.edu

HECHT, MICHAEL L.
PERSONAL Born 03/15/1949, m, 2 children **DISCIPLINE** COMMUNICATION **EDUCATION** Queens Col, BA, 71; MA, 73; Univ Ill, PhD, 76. **CAREER** Asst prof, Univ S Cal, 79-83; asst prof to prof, Ariz State Univ, 83-97; prof, PaState Univ, 97-. **HONORS AND AWARDS** Dist Schlp Awd, 89, 93, 97; Sliver Medallist Questar Awds; Article of Year Awd. **MEMBERSHIPS** SPR; ICA; NCA; ECA. **RESEARCH** Communication effectiveness; intergroup relations; culture and identity; adolescent drug prevention. **SELECTED PUBLICATIONS** Coauth, "Disclosure of sexual abuse by children and adolescents," J App Comm res 24 (96): 181-199; coauth, "Locating the voice of logic: Disclosure discourse of sexual abuse," West J Comm 61 (96): 1-13; coauth, "Ethnicity and gender similarities and differences in drug resistance," J App Comm Res 25 (97): 1-23; coauth, "Jewish American Identity," in Readings in Cultural Contexts, eds. JN Martin, TK Nakayama, Lisa A Forbes (Mountain View, CA: Mayfield, 98); ed, Communicating prejudice, Sage Pub (Newbury Park, CA), 98; coauth, Adolescent relationships and drug abuse, Erlbaum Pub (NY), 99; co-ed, The nonverbal communication reader: classical and contemporary perspectives, Waveland (Prospect Heights, IL), 99; coauth, "Ethnic and gender differences and similarities in adolescent drug use and the drug resistance process," Substance Use and Misuse 34 (99): 059-1083; coauth, "Being a Jewish mother/woman around the Christmas tree: The story of Sara," in Case studies in interpersonal communication: Process and Problems, eds. DO Braithwaite, JT Woods (Belmont, CA: Wadsworth, 00). **CONTACT ADDRESS** Dept Speech Communications, Pennsylvania State Univ, Univ Park, 234 Sparks Bldg, University Park, PA 16802-5201.

HECK, THOMAS F.
PERSONAL Born 07/10/1943, Washington, DC, m, 1968, 2 children **DISCIPLINE** MUSICOLOGY **EDUCATION** Univ Notre Dame, BA, 65; Yale Univ, PhD, 70; Univ Southern Calif, MLS, 77. **CAREER** Head, Music/Dance Lib, Ohio State Univ, 78-00; Emer Prof, 00-; asst prof, Mus Hist and Libr, Wis Conserv Mus, 77-78; Vis asst prof Mus Hist, Chapman Col, 75-76; vis asst prof mus, John Carroll Univ, 74-75; asst prof Mus Hist, Case Western Res Univ, 71-74. **HONORS AND AWARDS** Netherlands Inst Adv Stud Human and Soc Sci Fellow, 94-95; USIA Fac Exchange Fellow to the Univ Genoa, June 90; Fulbright Fellow, Italy, 85-86; Fulbright Fellow, Austria, 68-69. **MEMBERSHIPS** Am Musicol Soc; Mus Libr Asn; Inter Asn Mus Libr, Am Soc Theatre Res; Int Fed Theatre Res; Guitar Found Am. **RESEARCH** Music & Theatre History; Iconography; Commedia dell'arte; European cultural history in general; the history of the guitar. **SELECTED PUBLICATIONS** Mauro Giuliani: virtuoso guitarist and composer, Columbus, Editions Orphee, 95; The 'music information explosion' and its implications for college teachers and students, Missoula, Col Mus Soc, 92; Commedia dell'arte: a guide to the primary and secondary literature, NY, Garland, 88, xiv; The illustration of music periodicals, c.1880-1914: a question of halftones and 'whole'-tones, Fontes artis musicae 44, Dec 97, 307-330; The uses of music in Commedia performance, Theatre Symposium: A Jour Southeastern Theatre Conf, 1, 93, 7-12; The operatic Christopher Columbus: three hundred years of musical mythology, Annali d'italianistica, 10, 92, 236-278. **CONTACT ADDRESS** Ohio State Univ, Columbus, 1813 N High St, Columbus, OH 43210-3929. **EMAIL** insights@aya.yale.edu

HEDGEPETH, CHESTER MELVIN, JR.
PERSONAL Born 10/28/1937, Richmond, VA, m, 1969, 1 child **DISCIPLINE** ENGLISH **EDUCATION** Blackburn Coll, BA 1960; Wesleyan Univ, MA 1966; Harvard Univ, EdD 1977. **CAREER** Maggie Walker HS, teacher, 60-65; Macalester Coll, instr in English, 68-71; VA Union Univ, instr English, 66-68, 71-75; VA, Commonwealth Univ, coord of Afro-Amer studies, 78-; Univ of MD, dean arts & scis chmn, English & languages 83-95; African Language Project, principal investigator, 92-98. **HONORS AND AWARDS** Danforth Assoc Danforth Found 1980-86; Certificate of Merit, Goddard Space Flight Center, 1990; Distinguished Alumnus, Harvard University, 1986; Distinguished Alumnus, Blackburn College, 1992. **MEMBERSHIPS** Mem Phi Delta Kappa Harvard Chap 1976-; mem Sigma Pi Phi (Gamma Theta); mem S Atlantic Modern Lang Assn 1978-; president, VA Humanities Conf 1982-83. **SELECTED PUBLICATIONS** Author: Afro-American Perspectives in the Humanities, Collegiate Pub Co, 1980, Theories of Social Action in Black Literature, Peter Lang Pub, 1986, 20th Century African American Writers & Artists, ALA, 1991; senior editor, Maryland Review, 1986-96. **CONTACT ADDRESS** Dept English & Languages, Univ of Maryland, Eastern Shore, Princess Anne, MD 21853.

HEDGES, WILLIAM LEONARD
PERSONAL Born 02/16/1923, Arlington, MA, m, 1956 **DISCIPLINE** AMERICAN LITERATURE **EDUCATION** Haverford Col, BA, 46; Harvard Univ, PhD, 54. **CAREER** Teaching fel, Harvard Univ, 50-53; instr English, Univ Wis, 53-56; from asst prof to assoc prof, 56-67, chmn dept, 68-71, PROF ENGLISH, GOUCHER COL, 67-, CHMN AM STUDIES, 72-, Am Coun Learned Socs fel, 63-64. **MEMBERSHIPS** MLA. **RESEARCH** American Literature and intellectual history. **SELECTED PUBLICATIONS** Auth, Narrating Discovery--The Romantic Explorer in American Literature, 1790-1855, Am Lit, Vol 0066, 94. **CONTACT ADDRESS** Dept of Am Studies, Goucher Col, Towson, MD 21204.

HEDRICK, DONALD KEITH
PERSONAL Born 02/26/1947, Kansas City, MO, m, 1969, 2 children **DISCIPLINE** ENGLISH LANGUAGES AND LITERATURE **EDUCATION** Univ Kans, AB, 69; Cornell Univ, MA, 72, PhD(English), 74. **CAREER** Instr, Univ New Orleans, 73-76; ASST PROF ENGLISH, KANS STATE UNIV, 76-; Assoc, 82; Full Prof, 87. **HONORS AND AWARDS** Woodrow Wilson, 69; NEH Consortium, 80; Distinguished O'Connor Prof of Lit, Colgate Univ, 88-9; Ford Found Teaching Awd, 89; Cornell Soc for Humanities Fel, 81-2; Fulbright Teaching Awd, Charles Univ, Czech Rep, 98; Vis professorships, Amherst Col, 91; Univ Calif, Irvine, 01. **MEMBERSHIPS** MLA; Shakespeare Asn Am; Marxist Literary Group. **RESEARCH** Shakespearean drama; philosophy of language; film; critical and cultural theory. **SELECTED PUBLICATIONS** Auth, Cooking for the anthropaphagi: Jonson and his audience, Studies English Lit, spring 77; The masquing principle in Marston's The Malcontent, English Lit Renaissance, winter 78; Merry and weary conversation: textual uncertainty in As You Like It, English Lit Hist, 79; auth, "Berryman Text Dreams," in New Literary History, (81); auth, "An Enantiomorphous Hamlet," Shakespeare Quarterly, (84); co-ed, "Shakespeare Without Class: Misappropriations of Cultural Capital, St. Martin's/Palgrave, 00. **CONTACT ADDRESS** Dept of English, Kansas State Univ, Denison Hall, Manhattan, KS 66506-0701. **EMAIL** hedrick@ksu.edu

HEFFERNAN, CAROL F.
PERSONAL Born 11/17/1944, Brooklyn, NY, m, 1970, 1 child **DISCIPLINE** ENGLISH **EDUCATION** Barnard Col, AB, Univ Wis Madison, MA, 68; NY Univ, PhD, 73. **CAREER** Instr, Monmouth Col, 68-69; instr, Adelphi Univ, 69-72; instr, Nassau Community Col, 72-73; asst prof, US Merchant Marine Acad, 73-76; asst prof to prof, Rutgers Univ, 76-. **MEMBERSHIPS** New Chaucer Soc; MLA; Medieval Acad of Am. **RESEARCH** Chaucer, Middle English Romance Lit, Shakespeare. **SELECTED PUBLICATIONS** Ed, Le Bone Florence of Rome, Univ of Manchester Pr, (England), 76; auth, The Phoenix at the Fountain: Images of Woman and Eternity in Lactantius's 'Carmen de Ave Phoence' and the Old English 'Phoenix', Univ of Del Pr, (Newark), 88; auth, "The Disease of Love and Courtly Love in Chaucer's Troilus and Criseyde", Neophilogus 74, (90): 294-309; auth, The Melancholy Muse: Chaucer, Shakespeare, and Early Medicine, Duquesne Univ Pr, (Pittsburgh, PA), 95; auth, "Contraception and the Conclusion of Chaucer's Merchant's Tale", J of English and Ger Philology 94, (95): 31-41; auth, "Chaucer's Squire's Tale: The Poetics of Interlace of the 'well of English undefiled'", Chaucer Rev 32, (97): 32-45; auth, "The Medieval Tale of Florence and the East", S Asian Rev 19, (98): 1-10. **CONTACT ADDRESS** Dept English, Rutgers, The State Univ of New Jersey, Newark, 360 Dr Martin Luther King Blvd, Newark, NJ 07102-1803. **EMAIL** cfheff@andromeda.rutgers.edu

HEFFERNAN, CHARLES
DISCIPLINE MUSIC **EDUCATION** Univ Mich, BM, MM, PhD. **CAREER** Assoc prof. **HONORS AND AWARDS** Dir, Bach Soc Amherst. **SELECTED PUBLICATIONS** Auth, Choral Music: Technique and Artistry, 83; pubs on music education, vocal music, choral conducting, and aesthetics. **CONTACT ADDRESS** Music and Dance Dept, Univ of Massachusetts, Amherst, 720 Massachusetts Ave, Amherst, MA 01003.

HEFFERNAN, JAMES ANTHONY WALSH
PERSONAL Born 04/22/1939, Boston, MA, m, 1964, 2 children **DISCIPLINE** ENGLISH **EDUCATION** Georgetown Univ, AB, 60; Princeton Univ, PhD(English), 64. **CAREER** Instr English, Univ Va, 63-65; from asst prof to assoc prof, 65-76, chmn dept, 78-81, prof English, Dartmouth Col, 76-; Frederick Session Beebe prof in the art of writing, 97-. **HONORS AND AWARDS** Woodrow Wilson Fel, 60-61; Franklin Murphy Fel, 61-62; R. K. Root Fel, 62-63; Dartmouth Fac fel, 67-69; NEH Grant for Res Conf on Lit and Visual Arts, 84; dir, NEH Summer Seminar on Eng Romantic Lit and the Visual Arts, 87, 89; NEH Grant for Res Conf on the Fr Revolution, 89; NEH Fel, 91. **MEMBERSHIPS** MLA; North Am Soc for the Study of Romanticism; International James Joyce Found. **RESEARCH** English romantic poetry and painting; theory of literature and the visual arts; European Romanticism; James Joyce. **SELECTED PUBLICATIONS** Auth, Wordsworth's Theory of Poetry: The Transforming Imagination, Cornell Univ, 68; Reflections on Reflections in English Romantic Poetry and Painting, 79 & The Geometry of the Infinite: Wordsworth, Coleridge and Taylor, 82, Bucknell Rev; Writing: A College Handbook, Norton, 4th ed, 94; auth, The Re-Creation of Landscape: A Study of Wordsworth, Coleridge, Constable, and Turner, Univ Press of New Eng, 85; ed, Space, Time, Image, Sign: Essays on Literature and the Visual Arts, Peter Lang, 87; ed, Representing the French Revolution: Literature, Historiography, and Art, Univ Press of New Eng, 92; auth, Museum of Words: The Poetics of Ekphrasis from Homer to Ashbery, Univ Chicago, 93; Writing: A Concise Handbook, W.W. Norton, 96; auth, "Speaking for Pictures: The Rhetoric of Art Criticism," Word & Image, 98; coauth, Writing: A College Handbook, Norton, 00; auth, "Peter Milton's Turn: An American Printmaker Marks the Millennium," Word & Image. **CONTACT ADDRESS** Dept of English, Dartmouth Col, Hanover, NH 03755-3533. **EMAIL** jamesheff@dartmouth.edu

HEFFERNAN, MICHAEL
DISCIPLINE POETRY WRITING, CONTEMPORARY POETRY **EDUCATION** Univ Mass, PhD. **CAREER** English and Lit, Univ Ark. **SELECTED PUBLICATIONS** Auth, The Cry of Oliver Hardy, Ga, 79; To The Wreakers of Havoc, Ga, 84; The Man at Home, Ark, 88; Love's Answer, Iowa, 94; The Back Road to Arcadia, Poobeg, 94. **CONTACT ADDRESS** Univ of Arkansas, Fayetteville, Fayetteville, AR 72701.

HEFFERNAN, WILLIAM A.
PERSONAL Born 11/21/1937, Floral PK, NY, d, 3 children **DISCIPLINE** ENGLISH **EDUCATION** BA, 59, MA, 61, St. John's Univ; Fordham Univ, PhD, 70. **CAREER** Assoc Prof, 70-71, Immaculate Heart Col; Prof, 73-, Saddleback Col. **HONORS AND AWARDS** Fulbright, 72, Fulbright 89. **SELECTED PUBLICATIONS** Auth, Honda Dream, PSEUD Liam Patrick Galbraith. **CONTACT ADDRESS** Dept of Eng, Saddleback Col, 28000 Marguerite Pky, Mission Viejo, CA 92692. **EMAIL** bheffernan@saddleback.cc.ca.us

HEFLIN, RUTH J.
PERSONAL Born 06/19/1963, Pratt, KS, m, 1989, 1 child **DISCIPLINE** ENGLISH **EDUCATION** Kansas State Univ, BA, 85; MA, 88; Okla State Univ, PhD, 97. **CAREER** TA to lectr, Kansas State Univ, 86-89; adj prof, Univ of Kansas, 89; adj prof, William Jewell Col, 90-91; lectr, Kansas City Kansas Community Col, 90-92; adj prof, Univ of Miss, 90-92; teaching assoc to lectr, Okla State Univ, 92-98; asst prof, Kansas City Kansas Community Col, 98-. **HONORS AND AWARDS** Teaching Commendation, Okla State Univ, 95; Meritorious Serv as Honors Fac, Kansas City Kansas Community Col, 99; Distinguished mem of Honors Fac, 99. **MEMBERSHIPS** W Lit Assoc; MLA. **RESEARCH** American cultures: American Indian, Asian American, African American, especially. **SELECTED PUBLICATIONS** Auth, I Remain Alive: The Sioux Literary Renaissance, Syracuse Univ Pr, 00; auth, "Black Elk Passes on the Power of the Earth" in the Black Elk Reader, Syracuse Univ Pr, 00. **CONTACT ADDRESS** Dept Humanities, Kansas City Kansas Comm Col, 1234 Kiowa St, Leavenworth, KS 66048. **EMAIL** hefruth@toto.net

HEGEL, ROBERT E.
PERSONAL Born 01/09/1943, MI, m, 1974, 4 children **DISCIPLINE** LITERATURE **EDUCATION** Mich State Univ, BA, 65; Columbia Univ, MA, 67; PhD, 73. **CAREER** Asst prof, Case W Res Univ, 72-74; from asst prof to prof, Wash Univ St Louis, 75-. **HONORS AND AWARDS** Fac Mentor Awd, Wash Univ, 00; le prix Stanislas Julien of the Academie des Inscriptions et Belles-Lettres, Inst de France, 00. **MEMBERSHIPS** Asn for Asian Studies. **RESEARCH** Chinese narrative and literature, print culture in late Imperial China, representations of violence in writing and on the stage. **SELECTED PUBLICATIONS** Auth, The Novel in Seventeenth-Century China, Columbia Univ Press, 81; auth, "Traditional Chinese Fiction: The State of the Field," J of Asian Studies 53.2 (94); auth, Reading Illustrated Fiction in Late Imperial China, Stanford Univ Press, 98. **CONTACT ADDRESS** Dept Asian &

Near Eastern Lang, Washington Univ, 1 Brookings Dr, CB 1111, Saint Louis, MO 63130-4899. **EMAIL** rhegel@artsci.wustl.edu

HEIDENREICH, ROSMARIN
DISCIPLINE GERMAN AND ENGLISH LITERATURE **EDUCATION** Moorehead State Univ, BA, 64; Univ Man, MA, 66; Univ Toronto, PhD, 83. **CAREER** Prof, Schiller Univ, Ger, 68-69; prof, Univ Tubingen, Ger, 69; prof, Univ Freiburg, Ger, 69-74; Prof English & Translation, St. Boniface Col, Univ Manitoba, 93-. **HONORS AND AWARDS** Can Coun Doctoral Fel, 76-79. **MEMBERSHIPS** Can Asn Comp Lit; Can Asn Transl Studs. **SELECTED PUBLICATIONS** Auth, The Post-war Novel in Canada: Narrative Patterns and Reader Response, 89; auth, Recent Trends in Franco-Manitoban Fiction and Poetry, in Prairie Fire, 11, 90; auth, Causer l'amour dans le Far-West du Canada, in Poetiques de la Francophonie, 96. **CONTACT ADDRESS** Dept of English, St. Boniface Col, Winnipeg, MB, Canada R2H 0H7. **EMAIL** rheidenr@ustboniface.mb.ca

HEIDT, EDWARD RAYMOND
PERSONAL Born 10/20/1946, Rochester, NY, s **DISCIPLINE** ENGLISH **EDUCATION** St John Fisher Col, BA, 69; SUNY Brockport, MSc, 72; Toronto Sch Theol, MDiv, 75; Univ S Calif, PhD, 89. **CAREER** St Mark's Col, 89-92; session lectr, Univ Sask, 92-. **MEMBERSHIPS** CCCC; NCTE; MLA. **RESEARCH** Non-fiction; autobiography. **SELECTED PUBLICATIONS** Auth, Vision Voiced: Narrative in Autobiographical Writing, Peter Lang, 91; auth, The Image of the Church Minister in Lit, Edwin Mellon Pr, 94; auth, A Rhetoric for a Formation of Intention, 96. **CONTACT ADDRESS** 1411 Egbert St, Apt 207, Saskatoon, SK, Canada S7N 2L8. **EMAIL** heidt@duke.usask.ca

HEILBRUN, CAROLYN G.
PERSONAL Born East Orange, NJ, 3 children **DISCIPLINE** ENGLISH LITERATURE **EDUCATION** Wellesley Col, BA, 47; Columbia Univ, MA, 51, PhD(English), 59. **CAREER** Instr English, Brooklyn Col, 59-60; from instr to assoc prof, 60-72, PROF ENGLISH, COLUMBIA UNIV, 72-, Vis lectr, Union Theol Sem, 68-70; Swarthmore Col, 70-71; Guggenheim fel, 70-71; ed bd, Twentieth Century Lit, 72- & Signs, 74-; Radcliffe Inst fel, 76-; Rockefeller Found fel humanities, 76-77; mem exec coun, MLA, 76-79; vis prof, Princeton Univ, 82. **MEMBERSHIPS** MLA; Auth Guild; Auth League Am; PEN. **RESEARCH** Modern British literature, 1800-1950; English novel; biography; women. **SELECTED PUBLICATIONS** Auth, Is Biography Fiction, Soundings, Vol 0076, 93. **CONTACT ADDRESS** Dept of English, Columbia Univ, Philosophy Hall, New York, NY 10027.

HEILMAN, ROBERT BECHTOLD
PERSONAL Born 07/18/1906, Philadelphia, PA, m, 1935, 1 child **DISCIPLINE** ENGLISH LITERATURE **EDUCATION** Lafayette Col, AB, 27; Ohio State Univ, AM, 30; Harvard Univ, AM, 31, PhD, 35. **CAREER** Teaching fel, Tufts Col, 27-28; instr English, Ohio Univ, 28-30, Univ Maine, 31-33, 34-35; from instr to prof, La State univ, 35-48; prof English, Univ Wash, 48-76, chmn dept, 48-71; Arnold Prof, Whitman Col, 77., Bk Reviewer, Key Reporter, 59-; Guggenheim fel, 64-65, 75-76; SAtlantic Grad Educ lectr, 71; Nat Endowment for Humanities sr fel, 71-72; vis scholar, Univ Ala, Birmingham, 78-**HONORS AND AWARDS** Ariz Quart Best Essay Prize, 56; Explicator Bk Prize, 57; Longview Essay Awd, 60; NCTE distinguished lectr, 68; dlitt, lafayette col, 67; lld, grinnell col, 71; lhd, kenyon col, 73; dhum, whitman col, 77. **MEMBERSHIPS** MLA; NCTE; Philol Asn Pac Coast; Int Asn Univ Prof English; Shakespeare Asn Am. **RESEARCH** Criticism of drama; criticism of novel; history of English novel. **SELECTED PUBLICATIONS** Auth, The Southern Connection, LSU, 85; auth, The Workings of Fiction, 91; auth, We Scholars--Changing the Culture of the University, Am Scholar, Vol 0066, 97; The Fading Smile--Poets in Boston, From Robert Frost to Robert Lowell to Sylvia Plath, 1955-1960, Am Scholar, Vol 0065, 96; auth, The Professor and the Profession, Mo, 99. **CONTACT ADDRESS** Dept of English, Univ of Washington, Seattle, WA 98195.

HEIMAN, LAWRENCE FREDERICK
PERSONAL Born 08/24/1917, Decatur, IN **DISCIPLINE** CHURCH MUSIC **EDUCATION** Cath Univ Am, MA, 49; Pontifical Inst Sacred Music, Rome, LCG, 58, MCG, 59, DS Mus, 70. **CAREER** Prof Emeritus Music & Dir Emeritus Rensselaer Prog Church Music & Liturgy, St Joseph's Col, IN, 44. **HONORS AND AWARDS** Papal Gold Medal res for doctoral dissertation, 70; Nat Merit Awd, Nat Cath Music Educr Asn, 72; President's Fel, St Joseph's Col; Doctor of Letters, honoris causa, St. Joseph's Col, 96. **MEMBERSHIPS** Int Consociatio Sacred Music; N Am Acad Liturgy; Nat Asn Pastoral Musicians. **SELECTED PUBLICATIONS** Auth, The Rhythmic Value of the Final Descending Note After a Puncture in Codex 239 of Library of Laon, Etudes Gregoriennes, 72. **CONTACT ADDRESS** Saint Joseph's Col, Indiana, PO Box 815, Rensselaer, IN 47978-0815. **EMAIL** lheiman@saintjoe.net

HEIN, ROLLAND NEAL
PERSONAL Born 09/12/1932, Cedar Rapids, IA, m, 1954, 2 children **DISCIPLINE** ENGLISH, THEOLOGY **EDUCATION** Wheaton Col, BA, 54; Grace Theol Sem, BD, 57; Purdue Univ, PhD, 71. **CAREER** Assoc prof English, Bethel Col, Minn, 62-70; from Assoc Prof to Prof English, 70-97, Fac Emeritus, Wheaton Col, Ill, 97-. **MEMBERSHIPS** MLA. **RESEARCH** Life and writings of George MacDonald, 1824-1905. **SELECTED PUBLICATIONS** Auth, A biblical view of the novel, Christianity Today, 1/73; Lilith: theology through mythopoeia, Christian Scholar's Rev, 74; ed, Life Essential: The Hope of the Gospel, 74, Creation in Christ: The Unspoken sermons of George MacDonald, 76 & George MacDonald's World: An Anthology from the Novels, 78, H Shaw; The Harmony Within 1982; Sunrise, 89; George MacDonald: Victorian Mythmaker, 93; G.K. Chesterton: Myth, Paradox, and the Commonplace, Seven: An Anglo-Am J, 96; Lilith: A Variorum Edition, Johannesen, 97; Christian Mythmakers, Cornerstone, 98. **CONTACT ADDRESS** Dept of English, Wheaton Col, Illinois, 501 College Ave, Wheaton, IL 60187. **EMAIL** RollandNHein@Wheaton.edu

HEINEMAN, HELEN
PERSONAL Born 08/01/1936, Queens Village, NY, m, 1961, 4 children **DISCIPLINE** ENGLISH LITERATURE **EDUCATION** Queens Col, BA, 58; Columbia Univ, MA, 59; Cornell Univ, PhD, 67 **CAREER** Prof, Framingham St Col; pres, Framingham St Col, 99-. **HONORS AND AWARDS** Phi Bega Kappa; Woodrow Wilson Fel; Amer Assoc Univ Women Fel; Bunting Inst; Radcliffe Col Fel **RESEARCH** Victorian Literature **SELECTED PUBLICATIONS** Three Victorians in the New World: Dickens, Trollope and Mrs. Trollope In America, Lang, 90; Restless Angels: the Friendship of Six Victorian Women, Ohio Univ Pr, 84; Francees Trollope, GK Hall, 84 **CONTACT ADDRESS** Framingham State Col, 100 State, Framingham, MA 01701. **EMAIL** hheineman@frc.mass.edu

HEISE, URSULA K.
PERSONAL Born, Germany **DISCIPLINE** CONTEMPORARY LITERATURE, LITERARY THEORY, ECOCRITICISM, LITERATURE AND SCIENCE **EDUCATION** Univ Cologne, BA 81,82; Univ Calif, MA, 85; Univ Cologne, MA, 87; Stanford Univ, PhD, 93. **CAREER** English and Lit, Columbia Univ; assoc prof, English & comparative literature, Columbia Univ. **MEMBERSHIPS** MLA, SLS, ASLE, ACLA. **SELECTED PUBLICATIONS** Auth, Chronoschisms: Time, Narrative, Postmodernism; Cambridge Univ Press, 97. **CONTACT ADDRESS** Dept of English & Comparative Literature, Columbia Univ, 1150 Amsderdam Ave, MC 4938, New York, NY 10027-6902. **EMAIL** ukh2@columbia.edu

HEISSER, DAVID C. R.
PERSONAL Born 10/22/1942, Charleston, SC **DISCIPLINE** HISTORY, LIBRARY SCIENCE **EDUCATION** Col of Charleston, BS, 64; Univ NC, Chapel Hill, MA, 67, PhD, 72; Columbia Univ, MS, 75. **CAREER** Assoc prof, Head of Reference, Tufts Univ Library, 78-89; assoc prof & Government Documents Librarian, Univ Miami, 89-92; asst prof & Walterboro Librarian, Univ SC, Salkehatchie, 92-95; Asst Prof & Reference/Documents Librarian, The Citadel, 95-. **HONORS AND AWARDS** Fulbright fel; Woodrow Wilson fel; res grant, Cushwa Center for the Study of American Catholicism. **MEMBERSHIPS** Am Library Asn; Special Libraries Asn; SC Library Asn; SC Hist Soc; Am Cath Hist Asn. **RESEARCH** Government information; hist of SC; emblematica & symbolism. **SELECTED PUBLICATIONS** Auth, Marketing US Government Depository Libraries, Government Pubs Rev 13, 86; with Peter Hernon, GPO Regional Depositories, The Reference Librarian 32, 91; South Carolina's Mace and Its Heritage, House of Representatives of SC, 91; The State Seal of South Carolina: A Short History, SC Dept of Archives and Hist, 92; Warrior Queen of Ocean: The Story of Charleston and Its Seal, SC Hist Mag 93, 92; Jean Mayer: A Bibliography, 1948-1993, Tufts Univ Library, 98; Bishop Lynch's Civil War Pamphlet on Slavery, Cath Hist Rev 84, 98; Federal Depository Program at the Crossroads: The Library Administrator's Perspective, Government Information Quart 16, 99. **CONTACT ADDRESS** Daniel Library, The Citadel, The Military Col of So Carolina, Charleston, SC 29409. **EMAIL** David.Heisser@Citadel.edu

HEITZMANN, WILLIAM RAY
PERSONAL Born 02/12/1948, Hoboken, NJ, d, 2 children **DISCIPLINE** WRITING **EDUCATION** Villanova Univ, BS; Univ Chicago, MAT; Univ Del, PhD. **CAREER** Univ Chicago Lab High Sch; DuSable High Sch; North Chicago High Sch; Highland Falls High Sch; Villanova Univ; adj prof, Thomas Jefferson Univ. **HONORS AND AWARDS** Ford Found Scholar, Univ Chicago; NDEA Scholar, Calif State Univ at San Jose; NSF Scholar, Northwestern Univ; Teaching Awd (Honorable Mention), Univ Del; Grad Sch Scholar, Univ Chicago; Grad Sch Scholar, Calif State Univ at San Jose; Grad Sch Scholar, Northwestern Univ; Grad Sch Scholar, Univ Del; Harry A. Carman Awd, Middle States Coun for the Soc Studies; listed in Who's Who in America, Who's Who in Am Education, International Authors and Writers Who's Who, Contemporary Authors, Something About the Author, Community Leaders of America, and Men of Achievement; MSCSS Gold Medal; Outstanding Alumnus Awd, Univ Del; Outstanding Sci Awd, Nat Coun for the Soc Studies. **SELECTED PUBLICATIONS** Auth, Careers for Sports Nuts and Other Athletic Types, NTC/Contemporary Group; auth, Opportunities in Marine and Maritime Careers, NTC/Contemporary Group; auth, Opportunities in Sports and Athletics, NTC/Contemporary Group; auth, Opportunities in Sports Medicine, NTC/Contemporary Group; auth, Super Study Skills for Success 3rd Revision, Villanova Inst; auth, American Jewish Political Behavior: History and Analysis, R and E Res Associates; auth, 50 Political Cartoons for Teaching U.S. History, Villanova Inst. **CONTACT ADDRESS** Dept Educ, Villanova Univ, Villanova, PA 19085. **EMAIL** ray.heitzman@villanova.edu

HELD, DENNIS
PERSONAL Born 04/19/1958, Milwaukee, WI, s **DISCIPLINE** LITERATURE **EDUCATION** The Evergreen State Col, BA, 88; Univ Mont, MFA, 91. **CAREER** Asst prof, Lewis-Clark State Col, 93-. **HONORS AND AWARDS** Fuller Poetry Prize, 88; Martin Luther King, Jr. Essay Awd, 89; Acad of Am Poets Prize, 90. **MEMBERSHIPS** Assoc Writing Programs. **RESEARCH** Mark Twain, Sherwood Anderson, Contemporary Poetry. **SELECTED PUBLICATIONS** Auth of many works appearing in Poetry Magazine, Alaska Quarterly Review, Poets and Writers Magazine; Auth, Betting On the Night, Lost Horse Press (Spokane, WA), forthcoming. **CONTACT ADDRESS** Dept Lang & Lit, Lewis-Clark State Col, 500 8th Ave, Lewiston, ID 83501-2691. **EMAIL** dheld@lcsc

HELD, DIRK
PERSONAL Born 03/24/1939, New York, NY, m, 1962, 2 children **DISCIPLINE** CLASSICS **EDUCATION** Brown **CAREER** Instr Classics and Inst for Lib Arts, Emory Univ, 68-71; asst prof to prof of Classics, Conn Col, 71-; NEH fel for Interrelations Sci and Hum, 74-75. **HONORS AND AWARDS** Univ fel philos, Univ Penn, 66-67; NEH fel for Interrelations Sci and Hum, 74-75. **MEMBERSHIPS** Am Philol Asn; Soc Ancient Greek Philos; Int Soc Classical Tradition. **RESEARCH** Greek philosophy; Classical tradition 18th-19th Century. **SELECTED PUBLICATIONS** Auth Why Individuals didn't exist in classical Antiquity, N Eng Classical Newsl & Jour, 91; Megalopsychia in Nicomachean Ethics IV, Ancient Philos, 93; Bernard Williams Shame and Necessity, Int Jour Philos Stud, 95; Shaping Eurocentrism: The Uses of Greek Antiquity, Greeks and Barbarians: Essays on the Interactions between Greeks and Non-Greeks in Antiquity and the Consequences of Eurocentrism, CDL Press, 97; Plato and Aristotle on Memory, Knowledge and the Self, Memory, History and Critique, European Identity at the Millenium, Proceedings of the Fifth Conference of the International Society for the Study of European Ideas, Utrecht, 98. **CONTACT ADDRESS** Classics Dept, Connecticut Col, 270 Mohegan Ave, New London, CT 06320. **EMAIL** dthel@conncoll.edu

HELD, GEORGE
PERSONAL Born 01/28/1935, White Plains, NY **DISCIPLINE** ENGLISH & AMERICAN LITERATURE **EDUCATION** Brown Univ, AB, 58; Univ Hawaii, AM, 62; Rutgers Univ, PhD, 67. **CAREER** Instr English, Kamehameha Schs, 58-64; teaching asst, Rutgers Univ, 65-67; lectr, 67-68, asst prof English, 68-83, Assoc Prof, Queens Col, NY, 83-; Fulbright lectr, Univ Bratislava, 73-74; Fulbright lectr, Charles Univ, Prague, Czech, 74-76; co-ed, The Ledge Poetry Magazine, 91-. **HONORS AND AWARDS** A Directory of American Poets & Fiction Writers, 95-; Who's Who in America, 99; Winner of the 99 Talent House Press Poetry Chapbook Contest, 99. **MEMBERSHIPS** ALSC **RESEARCH** Poetry. **SELECTED PUBLICATIONS** Auth, Men on the moon: American novelists explore lunar space, Mich Quart Rev, spring 79; Heart to heart with nature: Ways of looking at A White Heron, Colby Libr Quart, 3/82; Conrad's Oxymoronic Imagination in The Secret Agent, Conradiana, 85; Brother Poets: The Relationship Between George and Edward Herbert, in Like Season'd Timber: Essays on George Herbert, Peter Lang, 87; In Defense of Homage to Catalonia, CN Rev, Dec/Jan 95-96; Poems in Commonweal, Confrontation, the fromalist, Modern Haiku, & dozens of other journals, 90-; Winged: Poems, Birnham Wood Graphics, 95; auth, My Night with Dasha (short story), Ignite, Dec 97; auth, Salamander Love & Others: Poems, Talent House Press, 98; auth, Open and Shut: Cinquains, Talent House Press, 99; auth, Beyond Renewal: Poems, Cedar Hill Publications, 00. **CONTACT ADDRESS** Dept of English, Queens Col, CUNY, 6530 Kissena Blvd, Flushing, NY 11367-1597. **EMAIL** geoheld7@aol.com

HELDMAN, JAMES M.
PERSONAL Born 07/15/1930, Durham, NC, m, 1952, 1 child **DISCIPLINE** ENGLISH **EDUCATION** Univ NC, BA, 56, MA, 58, PhD, 67. **CAREER** Instr English, Roanoke Col, 58-60, Univ Del, 64-66; asst prof, Univ Mo-Columbia, 66-72; chmn dept, 72-79, prof English, Western Ky Univ, 79- **MEMBERSHIPS** SAtlantic Mod Lang Asn. **RESEARCH** Victorian and British novel; Victorian prose and poetry; Edwardian novel. **SELECTED PUBLICATIONS** Auth, The last Victorian novel: technique and theme in Parade's End, Twentieth Century Lit, 72. **CONTACT ADDRESS** Dept of English, Western Kentucky Univ, 1 Big Red Way St, Bowling Green, KY 42101-3576.

HELDRETH, LEONARD GUY
PERSONAL Born 04/08/1939, Shinnston, WV, m, 1964, 2 children **DISCIPLINE** ENGLISH & AMERICAN LITERATURE& FILM **EDUCATION** WVa Univ, BS, 62, MA, 64; Univ Ill, PhD, 73. **CAREER** Abstract writer, NCTE/ERIC, 68-70; from instr to prof English, Northern Univ Mich, 70-; head, dept English, Northern Mich Univ, 88-91, 92-98; interim dean, Sch Arts & Sci, Northern Mich Univ, 91-92; assoc dean, Col Arts & Sci, Northern Mich Univ, 94-99; asst Vpres Undergrad Affairs, 98-00; interim assoc vpres, academic administration & planning, Northern Mich Univ, 99-00; provost, academic affairs, Northern Mich Univ, 00-. **HONORS AND AWARDS** English Dept fac merit award, 83, 87; Northern Mich Univ distinguished fac award, 87; bd mem, Mich Hum Coun, 89-93. **MEMBERSHIPS** Int Asn for Fantastic in the Arts; Am Cult Asn; Popular Cult Asn; Popular Cult Asn South. **RESEARCH** Film study; fantasy and science fiction. **SELECTED PUBLICATIONS** Auth, Films, Film Fantasies, and Fantasies: Spinning Reality from the Self in Kiss of the Spider Woman, J of the Fantastic in the Arts, 94; auth, Festering in Thebes: Elements of Tragedy and Myth in Cronenberg's Films, Post Script, 95; art, To Yokaichi and Beyond: part 1: The Yokaichi Experience; Getting to Know You, Marquette Monthly, 95; art, To Yokaichi and Beyond, part 2 Death, Life and Hiroshima Pizza, Marquette Monthly, 95; art, Architecture, Duality, and Personality: Mis-en-scene and Boundaries in Tim Burton's Films, Trajectories of the Fantastic, Greenwood, 97; auth, Anatomy of a Murder; From Fact to Fiction to Film, A Sense of Place, Northern Michigan, 97; auth, Memories! You're Talkin' About Memories! Retrofitting Blade Runner, Popular Pr, 98; co-ed, The Blood is the life: Vampires in Lit, Popular Pr, 99; guest ed, "Vampires in Film and Television," J of Popular Film and Television, summer 99. **CONTACT ADDRESS** Assoc Provost for Academic Affairs, No Michigan Univ, 1401 Presque Isle Ave, Marquette, MI 49855-5301. **EMAIL** lheldret@nmu.edu

HELDRICH, PHILIP J.
PERSONAL Born 11/06/1965, Chicago, IL, m, 1 child **DISCIPLINE** ENGLISH LITERATURE **EDUCATION** Univ Calif, San Diego, BA, 88; Kans State Univ, MA, 93; Okla State Univ, PhD, 97. **CAREER** Asst prof, Emporia State Univ, 97-. **HONORS AND AWARDS** First Place, Kans State Univ Awd in Fiction, 93; Edward Jones Studies Awd, Okla State Univ, 95; Paul Klemp Renaissance Studies Awd, Okla State Univ, 96; Janemarie Luecke Mem Prize for Poetry, Okla State Univ, 96; Clinton Keeler Fel, Okla State Univ, 96; Distinguished Grad Fel, Okla State Univ Found, 96; Clinton Keeler Fel for Outstanding Doctoral Student in English, Okla State Univ, 97; Honorable mention, Karamu Short Fiction Contest, 97; Honorable mention, New York Stories Int Fiction Contest, 98; Emporia State Univ Summer OOE Creativity Grant, 99; Semi-finalist, Col of the Redwoods Aleutian Goose Festival Poetry Awd, 99; First Place, Coun on Nat Lits Fiction Awd, 98; Herman M. Swafford Fiction Awd, Best Journal of the Year, 99; X. J,. Kennedy Poetry Prize, 99. **MEMBERSHIPS** Am Culture Asn, SW Am & Popular Culture Asns, Modern Lang Asn, Assoc Writing Progs. **RESEARCH** Twentieth century literature; American studies; Great Plains studies. **SELECTED PUBLICATIONS** Auth, "My Greatest Fear," Oasis 7.3 (99): 42-26; auth, "Reconciliation," Oasis 7.3 (99): 39-41; auth, "Everybody's Indian," Potpourri 10.4 (99): 6-10, reprinted in Potpourri: Tenth Anniversary Issue 11.1 (99): 74-78; auth, "Demolition," La Lit 16.2 (99): 46; auth, "Bread," North Am Rev 285.2 (2000): 20-23; auth, Good Friday, Huntsville: Tex Rev Press (forthcoming); auth, " 'Going to Indian Territory': Attitudes toward Native American s in Little House on the Prairie," Great Plains Quart (forthcoming); auth, "Re-Mapping the Spaces of Regionalism: An Expanded Definition," Kansas English (forthcoming); auth, "William Stafford's Mythopoetic Kansas," Midwest Quart (forthcoming); auth, "Connecting Surfaces: Gertrude Stein's Three Lives, Cubism, and the Metonymy of the Short Story Cycle," Studies in Short Fiction (forthcoming); coauth with Peter Donahue, "Soft Coal: The Sadness and Poetic Vision of Robert Hazel, " The Southern Quart, Special Issue: An American Romantic: Perspectives on Robert Hazel, (forthcoming); auth, "The Day I Became Jimmy Carter," Birmingham Poetry Rev (forthcoming); auth, "The Art of Throwing Snowballs," Birmingham Poetry Rev (forthcoming); auth, "Deep in the Interior," From Our Front Porch: New Western Poems of Kansas, Topeka: Woodley Memorial Press (forthcoming). **CONTACT ADDRESS** Dept English, Emporia State Univ, 1200 Commercial St, Emporia, KS 66801-5057. **EMAIL** Heldricp@emporia.edu

HELFAND, JODY
PERSONAL Born 04/22/1972, New York, NY **DISCIPLINE** ENGLISH **EDUCATION** Univ Haw, BA, 94. **CAREER** Instr, Chaminade Univ, 95-97; prof, Haw Pacific Univ, 99-; instr, Windward Community Col, 99-. **HONORS AND AWARDS** Phi Beta Kappa; Clark Awd. **MEMBERSHIPS** MLA. **RESEARCH** Gender Studies/Women Studies/Transsexual Studies. **SELECTED PUBLICATIONS** Auth, "The Food I Eat," Public Voices (97); auth, "Something is Lost," Rain Bird, (99); auth, "An Extension Of," "Foureen," and "Live As A Boy," Bamboo Ridge Pr, (99); auth, "The Day I Almost Lost Myself," "What Comes With An Attraction Between Cousins," Bamboo Ridge Pr, (00); auth, "How A Body Survives," Tinfish, (01); auth, "The Nature of Insects," Rio Grande Rev, (01); auth, "Her Taste," Illuminations, (01); auth, "Among The Stones Of Fire," Shades of December, (01). **CONTACT ADDRESS** Windward Community Col, 45 - 720 Keaahala Rd, Kaneohe, HI 96744. **EMAIL** jhrose22@hotmail.com

HELFAND, MICHAEL S.
PERSONAL Born 03/20/1942, New York, NY, m, 1965, 1 child **DISCIPLINE** VICTORIAN & MODERN ENGLISH LITERATURE **EDUCATION** Univ Va, BA, 64; Univ Iowa, PhD, 70. **CAREER** Asst prof English, 70-76, assoc prof English, Univ of Pittsburgh, 76-, Dir Grad Studies, 96-. **HONORS AND AWARDS** Fulbright Lectr Am Studies, China, 85-87, S Korea, 90-91. **MEMBERSHIPS** Northeast MLA. **RESEARCH** Modern fiction; victorian studies. **SELECTED PUBLICATIONS** Auth, Dickens at large, 1/72 & Architects of the self, 1/74, Novel: Forum on Fiction; Hemingway, a champ can't retire, Lost Generation J, 76; T H Huxley's Evolution and Ethics, Victorian Studies, 77; coauth, Anarchy and culture, Tex Studies Lit & Lang, 78; contribr, Victorian Poetry, yearly; coauth and co-ed, Oscar Wilde's Oxford Notebooks, Oxford Univ Press, 89. **CONTACT ADDRESS** Dept of English, Univ of Pittsburgh, 526 Cathedral/Learn, Pittsburgh, PA 15260-2504. **EMAIL** msh@pitt.edu

HELGERSON, RICHARD
PERSONAL Born Pasadena, CA, m, 1967, 1 child **DISCIPLINE** ENGLISH & COMP LIT **EDUCATION** Johns Hopkins Univ, PhD, 70. **CAREER** Prof, Eng, Univ Calif, Santa Barbara, Dept Chair 89-93. **HONORS AND AWARDS** Woodrow Wilson Fellowship, 63-63; NEH Fellowship, 79-80; 98-99; Huntington Library Fellowship, 84-85; Guggenheim Fellowship, 86; Folger Library Fellowship, 93-94; James Russell Lowell Prize, 94; British Council Prize in the Humanities 94; UCSB Faculty Research Lecturer 98; VC President's Fellowship 98-99. **MEMBERSHIPS** Modern Language Association; Renaissance Society of America, International Spenser Society; Shakespeare Association of America; North American Conference on British Studies. **RESEARCH** Early mod Europ drama and paint; Renaissance lit and cult. **SELECTED PUBLICATIONS** Auth, The Elizabethan Prodigals, Univ Calif Press, 77; Self-Crowned Laureates: Spenser, Jonson, Milton, and the Literary System, Univ Calif Press, 83; Tasso on Spenser: The Politics of Chivalric Romance, Yrbk Eng Stud, 88; "Writing Against Writing: Humanism and the Form of Coke's Institutes," Mod Lang Quart, 92; "Camoes, Hakluyt, and the Voyages of Two Nations," Cult and Colonial, 92; Forms of Nationhood, Univ Chicago Press, 92; Doing Literary History on a Large Scale, Eng Stud and Hist, 94; auth Adulterous Alliances: Home, State, and History in Early Modern European Drama and Painting, Univ Chicago Press, 00. **CONTACT ADDRESS** Dept of Eng, Univ of California, Santa Barbara, Santa Barbara, CA 93106-7150. **EMAIL** rhelgers@humanitas.ucsb.edu

HELLE, ANITA
DISCIPLINE ENGLISH EDUCATION **EDUCATION** Univ Puget Sound, BA, 70, MA, 72; Univ Ore, PhD, 86. **CAREER** Engl, Oregon St Univ. **SELECTED PUBLICATIONS** Auth, Reading Women's Autobiographies and Reconstructing Knowledge, Narrative and Dialogue in Education, Tchrs Col Press, 91; Reading the Rhetoric of Curriculum Transformation, NWSA Jour, 94; William Stafford: On the Poet, His vocation, and Cultural Literacy, NCTE, 94. **CONTACT ADDRESS** Oregon State Univ, Corvallis, OR 97331-4501. **EMAIL** ahelle@orst.edu

HELLEGERS, DESIREE
DISCIPLINE SIXTEENTH- AND SEVENTEENTH-CENTURY ENGLISH LITERATURE **EDUCATION** Univ Wash, PhD **CAREER** Asst prof, Washington State Univ. **RESEARCH** Literature and science, women writers, environmental issues in literature. **CONTACT ADDRESS** Dept of English, Washington State Univ, 1 SE Stadium Way, PO Box 645020, Pullman, WA 99164-5020. **EMAIL** hellegers@vancouver.wsu.edu

HELLENBRAND, HAROLD
DISCIPLINE EARLY AMERICAN LITERATURE, WORLD LITERATURES **EDUCATION** Stanford Univ, PhD. **CAREER** Prof, Dean, Col Liberal Arts, Univ Minn, Duluth. **SELECTED PUBLICATIONS** Auth, The Unfinished Revolution: Education and Politics in the Thought of Thomas Jefferson, Univ Del Press, 89. **CONTACT ADDRESS** Dept of Eng, California Polytech State Univ, San Luis Obispo, San Luis Obispo, CA 93433. **EMAIL** hhellenb@calpoly.edu

HELLER, DANA
DISCIPLINE AMERICAN LITERATURE **EDUCATION** MFA, PhD. **CAREER** Assoc Prof, Dir Institute; Engl, Old Dominion Univ. **RESEARCH** Gender Studies. **SELECTED PUBLICATIONS** Areas: Cross Purposes: Lesbians, Feminists, and the Limits of Alliance; Family Plots: The De-oedipalization of Popular Culture; The Feminization of Quest-Romance: Radical Departures. **CONTACT ADDRESS** Director Institute BAL, Old Dominion Univ, 4100 Powhatan Ave 4100 Powhatan Ave, Rm 432, Norfolk, VA 23529. **EMAIL** dheller@odu.edu

HELLER, DEBORAH
PERSONAL Born 07/08/1939, New York, NY, d, 2 children **DISCIPLINE** ENGLISH **EDUCATION** Cornell Univ, BA, 60; Harvard Univ, MA, 63; PhD, 70. **CAREER** Teaching fel, Harvard Univ, 62-69; vis asst prof to assoc prof, York Univ, 72-. **HONORS AND AWARDS** Phi Kappa Phi; NY State Scholar, 56-60; DAAD Fel, 60-61; Woodrow Wilson Nat Fel, 61-62; Fel, Harvard Univ, 63-67. **RESEARCH** Comparative literature, especially 19th and 20th century English and European (French, Italian, German) literature and writing by women. **SELECTED PUBLICATIONS** Co-ed, Jewish Presences in English Literature, Queen's Univ Press, 90; auth, "History, Art, and Fiction in Anna Banti's Artemisia," Contemporary Women Writers in Italy: A Modern Renaissance, (Univ Mass Press, 90), 45-61; auth, "Getting Loose: Women and Narration in Alice Munro's Friend of My Youth," Essays on Can Writing, (98): 60-81; auth, "Tragedy, Sisterhood and Revenge in Corinne," in Nineteenth Century Literature Criticism, (Gale Group, 01), 314-322. **CONTACT ADDRESS** Dept Humanities, York Univ, 4700 Keele St, 627 Atkinson Col, Toronto, ON, Canada M3J 1P3. **EMAIL** dheller@yorku.ca

HELLER, JANET
PERSONAL Born 07/08/1949, Milwaukee, WI, m, 1982 **DISCIPLINE** ENGLISH, LITERATURE, LINGUISTICS, CREATIVE WRITING, WOMEN'S STUDIES **EDUCATION** Oberlin Col, 67-70; Univ Wis at Madison, BA, 71; MA, 73; Univ Chicago, PhD, 87. **CAREER** Ed, Primavera, 73-92; coord of the Writing Prog, Univ of Chicago, 76-81; instr, Northern Ill Univ, 82-88; asst prof, Nazareth Col, 89-90; asst prof, Grand Valley State Univ, 90-97; asst prof, Albion Col, 98; asst prof, Western Mich Univ, 99-. **HONORS AND AWARDS** Winner, Friends of Poetry Contest, Kalamazoo, 89; listed in Directory of Am Poets & Fiction Writers, 79-. **MEMBERSHIPS** MLA, Mich Col English Asn, Soc for the Study of Midwestern Lit. **RESEARCH** Nineteenth-Century British Literature, Contemporary American Poetry, Prose Non-fiction, the Drama, Linguistics Applied to Literature, Women's Studies (Women Writers, Literature & Social Sciences, American Literature Since 1800). **SELECTED PUBLICATIONS** Auth, Coleridge, Lamb, Hazlitt, and the Reader of Drama, 90; articles have appeared in Poetics, Concerning Poetry, Lan and Style, Theatre J, Shakespeare Bulletin, The Eighteenth Century, PBSA, Libr Quart, Twentieth Century Lit, and others; poetry has appeared in Anima, Cottonwood, Organic Gardening, Ky Poetry Rev, Earth's Daughters, Lilith, Modern Maturity, and others. **CONTACT ADDRESS** Dept English, Western Michigan Univ, 1201 Oliver St, Kalamazoo, MI 49008-3804. **EMAIL** janet.heller@wmich.edu

HELLER, LEE ELLEN
DISCIPLINE ENGLISH **EDUCATION** Scripps Col, BA, 80; Brandeis Univ, MA, 82, PhD, 88. **CAREER** Asst prof, Eng, Mercer; current, Educ Consult. **MEMBERSHIPS** Am Antiquarian Soc; MLA; Western Asn of Col Admis Counselors (WACAC). **SELECTED PUBLICATIONS** Auth, "Cultural Criticism in the Classroom: Authority and Transcendent Truth after Poststructuralism," in College Literature, 90; auth, "Frankenstein and the Cultural Uses of Gothic," in Frankenstein: A Case Study in Contemporary Criticism, Bedford Books/St. Martin's Press, 91 & 92; auth, Instructor's Manual, Vol 1, Prentice-Hall Anthology of American Literature, 91; auth, "Recovering the Victorian Periodical," Nineteenth-Century Prose 20, 93; auth, "Conceiving the 'New' American Literature," Early Am Lit 29, 94. **CONTACT ADDRESS** Hamilton & Assocs Educ Consultants, PO Box 50724, Santa Barbara, CA 93150. **EMAIL** leeheller@worldnet.att.net

HELLER, TERRY L.
PERSONAL Born Geneseo, IL, m, 1969, 1 child **DISCIPLINE** ENGLISH **EDUCATION** North Cent Col, AB, 69; Univ Chicago, AM, 70; PhD, 73. **CAREER** Vis asst prof, Univ Mo, 73-74; lecturer, Univ of Turin, Italy, 74-75; asst prof to prof, Coe Col, 75-. **HONORS AND AWARDS** Assoc Col of the Midwest Newberry Library Fac Fel, 98; NEH Sem, 95; Coe Summer Res Grant, 89; Young Alumnus Merit Awd, 86; Coe Summer Res Grant, 83; Best Book Review Awd, 86. **MEMBERSHIPS** Mod Lang Asn of Am, Midwest Mod Lang Asn, Sci Fict Res Asn, Am Asn of Univ Prof. **RESEARCH** American fiction, fantasy and horror literature and film. **SELECTED PUBLICATIONS** Auth, The Delights of Terror: An Aesthetics of the Tale of Terror, Univ of Ill Press, 87; auth, Henry James's 'The Turn of the Screw': Bewildered Vision, Twayne, 89; ed, The Country of the Pointed Firs and Other Fiction, Oxford Univ Press, 96; ed, Tales of New England, Coe Review press, 97; ed, The King of Folly Island, Coe Review Press, 98; ed, The Sarah Orne Jewett Text Project, 97. **CONTACT ADDRESS** Dept English, Coe Col, 1220 1st Ave NE, Cedar Rapids, IA 52402-5008.

HELLINGER, BENJAMIN
PERSONAL Born 11/11/1933, Brooklyn, NY, m, 1969, 2 children **DISCIPLINE** ENGLISH LITERATURE **EDUCATION** Brooklyn Col, BA, 55, NYork Univ, MA, 57, PhD, 69. **CAREER** Lectr Eng, Lehman Col, 65-68; asst prof, 69-73, assoc prof eng, John Jay Col Criminal Justice, 74. **RESEARCH** Eighteenth century Eng lit; hist of criticism. **SELECTED PUB-**

LICATIONS Auth, The Editing of Jeremy Collier's Short View of the Immorality and Profaneness of the English Stage, Papers Bibliog Soc Am, 73; Jeremy Collier's courage: A dissenting view, Yearbk English Studies, 75; Jeremy Collier's false and imperfect citations, Restoration & 17th Century Theatre Res, 11/75. **CONTACT ADDRESS** Dept of Eng, John Jay Col of Criminal Justice, CUNY, 445 W 59th St, New York, NY 10019-1104.

HELLMANN, JOHN M.
PERSONAL Born 02/14/1948, Louisville, KY, m, 1968, 1 child **DISCIPLINE** ENGLISH **EDUCATION** Univ Louisville, BA, 70; MA, 73; Kent State Univ, PhD, 77. **CAREER** Prof of English, The Ohio State Univ at Lima. **HONORS AND AWARDS** Senior Fulbright Lectureships: Belgium 1985 and Germany, 92-93; Am Council of Learned Societies (ACLS), 82-83. **MEMBERSHIPS** Society for Cinema Studies. **RESEARCH** Post-1945 American Studies. **SELECTED PUBLICATIONS** Auth, The Kennedy Obsession: The American Myth of JFK, Columbia UP, 97; auth, Fables of Fact: The New Journalism as New Fiction, U of Illinois, P, 81; auth, American Myth and Legacy of Vietnam, Columbia UP, 86. **CONTACT ADDRESS** Dept Humanities, Ohio State Univ, Lima, 4240 Campus Dr, Lima, OH 45804-3576. **EMAIL** hellmann.1@osu.edu

HELLWIG, HAL
PERSONAL Born 11/19/1950, Salamanca, NY, m, 1988, 2 children **DISCIPLINE** ENGLISH LITERATURE **EDUCATION** UCLA, PhD, 85. **CAREER** Assoc prof; asst ch, Dept of Eng/Philos, 92-94; fac senate ch, 95-96; general ed, Idaho State Univ Accreditation Report, 94. **MEMBERSHIPS** Modern Lang Asn, NCTE. **RESEARCH** Am lit and computer applications in lit and in composition; Mark Twain. **SELECTED PUBLICATIONS** Auth, pubs on composition studies, graduate programs in English, Seventeenth century English literature, computational linguistics, and business communications. **CONTACT ADDRESS** Dept of English and Philosophy, Idaho State Univ, Pocatello, ID 83209. **EMAIL** hellharo@isu.edu

HELM, JAMES JOEL
PERSONAL Born 12/17/1937, Chicago, IL, m, 1960, 2 children **DISCIPLINE** CLASSICAL STUDIES **EDUCATION** Elmhurst Col, BA, 59; Union Theol Sem, MDiv, 63; Univ Mich, Ann Arbor, MA, 65, PhD(class studies), 68. **CAREER** Instr class studies, Univ Mich, Ann Arbor, 66-68; asst prof, 68-74, chmn dept, 76-82, 90-96, Assoc Prof Classics, Oberlin Col, 74-82, Prof 82-, Vis assoc prof classics, Scripps Col, 78-79; assoc dean, Oberlin Col, 86-89, Actg Dean, 91-92, 96-. **MEMBERSHIPS** Am Philol Asn; Archaeol Inst Am; Class Asn Mid West & South. **RESEARCH** Greek paleography; computer applications in classical studies; poetry of Catullus. **SELECTED PUBLICATIONS** Auth, Koros--From Satisfaction to Greed, Classical World, Vol 0087, 93. **CONTACT ADDRESS** Dept of Classics, Oberlin Col, 135 W Lorain St, Oberlin, OH 44074-1076. **EMAIL** james.helm@oberlin.edu

HELM, THOMAS EUGENE
PERSONAL Born 01/20/1943, Hammond, IN, m, 1966, 1 child **DISCIPLINE** RELIGION & LITERATURE **EDUCATION** Earlham Col, AB, 65; Havard Univ, STB, 68; Univ Chicago, AM, 72, PhD, 77. **CAREER** Asst prof, 74-80, assoc prof, 80-86, Prof Relig Studies, Western Ill Univ, 86-, dir Univ Honors, 98-, Res Coun grant, Western Ill Univ, 78; jr fel, Inst Med & Renaissance Studies, 79. **MEMBERSHIPS** Am Acad Relig; Midwest Am Acad Relig; Renaissance Soc; Soc Values Higher Educ. **RESEARCH** Renaissance and reformation studies; rhetoric. **SELECTED PUBLICATIONS** Auth, The warp of piety, the woof of politics: American civil religion, Perkins J, spring 78; Enchantment and the banality of evil, Relig Life, spring 80; The Christian Religion, Prentice Hall, 91. **CONTACT ADDRESS** Dept of Philos & Relig Studies, Western Illinois Univ, 1 University Cir, Macomb, IL 61455-1390. **EMAIL** te-helm@wiu.edu

HELMERS, MARGUERITE H.
PERSONAL Born 10/03/1961, Milwaukee, WI, m, 1987, 2 children **DISCIPLINE** ENGLISH **EDUCATION** Univ Wis, BA, 83; MA, 87; PhD, 92. **CAREER** Assoc prof, Univ of Wis, 92-01. **HONORS AND AWARDS** Outstanding Diss Awd, 93; Distinguished Teaching Awd, 98; Fel, Centre for 20th Century Studies, 99. **MEMBERSHIPS** MLA, NCTE, Rhetoric Soc of Am, Coun of Writing Program Admin. **RESEARCH** Rhetoric, visual arts, travel writing, literary criticism. **SELECTED PUBLICATIONS** Auth, Writing Students: Composition Testimonials and Representations of Students, SUNY Pr, 95; auth, "Foregrounding Ethical Awareness in Composition and English Studies," Heinemann, (98); auth, Dictionary of Literary Biography, British Travel Writers, 1910-1939, Bruccoli, Clark, Layman, 98; auth, Kitchen Cooks, Plate Twirlers, and Troubadours: Writing Program Administrators Tell Their Stories, Heinemann, 99; auth, Media, Discourse, and the Public Sphere, College English 63.4, 01. **CONTACT ADDRESS** Univ of Wisconsin, Oshkosh, 800 Algoma Blvd, Oshkosh, WI 54901. **EMAIL** helmers@uwosh.edu

HELMS, RANDEL
PERSONAL Born 11/16/1942, Montgomery, AL, m, 1985 **DISCIPLINE** ENGLISH **EDUCATION** Univ Calif, BA, 64; Univ Wash, PhD, 68. **CAREER** Asst Prof, UCLA, 68-76; Prof, Ariz State Univ, 76-. **RESEARCH** Bible literature; English Romanticism. **SELECTED PUBLICATIONS** Auth, Who Wrote the Gospels?, Millennium, 97. **CONTACT ADDRESS** Dept English, Arizona State Univ, Box 0202, Tempe, AZ 85287-0302. **EMAIL** www.Randel.Helms@asu.edu

HELSTERN, LINDA LIZUT
PERSONAL Born 08/21/1948, Philadelphia, PA, m, 1977, 1 child **DISCIPLINE** LITERATURE **EDUCATION** Hamline Univ, BA, 70; Univ NMex, MA, 95; Southern Ill Univ Carbondale, PhD, 01. **CAREER** Proj asst, Am Diabetes Assoc, 74-75; youth coordinator, Nat Multiple Schlerosis Soc, 75-76; commun mgr, Trans Union systems Corp, 76-77; proj dev, Shawnee Health Serv & Dev Corp, 77-79; corp dev asst, pub info specialist, asst to dean, S Ill Univ Carbondale, 82-. **HONORS AND AWARDS** Hon Mention, Bay Guardian Poetry Competition, 94; Fel, Vallecitos Retreat/Witter Bynner Found, 94; Hon Mention, Borderlands/Tex Poetry Rev, 95; AEGIS Awd, 98; Alan M Cohn Awd, Southern Ill Univ Carbondale, 98; Runner up, J Golden Taylor Awd, 97, 00. **MEMBERSHIPS** Assoc for the Study of Am Indian Lit, Assoc for the Study of Lit and the Environ, MLA, Western Lit Assoc, Hemingway Soc, Coun for Advan and Serv to Educ. **RESEARCH** Twentieth-Century Native/American literature, Twentieth-Centry Caribbean literature. **SELECTED PUBLICATIONS** Auth, "Indians, Woodcraft, and the Construction of White Masculinity: The Boyhood of Nick Adams," Hemingway Rev 20.1: 61-78; auth, ""'Nightland' and the Mythic West," SAIL 10.2: 61-78; auth, "Blue Smoke and Mirrors: Griever's Buddhist Heart," SAIL 9.1: 33-47; auth, "Gerald Vizenor: An Annotated Bibliography of Criticism," SAIL 11.1: 30-80; auth, "The Man Who Killed the Deer: Stories Within Stories," Studies in Frank Waters 20: 73-87; auth, "Gerald Vizenor's 'Griever: An American Monkey King in China': A Cross-Cultural Re-Membering," Loosening the Seams: Interpretations of Gerald Vizenor, ed A Robert Lee, (Bowling Green: Popular Pr, 00): 136-154; auth, "Sycorax Video Style: Kamau Brathwaite's Middle Passages," African Images: Recent Studies in Text and Cinema, (Trenton: Africa World Pr, 00): 139-52 **CONTACT ADDRESS** 289 Egret Lake Rd, Carbondale, IL 62901-8232. **EMAIL** helstern@engr.siu.edu

HELZLE, MARTIN
PERSONAL Born 08/17/1961, Stuttgart, Germany, m, 1987, 3 children **DISCIPLINE** CLASSICS **EDUCATION** Univ of Leeds, BA, 83; Univ of Cambridge, PhD, 88. **CAREER** Univ of Bristol, 80-87; Univ Wales, 87-88; Cleveland State Univ, 89, part time; John Carroll Univ, 89, part time; asst prof, 89-95; assoc prof, 96-, Case Western Reserve Univ. **HONORS AND AWARDS** Jopson research fel; RIG from State of Ohio; Humboldt Fel. **MEMBERSHIPS** APA; CAMWS; OCC; Mommsengesellschaft. **RESEARCH** Latin Poetry **SELECTED PUBLICATIONS** Auth, P Ouidii Nasonis Epistualarum ex Ponto liber IV: A commentary on Poems 1-7 and 16, 89; auth, Die Charakterisierung Scipios in Silius Italicus' Classica et Mediaevalia, 95; auth, Der Stil ist der Mensch, Redner und Reden im romischen Epos, 96. **CONTACT ADDRESS** Dept of Classics, Case Western Reserve Univ, 10900 Euclid Ave, Cleveland, OH 44106-7111. **EMAIL** mxh13@po.cwru.edu

HEMMINGER, WILLIAM
DISCIPLINE ENGLISH LITERATURE **EDUCATION** Ohio Univ, PhD. **CAREER** Fulbright prof, Madagascar. **SELECTED PUBLICATIONS** Auth, A Friend of the Family; articles on African lit. **CONTACT ADDRESS** Dept of Eng, Univ of Evansville, 1800 Lincoln Ave, Evansville, IN 47714. **EMAIL** bh35@evansville.edu.

HEMMINGWAY, BEULAH S.
PERSONAL Born 03/11/1943, Clarksdale, MS, m **DISCIPLINE** ENGLISH **EDUCATION** Coahoma Jr Coll, 1962; Alcorn State Univ, BS 1964; NC Central Univ, MA 1965; FL State Univ, PhD 1981. **CAREER** Southern University, teacher, 65-66; Voorhees College, teacher, 66-67; Benedict College, teacher, 67-72; Florida A&M University, associate professor, language & literature, beginning 1972, professor, currently. **HONORS AND AWARDS** Florida A&M University, Teacher of the Year, 1987-88, Meritorious Service Awd, 15-19 years, 1988; Teaching Incentive Awd Program (TIP), Winner, 1993. **MEMBERSHIPS** Natl Council of Teachers of English; College Language Association; FL College, English Teachers, Undergrad Council for the College of Arts & Science 1982-; Role & Scope Committee 1976; Library Resource Comm 1977; Curriculum Comm for Lang & Lit; Southern Association of Colleges & Schools Editing Committee; Homecoming Committee 1983; chairperson Poetry Festival 1975-82; advisor Lambda Iota Tau 1975-82; search comm for vp academic affairs FL A&M Univ 1982; Coll Level Acad Skills Test Task Force; reader for scoring state-wide essays holistically; board of directors LeMoyne Art Foundation 1980-82; Mothers March of Dimes 1982-; vice pres Natl Council of Negro Women 1982-; Jack & Jill of America 1979-81; prog chairperson 112th anniv Bethel Baptist Church; Tallahassee Urban League; NAACP; panelist FL Division of Cultural Affairs 1986; American Popular Culture Assn 1988; Drifters Inc 1989. **SELECTED PUBLICATIONS** Author, publications include: "Critics Assessment of Faulkners Black Characters FL A&M Univ" 1978; "A Comparative Pilot Study by Sex & Race of the Use of Slang" Soc for Gen Syst Rsch 1978; "Abyss-Gwendolyn Brooks Women" FL A&M Univ Bulletin; read paper 45th Annual Convention of Coll Lang Assoc 1985 "Can Computer Managed Grammar Make a Difference That Makes a Difference?"; Author Chapter 4, "Through the Prism of Africanity: A Preliminary Investigation of Zora Neale Hurston's Mules and Men," presented paper at American Popular Culture Assn 1989; "Through the Prism of Africanity," Zora in Florida, 1991; seminar: "Black Women Writers," 1983; workshop: "Teaching English Composition," Bay County English Teachers, Panama City, Florida; numerous other publications. **CONTACT ADDRESS** Dept of English, Florida A&M Univ, Tallahassee, FL 32307.

HENCH, MICHAEL
PERSONAL Born 05/14/1939, Chicago, IL, m, 3 children **DISCIPLINE** ENGLISH **EDUCATION** Univ Mass, Amherst, MA, PhD, 69. **CAREER** Asst prof, Thiel Col, Greenville, Pa, 86-88; Sr lect, Curry Col, 88-. **HONORS AND AWARDS** Jessie Neal Awd for Outstanding Journalism, 62; teaching dozens of different courses, 64-; coord, English, Univ of the Virgin Islands, 69-76; Secretary, Caribbean Col English Asn; many papers delivered. **RESEARCH** Learning motivation, moral education. **SELECTED PUBLICATIONS** Coauth with Jim Li, A Different Universe, Australian Children's Television Workshop; coauth with Jim Li, A Heart and Mind for Wanting to Learn (in press). **CONTACT ADDRESS** Dept Humanities, Curry Col, 1071 Blue Hill Ave, Milton, MA 02186-2302. **EMAIL** docmikeh@aol.com

HENDERSON, CAROL E.
PERSONAL Born 11/13/1964, Los Angeles, CA, 1 child **DISCIPLINE** ENGLISH **EDUCATION** Univ Calif, BA, 86; Calif State Univ, MA, 91; Univ Calif, PhD, 95. **CAREER** Teach asst, Univ Calif, 92; instr, Victor Val Col, 93-94; instr, Calif St, 94; teach assoc, Univ Calif, 94-95; asst prof, Univ Del, 95-. **HONORS AND AWARDS** Human Res Assistantship, Univ Cal, 92, 93; Grad Fee Fel, 91; Excel in Teach Awd, Outs New Fac, 96; Rebecca Diaz-West End Asn Schp, Kristine M. Scarano Schp, 92; Washington-Lincoln Alumni Schp, 90. **MEMBERSHIPS** MLA, CLA, PCA, ASA, Mid Atl Writers Asn, 19th C Women Writers Gp. **RESEARCH** African American Literature, American Literature from a Multi-cultural perspective, Women's Studies. **SELECTED PUBLICATIONS** Auth, "Boderlands: The Critical Matrix of Caste, Class, and Color in "Incidents in the Life of A Slave Girl," Legacy: A J of Am Women Writers 16 (99); auth, "Knee Bent, Body Bowed: (Re)Memory's Prayer of Spiritual Re(new)al," in Baldwin's "Go Tell It On The Mountain," Rel and Lit (95); rev, "The Sermon and the African American Literary Imagination," by Dolan Hubbard (95); rev, "Race, Modenity, Post modernity: A Look at the History of the Literatures of Peoples of Color since the 1960s," by W. Lawrence Hogue, Mod Fict Stud (98); rev, "Granny Midwives and Black Women Writers: Double-Dutched Readings" by Valerie Lee, Mod Fict Stud 45 (99); rev, "Places of Silence, Journeys of Freedom: The Fiction of Paule Marshall" by Eugenia C. DeLamotte, Mod Fict Stud (99); auth, "The Walking Wounded: Rethinking Black Women's Identity" in Ann Petry's "The Street," Mod Fict Stud 46 (00); auth, "Freedom to Self-Create: Identity and the Politics of Movement in Contemporary African American Fiction," Mod Fict Stud 46 (00); auth, "Bell Hooks," Dict of Lit Biog, 20th Cen Cult Theorists, ed, Paul Hansom (01). **CONTACT ADDRESS** Eng Dept, Univ of Delaware, 212 Memorial Hall, Newark, DE 19716. **EMAIL** ceh@udel.edu

HENDERSON, CHARLES, JR.
PERSONAL Born 08/22/1923, Lynchburg, VA, m, 1944, 5 children **DISCIPLINE** CLASSICS **EDUCATION** Davidson Col, AB, 42; UNC Chapel, MA, 46; PhD, 50. **CAREER** Instr, NYU, 50-55; asst prof, assoc prof, dean, UNC Chapel, 55-62; prof, asst pres, emeritus, Smith Col, 64-. **HONORS AND AWARDS** Fulbright, 53; Phi Beta Kappa, 42. **MEMBERSHIPS** APA; CANE; MAA. **RESEARCH** Ancient rhetoric; Latin literature. **SELECTED PUBLICATIONS** Co-auth, Latin for Americans, Macmillan, 68; McGraw Hill, 90; ed, Classical, Mediaeval and Renaissance Studies in honor of B. L. Ullman, Edizioni di Storia a Letteratura, 63; asst ed, Humanities in the South, 58-61; auth, "Cato's Pine Cone," TAPhA 86 (55): 256-67; auth, "The Career of the Younger Marcus Aemilius Scaurus," CJ 53 (58): 194-206; auth, "Quorum Parva Fui," TAPhA 130 (00). **CONTACT ADDRESS** 2 Dabney Lane, York Harbor, ME 03911. **EMAIL** chmn@cybertours.com

HENDERSON, JEFFREY
PERSONAL Born 06/21/1946, Montclair, NJ, m, 1996 **DISCIPLINE** CLASSICS **EDUCATION** Kenyon Col, BA, 68; Harvard Univ, MA, 70, PhD, 72. **CAREER** Asst prof, 72-78, Yale Univ; assoc prof, 78-82, Univ Mich; prof, 82-91, USC; prof, chmn, 91-, Boston Univ. **HONORS AND AWARDS** LHD, Kenyon Col, 94; Guggenheim fel, 97-98. **MEMBERSHIPS** APA; Asn of Literary Scholars & Critics. **RESEARCH** Greek lit, esp. drama; textual criticism. **SELECTED PUBLICATIONS** Auth, The Maculate Muse: Obscene Language in Attic

Comedy, Yale Univ Press, 75, Oxford Univ Press, 90; auth, Aristophanes: Essays in Interpretation, contr ed, Yale Classical Studies XXVI, Cambridge Univ Press, 80; ed with intro and commentary, Aristophanes Lysistrara, Clarendon Press, 87, 90; ed and transl, Aristophanes, Loeb Class Lib, Harvard Univ Press, 98. **CONTACT ADDRESS** Dept of Classical Studies, Boston Univ, 745 Commonwealth Ave, Boston, MA 02215. **EMAIL** jhenders@bu.edu

HENDERSON, JUDITH RICE
PERSONAL Born 09/24/1945, Bartlesville, OK, m, 1976, 3 children **DISCIPLINE** ENGLISH LITERATURE **EDUCATION** Univ Colo, BA, 67, BS, 67; Ind Univ, PhD(English lit), 74. **CAREER** Lectr, 71-74, from asst prof to prof, Univ Sask 74-, Can Coun res fel English, 75-76. **MEMBERSHIPS** MLA; Renaissance Soc Am; Int Soc Hist Rhet; Can Soc Renaissance Studies; Asn Can Univ Teachers English. **RESEARCH** Renaissance literature; stylistics; rhetoric. **SELECTED PUBLICATIONS** Auth, On Reading the Rhetoric of the Renaissance Letter, Renaissance-Rhetorik/Renaissance Rhetoric, ed. Heinrich F. Plett, (Berlin and NY: Walter de Gruyter, 93): 143-62; auth, Thomas Wilson (1523 or 1524 - 20 May 1581), Sixteenth Century British Nondramatic Writers, First Series, ed. David A. Richardson, Dictionary of Literary Biography 132, (Detroit: Gale Research, 93): 340-45; auth, Vain Affectations: Bacon on Ciceronianism in The Advancement of Learning, English Literary Renaissance 25, (95): 209-34; auth, Must a Good Orator Be a Good Man? Ramus in the Ciceronian Controversy, Rhetorica Movet: Studies in Historical and Modern Rhetoric in Honour of Heinrich F. Plett, ed. Peter L. Oesterreich and Thomas O. Sloane, Leiden: Brill, (99): 43-56; auth, John Heywood's The Spider and the File: Educating Queen and Country, Studies in Philology 96, (99): 241-74; auth, Angel Day (fl. 1583-99), British Rhetoricians and Logicians 1500-1660, First Series, ed. Edward A. Malone, Dictionary of Literary Biography, (Columbia, SC: Bruccoli Clark Layman); auth, Humanism and the Humanities: Erasmus' Opus de conscribendis epistolis in Sixteenth-Century Schools, Letter-Writing Manuals from Antiquity to the Present, ed. Carol Poster and Linda Mitchell (Columbia: U of South Carolina P). **CONTACT ADDRESS** Dept of English, Univ of Saskatchewan, 320 Arts Tower, 9 Campus Dr., Saskatoon, SK, Canada S7N 5A5. **EMAIL** hendrsnj@duke.usask.ca

HENDRIX, JERRY
DISCIPLINE COMMUNICATION **EDUCATION** Tex A&M-Commerce, BA; Univ Okla, MA; La State Univ, PhD. **CAREER** Asst prof, Univ Southwest La; Instr, Westmar Col, Le Mars, Iowa; Prof, Am Univ. **SELECTED PUBLICATIONS** Areas: public relations case studies, public speaking. **CONTACT ADDRESS** American Univ, 4400 Massachusetts Ave, Washington, DC 20016.

HENDRYX-BEDALOV, P.
PERSONAL Born 07/09/1955, Milwaukee, WI, d, 2 children **DISCIPLINE** COMMUNICATION DISORDERS **EDUCATION** Univ Wis Milwaukee, BS, 77; MS, 79; Northwestern Univ, PhD, 87. **CAREER** Assoc prof, Eastern Wash Univ, 94-. **MEMBERSHIPS** Am Speech-Lang-Hearing Assoc; Coun For Exceptional Children. **RESEARCH** Caregiving Relationships and Communication: Alzheimer, Speech and Language, Problems in Children. **SELECTED PUBLICATIONS** Coauth, "Diagnosis and treatment strategies for the latent sequelae of head trauma in children", J of Cognitive Rehab 3 (95): 8-12; auth, "Bridging a Gap Between Clinicians and Researchers", Treatment Res in Commun Disorders - Spec Interest Group Newsletter 1 (97): 3-5; auth, "Clinician-researcher: Bridge, Gap or Gully", Communique 3, (97); auth, "Assessment and intervention strategies for the latent sequelae of head trauma in children", Hearsay J of the Ohio Speech and Hearing Assoc 12 (98): 1; auth, "Ethnography: An introduction to method and application", J of Children's Commun Develop 20, (98): 1; auth, "Effects of caregiver communication on the outcome of requests in spouses with dementia of the Alzheimer type", Int J of Aging and Human Develop 49, (99): 127-149. **CONTACT ADDRESS** Commun Disorders, Eastern Washington Univ, 526 5th St, Cheney, WA 99004-1619. **EMAIL** pbedalov@ewu.edu

HENGEN, SHANNON
DISCIPLINE ENGLISH LITERATURE **EDUCATION** Univ Iowa, PhD. **RESEARCH** Canadian women's dramatic comedy; Margaret Atwood literature. **SELECTED PUBLICATIONS** auth, Whisper tangerine, Sudbury, ON: Laurentian Univ Press, (91): 143; auth, Margaret Atwood's power: mirrors, reflections and images in select fiction and poetry, Toronto, ON: Second Story Press, (93): 174; co-ed, Margaret Atwood's Power: Mirrors, Reflections and Images in Selected Fiction and Poetry, 93; auth, Approaches to Teaching Atwood's The Handmaid's Tale and Other Works, 94; auth, Theatre du Nouvel-Ontario and Francophone Culture in Sudbury, Ontario, Canada, Am Rev Can Studies, 91; art, 'your father the thunder / your mother the rain': Lacan and Atwood, Lit And Psychol, 86; coauth, Approaches to teachng Atwood's The Handmid's Tale and other works, New York, NY: Modern Language Asn of America, (96): 215. **CONTACT ADDRESS** English Dept, Laurentian Univ, 935 Ramsey Lake Rd, Sudbury, ON, Canada P3E 2C6. **EMAIL** shengen@nickel.laurentian.ca

HENIGHAN, THOMAS J.
PERSONAL Born 10/15/1934, New York, NY **DISCIPLINE** ENGLISH **EDUCATION** Columbia Univ, 56-57; Durham Univ, MLitt, 63; Univ Newcastle-upon-Tyne, PhD, 77. **CAREER** U.S. Foreign Ser, 59-61; instr, Central Mich Univ, 63-65; lectr to asst prof, 65-69, ASSOC PROF ENGLISH, CARLETON UNIV, 69-. **HONORS AND AWARDS** Can Coun fel, 69-70, grant, 83; Ont Arts Coun grants, 70, 72; Can Fedn Hum grant, 81. **SELECTED PUBLICATIONS** Auth, Natural Space in Literature, 82; auth, The Presumption of Culture, 96; auth, Ideas of North: A Guide to Canadian Arts and Culture, 97; contribur, Ottawa Rev, 76-79; ed/contribur, Brave New Universe, 80. **CONTACT ADDRESS** Dept of English, Carleton Univ, 1125 Colonel By Dr, Ottawa, ON, Canada K1S 5B6. **EMAIL** thomas_henighan@carleton.ca

HENNEDY, JOHN FRANCIS
PERSONAL Born 05/31/1936, Braintree, MA, m, 1963, 6 children **DISCIPLINE** ENGLISH **EDUCATION** Univ Notre Dame, BA, 58; Boston Univ, MA, 61; Univ Ill, Urbana, PhD(-English), 65. **CAREER** Asst prof English, 65-71, ASSOC PROF ENGLISH, PROVIDENCE COL, 71- **MEMBERSHIPS** MLA. **RESEARCH** Shakespeare; English Renaissance drama; 18th century. **SELECTED PUBLICATIONS** Auth, Launcelot Gobbo and Shylock's forced conversion, Tex Studies Lit & Lang, fall 73. **CONTACT ADDRESS** Dept of English, Providence Col, 549 River Ave, Providence, RI 02918-0002.

HENNESSY, MICHAEL
PERSONAL Born 03/09/1949, Yakima, WA, m, 1974, 4 children **DISCIPLINE** ENGLISH **EDUCATION** Marquette Univ, PhD. **CAREER** Univ of Memphis; Southwest Tex State Univ. **RESEARCH** Modern British Literature; Composition and Rhetoric. **SELECTED PUBLICATIONS** Coauth, The Borzoi Handbook for Writers; The Borzoi Practice Book for Writers; The Random House Practice Book; auth, articles and reviews on Auden, Tomlinson, Hughes, and other 20th century poets. **CONTACT ADDRESS** Southwest Texas State Univ, 601 University Dr, San Marcos, TX 78666-4604. **EMAIL** hennessy@swt.edu

HENSLEY, CARL WAYNE
PERSONAL Born 02/25/1936, Bristol, VA **DISCIPLINE** SPEECH COMMUNICATION **EDUCATION** Milligan Col, BA, 58; Christian Theol Sem, MDiv, 63; Butler Univ, MA, 66; Univ MN, PhD, 72. **CAREER** Minister, Christian Church, IN, 58-66; prof preaching, MN Bible Col, 66-73; aux prof, Bethel Theol Sem, 72-78; prof & chmn dept commun, Bethel Col, 73-, Consult, 77, mediator, 86. **MEMBERSHIPS** Speech Commun Asn; Int Asn Bus Communicators; Relig Speech Commun Asn; Cent States Speech Asn; Disciples of Christ Hist Soc. **RESEARCH** Hist and criticism of public address; intellectual hist of Am relig movement; 19th century revivalism; conflict mgmt. **SELECTED PUBLICATIONS** Auth, Harry S Truman: Fundamental Americanism in foreign policy speechmaking, Southern Speech Commun J, 75; Rhetorical vision and the Persuasion of a historical movement, Quart J of Speech, 75; Alexander Campbell and the second coming of Christ: A footnote to history, Discipliana, 76; Illustration: The sermonic workhorse, New Pulpit Digest, 77; That board meeting at Corinth, Princeton Sem Bull, 79; Rhetoric and reality in the Restoration movement, Mission J, 82. **CONTACT ADDRESS** Dept of Communication, Bethel Col, Minnesota, 3900 Bethel Dr, Saint Paul, MN 55112-6999. **EMAIL** w-hensly@bethel.edu

HERBECK, DALE A.
PERSONAL Born 06/14/1958, Chicago, IL, m, 1997 **DISCIPLINE** COMMUNICATION **EDUCATION** Augustana Col, BA, 80; Univ Iowa, MA, 82; PhD, 88. **CAREER** Asst Prof and Dir of Forensics, Boston Col, 85-91; Assoc Prof and Dir of Forensics, Boston Col, 91-94; Assoc Prof, Boston Col, 94-98; Assoc Prof and Chair, 98-. **HONORS AND AWARDS** Past President's Awd, Eastern Communication Assoc, 95; Service Awd, Am Debate Assoc, 94; Robert M. O'Neil Awd for Excellence in Research on Freedom of Expression, 93; Rev. John A. Trzaszka, S.J., Awd for Student Development, 89; Midwest Forensic Asn Research Awd, 87; Phi Beta Kappa; Omicron Delta Kappa; Mortar Board; Delta Sigma Rho-Tau Kappa Alpha. **MEMBERSHIPS** American Communication Assoc, 94, American Forensic Assoc, 82, Assoc for Education in Journalism and Mass Communication, 88, Central States Speech Assoc, 82, Eastern Communication Assoc, 87, International Communicatin Assoc, 96, National Communication Assoc, 82, Commission on Freedom of Expression, 97-00. **RESEARCH** Argument and debate, communication law, freedom of expression. **SELECTED PUBLICATIONS** Auth, Free Speech Yearbook, Cabondale: Southern Illinois Univ Press, 93; auth, Free Speech Yearbook, Carbondale: Southern Illinois Univ Press, 94; auth, Free Speech Yearbook, Carbondale: Southern Illinois Univ Press, 95; auth, Freedom of Speech in the United States, ed Thomas L. Tedford and Dale A. Herbeck (State College, PA: Strata, forthcoming in Spring of 2001); auth, "Presidential Debates as political Rituals: Clinton vs. Bush vs. Perot," in Clinton on Stump, State, and Stage: The Rhetorical Road to the White House, ed. Stephen A. Smith (Fayetteville, AR: Univ of Arkansas Press, 94), 249-72; auth, "Democratic Delusions: The Town Meeting in an Electronic Age, " in The Death of Discourse in a Wired World, ed. Rita Whillock and David Slayden (Thousand Oaks, CA: 98), 43-63; auth, "Cubby or Stratton Oakmont?: Defamatory Speech on Computer Bulletin Boards," forthcoming in Real Law Virtual Space: Communication Regulation in Cyberspace, ed. Susan Drucker and Gary Gumpert (Cresskill, NJ: Hampton, 99), 293-312; auth, "The Death of the Fan: Strikes, Consumers, and the Business of Baseball," Take Me Out to the Ballgame: Communication Baseball (Cresskill,NJ: Hampton Press, 00); auth, Criticial Legal Studies and Argumentation Theory," Argumentation 9 (95): 719-29; auth, "The First Amendment in Popular Culture: 'The People Vs. Larry Flynt,' forthcoming in Free Speech Yearbook (99). **CONTACT ADDRESS** Dept Communication, Boston Col, Chestnut Hill, Lyons Hall 215, Chestnut Hill, MA 02467-3804.

HERBERT, CHRISTOPHER
DISCIPLINE ENGLISH **EDUCATION** Yale Univ, PhD. **CAREER** Prof, Northwestern Univ. **HONORS AND AWARDS** 2 WCAS outstanding tchg awd(s); ACLS fel; NEH fel. **SELECTED PUBLICATIONS** Auth, Trollope and Comic Pleasure, Chicago, 87, Culture and Anomie, Chicago, 91; articles on, Dickens; George Eliot; Trollope; 19th-century scientific thought; auth, Victorian Relativity: Radical Thought and Scientific Discovery, Chicago, 01. **CONTACT ADDRESS** Dept of English, Northwestern Univ, Univ Hall 215, 1897 Sheridan Rd, Evanston, IL 60208. **EMAIL** c-herbert@northwestern.edu

HERENDEEN, WYMAN H.
DISCIPLINE ENGLISH LANGUAGE; LITERATURE **EDUCATION** Brown, BA, MA; Toronto Univ, PhD, 84. **CAREER** Prof; dept head. **HONORS AND AWARDS** Choice best acad bk designation. **RESEARCH** Cultural studies; history of ideas; persistence of the classical tradition; Renaissance, particularly Spenser, Shakespeare, Jonson, and Milton. **SELECTED PUBLICATIONS** Auth, From Landscape to Literature: The River and the Myth of Geography; co-ed, Ben Jonson's 1616 Folio. **CONTACT ADDRESS** Dept of English, Univ of Windsor, 401 Sunset Ave, Windsor, ON, Canada N9B 3P4. **EMAIL** whh@uwindsor.ca

HERING, FRANK G.
PERSONAL Born 05/09/1971, Chicago Hts, IL, m, 1993, 2 children **DISCIPLINE** ENGLISH **EDUCATION** Univ Chicago, BA, 93; Univ Fla, MA, 96; PhD, 00. **CAREER** Teaching asst, Univ Fla, 96-00; instr, St Stephen and St Agnes Sch, 00-. **HONORS AND AWARDS** Teaching Awd, Univ Fla; Phi Beta Kappa. **MEMBERSHIPS** ASA; MLA; Melville Soc. **RESEARCH** 19th and 20th Century American literature; 19th and 20th Century American reform movements. **SELECTED PUBLICATIONS** Auth, "Sneaking Around: Idealized Domesticity, Identity, Politics, and Games of Friendship in Neila Larson's Passing," Ariz Quart 57 (01): 35-60. **CONTACT ADDRESS** 4630 28th Rd S, Unit C, Arlington, VA 22206-1126. **EMAIL** fghering@aol.com

HERINGMAN, NOAH
PERSONAL Born 01/26/1969, Fargo, ND, s **DISCIPLINE** LITERATURE **EDUCATION** Garlham Col, BA, 91; Harvard Univ, PhD, 98. **CAREER** Asst prof, Univ of Mo, 98-. **HONORS AND AWARDS** Howard Mumford Dissertation prize, Harvard Univ, 98; Annual essay Prize, Keats-Shelley Asn of Am, 99; NEH Fel, Huntington Libr, 00-01. **MEMBERSHIPS** MLA, Am Comparative Lit Asn. **RESEARCH** British romanticism, history of geology. **SELECTED PUBLICATIONS** Auth, "Stones So Wonderous Cheap," Studies in Romanticism 37(1) (98): 43-61. **CONTACT ADDRESS** Dept English, Univ of Missouri, Columbia, 107 Tate Hall, Columbia, MO 65211-1500.

HERMAND, JOST
PERSONAL Born 04/11/1930, Kassel, Germany, m, 1956 **DISCIPLINE** MODERN GERMAN LITERATURE **EDUCATION** Univ Marburg, PhD, 55. **CAREER** From asst prof to prof Ger, 58-67, Vilas Res Prof, Univ Wis-Madison, 67-, Am Coun Learned Soc fel, 65-66; vis prof, Harvard Univ, 67, Univ Tex, Austin, 70, Free Univ W Berlin, 77 & 94, Univ Bremen, 78, Univ Giessen, 81, Univ Marburg, 81 & 91; Univ Essen, 86, Univ Kassel, 88; Univ Freiberg, 89; Univ Potsdam, 93; Univ Oldenburg, 94; Univ Munich, 98; Univ Cologne, 00. **HONORS AND AWARDS** Saxon Academy 85; Hilldale Awd Univ WI, 91; Honorary Mem of AATG, 97. **MEMBERSHIPS** MLA; Int Brecht Soc; Heine Soc. **RESEARCH** Cultural and intellectual history of Germany between 1870-1914; Heinrich Heine; lit after 1945. **SELECTED PUBLICATIONS** Auth, Literaturwissenschaft und Kunstwissenschaft, Metzler, Stuttgart, 65; Stilkunst um 1900, Akademie, Berlin, 67; Synthetisches Interpretieren, Nymphenburger, Munich, 68; Pop Int, Athenaum, Frankfurt, 71; ed, Heine's Reisebilder, Hoffmann & Campe, Hamburg, 73; auth, Streitobjekt Heine, Athenaum, Frankfurt, 75; Orte Irgendwo Formen utopischen Denkens, Athenaum, Koenigstein, 81; Konkretes Hoeren. Zum Inhalt der Instrumentalmusik, Argument, Berlin, 81; Kulturgeschichte der Bundesrepublik Deutschland, Nymphenburger, Munich, 86-88; Adolph Menzel, Rowohlt, Hamburg, 85; Arnold Zweig, Rowohlt, Hamburg, 90; Ueber Heinrich Heine, Lang, Frankfurd, 91; Gruene Utopien in Deutschland, Fischer, Frankfurt, 91; Old Dreams of a New Reich, Indiana, 91; Geschichte der Germanistik, Rowo-

hlt, Hamburg, 94; Judentum und deutsche Kultur, Boehlau, Cologne, 96; A Hitler Youth in Poland, Northwestern, Evanston, 97; Die deutschen Dichterbuende, Boehlau, Cologne, 98; auth, Formen des Eros in derkunst, 00. **CONTACT ADDRESS** Dept of Ger, Univ of Wisconsin, Madison, 1220 Linden Drive, Madison, WI 53706-1557. **EMAIL** jhermand@facstaff.wisc.edu

HERMANN, RICHARD
DISCIPLINE MUSIC **EDUCATION** Eastman School of Music, Yale Univ, New England Conseratory, Drake Univ. **CAREER** Prof, Eastman, Prof, Ithaca Col, Prof, Yale Univ, Prof, Berklee Col, Prof, Univ Nmex, Composers' Symposium, Las Cantantes. **HONORS AND AWARDS** Ed, Winds Quarterly. **MEMBERSHIPS** Arnold Schoengerg Institute, GAMUT, Music Theory Society of New York State, Rocky Mountain Society for Music Theory **SELECTED PUBLICATIONS** Ed, Concert Music, Rock, and Jazz since 1945: Essays and Analytical Studies (Rochester, NY), University of Rochester Press, 95. **CONTACT ADDRESS** Music Dept, Univ of New Mexico, Albuquerque, 1805 Roma NE, Albuquerque, NM 87131. **EMAIL** harhar@unm.edu

HERMANSSON, CASIE
PERSONAL Born 05/06/1968, Oakland, CA, m, 2000 **DISCIPLINE** 20TH CENTURY BRITISH LITERATURE **EDUCATION** Massey Univ, New Zealand, BA; Univ Toronto, MA, PhD. **CAREER** Full-time lectr. **HONORS AND AWARDS** Massey Scholar, 89; Univ of Toronto Connaught Scholar, 91-95; Univ of Toronto Woodhouse Prize for Best English Dissertation, 98, 00. **RESEARCH** Women's literature, postcolonial literature, detective fiction **SELECTED PUBLICATIONS** Auth, "The Great Gatsby," auth, "Canadian short story article on Northanger Abbey." **CONTACT ADDRESS** Dept of Eng, Pittsburg State Univ, 1701 S Broadway St, Pittsburg, KS 66762. **EMAIL** chermans@pittstate.edu

HERNDON, SANDRA L.
DISCIPLINE COMMUNICATION STUDIES **EDUCATION** Southern Ill Univ, PhD. **CAREER** Prof. **MEMBERSHIPS** Eastern Commun Asn. **SELECTED PUBLICATIONS** Auth, pubs on organizational communication, impact of new technologies on organizations, and workplace diversity. **CONTACT ADDRESS** Dept of Communication, Ithaca Col, 100 Job Hall, Ithaca, NY 14850.

HERNON, PETER
PERSONAL Born 08/31/1944, Kansas City, MO, m, 1972, 2 children **DISCIPLINE** LIBRARY AND INFORMATION SCIENCE **EDUCATION** Univ of Colo, BA, 66, MA, 68; Univ of Ill, advanced work in hist, 68-70; Univ of Denver, MA, 71; Ind Univ, PhD, 78. **CAREER** Ref libr, 71-75, instr, 71-74, asst prof, Univ of Nebr at Omaha, 74-75; assoc instr, Ind Univ, 75-78; vis lectr, Libr School, Univ of Wis at Madison, 78; ASSOC PROF, 81-83, ASST PROF, 78-81, PROF, GRAD SCHOOL OF LIBR AND INFOR SCI, SIMMONS COL, 86-; assoc prof, 83-85, prof, 85-86, vis prof, Grad Libr School, Univ of Az, 88; vis prof, Dept of Libr and Infor Studies, Victoria Univ of Wellington, 95-96. **HONORS AND AWARDS** Louise Maxwell Awd, Indian Univ School of Libr and Infor Sci Alumni Asn, 93; winner of res paper competition, Libr Res Round Table, 86; res grant, Asn of Libr and Infor Sci Ed, 85; Asn of Am Libr Schools' Res Paper Competition Awd, 82. **MEMBERSHIPS** Beta Phi Mu; Am Soc for Infor Sci; Am Libr Asn. **RESEARCH** Service quality; customer satisfaction; government information policy; research misconduct. **SELECTED PUBLICATIONS** Auth, Assessing Service Quality: Satisfying the Expectations of Library Customers, Am Libr Asn, 88; Research Misconduct: Issues, Implications, and Strategies, Ablex, 97; Federal Information Policies in the 1990s: Views and Perspectives, Ablex, 96; Service Quality in Academic Libraries, Ablex, 96; ed, Gov Infor Quart, J of Acad Librarianship, and Libr & Infor Sci Res. **CONTACT ADDRESS** Grad School of Libr & Infor Sci, Simmons Col, 300 The Fenway, Boston, MA 02115-5898. **EMAIL** peter.hernon@simmons.edu

HERREN, MICHAEL W.
PERSONAL Born 12/15/1940, Santa Ana, CA **DISCIPLINE** CLASSICS, MEDIEVAL STUDIES **EDUCATION** Claremont Men's Col, BA, 62; Pontif Inst Medieval Stud, MSL, 67; Univ Toronto, PhD, 69. **CAREER** High sch tchr, Calif, 62-64; asst to assoc prof, 69-78, PROF HUMANITIES AND CLASSICS, YORK UNIV, 78-, ch hum, 82-85; grad fac medieval stud, Univ Toronto, 90-. **HONORS AND AWARDS** Assoc fel, Clare Hall, Cambridge Univ, 74; SSHRCC leave fel, 80-81, 87-88; Alexander von Humboldt res fel, Munich, 81-82; Atkinson Col res fel, 86-87; sr res fel, class, King's Col London, 87-88; DAAD fel, 92; Killam res fel, 95-97. **MEMBERSHIPS** Medieval Acad Am; Medieval Latin Asn Am; Soc Promotion Eriugenian Stud; Soc Hiberno-Latin Stud. **RESEARCH** Classics and medieval studies. **SELECTED PUBLICATIONS** Auth, Hisperica Famina I: The A-Text, 74, II: Related Poems, 87; auth, Aldhelm: The Prose Works, 79; auth, Johannis Scotti Eriugenae Carmina, 93; ed, Insular Latin Studies, 82; ed, The Sacred Nectar of the Greeks, 88; ed, J Medieval Latin, 91-; comp, Latin Letters in Early Christian Ireland, 96. **CONTACT ADDRESS** York Univ, 4700 Keele St, North York, ON, Canada M3J 1P3. **EMAIL** aethicus@yorku.ca

HERRING, HENRY
DISCIPLINE AMERICAN LITERATURE **EDUCATION** Univ SC, BA, 61, MA, 64; Duke Univ, PhD, 68. **CAREER** Prof. **RESEARCH** Dept of Eng **SELECTED PUBLICATIONS** In the field of textual criticism. **CONTACT ADDRESS** The Col of Wooster, Wooster, OH 44691.

HERRING, PHILLIP F.
PERSONAL Born 06/30/1936, Fort Worth, TX, m, 1962, 2 children **DISCIPLINE** ENGLISH **EDUCATION** Univ of Tex, BA, 58, PhD, 66. **CAREER** Teaching asst and spec instr, Univ of Tex, 62-64; asst prof, Univ of Va, 65-70; from assoc prof to prof, Univ of Wis, 70-96; co-dir, Seventh Int James Joyce Symp , Zurich, 79; co-dir, NMex James Joyce Symp, 81; vis prof, Univ of NMex, 81-82; prog coord, Eight Int James Joyce Symp, Dublin, 82; adj prof, Univ of Tex, 96-. **HONORS AND AWARDS** A. Mellon Postdoctoral Fel, Univ of Pittsburgh, 68-69; Fel, Inst for Res in the Hums, 73; Romnes Fac Fel, 75-76; ACLS Travel Grant, 88; U.W.Fac Develop Grant, 89; NEH Summer Stipend, 91; Hilldale Undergrad Fac Awd, 93; Djuna, Choice selection for one of the best acad books of the year, 95. **MEMBERSHIPS** James Joyce Found; MLA; Madison Lit Club. **SELECTED PUBLICATIONS** Auth, Joyce's ULYSSES notesheets in the British Museum, 72; Joyce's Notes and Early Drafts for ULYSSES: Selections from the Buffalo, in TLS, 78; Joyce's Uncertainty Principle, 87; Reply to Grace Eckley, in J. Joyce Lit Suppl 5, 91; Joyce's Sourcebooks for Ulysses in the Manuscripts, in 'Ulysse' a l'article: Joyce aux marges du roman, 91; Dubliners: The Trials of Adolescence, in J. Joyce: A Collection of Critical Essays, 92; Djuna Barnes Remembers James Joyce, In J. Joyce Quart 30, 92, Djuna Barnes and the Songs of Synge, in Eire-Ireland 28:2, 93; Djuna Barnes, Behind the Heart, in Library Chronicle 23:4, 93; Zadel Barnes, Journalist, in Rev of Contemp Fiction 13:3, 93; Djuna Barnes and Thelma Wood: The Vengeance of Nightwood, in J of Modern Lit 18:1, 94; 'I know of no writer as mean as I would be'!: Djuna Barnes' The Antiphon, in De Gits, 95; Djuna: The Life and Work of Djuna Barnes, 95; ed, The Collected Stories of Djuna Barnes, 96; coed, James Joyce: The Centennial Symposium, 86 **CONTACT ADDRESS** Harry Ransom Humanities Research Center, Univ of Texas, Austin, PO Drawer 7219, Austin, TX 78713-7219. **EMAIL** PHerring@mail.utexas.edu

HERRON, CAROLIVIA
PERSONAL Born Washington, DC, s **DISCIPLINE** ENGLISH, AFRICAN-AMERICAN STUDIES **EDUCATION** Eastern Baptist College, BA, English lit, 1969; Villanova University, MA, English, 1973; University of Pennsylvania, MA, comparative lit & creative writing, 1983, PhD, comparative lit & lit theory, 1985. **CAREER** Harvard University, asst professor, African-American Studies and Comparative Literature, 86-90; Mount Holyoke College, assoc prof, English, 90-92; Hebrew College, visiting scholar, 94-95; Harvard University, visiting scholar, 95. **HONORS AND AWARDS** US Information Service, Fulbright Post-Doctoral Research Awd, 1985; NEH, Visit to Collections Awd, 1987; Radcliffe College, Bunting Institute Fellowship, 1988; Yale University, Beineke Library Fellowship, 1988; Folger Shakespeare Library, Post-Doctoral Research Awd, 1989. **MEMBERSHIPS** Classical Association of New England, 1986-93. **SELECTED PUBLICATIONS** Author: Thereafter Johnnie, novel, 1991; Selected Works of Angelina Weld Grimke, 1991. **CONTACT ADDRESS** Random House, 201 E 50th St, New York, NY 10022.

HERZ, JUDITH SCHERER
PERSONAL Born 01/15/1934, Brooklyn, NY, m, 1960, 2 children **DISCIPLINE** ENGLISH **EDUCATION** Barnard Col, BA, 54; Univ Rochester, MA, 55; PhD, 59. **CAREER** Instr, Cornell Univ, 60-69; asst prof to prof, Concordia Univ, 70-. **HONORS AND AWARDS** SSHRC Fel, 96-99. **MEMBERSHIPS** MLA, ACCUTE, Milton Soc of Am, John Donne Soc, Can Soc for Renaissance Studies, Humanites and Soc Sci Fed of Can. **RESEARCH** 17th-Century Writing, Early 20th Century Writing: Bloomsbury. **SELECTED PUBLICATIONS** Auth, "An Excellent Exercise of Wit: John Donne and the Poetics of Concealment" The Eagle and the Dove, Univ of Mo Pr, (86); auth, The Short Narratives of E M Forster, Macmillan Pr, 88; auth, "For Whom this Glorious Sight: Dante, Milton, and the Galileo Question," Milton and Italy, Medieval and Renaissance Text Soc, (91); auth, A Passage to India: Nation and Narration, Twayne, 93; auth, "Aemilia Lanyer and the Pathos of Literary History," Representing Women in renaissance England, Univ Mo Pr, (97); auth, "The Orphic and the Operatic in the Longest Journey," Queer Forster, Univ of Chicago Pr, (97); auth, "Under the Sign of Donne," Criticism, (01). **CONTACT ADDRESS** Dept English, Concordia Univ, Montreal, 1455 de-Maisonneuve Blvd W, Montreal, QC, Canada H3G 1M8. **EMAIL** jherz@vax2.concordia.ca

HERZBERG, BRUCE
PERSONAL Born 07/19/1949, Vineland, NJ, m, 1977, 2 children **DISCIPLINE** ENGLISH LITERATURE, RHETORIC **EDUCATION** Amherst Col, BA, 72; Rutgers Univ, PhD, 78. **CAREER** Instr English, Clark Univ, 78-80; educ dir comput programming & tech writing, John M Nevison Assocs, 80-81; from asst prof to prof English, Bentley Col, 81-; chair, Dept English, 00-. **HONORS AND AWARDS** Outstanding Bk Awd, CCCC, for Rhetorical Tradition, 92. **MEMBERSHIPS** MLA; NCTE; SBL; WPA. **RESEARCH** Rhetoric and compos theory; Bibl lit. **SELECTED PUBLICATIONS** Auth, Selected articles on Thomas Pynchon: An annotated bibliography, Twentieth Century Lit, 5/75; contribr, Thomas Pynchon & Gravity's Rainbow, In: Academic American Encycl, Arete Publ Co, 79; coauth, Some problems in E D Hirsch's Philosophy of Composition, Mod Lang Notes, 12/80; contribr, Hal Clement & George O Smith, In: Dict of Literary Biography: 20th Century American Science Fiction, BC Res Co, 81; auth, Breakfast, death, feedback: Thomas Pynchon and the technology of interpretation, Bucknell Rev, fall 82; auth, michel Foucault's Theory of Rhetoric, In: Contending with Words, MLA, 91; auth, Composition and the Politics of the Curriculum, In: Politics of Writing Instruction, Heinemann, 91; Rhetoric Unbound, In: the Social Perspective in Professional Communication, Sage, 92; Community Service and Critical Teaching, Col Compos Commun, 10/94; Co-auth, The Rhetorical Tradition, Bedford, 90; Co-auth, Bedford Bibliography for Teachers of Writing, Bedford, 96; Co-auth, Negotiating Difference, 96. **CONTACT ADDRESS** Dept of Eng, Bentley Col, 175 Forest St, Waltham, MA 02452-4705. **EMAIL** bherzberg@bentley.edu

HERZING, THOMAS WAYNE
PERSONAL Born 06/30/1939, St. Cloud, MN, m, 1961, 4 children **DISCIPLINE** BRITISH LITERATURE, ROMANTIC MOVEMENT **EDUCATION** St John's Univ, Minn, BA, 61; Marquette Univ, MA, 63; Univ Wis-Madison, PhD(English), 72. **CAREER** Instr English, St Joseph's Col, Ind, 62-67; from instr to asst prof, 67-74, assoc prof, 74-82, prof English, Univ Wis, Oshkosh, 82-, assoc dean, 96-, assoc, Ctr Activ Pub Sector, 74-; Emeritus, 00. **MEMBERSHIPS** MLA; Am Soc 18th Century Studies; NCTE. **RESEARCH** Rhetorical analysis; the intellectual history behind Blake's poetry; the psychology of creativity. **SELECTED PUBLICATIONS** Coauth, Introduction to Basic Photography, Univ Wis, 75; Opportunities in a Recovering Economy, 3/76 & Riding the Future Curve: Forecasting Short-Term Markets, 5/76, Treas Dig; An Interdisciplinary Approach to Marketing and Business Communication, Midwest Bus Admin Asn, 77; ed, Investment Fundamentals, Irwin, 80; ed, Marketing Channels and Strategies, Grid Publ, 81; Conducting Fundamentals, Prentice-Hall, 82; auth, Test bank, In: Investments, Dryden, 82; ed, Strategies in Personal Finance, McGraw Hill, 83, 85, 88, 92; auth, The Leach Co.: The First 100 Years, 87; Don't Shoot the Decoys, 93; co-auth, The University of Oshkosh: The First 100 Years, 98; auth, Splendor on the Grass, Schiffer Pblishing, 00. **CONTACT ADDRESS** Univ of Wisconsin, Oshkosh, 3864 Canlish Harbor Ln., Oshkosh, WI 54902. **EMAIL** herzing@uwosh.edu

HERZMAN, RONALD BERNARD
PERSONAL Born 11/17/1943, Brooklyn, NY, m, 1970, 2 children **DISCIPLINE** ENGLISH LITERATURE, MEDIEVAL STUDIES **EDUCATION** Manhattan Col, BA, 65; Univ Del, MA, 67, PhD(English), 69. **CAREER** Instr English, Univ Del, 68-69; asst prof, 69-79, ASSOC PROF ENGLISH, STATE UNIV NY, GENESEO, 79-, Fel in residence English, Univ Chicago, 78-79. **MEMBERSHIPS** Dante Soc Am. **RESEARCH** Dante; Chaucer; interdisciplinary medieval studies. **SELECTED PUBLICATIONS** Auth, Squaring the Circle--Exploring the Artistry of Dante in His 'Divine Commedia'--'Paradiso', and the Poetics of Geometry, Traditio-Studies Ancient Medieval Hist Thought Relig, Vol 0049, 94. **CONTACT ADDRESS** Dept of English, SUNY, Col at Geneseo, 1 College Cir, Geneseo, NY 14454-1401.

HERZOG, KRISTIN
PERSONAL Born 03/01/1929, Germany, w, 1 child **DISCIPLINE** ENGLISH **EDUCATION** Duke Univ, MA, 73; Univ of NC, PhD, 80; State of Lower Saxony, Germany, Studien Assessorin, 56; Univ of Gottingen, Germany, Studien Referendarin, 54. **CAREER** Tchr of Secondary Sch, Germany; Independent Scholar and Writer. **MEMBERSHIPS** Modern Lang Assoc, AAR, GAAS, MELUS, NCIS. **RESEARCH** Ethnic-Amer Lit; Womens Stud; Feminist Theol. **SELECTED PUBLICATIONS** Auth, Women, Ethnics, and Exotics: Images of Power in Mid-Nineteenth-Century American Fiction, Knoxville, Univ of Tennessee Press, 83; Finding Their Voice: Peruvian Women's Testimonies of War, Valley Forge, PA, Trinity Press International, 93; Contrib Ed to The Heath Anthology of American Literature, vol II and Instructor's Guide for this anthology, Lexington, MA, D.C. Heath, 90 & 94; Kraft des Uberlebens, Vielfaltige theologische Frauenforschung in den USA, Evangelische Kommentare, 97. **CONTACT ADDRESS** 2936 Chapel Hill Rd, Durham, NC 27707. **EMAIL** kristinberzog@compuserve.com

HERZOG, TOBEY C.
PERSONAL Born 10/16/1946, Peru, IL, m, 1967, 2 children **DISCIPLINE** ENGLISH **EDUCATION** Ill Wesleyan univ, BA, 68; Purdue Univ, MA, 72; PhD, 75. **CAREER** From asst prof to prof, Wabash Col, 76-. **HONORS AND AWARDS** Outstanding Young Alumnus, Ill Wesleyan Univ, 81; McLain-McTurnan Arnold Res Schol, Wabash Col, 88 & 92. **MEMBERSHIPS** MLA, Thomas Hardy Soc, Dickens Soc. **RESEARCH** Nineteenth-Century British Literature, American Literature about the Vietnam War. **SELECTED PUBLICATIONS**

TIONS Auth, Vietnam War Stories: Innocence Lost, Routledge, 92; auth, Tim O'Brien, Twayne, 97. **CONTACT ADDRESS** Dept English, Wabash Col, PO Box 352, Crawfordsville, IN 47933-0352. **EMAIL** herzogt@wabash.edu

HESLA, DAVID H.
PERSONAL Born 10/14/1929, Stevens Point, WI, m, 1956, 2 children **DISCIPLINE** LITERATURE; HISTORY OF IDEAS **EDUCATION** St Olaf Col, BA, 51; Univ Chicago, AM, 56, PhD, 64. **CAREER** Instr English, St Olaf Col, 55-56; from instr to asst prof, Cornell Col, 61-65; instr lit & theol, 65-70, assoc prof humanities, Emory Univ, 70-, consult, Miles Col, 71-72. **HONORS AND AWARDS** Fulbright lectr, US Educ Found, Finland, 72-73. **MEMBERSHIPS** Am Acad Relig. **RESEARCH** Religious dimensions of literature; modern British and American literature; literary criticism and theory. **SELECTED PUBLICATIONS** Auth, Theological ambiguity in the Catholic novels, In: Graham Greene, Univ KY, 63; The two roles of Norman Mailer, Adversity & Grace, 68; The Shape of Chaos: An Interpretation of the Art of Samuel Beckett, Univ Minn, 71. **CONTACT ADDRESS** Emory Univ, 1364 Clifton Rd NE, Atlanta, GA 30322-0001. **EMAIL** iladhh@emory.edu

HESS, WILLIAM HUIE
PERSONAL Born 12/24/1933, Arkadelphia, AR, m, 1954, 2 children **DISCIPLINE** CLASSICS **EDUCATION** Univ TX, BA, 55, MA, 59; Princeton Univ, MA, 62, PhD, 63. **CAREER** Spec instr class, 59-60, from instr to asst prof classics, Univ TX, 62-68; assoc prof, 68-78, Prof Lang & Chmn Dept, Univ UT, 78-83, Prof Emer, 98. **MEMBERSHIPS** Camus **RESEARCH** Greek comedy; ancient relig; hist of ideas. **CONTACT ADDRESS** 1860 Laurelwood Cir, Salt Lake City, UT 84121-1220.

HESSELGRAVE, DAVID J.
PERSONAL Born 01/03/1924, N Freedom, WI, m, 1944, 3 children **DISCIPLINE** RHETORIC AND PUBLIC ADDRESS **EDUCATION** Evangelical Free Church Sem, Dipl, 44; Univ Minn, BA, 56, MA, 56, PhD, 65. **CAREER** Prof, of Mission, 65-91, chr, Dept Missions & Evangelism, 65-88, dir, School World Mission & Evangelism, 67-88, prof, emeritus, 92-, Trinity Evangelical Divinity School; Exrc Dir, Evangelical Missiological Soc, 89-94. **HONORS AND AWARDS** Acad prize, Univ Alumni Asn **MEMBERSHIPS** Ministerial Asn Evangelical Free Chruch Amer; Evangelical Theol Soc; Evangelical Missiological; Amer Soc Missiology. **RESEARCH** Cross-cultural studies; World Missions; World religions **SELECTED PUBLICATIONS** Auth, Communicating Christ Cross-Culturally: An Introduction to Missionary Communication; Planting Churches Cross-Culturally: A Guide for Home and Foreign Missions; coauth, Contextualization: Meanings, Methods, and Models; Todays Choices for Tomorrows Mission; auth, Scripture and Strategy: The Use of the Bible in Postmodern Church and Mission; auth, Counseling Cross-Culturally: An Introduction to Theory and Practice for Christmas. **CONTACT ADDRESS** 4345 Terrace View Ln., Rockford, IL 61114. **EMAIL** DJHesselgrave@Juno.com

HESTER, KARLTON EDWARD
DISCIPLINE MUSIC **EDUCATION** Univ Tex at El Paso, BM; San Francisco State Univ, MM; City Univ NYork, PhD. **CAREER** Asst prof and Herbert Gussman dir Jazz Stud. **HONORS AND AWARDS** Mellon Postdoct fel, Cornell Univ, 91-92; Nat Endowment for the Arts, composition, 85, 89. **MEMBERSHIPS** Musicians Local 802; ASCAP. **RESEARCH** Contemporary composition; African American music innovators; world music. **SELECTED PUBLICATIONS** Auth, From Africa to Afrocentric Innovations Some Call 'Jazz' Vols 1-4, Hesteria Records and Pub, 00; The Melodious and Polyrhythmic Developments in John Coltrane's Spontaneous Compositions within a Racist Society, Edwin Mellen Press, 97; Video review of Tryin' to Get Home: A History of African American Song by Kerrigan Black, for Notes, quart jour Music Libr Asn, 95. **CONTACT ADDRESS** Dept of Music, Univ of California, Santa Cruz, 104 Lincoln Hall, Santa Cruz, CA 95064. **EMAIL** keh6@cornell.edu

HESTER, MARVIN THOMAS
PERSONAL Born 07/22/1941, Owensboro, KY, m, 1968, 1 child **DISCIPLINE** RENAISSANCE LITERATURE **EDUCATION** Centre Col, Ky, BA, 63; Univ Fla, MA, 65, PhD(English lit), 72. **CAREER** Instr English, Univ Fla, 64-67; instr English, 71-72, asst prof English lit, 72-77, fac res fel, 73-74, ASSOC PROF ENGLISH, NC STATE UNIV, 77-, Nat Endowment for Humanities fel, 72-73 & 81-82; faculty res fel, 75-76 & 76-77; Southeast Medieval and Renaissance Inst fel, 78; coed, Renaissance Papers, 79-; ed, John Donne J, 82; Prof English, NC State Univ, 83-. **HONORS AND AWARDS** Academy of Outstanding Teachers, 76; SE Medieval and Renaissance Institute Fellowship, 78; ACLS Fellowship, 84; President, John Donne Society of America, 88-89; Alumni Distinguished Undergraduate Teaching Awd, 89; NEH Fellowship, 92, 86, 82, 74; SAADE-SAMLA Outstanding Teacher Awd, 92; President, NCSU Phi Kappa Phi Honor Society, 93-94; Outstanding Publication in Donne Studies (John Donne Society of America), 94, 92; Recipient, UNC Board of Governors Awd for Excellence in Teaching, 96; Alexander Quarles Holladay Medal for Excellence, 97; Phi Kappa Phi, Southeast Regional Scholar, 99-. **MEMBERSHIPS** Southeastern Renaissance Soc; Renaissance Soc Am; SAtlantic MLA. **RESEARCH** English Renaissance; Donne. **SELECTED PUBLICATIONS** Auth, "A Fair Day in the Affections": Literary Essays, coed, with Jack Durant, 80; auth, Kinde Pitty and Brave Scorn: John Donne's Satyres, 82; auth, Seventeenth-Century British Nondramatic Poets, 3 vols, 92-93; auth, If-Thou-Regard-The-Same--Poem Between 'Amoretti' and 'Epithalamion'--Spenser Emblematic Centerfold, Anq, Vol 0006, 93; Miserrimum-Dictu, Donne Epitaph for His Wife, J English Germanic Philol, Vol 0094, 95; Donne and the Court-Of-Wards, Anq, Vol 0007, 94; Transfigured Rites in 17th-Century English Poetry, J English Germanic Philol, Vol 0092, 93; Let-Them-Sleep-- John Donne Personal Illusion in 'Holy Sonnet Iv', Papers Lang Lit, Vol 0029, 93; auth, "'let me love': Reading the Sacred 'currant' in Donne's Profane Lyrics," in Sacred and Profane, 95; auth, "Faeminae lectissimae: Reading Anne Donne," 96; auth, John Donne's "desire of more": The Subject of Anne Donne in His Poetry, 96; auth, Justus Lipsius: Epistolica institutio. Ed & transl with R.V. Young, 96; auth, "Herrick's Masque of Death," 99; auth, "'over reconing' the 'undertones': A Preface to 'some elegies' by Donne," 00; auth, "'like a spyed Spie': Donne's Baiting of Marlowe," 00. **CONTACT ADDRESS** No Carolina State Univ, Box 8105, Raleigh, NC 27695. **EMAIL** hester@unity.ncsu.edu

HEUCHEMER, DANE
DISCIPLINE MUSIC **EDUCATION** Univ Northern Colo, BM, 88; Ithaca Col, MM, 90; Univ Cincinnati, DPhil, 97. **CAREER** Asst prof mus, 97- ,vis inst mus, 95-97, Kenyon Col. **HONORS AND AWARDS** Presser Scholar, 94. **MEMBERSHIPS** AMS; Hist Brass Soc; Renaissance Soc of Am; Col Music Soc, MENC/OH, Music Edu Assn **RESEARCH** Renaissance Music, particularly in Germany and Italy; Performance Practice, Court Musical Patronage, conducting. **SELECTED PUBLICATIONS** Italian Musicians in Dresden in the Second Half of the Sixteenth Century, with an Emphasis on the Lives and Works of Antonio Scandello and Giovanni Battista Pinello di Ghirardi, Univ Cincinnati, 97. **CONTACT ADDRESS** Music Dept, Kenyon Col, Gambier, OH 43022. **EMAIL** heuchemerd@kenyon.edu

HEUETT, BRIAN L.
PERSONAL Born 04/14/1960, Spokane, WA, m, 1984, 6 children **DISCIPLINE** COMMUNICATION **EDUCATION** Wash State Univ, BA, 93; MA, 95; PhD, 98. **CAREER** TA, Wash State Univ, 93-98; asst prof, Southern Utah Univ, 98-. **HONORS AND AWARDS** SW Utah Sterling Scholar Judge, 99, 00; Chair, Commun Apprehension and Avoidance Comm, 99; Chair, IRB Comm, 99-00; State DEX Advisor of the Year, 00. **MEMBERSHIPS** Nat Commun Assoc; Western Speech Commun Assoc. **RESEARCH** Communication Apprehension. **SELECTED PUBLICATIONS** Coauth, "The relationship between visual imagery and public speaking apprehension", Commun Reports 10.1 (97); coauth, "Testing a refinement in an intervention for communication apprehension", Commun Reports 11.1 (98); coauth, "An examination of the impact of Performance Visualization", Commun Res Reports 16.1 (99): 29-39; coauth, "Imagery and public speaking apprehension in India", Commun Res Reports 16.2 (00): 131-137; coauth, "An examination of the long term effect of Performance Visualization", Commun Res Reports, (00). **CONTACT ADDRESS** Dept Commun Arts and Sci, So Utah Univ, 351 W Center St, Cedar City, UT 84720-2470. **EMAIL** heuett@suu.edu

HEWITT, AVIS GREY
PERSONAL Born 01/12/1951, Beckley, WV, m, 1970, 2 children **DISCIPLINE** ENGLISH **EDUCATION** Col Wooster, BA, 72; Ball State Univ, MA, 79; PhD, 93. **CAREER** Asst prof, Campbellsville Univ, 93; vis lectr, N Ariz Univ, 94-97; vis asst prof to asst prof, Grand Val State Univ, 98-. **HONORS AND AWARDS** Pinnacle Excellence, Teaching Awd, N Ariz Univ, 97. **MEMBERSHIPS** Christ and Lit; MLA; NCTE; MMLA; Jane Austen Soc. **RESEARCH** Contemporary American literature; global (postcolonial) literature. **SELECTED PUBLICATIONS** Auth, "The Minotaur as Mentor: Edmund Wilson's Role in the Career of Mary McCarthy," in Twenty Four Ways of Looking at Mary McCarthy: The Writer and Her Work, ed. Eve Stwertka (Conn: Greenwood, 96): 157-166; auth, "Hasidic Hallowing and Christian Consecration: Awakening to Authenticity in Denise Levertov's 'Matins,'" Renascence 50 (98): 97-107; auth, "'The Obligation to Live': Duty and Desire in John Univ Prdike's Self-Consciousness," in John Updike Religion: The Sense of the Sacred and the Motions of Grace, ed. James O. Yerkes (Grand Rapids: Erdmans, 99. 31-49; auth, "Intimations of Immortality: Mastered Irony in John Univ Prdike's 'Pigeon Feathers,'" Christian Lit 49 (00): 499-509. **CONTACT ADDRESS** English Dept, Grand Valley State Univ, 1 Campus Dr, Allendale, MI 49401-9403. **EMAIL** hewitta@gvsu.edu

HICKOK, KATHLEEN KLAIRE
PERSONAL Born 09/02/1946, Wichita, Kans **DISCIPLINE** ENGLISH **EDUCATION** Tulane Univ, BA, 68; Univ SW La, MA, 70; Univ Md, PhD, 77. **CAREER** Asst prof, Stetson Univ, 77-79; asst prof to prof, Iowa State Univ, 79-. **HONORS AND AWARDS** NEH Travel Grant, 84; ISU Carrie Chapman Catt Award, 92; ISU Outstanding Teaching Award, 89, 95. **MEMBERSHIPS** MLA; Nat Women's Studies Asn. **RESEARCH** Nineteenth Century British women writers; African American women writers. **SELECTED PUBLICATIONS** Auth, Representations of Women: Nineteenth-Century British Women's Poetry, Greenwood Press, 84. **CONTACT ADDRESS** Dept English, Iowa State Univ, 203 Ross Hall, Ames, IA 50011. **EMAIL** khickok@iastate.edu

HICKS, PATRICK
PERSONAL Born 04/12/1970 **DISCIPLINE** LITERATURE **EDUCATION** St John's Univ, BA, 92; DePaul Univ, MA, 94; Queen's Univ Belfast, MA, 95; Univ Sussex, PhD, 00. **CAREER** Lectr, Univ of Sussex, 98-99; vis asst prof, Univ of St Thomas, 01-02. **HONORS AND AWARDS** Minn Awd; Dept Dist in English. **MEMBERSHIPS** ACIS, MLA. **RESEARCH** Irish literature, gender studies, creative writing. **SELECTED PUBLICATIONS** Auth, "History and Masculinity in Brian Moore's The Emperor of Ice-Cream," Can Jour of Irish Studies, (99); auth, "Waiting for Jeannot: the (de) Construction of History in Brian Moore's 'No Other Life,'" Studies in Can Lit, (00); auth, "An Interview with Brian Moore," Irish Univ Rev, (00); rev, of "Brian Moore: The Chameleon Novelist," by Denis Sampson, Irish Univ Rev, (00); rev, of "Sam Hannah Bell: A Biography," by Sean McMahon, New Hibernia Rev, (00); rev of "Contemporary Irish Fiction: Themes, Tropes, Theories," eds Liam Harte and Michael Parker, New Hibernia Rev, (00). **CONTACT ADDRESS** Univ of St. Thomas, Minnesota, Saint Paul, MN 55105. **EMAIL** pj_hicks@hotmail.com

HICKSON, MARK
PERSONAL Born 08/10/1945, Macon, GA, m, 1986, 2 children **DISCIPLINE** COMMUNICATION **EDUCATION** Auburn Univ, BS, 66, MA, 68; S Ill, PhD, 71. **CAREER** Asst prof, Miss State Univ, 70-71; assoc prof, prof, chr, 74-87; prof, Univ of Ala at Birmingham, 87-. **HONORS AND AWARDS** S States Commun Assoc, Teaching Excellence Awd, 98; Telly Awd, 98. **MEMBERSHIPS** Nat Commun Assoc; Eastern Commun Assoc. **RESEARCH** Nonverbal communication; communication theory. **SELECTED PUBLICATIONS** coauth, NVC: Nonverbal communication studies and applications, Brown/Benchmark, 93; co-auth, Compatible theory and applied research: Systems theory and triangulation, Qualitative Res: Applications in organizational commun, Hampton, 93; auth, The ethos of an academic department, J of the Assoc of Commun Admin, vol 83, 67-70, 93; co-auth, Active prolific scholars in communication studies: Analysis of research productivity, II, Commun Educ, vol 42, 224-233, 93; coauth, Modeling cultures: Toward grounded paradigms, An integrated approach to communication theory and research, Erlbaum, 96; co-auth, qualitative/descriptive (participation-observation) methodology, Essentials of commun res, Longman, 98; coauth, Organizational communication in the personal context: From interview to retirement, Allyn and Bacon, 98. **CONTACT ADDRESS** 1004 Oak Tree Rd., Birmingham, AL 35244-2604. **EMAIL** hickson@uab.edu

HIEATT, ALLEN KENT
PERSONAL Born 01/21/1921, Indianapolis, IN, m, 1957, 2 children **DISCIPLINE** ENGLISH **EDUCATION** Univ Louisville, AB, 43; Columbia Univ, PhD(comp lit), 54. **CAREER** Instr English, Columbia Univ, 44-45; instr Col, 45-55, from asst prof to assoc prof, 55-69; vis prof, 68-69, PROF ENGLISH, UNIV WESTERN ONTARIO, 69-, Can Coun leave grant, 78. **MEMBERSHIPS** MLA; Renaissance Soc Am; Mod Humanities Res Asn; Asn Can Univ Teachers English. **RESEARCH** English; comparative literature and art history; 14th to 17th centuries. **SELECTED PUBLICATIONS** Ill, "Beowulf and Other Old English Poems," 88; ed, "The Canterbury Tales," 88; auth, "Chaucer, Spenser, Milton: Mythopoeic Continuities and Transformations," auth, "Short time's endless monument; the symbolism of the numbers in Edmund Spenser's Epithalamion. **CONTACT ADDRESS** Dept of English, Univ of Western Ontario, Univ College, Rm 173, London, ON, Canada N6A 3K7.

HIEATT, CONSTANCE B.
PERSONAL Born 02/11/1928, Boston, MA, m, 1958 **DISCIPLINE** LITERATURE **EDUCATION** Hunter Col (NYork), AB, 53, AM, 57; Yale Univ, PhD, 59. **CAREER** Lectr, City Col NY, 59-60; asst to assoc prof, Queensborough Commun Col, 60-65; assoc prof to prof, St John's Univ (Jamaica), 65-69; prof, 69-93, Prof Emer English, Univ Western Ontario, 93-. **HONORS AND AWARDS** Yale Univ fel, Lewis-Farmington fel, 57-59; Can Coun grants; SSHRCC grants; Fellow, Royal Soc of Canada. **MEMBERSHIPS** MLA; Medieval Acad Am; Int Soc Anglo-Saxonists; Canadian Soc of Mediev diets. **RESEARCH** Medieval culinary manuscripts. **SELECTED PUBLICATIONS** Auth, The Realism of Dream Visions, 67; auth, Essentials of Old English, 68; auth, An Ordinance of Pottage, 88; coauth, The Canterbury Tales of Geoffrey Chaucer, 64, rev ed, 81; ed/transl, Pleyn Delit: Medieval Cookery for Modern Cooks, 76, rev ed, 79, rev 2nd ed, 96; ed/transl, Curye on Inglysch: English Culinary Manuscripts of the Fourteenth Century, 85; ed/transl, La novele cirurgerie, 90; ed/transl, Beginning Old English, 94; ed/transl, The Tale of the Alerion (Guillaume de Machaut), 94; transl, Beowulf and Other Old English Poems, 67, 2nd ed, 83; transl, Karlamagnus Saga, vols I-II, 75, vol III, 80. **CONTACT ADDRESS** 335 Essex Meadows, Essex, CT 06426. **EMAIL** constancehieatt@yale.edu

HIEBERT, RAY ELDON
DISCIPLINE JOURNALISM **EDUCATION** Stanford Univ, BA, 54; Columbia Univ Grad School of Journalism, MS, 57; Univ of Maryland, MA, 61, PhD, 62. **CAREER** Inst, Dept of English, Univ of Minn, Duluth, 57-58; asst prof, Dept of Commun, 58-62, chemn, assoc prof & prof, Dept of Commun, Amer Univ, 62-66; founding dir, Washington Journalism Center, 65-68; chemn & prof, Dept of Journalism, 68-72, founding dean, Col of Journalism, Univ of Md 73-79; ed, Public Relations Review, 75-; ed, The Communicator, Radio Television News Dir Asn, 70-77; series ed, Longman Series in Public Commun, Longman Co, NY, 75-90; series ed, Contemp Issues in Journalism, Acropolis Books, Washington DC, 70-74; series ed, Wiley Series on Gov and Commun, John Wiley & Sons, NY, 68-70; Acad Advisor, Voice of Am, 83-91; founding dir, Am Journalism Center, Budapest, Hungary, 91-95; member, selection comt, Freedom Support Act Fels for Journalists from Eastern Europe, Int Res and Exchange Board, 95-96; consult on journalism ed in Eastern Europe, The Freedom Forum, 95-97; PROF, 68-98, prof emeritus, 98-, COL OF JOURNALISM, UNIV OF MD. **MEMBERSHIPS** Cosmos Club, Washington D.C.; Int Commun Asn; Asn for Ed in Journalism and Mass Commun. **SELECTED PUBLICATIONS** Coauth, Eastern European Journalism: Before, During, and After Communism, Hampton Press, 98; auth, Exploring Mass Media, Lawrence Erlbaum Asn, 98; coauth, Stages of Post-Communist Media Transition in Hungary, Hungary: A New Nation, European Centre for Traditional Culture, 98; coauth, Remedial Education: The Remaking of Eastern European Journalists, in Journalism Educ in Europe and North Am: An Int Comparison, Inst fur Publizistick, forthcoming; ed, Impact of Mass Media, Longman Co. Inc., 87, 91, 94, & 98; auth, Transition: From the End of the Old Regime to 1996, in Journalism and the Educ of Journalists in the New East/Central Europe, Hampton Press, 98; auth, Blarus, Estonia, Hungary, Latvia, Lithuania, Ukraine, in Looking to the Future: A Survey of Journalism Educ in Central and Easter Europe and the Soviet Union, Freedom Forum, 94; auth, Growth of Advertising and Public Relations in Post-Communist Hungary, in Public Relations Rev, winter 94; auth, The Difficult Birth of a Free Press in Hungary, in Amer Journalism Rev, 94. **CONTACT ADDRESS** College of Journalism, Univ of Maryland, Col Park, College Park, MD 20742. **EMAIL** rh27@umail.umd.edu

HIGDON, DAVID LEON
DISCIPLINE ENGLISH LITERATURE **EDUCATION** Univ KS, PhD, 68. **CAREER** Paul Whitfield Horn Prof Eng, TX Tech Univ; ed, Conradiana, 72-95. **HONORS AND AWARDS** Pres Excellence in Tchg Awd; AMOCO Excellence in Tchg Awd; YWES award. **RESEARCH** Postmodern narrative. **SELECTED PUBLICATIONS** Auth, Time and English Fiction, Shadows of the Past in Contemporary British Fiction. **CONTACT ADDRESS** Texas Tech Univ, Lubbock, TX 79409-5015. **EMAIL** L.Higdon@ttu.edu

HIGGINS, ELIZABETH J.
DISCIPLINE ENGLISH LITERATURE **EDUCATION** Univ Calif Los Angeles, PhD, 68. **CAREER** Fac, Atlanta Univ, 68; fac, Clark Atlanta Univ, 88. **RESEARCH** British romantic literature; American literature; Victorian novel and poetry. **SELECTED PUBLICATIONS** Auth, The Living Novel, 82; bk revs, Jour Col Lang Asn. **CONTACT ADDRESS** Clark Atlanta Univ, 223 James P Brawley Dr, SW, Atlanta, GA 30314.

HIGGINS, MARY ANNE
PERSONAL Born 01/22/1953, Barberton, OH, s **DISCIPLINE** COMMUNICATIONS **EDUCATION** Ohio State Univ, BS, 75; Univ Akron, MA, 85; Kent State Univ, PhD, 92. **CAREER** Vis inst, Kent State Univ, 91-92; Adj asst prof, 92-93; asst prof, Ind Purdue Ft Wayne, 93-97. **HONORS AND AWARDS** Finalist for Distinguished Teaching Awd, KSU, 91; Recipient of Res Awd, Kent State Univ, 92; Summer Grant Recipient, IPFW, 96. **MEMBERSHIPS** Nat Commun Assoc; Int Commun Assoc; Central States Commun Assoc. **RESEARCH** Rural/urban communication; health communication; communication with people with disabilities. **SELECTED PUBLICATIONS** Co-auth, Initiating and Reciprocating verbal aggression: Effects on credibility and credited valid arguments, Commun Studs, vol 43, 182-190, 93; auth, Common Ground, weekly newspaper column, The Independent, Massilon, OH, 92-94; New Trends, news values, and new models, NJ J of Commun, vol 4, (1)82-90, 96; auth, A critical rhetoric and the role of the critic, The Mich Academian, vol 29, 278-279, 97. **CONTACT ADDRESS** 14941 Marshallville Rd, Canal Fulton, OH 44614. **EMAIL** farmmah@aol.com

HIGGINS, WILLIAM E.
PERSONAL Born 01/18/1945, Newark, NJ, s **DISCIPLINE** CLASSICS **EDUCATION** Georgetown Univ, BA, 66; Harvard Univ, PhD, 71; New York Univ, MBA, 81. **CAREER** Asst prof, Brandeis Univ, 71-79. **HONORS AND AWARDS** Phi Beta Kappa, Jr Fel, Ctr for Hellenic Stud, Washington, DC, 77-78. **MEMBERSHIPS** Am Philol Asn. **RESEARCH** Greek literature; ancient history. **SELECTED PUBLICATIONS** Auth, Aspects of Alexander's Imperial Administration, Athenaeum, 80; Deciphering Time in the Herakles of Euripides, Quaderni Urbinati, 84; rev of Osborne, Demos, AHR, 86; rev of Hirsch, The Friendship of the Barbarians, AHR, 87; rev of Garner, Law and Society in Classical Athens, AHR, 89. **CONTACT ADDRESS** 489 Summit Ave, Maplewood, NJ 07040. **EMAIL** wehigg@bellatlantic.net

HIGLEY, SARAH
DISCIPLINE ENGLISH **EDUCATION** Univ CA at Berkeley, PhD. **CAREER** Assoc prof & dir Undergrad Stud; taught at, Univ CA at Berkeley & Univ Geneva, Switzerland. **RESEARCH** Medieval northern lang and lit, Old Eng, Middle Eng, Welsh, Middle Welsh, Old Norse; contemp popular cult. **SELECTED PUBLICATIONS** Auth, Between Languages: The Uncooperative Text in Early Welsh and Old English Nature Poetry; The Legend of the Learned Man's Android, in Retelling Tales, Cambridge: DS Brewer, 97; Old Llwarch's Jawbone: Mediating Old and New Translation in Middle Welsh Studies, in The Formation of Culture in Medieval Britain, Lewiston, 96 & The Spoils of Annwn: Taliesin and Material Poetry, in A Celtic Florilegium, Lawrence, 96; articles on, Beowulf, Old Eng elegies, medieval Welsh poetry and prose including The Mabinogion and The Bk of Taliesin, transl theory, ling, Old Norse, medieval magic, film and television, and science fiction. **CONTACT ADDRESS** Dept of Eng, Univ of Rochester, 601 Elmwood Ave, Ste. 656, Rochester, NY 14642. **EMAIL** slhi@troi.cc.rochester.edu

HIGONNET, MARGARET R.
PERSONAL Born 10/02/1941, New Orleans, LA, m, 3 children **DISCIPLINE** LITERATURE **EDUCATION** Bryn Mawr Col, AB, 63; Yale Univ, MPhil, 69; PhD, 70. **CAREER** Instr, George Wash Univ, 67-78; from asst prof to prof, Univ Conn, 70-; chemn of Comparative Literature Dept, Univ Conn, 76-80 & 99-00; guest prof, Univ Munich, 91-92, 93, & 00. **HONORS AND AWARDS** DAAD Fel, Tubingen, Gerany, 63-64; Woodrow Wilson Fel, Yal Univ, 64-65; Fulbright Scholar, Univ Col, 66-67; Rockefeller Grant, 85; Camargo Found Fel, 85; NEH Summer Fel, 88; Res Fel, Inst Juan March, 89; Vis Fel, Rutgers Ctr for Hist Analysis, 95; Bunting Inst Fel, Radcliffe Col, 95-96. **MEMBERSHIPS** MLA, Am Confr on Romanticism, Am Comparative Lit Asn, Children's Lit Asn. **RESEARCH** Nineteenth-Century European Literature, World War I, Feminist Theory, Children's Literature. **SELECTED PUBLICATIONS** Ed, The Sense of Sex: Feminist Perspectives on Hardy, Univ Ill Press (Champaign, IL), 93; ed, Borderwork: Feminist Engagements with Comparative Literature, Cornell Univ Press (Ithaca, NY), 94; co-ed, Reconfigured Spheres: Feminist Explorations of Literary Space, Univ Mass Press (Amherst, MA), 94; ed, Nineteenth-Century British Women Poets, Meridian, 96; ed, Lines of Fire: Women Writers on World War I, Dutton-Penquin, 99; coauth, Girls, Boys, Books, Toys, Johns Hopkins Univ (Baltimore, MD), 99. **CONTACT ADDRESS** Dept English, Univ of Connecticut, Storrs, 337 Mansfield Rd, Unit-25, Storrs, CT 06269-1025. **EMAIL** margaret.higonnet@uconn.edu

HILFER, TONY
PERSONAL Born 10/19/1936, Los Angeles, CA, m, 1994, 1 child **DISCIPLINE** AMERICAN LITERATURE **EDUCATION** Middlebury Col, BA, 58; Columbia Univ, MA, 60; Univ NC, Chapel Hill, PhD(English), 63. **CAREER** Asst prof, 63-69, assoc prof English 69-81; Prof, 82-; Univ Tex, Austin, 69-, lectr Am Studies, Keele Univ, 70-71; ed, Texas Studies in Literature and Language, 92-. **MEMBERSHIPS** MLA. **RESEARCH** American literature, popular culture. **SELECTED PUBLICATIONS** Auth, George and Martha: Sad, sad, sad, In: Seven Contemporary Authors, Univ Tex, 66; coauth, Baby doll: A study in comedy and social awareness, Ohio Univ Rev, 69; auth, The Revolt from the Village, 1915-1930, Univ NC, 69; Absurdist language: The foregrounding of the symbol system, Sci/Technol & Humanities, 78; The Crime Novel, A Deviant Genre, U of Texas, 90; American Fiction Since 1940, Longman-Addison Wesley, 92. **CONTACT ADDRESS** Dept of English, Univ of Texas, Austin, Austin, TX 78712-1026. **EMAIL** tonyhi@mail.utexas.edu

HILL, DAVID
DISCIPLINE ENGLISH LITERATURE **EDUCATION** IN Univ, PhD, 71. **CAREER** Prof Eng/dir lit studies, SUNY Oswego. **RESEARCH** 19th century Am lit; later 19th century Brit and Am fiction; lang and lit. **SELECTED PUBLICATIONS** Auth, essays on Emerson, James, Stevenson, and Eng compos; co-ed, The Journals and Miscellaneous Notebooks of Ralph Waldo Emerson (16 vol), Harvard UP, 60-82; The Poetry Notebooks of Ralph Walso Emerson, Univ MO P, 86. **CONTACT ADDRESS** SUNY, Oswego, Oswego, NY 13126. **EMAIL** dhill@Oswego.edu

HILL, EUGENE DAVID
PERSONAL Born 02/25/1949, New York, NY, m, 1987 **DISCIPLINE** RENAISSANCE LITERATURE, INTELLECTUAL HISTORY. **EDUCATION** Columbia Univ, BA, 70; Princeton Univ, PhD(English), 80. **CAREER** Instr, 78-80, asst prof Eng, Mt Holyoke Col, 80-86; from assoc prof to prof Eng, 86-94. **MEMBERSHIPS** Renaissance Soc Am. **RESEARCH** John Milton, John Donne, Thomas Kyd. **SELECTED PUBLICATIONS** Auth, The trinitarian allegory of the moral play of Wisdom, Mod Philol, 75; The place of the future, Sci Fiction Studies, 82; Parody and History in Arden of Feversham, Huntington Library Quarterly, 93. **CONTACT ADDRESS** Dept of English, Mount Holyoke Col, 50 College St, South Hadley, MA 01075-6421.

HILL, HOLLY
PERSONAL Born 11/16/1938, Cleveland, OH, d **DISCIPLINE** THEATRE **EDUCATION** Stanford Univ, BA, 59; Columbia Univ, MFA, 71; Grad School of CUNY, PhD, 77. **CAREER** NY Theatre Correspondent, The Times of London, 83-95; actress, on, off, & off-off Broadway, dinner theater, tours, 59-74; DIR & CO-FOUND, ARABIC THEATER PROJECT, O'NEILL THEATER CENTER, 97-; PROF OF SPEECH & THEATRE, JOHN JAY COL OF CUNY, 81-; FREELANCE THEATRE CRITIC, 74-. **HONORS AND AWARDS** Jury of Cairo Int Festival for Experimental Theatre, 97; five awards from the Res Found of CUNY; Richard Rodgers Fel, Columbia Univ. **MEMBERSHIPS** Am Theater Critics Asn; Drama Desk; Isben Soc of Am. **RESEARCH** History of acting; the well made play; Arabic theater. **SELECTED PUBLICATIONS** Auth, Actors Lives, Theatre Communs Group, 94; auth, Playing Joan, Theatre Communs Group, 87; assoc ed & contribu, Encyclopedia of the New York Stage 1920-29, Garland, 82. **CONTACT ADDRESS** 250 E 87th St, 190, New York, NY 10128-3115.

HILL, JAMES LEE
PERSONAL Born 12/10/1941, Meigs, GA, m **DISCIPLINE** ENGLISH **EDUCATION** Ft Valley State Col, BS, 63; Atlanta Univ, MA, 68; Univ Iowa, PhD, 76. **CAREER** Winder City Schs, instructor English 64-65; Hancock Central High, chmn Eng dept 65-68; Paine Coll, instructor English 68-71; Benedict Coll, chmn Eng dept 74-77; Albany State Coll, chmn Eng dept 77-96, Dean Arts & Sciences 81-00; Asst Vice Pres for Acad Affairs, 00-. **HONORS AND AWARDS** NEH Fellow Atlanta Univ 1969; NEH Fellow Univ of IA 1971-74; Governor's Awd in the Humanities, State of Georgia, 1987. **MEMBERSHIPS** Consultant, Natl Rsch Project on Black Women 1979-81; sec Albany Urban League Bd 1979-81; chair, assoc, asst chair, Conf on Coll Comp & Comm 1980-83; chair, vice chair GA Endowment for Humanities 1981-83; mem Exec Comm NCTE 1982-83; pres Beta Nu Sigma Phi Beta Sigma Frat 1983-; chair Academic Comm on English-GA 1983-84; vice pres S Atlantic Assn of Dept of English 1984-85; bd dir Natl Fed State Humanities Councils 1984-87; mem Coll Section Comm Natl Council of Teachers of English 1985-89, chair, 1993-95; Professional Service: dir NEA Writer-in-Resd Prog ASC 1982-91; dir NEH Summer Humanities Inst ASC, 1983, 1984, 1989; Regional dir Southern Region Phi Beta Sigma; visiting scholar Natl Humanities Faculty; Georgia Desoto Commission; Georgia Christopher Columbus Commission; NCTE Summer Inst for Teachers of Literature, dir, bd of dir, Georgia council of Teachers of English. **SELECTED PUBLICATIONS** Publications: "Migration of Blacks to Iowa," "The Apprenticeship of Chester Himes," "The Antiheroic Hero in the Novels of Frank Yerby," A Sourcebook for Teachers of Georgia History; editor, Studies in African and African-American Culture; "Interview with Frank Garvin Yerby;" "Frank Yerby;" "The Foxes of Harrow;" "A Woman of Fancy." **CONTACT ADDRESS** Office of Acad Affairs, Albany State Univ, 504 College Dr, Albany, GA 31705. **EMAIL** jhill@asurams.edu

HILL, JOHN WALTER
DISCIPLINE MUSIC **EDUCATION** Univ Chicago, BA; Harvard Univ, MA, PhD. **CAREER** Prof, 78-, Univ IL Urbana Champaign. **HONORS AND AWARDS** Nat Endowment for the Humanities, Grant, Am Coun of Learned Societies, Am Philosophical Soc, Am Fulbright Com. **MEMBERSHIPS** Am Musicol Soc. **RESEARCH** Music of the Baroque and Class periods. **SELECTED PUBLICATIONS** Auth, The Life and Works of Francesco Maria Veracini, Vivaldi's Ottone in Vill; auth, Roman Monody, Cantata, and Opera from the Circles around Cardialn Montalto, 97. **CONTACT ADDRESS** Dept of Music, Univ of Illinois, Urbana-Champaign, E Gregory Dr, PO Box 52, Champaign, IL 61820. **EMAIL** jwhill@uiuc.edu

HILL, L. BROOKS
PERSONAL Born 10/21/1943, Grenada, MS, m, 1961, 2 children **DISCIPLINE** SPEECH COMMUNICATION **EDUCATION** Univ of Memphis, BA, 64; Univ of Ala, MA, 65; Univ of Ill, PhD, 68. **CAREER** Prof, Univ of Okla, 68-88; prof & ch, Trinity Univ, 88-. **HONORS AND AWARDS** Phi Kappa Phi; local teaching awards. **MEMBERSHIPS** Nat Commun Assoc; Int Assoc for Intercultural Commun Studs (pres); Int Commun Assoc. **RESEARCH** Intercultural commun. **SELECTED PUBLICATIONS** Co-auth, The Needs of the International Student, Teaching and Directing the Basic Communication Course, Kendall/Hunt, 263-270, 93; co-auth, various articles in Organization and Behavior in Cross-Cultural Settings, Sanshusha, 193-218, 219-242, 289-312, 94; co-auth, articles in Cross-Cultural Communication and Aging in America, Erlbuam, 5-23, 1143-161, 97. **CONTACT ADDRESS** Dept of Speech & Drama, Trinity Univ, 715 Stadium Dr, San Antonio, TX 78212. **EMAIL** lhill@trinity.edu

HILL, LINDA MARIE
PERSONAL Born 07/13/1947, Vicksburg, MS **DISCIPLINE** 18TH CENTURY BRITISH LITERATURE **EDUCATION** Belhaven Col, BA, 69; Univ AR, MA, 71; Univ AL, PhD (18th Century British Lit), 89. **CAREER** English instr, L. B. Wallace Community Col, Andalusia, AL, 78-80; assoc prof English, Belhaven Col, Jackson, MS, 80-97; English Instr, Hinds Community Col, Rankin Campus, Pearl, MS, 97-. **HONORS AND AWARDS** Dean's Scholar, Univ AL Grad School. **MEMBERSHIPS** SE Soc for Eighteenth-Century Studies; MS Women's Political Network. **RESEARCH** Women's studies, 18th century; Am lit, 19th century. **SELECTED PUBLICATIONS** Auth, dissertation, The Dramatic Daring of Susanna Centlivre: A Feminist Study of the Foremost Woman Playwright of the Eighteenth Century, Univ AL, 89. **CONTACT ADDRESS** Hinds Comm Col, 3805 Hwy 80 E., Pearl, MS 39208-4295. **EMAIL** lmhill@hinds.cc.ms.us

HILL, MIKE K.
PERSONAL Born 07/31/1964, CA **DISCIPLINE** ENGLISH **EDUCATION** Humboldt State Univ, BA, 86; Univ Calif Santa Barb, MA, 88; SUNY Stony Brook, PhD, 94. **CAREER** Asst prof to assoc prof, Marymount Univ, 93-01; vis prof, Univ Mich, 98; asst prof, SUNY Albany, 99-. **HONORS AND AWARDS** Gustavas Myers Award, 97. **MEMBERSHIPS** MLA; ASECS; ASA; ASA. **RESEARCH** Race studies; popular culture studies; history of democracy; history of print; English novel. **SELECTED PUBLICATIONS** Auth, Whitness: A Critical reader, NYork Univ Pr, 97; auth, Masses, Classes and the Public Sphere, Verso, 00; auth, After Whitness: Identity, Ideology, Change, NYork Univ Pr (forthcoming). **CONTACT ADDRESS** English Dept, SUNY Albany, Humanities Bldg, Albany, NY 12222. **EMAIL** mikehill@csu.albany.edu

HILL, ORDELLE GERHARD
PERSONAL Born 09/04/1935, Brookings, SD, m, 1961 **DISCIPLINE** MEDIEVAL ENGLISH **EDUCATION** Augustana Col, BA, 57; Auburn Univ, MA, 59; Univ Ill, PhD(14th century English), 65. **CAREER** Instr English, Luther Col, 60-61; asst prof, Merrimack Col, 65-66; assoc prof, 66-68, PROF ENGLISH, EASTERN KY UNIV, 68- **MEMBERSHIPS** SAtlantic MLA; MLA. **RESEARCH** Medieval English literature. **SELECTED PUBLICATIONS** Auth, The Manor, The Plowman, and the Shepherd: A Gnarian Themes in Late Medieval and Early Renaissance Literature, Associated Univ Press, 93; auth, A Conduct Book For Richard II, Philol Quarterly, Vol 0073, 94. **CONTACT ADDRESS** Dept of English, Eastern Kentucky Univ, 521 Lancaster Ave, Richmond, KY 40475-3102. **EMAIL** enghill@acs.eku.edu

HILL, PATRICIA LIGGINS
PERSONAL Born 09/18/1942, Washington, DC, d **DISCIPLINE** ENGLISH **EDUCATION** Howard Univ Wash DC, BA cum laude 1965; Univ of San Francisco, MA English, 1970; Stanford Univ CA, PhD English/Amer Lit 1977. **CAREER** Univ of San Francisco, prof of English, 85-, assoc prof English, 79-84, dir ethnic studies, 77-, asst prof English, 77-79, English instructor, 71-77; Upper Midwest Tri-Racial Center, University of MN, resource consultant, 77-78; Urban Inst for Human Service Inc, research consultant, 76-80; Stanford University, teaching asst English, 74-77. **HONORS AND AWARDS** Recipient of fellowship, Natl Endowment for Humanities 1978; **MEMBERSHIPS** Bd dir Westside Mental Health Center 1971-78; SF Community College Bd 1972-78; CA Council of Black Educ 1973-. **SELECTED PUBLICATIONS** Roots for a Third World Aesthetic Found in Black & Chicano Poetry, De Colores 1980; "The Violent Space, An Interpretation of the Function of the New Black Aesthetic in Etheridge Knight's Poetry," Black Amer Lit Forum 1980; General editor, "Call & Response: The Riverside Anthology of the African American Literary Tradition," Houghton Mifflin, 1997; "The Dark/Black-Bad Light/White-Good Illusion in Joseph Conrad's 'Heart of Darkness' & 'Nigger of the Narcissus," Western Journal of Black Studies 1979. **CONTACT ADDRESS** English Department, Univ of San Francisco, 2130 Fulton St, San Francisco, CA 94117.

HILL, PHILIP GEORGE
PERSONAL Born 09/19/1934, Christiansburg, VA, m, 1957, 3 children **DISCIPLINE** DRAMA **EDUCATION** Univ Fla, BA, 56; Univ NC, Chapel Hill, MA, 60; Tulane Univ PhD(theatre), 64. **CAREER** Instr drama & speech, Allegheny Col, 60-62; PROF DRAMA, FURMAN UNIV, 64-98. **HONORS AND AWARDS** Suzanne M Davis Mem Awd, Southeastern Theatre Conf, 76. **MEMBERSHIPS** Am Theatre Asn (treas, 77-80); US Inst Theatre Technol; Southeastern Theatre Conf (vpres, 73-74, pres, 74-75). **SELECTED PUBLICATIONS** Auth, 7 books, 40+ articles. **CONTACT ADDRESS** Dept of Drama, Furman Univ, 3300 Poinsett Hwy, Greenville, SC 29613-0002. **EMAIL** phil.hill@furman.edu

HILL, SUSAN E. KOGLER
DISCIPLINE COMMUNICATIONS **EDUCATION** Bowling Green State Univ, BA, MA; Univ Denver, PhD. **CAREER** Dept ch, Cleveland State Univ. **SELECTED PUBLICATIONS** Co-auth, A Model of Mentoring and other Power Gaining Communication Strategies and Career Success, Organizational Communication: Emerging Perspectives, Vol IV, 94; The Impact of Mentoring and Collegial Support on Faculty Success: An Analysis of Support Behavior, Information Adequacy, and Communication Apprehension, Commun Edu, 38, 94. **CONTACT ADDRESS** Commun Dept, Cleveland State Univ, 83 E 24th St, Cleveland, OH 44115. **EMAIL** s.hill@csuohio.edu

HILL, THOMAS DANA
PERSONAL Born 05/06/1940, Boston, MA, d, 4 children **DISCIPLINE** ENGLISH **EDUCATION** Harvard Univ, BA, 61; Univ Ill, MA, 63; Cornell Univ, PhD(English), 67. **CAREER** From asst prof to fall prof English, 67-78, PROF ENGLISH & MEDIEVAL STUDIES, CORNELL UNIV, 78-, Soc Humanities fac fel, Cornell Univ, 70-71; Am Coun Learned Soc fel, 73-74. **HONORS AND AWARDS** Dir, NEH Summer Sem, 87, 93; Principal Investigator, The Sources of Anglo Saxon Literary Cult, 87-89; 90-92. **MEMBERSHIPS** Medieval Acad Am. **RESEARCH** Old and Middle English literature; Old French and Old Icelandic literature. **SELECTED PUBLICATIONS** Auth, Some remarks on the Site of Lucifer's Throne, Anglia, 69; Number and pattern in Lilja, J English & Gen Philol, 70; Sapiential structure and figural narrative in the Old English Elene, Traditio, 71; Vision and judgment in the Old English Christ III, 73 & Narcissas, Pygmalion, and the castration of Satan: Two mythographical themes in the Roman de la Rose, Studies Philol, 74; Parody and theme in the Middle English Land of Cockaygne, Notes & Queries, 75; The Accerbot charm and its Christian user, ASE, 77; Invocation of the Trinity and the Tradition of Lorica in Old English Poetry, Speculum, 81; The Prose Solomon and Saturn and Adrian and Rithess, Univ Toronto Press, 82. **CONTACT ADDRESS** Dept of English, Cornell Univ, 252 Goldwin Smith Hall, Ithaca, NY 14853-0001. **EMAIL** tdhi@cornell.edu

HILL, W. SPEED
PERSONAL Born 01/19/1935, Louisville, KY, m, 1984, 3 children **DISCIPLINE** ENGLISH **EDUCATION** Princeton Univ, AB (with Honors), 57; Harvard Univ, AM, PhD, 64. **CAREER** Asst prof, English, Case Western Reserve Univ, 64-69; asst prof, English, Univ Col, New York Univ, 69-73; assoc prof, English, 73-78, Prof, English, Lehman Col, CUNY 78-, Prof, English, Graduate Center, CUNY, 80-; vis prof, English, Univ British Columbia, Vancouver, 96. **HONORS AND AWARDS** Phi Beta Kappa; Woodrow Wilson Fel (honorary), 57-58; Am Philos Soc Grant-in-aid, 69-70; Folger Library fel, summer 69; Newberry Library fel, summer 69; ACLS grant-in-aid, 70-71; ACLS Sr fel, 73-74; Folger Library-British Academy fel, spring 73; NEH fel, 81-82; Honorary Doctorate of Humane Letters, Seabury-Western Theol Sem, 93; Honorary Doctorate of Humane letters, The University of the South, 95; listed in Who's Who in the East, 94-95, 95-96; Who's Who in American Education, 5th ed; Lehman Col, Awd for Res and Scholarship, 94; Honorary Doctorate of Letters, Sewanee: The Univ of the South, 95; grants to the Hooker Edition: NEH; Fac Res Awd Prog, CUNY. **SELECTED PUBLICATIONS** Ed, New Ways of Looking at Old Texts: Papers of the Renaissance English Text Soc, 1985-1991, English Renaissance: Nondramatic Literature, in Scholarly Editing: A Guide to Research, ed D. C. Greetham, MLA, 95; Scripture as Text, Text as Scripture: The Example of Richard Hooker, TEXT 9, 96; Where We Are and How We Got Here: Editing After Poststructuralism, Shakespeare Studies, 24, 96; Commentary on Commentary on Commentary: Three Historicisms Annotating Richard Hooker, for Margins of the Text, ed D. C. Greetham, Univ MI Press, 97; Richard Hooker in the Folger Edition: An Editorial Perspective & Richard Hooker: A Selected Bibliography, 1971-1993, compiled with Egil Grislis, for a volume of Hooker Conference papers, Richard Hooker and the Construction of a Texts & Studies, 97; New Ways of Looking at Old Texts, II: Papers of the Renaissance English Text Soc, 1992-1996, ed, numerous other articles, review articles, and reviews, also editor, co-ed, or supervisory editor of numerous volumes. **CONTACT ADDRESS** 33 C Tier St., Bronx, NY 10464. **EMAIL** wshlc@cunyvm.cuny.edu

HILL, WANDA W.
PERSONAL Born 03/01/1968, Concord, NC, m, 1997 **DISCIPLINE** ENGLISH **EDUCATION** Winston-Salem State Univ, BA, 90; Univ NC at Charlotte, MA, 94. **CAREER** Teacher, Cabarrus Co Sch, 91-96; Prof, Rowan-Cabarrus Community Col, 96-. **HONORS AND AWARDS** Excellence in Teaching Awd, Rowan-Cabarrus Community Col, 98; Young Careerist, Concord Bus and Prof Women's Orgn, 99. **MEMBERSHIPS** Delta Sigma Theta Sorority, Inc. **RESEARCH** African-American Literature, Southern Literature. **CONTACT ADDRESS** Dept Lib Arts, Rowan-Cabarrus Comm Col, PO Box 1595, Salisbury, NC 28145-1595. **EMAIL** rwhill@aol.com

HILL-LUBIN, MILDRED ANDERSON
PERSONAL Born 03/23/1933, Russell County, AL, m **DISCIPLINE** ENGLISH **EDUCATION** Paine Coll Augusta, GA, BA English Honors 1961; Western Reserve Cleveland, MA 1962; Indiana, 1964; Univ of Minnesota, 1965-66; Howard Univ & African-Amer Inst,1972; Univ of Illinois Urbana-Champaign, PhD English & African Studies 1974. **CAREER** Paine Coll, instructor/asst prof, 62-65 & 66-70; Hamline Univ, exchange prof, 65-66; Paine Coll, asst prof English/dir EPDA program, 70-72; Univ of IL, tchng asst/instructor, 72-74; Univ of Florida, assoc prof of English/dir English program for special admit students, 74-77, asst dean of graduate sch, 77-80, assoc prof of English & African Studies, 82-. **HONORS AND AWARDS** Alpha Kappa Mu Honor Soc Paine Coll 1960; Travel-Study Grant to W Africa African-Amer Intl 19; Trainer of Teachers Fellowship Univ of Illinois 1973-74; Gainesville Area Women of Distinction Awd, 1992; Univ of FL, Teacher of the Year, 1994; Gainesville Comm on the Status of Women, Susan B Anthony Awd, 1994. **MEMBERSHIPS** Proj assoc Council of Chief State School Officers Washington, DC 1981-82; consultant Amer Council on Educ 1981-; panel mem Adv Cncl Mellon Humanities Grant UNCF College Fund 1980-90; discipline comm in African Lit Fulbright Awards 1983-86; exec comm Coll Comp & Comm (CCCC) 1977-80; exec comm African Lit Assn 1983-89; pres Gainesville Chap of the Links 1985-87; pres FOCUS 1978-79; bd dir Gainesville/Alachua Co Center of Excell 1985-; Alpha Kappa Alpha Sor; pres, African Literature Assn 1987-88; dir, Gainesville-Jacmel Haiti Sister Cities Program, 1987-92; pres, The Visionaires, 1988-91; FL Humanities Council, bd of dirs, 1991-95; Santa Fe Community Coll District, bd of trustees, 1993-. **SELECTED PUBLICATIONS** Co-ed, "Towards Defining the African Aesthetic" and articles in, "Southern Folklore Quarterly," "Coll Lang Assn Journal"; "Presence Africaine"; "Okike"; Leadership and Achievement Award, Nu Eta Lambda Chapter Alpha Phi Alpha Fraternity 1988; articles, "The Black Grandmother in Literature," in Ngambika, 1986. **CONTACT ADDRESS** Univ of Florida, 4008 TUR, Gainesville, FL 32611.

HILL-MILLER, KATHERINE CECELIA
PERSONAL Born 01/24/1949, Granite City, IL, m, 1982, 1 child **DISCIPLINE** MODERN BRITISH & WOMEN'S LITERATURE **EDUCATION** Fordham Univ, BA, 71; Columbia Univ, MA, 72, MPhil, 74, PhD(English), 79. **CAREER** Teaching fel, Columbia Univ, 74; lect, Kingsborough Comm Col, 72-73; asst prof, Col William & Mary, 77-80; asst prof 80-84, assoc prof 84-89, PROF ENGLISH, CW POST CAMPUS LONG ISLAND UNIV, 89-; dir, poetry ctr, 82-85, DIR WRITING, CW POST CTR, 93-; guest lect, Rheinische Friedrich-Wilhelms-Universitat, Bonn, 86. **HONORS AND AWARDS** Dir, NEH Summr Sem; Virginia Woolf's Major Novels, 94,96,00. **MEMBERSHIPS** MLA; Virginia Woolf Soc. **RESEARCH** Virginia Woolf; experimental fiction; women writers. **SELECTED PUBLICATIONS** Auth, My Hideous Progeny: Mary SHelley, William Godwin, and the Father-Daughter Relaationship, Univ Del Press, 95; auth, The Bantam Book of Spelling, Bantam Books, 86; co-auth, Writing Effective Paragraphs, Harper and Row, 74; auth, Virginia Woolf's Places: A Guide to Some English Literary Landscapes, Duckworth Publishers, fothcoming; auth, Virginia Woolf and Leslie Stephen: History and Literary Revolution, Pubs of the Mod Lang Asn, 96, no 3, 81. **CONTACT ADDRESS** Dept of English, Long Island Univ, C.W. Post, Greenvale, NY 11548. **EMAIL** fkcmiller@aol.com

HILLARD, VAN E.
DISCIPLINE ENGLISH LITERATURE **EDUCATION** Univ Cincinnati, PhD, 87. **CAREER** Asst prof pract rhet; asst dir writing prog. **RESEARCH** Comp pedag; philos of rhetoric. **SELECTED PUBLICATIONS** Auth, publ(s) on rhet publ art; rhet photog; polit quilting. **CONTACT ADDRESS** Eng Dept, Duke Univ, Durham, NC 27706.

HILLIARD, JERRY
DISCIPLINE COMMUNICATION STUDIES **EDUCATION** Kent State Univ, BA, MA; Univ Tennessee, PhD. **CAREER** Prof. **MEMBERSHIPS** Public Rel Soc Am. **SELECTED PUBLICATIONS** Auth, pubs in Journalism & Mass Communication Quarterly, Newspaper Research Journal; co-auth, Pressing Issues; ed, History of Tennessee Newspapers, Tennessee, 96. **CONTACT ADDRESS** Dept of Communication, East Tennessee State Univ, PO Box 70717, Johnson City, TN 37614-0717.

HILLIARD, RAYMOND FRANCIS
PERSONAL Born 11/13/1943, Washington, DC, m, 1969, 1 child **DISCIPLINE** ENGLISH **EDUCATION** Univ MD, BA, 66; Univ Rochester, PhD, 76. **CAREER** From asst prof to assoc prof 76-91, prof eng, Univ Richmond, 91. **HONORS AND AWARDS** Phi Beta Kappa. **MEMBERSHIPS** MLA; Am Soc 18th Century Studies. **RESEARCH** Eighteenth-century British novel; narrative theory; psychoanalytic theory. **SELECTED PUBLICATIONS** Auth, "Emma: Dancing Without Space to Turn in," in Probability, Time, and Space in Eighteenth-Century Literature (AMS Press, 78); auth, Desire and the Structure of Eighteenth-century Fiction, Vol 9, Studies In Eighteenth Cent Cult, 79; auth, The Redemption of Fatherhood in The Vicar of Wakefield, Studies in Engl Lit, 83; auth, Pamela: Autonomy, Subordination, and the State of Childhood, Studies in Philol, 86; auth, Clarissa and Ritual Cannibalism, PMLA, 90; auth, Laughter Echoing from Mouth to Mouth: Symbolic Cannibalism and Gener in Evelina, Eighteenth Cent Life, 93. **CONTACT ADDRESS** Dept of Eng, Univ of Richmond, Richmond, VA 23173-0002. **EMAIL** rhilliar@richmond.edu

HILLIARD, STEPHEN SHORTIS
PERSONAL Born 06/20/1939, Framingham, MA **DISCIPLINE** ENGLISH **EDUCATION** Harvard Univ, AB, 61;

Princeton Univ, MA, 64, PhD(English), 67. **CAREER** Asst prof, 64-71, assoc prof English, Univ Nebr, Lincoln, 71-84; from assoc prof to prof English, 84. **MEMBERSHIPS** MLA. **RESEARCH** Renaissance literature; critical theory. **CONTACT ADDRESS** Dept of English, Univ of Nebraska, Lincoln, 303 Andrews Hall, Lincoln, NE 68588-0333. **EMAIL** shilliard1@unl.edu

HILLIGOSS, SUSAN
DISCIPLINE ENGLISH LITERATURE **EDUCATION** Univ Pa, PhD, 77. **CAREER** Dept Eng, Clemson Univ **RESEARCH** Professional communication; visual communication. **SELECTED PUBLICATIONS** Auth, Robert Coles in US Authors Series, Twayne, 97; co-ed, Literacy and Computers: The Complications of Teaching and Learning with Technology, MLA, 94; auth, "Visual Communication," Longman, 00. **CONTACT ADDRESS** Clemson Univ, 103 Strode, Clemson, SC 29634. **EMAIL** hillgos@clemson.edu

HILLIS, RICK
PERSONAL Born 03/02/1966, Nipawin, ON, Canada, m **DISCIPLINE** PHYSICAL EDUCATION, POETRY **EDUCATION** Univ Sask, BEd, 70; Univ Iowa, MFA, 84. **CAREER** Lectr, Stanford Univ, 90-93; writer in residence to asst prof, Reed Col, 94-00. **HONORS AND AWARDS** Stegner Fel; Drue Heinz Fiction Prize. **MEMBERSHIPS** PEN. **SELECTED PUBLICATIONS** Auth, The Blue Machines at Night, 88; auth, Limbo River, 90. **CONTACT ADDRESS** Dept English, Reed Col, 3203 SE Woodstock Blvd, Portland, OR 97202-8138. **EMAIL** rick.hillis@reed.edu

HILT, MICHAEL
DISCIPLINE COMMUNICATIONS **EDUCATION** Univ Kans, BS, 81, MS, 86; Univ Nebr, PhD, 94. **CAREER** Adj prof, Washburn Univ, 81-82; news producer/dir: KSNT-TV, Topeka, Kans, 82-86; adj prof, Rockhurst Col, 87; news producer: KCTV, Kansas City, Mo, 86-88; assoc prof, 88-, grad fel, Univ Nebr, Omaha, 93-; consult, Cox Commun, Omaha, Nebr, 97-. **SELECTED PUBLICATIONS** Auth, Television News and the Elderly: Broadcast Managers' Attitudes Toward Older Adults, Garland Publ Inc, 97. **CONTACT ADDRESS** Dept of Communication, Univ of Nebraska, Omaha, Omaha, NE 68182. **EMAIL** MHilt@cwis.unomaha.edu

HILTON, NELSON
PERSONAL Born 03/09/1950, Washington, DC, m, 1987, 2 children **DISCIPLINE** ENGLISH **EDUCATION** Univ Calif Santa Cruz, AB, 72; PhD, 79. **CAREER** Asst prof to assoc prof to prof, Univ Ga, 79-. **HONORS AND AWARDS** Fulbright/Hays, 76-77. **MEMBERSHIPS** MLA; SAMLA; ACH; ACM. **RESEARCH** 'Humanities computing'; Blake; romanticism. **SELECTED PUBLICATIONS** Auth, Literal Imagination: Blake's Vision of Words, Univ Calif Pr, 83; auth, Lexis Complexes: Literary Intentions, Univ Ga, 95; auth, Blake Digital Text Project, www.english.uga.edu/wblake. **CONTACT ADDRESS** English Dept, Univ of Georgia, Baldwin St, Athens, GA 30602. **EMAIL** nhilton@english.uga.edu

HIMELSTEIN, MORGAN Y.
PERSONAL Born 09/19/1926, Lebanon, CT, w, 1958, 2 children **DISCIPLINE** ENGLISH **EDUCATION** Wesleyan Univ, BA, 47; Columbia Univ, MA, 48; PhD, 58. **CAREER** Instr, Univ of Rochester, 48-50; Army of the US, 50-52; instr to prof emeritus, Adelphi Univ, 57- **HONORS AND AWARDS** Thorndike Fel, Wesleyan Univ; Merit Awd for Excellence in Scholarship, Adelphi Univ. **MEMBERSHIPS** AAUP, MLA, Opera Am. **RESEARCH** Drama and theatre of the 19th and 20th Centuries: Theatre and politics, 19th Century Operetta. **SELECTED PUBLICATIONS** Auth, Drama was a Weapon: The Left-Wing Theatre in New York, 1929-1941, Rutgers Univ Pr/Greenwood, 63, 76; transl, The Grand Duchess of Gerolstein, (Mapleson, 77, 82), transl, La Perithole, (Mapleson, 82); transl, Orpheus in the Underworld, (Mapleson, 85); transl, Die Fledermaus (Mapleson, 90). **CONTACT ADDRESS** 2401 Pennsylvania Ave, Apt 12B35, Philadelphia, PA 19130-3010. **EMAIL** myhimelstein@earthlink.net

HINCHCLIFFE, PETER
DISCIPLINE ENGLISH LITERATURE **EDUCATION** Univ British Columbia, BA, 58; Univ Toronto, MA, 60; PhD, 67. **CAREER** Ch, St. Jerome's Univ; assoc prof, St. Jerome's Univ; asst prof, St. Jerome's Univ; lectr, St. Jerome's Univ; lectr, Univ of Western Ontario. **SELECTED PUBLICATIONS** Auth, "Dennis Lee"; auth, "Dixon Scott"; auth, "Ethel Wilson"; auth, "Hopkins and C. Day Lewis"; auth, "Hopkins and Some Poets of the Thirties"; auth, "Isabella Valancy Crawford"; auth, "The Rainbow and Women in Love: From George Eliot to Thomas"; auth, "Hardy as Formal Models"; auth, "To Keep the Memory of So Worthy a Friend: Ethel Wilson As an Elegist"; auth, "Coming to Terms with Kipling: Puck of Pook's Hill, Rewards and Fairies and the Shape of Kipling's Imagination. **CONTACT ADDRESS** Dept of English, St. Jerome's Univ, Waterloo, ON, Canada N2L 3G3. **EMAIL** pmhinch@watarts.uwaterloo.ca

HINDEN, MICHAEL CHARLES
PERSONAL Born 06/05/1941, New York, NY **DISCIPLINE** ENGLISH & AMERICAN LITERATURE **EDUCATION** Ohio Univ, AB, 63; Sorbonne, Degre Superieur, 62; Brown Univ, PhD(English), 71. **CAREER** Instr English, Brown Univ, 68-69; asst prof, 70-75, assoc prof English, Univ Wis-Madison, 75-85, prof, 85-, chmn, Integrated Liberal Studies Prog, 80-84, assoc dean intl studies, 92-, dir, Bradley Learning Community, 95-, Fulbright prof Am lit, Univ Bucharest, Romania, 75-76. **HONORS AND AWARDS** Kiekhofer Distinguished Teaching Awd, Wis, 72. **MEMBERSHIPS** MLA; The Eugene O'Neill Soc (chmn & bd dirs, 82-). **RESEARCH** Modern drama; nature of tragedy; contemporary literature. **SELECTED PUBLICATIONS** Auth, Byrd Thou Never Wert: The Collected Poems and Post Cards of Emmett Byrd, Ten Speed Press, 80; Long Day's Journey into Night: Native Eloquence, Twayne, 90. **CONTACT ADDRESS** Dept of English, Univ of Wisconsin, Madison, 600 North Park St, Madison, WI 53706-1403. **EMAIL** hinden@macc.wisc.edu

HINDMAN, KATHLEEN BEHRENBRUCH
PERSONAL Born 09/22/1942, South Bend, IN, m, 1967, 7 children **DISCIPLINE** LITERATURE **EDUCATION** Valparaiso Univ, BA, 65; La State Univ, MA, 67; Pa State Univ, PhD(English), 80. **CAREER** Asst, La State Univ, 65-67, instr, 67-73, asst prof, 73-81; Assoc Prof, 81-94, PROF ENGLISH, MANSFIELD UNIV, 94-. **HONORS AND AWARDS** Honors Program at Valparaiso Univ; Sabbatticals, Spring 78, Fall 90, Fall 94; SSHE grant to attend NAWE Conf, March 95. **MEMBERSHIPS** English Asn of the Penn State Universities; Asn of Penn State Colleges and Universities; Asn of Lit Schol and Critics; Traditional Cosmology Soc. **RESEARCH** Graham Greene; the modern novel; the short story; curriculum development; mythology. **SELECTED PUBLICATIONS** Auth, Erratic Glints (poem), Modern Haiku, winter 70; Jack London's The Sea-Wolf: Naturalism with a spiritual bent, The Jack London Newsletter, 9-12/73; Graham Green, In: British Dramatists Since World War II, Bruccoli-Clark, summer 82; Graham Greene and the Medieval Morality, Proceedings: The 1988 Conference of the English Association of the Pennsylvania State Universities, WestChester Univ, Oct 14-15, 88; Graham Greene, Read More About It, Vol 3, Pierian Press, 89; The Technique of Comparison in Crane's The Monster, Proceedings: The 1993 Conference of the Pennsylvania Universities, Mansfield Univ, Oct 1-2, 93. **CONTACT ADDRESS** English Dept, Mansfield Univ of Pennsylvania, Belknap Hall, Mansfield, PA 16933-1308. **EMAIL** khindman@mnsfld.edu

HINES, JAMES ROBERT
PERSONAL Born 10/27/1937, Springfield, IL, d, 1 child **DISCIPLINE** MUSICOLOGY **EDUCATION** Old Dominion Univ, BA, 65; Va Commonwealth Univ, MM, 69; Univ NC, PhD(musicol), 74 **CAREER** Fac, Tidewater Community Col, 74-75; dir, Norfolk Camerata, 74-; music critic, Norfolk Virginian-Pilot, 74-77; dir music, 75-92, prof fine and performing arts, Christopher Newport Univ, 92-. **HONORS AND AWARDS** Outstanding Faculty **MEMBERSHIPS** Am Musicological Soc; Sonneck Soc Am Music **RESEARCH** Nineteenth century American music, folk music of Guyana. **SELECTED PUBLICATIONS** Ed, A performance practices bibliography, third supplement, Current Musicology, 73. **CONTACT ADDRESS** Christopher Newport Univ, 1 University Pl, Newport News, VA 23606. **EMAIL** jhines@cnu.edu

HINES, RANDY
DISCIPLINE COMMUNICATION STUDIES **EDUCATION** Kent State Univ, BA, MA; Tex Univ, PhD. **CAREER** Assoc prof, 91-. **MEMBERSHIPS** Public Rel Student Soc Am. **SELECTED PUBLICATIONS** Auth, pubs in Mid Atlantic Bulletin of the Newspaper Advertising Marketing Executives; Southern Newspaper Publishers Association Bulletin; Business Journal; ed, A History of Tennessee Newspapers. **CONTACT ADDRESS** Dept of Communication, East Tennessee State Univ, PO Box 70717, Johnson City, TN 37614-0717.

HINES, SUSAN CAROL
PERSONAL Born 08/06/1965, Atlanta, GA, s **DISCIPLINE** ENGLISH **EDUCATION** Univ Alaska, BA, 87; Univ Brit Colum, MA, 89; Ga State Univ, PhD, 98. **CAREER** Asst prof, Middle Ga Col, 93-98; asst prof, La Salle Univ, 98-00; developer, analysis, Eduprise.com, 00-. **HONORS AND AWARDS** Sorus Found Teaching Grant; Ga Humanities Coun Grant; Governer's Teaching Fel. **MEMBERSHIPS** AACE, MLA, ACM, ELO. **RESEARCH** Hypermedia, Instructional Design, New Media. **SELECTED PUBLICATIONS** Auth, "A Trial Reading of Robert Browning's 'The Ring and the Book,'" Studies in Browning and His Circle 18, (90): 28-33; auth, "The Body as Production in Shakespeare's 'Julius Caesar,'", Explicatun 52, (94): 135-137; auth, "What's Academic About Trek," Extrapolation 36, (95): 5-9; auth, "What Hypertext is Not Bound to Do," Etucause; auth, "A Matter of Course: What Trading Web Editing Can Do for Your Campus," Syllabus (99); auth, "Heim's 'Electric Language,'", H-Net Rev, Mich State Univ, (99); auth, "How To, and Why? What You Should Know About Course and Learning Management Systems," AACE, (Charlottesville, VA: 00). **CONTACT ADDRESS** 5 E Gleewood Pl, Durham, NC 27713. **EMAIL** shines@eduprise.com

HINKEL, HOWARD
DISCIPLINE BRITISH ROMANTICISM **EDUCATION** Tulane Univ, PhD, 68. **CAREER** Assoc prof & dept ch; past cha, campus Comt Undergrad Educ & Fac Develop Commt; past dir, Lower Div Stud & Campus Writing Program. **HONORS AND AWARDS** Purple Chalk awd, 86. **RESEARCH** Eighteeth-and nineteenth-century British natural philosophy; natural history; the romantic writers; natural history and the environment. **SELECTED PUBLICATIONS** Publ op, British Romanticism. **CONTACT ADDRESS** Dept of English, Univ of Missouri, Columbia, 236 Tate Hall, Columbia, MO 65211. **EMAIL** HinkelH@missiouri.edu

HINNANT, CHARLES H.
PERSONAL Born 03/18/1936, Cleveland, OH, m, 1968, 2 children **DISCIPLINE** ENGLISH **EDUCATION** Princeton Univ, BA, 59, Columbia Univ, MA, 60, PhD, 66. **CAREER** TA, Columbia Col, 62-65; asst prof, Univ of Mich, 65-72; assoc prof to prof, Univ of Mo Columbia, 72-. **HONORS AND AWARDS** Columbia Fel, 62-65; NEH Fel, 68; Grant, Univ of Mo, 75, 78; Univ of Mo, Fel, 87-88; Catherine Paine Middlebush Chair of English, 97-00; Gold Chalk Teaching Awd, 00. **MEMBERSHIPS** ASECS; Midwest ASECS. **RESEARCH** 18th Century. **SELECTED PUBLICATIONS** Auth, Thomas Hobbes, G.K. Hall, (Boston), 77; auth, Thomas Hobbes: A Reference Guide, G.K. Hall, (Boston), 80; auth, "Purity and Defilement in Gulliver's Travels", Macmillan/St. Martin's Pr, (London/NY), 87; auth, Samuel Johnson: An Analysis, Macmillan/St. Martin's Pr, (London/NY), 88; auth, The Poetry of Anne Finch: An Essay in Interpretation, Newark, Del, 94; rev, "Edward Tomarken", Papers on Lang and Lit 32.2, (Spring 96): 217-23; rev, "Brian Hanley", New Rambler 10, (94-95): 70-71; rev, "Thomas Woodman", British J for 18th Century Studies 19, (96): 113-14; rev, "Lionel Basney", Sewanee Rev 105, (97): 66-67; auth, Steel for the Mind: Samuel Johnson and Critical Discourse, Newark, Del, 94; coed, The Anne Finch Wellesley Manuscript Poems: A Critical Edition, Univ of Ga Pr, (Athens), 98. **CONTACT ADDRESS** Dept English, Univ of Missouri, Columbia, 107 Tate Hall, Columbia, MO 65211-1500. **EMAIL** hinnanth@missouri.edu

HINTZ, CARRIE
PERSONAL Born 08/23/1970, Edmonton, AB, Canada, s **DISCIPLINE** ENGLISH **EDUCATION** McGill Univ, BA, 92; Univ Toronto, MA, 93; PhD, 98. **CAREER** Adj lectr, Univ Toronto, 98-99; asst prof, Queens Col, CUNY, 99-. **HONORS AND AWARDS** PSC CUNY Res Grant; SSHRC Doctoral Fel. **MEMBERSHIPS** MLA; ASECS; Aphra Ben Soc; ACCUTE. **RESEARCH** Early modern women writers; Civil War literature; literary utopias. **SELECTED PUBLICATIONS** Auth, "But One Opinion: Fear of Dissent in Cavendish's New Blazing World," Utopian Stud 7 (96): 25-38; auth, "A Second Reference to Marin LeRoy de Gromberville's Polexandre in Dorothy Osborne's Letters," Note Queries (99); auth, "Utopian Writing," The Routledge Encyc of Women's Writings (00); auth, "All People Seen and Known: Dorothy Osborne and Early Modern Surveillance," Dalhousie Rev (00). **CONTACT ADDRESS** Dept English, Queens Col, CUNY, 6530 Kissena Blvd, Flushing, NY 11367-1575.

HINTZ, SUZANNE S.
DISCIPLINE SPANISH, LITERATURE **EDUCATION** Purdue Univ, BA, 67; Univ of Va, Med, 78; George Mason Univ, MA, 91; Cath Univ of Am, PhD, 93 **CAREER** Prof, 93-98, Germanna Cmnty Col; Div Chair, 98-, Northrn VA Cmnty Col **HONORS AND AWARDS** Embassy of Spain awd, 91; DeFerrari Sch, 90-93; Lee-Hatzfeld Sch, 90-92 **MEMBERSHIPS** MLA, SAMLA, LASA, MACLAS, AATSP **RESEARCH** Puerto Rican and Catalan lit. **SELECTED PUBLICATIONS** Auth, "Rosario Ferre, A Search for Identity," Literal books, 95; Essays in Honor of Josep M. Sola-Sole: Linguistic and Literary Relations of Catalan and Castilian, Peter Lang, 96; transl, "The War of the Christs and Amelia's Case, Peterlang, 92. **CONTACT ADDRESS** No Virginia Comm Col, Woodbridge, VA 22191. **EMAIL** shintz@nv.cc.va.us

HIROKAWA, RANDY Y.
PERSONAL Born 09/23/1953, HI, m, 1978, 3 children **DISCIPLINE** COMMUNICATION STUDIES **EDUCATION** Univ WA, PhD, 80. **CAREER** Asst prof, PA State Univ, 80-84; prof, Univ IA, 84-. **HONORS AND AWARDS** Burlington Northern Fac Achievement Awd, Univ IA, 89. **MEMBERSHIPS** Nat Commun Asn. **RESEARCH** Group decision-making. **SELECTED PUBLICATIONS** Ed, with M S Poole, Communication and Group Decision-making, Sage, 1st ed, 86, 2nd ed, 96; auth, Functional Approaches to the Study of Group Communication: Even Good Notions Have Their Problems, Small Group Res, 25, 94; Received Facilitators and Inhibitors of Effectiveness in Organizational Work Teams, Management Commun Quart, 8, 95; with L Erbert and A Hurst, Communication and Group Decision-Making Effectiveness, in Hirokawa and Poole, eds, Communication and Group Decision-making, 2nd ed, Sage, 96; with D S Gouran, Functional Theory and Communication in Decision-making and Problem-solving Groups, in Hirokawa and Poole, eds, Communication and Group Decision-making, 2nd ed, Sage, 96; with M S Poole, Communication and Group Decision-making, in Hirokawa and Poole, eds, Commu-

nication and Group Decision-making, Sage, 96; with A J Salazar, L Erbert, and R J Ice, Small Group Communication, in M B Salwen and D W Stacks, eds, An Integrated Approach to Communication Theory and Research, LEA, 96; with A J Salazar, An Integrated Approach to Communication and Group Decision-making, in L R Frey and J K Barge, eds, Managing Group Life: Communication in Decision-making Groups, Houghton-Mifflin, 97; auth, A Rose is a Rose By Any Other Name, But How Interdisciplinary Are Multi-professional Health Care Teams?, in E Swanson and R J Bulger, eds, Redefining Education in Primary Care, AAHC, in press; numerous other articles and book chapters, with several more publications forthcoming. **CONTACT ADDRESS** Dept of Commun Studies, The Univ of Iowa, 117 BCSB, Iowa City, IA 52242. **EMAIL** randy-hirokawa@uiowa.edu

HIRSCH, BERNARD ALAN

PERSONAL Born 10/03/1944, Chicago, IL, w, 1971, 1 child **DISCIPLINE** ENGLISH **EDUCATION** Univ Ill, Urbana, BS, 67, AM, 68, PhD, 75. **CAREER** Instr English, Northern Ill Univ, 68-70; lectr, Univ Ill, Urbana, 75-76; Asst Prof, 76-80, assoc prof English, Univ Kans, 80-. **HONORS AND AWARDS** Univ Kans res grant, 78; Edward F. Grier Teaching Award, 91; Vice-Chancellor's Fel, 97-98. **MEMBERSHIPS** MLA; Byron Soc; Keats-Shelley Asn; Western Lit Asn; NAm Soc Study Romanticism. **RESEARCH** English romantic movement; native American literature and culture. **SELECTED PUBLICATIONS** Co-ed, A Return to Vision, 71 & 74, The Shadow Within, 73 & The Essay: Structure and Purpose, 75, Houghton; auth, A want of that true theory: Julian and Maddalo as dramatic monologue, Studies Romanticism, winter 78; The Erosion of the Narrator's World View in Childe Harold's Pilgrimage, I-II, Mod Lang Quart, 12/81; Self-Hatred and Spritual Corruption in House Made of Dawn, Western Am Lit, 2/83; co-ed, The Essay: Readings for the Writing Process, Houghton Mifflin, 86; auth, The Telling Which Continues: Oral Tradition and the Written Word in Leslie Marmon Silko's Storyteller, Am Indian Quart, Winter 88, reprinted in Yellow Woman: Leslie Marmon Silko, Rutgers Univ Press, 93; Byron's Poetic Journal: Teaching Childe Harold's Pilgrimage, in Approaches to Teaching Byron's Poetry, MLA, 91. **CONTACT ADDRESS** Dept of English, Univ of Kansas, Lawrence, Lawrence, KS 66045-2115. **EMAIL** hirsch@falcon.cc.ukans.edu

HIRSCH, DAVID HARRY

PERSONAL Born 04/06/1930, Brooklyn, NY, m, 1954, 2 children **DISCIPLINE** ENGLISH & AMERICAN LITERATURE **EDUCATION** NYork Univ, BA, 51, MA, 53. **CAREER** From instr to prof English, 61-78, NICHOLAS BROWN PROF ORATORY & BELLES LETTRES IN ENGLISH & CHMN DEPT ENGLISH, BROWN UNIV, 78-, Vis lectr, Bar-Ilan Univ, Israel, 66-67; Soc Relig Higher Educ fel, 71-72. **MEMBERSHIPS** MLA. **RESEARCH** Nineteenth century English and American literature; Poe; Melville; the Bible in English literature. **SELECTED PUBLICATIONS** Auth, Reality and Idea in the Early American Novel, Mouton, The Hague, 71; John Barth's Freedom Road, Mediter Rev, spring 72; Linguistic structure and literary meaning, J Lit Semantics, fall 72; American Dionysian poetry and American poetics, Sewanee Rev, spring 75; Speech Acts and Fluid Language, J Lit Semantics, winter 76; Hamlet, Moby-Dick, and Passional Thinking, In: Aspects of Influence, Harvard Univ, 76; Deep metaphors and shallow structures, Sewanee Rev, winter 77. **CONTACT ADDRESS** Dept of English, Brown Univ, 1 Prospect St, Providence, RI 02912-9127.

HIRSCH, GORDON D.

PERSONAL Born 05/15/1943, Norwich, NY, m, 1972 **DISCIPLINE** ENGLISH **EDUCATION** Cornell Univ, AB, 65; Univ Calif, Berkeley, MA, 67, PhD(English), 71. **CAREER** From Asst Prof to Assoc Prof, 70-88, PROF ENGLISH, UNIV MINN, MINNEAPOLIS, 88-. **HONORS AND AWARDS** Horace T. Morse, Univ of Minn Alumni Assoc Awd for Outstanding Contrib to Undergraduate Educ, 99-00. **MEMBERSHIPS** MLA; Midwest Victorian Studies Asn. **RESEARCH** Victorian literature; the British novel; psychoanalytic literary criticism. **SELECTED PUBLICATIONS** Auth, Tennyson's Commedia, Victorian Poetry, 70; Charles Dickens' nurse's stories, Psychoanal Rev, 75; The mysteries in Bleak House: a psychoanalytic study, Dickens Studies Ann, 75; The monster was a lady: on the psychology of Mary Shelley's Frankenstein, Hartford Studies in Lit, 75; Organic imagery and the psychology of Mill's On Liberty, Mill News Lett, 75; The Laurentian double: images of D H Lawrence in the stories, D H Lawrence Rev, 77; Mr Pickwick's impotence, The Sphinx, 79; A psychoanalytic rereading of David Copperfield, Victorian Newslett, 80; Double Binds and Schizophrenogenic Conversations: Readings in Three Middle Chapters of Alice in Wonderland, Denver Quart, 84; History Writing in Carlyle's Past and Present, Prose Studies, 84; co-ed, Dr. Jekyll and Mr. Hyde After One Hundred Years, Univ Chicago Press, 88; auth, Shame, Pride, and Prejudice, Mosaic, 92; Robert Louis Stevenson, In: Dictionary of Literary Biography: British Travel Writers 1876-1909, 97; Ardor and Shame in Middlemarch, in: Scenes of Shame: Psychoanalysis, Shame and Writing, 99. **CONTACT ADDRESS** Dept of English, Univ of Minnesota, Twin Cities, 207 Church St SE, Minneapolis, MN 55455-0156. **EMAIL** hirsc002@tc.umn.edu

HIRSCH, JULIA

PERSONAL Born 01/01/1938, Antwerp, Belgium, 2 children **DISCIPLINE** ENGLISH **EDUCATION** Barnard Col, Columbia, Univ, BA, 59, MA, 60, PhD(English), 64. **CAREER** Lectr English & freshman adv, Barnard Col, Columbia Univ, 62-64; from instr to asst prof English, 64-73, Assoc Prof English, Brooklyn Col, 73-, Am Coun Learned Soc study fel, 67-68; vis sr lectr English lit, Haifa Univ, 70-71; Nat Endowment Humanities fel, 77-78. **RESEARCH** History of nationalism; translation theory; medieval iconography. **SELECTED PUBLICATIONS** Auth, In Search of Stature: Linguistic Theory and Practise in the Sixteenth Century, Inc Linguist, 1/69; Translation and cultural nationalism in the reign of Elizabeth, J Hist Ideas, 12/69; Eyeless in Gaza: Problems of teaching Renaissance literature in Israel, Col English, 1/73; Family Photographs, Oxford Univ Press, 6/81. **CONTACT ADDRESS** Dept of English, Brooklyn Col, CUNY, 2901 Bedford Ave, Brooklyn, NY 11210-2813.

HIRSCHBERG, STUART

PERSONAL Born 12/02/1942, Staten Island, NY, m **DISCIPLINE** ENGLISH **EDUCATION** Columbia Univ, AB, 65; Wagner Col, MA, 66; New York Univ, PhD, 72. **CAREER** Asst Prof, NDak State Univ, 70-74; Lect, Univ Cal, 74-76; Grants Off, Univ Ill, 76-77; Assoc Prof, Rutgers Univ, 77-. **HONORS AND AWARDS** Fulbright-Hayes, 77; Who's Who in the East, 95. **MEMBERSHIPS** MLA, NJCEA, PEN Am Center. **RESEARCH** Literary criticism, myth, semiotics, rhetoric, cultural studies. **SELECTED PUBLICATIONS** Auth, At the Top of the Tower: Yeats' Poetry Explored Through a Vision (Heidelberg), 79; Auth, Myth in the Poetry of Ted Hughes, Wolfhound Pr (Dublin), 81; Auth, Patterns Across the Disciplines, Macmillan, 88; Auth, The Many Worlds of Literature, Macmillan, 94; Auth, Strategies of Argument 2nd ed, Allyn and Bacon, 96; Auth, First Person Singular, Allyn and Bacon, 97; Auth, One World, Many Cultures, 3rd ed, Allyn and Bacon, 98; Auth, Reflections on Language, Oxford Univ Pr, 99; Auth, The New Millennium Reader 2nd ed, Prentice-Hall, 00; Auth, Reflections on Culture, One World, Many Cultures 4th ed, Allyn and Bacon (forthcoming). **CONTACT ADDRESS** Dept English, Rutgers, The State Univ of New Jersey, Newark, 360 MLK, Jr. Blvd, Hill Hall, #526, Newark, NJ 07102.

HIRSH, ELIZABETH

PERSONAL p **DISCIPLINE** ENGLISH **EDUCATION** Brown Univ, BA, 77; Univ Wis Chicago, MA, 80; PhD, 89. **CAREER** Instr, Univ Wis Madison, 90-92; asst prof to assoc prof, Univ S Fla, 92-. **MEMBERSHIPS** MLA; SAMLA. **RESEARCH** Modern and contemporary literature; gender studies; literary and cultural theory. **SELECTED PUBLICATIONS** Auth, Women Writing Culture, SUNY, 95. **CONTACT ADDRESS** English Dept, Univ of So Florida, Cpr 107, Tampa, FL 33620. **EMAIL** hirsh@chuma.cas.usf.edu

HIRSH, JAMES E.

PERSONAL Born 07/12/1946, Brooklyn, NY, m, 1969, 2 children **DISCIPLINE** ENGLISH **EDUCATION** Cornell Univ, BA, 68; Univ Wash, MA, 74; PhD, 78. **CAREER** Asst to assoc prof, Univ Haw, 80-90; assoc prof to prof, Ga State Univ, 90-. **HONORS AND AWARDS** Commun Awd, Ga State Univ; Distinguished Honors Prof Awd, Ga State Univ, 98. **MEMBERSHIPS** MLA, SAMLA, Shakespeare Assoc of Am, Medieval and Renaissance Drama Soc. **RESEARCH** Shakespeare, English Renaissance Drama, performance history, audience response, literary influence. **SELECTED PUBLICATIONS** Auth, The Structure of Shakespearean Scenes, Yale Univ Pr, 81; auth, "The 'to be or not to be' Scene and the Conventions of Shakespearean Drama," Mod Lang Quart, (81); auth, "Laughter at Titus Andronicus," Essays in Theatre, (88); auth, "Othello and Perception," Othello: New Perspectives, (Fairleigh Dickinson Univ Pr, 91); auth, "Samuel Clemens and the Ghost of Shakespeare," Studies in the Novel, (92); auth, "English Renaissance Drama and Audience Response," Studies in the Literary Imagination, (93); coauth, "Attributing A Funeral Elegy," PMLA, (97); ed, New Perspectives on Ben Jonson, Fairleigh Dickinson Univ Pr, 97; auth, "Shakespeare and the History of Soliloquies," Mod Lang Quart, (97); auth, "A Funeral Elegy, Shakespeare, and Elizabeth Cary," Ben Jonson Jour, (00). **CONTACT ADDRESS** Dept English, Georgia State Univ, University Plz, Atlanta, GA 30303-3083. **EMAIL** jhirsh@gsu.edu

HIRSH, JOHN CAMPION

PERSONAL Born 06/26/1944, Hartford, CT **DISCIPLINE** MEDIEVAL & AMERICAN LITERATURE **EDUCATION** Boston Col, AB, 65; Lehigh Univ, MA, 66, PhD(English), 70. **CAREER** Instr, Lehigh Univ, 69-70; from asst prof to assoc prof, 70-84, Prof English, Georgetown Univ, 84-. **HONORS AND AWARDS** Am Coun Learned Soc fel, 74-75; vis fel, Pembroke Col, Oxford, 93; Keeley Vis Fel, Wadham Col, Oxford, 00. **MEMBERSHIPS** Medieval Acad Am; Am Studies Asn; Arthurian Soc; Int Reading Asn. **RESEARCH** Chaucer and Middle English literature & spirituality; 19th and 20th century American literature; inner-city literacy. **SELECTED PUBLICATIONS** Auth, Western Manuscripts 12-16 Centuries in Lehigh Univ, 70; Medieval Manuscripts in Lehigh University Libraries. Western Manuscripts of the Twelfth through the Sixteenth Centuries in Lehigh University Libraries, Lehigh Univ, 70; Barlam and Iosaphat. A Middle English Life of Buddha, Edited from MS. Peterhouse 257, Early English Text Soc, OS 290, Oxford Univ Press, 86; Hope Emily Allen. Medieval Scholarship and Feminism, Pilgrim Books, 88; The Revelations of Margery Kemp. Paramystical Practices in Late Medieval England, Medieval and Renaissance Authors Series, Vol 10, E.J. Brill, 89; Sursum Corda. Teaching Urban Youth to Read, Georgetown Univ Press, 91; The Boundaries of Faith. The Development and Transmission of Medieval Spirituality, Studies in the Hist of Christian Thought, Vol LXVII, E.J. Brill, 96; auth, Chaucer and the Canterbury Tales: A Short Introduction, Blackwells, forthcoming, 02. **CONTACT ADDRESS** English Dept, Georgetown Univ, PO Box 571131, Washington, DC 20057-1131. **EMAIL** hirsh@gusun.georgetown.edu

HISE, PAT J.

PERSONAL Born Ft Riley, TX, 2 children **DISCIPLINE** ENGLISH **EDUCATION** Midwestern State Univ, BA, 85; MA, 88; Univ NTex, PhD, 98. **CAREER** TA, adj instr, Midwestern State Univ, 85-87, 88-89; teaching fel, Univ NTex, 87-89; lectr, El Paso Community Col, 90-94; teaching fel to adj prof, Univ NTex, 94-98; adj prof, N Central Tex Col, 00, 01-; adj prof, Central Tex Col, 00. **HONORS AND AWARDS** Alpha Chi; Alpha Lambda Delta; Kappa Delta Pi; Sigma Tau Delta; Who's Who in Teaching in America; Midwestern State Univ Fel, 85; Univ NTex Fel, 87, 94. **MEMBERSHIPS** MLA, Am Studies Asn Tex, Conf of Col Teachers of English. **RESEARCH** American literature, English composition, Creative writing. **SELECTED PUBLICATIONS** Auth, "The Greatness of The Great Gatsby," Voices, (Midwestern State Univ Pr, 87); auth, "3 a m Over the Second Cup," Green Fuse, (Univ NTex Pr, 89); auth, "The Pursuit of Nothingness in Play It as It Lays," CCTE Studies 56, (96): 75-84; auth, "Midsummer Dream," CCTE Studies 64, (99): 40-41; auth, "Wasted Modern Romantic Lyric," Amarillo Bay Vol 3, (01); auth, "Jim burden: Revealing the Common Meaning in Things in My Antonia," (forthcoming). **CONTACT ADDRESS** No Central Texas Col, 1500 N California, Corinth, TX 76240-4699. **EMAIL** pathise@airmail.net

HITCHCOCK, WALTER B.

PERSONAL Born 07/05/1941, Troy, Ala, m, 1966, 2 children **DISCIPLINE** ENGLISH **EDUCATION** Auburn Univ, BA, 63; Univ Ore, MA, 66; Duke Univ, PhD, 71. **CAREER** Asst prof to prof, Auburn Univ, 71-; Head, 77-90, Hargis Prof, 99-. **HONORS AND AWARDS** NDEA Fel; Rotory Found Fel; Phi Beta Kappa, Phi Kappa Phi; Awd for Fac Achievement in the Humanities, Auburn Univ. **MEMBERSHIPS** MLA; S Atlantic MLA; Soc for the Study of S Lit. **RESEARCH** Nineteenth-Century American Literature, Literature of the American South. **SELECTED PUBLICATIONS** Auth, Richard Malcolm Johnston, G.K. Hall, 78; coed; De Remnant Truth: The Tales of Jake Mitchell and Robert Wilton Burton, Univ of Ala Pr, 91; coed, American Short Stories, 5th and 6th Ed, Scott Foresman/Longman, 90, 97. **CONTACT ADDRESS** Dept English, Auburn Univ, Auburn Univ, Auburn, AL 36849-2900. **EMAIL** hitchwb@auburn.edu

HOAGLAND, EDWARD

PERSONAL d, 1 child **DISCIPLINE** CREATIVE WRITING, LITERATURE **EDUCATION** Harvard Univ, AB, 55. **CAREER** Instructor, Rutgers Univ, 66; Instructor, Sarah Lawrence, 67; Instructor, CUNY, 67-68; Instructor, Sarah Lawrence, 71; Instructor, Univ IA, 78; Instructor, The Writers Community, 79; Instructor, Columbia MFA, 80-81; Instructor, Univ IA, 82; Instructor, Bennington Col, 87-00. **HONORS AND AWARDS** Houghton Mifflin Literary Fel, 54; Longview Foundation Awd, 61; Prix de Rome, 64; Guggenheim Fel, 65; Grant, NY State Arts Coun, 72; Brandeis Univ Citation, 72; Guggenheim Fel, 75; Harold Vursell Awd, 81; NEH Grant, 82; Lannan Foundation Awd, 93; Nominated for Nat Book Awd, 74; Nominated for Nat Book Critics Circle Awd, 80; Nominated for Am Book Awd, 82; Nominated for NY Public Library Literary Lion, 88, 96; Nominated for Nat Magazine Awd, 89; Nominated for Boston Public Library Literary Light, 95; Elected to Am Acad and Inst of Arts and Letters, 82. **SELECTED PUBLICATIONS** Auth, City Tales, Capra Press, 86; auth, Seven Rivers West, Simon & Schuster, 86; auth, Heart's Desire, Simon & Schuster, 88; auth, The Final Fate of the Alligator, Capra Press, 92; auth, Balancing Acts, Simon & Schuster, 92; auth, Tigers and Ice, Lyons Press, 99. **CONTACT ADDRESS** PO Box 51, Barton, VT 05822.

HOBBS, WAYNE

DISCIPLINE MUSIC HISTORY AND LITERATURE **EDUCATION** FL State Univ, BME; New Orleans Baptist Theol Sem, MCM; Tulane Univ, PhD. **CAREER** Hd, dept Mus, Western KY Univ; ch, dept Mus, Univ New Orleans; prof Mus, dir, Sch Mus, Tex Tech Univ, 87-94. **RESEARCH** The early baroque; Am music. **SELECTED PUBLICATIONS** Publ articles in the fields of music administration, musicology, interdisciplinary arts, music theory, and choral music. **CONTACT ADDRESS** School of Music, Texas Tech Univ, Lubbock, TX 79409-5015. **EMAIL** whobbs@ttu.edu

HOBSON, CHRISTOPHER
PERSONAL Born 12/27/1941, New York, NY, s **DISCIPLINE** ENGLISH **EDUCATION** Harvard Univ, BA, 63; Univ Chicago, MA, 72; City U New York, Phd, 95. **CAREER** Vis Asst Prof, SUNY Col at Old Westbury, 96-97; Asst Prof, SUNY Col at Old Westbury. **MEMBERSHIPS** Modern Language Assoc, 92. **RESEARCH** William Blake; Literature and Social Protest; Literature and Homosexuality; African-American literature and homosexuality; African-American literature. **SELECTED PUBLICATIONS** Auth, "Unbound From Wrath: Orc and Blake's Crisis of Vision in The Four Zoas," Studies in English Literature 1500-1900 33, Autumn 93: 725-54; auth, "Political Motives and the 1935 Writers' Congress," Forum, PMLA 100:2, March: 281-82; auth, "Richard Wright's Communisms: Textual Variance, Intentionality, and Socialization in American Hunger, 'I Tried to Be a Communist,' and The God That Failed," Text 6, 94: 307-44; auth, "Country Mouse and Towny Mouse: Truth in Wyatt," Texas Studies in Literature and Language 39.3, fall 97: 230-58; auth, "The Radicalism of Felix Holt: George Eliot and the Pioneers of Labor," Victorian Literature and Culture 26.1, 98: 19-39; auth, "The Myth of Blake's 'Orc Cycle,' Blake, Politics, History, ed. Jackie DiSalvo, Christopher Z. Hobson, G. Anthony rosso Garland, 5-36; auth, "Trotskyism and the Dilemma of Socialism, With Ronald D. Tabor, Westport; Greenwood, 88; auth, "Blake, Politics, History, Co-editor with Jackie DiSalvo, George Anthony Rosso, New York: Garland, 98; auth, "The Chained Boy: Orc and Blake's Idea of Revolution," Lewisburg: Bucknell University Press, London: Associated University Presses, 99; auth, "Blake and Homosexuality," In press 00, St. Martin's Press Scholarly and Reference Division. **CONTACT ADDRESS** Dept English, SUNY, Col at Old Westbury, PO Box 210, Old Westbury, NY 11568-0210.

HOBSON, FRED C.
PERSONAL Born 04/21/1943, Winston-Salem, NC, d, 1 child **DISCIPLINE** ENGLISH **EDUCATION** Univ NC, AB, 65; PhD, 72; Duke Univ, MA, 67. **CAREER** Editorial Writer, Winston-Salem J and Sentinel, 69-70; From Asst Prof to Prof, Univ Ala, 72-86; Prof, La State Univ, 86-89; Prof, Univ NC, 89-. **HONORS AND AWARDS** Fel, Nat Endowment Humanities, 76-77; Lillian Smith Awd, 83; Jules F. Landry Awd, 83; State of Ala Authors Awd for Non-Fiction, 86; Fel, Univ NC, 91; Fel, Nat Humanities Ctr, 91-92; Jules F. Landry Awd, 99. **MEMBERSHIPS** MLA. **RESEARCH** Autobiography, biography, intellectual history. **SELECTED PUBLICATIONS** Auth, Serpent in Eden: H L Mencken and the South, Univ NC Pr (Chapel Hill, NC), 74; auth, Tell About the South: The Southern Rage to Explain, La St Univ Pr (Baton Rouge, LA), 83; auth, The Southern Writer in the Postmodern World, Univ Ga Pr (Athens, GA), 91; auth, Mencken: A Life, Random House (New York, NY), 94; auth, But Now I See: The White Southern Racial Conversion Narrative, La St Univ Pr (Baton Rouge, LA), 99. **CONTACT ADDRESS** Dept English, Univ of No Carolina, Chapel Hill, CB #3520, Chapel Hill, NC 27599-2319. **EMAIL** fhobson@email.unc.edu

HOCHMAN, WILL
DISCIPLINE CREATIVE WRITING, COMPOSITION, ADVANCED COMPOSITION, SALINGER SEMINAR, INDE **EDUCATION** Hobart Col, BA, 74; Univ MT, MFA, 76; NYork Univ, PhD, 94. **CAREER** Asst prof & dir, Writing, Univ of Southern CO. **HONORS AND AWARDS** Created, USC's 1st comput writing classroom. **RESEARCH** Writing; criticism; mod Am lit; computers and writing; writing centers; tchg teachers. **SELECTED PUBLICATIONS** Auth, Stranger Within, Boynton-Cook, 98; publ, Terminal Thinking; ed, War, Lit & the Arts. **CONTACT ADDRESS** Dept of Eng, Univ of So Colorado, 2200 Bonforte Blvd, Pueblo, CO 81001-4901. **EMAIL** hochman@meteor.uscolo.edu

HOCKS, RICHARD
PERSONAL Born 06/30/1936, Cincinnati, OH, m, 1957, 4 children **DISCIPLINE** ENGLISH **EDUCATION** Univ NC, PhD, 67. **CAREER** Prof & Catherine Paine Middlebush prof Humanities at Mizzou. **HONORS AND AWARDS** Finalist, Nat Bk awd; Purple Chalk awd & fac alumni awd. **SELECTED PUBLICATIONS** Auth, Henry James & Pragmatistic Thought, NC, 74 & Henry James: A Study of the Short Fiction, Twayne '90; co-ed, Norton critical ed of The Wings of the Dove. **CONTACT ADDRESS** Dept of English, Univ of Missouri, Columbia, 309 University Hall, Columbia, MO 65211. **EMAIL** hocksr@missouri.edu

HODGDON, BARBARA COVINGTON
PERSONAL Born 10/05/1932, Rochester, NY, 4 children **DISCIPLINE** ENGLISH LITERATURE, DRAMA **EDUCATION** Wellesley Col, BA, 53; Univ NH, MA, 70; PhD(English), 74. **CAREER** From asst prof to prof English, 74-81, Drake Univ, 80-, contrib ed, Shakespeare Newslett, 71-81, dir honor prog, 84-86, adv bd, Shakespeare on Film Newsl, 89-93; Shakespeare Interactive Hypermedia Archive Proj, 91-; Ed Board, Critical Survey, 94-; Ed Board, Essays in Theatre, 91-. **HONORS AND AWARDS** Madelyn Levitt Outstanding Teacher Awd, 94; Trustee, Shakespeare Assoc, 98-; Ellis and Nelle Levitt Distinguished prof of English, 92-; NEH Fel recipient, 91-92; Centennial scholar for Outstanding Undergraduate Teaching, 88; Nat Endowment for the Humanities Prof of English, 86-92. **MEMBERSHIPS** Shakespeare Asn Am; MLA; The Malone Soc; Soc for Cinema Studies. **RESEARCH** Shakespeare and performance; film. **SELECTED PUBLICATIONS** Auth, Henry IV, Part Two, Shakespeare in Performance Series, ed. James C. Bulman and J.R. Mulryne, Machester Univ Press, 93; auth, "The Critic, The Poor Player, Prince Hamlet, and The Lady in the Dark," in Close Reading Re-Visited, ed. Russ McDonald (Cornell Univ Press, 94); auth, "'Here Apparent:' Photography, History, and the Theatrical Unconscious," in Textual and Theatrical Shakespeare: Questions of Evidence, ed. Edward Pechter (Univ of Iowa Press, 96); auth, Henry IV, Part One: Texts and Contexts, Bedford-St Martin's, 97; auth, "Replicating Richard: Body Doubles, Body Politics," Theatre Journal (98); auth, The Shakespeare Trade: Performances and Appropriations, Univ of Penn Press, 98; auth, "Making it New: Katie Mitchell Refashions Shakespeare-History," in Transforming Shakespeare: Twentieth-Century Women's Re-visions, ed. Marianne Novy (St Martin's, 99); assoc general ed, Arden 3 Online Performance Project, 99-; auth, "William Shakespeare's Romeo + Juliet: Everything's Nice in America?," Shakespeare Survey 52 (99); ed, The Taming of the Shrew, Arden 3, forthcoming. **CONTACT ADDRESS** Dept of English, Drake Univ, 2507 University Ave, Des Moines, IA 50311-4505. **EMAIL** barbara.hodgdon@drake.edu

HODGES, LOUIS WENDELL
PERSONAL Born 01/24/1933, Eupora, MS, m, 1954, 2 children **DISCIPLINE** RELIGION & JOURNALISM **EDUCATION** Millsaps Col, BA, 54; Duke Univ, BD, 57, PhD, 60. **CAREER** From asst prof to assoc prof, 60-68, prof relig, 68-97, dir ethics, 74-97, Knight Prof Journalism, 97-, Univ Prog Soc & Professions, Washington & Lee Univ. **RESEARCH** Theology of race relations; theology and ethics, ethics and the press. **SELECTED PUBLICATIONS** Art, Christian Ethics and Non-Violence, Relig in Life, 62; art, The Roots of Prejudice, Christian Advocate, 62; coauth, The Christian and His Decisions, Abingdon, 69. **CONTACT ADDRESS** Dept of Journalism, Washington and Lee Univ, Lexington, VA 24450. **EMAIL** lhodgesl@wlu.edu

HODGINS, JACK S.
PERSONAL Born 10/03/1938, Comox, BC, Canada **DISCIPLINE** ENGLISH, WRITING **EDUCATION** Univ BC, BEd, 61, DLitt(hon), 95. **CAREER** High sch tchr, Nanaimo, BC, 61-80; writer-in-residence, Simon Fraser Univ, 77; writer-in-residence, 79, vis prof, Univ Ottawa, 81-83; vis prof, 83-85, prof, Univ Vicotoria, 85-. **HONORS AND AWARDS** Pres Medal, Univ Western Ont, 73; Eaton's BC Bk Awd, 77; Gov Gen Awd, 80; Can-Australia Awd, 86; Ethel Wilson Fiction Awd; Drummer General's Awd. **MEMBERSHIPS** Writers' Union Can; Int PEN. **SELECTED PUBLICATIONS** Auth, The Barclay Family Theatre, 81; auth, Innocent Cities, 90; auth, A Passion for Narrative, 93; auth, The Macken Charm, 95; auth, The Invention of the World; The Resurrection of Joseph Bourne; auth, The Honorary Parton; auth, Broken Gournd; auth, Spit Delaney's Island; auth, Over Forty in Borken Hill; auth, Left Behind in Squabble Bay. **CONTACT ADDRESS** Dept of Writing, Univ of Victoria, PO Box 1700, Victoria, BC, Canada V8W 2Y2. **EMAIL** jhodgins@uvic.ca

HOEFEL, ROSEANNE
DISCIPLINE AMERICAN LITERATURES, RHETORIC, POETRY AND WOMEN'S STUDIES **EDUCATION** Ohio State Univ, PhD. **CAREER** Assoc prof, Alma Col; assoc dean, Col of Letters and Science, Univ of Wisc, Osh Kosh. **HONORS AND AWARDS** Barlow Awd for Fac Excellence. **SELECTED PUBLICATIONS** Her articles have appeared in Stud in Short Fiction, Emily Dickinson J, Transformations, Phoebe, Feminisms and The Women's Stud Rev. **CONTACT ADDRESS** Letters & Sciences, Dean's Office, Univ of Wisconsin, Oshkosh, Alma, MI 48801. **EMAIL** hoefel@uwosh.edu

HOENIGER, FREDERICK J. D.
PERSONAL Born 04/25/1921, Goerlitz, Germany **DISCIPLINE** LITERATURE **EDUCATION** Univ Toronto, Victoria Col, BA, 46, MA, 48; Univ London, PhD, 54. **CAREER** Lectr, Univ Sask, 46-47; lectr to prof, 48-86, ch Eng, 69-72, dir, ctr Reformation & Renaissance stud, 64-69, 75-79, PROF EMER, VICTORIA COL, UNIV TORONTO. **HONORS AND AWARDS** Brit Coun scholar, 51-53; Guggenheim fel, 64-65. **MEMBERSHIPS** Can Soc Renaissance Stud; Int Shakespeare Asn. **RESEARCH** Shakespeare; Renaissance biology and medicine; drama, 1500-1700. **SELECTED PUBLICATIONS** Auth, Medicine and Shakespeare in the English Renaissance, 92; coauth, A Gathering of Flowers from Shakespeare, 97; gen ed, The Revels Plays, 71-85. **CONTACT ADDRESS** Dept of English, Univ of Toronto, Victoria Col, Toronto, ON, Canada M5S 1K7. **EMAIL** v.holmes@utoronto.ca; s.walton@utoronto.ca

HOFFMAN, ANNE
DISCIPLINE MODERN EUROPEAN FICTION, JEWISH LITERARY HISTORY **EDUCATION** Columbia Univ, PhD. **CAREER** Prof, Fordham Univ. **RESEARCH** Lit and psychoanalysis, feminist theory, contemp critical theory. **SELECTED PUBLICATIONS** Auth, A Book That Was Lost and Other Stories, Schocken Bk(s), 95. **CONTACT ADDRESS** Dept of Eng Lang and Lit, Fordham Univ, 113 W 60th St, New York, NY 10023.

HOFFMAN, DANIEL
PERSONAL Born 04/03/1923, New York, NY, m, 1948, 2 children **DISCIPLINE** ENGLISH **EDUCATION** Columbia Col, AB, 47; Columbia Univ, AM, 49, PhD, 56. **CAREER** Lectr English, Columbia Univ, 47-48 & Rutgers Univ, 48-50; instr, Temple Univ, 50-52 & Columbia Univ, 52-56; vis prof Am lit & hist, Univ Dijon, 56-57; from asst prof to assoc prof English lit, Swarthmore Col, 57-66; PROF ENGLISH, UNIV PA, 66-, POET IN RESIDENCE, 78-, Fel sch lett, Ind Univ, 59; Am Coun Learned Soc res fels, 61-62 & 66-67; Elliston lectr poetry, Univ Cincinnati, 64; lectr, Sixth Int Sch Yeats Studies, Sligo, Ireland: 65; Ingram Merrill Found poetry grant, 71-72; chancellor, Acad Am Poets, 72-; Consult poetry, Libr of Congr, 73-74; Nat Endowment Humanities res fel, 75-76; coun, Auth Guild, 81- **HONORS AND AWARDS** Awd, Yale Ser of Younger Poets, 53; Clarke F Ansley Awd, 57; Medal excellence, Columbia Univ, 64; Awd, Nat Inst Arts & Lett, 67; Poetry Mem Medal, Hungarian PEN, 80. **MEMBERSHIPS** MLA; PEN Club Am; English Inst; Auth Guild. **RESEARCH** Modern poetry, American literature. **SELECTED PUBLICATIONS** Auth, Bob, Hudson Rev, Vol 0047, 94; Blizzard, Hudson Rev, Vol 0047, 94; Scott Nearings Ninety-Eighth Year, Georgia Rev, Vol 0048, 94. **CONTACT ADDRESS** Dept of English, Univ of Pennsylvania, Philadelphia, PA 19174.

HOFFMAN, MICHAEL JEROME
PERSONAL Born 03/31/1939, Philadelphia, PA, m, 1988, 4 children **DISCIPLINE** ENGLISH **EDUCATION** Univ Pa, AB, 59, MA, 60, PhD(English), 63. **CAREER** Instr English, Washington Col, 62-64; from instr to asst prof, Univ Pa, 64-67; from asst prof to assoc prof, 67-75, PROF ENGLISH, UNIV CALIF, DAVIS, 75-; ASST VCHANCELLOR, ACAD AFFAIRS, 76-83, Vis prof English, Sorbonne, 72-73; **HONORS AND AWARDS** USAR, 57-61; Nat Defense Ed Act fel, 59-62. **MEMBERSHIPS** MLA; Am Studies Asn; Am Lit Group; MLA. **RESEARCH** Nineteenth and 20th century American literature; modern fiction; modernism; the Holocaust. **SELECTED PUBLICATIONS** Auth, The Development of Abstractionism in the Writings of Gertrude Stein, Univ Pa, 65; The Buddy System (novel), Holt, 71; The Subversive Vision: American Romanticism in Literature, Kennikat, 73; Themes, Topics, Criticism, Am Lit Scholar, 73-; Gertrude Stein, Twayne, 76; auth, Critical Essays on Gertrude Stein, 86; auth, Essentials of the Theory of Fiction, 88, rev, 96; auth, Critical Essays on American Modernism, 92. **CONTACT ADDRESS** Dept of English, Univ of California, Davis, Davis, CA 95616-5200. **EMAIL** mjhoffman@ucdavis.edu

HOFFMAN, TYLER B.
DISCIPLINE 19TH- AND 20TH-CENTURY AMERICAN LITERATURE AND CULTURE, POETRY, AND POETICS **EDUCATION** Univ Va, PhD. **CAREER** Instr, Rutgers, State Univ NJ, Camden Col of Arts and Sci; poetry reviewer, South Atlantic Rev. **RESEARCH** The rhetoric of Robert Frost. **SELECTED PUBLICATIONS** Auth, Emily Dickinson and the Limit of War, in The Emily Dickinson J; contribu, Robert Frost Encyclopedia. **CONTACT ADDRESS** Rutgers, The State Univ of New Jersey, New Brunswick, Camden Col of Arts and Sci, New Brunswick, NJ 08903-2101. **EMAIL** tbhlhh@crab.rutgers.edu

HOFFMANN, JOYCE
DISCIPLINE JOURNALISM **EDUCATION** NYork Univ, PhD. **CAREER** Engl, Old Dominion Univ. **HONORS AND AWARDS** Coordr, Journalism Emphasis. **RESEARCH** Reporting; media law and ethics; Vietnam & the press. **SELECTED PUBLICATIONS** Areas: Theodore H. White and Journalism as Illusion. **CONTACT ADDRESS** Old Dominion Univ, 4100 Powhatan Ave, BAL 313, Norfolk, VA 23058. **EMAIL** JHoffman@odu.edu

HOFFPAUIR, RICHARD
PERSONAL Born 10/08/1942, Bell, CA, m, 1970 **DISCIPLINE** ENGLISH LITERATURE **EDUCATION** Univ Calif, Berkeley, BA, 65, MA, 67; Univ London, PhD(English), 69. **CAREER** Asst prof, 69-76, ASSOC PROF ENGLISH, UNIV ALTA, 76- **MEMBERSHIPS** Can Asn Univ Teachers; Asn Can Univ Teachers English. **RESEARCH** Poetic tradition, 18th to 20th centuries; Romantic idology; literary criticism. **SELECTED PUBLICATIONS** Auth, The Art of Restraint: English Poetry from Hardy to Larkin. **CONTACT ADDRESS** Dept of English, Univ of Alberta, 3-5 Humanities Centre, Edmonton, AB, Canada T6G 2E5. **EMAIL** richard.hoffpauir@ualberta.ca

HOGAN, J. MICHAEL
PERSONAL Born 09/13/1953, Rapid City, SD **DISCIPLINE** COMMUNICATION **EDUCATION** Univ of Wis, Madison, PhD. **CAREER** Asst prof, Univ of Va, 81-86; Assoc prof, Prof, Ind Univ 86-97; Prof, Penn State Univ, 97-. **HONORS AND AWARDS** Winians-Wichelns Awd for Distinguished Scholar in Rhet & Public Address. **MEMBERSHIPS** Nat Commun

Assoc. **RESEARCH** Campaigns & social movements; public opinion & polling. **SELECTED PUBLICATIONS** Co-auth, Polling on the Issues: Public Opinion and the Nuclear Freeze, Public Opinion Quart, vol 55, 534-69, 91; auth, The Nuclear Freeze Campaign: Rhetoric and Foreign Policy in the Telepolitical Age, Mich State Univ Press, 94; auth, Eisenhower and Open Skies: A Case Study in Psychological Warfare, Eisenhower's War of Words: Rhetoric & Leadership, Mich State Univ Press, 94; co-auth, Woodrow Wilson, US Presidents as Orators: A Bio-Critical Sourcebook, Greenwood Press, 95; Demonization, Public Opinion, and the Gulf War, Argumentation and Values: Proceedings of the Ninth SCA/AFA Conf on Argumentation, Spch Commun Assoc, 96; co-auth, Defining the Enemy in Revolutionary America: From the Rhetoric of Protest to the Rhetoric of War, Southern Commun J, vol 61, 277-88, 96; Panama and the Panama Canal, The Encycl of US Foreign Rels, 97; auth, George Gallup and the Rhetoric of Scientific Democracy, Commun Monographs, vol 64, 161-79, 6/97; Ed, Rhetoric and Community: Studies in Unity and Fragmentation, Univ SC Press, 98; coauth, "Republican Carisma and the American Revolution," Quarterly Journal of Speech," vol. 86, 1-18. **CONTACT ADDRESS** Dept of Spch Commun, Pennsylvania State Univ, Univ Park, 234 Sparks Bldg, University Park, PA 16802-5201. **EMAIL** jmh32@psu.edu

HOGAN, ROBERT
PERSONAL Born 05/29/1930, Boonville, MO, m, 1950, 5 children **DISCIPLINE** ENGLISH **EDUCATION** Univ Mo, BA, 53, MA, 54, PhD(English), 56. **CAREER** Instr English, Univ Mo, 54-56 & Ohio Univ, 56-58; from instr to asst prof, Purdue Univ, 58-63; from asst prof to prof, Univ Calif, Davis, 63-70; PROF ENGLISH, UNIV DEL, 70-, Guggenheim fel, 61-62; vis prof Univ Rochester, 62-63; Fulbright vis prof, Univ Col, Dublin, 67-68; ed, J Irish Lit, 72- **RESEARCH** Anglo-Irish literature; modern drama. **SELECTED PUBLICATIONS** Auth, The Brave Timidity of Murray, Irish Univ Rev, Vol 0026, 96. **CONTACT ADDRESS** Dept of English, Univ of Delaware, Newark, DE 19711.

HOGGARD, JAMES MARTIN
PERSONAL Born 06/21/1941, Wichita Falls, TX, m, 1976, 2 children **DISCIPLINE** ENGLISH; CREATIVE WRITING **EDUCATION** Southern Methodist Univ, BA, 63; Univ Kans, MA, 65. **CAREER** From instr to assoc prof, 66-77, PROF ENGLISH, MIDWESTERN STATE UNIV, 77-. **HONORS AND AWARDS** Hardin Prof of the Year, 77; NEA Creative Writing Fel, 81; TIL Short Story Awd, 89; McMurty Dist Prof of English, 97; Soeurette Diehl Fraser Awd, 98; Stanley Walker Awd, 99. **MEMBERSHIPS** SCOLAS; ALTA; TACWT; TIL. **RESEARCH** Modern literature; tragedy and comedy. **SELECTED PUBLICATIONS** Auth, Mesquite, Southwest Rev, spring 69; But the daddy doesn't get to cry, Redbook Mag, 6/72; contribr, The New Breed, Prickly Pear, 73; Tragedy as mediation, Southwest Rev, summer 75; auth, No accounting shall be asked, Southwest Rev, summer 76; Eyesigns: Poems, Trilobite Press, 77; Trotter Ross: Novel, Thorp Springs Press, 81; The Shaper Poems, Cedarshouse Press, 83; Two Gulls, One Hawk: Poems, 83; Elevator Man: Nonfiction, 83; Breaking an Indelicate Statue: Poems, 86; The Art of Dying: Translations, 88; Love Breaks: Translations, 91; Chronicle of My Worst Years: Translations, 94; Riding the Wind & Other Tales, 97; Alone Against the Sea: Translations, 98; auth, Trotter Ross, rev ed, Wings Press, 99; auth, Medea in Taos: Poems, Pecan Grove Press, 00; auth, Stolen Verses: Translations, Northwestern UP, 00. **CONTACT ADDRESS** Dept of English, Midwestern State Univ, 3410 Taft Blvd, Wichita Falls, TX 76308-2096. **EMAIL** james.hoggard@nexus.mwsu.edu

HOGLE, JERROLD EDWIN
PERSONAL Born 05/15/1948, Los Angeles, CA, m, 1970, 2 children **DISCIPLINE** ENGLISH LITERATURE **EDUCATION** Univ Calif, Irvine, AB, 70; Harvard Univ, MA, 71, PhD(English), 74. **CAREER** Asst prof, 74-80, assoc prof English, Univ Az, 80-89; prof English, Univ Az, 89-; assoc dean, coll of humanities, Univ Az, 90-93; Univ Distinguished Prof, Univ Az, 96-; Chair of the Faculty, Univ Az, 97-. **HONORS AND AWARDS** Burlington Northern Foundation Faculty Achievement Awd, 88-89; Guggenheim Fellowship, 89-90; Mellon/Huntington Fellowship, 90; President, International Gothic Assoc, 95-97. **MEMBERSHIPS** MLA; NASSR; Keats-Shelley Assoc; International Gothic Assoc. **RESEARCH** Romantic literature; literary theory; 18th and 19th century novels; The Gothic. **SELECTED PUBLICATIONS** Shelley's Process, Oxford U P, 88; coed, Evaluating Shelley, Edinburgh, 96; articles in major essay collections and journals. **CONTACT ADDRESS** Dept of English, Univ of Arizona, PO Box 210067, Tucson, AZ 85721-0067. **EMAIL** hogle@u.arizona.edu

HOLBEIN, WOODROW LEE
PERSONAL Born 01/01/1929, Gallipolis, OH, m, 1956, 2 children **DISCIPLINE** ENGLISH & AMERICAN LITERATURE **EDUCATION** Baldwin-Wallace Col, AB, 53; Western Reserve Univ, MA, 54. **CAREER** Instr English, Marshall Univ, 55-56 & Bethany Col, 56-57; asst prof, 57-68, assoc prof English, The Citadel, 68- **MEMBERSHIPS** S Atlantic MLA; Shakespeare Asn Am; Southeast Renaissance Conf. **RESEARCH** Shakespeare; American stage history; Renaissance. **CONTACT ADDRESS** Dept of English, The Citadel, The Military Col of So Carolina, 171 Moultrie St, Charleston, SC 29409-0002.

HOLDEN, JONATHAN
PERSONAL Born 07/18/1941, Morristown, NJ, m, 1997, 2 children **DISCIPLINE** ENGLISH **EDUCATION** Oberlin Col, BA, 63; San Francisco State Col, MA, 70; Univ of Colo, PhD, 74. **CAREER** Stephens Col, 74-78; Kansas State Univ, 78-. **SELECTED PUBLICATIONS** Auth, The Rhetoric of the Contemporary Lyric, Ind Univ Pr, 80; auth, Style and Authenticity in Postmodern Poetry, Univ of Mo Pr, 86; auth, Brilliant Kids, Univ of Utah Pr, 92; auth, Ur-Math, State St Pr, 97; auth, "Mama's Boys", Men and Masculinities, 1.1 (Jul 98): 46-57; auth, "American Male Poetry of Sensibility", Poetry After Modernism ed Robert McDowell, Story Line Pr, (98): 268-277; auth, "Jinx", Midwest Quarterly, XL.4 (99): 429-430; auth, "The Public Nature of End-Rhymed Poems", The Writer's Chronicle 32.3 (Dec 99): 10-14; auth, The Old Formalism: Character in Contemporary American Poetry, Univ of Ark Pr, 00; auth, Knowing: New and Selected Poems, Univ of Ark Pr, 00. **CONTACT ADDRESS** Dept English, Kansas State Univ, 122 Denison Hall, Manhattan, KS 66506-0700. **EMAIL** jonhold@ksu.edu

HOLDITCH, WILLIAM KENNETH
PERSONAL Born 09/18/1933, Ecru, MS, s **DISCIPLINE** AMERICAN LITERATURE **EDUCATION** Southwestern at Memphis, BA, 55; Univ Miss, MA, 57, PhD, 61. **CAREER** From asst to instr, Univ Miss, 55-59; from instr to asst prof English, Christian Bros Col, Tenn, 61-65; from asst prof to prof, LA State Univ, New Orleans, 65-91; res prof, LA State Univ, New Orleans, 91-97; prof emeritus, LA State Univ, 97-; **MEMBERSHIPS** SCent MLA; Am Fedn Teachers; MLA; Soc Study Southern Lit. **RESEARCH** Novels of Dos Passos; William Faulkner; Tennessee Williams; literature of New Orleans. **SELECTED PUBLICATIONS** Auth, Tennessee Williams--A Descriptive Bibliography, Papers Bibliograph Soc Am, Vol 0090, 96; co-ed, Tennessee Williams volumes for Libr of Am; coauth, A More Congenial Climate: Tennessee Williams and the South. **CONTACT ADDRESS** 732 Frenchmen St, New Orleans, LA 70116.

HOLIAN, GAIL
PERSONAL Born 09/21/1948, Jersey City, NJ, m, 1998 **DISCIPLINE** ENGLISH **EDUCATION** St John's Univ, MA, 72; Drew Univ, PhD, 87. **CAREER** Instr, Neptune Sr High Sch, 77-80; adj instr, Ocean County Col, 74-81; from adj instr to prof, Georgian Court Col, 78-; Teaching Fel, NYork Univ, 79-80; adj prof, Monmouth Univ, 98-99. **HONORS AND AWARDS** Found for Independent Higher Educ Awd for Teaching Excellence and Campus Leadership, Nat Sears Roebuck Found, 89; grant, Univ Wales, 92; grant, Convegno Internazionale de Dante & Pound, 95; grant, Georgian Court Col, 93; grant, Florence J. Gould Found, 93. **MEMBERSHIPS** MLA, Medieval Acad of Am, Int Asn of Word and Image Studies, Ezra Pound Soc, Inst for the Psychol Study of the Arts. **RESEARCH** Medieval Literature, especially The Romance of the Rose and Illuminations of the Romance of the Rose. **SELECTED PUBLICATIONS** Auth, The Romance of the Rose Illuminated, 00; auth, Medieval & Renaissance Text and Studies, 00. **CONTACT ADDRESS** Dept English, Georgian Court Col, 900 Lakewood Ave, Lakewood, NJ 08701-2600. **EMAIL** gholian@georgian.edu

HOLLADAY, HILARY
PERSONAL Born 07/03/1961, Richmond, VA, s **DISCIPLINE** ENGLISH **EDUCATION** Univ of Va, BA, 83; Col of William & Mary, MA, 87; Univ of NC Chapel Hill, PhD, 93. **CAREER** Asst prof to assoc prof, Univ of Mass Lowell, 93-. **HONORS AND AWARDS** Awd, Acad of Am Poets, 89; Fel, Va Found for the Humanities, 98. **MEMBERSHIPS** MLA; George Moses Horton Soc for the Study of African-Am Poetry. **RESEARCH** African American literature, modern and contemporary (Lucille Clifton) poetry, beat literature. **SELECTED PUBLICATIONS** Auth, "Beth Henley", in Contemporary Poets, Dramatists and Non-Fiction Writers, eds Robert Bain and Joseph Flora, Greenwood Pr, 238-48; auth, Ann Petry, Twayne, 96; auth, "The Street: Lutie Johnson's Avenue of Escape", S Carolina Rev, (96): 22-31; auth, "The Language of Survival: Black Women Writers of the Civil War", Abafazi (96): 44-47; auth, "Narrative Space in Ann Petry's Country Place", Savier Rev, (96): 21-35; auth, "No Ordinary Woman: An Interview with Lucille Clifton", Poets & Writers Mag, (Apr 99): 30-35; auth, "i am not grown away from you: Lucille Clifton's Elegies for Her Mother", CLA J, (993): 430-44; auth, Baptism in the Merrimack, Loom Pr, 99; auth, "Song of Herself: Lucille Clifton's Poems About Womanhood", in The Furious Flowering of African American Poetry, ed Joanne V. Gabbin, Univ Pr of Va, (99): 281-97; auth, "'our lives are our line and we go on': Concentric Circles of History in Lucille Clifton's Generations" Xavier Rev (forthcoming). **CONTACT ADDRESS** Dept English, Univ of Massachusetts, Lowell, 61 Wilder St, Lowell, MA 01854-3049. **EMAIL** hilary_holladay@uml.edu

HOLLAHAN, EUGENE
PERSONAL Born 02/27/1933, Memphis, TN, m, 1963, 2 children **DISCIPLINE** ENGLISH & CONTINENTAL LITERATURE **EDUCATION** Memphis State Univ, AB, 59; Univ Tenn, MA, 61; Univ NC, PhD(English), 69. **CAREER** Instr English, NC State Univ, 62-69; asst prof, 69-77, ASSOC PROF ENGLISH, GA STATE UNIV, 77- **MEMBERSHIPS** MLA. **RESEARCH** Novel; poetry; structure and meaning in fiction. **SELECTED PUBLICATIONS** Auth, Irruption of nothingness: Sleep and freedom in Madame Bovary, Studies Philol, 73; The concept of crisis in Middlemarch, Nineteenth Century Fiction, 74; Stone Mountain Escape: A Book of Ten Poems, Work/Shop Press, 76; The path of sympathy: Abstraction and imagination in Camus' La Peste, Studies Novel, 77. **CONTACT ADDRESS** Dept of English, Georgia State Univ, 33 Gilmer St SE, Atlanta, GA 30303-3080.

HOLLAND, EUGENE W.
DISCIPLINE LITERATURE **EDUCATION** Yale Univ, BA, 74; Univ Calif at San Diego, PhD, 82. **CAREER** Dir of TA Training and Curriculum Development of the Muir Writing Prog, Univ of Calif at San Diego, 78-81; advisory ed, praxis, 82-84; transl consult, Palimpsest Press, 83-84; asst prof, Univ of Iowa, 84-85; vis prof, Univ of Calif at San Diego, 86; from asst prof to assoc prof, Ohio State Univ, 86-. **HONORS AND AWARDS** NEH Grant, Univ of Calif at San Diego, 76; Teaching Asst Development Prog Awd for Teaching Excellence, 78; Dissertation Fel, Univ of Calif at San Diego, 81-82; Bourse d'Etudes, French Govt, 81; Mellon Res Fel, Rice Univ, 82-84; Old Gold Summer Fel, Univ of Iowa, 85; Residency Fel, Univ of Calif at Santa Cruz, 96-97. **SELECTED PUBLICATIONS** Auth, "Schizoanalysis and Baudelaire: Some Illustrations of Decoding at Work," in Delueuze: A Critical Reader, ed. Paul Patton (Blackwells, 96), 240-256; auth, "Marx and Poststructualist Philosophies of Difference," S Atlantic Quart, 96.3 (97): 525-541; auth, "From Schizophrenia to Social Control," in Deleuze and Guattari: new Mappings in Politics, Philosophy, and Culture, ed. Eleanor Kaufman (MN: Univ of Minn Press, 98), 65-73; auth, Deleuze and Guattari's Anti-Oedipus: Introduction to Schizoanalysis, Rougtledge, 99; auth, "Infinite Subjective Representation and the Perversion of Death," Angelaki: J of the Theoretical Humanities (forthcoming); auth, "Nizan's Diagnosis of Existentialism and the Perversion of Death, in Deleuze and Literature, ed. Ian Buchanan (Edinburgh: Edinburgh Univ Press, forthcoming). **CONTACT ADDRESS** Dept French & Ital, Ohio State Univ, Columbus, 1841 Millikin Rd, Columbus, OH 43210-1229. **EMAIL** holland.1@osu.edu

HOLLAND, NORMAN N.
PERSONAL Born 09/19/1927, New York, NY, m, 1954, 2 children **DISCIPLINE** ENGLISH LITERATURE **EDUCATION** MIT, BS, 47; Harvard, LL.B, 50, PhD, 56; Boston Psychoanalytic Inst, Cert, 66. **CAREER** Inst, assoc prof, 55-66, MIT; prof, McNulty Prof, 66-83, SUNY Buf; Marston-Milbauer Eminent Scholar, Univ Florida, 83-. **HONORS AND AWARDS** Guggenheim Fel, 79-80; Amer Council of Learned Soc Sr Fel, 74-75. **MEMBERSHIPS** Shakespeare Asn of Amer; Intl Asn of Prof of Eng; Boston Psychoanlytic Soc and Inst; Amer Acad of Psychoanalysis; Asn Intl d'Esthetique Exp; Founder, Moderator, PSYART, online discus group; Founder, Ed in Chief, PSYART: A hyperlink Jour for the Psychology of the Arts. **RESEARCH** Psychoanalytic criticism; reader-response criticism; movies, Shakespeare. **SELECTED PUBLICATIONS** Auth, 5 Readers Reading, Yale Univ Press, 75; auth, The I, Yale Univ Press, 85; auth The Dynamics of Literary Response, Columbia Univ Press, 89; auth, The Critical I, Columbia Univ Press, 92; auth, Death In a Delphi Seminar: A Postmodern Mystery, SUNY Press, 95. **CONTACT ADDRESS** Dept of English, Univ of Florida, PO Box 3710, Gainesville, FL 32611-3710. **EMAIL** nholland@ufl.edu

HOLLANDER, JOHN
PERSONAL Born 10/28/1929, New York, NY, m, 1982, 2 children **DISCIPLINE** ENGLISH **EDUCATION** Columbia Univ, AB, 50, MA, 52; Ind Univ, PhD, 59. **CAREER** Lectr English, Conn Col, 57-59; from instr to assoc prof, Yale Univ, 59-66; prof English, Hunter Col & Grad Ctr, City Univ New York, 66-67; prof English, 77-86, A Bartlett Giamatti Prof English, 86-95, Sterling Prof English, 95-, Yale Univ; Poetry Ed, Partisan Review, 59-65; Christian Gauss Lecturer, Princeton Univ, 62; Visiting Prof, Linguistic Inst and School of Lettes, IN Univ, 64; Faculty, Salzburg Seminar in American Studies, 65; Ellisotn Poetry Prof, Univ of Cincinnati, 69; Contributing Ed, Harper's Magazine, 69-71; Residnet Guest Writer, City of Jerusalem, 80; Lecutrer, 81-82; Glasgow Lecturer, Washington and Lee Univ, 84; Advisory Ed, Word and Image, 85-92, Patten Lecturer, IN Univ, 86; Faculty, Sewanee Writers' Conference, 91, 93, 95, 97, 99. **HONORS AND AWARDS** Yale Series Younger Poets Awd, 58; Poetry Chap-Book Awd, 62; Levinson Awd, Poetry Mag, 74; Overseas Fellow, Churchill Col, Cambridge Univ, 67-68; Nat Inst Arts & Letters Awd in Literature, 63; Bollingen Prize, 83; Shenandoah Prize, 85; Melville Cane Awd, 90; Governor's Arts Awd for Poetry, Conn, 97; Morse Fel, Yale Univ, 62-63; MacArthur Fel, 90-95; Cleanth Brooks-Robert Penn Warren Awd, 97; Phi Beta Kappa, 81-82; Fellow, Inst for Advanced Study, IN Univ, 86; Awd in Literature, National Institute of Arts and Letters, 63; Levinson Prize, 74; Washington Monthly Prize, 76; Mina P. Shaughnessy Awd, Modern Lan-

guage Asn, 82; Bollingen Prize, 83; Ambassador Book Awd, The English Speaking Union, 94; Governor's Arts Awd for Poetry, State of Connecticut, 97; Morse Fellowship, Yale Univ, 62-63; Sr Fellowhsip, National Endowment for the Humanities, 73-74; Guggenheim Fellowship, 79-80; MacArthur Fellowship, 90-95; Marietta College, LittD, 82 DHL; IN Univ, 90; Maine Col of Art, DFA, 93; marietta col, littd, 82. **MEMBERSHIPS** Am Acad Arts & Sci; Am Acad Inst Arts & Letters; chancellor, Acad Am Poets; Asn of Literary Scholars and Critics, 00-01. **RESEARCH** Poetry and the other arts; the Renaissance; romantic poetry. **SELECTED PUBLICATIONS** Auth, The Untuning of the Sky, Princeton Univ Press, 61; auth, Vision and Resonance, Oxford Univ Press, 75; auth, The Figure of Echo Univ of CA Press, 81; auth, Melodious Guile, Yale Univ Press, 88; auth, Types of Shape, Expanded edition with notes and introduction, Yale Univ Press, 91; auth, Selected Poetry, Knopf, 93; auth, Tesserae and Oter Poems, Knopf, 93; auth, Selected Poetry, Knopf, 93; auth, Tesserae and Other Poems, Knopf, 93; auth, The Gazer's Spirit, Univ of Chicago Press, 95; auth, The Gazer's Spirit, Chicago, 95; ed, Animal Poems, Knopf, 96; ed, Garden Poems, Knopf, 96; ed, Nineteenth Century American Poetry, Library of America, 96; ed, Committed to Memory: 100 Best Poems to Memorize, Turtle Point, 96; ed, Marriage Poems, Knopf, 97; auth, the Work of Poetry, Columbia, 97; ed, Poems of Robert Frost, Knopf, 97; auth, The Work of Poetry, Columbia Univ Press, 97; auth, The Poetry of Everyday Life, Univ of MI Press, 98; auth, Figurehead and Other Poems, Knopf, 99; auth, Reflections on Espionage, 2nd ed with new notes and introduction, Yale Univ Press, 99; auth, Rhyme's Reason 3rd ed, expanded and revised, Yale Univ Press, 00. **CONTACT ADDRESS** PO Box 208302, New Haven, CT 06520-8302. **EMAIL** john.hollander@yale.edu

HOLLENBERG, DONNA KROLIK
PERSONAL Born 09/07/1942, Saskatoon, SK, Canada, m, 1989, 2 children **DISCIPLINE** ENGLISH **EDUCATION** Univ Manitoba, BA, 64; Boston Univ, MA, 68; Tufts Univ, PhD, 86. **CAREER** Instr, dept chmn, 70-, Mount Ida Jr Col; prof, 85-90, Simmons Col; prof, 91-, Univ Conn. **HONORS AND AWARDS** McGill Univ Scholar, 60-61; tuition scholar, Univ Stockholm, 61-62; HD Fel, Seinecke Lib, 91. **MEMBERSHIPS** AAUP; MLA; MELUE; ASCVS. **RESEARCH** Modern poetry; 20th century Amer lit; Canadian lit. **SELECTED PUBLICATIONS** Auth, Between History and Poetry: the Letters of H.D. and Norman Holmes Reneson, Univ Iowa Press, 97; auth, HD: The Poetics of Childbirth and Creativity, Northeastern Univ Press, 91. **CONTACT ADDRESS** Dept of English, Univ of Connecticut, Storrs, Storrs, CT 06269. **EMAIL** donna.hollenberg@uconn.edu

HOLLEY, LINDA TARTE
PERSONAL Born 10/06/1940, Darlington, SC, m, 1962, 2 children **DISCIPLINE** MEDIEVAL ENGLISH **EDUCATION** Winthrop Col, AB, 62; Tulane Univ, MA, 70, PhD(English), 76. **CAREER** ASST PROF PROF ENGLISH, NC STATE UNIV, 76-, Folger fel, 81. **MEMBERSHIPS** MLA; SAtlantic Mod Lang Asn; Southeastern Medieval Asn. **RESEARCH** Chaucer; Middle English. **SELECTED PUBLICATIONS** Auth, Design and focus in James Dickey's Deliverance, SC Rev, 4/78; The Abuse of Language in Three Canterbury Churchmen, Parergon, Nat Univ Australia Humanities Ctr, 80; The narrative speculum in Chaucer's Troilus & Criseyde, Col Lang Asn J, 12/81. **CONTACT ADDRESS** Dept of English, No Carolina State Univ, Raleigh, NC 27607.

HOLLEY, ROBERT P.
PERSONAL Born 05/01/1944, Toledo, OH, m, 1983 **DISCIPLINE** LITERATURE **EDUCATION** Xavier Univ, BA, 67; Yale Univ, PhD, 71; Columbia Univ, MLS, 73. **CAREER** Asst Dir, Univ Ut Libr, 79-88; From Dir to Assoc Prof, Wayne State Univ, 88- **HONORS AND AWARDS** Ut Libr Asn Res Awd, 87; Distinguished Alumnus, Columbia Sch of Libr Serv, 91. **MEMBERSHIPS** Am Libr Assoc, Assoc for Libr & Information Sci Educ, Mich Libr Assoc. **RESEARCH** Collection development, bibliographic control subject access to information. **SELECTED PUBLICATIONS** Auth, "Resource Sharing and Information Network Concerns at the 1992 IFLA Conference, New Delhi, India: A Bibliography with Abstracts," Resource Sharing and Information Networks, vol 9, no 1 (93): 131-149; auth, "Report on the IFLA Satellite Meeting 'Subject Indexing: Principles and Practices in the 90's,' August 17-18, 1993, Lisbon, Portugal," The Cataloging & Classification Quart, vol 9, no 1 (93): 131-149; auth, "Blackwell North America's Table of Contents Service," ISBN Rev, 15 (94): 55-66; auth, "IFLA and International Standards in the Area of Bibliographic Control," in Cataloging and Classification Standards and Rules, (Binghamton: Hayworth Pr, 96), 17-36; auth, "Results of a 'Survey on Bibliographic Control and National Bibliography, IFLA Section on Bibliography'," Int Cataloging and Bibliog Control, vol 27, no 1 (98): 3-7. **CONTACT ADDRESS** Dept Lit, Wayne State Univ, 3100 Adamany Library, Detroit, MI 48202. **EMAIL** aa3805@wayne.edu

HOLLEY, SANDRA CAVANAUGH
PERSONAL Born 03/30/1943, Washington, DC, 1 child **DISCIPLINE** SPEECH PATHOLOGY **EDUCATION** George Washington University, AB 1965, AM 1966; Univ of CT, PhD 1979. **CAREER** Southern CT State Univ, speech/language pathologist, prof 70-; Rehab Center of Eastern Fairfield Co, speech pathologist, 66-70; Dean, 98-. **HONORS AND AWARDS** Danforth fellow Southern CT State College 73-80; Leadership in Communications Awd Howard Univ 87; Honorary Doctor of Public Service degree George Washington Univ 89; Fellow, American Speech-Language-Hearing Association, 80; SCSU, Multicultural Founders Awd, 94; National Coalition of 100 Black Women, Milestone Awd, 94; Distinguished Alumna Awd, Dept. of Speech & Hearing, George Washington Univ, 97; Busines Times 20 Noteworthy Women Awd, 00. **MEMBERSHIPS** Chmn Humane Commission City of New Haven 77-86; bd of dir American Natl Red Cross S Central Chap 78-84; exec bd CT Speech & Hearing Assn 71-83; bd dir New Haven Visiting Nurse Assn 77-79; vice pres for adminstration, Amer Speech-Language-Hearing Assn 83-85; mem bd of dir The Foote School Association 85-89; pres American Speech-Language-Hearing Assn 88, Long Whard Theatre Bd of Dir, 98-. **CONTACT ADDRESS** Communication Disorders, So Connecticut State Univ, 501 Crescent St, New Haven, CT 06515. **EMAIL** holley@scsu.ctstateu.edu

HOLLIDAY, SHAWN P.
PERSONAL Born 05/21/1969, S Williamson, KY **DISCIPLINE** ENGLISH **EDUCATION** Ind Univ Pa, BA, 91; Marshall Univ, MA, 93; PhD, 99. **CAREER** Instr, Ind Univ of Pa, 97-98; instr, Marshall Col, 98-99; asst prof, Alice Lloyd Col, 99-. **HONORS AND AWARDS** Thomas Wolfe Student Prize. **MEMBERSHIPS** MLA, Thomas Wolfe Soc, Frank Norris sSoc, W Lit Assoc, Irish-Am Cult Inst, Phi Kappa Phi. **RESEARCH** American Literature since 1865, Western American Literature, Asian-American Literature, Modern Irish Literature, Shakespeare, Issues in Writing Across the Curriculum. **SELECTED PUBLICATIONS** Auth, "Sex and Comedy in Patrick Kavanagh's the Great Hunge," Notes on Modern Irish Literature, (95); auth, "Now for Our Irish Wars: Shakespeare's Warning Against the Usurpation of Ireland in the Lancastrian Tetralogy," Pa English, (96); auth, "The Pity, Terror, Strangeness, and Magnificence of It All: Landscape and Discourse in Thomas Wolfe's A Western Journal," Thomas Wolfe Rev, (97); auth, "Austin Clarke", "Patrick Kavanagh", "Thomas Kinsella", Modern Irish Writers: A Bio-Critical Sourcebook, Greenwood Pr, (97); auth, "John Fox", "Arthur Miller", "Mark Helprin", Encycl of Am War Lit, Greenwood Pr, (01); auth, Thomas Wolfe and the Politics of Modernism, Peter Lang, 01. **CONTACT ADDRESS** Alice Lloyd Col, PO Box 1, Edmond, WV 25837. **EMAIL** coriolanus31@aol.com

HOLLIDAY, VIVIAN LOYREA
PERSONAL Born 02/25/1935, Manning, SC **DISCIPLINE** CLASSICS, ANCIENT HISTORY **EDUCATION** Winthrop Col, AB, 57; Univ Mo, MA, 59; Univ NC, PhD(classics), 61. **CAREER** Instr classics, 61-63, from asst prof to assoc prof, 63-69, Aylesworth Prof Classics, Col Wooster, 69-, Dean Fac, 77-85, mem managing comt, Am Sch Class Studies, Athens, 67. **MEMBERSHIPS** Am Philol Asn; Am Inst Archaeol. **RESEARCH** Republican Rome; comparative literature; modern Greek literature. **SELECTED PUBLICATIONS** Auth, Pompey in Cicero's Letters and Lucan's Civil War, Mouton, The Hauge, 69; Kazantzakis, Odyssey, Neo-Hellenika, Vol III, 78; Job Satisfaction for the Faculty, Academic Job Satisfaction: Varieties and Values, 80; Classical and Modern Narratives of Leadership, (pub 1999). **CONTACT ADDRESS** Dept of Classics, The Col of Wooster, 1189 Beall Ave, Wooster, OH 44691-2363. **EMAIL** IN%vholliday@acs.wooster.edu

HOLLINGSWORTH, ANTHONY L.
PERSONAL Born 09/10/1967, Rockford, IL, m, 1995, 1 child **DISCIPLINE** CLASSICS, GERMAN LANGUAGE AND LITERATURE **EDUCATION** Univ Dallas, BA, 89; Brown Univ, AM, 93; PhD, 98. **CAREER** Asst prof, Roger Williams Univ, 97-; dept chair, 98-. **HONORS AND AWARDS** Fulbright Fel; DAAD Diss Fel; Den's Grad Fel; Rotary Schl; Cardinal Spellman Awd; Phi Beta Kappa. **MEMBERSHIPS** APA; CANE; RICA; ACL; ATFL. **RESEARCH** Latin and Greek literature; German language and literature; comedy and tragedy (ancient and modern); computing applications. **SELECTED PUBLICATIONS** Auth, "Let The Play Begin: The Origin of the Greek Theater," Class Calliope 8 (97); auth, "Octavian's Triple Triumph," Class Calliope 8 (97); auth, "Recitation and Senecan Tragedy: Where is The Similarity?," Class World (97); auth, "Love Leads to War: The Origins of The Trojan War," Class Calliope 9 (98); auth, "Defeat and Victory: Hannibal's March," Class Calliope (98); auth, "Hadrian: Emperor By Adoption," Classical Calliope (99); auth, "A Loud No to The Demand For Food & Water," Classical Calliope (99); auth, "Charlemagne, According to Einhard," Class Calliope (99); auth, "If You Build It, They Will Enroll: The Formation of a Language Department," NECJ (forthcoming). **CONTACT ADDRESS** Dept Humanities, Roger Williams Univ, 1 Old Ferry Rd, Bristol, RI 02809-2923. **EMAIL** alh@alpha.rwu.edu

HOLLINGSWORTH, MARGARET
PERSONAL Born Sheffield, England **DISCIPLINE** WRITING **EDUCATION** Loughborough Univ, ALA; Lakehead Univ, BA, 71; Univ BC, MFA, 74. **CAREER** Freelance journalist & foreign corresp, 66-90; asst prof, 81-93, asst prof, 92-93, Assoc Prof Creative Writing, Univ Victoria, 94-. **HONORS AND AWARDS** Jessie Awd, 95; Chalmers Awd, drama, 85; Dora Mavor Moore Awd, 86, 87; ACTRA Awd, radio drama, 86, 88. **MEMBERSHIPS** Writers' Union Can; Playwrights' Union; ACTRA; Libr Asn; PEN; Betty Lambert Soc. **SELECTED PUBLICATIONS** Auth, Willful Acts, 85; auth, Smiling Under Water, 89; auth, Why We Don't Write: Where Are Our Women Playwrights?, in Can Theatre Rev, 91; auth, Numbrains, 94. **CONTACT ADDRESS** Dept of Writing, Univ of Victoria, Victoria, BC, Canada V8W 2Y2. **EMAIL** mholling@finearts.uvic.ca

HOLLOWAY, KARLA F. C.
DISCIPLINE ENGLISH LITERATURE **EDUCATION** MI State Univ, PhD, 78. **CAREER** Prof, Duke Univ. **RESEARCH** Intersections between linguistics and lit. **SELECTED PUBLICATIONS** Auth, The Character of the Word, Greenwood, 87; New Dimensions of Spirituality, Greenwood, 87; Moorings and Metaphors: Figures of Culture and Gender in Black Women's Literature, Rutgers, 92; auth, Codes of Conduct: Race, Ethics, and the Color of Our Character. **CONTACT ADDRESS** Dept English, Duke Univ, 012 Allen Bldg., Box 90029, Durham, NC 27708. **EMAIL** kholloway@asdean.duke.edu

HOLLSTEIN, MILTON C.
DISCIPLINE COMMUNICATION STUDIES **EDUCATION** Univ Iowa, PhD, 55. **CAREER** Prof. **HONORS AND AWARDS** Deseret News First Contributors Awd, 92. **MEMBERSHIPS** Soc Prof Jour; Asn Edu Jour and Mass Commun. **SELECTED PUBLICATIONS** Auth, Editing with Understanding, Macmillan, 81; Magazines in Search of an Audience: A Guide to Starting New Magazines, Magazine Publ Asn, 69. **CONTACT ADDRESS** Dept of Communication, Univ of Utah, 100 S 1350 E, Salt Lake City, UT 84112.

HOLMER, JOAN OZARK
PERSONAL Born 07/11/1946, Minneapolis, MN, m, 1973, 2 children **DISCIPLINE** ENGLISH LITERATURE **EDUCATION** Univ Minn, BA; BS; Princeton Univ, MA, PhD. **CAREER** Prof, Georgetown Univ. **HONORS AND AWARDS** Edward B. Bunn Awd for Fac Excel, 88; Dean's Awd for Excel in Tchg, Georgetown Univ, 99. **MEMBERSHIPS** Shakespeare Asn of America; Phi Beta Kappa. **RESEARCH** Renaissance literature; source study; fairy mythology; fencing; biblical allusion; moral philosophy and ethics; performance phenomenology; dramatic structure and genre; intellectual, cultural, religious and economic history. **SELECTED PUBLICATIONS** Auth, The Merchant of Venice: Choice, Hazard and Consequence, MacMillan & St Martin's, 95. **CONTACT ADDRESS** English Dept, Georgetown Univ, 37th and O St, Washington, DC 20057. **EMAIL** homerj@georgetown.edu

HOLMES, BURNHAM
PERSONAL Born 07/23/1942, Grandville, NY, w, 1 child **DISCIPLINE** ENGLISH **EDUCATION** Univ Mo, BA, 64, MA, 65. **CAREER** Sch of Visual Arts, 81-95; Green Mountain Col, 96-98; Castleton State Col, 96-2000. **MEMBERSHIPS** Author's Guild, Literary Market Place Listing. **SELECTED PUBLICATIONS** Auth, Cesar Chavez: Farm Worker Activist, Austin, Tex: Raintree Steck-Vaughn (94); coauth, Yogi, Babe, and Magic, NY: Prentice-Hall (94); coauth, The TV Almanac, NY: Macmillan (94); auth, The Complete Book of Sports Nicknames, Los Angeles: Renaissance Books (98); auth, One Shining Moment, Avon Harper Collins (in press). **CONTACT ADDRESS** Dept English & Langs, Castleton State Col, Castleton, VT 05735. **EMAIL** Burnham.Holmes@castleton.edu

HOLMES, CHARLOTTE
PERSONAL Born 04/26/1956, GA, M, 1983, 1 child **DISCIPLINE** ENGLISH **EDUCATION** La State Univ, BA, 77; Columbia State Univ, MFA, 80. **CAREER** Assoc man ed, Ecco Press, 80-82; instr, Western Carolina Univ, 84-87; asst prof, Pa State Univ, 87-93; assoc prof, 93-. **HONORS AND AWARDS** Wallace Stegner Fel; Claire Woolrich Fel; Writers Exch Awd; PCA, Indv Fel; Bread Loaf Writers Conf Schl; George Atherton Teach Awd. **RESEARCH** Fiction writing; creative non-fiction writing. **SELECTED PUBLICATIONS** Auth, "The Impossible Man," Mademoiselle (77); auth, "Louisiana in Hurricane Season," Mag Poetry Prose (83); auth, Gifts and Other Stories, Confluence Press (Lewiston, Idaho), 94; auth, "Metropolitan," New Stories From The South: The Year's Best 1988, Algonquin Books (Chapel Hill, NC), 88; auth, "Invisible Babies," in Silent Parenting in The Academy, eds. Diana Hume, George and Constance Coiner (Evanston, IL: Univ of Ill Press, 97); auth, "Refrigerator," Mag Lit and Art 31 (99), 41-46; "Agnes Landowska: Her Art and Life," New Letters 64 (93), 105-124. **CONTACT ADDRESS** Dept English, Pennsylvania State Univ, Univ Park, 117 Burrows Bldg, University Park, PA 16802-6200. **EMAIL** cxh18@psu.edu

HOLMES, DAVID
DISCIPLINE COMPOSITION **EDUCATION** B.A. OK Christian Col, BA, 86; CA State Univ Dominguez Hills, MA, 93; Univ S CA, PhD, 97. **CAREER** Dir, Am Studies Prog; asst prof. **HONORS AND AWARDS** Irvine Teaching Fel, 93-97, Scholars for the Dream Awd, 95, Seaver Res Fel, 99-00, The

Carroll Awd, 99, Outstanding Young Men of Am, 87; 96. **SELECTED PUBLICATIONS** Auth, Nonfiction Prose, Encycl of Rhetoric, 95; auth, "Beyond Racially Reductive Compostion Theory," Race, Rhetoric, and Composition, Portsmouth: Heinemann-Boyton/Cook, (99), 53-66; auth, "The Fragmented Whole: Ralph Ellison, Kenneth Burke, and the Cultural Lieteracy Debate," Col Lang Assoc Journal vol 63, (00), 261-275. **CONTACT ADDRESS** Dept of Eng, Pepperdine Univ, 24255 Pacific Coast Hwy, Malibu, CA 90263. **EMAIL** dholmes@pepperdine.edu

HOLMES, MICHAEL E.
DISCIPLINE COMMUNICATION STUDIES **EDUCATION** Univ Minn, PhD, 91. **CAREER** Dept Comm, Utah Univ **MEMBERSHIPS** Int Commun Asn; Nat Commun Asn; NW Commun Asn; Western States Commun Asn. **RESEARCH** Organizational communication and nonroutine events; research methods and new communication technology; design theory. **SELECTED PUBLICATIONS** Auth, Optimal matching analysis of negotiation phase sequences in simulated and authentic hostage negotatiations, 97; Processes and patterns in hostage negotiations, Greenwood, 97; WinPhaser 1.0c: Interaction sequence description and analysis, 97; Naming virtual space in computer-mediated conversation, 95; Don't blink or you'll miss it: Issues in electronic mail research, 94; co-auth, Decision development in computer-assisted group decision making, Human Commun Res, 95; Negotiations in crisis, SUNY, 95. **CONTACT ADDRESS** Dept of Communication, Univ of Utah, 100 S 1350 E, Salt Lake City, UT 84112. **EMAIL** holmes@admin.comm.utah.edu

HOLOKA, JAMES P.
PERSONAL Born 01/19/1947, Rochester, NY, m, 1968, 3 children **DISCIPLINE** CLASSICS AND ANCIENT HISTORY **EDUCATION** Univ Rochester, BA, 69; SUNY-Binghamton, MA, 72; Univ Mich, PhD, 74. **CAREER** Teaching asst/fel, 69-72; lectr, Eastern Mich Univ, 74-76; from asst prof to prof, Eastern Mich Univ, 76-. **HONORS AND AWARDS** Rackham Prize Fel, Univ Mich, 73-74; NEH Summer Stipend, 76; Distinguish Fac Award for Excellence in Teaching and Commitment to Students, 80; Scholarly Recognition Award, 91. **MEMBERSHIPS** Am Philol Asn; Class Asn of the Mid West and South; Cen Intl d'Etudes Homeriques. **RESEARCH** Greek and Roman epic, lyric, and satire; Ancient history; Women in antiquity; Comparative literature and literary theory. **SELECTED PUBLICATIONS** Auth, "Homeric Originality: A Survey," 78; "Homer Studies 1971-1977," 79; "Looking Darkely: Reflections on Status and Decorum in Homer," 83; "Homer Studies 1978-1983 Pt. 1," 90; "Homer Studies 1978-1983 Pt. 2," 90; "Homer, Oral Poetry Theory and Comparative Literature: Major Trends and Controversies in Twentieth-Century Criticism," 91; World History, 91; "Nonverbal Communication in the Classics: Research Opportunities," 92; Lives and Times: A World History Reader, 95; trans, Homer: His Art and His World, 96; Co-auth, A Survey of Western Civilization, 97; auth, Marathon and the Myth of the Same-Day March 97, 00. **CONTACT ADDRESS** Foreign Language Dept, Eastern Michigan Univ, 7685 Paint Creek Dr, Ypsilanti, MI 48197. **EMAIL** fla_holoka@online.emich.edu

HOLTON, WILLIAM MILNE
PERSONAL Born 11/04/1931, Charlotte, NC, m, 1964 **DISCIPLINE** MODERN & AMERICAN LITERATURE **EDUCATION** Dartmouth Col, AB, 54, Harvard Univ, LLB, 57; Yale Univ, MA, 59, PhD, 65. **CAREER** From instr to assoc prof, 61-77, Prof English lit, Univ MD, College Park, 78-; Fulbright lectr, Univ Uppsala, 65-66; Fulbright prof, Univ Skopje, 70. **HONORS AND AWARDS** Golden Pen Awd, Macedonian Cult Comn (for transl), 77. **MEMBERSHIPS** MLA; S Atlantic Mod Lang Asn; James Joyce Soc; PEN Club; Fr Asn Am St. **RESEARCH** Modern American literature; modern and contemporary poetry; modern poetry in translation. **SELECTED PUBLICATIONS** Auth, Sparrow's fall and sparrow's eye: Stephen Crane's Maggie, Studia Neophilologica, 69; coauth, Private Dealings: Eight Modern American Writers, Almqvist & Wiksell, Stockholm, 69; auth, Cylinder of Vision: The Fiction and Journalistic Writings of Stephen Crane, La State Univ, 72; Notes on Macedonia, Contempora, 72; coauth, New Perspectives, 74; ed, The Big House and Other Stories of Modern Macedonia, Univ Mo, 74; co-ed, Reading the Ashes: An Anthology of Modern Macedonian Poetry, 77 & The New Polish Poetry: A Bilingual Collection, 78, Univ Pittsburgh, 78; Co-ed, Austrian Poetry Today, Schocleen, NY, 85; Serbian Poetry from the Beginnings to the Present, Yale, NY, 89; The Songs of the Serbian People: From The Collections of Vuk Stefaneric Karadzic, Univ Pitts, 97. **CONTACT ADDRESS** Dept English, Univ of Maryland, Col Park, 3101 Susquehanna Hill, College Park, MD 20742-8800. **EMAIL** wh25@umail.umd.edu

HOLTZ, WILLIAM
DISCIPLINE ENGLISH **EDUCATION** Univ Mich, PhD, 64. **CAREER** Prof; Catherine Paine Middlebush prof, 94; taught crs(es), sem in, Fielding, Sterne, Austen & Brontes. **HONORS AND AWARDS** 3 bk awds; ACLS & NEH fel. **SELECTED PUBLICATIONS** Auth, The Ghost in the Little House: A Life of Rose Wilder Lane, Univ Mo Press, 93; publ on, 18th-century lite, Engl novel & lit theory and criticism. **CONTACT ADDRESS** Dept of English, Univ of Missouri, Columbia, 309 University Hall, Columbia, MO 65211.

HOLUB, ROBERT C.
PERSONAL Born 08/22/1949, Neptune, NJ, m, 1998, 1 child **DISCIPLINE** GERMAN LITERATURE, LITERARY THEORY **EDUCATION** Univ Pa, BA, 71; Univ Wis, Madison, MA, 73, MA, 76, PhD, 79. **CAREER** Teaching asst, Univ Wis, Madison, 72-78; asst prof of German, Univ Calif, Berkeley, 79-. **HONORS AND AWARDS** Emmy Kleist Fel, Univ of Wis, Madison, 77; WARF Dissertation Fel, Univ Wis, Madison, 78-79; Alexander von Humboldt Fel, 83-85; Humanities Res Fel, Univ Calif, Berkeley, 89; DAAD Study Visit Grant, 95; NEH Summer Stipend, 95. **MEMBERSHIPS** MLA; Am Asn Teachers of German; Heinrich Heine Soc. **RESEARCH** German intellectual, cultural, and literary history of the 19th & 20th century. **SELECTED PUBLICATIONS** Auth, Heinrich Heine's Reception of German Grecophilia: The Function and Application of the Hellenic Tradition in the First Half of the Nineteenth Century, Carl Winter (Heidelberg), 81; auth, Reflections of Realism: Paradox, Norm, and Ideology in Nineteenth-Century German Prose, Wayne State Univ Press (Detroit, MI), 91; auth, J¤rgen Habermas: Critic in the Public Sphere, Routledge (London), 91; auth, Crossing Borders: Reception Theory, Poststructuralism, Deconstruction, Univ of Wis Press (Madison, WI), 92; coed, Impure Reason: Dialectic of Enlightenment in Germany, Wayne State Univ Press (Detroit, MI), 93; auth, Friedrich Nietzsche, Twayne Publishers (New York, NY), 95; coed, Responsibility and Commitment: Ethische Posulate der Kulturvermittlung: Festschrift f¤r Jost Hermand, Lang (Frankfurt), 96; coed, Heine's Contested Identities: Politics, Religion, and Nationalism in Nineteenth-Century Germany, Lang (New York, NY), 99. **CONTACT ADDRESS** Dept German, Univ of California, Berkeley, 5315 Dwinelle Hall, Berkeley, CA 94720-3243. **EMAIL** RCHolub@socrates.berkeley.edu

HOLZBERGER, WILLIAM GEORGE
PERSONAL Born 01/06/1932, Chicago, IL, m, 1965, 2 children **DISCIPLINE** ENGLISH **EDUCATION** Northwestern Univ, Evanston, PhB, 60, MA(Philos), 65, MA(English), 66, PhD(English), 69. **CAREER** Asst prof, 69-74, assoc prof, 74-81, prof English, 81-97, PROF EMER, 97- , BUCKNELL UNIV. **HONORS AND AWARDS** Am Philos Soc grant-in-aid, 70; Am Coun Learned Soc grant-in-aid, 72 & 73; Nat Endowment for Humanities fel, 75-76. **MEMBERSHIPS** MLA; AAUP; Soc Advan Am Philos; Santayana Soc. **RESEARCH** English and American literature and intellectual history; 20th century literature. **SELECTED PUBLICATIONS** Auth, The Unpublished Poems of George Santayana: Some Critical and Textual Considerations, Southern Rev, 1/75; co-ed, Perspectives on Hamlet, 76 & ed, The Complete Poems of George Santayana: A Critical Edition, 79, Bucknell Univ; auth, Remembering the Bard of Boar's Hill, Mich Quart, winter 80; Accentuating the Positive, Southern Rev, 7/81; What is an Educated Person?, Eidos, 85; A E Housman & George Santayana, In: The Dict of Literary Biography; auth, The Significance of the Subtitle in Santayana's Novel The Last Puritan: A Memoir in the Form of a Novel, in Price, ed, Critical Essays on George Santayana, G.K. Hall, 91; auth, A.E. Housman, 1859-1936, in Gay and Lesbian Literature, Gale, 93; auth, George Santayana, 1863-1952, in Payne, ed, A Dictionary of Cultural and Critical Theory, Blackwell, 95; co-ed, The Works of George Santayana, 4 v, MIT. **CONTACT ADDRESS** Dept of English, Bucknell Univ, Lewisburg, PA 17837. **EMAIL** holzbrgr@bucknell.edu

HONEYCUTT, JAMES M.
DISCIPLINE SPEECH COMMUNICATION **EDUCATION** Univ Ill, PhD. **CAREER** Assoc prof, La State Univ. **RESEARCH** Relational conflict; marital interaction. **SELECTED PUBLICATIONS** Published over a dozen studies in intrapersonal communication processes in terms of covert dialogues or imagined interactions. **CONTACT ADDRESS** Dept of Speech Commun, Louisiana State Univ and A&M Col, Baton Rouge, LA 70803. **EMAIL** sphone@lsu.edu

HONG, RAN-E
PERSONAL Born 05/20/1960, Seoul, South Korea, 1 child **DISCIPLINE** LITERATURE, FRENCH **EDUCATION** Ewha Woman's Univ, BA, 81; MA, 83; Univ Paris, Doct de 3e Cycle, 87; Brown Univ, PhD, 00. **CAREER** Lectr, Ewha Woman's Univ, 87-94; lectr, Hongik Univ, 92-93; lectr, Hankook Univ, 93-95; lectr, Konkuk Univ, 94-96; asst prof, Rivier Col, 00-01. **MEMBERSHIPS** MLA; NASSCFL; ASEF; CIBP; Soc du XVIIe Siecle; Soc des Amis de Port-Royal. **RESEARCH** 17th-century French literature and culture. **SELECTED PUBLICATIONS** Auth, "Le Paradoxe Dans les Premieres Liasses de L'Apologie," Cahiers de Asn Intl des Etudes (88); auth, "La Force et Ses Aspects Selon Pascal," Equinox (88); auth, "L'ideal de L'honnete Homme Selon Pascal et la Figure de L'homme de Qualite Selon Confucius Pascalienne," Pascal (90); auth, "La Recriture de Deux Contes de La Fontaine et Sq Signification," Fr 17th-Century Lit (00); auth, L'impossible Social Selon Moliere, Gunter Narr (forthcoming). **CONTACT ADDRESS** Dept Mod Lang, Grand Valley State Univ, 1 Campus Dr, Allendale, MI 49401-9403.

HOOD, MANTLE
DISCIPLINE ETHNOMUSICOLOGY **EDUCATION** Univ Calif, MA, BA; Univ Amsterdam, PhD. **CAREER** Prof emer, UCLA; vis prof; adj prof-. **HONORS AND AWARDS** Sr fel, NEH; Fulbright fel; Ford Found fel; former pres, soc ethnomusicology. **MEMBERSHIPS** Soc for Ethnomusicology. **RESEARCH** Indonesian music. **SELECTED PUBLICATIONS** Publ, twenty books and book chapters as well as over sixty articles in scholarly journals and encyclopedias. **CONTACT ADDRESS** Dept of Mus, West Virginia Univ, Morgantown, PO Box 6009, Morgantown, WV 26506-6009.

HOOPER, WILLIAM LOYD
PERSONAL m, 2 children **DISCIPLINE** MUSIC **EDUCATION** Southwest Bapt Col, cert, Bolivar, Mo, 51; William Jewell Col, BA, Philos, 53, Liberty, Mo; Univ Iowa, MA, music, 56; PhD, music, 66, minor in higher educ, George Peabody Col, Vanderbilt Univ, Nashville, Tenn; music composition study with, Philip Bezanson, 55-56, Univ Iowa, Philip Slates, 60-61, Peabody Col, Vanderbilt Univ, Humphrey Searle, 69-70, Royal Col of Music, London, England; training in psychotherapy, Westminster Pastoral Found, 82-83, London, England. **CAREER** Music tchr, K-12, Essex Pub Sch, Essex, Iowa, 53-55; music tchr, 9-12, Atalissa Pub Sch, Atalissa, Iowa, 55-56; pastor, Denver Bapt Church, Denver, Mo, 53-55; prof of music, Southwest Bapt Col, Bolivar, Mo, 56-60; minister of music and educ, First Bapt Church, Old Hickory, Tenn, 60-62; prof of music, New Orleans Bapt Sem, New Orleans, La, 62-74; acting dean, Sch of Church Music, New Orleans Bapt Sem, 64-65, dean, 65-74; head of music dept, Newstead Wood Sch for Girls, London Borough of Bromley England, 74-79; assoc pastor and minister of music, Emmanuel Bapt Church, Gravesend, Kent, England, 74-79; sr pastor, 79-83; chief examiner in music, Southeast Reg Examining Bd, Tunbridge Wells, Kent, England, 75-80; dean, prof of music, Sch of Fine Arts, Southwest Bapt Univ, 83-89; dir of assessment, dir of intl studies, prof of music, Southwest Bapt Univ, 89-98. **HONORS AND AWARDS** David Duce Awd in Philos, William Jewell Col, 53; Outstanding Young Men of Amer, 63; Citation for Achievement, William Jewell Col, 67; First Place winner, Delius Compos Competition, 73; First place winner, New Times Compos Competition, 74. **SELECTED PUBLICATIONS** Auth, Fundamentals of Music, Conv Press, 86; Ministry and Musicians, Broadman Press, 83; Music Fundamentals, Conv Press, 67; Church Music in Transition, Broadman Press, 63; compos, Jubilee, Cantata, Carl Fischer Co, Litany of Praise, Cantata, Carl Fischer Co, And He Shall Come, Cantata, Broadman Press, Sing Joyfully, choral collection, Broadman Press; incidental music for prof of Anouihl's Becket, Le Petit Theatre du Vieux Carre, New Orleans, La. **CONTACT ADDRESS** 116 W. Auburn St., Bolivar, MO 65613. **EMAIL** bhooper@sbuniv.edu

HOOPLE, ROBIN P.
DISCIPLINE ENGLISH LITERATURE **EDUCATION** Univ Syracuse, BA; MA; Univ Minn, PhD. **HONORS AND AWARDS** Co-ed, Mosaic; pres, Can Assn Am Studies. **RESEARCH** American Romanticism; American realism and naturalism. **SELECTED PUBLICATIONS** Auth, Distinguished Discord, 97; pub(s) on American literature. **CONTACT ADDRESS** Dept of English, Univ of Manitoba, Winnipeg, MB, Canada R3T 2N2. **EMAIL** hoople@cc.umanitoba.ca

HOOVER, DAVID LOWELL
PERSONAL Born 02/10/1949, Goshen, IN, m, 1974, 1 child **DISCIPLINE** MEDIEVAL LITERATURE, LINGUISTICS **EDUCATION** Manchester Col, BA, 71; Ind Univ, MA, 74, PhD(English lang), 80. **CAREER** Instr English, Ind Cent Univ, 80-81; ASST PROF ENGLISH, NY UNIV, 81- **MEMBERSHIPS** MLA. **RESEARCH** Medieval language and literature; metrics; stylistics. **SELECTED PUBLICATIONS** Auth, Theory, Fact, and Grammar, 2 Approaches to Old-English Meter, Modern Philol, Vol 0092, 94. **CONTACT ADDRESS** English Dept, New York Univ, 19 University Pl, New York, NY 10003-4556.

HOOVER, PAUL
PERSONAL Born 04/30/1946, Harrisonburg, VA, m, 1974, 3 children **DISCIPLINE** ENGLISH, CREATIVE WRITING, POETRY **EDUCATION** Manch Col, BA, 68; Univ Ill, MA, 73. **CAREER** Poet in Reside, Colum Col, 74-. **HONORS AND AWARDS** MAC, Art Gnt; Contem Poet Compet; Carl Sandburg Awd; NEA Fel; Gertrude Stein Awd; Shifting Found Gnts; CLMP Ed Gnt; Gwendolyn Brooks, Poet Laur Awd; GE Found Awd; LACL Fel. **MEMBERSHIPS** MLA. **RESEARCH** Contemporary American Poetry; African-American Interdisciplinary Arts. **SELECTED PUBLICATIONS** Auth, Letter to Einstein Beginning Dear Albert, The Yellow Press (Chicago), 79; auth, Somebody Talks a Lot, The Yellow Press (Chicago), 83; auth, Nervous Songs, L'Epervier Press (Seattle), 86; auth, Idea, The Figures (Great Barrington, MA), 87; auth, Saigon, Illinois, Vintage Contemporaries (NY), 88; auth, The Novel, New Directions (NY), 90; auth, Viridian, Univ Georgia Press (Athens, GA), 97; auth, Totem and Shadow: New and Selected Poems, Talisman House (Jersey City), 99; ed, Postmodern American Poetry, W W Norton (NY), 94; auth, "Pair of Figures for Eshu: Doubling of Consciousness in the Work of Kerry James Marshall and Nathaniel Mackey," Callaloo (99); auth, "Upper Limit Music (Counted Verse)," in An Exaltation of Forms, eds. Annie Finch, Katharine Varnes (Ann Arbor: Univ Mich Press, 99); rev, "Falling into the Sinister, Surreal World of Missing Persons," of The Artist of the Missing, by Paul Lafarge, San Fran

Chronicle (July, 99). **CONTACT ADDRESS** Dept English, Columbia Col, Illinois, 600 S Michigan Ave, Chicago, IL 60605-1900. **EMAIL** viridian@hotmail.com

HOOVER, POLLY
PERSONAL Born 08/28/1956, Yokosuka, Japan, m, 1986 **DISCIPLINE** CLASSICS **EDUCATION** Beloit Col, BA, 78; Univ Chicago, MA, 84; Univ Wisc, MA, 90; PhD, 95. **CAREER** Teaching Asst, Univ Chicago, 81-83; Teaching Asst to Instructor, Univ Wisc, 89-95; Visiting Instructor, Ohio State Univ, 95-97; part-time Instructor, Columbia Col, 97-98; Instructor, Wilbur Wright Col, 97-. **HONORS AND AWARDS** NEH Summer Sem Fel, 99; Pressey Honors Course Enrichment Fund, 96; Travel-Study Awd, CAMWS, 93; Distinguished Teaching Awd, 91-92; Univ Fel, 88-89. **MEMBERSHIPS** Am Philol Asn, Classical Asn of the Midwest and South. **RESEARCH** Literary Theory and Art; Technology in the Classroom. **SELECTED PUBLICATIONS** Auth, "Contextual Learning and the Latin Language Textbooks," Classical World, forthcoming; auth, The boundaries of Transgression, forthcoming. **CONTACT ADDRESS** Dept Humanities, Wilbur Wright Col N, 4300 N Narragansett Ave, Chicago, IL 60634-1591. **EMAIL** phoover@ccc.edu

HOPKINS, LEROY TAFT, JR.
PERSONAL Born 08/19/1942, Lancaster, PA **DISCIPLINE** RUSSIAN, GERMAN **EDUCATION** Millersville St Coll, BA 1966; Harvard U, PhD 1974. **CAREER** Millersville State Coll, asst prof of German, 79-; Prof of German, 92-; Chair Foreign Languages dept, 98-; Urban League of Lancaster Co Inc, acting exec dir, 79, asso dir, 76-79; Hedwig-Heyle-Schule (W Germany), instr English 74-76; NE Univ, instructor German, 71-72. **HONORS AND AWARDS** Received Travelling Fellowship Harvard Univ 1969-70; Study/Visit Grant for Research, German Academic Exchange Service, 1989; Member of Honor Society, Phi Kappa Phi, 1991. **MEMBERSHIPS** Adv Com on Black History PA Hist & Mus Commn 1979-; com person City of Lancasters Overall Econ Devel Prog; Bd Mem Lancastger Co Library/Lancaster Neighborhood Hlth Ctr 1977-; chmn PA Delegation to White House Conf on Libraries 1978-79; Past Pres, Lancaster Co. Historical Society, member of board 83-99, 00; 1st vice pres, Lancaster Historical Society, 1989-; mem, Pennsylvania Humanities Council, 1988-. **CONTACT ADDRESS** Dept of For Lang, Millersville Univ of Pennsylvania, Millersville, PA 17551. **EMAIL** leroy.hopkins@millersv.edu

HOPPER, PAUL
DISCIPLINE ENGLISH AND LINGUISTICS **EDUCATION** Univ Tex, PhD. **CAREER** Lit, Carnegie Mellon Univ. **HONORS AND AWARDS** Ed, Jour Lang Scis; 's Language, Collitz Prof LSA's Linguistics Inst, Fulbright Fel; Guggenheim Fel. **MEMBERSHIPS** MLAl; Ling Soc Am. **SELECTED PUBLICATIONS** Coauth, Grammaticalization, Cambridge, 93. **CONTACT ADDRESS** Carnegie Mellon Univ, 5000 Forbes Ave, Pittsburgh, PA 15213.

HORAN, ELIZABETH R.
PERSONAL Born 07/06/1956, Boston, MA, m, 1980, 1 child **DISCIPLINE** LITERATURE IN ENGLISH & SPANISH **EDUCATION** Barnard Col, BA 78; Univ Calif-Santa Cruz, MA, 84, PhD, 88. **CAREER** Lectr, Wheelock Col, 87-88; vis asst prof, Tufts Univ, 88-89; from asst prof to assoc prof, Ariz State Univ, 89-; vis assoc prof, Grand Valley State, 00-01. **HONORS AND AWARDS** Fulbright Schol, 85-87, 95-96; Gabriela Mistral Awd, Org Am States, 90. **MEMBERSHIPS** MLA; ACLA; Letras Feministas; Emily Dickinson Int Soc. **RESEARCH** US & Latin American women writers; translations; biography. **SELECTED PUBLICATIONS** Co-transl, Happiness, White Pine Press, 93; auth, Gabriela Mistral, an Artist and Her People, Org Am States, 94; To Market: The Dickinson Copyright Wars, Emily Dickinson J, 96; Santa Maestra Muerta: Body and Nation in Portraits of Gabriela Mistral, Taller de Letras, 97; Reading the Book of Memory, Always from Somewhere Else: A Memoir of My Jewish Father, The Feminist Press at CUNY, 98; auth, The Subversive Voice of Carmen Lyra, Univ Pr Florida, 00; author of numerous other articles and publications. **CONTACT ADDRESS** English Dept, Arizona State Univ, Tempe, AZ 85287-0302. **EMAIL** elizabeth.horan@asu.edu

HORNBACK, BERT
PERSONAL Born 12/22/1935, Bowling Green, KY, s **DISCIPLINE** ENGLISH LITERATURE **EDUCATION** Univ Notre Dame, AB, 57; AM, 61; PhD, 64. **CAREER** Instr, Univ Notre Dame, 63-64; prof, Univ Mich, 64-92; vis prof, Univ Col Dublin, 90-91; prof, Bellarmine Col, 92-00. **HONORS AND AWARDS** Distinguished Fac Awd, Univ Mich; Amoco Good Teaching Awd, Univ Mich; RUTN Sinclair Academic Counseling Awd (twice), Univ Mich; Ann Arbor Arts Awd. **MEMBERSHIPS** Dickens Soc, Ctr for the Advancement of Peripheral Thought. **RESEARCH** Dickens, Hardy, American Poetry, Irish Theatre, Homer, Sophocles. **SELECTED PUBLICATIONS** Auth, King Richard the Catsup, 72; auth, Minor Meditations for Campter, 72; ed, The Norton Critical Edition of Middlemarch, 77; auth, "The Hero of My Life": Essays on Dickens, 81; coauth, Our Mutual Friend: An Annotated Bibliography, 84; auth, Great Expectations: A Novel of Friendship, 87; auth, Middlemarch: A Novel of Reform, 88; coauth, Philophagos, 99; ed, The Norton Critical Edition of Middlemarch 2nd ed, 00; ed, Bright Unequivocal Eye: Poems, Papers, and Remembrances from the First Jane Kenyon Conference, 00. **CONTACT ADDRESS** Dept English, Bellarmine Col, 2001 Newburg Rd, Louisville, KY 40205-1863. **EMAIL** bghorn@bellsouth.net

HORNBY, RICHARD
PERSONAL Born 10/25/1938, Paterson, NJ, d, 2 children **DISCIPLINE** THEATRE **EDUCATION** Mass Inst Technol, BS, 62; Tulane Univ, MA, 65; PhD, 66. **CAREER** Asst prof, Bowdoin Col, 66-70; asst prof, Univ of British Columbia, 70-71; assoc prof to prof, Univ of Calgary, 71-80; prof, Fla State Univ, 91-00. **MEMBERSHIPS** Asn for Theatre in Higher Educ, Am Soc for Theatre Res, Actors Equity Asn, Ibsen Soc, O'Neill Soc. **RESEARCH** Shakespeare, modern drama, acting theory. **SELECTED PUBLICATIONS** Auth, Script into Performance, 77 & 95; auth, Patterns in Ibsen's Middle Plays, 81; auth, Drama, Metadrama, and Perception, 86; auth, The End of Acting, 92; auth, Mad about Theatre, 97. **CONTACT ADDRESS** Dept Theatre, Univ of California, Riverside, 900 University Ave, Riverside, CA 92521-0001. **EMAIL** dramacritic@cs.com

HORNE, DEE A.
PERSONAL Born 05/18/1959, New Rochelle, NY, m, 1982, 2 children **DISCIPLINE** LITERATURE **EDUCATION** McGill Univ, BA, 80; Univ Toronto, MA, 82; PhD, 90. **CAREER** Instr, McMaster Univ, 90-91; assoc prof, Univ Northern Brit Columb, 92-. **MEMBERSHIPS** MLA, Can Comp Lit Assoc, Am Cult Assoc. **RESEARCH** Creative Writing and Modern and Contemporary Literature. **SELECTED PUBLICATIONS** Auth, "Elizabeth Smart's Novel-Journal," Studies in Can Lit 16.2, (91, 92); auth, Biography in Disguise: Sylvia Plath's Journals," Wascana Rev 27.1, (92); auth, "To Know the Difference: Mimicry, Satire, and Thomas King's Green Grass, Running Water," Essays on Can Writing 56, (96): coed, Diverse Landscapes: Re-Reading Place Across Cultures in Contemporary Canadian Writing, UNBC Pr, 96; auth, "Listening to Silences," Studies in Can Lit, 23.2, (98); auth, Contemporary American Indian Writing: Unsettling Literature, Peter Lang, 99; auth, "Scaling Purdy," The Fiddlehead 202 (99); coed, "Interview with Jacqueline Baldwin," It's Still Winter 2.2, (99); auth, "A Postcolonial Reading of Louise Erdrich's Tracks," MLA, (01); auth, "Narratives as Testimony in Obasan and Snow Falling on Cedars," Changing Landscapes, Univ Mont Pr, (01). **CONTACT ADDRESS** Dept English, Univ of No British Columbia, 3333 University Way, Prince George, BC, Canada V2N 4Z9. **EMAIL** dee@unbc.ca

HORNER, BRUCE
PERSONAL Born 01/30/1957, New Brighton, PA, m, 1984, 1 child **DISCIPLINE** ENGLISH **EDUCATION** Univ of Pittsburgh, BA, 79; MA, 80; PhD, 88. **CAREER** From asst prof to assoc prof, Drake Univ, 88-94; assoc chair of English Dept, Drake Univ, 98-. **MEMBERSHIPS** Nat Coun of Teachers of English, Confr in Col Composition and Commun, Int Asn for the Study of Popular Music. **RESEARCH** Basic Writing, Work in Composition, Music Pedagogy, Politics of Literacy, Song Criticism. **SELECTED PUBLICATIONS** Co-ed, Key Terms in Popular Music and Culture, Blackwell, 99; coauth, Representing the "Other": Basic Writers and the Teaching of Basic Writing, Nat Coun of Teachers of English, 99; auth, Terms of Work for Composition: A Materialist Critique, SUNY Press, 00. **CONTACT ADDRESS** Dept English, Drake Univ, 2507 University Ave, Des Moines, IA 50311-4516. **EMAIL** brucehorner@drake.edu

HORNER, CARL S., III
PERSONAL Born 04/24/1945, Cleveland, OH, m, 1969, 2 children **DISCIPLINE** LITERATURE, WRITING **EDUCATION** Eastern Ky Univ, BA, 68; Ind Univ Bloomington, MA, 72; Fla State Univ, PhD, 89. **CAREER** Asst prof to assoc prof, director, Flagler Col, 89-. **HONORS AND AWARDS** Robert O Lawton Awd for Excellence in Teaching, Fla State Univ, 87; Phi Kappa Phi, 89; Sigma Tau Delta, 97. **MEMBERSHIPS** MLA, Phi Kappa Phi, Sigma Tau Delta. **RESEARCH** 19th and 20th Century American Literature, Vietnam War and World War II, Corporate Psycho Structure (socio-economics). **SELECTED PUBLICATIONS** Auth, The Boy inside the American Businessman: Corporate Darwinism in Twentieth-Century America Literature, 92; auth, Challenging the Law of Courage and Heroic Identification in Tim O'Brien's 'If I Die in a Combat Zone' and 'The Things They Carried', 99; auth, Principal, Perversion, and the American Power Dream: Misusing the 'Rite of Horatio Alger' in Ellison's 'Invisible Man', forthcoming. **CONTACT ADDRESS** Dept English, Flagler Col, PO Box 1027, Sainte Augustine, FL 32085-1027. **EMAIL** hornercs@flagler.edu

HORNING, ALICE S.
DISCIPLINE ENGLISH, LINGUISTICS **EDUCATION** Mich State Univ, 77, PhD, Boston Univ, BA, 71. **CAREER** Prof of Rhetoric and Linguistics, 94-, Oakland Univ; Assoc Prof, 88-94, Oakland Univ; Asst Prof, Oakland Univ, 82-88; Asst Prof, English, Wayne State Univ, 78-82. **HONORS AND AWARDS** Advising Excellence Awd, Oakland Univ, 85. **MEMBERSHIPS** NCTE; CCCC; Amer Assoc for Applied Linguistics, Michigan Linguistic Society, Assoc for Psychological Type. **RESEARCH** Language and Literacy acquisition, psycholinguistics; reading and writing processes. **SELECTED PUBLICATIONS** Auth, "The Psycholinguistics of Readable Writing," Ablex Publishing, 93; auth, "Understanding Literacy," co-edited with Ron Sudol, Hampton Press, 97; auth, "The Literacy Connection," co-edited with Ron Sudol, Hampton Press, 99. **CONTACT ADDRESS** Department Rhetoric, Oakland Univ, Rochester, MI 48309. **EMAIL** horning@oakland.edu

HORNSBY, ROGER ALLEN
PERSONAL Born 08/08/1926, Nye, WI, m, 1960 **DISCIPLINE** CLASSICS **EDUCATION** Western Reserve Univ, BA, 49; Princeton Univ, MA, 51, PhD(classics), 52. **CAREER** Instr Latin & Greek, 54-58, from asst prof to assoc prof classics, 58-67, chmn dept, 66-81, Prof Classics, Univ Iowa, 67-, Coun Learned Soc fel, 70-71; consult, Nat Endowment for Humanities, 71-72; ed, Text Book Series APA, 75-81, Am Acad Rome resident, 83. **HONORS AND AWARDS** Ovatio, Classic Asn Midwest & South, 80. **MEMBERSHIPS** Am Philol Asn; Classic Asn Midwest & South (pres, 68-69); Archaeol Inst Am; Am Numis Soc; Mediaeval Acad Am. **RESEARCH** Latin poetry; stoicism; Greek poetry. **SELECTED PUBLICATIONS** Auth, The Vergilian Simile as Means of Judgement, 60: 337-344, Classics J; The Armor of the Slain, Philol Quart, 4/66; The Works of Luther; Reading Latin Poetry, Okla Univ, 67; The Pastor in the Poetry of Vergil, Classics J, 1/68; Patterns of Action in the Aeneid, Univ Iowa, 70. **CONTACT ADDRESS** Dept Classics, Univ of Iowa, Iowa City, IA 52242.

HOROWITZ, SARA R.
PERSONAL Born New York, NY, m **DISCIPLINE** ENGLISH **EDUCATION** Brandeis Univ, PhD, 85. **CAREER** Asst Prof, Univ Del, 85-90; dir Jewish Studies prog, Univ Del, 90-. **HONORS AND AWARDS** Choice Awd for Outstanding Academic Book, 97. **MEMBERSHIPS** Mod Lang Asn, Asn for Jewish Studies. **RESEARCH** Holocaust Literature. **SELECTED PUBLICATIONS** Auth, Voicing the Void: Muteness and Memory in Holocaust Fiction, 97. **CONTACT ADDRESS** Dept English, Univ of Delaware, 42 Amstel Ave, Newark, DE 19716. **EMAIL** srh@udel.edu

HORTON, RONALD A.
PERSONAL Born 11/09/1936, Glendale, CA, m, 1968, 3 children **DISCIPLINE** ENGLISH **EDUCATION** Bob Jones Univ, BA, 58; UCLA, MA, 62; Univ NC Chapel Hill, PhD, 72. **CAREER** Instr, 60-66, prof, 69-, Bob Jones Univ. **HONORS AND AWARDS** Folger Shakespeare Libr Summer Fel, 70; S Atlantic Modern Lang Asn Book Awd, 76; pres, sc asn depts english, 76, 90; head, english div, bob jones univ, 69-. **MEMBERSHIPS** Modern Lang Asn; S Atlantic Modern Lang Asn; Renaissance Soc Am; Southeastern Renaissance Conference, Spenser Soc; Asn Literary Scholars and Critics. **RESEARCH** English Renaissance Literature. **SELECTED PUBLICATIONS** Auth, The Unity of The Faerie Queene, Univ GA Press, 78; "Aristotle and His Commentators," The Spenser Encyclopedia, Univ Toronto Press, 90; "The Argument of Spenser's Garden of Adonis," Love and Death in the Renaissance, Dovehouse, 91; "Spenser's Farewell to Dido: The Public Turn," in Classical, Renaissance, and Postmodern Acts of the Imagination: Essays Commemorating O.B. Hardison, Jr., Univ DE Press, 96; "Herbert's Thy Cage, Thy Rope of Sands: An Hourglass," George Herbert Jour, 97-98. **CONTACT ADDRESS** 407 Library Dr, Greenville, SC 29609. **EMAIL** rhorton@bju.edu

HORTON, SUSAN R.
PERSONAL Born 11/16/1941, Defiance, OH, d, 1 child **DISCIPLINE** ENGLISH; AMERICAN LITERATURE **EDUCATION** Brandeis Univ, PhD, 73. **CAREER** Prof English, Univ Mass at Boston, 72-. **HONORS AND AWARDS** Woodrow Wilson Dissertation Fel. **MEMBERSHIPS** MLA; Dickens Soc. **RESEARCH** 19th century cultural history; Dickens; African cross-cultural encounters. **SELECTED PUBLICATIONS** Auth, The Reader in the Dickens World, Macmillan Ltd/Univ Pittsburgh Press, 78; Interpreting Interpreting: Interpreting Dickens' Donkey, Johns Hopkins Univ Press, 79; Thinking Through Writing, Johns Hopkins Univ Press, 82, 85, 89; Literary Theory's Future, Literary Theory's Future, Univ Ill Press, 89; Difficult Women, Artful Lives: Olive Schreiner & Isak Dinesen, In and Out of Africa, Johns Hopkins Univ Press, 95; Victorian Optical Gadgetry, Modernist Selves, Victorian Literature & the Victorian Visual Imagination, Univ Calif Press, 97. **CONTACT ADDRESS** Harbor Campus, Univ of Massachusetts, Boston, Boston, MA 02125. **EMAIL** horton@umbsky.cc.umb.edu

HORVATH, BROOKE
PERSONAL Born 09/07/1953, Elyria, OH, m, 1975, 2 children **DISCIPLINE** ENGLISH **EDUCATION** Kent State Univ, BA, 75; SUNY, MA, 77; Purdue Univ, PhD, 87. **CAREER** Asst Prof, to Full Prof, Kent State Univ, 88-. **MEMBERSHIPS** Nat Book Critics circle, Sport Literature Asn, Midwest Mod Lang Asn, Asn of Literary Critics and Scholars. **RESEARCH** American literature; Writing (including creative writing); Contemporary world literature; Literary; Theory; Postmodernism. **SE-**

LECTED PUBLICATIONS Ed, Pynchon & Mason & Dixon, Univ Del Press, forthcoming; co-ed, The Finer Thread, the Tighter Weave: New Essays on Henry James's Short Fiction, Purdue Univ Press, forthcoming; co-ed, Line Drives: 162 Contemporary Baseball Poems, Southern Ill Univ Press, forthcoming; ed, Ed Sanders number, the Review of contemporary Fiction, 99; co-ed George Garrett's Elizabethan Trilogy, Texas Review Pub, 98; co-ed, A Goyen Companion: Appreciation of a Writer's Writer, Univ of Tex Press, 97; ed, Donilo Kis number, The Review of Contemporary Fiction, 94; auth, Consolation at Ground Zero, Eastern Washington Univ Press,95; auth, In a Neighborhood of Dying Light, Bottom Dog Press, 94; auth, "Poetry in Motion," Plain Dealer Sunday Magazine, (99): 8-9, 21' auth, "Why is the Woman in the Guess Jeans Ad Barefoot?," Texas Review, (99): 80-87; auth, "Brigid Brophy's It's all-right - I'm Only dying Comedy of Modern Manners: Notes on 'In Transit," The review of Contemporary Fiction, (95): 47-53; auth, "The Prose Poem and the Secret Life of Poetry," American Poetry Review, (92): 11-14; auth, "Reading The Gingerbread Man with My Daughter," Michigan Quarterly Review, (98): 392-395. **CONTACT ADDRESS** Dept English, Kent State Univ, 6000 Frank Ave NW, North Canton, OH 44720-7548. **EMAIL** bhorvath@stark.kent.edu

HORVATH, CARY W.
PERSONAL Born 08/19/1964, Youngstown, OH, m, 1981, 3 children **DISCIPLINE** COMMUNICATION ARTS **EDUCATION** Youngstown State Univ, BA, 89; Kent State Univ, MA, 93; Kent State Univ, PhD, 99. **CAREER** From Vis Instr to Asst Prof, Westminster Col, 00-. **HONORS AND AWARDS** Fel, Kent St Univ, 95-96; Who's Who Among Am Teachers, 98. **MEMBERSHIPS** NCA, ECA, CSCA. **SELECTED PUBLICATIONS** Auth, "Biological Origins of Communicator Style," Commun Quart 43 (95): 394-407; coauth, "Feelings About Verbal Aggression: Justifications for Sending and Hurt from Receiving Verbally Aggressive Messages," Commun Res Reports 13 (96): 19-26; coauth, "Counterattitudinal Advocacy: When High Argumentatives are More Persuasible," Commun Res Reports 14 (97): 79-87; coauth, "A Further Examination of Teacher Communicator Style and College Student Learning," J of the Ill Speech and Theatre Asn 48 (97): 37-48; auth, "Biological Origins of Communicator Style," in Commun and Personality: Trait Perspectives (Cresskill, NJ: Hampton Pr, 98), 69-94; auth, "The Role of the Basic Oral Communication Course in an Integrated First Year Program," Speech Commun Asn of Pa Annual 55 (99): 57-65. **CONTACT ADDRESS** Commun Arts, Westminster Col, Pennsylvania, 319 S Market St, New Wilmington, PA 16172-0002. **EMAIL** horvatcw@westminster.edu

HORVATH, RICHARD P.
DISCIPLINE MIDDLE ENGLISH LITERATURE **EDUCATION** Stanford Univ, PhD. **CAREER** Asst prof, Fordham Univ . **RESEARCH** Chaucer, 15th century lit. **SELECTED PUBLICATIONS** Auth, Critical Interpretation of The Canterbury Tales B23981, Eng Lang Notes 24, 86; History, Narrative, and the Ideological mode of the Peterborough Chronicle, Mediaevalia 18, 93. **CONTACT ADDRESS** Dept of Eng Lang and Lit, Fordham Univ, 113 W 60th St, New York, NY 10023.

HORWITZ, BARBARA
PERSONAL Born 03/29/1938, New York, NY, m, 1957, 3 children **DISCIPLINE** ENGLISH **EDUCATION** Barnard Col, BA, 57; Brooklyn Col, CUNY, MA, 60; SUNY, Stony Brook, PhD, 79. **CAREER** Prof, CW Post Campus, Long Island Univ, 20 years. **MEMBERSHIPS** MLA. **RESEARCH** Jane Austen; British novel in 18th and 19th Centuries. **SELECTED PUBLICATIONS** Auth, Jane Austen and the Question of Women's Education, Peter Lang (NY), 91; auth, "Structural Resemblances Between Pride and Prejudice and Framley Park," Persuasions (94); auth, "Women's Education During the Regency," Persuasions (95); auth, :The Unlikely Rebel in Mansfield Park," Ventures in Res (97); auth, British Women Writers, 1700-1850: An Annotated Bibliography, Salem/ Scarecrow (97). **CONTACT ADDRESS** Dept English, Long Island Univ, C.W. Post, 720 Northern Blvd, Greenvale, NY 11548-1319. **EMAIL** bjhorwitz@yahoo.com

HORWITZ, ROBERT
PERSONAL Born 04/16/1952, Los Angeles, CA, m, 2 children **DISCIPLINE** COMMUNICATIONS **EDUCATION** A B Stanford Univ, 74; Brandeis Univ, PhD, 82 **CAREER** Prof, Department of Communication, Univ of Cal, San Diego. **HONORS AND AWARDS** Ethics and Policy Awd for Communicaitons Research, 90; Fulbright Research fel, 95-96; Individual Research fel, Open Society Inst, 98. **RESEARCH** Communication institutions. **SELECTED PUBLICATIONS** Auth, The Irony of Regulatory Reform: The Deregulation of American Telecommunications, Oxford, 89; auth, Communication and Demographic Reform in South Africa, Cambridge Univ Press, 01. **CONTACT ADDRESS** Dept of Commun, Univ of California, San Diego, 9500 Gilman Dr, La Jolla, CA 92093. **EMAIL** rhorwitz@ucsd.edu

HOSKINS, ROBERT V.
PERSONAL Born 08/04/1942, Harlan, KY, m, 1965, 2 children **DISCIPLINE** ENGLISH **EDUCATION** Yale Univ, AB, 64; Univ Ky, MA, 69; PhD, 71. **CAREER** Asst prof to prof, James Madison Univ, 87-. **HONORS AND AWARDS** Edna Shaeffer Humanist Awd, James Madison Univ. **MEMBERSHIPS** MLA; Col Lit Assoc; NC VA CEA. **RESEARCH** 20th Century British Literature, Film. **SELECTED PUBLICATIONS** Auth, "Hale, Pinkie and the Pentecost Theme in Brighton Rock, Mod British Lit 3 (78):56-65; auth "Swift, Dickens, and the Horses in the End of the Road", James Madison Jour 37; (79):18-32; auth, "Through a Glass Darkly: Mirrors in The End of the Affairs", Notes on Contemp Lit 9, (79):3-5; auth, "Hamlet and A Severed Head", Am Notes and Queries 20, (81): 18-21; auth, "Greene and Wordsworth: the Ministry of Fear", S Atlantic Rev 48, (83):32-42; auth, "The Napoleonic Strategist of Brighton Rock", Col Lit 12, (85):11-17; auth, "Those Dreadful Clothes: the Meaning of Modern Sculpture and the Genesis of Greene's England Made Me", S Atlantic Rev 57 (92):73-91; auth, Graham Greene: A Character Index and Guide, Garland (NY), 91; auth, Graham Greene: An Approach to the Novels, Garland (NY:99). **CONTACT ADDRESS** Dept of English, James Madison Univ, 800 S Main St, Harrisonburg, VA 22807-0001. **EMAIL** hoskinrv@jmu.edu

HOSTETLER, MICHAEL J.
PERSONAL Born 08/19/1950, South Bend, IN, m, 1970, 3 children **DISCIPLINE** COMMUNICATION STUDIES **EDUCATION** Northwestern Univ, PhD, 93. **CAREER** Vis asst prof, Ind Univ Northwest, 93-94; S.U.N.Y. Oneonta; asst prof, St John's Univ, 95- . **MEMBERSHIPS** Nat Commun Asn; NY State Commun Asn; Relig Commun Asn. **RESEARCH** Am Pub Address; Relig and Rhet. **SELECTED PUBLICATIONS** Auth, John Calvin's Rhetorical Christianity and Sixteenth Century Religious Exiles: Constructing an Ethic of Refugees, Speech Commun Annual 10, 96; Liberty in Baptist Thought: Three Primary Texts, 1614-1856, The Am Baptist Quart 60, 96; Rethinking the War Metaphor in Religious Rhetoric: Burke, Black, and Berrigan's Glimmer of Light, The Jour of Commun and Relig 20, 97; The Enigmatic Ends of Rhetoric: Churchill's Fulton Address as Great Art and Failed Persuasion, Quart Jour of Speech 83, 97; Gov Al Smith Confronts the Catholic Question: The Rhetorical Legacy of the 1928 Campaign, Commun Quart 46, 98; William Jenning Bryan as Demosthenes: The Scopes Trial and the Undelivered Oration, On Evolution, Western Jour of Commun 62, 98; auth, "Constructing Audienes for Ecumenism: A Rhetoricalperspective," World Communication 27, 4, 98: 38-49. **CONTACT ADDRESS** Dept of Speech, St. John's Univ, 8000 Utopia Pky, Jamaica, NY 11439. **EMAIL** hostetlm@stjohns.edu

HOSTETLER, THEODORE J.
PERSONAL Born 02/07/1951, Canton, OH, m, 1975, 3 children **DISCIPLINE** LIBRARY SCIENCE, HISTORY **EDUCATION** Univ of IA, MA, 74; Bluffton Col, BA, 73 **CAREER** Libr Dir, 93-, Randolph-Macon Woman's Col; Head Access Svcs, 89-93, Univ of CA; Head Access Svcs, 79-89, Syracuse Univ; Head Circulation, 78-79 Univ of S FL **HONORS AND AWARDS** ALA, Univ of CA Achievement Awd, 92 **MEMBERSHIPS** VLA; ALA **RESEARCH** Reference; Undergraduate educ exp **SELECTED PUBLICATIONS** Auth, Introduction, 95; Coauth, Issue of Library Trends **CONTACT ADDRESS** Lipscomb Libr, Randolph-Macon Woman's Col, Lynchburg, VA 24503. **EMAIL** thostetler@rmwc.edu

HOUGH, MONICA
PERSONAL Born 10/30/1952, New York, NY, d, 2 children **DISCIPLINE** SPEECH **EDUCATION** Brooklyn Col, CUNY, VA, 76; Univ Fla, MA, 78; Kent State Univ, PhD, 88. **CAREER** Asst prof to prof, E Carolina Univ, 88-. **HONORS AND AWARDS** Fel, Kent State Univ, 87; Teaching Awd, E Carolina Univ, 92. **MEMBERSHIPS** Am Speech-lang and Hearing Assoc; NC Speech-Lang Hearing Assoc; Nat Aphasia Assoc. **RESEARCH** Semantic organization in brain-damaged adults, contextual influences in aphasia, apraxia of speech in adults. **SELECTED PUBLICATIONS** Coauth, "Contextual influences on comprehension of multiple meaning words by right hemisphere brain-damaged and non-brain-damaged adults", Aphasiology 11, (97): 447-459; rev, "Treatment of aphasia: From theory to practice", eds C. Code and D. Mueller, Clinical Ling and Phonetics 11 (97): 82-84; coauth, "Aphasic adults' knowledge of goal-directed action categories", J of Med Speech-Lang Pathology 5, (97): 167-180; auth, "Acquired adult language disorders", Nat Examination in Speech-Lang Pathology and Audiology, ed C. Nye, Singular Pub (San Diego, 98): 77-95; coauth, "Phonemic retrieval skills in apraxia of speech: Additional evidence for more than one type of impairment", Neuromotor Speech Disorders: Nature, Assessment, and Management, eds M. Cannito, K. Yorkston and D.R. Beukelman, Paul E. Brooks Pub (Baltimore, 98): 323-332; coauth, "Linguistic contextual influences on categorization skills after traumatic brain injury", Aphasiology 12 (98): 745-753; coauth, "Lip EMG activity during vowel production in apraxia of speech: Phrase context and word length effects", J of Speech-Lang-Hearing Res 41.4 (98): 786-801; coauth, "Phrase context effects on lip EMG activity during vowel production in apraxia of speech", J of Med Speech-Lang Pathology 7, (99): 145-154; auth, "Phonemic retrieval: Anomic aphasia revisited", J of Neurlinguistics 13, (00): 1-13; coauth, "Word Length effects on EMG/Vowel duration relationships in apraxic speakers", Folia Phoniatrica (forthcoming). **CONTACT ADDRESS** Dept Commun Disorders, East Carolina Univ, 1000 E 5th St, Greenville, NC 27858-2502. **EMAIL** houghm@mail.ecu.edu

HOUGHTON, EDWARD FRANCIS
PERSONAL Born 10/07/1938, New Brunswick, NJ, m, 1964, 3 children **DISCIPLINE** MUSICOLOGY **EDUCATION** Rutgers Univ, BA, 62; Univ Nev, MA, 63; Univ Calif, Berkeley, PhD(Music), 71. **CAREER** Asst prof Music, Rutgers Univ, 67-70; asst prof, 70-73, from assoc prof to prof Music, 81-; dean Arts Div, 92-; Univ Calif, Santa Cruz, 73-, dir, Univ Calif Educ Abroad Prog, Italy, 76-78. **HONORS AND AWARDS** NEH Fell, 80-81, 87. **MEMBERSHIPS** Am Musicol Soc. **RESEARCH** Music of the 15th century. **SELECTED PUBLICATIONS** Auth, Rhythm and meter in 15th century polyphony, J Music Theory, Spring 74; A new motet by Johannas Regis, Tijdschrift, 83; auth, "Ockeghem's scribes, then and now" in Johannas Ockeghem, Klincksieck, 98; auth, " A close reading of Compere's motet Sile Fragor" in Essys on Music and Culture, Kincksieck, 01. **CONTACT ADDRESS** Div of the Arts, Univ of California, Santa Cruz, 1156 High St, Santa Cruz, CA 95064-0001. **EMAIL** houghtn@cats.ucsc.edu

HOUSE, KAY S.
PERSONAL Born 05/18/1924, Payson, IL, d, 1946, 2 children **DISCIPLINE** ENGLISH **EDUCATION** Univ Ill, BA, 45; Wash Univ, MA, 45; Stanford Univ, PhD, 63. **CAREER** Prof, Eng, San Francisco State Univ; current, ED-in-CH, The Writings of James Fenimore Cooper. **MEMBERSHIPS** Am Antiquarian Soc **RESEARCH** James Fenimore Cooper **SELECTED PUBLICATIONS** Ed, James Fenimore Cooper's The Pilot, State Univ NY Press, 86, Lib Am, 91; auth, "Cooper's Indians After Yet Another "Century of Dishonor,'" in Letterature d'America, Univ Rome, 83; ed, James Fenimore Cooper's Satanstoe, State Univ NY Press, 90; auth, "The James Fenimore Cooper Collections at the American Antiquarian Society," in Serendipity and Synergy: Collection Development, Access and Research Opportunities at the American Antiquarian Society in the McCorison Era, Am Antiquarian Soc, 93; auth, "Four North American Writers and Their Terrain," Univ of Rome, in press. **CONTACT ADDRESS** PO Box 158, Payson, IL 62360-0158. **EMAIL** ksh4@webtv.net

HOUSTON, GEORGE W.
PERSONAL Born 11/15/1941, New York, NY, m, 1962, 2 children **DISCIPLINE** CLASSICS **EDUCATION** Haverford Col, BA, 63; Univ NC, PhD, 71. **CAREER** Instr to Prof and Dept Chair, Univ NC, 71-. **HONORS AND AWARDS** Fulbright Grant, Italy, 67-68; Rome Prize Fel, Am Acad, Rome, 67-69; Am Philos Soc Res Grant, 82; Bowman and Gordon Gray Assoc Prof, 86-89; Lurcy Fel, Inst for the Arts and Humanities, 89. **MEMBERSHIPS** Am Philol Asn; Archaeol Inst of Am; Am Soc of Greek and Latin Epigraphy; Vergilian Soc. **RESEARCH** Roman history and historiography; Latin Epigraphy; Roman social history and the history of technology. **SELECTED PUBLICATIONS** Auth, "A Revisionary Note on Ammianus Marcellinus 14.6.18: When Did the Public Libraries of Ancient Rome Close?" Library Quarterly, (88): 258-264; auth, "Ports in Perspective: Some Comparative Materials on Roman Merchant Ships and Ports," Am Journal of Archaeol, (88): 553-564; auth, "The State of the Art: Current Work in the Technology of Ancient Rome," Classical Journal (89): 63-80; auth, "What Uses Might Roman Farmers Have Made of the Loans They Received in the Alimenta Program?" Rivista Storica dell'Antichita, (93): 97-105; auth, "The Slave and Freedman Personnel in Roman Public Libraries," Preatti del CI Congresso Internazionale di Epigrafia Greca e Latina, (97): 819-827. **CONTACT ADDRESS** Dept Classics, Univ of No Carolina, Chapel Hill, CB 3145, Chapel Hill, NC 27599. **EMAIL** gwhousto@email.unc.edu

HOUSTON, VELINA H.
DISCIPLINE THEATRE, CINEMA, TELEVISION **EDUCATION** Kansas State Univ, BA, 79; Univ Calif, Los Angeles, MA, 81; Univ Southern Calif, PhD, 00. **CAREER** Playwright, screenwriter, 81-; vis asst prof to assoc prof, Univ of Southern Calif, 90-. **HONORS AND AWARDS** Rockefeller Found Fel, 87; San Diefo Drama Critics Circle Awd, 88; Sidney Brody Lit Fel, 88; Japanese Am Women of Merit, 1890-90; Remy Martin New Vision Awd, Am Film Inst, 92; Merit Fel, 94-96; Who's Who in Asian America, 94, 96; Po'okela Awd, 96; Japan Found Fel, 99-00; James Zumberge Fel, 99-00; Phi Beta Kappa. **MEMBERSHIPS** Writers Guild of Am; Dramatists Guild; Sacramento Theatre Co; Multiracial Am of S Calif; San Diego Asian Am Repertory Theatre; Pacific Asian Am Women Writers. **RESEARCH** Playwriting, screenwriting, poetry, modern and contemporary dramatic literature, teaching, dramaturgy, Asian American and Pacific Rim dramatic literature, cultural criticism and theory, multiracial-multiethnic-multicultural studies, Amerasian studies and selected Japanese and Japanese American literature and Japanese cinema. **SELECTED PUBLICATIONS** Auth, American Dreams, Negro Ensemble co, 84; auth, "Asa Ga Kimashita", (Morning Has Broken), East West Players, 84; auth, Tea, Manhattan Theatre Club, 85; auth, Japanese and Multicultural at the Turn-of-the-Century, Asia Soc Nat Public Radio, 94; auth, "Hula Heart", Eight Plays for Children: The New Generation Project, ed Coleman A. Jennings, Univ of Tex Pr, 99; auth, "The Soprano's Letter" and "Green Tea Girl in Orange Pekoe Country", Intersecting Circles: The Voices of Hapa Women in Poetry and Prose, eds Nora Okja Keller and Marie Hara, Bamboo Ridge Pr, 00; auth, "Ikebana", Pasadena Playhouse, 00; auth, "Shedding the Tiger",

Sacramento Theatre co, 01; auth, "Kokoro", Political Plays of the 1990s, ed Allan Havis, Univ of IL Pr, (forthcoming). **CONTACT ADDRESS** Sch of Theatre, Univ of So California, 1029 Childs Way, Los Angeles, CA 90089-0006. **EMAIL** vhouston@usc.edu

HOVANEC, EVELYN ANN
PERSONAL Born 12/23/1937, Uniontown, PA **DISCIPLINE** ENGLISH, FOLKLORE, HISTORY AND LORE OF COAL MINERS **EDUCATION** Duquesne Univ, BEd, 62, MA, 66; Univ Pittsburgh, PhD, 73. **CAREER** Teacher social studies & English, Pittsburgh pub jr high schs, 62-66; ASSOC prof English, PA State Univ, Fayette, 66-85 and 92-00, dir Acad Aff, PA State, McKeesport 85-92. **HONORS AND AWARDS** PSF Awd for Pub Svc, 94; PSM Awd for Svc, 89; PSF Awd for Teach Excel, 97; PSF Min Stu Org Fac Awd, 98. **MEMBERSHIPS** Nat Coun Teachers English; Col English Asn; MLA. **RESEARCH** Mining literature and lore; mythology; Henry James. **SELECTED PUBLICATIONS** Auth, 3 poems, Earth & You, 72; coauth, Making the humanities human, WVa Rev Educ Res, fall 73; auth, Horses of the Sun (2 poems), In: Cathedral Poets II, Boxwood, 76; coauth, Patch/Work Voices: The Culture & Lore of a Mining People, Harry Hoffman, 77; auth, Coal culture & communities, Pa Oral Hist Newslett, 77; The Sea (poem), In: Strawberry Saxifrage, Nat Soc Publ Poets, 77; coauth, Making the Humanities Human, West VA Review of Educ Res 1, 46-47, 73; auth, A Mythological Approach to Tomorrow, Assoc of Teach Educ Review 3, 78; auth, Reader's Guide to Coal Mining Fiction and Selected Prose Narratives, Bul of Biblio, 41-57, Sept, 86; auth, Marie Belloc Lowndes, An Encyclopedia of British Women Writers, Garland, 297-298, 88. **CONTACT ADDRESS** Pennsylvania State Univ, Fayette, PO Box 519, Uniontown, PA 15401-0519. **EMAIL** eah2@psu.edu

HOVENDICK, KELLY B.
PERSONAL Born 12/18/1970, Hanover, PA, m, 1996, 1 child **DISCIPLINE** HISTORY; ANTHROPOLOGY; LIBRARY SCIENCE **EDUCATION** E NM Univ, BS, 94; Univ Az, MA, 99. **MEMBERSHIPS** Amer Libr Assoc **RESEARCH** Gender & libr sci; technophobia. **CONTACT ADDRESS** E.S. Bird Libr, Syracuse Univ, Reference Dept, Room 210, Syracuse, NY 13244-2010. **EMAIL** kbhovend@library.syr.edu

HOVEY, KENNETH
DISCIPLINE LITERATURE **EDUCATION** Cornell Univ, BA; Grade Theol Union, Berkeley, MA; Univ VA, MA, PhD. **CAREER** Assoc prof; taught at, Univ Cincinnati, Univ NC at Greensboro & NC Wesleyan Col. **HONORS AND AWARDS** NEH fel; UTSA's President's Distinguished Achievement Awd for Tchg Excellence, 93; 2 fac fel, UNC & UTSA. **RESEARCH** Renaissance lit; Milton and 17th-century poetry; 17th-century philos and sci; early Am lit and cult, espec Poe; Bible as lit. **SELECTED PUBLICATIONS** Auth, Poe's Materialist Metaphysics of Man, in A Companion to Poe Stud, Greenwood Press, 96; publ on, Poe, Longfellow, Bradford, Bacon & Herbert; in, Am Quart, Am Transcendental Quart, Early Am Lit, PMLA, Renaissance Quart & Stud in Philol. **CONTACT ADDRESS** Col of Fine Arts and Hum, Univ of Texas, San Antonio, 6900 N Loop 1604 W, San Antonio, TX 78249. **EMAIL** khovey@lonestar.utsa.edu

HOWARD, ANNE BAIL
PERSONAL Born 11/19/1927, Albuquerque, NM, m, 1950, 2 children **DISCIPLINE** AMERICAN LITERATURE, COMPOSITION **EDUCATION** Univ NMex, MA, 53, PhD, 66. **CAREER** Teacher English, Espanola High Sch, 54-55 & Valley High Sch, Albuquerque, 55-57; instr & dir English A, Univ NMex, 59-63; from instr to asst prof, 63-71, dir Freshman English, 70-75, assoc prof, 71-85, Prof English, Univ Nev, Reno, 85-, Coord Women's Studies, 79-85; Emer English Prof. **HONORS AND AWARDS** Distinguished teaching award, 92; Distinguished Fac Awd, 00. **MEMBERSHIPS** MLA; NCTE; AAUP; Rocky Mountain Mod Lang Asn; Nat Women's Studies Asn. **RESEARCH** Women writers; biography. **SELECTED PUBLICATIONS** Coauth, A workbook for English A, Univ NMex, 62; The Long Campaign: A Biography of Anne Martin, Univ Nev Press, 85. **CONTACT ADDRESS** Dept of English, Univ of Nevada, Reno, Reno, NV 89557-0001. **EMAIL** abhoward@equinox.unv.edu

HOWARD, C. JERIEL
PERSONAL Born 03/14/1939, Wharton, TX **DISCIPLINE** ENGLISH **EDUCATION** Union Col, BA, 61; Tex Christian Univ, MA, 62, PhD(English), 67. **CAREER** Instr English, Southwestern Union Col, 62-64; instr, Union Col, 64-65, assoc prof, 65-66; instr, Tex Christian Univ, 66-67; guest instr, Tex Wesleyan Col, 67; chmn dept English, Tarrant County Jr Col, 67-68, chmn dept commun, 68-70; assoc prof, Bishop Col, 70-79; prof English, Northeastern Ill Univ, 79-. **MEMBERSHIPS** NCTE; Conf Col Compos & Commun; Conf Col Teachers English. **RESEARCH** Applied rhetoric; English methodology; American literature. **SELECTED PUBLICATIONS** Coauth, Contact: A Textbook in Applied Communications, 2nd ed, 74, 3rd ed, 78, Prentice-Hall; coauth (with Richard F Tracz), The Responsible Person, 2nd ed, Harper & Row, 75; Writing Effective Paragraph, Winthrop Press, 76; (with Elizabeth K Martin), Technique: Studies in Composition, 2nd ed, Harper & Row, 77; (with Dee Brock), Writing for a Reason, John Wiley & Sons, 77; Reprise: A Review of Basic Writing Skills, Goodyear Press, 80; (with Richard F Tracz), The Paragraph Book, Little-Brown, 82. **CONTACT ADDRESS** Dept of English, Northeastern Illinois Univ, 5500 N St Louis Ave, Chicago, IL 60625-4625. **EMAIL** CJerielH@aol.com

HOWARD, DIANE
PERSONAL Born 03/04/1947, Fort Lewis, WA, m, 1969, 3 children **DISCIPLINE** COMMUNICATION **EDUCATION** Univ Ore, BA, 69; Univ Wa, MEd, 87; Univ Tex, PhD, 96. **CAREER** Teacher, Tacoma, WA, 82-87; Teacher, Manhattan, Kans, 87-88; Univ of Mary Hardin-Baylor, 88-. **HONORS AND AWARDS** Phi Delta Kappa; Kappa Delta Pi; Phi Kappa Delta; Alpha Psi Omega; Sears-Roebuck Awd, 91, Piper Prof Nominee, 00, Univ of Mary Hardin-Baylor. **MEMBERSHIPS** NCA; PSI, Tex Educ Assoc. **RESEARCH** Qualitative and Quantitative Research. **SELECTED PUBLICATIONS** Auth, "Authentic Assessment", Int Educ Newsletter, John Dewey Soc; auth, Autobiographical Writing and Performing: An Introductory, Contemporary Guide to Process and Research in Speech Performance, McGraw Hill. **CONTACT ADDRESS** Sch Fine Arts, Univ of Mary Hardin-Baylor, 900 College St, Belton, TX 76513-2578. **EMAIL** dhoward@umhb.edu

HOWARD, HERBERT
PERSONAL Born 11/07/1928, Johnson City, TN, m, 1956, 1 child **DISCIPLINE** COMMUNICATIONS **EDUCATION** E Tenn State Univ, BS, 52; MS, 55; Oh Univ, PhD, 73. **CAREER** Announcer to Prog Dir, WJHL Radio Johnson City, 45-58; Instructor to Prof Emeritus, Univ Tenn, 59-. **HONORS AND AWARDS** Distinguished Broadcast Educ Awd, Broadcast Educ Asn, 00; Chancellor's Citation for Extraordinary Serv, Univ TN, 98; distinguished Service Awd, Col of Comm. **MEMBERSHIPS** Asn for Educ in Jounalism & Mass Comm; Broadcast Educ Asn; Soc of Prof Journalists; TN Asn of Broadcasters. **RESEARCH** Media ownership (TV, Cable, Radio, Newspaper); Economics of new media; Cable TV. **SELECTED PUBLICATIONS** Co-auth, Broadcast Adertising, Grid Pub, 78; auth, Multiple Ownership in Television Broadcasting, Arno Press, 79; co-auth, Radio and Television Programming, Grid Pub, 83; co-auth, Broadast Advertising, 2nd ed, Grid Pub, 84; co-auth, Broadcast Advertising, 3rd ed, Grid Pub, 91; co-auth, Radio, TV, and Cable Programming, Iowa State Univ Press, 94; auth, "Broadcast Media Research," in The Social Science Approach to Mass Media Research, Longman, 94; co-auth, "Economics of the Cable Industry," in Media Economics: Theory and Practice, Lawrence Erlbaum Assoc, 2nd ed, 98. **CONTACT ADDRESS** Dept Broadcasting, Univ of Tennessee, Knoxville, 1345 Circle Pk, Knoxville, TN 37996-0001. **EMAIL** hhoward@utk.edu

HOWARD, HUBERT WENDELL
PERSONAL Born 09/22/1927, Anderson, IN, m, 1956, 3 children **DISCIPLINE** ENGLISH LITERATURE, MUSIC **EDUCATION** DePauw Univ, AB, 49; Stanford Univ, MA, 52; Juilliard Sch Music, dipl, 58; Univ Minn, Minneapolis, PhD(English, music), 70. **CAREER** Dir relig educ, First Methodist Church, Anderson, Ind, 49-50; plant mgr, Paglo Labs, NY, 58-60; instr English, Univ Minn, Minneapolis, 60-64; from asst prof to assoc prof English & music, 64-74, prof English & music, St John Fisher Col, 74-, vis prof, Eve Sch, Monroe Community Col, 68-71 & 73-74. **HONORS AND AWARDS** Winton Found Excellence Awd, 62. **MEMBERSHIPS** MLA; Nat Asn Teachers Singing; NCTE; Northeast Am Soc 18th Century Studies. **RESEARCH** Renaissance British literature; 18th century British literature; Renaissance and Baroque music. **SELECTED PUBLICATIONS** Auth, He Loved Her (poem), Orphic Lute, spring 66; The Mystic (poem), Roanoke Rev, fall 72; The Parable, Col Compos & Commun, 12/73; Only Civil Disobedience, Alliance Witness, 4/74; Artistry or Snobbery, Sch Music News, 9/74; Aspasia & My Poem, Delta Epsilon Sigma Bull, 12/75; Becky and Bampfylde, Greyfriar, 77; Christina Rossetti: An Appreciation, Survivor, Arts and Lit Mag, July 77; Food and Drink as Subjects in the Literature, Painting , and Music of the Seventeenth and Eighteenth Centuries, Delta Epsilon Sigma Bull, Dec 78; Undermining the NFL, The Church Musician, Feb 79; Don't Just Get By, The Pioneer, St. John Fisher Col, Sept 80; Abraham Rothberg's The Song of David Freed, The Pioneer, Sept 80; An Answering Theology, Delta Epsilon Sigma Bull, Dec 80; Social Attitudes and Bad Writing, The Journal of English Teaching Techniques, winter 80; The Influence of the Music of Henry Purcell on the Poetry of Gerard Manley Hopkins, The Hopkins Quart, winter 82; Arthur Kober: 'No Regella Yenkee,' Polish American Studies, spring 83; A Good Dog Because It Has Hair, The College Board Review, summer 83; Songs For Learning, The College Board Review, summer 85; Progressive Education, Phi Delta Kappan, June 85; More Than a Name, Proteus, spring 85; Needed: A New Commitment to Public Service, Shared Purpose, The College Board News, summer 85; Bring Back Phil Silvers, The College Board Review, pp 6-9, fall 85; Hold the Phone, Young and Alive, March 86; Listen Up and Sound Off, American Way, April 86; Food and Drink as Subjects in the Paintings of the Eighteenth Century, Ball State Univ Forum, summer 86; Two Ways to Freedom, The College Board Rev, fall 86; Bach;s Detractors, Delta Epsilon Sigma Bull, March 87; The Filter of the Mind: The Edge Between the 'Written' and the 'Real," Midwest Quart, summer 87; Traditions, Col Brd Rev, summer 87; Jerome C. Hixson, Col Teaching, spring 88; The Enemy is Us, Col Brd Rev, fall 88; A Language With Spizzerinctum, Indiana English, spring 88; The Deeps Beneath the Depths, Ind English, winter 88; Guaranteed: The Right to Be A Student, Ind English, spring 89; A Context for Shock Art, City Newspaper (Rochester, NY), July 27, 89; A Re-reading of Ben Johnson's "Song to Celia," Col Lang Asn Journal, March 90; Lest We Forget: The Place of Roland Hayes in American Musical History, Delta Epsilon Sigma Journal, Oct 90; An English Professor's 'Spare' Time, Ind English, winter 90; Inside Communism and Zionism: Koestler's Darkness at Noon and Thieves in the Night, Delta Epsilon Sigma Journal, Jan 91; In Pursuit of the Real, San Jose Studies, spring 91; A Matter of Life and Death, Midwest Quart, autumn 91; Are Heroes Vanishing?, Forum for Honors, summer/fall 91; Hierarchic Systems as a Unifying Topic in the Writings of Arthur Koestler, Delta Epsilon Sigma J, Dec 91; The Fine Art of Baseball, DES Journal, March 92; Walcott MATCHED with Fisher, Nat Col Honors Council, NE Reg newsletter, summer 92; Making and Refining a Professor, Forum for Honors, summer/fall 92; Good Old American Politics, DES Journal, Oct 92; Quality Management, DES Journal, fall 93; Andrew Greeley's Literary Antecedents, DES Journal, winter 94; Technology: Artistic Medium and Muse, Research in Philosophy and Technology vol 14, 94; A Clockwork Shakespeare, Az English Bull, spring 94; Wings Instead of Clumsy Hooves, Ind English, spring 94; The Investigators, DES Journal, fall 94; The Mossad: The Enemy Within, DES Journal, fall 95; Remember the Sabbath, DES Journal, spring 95; The Creative Non-Fiction Essay, Ind English, fall 95; Paul Robeson Remembered, Midwest Quart, fall 96; Speaking of Editors.., DES Journal, fall 96; and author of many poems. **CONTACT ADDRESS** 3690 East Ave, Rochester, NY 14618-3597.

HOWARD, JEAN E.
PERSONAL Born 10/20/1948, Houlton, MA, m, 1972, 2 children **DISCIPLINE** DRAMA; RENAISSANCE LITERATURE **EDUCATION** Brown Univ, BA, 70; Univ London, MPhil, 72; Yale Univ, PhD, 75. **CAREER** Instr, Syracuse Univ, 75; prof; Asst prof, Syracuse Univ, 75-82; Assoc prof, Syracuse Univ, 82-88; Prof, Columbia Univ, 88-. **HONORS AND AWARDS** Marshall fel, 72; Danforth fel, 75; Wasserstrom prize, excellence tchr, Univ Syracusa, 75; NEH fel; Mellon fel; Folger fel; Newberry Library; Guggenheim Fellowship; ed bd, shakespeare quart; shakespeare stud; renaissance drama. **MEMBERSHIPS** Modern Language Assoc, Shakespeare Assoc of Am Pres, 99-00. **RESEARCH** Feminist and Marxist literary theory; Renaissance Literature. **SELECTED PUBLICATIONS** Auth, essays on Shakespeare, Pope, non-Shakespearean drama, contemporary criticism, new historicism, Marxism, postmodern political feminism; auth, Shakespeare's Art of Orchestration, 84; co-ed, Shakespeare Reproduced: The Text in History and Ideology, 87; NortonShakespeare, 97; coauth, The Stage and Struggle in Early Modern England, 1994; Engendering a Nation: A Feminist Account of Shakespeare's English Histories, 97; coed, Marxiest Shakespeares, 00. **CONTACT ADDRESS** Dept of Eng, Columbia Univ, 2960 Broadway, New York, NY 10027-6902. **EMAIL** jfh5@columbia.edu

HOWARD, LEIGH ANNE
PERSONAL Born 11/02/1964, Owensboro, KY, s **DISCIPLINE** ENGLISH, THEATRE **EDUCATION** Centre Col, BA, 86; Western Ky Univ, MA, 91; La State Univ, PhD, 95. **CAREER** Managing ed, Center Magazine, 86-90; ASST PROF OF COMMUN & COORD, PROG IN COMMUN STUDIES, SPALDING UNIV, 95-. **HONORS AND AWARDS** Outstanding Fac Member, Spalding Univ, 96-97. **MEMBERSHIPS** Nat Commun Asn; Southern States Commun Asn. **RESEARCH** Cultural/critical studies: film/media, women and body image, and ethnographic representation. **SELECTED PUBLICATIONS** Coauth, Krewe D'Elvis: LSU Folklore in the Making, La Folklore Miscellany, 93; coauth, The Political Correctness Controversy: Retreat from Argumentation and Reaffirmation of Critical Dialogue, The Am Behavioral Scientist, 95; auth, Playing Boal: Thetre, Therapy, Activism, Theatre Insight, 95; auth, Poetics and Petrochemicals: Organizational Performances of the Mississippi River, Corporate Advocacy: Rhetoric in the Communication Age, Greenwood Press, 97; auth, Ethics and Ethnography: Explicating Values in the Age of Postmodernity, The Am Behvioral Scientist, in press; auth, Stain Upon the Silence: Samuel Beckett's Deconstructive Inventions, Theatre Symposium, 97; auth, Learning to Recognize the Real Thing: Folklore as Persuasion in Magazine Advertising, Ky Journ of Commun, 98. **CONTACT ADDRESS** 501 Pine St, Apt. 1, Louisville, KY 40204-1131.

HOWARD, LILLIE PEARL
PERSONAL Born 10/04/1949, Gadsden, AL, d, 1979, 2 children **DISCIPLINE** ENGLISH **EDUCATION** Univ of South Alabama, Mobile, Al, BA, 1971; Univ of New Mexico, Albuquerque, NM, MA, 1972, PhD, 1975; Harvard University, Cambridge, MA, Grad of Institute for Educational Management, 1988 **CAREER** Assoc provost for Academic Affairs and Undergraduate Education, 94-95; Provost , Interim Position, 95; assoc prov for Academic Affairs, 95-99; assoc provost for Academic Affairs and Dean, Univ Col, 99-. **HONORS AND AWARDS** Woodrow Wilson Finalist, 1971; Ford Foundation Fellow, 1971-75; Grant Recipient, National Endowment for the

Humanities, 1987-90; Grant Recipient, Ohio Board of Regents, 1990. **MEMBERSHIPS** Member, Modern Languages Association; member, American Association of Higher Education; member, Ohio Board of Regents Committee on the Enhancement of Undergrad education; member, Ohio Board of Regents Commission on Articulation and transfer; member, The National Association of Women Deans, Administrators, and Counselors; member, The National Association of Academic Affairs Administrators; American Assoc of Higher Education. **SELECTED PUBLICATIONS** Auth, "Zora Neale Hurston, " Boston: Twayne Pub, 80; auth, "A Lack Somewhere: Nella Larsen's Quidksand and the Harlem Renaissance," Harlem Renaissance Re-examined, (A.M.S. Press, 88), 223-233; ed, alice Walker and Zora Neale Hurson: the Common Bond, Westpost, CT: Greenwood Press, 93; auth, "seraph on the Swanee," Henry Louis Gates, reprint from 1980 pub: Zora Neale Hurston, (Amistad Press, 93), 267-279. **CONTACT ADDRESS** Assoc Provost for Academic Affairs and Dean, Univ Col, Wright State Univ, Dayton, 3640 Colonel Glenn Highway, 270 Univ Hall, Dayton, OH 45435. **EMAIL** lillie.howard@wright.edu/patricia

HOWARD, SUSAN K.
PERSONAL Born 10/16/1958, Pittsfield, MA, d, 2 children **DISCIPLINE** ENGLISH **EDUCATION** Univ Mass, BA, 81; Univ Delaware, MA, 85; PhD, 91. **CAREER** Teaching Asst, Univ Delaware, 83-88; Visiting Instructor, Temple Univ, 88-90; Asst Prof to Assoc Prof, Duquesne Univ, 91-. **MEMBERSHIPS** Am Soc for 18th Century Studies; E Cent Am Soc for 18th Century Studies; NE Am Soc for 18th Century Studies. **RESEARCH** The novel of the 18th Century. **SELECTED PUBLICATIONS** Auth, "The Intrusive Audience in Fielding's Amelia," Journal of Narrative Technique, (87): 286-295; auth, "Amelia Opie," in The Dictionary of Literary Biography 116: Romantic Novelists, (Gale Research Press, 92), 228-233; auth, "Anna Laetitia Barbauld as Literary Biographer," in Dictionary of Literary Biography 142: British Literary Biographers, (Gale Research Press, 94), 12-23; auth, "Identifying the Criminal in Charlotte Lennox's Harriot Stuart," Eighteenth-Century Fiction, (93): 137-152; auth, A Critical Edition of Charlotte Lennox's The Life of Harriot Stuart, Fairleigh Dickinson Univ Press, 95; auth, A Critical Edition of Frances Burney's Evelina, Broadview Press, 00. **CONTACT ADDRESS** Dept Eng, Duquesne Univ, 600 Forbes Ave, Pittsburgh, PA 15282-0001. **EMAIL** howard@duq.edu

HOWARD, THARON
DISCIPLINE ENGLISH LITERATURE **EDUCATION** Purdue Univ, PhD, 92. **CAREER** Dept Eng, Clemson Univ **RESEARCH** Professional communication; rhetoric. **SELECTED PUBLICATIONS** Auth, Designing Computer Classrooms for Technical Communication Programs in Computer and Technical Communication: A Sourcebook for Teachers and Program Directors, Ablex, 98; The Rhetoric of Electronic Communities, Ablex, 97; Mapping the Minefield of Electronic Ethics, The Nearness of You: Students and Teachers Writing On-Line, Teachers and Writers Collab, 96; Who Owns Electronic Texts?, Electronic Literacies in the Workplace: Technologies of Writing, NCTE Series Comput Comp, 96. **CONTACT ADDRESS** Clemson Univ, Clemson, SC 29634. **EMAIL** tharon@clemson.edu

HOWARD, W. SCOTT
PERSONAL Born 11/06/1963, Englewood, NJ, m, 1988, 2 children **DISCIPLINE** ENGLISH **CAREER** Asst Prof of Poetics and Poetry, Dept of English, Univ of Denver, 98-; Graduate Teaching Asst, Dept of English, Univ of Washington, 94-98; Research Asst, Dept of English, Univ of Washington, 97; Summer Quarter Teaching Asst, Dept of English, Univ of Washington, 96; Pew/PFF Teaching Fellow, The Pew Charitable Trusts, Washington DC, and The Departments of English, Univ of Washington, and Seattle Pacific Univ, 96; Research Asst, Department of English, Univ of Washington, Univ of Washington, and Archives De Loire-Atlantique, Nantes, France, 95; Instructor, School of Extended Studies, Portland State Univ, 94; Graduate Reader, Department of English, Univ of Washington, 94; Graduate Teaching Asst, Dept of English, Portland State Univ, 89. **HONORS AND AWARDS** Faculty Research Fund Grant, SPAR Council, Univ of Denver, 99; Internationalization Research & Travel Grant, AHSS Committee, Univ of Denver, 99; Walter Rosenberry Research & Travel Grant, AHSS Committee, Univ of Denver, 99; Faculty Researh Fund Grant, Faculty Senate, Univ of Denver, 98; Humanities Dissertation Fellowship, School of Graduate Studies, Univ of Washington, 98; MLA Travel Grant, Modern Language Association, 97; Joan Webber Outstanding Teaching Prize, honorable mention, Dept of English, Univ of Washington, 97; Travel Grant, School of Graduate Studies, Univ of Washington, 97; Fowler Travel Grant, School of Graduate Studies, Univ of Washington, 97; Fowler Travel Grant, School of Graduate Studies, Univ of Washington, 95; Travel Grant, School of Graduate Studies, Portland State Univ, 89; Phi Kappa Phi, Portland State Univ, 89; Honors in English, Lewis & Clark College, 87; Research Grant, Lewis & Clark College. **SELECTED PUBLICATIONS** Auth, "Synergism: Blake's Dialectic of Self-Actualization in The Book of Thel," Interdisciplinary Nineteenth-Century Studies: April 6-7, 89, Portland State Univ; auth, "Anecdote as Reflexive Field in the Poetry of Susan Howe," Practicing Postmodernisms: May 6-8, 93, Univ of Oregon; auth, "Anecdote as Reflexive Field in the Poetry of Susan Howe," Articulation of Sound Forms in Time," Chimera: April 13-14, 94, Univ of Washington; auth, "signal escape wonderfl in themselves: Hope Atherton's Wanderings in Susan Howe's Articulation of Sound Forms in Time," Chimera: April 13-14, 94, Univ of Washington; auth, "Poetics of the Gift; or, Howe's hau, in Susan Howe's a bibliography of the king's book; or eikon basilike," Applied Derrida: July 19-22, 95, Univ of Luton, England; auth, "The Brevities: Formal Mourning, Transgression & Postmodern American Elegies," Talisman 20-21, 99; auth, "William Bronk: Metaphysician," William Bronk Memorial, Remarks Videocassette, Adirondack Community College, 99; auth, "Of Devotion and Dissent: An Collins' Divine Songs and Medications," Reading Early Women, Ed. Helen Ostovich, Ashgate Press, 00; auth, "An Collins and the Politics of Mourning," Speaking Grief in English Literary Culture, Shakepeare to Marvell, Ed. David Kent and Margo Swiss, Toronto: Univ of Toronto Press, 01. **CONTACT ADDRESS** Dept English, Univ of Denver, 2140 South Race St., Denver, CO 80210-4639. **EMAIL** showard@du.edu

HOWARD, WILLIAM J.
PERSONAL Born 05/21/1945, Prince George, BC, Canada **DISCIPLINE** ENGLISH **CAREER** Asst prof to assoc prof, 75-85, dept head, 84-87, 90-91, prof Eng, Univ Regina, 85-. **MEMBERSHIPS** Wordsworth/Coleridge Asn; John Clare Soc; Byron Soc; ACCUTE. **RESEARCH** Genre and nineteenth-century fiction and culture; eighteenth and nineteenth century shifts in the notion of genius and a genre of literary criticism she terms "normative interpretation"; twentieth century readings of the Victorian period, popular fiction, and the implications of political philos for literary theory. **SELECTED PUBLICATIONS** Auth, John Clare, 81; ed, Wascana Rev, 76-82; assoc ed, Prairie Forum, 77-81. **CONTACT ADDRESS** Dept of English, Univ of Regina, Regina, SK, Canada S4S 0A2. **EMAIL** johnstos@meena.cc.uregina.ca

HOWARTH, WILLIAM L.
PERSONAL Born 11/26/1940, Minneapolis, MN, d, 2 children **DISCIPLINE** ENGLISH **EDUCATION** Univ Ill, BA, 62; Univ Va, MA, 63; PhD, 67. **CAREER** Ed-in-Chief, The Writings of Henry D. Thoreau, 72-80; From Instr to Prof, Princeton Univ, 66-. **HONORS AND AWARDS** Phi Beta Kappa, 66; Dissertation Fel, Woodrow Wilson Found; Sr Res Fel, NEH, 77; Kellogg Found Fel, 89; Vis Scholar, Poynter Inst, 90; Best Am Essay, 93; Top 100 Works of 20th Century Jour, 99. **SELECTED PUBLICATIONS** Auth, Walden and Other Writings, Mod Libr (NY), 81; auth, Thoreau in the Mountains, Farrar, Straus & Giroux (NY), 82; auth, The Book of Concord: Thoreau's Life as a Writer, Viking (NY), 82; auth, Mountaineering in the Sierra Nevada, Penguin (NY), 89; auth, "The Mother of Literature: Journalism and The Grapes of Wrath," in Literary Journalism in Twentieth Century (Oxford, 91), and in New Essays on the Grapes of Wrath (Cambridge, 91); auth, "Putting Columbus in his Place," Southwest Rev 77-2/3 (Spring-Summer 92): 153-165; auth, The Ecocriticism, Univ of Ga Press (Athens), 96; auth, Reading the Earth: New Directions in the Study of Literature & Environment, Univ of Utah Press (Provo), 98; auth, "Imagined Territory: The Writings of Wetlands," New Lit Hist 30-3 (Summer 99): 509-539; auth, Textures of Place: Geographies of Imagination, Experience, and Paradox, Univ of Minn Press, 01. **CONTACT ADDRESS** Princeton Univ, 22 McCosh Hall, Princeton, NJ 08544.

HOWE, SONDRA WIELAND
PERSONAL Born 04/30/1938, Bridgeport, CT, m, 1961, 3 children **DISCIPLINE** MUSIC **EDUCATION** Wellesley Col, AB, 60; Radcliffe Col, AMT, 61; Univ Minn, MA, 85, PhD, 88. **CAREER** Independent Scholar **MEMBERSHIPS** ISME; MENC; MTNA; AMS; Sonneck Soc Am Mus; AGO. **RESEARCH** History of Music Education; Women composers. **SELECTED PUBLICATIONS** Luther Whiting Mason: International Music Educator, Warren, Mich, Harmonie Park Press, 97; Pauline Duchambge, Loisa Puget, Dora Pejacevic, Jane Vieu, Women Composers: Music Through the Ages, G.K. Hall, 96-99; **CONTACT ADDRESS** 135 Chevy Chase Dr, Wayzata, MN 55391. **EMAIL** howex009@tc.umn.edu

HOWELL, ALLEN C.
PERSONAL Born 03/18/1962, Portland, OR, m, 1997, 3 children **DISCIPLINE** MUSIC **EDUCATION** Whitman Col, BA, 84; Portland St Univ, MAT, 85; Univ Or, DMA, 93. **CAREER** Asst prof, Columbus St Univ, 94-96; dir, First Unit Methodist Church, Erie, Pa, 96- ;asst prof, Edinboro Univ Pa Edinboro, 96- . **HONORS AND AWARDS** Pi Kappa Lambda, Univ Or; Virginia Johnson Whitfield Mem Scholar, Univ Or; Rose M. Gross Scholar, Univ Or, 89; Presser Found Prize, Outstanding Musical Ability, Whitman Col, 84; David Campbell Awd, Outstanding Sr Recital, Whitman Col, 84; Sarah Johnson Mem Scholar, Outstanding Personal & Scholar Cal, Whitman Col, 80. **MEMBERSHIPS** Pi Kappa Lambda, Amer Choral Dir Assoc; Music Educ Nat Conf; Pa Music Educ Assoc; Orff Schulwerk Assoc; Col Music Soc. **RESEARCH** Choral methods; general music methods; conducting & rehearsal pedagogy; curriculum develop; res methods, tech in music educ **SELECTED PUBLICATIONS** Auth, Effect of Repeated Testing on Knowledge Acquisition of Secondary Choral Students, res paper symp & poster presentation, 92; Planning for Rehearsals: The Instructional Planning Thoughts and Practices of a Few Exemplary Public School Music Ensemble Teachers, res poster presentation, 93; Planning for Rehearsals: The Instructional Planning Thoughts and Practices of Selected High School and Middle School Band and Choral Directors, 96; copresenter, Assessing the Student Teaching Experience, 98. **CONTACT ADDRESS** Dept of Music, Edinboro Univ of Pennsylvania, Edinboro, PA 16444. **EMAIL** dr_howell36@yahoo.com

HOWELL, CHRISTOPHER L.
PERSONAL Born 08/29/1945, Portland, OR, m, 1988, 2 children **DISCIPLINE** CREATIVE WRITING, CONTEMPORARY LITERATURE **EDUCATION** Ore State Univ, BS, 68; Portland State Univ, MA, 71; Univ Mass, MFA, 73. **CAREER** Vis Writer, Pittsburgh State Univ, 86-87; vis writer, Whitman Col, 87-88; prof, Emporia State univ, 88-96; prof, Eastern Wash Univ, 96-. **HONORS AND AWARDS** Helen Bullis Prize, Poetry NW; Vachel Lindsey Prize; NEA Fel; Ore Arts Comm Fel; Wash State Governor's Prize; Book Proj Awd, Wash Arts Coun. **MEMBERSHIPS** Pacific NW Booksellers Assoc. **RESEARCH** Contemporary World Poetry, Scandinavian Literature. **SELECTED PUBLICATIONS** Auth, The Crime of Luck, Panache Books, (Sundeerland, MA), 77; auth, Why Shouln't I, L'Epervier, 78; auth, Through Silence: the Ling Wei Texts, L'Epervier, 81; auth, Sea Change, L'Epervier Pr, (Seattle), 85; auth, Sweet Afton, True Directions, (San Francisco), 91; auth, Memory and Heaven, Eastern Wash Univ Pr, (Cheney, WA), 97; auth, Lady of the Fallen Air, Trask House Books, (Portland, OR), 98; auth, Through Silence: the Ling Wei Texts, 2nd ed, Lost Horse Pr, (Spokane), 99; auth, Blessing's Precision, Lone Oak Pr, (Petersham, MA), (forthcoming). **CONTACT ADDRESS** Dept English, Eastern Washington Univ, EWU, 705 W First Ave, Spokane, WA 99204. **EMAIL** cnhowell@mail.ewu.edu

HOWELL, JOHN M.
PERSONAL Born 03/02/1933, Oshawa, ON, Canada, m, 1963, 1 child **DISCIPLINE** AMERICAN LITERATURE **EDUCATION** Millsaps Col, BA, 54; Univ Southern Calif, MA, 60; Tulane Univ, PhD(English), 63. **CAREER** Asst prof, 63-69, assoc prof, 69-80, Prof English, Southern Ill Univ, Carbondale, 81-, Chm Dept, 82-86, 95-98. **MEMBERSHIPS** MLA; NCTE. **RESEARCH** American literature. **SELECTED PUBLICATIONS** Auth, Hemingway's African Stories, Scribner, 69; auth, From Abercrombie & Fitch to The First Forty-Nine Stories: The Text of Ernest Hemingway's Francis Macomber, Proof: Yearbk Am Bibliog & Textual Studies, 72; Hemingway's Metaphysics in Four Stories of the Thirties: A Look at the Manuscripts, Southern Ill Univ, fall-winter 73; Hemingway, Faulkner, and The Bear, Am Lit, 3/80; John Gardner: A Bibliographical Profile, Southern Ill Univ Press, 80; Faulkner, Prufrock, and Agamemnon: Horses, Hell, and High Water, In: Faulkner: The Unappeased Imagination, Whitston, 80; The Wound and the Albatross: John Gardner's Apprenticeship, In: Thor's Hammer: Essays on John Gardner, Univ Cent Ark Press, 85; McCaslin and Macomber: From Green Hills to Big Woods, Faulkner J, Fall 86; John Barth: An Interview, Papyrus, Southern Ill Univ, Spring 87; Hemingway and Chaplin: Monkey Business in The Undefeated, Studies in Short Fiction, Winter 90; Salinger in the Waste Land, In: Critical Essays on Salinger's The Catcher in the Rye, G.K. Hall, 90; Understanding John Gardner, Univ of SC Press, 93. **CONTACT ADDRESS** Dept of English, So Illinois Univ, Carbondale, Carbondale, IL 62901-4300. **EMAIL** jmhowell@siu.edu

HOYT, CHARLES ALVA
PERSONAL Born 09/26/1931, Middletown, CT, m, 1974, 5 children **DISCIPLINE** ENGLISH LITERATURE **EDUCATION** Wesleyan Univ, AB, 53, MAT, 55; Columbia Univ, MA, 56, PhD(Eng), 61. **CAREER** Instr, Wayne State Univ, 57-60; from asst prof to assoc prof Eng, Bennett Col, 60-68, chmn dept, 68-77; assoc prof Eng, Marist Col, 77-79; Res & Writing, 79-, Consult hum, US govt, 72-; vis prof, State Univ NY Col New Paltz, 74. **RESEARCH** Ethnomusicology and jazz; Eng lit of the 19th century; contemp Eng and Am lit. **SELECTED PUBLICATIONS** Auth, Bernard Malamud and the new romanticism, In: Contemporary American Novelists, Southern Ill Univ, 64; Novelist or historian?, Columbia Univ Forum, 66; ed, Minor British Novelists, Southern Ill Univ, 67; auth, Contemporary British literature, In: Encycl Americana, Grolier, 68; ed, Minor American Novelists, Southern Ill Univ, 69; The Last Chance Jazz Band, Hudson Valley, 5/78; auth, Witchcraft, Southern Ill Univ Press, 81 & 82. **CONTACT ADDRESS** So Illinois Univ, Carbondale, PO Box 3697, Carbondale, IL 62901.

HOZESKI, BRUCE WILLIAM
PERSONAL Born 02/28/1941, Grand Rapids, MI, m, 1967, 1 child **DISCIPLINE** ENGLISH LITERATURE, HISTORY OF LANGUAGE, MEDIEVAL BRITISH LITERATURE **EDUCATION** Aquinas Col, BA, 64; Mich State Univ, MA, 66, PhD(medieval English lit), 69. **CAREER** Grad asst English, Mich State Univ, 64-69; instr, Lansing Community Col, 68-69; Prof English, Ball State Univ, 69-, Chair, University Senate, 96-, Dir Grad Programs in English, 98-01; Exec Secy and Treas of Lambda Iota Tau, The Nat Honor Soc for Lit, 90-; founder and president, Int Soc of Hildegard von Bingen Studies, 84-89, life-

time mem of exec coun; mem Bd of Dir, Christian Ministries of Delaware County, 97-03. **HONORS AND AWARDS** Outstanding Faculty Service Awd, 99-00. **MEMBERSHIPS** AAUP; MLA; Midwest Mod Lang Asn; NCTE; Medieval Acad Am. **RESEARCH** Medieval English literature; medieval drama; Hildegard of Bingen. **SELECTED PUBLICATIONS** Auth, Hildegard of Bingen's Ordo Virtutum: The earliest discovered liturgical morality play, Am Benedictine Rev, 75; A mathematical error in Jonathan Swift's A Modest Proposal, Am Notes & Queries, 76; The parallel patterns in Hrotsvitha of Gandersheim, a tenth century German playwright, and in Hildegard of Bingen, a twentieth century German playwright, Annuale Mediaevale, 78; The parallel patterns in Prudentia's Psychomachia and Hildegarde of Bingen's Ordo Virtutum, 14th Century, English Mystics Newslett, 82; Hildegard of Bingen's Scivias, 86; Hildegard von Bingen's Mystical Visions, 95; Hildegard of Bingen: The Book of the Rewards of Life: Liber Vitae Meritorum, 97; regular contribr to An Annotated Chaucer Bibliography - Studies in the Age of Chaucer, 91-present. **CONTACT ADDRESS** Dept of English, Ball State Univ, 2000 W University, Muncie, IN 47306-0460. **EMAIL** 00bwhozeski@bsuuc.edu

HUANG, GUIYOU
PERSONAL Born 12/24/1961, China, m, 1998 **DISCIPLINE** ENGLISH **EDUCATION** Qufu Teachers Univ, BA, 83; Peking Univ, MA, 89, Tex A & M Univ, PhD, 93. **CAREER** Instr, Qufu Teachers Univ, 83-88; instr, Peking Univ, 86-89; lectr, Tex A & M Univ, 93-95; assoc prof, Kutztown Univ, Pa, 95-; adjunct prof, Lehigh Univ, 2000-. **HONORS AND AWARDS** Tex A & M Univ Outstanding Diss Awd, 93; State System of Higher Ed of Pa Prof Develop Grant Awd, 98. **MEMBERSHIPS** MLA, Am Lit Asn, Am Studies Asn. **RESEARCH** 19th and 20th century American literature, Asian-American Studies, East/West Comparative Studies. **SELECTED PUBLICATIONS** Co-ed with Gu Zhengkun, et al, A Companion to Masterpieces in World Poetry, Beijing: Peking Univ Press (90); auth, "A Newer Realm of Poetry: Whitman and Ai Quing," Walt Whitman Quart Rev, 15.2 (spring 98): 1-58; auth, Whitmanism, Imagism, and Modernism in China and America, Selinsgrove: Susquehanna Univ Press, London: Assoc Univ Presses (97); auth, "The Parisians and Flemings: Pound's Perception of Modern French Literature," Paideuma 27.2 & 3 (fall & winter 98): 165-73; auth, five essays in The Walt Whitman Encyclopedia, ed J. R. LeMaster & Donald D. Kummings, New York: Garland Pub, Inc (98); auth, "A Newer Realm of Poetry: Whitman and Ai Qing," Walt Whitman Quart Rev, 15.2 (spring 98): 172-79; auth, "The Analects of Confucius," Encyclopedia of Literary Translation, London: Fitzroy Dearborn Pubs (2000); auth, "Maxine Hong Kingston," and "Frank Chin," in Asian-American Novelists: A Bio-Bibliographical Critical Sourcebook, ed Emmanuel S. Nelson, Westport, CT: Greenwood Press (Feb 2000); Auth, "Frank Chin," in Asian American Playwrights, ed Miles X. Liu, Westport, CT: Greenwood Press (2000); auth, Asian American Autobiographers: A Bio-Bibliographical Critical Sourcebook, Westport, CT: Greenwood Press (2001). **CONTACT ADDRESS** Dept English, Kutztown Univ of Pennsylvania, Kutztown, PA 19530. **EMAIL** huang@kutztown.edu

HUANG, SHAORONG
PERSONAL Born 03/12/1951, China, m, 1978, 1 child **DISCIPLINE** COMMUNICATION, INTERPERSONAL COMMUNICATIONS **EDUCATION** Bowling Green State Univ, PhD, 94. **CAREER** Asst prof, Univ Cincinnati, 96-. **MEMBERSHIPS** Nat Commun Asn. **RESEARCH** Intercultural communication and rhetoric. **SELECTED PUBLICATIONS** Coauth, "The cultural connotation and communicative function of China's kinship terms," Am Communication Journal, 00; auth, "Ten thousand businesses would thrive in a harmonious family: Chinese conflict resolution styles in cross-cultural families," Intercultural Communication Studies, 99; auth, "Filial piety is the root of all vitues: Cross-cultural conflicts and intercultural acceptance in Lee's two movies," Popular Culture Rev, 99; auth, Ritual, culture, and communication: Deification of Mao Zedong in China's cultural revolution movement, Politics, communication, and culture, Sage, Pub, 97; To rebel is justified: A rhetorical study of China's cultural revolution movement: 1966-1969, Univ Press of Am, 96; coauth, Expanding the knowledge base: Reconsidering the communication literature, J of the Asn for Commun Admin, 94; A brief survey of Chinese popular culture, J of Popular Culture, Bowling Green State Univ Popular Press, 93. **CONTACT ADDRESS** Univ of Cincinnati, 9555 Plainfield Rd, Cincinnati, OH 45236. **EMAIL** Huangsn@ucrwcu.rwc.uc.edu

HUBBARD, SUSAN S.
PERSONAL Born 09/06/1951, Syracuse, NY, m, 2 children **DISCIPLINE** ENGLISH, CREATIVE WRITING **EDUCATION** Syracuse Univ, BA, 74; MFA, 84. **CAREER** Reporter/columnist, The Binghamton Press, 74-76; reporter/columnist, The Evening Sentinel, 76-78; investigative reporter, The Journal-Courier, 78; reporter, The Herald-Journal, 79-80; instr, Syracuse Univ & Univ Col, 84-88; instr, SUNY Col of Environmental Sci and Forestry, 88; sr lectr, Cornell Univ, 88-95; vis writer in residence, Pitzer Col, 95; assoc prof, Univ of Central Fla, 95-. **HONORS AND AWARDS** Stephen Crane Prize, 83; Special Merit Awd for Exceptional Contributions in Teaching and Service to the Writing Prog, Syracuse Univ, 88; Asn Writing Prog Short Fiction Prize, 89; Dean's Prize for Excellence and Innovation in Teaching, Cornell Univ, 91;Master Writer Residency, National Writer's Voice, 97; Awd for Excellence in Undergraduate Teaching, Univ of Central Fla, 99; Resident Artist, Yaddo, 99; Resident Artist, Djerassi, 00; Outstanding Teaching Awd, South Atlantic Administrators' of Departments of English, 00. **MEMBERSHIPS** Assoc Writing Progs, Author's Guild. **RESEARCH** Creativity Studies Across the Arts, Gender and Fiction. **SELECTED PUBLICATIONS** Auth, Walking on Ice, Univ of Mo Press (Columbia, MO), 90; auth, "The Psychic Takes a Greyhound," Am W (97): 88; auth, "Selling the House," Am W (97): 90 & 92; auth, "Why I Have to Marry the Pool Guy," Miss Rev 26.3 (98): 213-215; auth, "Night Crossing," TriQuarterly 103 (98): 180-189; auth, "Birth of a Poet," Kalliope (99): 46-59; auth, Blue Money, Univ of Mo Press (Columbia, MO), 99; co-ed, 100 Percent Pure Florida Fiction, Univ Press of Fla (Gainsville, FL), 00; auth, "My Sister's Affair," Sundog: Southeast Rev 19.2 (00): 103-109. **CONTACT ADDRESS** Dept English, Univ of Central Florida, PO Box 161346, Orlando, FL 32816-1346. **EMAIL** shubbard@ucf.edu

HUBBARD, THOMAS K.
PERSONAL Born 07/19/1956, Oklahoma, OK, s **DISCIPLINE** LITERATURE **EDUCATION** Santa Clara Univ, BA, 75; Univ Calif Berkeley, MA, 77; Yale Univ, PhD, 80. **CAREER** Vis asst prof, Bard Col, 80-81; asst prof, Skidmore Col, 82-84, vis asst prof, Univ of Minn, 84-85; asst prof, Cornell Univ, 86-87; from vis lectr to prof, Univ of Tex, 85-86, 88-. **HONORS AND AWARDS** NEH; Alexander von Humboldt Fel. **MEMBERSHIPS** Am Philol Asn, Class Asn of Can, Class Asn of the Middle W & S. **RESEARCH** Greek and Roman poetry, homosexuality in the ancient world. **SELECTED PUBLICATIONS** Auth, The Pindaric Mind, E.J. Brill, 85; auth, The Mask of Comedy: Aristophanes and the Intertextual Parabasis, Cornell, 91; auth, The Pipes of Pan: Intertextuality and Literary Filiation in the Pastoral Tradition, Michigan, 98. **CONTACT ADDRESS** Dept Classics, Univ of Texas, Austin, 0 Univ of Texas, Austin, TX 78712-1013. **EMAIL** tkh@mail.utexas.edu

HUBERMAN, ELIZABETH LYLE
PERSONAL Born 11/30/1915, Gloucester, Mass, m, 1939, 4 children **DISCIPLINE** ENGLISH & AMERICAN LITERATURE **EDUCATION** Bryn Mawr Col, AB, 37; NY Univ, MA, 63, PhD(English), 69. **CAREER** From asst prof to assoc prof, 68-73, chmn dept English, 72-75, PROF ENGLISH, KEAN COL, NJ, 73-, CHMN DEPT, 81- **MEMBERSHIPS** MLA; Col English Asn (2nd vpres, 76-77, 1st vpres, 77-78, pres, 78-79). **RESEARCH** Contemporary British and American poetry; the short story. **SELECTED PUBLICATIONS** Co-ed, War: An Anthology, Wash Sq Press, 69; co-ed, 50 Great European Short Stories, Bantam, 71; auth, The Poetry of Edwin Muir, Oxford Univ, 71; Initiation and tragedy: A new look at Edwin Muir's The Gate, PMLA, 1/72; To Byzantium once more: A study of the structure of Yeats's Byzantium, Essays Lit, fall 74; MacKay Brown's Greenvoe: Rediscovering a novel of the Orkneys, Critique, 12/77; St Magnus Visited, Mass Rev, spring 80; George Mackey Brown's Magnus, Studies in Scottish Lit, XVI, 81. **CONTACT ADDRESS** 1382 Newtown Langhorne Rd, Pennswood Village, Apt J208, Newton, PA 18940-2401.

HUDDLE, DAVID R.
PERSONAL Born 07/11/1942, Ivanhoe, VA, m, 1968, 2 children **DISCIPLINE** ENGLISH **EDUCATION** Univ Va, BA, 68; Hollins Col, MA, 69; Columbia Univ, MFA, 71. **CAREER** Instr to Assoc Prof, Univ Vt, 71-81; Vis Prof, Middlebury Col, 81-82; Fac Member, Bread Loaf School, 79, 85-; Prof, Univ Vt, 82-. **HONORS AND AWARDS** Best Book of the Year, Los Angeles Times Book Review, 99; Distinguished Book of the Year, 99; Robert Frost Prof of Am Lit, Bread Loaf School of English, 91; NEH Fel, 87, 78; James Wright Prize, 82; Lawrence Foundation Prize, 79; William Raney Fel, Bread Loaf Writers' Conf, 77. **SELECTED PUBLICATIONS** Auth, La Tour Dreams of the Wolfgirl, Houghton Mifflin, forthcoming; auth, Not: A Trio-A Novella and Two Stories, Univ Notre Dame Press, 00; auth, The Story of a Million Years, Houghton Mifflin, 99; auth, Summer Lake: New & Selected Poems, La State Univ Press, 99; auth, Tenorman, Chronicle Books, 95; auth, A David Huddle Reader, Univ Press of N England, 94; auth, Intimates, David R Godine Pub, 93; auth, The Nature of Yearning, Peregrine Smith Books, 92; auth, The Writing Habit, Peregrine Smith Books, 92; auth, The High Spirits: Stories of Men and Women, David R Godine Pub, 89. **CONTACT ADDRESS** Dept English, Univ of Vermont, 425 Old Mill, Burlington, VT 05405-0001.

HUDGINS, CHRISTOPHER CHAPMAN
PERSONAL Born 03/22/1947, Richmond, VA, m, 1970, 1 child **DISCIPLINE** ENGLISH LITERATURE **EDUCATION** Davidson Col, AB, 68; Emory Univ, MA, 69, PhD, 76. **CAREER** Instr, Old Dominion Univ, 69-71; asst prof, 76-80, assoc prof English, 80-, chemn dept English, 83-94, chemn Nv Humanities Comm, 96, Univ Nv Las Vegas, 80-, Emory Univ Fel English, 68-69 & 71-75. **MEMBERSHIPS** MLA; Rocky Mt MLA; AAUP; Am Film Inst; vpres Harold Pinter Soc, 92; vpres David Monet Soc, 94. **RESEARCH** Harold Pinter; modern British and American drama; film studies. **SELECTED PUBLICATIONS** Auth, Dance to a cut-throat temper: Harold Pinter's poetry as index to intended audience response, Comp Drama, 12: 214-232; Inside out: Filmic technique and the theatrical depiction of a consciousness in Harold Pinter's Old Times, Genre, 13: 355-376; Intended audience response, The Homecoming, and the ironic mode of identification, Harold Pinter: A Collection of Critical Essays, Univ Mo, 90; co-ed, Gender and Genre: Essays on David Mamet, St. Martin's Pr, forthcoming. **CONTACT ADDRESS** Dept English, Univ of Nevada, Las Vegas, PO Box 455011, Las Vegas, NV 89154-5011. **EMAIL** hudginsc@nevada.edu

HUDSON, BARTON
PERSONAL Born 07/20/1936, m, 1959, 1 child **DISCIPLINE** MUSIC HISTORY & LITERATURE **EDUCATION** Midwestern Univ, BA; Ind Univ, MA, PhD. **CAREER** Ed, Early Keyboard Jour; prof-; New Obrecht Ed; Antoine Brumel, Opera Omnia: Thomas Crecquillon, Opera Omnia; Hayne van Ghizeghem, Opera Omnia; Ninot le Petit, Opera Omnia; New Josquin edition. **HONORS AND AWARDS** Fulbright scholar, Ger; Fulbright res fel, 92-93; maj Text/Editions grant, outstanding tchr and Benedum distinguished scholar, W Va Univ; mus ed, opera omnia of antoine brumel and thomas crecquillon. **MEMBERSHIPS** Am Musicological Society. **SELECTED PUBLICATIONS** Publ, articles in the Jour of Amer Musicol Soc, The Mus Quart, The New Grove Dictionary of Mus. **CONTACT ADDRESS** 473 Devon Rd., Morgantown, WV 26505. **EMAIL** bhudson@wvu.edu

HUDSON, G. ELIZABETH
PERSONAL Born 12/31/1961, Walnut Creek, CA, m, 1991, 2 children **DISCIPLINE** MUSICOLOGY **EDUCATION** Smith Col, BA, 86; Cornell Univ, MA, 90, PhD, 93. **CAREER** Asst prof, 91-98, assoc prof, Univ Va, 98- . **HONORS AND AWARDS** NEH Fellow, 95-96; AMS 50 Fellow, 91. **MEMBERSHIPS** AMS **RESEARCH** 19th and 20th century performance practice, analysis, and criticism; 19th century Italian opera; Feminist operatic criticism. **SELECTED PUBLICATIONS** Introduzione storica, in Donizetti's Maria Stuarda, ed. Anders Wiklund, Milan, Ricordi, 91. Gilda seduced: A tale untold, Cambridge Opera Jour, 4/3, 92; Les vpres siciliennes, Simon Boccanegra, Un ballo in maschera, La forza del destino, Macbeth, Don Carlos, Aida, Othello, and Falstaff, in Dict des oeuvres de l'art vocal, ed. Marc Honegger and Paul Prevost, Paris, Bordas, 92; Telling Tales: Verdi, Jago, and the Undoing of Otello, Royal Gala prog book, Royal Opera House, Covent Garden, 92. Entry on "Puccini" and each of his operas, in The Viking Opera Guide, London: Viking and Penguin, 93; Masking Music: A Reconsideration of Light and Shade in Un ballo in maschera, in Verdi's Middle Period: Source Studies, Analysis and Performance Practice (1849-59), ed Martin Chusid, Univ Chicago Press, 97; Ed, Critical Edition of Giuseppe Verdi's Il corsaro, Univ Chicago Press, 98. **CONTACT ADDRESS** Univ of Virginia, 112 Old Cabell Hall, Charlottesville, VA 22903. **EMAIL** eh6v@virginia.edu

HUDSON, GEORGE C., JR.
DISCIPLINE RENAISSANCE STUDIES **EDUCATION** Duke Univ, AB, 59, MA, 61; Univ MN, PhD, 74. **CAREER** Instr, Univ Louisville; prof, 69-. **RESEARCH** 17th century Brit poetry, post-16th century Japanese poetry. **SELECTED PUBLICATIONS** Auth, Expository Writing: Study and Practice; co-ed, Six Dark Questions, 66; articles, Kyoto Eng Cent News and Museum Travel. **CONTACT ADDRESS** Dept of Eng, Colgate Univ, 13 Oak Drive, Hamilton, NY 13346.

HUDSON, NICHOLAS
PERSONAL Born 12/02/1957, Montreal, QC, Canada, d, 1 child **DISCIPLINE** ENGLISH **EDUCATION** Univ W Ont, BA, 80; Univ Warwick, MA, 81; Univ Oxford, PhD, 84. **CAREER** Asst prof, Univ Toronto, 84-85; prof, Univ BC, 85-. **HONORS AND AWARDS** Fel, Humanities and Soc Sci Coun of Canada. **MEMBERSHIPS** MLA; Asn of Can Univ Teachers; Am Soc for Eighteenth-Century Studies; Can Soc for Eighteenth-Century Studies. **RESEARCH** Eighteenth-Century British Literature; Thought and Society; Samuel Johnson. **SELECTED PUBLICATIONS** Auth, Writing and European Thought, 1600-1820, Cambridge, 94; auth, "From 'Nation' to 'Race': The Origin of Racial Classification in Eighteenth-Century Thought," Eighteenth-Century Studies, 96; auth, "Oral Tradition: The Origins of an Eighteenth-Century Concept," in Tradition in Transition, Oxford, 97; auth, "The Nature of Johnson's Conservatism," ELH, 97; auth, "Britons Never Will Be Slaves: National Myth Conservatism, and the Beginnings of British Anti-Slavery," Eighteenth-Century Studies, 01. **CONTACT ADDRESS** Dept English, Univ of British Columbia, 397-1873 E Mall, Vancouver, BC, Canada V6T 1Z1. **EMAIL** nhudson@interchange.ubc.ca

HUDSON, ROBERT J.
PERSONAL Born 06/11/1921, Selma, AL, m, 1944, 1 child **DISCIPLINE** ENGLISH **EDUCATION** Tenn State Col, BA, 46; NYork Univ, MA, 47, PhD(English), 62. **CAREER** From instr to assoc prof English, 47-63, chmn dept, 71-77, asst dean, 68-74, PROF ENGLISH, TENN STATE UNIV, 63-, DEAN SCH ARTS & SCI, 74-, Prof English, Fisk Univ, 64-65, lectr

Shakespeare & Elizabethan drama, 67- **HONORS AND AWARDS** NY Univ Founder's Day Awd, 63. **MEMBERSHIPS** MLA; Col Lang Asn; NCTE; Shakespeare Asn Am; Conf Col Compos & Commun. **RESEARCH** Shakespeare, Elizabethan drama; sixteenth century non-dramatic literature. **SELECTED PUBLICATIONS** Auth, Publications by Cla Members, 1991-92, Cla J, Vol 0036, 92. **CONTACT ADDRESS** Dept of English, Tennessee State Univ, Nashville, TN 37203.

HUDSON, ROBERT VERNON
PERSONAL Born 08/29/1932, Indianapolis, IN, 2 children **DISCIPLINE** HISTORY OF MASS COMMUNICATION **EDUCATION** Ind Univ, Bloomington, BS, 54; Univ Ore, MS, 66; Univ Minn, Minneapolis, PhD(mass commun), 70. **CAREER** Sports writer, Indianapolis Stars, 51; City ed, News-Sentinel, Rochester, Ind, 54; staff corresp, United Press, Indianapolis, 54-56; reporter, Chicago Daily News, 56-57 & Fairchild Publ, Chicago, 57-58; serv exec, Pub Rels Bd, Chicago, 58-59; publ asst, Traffic Inst & Transp Ctr, Northwestern Univ, 60-61, news bur mgr, 61-63, info serv dir, 63; asst dir, News Bur, Ariz State Univ, 63-65; asst prof, 68-73, asst chmn, Sch Joun, 72-74, asst dean, Col Commun Arts, 74, assoc prof to prof Jour, Mich State Univ, 73-98, prof emeritus, 98-; freelance writer, 49-; staff writer, Traffic Dig & Rev, 60-61; TV prod-writer-anchorman, Phoenix, Ariz, 64-65; prof jour & head dept, Calif Polytech State Univ, San Luis Opispo, 75-76. **MEMBERSHIPS** Jack London Soc; Am Lit Asn. **RESEARCH** Biography; mass media history; The First Amendment; Literary Journalism; Will Irwin; Jack London. **SELECTED PUBLICATIONS** Coauth, Johnson's Information Strategy for Vietnam: An Evaluation, autumn 68, auth, Will Irwin's Pioneering Criticism of the Press, summer 70 & FoI Crusade in Perspective: Three Victories for the Press, spring 73, Jour Quart; Will Irwin's Crusade for the League of Nations, Jour Hist, autumn 75; The English roots of Benjamin Franklin's jour, Jour Hist, autumn 76; Non-indigenous Influences on Benjamin Franklin's Jour: Newsletters to Newspapers: Eighteenth-Century Jour, WVa Univ, 77; auth, The Writing Game: A Biography of Will Irwin, Iowa State Univ Press, 82; auth, Irwin, William Henry in: Biographical Dictionary of Internationalists, Greenwood, 83; auth, Will Irwin, in: American Newspaper Journalists, 1901-1925, Gale, 84; auth, Mass MediaL A Chronological Encyclopedia of Television, Radio, Motion Pictures, Magazines, Newspapers, and Books in the United States, Garland Publ, 87. **CONTACT ADDRESS** Michigan State Univ, 5420 Wild Oak Dr, East Lansing, MI 48823-7218.

HUDSON-WEEMS, CLENORA
PERSONAL Born 07/23/1945, Oxford, MS, m, 1989, 1 child **DISCIPLINE** ENGLISH **EDUCATION** LeMoyne Col, BA; L'Universite de Dejon, Cert in Fr studies; Atlanta Univ, MA; Univ Iowa, PhD. **CAREER** Prof, Univ Mo, -. **HONORS AND AWARDS** Ford Found Fels, Toni Morrison Soc Book Awd. **MEMBERSHIPS** African Heritage Studies Asn, Col Lang Asn, Asn for the Study of African-Am Life & Hist. **SELECTED PUBLICATIONS** Coauth, Toni Morrison, 90; auth, Africana Womanism: Reclaiming ourselves; auth, Emmett Till: The Sacrificial Lamb of the Civil Rights Movement, 94; auth, Africana Womanism: Theory and Practice, forthcoming; ed, Contemporary Africana Theory and Thought, Majority Pr, forthcoming; auth, Soul Mates, forthcoming. **CONTACT ADDRESS** Dept English, Univ of Missouri, Columbia, 107 Tate Hall, Columbia, MO 65211-1500.

HUESCA, ROBERT
DISCIPLINE COMMUNICATIONS **EDUCATION** CA State Univ, BA, 82; Univ TX-Austin, MA, 88; OHio State Univ, PhD, 94. **CAREER** Tchg asst, OH State Univ, 90-91; tchg assoc, OH State Univ, 91-93; grad fel, OH State Univ, 93-94; asst prof, 94-. **HONORS AND AWARDS** Ed clinic award, The Columbus Dispatch, 89; multi-yr minority stud fel, OH State Univ, 90; travel grant, OH State Univ, 92; res travel grant, Intl Stud Fel prog, 92; travel grant, Tinker found, OH State Univ, 93 Walter B Emery scholar award, OH State Univ, 94; fac summer develop grant, 96; res ch, assn edu in jour and mass commun, 95-96; v hd, assn edu in jour and mass commun, 96-97; hd, assn edu in jour and mass commun, 97-98; manuscript feferee, jour intl commun, 97; contribut ed, commun bknotes quart, l erlbaum assoc, 97. **MEMBERSHIPS** Mem, Assn Edu in Jour and Mass Commun; Intl Assn for Mass Commun Res; Intl Commun Assn Nat Assn of Hisp Jour(s); Union for Democratic Commun. **SELECTED PUBLICATIONS** Co-auth, Theory and practice in Latin American alternative communication research, Jour Commun 44, 94; auth, A procedural view of participatory communication: Lessons from Bolivian tin miners' radio, Media, Cult and Soc 17, 95; Dying to make the paper, Rhetorical criticism: Exploration & practice, Waveland, 95; Honda: The ultimate trip, Rhetorical criticism: Exploration & practice, Waveland, 95; Subject-authored theories of media practice: The case of Bolivian tin miners' radio, Commun Stud 46, 95; Diversity in communication for social change, Peace Rev 8, 96; New directions for participatory communication for developmentm, Media Devel 43, 96; Participation for development in radio: An ethnography of the reporteros populares of Bolivia, Gazette: Intl Jour for Mass Commun Stud 57, 96; Low-powered television in rural Bolivia: New directions for democratic media practice, Stud Latin Am Pop Cult 16, 97. **CONTACT ADDRESS** Dept of Commun, Trinity Univ, 715 Stadium Dr, San Antonio, TX 78212. **EMAIL** rhuesca@trinity.edu

HUFFMAN, CARL A.
PERSONAL Born 12/27/1951, Denver, CO, m, 1986, 3 children **DISCIPLINE** CLASSICS **EDUCATION** Univ Colo, BA, 74, MA, 76; Univ Tex, PhD, 81. **CAREER** From asst prof to assoc prof to prof, DePauw Univ, 81-. **HONORS AND AWARDS** John Simon Guggenheim Found Fel, 95-96; Howard Found Res Fel, 89-90; NEH Fel Independent Study & Res, 83-84; Bye Fel, Robinson Col, Cambridge Univ, 83-84. **MEMBERSHIPS** Am Philological Asn; Soc Ancient Greek Philos. **RESEARCH** Ancient philosophy. **SELECTED PUBLICATIONS** Auth, Philolaus of Croton: Pythagorean and Presocratic, 93; auth, The Pythagorean Tradition, Cambridge Companion to Early Greek Philos, 99; auth, Die Pythagoreer, Philosophen der Antike I, 96; auth, Pythagorisme, Le Savior Grec, 96; auth, Philolaus' Cosmogony, Ionian Philos, 89; auth, The Role of Number in Philolaus' Philosophy, Phronesis, 88; auth, The Authenticity of Archytas Fragment 1, Class Quart, 85. **CONTACT ADDRESS** Dept of Classics, DePauw Univ, 400 S Locust, Greencastle, IN 46135. **EMAIL** cahuff@depauw.edu

HUFFMAN, CLIFFORD CHALMERS
PERSONAL Born 06/05/1940, New York, NY, m, 1967 **DISCIPLINE** ENGLISH LITERATURE **EDUCATION** Columbia Univ, BA, 61, PhD(English), 69; Cambridge Univ, MA, 67. **CAREER** Instr English, Brandeis Univ, 68-70; asst prof, 70-73, ASSOC PROF ENGLISH, STATE UNIV NY, STONY BROOK, 73-93, full prof, 93-, DIR SUMMER SESSION, 76-78; Exec officer, Comt on Acadmic Standing and Appeals, 94-. **HONORS AND AWARDS** Nat Endowment Humanities grant, 76. **MEMBERSHIPS** MLA. **RESEARCH** History of ideas; Renaissance history; English and comparative Renaissance literatures. **SELECTED PUBLICATIONS** Auth, Coriolanus in Context, Bucknell Univ, 72; Titus Andronicus; Metamorphosis and Renewal, Mod Lang Rev, 72; History in Hawthorne's Custom-house, Clio, 73; Bassianus and the British History in Titus Andronicus, English Lang Notes, 74; The Christmas Prince; Univ and Popular Drama in the Age of Shakespeare, Costerus, 75; coauth, Firenzuola, Surrey and Thomas Watson Once More, Rev des Lang Vivautes, 76; ed, Tudor-Stuart Bibliography, Goldentree Bibliog, 78; auth, Unvalued jewels: The religious perspective in Richard III, Bucknell Rev, 82; auth, Pegasus Shakespeare Bibliography, 95. **CONTACT ADDRESS** Dept of English, SUNY, Stony Brook, 100 Nicolls Rd, Stony Brook, NY 11794-0002. **EMAIL** chuffman@notes.cc.sunysb.edu

HUFFMAN, JAMES RICHARD
PERSONAL Born 05/08/1944, Liberal, KS, m, 1965, 2 children **DISCIPLINE** ENGLISH, AMERICAN STUDIES **EDUCATION** Harvard Col, BA, 66; MI State Univ, MA, 67; PhD, 70. **CAREER** Asst prof Eng & Am lit, 70-75, assoc prof Eng, 75-85, prof eng, State Univ NY Col, Fredonia, 85, Dir Am Studies, 74-, Assoc prof, UER Des Pays Anglophones, Univ Paris III, Sorbonne Nouvelle, Paris, 76-77. **MEMBERSHIPS** Am Cult Asn; Popular Cult Asn. **RESEARCH** Am lit; popular cult; psychology and cult. **SELECTED PUBLICATIONS** Auth, Jesus Christ Superstar: Popular art and unpopular criticism, J Popular Culture, fall 72; The cuckoo clocks in Kesey's Nest, Mod Lang Studies, spring 77; A psychological redefinition of Styron's Confessions of Nat Turner, Literary Rev, winter 81; A psychological critique of American culture, Am J Psychoanalysis, 82; Murray Krieger and the impasse in contextualist poetics, In: Murray Krieger and Contemporary Critical Theory (Bruce Henriksen, ed), Columbia Univ, 86; Coauth (with Julie L Hoffman), Sexism and cultural lag: The rise of the jailbait song, 1955-1985, J Popular Culture, fall 87; Young Man Johnson, The Am J of Psychoanalysis, 9/89; A Norreyan approach to American literature, In: Dionysius in Literature: Essays on Literary Madness (Branimis M Rieger, ed), Bowling Green Univ Popular Press, 94. **CONTACT ADDRESS** American Studies Dept., SUNY, Col at Fredonia, Fredonia, NY 14063. **EMAIL** james.huffman@fredonia.edu

HUFFMAN, JOHN L.
DISCIPLINE COMMUNICATION STUDIES **EDUCATION** Univ IA, PhD, 73. **CAREER** Instr, Bowling Green State Univ, Pepperdine Univ, Univ Tulsa; prof, Univ NC, Charlotte. **RESEARCH** Commun law and policy; First Amendment theory. **SELECTED PUBLICATIONS** His research efforts have appeared in numerous jour(s), including Jour Quart, J of Broadcasting and Electronic Media, Free Speech Yearbk, J of Commun Law and Policy, Jour Monogr, and Intellect. **CONTACT ADDRESS** Univ of No Carolina, Charlotte, Charlotte, NC 28223-0001.

HUFMAN, MELODY J.
DISCIPLINE COMMUNICATION **EDUCATION** Wichita State Univ, BA, 77; Univ Denver, MA, 81, PhD, 83. **CAREER** Instr, Nat Col of Bus, Colorado, 82; instr, Metropolitan State Col, Colorado, 82; tchg fel, Univ Denver, 81-83; instr, Tarrant County Jr Col, Texas, 84; prof, Amber Univ, Texas, 84- . **MEMBERSHIPS** Natl Comm Asn; Western Comm Asn. **RESEARCH** Nonverbal communication; organizational communication; political communication. **SELECTED PUBLICATIONS** Auth, "Nonverbal Measures of self assessment," ERIC, 95; "Distance Learning Via a Modem," ERIC, 96; "Managerial Solutions," ERIC, 97; "Pet Adoption Experience a Dog-Gone Good Experience," Mansfield News Mirror, 97. **CONTACT ADDRESS** Gen Educ, Amber Univ, 1700 Eastgate Dr, Garland, TX 75041-5511. **EMAIL** drhufman@hotmail.com

HUGGINS, CYNTHIA
PERSONAL Born 06/23/1956, Greenville, SC, s **DISCIPLINE** ENGLISH **EDUCATION** Univ North Carolina at Greensboro, PhD, 97. **CAREER** Teaching asst, Univ North Carolina at Greensboro, 95-97; asst prof English, Univ Maine at Machias, 97-. **HONORS AND AWARDS** Lane Graduate Fel in English, Univ North Carolina at Greensboro; Mildred Kates Dissertation Awd, Univ North Carolina at Greensboro; Bronte Soc Res Grant; Graduate Teaching Awd, Dept of English, Univ North Carolina at Greensboro; Outstanding Graduate Teaching Asst Awd, Col of Arts and Sciences, Univ North Carolina at Greensboro. **MEMBERSHIPS** Bronte Soc; Mod Lang Asn; Victorians Inst; North Atlantic, Mod Lang Asn; 18th and 19th Century British Women Writers Asn. **RESEARCH** Brontes; Victorian fiction and poetry; literary biography; Romantics; 18th century novel. **SELECTED PUBLICATIONS** Auth, "Behind the Mask of Branwell Bronte", in Bronte Newsletter 9, 90; auth, "Adam Bede: Author, Narrator and Narrative", in George Eliot Review 23, 92; auth, "Review of Rose Macaulay: A Writer's Life", in English Literature in Transition 1880-1820 37, 94; coauth, "Review of 'The Letters of Charlotte Bronte. With a Selection of Letters by Family and Friends. Volume One, 1829-1847' Recent work on the Brontes", in Victorians Institute Journal 24, 96; auth, "Witnessing by Example: Southern Baptists in Clyde Edgerton's 'Walking Across Egypt' and 'Killer Diller'", in The Southern Quart 35, 97; auth, "A. Mary F. Robinson (1857-1944)", in Dictionary of Literary Biography: Victorian Women Poets, Gale Research, 98. **CONTACT ADDRESS** Univ of Maine, 9 O'Brien Ave., Machias, ME 046540. **EMAIL** CHUGGINS@ACAD.UMM.MAINE.EDU

HUGHES, ANDREW
PERSONAL Born 08/03/1937, London, England **DISCIPLINE** MUSIC, HISTORY **EDUCATION** BA, Bmus, MA, Dphil. **CAREER** Lectr, Queen's Univ (Belfast), 62-64; asst prof, Univ Ill, 64-67; assoc prof, Univ N Carolina, 67-69; prof, Univ Toronto, 69-. **HONORS AND AWARDS** Henry Hadow scholar, Oxford, 55; John Lowell Osgood Mem Prize, Oxford, 58; Guggenheim fel, 73-74; fel, Trinity Col, Univ Toronto, 80; Killam res fel, 93-95. **MEMBERSHIPS** Am Musicol Soc; Medieval Acad Am. **RESEARCH** Medieval liturgy, plainsong and other music, and liturgical manuscripts. **SELECTED PUBLICATIONS** Auth, Manuscript Accidentals: Ficta in Focus, 72; auth, A Bibliography of Medieval Music, 74, 2nd ed, 80; auth, Medieval Manuscripts for Mass and Office, 81, 86; auth, Style and Symbol: Medieval Music 800-1453, 89; auth, Late Medieval Liturgical Offices: Resources for Electronic Research: Texts, 94; auth, Late Medieval Liturgical Offices: Resources for Electronic Research: Sources and Chants, 96; ed, Fifteenth Century Liturgical Music, 68; co-ed, The Old Hall Manuscript, 69, 73. **CONTACT ADDRESS** Ctr Medieval Stud, Univ of Toronto, Toronto, ON, Canada M5S 1A1.

HUGHES, DIANA L.
PERSONAL Born 02/09/1947, Hannibal, MO, m, 1983 **DISCIPLINE** SPEECH LANGUAGE **EDUCATION** E Illinois Univ, BS, 69; S Illinois Univ, MS, 71, MS, 72; Univ Wash, PhD, 82. **CAREER** Col level tchng, Univ Wisc, 72-82; tchr, 82-, Central Mich Univ. **HONORS AND AWARDS** Mich Assn of Gov Bds, Dist Fac Mem, 88. **MEMBERSHIPS** Amer Speech-Lang-Hearing Assn; Mich Speech-Lang-Hearing Assn. **RESEARCH** Child lang disorders; assessment of narrative discourse; lang intervention. **SELECTED PUBLICATIONS** Auth, Language Treatment and Generalization: A Clinician's Handbook, College-Hill, 85; coauth, Developmental Sentence Scoring: Still Useful After All These Years, Topics in Lang Disorders, 92; art, Interest Area 6: Intervention Programming and Efficacy, ASHA Spec Int Div #10, Ed/Learn Correlates of Comm Disorders 2:2, 92; coauth, A Case Study of Phonological Development in Language Delayed Twins Not Enrolled in Therapy, J of Childhood Comm Disorders 15:2, 93; coauth, Two Approaches to the Facilitation of Grammar in Children with Language Impairment: An Experimental Evaluation, J of Speech & Hearing Res 36, 93; art, Intervention Programming and Efficacy SIC #10, Newsl, 93; coauth, Computer Technology: Use in Training Programs, Asha 38-39, 93; coauth, Vowel Use of Phonologically Disordered Identical Twin Boys: A Case Study, Perceptual Motor Skills 79, 94; coauth, Computer Assisted Instruction for Learning Developmental Sentence Scoring: An Experimental Comparison, Amer J of Speech-Lang Path 3:3, 94; coauth, Guide to Narrative Language: Procedures for Assessment, Thinking Publ, 97. **CONTACT ADDRESS** Central Michigan Univ, Moore 416, Mount Pleasant, MI 48859. **EMAIL** diana.l.hughes@cmich.edu

HUGHES, ELAINE W.
PERSONAL Born 04/03/1941, Graysville, AL, m, 1959, 3 children **DISCIPLINE** ENGLISH **EDUCATION** Ala Col, BA, 69; Univ Ala, PhD, 79. **HONORS AND AWARDS** NDEA Fel, 71-74; Carnegie Found CASE Prof the the Year,

Ala, 98-99. **MEMBERSHIPS** NCTE; ACETA; SAMLA; AAUW, Delta Kappa Gamma. **RESEARCH** Myth criticism, Alabama literature, Southern writers (contemporary). **SELECTED PUBLICATIONS** Coauth, "The Hero's Quest: A bibliographic Essay", Global Perspectives on Teaching Literature, NCTE, 93; auth, "Chapter on 70's", Our First Hundred Years, Montebello, 96; coed, Reading Our Lives: Southern Autobiography Anthology, Auburn Univ, 97. **CONTACT ADDRESS** Dept English, Univ of Montevallo, PO Box 6000, Montevallo, AL 35115-6000. **EMAIL** hughes@montevallo.edu

HUGHES, LINDA K.
PERSONAL Born 07/09/1948, Dodge City, KS, m, 1966, 1 child **DISCIPLINE** ENGLISH **EDUCATION** Wichita State Univ, BA, 70; Univ Mo Columbia, MA, 71, PhD, 76. **CAREER** Instr, 76-80, asst prof, 80-84, eng, Univ Mo Rolla; asst prof, 84-85, assoc prof, 85-88, eng, Washburn Univ; from assoc prof to Addie Levy Prof of Lit, Tex Christian Univ, 88-; dir grad studies, Texas Christian Univ, 92-99. **HONORS AND AWARDS** Phi Beta Kappa; Phi Kappa Phi; Phi Beta Delta; Dean's Teaching award; Honors Fac Recognition Awd; Chancellor's Medal for Distinguished Res and Creative Activity; Tex Christian Univ, 92; pres, Res Soc of Victorian Periodicals, 97-99. **MEMBERSHIPS** Mod Lang Asn; South Central Mod Lang Asn; Res Soc of Victorian Periodicals; Interdisciplinary 19th-century studies; 1890s Soc. **RESEARCH** Victorian literature and culture; Victorian periodicals; Poetry; Women poets; Aestheticism and gender; Arthurian studies; Serial literature; Authorship; Tennyson; Rosamund Marriott Watson; Elizabeth Gaskell. **SELECTED PUBLICATIONS** Auth, "A Fin-de-Siecle Beauty and the Beast: Configuring the Body in Works by Graham R. Tomson," Tulsa Studies in Women's Literature 14 (95): 95-121; auth, "Textual/Sexual Pleasure and Serial Publication," in Literature in the Marketplace: Nineteenth-Century British Publishing and Reading Practices (Cambridge Univ Press, 95), 143-64; guest ed, Victorian Poetry: Victorian Women Poets, Spring, 95; auth, "Fair Hymen Holdeth Hid a World of Woes: Myth and Marriage in Poems by Graham R. Tomson," in Victorian Women Poets: A Critical Reader (Basil Blackwell, 96), 162-85; monogr, Strange Bedfellows: W. E. Henley and Feminist Fashion History, occasional series no 3, Eighteen Nineties Soc, 97; auth, "Come Again, and Thrice as Fair" in The Modern Return, (Garland Publ, 98), 51-64; coauth, Victorian Publ and Mrs. Gaskell's Work, 99; co-ed, Biographical Passages: Essays in Victorian and Modernist Biography, 00. **CONTACT ADDRESS** Dept. of English, Texas Christian Univ, TW, Box 297270, Fort Worth, TX 76129. **EMAIL** l.hughes@tcu.edu

HUGHES, SHAUN FRANCIS DOUGLAS
PERSONAL Born 10/08/1944, Te Puke, NZ **DISCIPLINE** MEDIEVAL ENGLISH LANGUAGE & LITERATURE **EDUCATION** Victoria Univ Wellington, BA, 66; MA, 67; Univ Wash, PhD(English), 72. **CAREER** Jr lectr English, Massey Univ, NZ, 67-68; teaching asst, Univ Wash, 68-71, assoc 71-72; asst prof, 72-78, Assoc Prof English, Purdue Univ, West Lafayette, 78-, Vis lectr Scand, Dept Ger Lang & Lit, Harvard Univ, 78; corresp ed,Ger Lang & Lit Monogr, 78-; Am Coun Learned Soc fel, 79-80; humanities grant, Icelandic Sci Found, 80-81; guest ed, Mod Fiction Studies, 81; Gastprofessur, Englisches Seminar, Albert-Ludwigs-Univeritat, Freiburg im Breisgau, Germany, 98-99; guest ed, Modern Fiction Studies, 81, 84, 91; advisory ed, Modern Fiction Studies, 82-; consulting ed, Humor. **MEMBERSHIPS** Soc Advan Scand Studies. **SELECTED PUBLICATIONS** Auth, The Last Frontier: The Renaissance in Iceland 1550-1750, Parergon, 75; auth, John Cleland's Role in the History of Sanskrit Studies in Europe, Archivum Linguisticum, 76; auth, The Literary Antecedents of Ans Saga Bogsvergis, Mediaeval Scand, 76; The Ideal of Kingship in the Riddarasogur, Mich Acad, 78; auth, Mrs Elstob's Defence of Antiquarian Learning, in Her Rudiments of Grammar for the English-Saxon Tongue, 1715, Harvard Libr Bull, 79; auth, "Report on Rimur 1980," J English & Germanic Philol (80); auth, "Maori and Pakeha Behind the Tattooed Face: The Emergence of a Polynesian Voice in New Zealand Fiction," Mod Fiction Studies (81); auth, "The Anglo-Saxon Grammars of George Hickes and Elizabeth Elstob," in Anglo-Saxon Scholarship: The First Three Centuries (G K Hall, 82); auth, "Salutary Lessons from the History of Linguistics," in The Real World Linguist: Linguistic Applications in the 1980s (Ablex, 86); auth, "On 'Translating Contemporary Icelandic Poetry:' A Rebuff," Scand Studies (86); auth, "Sir Thomas Browne and Iceland," English Renaissance Prose (87); auth, "The Battle of Stamford Bridge and the Battle of Bouvines," Scand Studies (88); auth, "Aspects of Courtly literature in the Ridddarasogur," Forum (88); auth, "The Saga of An Bow Bender," in Medieval Outlaws: Ten Tales in Modern English (Sutton, 98). **CONTACT ADDRESS** Dept of English, Purdue Univ, West Lafayette, West Lafayette, IN 47907. **EMAIL** sfdh@omni.cc.purdue.edu

HULIT, LLOYD
PERSONAL Born 08/14/1945, Ashland, OH, m, 1966, 2 children **DISCIPLINE** SPEECH-LANGUAGE PATHOLOGY **EDUCATION** Ashland Col, BS, 67; Ohio State Univ, MA, 71, PhD, 72. **CAREER** Teacher, Glenwood High School, 67-68; teacher, L.J. Smith Elem School, 68-69; TA, Ohio State Univ, 71-72; prof, IL State Univ, 72-. **HONORS AND AWARDS** Distinguished Teaching Awd, IL State Univ, 83; Hon Mem, Golden Key Nat Honor Soc, IL State Univ, 88; Nat Distinguished Serv Registry: Speech, Lang and Hearing, 89; Who's Who in Am Educ, 89-90; Cert of Appreciation for Dedication to Teaching, Delta, Zeta, IL State Univ, 94; Golden Apple Awd, Am Speech-Lang-Hearing Assoc. 96. **MEMBERSHIPS** Am Speech-Lang-Hearing Assoc; IL Speech-Lang-Hearing Assoc. **RESEARCH** Stuttering, Phonology, Speech and Language Development. **SELECTED PUBLICATIONS** Auth, Straight Talk on Stuttering, Chares C Thomas, (Springfield, IL), 96; coauth, Born to Talk: An Introduction to Speech and Language Development, 2nd Edition, Allyn & Bacon, (Needham Heights, MA), 97; coauth, Instructor's Manual to Accompany Born to Talk, 2nd Edition, Allyn & Bacon, (Needham Heights, MA), 97; coauth, "The association of attitudes toward stuttering with selected variables", J of Fluency Disorders 19, (94): 247-267; coauth, A family bond, Stuttering Found of Am, 98. **CONTACT ADDRESS** Dept Speech Pathology and Audio, Illinois State Univ, 1 Campus Box 4720, Normal, IL 61790-0001. **EMAIL** lhulit@ilstu.edu

HULL, AKASHA GLORIA
PERSONAL Born Shreveport, LA **DISCIPLINE** ENGLISH **EDUCATION** Southern University, BA (summa cum laude), 1966; Purdue University, MA, 1968, PhD, 1972 **CAREER** Univ of Delaware, prof of English, 72-88; University of California, Santa Cruz, professor, women studies, 88-. **HONORS AND AWARDS** Fellowship, Rockefeller Foundation 1979-80; Outstanding Woman of Color, Natl Institute of Women of Color 1982; Ford Foundation, Postdoctoral Fellowship 1987-88; AAUW Fellowship 1990; Nat Humanities Ctr, 94-95; Semifinalist Ursula K. LeGuin Imaginative Fiction Contest, 00. **MEMBERSHIPS** Co-project dir, Black Women's Studies project 1982-84; Mellon Scholar, Wellesley Ctr for Rsch on Women 1983; Fulbright Senior Lectureship, Univ of the West Indies-Jamaica 1984-86; commission co-chair, Modern Language Assn; Natl Women's Studies Assn; advisor/consultant, Black American Literature Forum, Feminist Studies; Reviewer Women's Review of Books. **RESEARCH** Novel-in-progress **SELECTED PUBLICATIONS** All the Women are White, All the Blacks are Men, but Some of Us are Brave, Black Women's Studies 1982; Give Us Each Day, the Diary of Alice Dunbar-Nelson 1984; Color, Sex, and Poetry: Three Women Writers of the Harlem Renaissance 1987; Healing Heart: Poems 1973-1988, 1989; Works of Alice Dunbar-Nelson, 3 vols, 1988; auth, Soul Talk: The New Spirituality of African American Women, 01. **CONTACT ADDRESS** Kresge Col, Univ of California, Santa Cruz, Santa Cruz, CA 95064.

HULL, KENNETH
DISCIPLINE MUSIC **EDUCATION** Univ Waterloo, BA, 76; Univ Western Ontario, BM, 77; MM, 80; Princeton, PhD, 89. **CAREER** Assoc prof, Conrad Grebel Col. **MEMBERSHIPS** Can Liturgical Soc. **RESEARCH** Music of Brahms, musical allusion and twentieth century hymnody. **CONTACT ADDRESS** Dept of Music, Univ of Waterloo, Conrad Grebel Col, 200 Westmount Rd, Waterloo, ON, Canada N2L 3G6. **EMAIL** krhull@uwaterloo.ca

HULSE, CLARK
PERSONAL Born 01/01/1947, Pittsburgh, PA, m, 1969, 2 children **DISCIPLINE** ENGLISH, ART HISTORY **EDUCATION** Williams Col, BA, 69; Claremont Grad Sch, MA, 70, PhD(English), 74. **CAREER** Instr, 72-74, asst prof, 74-80, assoc prof, 80-90, prof, English and Art Hist,, 90-, interim dean, graduate college, 99-, Univ Ill Chicago, Acting Dir Center for Renaissance Studies, Newberry Libr, 86, 95, Visiting prof Art History, Northwestern Univ, 92. **HONORS AND AWARDS** Nat Endowment Humanities Newberry Libr fel, 79; Guggenheim fel, 87; Pres, Spencer Society, 90; British Academy Exchange fel, 93. **MEMBERSHIPS** MLA; Renaissance Soc Am, College Art Assoc. **RESEARCH** Sixteenth-century literature and visual culture; Shakespeare. **SELECTED PUBLICATIONS** Auth, Metamorphic Verse: The Elizabethan Minor Epic, 81; Stella's Wit: Penelope Devereux as reader of Sidney's Sonnets, in Rewriting the Renassaince: The Discourses of Sexual Difference in Early Modern Europe, 86; Shakespear's Sonnets and the Art of the Face, John Donne Jour, Vol 5, 86; Spenser, Bacon and the Myth of Power, in The Historical Renaissance: New Essays on Literature and History, 88; The Significance of Titian's Pastoral Scene, J. Paul Getty Museum Jour, Vol 17, 89; The Rule of Art: Literature and Painting in the Renaissance, 90; Dead Man's Treasure: The Cult of Thomas More, in The Production of English Renaissance Culture, 94; Early Modern Visual Culture: Representation, Race and Empire, 2000; Tudor Aesthetics, in Cambridge Companion to English Literature 1500-1600, 2000. **CONTACT ADDRESS** Dept of English, Univ of Illinois, Chicago, 601 S. Morgan, Chicago, IL 60607. **EMAIL** chulse@uic.edu

HUME, KATHRYN
PERSONAL Born 12/10/1945, Boston, MA, m, 1966 **DISCIPLINE** LITERATURE **EDUCATION** Radcliff, AB, 67; Univ of Pa, MA, 68; PhD, 71. **CAREER** Lectr, Univ of VA; Lectr, Asst Prof, Cornel Univ, 69-77; from Assoc Prof to Distinguished Prof, Pa State Univ, 77-. **RESEARCH** Contemporary fiction. **SELECTED PUBLICATIONS** Auth, 'The Owl and the Hightingale': the Poem and its Critics, The Univ of Toronto Press (Toronto), 75; auth, Fantasy and Mimesis: Responses to Reality in Western Literature, Methuen (London), 84; auth, Pynchon's Mythography: An Approach to 'Gravity's Rainbow', Soutehr Ill Univ Press (Carbondale), 87; auth, Calvino's Fictions: Cogito and Cosmos, Clarendon Press (Oxford), 92; auth, American Dream, American Nightmare: Fiction since 1960, Univ of Ill Press, forthcoming. **CONTACT ADDRESS** Dept English, Pennsylvania State Univ, Univ Park, 117 Burrowes Bldg., University Park, PA 16802-6200. **EMAIL** IAN@psu.edu

HUME, ROBERT DAVID
PERSONAL Born 07/25/1944, Oak Ridge, TN, m, 1966 **DISCIPLINE** ENGLISH LITERATURE **EDUCATION** Haverford Col, BA, 66; Univ Pa, PhD(English), 69. **CAREER** From asst prof to assoc prof English, Cornell Univ, 69-77; PROF ENGLISH, PA STATE UNIV, 77-, ASSOC HEAD DEPT, 79-83, distinguished prof, 90-91, Edwin Erle Sparks Prof, 91-98, Evan Pugh Prof, 98-. **HONORS AND AWARDS** Guggenheim Fel, 83-84. **MEMBERSHIPS** Soc Theatre Res; Am Soc 18th Century Studies; Am Soc Theatre Res. **RESEARCH** English drama, 1660-1800; 18th century novel and aesthetics; theory of literary criticism; history of opera. **SELECTED PUBLICATIONS** Auth, Dryden's Criticism, Cornell, 70; auth, Development of English Drama in the Late 17th Century, Oxford, 76; auth, Henry Fielding and the London Theatre, Oxford, 88; auth, Reconstructing Contexts, Oxford, 99; coauth, Producible Interpretation, Southern Ill, 85; coauth, A Register of English Theatrical Documents 1660-1737, Southern Ill, 91; coauth, Italian Opera in Late 18th Century London, vol 1, Oxford, 95, vol 2, Oxford, 00. **CONTACT ADDRESS** Dept of English, Pennsylvania State Univ, Univ Park, University Park, PA 16802. **EMAIL** rob-hume@psu.edu

HUMMA, JOHN BALLARD
PERSONAL Born 02/16/1940, Rosiclare, IL, m, 1982, 4 children **DISCIPLINE** NINETEENTH CENTURY AMERICAN LITERATURE **EDUCATION** George Washington Univ, BA, 63; Southern Ill Univ, Carbondale, MA, 65, PhD(English), 69. **CAREER** Assoc prof, 69-79, prof English, GA Southern Col, 80-. **HONORS AND AWARDS** Univ Excellence in Res Awd, 89. **MEMBERSHIPS** MLA. **RESEARCH** British fiction; American literature. **SELECTED PUBLICATIONS** Auth, Poe's Ligeia: Glanvill's Will or Blake's Will, Miss Quart, winter 72-73; The Art and Meaning of Sarah Orne Jewett's The Courting of Sister Wisby, winter 73 & Gabriel and the Bedsheets: The Ending of the Dead, spring 73, Studies Short Fiction; D. H. Lawrence as Friedrich Nietzche, Philol Quart, 1/74; Melville's Billy Budd and Lawrence's The Prussian Officer: Old Adams and New, spring 74 & Pan and The Rocking-Horse Winner, 78, Essays Lit; The Narrative Framing Apparatus of Scott's Old Mortality, Studies in the Novel, winter 80; The Interpenetrating Metaphor: Nature and Myth in Lady Chatterley's Lover, PMLA, Jan 83; John Fowles' The Ebony Tower: In the Celtic Mood, Southern Humanities Rev, Winter 83; Of Bits, Beasts, and Bush: The Interior Wilderness in D. H. Lawrence's Kangaroo; S Atlantic Rev, Jan 86; James and Fowles: Tradition and Influence, Univ of Toronto Quart, Fall 88; Metaphor and Meaning in D. H. Lawrence's Later Novels, Univ of Mo Press, 90; Realism and Beyond: The Imagery of Sex and Sexual Oppression in Elizabeth Stoddard's Lemorne Versus Huell, S Atlantic Rev, Jan 93; Lawrence in Another Light: Women in Love and Existentialism, Studies in the Novel, Winter 92; auth, Sister Carrie and Thomas Hardy, Regained, Dreiser Studies, Spring 92; auth, Jennie Gerhardt and the Dream of the Pastoral, Dreiser's Jennie Gerhardt: New Essays on the Restored Text, ed. James L. West III, 95. **CONTACT ADDRESS** Dept of English, Georgia So Univ, PO Box 8023, Statesboro, GA 30460-1000. **EMAIL** humma@gsaix2.cc.gasou.edu

HUMPHERYS, ANNE
PERSONAL Born 02/25/1937, Lehi, UT, d, 1 child **DISCIPLINE** ENGLISH LITERATURE **EDUCATION** Stanford Univ, BA, 59; Columbia Univ, MA, 62, PhD(English), 68. **CAREER** Prof, 82, prof English, Lehman Col and Grad Center, 80- **MEMBERSHIPS** MLA; Res Soc Victorian Periodicals; Northeast Victorian Studies Asn. **RESEARCH** Victorian literature; history of the English novel. **SELECTED PUBLICATIONS** Auth, Travels into the Poor Man's Country: The Work of Henry Mayhew, Univ of Georgia Press; auth, Dombey and Son: Carker the Manager, Nineteenth Century Fiction, 80; auth, The Geometry of the Modern City: G.W.M. Reynolds and The Mysteries of London, Browning Institute Studies, 83; auth, Henry Mayhew, Twayne English Authors Series, G.K. Hall, 84; auth, Popular Narrative and Political Discourse in Reynolds Weekly Newspaper, in Investigating Journalism: The Press in the Nineteenth Century, ed. By Aled Jones, Laurel Brake, and Lionel Madden, London and New York: Macmillan, 90; auth, Generic Stands and Urban Twists: The Victorian Mysteries Novel, Victorian Studies, 91; auth, Enoch Arden, the Fatal Return, and Annie's Silence, Victorian Poetry, 92; auth, Louisa Gradgrind's Secret: Marriage and Divorce in Hard Times' Dickens Studies Annual, 96; auth, Women Writers and the 19th Century Divorce Novel, in Women Novelists and the Woman Question, ed. Nicola Thompson, Cambridge, 99. **CONTACT ADDRESS** PhD Program in English, Graduate Sch and Univ

Ctr, CUNY, 365 Fifth Ave, New York, NY 10016. **EMAIL** Ahumphreys@gc.cuny.edu

HUMPHRIES, BETTYE
PERSONAL Born 03/13/1928, Wichita Falls, TX, w, 8 children **DISCIPLINE** ENGLISH, JOURNALISM **EDUCATION** Hardin Col, BA, 49; Midwestern State Univ, MEd, 72; Univ N Tex, EdD, 89. **CAREER** Teacher, Tex State, 69-75; Teacher, Vernon Reg Jr Col, 76-83; Training Specialist, Wayland Bapt Univ, 83-84; Training Specialist, Lackland AFB, 84-95; Instructor, Northwest Vista Col, 00-. **HONORS AND AWARDS** Teachers Cer, TX, 68; Master Instructor Cer, USAF, 79. **MEMBERSHIPS** Phi Delta Kappa; Toastmaster Intl; Intl Soc of Performance Improvement; TX Cmty Col Teachers Asn. **CONTACT ADDRESS** Dept Eng & Lang, Palo Alto Col, 1400 W Villaret Blvd, San Antonio, TX 78224-2417. **EMAIL** bhumphri@accd.edu

HUMPHRIES, TOM
DISCIPLINE CROSS CULTURAL COMMUNICATION **EDUCATION** Union Grad Sch, Cross-Cult Commun and Lang Learning, PhD, 77. **CAREER** Lectr, Univ Calif, San Diego. **SELECTED PUBLICATIONS** Co-auth, Deaf in America: Voices from a Culture, Harvard, 88; Deaf Culture and Cultures, Multicultural Issues in Deafness, Longman, 93; auth, Of Deaf Mutes, the Strange, and the Modern Deaf Self, Culturally Affirmative Psychotherapy with Deaf Persons, Erlbaum, 95. **CONTACT ADDRESS** Dept of Commun, Univ of California, San Diego, 9500 Gilman Dr, La Jolla, CA 92093. **EMAIL** thumphri@weber.ucsd.edu

HUNNING, ROBERT W.
DISCIPLINE ENGLISH LITERATURE **EDUCATION** Columbia Univ, BA, 58, PhD, 64; Oxford Univ, BA, 60, MA, 64. **CAREER** Instr, Middlebury Col; Yale Univ; Johns Hopkins Univ; NYU; Princeton Univ; dir, prof, Lincoln Col, Oxford, 80, 84, 86; prof, 63-. **HONORS AND AWARDS** ACLS fel; Guggenheim fel; NEH fel; elect fel, Medieval Acad Am, 86; dir, neh asummer sem, col tchr, 82, 85, 89; trustee, new chaucer soc, 97-01. **SELECTED PUBLICATIONS** Auth, books on medieval historiography and romance; co-ed, an anthology and two essay collections; co-transl, the Lais of Marie de France. **CONTACT ADDRESS** Dept of Eng, Columbia Col, New York, 2960 Broadway, New York, NY 10027-6902.

HUNT, ANTHONY
PERSONAL Born 12/03/1938, Philadelphia, PA, m, 1964, 2 children **DISCIPLINE** ENGLISH **EDUCATION** St Joseph's Univ, BA, 60; Univ Haw, MA, 66; Univ NMex, PhD, 71. **CAREER** Grad teaching asst, Univ NMex, 66-68; instr to asst prof, Colby Col, 68-72; WCar Univ, 73; asst prof to assoc prof to prof, Univ PR, 72-. **HONORS AND AWARDS** SR Fulbright-Hays Lectrshp, Univ Osijek, 86-87, Univ Wroclaw, 75-76; NEH 78, 93; Miller Prize, 97; Don D. Walker Prize, 80. **MEMBERSHIPS** MLA; ALS; NCTE; CEA; CCEA; ASLE; Phi Kappa Phi. **RESEARCH** Poetry of Gary Snyder; the long poem in modern literature; teaching of literature; multiple intelligences and poetry; creative writing. **SELECTED PUBLICATIONS** Auth, "Bubbs Creek Haircut: Gary Snyder's Great Departure in Mountains and Rivers Without End," West Am Lit 15 (80): 163-175; auth, "The Humpbacked Flute Player: The Structure of Emptiness in Gary Snyder's Mountains and Rivers Without End," ISLE (93): 1-23; co-auth, "Catherine Weldon: Derek Walcott's Visionary Telling of History," CEA Crit 59 (96): 8-20; auth, "Singing the Dyads: The Chinese Landscape Scroll and Gary Snyder's Mountains and Rivers Without End," J Mod Lit 23 (99): 7-34; auth, The Undertoad: Selected Poems of Anthony Hunt, Greenbird Pr, 98; auth, "Sailing the Metaphorical Seas of the Middle East: Gary Snyder's Boat of a Million Years," Atenea 20 (00): 67-75. **CONTACT ADDRESS** English Dept, Univ of Puerto Rico, Mayaguez, PO Box 9265, Mayaguez, PR 00681-9265. **EMAIL** ahunt@coqui.net

HUNT, CAROLINE C.
PERSONAL Born 06/03/1941, Bay Shore, NY, m, 1965, 2 children **DISCIPLINE** ENGLISH AND AMERICAN LITERATURE **EDUCATION** Harvard, BA, 63, PhD, 70; Oxford Univ, BA, 65. **CAREER** Assoc dean, Ratcliffe Col, 70; asst prof, Beaver Col, 70-74; asst to prof, 76- ; Col Charleston; Hunt Ed Consult, 99- . **HONORS AND AWARDS** Woodrow Wilson, 63; Fulbright, 63-65; Distinguished Adv Awd, 94, Col Charleston; Distinguished Res Awd, 96, Col Charleston; Distinguished Serv Awd, 98, Col Charleston. **MEMBERSHIPS** Int Res Soc Children's Lit; Children's Lit Asn; Children's Lit Assembly, NCTE; ALAN; USBBY. **RESEARCH** Children's literature, Literature for adolescents, Later Renaissance. **SELECTED PUBLICATIONS** Auth, British Children's Writers Since 1960, Gale Research, 96; auth, Four Women Writers for Children, Gale Research, 96. **CONTACT ADDRESS** Dept English, Col of Charleston, 84 Smith St, Charleston, SC 29401. **EMAIL** huntc@ccfc.edu

HUNT, JOHN DIXON
PERSONAL Born 01/18/1936, Gloucester, England, d, 2 children **DISCIPLINE** ENGLISH LITERATURE **EDUCATION** Bristol Univ UK, 57-59, PhD 64. **CAREER** Univ Michigan, tch fel, 59-60; Vassar Col, inst 60-62; Exeter univ, asst lectr, 62-64; Univ York, lectr 64-75; Univ London Bedford Col, reader, prof, 75-82; Leiden Univ Netherlands, prof, ch, 83-85; Univ E Anglia, prof, pub curator, 85-88; Dumbarton Oaks, dir, 88-91; Oak Spring Garden Library, acad adv, 91-94; Univ Penn, prof, ch, 94-. **HONORS AND AWARDS** Folger Shakespeare Lib Fel; John Hopkins Univ vis fel, vis prof; Leverhulme Trust Sr Fac Fel; Brit Acad Euro Ex Fund Gnt; Princeton Univ vis mem. **RESEARCH** Inter art Relationships; garden history and history. **SELECTED PUBLICATIONS** Editor since 81, Jour of Garden History, re-titled 98, Studies on the History of Gardens and Designed Landscapes; editor, Penn Studies in Landscape Architecture, Univ Penn Press, 96-; The Greater Perfection: A Theory of Gardens, Thames & Hudson conjunct with Univ Penn Press, forthcoming; The Oak Spring Hortis, Upperville VA, in press; Imagination: 1600-1750, J M Dent , 85, pbk, ed, Univ Penn Press, 96; The Italian Garden Art Design and Culture, essays by, Malcolm Campbell, Iris Lauterbach, Alessandro Tosi, Raymond Gastil, et al, Cambridge Univ Press, 93; Approaches New and Old to Garden History, in: Dumbarton Oaks Colloquim series, Garden Hist and Historiography, forthcoming; Garden Aesthetics, in: The Encycl of Aesthetics, ed Michael Kelly, OUP, forthcoming; Humphry Repton and Garden Historiography, Jour of Garden Hist, 96; Ruskin: The Design of Nature and the Transcription of its Manuscript, Assemblage, 97; The Garden as Virtual reality, Das Kunstliche Paradies, Gartenkunst im Spammungsfeld von Natur und Gesellschaft, ed, Marcus Kohler, spec issue, Die Gartenkunst, Hanover, 97. **CONTACT ADDRESS** Dept of Landscape Archit, Univ of Pennsylvania, 119 Meyerson Hall, Philadelphia, PA 19104-6311. **EMAIL** jdhunt@pobox.upenn.edu

HUNT, JOHN M., JR.
PERSONAL Born 09/21/1943, Bryn Mawr, PA, s **DISCIPLINE** CLASSICS **EDUCATION** Lafayette Col, AB, 65; Cornell Univ, Post-grad fel, 65-66; Bryn Mawr Col, MA, 68, PhD, 70 **CAREER** Inst, Lafayette Col, 70; Asst Prof, 70-76, Villanova Univ; Visit Assoc Prof, 78-80, Univ of CA, Santa Barbara; Assoc Prof, 84-90, Prof, 91-, Villanova Univ **HONORS AND AWARDS** Who's Who in Am Educ **MEMBERSHIPS** Soc of Mayflower Descendants in PA; Sons of the Revolution; PA Soc **RESEARCH** Latin lit; textual criticism **CONTACT ADDRESS** Dept of Mod Lang, Villanova Univ, Villanova, PA 19085. **EMAIL** john.hunt@villanova.edu

HUNT, LINDA
PERSONAL m **DISCIPLINE** WRITING II, ESSAY WRITING, AND JOURNAL WRITING AND AUTOBIOGRAPHY **EDUCATION** Whitworth Col, MAT, Gonzaga Univ, PhD, 97. **CAREER** Asso prof. **HONORS AND AWARDS** Dir, Whitworth's Freshman Composition Prog. **SELECTED PUBLICATIONS** Auth, Rare Beasts, Unique Adventures: Reflections for College Students, Harper/Collins: Zondervan; contribu, Seattle Times, Reader's Digest, Psychology Today, Christian Science Monitor. **CONTACT ADDRESS** Dept of Eng, Whitworth Col, 300 West Hawthorne Rd, Spokane, WA 99251. **EMAIL** lhunt@whitworth.edu

HUNT, MAURICE A.
PERSONAL Born 10/30/1942, Lansing, MI, m, 1978, 4 children **DISCIPLINE** ENGLISH **EDUCATION** Univ Mich, BA, 64; Univ Calif Berkeley, MA, 66; PhD, 70. **CAREER** Instr, Col of Marin, 70-73; lectr, Dominican Col, 74-75; asst prof to prof, Baylor Univ, 81-. **HONORS AND AWARDS** Phi Beta Kappa; Who's Who in Am; Greater Lansing Area Sports Hall of Fame; Baylor Univ Class of 1945 Centennial Prof. **MEMBERSHIPS** MLA; S Central Renaissance Assoc; Shakespeare Assoc of Am; Tex Conf of Col Teachers of English. **RESEARCH** Shakespeare, The Poetry of Edmund Spenser, English Renaissance Dramatists, The Poetry and Prose of Sir Philip Sydney. **SELECTED PUBLICATIONS** Auth, Shakespeare's Romance of the Word, Bucknell Univ Pr, 90; auth, Approaches to Teaching Shakespeare's The Tempest and Other Late Romances, MLA, (NY), 92; auth, The Winter's Tale: Critical Essays, Garland Pub, (NY), 95; auth, Shakespeare's Labored Art, Peter Lang Pub, (NY), 95; auth, Approaches to Teaching Shakespeare's Romeo and Juliet, MLA, (NY), 00; auth, "The Reclamation of Language in Much Ado About Nothing", Studies in Philology 97, (00): 166-92; auth, "Antimetabolic King John", Style 34.3 (00); auth, "Shakespeare's Pericles and the Acts of the Apostles", Christianity and Lit 49, (00): 1-14; auth, Cymbeline, MLA, (forthcoming); auth, "Qualifying the Good Steward of Shakespeare's Timon of Athens", English Studies 82, (forthcoming); auth, "Hellish Work in the Faerie Queene", Studies in English Lit 41 (forthcoming). **CONTACT ADDRESS** Dept English, Baylor Univ, Waco, PO Box 97404, Waco, TX 76798-7404. **EMAIL** maurice_hunt@baylor.edu

HUNT, PATRICK
DISCIPLINE CLASSICS **EDUCATION** BA, 77; Dallas Theol Sem, MA, 82; Univ London, PhD, 91. **CAREER** Lctr, Stanford Univ. **RESEARCH** Archaeol and papyrology. **SELECTED PUBLICATIONS** Auth, Holy Moountian, Sacred Stone, Precolumbian Art Res Inst, 94; Maya and Olmec Stone Contests: Basalt and Limestone Weathering Contrasts, Precolumbian Art Res Inst, 94; Sensory Images in the Song of Solomon, 95. **CONTACT ADDRESS** Stanford Univ, Bldg 20, Main Quad, Stanford, CA 94305.

HUNT, STEVEN B.
PERSONAL Born Dayton, OH **DISCIPLINE** COMMUNICATION **EDUCATION** Univ Kans, PhD, 73; Lewis & Clark NW Sch Law, JD, 85. **CAREER** Lewis & Clark Coll, 73-. **HONORS AND AWARDS** Editor, Pi Kappa Delta Forensic, 92-97; pres, Cross Examination Debate Asn, 94-95; Pi Kappa Delta Scholarship, 96; L E Norton award, 96. **MEMBERSHIPS** National Commun Asn; Western States Commun Asn; Phi Beta Kappa; Cross Examination Debate Asn; Am Forensics Asn. **RESEARCH** Political campaign commun; argumentation and debate; legal commun. **SELECTED PUBLICATIONS** various **CONTACT ADDRESS** Commun Dept, Lewis and Clark Col, 0615 SW Palatine Hill Rd, Portland, OR 97219. **EMAIL** hunt@lclark.edu

HUNT, TIM
PERSONAL Born 12/22/1949, Calistoga, CA, m, 1982, 2 children **DISCIPLINE** AMERICAN LITERATURE AND CREATIVE WRITING **EDUCATION** Cornell Univ, PhD. **CAREER** Prof, Wash State Univ. **RESEARCH** Modern American poetry; language and technology; textual theory; Robinson Jeffers; Jack Kerouac. **SELECTED PUBLICATIONS** Auth, Kerouac's Crooked Road: Development of a Fiction, 81; auth, Lake County Diamond, 86; ed, 5 vol, The Collected Poetry of Robinson Jeffers, 88-01. **CONTACT ADDRESS** Dept of English, Washington State Univ, 14204 Salmon Creek Ave., Vancouver, WA 98686. **EMAIL** hunt@vancouver.wsu.edu

HUNTER, DIANNE MCKINLEY
PERSONAL Born 10/04/1943, Cleveland, OH **DISCIPLINE** ENGLISH **EDUCATION** Alfred Univ, BA, 66; Purdue Univ, MA, 68; State Univ NYork, Buffalo, PhD(English), 72. **CAREER** Asst prof, 72-78, prof English, Trinity Col, Çonn, 78-89, Nat Endowment for Humanities fel, Univ Calif, 76; consult, Deakin Univ, Victoria, Australia. **MEMBERSHIPS** MLA; Int Shakespeare Assn.; Shakespeare Assoc of Am. **RESEARCH** Metatheater; psychoanalytic criticism; psychoanalysis of drama; feminism; hysteria. **SELECTED PUBLICATIONS** Auth, LeRoi Jones's Dutchman: Inter-racial ritual of sexual violence, American Imago, Fall 72 & In: The Practice of Psychoanalytic Criticism, Wayne State Univ, 76; co-ed, Gullibles Travels, Links Bks, 74; coauth (with Ian Reid), Myth in Literature and Society: Classical Antiquity, 79, auth, On Diving into the Wreck, In: The Makings of Modern Myth, 79, Is the Oedipus complex obsolescent?, In: Myth in Literature and Society: A Reader, 79 & Shakespearean mythmaking in Macbeth, In: Myth and Shakespeare: A Reader, 79, Deakin Univ Press; ed, Seduction and Theory, Univ of Ill Pr, 89; Hysteria, Psychoanalysis, and Feminism: The Case of Anna O, Writing on the Body, ed, Conboy et al, Columbia UP, 97; ed with intro and coauthor The Making of Dr Charcot's Hysteria Shows, Edwin Mellen, 98. **CONTACT ADDRESS** Dept of English, Trinity Col, Connecticut, 300 Summit St, Hartford, CT 06106-3186. **EMAIL** dhunter@mail.trincoll.edu

HUNTER, LINDA
DISCIPLINE AFRICAN LITERATURE **EDUCATION** Univ Ind, BA, 70, MA, 72, PhD, 76. **CAREER** Dept African Lang, Wisc Univ **RESEARCH** Hausa language, linguistics, and literature; language in society; stylistics. **SELECTED PUBLICATIONS** Auth, Transformation in African Verbal Art: Voice, Speech, Language, Jour Am Folklore, 96; Uvulectomy-the making of a ritual, S African Jour al of Med, 95. **CONTACT ADDRESS** Dept of African Languages and Literature, Univ of Wisconsin, Madison, 500 Lincoln Drive, Madison, WI 53706. **EMAIL** hunter@lss.wisc.edu

HURLEY, DAVID
DISCIPLINE MUSIC HISTORY AND OBOE **EDUCATION** Univ Mich, BA, 80; Univ Chicago, MA, PhD, 90, 91. **CAREER** Asst prof, 96- **RESEARCH** Seventeenth- and eighteenth-century music, G. Fl handel. **SELECTED PUBLICATIONS** Publ, articles and rev(s), The Jour of Musicol Res, The Mus Quart. **CONTACT ADDRESS** Dept of Mus, Pittsburg State Univ, 1701 S Broadway St, Pittsburg, KS 66762. **EMAIL** dhurley@pittstate.edu

HURT, JAMES RIGGINS
PERSONAL Born 05/22/1934, Ashland, KY, d, 1958, 3 children **DISCIPLINE** ENGLISH **EDUCATION** Univ Ky, AB, 56, MA, 57; Ind Univ, PhD(English), 65. **CAREER** Instr English, Univ Ky, 59-61; resident lectr, Ind Univ, 63-66; from asst prof to assoc prof, 66-73, prof English, Univ Ill, Urbana, 73-. **MEMBERSHIPS** MLA. **RESEARCH** Dramatic literature. **SELECTED PUBLICATIONS** Auth, Aelfric, Twayne, 72; Catiline's Dream: An essay on Ibsen's plays, Univ Ill, 72; Focus on Film and Theatre, Prentice, 74; Writing Illinois, Univ Ill, 92. **CONTACT ADDRESS** Univ of Illinois, Urbana-Champaign, 608 S Wright St, Urbana, IL 61801-3613. **EMAIL** j-hurt@uiuc.edu

HUSE, ANN A.
DISCIPLINE ENGLISH **EDUCATION** Amherst Col, BA, 87; Wash Univ, MA, 94; PhD. **CAREER** Res fel, Wash Univ, 99-00; asst prof, CUNY John Jay Col, 00-. **HONORS AND AWARDS** Lewis Walpole Lib Travel Fel, 01; Wash Univ

Teaching Award; Phi Beta Kappa. **MEMBERSHIPS** MLA; Renaissance Soc; SECS; NSECS; EMCS. **RESEARCH** 17th-century literature; Marvell, Milton, Dryden, Rochester; early modern women's literature; literature of the Vietnam War. **SELECTED PUBLICATIONS** Auth, "Cleopatra, Queen of the Seine: The Politics of Eroticism in Dryden's All For Love," Huntington Lib Quart 63 (00). **CONTACT ADDRESS** English Dept, John Jay Col of Criminal Justice, CUNY, 445 W 59th St, New York, NY 10019-1104. **EMAIL** aahuse@hotmail.com

HUSE, NANCY LYMAN
PERSONAL Born Newark, NJ **DISCIPLINE** ENGLISH **EDUCATION** Caldwell Col, BA, 65; Duquesne Univ, MA, 71; Chicago Univ, PhD(English), 75. **CAREER** Teacher English, Newark Archdiocesan Schs, 58-68 & District 214, Arlington Heights, Ill, 68-69; asst prof English, Augustana Col, Ill, 72-, item writer English, Educ Testing Serv, 76-; consult lit, Centrum, Inc, 77-. **HONORS AND AWARDS** Sabbatical Awd, Augustana Res Comt, 89-90; Harold T and Violet M Jaeke Awd for Leadership, Augustana, 94; Invited Keynote Speaker, The Work of Tove Jansson Conference, 94; Lois Lenski Distinguished Lecture Series, Ill State Univ, 95; Kerlan Collection Children's Lit Forum, Univ Minnesota, Letters as Literary Criticism, 94. **MEMBERSHIPS** MLA; NCTE; Children's Lit Asn; Women's Caucus, Mod Lang Asn. **RESEARCH** Adolescent literature; feminist criticism; composition. **SELECTED PUBLICATIONS** Auth, Jesus saves and sells: Popular fiction and the Messianic Forties, Proceedings Popular Cult Asn, 75; John Hersey and James Agee: A Critical Bibliography, G K Hall 78. Noel Streatfeild, Twayne's English Authors Series, MacMillan, 94; co-ed, The Critical Response to Tillie Olsen, Greenwood Press, 94; auth, Of Nancy Hanks Born: Meridel LeSueur's Abraham Lincoln, ChLA Q, Spring 93; Re-fabricating Culture, Changing Images of Women, 94-95; The Heavier Book Sack, intro to The Phoenix Award, 1990-1995, Scarecrow Press/ChLA, 95; Pioneer Myth Displaced: The Life of Rose Wilder Lane, The Lon and the Unicorn, 96. **CONTACT ADDRESS** Augustana Col, Illinois, 639 38th St, Rock Island, IL 61201-2210. **EMAIL** enhuse@augustana.edu

HUSEBOE, ARTHUR R.
PERSONAL Born 10/06/1931, Sioux Falls, SD, m, 1953 **DISCIPLINE** ENGLISH **EDUCATION** Augustana Col, BA; Univ SD, MA, 56; Ind Univ, PhD, 63. **CAREER** Instr, Univ SD, 60-61; prof to exec dir, Augustana Col, 61-. **HONORS AND AWARDS** Blue Key Nat Honor Soc, 53; Fel, Ind Univ, 57-59; D.H.L., 84; Alumni Achievement Award, Augustana Col, 85; NEH Prof of Reg Heritage, 89; Governor's Award, SD, 89. **MEMBERSHIPS** MLA; Norwegian Am Hist Asn; W Lit Asn. **RESEARCH** Restoration comedy; Western American Literature; Western American history. **SELECTED PUBLICATIONS** Auth, Poems and Essays of Herbert Frause, CWS, 90; auth, "Frederick Feikema Manfred," in Dictionary of Lit Biographies, Am Writers Asn, 99. **CONTACT ADDRESS** Dept English, Augustana Col, So Dakota, 813 E 38th St, Sioux Falls, SD 57105-5939. **EMAIL** huseboe@inst.augie.edu

HUSSEY, JOHN
DISCIPLINE ENGLISH LITERATURE **EDUCATION** Univ Detroit, AB and MA; Univ FL, PhD. **CAREER** Prof, 71-, Fairleigh Dickinson Univ. **RESEARCH** Am cult in the two decades prior to the Civil War; transcendentalists. **SELECTED PUBLICATIONS** Auth, Neighbors in Eden (vid). **CONTACT ADDRESS** Dept of English, Fairmont State Col, 1201 Locust Ave, Fairmont, WV 26554. **EMAIL** jhussy@mail.fscwv.edu

HUSSEY, MARK
PERSONAL Born 06/27/1956, London, England, m, 1992, 2 children **DISCIPLINE** ENGLISH LITERATURE **EDUCATION** Leeds Univ, BA, 78; Univ Nottingham, PhD, 82. **CAREER** Ed, English Tapes Prog, Sussex Publications, 76-82; asst to dir, Straus Thinking & Learning Ctr, 85-88; faculty, New School for Social Research, 87-90; oral Examiner, Gallatin Div., NY Univ, 88-90; faculty, Business Comm Prog, assoc prof to PROF ENGLISH, PACE UNIV, 84-; external examiner, honors thesis, Bates Col, 94; NY State Counc for the Humanities Speakers in the Humantities, 96-; **HONORS AND AWARDS** Faculty Recognition Awd, Adult Education, 92; founding editor, woolf studies annual, 94; organized first annual int virginia woolf conference at pace univ, 91 **MEMBERSHIPS** MLA, NCTE, Virginia Woolf Soc **RESEARCH** British modernism, feminist theory. **SELECTED PUBLICATIONS** Editor, Virginia Woolf Miscellany, 91-; Auth, Major Authors on CD-ROM: Virginia Woolf, Primary Source Media, 96; auth, Virginia Woolf A-Z: A Comprehensive Reference for Students, Teachers, and Common Readers to Her Life, Work and Critical Reception, Facts on File, 95; co-ed, Virginia Woolf: Emerging Perspectives. Selected Papers from the Third Annual Conference on Virginia Woolf, Pace UP, 94; auth, introduction to "Virginia Woolf: Themes and Variations. Selected Papers from the Second Annual Conference on Virginia Woolf, Pace UP, 93; auth, introduction to Virginia Woolf Miscellanies: Proceedings of the First Annual Conference on Virginia Woolf, Pace UP, 92; auth, "To the Lighthouse and Physics: The Corresponding Worlds of Virginia Woolf and David Bohm," in New Essays on Virginia Woolf, Contemporary Research Press, 95; auth, "A Violent Hunger for Lost Feelings," in Central Park, special issue, Spring 93; auth, "Refractions of Desire: The Early Fiction of Virginia and Leonard Woolf," in Modern Fiction Studies 38, Spring 92; auth, review of Defending Pornography: Free Speech, Sex, and the Fight for Women's Rights, in On the Issues, Summer 95; auth, review of Virginia Woolf: Critical Assessments, in Woolf Studies Annual, Routledge, 94; auth, review of No Man's Land and Letters from the Front in New York Times Book Review, Nov 6, 94. **CONTACT ADDRESS** Dept of English, Pace Univ, New York, 1 Pace Plaza, New York, NY 10038. **EMAIL** mhussey@pace.edu

HUSSMAN, LAWRENCE
PERSONAL Born 03/20/1932, Dayton, OH, d, 2 children **DISCIPLINE** ENGLISH; AMERICAN LITERATURE **EDUCATION** Univ Dayton, BA, 54; Univ Mich, MA, 57; EdD, 64. **CAREER** Asst prof, Univ Portland, 61-65; asst to full prof Emeritus, Wright State Univ, 65-93. **HONORS AND AWARDS** NEH grant, 84; Fulbright Teaching Awd, Poland, 93-94. **MEMBERSHIPS** MLA **RESEARCH** American literary naturalism. **SELECTED PUBLICATIONS** Auth, Dreiser and his Fiction: A Twentieth Century Quest, Univ Penn Press, (83); auth, Harbingers of a Century: The Novels of Frank Norris, Peter Lang, (99). **CONTACT ADDRESS** Dept English, Wright State Univ, Dayton, 440 Green St, Yellow Springs, OH 45387.

HUSTON, JOHN DENNIS
PERSONAL Born 09/21/1939, New York, NY, m, 1964, 2 children **DISCIPLINE** ENGLISH LITERATURE **EDUCATION** Wesleyan Univ, BA, 61; Yale Univ, MA, 64, PhD(English), 66. **CAREER** From instr to asst prof English, Yale Univ, 66-69; assoc prof, 69-79, PROF ENGLISH, RICE UNIV, 79- **MEMBERSHIPS** S Cent Mod Lang Asn; MLA. **RESEARCH** Elizabethan drama; Spenser; English Renaissance drama and poetry. **SELECTED PUBLICATIONS** Co-ed, Classics of the Renaissance Theater, Harcourt, 69; auth, The function of the mock hero in Spenser's Faerie Queene, Mod Philol, 2/69; Twelfth night and problems of identity, Mod Lang Quart, 9/72; Bottom waking, Studies English Lit 1500-1900, spring 73; To Make A Puppet, Shakespeare Studies, IX, 76; auth, Shakespeare's comedies of play, Columbia & Macmillan, 81. **CONTACT ADDRESS** Dept of English, Rice Univ, Houston, TX 77001.

HUTCHEON, LINDA
PERSONAL Born Toronto, ON, Canada **DISCIPLINE** ENGLISH, COMPARATIVE LITERATURE **EDUCATION** Cornell Univ , MA, 71; Univ Toronto, BA, 69, PhD, 75. **CAREER** Asst prof, 76-82, assoc prof, 82-85, prof, McMaster Univ, 85-88; Prof English, Univ Toronto, 88-. **HONORS AND AWARDS** Woodrow Wilson Fel, 69-79; Killam Postdoc fel, 78-79; John P. Robarts Ch Can Studs, 88-89; Guggenheim Fel, 92-93. **MEMBERSHIPS** MLA; Int Comp Lit Asn; Can Comp Lit Asn; Toronto Semiotic Circle; Ctr Italian Can Studs; Asn Can Col Univs Tchrs Eng. **RESEARCH** Interdisciplinary methodologies; comparative literary history. **SELECTED PUBLICATIONS** Auth, Narcissistic Narrative: The Metafictional Paradox, 80; auth, Formalism and the Freudian Aesthetic, 84; auth, A Theory of Parody, 85; auth, A Poetics of Postmodernism , 88; auth, The Canadian Postmodern: A Study of Contemporary English-Canadian Fiction, 88; auth, The Politics of Postmodernism, 89; auth, Irony's Edge: The Theory and Politics of Irony, 95; coauth, Opera: Desire, Disease, Death, 96; auth, Bodily charm: Living Opera, 00. **CONTACT ADDRESS** Dept of English, Univ of Toronto, Toronto, ON, Canada M5S 1A1.

HUTCHESON, THOM
DISCIPLINE MUSIC **EDUCATION** Univ Tex-El Paso, BA; Northwestern Univ, MA; Fla State Univ, PhD. **CAREER** Dept Muis, Middle Tenn State Univ **HONORS AND AWARDS** Composer-of-the-Yr, Tenn Mus Teachers Asn. **MEMBERSHIPS** Past dir, Amer Soc Univ Composers. **SELECTED PUBLICATIONS** Auth, Synvironment, Atlanta Int Film Festival; The Tightrope Walker March, for Concert Band; Macarena, for Jazz Ensemble & Multiphonix, for Percussion Ensemble. **CONTACT ADDRESS** Dept of Music, Middle Tennessee State Univ, 1301 E Main St, Murfreesboro, TN 37132-0001. **EMAIL** lthutch@frank.mtsu.edu

HUTCHINGS, WILLIAM
PERSONAL Born 09/13/1950, Lexington, KY, s **DISCIPLINE** TWENTIETH CENTURY BRITISH FICTION AND DRAMA **EDUCATION** Transylvania Univ, AB, 72; Univ of Kentucky, MA, 74; PhD, 81. **CAREER** Dept Eng, Univ Ala, 81-. **MEMBERSHIPS** MLA, 72-; James Joyce Foundation, Samuel Beckett Soc, Harold Pinter Soc. **SELECTED PUBLICATIONS** Auth, The Plays of David Storey: A Thematic Study, Southern Ill, 88; David Storey: A Casebook, Garland, 92. **CONTACT ADDRESS** Univ of Alabama, Birmingham, 1400 University Blvd, Birmingham, AL 35294-1150. **EMAIL** whutc3712@aol.com

HUTCHINS, CHRISTINE ELLEN
DISCIPLINE ENGLISH **EDUCATION** SUNY Buffalo, BA, 88; Columbia Univ, MA, 89; CUNY Grad Cen, PhD, 99. **CAREER** Asst prof, E Car Univ, 99-. **HONORS AND AWARDS** Col Arts Science Res Awd, ECar Univ, 01. **MEMBERSHIPS** MLA; SAA; RSA. **RESEARCH** 16th-century English print literature; drama; national identity. **CONTACT ADDRESS** English Dept, East Carolina Univ, 2201 Bate Bldg, Greenville, NC 27858. **EMAIL** hutchinsc@mail.ecu.edu

HUTCHINSON, KEVIN
DISCIPLINE COMMUNICATION **EDUCATION** Univ Richmond, BA, 75; Central Mich Univ, MA, 76; Univ Miss Columbia, PhD, 79. **CAREER** TA to instr, Univ of Miss Columbia, 76-79; instr, Columbia Col, 78; asst prof Univ of Maine Orono, 79-82; vis prof Macquarie Univ, 94; asst prof to prof, St Norbert Col, 82-. **HONORS AND AWARDS** Who's who Among Students in am Col and Univ, 74-75, 78-79; Outstanding Grad Student Teaching Awd, Univ of Miss, 77-78; Delta Epsilon Sigma, 95; Donald B. King Distinguished Scholar Awd, 95; Lambda Pi Eta, 98; Leonard Levina Outstanding Teaching Awd, St. Norbert Col, 98. **MEMBERSHIPS** Nat Commun Assoc; Int Commun Assoc. **SELECTED PUBLICATIONS** Coauth, "Body Accessibility re-revisited: The 60s, 70s, and 80s", Handbook of replication research in the behavioral and social sciences, ed J. Neuliep, Select Pr, (Corte Madera, 90): 341-352; coauth, "The effects of interviewer gender upon response bias in telephone survey research", J of Soc Behav and Personality 6.3 (91): 573-584; ed, Readings in organizational communication, Wm C. Brown Pub, (Dubuque, IA), 92; coauth, "The influence of parent modeling and peer modeling on the development of communication apprehension in elementary school children", Commun Quarterly 41.1 (93): 16-25; coauth, "Second thoughts about the measurement of communication apprehension at the elementary school level", Commun Rep 6.2 (93): 1-5; coauth, "The effects of eyeglasses upon perceptions of interpersonal attraction", J of Soc Behav and Personality 8.3 (93): 1-8; auth, "Encouraging undergraduate scholarship: Institutional strategies", J of the Assoc for Commun Admin 2 (94): 110-114; coauth, "Communication apprehension across cultures: A test of the PRCA-24 and comparisons between Australia and the United States", Australian J of Commun 22.1 (95): 1-9; auth, "Personnel administrator's preferences for resume content: Ten years after", Business Commun Quarterly 60.2 (97): 67-75; coauth, "Building trust through strategic planning", Planning for Higher Educ 27.2 (99): 21-27. **CONTACT ADDRESS** Dept Humanities and Fine Arts, St. Norbert Col, 100 Grant St, De Pere, WI 54115-2002. **EMAIL** hutckl@sncac.snc.edu

HUTCHISSON, JAMES M.
DISCIPLINE ENGLISH **EDUCATION** Radford Univ, BA, 82; Vir Poly Inst, MA, 84; Univ Del, PhD, 87. **CAREER** Asst prof, Wash Jeff Coll, 87-89; asst prof, Citadel, 89-94, assoc prof, 94-99, prof, 99-. **HONORS AND AWARDS** Phi Kappa Phi; Cit Fac Achiev Awd, 92, 95, 98; Sab Leave Gnt, 96-97; Univ Del, Diss Fel, 86-87. **MEMBERSHIPS** NLA; ALA; SSSL. **RESEARCH** American literature; Southern literature; contemporary British novels. **SELECTED PUBLICATIONS** Auth, "Poe, Anna Cora Mowatt, and T Tennyson Twinkle," Stud Am Renaissance 22 (93): 245-54; auth, "The Reviews: Evolution of a Critic," in A Companion to Poe Studies, ed. Eric W Carison (Westport, CT: Greenwood Press, 96), 296-22; auth, "Death and Dying in Jennie Gerhardt," in New Essays on Dreiser's Jennie Gerhardt, ed. James L W West III (Phil: Univ Penn Press, 95), 208-17; auth, "Dorothy Heyward: In the Shadow of Porgy," Carologue 15 (99): 3; ed, "Babbitt," by Sinclair Lewis, (NY: Penguin, 95); auth, "The Revision of Dreiser's Financier," J Mod Lit 20 (97): 201-15; auth, "Nathan West, Contempo Magazine, and The Composition of Miss Lonelyhearts," Reso Am Lit Study 24 (98): 84-100; ed, Sinclair Lewis: New Essays In Criticism, Whitston (Troy, NY: 97); auth, The Rise of Sinclair Lewis, 1920-1930, Penn State Univ Press (Univ Park, PA), 96; auth, DuBose Heyward: A Charleston Gentleman and The World of Porgy and Bess, Univ Press of Miss (Jackson, MS), 00. **CONTACT ADDRESS** Dept English, The Citadel, The Military Col of So Carolina, 171 Moultrie St, Charleston, SC 29409-0001. **EMAIL** hutchisson@citadel.edu

HUTTAR, CHARLES ADOLPH
PERSONAL Born 07/08/1932, Austin, TX, m, 1952, 7 children **DISCIPLINE** ENGLISH **EDUCATION** Wheaton Col, BA, 52; Northwestern Univ, MA, 53, PhD(English), 56. **CAREER** From asst prof to assoc prof English, Gordon Col, 55-66, from actg chmn to chmn dept, 55-66; chmn dept, 71-76, PROF ENGLISH, HOPE COL, 66-, Ed, Gordon Rev, 57 & 59, chmn, 65-66; Folger Shakespeare Libr grant-in-aid, 61; Am Philos Soc Penrose grant, 67, Johnson Fund grant, 78. **MEMBERSHIPS** MLA; Renaissance Soc Am; Conf Christianity & Lit (secy, 58-60; pres, 66-68); Milton Soc Am. **RESEARCH** Popular religious literature 1500-1700; Renaissance poetry. **SELECTED PUBLICATIONS** Auth, Poems by Surrey and others in a printed miscellany circa 1550, English Miscellany, 65; Wyatt and the several editions of The Court of Venus, Studies Bibliog, 66; The Christian basis of Shakespeare's Sonnet 146, Shakespeare Quart, 68; ed, Imagination and the Spirit, Eerdmans, 71; contribr, A Tolkien Compass, Open Court, 75; auth, Hymns, worship, and devotion, Reformed Rev, 75; contribr, The Longing for a Form: Essays in the Fiction of C S Lewis, Kent State Univ, 77; The Myth of David in Western Literature, Purdue Univ, (in press). **CONTACT ADDRESS** Dept of English, Hope Col, Holland, MI 49423.

HUTTENSTINE, MARIAN L.
PERSONAL Born 01/26/1940, PA, s **DISCIPLINE** MASS COMMUNICATION; ENGLISH EDUCATION **EDUCATION** Bloomsburg State Univ, BS, 61, MEd, 67; Univ of NC at Chapel Hill, PhD, 85. **CAREER** Tchr, Lake-Lehman High School, 61-63; dept ch Engl, Lake-Lehman High School, 63-66; instr, Lock Haven State Univ, 66-70; from asst prof to assoc prof, Lock Haven State Univ, 70-74; tchg asst, Univ of NC, 74-75; lectr, Univ of NC, 75-77; asst prof, Univ of Ala, 77-93; adj instr, Shelton State Comm Col, 93; assoc prof, Jacksonville State Univ, 93-95; assoc prof, Radford Univ, 95-97; dept head and assoc prof, Miss State Univ, 97-98, prof, 98-. **HONORS AND AWARDS** Newspaper Fund fel, 62; Nat Defense Educ fel, 63; Int Who's Who of Women, 84, 89, 91, 93; Who's Who of World, 84, 89, 91; Who's Who of Am Women, 85, 87, 89, 91, 93; Student Press Freedom Serv Awd, Ala Student Press Asn, 92; Sara Healey, Media Planning Bd Serv Awd, UA, 92; First Amendment Awd, Ala Media Professionals, 92; Cardinal Key Hon Soc, Hon Membership, 93; The Ken Knight Founder's Awd, Minorities for Careers in Commun, 93; Who's Who in the South and Southwest, 80, 82, 84, cont.; Who's Who of Personalities in the South, 81, 83, 85, 87, 89, 92, 94, 96; Who's Who in Commun and Entertainment, 95, 97; Who's Who in Education, 96, 98; Who's Who in the Media and Commun, 98; communicator of achievement, ala media professionals, 94. **MEMBERSHIPS** Nat Commun Asn; Asn for Educ in Journalism and Mass Commun; Investigative Reporters and Edits; Kappa Tau Alpha, Nat Fedn of Press Women; Ala Media Professionals; Miss Speech Commun Asn; Soc of Professional Journalists; Nat Asn of Exec Females; ACLU; PRAM. **RESEARCH** Commun Law, espec privacy, intellectual property, institutional liability; Journalism, espec writing styles; Media effectiveness, espec story structure effectiveness. **SELECTED PUBLICATIONS** Auth, Everywoman in the Journals of Joyce Maynard, 91; New roles, new problems, new concerns, NEW LAW, Southern Public Relations Jour 1/1, 93; coauth, How Public Relations Professionals View Men and Women Expert Source Credibility, 90; Nightmare in Copyright Law, 90; ADA: The Civil Rights Act for All, 92. **CONTACT ADDRESS** Dept of Communication, Mississippi State Univ, McComas Hall, PO Box PF, Mississippi State, MS 39762. **EMAIL** mhuttenstine@comm.msstate.edu

HUTTON, WILLIAM E.
PERSONAL Born 07/26/1961, Bellefonte, PA, m, 1991 **DISCIPLINE** CLASSICS **EDUCATION** Penn State Univ, BA, 82; Univ Tex Austin, MA, 85; PhD, 95. **CAREER** Vis asst prof, Univ Wis Madison, 91-92; instr, Univ Calgary, 92-96; vis asst prof, Truman State Univ, 96-97; vis asst prof, Coll of William and Mary, 97-. **HONORS AND AWARDS** Phi Beta Kappa; Phi Alpha Theta; Phi Kappa Phi; James R Wheeler Fel; Jacob Hirsch Fel; Eugene Vaderpool Fel, Am School of Classical Studies in Athens. **MEMBERSHIPS** Am Philol Asn; Archaeol Inst of Am; Classical Asn of the Middle W and S; Classical Asn of Va. **RESEARCH** Greek Prose; Greek History; Greek Historiography; Greek topography. **SELECTED PUBLICATIONS** Auth, The Meaning of ge-te-o in Linear B, Minos, 90-91. **CONTACT ADDRESS** Dept of Classical Studies, Col of William and Mary, Box 8795, Williamsburg, VA 23185-8795. **EMAIL** wehutt@wm.edu

HUXMAN, SUSAN S.
DISCIPLINE COMMUNICATION STUDIES **EDUCATION** Univ Kans, PhD. **CAREER** Asst prof, Wake Forest Univ; dir, basic course, Wichita State Univ; assoc prof-. **HONORS AND AWARDS** Awds tchg excellence, Univ Kans. **RESEARCH** Rhetorical criticism. **SELECTED PUBLICATIONS** Publ, in the field of rhetorical criticism and American Public. **CONTACT ADDRESS** Wichita State Univ, 1845 Fairmont, Wichita, KS 67260-0062. **EMAIL** shuxman@elliott.es.twsu.edu

HUYETT, PATRICIA
PERSONAL Born 04/27/1951, s **DISCIPLINE** ENGLISH **EDUCATION** Univ Mo at Kans City, BA; Univ Mo, MA. **CAREER** Prof, Kans city Art Inst, 84-91; coord of unity assessment, Univ Mo, 92-. **HONORS AND AWARDS** Sosland Awd for Teaching; Curators Fel. **MEMBERSHIPS** Nat Coun Teachers of English, Phi Kappa Phi. **RESEARCH** Writing Assessment, Student Portfolio. **SELECTED PUBLICATIONS** Auth, Eldorado Rosa: Voices from Midtown, Arvada House Press, 99; auth, "Stimulating Faculty Interest in Portfolios," Assessment in Practice; auth "Dymphia's Daughters," Survivor, 99. **CONTACT ADDRESS** Dept English, Univ of Missouri, Kansas City, 5100 Rockhill Rd, Kansas City, MO 64110-2446. **EMAIL** phuyett@umkc.edu

HYBELS, SAUNDRA
DISCIPLINE JOURNALISM **EDUCATION** Western Mich Univ, BA, 61; Univ Pa, MAC, 62; Univ Mich, PhD, 71. **CAREER** Asst prof, Jackson State Univ, 69-73; asst prof, Ithaca Col, 73-76; prof, Lock Haven Univ Pa, 76-; bd mem, Ross Libr. **HONORS AND AWARDS** NEH fel, Claremont Univ, 81; NEH fel, Univ Md, 86, Fullbright lectr, Fed States of Micronesia, 88-89; Johnson Found grant, 90; grant, State Syst of Higher Educ, 93; Who's Who in the East, 95; Fullbright Lectureship, Albania, 95. **MEMBERSHIPS** Asn for Educ in Jour and Mass Commun; Popular Cult Asn. **SELECTED PUBLICATIONS** Coauth, Speech Communication, D. Van Nostrand, 74; Broadcasting: An Introduction, D. Van Nostrand, 78; auth, Polish Gardens, Christian Sci Monitor, 87; The Listener, in Sam G. Riley, ed, Consumer Magazines of the British Isles, Greenwood Press, 93; Communicating Effectively, 4th ed, McGraw-Hill, 95. **CONTACT ADDRESS** Journalism Dept, Lock Haven Univ of Pennsylvania, Lock Haven, PA 17745. **EMAIL** shybels@eagle.lhup.edu

HYDE, VIRGINIA CROSSWHITE
PERSONAL Born Emporia, KS, m, 1987 **DISCIPLINE** ENGLISH **EDUCATION** Ariz State Univ, BA, 68; Univ Wis-Madison, PhD(English), 71. **CAREER** Asst prof, 70-75, assoc prof English, 75-93, Prof, Wash State Univ, Pullman, 93-. **MEMBERSHIPS** MLA; AAUP; Int Arthurian Soc; Browning Inst; D H Lawrence Soc of North Am; Phi Kappa Phi. **RESEARCH** Victorian poetry and fiction; early 20th century poetry and fiction; especially D H Lawrence; Authurian literature and art; religion and myth in literature. **SELECTED PUBLICATIONS** Auth, Heroes and ideology in Middlemarch, Papers on Language and Literature, 88; auth, The Risen Adam, D H Lawrence's Revisionist Typology, Penn State Univ, 92; contribr, Introduction and Essay, In, Women and the Journey, The Female Travel Experience, Wash State Univ, 93; contribr, Essay, In; Images of Persephone; Feminist Readings in Western Literature, Univ Press of Florida, 94; contribr, Introduction, Lawrences's The Plumed Serpent, Penguin, 95; ed with L D Clark, Lawrence's The Plumed Serpent, Penguin, 95; auth, Variants Covers of The Secret Rose, Yeats Annual, 98; auth, The sense of an ending in The Plumed Serpent with L D Clark, D H Lawrence Rev, 93-94; auth, Kate and the goddess, Subtexts in The Plumed Serpent, D H Lawrence Rev, 95-96; ed, A Prairie Soul, Poems of Hazel Clawson Crosswhite, Professional Press of Chapel Hill, 98; contrib, Essays, In, Approaches to Teaching D H Lawrence, MLA, 00; ed, Lawrence's Mornings in Mexico and Other Essays, Cambridge Univ, 2001 (contracted). **CONTACT ADDRESS** Dept of English, Washington State Univ, 1 SE Stadium Way, PO Box 645020, Pullman, WA 99164-5020. **EMAIL** hydev@wsunix.wsu.edu

HYDE, WILLIAM JAMES
PERSONAL Born 11/28/1924, Milwaukee, WI, m, 1950 **DISCIPLINE** ENGLISH **EDUCATION** Univ Wis, BS, 46; MA, 47; PhD, 53. **CAREER** Instr English, Univ Wis, Milwaukee, 46-47, Western Reserve Univ, 47-48 & State Univ Wash, 48-50; asst prof, Trinity Univ, San Antonio, 53-56; chmn dept, 60-64 & 67-72, prof, english, Univ Wis-La Crosse, 56-92, prof emeritus, 92-. **HONORS AND AWARDS** Honor Ten, Univ Wis, Milwaukee, 46; Knapp fel, Univ Wis, Madison, 52-53. **MEMBERSHIPS** MLA; Tennyson Soc. **RESEARCH** English novel; Victorian literature and history. **SELECTED PUBLICATIONS** Auth, "'Poor Frederick' and 'Poor Peter': Elizabeth Gaskell's Fraternal Deviants," The Gaskell Soc Journal 9 (95): 21-26; auth, "The Socialism of H.G. Wells in the Early Twentieth Century," Jour of the History of Ideas 17 (56): 217-234; auth, "George Eliot and the Climate of Realism," PMLA 72 (57): 147-164; auth, "Hardy's View of Realism: A Key to the Rustic Characters," Victorian Studies 2 (58): 45-59; auth, "Hardy's Response to the Critics of Jude," Victorian Newsletter 19 (61): 1-5; auth, "Jeanie Deans and the Queen: Appearance and Reality," Nineteenth-Century Fiction 28 (73): 86-92; auth, "The 'Craze for Collecting:' A Note on Hardy and Byron," Thomas Hardy Year Book19 (92): 63-65; auth, "Distinctive Realism: Wife Beating in Three Tales of the Victorian English Peasantry by Richard Jefferies," Victorian Review 25.1 (99): 50-63. **CONTACT ADDRESS** Dept of English, Univ of Wisconsin, La Crosse, La Crosse, WI 54601.

HYMAN, ROGER L.
DISCIPLINE ENGLISH LITERATURE **EDUCATION** York Univ, BA; Univ Toronto, MA, PhD. **RESEARCH** English-Canadian fiction; the novel. **SELECTED PUBLICATIONS** Art, Queen's Quarterly; art, Journal of Canadian Studies. **CONTACT ADDRESS** English Dept, McMaster Univ, 1280 Main St W, Hamilton, ON, Canada L8S 4L9. **EMAIL** hymanr@mcmaster.ca

HYNES, JENNIFER
DISCIPLINE ENGLISH **EDUCATION** Texas A&M, BS, 88; MA, 92; Univ So Carol, PhD, 96. **CAREER** Vis Inst, Eng, Univ W VA; inst, Univ SC. **MEMBERSHIPS** Am Antiquarian Soc **CONTACT ADDRESS** Col of Independent Learning, Univ of So Carolina, Columbia, Columbia, SC 29208. **EMAIL** jahynes@vm.sc.edu

HYNES, THOMAS J., JR.
PERSONAL Born 11/19/1949, Brighton, MA, d, 1 child **DISCIPLINE** COMMUNICATION STUDIES **EDUCATION** Univ Mass, BS, 71, PhD, 76; Univ NC- Chapel Hill, MA, 72. **CAREER** Full-time faculty member of Baylor Univ, Univ Louisville, and State Univ W Ga; Guest lecturer at over a dozen universities. **HONORS AND AWARDS** Outstanding Young Men of America: Debate Coach of the Year, 82, 83; Campus Impact Awd, Univ Louisville, 84; Oustanding Administrative Performance Awd, Univ Louisville, 90; Distinguished Service Awd, Jefferson County Public Sch, 96. **MEMBERSHIPS** Am Forensic Asn; Int Commun Asn; Southern Speech Commun Asn; Speech Commun Asn; Int Soc Study Argumentation; Am Asn Higher Educ; Coun Undergraduate Res. **RESEARCH** Argument and public policy; higher education and communication. **SELECTED PUBLICATIONS** Coauth, American Educational Reform, Nat Textbook Co, 81; What Price Defense, Nat Textbook Co, 82; One Justice for All, Nat Textbook Co, 83; An End to Poverty, Nat Textbook Co, 84; Not a Drop to Drink, Nat Textbook Co, 85; American Agricultural Policy, Nat Textbook Co, 86; auth, Paths to Peace in Latin America, Nat Textbook Co, 87; Counterplan: Theory and Practice, Griffin Press, 87; Aging in America, Nat Textbook Co, 88; The Last Frontier, Nat Textbook Co, 90; author of numerous articles and book chapters. **CONTACT ADDRESS** Vice President for Acad Affairs, State Univ of West Georgia, Carrollton, GA 30118. **EMAIL** thynes@westga.edu

I

IACOBUCCI, CHRISTINE
DISCIPLINE COMMUNICATION STUDIES **EDUCATION** Univ Albany, PhD. **CAREER** Asst prof. **SELECTED PUBLICATIONS** Auth, pubs on language use in social interactions, computer mediated communication, and human-computer interaction. **CONTACT ADDRESS** Dept of Communication, Ithaca Col, 100 Job Hall, Ithaca, NY 14850.

IADONISI, RICHARD A.
PERSONAL Born 11/09/1958, Dedham, MA **DISCIPLINE** ENGLISH **EDUCATION** Framingham State Col, BA 82; Boston Col, MA, 85; Ind Univ, PhD, 99. **CAREER** Instr, Framingham State Col, 87-89; foreign expert, S China Univ of Tech, 89-90; vis asst prof, Grand Valley State Univ, 94-. **MEMBERSHIPS** MLA, NCTE, Richard Wright Circle. **RESEARCH** American poetry, theories of otherness, theories of masculinities. **SELECTED PUBLICATIONS** Auth, "Bleeding History and Owning His (Father's) Story: Maus and Collaborative Autobiography," CEA Critic, (94); auth, "(In)Felicitous Space: The Interior Landscape of 'Snow,'" Robert Frost Rev, (96); auth, "Allen Ginsberg," Encycl of Am Poetry: The Twentieth Century, (01). **CONTACT ADDRESS** Grand Valley State Univ, 1 Campus Dr, Allendale, MI 49426. **EMAIL** iadonisr@gvsu.edu

IBELEMA, MINABERE
PERSONAL Born 12/09/1954, Bonny, Rivers State, Nigeria, m, 1994 **DISCIPLINE** JOURNALISM **EDUCATION** Wilberforce University, Wilberforce, OH, BA, 1979; Ohio State University, Columbus, OH, MA, 1980, PhD, 1984. **CAREER** Central State University, Wilberforce, OH, associate professor, 84-91; Eastern Illinois University, Charleston, IL, associate professor, 91-. **HONORS AND AWARDS** Honorable Mention, Munger Africana Library, African Thesis Competition, California Institute of Technology, 1982. **MEMBERSHIPS** NAACP member, association for Education in Journalism and Mass Communication, 1987-; member, Central States Communication Association, 1987-; member, Popular Culture Association, 1986-; corresponding secretary, American Association of University Professors, Central State University Chapter, 1990-. **SELECTED PUBLICATIONS** Author, Tribes and Prejudice: Coverage of the Nigerian Civil War, chapter in Africa's Media Image, 1991; author, Identity Crisis: The African Connection in African-American Sitcom Characters, chapter in Sexual Politics and Popular Culture, 1990. **CONTACT ADDRESS** Dept of Journalism, Eastern Illinois Univ, Buzzard Bldg, Charleston, IL 61920.

IMBODEN, ROBERTA
PERSONAL Born Buffalo, NY **DISCIPLINE** ENGLISH **EDUCATION** Mercyhurst Col, BA, 56, MA, 61; Univ Toronto, MA, 77. **CAREER** Instr and adj prof, Ryerson Polytechnic Univ, 65-. **MEMBERSHIPS** Can Hermeneutical Postmodern Soc. **SELECTED PUBLICATIONS** Auth, From the Cross to the Kingdom: Sartrean Dialectics and Liberation Theology, 87; auth, The Church, A Demon Lover: A Sartrean Critique of an Institution, 95. **CONTACT ADDRESS** Dept of English, Ryerson Polytech Univ, 350 Victoria St, Toronto, ON, Canada M5B 2K3. **EMAIL** rimboden@acs.ryerson.ca

IMBRIE, ANN ELIZABETH
PERSONAL Born 11/09/1950, Columbus, OH **DISCIPLINE** RENAISSANCE LITERATURE, LITERARY THEORY **EDUCATION** Smith Col, AB, 72; Univ NC, Chapel Hill, MA, 74, PhD(English), 79. **CAREER** Instr lit & writing, Univ NC, 78-79; ASST PROF ENGLISH, VASSAR COL, 79-, Nat Endowment for the Humanities fel, Brown Univ, 81-82. **MEMBERSHIPS** MLA. **RESEARCH** Nondramatic Renaissance literature, especially 17th century prose; Shakespeare; Renaissance literary theory and literary theory generally. **SELECTED PUBLICATIONS** Auth, What Shalimar Knew--Morrison, Toni 'Song of Solomon' as a Pastoral Novel, Col Engl, Vol 0055, 93. **CONTACT ADDRESS** Dept of English, Vassar Col, 124 Raymond Ave, Box 744, Poughkeepsie, NY 12604. **EMAIL** imbrie@vassar.edu

INBODEN, ROBIN L.
PERSONAL Born 03/02/1957, Logan, OH, m, 1994 **DISCIPLINE** LITERATURE **EDUCATION** Cornell Univ, PhD, 85, MA, 82; Kenyon Col, AB, 79 **CAREER** Dept Chair, 00-, Assoc Prof, 92-, Asst Prof, 89-92, Wittenberg Univ; Asst Prof, 85-89, Transylvania Univ **HONORS AND AWARDS** Sampson Excel in Tch Awd; phi beta kappa; nat merit schol **RESEARCH** Victorian lit; Romantic lit; Classic Hollywood Cinema **SELECTED PUBLICATIONS** Auth, "'The Valour of Delicate Women': The Domestication of Political Relations in Tennyson's Laureate Poetry," Victorian Poetry (98); auth, "The Ballad and History: Wordsworth's White Doe of Rylstone," in Selected Papers in Medievalism, ed Rebecca Cochran and James Goebel, Indiana Univ of Penn, 88. **CONTACT ADDRESS** Dept of English, Wittenberg Univ, PO Box 720, Springfield, OH 45501. **EMAIL** rinboden@wittenberg.edu

INGE, M. THOMAS
PERSONAL Born 01/18/1936, Newport News, VA, m, 2 children **DISCIPLINE** ENGLISH, LITERATURE **EDUCATION** Randolph Macon Col, BA, 59; Vanderbilt Univ, MA, 60; PhD, 64. **CAREER** Instr, Vanderbilt Univ, 62-64; asst prof, assoc prof, prof, Mich State Univ, 64-69; assoc prof, prof, ch, Virginia Commonwealth Univ, 69-80; dept hd, prof, Clemson Univ, 80-82; res schl, USIA, 82-84; ch, 84-, Randolph Macon Univ. **HONORS AND AWARDS** Fulbright-Hays Fel, 67, 71, 79, 88, 94; NEH Fel; Cragie Grants; Newberry Lib Stud Gnt; NEH Trv Gnt; Mednick Fel; SREB Gnt; VFH Gnt; USIA Gnt. **SELECTED PUBLICATIONS** Coauth, Russian Eyes on American Literature, (MS, 93); auth, Dark Laughter: The Satiric Art of Oliver W Harrington, (MS, 93); rev, "Why I left America and other Essays," by Oliver W Harrington (MS, 93); auth, William Faulkner: The Contemporary Reviews, Cambridge Univ Press, 94; auth, Sut Lovingood's Nat'ral Born Yarnspinner: Essays on George Washington Harris, (AL, 96); co rev, A Connecticut Yankee in King Arthur's Court, by Mark Twain (Oxford, 97); auth, Conversations with William Faulkner, (MS), 99; rev, Co Ayvtch, or a Side Show of the Big Show, by Samuel R Watkins, penguin, 99. **CONTACT ADDRESS** Dept Humanities, Randolph-Macon Col, PO Box 5005, Ashland, TX 23005-5505.

INGEBRETSEN, EDWARD J.
DISCIPLINE ENGLISH LITERATURE **EDUCATION** Loyola Univ, BA, MA; Duke Univ, PhD. **CAREER** Eng Dept, Georgetown Univ **RESEARCH** Edward American literature. **SELECTED PUBLICATIONS** Auth, Writing the Unholy: Lovecraft, Theology, and the 'Perfection of the Horrible', Fractal, 94; Psalms of the Still Country, 82; To Keep From Singing, 85; Love's Sentence: Domesticity as Religious Discourse in Robert Frost's Poetry, 89. **CONTACT ADDRESS** English Dept, Georgetown Univ, 37th and O St, Washington, DC 20057.

INGERSOLL, EARL G.
PERSONAL Born 05/06/1938, Spencerport, NY, m, 1960, 2 children **DISCIPLINE** ENGLISH **EDUCATION** Univ Wisc Madison, PhD. **CAREER** Prof English, SUNY Col at Brockport, 64 to pres; dept adv, English Majors, 81-89; mem, Dept Constitution Rev Comt, 80-82; participant, Commun Skills Workshops, 80-84; mem, Dept APT Comt, 79-80, 82-83, 92-93, 95-98, chmn, APT Comt, 89-90, 95-96; Dept Scheduler, 75-86; mem, Student Appeals Rev Comt, 72-73, 80-81, 95-96, 98-; mem, Dept Curriculum Comt, 71-86, chmn, 72-73, 80-81, 98-. **MEMBERSHIPS** MLA; Col English Asn; NY Col English Asn; D.H. Lawrence Soc of N Am; Margaret Atwood Soc; Lawrence Durrell Soc; Doris Lessing Soc. **RESEARCH** 19th and 20th century British literature; Irish literature; Canadian literature. **SELECTED PUBLICATIONS** Auth, Lawrence Durrell: Conversations, 98; Engendered Trope in Joyce's Dubliners, 96; Putting the Question Differently, 96; Doris Lessing: Conversations, 94; Representations of Science and Technology in British Literature Since 1880, 92; Conversations with May Sarton, 91; Margaret Atwood: Conversations, 90, rev, 92; coauth, The Post-Confessionals: Conversations with American Poets of the Eighties, 89, 92. **CONTACT ADDRESS** 173 Dewey St., Churchville, NY 14428. **EMAIL** eingerso@po.brockport.edu

INGLES, ERNIE B.
PERSONAL Born 12/30/1948, Calgary, AB, Canada **DISCIPLINE** BIBLIOGRAPHY, HISTORY **EDUCATION** Univ Calgary, BA, 70, MA, 73; Univ BC, MLS, 75. **CAREER** Head, Rare Bks & Spec Coll, Univ Calgary, 74-84; univ librn, Univ Regina, 84-90; dir libRs, 90-95, Assoc Vice Pres Learning Systems, Univ Alberta, 95-. **HONORS AND AWARDS** Marie Tremaine Medal Bibliog; Ruth Cameron Medal; Int Lib Sci Honour Soc, 74. **MEMBERSHIPS** Can Libr Asn; Bibliog Soc Can; Can Asn Col Univ Librs; Can Asn Res Librs. **SELECTED PUBLICATIONS** Auth, Canada: The Printed Record, 81, 82, 83, 84; auth, Canada: World Bibliography Series, 90; auth, Bibliography of Canadian Bibliographies, 94. **CONTACT ADDRESS** Univ of Alberta, University Hall 3-16, Edmonton, AB, Canada T6G 2J9. **EMAIL** ernie.ingles@ualberta.ca

INGRAHAM, VERNON LELAND
PERSONAL Born 10/01/1924, Milfrod, NH, d, 3 children **DISCIPLINE** ENGLISH **EDUCATION** Univ NH, BA, 49; Amherst Col, MA, 51; Univ PA, PhD(English), 65. **CAREER** Instr English, Univ Del, 60-62, Haverford Col, 62-63 & Gettysburg Col, 63-65; from asst prof to assoc prof, 65-72, chmn dept, 68-72, prof emer, English, Univ MA, Dartmouth, 71-. **HONORS AND AWARDS** assoc, Danforth Found, 73. **MEMBERSHIPS** MLA. **RESEARCH** Nineteenth and 20th century American literature; 20th century British literature. **SELECTED PUBLICATIONS** Auth, Survival: Readings on Environment, Holbrook, 71; ed, Literature from the Irish Literary Revival: An Anthology, Univ Press Am, 82. **CONTACT ADDRESS** Univ of Massachusetts, Dartmouth, 285 Old Westport Rd, North Dartmouth, MA 02747-2300.

INGRAM, WILLIAM
PERSONAL Born 11/23/1930, Chicago, IL, m, 1 child **DISCIPLINE** RENAISSANCE LITERATURE & SOCIETY **EDUCATION** Grinnell Col, BA, 53; Columbia Univ, MA, 56; Univ Pa, PhD, 66. **CAREER** Instr Eng, Drexel Inst Technol, 57-65; from asst prof to assoc prof, 66-78, prof eng, Univ MI, Ann Arbor, 78; Emeritus, 00. **HONORS AND AWARDS** Distinguished Tchg Awd, 69; Am Coun Learned Socs, Folger Libr, Huntington Libr & Univ MI grants; Nat Endowment for Hum fel, 80-81; Excellence in Education Awd, 97. **MEMBERSHIPS** Shakespeare Asn Am. **RESEARCH** Elizabethan drama; Renaissance cultl hist; computer-aided research. **SELECTED PUBLICATIONS** Co-ed, Concordance to John Milton's English Poetry, Clarendon, 73; auth, A London Life in the Brazen Age, Harvard Univ, 78; The Business of Playing, Cornell Univ Press, 92. **CONTACT ADDRESS** Dept of Eng, Univ of Michigan, Ann Arbor, Angell Hall, Ann Arbor, MI 48109-1003. **EMAIL** ingram@umich.edu

INMAN, BILLIE ANDREW
PERSONAL Born 05/16/1929, Thurber, TX, m, 1950, 2 children **DISCIPLINE** ENGLISH **EDUCATION** Midwestern Univ, BA, 50; Tulane Univ, MA, 51; Univ Tex Austin, PhD, 61. **CAREER** Teacher, Lubbock High School, 51-52; teacher, Borger High School, 52-54; instr, W Tex State Col, 55-57; instr, Univ Tex Austin, 61-62; instr to prof emerita, Univ of Ariz, 62-. **HONORS AND AWARDS** Scholar, Tulane Univ, 51-52; Fel, Univ Tex Austin, 54-60; NEH Fel, 82-83; Mortar Board Hall of Fame Awd, Univ Ariz, 86. **MEMBERSHIPS** MLA, Int Walter Pater Soc. **RESEARCH** British authors of the Victorian period, especially Walter Pater and William Money Hardinge. **SELECTED PUBLICATIONS** Auth, "The Organic Structure of 'Marius the Epicurean,'" Philol Quart 41, (62): 475-491; auth, "Pater's Appeal to His Readers: A Study of Two of Pater's Prose Styles," Tex Studies in Lit and Lang 14, (73): 643-665; auth, "Sebastian van Storck: Pater's Exploration into Nihilism," Nineteenth Century Fiction 30, (76): 457-476; auth, "The Intellectual Context of Walter Pater's 'Conclusion,'" Prose Studies 4, (83): 12-30; auth, Walter Pater's Reading: A Bibliography of His Library Borrowings and Literary References, 1858 - 1873, Garland Publ, (NY), 81; auth, Walter Pater and His Reading, 1874-1877, with a Bibliography of His Library Borrowings, 1878-1894, Garland Publ, (NY), 90; auth, "Estrangement and Connection: Walter Pater, Benjamin Howett, and William M Hardinge," Pater in the 1990s, ed Laurel Brake and Ian Small, ELT Pr, (Greensboro, NC, 91): 1-24; auth, "John 'Dorian' Grey and the Theme of Subservient Love in Walter Pater's Work of the 1890s," Comp Criticism vol 17, Walter Pater and the Culture of the Fin-de-siecle, (95): 85-107; auth, "Reaction to Saintsbury in Pater's Formulation of Ideas on Prose Style," Nineteenth Century Prose 24, (97): 108-126; auth, "Walter Pater, Walter Horatio Pater 1839-94," Cambridge Bibliog of English Lit, Vol IV: 1800-1900, ed Joanne Shattock, (Cambridge: Cambridge Univ Pr, 99): 2376-2384. **CONTACT ADDRESS** 5531 E North Wilshire Dr, Tucson, AZ 85711-4569. **EMAIL** bjainman@aol.com

INNES, CHRISTOPHER
PERSONAL Born 10/06/1941, Liverpool, England, m, 1972, 1 child **DISCIPLINE** ENGLISH, THEATRE **EDUCATION** Oxford Univ, BA, 65; BPh, 68; MA, 69; PhD, 69. **CAREER** Asst prof, Freie Univ, 68-69; vis emin scholar, New Castle Univ, 92; vis prof, Johannes Guttenburg Univ, 96; vis prof, Ohtani Univ, 00; asst prof, assoc prof, prof, York Univ, 69-; **HONORS AND AWARDS** Dist Res Prof, York Univ , 96-; Killam Fel, Can Coun, 98-00; Benian's Fel, St John's Col, 89-90. **MEMBERSHIPS** ASTR; ACUTE; CAIS; ITI; IAUPE; MLA; Soc for Theatre Res **RESEARCH** 20th-century drama and theatre. **SELECTED PUBLICATIONS** Auth, A Sourcebook on Naturalist Theatre, Routledge, 00; auth, British and American Twentieth-Century Theatre: A Critical Guide to Archives, Ashgate, 99; auth, Edward Gordon Craig: A Vision of Theatre, Harwood, 98; auth, Avant Garde Theatre: 1892-1992, Routledge, 93; auth, Modern British Drama: 1890-1990, CUP, 92; auth, Politics and the Playwright: George Ryga, S and P, 86; auth, Holy Theatre - Ritual and the Avant Garde, CUP, 81; auth, Modern German Drama: a Study in Form, CUP, 79; auth, Piscatpor's Political Theatre, CUP, 77. **CONTACT ADDRESS** Eng Dept, York Univ, 4700 Keele St, 208 Stong Col, Toronto, ON, Canada M3J 1P3. **EMAIL** cinnes@yorku.ca

INNESS, SHERRIE A.
PERSONAL Born 03/16/1965, Palo Alto, CA, s **DISCIPLINE** ENGLISH LITERATURE **EDUCATION** Wellesley Col, BA, 86; UC-San Diego, MA, 91; PhD, 93. **CAREER** Instr, 89-92, 93; Teach Asst, 90-92; UC San Diego;Miami Univ, Asst Prof English. 93-98; Assoc Prof, 99-. **HONORS AND AWARDS** Regents' Fel, 88; Tuition Fel, 90; NEH Fel, 95. **RESEARCH** Girls' culture; food studies; popular culture. **SELECTED PUBLICATIONS** Auth, Intimate Communities: Representation and Social Transformation in Women's College Fiction, 1895-1910, Bowling Green State Univ Popular Press, 95; Nancy Drew and Company: Culture, Gender, and Girls' Series, Bowling Green State Univ Popular Press, 97; The Lesbian Menace: Ideology, Identity, and the Representation of Lesbian Life, Univ Mass Press, 97; Breaking Boundaries: New Perspectives on Women's Regional Writing, Univ Iowa Press, 97; Tough Girls: Women Warriors and Wonder Women in Popular Culture, Univ Pa Press, 99; Delinquents and Debutantes: Twentieth-Century American Girls' Cultures, NY Univ Press, 98; Millenium Girls: Today' s Girls around the World, Rowman & Littlefield, 98; author of numerous articles and other publications. **CONTACT ADDRESS** English Dept, Miami Univ, 1601 Peck Blvd, Hamilton, OH 45011. **EMAIL** inness@muohio.edu

INSIGNARES, HARRIETTE B.
PERSONAL Born 10/24/1943, Savannah, GA, d, 4 children **DISCIPLINE** EDUCATION, ENGLISH **EDUCATION** Fisk Univ, BA, 64; Univ Wis, MST, 72; George Peabody Col, PhD, 80. **CAREER** Acad coun, Univ Wis, 70-72; asst cen dir, instr, 73-77; instr, Meharry Col, 75-76; instr, Geo Peabody Col, 76-77; instr, Am Baptist Col, 77-79; asst prof, Univ Tenn, 77-79; assoc prof, 80-88; prof, 88-; prog coord, 95-98. **HONORS AND AWARDS** Wis Leadershp Grant; Ford Fel; Sylvia Wilson Mem Fel; ASNE Fel; API Fel; Freedom Forum Fel; Outstand Teach Awd; David Eshelman Outstand Lead Awd; Trailblazer Awd; Adj Gen Dist Patriot Awd and Med; Poet of Merit Plaque and Med. **MEMBERSHIPS** Phi Beta Kappa; SPJ; NABJ; GKHS; Theta Alpha Phi; Pi Kappa Delta; ISP; Consortium of Doctors. **RESEARCH** Writing literacy; African-American rhetoric. **SELECTED PUBLICATIONS** Auth, Genesis, 76; auth, Juba's Folk Games: A Collection of Afo-American Children's Games; coauth, "Black Liberation and Legitimation: Rejection of the Mask," Writers Circle Mag, 75; auth, A Salute to the Heroes of Desert Storm; auth, "Tennessee Volunteers is No Idle Boast," Quill; auth, "Family Tree," in Last Goodbyes, Nat Lib of Poetry; auth, "No Unknown Soldiers," in America At the Millennium: Best Poets, Best Poems of the 20th Century; auth, "Sloe Gin," Old Hickory Rev; auth, "Blacks and the Bicentennial: A Response," Fisk Univ Herald; auth, "Gentle Georgian," Congressional Rec; auth, "Earth Sister," Trolley; auth, "A Juju of Their Own," Tenn Speech Comm J. **CONTACT ADDRESS** Dept Communications, Tennessee State Univ, 3500 John A Merritt Blvd, Nashville, TN 37209-1500. **EMAIL** hinsignare@aol.com

INSLEE, FORREST
PERSONAL Born 12/15/1961, Seattle, WA, s **DISCIPLINE** SPEECH **EDUCATION** Northwestern Univ, BA, 84, MA/PhD, 92; Regent Coll, MCS, 98 **CAREER** Asst Prof, Northwest Coll, 96-present. **MEMBERSHIPS** Natl Communication Assoc **RESEARCH** Cross-cultural Educ, leadership and management **CONTACT ADDRESS** Northwest Col, PO Box 579, Kirkland, WA 98083. **EMAIL** forrest.inslee@ncag.edu

IORIO, SHARON
DISCIPLINE MASS COMMUNICATION **EDUCATION** Okla State Univ, MS, PhD. **CAREER** Grad coord, MA Commun Prog; assoc prof. **SELECTED PUBLICATIONS** Publ, sociology and the history of mass communication. **CONTACT ADDRESS** Wichita State Univ, 1845 Fairmont, Wichita, KS 67260-0062.

IRMSCHER, CHRISTOPH
PERSONAL Born 11/25/1962, Tubingen, Germany, m, 1999, 1 child **DISCIPLINE** ENGLISH **EDUCATION** Univ of Bonn, MA, 88; PhD, 91; Habilitation, 98. **CAREER** Lectr, Univ Bonn, 92-93, 94-96; vis asst prof, Univ Tenn Knoxville, 93-94; lectr, Harvard Univ, 98-00; asst prof, Univ Md Baltimore County, 00-. **HONORS AND AWARDS** Fel, John F Kennedy Inst, 89; Fel, Ger Nat Scholar Found, 90-91; Fel, Stuttgart Sem, 92; Fulbright Grant, 93; Fel, Ger Res Coun, 96-98; Lit and Lang Award, Asn of Am Publ, 99; CUE Award for Distinction in Teaching, Harvard Univ, 99-00. **MEMBERSHIPS** MLA, Europ Asn of Am Studies. **RESEARCH** 19th-century American Literature, Literature and Science, Poetry. **SELECTED PUBLICATIONS** Auth, Masken der Moderne, Konigshausen and Neumann, 92; auth, The Poetics of Natural History, Rutgers Univ Pr, 99; ed, John James Audubon, Writings and Drawings, Libr of Am, 99. **CONTACT ADDRESS** Dept English, Univ of Maryland, Baltimore, Baltimore, MD 21250. **EMAIL** irmscher@umbc.edu

IRONS, GLENWOOD H.
DISCIPLINE COMMUNICATIONS **EDUCATION** Brock Univ, BA; SUNY, MA, PhD. **CAREER** Prof, Brock Univ. **RESEARCH** Popular narrative genres (Detectives, sci-fi, horror, romance, western, thriller) and woman detectives. **SELECTED PUBLICATIONS** Auth, Gender, Language and Myth: Essays on Popular Narrative, Univ Toronto Press, 92; Feminism in

Women's Detective Fiction, Univ Toronto Press, 95. **CONTACT ADDRESS** Dept of Applied Language Studies, Brock Univ, 500 Glenridge Ave, Saint Catharines, ON, Canada L2S 3A1. **EMAIL** girons@spartan.ac.BrockU.CA

IRSFELD, JOHN HENRY
PERSONAL Born 12/02/1937, Bemidji, MN, m, 1984, 1 child **DISCIPLINE** ENGLISH & AMERICAN LITERATURE & LANGUAGE **EDUCATION** Univ Tex, Austin, BA, 59, MA, 66, PhD(English), 69. **CAREER** From asst prof to assoc prof, 69-77, prof English & chemn dept, Univ Nevada, Las Vegas, 77- 84; Exec Asst to the Sr VP, Provost, 84-87; Deputy to the Pres, 87-90; VP and Deputy to the Pres, 90-95. **HONORS AND AWARDS** Barrick Scholar Awd, Univ Nev, Las Vegas, 85-86; Nev Governor's Arts Awd for Excellence in the Arts, 94. **MEMBERSHIPS** Nev Hum Comt, 81-87; NEH bd, 88, 89, 90, 92. **RESEARCH** Twentieth century English and American literature; poetry and poetics; fiction. **SELECTED PUBLICATIONS** Auth, Stop, rewind, and play (story), SDak Rev, 3/74; Ambivalence hardy fire (short story), Kans Quart, summer 74; The right thing: What it is, and how Theodore Roethke achieved it, Sparrow, 75; Coming Through (novel), 75 & Little Kingdoms (novel), 76, Putnam; The horse fountain (short story), Kans Quart, winter 76; Have you knocked on Cleopatra? (short story), 12/76 & The tourist (short story), 11/76, Las Vegas; auth, Rats Alley Novel, 87. **CONTACT ADDRESS** Dept of English, Univ of Nevada, Las Vegas, PO Box 455011, Las Vegas, NV 89154-5011. **EMAIL** irsfeldj@nevada.edu

IRVINE, CAROLYN LENETTE
PERSONAL Born 03/07/1947, Quincy, FL, m, 1977 **DISCIPLINE** SPEECH, ENGLISH **EDUCATION** Florida A&M University, Tallahassee, FL, BS, 1970; University of Florida, Gainesville, FL, MS, 1975; Florida State University, Tallahassee, FL, PhD, 1989. **CAREER** Shanks High School, Quincy, FL, speech & English teacher, 76-77; Florida A&M University, Tallahassee, FL, speech teacher, 75-76, 83-, English teacher, 78-83. **HONORS AND AWARDS** Certificate of Appreciation, Miracle Temple Daycare Center. **MEMBERSHIPS** Member, Jack and Jill of America, Inc, 1988-90; member, Associations of Teachers of America, 1989-90; member, Florida Speech Communication Association, 1984-91; member, Phi Delta Kappa, 1984-91; various others. **SELECTED PUBLICATIONS** "A Speech Recipe," The SGS Communicator, the School of General Studies, Florida A&M University, vol. 10, number 3, December 1990; "An Analysis of Speech," The SGS Communicator, the School of General Studies, Florida A&M University, vol. 8, number 4, December 1989; "Cooperative Education: Its Role and Scope in Vocational Education," ERIC Clearinghouse on Adult Career and Vocational Education, Research in Education, 1985; "Love," poem, in Anthology of Best Love Poetry, 1980. **CONTACT ADDRESS** Dept of English, Florida A&M Univ, Tallahassee, FL 32304. **EMAIL** carolyn.irvine@famu.edu

IRVINE, JAMES RICHARD
PERSONAL Born 03/04/1939, Port Arthur, TX, m, 1959 **DISCIPLINE** RHETORIC, SPEECH COMMUNICATION **EDUCATION** Stephen F Austin Univ, BS, 61, MA, 65; Univ Iowa, PhD(speech), 74. **CAREER** Teacher speech, Port Arthur pub schs, 61-63; teaching asst, Stephen F Austin Univ, 64-65; instr, Colo State Univ, 65-68; teaching asst rhetoric, Univ Iowa, 68-69; asst prof, 74-78, assoc prof, 78-82, PROF RHET & SPEECH, COLO STATE UNIV, 82-, Colo State Univ res grant, 76 & res sabbatical, 77. **HONORS AND AWARDS** Honors prof, Colo State Univ, 80. **MEMBERSHIPS** Speech Commun Asn Am; Rhet Soc Am; Western Speech Commun Asn; Conf Brit Studies. **RESEARCH** Rhetorical theory and criticism; 18th-century British rhetoric; enlightenment Scottish rhetorical theory. **SELECTED PUBLICATIONS** Auth, Campbell 'Philosophy of Rhetoric', bk-1, Associations With the Aberdeen-Philosophical-Society, Notes and Queries, Vol 0039, 92. **CONTACT ADDRESS** Dept of Speech Commun, Colorado State Univ, Fort Collins, CO 80523-0001.

IRVINE, LORNA MARIE
PERSONAL Born Ottawa, ON, Canada, m, 1962, 2 children **DISCIPLINE** ENGLISH LITERATURE **EDUCATION** McMaster Univ, BA, 59; Carleton Univ, MA, 65; Am Univ, PhD, 77. **CAREER** Lectr English, Carleton Univ, 65-67 & 69-72; lectr, Am Univ, 75-77, prof lectr, 77-78; Asst prof, George Mason Univ, 78-85; Assoc prof, 85-92; prof, 92-. **HONORS AND AWARDS** Nat Endowment for the Humanities; Canadian Studies Senior Fel; George Mason Univ Distinguished Fac Awd; Hon mem, Golden Key Honor Soc; Phi Kappa Phi. **MEMBERSHIPS** MLA; Asn Can Studies in US; Am Coun of Quebec Studies. **RESEARCH** Post-colonial studies; women's studies; cultural studies. **SELECTED PUBLICATIONS** Auth, Sub/Version: Canadian Fictions by Women, ECW Press (Toronto), 86; auth, Collecting Clues: Margaret Atwood's 'Bodily Harm,' ECW Press (Toronto), 93; auth, Critical Spaces: Margaret Laurence and Janet Frame, Camden House (South Carolina), 95; coauth, "Pre and Post-Mortem: Regendering and Serial Killing in Rioux, Dandurand, De, and Atwood," American Review of Canadian Studies, 99; auth, Recycling Culture: Kitsch, Camp, and Trash in Margaret Atwood's Fiction, in Margaret Atwood: Works and Impact, ed. Reingard Nischik, 00; auth, "Displacing the White Man's Burden in Michael Ondaatje's The English Patient," British Journal of Canadian Studies. **CONTACT ADDRESS** Dept English, George Mason Univ, Fairfax, Fairfax, VA 22030-4444. **EMAIL** lirvine@gmu.edu

IRVINE, MARTIN
DISCIPLINE ENGLISH LITERATURE **EDUCATION** State Univ NYork, BA; Brandeis Univ, MA; Harvard Univ, MA, PhD. **CAREER** Eng Dept, Georgetown Univ **RESEARCH** Media and cultural studies; Internet and information technology; educational technology; communications; literary theory; medieval literature; contemporary fiction. **SELECTED PUBLICATIONS** Auth, Grammatica and Literary Theory 350-1100, 93; Literate Subjectivity and Gender Conflicts in the Writings of Heloise and Abelard, 94; Medieval Textuality and the Archaeology of the Text, 90; Interpretation and the Semiotics of Allegory in the Works of Clement of Alexandria, Origen, and Augustine, 87; A Guide to the Sources of the Medieval Theories of Interpretation, Signs, and the Arts of Discourse; Aristotle to Ockham, 87. **CONTACT ADDRESS** English Dept, Georgetown Univ, 37th and O St, Washington, DC 20057.

IRVING, KARTINA M.
PERSONAL Born 01/16/1964, Ireland **DISCIPLINE** ENGLISH **EDUCATION** Trinity Col, BA, 86; CUNY Binghamton, MA, 88; PhD, 91. **CAREER** Asst prof, Bentley Col, 91-92; asst prof to assoc prof, George Mason Univ, 92-. **MEMBERSHIPS** PMLA. **RESEARCH** Literature of American immigration; nineteenth century American women writers; cultural studies. **SELECTED PUBLICATIONS** Auth, Immigrant Mothers: Narratives of Race and Maternity, 1890-1925, Univ Ill Pr, 00. **CONTACT ADDRESS** 102 Park Valley Rd, Silver Spring, MD 20910-5425. **EMAIL** kirving@gmu.edu

IRWIN, BONNIE D.
PERSONAL Born 08/19/1959, Chicago, IL, m, 1994 **DISCIPLINE** ENGLISH **EDUCATION** Univ Calif Berkeley, AB, 81; MA, 83; PhD, 91. **CAREER** Adj asst prof, Iowa State Univ, 91-94; assoc prof, Eastern Ill Univ, 94-. **HONORS AND AWARDS** NEH, 95. **MEMBERSHIPS** MLA, Am Folklore Soc, Medieval Acad of Am, Ill Philol Assoc, Ill Folklife Soc, Omicron Delta Kappa, Sigma Tau Delta. **RESEARCH** Medieval Storytelling, World Mythology, Medieval Arabic Literature, Medieval Spanish Literature. **SELECTED PUBLICATIONS** Auth, "What's in a Frame?: The Medieval Textualization of Traditional Storytelling," Oral Tradition, (95); auth, "Telling Tales: Medieval Narratives and the Folk Tradition, St. Martin's, (98); auth, Teaching Oral Traditions, MLA, 98; auth, Approaches to Teaching Boccaccio's Decameron, MLA, 00. **CONTACT ADDRESS** Dept English, Eastern Illinois Univ, Charleston, IL 61920. **EMAIL** bdirwin@eiu.edu

IRWIN, ELEANOR
PERSONAL Born Toronto, ON, Canada **DISCIPLINE** CLASSICS **EDUCATION** Univ Toronto, BA, 59, MA, 60, PhD, 67. **CAREER** Asst prof, 68-73, Assoc Prof, Scarborough Col, Univ Toronto, 73-, assoc ch, 80-82, 94-, vice prin & assoc dean, 89-93. **HONORS AND AWARDS** D.R. Campbell Awd Outstanding Contrib Scarborough Col, 84. **MEMBERSHIPS** Class Asn Can; Can Soc Patristic Studs; Int Soc Class Tradition. **RESEARCH** Flowering plants in the Classical Greek world; connections between medicinal plants and mythological figures; women and goddesses in the ancient world; reasons for the virginity of the Greek goddesses Hestia, Athena and Artemis. **SELECTED PUBLICATIONS** Auth, Colour Terms in Greek Poetry, 74; auth, Evadne, Iamos and Violets in Pindar's Sixth Olympian in Hermes, 96. **CONTACT ADDRESS** Dept of Humanities, Univ of Toronto, 1265 Military Trail, Scarborough, ON, Canada M1C 1A4. **EMAIL** irwin@scar.utoronto.ca

IRWIN, JOHN THOMAS
PERSONAL Born 04/24/1940, Houston, TX **DISCIPLINE** AMERICAN LITERATURE, HISTORY OF IDEAS **EDUCATION** Univ St Thomas, BA, 62; Rice Univ, MA & PhD, 70. **CAREER** Supvr pub affairs libr, Ling-Temco-Vought, NASA Manned Spacecraft Ctr, 66-67; asst prof Eng, Johns Hopkins Univ, 70-74; Ed, Ga Rev, Univ GA, 74-77; Prof Lit & English, 77-84, Decker Prof in the Humanities, The Writing Seminars, Johns Hopkins Univ, 84-, Chmn Dept, 77-96; ed, Johns Hopkins Fiction and Poetry Series, 79. **HONORS AND AWARDS** Danforth fel, Rice Univ, 70; Guggenheim fel, 91; Christian Gauss Prize, Phi Beta Kappa, 94; Scaglione Prize in Comparative Lit, MLA, 94. **MEMBERSHIPS** MLA; Asn of Literary; Scholars & Critics; Poe Studies Asn; Faulkner Soc. **RESEARCH** Mod Am poetry; 19th century Am novel; 20th century Am novel. **SELECTED PUBLICATIONS** Coauth, The structure of Cleanness: Parable as effective sign, Medieval Studies, 73; auth, Doubling and Incest/Repetition and Revenge, Johns Hopkins Univ, 75, expanded ed, Johns Hopkins Pr, 96; The Heisenberg Variations, Univ Ga, 76; American Hieroglyphics, Yale Univ Press, 80; The Mystery to a Solution, Johns Hopkins Press, 94; Just Let Me Say This About That, Overlook Press, 98. **CONTACT ADDRESS** Johns Hopkins Univ, Baltimore, 3400 N Charles St, Baltimore, MD 21218-2680.

ISAAC, LILY
DISCIPLINE ENGLISH **EDUCATION** BA, MA, PhD **CAREER** Assoc Prof, Liberty Univ, 92-. **RESEARCH** Distance Learning; ESL Pedagogy; Multiculturalism; TESL; Literary Criticism; Chaucer; Milton; World Literature; Christian Perspectives on Literature; Linguistics; International Studies. **SELECTED PUBLICATIONS** Auth, "Ruptured Relationships in Yasunari Kawabata's," The sound of the Mountain, Yama No Oto. **CONTACT ADDRESS** Dept English, Liberty Univ, PO Box 20000, Lynchburg, VA 24506-8001. **EMAIL** lisaac@liberty.edu

ISAAC, SAMUEL
DISCIPLINE ENGLISH **EDUCATION** BA, MA, BEd, PhD **CAREER** Assoc Prof, Liberty Univ, 89-. **RESEARCH** Dialogics; Metaphor; Literary Criticism; Multiculturalism; Shakespeare; Structuralism. **SELECTED PUBLICATIONS** Auth, The Marlovian Enigma: A Dialogic Resolution to a Structuralist Riddle. **CONTACT ADDRESS** Dept English, Liberty Univ, PO Box 20000, Lynchburg, VA 24506-8001. **EMAIL** csisaac@liberty.edu

ISAACS, NEIL D.
PERSONAL Born 08/21/1931, New York, NY, m, 1953, 4 children **DISCIPLINE** ENGLISH LITERATURE **EDUCATION** Dartmouth Col, AB, 53; Univ Calif, Berkeley, AM, 56; Brown Univ, PhD, 59. **CAREER** From inst to asst prof English, City Col New York, 59-63; from asst prof to assoc prof, Univ Tenn, 63-71; prof english, Univ MD, 71-. **MEMBERSHIPS** SAtlantic MLA. **RESEARCH** Old English and Middle English poetry; fiction; film. **SELECTED PUBLICATIONS** Auth, Jim Dandy, Va Quart Rev, Vol 0071, 95; Bathgate in the Time of Coppola + Doctorow, American Gangster Films, Lit-Film Quart, Vol 0024, 96; Malle Eye for Rose 'Storyville' + The Books Influence on 'Pretty Baby', Lit-Film Quart, Vol 0024, 96; Passing off, Va Quart Rev, Vol 0073, 97. **CONTACT ADDRESS** Dept of English, Univ of Maryland, Col Park, 4135 Susquehanna Hall, College Park, MD 20742-8821. **EMAIL** ndi821@aol.com

ISANG, S. AKPAN
PERSONAL Born Itak, Nigeria, 3 children **DISCIPLINE** ORGANIZATIONAL COMMUNICATION **EDUCATION** Howard Univ, PhD 96. **CAREER** Nyack College, asst prof, 97-. **HONORS AND AWARDS** Aids Short Story Awd; Aids Video Awd **MEMBERSHIPS** ICA; IMA; IPA **RESEARCH** Audience influence on media; mentoring in organization **SELECTED PUBLICATIONS** Auth, Mentoring as Interpersonal Communication: An Application of a Mentoring Model to a Black Cultural Environment. **CONTACT ADDRESS** Dept of Communication, Nyack Col, 1 South Blvd, Nyack, NY 10960-3698. **EMAIL** isang@nyack.edu

ISHMAN, SYBIL R.
PERSONAL Born 07/25/1946, Durham, NC, m **DISCIPLINE** ENGLISH **EDUCATION** Univ of NC (Greensboro), BA, 68; Univ of NC (Chapel Hill), MA, 71, PhD, 83. **CAREER** NC Central Univ, grad asst 1969-71, instr 1970-72; Instr of English, 72-76, asst prof of English, 79-85, NC State Univ, assist prof 1980-; Instr of English, Howard Univ, 76-77; Adj prof of English, 85-86; Chairperson, NTID English Dept, 86-91; asst prof, NTID Dept of Liberal Arts, 91-. **HONORS AND AWARDS** Nominee, Eisenhart Outstanding Teaching Awd, 92-93; Nominee, Eisenhart Outstanding Teaching Awd, 91-92; Teaching Effectiveness Recognition, North Carolina State Univ, 84; Who's Who Among Outstanding Black Collegians, 72. **MEMBERSHIPS** Mem Am Assn Univ Women; Modern Lang Assn; Natl Counc of Tchrs of English; mem TESOL; Natl Smart Set Durham Chpt. **CONTACT ADDRESS** Nat Technical Inst for the Deaf, Rochester Inst of Tech, One Lomb Memorial Dr, Rochester, NY 14623. **EMAIL** srince@rit.edu

ISKANDER, SYLVIA W.
PERSONAL Born 06/27/1940, Boston, MA, m, 1982, 2 children **DISCIPLINE** ENGLISH **EDUCATION** La State Univ, BS, 61; Univ SW La, MA, 65; Fla State Univ, PhD, 69. **CAREER** Asst prof to assoc prof, Univ SW La, 69-82; prof, Univ La Lafayette, 82-. **HONORS AND AWARDS** Distinguished Prof, Univ La Lafayette, 91. **MEMBERSHIPS** CLA; IRSCL; MLA. **RESEARCH** Young adult movies; Middle Eastern children's literature; censorship; fairy tales. **SELECTED PUBLICATIONS** Auth, "Reader, Realism and Robert Cormier," Children's Lit J 15 (87): 7-18; auth, "Arabic Detective Fiction for Adolescents," in Cross-culturism in Children's Literature (NYork: Child Lit Asn, 88): 75-77; auth, "Robert Cormier," (Univ Prdate) in Concise Dictionary of Literary Biography: Broadening Views, 1986-1989, ed. Laura Ingram (Detroit: Gale Group, 89): 35-51; auth, "Reading Challenges and Internet Censorship in the New Millennium: Presidential address," Child Lit Asn Qtly 24 (99): 174-78; auth, "Anne Franks Autobiographical Style," in A Scholarly Look at the Diary of Anne Frank, ed. Harold Bloom (PA: Chelsea, 99): 69-74; auth, "Robert Cormier," in Concise Dictionary of Literary Biography, Gale Lit Database (http://www.galenet.com/servlet/litRC/), 99; auth, "Anne Franks Reading: A Retrospective," in Anne Frank: Reflections on Her Life and Legacy, eds. Hyman A. Enzer, Sandra S. Enzer (Urbana: Ill Univ Pr, 00): 100-80. **CONTACT AD-**

DRESS English Dept, Univ of Louisiana, Lafayette, PO Box 44691, Lafayette, LA 70504-4691. **EMAIL** sylvia.iskander@juno.com

ISSAC, MEGAN
PERSONAL m **DISCIPLINE** ENGLISH **EDUCATION** Lawrence Univ, BA; Univ Calif at Los Angeles, MA; PhD. **CAREER** Assoc prof, Youngstown State Univ, 94-. **HONORS AND AWARDS** Phi Beta Kappa. **MEMBERSHIPS** MLA; Children's Lit Assoc; NCTE; Shakespeare Assoc of Am. **RESEARCH** Shakespeare, childrens and young adult literature. **SELECTED PUBLICATIONS** Auth, Heirs to Shakespeare: Reinventing the Bard in Young Adult Literature. **CONTACT ADDRESS** Dept English, Youngstown State Univ, 1 University Plz, Youngstown, OH 44555-0001.

IVERSON, STANLEY
PERSONAL Born 05/07/1940, Gays Mills, WI, m, 1972, 2 children **DISCIPLINE** CLASSICS **EDUCATION** Luther Col, BA, 62; Vanderbilt Univ, MAT, 63; MA, 69; PhD, 75. **CAREER** Teacher, Phoenix Union High Sch, 63-65; Prof, Concordia Col, 65-66, 69-. **MEMBERSHIPS** Am Philol Assoc, Am Classical League, Classical Assoc of Minn. **RESEARCH** Teaching of Latin. **SELECTED PUBLICATIONS** Co-ed, Fabulae Graecae: Longman's. **CONTACT ADDRESS** Dept Classics, Concordia Col, Minnesota, 3627 Rivershore Dr, Moorhead, MN 56560-5556. **EMAIL** iverson@gloria.cord.edu

IYER, NALINI
PERSONAL Born 02/15/1966, Bombay, India, m, 1991, 2 children **DISCIPLINE** ENGLISH **EDUCATION** Univ Madras, BA, 86; Purdue Univ, MA, 88, PhD, 93. **CAREER** Eng, Seattle Univ; assoc prof, of English. **MEMBERSHIPS** Midwest MLA; MLA. **SELECTED PUBLICATIONS** Auth, American Indian: Metaphors of the Self in Bharati Muckherjee's Holder of the World, Ariel, 96. **CONTACT ADDRESS** Dept of Eng, Seattle Univ, 900 Broadway, Seattle, WA 98122-4460. **EMAIL** niyer@seattleu.edu

J

JACKSON, ALLAN STUART
PERSONAL Born 04/24/1934, Pittsburgh, PA **DISCIPLINE** THEATER **EDUCATION** Univ Colo, BA, 56; Ohio State Univ, MA, 59, PhD(theater), 62. **CAREER** Instr theater, Ohio State Univ, 62; asst prof, 64-69, ASSOC PROF THEATER, STATE UNIV NY, BINGHAMTON, 69-. **MEMBERSHIPS** Am Educ Theater Asn; Am Soc Theater Res; Class Asn Am; Int Fed Theater Res. **RESEARCH** Theater **SELECTED PUBLICATIONS** Auth, Pizarro, Bridges and the Gothic Scene, Theatre Notebk, Vol 0051, 97. **CONTACT ADDRESS** 132 Annetta St, Vestal, NY 13850.

JACKSON, ARLENE M.
DISCIPLINE VICTORIAN LITERATURE **EDUCATION** Marygrove Col, AB, 60, Villanova Univ, MA, 62; Univ MI, PhD, 79. **CAREER** Engl, St. Joseph's Univ. **SELECTED PUBLICATIONS** Auth, Photography as Style and Metaphor, Art of Thomas Hardy, Thomas Hardy Annual 2, 84; The Question of Credibility in Anne Bronte's The Tenant of Wildfell Hall, Eng Studies 63, 82; Agnes Wickfield and the Church Leitmotif in David Copperfield, Dickens Studies Annual 9, 81; The Evolutionary Aspect of Hardy's Modern Men, Revue Belge de Philologie et d'Historie 56; Illustration and the Novels of Thomas Hardy, Rowman & Littlefield, 80. **CONTACT ADDRESS** Saint Joseph's Univ, 5600 City Ave, Philadelphia, PA 19131. **EMAIL** ajackson@sju.edu

JACKSON, BLYDEN
PERSONAL Born 10/12/1910, Paducah, KY, m, 1958 **DISCIPLINE** ENGLISH **EDUCATION** Wilberforce Univ, AB, 30; Univ Mich, AM, 38, PhD, 52. **CAREER** Teacher, pub schs, Ky, 34-45; from asst prof to assoc prof English, Fisk Univ, 45-54; prof English & chmn dept, Southern Univ, 54-62, dean grad sch, 62-69; assoc dean grad sch, 73-76, PROF ENGLISH, UNIV NC, CHAPEL HILL, 69-, SPEC ASST TO GRAD DEAN, 76-, Ed bull, Col Lang Asn, 59-; chmn col sect, NCTE, 71-73. **HONORS AND AWARDS** DH, Wilberforce Univ, 77; LIHD, Univ Louisville, 78. **MEMBERSHIPS** NCTE; MLA; Col Lang Asn (pres, 57-59); Col English Asn; Speech Commun Asn. **RESEARCH** Negro literature, Mich Alumni Rev; College Language Association, PMLA, 12/58. **SELECTED PUBLICATIONS** Coauth, Black Poetry in America, 74 & auth, The Waiting Years, 76, La State Univ. **CONTACT ADDRESS** Dept of English, Univ of No Carolina, Chapel Hill, Chapel Hill, NC 27514.

JACKSON, BRUCE
PERSONAL Born 05/21/1936, Brooklyn, NY, 3 children **DISCIPLINE** FILM, AMERICAN STUDIES **EDUCATION** Rutgers Univ, BA, 60; Ind Univ, MA, 62; Harvard Univ, JF, 63. **CAREER** Asst prof, 67-68, assoc prof, 69-71, prof English, Comp Lit & Folklore, 71-, SUNY distinguished prof, 90-, Samuel P. Capen Prof of Am Culture, 97-, SUNY Buffalo; dir, Ctr Stud Am Culture, 74-, sr consult, President's Crime Comn, Arthur D Little Co, 66; dir, Newport Folk Found, 65-72; Guggenheim Found fel, 71-72; adv bd, Nat Proj II, FIPSE, 75-77, New York Comn on Corrections, 76-77 & Inst Am West, 76-82; exec dir, Doc Res Inc, 78-; exec bd, Am Folklore Soc, 79-82. **HONORS AND AWARDS** Ed, J of Am Folklore, 86-90; pres, Am Folklore Soc, 84. **RESEARCH** Afro-American folklore; criminology; documentary. **SELECTED PUBLICATIONS** Auth, Law and Disorder; Criminal Justice in America, Illinois, 85; auth, Rainbow Freeware, New South Moulton Press, 86; ed, Feminism and Folklore, American Folklore Society, 87; auth, Fieldwork, Illinois, 87; auth, A User's Guide: Freeware, Shareware, and Public Domain Software, New South Moulton Press, 88; co-ed, The Centennial Index: 100 Years of Journal of American Folklore, American Folklore Society, 88; auth, Disorderly Conduct, Illinois, 92; co-ed, The World Observed: Reflections on the Fieldwork Process, Illinois, 96. **CONTACT ADDRESS** Ctr for Studies in Am Cult, SUNY, Buffalo, 610 Samuel Clemens Hall, Buffalo, NY 14260-7015. **EMAIL** bjackson@acsu.buffalo.edu

JACKSON, GORDON
PERSONAL Born, South Africa, m, 2 children **DISCIPLINE** COMMUNICATION STUDIES **EDUCATION** Wheaton Col, MA; Ind Univ, PhD. **CAREER** Prof. **RESEARCH** Media ethics in South Africa. **SELECTED PUBLICATIONS** Auth, bk, South African Press, 93. **CONTACT ADDRESS** Dept of Commun, Whitworth Col, 300 West Hawthorne Rd, Spokane, WA 99251. **EMAIL** gjackson@whitworth.edu

JACKSON, HEATHER J.
PERSONAL Born 12/25/1947, Birmingham, England, m, 1969, 2 children **DISCIPLINE** ENGLISH **EDUCATION** Univ Toronto, BA, 69; MA, 70; PhD, 73. **CAREER** Vis lectr to prof, dean, Univ of Toronto, 73-. **HONORS AND AWARDS** Woodrow Wilson Fel, 69-70; Connaught Res Fel, 94, 98; Assoc Fel Darwin Col, Cambridge, 94; Vis Fel, Magdalen Col, Oxford, 95; Vis Fel, Univ of London, 99; Killam Res Fel, 01-03. **MEMBERSHIPS** MLA, SHARP, ACCUTE, NASSR. **RESEARCH** Scholarly editing, ST Coleridge, Book History, Marginalia. **SELECTED PUBLICATIONS** Auth, "Coleridge, Etymology, and Etymologic," Jour of the Hist of Ideas, (83); ed, Samuel Taylor Coleridge, Oxford World Classics, 85; auth, "Turning and Turning: Coleridge on our Knowledge of the External World," PMLA, (86); ed, ST Coleridge: Selected Letters, Oxford Univ Pr, 88; auth, "The Immoderation of Samuel Johnson," Univ of Toronto Quart, (90); auth, "Coleridge's Women, of Girls, Girls, Girls Are Made to Love," Studies in Romanticism, (93); ed, Samuel Taylor Coleridge, Oxford Poetry Libr, (94); coed, ST Coleridge: Shorter Works and Fragments, Princeton Univ Pr, (95); ed, ST Coleridge: Marginalia Vols 3-6, Princeton Univ Pr, 92-01; auth, Marginalia, Yale Univ Pr, 01. **CONTACT ADDRESS** Dept English, Univ of Toronto, 7 King's Col Cir, Toronto, ON, Canada MTS 3K1. **EMAIL** heather.jackson@utoronto.ca

JACKSON, JACQUELINE DOUGAN
PERSONAL Born 05/03/1928, Beloit, WI, 4 children **DISCIPLINE** LITERATURE, CLASSICS **EDUCATION** Beloit Col, BA, 50, Univ Mich, Ann Arbor, MA, 51. **CAREER** Lectr lit, Kent State Univ, 66-68; Assoc Prof ,Univ Ill at Springfield, 70-83, prof, 83-; Consult, Rockford Teacher Develop Ctr, Ill, 68-70; radio lectr, Univ Wis, WHA Sch of the Air, 69-; Radio Lectr, Univ of Ill at Springfield, WUIS, 75-95. **HONORS AND AWARDS** Dorothy Canfield Fisher Awd, 67; dlitt, macmurray col, 76; dhl, beloit lcol, 77. **MEMBERSHIPS** MLA **RESEARCH** Creativity in children and adults; children's literature, current and historical; fantasy. **SELECTED PUBLICATIONS** Auth, the Taste of Spruce Gum, 66, Missing Melinda, 67, Chicken Ten Thousand, 68 & auth & illusr, the Ghost Boat, 69, Little; auth, Spring Song, Kent State Univ, 69; The Orchestra Mice, Reilly & Lee, 70; coauth, The Endless Pavement, Seabury, 73; auth, Turn Not Pale, Beloved Snail, Little, 74; auth, Stories from the Round Barn, Northwestern Univ Press, 97. **CONTACT ADDRESS** Dept of English, Univ of Illinois, Springfield, Brookens Rm 489, PO 19243, Springfield, IL 62794-9243. **EMAIL** jjackson@uis.edu

JACKSON, JAMES HARVEY
PERSONAL Born 06/24/1920, Stroll, SD, m, 1944, 2 children **DISCIPLINE** PUBLIC ADDRESS **EDUCATION** Pasadena Col, AB, 41, MA, 43; Univ Southern Calif, MA, 55, PhD, 57. **CAREER** Assoc prof speech, 49-57, chmn lett, 57-63, dean students, 60-78, PROF SPEECH, POINT LOMA COL, 57-, Danforth Found, teacher study grant, 55; mem acad coun, Speech Commun Asn. **MEMBERSHIPS** Western Speech Commun Asn. **RESEARCH** Evaluation of Speech delivery and content; speaking of Clarence Darrow. **SELECTED PUBLICATIONS** Auth, I Believe, Nazarene Publ House, 49; coauth, Too Young for Love?, Beacon Hill, 68. **CONTACT ADDRESS** Dept of Speech, Point Loma Nazarene Col, 3900 Lomaland Dr, San Diego, CA 92106-2810.

JACKSON, JAMES ROBERT DE JAGER
PERSONAL Born 07/14/1935, St. Andrew's, Scotland, m, 2 children **DISCIPLINE** ENGLISH **EDUCATION** Queen's Univ, BA, 57; MA, 58; Princeton Univ, AM, 60; PhD, 61; Univ London, PhD, 63. **CAREER** Vis res fel, Univ London, 62-63; asst prof, McMaster Univ, 63-64; asst prof to assoc prof to prof to Univ prof, Univ Toronto, 64-. **HONORS AND AWARDS** Can Coun Fel, 67-68; Guggenheim Fel, 72-73; Killam Sr Fel, 75-76; Killam Res Fel, 82-84; Connaught Fel, 85-86. **MEMBERSHIPS** MLA; ACCUTE. **RESEARCH** S.T. Coleridge; romantic poetry; bibliography; literary theory. **SELECTED PUBLICATIONS** Auth, Method and Imagination in Coleridge's Criticism, Harvard, 69; ed, Coleridge: The Critical Heritage, Routledge, 70, 91; auth, Poetry of the Romantic Period, Routledge, 80; ed, Logic, by S.T. Coleridge, Princeton, 81; auth, Annals of English Verse, 1770-1835, Garland, 85; auth, Historical Criticism and the Meaning of Text, London/NYork, 89; auth, Romantic Poetry by Women, Oxford, 93; co-ed, S.T. Coleridge, Shorter Works and Fragments, Princeton 95; co-ed, S. T. Coleridge Lectures 1818-1819: On the History of Philosophy, Princeton, 00. **CONTACT ADDRESS** English Dept, Univ of Toronto, Toronto, ON, Canada M5S 1K7.

JACKSON, KATHY MERLOCK
PERSONAL Born 08/27/1955, Pittsburgh, PA, m, 1983, 1 child **DISCIPLINE** COMMUNICATIONS **EDUCATION** West VA Univ, BA (magna cum laude), 77; OH State Univ, MA, 79; Bowling Green State Univ, PhD, 84. **CAREER** Prof and coordinator of Communications, Virginia Wesleyan Col, 84-. **HONORS AND AWARDS** Eleanor T Donley Awd, West VA Univ, 75-76; Graduate Col Dissertation res grant, Bowling Green State Univ, 83-84; Am Culture PhD prog non-service fel, Bowling Green State Univ, 83-84; VA Wesleyan Col fac development grant, 86, 88, 95-99; Mednick Found res grant, 86-00; One of fifty academmics nationwide invited to participate in the Int Radio and Television Soc Fac/Industry Seminar, New York City, 88, 89; Samuel Nelson Gray Distinguished Teaching award, V Wesleyan Col, 89; Walt Disney: A Bio-Bibliography awarded honorable mention for the Ray and Pat Browne Nat Book Awd of the Popular Culture Asn in the Text, Reference, and Resource Book Category. **MEMBERSHIPS** Am culture asn; Popular Culture Asn; VA Asn of Broadcast Educators. **RESEARCH** Media; children's culture. **SELECTED PUBLICATIONS** Auth, Reading the River: Film as a Socio-Cultural Artifact, with Gary Edgerton, J of Regional Cultures, 3,1, spring/summer 83; Harvey Comics: A Neighborhood of Little Girls and Boys, Media Sight 3, 1, summer 84; Book review of Children's Literature and the Movies ed by Douglas Street, The J of Popular Film and Television, 85; Images of Children in American Film: A Socio-Cultural Analysis, Scarecrow Press, 86; Frankie and Annette at the Beach: The Beach as a Locale in American Popular Film, in Beyond the Stars IV: Locals in American Popular Film, Popular Press, 93; Walt Disney: A Bio-Bibliography, Greenwood Press, 93; Oscar Wilde, The Dictionary of Literary Biography: British Children's Writers, 1880-1914, Bruccoli Clark Layman, Inc, 94; Mattel's TV Chatter: Selling Talking Dolls to Babyboom Children, in Childhood and Popular Culture, Popular Press, 94; book review of Out of the Garden: Toys and Children's Culture in the Age of Television Marketing by Stephen Kline in the J of Popular Film and Television, 95; co-auth, with Gary Edgerton, Redesigning Pocahontas: Disney, the White Man's Indian, and the Marketing of Dreams, J of Popular Film and Television, summer 96; auth, Introduction, in J of Popular Film and Television, summer 96; auth, Playing It Again and Again: Casablanca's Impact on American Mass Media and American Culture, J of Popular Film and Television, 00; numerous other articles and publications. **CONTACT ADDRESS** Communications, Virginia Wesleyan Col, 1584 Wesleyan Dr, Norfolk, VA 23502-5512. **EMAIL** kmjackson@vwc.edu

JACKSON, MARY E.
PERSONAL Born 11/20/1949, Oshkosh, WI, m, 1971 **DISCIPLINE** LIBRARY SCIENCE **EDUCATION** Carroll Col, BA (German and Sociology), 71; Drexel Univ, MLS, 74. **CAREER** Univ PA Libraries, 73-93, head, Interlibrary Loan Dept, 78-93; Asn of Res Libraries, 93-, Currently Senior Prog Officer for Access Services. **HONORS AND AWARDS** Beta Phi Mu; ALA Whitney-Carneghie Fund Awd; PA Library Asn Certificate of Merit. **MEMBERSHIPS** Am Library Asn. **RESEARCH** Academic/research libraries; interlibrary loan and document delivery; performance measures; Japanese studies. **SELECTED PUBLICATIONS** Auth, The NAILDD project and Interlibrary Loan Standards, SISAC News 11, summer/fall 96; Managing Resource Sharing in the Electronic Age, ed with Amy Chang, AMS Press, 96; Becoming a Published Author: Eight Simple Steps for Librarians, Library Administration & Management 11, winter 97; Copyright and Users: The Perspective of Users & Copyright in the United States: Current Developments & Initiatives, Copyright Issues in Libraries: Global Concerns, Local Solutions, IFLA Office for Universal Availability of Pubs and Int Lending, 97; The North American Interlibrary Loan and Document Delivery Project: Improving ILL/DD Services, Interlending and Document Supply 25, 97; Making Connections: An Update on Vendor Implementations of the ILL Protocol, ARL 194, Oct 97; Measuring the Performance of Interlibrary Loan and Document Delivery Services, ARL 195, Dec 97; ILL/DD: An Annual Review, co-ed, AMS Press, 00-; Loan Stars: ILL Comes of Age, Library J 123, Feb 98; Measuring the Performance of Interlibrary Loan Operations in North American Research and Academic Libraries, Asn of Res Libraries, 98; A

Spotlight on High-Performing ILL/DD Operations in Research Libraries, ARL 198, June 98; several other publications. **CONTACT ADDRESS** 21 Dupont Circle NW, Ste. 800, Washington, DC 20036. **EMAIL** Mary@arl.org

JACKSON, MICHELE
DISCIPLINE COMMUNCATION STUDIES **EDUCATION** Macalester Col, BA, 87; Univ Minn, MA, 90, PhD, 94. **CAREER** Asst prof. **RESEARCH** Group communication; computer based communication technology; philosophy of technology. **SELECTED PUBLICATIONS** Auth, Assessing the structure of communication on the World Wide Web, Jour Comput Mediated Commun, 97; The meaning of communication technology: The Technology Context scheme, 96; co-auth, Imagery on the World Wide Web: Representations of the former Yugoslavia, 97; Group decision support systems as facilitators of quality team efforts, 94; Communication theory and group support systems, 92. **CONTACT ADDRESS** Dept of Communication, Univ of Colorado, Boulder, Boulder, CO 80309. **EMAIL** jackson@colorado.edu

JACKSON, MILES MERRILL
PERSONAL Born 04/28/1929, Richmond, VA, m, 1954, 4 children **DISCIPLINE** LIBRARY AND INFORMATION SCIENCE; COMMUNICATIONS **EDUCATION** Virginia Union Univ, BA, 55; Drexel Univ, MS, 56. **CAREER** Free Library of Philadelphia, 56-58; head librn, Hampton Univ, 58-62; librn, Territorial Amer Samoa, 62-64; chief libn, Atlanta Univ, 64-69; assoc prof, State Univ New York, 69-75; prof to dean, SLIS, Univ Hawaii, 75-95. **HONORS AND AWARDS** Fulbright Scholar to Iran, 68-69; U.S. gvt. specialist to India and Pakistan, 84, 85. **MEMBERSHIPS** Amer Lib Assn; Assn Lib and Info Sci Edu. **RESEARCH** International flow of information. **CONTACT ADDRESS** PO Box 1602, Kaneohe, HI 96744. **EMAIL** jackson@hawaii.edu

JACKSON, PHILIP TAYLOR
PERSONAL Born 08/18/1937, Crawfordsville, IN, m, 1965, 1 child **DISCIPLINE** MUSICOLOGY **EDUCATION** Univ Richmond, Va, BA, 63; Univ NC, Chapel Hill, MA, 65, PhD(music), 68. **CAREER** Asst prof music, Occidental Col, 67-69; asst prof music hist, Conserv Music, Oberlin Col, 69-77; Assoc Prof Musicol, Baylor Univ, 77-80. Nat Endowment Humanities fel music, 67-69. **MEMBERSHIPS** Am Musicol Soc; Music Libr Asn; Int Musicol Soc; Col Music Soc; Renaissance Soc Am. **RESEARCH** Renaissance polyphonic Mass; Jachet of Mantua (16th century French composer active in Italy); Italian madrigal. **SELECTED PUBLICATIONS** Auth, Goostly Psalmes and Spirituall Songes--English and Dutch Metrical Psalms from Coverdale to Utenhove, 1535-1566, 16th Century J, Vol 0024, 93. **CONTACT ADDRESS** Ball State Univ, 1420 E Jackson, Muncie, IN 47306.

JACKSON, RICHARD P.
PERSONAL Born Lawrence, MA, m, 1999, 1 child **DISCIPLINE** ENGLISH **EDUCATION** Merrimack Col, BA, 69; Middlebury Col, MA, 72; Yale Univ, PhD, 76. **CAREER** Fac, Vermont Col, 87-; prof, Univ Tenn Chattanooga, 76-. **HONORS AND AWARDS** NEH Fel, 79; NEA Fel, 83; Fulbright Fel, 86; Pushcart Poetry Prize, 87, 92, 95-96; Juniper Prize, 88; Order of Freedom, Pres of Slovenia. **MEMBERSHIPS** Assoc Writing Programs, Acad of Am Poets, PEN, Poetry Soc of Am. **RESEARCH** Patriarchy & Italian renaissance, contemporary poetry, Eastern European poetry. **SELECTED PUBLICATIONS** Auth, Part of the Story, , Grove, 83; auth, Worlds Apart, Alabama, 87; auth, Alive All Day, Cleveland State UP, 92; auth, Heart Wall, Univ of Mass Press, 00. **CONTACT ADDRESS** Dept English, Univ of Tennessee, Chattanooga, 615 McCallie Ave, Chattanooga, TN 37403-2504. **EMAIL** svobodni@aol.com

JACKSON, RONALD, II
PERSONAL Born Cincinnati, OH, m, 2 children **DISCIPLINE** COMMUNICATIONS **EDUCATION** Univ Cincinnati, BA, 91; MA, 93; Howard Univ, PhD, 96. **CAREER** Adj Assoc Prof, Univ DC, 94-95; Asst Prof, Xavier Univ, 95-96; Asst Prof, Shippensburg Univ, 96-98; Asst Prof, Penn State Univ, 98-. **HONORS AND AWARDS** Who's Who in Am 00; Scholarly Productivity Awd, NCA, 98; Outstanding Young Men of Am; All Am Scholar's Awd. **MEMBERSHIPS** Nat Comm Asn; Intl Comm Asn; Nat Asn of African Am Studies; E Comm Asn. **RESEARCH** Public speaking; competitive Forensics; Communication theory; History of Rhetoric/Rhetoric theory; Intercultural Communication; African American communication. **SELECTED PUBLICATIONS** Auth, "Black manhood as xenophobe: An ontological exploration of the Hegelian dialectic," Journal of Black Studies, (97): 731-750; co-auth, "Tracing the evolution of race, ethnicity, and culture in communication studies," Howard Journal of communication, (98): 47-56; auth, "Mommy, there's a nigger at the door: Personal narratives, anecdotes and episodes of race," Journal of counseling & Development, 99; auth, "White Space, White Privilege: Mapping discursive inquiry into the self," Quarterly Journal of Speech, (99): 1-17; auth, The Negotiation of cultural Identity, Greenwood Pub Group, 99; auth, "So Real Illusions of Black Intellectualism; Exploring race, roles, and gender in the academy," communication Theory, (00): 48-63; co-auth, "Reasons for Closure Within the Vocational Rehabilitation System: What A Difference a Race Makes," American Rehabilitation, in press; co-ed, Innovations in African American Rhetoric, forthcoming; auth, Negotiation the Black Body: Intersections of Identity, Culture and Communication, SUNY Press, in press; co-auth, African American Communication, Sage Pub, forthcoming. **CONTACT ADDRESS** Dept Speech, Pennsylvania State Univ, Univ Park, 211 Sparks Bldg, University Park, PA 16808-1201.

JACKSON, WALLACE
DISCIPLINE ENGLISH LITERATURE **EDUCATION** PA Univ, PhD, 64. **CAREER** Prof, Duke Univ. **MEMBERSHIPS** MLA. **SELECTED PUBLICATIONS** Auth, The Probable and the Marvelous: Blake Wordsworth and the Eighteenth-Century Critical Tradition, Ga, 78; Vision and Re-vision in Alexander Pope, Wayne State, 83. **CONTACT ADDRESS** Eng Dept, Duke Univ, Durham, NC 27706.

JACOBI, MARTIN
DISCIPLINE RHETORIC AND ENGLISH LITERATURE **EDUCATION** Univ Ore, PhD, 84. **CAREER** Dept Eng, Clemson Univ **RESEARCH** Classical and modern rhetoric; American drama. **SELECTED PUBLICATIONS** Auth, Review of Rhetoric and Pluralism: Legacies of Wayne Booth, Rhetoric Soc Quart, 98; Professional Communication, Cultural Studies, and Ethics, S Atlantic Rev, 96; The Dramatist as Salesman: A Rhetorical Analysis of Miller's Intentions and Effects in Approaches to Teaching Miller's Death of a Salesman, MLA, 95; Ed Lemon: Prophet of Profit in Essays on Israel Horowitz, Greenwood, 94; The Monster Within in Lanford Wilson's Burn This, Lanford Wilson: A Casebook, Garland, 94; coauth, A Comprehensive Bibliography of Works by and about Richard M. Weaver, Rhetoric Soc Quart, 95; Richard Weaver in Encyclopedia of Rhetoric, Garlan, 96. **CONTACT ADDRESS** Clemson Univ, 806 Strode, Clemson, SC 29634. **EMAIL** mjacobi@clemson.edu

JACOBIK, GRAY
PERSONAL Born 05/21/1944, Newport News, VA, m, 1983, 2 children **DISCIPLINE** 19TH AND 20TH CENTURY AMERICAN POETRY **EDUCATION** Brandeis Univ, PhD. **CAREER** Prof Eng, Eastern Conn State Univ. **HONORS AND AWARDS** National Endowment for the Arts Fel in Creative Writing, 93; Artist's Fel, Conn Commission on the Arts, 96; The Yeats Prze, W.B. Yeats Soc of NYork, 97; The Juniper Prize, Univ Mass Pr, for "The Double Task," 98; "Dust Storm" and "The Circle Theatre" in The Best Am Poetry, 97, 99; X.J. Kennedy Poetry Prize for "The surface of Last Scattering," 99. **MEMBERSHIPS** Poetry Soc of Am; Academy of Am Poets; New England Poetry Club. **RESEARCH** Contemporary Am poetry. **SELECTED PUBLICATIONS** Poems in: Ploughshares; Prairie Schooner; Georgia Rev; Midwest Quart Rev; Southern Hum Rev; Am Lit Rev; N Am Rev; Alaska Quart Rev; Confrontation; auth, The Double Task, Univ Mass Pr, 98; auth, The Surface of Last Scattering, Texas Rev Pr, 99. **CONTACT ADDRESS** English Dept, Eastern Connecticut State Univ, 83 Windham Street, Willimantic, CT 06226. **EMAIL** jacobik@ecsuc.ctstateu.edu

JACOBS, DOROTHY HIERONYMUS
PERSONAL Born 03/13/1928, Hinsdale, IL, m, 1950, 2 children **DISCIPLINE** ENGLISH LANGUAGE & LITERATURE **EDUCATION** Univ Mich, Ann Arbor, AB, 50, AM, 60, PhD(English), 68. **CAREER** Prof English, Univ RI, 68-98. **HONORS AND AWARDS** Phi Kappa Phi; Regents-Alumni Scholar. **MEMBERSHIPS** MLA; AAUP; Milton Soc. **RESEARCH** Seventeenth century literature; modern drama. **CONTACT ADDRESS** Dept of English, Univ of Rhode Island, Kingston, RI 02881.

JACOBS, EDWARD
DISCIPLINE RESTORATION AND 18TH CENTURY BRITISH LITERATURE **EDUCATION** Univ Ill, PhD. **CAREER** Engl, Old Dominion Univ. **RESEARCH** 17th and 18th Century British Literature. **SELECTED PUBLICATIONS** Areas: The History of the Book; Cultural Historiography. **CONTACT ADDRESS** Old Dominion Univ, 4100 Powhatan Ave, BAL 202, Norfolk, VA 23058. **EMAIL** EJacobs@odu.edu

JACOBS, JOHN T.
DISCIPLINE ENGLISH **EDUCATION** Univ Notre Dame, PhD, 76. **CAREER** Prof & prog dir, Engl and Am Stud; Shenandoah's fac, 74-; site dir, 7th Willa Cather Int Sem, Shenandoah Univ, 97. **RESEARCH** Mod Southern fiction; nature writing; Willa Cather. **SELECTED PUBLICATIONS** Auth, The Western Journey: Exploration, Education, and Autobiography in Irving, Parkman, and Thoreau, 88; publ or presented papers on, Faulkner, Thoreau, Annie Dillard, Francis Parkman & Willa Cather. **CONTACT ADDRESS** Dept of Eng, Shenandoah Univ, 1460 University Dr., Winchester, VA 22601. **EMAIL** jjacobs@su.edu

JACOBS, KAREN
PERSONAL Born 01/06/1961, Stanford, CT **DISCIPLINE** ENGLISH **EDUCATION** Washington Univ, BA, 82; Univ Calif at Berkeley, 93. **CAREER** Teaching assoc, Univ Calif at Berkeley, 85-92; asst prof, Univ Colo at Boulder, 93-. **HONORS AND AWARDS** Outstanding Graduate Student Instr Awd, Univ Calif at Berkeley, 91; Dissertation Fel, Univ Calif at Berkeley Doreen B. Townsend Ctr for the Humanities, 91-92; Dissertation Fel, Univ Calif at Berkeley Dept of English, 92-93; Undergrad Res Opportunities Prog team grant, 99; Boulder Fac Assembly Awd for Excellence in Teaching, 00. **MEMBERSHIPS** MLA, Modernist Studies Asn. **RESEARCH** Twentieth-Century American Literature (especially modernism, postmodernism, the experimental novel, women authors, and African-American literature), Twentieth-Century American Intellectual and Cultural History (especially the rise of visual culture, art history, and political discourse), Twentieth-Century European Modernism, Literary, Critical and Narrative Theory, Feminist, Gender and Sexuality Theory. **SELECTED PUBLICATIONS** Auth, "The Eye's Mind: Henry James' The Sacred Fount and Vladimir Nabokov's The Eye," in Languages of Visuality: Crossings Between Science, Art, Politics, and Literature, ed. Beate Allert (Wayne State Univ Press, 96), 187-214; auth, "From 'Spy-glass' to 'Horizon': Tracking the Anthropological Gaze in Zora Neale Hurston," Novel (97): 329-360; auth, The Eye's Mind: Literary Modernism and Visual Culture, Cornell Univ Press, 00. **CONTACT ADDRESS** Dept English, Univ of Colorado, Boulder, PO Box 226, Boulder, CO 80309-0226. **EMAIL** kjacobs@spot.colorado.edu

JACOBS, NAOMI
DISCIPLINE ENGLISH **EDUCATION** Luther Col, BA, 75; Univ Mo, Columbia, MA, PhD, 82. **CAREER** Prof of English, Univ of Maine, 82-. **HONORS AND AWARDS** BA, summa cum laude, Luther Col, 75; Phi Kappa Phi; Outstanding Fac Member, Univ Maine, 97; President, Soc for Utopian Studies; D. R. Francis Fel in Creative Lit; G. Ellsworth Huggins Doctoral Fel; Mahan Awd for Fiction; Chancellor's Awd for Excellence in Teaching. **MEMBERSHIPS** Soc for Utopian Studies, MLA, William Morris Soc. **RESEARCH** Utopian literature, women's literature. **SELECTED PUBLICATIONS** Auth, "Meeting Places (short story)," The New Oneota Rev, 75; auth, "Geodesics (short story)," Midlands (spring 78); auth, "Now, then (short story)," Kennebec, 10 (86); auth, The Character of Truth: Historical Figures in Contemporary Fiction, Crosscurrents in Modern Fiction, Third Series, Carbondale: Southern Ill Univ Press (90); auth, "Islandia: Plotting Utopian Desire," Utopian Studies, 6.2 (95): 75-89; auth, "Garden Spot (poem)," Stolen Island Rev 3 (97): 23; auth, "Failures of the Imagination in 'Ecotopia'," Extrapolation, 38.4 (winter 97): 318-326; auth, "Beauty and the Body in 'News from Nowhere'," J of the William Morris Soc, 12.2 (spring 97): 26-30; auth, "Austin Tappan Wright: 'Islandia'," Dictionary of Literary Utopias, Paris: Champion-Slatkine (98); auth, "Memphis Symposium (poem)," Stolen Island Rev 4 (98): 25. **CONTACT ADDRESS** Dept English, Univ of Maine, 5752 Neville Hall, Orono, ME 04469-5752. **EMAIL** naomi_jacobs@umit.maine.edu

JACOBSON, HOWARD
PERSONAL Born 08/21/1940, Bronx, NY, m, 1965, 4 children **DISCIPLINE** CLASSICAL LITERATURE **EDUCATION** Columbia Col, NYork, BA, 62; Univ Chicago, AM, 63; Columbia Univ, PhD, 67. **CAREER** Instr Greek & Latin, Columbia Univ, 66-68; from Asst Prof to Assoc Prof, 68-80, Prof Classics, Univ Ill, Urbana, 80-; Lady Davis Vis Prof, Hebrew Univ, Jerusalem, Winter 83. **HONORS AND AWARDS** C.J. Goodwin Awd of Merit, 85. **MEMBERSHIPS** Am Philol Asn, Inst for Advanced Study, 93-94. **RESEARCH** Latin literature; Hellenistic Judaism; comparative literature. **CONTACT ADDRESS** Dept of Classics, Univ of Illinois, Urbana-Champaign, 707 S Mathews Ave, Urbana, IL 61801-3625.

JACOBSON, PAUL A.
PERSONAL Born 09/01/1957, Evanston, IL, s **DISCIPLINE** MUSIC **EDUCATION** Blackburn Col, BA, 79; Yale Univ Inst Sacred Mus, MM & MAR, 83; Grad Theol Union Berkeley, PhD, 96. **CAREER** Tchg asst, Blackburn Col, 77-79; tchg asst, Yale Divinity School, 81-83; interim choral conductor 85-86, donor campaign, 89-91, inst music, 84-91, Col St Catherine; interim choral conductor, St Paul Sem School Divinity, 98; adj fac, 92-95, asst to pres, 96-97, acting vp develop & publ rel, 97-, Jesuit School Theol Berkley; Assoc Dir of Development, San Francisco Oper, 99-. **HONORS AND AWARDS** George Marshall Fel, 79; Edwin Stanley Seder Scholar, 83; Alpha Chi **MEMBERSHIPS** N Amer Acad Liturgy; Soc Liturgica; Am Guild Organists; Asn Anglican Musicians; Col Mus Soc; Organ Hist Soc. **RESEARCH** Early Medieval (Carolingian) liturgy; Liturgy & music. **SELECTED PUBLICATIONS** Auth, The Benedictiones episcopales: A Case Study in the Gallicanization of the Roman Liturgy, 96; Sicut Samuhel unxit David: Early Carolingian Royal Anointings Reconsidered, Essays in Medieval Liturgy, Garland, 97; contrib Worship Music: A Concise Dictionary, Liturgical Press; auth, So That None Would Be Lost: Jacques de Vitry's Vita Mariae Oigniacensis, Int Medieval Cong, 97; Reform and Function: An Introduction to Visual Theology, San Anselmo Organ Festival, 97; rev, Ave verum Corpus: Misic & the Eucharist, CTSA, 97; auth, Contrib to New Catholic Encyclopedia, 00. **CONTACT ADDRESS** 1131-C

Mason Ct, San Francisco, CA 94130. **EMAIL** pajacobson@aol.com

JACOBSON, THOMAS L.
DISCIPLINE COMMUNICATIONS **EDUCATION** Western WA Univ, BA, 77; Univ WA, MA, 81; PhD 86. **CAREER** Vis asst prof, Northwestern Univ, 85-87; asst prof, SUNY Buffalo, 87-93; to assoc prof, 93-95; to ch, 95. **RESEARCH** Quality of international news coverage; mass and international commun. **SELECTED PUBLICATIONS** Auth, Old and New Approaches to Participatory Communication for Development in Participation: A Key Concept in Development Communication, Sage, 94; Electronic Mail Networks and Services in Third World Countries: Availability, Problems, Opportunities, Revue Tiers-Monde, 94; The Electronic Publishing Revolution is Not Global, JASIS: Jour Am Soc Info Sci, 94; coauth, Q-Analysis Techniques for Content Analysis, Quality & Quantity, 98; An Examination of the International Telecommunication Network, Jour Int Comm, 96; Non-commercial Computer Networks and National Development, Telematics Informatics, 93; A Pragmatist Account of Participatory Communication Research for National Development, Comm Theory, 93; co-ed, Participatory Communication Research for Social Change, Sage, 96. **CONTACT ADDRESS** Commun Dept, SUNY, Buffalo, 357 Baldy Hall, Buffalo, NY 14260. **EMAIL** jacobson@acsu.buffalo.edu

JACOBUS, LEE ANDRE
PERSONAL Born 08/20/1935, Orange, NJ, m, 1958, 2 children **DISCIPLINE** ENGLISH, PHILOSOPHY **EDUCATION** Brown Univ, AB, 57, AM, 59; Claremont Grad Sch, PhD(English), 68. **CAREER** Instr, Western Conn State Col, 60-68; PROF ENGLISH, UNIV CONN, 68-. **MEMBERSHIPS** MLA; James Joyce Soc; Milton Soc Am; Am Comt Irish Studies. **RESEARCH** Milton; 17th century English authors; modern Irish literature. **SELECTED PUBLICATIONS** Auth, Thaumaturgike in Paradise Lost, Huntington Libr Quart, 70; Self-knowledge in Paradise Lost, Milton Studies III, 71; Imamu Amiri Baraka: The quest for moral order, In: Modern Black Poets, Prentice, 73; John Cleveland: A Critical Study, Twayne, 75; Sudden Apprehension: Aspects of Knowledge in Paradise Lost, Mouton, 76; Humanities through the Arts, McGraw, 2nd ed, 78; ed, The Longman Anthology of Americn Drama, 82; Improving College Reading, Harcourt, 4th ed (in prep). **CONTACT ADDRESS** Dept of English, Univ of Connecticut, Storrs, 337 Mansfield Rd, Storrs, CT 06269. **EMAIL** jacobus@uconnvm.uconn.edu

JAHN-CLOUGH, LISA
PERSONAL Born 03/03/1967, Wakefield, RI, s **DISCIPLINE** ENGLISH **EDUCATION** Hampshire Col, BA, 88; Emerson Col, MFA, 93. **CAREER** Lecturer to Writer-in-Residence, Emerson Col, 94-. **HONORS AND AWARDS** Fac Author Awd, Emerson Col, 97, 98, 99, 00; Best Book of 1999, Child Magazine, 99. **MEMBERSHIPS** PEN. **RESEARCH** Children's literature: picture books through young adult - historical and contemporary. **SELECTED PUBLICATIONS** Auth, Missing Molly, Houghton Mifflin Co., 00; auth, My Friend and I, Houghton Mifflin Co, 99; auth, 1,2,3 Yippie, Houghton Mifflin Co, 98; auth, ABC, Yummy, Houghton Mifflin Co, 97; auth, My Happy Birthday Book!, Houghton Mifflin Co., 96; auth, Alicia has a Bad Day, Houghton Mifflin Co., 92; auth, Alicia's Evil Side, Arm-in-Arm Press, 92; auth, Alicia and Her happy Way of Life, Arm-in-Arm Press, 91. **CONTACT ADDRESS** Dept Writing, Emerson Col, 100 Beacon St, Boston, MA 02116-1501. **EMAIL** jahnclough@aol.com

JAHNER, ELAINE A.
DISCIPLINE ENGLISH LITERATURE **EDUCATION** IN Univ, PhD, 75. **CAREER** Prof, Dartmouth Col. **RESEARCH** Native Am lit. **SELECTED PUBLICATIONS** Auth, Indian Literature and Critical Responsibility, Studies in Am Indian Lit, 93; Lakota Myth, Univ Neb P, 83; Knowing All the Way Down to Fire in Feminist Measures: Soundings in Poetry and Theory, Women Cult Series, Univ Mich P, 95; coauth, Literary Themes in Indigenous Religions in HarperCollins Dictionary of Religion, 96. **CONTACT ADDRESS** Dept of English, Dartmouth Col, 6032 Sanborn House, Hanover, NH 03755. **EMAIL** Elaine.A.Jahner@dartmouth.edu

JAIMES, H.
PERSONAL Born 12/01/1964, Barcelona, Venezuela, d **DISCIPLINE** LITERATURE **EDUCATION** Central Univ Venezuela, BA, 89; NY Univ, MA, 92; Univ Pa, PhD, 98. **CAREER** Asst prof, NC State Univ. **HONORS AND AWARDS** Andrew W. Mellon Fel, Univ of Pa, 97; CHASS Res Awd, NC State Univ, 99. **MEMBERSHIPS** MLA. **RESEARCH** Nineteenth- and Twentieth-Century Latin American Literature, Literary Theory, Cultural Studies. **SELECTED PUBLICATIONS** Ed, Modernism y este'tica: cuaderno ine'dito, Fondo Editorial Tropykos, 99. **CONTACT ADDRESS** Dept For Lang, No Carolina State Univ, PO Box 8106, Raleigh, NC 27695-0001. **EMAIL** hjaimes@social.chass.ncsu.edu

JAMES, MICHAEL L.
PERSONAL Born 09/24/1946, Kennett, MO, m, 1970, 4 children **DISCIPLINE** COMMUNICATION **EDUCATION** Harding Univ, BA, 73; Ark State Univ, MSMC, 85; Fla State Univ, PhD, 92. **CAREER** Asst instr to assoc prof, Harding Univ, 78-; **HONORS AND AWARDS** Omicron Delta Kappa; Alpha Epsilon Rho; Kappa Tau Alpha, Alpha Phi Gamma; Distinguished Teacher Awd, Harding Univ, 89, 95; Malandro Schol, 91; Clarence Edney Teaching Fel, 91, 92; Col of Commun Fel, 91, 92. **MEMBERSHIPS** Ark Broadcast Educ Assoc; Broadcast Educ Assoc; ASCD; Speech Commun Assoc. **SELECTED PUBLICATIONS** Auth, "The Health Effects of Video Games", FSU Spectrum 3.2 (90); coauth, "Media Myopia", Interact 3.1 (91); coauth, "Interactive Compact Disc: Lessons Learned from IVD", Interact 3.1 (91); coauth, "Promoting the use of Interactive Media and Computer Assisted Learning: A Performance Management Perspective", Interact 3.2 (92); coauth, "Electronic Bulletin Board Uses and Media Effects", J of Broadcasting and Electronic Media, (95). **CONTACT ADDRESS** Dept Commun, Harding Univ, 900 E Center Ave, Searcy, AR 72149-0002.

JAMES, WILLIAM CLOSSON
PERSONAL Born 05/20/1943, Sudbury, ON, Canada, m, 1964, 3 children **DISCIPLINE** RELIGION, ENGLISH LITERATURE **EDUCATION** Queen's Univ, Ont, BA, 65, BD, 68; Univ Chicago, MA, 70, PhD(relig & lit), 74. **CAREER** Lectr, 73-75, asst prof, 75-80, chmn undergrad studies relig, 78-81, Assoc Prof Relig & Lit, Queen's Univ, Ont, 80-, Exec bd mem relig, Can Soc for Study Relig, 75-78; mem bd dirs relig, Can Corp for Studies Relig, 78-; book rev ed, Studies in Relig, 79-. **MEMBERSHIPS** Can Soc for Study Relig; Am Acad Relig. **RESEARCH** Religion and literature; modern Canadian fiction; heroism and the quest in literature; religious meaning of contemporary Canadian culture **SELECTED PUBLICATIONS** Auth, Nature and the Sacred in Canada + Role of Geography and Climate in Shaping a Canadian Identity, Stud in Religion Sciences Religieuses, Vol 0021, 92; auth, "The Canoe trip as Religious Quest;" auth, A Fur Trader's Photographs; auth, Locations of the Sacred: Essays on Religion, Literature, and Canadian Culture, Wilfried Laurier University Press, 98. **CONTACT ADDRESS** Dept of Religious Studies, Queen's Univ at Kingston, Theological Hall, Rm. 414, Kingston, ON, Canada K7L 3N6. **EMAIL** jameswc@post.queensu.ca

JAMES, WOODROW C.
PERSONAL Born 01/03/1936, Biloxi, MS, m, 1989 **DISCIPLINE** MUSIC **EDUCATION** La St Univ, BA, 58; Univ Ms, MM, 60; Mich St Univ, PhD, 66. **CAREER** Grad asst, 58-60, Univ Miss; grad asst, 61-64, Mich St Univ; asst prof, 64-65, Florence St Col; asst prof, 65-68, McNeese St Col; prof, 68-71, Univ Ok; prof, 72-73, Calif St Univ, Northridge; prof, 73-74, Calif St Univ, Pomona; prof, 74-90, Los Angeles City Col; vis prof, 98, E Los Angeles Col; vis prof, 99, Glendale Commun Col; prof, 90-, Los Angeles Valley Col. **HONORS AND AWARDS** First Place Composition Awd, 66, 67; Nat Endow for the Humanities fel, 78; Vocational Music Grant, 89; Jazz Educator of the Year, 93; first place composition award, 61. **MEMBERSHIPS** Amer Soc of Composers, Authors & Publ; Amer Federation of Musicians; Amer Federation of Teachers; Unit Prof of Calif; Music Assoc; Amer Soc of Music Arrangers & Composers. **RESEARCH** Music in England in the 18th cent; hist of jazz. **SELECTED PUBLICATIONS** Auth, Elegy for Trumpet and Band, Ludwig Music, 62; auth, The Use of the Harmonic Tritone in Twentieth-Century Music, Univ Mich, 65; auth, Brass Quartet (three movements), Mixomodian Music, 76; auth, Computer Assisted Instruction in the Fundamentals of Music, Los Angeles Commun Col, 88; auth, Professional Music in Los Angeles, 93, Los Angeles Commun Col, 94; recording, Jazz Crystallizations, Woody James Quintet, 78; recording, Hardcore Jazz, Woody James Septet, 82. **CONTACT ADDRESS** 18135 Hatton St, Reseda, CA 91335. **EMAIL** doctorjazz@earthlink.net

JAMESON, MICHAEL H.
PERSONAL Born 10/15/1924, United Kingdom, m, 1946, 4 children **DISCIPLINE** CLASSICS **EDUCATION** BA, 42; Univ Chicago, PhD, 49. **CAREER** Edward Clark Crossett Prof Emeritus Hum Studies and prof emeritus class. **RESEARCH** Greek hist; relig; epigraphy; archaeol. **SELECTED PUBLICATIONS** Auth, Sophocles, The Women of Trachis in Complete Greek Tragedies, 57; A Decree of Themistokles from Troizen, Hesperia, 60; Agriculture and Slavery in Classical Athens, CJ, 77-8; Sacrifice Before Battle in Hoplites, 91; coauth, A Greek Countryside: The Southern Argolid from Prehistory to Present Day, 92. **CONTACT ADDRESS** Stanford Univ, Bldg 20, Main Quad, Stanford, CA 94305. **EMAIL** michael.jameson@stanford.edu

JAMIL, S. SELINA
PERSONAL Born 02/03/1960, Bangladesh, m, 1983, 1 child **DISCIPLINE** ENGLISH **EDUCATION** Mich State Univ, Phd in English, 97; Mich State Univ, MA in English, 89; Univ Dhaka, BA & MA in English, 92. **CAREER** Asst Prof of English, Univ of Hartford, 97. **HONORS AND AWARDS** Univ of Hartford, International CtrFaculty Grant; Member of Phi Beta Delta Honor Society for International Scholar; Fulbright Scholarship. **MEMBERSHIPS** Modern Language Assoc; Editorial Advisory Board of Collegiate Press. **SELECTED PUBLICATIONS** Auth, "Awakenings," Form: A Magazine of the Arts 3, 84: 64; auth, "Why the Novel Matters," Harvest: Jahangirnagar Studies in Literature, 8, 87: 145-156; auth, "Uncle Tom's Cabin and the Covert Voice," Harvest: Jahangirnagar Studies in Literature, 11, 92: 36-58; auth, "Search," Short Stories Bimontly, June 98: 8; auth, "Exhaustion and Thoughts," Monsoon Magazine 1.2, 99; auth, "Moving," Of These Autumn Afternoon, 2.7, 99; auth, "Narrative Authority in the Jamesian Center of Consciousness," University Press of America, Forthcoming; auth, "The Inscrutable Silence of Women in Tagore's Short Stories," Journal of Commonwealth and Postcolonial Studies, Forthcoming; auth, "Silence: Woman's Burden or Triumph in Tagore's Short Stories," in Rabindranath Tagore in the New Millennium-Questions of Gender, Nation, Science and Tradition, Eds. Patrick Colm Hogan, Univ of Connecticut, and Lalita Pandit, Univ of Wisconsin, Forthcoming; auth, "Winging the Uncertain Flux of Time in Clear Light of Days," under consideration, Journal of Commonwealth Literatue. **CONTACT ADDRESS** Dept Basic Studies, Univ of Hartford, 200 Bloomfield Ave, West Hartford, CT 06117-1545.

JAMME, ALBERT W. F.
PERSONAL Born 06/27/1916, Senzeille, Belgium **DISCIPLINE** ENGLISH, FRENCH **EDUCATION** Cath Univ Louvain, DTheol, 47, DOr, 52; Pontif Bibl Comm, Rome, Lic, 48. **CAREER** Res Prof Semitics, Cath Univ Am, 55-, Epigraphical adv, Govt Saudi Arabia, 68-69. **MEMBERSHIPS** Cath Bibl Asn Am; Am Orient Soc. **RESEARCH** Pre-Islamic Arabian sci. **SELECTED PUBLICATIONS** Auth, Pieces Epigraphiques de Heid bin Aqil, la Necropole de Timna, (Hagr Kohlan), Biblio Mus, Louvain, 52; La Kynastie de Sarahbiil Yakuf et la documentation epigraphique sud-arabe, Ned Hist Archaeol Inst, Istanbul, 61; Sabaean inscriptions from Mahram Bilquis (Marib), Johns Hopkins Univ, 62; Miscellanees d'ancient arabe, I-XX, Washington, 71-98; Carnegie Museum 1974-1975 Yemen Expedition, Carnegie Natural Hist Spec Publ No 2, Pittsburgh, 76. **CONTACT ADDRESS** Dept of Semitics, Catholic Univ of America, 620 Michigan Ave N E, Washington, DC 20064-0002.

JANANGELO, JOSEPH
DISCIPLINE ENGLISH **EDUCATION** Manhattanville Col, BA, 81; NYork Univ, MA, 83, PhD, 88. **CAREER** Asst prof, english; dir, writing program. **RESEARCH** Rhetoric and composition; composition theory; computer-mediated instruction; autobiography. **SELECTED PUBLICATIONS** Co-ed, Resituating Writing: Constructing and Administering Writing Programs, Boynton, Cook, 95; Theoretical and Critical Perspectives on Teacher Change, Ablex, 93. **CONTACT ADDRESS** Dept of English, Loyola Univ, Chicago, 6525 N. Sheridan Rd., Chicago, IL 60626. **EMAIL** jjanang@wpo.it.luc.edu

JANDT, FRED E.
PERSONAL Born Seguin, TX **DISCIPLINE** COMMUNICATIONS **EDUCATION** Texas Lutheran Univ, BA,66; Stephen F Austin State Univ, MA, 67; Bowling Green State Univ, PhD, 70. **CAREER** Prof, Calif State Univ, San Bernadino, 83- . **MEMBERSHIPS** Nat Commun Asn Soc of Professionals in Dispute Resolution; So Calif Mediation Asn. **RESEARCH** Mediation; intercultural communication; computer-mediated communication. **SELECTED PUBLICATIONS** Auth, Win-Win Negotiating: Turning Conflict into Agreement, Wiley, 85; auth, Effective Interviewing for Paralegals, Anderson, 94; auth, Intercultural Communication: An Introduction, Sage, 95, 98; co-auth, Using the Internet and World Wide Web in Your Job Search, JIST, 97; coauth, Constructive Conflict Management: Asian-Pacific Cases, Sage, 96; auth, Alternative Dispute Resolution for Paralegals, Anderson, 97. **CONTACT ADDRESS** Communications Dept, California State Univ, San Bernardino, San Bernardino, CA 92407. **EMAIL** fjandt@csusb.edu

JANIK, DEL IVAN
PERSONAL Born 02/11/1945, Berwyn, IL, m, 1992, 2 children **DISCIPLINE** ENGLISH & AMERICAN LITERATURE **EDUCATION** Northwestern Univ, BA, 66; PhD, 71; Univ Mich, MA, 67. **CAREER** From Asst Prof to Assoc Prof, 71-81, Prof English, SUNY, Cortland, 81-. **HONORS AND AWARDS** SUNY Res Found fel, 77, 80. **MEMBERSHIPS** D.H. Lawrence Soc. **RESEARCH** D.H. Lawrence; modern American poetry; literature and the natural environment; modern english novel. **SELECTED PUBLICATIONS** Auth, Flann O'Brien: The artist as critic, Eire Ireland, 69; Toward Thingness: Cezanne's painting and Lawrence's poetry, Twentieth Century Lit, 73; The two infinites: D H Lawrence's Twilight in Italy, D H Lawrence Rev, 74; D H Lawrence's Future Religion: The unity of Last Poems, Tex Studies Lit & Lang, 75; D H Lawrence's Etruscan Places: The Mystery of Touch, Essays in Lit, 76; Poetry in the Ecosphere, Centennial Rev, 76; The Curve of Return: D H Lawrence's Travel Books, ELS, 81; auth, "History and the Here and Now: The Novels of Graham Swift," 20th Century Lit 35; auth, "No End of History: Evidence from the Contemporary english Novel," 20th Century Lit 41; auth, "A Cumbrian Rainbow: Melvin Bragg's Tallentire Trilogy," in D H Lawrence's Literary Inheritors (91). **CONTACT ADDRESS** Dept of English, SUNY, Col at Cortland, PO Box 2000, Cortland, NY 13045-0900. **EMAIL** janikd@cortland.edu

JANKOWSKI, THEODORA
DISCIPLINE EARLY MODERN LITERATURE , SPECIALTY IN DRAMA AND SHAKESPEARE **EDUCATION** Syracuse Univ, PhD. **CAREER** Asst prof, Washington State Univ. **RESEARCH** Cultural studies, feminist, Marxist, and queer theory; women writers of the early modern period. **SELECTED PUBLICATIONS** Auth, Women in Power in the Early Modern Drama, 92. **CONTACT ADDRESS** Dept of English, Washington State Univ, 1 SE Stadium Way, PO Box 645020, Pullman, WA 99164-5020. **EMAIL** tajankow@mail.wsu.edu

JANN, ROSEMARY
DISCIPLINE ENGLISH **EDUCATION** Duke Univ, BA, 71; MA, 72, PhD, 75, Northwestern Univ. **CAREER** Asst Prof, 75-79, Ripon Col; Asst Prof, 79-85, Assoc Prof, 85-86 Rutgers Univ; Assoc Prof 86-94, Prof, 94-, George Mason Univ. **CONTACT ADDRESS** Dept of English, George Mason Univ, Fairfax, Fairfax, VA 22030. **EMAIL** rjann@gmu.edu

JANNARONE, KIMBERLY M.
PERSONAL Born 10/24/1971, NC **DISCIPLINE** DRAMATIC HISTORY, THEORY, DIRECTING **EDUCATION** Emory Univ, BA, 93; Yale Sch Drama, MFA, 96; DFA, 00. **CAREER** Vis lectr, Smith Col, 98; pt act instr, Yale Univ, 97-00; act asst prof, Univ Wash, 00-01; asst prof, Univ Calif, 01-. **HONORS AND AWARDS** Bass Writ Fel, Yale, 98; Truman Capote Prize, 96; Emory Dean Acad Schl, 90-93; Phi Beta Kappa. **MEMBERSHIPS** MSTR, ATHE, MLA. **RESEARCH** French and German avant-garde theater; theater history; dramatic theory; revolution and theater; performance studies; performance theory. **SELECTED PUBLICATIONS** Auth, "Interview with Julie Harris," Yale Alum Mag (96); auth, "Puppetry and Pataphysics: Populism and the Ubu Cycle," New Thea Qtly (01). **CONTACT ADDRESS** Theater Arts Cen, Univ of California, Santa Cruz, 1156 High St, Santa Cruz, CA 95064. **EMAIL** kbymj@u.washington.edu

JANZEN, HENRY DAVID
DISCIPLINE ENGLISH LANGUAGE; LITERATURE **EDUCATION** Assumption Univ, BA; Univ Windsor, MA; Wayne State Univ, PhD, 70. **CAREER** Prof **RESEARCH** Renaissance literature; editing and textual criticism. **SELECTED PUBLICATIONS** Pub (s), Heywood, Middleton, Milton & Shakespeare; prepared ed 2 manuscript plays, Thomas Heywood's The Escapes of Jupiter and Francis Jaques's The Queen of Corsica. **CONTACT ADDRESS** Dept of English Language and Literature, Univ of Windsor, 401 Sunset Ave, Windsor, ON, Canada N9B 3P4. **EMAIL** janzen4@uwindsor.ca

JANZEN, LORRAINE
DISCIPLINE LITERATURE **EDUCATION** Brock, BA; McMaster, MA, PhD. **CAREER** Assoc prof, Nipissing Univ. **HONORS AND AWARDS** SSHRC 3 yr grant. **RESEARCH** Illustrated books. **SELECTED PUBLICATIONS** Auth, The Artist as Critic: Bitextuality in Fin-de-Sie cle Illustrated Books, Scolar, 95. **CONTACT ADDRESS** Dept of English, Nipissing Univ, 100 College Dr, Box 5002, North Bay, ON, Canada P1B 8L7. **EMAIL** lorraine@einstien.unipissing.ca

JARRED, ADA D.
PERSONAL Born 04/14/1937, Ruston, LA, d, 1962, 1 child **DISCIPLINE** LIBRARY AND INFORMATION STUDIES **EDUCATION** La Col, BA, 55; Univ Denver, MA, 61; Tex Women's Univ, PhD, 85. **CAREER** Reader Services, La Col Libry, 59-62; cat, Emory Univ Libry, 62-63; cat, LSU, 63-70; from vis asst prof to asst librn to sen librn to head librn and prof, 73-87, LSU at Alexandria; grad asst, Tex Women's Univ, 81, dir, librys, Northwestern State Univ, 87-. **HONORS AND AWARDS** Enhancement of Watson Libry, 90, Expanded CD-ROM Network for Business Databases, 93, Expanded Res Capability Hum, 94, Electronic Imaging Melrose Documents, 95, Technological Enhancement Tchr Educ, 96; Telecommunications Capabilities for Access to and Sharing of Nursing Resources, LEQSF; Micrographics Enhancement of Social Sciences, 97, Online Reserves For Business Edu, 99, La Board Regents. **MEMBERSHIPS** Am Libry Asn; Asn Col Res Librys; Col Libry Standards Committee; La Libry Asn; Acad Section Chair; Constitution and By-Laws Committee; Libry Development Committee; Continuing Educ Committee; La Lit Award Committee; La Acad Libry Infor Consortium; La Libry Network Commission; Beta Phi Mu; Delta Kappa Gamma; Phi Kappa Phi; Phi Alpha Theta. **RESEARCH** Library management. **SELECTED PUBLICATIONS** Auth, art, The Past is Prologue: Designing Information Services for Historic Preservationists, 95; auth, art, Connecting Historic Preservationists: A Proposed Partnership Based on the ERIC Model, 95; auth, art, Fee vs. Free: Maintaining the Balance, 95, auth, art, Eugene P. Watson Library, Northwestern State Univ, 99, and other prof articles. **CONTACT ADDRESS** 324 Mr Ed Ln, Natchitoches, LA 71457. **EMAIL** jarred@alpha.nsula.edu

JASKOSKI, HELEN
PERSONAL Born 05/13/1941, Tucson, AZ **DISCIPLINE** ENGLISH **EDUCATION** Mt St Mary's Col, Calif, BA, 63; Stanford Univ, MA, 67, PhD(English & Am lit), 69. **CAREER** Writer, Syst Develop Corp, 63-64; asst prof English, Calif State Univ, Los Angeles, 68-70; assoc prof, 70-80, Prof English, Calif State Univ, Fullerton, 80-, Fulbright lectr Am lit, Marie Curie-Sklodowska Univ, Poland, 73-74; co-dir, Calif State Univ Inst Prog, Florence, Italy, 82-83; mem adv bd, Poetry Therapy Inst, Los Angeles. **MEMBERSHIPS** MLA; Soc Study Multi-Ethnic Lit US. **RESEARCH** American ethnic literature; women's literature; psychology and literature. **SELECTED PUBLICATIONS** Auth, Power unequal to man: Conjure in works by 5 Afro-American authors, Southern Folklore Quart, 74; My heart will go out: Healing songs of native American women, Int J Women's Studies, No 4; Poetry, poetics and the poetry therapist, The Arts in Psychotherapy, No 7. **CONTACT ADDRESS** Dept of English & Comparative Literature, California State Univ, Fullerton, PO Box 6848, Fullerton, CA 92834-6848. **EMAIL** hjaskoski@fullerton.edu

JASON, PHILIP K.
PERSONAL Born 12/25/1941, m, 1962, 2 children **DISCIPLINE** LITERATURE **EDUCATION** New School for Social Res, BA, 63; Georgetown Univ, MA, 65; Univ of Md, PhD, 71. **CAREER** Instr to asst prof, Georgetown Univ, 66-73; asst prof to prof, US Naval Acad, 73-01. **MEMBERSHIPS** MLA. **SELECTED PUBLICATIONS** Ed, Anais Nin Reader, Swallow Pr, 73; auth, Nineteenth Century American Poetry: An Annotated Bibliography, Salem Pr, 89; coauth, Creative Writer's Handbook, Prentice Hall, 90; ed, Fourteen Landing Zones: Approaches to Vietnam War Literature, Univ of Iowa Pr, 91; auth, The Vietnam War in Literature: An Annotated Bibliography of Criticism, Salem Pr, 92; auth, Anais Nin and Her Critics, Camden House, 93; coed, Retrieving Bones: Stories and Poems of the Korean War, Rutgers Univ Pr, 99; auth, Acts and Shadows: the Vietnam War in American Literary Culture, Rowman and Littlefield, 00; coed, The Encyclopedia of American War Literature, Greenwood Pr. **CONTACT ADDRESS** Dept English, United States Naval Acad, Annapolis, MD 21402. **EMAIL** pjason@aol.com

JAUSS, DAVID
PERSONAL Born 02/25/1951, Windom, MN, m, 1971, 2 children **DISCIPLINE** CREATIVE WRITING **EDUCATION** Univ Iowa, PhD. **CAREER** English and Creative Writing, Univ Ark at Little Rock. **HONORS AND AWARDS** AWP Awd in Short Fiction; NEH grant; Pusheart Prize; O. Henry Prize. **SELECTED PUBLICATIONS** Auth, Black Maps; Improvising Rivers; Crimes of Passion; Ed, Strong Measures: Contemporary American Poetry in Traditional Forms; The Best of Crazyhorse: 30 years of Poetry and Fiction. **CONTACT ADDRESS** English Dept., Univ of Arkansas, Little Rock, 2801 S University Ave., Little Rock, AR 72204-1099.

JAY, GREGORY S.
PERSONAL Born 08/01/1952, North Hollywood, CA, m, 1979, 1 child **DISCIPLINE** ENGLISH **EDUCATION** Univ of Calif at Santa Cruz, BA, 75; State Univ of NYork, PhD, 80. **CAREER** Asst prof, Univ of Ala, 80-84; assoc prof, Univ of SC, 84-87; prof, Univ of Wis, 87- ; vis prof, Northwestern Univ, 91; schol in residence, Free Univ of Berlin, 91; contr ed, Am Lit Hist. **HONORS AND AWARDS** Summer Travel grant, Univ of Ala, 81; Summer Fac Res fel, Univ of Ala, 82; Res Conf grant, Nat Endowment for the Hums, 82; Summer Res grant, Univ of Ala, 83; Travel to Collections grant, Nat Endowment for the Hums, 83; NEH fel, 85; Ctr for 20th Centry Studies fel, 88-89; Res Incentive grant, UWM, 91; Ctr for 20th Century Studies, UWM, 94-95; Proj dir Rethinking American Studies: Connecting the Differnces, Nat Endowment for the Hums, 95-96; Res grant, Univ of Wis. **MEMBERSHIPS** Am Studies Asn; Midwest Modern Lang Asn; Mod Lang Asn; Multi-Ethnic Lit of the United States Soc. **SELECTED PUBLICATIONS** Auth, T.S. Eliot and the Poetics of Literary History, Baton Rouge: Louisiana State UP, 83; auth, After Strange Texts: The Role of Theory in the Study of Literature, Tuscaloosa: U of Alabama P, 85; auth, Modern American Critics; 1920-1955, vol. 63, Dictionary of Literary Biography, Detroit: Gale Res Co., 88; auth, Modern American Critics Since 1955, vol. 67, Dictionary of Literary Biography, Detroit: Gale Res Co., 88; auth, America the Scrivener: Deconstruction and the subject of Literary History, Ithaca: Cornell UP, 90; auth, American Literature and the Culture Wars, Ithaca: Cornell UP, 97; auth, "Jewish Writers in the Multicultural Literature Class," Heath anthology Newsletter, 16, (97): 8-11; coauth, "Where Do We Go From Here?" with Gerald Graff, In Political Correctness: A Response from the Cultural Left, By Richard Bernstein, Minneapolis: U of Minnesota Press, (97): 204-210; auth, "Women Writers and Resisting Readers," Legacy 15:1, (98): 104-110; auth, "Strategies and Challenges in High-Tech Teaching," Works and Days 16: 1-2, (98): 393-410. **CONTACT ADDRESS** Dept of English, Univ of Wisconsin, Green Bay, 876 E Birch Whitefish, Green Bay, WI 53217. **EMAIL** gjay@uwm.edu

JAY, PAUL
DISCIPLINE ENGLISH **EDUCATION** Univ Calif, Santa Cruz, BA, 75; Univ Calif, Berkeley, MA, 76; Univ Calif, Santa Cruz, PhD, 81. **CAREER** Prof. **RESEARCH** Literary criticism and theory; modernism and modernity; American literature; comparative literature of the Americas, border Stud. **SELECTED PUBLICATIONS** Auth, Contingency Blues: The Search for Foundations in American Criticism, Univ Wis Press, 97; Translation, Invention, Resistance: Rewriting the Conquest in Carlos Fuentes The Two Shores, Modern Fiction Stud 47, 97; Posing: Autobiography and the Subject of Philosophy in Postmodernism and Autobiography, Univ Mass Press, 94. **CONTACT ADDRESS** Dept of English, Loyola Univ, Chicago, 6525 N Sheridan Rd, Chicago, IL 60626. **EMAIL** pjay@orion.it.luc.edu

JEFCHAK, ANDREW TIMOTHY
PERSONAL Born 01/25/1936, East Chicago, IN, m, 1959, 3 children **DISCIPLINE** AMERICAN LITERATURE, FILM STUDY **EDUCATION** IN Univ, Bloomington, AB, 59; DePaul Univ, MA, 65; MI State Univ, PhD, 70. **CAREER** Instr Eng, Am Inst Banking, Chicago, 64-65; grad asst & asst to dir inquiry & expression, Justin Morrill Col, MI State Univ, 65-68; Prof Eng & Film Study, Aquinas Col, 68-, Kellogg Found-Asn Independent Cols & Univs of MI fel, 71-72; Danforth assoc, 77-83. **MEMBERSHIPS** Am Film Inst; AAUP; Univ Film Asn. **RESEARCH** Family relationships in mod fiction; lit and motion pictures, comp art forms; struct and irony in motion pictures. **SELECTED PUBLICATIONS** Film Critic, Grand Rapids Press, 1977. **CONTACT ADDRESS** Dept of Eng, Aquinas Col, Michigan, 1607 Robinson Rd S E, Grand Rapids, MI 49506-1799. **EMAIL** jefchand@aquinas.edu

JEFFERY, PETER
PERSONAL Born 10/19/1953, New York, NY, m, 1983, 2 children **DISCIPLINE** MUSIC HISTORY **EDUCATION** City Univ NYork, BA, 75; Princeton Univ, MFA, 77, PhD, 80. **CAREER** Hill Monastic Manuscript Libr, 80-82; asst prof, Univ Delaware, 84-87; assoc prof, 87- 93; Prof, Princeton Univ, 93-. **MEMBERSHIPS** SBC, Medieval Acad Am; Am Musicol Soc. **RESEARCH** Medieval Christian chant **SELECTED PUBLICATIONS** Auth, "A Proposal for a "Palaeographical Manual of the Byzantine Musical Notations'," in Palaeobyzantine Notations: A Reconstruction of the Source Material, A.A. Bredius Found, 95; auth, "Rome and Jerusalem: From Oral Tradition to Written Repertory in Two Ancient Liturgical Centers," in Essays on Medieval Music in Honor of David Hughes 207-47, 95. ed, Paths and Bridges: The Study of Liturgical Chant, East and West, Princeton Univ Press; co-auth, Ethiopian Christian Liturgical Chant: An Anthology, 93-97; **CONTACT ADDRESS** Music Dept, Princeton Univ, Princeton, NJ 08544. **EMAIL** jeffery@princeton.edu

JEFFRES, LEO
PERSONAL Born Bridgeport, NE **DISCIPLINE** MASS COM THEORY, JOURNALISM, INTERNATIONAL COM, METHODS **EDUCATION** Univ Idaho, BA; Univ Wash, MA; Univ Minn, PhD. **CAREER** Commun res ctr dir. **HONORS AND AWARDS** MAPOR fel; Fulbright scholar. **MEMBERSHIPS** Int Commun Asn; Nat Commun Asn; Asn for Educ in Jour and Mass Commun; Am Asn for Public Opinion Res; Fulbright Asn; Phi Beta Kappa; Soc of Professional Jour. **SELECTED PUBLICATIONS** Auth, Mass Media Processes, Waveland Press, 94; auth, Mass Media Effects, Waveland Press, 97; auth, The Impact of Ethnicity and Ethnic Media on Presidential Voting Patterns, Journalism & Communication Monographs, 99; auth, Ethnicity and Ethnic Media Use: A Panel Study, Communication Research, 00; coauth, The Television of Abundance Arrives: Cable Choices and Interest Maximiation, Telematics and Informatics, 00; auth, Urban Communication Systems: Neighborhoods & The Search for Community (forthcoming); coauth, Spirals of Silence: Expressing Opinions when the Climate of Opinion is Unambiguous. **CONTACT ADDRESS** Commun Dept, Cleveland State Univ, Cleveland, OH 44115. **EMAIL** l.jeffres@csuohio.edu

JEFFREY, DAVID LYLE
PERSONAL Born 06/28/1941, Ottawa, ON, Canada **DISCIPLINE** ENGLISH LITERATURE, ART HISTORY **EDUCATION** Wheaton Col, Ill, BA, 65; Princeton Univ, MA, 67, PhD(English), 68. **CAREER** Asst prof, Univ Victoria, BC, 68-69 & Univ Rochester, 69-72; assoc prof English & chmn dept, Univ Victoria, BC, 73-78; chmn dept, 78-81, Prof English, Univ Ottawa, 78-, Gen ed, Dict Biblical Tradition in English Lit, 77-; Can Coun leave fel, 77-78; adj prof, Regent Col, 78-, **HONORS AND AWARDS** Bk of Year Awd, Conf Christianity & Lit, 75; Solomon Katz Distinguished Lectr in Humanities, Univ Wash, 77. **MEMBERSHIPS** MLA; Conf Christianity & Lit; Mediaeval Acad Am; Asn Can Univ Teachers English; Am Acad Relig & Soc Biblical Lit. **RESEARCH** Medieval, modern and biblical literature. **SELECTED PUBLICATIONS** Ed, Dictionary of Biblical Tradition in English Literature, 93; auth, People of the Book: Christian Identity and Literary Culture, 96; co-ed, Rethinking the Future of the University (University of Ottawa Press Mentor Series), by David Lyle Jeffrey and Dominic Manganiello, 98; auth, English Spirituality in the Age of Wyclif; ed, A Burning and a Shining Light: English Spirituality in the Age of Wesley; ed, The Law of Love: English Spirituality in the Age of Wycliff. **CONTACT ADDRESS** Dept of English, Univ of Ottawa, Arts Bldg, 70 Laurier, Ottawa, ON, Canada K1N 6N5.

JEFFREYS, MARK
DISCIPLINE MODERNIST POETRY AND POETICS **EDUCATION** Emory, PhD, 90. **CAREER** Dept Eng, Univ Ala **SE-**

LECTED PUBLICATIONS Ed, New Definitions of Lyric, Garland, 97; Coauth, Teacher's Guide to the Norton Anthology of Poetry. **CONTACT ADDRESS** Univ of Alabama, Birmingham, 1400 University Blvd, Birmingham, AL 35294-1150.

JEHLEN, MYRA
DISCIPLINE ENGLISH LANGUAGE AND LITERATURE **EDUCATION** CUNY, BA; Univ Calif Berkeley, MA; PhD. **CAREER** Prof. **RESEARCH** Transatlantic cultural relations; literature and history; comparative literature. **SELECTED PUBLICATIONS** Auth, Caste and Class in Faulkner's South; auth, American Incarnation: The Individual, the Nation, and the Continent; auth, The English Literatures of America; ed, Papers of Empire. **CONTACT ADDRESS** Dept of English, Rutgers, The State Univ of New Jersey, New Brunswick, 510 George St, New Brunswick, NJ 08901-1167. **EMAIL** jehlen@rci.rutgers.edu

JEMIELITY, THOMAS J.
PERSONAL Born 12/17/1933, Cleveland, OH, m, 1965, 3 children **DISCIPLINE** ENGLISH **EDUCATION** John Carroll Univ, MA, 58; Cornell Univ, PhD, 65. **CAREER** Lectr English, Carleton Univ, Can, 62-63; from instr to asst prof, 63-70, chmn comt acad prog, Col Arts & Lett, 76-80, assoc prof to prof English, Univ Notre Dame, 70-. **HONORS AND AWARDS** Allen Seymour Olmsted fel, Cornell Univ, 60-61; Pres, Johnson Soc of the Cent Region, 85. **MEMBERSHIPS** Am Soc for Eighteenth-Century Studies; Jane Austen Soc of N Am; Eighteenth-Century Scottish Studies Soc; The Johnson Soc, Lichfield, England; The Johnson Soc of London; The Johnson Soc of the Cent Region; Midwest Am Soc for Eighteenth-Century Studies; NE Am Soc for Eighteenth-Century Studies. **RESEARCH** Mock-Biblical Satire; Alexander Pope and the Bible; satire; Samuel Johnson **SELECTED PUBLICATIONS** Auth, Savage Virtues and Barbarous Grandeur, Cornell Libr J, winter 66; I sing of a Maiden: God's courting of Mary, Concerning Poetry, 69; More in Notions Than Facts, Dalhousie Rev, fall 69; Dr Johnson and the Uses of Travel, Philol Quart, 4/72; Samuel Johnson, the Second Sight, and His Sources, Studies English Lit, summer 74; A Mock-Biblical Controversy: Sir Richard Blackmore in the Dunciad, PQ, 74; Post no bills (short story), Juggler, winter 78; Thomas Pennant's Scottish Tours and the Journey to the Western Islands of Scotland, In: Fresh Reflections on Samuel Johnson: Essays in Criticism, 87; More Disagreeable for Him to Teach or the Boys to Learn? The Vanity of Human Wishes in the Classroom, In: Teaching Eighteenth Century Poetry, AMS, 90; Satire and the Hebrew Prophets, 92; Teaching a Journey to the Western Islands of Scotland, In: Approaches to Teaching the Works of Samuel Johnson, MLA, 93; Gibbon Among the Aeolists: Islamic Credibility and Pagan Fanaticism in The Decline and Fall, In: Studies in Eighteenth-Century Culture; A Keener Eye on Vacancy: Boswell's Second Thoughts About Second Sight, Prose Studies. **CONTACT ADDRESS** Dept of English, Univ of Notre Dame, 356 Oshaugnessy Hall, Notre Dame, IN 46556. **EMAIL** Thomas.J.Jemielity.1@nd.edu

JENKINS, ANTHONY W.
PERSONAL Born 07/08/1936, Sutton Coldfield, England, m, 1960, 2 children **DISCIPLINE** MEDIEVAL LITERATURE **EDUCATION** Cambridge Univ, MA; Univ Calif, Berkeley, PhD. **CAREER** Adj prof **RESEARCH** Renaissance; 19th and 20th-century drama; the British novel. **SELECTED PUBLICATIONS** Auth, Modern British Drama, 1890-1990, Modern Drama, Vol 0036, 93. **CONTACT ADDRESS** Dept of English, Univ of Victoria, PO Box 3070, Victoria, BC, Canada V8W 3W1.

JENKINS, CHARLES M.
PERSONAL Born 05/31/1948, Denver, CO, m, 1969, 2 children **DISCIPLINE** ENGLISH **EDUCATION** Univ Calif, Santa Barbara, BA, 70, MA, 74; Claremont Grad Univ, PhD, 94. **CAREER** Sec Eng Teacher, 71-72, 85-90; ASSOC PROF, LOCK HAVEN UNIV, 94-. **RESEARCH** Mysticism, medieval lit; cognition & literacy. **SELECTED PUBLICATIONS** Auth, Bizarre Mnemonics: Implications for the Classroom, J Mental Imagery, 99. **CONTACT ADDRESS** English Dept, Lock Haven Univ of Pennsylvania, Lock Haven, PA 17745. **EMAIL** cjenkins@lhup.edu

JENKINS, JOYCE O.
DISCIPLINE AMERICAN LITERATURE **EDUCATION** Univ MI, BA, Ed, 71, MEd, 72; Bowling Green State Univ, PhD, 78. **CAREER** Assoc prof; co-ch, Black Hist Observance Comm, 93-94; hd lang(s). **HONORS AND AWARDS** Tchg fel, Bowling Green State Univ, 74-77; fel, NEH, Univ NC, 89; fel, Acad Leadership Acad, 93-95; recognition for excellence in leadership, off acad aff, 89; co-ch, annual black hist month scholar observance comm, 93-96. **MEMBERSHIPS** Mem, AAUP; Nat Coun Tchr(s) Eng; Mod Lang Assn; Nat Col Hon(s) Coun; S Reg Hon(s) Coun; Phi Delta Kappa; Eng Hon Soc; For Lang Assn Ga; Ga-SC Col Eng Assn. **SELECTED PUBLICATIONS** Auth, Black History Month, Artsline: Macon Arts Alliance, Calendar/Newsletter, 90; Readers Will Ask for More of Taulbert's Once Upon a Time, Review of Once Upon a Time When We Were Colored, 90; Fort Valley State College Cooperative Developmental Energy Program: The Only One of Its Kind, Macon Mag, 92. **CONTACT ADDRESS** Dept of Eng, Fort Valley State Univ, 600 Park St, Fort Valley, GA 310030.

JENKINS, KENNETH VINCENT
PERSONAL Born Elizabeth, NJ, d, 4 children **DISCIPLINE** ENGLISH, AFRICAN-AMERICAN LITERATURE **EDUCATION** Columbia Col NYork, AB; Columbia Univ NYork, AM; Columbia Univ, PhD candidate. **CAREER** South Side High School, Rockville Centre NY, chmn English dept 1965-72; Nassau Community Coll, Supvr Adjunct Faculty, Prof English and Afro-American Literature, Chmn Afro-Amer Studies Dept, 74-. **HONORS AND AWARDS** Baker Awd, Columbia Univ; community awards; Martin Luther King Jr Awd, Nassau County, 1989. **MEMBERSHIPS** Consultant in Eng, New York State Regents Comm; convener, chmn bd dir, Target Youth Centers Inc NY, 1973-75; Natl Bd Pacifica Found, mem 1973-80, chmn, pres 1976-80; chmn, Nassau County Youth Bd, 1979-; Phi Delta Kappa; Assn for the Study of Afro-Amer Life and History; Afro-Amer Inst NY; Mensa, 1968-70; Coun Black Amer Affairs; exec bd, NY African Studies Assn; African Heritage Studies Assn; mem, Governor's New York State Council on Youth, 1986-; advisory bd mem, Radio Station WBAI-FM NY, 1972-85; member, Schomburg Corp, 1989-; board member, Long Island Community Foundation, 1989-98; bd mem, New York State Youth Support Inc. **SELECTED PUBLICATIONS** Author of essays, "Last Day in Church"; reviews. **CONTACT ADDRESS** African-American Studies Dept, Nassau Comm Col, Garden City, NY 11530.

JENKINS, NICHOLAS
PERSONAL Born London, Britain **DISCIPLINE** ENGLISH **EDUCATION** Oxford Univ, BA, 84; MA, 97; PhD, 97. **CAREER** Instr to asst prof, Harvard Univ, 97-98; asst prof, Stanford Univ, 98-. **HONORS AND AWARDS** Harkness Fel, 86-88; ACLS Jr Fel, 00-01; Stanford Humanities Ctr Fel, 00-01. **RESEARCH** Modern and contemporary poetry; British culture; graphic arts. **SELECTED PUBLICATIONS** Ed, Lincoln Kirstein Reader, 91; series ed, Poetry in Translation Vols, Princeton Univ Pr; auth, The Island: W. H. Auden and the Making of a Post-National Poetry, Harvard Univ Pr (forthcoming). **CONTACT ADDRESS** English Dept, Stanford Univ, Stanford, CA 94305-2087. **EMAIL** njenkins@stanford.edu

JENKINS, RONALD BRADFORD
PERSONAL Born 11/14/1941, Rockingham, NC, m, 1973, 2 children **DISCIPLINE** RENAISSANCE LITERATURE **EDUCATION** Wake Forest Univ, BA, 64; NC State Univ, MA, 70; Univ NC, Chapel Hill, PhD(English), 76. **CAREER** Teacher English, E Southern Pines High Sch, NC, 64-66; instr, Vardell Hall Jr Col, 66-68, Winthrop Univ, SC, 70-72 & Univ NC, Chapel Hill, 75-76; asst prof, Campbell Col, 76-77, assoc prof, 77-78, Victor R Small prof & chmn dept, 78-79; Prof English & Chmn Dept English, Speech, and Journalism, GA Col & State Univ, 79-99; prof English, Dept English, Speech, and Journalism, GA Col and State Univ, 79-. **MEMBERSHIPS** MLA; SAtlantic Mod Lang Asn; Milton Soc Am; Renaissance Soc Am; Southeastern Renaissance Conf. **RESEARCH** Milton studies; Medieval and Renaissance theology; Victorian and Romantic poetic theory. **SELECTED PUBLICATIONS** Auth, A new look at an old tombstone (The Scarlet Letter), New Eng Quart, 9/72; Milton and the Theme of Fame, Studies English Lit Ser, Mouton, The Hague, 73; Invulnerable virtue in Wieland and Comus, SAtlantic Bull, 5/73; The Zerilla Dewey Subplot in The Rise of Silas Lapham, Explicator, spring 78; Robert Frost and the Agitated Heart, Notes on Contemp Lit, 3/80; The devil's advocate: A different approach to My Last Duchess, J English Teaching Tech, winter 80; Shakespeare's Measure for Measure: Cucullus non Facit Monachum, Explicator, summer 81; Four stages in the writing of expository prose, Freshman English Resource Notes, vol 7, no 1, 83; Henry Smith: England's Silver-Tongued Preacher, Mercer Univ Press, 83; Revelation in Paradise Regained, J of Evolutionary Psych, 85; The Case Against the King: The Family of Ophelia vs. His Majesty King Claudius of Denmark, J of Evolutionary Psych, 96. **CONTACT ADDRESS** P O Box 505, Milledgeville, GA 31061-0505. **EMAIL** rjenkins@mail.gcsu.edu

JENNE, NATALIE R.
PERSONAL Born 04/24/1934, Milwaukee, WI, s **DISCIPLINE** MUSIC **EDUCATION** Valparaiso Univ, BA, 56; Stanford Univ, MA, 57; DMA, 67. **CAREER** Lectr, Stanford Univ, 59; asst prof to prof, Concordia Col, 60-99. **HONORS AND AWARDS** Woodrow Wilson Dissertation Fel; Am Coun of Learned Soc Fel; Lutheran Brotherhood Fel. **MEMBERSHIPS** Am Musicological Soc, Am Bach Soc, Riemenschneider Bach Inst. **RESEARCH** Performance practices of Baroque music. **SELECTED PUBLICATIONS** Auth, Dance and the Music of J.S. Bach, Indiana Univ Press, 98; contribur, The Oxford Companion: J.S. Bach, Oxford Univ Press, 99; auth, Dance and the Music of J.S. Bach 2nd edition, forthcoming; contribur, Key Words in Church music, Concordia Pub House, forthcoming. **CONTACT ADDRESS** Dept Music, Concordia Univ, Illinois, 7400 Augusta St, River Forest, IL 60305-1402. **EMAIL** crfjennen@curf.edu

JENNINGS, MAUDE M.
PERSONAL Born 10/11/1927, New York, NY, m, 1948 **DISCIPLINE** ENGLISH LITERATURE **EDUCATION** Manhattanville Col, BA, 78; Ball State Univ, MA, 80; PhD, 86. **CAREER** Asst Prof, Ball State Univ, 86-. **HONORS AND AWARDS** Kellogg (leadership), 92; BSU Awd, 92, 93, 94; C-Span (leadership), 95. **MEMBERSHIPS** AAUW; Toni Morrison Soc; Penwomen. **RESEARCH** Literature of the migration from the south of African Americans during and after the 1900s. **SELECTED PUBLICATIONS** Auth, "Van Gogh & Hopkins," Van Gogh 100, 92; auth, Mary McLeod Bethune, Salem Press; auth, Barbara Jordan, Salem Press; auth, Adam Clayton Powell, Salem Press. **CONTACT ADDRESS** Dept English, Ball State Univ, 3408 N Benton Rd, Muncie, IN 47304. **EMAIL** maudeveronica@ameritech.net

JENSEN, EJNER JACOB
PERSONAL Born 01/28/1937, Omaha, NE, m, 2 children **DISCIPLINE** ENGLISH **EDUCATION** Carleton Col, BA, 59; Tulane Univ, MA, 60, PhD(English), 65. **CAREER** From instr to asst prof, 64-70, assoc prof, 70-79, Prof English, Univ Mich, Ann Arbor, 79- **MEMBERSHIPS** MLA; Malone Soc. **RESEARCH** English Renaissance drama; Shakespeare. **SELECTED PUBLICATIONS** Auth, Theme and imagery in The Malcontent, Studies English, Lit 70; The wit of Renaissance satire, Philol Quart, 72; The changing faces of love in English Renaissance drama, Comp Drama, 73; Lamb, Poel, and Our Post-War Theatre, Renaissance Drama, 79; John Marston, Dramatist, Salzburg, 79; Encounters with experience, New England Rev, 80; ed, The Future, UMI Press, 83; auth, Shakespeare and the Ends of Comedy, Indiana, 91; auth, Ben Jonson's Comedies on the Modern State, UMI. **CONTACT ADDRESS** Gayle Morris Sweetland Writing Center, Univ of Michigan, Ann Arbor, 435 S State St 11111 Angel Hall, Ann Arbor, MI 48109-1003. **EMAIL** ejjensen@umich.edu

JENSEN, H. JAMES
PERSONAL Born 06/07/1935, Albert Lea, MN, m, 1962, 2 children **DISCIPLINE** ENGLISH **EDUCATION** Univ Minn, BA, 55; MA, 62; Cornell Univ, PhD, 66. **CAREER** Asst prof to Prof Emeritus, Indiana Univ, 66-. **MEMBERSHIPS** Am Soc for Eighteenth Century Studies; Johnson Soc of the Central Region. **RESEARCH** History of Critical Theory and Rhetoric; 17th and 18th Century English, French, music, painting literature, philosophy, rhetoric; Composition Theory. **SELECTED PUBLICATIONS** Auth, A Glossary of John Dryden's Critical Terms, 69; auth, The Satirist's Art, 72; auth, The Muses Concord, 77; auth, Signs and Meaning in Eighteenth Century Art, 97; The Sensational Restoration, 97. **CONTACT ADDRESS** Dept English, Indiana Univ, Bloomington, 2315 E Moores Pl, Bloomington, IN 47401.

JENSEN, J. VERNON
PERSONAL Born 09/29/1922, Scandia, MN, m, 1954, 2 children **DISCIPLINE** SPEECH COMMUNICATION **EDUCATION** Augsburg Col, BA, 47; Univ Minn, MA, 48, PhD, 59. **CAREER** Instr speech & hist, Augsburg Col, 48-51; teaching asst hist, 51-53, instr commun, 53-59, from asst prof to assoc prof speech & commun, 59-67, dir, Commun Prog, 70-73, Prof to Prof Emer Speech & Commun, Univ Minn, Minneapolis, 67-, Fulbright lectr, State Training Col Teachers, Rangoon, Burma, 61-62. **MEMBERSHIPS** Speech Commun Asn; Am Asn Advan Humanities; Am Forensic Asn; Hist Sci Soc. **RESEARCH** Rhetorical criticism; British and Commonwealth public speaking; Thomas Henry Huxley as a communicator. **CONTACT ADDRESS** 1666 Coffman, Saint Paul, MN 55108. **EMAIL** jense003@umn.edu

JENSEN, KATHARINE
DISCIPLINE 17TH AND 18TH CENTURY LITERATURE, WOMEN'S WRITING, FEMINIST THEORY **EDUCATION** Columbia Univ, PhD, 88. **CAREER** Assoc prof, La State Univ. **SELECTED PUBLICATIONS** Auth, Male Models of Feminine Epistolarity, Writing the Female Voice, 88; The Inheritance of Masculinity and the Limits of Heterosexual Revision, 18th Century Life, 92; Writing Love: Letters, Women, and the Novel, 95. **CONTACT ADDRESS** Dept of Fr Grad Stud, Louisiana State Univ and A&M Col, Baton Rouge, LA 70803.

JENSEN, PETER
PERSONAL Born 08/19/1942, Brooklyn, NY, m, 1994, 1 child **DISCIPLINE** ENGLISH **EDUCATION** Univ Mich, BA, 64; New York Univ, MA, 65. **CAREER** Instr of English, Cleveland State Univ, 65-67; Univ of Oregon, 70; Lane Community Col, 86-98; Linfield Col, 98; Lynn-benton Community Col, 93-00. **HONORS AND AWARDS** Finalist for Book of Poetry, Oregon Book Awds, 93. **MEMBERSHIPS** Oregon Council of Teachers of English. **RESEARCH** Poetry; Fictions & Metafictions; Shakespeare; English Literature; Technical Writing; and Science. **SELECTED PUBLICATIONS** Auth, "Shakespeare: A Literary Friend," on Hamlet & Horatio, 98; auth, "Henry V" Something for everybody, Ashland Shakespeare Festival, 00. **CONTACT ADDRESS** Dept Liberal Arts, Linn-Benton Comm Col, 6500 Pacific Blvd Southwest, Albany, OR 97321-3755.

JENSEN, ROBERT W.
PERSONAL Born 07/14/1958, Devils Lake, ND, d, 1 child **DISCIPLINE** JOURNALISM, MASS COMMUNICATION **EDUCATION** Univ MN, PhD, 92. **CAREER** Asst prof, 92-98, assoc prof, Univ TX, 98-. **MEMBERSHIPS** AEJMC; ICA;

NCA. **RESEARCH** Freedom of speech; media law; feminism; sexuality; radical politics. **SELECTED PUBLICATIONS** Ed with David S Allen, Freeing the First Amendment: Critical Perspectives on Freedom of Expression, NY Univ Press, 95; coauth with Elvia R Arriola, Feminism and Free Expression: Silence and Voice, and auth, Embracing Uncertainty/Facing Fear, in Freeing the First Amendment, NY Univ Press, 95; auth, Pornography and the Limits of Experimental Research, in Gail Dines and Jean M Humez, eds, Gender, Race, and Class in Media: A Text Reader, Sage, 95; auth, The Politics and Ethics of Lesbian and Gay Wedding Announcements in Newspapers, Howard J of Commun, Jan-March 96; Knowing Poronography, Violence Against Women, March 96; What Are Journalists For?, Peace Rev, 96; Journalists and the Overtime Provisions of the Fair Labor Standards Act, Journalism and Mass Communications Quart, summer 96; Priviledge, Power, and Politics in Research, Int J of Qualitative Studies in Ed, 97; co-auth, with Gail Dines and Ann Russo, Pornography: The Production and Consumption of Inequality, Routledge, 98; auth, "First Amendment Potluck," Commun Law and Policy, 3:4, Autumn, (98): 563-588; numerous other publications and several forthcoming. **CONTACT ADDRESS** Dept of Journalism, Univ of Texas, Austin, Austin, TX 78712. **EMAIL** rjensen@uts.cc.utexas.edu

JERZ, DENNIS G.
DISCIPLINE ELECTRONIC TEXTS, TECHNICAL WRITING **EDUCATION** Univ Va, BA, 90; MA, 92; Univ Toronto, PhD, 01. **CAREER** Instr, Univ Toronto, 96-98; asst prof, Univ of Wis-Eau Claire, 98-. **HONORS AND AWARDS** Open Fellow, Univ Toronto, 93-97; Simcoe Special Fellow, Univ Toronto, 92-93. **MEMBERSHIPS** ATTW, NCTE, STC, MLA. **RESEARCH** Electronic texts; usability; technology in lit; online rhetoric; interactive fiction; public understanding of science. **SELECTED PUBLICATIONS** Auth, Towards a Pro-active Technical Writing Curriculum, Can Soc Mech Engineering Forum, 98; PSim 2.0: A Computer Simulation of Wagon Motion in the York Corpus Christi Pageant, (Re)Soundings: A World Wide Web Publication, 97; coauth, "Adapting Web Electronic Libraries to English Studies," with Christopher Douglas, Dennis G. Jerz, and Ian Lancashire, Surfaces, 99; auth, "Kairos Critique: Kudos and Catcalls for an Online Journal," Kairos: A Journal for Teachers of Writing in Webbed Environments 5.1, 00; auth, "PICK UP AX," Society for the Promotion of Adventure Games 22, (00). **CONTACT ADDRESS** Dept of English, Univ of Wisconsin, Eau Claire, Hibbard Hall 419, PO Box 4004, Eau Claire, WI 54702-4004. **EMAIL** jerzdg@uwec.edu

JETER, JOSEPH
PERSONAL Born 07/14/1946, Panama Canal **DISCIPLINE** ENGLISH, LITERATURE **EDUCATION** Memphis State Univ, BA, 68; MA/ 73; Univ Tenn, PhD, 89. **CAREER** TA, Memphis State Univ, 68-69, 71-72; instr, Hickman County Sch, 76-79; TA Univ of Tenn, 79-81; fac, Ala A&M Univ, 83-. **HONORS AND AWARDS** Fulbright Scholar, 93. **RESEARCH** Austrian Literature, History and Culture, European Studies. **SELECTED PUBLICATIONS** Auth, Adalbert Stifter's Bunte Steine: Theme, Structure, and Style in 3 Novellas. **CONTACT ADDRESS** Dept English and For Lang, Alabama A&M Univ, PO Box 333, Normal, AL 35762-0333. **EMAIL** jjeter@aamu.edu

JEWELL, JAMES EARL
PERSONAL Born 07/26/1929, Los Angeles, CA **DISCIPLINE** THEATER LIGHTING; ENGINEERING **EDUCATION** Univ of the Pacific, BA 51; Yale Univ, School of Drama. **CAREER** Holzmueller Corp SF, enginr div head, 57-67; Univ Cal Berke, sr lect, 63-67; Bolt Beranek Newmman SF & NY, sr consul, 67-69; Pacific Gas & Elec Co SF, Light Ser Admin, 69-87. **HONORS AND AWARDS** Lewis B Marks Awd; CIE; Coll Fell Amer Theater; CIE Dist Ser Awd. **MEMBERSHIPS** IES of NA; IES of China; SAH; AAAS; NTHP; NTS; ICI. **RESEARCH** History of lighting and lighting design; theater history. **SELECTED PUBLICATIONS** Auth, The Visual Arts in Bohemia: 125 Years of Artistic Creativity in the Bohemian Club, ed, Bohemian Club SF, CA, 97; Relighting Hearst Castle, SF Designers Light Forum, 96; Increasing fixture efficiency with connective venting in compact fluorescent downlights, Ninth Intl Conf, Varna Bulgaria, 93. Control system performance in a modern daylighted office building, with C. Benton, M. Fountain, S. Selkowitz, Proceedings of the 22nd CIE Sess, Melbourne Aus, Vic Aus, 91; Getting a Fix On Fixtures, APPA Lighting Wkshp, Omaha NE, Morgan Sys, Berkeley, 89; **CONTACT ADDRESS** 749 Rhode Island St, San Francisco, CA 94107-2629. **EMAIL** j_jewell@arch-light.com

JEWINSKI, EDWIN
DISCIPLINE CANADIAN PROSE; POETRY **EDUCATION** Waterloo, BA, MA; Toronto, PhD. **CAREER** Prof **RESEARCH** Canadian prose and poetry, postmodernism, Michael Ondaatje, Eli Mandel, creative writing, critical theory. **SELECTED PUBLICATIONS** Auth,: Milton Acorn: His Life and His Works, ECW Press, 91; The Politics of Art, Rudopi Press, 92; Co-ed, Joyce 'n Beckett, Fordham Press, 92; Auth, Joe Rosenblatt: His Life and His Works, ECW Press, 92; Michael Ondaatje: Express Yourself Beautifully, ECW Press, 94. **CONTACT ADDRESS** Dept of English, Wilfrid Laurier Univ, 75 University Ave W, Waterloo, ON, Canada N2L 3C5. **EMAIL** ejewinsk@mach1.wlu.ca

JIA, WENSHAN
PERSONAL Born 06/04/1961, Shaanxi, China, m, 1988, 2 children **DISCIPLINE** COMMUNICATION **EDUCATION** Xian For Lang Univ, BA, 85; MA, 94; Bowling Green Univ, MA, 94; Univ Mass, PhD, 00. **CAREER** Asst prof, Northwestern Univ, Xian, China, 88-92; asst prof, Truman State Univ, 98-00; asst prof, SUNY, 00-. **HONORS AND AWARDS** Best Paper Awd in Transl Studies, China Transl Assoc, 90; Top Five Paper Awd, NCA, 96; Nat Commun Asn Doctoral Honor, 98. **MEMBERSHIPS** Nat Commun Assoc; Assoc for Chinese Commun Studies. **RESEARCH** International Communication, Communication Theory, Asian Studies. **SELECTED PUBLICATIONS** Transl, "Xi'an's role in the regional modernization of Northwest China", Human Geog 3, (89): 86-92; coauth, Test of English as the Foreign Language Grammar Strategy, Northwest Polytechnic Univ Pub House, (China), 90; cotransl, A Handbook to Countertrade, Shaanzi Cultural and Tourism Pub House, (China), 92; auth, "African American population - an ethnocultural experience", Spectrum VII.1 (94): 2-4; auth, Remaking the Chinese character in the 21st century: the Chinese concepts of face, Ablex/Elsevier, (Stamford, CT), (forthcoming); coauth, Chinese Communication in the 20th and 21st Century: Advances, Challenges and Prospects, Ablex/Elsevier, (Stamford, CT), (forthcoming); auth, An Intercultural Communication Perspective on Sin-American Negotiations, Ablex/ Elsevier, (Stamford, CT), (forthcoming); auth, "Chinese face-oriented communication patterns", Intercultural Communication Reader, ed Larry Samovar, (forthcoming); auth, "A conceptual framework for cross-cultural studies of emotions", Intercultural Communication Reader, ed Thomas Steinflatt, (forthcoming); coauth, "Celebrating Bumper Harvest: A symbolic construction of a cultural community", J of Popular Culture, (forthcoming). **CONTACT ADDRESS** Dept Lang and Lit, Truman State Univ, 100 E Normal St, Kirksville, MO 63501-4200. **EMAIL** wjia@truman.edu

JIANG, NAN
PERSONAL Born Wujing, China **DISCIPLINE** ENGLISH **EDUCATION** Nanjiang Normal Univ, BA, 84; E China Normal Univ, MA, 87; Univ Ariz, PhD, 98. **CAREER** Lectr, Nanjing Normal Univ, 87-92; Grad Assoc, Univ Ariz, 92-98; Postdoc Fel, Penn State Univ, 98-99; Asst Prof, Auburn Univ, 99-. **MEMBERSHIPS** Teachers of English to Speakers of Other Lang; Am Asn for App Ling. **RESEARCH** Second language acquisition; Psycholinguistics; Second language teaching. **SELECTED PUBLICATIONS** Auth, "Testing processing explanations of asymmetry in cross-language priming," Bilingualism; Language and Cognition, 99; auth, "Lexical representation and development in a second language," Applied Ling, 00; auth, "Cross-language priming in episodic recognition," J of Memory and Lang, 01. **CONTACT ADDRESS** Dept English, Auburn Univ, Dept English, Auburn, AL 36849. **EMAIL** jiangna@auburn.edu

JIM, KIM SOON-JIN
DISCIPLINE WORLD JOURNALISM **EDUCATION** Univ MD, PhD, 82. **CAREER** Prof emer, Towson Univ, Baltimore. **HONORS AND AWARDS** 5 major grants from Tinker Found and US State Dept. **RESEARCH** China's world news agency, XINHU. **SELECTED PUBLICATIONS** Auth, "Hardback on Spain's world news agency, EFE, Greenwood, 89. **CONTACT ADDRESS** PSC 3, PO Box 5762, APO, AP 96266. **EMAIL** skim@towson.edu

JIMENEZ-RAMIREZ, TALIA
PERSONAL Born 02/25/1972, Mexico City, Mexico **DISCIPLINE** MUSIC, MUSICOLOGY **EDUCATION** Ithaca Col, BA, 93; NYork Univ, MA, 99. **CAREER** Admin Asst and Prof, Technol Inst Monterrey, Mexico City, 93-96; preceptor, College of Arts and Science , NYU, 99-. **HONORS AND AWARDS** Fullbright Travel Scholar, 89; Ithaca Col Scholar, 89-93; Truman Scholar 91, 93; Emerson Scholar, 92-93; Dana Intern, 90, 92; McCracken Scholar 96-99; Dean's Scholar, 96-99; DAAD Ger Stud Scholar, 97; NYU Summer Paper Travel Scholar, 98; Outstanding TA Awd, NYU, 00. **MEMBERSHIPS** Am Musicological Soc, First Performance at NYU, and International Asn for Semiotic Studies. **RESEARCH** Reception theory and music, Mexican concert and popular music, music philosophy. **SELECTED PUBLICATIONS** Auth, "The Vertical Dimensions of Musical Signification Shown by Jakobson's Model of Linguistic Communication," Institut fur Sozio-Semiotische Studien, Vienna, Austria, 14, 99, in process of publication by the ISSS (colloquium proceedings); auth, "Entre el juego y la ironia en la musica de Revueltas," paper read at the Ii Coloquio Internacional Silvertre Revueltas, Mexico City, 98; published in Pauta 70, 99; auth, "La Dimension social de los cuartetos de curedas de 1932: Estudio comparativo del Cuarto No 2 de Carlos Chavez y Musica de feria de Silvertre Revueltas", paper read ath the Chavez-Revueltas Centennial International Colloquium, Mexico City, 99; to be published by the National Institute of Fine Arts, Mexico City, Summer 00. **CONTACT ADDRESS** New York Univ, 24 Waverly Pl, 2nd Fl, New York, NY 10003. **EMAIL** tj201@is5.nyu.edu

JIMOH, A. YEMISI
DISCIPLINE AMERICAN LITERATURE **EDUCATION** Univ Houston, PhD. **CAREER** English and Lit, Univ Ark. **SELECTED PUBLICATIONS** Auth, African American Literature: The African Continuum--Folklore, Myths, and Legends, Western Jour Black Studies, 89. **CONTACT ADDRESS** Univ of Arkansas, Fayetteville, Fayetteville, AR 72701.

JIN, XUEFEI
DISCIPLINE ENGLISH LANGUAGE AND LITERATURE **EDUCATION** Brandeis Univ, PhD, 93. **CAREER** Asst prof **RESEARCH** Creative writing; poetry. **SELECTED PUBLICATIONS** Auth, Between Silences; Facing Shadows; Oceans of Words. **CONTACT ADDRESS** English Dept, Emory Univ, 1380 Oxford Rd NE, Atlanta, GA 30322-1950. **EMAIL** xjin@emory.edu

JOBE, STEVE
DISCIPLINE 19TH CENTURY AMERICAN LITERATURE, 18TH CENTURY BRITISH LITERATURE **EDUCATION** Univ S, BA, 78; Univ NC, Chapel Hill, MS, 81, PhD, 88. **CAREER** Assoc prof, Hanover Col, 90. **RESEARCH** 20th century Southern lit. **SELECTED PUBLICATIONS** Auth, The Discrimination of Stoicisms in The American, Stud in Am Fiction 16, 88; Henry James and the Philosophic Actor, Am Lit 62, 90; A Calendar of the Published Letters of Henry James, Henry James Rev 11, 90; Representation and Performance in The Tragic Muse, Am Lit Realism 1870-1910 26, 94; Henry James and the Innocence of Daisy Miller: A Corrected Text of the Letter to Eliza Lynn Linton, Am Lit Realism, 1870-1910 29, 97. **CONTACT ADDRESS** Hanover Col, Hanover, IN 47243. **EMAIL** jobe@hanover.edu

JOCKERS, MATTHEW L.
PERSONAL Born 11/28/1966, New York, NY, m, 1993, 1 child **DISCIPLINE** ENGLISH **EDUCATION** Montana State Univ, BA, 89; Univ Northern Colo, Greeley, MA, 93; Southern Ill Univ, Carbondale, PhD, 97. **CAREER** Grad teaching asst, Univ Northern Colo, Greeley, 90-93; asst ed, Colo North Rev, Greeley, Colo, 92-93; archives intern, Morris Library Irish Studies collection, Southern Ill Univ, Carbondale, fall 94, fall 95; grad teaching asst, Southern Ill Univ, Carbondale, 93-95; asst conf coordr, Am Conf for Irish Studies, Southern Ill Univ, Carbondale, Jan 96-April 96; asst to the Dir of Irish Studies, Dept English, Southern Ill Univ, Carbondale, 95-97; admin fac, English instr and coordr of Curriculum, Instruction, and Technology, Univ of Northern Colo, Center for Human Enrichment, Greeley, 97-. **HONORS AND AWARDS** Grad Sch Academic Fel, Univ Northern Colo, 91, 92; Sigma Tau Delta English Honor Soc, Univ Northern Colo, 92; Mae Cross Scholar, Univ Northern Colo, 92; Grad Dean's Citation for Excellence, Univ Northern Colo, 93; Who's Who in the Am West, 24th ed, New Jersey: Marquis, 94; nominated for the Outstanding Grad Teacher Awd, Southern Ill Univ, 95; Phi Kappa Phi Honor Soc, Southern Ill Univ, 95. **MEMBERSHIPS** Am Conf for Irish studies, Asn of Lit Scholars and Critics. **RESEARCH** British/ Irish literature, philosophy, Western tradition. **SELECTED PUBLICATIONS** Coauth with Craig Smith, "James Joyce's Ulysses," The Explicator, 50.4 (92): 235-237; auth, "Another 'Word Known to All Men' in Joyce's Ulysses," Notes on Modern Irish Lit, 8 (96): 38-40; auth, "A Literature of Good Fortune," in The Bay Area Irish, ed Donald Jordon, Univ Calif Press (forthcoming). **CONTACT ADDRESS** Center for Human Enrichment, Univ of No Colorado, 501 20th St, Greeley, CO 80639-0001. **EMAIL** mljocke@unco.edu

JOHANNESEN, RICHARD LEE
PERSONAL Born 08/14/1937, Davenport, IA, 2 children **DISCIPLINE** ENGLISH **EDUCATION** Augustana Col, Ill, BA, 59; Univ Kans, MA, 60, PhD(speech), 64. **CAREER** Instr speech, Univ Kans, 61-62; from instr to asst prof, Ind Univ, Bloomington, 64-71; assoc prof, 72-77, prof Commun Studies, Northern Ill Univ, 77-, dept chair, 88-96. **MEMBERSHIPS** Nat Comm Assoc. **RESEARCH** Contemporary theories of rhetoric; rhetorical criticism; ethical problems in communication. **SELECTED PUBLICATIONS** Ed, Ethics and Persuasion, Random, 67; co-ed, Language is Sermonic: Richard M Weaver on the Nature of Rhetoric, La State Univ, 70; ed, Contemporary Theories of Rhetoric, Harper, 71; auth, "The Jeremiad and Jenkin Jones," Communication Monographs, June 85; auth, "Collaborative Writing Interactions in One Ninth-Grade Classroom" Journal of Educational Research, 94, 334-344; auth, The Emerging Concept of Communication as Dialogue, Quart J Speech, 12/71; Ethics in Human Communication, Waveland Press, 4th ed, 96; auth, "Dilemmas of Fidelity: Qualitative Research in the Classroom," Invited chapter in Ethics and Representation in Qualitative Studies of Literacy, Urbana, IL: ncte, 96: 77-94; auth, "The Influence of Co-authoring on the Writing Process," Journal of Teaching Writing, 96, 65-79; auth, "Letters of Intent: Collaborative Self-Study as Reform in Teacher Education" in The Heart of the Matter: Teacher Education Reform Perspectives and Possibilities, Caddo Gap Press; 98: 81-99; auth, "Creating Literacy Communities: High School/University Partnership," English Journal 88.1, 98; co-ed, Contemporary American Speeches, Kendall-Hunt, 8th ed, 97, updated 9th ed., 00; articles, "Becoming Multicultural Supervisors: Lessons from a Collaborative Field Study" Journal of Curriculum and Supervision, 16.1, 00, 28-47; **CONTACT ADDRESS** Dept of Communication, No Illinois Univ, De Kalb, IL 60115-2825. **EMAIL** rjohannesen@niu.edu

JOHANNINGSMEIER, CHARLES
PERSONAL Born 11/27/1959, Lafayette, IN, m, 1989, 2 children **DISCIPLINE** AMERICAN STUDIES, ENGLISH **EDUCATION** Haverford Col, BA, 81; Ind Univ, MA, 88; PhD, 93. **CAREER** Instr, State Univ NYork at Cortland, 92-98; asst prof, Univ Nebr at Omaha, 98-. **HONORS AND AWARDS** Bibliog Soc of Am Fel, 94; CN Bibliog Soc of England Fel, 94. NEH Summer Stipend, 97. **MEMBERSHIPS** Res Soc for Am Periodicals; Soc for the Hist of Authorship Reading; Soc for Textual Scholar. **RESEARCH** Newspapers and Fiction, American Regionalism. **SELECTED PUBLICATIONS** Auth, Fiction and the American Literary Marketplace: The Role of Newspaper Syndicates in America, 1860-1900, Cambridge UP, 97. **CONTACT ADDRESS** Dept English, Univ of Nebraska, Omaha, 6001 Dodge St, Omaha, NE 68182-0001.

JOHANYAK, DEBRA L.
DISCIPLINE LITERATURE **EDUCATION** Univ Akron, BA, 77; MA, 82; Kent State Univ, PhD, 88. **CAREER** Univ Akron Wayne Col, 92-. **MEMBERSHIPS** MLA; NCTE. **RESEARCH** Shakespeare. **SELECTED PUBLICATIONS** Auth, "William Gilmore Simms: Deviant Paradigms of Southern Womanhood?" Miss Quart (93): 575-588; auth, "Poesian Feminism: Triumph or Tragedy?" Col Lang Asn J (95); auth, "The Maternal Heritage of Sex and Sin in Cooper's Leatherstocking Dark Ladies," Penn English (95); auth, "Visual Poster as Reading Quiz," Innov Abst (95); auth, "Cooper James Fennimore 1789-1851," and "Fiction: American 20thCentury," in Reader's Guide to Lit in English (London: Fitzroy Dearborn Pub, 96); auth, "Teaching Values as Valuable Teaching: Endorsing Personal Perspectives in the College Classroom," OATYC J (99): 26-28; auth, "Romanticism's Fallen Edens: The Malignant Contribution of Hawthorne's Literary Landscapes," Col Lang Asn J (99): 353-363. **CONTACT ADDRESS** English Dept, Univ of Akron, Wayne Col, 1901 Smucker Rd, Orrville, OH 44667-9192.

JOHN, BRIAN
DISCIPLINE ENGLISH LITERATURE **EDUCATION** Univ Wales, BA, MA, PhD. **RESEARCH** Mod Irish lit; mod British lit. **SELECTED PUBLICATIONS** Auth, Supreme Fictions: Studies in the Work of William Blake, Thomas Carlyle, W.B. Yeats, and D.H. Lawrence, 74; auth, The World as Event: the Poetry of Charles Tomlinson, 89. **CONTACT ADDRESS** English Dept, McMaster Univ, 1280 Main St W, Hamilton, ON, Canada L8S 4L9. **EMAIL** brianjhn@mcmaster.ca

JOHN, JUDITH A.
PERSONAL Born 05/30/1951, St Joseph, MO, d, 4 children **DISCIPLINE** ENGLISH **EDUCATION** Mo Western State Col, BS, 86; Kans State Univ, MA, 89; PhD, 92. **CAREER** Grad Teaching Asst, Kans State Univ, 86-92; Asst Prof to Assoc Prof, Southwest Mo State Univ, 92-. **HONORS AND AWARDS** Univ Service Awd, 99; Phi Kappa Phi Honor Soc, Kans State Univ, Grad Student Coun Scholarship, Kans State Univ, 87-92; Robert Greef Awd, Mo Asn of Teachers of English, 86; Nat Soroptimist Awd, 86; Am business Women's Asn Scholarship, 85; Kappa Delta Pi Honor Soc, Sigma Tau Delta English Honor Soc. **MEMBERSHIPS** Intl Children's Lit Asn, Mod Lang Asn, Nat Coun of Teachers of English, Mo Asn for Teachers of English, Lang Arts Dept of SW Mo, Intl Asn for Fantastic in the Arts, Midwest Mod Lang Asn. **RESEARCH** Children's literature; Fantasy; Adolescent literature; Renaissance literature. **SELECTED PUBLICATIONS** Auth, "From Death to rebirth: A Short History of Dragons and Their Presence in Modern Fantasy," in Flashes of the Fantastic: Selected Essays from the War of the Worlds Centennial, Nineteenth International Conference on the Fantastic in the Arts, forthcoming; auth, "Commands and Whispers: Maternal Voices in Early Advice books for children," ERIC, 93; auth, "John Rowe Townsend," in Dictionary of Literary Biography, forthcoming; auth, "Crescent Dragonwagon," in Cambridge Guide to Children's Literature, forthcoming; auth, "Catherine Sinclair," in Dictionary of Literary Biography: British Children's Writers, 1800-1880, Clark, Layman, 96; auth, "Philippa Pearce," in Dictionary of Literary Biography: British Children's Writers, 1800-1880, Clark, Layman, 96; auth, "Patricia Lynch," in Dictionary of Literary Biography: British Children's Writers, 1800-1880, Clark, Layman, 96; auth, "Dean Hughes," Twentieth Century Young Adult Writers, St. James, 94. **CONTACT ADDRESS** Dept English, Southwest Missouri State Univ, Springfield, 901 S National Ave, Springfield, MO 65804-0027. **EMAIL** jaj225f@mail.smsu.edu

JOHNSON, ALEX C.
PERSONAL Born 08/14/1943, Freetown, Sierra Leone, m, 1969, 2 children **DISCIPLINE** ENGLISH **EDUCATION** Univ Durham, BA, 68; Kent Univ, Canterbury, MA, 71; Univ Leeds, MPhil, 74; Univ Ibadan, PhD, 82. **CAREER** High Schls Tchr, 68-69, 71-72, Freetown, Sierra Leone; sr lectr, lectr, Eng dept, 74-88, FBC-USL; prof, Eng lang & Creole stud, 82-84, Univ Bayreuth, W Germany; sr lectr, actg head, class/phil dept, 87-88, assoc prof & head, Eng dept, 88-91, actg vice prin 89-90, dean, fac of arts, 89-91, Fourah Bay Col, Univ Sierra Leone; vis prof, 91-92, prof, Eng, 92-, SC St Univ. **HONORS AND AWARDS** Who's Who in Amer, 98; Who's Who in the South & Southwest, 97-98; Who's Who in the World, 98-99; Tchr of Year, 93, SCSU. **MEMBERSHIPS** CLA; ALA; NCTE; AAUP; WALS; SAMLA, South Eastern Renaissance Conference. **RESEARCH** Linguistic and sociolinguistic situation of Krio in Sierra Leone multilingualism; language of W African lit; Non-Native Varieties of English and Pidgins and Creoles. **SELECTED PUBLICATIONS** Auth, Creative Tension in West African Drama in English: The Linguistic Dimension, World Lit Written in Eng, 84; auth, The Development of Sierra Leone Krio, Bayreuth African Stud Ser: Towards African Authenticity, 85; auth, Multilingualism and Language Policy in Sierra Leone, Bayreuth African Stud Ser: Lang and Ed in Africa, 86; auth, The Role of the Languages of Minority Groups as Languages of Instruction and Vectors of Culture: Case Study of Sierra Leone, UNESCO, 89; auth, Chapters on Homer, Chaucer, the African Epic, African Oral Poetry in Literary Perspectives 2nd., ed Kendall Hunt, 98; auth, Krio Language in The Companion to African Literatures, Oxford: James Curry, 00; rev, in The African Book Publishing Record, (ABPR), 97,98,99,00; auth, Varieties of Krio and Standard Krio, Reading & Writing Krio, Uppsala, 92; auth, Two Historical Plays From West Africa, Komparatistische Heft 8, 83; auth, The Krio Language, in The Companion to Africa Literatures, 00. **CONTACT ADDRESS** Dept of Communications & Languages, So Carolina State Univ, 300 College St NE, Orangeburg, SC 29117. **EMAIL** Johnsonac@scsu.edu

JOHNSON, BOBBY HAROLD
PERSONAL Born 11/09/1935, Overton, TX, m, 1959, 2 children **DISCIPLINE** AMERICAN & JOURNALISM HISTORY **EDUCATION** Abilene Christian Col, BA, 58; Univ Okla, MA, 62, PhD(hist), 67. **CAREER** From asst prof to assoc prof, 66-77, Prof Hist, Stephen F Austin State Univ, 77-, Dir, Off Univ Info, Stephen F Austin State Univ, 79-82. **MEMBERSHIPS** Orgn Am Historans; Western Hist Asn **RESEARCH** American West, especially Oklahoma territory; history of American journalism; history of aviation. **SELECTED PUBLICATIONS** Auth, Booster attitudes of some newspapers in Oklahoma territory--the land of the fair god, autumn 65 & Reports of the governors of Oklahoma territory, winter 66-67, Chronicles Okla; Singing Oklahoma's praises: boosterism in the Soonerland, Great Plains J, fall 71; coauth, Wiley Post, his Winnie Mae, and the World's First Pressure Suit, Smithsonia, 71; auth, The Coushatta People Indian Tribal Series, 76; Doctors, druggists and dentists in the Oklahoma Territory, 1889-1907, Ariz & the West, summer 77. **CONTACT ADDRESS** Dept of Hist, Stephen F. Austin State Univ, Box 13013, Nacogdoches, TX 75962.

JOHNSON, CALVERT
PERSONAL Born 11/15/1949, MD **DISCIPLINE** MUSIC **EDUCATION** Kalamazoo Col, BA, 71; Northwestern Univ, MM; 72, DM, 76. **CAREER** From asst prof to assoc prof, Northeastern State Univ, 77-86; from assoc prof to prof, 86-, chair, Music Dept, 92-98, Agnes Scott Col. **HONORS AND AWARDS** Phi Beta Kappa; Pi Kappa Lambda; Int Who's Who in Music; 3rd annual award for CD recording, Soc for Am Music. **MEMBERSHIPS** Col Music Soc; Southeastern Hist Keyboard Soc; Am Guild of Organists; Organ Hist Soc; Early Music Am. **RESEARCH** Early keyboard music and performance practices especially Spain, England, and Italy, women composers especially for organ and harpsichord. **SELECTED PUBLICATIONS** Auth, "Spanish Keyboard Ornamentation, 1535-1626," The Diapason 69 (78): 1, 12-15; auth, "Early Italian Keyboard Fingering," Early Keyboard J 10 (92): 7-88; auth, "De la Registration de la musique anglaise pour orgue de 1660 a 1830," Orgues Meridionales (92): 1-34; auth, Spain: 1550-1830, Wayne Leopold Editions, 94; auth, "Amelie Julie Candeille," Women of Note Quart 7 (99): 12-25; auth, "Florence Beatrice Price: Chicago Renaissance Woman," The Am Organist 34 (00): 69-76; auth, England: 1730-1830, Wayne Leopold Editions, 00. **CONTACT ADDRESS** Dept of Music, Agnes Scott Col, 141 E Col Ave, Decatur, GA 30030. **EMAIL** cjohnson@agnesscott.edu

JOHNSON, CHRISTOPHER G.
DISCIPLINE ENGLISH LITERATURE **EDUCATION** Univ British Columbia, BA; MA; Leeds Univ, PhD. **CAREER** Prof. **HONORS AND AWARDS** Merit Awd; Outreach Awd. **RESEARCH** Theatrical production; dramatic theory; Canadian and Commonwealth drama. **SELECTED PUBLICATIONS** Auth, George F. Walker: Playing With Anxiety; pub(s) on Canadian and Commonwealth plays, playwrights, and theatres. **CONTACT ADDRESS** Dept of English, Univ of Manitoba, Winnipeg, MB, Canada R3T 2N2. **EMAIL** cjohns@cc.umanitoba.ca

JOHNSON, DAVID
PERSONAL Born 11/02/1944, Perth Arbor, NJ, m, 1983, 3 children **DISCIPLINE** ENGLISH **EDUCATION** Kansas State Col, BA, 66; Vanderbilt Univ, MA, 69; PhD, 72. **CAREER** Instr to prof, Univ of Nebr, 69-; chair, 89-92; Director, Bur of Sociol Res, 83-85, 95-. **HONORS AND AWARDS** NDEA Fel, 66-69; Grant, N Central Reg Ctr for Rural Develop, 79; Grant, Dept of Health and Human Serv, 80-82; Grant, Nat Inst of Aging, 83-86, 87-90; Grant, Nat Inst of Aging, 96-99; Fallup Professorship, 95-97; Grant, W.T. Grant Found, 97-98. **MEMBERSHIPS** Am Sociol Assoc; Midwest Sociol Soc; Psychol Assoc of Am; AAUP; Am Names Soc; Nat Coun on Family Relations; Population Assoc of Am; Am Assoc of Public Opinion Res. **RESEARCH** Quantum Methods, Family, Mental Health. **SELECTED PUBLICATIONS** Couth, "Rural-Urban women's experience of symptoms of depression related to economic hardship", J of women and Aging 10.3 (98); coauth, "Is marital quality a product of the dyadic environment or individual factors? Panel evidence from individuals in successive marriages", Soc Forces 76, (98): 883-904; coauth, "Attitudes toward marital naming", Names, (98); coauth, "Sampling Design Effects: Do They Affect the Analyses of Data from the National Survey of Families and Households (NSFH)?", J of Marriage and the Family 60, (98): 993-1001; coauth, "Testosterone and men's health", J of Behav Med 22, (99): 1-19; auth, "Testosterone and men's depression: The role of social behavior", J of Health and Soc Behav 40, (99): coauth, "Age and religiosity: Evidence from a three-wave panel analysis", J for the Sci Study of Relig 30.3 (99); auth, "Measuring marital relations", The Handbook of Family Measurement Techniques, Vol 2, eds J. Touliatos, B.F. Perlmutter, and G.W. Holden, Sage Pub, (Newbury Park, CA), 00; coauth, "Human aggression and enumerative measures of immunity", Psychosomatic Med, (forthcoming); coauth, "Trends in women's marital name choice: A content analysis of marriage announcements in the New York Times from 1966-1996", Names (forthcoming). **CONTACT ADDRESS** Dept Sociol, Univ of Nebraska, Lincoln, PO Box 880324, Lincoln, NE 68588-0324. **EMAIL** djohnson2@unl.edu

JOHNSON, DEWAYNE BURTON
PERSONAL Born 04/18/1920, Newman Grove, NE, m, 1942, 3 children **DISCIPLINE** JOURNALISM **EDUCATION** Univ Calif, Berkeley, BA, 48; Univ Calif, Los Angeles, MA, 50, EdD, 55. **CAREER** Corresp, United Press Asn, Tacoma, Wash, 48-49; res assoc, Univ Calif, Los Angeles, 51; instr English, El Camino Col, 52-53; asst prof English & dir pub rels, Southern Ore Col, 53-55; asst prof jour, San Diego State Col, 55-59; pub rels dir, La Mesa-Spring Valley Sch Dist, Calif, 59-60; instr English, San Diego City Col, 60; asst prof, 61-65, Prof Jour, Calif State Univ, Northridge, 61-, Fac Pres, 74-, Copy ed, San Diego Union, 55-59 & Los Angeles Times, 61-98. **HONORS AND AWARDS** Outstanding Prof Jour, Calif Newspaper Publ Asn, 73 & 77. **MEMBERSHIPS** Soc Prof Journalists. **RESEARCH** Photojournalism; future of the mass media; problems in mass communication. **SELECTED PUBLICATIONS** Auth, Historical analysis of the criticisms concerning teaching about the United Nations Educational, Scienfific and Cultural Organizations in the Los Angeles city schools. **CONTACT ADDRESS** 10118 Aldea Ave, Northridge, CA 91325. **EMAIL** dewayne.johnson@csun.edu

JOHNSON, ERIC
DISCIPLINE ENGLISH LITERATURE **EDUCATION** PhD, Univ Notre Dame. **CAREER** Prof, Dakota State Univ; Dean, Col Lib Arts, Dakota State Univ. **RESEARCH** Victorian literature & computers; literature; writing. **SELECTED PUBLICATIONS** Auth, Word Lengths, Authorship, and Four-Letter Words," TEXT Technol 6.1 (Spring 96): 15-23; auth, "Professor-Created Computer Programs for Student Research," Computers & the Humanities 30.2 (April 96), 171-179; auth, "The Kinds of Words used in the Novels of Jane Austen, Charles Dickens, and James Janke," TEXT Technol 6.2 (Summer 96): 91-96; auth, "World Wide Web Publishing with HTML 3.2," TEXT Technol 6.4 (Winter 96): 246-250; auth, "The World Wide Web, Computers, and Teaching Literature," in Annual Editions: Computers in Education: 00-01, eds Hirschbuhl & Bishop, Dushkin/McGraw-Hill, 99, 173-186 **CONTACT ADDRESS** Dakota State Univ, 820 N. Washington Ave, Madison, SD 57042. **EMAIL** johnsone@jupiter.dsu.edu

JOHNSON, J. THEODORE, JR.
DISCIPLINE NINETEENTH- AND TWENTIETH-CENTURY POETRY **EDUCATION** Univ Wis, PhD. **CAREER** Prof, Univ KS. **HONORS AND AWARDS** Chancellor's award for excellence in tchg; Mortar Board's recognition as an oustanding educator, 92; sr class HOPE award to hon an outstanding progressive educator; ed, proust res assn newsletter. **RESEARCH** Proust, and interrelations of lit and the visual arts. **SELECTED PUBLICATIONS** Publ(s), on Proust. **CONTACT ADDRESS** Dept of French and Italian, Univ of Kansas, Lawrence, Admin Building, Lawrence, KS 66045.

JOHNSON, JAMES WILLIAM
PERSONAL Born 03/01/1927, Birmingham, AL, m, 1957, 2 children **DISCIPLINE** ENGLISH LITERATURE **EDUCATION** Birmingham-Southern Col, AB, 50; Harvard Univ, AM, 50; Vanderbilt Univ, PhD, 54. **CAREER** Instr English, Vanderbilt Univ, 52-54; from instr to assoc prof, 55-65, prof eng, Univ Rochester, 65-70, prof Emeritus, 71-, Fulbright scholar, UK, 54-55; fel, Folger Libr, 63, Am Coun Learned Socs, 49-50, 66-67 & Guggenheim, 70-71. **HONORS AND AWARDS** Whos Who in Am; Matzdorf Award; ACLS fel; Folger Libr Fel, Guggenheim Fel. **MEMBERSHIPS** English Inst; MLA; Northeastern Am Soc 18th Century Studies. **RESEARCH** Women's lit; modern drama; eighteenth century English Restoration literature and Southern Literature. **SELECTED PUBLICATIONS** Auth, Logic and Rhetoric, Macmillan, 62; The For-

mation of English Neo-Classical Thought, Princeton Univ, 67; Utopian Literature, Random, 68; Concepts of Literature, Prentice-Hall, 71; What was neo-classicism?, J Brit Studies, 71; Prose in Practice, Harcourt, 72; Gibbon's architectural metaphor, J Brit Studies, 73; Letters from the Countess of Rochester, Rochester Libr Bull, 74; ed, The Plays of John Dennis, 80. **CONTACT ADDRESS** Dept of English, Univ of Rochester, 500 Wilson Blvd., RC Box 270451, Rochester, NY 14627-0451. **EMAIL** jsnj@mail.rochester.edu

JOHNSON, JEAN L.
PERSONAL Born 06/28/1938, Florence, AL, w, 1960, 2 children **DISCIPLINE** ENGLISH **EDUCATION** Univ Ala, BS, 60; MA, 61; Ind Univ Pa, PhD, 91. **CAREER** Teacher, Tuscaloosa County Public Sch System, 61-62; teacher, Florence City Public Sch System, 62-63 & 66-67; prof, Univ of N Ala, 67-00. **HONORS AND AWARDS** Outstanding Educator Awd, Gamma Chi Chapter of Delta Kappa Gamma Soc, 91; Laura M. Harrison Endowed Professorship in English, Univ of N Ala, 97-98; Outstanding Educ Awd, Girl Scouts of N Ala, 98. **MEMBERSHIPS** Nat Coun of Teachers of English, Confr on Col Composition and Commun, Am Dialect Soc, Phi Kappa Phi. **RESEARCH** Literacy, Sociolinguistics, Rhetoric. **SELECTED PUBLICATIONS** Auth, "Teaching Invention: A Pedagogy," The Delta Kappa Gamma Bull 53 & 54 (87): 27-32; auth, " A Descriptive Study of Gender Differences in Proscribed Language Behavior, Beliefs, and Attitudes," Md English J 28.2 (94): 16-20; auth, "A Comparative Study of What College Freshmen Report about Their Reading Backgrounds, Habits, and Preferences: 1976-1996," Ala English 2 (99): 27-31. **CONTACT ADDRESS** Dept English, Univ of No Alabama, 2 Univ North Ala, PO Box 5050, Florence, AL 35632-0001. **EMAIL** jjohnson@unanov.una.edu

JOHNSON, JEANNE M.
DISCIPLINE SPEECH-LANGUAGE PATHOLOGY **EDUCATION** Western Wash State Col, Bellingham, BA, 73; Western Wash Univ, Bellingham, MA, 78; Southern Ill Univ at Carbondale, PhD, 86. **CAREER** Actg dept ch, Wash State Univ, 96 and 97-98; Assoc prof, Grad Fac, Dept Speech & Hearing Sci, Wash State Univ, 93-; Adj assoc prof, Dept Commun Disorders, Eastern Wash Univ, 95; Asst prof, Grad Fac, Dept Speech & Hearing Sci, Wash State Univ, 87-93. **HONORS AND AWARDS** William F. Mullen Excellence in Teaching Award, College of Liberal Arts, Wash State Univ, 95; Tenure and Promotion to Assoc Prof, 93; Phi Kappa Phi Honor Soc, 86-; App to Grad Fac, Wash State Univ, 89; Doc Fel Award, Southern Ill Univ, 85-86; Delta Kappa Gamma Honor Soc, 80-83. **MEMBERSHIPS** Amer Speech-Lange-Hearing Asn; Wash State Speech and Hearing Asn; National Coun for Exceptional Children; Int Soc for Infant Stud; Soc for Res in Child Develop. **RESEARCH** Language development of children with prenatal drug exposure, augmentative communication, communication of individuals with severe, multiple disabilities, parent-child interaction, american sign language development and conversation. **SELECTED PUBLICATIONS** Coauth, Standardized Test Performance of Children with a History of Prenatal Exposure to Multiple Drugs/Cocaine, J Commun Disorders 30, 97 & Augmenting Basic Communication in Natural Contexts, Baltimore: Paul H. Brookes, 96. **CONTACT ADDRESS** Dept of Speech and Hearing Sciences, Washington State Univ, 201 Daggy Hall, Pullman, WA 99164-2420. **EMAIL** johnsjm@wsu.edu

JOHNSON, JEANNINE R.
PERSONAL Born 02/07/1968 **DISCIPLINE** POETRY, EXPOSITORY WRITING **EDUCATION** Haverford Col, BA, 90; Yale Univ, MA, 93; MPhil, 94; PhD, 98. **CAREER** Instr, Albertus Magnus Col, 95; instr, Yale Univ, 96-97; vis asst prof, Wake Forest Univ, 97-99; preceptor, Harvard Univ, 99-01. **HONORS AND AWARDS** Cert of Distinction in Teaching, Harvard Univ, 99-00. **RESEARCH** American poetry, 20th and 21st century American literature, African-American literature, British Romanticism, Modernism, poetics and aesthetic theory. **SELECTED PUBLICATIONS** Auth, "An Overview of Autobiography of Miss Jane Pittman," Novels for Students, (Gale, 97); auth, "An Overview of Those Winter Sundays," "An Overview of Ode to the West Wind," "An Overview of Funeral Blues," Poetry for Students, Vol 1/2/10, (97, 97, 00); auth, "Yusef Komunyakaa," Contemporary Southern Writers, (St James, 98); auth, "Adrienne Rich: To a Poet," Encycl of Aesthetics (Oxford, 99); auth, "A Companion to Twentieth-Century American Poetry (Facts on File)," Notes toward a Supreme Fiction, forthcoming.

JOHNSON, JEFFREY
DISCIPLINE 17TH AND 18TH CENTURY BRITISH LITERATURE **EDUCATION** Univ MS, PhD. **CAREER** Engl, Col Misericordia **SELECTED PUBLICATIONS** Contrib ed, The Variorum Edition of the Poetry of John Donne. **CONTACT ADDRESS** Dept of Humanities, Col Misericordia, 301 Lake St., Dallas, PA 18612-1098. **EMAIL** jjohnson@miseri.edu

JOHNSON, JULIE GREER
PERSONAL Born 09/06/1945, Hartford, CT, s **DISCIPLINE** SPANISH AMERICAN LITERATURE **EDUCATION** Memphis State Univ, BA, 67; Ind Univ, MA, 70, PhD(Span lit), 75. **CAREER** From instr to asst prof Span, Univ NC, Asheville, 74-77; from asst prof to full prof Span, Univ Ga, 77-. **HONORS AND AWARDS** John Carter Brown Fel, 84; Columbian Quincentennial Fel, 88; Outstanding Honors Prof, 88, 97; NEH Senior Fel, 99-00. **MEMBERSHIPS** MLA; Am Asn Teachers Span & Port; Latin Am Studies Asn; S Atlantic MLA; Southeastern Council for Latin Am Studies; Luso-Hispanic Humor Soc. **RESEARCH** Colonial Spanish American literature; Women, Satire, Printing, Theater **SELECTED PUBLICATIONS** Auth, Women in Colonial Spanish America: Literary Images, Greenwood Press, 83; auth, The Book in the Americas: The Role of Books and Printing in the Development of Culture and Society in Latin America, John Carter Brown Library, 88; auth, Satire in Colonial Spanish America: Turning the New World Upside Down, Texax, 93. **CONTACT ADDRESS** Dept Romance Lang, Univ of Georgia, Gilbert Hall, Athens, GA 30602. **EMAIL** jjohnson@arches.uga.edu

JOHNSON, KENNETH E.
DISCIPLINE ENGLISH LITERATURE **EDUCATION** Univ Ca, BA, 75; Brown Univ, MA, 77, PhD, 81. **CAREER** Instr, Rhode Island Jr Col, 78-80; instr, Stonehill Col, 76-81; asst prof, 81-82; assoc prof, Fla Int Univ, 82-. **HONORS AND AWARDS** Tchg Incentive Prog Awd, 96. **SELECTED PUBLICATIONS** Auth, Teaching to the Postmodern, Jour Curriculum Theorizing, 94; Point of View of the Wandering Camera, Cinema Jour, 93; Tina Howe's Feminine Discourse, 92; There's No Basement in the Alamo, or , Pee-wee's Hermeneutics, 92. **CONTACT ADDRESS** Dept of English, Florida State Univ, 11200 SW 8th St, Miami, FL 33174. **EMAIL** johnsonk@fiu.edu

JOHNSON, LEE MILFORD
PERSONAL Born 04/22/1944, Alexandria, MN, m, 1966, 4 children **DISCIPLINE** ENGLISH LITERATURE **EDUCATION** Hamline Univ, BA, 66; Princeton Univ, PhD(English), 70. **CAREER** From asst prof to prof English, Univ BC, 70-. **RESEARCH** Prosody; Romantic poetry, 17th century poetry. **SELECTED PUBLICATIONS** Auth, Wordsworth's Metaphysical Verse: Geometry, Nature, and Form, 82. **CONTACT ADDRESS** Dept of English, Univ of British Columbia, Vancouver, BC, Canada V6T 1W5.

JOHNSON, LEMUEL A.
PERSONAL Born 12/15/1941, Nigeria, m **DISCIPLINE** ENGLISH **EDUCATION** Oberlin Clg, BA 1965; PA St U, MA 1966; Univ of MI, PhD 1969. **CAREER** Dept of English Univ of MI, prof; English Univ of Sierra Leone Fourah Bay Clol, lecturer 1970-72; Radio Forum, host 1970-71. **HONORS AND AWARDS** Recipient hopwood awds for Short Story & Essay Cont 1967-68; Bredvold Prize for Scholar Publ; Dept of Eng Univ of MI awd 1972; pub num poems & translations. **MEMBERSHIPS** Sierra Leone Broad Serv Freetown; Pres African Lit Assc 1977-78. **SELECTED PUBLICATIONS** "The Devil, the Gargoyle & the Buffoon, The Negro as Metaphor in West Lit" 1971; Highlife for Caliban, 1973; "Hand on the Navel" 1978. **CONTACT ADDRESS** Univ of Michigan, Ann Arbor, Ann Arbor, MI 48109.

JOHNSON, LINCK CHRISTOPHER
PERSONAL Born 02/02/1946, Evanston, IL **DISCIPLINE** AMERICAN LITERATURE **EDUCATION** Cornell Univ, AB, 69; Princeton Univ, MA, 71, PhD(English), 75. **CAREER** Instr, 74-76, asst prof, 76-83, assoc prof, 83-88, prof English, Colgate Univ, 88- . **HONORS AND AWARDS** Henry E Huntington Libr vis fel, 76; NEH fel Am Antiq Soc, 85. **MEMBERSHIPS** MLA; Am Lit Asn; Ralph Waldo Emerson Soc; Margaret Fuller Soc; Thoreau Soc of Am; Soc for the Study of Am Women Writers. **RESEARCH** Emerson; Thoreau; antebellum reform movements; nineteenth-century American literature, culture, and society. **SELECTED PUBLICATIONS** Auth, Thoreau's Complex Weave: The Writing of A Week on the Concord and Merrimack Rivers, with the Text of the First Draft, Virginia, 86; auth, Revolution and Renewal: The Genres of Walden, in Critical Essays on Henry David Thoreau's Walden, G.K. Hall, 88; auth, Reforming the Reformers: Emerson, Throeau, and the Sunday Lectures at Amory hall, Boston, in, ESQ: A J of the Am Renaissance, 91; contribur, The Cambridge Companion to Henry David Thoreau, Cambridge, 95; auth, Walden and the Construction of the American Renaissance, in, Approaches to Teaching Thoreau's Walden and Other Writings, MLA, 96; contribur, Biographical Dictionary of Transcendentalism, and, Encyclopedia of Transcendentalism, Greenwood, 96; auth, Historical Introduction to A Week on the Concord and Merrimack Rivers, in the Princeton ed of The Writings of Henry D Thoreau, 80; auth, Emerson, Thoreau's Arrest, and the Trials of American Manhood, in The Emerson Dilemma: Essays on Emerson and Social Reform, GA, 00. **CONTACT ADDRESS** Dept of English, Colgate Univ, 13 Oak Dr, Hamilton, NY 13346-1379. **EMAIL** LJohnson@mail.colgate.edu

JOHNSON, LUCILLE MARGUERITE
PERSONAL Born 04/03/1919, Hatton, ND, m, 1948 **DISCIPLINE** ENGLISH LITERATURE, RHETORIC **EDUCATION** Concordia Col, Moorhead, Minn, BA, 40; Wash State Univ, MA, 43; Univ Mont, EdD(rhet & hist & philos of educ), 67. **CAREER** Chmn dept English, Austin Col, Minn, 43-46; asst prof, Ohio Univ, 46-48 & Univ Wash, 48-50; chmn dept, Centralia Col, 50-53; assoc prof, 53-67, Prof English & Chmn Dept, Pac Lutheran Univ, 67-, Consult, Teacher Educ Liaison Comt, Wash, 69-72; Can Embassy grant, 82. **MEMBERSHIPS** Am Asn Univ Women; MLA; NCTE Conf English Educ; Conf Col Compos & Commun. **RESEARCH** Chauceriana, Canadian literature. **SELECTED PUBLICATIONS** Auth, The Inner Life of Henry Vaughan as Revealed in His Religious Verse, Wash State Univ, 43; Teach them, 47 & The World's slow stain, 47, Lutheran Herald; A Neo-Aristotelian Study of Resources and Qualities of Descriptive Writing, Univ Mont, 67; Washington of the West, Wash State Hist Soc, 76. **CONTACT ADDRESS** Dept of English, Pacific Lutheran Univ, Park Ave, Tacoma, WA 98447.

JOHNSON, MICHAEL LILLARD
PERSONAL Born 06/29/1943, Springfield, MO, m, 1965 **DISCIPLINE** ENGLISH **EDUCATION** Rice Univ, BA, 65, PhD(English), 68; Stanford Univ, MA, 67. **CAREER** Lectr English, Rice Univ, 68-69; asst prof, 69-72, assoc prof, 72-78; Prof English, Univ Kans, 78-. **MEMBERSHIPS** Popular Cult Asn; Western Literature Association; NCTE. **RESEARCH** New journalism; lyric poetry; Western American literature; pedagogy; technology and literature. **SELECTED PUBLICATIONS** Auth, The New Journalism, Univ Kans, 71; Prometheus Reborn, 77 & Holistic Technology, 77, Libra; Dry season, 77 & The Unicorn Captured, 80, Cottonwood Rev; Familiar Stranger, 81; Ecphrases: Poem as Interpretations of the Other Arts, 89; Mind, Language, Machine, 87; The Birds form J. Know Where, 89; Violence and Grace, 93; Education on the Wild Side, 93; New Westers, 96. **CONTACT ADDRESS** Dept of English, Univ of Kansas, Lawrence, Lawrence, KS 66045-0001. **EMAIL** newwestr@eagle.cc.ukans.edu

JOHNSON, PATRICIA E.
PERSONAL Born 02/22/1951, m, 1989, 1 child **DISCIPLINE** ENGLISH **EDUCATION** Earlham Col, BA, 73; Univ Minn, PhD, 85. **CAREER** Asst prof, Univ Ala Huntsville, 85-89; asst to assoc prof, Pa State Harrisburg, 89-. **HONORS AND AWARDS** Univ Minn Fel, 84. **MEMBERSHIPS** MLA. **RESEARCH** Victorian literature, feminist criticism, the novel. **SELECTED PUBLICATIONS** Auth, "Hard Times and the Structure of Industrialism: the Novel as Factory," Studies in the Novel, (89); auth, "'This Heretic Narrative': The Strategy of the Split Narrative in Charlotte Bronte's Villette," SEL: Studies in Eng Lit, 1500-1900, (90); auth, "Charlotte Bronte and Desire (to Write): Pleasure, Power and Prohibition," Anxious Power: Reading, Writing, and Ambivalence in Narrative by Women, (93); auth, "The Gendered Politics of the Gaze: Henry James and George Eliot," Mosaic, (97): auth, "Art and Assassination in Elizabeth Gaskell's Mary Barton," Victorians Inst Jour, (99); auth, Hidden Hands: Working-Class Women and Victorian Social-Problem Fiction. **CONTACT ADDRESS** Sch of Humanities, Pennsylvania State Univ, Harrisburg, Middletown, PA 17057. **EMAIL** pelj@psu.edu

JOHNSON, RICHARD F.
PERSONAL Born 11/03/1961, Washington, DC, m, 1989, 3 children **DISCIPLINE** ENGLISH **EDUCATION** Georgetown Univ, BS, 84; NYork Univ, MA, 89; Northwestern Univ, PhD, 98. **CAREER** Teacher, US Peace Corp, 84-86; asst prof, DeVry Inst Tech, 89-91; adj instr, N Central Col, 89-95; adj instr, Col DuPage, 93-96; instr, Northwestern Univ, 92-96; asst prof, William Rainy Harper Col, 97-. **HONORS AND AWARDS** Grad Fel Northwestern Univ, 90-94; NEH Grant. **MEMBERSHIPS** MAA; ISAS; MLA; NATE; CCCC. **RESEARCH** Anglo-Saxon hagiography; Grendel Project; Beowulf; history, literature, art of the Middle Ages. **SELECTED PUBLICATIONS** Auth, "Archangel in the Margins: St. Michael in the Homilies of Cambridge, Corpus Christi Col," Traditio 53 (98): 63-91; auth, "Feasts of Saint. Michael the Archangel in the Liturgy of the Early Anglo-Saxon Church: Evidence from the Eighth and Ninth Centuries," Leeds Studies in English (00); auth, "General and Miscellaneous Subjects," in The Years Work in Old English Studies: 1998 (Old English Newsletter, 01); auth, St. Michael: Hero, Warrior, and Archangel, Boydell/Brewer (forthcoming). **CONTACT ADDRESS** English Dept, William Rainey Harper Col, 1200 W Algonquin Rd, Palatine, IL 60067. **EMAIL** rjohnson@harper.cc.il.us

JOHNSON, SIMON
DISCIPLINE CREATIVE WRITING **EDUCATION** Colo State Univ, BA, 62; Columbia Sch Journalism, MS, 63; Univ Iowa, MFA, 69, PhD, 72. **CAREER** Engl, Oregon St Univ. **SELECTED PUBLICATIONS** Auth, Modern Technical Writing, Pentice-Hall, 90. **CONTACT ADDRESS** Oregon State Univ, Corvallis, OR 97331-4501. **EMAIL** sjohnson@orst.edu

JOHNSON, TIMOTHY
DISCIPLINE MUSIC THEORY **EDUCATION** Univ Mass, BM; Univ Conn, MM; State Univ NYork, PhD. **CAREER** Asst prof. **MEMBERSHIPS** Col Music Soc; Soc Music Theory. **SELECTED PUBLICATIONS** Auth, pubs on Charles Ives, John Adams, minimalism, 17th-century theory, and technology. **CONTACT ADDRESS** Dept of Music History, Theory and Composition, Ithaca Col, 100 Job Hall, Ithaca, NY 14850. **EMAIL** tjohnson@ithaca.edu

JOHNSON, W. RALPH
PERSONAL Born Trinidad, CO, 2 children **DISCIPLINE** CLASSICS **EDUCATION** Univ Calif, BA, 61, MA, 63, PhD, 66. **CAREER** Asst to Assoc Prof, UC Berkeley, 66-74; Assoc Prof to Prof, Cornell, 74-81; Prof, Univ Chicago, 81-98; Emeritus. **HONORS AND AWARDS** Distinguished Tchg Awd; Christian Gauss Awd; Martin Lectures; Townsend Lectures. **SELECTED PUBLICATIONS** Auth, Luxuriance and Economy: Cicero and the Alien Style, Ucal Press,71; auth, Darkness Visible: A Study óf Vergil's Aeneid, Univ Calif Press,76; auth, The Idea of Lyric, Univ Calif Press, 82; auth, Momentary Monsters: Lucan and his Heroes, Cornell, 87; auth, Horace and the Dialectic of Freedom, Cornell Univ Press, 93; auth, Lucretius and the Modern World, Duckworth, 00. **CONTACT ADDRESS** Univ of Chicago, 1010 E 59th St, Chicago, IL 60637. **EMAIL** 1johnson@uchicago.edu

JOHNSON, WILLIE J.
PERSONAL Born 06/02/1953, Detroit, MI, m, 4 children **DISCIPLINE** COMMUNICATION, EDUCATION **EDUCATION** Hamline Univ, BA, 75; Univ Minn, MA, 80; PhD, 96. **CAREER** Instr, Normandale Community Col, 82-. **HONORS AND AWARDS** Fulbright Scholar; McKnight Fel; SPAN Fac Adv, Univ of Minn; Alpha Kappa Alpha Golden Apple Excellence in Educ Awd; Student Support Serv Fac Awd; Normandale Community Col Found Fac Awd; Distinguished Fac Awd. **MEMBERSHIPS** NEA; Educ Minn; Minn Community Col Fac Assoc. **RESEARCH** Minorities in Higher Education, Cross-Cultural Adoption, Intercultural Communication, Ethics in Education. **SELECTED PUBLICATIONS** Auth, "Being First Sometimes Too Heavy a Burden", St. Paul Pioneer Pr, June 99; auth, "Bringing 4-H to Chicago Was One Unusual Way Whites Have Done the Right Thing", St. Paul Pioneer Pr, Aug 99; auth, "Being a Person of Color Means Being Constantly On Your Guard, St. Paul Pioneer Pr, Sept 99; auth, "It's Time to Relearn Manners and Respect For Our Fellow Human Beings", St. Paul Pioneer Pr, Nov 99; auth, "Emotional Cost of Submerging Identity Is High", St. Paul Pioneer Pr, Nov 99; auth, "Christian Chauvinism Blocking Out Goodwill", St. Paul Pioneer Pr, Dec 99; auth, "Sometimes Love Isn't Enough: The Voices of Some Adult Korean Adoptees in Minnesota", Korean Am Hist Soc; Dec 99; auth, "For New Year, Resolve to be Agent of Change", St. Paul Pioneer Pr, Jan 00; auth, "The Loathsome 'N' Word: Time Young African Americans Quit Using It", St. Paul Pioneer Pr, Feb 00; auth, "Dive Into State's Cultural Kaleidoscope", St. Paul Pioneer Pr, Mar 00. **CONTACT ADDRESS** Dept Speech and Theatre, Normandale Comm Col, 9700 France Ave S, Minneapolis, MN 55431-4309.

JOHNSON-EILOLA, JOHNDAN
DISCIPLINE ENGLISH **EDUCATION** Mich Technol Univ, BS, 87; MS, 89; PhD, 93. **CAREER** Asst prof & dir of tech writing, NMex Inst of Mining and Technol, 93-94; asst prof, Purdue Univ, 94-98; dir of tech writing, Purdue Univ 97-98; dir of prof writing, Purdue Univ, 98- ; assoc prof, Purdue Univ, 98- ; assoc prof, Clarkson Univ, 00- ; dir, Ctr for Excellence in Commun, Clarkson Univ, 00- . **HONORS AND AWARDS** Outstanding Ph.D. Student, Mich Technol Univ, 93; Hugh Burns Awd, Comput and Compos. 94; Nell Ann Picket Awd, Asn of Tchr of Tech Writing, 96; Ellen Nold Awd, Comput and Compos, 97; curric develop grant, Purdue Univ, 97; reinvestment grant, Purdue Univ, 97 **MEMBERSHIPS** Alliance for Computers and Writing; Amer Asn of Univ Profs; Asn for Bus Commun; Asn for Computing Machinery; Asn for Tchrs of Advan Comp; Asn of Tchrs of Tech Writing; Council for Progs in Tech and Sci Commun; Conf on Col Comp and Commun; Soc for Tech Commun. **RESEARCH** Philosophies of instructional writing; intellectual property. **SELECTED PUBLICATIONS** Coauth, "The Tie that Binds: Bulding Discourse Communities and Group Cohesion Through Computer-Based Conferences," Collegiate Microcomputer VI.4 (Nov 88): 339-48; auth, "Control and the Cyborg: Writing and Being Written in hypertext," J of Advan Comp 13.2 (Fall 93): 381-400; coauth, "Contexts for Faculty Professional Development in the Age of Electronic Writing and Communication," Tech Commun 42.1 (Nov 95): 581-584; auth, "Accumulation, Circulation, and Association: Economies of Information in Online Spaces," IEEE Trans on prof Commun 38.4 (Dec 95): 228-238; auth, "Stories and Maps: Postmodernism and Professional Communication," Kairos 1.1 (Spring 96); coauth, "Online Suport Systems," ACM Computing Surveys 28.1 (March 96): 197-200; coauth, "Policing Ourselves: Defining the Boundaries of Appropriate Discussion in Online Forums," Computers and Comp 13.3 (96): 269-291; auth, "Relocating the Value of Work: Technical Communication in a Post-Industrial Age," Tech Commun Q 5.3 (96): 245-270; co-ed, Computers and Composition 15.4 (Aug 98), Greenwich, CT: Ablex; auth, Nostalgic Angels: Rearticulating Hypertext Writing, Ablex Pr (Greenwich, CT), 97. **CONTACT ADDRESS** Ctr for Excellence in Commun, Clarkson univ, Box 5762, Potsdam, NY 13699-5762. **EMAIL** johndan@clarkson.edu

JOHNSON-SHEEHAN, RICHARD
DISCIPLINE RHETORIC AND PROFESSIONAL COMMUNICATION **EDUCATION** Iowa State Univ, PhD, 95. **CAREER** Instr, Univ NMex, 95-. **RESEARCH** The rhetoric of modern physics. **SELECTED PUBLICATIONS** Publishing articles exploring the rhetoric of modern physics. **CONTACT ADDRESS** Univ of New Mexico, Albuquerque, Albuquerque, NM 87131. **EMAIL** rsheehan@unm.edu

JOHNSTON, ALEXANDRA F.
PERSONAL Born 07/19/1939, Indianapolis, IN **DISCIPLINE** ENGLISH, DRAMA **EDUCATION** Univ Toronto, BA, 61, MA, 62, PhD, 64; LLD(hon), Queen's Univ, 84. **CAREER** Asst prof, Queen's Univ, 64-67; asst prof to assoc prof, 67-77, Prof English, Victoria Col, Univ Toronoto 78-. **HONORS AND AWARDS** Fel, Royal Soc Can, 97. **MEMBERSHIPS** Index Middle Eng Prose (adv comt); Int Soc Medieval Theatre (pres, 82-92); Medieval Renaissance Drama Soc, MLA (pres, 89-91); dir, Records Early Eng Drama, 76-. **RESEARCH** Reed Volume on records of Berkshire, Buckinghamshire and Oxfordshire; Oxford City Section of REED Oxford City and University; History of Drama in Provinces; aspects of medieval and Tudour dramaturgy; the context of the York Cycles's compostion. **SELECTED PUBLICATIONS** Auth, "Acting Mary: the Emotional Realism of the Mature Virgin in the N- Town Plays," in From Page to Performance: Essays in Early English Drama, (Michigan, 95): 85-98; ed, English Parish Drama, Amsterdam and Atlanta, 96; auth, "The Continental Connection: a Reconsideration," in The Stage as Mirror: Civc Theatre in Late Medieval Europe, (Cambridge, 97): 6-24; coauth, Reformation and Resistance in Thames/Severn Parishes: The Dramatic Witness," in The Parish in English Life, (Manchester Univ Press, 97): 78-200; ed, Civic Ritural and Drama, (Amsterdam, 97): 7-14; auth, "At the Still Point of the Turning World: Augustinian roots of Medieval Dramturgy," European Medieval Drama, (Camerino, 97): 5-25; auth, "Vernacular Drama," in Garland's Medieval England: An Encyclopedia, (Kalamazoo, 98): 244-248; auth, William Revetour, Chaplain and Clerk of York, Testator," in Leeds Studies in English, (NS 29, 98) 153-172; auth, "The Robin Hood of the Records," in Robin Hood: The Legend as Performance, (Univ of Delaware Press, 98): 27-44; auth, "English Community Drama in Crisis: 1535-1580," in European Communities of Medieval Drama: a Collection of Essays, (Brepols, 99): 248-269. **CONTACT ADDRESS** Victoria Col, Univ of Toronto, 150 Charles St W, Toronto, ON, Canada M5S 1K9. **EMAIL** ajohnsto@chass.utoronto.ca

JOHNSTON, ARNOLD
PERSONAL m **DISCIPLINE** CREATIVE WRITING **EDUCATION** Univ Del, PhD. **CAREER** Prof, Creative Writing, W Mich Univ. **HONORS AND AWARDS** Two WMU Fac Res Fel; Two Mich Counc Arts Grants; Two NEA/Arts Fund Kalamazoo Grants; Irving S. Gilmore Found Emerging Artist Grant, Kalamazoo's Community Arts Medal; NMU Alumni Assn Excellence in Teaching Awd, 90. **MEMBERSHIPS** Dramatists' Guild. **RESEARCH** Fiction, and poetry. **SELECTED PUBLICATIONS** Auth, Of Earth and Darkness, Miss, 80; auth, What the Earth Taught Us, March Street Press, 96; auth, The Witching Voice, WMU Pr; auth, Scrimshaw; auth, The Edge of Running Water; auth, Suitors. **CONTACT ADDRESS** Dept of Engl, Western Michigan Univ, Sprau Tower, Kalamazoo, MI 49008-5092. **EMAIL** arnie.johnston@wmich.edu

JOHNSTON, CAROL ANN
DISCIPLINE RENAISSANCE LITERATURE **EDUCATION** Harvard Univ, PhD. **CAREER** Asst prof-. **RESEARCH** Relationship between poetry and visual culture during the seventeenth century in England. **SELECTED PUBLICATIONS** Auth, Eudora Welty's short fiction, 97. **CONTACT ADDRESS** Dept of Eng, Dickinson Col, PO Box 1773, Carlisle, PA 17013-2896.

JOHNSTON, GEORGIA
DISCIPLINE 20TH CENTURY BRITISH LITERATURE **EDUCATION** Rutgers Univ, PhD. **CAREER** Eng Dept, St. Edward's Univ; Assoc Prof. **RESEARCH** 20th Century British Literature, Autobiography, Creative Writing (Poetry). **SELECTED PUBLICATIONS** Auth, "Narratologies of Pleasure: Gertrude Stein's Autobiography of Alice. B. Toklas," Modern Fiction Studies 42.3 (96): 590-606; auth, "Virginia Woolf's Autobiographers: Sidonie Smith, Shoshanna Felman, and Shari Benstock," Virginia Woolf: Texts and Contexts, ed. Beth Rigel Daugherty and Eileen Barrett (NYork, Pace Univ, 96). 140-144; auth, "Virginia Woolf Revisiting Roger Fry into the Frames of 'A Sketch of the Past,'" Biography 20.3 (97): 284-301; auth, "Class Performance in Between the Acts: Audiences for Miss La Trobe and Mrs. Manresa," Woolf Studies Annual 3 (97): 61-75; auth, "Introduction: The Productions of Audience and Transgression," in Essays on Trangressive Readings: Reading Over the Lines, ed. Georgia Johnston (Lewiston, The Edwin Mellen Press, 97), ix-xxii; auth, "Introduction: Raising Community," in Proceedings of the Eight Annual Conference on Virigina Woolf, ed. Jeanette McVicker and Laura Davis (NYork, Pace Univ Press, 99), 1-5. **CONTACT ADDRESS** Saint Louis Univ, 221 N Grand Blvd, Saint Louis, MO 63103.

JOHNSTON, JOHN
DISCIPLINE ENGLISH LANGUAGE AND LITERATURE **EDUCATION** Columbia Univ, PhD, 84. **CAREER** Prof **RESEARCH** Modern fiction; British and American Poetry; critical theory. **SELECTED PUBLICATIONS** Auth, Carnival of Repetition; trans, On the Line; co-trans, In the Shadow of the Silent Majorities. **CONTACT ADDRESS** English Dept, Emory Univ, 1380 Oxford Rd NE, Atlanta, GA 30322-1950.

JOHNSTON, JOHN H.
PERSONAL Born 01/18/1921, Norfolk, VA, m, 1948, 7 children **DISCIPLINE** ENGLISH **EDUCATION** BA, 47; Univ Chicago, MA, 50; Univ Wis, PhD, 60. **CAREER** Instr, 54-56 & 57-60, from asst prof to assoc prof, 60-69, Prof Eng, W VA Univ, 69-89; Prof emer Eng, 89-. **MEMBERSHIPS** MLA; NCTE **RESEARCH** Eng poetry of World War I; Brit poetry, 1920-1939; urban poetics. **SELECTED PUBLICATIONS** Auth, Charles Sorley's bright promise, W VA Univ Philol Papers, 12/61; David Jones: The heroic vision, Rev Polit, 1/62; English Poetry of the First World War, Princeton Univ, 64; The Poet and the City, Univ GA Press, 84. **CONTACT ADDRESS** West Virginia Univ, Morgantown, Stansbury Hall, Morgantown, WV 26506. **EMAIL** jhj21@aol.com

JOHNSTON, KENNETH R.
PERSONAL Born 04/20/1938, Marquette, MI, m, 1961, 3 children **DISCIPLINE** ENGLISH **EDUCATION** Augustana Col, Ill, BA, 59; Univ Chicago, MA, 61; Yale Univ, AM, 62, PhD(-English), 66. **CAREER** Instr English, Augustana Col, Ill, 62-63; from asst prof to assoc prof English, 66-75, dir undergrad studies, 68-70, assoc dean col arts & sci, 73-74, Prof English, Ind Univ, Bloomington, 75-, Fulbright prof Am lit, Univ Bucharest, Romania, 74-75; mem, English Romantic Exec Comn, MLA, 78- **HONORS AND AWARDS** Distinguished Teaching Awd, Amoco Found, 73. **MEMBERSHIPS** MLA; Keats-Shelley Asn; Wordsworth-Coleridge Asn (pres, 74-76). **RESEARCH** English and American romantic poetry; Wordsworth; humanistic institutions. **SELECTED PUBLICATIONS** **CONTACT ADDRESS** Dept of English, Indiana Univ, Bloomington, Ballantine Rm 42, Bloomington, IN 47405. **EMAIL** johnstok@indiana.edu

JOHNSTON, MARK D.
PERSONAL Born 11/23/1952, Puyallup, WA, m, 1988, 2 children **DISCIPLINE** RHETORIC **EDUCATION** Univ Ore, BA, 74; John Hopkins Univ, MA, 76; PhD, 78. **CAREER** Asst prof, Wash Univ, 78-81; asst prof to assoc prof to prof, Ill State Univ, 83-97; dir Newberry Lib, 99-. **HONORS AND AWARDS** ACLS Fel, 82; Folger Shakespeare Lib NEH Fel, 88; NEH, 94; John Brown Prize, 91. **MEMBERSHIPS** MLA. **RESEARCH** Medieval Iberia; intellectual and cultural history; rhetoric; information technology. **SELECTED PUBLICATIONS** Auth, The Spiritual Logic of Ramon Llull, Clarendon Pr, 87; auth, "Mateo Aleman's Problem with Spelling," PMLA 103 (88): 759-69; auth, The Evangelical Rhetoric of Ramon Llull, Oxford Univ Pr, 96. **CONTACT ADDRESS** Info Tech, Newberry Library, 60 W Walton, Chicago, IL 60610. **EMAIL** johnstonm@newberry.org

JOHNSTON, PATRICIA A.
PERSONAL Born 07/30/1937, Chicago, IL, m, 1959 **DISCIPLINE** CLASSICS **EDUCATION** UCLA, AB, 67; Univ Calif Berkeley, MA, 72; PhD, 75. **CAREER** TA, Univ of Calif Los Angeles, 67-69; Univ Calif Berkeley, 70-75; asst prof to prof, Brandeis Univ, 75-. **HONORS AND AWARDS** Phi Beta Kappa; Sloan Fel. **MEMBERSHIPS** APA, Women's Class Caucus of APA, Vergilian Soc, Class Asn, CANE, CAMWS, Phi Beta Kappa. **RESEARCH** Greek and Latin Literature, specializing in Vergil and his precedessors, Religion, specializing in the Mystery Cults, Classical mythology, ancient Italy. **SELECTED PUBLICATIONS** Auth, "Eurydice and Proserpina in the Georgics," TAPA 107, (77): 161-172; auth, Vergil's Agricultural Golden Age: A Study of the Georgics, Leiden, 80; auth, "Poenulus I, 2 and Roman Women," TAPA 110 (80): 143-159; auth, "The Storm in Aeneid VII," Vergilius 27, (81): 23-30; auth, "Dido, Berenice, and Arsinoe," AJPh 108 (87): 649-654; auth, Traditio: An Introduction to the Latin Language and its Influence, Macmillan, 88; auth, "Love and Laserpicium in Catallus 7," CPh 88 (93): 329; auth, "Under the Volcano: Volcanic Myth and Metaphor in Vergil's Aeneid," Vergilius 42 (96): 55-65; auth, "Cybele and Her Companions on the Northern Littoral of the Black Sea," Cybele, Attis and Related Cults: Essays in Memory of MJ Vermaseren (Leiden, 96): 101-116; transl Vergil's Aeneid, Focus Publ, (forthcoming). **CONTACT ADDRESS** Dept Classics, Brandeis Univ, MS 016, Waltham, MA 02454-9110. **EMAIL** johnston@brandeis.edu

JOHNSTON, PAUL
DISCIPLINE ENGLISH **EDUCATION** Grand Valley State Col, BA; Univ MI Ann Arbor, MA; PhD,88. **CAREER** Chp, 97-99, Plattsburgh State Univ of NY. **RESEARCH** Am lit. **SELECTED PUBLICATIONS** Auth, publ(s) about representation of the environment in early Am lit and the relationship between cognitive sci and literary criticism. **CONTACT ADDRESS** SUNY, Col at Plattsburgh, 101 Broad St, Plattsburgh, NY 12901-2681.

JOHNSTON, STANLEY HOWARD
PERSONAL Born 04/28/1946, Cleveland, OH, m, 1976 **DISCIPLINE** ENGLISH LANGUAGE AND LITERATURE: ARCHIVES AND ACADEMIC LIBRARIES **EDUCATION** BA, Columbia Univ, 68; MA, 70, PhD, 77, Univ Western Ontario; MSLS Case Western Reserve Univ, 79. **CAREER** Tchg Asst, Dept English, Univ Western Ontario, 71-72; Asst ed, Spenser Newsletter, Univ Western Ontario, 72-73; Bibliog The Cleveland Herbals Proj Hist Div Cleveland Hea Sci Library, 84-90;

Cur of Rare Books, The Holden Arboretum, 90-. **HONORS AND AWARDS** Phi Beta Mu. **MEMBERSHIPS** The Bibilo Soc, Bibilo Soc Of Am, Council on Bot and Horticulture Libraries, Am Library Assoc(Rare Books and Manuscript Div), Soc for the Hist of Natural Hist. **RESEARCH** Analytical and Descriptive Biblio; Book and Printing Hist, Bot and Horticultural Hist; Medical Hist; Hist of Bot Illus. **SELECTED PUBLICATIONS** A Study of the Career and Literary Publications of Richard Pynson, Dissertation, UWO 1977; The Cleveland Herbal, Botanical and Horticultural Collections, Kent State Univ Press, 92; Cleveland's Treasures from the World of Cleveland; auth, Treasures from the World of Botanical Literature, Orange Frazer Press, 98; Inter column in CBHL Newsletter, 95. **CONTACT ADDRESS** Holden Arboretum, 9500 Sperry Rd, Kirtland, OH 44094. **EMAIL** stanley177@aol.com

JOLLY, ROSEMARY J.
DISCIPLINE ENGLISH LITERATURE **EDUCATION** Univ Toronto, PhD. **CAREER** Dept Eng, Queen's Univ **HONORS AND AWARDS** Frank Knox Awd. **RESEARCH** Postcolonial literatures and theory; theories of violence, philosophical, psychoanalytical and clinical; intersections between gender and nationalism in minority literatures; interdisciplinarity in the postcolonial context; African, especially South African literatures; status of oral testimony. **SELECTED PUBLICATIONS** Auth, Colonization, Violence and Narration in White South African Writing: Breyten Breytenbach, Andre Brink and J.M. Coetzee, Ohio Univ, 96; Bessie Head and homophobia in Cross Addressing: Discourse on the Border, SUNY, 96; co-ed, Writing South Africa, Cambridge, 97. **CONTACT ADDRESS** English Dept, Queen's Univ at Kingston, Kingston, ON, Canada K7L 3N6. **EMAIL** jollyr@post.queensu.ca

JOLY, RALPH ROBERT
PERSONAL Born 02/03/1940, Salem, MA, m, 1959, 2 children **DISCIPLINE** ENGLISH **EDUCATION** William Tyndale Col, BRE, 64; Eastern Mich Univ, MA, 65; Univ NC, Chapel Hill, PhD(English), 73. **CAREER** Asst prof English, Harrisburg Area Community Col, 67-68; asst prof, Bethel Col, 70-74; assoc prof, Northwestern Col, 76-77; assoc prof, 77-79, prof English, Asbury Col, 79-. **MEMBERSHIPS** MLA; NCTE. **RESEARCH** Literary archetypalism; James Joyce; compositional strategies. **CONTACT ADDRESS** Dept of English, Asbury Col, 1 Macklem Dr, Wilmore, KY 40390-1198. **EMAIL** rjoly@asbury.edu

JONES, ANNE HUDSON
PERSONAL Born 11/14/1944, El Dorado, AR, m, 1971 **DISCIPLINE** LITERATURE & MEDICINE **EDUCATION** La State Univ, BA, 65; Univ NC, PhD(comp lit), 74. **CAREER** Asst prof English, Va Wesleyan Col, 70-71; lectr, New River Community Col, 71-72; instr, Va Polytech Inst & State Univ, 73-75, asst prof, 75-78, asst dir, Ctr Prog in Humanities, 78-79; Asst Prof Lit & Med, Inst Med Humanities, Univ Tex Med Br, 79-, Assoc ed, Lit & Med, 80-; consult, Nat Bd Consult, Nat Endowment for the Humanities & Col Health Related Professions, Univ PR, 81- **MEMBERSHIPS** MLA; Am Comp Lit Asn; Southern Comp Lit Asn; Science Fiction Res Asn; Soc Health & Human Values. **RESEARCH** Medicine and the physician in American (popular) culture; feminist science fiction. **SELECTED PUBLICATIONS** Auth, A question of ethic: Materials and methods, Proc 27th Int Tech Community Conf, Inst Humanitic Studies, 80; Thomas Szasz' myth of mental illness and Peter Shaffer's Equus, Asclepius at Syracuse: Thomas Szasz, Libertarian Humanist, 81; Ethics and medical writing: A prolegomenon, Proc 28th Int Tech Community Conf, 81; Alexei Panshin's almost non-sexist Rite of Passage, in: Future Females: A Critical Anthology, Bowling Green Univ Press, 81; Salome: the decadent ideal, Comp Lit Studies, 81; Medicine and the physician in popular culture, in: The Handbook of American Popular Culture, Greenwood Press, 81; Women in science fiction: An annotated secondary bibliography, Extrapolation, spring 82; The cyborg (r)evolution in science fiction, in: The Mechanical God: Machines in Science Fiction, Greenwood Press, 82. **CONTACT ADDRESS** Inst Med Humanities, Univ of Texas, Med Branch at Galveston, 301 University Blvd, Galveston, TX 77550-2708.

JONES, BUFORD
DISCIPLINE ENGLISH LITERATURE **EDUCATION** Harvard Univ, PhD, 62. **CAREER** Bibliogr. **SELECTED PUBLICATIONS** Auth, articles on Melville, Thoreau, Poe and Hawthorne. **CONTACT ADDRESS** Eng Dept, Duke Univ, Durham, NC 27706.

JONES, CHARLENE DIEHL
DISCIPLINE ENGLISH LITERATURE **EDUCATION** Brandon Univ, BS, 82; Univ of Manitoba, MA, 86; PhD, 93; McGill Univ, Fel. **CAREER** Prof; teaching asst, Univ of Manitoba; teaching asst, Univ of Manitoba; lectr, Brandon Univ; marker, Univ of Manitoba; asst prof, St. Jerome's Univ. **HONORS AND AWARDS** SSHRC Post-Doctoral Fel; SSHRC Doctoral Fel; Colin Inkster Memorial Graduate Fel, Univ of Manitoba, 90; Dr. Bernon B. Rhodenizer Graduate Scholar, Univ of Manitoba, 90; Vis Fel, Univ of Manitoba, 90; Res Fel, Univ of Manitoba, 91; Drummond Fel, Univ of Manitoba, 91; Nominated - Alice Wilson Medal, Royal Soc of Canada, 92. **SELECTED PUBLICATIONS** Auth, Fred Wah; auth, "There's more nothing to say': Unspeaking Douglas Barbour's Story for a Saskatchewan Night,"; auth, "Sandra Birdsell's Agassiz Stories: Speaking the Gap"; auth, "Telling Secrets: Sinclaair Ross Sawbones Memorial"; auth, "All in the Family: Modernism and its Progeny"; auth, "Barbour's story for a Saskatchewan Night: Silence & Bliss & the Untenable Text"; auth, "Body/Language in Lola Lemire Tostevin's sophie"; auth, "Critical contamination, or going boudoir: a diallage"; auth, "Five Little Presses and How They Grew"; auth, "Remembering the Love Song: Ambivalence and Cohen's Take This Waltz". **CONTACT ADDRESS** Dept of English, St. Jerome's Univ, Waterloo, ON, Canada N2L 3G3. **EMAIL** cdiehljo@watarts.uwaterloo.ca

JONES, CHRISTOPHER A.
DISCIPLINE ENGLISH LITERATURE **EDUCATION** Univ Toronto, PhD, 95. **CAREER** Asst prof. **RESEARCH** Old English literature; Anglo-Saxon England **SELECTED PUBLICATIONS** Auth, Aelfric's Letter to the Monks of Eynsham. **CONTACT ADDRESS** Dept of English and Philos, Idaho State Univ, 921 S 8th Ave, PO Box 8056, Pocatello, ID 83209-0001. **EMAIL** jonechri@cwis.isu.edu

JONES, CHRISTOPHER P.
PERSONAL Born 08/21/1940, Chislehurst, England **DISCIPLINE** CLASSICS, ANCIENT HISTORY **EDUCATION** Oxon (Oxford), BA, 61, MA, 67; Harvard, PhD, 65. **CAREER** Lect, 65-66, Univ Toronto; asst prof, 66-68, assoc prof, 68-75, prof, 65-92, prof of class & hist, 92-97, George Martin Lane Prof of Classics & Hist, 97-, Harvard Univ. **HONORS AND AWARDS** Fel, Royal Soc of Canada; Corresp mem, Ger Archaeol Inst, 92; fel, Am Numismatic Soc, 93; The Am Philos Soc, 96; fel, Am Acad of Arts & Sci, 98. **MEMBERSHIPS** APA; Bd of Sr Fellows, Byzantine Stud, Dumbarton Oaks Res Lib & Collection, Harvard Univ; Class Asn of Canada; Inst for Advanced Stud, Princeton, Sch of Hist Stud; Soc for the Promotion of Hellenic Stud; Soc for Promotion of Roman Stud. **RESEARCH** Greek lit of the Roman period; Hellenistic and Roman hist; Greek epigraphy. **SELECTED PUBLICATIONS** Auth, Philostratus: Life of Apollonius of Tyana, Penguin Books, 71; auth, Plutarch and Rome, Oxford Univ Press, 71, 72; auth, The Roman World of Dio Chrysostom, Harvard Univ Press, 78; auth, Culture and Society in Lucian, Harvard Univ Press, 86; coed, Louis Robert, Le Martyre de Pionios, pretre de Smyrne, mis au point et complete par G. W. Bowersock et C. P. Jones, Dumbarton Oaks Res Lib & Collection, Wash, 94; auth, Kinship Diplomacy in the Ancient World, Harvard Univ Press, forthcoming 99. **CONTACT ADDRESS** Dept of Classics, Harvard Univ, 226 Boylston Hall, Cambridge, MA 02138. **EMAIL** cjones@fas.harvard.edu

JONES, DAN CURTIS
PERSONAL Born 12/18/1942, Chattanooga, TN, m, 1964, 1 child **DISCIPLINE** ENGLISH **EDUCATION** Carson-Newman Col, BA, 64; Vanderbilt Univ, MA, 67; Ind Univ Pa, PhD, 79. **CAREER** Instr, Univ Tenn, Nashville, 66-69; instr, Univ Tenn, Chattanooga, 69-72; Eng fac, 75-89, div chmn, 89-, Wytheville Community Col. **HONORS AND AWARDS** Woodrow Wilson Fel, 65 **MEMBERSHIPS** NCTE; Conf Col Compos & Commun; Two yr Col Eng Assoc Southeast. **RESEARCH** Literary reading process of inexperienced readers; comm col leadership. **SELECTED PUBLICATIONS** Auth, Preparing Students To Write About Poems, Col Compos & Commun, 5/79; art, Affective Response: A Plea For A Balanced View, Winter 80; Helping Students Enter The World Of The Poem, Fall 81. **CONTACT ADDRESS** Wytheville Comm Col, 1000 E Main St, Wytheville, VA 24382-3308. **EMAIL** wcjoned@wc.cc.va.us

JONES, DARYL
PERSONAL Born 07/26/1946, Washington, DC, m, 1979, 2 children **DISCIPLINE** ENGLISH **EDUCATION** Mich State Univ, BA, 68, MA, 70, PhD, 74. **CAREER** Grad Tchng Asst, Asst to the Dean, Mich State Univ, 68-73, 70-73; Asst to Assoc to Prof & Ch, Tex Tech Univ, 73-79, 79-82, 82-83, 83-86; Prof & Dean, Col of Arts & Sci, Boise State Univ, 86-91; Prof & Provost & VP for Acad Affairs, Boise State Univ, 91-. **HONORS AND AWARDS** Phi Beta Kappa; Phi Kappa Phi; Creative Writing Fellow Grant, NEA, 85; Pres Acad Ach Awd, Tex Tech Univ, 86; Natalie Ornish Poetry Awd, 90; Writer in Residence, State of Idaho, 92, 93; Lifetime Hon Member, Golden Key Honorary, 97-; elected member, tex inst of letters. **MEMBERSHIPS** WICHE NW Acad Forum; Tex Inst of Letters; Pres, Tex Asn of Creative Writing Tchrs, 84-86; Ch, S-Cent Asn of Dept of Eng, 83-84; Pres, S Plains Area Counc, 83-84. **RESEARCH** American literature; creative writing; the popular western novel. **SELECTED PUBLICATIONS** Auth, Someone Going Home Late, Texas Tech Univ Press, 90; Clenched Teeth and Curses: Revenge of the Dime Novel Outlaw Hero, J of Popular Culture, 652-65, 7, 73; auth, The Dime Novel Western, Bowling Green Univ Pop Press, 78; Two Years Behind the Lectern: On the Road as Idaho's Writer-in-Residence, Writer's NW Handbook, 6th ed, Media Weavers LLC, 75-77, 95. **CONTACT ADDRESS** Office of the Provost, Boise State Univ, 1910 Univ Dr, Boise, ID 83725. **EMAIL** aprjones@boisestate.edu

JONES, DOUGLAS GORDON
PERSONAL Born 01/01/1929, Bancroft, ON, Canada, 4 children **DISCIPLINE** CANADIAN & MODERN LITERATURE **EDUCATION** McGill Univ, BA, 52; Queen's Univ, Ont, MA, 54. **CAREER** Lectr English, Royal Mil Col, 54-55; asst prof, Ont Agr Col, 55-61; lectr, Bishop's Univ, Que, 61-63; assoc prof, 63-73, Prof Engl, Univ Sherbrooke, 73-. **HONORS AND AWARDS** Gov Gen Awd Poetry, 77; phd, univ guelph. **MEMBERSHIPS** Asn Can Univ Teachers English; League Can Poets; Asn Can & Que Literatures; fel Royal Soc Can. **RESEARCH** Canadian poetry in French and English. **SELECTED PUBLICATIONS** Auth, The sun is axeman (poetry), Univ Toronto, 61; Phrases from Orpheus (poetry), Oxford Univ, 67; Butterfly on Rock: A Study of Themes and Images in Canadian Literature, Univ Toronto, 70; in Search of America, Boundary, 74; transl, the Terror of the Snows (poetry), Univ Pittsburgh, 76; auth, Under the Thunder the Flowers Light up the Earth (poetry), Coach House, 77. **CONTACT ADDRESS** Dept of English Fac of Arts, Univ of Sherbrooke, Sherbrooke, QC, Canada J1K 2R1.

JONES, EDWARD T.
PERSONAL Born 07/05/1938, Clearfield, PA, m, 2 children **DISCIPLINE** LITERATURE **EDUCATION** Juniata Col, BA; Univ Md, PhD. **HONORS AND AWARDS** Sears-Roebuck Teaching Excellence and Campus Leadership Awd. **MEMBERSHIPS** MLA **RESEARCH** Literature, film. **SELECTED PUBLICATIONS** Auth, L.P. Hartley, 78; auth, Following Directions: A Study of Peter Brook, 85; auth, The Films of Mike Leigh, forthcoming. **CONTACT ADDRESS** York Col, Pennsylvania, York, PA 17405. **EMAIL** ejones@ycp.edu

JONES, ELLEN
DISCIPLINE TWENTIETH-CENTURY BRITISH AND IRISH LITERATURE **EDUCATION** Cornell Univ, PhD. **CAREER** Asst prof, St. Louis Univ **SELECTED PUBLICATIONS** Ed, Feminism & Mod Fiction; Feminist Readings Joyce, Virginia Woolf, Politics Modernism; auth, Feminist Readings of Joyce: Preface, Mod Fiction Studies, 89; The Letter Selfpenned to One's Other: Joyce's Writing, Deconstruction, Feminism, Ohio State Univ Press, 89; Figuring Woolf, Mod Fiction Studies, 92; Writing the Modern: The Politics of Modernism, Mod Fiction Studies, 92; Textual Mater: Writing the Mother in Joyce, Cornell Univ Press, 93; Commodious Recirculation: Commodity and Dream in Joyce's Ulysses, James Joyce Quart, 93; The Flight of a Word: Narcissism and the Masquerade of Writing in Virginia Woolf's Orlando, Women's Studies: Interdisciplinary Jour, 94; auth, " Figural Desire in Orlando," In Virginia Woolf: Emerging Perspectives, ed. Mark Hussey and Vera Neverow, Pace Univ Press (94): 108-14; auth, "Borderlines," Joyce: Feminism/Post/Colonalism, European Joyce Studies 8 (98): 7-22; auth, "Border Disputes," in Joyce and Language, ed. Laurent Milesi, Cambridge: Cambridge University Press (99); auth, "Empty Shoes," in Footnoes: On Shoes, ed. Shari Benstock and Suzanne Ferriss, Rutgers Univ Press (00). **CONTACT ADDRESS** Dept of English, Saint Louis Univ, 221 N Grand Blvd, Saint Louis, MO 63103. **EMAIL** jonese2@slu.edu

JONES, JAMES H.
PERSONAL Born 07/31/1929, Wheeling, WV, m, 1959, 5 children **DISCIPLINE** ENGLISH **EDUCATION** Kenyon Col, AB, 51; Univ Buffalo, MA, 57; Ind Univ, PhD(English), 65. **CAREER** From asst prof to assoc prof, 62-70, Prpf English, Northern Mich Univ, 70-, Nat Endowment for Humanities fel, 67-68. **MEMBERSHIPS** Shakespeare Asn Am; MLA. **RESEARCH** Shakespeare; ballads; Renaisssance Soc Am; Conf Christianity & Lit. **SELECTED PUBLICATIONS** Auth, Commonplace and memorization in the oral tradition of the English and Scottish popular ballad, J Am Folklore, 61; Lear and Leir: Matthew V: 30-37, the turning point and the rescue theme, Comp Drama, 70. **CONTACT ADDRESS** Dept of English, No Michigan Univ, 1401 Presque Isle Ave, Marquette, MI 49855.

JONES, JANE A.
PERSONAL Born 08/21/1948, Jamestown, NY, m, 1970, 2 children **DISCIPLINE** ENGLISH **EDUCATION** Hobart and William Smith Col, BA, 70; Case Western Reserve Univ, MA, 74; New York Univ, ABD, 79. **CAREER** Adj Lecturer, Queens Col, 81-82; Asst Prof to Prof, Manatee Community Col, 82-. **HONORS AND AWARDS** Fla Humanities Coun grant, 94; NEH Fac Study Project, 93; NEH Study Grant, 92; NEH Grant for Advancement in Humanities, 91; Sidney and Celia Siegel Fel, N Y Univ, 80. **MEMBERSHIPS** CCHA, Fla Col English Asn, Sarasota Inst of Lifetime Learning, Fl Asn of Cmty Col. **RESEARCH** Florida culture; Medieval literature; Women and literature. **SELECTED PUBLICATIONS** Ed, The Poetry of Florida: A History of the Imagination, Pineapple Press, 95; auth, Frida Kahol, Rourke Pub, 93 auth, "Florida in Renaissance Poetry," The Marjorie Kinnan Rawlings Journal of Florida Literature, 99; auth, "Literature and Families," in Encyclopedia of Family Life, Salem Press, 98; auth, "Bone by Fae Myenne Ng," in Masterpieces of Women's Literature, HarperCollins, 96; auth, "Juan Ponce de Leon's Voyages to Florida's Gulf Coast: Encounters with the Calusa," and "Seminole Wars 1816, 1835 1855," in Great Events from History: North America, Salem Press, 96; auth, "Baal by Bertolt Brecht," "for colored girls who

have considered suicide when the rainbow is enuf by ntozake shange," "The Wandering Scholar from Paradise by Hans Sachs," "Uncle Vanya by Anton Chekhov," and "The Lady's Not for Burning by Christopher Fry" in Masterplots: Twentieth Anniversary Revised Second Edition, Salem Press, 96; auth, "The Hour of the Star by Clarice Lispector," Masterpieces of Latino Literature, HarperCollins, 94. **CONTACT ADDRESS** Dept Humanities, Manatee Comm Col, 8000 Tamiami Trail S, Venice, FL 34293-5113. **EMAIL** jonesj@sc.mcc.cc.fl.us

JONES, JILL T.
PERSONAL Born 09/05/1947, Pontotoc, MS, m, 1998, 6 children **DISCIPLINE** ENGLISH **EDUCATION** Miss Univ for Women, BA, 69; Auburn Univ, MA, 73; Univ Miss, PhD, 84. **CAREER** Teacher, Nettleton High Sch, 69-70; teacher, Eddy Jr High Sch, 70-71; grad teaching asst, Auburn Univ, 71-74; teacher, Opelika Jr High Sch, 73-74; instr, S.D. Bishop State Jr Col, 75-78; part-time instr, San Jacinto Col System, 80-82; part-time instr, Alvin Community Col, 80-81; lectr, Univ of Houston System, 80-82; part-time instr, Northwest Jr Col, 82-84; grad teaching asst, Univ of Miss, 82-84; instr II, La State Univ, 84-89; acting asst prof, La Tech Univ, 89-90; prof, Southwestern Okla State Univ, 90-; dir of Freshman Composition, Southwestern Okla State Univ, 96-99. **HONORS AND AWARDS** Bernhardt Acad Excellence Awd; NDEA Fel; Phi Kappa Phi; Sigma Tau Delta. **MEMBERSHIPS** S Central MLA, Okla Coun Teachers of English, Popular Culture Asn. **RESEARCH** British literature 1890-1920. **SELECTED PUBLICATIONS** Auth, "Netta Syreft," The 1890s: An Encyclopedia of British Literature, Art, and Culture, Garland (New York), 93; auth, "Charlotte Mew," British Short Fiction Writers 1880-1914: The Realist Tradition in the Dictionary of Literary Biography series vol 135, Bruccoli Clark Layman, (Columbia, SC): 94; auth, "'Guilty or Not Guilty?': An Exercise in Critical Thinking," OCTE Exchange (94): 9-10; auth, "Arthur Machen's Supernaturalism: The Decadent Variety," Short Story Criticism, Gale Research (Detroit, MI), 95; auth, "Max Beerbohm," Encyclopedia of British Humorists: Geoffrey Chaucer to John Clesse, Garland (New York), 96; auth, "Netta Syreft," Late-Victorian and Edwardian British Novelists, Second Series, Bruccoli Clark Layman (Columbia, SC), 99. **CONTACT ADDRESS** Dept Lang Arts, Southwestern Oklahoma State Univ, Weatherford, 100 Campus Dr, Weatherford, OK 73096-3001. **EMAIL** jonesj@swosu.edu

JONES, JOHN H.
PERSONAL Born 03/13/1961, Newark, NJ, m, 1985 **DISCIPLINE** ENGLISH **EDUCATION** Randolph-Mason Col, BA, 83; Fordham Univ, MA, 88; PhD, 95. **CAREER** Asst prof, Jacksonville State Univ, 96-. **HONORS AND AWARDS** Phi Kappa Phi, 88-; Northeast Modern Lang Asn Grad Canons Paper Prize, 93. **MEMBERSHIPS** MLA, South Atlantic MLA, Nat Coun of Teachers of English, N Am Soc for the Study of Romanticism, Am Confr on Romanticism, Ala Coun of Teachers of English, Ala Col English Teacher Asn. **RESEARCH** William Blake, English Romantic Literature, Mikhail Bulchtin, Language Theory. **SELECTED PUBLICATIONS** Auth, "'Self-Annihilation' and Dialogue in Blake's Creative Process: Urizen, Milton, Jerusalem," Modern Lang Studies 24.2 (94): 3-10; auth, "Printed Performance and Reading The Book[s] of Urizen: Blake's Bookmaking Process and the Transformation of Late Eighteenth-Century Print Culture," Colby Quart 35 (99): 73-89. **CONTACT ADDRESS** Dept English, Jacksonville State Univ, 700 Pelham Rd North, Jacksonville, AL 36265-1602. **EMAIL** jhjones@jsucc.jsu.edu

JONES, LEANDER CORBIN
PERSONAL Born 07/16/1934, Vincent, AR, m, 1962, 3 children **DISCIPLINE** BLACK AMERICANA STUDIES, COMMUNICATIONS **EDUCATION** Univ of AR at Pine Bluff, AB 1956; Univ of IL, MS 1968; Union Graduate Institute, PhD 1973. **CAREER** Chicago Public Schools, English teacher 1956-68; Peace Corps Volunteer, English teacher 1964-66; City Colls of Chicago, TV producer 1968-73; Meharry Medical Coll, media specialist 1973-75; Western Michigan Univ, assoc prof Black Amer studies, 75-89, prof 1989-. **HONORS AND AWARDS** "Roof Over My Head" TV Series WDCN Nashville 1975; acted in and directed several plays Kalamazoo 1979-86; exec producer & host for TV series "Fade to Black" 1986. **MEMBERSHIPS** Mem Kappa Alpha Psi 1953-; mem exec comm DuSable Mus African Amer History 1970-; designer of programs in theatre andTV for hard-to-educate; pres TABS Ctr 1972-; mem AAUP 1973-; mem Natl Council of Black Studies 1977-, MI Council of Black Studies 1977-, Popular Culture Assoc 1978-; chmn Comm Against Apartheid 1977-; mem South African Solidarity Org 1978-; mem MI Org African Studies 1980-; commander Vets for Peace Kalamazoo 1980-; pres Black Theatre Group of the Kalamazoo Civic Players 1980-83; bd of dirs Kalamazoo Civic Players 1981-83, MI Commn on Crime and Delinquency 1981-83; pres Corbin 22 Ltd 1986; Lester Lake Corp, secretary of the bd, 1992. **SELECTED PUBLICATIONS** Author "Africa Is for Reel," Kalamazoo 1983. **CONTACT ADDRESS** Prof, Black Amer Studies, Western Michigan Univ, Kalamazoo, MI 49008. **EMAIL** jonesl@umich.edu

JONES, LOUIS CLARK
PERSONAL Born 06/28/1908, Albany, NY, m, 1932, 3 children **DISCIPLINE** HISTORY, LITERATURE **EDUCATION** Hamilton Col, BA, 30; Columbia Univ, MA, 31, PhD(Eng lit), 42. **CAREER** From instr to assoc prof English & Am lit, NY State Col Teachers, Albany, 34-46; dir, 46-72, Emer Dir, NY State Hist Asn & Farmers Mus, 72-; Prof Am Folk Art, Cooperstown Grad Prog, State Univ NY Col Oneonta, 73-, Guggenheim fel, 46; mem, NY Coun on Hist Sites, 54-58, NY Coun on Arts, 60-72 & NY State Hist Trust, 66-72; dir, Coopertown Grad Prog, State Univ NY col Oneonta, 64-72; Nat Endowment for Humanities res grant, 72-73. **HONORS AND AWARDS** Awd of Distinction, Am Asn State & Local Hist, 70; Katherine Coffee Prize, 81; lhd, hamilton col, 62. **MEMBERSHIPS** Am Asn Mus (vpres, 52-68); Am Asn State & Loal Hist (vpres, 50-57); fel Am Folklore Soc. **RESEARCH** Eighteenth century social history; New York state folklore; folklore of the supernatural; American folk art. **SELECTED PUBLICATIONS** Auth, Clubs of the Georgian Rakes, Columbia Univ, 42; Spooks of the Valley, Houghton, 48; Things that Bump in the Night, Hill & Wang, 59; ed, Growing up in the Cooper Country, Syracuse Univ, 65; Murder at Clearry Hill, 82; Three Eyes on the Past, Syracuse Univ Press, 82. **CONTACT ADDRESS** 11 Main St, Box 351, Cooperstown, NY 13326.

JONES, MARK
DISCIPLINE ENGLISH LITERATURE **EDUCATION** Columbia Univ, PhD. **CAREER** Dept Eng, Queen's Univ **HONORS AND AWARDS** Winner of ASUS Teaching Awd. **RESEARCH** Romantic poetry; literature and economics; pastoral; elegy; parody; history of literary criticism and theory. **SELECTED PUBLICATIONS** Auth, Lucy Poems, Univ Toronto, 95; Parody and its Containments, Representations, 96; Double Economics: Ambivalence in Wordsworth's Pastoral, PMLA, 93; Spiritual Capitalism: Wordsworth and Usury, JEGP, 93; Interpretation in Wordsworth, 91; co-auth, Wordsworth Scholarship: An Annotated Bibliography, Garland, 85; auth, Blake: An Illustrated Quarterly, Philological Quarterly; auth, Studies in English Literature; auth, Keats-Shelley Journal. **CONTACT ADDRESS** English Dept, Queen's Univ at Kingston, Kingston, ON, Canada K7L 3N6. **EMAIL** jonesmc@qsilver.queensu.ca

JONES, MARY ELLEN
DISCIPLINE AMERICAN LITERATURE; THE AMERICAN FRONTIER **EDUCATION** Duke Univ, AB, MA; Union Grad Sch, PhD. **CAREER** Prof/Eng; Dir/Am Stud prog. **HONORS AND AWARDS** Navy Commendation for work as liason, Sixth Fleet and people of Corf; fulbright scholar, greece. **SELECTED PUBLICATIONS** Auth, Christopher Columbus and His Legacy, 92; Seeds of Change: Readings on Cultural Exchange after 1492, 93; The American Frontier, 94; John Jakes: A Critical Companion, 96; Daily Life on the Nineteenth Century American Frontier, 98. **CONTACT ADDRESS** Wittenberg Univ, Springfield, OH 45501-0720.

JONES, NICHOLAS
DISCIPLINE ENGLISH LITERATURE **EDUCATION** Harvard Col, BA, 67; MA, 69; PhD, 73. **CAREER** Asso prof, Oberlin Coll, 76. **MEMBERSHIPS** Trustee, Northern Ohio Youth Orchestras. **RESEARCH** British Romantic period, Shakespeare and Renaissance drama, romantic women poets. **SELECTED PUBLICATIONS** Publ, anthology of 17th century New England sermons; articles on Milton and Herbert; biog essays on Felicia Hemans, Mary Russell Mitford, Mary Howitt, Hannah More in Dictionary of Lit Biog. **CONTACT ADDRESS** Dept of Eng, Oberlin Col, Oberlin, OH 44074. **EMAIL** Nicholas_Jones@qmgate.cc.oberlin.edu

JONES, RICHARD A.
PERSONAL Born 08/08/1953, London, England **DISCIPLINE** ENGLISH **EDUCATION** Univ Vir, BA, 75; MA, 76; Ver Col, MFA, 87. **CAREER** Prof, De Paul Univ, 87-. **HONORS AND AWARDS** IAC Lit Awd, 91, 95; Posner Awd, 86. **SELECTED PUBLICATIONS** Auth, Sonnets, Adastra Press (Easthampton) 90; auth, At Last We Enter Paradise, Copper Canyon (Port Townsend), 91; auth, A Perfect Time, Copper Canyon (Port Townsend), 94; auth, The Abandoned Garden, Tunheim Santrizos (Minn), 97; auth, 48 Questions, Telbot Bach (Los Angeles), 98; auth, The Blessing: New and Selected Poems, Copper Canyon (Port Townsend), 00. **CONTACT ADDRESS** Dept English, DePaul Univ, 802 West Belden, Chicago, IL 60614.

JONES, ROBERT ALSTON
PERSONAL Born 10/10/1938, Charleston, SC, m, 1961, 3 children **DISCIPLINE** MODERN GERMAN LITERATURE **EDUCATION** Duke Univ, AB, 60; Univ Tex, MA, 62, PhD(Ger), 66. **CAREER** Asst Prof Ger, Tufts Univ, 65-66; from Asst Prof to Assoc Prof, 66-98, Prof Ger and Assoc Dean, Univ Wis, Milwaukee, 98-; Assoc Dean for Research, Grad Sch, 90. **HONORS AND AWARDS** Alexander von Humbolt Found res fel, Ger, 77-78; DAAD, Univ of Turbingen, 62-63. **MEMBERSHIPS** Brecht Soc; Am Asn Teachers Ger; Kafka Soc; MLA. **RESEARCH** Elementary language instruction; German literature, especially of the modern period; modern German drama. **SELECTED PUBLICATIONS** Auth, Art and Entertainment: Jenian Literature and the Circus, 1890-1933, 85; coauth, Frank Wedekcud: A Bibliographic Handbook, 96. **CONTACT ADDRESS** Dept of Ger, Univ of Wisconsin, Milwaukee, PO Box 413, Milwaukee, WI 53201-0413. **EMAIL** rajones@uwm.edu

JONES, ROBIN A.
PERSONAL Born 08/16/1958, Anadarko, OK, m, 3 children **DISCIPLINE** COMMUNICATION; GENDER **EDUCATION** Okla State Univ, BS, 80; SW Baptist Theol Seminary, MA, 84; Okla Univ, PhD, 97. **CAREER** Adjunct Prof, Okla City Community Col, 97; Asst Prof, SWestern Okla State Univ, 97-. **HONORS AND AWARDS** Top Student Paper, Instructional Div, NCA, 96, CSCA, 96. **MEMBERSHIPS** Nat Commun Asn; AAUW; Central States Commun Asn; Delta Kappa Gamma. **RESEARCH** Gender issues; communication. **CONTACT ADDRESS** Southwestern Oklahoma State Univ, Weatherford, 100 Campus Dr., Weatherford, OK 73096-3098. **EMAIL** jonesra@swosu.edu

JONES, SIDNEY C.
PERSONAL Born 09/03/1934, Atlantic, IA, m, 1956, 2 children **DISCIPLINE** ENGLISH LITERATURE **EDUCATION** State Univ, Iowa, BA, 56; Univ Wis, MS, 59. **CAREER** Asst, dept polit sci, State Univ, Iowa, 55-56; asst, dept integrated lib studies, Univ Wis, 57-61; from asst prof to assoc prof, 61-67, prof English, Carroll Col, Wis, 67-, retired, 98-. **HONORS AND AWARDS** Johnson Memorial Prize, 56; Woodrow Wilson Fel 56-57; Sch of Criticism and Theory, 77. **MEMBERSHIPS** MLA **RESEARCH** Contemporary European literature; Renaissance literature; philosophy and literature. **CONTACT ADDRESS** 603 E Roberta Ave., Waukesha, WI 53186-5593. **EMAIL** sjones@carroll1.cc.edu

JONES, STANLEY E.
DISCIPLINE COMMUNCATION STUDIES **EDUCATION** State Univ Iowa, BA, 57, MA, 62; Northwestern Univ, PhD, 64. **CAREER** Prof. **RESEARCH** Nonverbal communication; applied communication; relationship of verbal and nonverbal codes. **SELECTED PUBLICATIONS** Auth, The Right Touch: Understanding and Using the Language of Physical Contact, Hampton, 94; Problems of validity in questionnaire studies of nonverbal behavior: Jourard's tactile body-accessibility scale, Southern Commun Jour, 92; co-auth, Touch attitudes and behaviors, recollections of early childhood touch, and social self confidence, Jour Nonverbal Behavior, 86. **CONTACT ADDRESS** Dept of Communication, Univ of Colorado, Boulder, Boulder, CO 80309. **EMAIL** Stanley.Jones@Colorado.edu

JONES, STEVEN
PERSONAL Born 03/02/1959 **DISCIPLINE** ENGLISH **EDUCATION** Univ Okla, BA, 80; Columbia Univ, PhD, 88. **CAREER** Prof; ed, Keats-Shelley J; coed, Romantic Circles Website. **HONORS AND AWARDS** Director, "Romantic Circles High School Project," NEH Teaching with Technology grant, 99-02 **RESEARCH** Romantic-period literature and culture; textual criticism; editing; hypertext theory. **SELECTED PUBLICATIONS** Auth, Shelley's Satire: Violence, Exhortation, and Authority, Northern Ill UP, 94; auth,The Black Dwarf as Satiric Performance, in Romanticism, Radicalism, and the Press, Wayne State UP, 97; auth,The Book of Myst in the Late Age of Print, Postmodern Culture, 97; auth, Satire and Countersatire in Crabbe and Wordsworth, The Wordsworth Circle, 98; auth, Satire and Romanticism, New York, St. Martin's Press, 00. **CONTACT ADDRESS** Dept of English, Loyola Univ, Chicago, 6525 N Sheridan Rd, Chicago, IL 60626. **EMAIL** sjones1@wpo.it.luc.edu

JONES, SUZANNE W.
PERSONAL Born 05/26/1950, Surry, VA, m, 1986, 2 children **DISCIPLINE** ENGLISH **EDUCATION** Col of William and Mary, BA 72, MA 75; Univ Virginia, PhD 84. **CAREER** Univ Richmond, co-or women's stud 85-94, asst prof, assoc prof, 84 to 92-. **HONORS AND AWARDS** Phi Beta Kappa; Dist EDU Awd; Outstanding Fac Awd; Tchg Awd. **MEMBERSHIPS** MLA; SSSL. **RESEARCH** Lit of the Am South; Twentieth Cent Women Writers and Lit. **SELECTED PUBLICATIONS** Ed, Growing Up in the South: An Anthology of Modern Southern Literature, NY, Mentor/Penguin USA, 91; Reading the Endings in Katherine Anne Porter's Old Mortality, Famous Last Words: Changes in Gender and Narrative Closure, ed Alison Booth, Charlottesville, VA UPV, 93, reprinted, in Critical Essays on American literature: Katherine Anne Porter, ed, Darlene Unrue, NY, G. K. Hall, 97; Edith Wharton's Secret Sensitiveness, The Decoration of Houses and Her Fiction, Jour of Modern Lit, 97; Reconstructing Manhood: Race, Masculinity, and Narrative Closure: Ernest Gaines's A Gathering of Old Men and A Lesson Before Dying, Masculinities, 95. **CONTACT ADDRESS** Dept of English, Univ of Richmond, Richmond, VA 23173. **EMAIL** sjones@richmond.edu

JONES, WARD
DISCIPLINE CLASSICAL STUDIES **EDUCATION** Univ Richmond, BA, 52; Univ NC at Chapel Hill, MA, 57, PhD, 59. **CAREER** Instr, Ohio State Univ, 59-61; assoc prof, 61-67; prof, 67- & Chancellor prof, 68-, Col William and Mary; vis

assoc prof, Tufts Univ in Naples, Italy, 65-66 & Univ NC, 66. **HONORS AND AWARDS** Ovatio awd, Class Asn Mid W and S, New Orleans, 88; Listed in Whols Who in Am, 85-; VP, 65-66 & pres, 66-67, Class Asn Va; sec-treas, 66-68 & pres, 80-82, Class Asn Mid W and S, Southern Sect; exec comt, Class Asn Mid W and S, 79-82; mng ed, Class J, 70-80; nominating comt, Class Asn Mid W and S; dir, 70-, VP, 78-80 & pres, 80-, Mediter Soc Am; VP, 86-88 & Marshal, 90-92, Alpha Chap of Phi Beta Kappa & pres, Alpha Delta Gamma, Hon Medieval and Renaissance Fraternity, 94-95; fel Inst Advanced Study in Arts and Humanities, Univ Minn, 67 - $300,00; fel Southeastern Inst Medieval and Renaissance Stud, Duke Univ & Univ NC, 66 - $600,00; 67 -600,00; 68 - $600.00 & 69-70 - $14,000,00; fac res assignments, William and Mary, 78 & 92-93. **RESEARCH** Vergil; Legend of the Sack of Troy; early history of the College of William and Mary. **SELECTED PUBLICATIONS** Auth, A New Latin Quitrent Poem of the College of William & Mary, Va Mag Hist and Biog, vol 96, 88; The So-Called Silvestris Commentary on the Aeneid and Two Other Interpretations, Speculum, 89 & A Latin Munusculum among the Papers of Francis Nicholson, Bodleian Libr Record, 93; coauth, The Commentary on the First Six Books of the Aeneid of Vergil Commonly Attributed to Bernardus Silvestris, Univ Nebr Press, 77 & An Aeneid Commentary of Mixed Type: the Glosses in MSS Harley 4946 and Ambrosianus GlII inf, The Pontifical Inst Mediaeval Stud, Toronto, 96; co-ed, Solomon Henning's Chronicle of Courland and Livonia, Baltic Stud Ctr, Madison, 92; rev, Schreiber and Maresca, Commentary on the First Six Books of Vergilis Aeneid by Bernardus Silvestris, in Vergilius, 80. **CONTACT ADDRESS** Dept of Classical Studies, Col of William and Mary, Morton Hall, Williamsburg, VA 23187-8795. **EMAIL** jwjone@facstaff.wm.edu

JOOMA, MINAZ
DISCIPLINE BRITISH LITERATURE **EDUCATION** Univ Surrey, BA, 85; Univ London, PGCE, 87; MA, 89; Mich State Univ, PhD, 95. **CAREER** Instr, Mich State Univ, 89-95; asst prof, St John's Univ, 96-97; independent scholar, 97-. **HONORS AND AWARDS** Fel, NE Am Soc for 18th Century Studies; All-University Excellence-in-Teaching Citation; Fel, Mich State Univ; John A Yunck Awd. **MEMBERSHIPS** MLA, Am Soc for 18th Century Studies, Col of Arts and Letters Fel Colloqium, Convocation, Group for Early Mod Cult Studies, Midwestern Am Soc for 18th Century Studies, Phi Betta Kappa, Phi Kappa Phi. **RESEARCH** British Studies, 18th Century English Narrative, 19th Century English Poetry and Narrative, 19th Century American Literature, Anthropology, Literary theory and criticism, Gender Studies, Education. **SELECTED PUBLICATIONS** Auth, "Spectating the spectator, re(ad)dressing the (ad)dressor," Am Transcendental Quart 4.7, (93): 321-333; auth, "The Alimentary Structures of Incest in 'Paradise Lost,'" Eng Lit Hist 63.1, (96): 25-43; auth, "Cannibalism, Incest, and Domestic Economy in 'Robinson Crusoe,'" Lit, Interpretation, Theory 18.1, (96); auth, "Cannibalism and Consumerism, or Robinson Crusoe Inc(orporates)," Eating Their Words: Cannibalism and the Boundaries of Cultural Identity, ed Kristen Leaver, frothcoming. **CONTACT ADDRESS** 11 George St, Apt 3, Summit, NJ 07901-4419.

JOOS, ERNEST
PERSONAL Born 01/06/1923, Uraiujfalu, Hungary, m, 1949, 6 children **DISCIPLINE** PHILOSOPHY, LITERATURE **EDUCATION** McGill Univ, MA, 59; Inst d'Etudes Medievales, Montreal, Lic en Phil, 66; Univ Montreal, PhD(medieval philos), 70. **CAREER** Asst prof philos, Loyola Col, Montreal, 67-75; PROF PHILOS, CONCORDIA UNIV, 75-, Vis prof philos, Univ Laval, Quebec, 77-78 & Univ de Montreal, 79-81. **MEMBERSHIPS** Can Philos Asn; Am Cath Philos Asn. **RESEARCH** Intentionality; metaphysics-ontology. **SELECTED PUBLICATIONS** Auth, Dialogue With Heidegger on Values: Ethics for Times of Crisis (American University Studies: Series V, Philosophy, Vol 127, December 92; ed, George Lukacs and His World: a Reassessment (American University Studies, Series XIX: General Literature, Vol 9, April 88; auth, Intentionlity, Source of Intelligibility: The Genesis of Intentionality (American University Studies, V: Philosophy, Vol 69), March 89. **CONTACT ADDRESS** Dept of Philosophy, Concordia Univ, Montreal, 1455 De Maisonneuve Blvd W, Montreal, QC, Canada H3G 1M8.

JORDAN, BORIMIR
PERSONAL Born 11/05/1933, Sofia, Bulgaria, m, 1961, 3 children **DISCIPLINE** CLASSICS **EDUCATION** Univ Calif, Berkeley, PhD, 68. **CAREER** Asst prof, Univ So Calif, 67-68; asst prof, assoc prof, prof, Univ Calif, Santa Barbara, 68- . **MEMBERSHIPS** APA. **RESEARCH** Ancient Greek history; Greek historical writers; Greek religion. **SELECTED PUBLICATIONS** Auth, The Athenian Navy, Berkeley, 75; Servants of the gods, Gottingen, 79. **CONTACT ADDRESS** Dept of Classics, Univ of California, Santa Barbara, Santa Barbara, CA 93106-3120. **EMAIL** bjordan@humanitas.ucsb.edu

JORGENS, JACK J.
PERSONAL Born 01/04/1943, Minneapolis, MN, m, 1965, 2 children **DISCIPLINE** ENGLISH, FILM STUDIES **EDUCATION** Carleton Col, BA, 65; City Col NYork, MA, 67; NYork Univ, PhD, 70. **CAREER** Asst prof Eng, Univ CT, 70-71 & Univ MA, Amherst, 71-75; Assoc prof eng. AM Univ, 75-, Prof, Shakespeare Inst, Univ Bridgeport, 76-77. **HONORS AND AWARDS** Outstanding Prog Develop Cinema Studies, Am Univ, 76. **MEMBERSHIPS** Am Film Inst; MLA; Soc Cinema Studies; Shakespeare Asn Am. **RESEARCH** Shakespeare in performance; film and theatre; video production. **SELECTED PUBLICATIONS** Auth, Alice Our Contemporary, Great Excluded: Critical Essays Children's Lit, 72; Champlain Shakespeare Festival, autumn 73, New York Shakespeare Festival, autumn 73, New York Shakespeare Festival, autumn 74, Champlain Shakespeare Festival, winter 76 & Champlain Shakespeare Festival, spring 77, Shakespeare Quart; Shakespeare on Film, Ind Univ, 77. **CONTACT ADDRESS** Dept of Lit, American Univ, 4400 Massachusetts Ave NW, Washington, DC 20016-8200. **EMAIL** accent2@accentmediainc.com

JORIS, PIERRE
PERSONAL Born 07/14/1946, Strasbourge, 2 children **DISCIPLINE** ENGLISH **EDUCATION** Bard Col, AB, 69; Univ Essex, MA, 75; State Univ NY (SUNY), PhD, 90. **CAREER** Asst Prof, Univ Constantine Algeria, 76-79; Lectr, Univ Md, 83; Instr, CIEE Paris, 85-87; Teaching Asst, State Univ NYork (SUNY), 88-89; Vis Lectr, Univ Calif, 89-90; Vis Lectr, San Diego State Univ, 91; Vis Lectr, Univ Calif, 92; Prof, State Univ NYork (SUNY), 92-. **HONORS AND AWARDS** Fac Res Awd Prog Grant, St Univ NY (SUNY), 93, 97; PEN Ctr USA W Awd, 94; Josephine Miles Awd for Excellence, 96; NEA Translation Grant, 99. **MEMBERSHIPS** LSV, HVWG, IAPL, PEN, MLA. **RESEARCH** Twentieth-Century experimental poetry and politics, theory and practice of translation. **SELECTED PUBLICATIONS** Coauth, The Selected Writings of Kurt Schwitters, Temple UP, 93; auth, Poems for the Millennium: The university of California Book of Modern and Postmodern Poetry, 2 vols Univ Calif Pr, 95, 98; auth, Towards a Nomadic Poetics, Spanner Ed (Hereford, UK), 99; auth, hjr, Earthwind Pr (Ann Arbor, MI), 99; auth, Out/Takes, Backwoods Broadsides Chaplet 46 (Ellsworth, ME), 99; ed, The Writings of Pablo Picasso, Exact Change Publ (Boston, MA), 00; auth, Poasis (Poems 1986-1999), Wesleyan UP, forthcoming. **CONTACT ADDRESS** Dept English, SUNY, 1400 Washington Ave, Albany, NY 12222-0100. **EMAIL** joris@csc.albany.edu

JOSLIN, KATHERINE
DISCIPLINE AMERICAN LITERATURE, AMERICAN STUDIES **EDUCATION** Northwestern Univ, PhD. **CAREER** Prof, English, W Mich Univ. **HONORS AND AWARDS** Western Mich Univ Alum; Fulbright Summer Inst for Intl Edu Grants. **MEMBERSHIPS** Am Asn for the Study of Lit and Environ; Am Studies Asn; Great Lakes Am Studies Asn; Edith Wharton Soc; Modern Lang Asn. **RESEARCH** Edith Wharton, literary criticism, Jane Addams as a writer, progressive era writers. **SELECTED PUBLICATIONS** Auth, Wretched Exotic: Essays on Edith Wharton in Europe, Peter Lang, 93; auth, Edith Wharton, in Women Writers Series, Macmillan Publs Limited & St. Martin's Press (London & NY), 91. **CONTACT ADDRESS** Dept of English, Western Michigan Univ, Sprau Tower, Kalamazoo, MI 49008. **EMAIL** joslin@wmich.edu

JOSLIN, MICHAEL E.
PERSONAL Born 05/20/1949, Philadelphia, PA, m **DISCIPLINE** ENGLISH **EDUCATION** Univ SC, BA, 73; PhD,77. **CAREER** Asst Prof, Jacksonville Univ, 78-82; Faculty, East Tenn State Univ, 85-89; Asst Prof to Prof, Lees-McRae Col, 89-. **HONORS AND AWARDS** Phi Beta Kappa, Phi Kappa Phi, McDuffy Sen English Awd, Havilah Babcock Creative Writing Awd, Fel, Ctr for Appalachian Studies and services, Third Place, Creative Journalism Awd, 92; Who's Who among Am teachers, Who's who in Media and Comm, Edgar Tufts Awd, Lees-McRae Col, 98 **MEMBERSHIPS** Appalachian Consortium. **SELECTED PUBLICATIONS** Auth, Our Living Heritage, Over mountain Press, 98; auth, "The Blacksmith," Appalachia Inside-Out: an anthology of Appalachian Literature, Univ Tenn Press, 95; auth, "Mountain Laure," The Draft Horse Journal, 95; auth, "Nothing New," multi-cultural Digest, 95; auth, "General Wilder's Home Still Labor of Love," The Tennessee Magazine, 97; auth, "Get Up, Nancy! Get Up Wendy!," The Draft Horse Journal, 97; auth, "Howard Burleson's Legacy," The Draft Horse Journal, 97; auth, "Veins of Ore: cranberry Mines Echo the Past," The Tennessee Magazine, 98. **CONTACT ADDRESS** Dept Humanities, Lees-McRae Col, PO Box 128, Banner Elk, NC 28604-0128. **EMAIL** joslin@lmc.edu

JOYCE, DONALD FRANKLIN
PERSONAL Born 11/04/1938, Chicago, IL, s **DISCIPLINE** LIBRARY SCIENCES **EDUCATION** Fisk Univ, BA 57; Univ Illinois, MS 60; Univ Chicago, PhD 78. **CAREER** Chicago Pub Lib, curator 60-81; Tenn State Univ Dwtnbr, coord 81-87; Austin Peay State Univ, dean libr and media 87-. **HONORS AND AWARDS** Distg Ser Awd; Black Caucus; Am Lib Asn. **MEMBERSHIPS** Am Lib Asn; Tenn Lib Asn. **RESEARCH** African Am Hist. **SELECTED PUBLICATIONS** Gatekeepers of Black Culture: Black Owned Book Publishing in the United States, 1817-1981, Westport Ct, Greenwood Press, 83; Black Book Publishers in the United States: A Historical Dictionary of the Presses, 1817-1990, Westport Ct, Greenwood Press, 91; Roated on the Chants of Slaves: Blacks in the Humanities, 1985-1997: A Selected Annotated Bibliography, 99. **CONTACT ADDRESS** Felix G Woodward Library, Austin Peay State Univ, Sixth and College Sts, Clarksville, TN 37044. **EMAIL** joyceD@apsu.edu

JOYCE, JANE W.
DISCIPLINE CLASSICS **EDUCATION** Bryn Mawr Col, BA; Univ Tex Austin, MA and PhD. **CAREER** Fac, 78-; prof. **HONORS AND AWARDS** Disting Prof Hum, Centre Col. **RESEARCH** Latin language and literature, ancient epic and lyric poetry, Greco-Roman drama, classical mythology and creative writing. **SELECTED PUBLICATIONS** Auth, Beyond the Blue Mountains; The Quilt Poems, Mill Springs Press, 84/86, Gnomon, 91; transl, Lucan's Pharsalia, Cornell Univ Press, 93. **CONTACT ADDRESS** Centre Col, 600 W Walnut St, Danville, KY 40422. **EMAIL** joycej@centre.edu

JRADE, CATHY L.
PERSONAL Born 03/12/1949, New York, NY, m, 1973, 1 child **DISCIPLINE** SPANISH AMERICAN LITERATURE **EDUCATION** Queens Col, CUNY, BA, 69; Brown Univ, AM, 71; PhD, 74. **CAREER** Asst prof, Vir Polytech Inst, 75-76; asst prof, assoc prof, Indiana Univ, 76-87; assoc prof, prof, Vanderbilt Univ, 87-; chmn dept span and port, Vanderbilt Univ, 98-. **HONORS AND AWARDS** Spence Wilson Fel; Fel and Co-Dir of the Fellows Prog of the Robt Penn Warren Cen for Human, 94-95, 00-01; Univ Res Coun Grnt, 97; Res Coun Fac Fel 89, 93; Kenan-Venture Fund Grnt, 88; Grnt-in-Aid of Res, Indiana Univ, 87; West Euro Fac Res Grnt, IN U, 86; Woodrow Wilson Fac Dev Grnt, 84-85; IN U Fac Fel, 79; Woodrow Wilson Dis Fel, 72, 73; Choice Mag, Outst Acad Title, 99; Exec Com of the MLA Div "Latin Am Literature from Independence to 1900, 82 and 97- 00; Hispania Awd, 79-80, 81; Phi Beta Kappa; Sigma Delta Pi; Summa Cum Laude, 69. **MEMBERSHIPS** MLA, AATSP, Inst of Intl de Lit Iberoamericana. **RESEARCH** Spanish American literature of the 19th and 20th centuries; modernisms; **SELECTED PUBLICATIONS** Auth, "Annotated Bibliography on Modernist Poetry," in The Cambridge History of Latin American Literature (Cambridge Univ Press, 96); auth, "Modernism on Both Sides of the Atlantic," Anales de la literatura espanola contemporanea 23 (98): 181-196; auth, "Modernist Poetry," in The Cambridge History of Latin American Literature (Cambridge Univ Press, 96); auth, Ruben Dario y la busqueda romantica de la unidad, Fondo de Cultura Economica (86); auth, Modernismo, Modernity, and the Development of Spanish American Literature Writings (Univ Tex Press, 98); auth, Modernismo, Modernity, and the Development of Spanish American Literature, netlibrary.com (00). **CONTACT ADDRESS** Dept. Spanish and Port, Vanderbilt Univ, PO Box 35-1616, Stn. B, Nashville, TN 37235. **EMAIL** cathy.1.jrade@vanderbilt.edu

JUDD, CATHERINE
PERSONAL Born Berkeley, CA, 1 child **DISCIPLINE** BRITISH LITERATURE, WOMEN'S STUDIES **EDUCATION** Univ Calif, Santa Cruz, BA, 82; Univ Calif Berkeley, MA, 85; PhD, 92. **CAREER** Asst to assoc prof, Univ of Miami, 92-. **HONORS AND AWARDS** NEH Summer Fel, 94; Univ of Miami Res Fel, 95; Univ of Miami Fel, 98, 99. **MEMBERSHIPS** MLA; Interdisciplinary Nineteenth-Century Studies Assoc; Nineteenth-Century Studies Assoc; Univ of Miami Women's Studies Assoc. **SELECTED PUBLICATIONS** Auth, "Nine Oils or the Balm of Gilead: Nursing and Social Healing in Hard Times", Reading Hard Times, ed Murray Baumgarten, Dickens Proj Pr, (Santa Cruz, 89); auth, "Male Pseudonyms and Female Authority in Victorian England", Literature and the Marketplace: Nineteenth-Century British Publishing and Reading Practices, eds John O Jordan and Robert L Patten, Cambridge Univ Pr, (Cambridge, 95); rev art on illness and mortality in Victorian fiction, Nineteenth-Century Contexts 19.4 (96): 109-112; rev art on Victorian prostitution, Nineteenth-Century Contexts, 20.1 (97): 115-118; auth, Bedside Seductions: Nursing and the Victorian Imagination, 1830-1880, St Martin's Pr, (NY), 98. **CONTACT ADDRESS** Dept English, Univ of Miami, PO Box 248106, Miami, FL 33124-8106. **EMAIL** catjudd@umiami.ir.miami.edu

JUHL, M. E.
PERSONAL Born 03/18/1957, El Dorado, AR, m, 1989 **DISCIPLINE** LIBRARIANSHIP **EDUCATION** Univ Texas, BA, 79; Columbia Univ, MLS, 86. **CAREER** Ref librn, N Y Pub Libr, 86-87; ref librn, Columbia Univ, 87-93; ref dir, Univ Arkansas Libr, 93- . **HONORS AND AWARDS** Magna cum Laude, 79. **MEMBERSHIPS** Am Philol Asn; ALA. **RESEARCH** Classics and computing; humanities computing. **SELECTED PUBLICATIONS** "Ex Machina: Electronic Resources for the Classics," Choice, 95; "Red, White, and Boolean," Choice, 98. **CONTACT ADDRESS** Library, Univ of Arkansas, Fayetteville, MULN 220J, Fayetteville, AR 72701. **EMAIL** bjuhl@comp.uark.edu

JUHNKE, JANET ANN
PERSONAL Born 11/26/1942, Halstead, KS, m, 1975, 2 children **DISCIPLINE** ENGLISH **EDUCATION** Bethel Col, BA, 64; Northwestern Univ, MAT, 65; Univ Kans, PhD(English), 74. **CAREER** Instr English, Bethel Col, 65-67; from Asst Prof

to Assoc Prof, 73-87, Prof English, 87-95, Asst Dean Fac, 80-82, VPres, Dean of Fac, Kans Wesleyan, 95-, Chmn Humanities Div, 75-79, 83-86, 89-92. **HONORS AND AWARDS** The Sears-Roebuck Found Teaching Excellence and Campus Leadership Awd, 91. **MEMBERSHIPS** AAHE; CIC. **RESEARCH** Satire; eighteenth century British literature; women's studies. **SELECTED PUBLICATIONS** Contribr, The Classic American Novel and the Movies, Ungar, 77; Inge's Women, Kans Quart, 86; contribr, Notable Women in the American Theater, Greenwood, 89. **CONTACT ADDRESS** Office of the Vice-President/Dean of Faculty, Kansas Wesleyan Univ, 100 E Claflin, Salina, KS 67401-6196. **EMAIL** juhnke@kwu.edu

JULIER, LAURA S.
PERSONAL Born New York, NY **DISCIPLINE** ENGLISH **EDUCATION** Univ Iowa, Phd, 88; Univ RI, MA, 79; SUNY Buffalo, BA, 70. **CAREER** Vis Asst Prof, Drake Univ, 88-90; Assoc Prof, Michigan State Univ, 90-. **HONORS AND AWARDS** Outstanding Fac, Michigan Campus Compact/Kellogg Foundation Community Service Learning Awd, March 95; Lily Endowment Teaching Fel, 93-94; University Awd for Exemplary Support of Women, Drake University, March 90; John C. Gerber Awd for Excellence in Teaching, Dept of English, Univ of Iowa, 87. **MEMBERSHIPS** MLA; NCTE; CCCC. **RESEARCH** Literary nonfiction; Indian captivity narratives; voice and representation in Am. Literary and cultural studies; rhetoric and composition studies. **SELECTED PUBLICATIONS** Auth, "Actual Experience, Preferred Narratives: Didion's After Henry," In The Critical Response to Joan Didion, Ed. Sharon Felton, Westport, CT: Greenwood Press, 93, 248-58; auth, "Private Texts and Social Activism: Reading the Clothesline Project," English Education December 94, 249-59, 249-59; auth, "The Difference It Makes to Speak: The Voice of Authority in Joan Didion," In Voices on Voice: Perspectives, Definitions, Inquiry, Ed. Kathleen Blake Yancey, Urbana, IL: NCTE, 94, 130-44; auth, "Us and Them: A Cautionary Essay about Restructuring Power in the Classroom," With David Cooper, Michigan Journal of Community Service Learning, 2, 95: 72-82; auth, "Democratic Conversations: Civic Literacy and Service-Learning in the American Grain," With David Cooper, In Writing the Community: Concepts and Models for Service-Learning in Composition, Eds Linda Adler-Kassner, Robert Crooks, and Ann Watters, American Association of Higher Education Series on Service-Learning in the Disciplines, Washington, DC: AAHE, 97; auth, "Voices from the Line: The Clothesline Project as Healing Text," Writing and Heaing: Towards an Informed Practice, Eds. Charles M. Anderson and Marian MacCurdy, Urbana, IL: NCTE Press, 00, 357-84. **CONTACT ADDRESS** Dept American Thought and Language, Michigan State Univ, 229 Bessey Hall, East Lansing, MI 48824-1033. **EMAIL** julier@ilot.msu.edu

JUNG, DONALD J.
DISCIPLINE COMMUNICATION STUDIES **EDUCATION** Univ Mo St Louis, BA; Univ Portland, MA; Purdue Univ, PhD. **CAREER** Asst prof, Castleton State Col, 78-91; asst prof, Univ MO-St. Louis, 91-. **SELECTED PUBLICATIONS** Auth, The Federal Communications Commission, the Broadcast Industry, and the Fairness Doctrine: 1981-1987, Univ Am; auth, Centering the Mass as a Social Condition: Technologies Mediate Humans Communicate, 95; auth, Is Interactivity a Function of Human Communication or Computer Mediation?, 95. **CONTACT ADDRESS** Communication Dept, Univ of Missouri, St. Louis, 8001 Natural Bridge Rd., Saint Louis, MO 63121.

JUNKINS, DONALD A.
PERSONAL Born 12/19/1931, Saugus, MA, m, 1958, 4 children **DISCIPLINE** AMERICAN LITERATURE, CREATIVE WRITING **EDUCATION** Univ Mass, BA, 53; Boston Univ, STB, 56, STM, 57, AM, 59, PhD(Am lit), 63. **CAREER** From instr to asst prof English, Emerson Col, 61-63; asst prof, Chico State Col, 63-66; from asst prof to assoc prof English, 66-74, dir MFA Grad Prog, 70-78, Prof English, Univ Mass, Amherst, 74-, Assoc poetry ed, Mass Rev, 68-70; NEA creative writing fel grant, 74, 79; poetry ed, New Am Rev, 81- **HONORS AND AWARDS** Jennie Tane Awd for poetry, 67; Nat Endowment for Arts award, 68; John Masefield Mem Awd, Poetry Soc Am, 72. **MEMBERSHIPS** Poetry Soc Am; Hemingway Soc. **RESEARCH** Creative writing, poetry; Poetry. **SELECTED PUBLICATIONS** Auth, Hawthorne's House of Seven Gables: A prototype of the Human mind, Lit & Psychol, 67; Should stars woo and lobster claws?: Edward Taylor's poetic theory, Early Am Lit, 11/68; The Graves of Scotland Parish (poetry), Heron, 69; Walden, 100 Years After Thoreau (poetry), Yorick, 69; And Sandpipers She Said (poetry), Univ Mass, 70; ed, The Contemporary World Poets, Harcourt, 76; auth, The Uncle Harry Poems and Other Maine Reminiscences, Outland Press, 77; Crossing by Ferry, Poems New and Selected Univ Mass, 78; auth, Playing for Keeps, Lynx House Press, 91; auth, Journey to the Corrida, Lynx House Press, 00; trans, Euripides Andromache (Euripides I), Pa Univ Press, 99. **CONTACT ADDRESS** 63 Hawks Rd., Deerfield, MA 01342. **EMAIL** djunk@english.umass.edu

JUNOD, SAMUEL A.
PERSONAL Born 06/07/1967, Geneva, Switz, s **DISCIPLINE** LINGUISTICS, LITERATURE **EDUCATION** Univ Geneva, 94, 96; John Hopkins Univ, PhD, 00. **CAREER** Asst prof, Univ Colo Boulder, 99-. **HONORS AND AWARDS** Jr Fac Dev Awd, 00. **MEMBERSHIPS** MLA; ACLA; SCSC. **RESEARCH** French renaissance; Rubelais; D'Aubigne; French Swiss literature. **SELECTED PUBLICATIONS** Auth, "Lectures du Physetere ou le Physetere se Degonfle," Etude Rabelaisiennes (98); auth, "Resingenies et Surgissement: Deux Modalites de la Parole Dam les Tragiques d'Agrippa d'Aubigne," Etude de Lettres (99). **CONTACT ADDRESS** Fr and Ital Dept, Univ of Colorado, Boulder, Boulder, CO 80309-0001. **EMAIL** junod@spot.colorado.edu

JUSDANIS, GREGORY
DISCIPLINE CLASSICAL LITERATURE, AESTHETICS **EDUCATION** McMaster Univ, BA, 78; Birmingham Univ, PhD, 83. **CAREER** Asst prof to assoc prof to prof, Ohio State Univ, 87-. **HONORS AND AWARDS** Guggenheim Fel, 92; Woodrow Wilson, 94. **MEMBERSHIPS** MLA; MGSA. **RESEARCH** Nationalism; Greek literature; globalization; aesthetics. **SELECTED PUBLICATIONS** Auth, The Poetics of Cavafy, Eroticism, Texuality, History, Princeton, 87; auth, Belated Modernity and Aesthetics, Culture, Inventing National Lit, 91; auth, The Necessary Nation, Princeton, 01. **CONTACT ADDRESS** Dept Classics, Ohio State Univ, Columbus, 230 N Oval Mall, 414 University Hall, Columbus, OH 43210.

JUSTICE, GEORGE L.
PERSONAL Born 11/16/1964, Philadelphia, PA, m, 1996 **DISCIPLINE** ENGLISH LITERATURE **EDUCATION** Wesleyan Univ, BA, 86; Univ Pa, MA, 90; PhD, 94. **CAREER** Vis asst prof, Univ Pa, 95; asst prof, Marquette Univ, 95-; vis asst prof, La State Univ, 00-01. **HONORS AND AWARDS** Winchester Fel, Wesleyan Univ, 88-95; Mellon Diss Fel, 92-93. **MEMBERSHIPS** MLA, Am Soc for 18th Century Studies, Johnson Soc of the Central Region. **RESEARCH** 18th-Century British Literature, Women's Writing, History of the Book, Literary Publishing. **SELECTED PUBLICATIONS** Auth, "The Eighteenth-Century Novel," Year's Work in English Studies, (98); auth, "Northanger Abbey as Anti-Courtship Novel," Persuasions, (99); auth, The Manufacturers of Literature: Writing and the Literary Marketplace in Eighteenth-Century England, Univ of Del Pr, 01; coed, Women's Writing and the Circulation of Ideas: Manuscript Publication in England, 1550-1800, forthcoming. **CONTACT ADDRESS** Dept English, Marquette Univ, Milwaukee, WI 53201-1881. **EMAIL** george.justice@marquette.edu

JUSTUS, JAMES HUFF
PERSONAL Born 04/22/1929, Newport, TN **DISCIPLINE** ENGLISH **EDUCATION** Univ Tenn, AB, 50, AM, 52; Univ Wash, PhD, 61. **CAREER** From instr to assoc prof, 61-69, Prpf English, Ind Univ, Bloomington, 70-, Contribr, American literary scholarship, an annual 1968-, Duke Univ, 70-. **MEMBERSHIPS** MLA; Soc Study Southern Lit; AAUP; SAtlantic Mod Lang Asn. **RESEARCH** Twentieth century American novel; American literature, 1800-1900. **SELECTED PUBLICATIONS** Auth, The epic design of Absalom, Absalom!, Tex Studies Lit & Lang, summer 62; Arthur Mervyn, American, 11/70 & Hawthorne's Coverdale: Character and art in the Blithedale romance, 3/75, Am Lit; On the restlessness of southerners, Southern Rev, winter 75; Not in defense but in memoriam, Miss Quart, fall 77; The unawakening of Edna Pontellier, Southern Lit J, spring 78; The Achievement of Robert Penn Warren, Louisiana State Univ Press, 81. **CONTACT ADDRESS** Dept of English, Indiana Univ, Bloomington, Bloomington, IN 47401.

JUSZCYK, FRANK
PERSONAL Born 07/13/1938, Laredo, TX, m, 1976, 2 children **DISCIPLINE** ENGLISH LITERATURE **EDUCATION** St Mary's Univ, BA, 63; Marquette Univ, MA, 65; Univ Wis Madison, PhD, 72. **CAREER** Instr, Univ of Wis, 69-72; teaching fel, W Mex Univ, 72-73; assoc prof, W NMex Univ, 92-. **HONORS AND AWARDS** Who's Who Among Am Teachers, 96. **MEMBERSHIPS** Da Engliscan Gesidas, Int Soc of Anglo-Saxonists. **RESEARCH** Northern European Mythology: Scandinavian, Germanic, Celtic, Anglo-Saxon Heroic Poetry, Hiberno-Norse Culture, Language and Literature, Scottish Historical Fiction. **SELECTED PUBLICATIONS** Auth, "Meeting Her," The Spirit That Wants Me: A New Mexico Anthology, Duff Inc, (91); auth, "The Os Rune and the Sword-Cult of Saxnot," Widowinde: The Periodical of Da Englican Gesidas, 115, (98). **CONTACT ADDRESS** Dept Humanities, Western New Mexico Univ, PO Box 680, Silver City, NM 88062-0680. **EMAIL** juszczykf@silver.wnmu.edu

K

KADLEC, DAVID
DISCIPLINE ENGLISH LITERATURE **EDUCATION** Univ Ind, BA; Univ Chicago, MA, PhD. **CAREER** Eng Dept, Georgetown Univ **RESEARCH** Modern British and American literature and culture; 20th century American poetry; literature and science; Victorian literature. **SELECTED PUBLICATIONS** Auth, pubs on Ezra Pound, James Joyce, Marianne Moore, Muriel Rukeyser and other 19th and 20th Century writers. **CONTACT ADDRESS** English Dept, Georgetown Univ, 37th and O St, Washington, DC 20057.

KAGAN, SUSAN
PERSONAL Born 12/27/1929, New York, NY, m, 1955, 2 children **DISCIPLINE** MUSICOLOGY **EDUCATION** Columbia Univ, BS, 51; Hunter Col CUNY, MA, 75; CUNY Grad School, PhD, 83. **CAREER** Pianist, St Louis Symphony Orchestra, 58-62 & Pitt Symphony Orchestra, 62-63; adj lectr, Bronx Comm Col, CUNY, 72-77; adj lectr, vis asst prof, substitute asst prof, PROF, HUNTER COL, CUNY; Am Asn Univ Women Diss Fel, 77; Rosa Riegelman Heintz Scholar, Hunter Col, 70. **MEMBERSHIPS** Am Musicol Soc; Local 802 Am Fedn Musicians; Int Franz Schubert Inst; Am Schubert Inst; Am Beethoven Soc; Berlioz Soc. **RESEARCH** 19th and 20th Century music. **SELECTED PUBLICATIONS** Ed Archduke Rudolph: Forty Variations on a Theme by Beethoven; Sonata in F for Violin and piano, 92; Archduke Rudolph: Variations in F for Violin and Piano, 95; Half and Half: Anthology of Work for Piano Four Hands, 98; discography Archduke Rudolph: Sonata in F Minor for Violin and Piano & Variations in F for Violin and Piano, Koch Int Classics, 92; Archduke Rudolph: Sonata in A for Clarinet and Piano: Trio in Eb for Clarinet, Cello, and Piano, Koch Int Classics, 95; W A Mozart: Piano Concertos K 413, 414, 449; Vox Classics, 95; W A Mozart: Piano Concertos K 246, 271 & Rondo in A, K 386, Koch Discover Int, 96; Edvard Grieg: Complete Sonatas for Violin and Piano, Koch Int Classics, 97. **CONTACT ADDRESS** Music Dept, Hunter Col, CUNY, 695 Park Ave, New York, NY 10021. **EMAIL** susankagan@AOL.com

KAGLE, STEVEN EARL
PERSONAL Born 09/15/1941, New York, NY, m, 1965, 2 children **DISCIPLINE** ENGLISH **EDUCATION** Cornell Univ, AB, 63; Univ Mich, MA & PhD(Am cult), 67. **CAREER** Asst prof English, Richmond Col, NY, 67-69; assoc prof, 69-80, Prof English, Ill State Univ, 80-, Chmn sem lit exploration, MLA, 72-. **MEMBERSHIPS** MLA; Am Studies Asn; Sci Fiction Res Asn. **RESEARCH** Autobiographical literature; American literary history; creative writing. **SELECTED PUBLICATIONS** Auth, Diary of John Adams & the motive of achievement, Hartford Studies Lit, 71; Societal quest, Extrapolation, 71; Heroism and the Scouring of the Shire, Muirgheal, 73. **CONTACT ADDRESS** Dept of English, Illinois State Univ, Stevenson Hall Rm 411, Normal, IL 61761. **EMAIL** sekagle@ilstu.edu

KAHANE, CLAIRE
PERSONAL Born New York, NY, 1 child **DISCIPLINE** ENGLISH **EDUCATION** City Col NYork, BA, 56; Univ Calif, Berkeley, MA, 63, PhD, 75. **CAREER** Assoc prof English, SUNY, 74-. **MEMBERSHIPS** MLA **RESEARCH** Psychoanalytic criticism; feminist criticism; British and American fiction. **SELECTED PUBLICATIONS** Auth, Flannery O'Connor's rage of vision, Am Lit, 3/74; Review: Essays in Creativity, Psychoanal Quart, 75; The artificial niggers, Mass Rev, 4/78; Comic vibrations and self-construction in grotesque literature, XXIX: 114-120 & The nuptials of metaphor and To the Lighthouse, XXX: 72-82, Lit and Psychol; The maternal legacy, the grotesque tradition in Flannery O'Connor's female gothic, Female Gothic, Eden Press Women's Publ, fall 81; coauth (with Janice Doane), Psychoanalysis and American fiction: The subversion of Q E D, Studies Am Fiction, 8/81; ed, Psychoanalyse und das Unheimliche: Essays aus der amerikanischen Literaturkritik, An anthology of Psychoanalytic Criticism, Bouvier Press, WGermany, 81; co-ed In Dora's Case: Freud-Hysteria-Feminism, Columbia UP, 85; The Mother Tongue: Essays in Feminist-Psychoanalytic Interpretation, Cornell UP, 85; auth, "Freud's Sublimation: Digust, Desire and the Female body." American Imago, vol 49, (92): 411-426; Auth, Passions of the Voice: Hysteria, Narrative and the Figure of the Speaking Woman, 1850-1915, Johns Hopkins, 95; auth, "The Aesthetic Politics of Rage," Literature, Interpretation, Theory, vol 3 (92): 19-31; rpt in States of Rage, ed Renee R. Curry and Terry L. Allison, (New York: New York Univ Press, 96), 126-145; auth, "Gender and Patrimony: Mourning the Dead Father" differences, vol 9 (97): 49-67. **CONTACT ADDRESS** Dept English, SUNY, Buffalo, PO Box 604610, Buffalo, NY 14260-4610. **EMAIL** ckahane@acsu.buffalo.edu

KAHN, COPPELIA
PERSONAL Born 08/17/1939, Seattle, WA, d, 1 child **DISCIPLINE** ENGLISH **EDUCATION** Barnard Col, BA (with honors), 61; Univ CA, Berkeley, MA, 64, PhD, 70. **CAREER** Teaching asst, acting instr, lect, English dept, Univ CA, Berkeley, 62-71; asst prof, English dept, Univ MA, 71-72; asst prof, assoc prof, prof, English dept, Wesleyan Univ, 73-86; vis assoc prof, Yale Univ, fall 83; vis prof, UCLA, 86-87; prof, English Dept, Brown Univ, 87-; vis prof, Universita' di Torino, April-May 96. **HONORS AND AWARDS** Fel, Oregon Center for the Humanities, 93; Fletcher Jones fel in the Humanities, Huntingdon Library, 88-89. **MEMBERSHIPS** Shakespeare Asn of

Am; Renaissance Soc of Am; MLA. **RESEARCH** Gender studies; English Renaissance lit; Shakespeare; cultural studies. **SELECTED PUBLICATIONS** Auth, Representing Shakespeare: New Psychoanalytic Essays, co-ed with Murray Schwartz, Johns Hopkins Univ, 80; Man's Estate: Masculine Identity in Shakespeare, Univ CA Press, 81; Shakespeare's 'Rough Magic': Renaissance Essays in Honor of C L Barber, co-ed with Peter Erickson, Univ DE Press, 85; Making a Difference: Feminist Literary Criticism, co-ed with Gayle Greene, Methuen, 85, trans into Jpanese, 91, Chinese trans forthcoming; Changing Subjects: The Making of Feminist Literary Criticism, co-ed with Gayle Greene, Routledge, 93; Magic of Bounty: Timon of Athens, Jacobean Patronage, and Maternal Power, rpt in Shakespearean Tragedy and Gender, ed Madelon Sprengnether and Shirley Nelson Garner, IN Univ Press, 95; The Rape in Shakespeare's Lucrece, rpt in Shakespeare and Gender: A History, ed Ivo Kamps and Deborah Barker, Verso Press, 95; Roman Shakespeare: Warriors, Wounds, and Women, in the series Feminist Readings of Shakespeare, ed Ann Thompson, Routledge, 98; Thomas Middleton and Thomas Dekker, The Roaring Girl, ed with intro, in The Complete Works of Thomas Middleton, ed Gary Taylor, Oxford Univ Press, forthcoming 99; Coming of Age in Verona, in Shakespeare's Early Tragedies: A Collection of Critical Essays, ed Mark Rose, Prentice-Hall, forthcoming. **CONTACT ADDRESS** Dept of English, Brown Univ, Box 1852, Providence, RI 02912. **EMAIL** coppelia_kahn@brown.edu

KAHN, MADELEINE
DISCIPLINE ENGLISH **EDUCATION** Swarthmore 'Col, BA, 77; Stanford Univ, PhD, 89. **CAREER** Assoc prof; Mills Col, 89-. **RESEARCH** 18th century English literature; the novel; feminist theory; gender studies; the Gothic and the sublime. **SELECTED PUBLICATIONS** Auth, Narrative Transvestism: Rhetoric and Gender in the Eighteenth-Century English Novel, Cornell UP, 91; A by-stander often sees more of the game than those that play: Ann Yearsley Reads The Castle of Otranto, in Questioning History: Postmodern Perspectives on 18th-Century Lit and Cult, Assoc UPresses, 97; Teaching Charlotte Charke: Pedagogy, Feminism, and the Construction of Self, in Now Introducing Charlotte Charke, Univ Ill Press, 97; The Milkmaid's Voice: Ann Yearsley and the Romantic Notion of the Poet, Approaches to Teaching Women Poets of the British Romantic Period, MLA Press, 97; Hannah More and Ann Yearsley: A Collaboration Across the Class Divide, Stud in 18th-Century Cult 25, 95; The Politics of Pornography, in American Women in the 90s: Today's Critical Issues, Northeastern UP, 93, sec ed, 94. **CONTACT ADDRESS** Dept of English, Mills Col, 5000 MacArthur Blvd, Oakland, CA 94613-1301. **EMAIL** mkahn@mills.edu

KAHN, SY M.
DISCIPLINE THEATRE ARTS **EDUCATION** Univ PA, BA; Univ CT, MA; Univ Wis, PhD. **CAREER** Fac, 63-87, dir and chair of theater, 68-81, exec dir of Fallon House, 70-84, prof emer, 87-, Univ of the Pacific. **HONORS AND AWARDS** Fulbright professorship; Order of the Pacific Awd. **SELECTED PUBLICATIONS** Auth, Between Tedium and Terror. **CONTACT ADDRESS** Pacific Ave, PO Box 3601, Stockton, CA 95211.

KAILING, JOEL
PERSONAL Born Atlanta, GA, m, 4 children **DISCIPLINE** SPEECH, INTERCULTURAL COMMUNICATION **EDUCATION** Univ Ky, PhD. **CAREER** Assoc prof, Lee Univ, 94-. **MEMBERSHIPS** Lee Comm Club; Lee Univ Vindagua, Missions Alive. **SELECTED PUBLICATIONS** Inside, Outside, Upside Down, Int Rev Missions, 88; A New Solution to the African Christian Problem; Missiology, 94. **CONTACT ADDRESS** Lee Col, Tennessee, 1120 N. Ocoee St, Cleveland, TN 37320-3450. **EMAIL** jkailing@leeuniversity.edu

KAIMOWITZ, JEFFREY H.
PERSONAL Born 11/03/1942, New York, NY, m, 1987, 1 child **DISCIPLINE** CLASSICS **EDUCATION** Johns Hopkins, AB, 64; Univ of Cincinnati, PhD, 70; Columbia Univ, MS, 76 **CAREER** Asst Prof, 69-73, Miami Univ, OH; Libr Trainee, 73-77, NY Pub Lib; Curator, 77-, Watkinson Lib, Trinity Col, Hartford **HONORS AND AWARDS** Phi Beta Kappa, 64; Woodrow Wilson Fel, 64-65; Fulbright Fel, 66-67 **MEMBERSHIPS** Am Lib Asc; Grolier Club **RESEARCH** Translating Latin poetry; Printing hist **CONTACT ADDRESS** Watkinson Lib, Trinity Col, Connecticut, Hartford, CT 06106. **EMAIL** jeffrey.kaimowitz@trincoll.edu

KAIRSCHNER, ANNE J.
PERSONAL d, 1 child **DISCIPLINE** ENGLISH **EDUCATION** Univ Calif Santa Cruz, BA; Univ Calif San Diego, MA, 82; CPhil, PhD. **CAREER** Instructor, Univ San Diego, 82-89; Instructor, SW Cmty Col, 82-89; Prof, Moorpark Col, 89-. **HONORS AND AWARDS** Fel, CA State Univ; Fel, San Diego; NEH Summer Sem; Sabbatical Year Awd, 95-96; Great Teachers Sem, Ventura Cmty Col, 93. **MEMBERSHIPS** MLA; NCTE. **RESEARCH** Shakespeare; Critical Theory; Renaissance History; Charles Dickens and Victorian History. **SELECTED PUBLICATIONS** Auth, "The Traces of Capitalist Patriarch of the Silences of The Golden Bowl," Henry James Review, 84. **CONTACT ADDRESS** Dept Lang Arts, Moorpark Col, 7075 Campus Rd, Moorpark, CA 93021-1605. **EMAIL** makirschner@vcccd.net

KAIVOLA, KAREN
DISCIPLINE ENGLISH LITERATURE **EDUCATION** Univ Wash, PhD. **CAREER** Assoc prof, 97-. **RESEARCH** 20th century literature; British Modernism; postcolonial literature; women's writing. **SELECTED PUBLICATIONS** Auth, Virginia Woolf, Vita Sackville-West, and the Question of Sexual Identity, 97; Reconstructing Androgyny's 'Blind Spot': Technology, Gender B(l)ending, and Emerging Liminal Identities, MOSAIC, 97. **CONTACT ADDRESS** English Dept, Stetson Univ, De Land, Unit 8378, DeLand, FL 32720-3771.

KALAIDJIAN, WALTER
DISCIPLINE ENGLISH LANGUAGE AND LITERATURE **EDUCATION** Univ Ill Urbana-Champaign, PhD, 92. **CAREER** Prof **RESEARCH** 20th-century American literature and culture. **SELECTED PUBLICATIONS** Auth, American Culture Between the Wars: Revisionary Modernism and Postmodern Critique; Languages of Liberation: The Social Text in Contemporary American Poetry; Understanding Theodore Roethke. **CONTACT ADDRESS** English Dept, Emory Univ, 1380 Oxford Rd NE, Atlanta, GA 30322-1950. **EMAIL** wkalaid@emory.edu

KALBFLEISCH, PAMELA J.
PERSONAL Born 10/05/1956, Twin Falls, ID, m, 1987 **DISCIPLINE** COMMUNICATION **EDUCATION** Michigan State Univ, PhD 85; Univ New Mexico, MA 79; Boise State Univ, BA cum laude 78. **CAREER** Univ Wyoming, assoc prof 94-99, prof, 99-; Univ Kentucky, asst prof 89-94; Cal State Univ, asst prof 87-89; Univ Montana, vis asst prof 86-87. **HONORS AND AWARDS** Phi Kappa Phi; Sec Vice WSCA. **MEMBERSHIPS** WSCA; NCA; ICA. **RESEARCH** Mentoring, social support; deceptive communication, gender. **SELECTED PUBLICATIONS** Auth, Interpersonal Communication, Needham Hts MA, Allyn & Bacon, under contract; Mentoring as a Personal Relationship, NY, Guilford, under contract; Gender Power and Communication in Human Relationships, co-ed, Mahwah NJ, Lawrence Erlbaum Assoc, 95; auth, Perceived Equity Satisfaction and Related Maintenance Strategies in Parent Adolescent Dyads, coauth, Jour of Youth Adolescence, in press; auth, Appeasing the Mentor, Aggressive Behavior, 97; auth, The Language of Detecting Deceit, Jour of Lang and Social Psychol, 94; auth, Communication in Interracial Relationships, Tina M Harris, ed, When I Look at You I Don't See Color, Newbury Park, Sage, forthcoming; Sex Differences in Presenting and Detecting Deceptive Messages, coauth, D Canary, K Dindia, eds, Sex Differences and Similarities, Mahwah NJ, Lawrence Erlbaum Assoc, 98; auth, Mentoring Across Generations: Culture Family and Mentoring Relationships, coauth, in: H Nooral-Deen ed, Cross Cult Comm and Aging in Amer, Mahwah NJ, Lawrence Erlbaum Assoc, 97; auth, Beyond Boundaries: Sex and Gender Diversity in Communication, rev, Women's Stud Comm, 97; auth, Women as Leaders, documentary, with Karen H Bonnell, in preparation. **CONTACT ADDRESS** Dept of Communication, Univ of Wyoming, PO Box 430, Laramie, WY 82070-0430. **EMAIL** pamelak@uwyo.edu

KALETA, KENNETH C.
PERSONAL Born 04/11/1948, Chicago, IL, w **DISCIPLINE** FILM **EDUCATION** New York Univ, PhD, 85. **CAREER** Prof, Rowan Univ, 88-. **MEMBERSHIPS** UFVA; BEA **RESEARCH** Independent filmmaking. **SELECTED PUBLICATIONS** David Lynch, Twayne Publ, 93; Hanif Kureishi: Postcolonial Storyteller, Univ Tx Press, 98. **CONTACT ADDRESS** Rowan Univ, 201 Mullica Hill Rd, Glassboro, NJ 08021. **EMAIL** kaleta@rowan.edu

KALLENDORF, CRAIG WILLIAM
PERSONAL Born 06/23/1954 **DISCIPLINE** CLASSICS, ENGLISH **EDUCATION** Valparaiso Univ, BA, 75; Univ NCar, MA, 77; PhD, 82. **CAREER** Asst prof to prof, 82-, interim dept head, Dept of Mod and Class Lang, 01-03, Tex A&M Univ. **HONORS AND AWARDS** NEH; ACLS; Delmar Found Fel; Teaching Awd; Res Awd. **MEMBERSHIPS** APA; MLA; RSA; IANLS; ISHR. **RESEARCH** Classical tradition; renaissance literature; history of the book. **SELECTED PUBLICATIONS** Auth, Virgil and the Myth of Venice; auth, In Praise of Aeneas. **CONTACT ADDRESS** Dept of English, Texas A&M Univ, Col Station, College Station, TX 77843-4227. **EMAIL** kalendrf@tamu.edu

KALPAKGIAN, MITCHELL A.
PERSONAL Born 06/24/1941, Milford, MA, w, 1972, 5 children **DISCIPLINE** ENGLISH, LITERATURE **EDUCATION** Bowdoin Col, BA, 63; Kansas Univ, MA, 65; Univ Iowa, PhD, 74. **CAREER** Prof, Simpson Col, 67-90, 92-; assoc prof, Christendom Col, 90-92. **HONORS AND AWARDS** NEH Fel, 81, 85; Andrew W. Mellon Fel, 85. **MEMBERSHIPS** Fel of Cath Scholars. **RESEARCH** Children's literature. **SELECTED PUBLICATIONS** Auth, The Marvelous in Fielding's Novels, Univ Pr of Am, 81; auth, "Why The Entertainment Industry Is Bad for Children", New Oxford Rev, Mar 96; auth, "Liberal Education and the Common Good", Faith and Reason, 96; auth, "Divorce: The Unnatural Termination of A Story", New Oxford Rev, Jan/Feb 97; auth, "If You Want an Uncomplicated Life, Seek the Simplicity of God's Truth", New Oxford Rev, June 97; auth, "The Modern World's Attempt to Beautify Sin and Death", New Oxford Rev, Feb 98; auth, "The Structures of Sin", Lay Witness, Apr 98; auth, "The Gospel of Adjustment, Common Ground, and Mediocrity", New Oxford Rev, Nov 98; auth, "The Perils of Multicultural Literature", St Croix Rev, Feb 99; auth, The Mysteries of Life in Children's Literature, Univ Pr of Am, (Lanham, MD), 99. **CONTACT ADDRESS** Dept English, Simpson Col, Iowa, 701 North C St, Indianola, IA 50125-1202. **EMAIL** kalpakgian@juno.com

KAMBOURELI, SMARO
DISCIPLINE 20TH-CENTURY CANADIAN LITERATURE **EDUCATION** Univ Thessaloniki, Greece, BA; Univ Manitoba, MA, PhD. **CAREER** Assoc prof; dir, Eng Grad Stud. **HONORS AND AWARDS** Fulbright Fel, 77-78; SSHRC Standard Res Grants, 92-95, 95-98. **RESEARCH** Literary; feminist, and postcolonial theory; women's writing. **SELECTED PUBLICATIONS** Ed, Making a Difference: Canadian Multicultural Literature, 96; On the Edge of Genre: The Contemporary Canadian Long Poem, 91; co-ed, A Mazing Space: Writing Canadian Women Writing, 87; auth, Scandalous Bodies: Diasporic Literature in English Canada, 99. **CONTACT ADDRESS** Dept of English, Univ of Victoria, PO Box 3070, Victoria, BC, Canada V8W 3W1. **EMAIL** kamboure@uvic.ca

KAMENISH, PAULA K.
DISCIPLINE WORLD LITERATURE, EUROPEAN LITERATURE, DRAMA, NOVELLA, AND NOVEL **EDUCATION** Ctr Col Ky, BA; Univ NC, Chapel Hill, MA, PhD. **CAREER** Assoc prof, Univ NC, Wilmington. **RESEARCH** German and French theatre of the 20th century; Dada movement. **SELECTED PUBLICATIONS** Published articles on Shakespeare, French Canadian author Roch Carrier, and various modern dramatists. **CONTACT ADDRESS** Univ of No Carolina, Wilmington, Morton Hall, Wilmington, NC 28403-3297. **EMAIL** kamenishp@uncwil.edu

KAMINSKI, THOMAS
PERSONAL Born 08/22/1950, Chicago, IL, m, 1980, 1 child **DISCIPLINE** EIGHTEENTH CENTURY ENGLISH LITERATURE **EDUCATION** Univ Ill, Urbana, BA, 72; Harvard Univ, AM, 73, PhD(English), 77. **CAREER** Asst prof English, Loyola Univ, Chicago, 77-86; assoc prof, 86-. **RESEARCH** Samuel Johnson; neo-classicism. **SELECTED PUBLICATIONS** Auth, Striving with Vergil: The Gennesis of Milton's Blind Mouths, Modern Philology 92, 95; Rehabilitating Augustanism: On the Roots of Polite Letters in England, Eighteenth-Century Life 20, 96; Opposition Augustanism and Pope's Epistle to Augustus, Studies in Eighteenth Century Culture, 26, 97. **CONTACT ADDRESS** Dept of English, Loyola Univ, Chicago, 6525 N Sheridan Rd, Chicago, IL 60626-5385. **EMAIL** tkamins@luc.edu

KAMINSKY, ALICE R.
PERSONAL Born New York, NY, w, 1 child **DISCIPLINE** LITERATURE **EDUCATION** NYork Univ, BA, 46, MA, 47, PhD, 52. **CAREER** Instr English, Hunter Col, 52-53, Cornell Univ, 54-57, 59-63; asst prof, 63-64, assoc prof, 64-68, Prpf English, State Univ NY Col, Cortland, 68-. **HONORS AND AWARDS** Fac exchange scholar, State Univ NY, New York. **MEMBERSHIPS** MLA; New Chaucer Soc. **RESEARCH** Philosophy of literature; Chaucer; Shakespeare. **SELECTED PUBLICATIONS** Auth, Lewes, G.H.--A Life, 19th-Century Lit, Vol 0047, 92; James, Henry, Stein, Gertrude, and the Biographical Act, English Lit in Transition 1880-1920, Vol 0040, 97; auth, The Victim's Song, Chaucer's Troilus & Grseyde; auth, Logic A Philosophical Introduction George Henry Lewis as Critic; auth, An Anthropology of his Criticism. **CONTACT ADDRESS** Dept of English, SUNY, Col at Cortland, Cortland, NY 13045.

KANE, PETER
PERSONAL Born 02/27/1932, Beverly Hills, CA, m, 1982, 4 children **DISCIPLINE** LIBERAL ARTS; COMMUNICATION **EDUCATION** Univ CA Santa Barbara, BA, 54; Univ CA Los Angeles, MA, 60; Purdue Univ, PhD, 67. **CAREER** Asst prof, speech, 61-65, St Joseph's College (Indiana); asst prof, rhetoric, 65-68, SUNY Binghamton; assoc prof, SUNY Brockport, 68-96, prof of communications emeritus 96-. **HONORS AND AWARDS** Franklyn Haiman Awd for Distinguished Scholarship Freedom of Expression, Natl Communication Assn, 93; Everett Lee Hunt Scholarship Awd, 87. **MEMBERSHIPS** Nat Communication Assn; Eastern Communication Assn. **RESEARCH** Freedom of Expression, Media Law **SELECTED PUBLICATIONS** Auth, Errors, Lies, and Libel, Southern Ill Univ Press, 92; Murder, Courts, and the Press, Southern Ill Univ Press 92. **CONTACT ADDRESS** 5268 County Rd. #11, Rushville, NY 14544. **EMAIL** kanepp@connecticom.com

KANELLOS, NICOLAS
PERSONAL 1 child **DISCIPLINE** LANGUAGE, LITERATURE, PUBLISHING **EDUCATION** Univ Autonoma Mex, Mex Lit & Cult, 64-65; Farleigh Dickinson Univ, BA, Span, 66; Univ Tex, MA, Roman Lang, 68; Univ Lisboa Portugal, Portuguese Lit & Cult, 69070; Univ Tex, PhD, Span & Portuguese, 74. **CAREER** PROF, UNIV HOUSTON, 80-. **SELECTED PUBLICATIONS** America's Hispanic People: Their Images Through History, 97; edr, Biographical Dictionary of Hispanic Literature in the United States, Greenwood Press, 89; Mexican-American Theater Legacy and Reality, Lat Am Rev Press, 87; Hispanic-American Almanac: A Reference Work on Hispanics in the United States, Gale Res, 93, Hispanic Firsts, Gale Res, 97; auth, Hispanic Periodicals in the United States: A Brief History and Comprehensive Bibliography, 00. **CONTACT ADDRESS** Dept Hisp & Class Lang, Univ of Houston, Houston, TX 77204-3128.

KANWAR, ANJU
PERSONAL Born 09/18/1962, Delhi, India, s **DISCIPLINE** ENGLISH **EDUCATION** Jesus & Mary Col, Univ of Delhi, BA (honors), 83; Univ of Delhi, MA, 86; Northern Ill Univ, PhD, 95. **CAREER** Lectr, Univ of Delhi, 86-88; tchg asst, 88-93, vis asst prof, Northern Ill Univ, 93-94; instr, Triton Col, 93; instr, Coll of Du Page, 93-94; vis lectr, North Central Col, 98 & 99; Instr, Waubonsee Community Col, 93 & 96-; Assoc Ed, 00-, Consumers Digest Online. **HONORS AND AWARDS** Outstanding Service Awd, Children's World, 95-96; Arnold B. Fox Awd for Res Writing, Northern Ill Univ, 90; International Woman of the Year, 99-00; International Biographical Assoc, Cambridge, England, Member, Advisory Council, 00-; International Biographical Assoc, Cambridge, England Service Awd, 99, Waubonsee Community College. **MEMBERSHIPS** MLA. **RESEARCH** Modern British Lit; issues of gender; pedagogy; Indian writing in English. **SELECTED PUBLICATIONS** Auth, The Sound of Silence Peter Lang Inc., 99; Gender in the Classroom: Boundaries Real or Imagined?, Thresholds in Education, 95; Briscoe's Alternative: Durga or Sati? Woolf and Hinduism in to the Lighthouse, Virginia Woolf: Texts and Contexts: Selected Papers from the 5th Annual Virginia Woolf Confr, Pace UP, 96; auth, Macbeth metamorphosed: Using to Teach in Studies in Literature and TESOL, I:1&2, Spring, 00. **CONTACT ADDRESS** 30W49 Granada Ct. #104, Naperville, IL 60563.

KAPLAN, CAREY
DISCIPLINE COLLABORATIVE COMPOSITION **EDUCATION** Univ MA, PhD. **CAREER** Eng, St. Michaels Col. **SELECTED PUBLICATIONS** Auth, The Canon and the Common Reader. **CONTACT ADDRESS** Saint Michael's Col, Winooski Park, Colchester, VT 05439. **EMAIL** ckaplan@smcvt.edu

KAPLAN, FRED
PERSONAL Born 11/04/1937, New York, NY, m, 1993, 3 children **DISCIPLINE** ENGLISH **EDUCATION** Brooklyn Col, BA, 59; Columbia Univ, MA, 61, PhD, 66. **CAREER** Instr English, Lawrence Univ, 62-64; asst prof, Calif State Univ, Los Angeles, 64-67; from asst to assoc prof, 67-75, Prof English, Queens Col, City Univ NY, 75-; Prof English, Grad Ctr, City Univ NY, 80-. **HONORS AND AWARDS** City Univ New York fac res grant, 68-69, 74-77 & 79-82, 84-98; Fulbright lectr, Univ Copenhagen, 73-74; Guggenheim Found Fel, 76-77; ed, Dickens Studies Annual, 79-94; NEH fel, Huntington Libr, 81-82; fel, Nat Humanities Center, 85-86; ed, Proj edition works Thomas Carlyle, 81-; Dickens Soc, pres, 91, 97. **MEMBERSHIPS** MLA; Dickens Fellowship; Dickens Soc. **RESEARCH** 19th and 20th century British and American literature; biography. **SELECTED PUBLICATIONS** Auth, Miracles of Rare Device: The poet's Sense of Self in Nineteenth-Century Poetry, Wayne State Univ, 72; Dickens and Mesmerism: The Hidden Springs of Fiction, Princeton Univ, 75; Thomas Carlyle, A Biography, Cornell Univ Press, 82; Sacred Tears: Sentimentality in Victorian Literature, Princeton, 87; Charles Dickens, A Biography, William Morrow, 88; Henry James, The Imagination of Genius, A Biography, William Morrow, 93; Gore Vidal, A Biography, Doubleday, 99. **CONTACT ADDRESS** Grad Ctr, Queens Col, CUNY, 33 W 42nd St, New York, NY 10016-4309.

KAPLAN, JUSTIN
PERSONAL Born 09/05/1925, New York, NY, m, 1954, 3 children **DISCIPLINE** AMERICAN LITERATURE **EDUCATION** Harvard Univ, BS, 44. **CAREER** Free-lance work with various NY publ, 46-54; ed, Simon & Schuster, 54-59; Writer, 59-, Vis lectr, Harvard Univ, 69, 73 & 76; writer-in-residence, Emerson Col, Boston, 77-78; Guggenheim Mem fel, 75-76. **HONORS AND AWARDS** Pulitzer Prize in Biography, 67; Nat Bk Awd in Arts & Lett, 67; Am Bk Awd, 81. **MEMBERSHIPS** Am Acad Arts & Sci; Mass Historical Soc; Am Acad Arts & Letters. **SELECTED PUBLICATIONS** Ed, With Toward Women, Dodd, 52; The Pocket Aristotle, Pocket Bks, 58; auth, Mr Clemens and Mark Twain, Simon & Schuster, 66; ed, Great Short Works of Mark Twain, Harper, 67; Mark Twain: Profile, Hill & Wang, 67; auth, Lincoln Steffens, a biography, 74 & Mark Twain and His World, 74, Simon & Schuster; Walt Whitman: A life, 80; gen ed, Bartlett's Familiar Quotation, 16th ed, 92; coauth, The Lang et Names, 97. **CONTACT ADDRESS** 16 Francis Ave, Cambridge, MA 02138. **EMAIL** jknames@aol.com

KAPLAN, LINDSAY
DISCIPLINE ENGLISH LITERATURE **EDUCATION** Johns Hopkins Univ, BA, 81; Univ Ca, PhD, 90. **CAREER** Eng Dept, Georgetown Univ **RESEARCH** Renaissance drama; Renaissance English law; race and gender in Renaissance culture; Jews in Early Modern England; Bible as literature. **SELECTED PUBLICATIONS** Auth, pubs on slander, women and slander; co-ed, Feminist Readings in Early Modern England, Cambridge, 96; The Culture of Slander in Early Modern England, Cambridge, 97. **CONTACT ADDRESS** English Dept, Georgetown Univ, 37th and O St, Washington, DC 20057.

KAPLAN, NANCY
DISCIPLINE LITERATURE **EDUCATION** Cornell, PhD. **CAREER** Assoc prof, Univ Baltimore. **RESEARCH** Computing technology. **SELECTED PUBLICATIONS** Auth, E-Literacies. **CONTACT ADDRESS** Commun Dept, Univ of Baltimore, 1420 N. Charles Street, Baltimore, MD 21201.

KAPLAN, SYDNEY JANET
PERSONAL Born 12/28/1939, Los Angeles, CA, 1 child **DISCIPLINE** ENGLISH **EDUCATION** Univ Calif, Los Angeles, AB, 61, MA, 66, PhD(English), 71. **CAREER** Asst prof, 71-78, Asspc Prof English, Univ Wash, 78-; Dir, Women Studies Prog, 82-92, Vis prof, Grad Inst Mod Letters, Univ Tulsa, summer, 80; Prof, English, 92-. **HONORS AND AWARDS** Nat Endowment for the Humanities Fellowship, 00-01. **MEMBERSHIPS** MLA; Women's Caucus for Mod Lang; Nat Women Studies Asn. **RESEARCH** British Modernism; Twentieth century women writers; Virginia Woolf, Katherine Mansfield; T.S. Eliot, J.M. Murry. **SELECTED PUBLICATIONS** Auth, Feminine Consciousness in the Modern Brithish Novel, Univ of IL Press, 75; auth, Katherine Mansfield and the Origins of Modernist Fiction, Cornell Univ Press, 91. **CONTACT ADDRESS** Dept of English, Univ of Washington, 354330, Seattle, WA 98195. **EMAIL** sydneyk@u.washington.edu

KARCHER, CAROLYN LURY
PERSONAL Born 02/25/1945, Washington, DC, m, 1965 **DISCIPLINE** AMERICAN LITERATURE & STUDIES **EDUCATION** Johns Hopkins Univ, MA, 67; Univ Md, PhD(Am studies), 80. **CAREER** Asst Prof English, Temple Univ, 1981-1988, assoc prof, 1988-1995, prof, 1995- **MEMBERSHIPS** MLA; Am Studies Asn; Melville Soc. **RESEARCH** Nineteenth and early 20th century American literature; women's studies; slavery. **SELECTED PUBLICATIONS** Auth, Shadow over the Promised Land: Slavery, Race, and Violence in Melville's America, 1980; The First Woman in the Republic: A Cultural Biography of Lydia Maria Child, 1994; Reconceiving 19th-Century American Literature--The Challenge of Women Writers, Amer Lit, Vol 0066, 1994; Margaret Fuller and Lydia Maria Child: Intersecting Careers, Reciprocal Influences, Essays on Margaret Fuller, ed. Fritz Fleischman, 2000; ed., HOBOMOK and Other Writings on Indians by Lydia Maria Child, 1986; An Appeal in Favor of that Class of Americans Called Indians by Lydia Maria Child, 1996; A Lydia Maria Child Reader, 1997; Hope Leslie by Catharine Maria Sedgwick, 1998. **CONTACT ADDRESS** Dept of English, Temple Univ, 1114 W Berks St, Philadelphia, PA 19122-6029.

KARI, DAVEN MICHAEL
PERSONAL Born 09/24/1953, Hot Springs, SD, m, 1988, 3 children **DISCIPLINE** ENGLISH LITERATURE **EDUCATION** Fresno Pacific Univ, BA, 75; Baylor Univ, MA, 83; Purdue Univ, MA, 85, PhD, 86; So Baptist Theol Sem, MDiv, 88, PhD, 91. **CAREER** Tchg asst, Baylor Univ, 78-79; tchg asst, Purdue Univ, 79-85; lectr Univ Louisville, Spalding Univ, Jefferson Commun Col, 86-90; asst prof, Missouri Baptist Col, 91; prof, Eng, Christian Stud, Fine Arts, Calif Baptist Univ, 91-98; Acad Dean, Washington Bible Col, 98- . **HONORS AND AWARDS** Fac Mem of the Year, 93; Outstanding Young Men of Am, 85; listed, Who's Who in Am, 99; listed, Contemporary Authors, 97; listed Who's Who in the World, 97, 98, 99. **MEMBERSHIPS** Am Acad Relig; Conf on Christianity and Lit. **RESEARCH** Christianity and the arts; Trinity and the visual arts; stained glass windows; T.S. Eliot's drama; Christianity and literature; Bible and literature. **SELECTED PUBLICATIONS** Founder and contribur, The English Accent: Newsletter for Purdue Univ Dept of Eng, 85; asst ed, Business Writing Strategies and Samples, Macmillan, 88; auth, T.S. Eliot's Dramatic Pilgrimage: Progress in Craft as an Expression of Christian Perspective, Edwin Mellen, 90; auth, A Bibliography of Sources in Christianity and the Arts, Edwin Mellen, 95; contribur and co-ed, Baptist Reflections on Christianity and the Arts: Learning from Beauty: A Tribute to William L. Hendricks, Edwin Mellen, 97. **CONTACT ADDRESS** Washington Bible Col, 6511 Princess Garden, Lanham Seabrook, MD 20706-3599. **EMAIL** dkari@bible.edu

KARMAN, JAMES
PERSONAL Born 08/12/1947, Moline, IL, m, 1968 **DISCIPLINE** ENGLISH, LITERATURE, ART, RELIGION **EDUCATION** Augustana Col, BA, 69; Univ Iowa, MA, 71; Syracuse Univ, PhD, 76. **CAREER** Postdoctoral fel, Syracuse Univ, 76-77; ast prof, 77-84, asoc prof, 84-87, prof coord, 87-, Calif St Univ, Chico. **HONORS AND AWARDS** Res fel, Nat Endowment Hum, 98-99; Book Club of California grnt, 99. **MEMBERSHIPS** Robinson Jeffers Tor House Found; Robinson Jeffers Asn; MLA; Col Art Asn; Am Acad Relig; Asn for Documentary Editing; Soc for Textua Scholar. **RESEARCH** Art; religion; literature; twentieth century history and culture; life and work of Robinson Jeffers. **SELECTED PUBLICATIONS** Ed, Critical Essays on Robinson Jeffers, GK Hall, 90; auth, Robinson Jeffers: Poet of California, rev., Story Line, 95; ed, Of Una Jeffers, Story Line, 98. **CONTACT ADDRESS** Dept of English, California State Univ, Chico, Chico, CA 95929-0830. **EMAIL** Jkarman@csuchico.edu

KAROLIDES, NICHOLAS J.
PERSONAL Born 08/05/1928, Albany, NY, m, 1962, 2 children **DISCIPLINE** ENGLISH **EDUCATION** NYork Univ, BS, 50, MA, 51, PhD(English), 63. **CAREER** Teacher & guid coun, Jr High Schs, NY, 54-64; from asst prof to assoc prof English, 64-69, asst dean Col Arts & Sci, 76-82, prof English, Univ Wis-River Falls, 69-, assoc dean, Col Arts & Sci, 82-, instr, NY Univ, 60-64; ed, Wis English J, 65-88, & JM Newsletter, 72-75. **HONORS AND AWARDS** Univ Wis-River Falls Distinguished Teaching Awd, 71; WCTE Awd for Meritorius Serv, 72-88; Myers Center Awd for the Study of Human Rights in North American for outstanding work on intolerance for Censored Books: Critical Viewpoints; 94; Univ of Wis Regents Excellance in Teaching Awd, State of Wis, 94; Outstanding Faculty Awd, Humanities Div, Univ Wisconsin-River Falls, 97; Wis Librn Asn Intellectual Freedom Awd, 98. **MEMBERSHIPS** NCTE; Conf English Educ. **RESEARCH** Literature; American pioneer related to American history and culture; teaching of minority literature in Wisconsin; censorship; application of literary theory. **SELECTED PUBLICATIONS** Auth, Banned Books: Literature Suppresses on Political Grounds, 98; co-auth, 100 Banned Books: Censorhsip History of World Literature, 99; auth/ed, "The Transactional Theory of Literature" in Reader Response in Secondary and College Classrooms, 00; auth/ed, "Role Playing Experiences: Expanding readers' responses to literature" in Reader Response in the secondary and college classrooms, 00; ed, Censored books: Critical Viewpoints, vol II, 01; auth, "Theory and practiee: An interview with Louise M Rosenblatt," in Language Arts, November 99; auth, "Teaching Literature as a reflective practitioner: Script and Spontaneity," in Reading Process: Transactional Theory in Action in A Guide to Curriculum Planning in English Language Arts, in press; auth, "Focus on the Sentence" in Strategies for Teaching First-Year Composition, in press; auth, Transactional Theory in Action in Reader Response in Elementary Classrooms, 96; Challenging Old Habits of Mind: Revisiting Reader's Stance, The New Advocate, Spring, 97. **CONTACT ADDRESS** Dept of English, Univ of Wisconsin, River Falls, 410 S 3rd St, River Falls, WI 54022-5013. **EMAIL** nicholas.karolides@uwrf.edu

KARPF, JUANITA
PERSONAL Born 10/31/1951, Rochester, NY **DISCIPLINE** MUSICOLOGY **EDUCATION** State Univ Col, Potsdam, NYork, BM, 73; Univ Ga, MM, 86, DMA, 92. **CAREER** Asst Prof, Music and Women's Stud, Univ of Ga, 95- . **MEMBERSHIPS** Am String Tchr Asn; Am Musicol Soc; Col Mus Soc, Mus Ed Nat Conf; Nat Women's Stud Assoc; Gender Res in Mus Ed; Sonneck Soc Am Mus. **RESEARCH** Feminist theory, women and music, African American history, American music history. **CONTACT ADDRESS** School of Music, Univ of Georgia, 250 River Rd, Athens, GA 30602-7287. **EMAIL** nkarpf@uga.cc.uga.edu

KARPINSKI, GARY S.
PERSONAL Born 07/20/1957, Philadelphia, PA, m, 1983, 2 children **DISCIPLINE** MUSIC **EDUCATION** Temple Univ, BM, MM; City Univ NYork, PhD. **CAREER** Asst prof of Music, Univ of Ore, 87-93; Assoc Prof of Music, Univ of Mass, 93-. **HONORS AND AWARDS** Ed, J Music Theory Pedagogy; pres, Asn Tech Music Instruction. **MEMBERSHIPS** Soc for Music Theory; Soc for Music Perception and Cognition; Am Musicological Soc. **RESEARCH** Musical Theory; aural skills; perception. **SELECTED PUBLICATIONS** Auth, Structural Functions of the Interval Cycles, Int J of Musicology, 95; Reviews of Recent Textbooks in Theory and Musicianship: Aural Skills, Music Theory Spectrum, 93; A Model for Music Perception and Its Implications in Melodic Dictation, J of Music Theory Pedagogy, 90; Hypercard: A Powerful Tchg Tool, The Computer and Music Educator, 90. **CONTACT ADDRESS** Dept of Music and Dance, Univ of Massachusetts, Amherst, Amherst, MA 01003. **EMAIL** garykarp@music.umass.edu

KARR, RONALD DALE
PERSONAL Born 04/19/1948, Pittsburgh, PA, m, 1974, 3 children **DISCIPLINE** LIBRARY SCIENCE **EDUCATION** Bucknell Univ, BA, 70; Boston Univ, MA, 72; Simmons Col; MS, 78; Boston Univ PhD, 81. **CAREER** Lectr, Northeastern Univ, 74-76, 78-79; res lib, U.S.Dept Trans, Cambridge, MA, 77-79; pub ser lib, Northwestern Univ Tran Lib, 79-85; lib, Univ of Massachusetts Lowell, 85-. **HONORS AND AWARDS** Beta Phi Mu, 79. **MEMBERSHIPS** AHA; OAH;

UHA. **RESEARCH** New England, Early America, Urban History, Social History, Railroads, Popular Culture. **SELECTED PUBLICATIONS** Auth, "William H. Wilson's The City Beautiful Movement: Book Review Essay," Hayes Historical J 10 (91): 67-71; auth, "Shelter the American Way: Federal Urban Housing Policy, 1900-1980," New England J of Public Policy 8 (92):169-84; auth, New England at a Glance: Profiles from the 1990 Census, Branch Line Press (Pepperell, MA), 93; auth, The Rail Lines of Southern New England: A Handbook of Railroad History, Branch Line Press (Pepperell, MA), 95; auth, "Publication Patterns of American Historians, 1950-1985," OAH Newsletter, 24 (96): 4-5; ed, The Turnpikes of New England, by Frederic J. Wood, Branch Line Press (Pepperell, MA), 97; auth "Why Should You Be So Furious? The Violence of the Pequot War." J American History 85 (98): 876-909; auth, Brookline" and "Social Structure of Suburbs" in Encyclopedia of Urban America: The Cities and Suburbs, ed. Neil Larry Shumsky (Santa Barbara: ABC-CLIO, 98), 1:103-04, 2: 720-23; ed, Indian New England, 1524-1674: A Compendium of Eyewitness Accounts of Native American Life, Branch Line Press (Pepperell, MA), 99. **CONTACT ADDRESS** O'Leary Library, Univ of Massachusetts, Lowell, 61 Wider St, Lowell, MA 01854-3098. **EMAIL** ronald_karr@uml.edu

KARRE, IDAHLYNN
DISCIPLINE INSTRUCTIONAL COMMUNICATION, COMMUNICATION IN EDUCATION, INTERPERSONAL COMM **EDUCATION** Univ CO, PhD, 70. **CAREER** Prof, 69-, ch, dept Speech Commun, Univ Northern CO. **SELECTED PUBLICATIONS** Wrote on tchg and learning in the col classroom. **CONTACT ADDRESS** Univ of No Colorado, Greeley, CO 80639.

KARTIGANER, DONALD M.
PERSONAL Born 05/29/1937, Brooklyn, NY, m, 1967, 3 children **DISCIPLINE** ENGLISH, LITERATURE **EDUCATION** Brown Univ, BA, 59; Columbia Univ, MA, 60; Brown Univ, PhD, 64. **CAREER** Asst Prof to Prof, Univ of Wash, 67-91; William Howry Prof, Univ of Miss, 91-. **HONORS AND AWARDS** Fulbright Lectr, Univ of Ljubljana Slovenia, 67-68; Fulbright Lectr, Jogiellanian Univ, Krakow Poland, 77-78; Fulbright Vis Prof, Univ of Tel-Aviv, Israel, 88. **RESEARCH** Modern English and American Literature, Faulkner, 19th Century English and American Literature. **SELECTED PUBLICATIONS** Auth, The Fragile Thread: The Meaning at Farm Faulkner's Novels; co-ed, Theories of American Literature; co-ed, 7 Volumes Faulkner and JoknaPaTawpha Conference Ser. **CONTACT ADDRESS** Dept English, Univ of Mississippi, University, MS 38677-1848.

KASKE, CAROL VONCKX
PERSONAL Born 02/05/1933, Elgin, IL, w, 1958, 1 child **DISCIPLINE** ENGLISH & COMPARATIVE LITERATURE **EDUCATION** Wash Univ, AB, 54; Smith Col, MA, 55; Johns Hopkins Univ, PhD(English), 64. **CAREER** Instr English, Duke Univ, 59-60, Women's Col, Univ NC, 61 & Univ Ill, Urbana, 61-64; from lectr to sr lectr, 64-73, asst prof English, Cornell Univ, 73-; from assoc prof to prof English, Cornell, 85-92. **HONORS AND AWARDS** Am Philos Soc grant-in-aid, 75, 86; Am Coun Learned Soc travel grant, 79, 86. **MEMBERSHIPS** MLA; Renaissance Soc Am; Spenser Soc; Int Assn Neo-Latin Studies; AAUP; Medieval Academy of Am; Int Asn of Univ Profs of English. **RESEARCH** Renaissance literature; theology; Edmund Spenser. **SELECTED PUBLICATIONS** Auth, The dragon's spark and sting and the structure of Red Cross's dragon fight, Studies Philol, 69; Mount Sinai and Dante's Mount Purgatory, Dante Studies, 71; contribr, Spenser's Pluralistic Universe, In: Contemporary Thought on Spenser, Univ Southern Ill, 75; Getting around the Parson's Tale, In: Chaucer at Albany, Burt Franklin, 75; auth, The Bacchus who wouldn't wash, Renaissance Quart, 76; Spenser's Amoretti and Epithalamion of 1595, English Lit Renaissance, 78; Religious Reverence doth Buriall Teene, Rev English Studies, 79; Auth, with John R Clark: Marsilio Ficino, Three Books on Life, a Critical Edition and Translation with Introduction and Notes, Binghamton, NY: Medieval and Renaissance Texts and Studies, 89; contribr, "How Spenser Really Used Stephen Hawes in the Legend of Holiness," in Unfolded Tales, ed. George Logan and Gordon Teskey (Ithaca: Cornell Univ Pr, 89), 119-136; auth, "The Audiences of the Faerie Queene: Iconoclasm and Related Issues in Books I, V, and VI," Lit and Hist 3 (94); auth, Spenser and biblical Poetics, Cornell Univ Pr (Ithaca, NYork), 99. **CONTACT ADDRESS** Dept of English, Cornell Univ, 250 Goldwin Smith Hall, Ithaca, NY 14853-0001. **EMAIL** cvk2@cornell.edu

KASS, ELAINE W.
PERSONAL Born 07/27/1947, Chicago, IL, m, 1979, 2 children **DISCIPLINE** SPEECH, THEATRE **EDUCATION** Marquette Univ, BA, 69; Univ Minn, MA, 71. **CAREER** Prince George's Community Col. **HONORS AND AWARDS** Advisor Awd, Prince Georges Community Col, 98-99. **MEMBERSHIPS** ECA; MCA. **RESEARCH** Voice and diction. **SELECTED PUBLICATIONS** Auth, USA Spoken English: The basics of U.S. American English pronunciation, SEAM Pub, 00; auth, Speaking American English: a rulebook and guide of USA pronunciation and spelling for the International Student, SEAM Pub, 00. **CONTACT ADDRESS** Dept Speech and Theatre, Prince George's Comm Col, 301 Largo Rd, Upper Marlboro, MD 20774-2109. **EMAIL** kassew@pg.cc.md.us

KASTAN, DAVID SCOTT
PERSONAL Born 01/04/1946, New York, NY, m, 1983, 1 child **DISCIPLINE** ENGLISH AND COMPARATIVE LITERATURE **EDUCATION** Princeton Univ, AB, 67; Univ Chicago, MA, 68 PhD, 74. **CAREER** Instr, Dartmouth Col, 73; prof, Columbia Univ, 87. **HONORS AND AWARDS** Gen ed, Arden Shakespeare; distinguished vis prof, Univ of Copenhagen, 98; distinguished vis prof, American Univ Cairo, 94. **SELECTED PUBLICATIONS** Auth, essays on Shakespeare and Renaissance lit, Daedalus, ELH, Renaissance Drama, Shakespeare Quarty, Shakespeare Stud, Stud in Philol; auth, Shakespeare and the Shapes of Time, 82; co-ed, Staging the Renaissance: Essays on Elizabethan and Jacobean Drama, 91; ed, Critical Essays on Shakespeare's Hamlet, 95; New History of Early English Drama, 97; A Companion to Shakespeare, 99; Shakespeare After Theory, 99. **CONTACT ADDRESS** Dept of Eng, Columbia Col, New York, 2960 Broadway, New York, NY 10027-6902. **EMAIL** dsk1@columbia.edu

KASTER, ROBERT A.
PERSONAL Born 02/06/1948, New York, NY, m, 1969, 2 children **DISCIPLINE** LATIN LANGUGE AND LITERATURE. **EDUCATION** Dartmouth Coll, AB, 69; Harvard Univ, MA, 71; PhD, 75. **CAREER** Harvard Univ: Tchg Fel, 72-73; Instr, Colby Col, 73-74; asst prof, 75-82, assoc prof, 82-89, prof, 89-97 Univ Chicago; prof, Princeton Univ; 97- **HONORS AND AWARDS** Nat Endowment Hum Fel, 80-81; John Simon Guggenheim Memorial Found Fel, 91-92; Charles J. Goodwin Awd of Merit, 91; Kennedy Found Prof of Latin, 97-; pres, am philol asn, 96; avalon found distinguished service prof, 96-97. **MEMBERSHIPS** Am Philol Asn; Asn Ancient Historians; Women's Class Caucus. **RESEARCH** Latin literature; Roman culture. **SELECTED PUBLICATIONS** Auth, Guardians of Language: The Grammarian and Society in Late Antiquity, TheTransformation of the Classical Heritage, /vik 11, Berkeley-Univ Calif Press, 88; Studies on the Text of Suetonius De Grammaticis et Rhetoribus, The American Philological Association: American Classical Studies, Scholars Press, 92; Suetonius: De Grammaticis et Rhetoribus, Clarendon Press, 95. **CONTACT ADDRESS** Dept of Classics, Princeton Univ, 104 East Pyne, Princeton, NJ 08544. **EMAIL** kaster@princeton.edu

KATASSE, CONNY
DISCIPLINE ENGLISH AS A GLOBAL LANGUAGE **EDUCATION** Union Inst, PhD. **CAREER** Univ Alaska. **SELECTED PUBLICATIONS** Area: Deaf children and English in Perspectives in Education and Deafness. **CONTACT ADDRESS** Univ of Alaska, Anchorage, 3211 Providence Dr., Anchorage, AK 99508.

KATZ, PHYLLIS
PERSONAL Born 05/23/1936, New Haven, CT, 4 children **DISCIPLINE** CLASSICS **EDUCATION** Wellesley Col, BA, 58; Univ Calif, Los Angeles, MA, 63; Columbia Univ, phD, 69. **CAREER** Lectr, Mount St Mary's Col, 62-63; Lectr, Barnard Col, 65- 66; asst prof, 69, instr, 68-69, Univ Ill; instr, CUNY, City College NY, 71-72; vis asst prof, Col New Rochelle, 74; lectr, 76, vis asst prof, 74-75; SUNY, Purchase; teach, 77-83, Miss Porter's Sch; lectr, fac mem, Class Asn New Eng, Summer Inst, summers 87-97; vis lectr, Univ Mass, 93; vis lectr, Wesleyan Univ, Grad Lib Stud Prog, 92; vis scholar, vis lectr, sen lectr, DARTMOUTH COL, 90-. **HONORS AND AWARDS** Barlow-Beach Awd, Classical Assoc of New England, 97; National Endowment for the Humanities; Reader's Digest Teacher Scholar, 90-91; National Endowment for the Humanities Faculty Adviser, Younger Scholar Awd, Summer 89; National Endowment for the Humanities Council for Basic Education Fellowship for Independent Study in the Humanities Summer 88; Miss Porter's School, Craven Summer Sabbatical, Columbia University, Summer 87; Columbia University, Woodbridge Honorary Fellowship, 65. **MEMBERSHIPS** Am Philogical Assoc, 86-; Am Classical League, 85-; Vergilian Society, 85-, Trustee, 97-00; Classical Assoc of New England, 83-, Pres, 89, Exec.Sec., 98-03; Women's Classical Caucus, 66-; Am Institute of Archaeology, 65-. **RESEARCH** Women in Antiquity: coming of age rituals of young girls, portrayals of girls and women in Greek poetry and on Attic and Corinthian pottery, literary and artistic depictions of gender and the body; women's voices in ancient and modern poetry. **SELECTED PUBLICATIONS** Auth, Hill-Stead 46.1.95: A Lost Work of the Painter of Athens, 931, BABESCH, No. 72, 97-1-20; auth, Io in the Prometheus Bound: A Coming of Age Paradigm for the Athenian Community, in Rites of Passage in Ancient Greece: Literature, Religion, Society, The Bucknell Review, 99, (Vol. XLIII, Number 1), 129-147; Selections from Ovid: Amores, Metamorphoses, with Charbra A. Jestin, 2nd Edition, Summber 00, Bolchazy-Carducci Press. **CONTACT ADDRESS** Dept of Classics, Dartmouth Col, HB 6086, Reed Hall, PO Box 1048, Hanover, NH 03755. **EMAIL** phyllis.b.katz@dartmouth.edu

KATZ, SANDRA
DISCIPLINE ENGLISH LITERATURE **EDUCATION** Smith Col, BA; Trinity Col, MA; Univ Mass, PhD. **CAREER** Prof, Hartford Univ. **RESEARCH** Biography ; American studies. **SELECTED PUBLICATIONS** Auth, biography of Elinor White Frost. **CONTACT ADDRESS** English Dept, Univ of Hartford, 200 Bloomfield Ave, West Hartford, CT 06117.

KAUFFMAN, BETTE J.
PERSONAL Born 05/14/1945, Washington, IA, w, 1998 **DISCIPLINE** COMMUNICATIONS **EDUCATION** Univ Iowa, BA, 80; Univ Pa, MA, 82; PhD, 92. **CAREER** Assoc prof, head, 97-,Univ of La-Monroe. **HONORS AND AWARDS** Pi Sigma Alpha Nat Honor Soc; Kappa Tau Alpha Nat Honor Soc; Omicron Delta Kappa Nat Leadership Honor Soc; Univ Iowa Hancher-Finkbine Medallion; Phi Beta Kappa; leon barnes commun j honor award, 79; ruth baty & maurice barnett jones scholar, 79, 80; cum laude grad, 80; tuition scholar, 80-86; grad teaching assistantships, 81-85; fac marshall for broadcast/cable, 91; faculty develop prog grant, 99. **MEMBERSHIPS** Assoc for Educ in Journ & Mass Commun; Publ Relations Soc of Amer; Int commun Assoc; founding member, Coalition for Multicultural Feminist Stud in Commun. **RESEARCH** Critical media stud; soc identity (race, class, gender) in culture & commun; visual commun. **SELECTED PUBLICATIONS** Auth, Feminist Facts: Interview Strategies and Political Subjects in Ethnography, Commun Theory, 92; art, Woman Artist: Between Myth and Stereotype, On the Margins of Art Worlds, Westview Press, 95; art, Missing Persons: Working Class Women and the Movies, 1940-1990, Feminism, Multiculturalism and the Media: Global Diversities, Sage Publ, 95; art, Media Realities: The Social Context of Visual Competence, J of Visual Literacy, 97; art, Angelica Kauffman, & Berenice Abbott, Women in World History, Yorkin Publ, 98. **CONTACT ADDRESS** Univ of Louisiana, Monroe, 120A Stubbs Hall, Monroe, LA 71209-0322. **EMAIL** jmckauffman@ulm.edu

KAVANAGH, PETER
PERSONAL Born 03/19/1916, Inniskeen, Ireland, m, 1963, 2 children **DISCIPLINE** ENGLISH **EDUCATION** Univ Col, Dublin, A BA, 40, HDE and MA, 41; Trinity Col, Dublin, PhD(English), 44. **CAREER** Master, Dublin Nat Schs, 37-45; asst prof English, St Francis Col, NY, 46-47, Loyola Univ, Ill, 47-49 and Gannon Col, 49-50; ed and writer, Encycl Amna, 50-53; eng, Cementation Co, London, 53-57; prof English, Fairleigh Dickinson Univ, 57-58; Res and Writing, 58-, Assoc prof English, Stout State Univ, 66-68. **MEMBERSHIPS** Assoc Brit Soc Engineers; MLA; Int Fedn Jists. **SELECTED PUBLICATIONS** Auth, Garden of the Golden Apples, 72; auth, Beyond Affection, 77; auth, Love's Tortunred Headland, 78; auth, Savage Rock, 78; auth, The Dancing Flame, 81; auth, Piling Up the Ricks, 89; auth, Pilgrimage of a Soul, 96; auth, Patrick Kavanagh; A Life Chronicle, 00. **CONTACT ADDRESS** Peter Kavanagh Hand Press, 33 Park Ave, New York, NY 10016. **EMAIL** peterkavanagh@mindspring.com

KAWIN, BRUCE FREDERICK
PERSONAL Born 11/06/1945, Los Angeles, CA **DISCIPLINE** FILM HISTORY; MODERN LITERATURE **EDUCATION** Columbia Univ, AB, 67; Cornell Univ, MFA, 69, PhD, 70. **CAREER** Asst prof English, Wells Col, 70-73; lectr English & Film, Univ Calif, Riverside, 73-75; specialist, Ctr for Advan Film Studies, Am Film Inst, 74; assoc prof, 75-80, prof English & Film, Univ Co, Boulder. **MEMBERSHIPS** MLA; SCS. **RESEARCH** Narrative theory; relations between literature and film. **SELECTED PUBLICATIONS** Auth, Slides (poem), Angelfish, 70; Telling It Again and Again: Repetition in Literature and Film, Cornell Univ, 72, repr Univ Press Co, 89; Faulkner and Film, Ungar, 77; Me Tarzan, you junk, Take One, 78; Mindscreen: Bergman, Godard and First-Person Film, Princeton Univ, 78; ed, To Have and Have Not--The Screenplay, Univ Wis, 80; The Mind of the Novel: Reflexive Fiction and the Ineffable, Princeton Univ, 82; Faulkner's MGM Screenplays, Univ Tenn, 82; How Movies Work, MacMillan, 87, repr Univ Ca Press, 92; co-auth, A short History of the Movies, 5th ed, MacMillan, 92; 6th ed, Allyn & Bacon, 96; 7th ed Allyn & Bacon, 99. **CONTACT ADDRESS** Dept of English, Univ of Colorado, Boulder, Box 226, Boulder, CO 80309-0226. **EMAIL** bkawin@aol.com

KAY, W. DAVID
PERSONAL Born 03/28/1939, Philadelphia, PA, m, 1959, 2 children **DISCIPLINE** ENGLISH LITERATURE **EDUCATION** Univ Pa, BA, 61; Princeton Univ, MA, 63, PhD, 68. **CAREER** Instr English, 65-68, asst prof, 68-78, assoc prof English, Univ Ill, Urbana, 78-; Danforth fel, Yale Div Sch, 69-70. **MEMBERSHIPS** Renaissance Soc Am; Shakespeare Asn Am. **RESEARCH** Renaissance humanism; Elizabethan and Jacobean drama; Ben Jonson. **SELECTED PUBLICATIONS** Auth, Bartholomew Fair: Ben Jonson in Praise of folly, English Lit Renaissance, spring 76; Erasmus learned joking: Ironic use of classical wisdom in Praise of Folly, Tex Studies in Lit & Lang, fall 77; Ben Jonson & Elizabethan dramatic convention, Mod Philol, 8/78; Ben Jonson: A Literary Life, Macmillan/St Martin's Press, 95; ed, John Marston, The Malcontent, New Mermaids, A&C Black/W.W. Norton, 98. **CONTACT ADDRESS** Dept of English, Univ of Illinois, Urbana-Champaign, 608 S Wright St, Urbana, IL 61801-3613. **EMAIL** w-kay@uiuc.edu

KAYE, FRANCES WELLER
PERSONAL Born 04/04/1949, Englewood, NJ, m, 1973 **DISCIPLINE** AMERICAN STUDIES AND AMERICAN LITERATURE **EDUCATION** Cornell Univ, BA, 70, MA, 72, PhD(Am studies), 73. **CAREER** Vis asst prof Am studies, Univ Iowa, 76-77; asst prof English, 77-80, Assoc Prof English, Univ Nebr-Lincoln, 81-, Assoc Ed, Great Plains Quart, 80- **RESEARCH** Great Plains studies; Aman studies; Canadian literature. **SELECTED PUBLICATIONS** Auth, Hamlin Garland & Frederick Philip Grove as self-conscious chroniclers of the pioneers, Can Rev Am Studies, 79; Bringing a symphony orchestra to Albion, Nebraska, Prairie Schooner, 81; The 49th Parallel and the 98th Meridian, Mosaic, 81; The Past is Prologue, 81 & Desert Places, 82, Prairie Schooner. **CONTACT ADDRESS** Dept of English, Univ of Nebraska, Lincoln, P O Box 880333, Lincoln, NE 68588-0333.

KEANEY, JOHN J.
DISCIPLINE CLASSICS **EDUCATION** Boston Coll, AB, 53; Harvard Univ, PhD, 59. **CAREER** Prof, Princeton Univ. **RESEARCH** Greek paleography and lexicography; Greek political theory. **SELECTED PUBLICATIONS** Auth, The Composition of Aristotle's Athenaion Politeia; ed, Harpocration: Lexeis of the Ten Orators; Contributing ed, Theophrastus of Eresus: Sources for his Life, Writings, Thought, and Influence. **CONTACT ADDRESS** Princeton Univ, 103 E Pyme, Princeton, NJ 08544.

KEARLY, PETER R.
PERSONAL Born 07/06/1972, Seoul, S Korea, m, 1998 **DISCIPLINE** ENGLISH LITERATURE **EDUCATION** Wayne State Univ, BA, 94; MA, 95. **CAREER** Adv, admin asst, Wayne State Univ, 92-98; GTA Wayne State Univ, 95-01; Instr, Henry Ford Communty Col, 00-01. **HONORS AND AWARDS** Rumble Fel; Fergusen Grad Essay Awd; Alumni Achievement Awd; Grant, Cornell Univ. **MEMBERSHIPS** MLA, Am Studies Assoc, Asian Am Studies Assoc. **RESEARCH** Asian American studies, Post-Colonial studies, Ethnic Studies, Gender Studies. **SELECTED PUBLICATIONS** Auth, "Toni Morrison and the Politics of Community," Jour of Am Cult, (00). **CONTACT ADDRESS** 19412 Mayfield Ave, Apt 202, Livonia, MI 48152-4247. **EMAIL** pkearly@wayne.edu

KEARNS, FRANCIS E.
PERSONAL Born 08/10/1931, Brooklyn, NY, m, 1960, 2 children **DISCIPLINE** ENGLISH **EDUCATION** NY Univ, AB, 53; Univ Chicago, MA, 54; Univ NC, PhD, 61. **CAREER** Instr, Univ NC, 54-60; Asst prof, Georgetown Univ, 60-65; Asst Prof to Prof and Dept Chair, Hunter Col, 68-. **HONORS AND AWARDS** Phi Beta Kappa; Res Grant, am Philos Soc; Grant, Bureau of Higher Educ; NEH Fel; Fulbright Prof, Univ Bergen Norway; Edward Douglas White Annual Awd, Georgetown Univ. **MEMBERSHIPS** am Lit Asn, Margaret Fuller Soc, Thoreau Lyceum. **RESEARCH** American literature of Vietnam War; Margaret Fuller; African American writers, Hawthorne, Fitzgerald. **SELECTED PUBLICATIONS** Auth, "Sex and the Literature of Black Experience: A Museum Piece," Delta epsilon Sigma Journal, (99): 15-23; auth, "The theme of Experience I Hawthorne's Blithedale Romance," in Geschicte und fiktion, Amerikanische Prosa Im 10. Jahrhundert, (72): 64-84; auth, "The Un-angry Langston Hughes," Yale Review, (70): 154-160; auth, The Black Experience in American Literature, The Viking Press, 70; auth, "Campus Activism," Yale Review, (68): 28-44; auth, "Social Consciousness and Academic Freedom in Catholic higher Education," in The Shape of Catholic Higher Education, Univ Chicago press, 67; auth, "Margaret Fuller and the Abolition Movement," Journal of the History of Ideas, (64): 120-127 **CONTACT ADDRESS** Dept English, Lehman Col, CUNY, 250 Bedford Park Blvd W, Bronx, NY 10468-1527. **EMAIL** francek@aol.com

KEARNS, NANCY
PERSONAL Born 10/07/1943, Huntsville, AL, w, 1966, 1 child **DISCIPLINE** ENGLISH **EDUCATION** Athens Col, BA, 66; Univ N Ala, MA, 79. **CAREER** Teacher, Hartselle High School, 66-68; Teacher, Decatur High School, 68-82; Teacher, Okaloosa-Walton Cmty Col, 83-90; Ala A & M Univ, 93-. **HONORS AND AWARDS** Teacher Fel, Nat Writing Project, Jacksonville State, Univ, 94; Advanced Fel, Nat Writing Project, AAMU, 96; Who's Who Among Am Teachers, 00 **MEMBERSHIPS** NCTE, ACTE. **SELECTED PUBLICATIONS** Auth, "'Band of Airy Thinness," Iowa Language Chronicle, 94; auth, "The I-Search paper," Indiana English, 96; auth, "Bartleby Revisited," Journal of Miss Council Teachers of English, 98. **CONTACT ADDRESS** Dept English, Alabama A&M Univ, PO Box 333, Normal, AL 35762-0333. **EMAIL** lilbit1025@aol.com

KEARNS, TERRANCE
PERSONAL Born 07/15/1946, State IS, NY, m, 1968, 2 children **DISCIPLINE** ENGLISH **EDUCATION** Col Holy Cross, Worcester, Mass, BA, 68; Ind Univ, Bloomington, Ind, PhD, 78. **CAREER** From Instr to Prof, Univ of Central Ark, Convey, 74-; Dept Chair, Univ of Central Ark, Convey, 90-98. **HONORS AND AWARDS** Hon Prog, Holy Crosss, 66-68; Fenwick Independent Study Scholar, Holy Cross, 67-68; Woodrow Wilson Fel, Ind Univ, 68-69; Dist Awd of Merit, Boy Scouts of Am, 89; Who's Who in Am, 53rd ed, 99. **MEMBERSHIPS** Asn of Lit Scholars and Critics, Ark Philol Asn. **RESEARCH** Shakespeare, English Renaissance Literature. **SELECTED PUBLICATIONS** Auth, "PAPA at Twenty: A Cumulative Indez," Publ of the Ark Philol Asn 21 (Fall 95): 91-118; auth, "Twenty-five Years of PAPA," Publ of the Ark Philol Asn 26 (Spring 00): 63-94. **CONTACT ADDRESS** Dept English, Univ of Central Arkansas, 201 Donaghey Ave, Conway, AR 72035-5001. **EMAIL** terrance@mail.uca.edu

KEATEN, JAMES A.
DISCIPLINE INTERCULTURAL COMMUNICATION **EDUCATION** PA State Univ, PhD, 70. **CAREER** Prof, Univ Northern CO. **MEMBERSHIPS** Speech Commun Asn; Western States Commun Asn; Japanese Psychol Asn. **RESEARCH** Commun apprehension; cross-cultural commun. **SELECTED PUBLICATIONS** Coauth, Teaching people to speak well: Training and remediation of communication reticence, Hampton Publ Co, 95; Komyunikeishon fuan to wa nanika? [A definition of communication apprehension and related constructs], Hokuriku Daiguku Kiyo, 20, 96; Development of an instrument to measure reticence, Commun Quart, 45, 97; Communication apprehension in Japan: Grade school through secondary school, Int J of Intercultural Rel, 21, 97; Assessing the cross-cultural validity of the Personal Report of Communication Apprehension scale (PRCA-24), Japanese Psychol Res, 40, 98; Fundamentals of communication: An intercultural perspective, Kawashima Shotem, 98. **CONTACT ADDRESS** Univ of No Colorado, Greeley, CO 80639. **EMAIL** jkeaten@bentley.unco.edu

KEATING, PATRICK
DISCIPLINE ENGLISH, SPEECH **EDUCATION** Univ Nebr, BS, 64; Colo State Univ, MA, 67; Ind Univ Pa, PhD, 87. **CAREER** Prof, Northeast Col, 69-. **HONORS AND AWARDS** NEH Awds. **MEMBERSHIPS** MLA. **RESEARCH** Communication Skills. **SELECTED PUBLICATIONS** Auth, Study of Nebraska Writers. **CONTACT ADDRESS** Dept Lib Arts, Northeast Comm Col, PO Box 469, Norfolk, NE 68702-0469.

KEEBLE, ROBERT L.
PERSONAL Born 07/03/1959, Tyler, TX, m, 1994 **DISCIPLINE** ENGLISH **EDUCATION** Tyler Jr Col, AA, 79; Stephen F. Austin State Univ, BS, 81; MA, 91; Univ Tulsa, PhD, 96. **CAREER** Lecturer, Stephen F. Austin State Univ, 89-91; Lecturer, Univ Tulsa, 91-95; Lecturer, Dade Cmty Col, 97-98. **MEMBERSHIPS** MLA; Sigma Tau Delta; S Cent MLA. **RESEARCH** 20th Century American Literature. **SELECTED PUBLICATIONS** Auth, "The Moviegoer as Psychotext," Southern Quarterly, 99; auth, "Nebulous Affair: Environment and Language," in Notes on Contemporary Literature, 97. **CONTACT ADDRESS** Dept Liberal Arts, Schreiner Col, 2100 Memorial Blvd, Kerrville, TX 78028-5611. **EMAIL** rkeeble@schreiner.edu

KEEFE, ROBERT
PERSONAL Born 03/11/1938, Framingham, MA, m, 1960 **DISCIPLINE** ENGLISH **EDUCATION** Brandeis Univ, AB, 64; Princeton Univ, PhD(English), 68. **CAREER** Asst prof, 67-77, Assoc Prof English, Univ Mass, Amherst, 78-, Guest prof, English lit, Univ Freiburg, Ger, 72-73 and 77-78. **MEMBERSHIPS** Soc Relig Higher Educ; MLA. **RESEARCH** Victorian literature; Matthew Arnold; 19th century concepts of time. **SELECTED PUBLICATIONS** Auth, Artist and Model, In: The Picture of Dorian Grey, Studies in the Novel, spring 73; Charlotte Bronte's World of Death, Univ Tex Press, Austin, 79; Entombed, Gothic, 5/79, reprinted in: The Year's Best Horror Stories: Series VIII, Daw Bks, 80; On Cowboys and Collectives: The Kennedy-Nixon Generation, The Mass Rev, fall 80. **CONTACT ADDRESS** Univ of Massachusetts, Amherst, Amherst, MA 01003.

KEEFER, JANICE KULYK
PERSONAL Born Toronto, ON, Canada **DISCIPLINE** ENGLISH **EDUCATION** Univ Toronto, BA, 74; Univ Sussex, MA, 76, DPhil, 83. **CAREER** Tutor, Univ Sussex, 77-78; lectr, 81-82, tchr, 82-83, asst prof, 83-84, postdoc fel, Univ Sainte-Anne, 84-86; Writer-in-Residence, Douglas Col, Vancouver, 87; Writer-in-Residence, Univ PEI, 89; assoc prof, 90-92, prof, Univ Guelph, 92-. **HONORS AND AWARDS** James Harris Entrance Scholar, 70-74; Woodhouse Scholar, 72, 73, 74; First Prize, PRISM Int Fiction Comp, 84; First prize & Top Prize, NS Writers' FedN, 85; Found Advan Can Letters Author's Awd, 86; Joseph B. Stauffer Prize, 88-89; Winning Entry, Malahat Long Poem Competition, 91. **MEMBERSHIPS** Eden Mills Writers' Festival Comt. **RESEARCH** Canadian lit and multiculturalism; creative writing. **SELECTED PUBLICATIONS** Auth, The Paris Napoli Express, 86; auth, Under Eastern Eyes: A Critical Reading of Canadian Maritime Fiction, 87; auth, Traveling Ladies, 90; auth, Rest Harrow, Harper Collins, 92; auth, The Green Library, 96; auth, Marrying the Sea, 98; auth, Honey and Ashes, Harper Collins, 98. **CONTACT ADDRESS** Dept of English, Univ of Guelph, Guelph, ON, Canada N1G 2W1.

KEEHNER, MARY
DISCIPLINE RHETORICAL THEORY AND CRITICISM **EDUCATION** Purdue Univ, PhD. **CAREER** Asst prof, Purdue Univ. **RESEARCH** Feminist and other ideological approaches to the study of discourse. **SELECTED PUBLICATIONS** Auth, The lost passages of Kenneth Burke's Permanence and Change, Commun Stud, 91; Arguing about fetal versus women's rights: An ideological evaluation, Warranting Assent: Case Stud in Argument Evaluation, 95. **CONTACT ADDRESS** Dept of Commun, Purdue Univ, West Lafayette, 1366 Lib Arts & Educ Bldg 2114, West Lafayette, IN 47907-1366. **EMAIL** keen@vm.cc.purdue.edu

KEEN, SUZANNE
PERSONAL Born 04/10/1963, Bethlehem, PA, m, 1992, 1 child **DISCIPLINE** ENGLISH **EDUCATION** Brown, AB, 84; AM, 86; Harvard, MA, 87; PhD, 90. **CAREER** Asst prof, Yale Univ, 90-95; asst prof, Washington & Lee Univ, 95-96, assoc prof, 97-. **HONORS AND AWARDS** Phi Beta Kappa, Rhode Island Alpha; Morse Fel, Yale Univ, 93-94; Individual Artist's Fel, Va Comn for the Arts, 97-98; John D. and Rose H. Jackson Fel, Beinecke Library, Yale Univ, 99; Nat Endowment for the Humanities Fel, 99-2000. **MEMBERSHIPS** MLA, Narrative Soc, Thomas Hardy Asn, Cath Comn for Intellectual & Cultural Affairs. **RESEARCH** The English novel, narrative theory, contemporary and Victorian literature. **SELECTED PUBLICATIONS** Auth, "Catching the Heart off Guard: the Generous Vision of Seamus Heaney," Cath Writers Series, Commonweal 17 (May 96): 10-14; auth, Victorian Renovations of the Novel: Narrative Annexes and the Boundaries of Representation, Cambridge Studies in Nineteenth-Century Literature and Culture 15, Cambridge Univ Press (98); "The Bad Wolf Returns," rev of While I was Gone, by Sue Miller, Commonweal 24 (Sept 99): 25-6; a portion of the fourth chapter of Victorian Renovations of the Novel appears in the new Norton Critical Edition of Thomas Hardy's The Mayor of Casterbridge, ed by Philip Mallet, Norton (forthcoming 2000); auth, " 'I cannot eat my words but I do': Food, Body and Word in the Novels of Jeanette Winterson," Scenes of the Apple: Hunger and Appetite as Metaphor in Nineteenth-and Twentieth-Century Women's Writing, ed Tamar Heller and Patricia Moran, SUNY Press (forthcoming); **CONTACT ADDRESS** Dept English, Washington and Lee Univ, Payne Hall, Lexington, VA 24450-2504. **EMAIL** skeen@wlu.edu

KEENAN, HUGH THOMAS
PERSONAL Born 01/16/1936, Humboldt, TN **DISCIPLINE** MEDIEVAL LITERATURE **EDUCATION** Memphis State Univ, BS, 57, MA, 60, BA, 63; Univ Tenn, PhD(English), 68. **CAREER** Instr English, Delta State Col, 60-62, Memphis State Univ, 62-63 & Univ Tenn, 63-67; assoc prof English, GA State Univ, 68-, Fel, Ctr Mediaeval & Renaissance Studies, Calif State Univ, 74; bk rev ed, SAtlantic Bull, 78-81. **MEMBERSHIPS** MLA; Mediaeval Acad Am; Mod Lang Soc Finland; SAtlantic Mod Lang Asn; Children's Lit Asn. **RESEARCH** Old English literature; Middle English Literature. **SELECTED PUBLICATIONS** Auth, The Ruin as Babylon, Tenn Studies Lit, 66; The of The Lord of the Rings, Tolkien & Critics, 68; Old English and Children's Literature, In: The Great Excluded, 71; ed, Typology and Medieval Literature, Studies in Lit Imagination, 75; auth, Christ and Satan: Some vagaries, Studies Medieval Cult, 75; The General Prologue, lines 345-346, Neuphilologische Mitteilungen, 78; ed, Dearest Chums and Partners, 93; Typology and English Medieval Literature, 92. **CONTACT ADDRESS** Dept of English, Georgia State Univ, 33 Gilmer St SE, Atlanta, GA 30303-3080.

KEENAN, J. G.
PERSONAL Born 01/19/1944, New York, NY, m, 2000 **DISCIPLINE** CLASSICS **EDUCATION** Col of the Holy Cross, AB 65; Yale Univ, MA 66, PhD 68. **CAREER** Univ Cal Berk, asst prof 68-73; Loyola Univ, assoc to full prof 74 to 98-. **HONORS AND AWARDS** NEH **MEMBERSHIPS** ASP; AIP; APA; ARCE; CAMWS **RESEARCH** Papyrology, ancient , social, economic and legal history; Byzantine and medieval Egypt. **SELECTED PUBLICATIONS** Auth, Egypt A.D. 425-600, Cambridge Ancient History, forthcoming; Review of Stanley Burstein, Ancient African Kingdoms, and Derek A. Welsby, The Kingdom of Kush, for The Classical Bull, forthcoming; Review of David Tandy, Warriors into Traders: The power of the Market in Early Greece, for Classical Bull, forthcoming; More From the Archive of the Descendents of Eulogius, with Todd Hickey, Analecta Papyrologica, 98; Gilgamesh: An Appreciation, in: Danny P. Jackson, trans, The Epic of Gilgamesh, rev ed, Bolchazy Carducci Pub, Wauconda Il, 97; George Sphrantzes: A Brief Review, The Ancient World, 96; The Aphrodito Murder Mystery: A Return to the Scene of the Crimes, BASP, 95; The Will of Gaius Longinus Castor, BASP, 94. **CONTACT ADDRESS** Dept of Classic Studies, Loyola Univ, Chicago, 6525 N Sheridan Rd, Chicago, IL 60626. **EMAIL** jkeenan@orion.it.luc.edu

KEENAN, RICHARD CHARLES
PERSONAL Born 04/28/1939, Philadelphia, PA, m, 1967, 2 children **DISCIPLINE** ENGLISH LITERATURE, CINEMA **EDUCATION** Temple Univ, BS, 62; St Joseph's Col, Pa, MA, 66; Temple Univ, PhD(English), 74. **CAREER** Instr, Devon

Prep Sch, Devon, Pa, 64-67, Temple Univ, 67-72, asst prof, 72-94, Prof English, Univ MD, Eastern Shore, 94-, Assoc ed, Lit/Film Quart, 77-. **MEMBERSHIPS** Literature/Film Asn; British Film Inst; MLA; Col English Asn **RESEARCH** American film studies; 19th century English & American literature. **SELECTED PUBLICATIONS** Auth, Browning and Shelley, 73 & coauth, Robert & Elizabeth Barrett Browning: An Annotated Bibliography for 1971, 73, Browning Inst Studies; auth, Cinema on Campus, Campus on Cinema, Lit/Film Quart, 4/73; Directors and Directions: Cukor, Ford and Kubrick, Lit/Film Quart, 74; Comments and Queries: No 5, (error in Browning biography by Irvine & Honan), Studies Browning & His Circle, spring 75; Negative Image: Black Actors and American Film, Lit/Film Quart, fall 75; coauth, Browning Without Words: D W Griffith's Filming of Pippa Passes, Browning Inst Studies, 76; The sense of an ending: Jan Kadar's distortion of Stephen Crane's The Blue Hotel, Lit/Film Quart, 88; Matthew Arnold, In: Survey of World Literature, Cavendish Press, 92; Colonial life and thought: Benjamin Rush, In: American Portraits: History through Biography Volume 1 to 1877, Kendall Hunt, 93; Salvador: Oliver Stone and the center of indifference, In: The Films of Oliver Stone, Scarecrow Press, 97. **CONTACT ADDRESS** Univ of Maryland, Eastern Shore, 11868 Academic Oval, Princess Anne, MD 21853-1299. **EMAIL** rkeenan@umes-bird.umd.edu

KEENER, FREDERICK M.
PERSONAL Born 12/28/1937, New York, NY, m, 1961, 2 children **DISCIPLINE** ENGLISH, COMPARATIVE LITERATURE **EDUCATION** St John's Univ, NYork, AB, 59; Columbia Univ, MA, 60, PhD(English), 65. **CAREER** From instr to asst prof English, St John's Univ, NY, 61-66; from asst prof to assoc prof, Columbia Univ, 66-72, dean summer session, 72-74; from assoc prof to prof, 74-78; Prof English, Hofstra Univ, 78-, Lectr, Hunter Col, 66; Nat Endowment for Humanities res fel, 76-77; vis prof, Columbia Univ, 81. **MEMBERSHIPS** MLA; Conf Brit Studies; Am Soc 18th Century Studies. **RESEARCH** Eighteenth century British literature; 18th century comparative literature. **SELECTED PUBLICATIONS** Critical Essays on Pope, Alexander, Scriblerian and the Kit-Cats, Vol 27, 95. **CONTACT ADDRESS** Dept of English, Hofstra Univ, 1000 Fulton Ave, Hempstead, NY 11550-1091.

KEEP, CHRISTOPHER J.
DISCIPLINE 19TH-20TH CENTURY BRITISH LITERATURE **EDUCATION** York Univ, BA, MA; Queen's Univ, PhD. **CAREER** Asst prof, Univ of Victoia. **HONORS AND AWARDS** Izaak Walton Killam Memorial post dr fel; post dr fel, SSHRC; AC Hamilton. **RESEARCH** Cultural studies; critical theory; film. **SELECTED PUBLICATIONS** Contrib, Dictionary of Literary Biography: Late-Victorian and Edwadian British Novelists, 95; ed, The Ambiguities of Empire, a special issue of the Victorian Review; auth, Litterature et informatique: La Litterature generee par ordinateur, (95); auth, Postmodern Apocalypse, 95; auth, Being on Line: Net Subjectivity, 97; auth, "Cyberspace Textuality: Computer Technology and Literary Theory, 99. **CONTACT ADDRESS** Dept of English, Univ of Victoria, PO Box 3070, Victoria, BC, Canada V8W 3W1. **EMAIL** ckeep@uvic.ca

KEESSEN, JAN
PERSONAL Born 12/21/1943, Hammond, IN, d **DISCIPLINE** LITERATURE, RHETORIC **EDUCATION** Purdue Univ, BA, 82; Univ Chicago, MA, 84; PhD, 90. **CAREER** Doctoral student, Univ Chicago, 84-86; instr, Purdue Calumet, 87-88; instr, Valparaiso Univ, 88-89; instr, Ga Inst of Technol, 89-90 **HONORS AND AWARDS** Literary Awds Campus Wide Contest, 79-81; Kneale Awd, 79; Univ Book Store Prize, Purdue Univ, 79 &80; Chancellor's Forum for Acad Honorees, 80-82; Best of Contest, Purdue Univ Annual Lit Awds Competition, 80; Merrill and Marjorie Swedland memorial Awd for Journalism, Wyo Wildlife, 80; Distinguished Student, Purdue Univ, 80-82; Delegate to the Chancellor's Forum for Acad Honorees, Purdue Univ, 80-82; Norman Maclean Scholar, Univ Chicago, 84-87; Britain Fel, Ga Inst of Technol, 89-91; NEH Grant, 93; Augustana Fac Res Grant, 93. **RESEARCH** Nineteenth-Century American Romanticism, American Realism, Myth and Reality in the American West, Rhetoric and Composition, Voice in Literature. **SELECTED PUBLICATIONS** Auth, "The Refiner," Skylark, 80; auth, "Ranching--Changing Livelihood in a Changing Land, Wyoming Wildlife (80): 12-15; auth, "The Sculptors," Skylark, 81; auth, "Writing Across the Curriculum: Wanted Guidelines for Teaching Writing in Non-Writing Courses," ERIC Clearinghouse on Reading and Communication Skills, Ind Univ, 91; rev, of "Animal Victims in Modern Fiction: From Sanctity to Sacrifice," by Scholtmeijer, Environmental Hist Rev 18.2 (94); auth, "A Word with Jan Keessen (weekly)," Rock Island Argus. **CONTACT ADDRESS** Dept English, Augustana Col, Illinois, 639 38th St, PO Box 239 B, Aledo, IL 61231. **EMAIL** enkeessen@augustana.edu

KEGL, ROSEMARY
DISCIPLINE 16TH AND 17TH CENTURY ENGLISH LITERATURE **EDUCATION** Cornell Univ, PhD. **CAREER** Assoc prof; taught at, Cornell Univ & WA Univ in St Louis. **HONORS AND AWARDS** Newberry Libr/Nat Endowment Humanities fel & Newberry Libr short-term fel. **RESEARCH** 16th and 17th century Eng lit; contemp marxist and feminist theory. **SELECTED PUBLICATIONS** Auth, Rhetoric of Concealment: Figuring Gender and Class in Renaissance Literature; articles on, Marvell, Puttenham, Shakespeare & 16th and 17th century women's intellectual activ. **CONTACT ADDRESS** Dept of Eng, Univ of Rochester, 601 Elmwood Ave, Ste. 656, Rochester, NY 14642. **EMAIL** kegl@troi.cc.rochester.edu

KEHL, DELMAR GEORGE
PERSONAL Born 09/12/1936, Mt Carroll, IL, m, 1963, 2 children **DISCIPLINE** AMERICAN LITERATURE **EDUCATION** Univ Wis-Madison, MS, 58; Univ Southern Calif, PhD(-English), 67. **CAREER** Instr English, Roosevelt Sch, Conn, 58-59; teaching asst, Univ Southern Calif, 61-64, lectr, 64-65; from asst prof to assoc prof, 65-70, Prof English, Ariz State Univ, 75-, Fac grants-in-aid, 69, 70, 72, 74, 76, 77 and 81; vis scholar, Harvard, 79; res fel, Yale, 79. **HONORS AND AWARDS** Elizabeth K Pleasants Awd Excellence in Teaching, Univ Southern Calif, 62. **MEMBERSHIPS** NCTE; MLA; Rocky Mountain Mod Lang Asn. **RESEARCH** Literature and theology; rhetoric; popular culture. **SELECTED PUBLICATIONS** Oconnor, Flannery 4th-Dimension, the Role of Sexuality in Her Fiction, Mississippi Quart, Vol 48, 95; The Southwest Viewed from the Inside-Out--A Conversation With Noble, Marguerite, J Southwest, Vol 36, 94. **CONTACT ADDRESS** Dept of English, Arizona State Univ, PO Box 870302, Tempe, AZ 85287-0302.

KEIL, CHARLES M. H.
PERSONAL Born 08/12/1939, Norwalk, CT, m, 1964, 2 children **DISCIPLINE** ANTHROPOLOGY, MUSIC **EDUCATION** Yale Univ, BA; Univ Chicago, MA, 64; PhD, 79. **CAREER** From asst prof to prof emer, Dept of Am Stud, SUNY Buffalo, 70- ; acting chemn, 78-89, 92, 94-95, Dir Undergrad Stud, 86-89, dir Grad Stud, 70-77, 79-82; vis prof, music, Univ Natal, 93; vis lectr, sociol of music, 82, 83. **HONORS AND AWARDS** Chicago Folklore Prize, co-winner, 80; Chicago Folklore Prize, 95; Woodrow Wilson Fel, 61-62; Ford Found Fel, 62-63; NIMH Fel, 63-64; Foreign Area Fel Prog, 65-67; Rockefeller Found Res Grant, 75; Guggenheim fel, 79-80. **SELECTED PUBLICATIONS** Auth, Urban Blues, Univ Chicago, 66; auth, Tiv Song: The Sociology of Art in a Classless Society, Univ Chicago, 79; coauth, Polka Happiness, Temple Univ, 92; co-ed, My Music, Wesleyan Univ, 93; coauth, Music Grooves: Essays and Dialogues, Univ Chicago, 94. **CONTACT ADDRESS** Dept of American Studies, SUNY, Buffalo, 1010 Clemens Hall, N Campus, Buffalo, NY 14260. **EMAIL** amsckeil@acsu.buffalo.edu

KEILLOR, ELAINE
DISCIPLINE BAROQUE AND CLASSICAL PERIODS, ETHNOMUSICOLOGY **EDUCATION** Univ Toronto, BA, MA, PhD. **CAREER** Lectr, York Univ, 75-76; instr, Queen's Univ, 76-77; asst prof, 77-82, assoc prof, 82-95, prof, Carleton Univ, 95-. **HONORS AND AWARDS** Chappell Medal, 58; Merit Awd, Fac Arts, Carleton Univ, 81; Canadian Women's Mentor Awd, 99; principal investigator, the can mus heritage soc; co-ch, another organized res unit. **MEMBERSHIPS** Can Musical Heritage; Am Musicol Soc; Int Musicol Soc; Soc Ethnomusicol; Can Univ Music Soc; Can Soc Traditional Music. **RESEARCH** Canadian music. **SELECTED PUBLICATIONS** Auth, monograph John Weinzweig and His Music: The Radical Romantic of Canada, 94; **CONTACT ADDRESS** Dept of Mus, Carleton Univ, 1125 Colonel By Dr, Ottawa, ON, Canada K1S 5B6. **EMAIL** elaine_keillor@carleton.ca

KEISER, GEORGE ROBERT
PERSONAL Born 02/26/1941, Pottsville, PA **DISCIPLINE** ENGLISH AND AMERICAN LITERATURE **EDUCATION** Lehigh Univ, BA, 62, MA, 64, PhD, 71. **CAREER** From instr to asst prof, Canisius Col, 67-73; asst prof, 73-75, assoc prof, 75-81, Prof English, Kans State Univ, 81-. **HONORS AND AWARDS** Am Philos Soc Grants, 73, 77; Am Coun Learned Soc fel, 79 and Huntington Libr fel, 82; Bibliog Soc of Am Fel, 87; Res Fel, Univ of London, 95; Bibliog Soc Res Grant, 95. **MEMBERSHIPS** Medieval Acad Am; Int Authurian Soc; Early English Text Soc; Soc for the Study of Mediaeval Langs and Lit, Cambridge Bibliog Soc; Bibliog Soc; Asn of Am Univ Professors; Early Bk Soc; Soc for the Hist of Authorship, Reading and Publishing. **RESEARCH** Medieval English literature. **SELECTED PUBLICATIONS** Auth, "A tretys of armes: A Revision of the Ashmolean Tract," The Coat of Arms ns 11 (96): 178-90; auth, "A New Text of, and New Light on, Supplement to the Index of Middle English Verse, 4106.5," Notes and Queries 241 ns 44 (96): 14-18; auth, "Reconstructing Robert Thornton's Herbal," Medium Aevum 65 (96): 35-53; auth, "Middle English Passion Narratives and their Contemporary Readers: The Vernacular Progeny of Mediatationes vitae Christi," The Mystical Tradition and the Carthusians, ed. J. Hogg Analecta Cartusiana 130 (96): 10.8-99; auth, Through a Fourteenth-Century Gardener's Eyes: Henry Daniel's Herbal," The Chaucer Review 31 (96): 58-75; auth, "Editing Scientific and Practical Writings," A Guide to Editing Middle English, ed. V.P. McCarren and D. Moffat, Univ of Mich Press (98): 109-122; auth, "Practical Books for Gentlement," The Cambridge History of the Book in Britain, Vol. III: 1400-1557, ED. L. Hellinga and J.B. Trapp, Cambridge: Cambridge Univ Press, (99): 470-90; auth, "The Conclusion of the Canon's Yeoman's Tale: Readings and (Mis)readings," The Chaucer Review 35 (00): 1-21; **CONTACT ADDRESS** Dept of English, Kansas State Univ, 106 Denison Hall, Manhattan, KS 66506-0701. **EMAIL** gkeiser@ksu.edu

KELLEGHAN, FIONA
PERSONAL Born 04/21/1965, West Palm Beach, FL, m, 1994 **DISCIPLINE** ENGLISH, LIBRARY & INFORMATION SCIENCE **EDUCATION** Univ Miami, BA, 87; Fla State Univ, MLS, 88; Univ Miami. MA. **CAREER** Regional Reporter, ACRL Newsletter, 94-98; Consult Ed, Sci Fiction Studies; librn, assoc prof, Univ Miami, 89-; book reviews ed, Journal of the Fantastic in the Arts, 99-. **MEMBERSHIPS** Am Libr Asn; Imagineering Interest Group; Sci Fiction Research Asn; Int Asn for the Fantastic in the Arts; Mythopoeic Soc. **RESEARCH** Lit criticism sci fiction, fantasy, horror fiction and film. **SELECTED PUBLICATIONS** Auth, "Lethem, Jonathan (Allen)" and "Williams, Walter Jon," in St. James Guide to Science Fiction Writers, St. James Press, 95; auth, "Good News from Outer Space (John Kessel)" and "The Deathworld Trilogy (Harry Harrison)," in Magill's Guide to Science Fiction and Fantasy Literature, Salem Press, 96; auth, "Kenrick, Tony" and "O'Connell, Carol," in St. James Guide to Crime & Mystery Writers, St. James Press, 96; coauth, "Fantasy Literature" and "Horror Literature," in Genre and Ethnic Collections: Collected Essays, JAI Press, 97; auth, "Roald Dahl," in Cyclopedia of World Authors, JAI Press, 97; auth, "Postcyberpunk Lost: The Pure Cold Light," in Nova Express, Winter/Spring 98; auth, "The Secret in the Chest: With Tests, Maps, Mysteries, & Intermittent Discussion Questions," in Realms of Fantasy, Oct 98; auth, "Coleridge Meets Carroll, in Mythprint: The Monthly Bulletin of the Mythopoeic Society, Jun 97, auth "Interview with John Kessel," in Science-Fiction Studies, Mar 93; auth, "Hell's My Destination: Imprisonment in the Works of Alfred Bester," in Science-Fiction Studies, Winter 94; auth, "Ambiguous News From the Heartland: John Kessel's Good News from Outer Space," in Extrapolation, Winter 94; auth, "Camouflage in Fantastic Fiction and Film," in Extrapolation, Summer 96; auth, "John Kessel's Screwball SF," in The New York Review of Science Fiction, Oct 97; auth, "Interview with Tim Powers," in Science- Fiction Studies, Spring 98; auth, "Getting a Life: Haunted Spaces in Two Novels of Tim Powers," in The New York Review of Science Fiction, Mar 98; auth, "Private Hells and Radical Doubts: An Interview with Jonathan Lethem," in Science-Fiction Studies, July 98; **CONTACT ADDRESS** Otto G. Richter Library, Univ of Miami, Coral Gables, FL 33124. **EMAIL** fkelleghan@library.miami.edu

KELLER, ARNOLD
DISCIPLINE ENGLISH LITERATURE **EDUCATION** Sir George Williams Univ, BA; Claremont Grad Sch, MA; Univ Concordia, PhD. **CAREER** Assoc prof **HONORS AND AWARDS** Co-developer, Computer Software: DynaMark, Intellimation, 93. **RESEARCH** Writing instruction; computer applications to the teaching of English; Web publishing; intelligent tutoring systems. **SELECTED PUBLICATIONS** Auth, Welcome to Logo: An Introduction for Teachers, Concordia Univ, 85; auth, when Machines Teach: Desinging Competer Courseware, Harper & Row, 87; auth, Curriculums Plural: The Case of Enlgish at the English CEGEPs. McGill J of Educ, 91; auth, English Simplified Exercises, Third Canadian ed, 96; coauth, English Simplified, Candian Edition, Harper & Row, 96; auth, Mordecai richlere, Encyclopedia of the Essay, ed by Tracy Chevalier, Chicago and London: Fizroy Dearborn Pub, 98. **CONTACT ADDRESS** Dept of English, Univ of Victoria, PO Box 3070, Victoria, BC, Canada V8W 3W1. **EMAIL** akeller@uvic.ca

KELLER, DALE
DISCIPLINE COMMUNICATIONS **EDUCATION** AR State Univ, BA, 72; Fuller Theol Sem, Mdiv, 79; Wheaton Col, MA, 85; Univ KS, PhD, 97. **CAREER** Asst prof, 89, Truman State Univ. **HONORS AND AWARDS** Co-adv, Intl Assn Bus Commun. **MEMBERSHIPS** Mem, Assn Bus Commun. **RESEARCH** Evaluating how an e-mail user's choice of lang may impact a reader's perceptions of the sender. **SELECTED PUBLICATIONS** Auth, A rhetorician ponders technology, or why Kenneth Burke never owned a personal computer, Electronic Jour Commun. **CONTACT ADDRESS** Dept of Commun, Truman State Univ, 100 E Normal St, Kirksville, MO 63501-4221. **EMAIL** Dkeller@Truman.edu

KELLER, EVE
DISCIPLINE ENGLISH LITERATURE **EDUCATION** Columbia Univ, PhD. **CAREER** Asst prof, Fordham Univ. **RESEARCH** Discourses of early mod sci, gender and sci. **SELECTED PUBLICATIONS** Auth, In the service of Truth and Victory: Geometry and Rhetoric in the Political Works of Thomas Hobbes, Prose Stud 15, 92; Mrs. Jane Sharp: Midwifery and the Critique of Medical Knowledge in Seventeenth-Century England, Women's Wrtg 2, 95. **CONTACT ADDRESS** Dept of Eng Lang and Lit, Fordham Univ, 113 W 60th St, New York, NY 10023.

KELLER, JILL LENETT
PERSONAL Born 05/11/1965, New York, NY, m, 1990, 2 children **DISCIPLINE** ENGLISH **EDUCATION** Brandeis Univ, BA, 87; Boston Univ, MA, 92. **CAREER** Vis instr, Salem State Col, 92-; adj instr, Middlesex Community Col, 92-. **HONORS AND AWARDS** Phi Beta Kappa. **MEMBERSHIPS** Assoc of Lit Scholars and Critics. **RESEARCH** 19th Century British Literature, Shakespeare. **SELECTED PUBLICATIONS** Rev, of ""Jane Austen's Novels: The Art of Clarity" by Roger Gard, Oxford Univ Pr J, Essays in Criticism, Oct 93. **CONTACT ADDRESS** Dept English, Middlesex Comm Col, 202 Springs Rd, Bedford, MA 01730-1114.

KELLETT, PETE
DISCIPLINE ORGANIZATIONAL COMMUNICATION **EDUCATION** Sheffield City Polytech, Eng, BA, 83; Southern IL Univ, Carbondale, MA, 85, PhD, 90. **CAREER** Asst prof, Univ NC, Greensboro; consult, Piedmont Triad area of NC. **MEMBERSHIPS** Speech Commun Asn; Int Commun Asn. **RESEARCH** Organizational commun; organizational change management. **SELECTED PUBLICATIONS** Author of approximately 20 book chapters, journal articles, and convention papers in organizational commun and related areas. **CONTACT ADDRESS** Communication (I), Univ of No Carolina, Greensboro, 109 James S Fergusen Bldg, Greensboro, NC 27412-5001. **EMAIL** pmkellet@uncg.edu

KELLEY, BEVERLY M.
PERSONAL Born Washington, DC, m, 1998, 3 children **DISCIPLINE** COMMUNICATION **EDUCATION** San Diego State Univ, BA, MA; Univ Calif at Los Angeles, PhD. **CAREER** Dir of Forensics, Calif Lutheran Univ, 77-84, asst prof to full prof, Dept of Commun,77-; TV Host/Producer, ETC TV, 86-87; TV Host/Writer, KADY-TV, 90; columnist, Ventura Co Star and Los Angeles Times, 97-; Radio Host, KCLM FM, 94-99. **HONORS AND AWARDS** Outstanding Woman of Ventura Co; Debate Coach of the Year, 83; Calif Lutheran Univ Prof of the Year, 86-87. **MEMBERSHIPS** Nat Commun Asn. **RESEARCH** Film, persuasion, pedagogy. **SELECTED PUBLICATIONS** Auth, "An Alternative to NDT Debate," Cross Examination Debate Asn J (April 81): 8-14; auth, "Great Ideas for Teaching Speech: Liar's Club and Rank Think Tank," Principles and Types of Speech Communication, 11th ed, ed by Raymond Zeuschner, Scott Foresman/Little Brown Higher Ed, Glenview, Ill (90); auth, "Feminist Perspective on Persuasion," Annual Conference of the Organization of the Study of Communication, Language and Gender, Marquette Univ Press, Milwaukee (91); auth, "Great Ideas for Teaching Speech: Liar's Club, Rank Think Tank, Who's on Tonight, Tonight?," Principles and Types of Speech Communication, 12tgh ed, ed by Raymond Zeuschner, Scott Foresman/Little Brown Higher Education, Glenview, Ill (94); auth, Reelpolitik: Political Ideologies in 30s and 40s Films, Praeger (Dec 98). **CONTACT ADDRESS** Dept Commun Arts, California Lutheran Univ, 60 W Olsen Rd, Thousand Oaks, CA 91360-2700. **EMAIL** kelley@clunet.edu

KELLEY, DELORES G.
PERSONAL Born 05/01/1936, Norfolk, VA, m **DISCIPLINE** ENGLISH **EDUCATION** VA State Coll, BA Philos 1956; New York Univ, MA Educ 1958; Purdue Univ MA Comm (grad tchg fellow) 1972; Univ of MD, PhD, Am Studies 1977. **CAREER** New York City Protestant Council, dir Christian Educ 1958-60; Plainview JHS, tchr of English 1965-66; Morgan State Univ, instr of English 1966-70; Purdue Univ, grad teaching fellow in speech 1971-72; Coppin State Coll, dept chmn lang lit & philos 1976-79, dean of lower div, 79-89, prof, communications, 90-; MD State Delegate (elected from 42nd district), 91-94; MD State Senator, 10th District, 95-. **HONORS AND AWARDS** Gov's apptmt State Com on Values Educ 1980; fellow Amer Council on Educ 1982-83; mem Baltimore Jewish Council Fact-Finding Mission to Israel 1987; Coppin Critical Reading Grant, National Endowment for the Humanities, 1988-89. **MEMBERSHIPS** Mem Alpha Kappa Alpha 1955-; vol host family Baltimore Council Intl Visitors 1976-; Roots Forum project grant MD Com on Humanities & Pub Policy 1977; mem evaluation team Hood Coll MD State Dept of Educ 1978; reviewer & panelist Natl Endowment for the Humanities 1979-80; chairperson adv council Gifted & Talented Educ Baltimore City Sch 1979-; bd mem Harbor Bank of MD 1982-; exec bd Baltimore Urban League; sec MD Dem Party 1986-90; pres, Black/Jewish Forum of Baltimore, 1990-92; chair, Baltimore Chapter, Natl Political Congress of Black Women, 1993-95; MD Commissioner on Criminal Sentencing Policy, 1996-98; bd, Institute Christian Jewish Studies, 1989-; pres-elect, Women Legislators of MD, 1997-98; pres, Women Legislators of MD, 1998-99. **CONTACT ADDRESS** 3100 Timanus Lane, Ste 101, Baltimore, MD 21244. **EMAIL** delores_kelley@senate.state.md.us

KELLEY, MICHAEL ROBERT
PERSONAL Born 08/20/1940, Washington, DC, m, 1994, 1 child **DISCIPLINE** ENGLISH LITERATURE, LINGUISTICS **EDUCATION** Cath Univ Am, BA, 62, MFA, 65, PhD(-English), 70. **CAREER** Asst prof, 70-75, assoc prof, 75-80, prof English, George Mason Univ, 80-, Contrib ed, Mod Humanities Res Asn Bibliog, 75-. **MEMBERSHIPS** MLA; Mediaeval Acad Am. **RESEARCH** Medieval English drama; Chaucer; literary aesthetics. **SELECTED PUBLICATIONS** Auth, Fifteenth Century Flamboyant Style and the Castle of Perseverance, Comp Drama, spring 72; English for Foreign Speakers--a Television Solution, AV instr, 11/72; Flamboyant Drama, Southern Ill Univ, 7; auth, "Antithesis as the Principle of Design in Chaucer's Parlement of Foules," Chaucer Rev 14 (79), 61-73. **CONTACT ADDRESS** George Mason Univ, Fairfax, Mail Stop 1D2, Fairfax, VA 22030-4444. **EMAIL** mkelley@gmu.edu

KELLEY, SAMUEL L.
DISCIPLINE COMMUNICATOIN STUDIES **EDUCATION** Univ Ark, BA, MA; Univ Mich, PhD. **CAREER** Prof. **SELECTED PUBLICATIONS** Auth, pubs on African Americans; films of Spike Lee; human communication. **CONTACT ADDRESS** Dept of Communication, SUNY, Col at Cortland, PO Box 2000, Cortland, NY 13045-0900. **EMAIL** Kelleys@cortland.edu

KELLNER, HANS
PERSONAL Born 05/12/1945, Pittsburgh, PA, m, 1980, 3 children **DISCIPLINE** RHETORIC **EDUCATION** Harvard Univ, AB, 66; Univ Rochester, PhD, 72. **CAREER** Prof, Mich State Univ, 77-91; prof, Univ Tex-Arlington, 91- . **HONORS AND AWARDS** Michigan State University Teacher-Scholar Awd, 80. **SELECTED PUBLICATIONS** Auth, "Language and Historical Representation: Getting the Story Crooked," University of Wisconsin Press, 89; coed, with F.R. Ankersmit, "A New Philosophy of History," and contributor of introductory essay, Reakton Press, London, and University of Chicago Press, Chicago, 95; auth, "Postmodern History and Tocqueville's God," in Festschrift for Jerzy Topolski, Poznan, Poland, 99; auth, "Hans Kellner, in Encounters: Philosophy of History After Postmodernism," ed. Ewa Domanska, Charlottesville: University Press of Virginia, 98; auth, "Never Again is Now," in History and Theory, 33:2, 94, 127-144; auth, "Who Is Reading the World as Text?" in Centennial Review, 38:1, 94, 33-48; auth, "After the Fall: October Reflections on the Histories of Rhetoric," ed. Victor Vitanza, Southern Illinois, Carbondale, 94; auth, "As Real as it Gets: Ricoeur and Historical Narrativity," in Meanings in Texts and Actions: Questioning Paul Ricoeur," ed. David E. Klemm & Will Schweiker, University of Virginia Press, Charlottesville & London, 93; auth, "Na¤ve and Sentimental realism: from advent to event," Storia della storiografia, 22, 92, 117-123; auth, "Beautifying the Nightmare: The Aesthetics of Postmodern History," Strategies: A Journal of Theory, Culture, and Politics, 91. **CONTACT ADDRESS** Dept. of English, Univ of Texas, Arlington, Arlington, TX 76019-0035. **EMAIL** kellner@uta.edu

KELLOGG, DAVID
DISCIPLINE ENGLISH LITERATURE **EDUCATION** UNC Chapel Hill, PhD, 94. **CAREER** Sr Lectr Fel, Duke Univ. **SELECTED PUBLICATIONS** Auth, publ(s) on contemp poetry; poetics; theory of poetic; Perloff's Wittgenstein: W(h)ither Poetic Theory?, Diacritics, 97. **CONTACT ADDRESS** Ctr for Tchg, Lrng, & Writing, Duke Univ, Durham, NC 27708. **EMAIL** kellogg@duke.edu

KELLY, ERNA
DISCIPLINE ENGLISH LITERATURE **EDUCATION** SUNY Albany, PhD. **CAREER** Fac, Univ Calif Los Angeles, 80-82; Univ Wis Eau Claire, 83-. **RESEARCH** Pre-19th Century women writers, poetry; non-fiction prose; drama. **SELECTED PUBLICATIONS** Auth, articles on writing and computers and 17th Century women poets. **CONTACT ADDRESS** Dept of English, Univ of Wisconsin, Eau Claire, Hibbard Hall 421, PO Box 4004, Eau Claire, WI 54702-4004. **EMAIL** ekelly@uwec.edu

KELLY, ERNECE BEVERLY
PERSONAL Born 01/06/1937, Chicago, IL, s **DISCIPLINE** ENGLISH **EDUCATION** University of Chicago, AB, 1958, MA, 1959; Northwestern University, PhD, 1972. **CAREER** University of Wisconsin, assistant professor, 78-81; Kingsborough Community College, associate professor, 84-. **HONORS AND AWARDS** Humanities Council of New York; Speakers in the Humanities, 1992-99; City University of New York, research grant, 1989; Schomburg Center for Research in Black Culture, scholar in residence, 1988; National Endowment on the Humanities, awarded summer seminar, 1978. **MEMBERSHIPS** College Language Association, 1972-; National Council of Teachers of English, director, task force on racism & bias in teaching of English, 1970-80; Conference on College Composition and Communication, executive committee, 1971-74. **SELECTED PUBLICATIONS** Film reviews, Crisis Magazine and New York area newspapers, 1991-; 138 Commonly Used Idioms, student booklet, 1989; Searching for America, National Council of Teachers of English, 1972; Points of Departure, John Wiley & Sons, 1972. **CONTACT ADDRESS** Kingsborough Comm Col, CUNY, 2001 Oriental Blvd, Brooklyn, NY 11235.

KELLY, HENRY ANSGAR
PERSONAL Born 06/06/1934, Fonda, IA, m, 1968, 2 children **DISCIPLINE** ENGLISH **EDUCATION** St. Louis Univ, AB, 59, AM, PhL, 61; Harvard Univ, PhD, 65. **CAREER** Asst prof, 67-69, assoc prof, 69-72, Prof, English Dept, UCLA, 72-, Dir, Center for Medieval and Renaissance Studies, 98-. **HONORS AND AWARDS** Guggenheim fel, 72; NEH fel, 80-81, 96-97. **MEMBERSHIPS** Fel, Medieval Academy of Am. **RESEARCH** Medieval and Renaissance lit and hist. **SELECTED PUBLICATIONS** Auth, The Devil, Demonology, and Witchcraft: The Development of Christian Beliefs in Evil Spirits, Doubleday, 68; Divine Providence in the England of Shakespeare's Histories, Harvard Univ Press, 70; Love and Marriage in the Age of Chaucer, Cornell Univ Press, 75; The Matrimonial Trials of Henry VIII, Stanford Univ Press, 76; Canon Law and the Archpriest of Hita, SUNY, 84; The Devil at Baptism: Ritual, Theology, and Drama, Cornell Univ Press, 85; Chaucer and the Cult of St. Valentine, Davis Medieval Texts and Studies no 5, E. J. Brill, 86; Tragedy and Comedy from Dante to Pseudo-Dante, Univ CA Press, 89; Ideas and Forms of Tragedy from Aristotle to the Middle Ages, Cambridge Univ Studies in Medieval Lit, Cambridge Univ Press, 93; Chaucerian Tragedy, Chaucer Studies no 24, D. S. Brewer, 97. **CONTACT ADDRESS** Dept of English, Univ of California, Los Angeles, Los Angeles, CA 90095. **EMAIL** kelly@humnet.ucla.edu

KELLY, JUSTIN J.
PERSONAL Born 03/19/1937, Cleveland, OH **DISCIPLINE** THEOLOGY AND LITERATURE **EDUCATION** Yale Univ, PhD, 74 **CAREER** Univ Detroit-Mercy, 72-. **HONORS AND AWARDS** Warren Prof, 91. **MEMBERSHIPS** AAR; CTSA; JASNA. **CONTACT ADDRESS** 10600 Fenkell, Detroit, MI 48238. **EMAIL** kellyjj@udmercy.edu

KELLY, R. GORDON
DISCIPLINE AMERICAN LITERATURE **EDUCATION** DePauw Univ, BA, 61; Claremont Grad Sch, MA, 62; Univ IA, PhD, 70. **CAREER** Am Stud Dept, Univ Md **RESEARCH** Lit works as evidence in the serv of cultl analysis. **SELECTED PUBLICATIONS** Auth, Mother Was a Lady: Self and Society in Selected American Children's Periodicals, 1865-1890, Greenwood Press, 74; Literature and the Historian, Amer Quart, 74, reprinted, John Hopkins UP, 98; Edited Children's Periodicals of the United States, Greenwood Press, 84; Children's Literature and Historical Fiction, Handbook of Amer Pop Cult, Greenwood Press, 98; Mystery Fiction and Modern Life, Univ Press Miss, 98. **CONTACT ADDRESS** Am Stud Dept, Univ of Maryland, Col Park, College Park, MD 20742. **EMAIL** rk12@umail.umd.edu

KELLY, REBECCA
DISCIPLINE COMMUNICATION STUDIES **EDUCATION** GA State Univ, MA; PhD. **CAREER** Prof, 81-, Southern Polytech State Univ. **MEMBERSHIPS** Am Med Writers Asn. **SELECTED PUBLICATIONS** Auth, publ(s) on tchg tech; lit; about William Golding; about Anne Tyler. **CONTACT ADDRESS** Hum and Tech Commun Dept, So Polytech State Univ, S Marietta Pkwy, PO Box 1100, Marietta, GA 30060. **EMAIL** rkelly@spsu.edu

KELLY, ROBERT LEROY
PERSONAL Born 02/06/1937, Shelton, NB, m, 1964, 2 children **DISCIPLINE** MEDIEVAL & RENAISSANCE LITERATURE **EDUCATION** St Benedict's Col, AB, 59; Univ Kans, MA, 62; Univ Ore, PhD, 69. **CAREER** Instr English, ID State Univ, 59-61 & Mt Angel Col, 66-68; asst prof, 68-74, assoc prof eng, Univ NC, Greensboro, 74. **MEMBERSHIPS** Mediaeval Acad Am; SAtlantic Mod Lang Asn; Southeastern Medieval Asn. **RESEARCH** Arthurian romance; Shakespeare; Spenser. **SELECTED PUBLICATIONS** Auth, Dactyls and curlews: Satire in A grammarian's funeral, Victorian Poetry, summer 67; Shakespeare's Scroops and the spirit of Cain, Shakespeare Quart, winter 69; Arthur, Galahad and the scriptural pattern in Malory, Am Benedictine Rev, 3/72; Hugh Latimer as Piers Plowman, Studies English Lit, 1500-1900, winter 77; Malory's Tale of Balin reconsidered, Speculum, 1/79; Malory and the Common Law: Hasty Judgement in the Tale of the Death of King Arthur, Medievalia et Humanistica, New Series, (95): 111-140; Patience as a Remedy for War in Malory's Tale of the Death of King Arthur, Studies in Philology, (94):111-135; Wounds Healing and Knighthood in Malorys Tale Lancelot and Guinevere, Studoes in Malory, Medieval Publ, (85): 183-199; auth, "Malory's Argument Against War with France: the Political Geography of France and the Anglo-French Alliance in the Morte Darthur," The Social and Literary Contexts of Malory's Morte Darthur, Arthurian Stud 42, (00): 111-33. **CONTACT ADDRESS** Dept of Eng, Univ of No Carolina, Greensboro, 1000 Spring Garden, Greensboro, NC 27412-0001. **EMAIL** rkelly@attglobal.net

KELLY, S.
PERSONAL Born 05/18/1944, Marlin, TX, m, 1965, 2 children **DISCIPLINE** SPEECH **EDUCATION** Baylor Univ, BA, 65; MA, 66; EdD, 97. **CAREER** Fac, McLennan Community Col. **HONORS AND AWARDS** Alpha Chi; Minnie Stevens Piper Prof, 90. **MEMBERSHIPS** Speech Commun Assoc; Tex Speech Commun Assoc. **RESEARCH** Interpersonal communication, business speech, gifted adult education. **SELECTED PUBLICATIONS** Auth, Study Guide and Activity Manual to Accompany DeVitos Messages, 1992-2000, Longman Pub,

York. **CONTACT ADDRESS** Dept Speech Commun, McLennan Comm Col, 1400 College Dr, Waco, TX 76708. **EMAIL** msk@mcc.cc.tx.us

KELLY, WILLIAM
PERSONAL Born 12/01/1953, Fall River, MA, m, 1975, 2 children **DISCIPLINE** ENGLISH **EDUCATION** Rhode Island Col, MA, 79; Univ RI, PhD, 87. **CAREER** Teacher, Fall River Public Schs, 75-84; from instr to prof, Bristol Community Col, 84-. **HONORS AND AWARDS** Case Carnegie Prof of the Year, 97. **MEMBERSHIPS** NCTE, MTA, NEA. **RESEARCH** Composition, Basic Writing. **SELECTED PUBLICATIONS** Auth, Models in Process: A Rhetoric and Reader, Macmillan, 88; auth, Beginnings: A Rhetoric and Handbook, Macmillan, 92; auth, Strategy & Structure: Short Readings for Composition, Allyn & Bacon, 96 & 99; coauth, Discovery: An Introduction to Writing, Allyn & Bacon, 97 & 00; coauth, Odyssey: A Guide to Better Writing, Allyn & Bacon, 98 & 00. **CONTACT ADDRESS** Dept Humanities & Fine Arts, Bristol Comm Col, 777 Elsbree St, Fall River, MA 02720-7307. **EMAIL** wkelly@bristol.mass.edu

KELVIN, NORMAN
PERSONAL Born 08/27/1924, New York, NY, m, 1956, 2 children **DISCIPLINE** ENGLISH LITERATURE **EDUCATION** Columbia Univ, AB, 48, MA, 50, PhD, 60. **CAREER** From Instr to Distinguished Prof English, City Col New York, 60-; from Prof to Distinguished Prof English, Grad Ctr, City Univ of New York, 84-. **HONORS AND AWARDS** Nat Endowment for Humanities sr fel, 67-68; Guggenheim fel, 74-75. **MEMBERSHIPS** MLA **RESEARCH** Nineteenth and 20th century British literature; letters of William Morris. **SELECTED PUBLICATIONS** Auth, A Troubled Eden: Nature and Society in the Works of George Meredith, Stanford Univ, 61; E M Forster, Southern Ill Univ, 67; The Collected Letters of William Morris, 4 vols, Princeton Univ Press, 84-96. **CONTACT ADDRESS** Dept of English, City Col, CUNY, 160 Convent Ave, New York, NY 10031-9198.

KEMMERER, KATHLEEN
PERSONAL Born 05/19/1952, PA, m, 1975, 4 children **DISCIPLINE** ENGLISH **EDUCATION** Fordham Univ, PhD, 93; Univ Scranton, MA, 88; Col Misericodia, 74. **CAREER** Asst Prof of English, Pa State, 98-; Lecturer, Pa State, 95-98; Adjunct Faculty, 93-95; Vis Asst Prof, Wilkes Univ, 90-92. **HONORS AND AWARDS** Royer Ctr Star Awd,99; Penn State Research & Development Grant, 99-00; Empower II, 98. **RESEARCH** Samuel Johnson, 18th Century Periodicals. **SELECTED PUBLICATIONS** Auth, "A neutral being between the Sexes: Samuel Johnson's Sexual Politics," Bucknell Press, Lewisburg, PA, 98. **CONTACT ADDRESS** Dept Liberal Arts, Pennsylvania State Univ, Hazleton, Hazleton, PA 18201-1202.

KEMP, FRED O.
DISCIPLINE RHETORIC AND COMPOSITION **EDUCATION** Univ TX, Austin, PhD, 88. **CAREER** Dir, Comput Writing Res Lab, Univ TX, Austin; assoc prof, dir, Compos and Rhet, TX Tech Univ; pres, The Daedalus Gp, Inc. **HONORS AND AWARDS** EDUCOM/NCRIPTAL award, 90; founder, the daedalus gp, inc, comput writing res lab, univ tx, austin. **MEMBERSHIPS** Co-dir, Alliance for Comput and Writing; NCTE Instr Technol Comt; CCCC Comput in Compos Comt. **SELECTED PUBLICATIONS** Writen about computer-based writing pedag(s); coauth of Daedalus Integrated Writing Environment (software). **CONTACT ADDRESS** Texas Tech Univ, Lubbock, TX 79409-5015. **EMAIL** F.Kemp@ttu.edu

KEMP, HENRIETTA J.
DISCIPLINE GERMAN, HISTORY, LIBRARY SCIENCE **EDUCATION** Univ Iowa, BA, 66; Univ Pittsburgh, MLS, 71. **CAREER** LIBR, 81-, SUPERV, FINE ARTS COLLECT, 89-, LUTHER COL. **CONTACT ADDRESS** Library, Luther Col, 700 College Dr, Decorah, IA 52101. **EMAIL** kempjane@luther.edu

KEMP, THERESA D.
DISCIPLINE LATE-MEDIEVAL AND EARLY MODERN BRITISH LITERATURE **EDUCATION** IN Univ, PhD, 94. **CAREER** Dept Eng, Univ Ala **HONORS AND AWARDS** Co-exec ed, Feminist Teacher; Prog Dir, UAB in Scotland. **SELECTED PUBLICATIONS** Articles: The Bloomsbury Guide Women's Lit, Shakespeare Quart, Sixteenth Century Studies, Renaissance Quart. **CONTACT ADDRESS** Univ of Alabama, Birmingham, 1400 University Blvd, Birmingham, AL 35294-1150.

KENDALL, CALVIN B.
PERSONAL Born 02/13/1935, Bronxville, NY, m, 1959, 2 children **DISCIPLINE** ENGLISH **EDUCATION** Bowdoin Col, BA, 56; Univ Calif, Berkeley, MA, 61, PhD(English), 66. **CAREER** Asst prof, 67-71, assoc prof, 71-82, prof English, Univ Minn, Minneapolis, 82-. **HONORS AND AWARDS** Horace T. Morse-Minnesota Alumni Assoc Awd for Outstanding Contributions to Undergraduate Education; Univ of Minnesota Acad of Distinguished Teachers. **MEMBERSHIPS** MLA, ISAS, ICMA, ALSC. **RESEARCH** Bede; Beowulf; medieval Latin poetics and rhetoric; Old English metrics; Romanesque verse inscriptions. **SELECTED PUBLICATIONS** Ed, Beda Venerabilis, De Arte Metrica et De Schematibus et Tropis, in Corpus Christianorum 123A, Turnout, 75; auth, Bede's Historia Ecclesiastica: The Rhetoric of Faith, in Medieval Eloquence: Studies in the Theory and Practice of Medieval Rhetoric, Berkeley and Los Angelos, 78; Imitation and the Venerable Bede's Historia Ecclesiastica, in Saints, Scholars, and Heroes, Collegeville, Mn, vol 1, 79; The Prefix un-- and the Metrical Grammar of Beowulf: in Anglo-Saxon England 10 (39-52), 82; The Metrical Grammar of Beowulf: Displacement, in Speculum 58, 83; Let us Now Praise a Famous City: Wordplay in the OE Durham and the Cult of St. Cuthbert, in Journal of English and Germanic Philology 87, 88; Dry Bones in a Cathedral: The Story of the Theft of Bede's Relics and the Translation of Cuthbert into the Cathedral of Durham in 1104, in Medievalia 10, 88; The Voice in the Stone: The Verse Inscriptions of Ste.-Foy of Conques and the Date of the Tympanum, in Hermeneutics and Medieval Culture, Albany, 89; Bede's Art of Poetry and Rhetoric: The Latin Text with an English Translation, Introduction, and Notes, Saarbrucken, 91; The Metrical Grammar of Beowulf, Cambridge, 91; ed, with Peter Wells, Voyage to the Other World: The Legacy of Sutton Hoo, Minneapolis, 92. Auth, The Gate of Heaven and the Fountain of Life: Speech-Act Theory and portal Inscriptions, in Essays in Medieval Studies 10, 93; The Plan of St. Gall: An Argument for a 320-Foot Church Prototype, In Medieval Studies 56, 94; Literacy and Orality in Anglo-Saxon Poetry: Horizontal Displacement in Andreas, in Journal of English and Germanic Philology 95, 96; The Verse Inscriptions of the Tympanum of Jaca and the PAX Anagram, Mediaevalia 19, 96; The Allegory of the Church: Romanesque Portals and Their Verse Inscriptions, Toronto, 98. **CONTACT ADDRESS** Dept of English, Univ of Minnesota, Twin Cities, 207 Church St S E, Minneapolis, MN 55455-0156. **EMAIL** kenda001@tc.umn.edu

KENDALL, KATHLEEN E.
PERSONAL Born Madison, WI **DISCIPLINE** COMMUNICATION **EDUCATION** Oberlin Col, BA, 58; Univ of Southern Miss, MA, 60; Ind Univ, PhD, 66. **CAREER** Instr, Allegheny Col, 60-62; assoc prof, SUNY Albany, 64-. **HONORS AND AWARDS** Grant, SUNY, Albany, 67, 70, 79, 83-84, 87-88, 94-95; Fac Develop Grant, C-SPAN, 91; Grant, Purdue Univ, 92; Goldsmith Res Awd, Harvard, 94; Res Fel, Shorenstein Center, Harvard Univ, 97. **MEMBERSHIPS** Nat Commun Assoc; Int Commun Assoc; Eastern Commun Assoc; Central States Commun Assoc; NY State Commun Assoc; Am Polit Sci Assoc. **RESEARCH** Communication in the presidential primaries, political campaign communication, debates, speeches and advertising of political candidates, media coverage of political campaigns. **SELECTED PUBLICATIONS** Coauth, "Sources of Political Information in a Presidential Primary Campaign", Journ Quarterly, (99): 148-151; auth, "Application of Communication Research to Political Contexts", Appl Commun Theory and Res, ed Dan O'Hair and Gary L Krebs, Lawrence Erlbaum Assoc, (90): 225-243; coauth, "Communication in the First Primaries: The Voice of the People in 1912", Pres Studies Quarterly 22 (92): 15-29; auth, "Public Speaking in the Presidential Primaries Through Media Eyes", Am Behav Sci 37, (93); 240-251; coauth, "Sex Differences in Political Communication During Presidential Campaigns", Commun Quarterly 43, (95): 131-141; ed, Presidential Campaign Discourse: Strategic Communication Problems, SUNY Pr, 95; coauth, "Political Images and Voting Decisions", Candidate Images in Presidential Elections, ed Kenneth L Hacker, Praeger, (NY, 95): 19-35; coauth, "Lyndon Johnson and the Problem of Politics: A Study in Conversation", The Future of the Rhetorical Presidency, ed Martin Medhurst, Tex A&M Univ Pr, (College Station, 96): 77-103; auth, "Presidential Debates Through Media Eyes", Am Behav Sci 40, (97): 1193-1207; auth, Communication in the Presidential Primaries: Candidates and the Media, 1912-200, Praeger, (Westport, CT), 00. **CONTACT ADDRESS** Dept Commun, SUNY Albany, 1400 Washington Univ, Albany, NY 12222-0100. **EMAIL** kk724@cnsvax.albany.edu

KENDRICK, CHRISTOPHER
DISCIPLINE ENGLISH **EDUCATION** Univ Ill at Urbana, BA, 75; Yale Univ, PhD, 81. **CAREER** Assoc prof. **RESEARCH** Milton; 16th and 17th-century British literature; Marxism and theory. **SELECTED PUBLICATIONS** Auth, Preaching Common Grounds: Winstanley and the Diggers as Concrete Utopians, in Writing and the English Renaissance, Longman, 96; Agons of the Manor: Symbolic Responses to the Agrarian Crisis in mid-Seventeenth-Century England,in The Production of Renaissance Culture, Cornell UP, 94. **CONTACT ADDRESS** Dept of English, Loyola Univ, Chicago, 6525 N Sheridan Rd, Chicago, IL 60626. **EMAIL** ckendri@wpo.it.luc.edu

KENDRICK, WALTER
DISCIPLINE VICTORIAN LITERATURE **EDUCATION** Yale Univ, PhD. **CAREER** Prof, Fordham Univ. **RESEARCH** Popular cult, pornography and censorship. **SELECTED PUBLICATIONS** Auth, The Thrill of Fear: 250 Years of Scary Entertainment, Grove Press, 91; Return to Sender: The Myth of the Death of the Letter, Village Voice Lit Supplement, 94. **CONTACT ADDRESS** Dept of Eng Lang and Lit, Fordham Univ, 113 W 60th St, New York, NY 10023.

KENNAN, WILLIAM R., JR.
DISCIPLINE ENGLISH **EDUCATION** Dartmouth, BA, 67; Harvard Univ, PhD, 72. **CAREER** Prof. **RESEARCH** Humor; comedy; Joyce; Shakespeare; Milton; 18th century; Kingsley Amis. **SELECTED PUBLICATIONS** Auth, Jocoserious Joyce: The Fate of Folly in Ulysses; Bertrand Russell and the Eliots; Metamorphoses of Spritual Autobiography; Blushing Like the Morn: Milton's Human Comedy in Paradise Lost; James Boswell's Notes Toward a Supreme Fiction; David Hume's Fables of Identity; Dryden's Aeneid as English Augustan Epic; Sterne's Etristramolgy; Rousseau: Prophet of Sincerity. **CONTACT ADDRESS** Dept of English, Williams Col, Oakley Center, Williamstown, MA 01267. **EMAIL** rbell@williams.edu

KENNEDY, CHRISTOPHER
DISCIPLINE ENGLISH LITERATURE **EDUCATION** Duke Univ, PhD, 79. **CAREER** Asst VP. **SELECTED PUBLICATIONS** Auth, articles on Old and Middle English lit; acad support spec admis students; intercollegiate athletics. **CONTACT ADDRESS** Eng Dept, Duke Univ, Durham, NC 27706.

KENNEDY, GEORGE A.
PERSONAL Born 11/26/1928, Hartford, CT, m, 1955, 1 child **DISCIPLINE** CLASSICS **EDUCATION** Princeton Univ, AB, 50; Harvard Univ, AM, 52, PhD, 54. **CAREER** Kennedy Traveling Fel, 54-55, instr and tutor of Classics, Hist, & Lit, 55-58, visiting asst prof, Harvard Univ, 59; asst prof of Greek, 58-59, asst prof of Classics, 59-63, assoc prof of Classics, 63-65, chemn, Haverford Col; prof of Classics & chemn, Dept of Classics, Univ of Pittsburgh, 65-66; prof of Classics, 66-72, dir, Am Office of L'Annee Philologique, 68-74, Paddison Prof of Classics, 72-95, chemn, Dept of Classics, 66-76, chemn, Dept of Linguistics, 75-76, chemn, Curriculum of Comparative Lit, 89-93, chemn of Univ fac, 85-88, Univ of NC at Chapel Hill; auth, Classical Rhetoric & Its Christian and Secular Tradition, Univ of NC Press, 99. **HONORS AND AWARDS** Fulbright fel, 64-65; Guggenheim fel, 64-65; Charles J. Goodwin Awd, Am Philological Asn; Distinguished Scholar Awd, Nat Commun Asn; Thomas Jefferson Awd, UNC-CH; Phi Beta Kappa, 50; member, National Humanities Council, 80-87, vice chemn, Board of Governors, Univ of NC Press, 73-88. **MEMBERSHIPS** Am Acad of Arts & Sci; Am Philosophical Soc; Am Philological Asn, 79-80; Int Soc for the Hist of Rhetoric, 79-80; National Humanities Council, 80-87, vice chemn, 83-85; chemn, Board of Governors, Univ of NC Press, 73-88 **SELECTED PUBLICATIONS** Auth, The Art of Persusion in Greece, Princeton Univ Press, 63; auth, Quintilian, Twayne Pubs, 69; auth, The Art of Rhetoric in the Roman World, Princeton Univ Press, 72; auth, Greek Rhetoric Under Christian Emperors, Princeton Univ Press, 83; auth, New Testament Interpretation through Rhetorical Criticism, Univ of NC Press, 84; auth, Aristotle, On Rhetoric: A Theory of Civic Discourse, Newly Translated with Introduction, Notes, and Appendices, Oxford Univ Press, 91; auth, A New History of Classical Rhetoric, Princeton Univ Press, 94; auth, Comparative Rhetoric: An Historical and Cross-Cultural Introduction, Oxford Univ Press, 98. **CONTACT ADDRESS** PO Box 271880, Fort Collins, CO 80527-1880.

KENNEDY, GEORGE E.
DISCIPLINE LITERATURE **EDUCATION** NYork Univ, PhD. **CAREER** Assoc prof & vice ch, Washington State Univ. **RESEARCH** Teaches technical writing, courses in the theory and methods of technical and professional communication. **SELECTED PUBLICATIONS** Coauth, Solving Problems Through Technical and Professional Writing, 93 & Correcting Common Errors in Writing, 96. **CONTACT ADDRESS** Dept of English, Washington State Univ, 1 SE Stadium Way, PO Box 645020, Pullman, WA 99164-5020. **EMAIL** gkennedy@mail.wsu.edu

KENNEDY, J. GERALD
PERSONAL Born 04/26/1947, Erie, PA, m, 1983, 2 children **DISCIPLINE** ENGLISH **EDUCATION** Grove City Col, BA, 69; Duke Univ, MA, 70; PhD, 73. **CAREER** Asst Prof, La State Univ, 73-78; Fulbright Lecturer, France, 78-79; Assoc Prof to Prof, La State Univ, 79-. **HONORS AND AWARDS** Phi Beta Kappa, Duke Univ, 73; Distinguished Fac Awd, LSU foundation, 93; Distinguished Res Master, LSU, 99. **MEMBERSHIPS** Mod Lang Asn, Poe Studies Asn, Hemingway Foundation and Soc, F Scott Fitzgerald Soc. **RESEARCH** American literature, 1815-1860; 20th Century American literature; The short story; Poe; Hemingway; Literary modernism; Expatriate writing; Story sequence; Literacy nationalism; Postmodern fiction; 1930 periodicals. **SELECTED PUBLICATIONS** Auth, French connections: Hemingway and Fitzgerald Abroad, St martins, 98; ed, Modern American Short Story Sequences, Cambridge, 95; auth, Imagining Paris: Exile Writing and American Identity, Yale, 93; auth, Poe, Death and the Life of Writing, Yale, 87; auth, The Narrative of Arthur Gordon and the abyss of Interpretation, Twayne, 95; auth, The Astonished Traveler: William Darby, Frontier Geographer and Man of Letters, LSU, 81. **CONTACT ADDRESS** Dept English, La State Univ, Baton Rouge, LA 70803-0104. **EMAIL** jgkenn@lsu.edu

KENNEDY, WILLIAM JOHN
PERSONAL Born 04/26/1942, Brooklyn, NY, m, 1967, 2 children **DISCIPLINE** RENAISSANCE & COMPARATIVE LITERATURE **EDUCATION** Manhattan Col, BA, 63; Yale Univ, PhD(comp lit), 69. **CAREER** Instr Eng, Fairleigh Dickinson Univ, 67-70; asst prof comp lit, 70-76, assoc prof, 76-82, Prof comp lit, Cornell Univ, 82-, Vis assoc prof comp lit, NY Univ, 82. **HONORS AND AWARDS** MLA Howard R. Marraro Prize, 83; Guggenheim fel 87-88; Villa Serbelloni, 98. **MEMBERSHIPS** MLA; Am Comp Lit Asn; Renaissance Soc Am. **RESEARCH** Lit theory; rhetorical criticism; lyric poetry. **SELECTED PUBLICATIONS** Auth, Rhetorical Norms in Renaissance Literature, Yale Univ Press, 78; Jacopo Sannazaro and the Uses of Pastoral, Univ New England Press, 83; Authorizing Petrarch, Cornell Univ Press, 94. **CONTACT ADDRESS** Comp Lit Dept, Cornell Univ, Ithaca, NY 14850. **EMAIL** WJK3@cornell.edu

KENNELLY, LAURA B.
PERSONAL Born Denton, TX, m, 1996, 5 children **DISCIPLINE** ENGLISH **EDUCATION** Univ N Texas, PhD, 75. **CAREER** Adj prof, Eng, Univ N Texas; current, asst editor, BACH: Journal of the Riemen Schneider Bach Institute, Baldwin-Wallace College. **HONORS AND AWARDS** Peterson Fellow; Am Antiquarian Soc; SCMLA Research Grant; AHA Kraus Awd. **MEMBERSHIPS** Am Antiquarian Soc. **RESEARCH** 18th Century Am Culture. **CONTACT ADDRESS** PO Box 626, Berea, OH 44017. **EMAIL** lkennelly@aol.com

KENT, CAROL FLEISHER
PERSONAL m, 1982 **DISCIPLINE** ENGLISH LITERATURE **EDUCATION** Univ NYork, MA; Bread Loaf Sch English, MA; Brown Univ, PhD; Univ of Fla, BA. **CAREER** Eng Dept, Georgetown Univ **RESEARCH** Modern literature and film. **SELECTED PUBLICATIONS** Auth, pubs on O'Connor and Hitchcock. **CONTACT ADDRESS** English Dept, Georgetown Univ, 37th and O St, Washington, DC 20057. **EMAIL** kentc@georgetown.edu

KERBY-FULTON, KATHRYN
DISCIPLINE MIDDLE ENGLISH LITERATURE **EDUCATION** Univ York, BA, Bed; York, Eng, PhD. **CAREER** Prof **RESEARCH** Medieval Latin religious writings; medieval women's literature. **SELECTED PUBLICATIONS** Auth, Reformist Apocalypticism and Piers Plowman, Cambridge UP, 90; Written Work: Langland, Labour and Authorship, U of Pennsylvania P; 97; Iconography and the Professional Reader: The Politics of Book Production in the Donce Piers Plowman, U of Minnesota P, 98. **CONTACT ADDRESS** Dept of English, Univ of Victoria, Clearihue Bldg, PO Box 3070, Victoria, BC, Canada V8W 3W1. **EMAIL** kerbyful@uvvm.uvic.ca

KERN-FOXWORTH, MARILYN L.
PERSONAL Born 03/04/1954, Kosciusko, MS, m, 1982 **DISCIPLINE** SPEECH **EDUCATION** Jackson State Univ, BS Speech 1974; FL State Univ, MS Mass Communications 1976; Univ of Wis-Madison, PhD Mass Communications 1982. **CAREER** FL State Univ, comm specialist 1974-76; General Telephone, personnel rep 1976-78; Univ of TN, asst prof 1980-87; Texas A&M Univ, assoc prof, 87-. **HONORS AND AWARDS** Valedictorian of graduate class 1974; Readers Digest travel grant 1979; 1st prize Alan Bussel Rsch Competition 1980; Leadership Awd Assn of Black Comm 1980; Kizzy Awd Black Women Hall of Fame Found 1981; PR Fellow Aloca Professional 1981; Amon Carter Evans Awd Scholar 1983; Women of Achievement Univ of TN 1983; Unity Awds in Media 2nd Place Lincoln Univ 1984. **MEMBERSHIPS** Exec comm Assn for Educ in Journalism 1980-; mem Natl Council of Negro Women 1980-; mem Assn of Black Communicators 1980-; mem Natl Comm Assn 1982-; mem Intl Platform Assn 1982-; advisor Campus Practitioners 1982; mem Public Relations Soc of Amer 1982-; consultant/assoc editor Nashville Banner 1983; minister of educ Mt Calvary Baptist Church 1983; staff mem Graduate Teaching Seminary 1983-; adviser Public Relations Student Soc of Amer 1983-; mem Natl Fed of Press Women 1983-; mem Natl Assn of Media Women 1983-; mem Natl Fed of Exec Women 1983-; advisory comm Phillis Wheatley YWCA 1983-; mem Black Media Assn; Black Faculty & Staff Assn newsletter editor; regional corres Still Here. **SELECTED PUBLICATIONS** "Helping Minorities, Student Organizations Can Fill Gaps in Minority Programs" Journalism Editor 1982, "Advertising More Than a Black Face" Black Journalism Review 1981, "A Challenge to Your Future GTE Automatic Electric" 1977, "All Minority Grads-Opportunity Is Knocking" 1982; 1st & only black in the nation to receive a PhD in Mass communications with a concentration in advertising & public relations; Speciaward Recognition of Excellence PRSA Chap Knoxville TN 1985; author Alex Haley's bio for Dictionary of Literary Biography, Afro-American Writers After 1955 published 1985; PRSA, advisor of the year 1985; Poynter Institute Fellow, 1988; Amer Press Institute Fellow, 1988; Pathfinder Award, Public Relation Institute, 1988; Agnes Harris AAUW Postdoctoral Fellow, 1991-92. **CONTACT ADDRESS** Texas A&M Univ, Col Station, 230 Reed McDonald Building, College Station, TX 77843-4111.

KERNER, HOWARD A.
DISCIPLINE ENGLISH **EDUCATION** SUNY at Albany, BA, 71; MA, 72. **CAREER** Prof, Jefferson Comm Col, 80-89; prof, Syracuse Univ, 85-87; prof, Polk Comm Col, 90-; prof, Nova SE Univ, 95-. **HONORS AND AWARDS** Who's Who among Teach of Am; NISOD Teach Awd. **RESEARCH** World literature; theater; holocaust. **SELECTED PUBLICATIONS** Auth, Biographical Critique on "Ray Bradbury," in Magill's Encyc Sci Fic and Fantasy Lit, Salem Press (Pasadena, CA), 96; auth, Biographical Critique on "Eugene O'Neil," in Identities and Issues in Lit, Salem Press (Pasadena, CA), 97; auth, Biographical Critique on "Anne Frank," in Encyc World Authors, Salem Press (Pasadena, CA), 97; auth, Biographical Critique on "Edward Lewis Walant," Salem Press (Pasadena, CA), 00. **CONTACT ADDRESS** Dept English, Polk Comm Col, 999Ave H Northeast, Winter Haven, FL 33881-4256. **EMAIL** hakerner@gte.net

KERSHNER, R. BRANDON
PERSONAL Born 11/17/1944, Cumberland, MD, d, 3 children **DISCIPLINE** ENGLISH AND COMPARATIVE LITERATURE **EDUCATION** Johns Hopkins Univ, BA, 66; MA, 66; Stanford Univ, MA, 68; PhD, 72. **CAREER** Grad tchg asst, Stanford Univ, 68-69; asst prof, 71-76; vis prof, Univ Utrecht, 78; vis prof, Univ Col Dublin, 84; vis prof, Univ Utrecht, 94; ch, SAMLA, 90; assoc prof, 76-90; prof, 90-. **HONORS AND AWARDS** Danforth fel, 66-72; Woodrow Wilson fel, 66; Amer Conf on Irish Stud award, 90; res grant, 93; Alumni Prof of English, 99. **MEMBERSHIPS** MLA; Intl James Joyce Found; Amer Conf Irish Stud. **RESEARCH** James Joyce. **SELECTED PUBLICATIONS** Auth, Dylan Thomas: The Poet and His Critics Chicago: Amer Lib Assn, 77; Joyce, Bakhtin and Popular Literature: Chronicles of Disorder, Univ NC Press, 89; ed, James Joyce, A Portrait of the Artist as a Young Man, St. Martin's Press, 92; The Twentieth-Century Novel: An Introduction, St Martin's Press, 97; ed, Joyce and Popular Culture, 96. **CONTACT ADDRESS** Dept of Eng, Univ of Florida, 226 Tigert Hall, Gainesville, FL 32611. **EMAIL** kershner@ufl.edu

KESHISHIAN, FLORA
PERSONAL Born 07/23/1954, Tehran, Iran **DISCIPLINE** COMMUNICATION **EDUCATION** NYork Univ, PhD, 95. **CAREER** Adj Asst Prof, 91-, NYU & Queens Coll, Asst Prof, 97-, Montclair State Univ; Visting Asst Prof, Queens Col, 00. **HONORS AND AWARDS** Reviewer, Critical Studies in Mass Communication. **MEMBERSHIPS** ICA, NCA, ECA, NYSCA. **RESEARCH** Culture & communication technology, language & culture, orality, politico-economic systems & culture. **SELECTED PUBLICATIONS** Auth, A Media Perspective: A Second point of view-A review of No Sense of Place, in: Communication Quartelry, 86; auth, Political Bias and Nonpolitical News, A Content Analysis of an Armenian and Iranian Earthquake in the New York Times and the Washington Post, in: Critical Studies in Mass Communication, 97; auth, Communication, and the U.S. Mass Media: The Experience of an Iranian Immigrant, in : The How and Journal of Communications, 00. **CONTACT ADDRESS** 167-09 65th Ave, Flushing, NY 11365. **EMAIL** fk6@is3.nyu.eud

KESSLER, CAROL
PERSONAL Born 05/09/1936, Grave City, PA, d, 2 children **DISCIPLINE** ENGLISH, LITERATURE **EDUCATION** Swarthmore Col, BA, 58; Harvard Grad Sch Educ, MA, 59; Univ Pa, PhD, 77. **CAREER** Prof, Pa State Univ Del Co; Coord of campus English Fac, 89-90, 99-; Coord of campus Women's Studies minor, 99-. **HONORS AND AWARDS** Residential Fel for Col Teachers, Univ of Md, 81-82; Summer Stipend, 87; Fel for Col Teachers and Independent Scholars, NEH, 88-89; Fulbright Sr Scholar in Am Studies, Presov, Slovakia, 95-96. **MEMBERSHIPS** MLA, Am Lit Asn, Soc for Utopian Studies, Soc for the Study of Multi-Ethnic Lit of the US, Soc for Study of Am Women Writers. **RESEARCH** 19th century New England women writers, late 20th century multi-ethnic US writers, literary study as consciousness-raising. **SELECTED PUBLICATIONS** Auth, Elizabeth Stuart Phelps, Twayne's United States Authors Series #434, G.K. Hall (Boston), 82; auth, The Story of Avis (1877) by Elizabeth Stuart Phelps(Ward). Introduced and Edited, Rutgers Univ Press (New Brunswick), 85, 88, 92, 95, NetLibrary.com, 99; auth, Charlotte Perkins Gilman: Her Progress Toward Utopia, with Selected Writings, Utopianism and Communitarianism Series, Univ of Syracuse Press (Syracuse), 95, Liverpool Science Fiction Texts Series, Liverpool Univ Press, 95; ed, Daring to Dream: Utopian Stories by United States Women, 1836-1919, Pandora Press/ Routledge & Kegan Paul (London), 84; compiler and ed, Daring to Dream: Utopian Stories by United States Women before 1950, Utopianism and Communitarianism Series, Univ of Syracuse Press (Syracuse), and HarperCollins (London), 95; auth, article in American National Biography, ed. J.A. Garrity, and M.C. Carnes (NY: Oxford Univ Press, 99), 428-430; auth, article in Women's Studies Encyclopedia, ed. H. Tierney (Westport, CT: Greenwood Press, 90 and Greenwood Electronic Media CD-ROM, 99); auth, article in The Cambridge Guide to Women's Writing in English, ed. L. Sage (Cambridge, England: Cambridge Univ Press, 99); auth, article in Dictionary of Literay Utopias, ed. V. Fortunati and R. Trousson (Paris: Champion-Sslatkine, 00); auth, article in The Mixed Legacy of Charlotte Perkins Gilman, ed. C.F. Golden and J.S. Zangrando (Newark: Univ of Del Press, 00). **CONTACT ADDRESS** Dept English, Pennsylvania State Univ, Delaware County, 25 Yearsley Mill Rd, Media, PA 19063-5522. **EMAIL** cfk1@psu.edu

KESSLER, JASCHA FREDERICK
PERSONAL Born 11/27/1929, New York, NY, m, 1950, 3 children **DISCIPLINE** ENGLISH **EDUCATION** NY Univ, BA, 50; Univ Mich, MA, 51; PhD, 54. **CAREER** Teaching Asst, Univ Mich, 51-54; Asst Prof, NY Univ, 54-55; Asst Prof, Hunter Col, 55-56; Asst Prof, Hamilton Col, 57-61; Prof to Prof Emeritus, UCLA, 61-92. **HONORS AND AWARDS** D.H. Lawrence Fel, 61; Fulbright Res Scholar, 63-64; Fel, Univ Calif, 63-64; Fulbright Sen Scholar, 70; Rockefeller Found Fel, 72; Fel, Playwrighting Am Place Theater, 67; Fel, Inst for Creative Arts, 74; Fel, NEH, 74; Regents Fel, Univ Calif, 77; Fel, Calif Arts Coun, 93-94; Major Hopwood Awd, 52; George Soros Found Awd, 89; Corvina Press Translation Prize; Shirley Collier Prize, 86; Artisjus Awd, 80; Hungarian PEN Club Memorial Medal; Translation Awd, 78; Grant, Finish Translation Centre, 01. **MEMBERSHIPS** ASCAP; Asn of Literary Scholars and Critics; PEN Center USA W. **RESEARCH** Writing Fiction; Poetry; Drama; Essay. **SELECTED PUBLICATIONS** Aut? Siren Songs & Classical Illusions: 50 Stories, McPherson & Co, 92; auth, The Face of Creation: 23 Contemporary Hungarian Poets, Coffee House Press, 93; auth, King Oedipus, a new translation, Univ Pa Press, 00; auth, Collected Poems, Xlibris Co, 00; auth, An Egyptian Bondage and Other Stories, Xlibris Co, 00; auth, Rapid Transit; 1948, Xlibris Co, 00; auth, Christmas Carols & Other Plays, Xlibris Co, 00; auth, Tataga's Children: Fairy Tales, Xlibris Co, 00; auth, Our Bearings at Sea: A Novel in Poems, Xlibris Co, 01; auth, Traveling Light: Selected Poems of Kirsti Simonsuuri, Xlibris Co, 01. **CONTACT ADDRESS** Dept English, Univ of California, 218 16th St, Santa Monica, CA 90402-2216. **EMAIL** jkessler@ucla.edu

KESSLER, ROD
PERSONAL Born 09/15/1949, Brooklyn, NY, m, 1990, 1 child **DISCIPLINE** ENGLISH **EDUCATION** Harvard, AB, 71; Univ Mass - Amherst, MS, 77; Univ Arizona, MFA, 81. **CAREER** Instr, 78, Greenfield Comm Col; writer in res, 82, Phillips Exeter Acad; prof, 83-00, Salem St Col. **CONTACT ADDRESS** English Dept, Salem State Col, 352 Lafayette St, Salem, MA 01970-5353. **EMAIL** rkessler@salemstate.edu

KESTERSON, DAVID B.
PERSONAL Born 02/19/1938, Springfield, MO, m, 1987, 2 children **DISCIPLINE** ENGLISH **EDUCATION** Southwest Mo State Univ, BSE, 59; Univ Ark, MA, 61; PhD, 65. **CAREER** Instr to Asst prof, NC State Univ, 64-68; Asst Prof to Prof and Vice Pres, Univ N Tex, 68-. **HONORS AND AWARDS** Phi Kappa Phi, 90; Distinguished Grad Alumnus Awd, Univ Ark, 88; House of Seven Gables Hawthorne Awd, Mass, 87; Sen Fulbright Lecturer, Germany, 85; Mortarborad Outstanding Prof, 80-81. **MEMBERSHIPS** Nathaniel Hawthorne Soc, Fulbright Asn, Mod Lang Asn of Am, S Central Mod Lang Asn, Melville Soc, Thoreau Soc, Mark Twain Circle of Am, Thomas Wolfe Soc, Poe Studies Asn. **RESEARCH** 19th Century American literature: Hawthorne, Melville, the transcendentalists, Mark Twain, Henry James; American novel; American humor; Southern literature. **SELECTED PUBLICATIONS** Auth, "Bill Nye," in American National Biography, Oxford Univ Press; 99; auth, "Josh Billings," in American National Biography, Oxford Univ Press, 99; auth, "Bill Nye," in Dictionary of Literary Biography: Nineteenth-Century American Western Writers, Gale Res co, 97; auth, "The 'Closed Portal's] of Happiness' in Washington Square," The south Carolina Review, (95): 85-90; ed, Critical Essays on Hawthorne's The Scarlet Letter, Hall and co, 88; auth, Bill Nye, Twayne Pub Co, 81; auth, Bill Nye: The western Writings, Western Writers Series, 76; auth, Josh Billings, Twayne Pub co, 73. **CONTACT ADDRESS** Dept English, Univ of No Texas, PO Box 311307, Denton, TX 76203-1307. **EMAIL** kesterson@unt.edu

KESTERSON, DAVID BERT
PERSONAL Born 09/02/1934, Dundonald, Northern Ireland, m, 1961, 1 child **DISCIPLINE** ENGLISH **EDUCATION** Univ Liverpool, BA, 56; Univ Birmingham, PhD(English), 63. **CAREER** Instr English, Univ MI, 59-61; lectr, Univ Western Ont, 61-63; from asst prof to assoc prof, Univ MI, 63-69; assoc prof, 69-75, Prof English, Gwent Allen Smith Prof English, Mt Holyoke Col, 75-; vis assoc prof English, Dartmouth Col, 68-69. **MEMBERSHIPS** Int Byron Soc; Renaissance Soc of Am; Renaissance English Text Soc; Byron Soc; Chesterton Soc. **RESEARCH** Shakespeare; Skelton; Southwell; music and literature. **SELECTED PUBLICATIONS** Auth, Two Shakespearean Sequences, Macmillan & Univ Pittsburgh, 77; Shakespeare, Harsnett, and the Devils of Denham, DE Univ Press, 93; Robert Southwell, Twayne, 96; ed, Skelton, The Book of the Laurel, DE Univ Press, 91. **CONTACT ADDRESS** Mount Holyoke Col, 50 College St, South Hadley, MA 01075-1461. **EMAIL** fbrownlo@mhc.mtholyoke.edu

KETNER, KENNETH LAINE
PERSONAL Born 03/24/1939, Mountain Home, OK, m, 1963, 1 child **DISCIPLINE** PHILOSOPHY, FOLKLORISTICS **EDUCATION** OK State Univ, BA, 61, MA, 67; Univ CA, Los An-

geles, MA, 68; Univ CA, Santa Barbara, PhD, 72. **CAREER** Instr philos, OK State Univ, 64-67; res asst folklore, Univ CA, Los Angeles, 67-68; teaching asst philos, Univ CA, Santa Barbara, 69-70; asst prof, 71-75, assoc prof, 75-77, Prof, 77-81, Peirce Prof Philos, TX Tech Univ, 81-, Dir Iinst Studies In Pragmaticism, 72-. **HONORS AND AWARDS** Res Merit Awd, TX Tech Univ, 80; NEH fel. **MEMBERSHIPS** Am Philos Asn; Charles S Pierce Soc. **RESEARCH** Am philos, philosophical anthropology; folkloristic method and theory. **SELECTED PUBLICATIONS** Auth, A Comprehensive Bibliography of the Published Works of Charles S Peirce, KTO Microform, 77; Charles S Peirce: Contributions to the Nation, TX Tech Univ, 78; Proceedings, Peirce Bicentennial Int Congress, TX Tech Univ, 81; The role of Hypotheses in Folkloristics, J Am Folklore, 86: 114-130; auth, Reasoning and the Logic of Things, Harvard Univ Press, 92; auth, A Thief of Peirce: The Letters of Kenneth Laine Ketner and Walker Percy, 95; auth, His Glassy Essence: An Autobiography of Charles Sanders Peirce, 98. **CONTACT ADDRESS** Institute for Studies in Pragmaticism, Texas Tech Univ, Lubbock, TX 79409-0002. **EMAIL** b9oky@ttacs.ttu.edu

KETROW, SANDRA M.
PERSONAL Born 05/20/1949, Indianapolis, IN **DISCIPLINE** COMMUNICATION STUDIES **EDUCATION** AB, 71, MS, 78, PhD, 82, Ind Univ. **CAREER** Teacher, Eng, Lawrenceburg High Sch, 76-78; assoc instr/ed asst, dept of speech comm, Ind Univ & Central States Speech Jour, 78-81; asst prof & dir of pub speaking, dept of speech, Univ Fla, 81-84; visiting asst & adjunct prof, dept of speech, Butler Univ, 84-86; asst prof, 86-92, assoc prof, 92-98, prof & dir of grad prog, 98-, dept of comm studies, Univ RI. **HONORS AND AWARDS** Fel, Teaching & Tech, Univ RI, 97-98; World Who's Who of Women, 95-; Who's Who of Intl Women, 94-; Who's Who of Bus & Professional Women, 93-; Who's Who of Amer Women, 93-. **MEMBERSHIPS** Nat Comm Asn; Intl Comm Asn; Eastern Comm Asn. **RESEARCH** Nonverbal communication; Argumentation in groups. **SELECTED PUBLICATIONS** Co-auth, Processes and Outcomes Related to Non-Rational Argument in Societal Groups, Argument in a Time of Change: Proceedings of the Tenth AFA/SCA Argumentation Conference, 103-109, Nat Comm Asn, 98; co-auth, Social Anxiety and Performance in an Interpersonal Perception Task, Psychological Reports, 81, 991-996, 97; co-auth, Improving Decision Quality in the Small Group: The Role of the Reminder, Small Group Communication, 404-410, 97; auth, Is it Homophobia, Heterosexism, Sexism, or Can I Pass?, Lesbians in Academia: Degrees of Freedom, 106-112, NY, Routledge, 97; co-auth, Improving Decision Making in the Group: Arguing with Constructive Intent, Proceedings of the Ninth AFA/SCA Argumentation Conference, Speech Comm Asn, 95; co-auth, Improving Decision Quality in the Small Group: The Role of the Reminder, Small Group Research, 26, 4, 521-541, 95; co-auth, Using Argumentative Functions to Improve Decision Quality in the Small Group, Argument and the Postmodern Challenge: Proceedings of the Eighth AFA/SCA Argumentation Conference, 218-225, Speech Comm Asn, 93. **CONTACT ADDRESS** Dept. of Communication Studies, Univ of Rhode Island, 60 Upper College Rd., Suite 1, Kingston, RI 02881-0812. **EMAIL** ketrow@uri.edu

KEY, WILSON BRYAN
PERSONAL Born 01/31/1925, Richmond, CA, m, 2000, 5 children **DISCIPLINE** COMMUNICATION **EDUCATION** Mex City Col, BA, 51; UCLA, MA, 53; Denver Univ, PhD, 71. **CAREER** Asst prof of Journalism, Boston Univ; res dir, Publicidad Badillo; pres, res & market development; assoc prof of mass commun, Univ of Western Ontario; Pres, Mediaprobe Inc. **MEMBERSHIPS** Mensa Int; Speech-Commun Asn; AAUP. **RESEARCH** Subliminal aspects of communication; general semantics. **SELECTED PUBLICATIONS** Auth, Age of Manipulation, Henry Holt; Clam-Plate Orgy, Prentice Hall; Media Sexploitation, Prentice Hall; Subliminal Seduction, Prentice Hall. **CONTACT ADDRESS** 150 E Laramie Dr., Reno, NV 89511.

KEYES, CLAIRE J.
PERSONAL Born 11/02/1938, Boston, MA, m, 1987 **DISCIPLINE** ENGLISH **EDUCATION** Boston State College, BS 60, MA 63; Univ Mass, PhD 80. **CAREER** Salem State College, prof eng, 66-96, prof emer, 96-. **HONORS AND AWARDS** Helene Wurlitzer Gnt; Poetry Finalist MA Artist Foun; Awd for Excell Grad Sch. **MEMBERSHIPS** MELUS; ASA; NEMLA; ASAIL; Phi Beta Phi. **RESEARCH** Amer Women Poets; American Indian Lit. **SELECTED PUBLICATIONS** Auth, I'm a Montano: Leslie Marmon Silko's Transformation of the Yellow Women Muth in Ceremony, Jour of Lit Stud, Capetown SA, 98; Pattian Rogers and the New Science, Sycamore, 98; Between Ruin and Celebration, Joy Hardjo's, in: In Mad Love and War, Borderlines, Swansea Wales, 97; Geronimo Jerome, Sextant, Jour of Salem State Coll, 96. **CONTACT ADDRESS** Dept of English, Salem State Col, 12 Higgins Rd, Marblehead, MA 01945. **EMAIL** CKEYES@salem.mass.edu

KEYISHIAN, HARRY
PERSONAL Born 04/09/1932, New York, NY, m, 1966, 4 children **DISCIPLINE** ENGLISH LITERATURE **EDUCATION** Queens Col (NYork), BA, 54; NYork Univ, MA, 57, PhD, 65. **CAREER** Asst instr English, Univ Md Overseas Proj, Newfoundland, 57-58; lectr, City Col New York, 59-60; instr, Bronx Community Col, 61 & Univ Buffalo, 61-64; from asst prof to assoc prof, 65-73, chmn dept, 72-74, Prof English, Fairleigh Dickinson Univ, Madison, 73-, dir, Fairleigh Dickinson Univ Press, 76-; ed, The Lit Rev, 76-. **HONORS AND AWARDS** Grants from NEH, NJ Coun on the Humanities, NJ Dept of Higher Educ, Mennen Found. **MEMBERSHIPS** MLA; Renaissance Soc Am; Shakespeare Asn Am. **RESEARCH** Elizabethan drama and Shakespeare; revenge themes in literature; 20th century fiction; film; performance criticism; advertising. **SELECTED PUBLICATIONS** Auth, Michael Arlen, Twayne, 75; Cross-Currents of Revenge in James's The American, in Mod Lang Studies, Spring 87; The NJ Shakespeare Festival's The Merchant of Venice: A Case Study, in On-Stage Studies, Spring 87; Vindictiveness and the Search for Glory in Frankenstein, in Am J Psychoanalysis, 9/89; The Shapes of Revenge: Victimization, Vengeance, and Vindictiveness in Shakespeare, Humanities Press, 95; ed, Critical Essays on William Saroyan, Twayne Publ, 95; Performing Violence in King Lear, in Shakespeare Bull, Summer 96; Michael Arlen, in Am Nat Biog, Oxford Univ Press, 98; author of several other journal articles. **CONTACT ADDRESS** Dept of English M105A, Fairleigh Dickinson Univ, Florham-Madison, 285 Madison Ave, Madison, NJ 07940-1099. **EMAIL** harry@alpha.fdu.edu

KEYSER, ELIZABETH
PERSONAL Born 04/16/1942, Marshalltown, IA, d **DISCIPLINE** ENGLISH **EDUCATION** Willamctle Univ, BA, 63; Claremont Grad Sch, PhD, 68; Univ Calif Berkeley, MLS, 78. **CAREER** Assoc prof, Hollins Univ, 88-00. **HONORS AND AWARDS** Children's Lit Asn Book Awd. **MEMBERSHIPS** MLA, ALA, ChLA, Am Studies Asn. **RESEARCH** Children's Literature, American Women's Literature, Henry James. **SELECTED PUBLICATIONS** Auth, Whispers in the Dark: The Fiction of Louisa May Alcott, 93; Little Women: A Family Romance, 99; ed, Children's Literature, 94-00; ed, Portable Louisa May Alcott, 00. **CONTACT ADDRESS** Dept English, Hollins Col, 7916 Williamson Rd, Roanoke, VA 24019-4421. **EMAIL** ekeyser@hollins.edu

KEYSSAR, HELENE
DISCIPLINE COMMUNICATIONS **EDUCATION** Univ Iowa, PhD, Mod Letters, 74. **CAREER** Prof, Commun, Univ Calif, San Diego. **RESEARCH** Feminist theatre. **SELECTED PUBLICATIONS** Auth, Feminist Theatre: An Introduction to Plays of Contemporary British and American Women, Macmillan, 85; Robert Altman's America, Oxford, 91; co-auth, Remembering War: A US-Soviet Dialogue on World War II, Oxford, 90. **CONTACT ADDRESS** Dept of Commun, Univ of California, San Diego, 9500 Gilman Dr, La Jolla, CA 92093. **EMAIL** hkeyssar@weber.ucsd.edu

KEZAR, DENNIS
DISCIPLINE ENGLISH RENAISSANCE LITERATURE **EDUCATION** Univ Va, PhD. **CAREER** Instr, Vanderbilt Univ. **RESEARCH** Shakespeare's poetic responses to early modern theatricalism; Milton's representations of death and violence. **SELECTED PUBLICATIONS** Auth, The Properties of Shakespeare's Globe, Eng Lit Renaissance; Shakespeare's Rome in Milton's Gaza?, Eng Lang Notes; Milton's 'Careful Ploughman', Notes & Queries; John Skelton's Fictive Text and the Manufacture of Fame, Renaissance Papers; Radical Letters and Male Genealogies in Johnson's Dictionary, Stud in Eng Lit; auth, Guilty Creatures, Oxford Univ Press, 01. **CONTACT ADDRESS** Vanderbilt Univ, Nashville, TN 37203-1727.

KHARPERTIAN, THEODORE
PERSONAL Born 01/21/1949, Jersey City, NJ, m, 1982, 2 children **DISCIPLINE** LITERATURE **EDUCATION** Univ of PA, Ba, 70; Mcgill Univ, MA, 71, PhD, 85 **CAREER** Prof, 79-, Hudson Co Comnty col; Lect, 88-93, Rutgers Univ **MEMBERSHIPS** Mod Lang Asn **RESEARCH** Satire **SELECTED PUBLICATIONS** Auth, A Hand to Turn the Time: The Menippean Satires of Thomas Pynchon, Associated Univ Presses, 90; Hagop: A Memoir of my Father, National Association for Armenian Studies and Research, forthcom **CONTACT ADDRESS** Dept of Eng and Humanities, Hudson County Comm Col, Jersey City, NJ 07306. **EMAIL** tkharpertian@hotmail.com

KHATIB, SYED MALIK
PERSONAL Born 05/07/1940, Trenton, NJ, m, 1965, 2 children **DISCIPLINE** COMMUNICATIONS **EDUCATION** Trenton State Coll, BA 1962; UCLA, diploma African Studies 1962; MI State Univ, MA 1966, PhD 1968. **CAREER** Stanford Univ, asst prof 69-75; SF State Univ, assoc prof 78-82; Princeton Univ, visiting lecturer 84; Trenton State Prison MCC, instructor 85; Rahway State Prison MCC, instructor 85; Mercer Coll, adjunct assoc prof; SUNY at New Paltz, Department of African-American Studies, associate professor, chairman, 85-88; Marist College, Assoc Prof of Communication, 88-. **HONORS AND AWARDS** Dean's Honor List Trenton State Univ 1960; NDEA Fellow MI State Univ 1965-67; Postdoctoral Fellow Univ of PA 1968; Issue Editor Journal of Social Issues vol 29, 1973; mem editorial bd Journal of Black Psychology, 1974-76; recipient, Comm Serv Awd Bay Area, 1975. **MEMBERSHIPS** Mem editorial bd Assn of Black Psychologists 1970; consultant SRI 1970; SSRC 1971; HEW 1972; 10 publications in the areas of methodology philosophy & psychology. **CONTACT ADDRESS** PO Box 878, New Paltz, NY 12561. **EMAIL** smksmksmk@aol.com

KHWAJA, WAQAS A.
PERSONAL Born 10/14/1952, Lahore, Pakistan, m, 1978, 4 children **DISCIPLINE** ENGLISH **EDUCATION** Govt Col, BA, 70; Punjab Univ, LLB, 74; Emory Univ, MA, 82; PhD, 95. **CAREER** Vis Fac, Income Tax Dir of Training, 92-93; Vis Prof, Quaid-e-Azam Law Col, 88-91; Vis Prof, Punjab Law Col, 88-93; Vis Fac, Lahore Col for Arts and Sci, 89-90; Vis Prof, Punjab Univ, 90-91; Vis Fac, Emory Univ, 95-96; Asst Prof, Agnes Scott Col, 95-. **HONORS AND AWARDS** Fel, Rotary Intl, 79-80; Fel, Univ Iowa, 88; Rotary Grant for Univ Teachers, 00-01; Professional Develop Grant, Agnes Scott Col, 00; Human Relations Awd, Agnes Scott Col, 00. **MEMBERSHIPS** MLA; S Atlantic MLA. **RESEARCH** Postcolonial literatures and cultures; Gothic literature; Nineteenth-century literature; Romantic poetry. **SELECTED PUBLICATIONS** Ed, Pakistani Short Stories, UPS Pub, 90; auth, Writers and Landscapes, Sang-e-Meel Pub, 91; auth, Mariam's Lament and Other Poems, Sang-e-Meel Pub, 92; auth, "The Gothic conventions and Henry James' Ghost Stories," J of the Dept English, 94; auth, The Aesthetics of Civilized Life: Interplay Between Artistic Design and Truth of Experience in Thackeray's Later Fiction, UMI Pub, 95. **CONTACT ADDRESS** Dept English, Agnes Scott Col, 2923 Evans Woods Dr, Atlanta, GA 30340-4815. **EMAIL** wkhwaja@agnesscott.edu

KIBLER, JAMES EVERETT, JR.
DISCIPLINE ENGLISH **CAREER** Prof of English, Univ GA. **HONORS AND AWARDS** Fel of Southern Writer Awd for Nonfiction in 99; Literary Achievement Awd from the Southern Heritage Soc. **SELECTED PUBLICATIONS** Ed, American Novelists Since World War II, Gale, 80; ed, Selected Poems of William Gilmore Simms, Univ Ga Press, 90; Poetry and the Practical, Univ Ark Press, 96; The Simms Review 1993-2001; auth, Our Fathers' Fields, Univ SC Press, 98; Poems From Scorched Earth, Charleston Press, 01. **CONTACT ADDRESS** Dept of English, Univ of Georgia, Park Hall 254, Athens, GA 30602. **EMAIL** jkibler@arches.uga.edu

KIEFER, FREDERICK P.
PERSONAL Born 01/03/1945, Providence, RI, s **DISCIPLINE** ENGLISH LITERATURE **EDUCATION** Loyola Col, BA, 67; Harvard Univ, MA, 68; PhD, 72. **CAREER** Vis asst prof, Univ of Wis, 72-73; prof, Univ of Ariz, 73-. **HONORS AND AWARDS** Mortar Board Awd for Teaching; Student Alumni Asn Awd for Teaching. **MEMBERSHIPS** Shakespeare Assoc; Renaissance Soc of Am. **RESEARCH** Renaissance Drama and Iconography. **SELECTED PUBLICATIONS** Auth, Fortune and Elizabethan Tragedy, Huntington Libr Pr, 83; auth, Writing on the Renaissance Stage, Univ of Del Pr, 96. **CONTACT ADDRESS** Dept English, Univ of Arizona, PO Box 210067, Tucson, AZ 85721-0067.

KIEFER, KATE
DISCIPLINE ENGLISH LITERATURE **EDUCATION** Univ Dayton, BA; Ohio State Univ, MA, PhD. **CAREER** Prof. **SELECTED PUBLICATIONS** Auth, pubs on computers and composition. **CONTACT ADDRESS** Dept of English, Colorado State Univ, Fort Collins, CO 80523. **EMAIL** kkiefer@vines.colostate.edu

KIEFER, LAUREN
DISCIPLINE ENGLISH **EDUCATION** Stanford Univ, BA; Cornell Univ, PhD, 93. **CAREER** Eng Dept, Plattsburgh State Univ **RESEARCH** Middle Eng, medieval Latin, and Old French lit(s), particularly from the 14th century. **SELECTED PUBLICATIONS** Auth, publ(s) on Medieval lit; articles on John Gower's Confession. **CONTACT ADDRESS** SUNY, Col at Plattsburgh, 101 Broad St, Plattsburgh, NY 12901-2681.

KIERNAN, KEVIN S.
PERSONAL Born 04/05/1945, New York, NY, m, 1969, 3 children **DISCIPLINE** ENGLISH, COMPUTING **EDUCATION** Fairfield Univ, AB, 67; Case Western Reserve Univ, MA, 68; PhD, 70. **CAREER** Asst prof, to prof, chair, Univ Ky, 70-. **HONORS AND AWARDS** NEH Fel, 75, 95; Fel, Am Philos Soc, 80; Choice Awd for Outstanding Book, 81; Libr Asn and Mecklermedia Awd, 94-95; Mellon Found Grant, 95-96; William S Ward Prize, 96; Distinguished Prof, Univ Ky, 98; IBM Shared Univ Res Grant, 98; Nat Sci Found Fel, 99-02; Int Res and Exchanges Board Fel, 99-00. **MEMBERSHIPS** MLA, Int Soc of Anglo-Saxonists, Int Assoc of Univ Prof of English. **RESEARCH** Old and Middle English Language and Literature, Electronic Editing, Humanities Computing, Manuscript Studies. **SELECTED PUBLICATIONS** Auth, The Rhorkelin Transcripts of Beowulf, Rosenkilde and Bagger, 86; auth, "digital Image-Processing and the Beowulf Manuscript," Lit and Ling Computing, (91); auth, "Digital Preservation, Restoration, and Dissemination of Medieval Manuscripts," Scholarly Publ, (94); auth, "The Legacy of Wiglaf: Saving a Wounded Beo-

wulf," Beowulf: Basic Readings, (94); auth, "Neil Ripley Ker," Dict of Medieval Scholarship, (98); auth, "King Alfred's Burnt Boethius," The Iconic Page in manuscript, Print, and Digital Culture, (98); auth, "The Conybeare-Madden Collation of Thorkelin's Beowulf," Anglo-Saxon Manuscripts and Their Heritage, (98); ed, The Electronic Beowulf, Brit Libr Publ, Univ Mich Pr, (99); auth, Beowulf and the Beowulf Manuscript, Brit Libr Publ, Univ Mich Pr, (99); auth, "The Reappearances of St Basil the Great in British Library MS Cotton Otho B x," Computers and the Humanities, (01). **CONTACT ADDRESS** Dept English, Univ of Kentucky, Lexington, KY 40506. **EMAIL** kiernan@pop.uky.edu

KIERNAN, MICHAEL TERENCE
PERSONAL Born 06/14/1940, New York, NY, m, 1964, 1 child **DISCIPLINE** ENGLISH LITERATURE **EDUCATION** Fairfield Univ, BA, 62; Marquette Univ, MA, 64; Harvard Univ, PhD(English), 71. **CAREER** Ed asst, Renascence, 62-64; teaching fel English, Harvard Univ, 67-71; Mather house resident tutor, 70-71, assoc mem grad fac, 73-79, asst prof, 71-77, assoc prof English, Pa State Univ, University Park, 77-, sr mem grad fac, 79-, Am Coun Learned Soc grant-in-aid, 72 & 78; Nat Endowment for Humanities-Folger Shakespeare Libr fel, 78; Am Philos Soc grant, 79, 87; Nat Endowment for Humanities-Huntington Libr res fel, 80; res fel, Huntington Libr, 86. **MEMBERSHIPS** Malone Soc; Renaissance Soc Am; Renaissance English Text Soc. **RESEARCH** Francis Bacon; Renaissance drama, especially Shakespeare; textual editing. **SELECTED PUBLICATIONS** Ed asst, The Plays of George Chapman: The Comedies: A Critical Edition, Univ Ill, Urbana, 70; auth, The order and dating of the 1613 editions of Bacon's Essays, Library, London, 12/74; ed, Henry the Fourth, Part One: A Bibliography to Supplement the New Variorum Edition of 1936 and the Supplement of 1956, Mod Lang Asn Am, 77; ed, Sir Francis Bacon: The Essayes or Counsels, Harvard Univ Press & Clarendon Press, 85; reissued as Sir Francis Bacon:The Essayes or Counsels Vol 15, The Oxford Francis Bacon, Oxford, 00; Sir Francis Bacon: The Advancement of Learning Vol 4, The Oxford Francis Bacon, Oxford, 00. **CONTACT ADDRESS** Dept of English, Pennsylvania State Univ, Univ Park, 117 Burrowes Bldg, University Park, PA 16802-6200. **EMAIL** mtk@psu.edu

KIERNAN, ROBERT F.
PERSONAL Born 10/21/1940, NJ, s **DISCIPLINE** ENGLISH **EDUCATION** Cath Univ Am, BA, 63; Manhattan Col, MA, 68; NY Univ, PhD, 71. **CAREER** Prof, Univ Sao Paulo, 91; Prof, Univ Brasilia, 92; Prof, Manhattan Col, 71-. **HONORS AND AWARDS** Phi Beta Kappa, 63; Finn Fel, Oxford Univ, 68; Am Participant Grant, US Information Agency, 88; Am Specialist Grant, US Information Agency, 89. **MEMBERSHIPS** Mod Lang Assoc of Am. **RESEARCH** Modern and contemporary American literature work in progress, a study of Reynolds Price to be entitled, The Amplificational Imperative. **SELECTED PUBLICATIONS** Auth, Katherine Anne Porter and Carson McCullers, Hall Pr (Boston, MA), 76; auth, Gore Vidal, Ungar (New York, NY), 82; auth, American Writing Since 1945, Ungar Pr (New York, NY), 83; auth, Noel Coward, Ungar Pr (New York, NY), 86; auth, Saul Bellow, Continuum Pr (New York, NY), 89; auth, Frivolity Unbound: Six Masters of the Camp Novel, Continuum Pr (New York, NY), 90; auth, "The New Southern Novel: A Bibliographical Essay," Ilha do Desterro: A J of Lang and Lit, no 30 (93): 13-27; auth, "The Styles of Saul Bellow," Saul Bellow and the Struggle at the Ctr (NY: AMS, 96), 91-100. **CONTACT ADDRESS** Dept English, Manhattan Col, 4513 Manhattan Col Pkwy, Bronx, NY 10471-4004. **EMAIL** rkiernan@manhattan.edu

KIESSLING, NICOLAS
DISCIPLINE MEDIEVAL AND RENAISSANCE LITERATURE **EDUCATION** Univ Wis, PhD. **CAREER** Prof & actg dir Grad Stud, Washington State Univ. **RESEARCH** The Library of Anthony Wood. **SELECTED PUBLICATIONS** Auth, The Incubus in English Literature, 77; The Library of Robert Burton, 88 & The Legacy of Democritus Junior, Robert Burton, 90; co-ed, 3 vol critical ed, Burton's The Anatomy of Melancholy, Clarendon Press, 88-94. **CONTACT ADDRESS** Dept of English, Washington State Univ, 1 SE Stadium Way, PO Box 645020, Pullman, WA 99164-5020. **EMAIL** kiesslin@wsu.edu

KIEVITT, F. DAVID
PERSONAL Born 08/30/1944, Peterson, NJ, s **DISCIPLINE** ENGLISH **EDUCATION** Seton Hall Univ, BA, 69; Columbia Univ, PhD, 75; Post Doctoral Studies, Princeton Univ, Yale Univ, Northwestern Univ, Univ Calif, Univ Minn, Univ Vienna. **CAREER** Preceptor, Columbia Univ, 73-75; Prof, Bergen Community Col, 75- **HONORS AND AWARDS** Distinguished Prof Awd, 95; Five NEH Fels; **MEMBERSHIPS** MLA, NEMLA, ASECS, AAR. **RESEARCH** Eighteenth-century literature, Reformation history. **SELECTED PUBLICATIONS** Coauth, "The School for Widows," Mid-Hudson Lang Studies 3 (80): 74-84; auth, "Tenure and Promotion in the Two-Year College," ADE Bulletin, Spring 1986 (86): 6-8; auth, "Three Times Three Penny: Brecht's versions of 'The Beggar's Opera,'" Mid-Hudson lang Studies 7 (84): 57-64; auth, "The Integration Project," Lesbian and Gay Studies Newsletter 17 (90): 29; auth, "Strategies for a Successful Faculty Development Program in the Two-Year College," The New Jersey Project: Integrating the New Scholarship on Gender, Rutgers Univ Pr (90): 39-42; auth, "The Sphere of Private Life: Hannah More's 'Bible Rhymes' and the Cult of Domestic Virtue," The Friend (92): 48-56. **CONTACT ADDRESS** Dept English, Bergen Comm Col, 400 Paramus Rd, Paramus, NJ 07652-1508. **EMAIL** dkievitt@bergen.cc.nj.us

KIJINSKI, JOHN
PERSONAL Born 07/06/1950, Cleveland, OH, m, 1972, 2 children **DISCIPLINE** ENGLISH LITERATURE **EDUCATION** Univ Wis, PhD, 85. **CAREER** Assoc prof, prof and char of dept of Eng and Philos. **MEMBERSHIPS** MLA; INCS; AAUP. **RESEARCH** Victorian literature. **SELECTED PUBLICATIONS** Auth, pubs in Victorian Literature and Culture, Victorian Studies, and English Literature in Transition. **CONTACT ADDRESS** Dept of English and Philosophy, Idaho State Univ, Pocatello, ID 83209. **EMAIL** kijijohn@isu.edu

KILCUP, KAREN L.
DISCIPLINE ENGLISH, AMERICAN LITERATURE **EDUCATION** Wellesley Col, BA, 75; Univ New Hampshire, Mass, MA, 77; Brandeis Univ, PhD, 86. **CAREER** Instr, Phillips Exeter Acad, New Hampshire, 83-87; lectr, Brandeis Univ, 87-89; vis asst prof, Colby Col, Waterville, Maine, 89-90; asst prof, Brandeis Univ, 90-93; vis asst prof, Tufts Univ, 991-93; lectr, The Univ of Hull, Kingston-upon-Hull, England, 93-97; assoc prof, Univ NC, Greensboro, 97-2000, prof, 2000-. **HONORS AND AWARDS** Distinguished Teacher, The White House Comn on Presidential Scholars and The Nat Educ Asn, Washington, DC, 87; Dorothy M. Healy Vis Prof of Am Studies (for res), Westbrook Col, Portland, ME, 96; Andrew W. Mellon Res Fel, Mass Hist Soc, Boston, 96-97; Edna and Jordan Davidson Eminent Scholar Chair in the Humanities (for res), Fla Int Univ, Miami, 2000. **MEMBERSHIPS** Modern Lang Asn, Am Studies Asn, Am Humor Studies Asn, Am Lit Asn, British Soc for Am Studies, Soc for the Study of Am Women Writers, Int 19th Century Am Women Writers Res Group. **RESEARCH** Nineteenth- and early twentieth-century American literature and culture. **SELECTED PUBLICATIONS** Ed, Nineteenth-Century American Women Writers: An Anthology, Cambridge, MA and Oxford, UK: Blackwell Pubs (97); auth, Robert Frost and Feminine Literary Tradition (monograph), Ann Arbor: Univ of Mich Press (98); ed, Nineteenth-Century American Women Writers: A Critical Reader, Cambridge, MA and Oxford, UK: Blackwell Pubs (97); ed, Questioning Jewett: Centennial Essays, Colby Quart Special Issue (98); ed, Nineteenth-Century American Women's Culture, Overhere: A European J of Am Culture Special Issue (98); ed, Soft Canons: American Women Writers and Masculine Tradition, Iowa City: Univ Iowa Press (99); co-ed, Jewett and Her Contemporaries: Reshaping the Canon, Gainesville: Univ Press of Fla (99); ed, Native American Women Writers c. 1800-1924: An Anthology, Cambridge, MA and Oxford, UK: Blackwell Pubs (2000). **CONTACT ADDRESS** Dept English, Univ of No Carolina, Greensboro, PO Box 26170, Greensboro, NC 27402-6170. **EMAIL** KlKilcup@uncg.edu

KILGOUR, MAGGIE
PERSONAL Born 01/09/1957, Toronto, ON, Canada, s **DISCIPLINE** ENGLISH **EDUCATION** Univ Toronto, BA, 81; Yale Univ, PhD, 86. **CAREER** Asst prof to prof and chair, McGill Univ, 87-. **HONORS AND AWARDS** Res Grant, SSHRCC, 92-96. **MEMBERSHIPS** MLA; RSA; IGA; ALSC; ACCUTE. **RESEARCH** Milton; Ovid; Classics and Renaissance literature; The Gothic novel; Cannibalism. **SELECTED PUBLICATIONS** Auth, From Communion to Cannibalism: An Anatomy of Metaphors of Incorporation, 90; auth, The Rise of the Gothic Novel, 95; auth, "Writing on Water," ELR, 287-305; auth, "The Function of Cannibalism at the Present Time," in Cannibalism and the Colonial World, (98): 238-259. **CONTACT ADDRESS** Dept English, McGill Univ, 853 Sherbrooke St W, Montreal, QC, Canada H3A 2T6. **EMAIL** mkilgo@pobox.mcgill.ca

KILLAM, G. DOUGLAS
PERSONAL Born 08/26/1930, New Westminster, BC, Canada **DISCIPLINE** ENGLISH **EDUCATION** Univ BC, BA, 54; Univ London, PhD, 64. **CAREER** Tchr, Sierra Leone, 63-65; tchr, Nigeria, 67-68; fac mem, York Univ, 68-73; tchr, Tanzania, 70-72; fac mem, 74-77, head Eng, 74-76, dean arts, Acadia Univ, 76-77; PROF ENGLISH, UNIV GUELPH, 77-. **MEMBERSHIPS** Asn Commonwealth Lit Lang Stud; Asn Can Univ Tchrs Eng; Can Asn African Stud; Int Asn Univ Profs Eng. **SELECTED PUBLICATIONS** Auth, Africa in English Fiction, 68; auth, Novels of Chinua Achebe, 68; auth, African Writers on African Writing, 72; auth, An Introduction to the Writings of Ngugi, 80; auth, Critical Perspectives on Ngugi, 85; ed, The Oxford Companion to African Literature: East and Central African Literatures in English, 79-89; co-ed, Can J African Stud, 79-81. **CONTACT ADDRESS** PO Box 112, Portland, ON, Canada K0G 1V0.

KILLORAN, HELEN
DISCIPLINE ENGLISH **EDUCATION** Gonzaga Univ, BA, 76; Univ Washington, MA, 87; PhD, 89. **CAREER** Post-Doctoral Fel, Univ Washington, 90; Asst prof, Ala State Univ, 91-93; Asst Prof to Assoc Prof, Ohio Univ, 93-. **HONORS AND AWARDS** Res Committee Grant, Ohio Univ, 96; Fac Fel, 00. **MEMBERSHIPS** MLA, ALA, Edith Wharton Soc, ALRC. **RESEARCH** Edith Wharton, Henry James. **SELECTED PUBLICATIONS** Auth, "Marie Louis de la Ramee," The New dictionary of Biography, forthcoming; auth, "Lionel Trilling and Ethan Frome," The Literary Imagination, forthcoming; auth, "Edith Wharton, Henri Bergson and the Aesthetics of Edith Wharton's The Glimpses of the Moon," Thalia, forthcoming; auth, "Meetings of Minds: Edith Wharton as Mentor and Guide," American Literary Mentors, 99; auth, Edith Wharton: Art and Allusion, Univ of Alabama Press paperback edition, 98; auth, Edith Wharton: Art and Allusion, Univ of Alabama Press hardback edition, 96; auth, "Xingu: Edith Wharton Instructs Literary Critics," Studies in American Humor, (96): 1-13; auth, "Sexuality and Abnormal Psychology in Edith Wharton's The lady's Maid's Bell," The CEA Critic, (94): 41-49; auth, "Edith Wharton's Reading in European Languages and its Influence on Her work," Wretched Exotic: Essays on Edith Wharton in Europe, New York, 93; auth, "Pascal, Bronte and Kerfol: The Horrors of a Foolish Quarrel," Edith Wharton Review, (93): 12-17. **CONTACT ADDRESS** Dept Arts & Sci, Ohio Univ, 1570 Granville Pike, Lancaster, OH 43130-1037. **EMAIL** killoran@ohiou.edu

KILPATRICK, ROSS S.
PERSONAL Born 10/03/1934, Toronto, ON, Canada, m, 1960, 3 children **DISCIPLINE** CLASSICS **EDUCATION** Univ Toronto, BA, 57, MA 64; Yale Univ, MA, 65, PhD, 67. **CAREER** Tchr, East York Collegiate, 57-64; instr, 67-68, asst prof, classics, 68-70, Yale Univ; assoc prof, 70-85, actg head dept, 84, asst to VP, 85, head dept, 85-95, prof, Queen's Univ, 85- . **HONORS AND AWARDS** OVATIO, Classical Assoc of the Middle West and South, 96. **MEMBERSHIPS** Am Philol Asn; Class Asn Can; Class Asn Middle West and South; Int Soc for Class Tradition; Ontario Class Asn; Soc of Fel of Am Acad in Rome; Vergilian Soc Am. **RESEARCH** Latin and Greek literature; classical tradition in Renaissance art and in English and Canadian literature. **SELECTED PUBLICATIONS** Ed, Smethurst, Classics at Queens: A Short History, Queen's Univ, 93; auth, In Praise of Nurses: T.R. Glover, Queen's Q, 94; auth, The Sea Took Pity, Studies, 95; auth, The Stuff of Doors and Dreams, Vergilius, 95; auth, Old Friends and Good Temper: T.R. Glover and Horace, Arethusa, 95; auth, Fortuna Regum: An Anonymous Landscape in the Bader Collection at Queen's, Int J for Class Trad, 97; auth, Yoshio Markino: A London Portfolio, Queen's Q, 97; auth, Yoshio Markino in the West London Hospital, J of Med Biog, 97; auth, A Missed Literary Source for Sir Charles G.D. Roberts' Out of Pompeii, Can Poetry, 97; auth, Giorgione's Tempest and the Flight of Hagar, Artibus et Historiae, 97; auth, Amicus Medicus: Medicine and Epicurean Therapy in Lucretius, Mem of the Am Acad in Rome, 97; ed, Sir Charles G D Roberts' Orion, and Other Poems, Canadian Poetry, forthcoming 98; auth, Education, Culture, and the Classics in Haliburton's Nova Scotia, Stud in Honor of Margaret Thomson, in Cahiers des Etudes Class, forth 98; auth, Nam Unguentum Dabo: Catullus 13 and Servius' Unguent of Phaon, Class Q, 98; auth, Horace, Vergil,and the Jews of Rome, Dionysius, forthcoming 98; auth, T R Glover at Queen's, Class Views, forthcoming 98; auth, Winnie-the-Pooh and the Canadian Connection, Queen's Q, forthcoming 98. **CONTACT ADDRESS** Dept of Classics, Queen's Univ at Kingston, 502 Watson Hall, Kingston, ON, Canada K7L 3N6. **EMAIL** kilpatri@post.queensu.ca

KILWEIN-GUEVARA, MAURICE A.
PERSONAL Born 11/05/1961, Belencito, Columbia, m, 1991, 2 children **DISCIPLINE** ENGLISH **EDUCATION** Univ Pittsburgh, BA, BS, 83; Bowling Green State Univ, MFA, 86; Univ Wisc-Milwaukee, PhD, 90. **CAREER** Prof, Indiana Univ, PA, 99-. **HONORS AND AWARDS** Devine Awd for Fiction, 85; Bread Loaf Scholar, 92; vis prof, Mex, 92; Fulbright Prof, Columbia, 93; Assoc Writing Progs, bd of dirs, 2000-2004. **MEMBERSHIPS** Assoc Writing Progs. **RESEARCH** Latina/o literature of the USA, creative writing pedagogy. **SELECTED PUBLICATIONS** Auth, Postmortem, Univ of GA Press (94); auth, Poems of the River Spirit, Univ Pittsburgh Press (96); auth, Autobiography of So-and-So, New Issues Press (2001). **CONTACT ADDRESS** Dept English, Indiana Univ of Pennsylvania, Indiana, PA 15705-0001. **EMAIL** mauricio@grove.iup.edu

KIM, MARGARET
PERSONAL Born 04/01/1969, Tainan, Taiwan **DISCIPLINE** ENGLISH **EDUCATION** Univ Wis, BA, 91; Harvard Univ, PhD, 00. **CAREER** Teach fel, Harvard Univ, 93-99; asst instr, Rutgers Univ, 00-01; asst prof, St John's Univ, 01-. **HONORS AND AWARDS** Mellon, 94, 95, 96, 97; Harvard Fel, 91-97. **MEMBERSHIPS** MLA; Langland Soc. **RESEARCH** Middle English literature; medieval history and culture; politics of dissent; the historical evolution of political organization. **SELECTED PUBLICATIONS** Auth, "Invisible Man, Oral Culture, and Postmodernism," EurAmerica (00). **CONTACT ADDRESS** Eng Dept., St. John's Univ, 8000 Utopia Pkwy, Jamaica, NY 11439. **EMAIL** msmkim@hotmail.com

KIME, WAYNE R.
PERSONAL Born 10/08/1941, Los Angeles, CA, m, 1965, 1 child **DISCIPLINE** ENGLISH **EDUCATION** Stanford Univ, BA, 63; Univ Del, MA, 65; PhD, 68. **CAREER** Instr, Univ Del, 67-68; Asst Prof, Univ Toronto, 58-77; Assoc Prof to Prof, Fairmont State Col, 78-. **HONORS AND AWARDS** Fel, Fairmont State Col, 99; Fel, WV Humanities Coun, 92; Fel, Newberry Library, 91-92; NEH Travel Grant, 91; Achievement Awd, Fairmont Arts and Humanities, 86; Grant, Am Coun of Learned Soc, CSE Seal of Merit, , 78; Fel, Canada Coun 74-75; Res Grant, Canada Coun, 69; Phi Beta Kappa. **MEMBERSHIPS** Western Hist Asn, Western Literature Asn. **RESEARCH** Military history; Western American history; American literature, Textual editing. **SELECTED PUBLICATIONS** Auth, Pierre M Irving and Washington Irving: A Collaboration in Life and Letters, Wilfrid Laurier Univ Press, 78; ed, Raising the Wind: The Legend of Lapland and Finland Wizards in literature, Univ Del,81; ed, Washington Irving, Miscellaneous Writings, 1803-1859, Twayne Pub, 81; ed, Washington Irving, Journals and Notebooks, Twayne Pub, 84; auth, Donald G Mitchell, Twayne Pub, 84; ed, The Plains of North America and Their Inhabitants: A Critical Edition, Univ Del Press,89; ed, The Powder River Expedition journals of Colonel Richard Irving Dodge, Univ Okla Press, 97; ed, The Black Hills Journals of Colonel Richard Irving Dodge, Univ Okla Press, 96auth, The Indian Territory Journals of Colonel Richard Irving Dodge, Univ Okla Press, forthcoming. **CONTACT ADDRESS** Dept Lang & Lit, Fairmont State Col, 1201 Locust Ave, Fairmont, WV 26554-2451. **EMAIL** wkime@mail.fscwv.edu

KIMMELMAN, BURT
PERSONAL Born 05/06/1947, Brooklyn, NY, m, 1989, 1 child **DISCIPLINE** ENGLISH **EDUCATION** SUNY, BA, 83; CUNY, MA, 87; PhD, 91. **CAREER** Teaching Fel, CUNY, 84-87; Adj Lecturer, SUNY, 87; Adj Lecturer, CUNY, 87-89; Adj Lecturer to Assoc Prof, NJ Inst Tech, 88-. **HONORS AND AWARDS** Prize Winner, Am Poetry Asn Nat Poetry Contest, 87; Finalist, Rainer Maria Rilke Nat Poetry Competition, 84; Mary Fay Poetry Awd, 82; Intl Who's Who in Poetry and Poets' Encyclopedia; 2000 Outstanding Intellectuals of the 20th Century. **MEMBERSHIPS** Asn of Literary Scholars and Critics, Asn for the Study of Lit and the Environment, Early Book Soc, Medieval Acad of Am, Medieval Club of NY, Mod Lang Asn, NJ Col English Asn, Soc for the History of Authorship, Reading and Publishing, Soc for Textual Scholarship. **RESEARCH** Modern and Postmodern Literature, especially poetry, interdisciplinary medieval studies; Technology and Culture, especially aesthetics; Textual scholarship; Communications Technology and Epistemology. **SELECTED PUBLICATIONS** Auth, The Pond at Cape May Point, New York, forthcoming; auth, First Life, Jersey City, forthcoming; auth, "Art as a Way: Absence and Presence, Aesthetics and Friendship in the William Bronk--Robert Meyer Correspondence," in The Body of this Life: Essays on the Work of William Bronk, Talisman House Pub, forthcoming; auth, "Objectist Poetics since 1970," in The World in Time and Space: Towards a History of Innovative American Poetry: 1970-2000, Talisman House Pub, forthcoming; auth, "Ockham, Chaucer, and the Emergence of Modern Poetics," in Rhetorical Poetics of the Middle Ages: Reconstructive Polyphony. Essays in Honor of Robert O. Payne, Fairleigh Dickinson Univ Press, 00; auth, "The Language of the Text: Authorship and Textuality in Pearl, The Divine Comedy and Piers Plowman," in The Medieval Book and the Magic of Reading, Garland Pub, 99; auth, The Poetics of Authorship in the Later Middle Ages: The Emergence of the Modern Literary Persona, Peter Lang Pub, 99; auth, The Winter Mind: William Bronk and American Letters, Fairleigh Dickinson Univ Press, 98; auth, "Analysis and Reflections about Preservation Week," Preservation Week Report, Spring 98. **CONTACT ADDRESS** Dept Humanities & Soc Sci, New Jersey Inst of Tech, 323 M L K Blvd, Newark, NJ 07102-1824. **EMAIL** kimmelman@njit.edu

KIMNACH, WILSON H.
DISCIPLINE ENGLISH **EDUCATION** Brown Univ, BA, 60; Univ Penn, MA, 62, PhD, 71. **CAREER** Affil prof, Eng, Clark; current, Prof, Eng & Presidential Prof, Hum, Bridgeport. **MEMBERSHIPS** Am Antiquarian Soc **SELECTED PUBLICATIONS** Ed, Sermons and Discourses, 1720-1723, vol 10 of the Works of Jonathan Edwards, Yale Univ Press, 92. **CONTACT ADDRESS** 59 Beecher Rd, Woodbridge, CT 06525.

KINDALL, SUSAN CAROL
PERSONAL Born 02/26/1967, Greenville, SC **DISCIPLINE** PIANO **EDUCATION** Bob Jones Univ, BM, 88, MM, 90; Univ Ok, DMA, 94. **CAREER** Prof, Bob Jones Univ, 98- **HONORS AND AWARDS** Gail Boyd DeStwolinski Awd, 93; OMTA Piano competition, 91; private study, alexander technique **MEMBERSHIPS** Music Teachers Assoc; Crescent Music Club. **RESEARCH** Twentieth-century Amer piano music; music tech & its application to piano pedagogy. **SELECTED PUBLICATIONS** Auth, The Twenty-Four Preludes for Solo Piano by Richard Cumming: A Pedagogical and Performance Analysis, UMI, 94. **CONTACT ADDRESS** Bob Jones Univ, PO Box 34444, Greenville, SC 29614. **EMAIL** kindall@gateway.net

KING, BEN L.
PERSONAL Born 01/31/1967, Bloomington, IN, s **DISCIPLINE** CLASSICS **EDUCATION** Princeton Univ, PhD, 97. **CAREER** Vis asst prof, Univ VA, 96-97; lectr, Univ Cal Riverside, 97-. **MEMBERSHIPS** Amer Philol Asn **RESEARCH** Greek intellectual history; Homer; Greek and Roman historigraphy. **SELECTED PUBLICATIONS** Auth, The Rhetoric of the Victim: Odysseus at the Swineherds Hut, Classical Antiquity, 99. **CONTACT ADDRESS** 600 Central Ave., #30, Riverside, CA 92507. **EMAIL** BENKING@verac1.ucr.edu

KING, JAMES
DISCIPLINE ENGLISH LITERATURE **EDUCATION** Univ Toronto, BA; Princeton Univ, MA, PhD. **RESEARCH** 20th century English lit and art; biography. **SELECTED PUBLICATIONS** Auth, William Cowper: a Biography, 86; auth, Interior Landscapes: a Life of Paul Nash, 87; auth, The Last Modern: a Life of Herbert Read, 90; auth, William Blake: His Life, 92; auth, Virginia Woolf, 94; auth, Margaret Laurence, 97. **CONTACT ADDRESS** English Dept, McMaster Univ, 1280 Main St W, Hamilton, ON, Canada L8S 4L9. **EMAIL** jking@mcmaster.ca

KING, KATHLEEN
DISCIPLINE ENGLISH LITERATURE **EDUCATION** Univ Nebr, PhD, 84. **CAREER** Assoc prof. **RESEARCH** Computers and education; the writing of fiction and poetry; online teaching; and distance learning. **SELECTED PUBLICATIONS** Auth, Cricket Sings; Going Online: Computerized Courses for Distant Learners. **CONTACT ADDRESS** Dept of English and Philosophy, Idaho State Univ, Pocatello, ID 83209. **EMAIL** kingkath@isu.edu

KING, PAUL E.
PERSONAL Born 10/07/1955, Fort Stockton, TX, m, 1977, 2 children **DISCIPLINE** SPEECH COMMUNICATION **EDUCATION** Univ North Tx, PhD, 85. **CAREER** Assoc Prof, TX Christian Univ, 85-. **HONORS AND AWARDS** Fine Arts & Commun Col Teaching Awd; Pi Kappa Delta; Pi Gamma Mu. **MEMBERSHIPS** ICA; SCA; SSCA. **RESEARCH** Information processing; interpersonal influence. **SELECTED PUBLICATIONS** Auth, Surviving an appointment as department chair, J of the Asn for Commun Admin, 97; coauth, Mindfulness, mindlessness, and communication instruction, Commun Ed, 98; A case study of the Weberian leadership of Joseph Smith, The J of Commun and Religion, 98; Compliance-gaining strategies, communication satisfaction, and willingness to comply, Commun Reports, 94; Contagion theory and the communication of public speaking anxiety, Commun Ed, 94. **CONTACT ADDRESS** Speech Commun Dept, Texas Christian Univ, Box 298000, Fort Worth, TX 76129.

KING, PETER
PERSONAL Born New York, NY **DISCIPLINE** CLASSICS, ANCIENT HISTORY **EDUCATION** Fordham Univ, MA; Univ NC, JD; PhD. **MEMBERSHIPS** Am Philol Asn. **RESEARCH** Roman Law, History and Society; Latin Language. **CONTACT ADDRESS** Dept Class, Temple Univ, 213 E 84th St, New York, NY 10028. **EMAIL** pking002@astro.temple.edu

KING, ROBERTA R.
PERSONAL Born 07/05/1949, CA, s **DISCIPLINE** MUSIC, MISSIOLOGY, ANTHROPOLOGY, ETHNOMUSICOLOGY **EDUCATION** Univ Calif Santa Barbara, BA, 72; Univ Ore, M Mus, 76, Fuller Theol Sem, MA, 82; PhD, 89. **CAREER** Lectr, Daustar Univ, Kenya, 78-99; ethnomusicologist, CBI Int, 82-99; Fuller Theol Sem, 00-. **HONORS AND AWARDS** David Allen Hubbard Awd, Fuller Sem; Regent Scholar, Univ of Calif. **MEMBERSHIPS** Soc for Ethnomusicology. **RESEARCH** African music, Communication (intercultural), ethnomusicology, Anthropology. **SELECTED PUBLICATIONS** Auth, Pathways in Christian Music Communication, Fuller Theol Sem, (Pasadena, CA), 89; auth, A Time to Sing, Evangel Pub (Nairobi, Kenya), 99. **CONTACT ADDRESS** School of World Mission, Fuller Theol Sem, 135 N Oakland Ave, Pasadena, CA 91182-0001. **EMAIL** rking@fuller.edu

KING, ROGER
PERSONAL Born 03/14/1947, London, England **DISCIPLINE** SOCIO-ECONOMICS; CREATIVE WRITER **EDUCATION** Univ Nottingham, UK, BSc, 69; Univ Mass, MS, 72; Univ Reading, UK, PhD, 77. **CAREER** Lectr, res fel, agric econ, Ahmadu/Bello Univ, Nigeria, 72-74; res off, rural develop, Univ Reading, UK, 74-79; consult, rural develop in Africa and Asia for UN, 79-90; vis prof, creative writing, Eastern Washington Univ, 90-91; assoc prof, creative writing, San Francisco State Univ, 94-97; self-employed writer, 97-. **HONORS AND AWARDS** Yaddo Fel; Breadloaf Fel. **MEMBERSHIPS** PEN. **RESEARCH** Relationship between international economic change, the lives of the poor, and the movement of people; relationship of social change, creative expression and freedoms. **SELECTED PUBLICATIONS** Auth, Horizontal Hotel, Andre Deutsch, 83; auth, The Development Game, Grantao, 86; auth, Written on A Stranger's Map, Grafton-Collins, 87; auth, Sea Level, Poseidon, 92. **CONTACT ADDRESS** 154 Shutesbury Rd, Leverett, MA 01054. **EMAIL** rogerking1@aol.com

KING, SHELLEY
DISCIPLINE ENGLISH LITERATURE **EDUCATION** Univ Toronto, PhD. **CAREER** Dept Eng, Queen's Univ **RESEARCH** Romantic and Victorian fiction; children's literature. **SELECTED PUBLICATIONS** Co-ed, Adeline Mowrbray, 98. **CONTACT ADDRESS** English Dept, Queen's Univ at Kingston, Kingston, ON, Canada K7L 3N6. **EMAIL** kings@qsilver.queensu.ca

KING, STEPHEN
DISCIPLINE SPEECH **EDUCATION** Boise State Univ, BA, 87; Univ NMex, MA, 90; Ind Univ, PhD, 97. **CAREER** Teaching Asst, Univ NMex, 88-90; Assoc Instr, Ind Univ, 90-95; Asst Prof, Delta State Univ, 95-. **HONORS AND AWARDS** Award for Teaching Excellence by a Grad Student, Int Commun Asn, 90. **MEMBERSHIPS** Nat Commun Asn, Southern States Speech Asn, Central States Speech Asn, Western States Speech Asn, Northwest Commun Asn. **RESEARCH** Rhetorical studies, intercultural communication, popular culture. **SELECTED PUBLICATIONS** Coauth, "The Sanctuary Movement: Criminal Trials and Religious Dissent," J of Commun and Relig, 15 (92): 15-28; coauth, "Bob Marley's 'Redemption Song': The Rhetoric of Reggae and Rastafari," J of Popular Cult, 29 (95): 17-36; auth, "International Reggae, Democratic Socialism and the Secularization of the Rastafarian Movement 1972-1980," Popular Music and Soc, 22(98): 39-60; auth, "The Co-Optation of a 'Revolution': Rastafari, Reggae and the Rhetoric of Social Control," Howard J of Commun, 10.2 (99): 77-95. **CONTACT ADDRESS** Dept Lang, Delta State Univ, 1003 W Sunflower Rd, Cleveland, OH 38733-0001. **EMAIL** sking@dsu.deltast.edu

KING, THOMAS L.
PERSONAL Born 09/23/1940, IN, m, 1963, 3 children **DISCIPLINE** THEATRE **EDUCATION** Indiana Univ, PhD, 70. **CAREER** Asst prof, Sweet Briar Col, 69-74; assoc prof, James Madison Univ, 74-85; prof, 85-. **HONORS AND AWARDS** Madison Schol, 96; Fulbright Lectr, Turkey, 96-97. **MEMBERSHIPS** ATHE; ARIT; TSA; PSI. **RESEARCH** American theater; Greek theater; Turkish and Ottoman performance. **SELECTED PUBLICATIONS** Auth, "Irony and Distance" in The Glass Menagerie, ETJ (73); auth, "Irony and Distance" in The Glass Menagerie, ed. RB Parker, Twentieth Century Interpretations of the Glass Menagerie (Yale, 83); auth, :The Theater in Islamic Tradition," CCHA Rev (97). **CONTACT ADDRESS** Dept Theater and Dance, James Madison Univ, 800 S Main St, Harrisonburg, VA 22807-0001.

KING, YVONNE
PERSONAL Born 05/30/1935, Clay Co., WV, d, 1 child **DISCIPLINE** LITERATURE **EDUCATION** Glenville State Col, AB, 57; West Virginia Univ, MSJ, 63. **CAREER** Teacher, Clay Co, Kanawha Co, Wood Co, WV Secondary Schools, 57-66; Journalism Prof, English Prof, Gstate Col, 66-; Advisor of Campus Weekly Newspaper, 66-90; Yearbook, intermittently, 66-99. **HONORS AND AWARDS** Who's Who (student); Who's Who in the East (teacher); Wall St. Newspaper Fund Fellow. **MEMBERSHIPS** Public Relations Society; Delta Kappa Gamma; National Council Teachers of English. **RESEARCH** Word Usage; Journalistic techniques; Grammatical tips. **SELECTED PUBLICATIONS** Auth, "Grammatically Speaking," 98. **CONTACT ADDRESS** Dept Language & Literature, Glenville State Col, 200 High St, Glenville, WV 26351-1200. **EMAIL** yking@rrol.net

KINNAMON, KENETH
PERSONAL Born 12/04/1932, Dallas, TX, 3 children **DISCIPLINE** ENGLISH **EDUCATION** Univ Tex, BA, 53; Harvard Univ, AM, 54; PhD, 66. **CAREER** Instructor, Tex Technol Col, 56-62; Instructor to Prof and Dept Head, Univ Ill, 65-82; Prof, Univ Ark, 82-. **HONORS AND AWARDS** Fel, Univ Ill; Phi Beta Kappa; NEH Summer Stipend; Fel, DuBois Inst. **MEMBERSHIPS** Mod Lang Asn, Am Literature Asn, The Hemingway Soc, Richard Wright Circle. **RESEARCH** African American Literature, especially Richard Wright; Ernest Hemingway. **SELECTED PUBLICATIONS** Auth, The Emergence of Richard Wright; auth, A Richard Wright Bibliography; co-auth, Black Writers of America; co-auth, Conversations with Richard Wright; auth, James Baldwin: A Collection of Critical Essays; auth, New Essays on Native Son; auth, Critical Essays on Richard Wright's Native Son. **CONTACT ADDRESS** Dept English, Univ of Arkansas, Fayetteville, 1 Univ of Ark, Fayetteville, AR 72701-1201.

KINNAMON, NOEL JAMES
PERSONAL Born 09/06/1943, Winston-Salem, NC **DISCIPLINE** ENGLISH **EDUCATION** Duke Univ, AB, 65; Univ NC, Chapel Hill, MA, 66, PhD(English), 76. **CAREER** Assoc Prof English, Mars Hill Col, 66- **MEMBERSHIPS** MLA; SAtlantic Mod Lang Asn; Southeastern Renaissance Conf. **RESEARCH** Renaissance English literature; medieval English literature. **SELECTED PUBLICATIONS** Auth, Recent Studies in Renaissance English Manuscripts, Eng Lit Renaissance 2, 97; God's Scholar: The Countess of Pembroke's Psalms and Beza's Psalmorum Davidis.. Libri Quinque, Notes and Queries, 1, 97; The Collected Works of Mary Sidney Herbert, Countess of Pembroke, Clarendon Press, 98; coed, "The Collected Works of

Mary Sidney Herbert," The Countess of Pembroke, 2 vols., Oxford Univ Press, 98. **CONTACT ADDRESS** Dept of English, Mars Hill Col, Mars Hill, NC 28754. **EMAIL** nkinnamon@mhc.edu

KINNEBREW, MARY JANE
PERSONAL Born 11/10/1944, Odessa, TX, m, 1965, 2 children **DISCIPLINE** ENGLISH **EDUCATION** Rice Univ, BA, 66; Lamar Univ, MA, 70; Univ Houston, PhD, 83. **CAREER** Prof, San Jacinto Col Central, 76-. **HONORS AND AWARDS** Distinguished Service Awd, Community Col Humanities Asn; Outstanding Fac Member, San Jacinto Col Central. **MEMBERSHIPS** Community Col Humanities Asn. **RESEARCH** British and American Literature. **SELECTED PUBLICATIONS** Auth, "From the heart of Reality: Non-Standard Dialect in the Fiction of Flannery O'Connor," Lang and Lit, 76; auth, "The Importance of Dialect Variation in The Member of the Wedding and The Heart Is A Lonely Hunter," Lang and Lit, 85. **CONTACT ADDRESS** Dept Lang Arts, San Jacinto Col, Central, 8060 Spencer Hwy, Pasadena, TX 77505-5903. **EMAIL** mjkinn@sjcd.cc.tx.us

KINNEY, ARTHUR F.
PERSONAL Born 09/05/1933, Cortland, NY **DISCIPLINE** ENGLISH **EDUCATION** Syracuse Univ, BA, 55; Columbia Univ, MS, 56; Univ Mich, Ann Arbor, PhD, 63. **CAREER** Act instr, Yale Univ, 63-66; from asst prof, 66-68, to assoc prof, 69-75, prof, 75- and Thomas W. Copeland Prof of Lit Hist, Univ Mass, Amherst; adj prof Engl, NY Univ; dir, Mass Ctr for Renaissance Stud, 97- . **HONORS AND AWARDS** Magna cum Laude, 55; Chancellor's Medal; Univ Res Fel; Distinguished Tchg Awd; Morse Fel; NEH Sr Fel; Folger Sr Fel; Huntington Sr Fel; Bread Loaf Scholar. **MEMBERSHIPS** Renaissance Eng Text Soc; Shakespeare Asn of Am; Renaissance Soc of Am; ed, Eng Lit Renaissance; ed, Mass Stud in Early Modern Culture series; ed, Twayne Eng Authors in the Renaissance series. **RESEARCH** English literary history and cultural studies; Faulkner and the American South. **SELECTED PUBLICATIONS** Auth, John Skelton: The Priest as Poet; auth, Rogues, Vagabonds, and Sturdy Beggars; auth, Renaissance Historicism; auth, Classical, Renaissance and Postmodernist Acts of the Imagination: Essays Commemorating O.B. Hardison, Jr.; auth, Poetics and Praxis: Understanding and Imagination: The Collected Essays of O.B. Hardison, Jr.; auth, Critical Essays on William Faulkner: The Sutpen Family; auth, Go Down, Moses: The Miscegenation of Time: auth, Approaches to Teaching The Sound and the Fury; ed, The Witch of Edmonton; ed, Cambridge Companion to English Literature, 1500-1600; auth, Dorothy Parker, Revisited, 2d ed; auth, "Humanist Poetics, 87; auth, "Continental Humanist Poetics," 89; auth, "Renaissance Drama," 99. **CONTACT ADDRESS** 25 Hunter Hill Dr, Amherst, MA 01002. **EMAIL** afkinney@english.umass.edu

KINNEY, JAMES JOSEPH
PERSONAL Born 03/11/1942, Utica, NY, m, 1968, 1 child **DISCIPLINE** ENGLISH **EDUCATION** St Bonaventure Univ, BA, 64; Univ TN, PhD(English), 72. **CAREER** Instr English, Univ TN, 69-71; div chm humanities, Columbia State Col, TN, 71-76; vis assoc prof English, Univ FL, 74-75; prof English, VA Commonwealth Univ, 77-; Nat Endowment for Humanities fel English, Univ MA, 76-77. **MEMBERSHIPS** Rhetoric Soc Am; MLA; Conf Col Compos & Commun; NCTE. **RESEARCH** Rhetoric; American literature; pedagogy. **SELECTED PUBLICATIONS** Auth, Training Teachers to Teach Composition, Freshman English News, fall 75; Tagmemic Rhetoric: A Reconsideration, Col Compos & Commun, 5/78; On Duty in an Age of Dilemma, Col English, 12/78; Classifying Heuristics, Col Compos & Commun, 12/79; Scientism and the Teaching of English, New Students in the Two-year Colleges, NCTE, 79; Composition Research and the Rhetorical Tradition, Rhet Soc Quart, summer 80; Why bother? The Importance of Critical Thinking, in: Fostering Critical Thinking, Jossey-Bass, 80; Understanding Writing, Random House, 82; Amalgamation!, Greenwood Press, 85. **CONTACT ADDRESS** Dept English, Virginia Commonwealth Univ, Box 842005, Richmond, VA 23284-2005. **EMAIL** jkinney@vcu.edu

KINNEY, JOSEPH
PERSONAL Born 05/14/1936, Philadelphia, PA, m, 1957, 4 children **DISCIPLINE** ENGLISH **EDUCATION** Villanova Univ, AB, 58; MA, 59; Bryn Mawr Col, PhD, 67. **CAREER** Instructor to Assoc Prof, Villanova Univ, 59-. **HONORS AND AWARDS** Founder's Awd, Villanova Univ Grad alumni Soc, 94. **RESEARCH** Shakespeare and Renaissance Drama **CONTACT ADDRESS** Dept English, Villanova Univ, 800 E Lancaster Ave, Villanova, PA 19085-1603. **EMAIL** joseph.kinney@villanova.edu

KINNEY, KATHERINE
DISCIPLINE AMERICAN AND AFRICAN AMERICAN LITERATURE **EDUCATION** Univ Wash, BA; Univ Pa, MA, PhD. **HONORS AND AWARDS** Fel, Post Nat Amer Stud Res Gp, Univ Calif Hum Res Inst, Irvine. **SELECTED PUBLICATIONS** Auth, "Foreign Affairs: Women, War, and the Post-National," Univ Calif Press; "Making Capital: War, Labor, and Whitman in Washington, D.C.," Breaking Bounds: A Whitman Centennial Volume; "Tim O'Brien's Going After Cacciato," Amer Lit Hist; Friendly Fire: American Identity and the Literature of the Vietnam War, 99. **CONTACT ADDRESS** Dept of Eng, Univ of California, Riverside, 1156 Hinderaker Hall, Riverside, CA 92521-0209. **EMAIL** kkinney@ucrac1.ucr.edu.

KINSMAN, LAWRENCE
PERSONAL Born 01/07/1953, New York, NY, s **DISCIPLINE** ENGLISH **EDUCATION** State Univ NYork at Oneonta, BA, 75; PhD, 83. **CAREER** Prof of English, New Hampshire Col, Manchester, 84-, Liberal Arts Coordr. **HONORS AND AWARDS** Fulbright Jr Lectureship in Am Lit, Univ of Oporto, Portugal, 86-87; Awd for Outstanding Emerging Writer, New Hampshire Writers & Pubs Proj, 96. **MEMBERSHIPS** Modern Lang Asn, Assoc Writing Programs, Fulbright Alumni Asn. **RESEARCH** The modernist short story; nineteenth-century French and Russian novels. **SELECTED PUBLICATIONS** Auth, "Legacies," NH Col J (spring 89); auth, "The Words I Wanted to Hear," Bay Windows (spring 90); "Father and Daughter," NH Col J (spring 94); auth, "Waking Hours," Compass Rose (95-96); auth, Water from the Moon and Other Love Stories, The Abelard Press (Dec 95); auth, "Visitations," NH Col J (spring 96); auth, "The Venus of the Douro," NH Col J (spring 97); auth, "Our Fallen Angel," By Windows (Oct 29, 97); auth, A Well-Ordered Life, The Abelard Press (Jan 98); auth, "Letter from Passey," New Laurel Rev (spring 99). **CONTACT ADDRESS** Dept Liberal Arts, New Hampshire Col, 2500 N River Rd, Hooksett, NH 03106-1067. **EMAIL** lkinsman@minerva.nhc.edu

KINZIE, MARY
DISCIPLINE ENGLISH **EDUCATION** Johns Hopkins Univ, PhD. **CAREER** Prof, Northwestern Univ; dir of the English Major in Writing. **HONORS AND AWARDS** Guggenheim fel; Koldyke outstanding tchg prof. **SELECTED PUBLICATIONS** Auth, Threshold of the Year, 82; Masked Women, 90; Summers of Vietnam, 90; Autumn Eros and Other Poems, 91; Ghost Ship, 96; The Cure of Poetry in an Age of Prose, 93; The Judge Is Fury: Dislocation and Form in Poetry, 94; auth, A Poet's Guide to Poetry, Chicago, 99. **CONTACT ADDRESS** Dept of English, Northwestern Univ, Univ Hall 215, 1897 Sheridan Rd, Evanston, IL 60208. **EMAIL** mkinzie@norhtwestern.edu

KIPLING, GORDON L.
PERSONAL Born Aurora, IL, m, 1965, 3 children **DISCIPLINE** ENGLISH **EDUCATION** Beloit Col, BA, 65; Univ Chicago, AM, 66; PhD, 71. **CAREER** Assoc Prof to Full Prof, UCLA, 69-. **HONORS AND AWARDS** Fel, NEH, 73; Fel, John Simon Guggenheim Found, 80; Fel, NEH, 89; Fulbright Res Fel, 90; Otto Grundler Prize f, 00; David Bevington Prize, 00. **RESEARCH** Medieval and early Renaissance theatre, including such forms of spectacular theatre as the royal entry and other festival drama. The artistic representation of medieval and renaissance theatres; Anglo-Dutch literary and theatrical relations; Drama and ritual, both religious and political. **SELECTED PUBLICATIONS** Ed, The Receyt of the Ladie Kateryne, Oxford Univ Press, 90; auth, "A Horse Designed by Committee: The Bureaucratics of the London Civic Triumph in the 1520s", in Research Opportunities in Renaissance Drama, Vol 31, 92; auth, "He That Saw It Would Not Believe It: Anne Boleyn's Royal Entry into London," in Civic Ritual and Drama in Medieval and Renaissance Europe, Rodopi, 97; auth, "Wonderful Spectacles: Theatre and Civic Culture," in A New History of Early English Drama, Columbia Univ Press, 97; auth, Enter the King: Theatre, Liturgy, and Ritual in the Medieval Civic Triumph, Clarendon Press, 98; auth, "Theatre as Subject and Object in Fouquet's 'Martyrdom of St Apollonia'," Medieval English Theatre, 99. **CONTACT ADDRESS** Dept English, Univ of California, Los Angeles, 2225 Rolfe Hall, Box 951530, Los Angeles, CA 90095-1530. **EMAIL** kipling@humnet.ucla.edu

KIPPERMAN, MARK
PERSONAL Born Brooklyn, NY, m, 1996 **DISCIPLINE** ENGLISH **EDUCATION** SUNY, BA, 72; Univ Penn, MA; PhD, 81. **CAREER** Asst Prof, Princeton Univ, 80-86; Assoc Prof, Northern Ill Univ, 86-. **HONORS AND AWARDS** Fel, Am Coun of Learned Soc, 82-83; Fel, NEH, 92-93; Honorable Mention Best Essay, Keats-Shelley Asn of Am, 91; Excellence in Teaching, Princeton Univ, 85; Phi Beta Kappa, 73. **MEMBERSHIPS** Mod Lang Asn, Keats-Shelley Asn of Am. **RESEARCH** English Romantic Poetry. **SELECTED PUBLICATIONS** Auth, Beyond Enchantment: German Idealism and English Romantic Poetry, Univ Penn Press, 86; auth, "History and Ideality: The Politics of Shelley's Hellas," Studies in Romanticism, 91; auth, "Absorbing a Revolution: Shelley becomes a Romantic," Nineteenth Century Literature, 92; auth, "Coleridge, Shelley, Dave, and Science's millennium," Criticism, 98. **CONTACT ADDRESS** Dept English, No Illinois Univ, 1425 W Lincoln Highway, Dekalb, IL 60115-2828. **EMAIL** makipper@niu.edu

KIRALYFALVI, BELA
DISCIPLINE THEATER AND DRAMA **EDUCATION** Univ Kans, PhD. **CAREER** Chp, speech commun; dir, Univ theatre; prof. **HONORS AND AWARDS** Adjudicator, ch, playwriting awards in the Amer Col Theatre Fest. **RESEARCH** Dramatic theory, criticism, and playscript analysis. **SELECTED PUBLICATIONS** Publ, aesthetics and theatre topics, nat and intl jour(s). **CONTACT ADDRESS** Dept of Commun, Wichita State Univ, 1845 Fairmont, Wichita, KS 67260-0062.

KIRBY, DAVID
PERSONAL Born 11/29/1944, Baton Rouge, LA **DISCIPLINE** AMERICAN LITERATURE, CREATIVE WRITING **EDUCATION** La State Univ, BA, 66; Johns Hopkins Univ, PhD, 69. **CAREER** Asst prof, 69-74, assoc prof, 74-79, dir writing prog, 73-77, asst exec vpres, 75-77, Prof English, Fla State Univ, 79-. **RESEARCH** Writings of Henry James; late 19th century American literature; modern poetry. **SELECTED PUBLICATIONS** Co-ed, Individual and Community: Variations on a Theme in American Fiction, Duke Univ, 75; auth, American Fiction to 1900: A Guide to Information Sources, Gale Res, 75; The Opera Lover, Anhinga Press, 77; Grace King, Twayne Publ, 80; America's Hive of Honey: Foreign Sources of American Fiction through Henry James, 80 & The Sun Rises in the Evening: Monism and Quietism in Western Culture, 82, Scarecrow. **CONTACT ADDRESS** Dept of English, Florida State Univ, 600 W College Ave, Tallahassee, FL 32306-1580. **EMAIL** dkirby@english.fsu.edu

KIRBY, JOHN T.
PERSONAL Born 05/09/1955, New Haven, CT, 2 children **DISCIPLINE** CLASSICS & COMPARATIVE LITERATURE **EDUCATION** Choate Sch, diploma, 73; Univ NC Chapel Hill, AB, 77; Univ NC Chapel Hill, MA, 81; Univ NC Chapel Hill, PhD, 85. **CAREER** Asst prof, class lang and lit, Smith Col, 85-87; founding chair, prog in class studies, Purdue Univ, 88-94; chair, prog in comparative lit, Purdue Univ, 94-. **HONORS AND AWARDS** Phi Eta Sigma, 74; Phi Beta Kappa, 76; Morehead Scholar, Univ NC, 73-77; Univ Res Asst, Univ NC, 80-81; Classics Teaching fel, Univ NC, 83-84; Software develop grant, ACIS Found of IBM, 85; Robert E. Frane Memorial Scholar, 85; Morris House fel, Smith Col, 86; Facul Teaching Awd nominee, Smith Col, 86; Libr Scholars grant prog award, Purdue Univ, 87; Facul teaching award nominee, Smith Col, 87, 88; XL Summer facul grant, Purdue Res Found, 88; Univ Outstanding Undergraduate Teaching Awd nominee, Purdue Univ, 88; XL summer facul grant, Purdue Res Found, 90; XL Intl Travel grant, Purdue Res Found, 91; res leave, dept foreign lang and lit, Purdue Univ, spring, 91; NEH fel, Univ Iowa, fall, 91; fel, Ctr for Humanistic Studies, Purdue Univ, spring, 93; Scholar-in-residence, Choate Rosemary Hall, fall, 93; Sch of Liberal Arts Outstanding Teaching award, Purdue Univ, 93; Amer Philol Asn award for Excellence in the Teaching of the Classics, 96; Twentieth Century award for achievement, Intl Bio Ctr, 97; man of the year, am biog inst, 96; international man of the year, int biog ctr, 96-97; listed in int dir of distinguished leadership, 7th ed, 97; listed in int who's who of intellectuals, 12th ed, 97. **MEMBERSHIPS** Mod Lang Asn; Amer Comparative Lit Asn; Amer Philol Asn; Calif Class Asn; Class Asn of the Middle West and South; Amer Soc for the Hist of Rhetoric. **RESEARCH** Classical Greek and Latin literature; Classical rhetoric and poetics; Literary theory. **SELECTED PUBLICATIONS** Auth, The Rhetoric of Cicero's Pro Cluentio, 90; ed, The Comparative Reader: A Handlist of Basic Reading in Comparative Literature, 98; jour articles, Amer Jour of Philol, 118, 517-554, 97; Philos and Rhetoric, 30, 190-202, 97; Voices in Italian Amer, 7, 207-211, 96; Ill Class Studies, 20, 77-81, 95; Voices in Italian Amer, 6, 71-76, 95; book chap, Ciceronian Rhetoric: Theory and Practice, 13-31, Roman Eloquence: Rhetoric in Society and Literature, 97; Classical Greek Origins of Western Aesthetic Theory, 29-45, 96; The Great Triangle in Early Greek Rhetoric and Poetics, 3-15, 94; The Neo-Latin Verse of Joseph Tusiani, 180-204, Joseph Tusiani: Poet, Translator, Humanist, 94; auth, Secret of the Muses Retold: Classical Influences on Itlaian Authors of the Twentieth Century, Chicago: University of Chicago Press, in press; ed, Landmark Essays on Ciceronian Rhetoric, Davis CA: Hermagoras Press/Erlbaum, in press. **CONTACT ADDRESS** Dept of For Lang and Lit, Purdue Univ, West Lafayette, 1080 Schleman Hall, West Lafayette, IN 47907-1354. **EMAIL** corax@purdue.edu

KIRBY-SMITH, H. T.
PERSONAL Born 01/11/1938, Sewanee, TN, m, 1970, 1 child **DISCIPLINE** ENGLISH **EDUCATION** Univ of the South, BA, 59; Harvard Univ, MA, 61. **CAREER** Instr, Univ of North Carolina at Greensboro, 67-70; Asst Prof, 70-76; Assoc Prof, 76. **HONORS AND AWARDS** Fulbright (France) 59-60; Woodrow Wilson, 60-61; Wallace Steaner Poetry Fellow, 62-63. **MEMBERSHIPS** SAMLA; MLA. **RESEARCH** Prosody; Modern Poetry. **SELECTED PUBLICATIONS** Auth, "The Origins of Free Verse," Ann Arbor: University of Michigan Press, 96, paper ed., 98: 304; auth, "A Philosophical Novelist: George Santayana and The Last Puritan," Carbondale: Southern Illinois University Press, 97: 208; auth, "Behind the Lines," (review essay), Southern Review, vol 35, no 3 Summer 99: 635-50; auth, "The Celestial Twins: Poetry and Music through the Ages," Amherst: Univ of Massachusetts Press, 99: 328. **CONTACT ADDRESS** Dept English, Univ of No Carolina, Greensboro, 1000 Spring Garden, Greensboro, NC 27412-0001. **EMAIL** htkirbys@uncq.edu

KIRK-DUGGAN, CHERYL ANN
PERSONAL Born 07/24/1951, Lake Charles, LA, m, 1983 **DISCIPLINE** THEOLOGY, MUSICOLOGY **EDUCATION** University of Southwestern Louisiana, BA 1973; University of Texas at Austin, MM 1977; Austin Presbyterian Theological Seminary, MDiv 1987; Baylor University, PhD, 1992. **CAREER** Univ of Tex at Austin, music of Black Am coach accomp 74-77; Austin Commun Col, music of Black Am 76-77; Prairie View A&M Univ, teacher 77-78; The Actor's Inst, teacher 82-83; Williams Inst CME Church, organist, choir dir 79-83; Self-employed, professional singer, voice teacher, vocal coach 80-85; Christian Methodist Church, ordained minister, deacons orders 84, elders orders 86; Baylor Univ, Inst of Oral Hist, grad asst, 87-89, Dept of Relig, teaching asst, 89-90; Meredith Col, asst prof, 93-96; Ctr For Women & Relig, Dir, Grad Theol Union, Asst Prof, 97-; Assoc Pastor, Phillips Temple CME, Berkeley, 97- ; Ed Bd, Contagion: J of Violence, Mimesis & Cult, 94-; Asn for Black Awareness, Meredith Col, Advisor, 94-96. **HONORS AND AWARDS** University of Southwestern Louisiana, Magna Cum Laude; University of Texas at Austin, University Fellowship, 1975-77; Fund for Theological Education, Fellowship for Doctoral Studies, 1987-88, 1988-89. **MEMBERSHIPS** Pi Kappa Lambda, 1976-; Omicron Delta Kappa, 1977-; associate pastor, Trinity CME Church, 1985-86; president, Racial Ethnic Faith Comm, Austin Seminary, 1986-87; Golden Key Honor Society, 1990; Colloquim On Violence & Religion; Society of Biblical Literature; American Academy of Religion; Center for Black Music Research; Society of Chritian Ethics; American Society for Aesthetics; Sigma Alpha Iota. **SELECTED PUBLICATIONS** Carnegie Hall debut, 81; featured: "Life, Black Tress, Das Goldene Blatte, Bunte," 81, 82; recording: "Third Duke Ellington Sacred Concert," Virgil Thompson's Four Saints in Three Acts, EMI Records, 81-82; author: Lily Teaching Fellow, 95, 96; Collidge Scholar with Asn for Religion & Intellectual Life, 96; "African-American Spirituals: Exorcising Evil Through Song," A Troubling in My Soul: Womanist Perspectives on Evil and Suffering, Orbis Press, 91; "Gender, Violence and Transformation," Curing Violence: The Thought of Rene Girard, Polebridge Press, 91; African-American Special Days: 15 Complete Worship Services, Abingdon Press, 96; It's In the Blood: A Trildgy of Poetry Harvested from a Family Tree, River Vision, 96; Exorcizing Evil: A Womanist Perspective on the Spirituals, Orbis, 97; auth, Refiner's Fire: A Religious Engagement with Violence, Fortress, 00. **CONTACT ADDRESS** Ctr for Women, Religion, 2400 Ridge Rd, Berkeley, CA 94709-5298. **EMAIL** kirkdugg@gtu.edu

KIRKWOOD, WILLIAM
DISCIPLINE COMMUNICATION STUDIES **EDUCATION** Northwestern Univ, BA, MA, PhD. **CAREER** Prof. **SELECTED PUBLICATIONS** Auth, pubs in Quarterly Journal of Speech, Communication Monographs, Communication Education, Journal of Communication, Rhetoric Society Quarterly, and Journal of Applied Communication Research. **CONTACT ADDRESS** Dept of Communication, East Tennessee State Univ, PO Box 70717, Johnson City, TN 37614-0717.

KIRSCHKE, JAMES J.
PERSONAL Born 08/10/1941, Norfolk, VA, m, 1969, 2 children **DISCIPLINE** ENGLISH **EDUCATION** La Salle Col, BA, 64; Temple Univ, MA, 70, PhD, 77. **CAREER** Captain, United States Marine Corp, retired (64-68, severely wounded); assoc ed and rev ed, J of Modern Lit, 70-78, Temple Univ; Dept of English, Villanova Univ, 77-. **HONORS AND AWARDS** Vice Pres of the Bd, Janits Fel Prog, 85-87; 2nd Dir, Oversight Comt, exec bd, SECAS, 92-. **MEMBERSHIPS** SECAS (now SEA), GEMCS, AAH. **RESEARCH** Lives and writings of the American Revolutionary Founders. **SELECTED PUBLICATIONS** Auth, Henry James and Impressionism (81); auth, Willa Cather and Six Writers from the Great War (91); auth, Governeur Morris (1752-1816): Author, Statesman and Man of the World (forthcoming); auth, Not Going Home Alone (forthcoming); author of articles, review essays and reviews in dozens of journals in the U.S. and abroad. **CONTACT ADDRESS** Dept English, Villanova Univ, 800 E Lancaster Ave, Bartley Hall, C & F, Villanova, PA 19085-1603. **EMAIL** James.Kirschke@villanova.edu

KIRSHENBLATT-GIMBLETT, BARBARA
PERSONAL Born 09/30/1942, Toronto, ON, Canada, m, 1964 **DISCIPLINE** PERFORMANCE ARTS **EDUCATION** Univ Toronto, BA, 65; Univ Calif, MA, 66; Ind Univ, PhD, 72. **CAREER** Assoc Prof, Univ Pa, 73-80; vis Prof, Intl School of Am, 83-84; Adj Prof, Univ Auckland, 98-; Prof and Chair, 81-. **HONORS AND AWARDS** Folklore Fel, Finnish Acad of Sci and Letters, 90-; Fel, NY Inst for the Humanities, 90-91; Fel, Am Folklore Soc, 85-; Fel, Am Anthropol Asn, Lindback Awd, Univ Penn, 76. **MEMBERSHIPS** Am Anthropol Asn, Asn for Jewish Studies, Am Studies Asn, Asn for Jewish Studies, Am Asn of Museums, ICOM, ICOFOM. **RESEARCH** Tourism, Heritage, Folklore, Museums, World fairs, Performance in everyday life, Food, Jewish culture. **SELECTED PUBLICATIONS** Auth, "Playing to the Senses: Food and Performance," Performance Research, (99): 1-30; auth, "Sounds of Sensibility," Judaism: A Quarterly Journal of Jewish Life and Thought, 98; auth, "Folklore's Crisis," Journal of American Folklore, (98): 111; auth, Destination Culture: Tourism, Museums, and heritage, Univ Calif Press, 98; auth, "The Moral Sublime: The Temple Emanuel fair and Its Cookbook, 1888," recipes for Reading: The community Cookbook and Its Stories, Univ Mass press, 97; auth, "A Place in the World: Jews and the Holy Land at World's Fairs," Encounters with the 'Holy Land': Place, Past and Future in American Jewish Culture, 97; auth, "The electronic Vernacular," Connected: Engagements with Media at Century's End, Univ Chicago Press, 96; auth, Image Before My Eyes: A Photographic History of Jewish Life in Poland, 1864-1939, Schocken, 94; auth, Fabric of Jewish Life: Textiles from the Jewish Museum Collection, Jewish Museum, 77; auth, Speech Play: Research and Resources for Studying Linguistic Creativity, Univ Penn Press, 76. **CONTACT ADDRESS** Dept Performance, New York Univ, 721 Broadway, Tisch School of the Arts, New York, NY 10003-6807. **EMAIL** bk3@nyu.edu

KISER, JOY
DISCIPLINE ART HISTORY, LIBRARY AND INFORMATION SERVICES **EDUCATION** Univ Akron, BA, 88; Case Western Reserve Univ, MA, 90; Kent State Univ, MLIS, 94. **CAREER** HEAD LIBR, CLEVELAND MUS NAT HIST; med libr Wooster Community Hosp. **CONTACT ADDRESS** Cleveland Mus of Nat Hist, Harold Terry Clark Lib, 1 Wade Oval Dr, Univ Cir, Cleveland, OH 44106-1767. **EMAIL** jkiser@cmnh.org

KISER, LISA J.
PERSONAL Born 07/21/1949, Chicago, IL, m, 1990 **DISCIPLINE** ENGLISH LITERATURE **EDUCATION** Univ Wis, BA 72; Univ VA, PhD 77 **CAREER** OH State Univ, asst prof 77-83, assoc prof 83-91, prof eng 91. **HONORS AND AWARDS** Alumni Distg Tch Awd; Honors Facul Ser Awd. **MEMBERSHIPS** Mod Lang Assn; Medieval Acad Am; Medieval Assn Midwest; New Chaucer Soc; Intl Court Lit Soc; AAUP. **RESEARCH** Medieval Lit and cult. **SELECTED PUBLICATIONS** Telling Classical Tales: Chaucer and the Legend of Good Women, Ithaca, Cornell Univ Press, 83; Truth and Textuality in Chaucer's Poetry, Hanover and London, Univ Press of New Eng, 91; several other books and articles. **CONTACT ADDRESS** Dept of Eng, Ohio State Univ, Columbus, 164 West 17th ST, Columbus, OH 43210. **EMAIL** kiser.1@osu.edu

KITCHELL, KENNETH F.
PERSONAL Born 10/24/1947, Brockton, MA, m, 1970, 1 child **DISCIPLINE** CLASSICAL STUDIES **EDUCATION** Coll of Holy Cross, BA, 69; Loyola Univ Chicago, MA, 73; PhD, 76. **CAREER** Loyola Univ, 74; Quigley Preparatory Sem S Chicago, 74-76; Cath High School Baton Rouge, 80-81; Am School of Class Studies Athens Greece, 89; co-dir, Program in Greece Vergilian Soc of Am, 90; instr, 76-78; asst prof, 83-94, assoc prof, 94-97, prof, LA State Univ, 97-; vis prof to full prof, Univ Mass, 98-. **HONORS AND AWARDS** Amoco Found award for Outstanding Undergraduate Techg, 80; Am Philol Asn Awd for excellence in Tchg of Classics, 83; LSU Student Govt Asn Fac Awd, 91; Robert L Amborski Distinguished Honors Prof Awd, 93; Ovatio, Clasical Asn of the Middle W and S, 94; Summer Scholar Centre for Hellenic Studies Wash DC, 97; LSU Alumni Asn Distinguished Fac Awd, 97; Who's Who in the South and Southwest; Who's Who of Emerging Leaders in America; Men of Achievement; Dictionary of International Biography; Who's Who in American Education; Full Prof, Classics, Univ of Mass, 99-. **MEMBERSHIPS** Am Philol Asn; Archaeol Inst Am; Am Class League; Asn of Ancient Hist; Class Asn of the Middle west and S; Class Asn of New England, Joint Asn of Class Tchrs; Mass Foreign Lang Asn; Class Asn of Mass; Class Asn of the Pacific Northwest Am Council on the Tchg of Foreign Lang. **RESEARCH** Latin and Greek Pedagogy; Crete. **SELECTED PUBLICATIONS** Entering the Stadium, Approaches to Ancient Greek Athletics, Class Bull, 98;coauth, A Trilogy on the Herpetology of Linnaeus's Systema Naturae X, Smithsonian Herpetological Service, 94; Albertus Magnus De Animalibus: A Medieval Summa Zoologica, 99. **CONTACT ADDRESS** The Dept of Classics, Univ of Massachusetts, Amherst, 520 Herter Hall, Amherst, MA 01003. **EMAIL** kkitchel@classics.umass.edu

KITELEY, BRIAN
PERSONAL Born 09/26/1956, Minneapolis, MN, m, 1991 **DISCIPLINE** WRITER **EDUCATION** Carleton Col, BA, 78; City Col of NY, MA, 85. **CAREER** Instr, Am univ in Cairo, 87-89; asst prof, Ohio Univ, 92-94; from asst prof to assoc prof, Univ of Denver, 94-. **HONORS AND AWARDS** NEA; Guggenheim; Whiting; Fine Arts Work Center. **SELECTED PUBLICATIONS** Auth, Still Life With Insects, 89; auth, I Know Many Songs, But I Cannot Sing, 96. **CONTACT ADDRESS** Dept English, Univ of Denver, 2140 S Race St, Denver, CO 80210-4639. **EMAIL** bkiteley@du.edu

KITTREDGE, WILLIAM ALFRED
PERSONAL Born 08/14/1932, Portland, OR, s, 2 children **DISCIPLINE** ENGLISH, CREATIVE WRITING **EDUCATION** Ore State Univ, BS, 53; Univ Iowa, MFA, 69. **CAREER** Regents Prof English, Univ Mont, 69-97. **HONORS AND AWARDS** Nat Endowment Arts award, 74, 82; Stegner fel, Stanford Univ, 73-74; Pacific Northwest Bookseller's Awds for Excellence, 84, 87; Montana Governor's Awd for the Arts, 86; co-winner of Montana Comt for the Humanities Awd for Humanist of the Year, 89; PEN West Awd, 92; Neil Simon Awd; Am Acad of Achievement, 93; co-winner of the Nat Endowment for the Humanities, 94. **SELECTED PUBLICATIONS** Auth, The Van Gogh Field and Other Stories, Univ of Miss Press, 79; auth, We Are Not In This Together, 84; auth, Hole in the Sky, Knoft 92; auth, Owning It All, Graywolf, 87; auth, Who Owns the West, Mercury House, 96; auth, The Portable Western Reader, 97; auth, Taking Care: Thoughts on Storytelling and Belief, 99; auth, Balancing Water: Restoring the Klamath Basin, 00; auth, The Nature of Generosity, 00. **CONTACT ADDRESS** Dept of English, Univ of Montana, Missoula, MT 59812.

KITTS, THOMAS M.
PERSONAL Born 10/05/1955, Staten Island, NY, m, 1977, 2 children **DISCIPLINE** ENGLISH **EDUCATION** St John's Univ, BA, 77; NYU, MA, 79; PhD, 91. **CAREER** Dir to adj instr to asst prof to assoc prof to act div chmn to chmn, St John's Univ, 83-. **HONORS AND AWARDS** Fac Achievement Medal, St John's Univ, 01; Teaching Year Hon Mention; St John's Summer Res Grant. **MEMBERSHIPS** MLA; PCA; ATDS; Dramatics Guild. **RESEARCH** Rock and roll culture; American drama; American literature. **SELECTED PUBLICATIONS** Auth, The Theatrical Life of George Henry Boker, Peter Lang, 94; auth, Gypsies (a play), Domestic Pr (NYork), 94; auth, "An Argument for Boker's Francesca da Rimini," Am Drama 3.2. (94): 53-70; auth, "The Individual vs. the Cult Leader: Don Delillo's Mao II, a Novel for the 1990s," Pop Cul t Rev 7 (96): 111-27; auth, "Unlikely Kinsman: Holmes and Iago," in Sherlock Holmes: Victorian Sleuth to Modern Hero, eds. Charles R. Putney, Sally Sugarman, Joseph A. Cutshall (Landham, MD: Scarecrow Pr, 96): 211-21; auth, "George Boker and Lawrence Barrett: Intersecting Theatrical Careers," Nineteenth Cent, VSA 17.1 (97): 27-34; auth, Instructor's Manual to Accompany Literature: Reading Fiction, Poetry, Drama and the Essay, McGraw-Hill, 98, rev 01, compact ed 00; auth, Instructor's Manual to Accompany The American Tradition in Literature, McGraw-Hill, 99. **CONTACT ADDRESS** 648 20th St, Brooklyn, NY 11218-1045. **EMAIL** tomkitts@aol.com

KIZER, ELIZABETH J.
DISCIPLINE COMMUNICATION STUDIES **EDUCATION** Angelo State Univ, BA; Tex Tech Univ, MA; Purdue Univ, PhD. **CAREER** Assoc prof **SELECTED PUBLICATIONS** Auth, The Women's Room: A Readers Theatre Script with Production Notes (rev), Univ Mo, 82; Protest Song Lyrics as Rhetoric, Popular Music Soc, 83; co-auth, Multi-Image and Live Performance: Some Connections, Storyboard, 85; Audio-Visual Effects in Readers Theatre: A Case Study, Int J Instructional Media, 87. **CONTACT ADDRESS** Communication Dept, Univ of Missouri, St. Louis, 590 Lucas Hall, Saint Louis, MO 63121. **EMAIL** sejkize@umslvma.umsl.edu

KLAGES, MARY
PERSONAL Born 01/29/1958, Columbus, OH, 2 children **DISCIPLINE** AMERICAN LITERATURE; CULTURAL STUDIES **EDUCATION** Dartmouth Col, AB, 80; Stanford Univ, MA, 82; PhD, 89. **CAREER** Assoc prof English, Univ Col-Boulder. **RESEARCH** 19th Century American literature & culture, Disability studies, Gender & sexaulity studies, Literacy theory. **SELECTED PUBLICATIONS** Auth, Woeful Afflictions: Disability & Sentimentality in Victorian America, Univ Penn Press, (99). **CONTACT ADDRESS** Dept English, Univ of Colorado, Boulder, CB 226, Boulder, CO 80309-0226. **EMAIL** Klages@spot.colorado.edu

KLAWITTER, GEORGE
DISCIPLINE RENAISSANCE LITERATURE **EDUCATION** Univ Notre Dame , AB, 63; Univ Mich, AM, 69; Univ Chicago, PhD, 81. **CAREER** Eng Dept, St. Edward's Univ **HONORS AND AWARDS** 3 NEH fel; Burlington-Northern Fac Awd Tchg Sch, 89, Tchr Year, 94; contrib ed, john donne variorum, brown univ women writers proj. **MEMBERSHIPS** MLA, Milton Soc, S Central Mod Lang Asn; John Donne Soc, Tex Medieval Soc; Medieval Acad Am; S Central Renaissance Asn, Renaissance Soc Am. **SELECTED PUBLICATIONS** Auth, The Poetry of Richard Barnfield. Selinsgrove: Susquehanna Univ Press, 90; Adapted to the Lake: Letters by the Brother Founders of Notre Dame, 1841-1849, Peter Lang, 93; The Enigmatic Narrator: The Voicing of Same-Sex Love in the Poetry of John Donne, Peter Lang, 94. **CONTACT ADDRESS** St. Edward's Univ, 3001 S Congress Ave, Austin, TX 78704-6489. **EMAIL** georgek@admin.stedwards.edu

KLEIN, JOAN LARSEN
PERSONAL Born Menominee, MI, 2 children **DISCIPLINE** ENGLISH LITERATURE **EDUCATION** Univ Mich, BA, 53; Harvard Univ, MA, 56, PhD(English), 58. **CAREER** Asst prof English, Univ Wis, 58-62; asst prof, Duquesne Univ, 63-64; lectr, Bryn Mawr Col, 64-70; asst prof, 70-79, Assoc Prof, Univ Ill, Urbana, 79-; Mellon fel English, Univ Pittsburgh, 61-62. **MEMBERSHIPS** MLA; Spenser Soc; Shakespeare Soc. **RESEARCH** Spenser; Shakespeare. **SELECTED PUBLICATIONS** Auth, Daughters, Wives, and Widows: Writings by Men About Women and Marriage in Renaissance England 1500-1640, Univ of Illinois Press, 92. **CONTACT ADDRESS** 2209 Vawter St, Urbana, IL 60801. **EMAIL** j-klein3@uiuc.edu

KLEIN, OWEN
DISCIPLINE THEATRE HISTORY; IMPROVISATION **EDUCATION** Villanova, MA; Ind Univ, PhD. **CAREER** Adj assoc prof. **SELECTED PUBLICATIONS** Pub (s), Theatre Hist in Can and 19th century Theatre Res; contrib ed, Oxford Companion to Canadian Drama and Theatre. **CONTACT ADDRESS** Dept of Dramatic Art, Univ of Windsor, 401 Sunset Ave, Windsor, ON, Canada N9B 3P4.

KLEIN, WILLIAM FRANCIS
PERSONAL Born 11/21/1936, Dwight, IL, m, 1962, 3 children **DISCIPLINE** ENGLISH LITERATURE, LITERARY THEORY **EDUCATION** Butler Univ, BA, 59; Univ Chicago, MA, 62, PhD, 75. **CAREER** Instr English, DePaul Univ, 62-64; asst prof, St Xavier Col, 65-67; assoc prof English, Kenyon Col, 68-. **MEMBERSHIPS** Medieval Acad Am. **RESEARCH** Anglo-Saxon poetry; Henry James; the English modal system. **SELECTED PUBLICATIONS** Auth, Purpose and the poetics of The Wanderer and The Seafarer, Anglo-Saxon Poetry, Univ Notre Dame, 75; Fiction and the figures of life, 76 & The story of Audun and the great bear, 77, Perspective; A Critic Nearly Anomalous, Sewanee Rev, 94. **CONTACT ADDRESS** Dept English, Kenyon Col, Sunset Cottage, Gambier, OH 43022-9623. **EMAIL** KLEIN@kenyon.edu

KLEINBERG, SEYMOUR
PERSONAL Born 01/05/1933, New York, NY, s **DISCIPLINE** ENGLISH LITERATURE **EDUCATION** City Col New York, BA, 53; Univ Conn, MA, 55; Univ Mich, PhD, 63. **CAREER** Instr, 59-62, Flint Jr Col; from asst prof to assoc prof, 62-72, prof Eng, 72-, Long Island Univ. **HONORS AND AWARDS** Nat Endowment for Humanities fel, 79, 84, 89, 96; Fel Yaddow Colony, 97; MacDowell Colony, 97. **MEMBERSHIPS** PEN **RESEARCH** Renaissance literature; gender studies; gay literature. **SELECTED PUBLICATIONS** Ed, The Other Persuasion, Vintage Books, 77; auth, Alienated Affections, St Martin's Press, 81; ed, Who's Who in Gay and Lesbian History, Routledge, 01. **CONTACT ADDRESS** Dept of English, Long Island Univ, Brooklyn, Brooklyn, NY 11201. **EMAIL** seymour.kleinberg@liu.edu

KLEINER, ELAINE LAURA
PERSONAL Born 05/02/1942, Portland, OR **DISCIPLINE** ENGLISH LANGUAGE & LITERATURE **EDUCATION** OR State Univ, BA, 64; Univ Chicago, MA, 66, PhD, 71. **CAREER** Tchg asst Eng, Univ WI-Madison, 67-68; from Asst Prof to Assoc Prof, 69-81, prof IN State Univ, 82, Dir, Interdisciplinary Univ Studies Gen Educ Prog, 76-85; Managing ed, Sch Rev, 68-70 & Sci-Fiction Studies, 72-74. **HONORS AND AWARDS** NDEA Fel, 65; Tchg Assistantship and Scholarship, Univ WI, 66; Ford Found Dissertation Year Schol, 68; Ellison Scholarship, Univ Chicago, 68; NEH Consult Grant, 77; Quality in Liberal Learning Grant, 78; NEH Summer Res Fel, Princeton Univ, 79; IN Arts Comn Grant, 83; IN Comt for the Hum Grant, 85; Fulbright Sr Scholarship Grant, Romania, 89-90; Univ Res Grant, IN State Univ, 95; Univ Arts Endowment Grant, IN State Univ, 96. **MEMBERSHIPS** IN Col Eng Asn; Asn Lit Scholarship & Critics; Soc Romanian Studies; IN Tchr(s) Writing; Nat Coun Tchr(s) Eng; IN Writers Asn; Asn Tchr(s) Tech Writing; **RESEARCH** Mod Eng lit; acad, creative, and professional writing; narrative theory; sci in lit. **SELECTED PUBLICATIONS** Auth, George Russell, In: Nationalism in Literature, New Brunswick, 96; Beside Great Waters: Poems from the Highlands and Islands, Avon Books, 97; This Sacred Earth and Other Poems, Mellen Poetry Press, 97; co-ed, Sacramental Acts: The Collected Love Poems of Kenneth Rexroth, Copper Canyon Press, 97; auth, Gadget Science Fiction: Technological Issues in Popular Culture, Simon and Schuster, 98; auth numerous other articles and publ. **CONTACT ADDRESS** Dept of Eng, Indiana State Univ, 210 N 7th St, Terre Haute, IN 47809-0002. **EMAIL** ejelk@root.indstate.edu

KLEINER, JOHN
DISCIPLINE ENGLISH **EDUCATION** Amherst Col, BA, 83; Cornell Univ, MS, 85; Stanford Univ, PhD, 90. **CAREER** Assoc prof. **RESEARCH** Classical and medieval literature; Latin, English, Italian traditions. **SELECTED PUBLICATIONS** Auth, Mismapping the Underworld: Error in Dante's Comedy. **CONTACT ADDRESS** Dept of English, Williams Col, Stetson d-25, Williamstown, MA 01267. **EMAIL** jkleiner@williams.edu

KLEINMAN, NEIL
PERSONAL Born Norfolk, VA, m, 1 child **DISCIPLINE** RENAISSANCE LITERATURE; COMMUNICATIONS DESIGN **EDUCATION** Univ Conn, PhD; Univ Pa, JD. **CAREER** Prof, Univ Baltimore. **HONORS AND AWARDS** Univ Maryland System Regents Awd for Distinguished Tchg, 98; dir, inst lang, technol, & publs design; codir, sch comm design; dir, doctorate coms design. **RESEARCH** Renaissance literature; propaganda; intellectual property; influence of new tecchnologies in modern society. **SELECTED PUBLICATIONS** Auth, The Dream that Was No More a Dream: A Search for Aesthetic Reality in Germany, 1890-1945. **CONTACT ADDRESS** Commun Dept, Univ of Baltimore, 1420 N. Charles Street, Baltimore, MD 21201. **EMAIL** nkleinman@ubmail.ubalt.edu

KLEINSASSER, JEROME
PERSONAL Born 03/28/1939, St. Paul, MN, m, 1980, 2 children **DISCIPLINE** MUSICOLOGY **EDUCATION** Univ Minn, PhD, 70. **CAREER** Prof Music, Calif State Univ, 72-. **MEMBERSHIPS** Am Musicol Soc, Col Mus Soc **RESEARCH** Opera **CONTACT ADDRESS** California State Univ, Bakersfield, 9001 Stockdale Hwy, Bakersfield, CA 93311-1099. **EMAIL** jkleinsasser@csub.edu

KLEMT, BARBARA
PERSONAL Born 09/07/1961, Ridgewood, NJ, s **DISCIPLINE** COMMUNICATIONS **EDUCATION** Ramapo Col, BA, 83; Univ SC, MA, 85; Middle Tenn State Univ, PhD, 94. **CAREER** News Ed, The Item, 86-88; Instr, Univ SC, 88-91; Asst Prof, Middle Tenn State Univ, 94-95; Copy Ed, News-Press, 96-97; Assoc Prof, Int Col Ft Myers, 97-99; Adj Prof, Edison Community Col, 95-. **HONORS AND AWARDS** Who's Who Among Students in Am Univ and Col, 83; Dept English Fel, Middle Tenn State Univ, 93; Phi Kappa Phi, Middle Tenn State Univ, 94. **MEMBERSHIPS** Am Scholastic Pr Asn, SC Pr Asn. **RESEARCH** Popular culture, women's studies, sports. **SELECTED PUBLICATIONS** Auth, "Judy Grahn's Edward the Dyke(s): Forsaking 'What is Female' for [Less] Power," New Growth Arts Rev (95): 41-49; auth, "Cardinals' Gant No Longer Feels Need to Prove Himself," The Item, 28 (96): 4D; auth, Pat Bradley: A True Champion," SPORTSfront (99): 28-29; auth, "Elite Golfer Honored in Naples," SPORTSfront, (00): 12-13; auth, "McMillon Hears Same Old Story," The Item, 23 (00); auth, "Shumate Under Control and Ready," The Messenger, 24 (00); auth, "Pendergrass in Pivotal Year," The Messenger, 24, (00). **CONTACT ADDRESS** Dept Commun, Edison Comm Col, PO Box 60210, Fort Myers, FL 33906-6210. **EMAIL** bklemt@edison.edu

KLENE, JEAN M.
PERSONAL Born 09/08/1929, Hannibal, MO, s **DISCIPLINE** ENGLISH **EDUCATION** St Marys Col, BA, 59, Univ Notre Dame, MA, 66, Univ Toronto, PhD, 70. **CAREER** Lectr to prof, St. Marys Col, 65-. **HONORS AND AWARDS** St Marys Col Res Grant, 74; 89; NEH Summer Sem, 77-78; 80; St. Marys Col Awd for Teaching & Service, 81; NEH Seminar, 83; 84; Lilley Fac Fel, 85-86; J. Roberts Awd for Best Edition, 97; **MEMBERSHIPS** MLA; Shakespeare Assoc of Am, Renaissance Soc of Am. **RESEARCH** Shakespeare, women writers of the early modern society and especially Lady Anne Southwell, art history. **SELECTED PUBLICATIONS** Ed, The Southwell-Sibthrope Commonplace Book: Folger MS, Medieval & Renaissance Texts & Studies, (Tempe, AZ), 97. **CONTACT ADDRESS** Dept English, Saint Mary's Col, Indiana, 313 Madeleva Hall, Notre Dame, IN 46556. **EMAIL** jklene@saintmarys.edu

KLENOTIC, JEFFREY F.
PERSONAL Born 08/12/1963, New Castle, PA, m, 2000 **DISCIPLINE** COMMUNICATION **EDUCATION** Pa State Univ, BA, 85; Univ of Mass, Amherst, MA, 88, PhD, 96. **CAREER** From instr comm to assoc prof, Univ NH Manchester, 92-. **HONORS AND AWARDS** Excellence in Teaching Awd, Univ of NH Manchester, 97; Phi Beta Kappa, 85-. **MEMBERSHIPS** Soc for Cinema Studies; Domitor; Nat commun Asn; Int Commun Asn; Northeast Historic Film Asn. **RESEARCH** Film history; media audiences; cultural studies. **SELECTED PUBLICATIONS** Auth, The Sensational Acme of Realism: Talker Pictures as Early Cinema Sound Practice, 99; auth, The Sounds of Early Cinema, Indiana Univ Press, 99; auth, Class Markers in the Mass Movie Audience: A Case Study in the Cultural Geography of Moviegoing 1926-1932, The Commun Rev, 98; The Place of Rhetoric in New Film Historiography: The Discourse of Corrective Revisionism, Film Hist: An Int J, 94; auth, Milos Forman, The Encycl of Film, Perigee Books, 91; auth, Miklos Jancso, The Encycl of Film, Perigee Books, 91. **CONTACT ADDRESS** Dept of Commun, Univ of New Hampshire, Manchester, 400 Commercial St., Manchester, NH 03101. **EMAIL** klenotic@christa.unh.edu

KLIGERMAN, JACK
PERSONAL Born 08/28/1938, Atlantic City, NJ, m, 1960, 1 child **DISCIPLINE** ENGLISH **EDUCATION** Syracuse Univ, BA, 60; MA, 62; Univ Calif, PhD, 67. **CAREER** Prof and Dept Chair, Lehman Col, 67-. **HONORS AND AWARDS** Innovative Teaching Awd, Lehman Col, 91. **MEMBERSHIPS** John Burroughs Asn, ASLE. **RESEARCH** American Nature Writing; Nature Photography. **CONTACT ADDRESS** Dept English, Lehman Col, CUNY, 250 Bedford Park Blvd W, Bronx, NY 10468-1527. **EMAIL** jackkl@lehman.cuny.edu

KLIMAN, BERNICE W.
PERSONAL Born 07/22/1933, Buffalo, NY, m, 1951, 4 children **DISCIPLINE** ENGLISH **EDUCATION** Hofstra Univ, BA, 60; Hunter Col, MA, 63; CUNY, PhD, 69. **CAREER** Part-time to full-time instr, Stony Brook, 64-66; part-time instr, C. W. Post Col, 64, 67-68; part-time instr, Queens Col, 69-73; asst prof, Baruch Col, 74-75, adjunct asst prof, spring 74-fall 75; vis fel, Davenport Col, Yale Univ, fall 73, fall 75, spring 77, spring 79; prof, Nassau Community Col, 76-99, Prof Emeritus, 99-. **HONORS AND AWARDS** NEH Summer Inst, 82, 85, 87; NEH Travel grant, 87; NEH grant, 89; FIPSE grant, 87-90; SUNY Sabbatical Scholar Awd, 89-90; Folger Shakespeare Library Short-term Fel, summer 91and 92; Distinguished Achievement Awd, Nassau Community Col, 92, 93, 95, 99; NEH Res Fel, 93; Proj Dir, NEH Awd, Res Tools for New Variorum Hamlet, 94-97; Proj Dir, NEH Awd, Preservation and Access Project for New Variorum Hamlet, 97-2000; Sabbatical Awd, 97. **MEMBERSHIPS** Columbia Univ Shakespeare Sem; Community Col Humanities Asn; Int Shakespeare Asn; Kalamazoo, the Int Congress on Medieval Studies; MIT, The Shakespeare Interactive Res Group; NEMLA; Shakespeare Asn of Am; Shenandoah Shakespeare Express; SHARP; ADE; Women in the Renaissance Sem, CUNY. **RESEARCH** Shakespeare in performance (especially film); textual/editing issues. **SELECTED PUBLICATIONS** Auth, Hamlet: Film, Television and Audio Performance, Madison, NJ: Fairleigh Dickinson Univ Press (88); co-ed with Paul Bertram, The Three-Text Hamlet: Parallel Texts of the First and Second Quartos, and First Folio, NY: AMS Press (91); auth, MacBeth. Shakespeare in Performance Series, gen eds J. R. Mulryne and James Bulman, Manchester: Manchester Univ Press (92, paperback, 95); auth, "Gleanings: The Residue of Difference in Scripts: The Case of Polanski's Macbeth," in Illuminations: Essays in Honor of Marvin Rosenberg, Newark, Del: Univ of Del Press (98); auth, "Samuel Johnson and Tonson's 1745 Shakespeare: Warburton, Anonymity and the Shakespeare Wars," in Reading Readings: Essays on Shakespeare Editing in the Eighteenth Century, ed Joanna Gondris, Madison, NJ: Fairleigh Dickinson Univ Press (98); auth, "Cum Notis Variorum: Samuel Henley, Shakespeare Commentator in Bell's Annotations," Shakespeare Newsletter 48, 4 (winter 98/99): 91-2, 108, 110; auth, "Considering the Terminology of the New Bibliography and After," Analytical and Enumerative Bibliography (forthcoming 2000); auth, "Charles Jennens' Shakespeare and His Eighteenth-Century Competitors," Cahiers Elisabethains (forthcoming 2000); ed and coordr, The New Variorum Hamlet, The New Variorum Shakespeare, Modern Language Association, gen eds, Richard Knowles and Paul Werstine (forthcoming 2005 in print, electronic pub, 2003). **CONTACT ADDRESS** Dept English, Nassau Comm Col, 1 Education Dr, Garden City, NY 11530-6719. **EMAIL** Klimanb@sunynassau.edu

KLIMKO, RONALD
DISCIPLINE MUSIC **EDUCATION** Milton Col, BA; Univ Wis Madison, MA, PhD. **CAREER** Prof. Univ of Idaho, Moscow, emer, 00. **HONORS AND AWARDS** Ed, Int Double Reed Soc. **MEMBERSHIPS** Int Double Reed Soc; Am Fedn of Musicians. **SELECTED PUBLICATIONS** Auth, Bassoon Performance Practices & Teaching in the United States & Canada, 74; co-auth, Bassoon Performance & Teaching Materials, Techniques & Methods, 93; auth, Basson with A View, 99. **CONTACT ADDRESS** Lionel Hampton Sch Music, Univ of Idaho, 415 W 6th St, Moscow, ID 83844. **EMAIL** rjklimko@moscow.com

KLINE, DANIEL
PERSONAL Born 05/04/1961, s, 2 children **DISCIPLINE** MEDIEVAL LITERATURE **EDUCATION** Indiana Univ, PhD. **CAREER** Univ Alaska. **RESEARCH** Literary and cultural theory; religion and literature; web design and distance learning. **SELECTED PUBLICATIONS** Articles: Comparative Drama; Essays in Medieval Studies; MLA's Profession 95; Philological Quarterly; College Literature; Literary and Linguistic Computing; Chau Review. **CONTACT ADDRESS** Univ of Alaska, Anchorage, 3211 Providence Dr., Anchorage, AK 99508. **EMAIL** afdtk@uaa.alaska.edu

KLINE, JOHN A.
PERSONAL Born 07/24/1939, Marshalltown, IA, m, 1974, 5 children **DISCIPLINE** SPEECH COMMUNICATION **EDUCATION** Iowa St Univ, BS, 67; Univ of Iowa, MS, 68, PhD, 70; Federal Executive Inst, Sr Exec, 86. **CAREER** Tchr, 66-67, Iowa St Univ; Grad NDEA/Res Fel, 67-70 Univ of Iowa; Asst Prof, Dir, 70-71, Fundamentals of Speech Com, Univ of New Mexico; Asst Prof, Dir, 71-75, Grad Stud, Univ of Missouri-Columbia; Assoc Prof, Dean, Communication, 75-82, Prof, Dir, Academic Affairs, 82-92, Provost, 92-, United States Air Univ. **HONORS AND AWARDS** Undergrad Scholar Fel, Iowa St Univ, 65-67; NDEA Fel, Univ of Iowa, 67-70; Central States Speech Assoc Outstanding Tchr, 72; Phi Kappa Phi Honor Soc, 76; Fed Employee of the Year Montgomery AL, 79; Awd for Meritous Civilian Svc, 84; Whos Who in America 45th Ed, 88; Decoratin for Exceptional Civilian Svc, 88. **MEMBERSHIPS** Natl Comm Assoc; Phi Delta Kappa; Amer Coun on Ed **SELECTED PUBLICATIONS** Art, Indicators of Good Marriages, Home Life, 93; auth, Parlez Pour Quon Vous Ecoute (French Trans Speaking Effectively), 93; auth, Listening Effectively, Air Univ Press, 96. **CONTACT ADDRESS** United States Air Force Acad, 55 LeMay Plaza South, Maxwell AFB, AL 36112-6335. **EMAIL** jkline@hq.au.af.mil

KLINK, WILLIAM
PERSONAL Born 07/04/1945, Ft. Myers, FL, m, 1991, 1 child **DISCIPLINE** LITERATURE **EDUCATION** Montclair St Univ, BA, 67; Cathol Univ, MA, 71, PhD, 72 **CAREER** Prof, Charles Co Commun Col, 27 yrs **HONORS AND AWARDS** Authored approx 100 books, articles and scholarly presentations **MEMBERSHIPS** Popular Culture Asn **RESEARCH** Am lit **CONTACT ADDRESS** Charles County Comm Col, La Plata, MD 20646. **EMAIL** billk@charles.cc.md.us

KLINKOWITZ, JEROME
PERSONAL Born 12/24/1943, Milwaukee, WI, m, 1978, 2 children **DISCIPLINE** ENGLISH **EDUCATION** Marquette Univ, BA, 66; MA, 67; Univ Wis, PhD, 69. **CAREER** Asst Prof, Northern Ill Univ, 69-72; From Assoc Prof to Prof, Univ Northern Iowa, 72-. **HONORS AND AWARDS** Univ Distinguished Scholar, Univ N Iowa, 85-. **MEMBERSHIPS** PEN Am Ctr. **RESEARCH** Contemporary fiction and culture, narratology of World War II air combat memoirs, jazz music, baseball. **SELECTED PUBLICATIONS** Auth, Basepaths: A Novel, Johns Hopkins UP (Baltimore, MD), 95; auth, Yanks Over Europe: American Flyers in World War II, UP Ky (Lexington, KY), 96; auth, Here at Ogallala State U: Novel, White Hawk Pr (Madison, WI), 97; auth, Keeping Literary Company: Working with Writers Since the Sixties, St Univ NY (SUNY) Pr (Albany, NY), 98; co-ed, The North Anthology of American Literature, 5th Ed, Norton Publ (New York, NY), 98; auth, Vonnegut in Fact: The Public Spokesmanship of Personal Fiction, Univ SC Pr (Columbia, SC), 98; auth, Owning a Piece of the Minors: Writing the Life of Baseball, Southern Ill UP (Carbondale, IL), 99; auth, With the Tigers Over China, 1941-1942: The Narratology of an Air War, UP Ky (Lexington, KY), 99. **CONTACT ADDRESS** Dept English, Univ of No Iowa, 1 University of Northern Iowa, Cedar Falls, IA 50614-0502.

KLOTMAN, PHYLLIS RAUCH
PERSONAL Born Galveston, TX, m, 2 children **DISCIPLINE** AMERICAN LITERATURE **EDUCATION** Case Western Reserve Univ, BA, 61, MA, 63, PhD(English, Am and Afro-Am lit), 69. **CAREER** Instr English, Lawrence Inst Technol, 67-68; asst prof, Ind State Univ, Terre Haute, 69-70; asst prof Afro-Am studies, 70-73, assoc prof, 73-78, Prof Afro-Am Studies, Ind Univ, Bloomington, 78-; Vis prof, Univ Hamburg, Ger, 78. **MEMBERSHIPS** MLA; Col Lang Asn; Col English Asn; Nat Coun Black Studies; Soc Cinema Studies. **RESEARCH** Afro-American literature, fiction, drama, biography and autobiography; Blacks in films. **SELECTED PUBLICATIONS CONTACT ADDRESS** Dept of Afro-Am Studies, Indiana Univ, Bloomington, Bloomington, IN 47401.

KLOTZ, MARVIN
PERSONAL Born 02/06/1930, New York, NY, m, 1953, 2 children **DISCIPLINE** AMERICAN LITERATURE **EDUCATION** Columbia Univ, BS, 51; Univ Minn, MA, 52; NYork Univ, PhD, 59. **CAREER** Instr English, NY Univ, 56-59; from asst prof to assoc prof, 59-69, Prof English, Calif State Univ, Northridge, 69-; Fulbright lectr, Saigon, South Vietnam and Taipei, Taiwan, 67-68 and Univ Tehran, Iran, 75-76. **RESEARCH** Faulkner; fictional realism; American prose style. **SELECTED PUBLICATIONS** Auth, Stephen Crane: Tragedian or comedian: The Blue Hotel, Univ Kans City Rev, 9/61; coauth, Faulkner's People: Index to His Characters, Univ Calif, 63; auth, The triumph over time: Narrative form in William Faulkner and William Styron, Miss Quart, 3/64; Procrustean revision in Faulkner's Go Down, Moses, Am Lit, 3/65; co-ed, Literature: The Human Experience, 73 & The Experience of Fiction, 75, St Martin's. **CONTACT ADDRESS** Dept of English, California State Univ, Northridge, Northridge, CA 91324.

KLUMPP, JAMES F.
DISCIPLINE RHETORICAL THEORY **EDUCATION** Univ MN, PhD, 73. **CAREER** Assoc prof, Univ MD. **RESEARCH** Kenneth Burke and the Europ continental critics. **SELECTED PUBLICATIONS** Co-auth, Rhetorical Criticism as Moral Action, Quart Jour Speech 75, 89. **CONTACT ADDRESS** Dept of Commun, Univ of Maryland, Col Park, 4229 Art-Sociology Building, College Park, MD 20742-1335. **EMAIL** jk44@umail.umd.edu

KNAPP, GERHARD PETER
PERSONAL Born Bad Kreuznach, Germany, 4 children **DISCIPLINE** LITERARY CRITICISM, FILM **EDUCATION** Tech Univ, Berlin, MA, 68, Dr Phil, 70. **CAREER** Asst prof Ger, Tech Univ, Berlin, 68-70; asst prof, Lakehead Univ, 70-72; asst prof, 72-74, assoc prof, 74-79, Prof Ger & Comp Lit, Univ Utah, 79-; vis prof Ger, Univ Amsterdam, 77-78. **HONORS AND AWARDS** Phi Beta Kappa (hon mem, 95). **MEMBERSHIPS** MLA; Am Asn Tchr(s) Ger; Can Asn Univ Tchr(s) Ger; Int Brecht Soc. **RESEARCH** 19th and 20th century lit; theory of literary criticism; film studies. **SELECTED PUBLICATIONS** Auth & coauth of 21 books, auth of 65 articles & ed & co-ed of 42 bks on Ger & comp lit. **CONTACT ADDRESS** Dept of Lang & Lit, Univ of Utah, 255 S Central Campus Dr, Rm 1400, Salt Lake City, UT 84112-8916. **EMAIL** gerhard.knapp@m.cc.utah.edu

KNAPP, JAMES A.
PERSONAL Born 11/10/1968, Pittsburgh, PA, m, 1993, 2 children **DISCIPLINE** ENGLISH LITERATURE **EDUCATION** Drew Univ, BA, 90; Temple Univ, MA, 94; Univ Rochester, PhD, 98. **CAREER** TA, Temple Univ, 93-94; GTA to instr, Univ of Rochester, 95-98; TA, Rochester Inst of Tech, 97; asst prof, Eastern Mich Univ, 98-. **HONORS AND AWARDS** Mellon Found, 97; Eastern Mich Univ, 00-01; Grant, Folger Shakespeare Inst; Eastern Mich Univ, Provost's Fac Awd. **MEMBERSHIPS** MLA, Soc for the Hist of Authorship, Reading, and Publ, Sixteenth Century Studies Conf, Shakespeare Assoc of Am. **RESEARCH** 16th and 17th Century British Literature, Literature and the Visual Arts, Aesthetic Theory. **SELECTED PUBLICATIONS** Auth, "Essayistic Messages: Internet Newsgroups as an Electronic Public Sphere," Internet Culture, ed David Porter, Routledge, (NY, 97); auth, "Translating for Print: Continuity and Change in Caxton's Mirror of the World," Disputatio, (98); auth, Joyce and Matisse Bound: Modernist Aesthetics in the Limited Editions Club Ulysses", ELH, 00; auth, "That most barbarous Nacion: John Derricke's Image of Ireland the delight of the well disposed reader," Criticism, (00). **CONTACT ADDRESS** Dept English, Eastern Michigan Univ, Ypsilanti, MI 48197. **EMAIL** jaknapp@online.emich.edu

KNAPP, JAMES FRANKLIN
PERSONAL Born 10/10/1940, Chicago, IL, m, 1 child **DISCIPLINE** MODERN LITERATURE, MODERNISM, IRISH LITERATURE **EDUCATION** Drew Univ, BA, 62; Univ Conn, PhD(English), 66. **CAREER** Asst prof, 66-71, assoc prof English, Univ Pittsburgh, 71-89; prof Eng, 89-; assoc dean, Arts & Sci, 00-. **MEMBERSHIPS** MLA. **RESEARCH** Modern British and American poetry; contemporary poetry; myth theory. **SELECTED PUBLICATIONS** Auth, The meaning of Sir Orfeo, Mod Lang Quart, 68; Delmore Schwartz: Poet of the orphic journey, Sewanee Rev, 70; The poetry of R S Thomas, Twentieth Century Lit, 71; Proteus in the classroom: Myth and literature today, Col English, 3/73; Eliot's Prufrock and the form of modern poetry, Ariz Quart, Spring 74; Myth in the powerhouse of change, Centennial Rev, Winter 76; Ezra Pound, Twayne, 79; Literary Modernism and the Transformation of Work, Northwestern U Press, 89; Norton Poetry Workshop CD ROM, WW Norton, 96. **CONTACT ADDRESS** Dept of English, Univ of Pittsburgh, 526 Cathedral/Learn, Pittsburgh, PA 15260-2504. **EMAIL** jkna@pitt.edu

KNAPP, JOHN A., II
PERSONAL Born 09/09/1940, Binghamton, NY, m, 1972, 4 children **DISCIPLINE** ENGLISH **EDUCATION** Wheaton Col, AB, 63; Mich State Univ, MAT, 68; Western Mich Univ, PhD, **CAREER** Prof Science Education, State Univ of New York, 72-75; Prof of English, State Univ of New York, 75-99. **HONORS AND AWARDS** E-Dan Black Belt, United States Soo Bahk Doo Federation, 99, Finalists for the C.S. Lewis Medal, 91. **RESEARCH** Creation and Evolution; Children's Fantasy. **SELECTED PUBLICATIONS** Auth, The Burgomaster's Rain, Ephemeron Press, 90. **CONTACT ADDRESS** Dept English, SUNY, Oswego, 7060 St Rte 104, Oswego, NY 13126-3560. **EMAIL** knapp@oswego.edu

KNAPP, JOHN V.
PERSONAL Born 05/03/1940, Syracuse, NY, m, 1977, 4 children **DISCIPLINE** ENGLISH, LITERATURE **EDUCATION** State Univ of NY, BS, 63; MS, 66; Univ of Ill at Urbana-Champaign, PhD, 71; Univ of Wis at Madison, PhD, 00. **CAREER** Teacher, Chittenango Central High Sch, 63-66; teaching asst, Univ of Ill at Urbana-Champaign, 66-71; res assoc, Univ of Wis at Madison Nat Ctr on Effective Secondary Schools, 86-89; from asst prof to prof, Northern Ill Univ, 71-; coord of English Educ, Northern Ill Univ, 83-88; from assoc ed to co-ed of Style, Northern Ill Univ, 85-91. **HONORS AND AWARDS** NEH Summer award, 77. **MEMBERSHIPS** MLA, NCTE. **RESEARCH** Psychological Literary Criticism, English Education , Modern British and American Literature, Composition and Rhetoric. **SELECTED PUBLICATIONS** Auth, "Classy Questions: Raising Student Achievement Through Authentic Discourse," Ill English Bull 78 (91): 42-55; ed & contribur, Literary Character, Univ Press of Am (Lanham, MD), 93; auth, Striking at the Joints: Contemporary Psychology and Literary Criticism, Univ Press of Am (Lanham, MD), 96; auth, "Animal Farm Hegemony: An Interactive Game for the College Classroom," Col Lit 23 (96): 143-156; guest co-ed & contribur, Family Systems Psychotherapy and Literature, Style 31.2 (97). **CONTACT ADDRESS** Dept English, No Illinois Univ, 330 Reevis Hall, Dekalb, IL 60115. **EMAIL** tb0jvk1@corn.cso.niu.edu

KNAPP, MARK L.
PERSONAL Born 07/12/1938, Kansas City, MO, m, 1975, 3 children **DISCIPLINE** COMMUNICATION **EDUCATION** Univ Kans, BS, 62; MA, 63; Pa State Univ, PhD, 66. **CAREER** From instr to asst prof, Univ of Wis at Milwaukee, 65-70; from assoc prof to prof, Purdue Univ, 70-80; prof, State Univ of NYork Col at New Paltz, 80-83; distinguished vis prof, Univ of Vt, 83; prof, Univ of Tex at Austin, 87-89; Jesse H. Jones Centennial Prof in Commun, Univ of Tex at Austin, 89-; chemn of dept of speech commun, Univ of Tex at Austin, 89-96; distinguished teaching prof, Univ of Tex, 99-. **HONORS AND AWARDS** Outstanding Young Teacher Awd, Central States Speech Asn, 69; Uhrig Awd for Excellence in Teaching, Univ of Wis at Milwaukee, 69; Sigma Delta Chi Leather Medal Awd, Purdue Univ, 72-73; Best Teacher Awd, Purdue Univ, 74; Golden Anniversary Awd for best monograph, Nat Commun Asn, 74; ICA Fel, Int Commun Asn, 80; ECA Scholar, Eastern Commun Asn, 82-83; Chancellor's Awd for Excellence in Teaching, State Univ of NY, 83; Cecil and Ida Green Honors Prof, Tex Christian Univ, 87; Distinguished Scholar Awd, Nat Commun Asn, 93; Robert J. Kibler Memorial Awd, Nat Commun Asn, 93; Chancellor's Coun Outstanding Teaching Awd, Univ of Tex, 93-94; Acad of Distinguished Teachers, Univ of Tex, 99. **MEMBERSHIPS** Nat Commun Asn, Int Commun Asn, Int Soc for the Study of Personal Relationships, Int Network on Personal Relationships. **RESEARCH** Interpersonal Communication, Nonverbal Communication, Communication in Close Relationships. **SELECTED PUBLICATIONS** Co-ed, Handbook of Interpersonal Communication, Sage (Newbury Park, CA), 94; coauth, Nonverbal Communication in Human Interaction, Harcourt Brace (Ft Worth, TX), 97; coauth, Interpersonal Communication and Human Relationships, Allyn & Bacon (Boston, MA), 00. **CONTACT ADDRESS** Dept Commun Studies, Univ of Texas, Austin, Austin, TX 78712-1013. **EMAIL** mlknapp@mail.utexas.edu

KNAPP, PEGGY ANN
PERSONAL Born 07/06/1937, Brainerd, MN, m, 1967, 3 children **DISCIPLINE** ENGLISH & AMERICAN LITERATURE **EDUCATION** Univ Wis-Madison, BS, 59, MA, 61; Univ Pittsburgh, PhD, 65. **CAREER** Lectr English, Mt Mercy Col, 65-66 & Univ Pittsburgh, 66-68; asst prof, Univ Conn, 68-69; from asst prof to assoc prof, 70-88, prof English, Carnegie-Mellon Univ, 88-. **MEMBERSHIPS** Mediaeval Acad Am; MLA. **RESEARCH** Middle English literature; Shakespeare; drama. **SELECTED PUBLICATIONS** Auth, Alisoun Weaves a Text, Phitol Quart, 86; Alisoun of Bath and the Reappropriation of Tradition, Chaucer Rev 24, 89; Deconstruction and the Canterbury Tales, Studies in the Age of Chaucer, 87; Chaucer and the Social Contest, Routledge, 90; Time Bound Words: Semantic and Social Economies from Chaucer's England to Shakespeare's, St. Martin's Press, 00; author numerous other articles. **CONTACT ADDRESS** Dept of English, Carnegie Mellon Univ, 5000 Forbes Ave, Pittsburgh, PA 15213-3890. **EMAIL** pk07@andrew.cmu.edu

KNAPP, ROBERT C.
PERSONAL Born 02/12/1946, m, 1974, 2 children **DISCIPLINE** ANCIENT HISTORY, CLASSICS **EDUCATION** Cent MI Univ, BA, 68; Univ PA, PhD, 73. **CAREER** Vis asst prof classics, Colby Col, 73; asst prof of hist, Univ of Utah, 73-74; asst prof, 74-80, Assoc Prof Classics, Numismatics, Univ CA, Berkeley, 80-87; Prof 87. **HONORS AND AWARDS** Am Council of Learned Societies Fellowship, 82-83. **MEMBERSHIPS** Asn Ancient Historians; Am Philol Asn; Archaeological Institute of Am Fellow; Royal Numismatic Society. **RESEARCH** Roman Spain; Roman Cult Studies. **SELECTED PUBLICATIONS** Auth, Aspects of the Roman Experience in Iberia, 206-100 BC, Anejos IX Hisp Antiqua, 77; The date and purpose of the Iberian denarii, Numis Chronicle, 77; The origins of provincial prosopography in the West, Ancient Soc, 78; Cato in Spain, 195-194 BC, In: Studies in Latin Literature and Roman History II, C Deroux, Brussells, 80; La epigrafia y la historia de la Cordoba romana, Annario, de Filologia, 80; Festus 262L and Praefecturae in Italy, Athenaeum, 80; L Axius Naso and Pro legato, Phoenix, 81; Roman Cordoba, Univ Calif press, 83; Latin Inscriptions from Central Spain, Univ Calif, 92; Mapping Ancient Iberia: Progress and Perspectives, intro, ed (and contribution, Ptolemy Mapping Baetica, pp 29-36) Classical Bulletin, special issue, 96; auth, Finis Rei Publicae, Eyewitnesses to the End of the Roman Republic, with P. Baughn, Focus Publishing, 99; ed, Barrington Atlas of the Greek and roman World, ed. By R.J. A Talbert, Princeton, 00. **CONTACT ADDRESS** Dept Class, Univ of California, Berkeley, 7233 Dwinelle Hall, Berkeley, CA 94720-2520. **EMAIL** RCKNAPP@SOCRATES.Berkeley.edu

KNAPP, ROBERT STANLEY
PERSONAL Born 03/29/1940, Alamosa, CO, m, 1965 **DISCIPLINE** ENGLISH **EDUCATION** Univ Colo, BA, 62; Univ Denver, MA, 63; Cornell Univ, PhD, 68. **CAREER** From instr to asst prof English, Princeton Univ, 66-74, Donald A Stauffer bicentennial preceptor, 70-73; asst prof, 74-77, assoc prof English, Reed Col, 77-, fel, Nat Endowment Humanities, Univ Chicago, 78-79. **MEMBERSHIPS** MLA, SAA, RSA. **RESEARCH** Shakespeare; critical theory. **SELECTED PUBLICATIONS** Auth, Samuel Beckett's allegory of the uncreating word, Mosaic, winter 73; Horestes: The uses of revenge, J English Lit Hist, summer 73; The monarchy of love in Lyly's Endymion, Miscellaneous Papers, 5/76; Love allegory in Grange's Golden Aphroditis, English Lit Renaissance, 78; Penance, irony & Chaucer's Retraction, Assays, 83; Shakespeare: The Theater and The Book, Princeton, 89; There's Letters from my Mother, Reading & Writing on Shakespeare, Delaware, 96; Is It Appropriate for a Man to Fear His Wife: Joan Case on Marriage, English Lit Renaissance, 98. **CONTACT ADDRESS** Dept English, Reed Col, 3203 SE Woodstock Blvd, Portland, OR 97202-8199. **EMAIL** knapp@reed.edu

KNAPP, TERENCE R.
PERSONAL Born 02/14/1932, London, England, s **DISCIPLINE** THEATRE **EDUCATION** Royal Academy Dramatic Art, London, Dip Distinction and Medallist, 54; Liverpool Playhouse Scholar, 195_; Parmiters, London, 88. **CAREER** Royal Shakespeare Co, 61; Inaugural Chichester Festival Theatre, 62; Royal Nat Theatre, 63-65; Nottingham Playhouse, 66-68; prof, Univ Haw, Manoa, 70-. **HONORS AND AWARDS** Churchill Fel (Japan Theatre Arts), 68; Japan Found VIP Awd, 77; Univ Haw Bd of Regents Medal of Excellence, 77; Peabody Awd for

'Damien' Khet.Hi, 78; Clopton Awd for Distinguished Service, 80; Nat Soc Arts and Letters, Haw Laureate, 96. **MEMBERSHIPS** Screen Actors Guild, British Actors Equity, Int House of Japan. **RESEARCH** Occidental/Oriental 'Fusion' production; spiritual and religious aspects of theatre; music in and of the theatre. **SELECTED PUBLICATIONS** Auth, Training of the Young Actor in Japan, Shinbun Darts (74); auth, Karasawagi Journal, Onstage Studies, Colo Shakespeare Festival (82); auth, "Genesis of Damien," Hawaii Catholic Herald (96); auth, "Hawaii's Adopted World Class Actor, " Xlbris (2000). **CONTACT ADDRESS** Dept Theatre & Dance, Univ of Hawaii, Manoa, 1770 East West Rd, Honolulu, HI 96822-2317. **EMAIL** tknapp@hawaii.edu

KNAUER, GEORG NICOLAUS
PERSONAL Born 02/26/1926, Hamburg, Germany, m, 1951, 1 child **DISCIPLINE** CLASSICAL STUDIES **EDUCATION** Hamburg Univ, PhD, 52. **CAREER** Asst Prof to Prof, Freie Univ Berlin, 54-66; Vis Prof, Yale Univ, 65; Prof, Univ Pa, 75-88; Guest Prof, Columbia Univ, 76-. **HONORS AND AWARDS** Guggenheim Fel, 79-80; NEH Fel, 84-85. **MEMBERSHIPS** APA; Renaissance Soc of Am. **RESEARCH** Latin translations of Homer (1360-1620). **SELECTED PUBLICATIONS** Auth, Psalmenzitate in Augustins Konfessionen, 55; auth, Die Aeneis und Homer, 64. **CONTACT ADDRESS** Dept Class Studies, Univ of Pennsylvania, 3300 Darby Rd, Haverford, PA 19041-1070. **EMAIL** gknauer@sas.upenn.edu

KNIES, EARL ALLEN
PERSONAL Born 07/11/1936, White Haven, PA, m, 1959, 3 children **DISCIPLINE** ENGLISH **EDUCATION** Muhlenberg Col, BA, 58; Lehigh Univ, MA, 60; Univ IL, PhD (English), 64. **CAREER** From asst prof to assoc prof, 64-74, chm dept, 74-78, prof English, OH Univ, 74-. **MEMBERSHIPS** MLA; Tennyson Soc. **RESEARCH** Victorian novel; Tennyson. **SELECTED PUBLICATIONS** Auth, Art, Death and the Composition of Shirley, Victorian Newsletter, fall 65; The Artistry of Charlotte Bront%, OH Univ Rev, 65; The I of Jane Eyre, Col English, 4/66; The Art of Charlotte Bront%, OH Univ, 69; The Diary of James Henry Mangles, Tennyson Res Bull, 11/81; Tennyson at Aldworth, OH Univ, 84. **CONTACT ADDRESS** Dept of English, Ohio Univ, Athens, OH 45701-2979. **EMAIL** kniese@ohio.edu

KNIGHT, CHARLES
PERSONAL Born 09/03/1937, San Francisco, CA, m, 1958, 4 children **DISCIPLINE** ENGLISH **EDUCATION** Haverford Col, BA, 58; Univ Pa, MA, 60; PhD, 64. **CAREER** Instr, Catholic Univ of Am, 61-62; instr, Univ Mass Amherst, 62-65; asst prof to full prof, Univ Mass, 65-. **MEMBERSHIPS** Modern Lang Asn, Am Soc for Eighteenth-Century Studies. **RESEARCH** Eighteenth-Century British Literature, The novel, Satire. **SELECTED PUBLICATIONS** Auth, Joseph Addison and Richard Steele: A Reference Guide, New York, 94; auth, "The Images of Nations in Eighteenth-Century Satire," Eighteenth-Century Studies, (89): 489-511; auth, "Satiric Nationalism," Transactions of the Seventh International Conference on the Enlightenment, Studies on Voltaire and the Eighteenth Century, (89): 1653-1655; auth, "Listening to encolpius: Modes of confusion in the Satyricon," University of Toronto Quarterly, (89): 335-354; auth, "Imagination's Cerberus: Satire and the Definition of Genre," Philological Quarterly, (90): 131-151; auth, "Joseph Andrews and the Failure of Authority," Eighteenth-Century Fiction, (92): 109-124; auth, "Satire, Speech, and Genre," Comparative Literature, (92): 22-41; auth, "The Spectator's Generalizing discourse," Prose Studies, (93): 44-57; auth, "The Spectator's Moral economy," Modern Philology, (93): 161-179. **CONTACT ADDRESS** Dept English, Univ of Massachusetts, Boston, 100 Morrissey Blvd, Dorchester, MA 02125-3300. **EMAIL** charles.knight@umb.edu

KNIGHT, DENISE D.
PERSONAL Born 04/24/1954, Utica, NY, m, 1981 **DISCIPLINE** ENGLISH **EDUCATION** SUNY, Albany, BA (summa cum laude), 83, MA, 85, DA, 86. **CAREER** Lect, Sienna Col, English dept, Loudonville, NY, 88-90; lect, SUNY, Albany, English Dept, 86-90; asst prof, 90-94, assoc prof, 94-97, Prof, SUNY, Cortland, English Dept, 97-. **HONORS AND AWARDS** Outstanding Reference Source Awd, Am Library Asn, References and Adult Serv div, 93; Phi Kappa Phi, 94; Radcliffe Col Res Support Grant Recepient, 94-95; Who's Who in the East, 95-96; speaker, NY Coun for the Humanities Speakers Prog, 96-98; 98-01; Outstanding Book Awd for Nineteenth-Century Am Women Writers, Greenwood Press, 97, from CHOICE, 97; Found, Central NY Conf on Lang and Lit, SUNY Col at Cortland, 91; ed, Gilman Soc Newsletter, 95-98; selection comm, Nat Women's Hall of Fame, 95, 96; dir, Center for Multicultural and Gender Studies, SUNY Col, Cortland, 96-98; BBC Radio Interview on Charlotte Perkins Gilman, Jan 98. **MEMBERSHIPS** Modern Lang Asn; Northeast Modern lang Asn; Charlotte Perkins Gilman Soc (pres, 98-2001); Am Lit Asn. **RESEARCH** Charlotte Perkins Gilman (1860-1935); 19th century Am women writers. **SELECTED PUBLICATIONS** Ed., The Yellow Wall-Paper and Selected Stories of Charlotte Perkins Gilman, Univ DE Press, 94; The Diaries of Charlotte Perkins Gilman, a two-volume critical ed, Univ Press VA, 94; The Later Poetry of Charlotte Perkins Gilman, Univ DE Press, 96; Unpunished: A Detective Novel by Charlotte Perkins Gilman, co-ed with Catherine J. Golden, Feminist Press, 97; Auth, Charlotte Perkins Gilman: A Study of the Short Fiction, Twayne Studies in Short Fiction, Twayne Pubs, 97; Ed., Nineteenth-Century American Women Writers: A Bio-Bibliographical Critical Sourcebook, Greenwood Press, 97; The Abridged Diaries of Charlotte Perkins Gilman, Univ Press VA, 98; The Dying of Charlotte Perkins Gilman, Am Transcendental Quart, June 99; Herland and Selected Stories of Charlotte Perkins Gilman, Penguin Classics, 99; auth, " Charlotte Perkins Gilman's First Book: A Biographical Gap," in ANQ, 00. **CONTACT ADDRESS** English Dept, SUNY, Col at Cortland, Cortland, NY 13045. **EMAIL** knightd@cortland.edu

KNIGHT, FAWN
DISCIPLINE ENGLISH **EDUCATION** Pepperdine Univ, BA, 71; MA, 73; Oakland Univ, PhD, 85. **CAREER** Adj instr, Valparaiso Univ, 76-77; adj lectr, Univ of Mich, 86; adj lectr, Oakland Univ, 86-95; assoc prof, Mich Christian Col, 78-95; prof, Ky Christian Col, 95-. **HONORS AND AWARDS** NEH Grant, 99; Mellon Found Grant, Austria, 00. **SELECTED PUBLICATIONS** Auth, "Marquerite Loft de Angeli: Writer and Illustrator for Children, Historic Women of Michigan: A Sesquicentennial Celebration, ed Rosalei R. Troester, Womens Studies Assoc, (87): 205-216; auth, "Islands of Wisdom, Islands of Probation: Christian Piety in Victorian Robinsonnades for Children", Message in a Bottle: The Literature of Small Islands, Proceedings of the Inf Conf hosted by the Small Islands Inst and the Univ of Prince Edward Island, (forthcoming); auth, Double-Take Award Winners Selected for Both Adult and Children's Awards, (forthcoming). **CONTACT ADDRESS** Dept Arts and Sci, Kentucky Christian Col, 100 Academic Pky, Grayson, KY 41143-1123. **EMAIL** fknight@email.kcc.edu

KNIGHT, NICHOLAS WILLIAM
PERSONAL Born 04/18/1939, Mt. Vernon, NY, m, 1961, 4 children **DISCIPLINE** MEDIEVAL & RENAISSANCE ENGLISH **EDUCATION** Amherst Col, BA, 61; Univ Calif, Berkeley, MA, 63; Ind Univ, PhD, 68. **CAREER** From instr to asst prof, 66-73, Wesleyan Univ; asst chmn dept, 70-71, fel, 71-72, Ctr Humanities; prof legal & common law hist, 73-75, Univ Bridgeport; assoc prof, 75-77, prof, 77-, chmn human, 75-, Univ Mo-Rolla; consult Renaissance lit, Choice; Ford Found fel, 70-71; scholar-in-residence English, Wesleyan Univ, 74-75; chmn, Policy Bd Joint Ctrs Aging, Univ Mo Syst, 77-. **MEMBERSHIPS** MLA; NCTE; Renaissance Soc Am. **RESEARCH** Shakespearean revenge tragedy; Shakespearean biography; equity in law and drama. **SELECTED PUBLICATIONS** Auth, The Death of J K (play), London Rev, 70; auth, Equity and Mercy in English Drama 1400-1641, Comp Drama, 72; auth, Spenserian Chivalric Influence in Paradise Regained, Costerus Essays, 72; art, Toward Archetype in the Joseph Colombo Shooting, Brit J Soc Psychiat & Community Health, 72; auth, Shakespeare at the Law: A Hidden Life, 1585-1595, Mason & Lipscomb, 73; art, Equity, The Merchant of Venice, and William Lambarde, Shakespeare Sur, 74; art, Lady That In Her Prime--Identified, Mo Philol Assn, 76; art, Legal Relationships Between Shakespeare's Life And His Works Since Schoenbaum's Life Records, Ark Philol Assn, 76. **CONTACT ADDRESS** Dept of English, Univ of Missouri, Rolla, Rolla, MO 65409-1060. **EMAIL** knight@umr.edu

KNIGHTON, ROBERT TOLMAN
PERSONAL Born 02/23/1935, Bountiful, UT, m, 1958, 3 children **DISCIPLINE** ENGLISH LITERATURE; AMERICAN LITERATURE **EDUCATION** Utah State Univ, BS, 61, MS, 62; Univ Colo, Boulder, PhD(English), 72. **CAREER** Instr English, Utah State Univ, 61-62; asst prof, 67-73, assoc prof, 73-80, Prof English, Univ of The Pac, 80-. **HONORS AND AWARDS** Faye and Alex G. Spanos Outstanding Teaching Awd, 93. **RESEARCH** Restoration and 18th Century English Literature; English Romantic Poetry; Modern Critical Theory, Technical Writing. **SELECTED PUBLICATIONS** Auth, Radical sublimation: The structure of community growth and alienation, Pac Hist, 76. **CONTACT ADDRESS** Dept of English, Univ of the Pacific, Stockton, 3601 Pacific Ave, Stockton, CA 95211-0197. **EMAIL** rknighto@uop.edu

KNOBLAUCH, CYRIL H.
PERSONAL Born 10/05/1945, Minneapolis, MN, m, 1984, 1 child **DISCIPLINE** ENGLISH **EDUCATION** Brown Univ, PhD, 73. **CAREER** Asst prof, Columbia Univ, 73-79; NYU, 79-82; assoc prof, 82-91, prof, 91-98, interim dean, Col of Arts and Sciences, State Univ of New York at Albany, 94-98; Dept of English, Univ NC at Charlotte, 98-. **RESEARCH** Rhetoric; literary studies; pedagogy. **SELECTED PUBLICATIONS** Auth, Rhetorical Traditions and the Teaching of Writing, Boynton/Cook, 84; Critical Teaching and the Idea of Literacy, Heinneman, 94; author of thirty articles. **CONTACT ADDRESS** Dept of English, Univ of No Carolina, Charlotte, Charlotte, NC 28223. **EMAIL** knoblauch@email.uncc.edu

KNOELLER, CHRISTIAN
PERSONAL Born New York, NY **DISCIPLINE** ENGLISH LITERATURE **EDUCATION** Univ Calif Berkeley, PhD, 93. **CAREER** Fac, 93-. **HONORS AND AWARDS** Educ Yr, Alaska, 87; NCTE Tchr Res Found, 92; Russo Prize, Bucknell Univ, 76. **SELECTED PUBLICATIONS** Auth, Song in Brown Bear Country; publications include poetry, textbooks, school district curricula, and educational research. **CONTACT ADDRESS** Dept of Curriculum and Instruction, Purdue Univ, West Lafayette, West Lafayette, IN 47907-1440. **EMAIL** knoeller@purdue.edu

KNOEPFLMACHER, U. C.
PERSONAL Born 06/26/1931, Munich, Germany, m, 4 children **DISCIPLINE** ENGLISH LITERATURE **EDUCATION** Univ CA, Berkeley, AB, 55, MA, 57; Princeton Univ, PhD, 61. **CAREER** From instr to assoc prof, Univ CA, Berkeley, 61-69, prof, 69-79; prof, 79-87, PATON FOUND PROF OF ANCIENT & MODERN LIT, PRINCETON UNIV, 88-; Am Coun Learned Soc fel, 65; Humanities Res Prof, 66-67 & 77; Guggenheim fel, 69-70, 87-88; sr fel, Nat Endowment Humanities, 72-73, 91-92; Nat Humanities Center NC, 95-96; adv bd, Pub Mod Lang Asn, 77-81, ed bd, 83-85; vis prof, Harvard Univ, summer, 71, Tulsa Univ, Grad Prof, 79 & Bread Loaf Sch English, 81, 83, 85, 87; dir, NEH Summer Seminars for Col Teachers, 75, 84, 86, 89; dir, NEH Summer Seminars for School Teachers, 90, 91, 95, 99. **HONORS AND AWARDS** Distinguished Teaching Awd, Acad Senate, Univ CA, Berkeley, 77; Children's Literature Asn Best Essay, 84, 97. **MEMBERSHIPS** MLA; NCTE; NE Victorian Asn; CHLA. **RESEARCH** Nineteenth century English literature; English novel; children's literature. **SELECTED PUBLICATIONS** Auth, Religious Humanism and the Victorian Novel, Princeton Univ, 65; George Eliot's Early Novels: The Limits of Realism, Univ Calif, 68; ed, Francis Newman: Phases of Faith, Leicester Univ, 70; auth, Laughter and Despair: Readings in Ten Novels of the Victorian Era, 71, co-ed, Nature and the Victorian Imagination, 77; The Endurance of Frankenstein: Essays on Mary Shelley's Novel, Univ CA, 78; Forbidden Journeys: Fairy Tales and Fantasies by Victorian Women Writers, Chicago Univ, 93; auth, Wuthering Heights: A Study, OH Univ, 94; Cross-writing the Child and the Adult, Yale Univ, 97; auth, Ventures Into Childland: Victorians, Fairy Tales, and Femininity, Chicago Univ, 98; auth, The Complete Fairy Tales of George MacDonald, Penguin, 99. **CONTACT ADDRESS** Dept of English, Princeton Univ, Mccosh Hall 22, Princeton, NJ 08544-1098. **EMAIL** uknopf@princeton.edu

KNOLES, LUCIA
DISCIPLINE ENGLISH **EDUCATION** St Mary's Col, BA, 72; Rutgers, MA, 76, PhD, 79. **CAREER** Assoc Prof, Eng, Assumption Coll. **MEMBERSHIPS** Am Antiquarian Soc **CONTACT ADDRESS** Dept of English, Assumption Col, 500 Salisbury St, Worcester, MA 01615-0005. **EMAIL** lknoles@eve.assumption.edu

KNOPP, SHERRON ELIZABETH
PERSONAL Born 04/11/1947, Fort Worth, TX **DISCIPLINE** MEDIEVAL & COMPARATIVE LITERATURE **EDUCATION** Loyola Univ, Chicago, AB, 71; Univ Calif, Los Angeles, MA, 72, PhD(English), 75. **CAREER** Asst prof, 75-80, assoc prof, 80-86, prof English, Williams Col, 86-. **MEMBERSHIPS** Mediaeval Acad Am; MLA; New Chaucer Soc. **RESEARCH** Chaucer; medieval romance; medieval dream poetry. **SELECTED PUBLICATIONS** Auth, Chaucer and Jean de Meun as Self-Conscious Narrators, Comitatus, 73; Catullus 64 and the Conflict Between Amores and Virtutes, Class Philol, 76; Artistic design in the stanzaic Morte Arthur, English Literary Hist, No 45; The Narrator and His Audience in Chaucer's Troilus and Criseyde, Studies in Philol, 78; A Zeer Zernes Ful Zerne: Teaching Sir Gawain and the Green Knight in the Survey for Majors, Approaches to Teaching Sir Gawain and the Green Knight, MLA, 86; Augustinian Poetic Theory and the Chaucerian Imagination, The Idea of Medieval Literature, Univ of Del Press, 91. **CONTACT ADDRESS** Dept of English, Williams Col, 880 Main St, Williamstown, MA 01267-2600. **EMAIL** Sherron.E.Knopp@williams.edu

KNORR, ORTWIN
PERSONAL Born 02/12/1966, Bremen, Germany, m, 1994, 1 child **DISCIPLINE** CLASSICS **EDUCATION** Univ Gottingen, PhD, 99. **CAREER** Wissen asst, Univ Gott, 92-93; lectr, Univ Calif Berkeley, 95; instr, Univ Gott, 96-99; lectr, John Hopkins Univ, 00; vis asst prof, Georgetown Univ, 00-01; asst prof, Willamette Univ, 01-. **HONORS AND AWARDS** Univ Gott and Univ Calif Berkeley, Fel, 93-94; Georgetown Univ Sum Grnt, 01. **MEMBERSHIPS** AAP. **RESEARCH** Latin poetry; Roman satire; Roman comedy; Greek and Roman material, culture, customs, beliefs. **SELECTED PUBLICATIONS** Auth, "The Character of Bacchis in Terence's Heautontimorumenos," Am J Philo (95); auth, "Zur Oberlieferungsgeschichte des Liber de Haeresibus des Johannes von Damascus," Byzant Zeitsch (98); auth, "Die Paralleluberlieferung zum Panarion des Epiphanius," Wiener Stud (99). **CONTACT ADDRESS** Dept of Classics, Willamette Univ, 900 State St, Salem, OR 20720. **EMAIL** oknorr@willamette.edu

KNOTT, JOHN R.
DISCIPLINE ENGLISH LITERATURE **EDUCATION** Yale Univ, AB, 59; Harvard Univ, PhD, 65. **CAREER** Instr, Harvard Univ, 65-67; from asst prof to prof, Univ Mich, 67-; assoc dean Univ Mich Col of Lit, Sci, & the Arts, 77-80; acting dean,

Univ Mich Col of Lit, Sci, & the Arts,, 80-81; chemn of Dept of English, Univ Mich, 82-87; interim dir, Univ Mich Inst for the Humanities, 87-88. **HONORS AND AWARDS** Carnegie Fel, Yale Univ; Woodrow Wilson Fel; NEH Fel, Mich Humanities Awd. **MEMBERSHIPS** MLA, Milton Soc of Am, Renaissance Soc of Am, Asn for the Study of Lit & the Environment. **RESEARCH** English Renaissance Literature, Literature and the Environment. **SELECTED PUBLICATIONS** Auth, Milton's Pastoral Vision, univ Chicago Press, 71; auth, The Sword of the Spirit: Puritan Responses to the Bible, Univ Chicago Press, 80; auth, Discourses of Martyrdom in English Literature, 1563-1694, Cambridge Univ Press, 93; co-ed, The Huron River: Voices from the Watershed, Univ Mich Press, 00. **CONTACT ADDRESS** Dept English, Univ of Michigan, Ann Arbor, 505 South State St, 3062 Tisch Hall, Ann Arbor, MI 48109-1045. **EMAIL** jknott@umich.edu

KNOWLES, RICHARD ALAN JOHN

PERSONAL Born 05/17/1935, Southbridge, MA, m, 1958, 2 children **DISCIPLINE** ENGLISH RENAISSANCE **EDUCATION** Tufts Univ, BA, 56; Univ Pa, MA, 58, PhD, 63. **CAREER** From instr to assoc prof, 62-90, prof eng, Dickson-Bascom prof of hum, 90-; Univ WI-Madison, 75, Folger Shakespeare Libr fel, 68; Guggenheim Found fel, 76-77; NEH fel, 83-87, hum res inst, 90; mem, Variorum Shakespeare Comt, 72-; Gen ed, Variorum Shakespeare, 78-90. **MEMBERSHIPS** MLA; Shakespeare Asn Am; Intl Asoc Univ Profs of Eng; Assoc Lit Critics and Scholars. **RESEARCH** Shakespeare; Renaissance mythography. **SELECTED PUBLICATIONS** Auth, Myth and type in As You Like It, English Lit Hist, 66; Unquiet and the double plot of 2 Henry IV, Shakespeare Studies, 66; Rough notes on editions collated for As You Like It, Shakespearean Res & Opportunities, 68-69; coauth, Shakespeare Variorum Handbook, MLA, 71; co-ed, English Renaissance Drama: Essays in Honor of Madeleine Doran & Mark Eccles, S Ill Univ, 76; ed, A New Variorum Edition of As You Like It, MLA, 77; auth, The Printing of the Second Quarto (Q2) of King Lear, Studies in Bibliography, 82; auth, "Dates for Some Serially Published Shakespeares," studiens in Bibligraphy 40 (87): 187-201; ed, A New Variorum Editions of Measure for Measure, 80, Anthony and Cleopatra, 90, The Winters Tale, 00; gen. ed, New Variorum Supplementary Bibliographies of 1 Henry IV, 2 Henry IV, Julius Caesar, Richard II, 77, Twelfth Night, 84; auth, "ReVision Awry in Folio Lear 3.1," Shakespeare Quarterly 46 (95): 32-46; auth, "Two Lears? By Shakespeare?", In Lear form Study to Stage, ed. J. Ogden & A. H. Scouten, Assoc Univ Presses (97): 57-78; auth, "Cordelia's Return," Shakespeare Quarterly 50 (99): 33-50; auth, "Merging the Kingdoms,"Shakespeare International Yearbook 1 (99): 266-86. **CONTACT ADDRESS** Dept of Eng, Univ of Wisconsin, Madison, 600 North Park St, Madison, WI 53706-1403. **EMAIL** rknowles@facstaff.wisc.edu

KNUTH, DEBORAH

PERSONAL Born 07/12/1952, Forest Hills, NY, m, 1974, 2 children **DISCIPLINE** ENGLISH **EDUCATION** Smith Col, AB, 74; Yale Univ, MA; MPhil; PhD, 78. **CAREER** Instr to Prof, Colgate Univ, 78-. **HONORS AND AWARDS** Teaching Excellence, Sears-Roebuck Foundation Colgate Univ, 90. **MEMBERSHIPS** AAUP, MLA, Am and Intl Soc for 18th Century studies, NWSA, Jane Austen Soc of NA. **RESEARCH** Eighteenth and Nineteenth Century British satire and fiction. **SELECTED PUBLICATIONS** Auth, "Lady Susan: A Bibliographical Essay," in A Companion to Jane Austen Studies, Conn Greenwood Press, in press; auth, "There is so little real friendship in the world!: Distant civility, conversational treats and good advice in Persuasion," Persuasions: The Journal of the Jane Austen Society of North America, (93): 148-156; auth, "The Dunciad and Smart Students: Learning the Importance of Dunces," in Approaches to Teaching Alexander Pope, New York, 93; auth, "Diversity and/in the Canon," Vox Facultatis: Newsletter of the Colgate Chapter of the AAUP, (90): 6-7; auth, "Sisterhood and Friendship in Pride and Prejudice: Need happiness be 'Entirely a Matter of Chance?'," Persuasions, (89): 99-109. **CONTACT ADDRESS** Dept English, Colgate Univ, 13 Oak Dr, Hamilton, NY 13346-1338. **EMAIL** dknuth@mail.colgate.edu

KNUTSON, ROSLYN L.

DISCIPLINE ENGLISH RENAISSANCE LITERATURE **EDUCATION** Univ Tex, PhD. **CAREER** English and Lit, Univ Ark **HONORS AND AWARDS** Dir, Cooper Honors Prog. **SELECTED PUBLICATIONS** Auth, The Repertory of Shakespeare's Company; "Falconer to the Little Eyases, Shakespeare Quart, 95; A Caliban in St. Mildred Poultry, Shakespeare & Cult Traditions; Telling the Story of Shakespeare's Playhouse World, Shakespeare Survey; The Commercial Significance of the Payments for Playtexts, Medieval & Renaissance Drama England; Elizabethan Documents, Captivity Narratives, and the Market for Foreign History Plays, English Literary Renaissance, 96. **CONTACT ADDRESS** Univ of Arkansas, Little Rock, 2801 S University Ave., Little Rock, AR 72204-1099. **EMAIL** rlknutson@ualr.edu

KNUTSON, SUSAN

PERSONAL Born Vancouver, BC, Canada **DISCIPLINE** ENGLISH **EDUCATION** Simon Fraser Univ, BA, 75, MA, 83; Univ BC, PhD, 89. **CAREER** Proj Coordr & Ed, The Kootenay Community Printing Proj, Argenta, BC, 72; prod & script writer, WomenVision, CFRO FM, 80-81; asst prof, 88-93, ch, 93-, Assoc Prof English, Univ Sainte-Anne, 93-. **HONORS AND AWARDS** Morris & Tim Wagner Fel, 84-85. **MEMBERSHIPS** Asn Can Studs; Can Women's Studs Asn; Can Res Inst Advan Women; Asn Can Univ Tchrs Eng; Asn Can & Quebec Lits. **SELECTED PUBLICATIONS** Auth, Challenging the Masculine Generic in Contempory Verse, 88; auth, For Feminist Narratology, 89; auth, Not for Lesbians Only: Reading Beyond Patriarchal Gender in Weaving Alliances: Selected Papers Presented for the Canadian Women's Studies Association at the 1991 and 1992 Learned Societies Conferences, 93. **CONTACT ADDRESS** Dept of English, Univ Sainte-Anne, Pointe-de-l'Eglise, NS, Canada B0W 1M0. **EMAIL** knutson@ustanne.ednet.ns.ca

KOBLER, JASPER FRED

PERSONAL Born 04/06/1928, Niagara Falls, NY, m, 1952, 2 children **DISCIPLINE** ENGLISH, AMERICAN LITERATURE **EDUCATION** La State Univ, BS, 49, BA, 51; Univ Houston, MA, 59; Univ Tex, PhD(English), 68. **CAREER** Reporter, Shreveport La Times, 51-52; res analyst, Defense Dept, Washington, DC, 52-54; reporter, United Press, New Orleans, 55-56; indust ed, Shell Oil Co, Houston, 56-59; instr English, Univ Houston, 59-61; from instr to asst prof, 64-70, Assoc Prof English, NTex State Univ, 70-. **MEMBERSHIPS** Col English Asn (treas, 78-81); NCTE; SCent Mod Lang Asn; Am Asn Advan Humanities. **RESEARCH** Nineteenth century American short story; American writers of 20s and 30s, especially Hemingway and Faulkner. **SELECTED PUBLICATIONS** Auth, Soldiers Home Revisited, A Hemingway, Mea-Culpa, Studies in Short Fiction, Vol 0030, 93. **CONTACT ADDRESS** Dept of English, Univ of No Texas, Denton, TX 76203.

KOCH, CHRISTIAN HERBERT

PERSONAL Born 06/27/1938, St. Paul, MN, m, 1972 **DISCIPLINE** COMMUNICATION THEORY **EDUCATION** Northwestern Col, BA, 59; Univ Minn, Minneapolis, MA, 64; Southern Methodist Univ, MFA, 67; Univ Iowa, PhD (speech and drama), 70. **CAREER** Instr music, Dr Martin Luther Col, 59-60, 61-62 and Wis Lutheran Col, 62-66; asst prof, 70-74, Assoc Prof Commun Studies, Oberlin Col, 74-; Dir, Oberlin Int Conf Film Studies, 71-73. **MEMBERSHIPS** Speech Commun Asn; Int Asn Semiotic Studies; Soc Cinema Studies. **RESEARCH** Semiotics; general systems theory; non-mechanistic cybernetics. **SELECTED PUBLICATIONS** Auth, Administrative Presiding officials Today, Admin Law Rev, Vol 0046, 94; Landis,James in the Administrative Process, Admin Law Rev, Vol 0048, 96; **CONTACT ADDRESS** Dept of Commun Studies, Oberlin Col, 135 W Lorain St, Oberlin, OH 44074-1076.

KOCH, KENNETH

PERSONAL Born 02/27/1925, Cincinnati, OH, m, 1957, 1 child **DISCIPLINE** ENGLISH, COMPARATIVE LITERATURE **EDUCATION** Harvard Univ, AB, 48; Columbia Univ, MA, 53, PhD, 59. **CAREER** Asst, Univ Calif, Berkeley, 51; from instr to assoc prof, 59-71, Prof English and Comp Lit, Columbia Univ, 71-; Guggenheim fel, 61; Fulbright grant, 78, 82. **HONORS AND AWARDS** Harbison Awd, Danforth Found, 70. **RESEARCH** Twentieth century American poetry; modern European literature. **SELECTED PUBLICATIONS** Auth, The Villino, Raritan-a Quart Rev, Vol 0012, 93; One Train May Hide Another, NY Rev Books, 93; One Train May Hide Another, Parabola-Myth Tradition and the Search for Meaning, Vol 0019, 94; Introduction to the Green Lake is Awake, Selected Poems, Am Poetry Rev, Vol 0023, 94; A Heroine of the Greek Resistance, Am Poetry Rev, Vol 0023, 94; A New Guide, Am Poetry Rev, Vol 0023, 94; Your Genius Made Me Shiver, Am Poetry Rev, Vol 0025, 96; An Interview With Koch, enneth, Am Poetry Rev, Vol 0025, 96; The True Life, Am Poetry Rev, Vol 0025, 96; How in Her Pirogue She Glides, Am Poetry Rev, Vol 0025, 96; What Makes This Statue Noble Seeming, Am Poetry Rev, Vol 0025, 96; Au Coconut School, Am Poetry Rev, Vol 0025, 96; Allegheny Menaces, Am Poetry Rev, Vol 0025, 96; Might I Be the First, Am Poetry Rev, Vol 0025, 96; In Ancient Times, Am Poetry Rev, Vol 0025, 96; Vous Etes Plus Beaux Que Vous Ne Pensiez, Poetry, Vol 0168, 96; Diving Along, Am Poetry Rev, Vol 0025, 96; Lets Pour, Am Poetry Rev, Vol 0025, 96; They Say Prince Hamlets Found a Southern Island, Am Poetry Rev, Vol 0025, 96; Mediterranean Suns, Am Poetry Rev, Vol 0025, 96; Africa Paese Notturno, Am Poetry Rev, Vol 0025, 96; Let Us Praise The Elephant, Am Poetry Rev, Vol 0025, 96. **CONTACT ADDRESS** Dept of English, Columbia Univ, New York, NY 10027.

KOCHHAR-LINDGREN, GRAY M.

PERSONAL Born 01/15/1955, Memphis, TN **DISCIPLINE** ENGLISH **EDUCATION** Univ Colo, BA, 77; Yale Univ Div Sch, MAR, 82; Univ NC, MA, 87; Emory Univ, PhD, 90. **CAREER** Instr, Univ of NC, 85-87; vis asst prof, Emory Univ, 87-91, 93-94; lectr, Universitat Regensburg, Ger, 91-93; asst prof, Temple Univ, 94-98; asst prof, Central Mich Univ, 98-. **HONORS AND AWARDS** Phi Beta Kappa; First Prize for Short Stories, Elon Col, 85; First Prize for Essays, Emory Univ, 87; NEH Summer Sem, 94; ROCAD Teacher of the Year, 97; Grant, CMU, 98, 99; Am Psychoanalytic Asn Mentoring Prog, 99-00. **MEMBERSHIPS** MLA; Int Assoc of Philos and Lit; Soc for Critical Exchange; Assoc for the Psychoanalysis of Cult and Soc. **SELECTED PUBLICATIONS** Auth, "The Last Boat Back", Colonnades, 85; auth, Narcissus Transformed: The Textual Subject in Psychoanalysis and Literature, pa State Univ Pr, 93; auth, Starting Time: A True Account of the Origins of Creation, Sex, Death, and Golf, White Cloud Pr, 95; auth, "The Vertiginous Frame: Havel, Heidegger, and Life in a Disjointed Germany", Picturing Cultural Values in Postmodern America, ed William G Doty, Univ of Ala Pr, 95; auth, "The Fish are Running", In-fisherman, 97; coauth, "Michael Bishop", Science Fiction Writers, ed Richard Bleiler, Scribners, (NY, 98); auth, "Ethics, Automation, and the Ear: The Suspension of Animation in Ernst Junger's The Glass Bees", CTheory: Theory, Technology and Culture 21.3, (98): 1-29; auth, "Naming the Abyss: Aeschylus, the Law, and the Future of Democracy", Angelaki: A J of the Theoretical Humanities 4.1 (99): 127-134; auth, "Psycho-Telemetry: Oedipus, Freud, and the Technology of Surveillance", J for the Psychoanalysis of Cult and Soc 4.2 (99): 133-140; auth, "Binding Time, Genre, and Desire: Freud's Construction of the Oedipus in The Interpretation of Dreams", Psychoanalytic Studies, (forthcoming). **CONTACT ADDRESS** Dept English, Central Michigan Univ, 100 W Preston Rd, Mount Pleasant, MI 48859-0001.

KOEGEL, JOHN

DISCIPLINE MUSIC HISTORY **EDUCATION** Calif State Univ, Northridge, BA; Calif State Univ, Los Angeles, MA; CUNY, MA; Cambridge Univ, MA; Claremont Grad Sch, PhD. **CAREER** Asst prof; Univ Mo, 97-. **HONORS AND AWARDS** NEH, Univ Tex-Austin, 96. **RESEARCH** Latin American music; music of Mexico and the Hispanic southwest; Spanish music. **SELECTED PUBLICATIONS** Co-ed, Music in Performance and Soc. **CONTACT ADDRESS** Dept of Music, Univ of Missouri, Columbia, 140 Fine Arts Bldg, Columbia, MO 65211. **EMAIL** musicjk@showme.missouri.edu

KOEHLER, G. STANLEY

PERSONAL Born 03/27/1915, West Orange, NJ, m, 1951, 5 children **DISCIPLINE** ENGLISH **EDUCATION** Princeton Univ, BA, 36, MA, 38, PhD, 42; Harvard Univ, MA, 37. **CAREER** Instr English, Okla State Univ, 38-40, Univ Kans, 46 & Yale Univ, 46-50; from asst prof to assoc prof, 50-62, Prof English, Univ Mass, Amherst, 62-89, Vis prof English, Univ Feiburg, Ger, 76-77, 84-85. **MEMBERSHIPS** MLA; Milton Soc Am. **RESEARCH** Contemporary Poetry, John Milton. **SELECTED PUBLICATIONS** Auth, A Curious Quire, Univ Mass, 63; The Art of Poetry: William Carlos Williams, Paris Rev, Fall 64; The Perfect Destroyers: A Signature of Poems, Mass Rev, summer 66; Milton's Milky Stream, J Am Folklore, 4-6/69; auth, "Satan's Journey," Fabula (69); The Fact of Fall (poetry), Univ Mass, 69; Milton's Use of Color and Light, Milton Studies III, Pittsburgh Univ, spring 71; Milton and the Art of Landscape, Milton Studies VIII, 75; auth, "Contours of Greece," Mass Rev (82); auth, Countries of the Mind: The Poetry of William Carlos Williams, Bucknell, 98. **CONTACT ADDRESS** Dept of English, Univ of Massachusetts, Amherst, Amherst, MA 01002. **EMAIL** gsk@english.umass.edu

KOHAN, KEVIN M.

PERSONAL Born 09/20/1964, Regina, SK, Canada, m, 1991, 2 children **DISCIPLINE** ENGLISH **EDUCATION** Univ Sask, LLB, 88; Univ Regina, BA, 90; Univ Victoria, PhD, 98. **CAREER** Lectr, Univ BC, 99-. **HONORS AND AWARDS** Fel, SSHRC, 92-94; Fel, Univ Victoria, 91. **RESEARCH** 19th and 20th Century American Literature. **SELECTED PUBLICATIONS** Auth, "Victims of Metaphor in the 'Wings of the Dove'," Henry James Rev, 99; auth, "Re-reading the Book in Henry James's 'The ambassadors'," Nineteenth Century Lit, 00; auth, "'The Golden Bowl' and the Subversion of Miraculous Forms," Studies in the Novel, 00; auth, "James and the Sacrificial Origin," Henry James Rev, 01. **CONTACT ADDRESS** Dept English, Univ of British Columbia, 2075 Westbrook Mall, Vancouver, BC, Canada V6T 1Z1. **EMAIL** kkohan@interchange.ubc.ca

KOLB, GWIN JACK

PERSONAL Born 10/09/1946, Chicago, IL, m, 1999 **DISCIPLINE** ENGLISH **EDUCATION** Univ Chicago, BA, 67; Univ Va, PhD, 71. **CAREER** Asst prof, 71-76, ASSOC PROF, UNIV CALIF LOS ANGELES, 76-. **MEMBERSHIPS** ALSC; Tennyson Soc. **RESEARCH** Victorian poetry and prose; James Joyce. **SELECTED PUBLICATIONS** Ed, The Letter of Arthur Henry Hallam, Ohio State Univ Press, 81; auth, Laureate Envy: T.S. Eliot on Tennyson, ANQ 11, 98; auth, Tennyson, Carlyle, and the Morte d'Arthur, Carlyle Stud Ann 17, 97; auth, auth, New Light on Arthur Hallam and Anna Wintour, Tennyson Res Bull 6, 95; auth, On First Looking into Pope's Iliad: Hallam's Keatsian Sonnet, Victorian Poetry 29, 91; auth, The Love of Letters, underdone: Two Tennyson Studies, Victorians Inst J 15, 87; auth, Morte d'Arthur: The Death of Arthur Henry Hallam, Biog 9, 86; auth, Tennyson's Epithalamion: Another Account, Philol Q 64, 85; auth, Arthur Henry Hallam, Dictionary of Literary Biography 32: Victorian Poets Before 1850, 84; auth, Portraits of Tennyson, Modern Philol 81, 83; auth, Arthur Hallam and Emily Tennyson, Rev Eng Stud 28, 77; auth, The

Hero and His Worshippers: The History of Arthur Henry Hallam's Letters, Bull John Rylands Libr 56, 73. **CONTACT ADDRESS** Dept of English, Univ of California, Los Angeles, Los Angeles, CA 90095-1530. **EMAIL** kolb@ucla.edu

KOLB, GWIN JACKSON
PERSONAL Born 11/02/1919, Aberdeen, MS, m, 1943, 2 children **DISCIPLINE** ENGLISH **EDUCATION** Millsaps Col, BA, 41; Univ Chicago, MA, 46; PhD, 49. **CAREER** From instr to prof, English, 49-77, chmn dept, 63-72, Chester D. Tripp prof humanities, Univ Chicago, 77-90; vis assoc prof, Northwestern Univ, 58 and Standford Univ, 60; Am Coun Learned Soc grant-in-aid, 61-62; chmn comt advan test in lit, Educa Testing Serv, 69-78; coed, Mod Philol, 73-90; vis prof, Univ Wash, 73; Ohio State Univ, 87; Peking Univ, 94; Univ Evansville, 96; Huntingdon Col, 97; Univ Ga, 98; Berry Col, 00. **HONORS AND AWARDS** Guggenheim fel, 56-57. **MEMBERSHIPS** MLA; NCTE; Asn Dept Eng; Johnson Soc Midwest; Am Soc 18th Cent Studies. **RESEARCH** English literature of the 18th century. **SELECTED PUBLICATIONS** Coauth, Dr Johnson's Dictionary, 55; coed, English Literature, 1660-1800: A Bibliography of Modern Studies Vol 3-5, 62, 72; auth, "Dr. Johnson's Vision of Theodore: Context, Genre, Reception," in Johnson and His Age, ed. James Engell, 84; ed, Samuel Johnson, "Rasselas" and Other Tales, 90; coed, Approaches to Teaching the Works of Samuel Johnson, 93. **CONTACT ADDRESS** Dept of Eng, Univ of Chicago, 1050 E 59th St, Chicago, IL 60637. **EMAIL** gwinkolb@midway.uchicago.edu

KOLIN, PHILIP
PERSONAL Born 11/21/1945, Chicago, IL, d, 2 children **DISCIPLINE** ENGLISH LITERATURE **EDUCATION** Chicago State Univ, BS, 66; Univ of Chicago, MA, 67; Northwestern Univ, PhD, 73. **CAREER** Prof, Univ of S Miss, 74-. **HONORS AND AWARDS** Alumni Distinguished Prof in the Humanities, Univ S Miss. **MEMBERSHIPS** S Atlantic MLA. **RESEARCH** Shakespeare; Tennessee Williams, Business-Technical Writing, Christian Poetry. **SELECTED PUBLICATIONS** Auth, "Titus Andronicus: Critical Essays", Garland Shakespeare Criticism Series, Garland (NY), 95; coed, Speaking on Stage: Interviews with Contemp Am Playwrights, Univ of Ala Pr, (Tuscaloosa), 96; auth, "Venus and Adonis: Critical Essays", Garland Shakespeare Criticism Series, Garland (NY), 97; auth, Tennessee Williams: A Guide to Research and Performance, Greenwood, (Westport, CT), 98; auth, Tennessee Williams's A Streetcar Named Desire: Plays in Production Series, Cambridge Univ Pr, (Cambridge), 00; auth, Deep Wonder: Poems, Grey Owl, 00; auth, Successful Writing at Work, 6th Ed, Houghton Mifflin (forthcoming). **CONTACT ADDRESS** Dept English, Univ of So Mississippi, Hattiesburg, MS 39406-5037. **EMAIL** philip.kolin@usm.edu

KOLKER, DELPHINE
PERSONAL Born 04/12/1918, Dayton, OH **DISCIPLINE** ENGLISH **EDUCATION** Univ Dayton, BS, 42; Cath Univ Am, MA, 44, PhD(English), 52. **CAREER** Instr English and chmn dept, Immaculata Col, Ohio, 44-59; asst prof English and humanities, St Joseph Col, Ind, 59-61; from asst prof to prof English and philos, St John Col Cleveland, 61-75; Prof English, Cleveland State Univ, 75-; Consult, Choice, 64-. **MEMBERSHIPS** MLA; Am Cath Philos Asn. **RESEARCH** Translations; philosophy; childrens literature. **SELECTED PUBLICATIONS** Auth, To Pay or Not to Pay in Local Governments Stake in Legislation to Reauthorize Superfund, Urban Lawyer, Vol 0025, 93. **CONTACT ADDRESS** Dept of English, Cleveland State Univ, Cleveland, OH 44115.

KOLKO, BETH E.
DISCIPLINE RHETORIC AND COMPOSITION **EDUCATION** Oberlin Col, BA, 89; Univ TX at Austin, MA, 91, PhD, 94. **CAREER** Asst prof, Univ TX at Arlington, 96-; asst prof, Univ WY, Laramie, 94-96; adj asst instr, Univ TX, Austin, 91-94 & tchg asst, 89-91; tchg asst, Techn Commun, Mech Eng Dept, Univ TX, Austin, 90-92; asst dir, Lower Div Eng Off, Univ TX at Austin, 92-93; staff mem, Eng Dept Comp Writing and Res Lab, Univ TX at Austin, 92; lower div Eng Adv Bd, Univ TX at Austin, 90-92; manuscript rev, J Adv Composition, 96-; ed bd mem, Kairos: A J For Tchrs of Writing in Webbed Env, 97-; adv bd mem, CULTSTUD-L listserv, 96-; owner & moderator, Ada-l, Listserv for women in technol within Eng dept, 96-; mem, Rocky Mt ACW Exec Bd, 94-96; coordr, Front Range Composition Reading Gp, 95. **SELECTED PUBLICATIONS** Auth, Bodies in Place: Real Politics, Real Pedagogy, and Virtual Space, High Wired: On the Design, Use, and Theory of Educational MOOs, Univ Mich Press, Ann Arbor, 97; Building a World With Words: The Narrative Reality of Virtual Communities, Works and Days 25/26, 95; Intellectual Property in Collaborative Virtual Space, Computers and Composition, 98; Using Inter Change Transcripts Recursively in the Writing Classroom, Wings 1 1:4, 93; Written Argumentation, Hyperard application, Design team mem, Intellimation Libre Macintosh, Santa Barbara, 93. **CONTACT ADDRESS** Dept of Eng, Univ of Texas, Arlington, 203 Carlisle Hall, PO Box 19035, Arlington, TX 76019-0595.

KOLODNY, ANNETTE
PERSONAL Born 08/21/1941, New York, NY **DISCIPLINE** AMERICAN LITERATURE, WOMENS STUDIES **EDUCATION** Brooklyn Col, BA, 62; Univ Calif, Berkeley, MA, 65, PhD(Am lit), 69. **CAREER** Asst prof English, Yale Univ, 69-70 and Univ BC, 70-74; admin coordr womens studies prog, Univ BC, 72-74; assoc prof English, Univ NH, 74-82; Univ BC Sr Res Grants, 70-; Can Coun sr res grant, 73-74; Mem Adv Bd, AM Lit, 74-; consult grants and fels, Can Coun, 77; Nat Endowment Humanities, 75-; fel study women soc, Ford Found, 75-76; Rockefeller found, 78-79; Guggenheim found, 79-80; Prof, Univ of Ariz. **HONORS AND AWARDS** Florence Howe Essay Prize, 79. **MEMBERSHIPS** MLA; Am Studies Asn; Can Asn Am Studies; Nat Womens Studies Asn. **RESEARCH** Early and contemporary American literature; women writers. **SELECTED PUBLICATIONS** Auth, Inventing a Feminist Discourse, Rhetoric and Resistance in Fuller, Margaret Woman in the Nineteenth Century, New Literary Hist, Vol 0025, 94; Response to Hartman, Rome, New Literary Hist, Vol 0027, 96; 60 Minutes at the University of Arizona in the Polemic Against Tenure, New Literary Hist, Vol 0027, 96; auth, Failing the Future: A Dean books at Higher Education in the 20th Century, Duke Univ Pr, 98. **CONTACT ADDRESS** Comp Cult & Lit Studies, Univ of Arizona, 1239 N Highland, PO Box 210431, Tuscon, AZ 85721-0431.

KOMAR, KATHLEEN LENORE
PERSONAL Born 10/11/1949, Joliet, IL, m, 1988 **DISCIPLINE** COMPARATIVE LITERATURE; MODERN GERMAN; ENGLISH LITERATURE **EDUCATION** Univ Chicago, BA, 71; Princeton Univ, MA, 75; PhD, 77. **CAREER** From asst prof to full prof, Univ Calif, Los Angeles, 77-; chair, Prog in Comp Lit, Univ Calif, Los Angeles, 86-89; dir, Humanities Cluster Prog, Univ Calif, Los Angeles, 91-92; assoc dean, Grad Div, Univ Calif, Los Angeles, 92-. **HONORS AND AWARDS** Goethe Prize, Univ Chicago, 70; DAAD Fel, 71-72; Kent Fel, 74-77; Career Dev Grant for Jr Fac, Univ Calif, Los Angeles, 79, 81; Am Coun of Learned Soc Travel Grant, 86; Dist Teaching Awd for Fac, Univ Calif, Los Angeles, 88-89. **MEMBERSHIPS** MLA; Am Comp Lit Asn; Philol Asn Pac Coast; Western Asn Ger Studies. **RESEARCH** Fragmented, multilinear narratives in the early 20th century: German and American; the poetry of Rainer Maria Rilke and Wallace Stevens; the works of Hermann Broch; contemporary women writers. **SELECTED PUBLICATIONS** Auth, Pattern and Chaos: Multilinear Novels by Dos Passos, Faulkner, Doeblin, and Koeppen, Camden House Publ (Columbia, SC), 83; auth, Transcending Angels: Rainer Maria Rilke's "Duino Elegies," Univ Nebr Press (Lincoln, NE), 87; auth, "Christa Wolf," in Magell's Survey of World Literature, Supplement, ed. Frank N. Magill (NY: Marshall Cavendish Corp, 95), 2835-2843; auth, "Visions and Re-Visions: Contemporary Women Writers Re-present Helen & Clytemnestra," in Visions in History: Visions of the Other, ed. Margaret R. Higonnet and Sumie Jones (Tokyo: Univ Toyko Press, 95), 593-600; auth, "Rilke: Metaphysics in a New Age," in Rilke-Rezeptionen: Rilke Reconsidered, ed. Sigrid Bauschinger and Susan Cocalis (Toebingen/Basel: Francke Verlag, 95), 155-169; auth, "Seventh Duino Elegy," in Reference Guide to World Literature, ed. Laura Berger (MI: St James Press, 95), 1012-1013; auth, "Christa Wolf's 'Cassandra,'" in Masterplots II: Women's Literature, ed. Frank N. Magill (CA: Salem Press, 95), 318-323; auth, "Kassandra as a Rebel Against War: The Theme of Heroism in Christa Wolf's Re-Vision of the Trojan War," in Themes and Structures: Studies in German Literature from Goethe to the Present, ed. Alexander Stephan (SC: Camden House, 97), 234-253; coed, Lyrical Symbols and Narrative Transformations, Camden House Publ (Columbia, SC), 98. **CONTACT ADDRESS** Dept of Comp Lit, Univ of California, Los Angeles, Los Angeles, CA 90095-1536. **EMAIL** komar@ucla.edu

KOMECHAK, MICHAEL E.
PERSONAL Born 08/19/1932, Gary, IN **DISCIPLINE** ENGLISH & AMERICAN LITERATURE **EDUCATION** Univ Notre Dame, MA, 61; Cardinal Stritch Col, BFA, 78. **CAREER** Chmn dept English, St Procopius Acad, 59-65; chaplain, bldg coordr & teacher English, 65-75, assoc prof Fine Arts, Benedictine Univ, 80-98, chmn div, 78-96, retired May, 98, continues to be curator of the univ art collection and coordinator of campus art exhibitions. **RESEARCH** Nineteenth century American and English literature; contemporary journalism. **SELECTED PUBLICATIONS** Auth, Portfolio Format, Scholastic Ed, 12/62; Organize Student Press Bureau for Better Public Relations, Bull Columbia Scholastic Press Adv Asn, 1/66; Raise Funds Via Attractive Ad Book, Scholastic Ed, 12/66; Milwaukee's Pabst Theatre, 6/77 & Dart's Last Church, 10/77, Inland Architect. **CONTACT ADDRESS** Fine Arts Program, Benedictine Univ, 5700 College Rd, Lisle, IL 60532-0900.

KONEK, CAROL WOLFE
PERSONAL Born 01/06/1934, Meade, KS, 4 children **DISCIPLINE** WOMENS STUDIES, ENGLISH **EDUCATION** Univ Kans, BS, 60; Wichita State Univ, MA, 68; Univ Okla, PhD(admin), 77. **CAREER** Instr compos, 68-76, Asst Prof Womens Studies, Wichita State Univ, 70-; Proj dir, proj DELTA, Womens Educ Equity Act, Wichita State Univ, 76-78. **MEMBERSHIPS** Am Educ Asn; Nat Asn of Women Deans, Adminrs and Counr; Nat Womens Studies Asn. **SELECTED PUBLICATIONS** Auth, The Creation of Feminist Consciousness From the Middle Ages, Historian, Vol 0056, 94; Contemporary Western-European Feminism, Historian, Vol 0056, 94. **CONTACT ADDRESS** Dept of Womens Studies, Wichita State Univ, 1845 Fairmont St, Wichita, KS 67260-0001.

KONICK, STEVE
DISCIPLINE COMMUNICATIONS **EDUCATION** Univ Md, Col Park, BA, 82, MA, 89, PhD, 93. **CAREER** Tchg asst, Univ Md, 86-91; lectr, Towson State Univ, 91-92; asst prof, SUNY, Geneseo, 92-96; asst prof, 96-, gen mgr, fac adv, Linfield Col, 96-; exec producer/news ed, Tuesday Weekly TV, 86-91; gen mgr/fac dir, WGSU-FM, 93-96, fac adv, NBS-AERho Honors Soc, SUNY, Geneseo, 94-96. **HONORS AND AWARDS** Prince Georgians on Camera First Place Video Awd, Tuesday Weekly, 87; Geneseo Orgn Leadership Develop Awd, 94. **MEMBERSHIPS** Asn for Educ in Jour and Mass Commun,89-. **SELECTED PUBLICATIONS** Auth, A Visual Thematic Analysis of Network News Coverage of AIDS, in Media-Mediated AIDS, ed Linda Fuller, 96. **CONTACT ADDRESS** Dept Commun, Linfield Col, 900 SE Baker St, McMinnville, OR 97128-6894. **EMAIL** skonick@linfield.edu

KONIGSBERG, IRA
PERSONAL Born 05/30/1935, New York, NY, m, 1957 **DISCIPLINE** ENGLISH **EDUCATION** City Col NYork, BA, 56; Columbia Univ, MA, 57; Stanford Univ, PhD(English), 61. **CAREER** Instr English and Am lit, Brandeis Univ, 61-63; from asst prof to assoc prof, 63-74, Prof English Lang and Lit, Univ Mich, Ann Arbor, 74-; Fulbright-Hays lectr Am lit, Univ Vienna, 66-67. **MEMBERSHIPS** MLA; Am Soc Eighteenth-Century Studies; Am Film Inst. **RESEARCH** Critical theory; film; restoration and 18th century English literature. **SELECTED PUBLICATIONS** Auth, The Movies, Introduction, Mich Quart Rev, Vol 0034, 95; Cinema, Psychoanalysis, and Hermeneutics, Secrets of The Soul, Mich Quart Rev, Vol 0034, 95; The Movies, a centennial issue, 2, Introduction, Mich Quart Rev, Vol 0035, 96; Cave Paintings and the Cinema, Wide Angle Quart J Film Hist Theory Criticism and Pract, Vol 0018, 96; The Only I in the World in Religion, Psychoanalysis, and the Dybbuk, Cinema J, Vol 0036, 97. **CONTACT ADDRESS** Dept of English, Univ of Michigan, Ann Arbor, Ann Arbor, MI 48104.

KONKLE, LINCOLN ERNEST
PERSONAL Born 02/12/1959, South Bend, IN, m, 1982, 2 children **DISCIPLINE** ENGLISH **EDUCATION** Indiana Univ, BS, 81; Kans State Univ, MA, 85; Univ Wis Madison, PhD, 91. **CAREER** Asst prof to assoc prof, Col NJers, 92-. **MEMBERSHIPS** MLA; NEMLA. **RESEARCH** American drama. **SELECTED PUBLICATIONS** Auth, "Puritan Epic Theatre: A Brechtian Reading of Edward Taylor's Gods Determinations," Comm Int Brecht Soc 19 (90): 58-71; auth, "'Histrionic' vs. 'Hysterical': Deconstructing Gender as Genre in Xorandor and Herbivore," in Utterly Other Discourse: The Texts of Christine Brooke-Rose, eds. Ellen J. Friedman, Richard Martin (Ill: Dalkey Arch Pr, 95): 176-191; auth, "Richard Vaughn Moody," in American Playwrights 1880-1945, ed. William W. Demastes (Conn: Greenwood Pr, 95): 302-309; auth, "J.B. Priestley," in British Dramatists 1880-1956, eds. William W. Demastes, Katherine E. Kelly (Conn: Greenwood Pr, 96): 327-338; auth, "American Jeremiah: Edward Albee as Judgment Day Prophet in The Lady from Dubuque," Am Drama 7 (97): 30-49; auth, "Puritan Paranoia: Tennessee Williams's Suddenly Last Summer as Calvinist Nightmare," Am Drama 7 (98): 51-72; rev, The Collected Short Play of Thornton Wilder, Tool," Am Drama 8 (99): 79-82; auth, "Judgment Day in the Jazz Age: American Puritanism in Wilder's Early Plays and Novels," in Thornton Wilder: New Essays (Conn: Locust Hill Pr, 99): 51-91; auth, "Thornton Wilder," in The Dictionary of Literary Biography Vol 228: Twentieth-Century American Dramatists, Sec Series, ed. Christopher J. Wheatley (Detroit: Broccoli Clark Layman Bk, Gale Group, 00): 267-88. **CONTACT ADDRESS** 1 Bet Ann Way, Trenton, NJ 08638-1703. **EMAIL** konklel@tcnj.edu

KONSTAN, DAVID
PERSONAL Born 11/01/1940, New York, NY, m, 1994, 2 children **DISCIPLINE** CLASSICS **EDUCATION** Columbia Col, BA, 61; Columbia Univ, MA, 63, PhD, 67. **CAREER** Lectr classics, Hunter Col, 64-65, Brooklyn Col, 65-67; dir Hum prog, 72-74, chr, 75-77, 78-80, asst prof, 67-72, assoc prof, 72-77, Jane A. Seney prof Greek, 77-87, Wesleyan Univ; Dir Grad Stud, 88-89, CHR, 89-90, 92-94, 98-2001, Prof Classics & Comp Lit, 87- , John Rowe Workman Distinguished Prof Classics & Humanistic Trad, Brown Univ; vis prof, Am Univ Cairo, 81-83; vis schol Univ Texas-Austin, 86-90; vis prof, UCLA, 87; Fulbright lectr, 88; vis prof, Univ Sydney, 90-91; vis prof, Univ Natal, 93, Univ La Plata, 97. **HONORS AND AWARDS** President, American Philol. Assn., 99; Guggenheim, ACLS, NEH Fellowships. **MEMBERSHIPS** Am Philol Asn. **RESEARCH** Ancient literature; culture. **SELECTED PUBLICATIONS** Auth, Sexual Summetry: Love in the Anceint Novel and Related Genres, Princeton Univ Press, 94; Greek Comedy and Ideology, Oxford Univ, 95; Friendship in the Classical World, Cambridge Univ Press, 97; Philodemus on Frank Criticism: Introduction, Translation and Notes, Soc Bibl

Lit Texts & Transl, 98; The greek Commentaries on Aristotle's Nicomachean Ethics 8 and 9, Cornell Univ Press. **CONTACT ADDRESS** Dept Classics, Brown Univ, Providence, RI 02912. **EMAIL** dkonstan@brown.edu

KOOISTRA, JOHN
DISCIPLINE ENGLISH **EDUCATION** Brock Univ, BA; McMaster, MA, PhD. **CAREER** Lectr, Nipissing Univ; McMaster; King Saud Univ, Riyadh, Saudi Arabia; Niagara Col; Brock Univ, 82-94. **SELECTED PUBLICATIONS** Auth, Shoo-fly Dyck, Summertime Stories from Front Porch Al, Penguin, 95; auth, Wonderbaby and the Flying Bathroom. **CONTACT ADDRESS** Dept of English, Nipissing Univ, 100 College Dr, Box 5002, North Bay, ON, Canada P1B 8L7.

KOON, G. W.
PERSONAL Born 06/01/1942, Columbia, SC, m, 1991, 3 children **DISCIPLINE** ENGLISH LITERATURE **EDUCATION** Univ Ga, PhD, 73. **CAREER** Dept Eng, Clemson Univ **RESEARCH** Modern American and Southern literature. **SELECTED PUBLICATIONS** Auth, Hank Williams: A Bio-Bibliography, Greenwood Press, 83; auth, A Collectin of Classic Southern Humor, ed. Peachtree Pubs, 84; auth, A Collection of Classic Southern Humor II, ed. Peachtree Pub, 86; auth, Old Glory and The Stars and Bars, Univ SC Press, 95; Readings for a New Southern Renaissance, SCR, 93; 14 Types of Ambiguity, Southern Cult, 95. **CONTACT ADDRESS** Clemson Univ, 316 Strode, Clemson, SC 29634. **EMAIL** badk@clemson.edu

KOONTZ, CHRISTIAN
PERSONAL Born 06/22/1930, Juniata, PA, s **DISCIPLINE** ENGLISH LITERATURE, LINGUISTICS **EDUCATION** Mercyhurst Col, BA; Cath Univ Amer, MA, PhD. **CAREER** Prof, 80-. **RESEARCH** Writing to learn, heal, and create. **SELECTED PUBLICATIONS** Auth, Cultivating Multiple Intelligences through the Living Journal. **CONTACT ADDRESS** Dept of Eng, Univ of Detroit Mercy, 4001 W McNichols Rd, PO BOX 19900, Detroit, MI 48219-0900. **EMAIL** ckoontzrsm@juno.com

KOONTZ, THOMAS WAYNE
PERSONAL Born 07/09/1939, Ft. Wayne, IN, m, 1998, 5 children **DISCIPLINE** CREATIVE WRITING, LITERATURE; FOLKLORE **EDUCATION** Miami Univ, BA, 61; Ind Univ, Bloomington, MA, 65, PhD(English), 70. **CAREER** Instr English, George Washington Univ, 65-67; Prof English, Ball State Univ, 67-; Nat Endowment Humanities educ grant & proj dir, Ball State Univ, 72-73. **HONORS AND AWARDS** Ely Lilly Fel. **RESEARCH** American studies and poetry; Black American literature. **SELECTED PUBLICATIONS** Auth, To Begin With; Charms; In Such a Light; ed, The View From The Top of The Mountain: Poems After Sixty, Barnwood Press, 81. **CONTACT ADDRESS** Dept of English, Ball State Univ, 2000 W University, Muncie, IN 47306-0002. **EMAIL** TKOONTZ@GW.BSU.EDU

KOOREMAN, THOMAS EDWARD
PERSONAL Born 02/07/1936, St. Louis, MO, m, 1967, 2 children **DISCIPLINE** SPANISH, SPANISH AMERICAN LITERATURE **EDUCATION** Northeast Mo State Univ, BS, 59; Univ Mo, Columbia, MAT, 66, PhD(Span), 70. **CAREER** Asst prof, 70-74, assoc prof, 74-82, Prof Span, Butler Univ, 82-99, prof emer, 99-. **HONORS AND AWARDS** Foreign Lang Teacher of the Year, Indiana, 96; CIBER Workshop, U Ill, 98. **MEMBERSHIPS** Am Asn Teachers Span and Port; AAUP; Am Literary Translators Asn; Asn of Colombianists. **RESEARCH** Spanish American literature; Literary Translation; Spanish for Business. **SELECTED PUBLICATIONS** Auth, Manuel Zapata Olivella, A Saint Is Born in China, U Texas, 91; auth, "Poetic Vision and the Creation of Character in Elcoronel no tiene quien le escrio," Romance Notes 23 (93); ed, Breves Cuentos Hispanos, Prentice Hall, 00. **CONTACT ADDRESS** Dept of Mod Foreign Lang, Butler Univ, 4600 Sunset Ave, Indianapolis, IN 46208-3443. **EMAIL** tkoorema@butler.edu

KOPACZ, PAULA D.
DISCIPLINE ENGLISH **EDUCATION** Mt. Holyoke, AB, 69; Univ Conn, MA, 70; Columbia Univ, PhD, 75. **CAREER** Assoc prof, Prof & Found Prof, Eng, E Kentucky Univ. **MEMBERSHIPS** Am Antiquarian Soc **SELECTED PUBLICATIONS** Auth, "'To Finish What's Begun': Bradstreet's Last Words," Early Am Lit 23, 88; auth, "Men Can Do Best and Women Know It Well: Anne Bradstreet and Feminist Aesthetics," Kent Philological Rev 2, 87; auth, "Feminist at the Tribune: Margaret Fuller as Professional Writer," Studies in the American Renaissance, 91. **CONTACT ADDRESS** Eastern Kentucky Univ, 467 Case Annex, Richmond, KY 40475. **EMAIL** engkopac@acs.eku.edu

KOPER, RANDALL J.
PERSONAL Born 10/12/1952, Grand Rapids, MI, s, 1 child **DISCIPLINE** COMMUNICATION **EDUCATION** Mich State Univ, BA, 75; MA, 84; PhD, 85. **CAREER** Asst prof, Univ of the Pacific, 85-90, assoc prof, 91-98, prof, 98-; vis asst prof, Univ Haw at Manoa, spring 91. **HONORS AND AWARDS** Schnoor Educ Fund Scholar, 70-74; Mich Competitive Scholar, 70-74; Grad Office Master's Scholar, Mich State Univ, 80; Outstanding Grad Student Teaching Awd Int Commun Asn, 85; Achievement Awd, KUOP, Univ of the Pacific, 91; Scholarly Activity Grants, Office of Grad Studies, Univ of the Pacific, 88, 90, 92; nominee for the Gary and Janice Podesto Fund Awd for Teaching, Coaching, and Counseling, Univ of the Pacific, 94; Fac Develop Grant, Univ of the Pacific, 95; Curriculum Infusion Teaching Grant, Univ of the Pacific, 96. **MEMBERSHIPS** Int Commun Asn, Nat Commun Asn, Western State Asn. **SELECTED PUBLICATIONS** Coauth, "The impact of communication context and persuader gender on persuasive message selection," Women's Studies in Commun, 7 (84): 1-12; coauth, "Non-verbal and relational communication associated with reticence," Human Communication Res, 10 (84): 601-626; coauth, "The relationship between communication rewards, communication approach/avoidance, and compliance-gaining message selection," in D. O'Hair & B. R. Patterson, eds, Advances in Interpersonal Communication Research, Las Cruces, NM: CRC Pubs (86): 129-146; coauth, "The efficacy of powerful/powerless language on persuasiveness/credibility," in M. Allen & R. W. Preiss, eds, Persuasion: Advances through Metanalysis, Dubuque, IA: Brown and Benchmark (94): 235-256; coauth, "The relationship of student-faculty out-of-class communication to instructor immediacy and trust and to student motivation," Commun Educ, 48 (99): 41-47. **CONTACT ADDRESS** Dept of Commun, Univ of the Pacific, Stockton, 3601 Pacific Ave, Stockton, CA 95211-0110. **EMAIL** rkoper@uop.edu

KOPFMAN, JENIFER E.
DISCIPLINE COMMUNICATION **EDUCATION** Miami Univ, BA, 91; MI State Univ, MA, 94, PhD, 95. **CAREER** Adjunct asst prof, Univ AZ, 95-97; asst prof, Univ Toledo, 97-99. **HONORS AND AWARDS** Dissertation of the Year Awd for Health Commun from the Speech Commun Asn and the Int Commun Asn, 95. **MEMBERSHIPS** Nat Commun Asn; Int Commun Asn; Western States Commun Asn. **RESEARCH** Health commun; persuasion & cognition; nonverbal commun. **SELECTED PUBLICATIONS** Auth, with S W Smith, K Morrison, and L A Ford, The Influence of Prior Thought and Intent on the Memorability and Persuasiveness of Organ Donation Message Strategies, Health Commun, 16, 94; with S W Smith, C L Medendorp, S Ranck, and K Morrison, The Prototypical Features of the Outstanding Professor from the Female and Male Undergraduate Perspective: The Roles of Verbal and Nonverbal Communication, J on Excellence in Col Teaching, 5, 94; with K Witte, H Bidol, M Casey, K Maduschke, A Marshall, G Meyer, K Morrison, K Ribisl, and S Robbins, Bringing Order to Chaos: Communication and Health, Commun Studies, 47, 96; S W Smith, and J K Ah Yun, Encouraging Feedback in the Large College Class: The Use of a Question/Comment Box, J of the Asn for Commun Administration, 3, 96; with S W Smith, Understanding the Audiences of a Health Communication Campaign: A Discriminant Analysis of Potential Organ Donors Based on Intent to Donate, J of Applied Commun Res, 24, 96; Persuading Potential Organ Donors to Sign Donor Cards: A Case History in Developing Effective Campaigns, in R J Knecht & E M Wiley, eds, Professional Business Communication: An Audience Centered Approach, Simon & Schuster Custom Pub, 97; with S W Smith, J K Ah Yun, and A Hodges, Affective and Cognitive Reactions to Narrative Versus Statistical Evidence Organ Donation Messages, J of Applied Commun Res, 26, 98. **CONTACT ADDRESS** Dept of Communcation, Cleveland State Univ, Grad Sch, 1983 E 24th St, Cleveland, OH 44115.

KOPTAK, PAUL E.
PERSONAL Born 04/01/1955, Denville, NJ, m, 1983 **DISCIPLINE** COMMUNICATION, OLD TESTAMENT **EDUCATION** Rutgers Univ, BA, Psychology, with honors, 77; N Park Theol Seminary, Master of Divinity, highest honors, 86; Garrett-Evangelical Theol Seminary/Northwestern Univ, PhD, Philosophy, 90. **CAREER** Part time instr in biblical and commun studs, N Park Col, 88-93; visiting lecturer, Carib Grad Sch of Theol, Kingston, Jam, 89-90; part-time instr in biblical studs, N Park Theol Seminary, 89-93; Interim Dean of studs, N Park Theol Seminary, 93-94; Assoc prof of Commun & Biblical interpretation, Paul & Bernice Brandel Chr in Preaching, N Park Theol Seminary, 93-. **MEMBERSHIPS** Acad of Homeletics; Assoc for Commun in Theol Educ; Chicago Soc of Biblical Res; Evangelical Homeletic Soc; Inst for Biblical Res; Kenneth Burke Soc; Relig Speech and Commun Assoc; Soc of Biblical Lit; Nat Commun Assoc. **SELECTED PUBLICATIONS** auth, Rhetorical Identification in Paul's Autobiographical Narrative: Galatians 1:13-2:14, Journal for the Study of the New Testament, vol 40, 97-115, 90; auth, What's New in Interpreting Genesis? A Survey of Recent Commentaries and Books, Covenant Quarterly, vol 53 no 1, 3-16, 2/95; auth, Preaching Lawfully, Litany on Law and Liberty: A Response to Psalm 119, Ex Audita, vol 11, 145-152, 95; auth, The Temple, the Scribe, and the Widow, Preaching On-Line, 3/96; Rhetorical Criticism of the Bible: A Resource for Preaching, Covenant Quarterly, vol 54 no 3, 26-36, 7/96; On Namings and New Years, Preaching, 43-46, 11/96; co-ed, To Hear and Obey: Essays in Honor of Frederick Carlson Holmgren, Covenant Pubs, 84-94, 97; Rhetorical Identification in Preaching, Preaching, 11/98. **CONTACT ADDRESS** No Park Theol Sem, 3225 W Foster Ave, #14, Chicago, IL 60625-4895. **EMAIL** pkoptak@northpark.edu

KORABIC, EDWARD W.
DISCIPLINE AUDIOLOGY **EDUCATION** Siena Col, BS, 72; Col St Rose, MA, 74; Syracuse Univ, PhD, 81. **CAREER** Asst Prof to Prof and Chair and Program Dir, Marquette Univ, 79-; Consulting Audiologist, Occupational Hearing Conservation, 81-. **HONORS AND AWARDS** Training Grant, Rehabilitation Services, 75-77; Fel, Veteran's Admin, 78; Grant, Office of Educ, 78-79; Nominated Beltone Teaching Awd, 81, 82, 84, 86; Continuing Educ Awd, Am Speech Lang Hearing Asn, 85. **MEMBERSHIPS** Acoustical Soc of Am, Am Acad of Audiol, Am Speech-Lang-Hearing Asn, Computer Users in Speech and Hearing, Coun of Accreditation in Occupational Hearing Conservation, Nat Industrial Hygiene Asn, Wisc Alliance of Hearing Professionals, Wisc Speech-Lang-Hearing Asn. **SELECTED PUBLICATIONS** Co-auth, "Elderly listeners' estimates of vocal age in adult females," Journal of Acoustical Soc of Am, (86): 692-694; co-auth, "Analysis of pitch perturbation (jitter) using a Visi-Pitch and a microprocessor," Journal Computer Users Speech Hearing (85): 86-93; co-auth, "Use of an acoustic resonating device (ARD) with a 'reverse ski slope hearing loss'," Hearing Journal, (87): 22-25; co-auth, "Fundamental frequency stability characteristics of elderly female voices," Journal of Acoustical Soc of Am, (87): 1196-1199; co-auth, "An inexpensive single switch scanning communication aid, Journal Computer Users Speech Hear, (87): 34-38; co-auth, "Thalamic functional tuning of the cortex dichotic listening tasks," Applied Neurophysiology, (89): 457-458; co-auth, "The effect of thalamic stimulation in processing dichotic listening tests," Brain and Language, (89): 336-351; co-auth, "Intraproduction variability in jitter measures from elderly speakers," Journal Voice, (90): 45-51; co-auth, "Effect of bilateral thalamic stimulation on dichotic verbal processing," Journal Neurolinguistics, (91): 407-425; auth, "Using an electronic spreadsheet to calculate the articulation index," Hearing Instruments, (93): 28-29. **CONTACT ADDRESS** Dept Speech Pathol & Audiol, Marquette Univ, PO Box 1881, Milwaukee, WI 53201-1881.

KORCHECK, ROBERT
PERSONAL m, 1 child **DISCIPLINE** MEDIEVAL AND RENAISSANCE LITERATURE **EDUCATION** St Bonaventure Univ, BA; WVA Univ, Morgantown, MA, PhD. **CAREER** Instr, Duquesne Univ; instr, Fairmont State Col; instr, CA State Univ PA. **RESEARCH** Milton. **SELECTED PUBLICATIONS** Wrote a bk-length study of a coal mining community in southwestern PA (Nemacolin); also contrib an assortment of materials on coal mining to numerous organizations and publ. **CONTACT ADDRESS** California Univ of Pennsylvania, California, PA 15419. **EMAIL** korcheck@cup.edu

KORENMAN, JOAN SMOLIN
PERSONAL Born 09/05/1941, Brooklyn, NY, m, 1968, 1 child **DISCIPLINE** AMERICAN LITERATURE **EDUCATION** Brandeis Univ, BA, 63; Harvard Univ, AM, 64, PhD(English), 70. **CAREER** Asst prof, 69-76, Assoc Prof English, Univ MD Baltimore County, 76-97; Prof, 97-; Dir Womens Studies Program, 81-98; Dir, Center for Women and Infor Technology 98-. **MEMBERSHIPS** Assoc of Women in Computing; Lit; MLA; NCTE. **RESEARCH** Computer-mediated communication; American fiction; womens studies. **SELECTED PUBLICATIONS** Auth, African American Women Writers, Black Nationalism, and the Matrilineal Heritage, Cla J College Lang Asn, Vol 0038, 94; auth, Internet Resources on Women: Using Electronic Media in Curriculum Transformation, 97; auth, Email Forums a nd Women's Studies: The example WMST-L in Cyber Feminism: Connectivity, Critique, Creativity, ed. S. Hawthorne and R. Klein, 99. **CONTACT ADDRESS** Dept of English, Univ of Maryland, Baltimore County, Baltimore, MD 21250. **EMAIL** korenman@umbc.edu

KORG, JACOB
PERSONAL Born 11/21/1922, New York, NY, m, 1953, 1 child **DISCIPLINE** ENGLISH **EDUCATION** City Col New York, BA, 43; Columbia Univ, MA, 47, PhD, 52. **CAREER** Instr English, Bard Col, 47-49 and City Col New York, 51-55; from asst prof to prof, Univ Wash, 55-68; prof, Univ Md, 68-70; Prof English, Univ Wash, 70-; Exchange prof, Nat Taiwan Univ, 60; travel grant, Am Coun Learned Soc, 81. **MEMBERSHIPS** Int Asn Univ Prof English, MLA, ALSC. **RESEARCH** Victorian contemporary and comparative literature; auth, Ritual and Experiment in Modern Poetry, St. Martins Pr, 95. **SELECTED PUBLICATIONS** Auth, The Writings of Thoreau, Henry,D. J, Vol 3, 1848-1865, Nineteenth Century Prose, Vol 0020, 93; The Thoreau Log in a Documentary Life of Thoreau, Henry,David 1817-1862, Nineteenth Century Prose, Vol 0020, 93; The Writings of Thoreau, Henry,D. J, Vol 4, 1851-1852, Nineteenth Century Prose, Vol 0020, 93; Jewish Life in Renaissance Italy, Clio-A J Lit Hist Phil Hist, Vol 0024, 95; The Myth of the Renaissance in 19th-Century Writing, Clio-A J Lit History Phil Hist, Vol 0025, 95; Shakespeare and the Jews in Shapiro,J, Clio-A J Lit Hist Philos Hist, Vol 0025, 96; The Collected Letters of Gissing, George, Vol 3, 1886-1888, Vol 4, 1889-1891, Vol 5, 1892-1895, Vol 6, 1895-1897, Nineteenth-Century Lit, Vol 0051, 96. **CONTACT ADDRESS** Dept of English, Univ of Washington, Seattle, WA 98195. **EMAIL** korg@u.washington.edu

KORITZ, AMY
DISCIPLINE MODERN LITERATURE, DRAMA **EDUCATION** Univ NC, PhD, 88. **CAREER** Instr, 89. **SELECTED PUBLICATIONS** Auth, Dancing the Orient for England: Maud Allan's 'The Vision of Salome, Theatre Jour 46.1, 94; Gendering Bodies/Performing Art: Dance and Literature in Early Twentieth-Century British Culture, AnnArbor: Univ Mich Press, 95; (Re)Moving Boundaries: From Dance History to Cultural Studies, Moving Words: Dance Criticism in Transition, Routledge, 96. **CONTACT ADDRESS** Dept of Eng, Tulane Univ, 6823 St Charles Ave, New Orleans, LA 70118. **EMAIL** akoritz@mailhost.tcs.tulane.edu

KORN, KIM HAIMES
DISCIPLINE COMMUNICATION STUDIES **EDUCATION** FL State Univ, MA, PhD. **CAREER** Instr lit, Southern Polytech State Univ; Asst Prof of English; Dir of the Writing Program **RESEARCH** Response theory; composition pedagogy; collaborative learning; portfolios; literacy and multicultural pedagogies **SELECTED PUBLICATIONS** Auth, publ(s) on response theory; collaborative lrng; literacy; multi cult pedag; auth, Rememory in the Writing Classroom: Telling Untold Stories through Oral Tradition Projects and Extraordinary Readings of Ordinary Lives: Reading Personal and Cultural Ideologies. **CONTACT ADDRESS** Hum and Tech Commun Dept, So Polytech State Univ, S Marietta Pkwy, PO Box 1100, Marietta, GA 30060. **EMAIL** khaimesk@spsu.edu

KOROLENKO, A. MICHAEL
PERSONAL Born 12/27/1954, NJ, s **DISCIPLINE** COMMUNICATIONS **EDUCATION** Vassar Col, BA, 76; Boston Univ, MS, 79. **CAREER** Instr, Bellevue Community Col; producer, director, writer, Korry Productions Ltd. **HONORS AND AWARDS** Harriet Van Loor Awd, Vassar Col; Trustees Lifelong Learning Awd, Seattle Central Community Col. **MEMBERSHIPS** NEA. **RESEARCH** American History, Media. **SELECTED PUBLICATIONS** Auth, The Open Door video, Bellevue Community Col; auth, The Online Advantage video, Bellevue Community Col; auth, Looking Glass Worlds video, Bellevue Community Col; auth, coed, Walking With Grandfather, PBS Series, Corp for Public Broadcasting, auth, Homer's Odyssey, Korry Prod; auth, Nighters, Korry Prod; auth, Writing for Multimedia, Wadsworth Pub; ed, Retrospect 360; Microsoft; auth, Since '45 video, Korry Prod. **CONTACT ADDRESS** Dept Telecommunications, Bellevue Comm Col, 3000 Landerholm Cir SE, Bellevue, WA 98007-6406. **EMAIL** korry@uswest.net

KOROM, FRANK J.
PERSONAL Born 12/15/1957, Kikinda, Yugoslavia, s **DISCIPLINE** FOLKLORE AND FOLKLIFE **EDUCATION** Univ Col, BA, 84; Univ Penn, MA, 87, PhD, 92. **CAREER** Postdoc fel, Smithsonian Inst, 92-93; adj lec, Santa Fe Commun Col, 94-98; cur, Museum of Int Folk Art, 93-98; asst prof, Boston Univ, 98- **HONORS AND AWARDS** Phi Beta Kappa, Univ Col, 84. **MEMBERSHIPS** All India Folklore Cong; Am Acad of Relig; Am Folklore Soc; Asn of Asian Stud; Folklore Fels of Finland; Int Asn for Tibetan Stud; Int Soc for Folk Narrative Res; Int Union of Anthrop and Ethnol Sci; Phi Beta Kappa. **RESEARCH** Hinduism; Islam; Buddhism; ritual, muth, folklore and material culture. **SELECTED PUBLICATIONS** Auth, "A Festive Mourning: Moharram in Trinidad," India Mag, 93; Report on a Planned Exhibit of Tibetan Material Culture in Diaspora," Asian Folklore Stud, 94; "Community Process and the Performance of Muharram Observances in Trinidad," Drama Rev, 94; "Memory, Innovation and Emergent Ethnicities: The Creolization of an Indo-Trinidadian Performance," Diaspora, 94; "Transformation of Language to Rhythm: The Hosay Drums of Trinidad," World of Music, 94; "Recycling in India: Status and Economic Realities," Recycled, Reseen, Reseen: Folk Art from the Global Scrap Heap, Abrams, 96; "Oral Canon Formation in a Bengali Religious Community," Suomen Anthrop, 96; "Place, Space and Identity: The Cultural, Economic and Aesthetic Politics of Tibetan Diaspora," Tibetan Culture in the Diaspora, Austrian Acad of Sci, 97; "Old Age Tibet in New Age America," Constructing Tibetan Culture: Contemporary Perspectives, 97; "Tibetans," American Immigrant Cultures: Builders of a Nation, Macmillan, 97; "Language, Belief and Experience in Bengali Folk Deity," Western Folklore, 97; "Editing Dharmaraj: Academic Genealogies of a Bengali Folk Deity," Western Folklore, 97; Oral Exegesis, Western Folklore, 97; "Foreword," The Art of Exile, Mus of New Mexico Pr, 98 **CONTACT ADDRESS** Dept of Religion, Boston Univ, 745 Commonwealth Ave., Boston, MA 02215. **EMAIL** korom@bu.edu

KORSHIN, PAUL J.
PERSONAL Born 07/24/1939, New York, NY, m, 1998 **DISCIPLINE** ENGLISH **EDUCATION** City Col New York, AB, 61; Harvard Univ, AM, 62, PhD(English), 66. **CAREER** Asst prof, 66-71, assoc prof, 71-80, prof English, Univ Penn, 80- ; Am Philos Soc grant-in-aid, 70; Am Coun Learned Soc grant-in-aid, 71 & 77; Guggenheim fel, 87-88; fel, Bellagio Ctr, Rockefeller Found, 88; co-chmn, Anglo-Am Organizing Comt, 18th Century Short Title Catalogue, 76-80. **MEMBERSHIPS** MLA; Mod Humanities Res Asn; Am Soc 18th Century Studies (exec secy, 73-78); Bibl Soc Am; Bibl Soc London. **RESEARCH** Eighteenth century English literature and intellectual history; 18th century literary patronage; Samuel Johnson, 1709-1784. **SELECTED PUBLICATIONS** Ed & contribr, Studies In Change and Revolution: Aspects of English Intellectual History, 1640-1800, 72 & auth, From Concord to Dissent: Major Themes in English Poetic Theory, 1640-1700, 73, Scolar Press, England; ed, The Widening Circle, Univ Penn, 76; Typologies in England, 1650-1820, Princeton Univ, 82; ed & gen ed, The Eighteenth Century: A Current Bibliography, AMS Press, 82; ed, contribur, Johnson After 200 Years, Univ Penn, 86; ed, The Age of Johnson: A Scholarly Annual, 12 vols, AMS, 87- . **CONTACT ADDRESS** Dept of English, Univ of Pennsylvania, 3340 Walnut St, Philadelphia, PA 19104-6273. **EMAIL** pkorshin@english.upenn.edu

KOSAR, ANTHONY J.
DISCIPLINE MUSIC THEORY **EDUCATION** W Liberty State Col, BM; Southern Ill Univ, MM; Ohio State Univ, PhD. **CAREER** Assoc prof, Westminster, 84-. **HONORS AND AWARDS** Highest hon(s), BM. **MEMBERSHIPS** Mem, Soc Mus Theory; Pi Kappa Lambda and Phi Kappa Phi. **RESEARCH** Theory pedagogy and 19th-century theory. **SELECTED PUBLICATIONS** Publ, articles, The Jour of Mus Theory Pedag. **CONTACT ADDRESS** Dept of Music Theory and Lit, Westminster Choir Col of Rider Univ, 101 Walnut Lane, Princeton, NJ 08540-3819.

KOSHI, ANNIE
PERSONAL Born 04/30/1934, Keala, India, m, 1978 **DISCIPLINE** ENGLISH **EDUCATION** Kerala Univ, MA, 69, DePaul Univ, MA, 71; Columbia Univ, EdM, 76; EdD, 77. **CAREER** Lectr, Kerala Univ, 58-69; teacher, L.D. Brandeis High School, 77-82; assoc prof, CUNY, 82-. **HONORS AND AWARDS** Outstanding Community Leader, Fed of Kerala Asn of N Am, 94. **MEMBERSHIPS** Nat Teachers of Eng; Teaching Eng to Spakers of Other Lang; Soc of Indian Academics in Am. **RESEARCH** Second Language Acquisition. **SELECTED PUBLICATIONS** Auth, Discoveries: Reading, Thinking, Writing, Heinle & Heinle, 94; auth, "Holistic Grammar Through Socratic Questioning", Foreign Lang Annals XXXIX, 3 (403-414). **CONTACT ADDRESS** Dept Eng As a Second Lang, City Col, CUNY, 160 Convent Ave, New York, NY 10031-9101.

KOSKI, CHERYL A.
PERSONAL Born 04/04/1957, Milwaukee, WI **DISCIPLINE** COMMUNICATIONS **EDUCATION** Univ Wisc Whitewater, BS, 79; Iowa State Univ, MA, 83. **CAREER** Instr, La State Univ, 83-87; sr tech ed, U.S. Dept of Energy, 88-. **HONORS AND AWARDS** Hilton A. Smith Fel, Univ Tenn, 97-98; Grad Student Res Award, Univ Tenn, 97-98; Kappa Tau Alpha, 96; Travel Grant, Am Chemical Soc, 96; Travel Grant, Am Soc for Microbiol, 95; Cert of Appreciation, U.S. Dept of Energy, 95; Award of Achievement, Soc for Tech Comm, 92, 94, 95, 96; Focus Award, Iowa State Univ, 82; Critical Writing Award, Iowa State Univ, 81; Paul Grant Memorial Scholar, Univ Wisc, 79; John A Heide Scholar Award, Univ Wisc, 79; Outstanding Achievement Award, Univ Wisc, 79; Who's Who Among Students in Am Univ and Col, 78-79; Phi Kappa Phi, 78. **RESEARCH** Science communication; Literary journalism. **SELECTED PUBLICATIONS** Auth, "Down the Rabbit Hole: Exploring Health Messages on the World Wide Web," J of Tech Writing and Comm, 97; auth, "Science Writers as Characterized in medical Journals: What Are Physicians Saying About Us?" J of Tech Writing and Comm, 98; auth, "The Nonfiction Novel as Psychiatric Casebook: Truman Capote's 'In Cold Blood'," J of Tech Writing and Comm, 99. **CONTACT ADDRESS** U.S. Dept of Energy, Oak Ridge Facilities, 128-C Durwood Rd, Knoxville, TN 37922-3271. **EMAIL** koski@utk.edu

KOSTELANETZ, RICHARD
PERSONAL Born 05/14/1940, New York, NY **DISCIPLINE** AMERICAN CULTURE **EDUCATION** Brown Univ, AB, 62; Columbia Univ, MA, 66. **CAREER** Co-founder and president, Assembling Press, 70-82; Contrib Ed, NY Arts J, 80-; prog assoc thematic studies, John Jay Col Criminal Justice, 72-73; sr staff, Univ Indiana Writers Conf, 76; vis prof, Am Studies and English, Univ Tex, Austin, 77; co-ed, Precisely: A Critical Jour, 76-; Sole proprietor, Archaeol Editions, 78-. **HONORS AND AWARDS** Res and Writing, 62-; Guggenheim fel, 67-68; Pulitzer Fel, 65; Guggenheim Fel, 67; Best Books of 1976 by the American Inst of Graphic Arts, Nat Endowment for Arts grant, 76; Ludwig Vogelstein Foundation, 80; CCLM Editors Fel, 81; NEA Visual arts senior fel, 85; Fel, New Assoc of Sephardi/Mizrahi Artists and Writers Int, 00-02. **RESEARCH** Experimental literature, particularly in North America; arts and artists in America; criticism of avant- garde arts, particularly literature. **SELECTED PUBLICATIONS** Auth, Avant Garde American Radio Art, North Am Rev, Vol 0278, 93; Flood in a Novel in Pictures, Am Book Rev, Vol 0014, 93; The Roaring Silence in Cage, John, A Life, Notes, Vol 0049, 93; Caxton, Caxton, a Predating, A Definition, and a Supposed Derivation, Notes and Queries, Vol 0040, 93; Not Wanting to Say Anything About Cage, John 1912-92, Chicago Rev, Vol 0038, 93; Grrrhhhh, Amn Book Rev, Vol 0014, 93; The Phenomenology of Revelation, Am Book Rev, Vol 0014, 93; Minimal Audio Plays, Western Hum Rev, Vol 0048, 94; It Too Shall Pass, Modern Languages Association Rev, Am Book Rev, Vol 0016, 94; Hysterical Pregnancy , North Am Rev, Vol 0279, 94; The Boulez-Cage Correspondence, Am Book Rev, Vol 0016, 95; Literary Video, Visible Language, Vol 0029, 95; Postmodern American Poetry in a Norton Anthology, Am Book Rev, Vol 0016, 95; Preface to Solos, Duets, Trios, and Choruses Membrane Future, Midwest Quart-A J Contemporary Thought, Vol 0037, 95; A Poetry-Film Storyboard in Transformations, Visible Lang, Vol 0030, 96; Anarchist Voices in an Oral-History of Anarchism in America, Am Book Rev, Vol 0017, 96; Interview With Schwartz, Tony, American Horspielmacher, Perspectives New Mus, Vol 0034, 96; Conservative Subversion, Am Book Rev, Vol 0017, 96; Format And Anxiety, Am Book Rev, Vol 0017, 96; The Year of the Hot Jock and Other Stories, Am Book Rev, Vol 0019, 97; A Star in the Family, Am Book Rev, Vol 0019, 97; Newsreel, Am Book Rev, Vol 0019, 97; Jim Dandy, Am Book Rev, Vol 0019, 97; The File on Stanley Patton Buchta, Am Book Rev, Vol 0019, 97; Roar Lion Roar and Other Stories, Am Book Rev, Vol 0019, 97; The Steagle, Am Book Rev, Vol 0019, 97; The Winner of the Slow Bicycle Race, Am Book Rev, Vol 0018, 97; Willy Remembers, Am Book Rev, Vol 0019, 97; Foreign Devils, Am Book Rev, Vol 0019, 97; auth, Political Essays, Autonomedia, 99; auth, Thirty Years of Visible Writing, BGB, 00; auth, More On Innovative Music(ian)s, Fallen Leaf-Scarecrow, 01. **CONTACT ADDRESS** Prince St, PO Box 444, New York, NY 10013. **EMAIL** rkostelanetz@bigfoot.com

KOTLER, PHILIP
PERSONAL Born 05/27/1931, Chicago, IL, m, 1955, 3 children **DISCIPLINE** MARKETING **EDUCATION** Univ Chicago, MA, 53; PhD, MIT, 56; Hon Doctorate, DePaul Univ, 88. **CAREER** Asst then Assoc Prof, Roosevelt Univ, 57-61; Asst Prof to Prof, NW Univ, 62-69; A Montgomery Ward Prof, 69-73; Harold T Martin Prof, 73-88; SC Johnson & Son Dist Prof, 89-. **HONORS AND AWARDS** Graham & Dodd Awd Fin Analysts Fedn, 62; MacLaren Advt Res Awd, 64; McKinsey Awd, 65; Alpha Kappa Psi Found Awd, 78; Philip Kotler Awd for excellence in Health Care Marketing, 85; Charlse Coolidge Parlin Nat Mktg Awd, 89; Marketer of the Yr, 83; marketing ed, holt, rinehart & winston, 65-78; ch, col mktg, inst mgt sci. **MEMBERSHIPS** Am Mktg Asn (bd 70-72); Inst Mgt Sci, Mktg Sci Inst (trustee 74-84); Phi Beta Kappa. **RESEARCH** Marketing. **SELECTED PUBLICATIONS** Auth, Marketing Management: Analysis, Planning and Control, 10th ed, 00; auth, Strategic Marketing for Nonprofit Organizations, 5th ed, 96; auth, Principles of Marketing, 9th ed, 01. **CONTACT ADDRESS** 301 Keystone Ct., Glencoe, IL 60022-1957. **EMAIL** pkotler@aol.com

KOTZIN, JOSHUA BOAZ
PERSONAL Born 11/23/1970, Israel, m **DISCIPLINE** ENGLISH **EDUCATION** Stanford Univ, BA, 92; Univ Iowa, MA, 97; PhD, 00. **CAREER** Adj instr to lectr, Yeshiva Col, 98-. **HONORS AND AWARDS** Univ Iowa Fel; Nat Merit Scholar. **MEMBERSHIPS** MLA; ALA; CCCC; NEMLA. **RESEARCH** 19th to 20th-century American literature and culture. **SELECTED PUBLICATIONS** Auth, "Reading in Rome," Mickle Street Rev; auth, "Numismatics," Henry Street. **CONTACT ADDRESS** 289 Hoyt St, Brooklyn, NY 11231-4907. **EMAIL** kotzin@ymail.yu.edu

KOVACH, CHARLES
PERSONAL Born 03/10/1962, s **DISCIPLINE** ENGLISH **EDUCATION** San Diego State Univ, BA, 83; MA, 94. **CAREER** Adj prof, San Diego City Col, 94-; adj instr, Southwestern Col, 97-; instr, Univ Calif at San Diego, 98. **HONORS AND AWARDS** Certificate of Appreciation for Service and Dedication to Southwestern Col Students, Southwestern Col; Certificate of Achievement, San Diego City Col Mentoring Prog; Certificate of Achievement for Outstanding Tutor Training, San Diego City Col. **MEMBERSHIPS** Nat Coun of Teachers of English Assembly for the Teaching of English Grammar, Nat Coun of Teachers of English Assembly for Am Lit, Iowa Coun of Teachers of English/Language Arts. **RESEARCH** English Writing Pedagogy. **SELECTED PUBLICATIONS** Contribur, Teaching English in the Two-Year Col; contribur, Syntax in the Schools; contribur, TESOL Matters; contribur, ESL Notes; contribur, Iowa Language News. **CONTACT ADDRESS** Dept English/Humanities, San Diego City Col, 1313 12th Ave, San Diego, CA 92101-4712. **EMAIL** ckovach@swc.cc.ca.us

KOVACIK, KAREN
PERSONAL Born 07/21/1959, East Chicago, IN **DISCIPLINE** ENGLISH **EDUCATION** Ind Univ, BA, 81; Cleveland State Univ, MA, 90; Ohio State Univ, PhD, 97. **CAREER** Asst Prof, Ind Univ, 97-. **HONORS AND AWARDS** Pushcart Prize nomination, The Journal, 99; Poetry Open first Prize, Glimmer Train Magazine, 99; Stan and Tom Wick Poetry Prize, 98; Helen Earnhart Harley Prize, Ohio state Univ, 97; Winner of the Wick Chapbook Competition, Kent State Univ Press, Acad of Am Poets Prize, Ohio State Univ, 96; Phyllis Smart Young Prize, Madison Review, 94; Fel, Univ Wisc, 92; Grant, Ohio arts Coun, 92; Winner of Poetry Atlanta Chapbook Competition, 90. **RESEARCH** Working Class Women poets; Multicultural poetry; 20th Century American literature. **SELECTED PUBLICATIONS** Auth, Beyond the Velvet Curtain, Kent

state Univ Press, 99; auth, Nixon and I, Kent State Univ Press, 98; auth, Return of the Prodigal, Poetry Atlanta Press, 91; auth, "Words of fire for Our Generation: contemporary Working-Class Poets on the Triangle Fire," Women's Studies Quarterly, (98): 137-158; auth, "Thirteen Ways of Looking at a Working-Class Background," in Writing Work: Writers on Working-class Writing, Bottom Dog Press, 99; auth, "Songs for a Belgrade Baker," Glimmer Train Magazine, forthcoming; auth, "To Warsaw," Massachusetts Review, forthcoming; auth, "Revising Sylvia," The Journal, (990: 20-21; trans, "German Gothic," "Her," "Penelomedea," by Borun-Jagodzinska, Katarzyna, Graham House Review, 92; trans, "The Exorcist," "Museum of the automaton," in shifting Borders: Eastern European Poetries of the 1980s, Fairleigh Dickinson Univ Press, 92 **CONTACT ADDRESS** Dept English, Indiana Univ-Purdue Univ, Indianapolis, 425 Univ Blvd, Indianapolis, IN 46202-5208. **EMAIL** kkovacik@iupui.edu

KOVACS, P. DAVID
PERSONAL Born 11/12/1945, Kenosha, WI, m, 1969, 2 children **DISCIPLINE** CLASSICS **EDUCATION** Col Wooster, BA, 67; Harvard Univ, AM, 69; PhD, 76. **CAREER** Asst prof, Univ Va, 76-82, assoc prof, 82-90, prof, 90-. **HONORS AND AWARDS** NEH, 90-92, 96-97. **MEMBERSHIPS** AMA; CAMWS; CA. **RESEARCH** Greek tragedy; Ovid. **SELECTED PUBLICATIONS** Auth, The Andromache of Euripides: An Interpretation, Scholars Press (Chico, CA), 80; auth, The Heroic Muse: Studies in the Hippolytus and Hecuba of Euripides, Johns Hopkins Univ Press (Baltimore), 87; auth, Euripidea, E J Brill (Leiden), 94; Auth, Euripides. The Loeb Classical Library Euripides, Greek text and English translation, Harvard Univ Press (94) vol 1; auth, Euripides. The Loeb Classical Library Euripides, Greek text and English translation, Harvard Univ Press (95) vol vol2; auth, Euripides. The Loeb Classical Library Euripides, Greek text and English translation, Harvard Univ Press (98) vol 3; auth, Euripides. The Loeb Classical Library Euripides, Greek text and English translation, Harvard Univ Press (99) vol 4; Auth, "Euripides, Troa des 95-97: Is Sacking Cities Really Foolish?" Classical Quart 33 (1983), 334-338; auth, "On Mèdea's Great Monologue (Eur. Medea 1021-1080)," CQ 36 (86): 343-352; auth, "Ovid, Metamorphoses 1.2," CQ 37 (1987):458-465; auth, "Zeus in Euripides Medea," AJP 114 (93): 45-70; auth, "The Theology of Euripides' Trojan Trilogy," Colby Quarterly 33.2 (97): 162-76. **CONTACT ADDRESS** Dept Classics, Univ of Virginia, 401 New Cabell Hall, Charlottesville, VA 22903-3125.

KOVARIK, BILL
DISCIPLINE PRINT AND WEB MEDIA **EDUCATION** VA Commonwealth Univ, BS; Univ SC, MA; Univ MD, PhD. **CAREER** Assoc prof, Radford Univ. **SELECTED PUBLICATIONS** Publ a bk on the hist of environmental conflict in the mass media. **CONTACT ADDRESS** Radford Univ, Radford, VA 24142. **EMAIL** wkovarik@runet.edu

KOVARIK, EDWARD
DISCIPLINE MUSIC HISTORY **EDUCATION** Northwestern Univ, BM, BME, MM; Harvard, MA, PhD. **CAREER** Assoc prof; dir, Windsor Collegium & mus dir and conductor, Windsor Commun Orchestra; first violin, Coventry Quartet of Windsor. **SELECTED PUBLICATIONS** Auth, pub (s), 15th and 16th century music. **CONTACT ADDRESS** Dept of Music, Univ of Windsor, 401 Sunset Ave, Windsor, ON, Canada N9B 3P4. **EMAIL** kovarik@uwindsor.ca

KOVARSKY, DANA
DISCIPLINE COMMUNICATIVE DISORDERS **EDUCATION** Univ TX at Austin, PhD, 89. **CAREER** Asst prof; post doctoral fel, Univ KS in Lawrence. **RESEARCH** Lang and soc interaction in clinical contexts, including sch(s) and med settings. **SELECTED PUBLICATIONS** Publ on, interactional patterning of adult-centered and child-centered lang therapy; conflict talk in rural Appalachian day care ctr(s); gp lang therapy practices among adults with traumatic brain injury; ethnog of commun disorders & lange use in contexts of schooling. **CONTACT ADDRESS** Dept of Communicative Disorders, Univ of Rhode Island, 8 Ranger Rd, Ste. 1, 108 Adams , Kingston, RI 02881-0807. **EMAIL** dkovars@uriacc.uri.edu

KOWALCZYK, RICHARD L.
DISCIPLINE VICTORIAN AND MODERN BRITISH LITERATURE **EDUCATION** Wayne State Univ, PhD. **CAREER** Prof, 61-. **RESEARCH** Technical writing based on professional consulting and publications. **SELECTED PUBLICATIONS** Pub(s), articles on writers' response to cultural issues; ed reader, Mod Lit. **CONTACT ADDRESS** Dept of Eng, Univ of Detroit Mercy, 4001 W McNichols Rd, PO BOX 19900, Detroit, MI 48219-0900. **EMAIL** KOWALR@udmercy.edu

KOWALEWSKI, MICHAEL J.
PERSONAL Born 11/02/1956, San Francisco, CA, m, 1983, 3 children **DISCIPLINE** ENGLISH **EDUCATION** Amherst Col, BA, 78; Rutgers Univ, MA, 82; PhD, 86. **CAREER** Asst prof, Princeton Univ, 86-91; asst to assoc prof, Carleton Col, 91-. **HONORS AND AWARDS** ACLS Fel, 88-89; Awd of Merit, Am Assoc of State and Local Hist, 98. **MEMBERSHIPS** MLA; Western Lit Assoc; Assoc for Study of Lit and Environ; Calif Studies Assoc. **RESEARCH** American literature, American art and photography, American film, regionalism and place in the arts, Travel writing, Environmental Studies. **SELECTED PUBLICATIONS** Ed, Temperamental Journeys: Essays on the Modern Literature of Travel, Univ of Ga Pr, (Athens, Ga), 92; auth, Deadly Musings: Violence and Verbal Form in American Fiction, Princeton Univ Pr, (Princeton), 93; auth, Popular Classics of American Literature, Eihosha Ltd (Tokyo), 96; ed, Reading the West: New Essays on the Literature of the American West, Cambridge Univ Pr, (NY), 96; ed, Gold Rush: A Literary Exploration, Heyday Books, (Berkeley), 97. **CONTACT ADDRESS** Dept English, Carleton col, 1 N College St, Northfield, MN 55057-4001. **EMAIL** mkowalew@carleton.edu

KOWALKE, KIM H.
PERSONAL Born 06/25/1948, Monticello, MN, m, 1978, 1 child **DISCIPLINE** MUSICOLOGY **EDUCATION** Macalester Col, BA, 70; Yale Univ, MA, 72; Mphil, 74; PhD, 77. **CAREER** Conductor, 102nd Nat Guard Band, 71-77, Greater New Haven Youth Symphony, 73-75; musical dir, Yale Dramat and Yale Cabaret, 73-74; principal conductor, Col Light Opera Company, Falmouth, Mass, 74, 75, 77, 79; teaching fel, Yale Univ, 74-75; conductor, Collegiate Symphony Orchestra of Occidental Col and Calif Inst of Technol, 77-83; musical dir and conductor, many productions of musical theater, Occidental Col, 77-86; from asst prof to assoc prof, Occidental Col, 77-86; prof, Univ of Rochester, 86- ; conductor, Happy End, Univ of Rochester, Street Scene, Eastman Opera Theatre 91; music dir, A Salute to Stephen Sondheim, Univ of Rochester, 95; conductor, Eastman Opera Theatre: There Once Was A Girl Named Jenny: A Celebration of the Music of Kurt Weill, 95; coproducer and -conductor, Broadway: The George Abbott Way, Eastman Theatre, 97. **HONORS AND AWARDS** Nat Merit Scholar, 66-70; W. Wilson Nat Fel, 70; Yale Univ Fel, 71-75; Martha Baird Rockefeller Fund for Music Grant in Musicology, 75-76; Whiting Prize Dissertation Fel, 76-77; Theron Rockwell Field Prize, 78; Mellon Found Grant, 78; ACLS Res Grant for Recent Recipients of the PhD, 80; The Arnold L. and L. S. Graves Awd in the Hums, 84-85; 3-Time Winner of ASCAP's Deems Taylor Awd for excellence in writing about music, 86, 90, 97; Irving Lowens Prize, Sonneck Soc for Am Music, 97; George Friedley Awd for outstanding book in the performing arts, 97. **MEMBERSHIPS** Phi Beta Kappa; Sonneck Soc for Am Music; Int Brecht Soc; Col Music Soc, Am Musicological Soc; Kurt Weill Found for Music. **RESEARCH** Whitman and Music; Adorno and the aesthetics of modernism; Wagner; post-Wagnerian symphonists; neo-Classicism. **SELECTED PUBLICATIONS** Ed, A New Orpheus: Essays on Kurt Weill, 86; coed, A Stranger Here Myself: Kurt Weill Studien, 93; Street Scene: A Sourcebook, 94; Der Silbersee: A Sourcebook, 95; Aufstieg und Fall der Stadt Mahagonny: A Sourcebook, 95; Lady in the Dark: A Sourcebook, 97; auth, Kurt Weill in Europe, 81; The Threepenny Opera in America, in: Die Dreigroschenoper, ed. by S. Hinton, 90; Hin und zurueck: Kurt Weill at 90, in The Musical Times, 90; Singing Brecht vs. Brecht Singing: Performance in Theory and Practice, in Cambridge Opera Journal 5/1, 93; Dancing on a Volcano: Berg and Weill, in Stagebill, Dec., 93; Kurt Weill, Modernism, and Popular Culture: Oeffentlicheit als Stil, in Modernism/Modernity 2, 95; Ein Ehemaliger Deutscher: Kurt Weill in Amerika, in Kurt Weill: Berlin-Paris-New York , 95; Mahagonny and Robert W. Service, in Kurt Weill Newsletter 13, 95; Hindemith and Whitman: An American Requiem, in Stagebill, Sept., 95; Response to the 'Bourges Resolution', in The Brecht Yearbook 21, 96; Blitzstein and Bernstein: Remaking The Threepenny Opera, introductory essay for Vol. 1 of the Kurt Weill Edition, a facsimile of the Holograph Partitur of Die Dreigroschenoper, 96; Putting Sondheim in Musical Theater Focus, in The Sondheim Rev 3, 97; Orff and Weill: The Brecht Connection, in Stagebill, 97; For Those We Love: Hindemith, Whitman, and An American Requiem', in Journal of the Am Musicological Soc, 97. **CONTACT ADDRESS** The Col Music Program, Univ of Rochester, 210 Todd, Rochester, NY 14627. **EMAIL** kkwk@db1.cc.rochester.edu

KOZIKOWSKI, STANLEY JOHN
PERSONAL Born 04/16/1943, Fall River, MA, m, 1965, 2 children **DISCIPLINE** ENGLISH, COMMUNICATIONS THEORY **EDUCATION** Southeastern Mass Univ, BS, 65; Univ Mass, MA 68, PhD(English), 71. **CAREER** Instr English, Col of Our Lady of the Elms, 68-71, asst prof, 71-75; asst prof, 75-77, Dean of Undergrad Fac, Bryant Col, 78-. **MEMBERSHIPS** Am Bus Commun Asn; Am Inst Decision Sci; MLA; NCTE; New England Asn Instnl Res. **RESEARCH** English Renaissance drama and poetry; modern American literature; communications theory. **SELECTED PUBLICATIONS** Auth, Fortune and men's eyes in Romeo and Juliet, Concerning Poetry, spring 77; Shakespeare's Antony and Cleopatra, Explicator, summer 77; Comedy ecclesiastical and otherwise in Gammer Gurton's Needle, Greyfriar, 77; Wyatt's They Flee From Me and Churchyard's Complaint of Jane Shore, Notes & Queries, 78; A reconsideration of Poe's The Cask of Amontillado, Am Transcendental Quart, 78; The unreliable narrations in Henry James's The Two Faces' and Edith Wharton's The Dilettante, Ariz Quart, 78; The allegory of love and fortune: The lottery in The Merchant of Venice, In: Renascence: Essays on Values in Literature, 80; The Gowrie Conspiracy against James VI: A new source for Shakespeare's Macbeth, Shakespeare Studies, 81. **CONTACT ADDRESS** Dept of Humanities & English, Bryant Col, 1150 Douglas Pike, Smithfield, RI 02917-1291.

KRAABEL, ALF THOMAS
PERSONAL Born 11/04/1934, Portland, OR, m, 1956, 3 children **DISCIPLINE** RELIGIOUS STUDIES, CLASSICS **EDUCATION** Luther Col, BA, 56; Univ Iowa, MA, 58; Luther Theol Sem, BD, 61; Harvard Univ, ThD, 68. **CAREER** Asst prof classics and relig studies, 67-70, assoc prof classics and chmn relig studies, 70-76, Prof Classics and Relig Studies, Univ Minn, Minneapolis, 76-; Chmn Dept and Dir Grad Study, 80-; Assoc dir, Joint expedition to Khirbet Shema, Israel, 69-73; Sabbatical fel, Am Coun Learned Soc, 77-78. **MEMBERSHIPS** Soc Bibl Lit; Am Acad Relig; Am Soc Study Relig; Soc Values Higher Educ. **RESEARCH** Greco-Roman religions; archaeology. **SELECTED PUBLICATIONS** Auth, Jewish Communities in Asia-Minor, Cath Bibl Quart, Vol 0055, 93; Ancient Jewish Epitaphs in An Introductory Survey of a Millennium of Jewish Funerary Epigraphy Cath Bibl Quart, Vol 0055, 93; From Synagogue to Church in Public Services and offices in the Earliest Christian Communities Interpretation-A, J Bible Theol, Vol 0048, 94; Mission and Conversion in Proselytizing in the Religious History of the Roman Empire, J Early Christian Studies, Vol 0004, 96; Early Christian Epitaphs from Anatolia, Cath Bibl Quart, Vol 0058, 96. **CONTACT ADDRESS** Dept of Classics, Univ of Minnesota, Twin Cities, 310A Folwell Hall, Minneapolis, MN 55455.

KRABBE, JUDITH
DISCIPLINE GREEK, LATIN & SANSKRIT LANGUAGES & LITERATURES **EDUCATION** Cath Univ, PhD. **CAREER** Dept Classics, Millsaps Col **SELECTED PUBLICATIONS** Auth, The Metamorphoses of Apuleius; coauth, An Introduction to Sanskrit. **CONTACT ADDRESS** Dept of Classical Studies, Millsaps Col, 1701 N State St, Jackson, MS 39210. **EMAIL** krabbjk@orka.millsaps.edu

KRAFFT, JOHN M.
PERSONAL Born 01/09/1951, Springfield, OH, m, 1971 **DISCIPLINE** ENGLISH **EDUCATION** Miami Univ, BA, 73; SUNY Buffalo, MA, 76; PhD, 78. **CAREER** Vis asst prof, West Virginia Univ, 77; assoc prof, Suffolk Comm Col, 78-90; asst-assoc prof, Miami Univ Ham, 90-. **HONORS AND AWARDS** Woodburn Fel; Mellon Fel. **MEMBERSHIPS** MLA; CELJ; AAUP; Soc Stud Narr Lit. **RESEARCH** Contemporary American Fiction; American Literature; The Novel. **SELECTED PUBLICATIONS** Co-found, Co-ed, Pynchon Notes, 79-; coauth, "Thomas Pynchon," Dictionary of Literary Biography, vol 173. **CONTACT ADDRESS** Dept English, Miami Univ, Hamilton, 1601 Peck Blvd, Hamilton, OH 45011-3399. **EMAIL** krafftjm@muohio.edu

KRAFT, ELIZABETH A.
PERSONAL Born 10/05/1954, Atlanta, GA, d **DISCIPLINE** ENGLISH **EDUCATION** Ga Southern Col, AB, 75; Ga State Univ, MA, 78; Emory Univ, PhD, 85. **CAREER** Asst Prof, Univ SC, 85-87; From Asst Prof to Prof, Univ Ga, 87-. **HONORS AND AWARDS** Phi Beta Kappa; NEH Summer Fel; William Andrews Clark Libr Fel; Bibliog Soc Am Fel; Sandy Beaver Teaching Awd; Outstanding Honors Prof. **MEMBERSHIPS** Mod Lang Asn, Am Soc for Eighteenth-Century Studies. **RESEARCH** Restorahm and Eighteenth-Century Baptist literature. **SELECTED PUBLICATIONS** Co-ed, The Poems of Anna Letitia Barbauld, Univ Ga Pr (Athens, GA), 94; auth, Laurence Sterne Revisited, Twayne (New York, NY), 96; auth, "The Pentecostal Moment in 'A Sentimental Journey'," in Critical Essays on Laurence Sterne (New York: G K Hall, 98), 292-310; ed, The Young Philosopher, by Charlotte Smith, Univ Ky Pr (Lexington, KY), 99; co-ed, Anna Letitia Barbauld: Selected Poetry and Prose, Broadview Pr, forthcoming. **CONTACT ADDRESS** Dept English, Univ of Georgia, Athens, GA 30602-0002. **EMAIL** ekraft@uga.edu

KRAFT, RUTH NELSON
PERSONAL Born St. Louis, MO, m, 1966 **DISCIPLINE** ENGLISH, MUSIC **EDUCATION** Northwestern Univ, BM, 35, MM, 40; Columbia Univ, MA, 61. **CAREER** Teacher, Woodmere Acad, NY, 43-56; teacher English and creative writing, G W Hewlett High Sch, NY, 56-68, coordr Humanities, 68-74; Instr Mod Fiction and Hist Music, Five Towns Col, Merrick, 75-. **HONORS AND AWARDS** Nat Awd, Outstanding Sec Educr Am, 75. **SELECTED PUBLICATIONS** Auth, Humor in American Literature in A Selected Annotated-Bibliography, Metaphor Symbolic Activ, Vol 0008, 93; Illuminating Shadows in The Mythic Power of Film, Metaphor Symbolic Activ, Vol 0009, 94. **CONTACT ADDRESS** Beverly Rd, Douglaston, NY 11363.

KRAHNKE, KARL
DISCIPLINE ENGLISH LITERATURE **EDUCATION** Univ Mich, BA, MA, PhD. **CAREER** Assoc prof. **RESEARCH** Discourse analysis of ESL writing; function of non standard Englishes in business and industry. **SELECTED PUBLICATIONS** Auth, puns on language and language teaching. **CONTACT ADDRESS** Dept of English, Colorado State Univ, Fort Collins, CO 80523. **EMAIL** kkrahnke@vines.colostate.edu

KRAJEWSKI, BRUCE
DISCIPLINE ENGLISH LITERATURE **EDUCATION** Univ Iowa, PhD. **RESEARCH** Philos hermeneutics; hist of interpretation; film; rhetoric. **SELECTED PUBLICATIONS** Auth, Traveling with Hermes: Hermeneutics and Rhetoric, 92; auth, The Musical Horizon of Religion: Blumenberg's Matthieuspassion, Hist Human Sci, 93; auth, Postmodernism, Allegory, and Hermeneutics in Brazil, 89. **CONTACT ADDRESS** English Dept, Laurentian Univ, 935 Ramsey Lake Rd, Sudbury, ON, Canada P3E 2C6.

KRAMAN, CYNTHIA
PERSONAL Born 06/03/1950, New York, NY **DISCIPLINE** ENGLISH **EDUCATION** Univ Mass, BA, 72; Hunter Col, MA, 90; Univ London, PhD, 98. **CAREER** Tutor, Hudson Guild, 72-73; Teacher, Univ Washington, 75-77; Writing workshops, Oakland Public Library, 91; Asst Prof to Asst Prof, Col of New Rochelle, 87-97. **HONORS AND AWARDS** commonwealth Scholar, Univ Mass, 68-72; Phi Beta Kappa, 71; Claire Woolrich Memorial Awd, 74; Wesleyan Poetry Prize Selection, 76; Devoted Service Awd CLP Program, 1987-1996; Queen Mary & Westfield ravel grants, 95; Squaw Valley/UC Davis Scholarship, 96; Who's Who of am Women, 01. **SELECTED PUBLICATIONS** Auth, Taking on the local color, Wesleyan Univ Press, 77; auth, The Mexican Murals, EG Press, 86; auth, My Heart Was Like a Sword, forthcoming; auth, Ordinary Women/Mujeres communes, Avon Press, 80; auth, Rain in the Forest, Light in the Trees, Contemporary Poetry from the Northwest, Owl Creek Press, 83; auth, "Medieval women in Their communities, in Communities of Otherness in Chaucer's Merchant's Tale, 97. **CONTACT ADDRESS** Dept English, Col of New Rochelle, 29 Castle Pl, New Rochelle, NY 10805-2338.

KRAMER, DALE VERNON
PERSONAL Born 07/13/1936, Mitchell, SD, m, 1960, 2 children **DISCIPLINE** ENGLISH **EDUCATION** SDak State Univ, BS, 58; Western Reserve Univ, MA, 60, PhD(English), 63. **CAREER** From instr to asst prof English, Ohio Univ, 62-65; from asst prof to assoc prof, 65-71, prof English, Univ Ill, Urbana, 71-96; Vis prof English, Reading Univ, England, 66-67; Univ Ill fac study grant, 67; Am Philos Soc res grant, 69, 86; assoc fel, Ctr Advan Studies, Univ Ill, 71-72. **MEMBERSHIPS** MLA; AAUP; Midwest Mod Lang Asn. **RESEARCH** Textual scholarship; aesthetics of fiction; Thomas Hardy; Joseph Conrad. **SELECTED PUBLICATIONS** Auth, Marlow, myth and structure in Lord Jim, Criticism, 66; Revisions and vision: Thomas Hardy's The Woodlanders, Bull NY Pub Libr, 71; Charles Robert Maturin, Twayne, 73; Thomas Hardy: The Forms of Tragedy, Macmillan, 75; ed, Critical Approaches to the Fiction of Thomas Hardy, Macmillan, 79; The Woodlanders, Thomas Hardy, Oxford Univ Press, 81; ed, The Mayor of Casterbridge, Oxford, 87; ed, Critical Essays on Thomas Hardy, G.K. Hall, 90; ed, Hardy: Tess of the d'Urbervilles, Cambridge, 91; ed, Cambridge Companion to Hardy, Cambridge, 99. **CONTACT ADDRESS** Dept of English, Univ of Illinois, Urbana-Champaign, 608 S Wright St, Urbana, IL 61801-3613. **EMAIL** d-kramer@staff.uiuc.edu

KRAMER, JENNIFER
PERSONAL Born 08/19/1964, Newark, NJ, m, 1992 **DISCIPLINE** CINEMA AND MASS MEDIA **EDUCATION** Univ Chicago, MA, 94 **CAREER** Assoc ed, video reviews counterpoise, amer libr asn, 97-. **MEMBERSHIPS** Nat Coalition Independent Scholars **RESEARCH** Cognitive science; Geometric modeling; Mass media conglomerates. **SELECTED PUBLICATIONS** Auth, The Spherical Burning Mirror, Premonitions, 93; Schroedingers Albatross, Puck, 94; The Method of Exhaustion, Trivia: A Jour of Ideas, 95; auth, Fairyland in the Kitchen, Jour Unconventional Hist, 96; Ongoing Support & The World Wide Web, Multimedia Producers Bible, 96; The Weeping Icon: Gender and Generic Conventions in the Film Bram Stokers Dracula, Dracular 97; Shadowboxing, Cyber-Psychos AOD, Lammas 97; Cold Comfort: Stephen W Hawking and The Bible, The Montrous and the Unspeakable: The Bible as Fantastic Literature, Sheffield Acad Press, 97; rev, Teh Nobel Legacy, Event Horizon, 98. **CONTACT ADDRESS** PO Box 281, Caldwell, NJ 07006. **EMAIL** picpal@picpal.com

KRAMER, JOSEPH ELLIOT
PERSONAL Born 12/21/1934, New York, NY **DISCIPLINE** ENGLISH LITERATURE **EDUCATION** Princeton Univ, BA, 56, MA, 58, PhD, 65. **CAREER** Asst Prof English, Univ CA, Berkeley, 61-69; Assoc Prof, 69-88, prof eng, Bryn Mawr Col, 88. **HONORS AND AWARDS** Fulbright Fel, London Univ, 59-61. **RESEARCH** Shakespeare; Brit drama to 1642; mod drama; lit of sexual minorities. **SELECTED PUBLICATIONS** Auth, Damon and Pithias: An apology for art, ELH, 12/68; Titus Andronicus: The flykilling incident, Shakespeare Studies, 69. **CONTACT ADDRESS** Dept of Eng, Bryn Mawr Col, 101 N Merion Ave, Bryn Mawr, PA 19010-2899. **EMAIL** jkramer@brynmawr.edu

KRAMER, LAWRENCE ELIOT
PERSONAL Born 08/21/1946, Philadelphia, PA, m, 1973, 1 child **DISCIPLINE** MUSICOLOGY **EDUCATION** Univ Pa, AB, 68; Yale Univ, MPhil, 70, PhD, 72. **CAREER** Asst prof English, Univ Pa, 72-78; asst prof, 78-81, assoc prof Eng, Fordham Univ, 81-87, prof Eng and Comp Lit 87-95; prof Eng and Mus 95-. **MEMBERSHIPS** Am Music Soc; Soc for Music Theory. **RESEARCH** Western art music; Cultural history. **SELECTED PUBLICATIONS** Auth, Music and Poetry, the 19th Century and After, Univ Cal, 84; auth, Music as Cultural Practice, 1800-1900, Univ Cal, 90; auth, Classical Music and Postmodern Knowledge, Univ. Cal, 95; auth, After the Lovedeath: Sexual Violence and the Making of Culture, Univ Cal, 97; auth, Franz Schubert: Sexuality, Subjectivity, and Song, Cambridge Univ, 98; ed, Walt Whitman and Modern Music: War, Desire, and the Trials of Nationhood, Garland, 00; auth, Music and Meaning: Toward a Critical History, Univ Col, forthcoming. **CONTACT ADDRESS** Dept of English, Fordham Univ, 113 W 60th St, New York, NY 10023-7484. **EMAIL** lkramer@fordham.edu

KRAMER, MARY DUHAMEL
PERSONAL Born 06/12/1944, Columbus, WI, m, 1968, 2 children **DISCIPLINE** ENGLISH LITERATURE **EDUCATION** Univ Wis-Madison, BA, 66; Univ KS, MA, 67, PhD, 69. **CAREER** Prof eng, Univ MA Lowell, 69-, Fiction bk reviewer-freelance auth, lectr. **HONORS AND AWARDS** Phi Beta Kappa **MEMBERSHIPS** AAUP **RESEARCH** Medieval and Renaissance lit. **SELECTED PUBLICATIONS** Auth, The Roman Catholic Cleric on the Jacobean stage, 71 & The American Wild West Show and Buffalo Bill Cody, 72, Costerus; local & nat jour & newspapers; textbook, Human Values in Western Culture. **CONTACT ADDRESS** Dept of Eng, Univ of Massachusetts, Lowell, 1 University Ave, Lowell, MA 01854-2893. **EMAIL** mary_kramer@uml.edu

KRAMER, MAURICE
PERSONAL Born 04/04/1930, Philadelphia, PA, m, 1959 **DISCIPLINE** ENGLISH **EDUCATION** Univ Pa, AB, 51, AM, 53; Harvard Univ, PhD(English), 58. **CAREER** Instr English, Rutgers Univ, 57-61; from instr to assoc prof, Brooklyn Col, 61-73; chmn dept, Brooklyn Col, 70-75; exec off, Spec Baccalaureate Degree Prog Adults, Brooklyn Col, 77-78; dean, Sch Humanities, Brooklyn Col, 78-80, from prof English to prof emeritus, Brooklyn Col, 73-. **MEMBERSHIPS** MLA. **RESEARCH** American literature. **SELECTED PUBLICATIONS** Co-ed, Library of Literary Criticism: Modern American Literature, Ungar, 69 & 76; auth, Alone at Home with Elizabeth Stoddard, Am Transcendental Quart, 80. **CONTACT ADDRESS** Dept of English, Brooklyn Col, CUNY, 2900 Bedford Ave, Brooklyn, NY 11210-2813. **EMAIL** mkramer@brooklyn.cuny.edu

KRAMER, MICHAEL W.
DISCIPLINE COMMUNICATION **EDUCATION** Concordia Jr Col, AA, 74; Concordia Col, BS, 76; NE Ill Univ, MA, 82; Univ Tex, PhD, 8/91. **CAREER** Teacher, Martin Luther HS, NY, 76-78; dept ch, Eng dept, Luther High School S, 78-84; asst prof, Concordia Lutheran Col, 84-91; assoc prof, Dept Commun, Univ Mo-Columbia, 91-. **HONORS AND AWARDS** Phi Kappa Phi, 87; Top competitive papers in Org Commun, SCA, 92, 94, 96; Top Competitive paper in the Basic Course, NCA, 97; Provost Outstanding Jr Fac Awd, 95. **MEMBERSHIPS** Int Commun Asn; Nat Commun Asn; Acad of Management. **RESEARCH** Organizational communication; group communication; interpersonal communUnication. **SELECTED PUBLICATIONS** Auth, Communication and uncertainty reduction during job transfers: Leaving and joining processes, Commun Monographs, vol 60, 178-198, 93; auth, Communication after job transfers: Social exchange processes in learning new roles, Human Commun Res, vol 20, 147-174, 93; auth, Uncertainty reduction during job transitions: An exploratory study of the communication experiences of newcomers and transferees, Management Commun Quart, vol 7, 384-412, 94; co-auth, Information-giving and information-receiving during job transitions, Western J of Commun, vol 59, 151-170, 95; co-auth, Communication during employee dismissals: Social exchange principals and group influences on employee exit, Management Commun Quart, vol 9, 156-190, 95; auth, A longitudinal study of peer communication during job transfers: The impact of frequency, quality, and network multiplexity on adjustment, Human Commun Res, vol 23, 59-86, 96; co-auth, The differential impact of a basic public speaking course on percieved communication competencies in class, work, and social contexts, Basic Commun Course Ann, Am Press, vol 8, 1-25, 96; co-auth, The impact of brainstorming on subsequent group decision-making: Beyond generating ideas, Small Grp Res, vol 28, 218-242, 97; co-auth, The impact of self-directed videotape feedback on students' self-reported levels of communication competence and apprehension, Commun Educ, vol47, 151-161, 98; co-auth, A framework for the study of emotions in organizational contexts, Management Commun Quart, vol 11, 336-372, 98. **CONTACT ADDRESS** Dept of Commun, Univ of Missouri, Columbia, 115 Switzler Hall, Columbia, MO 65211. **EMAIL** kramerm@missouri.edu

KRAMER, VICTOR ANTHONY
PERSONAL Born 10/21/1939, Youngstown, OH, m, 1963, 1 child **DISCIPLINE** AMERICAN LITERATURE, LITERARY CRITICISM **EDUCATION** St Edwards Univ, AB, 61; Univ Tex, Austin, MA, 63, PhD(English), 66. **CAREER** Asst prof English, Marquette Univ, 66-69; asst prof, 69-76, assoc prof, 76-81, Prof English, GA State Univ, 81-; Am Philos Soc grant, 73; sr Fulbright lectr, Univ Regensburg, West Ger, 74-75. **MEMBERSHIPS** MLA; Am Studies Asn; SAtlantic Mod Lang Asn; AAUP; Conf Christianity and Lit. **RESEARCH** Modern American literature; American studies and literary criticism. **SELECTED PUBLICATIONS** Auth, James Agee, Twayne, 75; co-ed, Olmsted South, Greenwood, 79; Thomas Martin's published journals: The pardox of writing as a step toward contemplation, Studia Mystica, 80; Agee's skepticism about art and audience, The Southern Rev, 81; Peter Taylor, In: Dict of Literary Biography, Yearbk, 81, Gale, 81; coauth, Reference Guide for Andrew Lytle, Peter Taylor, and Walker Percy, G K Hall (in press); auth, Thomas Merton (Twayne United States Authors Series volume), Twayne (in press); ed, with introd, American Critics at Work: Examinations of Contemporary Literary Theories, Whitston Publ (in press). **CONTACT ADDRESS** Dept of English, Georgia State Univ, 33 Gilmer St SE, Atlanta, GA 30303-3080.

KRANIDIS, RITA
DISCIPLINE VICTORIAN STUDIES, CULTURAL STUDIES, FEMINIST THEORY AND CRITICISM, AND POS **EDUCATION** Mount Holyoke Col, BA; Long Island Univ, MA; SUNY, Stony Brook, PhD. **CAREER** Prof, Radford Univ. **SELECTED PUBLICATIONS** Auth, Subversive Discourse: The Cultural Production of Late Victorian Feminist Novels, St Martin's, 95; ed, Imperial Objects: Essays on Victorian Women's Emigration and the Unauthorized Imperial Experience, Twayne Publ, 97. **CONTACT ADDRESS** Radford Univ, Radford, VA 24142. **EMAIL** mkranidi@runet.edu

KRANTZ, MARY DIANE F.
PERSONAL Born 10/30/1943, Carbondale, PA, s **DISCIPLINE** ENGLISH **EDUCATION** Fairfield Univ, BS, 66; MA, 73; Univ Calif Davis, MA, 89; PhD, 94. **CAREER** Instr, Univ Calif Davis, 88-93; vis lectr, Johannes Gutenberg Univ, 93-94; lectr, Univ Calif Davis, 94-95; assoc prof, Weber State Univ, 95-. **HONORS AND AWARDS** Hemingway Grant, 99-00; Fulbright Travel Awd, 93-94; Regents Fel, 87-88; NSF Fel, 69-72, 79. **MEMBERSHIPS** MLA, RMMLA; MA; URMA; NAWS. **RESEARCH** Medieval mysticism; ESP; Julian of Norwich and Hildegard von Bingen; Medieval drama; poetry of Denise Leverton; Chopin's The Awakening. **SELECTED PUBLICATIONS** Auth, The Life and Text of Julian of Norwich: The Poetics of Enclosure, Peter Lang, 97. **CONTACT ADDRESS** 1113 Country Hills Dr, Apt H1, Ogden, UT 84403-2478. **EMAIL** dkrantz@weber.edu

KRAPF, NORBERT A.
DISCIPLINE AMERICAN POETRY **EDUCATION** Notre Dame, PhD; St Joseph's Col, DHL honoris causa, 95. **CAREER** Prof, Long Island Univ, C.W. Post Campus. **SELECTED PUBLICATIONS** Auth, Arriving on Paumanok; The Playfair Book of Hours; Lines Drawn from Durer; Heartwood, A Dream of Plum Blossoms; Circus Songs; ed, Under Open Sky: Poets on William Cullen Bryant; Beneath the Cherry Sapling: Legends from Franconia; Finding the Grain: Pioneer Journals, Franconian Folktales, Ancestral Poems; transl, Shadows on the Sundial: Selected Early Poems of Rainer Maria Rilke. **CONTACT ADDRESS** Long Island Univ, C.W. Post, Brookville, NY 11548-1300.

KRASNER, DAVID
PERSONAL Born 03/01/1952, Brooklyn, NY **DISCIPLINE** THEATER **EDUCATION** Carnegie-Mellon Univ, BFA, 74; Va Commonwealth Univ, 90; Tufts Univ, PhD, 96. **CAREER** Assoc prof, Yale Univ **HONORS AND AWARDS** Amer Soc for Theater Res Errol Hill Awd, 98; dir, undergraduate theater stud, yale univ **MEMBERSHIPS** ASTR; ATHE; MLA. **RESEARCH** African-American theater; performance. **SELECTED PUBLICATIONS** Auth, Whose Role Is It, Anyway?, African Amer Rev, 95; The Mirror Up To Nature: Modernist Aesthetics and Racial Authenticity in African American Theatre, 1895-1900, Theatre Hist Stud, 96; Re-writing the Body: Aida Overton Walker and the Social Formation of Cakewalking, Theatre Survey, 96; Walter Benjamin and the Lynching Play: Allegory and Mourning in Angelina Weld Grimke's Rachel, J of Comparative Drama, 97; Resistance, Parody, and Double Consciousness in African-American Theater, 1895-1910; ed., Method Acting Reconsidered: Theory, Practice, Future (NY: St. Martin's Press, 00); coed, African American Performance and Theater History: A Critical Reader (NY: Oxford University Press, 01. **CONTACT ADDRESS** Theater Studies, Yale Univ, 254 York St, New Haven, CT 06520-8296. **EMAIL** david.krasner@yale.edu

KRATZ, DENNIS
PERSONAL Born Baltimore, MD, m, 1964, 1 child **DISCIPLINE** LITERATURE STUDIES **EDUCATION** Harvard Univ, PhD, 70. **CAREER** Prof and Dean. **HONORS AND AWARDS** Pres, American Literary Translators Asn, 1987-9; Chancellors Council Outstanding Teaching Awd, 92. **MEMBERSHIPS** American Literary Translations Asn, Medieval Academy of America. **RESEARCH** Medieval literature; classical tradition; fantasy/science fiction; Effective Listening Skills Irwin. **SELECTED PUBLICATIONS** Auth, The Romances

of Alexander, Garland, 91; Waltharius and Ruodlieb, Garland, 84; Mocking Epic: Waltharius, Alexandreis and the Problem of Christian Heroism, Ediciones Jose Porrua Turanzas, 80; Development of the Fantastic Tradition through 1811, Garland, 90. **CONTACT ADDRESS** School of Arts and Humanities, Univ of Texas, Dallas, Richardson, TX 75080. **EMAIL** dkratz@utdallas.edu

KRAUS, MATTHEW A.
PERSONAL Born 08/21/1963, Cincinnati, OH, m, 1991, 3 children **DISCIPLINE** CLASSICS **EDUCATION** Harvard-Radcliffe, BA, 85; Hebrew Union Col, Jewish Inst of the Religion, Rabbinic ordination, 91; Univ MI, PhD, 96. **CAREER** Asst Prof Classics and Jewish Studies, Williams Col, 96-. **MEMBERSHIPS** AJS; AAR-SBL; APA. **RESEARCH** Jerome; Judaism and the Greco-Roman world; late Antique Latin lit. **CONTACT ADDRESS** Dept of Classics, Williams Col, Stetson Hall, Williamstown, MA 01267. **EMAIL** mkraus@williams.edu

KRAUS, SIDNEY
PERSONAL Born 04/10/1927, Chicago, IL, m, 1952, 3 children **DISCIPLINE** POLITICAL COMMUNICATION, MASS COMMUNICATION, PUBLIC RELATIONS **EDUCATION** Art Inst Chicago, BFA, MFA; Univ IA, PhD. **CAREER** Comm, Cleveland St Univ. **HONORS AND AWARDS** Over 25 honors and awards. **SELECTED PUBLICATIONS** Auth; Televised Presidential Debates and Public Policy, 2nd ed, Lawrence Erlbaum & Assoc, 00; Mass Communication and Political Information, Lawrence Erlbaum & Assoc, 90, 7 other books. **CONTACT ADDRESS** Commun Dept, Cleveland State Univ, 83 E 24th St, Cleveland, OH 44115. **EMAIL** s.kraus@csuohio.edu

KRAUSE, DAVID H.
DISCIPLINE AMERICAN LITERATURE **EDUCATION** Marquette Univ, BA; Yale Univ, MA, MPhil, PhD. **CAREER** Assoc Acad Dean, Ctr for Tchg Excellence, Columbia Col, 99-. **HONORS AND AWARDS** Nat Endowment Hum fel. **SELECTED PUBLICATIONS** Auth, Noon at Smyrna; Summer Storm; Soapstone Wall. **CONTACT ADDRESS** Columbia Col, Illinois, Center for Teaching Excellence, 600 S Michigan Ave, Chicago, IL 60605. **EMAIL** dkrause@popmail.colum.edu

KRAUSE, SYDNEY JOSEPH
PERSONAL Born 07/22/1925, Paterson, NJ, m, 1952 **DISCIPLINE** ENGLISH AND AMERICAN LITERATURE **EDUCATION** Univ Mo, BA, 49; Yale Univ, MA, 51; Columbia Univ, PhD(English), 56. **CAREER** Instr English, Univ Mo, 50-52; asst dir English prog foreign students, Col William and Mary, 53; instr, Ohio State Univ, 53-55, dir continuity, Wosu, 55; asst prof, Univ Akron, 55-62; assoc prof, 62-66, dir bibliog and textual ctr, 66-69, Prof English, Kent State Univ, 66-; Am Coun Learned Soc grant, 61; gen ed, C B Brown ed, Kent State Univ and MLA, 66-; Fulbright lectr, Copenhagen, 68-69 and Tİbingen, Gdr, 82; exchange prof, Leipzig, Gdr, 82. **MEMBERSHIPS** MLA. **RESEARCH** American literature; Mark Twain; Charles Brockden Brown. **SELECTED PUBLICATIONS** Auth, Penn Elm and Edgar Huntly in Dark Instruction to the Heart and The Staging of Pivotal Scenes at The Foot of Said Tree in The Brown, Charles, Brockden Novel Edgar Huntly and the Short Story Somnambulism A Fragment, Am Lit, Vol 0066, 94; Punishing the Press in Using Contempt of Court to Secure the Right to a Fair Trial, Boston Univ Law Rev, Vol 0076, 96. **CONTACT ADDRESS** Dept of English, Kent State Univ, Kent, OH 44240.

KREISWIRTH, MARTIN
PERSONAL Born 06/28/1949, Elizabeth, NJ, m, 1972, 3 children **DISCIPLINE** ENGLISH **EDUCATION** Hamilton Col, BA, 71; Univ Chicago, MA, 72; Univ Toronto, PhD, 79. **CAREER** Asst Prof, Univ Toronto, 79-82; Asst Prof to Assoc Dean, Univ W Ont, 82-. **HONORS AND AWARDS** Fel, Univ Va, 89-90; Res Fel, Soc Sci and Humanities Coun of Can, 92-97; Asn of Am Pub Awd, 97. **MEMBERSHIPS** MLA; Can Asn of Col and Univ Teachers of English; William Faulkner Soc; Am Comp Lit Asn; Can Comp Lit Asn; Can Asn of Am Studies. **RESEARCH** Narrative Theory (in different disciplinary contexts); William Faulkner; Literary Theory; American Fiction. **SELECTED PUBLICATIONS** Co-ed, Theory Between the Disciplines: Authority/Vision/Politics, Univ Mich Press, 90; auth, "Trusting the Tale: The Narrativist Turn in the Human Sciences," New Literary History, 92; co-ed, The Johns Hopkins Guide to Literary Theory and Criticism, Johns Hopkins Univ Press, 94; co-ed, Constructive Criticism: The Human Sciences in the Age of Theory, Univ Toronto Press, 95; auth, 'Paradoxical and Outrageous Discrepancy: Transgression, Auto-Intertextuality and Faulkner's Yoknapatawpha', Faulkner and the Artist, Univ Miss Press, 96; auth, "Merely Telling Stories? Narrative and Knowledge in the Human Sciences", Poetics Today, 00. **CONTACT ADDRESS** Dept English, The Univ of Western Ontario, 252 Wortley Rd, London, ON, Canada N6C3R2. **EMAIL** martyk@uwo.ca

KREJCI-PAPA, MARIANNA
PERSONAL Born 08/30/1964, Valley Stream, NY, m, 1992, 3 children **DISCIPLINE** ENGLISH **EDUCATION** Brown Univ, AB, 86; Yale Univ, PhD, 96. **CAREER** Lectr, Univ Md, 93-97; adj fac, Point Loma Nazarene Univ, 98-99; asst prof, E Nazarene Col, 99-. **HONORS AND AWARDS** Phi Beta Kappa. **MEMBERSHIPS** MLA; NCTE; RSA. **RESEARCH** Orality and oral epic; Shakespeare and popular print; 16th century prose narratives; collaborative learning pedagogy. **CONTACT ADDRESS** 40 Hemlock Dr, Milton, MA 02186-2321. **EMAIL** krejcipm@enc.edu

KREMER, S. LILLIAN
PERSONAL Born 06/30/1939, New York, NY, m, 1960, 2 children **DISCIPLINE** AMERICAN AND JEWISH-AMERICAN LITERATURE **EDUCATION** State Univ NYork Albany, BA, 59; City Univ NYork, MA, 64; Kans State Univ, PhD(English), 79. **CAREER** Prof American Literature, Kans State Univ, 75-78, 78-79. **HONORS AND AWARDS** N.EH Fellowships, Memorial Foundation for Jewish Culture Awd. **RESEARCH** Holocaust in American literature; Jewish American writers; American ethnic literature. **SELECTED PUBLICATIONS** Auth, Post-Alienation, Recent Directions in Jewish-American Literature, Contemp Lit, Vol 0034, 93; auth, Witness Through the Imagination: Jewish American Holocaust Literature, Detroit: Wayne State U.P. 89; auth, Women's Holocaust Writing: Memory and Imagination, Lincoln: U. of Nebraska Press, 99; Numerous journal articles. **CONTACT ADDRESS** Kansas State U., Kansas State Univ, 1615 Osage, Manhattan, KS 66506. **EMAIL** lillian@ksu.edu

KREPS, GARY L.
DISCIPLINE COMMUNICATION **EDUCATION** City Col of San Francisco, 71-73; Univ of Colo, BA, 75, MA, 76; Univ of Southen Calif, 79. **CAREER** Instr, Chapman Univ, 76-78; teaching assoc, Unif of Southern Calif, 77-78; asst prof, Purdue Univ Calumet, 78-80; assir prof, 80-81, assoc prof, 80-83, dir of Organizational Commun, acting chemn, dept of Communicaton & Theatre, 81; dir of Health Studies Prog & adjunct prof of nursing, Ind Univ at Indianapolis, 82-83; asst prof, dir of the Health Commun Res Group, grad fac member, fel of the Inst for Health, Rutgers Univ, 83-87; dir of grad studies, 88-89, assoc prof, 87-88, prof, Northern Ill Univ, 87-95; exec dir & prof, Greenspun School of Commun, Univ of Nevada at Las Vegas, 95-97; ADJUNCT PROF, DOCTORAL PROG FACULTY, UNION INT, 96-; FOUNDING DEAN & PROF, SCHOOL OF COMMUN, HOFSTRA UNIV, 97-. **HONORS AND AWARDS** Gerald M. Phillips Awd for Distinguished Applied Commun Scholar, nat Commun Asn; listed in Who's Who in Entertainment, 3rd edition, 98-99; honorary mem of Lambda Pi Eta, Nat Commun Honor Soc, 97; listed in Int Who's Who of Professionals, 96; Applied Commun Book of the Year Awd, NCA Applied Commun Section, 95. **MEMBERSHIPS** Asn for Commun Admin; Asn for Ed in J and Mass Commun; Broadcast Ed Asn; Central States Commun Asn; Commun Inst for Online Scholar; Int Commun Asn; Nat Commun Asn; Eastern Commun Asn; Public Relations Professionals of Long Island; Western States Commun Asn; World Commun Asn. **RESEARCH** Organizational communication, intervention, & learning; health communication; health education and promotion; interpersonal/group interaction; multicultural relations; communication theory; leadership & empowerment; conflict management; communication and public policy, research methods. **SELECTED PUBLICATIONS** Auth, Disability and Culture: Effects on Multicultural Relations in Modern Organizatons, Handbook of Commun and People with Disablities: Res and Application, Lawrence Erlbaum, 98; auth, Social Responsibility and the Modern Health Care System: Promoting a Consumer Orientation to Health Care, Organizational Commun and Change, Hampton Press, 98; auth, Information and Organizational Development: Enhancing Reflexivity at the Alexander Center, Case Studies in Organizational Commun, Guilford Press, 97; auth, Communicating to Promote Justice in the Modern Health Care System, J of Health Commun: Int Perspectives, 96; guest ed, The Interface Between Health Commun and Health Psychology, J of Health Psychology, 96; coauth, Preventing Sexual Harassment in Educational Organizations: A Communication Perspective, Organizational Commun for Human Resource Managers in Higher Ed: A Manual for Commun Behave, Col & Univ Personnel Asn, 98; coauth, The History and Development of the Field of Health Communication, Health Commun Res: A Guide to Developments and Direction, Greenwood Press, 98; coauth, Listening: A Crucial CommunicationCompetency for Effective Health Care Delivery, Listening in Everyday Life: A Personal and Professional Approach, Univ Press of Am, 97; coauth, Testing a Relational Model of Helth Communication Competence Among Caregivers for Individuals with Alzheimer's Disease, J of Health Psychology, 96. **CONTACT ADDRESS** School of Commun, Hofstra Univ, Dempster Hall, Hempstead, NY 11549. **EMAIL** comglk@hofstra.edu

KRETZSCHMAR, WILLIAM A., JR.
PERSONAL Born 09/13/1953, Ann Arbor, MI, m, 1976, 2 children **DISCIPLINE** ENGLISH, LINGUISTICS **EDUCATION** Univ Mich, AB, 75; Yale Univ, MA, 76; Univ Chicago, PhD, 80. **CAREER** Asst prof, Univ of Wis Whitewater, 82-86; asst to prof, Univ of Ga, 86-. **MEMBERSHIPS** MLA; LSA; ADS; Assoc Computers and the Humanities; AAAL; AAAS; Medieval Acad of AM; IAUPE. **RESEARCH** American English, Language Variation/Sociolinguistics, Humanities, Computing, Medieval Literature. **SELECTED PUBLICATIONS** Coed, Dialects in culture: Essays in General Dialectology by Raven I. McDavid, Jr., Univ of Ala Pr, 79; auth, "Isoglosses and Predictive Modeling", Am Speech 67 (92): 227-49; coed, Handbook of the Linguistic Atlas of the Middle and South Atlantic States, Univ of Chicago Pr, 93; coauth, "Spatial Analysis of Linguistic Data with GIS Functions", Int Jof Geog Info Systems 7, (93): 541-60; auth, "Quantitative Area Analysis of Dialect Features", Lag Variation and Change 8, (96): 13-39; coauth, Introduction to Quantitative Analysis of Linguistic Survey Data, Sage (Thousand Oaks, CA), 96; auth, "Foundations of American English", in Focus on the USA, ed Edgar Schneider (Philadelphia: John Benjamins, 96), 25-50; auth, "Dimensions of Variation in American English Vocabulary" English Worldwide 17, (96): 189-211; auth, "American English for the 21st Century", in Englishes Around the World, Vol 1, ed Edgar Schneider (Amsterdam: John Benjamins, 97), 307-23; coed, Concise Dictionary of Pronunciation, Oxford Univ Pr, (forthcoming). **CONTACT ADDRESS** Dept English, Univ of Georgia, Athens, GA 30602-0002. **EMAIL** billk@atlas.uga.edu

KREVANS, NITA
DISCIPLINE CLASSICS **EDUCATION** Yale Col, BA, 75; Cambridge Univ, BA, 77; Princeton Univ, PhD, 84. **CAREER** Assoc prof, Univ Minn, Twin Cities. **RESEARCH** Hellenistic and Latin lyric. **SELECTED PUBLICATIONS** Auth, Print and the Tudor Poets, in Reconsidering the Renaissance, ed. M.A. Di Cesare, Medieval and Renaissance Texts and Studies, 93, Binghamton, 92; Ilia's Dream: Ennius, Virgil, and the Mythology of Seduction, HSCP 95, 93; Fighting against Antimachus: the 'Lyde' and the 'Aetia' Reconsidered, in Hellenistica Groningana. 1. Callimachus, eds, M A Harder, R F Regtuit, and G C Wakker, Groningen, 93; Medea as Foundation-heroine, in Medea, eds, Clauss and Johnston, Princeton UP, 97. **CONTACT ADDRESS** Dept of Class and Near Eastern Studies, Univ of Minnesota, Twin Cities, 9 Pleasant St. SE, 330 Folwell Hall, Minneapolis, MN 55455. **EMAIL** nkrevans@tc.umn.edu

KREYLING, MICHAEL
DISCIPLINE AMERICAN AND SOUTHERN LITERATURE **EDUCATION** Cornell Univ, PhD. **CAREER** Prof Eng, Vanderbilt Univ. **RESEARCH** Southern intellectual and literary history. **SELECTED PUBLICATIONS** Auth, Eudora Welty's Achievement of Order, 80; Author and Agent: Eudora Welty and Diarmuid Russell, 91; The Figure of the Hero in Southern Narrative. **CONTACT ADDRESS** Vanderbilt Univ, Nashville, TN 37203-1727.

KRIEGEL, ABRAHAM DAVID
PERSONAL Born 02/15/1938, New York, NY, m, 1965, 2 children **DISCIPLINE** MODERN ENGLAND **EDUCATION** Hunter Col, BA, 58; Duke Univ, MA, 60, PhD, 65. **CAREER** From asst prof to assoc prof, 64-77, prof hist, Univ Memphis, 77-. **HONORS AND AWARDS** Am Philos Soc Grant, 66-67; John Simon Guggenheim fel, 79-80; Walter D Love Prize N Am Conf Brit Stud, 88. **MEMBERSHIPS** AHA; Conf Brit Studies; S Hist Asn; S Conf Brit Studies. **RESEARCH** Nineteenth century British politics; the English aristocracy. **SELECTED PUBLICATIONS** Auth, The Politics of the Whigs in Opposition 1834-1835, J Brit Studies, 5/68; The Irish Policy of Lord Grey's Government, Eng Hist Rev, 1/71; ed, The Holland House Diaries, 1831-1840, Routledge & Kegan Paul, 77; Liberty and Whiggery in Early Ninteenth Century England, J Modern Hist, 6/80; Edmund Burke and the Quality of Honor, Albion, 12/80; A Convergence of Ethnics: Saints and Whigs in British Antislavery, J Brit Studies, 87; Biography and the Politics of the Early Nineteenth Century, J Brit Studies, 90; Whiggery in the Age of Reform, J Brit Studies, 93; Up for Grabs, Va Quart Rev, 97. **CONTACT ADDRESS** Dept Hist, Univ of Memphis, 3706 Alumni St, Memphis, TN 38152-0001. **EMAIL** akriegel@memphis.edu

KRIEGEL, LEONARD
PERSONAL Born 05/25/1933, New York, NY, m, 1957, 2 children **DISCIPLINE** ENGLISH **EDUCATION** Hunter Col, BA, 55; Columbia Univ, MA, 56; NYork Univ, PhD(Am civilization), 60. **CAREER** Asst prof English, Long Island Univ, 60-61; from instr to assoc prof, 61-72, Prof English, City Col New York, 72-; Fulbright lectr, Neth, 64-65 and 68-69; Guggenheim fel, 71-72; Rockefeller fel, 76; Fulbright lectr, France, 81. **MEMBERSHIPS** Pen; MLA; Am Studies Asn. **RESEARCH** Politics and literature; creative writing; writing on education. **SELECTED PUBLICATIONS** Auth, From the Catbird Seat, Football, Baseball, and Language, Sewanee Rev, Vol 0101, 93; Supermarket Modern, Antioch Rev, Vol 0051, 93; Gender and Its Discontents and Sex and Gender Questions Increasingly Dominate Cultural Discourse, Partisan Rev, Vol 0060, 93; Imaginary Others, Blacks and Jews in New York, Partisan Rev, Vol 0060, 93; Graffiti, Tunnel Notes of a New Yorker, Am Scholar, Vol 0062, 93; The Face Beneath the Window, One Mans View of Abortion, Va Quart Rev, Vol 0069, 93; Geography Lessons and The Physical Landscape in Literary Fiction, Sewanee Rev, Vol 0102, 94; Walking Light in Essays and Memoirs, Sewanee Rev, Vol 0102, 94; Forgive Me, Mrs. Reil-

ly, or How a New York Jew Learned to Love the South, Kenyon Rev, Vol 0016, 94; Beaches in Winter, Va Quart Rev, Vol 0070, 94; Boundaries of Memory in Liberals, Patriotism, and Melting Pots, Va Quart Rev, Vol 0071, 95; North On 99 and California and New York Remain the Raw Alternatives for Our American Future, Partisan Rev, Vol 0062, 95; Confessions of a Might-Have-Been Conservative, Or, How Newt and Rush Helped 1 New-York Liberal See the Light wnd Keep the Faith, Va Quart Rev, Vol 0072, 96; Immigrants, Partisan Rev, Vol 0063, 96; New York Losers and Winners, Va Quart Rev, Vol 0072, 96. **CONTACT ADDRESS** 355 Eighth Ave, New York, NY 10001. **EMAIL** len7373@aol.com

KRIEGER, MURRAY

PERSONAL Born 11/27/1923, Newark, NJ, m, 1947, 2 children **DISCIPLINE** ENGLISH LITERATURE, LITERARY THEORY **EDUCATION** Rutgers Univ, 40-42; Univ Chicago, MA, 48; Ohio State Univ, univ fel, PhD, 52. **CAREER** Instr, English, Kenyon Coll, 48-49; instr, Ohio State Univ, 51-52; asst to assoc prof, Univ Minn, 52-58; prof, English, 58-63, assoc mem, Center Advanced Study, 61-62, Univ Ill; M. F. Carpenter Prof Lit Criticism, Univ Iowa, 63-66; prof, English, dir. program in criticism, Univ Calif Irvine, 66-85; prof, English, UCLA, 73-82; Univ prof, 74-94, co-dir, Sch Criticism and Theory, 75-77, dir, 77-81, hon sr fel, 81-, dir, Univ Calif Humanities Res Inst, 87-89; Univ Res Prof, 94-. **HONORS AND AWARDS** Postdoctoral fel, Amer Coun Learned Socs, 66-67; humanities fel, Rockefeller Found, 78; fel, Amer Acad Arts and Scis, counc and exec comm, 87-88; Research Prize, Humboldt Foundation, Germany; resident scholar, Rockefeller Study Center, Bellagio, 90. **MEMBERSHIPS** Mod Lang Asn; Intl Asn Univ Profs English; Am Acad Art and Scis. **RESEARCH** Literary theory **SELECTED PUBLICATIONS** Auth, New Apologists for Poetry, 56; auth, The Tragic Vision, 60; auth, A Window to Criticism, 64; auth, The Play and Place of Criticism, 67; auth, The Classic Vision, 71; auth, Theory of Criticism, 76; auth, Poetic Presence and Illusion, 79; auth, Arts and the Level, 81; auth, Wars About Words About Words; auth, Theory, Criticism and the Literary Test, 88; auth, A Reopening of Closure: Organicism against Itself, 89; auth, Ekphrasis: The Illusion of the Natural Sign, 92; auth, The Ideological Imperative: Repression and Resistance in Recent American Theory, 93; auth, The Institution of Theory, 94. **CONTACT ADDRESS** 407 Pinecrest Dr, Laguna Beach, CA 92651. **EMAIL** mkrieger@uci.edu

KRING, HILDA ADAM

PERSONAL Born 01/03/1921, Munich, Germany, m, 1946 **DISCIPLINE** FOLKLORE & FOLKLIFE, ENGLISH **EDUCATION** Millersville State Col, BS, 42; Univ Pittsburgh, MLitt, 52; Univ PA, PhD(folklore, folklife), 69. **CAREER** Teacher English, social studies & Ger, Salisbury Twp High Sch, Gap, PA, 42-46; teacher English, Westmont-Upper Yoder High Sch, Johnstown, 46-47, Adams Twp High Sch, Sidman, 47-48 & Conemaugh Twp High Sch, Davidsville, 48-56; suprv, Slippery Rock State Col, 56-68; teacher, Slippery Rock Area Joint High Sch, 58-64 & 66-67; Prof English & Commun Arts, Grove City Col, 67-. **HONORS AND AWARDS** PA Teacher of the Year, 67; Florence E. MacKenzie Campus-Community Awd, 83; Mercer Co Medical Soc -Benjamin Rush Awd for Outstanding Community Service, 87; A. G. Sikorsky Awd-Leadership through Education -United Community Hospital, 92; Grove City Area Chamber of Commerce, 96; Daughters of the Am Revolution, Excellence in Community Service, 96. **SELECTED PUBLICATIONS** Auth, The Bird That Couldn't Sing (playette), Plays, 57; Another Approach to Poetry, English J, 1/61; The Mountain Wreath, Delta Kappa Gamma J, winter 65; Mary Goes Over the Mountain, PA Folklife, summer 70; The Harmonists: A Folk Cultural Approach, Scarecrow, 73; The Cult of St Walburga in Pennsylvania, PA Folklife, winter 74-75; The Many Faces of Teaching, Univ SC, 78; The Harmonist Kuche, 98. **CONTACT ADDRESS** Dept of English, 5 Kring Dr., Grove City, PA 16127.

KRISE, THOMAS W.

PERSONAL Born 10/27/1961, Fort Sam Houston, TX, m, 1987 **DISCIPLINE** ENGLISH **EDUCATION** US Air Force Acad, BS, 83; Central Mich Univ, MSA, 86; Univ Minn, MA, 89; Univ Chicago, PhD, 95. **CAREER** Instr to Assoc Prof and Dir, 89-. **HONORS AND AWARDS** Fulbright Fel, Univ of the West Indies, 99; CBS Bicentennial Narrators Scholarship, Univ Chicago, 94; Teaching Excellence Awd, US Air Force Acad, 90. **MEMBERSHIPS** Mod Lang Asn, Am Soc for Eighteenth-Century Studies; Soc of Early Am; Omohundro Inst for Early Am Hist & culture; Inst of Jamaica; Jamaican Hist Soc, Barbados Museum & Hist Soc, Fulbright Asn. **RESEARCH** Early West Indian studies; Early am studies; 17th and 18th Century British studies; Representations of the West Indies, imperialism, Slavery; Descriptive bibliography. **SELECTED PUBLICATIONS** Ed, Caribbean: an anthology of English Literature of the West Indies, 1657-1777, Univ Chicago Press, 99; auth, "True Novel, False History: Robert Robertson's Ventriolquized Ex-Slave in The speech of Mr. John Talbot Campo-bell (1736)," in Early American Literature, (95): 152-164; ed, "The sugar-Cane: A Poem, In Four Books (1764), Book IV The Genius of Africa," in The Heath Anthology of American Literature, Heath & Co, 98; rev, or "The Grotesque Depiction of War and the Military in Eighteenth-Century English Fiction," by David McNeil, War, Literature & the Arts, 91; co-ed, Peace Operations: Doctrine, Law, Case Studies,' forthcoming; auth, "Irish Roots of West Indian Sugar," forthcoming. **CONTACT ADDRESS** Dept English, United States Air Force Acad, 2304 Cadet Dr, United States Air Force Academy, CO 80840-5099. **EMAIL** thomas.krise@usafa.af.mil

KROEBER, KARL

PERSONAL Born 11/24/1926, Oakland, CA, m, 1953, 3 children **DISCIPLINE** ENGLISH **EDUCATION** Univ CA, AB, 47; Columbia Univ, MA, 51, PhD, 56. **CAREER** Lectr & instr, Columbia Univ, 52-56; from instr to prof English, Univ Wis, 56-70, assoc dean grad sch, 63-65; chmn, dept English, 73-76, Prof English & Comp Lit, Columbia Univ, 70-; Fulbright res fel, Italy, 60-61; US Off Educ grant, 65-66, Guggenheim fel, 66-67; vis prof English, Univ Wash, 68; NEH fel, 76; ed, Newslett, Asn Study Am Indian Lit, 77-, Kiekhofer Teaching Award, 59. **HONORS AND AWARDS** Fulbright fel, Guggenheim fel, US Office Educat grant, NEH grant. **MEMBERSHIPS** MLA; Mod Humanities Res Asn, Gt Brit; Am Comp Lit Asn; Int Asn Univ Prof English. **RESEARCH** Nineteenth century English literature; native American Indian literature; theory and history of fiction. **SELECTED PUBLICATIONS** Auth, Romantic Narrative Art, 61 & The Artifice of Reality, 64, Univ Wis; Styles in Fictional Structure, Princeton Univ, 71; Constable and Wordsworth: Romantic Landscape Vision, Univ Wis, 74; Images of Romanticism: Verbal and Visual Affinities, Yale Univ, 78; Traditional Literature of the American Indian, Univ Nebr Press, 81, 2nd ed, 97; Retelling/Rereading, Rutgers, 92; Ecological Literary Criticism, Columbia, 94; Artistry in Native American Myths, NE, 98. **CONTACT ADDRESS** Dept of English & Comp Lit, Columbia Univ, 2960 Broadway, New York, NY 10027-6900. **EMAIL** kk17@columbia.edu

KROEGER, CATHERINE CLARK

DISCIPLINE CLASSICAL STUDIES **EDUCATION** Bryn Mawr Col, AB, 47; Univ Minn, MA, 82; PhD, 87. **CAREER** Prot Chaplain, Hamilton Col, 87-88; Adj Prof, Hamilton Col, 92-. **MEMBERSHIPS** Am Acad of Relig; Soc of Bibl Lit; Am Inst of Archaeol; Am Philol Asn; Evangel Theol Soc **RESEARCH** Women in the biblical world; Africans of the Bible and early Church; Biblical response to violence against women. **SELECTED PUBLICATIONS** Auth, I Suffer Not a Woman: Re-examining I Timoth 2: 9-15 in Light of Ancient Evidence, Baker Books, 92; ed, Women, Abuse and the Bible: How the Scriptures Can Be Used to Hurt or to Heal, Baker Books, 95; ed, A Study Bible for Women: The New Testament, Baker Books, 98; co-auth, No Place for Abuse, Downers Grove IVP, 01; ed, InterVarsityPress Women's Bible Commentary, forthcoming. **CONTACT ADDRESS** 1073 Stony Brook Rd, Brewster, MA 02631. **EMAIL** ckroeger@world.std.com

KROEGER, KARL D.

DISCIPLINE MUSIC HISTORY **EDUCATION** Univ Louisville, BM, 54; MM, 59; Univ Ill, MS, 61; Brown Univ, PhD, 76. **CAREER** Music Libr, Prof Emer, Univ Colo. **MEMBERSHIPS** Am Antiquarian Soc **RESEARCH** William Billings **SELECTED PUBLICATIONS** Auth, The Complete Works of William Billings, vol 4; auth, The Worcester Collection of Sacred Harmony, Isaiah Thomas as a Music Publisher, Procs of AAS 86, 76; auth, The Complete Works of William Billings, v. 4, Am Musol Soc and Coll Soc Mass, 90; auth, Catalog of the Musical Works of William Billings, Greenwood, 91; auth, The Complete Works of William Billings, vol 1, 80, vol. 3, 86; auth, Pelissier's Columbian Melodies; researches in American Music, vol 13-14, 84; auth, "Collected Works of Daniel Reed" in Music of the United States of America, vol 4, A-R Editions, 95; auth, Music of the New American Nation: Sacred Music 1780-1820, 15 vols, Garland Press, 95. **CONTACT ADDRESS** Univ of Colorado, Boulder, C. B. 301, Boulder, CO 80309. **EMAIL** karl.kroeger@spot.colorado.edu

KROETSCH, ROBERT P.

DISCIPLINE ENGLISH LITERATURE **EDUCATION** Univ Alberta, BA; Middlebury Univ, MA; Univ Iowa, PhD. **CAREER** Prof emer. **HONORS AND AWARDS** Governor General's Awd, 69; Fel, of the Royal Soc of Canada, 86. **RESEARCH** Canadian wirting; modern and comtemporary lit, creative writing. **SELECTED PUBLICATIONS** Auth, pubs about Canadian writing, modern and contemporary literature, and creative writing; nine novels and eight books of poems. **CONTACT ADDRESS** Dept of English, Univ of Manitoba, Winnipeg, MB, Canada R3T 2N2.

KRONENFELD, JUDITH Z.

PERSONAL Born 07/17/1943, New York, NY, m, 1964, 2 children **DISCIPLINE** ENGLISH **EDUCATION** Smith Col, BA, 64; Stanford Univ, MA, 66; PhD, 71. **CAREER** Lectr, Univ Calif, Riverside, winter and spring 71, 72-73; asst prof, Purdue Univ, 76-77; lectr, Univ Calif, Irvine, 78-79; vis asst prof, Univ Calif, Riverside, 80-81; vis lectr, Univ Calif, Irvine, winter 84, fall and winter 85-86, vis assoc prof, winter 87; vis asst prof, Univ Calif, Riverside, 88-89, lectr, fall 84-. **HONORS AND AWARDS** BA, summa cum laude, Smith Col, 64; Monetary Awd for the best undergrad thesis in English, Smith Col, 64; Phi Beta Kappa, 64; Leuerhulme Trust Fund Fel, 68-69; Fulbright grant Awded 68 (declined in favor of the Leuerhulme); Non-Senate Academic Distinguished Researcher Awd, Univ of Calif, Riverside, 96-97. **MEMBERSHIPS** MLA, ALSC, Assoc Writing Progs, RSA. **RESEARCH** Literature of the English Renaissance, particularly poetry; the metaphysicals; religious poetry and religious controversy; Shakespeare; Renaissance religious culture and Renaissance literature; historicism and historicisms. **SELECTED PUBLICATIONS** Auth, "The 'Communalistic' African and the 'Individualistic' Westerner: Some Comments on Misleading Generalizations in Western Criticism of Soyinka and Achebe," Res in African Lits, 6, No 2 (fall 75): 199-225; coauth with L. L. Thomas and D. B. Kronenfeld, "Asdiwal Crumbles: A Critique of Levi-Straussian Myth Analysis," The Am Ethnologist, 3 (Feb 76): 147-73; auth, "In Search of Mister Johnson: Creation, Politics and Culture in Joyce Cary's Africa," Ariel, 7, No 4 (Oct 76): 69-97; auth, "Social Rank and the Pastoral Ideals of 'As You Like It'," Shakespeare Quart, 29, No 3 (summer 78): 333-48; auth, "Herbert's 'A Wreath' and Devotional Aesthetics: Imperfect Efforts Redeemed by Grace," English Literary Hist, 48 (81): 290-309; auth, "Probing the Relation between Poetry and Ideology: Herbert's 'The Windows'," John Donne J, 2, No 1 (83): 55-80; auth, "Post-Saussurean Semantics, Reformation Religious Controversy, and Contemporary Critical Disagreement," Assays: Critical Approaches to Medieval and Renaissance Texts, V, Pittsburgh: The Univ of Pittsburgh Press (89): 135-165; auth, "Enlightening Linguistics, Actual Reference and the Social Nature of Language, or, Yes, Virginia, There IS a World," The Associated Writing Programs Chronicle, 25, No 2 (Oct/Nov 92: 15-18; auth, " 'So Distribution Should Undo Excess, and Each Man Have Enough': Shakespeare's King Lear--Anabaptist Egalitarianism, Anglican Charity, Both? Neither?," English Lit Hist, 59 (winter 92): 755-784; auth, King Lear and the Naked Truth: Rethinking the Language of Religion and Resistance, Duke Univ Press (98). **CONTACT ADDRESS** Dept Creative Writing, Univ of California, Riverside, 900 Univ Ave, Riverside, CA 92521-0001. **EMAIL** jkronen@citrus.ucr.edu

KRONICK, JOSEPH

PERSONAL Born 12/31/1953, New York, NY **DISCIPLINE** 19TH AND 20TH CENTURY AMERICAN LITERATURE **EDUCATION** UCLA, PhD, 81. **CAREER** Prof, La State Univ; coed, Horizons in Theory and Am Cult, LSU Press ser. **HONORS AND AWARDS** Summer grant, Ctr for Fr and Francophone Stud, 87; NEH summer stipend, 88. **RESEARCH** Am poetry and non-fiction prose; philosophy and lit. **SELECTED PUBLICATIONS** Auth, American Poetics of History: From Emerson to the Moderns, 84; Dr. Heidegger's Experiment, Boundary 2, 90; Resembling Pound: Mimesis, Translation, Ideology, Criticism, 93; Telling the Difference: Stanley Cavell's Resistance to Theory, Am Lit Hist, 93; Libra and the Assassination of JFK, Ariz Quart, 94; coed, Theorizing American Literature: Hegel, the Sign and History, 91; auth, "Edmond Jabes and the Poetry of the Jewish Unhappy Consciousness," MLN, 91; auth, America's Modernisms: Revaluing the Canon, 96; auth, Derrida and the Future of Literature, 99; Rev, "Emerson and the Division of Criticism," 99. **CONTACT ADDRESS** Dept of Eng, Louisiana State Univ and A&M Col, Allen Hall, Baton Rouge, LA 70803. **EMAIL** jkronic@lsu.edu

KROPF, CARL R.

PERSONAL Born 12/07/1939, Canton, OH **DISCIPLINE** EIGHTEENTH CENTURY LITERATURE **EDUCATION** Otterbein Col, BA, 61; Kent State Univ, MA, 63; Ohio State Univ, PhD(English), 68. **CAREER** Teaching asst English, Ohio State Univ, 63-68; asst prof, 68-72, assoc prof, 72-81, Prof English, GA State Univ, 81-. **MEMBERSHIPS** MLA; S Atlantic Mod Lang Asn; Am Soc 18th Century Studies. **RESEARCH** Restoration drama; 18th century novel and poetry. **SELECTED PUBLICATIONS** Auth, Editors Comment and After Genette, Current Directions in Narrative Analysis and Theory, Studies Literary Imagination, Vol 0025, 92. **CONTACT ADDRESS** Dept of English, Georgia State Univ, Atlanta, GA 30303.

KRUCKEBERG, DEAN A.

PERSONAL Born 12/25/1946, Owatonna, MN, d, 2 children **DISCIPLINE** COMMUNICATIONS **EDUCATION** Wartburg Col BA, 69; Northern Ill Univ, MA, 74; Univ Iowa, PhD, 85. **CAREER** PR, Lutheran General Hosp, Il, 69-73; instr, and extension infor spec, Univ Minn, 73-76; instr, jour, Univ Iowa, 76-79; asst prof, jour and PR, Northwest Mo State Univ, 79-83; prof, coord, PR Degree Prog, Univ Northern Iowa, 83- . **HONORS AND AWARDS** Public Rel Soc of Am, Natl Outstanding Educator Awd, 95; Pathfinder Awd, Inst for Public Rel Res and Educ, 97; Iowa Regents Awd for Fac Excellence, 97. **MEMBERSHIPS** Public Rel Soc Am; Int Commun Asn; Natl Commun Asn; Asn for Educ in Jour and Mass Commun; Central States Commun Asn. **RESEARCH** International public relations; international public relations ethics; public relations community building and other pr theories. **SELECTED PUBLICATIONS** Auth, Public Relations and Community, in Image Und PR: Kann Image Gegenstand Einer Public Relations-Wissenschaft Sein?, Westdeutscher Verlag, 93; auth, Professional Profile, in Journalism, Writing Conference, 94; co-auth, Principles of Public Relations, United Arab Emirates Univ Pr, 94; coauth, Case studies in Public Relations, United Arab Emirates Univ Pr, 94; auth, International Journalism Ethics, in Global Journalism: Survey of International Journalism, Longman, 95; coauth, This is PR: The Realities of Public Relations, Wadsworth, 95; coauth, European Public Relations: An Evolving Paradigm, in International Public Relations: A Comparative Analysis, Erlbaum, 96; auth, Transnational Corporate Ethical Responsibilities, in International Public Relations: A Comparative Analysis, Erlbaum, 96; auth, Public Relations, in Media Education Assessment Handbook, Erlbaum, 97; auth, Using the Case Study Method in the Classroom, in Learning to Teach: What You Need to Know to Develop a Successful Career as a Public Relations Educator, Public Relations Soc of Am, 98; auth numerous articles. **CONTACT ADDRESS** Dept of Communication Studies, Univ of No Iowa, 260 CAC, Cedar Falls, IA 50614-0357. **EMAIL** kruckeberg@uni.edu

KRUEGER, CHRISTINE L.
PERSONAL Born 04/27/1957, Wausau, WI **DISCIPLINE** ENGLISH **EDUCATION** Lawrence Univ, BA, 79; Princeton Univ, MA, 82; PhD, 86. **CAREER** Asst to assoc prof, Marquette Univ, 85-. **HONORS AND AWARDS** NEH Fel; ACLS Fel; Monticello Found Fel; Charlotte Newcombe Fel. **MEMBERSHIPS** Interdisciplinary Nineteenth Century Studies; MLA; AAUP. **RESEARCH** Gender, Literature and Law, Literature and Religion, 19th Century British Literature. **SELECTED PUBLICATIONS** Coauth, "Spenser and the Victorians", Spenser Encycl, ed A.C. Hamilton, Univ of Toronto Pr, (89): 1416-1419; auth, The Reader's Repentance: Women Preachers, Women Writers, and Nineteenth-Century Social Discourse, Univ of Chicago Pr, 92; auth, "The Female Paternalist as Historian: Elizabeth Gaskell's My Lady Ludlow", Rewriting the Victorians: Theory, History and the Politics of Gender, ed Linda Shires, Routledge, (London, 92): 166-183; auth, "Speaking Like a Woman: or, How to Have the Last Word on Sylvia's Lovers", Famous Last Words: Changes in Gender and Narrative Closure, ed Alison Booth, Univ Pr of Va, (Charlottesville, 93): 135-153; auth, "Witnessing Women: Trial Testimony in Novels by Tonna, Gaskell and Eliot", Representing Women: Feminism, Literature, and Law, ed Susan Sage Heinzelman and Zipporah Batshaw Wiseman, Duke Univ Pr, (Durham, 94): 337-355; auth, "Naming Privates in Public: Indecent Assault Depositions, 1830-60", Adversaria: Special Issue on Law and Lit of Mosaic 27, (Dec 94): 121-140; auth, "Literary Defenses and Medical Prosecutions: Representing Infanticide in Nineteenth-Century Britain", Victorian Studies 40.2 (Winter 97): 271-294; auth, "Walks of Life: Clerical", the Blackwell Companion to Victorian Literature and Culture, ed Herbert F. tucker, Blackwells, (Oxford, 98): 141-154; auth, "Victorian Narrative Jurisprudence", Law and Literature: Current Legal Issues 1999, ed Michael Freeman and Andrew Lewis, Oxford Univ Pr, (Oxford, 99): 437-461. **CONTACT ADDRESS** Dept English, Marquette Univ, PO Box 1881, Milwaukee, WI 53201-1881. **EMAIL** christine.krueger@marquette.edu

KRUK, LAURIE
DISCIPLINE ENGLISH **EDUCATION** York Univ, BA; McMaster, MA; Western Univ, PhD. **CAREER** Asst prof, Nipissing Univ; Post-Doctoral Scholar, Simon Fraser & Univ in Burnaby, BC. **HONORS AND AWARDS** Northern Prospects Poetry prize; organized a poetry celebration and fund-raiser for the league of canadian poets, the (w)rites of spring. **MEMBERSHIPS** North Bay's literary club, "The Conspiracy of Three." **RESEARCH** Canadian literature; women's writing; short story. **SELECTED PUBLICATIONS** Auth, Theories of the World, 92. **CONTACT ADDRESS** Dept of English, Nipissing Univ, 100 College Dr, Box 5002, North Bay, ON, Canada P1B 8L7. **EMAIL** lauriek@einstein.unipissing.ca

KRUMMEL, DONALD WILLIAM
PERSONAL Born 07/12/1929, Sioux City, IA, m, 1956, 2 children **DISCIPLINE** LIBRARY SCIENCE, MUSIC **EDUCATION** Univ Mich, BA, Music, 51, MA, 53, MA, MLS, 54; PhD, 58. **CAREER** Instr, Music Lit, Univ Mich, 52-56; Library of Congress, 56-61; hd ref dept, Newberry Libr, 62-69; assoc prof/prof, Univ Ill; PROF EMER, UNIV ILL, 70-. **HONORS AND AWARDS** Guggenheim fel, Univ Sholar. **MEMBERSHIPS** Music Libr Asn; Am Libr Asn; Am Antiquarian Soc; Am Musicolgical Soc. **RESEARCH** History bibliography and libraries; Music bibliography **SELECTED PUBLICATIONS** The literature of Music Bibliography, Fallen Leaf Press, 92; "The Variety and uses of Music Bibliography," Foundations in music Bibliography, Hayworth, 93; "The Bay Psalm Book Tercentenary, 1698-1998," 1998. **CONTACT ADDRESS** Univ of Illinois, Urbana-Champaign, 501 E Daniel St, Champaign, IL 61820. **EMAIL** donkay@uiuc.edu

KRUPAT, ARNOLD
PERSONAL Born 10/22/1941, NY, d, 2 children **DISCIPLINE** ENGLISH **EDUCATION** NYork Univ, BA, 62; Columbia Univ, PhD, 67. **CAREER** Prof, Sarah Lawrence Col **HONORS AND AWARDS** Flik, Sarah Law Col Field Gnt, 95; Mellon Found, 93, 81; NEH 90, 87, 70; Leopold Schepp Found fel, 78; Columbia Univ Woodbridge fel, 66; Columbia Pres fel, 65; Woodrow Wilson fel, 62; Fulbright fel; Phi Beta Kappa; NEH Summer Stipend, 00. **RESEARCH** Am Cult Stud; Native Am Lit. **SELECTED PUBLICATIONS** Auth, The Turn to the Native: Studies in Criticism and Culture, Lincoln, Univ Nebraska Pr, 96; Woodsmen or Thoreau and the Indians, a novel, Norman, Univ Oklahoma Press, 94; Native American Autobiography: An Anthology, ed, Madison Univ Wisconsin Press, 94; co-ed, Here First: Autobiographical Essays by Native American Writers, NYork, Random House, 00. **CONTACT ADDRESS** Sarah Lawrence Col, 1 Mead Way, Bronxville, NY 10708. **EMAIL** akrupat@mail.slc.edu

KUBIS, THERESA S.
PERSONAL Born 09/04/1939, Brooklyn, NY, s **DISCIPLINE** ENGLISH **EDUCATION** Col New Rochelle, BA, 61; Columbia Univ, MA, 63; PhD, 72. **CAREER** Asst Prof, Bronx Cmty Col. **MEMBERSHIPS** MLA; NCTE; Renaissance Soc of Am. **RESEARCH** 16th Century Non-Dramatic Literature. **CONTACT ADDRESS** Dept Eng, Bronx Comm Col, CUNY, 2155 Univ Ave., Bronx, NY 10453-2804.

KUCICH, JOHN RICHARD
PERSONAL Born 04/05/1952, San Francisco, CA, s **DISCIPLINE** VICTORIAN LITERATURE, LITERARY THEORY **EDUCATION** Univ CA, Santa Cruz, BA, 74; State Univ NYork, Buffalo, MA, 76, PhD, 78. **CAREER** From Asst Prof to Assoc Prof, 79-90, Prof Eng, Univ MI, Ann Arbor, 90. **HONORS AND AWARDS** Nat Endowment for Hum fel, 83; Guggenheim Fel, 87-88. **MEMBERSHIPS** MLA; Narrative Soc; Dickens Soc. **RESEARCH** The novel. **SELECTED PUBLICATIONS** Auth, Action in the Dickens ending: Bleak House and Great Expectations, 19th Century Fiction, 6/78; Death worship among the Victorians: The Old Curiosity Shop, Publ Mod Lang Asn, 11/80; The purity of violence: A Tale of Two Cities, Dickens Studies Annual, 80; Excess and Restraint in the Novels of Charles Dickens, Univ Ga Press, 81; Repression in Victorian Fiction, Univ Calif Press, 87; The Power of Lies: Transgression in Victorian Fiction, Cornell Univ Press, 94; co-ed, Victorian Afterlife, Univ Minn Pr, 00. **CONTACT ADDRESS** Dept of Eng, Univ of Michigan, Ann Arbor, 505 S State St, Ann Arbor, MI 48109-1003. **EMAIL** jkucich@umich.edu

KUEHL, LINDA KANDEL
DISCIPLINE AMERICAN LITERATURE AND WORLD DRAMA **EDUCATION** City Col NYork, BA and MA; Lehigh Univ, PhD. **CAREER** Prof, Delaware Valley Col. **RESEARCH** Southern writers; Peter Taylor; Robert Hazel; authoring fiction. **SELECTED PUBLICATIONS** Auth, criticism and fiction in sev j(s) and books including Studies in Short Fic, Contemp Lit, Reader's Encyclopedia of Am Lit, and The Cimarron Rev. **CONTACT ADDRESS** Delaware Valley Col, 700 E Butler Ave, Doylestown, PA 18901-2697. **EMAIL** KuehlL@devalcol.edu

KUEHMANN, KAREN MARIE
PERSONAL Born 12/28/1954, Monrovia, CA **DISCIPLINE** MUSIC **EDUCATION** Bob Jones Univ, BS, 76, MA, 78; Az St Univ, EdD, 87. **CAREER** SoundForth Music dir, prof, Bob Jones Univ, 79- **HONORS AND AWARDS** Who's Who in Amer Col & Univ, 76 **MEMBERSHIPS** Music Educ Nat Conf **RESEARCH** Music educ in Christian schools **SELECTED PUBLICATIONS** Auth, Music for Christian Schools, Bob Jones Univ Press; Perspectives in Music for Christian Schools, Bob Jones Univ Press; Since I Have Been Redeemed, SoundForth, 99. **CONTACT ADDRESS** Bob Jones Univ, Box 34581, Greenville, SC 29614. **EMAIL** kkuehman@bju.edu

KUENZLI, RUDOLF ERNST
PERSONAL Born 07/28/1942, Switzerland, m, 1968, 2 children **DISCIPLINE** ENGLISH LITERATURE, COMPARATIVE LITERATURE **EDUCATION** Univ Wis-Madison, MA-(English), 68, MA(Ger), 69, PhD(comp lit), 71. **CAREER** Asst prof 70-76, assoc prof, 76-82, Prof English and Comp Lit, Univ Iowa, 82-; Res fel English and comp lit, Univ Iowa, 76; fel, Sch Criticism and Theory, Univ Calif, 78; Dir, Dada Arch Res Ctr, 78-; Inst Res Humanities fel, 79-80; chmn program comp lit, Univ Paul Valery, 80-83; vis prof, Montpellier, France, 81-82. **MEMBERSHIPS** MLA; Midwestern Mod Lang Asn; Comp Lit Asn; Asn Study Lit and Philos; Asn Study Dada and Surrealism. **RESEARCH** Avant-garde; Nietzsche; philosophies of language. **SELECTED PUBLICATIONS** Auth, Identities and Introduction, J Midwest Mod Lang Asn, Vol 0028, 95. **CONTACT ADDRESS** Dept of Lit, Univ of Iowa, 308 English Phil Bld, Iowa City, IA 52242-1492.

KUFTINEC, SONJA
PERSONAL Born 10/15/1966, Lawrence, MA, s **DISCIPLINE** THEATRE ARTS **EDUCATION** Stanford Univ, PhD. **CAREER** Asst prof. **HONORS AND AWARDS** General Fel, Dartmouth Col; Jacob K. Javits Nat Fel; Artslink Nat Fel; Mellon Found Awd; Centennial Teaching Awd, Stanford; Grant-in-Aid of res. **MEMBERSHIPS** Am Soc of Theatre Res; Asn of Theatre in Higher Education; Performance Studies international; Radicl Alternative Theatre. **RESEARCH** Community-Based performance, youth theatre, womens theatre, performance and social change; 20th century alternative theatre. **SELECTED PUBLICATIONS** Auth, pubs on performance art, 19/20th century American theatre, performance theory, women in theatre, and alternative forms of theatre; auth, "Beyond Brecht: An Interview with Bill Rauch," Theater Insight (96): 35-41; rev, of Pax Bosnensis for Theatre Journal, (96): 495-496; auth, "A Cornerstone for Rethinking Community Theater," Theater Topics, (96): 91-104; auth, "Cornerstone's Community Chalk Circle" The Brecht Yearbook 22, (97): 239-251; auth, "Odakle Ste?, Where are You From?, Active Learning and Community Based Theater in Former Yugslavia and the US," Theatre Topics, (97): 171-186; rev, of 18th International Theater of Youth Festival in Mostar Theater Journal, (98): 111-113; auth, "Ghost Town: Cultural Hauntologie in Mostar, Bosnia-Herzegovina," Text and Performance Quarterly, (98): 81-95; auth, "Playing with the Borders: Dramaturging Ethnicity in Bosnia," Journal of Dramatic Theory and Criticism, (98): 143-156; auth, "Staging the City with the Good People of New Haven," (forthcoming, 01); auth, "The Art of Bridge Building in Mostar" an Article for the Anthology City Play Grounds, (forthcoming, 01). **CONTACT ADDRESS** Theatre Arts and Dance Dept, Univ of Minnesota, Twin Cities, 580 Rarig, 330 21st Ave S, Minneapolis, MN 55455. **EMAIL** skuftinec@aol.com

KUIN, ROGER
PERSONAL Born 02/10/1941, The Hague, Netherlands, m, 1985, 2 children **DISCIPLINE** ENGLISH **EDUCATION** Univ Amsterdam, BA, 62; Exeter Col, BA, 64; Univ Amsterdam, MA, 66; Oxford Univ, MA, 67; Univ Amsterdam, Litt D, 73. **CAREER** Dept Asst, Cambridge Univ, 66-67; Res Asst, Yale Univ, 67-69; Lectr to Full Prof, York Univ, 69-. **HONORS AND AWARDS** Fel, Yale Univ Beiinecke Libr, 97. **MEMBERSHIPS** Sidney Soc; MLA; Renaissance Soc of Am; Spenser Soc; Centre for Reformation and Renaissance Studies. **RESEARCH** Sir Philip Sidney; Philippe de Mornay du Plessis; Sixteenth-century Anglo-Continental relations; Sonnet-sequences. **SELECTED PUBLICATIONS** Auth, Chamber Music: Elizabethan Sonnet-Sequences and the Pleasure of Criticism, Univ Toronto Press, 98; rev, "Elective Affinities: Sir Philip Sidney and Hubert Languet," Sidney J, 98; auth, "Querre-Muhau: Sir Philip Sidney and the New World," Renaissance Quart, 99; auth, "Private Library as Public Danger: The Case of Duplessis-Mornay," in The 16C French Religious Book - St Andrews, 00. **CONTACT ADDRESS** Dept English, York Univ, 4700 Keele St, Toronto, ON, Canada M3J 1P3. **EMAIL** rkuin@yorku.ca

KUIST, JAMES MARQUIS
PERSONAL Born 04/21/1935, White Plains, NY, m, 1960, 1 child **DISCIPLINE** BRITISH LITERATURE **EDUCATION** Davidson Col, AB, 57; Duke Univ, MA, 59, PhD(English), 65. **CAREER** Instr English, Col of William & Mary, 59-61 & Univ NC, 64-65; asst prof, Univ Western Ont, 65-67; from asst prof to assoc prof, 67-78, Prof English, Univ Wis-Milwaukee, 78-00, prof emer, 00-, Nat Endowment for Humanities Younger Humanist fel, 72-73, Res Tools grant, 78-79. **MEMBERSHIPS** MLA; Am Soc for 18th Century Studies; Johnson Soc Cent Region. **RESEARCH** British Periodicals; Samuel Johnson; 18th century novel; 18th century women's poetry. **SELECTED PUBLICATIONS** Auth, New light on Sterne: An old man's recollections of the young vicar, Pmla, 65; ed, Cursory Observations on the Poems Attributed to Thomas Rowley, Augustan Reprint Soc, 66; auth, The Works of John Nichols: An Introduction, Kraus Reprint Corp, 68; co-ed, Essays in Eighteenth-Century Literature in Honor of Benjamin Boyce, 71 & auth, The conclusion of Gray's Elegy, 71, SAtlantic Quart; auth, The Gentleman's Magazine in the Folger Library: The history and significance of the Nichols family collection, Studies Bibliog, 76; The Nichols File of the Gentleman's Magazine, Wis Press, 82; auth, "A collaboration in learning: The Gentleman's Magazine and its ingenious contributors," Studies Bibliog (91); auth, The Novel Rising, Lineages of the Novel, Verlag Trier, 00. **CONTACT ADDRESS** Dept of English, Univ of Wisconsin, Milwaukee, PO Box 413, Milwaukee, WI 53201-0413. **EMAIL** jmkuist@uwm.edu

KULLMAN, COLBY HAIGHT
PERSONAL Born 05/22/1945, New York, NY **DISCIPLINE** ENGLISH LITERATURE **EDUCATION** DePauw Univ, BA, 66; Univ Chicago, MA, 68; Univ Kans, MPhil, 73, PhD(English), 81. **CAREER** Asst instr English, Univ Kans, 69-79; chief ed, Theatre Companies of the World: Selected Profiles, Greenwood Press, 79-; Bk Rever, Am Ref Bk Annual, 76-; prof of Eng. **HONORS AND AWARDS** Phi Beta Kappa, 67; Outstanding Reference Books of 1986, awarded by the Library Journal, 87; Oustanding Contribution to Scholarship Awd, Golden Key National Honor Soc, 88; Nominated by South Carolina Review for the Pushcart Awd, 89; Delta Delta Delta, 94; Achievement Awd, National Council of Teachers of English, 96; Teacher of the Year, 97. **MEMBERSHIPS** MLA; NCTE; Col English Asn; Am Soc 18th Century Studies; Am Theatre Asn. **RESEARCH** Restoration and Eighteenth-Century Studies; Dramatic Literature; Satire; Biography; Comedy; Tragedy. **SELECTED PUBLICATIONS** Co-ed, Theatre Companies of the World, 2 vols., Westport, Connecticut: Greenwood Press, 86; auth, "Rule by Power: Big Daddyism in the World of Tennessee Williams's Plays," Miss Quarterly 48, No. 4, (95): 667-676; auth, "Modern Drama and The Southern Tradition: An Interview," The Drama Journal 7, (95): 211-226; co-ed, Speaking on Stage: Interviews With Contemporary American Playwrights, Tuscaloosa, Alabama: The Univ of Alabama Press, 96; auth, "From Nathaniel Bailey and Samuel Johnson to the O.E.D.: Using Dictionaries in the Writing Workshop," The Journal of The Mississippi Council of Teachers of English 19, No. 1, (97): 10-19; auth, "The Significance of Oath-

Taking Scenes in the Journals of James Boswell," Rationality And The Liberal Spirit, Shreveport, Louisiana: A Centenary Publication, 97; auth, "The Red Devil Battery Sign, A Bibliographic Essay," Tennesse Willams: a Guide to Research And Performance, Westport, Connecticut: Greenwood Press, (98): 194-203; auth, "Death of a Salesman at Fifty: An Interview with Arthur Miller," Michigan Quarterly Rev 37, No. 4, (98): 624-634; auth, "Tennessee William's Mississippi Delta: A Photo Essay," Southern Quarterly 38, No. 1, (99): 124-140. **CONTACT ADDRESS** Dept of English, Univ of Mississippi, Bondurant Hall C128, PO Box 1848, University, MS 38677-1848. **EMAIL** egcolby@olemiss.edu

KUMMINGS, DONALD D.
PERSONAL Born 07/28/1940, Lafayette, IN, m, 1987, 2 children **DISCIPLINE** ENGLISH, AMERICAN STUDIES **EDUCATION** Pur Univ, BA, 62; MA, 64; Ind Univ, PhD, 71. **CAREER** Teach assoc, Pur Univ, 63-64; instr, Adrian Coll, 64-66; assoc instr, Ind Univ, 66-70; asst prof, Univ Wis, 70-75; assoc prof, 75-85; prof, 85-. **HONORS AND AWARDS** Prof of Year, Carnegie Found, 97; Reg Teach Excell Awd; Stella C Gray Dist Teach Awd, 77, 90; Posner Poet Prize, CWW, 90; **MEMBERSHIPS** AAP; ALA; MLAA; WWA; WWBA; WFP. **RESEARCH** Walt Whitman; American poetry and poetics; Nineteenth-Century American literature; American short stories. **SELECTED PUBLICATIONS** Auth, "The Poetry of Democracies: Tocqueville's Aristocratic View," Comp Lit Stud 11 (74): 306-319; auth, "The Issue of Morality in James's The Golden Bowl," Ariz Quart 32 (76): 381-391; auth, "Walt Whitman's Vernacular Poetics," Can Rev Am Stud 7 (76): 119-131; auth, "Williams Paterson: The Vernacular Hero in the Twentieth Century," Am Poet 4 (86): 2-21; auth, Walt Whitman, 1940-1975: A Reference Guide, G K Hall (Boston), 82; auth, The Open Road Trip: Poems, Geryon Press (NY), 89; ed, "Approaches to Teaching Whitman's 'Leaves of Grass'," MLA (90); co-ed, Walt Whitman: An Encyclopedia, Garland Pub (NY and London), 98. **CONTACT ADDRESS** Dept English, Univ of Wisconsin, Parkside, PO Box 2000, Kenosha, WI 53141-2000. **EMAIL** d-p.kummings@worldnet.att.edu

KUNITZ, STANLEY
PERSONAL Born 07/29/1905, Worcester, MA, m, 1930, 1 child **DISCIPLINE** ENGLISH **EDUCATION** Harvard Univ, AB, 26, AM, 27. LitD, Clark Univ, 61 and Anna Maria Col, 77. **CAREER** Mem fac lit, Bennington Col, 46-49; prof English, State Teachers Col, Potsdam, 49-50; lectr, New Sch Soc Res, 50-57; vis prof, Brandeis Univ, 58-59, Danforth vis lectr, 61-63; lectr, 63-66, Adj Prof Writing, Grad Sch Arts, Columbia Univ, 67-; Guggenheim fel, 45; Lowell Poetry traveling fel, 54; vis prof, Univ Wash, 55-57, Queens Col, NY, 56-57, Yale Univ, 72, Rutgers Univ, 74 and Vassar Col, 81; Ford Found grant, 58-59; ed, Yale Ser of Younger Poets, 69-77; Chancellor, Acad Am Poets, 70-; consult poetry, Libr Congr, 74-76, hon consult Am letts, 76-79; vis prof and sr fel humanities, Princeton Univ, 78, Vassar Col, 81. **HONORS AND AWARDS** Garrison Medal, Harvard Univ, 26; Blumenthal Prize, 41; Levinson Prize, 56; Harriet Monroe Awd, Univ Chicago, 58; Pulitzer Prize, poetry, 59; Brandeis Univ Creative Arts Medal for poetry, 65; Lenvre Marshall Awd, 80. **MEMBERSHIPS** Nat Acad Inst Arts and Lett. **RESEARCH** Creative writing; modern British and American literature. **SELECTED PUBLICATIONS** Auth, Take Our Advice ad Veteran Teachers Give Solutions to Common Teaching Problems, Clavier, Vol 0032, 93; Hornworm, Autumn Lamentation, Am Poetry Rev, Vol 0024, 95; Hornworm, Summer Reverie, Am Poetry Rev, Vol 0024, 95; An Interview With Kunitz, Stanley, Mich Quart Rev, Vol 0036, 97. **CONTACT ADDRESS** 37 W 12th St, New York, NY 10011.

KUNZ, DON
PERSONAL Born 11/23/1941, Kansas City, MO, m, 1965, 1 child **DISCIPLINE** ENGLISH LITERATURE **EDUCATION** Kans State Univ, BA, 64; Univ Tex, Austin, MA, 65; Univ Wash, PhD, 68. **CAREER** From asst prof to assoc prof, 68-82, prof English, Univ RI, 82-, dir Grad Studies English, 79-83, dir Univ Honors Prog, 84-87, Honors Fac Fel, 89-92, coordr, Film Studies Prog, 93-97. **MEMBERSHIPS** Am Asn Univ Prof; Acad Am Poets; Lit/Film Asn; Phi Kappa Phi. **RESEARCH** Creative Writing; 20th century Am Fiction; film. **SELECTED PUBLICATIONS** Auth, The Drama of Thomas Shadwell, Inst English Sprache & Lit, Univ Salzburg, 72; Oliver Stone's Film Adaptation of Born on the Fourth of July: Redefining Masculine Heroism, in War, Lit, and the Arts 2.2, 90; Singing the Blues in A Soldier's Story, in Lit/Film Quart 19.1, 91; Nutty Professors, in Forum for Honors, Summer/Fall 92; ed, The Films of Oliver Stone, Scarecrow Press, 97; Oliver Stone's Talk Radio, in Lit/Film Quart 25.1, 97; author of numerous other journal articles, poetry, and reviews. **CONTACT ADDRESS** English Dept, Univ of Rhode Island, Kingston, RI 02881-0812. **EMAIL** dkunz@uri.edu

KUPERSMITH, WILLIAM ROGER
PERSONAL Born 10/21/1941, Evanston, IL **DISCIPLINE** ENGLISH LITERATURE **EDUCATION** Georgetown Univ, AB, 63; Univ Tex, Austin, PhD, 69. **CAREER** Lectr English, Rice Univ, 69-70; asst prof, Gonzaga Univ, 70-72; asst prof, 72-76, assoc prof, 76-81, Prof English, Univ Iowa, 81-, Philol Quart managing ed, 73-75 & ed, 75- **MEMBERSHIPS** Am Soc Eighteenth-Century Studies; Mid-West Am Soc Eighteenth-Century Studies (pres, 76-77); MLA; Johnson Soc of the Central Region (pres, 87-88). **RESEARCH** Neoclassical literature; English satire. **SELECTED PUBLICATIONS** Co-ed, Henry Fielding Pasquin, Univ Iowa, 73; ed, From Chaucer to Gibbon: Essays in Memory of Curt A Zimansky, Philol Quart, 75; auth, Rhetorical structure in The Vanity of Human Wishes, Studies in Philol, 75; Vice and folly in neoclassical satire, Genre, 78; Augustan literature, Philological Quart, Vol 57, 473-491; What makes a paper publishable, Bull of Midwest Mod Lang Asn, Vol 12, 15-19; Juvenal amoung the whigs, Forum, Vol 17, 43-51; ed, George Chapman's Translation of the Fifth Satire of Juvenal, Windhover Press, 79; Roman Satirists in Seventeenth-Century England, Univ Nebr Press, 85. **CONTACT ADDRESS** Dept of English, Univ of Iowa, 308 English Phil Bld, Iowa City, IA 52242-1492. **EMAIL** william-kupersmith@uiowa.edu

KURATA, MARILYN J.
DISCIPLINE NINETEENTH-CENTURY BRITISH LITERATURE **EDUCATION** Carnegie-Mellon, BS; Univ Wis, PhD, 76. **CAREER** Grad dir, Univ AL. **SELECTED PUBLICATIONS** Auth, Models and Methods for Writing About Literature. **CONTACT ADDRESS** Univ of Alabama, Birmingham, 1400 University Blvd, Birmingham, AL 35294-1150.

KURITZ, PAUL
PERSONAL Born 10/01/1948, Hazleton, PA, s, 4 children **DISCIPLINE** THEATER **EDUCATION** Univ Va, AB, 70; Ind Univ, MA, PhD. **CAREER** Instr, Moorehead State Univ, 73-75; instr, Univ Pittsburgh, 75-78; from asst prof to prof, Bates Col, 78-. **SELECTED PUBLICATIONS** Auth, Playing, An Introduction to Acting; auth, The Making of Theater History; auth, Fundamental Acting. **CONTACT ADDRESS** Bates Col, 227 Main St., #2, Norway, ME 04268-5912. **EMAIL** pkuritz@abacus.bates.edu

KURIYAMA, CONSTANCE
PERSONAL Born 06/22/1942, Madison, IN, m, 1972, 1 child **DISCIPLINE** ENGLISH, RENAISSANCE, DRAMA, FILM **EDUCATION** Ind Univ, BA, 64; Univ Calif at Berkeley, MA, 66; PhD, 73. **CAREER** Asst prof, Univ Ariz, 73-76; asst prof, Univ Va, 76-82; assoc prof, Tex Tech Univ, 82-. **HONORS AND AWARDS** Newberry Lib Grant; Folger Shakespeare Lib Grant; ACLS Grant; NEH. **MEMBERSHIPS** MLAA; Chaplin Soc. **RESEARCH** Renaissance drama; Christopher Marlowe; comedy; Chaplin. **SELECTED PUBLICATIONS** Co-ed, A Poet and a Filthy Playmaker: New Essays on Christopher Marlowe, AMS Press (NY), 88; auth, Hammer or Anvil: Psychological Patterns in Christopher Marlow's Plays, Rutgers UP (NB, NJ), 80; auth, "Chaplin's Impure Comedy: The Art of Survival," Film Quart 45 (92): 26-38; auth, "Marlowe, Shakespeare, and the Nature of Biographical Evidence," Univ Hartford Studies in Lit 20 (88): 1-12; auth, "Dr Greg and Dr Faustus: The Supposed Originality of the 1616 Text," Eng Lit Renaissance 5 (75): 171-197; auth, " Oliver's Richard III: A Re-Evaluation," in Focus on Shakespearean Film, ed. Charles W Eckert (Englewood Cliffs, NJ: Prentice Hall, 72). **CONTACT ADDRESS** Dept English, Texas Tech Univ, Lubbock, TX 79409-0999. **EMAIL** cbcbk@ttacs.ttu.edu

KURLAND, STUART M.
PERSONAL Born 01/17/1955, NC, m, 1989, 2 children **DISCIPLINE** ENGLISH **EDUCATION** Dartmouth Col, AB, 77; Univ Chicago, MA, 78; PhD, 84. **CAREER** Instr, Univ Ill, 80-84; vis asst prof, Hamilton Col, 84-85; vis asst prof, Emory Univ, 85-86; vis asst prof, Col of William & Mary; vis asst prof, St. John's Univ, 87-88; asst prof to assoc prof, Duquesne Univ, 88-. **MEMBERSHIPS** Am Asn of Univ Prof, Mod Lang Asn of Am, Shakespear Asn of Am. **RESEARCH** Shakespeare, Early Modern English Drama, Literature and History. **SELECTED PUBLICATIONS** Auth, "The Care . . . of subjects' good': Pericles, James I, and the Neglect of Government," Comparative Drama 30 (96): 220-244; auth, "Hamlet and the Scottish Succession?" Studies in English Literature, 1500-1900 (94): 279-300; auth, "A Beggar's Book/Outworths a noble's blood: The Politics of Faction in Henry VIII," Comparative Drama 26 (92): 237-253; auth, "We Need No More of Your Advice: Political Realism in The Winter's Tale", Studies in English Literature, 1500-1900 31 (91): 356-386; auth, "No innocence is safe,/When power contests: The Factional Worlds of Caesar and Sejanus," Comparative Drama 22 (88): 56-67. **CONTACT ADDRESS** Dept English, Duquesne Univ, 600 Forbes Ave, Pittsburgh, PA 15282-0001. **EMAIL** kurland@duq.edu

KURPIUS, DAVID
DISCIPLINE MASS COMMUNICATION **EDUCATION** Ind Univ, BA; Univ Wis, MA, 95, PhD, 97. **CAREER** Teching asst, Univ Wis Madison, 92-95; Asst prof, La State Univ, 97-. **HONORS AND AWARDS** H.V. Kaltenborn Fel, Univ of Wis, 92; Abe Schecter Grad Schlarship, 96-97; Harold E. Fellows Scholarship, Broadcast Educators Asn (BEA, 96-97; Top Paper Awd, Asn for Educ in Jour and Mass Commun Nat Conv, 98. **MEMBERSHIPS** Asn for Education in Journalism and Mass Communication; Int Communications Asn; Broadcast Educators Asn; Nat Asn of Black Journalists; Radio-Television News Directors Asn; Nat Press Photographers Asn; Soc of Professional Journalists. **RESEARCH** Broadcast journalism practices and production; race and media; mass communication theory. **SELECTED PUBLICATIONS** Coauth, Diversity in the News: A Conceptual and Methodological Framework, in Jour and Mass Commun Quart, 95; The Synthetic Crisis: Media and Influences on Perception of Crime, Asn for Educ in Jour and Mass Commun Nat Conv, 95. **CONTACT ADDRESS** The Manship Sch of Mass Commun, Louisiana State Univ and A&M Col, B-6 Hodges Hall, Baton Rouge, LA 70803-7202. **EMAIL** kurpius@lsu.edu

KUSHNER, DAVID Z.
PERSONAL Born 12/22/1935, Ellenville, NY, m, 3 children **DISCIPLINE** MUSICOLOGY **EDUCATION** Boston Univ, BM, 57; Col-Conservatory of Music, Univ of Cincinnati, MM, 58; Univ of Mich, PhD, 66. **CAREER** Asst prof of Music, Miss Univ for Women, 64-66; assoc to full prof, Radford Univ, 66-69; Prof & grad prog head, Musicology, Univ Fla, 69-. **HONORS AND AWARDS** Teaching Incentive Prog and Professorial Excellence Prog Awds, Univ of Florida; Master Teacher Certificate in Music Hist, Music Teachers Nat Asn; Man of the Year, Am Bio Inst; Int Man of the Year, Int Bio Centre; Musician of the Year, Found for the Promotion of Music. **MEMBERSHIPS** Am Musicological Soc; 19th-Century Studies Asn; Col Music Soc, Soc for Am Music; Music Teachers Nat (Life) Asn; Pi Kappa Lambda. **RESEARCH** Life and music of Ernest Bloch and Jaromir Weinberger; nationalism in 19th- and 20th-century music; music criticism; American music. **SELECTED PUBLICATIONS** Auth, Jaromir Weinberger, Int Dictionary of Opera, St James Press, 93; Bloch's Macbeth, Int Dictionary of Opera, St Ernest Bloch: A Guide to Research, Garland Pub, 99; The Ernest Bloch Companion, Greenwood Publishing, (in production) 01; James Press, 93; Ellen Taaffee Zwilich, Great Lives from Hist: Am Women, Salem Press, 95; Creative Teaching and the Practical Applications of Knowledge, Proceedings of the Eighteenth-Nat Conf on Successful Col Teaching, Valdosta State Col, 95; numerous entries including: Ernest Bloch, John Powell, Marc Blitzstein, Scott Huston, and Jaromir Weinberger, The New Grove Dictionary of Music and Musicians, Macmillan, 00; **CONTACT ADDRESS** School of Music, Univ of Florida, Gainesville, FL 32611. **EMAIL** DZK777@gator.net

KUSTUS, GEORGE L.
DISCIPLINE CLASSICS **CAREER** Fac, Harvard Univ, 53; prof emer, SUNY Buffalo, present. **RESEARCH** Ancient rhetoric; Class and Medieval lit, drama, educational hist. **SELECTED PUBLICATIONS** Auth, Studies in Byzantine Rhetoric, Thessalonica, 73; publ on rhetoric. **CONTACT ADDRESS** Dept Classics, SUNY, Buffalo, 712 Clemens Hall, Buffalo, NY 14260.

KUTZER, M. DAPHNE
DISCIPLINE ENGLISH **EDUCATION** Mt Holyoke, BA; IN Univ, MA and PhD,79. **CAREER** Fac, Plattsburgh State Univ of NY. **HONORS AND AWARDS** NY State Univ Chancellor's Awd Excellence Tchg, 96; Phi Eta Sigma Disting Fac Awd, 97. **RESEARCH** Children's lit; writing by women; 19th century lit. **SELECTED PUBLICATIONS** Auth, children's lit; articles on women's writing and feminist literary theory. **CONTACT ADDRESS** SUNY, Col at Plattsburgh, 101 Broad St, Plattsburgh, NY 12901-2681.

KUYK, DIRK ADRIAAN, JR.
PERSONAL Born 04/27/1934, Roanoke, VA **DISCIPLINE** AMERICAN & ENGLISH LITERATURE **EDUCATION** Univ Va, AB, 55; Brandeis Univ, PhD(English), 70. **CAREER** Asst prof, 70-74, assoc prof, 74-78, Prof English, Trinity Col (Conn), 78-. **RESEARCH** Faulkner; Yeats; the symbolist movement. **CONTACT ADDRESS** Dept of English, Trinity Col, Connecticut, 300 Summit St, Hartford, CT 06106-3186.

KUYPERS, JIM A.
DISCIPLINE COMMUNICATION **EDUCATION** LA State Univ, PhD, 95. **CAREER** Dir of Speech, Dartmouth Col, 95-. **HONORS AND AWARDS** Outstanding Contribution to Ocmmunication Scholarship Award, Am Commun Asn, 99; Early Career Res Award, Soutehrn States Commun Asn, 99. **MEMBERSHIPS** Am Commun Asn; Southern States Commun Asn; Nat Commun Asn. **RESEARCH** Political communication; communication criticism; media framing. **SELECTED PUBLICATIONS** Auth, "Doxa and a Realistic Prudence for a Critical Rhetoric," Communication Quarterly 44.4 (96): 452-462; auth, Presidential Crisis Rhetoric and the Press in the Post-Cold War World, Praeger (Westport, CT), 97; auth, "La Communicacion presidencial en crisis y el papel de la prensa: el presidente Clinton y la crisis Bosnia de 1995," Peruvian Library of Congress, Noticias (99); auth, "From Science, Moral Poetics: Dr. James Dobson's Response to the Fetal Research Initiative," Quarterly Journal of Speech 86.2 (00): 146-167; auth, "Another Shot Heard Around the World?" Tiempos Del Mundo (forthcoming); auth, "How to Spot Press Bias," The Dartmouth Alumni Magazine (forthcoming); auth, Media Manipulation of Controversial Issues, Praeger, (Westport, CT), forthcoming; auth, "Must We All Be Social Activists? A Reply to Robert Ivie," The American Journal (forthcoming); coed, Twentieth-Century Roots of Rhetorical Studies, Praeger (Westport, CT),

forthcoming. **CONTACT ADDRESS** Dartmouth Col, 6046 Bartlett Hall, Hanover, NH 03755. **EMAIL** jim.kuypers@dartmouth.edu

KUZNETS, LOIS R.
PERSONAL Born 01/08/1935, New Haven, CT, m, 1973, 2 children **DISCIPLINE** ENGLISH **EDUCATION** Swarthmore Col, BA, 56; Yale Univ, MAT, 57; Ind Univ, PhD, 73. **CAREER** Asst prof, CUNY, 73-82; Teacher, Cranbrook-Kingswood Schools, 82-83; assoc prof to prof, San Diego State Univ, 85-96. **HONORS AND AWARDS** Int Res Soc for Childrens Lit; Children's Lit Assoc; Mythopreic Soc. **MEMBERSHIPS** MLA; Children's Lit Assoc; Int Res Soc for Children's Lit. **RESEARCH** Children's and Adolescent Literature, Women's Studies. **SELECTED PUBLICATIONS** Auth, Kenneth Graheme, Twayne, 87; auth, When Toys Come Alive: Narratives of Animations, Metamorphosis and Development, Yale Univ Pr, 94. **CONTACT ADDRESS** 2117 Brockman Blvd, Ann Arbor, MI 48104-4529. **EMAIL** lkuznets@mediagone.net

KWASNY, ANDREA
DISCIPLINE AMERICAN LITERATURE **EDUCATION** SUNY, PhD. **CAREER** English and Lit, Univ Ark **SELECTED PUBLICATIONS** Auth, On the Margins: Postmodernist positions in Faulkner's 'other' representation. **CONTACT ADDRESS** Univ of Arkansas, Little Rock, 2801 S University Ave., Little Rock, AR 72204-1099. **EMAIL** adkwasny@ualr.edu

KYDD, ELSPETH
DISCIPLINE THEATRE ARTS **EDUCATION** Northwestern Univ, MA, PhD. **CAREER** Asst prof, Univ Toledo. **RESEARCH** Film theory; film hist; film and video production. **SELECTED PUBLICATIONS** Auth, publ(s) on racial representation in film and television. **CONTACT ADDRESS** Univ of Toledo, Toledo, OH 43606. **EMAIL** ekydd@uoft02.utoledo.edu

L

L'ALLIER, LOUIS
PERSONAL Born 02/27/1961, PQ, Canada **DISCIPLINE** CLASSICAL STUDIES **EDUCATION** Univ Ottawa, MA, 89; Laval Univ, PhD, 96. **CAREER** Lectr, Laval Univ, 96-. **MEMBERSHIPS** Am Philol Asn; Class Asn of Can; Soc des Etudes Anciennes du Quebec. **RESEARCH** Ancient Greek literature. **SELECTED PUBLICATIONS** Auth, "Le Heros Xenophontique et les Femmes," 98; "Le Domaine de Scillonte; Xenophon et l'Exemple Perse," 98; "Xenophon's Park at Scillua: Some Ancient and Modern Views on Nature," 97. **CONTACT ADDRESS** 24 Benedict St, Hull, QC, Canada J8Y 5G1. **EMAIL** l.lallier@sympatico.ca

LA FEMINA, GERARD
PERSONAL Born 08/11/1968, Brooklyn, NY, m, 1999, 1 child **DISCIPLINE** LITERATURE, POETRY WRITING **EDUCATION** Sarah Lawrence Col, AB, 90; Western Mich Univ, MA, 93; MFA, 93. **CAREER** Teaching assoc, Western Mich Univ, 90-93; instr, Nazareth Col, 93; instr, Kirtland Community Col, 94-. **HONORS AND AWARDS** Creative Artist Grant, Mich Coun of Arts and Cultural Affairs; Irving Gilmore Emerging Artist Grant. **MEMBERSHIPS** Assoc Writing Prog, MLA. **RESEARCH** Pop culture. **SELECTED PUBLICATIONS** Auth, A Print of Wildflowers (Love Poems), Ridgeway Press (Roseville, MI), 97; auth, Shattered Hours: Poems 1988-94, Red Dancefloor Press (Lancaster, CA), 98. **CONTACT ADDRESS** Dept Lang and Lit, Kirtland Comm Col, 10775 N Saint Helen Rd, Roscommon, MI 48653-9634. **EMAIL** lafeming@kirtland.cc.mi.us

LA FORTE, ROBERT SHERMAN
PERSONAL Born 09/08/1933, Frontenac, KS, m, 1959, 3 children **DISCIPLINE** UNITED STATES HISTORY & BIBLIOGRAPHY **EDUCATION** Kans State Col Pittsburg, BSE & MS, 59; Univ Tex, Austin, MLS, 68; Univ Kans, PhD(hist), 66. **CAREER** From instr to asst prof hist, East Tex State Univ, 64-67; from asst prof to assoc prof, 68-74, prof hist, N Tex State Univ, 77-00, prof emer, 00-, dept chair, 89-93, Univ Archivist, 75-85, Higher Educ Act fel, 67-68. **HONORS AND AWARDS** UNT Pres Teaching Awd, 92; Shelton Teaching Awd, 94; 'Fessor' Graham Awd, 95. **MEMBERSHIPS** The Hist Soc. **RESEARCH** Nineteenth and Twentieth century United States; History of Kansas. **SELECTED PUBLICATIONS** Auth, Leaders in Reform, Kansas' Progressive Republicans, Univ Kans, 74; Down the Corridor of Years, A Centennial History of U.N.T., 1890-1990, UNT Press, 89; co-ed, Remembering Pearl Harbor, SR Books, 91; co-ed, Building the Death Railway, SR Books, 93; co-ed, With Only the Will to Live, SR Books, 94. **CONTACT ADDRESS** Dept of Hist, Univ of No Texas, PO Box 310650, Denton, TX 76203-0650. **EMAIL** cb36@jove.unt.edu

LA MOY, WILLIAM T.
PERSONAL Born 01/27/1953, Hartford, CT, s **DISCIPLINE** LIBRARY, INFORMATION SCIENCE **EDUCATION** Yale Univ, BA, 76; Simmons Col, MS, 88. **CAREER** James Duncan Phillips Libr, ed, dir of publ, Peabody Essex Mus Collections. **HONORS AND AWARDS** Seven publications design awards from the New England Museum Asn. **MEMBERSHIPS** International Honor Society for Librarianship and Information Service, Colonial Society of MA. **RESEARCH** Librarianship and info svc; colonial soc of Mass; colonial Amer hist & lit. **CONTACT ADDRESS** Phillips Library, Peabody Essex Mus, East India Square, Salem, MA 01970. **EMAIL** will_lamoy@pem.org

LA PRADE, DOUGLAS E.
PERSONAL Born 07/30/1956, Sagamihara, Japan, s **DISCIPLINE** ENGLISH **EDUCATION** Southern Methodist Univ, BA, 78; Univ IL Urbana Champaign, AM, 80; PhD, 88. **CAREER** Univ of Barcelona, 84-85, 86-93; Autonomous Univ of Barcelona, 87-88; Univ of Tex Pan Am 93-. **HONORS AND AWARDS** Sigma Delta Pi, 75; Phi Beta Kappa, 77; Fulbright Lectr, Univ of Barcelona, 86-88; Fulbright Res Grant, Spain, 01. **RESEARCH** Hemingway, Censorship. **SELECTED PUBLICATIONS** Auth, La censura de Hemingway en Espana, Ediciones Univ de Salamanca, 91; auth, "The Reception of Hemingway in Spain", Hemingway Rev, (92): 42-50. **CONTACT ADDRESS** Dept English, Univ of Texas, Pan American, 1201 W University Dr, Edinburg, TX 78539-2909. **EMAIL** dlaprade@panam.edu

LABOR, EARLE G.
PERSONAL Born 03/03/1928, Tuskahoma, OK, m, 5 children **DISCIPLINE** ENGLISH **EDUCATION** Southern Methodist Univ, AB, 49; MA, 52; Univ Wisc, PhD, 61. **CAREER** Instr, Southern Methodist Univ, 48-54; Recruit Training Instr, US Navy, 54-55; Asst Sales Mgr, Haggar Co, 55-56; Instr, Centenary Col La, 56-59; Teaching Asst, Univ Wisc, 59-62; Asst Prof to Full Prof, Centenary Col of La, 62-. **HONORS AND AWARDS** Phi Beta Kappa; Omicron Delta Kappa; NEH Sen Fel, 74-75, 99-00; Col English Asn distinguished Service Awd, 82; CEA Honorary Lifetime Membership, 90; Humanist of the Year Awd, La Endowment for the Humanities, 91. **MEMBERSHIPS** Col English Asn, Jack London Soc, Mod Lang Asn, Nat Asn of Scholars, Intl Asn of Univ Prof of English. **RESEARCH** Jack London, American Literary Naturalism, Critical Theory. **SELECTED PUBLICATIONS** Co-auth, A Handbook of Critical Approaches to Literature, Oxford Univ Press, 66, 79, 92, 99; auth, Jack London, Twayne, 94; co-ed, the Letters of Jack London, Stanford Univ Press, 88; co-ed, The Complete Short Stories of Jack London, Stanford Univ Pres, 93; co-ed, LIT: Literature & Interpretive Techniques, HarperCollins, 86; ed, The Portable Jack London, Viking/Penguin, 94. **CONTACT ADDRESS** Dept English, Centenary Col of Louisiana, Shreveport, LA 71134-1188. **EMAIL** elabor@centenary.edu

LABRIE, ROSS E.
PERSONAL Born 10/17/1936, Montreal, PQ, Canada, m, 1966, 2 children **DISCIPLINE** ENGLISH **EDUCATION** Loyola Col, BA, 57; McGill Univ, MA, 60; Univ Toronto, PhD, 66. **CAREER** Instr, Univ Sask, 62-63; Instr to Prof, Univ BC, 63-. **HONORS AND AWARDS** Fel, Soc Sci and Humanities Res Coun, 80-81; Choice Magazine Acad Book Awd, 80. **MEMBERSHIPS** Christianity and Lit Asn; Intl Thomas Merton Soc. **RESEARCH** Catholic American Literature. **SELECTED PUBLICATIONS** Auth, The Catholic Imagination in American Literature, Univ Mo Press, 97; auth, Thomas Merton and the Inclusive Imagination, Univ Mo Press, 01. **CONTACT ADDRESS** Dept English, Univ of British Columbia, 397-1873 E Mall, Vancouver, BC, Canada V7N 1N5. **EMAIL** labrie@interchange.ubc.ca

LABRIOLA, ALBERT C.
DISCIPLINE ENGLISH LITERATURE **EDUCATION** Duquesne Univ, BEd, 61; Columbia Univ, MA, 62; Univ VA, MA, 63, PhD, 66. **CAREER** Prof, Duquesne Univ; Prof of English. **HONORS AND AWARDS** Distinguished Univ Prof. **MEMBERSHIPS** Milton Soc; John Donne Soc. **SELECTED PUBLICATIONS** Co-auth, Biblia Pauperum, 90; co-ed, Milton's Legacy in the Arts, 88. **CONTACT ADDRESS** Dept of Commun, Duquesne Univ, Forbes Ave, PO Box 600, Pittsburgh, PA 15282. **EMAIL** labriola@duq.edu

LABUZ, RONALD
PERSONAL Born 11/17/1953, Utica, NY, m **DISCIPLINE** ADVERTISING DESIGN, GRAPHIC DESIGN **EDUCATION** SUNY, Oswego, BA, 75; Ohio State Univ, MA, 77; Syracuse, MA, 95; PhD, 97. **CAREER** Prof, adv des, Prof, Graphic Comm, Mohawk Vly Comm Coll, Dept Head/Prof, Art Mohawk Valley Community College. **HONORS AND AWARDS** State Univ of New York Chancellor's Awd for Excellence, 89, SUNY Faculty Exchange Scholar, 90-. **MEMBERSHIPS** AM Antiquarian Soc, Graphic Design Education Assoc, 89-94, American Center for Design, Royal Printing Historical Society, American Printing History Society. **RESEARCH** Am Graphic Des, 1830-70. **SELECTED PUBLICATIONS** Auth, Type on Paper: The History of the Typesetting Machine, 89; auth, Contemporary Graphic Design, Van Nostrand Reinhold, 92; auth, The Computer in Graphic Design, Van Nostrand Reinhold 93; auth, Digital Typography, Digital Design; auth, Contemporary Typography, 00. **CONTACT ADDRESS** Dept of Graphic Comm, Mohawk Valley Comm Col, 1101 Sherman Dr, Utica, NY 13501. **EMAIL** rlabuz@mvcc.edu

LACKEY, KRIS L.
PERSONAL Born 10/26/1953, Oklahoma City, OK, m, 1976, 1 child **DISCIPLINE** ENGLISH **EDUCATION** Okla Baptist Univ, BA, 75; Univ New Mexico, MA, 77; PhD, 82. **CAREER** Vis asst prof, Univ of Tex of the Permian Basin, 83; instr, Auburn Univ, 83-86; from asst prof to prof, Univ of New Orleans, 86-. **RESEARCH** American literature. **SELECTED PUBLICATIONS** Auth, Road Frames: The American Highway Narrative, Univ of Nebr Press, 97. **CONTACT ADDRESS** Dept English, Univ of New Orleans, 2000 Lakeshore Dr, New Orleans, LA 70148-0001. **EMAIL** klackey@uno.edu

LADD, BARBARA
PERSONAL Born 02/01/1954, Greensboro, NC, s **DISCIPLINE** ENGLISH **EDUCATION** UNC-Chapel Hill, AB, 76; PhD, 90; UNC-Greensboro, MFA, 81; Univ of Tex at Austin, MA, 85. **CAREER** From asst prof to assoc prof, Emory Univ, 90-. **HONORS AND AWARDS** Fel, Wa Ctr for the Humanities. **MEMBERSHIPS** Am Lit Asn, MLA, S Atlantic MLA, S Central MLA, Soc for the Study of S Lit. **RESEARCH** American literature, late 19th & 20th centuries, with particular interests in regionalism, Faulkner, Welty, literature and modernity, literary postmodernism and creolizations. **SELECTED PUBLICATIONS** Auth, "'The Direction of the Howling': Nationalism and the Color Line in Absalom, Absalom!" Am Lit 66.3 (94): 525-551; auth, Nationalism and The Color Line in the Work of George W. Cable, Mark Twain, and William Faulkner, La State UP, 96; auth, "'Philosophers and Other Gynecologists': Women and the Polity in Requiem for a Nun," Miss Quart 52.3 (99): 483-501. **CONTACT ADDRESS** Dept English, Emory Univ, 1364 Clifton Rd NE, Atlanta, GA 30322-1061. **EMAIL** bladd@emory.edu

LADEFOGED, PETER
PERSONAL Born 09/17/1925, Sutton, England, m, 1953, 3 children **DISCIPLINE** LINGUISTICS, ENGLISH **EDUCATION** Univ Edinburgh, MA, 51, PhD, 59. **CAREER** Lectr phonetics, Univ Edinburgh, 53-61; W African Lang Surv fel, 61-62; from asst prof to assoc prof English, 62-65, Prof Ling, Univ Calif, Los Angeles, 65-, Team leader, Uganda Lang Surv, 68. **MEMBERSHIPS** Acoust Soc Am; Int Phonetic Asn; Int Asn Voice Identification; Am Speech and Hearing Asn; Ling Soc Am (pres). **RESEARCH** Experimental phonetics; African languages; phonology. **SELECTED PUBLICATIONS** Auth, Another View of Endangered Languages, Lang, Vol 0068, 92; Clicks and Their Accompaniments, J Phonetics, Vol 0022, 94; The Status of Phonetic Rarities, Lang, Vol 0072, 96; Phonetic Structures of Banawa, an Endangered Language, Phonetica, Vol 0054, 97; Abercrombie, David and the Changing Field of Phonetics, J Phonetics, Vol 0025, 97. **CONTACT ADDRESS** Dept of Ling, Univ of California, Los Angeles, Los Angeles, CA 90024.

LADIN, JAY
PERSONAL Born 03/24/1961, Rochester, NY, m, 1982, 2 children **DISCIPLINE** LITERATURE, CREATIVE WRITING **EDUCATION** Sarah Lawrence Col, BA, 82; Univ Mass Amherst, MFA, 95; Princeton Univ, PhD, 00. **CAREER** Lectr, Princeton Univ, 00-01. **HONORS AND AWARDS** Fulbright Scholar, 01-02; Whiting Found Fel, 99-00; Porter Ogden Jacobus Fel, 99-00; Carton Fel, 99-00. **MEMBERSHIPS** MLA; NEMLA; MSA. **RESEARCH** American poetry; modernism; poetics and cognitive science; Biblical narrative; democracy and language. **SELECTED PUBLICATIONS** Auth, "Breaking the Line: Emily Dickinson and William Carlos Williams," Emily Dick J 3 (94); auth, "Fleshing Out the Chronotope," in Critical Essays on Mikhail Bakhtin, ed. Caryl Emerson (Crit Ess on World Crit, G. K. Hall, 99); auth, "Search Conditions: Find 'Auden' and 'Modernism,'" in Will Auden: A Legacy, ed. David Izzo (locust Hill Pr, 01); auth, "Goblin with a Gauge: Teaching Emily Dickinson," Emily Dick J 9 (00); auth, "Thirsting for the Absolute: American Poetry gets Religion," Parnassus: Poetry in Rev (00); auth, "The Prince and the Paupered: Medieval Hebrew Poetry Meets the Twenty-First Century," Parnassus: Poetry in Rev 25 (01). **CONTACT ADDRESS** 15 Gaylord St, Amherst, MA 01002-2223. **EMAIL** jayladin@princeton.edu

LAFAYE, A.
PERSONAL Born 03/09/1970, Hudson, WI, s **DISCIPLINE** ENGLISH **EDUCATION** Univ MN, BA, 92; Minn State Univ, MA, 94; Univ Memphis, MFA, 96; Hollins Univ, MA, 98. **CAREER** Adj Instructor, Koanoke Col, 97-98; Visiting Asst Prof, SUNY, 98-00; Asst Prof, Calif State Univ, 00-. **HONORS AND AWARDS** Best Books, Bank St School of Educ, 99; Best Books in the Middle, VOYA, 99; Best Books for Teen Readers, New York, 00. **MEMBERSHIPS** ChLA, SCBWI, MELUS **RESEARCH** Bicultural identity in Literature, Geroler images in Literature, Southern Gothic Literature. **CONTACT ADDRESS** Dept English, California State Univ, San Bernardino, 5500 Univ Pkwy, San Bernardino, CA 92407.

LAFFOON, ELIZABETH ANNE
DISCIPLINE COMMUNCATION STUDIES **EDUCATION** Rice Univ, BA, 86; Univ Houston, MA, 88; Northwestern Univ, PhD, 93. **CAREER** Asst Prof, Commun Dept Grad Fac. **RESEARCH** Rhetorical theory and criticism. **SELECTED PUBLICATIONS** Auth, Are those real? Reconsidering Habermas's conception of performance, Speech Commun, 95; Towards a rhetoric of indirection: Exploring the enthymematic character of Habermas's model of therapeutic critique, 95; The Rhetoric of Ecofeminism, 94. **CONTACT ADDRESS** Dept of Communication, Univ of Colorado, Boulder, Boulder, CO 80309. **EMAIL** Elizabeth.Laffoon@Colorado.edu

LAFLEUR, RICHARD ALLEN
PERSONAL Born 09/22/1945, Newburyport, MA, m, 1967, 3 children **DISCIPLINE** CLASSICAL STUDIES **EDUCATION** Univ Va, BA, 68, MA, 70; Duke Univ, PhD, 73. **CAREER** Asst prof, 72-77, Assoc Prof Classics, Univ GA, 77-, Head Dept, 80-, Ed, Class Outlook, 79-; chmn, comt Prom Latin, 79-81, exec comt, 79-83, S sect secy-treas, 78-; Class Asn Midwest & South. **HONORS AND AWARDS** Am Philol Asn Awd, Excellence in Teaching Classics, 84; Classical Asn Midwest & South, Ovatio, 85; Am Classical League, pres, 84-86, hon pres for life, 86-; Univ GA, Bronze Medallion, Public Service, 88; For Lang Asn Ga, Teacher of the Year, 88; Ga Governors Awd, Humanities, 89. **MEMBERSHIPS** Am Class League; Am Philol Asn; Archaeol Inst Am; Class Asn Mid W & S; Vergilian Soc. **RESEARCH** Juvenal; Roman satire; Latin pedagogy. **SELECTED PUBLICATIONS** Auth, The Teaching of latin in American Schools, Scholars Press, 87; Latin Poetry for the Beginning Student, Longman, 87; Wheelock's Latin, Harper Collins, 95; Love and Transformation: An Ovid Reader, Scott Foresman-Addison Wesley 98; Latin for the 21st Century: From Concept to Classroom, Scott Foresman-Addison Wesley, 98. **CONTACT ADDRESS** Dept Classics, Univ of Georgia, Athens, GA 30602-0001. **EMAIL** rlafleur@parallel.park.uga.edu

LAGO, MARY MCCLELLAND
PERSONAL Born 11/04/1919, Pittsburgh, PA, m, 1944, 2 children **DISCIPLINE** MODERN ENGLISH AND BENGALI LITERATURE **EDUCATION** Bucknell Univ, BA, 40; Univ Mo-Columbia, MA, 65, PhD(English), 69. **CAREER** Instr, 64-70, lectr, 70-75, res grants, 71-74, assoc prof, 75-78, Prpf English, Univ MO-Columbia, 78-, Am Philos Soc res grants, 67, 68 and 70; Am Coun Learned Soc/Ford Found Joint SAsia Prog grant, 72-73; Nat Endowment for Humanities grant, 80-83. **HONORS AND AWARDS** DLitt, Bucknell Univ, 81. **MEMBERSHIPS** MLA; Midwest Mod Lang Asn; Asn Asian Studies; Soc of Authors, London; Virginia Woolf Soc. **RESEARCH** Modern Indian literature; late 19th and early 20th century English literature and art history. **SELECTED PUBLICATIONS** Auth, A 'River Called Titash', World Lit Today, Vol 0069, 95. **CONTACT ADDRESS** Dept of English, Univ of Missouri, Columbia, Columbia, MO 65201.

LAHAIE, SCOTT
PERSONAL Born 01/10/1961, Tulsa, OK, m, 1985, 2 children **DISCIPLINE** THEATRE HISTORY **EDUCATION** Sam Houston State Univ, BFA, 85; Baylor Univ, MA, 96; MFA, 00. **CAREER** Stage director to artistic director, Keller Theater, Germany, 83-93; multimedia dev, lectr, Baylor Univ, 96-. **HONORS AND AWARDS** Best Director of a Play Awd, Europ Tournament of Plays, 88; Best Lighting for a Play Awd, 92. **MEMBERSHIPS** IIR, ICSA, SSSA, SWGA. **RESEARCH** Bertolt Brecht, Irwin Piscator, and the theatre of the Weimar Republic, The German Playwright Heinz Coubier, Ira Adridge and the acting traditions of the 19th century, Genre criticism and the fiction of C.S. Lewis, Hypertext theory and the new literature, Applied Technology in the Arts and Humanities. **SELECTED PUBLICATIONS** Cotransl, The Beloved, by Heinz Coubier, (Will Meisel Verlag, 90); rev, of "The Outrageous Idea of Christian Scholarship," by George Marsden, Jour of Interdisciplinary Studies, (98); rev, of "Reclaiming the Soul," by Jeffrey H. Boyd, Jour of Interdisciplinary Studies, (00); auth, 'Ira Aldridge: In Search of Recognition," Jour of African Studies, forthcoming. **CONTACT ADDRESS** Baylor Univ, Waco, PO Box 97262, Waco, TX 76707. **EMAIL** scot_lahaie@baylor.edu

LAHEY, CHRISTINE
PERSONAL Born 09/07/1949, Wyandotte, MI, m, 2 children **DISCIPLINE** LITERATURE **EDUCATION** Wayne State Univ, BA, 71; MA, 74. **CAREER** Instr, Detroit col of Business, 80; instr, Wayne State Univ, 76-82; instr to adj assoc prof, Center for Creative Studies, 82-. **HONORS AND AWARDS** Tomkins Awd for Poetry, Wayne State Univ, 71, 76, 77; Finalist, Mich Counc for the Arts Competition, 85; Grant, Mich Council of the Arts, 90; First Place, Poetry, Oakland Community Col, 96. **MEMBERSHIPS** Book Club of Detroit; Phi Beta Kappa; Assoc of Literary Scholars and Critics. **RESEARCH** Fairy Tales, Sitwelliana, the Norse presence in North America. **SELECTED PUBLICATIONS** Rev, "Triptych of Excellence", of The Sitwells: A Family's Biography by John Pearson, Ga Rev 33.4 (79): 923-926; auth, "Some Brief Observations on the Life and Work of William Sharp (Fiona MacLeod), Ball State Univ Forum 21.4 (80) 18-26; coed, Planet Detroit: An Anthology of Urban Poetry, 83; rev, "Korydon's Music", by David Hall, Gargoyle 27, (85): 123-124; auth, "Do It In Detroit", Mich Quarterly Rev, (86); auth, "Dan's Shoe Repair: 1959", Blood to Remember: American Poets on the Holocaust, ed Charles Fishman, Tex Tech Univ Pr, 91; auth, "Collecting the Sitwells: Three Intellectual and Eccentric Siblings", Speaking of Books 1.4 (99): 4-5. **CONTACT ADDRESS** Dept Lib Arts, Center Creative Studies, 201 E Kirby St, Detroit, MI 48202-4048.

LAHOOD, MARVIN JOHN
PERSONAL Born 03/21/1933, Auburn, NY, m, 1959, 3 children **DISCIPLINE** ENGLISH **EDUCATION** Boston Col, BS, 54; Univ Notre Dame, MA, 58, PhD(English), 62. **CAREER** From instr to assoc prof English, Niagara Univ, 60-64; from assoc prof to prof, State Univ NY Col Buffalo, 64-71, assoc acad develop, 68-71; prof English and acad dean, Col Misericordia, 71-72 and Salem State Col, 72-75; prof English and dean fac, D'Youville Col, 75-78; Prof English, State Univ NY Col, Buffalo, 78-95; Distinguished Teaching Prof, 95-. **MEMBERSHIPS** MLA. **RESEARCH** American fiction; modern fiction. **SELECTED PUBLICATIONS** Riding the Yellow Trolley Car, World Lit Today, Vol 0068, 94; Brazil, World Lit Today, Vol 0069, 95; The Collected Stories of Auchincloss, Louis, World Lit Today, Vol 0069, 95; Mr Vertigo, World Lit Today, Vol 0069, 95; Palimpsest--a Memoir, World Lit Today, Vol 0070, 96; Vidal, Gore--Writer Against the Grain, World Lit Today, Vol 0070, 96; Talking Horse--Malamud, Bernard on Life and Work, World Lit Today, Vol 0071, 97; The 'Flaming Corsage', World Lit Today, Vol 0071, 97; Mrs Ted Bliss, World Lit Today, Vol 0071, 97; ed, Stories of Tragedy and Triumph, Simon & Schuster, 97. **CONTACT ADDRESS** SUNY, Buffalo, 93 Parkhaven Dr, Amherst, NY 14222. **EMAIL** lahoodmj@buffalostate.edu

LAIRD, DAVID
PERSONAL Born 10/16/1927, Marshfield, WI, m, 1955, 1 child **DISCIPLINE** ENGLISH LITERATURE **EDUCATION** Univ Wis, BA, 50, MA, 51, PhD, 55. **CAREER** From instr to asst prof English, Oberlin Col, 55-58; From Asst Prof to Assoc Prof English, Calif State Univ, 58-78, Prof, 68-73, Chmn Dept, 69-72, Coordr Am Studies, 77-79. Fel, Nat Humanities Inst, Univ Chicago, 78-79; sr Fulbright lectr, Univ Tunis, Tunisia, 79-80; Inst Renaissance and 18th Century Studies fel, Folger Shakespeare Libr, 82. **MEMBERSHIPS** MLA; Philol Asn PACIFIC Coast; Am Studies Asn; Malone Soc **RESEARCH** Shakespeare; rhetoric and style; American literature and cultural history. **SELECTED PUBLICATIONS** Auth, Cather, Willa Women, Gender, Place, and Narrativity in 'O Pioneers' and 'My Antonia', Great Plains Quart, Vol 0012, 92; The Midwestern Ascendancy in American Writing, Amer Lit, Vol 0067, 95. **CONTACT ADDRESS** 565 N. Milton Dr., San Gabriel, CA 91775.

LAIRD, EDGAR
DISCIPLINE MEDIEVAL LITERATURE **EDUCATION** Southwest TX State Univ, BA, MA; Rutgers, PhD. **CAREER** Southwest Tex State Univ **RESEARCH** James Joyce. **SELECTED PUBLICATIONS** Auth, Astrology and Irony in Chaucer's Complaint of Mars, Chaucer Rev, 72; Chaucer's Complaint of Mars, 1.145: 'Venus valaunse,' Philol Quart, 72; Astronomical 'Proporcioneles' in the Franklin's Tale, Eng Lang Notes, 88; A Note on Planetary Tables and a Planetary Conjunction in Troilus and Criseyde, Chaucer Rev, 90; Boethius, Boece, and Bootes, Mod Philol, 90; "Robert Grosseteste, Albumasar, and Medieval Tidal Theory, Isis, 81; Mars in Taurus at the Nativity of the Wife of Bath, Eng Lang Notes, 90; "Astrology in the Court of Charles V of France , Manuscripta, 90; "Columbus and the Sky of January 17, 1493, Sky & Telescope, 91; Love 'Elemented' in John Donne's 'Valediction: Forbidding Mourning,' , Am Notes & Queries, 91; Pelerin de Prusse on the Astrolabe, Medieval and Renaissance Texts and Studies, Binghamton, 95; Cosmic Law and Literary Character in Chaucer's Knight's Tale, Mellen, 95; Right Ascension, Am Jour, Physics, 96. **CONTACT ADDRESS** Southwest Texas State Univ, 601 University Dr, San Marcos, TX 78666-4604.

LAIRD, PAUL
PERSONAL Born 10/26/1958, Louisville, KY, m, 1982, 1 child **DISCIPLINE** MUSIC HISTORY **EDUCATION** Ohio State Univ, BM, 80, MA, 82; Univ NC-Chapel Hill, PhD, 86. **CAREER** Asst Prof, 91-94, Assoc Prof, Univ Kans, 97-; Asst Prof, 91-94, Univ Denver; Asst Prof, SUNY-Binghamton, 88-91; Vis Asst Prof, Penn State Univ, 87-88. **HONORS AND AWARDS** Prog for Cultural Coop Between Spain's Ministry of Culture and US Univ Grant; NEH travel grant. **MEMBERSHIPS** Am Musicol Soc; Col Mus Soc; Early Mus Am; Soc Espanola de Musicol; Soc Am Mus. **RESEARCH** Spanish and Latin American villancico; music of Leonard Bernstein; Broadway musicals; early stringed instruments. **SELECTED PUBLICATIONS** Towards A History of the Spanish Villancico, Warren, MI, Harmonie Park Press, 97. **CONTACT ADDRESS** Dept Music and Dance, Univ of Kansas, Lawrence, 452 Murphy Hall, Lawrence, KS 66045-2279. **EMAIL** plaird@ukans.edu

LAKE PRESCOTT, ANNE
DISCIPLINE ENGLISH LITERATURE **EDUCATION** Barnard Col, BA, 59; Columbia Univ, MA, 61, PhD, 67. **CAREER** Prof, Bernard Col, 61; Columbia, 79-. **HONORS AND AWARDS** Trustee, Renaissance Soc of Am; past pres, Spenser Soc; ed bd, SEL; CLS; Spenser Stud; Amer Notes and Queries; Moreana; adv coun, PMLA. **RESEARCH** Anthology of Renaissance texts with focus on gender. **SELECTED PUBLICATIONS** Auth, French Poets, English Renaissance, and Imagining Rabelais in the English Renaissance, Yale UP, 98. **CONTACT ADDRESS** Dept of Eng, Columbia Col, New York, 2960 Broadway, New York, NY 10027-6902.

LAKIN, BARBARA
PERSONAL Born 08/06/1930, Denver, CO, m, 1952, 2 children **DISCIPLINE** ENGLISH LITERATURE **EDUCATION** Kansas State Univ, BS; Colo State Univ, MA; Univ of Colo-Boulder, PhD. **CAREER** Assoc prof. **HONORS AND AWARDS** CSU Advising Awdand Mortar Board Excellence in Univ Education **RESEARCH** New Historicism; occult in English Renaissance literature. **SELECTED PUBLICATIONS** Auth, pubs on Gender and Power in Macbeth, Othello, and The Merchant of Venice; influence of Giordano Bruno's thought on several English Renaissance writers; Graham Greene. **CONTACT ADDRESS** Dept of English, Colorado State Univ, Fort Collins, CO 80523. **EMAIL** blakin@vines.colostate.edu

LALONDE, GERALD VINCENT
PERSONAL Born 05/18/1938, Bellingham, WA, m, 1969, 2 children **DISCIPLINE** CLASSICS, ANCIENT HISTORY **EDUCATION** Univ Wash, BA, 62, MA, 64, PhD(classics), 71. **CAREER** Instr classics, Univ Wash, 68-69; from instr to asst prof, 69-74, assoc prof, 74-79, Prof Class, Grinnell Col, 80. **MEMBERSHIPS** Archaeol Inst Am; Am Philol Asn; Brit Class Asn. **RESEARCH** Greek epigraphy, history and archaeology. **SELECTED PUBLICATIONS** Auth, A fifth century Hieron southwest of the Athenian Agora, 68 & A Boiotien decree in Athens, 77, Hisperia. **CONTACT ADDRESS** Dept of Classics, Grinnell Col, P O Box 805, Grinnell, IA 50112-0805.

LAMAN, BARBARA
PERSONAL Born 01/27/1945, Austria, d, 3 children **DISCIPLINE** ENGLISH LITERATURE **EDUCATION** Fla Int Univ, BA, 86; Univ Miami, MA, 87; PhD, 90. **CAREER** Lectr, Univ Miami, 90-92; assoc prof, Dickinson State Univ, 92-. **MEMBERSHIPS** Int James Joyce Found, Arthur Schnitzler Soc, Keats-Shelley Asn of Am. **RESEARCH** James Joyce, Modern Austrian Literature. **CONTACT ADDRESS** Dept Lang & Lit, Dickinson State Univ, 291 Campus Dr, Dickinson, ND 58601-4853. **EMAIL** blaman@eagle.dsu.nodak.edu

LAMAY, J. LEO
PERSONAL Born 01/17/1935, Bristow, VA, m, 1965, 3 children **DISCIPLINE** ENGLISH **EDUCATION** Univ Maryland, BA, 57; MA, 62; Univ Penn, PhD, 64. **CAREER** Instr to asst prof, George Washington Univ, 63-65; asst prof to prof, Univ Cal, 65-77; prof, Univ Del, 77-. **HONORS AND AWARDS** NEH Sr Fel, 83-84, 94-95; Dist Fac Lectr, Univ Del; Inst Adv Stud Fel; Guggenheim Fel; Hon Schl EAL. **MEMBERSHIPS** MLAA; ALA; ASA. **RESEARCH** Benjamin Franklin; early American literature. **SELECTED PUBLICATIONS** Auth, The Canon of Benjamin Franklin 1722-1776: New Attributions and Reconsiderations Univ Delaware Press (newarek), 86; auth, Men of Letters in Colonial Maryland, Univ Tenn Press (Knoxville), 72; auth, "New England's Annoyances: America's First Folk Song, Univ Delaware Press (Newark), 85; auth, The American Dream of Captain John Smith, Univ Press Virginia (Charlottesville), 91; auth, Did Pocahontas Save Captain John Smith?, Univ Georgia Press (Athens), 92. **CONTACT ADDRESS** Dept English, Univ of Delaware, 42 Amstel Ave, Newark, NJ 19716-2799. **EMAIL** lemay@udel.edu

LAMB, MARGARET
DISCIPLINE DRAMATIC LITERATURE AND DRAMA THEORY **EDUCATION** NYork Univ, PhD **CAREER** Assoc prof, Fordham Univ. **RESEARCH** Creative writing and the writer's process. **SELECTED PUBLICATIONS** Auth, Garrick's Anthony and Cleopatra, Shakespearean Criticism, 17, 92. **CONTACT ADDRESS** Dept of Eng Lang and Lit, Fordham Univ, 113 W 60th St, New York, NY 10023.

LAMBERT, GREGG
PERSONAL Born 08/08/1961, Miami, FL, d, 2 children **DISCIPLINE** ENGLISH **EDUCATION** Comparative Literature, Univ California, Phd, 95; Comparative Literature, Univ California, 92; Pacific Univ, BA, 83. **CAREER** Asst Prof, Dept of English, Syracuse Univ, 96-; Vis Lecturer, Univ of California, Irvine, 95-96. **HONORS AND AWARDS** Dorothy and Donald Strauss Dissertation Fel, 95. **MEMBERSHIPS** Modern Language Assoc; Invitational Assoc of Philosophy and Literature. **SELECTED PUBLICATIONS** Auth, "The Deleuzian Critique of Pure Fiction," Sub-Stance 84, vol. 26, no. 3, Winter 97, 128-152; auth, "On the University in the Ears of its Publics," Crossings, vol. 1, no. 1, Spring 97, 55-107; auth, "On the Uses and Abuses of Literature for Life: Introduction to the Literary Clinic," Postmodern Culture, Volume 8, No. 3 May 98; auth,

"The Work of Art in an Age of Alien Reproduction," Journal of Cultural and Regligious Theory, November, 99; auth, "Shall We Gather at the River?: The Contemporary Eulogy of James Wright," Literature & Theology: An Interdisciplinary Journal of Theory and Criticism, Oxford University Press, Forthcoming, winter 00; auth, "What Graduate Students Want?: John Guillory and the Obscure Object of English Desire," minnesota review, NS. 52-3, spring 00; auth, "Either Law or Life: The Question of Literature Between Deleuze and Derrida," Angelaki, vol 5.1, summer 00; auth, "Cinema and the Outside," The Brain is the Screen: Gilles Deleuze and the Philosophy of Cinema, ed. Gregory Flaxman, Minneapolis: University of Minnesota Press, spring 00; auth, "On the Uses and Abuses of Literature for Life," revised version in Gilles Deleuze and Literature, eds. Ian Bucanan and John Marks, Edinburgh: University of Edinburgh Press, spring 00; auth, "The Culture of the Stranger: Reglections on Aesthetic Ideology from the Baroque to the Post-Colonial," Series in the Critical Humanities, Boulder, CO: Davies Publishing Group, Forthcoming, fall 00. **CONTACT ADDRESS** Dept English, Syracuse Univ, Hall of Languages, Syracuse, NY 13244-1170. **EMAIL** glambert@syr.edu

LAMBERT, LYNDA J.
PERSONAL Born 08/27/1943, PA, m, 1961, 5 children **DISCIPLINE** ART, LITERATURE **EDUCATION** Slippery Rock Univ Pa, BFA, MA; WV Univ, MFA **CAREER** Instr, Commun Col of Beaver Co, Monaca, Pa, 85-88; instr, Slippery Rock Univ Pa, 90; teaching asst, WV Univ, 89-91; exec dir, Hoyt Inst, New Castle, Pa, 92-96, asst prof, Geneva Col, Beaver Falls, Pa, present. **MEMBERSHIPS** Assoc Artists of Pittsburgh; Assoc for Integrative Stud; Group A; Amer Assoc of Museums; Inst of Museum Svcs; Nat Assoc of Women Artists Inc; Pa Rural Arts Alliance, Women's Caucus for Art; Cal Art Assoc; Handweaver's Guild of Amer. **RESEARCH** Viking glass; African Amer art & lit; African art; ancient art. **SELECTED PUBLICATIONS** Auth, MacLennan, Rosalind, Abstract art exhibition invites interpretation, Butler Eagle, 95; MacLennan, Rosalind, Painter, sculptor complement each other, Butler Eagle, 95; Mabin, Connie, Artists painting Aliquippa portrait as a city of pride, Beaver Valley Times, 95; Marcello, Patricia Cornin, Parade of 25 Successful women for 1996, Successful Women Mag, 96; Wilson, Gladys Blews, Painter chooses unusual medium for her prints, Beaver Valley Times, 96. **CONTACT ADDRESS** 104 River Rd, Ellwood City, PA 16117. **EMAIL** llambert@geneva.edu

LAMPARSKA, RENA A.
DISCIPLINE LITERATURE **EDUCATION** Univ Wroctaw, Poland, LLM; Catholic Univ of America, MA; Harvard Univ, PhD. **CAREER** Assoc prof, Boston College. **RESEARCH** Italian literature. **CONTACT ADDRESS** Dept of Romance Languages and Literatures, Boston Col, Chestnut Hill, Chestnut Hill, MA 02167.

LANCASHIRE, ANNE C.
PERSONAL Born 11/23/1941, Montreal, ON, Canada, m, 3 children **DISCIPLINE** ENGLISH, FILM STUDIES **EDUCATION** McGill Univ, BA, 62; Harvard Univ, AM, 63; PhD, 65. **CAREER** Lectr to prof, Univ Toronto, 65-. **HONORS AND AWARDS** Pres Shakespeare Asn, 88-89; Trafalgar Ross Lectr, 87; Can Coun Fel, 71-72; SSHRCC Fel, 86-87; Dir Guild Part. **MEMBERSHIPS** SAA; ACCUTE; FSAC; Malone Soc; MRDS; MLA. **RESEARCH** Medieval and Renaissance theater history and drama; contemporary popular American film. **SELECTED PUBLICATIONS** Ed, Gallathea and Midas, by John Lyly, 69; auth, "Chaucer and the Sacrifice of Isaac," Chaucer Rev 9 (75): 320-326; auth, Editing Renaissance Dramatic Texts: English, Ital, and Span, 76; auth, The Second Maiden's Tragedy, Revels Plays, 78; auth, "Complex Design in The Empire Strikes Back," Film Critic 5 (81): 38-52; auth, "The Witch: Stage Flop or Political Mistake?" in Accompanying the Players (83); ed, Christopher Marlowe: Poet for the Stage, by Clifford Leech, 86; auth, "Medieval to Renaissance: Plays and the London Draper's Company," in The Center and the Compass, ed. R. Taylor, et al (93); auth, "Continuing Civic Ceremonies of 1530s London," in Civic Ritual and Drama in Late Medieval and Renaissance Europe, eds. W. Husken, A. F. Johnston (97); auth, "The Phantom Menace: Repetition, Variation, Integration," Film Crit 24 (00): 23-44. **CONTACT ADDRESS** Humanities Soc Sci Dept, Univ of Toronto, 130 St George St, Roberts Library, Toronto, ON, Canada M5S 3H1. **EMAIL** anne@chass.utoronto.ca

LANCASHIRE, IAN
PERSONAL Born 11/27/1942, Winnipeg, MB, Canada, m, 1968, 2 children **DISCIPLINE** ENGLISH **EDUCATION** Univ Man, BA, 64; Univ Toronto, MA, 65, PhD(English), 69. **CAREER** Lectr, 68-69, asst prof, 69-74, Assoc Prof English, Erindale Col, Univ Toronto, 74-, Can Coun leave fel, 73, grant Reed, 76; proj bibliographer theatre hist, Rec Early English Drama, 75- **MEMBERSHIPS** Medaieval Acad Am; Early English Text Soc; MLA; Can Soc Renaissance Studies. **RESEARCH** Records of early English drama, minstrelsy and ceremony; Medieval and Tudor drama; bibliography. **SELECTED PUBLICATIONS** Auth, Representative Poetry On-line, 94-; auth, Early Modern English Dictionaries Database, 96-00; auth, "Phrasal Repetends in Literary Stylistics: Shakespeare's Hamlet III. 1", Research in Humanities Computing 4, 96; auth, Using TACT With Electronic Texts, MLA, 96; co-ed, Tracing the Trail of Time, 97; auth, Edmund Coote, The English School-Master (1596), co-ed, Renaissance Electronic Texts, 98; auth, "Paradigms of Authorship," Shakespeare Studies, 98; auth, "Probing Shakespeare's Idiolect in Troilus and Cressida, 1.3. 1-29," University of Toronto Quarterly 68.3 (99): 728-67. **CONTACT ADDRESS** Dept of English, Univ of Toronto, 7 King's Col Cir, Toronto, ON, Canada M5S 3K1. **EMAIL** ian@chass.utoronto.ca

LANDES, W. DANIEL
PERSONAL Born 04/26/1950, Harrisonburg, VA **DISCIPLINE** PERFORMING ARTS **EDUCATION** Shenandoah Conservatory of Music, BM, 72; Univ Md, MM, 77; Southern Baptist Theolog Sem, DMA, 83. **CAREER** Assoc prof, Belmont Univ, 83-. **MEMBERSHIPS** Hymn Society; Society Electro-Acoustic Music. **RESEARCH** Hymnology; music technology. **SELECTED PUBLICATIONS** Coed, Electronic Encyclopedia of Hymnology. **CONTACT ADDRESS** School of Music, Belmont Univ, 1900 Belmont Blvd, Nashville, TN 37212. **EMAIL** landesd@mail.belmont.edu

LANDOW, GEORGE PAUL
PERSONAL Born 08/25/1940, White Plains, NY, m, 1966, 2 children **DISCIPLINE** ENGLISH LITERATURE, DIGITAL CULTURE, ART HISTORY **EDUCATION** Brandeis Univ, MA, 62; Princeton Univ, AB, 61, MA, 63, PhD(English), 66; Brown Univ, MA, 72. **CAREER** Instr English, Columbia Univ, 65-68, asst prof, 69-70; vis assoc prof, Univ Chicago, 70-71; assoc prof, 71-78, Prof English & Artist Hist, Brown Univ, 78-; Fel, Soc for Humanities, Cornell Univ, 68-69; Guggenheim Found fels, 73 & 78; consult lit & art, Museum Art, RI Sch Design, 76-79; vis fel, Brasenose Col, Oxford Univ, 77; fac fel, Brown Univ Inst for Res in Information and Scholarship (IRIS), 85-92; NEA, 84-85; NEH Summer Inst, Yale, 88, 91; British Academy vis prof, Univ of Lancaster, vis res fel, Electronics and Computer Science, Univ of Southampton (UK), vis prof Univ of Zimbabwe, 97: IL SU, 98; Distinguished vis prof, Nat Univ of Singapore, 98; Dean, Univ Scholars Prog; Prof, Nat Univ of Singapore, 00-. **HONORS AND AWARDS** Gustave O Arldt Award, Coun Grad Schs US, 72; .EDUCOM/NCRIPTAL award innovative courseware in the humanities, 90; many awards for websites. **MEMBERSHIPS** ACM; Tennyson Soc; Trollope Soc. **RESEARCH** Hypertext and digital culture; Victorian British poetry and nonfiction; Victorian painting and visual arts; theology and literature; MLA; Univ Coun Board of trustees; NUS, 00-, Bovenring Board Singapore UP, 01. **SELECTED PUBLICATIONS** Auth, Your Good Influence on Me: The Correspondence of John Ruskin and W H Hunt, John Rylands Libr, England, 76; William Holman Hunt and Typological Symbolism, Yale Univ, 79; ed, Approaches to Victorian Autobiography, Ohio Univ, 79; Victorian Types, Victorian Shadows: Biblical Typology and Victorian Literature, Art and Thought, Routledge & Kegan Paul, 80; Images of Crisis: Literary Iconology 1750 to the Present, Routledge & Kegan Paul, 82; Ruskin, Oxford Univ Press, 85; ed with others, Pre-Raphaelite Friendship, UMI, 85; ed, Ladies of Shalott: A Victorian Masterpiece and its Contexts, Brown, 86; Elegant Jeremiahs: The Sage from Carlyle to Mailer, Cornell, 86; ed with P. Delany, Hypermedia and Literary Studies, MIT, 91; Hypertext: The Convergence of Contemporary Critical Theory and Technology, Johns Hopkins, 92; ed with P. delany, Digital Word: Text-Based Computing in the Humanities, MIT, 93; Hyper/Text/Theory, Johns Hopkins, 94; Hypertext 2.0, Johns Hopkins, 97. **CONTACT ADDRESS** Dept of English and Digital Culture, Nat Univ of Singapore, Singapore 119260. **EMAIL** george@landow.com/uspdean@nus.edu.sg

LANDRUM, LARRY N.
PERSONAL Born Huntington, IN, 2 children **DISCIPLINE** AMERICAN LITERATURE, POPULAR CULTURE **EDUCATION** Purdue Univ, BA, 65, MA, 67; Bowling Green State Univ, PhD, 73. **CAREER** Instr, Ctr Studies Popular Culture, Bowling Green State Univ, 70-73; from Asst Prof to Assoc Prof, 73-84, prof eng, MI State Univ, 84; Adv ed, J Popular Cult, 67-85; bibliogr, J Popular Film, 72-; bibliogr, Popular Culture Asn, 73-85. **MEMBERSHIPS** Midwest Popular Cult Asn (vpres & treas, 77-78); MLA; Popular Cult Asn. **RESEARCH** Am lit; Am studies; popular cult. **SELECTED PUBLICATIONS** Co-ed, Challenges in American Culture, Bowling Green State Univ, 71; Theories and Methodologies in Popular Culture, 76 & Dimensions of Detective Fiction, 76, Popular Press; auth, American Popular Culture, Gale, 82; auth, American Mystery and Detective Novels, Greenwood Press, 99. **CONTACT ADDRESS** Dept of Eng, Michigan State Univ, 201 Morrill Hall, East Lansing, MI 48824-1036. **EMAIL** landrum@pilot.msu.edu

LANDY, FRANCIS
PERSONAL Born 07/10/1947, London, England, m, 1995, 1 child **DISCIPLINE** ENGLISH, COMPARATIVE LITERATURE **EDUCATION** Cambridge Univ, BA, 69; Sussex Univ, PhD, 83; **CAREER** From Asst Prof to Prof, Univ Alta, 84-. **MEMBERSHIPS** Soc of Bible lit, Am Acad of Relig, Can Soc of the Old Testament/Hebrew Bible. **RESEARCH** Literary Study of the Old Testament and Hebrew bible. **SELECTED PUBLICATIONS** Auth, "In the Wilderness of Speech: Problems of Metaphor in Hosea," Bibl Interpretation, 3 (95): 35-59; auth, Sex and Sadism in Hosea," in Jewish Explorations of Sexuality (London: Duckworth, Providence: Berghahn, 95), 17-26; auth, "Hosea" in Readings (Sheffield: Sheffield Acad Pr, 95); auth, "Do We Want Our Children to Read This Book?" The Bible and the Ethics of Reading (97): 155-175; auth, "Strategies of Concentration and Diffusion in Isaiah 6," Bibl Interpretation, 6 (99): 58-86; auth, "Flood and Fludd," in Bibl Studies/Cult Studies: The Third Sheffield Colloquium (Sheffield: Sheffield Acad Pr, 98), 117-159; auth, "Seraphim and Poetic Process," in The Labour of Reading: Essays in Hon of Robert C. Culley at the Time of This Retirement (Atlanta, GA: ScholarsPress, 99); auth, "Isaiah," in An Anthrop of Bibl Autobiographies (Sheffield: Sheffield Acad Pr, forthcoming). **CONTACT ADDRESS** Dept Comparative Lit, Univ of Alberta, Old Arts Bldg, Edmonton, AB, Canada T6G 2E1. **EMAIL** francis.landy@ualberta.ca

LANDY, MARCIA
PERSONAL Born 06/24/1931, Cleveland, OH, m, 1953, 2 children **DISCIPLINE** ENGLISH **EDUCATION** Ohio Univ, AB, 53; Univ Rochester, MA, 61, PhD, 62. **CAREER** From instr to asst prof English, Univ Rochester, 63-67; asst prof, 67-70, assoc prof, 70-79, Prof English and Film Stud, Univ Pittsburgh, 79-, Ed, Milton Studies, 67-; Danforth Found Assoc, 75. **HONORS AND AWARDS** Distinguished Service Prof of Eng/Film Stud, 98. **MEMBERSHIPS** MLA. **RESEARCH** Milton; women studies; literary and film criticism. **SELECTED PUBLICATIONS** Auth, Fascism in Film: The Italian Commercial Cinema 1930-1943, Princeton, 86; British Genres: Cinema and Society 1930-1960, Princeton, 91; Imitations of Life: A Reader on Film and Television Melodrama, Wayne State, 91; Film, Politics and Gramsci, Minn, 94; Queen Christina, BFJ, 96; Cinematic Uses of the Past, Minn, 96; The Folklore of Consensus: Theatricality in the Italian Cinema 1930-1943, SUNY, 98; auth, Italian Film, Cambridge, 00. **CONTACT ADDRESS** Dept of English, Univ of Pittsburgh, 443 Cathedral/Lear, Pittsburgh, PA 15260-0001. **EMAIL** mlandy@pitt.edu

LANE, ALCYEE
DISCIPLINE TWENTIETH-CENTURY AMERICAN LITERATURE **EDUCATION** UCLA, PhD, 96. **CAREER** Asst Prof, Eng, Univ Calif, Santa Barbara. **RESEARCH** Gay and lesbian lit; queer, feminist, crit race theory; African Am lit and cult. **SELECTED PUBLICATIONS** Auth, "Black Bodies/Gay Bodies: The Politics of Race in the Gay/Military Battle," Callaloo, 95. **CONTACT ADDRESS** Dept of Eng, Univ of California, Santa Barbara, Santa Barbara, CA 93106-7150. **EMAIL** lane@humanitas.ucsb.edu

LANE, CHRISTOPHER
DISCIPLINE ENGLISH LANGUAGE AND LITERATURE **EDUCATION** Univ London, PhD. **CAREER** Fac, Univ Wisc Milwaukee; Mellon Fel Hum, Univ Penn, 95-96; assoc prof, 88-. **RESEARCH** Victorian literature; British colonial fiction; critical theory. **SELECTED PUBLICATIONS** Auth, The Ruling Passion, Duke UP, 95; The Burdens of Intimacy, Univ Chicago, 98; ed, The Psychoanalysis of Race, Columbia UP, 98. **CONTACT ADDRESS** English Dept, Emory Univ, 1380 Oxford Rd NE, Atlanta, GA 30322-1950. **EMAIL** clane2@emory.edu

LANE, EUGENE N.
DISCIPLINE EPIGRAPHY AND COMPARATIVE GRAMMAR **EDUCATION** Princeton Univ, AB; Yale Univ, PhD. **CAREER** Taught at Univ Va; Prof & dir Grad Stud; Univ Mo, 66-; Prof Emer. **RESEARCH** Ancient religion; comparative grammar; Late Antiquity. **SELECTED PUBLICATIONS** Auth, Corpus Monumentorum Religionis Dei Menis, 4 vols, Leiden, Brill, 71-78; Corpus Cultus Iovis Sabazii, vols 2 & 3, Leiden Brill, 85-89; coauth, Paganism and Christianity, 100-425 CE: a Sourcebook; ed, Cybele, Attis, and Related Cults: Essays in Memory of MJ Vermaseren. **CONTACT ADDRESS** Dept of Classical Studies, Univ of Missouri, Columbia, 420D General Classroom Bldg, Columbia, MO 65211. **EMAIL** LaneE@missouri.edu

LANE, PINKIE GORDON
PERSONAL Born 01/13/1923, Philadelphia, PA **DISCIPLINE** ENGLISH **EDUCATION** Spelman Col, BA, 49; Atlanta Univ, MA, 56; La State Univ, PhD(English), 67. **CAREER** Prof English, Southern Univ, Baton Rouge, 67-80, Chmn Dept, 74-80. Vpres, South and West, Inc, ed-in-chief, South and West: Int Lit Quart. **MEMBERSHIPS** Poetry Soc Am. **SELECTED PUBLICATIONS** Wind Thoughts (poems), 72; ed, Discourses on Poetry, VI, 72 & Poems by Blacks, III, 73, South & West; J Black Poetry, Negro Am Lit Forum, Jeopardy, La Rev, Hoo Doo I, South & West, Voices Int, Energy W, Pembroke Mag, Poet: India, Last Cookie; The Mystic Female (poems), 78, articles in Phylon. **CONTACT ADDRESS** So Univ and A&M Col, 2738 77th Ave, Baton Rouge, LA 70807.

LANG, CECIL Y.
PERSONAL Born 09/18/1920, NC, m, 1952, 1 child **DISCIPLINE** ENGLISH LITERATURE **EDUCATION** Duke Univ, AB, 41, MA, 42; Harvard Univ, PhD, 49. **CAREER** From instr

to asst prof English, Yale Univ, 49-57; assoc prof, Claremont Grad Sch, 57-59; prof, Syracuse Univ, 59-65 and Univ Chicago, 65-67; prof, Ctr Advan Studies, 67-70, Commonwealth Prof English, Univ VA, 70-, Guggenheim and Fulbright fels, 51-52; Morse fel, Yale Univ, 56-57; mem adv bd, Victorian Poetry, 63-; mem adv bd, Victorian Studies, 64-66; mem ed comt, Pmla, 68-73. **MEMBERSHIPS** MLA. **RESEARCH** Nineteenth century English literature. **SELECTED PUBLICATIONS** Ed, The Swinburne Letters (6 vols), Yale Univ, 59-62; New Writings by Swinburne, Syracuse Univ, 64; The Pre Raphaelites and their Circle, Houghton, 68, 2nd ed, Univ Chicago, 75; introd, Tennyson in Lincoln, Tennyson Res Ctr, Lincoln, Eng, 71; co-ed (with E F Shannon Jr), the Tennyson Letters, Harvard Univ, Vol 1, 81 and Clarendon Press, 82. **CONTACT ADDRESS** 1820 Edgewood Lane, Charlottesville, VA 22903.

LANG, ROBERT
PERSONAL Born 10/25/1957, Zimbabwe, s **DISCIPLINE** FILM **EDUCATION** Columbia Univ, PhD, 86. **CAREER** Assoc Prof of Cinema, Univ of Hartford. **HONORS AND AWARDS** Fulbright Sr Scholar Awd, Univ of Tunis, 93-94. **MEMBERSHIPS** Soc for Cinema Studies. **RESEARCH** Hollywood cinema; African cinema; queer studies; contemporary French studies. **SELECTED PUBLICATIONS** Auth, American Film Melodrama: Griffith Vidor, Minnelli, Princeton Univ Press, 89; ed, The Birth of a Nation: D.W. Griffith Director, Rutgers Univ Press, 94; auth, Masculine Interests: Male Erotics in Hollywood Film, Columbia Univ Press, forthcoming 01; auth, American Film Melodrama: Griffith, Vidor, Minnelli. **CONTACT ADDRESS** 25 Frederick St, 302, Hartford, CT 06105. **EMAIL** lang@mail.hartford.edu

LANG-PERALTA, LINDA
PERSONAL Born 07/13/1953, Coronado, CA, m, 1982 **DISCIPLINE** LITERATURE **EDUCATION** Calif State Univ Long Beach, BA, 80; MA, 83; Univ Calif Irvine, PhD, 91. **CAREER** Instr, Univ of Calif Irvine, 91-94; lectr, Univ of Nev Los Vegas, 94-97; assoc prof, Metropolitan State Col Denver, 97-. **HONORS AND AWARDS** Outstanding TA of the Year, Univ Calif Irvine; Outstanding Teacher of Year, Univ of Redlands, 94-95; Fulbright, Kenya, 98. **MEMBERSHIPS** MLA, Am Assoc for 18th Century Studies, Am Comp Lit Assoc, Sigma Tau Delta, Phi Kappa Phi. **RESEARCH** Late 18th and Early 19th Century Literature and Postcolonial Literature. **SELECTED PUBLICATIONS** Coed and contributor, Visions of Peace, Calif State Univ, (Long Beach), 82; auth, "Clandestine delights: Frances Burney's life - writing," Finding Voice/Building Community: Women's Life-Writing, ed L Coleman, Bowling Green State Univ Popular Pr, (Bowling Green, 97); ed, Women, Revolution and the Novels of the 1790s, Mich State Univ Pr, (E Lansing), 99; rev, "Consuming Subjects: Women, Shopping, and Business in the Eighteenth Century" and "The Conversational Circle: Rereading the English Novel, 1740-1755," Clio, 99; rev, "A Tale of a Maasai Girl," by Grace Mesopirr Sicard, Souvenir: Jour of African Lit Vol 1.1, ed George Odera Outa, (Nairobi, Kenya), 99; auth, "Cultural renaissance through the performing arts in Kenya," Modern Kenya: Social Issues and Perspectives, ed Mary Ann Watson, Univ Pr of Am, (Landham, Md), 00. **CONTACT ADDRESS** Metropolitan State Col of Denver, Campus Box 32, PO Box 173362, Denver, CO 80217-3362. **EMAIL** langpera@mscd.edu

LANGBAUM, ROBERT
PERSONAL Born 02/23/1924, New York, NY, m, 1950, 1 child **DISCIPLINE** ENGLISH **EDUCATION** Cornell Univ, AB, 47; Columbia Univ, MA, 49, PhD(English), 54. **CAREER** From instr English to asst prof, Cornell Univ, 50-60; from assoc prof to prof, 60-67, James Branch Cabell Prof English, Univ VA, 67-, Ctr Advan Studies Behav Sci fel, 61-62; vis prof, Columbia Univ, 65-66; Guggenheim fel, 69-70; sr fel, Nat Endowment for Humanities, 72-73; mem Supv Comt, English Inst, 70-71, chmn, 72. **MEMBERSHIPS** MLA; Aaup; Acad Lit Studies. **RESEARCH** Nineteenth and 20th century English literature; literary criticism. **SELECTED PUBLICATIONS** Auth, The Poetry of Experience: The Dramatic Monologue in Modern Literary Tradition, Random & Chatto & Windus, London, 57, 2nd ed, 72, Norton, 63, 2nd ed, 71 & Penguin, England, 74; ed, Shakespeare's The Tempest, New Am Libr, 64; New English Libr, 64 & In: Complete Signet Classic Shakespeare, Harcourt, 72; auth, The Gayety of Vision a Study of Isak Dinesen's Art, Chatto & Windus, London, 64, Gyldendal, Copenhagen, Danish transl, 64, Random, 65 & 2nd ed, Univ Chicago, 75; ed, The Victorian Age, Fawcett, 67 & Acad Chicago, 82; auth, The Modern Spirit: Essays on the Continuity of 19th and 20th century literature, Oxford Univ, 70, Chatto & Windus: London, 70; New Modes of characterization in The Waste Land, In: Eliot in His Time, Princeton Univ, 73; The art of Victorian literature, In: The Mind and Art of Victorian England, Univ Minn, 76; The Mysteries of Identity: A Theme in Modern Literature, Oxford Univ, 77 & Univ Chicago, 82. **CONTACT ADDRESS** Dept of English, Univ of Virginia, Charlottesville, VA 22903.

LANGDON, BARBARA TRACY
PERSONAL Born Omaha, NE **DISCIPLINE** ENGLISH **EDUCATION** Bellevue Univ, BA, 89; Univ Nebr-Omaha, MA, 92. **CAREER** Instr & humanities chair, SE Community Col, 93-. **RESEARCH** Native American & Melungeon studies. **SELECTED PUBLICATIONS** Auth, The Melungeons: An Annotated Bibliography: Reference in Both Fiction and Non-Fiction, Dogwood Press, 98. **CONTACT ADDRESS** Dept Humanities, Southeast Comm Col, Lincoln, 8800 O St, Lincoln, NE 68520-1227. **EMAIL** blangdon@sccm.cc.ne.us

LANGELLIER, KRISTIN M.
DISCIPLINE COMMUNICATIONS **EDUCATION** Southern IL Univ, PhD, 80. **CAREER** Mark and Marcia Bailey Prof, grad coordr, Univ ME. **RESEARCH** Personal narrative. **SELECTED PUBLICATIONS** Auth, Personal narratives: Perspectives on theory and research, Text and Performance Quart, 9, 89; Appreciating phenomenology and feminism: Researching quiltmaking and communication, Human Stud, 17, 94; Responding to ethnicity: Franco-American studies in Maine, in H. Barthel ed, Logon didonai. Marz: Voraussichtlicher Erscheinungstermin, 96; coauth, Spinstorying: An analysis of women storytelling, in E. Fine and J. Speer eds, Performance, cult, and identity, Praeger, 92; Family storytelling as a strategy of soc control, in D. Mumby, ed, Narrative and soc control, Sage, 93. **CONTACT ADDRESS** Univ of Maine, Orono, ME 04469-5752. **EMAIL** kristin@maine.edu

LANGER, LAWRENCE L.
PERSONAL Born 06/20/1929, New York, NY, m, 1951, 2 children **DISCIPLINE** LITERATURE **EDUCATION** City Col New York, BA, 51; Harvard Univ, AM, 52, PhD, 61. **CAREER** Instr English, Univ CT, 57-58; from instr to assoc prof, 58-72, prof English, Simmons Col, 72-, Alumnae Prof English, 76-92, Prof Emeritus, 92-; Fulbright lectr Am lit, Univ Graz, Austria, 63-64; Nat Endowment for Humanities advan study & res fel, 78-79, 89-90. **HONORS AND AWARDS** Nat Book Critics Circle Awd for Criticism, 91. **MEMBERSHIPS** MLA; Pen. **RESEARCH** Holocaust studies; literature of the holocaust. **SELECTED PUBLICATIONS** Auth, The Holocaust and the Literary Imagination, Yale Univ, 75; The Age of Atrocity: Death in Modern Literature, Beacon, 78; Versions of Survival: The Holocaust and the Human Spirit, State Univ NY, 82; Holocaust Testimonies: The Ruins of Memory, Yale, 91; Admitting the Holocaust: Collected Essays, Oxford, 95; Art from the Ashes: A Holocaust Anthology, Oxford, 95; Landscapes of Jewish Experience: The Painting of Samuel Bak, Univ Press of New England, 97; Preempting the Holocaust, Yale, 98; The Game Continues: Chess in the Art of Samuel Bak, Indiana, 99. **CONTACT ADDRESS** 249 Adams Ave., West Newton, MA 02465. **EMAIL** LLanger@world.std.com

LANGFORD, GERALD
PERSONAL Born 10/20/1911, Montgomery, AL, m, 1938, 2 children **DISCIPLINE** ENGLISH **EDUCATION** Univ Va, AB, 33, AM, 34, PhD, 40. **CAREER** Instr, Univ Ky, 36-38 & NC State Col, 38-40; assoc prof, Winthrop Col, 40-43; from asst prof to assoc prof, 46-50, prof English, Univ Tex, Austin, 62-. **RESEARCH** Creative writing; modern English and American literature. **SELECTED PUBLICATIONS** Auth, Alias O Henry a Biography of William Sidney Porter, Macmillan, 57; auth, The Richard Harding Davis Years, Holt, 61; auth, The Murder of Stanford White, Bobbs, 62; auth, Ingenue among the Lions: The Letters of Emily Clark to Joseph Hergesheimer, 65; auth, Faulkner's Revision of Absalom, Absalom!, Univ Tex, 71; auth, Faulkner's Revision of Sanctuary, 72, Univ Tex; auth, Destination, A Novel, Stonehenge, 81. **CONTACT ADDRESS** Dept of English, Univ of Texas, Austin, Austin, TX 78712.

LANGFORD, THOMAS
PERSONAL Born 10/20/1930, Alice, TX, m, 1953, 2 children **DISCIPLINE** ENGLISH VICTORIAN LITERATURE **EDUCATION** Univ CA, BA, 56; TX Tech Univ, MA, 63; TX Christian Univ, PhD, 67. **CAREER** Minister, Churches Christ, 56-59; tchr Eng, Chas Page High Sch, OK, 58-61; fel, US Off Educ, 67-68; asst prof, 67-70, asst dean, 68-71, prof eng, TX Tech Univ, 70-, Assoc dean, grad sch, 71-95, Dean, grad sch, 95-96, Consult & reviewer, US Off Educ, 68-72; reviewer educ, Nat Coun Accreditation Tchr Educ, 68. **HONORS AND AWARDS** Outstanding Contrib to Graduate Educ in the South, 97; TTU Fac Leadership Awd, 93; TTU Tchg Acad, 98. **MEMBERSHIPS** AASC; Col Eng Asn; Tennyson Res Soc; Browning Inst; Conf Christianity & Lit. **RESEARCH** Victorian lit; Milton studies; Christianity and lit. **SELECTED PUBLICATIONS** Auth, The temptations in Paradise Regained, Tex Studies Lang & Lit, spring 67; Johnson's Rasselas and The Vanity of Human Wishes, Christianity & Lit, fall 70; The phases of passion in Tennyson's Maud, SCent Mod Lang Asn Studies, winter 70; Prophetic imagination and the unity of Jane Eyre, Studies Novel, summer 74; John Ruskin and the doctrine of imperfection, Restoration Rev, 10/76; Assessing a new general studies master's program, Tex Tech J Educ, summer 78; Milton on ministry, Restoration Quart, Vol 22, 79; Literacy and belief, Lit & Belief, 1/81; Interdisciplinary study in the fine arts, Jour Aesthetic Educ, 82; Tennyson's The Hesperides and Milton, Victorian Inst Jour, 87; Trollope's satire, Stud in Novel, 87; A new letter from Matthew Arnold, Victorian Prose, 89; Cordelia and the rhetoric of righteousness, Lit and Belief, 91; Graduate Education in the South, 91. **CONTACT ADDRESS** College of Arts & Sciences, Texas Tech Univ, Lubbock, TX 79409-1030. **EMAIL** tom.langford@ttu,edu

LANGIULLI, NINO FRANCIS
PERSONAL Born 10/09/1932, Brooklyn, NY, m, 1959, 3 children **DISCIPLINE** PHILOSOPHY, ENGLISH **EDUCATION** Maryknoll Col, AB, 55; Hunter Col, MA, 60; NYork Univ, MA, 65, PhD(philos), 73. **CAREER** Instr English, St Augustine's High Sch, Brooklyn, 57-60; instr theol, 61-65, asst prof philos, 66-71, assoc prof, 72-76, Prof Philos, St Francis Col, NY, 76-, Danforth Assoc, 66-72. **HONORS AND AWARDS** Fulbright 60-61; Sears Roebuck Teaching Exc, 91; assoc ed, Measure, 89-96; book rev ed, Telos, 98. **MEMBERSHIPS** The Metaphysics Soc; Nat Asn of Scholars. **RESEARCH** Contemporary philosophy; history of philosophy; metaphysics. **SELECTED PUBLICATIONS** Auth, Machiavelli, In: Shakespeare Encycl, Crowell, 66; ed & translr, Critical Existentialism, 69 & ed, The Existentialist Tradition, 71, Doubleday; translr, Existentialism, In: Encycl Britannica, Univ Chicago, 73; Possibility, Necessity, and Existence, Temple, 92; European Existentialism, Transaction, 97; auth, Beauty: " The Qualities of the Beheld and the Eye of the Beholder, "Awer, Arts Quart, W of Sp, 00; auth, "Liberal Education: What to Resist," Academic Questions Summer, 00. **CONTACT ADDRESS** 32 Farnum St, Lynbrook, NY 11563.

LANGLEY, STEPHEN G.
PERSONAL Born 12/25/1938, Gardner, MA **DISCIPLINE** THEATRE, SPEECH **EDUCATION** Emerson Col, BA, 60, MA, 61; Univ Ill, Urbana, PhD, 65. **CAREER** Lectr speech, 63-65, from instr to assoc prof, 65-76, bus mgr, Theatre Div, 66, gem mgr, Ctr Performing Arts, 68-75, prof theatre, Brooklyn Col, 76-, dir div Performing Arts Mgt, 75-, grad dept chp, Theatre Dept, 78-. **MEMBERSHIPS** Dramatists Guild; Am Theatre Asn. **RESEARCH** Puritanism and the American drama; performing arts administration. **SELECTED PUBLICATIONS** Auth, Theatre management in America: Principle and practice, and producers on producing, Drama Bk Specialists, 73, rev ed, 80. **CONTACT ADDRESS** Performing Arts Ctr, Brooklyn Col, CUNY, 2901 Bedford Ave, Brooklyn, NY 11210-2813.

LANGSTRAAT, LISA R.
DISCIPLINE ENGLISH LITERATURE **EDUCATION** Purdue Univ, PhD, 96. **CAREER** Asst prof, Univ So Miss. **RESEARCH** Rhetoric and composition; cultural studies; feminist theory. **SELECTED PUBLICATIONS** Auth, pubs in Rhetoric and Composition, Composition Forum, and Works and Days. **CONTACT ADDRESS** Dept of English, Univ of So Mississippi, Box 5037, Hattiesburg, MS 39406-5037. **EMAIL** lisa.langstraat@usm.edu

LANHAM, RICHARD ALAN
PERSONAL Born 04/26/1936, Washington, DC, m, 1957 **DISCIPLINE** ENGLISH **EDUCATION** Yale Univ, AB, 56, MA, 60, PhD(English), 63. **CAREER** From instr to asst prof, Dartmouth Col, 62-65; from asst prof to assoc prof, 65-71, Prof English, Univ Calif Los Angeles, 71-; Prof Emeritus, 94-; Dir Writing Prog, 79-86; Sr fel, Nat Endowment for Humanities, 73-74; Sr Fel, Soc for the Humanities, Cornell Univ, 84; Guggenheim Fel, 87-88; Norman Freehling Vis Prof, Inst for the Humanities, Univ of Mich, 94; Int Scholar, George Eastman House, Rochester, NY, 94; Andrew W. Mellon Prof, Tulane Univ, 95; Pres, Rhetorica, inc., 82-. **MEMBERSHIPS** MLA. **RESEARCH** Medieval and Renaissance Literature; Rhetoric; Higher Education in America; Electronic Text. **SELECTED PUBLICATIONS** Auth, "Sidney's Old Arcadia," Yale Univ Press, 65; auth, "A Handlist of Rhetorical Terms," Univ of Calif Press, 68, 2nd ed 92; auth, "Tristram Shandy: The Games of Pleasure," Univ of Calif Press, 73; auth, "Style: An Anti-Textbook," Yale Univ Press, 74; auth, "The Motives of Eloquence: Literary Rhetoric in the Renaissance," Yale Univ Press, 76; auth, "Revising Prose," Allyn & Bacon, 4th ed, 00; auth, "Revising Business Prose," Allyn & Bacon, 4th ed, 00; auth, "Analyzing Prose," Scribner's, 86; auth, "Literacy and the Survival of Humanism," Yale Univ Press, 83; auth, "The Electronic Word: Democracy, Technology and the Arts," Univ of Chicago Press, 93. **CONTACT ADDRESS** 927 Bluegrass Lane, Los Angeles, CA 90049. **EMAIL** lanham@ucla.edu

LANIER, DOUGLAS M.
DISCIPLINE ENGLISH **EDUCATION** Stetson Univ, BA, 77; Duke Univ, MA, 80; PhD, 87. **CAREER** Instr, Duke Univ, 84-85; vis lectr, UCLA, 86-87; asst prof, Allegheny Col, 87-90; asst prof to assoc prof to dir grad studies, Univ NHam, 90-. **HONORS AND AWARDS** NEH Fel, 91; Gustafson Fac Fel, 92; Teaching Excellence Awd, 00; Folger Fel, 01. **MEMBERSHIPS** MLA; RSA; SAA; NEMLA; Malone Soc. **RESEARCH** Shakespeare and early modern drama; film; cultural studies and cultural theory. **SELECTED PUBLICATIONS** Auth, "Stigmatical in Making: The Material Character of the Comedy of Errors," ELR 23 (93): 81-112; auth, "Reading Milton, Reading Jonson, Reading Shakespeare," in Reading and Writing in Shakespeare, ed. David Bergeron (Univ Del, 95): 220-50; auth, "Drowning the Book: Prospero's Books and the Textual Shakespeare, in Shakespeare, Theory and Performance, ed. James Bulman (96): 187-209; auth, "Fertile Visions: Jacobean Revels and the Erotics of Occasion," SEL 39 (99): 327-56; auth, "The Idea of a John Barrymore," Colby Quart 37 (01): 31-54; "Art thou base, common and popular?: Cultural Politics of Branagh's Hamlet," in Spectacular Shakespeare, eds. Lisa

Starks, Courtney Lehmann (Fairleigh Dick Pr, 01). **CONTACT ADDRESS** English Dept, Univ of New Hampshire, Durham, Durham, NH 03824. **EMAIL** doug.lanier@unh.edu

LANIER, PARKS
PERSONAL Born, GA **DISCIPLINE** BRITISH ROMANTICISM, APPALACHIAN STUDIES **EDUCATION** Pfeiffer Col, AB; Univ TN Knoxville, MA, PhD. **CAREER** Prof, Radford Univ. **SELECTED PUBLICATIONS** Ed, Poetics of Appalachian Space. **CONTACT ADDRESS** Radford Univ, Radford, VA 24142. **EMAIL** planier@runet.edu

LANKEWISH, VINCENT A.
DISCIPLINE ENGLISH **EDUCATION** NYork Univ, BA, 84; Merton Col, Oxford, MPhil, 86; Rutgers Univ, New Brunswick, PhD, 97. **CAREER** Asst Prof Eng, PA State Univ, Univ Park, 98-. **CONTACT ADDRESS** English Dept, Pennsylvania State Univ, Univ Park, Burrowes Bldg, University Park, PA 16802-6200. **EMAIL** val4@psu.edu

LANOUETTE, WILLIAM JOHN
PERSONAL Born 09/14/1940, New Haven, CT, m, 1969, 2 children **DISCIPLINE** ENGLISH LITERATURE **EDUCATION** Fordham Col, AB, 63; London Sch of Econ, MSc, 66, PhD, 73. **CAREER** Res and reporter, Newsweek, 61-64; professional staff mem and legis asst, Res and Tech Prog Subcomt, US House of Representatives, 67-68; staff writer, The Nat Observ, Dow Jones & Co, 69-70, 72-77; staff correspondent and contrib ed, Nat Jour, 77-83; comm dir and sr assoc, World Resources Inst, 83-85; auth, Genius in the Shadows: A Biography of Leo Szilard, The man Behind the Bomb, 86-89; Wash correspondent, Bull of the Atomic Sci, 89-90; sr eval, Energy and Sci Issues, US General Acctg Office, 91-. **HONORS AND AWARDS** Guest scholar, Woodrow Wilson Intl Ctr for Scholars, Smithsonian Inst, 89; fel, John F. Kennedy Sch of Govt, Harvard Univ, 88-89; Forum award, 74. **RESEARCH** Interactions of science and politics, especially relating to the military and civilian applications of atomic energy; The rise and corruption of professional rowing in 19th Century America. **SELECTED PUBLICATIONS** Auth, Leo Szilard: A Comic and Cosmic Wit, Leo Szilard Centenary Volume, Eotvos Physical Soc, Budapest, 98; auth, Why We Dropped the Bomb, Civilization, Mag of the Libr of Congress, Jan/Feb, 95; auth, Reporting on Risk: Who Decides What's News?, Risk: Health, Safety & Environment, Quart, Franklin Pierce Law Ctr, vol 5, no 3, Summer, 94; auth, Genius in the Shadows: A Biography of Leo Szilard, The Man Behind the Bomb, Charles Scribner's Sons, 92, Univ Chicago Press, 94. **CONTACT ADDRESS** 326 Fifth St. SE, Washington, DC 20003. **EMAIL** lanouettew.rced@gao.gov

LAPP, ROBERT KEITH
PERSONAL Born 12/10/1956, Toronto, ON, Canada, m, 1985, 2 children **DISCIPLINE** ENGLISH LITERATURE **EDUCATION** Univ Toronto, BA, 78; MA, 85; Dalhousie Univ, PhD, 97. **CAREER** Asst prof, Mt Allison Univ, 97-. **HONORS AND AWARDS** Fel, Soc Sci and Humanities Res Coun of Can, 92-94; Crake Found Res Awd, 01. **MEMBERSHIPS** MLA, NASSR, RSVP, ACCUTE. **RESEARCH** 19th Century Periodicals, Literature of the 1830's, Romantic Historicisism, Information theory. **SELECTED PUBLICATIONS** Auth, Contest for Cultural Authority: Hazlitt, Coleridge and the Distresses of the Regency, Wayne State Univ Pr, 99. **CONTACT ADDRESS** Dept English, Mount Allison Univ, Sackville, NB, Canada E4L 1G9. **EMAIL** rlapp@mtu.ca

LARDINOIS, ANDRE P. M. H.
PERSONAL Born 06/14/1961, Watford, England **DISCIPLINE** CLASSICS **EDUCATION** Free Univ, Neth, BA, 84; MA, 88; Princeton Univ, MA, 91; PhD, 95. **CAREER** Asst prof, Univ Minn, Twin Cities. **RESEARCH** Archaic Greek poetry; greek tragedy; greek and roman mythology. **SELECTED PUBLICATIONS** Auth, Lesbian Sappho and Sappho of Lesbos, in J N Bremmer, ed, From Sappho to de Sade: Moments in the History of Sexuality, London-NY, 89; Greek Myths for Athenian Rituals: Religion and Politics in Aeschylus' Eumenidesand Sophocles' Oedipus Coloneus, GRBS 33/4, 92; Subject and Circumstance in Sappho's Poetry, TAPA 124, 94; Who Sang Sappho's Songs?, in E Greene, ed, Reading Sappho: Contemporary Approaches, Berkeley, 96; Modern Paroemiology and the Use of Gnomai in Homer's Iliad, CP 92, 97; coauth, Tragic Ambiguity: Anthropology, Philosophy and Sophocles' Antigone, Leiden, 87; coedit, Making Silence Speak: Women's Voices in Greek Literature and Society, Princeton Univ Press, 01. **CONTACT ADDRESS** Dept of Class and Near Eastern Studies, Univ of Minnesota, Twin Cities, 9 Pleasant St. SE, 330 Folwell Hall, Minneapolis, MN 55455-0125. **EMAIL** lardi001@tc.umn.edu

LARES, JAMEELA
PERSONAL Born 06/03/1950, Glendale, CA, s **DISCIPLINE** ENGLISH **EDUCATION** Cal State Univ, BA, 80; Univ Calif at Los Angeles, MA, 87; Univ So Cal, PhD, 94. **CAREER** Asst prof, Azusa Pac Univ, 94-95; asst prof, Univ S Miss, 95-99; assoc prof, 99-. **HONORS AND AWARDS** Lucas Endow, Fac Excel; Williams Andrew Clark Mem Lib Fel; All Univ Fel; Univ Calif, Los Angeles, Fel; Phi Beta Kappa res Mentor Awd. **MEMBERSHIPS** Milton Soc Am; Intl Milton Symp; Intl John Bunyan Soc; John Donne Soc; MLA; ISHR; ASHR; CSSR; CBHS; Beatrix Potter Soc. **RESEARCH** Milton' seventeenth century literature; history of rhetoric; preaching and biblical style; children's literature. **SELECTED PUBLICATIONS** Auth, "The Duchess of Malfi and Catherine of Valois," Notes and Queries 40 (93): 208- 211; auth, "Christian Knights and the Rhetoric of Religious Controversy, 1500-1800," in Rhetoric in the Vortex of Cultural Studies, ed. Arthur Walzer (Minneapolis: Burgess, 93), 131-38; auth, "Chaucer's Retractions: A ' Verray Parfit Penitence,' " Cithara 34 (94): 18-33; auth, "Biblical Metaphor and the Development of Prose Style," Can Jo Rhet Stud 7 (96): 83-93; auth, "Paradise Lost, XI and XII and the Homiletic Tradition," Milton Stud 34 (96): 99-116; auth, "Milton and the 'Office of a Pulpit,"' Ben Jonson J 3 (96): 109-126; auth, "Classical and Christian Conflicts in Keckennann's De rhetoricae ecclesiasticae utilitate," Adv the Hist Rhet 3 (1998): 57-66; auth, " "William Ames" and "Matthew Sutcliffe"," in British Rhetoricians, 1500-1660, Dictionary of Literary Biography, ed. Edward Malone (forthcoming); auth, Milton and the Preaching Arts, Duq Univ Press, (forthcoming). **CONTACT ADDRESS** Dept English, Univ of So Mississippi, PO Box 5037, Hattiesburg, MS 39406. **EMAIL** jlares@ocean.otr.usm.edu

LAROCHE, ROLAND ARTHUR
PERSONAL Born 03/04/1943, Berlin, NH, m, 1965, 3 children **DISCIPLINE** CLASSICS **EDUCATION** Boston Col, BA, 65; Tufts Univ, MA, 66, PhD(classics), 72. **CAREER** Teacher French, Latin and Greek, Pingree Sch, S Hamilton, Mass, 66-70; asst prof classics, State Univ NY, Potsdam, 70-77; teacher Latin and French, Cheshire Acad, Conn, 77-81; Teacher Latin and Greek and Chmn, Foreign Lang Dept, Albany Acad, 81-. **MEMBERSHIPS** Am Class League; Class Asn Atlantic States. **RESEARCH** Greek and Roman numerical practices; Livy; early Roman historiography. **SELECTED PUBLICATIONS** Auth, Popular Symbolic-Mystical Numbers in Antiquity, Latomus, Vol 0054, 95; Number Symbolism, Latomus, Vol 0055, 96. **CONTACT ADDRESS** Albany Acad, Albany, NY 12210.

LARSON, CHARLES RAYMOND
PERSONAL Born 01/14/1938, Sioux City, IA, m, 1971, 2 children **DISCIPLINE** LITERATURE **EDUCATION** Univ Colo, BA, 59, MA, 61; Ind Univ, PhD, 70. **CAREER** Tchr, 62-64, US Peace Corps, Oraukwu, Nigeria; instr, 65-67, Am Univ; lectr, 67-70, Ind Univ; assoc prof, 70-74, prof, 74-, Am Univ; gen ed, Collier Bks African-Am Libr, 68-; prin juror, English-Speaking Union Lit Award for Third World Writers, 72-; ; fiction & bk rev ed, 96-, Worldview. **HONORS AND AWARDS** Fulbright lectr, Africa, 72; Younger Humanist fel, NEH, 74-; Guggenheim fel, 76-77; individual res fel, NEH, 85-86. **MEMBERSHIPS** African Lit Asn, African Skies Library Foundation, 99-. **RESEARCH** African literature, Third World fiction, American Indian fiction. **SELECTED PUBLICATIONS** Auth, The Emergency of African Fiction, Indiana Univ Pr, 72; auth, The Novel in the Third World, Inscape, 76; auth, Academia Nuts, Bobb-Merrill, 77; auth, The Insect Colony, Holt, Rinehart, 78; auth, American Indian Fiction, Univ of New Mexico Pr, 78; auth, Arthur Dimmesdale, A & W Publ, 82; co-ed, Worlds of Fiction, Macmillan, 93; auth, Invisible Darkness: Jean Toomer and Nella Larsen, Univ Iowa Press, 93; auth, Under African Skies: Modern African Stories, FSG & Payback, 97; auth, The Ordeal of the African Writer, Zed Books, 01. **CONTACT ADDRESS** American Univ, Washington, DC 20016. **EMAIL** clarson@american.edu

LARSON, DAVID MITCHELL
PERSONAL Born 10/21/1944, Marshall, MN, m, 1967, 1 child **DISCIPLINE** AMERICAN & BRITISH LITERATURE **EDUCATION** Univ Minn, Morris, BA, 66; Univ Minn, Minneapolis, MA, 69, PhD, 73. **CAREER** Asst prof English, Franklin & Marshall Col, 71-75; asst prof Eng, Cleveland State Univ, 75-79; Assoc Prof, Eng, Cleveland State Univ, 79-. **MEMBERSHIPS** AAUP; CSA. **RESEARCH** Early American literature, especially writers of the later eighteenth century; contemporary science fiction. **SELECTED PUBLICATIONS** Art, Eighteenth Century Tales Of Sheep's Tails And One of Benjamin Franklin's American jokes, Philol Quart, spring 80; art, Thematic structure and conventions in science fiction, The Sphinx, 81; art, Behevolent Persuaasion: the Art of Benjamin Franklin's Philanthropic Papaers, PMHB, CX, 86; art, Benjamin Franklin's touth, His Biographers, and the Autobiography, PMHB CXIX, 95 **CONTACT ADDRESS** Dept of English, Cleveland State Univ, 1983 E 24th St, Cleveland, OH 44115-2440. **EMAIL** d.larson@csaohio.edu

LARSON, DORAN
DISCIPLINE FICTION WRITING **EDUCATION** Univ CA at Santa Cruz, BA; SUNY at Buffalo, MA, PhD. **CAREER** Asst prof; taught at, SUNY Buffalo, Univ Paris & Univ WI Madison and Richland campuses. **HONORS AND AWARDS** Over 10 grants & awd(s) for tchg excellence, tchg develop & fiction writing. **SELECTED PUBLICATIONS** Auth, 2 novels, Bantam, 85 & Permanent, 97; articles in, Mod Lang Stud, AR Quart, Cinema J; stories in, IA Rev, Boulevard, Va Quart Rev, Other Voices. **CONTACT ADDRESS** Col of Fine Arts and Hum, Univ of Texas, San Antonio, 6900 N Loop 1604 W, San Antonio, TX 78249. **EMAIL** dlarson@lonestar.utsa.edu

LARSON, GEORGE S.
PERSONAL Born 07/28/1939, Willmar, MN, m, 1971 **DISCIPLINE** ENGLISH **EDUCATION** Augsburg Col, BA, 61; Duke Univ, MA, 62; Univ Mass, PhD, 69. **CAREER** Instr to asst prof to assoc prof to prof, Concordia Col, 62-. **HONORS AND AWARDS** Woodrow Wilson Fel, 61-62; Nat Defense Edu Act Fel, 66-68. **MEMBERSHIPS** MLA; NCTE; Dickens Soc. **RESEARCH** Charles Dickens; music; literature. **SELECTED PUBLICATIONS** Auth of several critical essays in Minn English J. **CONTACT ADDRESS** English Dept, Concordia Col, Minnesota, Moorehead, MN 56562-0001.

LARSON, ORVILLE K.
PERSONAL Born 03/07/1914, Chicago, IL, m, 1946, 4 children **DISCIPLINE** DRAMA **EDUCATION** Univ Wis, BS, 41; Western Reserve Univ, MA, 42; Univ Ill, PhD(speech), 56. **CAREER** Instr speech and theatre, Univ Md, 46-49; instr speech and drama, Univ Conn, 51-56; asst prof speech, Mich State Univ, 56-59; assoc prof fine arts, Ohio Univ, 59-61; assoc prof speech and theatre and head div theatre, Univ Mass, 61-65; prof speech and theatre and chmn dept, Univ Bridgeport, 65-67; Prof Speech and Theatre, Kent State Univ, 69-. **MEMBERSHIPS** Am Soc Theatre Res; Am Theatre Asn; Col Art Asn Am; Speech Commun Asn. **RESEARCH** Stage machinery and spectacle in the theatre of the Renaissance; history of theatrical art in 20th century American theatre; relationship between art and theatre of the Renaissance. **SELECTED PUBLICATIONS** Auth, The James Adams Floating Theater, Theatre Survey, Vol 0033, 92; The Simple Stage, its Origins in the Modern American Theater, Theatre Survey, Vol 0035, 94. **CONTACT ADDRESS** Theatre Div Dept of Speech, Kent State Univ, Kent, OH 44242.

LARSON, RICHARD LESLIE
PERSONAL Born 01/19/1929, Stevens Point, WI, m, 1962 **DISCIPLINE** ENGLISH **EDUCATION** Harvard Univ, AB, 49, AM, 50, PhD(English), 63. **CAREER** Instr, Harvard Univ, Grad Sch Bus Admin, 56-59, lectr, 59-63; from asst prof to prof English, Univ Hawaii, 63-73; assoc dean educ, 73-75, actg dean, 75-78, dean, 78, Prof Educ, Lehman Col, 73-, Dean Prof Studies, 78-, Compiler ann bibliog on teaching of compos, Col Compos and Commun, 75-78. **MEMBERSHIPS** NCTE; Nat Conf Res English; MLA; Conf Col Compos and Commun; Speech Commun Asn. **RESEARCH** Rhetoric; teacher education in English; evaluation of teaching in English composition. **SELECTED PUBLICATIONS** Auth, Rhetorical Guide to the Borzoi College Reader, Knopf, 67; Discovery through questioning: a plan for teaching rhetorical invention, Col English, 11/68; Toward a linear rhetoric of the essay, Com Compos and Commun, 5/71; The evaluation of teaching: College English, MLA, 71; Process or product: the evaluation of teaching or the evaluation of learning, Bull Asn Depts English, 12/72; ed, Children and Writing in the Elementary School: Theories and Techniques, Oxford Univ, 75; auth, Structure and form in nonfiction prose, in: Teaching Composition: Ten Bibliographical Essays, Tex Christian Univ, 76. **CONTACT ADDRESS** 30 Greenridge Ave Apt 5-M White, Plains, NY 10605.

LARSSON, DONALD
PERSONAL Born 01/25/1949, Presque Isle, ME, m, 1975, 1 child **DISCIPLINE** ENGLISH **EDUCATION** George Washington Univ, BA, 71; Univ Wisc Madison, MA, 74; PhD, 80. **CAREER** TA, Univ of Wis Madison, 75-80; adj asst prof, Univ of Wis Eau Claire, 80-81; asst prof to prof, Minn State Univ, 81-. **HONORS AND AWARDS** NEH Fel, 81, 89, 95; Fac Res Grant, Mankato State Univ, 90; Teaching Scholar Fel, Mankato State Univ, 97. **MEMBERSHIPS** MLA; Midwest MLA; Soc for Cinema Studies; Soc for the Study of Narrative Lit; Nat Assoc for Humanities Educ; NCTE. **RESEARCH** Film theory and criticism, literary theory and criticism, Thomas Pynchon, issues in higher education, interdisciplinary humanities. **SELECTED PUBLICATIONS** Auth, "The Camera Eye: Cinematic Narration in U.S.A. and Gravity's Rainbow", Idea of Order in Literature and Film, ed Peter Ruppert, Fla State Univ Pr, (80): 94-105; auth, "The Formal Structure of Red River and the Hawksian Woman", Heritage of the Great Plains 13 (80): 1-7; auth, "Novel into Film: Some Preliminary Reconsiderations", Transformations in Literature and Film, ed Leon Golden, Fla State Univ Pr, (83): 69-83; auth, "Stella Dallas and American Motherhood, 1923-1937", Proceedings of the 6th annual Purdue Conf on film, Purdue Univ Pr, (83): 63-69; auth, "Caught in the Crossfire: The Interweaving of Identifications in a film noir", Proceedings of the 6th annual Purdue Conf on Film, Purdue Univ Pr, (83): 273-278; auth, "From the Berkshires to the Brocken: Transformations of a Source in the Secret Integration and Gravity's Rainbow", Pynchon Notes, (90): 87-98; auth, "a History of a Dream: A Tribute to Djibril Diop Mambety, Orange Light (June-July 99). **CONTACT ADDRESS** Dept English, Minnesota State Univ, Mankato, PO Box 8400, Mankato, MN 56002-8400. **EMAIL** donald.larsson@mankato.msus.edu

LARY, NIKITA
PERSONAL Born 07/06/1940, Washington, DC **DISCIPLINE** ENGLISH **EDUCATION** Haverford Col, BA, 60; Cambridge Univ, BA, 63; Univ Sussex, DPhil, 69. **CAREER** Asst prof to assoc prof, York Univ, 69-; vis assoc prof, Univ

Victoria, 81-82. **HONORS AND AWARDS** Stipend, SSHRCC, 88-89; Res Grant, SSHRCC, 93-96. **RESEARCH** Soviet film of the twenties and thirties. **SELECTED PUBLICATIONS** Auth, "Russian Film," in Russia and the Arts, Cambridge Univ Press, 99. **CONTACT ADDRESS** Dept English, York Univ, 4700 Keele St, 208 Stong Col, Toronto, ON, Canada M3J 1P3. **EMAIL** nlary@yorku.ca

LASARENKO, JANE
DISCIPLINE ENGLISH **EDUCATION** SUNY, Binghamton, BA, 72, MA, 74; OH State Univ, Columbus, PhD, 88. **CAREER** Asst prof, WTX A & M Univ, 91- & St Anselm Col, Manchester, 88-91; tchg asst, OH State Univ, Columbus, 84-88. **HONORS AND AWARDS** Dir, Writing-Across-the-Curric Prog, Webmistress, Slippery Rock Univ, 91-96; ed, TX Voices, TX Coun Tchr(s) Engl newsl, WTAMU, 95-97; Webmistress, dept Engl and Mod Lang, WTAMU; taught 1st univ completely online crse in, 96, WTAMU. **SELECTED PUBLICATIONS** Auth, Wired for Learning, Que Corp, 97; Teaching Literature in Cyberspace, Chapter for Integrating Information Technology Tools in Instruction, Microsoft Corp CD-ROM, 97; Collaborative Strategies in A Networked Classroom, Tchg in The Commun Col Elec J 1 3, 96; So, You Wanna MOO, Kairos 1 2, 96; Prowling Around, Kairos 1 1, 96; Computers and Writing: A Student's Perspective, Epiphany Guidebk, The Epiphany Gp, 96; Teaching Plagiarism, Paraphrase, and Summary: A Computer-Based Integrated Approach, The Exercise Exch 41 2, 96; The Red Scream: A Mystery Lover's Dream, Bk(s) in Tex, 96; Under The Beetle's Cellar, Bk(s) in Tex, 96; Horseshoe Sky, Women in Libr 25 1, 95; From Invitation to Experience: A Narrative of (Dis)Engagement, Midwest Quarterly 36 1, 94; coauth, Traveling the Virtual Terrain: Practical Strategies for Survival in the Electronic Classroom, The Online Classroom, Hampton Press, 98; Publishing on The World Wide Web: A Call for Standards and Guidelines, Kairos 1 3, 96. **CONTACT ADDRESS** Dept of Eng, Slippery Rock Univ of Pennsylvania, 102 Maltby Center, Slippery Rock, PA 16057.

LASS, NORMAN J.
PERSONAL Born 09/20/1943, New York, NY, m, 1967, 2 children **DISCIPLINE** SPEECH PATHOLOGY, AUDIOLOGY **EDUCATION** Brooklyn Col, BA, 65; Purdue Univ, MS, 66; PhD, 68. **CAREER** Post-doctoral res fel, Univ Kans Medical Ctr Bureau of Child Res, 68-69; from asst prof to prof, W Va Univ, 69-; chemn of Dept of Speech Pathology and Audiology, W Va, Univ, 74-83. **HONORS AND AWARDS** Outstanding Teacher Awd, W Va Univ, 70-71 & 72-73; Exxon Educ Found Awd, W Va Univ, 72-73; Outstanding Teacher of 1987-1988 in the Dept of Speech Pathology and Audiology Awd, W Va Univ Chapter of the Nat Student Speech-Language-Hearing Asn; Outstanding Teacher Awd, W Va Univ Col of Human Resources and Educ, 89-90; Outstanding Teaching Awd, W Va Univ Found, 90-91; Most Outstanding Prof Awd, W Va Univ Panhellenic Coun, 93; Golden Apple Awd for Outstanding Teaching, W VA Univ Chapter of Golden Key Nat Honor Soc, 98-99. **MEMBERSHIPS** Am Speech-Language-Hearing Asn, Acoustical Soc of Am, Am Asn of Phonetic Sci, Int Soc of Phonetic Sci, W Va Speech-Language-Hearing Asn. **RESEARCH** Speech perception, speech production. **SELECTED PUBLICATIONS** Coauth, "Academic procrastination by speech-language pathology and audiology students," NSSLHA J 23 (96): 42-45; coauth, "Selecting a doctoral program in communication sciences and disorders," NSSLHA J 23 (96): 59-62; coauth, "The acoustic characteristics of American English," in Principles of Experimental Phonetics, ed. N. J. Lass (MO: Mosby, 96), 185-225; ed, Principles of Experimental Phonetics, Mosby (St. Louis, MO), 96; coauth, Fundamentals of Speech Science, Allyn & Bacon (Boston, MA), 99. **CONTACT ADDRESS** Dept Speech Pathology & Audiology, West Virginia Univ, Morgantown, 805 Allen Hall, Morgantown, WV 26506-6122. **EMAIL** nlass@wvu.edu

LASSLO, ANDREW
PERSONAL Born 08/24/1922, Mukacevo, Czechoslovakia, m, 1955, 1 child **DISCIPLINE** MEDICINAL CHEMISTRY AND LIBRARY SCIENCE **EDUCATION** Univ Il, MS, 48, PhD, 52, MSLS, 61. **CAREER** Res chemist, Monsanto Chemical Co, St. Louis, Mo, 52-54; asst prof, Emory Univ, Atlanta, Ga, 54-60; prof to emeritus prof, chair, dir, 60-, Univ Tn. **HONORS AND AWARDS** Fel, Univ Il, Chicago, 51-52; Americanism Medal, Daughters of the Amer Revolution, 76; Sigma Xi Excellence in Res Awd, Univ Tn, 89; Alumni Distinguished Svc Prof & Chairman, Univ Tn, 89-90; Beta Phi Mu; Rho Chi; Phi Lambda Sigma; Sigma Xi; awardee, res and training grants, Nat Inst of Health, 58-64, 66-72, 82-89, National Sci Found, 64-66, Geschickter Fund for Medical Res, 59-65, Gustavus and Louise Pfeiffer Res Found, 81-87. **MEMBERSHIPS** Fellow, Acad Pharm Res & Sci; Fellow, Amer Assoc Advan of Sci; Fellow, Amer Assoc of Pharm Scientists; Fellow, Amer Inst of Chemists; Sr. Member, Amer Chem Soc, Amer Life Member, Libr Assoc, Amer Pharm Assoc, Amer Soc for Pharm & Experimental Therapeutics. **RESEARCH** Science information & library resources. **SELECTED PUBLICATIONS** Ed, Blood Platelet Function and Medicinal Chemistry, 84; coauth, Inhibition of Thrombus Formation in Vivo by a Novel Antiplatelet Agent, Arterosclerosis, 90; art, Inhibition of Platelet Adhesion and Thrombus Formation on a Collagen-Coated Surface by Novel Carbamoylpiperidine Antiplatelet Agents, 92; auth, Research, Relevance and Reason, Res Commun in Psychol, Psych & Behavior, 94; auth, Travel at Your Own Risk - Reflections on Science, Research, and Education, PJD Publ, 98; auth, Molecules, Miracles and Medicine, Warren H. Green, 00. **CONTACT ADDRESS** 5479 Timmons Ave, Memphis, TN 38119. **EMAIL** alasslo.Memphis.24822@worldnet.att.net

LASSNER, PHYLLIS
PERSONAL Born 05/14/1936, New York, NY, m, 1972, 2 children **DISCIPLINE** GENDER STUDIES, WRITING **EDUCATION** Wayne State Univ, BA, 58; PhD, 83. **CAREER** Lectr, Univ of Mich, 80-93; sr lectr, Northwestern Univ, 93-. **HONORS AND AWARDS** Northwestern Univ Humanities Ctr Fel; Panhellenic Distinguished Teaching Awd. **MEMBERSHIPS** MLA, Modernist Studies Assoc, Soc for the Study of the Space Between 1914-1945. **RESEARCH** British women interwar and World War II writers, British women writers at the end of the Empire, Women's Writing of the Holocaust. **SELECTED PUBLICATIONS** Auth, Elizabeth Bowen, Macmillan, 90; auth, Elizabeth Bowen: A Study of the Short Fiction, GK Hall, 91; auth, British Women Writers of World War II, Macmillan, 98. **CONTACT ADDRESS** 2111 Orrington Ave, Evanston, IL 60201-2913. **EMAIL** phyllisl@northwestern.edu

LATEINER, DONALD
PERSONAL Born 06/01/1944, New Rochelle, NY, m, 1976, 2 children **DISCIPLINE** CLASSICAL STUDIES, ANCIENT HISTORY **EDUCATION** Univ Chicago, BA, 65; Cornell Univ, MA, 67; Stanford Univ, MA, 70, PhD(classics), 72. **CAREER** Lectr hist, San Francisco State Col, 68-69; acting asst prof classics, Stanford Univ, 71-72; asst prof class studies, Univ PA, 72-79; asst prof, 79-82, Assoc Prof Humanities-Classics, 82-85, prof, 85-92, JOHN WRIGHT PROF GREEK & HUMANITIES, OH WESLEYAN UNIV, 93-. **HONORS AND AWARDS** Am School of Classical Studies @ Athens, Seymour fel, 69-70; Center for Hellenic Studies, Washington, D.C., vis Sr Scholar, 99. **MEMBERSHIPS** Am Philol Asn; Am Asn Ancient Historians; Archaeol Inst Am; Friends Ancient Hist. **RESEARCH** Greek epic; nonverbal behaviors in ancient lit; Greek historiography; Latin elegy; Greek oratory. **SELECTED PUBLICATIONS** Auth, The Speech of Teutiaplus, Greek, Roman & Byzantine Studies, 75; Tissaphernes and the Phoenician fleet, Trans Am Philol Asn, 76; Obscenity in Catullus, Ramus, 77; No Laughing Matter: A Literary Tactic in Herodotus, Trans Am Philol Asn, 77; An Analysis of Lysias' Defense Speeches, Rivista Storica dell' Antichita, 81; The Historical Method of Herodotus, Toronto, 89; The Failure of the Ionian Revolt, Historia, 82; Mimetic Syntax: Metaphor from World Order, Am J of Philol, 90; Sardonic Smile, Nonverbal Behavior in Homeric Epic, Ann Arbor, 95; auth, "Abduction Marriage in Heliodorus' Aethiopica," GRBS (97). **CONTACT ADDRESS** Dept of Humanities-Classics, Ohio Wesleyan Univ, 61 S Sandusky St, Delaware, OH 43015-2398. **EMAIL** dglatein@cc.owu.edu

LATHAM, ANGELA
PERSONAL Born 06/11/1961, Corydon, IN, m, 1995, 1 child **DISCIPLINE** THEATRE, PERFORMANCE STUDIES **EDUCATION** Univ N Tex, MS, 85; Univ Ill Urbana-Champaign, PhD, 97. **CAREER** Instr, Univ N Tex, 85-87; instr, Richland Col, 86-87; grad instr, Univ Ill Urbana-Champaign, 94-96; prof & dir of theatre, Triton Col, 97-. **HONORS AND AWARDS** Cultural Values & Ethics Fel, 96-97; Outstanding Dissertation, Nat Commun Asn, 97. **MEMBERSHIPS** Nat Commun Asn, Am Theatre in Higher Educ. **RESEARCH** Women's History, Fashion History, Performance Studies, American Theatre History. **SELECTED PUBLICATIONS** Auth, Posing A Threat: Flappers, Chorus Girls and Other Brazen Performers of the American 1920s. **CONTACT ADDRESS** Dept Fine Arts, Triton Col, 2000 5th Ave, River Grove, IL 60171-1907. **EMAIL** alatham@triton.cc.il.us

LATHAM, SEAN
PERSONAL Born 12/31/1971, Colorado Springs, CO, m, 1995, 1 child **DISCIPLINE** ENGLISH LITERATURE **EDUCATION** Swarthmore Col, BA, 94; Brown Univ, AM, 96; PhD, 00. **CAREER** TA to asst prof, Brown Univ, 95-01; asst prof, Univ of Tulsa, 01-. **HONORS AND AWARDS** Phi Beta Kappa Fel, 94; Malcolm Forbes Ctr Res Fel, 98, 99; R and E Salomon diss Fel, 99; Joukowsky Awd, 00. **MEMBERSHIPS** MLA, Modernist Studies Assoc, Int James Joyce Found. **RESEARCH** Literary modernism, James Joyce, material culture, digital studies, cultural theory. **SELECTED PUBLICATIONS** Auth, "Jim Bond's America," Miss Quart, (98); auth, "Introduction to the New Age, Vol 1," Modernist Jour Project, ed Robert Scholes, (00); auth, "Culture Beyond the Coteries: the New Age and the New Modernisms," Jour of Mod Lit, (02); auth, "A Portrait of the Snob: James Joyce and the Anxieties of Cultural Capital," Mod Fiction Studies, (02). **CONTACT ADDRESS** Dept English, Univ of Tulsa, 600 S College Way, Tulsa, OK 74104. **EMAIL** sean_latham@brown.edu

LATIMER, DAN RAYMOND
PERSONAL Born 07/15/1944, San Angelo, TX, m, 1970, 1 child **DISCIPLINE** COMPARATIVE LITERATURE, ENGLISH STUDIES **EDUCATION** Univ Tex, Austin, BA, 66; Univ Mich, Ann Arbor, MA, 67, PhD(comp lit), 72. **CAREER** Asst prof, 72-78, assoc prof Eng, Auburn Univ, 78-; Res and Writing, 82-, Asst Ed, Southern Humanities Rev. **MEMBERSHIPS** MLA; Am Comp Lit Asn; Southern Comp Lit Asn. **RESEARCH** Symbolism; modern criticism; Goethe. **SELECTED PUBLICATIONS** Auth, Contemporary Critical Theory, 89; auth, "Oedipus in the South Seas: The Case of Herman Melvilles Typee," Essays in Lit, 94; auth, "Piracopuios Missing Finger: Schiler, Batarille, and the Fate of English Studies," The Comparatist, 98. **CONTACT ADDRESS** Dept of English, Auburn Univ, University, AL 36849.

LATOUSEK, ROB
PERSONAL Born 07/10/1956, Evanston, IL **DISCIPLINE** CLASSICS **EDUCATION** Holy Cross Col, BA, 78; Loyola Univ, Chicago, MA, 85. **CAREER** Univ Wisconsin, Madison, proj asst, 86-88, Centaur Systems Ltd, Pres, 84-. **HONORS AND AWARDS** HCC, Bean Scholarship, 74-78, Loyola Univ., Condon Fel, 82-84 **MEMBERSHIPS** APA, ACL, CAMS **RESEARCH** Classical computing **SELECTED PUBLICATIONS** Auth, Software Directory for the Classics, ACL, 93-95, Random Access, Classical Outlook, ACL, 89-, Survey of latin Instructional Software for the Microcomputer, ACL, 85-91, software pub, Tutrix, 88; Latin Vocab Drill, 87; Latin Flash Drill, 85; Centaur Sys Ltd. **CONTACT ADDRESS** Centaur Systems Ltd, 407 North Brearly St, Madison, WI 53703-1603. **EMAIL** Latousek@centaursystems.com

LATTA, KIMBERLY
DISCIPLINE SEVENTEENTH-CENTURY BRITISH LITERATURE **EDUCATION** Rutgers Univ, PhD. **CAREER** Asst prof, St. Louis Univ. **SELECTED PUBLICATIONS** Auth, Such is My Bond: Maternal and Paternal Debt in Anne Bradstreet, Univ KY Press. **CONTACT ADDRESS** Dept of English, Saint Louis Univ, 221 N Grand Blvd, Saint Louis, MO 63103. **EMAIL** lattak@slu.edu

LATTA, SUSAN M.
DISCIPLINE ENGLISH LITERATURE AND LINGUISTICS **EDUCATION** Ind State Univ, BA, MA; Purdue Univ, PhD. **CAREER** Dir, wrtg prog; asst prof, 96-. **RESEARCH** Participatory action research and computer assisted instruction. **SELECTED PUBLICATIONS** Pub(s), essays on mass media in the classroom, student self-assessment, and critical research methodologies. **CONTACT ADDRESS** Dept of Eng, Univ of Detroit Mercy, 4001 W McNichols Rd, PO BOX 19900, Detroit, MI 48219-0900. **EMAIL** LATTAS7@udmercy.edu

LATTIMORE, STEVEN
PERSONAL Born 05/25/1938, Bryn Mawr, PA **DISCIPLINE** CLASSICS, CLASSICAL ARCHEOLOGY **EDUCATION** Dartmouth Col, AB, 60; Princeton Univ, MA, 64, PhD(class archaeol), 68. **CAREER** Instr class archaeol, Dartmouth Col, 64; instr Greek, Haverford Col, 65-66; asst prof classics and class archaeol, Intercol Ctr Class Studies, Rome, 66-67; asst prof, 67-74, Assoc Prof Classics, Univ Calif, Los Angeles, 74-, Guggenheim Found fel, 75-76. **MEMBERSHIPS** Archaeol Inst Am; Am Philol Asn. **RESEARCH** Classical sculpture; Greek literature; mythology. **SELECTED PUBLICATIONS** Auth, The bronze apoxyomenos from Ephesos, Am J Archaeol, 72; Battus in Theocritus' fourth Idyll, Greek, Roman & Byzantine Studies, 73; A Greek pediment on a Roman temple, Am J Archaeol, 74; The Marine Thiasos in Greek Sculpture, Archaeol Inst Am, 76. **CONTACT ADDRESS** Dept of Classics, Univ of California, Los Angeles, Los Angeles, CA 90024.

LAUBACH, DAVID C.
PERSONAL Born 04/24/1939, Danville, PA, m, 1969, 2 children **DISCIPLINE** ENGLISH **EDUCATION** Univ Mass, EdD, 85. **CAREER** Dir of Lang Arts, Westfield, 84-85; dir of Lang Arts, Colonial Schs, 85-87; assoc prof, Kutztown Univ, 87-. **HONORS AND AWARDS** Fulbright, Eng, 69-70; Nat Endowment for Humanities Grant, 84-85. **MEMBERSHIPS** NCTE, MLA. **RESEARCH** Faulkner, folklore, teaching of literature. **SELECTED PUBLICATIONS** Auth, Growing Up Amish, Univ Eds, 97; auth, Introduction to Folklore, Harcourt Brace, 97. **CONTACT ADDRESS** Dept English, Kutztown Univ of Pennsylvania, Kutztown, PA 19530.

LAUBENTHAL, PENNE J.
PERSONAL Born 08/02/1944, Athens, AL, s, 1961, 2 children **DISCIPLINE** ENGLISH; SPEECH; CONFLICT MANAGEMENT; BIBLIOTHERAPY **EDUCATION** Athens Col, Ala, BA, 65, MAT, 68; George Peabody Col, PhD(English), 72. **CAREER** Tutor & instr, 65-68, from asst prof to assoc prof, 68-72, Prof English, Athens Col, ALA, 72-, Chairperson Humanities Dept, 80-. **HONORS AND AWARDS** Outstanding Commitment to Teaching, 91; NEH Fel, 80, 88, 97. **MEMBERSHIPS** MLA; AAUP; SAtlantic Mod Lang Asn; Speech Commun Asn. **RESEARCH** Modern drama; comparative literature **SELECTED PUBLICATIONS** Auth, A Humanist Looks at the Mind-Body Connection, J Med Asn Ga, 11/94; Biography of C. Eric Lincoln, In: A Bibliographical Guide to Alabama Literature; author of poetry published in Poet magazine and Elk River Review; reviews published in Myhtosphere and J Poetry Therapy; auth, "The Gathering" in Chocolate for a Woman's Blessing edited by Kay Allenbaugh (Simon and Shuster, 00); auth, "Midlife Crisis," in Fabulous After Fifty by Shirley Mitchell (New Leaf Press, 00). **CONTACT ADDRESS** Dept of English, Athens State Univ, 300 N Beaty St, Athens, AL 35611-1999. **EMAIL** laubepj@athens.edu

LAUDON, ROBERT TALLANT
PERSONAL Born 12/30/1920, St. Paul, MN **DISCIPLINE** MUSICOLOGY AND MUSIC **EDUCATION** Univ Minn, BA, 47, MA, 50; Univ Ill, PhD, 69. **CAREER** Assoc Prof, Jamestown Col, 52-55; Asst Prof, St Cloud State Col, 55-62; Prof, Univ Minn, 62-86, Prof Emeritus, 86- . **HONORS AND AWARDS** BA magna cum laude, Phi Beta Kappa; Pi Kappa Phi; Pi Kappa Lambda; Phi Mu Alpha Sinfonia. **MEMBERSHIPS** Am Musicol Soc; Minn Mus Tchr Assoc; Nat Mus Tchr Assn; Minn Hist Soc. **RESEARCH** 19th-century symphony; Minn music and musicians. **SELECTED PUBLICATIONS** Symphonic Genres, Current Musicol, 78; Sources of the Wagnerian Synthesis, Munich, 79; Eduard Sobolewski, Frontier Kapellmeister, Mus Quart, 89; Visual Image and Couperin's Harpsichord Music, Alexander L Ringer Festschrift, 91; Debate about Consecutive Fifths, A Context for Brahm's Manuscript, Music and Letters, 92; auth, Minnesota Music Teachers Association; auth, The Profession and the Community, 1901-2000, St. Paul, 00. **CONTACT ADDRESS** 924-18th Ave SE, Minneapolis, MN 55414. **EMAIL** laudo001@tc.umn.edu

LAUDUN, JOHN
DISCIPLINE FOLKLORE, LITERATURE **EDUCATION** La State Univ, BA, 86; Syracuse Univ, MA, 89; Ind Univ, PhD, 99. **CAREER** Asst prof, Univ of La Lafayette, 99-. **HONORS AND AWARDS** Jacob K Javitz Fel, 87-92; Delmore Schwartz Prize for Poetry, 89; MacArthur Scholar, 92-93. **MEMBERSHIPS** Am Folklore Soc, La Folklore Soc, MLA, Soc for Ling Anthrop. **RESEARCH** Material folk culture, folk life, folk art, verbal art. **SELECTED PUBLICATIONS** Auth, "Talking Shit in Reyne", La Folklore (99); auth, "The Poetrics of Vernacular Spaces," S Folklore 57.2 (00); auth, Louisiana Gumbos, forthcoming. **CONTACT ADDRESS** Dept English, Univ of Louisiana, Lafayette, Box 44691, Lafayette, LA 70504-0001. **EMAIL** laudun@louisiana, edu

LAUER, JANICE M.
PERSONAL Born Detroit, MI **DISCIPLINE** RHETORIC, LINGUISTICS **EDUCATION** Marygrove Col, BA, 54; St Louis Univ, MA, 61; Univ Mich, EdD(English rhetoric), 67. **CAREER** Prof English, Marygrove Col, 62-; Dir Writing Prof English, Univ Detroit, 72-, Bd dirs, Rhetoric Soc Am, 78-78; dir writing, Cranbrook Writers Conf, 76-. **MEMBERSHIPS** Rhetoric Soc Am; Conf Col Compos and Commun; NCTE. **RESEARCH** Heuristics; creative process; rhetoric. **SELECTED PUBLICATIONS CONTACT ADDRESS** Dept of English, Univ of Detroit Mercy, Detroit, MI 48221.

LAUINGER, JOSEPH
PERSONAL Born 04/26/1947, Philadelphia, PA, m, 1970, 1 child **DISCIPLINE** LITERATURE **EDUCATION** Univ Pa, BA, 68; Oxford Univ, BA, 70, MA, 75; Princeton Univ, MA, 72, PhD, 74. **CAREER** Asst prof, Vassar Col, 73-74; asst prof to prof, Mercer Col, 74-96; prof, Sarah Lawrence Col, 88-. **HONORS AND AWARDS** NEH grant, 75; New York State Teachers Excellence Awd, 84. **MEMBERSHIPS** Dramatists Guild, AAUP. **RESEARCH** Dramatic literature: medieval, Roman, ancient Greek. **CONTACT ADDRESS** Dept Gen Lit, Sarah Lawrence Col, 1 Meadway, Bronxville, NY 10708-5931. **EMAIL** jlauin@mail.slc.edu

LAURENT, DIANNA V.
PERSONAL Born 10/16/1955, Topeka, KS, d, 1 child **DISCIPLINE** ENGLISH **EDUCATION** Southeastern La Univ, BA, 77; MA, 80; Univ Miss, PhD, 93. **CAREER** Instr, Southeastern La Univ; dir of training, Fla Parishes Soc Sci Res Ctr. **MEMBERSHIPS** MLA. **RESEARCH** Research methodology. **SELECTED PUBLICATIONS** Auth, Net Quest: Exploring Zoology, William C. Brown Pub, 97; auth, Internet Research Methodologies for the Social Sciences, Sage Pub, forthcoming. **CONTACT ADDRESS** Dept English, Southeastern Louisiana Univ, 500 Western Ave, Hammond, LA 70402-0001. **EMAIL** dlaurent@selu.edu

LAUTERBACH, CHARLES EVERETT
PERSONAL Born 03/08/1934, Denver, CO, m, 1962 **DISCIPLINE** DRAMA **EDUCATION** Univ Colo, BA, 56, MA, 61; Mich State Univ, PhD(Theatre), 66. **CAREER** Instr Drama, Univ Colo, 61; asst instr, Mich State Univ, 63-64; asst prof, Cent Wash State Col, 64-66 & Univ Calif, Riverside, 66-71; prof Theatre, Boise State Univ, 71-. **MEMBERSHIPS** Am Theatre Asn; Am Soc Theater Res. **RESEARCH** The drama of Thornton Wilder; trends in dramatic styles in American drama of the 1920's; 19th century American theatre history. **CONTACT ADDRESS** Dept of Theatre, Boise State Univ, 1910 University Dr, Boise, ID 83725-0399. **EMAIL** clauter@micron.net

LAUZEN, MARTHA M.
DISCIPLINE GENDER AND MASS COMMUNICATION **EDUCATION** Univ IA, BA, MA; Univ MD, PhD. **CAREER** Comm, San Diego St Univ. **MEMBERSHIPS** Mem, ICA, Women in Film. **RESEARCH** Women in television and film. **SELECTED PUBLICATIONS** Auth, numerous articles on Women in television, Jour of Broadcasting and Electronic Media, Jour of Commun Inquiry, Mass Commun and Society and issues mgt and pub rel(s), Jour Pub Rel(s) Res; Mgt Commun Quart; Jour Quart. **CONTACT ADDRESS** San Diego State Univ, School of Commun, 5500 Campanile Dr, San Diego, CA 92182. **EMAIL** comments@sdsu.edu

LAVALLEY, ALBERT J.
PERSONAL Born 07/08/1935, Springfield, MA **DISCIPLINE** FILM STUDIES **EDUCATION** Yale Univ, English, PhD, 61. **CAREER** Fac, Yale Univ; fac, San Francisco State Univ; fac, Rutgers Univ; fac, Univ CA Santa Barbara; chr film studies, Dartmouth Col, 84-95; prof. **HONORS AND AWARDS** Founder, Limelight film and theatre bookstore. **RESEARCH** Billy Wilder and Fritz Lang. **SELECTED PUBLICATIONS** Co-ed, Eisentein at 100, Rutgers Univ Press, 01. **CONTACT ADDRESS** Dartmouth Col, 3529 N Main St, #207, Hanover, NH 03755. **EMAIL** allavalley@dartmouth.edu

LAVASSEUR, DAVID G.
PERSONAL Born 02/23/1966, Baltimore, MD, s **DISCIPLINE** COMMUNICATION STUDIES **EDUCATION** Univ Md, BA, 88; Univ Md, MA, speech and comm, 90; Univ Kans, PhD, comm studies, 94. **CAREER** Asst prof, Villanova Univ, 94-97; asst prof, West Chester Univ, 97-. **HONORS AND AWARDS** Phi Beta Kappa Top Academic Jr Awd, 87; Nat Speakers' An Scholarship Recipient, 90-91; Excellence in Teahcng Awd, Univ of Kansas, 92; Outstanding Communication Prof award, Nat Speakers Asn, 98; Univ Development Awd for New Faculty, 98. **MEMBERSHIPS** Nat Comm Asn. **RESEARCH** Public policy communication. **SELECTED PUBLICATIONS** Auth, A defense of questions in rhetorical criticism, National Forensic Journal, 7, (89): 151-158; auth, Justice and the balance, In Principles and types of speech communication, 11th ed., Glenview, Il: Scott, Foresman/Little, Brown Higher Education, 90; auth, Edifying arguments and perspective by incongruity: The perplexing argumentation method of Kenneth Burke, Argumentation and Advocacy, 29, (93): 195-203; auth, The use of evidence in presidential debates: What level and type of evidence maximize a candidate's effectiveness? Argumentation and Advocacy 32, (96): 129-142; auth, The Dole humor myth and the risks of recontextualizing rhetoric, Southern Journal of Communication, 62, (96): 56-72; auth, A reconsideration of Edmund Burke's rhetorical art: A rhetorical struggle between purdence and heroism, Quarterly Journal of Speech, 83, (97): 332-350; auth, Accounting for Dol's humor in the 1976 vice presidential debate: A response to Gurner, Soutehrn Journal of Communication, 64, (97):243-247; auth, Understanding audience elaboration, IN L.W. Hugenberg & B.S. Moyer, eds., Teaching ideas for the basic communication course, New York: Kendall/Hunt, (99): 29-39; auth, How juries hear hearsay evidence, Court Call, (99): 1-3; auth, The rhetorical constructions of economic policy: Political judgment and the 1995 budget debate, Rehtoric and Public Afairs, 3, (00)183-209. **CONTACT ADDRESS** Dept. of Communication Studies, West Chester Univ of Pennsylvania, West Chester, PA 19383. **EMAIL** dlevasseur@wcopa.edu

LAVEZZO, KATHY
DISCIPLINE ENGLISH **EDUCATION** Univ Calif-Santa Barbara, PhD, 99. **CAREER** Asst prof English, Univ Iowa, 99- . **HONORS AND AWARDS** Mayers fel, Huntington Libr. **MEMBERSHIPS** MLA; Soc Medieval Fem Schol; New Chaucer Soc; Medieval Acad. **RESEARCH** Medieval literature and culture, Nationalism, Sex/gender system, Cultural geography. **SELECTED PUBLICATIONS** Auth, "Sobs and Sighs Between Women: the Humuertics of Compassion in the book of Margery Kenpe," Premodern Sexualities, Routledge, (96); auth, "Another Country:____ and the Production of English Identity," New Medieval Lit, pp 67-93, (99). **CONTACT ADDRESS** Dept English, Univ Iowa, 308 English Philosophy Bld, Iowa City, IA 52242-1408. **EMAIL** Kathy-Lavezzo@uiowa.edu

LAW, JULES
DISCIPLINE ENGLISH **EDUCATION** Johns Hopkins Univ, PhD. **CAREER** Assoc Prof, Northwestern Univ. **HONORS AND AWARDS** ACLS Fel, 86. **SELECTED PUBLICATIONS** Auth, The Rhetoric of Empiricism from Locke to I. A. Richards, 93; articles on, James Joyce; George Eliot; Derrida; Wittgenstein Hardy. **CONTACT ADDRESS** Dept of English, Northwestern Univ, 1897 Sheridan, Evanston, IL 60208.

LAW, RICHARD
PERSONAL Born 04/04/1933, Philadelphia, PA, m, 1955, 5 children **DISCIPLINE** ENGLISH LITERATURE **EDUCATION** W Chester Univ, BSEd, 58; Lehigh Univ, MA, 62; Temple Univ, PhD, 74. **CAREER** Asst prof to prof, Kutztown Univ, 62-91; assoc prof, Albernia Col, 96-. **HONORS AND AWARDS** Commonwealth of Pa Distinguished Teaching Chair, 76. **MEMBERSHIPS** Col English Assoc; Mid-Atlantic Am/Popular Culture Assoc. **RESEARCH** Related Arts Critical Theory. **SELECTED PUBLICATIONS** Coauth, Starmont Guide to Suzy McKee Charnas, Joan Vinge, and Octavia Butler, 86; auth, "The Heroic Ethos in Dryden's Heroic Plays" Studies in English Lit, 82; auth, "The Proslogion and St. Anselm's Audience", Selected Papers from the Centennial Celebration of St. Anselm's Col, 91. **CONTACT ADDRESS** Dept Humanities, Alvernia Col, 400 St Bernadine St, Reading, PA 19607-1737.

LAW, RICHARD G.
PERSONAL Born 04/05/1943, Fairbury, NE, m, 1968, 4 children **DISCIPLINE** MODERN AMERICAN LITERATURE **EDUCATION** Wash Univ, PhD. **CAREER** Prof & dir Gen Educ, Wash State Univ. **MEMBERSHIPS** Golden Key honorary, 95; Phi Kappa Phi, 93; Nat Defense Education Act, Title IV Fel, 66-69; Woodrow Wilson Fel, 65-66; Phi Beta Kappa, 64; Phi Eta Sigma, 62. **RESEARCH** Literature of the American South; General Eduation Reform. **SELECTED PUBLICATIONS** Contrib ed, Time's Glory: Original Essays on Robert Penn Warren, 86. **CONTACT ADDRESS** Dept of English, Washington State Univ, 1 SE Stadium Way, PO Box 645020, Pullman, WA 99164-5020. **EMAIL** rlaw@wsu.edu

LAWALL, GILBERT WESTCOTT
PERSONAL Born 09/22/1936, Detroit, MI, m, 1957, 2 children **DISCIPLINE** CLASSICS **EDUCATION** Oberlin Col, AB, 57; Yale Univ, PhD, 61. **CAREER** Instr classics, Yale Univ, 61-63 & 64-65, jr fel, Ctr Hellenic Studies, 63-64; asst prof classics, Amherst Col, 65-67; from asst prof to assoc prof, 67-72, Prof Classics, Univ MA, Amherst, 72-. **HONORS AND AWARDS** Barlow-Beach Awd Distinguished Serv, Class Asn New England, 79; Oustanding contrib For Lang Educ, Class Asn Empire State, 79. **MEMBERSHIPS** Am Philol Asn; Class Asn New Eng (vpres, 72-73, secy-treas, 80-87); Vergilian Soc; Archaeol Inst Am; Am Class League (pres, 76-80). **RESEARCH** Hellenistic Greek poetry; Senecan tragedy; Catullus; Horace; Latin pedagogy. **SELECTED PUBLICATIONS** Auth, Theocritus' Coan Pastorals: A Poetry Book, Ctr Hellenic Studies, 67; The Phaedra of Seneca: Latin Text and Study Materials, Bolchazy-Carducci Publ, 81; Petronius: Selections from the Satyricon: Introduction, Notes, and Vocabulary by Gilbert Lawall, Bolchazy-Carducci Pubs, 3rd rev ed, 95; Plautus' Menaechmi: ed with Introduction and Running Vocabularies by Gilbert Lawall and Betty Nye Quinn, Bolchazy-Carducci Pubs, Chicago, 81; Euripides Hippolytus: A Companion and Translation by Gilbert and Sarah Lawall, Bristol Classical Press, 86; ed and coauth, Cicero's Somnium Scipionis: The Dream of Scipio, Sally Davis and Gilbert Lawall, Prentice Hall, 88; The Aulularia of Plautus: The Pot of Gold, Gilbert Lawall and Betty Nye Quinn, Prentice Hall, 88; ed, The Romans Speak for Themselves: Books I and II, Prentice Hall, 89, rev ed, 95; coauth, Maurice Balme and Gilbert Lawall, Athenaze: An Introduction to Ancient Greek, Book I, NY: Oxford Univ Press, 90, Book II, NY: Oxford Univ Press, 91; coauth rev, Fabulae Graecae: A Revised Edition of Richie's Fabulae Faciles, ed by Gilbert Lawall, Stanley Iverson, and Allen Wooley, Prentice Hall, 91; coauth rev and ed with David Perry, Fabulae Romanae: Stories of Famous Romans, Prentice Hall, 93; chief rev ed, Ecce Romani: A Latin Reading Program, 3rd ed, Prentice Hall, 00; auth, Love and Betrayal: A Catullus Reader by Bruce Arnold, Andrew Aronson, and Gilbert Lawall, Prentice Hall, 00. **CONTACT ADDRESS** Dept of Classics, Univ of Massachusetts, Amherst, Amherst, MA 01003-3905. **EMAIL** glawall@classics.umass.edu

LAWLER, TRAUGOTT
PERSONAL Born 03/08/1937, Nyack, NY, m, 1958, 4 children **DISCIPLINE** ENGLISH **EDUCATION** Col Holy Cross, AB, 58; Univ Wis, MA, 62; Harvard Univ, PhD(English), 66. **CAREER** From instr to asst prof English, Yale Univ, 66-72; from assoc prof to prof, Northwestern Univ, Evanston, 72-81; Prof English, Yale Univ, 81-, Am Coun Learned Sic fel, 77-78. **HONORS AND AWARDS** Guggenheim Fel, 83-84. **MEMBERSHIPS** Medieval Acad Am; Soc Study Medieval Lang and Lit. **RESEARCH** Old and middle English; medieval Latin; Chaucer; Langland. **SELECTED PUBLICATIONS** Ed & transl, The Parisiana Poetria of John of Garland, 74; auth, The One and the Many in the Canterbury Tales, 80; coed and cotransl, Jankyns Book of Wikked Wyves, 97. **CONTACT ADDRESS** Dept of English, Yale Univ, P O Box 208302, New Haven, CT 06520-8302. **EMAIL** traugott.lawler@yale.edu

LAWRENCE, ELIZABETH ATWOOD
PERSONAL Born 10/01/1929, Boston, MA, m, 1957, 2 children **DISCIPLINE** ENGLISH **EDUCATION** Mt Holyoke Col, BA, 51; Univ Pa, Sch of Vet Med, VMD, 56; Brown Univ, MA, 76, PhD, 79. **CAREER** Vet med practice, 56-80; full-time fac mem, Tufts Univ, Sch of Vet Med, 81-; prof, dept of environ & population health, Tufts Univ Sch of Vet Med. **HONORS AND AWARDS** James Mooney award, Southern Anthrop Soc; Woman Vet of the Yr award, Asn for Women Vet; Intl Distinguished Scholar award, Intl Asn of Human-Animal interactions Orgn. **MEMBERSHIPS** Amer Vet Med Asn; Amer Anthrop Asn; Amer Vet Hist Soc. **RESEARCH** Human relationships with animals and nature; Human-animal continuity; Animal symbolism. **SELECTED PUBLICATIONS** Auth, A Woman Veterinary Students in the 50s: The View from the Millennium, Anthrozoos, vol 10, no 4, 97; auth, Human and Horse Medicine Among Some Native America Groups, Agr and Human Values, Jun, 98; auth, Cultural Perceptions of Differences Between People and Animals: A Key to Understanding Human-Animal Relationships, Jour of Amer Culture, vol 18, no 3, 95; auth, Love For Animals and the Veterinary Profession, Jour of the Amer Vet Med Asn, vol 205, no 7, 94; auth, Seeing in Nature What Is Ours: The Human-Animal Bond in Poetry, Jour of Amer Culture, vol 17, no 4, 94; auth, Conflicting Ideologies: Views of Animal Rights Advocates and Their Opponents, Soc and Ani-

mals, vol 2, no 2, 94; auth, Euthanasia and the Human-Equine Bond, Equine Practice, vol 15, no 10, 93; auth, A Seventh Cavalry Veterinarian, Custer, and Rain-in-the-Face: The Story Behind A Legend, Jour of the West, vol 32, no 2, 93. **CONTACT ADDRESS** PO Box 35, Adamsville, RI 02801.

LAWRENCE, KATHLEEN
DISCIPLINE COMMUNICATOIN STUDIES **EDUCATION** Boston Col, BA, 80; Univ Ind, MA; 84, PhD. **CAREER** Assoc prof. **SELECTED PUBLICATIONS** Auth, pubs on intercultural, rhetorical, and health communication. **CONTACT ADDRESS** Dept of Communication, SUNY, Col at Cortland, PO Box 2000, Cortland, NY 13045-0900. **EMAIL** lawrencek@cortland.edu

LAWRENCE, SAMUEL G.
DISCIPLINE INTERPERSONAL AND INTERCULTURAL COMMUNICATION **EDUCATION** PhD. **CAREER** Univ Albany - SUNY **SELECTED PUBLICATIONS** Auth, Normalizing stigmatized practices: Achieving co-membership by 'doing being ordinary, Res Lang & Soc Interaction, 96. **CONTACT ADDRESS** SUNY, Albany, 1400 Washington Ave, Albany, NY 12222.

LAWRENCE, SEAN
PERSONAL Born 10/27/1971, Moose Factory, ON, Canada, m, 1996 **DISCIPLINE** ENGLISH **EDUCATION** Univ King's Col, BA, 93; Dalhousie Univ, MA, 94; Univ BC, PhD, 01. **CAREER** Instr, Simon Fraser Univ, 96-98; lectr, Univ BC, 00-. **HONORS AND AWARDS** Gilean Douglas Awd; James W. Tupper Grad Fel. **MEMBERSHIPS** Renaissance Soc of Am; Shakespeare Asn of Am; soc Francaise Shakespeare; Asn of Can Col and Univ Teachers of English; Pac NW Renaissance Soc; Can Soc for Hermeneutics and Postmodern Thought. **RESEARCH** Shakespeare; Renaissance Literature; Ethics; Continental Philosophy. **SELECTED PUBLICATIONS** Auth, "As a Stranger Give it Welcome: Alterity and Ethics in Hamlet and the New Historicism," Europ J of English Studies, (00): 155-169. **CONTACT ADDRESS** Dept English, Univ of British Columbia, 397-1873 E Mall, Vancouver, BC, Canada V6T 1Z1. **EMAIL** seanlawrence@writeme.com

LAWSON, LEWIS ALLEN
PERSONAL Born 11/13/1931, Bristol, TN, m, 1957, 2 children **DISCIPLINE** ENGLISH **EDUCATION** ETenn State Col, BS, 57, MA, 59; Univ Wis, PhD(English), 64. **CAREER** From instr to assoc prof, 63-71, prof Eng, Univ MD, Col Park, 72-, Fulbright prof English, Univ Copenhagen, 71-72. **MEMBERSHIPS** Soc Study Southern Lit; SAtlantic Mod Lang Asn. **RESEARCH** Southern and American literature. **SELECTED PUBLICATIONS** Auth, The Art and Mind of Flannery O'Connor, 66; auth, Kierkegaard's Presence in Contemporary American Life, Scarecrow, 71; auth, Conversions with Walker Persy, Mississippi, 85; auth, More Conversations with Walker Percy, Mississippi, 93; auth, Walker Percy and His Feminine Characters, 95; auth, Another Generation, Mississippi, 84; auth, Wheeler's Last Raid, Penkevill, 86; auth, Following Percy, Whitson, 88; auth, Still Following Percy, Whitson, 96. **CONTACT ADDRESS** Dept of English, Univ of Maryland, Col Park, College Park, MD 20742-0001. **EMAIL** ll5@umail.umd.edu

LAY, MARY M.
DISCIPLINE RHETORIC STUDIES **EDUCATION** Univ NMex, MA, PhD. **CAREER** Prof **RESEARCH** Gender and communication; reproductive technologies; feminist theory and rhetoric of science and technology. **SELECTED PUBLICATIONS** Co-auth, The Rhetoric of Midwifery: Conflicts and Conversations in the Minnesota Home Birth Community in the 1990s, Quarterly J Speech, 96; The Emergence of the Feminine Voice, 1526-1640: The Earliest Published Books by English Renaissance Women, J Advanced Composition, 95. **CONTACT ADDRESS** Rhetoric Dept, Univ of Minnesota, Twin Cities, 64 Classroom Office Bldg, 1994 Buford Ave, Saint Paul, MN 55108. **EMAIL** mmlay@maroon.tc.umn.edu

LAYMAN, LEWIS M.
DISCIPLINE ENGLISH LITERATURE **EDUCATION** Middlebury Univ, BA; Univ Minn, MA; Univ British Columbia, PhD. **CAREER** Assoc prof **RESEARCH** William Faulkner. **SELECTED PUBLICATIONS** Auth, pub(s) on Whitman, Joyce and Faulkner. **CONTACT ADDRESS** Dept of English, Univ of Manitoba, Winnipeg, MB, Canada R3T 2N2.

LAYMAN, RICHARD
PERSONAL m, 1973, 2 children **DISCIPLINE** ENGLISH, AMERICAN LITERATURE, AMERICAN SOCIAL HISTORY **EDUCATION** Ind Univ, BA, 71; Univ Louisville, MA, 72; Univ SC, PhD, 75. **CAREER** Manly Inc, VPres, 83-; Bruccoli, Clark, Laymen, VPres, 76-. **SELECTED PUBLICATIONS** Numerous. **CONTACT ADDRESS** Bruccoli Clark Layman, Inc, 2006 Sumter St, Columbia, SC 29201. **EMAIL** rlayman@BCL-Manly.com

LAZAR, MOSHE
DISCIPLINE DRAMA AND COMPARATIVE LITERATURE **EDUCATION** Sorbonne, Paris, PhD. **CAREER** Prof, Univ Southern Calif; diplomado de Filologia Hispanica, Salamanca, Spain; res assoc, Ctr for Medieval and Renaissance Stud, UCLA. **RESEARCH** Spanish and Judeo-Spanish biblical and para-biblical texts. **SELECTED PUBLICATIONS** Auth, Provencal literature: Amour Courtois et Fin'Amors; Bernard de Ventadour; Lo Jutgamen General. **CONTACT ADDRESS** Col Letters, Arts & Sciences, Univ of So California, University Park Campus, Los Angeles, CA 90089. **EMAIL** lazar@.usc.edu

LAZAREVICH, GORDANA
PERSONAL Born Belgrade, Yugoslavia **DISCIPLINE** MUSIC **EDUCATION** Univ Toronto, Art & Lic dipl, 60; Juilliard Sch Music, BS, 62, MS, 64; Columbia Univ, PhD, 70. **CAREER** Instr, Barnard Col, 69-71; asst prof, 71-74, Columbia Univ; asst prof, 74-76, assoc prof, 76-83, Prof Musicology, Univ Victoria, 83-, dean grad stud, 92-97. **MEMBERSHIPS** Mem, SSHRC Adjudicating Ctte Art Hist; Soc 18th Century Studs; Can Asn Univs Schs Music; Can Univ Music Soc; Can Fedn Hum. **SELECTED PUBLICATIONS** Auth, Music in the Preclassic and Classic Era for the Schirmer History of Music, MacMillan, 83; auth, The Musical World of Frances James and Murray Adaskin, Univ of Toronto Press, 88; auth, The Musical World of Frances James and Murray Adaskin, 88. **CONTACT ADDRESS** Sch of Music, Univ of Victoria, PO Box 1700, Victoria, BC, Canada V8W 2Y2. **EMAIL** srsgs01@uvvm.uvic.ca

LAZARUS, CATHY LYNN
PERSONAL Born 07/30/1956, Chicago, IL **DISCIPLINE** SPEECH PATHOLOGY **EDUCATION** Northwestern Univ, PhD 97. **CAREER** Northwestern Univ, assoc dir, voice speech lang serv, 80 to 98-. **MEMBERSHIPS** ASHA; ISHA; CASLA; Dysphagia Res Soc. **RESEARCH** Swallowing disorders, head neck cancer patients; management of swallowing disorders. **SELECTED PUBLICATIONS** Swallow recovery in an oral cancer patient following surgery radiotherapy and hyperthermia , coauth, Head and Neck, 94;Effects of a sour bolus on oropharyngeal swallow measures in patients with neurogenic dysphagia, coauth, Jour of Speech and Hearing Research, 95; auth, Communication problems in individuals with head and neck cancer, in: L. Cherney ed, Topics in Geri Rehab, in press; coauth, Swallowing disorders in head neck patients treated with radiotherapy and adjuvant chemotherapy, 96; Comments on effects of cold touch and chemical stimulation of the anterior faucial pillar on human swallowing, ed, Dysphagia, 96; auth, Swallowing and tongue function following treatment for oral and oropharyngeal cancer, 00; auth, Manaagement of swallowing disorders in head and neck cancer patients: optimal patterns of care, 00; coauth, Journal of Speech-Language and Hearing Resarch, 1011-1023. **CONTACT ADDRESS** Medical Sch, Northwestern univ, 201 E Huron St, Suite 10-205, Chicago, IL 60611. **EMAIL** claz@northwestern.edu

LEACH, ELEANOR W.
DISCIPLINE CLASSICAL STUDIES **EDUCATION** Bryn Mawr Col, BA, 59; Yale Univ, PhD, 63. **CAREER** Prof, Ind Univ, Bloomington. **RESEARCH** Latin texts. **SELECTED PUBLICATIONS** Auth, Absence and Desire in Cicero's De Amicitia, CW, 93; Oecus on Ibycus: Investigating the Vocabulary of the Roman House, Oxbow, 97; auth, "Personal and Communal Time in the Reading of Horace's 'Odes,' Books 1-3," Arethusa (98). **CONTACT ADDRESS** Dept of Classical Studies, Indiana Univ, Bloomington, 1020 E Kirkwood Ave, 547 Ballantine Hall, Bloomington, IN 47405. **EMAIL** leach@indiana.edu

LEACH, JIM
DISCIPLINE COMMUNICATIONS **EDUCATION** Univ Exeter, BA; Univ Birmingham, MA, PhD. **CAREER** Prof, Brock Univ. **RESEARCH** Canadian cinema, European cinema, film theory, and cultural theory. **SELECTED PUBLICATIONS** Auth, A Possible Cinema: The Films of Alain Tanner, Scarecrow Press, 84; Everyone's an American now: Thatcherist Ideology in the Films of Nicolas Roeg, Fires Were Started: British Cinema and Thatcherism, Univ Minn Press, 93; North of Pittsburgh: Genre and National Cinema in the Canadian Context, Film Genre Reader, Univ Tex Press, 95; coauth, Understanding Movies, (Canadian Edition), Toronto: Prentice-Hall, 98; auth, Claude Jutra, Filmmaker, Montreal: McGill-Queen's Univ Press, 99. **CONTACT ADDRESS** Dept of Film Stud, Dramatic and Visual Arts, Brock Univ, 500 Glenridge Ave, Saint Catharines, ON, Canada L2S 3A1. **EMAIL** jimleach@spartan.ac.BrockU.CA

LEACH, JOSEPH
PERSONAL Born 05/02/1921, Weatherford, TX **DISCIPLINE** AMERICAN LITERATURE **EDUCATION** Southern Methodist Univ, AB, 42; Yale Univ, PhD, 48. **CAREER** Assoc prof, 47-55, Prof English, Univ Tex, El Paso, 55-, Head Dept, 60-. **MEMBERSHIPS** Am Folklore Soc; Rocky Mountain Mod Lang Asn; NCTE; Col Conf Compos and Commun; MLA. **RESEARCH** American cultural history. **SELECTED PUBLICATIONS** Auth, The typical Texan; Farewell to Horseback, Muleback, Footback and Prairie Schooner; Bright Particular Star, Yale Univ, 70. **CONTACT ADDRESS** Dept of English, Univ of Texas, El Paso, El Paso, TX 79968.

LEAHY, DAVID G.
DISCIPLINE CLASSICS **EDUCATION** St. Peter's Col, BA, 59; Fordham Univ, MA, 64. **CAREER** Lectr, Iona Col, 63-64; Assoc Prof, NY Univ, 64-72; Assoc Prof, C.W. Post Col LIU, 72-76; Mgt Consult, 76-89; Adj Assoc Prof, Brooklyn Col CUNY, 85-92; Vis Assoc Prof & Dir Undergrad Relig Studies, NY Univ, 91-98; Distinguished Vis Prof Philos, Loyola Col Md, 98-; Vis Assoc Prof, SUNY - Stony Brook, 95. **HONORS AND AWARDS** Scholarship to St. Peter's Col; Nat Oratorical Contest Col & Univ Scholarships; Scholarship to Fordham Univ; NYU Lindback Found Awd for Distinguished Teaching; **MEMBERSHIPS** Am Philos Asn; Soc Advancement Am Philos; Am Acad Relig. **SELECTED PUBLICATIONS** Auth, To Create The Absolute Edge, J Am Acad Relig, 89; The New Beginning: Beyond the Post-Modern Nothingness, J Am Acad Relig, 94; Novitas Mundi: Perception of the History of Being, SUNY Press, repr, 94; Foundation: Matter The Body Itself, SUNY Press, 96; The Golden Bowl Structure, Geodesic Math Links, Geodesic Designs, Inc, 96-98 (http://www.geod.com/main/geomath.htm) **CONTACT ADDRESS** 104 Yorkleigh Rd., Towson, MD 21204. **EMAIL** dgl@dgleahy.com

LEARS, T. J. JACKSON
PERSONAL Born 07/26/1947, Annapolis, MD, m, 1969, 1 child **DISCIPLINE** AMERICAN HISTORY & LITERATURE **EDUCATION** Univ Va, BA, 69; Univ NC, Chapel Hill, MA, 73; Yale Univ, PhD, 78. **CAREER** Instr Am studies, Yale Univ, 77-79; Asst Prof US Hist, Univ MO, Columbia, 79-; prof, Rutgers Univ. **MEMBERSHIPS** Am Studies Asn. **RESEARCH** American advertising; literary modernism; cultural impact of modernization. **SELECTED PUBLICATIONS** Auth, Making Fun of Popular Culture, Amer Hist Rev, 92. **CONTACT ADDRESS** Dept of Hist, Rutgers, The State Univ of New Jersey, New Brunswick, 16 Seminary Place, New Brunswick, NJ 08901. **EMAIL** tjlears@rci.rutgers.edu

LEAVELL, LINDA
DISCIPLINE LATE 19TH THROUGH CONTEMPORARY AMERICAN LITERATURE **EDUCATION** Rice Univ, PhD, 86. **CAREER** Engl, Okla St Univ; Rhodes Col, 85-86; Oklahoma State Univ, 01-. **HONORS AND AWARDS** SCMLA book award. **MEMBERSHIPS** SCMLA, MLA, MSA, Modernist Studies Asn. **RESEARCH** Marianne Moore, Biography, Literature and the visual arts. **SELECTED PUBLICATIONS** Auth, Marianne Moore and the Visual Arts: Prismatic Color, La State Univ Press, 95. **CONTACT ADDRESS** Oklahoma State Univ, Stillwater, 205 Morrill Hall, Stillwater, OK 74078. **EMAIL** leavell@okstate.edu

LEAVER, ROBIN A.
PERSONAL Born 05/12/1939, Aldershot, England, m, 1988 **DISCIPLINE** SACRED MUSIC **EDUCATION** Trinity Col, Theol Dip, Bristol, England; Rijksuniversiteit Groningen, Dtheol cum laude **CAREER** Pres, Intl Arbeitsgemeinschaft fur Hymnologie, 85-89; bd dir(s), Charles Wesley Soc, 89-; contrib ed, Jahrbuch fur Liturgik und Hymnologie, 76-; The Hymnology Annual, 89-; lectr, Taverner Choir and Players; Early Mus Ctr; Eng Bach Fest; The Gabrieli Consort; The Bach Choir Bethlehem; The Berkeley Fest; consult, Brit Broadcasting Corporation, Oxford UP; vis prof, Drew Univ, 88-. **HONORS AND AWARDS** Winston Churchill fel, 71; ed, Studies in Liturgical Musicol; co-editor, Drew Liturgical Studies; listed, contemp auth(s), dictionary of intl biog, who's who in the world, latimer house, oxford, 77-84; wycliffe hall, oxford, 84-85. **MEMBERSHIPS** Hon mem, Riemenschneider Bach Inst, 73; mem, Scholarly Adv Comm Kessler Reformation Coll, Emory University, 95-. **RESEARCH** Theory pedagogy and 19th-century theory. **SELECTED PUBLICATIONS** Auth, Bachs theologische Bibliothek, 83; J S Bach and Scripture, 85; The Theological Character of Music in Worship, 89; Goostly psalmes and spirituall songes: English and Dutch Metrical Psalters from Coverdale to Utenhove 1535-1566, 91; Come to the Feast: The Original and Translated Hymns of Martin H. Franzman, 94; co-auth, Liturgy and Music: Lifetime Learning, 98. **CONTACT ADDRESS** Sacred Music, Westminster Choir Col of Rider Univ, 101 Walnut Lane, Princeton, NJ 08540-3819. **EMAIL** Leaver@enigma.rider.edu

LEBARON, CURTIS D.
DISCIPLINE COMMUNCATION STUDIES **EDUCATION** Young Univ, BA, 89; Univ Utah, MA, 93; Univ Tex, PhD, 97. **CAREER** Asst prof. **HONORS AND AWARDS** Top Three Paper Awd; Orea B. Tanner Memorial Awd, 88. **MEMBERSHIPS** Int Commun Asn; Speech Commun Asn; Western States Commun Asn; Int Pragmatics Asn. **RESEARCH** Language and social interaction within institutional settings; multimedia analysis of communication processes; micro ethnography of communication; deceptive communication. **SELECTED PUBLICATIONS** Co-auth, Looking for Verbal Deception in Clarence Thomas's Testimony, Univ Ill, 96. **CONTACT ADDRESS** Dept of Communication, Univ of Colorado, Boulder, Boulder, CO 80309. **EMAIL** Curtis.Lebaron@Colorado.edu

LEBLANC, ALBERT
PERSONAL Born 09/18/1942, Baton Rouge, LA, m, 1971 **DISCIPLINE** MUSIC EDUCATION **EDUCATION** Univ Il-

linois, MS 69, PhD 75; Louisiana State Univ, B Mus Ed 65. **CAREER** Michigan state Univ, prof 76-; Cemrel Inc, eval specialist, 73-76; Thibodaux LA, HS band dir, 65-70. **HONORS AND AWARDS** Mus Educ Nat Conf Sr res awd. **MEMBERSHIPS** MENC; SAH. **RESEARCH** Music listening preferences; music performance anxiety. **SELECTED PUBLICATIONS** Auth, Effects of style tempo and performing medium on children's music preference, in: Music edu research: An anthology from the Jour of Research in Music edu, ed, Harry E Price, Reston VA, MENC, 98; Effect of audience on music performance anxiety, coauth, Jour of res in Music Edu, 97; rev of, Experiencing music technology: Software and Hardware, by David Brian Williams, Peter Richard Webster, Music Edu Jour, 97; Building theory in music education: A personal account, Philo of Music Edu Rev, 96; Music style preferences of different age listeners, Jour of Res in Music Edu, 96; rev of, Music matters: A new philosophy of music education, by David J. Elliott, Music Edu Jour, 96; Differing results in research on preferences for music tempo, Perceptual and Motor Skills, 95; A theory of music performance anxiety, Quart Jour of Music teaching and Learning, 94. **CONTACT ADDRESS** School of Music, Michigan State Univ, East Lansing, MI 48824-1043. **EMAIL** aleblanc@pilot.msu.edu

LEBOFSKY, DENNIS STANLEY
PERSONAL Born 10/28/1940, Philadelphia, PA, m, 1965, 5 children **DISCIPLINE** LINGUISTICS; ENGLISH **EDUCATION** Temple Univ, BA, 61; Princeton Univ, MA, 65, PhD(ling), 70. **CAREER** From Instr to Asst Prof, 65-84, Assoc Prof English, Temple Univ, 84-. **RESEARCH** Philadelphia English. **CONTACT ADDRESS** Dept of English, Temple Univ, 1114 W Berks St, Philadelphia, PA 19122-6029. **EMAIL** dlebofsk@nimbus.temple.edu

LECHE, EMMA JEAN GHEE
PERSONAL Born Mobile, AL **DISCIPLINE** COMMUNICATION; BUSINESS **EDUCATION** Howard Univ, PhD, 94. **CAREER** US Federal Government Wash DC, program and management, 78-94. **MEMBERSHIPS** AOM, ABC, NCA, SVHE. **RESEARCH** Industrial Chaplaincy. **SELECTED PUBLICATIONS** Auth, Industrial Chaplains as Change Agents and Ethics Officers, forthcoming. **CONTACT ADDRESS** Bon Wit Plaza, 2401 H St NW, #808, Washington, DC 20037-2541. **EMAIL** ejlisadove@aol.com

LEDERER, KATHERINE
PERSONAL Born Trinity, TX, 2 children **DISCIPLINE** ENGLISH **EDUCATION** Sam Houston State Univ, BA, 52; Univ Ark, MA, 58, PhD, 67. **CAREER** Teacher pub schs, Tex, 54-56; asst English, Univ Ark, 56-59, instr, 59-60; from instr to assoc prof, 60-68, Prof English, Southwest MO State Univ, 68-. **HONORS AND AWARDS** Governor's Humanities Awd, Missouri Humanities Council, 99; Univ Awd for Teaching, 99; SMSU Excellence in Community Service Awd, 99; Univ Awd for Service, 98; SMSU Foundation Excellence in Res Awd, 90. **MEMBERSHIPS** MO-RARE, St Louis, Missouri; Tony Morrison Soc; Col Lang Asn. **RESEARCH** Modern and comtemporary Am and British lit: African Am hist and lit. **SELECTED PUBLICATIONS** Auth, Lillian Hellman, G.K. Hall, 79, 90; auth, Many Thousand Gone, Missouri Committee for the Humanities, 86; auth, guest ed, Ozarks Watch, " African Ameicans of the Ozarks," 99. **CONTACT ADDRESS** Dept of English, Southwest Missouri State Univ, Springfield, 901 S National, Springfield, MO 65802. **EMAIL** kg1952f@mail.smsu.edu

LEE, ALVIN A.
PERSONAL Born 09/30/1930, Canada, w, 1957, 5 children **DISCIPLINE** ENGLISH **EDUCATION** Univ Toronto, BA, 53; Victoria Univ, MDiv, 57; Univ Toronto, MA, 58; PhD, 61. **CAREER** Teaching fel, Univ Toronto, 57-59; asst prof to assoc prof to prof to emer to asst dean to dean, McMaster Univ, 60-; gen ed, Col Wks Northrop Frye, 93-. **HONORS AND AWARDS** Sanford Div Gold Medal, 57; Can Coun Predoct and Sr Fel, 59; Hon Prof, Univ Sci Tech, Beijing, 81, Heilongjiang Univ, 86, Peking Univ, 93; Hon D Litt, 86, 93; Northrop Frye Medal, 96; Hamilton Gall Dist, 96; Pres Teaching Excellence Awd, McMaster Univ, 96. **MEMBERSHIPS** MLA; ACCUTE; Frye Centre. **RESEARCH** Old English poetry; Canadian poetry; English literature; Bible and literature; literary criticism; literary theory; life and writings of Northrop Frye. **SELECTED PUBLICATIONS** Co-auth, Uses of Imagination, 6 vols, Harcourt Brace, 72-74; auth, James Reaney, 68; auth, The Guest-Hall of Eden: Four Essays on the Design of Old English Poetry, Yale, 72; auth, Gold-Hall and Earth-Dragon: Beowulf as Metaphor, Toronto Univ Pr, 98; co-ed, NorthrUniv Pr Frye on Religion, Toronto Univ Pr, 00. **CONTACT ADDRESS** English Dept, McMaster Univ, 1280 Main St W, Hamilton, ON, Canada L8S 4L9. **EMAIL** alvinlee@mcmaster.ca

LEE, CHIN-CHUAN
PERSONAL Born 09/20/1946, m, 1792 **DISCIPLINE** MASS COMMUNICATION STUDIES **EDUCATION** Univ Hawaii, MA; Univ Mich, PhD. **CAREER** Prof; Founding Pres, Chinese Communication Assoc. **RESEARCH** Political Communication, Political Economy of the Media, Social Theories and Media Studies. **SELECTED PUBLICATIONS** Auth, Sparking a Fire: The Press and the Ferment of Democratic Change in Taiwan, J Monographs, 93; Media Imperialism Reconsidered, 80; co-auth, Hong Kong Journalists in Transition, 95; Mass Media and Political Transition: The Hong Kong Press in China's Orbit, 91; ed, China's Media, Media's China, 94; Voices of China: The Interplay of Politics and Journalism, 90; ed, Power, Money, and Media: Communication Patterns and Bureaucratic Control in Cultural China, 00. **CONTACT ADDRESS** Mass Communication Dept, Univ of Minnesota, Twin Cities, 111 Murphy Hall, 206 Church St SE, Minneapolis, MN 55455. **EMAIL** leexx010@umn.edu

LEE, DAVID
PERSONAL Born 08/13/1944, Matador, TX, m, 1971, 2 children **DISCIPLINE** 17TH AND 18TH CENTURY BRITISH LITERATURE **EDUCATION** Colorado State Univ, BA, 67; Idaho State Univ, MA, 70; Univ of Utah, PhD, 73. **CAREER** Prof of English, Dept Head, Southern Utah Univ, 71-. **HONORS AND AWARDS** Outstanding Educator, 74, 81 & 94; Prof of the Year, 96 and 00; Governor's Awd for Lifetime Achievement in the Arts; Poet Laureate, 97; Western States Book Awd, 96; Critic's Choice Awd, 96; Mountain and Plains States Bookseller's Awd, 97. **MEMBERSHIPS** Utah Acad of Arts and Sci; Rocky Mountain Modern Language Asn; Assoc Writing Programs. **RESEARCH** Modern poetry; Pound and the development of modern poetics. **SELECTED PUBLICATIONS** Auth, The Porcine Legacy, Copper Canyon Press; Driving and Drinking, Copper Canyon Press; The Porcine Canticles, Copper Canyon Press; Shadow Weaver, Brooding Heron Press; Paragonah Canyon Autumn, Brooding Heron Press; Wayburne Pig, Brooding Heron Press, The Fish, Wood Works Press; Day's Work, Copper Canyon Press; My Town, Copper Canyon Press. **CONTACT ADDRESS** Dept of Language and Lit, So Utah Univ, Ceder City, UT 84720. **EMAIL** leed@suu.edu

LEE, DOROTHY A. H.
PERSONAL Born 01/22/1925, Columbia, MO, w, 1950 **DISCIPLINE** ENGLISH **EDUCATION** Wayne State Univ, BA, 1945, MA, 1947; Radciiffe College, MA, 1948; Radcliffe College & Harvard Univ, PhD, 1955. **CAREER** Wayne State Univ, asst professor, 52-62; Henry Ford Comm College, instructor, 63-72; Univ of MI-Dearborn, professor, 72-93. **HONORS AND AWARDS** Univ of MI-Dearborn, Susan B Anthony Awd, 1985; Distinguished Teaching Awd, 1985; MI Assn of Governing Boards of Colleges & Universities, Distinguished Facility Awd, 1987; F Cousens Retired Person Awd, U of M-Dearborn, 1993. **SELECTED PUBLICATIONS** Essays published in Michigan Quarterly Review, Black Women Writers; Callaloo Black American Literary Forum; College Language Assn Journal; Journal of Spanish Studies-Twentieth Century; Critique; Modern Drama. **CONTACT ADDRESS** Professor Emeritus, Univ of Michigan, Dearborn, 4901 Evergreen Rd, Dearborn, MI 48128. **EMAIL** dahl@umich.edu

LEE, DOUGLAS
PERSONAL Born 11/03/1932, Carmel, CA, m, 1961 **DISCIPLINE** MUSIC, MUSICOLOGY **EDUCATION** DePauw Univ, BMus, 54; Univ Mich, MMus, 58 PhD, 68. **CAREER** Asst prof, Mt. Union Col, 59-61; Rackham Fel, Univ Mich, 61-63; Wichita State Univ, prof, chmn, musicol, 64-86; prof, chmn, musicol, Vanderbilt Univ, 86-98. **HONORS AND AWARDS** Rector Scholar, Depauw U, 50-54 Rackham Fel, Univ Mich, 61-63; Res grant, NEH, 79-80; Am Philosophical Soc, 80; res grants Wichita State Univ, Vanderbilt Univ; Kansas Arts Council; Tennessee Arts Commission; Outstanding Educators of Am, 75; Who's Who in Am; Int'l Dir of Music and Musicians; other biographical citations. **MEMBERSHIPS** Am Musicol Soc; Sonneck Soc for Am Music; Mus Teachers Nat Assoc; Am Soc for 18th Century Studies. **RESEARCH** Early classic 19th cent instrumental music; hist keyboard concerto; Am music 19th cent; Am Symphony Orchestra. **SELECTED PUBLICATIONS** A Musician at Court, 98; Christoph Nichelmann and the Free Fantasia, in CPE Bach Studies, 88; ed, 6 kb concertos for The C.P.E.Bach Edition (awaiting publication); articles in Groves Dictionary of Music and Musicians, 80; Groves Dictionary of Am Music, 84; ca 50 articles in Musical Quarterly; Sonneck Soc Bulletin; European Studies J; Studies in Biography. **CONTACT ADDRESS** Vanderbilt Univ, 2400 Blakemore Ave, Nashville, TN 37212. **EMAIL** douglas.lee@vanderbilt.edu

LEE, HELEN ELAINE
PERSONAL Born 03/13/1959, Detroit, MI, s, 1 child **DISCIPLINE** LITERATURE **EDUCATION** Harvard College, BA, 1981; Harvard Law School, JD, 1985. **CAREER** Various law-related and attorney jobs, 85-94; Univ of Mich, Dearborn, adjunct lecturer, 95; MA Institute of Technology, Assoc Prof, Writing & Humanistic Studies, currently. **HONORS AND AWARDS** American Library Assn, Black Caucus, First Novel Awd, 1994, 1995; DC Commission on the Arts and Humanities, $5,000 Grant-in-Aid Awd, 1991; Phi Beta Kappa. **RESEARCH** Prison **SELECTED PUBLICATIONS** Author, novel, The Serpent's Gift, Atheneum Publishers, 1994, London Headline Press, 1994; Marriage Bones, The African Diaspora in Short Fiction, ed; Charles Rowell Westview Press, 1995; Silences, The Best Short Stories by Black Writers vol II, ed, Gloria Naylor, Little, Brown and Co, 1995; novel Water Marked, Scirbner, 99. **CONTACT ADDRESS** Program in Writing and Humanistic Studies, Massachusetts Inst of Tech, Rm 14E-303, Cambridge, MA 02139-4307.

LEE, HSIAO-HUNG
PERSONAL Born 09/11/1953, Shanghai, China, m, 1979, 1 child **DISCIPLINE** ENGLISH LITERATURE; LIBRARY SCIENCE **EDUCATION** Shangai Tchrs Univ, BA, 76; Drew Univ, Mphil, 88 PhD, 90; Rutgers Univ, MLS, 91. **CAREER** Ref librn, Univ Central Ark, 91-95; asst prof, Troy State Univ, 96-. **HONORS AND AWARDS** Buckminster Fuller Scholar, 84-85; United Nations Scholar, 84-85; Drew Univ Full Scholar, 85-89. **MEMBERSHIPS** Ala Libr Asn; Am Libr Asn; Modern Language Asn. **RESEARCH** Victorian literature; uterary theory; information science. **SELECTED PUBLICATIONS** Auth, Chinese Herbal Medicine, Handbook of Popular Culture in China, Westport: Greenwood Press, 94; auth, The Possibilities of Hidden Things, Narrative Transgressions in Victorian Fictional Autobiographies, Peter Lang Publishing, 96. **CONTACT ADDRESS** 3663 N. Trainer Rd., Rockford, IL 61114. **EMAIL** ader1@rvc.cc.il.us

LEE, HUGH MING
PERSONAL Born 02/10/1945, Honolulu, HI **DISCIPLINE** CLASSICS **EDUCATION** St Mary's Col, Calif, BA, 66; Stanford Univ, MA, 71, PhD(classics), 72. **CAREER** Instr classics, Ind Univ, Bloomington, 71-72, asst prof, 72-78; asst prof, Miami Univ, Ohio, 78-79; Asst Prof Classics, Univ MD, College Park, 79-, Nat Endowment for Humanities fel, 79-80. **HONORS AND AWARDS** Year-long res fel from the Fulbright Found (Rome); NEH; Am Coun of Learned Societies (Cologne). **MEMBERSHIPS** Am Philol Asn; Archaeol Inst Am; Vergilian Soc; Classical Asn Atlantic States. **RESEARCH** Greek and Roman athletics. **SELECTED PUBLICATIONS** Auth, "Running and the Stadium," Archaeology, (96): 35; auth, "Yet Another Scoring System for the Ancient Pentathlon," Nikephoros 8, (96): 41-55; auth, "The Later Greek Boxing Glove and the Roman Caestus: A Centennial Reevaluation of Juthner's Uber antike Turngerathe, Nikephoros 10, (forthcoming). **CONTACT ADDRESS** Dept of Classics, Univ of Maryland, Col Park, Marie Mount Hall, Rm 2407, College Park, MD 20742-7532. **EMAIL** hlee@deans.umd.edu

LEE, JAE-WON
PERSONAL Born 01/30/1940, Chinju, South Korea, m, 1997, 2 children **DISCIPLINE** JOURNALISM, POLITICAL COM, INTERNATIONAL COMMUNICATION **EDUCATION** Seoul Nat Univ, BA, MA; Marquette Univ, MA; Univ IA, PhD. **CAREER** Comm, Cleveland St Univ; prof of Journalism Cleveland State Univ, 73; reporter, The Korea Times, 63-67; vis prof, Institute of Foreign Affairs and Nat Security, 80-81; exec dir, Olympic Media Awards, 95-00; asst to provost, Cleveland State Univ, 93-. **HONORS AND AWARDS** Ffulbright scholarship, 67-69; Nat Teaching Award for Excellence in Journalism Teaching, 87; Fulbright professorship, 88; Fellows at the East-West Ctr, Poynter Institute and AM Press Institute. **MEMBERSHIPS** Asn for Education in Journalism and Mass Commun; International Commun Asn; International Asn for Media Commun Res; Soc of Professional Journalists; Fulbright Asn. **RESEARCH** News and reality, public opinion, international flow of news, media and politics/elections. **SELECTED PUBLICATIONS** Ed, Seoul Olympics and the Global Media, Seoul Olympics Memorial Asn, 92; co-auth, A Critical Look at Mass Communication in Korea, Nanam Publ, 94; Modernization vs Revolution, Sung Kyon Kwan UP, 93. **CONTACT ADDRESS** Commun Dept, Cleveland State Univ, 2001 Euclid Ave, Cleveland, OH 44115. **EMAIL** j.lee@csuohio.edu

LEE, JAI HYON
PERSONAL Born 05/29/1926, Korea, m, 1951, 4 children **DISCIPLINE** JOURNALISM **EDUCATION** Seoul Nat Univ, MA 62; Syracuse Univ, PhD, 65. **CAREER** Journalist, 53-60; Press Sec to the President of the Republic of Korea, 60; Dep director of Res, Korean Nat Reconstruction Agency, 60-61; Gen Director, Radio Voice of Free Korea, 63-65; Director of Public information, Korean Ministry of Culture and Information, 61-63; Delegate to UNESCO and chief cultural and information attache, Korean Embassy in Paris, 65-69; Chief cultural and information attache, Korean embassy in Washington, 70-73; Assoc Prof to Prof, Western Ill Univ, 73-. **HONORS AND AWARDS** Fulbright Scholar, 63; Medal of Honor for Distinguished Civil Service, Korean Govt, 70; Korea Peace and Reunification Awd of NCCCUSA Korea Church coalition for Peace, Justices and Reunification, 91. **MEMBERSHIPS** Soc of Professional Journalists, Asn for Educ in Journ and Mass Comm, Journal of Developing Areas, Korean Am Comm Asn. **RESEARCH** The press and foreign policy; the press and government; the press and public opinion; the issues of mass communication; international communication. **SELECTED PUBLICATIONS** Auth, "Human Rights and Politics in US-Korean Relations," in Korean American Relations at Crossroads, 82; auth, "A Chronology of Korean Affairs under park Chung-Hee's Rule with reference to the United States and the World," in Investigation of Korean-American Relations, Appendixes Vol I, 78; auth, "The Politics of Moon," in Science, Sin and Scholarship, 78; auth, A Handbook of Korea, 56; auth, Korean perspective, 54; auth, Korean lore, 53. **CONTACT ADDRESS** Dept English & Journalism, Western Illinois Univ, 1 Univ Circle, Macomb, IL 61455-1367. **EMAIL** jh-lee1@wiu.edu

LEE, JAMES WARD
PERSONAL Born 02/12/1931, Birmingham, AL, d, 2 children **DISCIPLINE** ENGLISH **EDUCATION** Mid TN State Univ, BS, 56; Auburn Univ, MA, 57, PhD, 64. **CAREER** Prof, Eng, Univ N TX, 70-99, ch, Eng, 86-92, Dir, Center TX Studies, 86-94, Dir UNT Press, 88-90, Ed, Studies in Novel, 66; ed, New TX, 91-; Ed, Amer Lit Review, 88-90; Ed, TX Studies, 92-94; Ed, TX Traditions Series, 85-; Acquisitions consult, TCU Press, 97-; Member Natl Faculty, 73-; TX Inst Letters, 74-. **HONORS AND AWARDS** St Andrews Acad of Distinguished Scholars; President's Awd UNT, 87; **MEMBERSHIPS** TX Folklore Soc; SCMLA; CCTE; Swestern Historical Assoc. **RESEARCH** Novel; folklore; TX Lit and cult. **SELECTED PUBLICATIONS** Coauth, J D Salinger and the Critics, Wadsworth, 62; auth, William Humphrey, Steck, 67; John Braine, Twayne, 68; Poetry: A Thematic Approach, Wadsworth, 68; co ed, Swestern American Literature: A Bibliography, OH univ Press, 80; Classics of Texas Fiction, E-Heart, 86; Texas: My Texas, UNT Press, 93; ed, 1941: Texas Goes to War, UNT Press, 91.

LEE, M. OWEN
PERSONAL Born 05/28/1930, Detroit, MI **DISCIPLINE** CLASSICS **EDUCATION** Univ Toronto, BA, 53, MA, 57; St Michael's Col, Univ Toronto, STB, 57; Univ BC, PhD, 60. **CAREER** From lectr to asst prof classics, St Michael's Col, Univ Toronto, 60-68; from assoc prof to prof, Univ St Thomas, Tex, 68-72; assoc prof, Loyola Univ Chicago, 72-75; assoc prof, 75-79, Prof Classics, Univ Toronto, 79-. **MEMBERSHIPS** Am Philol Asn. **RESEARCH** Myth of Orpheus; Roman poets; Wagner. **SELECTED PUBLICATIONS** Auth, Correspondence + Amara, Lucine, Opera Quart, Vol 0009, 92; Die 'Aeneis' as the Subject of Opera--Dramaturgical Changes From the Early Baroque to Berlioz, Phoenix-J Class Assoc of Can, Vol 0046, 92; Correspondence + Burroughs, Bruce, Opera Quart, Vol 0009, 93; Wagner 'Schwarzschwanenreich' + Johanning, Raffeiner, Quandt, Bach--Marco Polo 8 223777 8, Opera Quart, Vol 0012, 96; Correspondence + Farkas Rev of Lee 'First Intermissions'--Comment, Opera Quart, Vol 0012, 96; Wagner die 'Meistersinger Von Nurnberg' + Wiener, Thomas, Watson, Keilberth-Eurodisc 69008 2 Rg, Opera Quart, Vol 0012, 96; Wagner 'Tristan Und Isolde' + Jerusalem, Meier, Barenboim--Teldec 94568 2, Opera Quart, Vol 0013, 96; Wagner die 'Meistersinger Von Nurnberg' + Schoffler, Seider, Seefried, Bohm Preiser 90234, Opera Quart, Vol 0012, 96. **CONTACT ADDRESS** St. Michael's Col, 81 St Mary St, Toronto, ON, Canada M5S 1A1.

LEE, RONALD E.
PERSONAL Born 02/07/1952, Wyandotte, MI, m, 1980, 1 child **DISCIPLINE** COMMUNICATION STUDIES **EDUCATION** Wayne Univ (Detroit), BA, 74, MA, 76; Univ Iowa, PhD, 81. **CAREER** Asst prof, Ind Univ-Bloomington, 83-91; Assoc prof, Univ Nebr-Lincoln, 91-. **HONORS AND AWARDS** Obermann Fellow, Iowa Ctr for Adv Studs, Univ Iowa, 91; Recipient of Medwest Forensic Assoc Award for Outstanding Schol, 89, 92; Outstanding Young teach, Cent States Commun Assoc, 87. **MEMBERSHIPS** Am Forensic Assoc; Cent States Commun Assoc; DSR-TKA; Nat Commun Assoc. **RESEARCH** Contemporary rhetorical theory; rhetorical criticism; contemporary American public discourse. **SELECTED PUBLICATIONS** Auth, Humility and the political servant: Jimmy Carter's post-presidential rhetoric of virtue and power, Southern Commun J, vol 60, 120-130, 95; co-auth, Christian tradition, Jeffersonian democracy, and the myth of the sentimental family: An exploration of the premises of social-conservative argumentation, Argumentation and Values, Speech Commun Assoc, 36-42, 95; co-auth, Technical discourse in defense of public virtue: Ronald Reagan's explanation of the Iran/Contra affair, Pol Commun, vol 13, 115-129, 96; co-auth, The environmental rhetoric of balance: A case study of regulatory discourse and the colonization of the public, Tech Commun Quart, vol 6, 25-40, 97; auth, Governing without passion: Willard's call for a rhetoric of competence, Argumentation and Advocacy, vol 33, 135-146, 97; co-auth, Myths of blood, property, and maternity: Exploring the public argumentation of anti-adoption advocates, Argument in a time of change: Definitions, frameworks, and critiques, Nat Commun Assoc, 256-261, 98; Getting down to the meat: Associational clusters and symbolic alignments in the discourse of meat consumption, Commun Studs, 98; co-auth, Multicultural education in the little red schoolhouse: A rhetorical exploration of ideological justification and mythic repair, Commun Studs, 98; ed, Political communication ethics: An oxymoron?, (00): 23-50; ed, Argument at century's end: Reflecting on the past and envisioning the future, (00): 133-142. **CONTACT ADDRESS** Univ of Nebraska, Lincoln, 437 Oldfather Hall, Lincoln, NE 68588. **EMAIL** rlee1@unl.edu

LEE, WILLIAM DAVID
PERSONAL Born 08/13/1944, Matador, TX, m, 1971, 2 children **DISCIPLINE** LITERATURE **EDUCATION** CO St Univ, BA, 67; ID St Univ, MA, 70; Univ of UT, PhD, 73 **CAREER** Head Prof, 71-, S UT Univ **HONORS AND AWARDS** Poet laureate of UT, 97; Nat Endow for Humanities Fels; Prof of the Year; Net Endow for Arts Fellowships; nat endow for humanities fels; prof of the year **MEMBERSHIPS** RMMLA, AWP **RESEARCH** Contemp poetry **SELECTED PUBLICATIONS** Auth, Covenants, Spoon River Press, 96; The Fish, Woodworks Press, 97; The Wayburne Pig, Brooding Heron Press, 98; A Legacy of Shadows: Selected Poems, Copper Canyon, 99; News from Down to the Caf¤: New Poems, Copper Canyon, 99. **CONTACT ADDRESS** Dept of English, So Utah Univ, Cedar City, UT 84790. **EMAIL** lee-d@suu.edu

LEE, WILLIAM L.
PERSONAL Born 10/17/1947, Amarillo, TX, m, 1981, 1 child **DISCIPLINE** ENGLISH LITERATURE **EDUCATION** Dartmouth Col, BA, 69; Oxford Univ, BA, 71; MA, 86; Yale Univ, MPhil, 73; PhD, 80. **CAREER** ESL instr, Oxford Univ, 72-73; instr, Yale Univ, 73-74; instr, Colby Col, 74-77; instr, Tufts Univ, 78-79; lectr, Harvard Univ, 80-83; asst to assoc prof, Yeshiva Univ, 83-. **HONORS AND AWARDS** Nat Merit Scholarship, 65-69; Phi Beta Kappa; Kent Fel, 71-76; Prize Teaching Fel, 73-4; Mellon found Grant, 84; Senior Prof Awds, 85, 87, 89; Who's Who in Am Educ, 89-90; Who's Who in the East, 93-94; Who's Who Among Am Teachers, 00. **MEMBERSHIPS** MLA, William Morris Soc, NE Victorian Studies Assoc. **RESEARCH** Victorian Studies, Critical Theory, Poetry, Educational Theory and Practice, Pedagogy. **SELECTED PUBLICATIONS** Auth, "The Kelmscott Press (London: 1891-1898)" and "The Studio (London: 1893-1963); Studio Vista (London 1963-)," British Literary Publishing Houses, 1881-1965, Gale Res, (Detroit, London, 91): 178-86, 318-325; ed, Englewood's Liberty Square: From the 1766 Liberty Pole to the 1999 Centennial, Yale Univ, 98; ed, Celebrating Englewood's Centennial, EHPAC, 99. **CONTACT ADDRESS** Yeshiva Col, 163 W Demarest Ave, Englewood, NJ 07631-2240. **EMAIL** leewill@ymail.yu.edu

LEE-RIFFE, NANCY M.
PERSONAL Born 01/16/1933, Danville, KY, d, 1955, 5 children **DISCIPLINE** ENGLISH **EDUCATION** Agnes Scott Col, BA, 54; Radcliffe Col, AM, 55; Univ Ky, PhD, 63. **CAREER** Instr English, Temple Univ, 60-64; prof asst test develop, Educ Testing Serv, 64-65; asst prof English, Ursinus Col, 65-67; assoc prof, LaSalle Col, 67-68; assoc prof, 68-71, Prof English, 71-98, Eastern KY Univ; Mem col bd, Consult writing exam questions English Compos Test & reader advan placement English exams & English compos essay exams, 65-; Henry E Huntington Libr fel, 77. **HONORS AND AWARDS** Outstanding Young Women in Am Awd, 67. **MEMBERSHIPS** ASECS, SEASECS, Milton Soc. **RESEARCH** Shakespeare, Milton, 18th century English periodicals, Jane Austen. **SELECTED PUBLICATIONS** Auth, The Elizabethan stage: A bibliography, Shakespeare Newslett, 63; A finding list of some 18th century periodicals, Bull NY Pub Libr, 63; A fragment of Milton, from the Italian, Mod Philol, 66; Shall and will, Am Speech, spring-summer 76; Anecdotes about Scriblerians and Kit-Cats, Scriblerian, spring 77; The heavenly plantation: A seventeenth century mention of Florida, Fla Hist Quart, 10/77; auth, Jane Austen and English Country Dance, 98. **CONTACT ADDRESS** 406 Jackson St, Berea, KY 40403-1726. **EMAIL** retleeri@acs.eku.edu

LEEDOM, TIM C.
PERSONAL Born 04/23/1945, Plainfield, NJ, d, 1 child **DISCIPLINE** POLITICAL SCIENCE, JOURNALISM **EDUCATION** Univ KS; Univ Hawaii, BS, 69. **CAREER** Aide, Gov John A. Burns, St of Hawaii; aide, Lt. Gov Thomas P. Gill, St of Hawaii; aide, Off of Sen John Leopold, St of Hawaii; ed, The Truthseeker, Freethought J. **HONORS AND AWARDS** Ford Found Legisl Internship; Exec Internship; PBS Internship, Univ Hawaii; Bk of Yr, 94. **RESEARCH** Religion; history. **SELECTED PUBLICATIONS** Auth, The Book Your Church Doesn't Want You To Read; auth, World's Apart; The Main Man. **CONTACT ADDRESS** PO Box 5009, Balboa Island, CA 92662.

LEEDS, BARRY H.
PERSONAL Born 12/06/1940, New York, NY, m, 1968, 2 children **DISCIPLINE** ENGLISH **EDUCATION** Columbia Univ, BA, 62; MA, 63; Ohio Univ, PhD, 67. **CAREER** Lectr, CUNY, 63-64; instr, Univ Tex, 64-65; teaching fel, Ohio Univ, 65-67; asst prof to assoc prof, 68-71, prof, 76-, dist prof, 91-, Central Conn St Univ, Consult Am lit, Choice Mag, 68-; consult, Am Lit, Univ Tex Press, 79. **HONORS AND AWARDS** Distinguished Serv Awd, 82; Distinguished Univ Prof, 91-. **MEMBERSHIPS** AAUP; PCA. **RESEARCH** Contemporary American Novel, notably Norman Mailer and Ken Feseu. **SELECTED PUBLICATIONS** Auth, The Structured Vision of Norman Mailer, NY Univ Pr, 69; auth, Ken Kesey, Ungar, 81. **CONTACT ADDRESS** Dept English, Central Connecticut State Univ, 200 Blekeslee St, Apt 121, Bristol, CT 06010. **EMAIL** leeds@mail.ccsu.edu

LEEDS-HURTWITZ, WENDY
PERSONAL Born 06/17/1953, IN, m, 1979 **DISCIPLINE** COMMUNICATION **EDUCATION** SUNY, BA, 75; Univ Pa, MA, 80; PhD, 83. **CAREER** Asst Prof to Prof, Univ Wis, 82-. **HONORS AND AWARDS** Stella C Gray Excellence in Teaching Awd, 95; Univ Wisc System Admin Fel, 90-91. **MEMBERSHIPS** Nat Comm Asn, Intl Comm Asn. **RESEARCH** Communication theory, Semiotics, Language and social interaction, Intercultural communication, Childhood socialization. **SELECTED PUBLICATIONS** Ed, Social Approaches to Communication, New York, 95; auth, Semiotics and communication, New York, 93; auth, communication in Everyday Life, Ablex, 89. **CONTACT ADDRESS** Dept Comm, Univ of Wisconsin, Parkside, 900 Wood Rd, Kenosha, WI 53141-2000. **EMAIL** wendy.leeds-hurwitz@uwp.edu

LEEMAN, RICHARD W.
PERSONAL Born 06/16/1955, Oak Park, IL, m, 1990, 2 children **DISCIPLINE** COMMUNICATION STUDIES **EDUCATION** Shippensburg State Col, BS, 77; Univ Md, MA, 82; PhD, 90. **CAREER** Instr, Clemson Univ, 85-89; from asst prof to assoc prof, Univ NC at Charlotte, 89-. **HONORS AND AWARDS** Daniel M. Rohrer Awd for Best Argumentation Article, Am Forensic Asn, 91; Betty Jo Welch Service Awd, Carolinas Commun Asn, 99. **MEMBERSHIPS** Nat Commun Asn, Southern States commun Asn, Carolinas Commun Asn. **RESEARCH** African American Oratory, Oratory of the Nineteenth-Century, Rhetoric of Terrorism. **SELECTED PUBLICATIONS** Auth, "The Rhetoric of Terrorism and Counterterrorism, Greenwood Press, 91; auth, "Do Everything" Reform: The Oratory of Francis F. W. Willard, Greenwood Press, 92; auth, African-American Orators, Greenwood Press, 96. **CONTACT ADDRESS** Dept Commun, Univ of No Carolina, Charlotte, 9201 University City Blvd, Charlotte, NC 28223-0001. **EMAIL** rwleeman@email.uncc.edu

LEEPER, JILL M.
PERSONAL Born 11/02/1960, Bremen, Ind, s **DISCIPLINE** ENGLISH **EDUCATION** Ball State Univ, BS, 83; MA, 87; Univ Rochester, MA, 92. **CAREER** Instr, Ball State Univ, 85-86; Adj Instr, Ind Univ E, 87; Adj Instr, Ind Univ-Purdue Univ, 87-88; Instr, Univ Rochester, 90-92; Instr, Ind Univ at Kokomo, 92-95; Instr, DePaul Univ, 93-98; Lectr, Butler Univ, 98-99; Lectr, Ind Univ-Purdue Univ, 99-00; Instr, Ball State Univ, 00-. **HONORS AND AWARDS** Hon Hoosier Scholar, 79; State Acad Scholar, Ball State Univ, 79-83; Grad Asst, Ball State Univ, 85-87; Grad Asst, Univ Rochester, 89-92. **MEMBERSHIPS** MLA; Soc for Cinema Studies; Nat Coun of Teachers of English. **RESEARCH** Modern and contemporary American literature; Composition and Rhetoric; Humanities; Film and Television; Cultural Studies; Disability Studies; Body Image. **SELECTED PUBLICATIONS** Auth, "Crossing Musical Borders: The Soundtrack for Touch of Evil," in Soundtrack Available: Essays on Film and Pop Music, Duke Univ Press, 00. **CONTACT ADDRESS** Dept English, Ball State Univ, 4824 Victoria Rd, Indianapolis, IN 46288. **EMAIL** jmleeper@netscape.com

LEER, NORMAN ROBERT
PERSONAL Born 02/25/1937, Chicago, IL **DISCIPLINE** ENGLISH, COMPARATIVE LITERATURE **EDUCATION** Grinnell Col, AB, 58; Ind Univ, MA, 60, PhD(English), 64. **CAREER** Instr English, State Univ NY Stony Brook, 63-65; asst prof, Beloit Col, 65-67; assoc prof Roosevelt Univ, 67-72, assoc prof, 72-78, prof English, 78-, mem bd, Urban Life Ctr, 72-; coordr, Educ Network, Asn Humanistic Psychol, 72-74 & Midwest Regional Newslett, 78-; Fulbright lectr English, Odense Univ, Denmark, 74-75; lectr, Center for Older Adults, Fourth Presbyterian Church of Chicago, 96-. **HONORS AND AWARDS** Phi Beta Kappa, Grinnell College, 58; Poetry Prize, All Nations Poetry Contest, Triton Col, 76, 77, 78, 79 & 81; Burlington Northern Awd, Roosevelt Univ (for teaching and scholarship), 86; Illinois Significant Poet's Awd, 90; Samuel Ortrowski Awd, Roosevelt Univ (for best creative work), 98. **RESEARCH** Modern literature in the light of existential philosophy and humanistic psychology; writing poetry; application of some of the techniques of humanistic psychology to college teaching. **SELECTED PUBLICATIONS** Auth, Escape and Confrontation in the Stories of Philip Roth, Christian Scholar, summer 66; The Limited Hero in the Novels of Ford Madox Ford, Mich State Univ, 67; The Double Theme in Malamud's Assistant: Dostoevsky with Irony, Mosaic, spring 71; Innovation and power struggles: An Experiential Deadlock, J Humanistic Psychol, winter 73; To Doris Lessing: Inside the Apocalypse, Oyez Rev, spring 75; Riding Commas to the Moon: Teaching Maleness and Imagination, New Directions in Teaching, winter 78; Slightly Crumpled Survival Flower (poems), Spoon River Poetry Press, 85; I Dream My Father in a Stone (poems), Mellen Poetry Press, 91; Second Lining (poems), Mellen Poetry Press, 97; Over 100 individual poems in Spoon River Quart, Willow Review, Rhino, Oyez Review, The Wolf Head Quart, Poetry Digest, and American Poets and Poetry. **CONTACT ADDRESS** Dept of English, Roosevelt Univ, 430 S Michigan Ave, Chicago, IL 60605-1394.

LEESON, TED
DISCIPLINE WRITING **EDUCATION** Marquette Univ, BA, 76; Univ Va, MA, 79, PhD, 84. **CAREER** Engl, Oregon St Univ. **SELECTED PUBLICATIONS** Auth, The Habit of Rivers. Lyons & Burford, 94. **CONTACT ADDRESS** Oregon State Univ, Corvallis, OR 97331-4501. **EMAIL** tleeson@orst.edu

LEFCOWITZ, BARBARA
PERSONAL Born 01/15/1935, New York, NY, d, 2 children **DISCIPLINE** ENGLISH **EDUCATION** Smith, BA, 56; SUNY Buffalo, MA, 64; Univ MD, PhD, 70. **CAREER** Prof

Anne Arundel Community Col, 71-. **HONORS AND AWARDS** Smith, BA, cum laude, 56; Nat Endowment for the Arts; Nat Endowment for the Humanities; Rockefeller Found. **RESEARCH** Creative writing, international studies. **SELECTED PUBLICATIONS** Auth of six books of fiction and poetry, articles, stories, and poems in over 350 journals. **CONTACT ADDRESS** Dept Humanities, Anne Arundel Comm Col, 101 Col Pky, Arnold, MD 21012-1857. **EMAIL** Blefcowitz@aol.com

LEFEW-BLAKE, PENELOPE
DISCIPLINE ENGLISH LITERATURE **EDUCATION** Carthage Col, BA, 79; Northern Illinois Univ, MA, 84; PhD, 92. **CAREER** Teaching Asst, Northern Ill Univ, 82-84; Instr, Northern Ill Univ, 84-92; Vis Prof, Christ Church Col, 97; Prof, Rock Valley Col, 89-. **HONORS AND AWARDS** Who's Who Among America's Teachers, 96-99, Teacher of the Year Nominee, 97-99. **MEMBERSHIPS** MLA, Sigma Tau Delta, NEMLA. **RESEARCH** German Philosophy and British Literature, WWII, Women's Studies. **SELECTED PUBLICATIONS** Auth, Schopenhauer and Women's Literature, Mellen Press, 00; auth, "'A Striving and A Striving' Schopenhauerian Pessimisms in Olive Schreiner's 'The Story of an African Form' and 'From Man to Man,'" English Lit in Transition 37-3 (Sept 94). **CONTACT ADDRESS** Div Communications, Rock Valley Col, 3301 N Mulford Rd, Rockford, IL 61114-5640. **EMAIL** faco3pb@rvc.cc.il.us

LEFF, LEONARD J.
PERSONAL Born 01/23/1942, Houston, TX, m, 1969, 1 child **DISCIPLINE** FILM STUDIES **EDUCATION** Univ Tex Austin, BA, 63; Univ Houston, MA, 65; Northern Ill Univ, PhD(English), 71. **CAREER** Instr English Lit, McNeese State Univ, 65-68 & Northern Ill Univ, 68-69; asst prof English Lit & Film, Bellevue Col, 73-79; asst prof English Lit & Film, Okla State Univ, 79-; prof English, 91-. **HONORS AND AWARDS** The Dame in the Kimono, New York Times Book Review Notable Books of the Year, 90. **MEMBERSHIPS** MLA; Soc Cinema Studies. **RESEARCH** Film hist; film criticism; film writing. **SELECTED PUBLICATIONS** Auth, Hollywood lives, Southern Quart, 4/78; Who's Afraid of Virginia Woolf?: A test of American film censorship, Cinema J, Spring 80; I hear America typing: A survey of scriptwriting manuals, Quart Rev Film Studies, Summer 81; Instant movies: The short, unhappy life of William Sargent's Electronovision, J Popular Film & TV, Spring 81; Play into film: Warner Brothers' Who's Afraid of Virginia Woolf?, Theatre J, 12/81; Hemingway and His Conspirators: Hollywood, Scribners, and the Making of American Celebrity Culture, Rowman & Littlefield, 97; Hitchcock and Selznick: The Rich and Strange Collaboration of Alfred Hitchcock and David O Selznick in Hollywood, Weidenfeld & Nicolson, 87, rpt University of California Press, 98; auth, "Cutting Notorius," (99): 26-29; auth, "What in the World Interests Women?, (97): 385-405. **CONTACT ADDRESS** Dept of English, Oklahoma State Univ, Stillwater, Stillwater, OK 74078-0002. **EMAIL** leff_osu@osu.net

LEFKOWITZ, MARY ROSENTHAL
PERSONAL Born 04/30/1935, New York, NY, m, 1982, 2 children **DISCIPLINE** CLASSICS **EDUCATION** Wellesley Col, BA, 57; Radcliffe Col, MA, 59, PhD, 61. **CAREER** Instr Greek, 59-63, from asst prof to assoc prof Greek & Latin, 63-75, chemn dept, 70-72, 75-78, 81-87, 91-94, & 96-, prof Greek & Latin, Wellesley Col, 75-; Andrew W Mellon prof humanities, 79-; fel, Radcliffe Inst, 66-67, 72-73, Am Coun Learned Soc fel, 72-73; mem managing comt, Am Sch Class Studies, Athens, 71-; vis prof, Univ Calif, Berkeley, 78; vis fel, St Hilda's Col, Oxford, 79-80; dir Nat Endowment Summer Seminar, 84-85; Nat Endowment for Humanities fel, 79-80, 91. **HONORS AND AWARDS** Honorary Fel, St. Hilda's Col, 94-; LHD, Trinity College, 96; Honorary Ph.D., Univ of Patras, 99; L.H.D., Grinnell Col, 00. **MEMBERSHIPS** Am Philol Asn; Archaeol Inst Am. **RESEARCH** Greek poetry; classical mythology; ancient biography. **SELECTED PUBLICATIONS** Auth, The Victory Ode, Noyes, 76; Heroines and Hysterics, St Martin's, 81; The Lives of the Greek Poets, 81; co-ed, Women's Life in Greece and Rome, Johns Hopkins, 82, 2nd ed, 92; auth, Women in Greek Myth, John's Hopkins, 86; First-Person Fictions, Oxford, 91; Not Out of Africa, Basic Books, 96; co-ed Black Athena Revisited, North Carolina, 96. **CONTACT ADDRESS** Dept of Classical Studies, Wellesley Col, 106 Central St, Wellesley, MA 02481-8252. **EMAIL** mlefkowitz@wellesley.edu

LEGGETT, B. J.
PERSONAL Born 02/25/1938, Alamo, TN, m, 1960, 2 children **DISCIPLINE** MODERN LITERATURE **EDUCATION** Lambuth Col, BA, 60; Univ Fla, MA, 62, PhD(English), 65. **CAREER** From asst prof to assoc prof, 65-77, Prof English, Univ Tenn, Knoxville, 77-, Nat Found Arts and Humanities fel 67; Hunington Libr fel, 81. Lindsay Young Prof English, 82-83. **MEMBERSHIPS** SAtlantic Mod Lang Asn; MLA. **RESEARCH** Modern poetry. **SELECTED PUBLICATIONS** Auth, Larkin Blues--Jazz and Modernism, 20th Century Lit, Vol 0042, 96. **CONTACT ADDRESS** Dept of English, Univ of Tennessee, Knoxville, Knoxville, TN 37916. **EMAIL** legg@utkux.utcc.ukt.edu

LEHMAN, PAUL ROBERT
PERSONAL Born 04/18/1941, Mansura, LA, m **DISCIPLINE** ENGLISH **EDUCATION** LA City Coll, AA 1966; Central State Coll, BA 1969; Central State U, ME 1971; Lehigh U, PhD 1976. **CAREER** Central State U, dean of grad coll 1985-88, prof dept of English 1984, 88-, assoc prof dept of Eng 1976-; NCACC, adjunct prof 1974-76; CSU, instr 1971-73;CSU, lecturer 1969-71; KWTV, newsman reporter writer editor photographer producer & weekend anchorman 1968-70; KOFM radio, music newsman 1968-69; Standard Oil of CA, credit dept 1966-67; Western Electric Co, tester insptct 1963-66; Northampton Co Area Community Coll, dev co-ordinated coll orientation wkshp for minority stud 1975; Blk Am Lit, vol lecturer coll pub private sch (Jr & Sr) churches on Radio/TV News 1974-75; member, Edmond Arts & Humanities, 91-; board member, Oklahoma Arthritis Foundation, 91-; board member, Oklahoma Alliance for Art Education, 89-. **HONORS AND AWARDS** Best actor in minor roll CSC 1968; dean's honor roll CSC 1968; 1st blk Am to rec PhD in Eng from Lehigh 1976; 1st blk Am to teach at CSU 1969; 1st blk in OK to anchor weekend TV news 1969; listed in Contemporary Authors for 1977-78; Lehigh Univ Fellowship 1973-76; 1st dissertation on John Oliver Killens 1976; 2nd place all-coll speech contest 1965; Awd for Serv to Urban League of Greater Okla City 1984; Awd for Serv to Boy Scouts of Amer 1985. **MEMBERSHIPS** Natl Jay-Cees; NAACP; Urban League; Heart Assn Natl Assn of Press Photographers; stud exec officer LACC 1966; mem NEA, OEA, CSEA, NCTE; vice chmn, Oklahoma Foundation for the Humanities 1988-89; treasurer, Oklahoma Alliance for Arts Education 1988-; Oklahoma Folklife Council; Edmond Community Housing Resource Board; Afro-American Southern Assn; Edmond Arts & Humanities, 1991-; Oklahoma Arthritis Foundation, 1991-. **CONTACT ADDRESS** Dept of English, Central State Univ, Oklahoma, 100 University Dr, Edmond, OK 73034.

LEIBOWITZ, HERBERT
PERSONAL Born 04/26/1935, Staten Island, NY, m, 1978, 1 child **DISCIPLINE** ENGLISH **EDUCATION** Brooklyn Col, BA, 56; Brown Univ, MA, 58; Columbia Univ, PhD, 66. **CAREER** Asst prof, Columbia Univ, 65-70; vis assoc prof, Wash Univ St Louis, 69-70; assoc prof, Richmond Col, 70-76; assoc prof, Col of Staten Island CUNY, 76-91; prof, Grad Center CUNY, 86-91. **HONORS AND AWARDS** Sen Fulbright Prof, Univ Barcelona, 99; Nora Magid Award, Am CTR, 95; Guggenheim Fel, 91-92; Fannie Hurst Prof, Wash Univ, 95. **MEMBERSHIPS** NY Inst for the Humanities; MLA. **RESEARCH** American Autobiography; American poetry; Contemporary poetry; Biography; Style; Poetics. **SELECTED PUBLICATIONS** Auth, Fabricating Lives: Explorations in American Autobiography, 89; ed, Musical Impressions: Selected Music Criticism of Paul Rosenfeld; ed, Parnassus: Twenty Years of Poetry, (forthcoming). **CONTACT ADDRESS** Grad Center, Graduate Sch and Univ Ctr, CUNY, 205 W 89th St, New York, NY 10024-1828. **EMAIL** parenw@aol.com

LEIDHOLDT, ALEX S.
DISCIPLINE JOURNALISM HISTORY, MESSAGE DESIGN AND PRODUCTION **EDUCATION** Old Dominion Univ, PhD, 91. **CAREER** Asst prof, Purdue Univ. **SELECTED PUBLICATIONS** Auth, Standing Before the Shouting Mob: Lenoir Chambers and Virginia's Massive Resistance to Public School Integration, Univ Ala Press; USA/USSR Youth Summit Series, PBS; Doing Business with the Soviet Union, PBS ALSS; Prophets and Translators; Symbols, Stories and Visual Images, PBS ALSS. **CONTACT ADDRESS** Dept of Commun, Purdue Univ, West Lafayette, 1366 Lib Arts & Educ Bldg 2114, West Lafayette, IN 47907-1366. **EMAIL** aleidhol@purdue.edu

LEIGH, DAVID J.
PERSONAL Born 04/16/1937, Seattle, WA, s **DISCIPLINE** ENGLISH **EDUCATION** Gonzaga Univ, BA, 61; MA, 62; Regis Col, MA, 69; Yale Univ, PhD, 72. **CAREER** Assoc prof, Gonzaga Univ, 72-83; inst dir, 76-82; prof, Seat Univ, 83-. **HONORS AND AWARDS** Grad Fel Yale Univ; NEH, 82. **MEMBERSHIPS** MLA; Con Christ and Lit; Soc Stud Hum Ideas of Ult Reality and Mean. **RESEARCH** Autobiography; apocalyptic themes in literature; 18th and 19th C British literature. **SELECTED PUBLICATIONS** Auth, Circuitous Journeys: Modern Spiritual Autobiography, Fordham Univ Press, 00. **CONTACT ADDRESS** Dept English, Seattle Univ, 901 12th Ave, Seattle, WA 98122-4411. **EMAIL** dleigh@seattleu.edu

LEIGHTON, LAUREN GRAY
PERSONAL Born 06/21/1934, Virginia, MN, m, 1991, 2 children **DISCIPLINE** RUSSIAN LITERATURE, ROMANTICISM **CAREER** Instr Russian, Mercer Univ, 62-63; instr, Grinnell Col, 63-64; asst prof Slavic, Univ Va, 67-72; assoc prof, Northern Ill Univ, 72-78; Prof Slavic, Univ Ill, Chicago, 78-97, US-USSR Acad Exchange, IREX-USSR Ministry Higher Educ, 70 and IREX-USSR Acad Sci, 77, 89-90; ed, Slavic and East Europ J, 76-80. **MEMBERSHIPS** Asn Advan Slavic Studies; Am Asn Univf, Am Asn Teachers Slavic and East Europ Lang. **RESEARCH** Russian romanticism; Pushkin; translation theory. **SELECTED PUBLICATIONS** Auth, Literary Translation in Russia and America, 19: The Esoteric tradition in Russian Romantic Literature, 1994; A bibliography of Alexander Pushkin in English, 1999. **CONTACT ADDRESS** Dept of Slavic Lang and Lit, Univ of Illinois, Chicago, 601 S Morgan, Chicago, IL 60607. **EMAIL** laurengl@ptwi.net

LEINIEKS, VALDIS
PERSONAL Born 04/15/1932, Liepaja, Latvia **DISCIPLINE** CLASSICS **EDUCATION** Cornell Univ, BA, 55, MA, 56; Princeton Univ, PhD, 62. **CAREER** From instr to asst prof classics, Cornell Col, 59-64; assoc prof, Ohio State Univ, 64-66; assoc prof, 66-71, Prof Classics, Univ Nebr, Lincoln, 71-, Chm Dept, 67-95, Chm Comp Lit Prog, 70-86. **MEMBERSHIPS** Am Philol Asn; Am Classical League; Classical Asn of the Middle West and South. **RESEARCH** Greek and Latin literature and linguistics; linguistic theory. **SELECTED PUBLICATIONS** Auth Morphosyntax of the Homeric Greek Verb, Mouton, 64; The Structure of Latin: An Introductory Text Based on Caesar and Cicero, MSS Educ Publ, 75; Index Nepotianus, Univ Nebr, 76; The plays of Sophokles, Grîner, 82; The City of Dionysos, Teubner, 96. **CONTACT ADDRESS** Dept of Classics, Univ of Nebraska, Lincoln, 234 Andrews, Lincoln, NE 68588-0337. **EMAIL** vleinieks2@unl.edu

LEISSNER, DEBRA
PERSONAL Born 08/21/1957, Dallas, TX, m, 1980, 2 children **DISCIPLINE** ENGLISH **EDUCATION** Univ N Tex, BS, 91, MA, 93; PhD, 98. **CAREER** Asst prof, Lousiana Tech Univ, 98- . **HONORS AND AWARDS** Eugene P. Wright Outstanding Studententententent Grad Studententententent Awd; Meadows Exc Tchg Schol; Carl B. & Florence E. King Found Schol. **MEMBERSHIPS** Soc Tech Commun; Mod Lang Asn; S Cent Soc Eighteenth-Century Student; Am Soc Eighteenth-Century Student. **RESEARCH** Restoration and Eighteenth-century drama, Eighteenth-Century novels, Gender studies, Literary theory. **SELECTED PUBLICATIONS** Auth, "Pope, Petrarch, and Shakespeare: Renaissance Influences in Eloisa to Abelard", Philol Quart 74, 173-187, (95); auth, "Divided Nation, Divided Self: The Language of Capitalism and Madness in Otway's Venice Preserved," Studies in Literary Imagination (99). **CONTACT ADDRESS** Dept English, Louisiana Tech Univ, 305 Wisteria St, Ruston, LA 71270-4235. **EMAIL** leissner@garts.latech.edu

LEITAO, DAVID
PERSONAL Born 06/18/1964, CT, m, 1988 **DISCIPLINE** CLASSICS **EDUCATION** Dartmouth, AB, 86; Univ Mich, MA, 90, PhD, 93. **CAREER** Vis asst prof, 93-95, Ohio St Univ; asst prof, 95-, San Francisco St Univ. **RESEARCH** Gender and sexuality; anthropology of ancient world; computers in classics. **SELECTED PUBLICATIONS** Art, Classical Antiquity; art, Mnemosyne; art, Bucknell Review; art, Neue Parly; auth, Materialie Discussion. **CONTACT ADDRESS** 1600 Holloway Ave, San Francisco, CA 94132. **EMAIL** dleitao@sfsu.edu

LEITCH, THOMAS
PERSONAL Born 06/23/1951, Orange, NJ, m, 1977, 2 children **DISCIPLINE** ENGLISH **EDUCATION** Columbia Col, BA, 72; Yale Univ, PhD, 76. **CAREER** Asst Prof English, Yale Univ, 76-83; Asst Prof English, Univ of Delaware, 83-86; Assoc Prof English, Univ of Delaware, 86-91; Prof English, Univ of Delaware, 94. **HONORS AND AWARDS** Senior Fulbright Lectureship, Hebrew Univ of Jerusalem, 89-90 **MEMBERSHIPS** Modern Language Assn, Society for Cinema Studies, Literature/Film Assn, Mystery Writers of America, Sisters in Crime. **RESEARCH** Literacy and Cultural Theory, Film and Popular Culture. **SELECTED PUBLICATIONS** Auth, What Stories Are: Narrative Theory and Interpretation (86); auth, Find the Director and Other Hitchcock Games (91); auth, Lionel Trilling: An Annotated Bibliography (92). **CONTACT ADDRESS** Dept English, Univ of Delaware, 212 Memorial Hall, Newark, DE 19716-2799. **EMAIL** tleitch@udel.edu

LEITCH, VINCENT B.
PERSONAL Born 09/18/1944, Hempstead, NY, d, 2 children **DISCIPLINE** LITERARY CRITICISM AND THEORY **EDUCATION** Hofstra Univ, BA, 66; Villanova Univ, MA, 67; Univ Fla, PhD, 72. **CAREER** Asst prof to prof, Mercer Univ, 73-86; prof, Purdue Univ, 86-97; Paul and Carol Daube Sutton Chair, Univ of Okla, 97-. **HONORS AND AWARDS** Res Grant, Am Philos Assoc, 74; NEH Fel, 76, 80; ACLS Fel, 85-86; Excellence in Teaching Awds, 88, 89, 92, 93, 94, 96; Outstanding Academic Book, Choice Awd, Asn of Col and Res Libr, 88; Vis Fac Fel, Big 12 Univ, Univ of Miss, 00. **MEMBERSHIPS** Am Comp Lit Assoc; Int Assoc for Philos and Lit; MLA; PEN Am Center; Soc for Critical Exchange. **RESEARCH** Contemporary Literary Criticism and Theory, History of Criticism, Cultural Studies, Theories of Postmodern Culture, Twentieth-Century American Poetry and Poetics, History of Poetry and Poetics, Continental Philosophy, Theories of Pedagogy, Postwar Visual Culture. **SELECTED PUBLICATIONS** Auth, Deconstructive Criticism: An Advanced Introduction, Columbia Univ Pr, 83; auth, American Literary Criticism from the 1930s to 1980s, Columbia Univ Pr, (NY), 88; auth, Cultural Criticism, Literary Theory, Poststructuralism, Columbia Univ Pr, (NY), 92; auth, Postmodernism - Local Ef-

fects, Global Flows, SUNY Albany, 96; ed, The Norton Anthology of Theory and Criticism, W.W. Norton, (NY), (forthcoming). **CONTACT ADDRESS** Dept English, Univ of Oklahoma, 900 Asp Ave, Norman, OK 73019-4050. **EMAIL** vbleitch@ou.edu

LEITER, SAMUEL LOUIS
PERSONAL Born 07/20/1940, Brooklyn, NY, m, 1963, 2 children **DISCIPLINE** THEATRE **EDUCATION** Brooklyn Col, BA, 62; Univ Hawaii, MFA, 64; NYork Univ, PhD(dramatic art), 68. **CAREER** Lectr theatre, 65-68, from asst prof to assoc prof, 68-76, Prof Theatre, Brooklyn Col, 77-, **HONORS AND AWARDS** Fulbright Senior Res Sch, 74-75, Choice Awd Outstand Acad Book, Claire and Leonard Tow Prof 97-98 **MEMBERSHIPS** Am Soc Theatre Res; Asn for Theatre in Higher Educ; Cnl of Ed of Learned Jou; Int Fed of Theatre Res **RESEARCH** Japanese theatre; American theatre history; directing theory. **SELECTED PUBLICATIONS** auth, Four Interviews with Kabuki Actors, Educ Theater Jou, 66; auth, The Frozen Moment: A Kabuki Technique, Drama Survey, 67; auth, Brooklyn as an American Theater City 1861-1898, Jou of Long Island Hist, 68; auth, The Depiction of Violence on the Kabuki Stage, Educ Theater Jou,69; auth, Theater in the City of Churchesm Players, 69; auth, Keren: Spectacle and Trickery on the Kabuki Stage, Educ Theater Jou, 76; auth, Tha Kabuki Juhachiban, Lit East and West, 76; auth, Ichikawa Danjuro IX, A Life in Kabuki, Educ Theater Jou, 77; auth, Get Someone to Teach You How to Act! Sir John Gielgud Directs, Theater Hist Stu, 88; auth, Kumagai's Battle Camp: Form and Tradition in Kabuki Acting, Asian Theater Jou, 91; auth, The International Symposium of Traditional Theaters of Asia, Beijing, 91, Asian Theater Jou, 92; auth, Theater on the Homefront: World War II on New York's Stages, 1941-1945, Jou of Am Drama and Theater, 93; auth, Daniel S.P. Yang of the Hong Kong Repertory Theater, Asian Theater Jou, 93; The Kanamaru-za: Japan's Oldest Kabuki Theater, Asian Theater Jou, 97; auth, What really Happens Backstage: A Nineteenth-Century Kabuki Document, Theater Survey, 97; auth, From the London Patents to the Edo Sanza: A Partial Comparison of British Theater and Kabuki, ca. 1650-1800, Theater Symposium VI, 98; auth, Trans and Commentary of the Birth of the Hanamichi, Theater Res Int, 99; auth, Japan: In the History of the Theater, 68; auth, Brooklyn Academy of Music: When Theater spelled SIN at BAM, In Brooklyn, 79; auth, Kabuki: An Introduction, In Kabuki, 82; auth, Brooklyn Theater Co, 1871-1875, Brooklyn Theater Co; auth, Brooklyn Theater Co, 1875-1876, Park Theater Co in American Theater Companies, 1749-1887, 86; auth, Kabuki: What's in it for us? Proceedings: East Asian Festival, Sta Univ of NY Brockport, 91; auth, Sol Hurok, Wiliam Inge, Diana Sands, Herman Shumlin, Samuel Spewack, and Margret Webster, Dictionary of American Biography, 94; auth, Kermit Bloomgarden, Alfred Lunt, Mary Pickford, Rosalind Russell, and Herman Shumlin, Dictionary of Americanb Biography, 95; auth, David Belasco and James A. Herne, American National Biography, 96; auth, Bando Mitsugoro, Bando Tamasaburo, Bunraku, Hanamichi, Ichikawa Danjuro, Ichikawa Ennosuke, Japanese Traditional Schools, Jidaimono, Kabuki Theater, Kurogo, Kataoka Tako, Matsumoto Joshiro, Nakamura Ganjiro, Nakamura Kankuro, Nakamura Kanzaburo, Nakamura Kichiemon, Nakamura Tomijuro, Nakamura Utaemon, Okuni Onnagata, Onoe Baiko, Onoe Kikugoro, One Shoroku, Sewamono, and Shishimai, Oxford Int Encyc of Dance, 98; auth, Directors and Directing: 1945- present, Cambridge History of the American Theater, 99; auth, Ethel Merman, Bette Davis, Lotte Lenya, Alan Schneider, Joshua Logan, Charles Ludlam, Lee Strasberg, Geraldine Page, and Danny Kaye, Scribner Encyclopedia of American Lives, 99; auth, The Art of Kabuki: Famous Plays, Performance, Univ of Calif Press, 79, reprint, Dover, 99; auth, Kabuki Encyclopedia: An English-Language Adaptation of Kabuki Jiten, Grenwood, 79; auth, The Encyclopedia of the New York Stage, 1920-1930, Greenwood, 86; ed, Shakespeare Around the Globe: A Guide to Notable Postwar Productions, Greenwood, 86; auth, Ten Seasons: New York Theater in the Seventies, Greenwood, 86; auth, From Belasco to Brook: Representative Directors of the English-Speaking Stage, Greenwood, 91; auth, From Stanislavsky to Barrault: Representative Directors of the European Stage, Greenwood, 91; auth, The Encyclopedia of the New York Stage, 1940-1950, Greenwood, 92; auth, The Great Stage Directors: 100 Distinguised Careers of the Theater, Facts on File, 94; auth, New Kabuki Encyclopedia: A Revised Adaptation of Kabuki Jiten, Greenwood, 97; ed, Japanese Theater in the World, Japan Society, 97; ed, Zeami and the No Theater in the World, 98; ed, Asian Theater Jou, 91-. **CONTACT ADDRESS** Dept of Theatre, Brooklyn Col, CUNY, 2900 Bedford Ave, Brooklyn, NY 11210-2813. **EMAIL** sleiter@brooklyn.cuny.edu

LEITH, LINDA J.
PERSONAL Born 12/13/1949, Belfast, Northern Ireland **DISCIPLINE** ENGLISH **EDUCATION** McGill Univ, BA, 70; Univ London(Eng), PhD, 76. **CAREER** Teacher English, John Abbott Col, 75-; lectr, Concordia Univ, 82-83; lectr, McGill Univ, 88. **MEMBERSHIPS** Dir, Que Soc Promotion Eng Lang Lit, 88-94, 96-98; vice pres, Fedn Eng Lang Writers Que, 93-94, 97-98; mem, exec, Can Asn Irish Stud, 92-95; nat coun, Writers Union Can, 94-96; mem, Union des crivaines et ecrivains quebecois, 95-. **SELECTED PUBLICATIONS** Auth, Introducing Hugh MacLennan's Two Solitudes, 90; ed, Matrix, 88-94; ed, Telling Differences: New English Fiction from Quebec, 89; ed, Vehicule Fiction Ser, 89-94; founding assoc ed, Montreal Rev, 78-79, mem, bd consult, Science-Fiction Stud, 81-91. **CONTACT ADDRESS** Dept of English, John Abbott Col, PO Box 2000, Ste. Anne de Bellevue, QC, Canada H9X 3L9.

LEITZ, ROBERT C.
PERSONAL Born 10/28/1944, New Orleans, LA, m, 1968 **DISCIPLINE** ENGLISH **EDUCATION** Univ New Orleans, BA, 67; Texas A&M Univ, MA, 69; Texas A&M, PhD, 73 **CAREER** Asst prof, Louisiana State Univ, 73-77; assoc prof, Louisiana State Univ, 77-82; prof, Louisiana State Univ, 82-; Curator, James Smith Noel Collection, Noel Memorial Libr, Ruth Herring Noel Distinguished Prof, 00-. **HONORS AND AWARDS** Henry E Huntington Libr Fel, 79; LSU Distinguished Fac Fel, 85 **MEMBERSHIPS** Frank Norris Soc; Jack London Soc; Assoc Documentary Editing **RESEARCH** Documentary Editing; American literature **SELECTED PUBLICATIONS** Coauth, The Letters of Charles W. Chestnutt, 1906-1932, Stanford Univ; coauth, The Essays and Speeches of Charles W. Chestnutt, Stanford Univ, 99; coauth, To Be an Author! The Letters of Charles W. Chestnutt, 1889-1905, Princeton Univ, 97 **CONTACT ADDRESS** Dept Eng, Louisiana State Univ, Shreveport, 1 University Pl, Shreveport, LA 71115. **EMAIL** rleitz@pilot.lsus.edu

LELAND, CHARLES WALLACE
PERSONAL Born 03/22/1928, Culver, IN **DISCIPLINE** ENGLISH LITERATURE, SCANDANAVIAN DRAMA **EDUCATION** Oberlin Col, AB, 50; Oxford Univ, BA, 53, MA, 56; Univ Toronto, STB, 58. **CAREER** Lectr English, 59-62, asst prof, 62-69, Assoc Prof English, Univ Toronto, 69-, Roman Cath priest, Congregation of St Basil, 59-. **MEMBERSHIPS** Asn Advan Scand Studies Can; Ibsen Soc Am; Soc Advan Scand Study. **RESEARCH** Ibsen; Strindberg; literature of the English Renaissance. **SELECTED PUBLICATIONS** Auth, Catiline and the Burial Mound, Mod Drama, Vol 0038, 95. **CONTACT ADDRESS** St. Michael's Col, Toronto, ON, Canada M5S 1J4.

LELAND, CHRISTOPHER
PERSONAL Born 10/17/1951, Tulsa, OK **DISCIPLINE** CREATIVE WRITING, LITERARY HISTORY **EDUCATION** Pomona Col, Baccalaureate, 73; Univ Nac de Cuyo, Post-Baccalaureate, 74; Univ Calif, MA, 80; PhD, 82. **CAREER** Briggs-Copeland asst prof, Harvard Univ, 83-88; fac member, Bennington Col, 88-90; prof, Wayne State Univ, 90-; fac member, Bennington Summer Writing Workshop, 91; head of creative writing section, Wayne State Univ, 94-. **HONORS AND AWARDS** Fulbright Teaching Fel, Univ Autonoma de Madrid, 96; Board of Governors Distinguished Fac Awd, Wayne State Univ, 97; For Travel Grant, Wayne State Univ, 98; Board of Governors Fac Recognition Awd, Wayne State Univ, 98; President's Awd for Excellence in Teaching, Wayne State Univ, 99. **MEMBERSHIPS** PEN, MLA, Poets and Writers, Inc., Assoc Writing Prog. **RESEARCH** Gay and Lesbian Studies, Latin American Literature, American Social History, American Literature. **SELECTED PUBLICATIONS** Auth, Mean Time, Random House (New York, NY), 82; auth, The Last Happy Men: The Generation of 1922, Fiction, and the Argentine Reality, Syracuse Univ Press (Syracuse, NY), 86; auth, Mrs. Randall, Houghton Mifflin (Boston, MA), 87; transl, Open Door: Stories by Luisa Valenzuela (pp. 9-19 & 24-86), North Point Press (Berkeley, CA), 88; auth, The Book of Marvels, Charles Scribner's Sons (New York, NY), 90; transl, The Censors: A Bilingual Selection of Stories by Luisa Valenzuela, Curbstone Press (Willimantic, CT), 92; auth, The Professor of Aesthetics, Zoland Books (Cambridge, MA), 94; auth, Letting Loose, Zoland Books, (Cambridge, MA), 96; auth, The Art of Compelling Fiction: How to Write a Page-Turner, Story Press (Cincinnati, OH), 98. **CONTACT ADDRESS** Dept English, Wayne State Univ, 51 W Warren Ave, Detroit, MI 48201-1305.

LEMASTER, JIMMIE R.
PERSONAL Born 03/29/1934, Pike County, OH, m, 1966, 3 children **DISCIPLINE** ENGLISH LANGUAGE AND LITERATURE **EDUCATION** Defiance Col, BS, 59; Bowling Green State Univ, 62, PhD(English), 70. **CAREER** Teacher English, Stryker High Sch, 59-61; teacher, Bryan High Sch, 61-62; prof and chmn dept, Lang and Lit, Defiance Col, 62-77; Dir Am Studies Prog, Baylor Univ, 77-, Ed, Tex Writers Newsletter, 79-80; lectr Am lit, Second Foreign Lang Inst, Peking, 80-81; Executive Secy, Southwest Conf Humanities Consortium, 81-. **HONORS AND AWARDS** Publs Awd, South and West, Inc, 70; Ohio Poet of Year, 76; Dean of Col Awd Acad Excellence, 77. **MEMBERSHIPS** MLA; Aaup; Am Studies Asn; SCent Mod Lang Asn; Conf Col Teachers English. **RESEARCH** Twentieth century American literature; Jesse Stuart. **SELECTED PUBLICATIONS** Auth, A Chinese London Connection + A Conversation With Zhang, Bao, Anq-Quart J Short Articles Notes And Rev(s), Vol 0010, 97. **CONTACT ADDRESS** English Dept, Baylor Univ, Waco, Waco, TX 76798. **EMAIL** j_r_lemaster@baylor.edu

LEMIRE, ELISE V.
DISCIPLINE ENGLISH **EDUCATION** Yale Univ, BA, 86; Rutgers Univ, MA, 90, MPhil, 92, PhD, 96. **CAREER** Asst Prof, Lit, State Univ NY-Purchase. **HONORS AND AWARDS** Charlotte W. Newcombe Fellowship **MEMBERSHIPS** Am Antiquarian Soc **SELECTED PUBLICATIONS** Auth, "Making Miscegenation: Discourses of Interracial Sex and Marriage in the U.S., 1790-1865" **CONTACT ADDRESS** Hum Div, SUNY, Col at Purchase, 735 Anderson Hill Rd, Purchase, NY 10577-1400. **EMAIL** Lemire@Brick.Purchase.Edu

LEMIRE, MAURICE
PERSONAL Born 01/21/1927, Saint-Gabriel-de-Brandon, PQ, Canada **DISCIPLINE** LITERATURE **EDUCATION** Col Jean-de-Brebeuf, BA, 49; Univ Montreal, LTh, 53; Sorbonne, LL, 57; Univ Laval, DES, 62, DL, 66. **CAREER** Fac, Univ Montreal, 60-64; ch Fr dept, Univ Sherbrooke, 64-66; prof, 69-93, ch Can stud, 71-72, Prof Emer Litteratures, Univ Laval, 94-. **HONORS AND AWARDS** Medaille Lorne Pierce, SRC, 89; Prix Raymond Klibansky, 92; Medaille de l'Academie des Lettres du Que, 94; Prix du Conseil Int des etudes canadiennes, 96. **MEMBERSHIPS** Soc d'histoire du theatre du Que; Asn des etudes canadiennes; Asn pour l'etude de l'imprime. **SELECTED PUBLICATIONS** Auth, Les grands themes nationalistes du roman historique canadien -francais, 70; auth, Charles Guerin de P.J.O. Chaveau, 75; auth, Les Contes de Louis Frechette, 2 vols, 76, 78; auth, Introduction a la litterature quebecoise 1900-1940, 80; auth, L'Institution litteraire, 86; auth, Le poids des politiques culturelles, 87; auth, Formation de l'imagination litteraire quebecoise, 93; auth, La litterature quebecoise en projet, 94; dir, Dictionnaire des oeuvres litteraires du Quebec, 5 vols, 71-85; dir, La Vie litteraire au Quebec, 3 vols, 91-95. **CONTACT ADDRESS** Dep litteratures, Univ of Laval, Ste. Foy, QC, Canada G1K 7P4.

LENARD, MARY
DISCIPLINE RHETORIC, PROSE, AND BRITISH LITERATURE **EDUCATION** Univ Tex, Austin, PhD. **CAREER** Vis instr, Alma Col; lecturer, Univ Wisc, Parkside, 98--. **RESEARCH** Women's literature; feminist and cultural criticism. **SELECTED PUBLICATIONS** Published work in 19th-century British literature. **CONTACT ADDRESS** Dept. of English, Univ of Wisconsin, Parkside, Kenosha, WI 53141-2000. **EMAIL** lenard@uwp.edu

LENNON, J. MICHAEL
PERSONAL Born 06/13/1942, Fall River, MA, m, 1968, 3 children **DISCIPLINE** ENGLISH **EDUCATION** Stonehill Col, AB, 63; Univ RI, MA, 69; PhD, 75. **CAREER** Prof and exec dir, Univ Ill Springfield, 72-91; prof and vp, Wilkes Univ, 92-. **HONORS AND AWARDS** Phi Kappa Phi; NEH Fel; Literary Executor, Norman Mailer Papers. **MEMBERSHIPS** MLA; NEMLA; James Jones Literary Soc. **RESEARCH** Norman Mailer; Nonfiction theory; Nineteenth Century American literature. **SELECTED PUBLICATIONS** Auth, The James Jones Reader, Birch Lane, 91; auth, Norman Mailer: Work and Days, Sligo Press, 00. **CONTACT ADDRESS** Dept English, Wilkes Univ, 67 S Pioneer Ave, Shavertown, PA 18708-1328. **EMAIL** lennon@wilkes.edu

LENNOX, JOHN W.
PERSONAL Born 06/14/1945, Toronto, ON, Canada **DISCIPLINE** ENGLISH **EDUCATION** York Univ, BA, 67; Univ Sherbrooke, MA, 69; Univ NB, PhD, 76. **CAREER** Lectr, 70-77, assoc prof, 77-90, dir Robarts ctr Can stud, 85-88, dir grad prog Eng, 87-90, prof Eng, York Univ, 91-; assoc dean, Fac of Graduate Studies. **MEMBERSHIPS** Asn Can Que Lit (pres 82-84); Asn Can Stud (pres 92-94); Int Coun Can Stud (pres 95-97). **RESEARCH** Canadian life-writing, fiction, and literary hist. **SELECTED PUBLICATIONS** Coauth, William Arthur Deacon: A Canadian Literary Life, 82; ed, Margaret Laurence-Al Purdy: A Friendship in Letters, 93; co-ed, Dear Bill: The Correspondence of William Arthur Deacon, 88; co-ed, Selected Letters of Margaret Laurence and Adele Wiseman, 97. **CONTACT ADDRESS** Dept of English, York Univ, 4700 Keele St, North York, ON, Canada M3K 1P3. **EMAIL** jlennox@yorku.ca

LENOSKI, DANIEL S.
DISCIPLINE ENGLISH LITERATURE **EDUCATION** Univ Manitoba, BA; MA; Queen's Univ, PhD. **CAREER** Assoc prof **RESEARCH** Aesthetic theories of W. B. Yeats; Anglo-Irish lit, late Victorian and early 20th century British lit, and the Canadian novel. **SELECTED PUBLICATIONS** Auth, pub(s) on Anglo-Irish literature, late Victorian and early 20th century British literature, and Canadian novel; ed, Mosaic, The Canadian Journal of Irish Studies. **CONTACT ADDRESS** Dept of English, Univ of Manitoba, Winnipeg, MB, Canada R3T 2N2. **EMAIL** lenoski@cc.umanitoba.ca

LENT, JOHN ANTHONY
PERSONAL Born 09/08/1936, East Millsboro, PA, 5 children **DISCIPLINE** MASS COMMUNICATIONS, ASIAN STUDIES **EDUCATION** Ohio Univ, BSJ, 58, MS, 60; Univ Iowa, PhD, 72. **CAREER** Instr English & J, WVa Inst Technol, 60-62; lectr jour, De La Salle Col, Manila, Philippines, 64-65;

asst prof English & jour, WVa Inst Technol, 65-66; asst prof jour, Wis State Univ-Eau Claire, 66-67 & Marshall Univ, 67-69; vis assoc prof jour, Univ Wyo, 69-70; assoc ed, Int Commun Bull, Univ Iowa, 70-72; coordr mass commun prog, Univ Sains Malaysia, Penang, 72-74; assoc prof, 74-76, Prof Mass Commun, Temple Univ, 76-; ed, Berita; chair, Asian Cinema Studies Soc; ed, Asian Cinema; managing ed, WittyWorld; assoc ed, Asian Thought and Soc; chair, IAMCR Comic Art Working Group; Rogers distinguished prof, Univ of Western Ontario, 00; ed, Int J of Comic Art; Chair, Asian Pop Cult group of Pop Cult Asn. **HONORS AND AWARDS** Paul Eberman res award; 2 Broadcast Preceptor awards; Ray and Pat Browne Nat Book award; founder, Malaysia/Singapore/Brunei Studies Group; Fulbright grant, Philippines, 64-65. **MEMBERSHIPS** Asn Asian Studies; Int Asn Mass Commun Res **RESEARCH** Comic Art; animation; Mass media in Third World, especially in Caribbean and Asia; use of folk media; history of mass communications. **SELECTED PUBLICATIONS** Ed, The Asian Newspapers' Reluctant Revolution, Iowa State Univ/Azumi Shoppan, 71, 72; auth, Philippine Mass Communications .., Philippine Inst, 71, 72; Asian Mass Communications: A Comprehensive Bibliography, Temple Univ, 75, Suppl, 78; ed, Cultural Pluralism in Malaysia, Northern Ill Univ, 77; auth, Third World Mass Media and Their Search for Modernity, Bucknell Univ/Assoc Iniv Presses, 77; ed, Broadcasting in Asia and the Pacific, Temple Univ/Heinemann, 78; Asian Popular Culture, Different Road Taken, Global Productions (with G Sussman), Transnational Commun, and 40 others and over 500 journal articles; ed, International Journal of Comic Art. **CONTACT ADDRESS** 669 Ferne Blvd, Drexel Hill, PA 19026.

LENTRICCHIA, FRANK, JR.
PERSONAL Born 05/23/1940, Utica, NY, m, 1973, 2 children **DISCIPLINE** LITERATURE, ENGLISH **EDUCATION** Utica Col of Syracuse Univ, BA, 62; Duke Univ, MA, 63; PhD, 66. **CAREER** Asst prof, Univ of Calif, Los Angeles, 66-68; from asst prof to prof, Univ of Calif, Irvine, 68-82; Autrey Prof of Humanities, Rice Univ, 82-84; Katherine Everett Gilbert Prof of English and Lit, Duke Univ, 84-. **HONORS AND AWARDS** Grad scholar, Duke Univ, 62. **MEMBERSHIPS** Mod Lang Asn of Am. **RESEARCH** American literature, history of poetry, modernism, the role of the intellectual in culture, the history of theory of criticism. **SELECTED PUBLICATIONS** Auth, The Gaiety of Language: An Essay on the Radical Poetics of W.B. Yeats and Wallace Stevens, Univ of Calif Press, 68; auth, Robert Frost: Modern Poetics and the Landscapes of Self, Duke Univ Press, 75; auth, After the New Criticism, Univ of Chicago Press, 80; auth, Criticism and Social Change, Univ of Chicago Press, 84; auth, Ariel and the Police, Harvester, 88; auth, The Edge of Night, Random House, 94; auth, Johnny Critelli, Scribner, 96; auth, The Knifeman, Scribner, 96; auth, The Music of the Inferno, SUNY Press, 99; auth, Lucchesi and the Whale, Duke Univ Press, 01. **CONTACT ADDRESS** Prog in Lit, Duke Univ, Durham, NC 27708.

LENZ, JOHN RICHARD
PERSONAL Born 07/03/1957, New York, NY, m, 1994, 1 child **DISCIPLINE** CLASSICAL STUDIES **EDUCATION** Columbia Univ, PhD, 93. **CAREER** 90-91, Union College; 91-94, Chmn 94-, Drew Univ. **HONORS AND AWARDS** Fulbright Travel Grant, Greece, 88-89. **MEMBERSHIPS** Bertrand Russell Society, Pres; NJ Classical Assoc, VP. **RESEARCH** Bertrand Russell; ancient Greece. **CONTACT ADDRESS** Dept of Classics, Drew Univ, Madison, NJ 07940. **EMAIL** jlenz@drew.edu

LENZ, WILLIAM ERNEST
PERSONAL Born 06/26/1950, New York, NY, m, 1975, 2 children **DISCIPLINE** ENGLISH AND AMERICAN LITERATURE **EDUCATION** BA magn cum laude Amherst College 73, MA Univ of Virginia 74, PhD Univ of Virginia 80. **CAREER** Prof and Chair Dept of English Chatham College. **HONORS AND AWARDS** Prof of English 97-98, NEH Project Director 96-97. **MEMBERSHIPS** MLA; ASA; NEMLA; SHARP; ALA. **RESEARCH** Explanations and Travel Literature. **SELECTED PUBLICATIONS** The Poetics of the Antarctic; A Study in Nineteenth-Century American Cultural Perceptions "Garland Studies in Nineteenth-American Literature", New York Garland, 95; Fast Talk and Flush Time: The Confidence Man As A Literary Convention, Columbia Univ of Missouri Press, 85; Identity in John Lloyd Stephen's Incidents of Travel in Central America,Chiapas and Yucatan in Travel Culture: Essays on What Makes Us Go; ed, Carol Traynor Williams Westport Connecticut and London Praeger, 79-87, 98; The Function of Wonem in Old Southwestern Humor:Re-reading Porter's Big Bear and Quarter Race Collections Mississippi Quarterly XLVI, 4, 598-600, 93; Poe's Arthur Gordon Pym and the Narrative Techniques of Antarctic Gothic, CEA Critic 53, 3, 41-63, 91; The Galapagos Islands: The Encantadas of Darwin and Melville Animal Talk, 9, 1, 26 91. **CONTACT ADDRESS** Dept of English, Chatham Col, Woodland Rd., Pittsburgh, PA 15232. **EMAIL** lenz@chatham.edu

LEON, PHILIP WHEELER
PERSONAL Born 12/28/1944, Memphis, TN, m, 1967, 1 child **DISCIPLINE** AMERICAN LITERATURE **EDUCATION** Wake Forest Univ, BA, 66, MA, 70; Vanderbilt Univ, PhD(English), 74. **CAREER** Instr English, Winston-Salem State Univ, 69-71, asst prof, 73-75; asst prof, 75-80, Assoc prof to Prof of English, The Citadel, 80-. **MEMBERSHIPS** South Atlantic Modern Language Assoc; American Osler Soc; Walt Whitman Assoc; Mark Twain Circle. **RESEARCH** American fiction; bibliographic study. **SELECTED PUBLICATIONS** Auth, Composition as a Human Enterprise, NC English Teacher, spring 75; Joseph Seamon Cotter's Short Stories, Filson Club Hist Quart, 10/75; The Lost Boy and a Lost Girl, Southern Lit J, fall 76; Teaching the Old, the New and the Discovery of Both, Notes on Teach English, 12/77; William Styron: An Annotated Bibliography of Criticism, Greenwood, 78; A Vast Dehumanization, Va Quart Rev, autumn 79; Styron's Narrative Technique in the Achievement of William Styron, Univ GA Press, 82; Walt Whitman and Sir William Osler, ECW Press, (Toronto), 95; Mark Twain and West Point, ECW Press, (Toronto), 96; Bullies and Cowards: The West Point Hazing Scandal, 1898-1901, Greenwood Press, (Westport, CT), 00. **CONTACT ADDRESS** Dept of English, 171 Moultrie St, Charleston, SC 29409-6310. **EMAIL** leonp@citadel.edu

LEONARD, JAMES S.
PERSONAL Born 07/02/1947, Bristol, VA, m, 1979, 1 child **DISCIPLINE** ENGLISH **EDUCATION** Univ Tenn, BA, 69; MA, 79; Brown Univ, PhD, 83. **CAREER** Asst prof, 83-88; assoc prof, 88-93; prof, 93-, Citadel. **HONORS AND AWARDS** SAMLA Stud Awd, 84; Citadel Fac Ach Awds, 88, 89, 90, 92, 93, 97. **MEMBERSHIPS** MLA; ALA; AHSA; SAMLA; Mark Twain Cir; Wallace Stevens Soc. **RESEARCH** Mark Twain; Wallace Stevens. **SELECTED PUBLICATIONS** Coauth, The Fluent Mundo: Wallace Stevens and the Structure of Reality, Univ Georgia Press (Athens), 88; auth, afterward, A Tramp Abroad, The Oxford Mark Twain, Oxford Univ Press, 97; co-ed, Satire or Evasion? Black Perspectives on Huckleberry Finn, Duke Univ Press (Durham), 92; co-ed, Author-ity and Texuality: Current Views of Collaborative Writing, Locusthill Press (West Cornwall, CT), 94; ed, Making Mark Twain Work in the Classroom, Duke Univ (Durham), 99; ed, Mark Twain Circular, MTCA (87-). **CONTACT ADDRESS** Dept English, The Citadel, The Military Col of So Carolina, 171 Moultrie St, Charleston, SC 29409-0001. **EMAIL** leonardj@citadel.edu

LEONARDI, SUSAN J.
PERSONAL Born 04/27/1946, CA, 4 children **DISCIPLINE** ENGLISH LITERATURE **EDUCATION** Univ Cal, Davis, PhD, 86, MA, 82, eng lit; Immaculata Col, PA, BA, 68. **CAREER** Univ MD, Col Pk, asst prof, 87-89, assoc prof, 90-97, prof, 98-. **HONORS AND AWARDS** Students Awd for Excellence in Teaching, 89; ch, Comt on Lesbian, Gay, and Bisexual Studies, 92-94; NEH Summer Grant for Seminar, Brown Univ, 94; Curriculum Dev Grant, 94-95. **SELECTED PUBLICATIONS** The Diva's Mouth: Body, Voice, Prima Donna Politics, with Rebecca A Pope, Rutgers Univ Press, 96; Dangerous By Degrees: Women at Oxford and the Summerville College Novelists, Rutgers Univ Press, 89; auth, Opera: Nationalities/Ideologies/Sexualities; Tulsa Studies in Women's Literature. **CONTACT ADDRESS** Dept Eng, Univ of Maryland, Col Park, Susquehanna Hall, Rm 4135, College Park, MD 20742-8815. **EMAIL** sl18@umail.umd.edu

LEPLEY, DOUG
DISCIPLINE ENGLISH LITERATURE **EDUCATION** Susquehanna Univ, BA; Bucknell Univ, MA; Lehigh Univ, PhD. **CAREER** Prof, 78, vice-pres, Acad Aff, Thomas Col. **SELECTED PUBLICATIONS** Publ articles on Geoffrey Chaucer and John Gower. Also edited for Shoestring Press and Mainely Local. **CONTACT ADDRESS** Thomas Col, Maine, Admin Bldg, Waterville, ME 04901-5097. **EMAIL** lepley@thomas.edu

LESK, ANDREW J.
PERSONAL Born Sudbury, ON, Canada **DISCIPLINE** ENGLISH **EDUCATION** Univ Toronto, BA, 93; Univ Guelph, MA, 94; Univ Montreal, PhD, 01. **CAREER** Instr, Univ Montreal, 95-00. **HONORS AND AWARDS** Dept Scholar, Univ Montreal, 95-98; Joseph Wesley MacCallum Scholar, 92; YMCA Mem Scholar, Khaki Univ, 92; R. G. Riddell Mem Bursary, 92; Webster Prize, Univ Toronto, 90. **MEMBERSHIPS** MLA; NEMLA; ACCCUTE; ACS. **RESEARCH** Canadian literature; gay and lesbian studies; queer theory and gender studies; post colonialism. **SELECTED PUBLICATIONS** Auth, "Achebe and His Critics: Racism in Heart of Darkness," Essay/Studies Lit Critic 3 (94); auth, "Something Queer Going on Here: Desire in the Short Fiction of Sinclair Ross," Essays Can Writing 61 (97); auth, "Leonard Cohen's Traffic in Alterity in Beautiful Losers," Studies Can Lit 22 (97); auth, "Untenable Imaginings and Imagined Communities: Robert Lecker on the Failings of Criticism," Henry Street 7 (98); auth, "On Sinclair Ross's Straight(ened) House," English Studies Can (01); auth, "Having a Gay Old Time in Paris: John Glassco's Not-So-Queer Adventures," in In a Queer Country: Gay and Lesbian Studies in the Canadian Context, ed. Terry Goldie (Arsenal Pulp Pr, 01); co-auth, "Gender Trespass and Masculine Privilege: 'Male Trouble' on Spit Delaney's Island," Studies Can Lit (forthcoming). **CONTACT ADDRESS** 318 Albany Ave, Toronto, ON, Canada M5R 3C9. **EMAIL** andrew.lesk@umontreal.ca

LESSER, WENDY
PERSONAL Born 03/20/1952, CA, m, 1985, 1 child **DISCIPLINE** ENGLISH **EDUCATION** Harvard, BA, 73; Univ Cal Berkeley, PhD, 82. **CAREER** Ed, The Threepenny Review, 80-; Guggenheim fel; ACLS fel; NEH fel; OSI fel; fel Am Acad Arts & Sci; Morton Darwen Zabel Award. **RESEARCH** Literature; Visual arts; Performing arts. **SELECTED PUBLICATIONS** His Other Half; Pictures at an Execution; The Amateur. **CONTACT ADDRESS** Threepenny Review, PO Box 9131, Berkeley, CA 94709.

LESTER, JAMES
PERSONAL Born 03/05/1935, Fort Smith, AK, m, 1958, 2 children **DISCIPLINE** ENGLISH **EDUCATION** E Cent Univ Okla, BA, 57; Okla State Univ, MA, 63; Univ Tulsa, PhD, 70. **HONORS AND AWARDS** Parriott Fel. **MEMBERSHIPS** MLA; NCTE; SMLA. **RESEARCH** Compostion. **SELECTED PUBLICATIONS** Auth, A Writer's Guide to Figurative Language: Making Language Work Effectively in Poetry, Fiction and Nonfiction, Lester Pub, 94; auth, Writing: Style and Grammar, GoodYearBooks, 94; auth, Of Bunsen Burners, Bones, and Belles Lettres: Classic Essays across the Curriculum, NTC Pub Group, 96; auth, Plato's Heirs: Classic Essays, NTC Pub Group, 96; auth, Daughters of the Revolution: Classic Essays by Women, NTC Pub Group, 96; auth, Diverse Identities: Classic Multicultural Essays, NTC Pub Group, 96; auth, Writing Research Papers: A Complete Guide, HarperCollins Pub, 96; auth, Citing Cyberspace, Addison, 97; auth, Writing Research Papers: A Complete Guide, 9th ed, New York, 99; auth, The Essential Guide to Writing Research Papers, New York, 99. **CONTACT ADDRESS** Dept Lang & Lit, Austin Peay State Univ, 601 College St, Clarksville, TN 37044-0001. **EMAIL** lesterjd@knighthouse.com

LESTER, MARK
DISCIPLINE ENGLISH **EDUCATION** Univ CA, PhD. **CAREER** Found ch, dept Eng Sec Lang, Eastern WA Univ . **SELECTED PUBLICATIONS** Auth, Grammar in the Classroom. **CONTACT ADDRESS** Eastern Washington Univ, Cheney, WA 99004-2431.

LESTOURGEON, DIANA E.
PERSONAL Born 04/06/1927, Covington, KY **DISCIPLINE** ENGLISH **EDUCATION** Univ Pa, AB, 49, AM, 50, PhD(English), 60. **CAREER** Instr, Ala Polytech Inst, 53-54 & Univ Mo, 54-55; asst instr, Pa State Univ, 55-56; from asst instr to instr, Univ Pa, 56-63; from asst prof to assoc prof, 65-77, Prof English, Widener Univ, 77- . **MEMBERSHIPS** MLA **RESEARCH** Twentieth century British fiction; psychological fiction; Victorian LIT **SELECTED PUBLICATIONS** Auth, Rosamond Lehmann, Twayne, 65; coauth, The Figure in The Carpet, Albion, 76. **CONTACT ADDRESS** Dept of English, Widener Univ, Pennsylvania, 1 University Pl, Chester, PA 19013-5792.

LETTIS, RICHARD
PERSONAL Born 06/30/1928, Springfield, MA, m, 1951, 5 children **DISCIPLINE** ENGLISH **EDUCATION** Univ Mass, BA, 52; Yale Univ, MA, 53, PhD(English), 57. **CAREER** Instr English, Ohio Univ, 56-60; from asst prof to assoc prof, 60-67, exec dean, 71-73, Prof English, C W Post Col, Long Island Univ, 67-, Humanities ed, Pennant Studies Guides, Educ Res Assoc and Bantam, 66-67. **RESEARCH** English novel of 18th and 19th centuries. **SELECTED PUBLICATIONS** Auth, How I Work, Dickens in the Writers Chair, Dickensian, Vol 0089, 93. **CONTACT ADDRESS** Long Island Univ, C.W. Post, Greenvale, NY 11548.

LETZRING, MONICA
PERSONAL Born 02/01/1935, Grafton, ND **DISCIPLINE** ENGLISH AND COMPARATIVE LITERATURE **EDUCATION** Col St Scholastica, BA, 57; Univ Md, MA, 60, PhD, 63. **CAREER** Instr English lit, Col Notre Dame, Md, 63; instr English, Ctr Ling, Bergamo, Italy, 63-65; asst prof, 65-75, Assoc Prof English, Temple Univ, 75-. **MEMBERSHIPS** MLA; Am Soc 18th Century Studies. **RESEARCH** Eighteenth century English literature. **SELECTED PUBLICATIONS** Auth, Influence of Camoens in English literature, Rev Camoneana, 64, 65, 71; Strangford's poems from the Portuguese of Camoens, Comp Lit, fall 71; The Adamastor episode and 18th century theory of the sublime in England, Actas da I Reuniao Int de Camonistas, 73; Mickle, Boswell, Liberty and the Prospects of Liberty and Slavery, Mod Lang Rev, 74; Sarah Prince Gill and the John Adams-Catharine Macaulay correspondence, Proc Mass Hist Soc, 76. **CONTACT ADDRESS** Dept of English, Temple Univ, 1114 W Berks St, Philadelphia, PA 19122-6029.

LEUBSDORF, JOHN
PERSONAL Born 02/11/1942, New York, NY, m, 1998, 1 child **DISCIPLINE** LAW, LITERATURE **EDUCATION** Harvard Univ, BA, 63; Stanford Univ, MA, Eng, 64; Harvard Law Sch, JD, 67. **CAREER** Assoc prof and prof, Boston Univ, 75-84; vis prof, Columbia Univ, 90-91; Univ Calif Berkeley, 93; Cornell Univ, 95; prof, Rutgers Law Sch, Newark, 84-. **HONORS AND AWARDS** Fulbright scholar, Paris, 95. **MEMBERSHIPS** Amer Law Inst. **RESEARCH** Legal Ethics,

Civil Procedure, and Law & Literature. **SELECTED PUBLICATIONS** Auth, Civil Procedure, 4th ed, with F. James and G. Hazard, 92; auth," Man In His Original Dignity," Legal Ethics In France, 00; auth, " Restatement of the Law Governing Lawyers," Assoc Reporter, 00. **CONTACT ADDRESS** Rutgers, The State Univ of New Jersey, Newark, 15 Washington St., Newark, NJ 07102. **EMAIL** leubsdorf@kinoy.rutgers.edu

LEUPIN, ALEXANDRE
PERSONAL m, 4 children **DISCIPLINE** MEDIEVAL LITERATURE, LITERARY CRITICISM AND THEORY, PSYCHOANALYSIS, EPISTEM **EDUCATION** Univ Geneva, Doctorat, 71. **CAREER** Asst prof, Dept of Fr and Italian, Miami Univ, Oxford, Ohio, 82-83; assoc prof, 83-84, prof, 85-. Dept of Fr and Italian, La State Univ; full mem, Program of Comparative Lit, LSU, 92-; Acting dir of graduate studies, Dept of Fr and Italian, LSU, fall 96. **HONORS AND AWARDS** Dow Healey Memorial fel, 91; Summer grant for res, LSU, 92, 94; Stipend for Travel Abroad, College of Arts and Sciences, LSU, 94. **RESEARCH** Theoretical psychoanalysis; theology; art history; epistemology; Lacan. **SELECTED PUBLICATIONS** Auth, Le Graal et la litterature: etude sur la vulgate arthurienne en prose, L'Age d'Homme (Lausanne), 83; auth, Barbarolexis: Medieval Literature and Sexuality, Harvard Univ Press, 89; ed, Lacan and the Human Sciences, Univ of Nebraska Press, 91; auth, Fiction et incarnation, theologie et litterature au Moyen Age, Flammarion (Paris), 93; auth, "Edouard Glissant: l'oeuvre-mangrove," Art Press (97); auth, "Les temps dans le 'Roman de la Rose,'" Melanges Lorenzo Renzi (Padova, 99); auth, "The Impossibe Copula," Rhetoric Society Quarterly (99): 11-20. **CONTACT ADDRESS** Dept of Fr Grad Stud, Louisiana State Univ and A&M Col, Baton Rouge, LA 70803. **EMAIL** frleup@lsu.edu

LEUTHOLD, STEVEN M.
PERSONAL Born 05/24/1957, Houston, TX, m, 1981, 2 children **DISCIPLINE** COMMUNICATIONS **EDUCATION** Univ Montana, BA, 80; Wash State Univ, MA, 89; Univ Penn, PhD, 92. **CAREER** Instr, Intensive Am Lang Ctr, 88, instr, Murrow Sch for Commun, 87-89, Wash State Univ; instr, Annenberg Sch for Commun, Univ Penn, 89-92; asst prof, Syracuse Univ Sch of Art and Design, 92-99; asst prof, Northern Mich Univ, 99-. **MEMBERSHIPS** Col Art Asn. **RESEARCH** Art theory; aesthetics; indigenous issues; color; media studies. **SELECTED PUBLICATIONS** Auth, An Indigenous Aesthetic? Two Noted Native Videographers: George Burdeau and Victor Masayesva, Wicazo Sa: A Rev of Native Am Stud, 94; auth, Social Accountability and the Production of Native American Film and Video, Wide Angle, 94; auth, Native American Responses to the Western, Am Indian Cult and Res Jour, 95; auth, Native American Art and Artists in Visual Arts Documentaries from 1973-1991, On the Margins of Artworlds, Westview, 95; auth, The Book and the Peasant: Visual Representation and Social Change in German Woodcuts, 1521-1525, Printing Hist, 95; auth, Is There Art in Indigenous Aesthetics? Jour of Arts Mgt, Law and Soc, 96; auth, Representing Truth and History in Native American Documentary, Film and Hist, 97; auth, Native American Documentary: An Emerging Genre, Film Criticism, 97; auth, Native Media's Communities, Am Indian Cult and Res Jour, 97; auth, Indigenous Aesthetics: Representation and Conditions of Reception, Dialogue and Universalism, 97; auth, Crossing the Lines: Toward a Curriculum of Comparative Deisign, Multicultural Educ, 97; auth, Historical Representation in Native American Documentary: A Review Essay, Ethnohistory, 97; auth, Genre-lizing about Realism, Art Criticism, 98; auth, Indigenous Aesthetics: Native Art, Media and Identity, Texas, 98. **CONTACT ADDRESS** Dept of Art and Design, No Michigan Univ, 1401 Presque Isle Ave, Marquette, MI 49885-5339. **EMAIL** sleuthol@nmu.edu

LEV, PETER
PERSONAL Born 06/15/1948, Cleveland, OH, m, 1976, 1 child **DISCIPLINE** MASS COMMUNICATION **EDUCATION** Wesleyan Univ, BA, 70; Univ Calif, Los Angeles, MA, 74, PhD, 80. **CAREER** Vis Asst Prof, Univ Tex at Dallas, 80-82; Asst Prof, 83-88, Assoc Prof, 88-93, Prof Mass Commun, Towson Univ. **HONORS AND AWARDS** Fac Excellence Awd, Towson, 96-97; past pres, lit/film asn; ed bd, lit film quart; crse file ed, j of film & video. **MEMBERSHIPS** Lit/Film Asn; Int Asn for Media & Hist; Univ Film & Video Asn; Soc for Cinema Stud. **RESEARCH** History of American & European film; international film & television; film & ecology. **SELECTED PUBLICATIONS** Auth, The Euro-American Cinema, Univ Tex Press, 93; auth, Whose Future?, Lit/Film Quart, 26.1, 98; 7 essays in The Encyclopedia of Novels into Film, 98; auth, Conflicting Visions: American Films of the 1970s, Univ Tex Press, 00. **CONTACT ADDRESS** Dept of Electronic Media & Film, Towson State Univ, Towson, MD 21252. **EMAIL** plev@towson.edu

LEVANDER, CAROLINE FIELD
DISCIPLINE ENGLISH, LITERATURE **EDUCATION** Rice Univ, PhD, 95. **CAREER** Asst prof, Trinity Univ, 95-00; assoc prof, Rice Univ, 01-. **MEMBERSHIPS** ALA; MLA. **RESEARCH** 19th century American literature; women and gender studies. **SELECTED PUBLICATIONS** Auth, Voices of the Nation: Women and Public Speech in 19th-Century American Culture, Cambridge Univ Pr, 98. **CONTACT ADDRESS** English Dept, Rice Univ, 6100 Main St, MS30, Houston, TX 77005-1827. **EMAIL** clevander@rice.edu

LEVENDUSKI, CRISTINE
DISCIPLINE ENGLISH LANGUAGE AND LITERATURE **EDUCATION** Univ Minn, PhD, 89. **CAREER** Assoc prof/dir grad studies. **RESEARCH** American studies; early American literature. **SELECTED PUBLICATIONS** Auth, Peculiar Power: A Quaker Woman Preacher in 18th Century America, Smithsonian, 96. **CONTACT ADDRESS** English Dept, Emory Univ, 1380 Oxford Rd NE, Atlanta, GA 30322-1950. **EMAIL** cmleven@emory.edu

LEVENSON, CARL
DISCIPLINE ENGLISH LITERATURE **EDUCATION** Univ Chicago, PhD, 86. **CAREER** Assoc prof. **RESEARCH** Plato; Old Testament; continental philosophy. **SELECTED PUBLICATIONS** Auth, Socrates and the Corybantes; Dionysian Spirituality in the Philosophy of Plato; co-ed, Reality of Time and of Life and Death. **CONTACT ADDRESS** Dept of English and Philosophy, Idaho State Univ, Pocatello, ID 83209.

LEVENSON, JACOB CLAVNER
PERSONAL Born 10/01/1922, Boston, MA, m, 1946, 3 children **DISCIPLINE** ENGLISH **EDUCATION** Harvard Univ, AB, 43, PhD, 51. **CAREER** Tutor, 46-50, Harvard Univ; instr, 50-54, Univ Conn; from asst prof to prof, 54-67, chmn prog Am studies, 63, Univ Minn; chmn dept, 71-74, Edgar Allan Poe Prof English, 67-, Univ Va; mem fac Am Studies Sem, Salzburg, Austria, 47 & 49; vis lectr English & gen educ, 51-52, Harvard Univ; Am Philos Soc Penrose grant, 56; fac res grant, Univ Minn, 56; Guggenheim fel, 58-59; Am Coun Learned Soc fel, 61-62; mem English Inst; mem comt consult, Notable American Women, 1607-1950, Radcliffe Col, 63-72. **HONORS AND AWARDS** E Harris Harbison Distinguished Tchng Awd, Danforth Found, 66; Univ Va Soc of Fels, 78-. **MEMBERSHIPS** MLA; Am Studies Assn. **RESEARCH** American literature; American cultural history. **SELECTED PUBLICATIONS** Auth, The Sadness of Sister Carrie, Morphologies of Faith, Scholars Press, 90; auth, American Literature 1865-1914, Reader's Encycl of Amer Hist, Houghton, 91; auth, Passage to Modernity: Crane's Red Badge and Norris's McTeague, Cambridge Companion to American Realism and naturalism, Cambridge, 95. **CONTACT ADDRESS** Univ of Virginia, 219 Bryan Hall, Charlottesville, VA 22903. **EMAIL** jcl3g@virginia.edu

LEVENSON, JILL
DISCIPLINE ENGLISH **EDUCATION** Queen's Col City, Univ New York, BA, 63; Harvard Univ, MA, 64, PhD, 67. **CAREER** Lectr, Queen's Col City, Univ New York, 64; tutor, Harvard Univ, 65-66; asst prof, Trinity Col, 67-74, assoc prof, 74-82, Prof English, Univ Toronto 82-. **HONORS AND AWARDS** Cert Merit, Conf Ed Learned J, 86; Outstanding Tchr Awd, Fac Arts Sci, Univ Toronto, 94. **MEMBERSHIPS** MLA; Shakespeare Asn Am; Int Shakespeare Asn; Am Soc Theatre Res. **RESEARCH** Shakespeare and modern drama; bibliography for Romeo and Juliet and Othello; the construction of narrative in second-tier (I.e, non-Shakespearean, non-Marlovian) history plays of the english Renaisssance. **SELECTED PUBLICATIONS** Auth, Romeo and Juliet (Shakespeare in Performance), 87; auth, "Comedy," in Cambridge Companion to English Renaissance Drama (90); coed, Shakespeare and the Twentieth Century, 98; contributor, Shakespeare: Text and Theater, ed. Lois Potter and Arthur F. Kinney, 99; ed, Romeo and Juliet, Oxford Univ Press (NY), 00; contributor, Cambridge Companion to Tom Stoppard (forthcoming). **CONTACT ADDRESS** Trinity Col, Univ of Toronto, Toronto, ON, Canada M5S 1H8. **EMAIL** jilleven@trinity.toronto.edu

LEVERNIER, JAMES ARTHUR
PERSONAL Born 07/26/1949, Highland Park, IL **DISCIPLINE** ENGLISH, AMERICAN STUDIES **EDUCATION** Marquette Univ, BA, 71; Univ Pa, MA, 73; PhD, 75. **CAREER** Asst prof, 76-80, Assoc Prof English, Univ Ark, Little Rock, 80-, Dir, Am Studies, 78-. **MEMBERSHIPS** MLA; Children's Lit Asn; Am Studies Asn. **RESEARCH** Early American literature; native American studies; folklore. **SELECTED PUBLICATIONS** Co-ed, The Indians and Their Captives, Greenwood Press Contrib Am Studies, 77; auth, The captivity narrative as regional, military and ethnic history, 77; Introd to Increase Mather's An Essay for the Recording of Illustrious Providences, Scholars Facsimiles & Reprints, 77; Calvinism and transcendentalism in the poetry of Jones Very, ESQ: J Am Renaissance, 78; ed, Soldiery Spiritualized: Nine Sermons Preached Before the Artillery Companies of New England, 1672-1772, Scholars Facsimiles & Reprints, 80; coauth, Structuring Paragraphs: A Guide to Effective Writing, St Martins Press, 81; co-ed, Sermons and Cannonballs: Eleven Sermons on Military Events of Historic Significance During the French and Indian Wars, 1689-1760, Scholars' Facsimiles & Reprints, 82; The captivity narrative as children's literature, Markham Rev (in press). **CONTACT ADDRESS** Univ of Arkansas, Little Rock, 2801 S University Ave, Little Rock, AR 72204-1000.

LEVIN, CHARLES
DISCIPLINE COMMUNICATION STUDIES **EDUCATION** McGill Univ, BA, MA; Concordia Univ, PhD. **CAREER** Fac lectr, McGill Univ. **HONORS AND AWARDS** SSHRC Doctoral and Postdoctoral Fel; Concordia fel; Governor General's Gold Medal; Prix d'Excellence de l'Acadmie des Grands Montralais. **MEMBERSHIPS** Can Psychoanalytic Soc. **RESEARCH** European social thought and aesthetics since the enlightenment. **SELECTED PUBLICATIONS** Auth, "The Epicenity of the Text: Lacanian Psychoanalysis and Feminist Metatheory," Borderlines 7, 87; auth, "Time and Post modernism: A Capsule," Communication 10, (88): 311-330; auth, "Thinking through the Hungry Baby: Towards a New Pleasure Principle," Psychoanalytic Study of the Child, 47, 92; auth, "Entre la Chaire et l'Esprit: le Corps Social du Nouveau-ne," Sociologie et Societe, 24:1, 92; auth, Jean Baudrillard: A Study in Cultural Metaphysics, London: Prentice Hall, 96. **CONTACT ADDRESS** Dept Communications, McGill Univ, 845 Sherbrooke St, Montreal, QC, Canada H3A 2T5. **EMAIL** cxcl@musica.mcgill.ca

LEVIN, JONATHAN
DISCIPLINE 19TH-AND 20TH-CENTURY AMERICAN LITERATURE **EDUCATION** Mich, BA, 83; UCLA, MA, 85; Rutgers, PhD, 95. **CAREER** English and Lit, Columbia Univ **HONORS AND AWARDS** Fel, Nat Hum Ctr; Assoc ed, Raritan Rev. **SELECTED PUBLICATIONS** Auth, Walt Whitman, an illustrated selection of Whitman's poetry, 97. **CONTACT ADDRESS** Columbia Univ, 2960 Broadway, New York, NY 10027-6902.

LEVIN, RICHARD A.
PERSONAL Born 04/04/1944, Brooklyn, NY, m, 1975, 2 children **DISCIPLINE** ENGLISH LITERATURE **EDUCATION** Univ NC, Chapel Hill, BA, 65; Oxford Univ, BA, 67; Stanford Univ, PhD, 72. **CAREER** From instr to asst prof Eng, Univ New Orleans, 71-74; asst prof, 74-81, Assoc Prof Eng, Univ CA, Davis, 81. **MEMBERSHIPS** MLA; Shakespeare Asn Am. **RESEARCH** Early mod Eng Lit. **SELECTED PUBLICATIONS** Love and Society in Shakespear Comedy, Univ of DE Press, 85; articles on Sponsor Sidney Shakespears dramatic contemporaries. **CONTACT ADDRESS** Dept of Eng, Univ of California, Davis, Davis, CA 95616-5200. **EMAIL** ralevin@ucdavis.edu

LEVIN, RICHARD L.
PERSONAL Born 08/21/1922, Buffalo, NY, m, 1952, 2 children **DISCIPLINE** ENGLISH **EDUCATION** Univ Chicago, BA, 43; MA, 47; PhD, 57. **CAREER** Instr to asst prof, Univ Chicago, 49-57; prof, SUNY Stony Brook, 57-94. **HONORS AND AWARDS** ACLS Fel, 63-64; NEH Sr Fel, 74; Guggenheim Fel, 78-79; Fulbright Lectrshp, 84-85; NHC Fel, 87-88; Explicator Awd, 71; Fac Exchange Scholar, 81-90. **MEMBERSHIPS** MLA; SAA; MRDS; Joseph Crabtree Found; Shakespeare Globe Cen; Columbia Shakespeare Sem. **RESEARCH** English renaissance drama; literary criticism and critical theory; wise women and witches; ballads; proverbs. **SELECTED PUBLICATIONS** Auth, The Question of Socrates, Harcourt, 61; ed. Tragedy: Plays, Theory and Criticism, Harcourt, 65; auth, The Multiple Plot in English Renaissance Drama, Univ Chicago, 71; auth, New Readings vs. Old Plays: Recent Trends in the Reinterpretation of English Renaissance Drama, Univ Chicago, 79; auth, "Feminist Thematics and Shakespearean Tragedy," PMLA (88); auth, "The Poetics and Politics of Bardicide," PMLA (91); auth, The New and the Old Historicizing of Shakespeare," REAL (95); auth, "Silence is Consent," Col English(97); auth, "The Old and the New Materializing of Shakespeare," Shake Int Yearbk (99). **CONTACT ADDRESS** English Dept, SUNY, Stony Brook, Stony Brook, NY 11794-5350. **EMAIL** rlevins@ms.cc.sunysb.edu

LEVIN, SAUL
PERSONAL Born 07/13/1921, Chicago, IL, m, 1951, 6 children **DISCIPLINE** CLASSICS **EDUCATION** Univ Chicago, AB, 42; PhD, 49. **CAREER** Instr, Univ Chicago, 49-51; from asst prof to assoc prof, Wash Univ, 51-61; prof, SUNY Binghamton, 61-; Dist Prof of Ancient Lang, 90-00; prof emer, 00-. **HONORS AND AWARDS** Fac Fel, Ford Found, 53-54; grants & fels, Res Found and Joint Awds Coun, SUNY, 61, 63, 65, 66, 68, 69, 75. **MEMBERSHIPS** Am Philol Asn; Soc Bibl Lit; Ling Asn Can and US; Class Asn of the Atlantic States; Class Asn of the Empire State; Int Orgn for Septuagint and Cognate Studies; Asn for the Study of Lang in Prehistory; Soc for Ancient Greek Philos; Golden Key Nat Honor Soc. **RESEARCH** Comparison of Semitic and Indo-European languages; Classical Greek, especially the Homeric dialect; Hebrew scriptures. **SELECTED PUBLICATIONS** Auth, Guide to the Bible, Part I: Genesis to Malachi (The Pentateuch, the Former Prophets or Historical Books, the Latter Prophets), SUNY-Binghamton, 87; auth, Guide to the Bible, Part II: The Hagiographia (or "Writings"), selected Apocrypha, the New Testament, SUNY-Binghamton, 87; auth, Guide to the Bible: The Hebrew Scriptures (or Old Testament), selected Apocrypha, the New Testament, 2nd ed, SUNY-Binghamton, 89; cotransl, Rerum senilium libri, by Petrarch (Baltimore: Johns Hopkins Univ Press, 92); auth, Semitic and Indo-European: The principal etymologies, with observations on Afro-Asiatic, John Benjamins

(Amsterdam), 95; auth, "Greek as the Superstrate Written Language of Jews and Other Semitic Populations," Israel Oriental Studies 15 (95): 265-279; auth, "Rejoinder to Lamberti," Anthropos 94 (99): 646-647; auth, "'Achilles' Grudge' and 'Groveling before the Lord': Some Impediments to an Accurate Translation," LACUS Forum 25 (98): 421-431; auth, "The Forerunners of Scientific Phonology: Diacritical Marks and Other Reforms in Orthography," in Functional Approaches to Language, Culture and Cognition, ed. David G. Lockwood et al (Amsterdam: John Benjamins, 00), 569-592; auth, "How Polyglots Enlarge the Lexicon of Their Primary Language," LACUS Forum 26 (99). **CONTACT ADDRESS** Dept of Class and Near Eastern Studies, SUNY, Binghamton, Binghamton, NY 13902-6000. **EMAIL** slevin@binghamton.edu

LEVINE, BERNARD
PERSONAL Born 07/15/1934, Boston, MA, m, 1963 **DISCIPLINE** ENGLISH LITERATURE **EDUCATION** Harvard Univ, AB, 56; Brown Univ, PhD, 65. **CAREER** Asst English, Brown Univ, 61-63; from instr to asst prof, 63-71, assoc prof English, Wayne State Univ, 71-. **MEMBERSHIPS** MLA **RESEARCH** Nineteenth and twentieth century romantic poetry; W B Yeats. **SELECTED PUBLICATIONS** Auth, High talk: Concentrative analysis of a poem by Yeats, James Joyce Quart, winter 66; Yeats' Aesthetics and His Concept of Self, 66 & The Dissolving Image: Yeats' Spiritual-Aesthetic Development, 69, Wayne State Univ; Yeats' Leda and the Swan: A psychopoetic analysis, Bucknell Rev, 69. **CONTACT ADDRESS** Dept of English, Wayne State Univ, 431 State Hall, Detroit, MI 48202-1308.

LEVINE, DANIEL BLANK
PERSONAL Born 09/22/1953, Cincinnati, OH **DISCIPLINE** CLASSICAL LANGUAGE AND LITERATURE **EDUCATION** Univ Minn, BA, 75; Univ Cincinnati, PhD(classics), 80. **CAREER** Asst Prof Classics, Univ Ark, 80-, Ed, Ark Class Newslett, 80-. **MEMBERSHIPS** Class Asn Mid West and South; Am Philol Asn. **RESEARCH** Epic poetry; archaic Greek history. **SELECTED PUBLICATIONS** Auth, "Counterfeit Man," (in Greek and Hebrew Literature) in Classical Texts and their Traditions: Studies in Honor ofo C.R. Trahman, (Scholars Press: Chico, Calif, 84): 125-137; auth, "Symposium and Polis," in Theognis of Megara: Poetry and the Polis, eds. T.J. Figueira and G. Nagy, (Johnss Hopkins: Baltimore, 85): 176-196; auth, "Pittacus of Mytilene," in Great Lives from History: Ancient and Medieval Series, ed. F.N. Magil, (Salem Press: Pasadena, 88): 1644-1649; auth, "Phidias," in Great Lives from History: Ancient and Medieval Series, ed. F.N. Magill, (Salem Press: Pasadena, 88): 1592-1597; auth, "Eupalinus of Megara," in Great Lives from History: Ancient and Medieval Series, ed. F.N. Magill, (Salem Press: Pasaden, 88): 704-708; auth, "Acorns and Primitive Life in Greek and Latin Literature," Classical and Modern Literature 9, (89): 87-95; auth, "Uses of Classical Mythology in Rita Mae Brown's Soutehrn Discomfort," Classical and Modern Literature 10, (89): 63-70; auth, "John Clinton Futrall," "Henry Harrison Strauss," biographical essays Some illustious Educators of Old Main, Univ of Ark, 91; auth, "Hubris in Josephus Jewish Antiquities 1-4," Hebrew Union Col Annual, 64, (93): 51-87; auth, "Classica Americana Troglodytica: V.T. Hamlin' Alley Oop April 1939-Febrary 1940, The Epics Meet the Comics," Classical and Modern Literature: A Quarterly 14.4, (94): 365-386. **CONTACT ADDRESS** Dept of Foreign Lang, KIMP 425, Univ of Arkansas, Fayetteville, 904 Park Ave, Fayetteville, AR 72701. **EMAIL** dlevine@comp.uark.edu

LEVINE, GEORGE L.
DISCIPLINE ENGLISH LANGUAGE AND LITERATURE **EDUCATION** NYork Univ, BA; Univ Minn, MA; PhD. **CAREER** Kenneth Burke Prof Engl. **HONORS AND AWARDS** Guggenheim Fel; NEH Fel; Rockefeller Found Fel. **RESEARCH** Victorian literature and culture; novel and narrative; science and culture; Darwin. **SELECTED PUBLICATIONS** Auth, Darwin and the Novelists; auth, The Realistic Imagination; Lifebirds. **CONTACT ADDRESS** CCACC, Rutgers, The State Univ of New Jersey, New Brunswick, 8 Bishop Place, New Brunswick, NJ 08901-1167. **EMAIL** georlevine@cs.com

LEVINE, GEORGE RICHARD
PERSONAL Born 08/05/1929, Boston, MA, m, 1958, 2 children **DISCIPLINE** ENGLISH **EDUCATION** Tufts Col, BA, 51; Columbia Univ, MA, 52, PhD(English), 61. **CAREER** Instr, Northwestern Univ, 59-63; from asst prof to assoc prof, 63-70, assoc provost fac Arts & Lett, 71-72, provost & dean fac Arts & Lett, 75-81, prof English, State Univ NY Buffalo, 70-, Fulbright lectr, Univ Cologne, 69-70, Chancellor's Award for Excellence in Teaching, State Univ NY, 74. **MEMBERSHIPS** MLA; Am Soc 18th Century Studies. **RESEARCH** Eighteenth century English lit; English novel; dynamics of the teaching-learning process. **SELECTED PUBLICATIONS** Coauth, Riverside Readings, Columbia Univ, 58; Readings in American English, Prentice-Hall Int, 60; auth, Henry Fielding and the Dry Mock: A Study of the Techniques of Irony in his Early Works, Mouton, 67; coauth, Poetic and pictorial design in Two Songs of Innocence, Pmla, 5/67; auth, Dryden's Inarticulate Poesy: music and the Davidic King in Absalom and Achitophel, 18th Century Studies, Summer 68; Satiric intent and Baroque design in Donne's Go and Catch a Falling Star, Neuren Sprachen, 71; coauth, Poetry and the group process: an experiment in classroom dynamics, New Directions in Teaching, Winter 74; Introduction to Jonathan Swift, A Modest Proposal and Other Satires, Prometheus Press, 95; coauth, co-ed, Harp on the Shore: Thoreau and the Sea, SUNY Press, 85. **CONTACT ADDRESS** Dept of English, SUNY, Buffalo, PO Box 604610, Buffalo, NY 14260-4610. **EMAIL** grlevine@acsu.buffalo.edu

LEVINE, MOLLY MYEROWITZ
PERSONAL Born 12/18/1942, Hartford, CT, m, 2 children **DISCIPLINE** CLASSICS **EDUCATION** Radcliffe Col, BA, 64; Yale Univ, MPhil , 71; Bar-Ilan Univ, PhD, 80. **CAREER** Instr to asst prof, Bar-Ilan Univ, 66-83; lectr to prof, Howard Univ, 84-. **HONORS AND AWARDS** Women's Class Caucus Award, Howard Univ, 90-91, 96-97, 99-00; Blegen Res Fel, Vassar Col, 90-91; Andrew W. Mellon Fac Enrichment Stipend, Howard Univ, 86; NEH summer seminar, Am Acad Rome, 86. **MEMBERSHIPS** Am Philol Asn; Class Asn of the MidAtlantic States; Wash Class Soc. **RESEARCH** Augustan poetry; Myth and religion; Gender; Cultural studies; Greece and the Near East; Translation theory. **SELECTED PUBLICATIONS** Auth, "Multiculturalism and the Classics," Arethusa, (92): 215-220; auth, "The Domestication of Desire: Ovid's Parva Tabella and the Theater of Love," in Pornography and Representation in Greece and Rome, (Oxford, 92(, 131-157; rev, of "The Use and Abuse of Black Athena," in The Am Hist Rev, (92): 440-460; auth, "The Gendered Grammar of Ancient Mediterranean Hair," in Off With Her Head: The Denial of Women's Identity in Myth, Religion, and Culture, (Univ Calif Press, 95), 76-130; auth, "Bernal and the Athenians in the Multicultural World of the Ancient Mediterranean," in Classical Studies in Honor of David Sohlberg, (Bar-Ilan Univ Press, 96), 1-56; auth, "Women Who Wait: Akiva's Rahel and Odysseus' Penelope," in Papers from the Howard Gilman Intl Conf, (Tel-Aviv Univ Press, 98), 303-335; rev, of "The Marginalization of Martin Bernal," Class Philol, (98): 345-363. **CONTACT ADDRESS** Dept Class, Howard Univ, 6106 Dunleer Ct, Bethesda, MD 20817. **EMAIL** myerowitz@aol.com

LEVINE, PHILIP
PERSONAL Born 01/10/1928, Detroit, MI, m, 1945, 3 children **DISCIPLINE** CREATIVE WRITING **EDUCATION** Wayne State Univ, BA, 50, MA, 55; Univ Iowa, Mfa, 57. **CAREER** Instr English, Univ Iowa, 55-57; Stegnar fel, Stanford Univ, 57-58; Prof English, Calif State Univ, Fresno, 58-, Guggenheim fel, 73; Nat Endowment for the Arts grant, 76. **HONORS AND AWARDS** Joseph Henry Jackson Awd, 63; Chaplebrook Awd, 68; Frank O'Hara Mem Awd, 72; Nat Inst Arts and Lett Awd, 73; Lenore Marshall Awd, Saturday Rev and New Hope Found, 76. **RESEARCH** Poetry; contemporary Spanish and Spanish American poetry; translation. **SELECTED PUBLICATIONS** Auth, 1933, Atheneum, 74; on the Edge and Over, Cloud Marauder, 76; The Names of the Lost, 76, Seven Years from Somewhere, 79 and Ashes: Poems New and Old, 79, Atheneum; Pili's Wall, Unicorn Press, rev ed, 80; Don't Ask, Univ Mich Press, 81; One for the Rose, Atheneum, 81. **CONTACT ADDRESS** Dept of English, California State Univ, Fresno, Fresno, CA 93710.

LEVINE, RICHARD ALLAN
PERSONAL Born 05/13/1932, Malden, MA, m, 1954, 2 children **DISCIPLINE** ENGLISH **EDUCATION** Univ Mass, BA, 53; Univ Conn, MA, 55; Ind Univ, PhD, 61. **CAREER** Assoc, Ind Univ, 55-57, resident lectr English, 57-59; from instr to asst prof, Miami Univ, 59-64; asst prof, Univ Calif, Riverside, 64-69; assoc prof, 69-72, dir grad studies, 70-73, Prof English, State Univ NY Stony Brook, 72-, Chmn Dept, 75-. **MEMBERSHIPS** MLA; NCTE; Int Asn Univ Prof English. **RESEARCH** Victorian literature; the English novel; literature and society. **SELECTED PUBLICATIONS** Auth, Backgrounds to Victorian Literature, Chandler, 67; Disraeli's Tancred and The Great Asian Mystery, Nineteenth Century Fiction, 6/67; Benjamin Disraeli, Twayne, 68; Dickens, The two nations and and Individual possibility, Studies Novel, summer 69; The Victorian Experience: The Novelists, 76, The Victorian Experience: The Poets, 82 & The Victorian Experience: The Prose Writers (in press), Ohio Univ. **CONTACT ADDRESS** Dept of English, SUNY, Stony Brook, Stony Brook, NY 11794.

LEVINE, ROBERT
PERSONAL Born 05/09/1933, New York, NY, m, 1958, 3 children **DISCIPLINE** ENGLISH **EDUCATION** City Col NYork, BA, 54; Columbia Univ, MA, 58; Univ CA, Berkeley, PhD, 63. **CAREER** Instr Eng, Rensselaer Polytech Inst, 58-59 & Cornell Univ, 62-64; from Asst Prof to Assoc Prof, 64-88, Prof English, Boston Univ, 88-, Actg Chmn, Classics Dept, 71-73, Chmn, Medieval Studies Comt, 74-76, Asst Dean, Advising Office, Col Liberal Arts, 78-79, Spring 87, 89-95; Vis Asst Prof English, Brown Univ, Spring 66; Vis Assoc Prof, Universite Paul Valery, France, Fall 84. **MEMBERSHIPS** MLA. **RESEARCH** Old Eng; Middle Eng; Medieval Latin. **SELECTED PUBLICATIONS** Transl, France Before Charlemagne, Mellen Press, 90; A Thirteenth-Century Minstrel's Chronicle, Mellen Press, 90; A Thirteenth-century Life of Charlemagne, Garland Press, 91; The Deeds of God through the Franks, Boydell & Brewer, 97; auth, Gower as Gerontion: Oneiric Autobiography in the Confessio Amantis, Medieaevistik 5, 92; Who composed Havelok for whom?, Yearbook for English Studies XXII, 92; The Pious Traitor: the Man who Betrayed Antioch, Mittellateinisches Jahrbuch XXXIII, 98; author or numerous other articles. **CONTACT ADDRESS** Dept of Eng, Boston Univ, 236 Bay State Rd, Boston, MA 02215-1403. **EMAIL** bobl@bu.edu

LEVINE, VICTORIA LINDSAY
PERSONAL Born 09/08/1954, Palo Alto, CA, m, 1982, 2 children **DISCIPLINE** ETHNOMUSICOLOGY, AMERICAN INDIAN STUDIES **EDUCATION** San Francisco State Univ, BMUS, BA, 77; MA, 80; Univ Ill Urbana, PhD, 90. **CAREER** W.M. Keck Foundation dir of the Hulbert Center for Southwestern Studies; Assoc prof, Colorado Col. **HONORS AND AWARDS** John D. & Catherine T. McArthur prof, 91-93; Am Council of Learned Soc Sr Fellow, 94-95; Ida Halpern Fellow and Awd, 99. **MEMBERSHIPS** Soc for Ethnomusicology; Col Music Soc; Soc for Am Music. **RESEARCH** Am Indian musics & cultures; Latino musics & cultures; Balinese music. **SELECTED PUBLICATIONS** Auth, pubs on Ethnomusicology, American Indian Musical Cultures, Music of the American Southwest, and Latino Music of the US; co-auth, book on Choctaw Indian Music; co-ed; Catalogue of Music in the Ruben Cobos Collection of New Mexican Folklore. **CONTACT ADDRESS** Music Dept, Colo Col, 14 E Cache La Poudre St, Colorado Springs, CO 80903. **EMAIL** vlevine@coloradocollege.edu

LEVITIN, ALEXIS
PERSONAL Born 11/27/1942, New York City, NY, s, 2 children **DISCIPLINE** ENGLISH **EDUCATION** Columbia Univ, BA, 63; MA, 64; PhD, 71. **CAREER** Fac, Plattsburgh State Univ of NY. **HONORS AND AWARDS** SUNY-Plattsburgh Presidential Res Award, summer, 99; Rockefeller Found Study Ctr Residency at Bellagio, July, 97; Witter Bynner Found for Poetry Translation Grant, 96-97; Nat Endowment for the Arts Translation Fel Grant, 93; Fernando Pessoa Award from the Translation Ctr at Columbia Univ for Slopes of a Gaze, 92; Calouste Gulbenkian Res fel, 92; Portuguese Cultural Inst Res Grant, 92; New York State Council on the Arts Translation Grant, 84-88, 90-91; PDQWL-NYS/WP Experienced Fac Development Award, 85, 87, 91; Fulbright Junior Lecturer Award to Oporto, Portugal, 80; National Endowment of the Humanities, Summer Seminar in Greek Tragedy, 79; Fulbright Senior Lecturer Award to Santiago, Chile, 76; Columbia Univ President's fel, 65-66; New York State Regents fel, 59-63. **RESEARCH** Creative writing; Shakespeare; world lit. **SELECTED PUBLICATIONS** Auth, transl(s) of poetry from the Portuguese. **CONTACT ADDRESS** Dept of English, SUNY, Col at Plattsburgh, 101 Broad St, Plattsburgh, NY 12901. **EMAIL** alexis.levitin@plattsburgh.edu

LEVITT, MORTON PAUL
PERSONAL Born 12/22/1936, Brooklyn, NY, m, 1963 **DISCIPLINE** ENGLISH **EDUCATION** Dickinson Col, BA, 58; Columbia Univ, MA, 60; Pa State Univ, PhD(English), 65. **CAREER** Instr English, Pa State Univ, 60-62; from instr to prof English, Temple Univ, 62-; vis prof, Univ Granada, Spain 83; vis prof, Concordia Univ, Montreal, 83; ed, J of Modern Lit, 86-; vis prof, Univ British Columbia, Vancouver, 90, 95. **HONORS AND AWARDS** Fulbright lectr Am lit, Zagreb Univ, Yugoslavia, 74-75; Carnegie Found Fel, 90, 98; Fulbright lectr comp lit, Univ Lisbon, Portugal, 95. **RESEARCH** Literary modernism; the Modernist arts. **SELECTED PUBLICATIONS** Auth, Bloomsday: An Interpretation of James Joyce's 'Ulysses,' 72; auth, The Cretan Glance: The World and Art of Nikos Kazantzakis, 80; auth, Modernist Survivors: The Contemporary Novel in England, the US, France and Latin Am, 87; auth, James Joyces and Modernism: Beyond Dublin, 00; ed, Joyce and the Joyceans, forthcoming. **CONTACT ADDRESS** Dept of English, Temple Univ, 1114 W Berks St, Philadelphia, PA 19122-6029.

LEVITT, STEVEN R.
DISCIPLINE COMMUNICATION **EDUCATION** MT State Univ, BA, 82; WV Univ, MA, 83; OH State Univ, PhD, 88. **CAREER** Assoc prof, Univ TX at San Antonio, 97-& asst prof, 91-97; asst prof, Univ KY, 86-91; grad tchg asst, OH State Univ, 83-86 & W V Univ, 82-83; undergrad tchg asst, MT State Univ, 82. **HONORS AND AWARDS** Phi Kappa Phi Nat Hon Soc, WV Univ, 83; Nat Commun Forum Univ Fac Grant, 89; President's Distinguished Achievement Award in Univ Service, 00; formed, 1st publ relations stud soc chap in san antonio. **SELECTED PUBLICATIONS** Auth, "Designing videoconferencing facilities for improved eye contact: A case study in technological development," J Broadcasting and Electronic Media, 31 2, 87; auth, "Risky shift and gender of the advocate: Information theory versus normative theory," Gp and Organizational Stud, 9 2, 84; auth, rev, Issues in new information technology, 89; auth, "Measuring the information society," J Broadcasting & Electronic Media, 33 2, 89; auth, Technology transfer and media imperialism: The US-Canadian case, Media criticism: Journeys in interpretation, Dubuque, Kendall/Hunt Publ Comp, 92; coauth, Inforrmation technology, gender and power in organizations, Oablex Publications, 96; coauth, Women in Orrganizations: Perspectives of Power, Creskill, N.J.: Hampton Press, Inc., (99): 273-288; coauth, Visual and statistical

thinking: An essential communication curriculum for engineers, Proceedings: Engineering Education for the 21st Century, (00): 155-158; coauth, Using new technology to provide access and match engineering educaiton to the needs of business, Proceedings: Engineering Education for the 21st Century, (00): 151-154. **CONTACT ADDRESS** Dept of Communication, Univ of Texas, San Antonio, 6900 N Loop 1604 W, San Antonio, TX 78249. **EMAIL** slevitt@utsa.edu

LEVY, ALFRED J.
PERSONAL Born 11/15/1926, Boston, MA, m, 2 children **DISCIPLINE** ENGLISH & AMERICAN LITERATURE **EDUCATION** Clark Univ, AB, 49; Univ Wis, AM, 50, PhD(English), 57. **CAREER** Assoc English, IN Univ, 55-57, from instr to asst prof, 57-61; from asst prof to assoc prof, 61-71, assoc dean arts & sci, 68-76, prof English, Univ Hawaii, Manoa, 71-. **MEMBERSHIPS** AAUP. **RESEARCH** American prose fiction; world literature. **SELECTED PUBLICATIONS** Coauth, Manuscripts of Hawthorne's short stories, Studies Bibliog, 61; auth, Ethan Brand and the unpardonable sin, Boston Univ Studies English, autumn 61; The House of the Seven Gables: the religion of love, 19th-Century Fiction, 12/61. **CONTACT ADDRESS** Dept English, Univ of Hawaii, Manoa, 1733 Donaghho Rd, Honolulu, HI 96822-2368.

LEVY, ANITA
DISCIPLINE 19TH CENTURY NOVEL, GOTHIC FICTION, EARLY MODERN AND VICTORIAN CULTURE **EDUCATION** Univ CA at San Diego, PhD. **CAREER** Asst prof; taught at, Williams Col & Univ CA at San Diego. **RESEARCH** Late-18th and 19th century Brit lit, espec the novel, gender studies, and cult studies. **SELECTED PUBLICATIONS** Auth, Other Women: The Writing of Class, Race, and Gender, 1832-1898; articles on, early mod print cult, Brontes, Victorian anthrop, Dorothy Richardson & gendered labor. **CONTACT ADDRESS** Dept of Eng, Univ of Rochester, 601 Elmwood Ave, Ste. 656, Rochester, NY 14642. **EMAIL** levy@db1.cc.rochester.edu

LEVY, ANITA B.
PERSONAL Born 06/06/1955, New York, NY, m, 1990, 2 children **DISCIPLINE** ENGLISH **EDUCATION** Univ Roch, BA, 77; Univ Calif, MA, 82; PhD, 88. **CAREER** Lectr, George Wash Univ, 88-89; vis asst prof, Williams Col, 89-90; res ed, Howard Univ, 91-92; asst prof, , assoc prof, Univ Roch, 93-00; prog off, Phi Beta Kappa Soc, 00-. **HONORS AND AWARDS** Hum Res Bd, Brit Acad and Vict Stud Cen, Univ Leicester, 96; Susan B. Anthony Inst Gen and Wom Stud, 95; Vis Schl Eng, Georgetn Univ; Ed Bd, GENDERS, 90-94; Michel de Certeau Mem Prize for Out Dis, Dept Eng Am Lit, Univ Cal. **MEMBERSHIPS** MLA; NACBS; ENCSA. **RESEARCH** Nineteenth-century fiction; gender studies; history of the novel. **SELECTED PUBLICATIONS** Auth, Other Women: the Writing of Class, Race and Gender, 1832-1898, Princeton UP, 90; auth, "Jane Eyre, the Woman Writer and the History of Experience," Mod Lang Qtly (95); auth, "Clarence Rook," Dict Lit Biog: Brit Short Fic, 94; auth, "Tendered Labor, the Woman Writer and Dorothy Richardson," Novel, 91; auth, "Other Women and New Women: Writing Race and Gender," in The Story of an African Farm, in The Victorians and Race, ed. Shearer West, 97; auth, "Reproductive Urges: Popular Novel Reading, Sexuality and the English Nation," in Inventing Maternity: Biology, Politics, Literature, eds. Carole Barash, Susan Greenfield, 98; auth, Reproductive Urges: Popular Novel-Reading, Sexuality, and the English Nation, Univ Penn Press, 99; auth, "Public Spaces, Private Eyes: Gender and the Social in Villette," Nineteenth-Cen Con (00). **CONTACT ADDRESS** The Phi Beta Kappa Soc, 1785 Massachusetts Ave. NW, 4th Fl., Washington, DC 20009. **EMAIL** anitalevy@yahoo.com

LEVY, DAVID BENJAMIN
PERSONAL Born 03/29/1948, New York, NY, m, 1968, 2 children **DISCIPLINE** MUSIC **EDUCATION** Eastman Sch of Music, BM, 69, MA, 71; Univ Rochester, PhD, 80. **CAREER** Prof, Chair, Wake Forest Univ, 76- . **HONORS AND AWARDS** Advisory Bd, Amer Beethoven Soc; Outstanding Acad Book, Choice, 96. **MEMBERSHIPS** Amer Musicological Soc; Amer Beethoven Soc. **RESEARCH** Beethoven stud; Berlioz; Wagner; nineteenth century music. **SELECTED PUBLICATIONS** Auth, Ritter Berlioz' in Germany, Berlioz Stud, Cambridge Univ Press, 92; The Contrabass Recitative in Beethoven's Ninth Symphony Revisited, Hist Performance, 92; To the Ninth, Power, Wake Forest Univ Mag, 95; Beethoven: The Ninth Symphony, Schirmer Books, 95; assoc ed, Historical Performance, 93-95. **CONTACT ADDRESS** Dept of Music, Wake Forest Univ, Box 7345, Winston-Salem, NC 27109. **EMAIL** levy@wfu.edu

LEVY, EMANUEL
PERSONAL Born 02/04/1947, Israel, d **DISCIPLINE** SOCIOLOGY, CULTURAL FILM STUDIES **EDUCATION** Tel-Aviv Univ, BA, 71; MA, 73; Columbia Univ, MPhil, 75; PhD, 78. **CAREER** Assoc prof, CUNY and Columbia, 81-85; assoc prof, Wellesley Col, 86-89; ten prof, Ariz State Univ, 90-. **HONORS AND AWARDS** Nat Jewish Bk Awd; Fac Res Creat Awd; Who' Who in Am, World; Outstand People of 20th Century. **MEMBERSHIPS** NSFC. **RESEARCH** Film; popular culture; global cinema; mass communications. **SELECTED PUBLICATIONS** Auth, John Wayne: Prophet of the American Way of Life, 88, 99; auth, The History and Politics of the Oscar Awards, 86, 91; auth, Small-Town America in Film, 91; auth, George Cukor, Master of Elegance, 94; auth, Cinema of Outsiders: The Rise of American Independent Film, NYUP, 99; auth, Andrew Sarris: American Film Critic, forthcoming. **CONTACT ADDRESS** Dept Sociology, Arizona State Univ, West, PO Box 37100, Glendale, AZ 85306.

LEVY, JACQUES
DISCIPLINE THEATER **EDUCATION** BA CCNY, BA, 56; MI State Univ, MA, 58, PhD, 61. **CAREER** Dir, writer, prof theater, 30 yr(s); instr, Yale, Columbia Univ, Hunter Col; prof; dir, the Theater, 92. **HONORS AND AWARDS** Obie award; Drama Desk and Outer Critics Circle award; 4 BMI awards for bk and lyrics of a produced musical; grammy nominations. **SELECTED PUBLICATIONS** Auth, Fame..The Musical, Lyricist, 95. **CONTACT ADDRESS** Dept of Eng, Colgate Univ, 13 Oak Drive, Hamilton, NY 13346.

LEVY, MICHAEL MARC
PERSONAL Born 04/15/1950, Chicago, IL, m, 1983, 2 children **DISCIPLINE** SCIENCE FICTION, RENAISSANCE, AND CHILDREN'S LITERATURE **EDUCATION** Univ IL, Champaign, BA, 72; OH State Univ, MA, 74; Univ MN, Minneapolis, PhD(English), 82. **CAREER** Lectr English, 80-84, assist prof, 85-86, assoc prof, 87-89, PROF, UNIV WI-STOUT, 90-. **MEMBERSHIPS** MLA; Sci Fiction Res Asn; Children's Lit Asn; MMLA; International Association for the Fantastic in the Arts. **RESEARCH** Science fiction, particularly when related to gender; children's lit, particularly when related to science fiction, gender, and Southeast Asian children's lit. **SELECTED PUBLICATIONS** Auth, Philip Francis Nowlan & Gary K Wolf, 20th Century Sci Fiction Writers, 81; coauth, Modern Science Fiction and Fantasy: A Study Guide, Univ Minn Exten, 81; auth, Sir William Davenant, Francis Beaumont, Thomas Middleton & Thomas Randolph, Critical Survey of Poetry, 82; Who, What, and Why? Character Motivation in Doctor Who, Children's Lit Asn Quart, 85; Paradise Lost in Northern Wisconsin, Approaches to Paradise Lost, 86; Modern Science Fiction and Fantasy: A Study Guide, 3rd ed, with Patricia C. Hodgell, 94; From Darkness to Light: Judy Chicago's Holocaust Project, with Sandra Lindow, Kaleidoscope, 94, Natalie Babbitt, 91; The New Wave, Cyberpunk and Beyond, Anatomy of Wonder, 95; George R. R. Martin: I Want to Provide a Journey We Haven't Taken Before, Pubs Weekly, 96; Lois McMaster Bujold: Science Fiction and Disability, Kaleidoscope, 97; Who Killed Science Fiction? A Spectrum of Responses, NY Review of SF, 97; Lois Lowry's The Giver: Interrupted Bildungsroman or Ambiguous Dystopia?, Foundation, 97; Science Fiction in 1997, What Do I Read Next?, 98; Ophelia Triumphant: the Survival of Adolescent Girls in Recent SF by Butler and Womack, Foundation, 98; Annotated Bibliography of Young Adult Science Fiction: History and Criticism, Young Adult Science Fiction, 99; Young Adult Science Fiction as Bildungsroman, 99; Portrajal of SE Asian Refugees in Recent American Children's Books, 00; What If Your Fairy Godmother were an Ox? The Many Cinderellas of SEAsia, 00; Tull Tide Night: J.R. Dunn's Science Fictional Revenge Tragedy, 02. **CONTACT ADDRESS** Dept English, Univ of Wisconsin, Stout, Po Box 790, Menomonie, WI 54751-0790. **EMAIL** levym@uwstout.edu

LEVY, STEPHEN
PERSONAL Born 10/24/1945, Philadelphia, PA, m, 1977, 1 child **DISCIPLINE** ENGLISH **EDUCATION** Temple Univ, BA, 66; Duke Univ, MA, 68; Fordham Univ, PhD, 81. **CAREER** prof, Mo State Univ, 71-73; prof, Pace Univ, 79-81; mathematician, Wall St, 82-83; computer sci, AT&T Bell Labs, 85-89; computer sci, A. Monmouth, 90-93; prof, Col of Morris, 94-. **HONORS AND AWARDS** Fel, Nat Found Fel, Duke, 66-68; Johns Hopskins Univ Fel, 68-71; Grant, NEH, 95; Acad Excellence Awd, Col of Morris, 97; Grant, NJCH, 98, 99. **MEMBERSHIPS** Am Philos Assoc; Soc for Advan of Am Philos; Am Soc of Philos Teachers. **RESEARCH** Logic, philosophy or mathematics, ethics, cognitive science. **SELECTED PUBLICATIONS** Auth, "Peirce's Theory of Infinitesimals", Int Philos Quarterly 91; rev, of "Reasoning and the Logic of Things", ed K. Ketner and H. Putnam, Transactions Peirce Soc, Winter 94; rev, of "Descriptions" by S. Neale, Modern Logic, Fall 95; auth, "The Mining of Bertrand Russell", Modern Logic, Winter 96; auth, "The Interconnections between Mathematics and Logic", in Studies in the Logic of Peirce, ed Houser et al, Ind Univ Pr, 97; rev of "The Essential Peirce II", ed Peirce Edition Project, Soc for Advan of Am Philos News, Summer, 99; Auth, Strain Your Brain: Puzzles in Logic, 00; auth, "Theories of Reference" Modern Logic, Autumn 00. **CONTACT ADDRESS** Dept English, County Col of Morris, 214 Center Grove Road, Randolph, NJ 07869-2007. **EMAIL** stephlevy@juno.com

LEVY, WILLIAM TURNER
PERSONAL Born 11/03/1922, Far Rockaway, NY **DISCIPLINE** ENGLISH **EDUCATION** City Col New York, BA, 42; Columbia Univ, MAj 47, PhD, 52. **CAREER** From instr to assoc prof English, Baruch Col, 46-77; priest, Protestant Episcopal Church, 52-; sr ed, The Churchman, 59-76; Provost, Viewpoint Sch, Calabasas, Calif, 79-. **SELECTED PUBLICATIONS** Auth, The Idea of the Church in T S Eliot, Christian Scholar, 58; auth, William Barnes: The Man and the Poems, Longmans Ltd, Dorchester, 60;art, Jeffers as prophet, Robinson Jeffers, Grabhorn, 62; coauth, Affectionately, T S Eliot, Lippincott, 68; coauth, The Films of Frank Capra, Citadel, 77; coauth, The Complete Films of Frank Capra, Citadel, 92; coauth, The Extraordinary Mrs R Wiley, 99. **CONTACT ADDRESS** 22121 Lanark St, Canoga Park, CA 91304.

LEWALSKI, BARBARA KIEFER
PERSONAL Born 02/22/1931, Chicago, IL, m, 1956, 1 child **DISCIPLINE** ENGLISH LITERATURE, RENAISSANCE **EDUCATION** Kans State Teachers Col, Emporia, Bsed, 50; Univ Chicago, AM, 51, PhD, 56. **CAREER** From prof to William R Kenan Prof Eng, Harvard Univ, 82-, dir grad studies, Harvard Univ, 97-. **HONORS AND AWARDS** MLA James Russell Lowell Prize, 79; Milton Society, James Holly Hanford Awd, 83, 85; Am Acad Arts & Scis; Am Philos Soc; Intl Asn Univ Prof Eng. **MEMBERSHIPS** MLA; Milton Soc Am; Renaissance Soc Am; Soc Study Early Mod Women. **RESEARCH** Milton; 17th cent lit; early modern women's writing. **SELECTED PUBLICATIONS** Auth, Milton's Brief Epic; The Genre, Meaning, and Art of Paradise Regained, Methuen and Brown Univ Press, 66; auth, Donne's Anniversaries and the Poetry of Praise: The Creation of a Symbolic Mode, Princeton Univ Press, 73; auth, Protestant Poetics and the Seventeenth-Century Religious Lyric, Princeton Univ Press, 79, paperback 84, reprint 86; auth, Paradise Lost and the Rhetoric of Literary Forms, Princeton Univ Press, 85, paperback, 86; auth, Writing Women in Jacobean England, 1603-1625, Harvard Univ Press, 93, paperback, 95; auth, Rensaissance Genres: Essays on Theory, History, and Interpretation, Harvard English Studies 14, Harvard Univ Press, 86; auth, Norton Anthology of English Literature, Seventeenth Century Seciton, Norton, 86, 93, 00; auth, The Polemics and Poems of Rachel Speght, Oxford Univ Press, 96; auth, The Life of John Milton: A Critical Biography, Blackwell, 00. **CONTACT ADDRESS** Dept of Eng, Harvard Univ, Barker Ctr #215, Cambridge, MA 02138. **EMAIL** lewalski@fas.harvard.edu

LEWES, ULLE ERIKA
PERSONAL Born 03/22/1942, Tallinn, Estonia, w, 1989 **DISCIPLINE** MEDIEVAL & COMPARATIVE LITERATURE **EDUCATION** Cornell Univ, AB, 64; Harvard Univ, MA, 65, PhD, 72. **CAREER** Instr, Temple Univ, 71-72, asst prof, 72-78; Assoc Prof, 78-82, Prof English, Ohio Wesleyan Univ, 82-, Dir Writing Ctr, Ohio Wesleyan Univ; writing consult, Muskingum Col, Denison Col, Col DuPage & Rice Univ; Dir, Project Writing across the Curriculum, Mellon Found Grant, 79-82; Lead Prof, NEH Summer Inst on Renaissance Drama, Secondary School Teachers-Ohio Wesleyan, 86; dir, various Ohio Wesleyan grants, 84, 85, 86, 94. **HONORS AND AWARDS** Phi Beta Kappa, 63; S.A. Potter Awd, Harvard Univ, 72; Medieval Acad Younger Schol grant, Int 12th Century Renaissance Conf, Medieval Acad, 77; Benjamin T. Spencer Lectureship, 94-96. **MEMBERSHIPS** MLA; Medieval Acad Am; Asn Teachers Advanc Compos; Conf Col Comp and Commun; Coun Writing Prog Admin; Estonian Learned Soc; Nat Coun Teachers English; Tristan Soc. **RESEARCH** The Tristan legend; Women's Studies; Shakespeare Studies; the theory and practice of teaching composition. **SELECTED PUBLICATIONS** Auth, Is America Losing Her Folklore Heritage?, Town and Country, 78; The Life in the Forest: Influence of the Saint Giles Legend on the Courtly Tristan Story, Univ Tenn, Chattanooga, 79; A Rejoinder to C.S. Jaeger on the Tristan Story, Tristania, 81; The Uses of Peer Editing in Advanced Writing Courses, J Advanced Comp, 85; The Originality of the Farewell Scene in Gottfield's Tristan, Tristania, 89; Writing as Learning: A Workbook for Teachers of Jefferson County Schools, 90. **CONTACT ADDRESS** Dept of English, Ohio Wesleyan Univ, 61 S Sandusky St, Delaware, OH 43015-2398. **EMAIL** uelewes@cc.owu.edu

LEWIS, CYNTHIA
PERSONAL Born 10/11/1951, Middleton, OH, m, 4 children **DISCIPLINE** ENGLISH **EDUCATION** Ohio State Univ, BA, 74; Harvard Univ, MA, 75, PhD, 80. **CAREER** From asst prof to assoc prof to prof to chemn, 80-, Davidson Col. **HONORS AND AWARDS** Omicron Delta Kappa; Best Tchr Awd; CASE; Love of Tchg Awd. **MEMBERSHIPS** Shakespeare Asn Am **RESEARCH** Shakespeare in Renaissance drama **SELECTED PUBLICATIONS** Auth, art, Dark Deeds Darkly Answered, 83; auth, art, With Simular Proof Enough, 91; auth, art, Heywood's Gunaikeion and Women-Kind in A Women Killed With Kindness, 94; auth, Particular Saints: Shakespeare's Four Antonios, Their Context and Their Plays, 97. **CONTACT ADDRESS** Dept of English, Davidson Col, PO Box 1719, Davidson, NC 28036. **EMAIL** cylewis@davidson.edu

LEWIS, GLADYS S.
DISCIPLINE ENGLISH **EDUCATION** Tex Christian Univ, AB, 55; Univ Central Okla, MA, 85; Okla State Univ, PhD, 92. **CAREER** Asst Prof to Prof, Univ Central Okla, 91-. **HONORS AND AWARDS** Scholar Leadership Sem, 88; NEH Summer Sem, 95; UCO Pres's Excellence in Teaching Awd, 97. **MEMBERSHIPS** MLA, Am Studies Asn, John Buayan Soc, Am Lit

Asn, Hemingway Soc, Stowe Soc. **RESEARCH** 19th century American and British fiction. **SELECTED PUBLICATIONS** Auth, Messenger, Message, and Response, UPA, 94; ed, The Jewish Roots of Christological Monotheism. **CONTACT ADDRESS** Dept English, Univ of Central Oklahoma, 100 N Univ Dr, Edmond, OK 73034-5207. **EMAIL** GSLPHD@aol.com

LEWIS, JAYNE ELIZABETH
PERSONAL Born 08/24/1961, Kansas City, MO, m, 1998, 1 child **DISCIPLINE** ENGLISH **EDUCATION** Univ Colo, BA, 83; Col Wm & Mary, MA, 84; Princeton Univ, PhD, 88. **CAREER** Asst prof, 88-94, ASSOC PROF, ENG, 94-, UNIV CALIF, LOS ANGELES. **HONORS AND AWARDS** NEH summer stipend, 90; NEH fel, 97-98; ACLS fel, 90; Univ Calif Pres fel, 90; ed bd, journalx **MEMBERSHIPS** Mod Lang Asn; Am Soc 18th cent Stud. **RESEARCH** 18th cent Br lit; lit & hist. **SELECTED PUBLICATIONS** Auth, The English Fable: Aesop and Literary Culture, 1651- 1740, Cambridge Univ Press, 96; auth, The Trial of Mary Queen of Scots, Bedford, 98; auth, Mary Queen of Scots: Romance and Nation, Routledge, 98. **CONTACT ADDRESS** Dept of English, Univ of California, Los Angeles, Los Angeles, CA 90095. **EMAIL** jlewis@humnet.ucla.edu

LEWIS, JON
PERSONAL Born 05/08/1955, NY, m, 1987, 2 children **DISCIPLINE** FILM STUDIES **EDUCATION** Hobart Col, BA, 77; SUNY, MFA, 79, UCLA, PhD, 83. **CAREER** Engl, Oregon St Univ. **MEMBERSHIPS** Soc for Cinema Studies; MLA; Pacific Northwest Am Studies Asn. **SELECTED PUBLICATIONS** Auth, Punks in L.A.: It's Kiss or Kill, Jour Popular Cult, 88; Voices From a Steeltown: Tony Buba's Lightning Over Braddock Aferimage, 89; The Road to Romance and Ruin: Teen Films and Youth Culture, Routledge, 92; The Crisis of Authority in Francis Coppola's Rumble Fish, in Crisis Cinema, Maisonneuve Press, 92; Disney After Disney: From Family Business to the Business of Family, in Disney Discourses, Routledge ,94; Whom God Wishes to Destroy.. Francis Coppola and The New Hollywood Duke Univ Press, 95; The New American Cinema, Duke Univ Press, 98; auth, "We do not ask you to condone this..How the Blacklist Saved Hollywood, " Cinema J (00); auth, Hollywood v. Hosokofe, NYork Univ Press, 00. **CONTACT ADDRESS** English Dept, Oregon State Univ, Corvallis, OR 97331-4501. **EMAIL** jlewis@orst.edu

LEWIS, KEVIN
PERSONAL Born 07/13/1943, Asheville, NC, m, 1976, 2 children **DISCIPLINE** ARTS, LITERATURE, RELIGION; RELIGIOUS STUDIES **EDUCATION** Harv Col, BA, 65; St Johns Col, BA, 67; MA, 71; Univ Chic, MA, 69, PhD, 80. **CAREER** Instr, Valpar Univ, 70; asst prof, assoc prof, Univ S Car, 73-; prin, Prest Res Col, 95-98. **HONORS AND AWARDS** Fulbright Sr Lectr, Poland, 88, Gaza, 98; Vis Res Fel Trev Coll, Wolfson Coll. **MEMBERSHIPS** AAR; MLA; SLA; ASA. **RESEARCH** Images of lonesomeness in the American Arts; Muggletonians; Biblical literalism; 19th and 20th century British and American poets. **SELECTED PUBLICATIONS** Auth, The Appeal of Muggletonianism, 86; co-ed, The Changing Shape of Protestantism in the South, 96. **CONTACT ADDRESS** Dept Religious Studies, Univ of So Carolina, Columbia, Columbia, SC 29208. **EMAIL** kevin@sc.edu

LEWIS, LISA
DISCIPLINE CREATIVE WRITING & POETRY **EDUCATION** Univ Houstin, PhD, 93. **CAREER** Engl, Okla St Univ. **HONORS AND AWARDS** Univ Wis Press' Brittingham Prize Poetry; Jessica Nobel Maxwell prize; Lynda Hull Memorial prize; Best Am Poetry, The Pushcart Prize anthology. **SELECTED PUBLICATIONS** Auth, The Unbeliever; Silent Treatment, Viking/Pelikan, 98. **CONTACT ADDRESS** Oklahoma State Univ, Stillwater, 101 Whitehurst Hall, Stillwater, OK 74078.

LEWIS, MARTHA HOFFMAN
PERSONAL Born 11/08/1922, Newton, MA, m, 1954, 2 children **DISCIPLINE** CLASSICS **EDUCATION** Univ Calif, Berkeley, AB, 43; Bryn Mawr Col, MA, 49, PhD, 51. **CAREER** Teacher Latin and English, Red Bluff High Sch, Calif, 44-45, Piedmont High Sch, 45-48; asst prof classics and educ, Univ Ill, 53-56; asst prof Latin, 63-66; assoc prof Latin and English, Rockhurst Col, 66-82. **HONORS AND AWARDS** Fulbright scholar and fel, Am Acad Rome, 51-53. **MEMBERSHIPS** Am Philol Asn; Am Asn Ancient Historians. **RESEARCH** Roman history, especially late republic and early empire; modern poetry. **SELECTED PUBLICATIONS** Auth, The Official Priests of Rome Under the Julio-Claudrasus, Am Acad in Rome, Papers and Monographs 16, 55. **CONTACT ADDRESS** 716 W 109th Terr, Kansas City, MO 64114.

LEWIS, MITCHELL R.
PERSONAL Born 10/08/1966, Washington, DC **DISCIPLINE** ENGLISH **EDUCATION** Calif State Univ Fullerton, BA, 91; MA, 93; Univ Okla, PhD, 01. **CAREER** Teach asst to res asst to vis asst prof, Univ Okla, 95-. **HONORS AND AWARDS** Roy and Florena Hadsell Scholar. **MEMBERSHIPS** MSA; MLA. **RESEARCH** Modernism; postmodernism; 20th-century British literature; literary and cultural theory. **SELECTED PUBLICATIONS** Auth, "Timely Materialisms: New Combinations of Postructuralism and Cultural Critique," Mod Fiction Studies 46 (00); co-auth, "US Cultural Studies," in The Johns Hopkins Guide to Literary Theory and Criticism, eds. Michael Groden, Martin Kreiswirth, Imre Szeman (Baltimore: Johns Hopkins Univ Pr, forthcoming); auth, "Gyorgy Lukacs," in The Edinburgh Encyclopedia of Modern Criticism and Theory, ed. Julian Wolfreys (Edinburgh: U of Edinburgh Pr, forthcoming); auth, "Angela Margaret Thirkell" and "Sybille Bedford," in Twentieth-Century British Women Writers, eds. Vicki/Del Janik (Westport, Conn: Greenwood Pr, forthcoming). **CONTACT ADDRESS** English Dept, Univ of Oklahoma, 113 Gittinger Hall, Norman, OK 73019. **EMAIL** mrlewis333@juno.com

LEWIS, NATHANIEL
DISCIPLINE AMERICAN LITERATURE AND IMAGES OF THE WEST **EDUCATION** Harvard Univ, PhD. **CAREER** Eng, St. Michaels Col. **SELECTED PUBLICATIONS** Area: cult of the Am West. **CONTACT ADDRESS** Saint Michael's Col, Winooski Park, Colchester, VT 05439. **EMAIL** nlewis@smcvt.edu

LEWIS, PERCILES
PERSONAL Born 09/13/1968, Toronto, ON, Canada, m **DISCIPLINE** ENGLISH **EDUCATION** McGill Univ, BA, 90; Stanford Univ, MA, 91; PhD, 97. **CAREER** Assoc prof, Yale Univ, 98-. **HONORS AND AWARDS** Res Coun Can Dept of Soc Sci and Hum postdoc fel, 96-98; Whiting Fel. **MEMBERSHIPS** ACLA, MLA, CAUT, AAUP. **RESEARCH** The modern novel; literary theory; literature and philosophy. **SELECTED PUBLICATIONS** Auth, "Modernism, Naturalism and the Novel," Cambridge Univ Press (00). **CONTACT ADDRESS** Dept of English, Yale Univ, PO Box 208302, New Haven, CT 06520-8302. **EMAIL** pericles.lewis@yale.edu

LEWIS, ROBERT WILLIAM
PERSONAL Born 12/15/1930, Elrama, PA, s, 2 children **DISCIPLINE** ENGLISH **EDUCATION** Univ Pittsburgh, BA, 52; Columbia Univ, MA, 58; Univ Ill, PhD, 63. **CAREER** Asst, Columbia Univ, 55; instr English, Univ Nebr, 55-58; asst, Univ Ill, 58-63; from instr to asst prof, Univ Tex, Austin, 63-69; chmn dept, 69-78, 96-00, assoc prof, 69-71, Prof English, 71-90, distinguished prof, 90-, Univ North Dak; asst ed, Abstr English Studies, 65-66; coordr Peace Corps, Univ Tex, 65-67; Fulbright-Hays lectr, Italy, 67-68; consult, Nat Endowment for Humanities, 71-77; res prof, Univ NDak, 71; vis prof Am studies & Fulbright-Hays lectr, Ain Shams Univ, Cairo, 75-76; vis prof English, Am Univ in Cairo, 75-76. **MEMBERSHIPS** MLA; NCTE; Aaup; Hemingway Soc. **RESEARCH** American literature; literary criticism; American Indian literature. **SELECTED PUBLICATIONS** Auth, Hemingway on Love, Texas 65, Maskell House, 73; auth, Art, Hemingway in Italy: Making It Up, J Mod Lit, 4/82; ed, Hemingway in Italy and Other Essays, Praeger, 90; auth, A Farewell to Arms: The War of the Words, Twayne, 92. **CONTACT ADDRESS** Dept of English, Univ of No Dakota, PO Box 7209, Grand Forks, ND 58202-7209. **EMAIL** robert_lewis@und.nodak.edu

LEWIS, THOMAS SPOTTSWOOD WELLFORD
PERSONAL Born 05/29/1942, Philadelphia, PA, m, 1964, 1 child **DISCIPLINE** ENGLISH & AMERICAN LITERATURE **EDUCATION** Univ New Brunswick, CAN, BA, 64; Columbia Univ, MA(honors), 65, PhD, 70. **CAREER** Instr English, Iona Col, 67; res asst English, Columbia Univ, 67-68; from instr to asst prof, 68-75, assoc prof English, 75-82, Prof, Skidmore Col, 83-; Am Philos Soc res grant, 71 & 75; NY Coun for Humanities grant, 77, 87; dir, Brooklyn Bridge and Am Cult Symposium, 77; Consult, Florentine Films, 78-; NEH grants, 85, 86, 89, 93, 95-96, 97; Corp for Public Broadcasting grant, 89; various grants for The Empire of the Air radio prog, private donor, WETA, Wash, 88, General Motors, 90, 91, Am Public Radio, 90; support, WETA, 92; OR Coun for the Humanities grant, 93; TX Coun for the Humanities grant, 93; Arthur Vining Davis Found grant, 95-96; Quadralli Prof of Social Responsibility, 97. **HONORS AND AWARDS** Fac fel, Columbia Univ, 64-68; Paul Klingenstein fel, Columbia Univ, 65-66; Woodrow Wilson Dissertation fel, 68; Skidmore Col Fac Res Lect, 85; W. C. D. Pacey Lect, Univ New Brunswick, 90; Harry Houck Awd, Antique Radio Club of Am, 92; fel, Radio Club of Am, 92; Marconi Awd, Veteran Wireless Operators Asn, 92; Divided Highways film, 98: George Foster Peabody Awd; Best Documentary, New England Film Festival; Bronze Apple, Nat Ed Asn; honorable mention, San Francisco Film Festival & Chicago Film Festival; Academy of Television Arts and Sciences Emmy, Best Historical Documentary. **MEMBERSHIPS** MLA. **RESEARCH** Biography; modern British and American literature; literature and technology. **SELECTED PUBLICATIONS** Auth, Hart Crane and His Mother: A Correspondence, Salmagundi, no 9, spring 69; Some new letters of John Butler Yeats, in Modern Irish Literature, Twayne, 72; The Letters of Hart Crane and His Family, Columbia Univ Press, 74; ed, Virginia Woolf: A Collection of Criticism, McGraw-Hill, 75; auth, The Brooklyn Bridge: Lewis Mumford and Hart Crane, Hart Crane Newlett, 4/78; Lewis Mumford and the Academy, Salmagundi, 80; Homeric Epic and the Greek Vase, in The Greek Vase, Hudson-Mohawk Asn Cols & Univs, 81; The Brothers of Ganymede, Salmagundi, 82; Virginia Woolf and the Sense of the Past, Salmagundi, no 68-69, 85-86; Radio Revolutionary: Edwin Howard Armstrong's Invention of FM Radio, Am Heritage of Invention and Technology, fall 85, reprinted, Skidmore Voices, fall 86; To Do, To Be, To Suffer: The Memoirs of Ulysses S. Grant, Saratoga Springs, Skidmore Col Fac Res Lect, 87; Rudolph Arnheim's Snippets and Seeds, Salmagundi, no 78-79, spring/summer 88; Rev of Ruth Hoberman, Modernizing Lives: Experiments in English Biography, vol 11, no 3, summer 88; Empire of the Air: The Men Who Made Radio, NY, Harper/Burlingame Books, 91; A Godlike Presence: The Impact of Radio on the Nineteen Twenties and Thirties, Magazine of History, vol 6, no 4, spring 92; Triumph of the Idol - Rush Limbaugh and a Hot Medium, Media Studies J, vol 7, no 3, summer 93; Divided Highways: The Interstate Highway System and the Transformation of American Life, NY, Viking Books, 97; various positions on several films and radio broadcasts. **CONTACT ADDRESS** Dept of English, Skidmore Col, 815 N Broadway, Saratoga Springs, NY 12866-1698.

LEWIS, TODD VERNON
PERSONAL Born 01/12/1949, Lynwood, CA, m, 1991, 2 children **DISCIPLINE** SPEECH COMMUNICATION **EDUCATION** Biola Univ, BA, 72; Ohio State Univ, MA, 74; Louisiana State Univ, PhD, 80. **CAREER** Teaching asst speech, Ohio State Univ, Columbus, 73-74; teaching asst, Louisiana State Univ, Baton Rouge, 77-78; prof & chm, commun, Biola Univ, La Mirada, Calif, 74-. **HONORS AND AWARDS** AFA-NIET Distinguished Serv Awd, 90 **MEMBERSHIPS** Nat Commun Assn; Am Forensics Assn; Relig Commun Assn; Nat Forensics Assn. **RESEARCH** Religious communication (rhetoric); readers theatre; forensics; film history. **SELECTED PUBLICATIONS** Auth, Communicating Literature, 3rd ed, Kendall/Hunt Pub co, 00. **CONTACT ADDRESS** Dept of Communication, Biola Univ, 13800 Biola Ave, La Mirada, CA 90639-0001. **EMAIL** todd_lewis@peter.biola.edu

LEYASMEYER, ARCHIBALD I.
PERSONAL Born 12/15/1935, Riga, Latvia, m, 1964 **DISCIPLINE** ENGLISH **EDUCATION** Harvard Univ, BA, 57; Eastern Baptist Theol Sem, Mre, 60; Princeton Univ, MA, 64, PhD(-English), 67. **CAREER** From instr to asst prof, 64-68, Morse-Alumni Dist Tchg Prof, 96-, Faculty Dir, 79, Assoc Prof English, Univ Minn, Minneapolis, 68-, Fac Dir, Univ Without Walls, 79-, Morse-Amoco Award, 82. **HONORS AND AWARDS** Danforth Assoc, Gordon L. Starr Awd, Univ Col Disting Tchg Awd, Ruth Christie Tchg Awd. **MEMBERSHIPS** Asn Eighteenth Century Studies; Asn Advan Baltic Studies; Johnsonian Soc; MLA. **RESEARCH** Modern drama; eighteenth century; satire. **CONTACT ADDRESS** Dept of English, Univ of Minnesota, Twin Cities, 207 Church St S E, Minneapolis, MN 55455-0156. **EMAIL** leyas002@umn.edu

LHAMON, W. T., JR.
PERSONAL m, 2 children **DISCIPLINE** ENGLISH **EDUCATION** Johns Hopkins Univ, BA, 66; Univ Ind, PhD, 73. **CAREER** Prof, Eng, Fla State Univ. **HONORS AND AWARDS** NEH Fellowships, 92, 98. **MEMBERSHIPS** Am Antiquarian Soc **CONTACT ADDRESS** Dept of Eng, Florida State Univ, PO Box Washington, DC, Tallahassee, FL 32306-1036. **EMAIL** wlhamon@english.fsu.edu

LIBERMAN, TERRI
PERSONAL Born Brooklyn, NY **DISCIPLINE** AMERICAN AND MODERN LITERATURE **EDUCATION** William Smith Col, BA, 64; Purdue Univ, MA, 66; Case Western Reserve Univ, PhD(English), 76. **CAREER** Instr English, Col Wooster, 66-68; Prof English, Norwich Univ, 76- **MEMBERSHIPS** MLA; Pop Cult Asn; Phi Beta Kappa. **RESEARCH** Contemporary literature; women's studies; popular culture. **CONTACT ADDRESS** Dept of English, Norwich Univ, Northfield, 65 S Main St, Northfield, VT 05663-1035.

LIBIN, KATHRYN
DISCIPLINE MUSIC HISTORY AND THEORY **EDUCATION** Oberlin Conserv, BM; NYork Univ, PhD. **CAREER** Vis Instr, Vassat Col; recitals, Boston Early Mus Festival, Metropolitan Mus Art, Moravian Mus in Bethlehem, Pa, Vassar Col. **RESEARCH** Music of the late 18th and early 19th centuries; the history and performance practice of early keyboard instruments. **SELECTED PUBLICATIONS** Contribu, Metropolitan Mus Art; notes have appeared in Stagebill for Great Performers, Lincoln Center; auth, liner notes for complete cycles of the Mozart solo keyboard works & sonatas for violin and keyboard. **CONTACT ADDRESS** Classics Dept, Vassar Col, 124 Raymond Ave., Poughkeepsie, NY 12604.

LICKONA, THOMAS E.
PERSONAL Born 04/04/1943, Poughkeepsie, NY, m, 1966, 2 children **DISCIPLINE** ENGLISH, PSYCHOLOGY **EDUCATION** Siena Col, BA, 64; Ohio Univ, MA, 65; State Univ NYork, Albany, PhD, 71. **CAREER** Prof, Educ, State Univ NY, Cortland, 70-; vis prof, Harvard Univ, Boston Univ, 78-79; Dir, Ctr 4th, 5th R's, State Univ NY, Cortland, 94-. **MEMBERSHIPS** Character Education Partnership; Nat Asn Scholars; Soc

of Cath Soc Scientists. **RESEARCH** Moral development, character education. **SELECTED PUBLICATIONS** Moral Development and Behavior, 76; Raising Good Children, 83; Educating for Character: How Our Schools Can Teach Respect and Responsibility, 91; Character Development in Schools and Beyond, 92; Sex, Love, and You: Making the Right Decision, 94. **CONTACT ADDRESS** Educ Dept, SUNY, Col at Cortland, Cortland, NY 13045. **EMAIL** C4n5RS@Cortland.edu

LIDDELL, JANICE LEE

DISCIPLINE ENGLISH LITERATURE **EDUCATION** Univ Mich, MA and PhD. **CAREER** Chp Dept Eng. **RESEARCH** African women's literature, particularly African American and Caribbean. **SELECTED PUBLICATIONS** Auth, Imani: and the Flying Africans; various children's books. **CONTACT ADDRESS** Clark Atlanta Univ, 223 James P Brawley Dr, SW, Atlanta, GA 30314.

LIDOV, JOEL

PERSONAL Born 03/13/1945, Chicago, IL, m, 2 children **DISCIPLINE** GREEK & LATIN LANGUAGE & LIT **EDUCATION** Columbia Coll, BA, 66; Columbia Univ, MA, 67, PhD, 72. **CAREER** Visiting/acting, asst prof, Univ of CA Berkely, 70-73; Visiting asst prof, 73-75, Stanford Univ; asst to assoc prof, Queens College & graduate sch, City Univ of NY, 75-. **HONORS AND AWARDS** Phi Beta Kappa, 65; Earle Prize in classics, 66; Woodbridge distinguished fel, 70; Gildersleev prize (John Hopkins Univ Press), 93. **MEMBERSHIPS** Amer Philogical Assn **RESEARCH** Classical Greek Lit (especially Archaic, classical poetry) **SELECTED PUBLICATIONS** Auth, Alternating Rhythm in Archaic Greek Poetry, Trans, American Philological Assoc, 89; What am I? What am I not?: Three Recent Pindars, Classical Journal, 93; The Second Stanza of Sappho 31, Another Look, American Journal of Philology, 93; Pindar's Hym to Cybele, Meter, Form and Syncretism, Greek, Roman and Byzantine Studies, 96. **CONTACT ADDRESS** Dept of Classical Middle-Eastern & Asian Langs, Queens Col, CUNY, 6530 Kissena Blvd, Flushing, NY 11367. **EMAIL** joel_lidov@qc.edu

LIEB, MICHAEL J.

DISCIPLINE ENGLISH **EDUCATION** Rutgers Univ, AB, 62; AM, 64; PhD, 67. **CAREER** Asst Prof, William & Mary Col, 67-70; Assoc Prof, Univ Ill, 70-75; From Vis Prof to Prof, Univ Chicago, 79-. **HONORS AND AWARDS** Alan M Hallene Sr Univ Scholar Awd, Univ Ill, 88-90; NEH Fel for Univ Teachers, 91-92; Irene Samuel Mem Awd, 94, 97. **MEMBERSHIPS** ACLS, APS, Milton Soc of Am. **SELECTED PUBLICATIONS** Auth, The Visionary Mode: Biblical Prophecy, Hermeneutics and Cultural Change, Cornell UP (Ithaca), 91; co-ed, Literary Milton: Text, Pretext, Context, Duquesne UP (Pittsburgh, PA), 94; auth, Milton and the Culture of Violence, Cornell UP (Ithaca), 94; co-ed, The Miltonic Samson, Pittsburgh UP (Pittsburgh, PA), 96; auth, Children of Ezekiel: Aliens, UFOs, the Crisis of Race and the Advent of End Time, Duke UP (Durham), 98; co-ed, John Milton: The Author in His Works, Pittsburgh UP (Pittsburgh, PA), 00. **CONTACT ADDRESS** Dept English, Univ of Illinois, Chicago, 601 S Morgan St, Chicago, IL 60607-7100. **EMAIL** mlieb@uic.edu

LIEBERMAN, LAURENCE

PERSONAL Born 02/16/1935, Detroit, MI, m, 1956, 3 children **DISCIPLINE** ENGLISH, MODERN POETRY **EDUCATION** Univ Mich, BA, 56, MA, 58. **CAREER** Instr English, Orange Coast Col, 60-64; from asst prof to assoc prof, Col Virgin Islands, 64-68; assoc prof, 68-70, Prof English, Univ Ill, Urbana, 70-; consult & poetry ed, Univ Ill Press, 70-; poetry reviewer, Yale Rev, 71-75. **HONORS AND AWARDS** Major Hopwood Awd poetry writing, 58; Fel, Yaddo, NY, 63 & 67; Huntington-Hartford Found fel, 64; Nat Endowment for Arts Awd for poem, 67; assoc fel, Univ Ill Ctr Advan Study, Japan & Hawaii, 71-72, 90-91, 00-01; Ill Arts Coun Proj Completion grant, 80, writing fel, 82-83; NEA Fel, 86; Jerome Stesack Awd, Am Poetry Rev, 86. **MEMBERSHIPS** MLA.; AWP; PSA. **RESEARCH** Contemporary American poetry; poetry criticism. **SELECTED PUBLICATIONS** Auth, The Osprey Suicides (a volume of poems), Macmillan & Collier, 73; The Osprey Suicides (poem), New Yorker, 11/72; Whispers out of time: A reading of John Ashbery's Self-Portrait in a Convex Mirror, Am Poetry Rev, 5/77; Unassigned Frequencies: American Poetry in Review (1964-77), Univ Ill, 12/77; Joren: The Volcanic Falls, a long poem, Hudson Rev, winter 77-78; Sea Caves of Dogashima, a long poem, Am Poetry, fall 78; God's Measurements (a volume of poems), 80 & Eros at the World Kite Pageant: Poems (1979-82), 83, MacMillan; The Mural of Wakeful Sleep, poems, Macmillan, 85; The Creole Mephistopheles, Macmillan, 89; New and Selected Poems, Univ Ill Press, 93; The St. Kitts Monkey Feuds, book-length poem, The Cummington Press, 95; Beyond the Muse of Memory: Essays on Contemporary American Poets, Univ Mo Press, 95; Dark Songs: Slave House and Synagogue, Univ Ark Press, 96; Compass of the Dying, Univ Ark Press, 98; The Regatta in the Skies: Selected Poems, Univ Ga Press, 99; auth, Flight From The Mother Stone, Univ Ark Press, 00. **CONTACT ADDRESS** Dept of English, Univ of Illinois, Urbana-Champaign, 608 S Wright St, Urbana, IL 61801-3613.

LIEBLER, MICHAEL L.

PERSONAL Born 08/24/1953, Detroit, MI, m, 1926, 2 children **DISCIPLINE** ENGLISH **EDUCATION** Oakland Univ, BA, 76; Oakland Univ, MA, 80. **CAREER** Senior Lecturer, Wayne State Univ, 80-; Adjunct Prof, Macomb Community Col, 89-; YMCA of USA National Arts & Humanities Faculty, 97-; Adjunct Prof, Center for Creative Studies, 85-90; Adjunct English instr, Henry Ford Community Col, 80-86; **HONORS AND AWARDS** Received Poet-In-Residence Awd at Northern Michigan Univ-Summer 00; Nominated for Wayne State University Awd for Community Involvement, 00; Nominated for Pushcart Literary Awds in 98, 95 & 90; Received Wayne State Univ Excellence in Teaching Awds, 93, 94, & 96; Received Wayne State Univ Quality Service Awd, 93; Nominated for Governor of Michigan's 98 &99 Arts & Cultural Leader Awd; Nominated for YMCA Arts Program for Governor of Michigan's 98 & 99 Awd; Honorable Mention-Canda's Cranberry Press Chapbook Contest 97; Honorable Mention Poet's Magazine's Poetry Contest 96. **MEMBERSHIPS** AAOP; AWP; MLA. **RESEARCH** Vietnam War through Literature; Performance Poetry; Labor History & Lit. **SELECTED PUBLICATIONS** Auth, "The Martyr of Pig: Dada Poems, Ridgeway Press, 74; auth, "Knit Me A Pair of Your Shoes, Ridgeway Press, 75; auth, "Unfinished Man in the Perfect Mirror, Casterbridge Press, 76; auth, "Measuring Darkness, Ridgeway Press, 80; auth, "Whispers by the Lawn-Volume I, 85; auth, Whisper by the Lawn-Volume II, Ridgeway Press, 87; Breaking the Voodoo, Parkville Press, 90; Deliver Me, Ridgeway Press, 92; auth, "Stripping the Adult Century Bare, Viet Nam Generation Press, 95; auth, Brooding the Hearlands, Bottom Dog Press of Firelands College, 98; auth, Written In Rain: New & Selected Poems 85-00, 00. **CONTACT ADDRESS** Dept English, Wayne State Univ, 51 West Warren Ave, Detroit, MI 48201-1305. **EMAIL** mlliebler@aol.com

LIEPE-LEVINSON, KATHERINE

DISCIPLINE THEATER-ACADEMIC AND PRACTICAL **EDUCATION** Empire State Col, BA, 84; Hunter Col, MA, 86; CUNY, PhD, 93. **CAREER** Art dir, Terra Firma Studiotheatre; dir, Synergy Performance Group; instr, Hunter Col, Empire State Col; vis asst prof, 93. **HONORS AND AWARDS** Arts grants, NY State Coun; grant, NYSCA; John Golden playwriting award, Hunter Col. **SELECTED PUBLICATIONS** Auth, Aphrodite's Last Visit: A Period Piece, Twenty-three Plays from the New Play Development Workshop, Miss State UP, 94; Multiple Perspectives in Motion, Peer Helping: The Vision, The Mission, MIT Press, 93; rev(s), Biomechanics: Meyerhold's System of Movement Training, Taking the Myster out of Sensory Technique, Theatre Service, 94. **CONTACT ADDRESS** Dept of Eng, Colgate Univ, 13 Oak Drive, Hamilton, NY 13346.

LIGGETT, SARAH

DISCIPLINE WRITING **EDUCATION** Purdue Univ, PhD, 82. **CAREER** Prof, La State Univ. **HONORS AND AWARDS** Phi Beta Kappa; NCTE Awd, Comput & Composing, 86. **RESEARCH** Technical writing; research methodology in composition and writing pedagogy. **SELECTED PUBLICATIONS** Auth, Preventing Meltdown: Licensee Event Reports in the Nuclear Energy Industry, Stud in Tech Commun, 90; Creativity and Non-Literary Writing: The Importance of Problem Finding, J of Tchg Writing, 91; coauth, Computers & Composing: How the New Technologies Are Changing Writing, 84; Power Relations, Technical Writing Theory, and Workplace Writing, J of Bus and Tech Commun, 93; Changing Institutions, Changing Teachers, ADE Bull, 96; coauth, "Technical and Political Literacy: Training and Communicating in the Nuclear Powers Industry," in Expanding Literatures: English Teaching and the New Workplace (98); auth, "After the Practicum: Assesing Teacher Preparation Programs," in The Writing Program Administrator as Researcher: Inquiry in Actions and Reflection (99). **CONTACT ADDRESS** Dept of Eng, Louisiana State Univ, B-31 Coates Hall, Baton Rouge, LA 70803. **EMAIL** enligg@lsu.edu

LIGHTFOOT, DAVID

PERSONAL Born 02/10/1945, Looe, United Kingdom, m, 1982, 4 children **DISCIPLINE** COMMUNICATIONS **EDUCATION** King's Col, BA, 66; Univ Mich, MA; PhD, 70. **CAREER** Teaching Fel, Univ MI, 67-70; Asst Prof to Assoc Prof, McGill Univ, 70-78; Prof to Extraordinary Prof, Univ Utrecht, 78-86; Prof and Chair, Univ Md, 83-; Adj Prof, Johns Hopkins Univ, 90-98; Assoc Fir, Neural and Cognitive Sci Prog, Univ Md, 98-. **HONORS AND AWARDS** Res Grant, Am Philos, 72; Res Grant, Mcgill Humanities Div; Canad coun Leave Fel, 76-77; Associateship, Cambridge Univ, 76-77; Res Grant, Dutch org for the Adv of Pure Sci Res, 82-83; Fel, Am coun of Learned Soc, 88; Grants, Nat Sci Foundation, 88-90, 89-91, 99-00; Res Awd, Univ MD, 89; Distinguished Rac Res Fel, Univ MD, 96-97; Summer Res Awd, Univ MD, 98. **MEMBERSHIPS** Canadian Ling Asn; Intl Soc for Hist Ling; Ling Soc of Am; Nat Res Coun. **RESEARCH** Syntax, language change, language acquisition. **SELECTED PUBLICATIONS** Auth, How to set parameters: Arguments from language change, MIT Press, 91; ed, Verb Movement, Cambridge Univ Press, 94; auth, The development of language: Acquisition, change and evolution, Oxford Univ Press, 99; auth, "The spandrels of the linguistic genotype," in The evolutionary emergence of language, Cambridge Univ Press, 00; auth, "Grammatical approaches to syntactic change," in Handbook of historical linguistics, Oxford Univ Press, 00; co-auth, "The human language faculty as an organ," Annual Review of Physiology, 00; co-auth, "Intact grammars but intermittent access," Behavioral and Brain Sciences, 00; co-auth, The language organ: Linguistics as cognitive physiology, forthcoming; auth, "How long was the nineteenth century?," in Festschrift for Mary Kat, in press; auth, "Myths and the prehistory of grammars," in Syntactic reconstruction, Amsterdam, in press; auth, "Plato's problem, UG and the language organ," in Companion to Noam Chomsky, Cambridge Univ Press, in press. **CONTACT ADDRESS** Dept Ling, Univ of Maryland, Col Park, 1401 Marie Mount Hall, College Park, MD 20742-7505. **EMAIL** dlight@deans.umd.edu

LIGHTFOOT, JEAN HARVEY

PERSONAL Born 11/29/1935, Chicago, IL, d **DISCIPLINE** ENGLISH **EDUCATION** Fisk Univ, BA 1957; Univ of Chgo, MA 1969; Northwestern Univ Evanston IL, PhD 1974. **CAREER** Chicago Public Schools, English teacher 1957-69; Kennedy King Campus Chicago City Coll, prof English 1969-; Citizens Comm on Public Educ, exec dir 1975-76; Comm on Urban Affair Spec Projects AME Church, exec dir 1978-80; The Neighborhood Inst, educ coordinator 1979-. **HONORS AND AWARDS** Outstanding Young Women of Amer 1968; Ford Fellowship Univ of Chicago 1968-69; TTT Fellowship Northwestern Univ 1972-73. **MEMBERSHIPS** Counselor Hillcrest Ctr for Children NY 1958-61; asst prof ed Northeastern Univ Chicago 1974-76; consult Prescription Learning Inc 1977-; featured soloist Park Manor Cong Church 1958-, John W Work Chorale 1959-; staff dir, convener The S Shore Schools Alliance 1979-80. **CONTACT ADDRESS** Education Coordinator, Neighborhood Inst, 1950 E 71st St, Chicago, IL 60649.

LIGHTFOOT, MARJORIE JEAN

PERSONAL Born 04/24/1933, Oak Park, IL **DISCIPLINE** CONTEMPORARY ENGLISH, AMERICAN LITERATURE **EDUCATION** Brown Univ, AB, 55; Northwestern Univ, MA, 56, PhD(English), 64. **CAREER** Instr freshman English, Univ Ariz, 60-63, asst prof Am lit & humanities, 64-69, assoc prof English, 69-74, Prof English, Ariz State Univ, 74- **MEMBERSHIPS** MLA; Rocky Mountain Mod Lang Asn; Western Humor & Irony; WestCent Mod Lang Asn. **RESEARCH** Twentieth century British and American literature; Chaucer and the Bronte's; 20th century women authors. **SELECTED PUBLICATIONS** Auth, Prosody and Performance, Quart J Speech, 2/67; The Uncommon Cocktail Party, Mod Drama, 2/69; Numerical Sequential and Temporal Patterns in English Verse, Quart J Speech, 4/71; Description and Transcription of Temporal Patterns of Rhythm in English Verse, summer 74 & Temporal Prosody, fall 74, Lang & Style; Breakthrough in Doris Lessing's The Golden Notebook, Studies in the Novel, summer 75; Fiction vs Reality: Clues and Conclusions in The Golden Notebook, Mod Brit Lit, fall 77; Geoffrey Chaucer's Troilus and Criseyde: A Dramatic Adaptation and Translation of the Poem, 2nd ed, 1/78; Glimpses of the Brontes: A Biography on Stage, privately publ, 79, 2nd ed, 80. **CONTACT ADDRESS** Dept of English, Arizona State Univ, PO Box 870302, Tempe, AZ 85287-0302.

LIKES, TERRY

PERSONAL m **DISCIPLINE** BROADCAST JOURNALISM **EDUCATION** Maryville Univ, St. Louis BA 88; W Ky Univ, MA, 88; Univ Ky, PhD, 96. **CAREER** Asst prof, Western Ky Univ, 88-; Radio/TV news/ sports announcer, broadcast consult, 88-. **HONORS AND AWARDS** Ky Press award for news coverage, 86, 87, 98, 99; BEA, 99. **MEMBERSHIPS** RTNDA. **RESEARCH** News reporting, Radio/TV performance, writing; producing/directing WKU NewsChannel 12/WKYU-TV. **SELECTED PUBLICATIONS** Areas: Radio and Television. **CONTACT ADDRESS** School of Journalism and Broadcasting, Western Kentucky Univ, 1 Big Red Way Street, Bowling Green, KY 42101. **EMAIL** terry.likes@wku.edu

LILES, BETTY Z.

DISCIPLINE COMMUNICATION SCIENCES **EDUCATION** Lady of the Lake Univ, MA, 68; Univ Minn, PhD, 73. **CAREER** Prof emer, Univ Conn; past Speech and Lang Consult, ACES, North Haven, CT. **RESEARCH** Normal and disordered child language. **SELECTED PUBLICATIONS** Auth, Narrative Discourse in Children with Language Disorders and Children with Normal Language: A Critical Review of the Literature, JSHR, 93; The Measurement of Narrative Discourse in Children with Language Disorders, JSHR, 95. **CONTACT ADDRESS** Dept of Communication Sci, Univ of Connecticut, Storrs, 1097 Storrs Rd, Storrs, CT 06269-1085.

LILLY, PAUL R., JR.

DISCIPLINE ENGLISH **EDUCATION** Holy Cross Col, BA; Boston Col, MA; Fordham Univ, PhD. **CAREER** Dept Eng, SUNY Col at Oneonta **HONORS AND AWARDS** Fulbright Lectureship, Spain 73-75, Belgium 85-86, India 95; fellow, NEH; 78-79; NEH Summer Inst, 95; SUNY res grant. **RESEARCH** Contemp and mod Am fiction, the Am Renaissance, and Am humor. **SELECTED PUBLICATIONS** Auth, Words in Search of Victims: The Achievement of Jerzy Kosinski, Kent State UP, 88; articles on William Faulkner, Richard Bausch,

Elizabeth Tallent, Mary Gordon, John Updike, Jerzy Kosinski, 19th century humorists Augustus Baldwin Longstreet, William Tappan Thompson, Petroleum V. Nasby, and others. **CONTACT ADDRESS** SUNY, Col at Oneonta, 304 Fine Arts Bldg, Oneonta, NY 13820.

LIM, SHIRLEY G.
PERSONAL Born 12/27/1944, Malaysia, m, 1972, 1 child **DISCIPLINE** ENGLISH **EDUCATION** Univ of Malaya, Kuala Lumpur, BA, 67; Brandeis Univ, MA, 71; PhD, 73. **CAREER** Asst prof, Hostos Community Col, 73-76; assoc prof, Westchester Col, 76-90; prof, Univ of Calif Santa Barbara, 93-. **HONORS AND AWARDS** Fulbright Scholar, 69-72, Lectr, 96; Univ of Malaya Prizes, 65, 67; NEY Seminar, 78, 87; Mellon Fel, 83; SUNY Chancellor's Awd for Excellence in Teaching, 81; Asia Found Fel, 89; NEH Consultant, 95; Am Book Awd, 97; JT Stewart Awd, 99; Distinguished Lect, Univ of W Australia, 99. **MEMBERSHIPS** MLA; Am Studies Assoc; Assoc of Commonwealth Lang and Lit; Nat Women Studies Assoc; Fulbright Assoc. **RESEARCH** Ethnic American/Asian American Literary Studies, US Feminism. **SELECTED PUBLICATIONS** Auth, Monsoon History: Selected Poems, Skoob Pacifica, (London), 94; auth, Writing Southeast/Asia in English: Against the Grain, Skoob Pacific (London), 94; auth, Life's Mysteries: The Best of Shirley Lim, Times Books Int, (Singapore), 95; auth, Among the White Moon Faces: An Asian-American Memoir of Homelands, Feminist Pr, (NY), 96; auth, "Theory and Postcolonial Studies", New Lit in English, 96; auth, Two Dreams: Short Stories, Feminist Pr, (NY), 97; auth, "Ain't I a Feminist?: Re-forming the Circle", Live, From Feminism: Memoirs of Women's Literature, eds Rachel Blau DuPlessis and Ann snitow, Crown Books, 98; auth, What the Fortune Teller Didn't Say, West End Pr, (Albuquerque, NMex), 98; ed, Asian American Literature, NTC Pr, 99; coed, Power, Race and Gender in Academe: Strangers in the Tower?, MLA Pr, 00. **CONTACT ADDRESS** Dept English, Univ of California, Santa Barbara, 552 University Rd, Santa Barbara, CA 93106. **EMAIL** slim@humanitas.ucsb.edu

LIMBACHER, JAMES L.
PERSONAL Born 11/30/1926, St. Marys, OH **DISCIPLINE** DRAMA, FILM **EDUCATION** Bowling Green State Univ, BA, 49, MA, 54; Ind Univ, MS, 55; Wayne State Univ, MS in LS, 72. **CAREER** Mem Audio-Visual Div, Dearborn Dept Libr, 55-; Instr Film Hist, Wayne State Univ, 73-. **MEMBERSHIPS** Am Fed Film Soc (pres, 62-65); Educ Film Libr Asn (pres, 66-69); Soc Cinema Studies. **RESEARCH** History and appreciation of the motion picture; audio-visual media. **SELECTED PUBLICATIONS** Auth, Lulu in Berlin, J Popular Film and Television, Vol 0020, 92; Almonds and Raisins, J Popular Film and Television, Vol 0020, 92; Pioneers of the French Cinema, Vol 1, J Popular Film and Television, Vol 0020, 92; Dead of Night, J Popular Film and Television, Vol 0020, 92; The 'Whales of August', J Popular Film and Television, Vol 0022, 94; 'Orphans of the Storm', J Popular Film and Television, Vol 0022, 94; 'Indianapolis--Ship of Doom', J Popular Film and Television, Vol 0022, 94; Grey Gardens, J Popular Film and Television, Vol 0022, 94; 'Dizzy Gillespie--a Night in Tunisia', J Popular Film and Television, Vol 0022, 94; The 'Patti Page Songbook', J Popular Film and Television, Vol 0022, 94; Color Adjustment, J Popular Film and Television, Vol 0022, 94; Night of the Hunter, J Popular Film and Television, Vol 0022, 94; The 'Man You Loved to Hate', J Popular Film and Television, Vol 0022, 94; The 'Origins of American Films', J Popular Film and Television, Vol 0023, 95. **CONTACT ADDRESS** 21800 Morley Ave, Dearborn, MI 48124.

LIMON, JOHN
DISCIPLINE ENGLISH **EDUCATION** Harvard Univ, BA, 73; Univ Calif Berkeley, PhD, 81. **CAREER** Prof, Eng lit. **RESEARCH** Am Lit and the hist and philos of science and of war; stand-up comedy; Kafka. **SELECTED PUBLICATIONS** Auth, "Stand-up Comedy in Theory, or, Abjection in America" (Duke: 00). **CONTACT ADDRESS** Dept of English, Williams Col, Stetson d-16, Williamstown, MA 01267. **EMAIL** jlimon@williams.edu

LIN, CAROLYN
DISCIPLINE ADVERTISING, MASS COM THEORY, TELECOMMUNICATIONS **EDUCATION** Nat Cent Univ, BA; IA State Univ, MS; MI State Univ, PhD. **CAREER** Grad prog dir, Cleveland State Univ; dir, Multimedia Advertising Certificate Prog; founder, Communication Technology & Policy Division at the Asn for Education of Journalism & Mass Communication. **HONORS AND AWARDS** Nat Asn of Television Program Executive Fac Fel; Nat Asn of Broadcasters res grants; cited as the 11th most productive mass commun schoalr in the U.S., 85-90, Southwest Education Council, 90; cited as third most prolific telecommunication scholar in peer-review journals, 85-94, Jour of the Asn for Commun Admin, 98. **MEMBERSHIPS** Int Commun Asn; Asn for Educ in Journalism & Mass Commun; Am Advertising Acad; Broadcast Educ Asn. **RESEARCH** Uses, content and effects of new communication technology and new media advertising; media economics; communication technology and policy. **SELECTED PUBLICATIONS** Auth, "Predicting Online Services Adoption Likelihood Among Potential Subscribers: A Motivational Approach," Journal of Advertising Research 39 (99); auth, "The Role of the VCR in Family Television Viewing," in Television and the American Family, 2nd edition, ed. J. Bryant and J.A. Bryant (Hillsdale, NJ, Lawrence Erlbaum, Inc., 00); auth, "Audience Attributes, Media Supplementation, and Likely Online Service Adoption," Mass Commun and Soc, forthcoming; coauth, Communication Technology and Society: Audience, Adoption and Uses, forthcoming; auth, "Global Communication Technology Diffusion" and "Globalization of Media Industries," in International Communication: Theory and Cases, ed. K. Anokawa, C.A. Lin, and M.B. Salwen (Wadsworth Publishing, forthcoming); coed, International Communications: Issues and Cases, forthcoming; auth, "Satellite Communication," in Communication Technology Update, 7th edition, ed. A.E. Grant (Boston, Focal Press, forthcoming), 223-233; auth, "Theory and Research Implications for the Multimedia Technology Environment," in Communication Technology and Society: Audience Adoption and Uses, ed. C.A. Lin and D.J. Atkin (Cresskill, NJ, Hampton Press, Inc., forthcoming). **CONTACT ADDRESS** Commun Dept, Cleveland State Univ, 83 E 24th St, Cleveland, OH 44115. **EMAIL** c.a.lin@csuohio.edu

LIN, YI-CHUN TRICIA
PERSONAL Born 04/04/1960, Miaoli, Taiwan, s **DISCIPLINE** ENGLISH **EDUCATION** Nat Taiwan Normal Univ, BA, 82; Tamkang Univ, MA, 87; SUNY, PhD, 97. **CAREER** ESL Instr, Fu-Ying High School, 82-84; Teaching Asst, SUNY, 87-91; Adj Lecturer, CUNY, 92-93; Adj Lecturer, Columbia Univ, 94; Instr, CUNY, 94-96; Faculty, Vassar Col, 97-98; Asst Prof, Boro of Manhattan Cmty Col, 96-. **HONORS AND AWARDS** Grant, BMCC Title II, 00; Fac Res Awd, CUNY, 98-99; Fac Development Awd, BMCC, 98; Who's Who among Am Teachers, 98; Grad Res Assistantship, Humanities Institute at Stony Brook, 91-92; Exemplary Grad Teaching Asst, 91; Phi Tau Phi scholastic Honor Soc, 86. **MEMBERSHIPS** Asian Am Writers' Workshop, Asn for Asian Am Studies, The community Col Humanities Asn, The Intl Asn for Philos and Lit, Mod Lang Asn, Soc for the Study of the Multi-Ethnic Lit of the US. **RESEARCH** Asian/Pacific American literature; composition and literature; Cultural studies; Images of women in Chinese and Western literatures; Modernist fiction--East & West; Feminism & psychoanalysis; Hermeneutics and deconstruction in literature; Chinese literature and language; Taiwanese literature, 1930-present. **SELECTED PUBLICATIONS** Auth, "Theresa Hak Kyung cha," Asian American Novelists: A Bio-Bibliographical Critical Sourcebook, 00; rev, of "Beyond the Limbo silence, Il Tolomeo," by Elizabeth Nunez, forthcoming; auth, "Translation as empowerment in Developmental Writing and beyond," Inquirer, 99; rev, of "An Interethnic Companion to Asian American Literature," by King-Kok Cheung, Journal of American Ethnic History, forthcoming; auth, Selected Poems of Madison Morrison: A Bilingual Edition, Taipei, 85; rev, of "Growing Up Asian American: An anthology," by Maria Hong, Amerasian, (94): 111-112 **CONTACT ADDRESS** Dept English, Borough of Manhattan Comm Col, CUNY, 199 Chambers St, New York, NY 10007-1044. **EMAIL** tricia_lin_ny@yahoo.com

LINCOLN, HARRY B.
PERSONAL Born 03/06/1922, Fergus Falls, MN, m, 1947, 3 children **DISCIPLINE** MUSIC HISTORY **EDUCATION** Macalester Col, BA, 46; Northwestern Univ, M Mus, 47, PhD(music hist), 51. **CAREER** From instr to assoc prof, 51-63, chmn dept, 73-76, prof music, 63-87, Dist Serv Prof Emer, State Univ NY Binghamton, 87-; US Off Educ grants, 67-69; Nat Endowment for Humanities res grants, 77-78 & 79-80; res grants, ACLS, Am Phil Soc, 92. **MEMBERSHIPS** Col Music Soc (pres, 68-70); Am Musicol Soc; Music Libr Asn; Int Musicol Soc. **RESEARCH** Sixteenth century Italian music; development of computer techniques for thematic indexing. **SELECTED PUBLICATIONS** Auth, I manuscritti Chigiani di Musica organocembalistica, L 'Organo, 67; Some criteria and techniques for developing computerized thematic idices, Elecktronische Datenverarbeitung Musikwissenschaft, 67; The Madrigal Collection L'Amorosa Ero: Brescia, 1588, State Univ NY, 68; Early Seventeenth-Century Keyboard Music in the Vatican Library Chigi Manuscripts, Am Inst Musicol, 68; ed, The Computer and Music, Cornell Univ, 70; auth, Uses of the computer in music composition and research, In: Advances in the Computer, Acad Press, 72; Encoding, decoding and storing melodies for a data base of Renaissance polyphony, Proc Third Int Conf on Very Large Data Bases, Tokyo, 10/77; auth, The Italian Madrigal and Related Repertories, Yale Univ Press, 88; The Latin Motet, Inst Mediaeval Music, 93; co-auth, Study Scores of Historical Styles, Prentice Hall, 86; Dir Music Faculties in American Col and Univ, 4 eds, 67-72. **CONTACT ADDRESS** Dept of Music, SUNY, Binghamton, Binghamton, NY 13901. **EMAIL** BG0056@bingvmb.cc.binghamton.edu

LINCOLN, KENNETH
PERSONAL Born 07/22/1943, Lubbock, TX, 1 child **DISCIPLINE** ENGLISH LITERATURE **EDUCATION** Stanford Univ, BA, 65; Indiana Univ, MA, 67, PhD, 69. **CAREER** Prof English and American Indian Studies, UCLA, 69- . **HONORS AND AWARDS** Fulbright res and lectr, Italy, 84; delegate, Sino-American Writers' Conf, China, 88; Professore Contratto, Univ Piza, 90, Univ Florence, 93, Univ Rome, 97; Distinguished tchg award, 91; Rockefeller res, Bellagio, Italy, 92; USIS German lect tour, 93. **RESEARCH** Native American studies; modern poetry. **SELECTED PUBLICATIONS** Auth, Indi'n Humor: Bicultural Play in Native America, Oxford, 93; auth, Men Down West, Capra, 97; auth, A Writer's China: Bridges East & West, Capra, 99; auth, Sing with the Heart of a Bear: Fusions of Native and American Poetry 1890-1999, California, 99. **CONTACT ADDRESS** Dept of English, Univ of California, Los Angeles, 405 Hilgard Ave, Los Angeles, CA 90095-1530. **EMAIL** lincoln@humnet.ucla.edu

LIND, REBECCA
PERSONAL Born 11/18/1955, Tripoli, Libya, s **DISCIPLINE** COMMUNICATIONS **EDUCATION** Humboldt State Univ, BA, 87; Univ Minn, MA, 89; PhD, 92. **CAREER** Teaching Asst to Vis Asst Prof, Univ Minn, 87-97; Assoc Prof, Univ Ill, 92-. **HONORS AND AWARDS** Silver Circle Awd finalist, UIC, 99; Awd for top three paper, Speech Comm Asn, 95; Intl Professional and Business Women's Hall of Fame Inductee, 99; Outstanding Young Woman of Am, Robert L Scott Book Awd, Grant Norman & Mary Pattiz Foundation, 98; Grant, Nat Asn of Broadcaster, 91. **MEMBERSHIPS** Intl Comm Asn, Speech Comm Asn, Asn for Educ in Journalism and Mass Comm, Broadcast Educ Asn, Phi Kappa Phi; Omicron Delta Kappa; Kappa Tau Alpha; Alpha Lambda Delta. **SELECTED PUBLICATIONS** Co-auth, "Radio stations and the world Wide Web," Journal of radio Studies, (00): 203-221; co-auth, "A computer content analysis of candidates' gender related electronic news story content in relation to tracking polls," in New Directions in computer Content Analysis: Theory, Method, Practice, in press; co-auth, "The representation of the homeless in US electronic media: a computational linguistic analysis," in Representing the Homeless: Media's Image of Homeless Culture, 99; co-auth, "Viewer sensitivity to ethical issues in TV Coverage of the Clinton-Flowers scandal," Political communication, (99): 169-181; co-auth, "Identifying patterns of ethical sensitivity in TV news viewers: An assessment of some critical viewing skills," Journal of Broadcasting and Electronic Media, (98): 507-519; auth, "The representation of Arabs in US electronic media," in Cultural Diversity and the US Media, (98): 157-167; auth, "Ethical sensitivity in viewer evaluations of TV news," Human communication Research, (97): 535-561; co-auth, "Cognitive maps assess news viewer ethical sensitivity," Journal of Mass Media Ethics, (97): 133-147; auth, 'Viewers evaluate the usefulness of advisory warnings about violent television content," communication and Theater Association of Minnesota Journal, 97; auth, "Care and justice in audience evaluations of ethics in TV news," Journal of Mass Media Ethics, (96): 82-94. **CONTACT ADDRESS** Dept Comm, Univ of Illinois, Chicago, 1007 W Harrison St, Chicago, IL 60607-7137. **EMAIL** rebecca@uic.edu

LINDAHL, CARL
PERSONAL Born 12/02/1947, Boston, MA **DISCIPLINE** FOLKLORE, ENGLISH, MEDIEVAL STUDIES **EDUCATION** Harvard Univ, BA, 71; Indiana Univ, Bloomington, MA, 76, PhD, 80. **CAREER** Asst prof, 80-86, assoc prof, 86-97, prof, 97- , English Dept, Univ Houston. **HONORS AND AWARDS** Magna Cum Laude, 71; fel, Am Coun Learned Soc, 83; tchg excellence awd, 93; Alcee Fortier Awd, Am Folklore Soc, 96; fel, Virginia Found for Hum, 97; Lib of Cong Parsons Grant, 98; Founder and ed, World Folktale Library, Garland and Univ Pr Miss; editorial bd, Folklore; dist ed bd, Medieval Folklore. **MEMBERSHIPS** Am Folklore Soc; Folklore Soc, London; Int Soc for Contemp Legend Res; Int Soc for Folk Narrative Res; New Chaucer Soc; Nordic Inst of Folklore. **RESEARCH** Folk narrative; medieval literature; medieval folklore; American folklore. **SELECTED PUBLICATIONS** Auth, the Oral Undertones of Late Medieval Romance, in Oral Tradition in the Middle Ages, Medival and Renaissance Texts Series, 95; auth, Bakhtin's Carnival Laughter and The Cajun Country Mardi Gras, in Folklore, 96; ed, Outlaws and Other Medieval Heroes, Southern Folklore, 96; co-ed, Swapping Stories: Folktales from Louisiana, Mississippi, 97; co-auth, Cajun Mardi Gras Masks, Mississippi, 97; auth, the Presence of the Past in the Cajun Country Mardi Gras, in J of Folklore Res, 96; auth, Some Uses of Numbers, in J of Folklore Res, 97; auth, the Oral Aesthetic and the Bicameral Mind, in Gilgamesh: A Reader, Bolchazy-Carducci, 97; auth, the Power of Being Outnumbered, in La Folklore Miscellany, 97; auth, Chaucer and the Shape of Performance, in Critical Essays on Geoffrey Chaucer, GK Hall, 98; auth, Sir Gawain and the Green Knight, Robert Burns's 'Halloween,' and Myth in its Time, in telling Tales, Medieval Narratives and the Folk Tradition, St Martins, 98; coed, Medieval Folklore: An Encyclopedia of Myths, Legends, Tales, Beliefs, and Customs, ACB-CLIO, 00. **CONTACT ADDRESS** Dept of English, Univ of Houston, Houston, TX 77204-3012. **EMAIL** clindahl@uh.edu

LINDBERG, JOHN
PERSONAL Born 10/22/1955, Merrill, WI, m, 1980, 3 children **DISCIPLINE** MUSICOLOGY **EDUCATION** Univ Fla, BM, 76; Univ Mo-Columbia, MA, 79; Univ Cincinnati, PhD, 89. **CAREER** Assoc prof music, Mankato State; asst prof, music, Univ Northern Iowa; prof, Minn State Univ, Mankato. **HONORS AND AWARDS** Fulbright Scholar, Frankfurt-am-Main, 79-80; Fulbright Fel, Nuremberg, 87-88. **MEMBERSHIPS** Col Mus Soc; Am Musicol Soc. **RESEARCH** Music of Germany before 1800, the Bassoon **SELECTED PUBLICATIONS** The Lied before 1800, in Reader's Guide to Music:

History, Theory, and Criticism; Christoph Graupner, Concerti grossi for 2 violins, 96; Christoph Graupner, Concerto grosso for 2 oboes, 98. **CONTACT ADDRESS** Music Dept, Minnesota State Univ, Mankato, Mankato, MN 56001. **EMAIL** john.lindberg@mankato.msus.edu

LINDEN, STANTON J.
DISCIPLINE MILTON AND SEVENTEENTH-CENTURY NONDRAMATIC LITERATURE **EDUCATION** Univ Minn, PhD. **CAREER** Prof, Washington State Univ. **RESEARCH** 15th-century alchemist George Ripley and the Ripley Scrolls. **SELECTED PUBLICATIONS** Auth, Darke Hierogliphicks: Alchemy in English Literature from Chaucer to the Restoration, 96; ed, William Cooper's A Catalogue of Chymicall Books, 1673-88, 87 & The Mirror of Alchemy, attributed to Roger Bacon, 92; gen ed, rep series English Renaissance Hermeticism & ed, Cauda Pavonis: Studies in Hermeticism; co-ed, Emblems and Alchemy, 98; ed, George Ripley's "Compound of Alchymy", 01. **CONTACT ADDRESS** Dept of English, Washington State Univ, 1 SE Stadium Way, PO Box 645020, Pullman, WA 99164-5020. **EMAIL** linden@wsu.edu

LINDENBURGER, HERBERT S.
PERSONAL Born 04/04/1929, Los Angeles, CA, m, 1961, 2 children **DISCIPLINE** ENGLISH, COMPARATIVE LITERATURE **EDUCATION** Antioch Col, BA, 51; Univ Washington, PhD, 55. **CAREER** Instr to prof, Univ of Calif, Riverside, 54-66; prof, Washington Univ, 66-69; Avalon Prof of Humanities, Stanford Univ, 69-. **HONORS AND AWARDS** Guggenheim Fel, 68-69; Nat Endowment for Humanities Fel, 75-76, 82-83; Stanford Humanities Ctr Fel, 82-83; Pres, MLA, 97. **MEMBERSHIPS** MLA, Am Comp Lit Asn. **RESEARCH** Romanticism, modernism, relation of literature to other arts, opera. **SELECTED PUBLICATIONS** Auth, On Wordsworth's Prelude, Princeton Univ Press (63); auth, Historical Drama, Univ Chicago Press (75); auth, Saul's Fall, Johns Hopkins Univ Press (79); auth, Opera: The Extravagant Art, Cornell Univ Press (84); auth, The History in Literature, Columbia Univ Press (90); auth, Opera in History: From Monteverdi to Cage, Stanford Univ Press (98); auth, Literature and the Other Arts, Cambridge History of Criticism (2000). **CONTACT ADDRESS** Dept English Bldg 460, Stanford Univ, Stanford, CA 94305-2087. **EMAIL** Lindenberger@stanford.edu

LINDER, LAURA R.
PERSONAL Born 07/13/1954, Albuquerque, NM, m, 1991, 1 child **DISCIPLINE** MASS COMMUNICATION **EDUCATION** Univ of NC, PhD, 97. **CAREER** Asst prof, Univ of NC. **MEMBERSHIPS** NCA; ICA; UFVA; BEA; IRTS; ACM; ACJMC; AAUP; AAUW; RTWOA. **RESEARCH** Public access television; Situation comedies. **SELECTED PUBLICATIONS** Auth, Now on the Net, Tune-In, fall, 95; Video User's Guide for Mass Communication, 96; Thomas Edison, The Hist of Mass Media in the United States: An Encycl, ed M.A. Blanchard, 98; Radio Corporation of America, The Hist of Mass Media in the U.S.: An Encycl, ed M.A. Blanchard, 98; Community Access Television, The Hist of Mass Media in the U.S.: An Encycl, ed M.A. Blanchard, 98; auth, Public Access Television: America's Electronic Soapbox, 99. **CONTACT ADDRESS** Dept of Broacasting & Cinema, Univ of No Carolina, Greensboro, 211 Brown Bldg, PO Box 26170, Greensboro, NC 27402-6170. **EMAIL** lrlinder@uncg.edu

LINDERSKI, JERZY
DISCIPLINE CLASSICS **EDUCATION** Univ Cracow, MA, 55, PhD, 60. **CAREER** Prof, Univ NC, Chapel Hill; vis mem, Inst for Advan Stud, Princeton Univ, 77-78. **HONORS AND AWARDS** Ford Found fel, 62-63; Deut Forschungsgemeinschaft fel, Univ Cologne, 70-71; Guggenheim fel, 77-78; NEH fel, 85-86. **RESEARCH** Cicero; Roman law. **SELECTED PUBLICATIONS** Auth, Broughton, Thomas Robert Shannon, in W.W. Briggs, Jr, ed, Biog Dictionary of N Am Classicists, Westport, Ct., 94; Zum Wandel d/l: medulla / melila, Glotta 71 93, 94; Thomas Robert Shannon Broughton, Gnomon 67, 95; A Missing Ponticus, Am J of Ancient Hist 12, 87, 95; Games in Patavium, Ktema 17, 92, 96; Q. Scipio Imperator, in Jerzy Linderski, ed, Imperium Sine Fine: T.R.S. Broughton and the Roman Republic, Hist Einzelschriften 105, 96; Cato Maior in Aetolia, in Robert W. Wallace and Edward M. Harris, eds, Transitions to Empire. Essays in Greco-Roman History 360 -146 B.C. in Honor of Ernst Badian, Norman, OK, 96; Agnes Kirsopp Michels and the Religio, Class J 92.4, 97; Fatalis: A Missing Meretrix, Rheinisches Mus 140, 97; ed, Imperium Sine Fine: T.R.S. Broughton and the Roman Republic, Hist Einzelschriften 105, Steiner Verlag, 96; coauth, T. Robert S. Broughton, In Memoriam, Am Philol ASn Newsl 17.2, 94. **CONTACT ADDRESS** Univ of No Carolina, Chapel Hill, Chapel Hill, NC 27599.

LINDHEIM, SARA H.
DISCIPLINE CLASSICS **EDUCATION** Brown Univ, PhD, 95. **CAREER** Asst Prof. **MEMBERSHIPS** Am Philol Asn; Women's Classical Caucus. **RESEARCH** Latin poetry, Sappho, critical and feminist theory. **SELECTED PUBLICATIONS** Auth, "Hercules Cross-Dressed, Hercules Undressed: Unmasking the Construction of the Propertian Amator in Elegy 4.9," in Am Jour of Philology 119.1 (98), 43-66; auth, I Am Dressed, Therefore I Am?: Vertumnus in Propertius 4.2 and in Metamorphoses 14.662-771, Ramus 27.1 (98), 27-38; auth, Omnia Vincit Amor: Or, Why Oenone Should Have Known It Would Never Work Out (Eclogue 10 and Heroides 5), Material e discussioni per l'analisi dei testi classici 44 (00), 83-101. **CONTACT ADDRESS** Dept of Classics, Univ of California, Santa Barbara, Santa Barbara, CA 93106-7150. **EMAIL** lindheim@humanitas.ucsb.edu

LINDHOLDT, PAUL
PERSONAL Born 05/04/1954, Seattle, WA, m, 1994, 2 children **DISCIPLINE** AMERICAN LITERATURE **EDUCATION** Western Wash Univ, BA, 78; MA, 80; Pa State, PhD, 85. **CAREER** Idaho State Univ, 84-87; Western Wash Univ, 87-90; Univ of Idaho, 90-94; Eastern Wash Univ, 94-. **HONORS AND AWARDS** Acad of Am Poets Awd, First Place, Pa State Univ, 84. **MEMBERSHIPS** Assoc for the Study of Lit and Environ. **RESEARCH** Early American Literature and Culture, Nature Writing, Environmental Literature. **SELECTED PUBLICATIONS** Auth, John Josselyn, Colonial Traveler, 88; auth, Cascadia Wild, 93. **CONTACT ADDRESS** Dept English, Eastern Washington Univ, M/S 25, Cheney, WA 99004. **EMAIL** plindholdt@ewu.edu

LINDNER, CARL MARTIN
PERSONAL Born 08/31/1940, Brooklyn, NY, 2 children **DISCIPLINE** AMERICAN LITERATURE AND CULTURE **EDUCATION** Univ Wis-Madison, PhD. **CAREER** Prof, Univ of WI, Parkside. **HONORS AND AWARDS** UW-Parkside Awd, Exellence in Res and Creative Act 96; Univ WI Regents Tchg Exellence Awd, 92; Stella C Gray Distinguished Tchg Awd, 90-91; Ragdale Found fel, 90; WI Arts Bd Creative Writing fel for Poetry, 80; Standard Oil Distinguished Tchr Awd, 69-70. **SELECTED PUBLICATIONS** Essays on, lit; publ approx 200 poems in var lit jour, 2 chapbks of poetry, Vampire & The Only Game; bk of poetry, Shooting Baskets in a Dark Gymnasium. **CONTACT ADDRESS** Dept of Eng, Univ of Wisconsin, Parkside, 900 Wood Rd, 218 Commun, PO Box 2000, Kenosha, WI 53141-2000. **EMAIL** carl.lindner@uwp.edu

LINDSAY, STAN A.
PERSONAL Born 12/09/1949, Canton, IL, m, 1970, 4 children **DISCIPLINE** RHETORIC **CAREER** Lectr and vis instr, Purdue Univ, 87-98; vis lectr, Indiana Univ, 97-98; instr, Loyola Univ-Chicago, 98-. **MEMBERSHIPS** Nat Commun Asn; Rhetoric Soc Am; Kenneth Burke Soc; Cent States Commun Asn; Am Acad Relig; Soc Bibl Lit. **RESEARCH** Exploring the implications of Kenneth Burkes concept of entelechy. **SELECTED PUBLICATIONS** Auth Prayer as Proto-Rhetoric, The Jour of Commun and Relig, 97; Implicit Rhetoric: Kenneth Burkes Extension of Aristotles Concept of Entelchy, Univ Press Am, 98; The Twenty-One Sales in a Sale, Oasis Books, 98. **CONTACT ADDRESS** PO Box 2421, West Lafayette, IN 47906. **EMAIL** slindsa@luc.edu

LINDSKOLD, JANE M.
PERSONAL Born 09/15/1962, Washington, DC, m, 1997 **DISCIPLINE** ENGLISH **EDUCATION** Fordham Univ, BA, 84, MA, 86, PhD, 89. **CAREER** Teaching Fel, 86-88, Adj Prof, Fordham Univ, 88, 89; Vis Asst Prof, 89-91, Asst Prof, Lynchburg Col, 91-94; Full-time author, 94-. **HONORS AND AWARDS** Dean's List, 82-83, 83-84; Henry Luce Fel, 84-85, 85-86; Presidential Fel, 86-87, 87-88; Zia Awd, 00. **RESEARCH** Modern British, Medieval, and Renaissance literature; science fiction; mythology; drama; composition and computers. **SELECTED PUBLICATIONS** Auth, Brother to Dragons, Companion to Owls, AvoNova, 94; Marks of Our Brothers, AvoNova, 95; Pipes of Orpheus, AvoNova, 95; Chronomaster (authored the novel, computer game, and strategy guide), Prima, 96; Smoke and Mirrors, AvoNova, 96; When the Gods Are Silent, AvoNova, 96; coauth, Donnerjack, AvoNova, 97; auth, Changer, Avon Eos, 98; coauth, Lord Demon, Avon Eos, 99; auth, Legends Walking, Avon Eos, 99; author of numerous other publications. **CONTACT ADDRESS** 3900 75th St. NW, Albuquerque, NM 87120.

LINK, FREDERICK M.
PERSONAL Born 09/02/1930, Reno, NV **DISCIPLINE** ENGLISH LITERATURE **EDUCATION** Southwestern at Memphis, AB, 52; Boston Univ, MA, 54, PhD(English), 57. **CAREER** Asst prof English, Boston Univ, 60-63; asst prof, 63-65, assoc prof, 65-68, Prof English, Univ Nebr-Lincoln, 68-, Chmn Dept English, Univ Nebr-Lincoln, 81-. **MEMBERSHIPS** MLA; Midwest Mod Lang Asn; Aaup. **RESEARCH** English drama, 1660-1837; English poetry, 1660-1798. **SELECTED PUBLICATIONS** Auth, Editing Cather, Stud in the Novel, Vol 0027, 95. **CONTACT ADDRESS** Dept of English, Univ of Nebraska, Lincoln, Lincoln, NE 68588.

LINK, JAMES R.
PERSONAL Born 08/31/1941, Washington, DC, s **DISCIPLINE** ENGLISH **EDUCATION** Univ Notre Dame, BA, 63; Univ Md, MA, 72. **CAREER** Asst Prof, Prince Georges Cmty Col, 89-. **HONORS AND AWARDS** Fulbright Grant. **CONTACT ADDRESS** Dept Dev Studies, Prince George's Comm Col, 301 Largo Rd, Upper Marlboro, MD 20774-2109. **EMAIL** linkjr@pg.cc.md.us

LINN, MICHAEL D.
PERSONAL Born 03/07/1936, Aberdeen, SD, m, 1962, 1 child **DISCIPLINE** LINGUISTICS, AMERICAN ENGLISH **EDUCATION** Univ Mont, BA, 60, MA, 62; Univ Minn, MA, 70, PhD(commun), 74. **CAREER** Instr English, Lamara State Col of Tech, 63-65; res asst ling, Univ Minn, 68-71 and Cent Midwest Regional Educ Lab, 71-72; from instr to asst prof English, Va Commonwealth Univ, 72-77; asst prof, 77-80, Assoc Prof English and Anthrop, Univ Minn, Duluth, 80-, Consult, Cent Midwest Regional Educ Lab, 72-73, Richmond Pub Sch, 74-75 and Va State Dept of Educ, 74-75; tape collector, US Dialect Tape Depository, 75-78; reader and consult, Choice, 75-; lectr, Arrowhead Speaker Serv, 78-81; manuscript reader, Halcyon, 78-; res fel, Mass Inst of Technol, 78; manuscript referee, J Teacher Educ, 79-81. **MEMBERSHIPS** NCTE; Am Dialect Soc; MLA; Ling Soc Am; Asn Appl Ling. **RESEARCH** American dialects; language variation; the teaching of writing. **SELECTED PUBLICATIONS** Auth, Papers From the Special Session in Honor of Professor Sibata, Takesi--Introduction, Amer Speech, Vol 0071, 96. **CONTACT ADDRESS** English Dept, Univ of Minnesota, Duluth, 10 University Dr, Duluth, MN 55812-2496.

LINN, WILLIAM JOSEPH
PERSONAL Born 10/10/1943, Pittsburgh, PA, m, 2 children **DISCIPLINE** ENGLISH LITERATURE **EDUCATION** Long Island Univ, BA, 65; Hunter Col, MA, 67; NYork Univ, PhD, 70. **CAREER** Lectr Eng, Hunter Col, 70-74; asst prof, Brooklyn Col, City Univ NY, 74-77; coordr, Learning Ctr, Passaic County Community Col, 77-78; Asst Prof Eng & Dir Core Writing Prog, Univ MI, Dearborn, 79-81; assoc prof eng, Univ of MI-Dearborn, 81. **HONORS AND AWARDS** Fulbright lectr, Am lit, Univ of Yaounde (Cameroon), 85; Fulbright lectr, Am lit, Univ of Veliko-Turnovo (Bulgaria), 88-90; Fulbright lectr, Am lit, Univ of Ouagadougou (Burkina Fusa), 95-96; Creative Artists Public Service, Grant in Fiction, 79; Michigan Council for the Arts, Grant in Fiction, 84. **MEMBERSHIPS** AAUP **RESEARCH** Anglo-Irish lit; Psych of learning. **SELECTED PUBLICATIONS** Auth, The pendulum of power: dynamics within the classroom & Remediation and the remedial process, In: Yearbook (1975) of Improving College and University Teaching; Contrastive approaches: An experiment in pedagogical technique, Col Engl, 10/76; The war veteran's reaction to Conrad's The Tale, Teaching Engl in the 2-year college, fall 77; Creativity and remediation: The nexus of change, Col Engl, 12/77; Psychological variants of success, Col Engl, 4/78; The use of personality and taste in teaching writing, Teaching English in the 2-year college, winter 78; Numbers and Angela II, Col Engl, 1/81; Zen and the art of composing, Teaching Engl in the 2-year college, fall 81; Shamrocks and semicolons, AZ Engl Bull, winter 85; various entries in Dictionary of Irish Literature (orig and rev ed), Greenwood Press, 79 & 96; Missing in Action (novel), Avon Books (USA) and Sphere Books (Gr Brit), 81 & 83; Kambe Hai (novel), Sphere Books (Gr Brit), 87. **CONTACT ADDRESS** Eng Dept, Univ of Michigan, Dearborn, 4901 Evergreen Rd, Dearborn, MI 48128-1491. **EMAIL** wjlinn@ca-fl.umd.umich.edu

LINTON, CALVIN DARLINGTON
PERSONAL Born 06/11/1914, Kensington, MD, m **DISCIPLINE** ENGLISH LITERATURE **EDUCATION** George Washington Univ, AB, 35; Johns Hopkins Univ, AM, 39, PhD, 40. **CAREER** From jr instr to instr English, Johns Hopkins Univ, 39-40; prof & head dept, Queens Col, NC, 40-41; from asst dean to assoc dean, 45-57, Prof English, George Washington Univ, 47-84, prof emer, 84-; Dean, Columbian Col Arts & Sci, 57-84, dean emer, 84-; Consult report writing, Nat Security Agency, US Air Force, US Civil Serv Comn & US Army Chem Corps; comnr, Comn Insts of Higher Educ, Mid States Asn Cols & Sec Schs, 62-71, vchm, 67-71; lectr, Folger Inst Renaissance & 18th Century Studies. **HONORS AND AWARDS** DHumLett, Erskine Col, 95. **MEMBERSHIPS** MLA; Mod Humanities Res Asn, Gt Brit (Am secy, 63-); Eastern Asn Deans; Am Conf Acad Deans. **RESEARCH** Milton; government writing; T S Eliot. **SELECTED PUBLICATIONS** Auth, How to Write Reports: Effective Revenue Writing, US Govt Printing Off, 61; The Bible As Literature, In: The Expositor's Commentary, Zondervan, 74; The Bicentennial Almanac, 75 & The American Almanac, 77, Thomas Nelson; Humor in the Bible, In: The International Standard Bible Encycl, Eerdmans, 82. **CONTACT ADDRESS** 5216 Farrington Rd Westmoreland Hills, Bethesda, MD 20816.

LINTON, PATRICIA
DISCIPLINE CONTEMPORARY LITERATURE **EDUCATION** Indiana Univ Pa, PhD. **CAREER** Univ Alaska. **SELECTED PUBLICATIONS** Auth, " Modern Fiction Studies", Melus; Sail. **CONTACT ADDRESS** Univ of Alaska, Anchorage, 3211 Providence Dr., Anchorage, AK 99508.

LIONARONS, JOYCE T.
PERSONAL Born 11/19/1952, Chicago Heights, IL **DISCIPLINE** ENGLISH **EDUCATION** Univ Colo, BA, 74; Univ Denver, MA, 78; PhD, 83. **CAREER** Vis asst prof, Ill Col, 83-84; asst prof to prof, Ursinus Col, 94-. **HONORS AND AWARDS** Summer Grant, Ursinus Col, 96, 89; NEH Sem, 97; Pearlstine Grant, Ursinus Col, 98; Laughlin Prof Achievement

Awd. **MEMBERSHIPS** MLA, Int Soc of Anglo-Saxonists, Medieval Acad, SE Medieval Assoc, Del Valley Medieval Assoc. **RESEARCH** Old English and Old Norse Literature, particularly the works of Wulfstan of York. **SELECTED PUBLICATIONS** Auth, "Magic, Machines, and Deception: Technology in the Canterbury Tales," Chaucer Rev, (93); auth, "Bodies, Buildings, and Boundaries: Metaphors of Liminality in Old English and Old Norse Literature," Essays in Medieval Studies, (94); auth, "Beowulf: Myth and Monsters," English Studies, (96); auth, The Medieval Dragon: The Nature of the Beast in Germanic Literature, Hisarlik Pr, 98; auth, "Cultural Syncretism and the Construction of Gender in Cynewulf's Elene," Exemplaria, (98); auth, "The Otherworld and Its Inhabitants in Das Nibelungenlied," A Companion to the Nibelungenlied, ed Winder McConnell, (Camden House, 98). **CONTACT ADDRESS** Dept English, Ursinus Col, Collegeville, PA 19426-1000. **EMAIL** jlionarons@urinus.edu

LIPKING, LAWRENCE
PERSONAL Born 04/28/1934, New York City, NY, m, 1965 **DISCIPLINE** ENGLISH **EDUCATION** Cornell Univ, PhD, 62; Western Reserve, BA, 55. **CAREER** Princeton Univ, 60-79; Chester D. Tripp prof Humanities, Northwestern Univ, 79-. **HONORS AND AWARDS** Christian Gauss Awd, William Riley Parker prize, MLA; NEH; Guggenheim; ACLAS, etc; The Gauss Awd was for The Life of the Poet, 82. **MEMBERSHIPS** Am Acad of Arts and Sciences; MLA; ASECS. **RESEARCH** 18th century literature; science and imagination. **SELECTED PUBLICATIONS** Auth, The Ordering of the Arts in Eighteenth-Century England 70; The Life of the Poet: Beginning and Ending Poetic Careers, 81; Abandoned Women and Poetic Tradition, 88; Samuel Johnson: The Life of an Author, 98; ed; Norton Anthology of English Literature; The Genius of the Shore: Lycidas, Adamastor, and the Poetics of Nationalism, 96. **CONTACT ADDRESS** Dept of English, Northwestern Univ, 1801 Hinman, Evanston, IL 60208. **EMAIL** lipking@northwestern.edu

LIPPMAN, EDWARD
PERSONAL Born 05/24/1920, New York, NY, m, 1942, 2 children **DISCIPLINE** HISTORY OF MUSIC **EDUCATION** City Col NYork, BS, 42; NYork Univ, MA, 45; Columbia Univ, PhD(musicol), 52. **CAREER** From instr to assoc prof, 54-69, Prof Music, Columbia Univ, 69-, Guggenheim fel, 58-59; Columbia Univ Coun Res Humanities grants, 60, 63, 65; Am Coun Learned Soc fel, 67-68; lectr, Bryn Mawr Col, 72-73. **HONORS AND AWARDS** Harriet Cohen Int Music Awd, 54. **MEMBERSHIPS** Intenational Musicol Soc; Am Musicol Soc; Am Soc for Aesthetics. **RESEARCH** Philosophy and aesthetics of music; 19th century history of music; ancient Greek conceptions of music. **SELECTED PUBLICATIONS** Auth, Musical Thought in Ancient Greece, 64; auth, A Humanistic Philosophy of Music, 77; auth, Musical Aesthetics: A Historical Reader, 3v., 85; auth, A History of Western Musical Aesthetics, 92; auth, Wagner and Beethoven--Wagner, Richard Reception of Beethoven, Opera Quart, Vol 0009, 93; auth, The Philosophy and Aesthetics of Music, 99. **CONTACT ADDRESS** Dept of Music, Columbia Univ, New York, NY 10027. **EMAIL** eval424@aol.com

LIPS, ROGER C.
DISCIPLINE AMERICAN LITERATURE, WORLD LITERATURE **EDUCATION** Univ Wis, Madison, PhD. **CAREER** Assoc prof, Univ Minn, Duluth. **SELECTED PUBLICATIONS** Auth, Orestes A. Brownson, in American Literary Critics and Scholars,1800-1850, Gale, 87; Francis Fisher Browne, in American Magazine Journalists, 1850-1900. Gale. 89. **CONTACT ADDRESS** Dept of Eng, Univ of Minnesota, Duluth, Duluth, MN 55812-2496.

LIPSCHULTZ, JEREMY HARRIS
DISCIPLINE COMMUNICATIONS **EDUCATION** Southern Ill Univ, PhD, 90. **CAREER** Prof, 89-, grad prog ch, dept Commun, Univ Nebr, Omaha. **HONORS AND AWARDS** Ed bd, J of Broadcasting & Electronic Media; ed bd; J & Mass Communication Educaor; ed bd, J of Radio Studies. **RESEARCH** Broadcast regulation. **SELECTED PUBLICATIONS** Broadcast Indecency: FCC Regulation and the First Amendment, Focal Press, 97; auth, "New Technologies," in Communication and the Law, 4th ed, 01. **CONTACT ADDRESS** Dept of Communication, Univ of Nebraska, Omaha, Omaha, NE 68182. **EMAIL** jeremy@unomaha.edu

LIPSCOMB, DREMA RICHELLE
DISCIPLINE ENGLISH **EDUCATION** Rensselaer Polytech Inst, PhD. **CAREER** Asst prof; taught at Northern MI Univ, SUNY at Albany, Siena College & Rensselaer Polytech Inst. **HONORS AND AWARDS** Univ of Rochester Student Association's Women of the Year Awd; Center for Women in Government Fellow; National Women's Studies Association and Pergamon Press Scholarship Awd; Philip Morris Minority Women's Training Awd; Schesinger Library Grant from the Mary Lizzie Saunders Clapp Fund. **RESEARCH** Literary studies; rhetorical and cult criticism; African Am feminist theory. **SELECTED PUBLICATIONS** Publ on, rhetorical criticism; discourse and soc; race and writing & African Am feminist theory. **CONTACT ADDRESS** Dept of English, Univ of Rochester, 500 Wilson Blvd, RC Box 270451, Rochester, NY 14627-0451. **EMAIL** dbbe@mail.rochester.edu

LISBY, GREGORY C.
DISCIPLINE MASS COMMUNICATION, JOURNALISM **EDUCATION** Auburn Univ, BA; Univ Miss, MA; Univ Tenn, doctorate, 88. **CAREER** Assoc prof, dir, Grad Stud, Ga State Univ; ed bd, Am Jour. **HONORS AND AWARDS** Outstanding Jr Fac Awd, Ga State Univ; Henry W Grady Prize for Res in Jour Hist, 90. **MEMBERSHIPS** Past hd, Law Div, Asn for Educ in Jour & Mass Commun. **RESEARCH** Communication law and legal history. **SELECTED PUBLICATIONS** Auth, Mass Communication Law in Georgia, New Forums Press, 95. **CONTACT ADDRESS** Georgia State Univ, Atlanta, GA 30303. **EMAIL** glisby@gsu.edu

LISTON, WILLIAM T.
PERSONAL Born 10/07/1930, Mt Kisco, NY, d, 1958, 5 children **DISCIPLINE** ENGLISH **EDUCATION** SUNY, Albany, BA, 57; Univ Ill, MA, 60, PhD, 66. **CAREER** Asst prof, Ball State Univ, 65, assoc prof, 70, prof, 80-; Dir, Ball State Univ London Centre, 79-80; exchange prof, Yeungnam Univ, spring 84; exchange prof, Bucknell Univ, 87-88. **MEMBERSHIPS** Shakespeare Asn Am, Int Shakespeare Soc, Am Theatre Critics Asn, Am Assoc Univ Profs. **RESEARCH** Shakespeare in performance. **SELECTED PUBLICATIONS** Auth, Francis Quarles' Divine Fancies: A Critical Edition, New York: Garland (92); auth, "Paraphrasing Shakespeare," Teaching Shakespeare Into the Twenty-First Century, ed Ronald E. Salomone and James E. Davis, Athens: Ohio Univ Press (97); auth, "Shakespeare's Plays in Performance from 1970," Appendix B, The Riverside Shakespeare, 2nd ed, Boston: Houghton Mifflin (97); numerous theatre and book reviews in Shakespeare Bull, Shakespeare Quart, Theatre J, Cahiers Elisabethains, and other pubs. **CONTACT ADDRESS** Dept English, Ball State Univ, Muncie, IN 47306-0460. **EMAIL** 00wliston@bsu.edu

LITTLE, ANNE COLCLOUGH
PERSONAL Born 08/04/1944, Florence, SC, m, 1965, 2 children **DISCIPLINE** ENGLISH **EDUCATION** Univ So Carolina, BA, 65; Auburn Univ, MA, 80; Univ So Carolina, PhD, 89. **CAREER** Asst prof, 89-95, assoc prof, 95- , Auburn Univ, Montgomery. **MEMBERSHIPS** So Atlantic MLA; F. Scott Fitzgerald Soc; Asn of Col English Tchrs of Ala. **RESEARCH** Twentieth-century American poetry; twentieth-century American fiction; women's literature. **SELECTED PUBLICATIONS** Auth, The Crystal Lens of Time: Andrew Hudgins' The Glass Hammer, Chattahoochee Rev, 95; auth, The Manuscripts of James Gould Cozzens' By Love Possessed, Resources for Am Lit Stud, 95; co-ed, The Muses Female Are; Martha Moulsworth and Other Women Writers of the English Renaissance, Locust Hill, 95; auth, Alice Perrin, in Naufftus, ed, British Short Fiction Writers, 1880-1914: The Romantic Tradition, Dict of Lit Biog, v. 156, Gale, 96; coauth, Short Fiction: A Critical Companion, Locust Hill, 97; auth, Old Impulses, New Expressions: Duality and Unity in the Poetry of Denise Levertov, Renascence, 97; co-ed, Denise Levertov: New Perspectives, Locust Hill, 00. **CONTACT ADDRESS** Dept of English and Philosophy, Auburn Univ, Montgomery, Montgomery, AL 36124-4023. **EMAIL** alittle@mickey.aum.edu

LITTLE, GRETA D.
PERSONAL Born 12/03/1943, Asheville, NC **DISCIPLINE** ENGLISH, LINGUISTICS **EDUCATION** Carleton Col, BA, 65; Univ NC, MA, 69, PhD(ling), 74. **CAREER** Peace Corps teacher English, Haile Selassie 1st Sch, Ethiopia, 65-67; teaching asst Swahili, Univ NC and Duke Univ, 72; inst ling, Univ NC, 72-73; Fulbright lectr English, Cyril and Methodius Univ, Skopje, 73-74; dir English for Foreign Students, 77-79, Asst Prof English and Ling, Univ SC, 74-, Assoc Ed, Southeastern Conf Ling Rev, 77-. **MEMBERSHIPS** Ling Soc Am; Ling Asn Can and US; Southeastern Conf Ling; Southern Asn Africanists; Teachers English to Speakers Other Lang. **RESEARCH** Syntactic change; African languages. **SELECTED PUBLICATIONS** **CONTACT ADDRESS** English Dept, Univ of So Carolina, Columbia, Columbia, SC 29208.

LITTLE, JONATHAN D.
PERSONAL Born 09/12/1959, Boston, MA, m, 1988, 2 children **DISCIPLINE** ENGLISH, LITERATURE **EDUCATION** Univ Va, BA, 81; Hunter Col, MA, 84; Univ Wis Madison, PhD, 88. **CAREER** Assoc prof to prof to dept chmn, Alverno Col, 94-. **HONORS AND AWARDS** Norman Knox Award. **MEMBERSHIPS** MLA; MELUS. **RESEARCH** Ethnic literature; religion and literature. **SELECTED PUBLICATIONS** Auth, Charles Johnson's Spiritual Imagination, 97; auth, "Beading the Multicultural World: Louise Erdrich's The Antelope Wife and the Sacred Metaphysic," Contemp Lit (00); auth The Dolphin Life, 01. **CONTACT ADDRESS** English Dept, Alverno Col, 3401 S 39th St, Milwaukee, WI 53215-4020. **EMAIL** jonathan.little@alverno.edu

LITTLEFIELD, DANIEL F.
PERSONAL Born 05/23/1939, Salina, OK **DISCIPLINE** NATIVE AMERICAN LITERATURE & HISTORY **EDUCATION** Oklahoma State Univ, PhD. **CAREER** Lit and Am Native Press Arch Dir, Univ of Ark at Little Rock. **HONORS AND AWARDS** Phi Beta Kappa; Oklahoma Hist Hall of Fame. **SELECTED PUBLICATIONS** auth, Africans and Seminoles; auth, Africans and Creeks; auth, The Cherokee Freedmen; auth, The Chicksaw Freedmen; auth, Alex Posey: Creek Poet, Journalist, and Humorist; auth, Seminole Burning; co-auth, A Bibliography of Native American Writers; co-auth, A Bibliography of Native Writers: A Supplement; co-auth, American Indian and Alaska Native Newspapers and Periodicals, 1826-1924; co-auth, American Indian and Alaska Native Newspapers and Periodicals, 1925-70; co-auth, American Indian and Alaska Native Newspapers and Periodicals, 1971-1985; ed, The Life of Okah Tubbee; co-ed, The Fus Fixico Letters; co-ed, Kemaha: The Omaha Stories of Francis LaFlesche; co-ed, Tales of the Bark Lodges; co-ed, Native American Writing in the Southeast: An Anthology. **CONTACT ADDRESS** Univ of Arkansas, Little Rock, 2801 S University Ave., Little Rock, AR 72204-1099. **EMAIL** dflittlefiel@ualr.edu

LITTLEFIELD, DAVID J.
PERSONAL Born 08/22/1928, Tupper Lake, NY, m, 1953, 4 children **DISCIPLINE** ENGLISH **EDUCATION** Spring Hill Col, AB, 51; Yale Univ, MA, 53, PhD, 61. **CAREER** Instr Eng, 53-56 & 59-61, from asst prof to prof, 61-71, dir freshman Eng, 64-65 & 66-68, chmn, Div Hum, 67-70, chmn, Dept Eng & Drama, 71-74, Stewart Prof Eng, Middlebury Col, 71-95, Vis fel classics, Princeton Univ, 65-66; educ consult, Kinney Nat Serv, Inc, 68-; chmn, Vt Coun on Hum & Pub Issues, 72-76; consult-panelist, Media Prog, Div Pub Progs, Nat Endowment for Hum, 75-; summer fel, Stanford Univ, 75; vis prof, Antioch Sch Law, summer, 76 & fall, 78. **MEMBERSHIPS** MLA; Am Philol Asn. **RESEARCH** Aristophanes; Ovid; Eng neoclassical lit; law and lit. **SELECTED PUBLICATIONS** Auth, Pomona and Vertumnus: A fruition of hist in Ovid's Metamorphoses, Arion, 65; ed, Twentieth Century Interpretations of the Frogs, Prentice-Hall, 68; auth, Metaphor and myth: The unity of Aristophanes' Knights, Studies Philol, 68. **CONTACT ADDRESS** 346 Sperry Rd, Cornwall, VT 05753-9447. **EMAIL** djl@shoreham.net

LITTMAN, ROBERT J.
PERSONAL Born 08/23/1943, Newark, NJ, m, 1966, 3 children **DISCIPLINE** ANCIENT HISTORY, CLASSICS **EDUCATION** Columbia Univ, BA, 64, PhD(class philol), 70; Oxford Univ, BLitt, 68. **CAREER** Instr hist, Rutgers Univ, 67-68; instr classics, Brandeis Univ, 68-70; asst prof, 70-75, assoc prof, 75-79, Prof Classics, Univ Hawaii, Manoa, 79-, Herodotus fel and vis mem, Inst Advan Study, Princeton, 77. **MEMBERSHIPS** Am Philol Asn; Am Hist Asn; Soc Prom Hellenic Studies, Friends Ancient Hist. **RESEARCH** Greek history; historiography; Greek literature. **SELECTED PUBLICATIONS** Auth, Epidemiology of the Plague of Athens, Transactions of the American Philol Asn, Vol 0122, 92; Athens, Persia and the Book of Ezra, Transactions of the Amer Philol Asn, Vol 0125, 95; Kinship and Politics in Athens, 90; Jewish History in 100 Nutshells, 96. **CONTACT ADDRESS** Dept of Europ Lang and Lit, Univ of Hawaii, Manoa, 1890 E. West Rd., Honolulu, HI 96822-2362. **EMAIL** littman@hawaii.edu

LITZ, ARTHUR WALTON
PERSONAL Born 10/31/1929, Nashville, TN **DISCIPLINE** ENGLISH **EDUCATION** Princeton Univ, BA, 51; Oxford Univ, DPhil, 54. **CAREER** Assoc prof, 56-67, chmn dept 75-81, Prof English, Princeton Univ, 67-, Am Coun Learned Soc fel, 60-61; Nat Endowment for Humanities sr fel, 74-75; ed, the James Joyce Archive, 78-80. **HONORS AND AWARDS** Danforth Gifted Teaching Awd, 72. **MEMBERSHIPS** MLA; English Inst. **RESEARCH** James Joyce; 19th century novel; modern poetry and fiction. **SELECTED PUBLICATIONS** Auth, The Art of James Joyce, 61, Modern American Fiction: Essays in Criticism, 63, Jane Austen, 65 & The Poetic Development of Wallace Stevens, 72, Oxford Univ; ed, Modern Literary Criticism, 1900-1970, Atheneum, 72; Eliot in His Time, Princeton Univ, 73; Major American Short Stories, Oxford Univ, 75 & 80; Scribner Quarto of Modern English and American Literature, Scribner's, 78. **CONTACT ADDRESS** Dept of English, Princeton Univ, Princeton, NJ 08544.

LIU, ALAN
DISCIPLINE ENGLISH LITERATURE **EDUCATION** Stanford Univ, PhD, 80. **CAREER** Prof, Eng, Univ Calif, Santa Barbara. **RESEARCH** Cultural criticism and postmodernism. **SELECTED PUBLICATIONS** Auth, "The Voice of the Shuttle: Web Page for Humanities Research," Wordsworth: The Sense of History, Stanford Univ Press, 89; "The Power of Formalism: The New Historicism," ELH, 89; "Wordsworth and Subversion, 1793-1804: Trying Cultural Criticism," The Yale Jour of Criticism, 89; "Local Trancendence: Cultural Criticism, Postmodernism, and the Romanticism of Detail," Representations; 89. **CONTACT ADDRESS** Dept of Eng, Univ of California, Santa Barbara, Santa Barbara, CA 93106-7150. **EMAIL** ayliu@humanitas.ucsb.edu

LIU, CATHERINE
DISCIPLINE EARLY MODERN FRENCH NOVEL; LITERARY THEORY; PSYCHOANALYSIS; COMPARATIVE LITERATURE **EDUCATION** CUNY, PhD. **CAREER** Instr, Univ Minn, Twin Cities. **HONORS AND AWARDS** McKnight Land-grant prof. **MEMBERSHIPS** MLA; AAUW. **RESEARCH** The fiction of Lafayette; historiography; psychoanalytic theory; modernism and modernity. **SELECTED**

PUBLICATIONS Published in the fields of psychoanalytic theory and art criticism. **CONTACT ADDRESS** Dept of Cult Studies and Comp Lit, Univ of Minnesota, Twin Cities, 9 Pleasant St. SE, 350 Folwell Hall, Minneapolis, MN 55455. **EMAIL** liuxx@tc.umn.edu

LIU, T.
PERSONAL Born 10/02/1965, San Jose, CA, s **DISCIPLINE** ENGLISH **EDUCATION** Brigham Young Univ, BA, 89; Univ Houston, MA, 91. **CAREER** Asst Prof, Cornell Univ, 94-98; Asst Prof, William Paterson Univ, 98-. **HONORS AND AWARDS** Norma Farber First Book Awd, Poetry Soc of Am, 92; Holloway Lect, Univ Calif, 97. **RESEARCH** Associated writing programs, pen American Center poetry. **SELECTED PUBLICATIONS** Auth, Vox Angelica, Slite James Books, 92; auth, Burnt Offerings, Copper Canyon Pr, 95; auth, Say Goodnight, Copper Canyon Pr, 98; auth, Word of Mouth: An Anthropology of Gay American Poetry, Talisman House Pr, 00. **CONTACT ADDRESS** Dept English, William Paterson Univ of New Jersey, 300 Pompton Rd, Wayne, NJ 07470-2103. **EMAIL** liut@wpunj.edu

LIU, YAMENG
DISCIPLINE CONTEMPORARY RHETORICAL STUDIES **EDUCATION** Univ Southern Calif, PhD. **CAREER** Lit, Carnegie Mellon Univ. **SELECTED PUBLICATIONS** Areas: Aristotle and John Donne. **CONTACT ADDRESS** Carnegie Mellon Univ, 5000 Forbes Ave, Pittsburgh, PA 15213.

LIU, YU
PERSONAL Born, China **DISCIPLINE** ENGLISH **EDUCATION** Loyang For Lang Inst, BA, 78; Lancaster Univ, MA, 80; Edinburgh Univ, MSc, 81; SUNY Buffalo, PhD, 94. **CAREER** Asst lectr, Loyang For Lang Inst, 81-85; instr, asst prof, Niagara Cnty Comm Col, 94-. **HONORS AND AWARDS** NEH, 97, 00; NYS Hum Coun Sem Fel, 98; Huntington Lib Fel, 01. **MEMBERSHIPS** MLA; ASA. **RESEARCH** English romantic poetry; the aesthetics, ethics and politics of Kant; European enlightenment philosophy and history; metaphysics of Confucianism. **SELECTED PUBLICATIONS** Auth, Poetics and Politics: The Revolutions of Wordsworth, Peter Lang (New York), 99; auth, "The Politics of Compassion: 'The Discharged Soldier and the Old Cumberland Begga,'" Eng Lang Notes (00); auth, "The Ambiguity of Sound and Silence: The Prelude," Ess in Lit (94); auth, "Crisis and Recovery: The Wordsworthian Poetics and Politics," Pap on Lang and Lit (00); auth, "Revaluating Revolution and Radicalness in the Lyrical Ballads," Stud Eng Lit (96). **CONTACT ADDRESS** Eng Dept., Niagara Cnty Comm Col, 3111 Saunders Settlement Rd, Sanborn, NY 14132. **EMAIL** yuliu@hotmail.com

LIUZZA, ROY
DISCIPLINE ANGLO-SAXON LITERATURE, MEDIEVAL LITERATURE **EDUCATION** Northeast La Univ, BA, 78; Yale University, MA, 79, PhD, 88. **CAREER** Instr, 90, Tulane Univ. **SELECTED PUBLICATIONS** Auth, The Old English Version of the Gospels Early English Text Society, EETS O.S. 304, Oxford, 94; Representation and Readership in the Middle English Havelok, JEGP 93, 94; The Return of the Repressed: New and Old Theories in Old English Literary Criticism, Old English Shorter Poems: Basic Readings on Anglo-Saxon Lit 3, Garland Press, 94; On the Dating of Beowulf, Beowulf: Basic Readings on Anglo-Saxon Lit 1, Garland Press, 95; Orthography and Historical Linguistics, Jour Eng Ling 24, 96; co-ed, Anglo-Saxon Manuscripts in Microfiche, Facsimile vol 6: Gospels, MRTS, 95. **CONTACT ADDRESS** Dept of Eng, Tulane Univ, 6823 St Charles Ave, New Orleans, LA 70118. **EMAIL** rliuzza@mailhost.tcs.tulane.edu

LIVATINO, MELVIN W.
PERSONAL Born 06/27/1940, Chicago, IL, d, 1966, 3 children **DISCIPLINE** ENGLISH **EDUCATION** Univ Ill, BA, 66; Loyola Univ Chicago, MA, 68. **CAREER** Inst, 68-71, asst prof, 71-76, Wright Col, City Col Chicago; asst prof, 76-86, assoc prof, 86-91, PROF ENG, 91-, TRUMAN COL, CITY COL CHICAGO. **HONORS AND AWARDS** Phi Theta Kappa, 62; Ford Foundation Fel, 86-87; Kellogg Fel, 91; Truman Col Distinguished Prof Awd, 99 ; ed, discourse, city cols chicago fac magazine, 90-94. **MEMBERSHIPS** ALSC; C.G. Jung Inst Chicago, Jos Campbell Soc. **RESEARCH** Teaching creative writing; creative nonfiction; John Cheever, Raymond Carver; 20th cent Am lit; film studies. **SELECTED PUBLICATIONS** Ed, pub, classroom anthology student writing, 88-; ed, pub, chapbook series students' work, 98-; ed, pub These Foreign Shores, Eng Sec Lang mag, 97, columnist, Keen-ager, 71-95. **CONTACT ADDRESS** English Dept, City Cols of Chicago, Harry S. Truman Col, 1145 Wilson Ave, Chicago, IL 60640. **EMAIL** mlivatino@ccc.edu

LIVINGSTON, JAMES L.
PERSONAL Born 10/21/1940, Detroit, MI, m, 1962, 4 children **DISCIPLINE** RENAISSANCE LITERATURE **EDUCATION** Univ Detroit, AB, 62; Univ NC, Chapel Hill, MA, 65; Univ Buffalo, PhD, 70. **CAREER** Instr, Detroit Country Day Sch, 65-66; instr, Clemson Univ, 66-67; inst, Fredonia State Col, 67-68; asst prof, 69-73, assoc prof, 73-82, prof English, 82-, Northern Mich Univ. **HONORS AND AWARDS** Woodrow Wilson Fel, 62; NEH grants, 85, 88, 91, 94. **MEMBERSHIPS** Renaissance Soc Am; Milton Soc. **RESEARCH** Mythology; Shakespeare; Ben Jonson; poetry and music. **SELECTED PUBLICATIONS** Auth, Walt Whitman's Epistle to the Americans, Am Lit, 1/69; art, With Whitman Around the Campfire, Walt Whitman Rev, 6/70; Auth, Names in Twain's Mysterious Stranger, Notes & Queries, 6/71. **CONTACT ADDRESS** Dept of English, No Michigan Univ, 1401 Presque Isle Ave, Marquette, MI 49855-5301. **EMAIL** jlivings@nmu.edu

LJUNGQUIST, KENT PAUL
PERSONAL Born 06/22/1948, Worcester, MA **DISCIPLINE** AMERICAN LITERATURE **EDUCATION** Clark Univ, BA, 70; Univ Conn, MA, 72; Duke Univ, PhD(English), 75. **CAREER** Asst prof English, Bluefield Col, 75-77; asst prof, 77-81, assoc prof to prof English, Worcester Polytech Inst, 81-, co-ed, Passing of fairyland, Poe Studies Asn Newslett, 78-84, 91-97. **MEMBERSHIPS** Poe Studies Asn; Hawthorne Soc; Soc Study Southern Lit. **RESEARCH** Poe; Melville; literary attitudes toward landscape; New England writers. **SELECTED PUBLICATIONS** Auth, Poe's Raven and Bryant's Mythology, Am Transcendental Quart, winter 76; coauth, Monsieur Dupin: Further Details on the Reality Beyond the Legend, Southern Lit J, fall 76; auth, The Influence of Adonais on Eleonora, Poe Studies, 6/77; Poe's The Island of the Fay: The Passing of Fairyland, Studies Short Fiction, summer 77; Burke's Enquiry and The Pit and the Pendulum, Poe Studies, 6/78; How to write a Poe thriller, Southern Literary J, spring 80; Jack Burden's Kingdom by the Sea, Notes on Comtemp Lit, 1/80; Uses of the Daeman in Selected Works by Poe, Interpretations, 80; The Grand and the Fair: Poe's Landscape Aesthetics and Pictorial Techniques, 84; co-ed, J. F. Cooper's The Deerslayer, 87; auth, The Identity of Outis: A Further Chapter in the Poe-Longfellow War, Am Lit, 88; ed, Facts on File Bibliography of America Fiction to 1865, 94; auth, Surveys of Poe Criticism, American Literary Scholarship 1983-86, 95; The Little War and Longfellow's Dilemna: New Documents in the Plagiarism Controversy of 1845, Resources for Am Lit Study, 97. **CONTACT ADDRESS** Dept of Humanities, Worcester Polytech Inst, 100 Institute Rd, Worcester, MA 01609-2247. **EMAIL** kpl@wpi.edu

LLOYD, DAVID T.
PERSONAL Born 02/25/1954, Utica, NY, m, 1990 **DISCIPLINE** ENGLISH LITERATURE **EDUCATION** St Lawrence Univ, BA, 75; Univ Vermont, MA, 78; Brown Univ, MA, 85; PhD, 85. **CAREER** Adjunct instr, Univ Vermont, 78-81; adjunct instr, Brown Univ, summers 84, 85; asst prof, 85-91, assoc prof, 91-95, prof, Le Moyne Col, 95-, Rev Francis J. Fallon,, SJ, Prof, 98-2001, Dir, The S.I. Newhouse Writing Center, 85-91, chair, Dept of English, 92-96, Dir, Creative Writing Prog, 97-98. **HONORS AND AWARDS** Tupper Awd, Univ Vermont, 79; NEH Summer Sem, 81, 89, 93; Scholar of the Year, Le Moyne Univ, 95; Rev. Francis J. Fallon Endowed Prof, 98-2001; Individual Artist Grant, Awd, Cultural Resources Coun Community Arts Grant Prog; First prize for two poems, Tallgrass Anthology/Contest; Robert H. Winner Memorial Awd, Poetry Soc of Am, co-winner. **MEMBERSHIPS** North Am Asn for the Study of Welsh Culture and Hist, The Assoc Writing Progs, Celtic Studies Asn of North Am, The Am Conf for Irish Studies, The Modern Lang Asn. **SELECTED PUBLICATIONS** Auth, "The Public and Private Realms of Geoffrey Hill's Mercian Hymns," in Self, World, Poem: Essays on Contemporary Poetry, ed Leonard Trawick, Kent, Ohio: Kent State Univ Press (90); auth, "Poetry in Post War Britain: The Two Generations," in Contiguous Traditions in Post-War British poetry., ed C. C. Barfoot, Dutch Quart Rev Studies in Lit (94); ed, The Urgency of Identity: Contemporary English-Language Poetry from Wales, Evanston, Il: TriQuarterly Books/Northwestern Univ Press (94); auth, "Fusions in Seamus Heaney's North," in Seamus Heaney: The Shaping Spirit, ed Catherine Malloy and Phyllis Carey, Newark: The Univ of Del Press (96); auth, Writing on the Edge: Interviews with Writers and Editors of Wales, Amsterdam and Atlanta: Costerus Series, Rodopi (97); auth, "Back to the Future: the Latest Anthology of Anglo-Welsh Literature," commissioned review article on Twentieth Century Anglo-Welsh Poetry, ed by Dannie Abse, Planet 127 (Feb/March 98): 76-71; contribur to "Books 98: Planet's Contributors Make Their Selection," Planet, No 132 (Dec/Jan 99): 78; auth, "Articulate to the End: R. S. Thomas and the Crisis of Language," (Ariel (forthcoming). **CONTACT ADDRESS** Dept English, Le Moyne Col, 1419 Salt Springs Rd, Syracuse, NY 13214-1302. **EMAIL** lloyd@maple.lemoyne.edu

LOACH, DONALD
DISCIPLINE MUSIC **EDUCATION** Yale Univ, MM; Univ Ca, PhD. **CAREER** Dept Music, Va Univ **RESEARCH** Choral conducting; counterpoint; medieval and renaissance music. **SELECTED PUBLICATIONS** Auth, A Stylistic Approach to Species Counterpoint, Journal Music Theory; Basic Counterpoint (rev), Jour Music Theory; The Study of Fugue (rev), Jour Music Theory. **CONTACT ADDRESS** Dept of Music, Univ of Virginia, Charlottesville, VA 22903. **EMAIL** dgl@virginia.edu

LOBB, EDWARD
DISCIPLINE ENGLISH LITERATURE **EDUCATION** Princeton Univ, PhD. **CAREER** Dept Eng, Queen's Univ **HONORS AND AWARDS** ASUS Tchg Awd. **RESEARCH** Modern literature; T.S. Eliot; modern art and photography. **SELECTED PUBLICATIONS** Auth, T.S. Eliot and the Romantic Critical Tradition; pubs on modern fiction and poetry, ed, Words in Time; New Essays on Eliot's Four Quartets. **CONTACT ADDRESS** English Dept, Queen's Univ at Kingston, Kingston, ON, Canada K7L 3N6. **EMAIL** rel@qsilver.queensu.ca

LOCHHEAD, DOUGLAS GRANT
PERSONAL Born 03/25/1922, Guelph, ON, Canada, w, 1949, 2 children **DISCIPLINE** ENGLISH **EDUCATION** McGill Univ, BA, 43; BLS, 51; Univ Toronto, MA, 47. **CAREER** Librn and lectr sociol, Univ Victoria, BC, 51-52; librn cataloguer, Cornell Univ, 52-53; chief librn and prof, Dalhousie Univ, 53-60; chief librn and prof English, York Univ, Ont, 60-63; Librn, Massey Col, Univ Toronto, 63-75, prof English, bibliog and palaeography, Univ Col, 65-75; Davidson Prof Can Studies, Mt Allison Univ, 75-, Dir Ctr for Can Studies, 77-, Sr fel, Massey Col, Univ Toronto, 64-75, emer fel, 75-, spec lectr fac libr sci, 65-75; Can Coun Res grants, 67, 68, 78 and 79; mem bd, Inst of Can Hist Reproductions, Ottawa, 78-. **HONORS AND AWARDS** Canada Council Res Grant, 67; Royal Soc of Canada, Fel, 76; Queen's Silver Medal, 77; Massey Col, Univ of Toronto, Sr Fel, 65-; Massey Col, Fel Emer, 81-; Canada Council Short-Term Writers Grant, 78, 79, 80; Awd of Merit, 87; Merit Awd, 90. **MEMBERSHIPS** Asn Can Univ Teachers English; fel Royal Soc Can; Bibliog Soc Can; Bibliog Soc Am; League Can Poets. **RESEARCH** Canadian printing history; 19th century Canadian literature. **SELECTED PUBLICATIONS** Auth, 'Silvester Tiffany' in Dictionary of Canadian Biography, Toronto, Univ of Toronto Press, (80): 814-816; auth, "A New Athens Rising Near the Pole': Evidences of a culture in 1th Century Quebec Inprints," Bulletin of Canadian Studies, 1, (84): 72-82; auth, 'Essays in Canadian Bibliography: Bibliographical Studies in Reprint,' in Papers of the Bibliographical Society of Canada, (84): 30-31; auth, Something Still to Find: Unexplored Fields of Canadian Literature, Edinburgh, ed, Douglas Lochhead, Centre of Canadian Studies, Univ of Edinburgh, (84): 14; auth, Windflower: Selected Poems of Bliss Carman, ed, Douglas Lochhead, Ottawa, Tecumseh Press, (85): 251; auth, Powassan's Drum: Selected Poems of Duncan Campbell Scott, ed, Douglas Lochhead, Ottawa, Tecumseh Press, (85): 208; auth, St. Ursula's Convent or The Nun of Canada, by Julia Catherin Beckwith Hart, ed, Douglas Lochhead, Ottawa, Carleton Univ Press, (91): 237; auth, Black Festival, Sackvile, Harrier Editions, (91): 54; auth, Homage to Henry Alline and Other Poems, Fredericton, Goose Lane Editions, (92): 122. **CONTACT ADDRESS** Ctr Can Studies, Mount Allison Univ, Sackville, NB, Canada E0A 3C0.

LOCHMAN, DANIEL
PERSONAL Born 09/19/1953, Springfield, IL, m, 3 children **DISCIPLINE** MEDIEVAL AND EARLY MODERN LITERATURE **EDUCATION** Loyola Univ Chicago, BA, MA; Univ Wis, PhD. **CAREER** Southwest Tex State Univ **RESEARCH** Tudor humanists, espec John Colet and Thomas More, Elizafethans, Milton. **SELECTED PUBLICATIONS** Areas: Milton; John Colet; Thomas More; Desiderius Erasmus. **CONTACT ADDRESS** Southwest Texas State Univ, 601 University Dr, San Marcos, TX 78666-4604. **EMAIL** dl0z@swt.edu

LOCHRIE, KARMA D.
PERSONAL Born 01/01/1955 **DISCIPLINE** ENGLISH LITERATURE **EDUCATION** DePauw Univ, BA, 77; Princeton Univ, MA, 78; PhD, 81. **CAREER** Asst prof, Univ Haw Manoa, 81-88; asst to assoc prof, Loyola Univ Chicago, 88-99; prof, Ind Univ, 99-. **HONORS AND AWARDS** NEH Fel, 90; Res Fel, UC Santa Cruz, 97; Choice Awd for Outstanding Academic Book, 99. **MEMBERSHIPS** MLA, New Chaucer Soc, Medieval Acad of Am, Soc for Medieval Feminist Scholar, Soc for the Study of Homosexuality in the Middle Ages. **RESEARCH** Medieval literature and culture, gender, queer theory. **SELECTED PUBLICATIONS** Auth, "Margery Kempe," Encyl of the Middle Ages, ed Szarmach and tavormina, (88); auth, "The Language of Transgression: Body, Word, and Mystical Discourrse," Speaking Two Languages, ed Frantzen, (91); auth, Margery Kempe and Translations of the Flesh, Univ of Pa Pr, 91; auth, "Gender, Sexual Violence, and the Politics of War in the Old English Judith," Class and Gender in Early English Literature: Intersections, ed Britton J Harwood and Gillian R Overing, (94); auth, "Don't Ask, Don't Tell: Murderous Plots and Medieval Secrets", Premodern Sexualities, ed Frandenburg and Freccero, (96); auth, "Desiring Foucault," Jour of Medieval and Early Mod Studies 27.1 (97): 3-16; coed, Constructing Medieval Sexuality, Univ Min Pr, 97; auth, Covert Operations: The Medieval Uses of Secrecy, Univ Pa Pr, 99; auth, "Presidential Improprieties and Medieval Categories: The Absurdity of Heterosexuality," Queering the Middle Ages, ed Glenn Burger and Steven F Kruger, (01). **CONTACT ADDRESS** Dept English, Indiana Univ, Bloomington, 1020 E Kirkwood Ave, 442 Ballantine Hall, Bloomington, IN 47405. **EMAIL** klochrie@indiana.edu

LOCK, F. P.
DISCIPLINE ENGLISH LITERATURE **EDUCATION** McMaster Univ, PhD. **CAREER** Dept Eng, Queen's Univ **RESEARCH** Restoration and eighteenth century literature; politics; intellectual history; Jonathan Swift; Edmund Burke. **SELECTED PUBLICATIONS** Auth, Susanna Centlivre, The Politics of 'Gulliver's Travels', Reflections on the Revolution in France, (rev); pubs on Swift, Burke, and Austen; co-ed, Collected Poems of Thomas Parnell. **CONTACT ADDRESS** English Dept, Queen's Univ at Kingston, Kingston, ON, Canada K7L 3N6. **EMAIL** lockfp@qsilver.queensu.ca

LOCKE, RALPH PAUL
PERSONAL Born 03/09/1949, Boston, MA, m, 1979, 2 children **DISCIPLINE** MUSICOLOGY, MUSIC, HISTORY, SOCIOLOGY **EDUCATION** Harvard Univ, BA, 70; Univ Chicago, MA, 74, PhD, 80. **CAREER** Prof, Eastman School Music, 75-. **HONORS AND AWARDS** ASCAP Deems Taylor Awd, 92, 96, and 99. **MEMBERSHIPS** Am Musicol Soc; Sonneck Soc Am Music. **RESEARCH** Music and society; Music and gender; Music in France & Italy; Music patronage in the US; Musical exoticism and Orientalism. **SELECTED PUBLICATIONS** Auth Music, Musicians, and the Saint-Simonians, Univ Chicago Press, 86; Paris: Centre of Intellectual Ferment (1789-1852), Man & Music: The Early Romantic Era, Between Revolutions: 1789 and 1848, Prentice-Hall, 91; What Are These Women Doing in Opera? En travesti: Women, Gender Subversion, Opera, Columbia Univ Press, 95; Cultivating Music in America: Women Patrons and Activists since 1860, Univ Cal Press, 97; Constructing the Oriental 'Other': Saint-Saens's Samson et Dalila, The Work of Opera: Genre, Nationhood, and Sexual Difference, Columbia Univ Press, 97; The French Symphony: David, Gounod, and Bizet to Saint-Saens, Franck, and Their Followers, The Nineteenth-Century Symphony, Schirmer Books, 97; Cutthroats and Casbah Dancers, Muezzins and Timeless Sands: Musical Images of the Middle East, The Exotic in Western Music, NE Univ Press, 98; Musicology and/as Social Concern: Imagining the Relevant Musicologist, Oxford Univ Press, 98; Auth, Musical Exoticism and Orientalism: Problems for the Worldly Critic, Edward Said and the Work of the Critic, Duke Univ Press, 00. **CONTACT ADDRESS** Eastman Sch of Music, 26 Gibbs St, Rochester, NY 14604-2599. **EMAIL** RLPH@MAIL.ROCHESTER.EDU

LOCKETTE, AGNES LOUISE
PERSONAL Born 04/21/1927, Albany, GA, m **DISCIPLINE** ENGLISH **EDUCATION** Albany State Coll, Albany, GA, BS, 1948; Univ of Nevada, Las Vegas, MEd, 1967; Univ of Arizona, Tucson, EdD, 1972. **CAREER** Carver HS Dawson, GA, teacher, 48-49; Clark County School Dist, Las Vegas, NV, teacher, 52-70; Univ of Nevada, Las Vegas, prof of educ, 72-84, prof, 71-. **HONORS AND AWARDS** Honors Hazard Training School, Albany State Coll, GA; diploma, Albany State Coll HS Albany State Coll, GA; class valedictorian; first woman appointed to Clark County Air Pollution Hearing Bd, 1972-; Keynote speaker Annual Honor Convocation Univ of NV Las Vegas 1984; Disting Teaching Awd Coll of Educ Univ of NV Las Vegas 1984; Outstanding Service Awd, Westside School Alumni Assn, 1988; Recipient of one of UNLV's First Master's Degrees, Elem Educ, MEd, 1967. **MEMBERSHIPS** Kappa Delta Pi; Delta Kappa Gamma Soc; Natl Concil of Teachers of English; Amer Assn Univ Women; mem, Phi Kappa Phi; Assn of Childhood Educ Intl; Natl Soc of Profs; Natl Educ Assn; Grace Community Church, Boulder City, NV, church council, mem, financial section, 1989-; chairperson, Clark Co Air Pollution Hearing Bd, Las Vegas, NV. **CONTACT ADDRESS** Education, Univ of Nevada, Las Vegas, 4505 Maryland Parkway, Las Vegas, NV 89154.

LOCKFORD, LESA
PERSONAL Born 06/01/1958, Salt Lake City, UT, d **DISCIPLINE** THEATRE **EDUCATION** Univ Calif, BA, 80; Calif State Univ, MA, 93; Southern Ill Univ, PhD, 98. **CAREER** Asst Prof, Centenary Col, 98-00; Asst Prof, Bowling Green State Univ, 00-. **MEMBERSHIPS** Nat Comm Asn, British Equity, Asn of Theatre in Higher Educ. **RESEARCH** Performance theory and methodology; Feminist theory and gender studies; Qualitative methods of inquiry (ethnography, phenomenology, hermeneutics); Performance composition. **SELECTED PUBLICATIONS** Auth, "An Ethnographic Ghost Story; Adapting 'What's a Nice Commodity Like You Doing in a Spectacle Like This?," Text and performance Quarterly, in press; auth, Performing Femininity, AltaMira Pub, in press; co-auth, "Toward a Poetic Phenomenology of Performance," On Stage Studies, (99): 64-77; auth, "reclamation and revaluation: The discursive dominion and Critical Poetics of erotic Teachers," Text and performance Quarterly, (98): 380-400; auth, "Emergent Issues in the Performance of a Border-Transgressive Narrative," in The Future of Performance Studies: Visions & Revisions, 98; auth, "Social Drama in the Spectacle of femininity: The Performance of Weight Loss in the Weight Watchers' Program," Women's Studies in communication, (96): 291-312; co-auth, "Process and Practice: Developing the Performance," HIV Education: Performing Personal Narratives (Proceedings of a Conference Funded by the US Centers for Disease Control and prevention and Arizona State University, Ariz State Univ Press, 93. **CONTACT ADDRESS** Dept Theatre Arts, Bowling Green state Univ, 322 South Hall, Bowling Green, OH 43403.

LOCKHART, PHILIP N.
PERSONAL Born 05/03/1928, Smicksburg, PA, m, 1959, 2 children **DISCIPLINE** CLASSICAL STUDIES **EDUCATION** Univ Pa, BA, 50; Univ NC, MA, 51; Yale Univ, PhD(classical lang), 59. **CAREER** Teacher, Ezel Mission Sch, Ky, 51-52; instr class lang, Univ Mo, 54-56; instr class studies, Univ Pa, 57-61, asst prof, 61-63; assoc prof class lang and chmn dept, 63-68, prof, 68-71, Asbury J Clarke Prof Latin and Chmn Dept, Dickinson Col, 71- , prof emer, 90-; Vis prof, Ohio State Univ, 69-70. **HONORS AND AWARDS** Ganoe Awd Teaching, Dickinson Col, 69, 73, 81; 2000 Outstanding Scholars, Who's Who, 00. **MEMBERSHIPS** Am Philol Asn; Archaeol Inst Am; Am Class League; Vergilian Soc Am. **RESEARCH** Latin poetry; fourth century AD; Homeric background. **SELECTED PUBLICATIONS** Auth, Moser, Mary, E. 1950-1996--in Memoriam, Class World, Vol 0089, 96. **CONTACT ADDRESS** Dept of Class Lang, Dickinson Col, Carlisle, PA 17013. **EMAIL** lockhart@dickinson.edu

LOCKLIN, GERALD IVAN
PERSONAL Born 02/17/1941, Rochester, NY, 7 children **DISCIPLINE** ENGLISH **EDUCATION** St John Fisher Col, BA, 61; Univ Ariz, MA, 63, PhD, 64. **CAREER** Prof English, Calif State Univ, Long Beach, 65-. **HONORS AND AWARDS** Borestone Mt Best Poem Awd, 67. **RESEARCH** Twentieth century literature; poetry. **SELECTED PUBLICATIONS** Auth, Locklin Biblio: A Bibliography on the Work of Gerald Locklin, 1963-1990, Zerx Press, 91; co-ed, A New Geography of Poets, Univ Ark Press, 92; Charles Bukowski: A Sure Bet (essays, memoirs, and poems), Water Row Books, 3/96; Locklin Biblio 2: A Bibliography on the Work of Gerald Locklin, Vol 2, 1990-1997, Zerx Press, 97; The First Time He Saw Paris, In: Two Novellas, Event Horizon Press, 97; auth of over 2000 articles, essays, reviews, books of poetry, poetry in anthologies, and other works including audio, video, and alternative media; auth, Down and Out: A Novel, Event Horizon Press, 98; auth, Go West, Young Tord: Selected Writings, Water Row Press, 98; auth, The Firebird Poems, Event Horizon Press, 99; auth, Hemingway Colloquium: The Poet Goes to Cuba, Event Horizon Press, 99; auth, A Simpler Time A Simpler Place: Three Mid-Century Stories, Event Horizon Press, 00; auth, Candy Bars, Selected Stories, Water Row Press, 00. **CONTACT ADDRESS** Dept of English, California State Univ, Long Beach, 1250 N Bellflower, Long Beach, CA 90840-0001. **EMAIL** glocklin@csulb.edu

LOCKRIDGE, LAURENCE SHOCKLEY
PERSONAL Born 07/01/1942, Bloomington, IN **DISCIPLINE** ENGLISH LITERATURE; AMERICAN LITERATURE **EDUCATION** Ind Univ, AB, 64; Harvard Univ, MA, 68, PhD(English), 69. **CAREER** Asst prof, Rutgers Univ, New Brunswick, 69-76; vis lectr English, Northwestern Univ, 77-78; Assoc Prof to Prof English, NY Univ, 78-. **HONORS AND AWARDS** Phi Beta Kappa, 63; Woodrow Wilson Fel, 64-65; Danforth Fel, 64-69; NEH Summer Stipend, 78; Guggenheim Fel, 84-85; The MidAmerica Awd, 98. **MEMBERSHIPS** NY Inst for the Humanities; The Biog Seminar; PEN Am Ctr; Authors' Guild; The Manuscript Soc; Soc for the Study of Midwestern Lit; Am Asn of Suicidologists; Am Suicide Found. **RESEARCH** Literature and philosophy; biography and autobiography; ethics and literature; British and American Romanticism; history of critical theory. **SELECTED PUBLICATIONS** Auth, Coleridge the Moralist, Cornell Univ, 77; The Ethics of Romanticism, Cambridge Univ Press, 89; Shade of the Raintree: The Life and Death of Ross Lockridge, Jr., Viking, Penguin, 94, Penguin Books, 95; ed, Raintree County, Penguin Books, 94; co-ed, Nineteenth-Century Lives, Cambridge Univ Press, 89. **CONTACT ADDRESS** Dept of English, New York Univ, 19 University Pl, Rm 200, New York, NY 10003-4556. **EMAIL** lawrence.lockridge@nyu.edu

LOCKWOOD, LEWIS HENRY
PERSONAL Born 12/16/1930, New York, NY, m, 1977, 2 children **DISCIPLINE** MUSICOLOGY **EDUCATION** Queens Col, NYork, BA, 52; Princeton Univ, MFA, 55, PhD(music), 60. **CAREER** From instr to prof, Princeton Univ, 58-72; chmn dept, Princeton Univ, 70-73; Robert Schirmer '21 prof music, Princeton Univ, 72-80; prof Music, Harvard Univ, 80-, ed of jour, 63-66, Am Musicol Soc, Am Coun Learned Soc deleg, 66-68, fel, 68-69; consult ed, Grove's Dict of Music & Musicians, 70-; **HONORS AND AWARDS** Einstein Awd, Am Musicol Soc, 70; Nat Endowment for Humanities sr fel, 73-74; Guggenheim Found fel, 77-78; vis, Inst Advan Study, 77-78; Hon Doctorate, Universita Degli Studi, Ferrara, 91; Hon Doctorate, New England Conservatory of Music, 97; ma, harvard univ. **MEMBERSHIPS** Am Musicol Soc (vpres, 70-72, pres, 87-88), Renaissance Soc Am. **RESEARCH** Renaissance music; music of Beethoven; history of opera. **SELECTED PUBLICATIONS** Auth, The autograph of Beethoven's Sonata for Violoncello and Piano, Op 69, Music Forum; The Counter-Reformation and the Masses of Vincenzo Ruffo, Fondazione Giorgio Cini, 70; On Beethoven's sketches and autographs: Some problems of definition and interpretation, Acta Musicol, 70; Music at Ferrara in the period of Ercole I d'Este, Studi Musicali, 72; Josquin at Ferrara: New documents and letters, Proc Int Josquin Festival-Conf, 73; Aspects of the L'homme Arme Tradition, Proc Royal Musical Asn, 73-74; ed, Palestrina: Pope Marcellus Mass, Norton Critical Scores, Norton, 75; auth, Dufay and Ferrara, Papers of the Dufay Quincentenary Conf, 76; Music in Renaissance Ferrara, Oxford, 84; Beethoven; Studies in the Creative Process, Cambridge, Mass, 92. **CONTACT ADDRESS** Dept of Music, Harvard Univ, Music Bldg, Cambridge, MA 02138-3800. **EMAIL** llockw@fas.harvard.edu

LOCKYER, JUDITH ANN
PERSONAL Born 11/03/1949, Georgetown, KY, m, 1999 **DISCIPLINE** LITERATURE **EDUCATION** Univ Ky, BA, 71; MA, 79; Univ Mich, PhD, 84. **CAREER** Prof/chmn, Albion Col, 85-. **HONORS AND AWARDS** NEH Seminar, 91; AAC Resource Consult. **MEMBERSHIPS** MLA; MMLA. **RESEARCH** Southern literature by women; Faulkner book on Ellen Douglas, Roselle Brown, Kaye Gibbons, Vicki Covington. **SELECTED PUBLICATIONS** Auth, Ordered by Words: Languages and Narration in the Novels of William Faulkner, Univ Southern Ill, 91; auth of articles in Ariz Quart, Chiba Rev. **CONTACT ADDRESS** 29196 Albion Rd, Albion, MI 49224-9736. **EMAIL** jlockyer@albion.edu

LOE, THOMAS BENJAMIN
PERSONAL Born 06/14/1943, Perham, MN, m, 1964, 3 children **DISCIPLINE** ENGLISH LITERATURE **EDUCATION** St Olaf Col, BA, 65; Univ Iowa, MA, 71; PhD, 74. **CAREER** From instr to asst prof, 71-77, actg chmn dept, 78-80, 96, assoc prof, 77-89, prof, 89-, English, State Univ NY Col Oswego; vis res schol, Cambridge Univ 87-88. **HONORS AND AWARDS** SUNY Chancellor's Awd for Excel in Tchg. **MEMBERSHIPS** NEMLA. **RESEARCH** 19th and 20th century English novel; narrative theory. **SELECTED PUBLICATIONS** Auth, Modern Allegory and the Form of Seize the Day, Saul Bellow Journal, 7:1, (88): 57-66; auth, Gothic Plot in Great Exectations, Dickens Quarterly 6:3, (89): 102-10; auth, Mythic Descent in Dances with Wolves, Literature/Film Quarterly, 20:3, (92): 199-204; auth, Gothic Plot in Gret Expectations, Dickens Quarterly 6:3, (89): 102-10, rep. in Great Expectations, New York, St. Martin's Press, (94): 203-215; auth, Design and Meaning in The Ebony Tower, Journal of the Short Story in English/Les Cahiers de la Nouvelle, L'Universite Angers 25:4, (95): 32-47; auth, Jamaica Kincaid's Lucy as a Short Story Sequence, Notes on Contempory Lit 26.1, (96): 2-5; auth, Hartwick Classic Film Leadership Cases: The Flight of the Phoenix, Oneonta: Hartwick, 97; auth, Hartwick Classic Film Leadership Cases: The Man Who would Be King, Oneonta: Hartwick, 97; auth, The Strange Modernism of Le Fanu's Green Tea, That Other World: The Supernatural and the Fantastic in Irish Literature and its Contexts, vol. 1, Gerrards Cross, England: Colin Smythe, (98): 293-306. **CONTACT ADDRESS** Dept of English, SUNY, Oswego, 7060 State Route 104, Oswego, NY 13126-3599. **EMAIL** loe@oswego.edu

LOEFFLER, DONALD LEE
PERSONAL Born 05/30/1930, Piqua, OH, s **DISCIPLINE** COMMUNICATIONS; THEATER **EDUCATION** Univ of Dayton, BS, 52; Teachers Col, Columbia Univ, MA, 53; State Univ of Iowa, 60; Bowling Green State Univ, PhD, 69. **CAREER** Teacher, public schools of Durand, Mich, 55-57; U.S. Army, Personnel Sergeant Major (E-5), 53-55; teacher, Gunston Jr High School, 57-58; chief speech therapist, Barney Children's Medical Center, 60-64; asst prof of speech, Mass State Col at Worcester, 64-67; part-time speech therapist, Public Schools of New Reigel, 67-68; teaching fel, supervisor of Speech Instructional Center, visiting instr, Bowling Green State Univ, 68-69; dir of theatre, 69-92, tenured, 74; assoc prof, 69-75, prof, 75-92, head, Dept of Speech and Theatre Arts, Western NC Univ, 70-88. **HONORS AND AWARDS** Alpha Psi Omega; Boss of the Year, NCAEOP, 80-81; Secretary Suzanne M. Davis Memorial Awd for Outstanding Service to Theatres in the Southeast, 88; Exceptional Service Trophy, 88, Herman Middleton Distinguished Career Awd, 92. **MEMBERSHIPS** Am Asn of Univ Prof; Am Speech and Hearing Asn; Nat Asn Schools of Theatre; Asn of Commun Admin; Am Theatre Asn; Am Theatr in Higher Education; Carolina Speech Commun Asn; NC Theatre Conf; Southeastern Theatre Conf; Speech Commun Asn; Univ and Col Theatre Asn. **SELECTED PUBLICATIONS** Auth, Homosexual Character in Drama, Arno Press, 75; auth, Coming Out-1950-1970, Southern Theatre, 74; auth, Theatre Perspectives on the Field of Communication, ACA Bull, 84; auth, Figuring Workload Equivalencies of Performance/Production Assignments for Theatre Faculty, ACA Bull, 84; auth, Strategies for Tenure/Promotion of Technical Theatre Faculty, ACA Bull, 85; auth, Censorship in College and University Theatres: the Administrative Point of View, ACA Bull, 86; auth, The Tenuring of Technical Theatre Faculty: A Call for Assistance, ACA Bull, 86; auth, Departmental Administrations: Chairing, Managing, and Running the Academic Enterprise, ACA Bull, 87; auth, Closing the Gap: How Colleges and Universities Can Help Improve Secondary Theatre Education, ACA Bull, 87. **CONTACT ADDRESS** Dept of Commun and Theatre Arts, Western Carolina Univ, 2705 W. Cluster Ave., Tampa, FL 33014-4387. **EMAIL** dllcfm@gte.net

LOESBERG, JONATHAN
DISCIPLINE BRITISH LITERATURE **EDUCATION** Cornell Univ, PhD, 77; Cornell Univ, MA, 75; Brown Univ, AB, 72. **CAREER** Ch, Amer Univ Dept Lit, 96- dir, Univ Honors

Program, Amer Univ, 92-95; prof, Amer Univ, 91-; deputy chair, Amer Univ Dept Lit, 90-92; dir, MA Program Lit, Amer Univ, 84-86, 91; assoc prof, Amer Univ, 86-91; asst prof, Amer Univ, 82-86; asst prof, Col of Holy Cross, 80-82; vis asst prof, Brandeis Univ, 79-80; asst prof, Cornell Univ, 77-79. **HONORS AND AWARDS** ACLS Fel, 95-96; Amer Univ CAS Awd for Achievement in Scholarship, 91; NEH Summer Inst Co-Dir, 90; AU NEH Colloquium Participant, 88; Amer Univ Summer Grant, 87; Mellon Grant, 85; NEH Summer Stipend, 84; NEH Summer Sem Fel, 82; School of Criticism & Theory Fel, 81; Cornell Summer Fel, 73, 74, 75, 76; Phi Kappa Phi, 76; Cornell Grad Fel, 72-73; Phi Beta Kappa, 71. **MEMBERSHIPS** Northeast Victorian Studies Assod Prog Ch, 96-97, pres, 00-; Duke Univ Pr Reader; Univ Virginia Pr Reader; Univ Ga Pr Reader; Columbia Univ Pr Reader. **RESEARCH** Literary theory, connections between literature and philosophy. **SELECTED PUBLICATIONS** Cultural Studies, Victorian Studies and Formalism, Victorian Literature and Culture, 99; Materialism and Aesthetics: Paul de Man's Aesthetic Ideology, Diacritics, 98; Dickensian Deformed Children and the Hegelian Sublime, Victorian Studies, 97; Aestheticism and Deconstruction: Pater, Derrida and de Man, Princeton Univ Pr, 91. **CONTACT ADDRESS** Dept of Literature, American Univ, 3717 Windon Pl, NW, Washington, DC 20016. **EMAIL** jloesbe@american.edu

LOEWENSTEIN, DAVID
PERSONAL Born 09/20/1955, Boston, MA, m, 1997 **DISCIPLINE** ENGLISH LITERATURE **EDUCATION** Oberlin Col, BA, 77, Univ Va, MA, 79; PhD, 85. **CAREER** Asst prof, Loyola Univ of Chicago, 85-89; asst prof to prof, Univ of Wisc-Madison, 89-. **HONORS AND AWARDS** Guggenheim Fel, 95-96; James Holly Hanford Awd for Distinguished Book, 91; Overseas Fel, Churchill Col, Cambridge, 99; NDH Fel, Newberry Libr, 89-90. **MEMBERSHIPS** MLA; Renaissance Soc of Am; Milton Soc of Am; Int Assoc of Univ Prof of English. **RESEARCH** Renaissance or early modern English literature, Milton, literature and heresy in early modern England. **SELECTED PUBLICATIONS** Auth, Milton and the Drama of History: Historical Vision, Iconoclasm and the Literary Imagination, Cambridge Univ Pr, 90; auth, Milton: Paradise Lost, Cambridge Univ Pr, 93; auth, Representing Revolution in Milton and His Contemporaries: Religion, Politics, and Polemics in Radical Puritanism, Cambridge Univ Pr, 00. **CONTACT ADDRESS** Dept English, Univ of Wisconsin, Madison, 600 N Park St, Madison, WI 53706-1403. **EMAIL** daloewen@facstaff.wisc.edu

LOFTIS, JOHN E.
PERSONAL Born 02/28/1945, Sioux City, IA, m, 1966, 3 children **DISCIPLINE** ENGLISH **EDUCATION** Univ of the South, BA, 66; Emory Univ, MA, 69; PhD, 71. **CAREER** From instr to prof, Univ of Northern Colo, 70-. **HONORS AND AWARDS** NEH Summer Sem, 76 & 85. **MEMBERSHIPS** MLA, RMMLA, ASECS. **RESEARCH** Eighteenth-Century English Literature, The Novel, Law and Literature. **SELECTED PUBLICATIONS** Auth, "Engineering Democracy: Departmental Organization," ADE Bullet 110 (Spring 95): 20-23; auth, "Congreve's Way of the World and Popular Criminal Literature," Studies in English Lit 1500-1900 (Summer 96): 561-578; rev, of "The business of Common Life: Novels and Classical Economics between Revolution and Reform," by David Kaufmann, Rocky Mountain Rev 50 (Fall 96): 78-80; rev, "I'd Rather Be Reading Jane Austen: The Appeal of the Augustans," by Alan Downie, Scriblerian 29 (Autumn 96): 50; rev, "Swift's political Satire," by Ronald Knowles, Scriblerian 30 (Spring 98): 48-51; rev, "The Conversational Circle: Rereading the English Novel, 1740-1775," by Betty Schellenberg, Rocky Mountain Rev 52 (Spring 98): 81-82. **CONTACT ADDRESS** Dept English, Univ of No Colorado, 501 20th St, Greeley, CO 80639-0001. **EMAIL** jelofti@bentley.unco.edu

LOGAN, DEBORAH
PERSONAL Born Scranton, PA, 3 children **DISCIPLINE** NINETEENTH-CENTURY BRITISH LITERATURE **EDUCATION** Hamilton Col, BA; Univ NC Chapel Hill, MA, PhD. **CAREER** Prof **RESEARCH** Romantic and Victorian Literature; Harriet Martineau, Thomas Hardy. **SELECTED PUBLICATIONS** Auth, Fallenness in Victorian Women's Writing, Univ Missouri Press, 98. **CONTACT ADDRESS** Western Kentucky Univ, 1526 Big Red Way Street, Bowling Green, KY 42101. **EMAIL** deborah.logan@wku.edu

LOGAN, GEORGE
DISCIPLINE ENGLISH LITERATURE **EDUCATION** Harvard Univ, PhD. **CAREER** Dept Eng, Queen's Univ **RESEARCH** Renaissance humanism; English literary Renaissance. **SELECTED PUBLICATIONS** Auth, The Meaning of More's 'Utopia'; pubs on Renaissance literature, Renaissance humanism, and computer applications to literary studies; co-ed,The Norton Anthology of English Literature; Utopia; Unfolded Tales: Essays on Renaissance Romance. **CONTACT ADDRESS** English Dept, Queen's Univ at Kingston, Kingston, ON, Canada K7L 3N6. **EMAIL** logang@qsilver.queensu.ca

LOGGINS, VERNON P.
PERSONAL Born 08/18/1952, Birmingham, AL, m, 1992, 1 child **DISCIPLINE** ENGLISH **EDUCATION** Purdue Univ, BA, 75; Ball State Univ, MA, 78; Purdue Univ, PhD, 87. **CAREER** Asst Prof, Valdosta State Univ, 89-92; Assoc prof, Purdue Univ, 92-. **MEMBERSHIPS** MLA, CLA, Shakespeare Asn of Am. **RESEARCH** Shakespeare studies; Renaissance literature; Modern British and American Poetry. **SELECTED PUBLICATIONS** Co-auth, Shakespeare's Deliberate Art, Univ Pres of Am, 96; auth, The Life of Our design, Univ Press of Am, 92. **CONTACT ADDRESS** Dept Letters & Lang, Purdue Univ, No Central, 1401 S US Hwy 421, Westville, IN 46391-9542. **EMAIL** mick.loggins@worldnet.att.net

LOGSDON, LOREN
DISCIPLINE ENGLISH LITERATURE **EDUCATION** Eureka Col, BA; Univ IL, MA; OH Univ, PhD. **CAREER** Prof, Eureka Col . **HONORS AND AWARDS** Ed, Eureka Lit Mag. **RESEARCH** Am lit. **SELECTED PUBLICATIONS** Ed, The Eureka Literary Magazine; ed, Eureka Studies in Teaching Short Fiction. **CONTACT ADDRESS** Eureka Col, 300 E College Ave, PO Box 280, Eureka, IL 61530. **EMAIL** llogsdon@eureka.edu

LOHAFER, SUSAN
PERSONAL Born 06/23/1942, Goshen, NY, m **DISCIPLINE** SHORT FICTION THEORY, LITERARY NONFICTION **EDUCATION** Radcliffe Col, AB, 64; Stanford Univ, MA, 66; NYork Univ, PhD, 70. **CAREER** Vis asst prof English, Ohio State Univ, 72-73; asst prof, 73-77, Assoc Prof 77- 82, prof, English, Univ Iowa, 82-. **MEMBERSHIPS** MLA; M/MLA; Soc for the Stu of the Short Story. **RESEARCH** Short fiction theory. **SELECTED PUBLICATIONS** Auth, Knave, Fool, and Genius, Univ NC, 73; auth, Coming to terms with the Short Story, LSUP, 83; co-ed, Short Story Theory at a Crossroads, LSUP, 89; co-ed, The Tales We Tell, Greenwood, 98. **CONTACT ADDRESS** Dept of English, Univ of Iowa, 308 English Phil Bldg., Iowa City, IA 52242-1492. **EMAIL** slohafer@compuserve.com

LOHMANN, CHRISTOPH KARL
PERSONAL Born 10/06/1935, Berlin, Germany, m, 1961, 2 children **DISCIPLINE** ENGLISH, AMERICAN STUDIES **EDUCATION** Swarthmore Col, BA, 58; Columbia Univ, MA, 61; Univ Pa, PhD(Am civilization), 68. **CAREER** Asst prof, 68-73, assoc prof, 73-81, Prof English, Ind Univ, Bloomington and Assoc Dean Fac, 81-, Assoc ed, a Selected Edition of W D Howells, Ind Univ, 72-; Fulbright Comn sr res fel, Fed Repub Ger, 76-77. **MEMBERSHIPS** MLA; Am Studies Asn. **RESEARCH** Nineteenth century American literature; American studies. **SELECTED PUBLICATIONS** Auth, The burden of the past in Hawthorne's American romances, SAtlantic Quart, winter 67; The agony of the English romance, Nathaniel Hawthorne J, 72; Jamesian irony and the American sense of mission, Tex Studies Lit & Lang, 74; coauth, Commentary on Henry James Letters, Nineteenth-Century Fiction, 9/76; coed, Selected Letters of W D Howells, vols I-V, Twayne, 82; E L Doctorow's Historical Romances, The Contemporary American Novel, Adler Foreign Books, 82. **CONTACT ADDRESS** Dept of English, Indiana Univ, Bloomington, Bloomington, IN 47401.

LOHRLI, ANNE
PERSONAL Born 02/09/1906, Bake Oven, OR **DISCIPLINE** ENGLISH LANGUAGE AND LITERATURE **EDUCATION** Occidental Col, AB, 27, AM, 28; Columbia Univ, AM, 32; Univ Southern Calif, PhD, 37. **CAREER** Res and collaboration, 27-37; teacher, Los Angeles City Schs, 38-45; prof, 45-65, Emer Prof English, N Mex Highlands Univ, 65-, Vis prof, Univ Trieste, 54. **MEMBERSHIPS** MLA. **RESEARCH** Victorian periodicals. **SELECTED PUBLICATIONS** Auth, Fresh Fields and Pastures New + Misquoting Milton Line From 'Lycidas', Notes and Queries, Vol 0041, 94; The Divine Williams--Query, Notes and Queries, Vol 0044, 97. **CONTACT ADDRESS** New Mexico Highlands Univ, 790 Baylor Ave, Claremont, CA 91711.

LOISELLE, ANDRE
DISCIPLINE FILM **EDUCATION** Univ Brit Columbia, PhD. **CAREER** Asst prof. **RESEARCH** Canadian and Quebecois cinema. **SELECTED PUBLICATIONS** Co-ed, Auteur/Provocateur: The Films of Denys Arcand, Flicks Bk(s)/Praeger, 95; pub(s), articles on film and theatre in jour(s), The Can Jour of Film Stud; Quebec Stud; Post Script; Theatre Res in Can; Essays in Theatre and L'Annuaire theatral; auth, articles on Michel Brault's Les Ordres; auth, bk on Anne Claire Poirier's film Mourir a tue-tete, Flicks Bk(s). **CONTACT ADDRESS** Dept of Art and Cult, Carleton Univ, 1125 Colonel By Dr, Ottawa, ON, Canada K1S 5B6. **EMAIL** andre_loiselle@carleton.ca

LOIZEAUX, ELIZABETH BERGMANN
PERSONAL Born 12/16/1950, New York, NY, m, 1982 **DISCIPLINE** ENGLISH LITERATURE **EDUCATION** Mt Holyoke Col, BA, 72; Univ Mich, Ann Arbor, MA, 74, PhD(English), 80. **CAREER** Asst prof Eng, Univ MD, Col Park, 80-. **HONORS AND AWARDS** NEH Summer Stipend, 82. **MEMBERSHIPS** MLA; SAtlantic Modern Lang Asn; Victorians Inst. **RESEARCH** William Butler Yeats; relations of poetry and the visual arts; modern poetry. **SELECTED PUBLICATIONS** Auth, Yeats and the Visual Arts, Rutgers, 86; auth, Yeats: An Annual of Critical and Textual Studies, Word & Image, and Review. **CONTACT ADDRESS** 51 Walnut Ave, Takoma Park, MD 20912. **EMAIL** el18@umail.umd.edu

LOMAS, RONALD LEROY
PERSONAL Born 05/21/1942, Rock Island, IL **DISCIPLINE** SPEECH **EDUCATION** Western IL Univ, BA 1965, MA 1967; Bowling Green State Univ, PhD 1976. **CAREER** Western IL Univ, grad asst dept of speech 1965-66; Bowling Green State Univ, grad asst dept of speech 1969-70; Lorain Cty Comm Coll instr speech & dir forensics, reg adv 1969; Bowling Green State Univ, instr speech & ethnic studies 1970-, asst to dir of ethenic studies 1970-75; Univ of Cincinnati Med School, coord of supportive serv 1975-76; TX So Univ Houston, assoc prof speech comm. **HONORS AND AWARDS** Foreign Serv Scholar 1964; Omicron Delta Kappa 1973; Disting Faculty Awd 1974; Outstanding Instr TSU 1980. **MEMBERSHIPS** Chmn faculty eval comm Lorain Cty Comm Coll 1968-69; chmn Minority Affairs Comm 1968-69; adv Black Progressives 1968-69; consult & lectr Black Culture St Pauls Episcopal Church Maumee OH 1972-73; leadership consult B'nai B'rith Youth Org S Euclid OH 1972-73, Lorain Council 1970-71, MI Council 1973; communication consult Title I Grant Toledo Minority Businessmen 1974-75; mem Intl Commun Assoc, Speech Commun Assoc; producer Black Perspectives WBGU Channel 70 1971;producer, host & writer of prog WBGU Channel 57 1973. **CONTACT ADDRESS** Texas So Univ, 3100 Cleborne St, Houston, TX 77004.

LONDON, BETTE
DISCIPLINE ENGLISH **EDUCATION** Univ CA at Berkeley, PhD. **CAREER** Assoc prof & dept ch; taught at, Univ CA at Berkeley. **RESEARCH** 19th and 20th century Brit lit; feminist and postcolonial theory; gender studies; hist of authorship. **SELECTED PUBLICATIONS** Auth, The Appropriated Voice: Narrative Authority in Conrad, Forster, and Woolf; Mary Shelley, Frankenstein, and the Spectacle of Masculinity, PMLA 108, 93; Of Mimicry and English Men: EM Forster and the Performance of Masculinity, in A Passage to India, Theory in Practice Series, Open UP, 94; Writing Double: Women's Literary Partnerships. **CONTACT ADDRESS** Dept of English, Univ of Rochester, 500 Wilson Blvd, RC Box 270451, Rochester, NY 14627-0451. **EMAIL** bldn@mail.rochester.edu

LONDRE, FELICIA HARDISON
PERSONAL Born 04/01/1941, Fort Lewis, WA, m, 1967, 2 children **DISCIPLINE** THEATER HISTORY, DRAMATIC LITERATURE **EDUCATION** Univ Mont, Missoula, BA, 62; Univ Wash, Seattle, MA, 64; Univ Wis-Madison, PhD(theater), 69. **CAREER** Asst prof speech & theater, Univ Wis-Rock County, 69-75; Wis Arts Bd, theatre & film adv bd, 74-75; dramaturg, Mo Repertory Theatre, 75-; asst prof theater & film, Univ Tex, Dallas, 75-78; assoc prof to prof, 78-87, partic, Avant Garde Theatre, 79; traveling respondant, Am Col Theatre Festival, Region 5-S, 80-; app, Comn Theatre Res, Am Theatre Asn, 81-84; partic, Soviet & Polish drama, 82; Curator's Prof Theater, Univ Mo-Kansas City, 87-; **HONORS AND AWARDS** Daughter of Mark Twain Soc, elected 81; Recipient of Grants and fel(s) from UMKC, NEH, Mo Humanities Coun; Distinguished Alumna Awd from the Univ of Montana, 98; Col of Fel of the Am Tehatre: inducted as Fel at the J.F.K Ctr in Washington D.C., 99; Honorary Co-Found, Heart of Am Shakespeare Festival, 91-. **MEMBERSHIPS** Am Soc Theatre Res; Mark Twain Soc; Asn for Theatre in Higher Educ. **RESEARCH** Nineteenth & 20th century French, Spanish and Russian theatre history and dramatic literature; American entertainment of the silent film era, 1895-29; playwriting and dramaturgy. **SELECTED PUBLICATIONS** Auth, Tenessee Williams, New York: Frederick Ungar Pub, 79; auth, Tom stoppard, Frederick Ungar Pub, 81; trans, The Show-Man, Andree Chedid, Ubu Repertory theater Pub, 84; auth, Federico Garcia Lorca, frederick Ungar Pub, 84; coed, Shakespeare Around the Globe: A Guide to Notable Postwar Revivals, Westport, CT: Greenwood Press, 86; auth, Tennessee Williams: Life, Work, and Criticism, York Press, 89; auth, The History of World Thearter: From the English Restoration to the Present, Continium, 91; co-auth, Shakespeare companies and Festivals: an International Guide, Westport, CT: Greenwood Pub Group, 95; auth, Editor, Love's Labour's Lost: Critical essays, Garland Pub, 97; co-auth, The History of North American theater: the Unitedc States, Canada, and Mexico from Pre-Columbian Times to the Present, Continuum, 98. **CONTACT ADDRESS** Dept of Theatre, Univ of Missouri, Kansas City, 528 e. 56th St, Kansas City, MO 64110. **EMAIL** LondreF@umkc.edu

LONEY, GLENN MEREDITH
PERSONAL Born 12/24/1928, Sacramento, CA, s **DISCIPLINE** THEATRE & SPEECH **EDUCATION** Univ Calif, Berkeley, AB, 50; Univ Wis-Madison, MA, 51; Stanford Univ, PhD, 54. **CAREER** Instr, 55-56, San Francisco State Col; instr, 56, Univ Nev, Las Vegas; lectr, Europe, 56-59, Univ Md; instr, 59-61, Hofstra Univ; from asst prof to assoc prof, 61-70, prof, 70-, Brooklyn Col; prof, 70-, emeritus prof, 91, Grad Ctr, CUNY; hon fel, 60, Am Scand Found. **MEMBERSHIPS** Am Theatre Assn; Am Soc Theatre Res; Theatre Libr Assocs; Int Fed Theatre Res; Theatre Hist Soc; AAUP; Am Music Critics Assn, Am Theatre Critics Assn; Drama Desk; Outer Critics Circle; Muni Art Soc NY; Phi Beta Kappa; Alpha Mu Gamma, Phi Eta Sigma, Phi Delta Phi. **RESEARCH** Opera as theatre; preservation of historic theatres; dance theatre. **SELECTED PUBLICATIONS** Auth, Your Future in the Performing Arts, Rosen, 80; The House of Mirth-the Play of the Novel, Assoc

Univ Presses, 81; auth, 20th Century Theatre, Facts on File, 82; auth, California Gold Rush Drama, Musical Theatre in America, 84; auth, Creating Careers in Music Theatre, 88; auth, Staging Shakespeare, 90; auth, Peter Brook: Oxford To Orghast, 98; ed, Art Deco News & The Modernist, 81-94; chief corresp, New York Theatre - Wire, NY Museum Wire, online, 96. **CONTACT ADDRESS** 3 E 71st St, New York, NY 10021.

LONG, ADA
DISCIPLINE EIGHTEENTH-CENTURY LITERATURE AND WOMEN'S LITERATURE **EDUCATION** Stanford, BA, 67; SUNY, PhD, 76. **CAREER** Dir, Univ honors prog, Univ AL. **SELECTED PUBLICATIONS** Auth, Off the Map: Selected Poems of Gloria Fuertes; Stepping Out: An Introduction to the Arts; A Handbook for Honors Directors. **CONTACT ADDRESS** Univ of Alabama, Birmingham, 1400 University Blvd, Birmingham, AL 35294-1150.

LONG, ANTHONY A.
PERSONAL Born 08/17/1937, Manchester, United Kingdom, m, 2 children **DISCIPLINE** CLASSICS **EDUCATION** Univ Col London, BA, 60; Univ London, PhD, 64. **CAREER** Prof, Univ Liverpool, 73-83; Prof, Univ Calif, 83-. **HONORS AND AWARDS** Guggenheim Fel, 86; NEH Fel, 91; Fel, Am Acad of Arts & Sci, 89-; Corresponding Fel of Brit Acad, 92-. **RESEARCH** Ancient Greek and Roman philosophy, Greek literature. **SELECTED PUBLICATIONS** Auth, Language and Thought in Sophacles, 68; auth, Problems in Stoicism, 71; auth, Hellenistic Philosophy, 74, 2nd Ed, 86; , The Hellenistic Philosphies, 87; auth, The Question of Eclecticism, 88; coauth auth, Stoic Studies, 96; ed, The Cambridge Companion to Early Greek Philosophy, 99. **CONTACT ADDRESS** Dept Classics, Univ of California, Berkeley, 5303 Dwinelle Hall, Berkeley, CA 94720-2520. **EMAIL** aalong@uclink4.berkeley.edu

LONG, RICHARD ALEXANDER
PERSONAL Born 02/09/1927, Philadelphia, PA **DISCIPLINE** ENGLISH **EDUCATION** Temple Univ, AB, 47, MA, 48; Univ Poitiers, DesL, 65. **CAREER** Instr, WVa State Col, 49-50; asst prof English, Morgan State Col, 51-64; lectr, Univ Poitiers, 64-65; prof English and French, Hampton Inst, 66-68; Prof English, Atlanta Univ, 68-, Fulbright scholar, Univ Paris, 57-58; vis lectr, Harvard Univ, 70-71; Adj Prof, Emory Univ, 72-. **MEMBERSHIPS** MLA; Mod Humanities Res Asn; Mediaeval Acad Am; Col Lang Asn (pres, 69-71); Ling Soc Am. **RESEARCH** Theory of art; Afro-American culture; medieval literature. **SELECTED PUBLICATIONS** Auth, Race Contacts and Interracial Relations, African Amer Rev, Vol 0029, 95. **CONTACT ADDRESS** Emory Univ, Atlanta, GA 30322.

LONG, THOMAS L.
DISCIPLINE ENGLISH **EDUCATION** Catholic Univ America, BA, 75; MA, 81; Univ Illinois, AM, 77; Indiana Univ Pa, PhD, 97. **CAREER** Assoc/Pastor, Catholic Diocese of Richmond, 80-88; Asst/Assoc Prof of English, Thomas Nelson Community Col, 89-. **MEMBERSHIPS** ASA, MLA, ATTW, SAMLA, NCTE. **RESEARCH** Gender, Lesbian & Gay Studies, Apocalypticism and Millennialism. **SELECTED PUBLICATIONS** Auth, "Larry Kramer," and "Literary Theory and Homosexuality," Readers Guide to Lesbian and Gay Studies, ed. Timothy Murphy, Fitzroy Dearborn Publishers, 00; auth, "Defilement", "Maps of Apocalyptic Time," "Mysticism," "Plague & Pestilence," "Sexuality," "Sodom," "Utopia", The Encyclopedia of Millennialism and Millennial Movements, ed. Richard Landes, Routledge, 00. **CONTACT ADDRESS** Dept Humanities, Thomas Nelson Comm Col, PO Box 9407, Hampton, VA 23670-0407. **EMAIL** longt@tncc.cc.va.us

LONG, TIMOTHY
PERSONAL Born 01/31/1943, Cincinnati, OH, s **DISCIPLINE** CLASSICS **EDUCATION** Xavier Univ, BA, 65; Princeton Univ, MA, 67; PhD, 71. **CAREER** Lectr to prof, Ind Univ, 69-; Chair, 93-97. **HONORS AND AWARDS** Alexander von Humboldt Fel, Ger, 77-78; Fulbright Lectr, Ger, 87-88. **MEMBERSHIPS** Am Philol Assoc; Class Assoc of the Middle West and South; Am Class League. **RESEARCH** Ancient comedy, comic theory. **SELECTED PUBLICATIONS** Auth, Barbarians in Greek Comedy, Univ of Southern Il Pr, 87; auth, Repetition and Variation in the Short Stories of Herodotous, Atheneaeum, (Frankfurt), 87. **CONTACT ADDRESS** Dept Class Studies, Indiana Univ, Bloomington, 1020 E Kirkwood Ave, Bloomington, IN 47405-7103. **EMAIL** longt@indiana.edu

LONGENBACH, JAMES
DISCIPLINE ENGLISH **EDUCATION** Princeton Univ, PhD. **CAREER** Joseph Henry Gilmore prof; taught at, Princeton Univ & Oxford Univ. **HONORS AND AWARDS** Guggenheim & Mellon fel; NEH st fel. **RESEARCH** Mod lit.; problem of postmodernism in Ameircan poetry. **SELECTED PUBLICATIONS** Auth, Modern Poetry After Modernism, Wallace Stevens: The Plain Sense of Things; Stone Cottage: Pound, Yeats, and Modernism, Modernist Poetics of History. **CONTACT ADDRESS** Dept of English, Univ of Rochester, 500 Wilson Blvd, RC Box 270451, Rochester, NY 14627-0451. **EMAIL** jlgb@mail.rochester.edu

LONGEST, GEORGE CALVIN
PERSONAL Born 02/17/1938, Richmond, VA, 4 children **DISCIPLINE** AMERICAN LITERATURE **EDUCATION** Univ Richmond, Ba, 60, MA, 61; Univ GA, PhD(Am lit), 69. **CAREER** Instr Eng, VA Polytech Inst & State Univ, 62-63; from instr to asst prof, 63-77, asst chmn dept, 73-80, actg chmn dept, 80-82, Assoc Prof Eng, VA Commonwealth Univ, 77-, Assoc Chmn Dept, 82-, Managing ed, Resource for Am Literary Study, 78-81; Ed, Annual Bibliog in Southern Lit, Miss Quart. **HONORS AND AWARDS** Tchg Excellence Awd, Asn Dept Eng & MLA, 73. **MEMBERSHIPS** S Atlantic Mod Lang Asn; Soc Study Southern Lit. **RESEARCH** Southern and mod Am lit; nineteenth century Am lit. **SELECTED PUBLICATIONS** Contribr, Soc Study, 76-82; Annual bibliography Southern literature, Miss Quart, winter 77; auth, Three Virginia Writers: Mary Johnston, Thomas Nelson Page, Amelie Rives Trochetzkoy, G K Hall, 78; Genius in the Garden: Chartes F. Gillette and Landscape Architecture in Virginia, 92. **CONTACT ADDRESS** 1136 West Ave, Richmond, VA 23220. **EMAIL** glongest@vcu.edu

LONGMIRE, SAMUEL
DISCIPLINE ENGLISH LITERATURE **EDUCATION** Ind Univ, PhD. **CAREER** Fulbright lectr, Romania; dept ch; dean, Col Arts and Sci; prof, Univ Evansville. **HONORS AND AWARDS** Founder, UE Chapter, Samuel Johnson Soc. **SELECTED PUBLICATIONS** Auth, scholarly articles on eighteenth century literary figures; pub(s), short fiction, in Cottonwood, The Flying Island, And Down The River; **CONTACT ADDRESS** Dept of Eng, Univ of Evansville, 1800 Lincoln Ave, Evansville, IN 47714. **EMAIL** sl27@evansville.edu.

LONGO, BERNADETTE
DISCIPLINE PROFESSIONAL COMMUNICATION **EDUCATION** Rensselaer Polytech Inst, PhD, 96. **CAREER** Dept Eng, Clemson Univ **RESEARCH** Technical commun, cultural stud, and hist of computing. **SELECTED PUBLICATIONS** Auth, Design Collaboration Network User Manual, Rensselaer Polytech Inst, 94; Advanced System Operation Courseware Trainer's Manual, Power Tech, 93; Technical Communication Constituted as an Object of Cultural Study, Tech Comms Quart, 98; From Secrets to Science: Technical Writing, Utility, and the Hermetic Tradition in Agricola's De Re Metallica, Jour Tech Writing Comm, 97; Who Makes Engineering Knowledge?, IEEE Int Prof Comm Conf Proceedings, 97; coauth, Extending the Boundaries of Rhetoric in Legal Pedagogy, Jour Bus Tech Comm, 96; auth, Spurious Coin: A Hist of Science, Management, and Technical Writing, SUNY Press, 00. **CONTACT ADDRESS** Clemson Univ, Clemson, SC 29634. **EMAIL** blongo@clemson.edu

LONGYEAR, REY MORGAN
PERSONAL Born 12/10/1930, Boston, MA, m, 1959 **DISCIPLINE** MUSICOLOGY **EDUCATION** Calif State Col Los Angeles, AB, 51; Univ NC, MA, 54; Cornell Univ, PhD(musicol), 57. **CAREER** Teacher, High Sch, Md, 57-58; from asst prof to assoc prof music, Univ Southern Miss, 58-63; assoc prof, Univ Tenn, 63-64; assoc prof, 64-70, Prof Music, Univ KY, 70-, Bk rev ed, J Res Music Educ, 65-70; consult, Exploratory Comt for Assessing Progress in Educ, 67-68 and Nat Assessment of Educ Progress, 67-; Guggenheim fel, 71; bd mem, Univ Prof Acad Order, 81- **MEMBERSHIPS** Am Musicol Soc; Col Music Soc; Int Musicol Soc; Gesellschaft fur Musikforschung; Soc Ital Musicol. **RESEARCH** Eighteenth and 19th century music; music and German literature. **SELECTED PUBLICATIONS** Auth, Music and Musicians in 19th Century Italy, Notes, Vol 0049, 93. **CONTACT ADDRESS** Sch of Music, Univ of Kentucky, Lexington, KY 40506.

LONIGAN, PAUL R.
PERSONAL Born 05/27/1935, New York, NY, m, 1965, 4 children **DISCIPLINE** CLASSICS **EDUCATION** Queens Col, BA, 60; Johns Hopkins Univ, PhD, 67. **CAREER** Instructor, Russell Sage Col, 63-65; Assoc Prof, SUNY, 65-67; Prof, Queens Col, 67-. **HONORS AND AWARDS** Nat Defense Fel; Phi Beta Kappa; Nat German Honor Soc; Men of Achievement; Presidential Cert, Queens Col; Plaque of Distinction, Queens Col; Intl Order of Merit, 99. **MEMBERSHIPS** Phi Beta Kappa; Circulo de Cultura Panamerican; Cumann na Scribheann nGaedhilge; Irish Am cultural Inst; Delta Phi Alpha; Asn of Literary Scholars and critics; Archaeol Inst of Am; Biblical Archaeol Soc; Intl Order of Merit. **RESEARCH** Medieval literature; Renaissance literature; Classics; Mythology; Philology; Celtic Studies; Indo-European Studies. **SELECTED PUBLICATIONS** Auth, The Druids: Priests of the Ancients Celts, Greenwood Pub Groups, 96; ed, Maria Victoria Carreno Montas, Santo Domingo, 99; auth, "Napoleon Bonaparte: sus estrategias de expansion en America y el Caribe," forthcoming. **CONTACT ADDRESS** Dept Romance Lang, Queens Col, CUNY, 6530 Kissena Blvd, Flushing, NY 11367-1575. **EMAIL** garwaf@juno.com

LONT, CYNTHIA M.
PERSONAL Born 05/25/1951, Geneva, NY **DISCIPLINE** COMMUNICATIONS **EDUCATION** Auburn Cmty Col, AA, 72; SUNY Oswego, BA, 75; S Ill Univ, 76; Univ Iowa, PhD, 84. **CAREER** Director, Student Video Center at George Mason Univ, 90-96; director, Student Tech and Resource Center, 96-99; dept chair, George Mason Univ, 99-. **HONORS AND AWARDS** Best Take Awd, Wash DC, 98; Awd of Distinction, Nat Communicator Awd, 96,98; Fac Grant, Col of Arts and Sci, 97; Video Awd of Excellence, Nat Communicator Awd, 97. **MEMBERSHIPS** Intl comm Asn, Asn for Educ in Journalism Mass comm, Speech Comm Asn, E Comm Asn, S States comm Asn, Media Report to Women, VA Speech Comm Asn, Org for Res on Women and Comm. **RESEARCH** Women and media, Visual communication, Women's music, Mass communication theory. **SELECTED PUBLICATIONS** Auth, "Using technology to increase face-to-face interaction," The Speech Communication Teacher, 97; auth, "Analysis of the terms surrounding the commodification process," Communication Quarterly, 90; auth, Roles assigned females and males in non-music radio programming," Sex Roles, 90; auth, "The capstone course in speech communication: format and purpose," Association for Communication Administration Bulletin, 90; auth, "Subcultural persistence: The case of Redwood Records," Women's Studies in Communication, 88; auth, "Women's music in the United States," International Association for the Study of Popular Music, 85; auth, "Between the Covers: a review of Cris Williamson and Tret Fure's album," Women and Language, 00; auth, "Women and media: Special issue," Women and Language, 91; auth, "Not again! A review essay of William A Rusher's The Coming Battle for the Media: curbing the Power of the Elite," International Journal of Group Tensions, 90; auth, "An industry of its own: Women's music," Onetwothreefour: a rock 'n' roll Quarterly, 86. **CONTACT ADDRESS** Dept Comm, George Mason Univ, Fairfax, 4400 Univ Dr, Fairfax, VA 22030-4422. **EMAIL** clont@gmu.edu

LOOKER, MARK S.
PERSONAL Born 01/19/1952, Detroit, MI **DISCIPLINE** ENGLISH LITERATURE **EDUCATION** Concordia Col, BA, 73; Washington Univ, MA, 74; Univ Mich, PhD, 84. **CAREER** Instr, St John's Col, 74-75; asst prof to prof, Concordia Col, 75-. **MEMBERSHIPS** MLA, NCTE, NA Coun on Brit Studies, Midwest Victorian Studies Assoc, Caribbean Studies Assoc, Assoc for Integrative Studies. **RESEARCH** Victorian Literature and Culture, Literature and Culture of the Caribbean, Black British Writing of Post WWII, Urban Studies, Literature and the Other Arts. **SELECTED PUBLICATIONS** Auth, "Victoria's Jubilees and the Religious Press," Victorian Periodicals Rev, (88); coauth, Victorian Britain, Garland Publ, 89; rev, of "Benjamin Disraeli Letters", Victorian Periodicals Rev, (90); rev, of "The Caribbean Artists Movement", Albion, (95); auth, Atlantic Passages, Peter Lang Publ, 96; rev, "Into the Light of Things: The Art of the Commonplace from Wordsworth to John Cage," Assoc for Integrative Studies, (99). **CONTACT ADDRESS** Concordia Univ, Michigan, 409 Mark Hannah Pl, Ann Arbor, MI 48103. **EMAIL** lookerm@ccaa.edu

LOOSER, DEVONEY K.
PERSONAL Born 04/11/1967, St Paul, MN, m, 1996 **DISCIPLINE** ENGLISH, WOMEN'S STUDIES **EDUCATION** Augsburg Col, BA, 89; SUNY Stony Brook, PhD, 93. **CAREER** Instr to asst to dir, SUNY, 89-93; asst prof, Ind State Univ, 93-98; asst prof, Univ of Wis, 98-00; vis asst prof, Ariz State Univ, 00-01; asst prof, La State Univ, 01-. **HONORS AND AWARDS** NEH Fel, 97; William Andrews Clark Mem Libr Fel, 97. **MEMBERSHIPS** MLA, Am Soc for Eighteenth Century Studies, Jane Austen Soc of NA, NA Soc for the Study of Romanticisim, Nat Women's Studies Assoc. **RESEARCH** British women writers, feminist theory, histories of aging, historiography, Jane Austen. **SELECTED PUBLICATIONS** Ed, Jane Austen and Discourses of Feminism, St. Martin's Pr, 95; coed, Generations: Academic Feminists in Dialogue, Univ of Minn Pr, 97; auth, British Women Writers and the Writing of History, 1670-1820, Johns Hopkins Univ Pr, 00. **CONTACT ADDRESS** Dept English, La State Univ, Baton Rouge, LA 70803-5001. **EMAIL** devoney@mac.com

LOPEZ, CARLOS
PERSONAL Born 06/02/1950, Uruguay, m, 1984, 3 children **DISCIPLINE** LATIN AMERICAN LITERATURE, CULTURE **EDUCATION** Instituto Profesores Artigas, Uruguay, Prof and Literatura, 76; Ohio State Univ, PhD, 95. **CAREER** Instituto profesores Artigan, Uruguay, 91-92; asst prof, Marshall Univ, 95-00. **MEMBERSHIPS** LASA; MLA; LAILA. **RESEARCH** Popol Vuh, Colonial Literature, Globalization and Latin American Cultures. **SELECTED PUBLICATIONS** Auth, El Popol Wuj y sus epistemologieas. Las diferencias, el conociniento y los ciclos del infinito (The POPOL WUJ and Their Epistemologies. Differences, Knowledge and the Cycles of infinite). **CONTACT ADDRESS** Dept Mod Lang, Marshall Univ, 400 Hal Greer Blvd, Huntington, WV 25755-0001. **EMAIL** lopez@marshall.edu

LOPEZ, DEBBIE
PERSONAL Born 06/25/1955, Evanston, IL, m, 2000 **DISCIPLINE** LITERATURE **EDUCATION** Univ S, BA; Middlebury College's Bread Loaf Sch Engl, MA; Harvard Univ, AM, PhD, 94. **CAREER** Prof; taught at, Univ AL at Birmingham, Birmingham-Southern Col & Harvard Univ; asst grad adv; assoc prof, at UTSA, assis graduate adivsor of record. **HONORS AND AWARDS** UTSA Int Travel Grant, 96; Harvard's

Howard Mumford Jones Prize, 94; Ford Foundation Fel. **RESEARCH** British and American Romanticism; 19th-century British poetry; late 19th and early 20th-century American novels. **SELECTED PUBLICATIONS** Presented invited papers at, Harvard University's Seminar on Environmental Ethics, 94 & 95; auth, Twain, Kents, Melville, Hawthorne, Morrison, London, and M.G. Brooks. **CONTACT ADDRESS** Col of Fine Arts and Hum, Univ of Texas, San Antonio, 6900 N Loop 1604 W, San Antonio, TX 78249.

LOPEZ, OSCAR R.
PERSONAL Born Medellen, Columbia, m, 1994 **DISCIPLINE** LITERATURE, SPANISH **EDUCATION** BEd, Ude A Medellin, Colombia, 78; BPh, 86; Wash Univ, MA, 90; Univ Cincinnati, PhD, 98. **CAREER** prof, Univ de Antioquia, Colombia, 86-90, 92-94; dir, Univ Medellin, 92-94; asst prof, St Louis Univ. **HONORS AND AWARDS** Book Publication Awd, Medellin, 96; Fel, Wash Univ, 90; Res Fel, Univ of Cincinnati, 96; Taft Mem Res, Univ of Cincinnati, 97; Mellon Res, St Louis Univ, 00. **MEMBERSHIPS** MLA; INTI; Revista of Lit. **RESEARCH** Contemporary Latin American Literature. **SELECTED PUBLICATIONS** Auth, "El carnero: o de la tecnica narrativa", Con-textos, Revista de semiotica literaria 16, (95): 19-31; auth, "Acerca del cuento: o de las mudanzas de la narracion", Dominical, (Dec 95): 9-13; auth, La critica latinoaericana: o del dialogo cultural con los otros, Martin Vieco Ltda, (Medellin), 96; auth, "Una carta a Martin Romana: La realidad ficcionalizada, La ficcion Real (izada)", Cincinnati Romance Review 15, (96): 166-173; auth, "Algunas contradicciones en las ideas ilustradas de Jose Cadalso", Con-Textos: Revista de semiotica literaria 19, (April 97): 25-40; auth, "Las sagas literarias: de los griegos a Armando Romero", Domincal (Nov 97): 9-12; auth, "Un bel morir: novela clave en el ciclo del Gaviero", Hojas Univ 44 (Nov 97): 86-93; auth, "El vampiro de la colonia Roma: o del travestismo posmoderno", Revists de Lit Mexicana Contemporanea 10 (99). **CONTACT ADDRESS** Dept Mod and Class Lang, Saint Louis Univ, 221 N Grand Blvd, Saint Louis, MO 63103-2006. **EMAIL** arieslop@yahoo.com

LOPEZ, TIFFANY ANA
PERSONAL Born San Gabriel, CA **DISCIPLINE** US LATINO LITERATURE & PERFORMANCE, 20TH CENTURY AMERICAN DRAMA, MULTI-ETHNIC CHILDREN'S LITERATURE **EDUCATION** Calif State Univ, BA; Univ Calif-Santa Barbara, PhD. **CAREER** Ast Prof, Univ Calif, Riverside. **HONORS AND AWARDS** Univ of Calif President's Research Fel in the Humanities; Co Principal Investigator Rockefeller Found; Humanities Fel Residency Site, 00. **MEMBERSHIPS** Am Literature; Assoc Latina/o Literary Affiliate. **RESEARCH** Chicana/o and Latina/o popular culture, and feminist and minority discourses. **SELECTED PUBLICATIONS** Ed, anthol, Growing Up Chicana/o, William & Morrow, 93; auth, "Imaging Community: Video in the Installation Work of Pepo Osorio," Art Jour, 95; "A Tolerance for Contradictions: The Short Stories of Mare Cristina Mena," 19th Century Amer Women Writers: A Critical Reader, Oxford Univ Press, 98; "Performing Aztlam: The Female Body as Cultural Critique in the Teatro of Cherre Moraga," Performing America: Cultural Nationalism in American Theatre, Univ Mich Press, 98. **CONTACT ADDRESS** Dept of Eng, Univ of California, Riverside, 1202 Humanities and Social Sciences, Riverside, CA 92521-0209. **EMAIL** tiffany.lopez@ucr.edu

LORBE, RUTH ELISABETH
PERSONAL Born 05/02/1925, Nuremberg, Germany **DISCIPLINE** MODERN GERMAN LITERATURE **EDUCATION** Univ Erlangen, PhD, 52. **CAREER** Student Raetin Ger, hist and English, intermediate sch, Nuremberg, 52-54, 55-60 and 62-64; lectr Ger, Univ Col North Staffordshire, 54-55; from instr to assoc prof, 60-72, Prof Ger, Univ Ill, Urbana, 72-. **MEMBERSHIPS** MLA; Am Asn Teachers Ger; Am Comp Lit Asn; Hofmannsthal-Gesellschaft; Int Brecht Soc. **RESEARCH** Children's songs, especially nursery rhymes; modern German poetry; German literataure after 1850. **SELECTED PUBLICATIONS** Auth, Hofmannsthal or the Geometry of the Subject--Psychostructural and Iconographic Studies on the Prose Works, J Engl and Ger Philol, Vol 0092, 93; Morike Muses--Critical Essays on Morike, Eduard, Ger Rev, Vol 0069, 94; Carossa, Hans--13 Essays on his Works, J Engl and Ger Philol, Vol 0095, 96. **CONTACT ADDRESS** Dept of Ger Lang and Lit, Univ of Illinois, Urbana-Champaign, Urbana, IL 61801.

LOSADA, LUIS ANTONIO
PERSONAL Born 01/07/1939, New York, NY, m, 1966 **DISCIPLINE** CLASSICS, ANCIENT HISTORY **EDUCATION** Hunter Col, AB, 60; Columbia Univ, MA, 62, PhD(Greek and Latin), 70. **CAREER** From lectr to asst prof classics, 68-74, Assoc Prof Classics, Lehman Col, 74-, Chmn Dept Class and Orient Lang, 73-, Assoc mem, Univ Sem Class Civilization, Columbia Univ, 72-. **MEMBERSHIPS** Am Philol Asn; Petronian Soc; Am Inst Archaeol. **RESEARCH** Greek history and numismatics; the teaching of classical languages. **SELECTED PUBLICATIONS** Auth, The Aetolian indemnity of 189 and the Agrinion hoard, Phoenix, 65; coauth, The time of the shield signal at Marathon, Am J Archaeol, 70; auth, Fifth columns in the Peloponnesian War: How they worked and the defense against them, Klio, 72; The Fifth Column in the Peloponnesian War, E J Brill, 72. **CONTACT ADDRESS** Lehman Col, CUNY, Bronx, NY 10468.

LOTT, RAYMOND
PERSONAL Born 07/07/1936, Orlando, FL, m, 1958, 2 children **DISCIPLINE** ENGLISH LITERATURE **EDUCATION** Univ Miami, BA, 58, MA, 59; Duke Univ, PhD, 62. **CAREER** Res asst, Duke Univ, 61; from instr to assoc prof, 61-73, Prof English, Fla Southern Col, 73-. **MEMBERSHIPS** NCTE; Col English Asn; MLA. **RESEARCH** Shakespeare; English, American and French novel; modern drama. **SELECTED PUBLICATIONS** Auth, The 'Crucifix Fish', Lit Rev, Vol 0037, 93. **CONTACT ADDRESS** Dept of English, Florida So Col, Lakeland, FL 33802.

LOUCKS, JAMES F.
PERSONAL Born 02/07/1936, Lakewood, OH, m, 1989, 2 children **DISCIPLINE** ENGLISH **EDUCATION** Yale Univ, BA 57; Ohio State Univ, PhD 67. **CAREER** Ohio State Univ, assoc prof, asst vpres reg ser, 78-83, OSU Newark Campus; Coor of English, 77-78, 83-; assoc dean, 77 to 83-; Val Univ IN, ch, assoc prof, 71-77; Drexel Univ PA, assoc prof 70-71; Univ VA, asst prof, dir soph eng prog, 67-70; Ohio State Univ Colum, tchg asst, instr, 60-67. **HONORS AND AWARDS** Univ Prof Val Univ. **MEMBERSHIPS** TS Eliot Soc. **RESEARCH** Victorian and 20th Cent Poetry. **SELECTED PUBLICATIONS** Coauth, Browning's Roman Murder Story: A Reading of the Ring and the Book, with R.D. Altick, Chicago, 68; auth, Robert Brownings Poetry: A Norton Critical Edition, NY, Norton, 79 reprint, 83; auth, The Exile's Return: Fragment of a TS Eliot Chronology, ANQ, 96; auth, Eliot's Burbank with a Baedeker: Bleistein with a Cigar, ANQ, 95; Eliot's Ash Wednesday, ANQ, 95; auth, The Ring and the Book and the Land and the Book, ANQ, 94; rev, The Varieties of Metaphysical Poetry, by TS Eliot, ed, Ronald Schchard, London, Faber, 93, ANQ, 96; auth, TS Eliot at 110: Fin-de-siecle Studies, Parts I/II, ANQ, 98. **CONTACT ADDRESS** Dept of English, Ohio State Univ, Newark, 1179 University Dr, Newark, OH 43055-1797. **EMAIL** loucks.1@osu.edu

LOUDEN, BRUCE
PERSONAL Born 11/08/1954 **DISCIPLINE** CLASSICS, COMPARATIVE LITERATURE **EDUCATION** Univ Calif at Santa Cruz, BA, 77; San Francisco State Univ, MA, 83; Univ of Calif at Berkeley, PhD, 90. **CAREER** Vis asst prof, Univ Wis Madison, 90-91; from asst prof to assoc prof, Univ Tex at El Paso, 91-. **HONORS AND AWARDS** Summer Scholar, The Ctr for Helenic Studies, 96 & 00. **RESEARCH** Epic Poetry, Mythology, the Bible. **SELECTED PUBLICATIONS** Auth, The Odyssey: Structure, Narration and Meaning, Johns Hopkins Univ Pr, 99. **CONTACT ADDRESS** Dept Lang & Ling, Univ of Texas, El Paso, 500 W Univ Ave, El Paso, TX 79968-8900. **EMAIL** blouden@miners.utep.edu

LOUGY, ROBERT E.
PERSONAL Born 09/11/1940, San Francisco, CA, m, 1962, 2 children **DISCIPLINE** ENGLISH **EDUCATION** Univ Calif, Davis, AB, 62, MA, 64, PhD(English), 66. **CAREER** Asst, Univ Calif, Davis, 62-65, fel, 65-66; asst prof, 66-72, Assoc Prof English, PA State Univ, University Park, 72-, Asst ed, Seventeenth-Century News, 66-67, abstr ed, 67-68; jr fel, Inst Arts and Humanistic Studies, Pa State Univ, 70-73; Nat Endowment for Humanities fel, 73-74. **MEMBERSHIPS** MLA. **RESEARCH** Nineteenth century British novel and theory of the novel; aesthetics and poetic theory of the 19th and 20th centuries; British Romantic Poetry. **SELECTED PUBLICATIONS CONTACT ADDRESS** Dept of English, Pennsylvania State Univ, Univ Park, 117 Burrowes Bldg, University Park, PA 16802-6200.

LOUIS, MARGOT K.
DISCIPLINE ENGLISH LITERATURE **EDUCATION** Univ Toronto, PhD. **CAREER** Assoc prof **RESEARCH** 19th-century poetry; 19th-century women poets. **SELECTED PUBLICATIONS** Auth, "Victorian Poetry, Victorian Newsletter, Nineteenth-Century Lit, Explicator, Mythlore, Victorian Lit and Cult"; auth, Swinburne and his Gods: The Roots and Growth of an Agnostic Poetry, McGill-Queen's UP; co-ed, Influence and Resistance in Nineteenth-Century English Poetry, Macmillan. **CONTACT ADDRESS** Dept of English, Univ of Victoria, PO Box 3070, Victoria, BC, Canada V8W 3W1. **EMAIL** mlouis@uvic.ca

LOUNSBERRY, BARBARA S.
PERSONAL Born 11/23/1946, Cedar Falls, IA, m, 1968, 1 child **DISCIPLINE** ENGLISH **EDUCATION** Univ N IA, BA, 69; MA, 71; Univ IA, PhD, 78. **CAREER** Asst Prof to Prof, 78-. **HONORS AND AWARDS** Distinguished Scholar Awd, Univ N IA, 94; Outstanding Teacher Awd, Univ IA, 98; Creative Intelligence Awd, Maharishi Univ, 94; Fac Excellence Awd, IA State Board of Regents, 92. **MEMBERSHIPS** MLA; Midwest MLA; Intl Virginia Woolf Soc, Asn for Literature & the Environment; Loren Eisley Asn; Ruth Suckow Memorial Asn; Nat Educ Asn; IA State Educ Asn. **RESEARCH** Literary or Creative Nonfiction, including: memoir and autobiography, biography, nature, travel, and science writing. **SELECTED PUBLICATIONS** Auth, The Art of Fact: Contemporary Artists of Nonfiction, Greenwood Press, 90; auth, The Writer in You, HarperCollins, 92; co-ed, Writing Creative Nonfiction: The Literature of Reality, HarperCollins, 96; co-ed, A University in Pursuit of Quality: The Future of Learning and Teaching at the University of Northern Iowa, Cedar Falls, 96; auth, "Woolf's Diaries and Letters as Texts/Contexts," in Virginia Woolf: Texts and Contexts, (Pace Univ Press, 96), 93-98; coauth, "Supporting Curriculum Development", in Handbook of the Undergraduate Curriculum, (Jossey-Bass, 97), 661-683; coed, Telling Tales: Perspectives on the Short Story, Greenwood Press, 98; ed, Time and Chance: An Iowa Murder Mystery, Cedar Falls, 98; ed, 16,000 Suspects: An Iowa Mystery, Cedar Falls, 99; auth, "Virginia Woolf and the Community of Diarist," in Virginia Woolf and Communities, (Pace Univ Press, 99), 202-211. **CONTACT ADDRESS** Dept Eng, Univ of No Iowa, 1 Uni of N IA, Cedar Falls, IA 50614-0027. **EMAIL** Barbara.Lounsberry@uni.edu

LOVE, GLEN A.
PERSONAL Born 07/04/1932, Seattle, WA, m, 1956, 2 children **DISCIPLINE** ENGLISH **EDUCATION** Univ Wash, BA, 54, MA, 59, PhD(Am lit), 64. **CAREER** Teacher pub schs, Seattle, Wash, 55-59; asst English, Univ Wash, 59-60, asst dean students, 60-63; asst prof English, San Diego State Col, 63-65; from asst prof to assoc prof, 65-74, dir compos, 65-70 and 73-74, assoc dean grad sch, 70-71, actg head dept, 78, Prof English, Univ Ore, 74-00, Fulbright lectr, Univ Regensburg, WGer, 78-79; Univ Tubingen, 86. **HONORS AND AWARDS** Walker Prize, Western Lit Assn, 90, Wylder Awd, Western Lit, Assn, 95. **MEMBERSHIPS** Assoc for Study of Lit and Environment; Am Studies Asn; PACIFIC Northwest Am Studies Asn (pres, 76-78); Western Lit Asn. **RESEARCH** Ecocriticism, American literature; Western American literature. **SELECTED PUBLICATIONS** Auth, Et in Rcadia Ego--Pastoral Theory Meets Ecocriticism, Western Amer Lit, Vol 0027, 92; auth, Babbitt: An American Live Twayne, 93; auth, "Ecocriticism and Science: Toward Consilience; auth, New Lit History Vol 30, 99. **CONTACT ADDRESS** Dept of English, Univ of Oregon, Eugene, OR 97403. **EMAIL** rglove@oregon.uoregon.edu

LOVELADY, EDGAR JOHN
PERSONAL Born 11/12/1937, Grand Rapids, MI, m, 1958, 2 children **DISCIPLINE** ENGLISH, GREEK **EDUCATION** Toronto Bible Col, dipl bible, 58; Grace Col, BA, 60; Grace Theol Sem, MDiv, 63; St Francis Col, MA, 66; Purdue Univ, PhD(English), 74; Grace Theol Sem, ThM, 76. **CAREER** Teacher English, W Noble Sch Corp, 63-66; Prof English & Greek, Grace Col, 66-. **HONORS AND AWARDS** Alva J McClain Awd, Grace Col, 75; Distinguished Alumnus, 75; Delta Epsilon Chi; Phi Kappa Phi; Int Who's Who in Educ. **MEMBERSHIPS** MLA; Ind Coun of Teachers of English. **RESEARCH** Old English grammar; Greek grammar. **SELECTED PUBLICATIONS** Auth, The Logos concept in John 1:1, Grace J, spring 63; The rise of Silas Lapham as problem novel, Ind English J, 73-74. **CONTACT ADDRESS** Grace Col, 200 Seminary Dr., Box 397, Winona Lake, IN 46590-1294. **EMAIL** lovelaej@grace.edu

LOVERIDGE-SANBONMATSU, JOAN
PERSONAL Born 07/05/1938, Hartford, CT, m, 1964, 2 children **DISCIPLINE** RHETORIC AND COMMUNICATION; BRITISH AND IRISH HISTORY. **EDUCATION** Univ Vermont, BA, 60; Ohio Univ, MA, 63; Penn State Univ, PhD, 71. **CAREER** Tchg asst, Commun Stud, Ohio Univ, 62-63; instr Commun Stud & ESL, Penn State Univ, 66-67; vis asst prof Commun Stud, RIT, 71; adj prof Commun Stud, Monroe Commun Col, 72-76; asst prof Commun Stud & Womens Stud, SUNY Brockport, 63-77; Prof Commun Stud & Women,s Stud, SUNY Oswego, 77-98; Co-coord, Women's Studies Prog, 78-80 & 82; Prof emer, 99; instr Intensive Eng Summer Prog, 92-. **HONORS AND AWARDS** Postdoctoral fel Multicult Womens Summer Inst, Univ of IL at Chicago, 83; Trailblazer Higher Educ Awd, Nat Orgn Women, Cent NY State, 87; Womens Ctr Awd Extraordinary Commitment Womens Issues, 96, Womens Ctr Awd Outstanding Dedication to Womens Ctr, 98, SUNY Oswego ; SUNY Oswego Intensive Eng Prog, 95, 96; SEED Awd, 98; Am Red Cross Overseas Asn Pres Citation Awd Soc Change, 98; research grant, PA State Univ, 70; research grants SUNY Oswego, 78, 91, 92, 94, 95, 96; Working Life grantee, 85, 87, 93, 94, 98; Coalition for Peace Edu Awd. **MEMBERSHIPS** Nat Commun Asn; Nat Womens Stud Asn; E Commun Asn; NY State Speech Asn; Soc Int Educ, Trng & Res; Am Red Cross Overseas Asn; Speech Commun Asn Puerto Rico. **RESEARCH** Japanese American women interned at Poston in World War II; Womens studies, English as a second language; Rhetoric and social change poet selected. **SELECTED PUBLICATIONS** contrib-auth, Multicultural Dilemnas of Language Usage, Why Don't You Talk Right, Multicultural Commun Perspectives, Kendall Hunt, 92; Benazir Bhutto: Feminist Voice for Democracy in Pakistan, Howard Jour Commun, 94; Helen Broinowski, Caldicott: pediatrician, peace activist, catalyst for the nuclear disarmament movement, Women Public Speakers in the United States, Greenwood Press, 94; coauth Feminism and Womans Life, Minerva Publ Co, 95. **CONTACT ADDRESS** 23 McCracken Dr, Oswego, NY 13126. **EMAIL** sanbonma@oswego.edu

LOVERING, JOSEPH PAUL
PERSONAL Born 02/16/1921, Calais, ME, m **DISCIPLINE** ENGLISH **EDUCATION** Col Holy Cross, AB, 43; Boston Univ, MA, 48; Ottawa Univ, PhD, 56. **CAREER** Instr English, St Anselm's Col, 46-48; asst prof, St Michael's Col, 48-56, assoc prof, 56-60, prof english & chm dept, Canisius Col, 60-, chm fac senate, 73-, Dir Grad English, 76- **MEMBERSHIPS** Col English Asn. **RESEARCH** American novel and poetry. **SELECTED PUBLICATIONS** Auth, S Weir Mitchell, Twayne, 71; Dorothy Canfield Fisher, Vt Hist; Gerald Warner Brace, S K Hall, 81. **CONTACT ADDRESS** Dept of English, Canisius Col 2001 Main St, Buffalo, NY 14208.

LOVING, JEROME M.
PERSONAL Born 12/25/1941, Philadelphia, PA, m, 1965, 2 children **DISCIPLINE** ENGLISH **EDUCATION** Penn State Univ, BA, 64; Duquesne Univ, MA, 70; Duke Univ, PhD, 73. **CAREER** From asst prof to prof, Tex A & M Univ, 73-; vis prof, Sorbonne, 84; vis prof, Univ Tex, 86; vis prof, Sorbonne Nouvelle, 89. **HONORS AND AWARDS** Fulbright, 78 & 89. **MEMBERSHIPS** Am Lit Asn, Int Asn of Univ Professors of English. **RESEARCH** Nineteenth- and Early Twentieth-Century American Literature, Walt Whitman, Theodore Dreiser. **SELECTED PUBLICATIONS** Auth, Civil War Letters of George Washington Whitman, Duke Univ, 75; Walt Whitman's Champion: William Douglas O'Connor, Tex A&M Univ, 78; Emerson, Whitman and the American Muse, Univ NC, 82; Whitman and Dickinson, Am Lit Scholar, 80-85; auth, Emily Dickinson: The Poet on the Second Story, 86; auth, Lost in the Customhouse: Authorship in the American Renaissance, 93; auth, Walt Whitman: The Song of Himself, 99 (in press); ed, walt Whitman: Leaves of Grass, Oxford Univ Press, 90; Frank Norris' McTeague, Oxford Univ Press, 95; auth, of numerous journal articles. **CONTACT ADDRESS** Dept English, Texas A&M Univ, Col Station, MSC 4227, College Station, TX 77843-0001. **EMAIL** j-loving@tamu.edu

LOVITT, CARL
DISCIPLINE ENGLISH LITERATURE **EDUCATION** Univ Wis, PhD, 81. **CAREER** Dept Eng, Clemson Univ **RESEARCH** International professional communication. **SELECTED PUBLICATIONS** Auth, The Rhetoric of Murderers' Confessional Narratives: The Model of Pieere Rivdere's Memoir, Jour Narr Techs, 92; Using Journals to Redefine Public and Private Domains in the Literature Classroom, When Writing Teachers Teach Literature, Boynton/Cook, 95; Defoe's Almost Invisible Hand: Narrative Logic as a Structuring Principle in Moll Flanders, 18th Century Fic, 93; coauth, Helping Student Writers Get Things Done: Teaching Genre in the First-Year Composition Course, MLA, 97; Portfolios in the Disciplines: Sharing Knowledge in the Contact Zone, New Directions in Portfolio Assessment, Boynton/Cook, 94. **CONTACT ADDRESS** Clemson Univ, Clemson, SC 29634. **EMAIL** lcarl@clemson.edu

LOW, ANTHONY
PERSONAL Born 05/31/1935, San Francisco, CA, m, 1961, 13 children **DISCIPLINE** ENGLISH LITERATURE **EDUCATION** Harvard Univ, AB, 57, MA, 59, PhD(English), 65. **CAREER** Asst prof, Seattle Univ, 65-68; from asst prof to assoc prof, 68-78, prof English, NY Univ, 78-, asst ed, Seventeenth-Century News, 68-73; vis scholar, Jesus Col, Cambridge, 74-75. **HONORS AND AWARDS** Pew Evangelical Fel 95; Honored Milton Scholar, 95. **MEMBERSHIPS** MLA; Milton Soc Am; Spenser Soc Am; Mod Humanities Res Asn; Renaissance Soc Am. **RESEARCH** Milton; Renaissance and 17th century literature; modern literature. **SELECTED PUBLICATIONS** Auth, Action and suffering: Samon Agonistes and the irony of alternatives, Pmla, 5/69; The image of the tower in Paradise Lost, Studies English Lit, Winter 70; Augustine Baker, Twayne, 70; Milton's God: Authority in Paradise Lost, Milton Studies, 72; The Blaze of Noon: A Reading of Samson Agonistes, Columbia Univ, 74; Milton's Samson and the Stage, with implications for dating the play, Huntington Libr Quart, 8/77; Love's Architecture: Devotional Modes in Seventeenth-Century English Poetry, NY Univ, 78; The unity of Milton's Elegia Sexta, English Lit Renaissance, Spring 81; The Reinvention of Love: Poetry, Politics and Culture from Sidney to Milton, Cambridge Univ, 93. **CONTACT ADDRESS** Dept of English, New York Univ, 19 University Pl, New York, NY 10003-4556. **EMAIL** low@compuserve.com

LOW, LISA
PERSONAL Born 05/20/1952, Boston, MA, m, 1991, 2 children **DISCIPLINE** ENGLISH **EDUCATION** Univ Wisc, BA, 74; Univ Mass, MA, 84; PhD, 86. **CAREER** Asst Prof, Cornell Col, 86-87; Visiting Asst Prof, Colby Col, 87-89, Asst Prof to Prof, Pace Univ 89-. **HONORS AND AWARDS** Kenan Grant; Charles Peters Shakespeare Awd, first runner-up; Dist Qualifying Exam, Univ of Mass, 82. **MEMBERSHIPS** Intl Virginia Woolf Soc, Milton Soc, Milton Soc of Am. **RESEARCH** Milton in the context of feminism and feminist history; Virginia Woolf's reading of Milton. **SELECTED PUBLICATIONS** Auth, "Listen and Save: Woolf's Allusions to Comus in Her Revolutionary First Novel," in Virginia Woolf: Reading the Renaissance, Ohio Univ Press, 99; auth, "Woolf's Allusions to Hedda Gabler in The voyage Out," Virginia Woolf Miscellany, (97): 3-4; auth, "Refusing to Hit Back: Virginia Woolf and the Impersonality Question," in Virginia Woolf and the Essay, Bedford, 97; auth, "Two figures in Dense Violet Night: Virginia Woolf, John Milton, and the epic vision of Marriage," Woolf Studies annual, (95): 65-88; auth, "Milton and Woolf in the women's Studies and English Literature classroom," in (Re)Reading, (Re)Writing, (Re)Thinking Virginia Woolf, Pace Univ Press, 95; auth, Milton, the Methphysicals, and romanticism, Cambridge Univ Press, 94; auth, "Thou Canst Not touch the Freedom of My Mind: fascism, Female Consciousness, and Narrative innovation in Mrs. Dalloway," in Virginia Woolf and Fascism, Macmillan Press, forthcoming; auth, "When Woolf Reads Milton: A Study in Feminist Intertextuality, Cambridge Univ Press; auth, Virginia Woolf and Literary History, St. Martin's Press, forthcoming; auth, "Undoing the Binaries: The Question of the Feminine in Paradise Lost," in Milton and Sexual Politics, Johns Hopkins, forthcoming; auth, "Ridding Ourselves of Macbeth", ed. Harold Bloom, Chelsea House, 91; auth, "In Defense of Hedda" in Drama Criticism (Detroit: Gale Research, 92). **CONTACT ADDRESS** Dept English, Pace Univ, New York, 1 Pace Plaza, New York, NY 10038-1502. **EMAIL** lisalow@aol.com

LOWANCE, MASON IRA
PERSONAL Born 06/02/1938, Atlanta, GA, m, 1963, 2 children **DISCIPLINE** ENGLISH AND AMERICAN LITERATURE **EDUCATION** Westminster School, 56-60; Princeton Univ, AB (cum laude), 60; Oxford Univ, BA, 64, MA, 67; Emory Univ, PhD, 67. **CAREER** Consult to Office of Ed, 65-78; instr in religion and English, Punahou School, 60-61; instr in English, Morehouse Col, 64-67; ASST TO PROF OF ENGLISH, UNIV OF MASS. **HONORS AND AWARDS** Guggenheim Fel, 82-83; Am Antiquarian Soc NEH Fel, 77; Nat Humanities Inst, Yale, 77-78; Distinguished Alumnus Awd, Westminster School, 92. **MEMBERSHIPS** MLA; Am Antiquarian Soc; Am Studies Asn; Soc of Early Americanists. **RESEARCH** American religion and literature; American religious history; nineteenth century American slavery and abolitionism; metaphor and symbolism in American literature. **SELECTED PUBLICATIONS** Auth, The Typological Writings of Jonathan Edwards, Yale Univ Press, 93; auth, The Stowe Debate: Rhetorical Strategies in Uncle Tom's Cabin, Univ of Mass Press, 94; auth, Spirituals, Encyclo of Am Poetry, Chicago, 98; Against Slavery: An Abolitionist Reader, Penguin, 00; auth, A House Divided: the Antebellum Slavery Debates in America 1776-1865, Princeton Univ Press, forthcoming. **CONTACT ADDRESS** Dept of English, Univ of Massachusetts, Amherst, Bartlett Hall, Amherst, MA 01003.

LOWE, JOHN
DISCIPLINE AFRICAN AMERICAN, SOUTHERN, AND ETHNIC LITERATURE **EDUCATION** Columbia, PhD, 81. **CAREER** Prof, La State Univ. **HONORS AND AWARDS** Fulbright scholar, India, 83; NEH summer sem, Berkeley, 84; Andrew W. Mellon Fac Fel in the Hum, Harvard Univ, 85-86; fac fel, Ford Found, 86-87; LSU Fac Res Awds, Summer, 89, 91; NEH travel to collections grant, 90; La Endowment for the Hum grant, 92; fel, Am Coun of Learned Soc, 92-93; Sr Fulbright Professorship, Univ Munich, Germany, 95-96. **MEMBERSHIPS** Pres, La Folklore Soc, 91-92; pres, MELUS, 97-. **RESEARCH** Humor; Hurston; Wright; Faulkner; Gaines; Louisiana literature; native American literature. **SELECTED PUBLICATIONS** Auth, Jump at the Sun: Zora Neale Hurston's Cosmic Comedy, 94; Coyote's Jokebook: Humor in Native American Literature and Culture, The Dictionary of Native Am Lit, 94; Wright Writing Reading: Narrative Strategies in Uncle Tom's Children, in The Modern American Short Story: Sequence as a Genre, 94; An Interview with Brenda Marie Osbey, The Southern Rev, 94; From Mule Bones to Funny Bones: the Plays of Zora Neale Hurston, Southern Quart, 95; I am Joaquin! Space and Freedom in Yellow Bird's Joaquin Murieta, Early Native Am Lit, 96; Humor and Ethnicity in Ethnic Autobiography: Zora Neale Hurston and Jerre Mangione, in Cul Difference and the Lit Text, 96; 'Change the Joke and Shift the Yoke': The Tradition of African American Humor, Presses Universitaires, 96; ed, Conversations with Ernest Gaines; coed, The Future of Southern Letters, 96. **CONTACT ADDRESS** Dept of Eng, Louisiana State Univ and A&M Col, 240C Allen Hall, Baton Rouge, LA 70803. **EMAIL** jlowe@unix1.sncc.lsu.edu

LOWE, WALTER G.
PERSONAL Born 01/10/1948, Seattle, WA, m, 1982, 5 children **DISCIPLINE** ENGLISH **EDUCATION** Univ Wash, BA, 70; Buffalo State Col, MA, 75; Unification Theol Sem, MReligEd, 91. **CAREER** English dept, Nangrahar Med Univ, 73-75; adj, Marist Col, 90-91; adj, Unification Theol Sem, 90-91; adj, Bellevue Community Col, 92-99; English instr, Green River Community Col, 93- . **MEMBERSHIPS** WAESOL, NCTE. **RESEARCH** American literature, English grammar. **CONTACT ADDRESS** Dept English, Green River Community Col, 12301 SE 320 St, Auburn, WA 98092-3622. **EMAIL** wlowe@grcc.ctc.edu

LOWNEY, JOHN
DISCIPLINE ENGLISH **EDUCATION** Univ MA, 79; MA, 86; Brown Univ, PhD, 91. **CAREER** Teaching Asst, Univ Mass, 85-86; Adv Teaching Fel to Adj Lecturer, Brown Univ, 87-92; Asst Prof, Ill Benedictine Col, 92-96; Asst Prof, St. John's Univ, 96-. **HONORS AND AWARDS** Grant, St John's Univ, 97, 98; NEH Grant, 94; Untermeyer Fel, Brown Univ, 89; Fel, Brown Univ, 86. **MEMBERSHIPS** Mod Lang Asn; William Carlos Williams Soc; Am Lit Asn; Am Studies Asn; Soc for the Study of the Multi-ethnic Lit of the US; NY Metro Am Studies Asn; NE Mod Lang Asn; NY Col Eng Asn; Am Culture Asn; N Eng Am Studies Asn. **SELECTED PUBLICATIONS** Auth, The American Avant-Garde Tradition: William Carlos Williams, Postmodern Poetry and the Politics of cultural Memory, Bucknell Univ Press, 97; auth, "Homesick for those memories: The Gendering of Historical Memory in Women's Narratives of the Vietnam War," in Burning Down the House: Recycling Domesticity, (Westview, 98), 257-278; auth, "A material collapse that is Construction: Gwendolyn Brooks' In the Mecca and the Poetics of Counter-Memory," MELUS, (98): 3-20; auth, "Truths of Outrage, Truths of Possibility: Muriel Rukeyser's The Book of the Dead," in How Shall We Teach Each Other of the Poet?: The Life and Writing of Muriel Rukeyser, (St. Martin's, 99), 195-208; auth, "Littered with Old correspondences: Elizabeth Bishop, Wallace Stevens, and the 1930s," Arizona Quarterly, (990: 87-114; auth, "Poetry, Property, and Propriety: Lorine Niedecker and the Legacy of the Great Depression," Sagetrieb, forthcoming; auth, "The Desert Music and Journey to Love," in The William Carlos Encyclopedia, Greenwood, forthcoming; auth, "Reading the Borders of 'The Desert Music'," in The William Carlos Williams Review, forthcoming; auth, "Langston Hughes and the 'Nonsense' of Bebop," American Literature, forthcoming; auth, "Haiti and Black Transnationalsim: Remapping the Migrant Geography of Hoe to Harlem," African American Review, forthcoming. **CONTACT ADDRESS** Dept Eng, St. John's Univ, 8000 Utopia Pkwy, Jamaica, NY 11439. **EMAIL** lowneyj@stjohns.edu

LOWRIE, MICHELE
PERSONAL Born 04/24/1962, New Haven, CT, m, 1988, 1 child **DISCIPLINE** CLASSICS **EDUCATION** Yale Univ BA 84; Harvard Univ PhD 90; Institute for Advance Study. **CAREER** New York Univ, asst prof 90-96, assoc prof, 97-. **HONORS AND AWARDS** Presidential Fell NYU; Burkhardt Fellowship, ACLS; Inst for Advanced Study. **MEMBERSHIPS** CS **RESEARCH** Latin lit; Augustan poetry. **SELECTED PUBLICATIONS** Auth, Horace's Narrative Odes, Oxford, Clarendon Press, 97, rev by Bryn Mawr Classical Rev 98; Spleen and the Monumentum: Memory in Horace and Baudelaire, Comp Lit, 97; A Parade of Lyric Predecessors, Horace Odes, Phoenix, 95; Lyric's Elegos and the Aristotelian Mean: Horace Odes, Class World, 94; Myrrha's Second Taboo, Ovid Metamorphoses, Class Philology, 93; Classical Review, Classical Philology, 99; Journal of Roman Studies, 99. **CONTACT ADDRESS** Dept of Classics, New York Univ, 25 Waverly Pl, New York, NY 10003. **EMAIL** michele.lowrie@nyu.edu

LOWRY, DAVID
PERSONAL Born 03/15/1953, Abilene, TX, m, 1976, 2 children **DISCIPLINE** MASS COMMUNICATION **EDUCATION** Abilene Christian Univ, BA, 76; MA, 78; Univ N TX, PhD, 82. **CAREER** Ex-instr, OK Christian Univ; dir, Edu Tech, Pepperdin; prof, 85-. **HONORS AND AWARDS** Freshman Seminiar Teaching Awd; Pres Seaver Fac Asn 00-01. **MEMBERSHIPS** Mem, Univ Acad Coun; Seaver Acad Coun; tchg, Pepperdine Overseas Intl Coun. **RESEARCH** Family communication, impact of new technology upon a variety of communication variables. **SELECTED PUBLICATIONS** Publ, area of interpersonal commun. **CONTACT ADDRESS** Pepperdine Univ, 24255 Pacific Coast Hwy, Malibu, CA 90263. **EMAIL** dlowry@pepperdine.edu

LU, XING L.
PERSONAL Born 05/26/1956, Beijing, China, m, 1981, 1 child **DISCIPLINE** RHETORIC, COMMUNICATION **EDUCATION** Beijing Second Foreign Lang Inst, China, BA, 82; Canberra Col, Australia, MA, 84; Univ of Ore, PhD, 91. **CAREER** Vis prof, Univ of Puget Sound, 91-91; from asst prof to assoc prof, DePaul Univ, 92- . **HONORS AND AWARDS** Ola Love Fel Am Asn of Univ Women, 88; James A. Winans-Herbert A. Wichelns Memorial Awd for Distinguised Scholarship in Rhetoric and Public Address for Rhetoric in Ancient China, Fifth to Third Century B.C.E.: A Comparison with Greek Rhetoric, 99. **MEMBERSHIPS** Nat Commun Asn; Am Soc of the Hist of Rhet; Asn of Chine Commun Studies. **RESEARCH** Class Chinese Rhetoric; Chinese commun studies; Interculture communication; Language and culture; Political discourse. **SELECTED PUBLICATIONS** Auth, On the Study of Chinese Rhetoric, The Western Jour of Commun, vol 57, 93; auth, Theory of Persuasion in Han Fei Tzu and Its Impact on Chinese Communication Behaviors, The Howard Jour of Communs, vol 5, 93; auth, Identity Negotiation in the Classroom, I Have a Story to Tell, ed. S. Jackson and J. Solis, 98; auth, Rhetoric and Philosophy in Ancient China: A Comparison with Ancient Greek Rhetoric from 5th-3rd Centuries BCE, 98; auth, In Interface Between Individualistic and Collectivistic Orientations in Chinese Cultural Values and Social Relations, The Howard Jour of Communs, vol 9(2), 98; auth, An Ideological/ Cultural Analysis of Political Slogans in Communist China, Discourse & Soc, Vol.10(4) (99): 487-508; auth, "A Rhetoric of Nationalism and Anti-Americanism in China Can Say No," Intercultural Communcation Studies, Vol. VIII-2 (99): 163-

176; auth, "A Sent Down Girl Speaks," Chicago Reader (99); auth, "The Influence of Classical Chinese Theories on Contemporary Communication," in Chinese Perspectives on Rhetorical and Communication, ed. D. Ray Heisey (Ablex Publishing Company, 00): 3-24. **CONTACT ADDRESS** 408 W Wilshire Dr., Wilmette, IL 60091-3154. **EMAIL** llu@wppost.depaul.edu

LUBBEN, JOSEPH
DISCIPLINE MUSIC THEORY **EDUCATION** Univ Notre Dame, BA, 85; Brandeis Univ, MFA, 89; Brandeis Univ, PhD, 95. **CAREER** Vis fac, Univ Notre Dame, 90-92; Brandeis Univ, 92-93; Visiting asst prof, Oberlin Coll, 95. **HONORS AND AWARDS** AMS50 Dissertation Fel, Am Musicol Soc, 93. **SELECTED PUBLICATIONS** Contribu, Mus Theory Spectrum, 93. **CONTACT ADDRESS** Dept of Mus, Oberlin Col, Oberlin, OH 44074.

LUBETSKI, EDITH
PERSONAL Born 07/16/1940, Brooklyn, NY, m, 1968, 3 children **DISCIPLINE** LIBRARY SCIENCE, JEWISH STUDIES **EDUCATION** Brooklyn Col, BA, 62; Columbia Univ, MSL, 65; Yeshiva Univ, MA, 68. **CAREER** Judaica Librarian, Stern Col for Women, 65-66, acquistion librarian, 66-69, head librarian, 69-. **HONORS AND AWARDS** Asn of Jewish Libraries Fanny Goldstein Merit Awd, in recognition of Outstanding Contribution to the Asn and Judaica librarianship, 93; Asn of Jewish Libraries: Nat Corresp Sec, 80-84, Pres, NY Chapter, 84-86, Nat Pres, 86-88. **MEMBERSHIPS** ALA, Asn of Jewish Librs. **RESEARCH** Judaica. **SELECTED PUBLICATIONS** Coauth with Meir Lubetski, Building a Judaica Library Collection (83); auth, The Jewish Woman: Recent Books (95); contributed articles to professional journals. **CONTACT ADDRESS** Hedi Steinberg Libr, Head Librarian, Stern Col for Women, 245 Lexington Ave, New York, NY 10016.

LUCAS, BRAD E.
PERSONAL Born 10/14/1969, Highland Park, IL, m, 1993 **DISCIPLINE** ENGLISH **EDUCATION** Univ Ill, BA, 92; SW Tex State Univ, MA, 94; Univ Tex, MLS, 96; Univ Nev, PhD, 01. **CAREER** Lectr, SW Tex State Univ, 94; lectr, Tex Lutheran Univ, 96; teaching fel, Univ of Nev, 96-01. **HONORS AND AWARDS** Outstanding Student Awd, UCCSN, 99; Outstanding TA Awd, UNR, 00; Scott Gordon Douglass Mem Teaching Scholarship, 00-01. **MEMBERSHIPS** Conf on Col Comp and Commun, NCTE, MLA, Assoc of Teachers of Advan Comp, Rhetoric Soc of Am, AAUP, Oral History Assoc, SW Oral Hist Assoc, RMMLA, Assoc of Teachers of Tech Writing, Grad Student Assoc, Holocaust Educ Found. **RESEARCH** Composition, Rhetoric, Pedagogy, Oral History, Academic Freedom, Cultural Trauma. **SELECTED PUBLICATIONS** Auth, "Bakhtinian Carnival, Corporate Capital, and the Last Decade of the Dead," Perspectives on the Grateful Dead: Critical Writings, (99); auth, "Traumatic Narrative, Narrative Genre, and the Exigencies of Memory," Utah For Lang Rev, (99); coauth, "Emerging (Web) Sites for Writing Centers: Practicality, Usage, and Multiple Voices under Construction," Taking Flight with OWLs: Examining Technology Use in Writing Centers, (00); auth, "Rude and Raucous Catcalls: Governor's Day, 1970," Nev Hist Soc Quart, (01). **CONTACT ADDRESS** Dept English, Univ of Nevada, Reno, Reno, NV 89557-0031. **EMAIL** brad@unr.edu

LUCAS, JAMES L.
PERSONAL Born 10/20/1923, Canton, OH, d **DISCIPLINE** ENGLISH **EDUCATION** Boston Univ, AB 1947; Cornell Univ Law School, LLB 1950; Univ of Chgo, MA English 1965; Univ of Chicago Divinity School, MA 1970; No IL Univ, PhD 1980. **CAREER** OH Indust Commiss, atty examiner 1953-57; Wittenberg Univ Springfield OH, instr english & humanites 1957-60; Harper Coll Palatine IL, instr english 1967-; TV Coll Chicago City Coll,TV instr 1970-74,84-; Chicago City Coll Wilbur Wright Coll, prof english 1965-. **HONORS AND AWARDS** Martin Luther Fellow United Lutheran Church of Amer 1950; author 2 manuals in Amer Literature for televised college courses publ by Chicago Ed TV Assoc 1970-,71; author The Religious Dimension of Twentieth-Century & Amer Lit publ by Univ Press of Amer 1982-; listed in Men of Acheivement 1977; author Executive Seizure Power Constitutional Power of the President to Seize Private Industry publ JAG Bulletin USAF 1959. **MEMBERSHIPS** Mem Bar of US Supreme Court 1955-, US Court of Military Appeals 1955-, Supreme Court of OH 1952-; lecturer fine arts, lit, humanites Chgo-Area Orgs 1965-; mem United Lutheran Church of Amer 1960, Sigma Tau Delta Natl English Honors Soc; Modern Lang Assoc 1975-, Natl Council of Teachers of English 1980-. **CONTACT ADDRESS** Wilbur Wright Col, City Cols of Chicago, Wilbur Wright Col, 3400 N Austin Ave, Chicago, IL 60634.

LUCAS, MARK T.
PERSONAL Born 06/05/1953, Georgetown, KY, m, 1978, 2 children **DISCIPLINE** ENGLISH LITERATURE **EDUCATION** Centre Col, BA, 75; Univ NC Chapel Hill, PhD. **CAREER** Fac 81, prof, current. **HONORS AND AWARDS** Hughes and Kirk Awds, Centre Col; Sears Found Tchg Prize; NEH Fellow; Hartsell Awd, Univ NC. **RESEARCH** Southern literature; William Faulkner. **SELECTED PUBLICATIONS** Auth, The Southern Vision of Andrew Lytle, La State Univ Press, 87; contrib, Fifty Southern Writers after 1900, Greenwood, 87; Companion to Southern Literature, La State Univ Press, 99; ed, Home Voices: A Sampler of Southern Writing, Univ Press of KY, 91. **CONTACT ADDRESS** Centre Col, 600 W Walnut St, Danville, KY 40422. **EMAIL** lucasmrk@centre.edu

LUCAS, STEPHEN E.
PERSONAL Born 10/05/1946, White Plains, NY, m, 1969, 2 children **DISCIPLINE** COMMUNICATION **EDUCATION** Univ CA, Santa Barbara, BA, 68; PA State Univ, MA, 71, PhD, 73. **CAREER** Asst prof, 72-76, assoc prof, 76-82, prof, Dept Commun Arts, Univ WI, 82-; vis assoc prof, Univ VA, 79. **MEMBERSHIPS** Pulitzer Prize nomination for Portents of Rebellion, 76; Speech Commun Asn Golden Anniversary Award for Portents of Rebellion: Rhetoric and Revolution in Philadelphia, 1765-1776, 77; Chancellor's Award for Excellence in Teaching, Univ WI, 88; IW Student Asn Excellence in Teaching Award, 92; elected to WI Teaching Academy, 97. **RESEARCH** Am political rhetoric; rhetorical criticism. **SELECTED PUBLICATIONS** Auth, Portents of Rebellion: Rhetoric and Revolution in Philadelphia, 1765-1776, Temple Univ Press, 76; The Schism in Rhetorical Scholarship, Quart J of Speech, Feb 81; Genre Criticism and Historical Context: The Case of George Washington's First Inaugural Address, Southern Commun J, summer 86; The Renaissance of American Public Address: Text and Context in Rhetorical Criticism, Quart J of Speech, May 88; Justifying America: The Declaration of Independence as a Rhetorical Document, in Thomas W Benson, ed, American Rhetoric: Context and Criticism, Southern IL Univ Press, 89; The Stylistic Artistry of the Declaration of Independence, Prologue, spring 90; The Art of Public Speaking, 6th ed, McGraw-Hill, 98; The Rhetorical Ancestry of the Declaration of Independence, Rhetoric and Public Affairs, summer 98; George Washington: The Wisdom of an Anmerican Patriot, Madison Housem 98. **CONTACT ADDRESS** Dept of Commun Arts, Univ of Wisconsin, Madison, Madison, WI 53706. **EMAIL** selucas@facstaff.wisc.edu

LUCID, ROBERT FRANCIS
PERSONAL Born 06/25/1930, Seattle, WA, m, 1954, 1 child **DISCIPLINE** ENGLISH **EDUCATION** Univ Wash, BA, 54; Univ Chicago, MA, 55, PhD, 58. **CAREER** Instr English, Univ Chicago, 57-59; asst prof, Wesleyan Univ, 59-64; from asst prof to assoc prof, 64-75, prof Eng, Univ Pa, 75-, Chmn Dept, 80-. **MEMBERSHIPS** Am Studies Asn (exec secy, 64-69); MLA; Aaup. **RESEARCH** Am lit; modern lit. **SELECTED PUBLICATIONS** Auth, "The Journals of Richard Henry Dana, Jr. 3 vols., The Belknap Press of the Harvrad Univ Press, 68; auth, Norman Mailer, the Man and his Work Little Brown, Boston, 71; auth, The Long Patrol, Twenty Five Years of Writing from the Work of Normn Mailer, World Publishing Company, 71; auth, "Aldridge and Fiedler: Presiding at the End," Michigan Quarterly Rev, (84): 289-293; rev, "Aesthetic Sensibility and the Idea of the Imagination in America," vol. 7, (85): 113-118; ed, "Prolegomenon to a Biography of Norman Mailer," in Critical Essays on Norman Mailer, G.K. Hall & Co., Boston, (86): 174-184; auth, "In Memoriam Robert E. Spiller: 1896-1988," Am Quarterly, (89): 522-525; co-ed, "In Honor of E. Sculley Bradley: 1897-1987," in Margin to Mainstream: The Broadening of the American Literary Canon, ed. Eugene A. Boldt, Jr., and Constance Harsh, (Philomathean Soc Press, Philadelphia, 92): 95-97. **CONTACT ADDRESS** Dept of English, Univ of Pennsylvania, Philadelphia, PA 19104. **EMAIL** rlucid@english.upenn.edu

LUDLOW, JEANNIE
PERSONAL Born 06/02/1961, Fountain County, IN, p, 1995, 1 child **DISCIPLINE** AMERICAN CULTURE STUDIES **EDUCATION** Bowling Green State Univ, PhD, 92. **CAREER** Instr, 90-98; prof, 98-, Bowling Green State Univ. **HONORS AND AWARDS** Diss Res Fel; Shankin Awd, Res Excel. **MEMBERSHIPS** NWSA; ASA; MMLA. **RESEARCH** Cultural studies approaches to various aspects of American Women's lived experiences and cultural expressions. **SELECTED PUBLICATIONS** Auth, "Working (In) the In-Between: Poetry, Criticism, Interrogation and Interruption," SML: Studies in American Indian Literatures (94); auth, "Priorities and Power: Adjuncts in the Academy," Thought & Action (98); auth, "Seaming Meanings: Wendy Rose, Diane Glancy and Carol Sanchez Writing In Between," forthcoming. **CONTACT ADDRESS** American Culture Studies, Bowling Green State Univ, 910 N Main St, Bowling Green, OH 43402-1819. **EMAIL** jludlow@bgnet.bgsu.edu

LUDWIG, RICHARD MILTON
PERSONAL Born 11/24/1920, Reading, PA **DISCIPLINE** ENGLISH **EDUCATION** Univ Mich, AB, 42; Harvard Univ, Am, 43, PhD(English), 50. **CAREER** From instr to assoc prof, 50-68, Prof English, Princeton Univ, 68-, Asst Librn Rare Bks & Spec Collections, 74-, Princeton preceptor, 54-57, Eng, 55-56, McCosh fac fel, 67-68. **MEMBERSHIPS** Am Studies Asn; MLA; Grolier Club. **RESEARCH** American and English novel; American poetry; American drama. **SELECTED PUBLICATIONS** Co-ed, Major American Writers, Harcourt, 52; ed, Aspects of American Poetry, Ohio State Univ, 63; Letters of Ford Madox Ford, Princeton Univ, 65; auth, Guide to American Literature and Its Backgrounds since 1890, Harvard Univ, 72; co-ed, Literary History of the United States, Macmillan, 74; ed, Dr Panofsky & Mr Tarkington, Princeton Univ Libr, 74; co-ed, Advanced Composition, Harcourt, 77. **CONTACT ADDRESS** Princeton Univ, 22 McCosh Hall, Princeton, NJ 08540.

LUEBKE, STEVE
PERSONAL Born 12/29/1957, Green Bay, WI, m, 1989, 1 child **DISCIPLINE** ENGLISH LITERATURE **EDUCATION** Univ Wis, MA, PhD. **CAREER** Prof, Univ of WI. **HONORS AND AWARDS** Wisconsin Teaching Fel. **RESEARCH** Contemp Am lit; fiction and poetry writing; lit and music; travel lit. **SELECTED PUBLICATIONS** Auth, Using Music and Television in the Fresman English Classics; auth, Contemporary Am Travel Fiction; auth, Original Poetry and Fiction; auth, Robert Silverberg; auth, pubs on Paul Theroux, Stephen Minot, Jack London; critical thinking. **CONTACT ADDRESS** Eng Dept, Univ of Wisconsin, River Falls, 410 S. 3rd St., PO Box 410, River Falls, WI 54022-5001. **EMAIL** steven.r.luebke@unrf.edu

LUEY, BETH EDELMANN
PERSONAL Born 02/23/1946, Columbus, OH, m, 1967, 1 child **DISCIPLINE** SCHOLARLY PUBLISHING **EDUCATION** Radcliffe Col, BA, 67; Harvard Univ, AM, 68; Nat Hist Publ & Records Comn, cert, 81. **CAREER** Managing ed, World Law Fund; asst & assoc ed, Univ Pittsburgh Press, 73-77; dir sch publ prog, Ariz State Univ, 80-. **MEMBERSHIPS** Asn Doc Ed; Women in Scholarly Publ; Soc Hist Authorship, Reading, and Publ. **SELECTED PUBLICATIONS** Auth, Handbook for Academic Authors, Cambridge Univ Press, 87, 90, 95; Editing Documents and Texts, Madison House, 90; coauth, The Structure of International Publishing in the 1990's, Transaction, 92. **CONTACT ADDRESS** Dept of Hist, Arizona State Univ, PO Box 872501, Tempe, AZ 85287-2501. **EMAIL** beth.luey@asu.edu

LUHR, WILLIAM
PERSONAL Born 03/03/1946, Brooklyn, NY, m, 1981, 1 child **DISCIPLINE** ENGLISH **EDUCATION** Fordham Univ, BA, 67; NY Univ, MA, 69; PhD, 76. **CAREER** Prof, St Peters Col, 76-. **HONORS AND AWARDS** Ariel Durant Fel, St Peters Col, 87, 90; NEH Fac Resources Fel, NY Univ, 93; Hon Scholar-in Residence, NY Univ, 98; Who's Who in the East; Who's Who in the World; Dict of Int Biog; Who's Who in Entertainment; Int Authors and Writers Who's Who. **MEMBERSHIPS** MLA, SCS, MEA, UFVA, Forum for the Psychoanalytic Study of Film. **RESEARCH** Media and society, fiction in film, developmental writing, broadcast studies. **SELECTED PUBLICATIONS** Auth, "The Scarred Woman Behind the Fun: Gender, Race and History in Recent Westerns," The Bilingual Rev/La Revista Bilingue, vol XX, No 1 (95): 37-44; ed, The Maltese Falcon: John Huston, Director (Rutgers Films in Print Series), Rutgers UP (New York), 95; auth, "Reception, Representation and the O K Corral: Shifting Images of Wyatt Earp," in Authority and Transgression in Lit and Fiom (Gainesville, FL: UP Fla, 96), 23-44; auth, "'Is That Supposed to be Funny?' -- Visual Humor in Film," Persistence of Vision, No 14 (97): 88-95; auth, "Border Crossings in 'Out of the Past' and 'L A Confidential'," The Bilingual Rev/La Revista Bilingue, vol XXIII, no 3 (98): 230-236; coauth, "Writing a Biography of Blake Edwards,: Biog and Source Studies, 4 AMS Press (98): 71-86; auth, "Mutilating Mel: Martyrdom and Masculinity in 'Braveheart'," in Mythologies of Violence in Postmod Media (Wayne St Pr, 99), 227-246; coauth, Thinking About Movies: Watching, Questioning, Enjoying, Harcourt, Brace and Co (Fort Worth, TX), 99; coauth, The Life of Blake Edwards, forthcoming; coauth, Blake Edwards: An Oral History, forthcoming. **CONTACT ADDRESS** Dept English, Saint Peter's Col, 2641 Kennedy Blvd, Jersey City, NJ 07306-5943. **EMAIL** luhr_w@spcvxa.spc.edu

LUKACHER, NED
PERSONAL Born 09/03/1950, York, PA, m, 1978 **DISCIPLINE** ENGLISH LITERATURE, COMPARATIVE LITERATURE **EDUCATION** Dickinson Col, BA, 72; Univ Ariz, MA, 74; Duke Univ, PhD(English), 78. **CAREER** Asst Prof English, Univ Ill, Chicago, 80-. **SELECTED PUBLICATIONS** Auth, K(Ch)ronosology, Sub-stance, Vol 25, 80; Notre-Homme-des-Fleurs: Wolf Solent's Metaphoric Legends, Powys Rev, Vol 6, 80; Schreber's juridical opera: A reading of the Denkwsrdigkeiten Eines Nervenkranken, Structuralist Rev, Vol 2, 81; Freud's Phantom, In: Psychoanalysing Psychoanalysis: Freud and the Hidden Fault of the Father, Johns Hopkins Univ Press, 82. **CONTACT ADDRESS** Univ of Illinois, Chicago, Chicago, IL 60680.

LUKENBILL, WILLIS B.
PERSONAL Born 03/27/1939, Smith Cty, TX, m, 1968, 1 child **DISCIPLINE** LIBRARY AND INFORMATION SCIENCE **EDUCATION** Indiana Univ, PhD, 73, Library Science (major), Instructural Systems Technology (minor); Dissertation title: Library/Media Technological Assistants in Louisiana; An Analysis of Needs, Problems and Prospects for Future Development, 73; Oklahoma Univ, M.L.S., 64, Library Science, (major), History (secondary field), Univ of North Texas State B.S. in Ed., Education, Hisotry, (major and teaching field),

Tyler Junior College, A.A., 59; History and Education areas of interest. **CAREER** Prof, Graduate School of Library and Information Science, Univ of Texas at Austin, 96-; Assoc Prof, Graduate School of Library and Information Science, Univ of Texas at Austin, 81-96; Asst Prof, Graduate School of Library and Information Science, Univ of Texas at Austin, 75-81; Asst Prof and Coordinator, Library Science Education (undergraduate program), College of Library and Information Services and College of Education, Univ of Maryland, College Park, 72-74; Instructor of Library Science, College of Education, Louisiana Tech Univ, Ruston, La., 64-69; Reference Librarian (Circulation, Reference, and Government Documents Supervisor), Austin College, Sherman, Texas, 64; Librarian, Seguin High School, Seguin, Texas, 61-63. **HONORS AND AWARDS** Temple Tchng Fel, Univ Tex, 87-88; Hall of Fame, Grad Sch Lib & Inf Sci, Univ N Tex. **MEMBERSHIPS** Am Lib Asn; Tex Lib Asn. **RESEARCH** Popular culture; youth media & literature; sociology of information delivery; AIDS-HIV information delivery. **SELECTED PUBLICATIONS** Auth, "AIDS Information Services in American Public Library: A National Comparison of Attitudes Held by Public Library and AIDS Service Directors," Library and Information Science Research 12, (90), 183-216; auth, "Interagency Cooperation in Providing AIDS-HIV Information: An Action Agenda for Public Libraries," AIDS Service Agencies, and Other Health Information Providers, Resource Sharing & Information Networks 9, (94), 45-54; auth, "Providing HIV-AIDS Information for Youth in Libraries A Community Psychology and Social Learning Approach," J of Youth Services in Libraries, 9, Winter, (95), 55-67; auth, AIDS-HIV Information Services and Programs in Libraries, Lib Ultd, 94; auth, Providing HIV-AIDS Information for Rural Communities: A Role for the Rural Public Library, Pub Libraries, 34, 284-290, 10, 95; auth, AIDS-HIV Services and Programs in Libraries, Encycl of Lib & Info Sci, vol 60, Marcel Dekker, Inc, 97; auth, "Erotized AIDS-HIV Information on Cable Television: A Study of Obscenity," State Censorship and Cultural Resistance, AIDS Educ & Prevention, 10, (98), 229-244; auth, "Historical Resources in the Local Church: A Field Report on the Largely Gay and Lesbian Congregation," American Archivist, 61, (98), 384-99; auth, "Information Resources Centers for Community-Based Organizations: A Field Study of an AIDS-HIV Service Agency," J of Interlibrary Loan, Documentt Delivery & Information Supply 9, no. 1, (98), 37-56; auth, "Observations on the Corporate Culture of a Gay and Lesbian Congregation," J for the Scientific Study of Religion, 37, (98), 440-452; auth, "Incestuous Sexual Abuse Themes in Contemporary Novels for Adolescence: A Culture Study," The New Review of Children's Literature and Librarianship, Vol 5, (99), 151-167. **CONTACT ADDRESS** Grad Sch of Lib & Info Sci, Univ of Texas, Austin, SZB 564, D7000, Austin, TX 78712. **EMAIL** luke@gslis.utexas.edu

LUMSDEN, LINDA

PERSONAL Born 12/22/1953, Hartford, CT, 2 children **DISCIPLINE** MASS COMMUNICATION **EDUCATION** Central Ct St Univ, BA, 78; Syracuse Univ, MA, 89; Univ NC Chapel Hill, PhD, 95. **CAREER** Asst prof, W Ks Univ, 96- **HONORS AND AWARDS** Minnie Rubinstein Grad Res Fel, 94 **MEMBERSHIPS** AEJMC; AJHA. **RESEARCH** Women's hist; jour hist; first amendment hist. **SELECTED PUBLICATIONS** Auth, Adirondack Craftspeople, Adirondack Publ Co, 83; Playing with Fire: A legal Analysis of Cross Burning in RAV w. St. Paul, Free Speech Yearbook, 93; Rampant Women: Suffragists and the Right of Assembly, Univ Tn Press, 97; Suffragist, Equal Rights, in Women's Periodicals of the US, Greenwood Press, 97; Feminist Press, New York Times, New York Herald Tribune, Suffrage Press, in History of the Mass Media in the US, Fitzroy Dearborn, 98. **CONTACT ADDRESS** Dept of J, Western Kentucky Univ, Bowling Green, KY 42101. **EMAIL** linda.lumsden@wku.edu

LUNARDI, EGIDIO

PERSONAL Born 06/09/1938, Lucca, Italy, d, 4 children **DISCIPLINE** LITERATURE **EDUCATION** Brown Univ, PhD, 76; MA, 69; Providence Col, BA, 64. **CAREER** Full Prof of Italian, Lake Erie Col, 88-; Assoc Prof of Italian, 82-88; Asst Prof, 75-81. **HONORS AND AWARDS** National Endowment for the Humanities, Dartmouth College, 86; Univ Calif, Los Angeles, 82; Stanford Univ, 79. **MEMBERSHIPS** AAUP; AATI. **RESEARCH** 20th Century Italian Literature; Dante Alighieri. **SELECTED PUBLICATIONS** Auth, "Giovanni Pascoli: Convival Poems Part I," Introd, Translation, Commentary, 79; auth, "Giovanni Pascoli: Convival Poems Part II," Introd, Translation, Commentary, 81. **CONTACT ADDRESS** Dept Arts & Sciences, Lake Erie Col, 391 West Washington St, Painesville, OH 44077-3309. **EMAIL** lunardi@lakeerie.edu

LUNDE, ERIK SHELDON

PERSONAL Born 10/16/1940, Hanover, NH, m, 1963, 2 children **DISCIPLINE** AMERICAN HISTORY, FILM HISTORY, FILM STUDIES **EDUCATION** Harvard Univ, AB, 63; Univ Md, MA, 66, PhD(Am Hist), 70. **CAREER** Asst prof Am Hist, Marquette Univ, 69-70; asst prof, 70-74, assoc prof, 74-79, prof Am Thought & Lang, Mich State Univ, 79-. **HONORS AND AWARDS** Outstanding Teacher Awd, Mich State Univ Chapter, Golden Key National Honor Society, 94. **MEMBERSHIPS** Am Film Institute. **RESEARCH** William Wyler; Alfred Hitchcock; D.W. Griffith; silent film. **SELECTED PUBLICATIONS** Auth, Horace Greeley, G K Hall, 81; co-ed with Douglas Noverr, Film Studies and Film History, Markus Wiener, 89; **CONTACT ADDRESS** Dept of American Thought & Lang, Michigan State Univ, 289 Bessey Hall, East Lansing, MI 48824-1033. **EMAIL** lundee@pilot.msu.edu

LUNDIN, ANNE

PERSONAL Born 11/27/1944, NJ, d, 2 children **DISCIPLINE** LIBRARY, INFORMATION STUDIES **EDUCATION** Ohio Wesleyan Univ, BA, 66; Univ Mich, MA, 67; La State Univ, MLS, 86; Univ Ala, PhD, 92. **CAREER** Assoc Prof, Univ Wis, 93-. **HONORS AND AWARDS** NEH Fel. **MEMBERSHIPS** MLA, ALA, Soc for the Hist of Arthurship and Publ. **RESEARCH** Victorian children's literature, library history, reading history. **SELECTED PUBLICATIONS** Auth, "In a Different Place: Feminist Aesthetics of the Picture Book," in Ways of Knowing: The Intellectual Life of Young People (Scarecrow Pr, 96), 203-231; auth, "The Pedagogical Context of Women in Children's Services and Literature Scholarship," Libr Trends 44:4, Univ Ill Pr (96): 840-850; auth, "Could Caldecott have Won the Caldecott? Victorian Views of Selection and Evaluation," J of Children's Lit 24:1, Ohio St UP: 28-40; auth, "Writing Kate Greenaway: Carrier Bag Autobiography," Children's Lit 26, Yale UP (98): 169-184; "Sensational Designs: The Cultural Work of Kate Greenaway," in Lit and the Child: Romantic Continuities/Postmodern Contestations, Univ Iowa Pr (forthcoming); auth, Victorian Horizons: The Reception of the Picture Books of Walter Crane, Randolph Caldecott and Kate Greenaway, Scarecrow Pr, forthcoming; auth, Defining Print Culture for Youth: The Cultural Work of Children's Literature, Ohio St UP, forthcoming. **CONTACT ADDRESS** Dept Libr & Information Studies, Univ of Wisconsin, Madison, 600 N Park St, Madison, WI 53706-1403. **EMAIL** alundin@facstaff.wisc.edu

LUNSFORD, ANDREA A.

PERSONAL Born 09/17/1942, Ardmore, OK, s **DISCIPLINE** ENGLISH **EDUCATION** Univ Fla, BA, 63; MA, 64; Ohio State Univ, PhD, 77. **CAREER** Asst prof to assoc prof, Univ British Columbia, 77-86; prof, Ohio State Univ, 87-00; prof to dir, Stanford Univ, 00-. **HONORS AND AWARDS** Regents Distinguished Prof Awd; Distinguished Scholar Awd; MLA Shaughnessy Awd; Best Essay Braddock Awd. **MEMBERSHIPS** MLA; ISHR; RSA; NCTE. **RESEARCH** History and theory of writing; collaboration and writing; gender and rhetoric; contemporary rhetorical theory and practice. **SELECTED PUBLICATIONS** Auth, Singular Texts, Plural Authors: Perspectives on Collaborative Writing; auth, Essays on Classical Rhetoric and Modern Discourse; auth, Reclaiming Rhetorica: Women in the History of Rhetoric; auth, Everything's an Argument; co-auth, The St. Martin's Handbook. **CONTACT ADDRESS** English Dept, Stanford Univ, Bldg 460, Stanford, CA 94305. **EMAIL** lunsford@stanford.edu

LUPACK, ALAN

PERSONAL Born 08/13/1946, New York City, NY **DISCIPLINE** ENGLISH **EDUCATION** Univ PA, PhD. **CAREER** Cur, Rossell Hope Robbins Libr & Koller-Collins grad ctr; taught at, St John's Univ, Wayne State Col NE & Univ Wroclaw Poland. **HONORS AND AWARDS** Elected Pres of the N Am Branch of the Int; developer, camelot proj www. **MEMBERSHIPS** Ed bd, Arthuriana and TEAMS Middle Eng Texts. **RESEARCH** Mod versions of the Arthurian legends, particularly the Arthurian legend in Am; medievalism in lit and the arts. **SELECTED PUBLICATIONS** Auth, The Dream of Camelot, poems; ed, Three Middle English Charlemagne Romances, Arthur the Greatest King: An Anthology of Modern Arthurian Poetry; Arthurian Drama: An Anthology, Lancelot of the Laik and Sir Tristrem, A Round Table of Contemporary Arthurian Poetry & special issue of Arthuriana on King Arthur in America; articles on, Sir Tristrem, Amer Arthurian lit & Arthurian youth groups. **CONTACT ADDRESS** Dept of Eng, Univ of Rochester, 601 Elmwood Ave, Ste. 656, Rochester, NY 14642. **EMAIL** alupack@rcl.lib.rochester.edu

LURIE, ALISON

PERSONAL Born 09/03/1926, Chicago, IL, m, 1996, 3 children **DISCIPLINE** CHILDREN'S LITERATURE, FOLKLORE **EDUCATION** Radcliffe Col, AB, 47. **CAREER** Lectr Eng, 69-73, adj assoc prof, 73-76, assoc prof, 76-79, Prof Eng, Cornell Univ, 79-, Frederic J Whiton Prof Am Lit, Cornell Univ, Yaddo Found fel, 63, 64 & 66; Guggenheim fel, 65; Rockefeller Found fel, 67. **HONORS AND AWARDS** New York State Cultural Coun Found Grant (CAPS), 72-73; Am Ac Arts & Lett Awd, Fiction, 84; Pulitzer Prize, Fiction, 85; Radcliffe Col Alumnae Recognition Awd, 87; Prix Femina Etranger, 89 **MEMBERSHIPS** MLA; Aaup; Children's Lit Asn; Pen Club; Author's Guild. **SELECTED PUBLICATIONS** Auth, Love and Friendship, Macmillan, 62; The Nowhere City, Coward McCann, 65; Imaginary Friends, 67, Coward McCann; Real People, 69 & The War Between the Tates, 74, Random House; V R Lang: Poems and Plays, with Memoir by Alison Lurie, Random House, 75; co-ed, The Garland Library of Children's Classics (73 vols), Garland Publ, 76; auth, Only Children, Random House, 79; Clever Gretchen and Other Forgotten Folk Tales, Crowell, 80; The Heavenly Zoo, Farrar Strauss, 81; The Language of Clothes, Random House, 81; Foreign Affairs, Random House, 84; The Truth abut Lorin Jones, Little Brown, 88; Don't Tell the Grownups: Subversive Children's Literature, Little Brown, 90; Women and Ghosts, Doubleday, 94; The Last Resort, Holt, 98; ed, The Oxford Book of Modern Fairy Tales. **CONTACT ADDRESS** Eng Dept, Cornell Univ, 252 Goldwin Smith Hall, Ithaca, NY 14853-0001. **EMAIL** al28@cornell.edu

LUSARDI, JAMES P.

PERSONAL Born 09/03/1931, Morristown, NJ, m, 1953, 2 children **DISCIPLINE** ENGLISH **EDUCATION** Lafayette Col, AB, 55; Yale Univ, MA, 57, PhD(English), 63. **CAREER** Instr English, Williams Col, 58-61; asst prof, Wesleyan Univ, 62-66; from assoc prof English to Francis A. March Prof of English, Lafayette Col, 66-. **HONORS AND AWARDS** Am Coun Learned Soc grant, 65; Jones Teaching Awd, 68; Senator of Phi Beta Kappa, 91-. **MEMBERSHIPS** MLA; Shakespeare Asn of Am; Int Shakespeare Asn; Columbia Shakespeare Seminar, exec bd; Am Philos Soc; NEH, 88. **RESEARCH** English Renaissance; dramatic and non-dramatic literature, especially Shakespeare. **SELECTED PUBLICATIONS** Co-ed, Yale Edition of 'St. Thomas More,' 73; co-ed, Shakespeare Bulletin, 84-; auth, Reading Shakespeare in Performance: King Lear, 91; auth, The Pictured Playhouse, Reading the Utrecht Engraving of Shakespeare London, Shakespeare Quart, Vol 0044, 93; articles in Shakespeare Quart, Shakespeare Yearbook, Hamlet Studies, Shakespeare on Film Newsletter, CEA Critic, On-Stage Studies, and various anthologies. **CONTACT ADDRESS** Dept of English, Lafayette Col, Easton, PA 18042. **EMAIL** lusardij@lafayette.edu

LUSCHER, ROBERT M.

PERSONAL Born San Diego, CA, m, 1975, 2 children **DISCIPLINE** AMERICAN LITERATURE **EDUCATION** Univ Calif, San Diego, BA; Duke Univ, MA, PhD. **CAREER** Instr, La State Univ; instr, dir, honors, ch, dept Eng, Catawba Col; prof, ch, dept Eng, Univ Nebr, Kearney. **HONORS AND AWARDS** NEH Summer Study Grant. **MEMBERSHIPS** MLA; MMLA; Soc for the Study of the Short Story. **RESEARCH** John Updike, the short story sequence. **CONTACT ADDRESS** Dept of Eng, Univ of Nebraska, Kearney, Kearney, NE 68849-1320. **EMAIL** luscherr@unk.edu

LUSHNIG, CECILIA EATON

PERSONAL Born New York, NY, m, 1970 **DISCIPLINE** CLASSICS **EDUCATION** City Col NYork, BA, 62; Univ Cincinnati, MA, 63; PhD, 72. **CAREER** Instr, Ohio Univ, 66-70; asst prof, Univ Wash, 73-74; prof, Univ Idaho, 75-. **HONORS AND AWARDS** APA Teach Awd; Phi Kappa Phi; Cen Hellenic Studies Scholar. **MEMBERSHIPS** CAPN; WCC; AFT. **RESEARCH** Greek Tragedy; language teaching. **SELECTED PUBLICATIONS** Auth, An Introduction to Ancient Greek: A Literary Approach, Charles Scribner's Sons, 76; auth, Latin and Literacy: An Essay on How and Why to Revive Latin in the Schools, Am Class League, 78; coauth, ETYMA: An Introduction to Vocabulary Building from Latin and Greek, UP Am, 82; auth, Vocabula: A Course in Latin Vocabulary Building, Class Asn New Eng Pub, 87; auth, Time Holds the Mirror: A Study of Knowledge in Euripides Hippolytus, EJ Brill, 88; auth, Tragic Aporia: A Study of Euripides' Iphigenia at Aulis, Ramus Monographs, 89; auth, Etymidion, rev ed, UPA, 94; auth, The Gorgon's Severed Head: A Study of Euripides' Alcestis, Electra, and Phoenissae, EJ Brill, 95. **CONTACT ADDRESS** Dept Foreign Lang, Univ of Idaho, 375 S Line St, Moscow, ID 83844-0001. **EMAIL** luschnig@uidaho.edu

LUSTIG, MYRON W.

DISCIPLINE INTERCULTURAL COMMUNICATION **EDUCATION** Univ Wis, PhD. **CAREER** Comm, San Diego St Univ; ed, Commun Reports; assoc ed, W Jour Commun. **MEMBERSHIPS** NCA, WSCA **RESEARCH** Interpersonal and Intercultural Communication. **SELECTED PUBLICATIONS** Auth, Intercultural Competence: Interpersonal Communication Across Cultures, 99. **CONTACT ADDRESS** School of Commun, San Diego State Univ, 5500 Campanile Dr, San Diego, CA 92182-4561. **EMAIL** rlustig@mail.sdsu.edu

LUTKUS, ALAN

PERSONAL Born 09/28/1940, East Chicago, IN, m, 1966 **DISCIPLINE** ENGLISH, LINGUISTICS **EDUCATION** Harvard Univ, BA, 62; Ind Univ, MA, 66, PhD, 75. **CAREER** Ndea Lectr Ling, Trinity Col, Conn, 68; Instr Eng & ling, Northern IL Univ, 69-71; Assoc Prof Eng & Ling, State Univ NY Col Geneseo, 73-; Chief Ling Consul, Amer Inst Tech, vocab series Wordscape, 90; media consult, NEH Amer radio Project, 96-97. **RESEARCH** Stylistics; film. **SELECTED PUBLICATIONS** Coauth, Arts and Skills of English: Daybook, Grades 3-6, Holt, 72-73; auth, Troublespeaking the approach to public doublespeaking: Purism and our concept of language, Col English, 76; coauth, Spelling Matters, 77 & The World of Spelling, Grades 1-8, 78, Heath; coauth, Spelling Worlds, Grades 2-6, Ditto Master Series, Heath, 79; Composition Theory Meets Practice and They Pretty Well Get Along Twice, Journal of Teaching Writing, 3, 84; Literacy Reconsidered For Better and Worse, Review essay, Journal of Teaching Writing, 2, 83. Buster Keaton, p265-272, Sir John Falstaff, p176-184, Touchstone, p466-470, in Fools and jesters in Literature, Art, and History: A Bio-Biographical Sourcebook, Greenwood Press, 98; **CONTACT ADDRESS** Dept of Eng, SUNY, Col at Geneseo, 1 College Cir, Geneseo, NY 14454-1401. **EMAIL** lutkus@genesco.edu

LUTZ, MARY ANNE
DISCIPLINE ENGLISH **EDUCATION** LaSalle, BA, 75; Rutgers, MA, 82, PhD, 86. **CAREER** ASSOC PROF, ENG, FROSTBURG STATE UNIV **MEMBERSHIPS** Am Antiquarian Soc **CONTACT ADDRESS** Dept of Eng, Frostburg State Univ, Frostburgh, MD 21532-1099.

LUTZ, REINHART
DISCIPLINE ENGLISH LITERATURE **EDUCATION** Univ Berlin, BA, 83; Univ CA, MA, 85; PhD, 91. **CAREER** Assoc prof, Univ Pacific. **MEMBERSHIPS** MLA; UOP; Soc Cinema Studies. **SELECTED PUBLICATIONS** Auth, publ(s) on Barry Malzberg; J.G. Ballard; Ohm Krueger. **CONTACT ADDRESS** Eng Dept, Univ of the Pacific, Stockton, Pacific Ave, PO Box 3601, Stockton, CA 95211.

LUTZ, WILLIAM
PERSONAL s, 1 child **DISCIPLINE** RHETORIC AND COMPOSITION, 19TH-CENTURY BRITISH LITERATURE **EDUCATION** Rutgers Sch Law, JD; Nev, Reno, PhD. **CAREER** Instr, Rutgers, State Univ NJ, Camden Col of Arts and Sci; ed, Quart Rev of Doublespeak 80-94. **HONORS AND AWARDS** Warren I. Sussman Awd for Excellence in Tchg, 91; George Orwell Awd for Distinguished Contribution to Honesty and Clarity in Pub Lang, 96; Rutgers Univ President's Awd for Public Service, 00. **SELECTED PUBLICATIONS** Auth, Beyond Nineteen Eighty-Four, NCTE, 89; Doublespeak , Harper-Collins, 89; The New Doublespeak, HarperCollins, 96; The Assessment of Writing: Politics, Policies, and Practices, Mod Lang Asn, 96; ed, Webster's New World Thesaurus, Simon and Schuster, 86; The Cambridge Thesaurus of American English, Cambridge, 94; auth, Doublespeak Defined, Harper Collins, 00. **CONTACT ADDRESS** Rutgers, The State Univ of New Jersey, Camden, Camden Col of Arts and Sci, Camden, NJ 08102-1405. **EMAIL** wlutz@crab.rutgers.edu

LUXON, THOMAS H.
PERSONAL Born 04/26/1954, Darby, PA, m, 1988, 2 children **DISCIPLINE** ENGLISH, LITERATURE **EDUCATION** Brown Univ, AB, 77; Univ Chicago, AM, 78, PhD, 84. **CAREER** William Rainey Harper Instr, 84-85, Univ Chicago; vis asst prof, 85-86, St. Lawrence Univ, NY; asst prof, 87-88, Franklin and Marshall Col; asst prof, 88-94, assoc prof, 94-, Dartmouth Col. **HONORS AND AWARDS** The Robinson Potter Dunn Premium in Eng, Brown Univ, 76; The Ratcliffe Hicks Premium in Eng, Brown Univ, 77; Univ Chicago Scholar for Grad Stud, 78-79, 81-82, 83-84; The Charlotte W. Newcombe Diss fel, The Woodrow Wilson Fel Found, 83-84; Nat Endowment for the Hum Fel for Independent Stud & Res, 86-87; Jr Fac fel, Dartmouth Col, 92; Venture Fund for Acad Computing, Dartmouth Col, 97. **MEMBERSHIPS** Modern Lang Asn; John Bunyan Soc of North Am; John Milton Soc; Renaissance Soc of Am. **RESEARCH** Early modern culture, especially relig and lit; critical theory; teaching writing; electronic editions of literary works. **SELECTED PUBLICATIONS** Auth, Other Men's Words and Bunyan's New-Birth, Texas Stud in Lang & Lit, 36, 94; auth, Literal Figures: Puritan Allegory and the Reformation Crisis in Representation, Univ Chicago Press, 95; auth, Rough Trade: Milton as Ajax in the Place of Punishment, Prose Stud: Lit, Hist, Theory 19, 96; auth, Single Imperfection: Manliness in the Age of Milton, Univ Chicago Press; A Second Daniel: The Jew and the True Jew in The Merchant of Venice, Early Modern Lit Studies 4.3, 99; Not Words Alone: Milton and Carnal Conversation. **CONTACT ADDRESS** Dartmouth Col, 6032 Sanborn House, Hanover, NH 03755. **EMAIL** thomas.h.luxon@dartmouth.edu

LVOVICH, NATASHA
PERSONAL Born 06/11/1956, Moscow, Russia, m, 1980, 2 children **DISCIPLINE** ENGLISH **EDUCATION** Moscow Ling Univ, BA, 76, MA, 78; Union Grad School, PhD, 95. **CAREER** Instr, Moscow Lang Training Ctr, 80-88; transl, Hebrew Immigrant Aid Soc, 88-89; instr, Sutton Bus School, 89-90; instr, Michel Thomas Lang Ctr, 89-94; instr, Touro Col, 90-94; consult, Jews for Racial & Econ Justice, 94-96; adj asst prof Dept Tchg & Learning, NY Univ, 95-97; adj lectr, 91-94, substitute instr, 94-95, adj asst prof, 95-97, substitute asst prof English, 97, ASST Prof English, 97- , Kingsborough Comm Col, CUNY. **MEMBERSHIPS** MLA; TESOL Int; NYS TESOL; CUNY ESL Coun; Ctr Appl Ling. **RESEARCH** Second language acquisition: Psycho-and sociolinguistic perspectives; Inter-cultural and affective dimensions of bilingualism; Acculturation and language learning; Socio-cultural identity and language. **SELECTED PUBLICATIONS** Auth, The Effect of the Affect: Psychosocial Factors in Adult ESL Student Language Performance, College ESL, CUNY, 95; The Multilingual Self: An Inquiry into Language Learning, Lawrence Erlbaum Assoc Publi, 97; Acculturation and Learning: A Multilingual View, CenterPieces, Kingsborough Comm Col, CUNY, 98. **CONTACT ADDRESS** Dept of English, Kingsborough Comm Col, CUNY, 2001 Oriental Blvd, Brooklyn, NY 11235. **EMAIL** NLvovich@kbcc.cuny.edu

LYDA, PAUL
PERSONAL Born 08/17/1946, Asheville, NC, m, 1969, 2 children **DISCIPLINE** ENGLISH **EDUCATION** Berea Col, BA; Univ NC at Charlotte, Med; Bob Jones Univ, EdD. **CAREER** Teacher, grades K-12, 4 years; Principal, 10 years; Col Teacher, 11 years; Academic Dean, 2 years. **HONORS AND AWARDS** Helped to establish several Christian Schools; reorganized an international Christian School in Seoul, Korea. **MEMBERSHIPS** Am Asn of Christian Schools, Am Conf of Academic Deans. **RESEARCH** Emotional handicaps, learning disabilities, special education. **CONTACT ADDRESS** Dept Ed, Pillsbury Baptist Bible Col, 315 S Grove Ave, Owatonna, MN 55060. **EMAIL** lydas@rconnect.com

LYLAK, EUGENE
PERSONAL Born 10/18/1946, Rothenburg, Germany, m, 1975, 3 children **DISCIPLINE** ENGLISH **EDUCATION** SUNY Buffalo, BA, 71; St. Michael's Col, MEd, 76; Univ Rochester, EdD, 95. **CAREER** Nat Tech Inst for the Deaf, Rochester Inst of Tech. **HONORS AND AWARDS** Outstanding Staff Member, RIT/NTID. **MEMBERSHIPS** TESOL; AERA; CAID. **RESEARCH** Deafness, Language Acquisition, English as a Second Language. **SELECTED PUBLICATIONS** Auth, "Commemoration and independence for Ukraine", Credit Union Opinion 118.2, UFCU, (Rochester, 85): 21; auth, "A response to current demographic studies within the Soviet Union", The Soviet Realities Project, eds L. Andolino and R. McKinney, RAUN, (NY, 85): 40-46; coed, The Art of Irene Banach-Twerdochlib, Harmony Pr, (Toronto), 87; auth, Deaf students' understanding of because and so, Univ Microfilms Int, 95; auth, "Film Review: The Key", J of Acad Media Libr, 97; ed, Mindscapes by Jack Slutzky, Oatka Creek Studios (Rochester, NY), 98; auth, "Resources for Teaching ESL Students Who Are Deaf", ESL Magazine, Nov/Dec 99. **CONTACT ADDRESS** Dept English, Nat Tech Inst for Deaf, 1 Lomb Memorial Dr, Rochester, NY 14623-5603. **EMAIL** exlnce@rit.edu

LYNCH, KATHRYN
PERSONAL Born 03/30/1951, Los Angeles, CA, m, 1974, 3 children **DISCIPLINE** ENGLISH **EDUCATION** Stanford Univ, BA, 73; Univ Virginia, MA, 78, PhD, 82. **CAREER** Asst Prof, Assoc Prof, Prof, 83 to 98-, Wellesley College; Lectr, 82-83, UCLA. **HONORS AND AWARDS** NEH 87, 97. **MEMBERSHIPS** MLA; MAA; Chaucer Soc. **RESEARCH** Chaucer; Medieval Lit; Dreams in Lit. **SELECTED PUBLICATIONS** Auth, Chaucer's Philosophical Visions, D.S. Brewer (Cambridge), 00; auth, The Logic of the Dream Vision in Chaucer's, House of Flame, Literary Nominalism and the Theory of Rereading Medieval Texts, Lewiston NY, 95; auth, East Meets West in Chaucer's Squire's and Franklin's Tales, Speculum, 95; Partitioned Fictions: The Meaning and Importance of Walls in Chaucer's Poetry, Art and the Context in Late Medieval English Narrative, ed, R R Edwards, Cambridge, 94; auth, The High Medieval dream Vision: Poetry Philosophy and Literary Form, Stanford, 88. **CONTACT ADDRESS** Dept of English, Wellesley Col, Wellesley, MA 02481. **EMAIL** klynch@wellesley.edu

LYNCH, ROSE MARIE
PERSONAL Born 09/09/1942, Linton, IN, m, 1977, 2 children **DISCIPLINE** ENGLISH **EDUCATION** Ind State Univ, BS, 64, MS, 64; Ball State Univ, PhD(English), 75. **CAREER** Instr English, Olney Central Col, 64-68; teaching fel, Ball State Univ, 68-70; Instr English & Jour, Ill Valley Community Col, 70-, newspaper advisor, Tech Prep team leader. **HONORS AND AWARDS** Connections 2000, Ill State Board of Educ, 93; Outstanding Fac Mem Award, Ill Comm Col Trustees Asn, 94; Illinois Prof of the Year, Carnegie Found for the Advanc of Teaching, 99; Connections 2000, Ill State Board of Educ, 99. **MEMBERSHIPS** Nat Sch Board Asn; Am Fedn of Teachers; LaSalle-Perm High Sch Board of Educ. **RESEARCH** Freshman composition programs, particularly in junior colleges. **SELECTED PUBLICATIONS** Auth, We Can't wish it away, ADE Bull, 5/76; auth, Junior college instructors do need special training, Conf Col Compos & Commun, 5/76; auth, The Advisor's Nightmare, Community Col Journalist, 88; auth, Reliving the past, Col English, 9/77; auth, Did I Miss Anything, Eng J, 4/91; coauth, Style Book, Illinois Valley Comt Col, 96; auth, "Tech Prep That Works," Tech Prep Notes: An ICCB e-Publication, 00. **CONTACT ADDRESS** Illinois Valley Comm Col, 2578 E 350th Rd, Oglesby, IL 61348-1074. **EMAIL** rmlynch@ivcc.edu

LYNCH, THOMAS PATRICK
PERSONAL Born 08/19/1930, Brooklyn, NY **DISCIPLINE** ENGLISH LITERATURE **EDUCATION** Fordham Univ, MA, 58; Columbia Univ, MA, 64, PhD, 69. **CAREER** Prof Eng, Greek & Latin, San Jose Sem, Quezon City, Philippines, 55-58; ch Eng, Ateneo Davao, Davao City, Philippines, 64-66; asst prof, Ateneo Manila, Philippines, 70-74; Prof Eng, St Peter's Col, Jersey City, NJ, 74-, Chmn Dept, 78. **MEMBERSHIPS** MLA; Col Eng Asn. **RESEARCH** Nineteenth and 20th century Am; Brit 20th century; Chaucer. **SELECTED PUBLICATIONS** Auth, Still needed: A Tuckerman text, Papers Bibliog Soc Am, 75. **CONTACT ADDRESS** Dept of English, Saint Peter's Col, 2641 Kennedy Blvd, Jersey City, NJ 07306-5997.

LYNGSTAD, SVERRE
PERSONAL Born 04/30/1922, Norway, 1 child **DISCIPLINE** ENGLISH **EDUCATION** Univ Oslo, Norway, BA(English), 43, BA(hist), 46; Univ Wash, MA, 49; NYork Univ, PhD(English), 60. **CAREER** Asst English compos, NY Univ, 49-53; lectr English compos and lit, City Col New York, 54-55; instr English, Hofstra Col, 55-60 and Queens Col, NY, 60-62; from asst prof to assoc prof, 62-68, Prof English, NJ Inst Technol, 68-, Ed consult Scand lit, Grove Press, NY, 63-68. **MEMBERSHIPS** MLA; Am Comp Lit Asn; Soc Advan Scand Studies; Int Soc Study Time. **RESEARCH** The novel, especially British, Scandinavian and Russian; time in literature; technology and human values. **SELECTED PUBLICATIONS** Auth, Helvetesfabel, World Lit Today, Vol 0066, 92; Min Steilende Love, Noveller Om Kjaerlighet, World Lit Today, Vol 0067, 93; 'Brekasjer'--Collected Poems 1970-1985, World Lit Today, Vol 0067, 93; A History of Norwegian Literature, World Lit Today, Vol 0068, 94; Dikt Og Spelmannsmusikk 1968-1993, World Lit Today, Vol 0068, 94; 'Dimension'--Special Issue, Scand Stud, Vol 0067, 95; Frokost I Det Skjonne, World Lit Today, Vol 0069, 95; Omrade Aldri Fastlagt, World Lit Today, Vol 0069, 95; Fimbul, World Lit Today, Vol 0069, 95; Kalenderdikt, World Lit Today, Vol 0070, 96; En 'Annen Vei', World Lit Today, Vol 0071, 97. **CONTACT ADDRESS** Dept of Humanities, New Jersey Inst of Tech, 323 High St, Newark, NJ 07102.

LYON, JANET W.
PERSONAL Born 10/30/1954, Springfield, MA, m, 1985, 2 children **DISCIPLINE** ENGLISH, LITERATURE, WOMEN'S STUDIES **EDUCATION** Yale Univ, New Haven, RN, 75; Trinity Col, BA, 82; Univ Vir, MA, 84; PhD, 92. **CAREER** Assoc prof, Univ Ill, 99-01; assoc prof, Penn State Univ, 01-. **HONORS AND AWARDS** Campus Wide Teaching Awd, Col Wide Teaching Awd, Univ Ill, 99. **MEMBERSHIPS** MLA; MSA; SDS. **RESEARCH** British modernism; feminist theory; women's literature; modern studies; disability studies. **SELECTED PUBLICATIONS** Auth, Manifestoes: Provocations of the Modern, Cornell UP, 99. **CONTACT ADDRESS** English Dept, Penn State Univ, 813 W Forester Ave, State College, PA 16801.

LYONS, BONNIE
PERSONAL Born New York City, NY, m, 1 child **DISCIPLINE** LITERATURE **EDUCATION** Newcomb Col, BA; Tulane Univ, MA, PhD. **CAREER** Prof; taught at, Newcomb Col, Boston Univ; Fulbright vis prof, Inst for Am Stud in Rome, Univ Haifa & Univ Tel Aviv; Fulbright sr lectr, Aristotelian Univ, Thessaloniki, Greece, Ctr Univ & Autonoma Univ Barcelona, Spain. **HONORS AND AWARDS** UTSA Res Leave; 3 UTSA Fac Res Awd(s); 2 Fulbright Prof; UTSA President's Distinguished Achievement Awd, Tchg Excellence, 91 and 98; AMOCO Tchg Awd, 85. **RESEARCH** 19th and 20th-century Am lit; 20th-century Brit and Continental lit; mod drama; the Eng Novel; Am Jewish lit; women in lit; drama as a genre. **SELECTED PUBLICATIONS** Auth, Henry Roth: The Man and His Work, Cooper Square Publ, 77; Philip Roth, Hellman, Bellow, Schwartz, Olsen, Chopin, Atwood; auth, "Passion and Craft: Interviews with Notable Writers, 98," Univ of Illinois. **CONTACT ADDRESS** Col of Fine Arts and Hum, Univ of Texas, San Antonio, 6900 N Loop 1604 W, San Antonio, TX 78249. **EMAIL** blyons@lonestar.utsa.edu

LYONS, BRIDGET G.
PERSONAL Born 08/28/1932, Prague, Czechoslovakia, m, 1971 **DISCIPLINE** ENGLISH LANGUAGE AND LITERATURE **EDUCATION** Radcliffe Univ, BA; Oxford Univ, MA; Columbia, PhD. **CAREER** Prof. **RESEARCH** 16th-17th century English literature; European Renaissance. **SELECTED PUBLICATIONS** Auth, Orson Welles: Chimes at Midnight, Reading in an Age of Theory; ed, Voices of Melancholy. **CONTACT ADDRESS** Dept of English, Rutgers, The State Univ of New Jersey, New Brunswick, 510 George St, Murray Hall, New Brunswick, NJ 08901-1167. **EMAIL** lyons@fas-english.rutgers.edu

LYONS, DECLAN P.
PERSONAL Born 12/03/1961, Galway, Ireland **DISCIPLINE** ANCIENT CLASSICS, FRENCH **EDUCATION** Nat Univ Ireland, BA; Univ Dublin, MLitt, 90; SUNY-Buffalo, PhD, 98. **CAREER** Tchg asst, SUNY-Buffalo, 88-92; res scholar, Univ de Geneve-Suisse, 92-93; asst prof Classics, Franciscan Univ, 94- . **HONORS AND AWARDS** Coun Euro res fel, Switz, 92-93; Ital Cult inst res awd, 98. **MEMBERSHIPS** APA; CAAS. **RESEARCH** Hellenistic Philosophy; Neronian Rome; SENECA; Hellenistic Poetry; Psychology and Classics. **CONTACT ADDRESS** Dept of Mod & Classical Lang, Franciscan Univ of Steubenville, 1235 Univ Blvd, Steubenville, OH 4395 **EMAIL** lyons@fran.u.edu

LYONS, TIMOTHY JAMES
PERSONAL Born 07/06/1944, Framingham, MA, m children **DISCIPLINE** FILM HISTORY AND HI RAPHY **EDUCATION** Univ Calif, Santa Barb MA, 68; Univ Iowa, PhD(speech and dramatic **REER** From instr to asst prof radio, TV and fil 72-76, chmn dept, 76-78, assoc prof, 76-80

Asn 76-. **MEMBERSHIPS** Soc Cinema Studies (secy, 75-77, pres, 77-79); Univ Film Asn. **RESEARCH** American silent film; Charles Chaplin. **SELECTED PUBLICATIONS** Auth, The Complete Guide to American Film Schools and Cinema and Television Programs, J Film and Video, Vol 0047, 95. **CONTACT ADDRESS** 2534 Poplar, Philadelphia, PA 19130.

LYONS-CHASE, ROSEMARY
PERSONAL Born 11/30/1948, New York, NY **DISCIPLINE** ENGLISH **EDUCATION** Manhattanville Col, BA, 70; Vassar Col, MA, 73; SUNY, DA, 00. **CAREER** Instructor to Assoc Prof, Columbia-Greene Cmty Col, 81-. **HONORS AND AWARDS** President's Awd for Excellence, 98. **MEMBERSHIPS** Mod Lang Asn. **RESEARCH** Literature against the grain: by women, minority writers, outsiders. **CONTACT ADDRESS** Dept Humanities & Fine Arts, Columbia-Greene Comm Col, 4400 Rte 23, Hudson, NY 12534-2907.

LYTAL, BILLY D.
PERSONAL Born 10/01/1939, Prentiss County, MS, m, 1961, 2 children **DISCIPLINE** COMMUNICATIONS **EDUCATION** Miss Col, BA, 61; Univ Miss, MA, 64; Univ Southern Miss, PhD, 80. **CAREER** Instr of Comm, Chairman Dept. of Comm, Miss Col, 65-. **HONORS AND AWARDS** Chemn, Advertising comm, Public Relations comm; chemn, Miss Col. **MEMBERSHIPS** Miss Speech; Comm Asn. **RESEARCH** Audience profile **CONTACT ADDRESS** 115 E Lakeview, Clinton, MS 39056. **EMAIL** lytal@mc.edu

M

MA, QIAN
DISCIPLINE ENGLISH LITERATURE **EDUCATION** Emory Univ, PhD. **CAREER** Dept Eng, Clark Atlanta Univ **RESEARCH** Comparative literature (Chinese and English); feminist literary criticism, especially feminist utopian studies; Chinese literature; 18th century British literature. **SELECTED PUBLICATIONS** Auth, published a book in China on the history of English literature. **CONTACT ADDRESS** Clark Atlanta Univ, 223 James P Brawley Dr, SW, Atlanta, GA 30314.

MACCHIARULO, LOUIS
PERSONAL Born 01/04/1958, Queens, NY, m, 1983, 2 children **DISCIPLINE** CLASSICS **EDUCATION** Fordham Univ, PhD, 86. **CAREER** Instr Latin, Greek & Italian, Regis High School. **HONORS AND AWARDS** Assistantship, Fordham Univ, 79-81; Fordham Univ Fel, 81-83. **MEMBERSHIPS** APA; Virgilian Soc **RESEARCH** Homer; Virgil, Dante, Roman History **SELECTED PUBLICATIONS** The Life and Times of Fortunato, PhD Thesis. **CONTACT ADDRESS** 55 E 84th St, New York, NY 10028.

MACCOULL, LESLIE
PERSONAL Born 08/07/1945, New London, CT, s **DISCIPLINE** CLASSICS; SEMITICS (COPTIC) **EDUCATION** Vassar Col, AB, 65, summa cum laude; Yale Univ, MA, 66; Catholic Univ of Amer, PhD with distinction, 73. **CAREER** Curator, 74-78, Inst of Christian Oriental Research, Catholic Univ; dir of studies, 78-84, Soc for Coptic Archaeology Cairo; senior research scholar (North Am), 84- , adjunct, 97, AZ Ctr for Medieval and Renaissance Studies, AZ State Univ. **HONORS AND AWARDS** Phi Beta Kappa 64; Dumbarton Oaks jr fel 69-71; summer fel, 83; fel, 90-91; fel, Ameri Research Ctr in Egypt, 78-79; NEH Fel, 93-94. **MEMBERSHIPS** Amer Soc of Papyrologists; Intl Assn for Coptic Studies; US Natl Committee for Byzantine Studies, Mensa. **RESEARCH** Coptic papyrology; Byzantine papyrology; social and cultural hist of lat antiquity. **SELECTED PUBLICATIONS** Auth, Dated and datable Coptic documentary hands before A.D. 700, Le Museon, 97; auth, The Triadon: an English translation, Greek Orthodox Theological Review, 97; auth, Chant in Coptic pilgrimage, in Pilgrimage and Holy Space in Late Antique Egypt, 98; auth, BM 1075: A Sixth-Century Tax Register from the Hermopolite, in press; coauth, Catalogue of the Illustrated Manuscripts in the Coptic Museum, in press; auth, The Historical Background of John Philoponus' De Opificio Mundi in the Culture of Byzantine-Coptic Egypt, Zeitshrift fur Autkes Christeutum, in press. **CONTACT ADDRESS** 914 E Lemon St, #137, Tempe, AZ 85281. **EMAIL** haflele@imap4.asu.edu

MACCURDY, MARIAN
DISCIPLINE ENGLISH **EDUCATION** Syracuse Univ, PhD, 80. **CAREER** Istructor, Syracuse Univ, 80-85; Asst Prof to Assoc Prof and Chair, Ithaca Col, 85-. **HONORS AND AWARDS** Pearl Muse Awd, Muse Nat Poetry competition, 89. **MEMBERSHIPS** NCTE, CCCC, Assoc Writing Programs. **RESEARCH** Writing and healing; Personal essay and memoir; Women's studies. **SELECTED PUBLICATIONS** Auth, "Truth, Trauma, and Justice in Gillian Slovo's Every Secret Thing," Literature and Medicine, 00; auth, "Writing and Healing, Nat Coun of Teachers of English Press, 00; auth, "Food for the Gods," Ararat, (98): 9-12; auth, "Monsters from the Id," Ararat, (97): 12-14; auth, "The Grape Arbor," "For the Women Warriors," "Apparition," and "Shooting Star," (poems) in Ararat, (96): 12; auth, "From Image to Narrative: The Politics of the Personal," Journal of Teaching Writing, (95): 75-108; auth, "The four women of the apocalypse: Feminine Images in Magazine advertisements," in Utopia and Gender in advertising: a Critical Reader, Syracuse Univ Press, 94; auth, "Irony" and "Healing" (poems), Journal of Poetry Therapy, (92): 132-133; auth, "Bitch or Goddess; Polarized Images of Women in Arthurian Film," Platte Valley Review, (90): 3-24. **CONTACT ADDRESS** Dept Writing, Ithaca Col, 953 Danby Rd, Ithaca, NY 14850-7000. **EMAIL** maccurdy@ithaca.edu

MACDONALD, MARGARET READ
PERSONAL Born 01/21/1940, Seymour, IN, m, 1965, 2 children **DISCIPLINE** FOLKLORE; CHILDREN'S LITERATURE **EDUCATION** Ind Univ, AB, 62, PhD, 79; Univ Wash, Seattle, MLS, 64; Univ Hawaii, MEdEc, 68. **CAREER** Children's Specialist, 64-72, Childrens Lbn, 77-, King Co Lib System, Seattle, Wash; Vis Lecturer, Univ Wash, Seattle, 75-79, 96-. **HONORS AND AWARDS** Fulbright Schol, 95-96; Nat Storytelling Asn Leadership Awd, 98. **MEMBERSHIPS** Am Folklore Soc; Am Library Asn; Nat Storytelling Asn; Int Bd on Books for Youth; Soc of Children's Book Writers & Illustrators. **RESEARCH** Personal narrative; performance theory; the folktale. **SELECTED PUBLICATIONS** Auth, The Storyteller's Sourcebook: A Subject, Title, and Motif Index to Folklore Collections for Children, Gale, 82; auth, Scipio, Indiana: Threads from the Past, Ye Galleon, 88; auth, The Folklore of World Holidays, Gale, 91; auth, The Storyteller's Start-up Book: Finding, Learning, Performing, and Using Folktales, Aug Hse, 93; auth, Scipio Storytelling: Talk in a Southern Indiana Community, Univ Press of Am, 96; ed, Thai Tales: Folktales of Thailand by Supaporn Vathanaprida, Libraries Unltd, 94; auth, Traditional Storytelling Today: An International Sourcebook, Fitzroy Dearborn, 99. **CONTACT ADDRESS** 11507 NE 104th, Kirkland, WA 98083. **EMAIL** margmacd@kcls.org

MACDONALD, ROBERT HUGH
PERSONAL Born 06/15/1934, Manchester, England, m, 1959, 2 children **DISCIPLINE** ENGLISH LITERATURE **EDUCATION** NY Univ, AB, 59; Univ Edinburgh, dipl English studies, 63, PhD(English), 69. **CAREER** Asst prof, 68-71, assoc prof, 71-79, Prof English, Carleton Univ, 79-. **RESEARCH** The novel; myth and symbol. **CONTACT ADDRESS** Dept of English, Carleton Univ, 1125 Colonel By Dr, Ottawa, ON, Canada KIS 5B6.

MACE, SARAH
DISCIPLINE CLASSICS **EDUCATION** Colby Col, BA, 82, Univ Penn, MA, 85; Yale Univ, PhD, 92. **CAREER** Lectr, Univ Penn, 92-93; vis asst prof, Columbia Univ, 93-94; vis asst prof, Dartmouth Col, 94-95; vis asst prof, 95-97, asst prof, 97-, Union Col. **HONORS AND AWARDS** Charles C Sherman fel, 86-87; Yale Univ fel, 87-89; 85-86; Whiting Diss Fel, 90-91. **RESEARCH** Homer, Hesiod and the epic tradition; Presocratica; Archaic Greek lyric; Epinician; Aeschylus; Lucretius. **SELECTED PUBLICATIONS** Auth, Utopian and Erotic Fusion in a New Elegy of Simonides, APE, 96; rev of Lesbian Desire in the Lyrics of Sappho by Snyder, AJP, forthcoming. **CONTACT ADDRESS** Dept of Classics, Union Col, New York, Schenectady, NY 12308. **EMAIL** maces@idol.union.edu

MACEWEN, SALLY
PERSONAL Born Abington, PA **DISCIPLINE** CLASSICAL LANGUAGES AND LITERATURES **EDUCATION** Mt Holyoke Col, BA, 70; Univ Pa, PhD, 81. **CAREER** Vis Lectr, Univ Ut, 79-82; Asst Prof to Assoc Prof, Agnes Scott Col, 82-. **HONORS AND AWARDS** Human Relations Awd, Agnes Scott Col; Liberty Bell Awd, Decatur-DeKalb Bar Asn; DuPont Fac Develop Grant; Grant, NEH. **MEMBERSHIPS** Am Philol Asn; Class Asn of the Middle W and S; Ga Class Asn; Am Class League; Women's Class Caucus; Asn for Moral Educ. **RESEARCH** Greek Drama; Greek history; Diversity studies; Latin poetry; Gender studies. **SELECTED PUBLICATIONS** Auth, "Classical Drama and the American Western," Classical Bulletin, 97; auth, "Observations by a Classicist on Teaching Diversity on a Predominantly White Campus," Classical World, 02. **CONTACT ADDRESS** Dept Lang, Agnes Scott Col, 141 E College Ave, Decatur, GA 30030. **EMAIL** smacewen@agnesscott.edu

MACHANN, CLINTON J.
PERSONAL Born 07/18/1947, Bryan, TX, m, 1974, 3 children **DISCIPLINE** ENGLISH **EDUCATION** Tex A & M Univ, BA, 69; Univ Tex, PhD, 76. **CAREER** Prof, Tex A & M Univ, 76-. **HONORS AND AWARDS** Fulbright lectureship, Charles Univ Prague, 90. **MEMBERSHIPS** Mod Lang Asn, Czechoslovak Soc of Arts and Sci, Czech Educ Foundation of Tex. **RESEARCH** British Victorian Literature; Am Ethnic Literatures and Cultures; Slavic Studies. **SELECTED PUBLICATIONS** Auth, Matthew Arnold: A Literary Life, Macmillan, 98; auth, The Genre of Autobiography in Victorian Literature, Univ Mich Press, 94; auth, Czech-Americans in Transition, Eakin Press, 99. **CONTACT ADDRESS** Dept English, Texas A&M Univ, Col Station, MSC 4227, College Station, TX 77843-4227. **EMAIL** c-machann@tamu.edu

MACHANN, VIRGINIA
PERSONAL Born 12/04/1945, NE, m, 1974, 3 children **DISCIPLINE** ENGLISH **EDUCATION** Univ Neb, BA, 67; MA, 71; Univ Tex, PhD, 79. **CAREER** Teachers Aid, Univ Tex Austin, 71-78; Visiting Asst Prof, Tex A&M, 78; CEO, On the Double Inc, 79-92; Instructor, Blinn Col, 93-. **CONTACT ADDRESS** Dept Humanities, Blinn Col, PO Box 6030, Bryan, TX 77805-6030. **EMAIL** gmachann@ucmail.blinncol.edu

MACHOR, JAMES
PERSONAL Born 10/13/1950, Cleveland, OH, m, 1972, 1 child **DISCIPLINE** AMERICAN, ENGLISH LITERATURE **EDUCATION** Oh Univ, BA, 72; Univ Idaho, MA, 74; Univ Ill, PhD, 80. **CAREER** Asst prof, 80-86; assoc prof, 86-90, Ohio State Univ; vis sr lectr, Univ Brussels, 91; assoc prof, Kansas State Univ, 90-95; prof, Kansas State Univ, 95-. **HONORS AND AWARDS** Fulbright Fel, ALAS, Univ Brussels, 91; Outstand Schl Awd, Ohio State Univ, 88; NEH Fel, 86; Clifford Prize, ASECS, 82-83. **MEMBERSHIPS** MLA; ASA; ALA. **RESEARCH** 19th C American fiction; reader-response and reception criticism and theory; feminist criticism; Colonial American writing and culture. **SELECTED PUBLICATIONS** Auth, "Poetics as Ideological Hermeneutics: American Fiction and the Historical Reader of the Early Nineteenth Century," Reader: Essays in Reader-Oriented Theory, Criticism, and Pedagogy 25 (91): 49-64; auth, Informed Reading and Early Nineteenth-Century American Fiction," Nineteenth-Century Literature 47 (92): 320-48; ed, "Historical Hermeneutics and Antebellum Fiction: Gender, Response Theory, and Interpretive Contexts." Readers in History (Baltimore: Johns Hopkins UP, 93), 54-84; auth, "Searching for Targets with a Loaded Canon," ESQ: J American Renaissance 39 (93): 185-206; ed, Readers in History: Nineteenth-Century American Literature and the Contexts of Response (Baltimore: Johns Hopkins Univ Press, 93); auth, "Canon Exchanges and the Changing Profession," J Midwest Modern Language Association 31.2 (98): 24-30; co-ed, Reception Study: From Literary Theory to Cultural Studies (New York: Routledge, 00). **CONTACT ADDRESS** Dept English, Kansas State Univ, 122 Dennison Hall, Manhattan, KS 66506-0700. **EMAIL** machor@ksu.edu

MACK, MICHAEL
PERSONAL Born 08/11/1963, Detroit, MI, s **DISCIPLINE** ENGLISH **EDUCATION** Harvard Univ, AB, 85; Manhattanville Univ, MA, 89; Columbia Univ, MA, 91; M Phil, 94; PhD, 98. **CAREER** Teach asst, Columbia Univ, 91-92; prece, 92-96; instr, Catholic Univ, 97-98; asst prof, 98-. **MEMBERSHIPS** Shakespeare Asn Am. **RESEARCH** Shakespeare; 16th and 17th C English literature. **SELECTED PUBLICATIONS** Auth, "The Analogy of God and Man in Sidney and Shakespeare," Columbia Univ (98). **CONTACT ADDRESS** Dept English, Catholic Univ of America, 620 Michigan Ave, Washington, DC 20064-0001. **EMAIL** mackm@cua.edu

MACK, ROBERT
DISCIPLINE 18TH-CENTURY BRITISH LITERATURE **EDUCATION** Princeton Univ, PhD. **CAREER** Instr, Vanderbilt Univ. **RESEARCH** Biography of Thomas Gray. **SELECTED PUBLICATIONS** Ed, Oriental Tales; Arabian Nights' Entertainments; Horace Walpole's The Castle of Otranto; co-ed, Frances Burney's The Wanderer. **CONTACT ADDRESS** Vanderbilt Univ, Nashville, TN 37203-1727.

MACK, S. THOMAS
DISCIPLINE AMERICAN LITERATURE **EDUCATION** W Chester Univ, BA, 69; John Carroll Univ, MAT, 70; Villanova Univ, MA, 73; Lehigh Univ, PhD, 76. **CAREER** Prof, Univ SC Aiken, 76- ; lectr, Shanxi Univ, Taiyuan, People's Repub of China. **HONORS AND AWARDS** Outstanding Teacher of the Year, 79-80; Amoco Found Outstanding Teaching Awd, 80; Univ Svc Awd, 88-89; Comm Svc Awd, 92-93. **SELECTED PUBLICATIONS** Auth, A Measure of Time, Masterpieces of African Am Lit, Harper Collins, 92; auth, Christopher Coe, Identitites and Issues in Lit, Salem Pr, 97; auth, Percival Everett, in Contemporary Southern Writers, St. James Press, 98; Alnilam, in Cyclopedia of Literary Characters, Salem Press, 98. **CONTACT ADDRESS** 53 Deerwood Ct, Aiken, SC 29803. **EMAIL** tomm@aiken.sc.edu

MACK, SARA
PERSONAL Born 05/01/1939, New Haven, CT, w, 2 children **DISCIPLINE** CLASSICS **EDUCATION** AM, 64, PhD, 74, Harvard Univ. **CAREER** Asst/Assoc/Full Prof, 76-, UNC-Chapel Hill. **HONORS AND AWARDS** Bowman and Gordon Gray Professorship, 94-97; Fellowship, Natl Humanities Ctr. **MEMBERSHIPS** Amer Philological Assoc; Assoc of Literary Scholars and Critics; Classics Assoc of the Midwest and South; NC Classical Assoc; Virgilian Soc. **RESEARCH** Latin Poetry; Greek and Latin epic; Euripides. **SELECTED PUBLICATIONS** Auth, Ovid (Hermes Books), 88; reviews, Allen Mandelbaum, The Metamorphoses of Ovid: A New Verse Translation, 94; Carole Newlands, Playing with Time, Ovid and the Fasti, 97; auth, "Pattern of Time in Vergil's Aeneid, Oklahoma 99; auth, "Ruit Oceano Nox," cq 80; auth, "The Single Supplie" Ramus 81; auth, "Teaching Ovid's Orpheus to Beginners" CJ 96; auth, "Acis and Galatea," Arion 99; rev, "Wiltshire, Public & Private in Vergil's Aenerd," 90; auth, "Cairs, Virgil's Augus-

tan Epic," 92; auth, "Farreu, Virgil's Georgies & The Traditaes or Aenerd Epic, Mynas, Virgil Geargics, 94. **CONTACT ADDRESS** Univ of No Carolina, Chapel Hill, 212 Murphey Hall, CB #3145, Chapel Hill, NC 27599-3145. **EMAIL** smack@email.unc.edu

MACKAY, CAROL HANBERY
PERSONAL Born 07/01/1944, San Francisco, CA **DISCIPLINE** ENGLISH LITERATURE, RHETORIC AND COMPOSITION **EDUCATION** Stanford Univ, BA, 66, MA, 67; Univ Calif, Los Angeles, PhD(English), 79. **CAREER** Asst Prof English, Univ Tex, Austin, 79-, Teach assoc and fel, Univ Calif, Los Angeles, 74-78; consult, Nat Inst Educ Writing Proficiency Assessment, 80-. **HONORS AND AWARDS** Outstanding New Teacher, Amoco Found, 81. **MEMBERSHIPS** MLA; NCTE; Conf Col Compos and Commun. **RESEARCH** The novel; 19th century English literature. **SELECTED PUBLICATIONS** Auth, Soaring Between Home and Heaven + Victorian Photography--Cameron, Julia, Margeret Visual Meditations on the Self, Libr Chronicle of the Univ Tex at Austin, Vol 0026, 96. **CONTACT ADDRESS** Dept English, Univ of Texas, Austin, 0 Univ of Texas, Austin, TX 78712-1026.

MACKENDRICK, LOUIS KING
DISCIPLINE ENGLISH LANGUAGE; LITERATURE **EDUCATION** Western Ontario, BA, MA; Toronto, PhilM, PhD, 71. **CAREER** Prof **RESEARCH** Canadian short story. **SELECTED PUBLICATIONS** Auth, Robert Harlow and His Works; Al Purdy and His Works & Some Other Reality: Alice Munro's Something I've Been Meaning to Tell You; ed, Probable Fictions: Alice Munro's Narrative Acts & issue of Essays on Canadian Writing on Al Purdy. **CONTACT ADDRESS** Dept of English Language and Literature, Univ of Windsor, 401 Sunset Ave, Windsor, ON, Canada N9B 3P4. **EMAIL** mackena@uwindsor.ca

MACKENZIE, RAYMOND
PERSONAL Born Beloit, WI **DISCIPLINE** ENGLISH **EDUCATION** Concordia Col, BA, 73; Kans State Univ, MA, 75; PhD, 81. **CAREER** Asst to assoc prof, Mankato State Univ, 81-86; Pub Manager, Cray Research, 86-89; prof, Univ of St Thomas, 89-. **MEMBERSHIPS** MLA; SHARP; STSS; RSVP. **RESEARCH** 19th - 20th Century British and French Literature. **SELECTED PUBLICATIONS** Auth, "Viola Meynell", Late Victorian and Edwardian British Novelists, 1890-1918, ed George M Johnson, Bruccoli Clark Layman, (Sumter, 95); auth, "Advertising", "Allen Lane and Penguin Books", "The Manchester Guardian", and "Periodicals", Encycl of 20th Century Britain, ed F Leventhal, Garland Pr, 95; auth, "Edmund Curll", and "Archibald Constable", British Literary Book Trade, 1700-1820, ed J Bracken, Bruccoli Clark Layman, 95; auth, "The Tonsons", and "Bernard Lintot", British Literary Book Trade, 1600-1700, ed J Bracken, Bruccoli Clark Layman, 95; auth, "Edwin Muir", British Novelists Between the Wars, ed George M Johnson, Bruccoli Clark Layman, 98; auth, "Lady Cynthia Asquith", Encycl of British Women Writers, Rutgers Univ Pr, 98; auth, "Selling Dreams: Catholicism and the Business Communicator", Logos, 99. **CONTACT ADDRESS** Dept English, Univ of St. Thomas, Minnesota, 2115 Summit Ave, Saint Paul, MN 55105-1048. **EMAIL** rnmackenzie@stthomas.edu

MACKETHAN, LUCINDA HARDWICK
PERSONAL Born 09/12/1945, Akron, OH, m, 1969, 2 children **DISCIPLINE** AMERICAN LITERATURE, BRITISH LITERATURE **EDUCATION** Hollins Col, BA, 67; Univ NC, Chapel Hill, MA, 69, PhD(English), 74. **CAREER** Instr, 71-74, asst prof, 74-79, Assoc Prof English, NC State Univ, 80-, Nat Endowment for Humanities fel, 81. **MEMBERSHIPS** MLA; Soc Study Southern Lit; S Atlantic MLA. **SELECTED PUBLICATIONS** Auth, Redeeming Blackness--Urban Allegories of Oconnor, Percy, and Toole, Stud in the Lit Imagination, Vol 0027, 94. **CONTACT ADDRESS** Dept of English, No Carolina State Univ, Raleigh, NC 27695.

MACKEY, BARBARA S.
PERSONAL Born 01/27/1941, Los Angeles, CA, d, 1971, 1 child **DISCIPLINE** SPEECH **EDUCATION** U of Mich, BA, 62, MA, 95; Bowling Green State Univ, PhD, 96. **CAREER** Head of English and Speech div, John Woolman School, Nevada city, CA, 63; instr, Southern Univ LA, 65-67; Dir of Hancock County Speech Improvement Prog (GA), 67-68; asst prof, Shippensburg State Col, 68-69; teaching asst, PA State Univ, 69-71; instr, PA State Dept of Continuing Ed, 71-73; instr, Shippensburg State Col, 76-77; Lecturor, Penn State/York, 86-93; Int vis prof, Kolej Damansara Utama, Malaysia, spring 89; instr, Millersnvilee Univ, spring 93; Bowling Green State Univ, 93-96; currently part-time at Univ of Toledo, Owens Community Col, and Univ of Findlay. **HONORS AND AWARDS** First managing dir of Old Bedford Village Opera House, 82-84; creator and dir, Oral Interpretors Project, Old Bedford Village, 82-84. **MEMBERSHIPS** Asn for Theatre in Higher Ed; Speech Commun Asn; Central States Commun Asn; Theatre Asn of PA; Am Soc for Eighteenth-Century Studies. **RESEARCH** Theatre hist; 18th century; dramalurgy; dramatic lit. **SELECTED PUBLICATIONS** Auth, Classroom Across the World, Univ MI School of Ed Innovator, vol 23, no 1, spring-summer 92; Personality Assessments as a Guide to Acting Pedagogy, Communication and Theatre Asn of MN J, vol 22, summer 95; book review of The First English Actresses: Women and Drama 1660-1700, by Elizabeth Howe, Restoration and Eighteenth Century Theatre Research, series 2, vol 10, no 2, winter 95; The Antigone TV Interviews: An Activity for the Introductory Theatre Class, Commun and Theatre Asn of MN J, vol 24, 97; book review of Getting Into the Act: Women Playwrights in London 1776-1829, by Ellen Donkin, Restoration and Eighteenth Century Theater Research, series 2, vol 12, no 1, summer 97; book review of John Barrymore, Shakespearean Actor, by Michael A Morrison, in Text and Performance Quart, July 98; book review, Broken Boundaries: Women and Feminism in Restoration Drama, ed by Katherine M Quinsey, Restoration and Eighteenth Century Theatre Research, summer 98; The Lost Acting Treatise of Charles Manklin, Speech and Theatre Asn of MN, Aug 98; book review, Playwrights and Plagiarists in Early Modern England, by Laura J Rosenthal, Theatre J, Oct 98; numerous other publications. **CONTACT ADDRESS** 1510 Westfield Ave., Ann Arbor, MI 48103-5740. **EMAIL** bmackey@provid.net

MACKIE, HILARY S.
DISCIPLINE CLASSICS **EDUCATION** BA, 87; Princeton Univ, PhD, 93. **CAREER** Vis prof, Stanford Univ. **RESEARCH** Archaic Greek poetry; lit theory; Augustan poetry. **SELECTED PUBLICATIONS** Auth, Talking Trojan: Difference and Conversational Style in the Iliad, 96. **CONTACT ADDRESS** Dept of Span and Class, Rice Univ, 6100 Main St., Houston, TX 77005-1892.

MACKLIN, F. ANTHONY
PERSONAL Born 12/30/1937, Philadelphia, PA, m, 1995, 2 children **DISCIPLINE** ENGLISH **EDUCATION** Villanova Univ, BA, 60; MA, 63. **CAREER** Juror, Sight and Sight, American Film Institute. **RESEARCH** Contemporary Fiction (deLillo), Contemporary Drama (Albee, Mamet, Shepherd et al), Film (Hitchcock et al). **SELECTED PUBLICATIONS** Auth, Voices from the Set, Scarecrow Press, 00; auth, "American Pastime", North American Review (99); auth, "Benund Justice", (95). **CONTACT ADDRESS** Dept English, Univ of Dayton, 300 College Park, Dayton, OH 45469-0001. **EMAIL** macklin@checkov.hm.udayton.edu

MACKSEY, RICHARD ALAN
PERSONAL Born 07/25/1931, Glen Ridge, NJ, m, 1956, 1 child **DISCIPLINE** COMPARATIVE LITERATURE, ENGLISH **EDUCATION** Johns Hopkins Univ, MA, 53, PhD, 57. **CAREER** Jr instr English, Johns Hopkins Univ, 53-55; from instr to asst prof, Loyola Col, 56-58; asst prof writing sem, 58-63, assoc prof humanistic studies, 64-73, Carnegie lectr sem hist ideas, 62-64, chmn sect lang, lit and cult, 66-72, actg dir humanities ctr, 68-69, Prof Humanistic Studies and Chmn Humanities Ctr, Johns Hopkins Univ, 73-, Chmn comt internal evidence, Bibliog Conf, 62; lectr, Baltimore Mus Art, 64-65; dir, Bollingen Poetry Festival, Turnbull lect, Theatre Hopkins, Center Stage, Tantamount Films, Carroll House and Levering Hall; moderator, Dialogue of the Arts, CBS; ed comp lit, Mod Lang Notes and Structure. **MEMBERSHIPS** MLA; Am Soc Aesthet; Renaissance Soc Am; Mediaeval Acad Am; Col English Asn. **RESEARCH** European and English novel; poetics, rhetoric, and theory of literature; interrelation of arts, comparative methodology and intellectual history. **SELECTED PUBLICATIONS** Auth, Poems from the Hungarian Revolution, Cornell Univ, 66; Forerunners of Darwin, 2nd ed, 68, The Languages of Criticism and the Sciences of Man, 69 & Interpretation: Theory and Practice, Johns Hopkins, 69; coauth, Negative metaphor and Proust's rhetoric of absence, Mod Lang Notes, 70; co-ed, The Structuralist Controversy, 72 & auth, Velocities of Change, Johns Hopkins; Gloria Victis, Nemzetor, Munich, 66. **CONTACT ADDRESS** Ctr for Humanities, Johns Hopkins Univ, Baltimore, 3400 N Charles St, Baltimore, MD 21218-2680.

MACKY, NANCY
PERSONAL Born 06/23/1937, Rochester, NY, w, 2 children **DISCIPLINE** DRAMA AND IRISH LITERATURE **EDUCATION** Kent State Univ, PhD. **CAREER** Assoc prof, English, Westminster Col; vis schlr, Oxford Univ, 01-02. **HONORS AND AWARDS** Lady Gregory, schlr; NEH Lilly Fel. **RESEARCH** Approaches to teaching; W. B. Yeats; Lady Gregory; Jon Stallworthy; Peter W. Macky. **SELECTED PUBLICATIONS** Co-auth, "Sculpting the Text," in Learning Literature in an Era of Change: Innovations in Teaching, ed Dona Hickey and Donna Reiss, Stylus Pub, 00. **CONTACT ADDRESS** Dept of Eng, Westminster Col, Pennsylvania, New Wilmington, PA 16172-0001. **EMAIL** nmacky@westminster.edu

MACLAINE, ALLAN HUGH
PERSONAL Born 10/24/1924, Montreal, PQ, Canada, m, 1949 **DISCIPLINE** ENGLISH **EDUCATION** McGill Univ, BA, 45; Brown Univ, PhD(English), 51. **CAREER** Instr English, McGill, 46-47, Brown Univ, 47-50 & Univ MA, 51-54; from asst prof to prof, TX Christian Univ, 54-62; PROF ENGLISH, UNIV RI, 62-, DIR GRAD STUDIES ENGLISH, 71-, Chmn dept English, 66-67, actg dean div univ exten, 67-68, dean, 68-71. **MEMBERSHIPS** MLA; Col English Asn (dir, 61-, pres, 65-66); Int Asn Univ Prof English; fel Nat Univ Exten Asn; Asn for Scottish Literary Studies. **RESEARCH** Scottish poetry, especially Burns; middle English literature, especially Chaucer; 18th century English literature. **SELECTED PUBLICATIONS** Auth, Burn's use of Parody in Tam O'Shanter, Criticism, 59; The Student's Comprehensive Guide to the Canterbury Tales, Barron's, 64; Robert Fergusson, Twayne, 65; The Christis Kirk tradition: Its evolution in Scots poetry to Burns, Studies in Scottish Lit, 65-66; Allan Ramsay, Twayne, 85; ed, The Christis Kirk Tradition: Scots Poems of Folk Festivity, Asn for Scottish Literary Studies, 96. **CONTACT ADDRESS** Dept of English, Univ of Rhode Island, Kingston, RI 02881.

MACLEAN, HUGH NORMAN
PERSONAL Born 03/24/1919, Aguilas, Spain, m, 1949, 2 children **DISCIPLINE** ENGLISH **EDUCATION** Princeton Univ, BA, 40; Univ Toronto, MA, 47, PhD(English), 50. **CAREER** Lectr English, Univ Toronto, 49-50; asst prof, Royal Mil Col, 50-56, Univ Cincinnati, 56-60 and York Univ, 60-63; prof, 63-74, Distinguished Teaching Prof English, State Univ NY Albany, 74-, Huntington Libr res fel, 54-55; Ed, Spenser Newsletter, 82-. **MEMBERSHIPS** MLA; Renaissance Soc Am; Int Asn Univ Profs English; Shakespeare Asn Am; Spenser Soc; Milton Soc. **RESEARCH** Literature of the English Renaissance. **SELECTED PUBLICATIONS** Ed, Edmund Spenser's Poetry, 69, 82 and Ben Jonson and the Cavalier Poets, 74, Norton. **CONTACT ADDRESS** Dept of English, SUNY, Albany, Albany, NY 12222.

MACLEOD, ALISTAIR
DISCIPLINE ENGLISH LANGUAGE; LITERATURE **EDUCATION** St Francis Xavier, BA; BEd; LLD, 69; New Brunswick, MA; Univ Notre Dame, PhD. **CAREER** Prof; fiction ed, The Windsor Review; tchr, advanced writing in the summer prog at, Banff; Can participant in the Can Scotland Writers-in-Residence Exchange Prog, 84-85. **RESEARCH** 19th-century literature; Creative Writing. **SELECTED PUBLICATIONS** Auth, The Lost Salt Gift of Blood, 76; As Birds Bring Forth the Sun, 86. **CONTACT ADDRESS** Dept of English Language and Literature, Univ of Windsor, 401 Sunset Ave, Windsor, ON, Canada N9B 3P4. **EMAIL** alistar@uwindsor.ca

MACLEOD, GLEN
PERSONAL Born 10/10/1948, Berea, OH, s **DISCIPLINE** ENGLISH **EDUCATION** Wesleyan Univ, BA, 71; Princeton Univ, MA, 78, PhD, 81. **CAREER** Instr, Southampton Col of Long Island Univ, 80-81, asst prof, 81-83; asst prof, Univ Conn, Waterbury, 83-87, assoc prof, 87-94, prof, 94-. **HONORS AND AWARDS** NEH fel for col teachers, 83; J. Paul Getty Fel in the Hist of Art and the Humanities, 87-88. **RESEARCH** American literature, modern poetry, literature and the visual arts. **SELECTED PUBLICATIONS** Auth, " A New Version of Wallace Stevens," Princeton Univ Library Chronicle, 41:1 (fall 79): 22-29; auth, "Stevens at the Front: 'Lettres d'un Soldat'," The Wallace Stevens J, 5:3-4 (fall 81): 46-55; auth, Wallace Stevens and Company: The "Harmonium Years, 1913-1923, UMI Res Press (83); auth, "Fairfield Porter and Wallace Stevens: Kindred Spirits of American Art," Archives of Am Art J, 24:1 (fall 84): 2-12; auth, "Stevens and Surrealism: The Genesis of 'The Man with the Blue Guitar'," Am Lit, 59:3 (Oct 87): 359-377; auth, " 'Notes toward a Supreme Fiction' and Abstract Art," J of Modrn Lit, 16:1 (summer 89): 31-48; auth, "Surrealism and the Supreme Fiction: 'It Must Give Pleasure'," The Wallace Stevens J, 14:1 (spring 90): 33-38; auth, Wallace Stevens and Modern Art: From the Armory Show to Abstract Expressionism, Yale Univ Press (93); auth, "Painting in Poetry/ Poetry in Painting: Wallace Stevens and Modern Art," art exhibition catalogue, Sidney Mishkin Gallery, Baruch Col, CUNY (95); auth, "The Influence of Wallace Stevens on Contemporary Artists," The Wallace Stevens J, 20:2 (fall 96): 139-180. **CONTACT ADDRESS** Dept English, Univ of Connecticut, 32 Hillside Ave, Waterbury, CT 06710-2217.

MACMILLAN, CARRIE H.
PERSONAL Born 11/03/1945, Fredericton, NB, Canada **DISCIPLINE** ENGLISH **EDUCATION** Univ NB, BA, 67; Dalhousie Univ, MA, 70; McMaster Univ, PhD, 77. **CAREER** Asst prof, 77-83, assoc prof, 84-93, head dept, 94-, Prof English, Mt Allison Univ 94-. **HONORS AND AWARDS** Tucker Tchr Awd, Mt Allison Univ, 90. **MEMBERSHIPS** Asn Can Col Univ Tchrs Eng; Asn Can Que Lits; Hum Asn Can. **SELECTED PUBLICATIONS** Coauth, Silenced Sextet: Six Nineteenth-Century Canadian Women Novelists, 93. **CONTACT ADDRESS** Dept of English, Mount Allison Univ, Sackville, NB, Canada E4L 1B8. **EMAIL** cmacmillan@mta.ca

MACNAUGHTON, WILLIAM ROBERT
PERSONAL Born 11/14/1939, Moncton, NB, Canada, m, 1962, 3 children **DISCIPLINE** ENGLISH, AMERICAN LITERATURE **EDUCATION** Univ Toronto, BA, 62; Univ Wis, MA, 63, PhD(English), 69. **CAREER** Asst prof, 70-75, Assoc Prof English, Univ Waterloo, Ont, 75-, Chmn, 79-, Can Coun res fel, 71 and 76. **MEMBERSHIPS** Asn Can Univ Teachers English; Can Asn Am Studies. **RESEARCH** Nineteenth and 20th century American literature, particularly writers of realistic and naturalistic fiction. **SELECTED PUBLICATIONS** Auth, Mark Twain's Last Years as a Writer; auth, Henry James: The Later Novels; ed, Critical Essays on John Updike. **CONTACT ADDRESS** Dept of English, Univ of Waterloo, 200 Univ Ave W, Waterloo, ON, Canada N2L 3G1.

MACNEALY, MARY SUE
PERSONAL Born Newark, OH **DISCIPLINE** RHETORIC, COMPOSITION **EDUCATION** Ohio State Univ, BA, 79; MA, 82; Carnegie Mellon, PhD, 88. **CAREER** Asst prof, Univ Memphis, 88; assoc prof, 93; prof, 99-. **HONORS AND AWARDS** Outstand Instr, 87. **MEMBERSHIPS** NCTE; ATWT; STC; ABC. **RESEARCH** Rhetoric; technical writing; composition. **SELECTED PUBLICATIONS** Co-ed, Empirical Approaches to Literature and Aesthetics, Ablex (Norwood, NJ), 96; auth, Strategies for Empirical Research in Writing, Allyn and Bacon (Boston), 99. **CONTACT ADDRESS** Dept English, Univ of Memphis, 3706 Alumni St, Memphis, TN 38152-0001. **EMAIL** macnealy@memphis.edu

MACNEIL, ANNE
DISCIPLINE MUSIC HISTORY **EDUCATION** Univ Chicago, PhD. **CAREER** Asst prof; Am Acad fel in Rome, 92; ed, Socy for 17th-century Music Newsletter. **MEMBERSHIPS** Comt on the Status of Women, Am Musicol Soc. **RESEARCH** Renaissance; early mod studies. **SELECTED PUBLICATIONS** Auth, book on the Andreini family and music in the commedia dell'arte, Oxford UP, 99; The Divine Madness of Isabella Andreini, Proc Royal Musical Asn 120, 95 & The Virtue of Gender, La femme lettre la Renaissance: XIIth Colloque Int de L'Institut Interuniversitaire Renaissance et Humanisme, Bruxelles, 96, Brussels: Inst Interuniversitaire Renaissance et Humanisme, 97; coauth, The New International Dictionary of Music, NY, Meridian, 92. **CONTACT ADDRESS** School of Music, Univ of Texas, Austin, 2613 Wichita St, Austin, TX 78705.

MACOVSKI, MICHAEL
DISCIPLINE LITERATURE OF THE ROMANTIC PERIOD **EDUCATION** Univ CA, Berkeley, PhD. **CAREER** Assoc prof, Fordham Univ. **RESEARCH** Byron, M. Bakhtin. **SELECTED PUBLICATIONS** Auth, Byron, Bakhtin, and the Translation of History, Re-reading Byron, Garland Press, 93; Dialogue and Literature: Apostrophes, Auditors, and the Collapse of Romantic Discourse, Oxford UP, 94. **CONTACT ADDRESS** Dept of Eng Lang and Lit, Fordham Univ, 113 W 60th St, New York, NY 10023.

MACPHEE, LAURENCE EDWARD
PERSONAL Born 12/02/1934, Jersey City, NJ, m, 1960, 3 children **DISCIPLINE** ENGLISH **EDUCATION** St Peter's Col, NJ, BS, 56; NYork Univ, MA, 59; Rutgers Univ, PhD(English), 67. **CAREER** From instr to assist prof, 59-68, Assoc Prof English, Seton Hall Univ, 68- **HONORS AND AWARDS** Swiss Government Fel, 56-57; Woodrow Wilson Fel, 58-59; Danforth Fel, 58-61. **MEMBERSHIPS** MLA; AAUP. **RESEARCH** J F Cooper; 19th century American novel. **SELECTED PUBLICATIONS** Auth, The Great Gatsby's romance of motoring: Nick Carraway and Jordan Baker, Mod Fiction Studies, summer 72. **CONTACT ADDRESS** Dept of English, Seton Hall Univ, So Orange, 400 S Orange Ave, South Orange, NJ 07079-2697.

MACPHERSON, JAY
PERSONAL Born 06/13/1931, London, England **DISCIPLINE** ENGLISH **EDUCATION** Carleton Col, Ont, BA, 51; McGill Univ, BLS, 53; Univ Toronto, MA, 55, PhD(English), 64. **CAREER** Lectr, 57, from asst prof to assoc prof, 58-73, Prof English, Victoria Col, Univ Toronto, 73-. **MEMBERSHIPS** Asn Can Univ Teachers English; League Can Poets. **RESEARCH** Eighteenth century to present romance fictions. **SELECTED PUBLICATIONS** Auth, A Dictionary of Biblical Tradition in English Literature, Univ Toronto Quart, Vol 0065, 95; Sparshott, Francis, Poet, J Aesthet Educ, Vol 0031, 97. **CONTACT ADDRESS** Victoria Col, Univ of Toronto, Toronto, ON, Canada M5S 1A1.

MACRAE, SUZANNE H.
DISCIPLINE MEDIEVAL LITERATURE **EDUCATION** Univ N Carolina, PhD. **CAREER** English and Lit, Univ Ark. **SELECTED PUBLICATIONS** Auth, Thomas Berger's Mythical Arthur Rex, Popular Arthurian Traditions, 92; Yeelen: A Political Fable of the Komo Blacksmiths/Sorceres, Res African Lit, 95; Mature and Older Women in African Film, Res African Lit, 96. **CONTACT ADDRESS** Univ of Arkansas, Fayetteville, Fayetteville, AR 72701.

MADDEN, DAVID
PERSONAL Born 09/10/1950, San Francisco, CA, m, 1977, 2 children **DISCIPLINE** ENGLISH **EDUCATION** Univ of Calif at Davis, BA, 72; MA, 74; PhD, 80. **CAREER** Lectr, Univ of Pisa, 77-78; lectr, Univ of Calif at Davis, 80-82; from asst prof to prof, Calif State Univ at Sacramento, 82-. **HONORS AND AWARDS** Phi Kappa Phi; Fulbright Teaching Fel, 77-78; Exceptional Merit Services Awd, Calif State Univ at Sacramento, 84; Meritorious Performance and Professional promise Awd, Calif State Univ at Sacramento, 86; res grant, Calif State Univ at Sacramento, 89-94; Outstanding Teacher, Calif State Univ at Sacramento, 99. **MEMBERSHIPS** Am Confr for Irish Studies, Irish Am Cultural Inst. **RESEARCH** Contemporary American fiction, Irish literature. **SELECTED PUBLICATIONS** Auth, Understanding Paul West, Univ of SC Press (Columbia, SC), 93; ed, Critical Essays on American Literature: Thomas Berger, G.K. Hall (New York, NY), 95; guest ed, The Review of Contemporary Fiction XVII (summer 97); auth, "Alan Burns," The Dictionary of Literary Biography: Contemporary British Novelists 1960-Present, The Gale Group (Farmington Hills, MI), 98; auth, "Indoctrination to Pariahdom: Liminality in the Fiction of Paul West," Critique 40 (98): 49-70; auth, "Jacob Steendam," American National Biography vol 20, Oxford Univ Press (New York), 99; auth, "Paul West and the Postmodern Sensibility," Postmodernism: Key Figures, Blackwell (Malden, MA) forthcoming. **CONTACT ADDRESS** Dept English, California State Univ, Sacramento, 6000 J St, Sacramento, CA 95819-2605. **EMAIL** maddendw@csus.edu

MADDEN, DAVID
PERSONAL Born 07/25/1933, Knoxville, TN, m, 1956, 1 child **DISCIPLINE** ENGLISH **EDUCATION** Univ Tenn, BS, 57; San Francisco State Col, MA, 58; Yale Drama School, 60. **CAREER** Instructor, Appalachian State Teachers Col, 58-59; Instructor, Center Col, 60-62; Instructor, Univ Louisville, 62-64; Instructor, Kenyon Col, 64-66; Writer-in-residence to Prof, La State Univ, 68-. **HONORS AND AWARDS** Distinguished Fac Awd; LSU Alumni Asn; Nat Coun of the Arts Awd; Pearl Setzer Deal Awd; Jack Conroy Awd for the short Story; New Letters Awd; Best Am Short Stories; Nat Coun of the Arts Awd; William Raney Fel; John Golden Fel. **MEMBERSHIPS** Assoc Writing Prog, Popular Culture Asn, Soc of Cinematol, Popular Culture Asn, Thomas Wolfe Soc. **RESEARCH** Psychology of the act of reading; The art of writing; Major and emerging male and female, American including Southern English, and French writers. **SELECTED PUBLICATIONS** Ed, Beyond the Battlefield: The Ordinary Life and Extraordinary Times of the civil War soldier, Simon & Schuster, 00; ed, The Legacy of Robert Penn Warren, LSU Press, 00; ed, Classic of Civil War Fiction, Univ Miss Press, 91; auth, sharpshooter: A Novel of the Civil War, Univ Tenn Press, 96; auth, The fiction Tutor: The art of Writing and reading Fiction, Harcourt Brace, 90; auth, A Pocketful of Essays, forthcoming; auth, A Pocketful of Plays, Harcourt, 96; auth, a Pocketful of Poems, Harcourt, 96; auth, A Pocketful of Prose: Vintage II, Harcourt, 92. **CONTACT ADDRESS** Dept English, La State Univ, Baton Rouge, LA 70803-0104. **EMAIL** dmadden@lsu.edu

MADDEN, DEIDRE
PERSONAL Born 01/08/1936, Washington, DC, m, 3 children **DISCIPLINE** SPEECH & LANGUAGE **EDUCATION** Ohio Univ, BA, 58; Western Reserve, MA, 67; Kent State Univ, PhD, 82. **CAREER** Speech Pathol, 60-68, Parochial; Lect, 67-68, Com Col; Asst, Full Prof, 67-98, Baldwin-Wallace Col **HONORS AND AWARDS** Chair-Dept-BW; Co-Chair, Faculty-BW; Chair-Sexual Harrassment Com-BW **MEMBERSHIPS** ASHA; OSHA; ASTD **CONTACT ADDRESS** Dept of Speech Commun & Theatre, Baldwin-Wallace Col, 275 Eastland Rd., Berea, OH 44017. **EMAIL** dmadden@bw.edu

MADDEN, ETTA M.
PERSONAL Born 04/02/1962, New Orleans, LA, m, 1986, 2 children **DISCIPLINE** ENGLISH **EDUCATION** Hardinv Univ, BA, 84; Univ Va, MA, 86; Univ NHamp, PhD, 95. **CAREER** Assoc prof, SMSU, 95-01. **HONORS AND AWARDS** NEH Awd, 87-88; SMSU Fel, 96; Mellon Fel, 00. **MEMBERSHIPS** MLA, Am Studies Assoc, Soc of Early Americanists, Soc for the Hist of Authorship, Reading and Publ, NCTE, Soc for Lit and Sci, Soc for Utopian Studies, Communal Studies Assoc. **RESEARCH** Religion and literature, utopian societies, autobiographies, spiritual narratives, science and literature, food, drink and literature. **SELECTED PUBLICATIONS** Auth, "Resurrecting Life through Rhetorical Ritual: A Buried Value of the Puritan Funeral Sermon," Early Am Lit, (91); rev, of "Nellie Brown, or the Jealous Wife, with other Sketches," Borderlines: Studies in Am Cult, (96); auth, "Reading, Writing and the Race of Mother Figure: Shakers Rebecca Cox Jackson and Alonzo giles Hollister," A Mighty Baptism: Race, Gender, and the Creation of American Protestantism, (96); auth, "Sarah Wister," Am Women Prose Writers to 1820, (98); auth, Bodies of Life: Shaker Literature and Literacies, Greenwood, 98; auth, "Quaker Elizabeth Ashbridge as 'the Spectacle and discourse of the Company': Metaphor, Synecdoche, and Synthesis," Early Am Lit, (99); rev, "Making the American Self: Jonathan Edwards to Abrham Lincoln," Borderlines: Studies in Am Cult, (99); rev, of "In the Valley of the Shadow: An Elegy to Lancaster County," Utopian Studies, (99). **CONTACT ADDRESS** Southwest Missouri State Univ, Springfield, 901 S National Ave, Springfield, MO 65804. **EMAIL** emm605@smsu.edu

MADDEN, KATE
DISCIPLINE COMMUNICATION STUDIES **EDUCATION** Colby Col, BA; Univ Pa, MA; Pa State Univ, PhD. **CAREER** Asst prof, SUNY. **RESEARCH** International mass communication; media and cultural diversity; communication technology and cultural change. **SELECTED PUBLICATIONS** Auth, Video and Cultural Identity: the Inuit Broadcasting Corporation Experience. **CONTACT ADDRESS** Dept of Communication, SUNY, Col at Brockport, Brockport, NY 14420. **EMAIL** kmadden@po.brockport.edu

MADDOCK, LAWRENCE H.
PERSONAL Born 07/14/1923, Ogden, UT, s **DISCIPLINE** ENGLISH **EDUCATION** George Peabody Col, BA, 46; Univ S Calif, 46; George Peabody Col, PhD, 65. **CAREER** Teacher, Jacksonville Fla, 49-52; instr, Univ Fla, 52-53; asst prof to assoc prof, Calif State Col, 55-64; assoc prof, NE La State Col, 64-67; assoc prof, Univ W Fla, 67-90 **MEMBERSHIPS** MLA; Thomas Wolfe Soc; Mormon Hist Asn. **RESEARCH** Samuel Taylor Coleridge; Thomas Wolfe. **SELECTED PUBLICATIONS** Auth, The Door of Memory, 74; auth, John Maddock, Mormon Pioneer, 96. **CONTACT ADDRESS** Dept English, Univ of West Florida, 1012 Gerhardt Dr, Pensacola, FL 32503-3222.

MADDOX, LUCY
DISCIPLINE AMERICAN LITERATURE **EDUCATION** Furman Univ, BA; Duke Univ, MA; Univ Va, PhD. **CAREER** Eng Dept, Georgetown Univ **RESEARCH** 19th and 20th century American literature; Native American literature. **SELECTED PUBLICATIONS** Auth, Susan Fenimore Cooper and the Plain Daughters of America, 88; Gilbert White and the Politics of Natural History, 86; Nabokov's Novels in English, 83; Removals: Nineteenth-Century American Literature and the Politics of Indian Affairs, 91. **CONTACT ADDRESS** English Dept, Georgetown Univ, 37th and O St, Washington, DC 20057. **EMAIL** maddoxl@gusun.georgetown.edu

MADGETT, NAOMI LONG
PERSONAL Born 07/05/1923, Norfolk, VA, w, 1972, 1 child **DISCIPLINE** ENGLISH **EDUCATION** VA State Coll, BA 1945; Wayne State Univ, MEd 1955; Intl Inst for Advanced Studies (Greenwich Univ), PhD 1980. **CAREER** Poet and author, 41-; Prof, publisher-editor; MI Chronicle, staff writer 1946-47; MI Bell Tel Co, serv rep 1948-54; Detroit Pub Sch, teacher 1955-65, 66-68; public speaker, poetry readings only 1956-; Oakland Univ, res assoc 1965-66; East MI Univ, assoc prof English 1968-73; Univ of MI, lectr 1970; East MI Univ, prof 1973-84, Prof Emeritus 1984-; Lotus Press, publ & editor 1974-; editor, Lotus Poetry Series, MI State Univ Press, 93-98. **HONORS AND AWARDS** Distinguished English Teacher of the Year, Met Detroit; 1st recipient Mott Fellowship in English 1965; Disting Soror Awd, Alpha Rho Omega Chap, Alpha Kappa Alpha Sor, 1969; papers being collected in Special Collections Libr Fisk Univ; Resolutions from Detroit Cty Cncl 1982 and MI State Legisl 1982 & 1984; Key to the City of Detroit 1980; Recognition by Black Caucus of Natl Cncl of Teachers of English 1984; Natl Coalition of 100 Black Women 1984; Induction into Stylus Society Howard Univ 1984; Disting Artist Awd, Wayne State Univ, 1985; Robert Hayden Runagate Awd, 1985; Creative Artist Awd, MI Council for the arts, 1987; Creative Achievement Awd, College Language Assn, 1988; "In Her Lifetime" Awd, Afrikan Poets Theatre Inc, 1989; Literature Awd, Arts Foundation of Michigan, 1990; Honorary Degree, Loyola University, Chicago, 1993; Recognition by Black Caucus of American Library Assn, 1992; honorary degree, MI State Univ, 1994; MI Artist Awd, 1993; Amer Book Awd, 1993; George Kent Awd, 95; Induction into Nat Literary Hall of Fame for Writers of African Descent, 99. **MEMBERSHIPS** Coll Language Assn; Alpha Kappa Alpha Sor; Detroit Women Writers; Southern Poverty Law Center; Langston Hughes Society; Zora Neale Hurston Society. **SELECTED PUBLICATIONS** Editor of two anthologies including: Adam of Ife: Black Women in Praise of Black Men, 1992; eight books published including: Remembrances of Spring: Collected Early Poems, 1993; Octavia and Other Poems, 1988; Star by Star; Pink Ladies in the Afternoon; Exits & Entrances; poems widely anthologized & translated. **CONTACT ADDRESS** Lotus Press Inc, PO Box 21607, Detroit, MI 48221. **EMAIL** nlmadgett@aol.com

MADIGAN, MARK J.
PERSONAL Born 01/16/1961, Harford, CT, s **DISCIPLINE** ENGLISH **EDUCATION** St Michael's Col, BA, 83; Univ VT, MA, 87; Univ MA, PhD, 91. **CAREER** Lecturer, Univ VT, 91-96; Asst Prof, Nazareth Col, 96-. **HONORS AND AWARDS** Fel , Intl Willa Cather colloquium, New York, 98; Fel, Eighth Intl Sem on Willa Cather, NE, 00; Sem Fel, Sixth Intl Seminar on Willa Cather, Quebec City, 95; Phi Kappa Phi, 91. **MEMBERSHIPS** Dorothy Canfield Fisher Soc; Willa Cather Soc; NE Popular Culture Asn; John Edgar Wideman Soc; Richard Wright Circle **RESEARCH** African American Literature; Modern and contemporary American Literature; Popular Culture. **SELECTED PUBLICATIONS** Auth, "Miscegenation and 'The Dicta of Race and Class': The Rhinelander Case and Nella Larsen's Passing," Modern Fiction Studies, (90): 523-529; auth, "Willa Cather and Dorothy Canfield fisher: Rift, Reconciliation, and One of Ours," in Cather Studies I, (Univ NE Press, 90), 115-129; ed, Fisher, Dorothy Canfield. Keeping Fires Night and Day: Selected Letters of Dorothy Canfield fisher, Univ MO Press, 93auth, "'As True and direct as a Birth or Death Certificate': Richard Wright on Jim Thompson's Now and On Earth," Studies in American Fiction, (94): 105-110; ed, Fisher, Dorothy Canfield. Seasoned Timber, UP of N Eng, 96; ed, Fisher, Dorothy Canfield. The Bedquilt and Other Stories, Univ MO Press, 96. **CONTACT ADDRESS** Dept Eng, Nazareth Col of Rochester, 4245 E Ave, Rochester, NY 14618-3703. **EMAIL** mjmadiga@naz.edu

MADIGAN, MARY

PERSONAL Born 07/25/1922, Chicago, IL **DISCIPLINE** MEDIEVAL ENGLISH **EDUCATION** DePaul Univ, BA, 52; Univ Detroit, MA, 58; St Louis Univ, PhD(English), 67. **CAREER** Asst prof English, St Procopius Col, 65-69; assoc prof, Duquesne Univ, 69-72; Assoc Prof English, St Michael's Col, Univ Toronto, 72-. **MEMBERSHIPS** Mediaeval Acad Am; MLA. **RESEARCH** Middle English prose; English drama; literary criticism. **SELECTED PUBLICATIONS** Auth, Sidney, Amer Scholar, Vol 0065, 96. **CONTACT ADDRESS** 2 S 304 Hawthorne Lane, Wheaton, IL 60187.

MAERTZ, GREGORY

PERSONAL Born 11/28/1958, Buffalo Lake, MN, m, 2000 **DISCIPLINE** ENGLISH **EDUCATION** Northwestern Univ, BA, 81; Harvard Univ, MA, 83; PhD, 88. **CAREER** Asst prof to assoc prof, St John's Univ, 90-. **HONORS AND AWARDS** Phi Beta Kappa, 81; Fulbright Fel, Univ of Heidelberg, 86-88; Mellon Fel, 88-90; NEMLA, 93; Beineck, 95-96; AAS, 96-97; DAAD, 98; Inst for Advan Study, 00-01. **MEMBERSHIPS** MLA; ASECS; GSNA; NASSR. **RESEARCH** Romanticism, the afterlife of Nazi culture, Anglo-German and German-American cultural relations. **SELECTED PUBLICATIONS** Ed, Cultural Interactions in the Romantic Age: Critical Essays in Comparative Literature, SUNY Pr, (Albany), 98; ed, George Eliot Middlemarch, Broadview Lit Arts (Peterborough, ON), (forthcoming); auth, Literature and the Cult of Personality: Goethe and the Formation of high Culture in Britain and the United States, 1790-1950 (forthcoming); auth, Nazi Art: The Secret Postwar History (forthcoming); auth, Children of Prometheus (forthcoming). **CONTACT ADDRESS** Dept English, St. John's Univ, 8000 Utopia Pky, Jamaica, NY 11439-0001. **EMAIL** maertzg@stjohns.edu

MAGER, DONALD

PERSONAL Born 08/24/1942, Santa Rita, NM, d, 2 children **DISCIPLINE** ENGLISH, PHILOSOPHY **EDUCATION** Drake Univ, BA, 64; Syracuse Univ, MA, 66; Wayne State Univ, PhD, 86. **CAREER** Prof of English, Johnson C. Smith Univ, 86-. **HONORS AND AWARDS** The Mott Univ Distinguished Prof, 99; Winner, Union County Writers Club 1998 Chapbook Contest for Borderins, 98; Finalist for Beholders in the Brickhouse Books annual Stonewall Chapbook Contest for Borderings, 97; Associate Artist Residency, Atlantic Cente For The Arts, New Smyrna Beach, Florida, 6-26, March 94; Reader on the Blumenthal Readers and Writers Series of the North Carolina Poetry Network, 94; Par Excellence Teaching Awd, Divisional Nominee, 96; Par Excellence Teaching Awd, Divisional Nominee, 95; Par Excellence Teaching Awd Divisional Nominee, 94; Par Excellence Teaching Awd, Divsional Nominee, 93; First Prize, The Lyricist Statewide Poetry Competition, Campbell Univ, 92; Par Excellence Teaching Awd, Divisional Nominee, 92; Par Excellence Teaching Awd, Divisional Nominee, 91; Tompkins Awd, first prize for poetry, Wayne State University, 86; Thomas A. Rumble Graduate Fel, Wayne State Univ, 84, 85, 86; Michigan Organization for Human Rights Awd for community service, 77. **MEMBERSHIPS** MLA; NC Poetry Society; Phi Beta Kappa, 64; Poetry Society of America, 99; Charlotte Writers Club, 96; North Carolina Poetry Society, Raleigh, NC, 95; Appointed to The Academy of American Poets as an Assciate, 94; The Writers' Workshop, Asheville, North Carolina, 94; Modern Language Assoc, 84. **RESEARCH** Renaisance Drama; Gay/Lesbian Studies; Twentieth Century Czech; Russian Poetry. **SELECTED PUBLICATIONS** Auth, "To Track The Wounded: A Journal," Poetry chapbook, (Roseville, MI): Ridgeway Press; auth, "John Bale and Early Tudor Sodomy Discourse," Queering The Renaissance, Ed, Jonathan Goldberg, Durham: Duke Univ Press, 93; auth, "Glosses: Twenty-four Preludes and Etudes," Poetry volume, St. Andrews Presbyterian College Press; auth, "Teaching About Homophobia at a Historically Black University: A Role Play for Undergraduate Students," with Robert Sulek, Overcoming Heterosexism and Homophobia: Strategies That Work, ed, James T. Sears and Walter L. Williams, (New York): Columbia U. Press, 97: 182-196; auth, "That Which Is Owed To Death," Poetry bolume, (Charlotte, NC): Main Street Rag Press; auth, "Borderings," Poetry volume, (Monroe, NC): Union County Writers Press, 98 Winter of the Union County Writers Press National Chapbook Contest; auth, "Deathwatch," Chapter in The Isherwood Century: Essays on the Life and Work of Christopher Isherwood, ed, James J. Berg and Chris Freeman, (Madison): Univ of Wisconsin Press, 00. **CONTACT ADDRESS** Dept English & Philosophy, Johnson C. Smith Univ, 100 Beatties Ford Rd, Charlotte, NC 2816-5302. **EMAIL** dmager@jcsu.edu

MAGNUSON, PAUL ANDREW

PERSONAL Born 04/10/1939, Newton, MA, m, 1965, 2 children **DISCIPLINE** ENGLISH LITERATURE **EDUCATION** Brown Univ, AB, 61; Univ Minn, PhD, 69. **CAREER** Asst prof English, Univ Pa, 69-74, asst prof, 74-76; assoc prof English, 76-88, prof, 88-, NY Univ, 76-. **MEMBERSHIPS** MLA; Wordsworth-Coleridge Asn; Keats-Shelley Asn. **RESEARCH** English Romantic lit. **SELECTED PUBLICATIONS** Auth, Coleridge's Nightmare Poetry, Univ Va, 74; Coleridge and Wordsworth: A Lyrical Dialogue, Princeton, 88; Reading Public Romanticism, Princeton, 98. **CONTACT ADDRESS** Dept of English, New York Univ, 19 University Pl, New York, NY 10003-4556. **EMAIL** pm1@is3.nyu.edu

MAGUIRE, JAMES HENRY

PERSONAL Born 04/02/1944, Denver, CO, m, 1967, 2 children **DISCIPLINE** AMERICAN LITERATURE AND STUDIES **EDUCATION** Univ Colo, Boulder, BA, 66; Ind Univ, Bloomington, MA, 69, PhD(English and Am studies), 70. **CAREER** Asst prof, 70-75, ASSOC PROF, 75-87, Prof, English and Am Lit, Boise State Univ, 87-, Co-Ed, Boise State Univ Western Writers Ser, 72-98; Co-Ed, Lit Hist Am West, 87-. **HONORS AND AWARDS** Distinguished Achievement Awd; Western Literature Assoc, 94. **MEMBERSHIPS** MLA; Am Studies Asn; Western Lit Asn. **RESEARCH** American realism; Western American literature; the novel. **SELECTED PUBLICATIONS** Auth, Mary Hallock Foote, 72; ed, The Literature of Idaho: an Anthology, 86; co-ed, Into the Wilderness and Dream, 94; coed, A Rendezvous Reader, 97. **CONTACT ADDRESS** Dept of English, Boise State Univ, Boise, ID 83725. **EMAIL** jmaguire@boisestate.edu

MAHONEY, DHIRA B.

PERSONAL Born 12/03/1938, Calcutta, India, m, 1970 **DISCIPLINE** ENGLISH **EDUCATION** Oxford Univ, BA, 60; MA, 64; Univ Calif Santa Barbara, 74. **CAREER** Sen Asst Lectr, Loreto Col, 61-66; Assoc and Teaching Fel, Univ Calif, Santa Barbara, 66-70; Lectr, Kent State Univ, 75-76; Adj Lectr to Asst Prof, Univ Ariz, 76-88; Vis Asst Prof to Assoc Prof, Ariz State Univ, 88-. **HONORS AND AWARDS** NEH Summer Inst, 83; ASU Humanities Release-Time Awd, 91; Intl Travel Grant, Col of Liberal Arts and Sci, 94. **MEMBERSHIPS** Medieval Acad of Am; MLA; Medieval Asn of the Pacific; Intl Arthurian Soc; Intl Courtly Lit Soc; New Chaucer Soc; Medieval Feminist Newsletter; John Gower Soc; Rocky Mountain Medieval and Renaissance Asn. **RESEARCH** Self-fashioning in medieval prologues and epilogues; Malory's Morte Darthur; Arthurian literature (medieval to modern). **SELECTED PUBLICATIONS** Auth, "Malory's Tale of Gareth and the Comedy of Class," The Arthurian Yearbook, 91; auth, "Malory's Great Guns Revisited," BBBIAS 44, 93; auth, "Courtly Presentation and Authorial Self-Fashioning," Mediaevalia 21, 96; auth, "Gower's Two Prologues to Confessio Amantis" in Revisioning Gower, Pegasus Press, 98; ed, The Grail: A Casebook, Garland Pub, 00. **CONTACT ADDRESS** Dept English, Arizona State Univ, PO Box 870302, Tempe, AZ 85287-0302. **EMAIL** Dhira.Mahoney@asu.edu

MAHONEY, IRENE

PERSONAL Born 05/05/1921, Brooklyn, NY **DISCIPLINE** ENGLISH **EDUCATION** Col New Rochelle, BA, 41; Fordham Univ, MA, 48; Cath Univ Am, PhD, 58. **CAREER** Assoc prof, 62-69, prof English, 69-, Writer-In-Residence, 70-, Col New Rochelle. **RESEARCH** French Renaissance; contemporary fiction. **SELECTED PUBLICATIONS** Auth, Marie of the Incarnation: Mystic and Missionary, Doubleday, 64; auth, Royal Cousin: Life of Henry IV of France, Doubleday; auth, Life of Catherine de Medici, Coward, 74. **CONTACT ADDRESS** Dept of English, Col of New Rochelle, New Rochelle, NY 10801.

MAHONEY, JOHN FRANCIS

PERSONAL Born 05/19/1929, Detroit, MI, m, 1980, 4 children **DISCIPLINE** ENGLISH, CLASSICS **EDUCATION** Univ Detroit, BA, 50, MA, 52; Univ NC, PhD, 56. **CAREER** Instr English, Univ NC, 53-56; instr Latin, Duke Univ, 54-56; asst prof Mid English, Duquesne Univ, 56-59, assoc prof English & chm grad studies, 59-61; assoc prof English & comp lit, Univ Detroit, 61-63, chm grad comt, 61-64, prof, chem dept and English, 64-69, dean col arts & sci, 69-73; dean, Walden Univ, 73-74; vpres acad affairs, William Paterson Col NJ, 74-78; Dean, Walden Univ, 79-, Southern Fels Fund fel, 56; mem bd, Am Grad & Prof Comn, 66-; pres, Vri, Inc, 79-90; admin dir, Beli-Laddi farm, 80- ; ed & publ Imperial Beach & South County Times, 85-98; columnist, Imperial Beach Eagle & Times, 98- ; Project Develop Officer, B.E.L.I., Inc., 96- . **MEMBERSHIPS** MLA; Mediaeval Acad Am; Dante Soc Am; Soc Exceptional Children. **RESEARCH** Mixed media; mediaeval languages; Dante. **SELECTED PUBLICATIONS** Ed, The Structure of Purgatorio, Dante Soc Bull, 62; Chaucerian Tragedy and the Christian Tradition, Ann Mediaevale, 62; American Authors and Critics (12 vols), Holt, 62-; coauth, Studies in Honor of U T Holmes, Jr, Univ NC, Chapel Hill, 66; The Insistent Present, Houghton, 70; co-ed, New Poets, New Music, Winthrop, 71; coauth, Early Help (film), Medianovations, 73; The House of Tenure (play), Medianovations, 80. **CONTACT ADDRESS** PO Box 5429, Playa del Rey, CA 92293. **EMAIL** mahwis@gte.net

MAHONEY, JOHN L.

PERSONAL Born 02/04/1928, Somerville, MA, m, 1956, 3 children **DISCIPLINE** ENGLISH **EDUCATION** Boston Col, BA, 50; MA, 52; Harvard Unv, PhD, 57. **CAREER** Instr to prof, Boston Col, 95-. **HONORS AND AWARDS** Mass Prof of the Year, 89; Phi Beta Kappa Teaching Awd, Boston Col, 94; Thomas F. Rattigan Chair of English, 94-. **MEMBERSHIPS** MLA; Keats-Shelley Assoc; Wordsworth-Coleridge Assoc; The Johnsonians. **RESEARCH** British Enlightenment and Romantic Literature, Literature and Religion. **SELECTED PUBLICATIONS** Ed, The English Romantics: Major Poetry and Critical Theory, D.C. Heatland (Lexington and Toronto), 78; ed, The Enlightenment and English Literature, Health and co, (Lexington and Toronto), 81; auth, The Persistence of Tragedy: Episodes in the History of Drama", Boston Public Libr, NEH, 85; auth, The Whole Internal Universe: Imitation and the New Defense of Poetry, 1660-1830, Fordham Univ Pr, (NY), 85; coed, Coleridge, Keats and the Imagination: Romanticism and Adam's Dream, Univ of Miss Pr, (Columbia), 89; auth, Wordsworth: A Poetic Life, Fordham Univ Pr, (NY), 97; auth, "William Hazlett",Encycl of the Essay, ed Tracy Chevalier, Fitzroy Dearborn (London), 97; auth, "Literature and Religion: Theory to Practice", Perspectives on the Unity and Integration of Knowledge, ed Ronald Glasberg, Peter Lang (NY), 97; ed, Seeing Into the Life of Things: Essays on Religion and Literature, Fordham Univ Pr, (NY), 98, auth, "The Rydal Mount Ladies Boarding School: Wordsworthean Education in America", Cult Interaction in the Romantic Age, ed Gregory Maertz, State Univ of NY Pr, 98. **CONTACT ADDRESS** Dept English, Boston Col, Chestnut Hill, 140 Commonwealth Ave, Chestnut Hill, MA 02467-3800. **EMAIL** mahoneyj@bc.edu

MAHONY, ROBERT E. P.

PERSONAL Born 09/08/1946, Bronxville, NY, m, 1973, 1 child **DISCIPLINE** ENGLISH LITERATURE & IRISH STUDIES **EDUCATION** Georgetown Univ, AB, 68; Trinity Col, Dublin, PhD, 74. **CAREER** Asst prof, Univ IL, Chicago Circle, 74-79; asst prof, 79-82, Assoc Prof Eng, Cath Univ Am, 82. **MEMBERSHIPS** Am Center for Irish Studies; Int Soc for Study of Irist Lit; Am Soc 18th Century Studies. **RESEARCH** Eighteenth century poetry and poetics; Anglo-Irish lit; bibl; Swift. **SELECTED PUBLICATIONS** Auth, Ed, Different Styles of Poetry, Cadenus, Dublin, 78; coauth (with Betty Rizzo), Christopher Smart: An Annotated Bibliograhy, Garland, 84; The Annotated Letters of Christopher Smart, Southern Ill Univ Press, 91; Jonathan Swift: The Irish Identity, Yale, 95. **CONTACT ADDRESS** Dept of Eng, Catholic Univ of America, 620 Michigan Ave N E, Washington, DC 20064-0002. **EMAIL** mahony@cua.edu

MAIER, JOHN

PERSONAL Born 06/14/1943, Charleston, WV, m, 1966, 1 child **DISCIPLINE** ENGLISH **EDUCATION** Duquesne Univ, BA, 65, PhD, 70; Univ Pa, AM, 66. **CAREER** Instr Eng, Duquesne Univ, 66-69; asst prof, Clarion State Col, 69-71; from Asst Prof to Assoc Prof, 71-85, Prof Eng, State Univ Ny Col Brockport, 85-99, Distinguished Teaching Prof, 99-. Co-ed, Lit Onomastics Studies, 74-78; Fulbright-Hays lectr, Syria & Jordan, 79-80, Morocco, 89-; Dir, NEH Summer Seminar, 86, 93. **HONORS AND AWARDS** State Univ NY Res Found grants, 76, 79, 81 & 82; Nat Endowment of Humanities fel, 77; SUNY Chancellor's Awd for Excellence in Tchg, 96. **MEMBERSHIPS** Soc Bibl Lit; Am Orient Soc; MLA; Int Asn Philos & Lit; Mediaeval Acad Am. **RESEARCH** Eng Renaissance lit; lit of the ancient Near East; lit theory and criticism. **SELECTED PUBLICATIONS** Auth, Mesopotamian names in The Sunlight Dialogues, or, Mama makes it to Batavia, New York, Lit Onomastics Studies, 77; Image and Paradox in Venus and Adonis and The Rape of Lucrece, English Studies Collections, 77; The file on Leonidas Le Cenci Hamilton, Am Lit Realism, 1870-1910, 78; co-ed, The Bible in Its Literary Milieu: Contemporary Essays, Eerdmans, 80; Is Tiamat really Mother Huber?, Lit Onomastics Studies, 82; The Truth of a most ancient work: Interpreting a poem addressed to a holy place, Centrum, 82; coauth, Gilgamesh, Translated from the Version of Sinleqi unninni, 84; Myths of Enki, The Crafty God, 89; co-ed, Mappings of the Biblical Terrain: The Bible as Text, 90; auth, Desert Songs: Western Images of Morocco and Moroccan Images of the West, 96; ed, Gilgamesh: A Reader, 97; author of numerous other articles. **CONTACT ADDRESS** Dept of Eng, SUNY, Col at Brockport, 350 New Campus Dr, Brockport, NY 14420-2914. **EMAIL** jmaier@rochester.rr.com

MAIER, LINDA

PERSONAL Born 11/01/1957, Jefferson City, MO **DISCIPLINE** SPANISH AMERICAN LITERATURE **EDUCATION** WA Univ, AB, 80; Univ VA, MA, 82; PhD, 87. **CAREER** Univ Ala in Huntsville. **MEMBERSHIPS** Am Asn of Teachers of Span and Port; Int Asn of Hispanists; MLA; South American MLA. **SELECTED PUBLICATIONS** Auth, Borges and the European Avant-garde, Lang, 96. **CONTACT ADDRESS** Univ of Alabama, Huntsville, Huntsville, AL 35899. **EMAIL** maierl@email.uah.edu

MAIERS, JOAN

PERSONAL Born Washington, DC **DISCIPLINE** ENGLISH, POETRY **EDUCATION** Univ Washington, BS. **CAREER** Instr, HS's, Elder Hostel; Oasis; instr, Marylhurst Univ; pharm, non-profit org. **MEMBERSHIPS** PSOP; OSPA; PEN USA. **RESEARCH** Poetry manuscripts. **SELECTED PUBLICATIONS** Coauth, Blooming in the Shade; auth, If I Had a Hammer; auth, Twelve Oregon Poets 1, 2, 3, (Chap Books). **CONTACT ADDRESS** Dept Humanities, Marylhurst Col, PO Box 33, Marylhurst, OR 97036.

MAIO, SAMUEL

PERSONAL Born 05/16/1955, Raton, NM, m, 1978, 4 children **DISCIPLINE** ENGLISH **EDUCATION** Univ Utah, BA, 77; MA, 79; Univ Southern Calif, PhD, 86. **CAREER** Lectr,

Univ of Calif, 85-90; lectr to prof, San Jose State Univ, 90-. **HONORS AND AWARDS** Calif State Univ Grants, 92, 94; Grant, San Jose State Univ, 96; Christian Gauss Awd, 96; Teaching Awd, San Jose State Univ, 97; Pulitzer Prize nomination, 98. **SELECTED PUBLICATIONS** Auth, Creating Another Self: Voice in Modern American Personal Poetry, Thomas Jefferson Univ Pr, 95; auth, "Writing Assignments on W H Auden's Musee des Beaux Arts",Teaching Composition with Literature: Writing Exercises and Ideas, ed Dana Gioia, Harper-Collins, (NY, 95): 84-85; auth, "The Word Lunacy was Never Employed: A Defense of the Structure of Poe's Narrative of Arthur Gordon Pym", SDak Rev 35.1 (97): 54-67; auth, The Burning of Los Angeles, Thomas Jefferson Univ Pr, 97; auth, "Edwin Muir, Scottish Bard", Formalist 9.1 (98); auth, "Arrivato!", Ital Americana 16.1 (98); auth, Counter-Measures; Metrical Poetry in the Modern Age, Thomas Jefferson Univ Pr, 00. **CONTACT ADDRESS** Dept English, San Jose State Univ, 1 Washington Sq, San Jose, CA 95192-0001.

MAITZEN, ROHAN AMANDA
DISCIPLINE 19TH-CENTURY BRITISH NOVEL, VICTORIAN LITERATURE **EDUCATION** Univ Brit Columbia, BA, 90; Cornell Univ, MA, 93, PhD, 95. **CAREER** Tchg asst, Cornell Univ; asst prof, 95-. **HONORS AND AWARDS** Mellon Dissertation Yr fel, 94-95; Sage grad fel, 93-94; Mellon fel, 90-92; Commonwealth scholar, Cambridge Univ, 90; Eng hon(s) medal and prize, Univ Brit Columbia, 90; ch, nominating comm, 97-98; undergrad comm, 96-97; undergrad adv, dept eng, 96-97; **MEMBERSHIPS** Mem, Inter Unit Rev Comm, 98; Acad Develop Comm, 98-01; Adv Comm, 98-01; Undergrad Comm, 98-99; Acad Fin and Plan Comm, 97-98; Lib and Arch Comm, Univ King's Col, 96-98; Int Unit Rev Comm, 96-97. **SELECTED PUBLICATIONS** Auth, "This Feminine Preserve: Historical Biographies By Victorian Women," Victorian Stud, 95; "By No Means An Improbable Fiction: Redgauntlet's Novel Historicism," Stud in the Novel, 93; rpt, Critical Essays on Sir Walter Scott: The Waverley Novels, G.K. Hall, 96; Gender, Genre, and Victorian Historical Writing, Garland, 98; rev, Review of Rosemarie Bodenheimer, The Real Life of Mary Ann Evans: George Eliot, Her Letters and Fiction, Cornell UP, 94; Victorian Rev, 95. **CONTACT ADDRESS** Dept of Eng, Dalhousie Univ, Halifax, NS, Canada B3H 3J5. **EMAIL** rohan.maitzen@dal.ca

MAJOR, CLARENCE
PERSONAL Born 12/31/1936, Atlanta, GA, m, 1980 **DISCIPLINE** ENGLISH **EDUCATION** State Univ of New York at Albany, BS; Union Institute, PhD. **CAREER** Writer; Sarah Lawrence College, Bronxville, NY, lecturer, 72-75; Howard University, Washington, DC, lecturer, 75-76; University of Washington, Seattle, WA, assistant professor, 76-77; University of Colorado, Boulder, CO, associate professor, 77-81, professor, 81-89; University of California at Davis, Prof, 89-; has held numerous other positions as visiting professor, consultant, and lecturer. **HONORS AND AWARDS** Nat'l Council on the Arts Awd, Assn of Univ Presses, 1970; Pushcart prize for poem "Funeral," 1976; Fulbright-Hays Inter-Univ Exchange Awd, Franco-Amer Comm for Educational Exchange, 1981-83; Western State Book Awd for Fiction (My Amputations), 1986. **SELECTED PUBLICATIONS** All-Night Visitors (novel), 1969; Dictionary of Afro-American Slang, 1970; Swallow the Lake (poetry), 1970; Symptoms and Madness (poetry), 1971; Private Line (poetry), 1971; The Cotton Club: New Poems, 1972; No (novel), 1973; The Dark and Feeling: Black American Writers and Their Work (essays), 1974; The Syncopated Cakewalk (poetry), 1974; Reflex and Bone Structure (novel), 1979; Emergency Exit (novel), 1979; Inside Diameter: The France Poems, 1985; My Amputations: A Novel, 1986; Such Was the Season: A Novel, 1987; Surfaces and Masks (poetry), 1987; Some Observations of a Stranger at Zuni in the Latter Part of the Century (poetry), 1988; Painted Turtle: Woman with Guitar (novel), 1988; Juba to Jive: A Dictionary of African-American Slang, Penguin, 1994; Calling the Wind, Anthology, 1993; The Garden Thrives, Anthology, 1996; Dirty Bird Blues, Novel, 1996; Configurations: New and Selected Poems: 1958-1998; author of numerous articles, reviews and anthologies; editor. **CONTACT ADDRESS** Dept of English, Univ of California, Davis, Davis, CA 95616.

MAJOR, WILFRED E.
DISCIPLINE CLASSICS **EDUCATION** Southern IL Univ Carbondale, BA, 89; IN Univ, MA, 91; IN Univ, PhD, 96. **CAREER** Assoc instr, IN Univ, 90-94; instr, Hobart and William Smith Col, 94-96; instr, Loyola Univ New Orleans, 95-97; adj instr, Tulane Univ, 96-97; asst prof, St Anselm Col, 97-00; vis asst prof, Loyola Univ, 00-. **HONORS AND AWARDS** Phi Kappa Phi, Southern Ill Univ, 88; Indiana Univ Grad Sch Fel, 89; Dr. Lola Case Bk Awd, 93; Grad Student Travel Awd, 95; Help Our Peers Execl (HOPE) Awd for Teaching Excellence, 97 **MEMBERSHIPS** Am Philological Asn; Classical Asn of New England; Classical Asn of the Middle West and South; Lousiana Classical Asn. **SELECTED PUBLICATIONS** Auth, Gorgias' Undeclared Theory of Arrangement Revisited, Southern Comm Jour, 97; Gorgias' "Undeclared" Theory of Arrangement: A Postscript to Smeltzer, Southern Comm Jour, 96; ed, Euripides: Andromache in Aris and Phillips 1994, Didaskalia, 95; auth, "Menander in Macedonian World," Greek Roman and Byzantine Studies 38 (97): 41-73; auth, "Social Class System and the Economy," The Roman Republic and Empire 264 BCE-476CE, World Eras Series, (Columbia, SC: Manly, 01); auth, "Antiphon, Crates, Cratinus," "Demetrius Phalereus," "Diocles of Carystus," "Eupolis," "Gelon of Syracuse," "Menander," and "Theron of Acragas," in Encyclopedia of the Ancient World, (Salem Press, forthcoming). **CONTACT ADDRESS** Dept of Classical Studies, Loyola Univ, New Orleans, 6363 St Charles Ave, Box 113, New Orleans, LA 70118. **EMAIL** wemajor@loyno.edu

MAKAU, JOSINA M.
PERSONAL Born 04/11/1950, Oostzahn, Netherlands **DISCIPLINE** RHETORIC, PHILOSOPHY **EDUCATION** Calif State Univ, Northridge, BA, 73; Univ Calif, Los Angeles, MA, 73; Univ Calif, Berkeley, MA, 76, PhD(rhetoric), 80. **CAREER** Asst Prof Commun, Ohio State Univ, 79-. **MEMBERSHIPS** Speech Commun Asn; Rhetoric Soc Am; Int Soc Hist Rhetoric; Cent States Speech Asn. **RESEARCH** Rhetoric and philosophy of law; modern theories of argumentation; rhetorical criticism. **SELECTED PUBLICATIONS CONTACT ADDRESS** Dept of Commun, Ohio State Univ, Columbus, Columbus, OH 43210.

MAKINO, YASUKO
PERSONAL Born 04/08/1937, Tokyo, Japan, m, 1963, 1 child **DISCIPLINE** LIBRARY SCIENCE; JAPANESE STUDIES **EDUCATION** Tokyo Women's Christian Univ, BA; Univ IL, MA, 70, MLS, 72. **CAREER** Univ IL, Urbana-Champaign, 72-91; Columbia Univ, 91-98; Princeton Univ Library, 98-. **MEMBERSHIPS** Asn for Asian Studies. **RESEARCH** Japanese bibliography and reference works. **SELECTED PUBLICATIONS** Auth, Japan Through Children's Literature, Greenwood Press, 85; Student Guide to Japanese Sources in the Humanities, Center for Japanese Studies, Univ MI, 94; Japan and the Japanese: A Bibliographical Guide to Reference Sources, Greenwood Press, 96. **CONTACT ADDRESS** Princeton Univ, Gest Libr, Princeton, NJ 08544. **EMAIL** ymakino@princeton.edu

MALACHUK, DANIEL S.
PERSONAL Born 05/18/1967, Plainfield, NJ, m **DISCIPLINE** ENGLISH, LITERATURE **EDUCATION** Bowdoin Col, BA, 89; Rutgers Univ, MA, 94; PhD, 96. **CAREER** Asst Prof, Daniel Webster Col, 97-. **HONORS AND AWARDS** Phi Beta Kappa. **RESEARCH** Nineteenth-Century English and American literature, American pragmatism, jazz. **SELECTED PUBLICATIONS** Auth, "The Republican Philosophy of Emerson's Early Lectures," The New England Quarterly 71,3 (98): 404-428; auth, "Walt Whitman and the Culture of Pragmatism," Walt Whitman Quart Rev 17,1/2 (99): 62-70; auth, "'Loyal to a Dream Country': Republicanism and the Pragmatism of William James and Richard Rorty," J of Am Studies (forthcoming); auth, "Coleridge's Republicanism and the Aphorism in 'Aids to Reflection'," Studies in Romanticism (forthcoming). **CONTACT ADDRESS** Dept Soc Sci, Daniel Webster Col, 20 University Dr, Nashua, NH 03063-1323. **EMAIL** malachuk@dwc.edu

MALAMUD, MARTHA A.
PERSONAL Born Boston, MA, m, 2 children **DISCIPLINE** CLASSICS **EDUCATION** Bryn Mawr, BA, 78; Cornell, PhD, 85. **CAREER** Asst, assoc prof, Univ of Southern Cal, 84-92; assoc prof, classics dept, Univ of Buffalo (SUNY), 92-. **HONORS AND AWARDS** Mellon fel; Rome prize: NEH sr fel, Amer Acad in Rome, 88-89; ACLS grant. **MEMBERSHIPS** Amer Philol Asn. **RESEARCH** Late antique lit; Latin epic; Allusion and the development of the Roman Imperial period **SELECTED PUBLICATIONS** Ed, Arethusa;m auth, A Poetics of Transformation: Prudentius and Classical Mythology **CONTACT ADDRESS** Classics Dept., SUNY, Buffalo, Clemens Hall, Buffalo, NY 14260. **EMAIL** malamud@acsu.buffalo.edu

MALAND, CHARLES J.
PERSONAL Born 09/21/1949, Albert Lea, MN, m, 1973, 1 child **DISCIPLINE** AMERICAN CULTURE **EDUCATION** Augsburg Col, BA, 71; Univ Mich, MA, 72; PhD, 75. **CAREER** Lake Forest Col, 76-78; asst prof, 78-83; assoc prof, 83-90; prof, 90-, Univ Tenn. **HONORS AND AWARDS** AFI, Rockefeller Found Sem; Lilly Found Fel; Fulbright Fel; Hodges Teach Awd; AA Outstand Teach Awd. **MEMBERSHIPS** ASA; SCS; IAMHIST. **RESEARCH** American film and its relationship to American culture. **SELECTED PUBLICATIONS** Auth, American Visions: The films of Chaplin, Ford, Capra and Welles, 1936-1941, 71; rev, ed, Frank Capra, 95; auth, Chaplin and American Culture: The Evolution of a Star Image, 89. **CONTACT ADDRESS** Dept English, Univ of Tennessee, Knoxville, 1345 Circle Park, Knoxville, TN 37996-0001.

MALANDRA, WILLIAM
DISCIPLINE CLASSICAL AND NEAR EASTERN STUDIES **EDUCATION** Haverford Col, BA, 64; Brown Univ, BA, 66; Univ Pa, PhD, 71. **CAREER** Assoc prof, Univ Minn, Twin Cities. **RESEARCH** Indo-Iranian philological studies. **SELECTED PUBLICATIONS** Auth, Avestan zanu-drajah: an Obscene Gesture, Indo-Iranian J 22, 80; An Introduction to Old Iranian Religion, Univ Minn Press, 83; Rasnu and the Office of Divine Judge: Comparative Reconstructions and the Varuna Problem, Festschrift for Ludo Rocher, Madras: Adyar Libr, 87. **CONTACT ADDRESS** Univ of Minnesota, Twin Cities, 9 Pleasant St. SE, 330 Folwell Hall, Minneapolis, MN 55455.

MALEK, ABBAS
PERSONAL Born 07/02/1945, Iran, m, 1997, 1 child **DISCIPLINE** COMMUNICATIONS **EDUCATION** Amer Univ, PhD. **CAREER** Assoc prof. **MEMBERSHIPS** Pres, Int Commun sect, IAMCR. **RESEARCH** International communication; cross cultural communication; communication policy. **SELECTED PUBLICATIONS** Auth, News Media & Foreign Relations, Ablex, 97; ed, bk series, Contemp Stud in Int Political Commun; Global Dynamic of News, ed, Ablex, 00. **CONTACT ADDRESS** School of Communications, Howard Univ, 2400 Sixth St NW, Washington, DC 20059. **EMAIL** amalek@erols.com

MALICOTE, S.
PERSONAL Born 02/24/1947, IN, s, 3 children **DISCIPLINE** LITERATURE, INTERDISCIPLINARY STUDIES **EDUCATION** Butler Univ, BA, 68; Ind Univ, MA, 70; PhD, 74. **CAREER** Vis asst prof, Purdue Univ, 74-76; asst prof, Wabash Col, 76-79; asst prof, Marshtill Col, 79-85; from assoc prof to prof & chair, Univ of NC at Asheville, 85- **HONORS AND AWARDS** NEH Summer Stipend, Harvard, 78; Feldman Distinguished Prof, UNCA, 92; NEH Summer Stipend, Cornell, 93. **MEMBERSHIPS** Am Asn of Teachers of French, Asn of Integrative Studies **RESEARCH** Medieval French literature, old French epic (13th century), word and image in the medieval French epic. **SELECTED PUBLICATIONS** Auth, "The Role of Manuscript illumination in 'The Chanson de Jeste, Aiol,'" Romania 114 (96): 316-334; auth, "The Illuminated Geste de Saint Gilles," Romanic Review (Forthcoming). **CONTACT ADDRESS** Dept For Lang, Univ of No Carolina, Asheville, 1 Univ Heights, Asheville, NC 28804-3251. **EMAIL** malicote@unca.edu

MALLARD, HARRY
DISCIPLINE MUSIC HISTORY **EDUCATION** Sam Houston State Univ, BM, MA; Univ Tex, PhD. **CAREER** Coordr, Hist and Lit Stud, prof, Sam Houston State Univ. **HONORS AND AWARDS** NEH grant recipient. **RESEARCH** 18th-century musical thought. **CONTACT ADDRESS** School of Music, Sam Houston State Univ, 1801 Ave I, Suite 225, Huntsville, TX 77341-2208. **EMAIL** mus_jhm@shsu.edu

MALLIN, DEA Z.
PERSONAL Born 04/01/1942, Philadelphia, PA, w, 1977, 1 child **DISCIPLINE** ENGLISH **EDUCATION** Univ Pa, BA, 64; MA, 68. **CAREER** Assoc Prof, Community Col of Philadelphia, 70-. **HONORS AND AWARDS** Christian R. and Mary F. Lindback Found Awd for Distinguished Teaching, 93; Who's Who in the E; Who's Who in Writers, Editors, and Poets; Phi Beta Kappa. **MEMBERSHIPS** Phi Beta Kappa, Mortanboard, Am Asn of Univ Women. **RESEARCH** Long-term effects of loss in childhood upon literary output. **SELECTED PUBLICATIONS** Auth, chap in The Day My Father Died (Running Press, 93); auth, chap in Creativity and Madness; Psychological Studies of Art and Artists, (Edgar Allan Poe: Descent into Madness?) (AIMED Press, 94); articles in Islands, Wash Post, Philadelphia Inquirer, Boston Globe, Baltimore Sun, Burlington Co Times. **CONTACT ADDRESS** Dept English, Comm Col of Philadelphia, 1700 Spring Garden St, Philadelphia, PA 19130-3936. **EMAIL** dmallin@ccp.cc.pa.us

MALM, WILLIAM P.
PERSONAL Born 03/06/1928, LaGrange, IL, m, 1954, 3 children **DISCIPLINE** ETHNOMUSICOLOGY **EDUCATION** Northwestern Univ, BA, 49, MM, 50; Univ Calif, Los Angeles, PhD, 59. **CAREER** Instr music, Univ Ill, 50-51; instr, US Naval Sch Music, 51-52; lectr, Univ Calif, Los Angeles, 57-60; from asst prof to assoc prof, 60-66, PROF MUSIC, UNIV MICH, ANN ARBOR, 66-94, Am Coun Learned Soc grant, 63; sr fel, Cult Learning Inst, EAst-West Ctr, Hawaii, 73; Ernest Bloch prof music, Univ Calif, Berkeley, 80; dir, Stearns Collection, 81-94; Univ of Haw, 00. **HONORS AND AWARDS** Henry Russel Awd, 65; Koizumi Fumio Prize, 93. **MEMBERSHIPS** Soc Ethnomusicol (pres, 77-79); Soc Asian Music; Asn Asian Studies; Int Folk Music Coun. **RESEARCH** Japanese music; holography; computer data banks in organology. **SELECTED PUBLICATIONS** Auth, Comparative Musicology and Anthropology of Music--Essays on the History of Ethnomusicology, Music and Letters, Vol 0074, 93; auth, Music Cultures of the Pacific, Near East and Asia, Prentice-Hall, 3rd ed, 96; auth, Japanese Traditional Music and Musical Instrument, Kodansua, 00. **CONTACT ADDRESS** 1530 Cedar Bend Dr, Ann Arbor, MI 48105. **EMAIL** malm@umich.edu

MALOF, JOSEPH FETLER
PERSONAL Born 05/26/1934, Riga, Latvia, m, 1957, 3 children **DISCIPLINE** ENGLISH **EDUCATION** Kenyon Col, BA, 56; Univ Calif, Los Angeles, MA, 57, PhD(English), 62. **CAREER** Asst English, Univ Calif, Los Angeles, 60-61; from

instr to assoc prof, 61-73, Prof English, Univ Tex, Austin, 73-, E Harris Harbison Prize, Danforth Found, 70. **RESEARCH** Twentieth century poetry in English; American literature; English versification. **SELECTED PUBLICATIONS** Auth, The native rhythm of English meters, Tex Studies Lit & Lang, Winter 64; Meter as organic form, Mod Lang Quart, 3/66; A Manual of English Meters, Ind Univ, 70; Haiku in heroics, Lit East & West 3/71. **CONTACT ADDRESS** Dept of English, Univ of Texas, Austin, Austin, TX 78712-1026.

MALONE, DUMAS
PERSONAL Born 01/10/1902, Coldwater, MS, m, 1925, 2 children **DISCIPLINE** HISTORY, BIOGRAPHY **EDUCATION** Emory Univ, BA, 10; Yale Univ, BA, 16, MA, 21, PhD, 23. **CAREER** Instr hist, Yale Univ, -23, asst prof, 23; from assoc prof to prof, Univ Va, 23-29; ed, Dict Am Biog, 29-31, ed-in-chief, 31-36; dir and chmn bd Syndics, Harvard Univ Press, 36-43; prof hist, Columbia Univ, 45-59; Jefferson Found prof hist, 59-62, BIOGRAPHER IN RESIDENCE, UNIV VA, 62-, Vis prof, Yale Univ, 27, Sterling sr fel, 27-28; ed, Hist Bk Club, 48-; Guggenheim fels, 51-52 and 58-59; managing ed, Polit Sci Quart, 53-58; hon consult, Am hist, Libr Congr, 68. **HONORS AND AWARDS** Porter Prize, Yale Univ, 23, Wilbur L Cross Medal, 72; Thomas Jefferson Awd, Univ Va, 64; John F Kennedy Medal, Mass Hist Soc, 72; Pulitzer Prize in Hist, 75; dlitt, emory univ and rochester univ, 36, dartmouth col, 37 and col william and mary, 77; lld, northwestern univ, 35 and univ chattanooga, 62. **MEMBERSHIPS** AHA; Southern Hist Asn(pres, 67-68); Am Antiq Soc; Am Acad Arts and Sci; Soc Am Hist. **RESEARCH** Early American history. **SELECTED PUBLICATIONS** Auth, A Linguistic Approach to the Bakhtinian Hero in Martin, Steve 'Roxanne', Lit-Film Quart, Vol 0024, 96. **CONTACT ADDRESS** Alderman Libr, Univ of Virginia, Charlottesville, VA 22901.

MALONE, EDWARD A.
PERSONAL Born 06/03/1962, Redbank, NJ, m, 1995, 2 children **DISCIPLINE** ENGLISH **EDUCATION** Southwest Mo State Univ, BSEd, 84; MA, 87; S Ill Univ, PhD, 93. **CAREER** Teacher, CAEL, Brazil, 79; teacher, Mansfield, MO, 84-85; GTA, S Ill Univ, 87-92; adj lectr to lectr, Univ of Mo, 93-96; asst prof to assoc prof, Mo Western State Col, 96-. **HONORS AND AWARDS** Mildred Henderson Ewsing Awd, SMSU, 84; LAS Coun of Chairpersons Awd, MWSC, 97; Dr. James V. Mehl Outstanding Fac Scholarship Awd, MWSC, 01. **MEMBERSHIPS** MLA, Renaissance Soc of Am, Soc for Tech Communicators, Edmund Spenser Soc, Vladimir Nabokov Soc. **RESEARCH** Renaissance rhetoric and literature, Edmund Spenser, John Milton, History of the English Language. **SELECTED PUBLICATIONS** Auth, The Cartomancer, Macguffin, 89; auth, "Nabokov on Faulkner," Faulkner Jour, (00); auth, "Doubting Thomas and John the Carpenter's Oaths in the Miller's Tale," English Lang Notes, (91); coauth, "Nabokov in Letters: An Annotated Bibliogr, " The Nabokovian, (94); ed, The Project Gutenberg Edition of the Blue Lagoon: A Romance, by H. de Vere Stacpool, Project Gutenberg, (96); rev, of Milton and Spenser, Milton Quart, (96); auth, "Marriane Postans," British Travel Writers, 1837-1975: Victorian Period, (96); coauth, "Sydney and Moorehouse's Metropolitan Trilogy," Anglistik, (00); coauth, "Technology and Society; Redefining Human Life: Characterizing Human Life in the Age of Technology," Jour of Col Sci Teachers, (01); ed, British Rhetoricians and Logicians, 1550-1600, First Series, Dict of Lit Biogr, Gale, 01. **CONTACT ADDRESS** Missouri Western State Col, 4525 Downs Dr, Saint Joseph, MO 64507. **EMAIL** malone@mwsc.edu

MALOUF, MELISSA
DISCIPLINE ENGLISH LITERATURE **EDUCATION** Univ CA Irvine, PhD, 79. **CAREER** Prof, Duke Univ. **HONORS AND AWARDS** Pushcart Prize, 89. **SELECTED PUBLICATIONS** Auth, It Had to Be You, Press, 97; No Guarantees, William Morrow, 90. **CONTACT ADDRESS** Eng Dept, Duke Univ, Durham, NC 27706.

MALSBARY, GERALD HENRY
PERSONAL Born 11/06/1952, Oakland, CA, m, 1979, 5 children **DISCIPLINE** CLASSICS **EDUCATION** Univ Calif, Berkeley, BA, 74, MA, 76; Univ Toronto, PhD, 88. **CAREER** Asst prof, St. Michael's Col, 87-89; res, Thesaurus Linguae Latinae, Munich, 89-91; prof, St. Charles Borromeo Sem, 91- . **HONORS AND AWARDS** Am Philol Asn, TLL fel, 89. **MEMBERSHIPS** APA; NAMLA. **RESEARCH** Trivium; ethics; metaphysics; education history; Vatican II doctrines; Chinese and Indian philosophy. **SELECTED PUBLICATIONS** Three articles on Early Christian Latin; four books translated from German and Italian. **CONTACT ADDRESS** 260 Ballymore Rd, Springfield, PA 19064. **EMAIL** drmalsbary@juno.com

MALTZ, DIANA F.
PERSONAL Born 06/18/1965, NY **DISCIPLINE** ENGLISH **EDUCATION** Bennington Col, BA, 87; Stanford Univ, MA, 90, PhD, 97. **CAREER** Lectr, Stanford Univ, 97-98; asst prof, S Ore Univ, 99-. **HONORS AND AWARDS** Yale Cen British Art and Paul Mellon Cen British Art, 00; Ahmanson-Getty Postdoct Fel UCLA, 99; Dept Fem Stud, Stanford Univ, Res Fel/Teach Asst, 96; Colin V. Higgins Mem Dis Fel, 95. **MEMBERSHIPS** MLA, INCS, PCCBS. **SELECTED PUBLICATIONS** Auth, "Octavia Hill and The Aesthetics of Victorian Tenement Reform," in Homes and Homelessness in the Victorian Imagination: AMS Studies in Nineteenth-Century Literature and Culture, eds. H. M. Daleski and Murray Baumgarten (AMS Press, 99); auth, "Engaging Delicate Brains: From Working-Class Enculturation to Upper-Class Lesbian Liberation in Vernon Lee and Kit Anstruther-Thomson's Psychological Aesthetics," in Women and British Aestheticism, eds. Talia Schaffer and Kathy Psomiades (Univ Press of Vir, 99); auth, "Practical Aesthetics and Decadent Rationale in George Gissing," Vict Lit and Cult 28 (00); rev, Suzanne Keen's Renovations of the Victorian Novel: Narrative Annexes and the Boundaries of Representation, Nineteenth-Cen Lit 55 (00); auth, "Wilde's Woman's World and the Culture of Aesthetic Philanthropy" in Wilde Writings: Contextual Criticisms, ed. Joseph Bristow (Univ Toronto Press, 01). **CONTACT ADDRESS** Eng Dept., So Oregon Univ, 1250 Siskiyou Blvd, Ashland, OR 97520. **EMAIL** maltzd@sou.edu

MAMA, RAOUF
DISCIPLINE AFRICAN LITERATURE **EDUCATION** Univ MI, PhD. **CAREER** Eng Dept, Eastern Conn State Univ **SELECTED PUBLICATIONS** Tales in: Storytelling Mag; Parabola; CT Rev; Facts & Fiction. **CONTACT ADDRESS** Eastern Connecticut State Univ, 83 Windham Street, Willimantic, CT 06226. **EMAIL** MAMA@ECSU.CTSTATEU.EDU

MAMAN, MARIE
PERSONAL Born 12/27/1931, Norway, m, 1957, 4 children **DISCIPLINE** INFORMATION SCIENCE **EDUCATION** Degree, Stockholms Tekniska Inst, 54; Rutgers Univ, BA, 74, MLS, 76. **CAREER** Chem Techn, Norwegian Col Agriculture, 55-56; chem techn, Inst Nat de la Recherche Agronomique, 57; ref librn, 82-, circ libr, 84- Rutgers Univ. **MEMBERSHIPS** ALA; USAIN **RESEARCH** Women-bibliography **SELECTED PUBLICATIONS** Coauth, Women in Agriculture: A Guide to Research, 96; auth, art, Survey of the Literature on Women in Agriculture at the Rutgers University Libraries, 93; auth, art, Elise Boulding: A Bibliography, 92; coauth, art, Aims of User Education: Special Library Results, 92; auth, art, Cora Sandel (1890-1947), 91. **CONTACT ADDRESS** Mabel Smith Douglass Library, Rutgers, The State Univ of New Jersey, New Brunswick, 8 Chapel Dr, New Brunswick, NJ 08901-8521.

MAMOOJEE, ABDOOL-HACK
DISCIPLINE CLASSICS **EDUCATION** Merton Col, Oxford, BA, 65, MA, 68; Univ Ottawa, PhD, 78. **CAREER** Instr, Royal Col, Port-Louis, Mauritius; Univ Quebec, Univ Ottawa; prof, 69-. **HONORS AND AWARDS** Ch, dept lang; deputy-dean, Fac Arts; corresponding mem, Can Fed for the Hum; act mem, Class Assn Can. **MEMBERSHIPS** Classical Asn of Canada. **RESEARCH** Works of Cicero and the history of the Late Roman Republic. **SELECTED PUBLICATIONS** Auth, "Le proconsulat de Q. Ciceron en Asie," Echos du monde classique, vol. 38, (94): 23-50; auth, "Cicero, in togo candida fr. 8", Classical Views, vol. 39.3, (95): 401-412; rev, of A. Vasaly, representations: Images of the world in Ciceronian oratory, Classical Views, vol. 49.33, (95): 428-432; auth, Le proconsulat de Q. Ciceron en Asie, Echos du monde classique, 94; Cicero, In toga candida fr 8, Class Views, 95; rev, of J. W. Crawford, Cicero: the fragmentary speeches, Phoenix vol. 49.2, (95): 168-170, vol. 50.2, (96): 167; auth, "Cicero, ad Atticum 11.8.2: a note on Furnius", Classical Views, vol. 41.2, (97): 317-324; auth, "Cicero's choice of a deputy in Cilicia: the Quintus option," Ancient History Bulletin, vol. 12.1-1, (98): 19-28; auth, "Cicero: agrestis versus rusticus," Melanges Margaret Thomson, Cahier des etudes anciennes, vol. 34, (98): 95-102; auth, "Gratiarum actio iv Kal. Iun. Habita A.D. MIM", Classical Views, vol. 43.1, (99): 163-164. **CONTACT ADDRESS** Dept of Lang, Lakehead Univ, 955 Oliver Rd, Thunder Bay, ON, Canada P7B 5E1. **EMAIL** aketonen@sky.lakeheadu.ca

MANCHEL, FRANK
PERSONAL Born 07/22/1935, Detroit, MI, m, 1958, 2 children **DISCIPLINE** ENGLISH, COMMUNICATION **EDUCATION** Oh State Univ, BA, 57; Hunter Col, MA, 60; Columbia Univ, EdD, 66. **CAREER** Instr high sch, NY, 58-64; asst prof English, Southern Conn State Col, 64-67; assoc prof, 67-72, Prof Commun, Univ Vt, 72-, Assoc Dean, Col Arts & Sci, 77-88, Prog Coord, Commun Dept, 81-83, Dir grad English inter prof, Univ Vt, & La Mancha proj, 68; prof Eng, Univ VT, 88-00, prof emer, 00; mem nat comt innovative practices in English educ, 68; critic-at-large, WEZF-TV, 81-83. **MEMBERSHIPS** Soc Cinema Studies; Brit Film Inst; Univ Film & Video Asn. **RESEARCH** Motion picture; Black studies; comedy. **SELECTED PUBLICATIONS** Auth, Terrors of the Screen, 70 & Cameras West, 71, Prentice-Hall; Film Study: A Resource Guide, Fairleigh Dickinson Univ, 73; Yesterday's Clowns, 73, The Talking Clowns, 76, An Album of Great Science Fiction Films, 76, Women on the Hollywood Screen, 77 & Gangsters on the Screen, 78, Watts; Box-Office Clowns, 79 & An Album of Great Sports Movies, 80, Watts; Film Study: An Analytical Bibliography, 4 vol, 90. **CONTACT ADDRESS** 682 Forest Rd., Saint George, VT 05495-8046. **EMAIL** fmanchel@zoo.uvm.edu

MANCINI, ALBERT NICHOLAS
PERSONAL Born 09/15/1929, Trenton, NJ, m, 1968, 2 children **DISCIPLINE** LITERARY HISTORY **EDUCATION** Univ Naples, DLett, 57; Univ Calif, Berkeley, PhD(Romance lit), 64. **CAREER** Teaching asst Ital lang, Univ Calif, Berkeley, 57-61; instr Ital lang and lit and comp lit, Princeton Univ, 62-64; from asst prof to assoc prof, 64-67, consult, Sch Educ, 65-66, to assoc prof, 67-72, prof ital lang and lit, Ohio State Univ, 72-, Assoc ed, Forum Italicum, 78-; consult, Univ Toronto Press, Univ Calif Press, Princeton Univ Press and Ohio State Univ Press; evaluator, Nat Endowment for Humanities; vis prof, Ital Sch Middlebury Col, 78, 82, 85, 87, 89, 91; assoc ed, Italica, 94-; consult ed, Esperienze letterarie, 82-. **HONORS AND AWARDS** Distinguishing Prof Series, Univ Wis - Madison, 92; prof, NEH Summer Inst, Florence, Italy, 94; scholar in residence, Ital Sch, Middlebury Col, 95; Awd Ital Ministry of Educ, 95. **MEMBERSHIPS** Am Asn Teachers Ital; Dante Soc Am; Renaissance Soc Am; Am Asn for Ital Studies. **RESEARCH** Italian literature of the 15th, 16th and 17th centuries; cross-influences in Romance literatures in the same periods; bibliography. **SELECTED PUBLICATIONS** Auth, "Seicento Theatre, Seicento Narrative," in Cambridge History of Ital Lit, 97. **CONTACT ADDRESS** Dept of French and Ital, Ohio State Univ, Columbus, 1841 Millikin Rd, Columbus, OH 43210-1229. **EMAIL** mancini.1@osu.edu

MANDEL, OSCAR
PERSONAL Born, Belgium **DISCIPLINE** LITERATURE **EDUCATION** New York Univ, BA, 47; Columbia Univ, MA, 48; OSU, PhD, 51. **CAREER** Prof, Calif Inst of Technol, 61-. **RESEARCH** Drama; Aesthetics. **SELECTED PUBLICATIONS** Auth, The Art of Alessandro Magnasco, 94; auth, The Cheerfulness of Dutch Art: A Rescue Operation, 96; auth, Fundamentals of the Art of Poetry, 98; auth, August von Kotzebue: the Comedy, the Man, 90; auth, The 'Ariadne' of Thomas Corneille, 82; auth, Philoctetes and the Fall of Troy, 81 **CONTACT ADDRESS** Dept Humanities, California Inst of Tech, 1201 E Calif Blvd, Pasadena, CA 91125-0001. **EMAIL** om@hss.caltech.edu

MANDL, BETTE
PERSONAL Born 08/19/1940, Brooklyn, NY, m, 1960, 2 children **DISCIPLINE** ENGLISH **EDUCATION** Brooklyn Col, BA, 61; NY Univ, MA, 65; Boston Univ, EdD, 81. **CAREER** Instr, Cambridge Ctr for Adult Educ, 71-; from instr to prof, Suffolk Univ, 80-. **HONORS AND AWARDS** Res Scholar Awd, Boston Univ; Phi Beta Kappa; Outstanding Fac Member of the Year, 98. **MEMBERSHIPS** MLA, Nat Coun of Teachers of English, Eugene O'Neill Soc. **RESEARCH** Modern and Contemporary Drama, Women and Literature. **SELECTED PUBLICATIONS** Auth, "Disturbing Women: Wendy Kesselman's My Sister in this House," in Modern Am Drama: The Female Canon, ed. June Schlueter (NJ: Fairleigh Dickenson UP, 90), 246-253; auth, "Absence as Presence: The Second Sex in The Iceman Cometh," The Critical Response to Eugene O'Neill, ed. John Houchin (CT: Greenwood UP, 93), 184-190; auth, "Desire Under the Elms," Twentieth-Century Literary Criticism Vol 49, ed. Laurie Di Mauro (MI: Gale Res Inc., 93), 296-290; auth, "Gender and Design in Eugene O'Neill's Strange Interlude," The Eugene O'Neill Rev 19 (95): 123-128; auth, "'Alive Still in You': Memory and Silence in A Shayna Maidel," Staging Difference: Cultural pluralism in American Theatre and Drama," ed. Marc Maufort (NY: Peter Lang Pub, 95); auth, "Beyond Laughter and Forgetting: Echoes of the Holocaust in Neil Simon's Lost in Yonkers," in Neil Simon: A Casebook, ed. Gary Konas (Garland, 97); auth, "Women's Movement: The Personal as Political in the Plays of Wendy Wasserstein," Wendy Wasserstein: A Casebook, ed. Claudia Barnett (Garland, 99). **CONTACT ADDRESS** Dept English, Suffolk Univ, 8 Ashburton Place, Boston, MA 02108-2701. **EMAIL** bmandl@acad.suffolk.edu

MANER, MARTIN
PERSONAL Born 06/16/1946, Sturgis, MI, m, 1982, 2 children **DISCIPLINE** ENGLISH, LITERATURE **EDUCATION** Occidental Col, BA (cum laude), 68; Univ Virginia, MA, 72; PhD, 75. **CAREER** Teaching Asst, Univ of Virginia, 74-75; Lecturer, Univ of Virginia, 75-76; Asst Prof, Wright State Univ, 76-81; Assoc Prof, Wright State Univ, 81-89; Prof, Wright State, 89-. **HONORS AND AWARDS** NCTE Awd for Writing, 1964; Danforth Career Teaching, Fel, Univ of Virginia, 68-69; 71-74; Presidential Awd for Excellence in Research, Wright State Univ, 99. **MEMBERSHIPS** Modern Language Assn, Am Soc. For 18th Century Studies, AAUP. **RESEARCH** Eighteenth-Century British Lit, Research Writing, Satire, Samuel Johnson. **SELECTED PUBLICATIONS** Auth, The Philosophical Biographer, Univ of Georgia P (Athens, GA), 88; auth, The Spiral Guide to Research Writing, Mayfield (Mountain View, CA), 96; auth, The Research Process, Mayfield (Mountain View, CA), 00 **CONTACT ADDRESS** Dept English, Wright State Univ, Dayton, 3640 Colonel Glenn Hwy, Dayton, OH 45435-0001. **EMAIL** martin.maner@wright.edu

MANGANARO, ELISE SALEM
DISCIPLINE ENGLISH LITERATURE **EDUCATION** Univ NC, PhD. **CAREER** Fac, Fairleigh Dickinson Univ . **RESEARCH** 16th-18th century Brit lit, world lit, contemp Arab

writers, ethnic Am lit, cult studies, and mass media. **SELECTED PUBLICATIONS** Auth, essays in Engl Studies, MELUS, Biog East and West. **CONTACT ADDRESS** Fairleigh Dickinson Univ, Teaneck-Hackensack, 1000 River Rd, Teaneck, NJ 07666.

MANGANIELLO, DOMINIC
PERSONAL Born 11/04/1951, Cimitile, Italy, m, 1979, 1 child **DISCIPLINE** MODERN ENGLISH LITERATURE **EDUCATION** McGill Univ, BA, 74; Univ Oxford, DPhil, 78. **CAREER** Lectr, Univ Laval, 78-79; Asst Prof English Lit, Univ Ottawa, 79-. **MEMBERSHIPS** Dante and Modern Lit, the Inklings, Dorothy Sayers. **RESEARCH** T S Eliot and Dante. **SELECTED PUBLICATIONS** Auth, Joyce's Politics, London: Routledge and Kegan Paul, 80; auth, T.S. Eliot and Dante, London: Macmillan, New York: St. Martin's P, 89; coed, Rethinking the Future of the Univ, D. Jeffrey, Ottawa: Univ of Ottawa Press, 98. **CONTACT ADDRESS** Dept of English, Univ of Ottawa, 70 Laurier, Ottawa, ON, Canada K1N 6N5. **EMAIL** domeng@uottawa.ca

MANHEIM, MICHAEL
PERSONAL Born 03/04/1928, New York, NY, m, 1955, 2 children **DISCIPLINE** ENGLISH **EDUCATION** Columbia Col, AB, 49; Columbia Univ, MA, 51, PhD, 61. **CAREER** Instr English, Univ Del, 53-61; from asst prof to assoc prof, 61-67, assoc dean humanities, 63-66, chmn dept English, 66-72 and 79-82, Prof English, Univ Toledo, 67-, Danforth grant, 59-60; proj dir, Nat Endowment for Humanities Planning Proj, WGTE-TV-FM, Toledo, 76-78; mem, Chancellor's adv comt telecommun higher educ, 81. **HONORS AND AWARDS** Outstanding Teachers Awd, Univ Toledo, 74. **MEMBERSHIPS** Shakespeare Asn Am; Aaup; MLA; Midwest Mod Lang Asn. **RESEARCH** Shakespeare; Elizabethan drama; modern drama. **SELECTED PUBLICATIONS** Auth, Oneill, Eugene Creative Struggle, the Decisive Decade, 1924-1933, Mod Drama, Vol 0037, 94; The Function of Battle Imagery in Kurosawa Histories and the 'Henry V' Films, Lit-Film Quart, Vol 0022, 94. **CONTACT ADDRESS** Dept of English, Univ of Toledo, Toledo, OH 43606.

MANIATES, MARIA RIKA
PERSONAL Born 03/30/1937, Toronto, ON, Canada **DISCIPLINE** MUSICOLOGY, PHILOSOPHY **EDUCATION** Univ Toronto, BA, 60; Columbia Univ, MA, 62, PhD(musicol), 65. **CAREER** From lectr to assoc prof, 65-74, chmn dept, 73-78, PROF MUSICOL, UNIV TORONTO, 74-, Am Coun Learned Socs grant-in-aid musicol, 66-67; vis prof music, Columbia Univ, 67 and 76; appln appraiser musicol, Can Coun, 69-, res fel, 70-72; Einstein Award Comt, Am Musicol Soc, 76-79; Can Coun travel grants, 73, 75, 77, 78, 79, and 80; Univ Toronto humanities res grants, 78-79 and 79-80. **MEMBERSHIPS** Int Musicol Soc; Am Musicol Soc; Renaissance Soc Am; Can Renaissance Soc; Int Soc Hist Rhetoric. **RESEARCH** Renaissance music and culture; mannerism; philosophy and aesthetics. **SELECTED PUBLICATIONS** Auth, Musica Scientia--Musical Scholarship in the Italian Renaissance, Notes, Vol 0050, 93; The Politicized Muse--Music for Medici Festivals, 1512-1537, Renaissance and Reformation, Vol 0018, 94; Music in Renaissance Magic--Toward a Historiography of Others, J Amer Musicol Soc, Vol 0048, 95; **CONTACT ADDRESS** Fac of Music, Univ of Toronto, Toronto, ON, Canada M5S 1A1.

MANIQUIS, ROBERT MANUEL
PERSONAL Born 09/04/1940, Newark, NY, m, 1961, 2 children **DISCIPLINE** ENGLISH LITERATURE, COMPARATIVE LITERATURE **EDUCATION** Rutgers Univ, BA, 62; Columbia Univ, MA, 63, PhD(English), 67. **CAREER** Asst prof English, 66-77, dir freshman English, 75-76, Assoc Prof English, Univ Calif, Los Angeles, 77-, Am Coun Learned Soc fel, 72-73. **MEMBERSHIPS** MLA; Philol Asn PACIFIC Coast. **RESEARCH** Nineteenth century Romanticism, English, French, and German; 19th century novel, English, French, and German. **SELECTED PUBLICATIONS** Auth, Comparison, intensity, and time in Tintern Abbey, Criticism, fall 69; The puzzling Mimosa: Sensitivity and plant symbols in Romanticism, Studies Romanticism, spring 69; Lonely empires: Personal and public visions of Thomas De Quincey, In: Literary Monographs, Univ Wis, 76. **CONTACT ADDRESS** Dept of English, Univ of California, Los Angeles, Los Angeles, CA 90024.

MANLEY, FRANK
DISCIPLINE ENGLISH LANGUAGE AND LITERATURE **EDUCATION** Johns Hopkins Univ, PhD, 59. **CAREER** Charles Howard Candler Prof Ren Lit. **RESEARCH** Shakespeare; Donne; Renaissance drama and poetry. **SELECTED PUBLICATIONS** Ed/Trans, Epistola Ad Pomeranum; ed, All Fools; The Anniversaries; co-ed/trans, De Fructu qui ex Doctrina Percipitur. **CONTACT ADDRESS** English Dept, Emory Univ, 1380 Oxford Rd NE, Atlanta, GA 30322-1950. **EMAIL** fmanley@emory.edu

MANN, ALFRED
PERSONAL Born 04/28/1917, Hamburg, Germany, m, 3 children **DISCIPLINE** MUSIC **EDUCATION** State Acad Music, dipl, 37; Curtis Inst Music, dipl, 42; Columbia Univ, AM, 50, PhD, 55. **CAREER** Instr, State Acad, Berlin, 37; instr and res asst, Curtis Inst Music, 39-41; from asst prof to assoc prof, 47-56, prof, 56-79, EMER PROF MUSIC, RUTGERS UNIV, 80-; PROF MUSCICOL, EASTMAN SCH MUSIC, UNIV ROCHESTER, 80-, Conductor, Cantata Singers, NY, 52-59; dir publ, Am Choral Found, Inc and ed, Am Choral Rev, 61-; mem bd dirs, Georg Friedrich Handel Ges, Halle, 67-; Gottinger Handelges, 67-; mem, Bach Choir of Bethlehem, 69-81. **HONORS AND AWARDS** MusD, Spokane Conserv Music, 47, Baldwin-Wallace Col, 81. **MEMBERSHIPS** Am Musicol Soc; Int Musicol Soc; Neve Bachgesellschaft (secy, Am Chap, 72-). **RESEARCH** History of music theory and choral music. **SELECTED PUBLICATIONS** Coauth, Thomas Attwoods Theorie--und Kompositionsstudien bei Mozart, 65 and auth, J J Fux, Gradus ad Parnassum, 67, Barenreiter; coauth, the present state of Handel research, Acta Musicologica, 69; auth, Beethoven's contrapuntal studies with Haydn, Musical Quart, 70; Haydn's Elementarbuch, Music Forum, 73; Hanuel's Composition Lessons, Bareureiter, 79; Zur Kontrapunktlehre Haydons Und Mozarts, Mozart-Jahrbuch, 78, 79; Zu Schubert's Studien im Strengen Satz, Schuburt Congr Report, 78. **CONTACT ADDRESS** Eastman Sch of Music, Rochester, NY 14604.

MANN, BRIAN
PERSONAL Born San Francisco, CA **DISCIPLINE** MUSIC HISTORY **EDUCATION** Univ Edinburgh, BMus; Univ Calif, Berkeley, MA, PhD. **CAREER** Assoc prof, Vassar fac, 87-. **RESEARCH** Vocal music of the Italian Renaissance. **SELECTED PUBLICATIONS** Auth, monograph on the secular madrigals of the Flemish composer Filippo di Monte, 1521-1603, UMI Press, 83; res, Jagellonian Library, Kracow, Poland; Mus Libry Asn Notes, 92; ed, Complete Works, Filippo di Monte; Univ Leuven Press; Ensemble Mus of Paolo Quagliati, 94. **CONTACT ADDRESS** Classic Dept, Vassar Col, 124 Raymond Ave., Poughkeepsie, NY 12604. **EMAIL** mann@vassar.edu

MANN, DAVID D.
PERSONAL Born 09/13/1934, Oklahoma City, OK, m **DISCIPLINE** LITERATURE **EDUCATION** Okla State Univ, BS, 56; MA, 63; Ind Univ, PhD, 69. **CAREER** Instr, Wabash Col, 65-67; asst prof to assoc prof to prof, Miami Univ, 68-. **HONORS AND AWARDS** Folger Lib, 70; BSA, 88; Beinecke Lib, Yale Univ, 89; Lilly Lib, 91. **MEMBERSHIPS** ASES; MLA; SJSM; STS; SOME. **RESEARCH** 18th-century drama literature; Robert Louis Stevenson; Arthur Conan Doyle; textural criticism; children's literature. **SELECTED PUBLICATIONS** Ed, "The Enchantress," in A Concordance to the Plays and Poems William Congrere (Cornell Univ Pr, 73); auth, Sir George Etherege: A Reference Guide, GK Hall, 81; ed, A Concordance to the Plays and Poems of Sir George Etherege, Greenwood, 85; co-auth, Women Playwrights in England, Ireland, and Scotland, Ind Univ Pr, 96; ed, The Plays of Theophilus and Susannah Cibber, Garland, 98. **CONTACT ADDRESS** 2101 Twin Hill Rd, Louisville, KY 40207-1144. **EMAIL** ddmann@iglou.com

MANN, HARVEEN SACHDEVA
DISCIPLINE ENGLISH **EDUCATION** Government Col, India, BA, 77; Panjab Univ, India, MA, 79; Purdue Univ, West Lafayette,PhD, 86. **CAREER** Assoc prof. **RESEARCH** Postcolonial Stud; south Asian Stud; third world feminism; literary criticism and theory; Asian and Asian American Stud. **SELECTED PUBLICATIONS** Auth, Being Borne across: Translation and Salman Rushdie's The Satanic Verses, Criticism 37.2, 95; Women's Rights versus Feminism Postcolonial Perspectives, in Postcolonial Discourse and Changing Cultural Contexts: Theory and Criticism, Greenwood, 95; Bharat mein Mahila Lekhana, or Women's Writing in India: Regional Literatures, Translation, and Global Feminism, Socist Rev 24.4, 94; Cracking India: Minority Women Writers and the Contentious Margins of Indian Nationalist Discourse, The J Commonwealth Lit 29.2 , 94; articles on, gender and Sikh nationalism; ethics and Third World lit Stud; Saadat Hasan Manto and Mahasweta Devi. **CONTACT ADDRESS** Dept of English, Loyola Univ, Chicago, 6525 N. Sheridan Rd., Chicago, IL 60626. **EMAIL** hmann@wpo.it.luc.edu

MANN, JEFFREY A.
PERSONAL Born 08/08/1959, Clifton Forge, VA, s **DISCIPLINE** ENGLISH **EDUCATION** W Va Univ, BA, 81; BS, 81; MA, 84. **CAREER** Instr, W Va Univ, 87-89; Instr, Va Tech, 89-. **HONORS AND AWARDS** Phi Beta Kappa; Gamma Sigma Delta; Xi Sigma Pi, 81; Teaching Awd, Va Tech, 93; Winner, Stonewall Chapbook Competition, 97; Winner, Poetic Matrix Chapbook Series, 99; Winner, Gival Pr Chapbook Competition, 001 **MEMBERSHIPS** Appalachian Studies Assoc. **RESEARCH** Gay life in appalachia, the vampire in literature and film. **SELECTED PUBLICATIONS** Auth, Bliss, (Baltimore: BrickHouse Books) 98; auth, "Clematis" in Weeping with Those Who Weep: Poems of Bereavement, ed Barbara Smith and Arline Thorn, 98; auth, "The Misanthrope Grows Habanero Peppers" in Pine Mountain Sand and Gravel: Contemporary Appalachian Writing, 98; auth, "West Virginia Towns and Turnip Greens" in Pine Mountain Sand and Gravel: Contemporary Appalachian Writing, 99; auth, "Bones Washed with Wine" in L'Attitude, 99; auth, "Watering Broccoli", Potomac Review, 99; auth, "Mountain Fireflies and Creecy Greens", The Jour of Ky Studies, 99; auth, "Stonewall and Matewan: Some Thoughts on Gay Life in Appalachia", Jour of Appalachian Studies, 00; auth, Flint Shards from Sussex, Gival Pr, (Arlington, VA) 00; auth, Mountain Fireflies, Poetric Matrix (Yosemite, CA), 00. **CONTACT ADDRESS** Dept English, Virginia Polytech Inst and State Univ, 100 Virginia Tech, Blacksburg, VA 24061-0001.

MANN, JOHN STUART
PERSONAL Born 09/12/1945, Washington, DC, m, 1969, 2 children **DISCIPLINE** ENGLISH & AMERICAN LITERATURE **EDUCATION** Col Wooster, BA, 67; Univ PA, MA, 68, PhD, 72. **CAREER** Asst prof, 71-77, dir grad studies, dept Eng, 78-82, Assoc Prof Eng, Western IL Univ, 77-, Poetry & Ed ed, Miss Valley Rev Creative Writing, 73-95. **MEMBERSHIPS** MLA; Col Eng Asn; Am Asn Univ Prof. **RESEARCH** Nineteenth century Am fiction and poetry; contemp Ampoetry. **SELECTED PUBLICATIONS** Auth, Dream in Emily Dickinson's poetry, Emily Dickinson Bull, 78; Dickinson's Letters to Higginson: Motives for Metaphor, Higginson J Poetry, 78; The theme of the double in The Call of the Wild, Markham Rev, 78; Emily Dickinson, Emerson, and the poet as namer, New Eng Quart, 78; Carolyn Forche: Poetry & Survival in America, Poetry, 86; numerous poems in lit mags. **CONTACT ADDRESS** Dept of Eng, Western Illinois Univ, 1 University Circle, Macomb, IL 61455-1390. **EMAIL** john_mann@ccmail.wiu.edu

MANN, KAREN BERG
PERSONAL Born 04/20/1945, Waukegan, IL, m, 1969 **DISCIPLINE** ENGLISH **EDUCATION** Northwestern Univ, BA, 67; Univ Pa, MA, 68, PhD(English), 71. **CAREER** Asst prof, 71-76, Assoc Prof English, Western Ill Univ, 77-. **MEMBERSHIPS** NCTE. **RESEARCH** Nineteenth century British literature; prose fiction; women's studies; FILM. **SELECTED PUBLICATIONS** Auth, The Matter With Mind--Violence and the 'Silence of the Lambs', Criticism-Quart for Lit and the Arts, Vol 0038, 96. **CONTACT ADDRESS** Dept of English, Western Illinois Univ, 1 University Cir, Macomb, IL 61455-1390. **EMAIL** kb-mann@wiu.edu

MANN, THOMAS J.
PERSONAL Born 02/21/1948, Chicago, IL, s **DISCIPLINE** LIBRARY SCIENCE **EDUCATION** Saint Louis Univ, BA, 70; Loyola Univ Chicago, PhD, 75; LA State Univ, MLS, 79. **CAREER** Private investigator, 76-77; reference librarian, 80, LSU; Catholic Univ of Amer, 80-81; Library of Congress, 81-. **MEMBERSHIPS** Amer Library Assn, Cosmos Club. **SELECTED PUBLICATIONS** Auth, A Guide to Library Research Methods, 87; auth, Library Research Models, 93; auth, The Oxford Guide to Library Research, 98. **CONTACT ADDRESS** Humanities and Social Sciences Div, Library of Congress, 101 Independence Ave, SE, Washington, DC 20540-4660. **EMAIL** tman@loc.gov

MANNING, JOSEPH G.
DISCIPLINE CLASSICS **EDUCATION** BA, 81; Univ Chicago, PhD, 92. **CAREER** Asst prof, Stanford Univ. **RESEARCH** Papyrology; Hellenistic, Near Eastern, and Egyptian hist. **SELECTED PUBLICATIONS** Auth, Land and Social Status in Hellenistic Egypt in Grund und Boden in Altagypten, Tubingen, 95; Demotic Egyptian Instruments of Conveyance as Evidence of Ownerswhip of Real Property in Chicago-Kent Law Review, 96; The Hauswaldt Papyri: A Third Century Family Archive from Edfu, Upper Egypt , Demotische Studien, 96. **CONTACT ADDRESS** Stanford Univ, Bldg 20, Main Quad, Stanford, CA 94305. **EMAIL** jmanning@stanford.edu

MANNING, PETER J.
PERSONAL Born 09/27/1942, New York, NY, m, 1998, 3 children **DISCIPLINE** ENGLISH **EDUCATION** Harvard Univ, BA, 63; Yale Univ, MA, 65, PhD(English), 68. **CAREER** Asst prof English, Univ Calif, Berkeley, 67-75; Assoc Prof English, Univ Southern Calif, 77-, Guggenheim fel, 81-82; Prof and Chair of English, SUNY at Stony Brook, 00-. **HONORS AND AWARDS** NEH Fellowship, 93-94; Keats-Shelly Assn Distinguished Scholar Awd. **MEMBERSHIPS** MLA; Byron Soc; Wordsworth-Coleridge Asn; Keats-Shelley Asn. **RESEARCH** English romantic poetry. **SELECTED PUBLICATIONS** Auth, Childe Harold in the Marketplace + 'Childe Harolds Pilgrimage' by Byron, George, Gordon--From Romaunt to Handbook, Mod Lang Quart, Vol 0052, 91; ed, "Longman Anthology of British Literature," 99; auth, "Byron, George Gordon Lord," Selected Poems, 96; auth, "Reading Romantics," 90; auth, "Cleansing the Images: Wordsworth, Rome, and The Rise of Historicism," Texas Studies in Language and Literature, 33, 91. **CONTACT ADDRESS** Dept of English, SUNY, Stony Brook, Stony Brook, NY 11794.

MANNING, SUSAN
DISCIPLINE ENGLISH **EDUCATION** Columbia Univ, PhD. **CAREER** Prof, Northwestern Univ. **RESEARCH** 19th- and 20th-century dance, theatre and drama in Europe and the United States. **SELECTED PUBLICATIONS** Auth, Ecstasy and the Demon: Feminism and Nationalism in the Dances of Mary Wigman, 93. **CONTACT ADDRESS** Dept of English, Northwestern Univ, 1801 Hinman, Evanston, IL 60208. **EMAIL** s-manning@northwestern.edu

MANNINO, MARY ANN V.
PERSONAL Born 08/03/1943, Philadelphia, PA, d, 2 children **DISCIPLINE** ENGLISH **EDUCATION** Univ Pa, AB, 65; Temple Univ, MA, 86; PhD, 95. **CAREER** Vis asst prof, Temple Univ, 95-. **HONORS AND AWARDS** Merit of Teaching, 96, 97, 98. **MEMBERSHIPS** MLA; Am Hist Asn. **RESEARCH** American Women's Literature. **SELECTED PUBLICATIONS** Auth, Revisionary Identities; Strategies of Empowerment in the Writing of American Women. **CONTACT ADDRESS** Dept Hist, Temple Univ, 8120 Winston Rd, Philadelphia, PA 19118-2917.

MANOGUE, RALPH ANTHONY
PERSONAL Born 08/05/1935, New York, NY **DISCIPLINE** ENGLISH LITERATURE **EDUCATION** Georgetown Univ, BS, 58; Univ Va, MA, 60; NYork Univ, PhD(English), 71. **CAREER** Teacher and dept head, Congressional High Sch, Falls Church, Va, 59-64; adj lectr, Queens Col, NY, 64-72; Prof English, Middlesex County Col, NJ, 71-. **MEMBERSHIPS** Wordsworth-Coleridge Asn; Keats-Shelley Asn; Conf Brit Studies. **RESEARCH** British Romantics; freedom of the press: England 1780-1832; radical English publishers 1780-1832. **SELECTED PUBLICATIONS** Auth, Study guide for Arthur Miller's The Price, Group Sales Publ, summer 79; Robert Southey & William Winterbotham: New lights on an old quarrel, Charles Lamb Bull, 4/82; Theatrical history of Robert Southey's Wat Tyler, Theatre Notebk, London (in press). **CONTACT ADDRESS** Middlesex County Col, Edison, NJ 08818.

MANSELL, DARRELL L.
PERSONAL Born 04/09/1934, Canton, OH, m, 1979, 1 child **DISCIPLINE** ENGISH **EDUCATION** Oberlin Col, BA, 56; Oxford Univ, 61-62; Yale Univ, PhD, 63. **CAREER** Instructor to Prof Emeritus, Dartmouth Col, 62-. **MEMBERSHIPS** Jane Austen Soc of N Am; NE Victorian Studies Asn; Jane Austen Soc of N New England. **RESEARCH** Victorian and Brit lit. **SELECTED PUBLICATIONS** Auth, "The Jazz History of the World in The Great Gatsby," English Language Notes, (87): 57-62; auth, "The Difference Between a Lump and a Text," Poetics Today, (88): 791-805; auth, "Trying to Bring Literature Back Alive: The Ivory in Joseph Conrad's Heart of Darkness," Criticism, (91): 205-215; auth, "Metaphor as Matter," Language and Literature, (92): 109-120; auth, "Telling It Like It Was in English 83," AWP Chronicle, (93): 20-23; auth, "The Intelligence of Material Objects in a Literary Text," Language and Style, (90): 195-205; auth, "Dying into the Type: Tennyson's Surrender to Public Language in 'The Lover's Tale,'" Texas Studies in Literature and Language, (97): 296-320; auth, "Words Lost in In Our Time," The Hemingway Review, (97): 5-14; auth, "Displacing Hallam's Tomb in Tennyson's In Memoriam," Victorian Poetry, (98): 97-111; auth, "Language in an Image," Criticism, (99): 187-205. **CONTACT ADDRESS** Dept Eng, Dartmouth Col, 6032 Sanborn Hall, Hanover, NH 03755-3533. **EMAIL** Darrell.Mansell@Dartmouth.edu

MANSO, LEIRA ANNETTE
DISCIPLINE LITERATURE **EDUCATION** Univ Puerto Rico, BA, 87; New York Univ, MA, 89; SUNY (Binghamton), PhD, 96. **CAREER** Adjunct Prof, 96-, Broome Community Col. **CONTACT ADDRESS** 2452 High Ave, Vestal, NY 13850-2740. **EMAIL** manso_l@sunybroome.edu

MANY, PAUL
DISCIPLINE COMMUNICATION STUDIES **EDUCATION** St John's Univ, BA; OH State Univ, MA, PhD. **CAREER** Prof, Univ Toledo. **SELECTED PUBLICATIONS** Auth, These Are the Rules, 97; The Fine Art of Saying No, Academe, 96; Literary Journalism: Newspapers' Last, Best Hope, Conn Rev, 96; Rabbits, Live and Dressed. **CONTACT ADDRESS** Dept of Commun, Univ of Toledo, Toledo, OH 43606. **EMAIL** pmany@uoft02.utoledo.edu

MAPP, EDWARD C.
PERSONAL Born 08/17/1929, New York, NY **DISCIPLINE** THEATER **EDUCATION** City Coll of NYork, BA 1953; Columbia Univ, MS 1956; NYork Univ, PhD 1970. **CAREER** NY City Bd of Educ, tchr 1957-64; NY City Tech Coll, dir of Library Learning Resources Center 1964-77; Borough of Manhattan Community Coll, dean of faculty 1977-82; City Colleges of Chicago, vice chancellor, 82-83; Borough of Manhattan Community Coll, prof 1983-92, Prof Emeritus, 94-. **HONORS AND AWARDS** Founders Day Awd for Outstanding Scholarship NY Univ 1970; Distinguished Serv Awd Borough of Manhattan Community Coll The City Univ of NY 1982; elected to NY Acad of Pub Educ 1978; Black Collectors Hall of Fame, 1992. **MEMBERSHIPS** Dir Natl Serv Corp 1984-87; bd of dir United Nations Assoc of NY 1975-78; bd of trustees NY Metro Ref & Rsch Agency 1980-81; feature columnist Movie/TV Mktg 1979-91; 100 Black Men Inc 1975-85; bd mem (Brooklyn Region) Natl Conf of Christians & Jews 1975-81; treas City Univ of NY Fac Senate 1972-77; Brooklyn Borough Pres Ed Adv Panel 1981; commissioner, New York City Human Rights Commission, 1988-94, vice chair, 1992-94. **SELECTED PUBLICATIONS** Author: Blacks in American Films, 1972; Puerto Rican Perspectives, 1974; Blacks in Performing Arts, 1978, 2nd edition, 1990; co-author: A Separate Cinema, 1992; curator: Edward Mapp African-American Film Poster Collection, presented to Center for Motion Picture Study of the Academy of Motion Picture Arts and Sciences, 1996. **CONTACT ADDRESS** Borough of Manhattan Comm Col, CUNY, New York, NY 10007.

MAQBOOL, AZIZ
DISCIPLINE ENGLISH LITERATURE **EDUCATION** Punjab Univ, BA, MA; Oxford Univ, PhD. **RESEARCH** Nineteenth and twentieth century literature; Henry James; modern fiction; critical theory; textual criticism. **SELECTED PUBLICATIONS** Auth, The Tales of Henry James, 84. **CONTACT ADDRESS** English Dept, McMaster Univ, 1280 Main St W, Hamilton, ON, Canada L8S 4L9. **EMAIL** azizm@mcmaster.ca

MARBAIS, PETER C.
PERSONAL Born 07/01/1973, East Liverpool, OH, m, 1997 **DISCIPLINE** ENGLISH **EDUCATION** Ohio Wesleyan Univ, BA, 95; Kent State Univ, MA, 98. **CAREER** Teaching fel, Kent State Univ, 96-00; asst prof, Bethany Col, 00-01; instr, Hutchison Comm Col, 01-. **HONORS AND AWARDS** Teaching Fel, Kent State, 98. **MEMBERSHIPS** ASECS; MLA; John Bunyan Soc. **RESEARCH** 18th-century British novel; continental literature; science fiction; feminist studies. **SELECTED PUBLICATIONS** Rev, "Transformations of Language in Modern Dystopias," by David W. Sisk, Extrapolation (98); rev, "Arthur C. Clarke: A Critical Companion," by Robin Ann Reid, Extrapolation (98); auth, "The Tormented Body in the Life and Death of Mr. Badman," in Reading Dissenting Writing, ed. N. H. Keeble (Bern: Peter Lang, (forthcoming)). **CONTACT ADDRESS** 5316 County Road 56, Toronto, OH 43964-7928. **EMAIL** marbaisp@bethany16.edu

MARCELLO, LEO L.
PERSONAL Born 08/06/1945, DeRidder, LA **DISCIPLINE** POETRY **EDUCATION** Tulane Univ, BA, 67; La State Univ, MA, 70; PhD, 76. **CAREER** Asst prof, McNeese State Univ, 82-85; lectr, Cath Univ of Am, 87-88; instr, Howard Univ, 88-89; asst prof to prof, McNeese State Univ, 89-. **HONORS AND AWARDS** 1st Prize for Poetry, Deep S Writers Conf, 80; Acme Fiction Awd, 82; David Lloyd Kreeger Awd, 87; Shearman Fel, 89-91; Shearman Acad Prof, 92-93; La Endowment for the Humanities Grant, 93; McNeese State Univ Distinguished Prof of the Year, 93. **MEMBERSHIPS** SCMLA; SCCCL; AWP; CCL; AIHA; Phi Eta Sigma; Alpha Psi Omega; Arba Sicilia. **RESEARCH** Poetry, spirituality and the arts. **SELECTED PUBLICATIONS** Auth, Nothing Grows in One Place Forever; auth, Silent Film; auth, Blackrobe's Love Letter; auth, The Secret Proximity of Everywhere. **CONTACT ADDRESS** Dept Lang Arts, McNeese State Univ, PO Box 5508, Lake Charles, LA 70606-5508.

MARCHANT, PETER L.
PERSONAL Born 05/14/1928, London, England, m, 1961, 2 children **DISCIPLINE** ENGLISH **EDUCATION** Cambridge, BA, 53, MA, 56; Univ Iowa, PhD(English), 66. **CAREER** Lectr English, Univ BC, 54-55; instr Coe Col, 57-58; from instr to asst prof, Pa State Univ, 63-68; from asst prof to assoc prof, 68-74, prof English, State Univ NY Col Brockport, 74-; prof Emeritus, ret, 93. **HONORS AND AWARDS** Chancellor's Awd for Excellence in Teaching, 78. **RESEARCH** Fiction; the English novel; teaching English to the disadvantaged. **SELECTED PUBLICATIONS** Auth, Give Me Your Answer, Do, Michael Joseph, 60. **CONTACT ADDRESS** SUNY, Col at Brockport, 350 New Campus Dr, Brockport, NY 14420-2914. **EMAIL** pmarchant@alsbrockport@edu

MARCUS, LEAH S.
PERSONAL Born 09/12/1945, Valparaiso, IN, m, 1974, 2 children **DISCIPLINE** RENAISSANCE LITERATURE, EARLY MODERN LITERATURE, SHAKESPEARE, TEXTUAL STUDIES **EDUCATION** Carleton Col, BA, 67; Columbia Univ, MA, 68; PhD, 71. **CAREER** From asst prof to assoc prof, Univ of Ill at Chicago, 72-84; fac, Univ of Wis, Madison, 84-88; fac, 88-95, Jane and Roland Blumberg Prof in English, 95-98, Univ of Tex, Austin; Edwin Mims Prof of English, Vanderbilt Univ, 98-. **HONORS AND AWARDS** NEH fel, 73, 78; Guggenheim fel, 86-87; Marlowe Soc Prize for best article, 92. **MEMBERSHIPS** MLA; Milton Soc Am. **RESEARCH** The writings of Queen Elizabeth I, seventeenth century English literature, medieval literature, literature and social organization. **SELECTED PUBLICATIONS** Auth, The Christ child as sacrifice: Medieval tradition and the Corpus Christi plays, Speculum, 7/73; Vaughan, Wordsworth, Coleridge, and the Encomium Asini, ELH, Vol 42, 75; Herrick's Noble Numbers and the politics of playfulness, English Lit Renaissance, Vol 7, 77; Childhood and Cultural Despair: A Theme and Variations in 17th Century Literature, Univ Pittsburgh, 78; Present occasions and the shaping of Ben Jonson's masques, Elh, Vol 45, 78; auth, Childhood and Cultural Despair, 78; The Politics of Mirth, 86; Puzzling Shakespeare, 88; Unediting the Renaissance, 96. **CONTACT ADDRESS** Dept of English, Vanderbilt Univ, Nashville, TN 37203-1727. **EMAIL** l.marcus@vanderbilt.edu

MARCUS, MORDECAI
PERSONAL Born 01/18/1925, Elizabeth, NJ, m, 1955, 2 children **DISCIPLINE** ENGLISH **EDUCATION** Brooklyn Col, BA, 49; NYork Univ, MA, 50; Univ Kans, PhD, 58. **CAREER** Asst, Rutgers Univ, 51-52; from asst instr to instr, Univ Kans, 52-58; from instr to asst prof, Purdue Univ, 58-65; from asst prof to assoc prof, 65-72, Prof English, Univ Nebr, Lincoln, 72-. **MEMBERSHIPS** MLA. **RESEARCH** Modern poetry; literature and psychology; writing of poetry. **SELECTED PUBLICATIONS** Auth, What is an initiation story?, J Aesthet Art Criticism, winter 60; Walt Whitman and Emily Dickinson, Personalist, autumn 62; Five Minutes to Noon (poems), Best Cellar, 71; The whole pattern of Robert Frost's Two Witches, Lit and Psychol, No 2, 76; Return from the Desert (poems), Newedi, 77; Conversational Basketball (poems), Nebr Rev, 80; Talisman (poems), Sparrow, 81; A Midsummer Night's Dream: the Dialectic of Eros-Thanatos, Am Imago, fall 81. **CONTACT ADDRESS** Dept of English, Univ of Nebraska, Lincoln, Lincoln, NE 68588.

MARCUS, SHARON
DISCIPLINE ENGLISH AND COMPARATIVE LITERATURE **EDUCATION** Brown Univ, BA, 86; Johns Hopkins Univ, PhD, 95. **CAREER** Assoc prof, eng dept, Univ Calif Berkeley. **RESEARCH** 19th century British and French novel; Feminist theory; Lesbian and gay studies; Urban and architectural history. **SELECTED PUBLICATIONS** Auth, Apartment Stories: City and Home in Nineteeth Century, Paris and London. **CONTACT ADDRESS** Dept. of English, Univ of California, Berkeley, Berkeley, CA 94720-1030. **EMAIL** smarcus@socrates.berkeley.edu

MARCUS, STEVEN
DISCIPLINE 19TH-CENTURY LITERATURE AND CULTURE **EDUCATION** Columbia Univ, AB, 48, AM, 49, PhD, 61; Clark Col, DHL, 86. **CAREER** Sci assoc, Am Acad psychoanalysts.George Delacorte prof. **HONORS AND AWARDS** Fel, Am Acad Arts and Sci; Acad Lit Stud; Fulbright fel; Am Coun Learned Soc; Guggenheim award; Ctr Advan Stud Behav Sci; Rockefeller grant; Mellon grants; Ch, exec comm Bd Trustees, NEH; hon mem, Am Psychoanalytic Asn, 79; Inst psychoanalytic training and res, 91; assoc ed, Partisan Rev; ed bd, Prose; Stud,Psychoanalysis and Contemporary Thought; Psychoanalytic Bk, Psyche. **SELECTED PUBLICATIONS** Auth, 200 publ; Freud and the Culture of Psychoanalysis, 84; Medicine and Western Civilization, 95; Dickens From Pickwick to Dombey; The Other Victorians; Engels; Manchester and the Working Class; Doing Good; Representations: Essays on Literature and Society; co-ed, Ernest Jones's The Life; Work of Sigmund Freud; auth, Freud and the Culture of Psychoanalysis. **CONTACT ADDRESS** Dept of English, Columbia Col, New York, 2960 Broadway, New York, NY 10027-6902. **EMAIL** sm50@columbia.edu

MARDER, HERBERT
DISCIPLINE ENGLISH **EDUCATION** Columbia Univ, PhD(English), 64. **CAREER** Assoc Prof English, Univ Ill, Urbana, 65-. **RESEARCH** Modern fiction; feminist literature; improvisation in contemporary poetry. **CONTACT ADDRESS** Univ of Illinois, Urbana-Champaign, Champaign, IL 61820. **EMAIL** marder@uiuc.edu

MARES, CHERYL
DISCIPLINE ENGLISH **EDUCATION** Univ CO, BA; Princeton Univ, MA; PhD. **CAREER** Assoc prof, Sweet Briar Col. **HONORS AND AWARDS** Stu Govt Assn Excellence Tchg Awd, Sweet Briar Col, 88. **RESEARCH** Literary theory; 20th century women writers; Virginia Woolf. **SELECTED PUBLICATIONS** Auth, articles on Virginia Woolf. **CONTACT ADDRESS** Sweet Briar Col, Sweet Briar, VA 24595.

MARES, E. A.
DISCIPLINE CREATIVE WRITING, POETRY **EDUCATION** Univ NMex, PhD, 74. **CAREER** Instr, Univ NMex. **SELECTED PUBLICATIONS** Auth, The Unicorn Poem and Flowers and Songs of Sorrow, 92; There Are Four Wounds, Miguel, 94. **CONTACT ADDRESS** Dept of Hist, Univ of New Mexico, Albuquerque, Albuquerque, NM 87131. **EMAIL** tmares@unm.edu

MARGOLIES, ALAN
PERSONAL Born 10/12/1933, New York, NY **DISCIPLINE** ENGLISH AND AMERICAN LITERATURE **EDUCATION** City Col New York, BA, 54; NYork Univ, MA, 60, PhD(English), 69. **CAREER** Lectr English, Brooklyn Col, 61-68; lectr, City Col New York, 69-70; asst prof, 70-75, assoc prof, 76-80, Prpf English, John Jay Col Criminal Justice, 81-, City Univ New York fac res award, 71-74 and 81-82; Am Coun Learned Soc grant-in-aid, 72; Nat Endowment for Humanities grant, 79-81. **MEMBERSHIPS** MLA; Bibliog Soc Am; Am Lit Sect, MLA; Am Studies Asn; Northeast Mod Lang Asn. **RESEARCH** American literature; bibliography; film. **SELECTED PUBLICATIONS** Auth, The Maturing of Fitzgerald, F. Scott, 20th Century Lit, Vol 0043, 97. **CONTACT ADDRESS** Dept of English, John Jay Col of Criminal Justice, CUNY, 445 W 59th St, New York, NY 10019.

MARGOLIN, URI
PERSONAL Born 12/22/1942, Tel Aviv, Israel, m, 1968, 1 child **DISCIPLINE** COMPARATIVE LITERATURE, POETICS **EDUCATION** Hebrew Univ, Jerusalem, BA, 64; Cornell Univ, MA, 70, PhD(comp lit); 72. **CAREER** Teaching Asst, Cornell Univ, 69-70; Asst Prof, Univ of Alberta, 72; Assoc Prof, 76; Prof, 83. **HONORS AND AWARDS** Univ of Alberta Res Grant, 72; Univ of Alberta Res Grant, 75; CRF travel grant, 89, 90, 92, 94, 95, 97. **MEMBERSHIPS** Int Comp Lit Asn; Can Comp Lit Asn. **RESEARCH** Poetics; theory of genres; literary methodology. **SELECTED PUBLICATIONS** Auth, "Narrative 'You' Revisited" Language and Style, 23, 4, (90): 425-446, published Dec 95; auth, "Characters and their Versions" in Fiction Updated, eds, Calin-Andrei Mihailescu and Wand Hamarneh, Univ of Toronto Press, (96): 113-132; auth, "Telling Our Story: On 'We' Literary Narratives" Language and Literature, 5, 2 (96): 115-33; auth, "Formal, Sematic and Pragmatic Aspects of Metatetuality: Comparatism Revisited," eds, de Zepetnek and Dimic, Comparative Literature Today: Theroies and Practice, Paris: Honore Champion, 99; auth, "Collective Perspective, Individual Perspective and the Speaker in between: On 'We' Literary Narratives," eds, Chatman & van Peer, Narrative Perspective Cognition and Emotion, SUNY Press, 99; auth, "Character, Types of" & "Person in Narrative" in Encyclopedia of the Novel, Fitzroy Dearborn Publishers, Chicago, 88. **CONTACT ADDRESS** Dept of Comp Lit, Relig, & Film/Media Studs, Univ of Alberta, 347 Arts, Edmonton, AB, Canada T6G 2E6. **EMAIL** uri.margolin@ualberta.ca

MARGULIES, IVONE
DISCIPLINE FILM STUDIES **EDUCATION** Univ do Estado do Rio de Janeiro, BA; Univ Federal do Rio de Janeiro, MA; NYork Univ, 92. **CAREER** Taught at, NY Univ, Barnard Col & Sch Visual Arts; past ed, Motion Picture J; **HONORS AND AWARDS** Soc Cinema Stud awd, 92-93. **RESEARCH** Feminist film practice; Independent film; performance in film and video and cinema verite strategies. **SELECTED PUBLICATIONS** Auth, Nothing Happens: Chantal Akerman's Hyperrealist Everyday, Duke UP, 96. **CONTACT ADDRESS** Dept of Film and Media Studies, Hunter Col, CUNY, 695 Park Ave, New York, NY 10021. **EMAIL** imarguli@hunter.cuny.edu

MARIANI, PAUL L.
PERSONAL Born 02/29/1940, New York, NY, m, 1963, 3 children **DISCIPLINE** MODERN POETRY, BIOGRAPHY **EDUCATION** Manhattan Col, BA, 62; Colgate Univ, MA, 64; City Univ New York, PhD(English), 68. **CAREER** Lectr English, Colgate Univ, 63; from instr to asst prof, John Jay Col, 66-68; from asst prof to assoc prof, 68-71, dir grad studies, 72-74, prof English, Univ Mass, 75-; assoc ed, William Carlos Williams Rev; Sagetribe, Bread Loaf Sch of English, 82-84; Bread Loaf Writer's Conf, Poetry Staff, 85-96; dir, The Glen, 95, 96, & 98. **HONORS AND AWARDS** Dist Univ Prof, Univ Mass/ Amherst; NEH Fel for Independent Res, 72, 73, 81 & 82; New Jersey Writers' Awd for Williams Bio, 82; NEA Fel, 84; Guggenheim Fel, 85 & 86; Healy Res Grant, 84; Univ Mass Res Fel, 86 & 87; Choice Awd from Prairie Schooner, 89 & 95. **MEMBERSHIPS** MLA; Hopkins Soc; Poetry Soc Am. **RESEARCH** Twentieth century American poetry and poetics; Gerard Manley Hopkins; William Carlos Williams; John Berryman; Robert Lowell; Hart Crane. **SELECTED PUBLICATIONS** Auth, William Carlos Williams: A New World Naked, McGraw-Hill, 81; Dream Song: The Life of John Berryman, William Morrow, 90; Timing Devices: Godline, 79; Crossing Cocytus, Grove Press, 82; Prime Mover: Grove Press, 85; Salvage Operations: New and Selected Poems, WW Norton & Co, 90; The Great Wheel, WW Norton, 96; The Broken Tower: A Life of Hart Crane: WW Norton, 99. **CONTACT ADDRESS** Dept of English, Univ of Massachusetts, Amherst, Amherst, MA 01003. **EMAIL** pmarian@english.umass.edu

MARINCOLA, JOHN
PERSONAL Born 12/14/1954, Philadelphia, PA, s **DISCIPLINE** CLASSICS **EDUCATION** Swarthmore Col, BA, 79; Brown Univ, PhD, 85. **CAREER** Instr to asst prof, Col of the Holy Cross, 84-86; vis asst prof to assoc prof, Union Col, 86-97; exec dir, Am Philol Asn, 97-98; assoc prof, NY Univ, 00-. **HONORS AND AWARDS** Fel, Center for Hellenic Studies, 99-00. **MEMBERSHIPS** Am Philol Asn, Asn of Ancient Hist, Cambridge Philol Soc, Class Asn, Class Asn of the Atlantic States, Class Asn of the Middle W and S. **RESEARCH** Greek and Roman historiography, Ancient Rhetoric, Greek History. **SELECTED PUBLICATIONS** Transl, Herodotus: The Histories, Penguin Books, 96; auth, "Odysseus and the Historians," Histos 1, (97); auth, Authority and Tradition in Ancient Historiography, Cambridge, 97; auth, "Genre, Convention and Innovation in Greco-Roman Historiography,", The Limits of Historiography: Genre and Narrative in Ancient Historical Texts, ed C Kraus, (Leiden, 99): 281-324; auth, Greek Historians, Greece and Rome New Surveys in the Classics, Oxford, 01. **CONTACT ADDRESS** Dept Classics, New York Univ, New York, NY 10003. **EMAIL** john.marincola@nyu.edu

MARINELLI, PETER V.
PERSONAL Born 07/30/1933, New York, NY **DISCIPLINE** ENGLISH **EDUCATION** Fordham Univ, BA, 55, MA, 60; Princeton Univ, PhD(English), 64. **CAREER** Prpf English, Univ Col, Univ Toronto, 63-. **RESEARCH** Medieval period; English and Italian Renaissance. **SELECTED PUBLICATIONS** Auth, Selections From Boiardo 'Orlando Innamorato', Italica, Vol 0069, 92. **CONTACT ADDRESS** Univ of Toronto, English Sect Univ Col, Toronto, ON, Canada M5S 1A1.

MARISSEN, MICHAEL
PERSONAL Born 06/31/1960, Hamilton, Canada, m, 1981, 2 children **DISCIPLINE** MUSIC HISTORY **EDUCATION** Calvin Col, BA; Brandeis Univ, PhD. **CAREER** Vis prof, Princeton Univ, 92-93; assoc prof, Swarthmore Col, 89. **HONORS AND AWARDS** Alexander von Hmboldt Stiftung, Am Coun of Learned Doc, Nat Endowment for the Humanities, Soc Sci and Humanitites Res Coun of Canada, Deutscher Akademischer Austauschdienst **MEMBERSHIPS** Am Musicological Soc, Am bach soc, Int Arbeitsgemeinschaft fur theologische Bachforschung **RESEARCH** Music hist; early music performance, music and theology/bibilical. **SELECTED PUBLICATIONS** Auth, "Religious aims in Mendelssohn's 1829 Berlin-Singakademi performances of Bach's St Mathew Passion," Musical Quarterly 77, (93); auth, The Social and Religious Designs of J. S. Bach's Brandenburg Concertos, Princeton UP, 95; auth, "The theological character of J.S. bach's Musical Offering," Bach-Studies, Cambradge: Cambridge Univ Press, 95; Lutheranism, Anti-Judaism, and Bach's St John Passion, Oxford UP, 98; coauth, An Introduction to Bach Studies, Oxford UP, 98; ed, Creative Responses to the Music of J. S. Bach from Mozart to Hindemith, U Neb P, 98; auth, A critical reappraisal of J.S. Bach's A-major jlute sonata," J of Musicology 6, (98), 367-386. **CONTACT ADDRESS** Swarthmore Col, Swarthmore, PA 19081-1397. **EMAIL** mmariss1@swarthmore.edu

MARK, REBECCA
DISCIPLINE PERFORMANCE STUDIES, SOUTHERN LITERATURE **EDUCATION** B.A.: SUNY Col at Purchase, 1978 Ph.D, Stanford Univ, 1986. **CAREER** Instr, 89, Tulane Univ. **SELECTED PUBLICATIONS** Auth, The Dragon's Blood: Feminist Intertextuality, Eudora Welty's The Golden Apples. **CONTACT ADDRESS** Dept of Eng, Tulane Univ, 6823 St Charles Ave, New Orleans, LA 70118. **EMAIL** rmark@mailhost.tcs.tulane.edu

MARKELS, JULIAN
PERSONAL Born 06/24/1925, Chicago, IL, m, 1963, 3 children **DISCIPLINE** ENGLISH **EDUCATION** Univ Chicago, BS, 48; Univ Minn, MA, 52, PhD(English), 57. **CAREER** Instr English, Univ Minn, 52-56; from instr to assoc prof, 56-67, Prof English, Ohio State Univ, 67-, Chmn Dept, 76-; emer. **HONORS AND AWARDS** Elizabeth Clay Howald fel, 65-66. **RESEARCH** Shakespeare; American literature; American cultural history. **SELECTED PUBLICATIONS** Auth, The Liberal Bombast of Billy Budd, Essays in Arts and Sciences, Vol 15, 86; auth, Melvilles Sexual Politics, Review, Vol 9, 87; auth, King Lear, Revolution, and the New Historian, Mod Languange Studies, Vol 21, 91; auth, Shakespeare's Materialism in King Lear, Rethinking Marxism, Vol 4, 91; auth, The Moby-Dick White Elephant, Ameican Lit, Vol 66, 94; auth, Textualized Absence as Professional Practice, Minnesota Rev, Vol 45/46, 96; auth, Toward a Marxian Reentry to the Novel, Narrative, vol 4, 96; auth, Negotiating and Audience for American Exceptionalisnm: Redburn and Roughing It, in Reciprocal Influences, Columbus, Ohio State Univ Press, 99; auth, the Representation of Class in the Realist Novel, Rethinking Marxism, Vol 11, 99; auth, Socialism-Anxiety: The Princess Casamassima and Its New York Critics, College Literature, Vol 27, 00. **CONTACT ADDRESS** Dept of English, Ohio State Univ, Columbus, 164 W 17th Ave, Columbus, OH 43210.

MARKEN, JACK WALTER
PERSONAL Born 02/11/1922, Akron, OH, m, 1946, 3 children **DISCIPLINE** ENGLISH **EDUCATION** Univ Akron, BA, 47; Ind Univ, MA, 50, PhD(English), 53. **CAREER** Instr, Univ Ky, 52-54; asst prof English and humanities, Ohio Wesleyan Univ, 54-55; asst prof, Cent Mich Univ, 55-60; prof English, Slippery Rock State Col, 60-67; Prof English, S Dak State Univ, 67-, Am Philos Soc grant, 59, res grants, 65, 67; Fulbright lectr, Univ Jordan, 65-66; US Info Serv-Finnish-Am Soc lectr Am Indian lit, Finland, 70; lectr, Univ Jordan, 82; Gen Ed, Native Am Bibliog Series, Scarecrow Press, 80-, Distinguished Award in Humanities, SDak Comt on Humanities, 77. **MEMBERSHIPS** MLA; Aaup. **RESEARCH** The late 18th century; literature of the American Indian. **SELECTED PUBLICATIONS** Auth, Walking the Rez Road, Amer Indian Culture and Res J, Vol 0017, 93. **CONTACT ADDRESS** So Dakota State Univ, Brookings, SD 57007.

MARKI, IVAN
PERSONAL Born 06/14/1934, Budapest, Hungary, m, 1965, 2 children **DISCIPLINE** LITERARY CRITICISM, AMERICAN LITERATURE **EDUCATION** Univ Alta, BA, 61; Columbia Univ, MA, 63, PhD(English), 74. **CAREER** From instr to asst prof, 65-75, assoc prof, 75-77, Margaret Bundy Scott Assoc Prof, 77-83, prof, 83-99, Edmund A. Lefevre prof, 99-, English, Hamilton Col; Fulbright Visit Prof, KLTE, Debrecen, Hungary, 91-92. **MEMBERSHIPS** MLA; Am-Hungarian Educr Asn; ALSC **RESEARCH** Nineteenth-century American literature; twentieth-century American literature; critical theory. **SELECTED PUBLICATIONS** Auth, The Trial of the Poet: An Interpretation of the First Edition of Leaves of Grass, Columbia Univ, 76. **CONTACT ADDRESS** Dept of English, Hamilton Col, New York, 198 College Hill Rd, Clinton, NY 13323-1292. **EMAIL** imarki@ruby.hamilton.edu

MARKLEY, ARNOLD A.
PERSONAL Born 03/24/1964, Greenville, SC, p **DISCIPLINE** ENGLISH **EDUCATION** Guilford Col, BA, 86; Univ NC, MA, 90; PhD, 96. **CAREER** Teaching asst, Univ Pa, 88; instr, Durham Tech Community Col, 90-91; teaching asst and instr, Univ NC, 91-96; asst prof, Pa State Univ, 96-. **HONORS AND AWARDS** Aleine McLeod McLaurin Dissertation Fel, Univ NC, 93; Res Grant, Pa State Univ, 97, 00, 01; George W. Atherton Award, Pa State Univ, 01 **MEMBERSHIPS** MLA; Tennyson Soc; Keats-Shelley Asn; NASSR; E Cent Am Soc for Eighteenth Century Studies; Eighteenth and Nineteenth Century British Women Writers Asn. **RESEARCH** British romantic, Victorian and early 20th Century literature; British Jacobean fiction; William Godwin; Mary Wollstonecraft; Mary Shelley; Gothic fiction; Poetry of Tennyson and the Pre-Raphaelites; Classical Mythology and British literature; Textual editing. **SELECTED PUBLICATIONS** Auth, "Laughing That I May Not Weep: Mary Shelley's Short Fiction and Her Novels," Keats-Shelley J, (97): 97-124; auth, "Barbarous Hexameters and Dainty Meters: Tennyson's Uses of Classical Versification," Studies in Philol, (98): 456-486; auth, "Tennyson's Classical Dramatic Monologues and the Approximation of Greek and Latin Poetry," Victorian Rev, (99): 35-49; auth, "Tainted Wethers of the Flock: Homosexuality and Homosocial Desire in Mary Shelley's Novels," Keats-Shelley Rev, (99): 35-49; auth, "The Truth in Masquerade: Cross-dressing and Disguise in Mary Shelley's Short Stories," in Mary Shelley: Fictions from Frankenstein to Falkner, (Basingstoke: Macmillan, 00), 109-126; auth, "Eliza Ogilvy, Highland Minstrelsy, and the Perils of Victorian Motherhood," Studies in Scottish Lit, (forthcoming); auth, "E.M. Forster's reconfigured Gaze and the Creation of a Homoerotic Subjectivity," Twentieth Century Lit, (forthcoming); co-ed, Fleetwood: or, The New Man of Feeling, Broadview Press, 01; co-ed, Caleb Williams, Broadview Press Lit Texts Series, 00; ed, Poems, Translations, and Other Uncollected Writings. Mary Shelley's Literary Lives and Other Writings, Pickering and Chatto, (forthcoming). **CONTACT ADDRESS** Dept English, Pennsylvania State Univ, Delaware County, 25 Yearsley Mill Rd, Media, PA 19063. **EMAIL** aam2@psu.edu

MARKOS, LOUIS
PERSONAL Born, NJ, m, 1989, 2 children **DISCIPLINE** ENGLISH **EDUCATION** Colgate Univ, BA, 86; Univ of Mich, MA, 87; Univ of Mich, PhD, 91. **CAREER** Assoc prof; fac, Houston Baptist Univ, 9 yrs. **HONORS AND AWARDS** Who's Who Among Amer Tchr(s), 96; NEH Summer Inst Virgil's Aeneid, Emory Univ, 94; Opal Goolsby Outstanding tchg awd, 92; Outstanding Teaching Asst Award, Univ of Mich, 90; Departmental Teaching Award, Univ of Mich, 90. **MEMBERSHIPS** Phi Beta Kappa. **RESEARCH** Marriage of his evangelical Christian faith and his love for humanistic pursuits. **SELECTED PUBLICATIONS** Auth, From Plato to Postmodernism: Understanding the Essence of Literature and the Role of the Author, Series of 24 lectures, The Teaching Company, 99; speech, Heroes of Greek Mythology: Perseus, Jason, Theseus, and Hercules, AHEPA, 00; auth, The Life and Writings of C.S. Lewis, 12 lectures, Teaching Company, 00; speech, Pressing Forward: Tennyson and the Victorian Spirit of Progress, Mus of Printing History Lyceum, Houston, Tex, 00; auth, Confessions of a Humanist Christian, forthcoming; auth, Life to the Full: The Search for Joy in a Fallen World, forthcoming; My Icon Case: Literary Sketches of a Greek-American Family, forthcoming; coauth, Witness to the Truth, A Literary Analysis of John, forthcoming. **CONTACT ADDRESS** Language Dept, Houston Baptist Univ, 7502 Fondren Rd, Houston, TX 77074. **EMAIL** lmarkos@hbu.edu

MARKS, LAURA U.
DISCIPLINE FILM STUDIES **EDUCATION** Univ Rochester, MA, PhD. **CAREER** Asst prof, Carleton Univ. **RESEARCH** Interested in the ways artists work with established or even obsolete technologies. **CONTACT ADDRESS** Dept of Art and Cult, Carleton Univ, 1125 Colonel By Dr, Ottawa, ON, Canada K1S 5B6. **EMAIL** laura_marks@carleton.ca

MARKS, PATRICIA
DISCIPLINE BRITISH NOVEL, VICTORIAN POETRY AND PROSE, RESEARCH AND CRITICISM **EDUCATION** Douglass Univ, BA, 65; Mich State Univ, PhD, 70. **CAREER** Prof Eng, fac senate, acad comt, grad exec comt, grievance comt, core curric subcomt, Women's Stud comt, Valdosta State Univ; Regents Distinguished Prof for Tchg and Lrng, Asheville Inst, 96; fac develop adv comt, fac develop comt, Univ Syst of Ga. **HONORS AND AWARDS** NDEA Title IV fel, Mich State Univ, 67-70; NEH fel in Residence, Univ Pa, 77-78; fac develop grants and res grants, Valdosta State Univ fac, 85-; IISP travel sem, 89; NEH summer sem, Univ Calif, Berkeley, 93; Am Asn of Higher educ Faculty Citizenship Awd, 94; NEH summer stud grant, 95. **MEMBERSHIPS** Trustee, Dickens Soc, 94; secy, Hawthorne Soc, 97. **SELECTED PUBLICATIONS**

Auth, American Literary and Drama Reviews: An Index to Late Nineteenth Century Periodicals, G K Hall, 84; Bicycles, Bangs, and Bloomers: The New Woman in the Popular Press, UP Kentucky, 90; coauth, The Smiling Muse: Victoriana in the Comic Press, Assoc UP/Art Alliance, 85; Paul Dombey and the Milk of Human Kindness, in Dickens Quart 9.1, 94; Rev of Victorian American Women 1840-1880: An Annotated Bibliography, by Karen Rae Mehaffey, in Victorian Per Rev 27, 94; Rev of George Cruikshank's Life, Times, and A rt, Vol I: 1792-1835, by Robert Patten, in Victorian Per Rev 27, 94; The Boy on the Wooden Horse: Robert Audley and the Failure of Reason, in Clues, 94; Rev of Parentage and Inheritance in the Novels of Charles Dickens, by Anny Sadrin, in Dickens Quart 12, 95; Rev of Dickens and the Grown-up Child, by Malcolm Andrews, in S Atlantic Rev 60, 95; Rev of The Afterlife of Property: Domestic Security and the Victorian Novel, by Jeff Nunokawa, in ANQ, 95; Americanus Sum: Life Attacks Anglomania, in Victorian Per Rev 28, 95; 'Mon Pauvre Prisonnier': Becky Sharp and the Triumph of Napoleon, in Stud in the Novel 28.1, 96; Painting a Classroom, Reaching Through Tchg 10.1, 97. **CONTACT ADDRESS** Dept of Eng, Valdosta State Univ, 1500 N. Patterson St, Valdosta, GA 31698. **EMAIL** pmarks@valdosta.edu

MARLANE, JUDITH
DISCIPLINE COMMUNICATION **EDUCATION** Columbia Univ, BFA, 58; MA, 62, EdD, 74. **CAREER** WNET Television, 62-66; founder, pres, JSG Prod, 66-82; producer, MCA/WWOR-TV, NYork, 82-87; pres, Juroco, 89- ; chair, prof, Calif St Univ Northridge, 87- . **HONORS AND AWARDS** Who's Who; Broadcast Preceptor Awd, 77; Front Page Awd Judge, 80; Int Film & Television Festival Silver Medallion, 83; Silver Angel Awds, 82, 83, 84, 85, 86 **MEMBERSHIPS** Nat Acad of Television Arts & Sci; Int Radio & Television Soc; Broadcast Educ Assoc; Hollywood Radio & Television Soc; Nat Pr Club; Pen Center USA, West; Amer Women in Radio & Television; Amer Assoc of Univ Prof; Nat Assoc of Broadcasters; Nat Educ Assoc; Pi Lambda Theta; Kappa Delta Pi. **SELECTED PUBLICATIONS** Auth, Lawyer Advertising on Television, Trial Diplomacy J, 89; auth, The world of Chinese Television, Television Quart, 92; auth, Women in Television News, Columbia Univ Press, 76; auth, Women in Television News Revisited, Univ Tx Press, 99. **CONTACT ADDRESS** Dept of Radio-Television-Film, California State Univ, Northridge, 18111 Nordhoff St, Northridge, CA 91330-8317. **EMAIL** judith.marlane@csun.edu

MARLIN, JOHN
DISCIPLINE ENGLISH **EDUCATION** US Mil Acad, BS; Univ Chicago, AM, PhD. **CAREER** Asst prof, Col St. Elizabeth. **RESEARCH** Medieval drama. **SELECTED PUBLICATIONS** Auth, Virtual Ritual: History, Drama, and the Spirit of the Liturgy in the Flenny Playbook, Amer Benedictine Rev, Dec 97; auth, Monastic Spirituality and 12th century Drama, Int Medieval Cong, 97. **CONTACT ADDRESS** Dept of Eng, Col of Saint Elizabeth, 2 Convent Rd., Morristown, NJ 07960. **EMAIL** jmarlin@liza.st-elizabeth.edu

MARLING, WILLIAM H.
DISCIPLINE AMERICAN LITERATURE, MODERNISM **EDUCATION** Univ Utah, BA, MA, Univ Calif, PhD. **CAREER** English, Case Western Reserve Univ. **HONORS AND AWARDS** Dir, Grad Studies. **SELECTED PUBLICATIONS** Auth or ed, The American Roman Noir; Raymond Chandler; Dashiell Hammett; William Carlos Williams and the Painters. **CONTACT ADDRESS** Case Western Reserve Univ, 10900 Euclid Ave, Cleveland, OH 44106. **EMAIL** wxm3@po.cwru.edu

MARLOW, JAMES ELLIOTT
PERSONAL Born 02/14/1938, Belle Rive, IL, m, 1988, 2 children **DISCIPLINE** ENGLISH LITERATURE **EDUCATION** Dartmouth Col, BA, 60; Univ Calif, Davis, MA, 68, PhD, 72. **CAREER** Asst prof English, Col William & Mary, 69-73; asst prof, 73-76, assoc prof, 76-80, prof English, Univ Mass, Dartmouth, 80-. **HONORS AND AWARDS** Dartmouth Class of 1960 Poet; NEH Seminar, 73, 80. **MEMBERSHIPS** MLA; Dickens Soc; Victorian Inst. **RESEARCH** Novels of Charles Dickens; semiotics; playwriting. **SELECTED PUBLICATIONS** Auth, Franklin, Dickens, and solitary monster, Dickens Studies Newslett, 81; The response of Victorian periodicals to the fate of Franklin, Victorian Periodicals Rev, 82; Pickwick, Pugilism, and Popular Culture, J Popular Culture, 82; The Second Disk, Am Heritage, 12/82; English Cannibalism: Dickens After 1859, Studies in English Lit 23, 83; Pickwick's Writing: Propriety and Language, English Lit Hist 53, 86; Social Harmony and Dickens' Revolutionary Cooking, Dickens Studies Annual 17, 89; Charles Dickens: The Uses of Time, Am Univ Presses, 94. **CONTACT ADDRESS** Dept of English, Univ of Massachusetts, Dartmouth, 285 Old Westport Rd, North Dartmouth, MA 02747-2300. **EMAIL** jmarlow@umassd.edu

MARLOWE, ANN
PERSONAL Born 12/29/1939, Garrett, IN, s **DISCIPLINE** ENGLISH **EDUCATION** St Francis Col, Ind, BA; Univ Dayton, MA; Univ NMex, PhD. **CAREER** Teaching fel, Univ Dayton, 64-65; instr, Tri-State Univ, 65-67, 70-71; teaching fel, Univ Nmex, 67-68, 69-70; prof, Mo Southern State Col, 71-. **HONORS AND AWARDS** NEH Fac Seminars, Berkeley, Dartmouth; NEH referee, panelist for grants. **MEMBERSHIPS** Am Friends of Wordsworth, Mo Asn of Teachers of English, Nat Ed Asn, Sigma Tau Delta English Honorary. **RESEARCH** Techniques of creativity and analysis of writing, techniques of poetry, early American novel. **SELECTED PUBLICATIONS** Auth, "Wieland, A Story With A Moral," RE: Artes Liberales (Spring 81); auth, "The Pond That Mirrors the College," The Joplin Globe (Nov 5, 99); auth of 4 poems published by Int Poetry Asn. **CONTACT ADDRESS** Dept English, Missouri So State Col, 3950 Newman Rd, Joplin, MO 64801-1512. **EMAIL** Marlowe-A@mail.mssc.edu

MAROCCHINO, KATHRYN D.
PERSONAL Born 05/05/1953, Indianapolis, IN, m, 1974 **DISCIPLINE** ENGLISH, LITERATURE, SPEECH COMMUNICATION **EDUCATION** Technic Inst for Experts in Bus, grad, 72; Univ Turin, PhD, 79. **CAREER** Lectr, Stanford Univ, 83-87; Instr, Paden Adult Educ Ctr, 84-88; Instr, Col of Alameda, 87-88; Lectr, Univ Calif, 88-89; Prof, Calif Marine Acad, 90- **HONORS AND AWARDS** Who's Who Registry of Bus Leaders; Int Auths and Writers Who's Who. **MEMBERSHIPS** Int Asn for the Fantastic in the Arts, Bram Stoker Soc, Gothic Soc, Am Transl Asn, Northern Calif Transl Asn, Am Lit Transl Asn, Asn for Death Educ and Coun. **RESEARCH** Translation, thanatology, humanities, speech communication. **SELECTED PUBLICATIONS** Auth, Avviamento alla lettura in lingua inglese, Giappichelli (Turin), 82; auth, Instructor's Manual and Testing Program for Ciao! Holt, Rinehart & Winston Publ (New York, NY), 86; auth, "Goblin Market," in Masterplots: Revised Second Ed (Pasadena: Salem Pr, 96); auth, "Dracula," in Masterplots: Revised Second Ed (Pasadena: Salem Pr, 96); auth, "The Nikki Hospice Foundation for Pets: Making Animal Hospice Care a Reality," The Pet Companion (97); auth, "Bringing Hopice Home," Veterinary Econom (98); auth, "The Nikki Hospice Foundation for Pets: A Humane Option for Companion Animals," Four Paws Pr, A Publ of the Benicia Vallejo Humane Soc, vol 2, issue 3 (99). **CONTACT ADDRESS** Dept English, California Maritime Acad, PO Box 1392, Vallejo, CA 94590-0644. **EMAIL** kmarocchino@csum.edu

MAROTTI, ARTHUR FRANCIS
PERSONAL Born 04/03/1940, New York, NY, m, 1964, 2 children **DISCIPLINE** ENGLISH **EDUCATION** Fordham Univ, AB, 61; Johns Hopkins Univ, PhD, 65. **CAREER** Asst prof English, Wash Univ, 65-70; assoc prof English, full prof English, 85-, Wayne State Univ, 70-85, Fel, Humanities Ctr, Johns Hopkins Univ, 70-71; Guggenheim fel, 75-76; fac res award, Wayne State Univ, 78, 88. **HONORS AND AWARDS** ACLS Fel, 88-89; Wayne State Univ Charles Gershenson Distinguished Fac Fel, 95-97; NEH Fellowship, 00; Wayne St. U. Distinguished Grad Faculty Awd, 00. **MEMBERSHIPS** Mla; Midwest Mod Lang Asn; Renissance Soc Am; Meton Soc Am; Renaissance Eng Text Soc; Soc Textual Scholar. **RESEARCH** Sixteenth and 17th century poetry and drama; John Donne's poetry; Transmission of texts in manuscript & print; Religious discourses in early modern England. **SELECTED PUBLICATIONS** Auth, All about Jonson's poetry, ELH, 72; contribr, Donne and the extasie, The Rhetoric of Renaissance Poetry, Univ Calif, 74; auth, Countertransference, the communication process, and the dimensions of psychoanalytic criticism, Critical Inquiry, 78; John Donne and the Rewards of Patronage, Patronage in the Renaissance, Princeton Univ, 81; Love is not love: Elizabethan Sonnet Sequences and the Social Order, Elh, 82; co-ed,Reading With a Difference: Gender, Race, and Cultural Identity, Wayne State Univ, 93; ed, Critical Essays on John Donne, GK Hall, 94; Manuscript, Print, and the English Renaissance Lyric, Cornell Univ, 95; coed, Texts and Cultural Change in Early Modern England, MacMillan, 97; ed., "Catholicism and Anti-Catholicism in Early Modern English Texts," 99; coed, "Print, Manuscript, and Performance: The Changing Relations of the Media in Early Modern England, 00. **CONTACT ADDRESS** Dept of English, Wayne State Univ, 51 W Warren, Detroit, MI 48202-1308. **EMAIL** a.marotti@wayne.edu

MAROVITZ, SANFORD E.
PERSONAL Born 05/10/1933, Chicago, IL, m, 1964 **DISCIPLINE** ENGLISH **EDUCATION** Lake Forest Col, BA, 60; Duke Univ, MA, 61; PhD, 68. **CAREER** Instr English, Temple Univ, 63-65; Fulbright lectr, Univ Athens, Greece, 65-67; from asst prof, 67-70, to assoc prof, 70-75, to full prof, 75-96, to prof emeritus, Kent State Univ, 96-; vis prof English, Shimane Univ, Matsue, Japan, 76-77; chair dept English, Kent State Univ, 87-92. **HONORS AND AWARDS** Woodrow Wilson fel, 60; Fulbright Teaching Awd, Greece, 65-67; Dist Service Awd, Lake Forest Col, 85; Dist Teaching Awd, Kent State Univ, 85; Pres Citation, Shimane Univ, Japan, 98; Pres Medal, Kent State Univ, 99. **MEMBERSHIPS** MLA; Col English Asn; Melville Soc; Western Lit Asn; W.D. Howells Soc; Nathaniel Hawthorne Soc; Am Studies Asn; AAUP; Aldous Huxley Soc; Ralph Waldo Emerson Soc; Saul Bellow Soc. **RESEARCH** Nineteenth century American literature with special interests in Melville, Howells, Jewish literature, and Western writing; Aldous Huxley's life and writing. **SELECTED PUBLICATIONS** Coed, Artful Thunder: Versions of the Romantic Tradition in American Literature in Honor of Howard P. Vincent, Kent State Univ Press (Kent, OH), 75; auth, "Emerson's Shakespeare: From Scorn to Apotheosis," in Emerson Centenary Essays, ed. Joel Myerson (IL: S Ill Univ Press, 82), 122-155; coauth, Bibliographical Guide to the Study of the Literature of the U.S.A., 5th ed., Duke Univ Press (Durham, NC), 84; auth, "Toward 'Moby-Dick': A Freshman Honors Course," in Approaches to Teaching Melville's Moby-Dick, ed. Martin Bickman (NY: Mod Lang Asn, 85), 56-65; auth, "Herman Melville: A Writer for the World," in A Companion to Melville Studies, ed. John Bryant (CT: Greenwood Press, 86), 741-780; auth, "Romance and Realism: Children of the New Colossus and the Jewish Struggle Within," in American Realism and the Canon, ed. Tom Quirk and Gary Scharnhorst (DE, London, Toronto: Del Univ Press/Assoc Univ Presses, 94), 102-126; auth, Abraham Cahan, Twayne Publ (New York, NY), 96; auth, "From Mythic Visions to a Shattered American Dream: Nature Expropriated in the Buckskin Man Tales," in The Lizard Speaks: Essays on the Writings of Frederick Manfred, ed. Nancy Owen Nelson (SD: Center for Western Studies, 98), 130-154; auth, "Back to the Beginning: A Late Look at Bellow's Early Stories," in Small Planets: Saul Bellow and the Art of Short Fiction, ed. Gerhard Bach and Gloria L. Cronin (MI: Michigan State Univ Press, 00), 3-17; coed, Melville "Among the Nations": Proceedings of an International Conference, Volos, Greece, July 2-6, 1997, Kent State Univ Press (Kent, OH), 01. **CONTACT ADDRESS** Dept of English, Kent State Univ, Kent, OH 44242. **EMAIL** smarovit@kent.edu

MARQUEZ, ANTONIO
DISCIPLINE AMERICAN AND COMPARATIVE LITERATURE **EDUCATION** Univ Nmex, PhD, 77. **CAREER** Instr, Univ NMex, 77-. **HONORS AND AWARDS** Fulbright scholar/lectr. **SELECTED PUBLICATIONS** Auth, Richard Rodriguez's Hunger of Memory and New Perspectives on Ethnic Autobiography, Tchg Am Ethnic Lit, UNM, 95. **CONTACT ADDRESS** Univ of New Mexico, Albuquerque, Albuquerque, NM 87131. **EMAIL** amarquez@unm.edu

MARRA, KIM
PERSONAL Born 08/24/1957, Cleveland, OH, s **DISCIPLINE** THEATRE STUDIES **EDUCATION** Dartmouth, BA, 81; Brown Univ, MA, 83; Univ Wis-Madison, PhD, 90. **CAREER** Asst prof to assoc prof theatre arts, Univ Iowa, 90- . **HONORS AND AWARDS** Col Teaching Awd, Univ Iowa, 98; Dean's Schol Awd, Univ Iowa, 99-00. **MEMBERSHIPS** Am Soc Theatre Res; Asn Theatre Higher Educ; Mid-Am Theatre Conf. **RESEARCH** US theatre history, 1865-1930. **SELECTED PUBLICATIONS** Ed, Passing Performances: Queer Readings of Leading Players in American Theatre History, Univ Mich Press, (98). **CONTACT ADDRESS** Dept Theatre Arts, Univ Iowa, 104 Theatre Building, Iowa City, IA 52242-1705. **EMAIL** kim-marra@uiowa.edu

MARREN, SUSAN M.
DISCIPLINE MODERN AMERICAN FICTION **EDUCATION** Univ Mich, PhD. **CAREER** English and Lit, Univ Ark. **SELECTED PUBLICATIONS** Auth, Subversive Mothering in Harriet Jacob's Incidents in the Life of a Slave Girl and Toni Morrison's Beloved, Mich Feminist Studies, 91; Between Slavery and Freedom: The Transgressive Self in Olaudah Equiano's Autobiography, PMLA, 93. **CONTACT ADDRESS** Univ of Arkansas, Fayetteville, Fayetteville, AR 72701.

MARRON, MARIA B.
DISCIPLINE COMMUNICATIONS **EDUCATION** Univ Col Dublin, BA; OH Univ, MA, PhD. **CAREER** Comm Dept, Southwest Tex State Univ **SELECTED PUBLICATIONS** Auth, The Founding of Investigative Reporters and Editors, Inc., and the Fledgling Organization's Conduct of the Arizona Project: A Time of Trial and Triumph, Asn Educ Journalism & Mass Comm Annual Conf, 93; Investigative Journalism, Journalism Professionalism, and Professional Efficacy in Ireland, Int Comm Asn, 94. **CONTACT ADDRESS** Southwest Texas State Univ, 601 University Dr, San Marcos, TX 78666-4604.

MARRS, SUZANNE
DISCIPLINE COMPOSITION, 19TH AND 20TH CENTURY AMERICAN LITERATURE **EDUCATION** Univ Okla, PhD. **CAREER** Welty Scholar-in-Residence, Miss Dept Archives and Hist, 85-86; lectr, in Russia & Fr; consul, BBC documentary on Eudora Welty, 87. **RESEARCH** South. **SELECTED PUBLICATIONS** Auth, bk The Welty Collection & articles on Eudora Welty's fiction. **CONTACT ADDRESS** Dept of English, Millsaps Col, 1701 N State St, Jackson, MS 39210.

MARRUS, FRANCINE E.
DISCIPLINE COMMUNICATION THEORY **EDUCATION** Ohio Univ PhD 89. **CAREER** Living Legacy, researcher; writer, 98-; Clemson Univ, asst prof 90-98; FU, vis asst prof 90; UT, instr 85-88. **HONORS AND AWARDS** Appreciation Awd; Community Serv Awd. **MEMBERSHIPS** NCA; SCW. **RESEARCH** Spiritual Communications; half contexts and representations; ethnomorphic methods. **SELECTED PUBLICATIONS** Auth, Living in the Light: Myths in Alcoholics Anonymous that communicate a member's view of wellness in recovery, Communication in Recovery: Studies in Personal

Transformation, eds, L Eastland, S. Herndon, J. Barr, Hampton Press, in progress; auth, In the Spirit: Communication Performance in a twelve step program, Communication in Recovery: Studies in Personal Transformation, eds, L. Eastland, S. Herndon, J. Barr, Hampton Press, in progress; auth, Leading classroom discussion in the basic course, Teaching and directing the basic comm course, eds, L.W. Hugenberg, P.L. Gray, D.N. Trank, Dubuque IA, Kendall and Hunt Pub, 93. **CONTACT ADDRESS** 167 Cedar Creek Circle, Central, SC 29630-9467. **EMAIL** learnangel@aol.com

MARSHALL, ALICIA A.
DISCIPLINE HEALTH COMMUNICATION **EDUCATION** Purdue Univ, PhD. **CAREER** Asst prof, Texas A&M Univ. **HONORS AND AWARDS** National Inst Health grant; US Army Dept grant. **SELECTED PUBLICATIONS** Publ in, Health Commun; Commun Monographs; Acad Med; J Gen Internal Med; contribur, Health Communication and the Disenfranchised; Integrated Approaches to Communication Theory and Research; Case Studies in Health Communication. **CONTACT ADDRESS** Dept of Speech Communication, Texas A&M Univ, Col Station, College Station, TX 77843-4234.

MARSHALL, CYNTHIA
PERSONAL Born 08/16/1956, Penn, m, 1981 **DISCIPLINE** ENGLISH **EDUCATION** Slippery Rock Univ, BS, 78; MA, 80; Univ Pittsburgh, PhD,87. **CAREER** Prof, Cmty Col of Beaver County, 90-. **HONORS AND AWARDS** Who's Who Women, Who's Who Teachers, Ernest Brennecke Awd, Slippery Rock Univ, 80. **MEMBERSHIPS** Penn State Teachers Asn, Nat Educ Asn, Mod Lang Asn, Asn of Am Indian, Alaska Native prof, Recorder Soc of Am. **RESEARCH** Poetry, Native American poetry and studies. **SELECTED PUBLICATIONS** Auth, "A Boxing Day Celebration," The Gilded Age, Victorian monthly, 88; auth, "Agnes DeMille," The Research Guide to American Historical biography, 91; auth, "Angela Davis," The Research guide to American Historical biography, 91; auth, "The Bat" and "Samhain Celebration", in The Pittsburgh Quarterly, 92; auth, "The championing of the Liberal Arts: Creating Courses for the Next Millenium," The Penn Asn of Two Year Col , 93; auth, "Beltaine," Wise Women's Journal, 95; auth, "Cold Rain," The Laurel Wreath; auth, "White Buffalo," The Native American Newsletter; auth, "A Proper Sacrifice" in Red Ink, University of Arizona Journal, 96; auth, Monaca Bridge, 97; auth, "My Guardian Angel," in A New Song, 98. **CONTACT ADDRESS** Dept Arts & Sci, Comm Col of Beaver County, 1 Campus Dr, Monaca, PA 15061-2566. **EMAIL** cynthia-marshall@ccbc.cc.pa.us

MARSHALL, DAVID
DISCIPLINE ENGLISH **EDUCATION** Johns Hopkins Univ, PhD. **CAREER** Prof, Northwestern Univ. **RESEARCH** 18th century fiction and aesthetics, narrative theory; Shakespeare; lyric poetry; autobiography; Philosophy and literature. **SELECTED PUBLICATIONS** Auth, The Figure of Theater: Shaftesbury, Defoe, Adam Smith and George Eliot, Columbia Univ Press, 86; The Surprising Effects of Sympathy: Marivaux, Diderot, Rousseau and Mary Shelley, Univ Chicago Press, 88. **CONTACT ADDRESS** Dept of English, Northwestern Univ, 1801 Hinman, Evanston, IL 60208.

MARSHALL, DONALD G.
PERSONAL Born 09/09/1943, Long Beach, CA, m, 1975, 2 children **DISCIPLINE** ENGLISH **EDUCATION** Harvard Univ, AB, 65; Yale Univ, PhD, 71. **CAREER** Asst prof, UCLA, 69-75; from assoc prof to prof, 75-90, Univ Iowa; prof, UIC, 90-. **HONORS AND AWARDS** NEH Fel, 73-74 **MEMBERSHIPS** Modern Lang Asn; Conference on Christianity and Literature. **RESEARCH** Literary theory and its history; Wordsworth; literature and religion. **SELECTED PUBLICATIONS** Ed, Literature as Philosophy, Philosophy as Literature, 87; ed, Hans-Georg Gadamer. Truth and Method, 89; auth, Contemporary Critical Theory: A Selective Bibliography, 93. **CONTACT ADDRESS** Dept of English, Univ of Illinois, Chicago, 601 S Morgan, Rm 2027, Chicago, IL 60607-7120. **EMAIL** marshall@uic.edu

MARSHALL, LINDA EDITH
PERSONAL Born 04/25/1941, London, ON, Canada, m, 1965, 1 child **DISCIPLINE** ENGLISH **EDUCATION** Univ Western Ont, BA, 63, MA, 65; Univ Toronto, PhD(Medieval studies), 74. **CAREER** Lectr, 65-72, asst prof, 72-79, Assoc Prof English, Univ Guelph, 79-, Can Coun leave fel Medieval poetic theory, 77. **MEMBERSHIPS** Medieval Acad Am; Asn Can Univ Teachers English; Keats-Shelley Asn Am. **RESEARCH** Poetic theory, Medieval and Romantic. **SELECTED PUBLICATIONS** Auth, Transfigured to his Likeness, Sensible Transcendentalism in Rossetti, Christina 'Goblin Market', Univ Toronto Quart, Vol 0063, 94; Abstruse the Problems, Unity and Divisions in Rossetti, Christina 'Later Life, a Double Sonnet of Sonnets', Victorian Poetry, Vol 0032, 94. **CONTACT ADDRESS** Dept of English, Univ of Guelph, Guelph, ON, Canada N1G 2W1.

MARSHALL, W. GERALD
PERSONAL Born Statesville, NC **DISCIPLINE** ENGLISH **EDUCATION** Lenoir-Rhyme Col, BA; Appalachian State Univ, MA; State Univ NYork at Binghamton, PhD. **CAREER** Assoc prof, Univ of Hawaii **MEMBERSHIPS** MLA **RESEARCH** Restoration and Eighteenth Century Lit and Culture **SELECTED PUBLICATIONS** Auth, A Great Stage of Fools: Theatricality and Madness in the Plays of William Wycherley, AMS Press, 94; The Restoration Mind, Univ of Delaware Press, 97. **CONTACT ADDRESS** Dept of English, Univ of Hawaii, Manoa, Honolulu, HI 96822-2453.

MARSILIO, MARIA S.
PERSONAL Born 05/21/1963, Glenside, PA, m, 2001 **DISCIPLINE** CLASSICAL STUDIES **EDUCATION** Col New Rochelle, BA, 85; Univ Pa, MA, 89; PhD, 93. **CAREER** Lectr, Univ of Pa, 93-95; vis asst prof to asst prof, Saint Joseph's Univ, 95-. **HONORS AND AWARDS** Grant, St Joseph's Univ, 98; Awd for Res, St Joseph's Univ, 00. **MEMBERSHIPS** Am Philog Assoc, Classical Assoc of the Atlantic States, Am Classical League, Pa Classical Assoc, Philadelphia Classical Soc. **RESEARCH** Greek Epic and Lyric Poetry, Greek and Roman Drama, Gender and Sexuality in Antiquity. **SELECTED PUBLICATIONS** Auth, "Hesiod's Winter Maiden," Helios 24.2, (97): 101-111; auth, "The Poetics of Hesiod's Winter," Annali della Scuola Normale Superiore di Pisa, IV.II.2, (97): 411-425; auth, "Two Ships in the Menaechmi," Classical World 92.2, (98): 131-139; auth, Farming and Poetry in Hesiod's Works and Days, Univ Pr of Am (Lanham), 00. **CONTACT ADDRESS** Sch of Arts and Sciences, Saint Joseph's Univ, 5600 City Ave, Philadelphia, PA 19131. **EMAIL** marsilio@sju.edu

MARSLAND, AMY
PERSONAL Born 03/23/1924, Saskatoon, Canada, m, 1951, 4 children **DISCIPLINE** ENGLISH LITERATURE **EDUCATION** Univ Saskatchewan, BA, 44; Univ Mich, MA, 45, PhD, 50. **CAREER** Instr, Carleton Col, 50-51; lectr, SUNY Binghamton, 61-65; ed Chenango Am, 58-62; treas Twin Valley Publ, 65-86; Phi Beta Kappa; Phi Kappa Phi. **RESEARCH** Comparative Cultures. **SELECTED PUBLICATIONS** Venezuela Through Its History, 54; Cache-Cache, 80; Snow White, the Wolf and the Unicorn: Structural Origins of Western Culture, 81; A Classic Death, 85; Symbols in Art, 30,000 BC to the Present, http://members.aol.com/symartamym, 98. **CONTACT ADDRESS** 12 S Chenango St, Greene, NY 13778. **EMAIL** MarslandSr@AOL

MARTIN, BRUCE KIRK
PERSONAL Born 05/28/1941, Jersey City, NJ, m, 1965, 2 children **DISCIPLINE** ENGLISH AND AMERICAN LITERATURE **EDUCATION** Univ Cincinnati, AB, 63, MA, 66, Ph-D(English), 67. **CAREER** From asst prof to assoc prof, 67-78, Prof English, Drake Univ, 78-, Summer sem, Nat Endowment for Humanities, 78; Dept Chair, 83-89, vis prof of english, Nat Univ of Singapore, 91-92. **HONORS AND AWARDS** Fulbright lectureships: Nat Univ of Singapore, 86-87, and Kwangju Univ (South Korea), 95-96; Ellis and Nelle Levitt Distinguished Prof of English, Drake Univ, 00-. **MEMBERSHIPS** MLA **RESEARCH** Nineteenth and 20th-century British literature; literary theory. **SELECTED PUBLICATIONS** Auth, Vincy, Fred and the Unraveling of 'Middlemarch', Papers on Lang and Lit, Vol 0030, 94; auth, Philip Larkin, Twayne, 78; auth, British Poetry Since 1939, Twayne, 85; auth, David Lodge, Twayne, 99. **CONTACT ADDRESS** Dept of English, Drake Univ, 2507 University Ave, Des Moines, IA 50311-4505. **EMAIL** bruce.martin@drake.edu

MARTIN, DONALD R.
DISCIPLINE COMMUNICATIONS, TELECOMMUNICATIONS **EDUCATION** OH State Univ, PhD. **CAREER** Instr, Ohio Wesleyan Univ, 65-68; asst prof, Calif State Polytechnic Univ, 68-69; assoc prof, San Diego State Univ, 69-; instr, CA Polytechnic State Univ; OH Wesleyan Univ; assoc prof, 93-; interim dir, San Diego State of Commun, 00-01. **HONORS AND AWARDS** Telecommun mgr, KPBS. **RESEARCH** Telecommunications management and the deployment of new telecommunications technologies. **SELECTED PUBLICATIONS** Auth, bk chapters and jour articles in area of new telecommun technol. **CONTACT ADDRESS** Dept of commun, San Diego State Univ, 5500 Campanile Dr, San Diego, CA 92182-4561. **EMAIL** dmartin@mail.sdsu.edu

MARTIN, HERBERT WOODWARD
PERSONAL Born 10/04/1933, Birmingham, AL, m, 1979, 2 children **DISCIPLINE** MODERN POETRY, CREATIVE WRITING **EDUCATION** Univ Toledo, BA, 64; Middlebury Col, MLitt, 72; Carnegie-Mellon Univ, DA, 79. **CAREER** Tchg fel freshman compos, State Univ NY, Buffalo, 64-67; from instr to asst prof freshman compos, sophmore English & creative writing, Aquinas Col, 67-70; from asst to assoc prof, 70-80, prof poet in residence, creative writing, Drama, mod poetry & mod drama, Univ Dayton, 70; distinguished visiting prof, central MI univ, 73-; Fulbright fell, Janus Pannonius univ, Pecs, ungary, 90-91. **HONORS AND AWARDS** Paul Laurence Dunbar humanitarian award, 96; Opus award, Poetry and performance, 96; Elmer Lackner award, Univ sevice, 96; OH Hum couns Bjornson Hum award, 96; First writer in residence at Paul Laurence Dunbar Memorial House, 96; Paul Laurence Dunbar Laureate Peot for Dayton, OH, 96; Hon PhD of Humane letters from Urbana univ, 98; Ohioana Awd for Theatrical Performance, 98. **RESEARCH** In His Own Voiuce: The Dramatic and Other Uncollected Works of Paul Laurence Dunbar. **SELECTED PUBLICATIONS** Auth, New York, The Nine Million and other Poems, Abracadabra Press, 68; The Shit-Storm Poems, Pilot Press, 72; The Persistence of the Flesh, 76 & The Forms of Silence, 80, Lotus Press; Paul Laurence Dunbar: A Singer of Songs, State of Ohio Libr, 79; Paul Laurence Dunbar: Common Ground, opera, 95; It Pays to Advertise, opera, 96; auth, Galileo's Suns, 99; auth, The Log of the Vigilante, 00. **CONTACT ADDRESS** Univ of Dayton, 300 College Park, Dayton, OH 45469-0002. **EMAIL** Martinh@checkov.hm.udayton.edu

MARTIN, JANET MARION
PERSONAL Born 10/24/1938, Bogalusa, LA **DISCIPLINE** CLASSICS **EDUCATION** Radcliffe Col, AB, 61; Univ MI, MA, 63; Harvard Univ, PhD, 68. **CAREER** From instr to asst prof classics, Harvard Univ, 68-72; asst prof, 73-76, Assoc Prof Classics, Princeton Univ, 76-, Fel Post-classical & humanistic studies, Am Acad Rome, 71-73. **MEMBERSHIPS** Am Philol Asn; Mediaeval Acad Am. **RESEARCH** Medieval Latin lit: ancient and medieval rhetoric and poetics; the class tradition. **SELECTED PUBLICATIONS** Ed, Peter the Venerable: Selected Letters, Pontifical Inst Mediaeval Studies, 74; auth, John of Salisbury's manuscripts of Frontinus and of Gellius, J Warburg & Courtauld Insts, 77; Uses of tradition: Gellius, Petronius, and John of Salisbury, Viator, 79; contribr, chap, In: The Renaissance of the Twelfth Century, Harvard Univ, 82. **CONTACT ADDRESS** Dept of Class, Princeton Univ, 104 E Pyne, Princeton, NJ 08544-1098. **EMAIL** jmmartin@princeton.edu

MARTIN, JAY
PERSONAL Born 10/30/1935, Newark, NJ, m, 1956, 3 children **DISCIPLINE** LITERATURE, AMERICAN STUDIES, PSYCHOANALYSIS **EDUCATION** Columbia Col, AB, 56; Ohio State Univ, MA, 57; PhD, 60; Southern Calif Psychoanalytic Inst, PhD, 83. **CAREER** From instr to assoc prof, Yale Univ, 60-68; prof, Univ of Calif at Irvine, 68-79; prof, Moscow State Univ, 76; prof, Univ of Southern Calif, 79-96; Edward S. Gould Prof and Prof of Govt, Claremont McKenna Col, 96-; Dai Ito Chun Distinguished Prof, Univ of Hawaii, 00-01. **HONORS AND AWARDS** Morse Fel; Am Philos Soc Fel, Guggenheim, NEH Sr Res Fel, Rockefeller Found Sr Fel, Bellasio Rockefeller Found Study Ctr, DURFEE Fel, USC Res Grant Prizes, Burlington Northern Found Res Prize, Marie H. Briehl Prize in Child Psychoanalysis, USC Distinguished Emritus Prof Prize, Alexander Prize in Adult Psychoanalysis, Seattle Psychoanalytic Prize for Research, Phi Kappa Phi Book Awd. **MEMBERSHIPS** Southern Calif Psychoanalytic Soc. **RESEARCH** American Culture, Government & Political Science, American Literature, Biography, American Philosophy. **SELECTED PUBLICATIONS** Auth, Conrad Aiken; auth, Harvest of Change, auth, Nathanael West; auth, Always merry and Bright; Auth, Winter Dreams: An American in Moscow; auth, Robert Lowell: Who Am I This Time? **CONTACT ADDRESS** Dept of Govt, Claremont McKenna Col, 500 E 9th St, Claremont, CA 91711-5903. **EMAIL** jmartin@mckenna.edu

MARTIN, JOHN SAYRE
PERSONAL Born 11/25/1921, England, m, 1956, 3 children **DISCIPLINE** ENGLISH **EDUCATION** Univ Calif, Berkeley, AB, 43, MA, 48, PhD(English), 58. **CAREER** Lectr English, Univ Calif, Berkeley, 55-56; instr, Univ Ill, Urbana, 57-62; asst prof, Hiram Col, 62-65; assoc prof, 65-79, Prof English, Univ Calgary, 80-. **MEMBERSHIPS** MLA; Philol Asn Pac Coast; Asn Can Univ Teachers English. **RESEARCH** Nineteenth and twentieth century literature. **SELECTED PUBLICATIONS** Auth, Mrs Moore and the Marabar Caves, Mod Fiction Studies, winter 65-66; Peter Bayley and the lyrical ballads, English Studies, 12/67; Wordsworth's echoes, English Lang Notes, 3/68; E M Forster, the Endless Journey, Cambridge Univ, 76. **CONTACT ADDRESS** Dept of English, Univ of Calgary, Calgary, AB, Canada T2N 1N4. **EMAIL** martinj@ucalgary.ca

MARTIN, RONALD EDWARD
PERSONAL Born 06/30/1933, Chicago, IL, m, 1956, 3 children **DISCIPLINE** ENGLISH; AMERICAN STUDIES **EDUCATION** Carroll Col, Wis, BA, 55; Boston Univ, AM, 57, PhD(Am lit), 63. **CAREER** Instr English, Boston Univ, 61-62; from instr to asst prof, 62-68, assoc prof, 68-81, Prof English, Univ Del, 81-99; Am Coun Learned Soc grant-in-aid, 67-68; dir, Ctr Sci & Cult, 81-85; Fulbright Distinguished Chr, Am Stud, Odense Univ, Denmark, 93-94; emeritus prof English, Univ Del, 99-. **MEMBERSHIPS** AAUP; AAAS. **RESEARCH** American literature since 1880; relationships of science, philosophy, and literature; American literature and anthropology, 1870-1940. **SELECTED PUBLICATIONS** Auth, The Fiction of Joseph Hergesheimer, Univ Pa, 65; American Literature and the Universe of Force, Duke Univ, 81; American Literature and the Destruction of Knowledge, Duke Univ, 91. **CONTACT ADDRESS** 234 W Main, Newark, DE 19711. **EMAIL** rmartin@udel.edu

MARTIN, RUSSELL L.
PERSONAL Born, TS, m, 1982, 3 children **DISCIPLINE** ENGLISH **EDUCATION** S Methodist Univ, BA, 78, MA, 86; PhD, Virginia, 94; Il, MS, IL, 95. **CAREER** NAIP CATALOGUER, RES ASST, A HISTORY OF THE BOOK IN AMERICA, AAS, Curator of Newspapers. **SELECTED PUBLICATIONS** Auth, Mr, Jefferson's Business: The Farming Letters of Thomas Jefferson and Edmund Bacon, 1806-1826; auth, Two American Farmers: Thomas Jefferson and Edmund Bacon, Mag of Albemarle Co Hist 50, 92. **CONTACT ADDRESS** Am Antiquarian Soc, 185 Salisbury St, Worcester, MA 01609. **EMAIL** rmartin@mwa.org

MARTIN, SEAN ELLIOT
PERSONAL Born 03/30/1970, Metropolis, IL, s **DISCIPLINE** ENGLISH **EDUCATION** Univ Toledo, BA, 92; E Mich Univ, MA, 95. **CAREER** Grad asst, E Mich Univ, 94-95; instr, Univ of Toledo Community Col Br, 95; grad asst and adj instr, Duquesne Univ, 98-. **HONORS AND AWARDS** Presidential Scholar Awd, Univ of Toledo; Inductee, EUSAIMA Int. Black Belt Hall of Fame. **MEMBERSHIPS** MLA, Pa Col Eng Assoc, Community Col Humanities Assoc, E USA Int Martial Arts Assoc. **RESEARCH** Literature, film and visual art relating to the night-time world, the mysterious or paranormal, gender issues, mystic and spiritual traditions and science-fiction/fantasy/horror. **SELECTED PUBLICATIONS** Auth, The Border of Twilight: Representations of Nocturnal America; auth, Iconography of a Holocuast: Nazi Imagery in the Poems of American Women; auth, The Female Beastiary; Representations of Woman as Monster; auth, The Gate of the Devil: The Demonizing of Female Sexuality in Bram Stoker's 'Dracula'. **CONTACT ADDRESS** 1510 Alabama Ave, Pittsburgh, PA 15216-1802.

MARTIN, SHERRILL V.
DISCIPLINE MUSIC HISTORY **EDUCATION** Univ NC, Chapel Hill, PhD. **CAREER** Prof, Univ NC, Wilmington; nat musicol ed, Am Mus Tchr; nat bk rev ed, Sonneck Soc Bull. **SELECTED PUBLICATIONS** Auth, Feel the Spirit, 88; Henry Gilbert: A Bio-Bibliography; one essay in Time, Talent, Tradition. **CONTACT ADDRESS** Univ of No Carolina, Wilmington, Kenan Hall, Wilmington, NC 28403-3297. **EMAIL** martins@uncwil.edu

MARTIN, SUSAN D.
PERSONAL Born 11/30/1951, Berkeley, CA, m, 1989 **DISCIPLINE** CLASSICS **EDUCATION** Univ Calif, BA, 73; BA, 76; Univ Mich, PhD, 81. **CAREER** Asst prof to assoc prof to dept head to assoc dean to prof, Univ Tenn, 81-. **HONORS AND AWARDS** Chancellor's Citation; Public Serv Award, Univ Tenn; NEH Fel, 91; Harvard Law Sch Fel, 88-89; Am Acad Rome Fel, 80-81; Horace Rackham Fel, 79-80. **MEMBERSHIPS** APA; CAMWS; ASLH; ACVAAR; AIA; CSAAR; TFLTA; TCA; SFAAR. **RESEARCH** Roman law; Roman social and economic history; women in antiquity. **SELECTED PUBLICATIONS** Auth, "A Reconsideration of Probatio Operis," APA 103 (86); auth, The Roman Jurists and the Organization of Private Building in the Late Republic and Early Empire, Collection Latomas (Brussels), 89; auth, "Servum Meum Mulionem Donduxisti: Mules, Muleteers and Transport in Classical Roman Law," MLA 120 (90); auth, "Imeritia: The Responsibility of Skilled Workers in Classical Roman Law," Am J Philol 122 (01); auth, "Roman Law and the Study of Land Transportation," in Speculum Iuris: Roman Law as a Reflection on Economic and Social Life in Antiquity, eds. J. J. Aubert, B. Sirks (01); auth, Roman Land Transportation, Univ Mich Pr (forthcoming). **CONTACT ADDRESS** Class Dept, Univ of Tennessee, Knoxville, 1101 McClung Tower, Knoxville, TN 37996-0413. **EMAIL** sdmartin@utk.edu

MARTIN, TERRY J.
PERSONAL Born 10/26/1958, Berkeley, CA, m, 1982, 2 children **DISCIPLINE** ENGLISH **EDUCATION** SUNY, Buffalo, PhD, 88. **CAREER** Instr, Universidad Industrial de Santander, Colombia, 81-82; asst prof, Idaho State Univ Pocatello, 88-89; assoc prof, Baldwin-Wallace Coll, 89-. **HONORS AND AWARDS** Phi Beta Kappa, 79; Chancellor's Awd for Excellence in Teaching, SUNY/Buffalo, 86; Omicron Delta Kappa, 95; Sigma Delta Pi, 00. **MEMBERSHIPS** Soc Study of the Short Story; Midwest MLA. **RESEARCH** 19th-century American literature; African-American literature; literary theory. **SELECTED PUBLICATIONS** Auth, "A Slave in Form. . .[But Not] in Fact': Frederick Douglass and the Paradox of Transcendence," Proteus, A Journal of Ideas: The Legacy of Frederick Douglass, spring 95; auth, "John Barth's 'Petition' as Micro-cosm," Short Story, spring 96; auth, "Harriet Jacobs," Nineteenth-Century American Women Writers, 97; auth, "John Barth," An International Companion to the Contemporary Short Story in English, 98; auth, Rhetorical Deception in the Short Fiction of Hawthorne, Poe, and Melville, Edwin Mellen, 98. **CONTACT ADDRESS** Dept of English, Baldwin-Wallace Col, Berea, OH 44017. **EMAIL** tmartin@bw.edu

MARTIN, TIMOTHY
PERSONAL Born 09/21/1950, Thomaston, CT, m, 1991 **DISCIPLINE** MODERN BRITISH LITERATURE, IRISH LITERATURE, JAMES JOYCE **EDUCATION** Univ Pa, PhD. **CAREER** Instr, Rutgers, State Univ NJ, Camden Col of Arts and Sci; dir, James Joyce Conf, Philadelphia, 89; invited lectr, James Joyce Summer Sch, Dublin, 93, 95, 96, 99; invited lectr, Trieste Joyce Sch, 97, 98; Chair, North Am Academic Program, 17th Int James Joyce Symposium, 00. **RESEARCH** James Joyce **SELECTED PUBLICATIONS** Auth, Joyce and Wagner: A Study of Influence, Cambridge, 91; coed, Joyce in Context, Cambridge, 92. **CONTACT ADDRESS** Camden Col of Arts and Sci, Rutgers, The State Univ of New Jersey, Camden, Camden, NJ 08102. **EMAIL** timartin@crab.rutgers.edu

MARTIN, WANDA
DISCIPLINE COMPOSITION AND RHETORIC **EDUCATION** Univ Louisville, PhD, 87. **CAREER** Instr, dir, freshman Eng prog, Univ NMex. **SELECTED PUBLICATIONS** Recent articles on teaching an ethical approach to argumentation have appeared in Tech Commun Quart and Issues in Writing. **CONTACT ADDRESS** Univ of New Mexico, Albuquerque, Albuquerque, NM 87131. **EMAIL** wmartin@unm.edu

MARTIN, WILLIAM BIZZELL
PERSONAL Born 05/12/1926, Waxahachie, TX, m, 1950, 2 children **DISCIPLINE** ENGLISH LITERATURE **EDUCATION** Southern Methodist Univ, BA, 48; Univ Edinburgh, Scotland, dipl, 50, PhD, 53. **CAREER** Instr English, Tarleton State Col, 50-51; from instr to asst prof, Agr & Mech Col Tex, 52-55; assoc prof, Northeast Mo State Teachers Col, 55-56; prof English & dept head, Tarleton State Univ, 56-86, prof emeritus, 87-, Smith-Mundt lectr English & Am lit, Lebanese Nat Univ, 60-61. **MEMBERSHIPS** MLA; S.C. M.L.A. **RESEARCH** Eighteenth century English drama, Modern British and American drama. **SELECTED PUBLICATIONS** Ed, Texas Plays, SMU Press, 90; Chapters in Grider and Rodenberger, Texas Women Writers: A Tradition of Their Own, Tx A&M Univ Press, 97 and in Updating the American West (a supp to A Literary History of the American West), Tx Christian Univ Press, 97. **CONTACT ADDRESS** Dept of English & Lang, Tarleton State Univ, PO Box T-0300, Stephenville, TX 76402-0002. **EMAIL** martin@tarleton.edu

MARTIN-MURREY, LORETTA
PERSONAL Born 05/16/1954, Glasgow, KY, m, 1977, 1 child **DISCIPLINE** ENGLISH **EDUCATION** Western Ky Univ, BA, MA; Univ Ky, PhD, 91. **CAREER** Assoc Prof, 83-; Prof, Western Ky Univ, 84-. **HONORS AND AWARDS** Dir W Ky Univ-Glasgow Writing Center; ed, Broomsedge Chronicles. **MEMBERSHIPS** Rawsticks, Bale Boone Poetry Group, Rainsticks Poetry Group. **RESEARCH** Quilting in Southern Literature, writing, poetry, and Japanese language and culture. **SELECTED PUBLICATIONS** Areas: Eudora Welty, Mary Lee Settle, and Joy Bale Boone. **CONTACT ADDRESS** Western Kentucky Univ, Glasgow Campus, 213 Liberty St, Glasgow, KY 42141. **EMAIL** loretta.murrey@wku.edu

MARTINE, JAMES JOHN
PERSONAL Born 07/23/1937, Philadelphia, PA, m, 1961, 3 children **DISCIPLINE** AMERICAN LITERATURE, ENGLISH **EDUCATION** Temple Univ, BA, 67; Pa State Univ, MA, 68, PhD(English), 71. **CAREER** Asst prof, 71-74, assoc prof, 74-79, prof am lit, St Bonaventure, 80-, Reviewer, Philadelphia Sunday Bull Bk Sect, 71-82 & Libr J, 73-; adv ed, Studies Am Fiction, 72-; Nat Endowment for Humanities grant, summer, 76. **MEMBERSHIPS** MLA; Aaup; Northeast Mod Lang Asn. **RESEARCH** Twentieth century American fiction; 19th century American literature; history of American literature. **SELECTED PUBLICATIONS** Auth, The Courage to Defy, In: Critical Essays on Catch-22, Dickenson, 73; Fred Lewis Pattee and American Literature, Pa State Univ, 73; American Literature: Student Guide 1 & 2, Intext, 77; All in a boiling soup: An interview with Arthur Miller, In: Critical Essays on Arthur Miller, 79 & ed, Critical Essays on Arthur Miller, 79, G K Hall; Dict of Literary Biography: American Novelists 1910-1945, Vol 9, Part 1-3, Gale, 81; Rich boys and Rich Men: The Bridal Party, In: The Short Stories of F Scott Fitzgerald: New Approaches in Criticism, Univ Wis Press, 82; The Window, Delta Epsilon J, 82; auth, The Crucible: Politics, Poverty, and Prestense, Twayne, 93; Drama, In: Am Lit Scholar, 93-98. **CONTACT ADDRESS** Dept of English, St. Bonaventure Univ, Saint Bonaventure, NY 14778-9999. **EMAIL** jmartine@sbu.edu

MARTINEZ, INEZ A.
PERSONAL Born 09/29/1939, Albuquerque, NM, s **DISCIPLINE** ENGLISH **EDUCATION** St. Louis Univ, BS, 64; MA, 65; Univ Wis Madison, PhD, 79. **CAREER** Coinstr, City of NYork Univ Grad Sch, 97, 98; Instr to Prof, Kingsborough Community Col, 70-; Coordr, English Col Non Collab Prog, Kingsborough Community Col, 87-; Co-dir, Women's Studies, Kingsborough Community Col, 94-. **HONORS AND AWARDS** Post-Doctoral Mellon Fel, Grad Sch of City Univ of NY, 83, 89; Ford Fel, 64-65; Kent Fel, 67-70; NY Found for the Arts Fel for Fiction, 87; PSC Res Grant, 86, 97, 98. **MEMBERSHIPS** MLA, Am Lit Caucus of the MLA, Caucus of the MLA, Lesbian and Gay Caucus of the MLA, The Nat Women's Studies Asn, The Women of Color Caucus of the Nat Women's Studies Asn. **RESEARCH** Psychological criticism of literature from a Jungian perspective. **SELECTED PUBLICATIONS** Auth, "Roots," in Linking Roots, ed. Bryce Milligan (San Antonio: M&A Editions, 93); auth, To Know the Moon, Sandia Press (Brooklyn), 93; auth, "The Singing Antelope," in Daughters of the Fifth Sun: A Collection of Latina Fiction and Poetry (NY: Riverhead Books, 95), 254-258; auth, "Voices: A Shared Jungian Experience," The Round Table Rev IV (Nov/Dec 96): 9-16; auth, "The Singing Antelope and the Genesis of the Singing Antelope," in From the Listening Place, ed. Margaret Blanchard (Portland, Maine: Astarte Shell Press, 97), 27-30; auth, "Framing Questions About Access to CUNY," Community REV XV (97): 22-27; auth, "The Feminine' Revisited: A Reply to Sylvia Senesky's 'The Labyrinth: A Woman's Jouney'," The Round Table Rev V (Nov/Dec 97): 11-15; auth, "The Feminine Principle: A Relic," The Round Table Rev V (Mar/Apr 98): 3, 15; auth, "Bridging Conceptual Worlds, a review of 'Lesbians and Lesbianisms: A Post-Jungian Perspective' by Claudette Kulkarni," The Round Table Rev V (May/June 98): 18-20; auth, "An Odyssey," in Mothers of Women's Studies (NY: Feminist Studies, in press). **CONTACT ADDRESS** Dept English, Kingsborough Comm Col, CUNY, 2001 Oriental Blvd, Brooklyn, NY 11235-2333. **EMAIL** iiamm@aol.com

MARTINEZ, JACQUELINE M.
DISCIPLINE SEMIOTICS, PHENOMENOLOGY, FEMINIST THEORY, INTERCULTURAL COMMUNICATION **EDUCATION** Southern Ill Univ, PhD, 92. **CAREER** Asst prof, Purdue Univ. **SELECTED PUBLICATIONS** Auth, Radical Ambiguities and the Chicana Lesbian; Body Topographies on Contested Lands, in Spoils of War: Women of Color, Cultures, Revolutions, 97; coauth, Signifying Harassment: Communication, Ambiguity, and Power, Human Stud, 95. **CONTACT ADDRESS** Dept of Commun, Purdue Univ, West Lafayette, 1080 Schleman Hall, West Lafayette, IN 47907-1080. **EMAIL** martinez@purdue.edu

MARTINEZ, NANCY CONRAD
PERSONAL Born 03/25/1944, Corvallis, OR, m, 1971 **DISCIPLINE** BRITISH LITERATURE **EDUCATION** Southern Ore State, BA, 71; Univ NMex, MA, 72, PhD(English), 76. **CAREER** Adj asst prof English, 77-79, dir, Develop Acad Prog & asst prof English, 80-81, Assoc Dean, Col Gen Studies, Univ Albuquerque, 82-. **MEMBERSHIPS** Conf Col Compos & Commun; NCTE; SCent Soc Eighteenth Century Studies; Western Col Reading Asn. **RESEARCH** Satire; composition. **SELECTED PUBLICATIONS** Auth, Shakespeare Sonnet-99, a Blighted Flower Garden in a Winters Tale, Explicator, vol 0051, 93. **CONTACT ADDRESS** Univ of New Mexico, Albuquerque, Albuquerque, NM 87131.

MARTINEZ, YOLANDA
PERSONAL Born 05/10/1966, Santurce, Puerto Rico, m, 1988 **DISCIPLINE** LITERATURE **EDUCATION** Univ Puerto Rico, BA, 89; Univ Calif, Berkeley, MA, 91; PhD, 96. **CAREER** Asst Prof, Univ of Puerto Rico, 96-97; Vis Prof, Univ of Calif, Berkeley, 97; Asst Prof, Princeton Univ, 97-. **HONORS AND AWARDS** Ford Found Predoctoral Fel; Ford Found Postdoctoral Fel; Ford Found Dissertation Fel; Chancellor's Minority Fel Univ of Calif; Who's Who in Am Univ(s) and Col(s). **MEMBERSHIPS** MLA, Latin Am Studies Asn, Caribbean Studies Asn. **RESEARCH** Latin American Literature: Colonial, Hispanic Caribbean and Latino Literature, Literary Theory, Colonial and Postcolonial Theory. **SELECTED PUBLICATIONS** Auth, "Deconstructing Puerto Ricans Through Sexuality: Female Counter-narratives on Puerto Rican Identity (1894-1934)," in Puerto Rican Jam: Rethinking Colonialism and Nationalism, ed. Frances Negron Muanter and Ramon Grosfoguel (Minneapolis: Univ of Minn Press, 97), 127-139; auth, "Sabere americanos: la constitucion de una subjetividad colonial en los villancicos de Sor Juana," Revista Iberoamericana 63-181 (Oct/Dec 970: 631-648; auth, "De ilegales e indocumentados: representaciones culturales de la migracion dominicana en Puerto Rico," Revista de Ciencias Sociales, Univ of Puerto Rico Nueva Epoca 4 (Jan 98): 147-173; auth,"In & Out: logicas de la representacion politica y cultural," Dialogo (May 98): 38-39; auth, "hacia unos estudios culturales latinoamericanos: algunas notas sobre el impacto en la ensenanza," Revista de Ciencias Sociales, Univ of Puerto Rico Nueva Epoca 4 (June 98): 113-136; auth, "Cuban Migration Today: The Reconstruction of a Transnational Community?," Prog of Latin Am Studies Bull, Princeton Univ (Fall 98): 3-4; auth, "Cartografias pancaribenas: representaciones culturales de los enclaves caribenos en Puerto Rico y Estados Unidos," Revista de Estudios Hispanicos 25-1/2 (98): 65-90; auth, "Saberes americanos: constitucion de una subjetividad intelectual femenina en la poesia lirica de Sor Juana," Revista de Critica Literaria Latinoamericana 25-49 (99): 79-98; auth, "Caribbean Displacements: Migrations or Diasporas?," Prog of Latin Am Studies Bull, Princeton Univ (Spring 99): 6-7; auth, Saberes americanos: subalternidad y epistemologia en los escritos de Sor Juana, Ins Int de Lit Iberamericana- Serie Nuevo Siglo (Pittsburgh), 99. **CONTACT ADDRESS** Dept Romance Languages, Princeton Univ, 201 E Pyne Hall, Princeton, NJ 08544-0001. **EMAIL** yolanda@princeton.edu

MARTONE, MICHAEL
PERSONAL Born 08/22/1955, Fort Wayne, IN, m, 1984, 2 children **DISCIPLINE** ENGLISH **EDUCATION** Butler Univ;

Ind Univ, AB, 77; Johns Hopkins, MA, 79. **CAREER** Instr, Johns Hopkins, 79-80; Asst to Assoc Prof, Iowa State Univ, 80-87; Instr to Asst Prof, Harvard Univ, 87-90; Assoc Prof, Syracuse Univ, 90-96; Prof, Ala State Univ, 96-. **HONORS AND AWARDS** NEA, 84, 88; Winner, Best Short Short Story Contest, 88. **MEMBERSHIPS** Nat Writers Union. **SELECTED PUBLICATIONS** Auth, Fort Wayne is Seventh on Hitler's List, Ind Univ Press, 90; auth, Townships, Univ Iowa Press, 92; auth, Pensees: The Thoughts of Dan Quayle, Broad Ripple Press, 94; auth, Seeing Eye, Zoland Press, 95; auth, The Sex Life of the Fantastic Four, Strode Cabin Press, 99; auth, The Scribner's Anthology of Contemporary Short Fiction, Scribner's, 00; auth, The Death Tour, Wing and Wheel Press, 00; auth, The Flatness and Other Landscapes, Univ Ga Press, 00. **CONTACT ADDRESS** Dept English, Univ of Alabama, Tuscaloosa, PO Box 877240, Tuscaloosa, AL 35402. **EMAIL** mmartone@english.as.ua.edu

MARTZ, LOUIS LOHR

PERSONAL Born 09/27/1913, Berwick, PA, m, 1941, 3 children **DISCIPLINE** ENGLISH **EDUCATION** Lafayette Col, AB, 35; Yale Univ, PhD, 39. **CAREER** From instr to prof English, 38-57, Douglas Tracy Smith prof English & Am lit, 57-71, dir Beinecke Rare Bk & Manuscript Libr, 72-77, Sterling Prof English, Yale Univ, 71-, Guggenheim fel, 48-49; William Lyon Phelps lectr, Yale Univ, 67; Ward-Phillips lectr, Notre Dame Univ, 68; Nat Endowment for Humanities fel, 77-78. **HONORS AND AWARDS** LittD, Lafayette Col, 60. **MEMBERSHIPS** Am Acad Arts & Sci; MLA; Renaissance Soc Am; Antiqn Soc; Amici Thomae Mori. **RESEARCH** Renaissance; 17th and 20th centuries. **SELECTED PUBLICATIONS** Auth, The Paradise Within, Yale Univ, 64; A greenhouse Eden, In: Theodore Roethke, Univ Wash, 65; The rising poet, In: Lyric and Dramatic Milton, Columbia Univ, 65; The Poem of the Mind, Oxford Univ, 66; Portrait of Miriam, In: Imagined Words, Methuen, 68; The Wit of Love, Univ Notre Dame, 69; co-ed, Thomas More's Prayer Book, Yale Univ, 69; ed, Marlowe's Hero and Leander, Folger Shakespeare Libr, 72. **CONTACT ADDRESS** Yale Univ, 994 Yale Station New, Haven, CT 06520.

MARVIN, ELIZABETH W.

PERSONAL Born 11/10/1955, Denton, TX, m, 2 children **DISCIPLINE** PERFORMING ARTS **EDUCATION** Col Wooster, BA, 77; Eastman Sch Music, MA, 81, PhD, 89. **CAREER** Instr, Marymount Palos Verdes Col, 80-82; from tchg asst to instr to asst prof to assoc prof to chemn, Eastman Sch Music, 82-. **HONORS AND AWARDS** NEH; Nat Grad Fel Prog Fel, US Dept Edu, 86-87; Young Scholar Awd, 93; Bridging Fel, 93; Res leave, 94, 98. **MEMBERSHIPS** Col Music Soc; Music Theory Soc of NY State; Soc Music Perception & Cognition; Phi Beta Kappa; Pi Kappa Lambda; Soc Music Theory. **RESEARCH** Empirical testing of melodic and rhythmic perception in tonal and non-tonal contexts; cognitive differences among musicians, non-musicians, and absolute pitch listeners; the relation between music cognition and aural skills pedagogy; theories of rhythmic stucture; analysis of twentieth-century music; the relaitonships among analysis, performance, and perception. **SELECTED PUBLICATIONS** Coed, Concert Music, Rock, and Jazz since 1945: Essays and Analytical Studies, Univ of Rochester Press (Rochester, NY), 95; auth, "A Generalization of Contour Theory to Diverse Musical Spaces: Analytical Applications to the Music of Dallapiccola and Stockhausen," in Concert Music, Rock, and Jazz since 1945: Essays and Analytical Studies, ed. Elizabeth West Marvin and Richard Hermann (Rochester, NY, Rochester Univ Press, 95), 135-171; auth, "On Preparing Anton Webern's Early Songs for Performance: A Collaborators' Dialogue," Theory and Practice 20 (95): 31-124; auth, "Research on Tonal Perception and Memory: What Implications for Music Theory Pedagogy?," Journal of Music Theory Pedagogy 9 (95): 31-70; coauth, "Absolute Pitch and Sex Affect Event-Related Potential Activity for a Melodic Interval Discrimination Task," Journal of the Acoustical Society of America 102 (97): 451-460; auth, Tonal/Atonal: Cognitive Strategies for Recognition of Transposed Melodies," in Music Theory in Concept and Practice, ed. James Baker, David Beach, and Jonathan Bernard (Rochester, NY, Rochester Univ Press, 97), 217-236; coauth, "Absolute Pitch: Prevalence, Ethnic Variation, and the Estimation of the Genetic Component," The American Journal of Human Genetics 65.3 (99): 911-913; coauth, "The Effect of Modulation and Formal Disruption on Perception of Tonic Closure by Expert Listeners," Music Perception 16.4 (99): 389-408; coauth, A Musician's Guide to Theory and Analysis, W.W. Norton, forthcoming. **CONTACT ADDRESS** Eastman Sch of Music, 26 Gibbs St, Rochester, NY 14604. **EMAIL** betsy@theory.esm.rochester.edu

MARVIN, JULIA

PERSONAL Born 07/12/1966, Towanda, PA, s **DISCIPLINE** MEDIEVAL ENGLISH LITERATURE **EDUCATION** Princeton Univ, BA, 98; MA, 92; PhD, 97. **CAREER** Instr, Princeton, 95; lectr, Southern IL Univ, 96-97; asst prof, Univ of Notre Dame, 97-. **HONORS AND AWARDS** Presidential Scholar, 84; Fulbright Grant, UK, 93-94; Charlotte W. Newcombe Fel, 95-96. **MEMBERSHIPS** Medieval Acad; ACLA; Chronicle Soc; Phi Beta Kappa. **RESEARCH** Anglo-Norman language and literature, medieval historiography, Arthurian literature, manuscript studies, Chaucer. **SELECTED PUBLICATIONS** Auth, "Cannibalism as an Aspect of Famine in Two English Chronicles", Food and Eating in Medieval Society, eds Martha Carlin and Joel T. Rosenthal, Hambledon, (98): 73-86. **CONTACT ADDRESS** Prog of Lib Studies, Univ of Notre Dame, 102 O'Shaughnessy Hall, Notre Dame, IN 46556-5639.

MARX, PAUL

PERSONAL Born 12/24/1930, New York, NY, m, 1955, 2 children **DISCIPLINE** ENGLISH **EDUCATION** Univ MI, BA, 53; Univ IA, MFA, 57; New York Univ, PhD, 66. **CAREER** Lectr Eng, Southern IL Univ, 57-60; asst prof, Lehigh Univ, 63-67; assoc prof, 67-73, Prof Eng & Chmn Dept, Univ New Haven, 73. **MEMBERSHIPS** MLA; NCTE. **RESEARCH** Romantic, Victorian and mod Brit lit. **SELECTED PUBLICATIONS** Ed, Twelve Short Story Writers, Holt, 70; auth, Eduora Welty & Harvey Swados, In: Contemporary Novelists, St James Press, 72; Modern and Classical Essayists, Mayfield, 96. **CONTACT ADDRESS** Dept of English, Univ of New Haven, 300 Orange Ave, West Haven, CT 06516-1999. **EMAIL** pmarx@snet.net

MARZEC, MARCIA SMITH

PERSONAL Born 02/28/1948, Joliet, IL, m, 1975, 4 children **DISCIPLINE** ENGLISH **EDUCATION** Northern Ill Univ, BA, 70; MA, 73; PhD, 80. **CAREER** Instr to Asst Prof, Ill State Univ, 77-82; Asst Prof, Ill Wesleyan Univ, 82; Asst Prof, Millikin Univ, 84-85; Asst Prof to Prof, Univ St Francis, 85-. **HONORS AND AWARDS** Delta Kappa Soc Intl Ill, 98; Fac Awd of Distinction, Univ St Francis, 87, 97; Outstanding Prof, Chicago Tribune, 94; Fac Awd, Unit St Francis, 93. **MEMBERSHIPS** Asn for documentary Editing, Intl Boethius soc, Medieval Acad of Am, Mod Lang Asn of am, New Chaucer Soc, Soc for Textual Scholarship, Soc for Medieval Archaeol. **RESEARCH** Old and Middle English literature; Film. **SELECTED PUBLICATIONS** Auth, "I wol you seyn the lyf of Seint Edward: Evidence for Consistency I the Character of Chaucer's Monk," In Geardagum, (94): 85-96; auth, "Mr. Head's Journey to the Cross: Character, Structure, and Meaning in O'Connor's 'The Artificial Nigger," Logos, (97): 51-68. **CONTACT ADDRESS** Dept English & Lang, Univ of St. Francis, 500 Wilcox St, Joliet, IL 60435-6169. **EMAIL** mmarzec@stfrancis.edu

MASLAN, MARK

DISCIPLINE AMERICAN LITERATURE **EDUCATION** Univ Calif-Berkeley, PhD, 91. **CAREER** Assoc prof, Eng, Univ Calif, Santa Barbara. **MEMBERSHIPS** MLA. **RESEARCH** Nineteenth-Century Am Lit; Post-War Am Lit; Am Poetry; Theories of Sexuality. **SELECTED PUBLICATIONS** Auth, "Foucault and Pragmatism," Raritan, 88; "Whitman's 'Strange Hand': Body as Text in Drum-Taps," ELH, 91; "Whitman and his Doubles," Amer Lit Hist, 94; auth, "Whitman, Sexuality, and Poetic Authority," Raritan 17:4, (98): 98-119; auth, Whitman Possessed: Poetry, Sexuality, and Popular Authority, Johns Hopkins Univ Press, (forthcoming, 01). **CONTACT ADDRESS** Dept of Eng, Univ of California, Santa Barbara, Santa Barbara, CA 93106-7150. **EMAIL** mmaslan@humanitas.ucsb.edu

MASON, ABELLE

PERSONAL Born 01/10/1929, Norwalk, CT, m, 1948, 2 children **DISCIPLINE** ENGLISH **EDUCATION** Harvard, Radcliffe Col, AB, 50; Columbia Univ, MA, 67. **CAREER** Preceptor, Columbia Univ, 67-68; instr, NYork Univ, 68-71; lectr, Boston Univ, 72-77; lectr, Mass Inst of Tech, 77-82; lectr, Georgetown Univ, 87-. **HONORS AND AWARDS** Fred W. Malkemes Awd, NY Univ, 98. **MEMBERSHIPS** TESOL; WATESOL. **RESEARCH** Academic Listening, Language/Culture Issues of Foreign Graduate Students, Faculty Integration of Native and Non-Native Graduate Students into the Course Work. **SELECTED PUBLICATIONS** Auth, Understanding Academic Lectures, Prentice-Hall, 83; auth, Ports of Entry: Ethnic Concerns, Harcourt Brace Jovanich, 84; auth, Ports of Entry: Social Concerns, Harcourt Brace Jovanich, 85; auth, Ports of Entry: Scientific Concerns, Harcourt Brace Jovanich, 86. **CONTACT ADDRESS** Dept English As a Second Lang, Georgetown Univ, 1421 37th St NW, Washington, DC 20057-0001. **EMAIL** masona115@aol.com

MASON, BOBBIE ANN

PERSONAL Born 05/01/1940, Mayfield, KY, m, 1969 **DISCIPLINE** ENGLISH **EDUCATION** Univ Conn, PhD, 72. **CAREER** Writer; fiction. **HONORS AND AWARDS** PEN Hemingway Awd; Southern Book Awd. **MEMBERSHIPS** PEN; Author's Guild. **RESEARCH** American and Irish Literature 20th Century. **SELECTED PUBLICATIONS** Auth, In Country; Feather Crowns; Shiloh and Other Stories; Clear Springs. **CONTACT ADDRESS** Creative Mgt, 40 W 57th St, c/o Amanda Urban, New York, NY 10019.

MASON, DAVID

PERSONAL Born 12/11/1954, Bellingham, WA, m, 1988, 1 child **DISCIPLINE** ENGLISH **EDUCATION** Colorado Col, BA, 78; Univ Rochester, MA, 86; PhD, 89. **CAREER** Instr, Univ of Rochester, 86-88; asst prof to assoc prof, Moorhead State Univ, 89-98; asst prof, Colo Col, 98-. **HONORS AND AWARDS** Fulbright Fel, Greece, 77; Fel, Wesleyan Univ, 85; Nicholas Roerich Poetry Prize, 91; Fac Res Grants, Moorhead State Univ, 90, 92, 93, 95; Alice Fay Di Castagnola Awd, Poetry Soc of Am, 93; Minn Prof of the Year, Carnegie Found, 94; Fel, Minn State Arts Board, 95; President, Poet's Prize Committee, 96-. **SELECTED PUBLICATIONS** Auth, Small Elegies, Dacotah Territory Pr, 90; auth, The Buried Houses, Story Line Pr, 91; auth, Three Characters from a Lost Home, Jones Alley Pr, 95; auth, Land Without Grief, Jones Alley Pr, 96; auth, The Country I Remember, Story Line Pr, 96; coed, Rebel Angels: 25 Poets of the New Formalism, Story Line Pr, 96; auth, "Other Voices, Other Lives", After New Formalism, ed Annie Finch, Story Line Pr, 99; transl, "Seven Poems by Yorgos Houliaras", Agenda (England, 99): 109 - 115; coed, Western Wind: An Introduction to Poetry, 4th Ed, McGraw-Hill, 00; auth, The Poetry of Life, Story Line Pr, 00. **CONTACT ADDRESS** Dept English, Colorado Col, 14 E Cache La Poudre St, Colorado Springs, CO 80903-3243. **EMAIL** dmason@coloradocollege.edu

MASON, H. J.

PERSONAL Born 07/29/1943, Norwich, United Kingdom, m, 1970, 3 children **DISCIPLINE** CLASSICS **EDUCATION** McGill Univ, BA, 64; AM, 65, PhD, 68, Harvard Univ. **CAREER** Teaching Fel, Harvard Univ, 65-66, 67-68; Asst Prof, 68-72, Assoc Prof, 72-, Undergrad coordinator, 95-, Univ Toronto. **RESEARCH** Ancient novel; classical linguistics; topography. **SELECTED PUBLICATIONS** Auth, "The distinction of Lucius," Phoenix 37, (83): 135-43; auth, "The literature of Classical Lesbos and the Fiction of Stratis Myrivilis," C&ML 9, (89): 347-57; auth, Salmonella typhi and the Throne of Spain, Canadian Bulletin of Medical History, 90; Ancient Novels and Opera libretti, The Ancient Novel: Classical Paradigms and Modern Perspectives, 90; auth, "Mytilene and Methymna," EMC 37, (93): 225-50; auth, "Greek and Latin Versions of the Ass-Story," ANRW 34.2, (94): 1665-1770; auth, "Romance in a limestone landscape, CP 90, (95): 263-66; auth, "The End of Antissa," AJP 116, (95): 399-410 **CONTACT ADDRESS** Dept of Classics, Univ of Toronto, 97 St. George St, Toronto, ON, Canada M5S 2E8. **EMAIL** hmason@chass.utoronto.ca

MASON, WILLIAM E.

PERSONAL Born 06/10/1945, Tupelo, MS, m, 1967, 2 children **DISCIPLINE** ENGLISH **EDUCATION** Blue Mt Col, BA, 68; Southern Bapt Theol Sem, Mdiv, 77; Univ Ms, Med, 87; PhD, 93. **CAREER** English teacher, Public School system, 68-84; prof, 93- . **MEMBERSHIPS** NCTE; SADE; Phi Delta Kappa. **RESEARCH** Assessment of student writing. **SELECTED PUBLICATIONS** Auth, Biography of Mississippi Baptist Pastors. **CONTACT ADDRESS** Dept Gen Educ, Mid-Continent Baptist Bible Col, 334 Sawyer Rd E, Hickory, KY 42051. **EMAIL** bmason@apex.net

MASSA, RICHARD WAYNE

PERSONAL Born 05/02/1932, Carona, KS, m, 1971, 3 children **DISCIPLINE** ENGLISH **EDUCATION** Univ Mo-Columbia, BJ, MA, 54. **CAREER** Instr jour, Univ Mo, 55; instr, Miss State Col Women, 57-58; assoc prof Eng, Okla Col Lib Arts, 58-69; consult & vpres, Interpersonal Commun Consults, 69-72; prof jour, Mo Southern State Col, 72-, head, dept commun, 80-, spec instr jour, Northeast Mo State Univ, 72; dir, intl studies, 96. **HONORS AND AWARDS** Govenor's Awd for Excellence in Education, 96-99. **RESEARCH** Communications; crime reporting; international journalism. **SELECTED PUBLICATIONS** Coauth & co-ed, Contemporary Man in World Society, 69; co-ed, Aesthetic Man, 69; auth, Philosophical Man, McCutcheon, 69; auth, Inquisitive Man, McCutcheon, 70. **CONTACT ADDRESS** Inst of Int Studies, Missouri So State Col, 3950 Newman Rd, Joplin, MO 64801-1512. **EMAIL** massar@mail.mssc.edu

MASSE, MICHELLE

DISCIPLINE NARRATIVE, FEMINIST AND PSYCHOANALYTIC THEORY, FICTION **EDUCATION** Brown Univ, PhD, 81. **CAREER** Assoc prof, La State Univ; assoc ed, NOVEL: A Forum on Fiction, 77-81; ser ed, Feminist Theory and Criticism (SUNY Press). **HONORS AND AWARDS** NEH Fel, 83-84; fel, Newberry Libr, Monticello Col Found, 89; La Enhancement grant, 91, 94; Nat Humanities Center, 00-01. **RESEARCH** Narcissism and the bildungsroman. **SELECTED PUBLICATIONS** Auth, In the Name of Love: Women, Masochism, and the Gothic, 92. **CONTACT ADDRESS** Dept of Eng, Louisiana State Univ and A&M Col, 212P Allen Hall, Baton Rouge, LA 70803. **EMAIL** mmasse@unix1.sncc.lsu.edu

MASSELINK, NORALYN

PERSONAL Born 04/27/1959, m, 3 children **DISCIPLINE** 17TH CENTURY ENGLISH LITERATURE **EDUCATION** Calvin Coll, BA, 81; Univ Ill, Urbana, MA, 83, PhD, 87. **CAREER** Lectr, Interboro Inst, 87; asst prof, Hofstra Univ, 87-88; ASSOC PROF ENGLISH, SUNY, CORTLAND, 88-. **MEMBERSHIPS** John Donne Soc. **RESEARCH** John Donne **SELECTED PUBLICATIONS** Auth, Donne's Epistemology and the Art of Memory, The John Donne J, 8.1, 89; auth, Apparition Head vs. Body Bush: The Prosodical Theory and Practice of John Crowe Ransom, The Southern Q, winter 91; auth, Wormseed Revisited: Glossing Line Forty of Donne's Farewell to Love, Eng Lang Notes, 30.2, Dec 92; auth, A Matter of Interpretation: Example and John Donne's Role as Preacher and as Poet, The John Donne J, 11.1&2, 92; co-ed, The Cortland Composition Handbook, McGraw-Hill, 96; auth, Teaching Donne's Devotions Through the Literature of AIDS, Studies in Medieval and Renaissance Teaching, 6.1, spring 98; auth, Memory in John Donne's Sermons: Readie or Not? S Atlantic Rev, 63.2, spring 98. **CONTACT ADDRESS** Dept of English, SUNY, Col at Cortland, PO Box 2000, Cortland, NY 13045. **EMAIL** masselinkn@snycorva.cortland.edu

MASTELLER, RICHARD N.

PERSONAL Born 04/10/1945, Reading, PA, m, 1 child **DISCIPLINE** TWENTIETH-CENTURY AMERICAN LITERATURE, AMERICAN STUDIES **EDUCATION** Univ Rochester, BA; Univ Va, MA; Univ Minn, PhD. **CAREER** Instr, Univ Minn; Ill State Univ; Prof, Whit man College, 78-; Phi Beta Kappa. **HONORS AND AWARDS** Postdoc fel, Smithsonian's Nat Mus Amer Art; cur, exhib photography and of satiric graphic art of the 30s. **MEMBERSHIPS** Am Studies Assoc, MLA. **RESEARCH** Relations between literature and visual art in an American studies context. **SELECTED PUBLICATIONS** Publ, essays on the vision of the American purveyed by western stereographs of the late nineteenth century; satiric vision of Reginald Marsh and John Dos Passos in the era of the 30s; auth, seeing through photography; auth, Constantin Branwsi and versions of modernism; auth, The poetic search for community in "little" magazines. **CONTACT ADDRESS** Dept of Eng, Whitman Col, 345 Boyer Ave, Walla Walla, WA 99362-2038. **EMAIL** mastellerr@whitman.edu

MASTERS, HILARY

PERSONAL Born 02/03/1928, Kansas City, MO, m, 1994, 3 children **DISCIPLINE** ENGLISH **EDUCATION** Brown Univ, 52. **CAREER** Drake Univ, 75-77; Clark Univ, 79; Drake Univ, 80-82; Denver Univ, 82; Vis Writer, Ohio Univ, 80-82; Univ of NC Greensboro, 90-Fulbright Scholar, Finland; Prof, Carnegie Mellon Univ, 83-. **HONORS AND AWARDS** Best Essay, 98; Balch Awd, Best Am Essay, 99; Fulbright Scholar, Finland. **MEMBERSHIPS** Authors Guild. **SELECTED PUBLICATIONS** Auth, Home in the Exile, 96; auth, In Montaigne's Town, 00; Essays and stories in Wash Post, Ohio Rev, Va Quart, New Letter. **CONTACT ADDRESS** Dept English, Carnegie Mellon Univ, 5000 Forbes Ave, Pittsburgh, PA 15213-3815. **EMAIL** hm05@andrew.cmu.edu

MATABANE, PAULA W.

DISCIPLINE COMMUNICATIONS **EDUCATION** Howard Univ, PhD. **CAREER** Assoc prof. **RESEARCH** TV audience characteristics; social learning from tv; African Americans in tv and film. **SELECTED PUBLICATIONS** Documentary producer-writer, Africa in the Holy Land: Significant Connections, producer of informational video/film programs. **CONTACT ADDRESS** School of Communications, Howard Univ, 2400 Sixth St NW, Washington, DC 20059.

MATANLE, STEPHEN

DISCIPLINE COMMUNICATIONS **EDUCATION** Johns Hopkins Univ, MA; Am Univ, PhD. **CAREER** Assoc prof, Univ Baltimore; ch, Div Lang, Lit & Comm Design, 95-. **CONTACT ADDRESS** Commun Dept, Univ of Baltimore, 1420 N. Charles Street, Baltimore, MD 21201.

MATAR, NABIL

PERSONAL Born 11/04/1949, Beirut, Lebanon, m, 1986, 2 children **DISCIPLINE** ENGLISH **EDUCATION** Cambridge Univ, PhD, 76. **CAREER** Prof, Florida Inst Technol, 88- ; dept head, 97- . **RESEARCH** Anglo-Islamic relations; the Renaissance. **SELECTED PUBLICATIONS** Auth, Muslims in Seventeenth-Century England, J Islamic Studies, 97; auth, Wives, Captive Husbands and Turks: The First Women Petitioners in Caroline England, Explor in Renaissance Cult, 97; auth, Alexander Ross and the First English Translation of the Qur'an, The Muslim World, 98; auth, Islam in Britain: 1558-1685; auth, The Renaissance Triangle: Muslims, Britons and American Indians, 98. **CONTACT ADDRESS** Humanties Dept, Florida Inst of Tech, Melbourne, FL 32901. **EMAIL** nmatar@fit.edu

MATCHETT, WILLIAM H.

PERSONAL Born 03/05/1923, Chicago, IL, m, 1949, 3 children **DISCIPLINE** ENGLISH **EDUCATION** Swarthmore Col, AB, 49; Harvard Univ, MA, 50; PhD, 57. **CAREER** Instr to asst prof to assoc prof to prof to emer, Univ Wash, 54-; ed, MLA, 64-82. **HONORS AND AWARDS** Hayes Prize, 48; Furioso Prize, 52; Wash Gov Awd, 82. **MEMBERSHIPS** MLA. **RESEARCH** Shakespeare; Emily Dickenson. **SELECTED PUBLICATIONS** Auth, Water Ouzel and Other Poems, Houghton- Mifflin, 55; auth, "Dickinson's Revisions of 'Two Butterflies,'" PMLA 9 (62); auth, The Phoenix and the Turtle: Shakespeare's Poem and Chester's 'Loues Martyr', Mouton, 65; co-auth, Poetry: From Statement to Meaning, Oxford, 65; ed, Shakespeare's King John, Signet, 66; auth, "Some Dramatic Techniques in The Winter's Tale," Shakes Sur (69); auth, "Shylock, Iago and Sir Thomas More: with some further discussion of Shakespeare's imagination," PMLA (77); auth, "Some Dramatic Techniques in King Lear," in Shakespeare: The Theatrical Dimension (AMS Pr, 79); auth, Fireweed and other Poems, Tidal Pr, 80; auth, "Reversing the Field: Anthony and Cleopatra in the Wake of King Lear," MLQ (84). **CONTACT ADDRESS** 1017 Minor Ave, Apt 702, Seattle, WA 98104-3531.

MATES, JULIAN

PERSONAL Born 06/24/1927, New York, NY, m, 3 children **DISCIPLINE** DRAMATIC LITERATURE **EDUCATION** Brooklyn Col, BA, 49; Columbia Univ, MA, 50, PhD, 59. **CAREER** Lectr Eng, City Col NY, 51-52; lectr, Hofstra Col, 52-53, instr, 53-58; asst prof, 59-61, assoc prof, 62-66, Prof Eng, C W Post Col, Long Island Univ, 67-, Dean Sch Of Arts, 68-87, Dir, Am Theatre Festival; Prof Emer, CW Post Col of LIU, 97-. **HONORS AND AWARDS** Oscar G. Sonnick Library of Congress Awd. **MEMBERSHIPS** Am Soc Theatre Res, Theatre Libr Asn, Assoc for Theatre in Higher Educ. **RESEARCH** Am lit; musical theatre. **SELECTED PUBLICATIONS** Auth, The American Musical Stage before 1800, Rutgers Univ, 62; coauth, Renaissance Culture: A New Sense of Order, Braziller, 66; auth, Dramatic anchor: Research opportunities in the American drama before 1800, Early American Lit, 71; American musical theatre: Beginnings to 1900, In: American Theatre: The Sum of Its Parts, Samuel French, 72; Sam Harris, In: Dictionary of Am-Biography, Scribner, 73; contribr, Renaissance literature, In: Europe Reborn, Mentor, 75; ed, William Dunlap: 4 Plays, Scholars' Facsimiles & Reprints, 76; contribr, Theatre vs drama: popular entertainment in early America, In: Discoveries & Considerations, State Univ NY, 76; ed, Musical works of William Dunlap, Scholars Facsimiles & Reprints, 80; auth, America's Musical Stage: 200 Years of Musical Theatre, Greenwood, 85. **CONTACT ADDRESS** Eng Dept, Long Island Univ, C.W. Post, 720 Northern Blvd, Greenvale, NY 11548-1300. **EMAIL** jmates@earthlink.net

MATHENY, DAVID LEON

PERSONAL Born 10/15/1931, El Reno, OK, m, 1954, 2 children **DISCIPLINE** SPEECH **EDUCATION** Kans State Teachers Col, Ba, 53, MS, 57; Univ Okla, PhD(speech), 65. **CAREER** From instr to asst prof speech, Tex Christian Univ, 57-67; Prof Speech, Enporia State Univ, 67-, Ed, The Presumption, 77-. **MEMBERSHIPS** Speech Commun Asn; Am Forensic Asn; Cent States Speech Asn. **RESEARCH** American public address; argumentation and debate. **SELECTED PUBLICATIONS** Auth, Douglass, Frederick, Abolition Orator, Proteus, vol 0012, 95. **CONTACT ADDRESS** Dept of Speech, Emporia State Univ, Emporia, KS 66801.

MATHEWSON, DAVE L.

PERSONAL Born 11/06/1963, Wellsboro, PA, m, 3 children **DISCIPLINE** ENGLISH **EDUCATION** Colo Crhsitian Col, BA, 86; Denver Sem, MA, 89; Univ Aberdeen, Scotland, PhD, 98. **CAREER** Lect, Univ Aberdeen, Scotland, 97; INST, NEW TESTAMENT, OAK HILLS CHRISTIAN COL, 98. **MEMBERSHIPS** Evangelical Theol Soc. **SELECTED PUBLICATIONS** Auth, Revelation in Relent Genre Criticism: Some Implications for Interpretation, Trinity Journal, 13, (92): 193-213; auth, The Parable of the Unjust Steward (Luke 16:1-13): A Reexamination of the Traditional View in Light of Recent Challenges; auth, Journal of the Evangelical Theological Society, 38, (95): 29-39; auth, Verbal Aspect in Imparatival Constructions in Pauline Ethical Injunction, Filologia Neotestmentaria 17, (Mayo, 96), 21-35; auth, Reading Hebrews 6:4-6 in Lights of the Old Testament, Westminster Theological Journal, 61, (99): 209-25. **CONTACT ADDRESS** Oak Hills Bible Col, 1600 Oak Hills Rd SW, Bemidji, MN 56601. **EMAIL** d_mathewson@hotmail.com

MATHIESEN, THOMAS J.

PERSONAL Born 04/30/1947, Roslyn Heights, NY, m, 1971 **DISCIPLINE** MUSIC **EDUCATION** Willamette Univ, BA, 68; Univ South Cal, MM, 70, DMA, 71. **CAREER** Willamette Univ, tchg asst, 66; Univ S Cal, tchg asst, 69-71, lectr, 71-72; Brigham Young Univ, inst, asst prof, assoc prof, prof, assoc dean, head musicology, 72-88; Indiana Univ, Sch of Mus, prof, dist prof, 88-. **HONORS AND AWARDS** NEH, sr fel, 85-86; MLA, Vincent Duckles Awd, 90; Guggenheim fel, 90-91; AMS & IMS Awds 96-. **MEMBERSHIPS** IMS, AMS, MLA, APA, AAUP. **RESEARCH** Musicology; ancient Greek music and music theory **SELECTED PUBLICATIONS** Auth, Greek Views of Music, in: Source Readings in Music History, ed by Leo Treitler, NY: W.W. Norton, 97; Ancient Greek Music Theory: A Catalogue raisonne of Manuscripts, G. Henle Verlag, 88; Aristides Quintilianus on Music in Three Books: Translation, with Introduction, Commentary, and Annotations, ed by Claude V. Palisca, Yale Univ Press, 83;A Bibliography of Sources for the Study of Ancient Greek Music, ed by G.R. Hill, Boonin, 74; Greek and Latin Music Theory, Founding & Gen Editor, Univ Nebraska Press, 92-. **CONTACT ADDRESS** School of Music, Indiana Univ, Bloomington, Musicology Dept, 1201 E Third St, Bloomington, IN 47405. **EMAIL** mathiese@indiana.edu

MATHISEN, RALPH WHITNEY

PERSONAL Born 02/17/1947, Ashland, WI, m, 1979 **DISCIPLINE** ANCIENT HISTORY, CLASSICS **EDUCATION** Univ Wis, BS, 69, MA, 73, PhD(hist), 79; Rensselaer Polytech Inst, MS, 72. **CAREER** Vis asst prof Roman hist, Univ Ill, Chicago Circle, 79-80; ASST PROF ANCIENT & BYZANTINE HIST, UNIV SC, 80-. **MEMBERSHIPS** Asn Ancient Historians; Am Philol Asn; Am Hist Asn; Soc Ancient Numis. **RESEARCH** Late Roman society and religion; late Roman prosopography; Greek and Roman numismatics. **SELECTED PUBLICATIONS** Auth, Hilarius, Germanus and Lupus: The aristocratic background of the Chelidonius affair, Phoenix, 79; Resistance and reconciliation: Majorian and the Gallic aristocracy, Francia, 79; Sidonius on the reign of Avitus: A study in political prudence, 79 & Epistolography, literary circles and family ties in late Roman Gaul, 81, Trans Am Philol Asn; Antigonus Gonatas and the silver coinages of Macedonia circa 280-270 BC, Am Numis Soc Mus Notes, 81; Avitus, Italy and the East in AD 455-456, Byzantion, 81; The last year of Saint Germanus of Auxerre, Analecta Bollandiana, 81; Petronius, Hilarius and Valerianus: Prosopographical notes on the conversion of the Roman aristocracy, Hist, 81. **CONTACT ADDRESS** Dept of Hist, Univ of So Carolina, Columbia, Columbia, SC 29208.

MATIN, A. MICHAEL

PERSONAL Born 04/18/1963, Baltimore, MD, m, 1996, 1 child **DISCIPLINE** ENGLISH **EDUCATION** Vassar Col, BA, 86; Columbia Univ, MA, 88; MPhil, 91; PhD, 97. **CAREER** Instr to adj prof, Columbia Univ, 90-98; adj prof, CUNY, 97-98; adj prof, Univ NC Asheville, 98; prof, Warren Wilson Col, 99-. **HONORS AND AWARDS** Pres Dissertation Fel, Columbia Univ, 92-93; Pres Fel, Columbia Univ, 88-89, 89-90, 91-92; Shamonsey Fel, Columbia Univ, 90-91. **MEMBERSHIPS** MLA; SAMLA. **RESEARCH** Late-Nineteenth and Twentieth Century British Literature; Anglophone Colonial and Postcolonial Literature. **SELECTED PUBLICATIONS** Auth, "David Lodge," in British Writers, (Scribners, 97), 363-387; auth, "We Aren't German Slaves Here, Thank God: Conrad's Transposed Nationalism and British Literature of Espionage and Invasion," J Mod Lit, (97): 251-280; auth, "Anita Desai," in British Writers, (Scribners, 99), 53-76; auth, "The Hun is at the Gate: Historicizing Kipling's Militaristic Rhetoric, from the Imperial Periphery to the National Center," Studies in the Novel, (99): 432-470; auth, "W.H. Auden," and "T.S. Eliot," in World Poets, (Scribners, 00), 35-46 and 345-357; auth, "Kim, Invasion-Scare Literature, and the Russian Threat to British India," (forthcoming). **CONTACT ADDRESS** Dept English, Warren Wilson Col, 39 Timber Park Dr, Black Mountain, NC 28711-9460. **EMAIL** mmatin@warren-wilson.edu

MATOTT, GLENN

DISCIPLINE ENGLISH LITERATURE **EDUCATION** Tufts Univ, BA; Univ Mont, MA; Univ Nothern Colo, PhD. **CAREER** Prof emer. **SELECTED PUBLICATIONS** Auth, pubs on philosophy, practice of teaching writing. **CONTACT ADDRESS** Dept of English, Colorado State Univ, Fort Collins, CO 80523-1773. **EMAIL** gmattot@vines.colostate.edu

MATRO, THOMAS G.

PERSONAL Born Hammonton, NJ, m, 4 children **DISCIPLINE** ENGLISH **EDUCATION** Rutgers Univ, BS, 62: MA, 66, PhD(English), 75. **CAREER** Instr English, Rutgers Col, Rutgers Univ, 70-71, lectr, 71-73; lectr, 73-74, asst prof, 74-80, Assoc Prof English, Cook Col, Rutgers Univ, 80-. **MEMBERSHIPS** MLA; Virginia Woolf Soc; Humanities & Techol Asn (pres, 97-99). **RESEARCH** Modern British literature; literature and technology; Am lit of 19th and 20th centuries. **SELECTED PUBLICATIONS** Auth, Only Relations: Vision & Achievement, In: To the Lighthouse, PMLA, 3/84; Constituting Tension & Uncertainty in Walker Percy's The Thanates Syndrome, Humanities and Technol Rev, Fall 94. **CONTACT ADDRESS** Dept of Humanities & Commun, Rutgers, The State Univ of New Jersey, New Brunswick, 70 Lipman Dr., New Brunswick, NJ 08901-8525. **EMAIL** matro@aesop.rutgers.edu

MATSEN, WILLIAM

PERSONAL Born 04/22/1948, Hibbing, MN, d, 2 children **DISCIPLINE** ENGLISH, AMERICAN LITERATURE **EDUCATION** Univ Minn, BA, 70; MA, 72; Univ NDak, PhD, 90. **CAREER** Instr, Northland Col, 72-74; instr, Ky State Univ, 75-81; instr, Bemidji State Univ, 86-88; grad teaching asst, Univ of NDak, 88-90; instr, N Hennepin Community Col, 90-; prof, Concordia Int Univ, 96-97. **HONORS AND AWARDS** Board of Higher Educ Scholar, Univ of NDak, 89; Grant, N Hennepin Community Col, 95. **MEMBERSHIPS** Educ Minn, Nat Educ Asn. **RESEARCH** American Literature (Twentieth-Century), Narrative Theory, Interdisciplinary Studies, Eastern European Literature. **SELECTED PUBLICATIONS** Auth, "The Battle of Sugar Point: A Re-examination," Minn Hist (87); auth, "Professor William Schaper, War Hysteria, and the Price of Academic Freedom," Minn Hist (88); auth, "Atrocities Propaganda: How the Media Drummed Up War Fever in World War I," Media Hist (92); auth, The Great War and The American Novel: Versions of Reality in the Writer's Craft in Selected Fiction of the First World War, Peter Lang, Inc. (Berlin, Germany), 93. **CONTACT ADDRESS** Dept English, No Hennepin Comm Col, 7411 85th Ave N, Minneapolis, MN 55445-2231. **EMAIL** bmatsen@nh.cc.mn.us

MATSUDA, PAUL KEI
PERSONAL Born 09/11/1970 **DISCIPLINE** COMPOSITION STUDIES, APPLIED LINGUISTICS **EDUCATION** Univ Wis, BA, 93; Miami Univ, MA, 95; Purdue Univ, PhD, 00. **CAREER** Asst prof, Miami Univ, 00-01; asst prof, Univ of NHamp, 01-. **MEMBERSHIPS** MLA, NCTE, Conf on Col Comp and Commun, Teachers of Eng to Speakers of Other Lang, Am Assoc for Appl Ling, Coun of Writing Program Admin, Soc for the Hist of Ling and Lang Studies, N New Eng TESOL, Japan Assoc for Lang Teaching, Ohio Teachers of Eng to Speakers of Other Lang. **RESEARCH** Second language writing, contrastive rhetoric, written discourse analysis. **SELECTED PUBLICATIONS** Auth, "Contrastive Rhetoric in Context: A Dynamic Model of L2 Writing," Jour of Second Lang Writing, (97); auth, "Situating ESL Writing in a Cross-Disciplinary Context," Writing Commun, (98); auth, "Composition Studies and ESL Writing: A Disciplinary Division of Labor," Col Comp and Commun, (99); coauth, "Cross-cultural Composition: Mediated Integration of US and International Students," Composition Studies, (99); coauth, "Beyond the L2 Metaphor: Towards a Mutually Transformative Model of ESL/WAC Collaboration," Acad Writing, (00); coauth, "On the Future of Second Language Writing: A Colloquium," Jour of Second Lang Writing, (00); auth, "Re-examing Audiolingualism: On the Genesis of Reading and Writing in L2 Studies," Linking Literacies: Perspectives on Second Language Reading/Writing Connects, ed Diane Belcher and Alan Hirvele, Univ of Mich Pr, (Ann Arbor, 01); coed, Landmark Essays on ESL Writing, Lawrence Erlbaum Assoc, 01; coed, On Second Language Writing, Lawrence Erlbaum Assoc, 01. **CONTACT ADDRESS** Dept English, Univ of New Hampshire, Durham, 95 Main St, Hamilton Smith Hall, Durham, NH 03824-3574. **EMAIL** matsuda@jslw.org

MATTESON, ROBERT STEERE
PERSONAL Born 11/19/1931, New Paltz, NY, m, 1958, 3 children **DISCIPLINE** ENGLISH **EDUCATION** Haverford Col, BA, 53; Univ Pa, MS, 59, MA, 61; Univ Okla, PhD(English), 68. **CAREER** Spec instr English, Univ Okla, 63-64; from instr to assoc prof, 65-75, Prof English, St Lawrence Univ, 75-. **RESEARCH** ABP William King, private librarius in Oreland. **SELECTED PUBLICATIONS** Auth, King, William, Basiraeana and Lanaeana, Libr, vol 0017, 95. **CONTACT ADDRESS** 33 Judson, Canton, NY 13617.

MATTHEWS, JACK
PERSONAL Born 06/17/1917, Winnipeg, MB, Canada, m, 1942, 2 children **DISCIPLINE** COMMUNICATION & PSYCHOLOGY **EDUCATION** Heidelberg, AB, 38; Ohio Univ, MA, 40, PhD, 46 **CAREER** Asst Dir, 46-48, Purdue Univ; Asst Prof, Prof, 48-88, Univ of Pittsburgh **HONORS AND AWARDS** Dr Sci, Heidelberg **MEMBERSHIPS** Am Phychol Assoc; Speech Assoc of Am **RESEARCH** Speech Pathology; Social Psychology **SELECTED PUBLICATIONS** Auth, The Speech Communications Process, Scott, Foresmans; The Emeritus Professor: Old Rank-New Meaning, George Washington U Press & ASHE; The Professions of Speech-Language Pathology in Human Communications Disorders, McMillan; Communication Disorders in the Mentally retarded, Appleton Century Crofts **CONTACT ADDRESS** Verona, PA 15147-3851. **EMAIL** jmatthws@pitt.edu

MATTHEWS, JACK
PERSONAL Born 07/22/1925, Columbus, OH, m, 1947, 3 children **DISCIPLINE** ENGLISH LITERATURE **EDUCATION** Ohio State Univ, BA; MA. **CAREER** Prof, Ohio Univ, 71-. **HONORS AND AWARDS** Guggenheim Awd; Ohio Arts Counc Awd; Distinguished Professor of English, Ohio Univ, 77-. **MEMBERSHIPS** Phi Beta Kappa. **RESEARCH** Writing fiction, essays, poetry, the world of rare books. **SELECTED PUBLICATIONS** Ed, Archetypal Themes in the Modern Story, St Martins Pr, 73; auth, Sassafras, Houghton Mifflin, 83; auth, Memoirs of a Bookman, Ohio Univ Pr, 89; auth, Dirty Tricks, Johns Hopkins Univ Pr, 90; auth, On the Shore of That Beautiful Shore, Dramatic Pub, 91; ed, Rare Book Lore: Selected Letters of Ernest J Wessen, Ohio Univ Pr, 91; auth, Storyhood as We Know It and Other Stories, Johns Hopkins Pr, 93; auth, Booking Pleasures, Ohio Univ Pr, 95; auth, Reading Matters, Oak Knoll Pr, (forthcoming). **CONTACT ADDRESS** Dept English, Ohio Univ, 1 Ohio Univ, Athens, OH 45701-2942. **EMAIL** matthej1@ohiou.edu

MATTHEWS, JOHN F.
PERSONAL Born 02/15/1940, Leicester, England, m, 1965, 2 children **DISCIPLINE** CLASSICS, ANCIENT HISTORY **EDUCATION** Oxford Univ, BA, 63; MA, 67; PhD, 70. **CAREER** Res Fel, Balliol Coll, Oxford, 65-69; Univ Lecturer, Univ of Oxford, 69-90; reader, 90-92: prof, 92-96. **HONORS AND AWARDS** Fel of Brit Acad; Fel of Royal Hist soc; Fel of Soc of Antiquaries of London. **MEMBERSHIPS** Soc for the Promotion of Roman Studies London; Am Philol Asn, Byantine Studies Asn. **RESEARCH** Late Roman History. **SELECTED PUBLICATIONS** Auth, Western Aristocracitsand Imperial Court, 75,90; Political Life and Culture in Late Roman Society, 85; The Roman Empire of America, 89; Laying down the Law: a Study of the Theodosian Code, 00; coauth, Atlas of Roman World, 82; The Goths in the Fourth Century, 91. **CONTACT ADDRESS** 160 McKinley Ave, New Haven, CT 06515. **EMAIL** john.matthews@yale.edu

MATTHEWS, REBECCA
PERSONAL Born 12/23/1953, Salem, MO, m, 1991, 5 children **DISCIPLINE** ENGLISH, HISTORY **EDUCATION** SW Tex State Univ, BA, 86; Tex Tech Univ, MA, 89. **CAREER** From TA to lectr, Tex Tech Univ, 86-92; instr, New Mex State Univ, 92-98; adj fac, San Antonio Col, 98-. **MEMBERSHIPS** W Tex Hist Asn, Western Lit Asn, Tex Kolflore Soc, Tex/SW Popular Culture Asn. **RESEARCH** Southwestern literature, folklore **SELECTED PUBLICATIONS** Auth, "When Fact Becomes Legend: West Texas Folk Heroes," W Tex Hist Asn Year Book LXVII (91): 84-93; auth, "Roping Yarns," The Permian Hist Annual (91): 13-22; auth, "The West Texas Ribbon Wars," True West (93): 34-43; auth, "The Town That Cereal Built," True West (94): 38-43; auth, "Elmer Kelton's Women: Hummingbirds with Hard-Steel Strength," J of the West 37.1 (98): 19-24; auth, "Pearl Nance, a Remarkable Ranchwomen," W Tex Hist Asn Year Book LXXIV (98): 122-127; auth, "Jane Gilmore Rushing: A West Texas Romanticist," RE:AL, The J of Lib Arts XXIII.I (98): 108-115; auth, "The Dialect Joke Rides the Range: The Emergence of Dialect Humor in Cowboy Poetry," Southwestern Am Lit 24.2 (99): 25-33; auth, "Elmer Kelton's Most Unusual Villians," in Elmer Kelton: A Half Century in Print, ed. Preston Lewis (Lubbolk, TX: Tex Tech Press, 00); auth, "Writing the Un-Western: Jane Gilmore Rushing and Mary Dove," Concho River Review (00). **CONTACT ADDRESS** Dept English, San Antonio Col, 1300 San Pedro Ave, San Antonio, TX 78212-4201. **EMAIL** jbmatthews2@juno.com

MATTHEWS, VICTOR J.
PERSONAL Born 01/29/1941, Londonderry, Northern Ireland, m, 1967, 1 child **DISCIPLINE** CLASSICS **EDUCATION** Queen's Univ, Belfast, BA, 63; Queen's Univ, Belfast, Dip Educ, 64; McMaster Univ, Hamilton, Ontario, MA, 65; Queen's Univ, Belfast, PhD, 68. **CAREER** Lectr, 65-69, asst prof, 69-74, assoc prof, 74-94, prof, 94-, classics, Univ Guelph. **HONORS AND AWARDS** Nat Humanities Ctr fel, 86-87; SSHRC leave fel, 86-87. **MEMBERSHIPS** Ontario Class Asn; The Class Asn of Can; The Amer Philol Asn; The Israel Soc for the Promotion of Class Studies. **RESEARCH** Greek epic; Hellenistic literature; Greek athletics. **SELECTED PUBLICATIONS** Auth, Antimachus of Colophon: Text and Commentary, Leiden, 96; auth, Aphrodite's Hair: Colluthus and Hairstyles in the Epic Tradition, Eranos 94, 96; auth, The Greek Pentathlon Again, Zeitschrift fur Papyrologie und Epigraphik 100, 94; auth, In Defense of the Artemis of Antimachos, Liverpool Class Mth, 18.6, 93. **CONTACT ADDRESS** School of Languages & Lits, Univ of Guelph, Guelph, ON, Canada N1G2W1. **EMAIL** vjmatthe@uoguelph.ca

MATTHIAS, JOHN EDWARD
PERSONAL Born 09/05/1941, Columbus, OH, m, 1967, 2 children **DISCIPLINE** ENGLISH LITERATURE **EDUCATION** OH State Univ, BA, 63; Stanford Univ, MA, 66. **CAREER** Assoc prof, 67-79, Prof Eng, Univ Notre Dame, 80-; Mem, London Poetry Secretariat, London Arts Asn, poets & writers prog, NY State Coun Arts & prog poetry readings, Ill Arts Coun, 70-; vis fel, Clare Hall, Cambridge Univ, England, 76-77, assoc, 77-; vis prof, Skidmore Col 78 & Univ Chicago, 80. **HONORS AND AWARDS** O-Brien Awd, Ctr for Study Man, Notre Dame, 75; Columbia Univ Transl Ctr Awd, 78; Swedish Inst Awd, 81; Poetry Awd, Soc Midland Authors, 84; Ingram Merrill Found Awd, 84, 90; Slobodan Janovic Literary Prize in Translation, 89; George Bogin Awd, Poetry Soc Am, 90; Lily Endowment Fel, 93; Ohio Libr Asn Poetry Awd: Best volume of poetry publ, 95, 96. **RESEARCH** Mod Brit poetry; mod Am poetry; creative writing. **SELECTED PUBLICATIONS** Auth, Bucyrus, 70 & ed, Twenty-Three Modern British Poets, 71, Swallow; Contemporary British Poetry, Northwestern Univ, 71; auth, Turns, 74 & Crossing, 79, Swallow; ed, Introducing David Jones, Faber & Faber, 80; Five American Poets, Carcanet, 80; co-ed, Contemporary Swedish Poetry, Anvil, 80; Bathory & Lermontov, Kalejdoskop forlag, 80; auth, Nothern Summer, Swallow Press, 84; co-ed & transl, The Battle of Kosovo, Swallow Press, 87; ed, David Jones: Man and Poet, Nat Poetry Found, 89; auth, Tva Dikter, Ellerstrom Publ, 89; ed, Selected Works of David Jones, Nat Poetry Found, 93; auth, Swimming at Midnite: Selected Shorter Poems, Swallow Press, 95; Beltane at Aphelion: Collected Longer Poems, Swallow Press, 95; Pages: New Poems & Cutting's, Swallow Press, 00. **CONTACT ADDRESS** Dept of Eng, Univ of Notre Dame, 356 Oshaugnessy Hall, Notre Dame, IN 46556. **EMAIL** John.E.Matthias.1@nd.edu

MATTINGLY, CAROL
DISCIPLINE HISTORY OF RHETORIC, COMPOSITION THEORY AND PRACTICE, AMERICAN LITERATURE **EDUCATION** Univ Louisville, PhD, 92. **CAREER** Assoc prof, dir, Nat Writing Proj, La State Univ. **HONORS AND AWARDS** Phi Kappa Phi Awd, 97. **RESEARCH** 19th century American women writers; 19th-century women and rhetoric. **SELECTED PUBLICATIONS** Auth, Women in Louisville: Moving Toward Equal Rights, The Filson Club Hist Quart 55, 81; Valuing the Personal: Feminist Concerns for the Writing Classroom: Gender and Academe: Feminist Pedagogy and Politics, Rowman and Littlefield, 94; Pin-the Condom-on the Man: Strategies for Selling Safe Sex, Popular Cult Rev VI.2, 95; Women-Tempered Rhetoric: Public Presentation and the WCTU, Rhet Rev 14.1, 95. **CONTACT ADDRESS** Dept of Eng, Louisiana State Univ and A&M Col, 232B Allen Hall, Baton Rouge, LA 70803. **EMAIL** enmatt@unix1.sncc.lsu.edu

MATUKA, YENO M.
PERSONAL Born 03/17/1948, Mboto, Congo, m, 1981 **DISCIPLINE** ENGLISH **EDUCATION** UNAZA Congo, BA, 75; Reading Univ, MA, 78; Ball State Univ, MA, 87; PhD, 91. **CAREER** Elementary sch teacher, Congo, 68-70; instr, UNAZA/IPN Congo, 78-85; vis prof to asst prof, Ball State Univ, 92-. **HONORS AND AWARDS** Brit Coun Fel, 76-78; Fulbright Scholar Fel, 85-88. **MEMBERSHIPS** Ind Teachers of Writing; Asn for Curriculum Design. **RESEARCH** Language and Culture; Crosscultural Pragmatics and the Universal Mind; English Language Teaching Methods; Kikongo Linguistics. **SELECTED PUBLICATIONS** Auth, "The Palaver: A System of Conflict Management," in Pana-Africanism and Cross-Cultural Understanding, (Ginn Press, 93), 267-274; auth, "Kikongo," in Encyclopedia of World's Major Languages, 01. **CONTACT ADDRESS** Dept English, Ball State Univ, Dept English, Muncie, IN 47306. **EMAIL** 01ymmatuka@bsu.edu

MAUD, RALPH N.
PERSONAL Born 12/24/1928, Yorkshire, England **DISCIPLINE** ENGLISH **EDUCATION** Harvard Col, AB, 53; Harvard Univ, PhD, 58. **CAREER** Teaching Fel, Harvard Univ, 54-58; instr to assoc prof, SUNY, Buffalo, prof to prof emeritus, Simon Fraser Univ, 65-. **HONORS AND AWARDS** Guggenheim Fel. **MEMBERSHIPS** MLA, ALSC. **RESEARCH** Dylan Thomas, Charles Olson, Northwest Coast Native Literature. **SELECTED PUBLICATIONS** Auth, Introduction to Dylan Thomas' Poetry, 63; ed, The Notebooks of Dylan Thomas, 67, 89; auth, Dylan Thomas in Print, 70; ed, The Salish People, 78; auth, A Guide to BC Indian Myth and Legend, 82; ed, Dylan Thomas The Broadcasts, 91; auth, Charles Olson's Reading: A Biography, 96; auth, What Does Not Change, 98; auth, Transmission Difficulties, 00; auth, Selected Letters of Charles Olson, 00. **CONTACT ADDRESS** 1104 Maple St, Vancouver, BC, Canada V6J 3R6.

MAULTSBY, PORTIA K.
PERSONAL Born 06/11/1947, Orlando, FL, s **DISCIPLINE** MUSIC **EDUCATION** Mount St Scholastica Coll, Atchison, KS, BM, piano/theory composition, 68; Univ of Wis, Madison, Wis, MM, musicology, 1969, PhD, ethnomusicology, 1974. **CAREER** IN Univ, Bloomington, IN, prof, Afro-American Studies, 71-. **HONORS AND AWARDS** Selected as one of 8 American performers/scholars to participate in workshop/conference on African American Sacred Music in Havana, Cuba, 90; selected as one of 6 American ethnomusicologists to participate in an American-Soviet Research Conference in the Soviet Union, 1988; Awded Honorary Doctor of Music Degree, Benedictine, KS, 1985; Portia K Maultsby Day proclaimed by the Mayor of Orlando, FL, 1975; Utrecht Univ, Netherlands, apptd prof to "Belle van Zuylen" Chair, Distinguished Visiting Professor, 1997-98; Center for Advanced in the Behavioral Sciences, Fel, 99-00. **MEMBERSHIPS** Exec bd, Int Assn for the Study of Popular Music, 1987-95, editorial bd, 1989-; council mem, Society for ethnomusicology, 1973-76, 1977-80, 1988-91. **SELECTED PUBLICATIONS** Delivered keynote address for GATT Conference on the exchange of culture between America and Europe in Tilburg, The Netherlands, 1994; auth, sub-ed, "African-American music "Sections, Garland Encycopedia of World Music, 00. **CONTACT ADDRESS** Dept of Folklore and Ethrousicology, Indiana Univ, Bloomington, 504 N Fess, Bloomington, IN 47405. **EMAIL** maultsby@indiana.edu

MAURER, A. E. WALLACE
PERSONAL Born 09/11/1921, Grenfell, SK, Canada, m, 1963, 2 children **DISCIPLINE** ENGLISH **EDUCATION** Univ Man, BA, 42, MA, 48; Univ Wis, PhD, 54. **CAREER** Teaching asst English, Univ Wis, 48-53; from asst instr to prof English, Ohio State Univ, 53-. **MEMBERSHIPS** MLA. **RESEARCH** John Dryden and the Restoration. **SELECTED PUBLICATIONS** Auth, Shaw, the Annual of Shaw Studies, vol 11, Shaw and Politics, Mod Drama, vol 0037, 94; co-ed, The Works of John Dryden, vols XVII, XX, Univ Calif. **CONTACT ADDRESS** Dept of English, Ohio State Univ, Columbus, Columbus, OH 43210. **EMAIL** maurer.6@osu.edu

MAURER, MARGARET
PERSONAL Born 10/21/1947, Canton, OH, m, 1978, 1 child **DISCIPLINE** SHAKESPEARE, 16TH AND 17TH CENTURY ENGLISH LITERATURE **EDUCATION** Seton Holl Col, BA, 69; Cornell Univ, PhD, 73. **RESEARCH** 16th and early 17th century Eng lit. **SELECTED PUBLICATIONS** Publ, Mod Lang Quart, Studies in Philogy, Studies in Eng Lit, ELH, Genre, Style. **CONTACT ADDRESS** Dept of Eng, Colgate Univ, 13 Oak Drive, Hamilton, NY 13346. **EMAIL** mmaurer@mail.colgate.edu

MAUS, FRED EVERETT
DISCIPLINE MUSIC HISTORY **EDUCATION** Oxford Univ, ML; Princeton Univ, PhD. **CAREER** Assoc prof, Dept Music, Va Univ. **HONORS AND AWARDS** NEH Fel, 92-93.

RESEARCH Dramatic and narrative aspects of instrumental music; relations between musical analysis and musical aesthetics; gender studies; recent American music. **SELECTED PUBLICATIONS** Auth, Music as Drama, 88; Recent Ideas and Activities of James K. Randall and Benjamin Boretz, 88; Music as Narrative, Ind Theory Rev, 91; Hanslickos Animism, Jour Musicol, 92; Masculine Discourse in Music Theory, 93. **CONTACT ADDRESS** Dept of Music, Univ of Virginia, Cabell Hall No 113, PO Box 400176, Charlottesville, VA 22904-4176. **EMAIL** fem2x@virginia.edu

MAUS, KATHARINE E.
DISCIPLINE ENGLISH **EDUCATION** Cornell Univ, BA, 76; Johns Hopkins Univ, MA, 78; PhD, 82. **CAREER** Instr to asst prof, Princeton Univ, 81-88; assoc prof to prof, Univ Va, 88-. **HONORS AND AWARDS** Folger Inst Fel, 79, 86; NEH Fel, 84-85; Princeton Univ Preceptorship, 85-88; Univ Va Fel, 95, 02; Harrison Fund Fac Awd, 96; Roland Bainton Book Prize, 96; ACLS Fel, 00-01; Guggenheim Mem Fel, 00-01; Leverhulme Vis Res Prof, 02. **MEMBERSHIPS** MLA, Shakespeare Assoc of Am. **RESEARCH** English literature of the 16th and 17th centuries. **SELECTED PUBLICATIONS** Auth, Ben Jonson and the Roman Frame of Mind, Princeton Univ Pr, 85; coed, Soliciting Interpretation: Literary Theory and English Seventeenth-Century Poetry, Univ of Chicago Pr, 91; ed, Four Revenge Tragedies of the English Renaissance, Oxford Univ Pr, 95; auth, Inwardness and Theater in the English Renaissance, Univ of Chicago Pr, 95; coed The Norton Shakespeare, WW Norton, 97; coed, The Norton Anthology of Renaissance Drama, WW Norton, 02. **CONTACT ADDRESS** Dept English, Univ of Virginia, PO Box 400121, Charlottesville, VA 22903. **EMAIL** kem6v@virginia.edu

MAXFIELD, JAMES F.
PERSONAL Born 12/25/1936, Omaha, NE, m, 1958, 3 children **DISCIPLINE** ENGLISH **EDUCATION** Knox Col, BA, 59; Univ Iowa, MA, 61, Phd(English), 67. **CAREER** Instr English, Knox Col, 64-66; from instr to asst prof, 66-71, assoc prof, 71-82, Prof English, Whitman Col, 82-. **HONORS AND AWARDS** Graves Awd, 70-71. **MEMBERSHIPS** MLA; Am Film Inst. **RESEARCH** Victorian novel, Dickens, Hardy; 20th century literature; cinema. **SELECTED PUBLICATIONS** Auth, Out of the Past--The Private Eye as Tragic Hero, New Orleans Rev, vol 0019, 92; The Worst Part + Scorsese, Martin 'Mean Streets', Lit-Film Quart, vol 0023, 95. **CONTACT ADDRESS** Dept of English, Whitman Col, Walla Walla, WA 99362.

MAXMIN, JODY
DISCIPLINE CLASSICS **EDUCATION** Oberlin Col, BA, 71; Oxford Univ, 73; Oxford Univ, 79. **CAREER** Acting asst prof, Stanford Univ, 79-80; asst prof, Stanford Univ, 80-88; assoc prof, Stanford Univ, 88-. **HONORS AND AWARDS** Phi Beta Kappa, Oberlin Col, 70; Danforth Found Fel, 71; Woodrow Wilson Found Fel, 71; Leonard and Katherin Woolley Fel, Oxford Univ, 73; Junior Res Fel, Oxford Univ, 75-79; Millard Meiss Found Award, 82; Dean's Award for Distinguished Teaching, Stanford Univ, 83; Hoagland Award for Undergraduate Teaching, Stanford Univ, 89; Associated Students of Stanford Univ Award for Teaching Excellence, 91; Phi Beta Kappa, Northern California Asn, Excellence in Teaching Award; Bing Teaching Initiative Grant, 92; Phi Beta Kappa, Undergraduate Teaching Prize; Associated Students of Stanford Univ Award for Teaching Excellence, 96-97. **RESEARCH** Greek and Roman art; Greek vase-painting and sculpture; Archaeological Institute of America; College Art Association; Society for the Promotion of Hellenic Studies (London). **SELECTED PUBLICATIONS** Auth, "The Anatomy Lesosn of Miss Richter," in Arion, (74): 740-44; auth, Meniskoi and the Birds," Journal of Hellenic Studies, (75): 175-80; auth, "Betes Noires from Amathus," Report of the Department of Antiquities of Cyprus, (82): 183-86; Articles on Exekias, The Amasis Painter, Lydos and Sophilos in The Encyclopedia of Visual Art, vol. II, A Biographical Dictionary, ed. Sir Lawrence Gowing, Englewood Cliffs, (83): 12-13, 208, 400, 647-48; auth, "A Hellenistic Echo in Daumier's Penelope?" Art International, 84; auth, "The Painter of Berlin 1686 Comes to Stanford," notice in The Committee for Art Calendar, 86; auth, "A New Amphora by the Painter of Berlin 1686," Studien zur Mythologie und Vasenmalerei, Festschrift for Knorad Schauenburg, Mainz, (86): 35-40; auth, Addendum to an article by Edward Courtney, "Two Catullian Questions," Prometheus, 89; auth, The Painter of Acropolis 606, the painters of Group E and the Swing Painter in The Dictionary of Art, vol. 32, ed. Jane Turner, Grovve's Dictionaries, Inc., New York, 96; coauth, "Euphronios: A Presbyope in Ancient Athens?" Marmor and Ravin, eds., The Eye of the Artist, Mosby-Year Book, Inc. St. Louis, (97): 48-57. **CONTACT ADDRESS** Dept of Art, Stanford Univ, Stanford, CA 94305-2018.

MAXWELL, DAVID LOWELL
DISCIPLINE ANATOMY AND PHYSIOLOGY OF SPEECH AND HEARING **EDUCATION** Southern IL Univ, BS, MS, PhD. **CAREER** Emerson Col. **MEMBERSHIPS** Boston Naval Hosp; Depart Behav Neurology Eunice Kennedy Shriver Ctr, Mass Gener Hospital; Craniofacial Study Gp; Harvard Med Sch; Boston Univ Medic Sch; Boston Univ Grad Sch Dental Med; Instit Correction Facial Deformities; Univ Hospital; New England Med Ctr; Cognitive Behav Assessment Unit Douglas Thom Clinic. **SELECTED PUBLICATIONS** Auth, Research and Statistical Meghods in Communication Disorders, Maxwell & Satake, 97; Theory of Probability for Clinical Diagnostic Testing, Satake & Maxwell, 93. **CONTACT ADDRESS** Emerson Col, 100 Beacon Street, Boston, MA 02116-1596.

MAXWELL, RICHARD
PERSONAL Born 10/15/1948, Grand Forks, ND, m, 1995, 2 children **DISCIPLINE** LITERATURE, ENGLISH **EDUCATION** Univ Calif Riverside, BA, 70; Univ Chicago, PhD, 76. **CAREER** Asst prof to assoc prof to prof, Valparaiso Univ, 78-. **HONORS AND AWARDS** Am Acad Berlin Fel, 01; Univ Res Profshp, Valparaiso Univ, 80, 94; Harper Fel, 75. **MEMBERSHIPS** MLA; PSNA. **RESEARCH** Urban life in literature; art and film; historical fiction; cultural relations between England and France. **SELECTED PUBLICATIONS** Auth, The Mysteries of Paris and London, 92; auth and ed, The Victorian Illustrated Book, forthcoming; auth, "Pretenders. in Sanctuary," MLO (00); auth, "Inundations of Time," ELH (01). **CONTACT ADDRESS** English Dept, Valparaiso Univ, Valparaiso, IN 46383. **EMAIL** richard.maxwell@valpo.edu

MAY, CHARLES EDWARD
PERSONAL Born 02/18/1941, Paintsville, KY, m, 1980, 3 children **DISCIPLINE** ENGLISH & AMERICAN LITERATURE **EDUCATION** Morehead State Univ, BA, 63; Ohio Univ, MA, 64, PhD(English), 66. **CAREER** Asst prof English, Ohio Univ, 66-67; from asst prof to assoc prof, 67-77, Prof English, Calif State Univ, Long Beach, 77-. **HONORS AND AWARDS** Outstanding Prof Awd, 84; Fulbright fel, Dublin, Ireland, 96-97. **RESEARCH** The short story. **SELECTED PUBLICATIONS** Auth, Short Story Theories, Ohio Univ, 76; The Modern European Short Story, 89; Edgar Allan Poe: A Study of the Short Fiction, 91; Fiction's Many Worlds, 93; The New Short Story Theories, 94; The Short Story: The Reality of Artifice, 94; Interacting with Essays, 96. **CONTACT ADDRESS** Dept of English, California State Univ, Long Beach, 1250 N Bellflower, Long Beach, CA 90840-0001. **EMAIL** cmay@csulb.edu

MAY, ERNEST
DISCIPLINE MUSIC **EDUCATION** Harvard Univ, BA; Princeton Univ, PhD. **CAREER** Prof. **HONORS AND AWARDS** Pres, Am Musicol Soc, 88-90. **SELECTED PUBLICATIONS** Auth, pubs on Bach organ music; ed, New Bach Edition; co-ed, J. S. Bach as Organist, Univ Ind, 86. zGEN **CONTACT ADDRESS** Music and Dance Dept, Univ of Massachusetts, Amherst, 720 Massachusetts Ave, Amherst, MA 01003.

MAY, JAMES M.
PERSONAL Born 09/02/1951, Youngstown, OH, m **DISCIPLINE** GREEK AND ROMAN RHETORIC **EDUCATION** Kent State Univ, BS, 73; Univ NC, PhD, 77. **CAREER** St. Olaf Col. **HONORS AND AWARDS** NEH Fel for Col Teachers, 83-84; The Am Philological Asn Nat Awd for Excellence in the Teaching of the Classics, 86-87; NEH Grant to conduct a Summer Seminar for School Teachers; NEH Grant to conduct a Summer Seminar for School Teachers at St. Olaf Col; NEH Fel for Col Teachers, 91-92; Sears-Roebuck Found Teaching Excellence and Campus Leadership Awd, 91. **MEMBERSHIPS** The Am Plilological Asn Committee on Awards for the Excellence of the Teaching of Classics, 89-92; Editorial Bd for Textbooks, 90-94; Ad Hoc Committee on Campus Advisory Service, 92-95; Vice Pres for Education, 93-97; Bd of Directors, 93-97; Executive Committee of the Bd of Directors, 95-96; Dir of the Campus Advisory Service, 00-; The Am Classical League; The Classical Asn of Minn; Ch, Nomination Committee, 81; Pres, 83-85; The International Soc for the Hist of Rhetoric. **RESEARCH** Greek & Roman Rhetoric and Oratory; Republican & Golden Age Latin Poetry; Rhetoric in the Middle Ages; Liturgy & Music (Gregorian Chant) of the Middle Ages; Educational Methods, Means, & Curricula in the teaching of Classics. **SELECTED PUBLICATIONS** Coauth, Thirty Eight Latin Stories, with Anne Groton, Chicago: Bolchazy-Carducci Publishers, 86, 3rd, revised ed, 89, 4th revised ed, 94, 5th revised ed, 95; auth, Trials of Character: The Eloquence of Ciceronian Ethos, Univ N Carolina Press, 88; auth, "Patron and Client, Father and Son in Cicero's Pro Caelio," The Classical Journal 90, (95): 433-441; auth, "Cicero and the Beasts, "Sylecta Classica 7, (96): 143-153; auth, "Cicero," in the Dictionary of Literary Biography, Bruccoli-Clark-Layman, 99; Cicero: On the Ideal Orator, with Jakob Wisse, Oxford and New York: Oxford Univ Press, 01. **CONTACT ADDRESS** St. Olaf Col, 1520 St Olaf Ave, Northfield, MN 55057. **EMAIL** may@stolaf.edu

MAY, JILL P.
PERSONAL Born 08/23/1943, Rocky Ford, CO, m, 1967, 2 children **DISCIPLINE** CHILDREN'S LITERATURE, LIBRARY EDUCATION **EDUCATION** Wis State Univ-Eau Claire, BA, 65, Univ Wis-Madison, Msls, 66. **CAREER** Vis asst prof, 70-75, asst prof, 75-82, assoc prof, 82-91, prof, Children's Lit, Purdue Univ, 91- ; **HONORS AND AWARDS** Nat Endowment for the Humanities, Ind Libr Asn, 79; ed, Ind Libraries: A Quart J, 80-82; Pub Ch, Children's Lit Asn, 83-89; vpres, Children's Lit Asn, 88-89; Mod Lang Asn, Children's Lit Div Ch, 87-88. **MEMBERSHIPS** Children's Lit Asn; MLA; NCTE; Col Engl Asn. **RESEARCH** Historical children's literature; film in children's literature; minority children's literature. **SELECTED PUBLICATIONS** Auth, Feminism and Childrens Literature, Fitting 'Little Women' Into the American Literary Canon, Cea Critic, vol 0056, 94; auth, Children's Literature and Critical Theory: Reading and Writing for Understanding, Oxford Univ Pr, 95; auth, Theory and Textual Interpretation--Childrens Literature and Literary Criticism, J Midwest Mod Lang Asn, vol 0030, 97. **CONTACT ADDRESS** Lit & Lang Dept, Purdue Univ, West Lafayette, 4168 LAEB, West Lafayette, IN 47907-1968. **EMAIL** jillmay@purdue.edu

MAY, JOHN RICHARD
PERSONAL Born 09/16/1931, New Orleans, LA, m, 1977, 4 children **DISCIPLINE** LITERATURE & RELIGION, FILM CRITICISM, ENGLISH **EDUCATION** Loyola Univ, La, BBA, 51; Spring Hill Col, MA, 57; St Louis Univ, STL, 65; Emory Univ, PhD(Lit & Theol), 71. **CAREER** Lectr Humanities, Spring Hill Col, 65-68; from asst prof to assoc prof Relig Studies, Loyola Univ, La, 71-76, dir Mat Social Studies, 74-76; assoc prof & chmn Freshman English, 76-81, prof English, La State Univ, Baton Rouge, 81-; dept chmn, 83-92; alumni prof, 88; assoc ed, Horizons, 74-80; prog dir, La Comt on Humanities, 75-77. **HONORS AND AWARDS** Alpha Sigma Nu; Phi Kappa Phi. **MEMBERSHIPS** Col Theol Soc; Conf Christianity & Lit; Southeastern Am Acad Relig; Walker Percy Soc; Flannery O'Connor Soc. **RESEARCH** Theological literary criticism; American literature; religion and film. **SELECTED PUBLICATIONS** Auth, Toward a New Earth; Apocalypse in the American Novel, Univ Notre Dame, 72; contribr, Mark Twain, 74; Disguises of the Demonic, Association, 75; auth, The Pruning Word: The Parables of Flannery O'Connor, Univ Notre Dame, 76; coauth, Film Odyssey: The Art of Film as Search for Meaning, 76 & The Parables of Lina Wertmuller, 77, Paulist; ed, The Bent World: Essays on Religion and Culture, Scholars Press, 81; co-ed, Religion in Film, Univ Tenn Press, 82; ed, Image and Likeness: Religious Visions in Am Film Classics, Paulist, 92; ed, New Image of Religious Film, Sheed & Ward, 97. **CONTACT ADDRESS** Dept of English, Louisiana State Univ and A&M Col, Baton Rouge, LA 70803-0001. **EMAIL** jmay2@lsu.edu

MAY, STEVEN W.
PERSONAL Born 10/25/1941, Indianapolis, IN, 1 child **DISCIPLINE** ENGLISH LITERATURE **EDUCATION** Rockford Col, BA, 63; Univ Chicago, MA, 64; PhD, 68. **CAREER** Instr, Augustana Col, 64-65; asst prof, Northern Ill Univ, 68-69; assoc prof to prof, Georgetown Col, 69-. **HONORS AND AWARDS** Phi Beta Kappa; NEH Ref Materials grant, 93-96; Cawthorne Teaching Awd, 91; Mellon Fel. **MEMBERSHIPS** AAUP, MLA, Renaissance Eng Text Soc, Soc for Textual Scholarshp. **RESEARCH** Bibliography and First-Line Index of English Verse, 1559-1603, The Elizabethan Court, English Renaissance Manuscripts. **SELECTED PUBLICATIONS** Auth, Sir Walter Raleigh, Twayne's English, Boston, 89; auth, The Elizabethan Courtier Poets, Univ of Miss Press, 91; auth, Henry Stanford's Anthology, Cambridge Univ. **CONTACT ADDRESS** Dept English, Georgetown Col, 400 Est College St, Georgetown, KY 40324-1628. **EMAIL** smay@georgetowncollege.edu

MAYER, ROBERT
DISCIPLINE EIGHTEENTH-CENTURY BRITISH LITERATURE **EDUCATION** Northwestern Univ, PhD, 87. **CAREER** Engl, Okla St Univ; assoc prof. **RESEARCH** Historiography and fiction and the links between them. **SELECTED PUBLICATIONS** Auth, History and the Early English Novel: Matters of Fact from Bacon to Defoe, Cambridge Univ Press, 97; auth, The Illogical Status of Fictional Discourse: Scott's Footnotes for the Waverley Novels," (forthcoming); auth, "Did You Say Middle Class? The Question of Taste and the Rise of the Novel," (forthcoming). **CONTACT ADDRESS** Oklahoma State Univ, Stillwater, 101 Whitehurst Hall, Stillwater, OK 74078.

MAYEUX, PETER
PERSONAL Born 09/20/1942, New Iberia, LA, m, 1965, 1 child **DISCIPLINE** JOURNALISM **EDUCATION** Univ Southwestern La, BA, 65; Univ Iowa, MA, 67. **CAREER** Instr, Univ of Southwestern La, 67-69; prof, Univ of Nebr Lincoln, 69-. **HONORS AND AWARDS** Teaching Awd, Col of Jour and Mass Commun, 90; Leyman Awd for Res, 96. **MEMBERSHIPS** Nebr Broadcasters Assoc; Radio-TV News Directors Assoc; Broadcast Educ Assoc; Am Jour Hist Assoc. **RESEARCH** Mass Media History, Electronic Media Writing, Convergence. **SELECTED PUBLICATIONS** Auth, Broadcast News Writing and Reporting, McGraw-Hill, (NY), 96; auth, "Local Media Collaboration: Possibilities, Benefits, Pitfalls", Editor and Publisher, (Dec 96): 36, 37, 48; auth, "A History of Nebraska Media", Univ La, 97; auth, "Broadcast Pioneers", Hist of the Mass Media in the US: An Encyclopedia, ed Margaret A Blanchard, Fitzroy Dearborn, (Chicago/London, 98); "Designing and Producing A History of Nebraska Media CD-ROM", Hist Computer Rev 14.2 (98): 21-34; auth, "Floyd Kalber", Encyclopedia of Television News, ed Michael D Murray, Oryx Pr, (Phoenix, 99); auth, "Doris Fleischman Bernays",

Am National Biography, eds John A Garraty and Mark C Carnes, Oxford Univ, (NY), 99; auth, "War of the Worlds", The Media in America: A History, Vision Pr, eds W.D. Sloan and J.D. Startt, (Northport, 99). **CONTACT ADDRESS** Col of Jour, Univ of Nebraska, Lincoln, PO Box 880127, Lincoln, NE 68588-0127. **EMAIL** pmayeux@unlserve.unl.edu

MAYFIELD, JOHN R.
PERSONAL Born 11/06/1945, Lubbock, TX, m, 1 child **DISCIPLINE** HISTORY, LITERATURE **EDUCATION** Columbia Univ, BA, 68; Johns Hopkins Univ, PhD, 73. **CAREER** Asst prof, Unif of Ky, 72-82; assoc prof, Univ of Baltimore, 85-95; prof, Samford Univ, 95-. **HONORS AND AWARDS** Distinguished Prof in Teaching, Univ of Baltimore, 91; Ford Fel, 72. **MEMBERSHIPS** Southern Hist Asn, Soc for Historians of the Early Am Republic. **RESEARCH** Southern U.S. literature and humor, Southern intellectual history. **SELECTED PUBLICATIONS** Auth, The New Nation: 1800-1845; auth, Rehearsal for Republicanism. **CONTACT ADDRESS** Dept Hist & Polit Sci, Samford Univ, 800 Lakeshore Dr, Birmingham, AL 35229-0001. **EMAIL** jrmayfie@samford.edu

MAYNARD, JOHN ROGERS
PERSONAL Born 10/06/1941, Williamsville, NY, d, 1 child **DISCIPLINE** ENGLISH LITERATURE, BIOGRAPHY **EDUCATION** Harvard Col, BA, 63; Harvard Univ, PhD(English), 70. **CAREER** From English tutor to asst prof English, hist, lit, Harvard univ, 65-74; from asst prof English to prof English, NYork Univ, 74-. **HONORS AND AWARDS** Nat Endowment Humanities sr res grant, Robert Browning Biog, 72-73; Thomas J Wilson Prize, Bd Syndics, Harvard Univ Press, 76; Guggenheim fel, 80-81; **MEMBERSHIPS** PEN; MLA; Browning Inst. **RESEARCH** Nineteenth and twentieth-century English literature; biography; sexuality in literature; reading theory. **SELECTED PUBLICATIONS** Auth, Brownings Youth (Harvard), 77; auth, Charlotte Bronte and Sexuality (Cambridge), 84; coed, Victorian Lit and Culture, 91; auth, Victorian Discourses on Sexuality and Lit (Cambridge), 93; coed, Anne Thacktray Ritchie: Journals and Letters (Ohio), 94; auth, Browning Reviewed: Review Essays 1980-1995, Lang, 98. **CONTACT ADDRESS** Dept of English, New York Univ, 19 University Pl, New York, NY 10003-4556. **EMAIL** jrm4@is2.nyu.edu

MAYO, CHARLES M.
DISCIPLINE PUBLIC RELATIONS AND ADVERTISING **EDUCATION** Univ Ala, PhD, 93. **CAREER** Asst prof, La State Univ, hosp dir, Commun, dir, col PR. **RESEARCH** Public relations; advertising; organizational communication. **SELECTED PUBLICATIONS** Coauth, Changes in Global Focus of U.S. Business Magazines, in Jour Quart, 91; Measuring Advertising's Effectiveness, Franchising Update, 92; Game Time, Soap Time, and Prime Time TV Ads: Treatment of Women in Sunday Football and Rest-of-Week Commercials, in Jour Quart, 93. **CONTACT ADDRESS** The Manship Sch of Mass Commun, Louisiana State Univ and A&M Col, Baton Rouge, LA 70803.

MAZEL, DAVID
PERSONAL Born 03/06/1956, Los Angeles, CA, d **DISCIPLINE** ENGLISH **EDUCATION** Adams State Col, BA, 85; MA, 87; La State Univ, PhD, 96. **CAREER** Asst prof, Univ of Western Ala, 96-97; asst prof, Adams State Col, 97-. **HONORS AND AWARDS** J. Golden Taylor Awd, Western Lit Asn; Board of Regents Fel, La State Univ, 91-95. **RESEARCH** Environmentalism and American Literature. **SELECTED PUBLICATIONS** Auth, Pioneering Ascents, Stackpole Books (Harrisburg, PA), 91; auth, Mountaineering Women, Tex A&M Univ Press (College Station, TX), 94; auth, American Literary Environmentalism, Univ of Ga Press (Athens, GA), 00. **CONTACT ADDRESS** Dept Commun, Adams State Col, Alamosa, CO 81102. **EMAIL** dbmazel@adams.edu

MAZER, CARY M.
PERSONAL Born 02/22/1953, New York, NY, m, 1993 **DISCIPLINE** THEATRE **EDUCATION** Princeton Univ, AB, 74; Columbia Univ, MA, 76; PhD, 80. **CAREER** Asst to assoc prof, Univ Pa, 79-. **HONORS AND AWARDS** ACLS Fel, 81-82; Awd for Mentorship, 01. **MEMBERSHIPS** Am Soc for Theatre Res, Soc for Theatre Res, Int Fed for Theatre Res, Assoc for Theatre in Higher Educ, MLA, Am Theatre Critics Assoc. **RESEARCH** Shakespeare Performance History, Shakespeare Performance Pedagogy, Victorian and Edwardian Drama and Theatre. **SELECTED PUBLICATIONS** Auth, Shakespeare Refashioned: Elizabethan Plays on Edwardian Stages, UMI Res Pr, 81; auth, "The Criminal as Actor: HB Irving as Criminologist and Shakespearean," Shakespeare and the Victorian Stage, ed Richard Foulkes, (Cambridge Univ Pr, 86); auth, "The Voysey Inheritance," Harley Granville Barker: An Edinburgh Retrospective, ed Jan MacDonald and Leslie Hill, (Glasgow: Theatre Studies Publ, 93); auth, "Historicizing Alan Dessen: Scholarship, Stagecraft and the 'Shakespeare Revolution,'" Shakespeare, Theory, and Performance, ed James C Bulman (Routledge, 96); auth, "Rebottling: Dramaturgs, Scholars, Old Plays, and Modern Directors," Dramaturgy in American Theatre: A Casebook, ed Susan Jonas, Geoffrey Proehl, and Michael Lupu, (Harcourt Brace, 97); auth, "Master Class and the Paradox of the Diva," Terrence McNally: A Casebook, ed Toby Silverman Zinman, (Garland Pr, 97); auth, "Statues: Mary Anderson, Shakespeare, and Statuesque Acting," Shakespearean Illuminations Essays in Honor of Marvin Rosenberg, ed Jay Halio, (Univ Del Pr, 98); auth, "Playing the Action: Building and Interpretation from the Scene Up," Shakespeare Through Performance, ed Milla Cozart Riggio, (MLA, 99); auth, "New Theatres for a New Drama," Cambridge Companion to Victorian and Edwardian Theatre," ed Kerry Powell, (Cambridge Univ Pr, 03). **CONTACT ADDRESS** Theatre Arts Prog, Univ of Pennsylvania, Philadelphia, PA 19104-6219. **EMAIL** cmazer@english.upenn.edu

MAZZARO, JEROME L.
PERSONAL Born 11/25/1934, Detroit, MI **DISCIPLINE** RENAISSANCE AND CONTEMPORARY LITERATURE **EDUCATION** Wayne State Univ, AB, 54, PhD(English), 63; Univ Iowa, MA, 56. **CAREER** Instr English, Univ Detroit, 58-61; asst prof, State Univ NY Col Cortland, 62-64; From Asst Prof to Assoc Prof, State Univ NY Buffalo, 64-72, Prof English, 72-80; prof emer, 80-. **HONORS AND AWARDS** Guggenheim fel, 64-65. **MEMBERSHIPS** Dante Soc Am. **RESEARCH** Contemporary poetry; Renaissance poetry. **SELECTED PUBLICATIONS** Auth, The Arts of Memory and Hogarth, William Line of Beauty, Essays in Lit, vol 0020, 93; Mnema and Forgetting in Euripides the 'Bacchae', Comp Drama, vol 0027, 93; Morality in Pirandello 'Come Tu Mi Vuoi', Mod Drama, vol 0036, 93; Whitman, Walt and the Citizens Eye, Sewanee Rev, vol 0102, 94; Play and Pirandello Il 'Giuoco Delle Parti', Comp Drama, vol 0027, 94; The Growth of 'Leaves of Grass', Sewanee Rev, vol 0102, 94; Whitman and the American Idiom, Sewanee Rev, vol 0102, 94; Tapping God Other Book, Wordsworth at Sonnets, Stud in Romanticism, vol 0033, 94; Disseminating Whitman, Sewanee Rev, vol 0102, 94; Mathematical Certainty and Pirandello 'Cosi E Se Vi Pare, Comp Drama, vol 0028, 95; Euripides and the Poetics of Sorrow, Comp Drama, vol 0029, 95; Pirandello I 'Giganti Della Montagna' and the Myth of Art, Essays in Lit, vol 0022, 95; Pirandello and Film, Comp Drama, vol 0030, 96; Whitman, Walt America--A Cultural Biography, Sewanee Rev, vol 0104, 96; Road Thoughts, Hudson Rev, vol 0049, 96; Pirandellos 'Sei Personaggi' and Expressive Form, Comp Drama, vol 0030, 96; Duets, Hudson Rev, vol 0050, 97. **CONTACT ADDRESS** Dept of Modern Lang and Lit, SUNY, Buffalo, 910 Clemens Hall, North Campus, Buffalo, NY 14260.

MBABUIKE, MICHAEL C.
PERSONAL Born 08/15/1943, Nigeria, m, 1981, 6 children **DISCIPLINE** LITERATURE, ANTHROPOLOGY **EDUCATION** Univ Nigeria, BA, 71; Univ Sorbonne, Paris, MA, 73; D Lit, 75. **CAREER** Prof, City Univ NYork, Hostos Comm Col, 86-. **HONORS AND AWARDS** Dist Merit Awd, UNN Alumnus, 98; Dist Lead Awd, NYASA, 99. **MEMBERSHIPS** ASA; ALA; NYASA. **RESEARCH** Literature; anthropology and the dispossessed. **SELECTED PUBLICATIONS** Auth, Poems of Memory Trips (98), vol 1; auth Poems of Memory Trips (99), vol 2. **CONTACT ADDRESS** Dept Humanities, City Univ NY, Hostos Comm Col, 475 Grand Concourse, Bronx, NY 10451-5307.

MC CAULEY, BARBARA L.
PERSONAL Born 03/02/1951, Kansas City, MO, s **DISCIPLINE** ENGLISH **EDUCATION** Central Mo State Univ, BSE, 73; MA, 76; Fla State Univ, PhD, 93. **CAREER** Southeastern Community Col, 77-78; prof tutor, Park Col, 78-79; Macon Jr Col, 79-83; Gainesville Jr Col, Ga, 86-87; grad asst, Fla State Univ, 83-86, 87-88, vis instr, 88-89; adjunct instr, Tallahassee Community Col, 89-93; instr, North Fla Community Col, 93-. **HONORS AND AWARDS** Phi Kappa Phi, Sigma Tau Delta, Kappa Delta Pi, Alpha Pi Omega, Who's Who of Am Teachers, Who's Who in Am. **MEMBERSHIPS** Fla Col English Asn, Int Arthurian Soc, Mythpoeic Soc, Int Asn of the Fantastic in the Arts. **RESEARCH** Medieval language, literature; teaching the Middle Ages; fantasy and the arts; Tolkien. **SELECTED PUBLICATIONS** Auth, "Pas de Deux, Ufa 1951: For Nureyev," in Col Poetry (76); auth of numerous feature articles on dance for Macon Telegraph (79-820; auth, "La Demoiselle Argente," in Tournaments Illuminated (fall 84); auth, auth, "Giraldus 'Silvestre' of Wales and His Prophetic History of Ireland: Merlin's Role in the Expugnatio Hiberica," Quodam et Futuris, 3.4 (93): 41-62. **CONTACT ADDRESS** Dept Business/Soc Sci & Humanities, No Florida Comm Col, 1000 Turner Davis Dr, Madison, FL 32340-1602.

MC GLAMERY, GAYLA
PERSONAL Born 04/24/1954, Stillwater, OK, m, 1990, 1 child **DISCIPLINE** ENGLISH **EDUCATION** Baylor Univ, BA, 76; Emory Univ, PhD, 83. **CAREER** Co-Dir, Loyola Hon Prog, 91-96; Co-Dir, Study Abroad Prog, Luven, Belgium, 96-97; Assoc Prof, Loyola Col Baltimore, 91-. **MEMBERSHIPS** Southwestern 19th Century Studies Asn. **RESEARCH** Victorian Literature, The Novel. **SELECTED PUBLICATIONS** Articles on Charlotte Bronte, George Meredith, and Andrew Marvell. **CONTACT ADDRESS** Dept English, Loyola Col, 4501 N Charles St, Baltimore, MD 21210-2601.

MC MASTER, MICHELE
DISCIPLINE PSYCHOLOGY, COMMUNICATION **EDUCATION** Knox Col, BA, 71; Governors State Univ, MA, 75; MA, 89; Union Institute, PhD, 99. **CAREER** Educator, Tinley Park Mental Health Ctr, 71-78; Coordinator of Out-Patient Psychiatric Svcs, 79-90; Dir of Women's Svcs, 81-82; Psychotherapist, 82-94; Univ Lecturer, Governors State Univ, 92-. **HONORS AND AWARDS** Who's Who in the Human Services, Who's Who of America's Teachers, 94-95; Who's Who of America's Teachers, 96-97; Fac Appreciation Awd; Fac Appreciation Awd; Who's Who of America's Teachers, 98-99; Who's Who of Am Women, 99-00; Who's Who of Am Women, 00-01. **MEMBERSHIPS** Jean Gebser Society. **RESEARCH** Intrapersonal Communication, Consciousness, Learning. **SELECTED PUBLICATIONS** Auth, "Alternative Intercultural Learning," Proceedings of the 26th Annual Third World Conference; auth, "An Intrapersonal System View of Communication," Doctoral dissertation, The Union Institute, 99; auth, "Study Guide (for the correspondence for Concepts in Human Communication), 92-. **CONTACT ADDRESS** Dept Liberal Arts, Governors State Univ, 1 Univ Pkwy, Park Forest, IL 60466. **EMAIL** gmmcmast@govst.edu

MC MILLIN, BARBARA C.
PERSONAL Born 09/08/1959, Ripley, MS, m, 1983, 1 child **DISCIPLINE** ENGLISH **EDUCATION** Northeast MS Community Col, AA, 99; Union Univ, BA, 81; Univ MS, MA, 82; DA, 87. **CAREER** English Instr, Northeast MS Community Col, 87-92; Dept. Chair, 91-92; Asst. Prof of English, Union Univ, 92-96; Dept Chair, Union Univ, 93-99; Assoc Prof of English, Union Univ, 96-. **HONORS AND AWARDS** Who's Who in the World, 99; Who's Who in America, 99; Fac of the Year, 98-99; Who's Who in the South & Southwest, 98; Who's Who Among America's Teachers, 98; Outstanding Young Women of America, 98. **MEMBERSHIPS** Coll English Assn; South Central Modern Language Assn; Tennessee Philogical Assn. **CONTACT ADDRESS** Dept English, Union Univ, 1050 Union Univ Dr, Jackson, TN 38305-3656. **EMAIL** bmcmilli@uu.edu

MCALEAVEY, DAVID WILLARD
PERSONAL Born 05/27/1946, Wichita, KS, m, 1977, 2 children **DISCIPLINE** ENGLISH & AMERICAN LITERATURE **EDUCATION** Cornell Univ, BA, 68, MFA, 72, PhD(English), 75. **CAREER** Instr, 74-75, asst prof, 75-88, prof, George Wash Univ, 89-. **MEMBERSHIPS** MLA. **RESEARCH** Creative writing, twentieth century English and American poetry and poetics. **SELECTED PUBLICATIONS** Auth, Sterling 403, Ithaca House, 71; auth, The Forty Days, Ithaca House, 75; auth, Shrine, Shelter, Cave, Ithaca House, 80; auth, "Evidence of Community: Writing from the Jenny McKean Moore Community Workshops at George Washington University," GW Wash Studies (84); auth, Holding Obsidian, Wash Writer's Publ House, 85; auth, "The Oppens: Remarks Towards Biography," Ironwood (85); auth, "Oppen on Oppen: Extracts from Interviews," Sagetrib (86); auth, "Washington and Washington Writing," GW Wash Studies (86); auth, "Oppen on Literature and Literary Figures and Issues," Sagetrib (87). **CONTACT ADDRESS** Dept of English, The George Washington Univ, 801 22nd St NW, Washington, DC 20052-0001. **EMAIL** dmca@gwu.edu

MCALEXANDER, HUBERT H.
PERSONAL Born 10/27/1939, Holly Springs, MS, m, 1970, 1 child **DISCIPLINE** ENGLISH **EDUCATION** Univ of Miss, BA, 61; MA, 66; Univ of Wis at Madison, PhD, 73. **CAREER** Instr, Univ of Miss, 66-69; asst prof, Tex A & M Univ, 73-74; asst prof to prof, Univ of Ga, 93-. **HONORS AND AWARDS** Josiah Meigs Awd for Excellence in Teaching, Univ of Ga, 97. **MEMBERSHIPS** MLA, Southeastern MLA, Am Lit Asn, Soc for the Study of Southern Lit. **RESEARCH** Literary biography, Southern literature and culture, American literature. **SELECTED PUBLICATIONS** Auth, The Prodigal Daughter: A Biography of Sherwood Bonner, La State Unive Press (Baton Rouge, LA), 81 and Univ of Tenn Press, 99; auth, Conversations with Peter Taylor, Univ Press of Miss (Jackson, MS), 87; auth, Critical Essays on Peter Taylor, G.K. Hall (New York), 93; auth, "History, Gender, and the Family in A Stand in the Mountains," The Craft of Peter Taylor, Univ of Ala press (Tuscaloosa, AL), 95; auth, "Peter Taylor: The Undergraduate Years at Kenyon," Kenyon Rev 21 (99): 43-57. **CONTACT ADDRESS** Dept English, Univ of Georgia, Athens, GA 30602-0002. **EMAIL** hmcalexa@uga.edu

MCALEXANDER, PATRICIA JEWELL
PERSONAL Born 01/26/1942, Johnstown, NY, m, 1970, 1 child **DISCIPLINE** ENGLISH **EDUCATION** State Univ NYork, Albany, BA, 64; Columbia Univ, MA, 66; Univ Wis-Madison, PhD, 73. **CAREER** Instr English, Univ Colo, 66-68; Lectr to assoc prof English, Univ GA, 77-. **MEMBERSHIPS** MLA; S Atlantic Mod Lang Asn. **RESEARCH** American literature; literature of the early republic; Charles Brockden Brown. **SELECTED PUBLICATIONS** Auth, Faking It--A Look Into the Mind of a Creative Learner, Coll Compos and Commun, 93; Written Language Disorders, Coll Compos and Commun, 93. **CONTACT ADDRESS** Dept of English, Univ of Georgia, 226 Milledge Hall, Athens, GA 30602-5554. **EMAIL** pmcalex@uga.edu

MCALLISTER, MATTHEW P.
DISCIPLINE ADVERTISING **EDUCATION** Purdue Univ, BA, 83, MA, 86; Univ IL, Phd, 90. **CAREER** Grad Tchg Asst, Purdue Univ, 83-85; Grad Tchg Asst, Univ IL, 85-90; Adj Fac Mem, 89, 90; Vis Asst Prof, Denison Univ, 90-91; Asst Prof, VA Tech, 91-97; Assoc Prof with tenure; VI Tech, 97-. **HONORS AND AWARDS** Outstanding Academic Bk 96; Certificate Tchg Excellence Awd; Adv Year, VA Tech Univ Student Leadership Awds, Cited tchg excellence Comm 220 Cited tchg excellence Speech Comm 112; Nat Sci Found fel, Purdue Univ; ed board, crit studies mass comm, 96-; vice-chair, int comm asn, 96-; secy, int comm asn, 94-96; panel respondent,int comm asn; 93, 95, 96; panel chair, int comm asn. **MEMBERSHIPS** Kappa Tau Alpha, National Commun(s) Honorary. **SELECTED PUBLICATIONS** Auth, The Commercialization Am cult: New advertising, control and democracy. Thousand Oaks, CA: Sage Publs, Inc. Hardback and paperback ed, 96. **CONTACT ADDRESS** Virginia Polytech Inst and State Univ, Blacksburg, VA 24061. **EMAIL** mattm@vt.edu

MCALPIN, SARA
DISCIPLINE ENGLISH **EDUCATION** Clarke Col, BA, 56; Marquette Univ, MA, 64; Univ Pa, PhD, 71. **CAREER** St Joseph Acad, 59-61; teach fel, Univ Pa, 67-71; CLARK COL, 61-67, 71-. **CONTACT ADDRESS** 1550 Clark Dr, Dubuque, IA 52001. **EMAIL** smcalpin@keller.clarke.edu

MCALPINE, MONICA ELLEN
PERSONAL Born 08/14/1940, Rochester, NY, m, 1974, 1 child **DISCIPLINE** ENGLISH LITERATURE **EDUCATION** Nazareth Col, Rochester, BA, 62; Univ Rochester, MA, 67, PhD, 72. **CAREER** Instr Eng, Univ Rochester, 67-68; from instr to asst prof, 68-77, assoc prof, 77-91, Prof Eng, Univ MA, Boston, 91; dir, Univ Honors Program, 94-. **MEMBERSHIPS** MLA; Mediaeval Acad Am; New Chaucer Soc. **RESEARCH** Chaucer; Middle Eng lit. **SELECTED PUBLICATIONS** Auth, The Genre of Troilus and Criseyde, Cornell Univ, 78; The pardoner's homosexuality and how it matters, Pmla, 95:8-22; Chaucer's Knight't Tale: An Annotated Bibliography, 1900-1985, Toronto Univ, 91. **CONTACT ADDRESS** Univ of Massachusetts, Boston, 100 Morrissey Blvd, Boston, MA 02125-3300. **EMAIL** monica.mcalpine@umb.edu

MCBANE, JOHN SPENCER
PERSONAL Born Atlanta, GA, m, 3 children **DISCIPLINE** ENGLISH **EDUCATION** Presbyterian Col, BA, 68; Emory Univ, MA, 73; PhD, 74. **CAREER** Asst prof to assoc prof, Troy State Univ, 74-84; asst prof to prof and assoc dean, Univ Ala Huntsville, 84-97. **HONORS AND AWARDS** Woodrow Wilson Fel, 68; Phi Kappa Phi; Danforth Fel, 70-74. **MEMBERSHIPS** MLA; S Atlantic MLA; Shakespeare Asn of Am; Nat Coun of Teachers of English. **RESEARCH** Shakespeare; Renaissance literature and culture; Literary theory. **SELECTED PUBLICATIONS** Auth, "Olivier's King Lear and the 'Feminine' Virtues in Shakespearean Tragedy," Shakespeare Yearbook, (92): 143-166; auth, Renaissance Magic and the Return of the Golden Age: The Occult Tradition and Marlowe, Jonson, and Shakespeare, reprint, Univ Nebr Press, 92; auth, "Pluralism, Relativism, and the Question of Evidence in Shakespearean Studies," Col English, (96): 517-540; auth Cymbeline, The Winter's Tale, and The Tempest: An Annotated Bibliography of Shakespeare Studies, 1864-1999, Pegasus Press, 01. **CONTACT ADDRESS** Dept English, Univ of Alabama, Huntsville, 11314 Mountaincrest Dr SE, Huntsville, AL 35803-1616. **EMAIL** mebanej@email.uah.edu

MCBRIDE, MARGARET
DISCIPLINE LITERATURE **EDUCATION** Univ KS, BA; Univ PA, MA, PhD. **CAREER** Assoc prof; dir, Grad Prog & Grad Adv Record, 78-81 & 88-. **HONORS AND AWARDS** Facu Res Leave, 97; UTSA Fac Res Awd, 83; Col of Fine Arts Awd, 92; Hum Travel Grant, 93; AMOCO Awd, 87. **RESEARCH** James Joyce. **SELECTED PUBLICATIONS** Publ on James Joyce, in The James Joyce Quart, Joyce Stud Annual, JEGP. **CONTACT ADDRESS** Col of Fine Arts and Hum, Univ of Texas, San Antonio, 6900 N Loop 1604 W, San Antonio, TX 78249.

MCBRIDE, WILLIAM
DISCIPLINE ENGLISH LITERATURE **EDUCATION** Colo State Univ, BA; Univ Nothern Colo, MA; Univ Nebr, PhD. **CAREER** Prof emer, Colo State Univ. **SELECTED PUBLICATIONS** Auth, pubs on Charles Dickens; co-auth, Young Adult Literature: Background, Selection & Use. **CONTACT ADDRESS** Dept of English, Colorado State Univ, Fort Collins, CO 80523-1773.

MCCABE, BERNARD
PERSONAL Born 08/09/1923, Middlesbrough, England, m, 1952, 8 children **DISCIPLINE** ENGLISH **EDUCATION** Univ Manchester, Llb, 45; Stanford Univ, MA, 59, PhD(English), 61. **CAREER** Asst prof, 61-66, chmn, 72-76, assoc prof, 66-79, Prof English, Tufts Univ, 79-. **MEMBERSHIPS** MLA. **RESEARCH** Novel of social protest; modern fiction; the eighteen-thirties and forties. **SELECTED PUBLICATIONS** Auth, End-End Heat + An Interview With Bird, Antonia on 'Face', Sight and Sound, vol 0007, 97. **CONTACT ADDRESS** Dept of English, Tufts Univ, Medford, Medford, MA 02155.

MCCABE, NANCY
PERSONAL Born 11/10/1962, Wichita, KS, s, 1 child **DISCIPLINE** ENGLISH **EDUCATION** Wichita St Univ, BA, 84; Univ Ark, MFA, 89; Univ Neb, PhD, 95. **CAREER** Instr, Southwest Mo St Univ, 89-92; Instr, Univ Neb, 92-96; Asst Prof, Presbyterian Col, 96-. **HONORS AND AWARDS** Lily Peter Fel, 86-89; Bancum Falkerson Awd, 88; 1st Pl for Fiction, 88; John Gould Fletcher Awd, 89; Prairie Schooner Reader's Choice Awd, 00. **RESEARCH** Creative writing, women's literature in the 20th Century. **SELECTED PUBLICATIONS** Auth, "Lucy's House," Lincoln Rev (97): 72-87; auth, "Dangerous Secrets at Large: Four Small Press Novels," in Am Lit Rev (99): 143-152; auth, "Waiting to Adopt," in Touched by Adoption (Santa Barbara, CA: Green River Pr, 99), 201; auth, "Chinese Class," in The Red Thread Mag (forthcoming); auth, "Leaving Sparta," Phoebe: An Interdisciplinary J of Feminist Scholarship (forthcoming); auth, "The Art of Being Human," Puerto del Sol (forthcoming); auth, "One Mean Bad Kid: A Week in the Life of a Writer in the Schools," Writing on the Edge (forthcoming). **CONTACT ADDRESS** Dept English, Presbyterian Col, 503 S Broad St, Clinton, SC 29325-2865.

MCCAFFREY, DANIEL
PERSONAL Born Teaneck, NJ, m, 1971, 2 children **DISCIPLINE** CLASSICS **EDUCATION** Fordham Univ, AB, 68; Univ Mich, PhD, 74. **CAREER** Vis asst prof, Hope Col, 74-75; prof, Randolph-Macon Col, 75-. **HONORS AND AWARDS** NEH Summer Inst, Ohio State Univ, 83; NEH Summer Inst, Univ Southern Calif, 87; Dana fel, Carnegie Mellon Univ, 88-89; mem, va's lat textbk adoption comt, 90. **MEMBERSHIPS** Mem, Bd of Dir, Class Asn of Va 91-95; mem, APA Comt on Comput Activ, 91-94; mem, APA Subcomt on Assessment, 91-95; Comt mem, For Lang Asn of Va, 96-97. **SELECTED PUBLICATIONS** Auth, Some Dangers in the Uncritical Use of CAI in the Classroom, in Computer-Aided Instruction in the Humanities, ed by Solveig Olsen, MLA, 85; Teaching Ancient Languages with the Computer, Prospects, Summer, 92; coauth, Building Collegiality through Co-operative Programs, CJ 83, 88. **CONTACT ADDRESS** Dept of Class, Randolph-Macon Col, Ashland, VA 23005-5505.

MCCAFFREY, JERRINE A.
PERSONAL Born Sioux City, IA **DISCIPLINE** LITERATURE **EDUCATION** Univ ofNE, PhD, 96 **CAREER** Tchr, 90-, Des Moines Area Cmty Col **HONORS AND AWARDS** Ron Howard Master Tchr Awd **MEMBERSHIPS** WLA **CONTACT ADDRESS** Dept of Humanities and English, Des Moines Area Comm Col, 906 N Grant Rd, Carroll, IA 51401-2525. **EMAIL** jamccaffrey@dmacc.cc.ia

MCCALEB, JOSEPH L.
DISCIPLINE COMMUNICATIONS **EDUCATION** Univ TX, PhD, 76. **CAREER** Assoc prof, Univ MD. **RESEARCH** Tchr effectiveness in the develop of their personal authority. **SELECTED PUBLICATIONS** Auth, How Do Teachers Communicate, Amer Assn Col Tche Edu, 87; Evaluating Teachers' Communications, Future of Speech Commun, SCA, 89. **CONTACT ADDRESS** Dept of Commun, Univ of Maryland, Col Park, 4229 Art-Sociology Building, College Park, MD 20742-1335. **EMAIL** jm33@umail.umd.edu

MCCALL, MARSH H., JR.
DISCIPLINE CLASSICS **EDUCATION** BA, 60; Harvard Univ, PhD, 65. **CAREER** Prof class and dean cont studies/ summer sess, Stanford Univ. **RESEARCH** Greek lit; Greek tragedy; rhetoric; lit and textual criticism. **SELECTED PUBLICATIONS** Auth, Ancient Rhetorical Theories of Simile and Comparison,69; The Chorus of Aeschylus' Choephori in Cabinet of Muses: Essays in Honor of Thomas G. Rosenmeyer, 90; ed, Aeschylus, A Collection of Critical Essays, 72. **CONTACT ADDRESS** Stanford Univ, Bldg 20, Main Quad, Stanford, CA 94305.

MCCANN, JANET P.
PERSONAL Born, NJ, m, 4 children **DISCIPLINE** ENGLISH **EDUCATION** Otterbein Col, BA, 63; Univ Pittsburgh, MA, 64; PhD, 74. **CAREER** Grad teaching asst, Univ Pittsburgh, 64-65; instr, George Williams Col, 64-68; from instr to prof, Tex A & M Univ, 69-. **HONORS AND AWARDS** NEA Creative Writing Grant, 89. **MEMBERSHIPS** AAUP, SCMLA, Wallace Stevens Soc. **RESEARCH** Wallace Stevens, Women's Novels. **SELECTED PUBLICATIONS** Coauth, Creative and Critical Thinking, Houghton Mifflin, 85; auth, How They Got Here, Pudding Pub, 85; auth, Dialogue with the Dogcatcher, Slough Press, 87; auth, Ghosts of Christmas, Chimera Connections Press, 90; auth, "Wallace Stevens, Computers, and Creative Writing," in Teaching Wallace Stevens: Practical Essays, eds. John Serio and B. J. Leggett (TN: Univ Tenn Press, 94); co-ed, Odd Angles of Heaven: Contemporary Christian poetry, Harold Shaw Pub, 94; auth, Wallace Stevens Revisited: The Celestial Possible, Twayne/MacMillan, 95; auth, Looking for Buddha in the Barbed-Wire Garden, Avission Press, 96; co-ed, The Dove of the millennium: Contemporary Catholic Poetry, Story Line, 00. **CONTACT ADDRESS** Dept English, Texas A&M Univ, Col Station, College Station, TX 77843-0001. **EMAIL** jpm9243@acs.tamu.edu

MCCANN, RICHARD
DISCIPLINE CREATIVE WRITING **EDUCATION** Va Commonwealth Univ, BA; Hollins Col, MA; Univ Iowa, MA; PhD. **CAREER** Asst prof, codir, MFA program, creative writing, Am Univ. **HONORS AND AWARDS** Beatrice Hawley Awd, 94, Capricorn Poetry Awd, 93; NEA, Creative Writ Fel. **MEMBERSHIPS** Board of Trustees Jenny McKean Moore Fund Writers. **SELECTED PUBLICATIONS** Auth, Ghost Letters; Nights of 1990; Dream of the Traveler; Worlds of Fiction; Co-ed, Landscape and Distance: Contemporary Poets from Virginia; coed, Things Shaped in Passing: More 'Poets for Life' Writing from the AIDS Pandemic. **CONTACT ADDRESS** Dept of Lit, American Univ, 4400 Massachusetts Ave, Washington, DC 20016. **EMAIL** rmccann@american.edu

MCCARREN, VINCENT PAUL
PERSONAL Born 03/22/1939, New York, NY, m, 1968 **DISCIPLINE** CLASSICAL STUDIES, MEDIEVAL LITERATURE, GLOSSOGRAPHY, TEXTUAL CRITICISM, PALAEOGRAPHY **EDUCATION** Fordham Univ, AB, 60; Columbia Univ, AM, 67; Univ Mich, PhD, 75. **CAREER** Lectr Greek & Latin, Brooklyn Col, 63-68; instr, Hunter Col, 68-69, class lang & lit, Herbert H Lehman Col, 69-70; lectr Greek & Latin, 75-76, Univ Mich, acad coun gen acad areas, 77-78, researcher, Middle English Dict, Univ Mich, 79-01. **MEMBERSHIPS** Am Soc Papyrologists; Am Philol Soc; Medieval Acad of Am; Medieval Latin Asn of North Am. **RESEARCH** Documentary papyrology; Greek and Latin etymological studies; Medieval Glossology. **SELECTED PUBLICATIONS** Auth, A Critical Concordance to Catullus, E. J. Brill (Leiden), 77; auth, Michigan Papyri XIV, Scholars Press (Chico, CA), 80; coauth, "P.HAUN.14, P.MICH.679, and P.HAUN.15 - A Re-Edition," Zeitschrift Fur Papyrologie Und Epigraphik 58 (85): 71-79; auth, "Two Receipts for Payment of Poll Tax," Zeitschrift fur Papyrologie und Epigraphik 61 (85): 58-60; coauth, "The Abecedarium from B.M. Cotton MS.TITUS D18," Modern Philology 87 (90); auth, P.Michigan Koenen (P.MICH XVIII) - festschrift edition, V.McCarren #792 (P.MICH. Inventory 258): Receipt for Advamces Occassioned by the Lease of Vineyard Properties, 285-295, J.C. Geiben (Amsterdam), 96; coed and contributor, A Guide to Editing Middle English, Univ Mich Press, 98; auth, "Gloucester Fragement of the Medulla Grammatice: GDR/Z1/31: a critical edition," The Journal of Medieval Latin 10, BREPOLS, 01. **CONTACT ADDRESS** 302 Memory Lane, Brookings, OR 97415. **EMAIL** VPM@umich.edu

MCCARTHY, B. EUGENE
PERSONAL Born 05/03/1934, Grand Haven, MI, m, 1962, 3 children **DISCIPLINE** ENGLISH **EDUCATION** Univ Detroit, AB, 58, MA, 61; Univ Kans, PhD(English), 66. **CAREER** Instr English, Univ Detroit, 60-61; from instr to asst prof, 65-72, Assoc Prof English, Col of the Holy Cross, 72-. **RESEARCH** Milton; literary criticism of Restoration drama. **SELECTED PUBLICATIONS** Auth, Gray Music for the 'Bard' + Autograph Manuscript by Gray, Thomas, Revf Engl Stud, vol 0048, 97. **CONTACT ADDRESS** 422 Lovell, Worcester, MA 01602.

MCCARTHY, GERALD
PERSONAL Born 11/28/1947, m, 3 children **DISCIPLINE** ENGLISH **EDUCATION** SUNY Geneseo, BA, 74; Univ Iowa, MFA, 76. **MEMBERSHIPS** AUUP; Poets and Writers. **RESEARCH** African Americans in Vietnam War. **SELECTED PUBLICATIONS** Auth, War Story, 77; auth, Shoetown, 92; auth, Throwing the Headlines, 00. **CONTACT ADDRESS** Dept Humanities, St. Thomas Aquinas Col, 125 Route 340, Sparkill, NY 10976-1041.

MCCARTHY, JOHN F.
PERSONAL Born 02/25/1930, Newton, MA **DISCIPLINE** ENGLISH **EDUCATION** Harvard Univ, BA, 51; Yale Univ, MA, 53, PhD(English), 63. **CAREER** Instr English, Univ NH, 56-59; from instr to asst prof, 59-69, Assoc Prof English, Boston Col, 69-. **MEMBERSHIPS** MLA. **RESEARCH** Nineteenth century English poetry. **SELECTED PUBLICATIONS** Auth, The Canonical Meaning of the Recent Authentic Interpretation of Canon-230.2 Regarding Female Altar Servers, Sacred Mus, vol 0122, 95. **CONTACT ADDRESS** Dept of English, Boston Col, Chestnut Hill, 140 Commonwealth Ave, Chestnut Hill, MA 02167-3800.

MCCARTHY, PATRICK A.
PERSONAL Born 07/12/1945, Charlottesville, VA, m, 1997, 3 children **DISCIPLINE** ENGLISH **EDUCATION** Univ Virginia, BA, 67, MA, 68; Univ Wisc - Milwaukee, PhD, 73. **CAREER** Asst prof, 76-81, assoc prof, 81-84, prof, 84-, dir, grad stud, 86-95, dir, undergrad stud, Engl, 98-99, Univ Miami. **HONORS AND AWARDS** Nat Merit Scholar; Echols Scholar, Univ of Virginia, 63-67; Grad Teaching Assistantship, Univ of Wisconsin-Milwaukee, 69-72; Am Coun of Learned Societies Travel Grant, 77; Max Orovitz Summer Fellowships, Univ of Miami, 80, 82, 85, 90, 92; General Res Support Awds, Univ of Miami, 90, 92, 93, 97. **MEMBERSHIPS** Am Conf for Irish Studies; Asn of Literary Scholars and Critics; Int James Joyce Found; MLA; Samuel Beckett Soc; South Atlantic Modern Language Asn. **RESEARCH** Modern British & Irish lit, Irish

stud, sci fiction. **SELECTED PUBLICATIONS** Auth, The Riddles of Finnegans Wake, Fairleigh Dickinson Univ Press, 80; auth, Olaf Stapledon, Twayne Publishers, 82; auth, Ulysses: Portals of Discovery, Twayne Publishers, 90; auth, Forests of Symbols: World, Text, and Self in Malcolm Lowry's Fiction, Univ of Georgia Press, 94; ed, Critical Essays on Samuel Beckett, GK Hall, 86; coed, The Legacy of Olaf Stapledon: Critical Essays and an Unpublished Manuscript, Greenwood Press, 89; ed, Critical Essays on James Joyce's Finnegans Wake, GK Hall, 92; auth, Malcolm Lowry's La Mordida: A Scholarly Edition, Univ of Georgia Press, 96; coed, Joyce/Lowry: Critical Perspectives, Univ Press of Kentucky, 97. **CONTACT ADDRESS** Dept of English, Univ of Miami, Coral Gables, FL 33124. **EMAIL** p.mccarthy@miami.edu

MCCARTHY, PATRICK J.
PERSONAL Born 08/03/1922, New York, NY, m, 1951 **DISCIPLINE** ENGLISH LITERATURE **EDUCATION** Columbia Univ, PhD, 60. **CAREER** Prof Emer, Univ Calif, Santa Barbara. **HONORS AND AWARDS** Trustee, Dickens Soc; adv bd, nineteenth-century prose; ed, dickens-l, the e-group for dickensians. **RESEARCH** Stud of the lang of value in Dickens. **SELECTED PUBLICATIONS** Auth, Matthew Arnold and the Three Classes, Columbia Univ Press, 64. **CONTACT ADDRESS** Dept of Eng, Univ of California, Santa Barbara, Santa Barbara, CA 93106-7150. **EMAIL** mccarthy@humanitas.ucsb.edu

MCCARTHY, WILLIAM B.
PERSONAL Born 10/10/1939, Washington, DC, m, 1982, 3 children **DISCIPLINE** ENGLISH **EDUCATION** Spring Hill Col, AB, 64; MA, 69; La State Univ, MA, 71; Ind Univ, PhD, 78. **CAREER** Asst prof, Monmouth Col, 77-79; asst prof, Pikeville Col, 79-80; instr, Lincoln Memorial Univ, 80-81; instr, Salisbury State Col, 81-84; assoc prof, Univ of the Ozarks, 84-89; prof, PaState Univ, 89-. **HONORS AND AWARDS** President, Mid_Am Folflore Soc, 88; MLA Exec Comt on Folklore and Lit, 90-94; Sigma Tau Delta English Honor Soc; Who's Who in the E, 91; Who's Who in Am Educ, 92; Who's Who in the World, 00. **MEMBERSHIPS** MLA, Asn of Lit Scholars and Critics, Am Folklore Soc, Ballad Comn, Soc Int d'Ethnologie et de Folklore, Int Soc for Folk Narrative Res, English Folk Dance and Song Soc. **RESEARCH** Folk tales, oral tradition, American religion. **SELECTED PUBLICATIONS** Auth, The Ballad Matrix, Ind Univ Press (Bloomington), 90; auth, Jack in Two Worlds, Univ of NC Press (Chapel Hill), 94; auth, "The Polarization of Scots Society and Ballad collecting in Early Nineteenth Century," Lore and Lang 12 (94): 131-148; auth, "Transcribing Tales: For the Eye or For the Ear?" The Yearbook of English Studies 25 (95): 80-102; auth, "The Expressive Resources of Anglo-American Balladry," in Oral Tradition and Hispanic Studies: essay in Honor of Samuel G. Armistead, eds. Mishael Caspi and John Miles Foley (New York, NY: Garland, 95); auth, "The Stanza Concept as a Compositional Tool in Scots Ballad," in Visions and Identities, ed. Eydun Andreassen (Torshavn, Faroe Islands: Tungulist, 96); auth, "Olive Dame Campbell and Appalachian Tradition," in F.J. Child and the Ballad in English, eds. Thomas Cheeseman and Sigrid Riuwerts (Bern: Peter Lang, 97); auth, "Using Oral Tradition in the Composition Classroom," in Teaching Oral Traditions, ed. John Miles Foley (NY: MLA, 98). **CONTACT ADDRESS** Dept English, Pennsylvania State Univ, Dubois, 1 College Pl, Du Bois, PA 15801-2533. **EMAIL** wbm3@psu.edu

MCCARTHY, WILLIAM PAUL
PERSONAL Born 08/25/1942, Bronxville, NY **DISCIPLINE** EIGHTEENTH CENTURY BRITISH LITERATURE **EDUCATION** Hobart Col, BA, 64; Rutgers Univ, PhD, 74. **CAREER** From instr to assoc prof, 72-87, prof english, La State Univ, 87-. **HONORS AND AWARDS** NEH Fel, 88. **MEMBERSHIPS** MLA; Am Soc Eighteenth-Century Studies. **RESEARCH** Eighteenth century British Literature; British women writers, 1760-1815. **SELECTED PUBLICATIONS** Auth, Hester Thrale Priozzi, North Carolina, 85; coed, The Meridian Anthology of Early Women Writers: British Literary Women from Aphra Behn to Maria Edgeworth, New American Library, 87; coed, The Poems of Anna Letitia Barbauld, Georgia, 94. **CONTACT ADDRESS** Iowa State Univ, Ames, IA 50011-0002. **EMAIL** Wpmccarthy@aol.com

MCCARTNEY, JESSE FRANKLIN
PERSONAL Born 11/29/1939, Duncan, OK, m, 1959, 2 children **DISCIPLINE** ENGLISH **EDUCATION** OK State Univ, BS, 63; Univ AR, MA, 65, PhD, 71. **CAREER** From asst prof to assoc prof Eng, Univ Southern MS, 68-77; dir, Off Instr Develop, Ball State Univ, 77-82; Prof Eng & Vpres Instnl Serv, Catawba Col, 82-85, Vpres Acad Affairs & Dean, 85-92; Chmn, Eng Dept & dir Inst Res, 92. **MEMBERSHIPS** MLA; South Cent Mod Lang Asn; Prof & Organizational Develop Network; Am Asn Higher Educ. **RESEARCH** Mod Brit and Am lit; tchg in the hum. **SELECTED PUBLICATIONS** Guest-ed & contribr, Special Issue on Teaching the Humanities, Southern Quart, 1/74; auth, The Frank Arthur Swinnerton collection: A special literary collection, English Lit Transition, 75; The pedagogical style of T H Huxley in On the Physical Basis of Life, Southern Quart, 1/76; Barry Hannah, Miss Libr Comn, 77; The contributions of faculty development to humanistic teaching, Lib Educ, 12/77; Politics in Graham Green's The Destructors, Southern Humanities Rev, winter 78; Faculty Development: Planning for Individual and Institutional Renewal, Planning for Higher Educ, winter 80. **CONTACT ADDRESS** Eng Dept, Catawba Col, 2300 W Innes St, Salisbury, NC 28144-2488. **EMAIL** jmccartn@catawba.edu

MCCASKILL, BARBARA ANN
PERSONAL Born 09/14/1960, Fort Dix, NJ **DISCIPLINE** AMERICAN LITERATURE **EDUCATION** Columbus State Univ, BA, 82; Emory Univ, MA, 86; PhD, 88. **CAREER** Asst prof, SUNY Albany, 88-91; asst prof to assoc prof, Univ Ga, 93-. **HONORS AND AWARDS** DuBois Inst Fel, Harvard Univ; Fel, Columbia Univ; Fel, Ford Found; Dissertation Fel; AAUW; Fel, Rockefeller Found. **MEMBERSHIPS** MLA; ALA; ASA; MELUS; SSAWW; SAMLA. **RESEARCH** Literature of American slavery and abolition; Slave narratives; 19th Century African American women writers; Black Feminism. **SELECTED PUBLICATIONS** Ed, Running 1,000 Miles for Freedom; auth, Multicultural Literature and Literacies: Making Space for Difference; auth, Womanist Theory and Research. **CONTACT ADDRESS** Dept English, Univ of Georgia, 237 Jasmine Trl, Athens, GA 30606-6505. **EMAIL** bmccask@arches.uga.edu

MCCAULEY, REBECCA J.
DISCIPLINE COMMUNCATION SCIENCES **EDUCATION** Univ Chicago, PhD, 81. **CAREER** Dept Comm, Vermont Univ **MEMBERSHIPS** ASHA; VSHA; Acoust Soc Am. **RESEARCH** Normal and disordered speech; testing and measurement of speech and language. **SELECTED PUBLICATIONS** Auth, Familiar strangers: criterion-referenced measures in communication disorders, 96; Phonologic Disorders, 94; A comprehensive phonological approach to assessment and treatment of sound system disorders, 93; coauth, Intelligibility and analysis of phonetic contrast errors in speakers with amyotrophic lateral sclerosis, Jour Speech Hearing Res, 95. **CONTACT ADDRESS** Dept of Communication Sciences, Univ of Vermont, 360 Waterman Bldg, Burlington, VT 05405. **EMAIL** rmccaule@zoo.uvm.edu

MCCLAIN, E.
PERSONAL Born 04/18/1951, Boulder, CO, m, 1984, 2 children **DISCIPLINE** ENGLISH **EDUCATION** St Edwards Univ, BA, 74; Univ West Fla, Pensacola, MAT, 82. **CAREER** Assoc prof, Pensacola Jr Col, 86-96; prof, St Johns River Community Col, 96-. **HONORS AND AWARDS** Pensacola Jr Col Teaching Excellence Awd, 86; Adelia Rosasco-Soule Literary Art Outstanding Achievement Awd, 94. **MEMBERSHIPS** Kappa Delta Pi. **RESEARCH** Folklore. **SELECTED PUBLICATIONS** Auth, "Smoke Screen" (short story), Half Tones to Jubilee (93); auth, "Recovery," (poem), The Emerald Coast Rev (94); auth, "Undergrowth," (poem) The Emerald Coast Rev (95); auth, "Closed," (poem) Half Tones to Jubilee (97); auth, "Warfare," The International Library of Poetry Anthology (Oct 99); auth, "Karma Concession," The International Library of Poetry Anthology (Dec 99); auth, "Riven Spirit," The International Library of Poetry Anthology (Feb 2000). **CONTACT ADDRESS** Dept General Educ, St. Johns River Comm Col, 283 Col Dr, Orange Park, FL 32065-7639.

MCCLARTY, WILMA KING- DOERING
PERSONAL Born 07/21/1939, w, 1962, 2 children **DISCIPLINE** ENGLISH, ENGLISH EDUCATION **EDUCATION** Andrews Univ BA, 61, MA, 62; Univ MT, DEduc, 68. **CAREER** Asst prof Eng & educ, Southwestern Union Col, 68-72; assoc prof, 72-80, Prof Eng & Chmn Dept, Southern Adventist University, 80-; Coord, Seventh-day Adventist Sec Sch Eng Tchrs Conv, Southern Missionary Col, 73. **MEMBERSHIPS** NCTE. **SELECTED PUBLICATIONS** Auth, Why are you so peculiar?, Rev & Herald, 8/71; Open-minded or just empty headed, J Adventist Educ, 2-3/72; Urgency (poem), Ministry, 2/72. **CONTACT ADDRESS** Dept of Eng, So Adventist Univ, PO Box 370, Collegedale, TN 37315-0370. **EMAIL** wmclarty@southern.edu

MCCLARY, BEN HARRIS
DISCIPLINE ENGLISH **EDUCATION** Univ Tenn, BA, 55; MA, 57; Sussex, PhD, 66. **CAREER** Prof, PROF EMER ENG, MIDDLE GEORGIA COLL **MEMBERSHIPS** Am Antiquarian Soc **SELECTED PUBLICATIONS** Auth, "William Cullen Bryant's Sketch of His Father in American Biography, " Am Lit 55, 83; "George Washington Harris's New York Atlas Series: Three New Items," Stud in Am Humor 2, 84; "Samuel Lorenzo Knapp and Early American Biography," Procs of the AAS 95, 85. **CONTACT ADDRESS** PO Box 80082, Chattanooga, TN 37414.

MCCLELLAND, JOHN FLEMING
PERSONAL Born 10/28/1946, Atlanta, GA, m, 1979 **DISCIPLINE** ENGLISH **EDUCATION** Vanderbilt Univ, BA, 68; Univ Ga, MA, 74; PhD, 81. **CAREER** From teaching asst to instr, Univ Ga, 74-81; from asst prof to prof, Univ La at Monroe, 81-. **HONORS AND AWARDS** Sigma Tau Delta; Phi Kappa Phi; Col of Liberal Arts Researcher of the Year, 84, 86, 87, & 89; Univ Outstanding Researcher, 89; Thomas & Mary Barham Prof of English, 99-01. **MEMBERSHIPS** MLA, SAMLA, Keats-Shelley Asn, Carlyle Soc. **RESEARCH** Nineteenth-Century British Literature & Culture. **SELECTED PUBLICATIONS** Ed, The Collected Poems of Thomas & Jane Welsh Carlyle, 86. **CONTACT ADDRESS** Dept English, Univ of Louisiana, Monroe, 700 Univ Ave, Monroe, LA 71209-9000. **EMAIL** enmcclelland@ulm.edu

MCCLUNG, WILLIAM A.
PERSONAL Born 01/22/1944, Norfolk, VA, s **DISCIPLINE** ENGLISH **EDUCATION** Williams Col, BA, 66; Harvard Univ, AM, 67, PhD, 72. **CAREER** Asst prof to assoc prof to Prof Eng, Miss State Univ, 71-. **HONORS AND AWARDS** Dexter Fel, Harvard Univ, 70; Am Phil Soc Grantee, 85; vis fel, The Huntington Libr, 85; ACLS Fel, 88; Andrew W. Mellon Fel, The Huntington Libr, 91. **MEMBERSHIPS** Phi Beta Kappa, Phi Kappa Phi, Am Asn Univ Prof; Mod Lang Asn, Soc of Arch Hist; Renaissance Soc of Am; Milton Soc of Am, John Donne Soc of Am, Nat Trust for Hist Pres. **RESEARCH** Literary/architectural relations **SELECTED PUBLICATIONS** Auth, "The Country House in English Renaissance Poetry, U of California, p, 77; auth, The Architecture of Paradise: Survivals of Eden and Jerusalem, U of California P, 83; auth, "Designing Utopia," Moreana: Bulletin Thomas More (France), 94ed, commentary, The Variorum Edition of the Poetry of John Donne, Vol VIII: The Epigrams, Epithalamions, Epitaphs and Inscriptions, Indiana UP, 95; auth "The Decor of Power in Naples, 1747," Jour of Arch Educ 52.1, 98; auth, Landscapes of Desire: Anglo My Thologies of Los Angeles, U of California p, 00. **CONTACT ADDRESS** Mississippi State Univ, PO Drawer E, Mississippi State, MS 39762-5505. **EMAIL** wam3@ra.msstate.edu

MCCLURE, CHARLES R.
PERSONAL Born 05/24/1949, Syracuse, NY, m, 1970, 1 child **DISCIPLINE** INFORMATION STUDIES **EDUCATION** OK State Univ, BA (Spanish), 71; MA (Hist), 73; Univ OK, MLS (Library Science), 74; Rutgers Univ, PhD (Information Studies), 77. **CAREER** Prof, Univ OK, School of Library Science, 78-86; distinguished prof, Syracuse Univ, School of Information Studies, 86-99; Francis Eppes prof, Florida State Univ, 99-. **HONORS AND AWARDS** Best Book of the Year, Am Soc for Information Science, 87; Distinguished Researcher, Nat Commission on Libraries and Information Science, 94; Am Libr Asn, Jesse H. Shera award, 90. **MEMBERSHIPS** Am Library Asn; Information Industry Asn; Asn of Library and Information Science. **RESEARCH** Information policy; planning/evaluation of information services. **SELECTED PUBLICATIONS** Coauth, Libraries in the Internet/National Research and Education Network (NREN): Perspectives, Issues and Strategies, Meckler Pub, 94; coauth, Internet Costs and Cost Models for Public Libraries, Nat Commission on Libraries and Information Science, 95; coauth, Assessing the Academic Networked Environment: A Manual of Strategies and Options, Coalition for Networked Information, 96; coauth, The 1996 National Survey of Public Libraries and the Internet: Issues Progress and Issues, Nat Commission on Libraries and Information Science, 96; co-ed and contrib, Federal Information Policies in the 1990's: Issues and Conflicts, Ablex Pub Corp, 96; coauth, An Evaluation of the Federal Government's Implementation of the Government Information Locator Service (GILS), Government Printing Office, 97; coauth, The 1997 Survey of Public Libraries and the Internet: Costs and Capabilities for the Electronic Networked Environment, Am Library Asn, 98; coauth, Policy Issues and Stategies Affecting Public Libraries in the National Networked Environment, Nat Commission on Libraries and Information Science, 98; coauth, The 1998 National Survey of Public Library Outlet Internet Connectivity, Nat Commission on Libraries and Information Science, 99. **CONTACT ADDRESS** School of Information Studies, Florida State Univ, Louis Shores Bldg., Room 226, Tallahassee, FL 32306-2100. **EMAIL** cmcclure@lis.fsu.edu

MCCLURE, JOHN
DISCIPLINE ENGLISH LANGUAGE AND LITERATURE **EDUCATION** Tufts Univ, BA; Stanford, MA; PhD. **CAREER** Prof. **RESEARCH** Colonial cultural studies; religious cultural studies; contemporary fiction. **SELECTED PUBLICATIONS** Auth, Kipling and Conrad: The Colonial Fiction, Late Imperial Romance. **CONTACT ADDRESS** Dept of English, Rutgers, The State Univ of New Jersey, New Brunswick, 510 George St, Murray Hall, New Brunswick, NJ 08901-1167. **EMAIL** jmcclure@rci.rutgers.edu

MCCLURE, LAURA KATHLEEN
PERSONAL Born 12/26/1959, Wichita Falls, TX, m, 1988, 3 children **DISCIPLINE** CLASSICS **EDUCATION** Bard Col, BA, 82; St. John's Col, MA, 84; Univ Chicago, MA, 86, PhD, 91. **CAREER** Univ Wisconsin, Madison, asst prof, classics, 91-99; Assoc Prof, 99-. **HONORS AND AWARDS** Univ of WI Distinguished Teaching Awd, 99; Associate Res Awd, 99-00. **MEMBERSHIPS** APA, CAMS, WCC **RESEARCH** Athenian drama; women in antiquity; classical tradition. **SELECTED PUBLICATIONS** Auth, Spoken Like a Woman: Speech and Gender in Athenian Drama, Princeton Univ Press, forthcoming/99; ed, Blackwell Reader on Sexuality and Gender in the Classical World; auth, "'The Worst Husband': Discourses of Praise

an Blame in Euripidess' Media," 99; co-edit, Making Silence Speak: Women's Voices in Ancient Greece, forthcoming, PUP, fc; He Is and Is Not: Euripides as a Comic Character, in: Approaches to Teaching World Literature; ed R. Mitchell-Boyask, fc; Gunaikos Logos: Speech, Gender and Spectatorship in Aeschylus' Agamemnon, Helios, 97; Teaching a Course on Gender in the Classical World, Class Jour, 97; Clytemnestra's Binding Song, Class Jour, 97; Female Speech and Characterization in Euripides, in: Lo spettacolo delle voci, ed A.H. Sommerstein and F. de Martino, Bari, 95; On Knowing Greek: George Eliot and the Classical Tradition, in: Clas & Mod Lit, 93. **CONTACT ADDRESS** Dept of Classics, Univ of Wisconsin, Madison, 1220 Linden Dr, Madison, WI 53706. **EMAIL** lmcclure@facstaff.wisc.edu

MCCLUSKEY, JAMES J.
PERSONAL Born 07/16/1953, Brockville, ON, Canada **DISCIPLINE** BROADCASTING **EDUCATION** Univ Mich, BGS, 75; MA, 76; Kans State Univ, PhD, 93. **CAREER** Asst teacher, Univ of Mich, 75-76; asst prof, Oakland Community Col, 77-83; asst prof, Kans State Univ, 90-92; asst prof and sequence coord, Univ of Okla, 92-; asst prof, Central Mich Univ, 97-. **HONORS AND AWARDS** Grant, Cental Mich Univ, 00. **MEMBERSHIPS** Broadcast Educ Asn, Mich Asn of Broadcasters, Midwestern Educ Res Asn Coun. **RESEARCH** Broadcasting, Radio & TV, New Technologies including Virtual Reality. **SELECTED PUBLICATIONS** Auth, Starting a Student Radio Station, Simon & Schuster Custom Pub, Inc. (Needham Heights, MA), 98; auth, Advising, Managing and Operating a Student Radio Station, Simon & Schuster Custom Pub, Inc. (Needham Heights, MA), 98; auth, Broadcast Station Management and Ownership: The Professional Perspective, Simon & Schuster Custom Pub, Inc. (Needham Heights, MA), forthcoming. **CONTACT ADDRESS** Dept Broadcast & Cinematic Art, Central Michigan Univ, 100 W Preston Rd, Mount Pleasant, MI 48859-0001. **EMAIL** james.j.mccluskey@cmich.edu

MCCLYMONDS, MARITA P.
DISCIPLINE MUSIC **EDUCATION** Univ Ca, PhD. **CAREER** Assoc prof, Dept Music, Va Univ. **HONORS AND AWARDS** ACLS Fel, 84-85; NEH Travel Grant, 89. **RESEARCH** 18th century opera especially Italian opera. **SELECTED PUBLICATIONS** Auth, La morte di Semiramide ossia La vendetta di Nino and the Restoration of Death and Tragedy to the Italian Operatic Stage in the 1780s and 90s, 87; The Venetian Role in the Transformation of Italian Opera Seria during the 1790s, 89. **CONTACT ADDRESS** Dept of Music, Univ of Virginia, Cabell Hall No 113, PO Box 400176, Charlottesville, VA 22904-4176. **EMAIL** mpm3c@virginia.edu

MCCOLLEY, DIANE K.
DISCIPLINE 17TH CENTURY POETRY, RENAISSANCE AND REFORMATION CULTURAL CONTEXTS **EDUCATION** Univ Ill, PhD. **CAREER** Instr, Rutgers, State Univ NJ, Camden Col of Arts and Sci; ed bd, Milton Stud. **HONORS AND AWARDS** James Holly Hanford Awd, 93. **MEMBERSHIPS** Pres, Milton Soc. **RESEARCH** Environmental poetics in early modern and modern poetry. **SELECTED PUBLICATIONS** Auth, Milton's Eve, Ill, 83; Milton and the Sexes, The Cambridge Companion to Milton, Cambridge, 92; A Gust for Paradise: Milton's Eden and the Visual Arts, Ill, 93; The Copious Matter of My Song, Literary Milton: Text, Pretext, Context, Duquesne Univ Press, 94; Beneficent Hierarchies: Reading Milton Greenly, Spokesperson Milton: Voices in Contemporary Criticism, Susquehanna, 94; Poetry and Music in Seventeenth-Century England, Cambridge Univ Press, 97. **CONTACT ADDRESS** Rutgers, The State Univ of New Jersey, New Brunswick, 311 N 5th St, Camden, NJ 08102. **EMAIL** mccolley@crab.rutgers.edu

MCCOLLEY, KATHLEEN
DISCIPLINE ENGLISH **EDUCATION** Univ Puget Sound, BA, 91; Univ Haw, MA, 98. **CAREER** Assoc fac, Pac Rim Bible Inst, 99; grad asst, Univ Haw, 98-00; assoc fac, Cascadia Community Col, 01. **HONORS AND AWARDS** CCCC Scholar Dream. **MEMBERSHIPS** MLA; CCC; MTNA; WSMTA; AAUN; NCTE. **RESEARCH** Sensational Victorian novels; modernism. **SELECTED PUBLICATIONS** Auth, Poem in Intersecting Circles: The Voices of Hapa Women in Poetry and Prose, eds. Marie Hara, Nora Keller (Haw: Bamboo Ridge Pr, 99); auth, "Claiming Center Stage: Speaking Out for Homoerotic Empowerment in the Bostonians," Henry James Rev 21 (00). **CONTACT ADDRESS** PO Box 98014, Des Moines, WA 98198-0014. **EMAIL** kmccolley@hotmail.com

MCCOMBS, MAXWELL E.
PERSONAL Born 12/03/1938, Birmingham, AL, m, 4 children **DISCIPLINE** COMMUNICATION **EDUCATION** Tulane Univ, BA, 60; Stanford Univ, 61; PhD, 66. **CAREER** Lectr, Univ Calif, Los Angeles, 65-66; asst prof, 66-67; asst prof, Univ NC, 67-69; assoc prof, 69-73; dir ANPA, 75-84; prof, Syracuse Univ, 73-85; prof, Cath Univ of Chile, 00-; adj prof, Univ Navarra, 94-; chair, prof, Univ Tex at Austin, 85-. **HONORS AND AWARDS** Paul J Deutschmann Awd; Murray Edelman Awd; Best Res Article; ICA Fel; Edward Trayes Prof of Year Awd; Sydney S Goldish Awd; Phi Beta Kappa; Omicron Delta Kappa; Kappa Tau Alpha. **MEMBERSHIPS** AEJMC; AAPOR; ICA; WAPOR. **RESEARCH** Mass communication and public opinion. **SELECTED PUBLICATIONS** Coauth, Contemporary Public Opinions: Issues and News, Lawrence Erlbaum (Hillsdale, NJ), 91; coauth, Communication and Democracy: Exploring the Theoretical Frontiers in Agenda Setting Theory, Lawrence Erlbaum (Mahwah, NJ), 97; coauth, The National Issues Convention Experiment in Political Communication, Lawrence Erlbaum (Mahwah, NJ), 99; coauth, Research in Mass Communication: A Practical Guide, St Martin's Press (Boston), 00. **CONTACT ADDRESS** Dept Journalism, Univ of Texas, Austin, Austin, TX 78712-1013.

MCCONNELL, KATHLEEN
PERSONAL Born 07/17/1961, Peterborough, ON, Canada, s **DISCIPLINE** ENGLISH, LITERATURE, CREATIVE WRITING **EDUCATION** Mt St Vincent Univ, BA, 93; Wilfrid Laurier Univ, MA, 94; Dalhousie Univ, PhD, 00. **CAREER** Part time instr, Dalhousie Univ and Mt St Vincent Univ. **HONORS AND AWARDS** RCCA Soc Sci Humanities Awd, 96-98; Dalhousie's Pres Grad Teaching Awd, 95. **MEMBERSHIPS** MLA; IGA; ACCUTE; NASSR; WFNS. **RESEARCH** 18th century romantics; critical theory; creative writing. **SELECTED PUBLICATIONS** Auth, "Unnatural Habitats," Eastgate Quart (95); auth, "Textile Tropes in the Afterlife of George Cartwright," Can Lit 149 (96); auth, Enquiries Concerning Human Misunderstanding: Theory, Speculation, Practice," Henry St 7 (98); auth, "Praise Between Peers: Felicia Hemans in the Wordsworth Household," in Relocating Praise: Literary Modalities and Rhetorical Contexts, ed. Alice G. den Otter (Toronto: Can Scholar Pr, 00); auth, "Chaos at the Mouth of Hell: Why the Columbine High School Massacre had repercussions for Buffy the Vampire Slayer," Gothic Study 2 (00); auth, "Faith," Can Lit (forthcoming). **CONTACT ADDRESS** 1382 Ketch Harbour Rd, Sambro Head, NS, Canada B3V 1L1. **EMAIL** kathymac@is2.aol.ca

MCCORD, HOWARD
PERSONAL Born 11/03/1932, El Paso, TX, m, 1975, 4 children **DISCIPLINE** ENGLISH **EDUCATION** Univ Tex, El Paso, BA, 57; Univ Utah, MA, 58. **CAREER** Assoc prof English & humanities, Washington State univ, 60-71; dir creative writing prog, 71-80, 90-98; prof English, Bowling Green State Univ, 71-98; prof Emeritus, 98-, D H Lawrence fel, Univ NMex, 71; secy exec comn bd dir, Coord Coun Lit Mag, 72-77; adj prof, Union Grad Sch, 73-; res associateship for study in Iceland, Bowling Green Univ, 73; Nat Endowment arts fel, 76, 83; mem lit adv panel, 77-79; vis prof, Calif State Univ, 76; distinguished lectr, Univ Alaska, 78-81; chmn lit panel, Ohio Arts Coun, 79-81. spec achievement award, Bowling Green Univ, 75. **MEMBERSHIPS** MLA; Pen Club; Poetry Soc Am; Arctic Inst. **RESEARCH** Poetry; fiction; criticism. **SELECTED PUBLICATIONS** Auth, Fables and Transfigurations, 67, Longjaunes his Periplus, 68 & Maps, 71, Kayak; Selected Poems, 1955-1971, 75 & The Great Toad Hunt and Other Expeditions, 78, Crossing; The Arctic Desert, Stonemarrow, 78; The Arcs of Lowitz, Saltworks, 80; Walking Edges, Raincrow, 82; Dake of Chemical Birds, Bloody Twin, 89; The Man Who Walked to the Moon, McPherson, 97; Bone/Hueso, Logan Elim, 99. **CONTACT ADDRESS** Creative Writing Prog, Bowling Green State Univ, 1001 E Wooster St, Bowling Green, OH 43403-0001. **EMAIL** mccord@bgnet.bgsu.edu

MCCORDUCK, EDWARD SCOTT
PERSONAL Born 07/27/1962, Utica, NY, m, 1994, 2 children **DISCIPLINE** ENGLISH **EDUCATION** Syracuse Univ, AB; MA, 91; ABD; Cornell Univ, PhD. **CAREER** Instr, Univ of Maine, 89-90; Instr, State Univ of NYork at Syracuse, 90-95; Lectr, State Univ of NYork at Cortland, 95-. **HONORS AND AWARDS** Awards, NY State Univ, 93, 94, 95. **MEMBERSHIPS** Dict Soc of N Am; Ling Soc of Am; NY State Teachers of English to Speakers of Other Lang. **RESEARCH** English grammar, linguistics, history of the English language, lexiograph, English as a second/foreign language, education applications of computers in the World Wide Web. **SELECTED PUBLICATIONS** Auth, Grammatical Information in ESL Dictionaries, Max Niemeyer verlag, (Tubingen), 93; auth, "What Happened to the Dinosaurs?", SLE Newsworld, 94; auth, "Review of the Longman Dictionary of American English for Microsoft Windows, Int Jour of Lexicography 8.1 (95); auth, "Review of the Longman Interactive English Dictionary", Dictionaries 17, (96); auth, "Computerized EFL Dictionaries", EFL Gazette, 96; auth, "Electronic Dictionaries Will Power Learning Techniques", Am Lang Rev, 97; auth, "Making the Most of Multimedia Tools", Am Lang Rev, 97; auth, "Review of the Collins COBUILD on CD-ROM", Lexicographica 13, 97; auth, Understanding American Football, NTC Pub (Lincolnwood, IL), 98. **CONTACT ADDRESS** Dept English, SUNY, Col at Cortland, PO Box 2000, Cortland, NY 13045-0900. **EMAIL** mccorduc@cortland.edu

MCCORKLE, W. BENSON
PERSONAL Born 03/07/1974, Augusta, GA, s **DISCIPLINE** ENGLISH **EDUCATION** Augusta Col, BA, 96; Ohio State Univ, MA, 00. **CAREER** Writer, Metropolitan Spirit, Ga, 96-97; supvr, Athens Daily News, 97-98; grad teach assoc to writing prog admin, Ohio State Univ, 99-. **HONORS AND AWARDS** McCrary Eng Awd, 96; Ohio State Univ Fel, 98. **MEMBERSHIPS** NCTE, MLA, Phi Kappa Phi, Ga Continental Philos Circle. **RESEARCH** Rhetoric, media theory, digital culture. **SELECTED PUBLICATIONS** Auth, "The Simpsons: Mirror of Society," Everything's an Argument, ed Andrea Lunsford, (NY: St. Martins Pr), (00); coed, Writing Lives, (forthcoming). **CONTACT ADDRESS** 5323 Stock Rd, Columbus, OH 43229-5033. **EMAIL** mccorkle.12@osu.edu

MCCORMACK, ERIC
DISCIPLINE ENGLISH LITERATURE **EDUCATION** Univ of Glasgow, MA; Univ Manitoba, PhD. **CAREER** Assoc prof and chair, Dept of Eng, St. Jerome's Univ. **HONORS AND AWARDS** Commonwealth Writers Prize, 88; Arts Council Bk Prize; Governor General's Awd Fiction, 97. **MEMBERSHIPS** Writers Union of Can; PEN. **SELECTED PUBLICATIONS** Auth, Black Water 2; First Blast of the Trumpet Against the Monstrous Regiment of Women; Gates of Paradise; I Shudder at Your Touch-Tales of Sex and Horror; Inspecting the Vaults; Likely Stories: A Postmodern Sample; Oxford Book of Canadian Detective Fiction; Oxford Book of Canadian Ghost Stories; Oxford Book of Scottish Short Stories; Paper Guitar; Short Fiction; The Mysterium; The Paradise Motel; The Story Begins The Story Ends. **CONTACT ADDRESS** Dept of English, St. Jerome's Univ, Waterloo, ON, Canada N2L 3G3. **EMAIL** epmccorm@watarts.uwaterloo.ca

MCCORMICK, EDGAR LINDSLEY
PERSONAL Born 03/12/1914, Wadsworth, Ohio, m, 1945, 1 child **DISCIPLINE** ENGLISH **EDUCATION** Kent State Univ, AB, 36; Univ Mich, MA, 37, PhD, 50. **CAREER** Head dept, Ala State Teachers Col, Florence 46-50 & Bethany Col, 50-54; from asst prof to assoc prof English, 54-64, prof, 64-79, chmn freshman English, 56-60, from asst dean to assoc dean, Col Arts & Sci, 64-70, coord Am studies, 70-78, prof emer, Kent State Univ, 79- . **MEMBERSHIPS** MLA; NCTE; Am Studies Asn. **RESEARCH** American literature; T W Higginson as literary historian; Western Reserve history. **SELECTED PUBLICATIONS** Coauth, Life on a Whaler, Heath, 60; co-auth, Imagination and intellect, Prentice-Hall, 62; co-auth, Nantucket migration to Portage County, Ohio, Hist Nantucket, 63; co-auth, Creatures Here Below, 72; co-authHome Place and Other Poems, Old Forge Press, 81; auth, Brimfield and Its People, Shoestring Pr, 88; auth, They Also Served, 93. **CONTACT ADDRESS** 1106 Old Forge Rd, Kent, OH 44240.

MCCOY, GARY W.
PERSONAL m, 3 children **DISCIPLINE** CHURCH MUSIC **EDUCATION** Cent Mo State Univ, BME; Southwestern Baptist Theol Sem, MCM; Southwestern Baptist Theol Sem, DMA; addn stud, Midwestern Baptist Theol Sem; Myong Dong Inst, Seoul, degree Korean Lang Stud. **CAREER** Prof, Korea Baptist Col/Sem, 85-89; dir, Area Mus Dept, Korea Baptist Col/Sem, 86-89; church mus consult, 75-79; assoc prof, 91; dir, Bill and Pat Dixon Sch of Church Mus, Golden Gate Baptist Theol Sem. **HONORS AND AWARDS** Missionary, For Mission Bd, 74; minister of mus, Concord Korean Baptist Church. **SELECTED PUBLICATIONS** Auth, Come to the Manger; Easter Praises and Jesus; the Very Thought of Thee, Jordan Press Seoul, Korea; Hymn Arrangements for the Korean Church Pianist and His Only Son: God's Gift at Christmas; pub(s), S Baptist keyboard mag; Pedalpoint. **CONTACT ADDRESS** Golden Gate Baptist Theol Sem, 201 Sem Dr, Mill Valley, CA 94941-3197. **EMAIL** GaryMcCoy@ggbts.edu

MCCOY, KEN W.
PERSONAL Born, AL, m, 1993 **DISCIPLINE** THEATRE **EDUCATION** Univ AL, Birmingham, BA, 82; Southern Ill Univ Carbondale, MFA, 84; Bowling Green St Univ, PhD, 94. **CAREER** Asst prof to assoc prof, Dept of Communication Stud and Theatre Arts, 94-, Stetson Univ, FL. **HONORS AND AWARDS** BGSU; Outstanding Grad Stud; Shanklin Res Awd Finalist; Graduate Fellow; UAB: Omicron Delta Kappa. **MEMBERSHIPS** NCA; Asn for Theatre in Higher Education. **RESEARCH** Hispanic and Latin American theatre, internet and performance. **SELECTED PUBLICATIONS** Auth, "A Brief Guide to Internet Resources in Theatre and Performance Studies" 1993-2001; contribur, Who's Who in the Contemporary World Theatre, Rutledge Publ, 00; art, Strategies for Liberation in the Latin American Popular Theatre, Theatre InSight, 95; auth, Liberating the Latin American Audience: The Conscientizacao of Enrique Buenaventura and Augusto Boal, 95; art Book Rev, Diana Taylors Theatre of Crisis, Theatre InSight, 95; art, A Guide to Internet Resources in Theatre and Performance Studies, The Internet Comp Subject Guides to Humanities Res, 95; art, The Theatre of Mario Vargas Llosa A Bibliography and Production History 1981-1994, Latin Amer Theatre Rev, 95; art, A Brief Bibliograpy of Internet Theatre Resources Beyond Email, Theatre Topics, 95. **CONTACT ADDRESS** Stetson Univ, De Land, 421 N Woodland Blvd, Unit 8374, DeLand, FL 32720. **EMAIL** kmccoy@stetson.edu

MCCRACKEN, DAVID
PERSONAL Born 05/07/1939, Cincinnati, OH **DISCIPLINE** ENGLISH **EDUCATION** Oberlin Col, BA, 61; Univ Chicago, MA, 62, PhD(English), 66. **CAREER** Asst prof, 66-71, assoc prof, 71-80, Prof English, Univ Wash, 80-. **MEMBERSHIPS** MLA; Am Soc 18th century Studies; Wordsworth-Coleridge

Asn. **RESEARCH** Late eighteenth century literature; Wordsworth. **SELECTED PUBLICATIONS** Ed, Caleb Williams, Oxford, 69; auth, Godwin's literary theory, Philol Quart, 69; The drudgery of defining: Dr Johnson's debt to N Bailey, Mod Philol, 69; Godwin's Caleb Williams: A fictional rebuttal of Burke, Studies in Burke & His Time, 70; The development of Edmund Burke's reflections, Western Speech Commun, summer 76; auth, Junius and Philip Francis, Twayne, 79; Goldsmith and the natural revolution of things, J English and Germanic Philol, 79; Wordsworth on human wishes and poetic borrowing, Mod Philol, 5/82. **CONTACT ADDRESS** Dept of English, Univ of Washington, Seattle, WA 98195.

MCCRAY, JAMES
PERSONAL Born Kankakee, IL, d, 2 children **DISCIPLINE** MUSIC **EDUCATION** Ill Wesleyan Univ, BME; Southern Ill Univ, MM; Univ Iowa, PhD. **CAREER** Prof, Colo State Univ. **HONORS AND AWARDS** Prof of the Year, Longwood Col; Prof of the Year, Univ So Fla; Orpheus Awd; Outstanding Educator Awd, 92-93. **SELECTED PUBLICATIONS** Auth, pubs on composition, choral methods, and conducting. **CONTACT ADDRESS** Music, Theatre, and Dance Dept, Colorado State Univ, Fort Collins, CO 80523. **EMAIL** jmccray@vines.colostate.edu

MCCULLEN, MAURICE
DISCIPLINE ENGLISH LITERATURE **CAREER** Prof, Univ Pacific. **HONORS AND AWARDS** Fulbright lecturer, Fudan Univ, Shanghai, China, 91-93. **SELECTED PUBLICATIONS** Auth, E. M. Delafield, 85; co-auth, George Meredith: Characters and Characteristics, Garland, 79. **CONTACT ADDRESS** Eng Dept, Univ of the Pacific, Stockton, Pacific Ave, PO Box 3601, Stockton, CA 95211.

MCCULLOH, WILLIAM EZRA
PERSONAL Born 09/08/1931, McPherson, KS, m, 1956, 2 children **DISCIPLINE** CLASSICAL LANGUAGES & LITERATURES **EDUCATION** Ohio Wesleyan Univ, AB, 53; Oxford Univ, BA, 56; Yale Univ, PhD, 62. **CAREER** Instr classics, Wesleyan Univ, 56-61; from instr to assoc prof, 61-68, prof classics, Kenyon Col, 68-99, prof emer, 99-. **HONORS AND AWARDS** Am Philological Assoc Awd for Excellence in Teaching, 85; Nat Endowment for the Humanitites Fel for Col Teachers, 84-85; Ohio Prof of the Year, Carnegie Fund for the Advancement of Teaching and Council for Advancement and Support of Educ, 95. **MEMBERSHIPS** Am Philol Asn; Class Asn Mid W & S; Soc Ancient Greek Philos; NAm Patristics Soc; Int Soc for Neoplatonic Studies. **RESEARCH** Greek poetry and philosophy; the ancient novel; Greek patristics. **SELECTED PUBLICATIONS** Auth, Introduction to Greek Lyric Poetry, Bantam, 62; Metaphysical solace in Greek tragedy, Class J, 12/63; Aristophanes seen whole, Sewanee Rev, fall 65; Longus, Twayne, 70. **CONTACT ADDRESS** Dept of Classics, Kenyon Col, Ascension Hall, Gambier, OH 43022-9623. **EMAIL** mcculloh@kenyon.edu

MCCULLOUGH, JOSEPH B.
PERSONAL Born 09/08/1943, Spokane, WA, m, 1980 **DISCIPLINE** AMERICAN LITERATURE & HUMOR **EDUCATION** Gonzaga Univ, BEd, 66; Ohio Univ, MA, 67, PhD(English), 69. **CAREER** Asst prof, 69-72, assoc prof, 72-79, actg dean, Grad Col, 77-80, prof English, Univ Nev, Las Vegas, 79-98, Fulbright lectr Am Lit, Helsinki Univ, 80-81; U of Athens, 85-86; Distinguished Prof, UNVL, 98-. **HONORS AND AWARDS** UNLV Alumni Distinguished Faculty of the Year Awd, 93; Barrick Distinguished Scholar, UNLV, 97; Rita Deanin Abbey Teacher of the Year in Liberal Arts, 00. **RESEARCH** Hamlin Garland; American literarey realism and Mark Twain. **SELECTED PUBLICATIONS** Auth, Mark Twain and the Hy Slocum-Carl Byng controversy, Am Lit, 3/71; A listing of Mark Twain's contributions to the Buffalo Express, 1869-1871, Am Lit Realism, Winter 72; co-ed (with Robert K Dodge), Voices From Wah 'Kon-Tah: Contemporary Poetry of Native Americans, Int Publ, 74; auth, Madam Merle: Henry James' White Blackbird, Papers Lang & Lit, Summer 75; coauth (with Robert K Dodge), The Puritan myth and the Indian in the early American novel, Pembroke Mag, Summer 76; Pudd'nhead Wilson: A search for identity, Mark Twain J, Summer 77; Hamlin Garland, Twayne, 78; Hamlin Garland's romantic fiction, In: Critical Essays on Hamlin Garland, G K Hall, 82; Selected Letters of Hamlin Govland, co-ed with Keith Newlin, U of Neb Press, 98; auth, The Bible According to Mark Twain, co-ed, Howard Baetzhold, U. of Georgia Press; auth, Mark Twain at the Buffalo Express, co-ed, Janice McIntire-Strasburg, Northern Illinois U. Press. **CONTACT ADDRESS** Dept of English, Univ of Nevada, Las Vegas, PO Box 455011, Las Vegas, NV 89154-5011. **EMAIL** JoeMcc@nevada.edu

MCCUTCHEON, ELIZABETH NORTH
PERSONAL Born 11/13/1932, New York, NY, m, 1959, 2 children **DISCIPLINE** ENGLISH LITERATURE **EDUCATION** William Smith Col, BA, 54; Univ Wis, MA, 56, PhD(English), 61. **CAREER** From asst prof to assoc prof, 66-74, Prof English, Univ Hawall, 74-95; prof Emeritus; Guggenheim fel, 79-80. **HONORS AND AWARDS** DHL, Hobart & William Smith Col, 80. **MEMBERSHIPS** MLA; Bibliog Soc Eng; Renaissance Soc Am; Amici Thomae Mori; Int Asn Neo-Latin Studies. **RESEARCH** English literature of the 16th and 17th centuries; Neo-Latin literature; rhetoric. **SELECTED PUBLICATIONS** Auth, Lancelot Andrewes' Preces Privatae: A journey through time, Studies Philol, 68; Thomas More, Raphael Hythlodaeus, and the Angel Raphael, Studies English Lit, 69; Denying the contrary: More's use of litotes in the Utopia, Moreana, 71; Bacon and the Cherubim: An iconographical reading of the New Atlantis, English Lit Renaissance, 72; Sir Nicholas Bacon's Great House Sententiae (Latin text with first English transl & introd, notes and bibliog), English Lit Renaissance Suppl No 3, 77; Recent studies in Andrewes, Eng Lit Renaissance, 81; The Apple of My Eye: Thomas More to Antonio Bonvisi: A Reading and a Translation, Moreana, 81; My Dear Peter: More's Ars Poetica and Hermeneutics for Utopia, Angers, France, 82. **CONTACT ADDRESS** Dept of English, Univ of Hawaii, Manoa, 1733 Donaghho Rd, Honolulu, HI 96822-2368. **EMAIL** mccutch@aloha.net

MCDANIEL, GERALD
PERSONAL Born 10/09/1945, Wichita Falls, TX, s **DISCIPLINE** ENGLISH **EDUCATION** Midwestern State Univ, BA, 66; MA, 68; Univ Tex at Austin, PhD, 76. **CAREER** Prof, E Tex State Univ, 68-71; prof, McMurry Univ, 76-93; prof, N Central Tex Col, 93-. **HONORS AND AWARDS** NEH Fel, Univ NC Chapel Hill, 83; Outstanding Teacher Awd, McMurry Univ, 83; Outstanding Teacher Awd, N Central Tex Col, 95. **MEMBERSHIPS** Thomas Lovell Beddues Int Soc. **RESEARCH** Nineteenth-Century British Literature and History, Twentieth-Century American (Southern) Literature History. **SELECTED PUBLICATIONS** Coauth, Leigh Hunt: A Comprehensive Bibliography, Garland Press, 85. **CONTACT ADDRESS** Dept Commun, No Central Texas Col, 1525 W California St, Gainesville, TX 76240-4636. **EMAIL** gmcdanie@nctc.cc.tx.us

MCDANIEL, REBECCA M.
DISCIPLINE ENGLISH, COMMUNICATION **EDUCATION** Ball State Univ, BS, 71; MA, 72. **CAREER** Adjunct Instr of English, Univ of Cincinnati, 72-73; Instr of English and Speech, 73-77; Asst Prof of English & Speech, 77-91; Assoc Prof of English & Communication 91-. **MEMBERSHIPS** National Communication Assoc. **RESEARCH** Cross Cultural Nonverbal Communication. **SELECTED PUBLICATIONS** Auth, "Scared Speechless: Public speaking step by step," by McDaniel, Rebecca, sage Publications Inc.: Thousand Oaks, CA; auth, "Simplified Sentence Skills," by Hansen, Barbara and Rebecca McDaniel, Lincolnwood: Natural Textbook Company. **CONTACT ADDRESS** Dept English, Univ of Cincinnati, Raymond Walters Col, 9555 Plainfield Rd, Cincinnati, OH 45236-1007. **EMAIL** mcdanirm@urwcu.rwc.uc.edu

MCDERMOTT, DOUGLAS
PERSONAL Born 09/25/1936, Los Angeles, CA, m, 1958, 6 children **DISCIPLINE** DRAMATIC ART **EDUCATION** Pomona Col, AB, 58; Univ NC, MA, 60; Univ Iowa, PhD(drama), 63. **CAREER** From asst to assoc prof dramatic art, Univ Calif, Davis, 63-70; Prof Drama, Calif State Univ, Stanislaus, 70-00. **MEMBERSHIPS** Am Soc Theatre Res. **RESEARCH** 19th century American and British theatre history. **SELECTED PUBLICATIONS** Auth, The Impact of Working Conditions Upon Acting Style, Theatre Res Int, vol 0020, 95. **CONTACT ADDRESS** Dept of Drama, California State Univ, Stanislaus, Turlock, CA 95380. **EMAIL** mcdermott@charter.net

MCDONALD, KELLY M.
PERSONAL Born 10/28/1970, Auburn, WA, s **DISCIPLINE** COMMUNICATION STUDIES **EDUCATION** Kansas Univ PhD 98. **CAREER** Kansas Univ, grad tchg asst, 94-97; Western Washington Univ, asst prof, 97-. **MEMBERSHIPS** AFA; ASR; CSSA; ICA; NCA. **RESEARCH** Criticism; political communication; argumentation and persuasion. **SELECTED PUBLICATIONS** Auth, Getting the Story Right: The Role of Narrative in Academic Debate, coauth, Rostrom, 98; auth, Extending the Conversation: Continuity and Change with Debate and Forensics Organizations Entering the 21st Century, Argumentation and Advocacy, 96; auth, Arguing Across Spheres: The Impact of Electronic LISTSERV'S on the Public Sphere Argument, coauth, Proceedings of the Ninth SCA/AFA Conf on Argumentation, 95. **CONTACT ADDRESS** Dept of Communication, Western Washington Univ, Bellingham, WA 98225-9102. **EMAIL** kmmcdon@cc.wwu.edu

MCDONALD, MARIANNE
PERSONAL Born 01/02/1937, Chicago, IL, 6 children **DISCIPLINE** THEATRE **EDUCATION** Bryn Mawr Univ, BA, 58; Univ Chicago, MA, 60; Univ Calif Irvine, PhD, 75. **CAREER** Teaching asst, Univ Calif Irvine, 72-75; adj assoc prof to prof, Univ Calif Irvine, 90-; vis prof, Univ Ulster, 97; vis prof, Univ Cork, 99-; **HONORS AND AWARDS** Ellen Browning Scripps Humanitarian Award, 75; Distinguished Serv Award, Univ Calif Irvine, 82; Philanthropist of the Year, 85; Irvine Medal, Univ Calif, 87; Third Prize, Midwest Poetry Center Contest, 87; Woman of the Year, AHEPA, 88; Bravissimo Gold Medal, San Diego Opera, 90; Woman of Distinction, San Diego, 90; Woman of the Year, Am Biographical Asn, 90; Gold Medal, Soc for the Internationalization of the Greek lang, 90; Gold Medal, Mayor of Athens, 91; Gold Medal, Mayor of Piraeus, 91; Woman of the Year, 91; Acad of Achievement Award, AHEPA, 92; Most Admired Woman of the Decade, Am Biographical Inst, 92; Hypatia Award, Hellenic Asn of Univ Women, 93; Intl Order of Merit, 93; Civis Universitatis Award, Univ Calif San Diego, 93; Woman of Delphi Award, 93; Am Ireland Fund Heritage Award, 94; Volunteer of the Year, Women's Intl Center, 94; God medal, Delphi, 95; Education Award, San Diego Bus J, 95; Alexander the Great Award, Hellenic Cultural Soc, 95; Gold Star Award, San Diego Arts League, 97; Eschilo d'Oro Award, Instituto Nazionale del Dramma Antico, 98; Fulbright Fel, 99; Ellis Island Award, New York, 99; Spirit of Scripps Award, 99; Medal for Distinguished Serv, Am Philol Asn, 99; Am Hellenic Coun Award, 00; KPBS Patte Award, 01; Distinguished Alumni and Friends Leadership Award, Univ Calif Irvine, 01. **MEMBERSHIPS** Am Philol Asn; MLA: Am Sch of Class Studies; Royal Irish Acad. **RESEARCH** Plays; Filma; Operas based on the classics; Irish studeis; South Africa: Work of Athol Fugard. **SELECTED PUBLICATIONS** Auth, Ancient Sun, Modern Light: Greek Drama on the Modern Stage, Columbia Univ Press, 92; auth, "Elektra's Kleos Aphthition: Sophokles into Opera," in Modern Critical Theory and Classical Literature, (Leiden, 94), 103-126; auth, "Democratic Disenfranchisement: Women Metics and Slaves in Fifth-Century Athens," in A Challenge to Democracy: Proceedings from a Symposium, Washington, 94; auth, Star Myths: Tales of the Constellations, Michael Friedman Pub Group, 96; auth, "Medea as Politician and Diva: Riding the Dragon into the Future," in Medea: Essays on Medea in Myth, Literature, Philosophy and Art, (Princeton Univ Press, 97), 297-323; auth, "When Despair and History Rhyme: Colonialism and Greek Tragedy," New Hibernia Rev, (97): 57-70; auth, Mythology of the Zodiac: Tales of the Constellations, MetroBooks, 00; auth, "Classics as Celtic Firebrand: Greek Tragedy, Irish Playwrights, and Colonialism," in Theatre Stuff: Critical Essays on Contemporary Irish Theatre, (Carysfort Press, 00), 16-26; auth, "Medea e mobile: The Many Faces of Medea in Opera," in Medea in Performance 1500-2000, (Oxford Unv Press, 00), 100-118. **CONTACT ADDRESS** Dept Theatre and Class, Univ of California, San Diego, PO Box 929, Rancho Santa Fe, CA 92067. **EMAIL** mmcdonald@ucsd.edu

MCDONALD, R.
PERSONAL Born 02/21/1966, New York, NY, m, 1988, 2 children **DISCIPLINE** BRITISH LITERATURE **EDUCATION** Univ Fla, BA, 88; MEd, 89; Univ S Fla, MA, 93; PhD, 97. **CAREER** Asst prof, Utah Valley State Col, 98-. **HONORS AND AWARDS** Harriet & Irving Deer Awd for Excellence; Phi Beta Kappa. **MEMBERSHIPS** MLA; Rocky Mountain MLA; AFL; Nat Counc of Teachers of English; SE Medieval Assoc; Int Congress on Medieval Lit. **RESEARCH** Anglo Saxon Literature, Internet Pedagogy, Medieval Mysticism, Chaucer. **SELECTED PUBLICATIONS** Auth, "The Reve Was a Sclendre Colerik Man", Chaucer's Pilgrims: An Historical Guide to the Pilgrims in the Canterbury Tales, Greenwood, (Westport, CT, 96): 288-99; auth, "Review of S.H. Rigby's Chaucer in Context", In-Between: Essays and Studies in Criticism 6.2 (Sept 97): 175-78; auth, "Chronicles and Annals", Encylop of Med Lit, Greenwood, (Westport, CT), 98; auth, "Exploring Chaucer's Theories of Language: Englyssh Suffissant and Slydengness of Tounge", In Between: Essays and Studies in Criticism 13.1 (Mar 98): 31-48; auth, "Review of Carolyne Larrington's Women and Medieval Writing in Medieval Europe", In-Between: Essays and Studies in Criticism 7.2 (Sept 98): 211-15; auth, "The Christianization of Pagan Myth: Chaucer's Use of Ovid in the Book of the Duchess", Encyclia, 98; auth, "Emma: Reception and Criticism", A Companion to Jane Austen Studies, Greenwood (Westport, CT), 99; auth, "Epic Poetry in the Medieval World", A Companion to Old and Middle English Literature, Greenwood, (Westport, CT), (forthcoming). **CONTACT ADDRESS** Dept English, Utah Valley State Col, 800 W University Pky, Orem, UT 87097-8295. **EMAIL** mcdonari@uvsc.edu

MCDONALD, SHEILA
DISCIPLINE ROMANTIC POETRY, BLACK AMERICAN LITERATURE **EDUCATION** SUNY, Stony Brook, PhD. **CAREER** Assoc prof, Long Island Univ, C.W. Post Campus. **SELECTED PUBLICATIONS** Auth, The Impact of Libertinism on Byron's Don Juan. **CONTACT ADDRESS** Long Island Univ, C.W. Post, Brookville, NY 11548-1300.

MCDONALD, VERLAINE
DISCIPLINE COMMUNICATION **EDUCATION** Seattle Pac Univ, BA, 87; USC, MA, 93; Univ Southern Calif, PhD, 94. **CAREER** Asst Prof, Seattle Pac Univ, 94-95; Asst Prof, Berea Col, 95-. **MEMBERSHIPS** Nat Commun Asn; Southern States Commun Asn. **RESEARCH** Rhetorical theory & criticism; the history of American Communism. **CONTACT ADDRESS** Berea Col, CPO 1333, Berea, KY 40404-0001. **EMAIL** verlaine_mcdonald@berea.edu

MCDONALD, WALTER ROBERT
PERSONAL Born 07/18/1934, Lubbock, TX, m, 1959, 3 children **DISCIPLINE** ENGLISH **EDUCATION** Tex Technol Col, BA, 56, MA, 57; Univ Iowa, PhD(English) 66. **CAREER** Instr English, US Air Force Acad, 60-62 & 65-66, from asst prof to assoc prof, 66-71; assoc prof, 71-75, Prof English, Tex

Tech Univ, 75-87, lectr, Univ Colo, 67-69; horn prof of Eng, 87-. **HONORS AND AWARDS** Texas Prof of the Year, CASE, 92; Four National Cowboy Hall of Fame's Western Heritage Award for All That Matters; Ohio State Univ Press/The Journal Award for Blessings the Body Gave, 98; Tex State Poet Laureate, 01. **MEMBERSHIPS** MLA; The Texas Instit of Letters; Western Writers of America; PEN; Assoc Writing Progs; Texas Assoc of Creative Writing Teachers. **RESEARCH** Creative Writing; modern Am fiction and poetry. **SELECTED PUBLICATIONS** Auth, A Band of Brothers: Stories from Vietnam, Texas Tech; auth, Whatever the Wind Delivers: Celebrating West Texas and the Near Southwest, Tex Tech Univ Press; auth, After the Noise of Saigon, Massachusetts; autah, Night Landings, Harper & Row; auth, Counting Survivors, Pittsburgh; auth, Blessings the Body Gave, Ohio State; auth, All Occasions, Univ of Notre Dame Press, 00. **CONTACT ADDRESS** Dept of English, Texas Tech Univ, Lubbock, TX 79409-3091. **EMAIL** walt.mcdonald@ttu.edu

MCDONNELL, CLARE I.

PERSONAL Born 02/07/1920, Philadelphia, PA **DISCIPLINE** ENGLISH **EDUCATION** Catholic Univ, MA, 57; Penn State Univ, Mhum, 78; Hon PhD, 98. **CAREER** Fac, Neumann Col, 84-; Franciscan Scholar in Res, Neumann Inst, 94-. **HONORS AND AWARDS** NEH Fels, Fordam Univ, Georgetown Univ, Univ Md, Haverford Univ, Univ Tenn, Princeton Univ; Res Scholar, St. Deniol's Libr of Wales. **RESEARCH** Medieval and renaissance art and literature, Franciscan studies. **SELECTED PUBLICATIONS** Auth, The Cord, Neumann Col Accent Publ, Delta Epsilon Sigma J. **CONTACT ADDRESS** Dept Arts and Sci, Nuemann Col, One Neumann Dr, Aston, PA 19014-1298. **EMAIL** cmcdonne@smtpgate.neumann.edu

MCDONOUGH, ANN

DISCIPLINE THEATRE **EDUCATION** Univ Minn, PhD. **CAREER** Hd, sr adult theatre prog, Univ Nev, Las Vegas; Director of Gerontology and Head of Senior Adult Theatre. **SELECTED PUBLICATIONS** Auth, The Golden Stage: Dramatic Activities For Older Adults, Kendall-Hunt Publ, 95; auth, "New Monologues for Mature Actors, 95, Dramatic Publishing Co.; auth, "Ten to Twenty Minute Plays for Mature Actors, 98, Dramatic Publishing; auth, "A Grand Entrance: Scenes and Monologues for Mature Actors, 00, Dramatic Publishing Co. **CONTACT ADDRESS** Univ of Nevada, Las Vegas, Las Vegas, NV 89154. **EMAIL** mcdonoua@nevada.edu

MCDONOUGH, C. J.

PERSONAL Born 04/10/1942, United Kingdom, m, 1967, 2 children **DISCIPLINE** CLASSICS **EDUCATION** Univ Col London, BA, 63, MA, 65; Univ Toronto, PhD, 68. **CAREER** Prof, Univ Toronto, 67- **MEMBERSHIPS** APA, Medieval Acad Am. **RESEARCH** Latin satire; medieval latin lit; textual criticism and editing. **SELECTED PUBLICATIONS** ed, Warner of Rouen, Pims, 95. **CONTACT ADDRESS** Dept of Classics, Univ of Toronto, 97 St. George St., Toronto, ON, Canada M5S 2E8. **EMAIL** mcdonough@trinity.utoronto.ca

MCDOUGALL, WARREN

DISCIPLINE ENGLISH **EDUCATION** Western Ontario, BA; Edinburgh, PhD. **CAREER** HON FELL, ENG LIT, EDINBURGH. **MEMBERSHIPS** Am Antiquarian Soc

MCDOWELL, EARL E.

PERSONAL Born 05/06/1942, Columbus, OH, m, 1973, 2 children **DISCIPLINE** RHETORIC STUDIES **EDUCATION** WVa Univ, MA; Univ Nebr, PhD. **CAREER** Prof **MEMBERSHIPS** STC; NCN; CSCA; NACTA. **RESEARCH** Technical communication apprehension; technical communication programs; employment cycle interviewing; conflict; gender and psychological sex. **SELECTED PUBLICATIONS** Auth, Interviewing Practices for Technical Writers, Baywood, 91; Research in Scientific and Technical Communication, Burgess Int, 93; Scientific and Technical Communicators' Perceptions of the Performance Appraisal Interview, J Tech Writing Commun, 95; co-auth, An Exploratory Study of the Communication Behaviors of Japanese and US College Students, 97. **CONTACT ADDRESS** Rhetoric Dept, Univ of Minnesota, Twin Cities, 64 Classroom Office Bldg, 1994 Buford Ave, Saint Paul, MN 55108. **EMAIL** mcdow0012@mail.umin.edu

MCDOWELL, FREDERICK PETER WOLL

PERSONAL Born 05/29/1915, Philadelphia, PA, m, 1953, 5 children **DISCIPLINE** ENGLISH **EDUCATION** Univ Pa, BS, 37, MA, 38; Harvard Univ, PhD(English), 49. **CAREER** Instr English, Washington & Jefferson Col, 38-39 & Univ Del, 39-41; from instr to assoc prof, 49-63, Prof English, Univ Iowa, 63-, exchange prof, Universite Paul Valery, Montpellier, France, 80-81; Emer, 85-. **HONORS AND AWARDS** Nat Endowment for Humanities sr fel, 73-74. **MEMBERSHIPS** MLA; Ellen Glasgow Soc (pres, 77); Virginia Woolf Soc; Joseph Conrad Soc; Am Shaw Soc. **RESEARCH** British and American literature since 1850; George Bernard Shaw; Bloomsbury group. **SELECTED PUBLICATIONS** Auth, Heartbreak House--Preludes and Apocalypse, Engl Lit in Transition 1880-1920, vol 0038, 95; 'Pygmalion'--Shaw Spin on Myth and Cinderella, Engl Lit in Transition 1880-1920, vol 0039, 96. **CONTACT ADDRESS** Univ of Iowa, 3801 Grand Ave, Apt 301, Des Moines, IA 50312-2845.

MCELRATH, JOSEPH R., JR.

PERSONAL Born 06/10/1945, Jesup, GA, m, 1966, 2 children **DISCIPLINE** ENGLISH **EDUCATION** LeMoyne Col, BA, 67; Duquesne Univ, MA, 69; Univ of South Carolina, PhD, 73. **CAREER** Asst Prof, 73-74, SUNY; Asst Prof, 74-77, Assoc Prof, 77-81, Prof, 81-00, Florida St Univ.; William Hudson Rogers Prof. 00. **HONORS AND AWARDS** John Frederick Lewis Awd of the Amer Philos Soc, 96; Lyman H. Butterfield Awd of the Assoc for Documentary; Editing, 98; Sylvia Lyons Render Awd of the Charles Waddell Chesnutt Assoc, 99 **MEMBERSHIPS** Stephen Crane Soc; Frank Norris Soc; Assoc for Documentary Editing; Soc for Textual Scholarship; Charles Waddel Chesnutt Assoc **RESEARCH** Amer lit 1870-1910. **SELECTED PUBLICATIONS** Auth, Frank Norris Revisited, Twayne, 92; auth, Frank Norris A Descriptive Bibliography, Univ of Pit Press, 92; auth, John Steinbeck The Contemporary Reviews, Cambridge Univ Press, 96; auth, The Apprenticieship Writings of Frank Norris, Amer Philosophical Soc, 96; auth, To Be An Author: Letters of Charles W Chesnutt, Princeton Univ Press, 97; auth, Charles W. Chesnutt: Essays and Speeches, Stanford Univ Press, 99; auth, Critical Essays on Charles W. Chesnutt, Hall, 99. **CONTACT ADDRESS** Florida State Univ, Dept of English, Tallahassee, FL 32306. **EMAIL** jmcelrath@english.fsu.edu

MCELREATH, MARK

DISCIPLINE COMMUNICATION, PUBLIC RELATIONS **EDUCATION** Univ Wis, Madison, PhD, 75. **CAREER** Instr, fac adv, PR Gp, Towson Univ; ed bd, J of PR Res. **MEMBERSHIPS** Hd, Ethics Comt, Int Asn of Bus Communicators. **SELECTED PUBLICATIONS** Auth, The Management of Systematic Ethical Public Relations Campaigns. **CONTACT ADDRESS** Towson State Univ, Towson, MD 21252-0001. **EMAIL** mmcelreath@towson.edus

MCELROY, COLLEEN J.

PERSONAL Born 10/30/1935, St Louis, MO, d **DISCIPLINE** ENGLISH **EDUCATION** Kansas State Univ, Manhattan KS, BS, 1958, MS, 1963; Univ of Washington, Seattle WA, PhD, 1973. **CAREER** Rehabilitation Inst, Kansas City MO, chief, Speech & Hearing Serv, 63-66; Western Washington Univ, Bellingham WA, asst prof, Speech, 66-74; Univ of Washington, Seattle WA, supvr, EOP Composition, 72-83, dir, Creative Writing, 84-87, prof of English, 83-. **HONORS AND AWARDS** NEA Creative Writing Fellowship for Poetry, 1978; Fiction 1st place, Callalvo Magazine, 1981; Poetry 1st place, Cincinnati Poetry R, 1983; Creative Writing Residency, MacDowell Colony, New Hampshire, 1984, 1986; Before Columbus Amer Book Awd, 1985; Women of Achievement, Theta Sigma Phi, 1985; Creative Writing Residency Yugoslavia, Fulbright Fellowship, 1988; Washington State Governor's Awd for Fiction and Poetry, 1988; NEA Creative Writing Fellowship for Fiction, 1991; Rockefeller Fellowship to Bellagio Institute, Lake Como, Italy, 1991; DuPont Distinguished Scholar in Residence, Hollins College, Virginia, 1992; Fulbright Research Fellowship, Madagascar, 1993; Arts America, Jordan & Morocco, 1996. **MEMBERSHIPS** Mem, Writers Guild of Amer East, 1978-, Dramatists Guild, 1986-, PEN Writers, 1989-; member, Author's Guild, 1989-; member, Writer's Union, 1989-. **SELECTED PUBLICATIONS** The Wild Gardens of the Loup Garou, 1983; Queen of the Ebony Isles, 1984; Jesus and Fat Tuesday, 1987; Follow the Drinking Gourd, 1987; Driving Under the Cardboard Pines, 1990; What Madness Brought Me Here, 1990; A Long Way from St Louie, 1997; auth, Travelling Music, 98; auth, Over the Lip of the World, 99. **CONTACT ADDRESS** Professor of English, Univ of Washington, Seattle, WA 98109.

MCELROY, JOHN HARMON

PERSONAL Born 03/28/1934, Parker's Landing, PA, m, 1957, 4 children **DISCIPLINE** AMERICAN LITERATURE **EDUCATION** Princeton Univ, AB, 56; Duke Univ, MA, 62, PhD(Am lit), 66. **CAREER** Instr English, Punahou Sch, 58-60; asst prof Am lit, Univ Wis-Madison, 66-70; from asst prof to assoc prof, 70-76, Prof Am Lit, Univ Ariz, 76-, Fulbright lectr Am lit, Univ Salamanca, 68-69. **MEMBERSHIPS** MLA; Melville Soc; Poe Soc. **RESEARCH** Textual criticism; literary criticism; American literature, 1760-1860. **CONTACT ADDRESS** Dept of English, Univ of Arizona, 1 University of Az, Tucson, AZ 85721-0001. **EMAIL** jmcelroy@u.arizona.edu

MCFAGUE, SALLIE

PERSONAL Born 05/25/1933, Quincy, MA **DISCIPLINE** THEOLOGY, RELIGION AND LITERATURE **EDUCATION** Smith Col, BA, 55; Yale Divinity Sch, BD, 59; Yale Grad Sch, PhD(theol), 64. **CAREER** Asst prof, 72-75, dean, 75-79, assoc prof, 75-79, Prof Theol, Vanderbilt Divinity Sch, 80-. Ed, Soundings, 67-75; Nat Endowment for Humanities fel, Oxford, 80-81. **MEMBERSHIPS** Am Acad Relig; Soc Values Higher Educ; Soc Arts, Relig & Contemp Cult; Am Theol Soc. **RESEARCH** Religious language; contemporary theology, religion and literature. **SELECTED PUBLICATIONS** Auth, Barbour, Ian--Theologians Friend, Scientists Interpreter, Zygon, vol 0031, 96; The Loving Eye Versus the Arrogant Eye--Christian Critique of the Western Gaze on Nature and the Third World, Ecumenical Rev, vol 0049, 97. **CONTACT ADDRESS** Vanderbilt Univ, 221 Kirkland Hall, Nashville, TN 37232.

MCFARLAND, DOUGLAS D.

PERSONAL Born 07/18/1946, Portland, OR, m, 1973, 4 children **DISCIPLINE** LAW, SPEECH **EDUCATION** Macalester Col, BA, 68; NY Univ, JD, 71; Univ Minn, PhD, 83. **CAREER** Lawyer, Dorsey & Whitney, 71-74; prof Hamline Univ, 74-; admin asst to Chief Justice, Supreme Court of US, 84-86. **HONORS AND AWARDS** Phi Beta Kappa; Professor of the Year (2). **RESEARCH** Civil procedure, evidence. **SELECTED PUBLICATIONS** Coauth, Minnesota Civil Practice, 79; "Diversity Jurisdiction: Is There Fear of Local Prejudice?, 7 Lit 38, Fall 80; auth, "Lerias: A Socratic Dialogue", 67 ABAJ 867, 81; auth, "Dead Men Tell Tales: Thirty Times Three Year of the Judicial Process After Hillmon", 30 Vill L. Rev 1, 85; auth, "Self-Images of Law Professors: Rethinking the Schism in Legal Education, 35 J. Legal Educ 232, 85; auth, "Students and Practicing Lawyers Identify the Ideal Law Professor", 36 J. Legal Educ 93, 86; coauth, "The Need for a New National Court,", 100 Harv L Rev 1400, 87; auth, "The Unconstitutional Stub of 1441¤", 54 Ohio St LJ 1059 (93); auth, "Chief Justice Warren E. Burger: A Personal Tribute", 19 Hamline L. Rev 1, 95. **CONTACT ADDRESS** School of Law, Hamline Univ, 1536 Hewitt Ave, Saint Paul, MN 55104-1205. **EMAIL** dmcfarland@gw.hamline.edu

MCFARLAND, KATHARINE

PERSONAL Born 11/17/1952, Baltimore, MD, s **DISCIPLINE** ENGLISH **EDUCATION** NC Wesleyan Col, BA, 74; Towson State Univ, MA, 82; Tex A & M Univ, PhD, 92. **CAREER** Vis Fac, Sam Houston state Univ, 94-95; Lecturer and Supervisor, Tex A & M Univ, 95-97; Asst Prof, Shippensburg Univ, 97-. **MEMBERSHIPS** Phi Delta Kappa; Nat Coun of Teachers of English, Penn Coun of Teachers of English Lang Arts, Nat Asn of Teachers of English to Speakers of Other Lang, Nat Asn of Multicultural Educ, Nat Coun of Teacher Educators. **RESEARCH** Secondary literacy; Teacher-as-researcher; reading and writing across the curriculum. **SELECTED PUBLICATIONS** Auth, "A Quick History and Some Gentle guidelines for a Teacher-as-Researcher Project," ERIC Document Reproduction Service, forthcoming; auth, "Student Teacher Portfolios: Choose Three Goals," ERIC Document Reproduction Service, forthcoming; auth, "Student Teachers as Reflective Practitioner in Facilitating change," ERIC Document Reproduction Service, forthcoming; auth, "Designing an Effective Action research Project in the Language Arts classroom," Penn State Univ, 97; auth, "Procedures for comprehensible Input for Limited English Proficient Students," ERIC Document Reproduction Service, forthcoming; auth, "Language Acquisition & development for bilingual/ESL Programs," ERIC Document Reproduction Service, 96; auth, "student Research papers: Instead of One, Assign Seven!," Across-the writing program Newsletter, 94; co-auth, "The Teacher as Researcher: Historical perspectives," in Teachers Are Researchers: reflection in action, 93; co-auth, "Using Qualitative Observation to Document Group Processes in Accelerated Schools Training: Techniques and Results," ERIC Document Reproduction Service, 92; auth, "Case Studies of the dialogue Journal in Multicultural Education, ERIC Document Reproduction Service, 92. **CONTACT ADDRESS** Dept English, Shippensburg Univ of Pennsylvania, 1871 Old Main Dr, Shippensburg, PA 17257-2200. **EMAIL** kpmcfa@ship.edu

MCFARLAND, RONALD E.

PERSONAL Born 01/29/1942, Bellaire, OH, m, 1966, 3 children **DISCIPLINE** ENGLISH & AMERICAN LITERATURE; CREATIVE WRITING **EDUCATION** Brevard Jr Col, AA, 62; FSU, BA, 63; MA, 65; Univ of Ill, PhD, 70. **CAREER** Instr, Sam Houston State Col, 65-67; asst prof to prof, Univ of ID, 70-; exchange prof, OH Univ, 85-86. **HONORS AND AWARDS** Univ ID Lib Fac Awd, 84; Idaho State Writer-in-Residence, 84-85; Burlington-Northern Fac Achievement Awd, 90; Alumni Awd for Fac Excellence, 91; Distinguished Alumnus, Brevard CC, 96; Student Orgn Adv Awd, 98. **MEMBERSHIPS** Hemingway Soc, Pac NW Am Studies Asn, Acad of Am Poets; Soc, Pac NW Am Studies Assoc. **SELECTED PUBLICATIONS** Auth, David Wagoner, Western Writers Series, 89; auth, The Haunting Familiarity of Things, Singular Speech, 93; auth, Norman Maclean, Western Writers Series, 93; auth, Tess Gallagher, Western Writers Series, 95; auth, The World of David Wagoner, Univ of ID, 97; auth, Ballgloves, Polo Grounds, 00; auth, The Mad Waitress Poems, Permafrost, 00; auth, The Hemingway Poems, Pecan Grove, 00; auth, Stranger in Town: New & Selected Poems, Confluence, 00. **CONTACT ADDRESS** Dept English, Univ of Idaho, 375 S Line St, Moscow, ID 83844-1102. **EMAIL** ronmcf@uidaho.edu

MCGEE, CHRISTOPHER EDWARD

DISCIPLINE ENGLISH LITERATURE **EDUCATION** Univ Toronto, BA; MA; PhD. **CAREER** Assoc prof, St. Jerome's Univ. **HONORS AND AWARDS** Sir Bertram Windle Gold Medal in Eng, Univ of Toronto, 71; Open Fel and Ontario Government Scholarship, Univ of Toronto, 75; Nominated Distinguished Teacher Awd, Univ of Waterloo, 81. **SELECTED PUBLICATIONS** Auth, Strangest consequence from remotest cause: The Second Performance of The Triumph of Peace; The Visit of the Nine Goddesses: A masque at Sir John Crofts' House; A Canadian Reports on the Stratford Festival (rev); A Matter of Time (rev); ABCs of ABCs: Two Canadian Exemplars; Against the Stream (rev); An Entertainment for Elizabeth I at Greenwich; The Elizabethan Theatre X, XI, XII, XIII; The Elizabethan Theatre XIV: (Women and the Elizabethan Theatre). **CONTACT ADDRESS** Dept of English, St. Jerome's Univ, Waterloo, ON, Canada N2L 3G3. **EMAIL** cemcgee@watarts.uwaterloo.ca

MCGEEVER, KATHLEEN
PERSONAL Born Bakersfield, CA **DISCIPLINE** THEATRE, STAGE DIRECTION **EDUCATION** San Diego State Univ, BA, 81; Sand Diego State Univ, Teaching Credential, 86; Humboldt State Univ, MFA, 96. **CAREER** Grad asst, Humboldt State Univ, 93-96; Vis instr, N Ariz Univ, 96-98; asst prof, Univ of Montevallo, 98-. **HONORS AND AWARDS** Fac Dev Grant; Grad Equity Fel; Skull & Dagger Hon Soc; Outstanding Young Woman of Am; John Van Duzer Fel; Phi Kappa Phi Pres Scholars and Artists Awd; John & Ethelyn Paulley Fel; Irene Ryan Nomination. **MEMBERSHIPS** ATHE; ATA; ETA; ACTS; Phi Kappa Phi; Alpha Psi Omega; TCAP; CETA; SCETA. **RESEARCH** New Play development; Virtual Technology. **SELECTED PUBLICATIONS** Auth, "Exiles in 'No Man's Land' and 'The Caretaker' A Comparison of Two of Pinter's Tramps," Cycnos 14(April 97). **CONTACT ADDRESS** Dept Commun Arts, Univ of Montevallo, Div of Theatre, PO Box 6000, Montevallo, AL 35115-6000. **EMAIL** mcgeevk@montevallo.edu

MCGHEE, JAMES
PERSONAL 3 children **DISCIPLINE** THEATER **EDUCATION** Montclair State Col, AB; Bowling Green State Univ, PhD. **CAREER** Prof; dir, theater. **SELECTED PUBLICATIONS** Area: critical study of Sam Shepard. **CONTACT ADDRESS** York Col, Pennsylvania, 441 Country Club Road, York, PA 17405-7199.

MCGILLIVRAY, MURRAY D.
PERSONAL Born 07/24/1953, Moose Jaw, SK, m, 1987, 2 children **DISCIPLINE** ENGLISH **EDUCATION** Nova Scotia Col, BFA, 75; McGill Univ, BA, 79; MA, 81; Univ Toronto, PhD, 87. **CAREER** Ed, Concordia Univ, 78-81; lectr, Univ Toronto, 86-87; asst prof, Brock Univ, 87-88; asst prof to assoc prof to dept chmn to prof, Univ Calgary, 88-. **MEMBERSHIPS** CSM; New Chaucer Soc; MLA; MAP. **RESEARCH** Old and Middle English literature; electronic scholarly editing; manuscript studies. **SELECTED PUBLICATIONS** Auth, Memorization in the Transmission of the Middle English Romances, Garland, 90; auth, Electronic Representation of Manuscript Text: Possibilities and Limitations, Univ Toronto Pr, 93; auth, "Creative Anachronism: Marx's Problem With Homer, Gadamer's Discussion of 'The Classical,' and Our Understanding of Older Literatures," New Lit Hist (94); auth, "Towards a Post-Critical edition: Hypertext, Theory, and the Presentation of Middle English Works," Text (95); auth, Geoffrey Chaucer's Book of the Duchess: A Hypertext Edition, Univ Calgary Pr, 97, 2nd ed, 99. **CONTACT ADDRESS** English Dept, Univ of Calgary, 2500 University Dr NW, Calgary, AB, Canada T2N 1N4. **EMAIL** mmcgilli@ucalgary.ca

MCGINTY, CAROLYN
PERSONAL Born 01/07/1921, Chicago, IL **DISCIPLINE** LITERARY CRITICISM, AMERICAN LITERATURE **EDUCATION** Loyola Univ Chicago, PhB, 43, MA, 49; Cath Univ Am, PhD(English), 63. **CAREER** From instr to asst prof, 63-75, assoc prof English & chemn dept, Rosary Col, 76-; res dir semester in London, 73, 73-75; consult, Scholastic Testing Serv, Bensenville, IL, 67-. **MEMBERSHIPS** Aaup; Col English Asn; MLA; NCTE. **RESEARCH** Linguistics and stylistics; Henry James' prose style. **CONTACT ADDRESS** Dept of English, Rosary Col, River Forest, IL 60305.

MCGIVERON, RAFEEQ O.
PERSONAL Born 01/29/1967, Lansing, MI, m, 1988, 3 children **DISCIPLINE** ENGLISH **EDUCATION** Mich State Univ, BA, 89; MA, 92. **CAREER** Instr, Mich State Univ, 89-91; Instr and fac adv, Lansing CC, 92-. **MEMBERSHIPS** Popular Culture Asn **RESEARCH** Modern American literature, Willa Cather, science fiction. **SELECTED PUBLICATIONS** Auth, "'The Patterns of' Lowell's 'Patterns'," The Explicator 55 (97): 142-144; auth, "'Do You Know the Legend of Hercules and Antaeus?' The Wilderness in Ray Bradbury's "Fahrenheit 451,"" Extrapolation 38 (97): 102-109; auth, "A Relationship . . . More than Six Inches Deep': Lust and Love in Silverberg's Science Fiction," Extrapolation 39 (98): 40-51; auth, "'To Build a Mirror Factory': The Mirror and Self-Examination in Ray Bradbury's "Fahrenheit 451,"" Critique: Studies in Contemporary Fiction 39 (98): 282-287; auth, "'Social Disconnection in' Yellen's "Nighthawks,"" The Explicator 56 (98): 148-149; auth, "'Names in' Huxley's "Brave New World,"" The Explicator 57 (98): 27-30; auth, "Starry-Eyed Internationalists' versus the Social Darwinists: Heinlein's Transnational Governments," Extrapolation 40 (99): 53-70; auth, "From a 'Stretch of Grey Sea' to the 'Extent of Space': The Gaze across Vistas in Cather's "The Professor's House,"" W Am Lit 34 (00): 388-408. **CONTACT ADDRESS** Dept Humanities, Lansing Comm Col, PO Box 40010, Lansing, MI 48901-7210.

MCGLINN, JEANNE
PERSONAL Born 10/06/1948, Chicago, IL, m, 1973, 3 children **DISCIPLINE** ENGLISH **EDUCATION** Clarke Col, BA, 70; Univ Kans, MA, 72; PhD, 79. **CAREER** Instr, Ottawa Univ, 79; instr, Baker Univ, 80; adj instr, Ottawa Univ, 83; lectr, Univ of Kans, 79-84; adj asst prof to assoc prof, Univ NC Asheville, 84-. **HONORS AND AWARDS** Univ Res Counc Fel, 88; Grant, Distinguished Vis Scholars Prog, 91; Grant, NC School-Based Res Prog, 93-94; Grant, UNCA, 94, 95. **MEMBERSHIPS** IRA; NCTE; ALAN; LESIG; NCIRA; Smoky Mt Counc of IRA. **RESEARCH** Adolescent literature, multicultural literature, teacher preparation, methods of teaching. **SELECTED PUBLICATIONS** Auth, "Their Own Story: Literature for African American Children", Reading Horizons 34.4, (94): 208-215; coauth, "Teachers' Knowledge of African American Children's Literature: A Case Study", Reading Instruction J (95): 15-20; auth, "Power Books: Literature for African American Boys", Book Links (Jan 96): 21-23; auth, "The Impact of Title IX on Women's Education and Athletics", Ready Ref, Women's Issues, ed Margaret McFadden, Salem Pr, (97): 868-870; auth, "Working for Change Within the Elementary School: A Staff Development Case Study", NC J of Teacher Educ, IX.2 (98): 70-79; auth, "Teaching in Ecuador and Its Impact on Literacy", Literacy: Issues and Practices, 98; coauth, A Teacher's Guide to the signet Classic Edition of Shakespeare's Richard III, Penguin, 98; auth, Ann Rinaldi: Historian and Storyteller, Scarecrow, 00; auth, Teacher's Guide to the Signet Classic Edition of As You Like it, Penguin, 00; auth, Teacher's Guide to the Novels of Ann Rinaldi, Scholastic, 00. **CONTACT ADDRESS** Dept Educ, Univ of No Carolina, Asheville, 1 University Heights, Asheville, NC 28804-3251. **EMAIL** jmcglinn@unca.edu

MCGLONE, EDWARD L.
PERSONAL Born 09/20/1941, Athens, OH **DISCIPLINE** COMMUNICATION STUDIES **EDUCATION** Univ Ohio, BA, PhD. **CAREER** Prof, 87-. **HONORS AND AWARDS** Outstanding Young Tchr Awd; Paideia Awd; **MEMBERSHIPS** Central States Commun Asn; Speech Commun Asn. **SELECTED PUBLICATIONS** Auth, pubs on communication theory and interpersonal communication. **CONTACT ADDRESS** Div of Communcation and Theatre Arts, Emporia State Univ, 1200 Commercial St, Emporia, KS 66801-5087. **EMAIL** mcglonee@emporia.edu

MCGLYNN, PAUL DUMON
PERSONAL Born 07/11/1937, Detroit, MI, m, 1963, 2 children **DISCIPLINE** ENGLISH **EDUCATION** Univ Detroit, PhB, 59, MA, 61; Rice Univ, PhD, 67. **CAREER** Instr Eng, Univ Detroit, 61-62; from instr to assoc prof, 64-77, Prof Eng, Eastern MI Univ, 77. **MEMBERSHIPS** MLA; Midwestern Mod Lang Asn. **RESEARCH** Eighteenth century Brit lit; the novel; cinema; Irish lit. **SELECTED PUBLICATIONS** Auth, Orthodoxy versus anarchy in Sterne's Sentimental Journey, Papers on Lang & Lit, summer 71; Point of view and the craft of cinema: Notes on some devices, J Aesthet & Art Criticism, winter 73; Rhetoric as metaphor in The Vanity of Huamn Wishes, Studies English Lit, summer 75; since 1987, a published poet. Over 200 poems in over 92 journals in the U.S., Canada, and Great Britain, including Chiron Rev, Bouillabaisse, Windsor Rev, Sepia, Poetry Motel, and Santa Barbara Rev. **CONTACT ADDRESS** Dept of Eng, Eastern Michigan Univ, 612 Pray Harrold, Ypsilanti, MI 48197-2201. **EMAIL** eng_mcglynn@online.emich.edu

MCGOWAN, JOHN P.
PERSONAL Born 07/21/1953, Rockville Centre, NY, m, 1984, 2 children **DISCIPLINE** ENGLISH, COMPARATIVE LITERATURE **EDUCATION** Georgetown Univ, AB, 74; SUNY at Buffalo, PhD, 78. **CAREER** Asst prof, Univ of Mich, 79-82; ed asst, Univ of Calif Pr, 83-84; asst prof to assoc prof, Univ of Rochester, 84-92; prof, Univ of NC, 92-. **HONORS AND AWARDS** NEH Fel, 89; NEH Seminar, 97; Chapman Family Teaching Awd, Univ NC, 99. **MEMBERSHIPS** MLA. **RESEARCH** Literary Theory, American Pragmatism, Victorian Literature, Political Philosophy. **SELECTED PUBLICATIONS** Auth, Representation and Revelation: Victorian Realism from Carlisle to Yeats, 86; auth, Postmodernism and its Critics; coed, Hannah Arendt and the Meaning of Politics, 91; coed, Hannah Arendt and the Meaning of Politics, 97; auth, Hannah Arendt: An Introduction, 98; coed, Norton Anthology of Theory and Criticism, (forthcoming). **CONTACT ADDRESS** Dept English, Univ of No Carolina, Chapel Hill, CB # 3520, Chapel Hill, NC 27599-3520. **EMAIL** jpm@email.unc.edu

MCGOWAN, JOSEPH P.
DISCIPLINE ENGLISH **EDUCATION** Villanova Univ, BA, 88; Univ PA, PhD, 91. **CAREER** Asst prof, Univ San Diego, 93-; instr, Villanova Univ, 92-93; tchg fel, Univ Pa, 89-92; tchg apprentice, Univ PA, 88-89. **SELECTED PUBLICATIONS** Auth, Anglo-Saxon Manuscripts in Microfiche Facsimile: Legal and Grammatical Manuscripts at London & Oxford, Binghamton, NY:SUNY/Medieval & Renaissance Texts & Stud, 98; More Glosses from Early Medieval English Manuscripts, Notes & Queries, 98; Anglo-Saxon Manuscripts in Microfiche Facsimile, vol 8: Manuscripts in Switzerland, Binghamton, SUNY/Medieval & Renaissance Texts & Stud, 98; Augustine of Ancona, Sermones dominicales, Sermones de sanctis adclerum, Collationes pro defunctis 2 vols, Rome/Villanova:Augustinian Press, 98 & Readings from the Beowulf Manuscript, fols. 94r-98r, the St Christopher folios, Manuscripta, 97; coauth, Four Unedited Prayers from British Library,MS Cotton Tiberius A. iii, Mediaeval Stud 56, 94; rev, Apollonius of Tyre: Medieval and Renaissance Themes and Variations, in J of Medieval Latin 7, 97. **CONTACT ADDRESS** Dept of Eng, Univ of San Diego, 5998 Alcal Park, San Diego, CA 92110-2492. **EMAIL** mcgowan@teetot.acusd.edu

MCGRAIN, JOHN W.
PERSONAL Born 07/25/1931, Baltimore, MD, s **DISCIPLINE** ENGLISH **EDUCATION** Loyola Col, 49. **CAREER** Technical Publ, Bendix Corp, Technical Service Corp DMS-Int, 55-70; County Historian & Hist Preservation Planner, Office of Planning, Baltimore County, Md, 76-98. **MEMBERSHIPS** Soc Archit Hist; Soc Industrial Archeol; Md Hist Soc. **RESEARCH** State and local history; gristmills; industries; agriculture; architecture. **SELECTED PUBLICATIONS** Auth, Lewis Mill Goes to Pottery, Old Mill News, 4/84; Pig Iron/Cotton Duck: The Company Towns of Baltimore County, Baltimore County Public Libr, 85; The Man Who "Invented" Automation, Evening Sun, 5/23/87; The English Consul Mansion and Its Owners, Md Hist Mag, Spring 89; History of Agriculture in Baltimore County, limited edition, Towson Libr & Md Hist Soc, 90; Pig Iron/Cotton Duck, vol 2 (in prep); author of numerous other articles and publications. **CONTACT ADDRESS** Office of Planning, 401 Bosley Ave, Towson, MD 21204. **EMAIL** jmcgrain@co.ba.md.us

MCGRATH, FRANCIS C.
PERSONAL Born 07/22/1942, Malden, MA, 2 children **DISCIPLINE** LITERATURE **EDUCATION** Dartmouth Col, BA, 64; Univ Tex Austin, PhD, 73. **CAREER** Asst prof, Univ Pa, 73-79; asst prof, Rutgers Univ, 79-85; prof to col dean, Univ S Maine, 85-. **HONORS AND AWARDS** Woodrow Wilson Found, 71-72; ACLS, 90. **MEMBERSHIPS** MLA; ACIS; IJJF. **RESEARCH** Irish literature and culture; aesthetics and literary theory; postcolonial literature and theory; 19th and 20th-century British literature. **SELECTED PUBLICATIONS** Auth, The Sensible Spirit: Walter Pater and the Modernist Paradigm, Univ Pr Fla; auth, Brian Friel's (Post) Colonial Drama: Language, Illusion and Politics, Syracuse Univ Pr. **CONTACT ADDRESS** Col Arts Sci, Univ of So Maine, PO Box 9300, Portland, ME 04104-9300. **EMAIL** mcgrath@maine.maine.edu

MCGUIRE, CHARLES
PERSONAL Born 11/24/1969, Minneapolis, MN, m **DISCIPLINE** MUSICOLOGY **EDUCATION** Oberlin Col, BA, 92; Oberlin Conserv, BMus, 92; Harvard Univ, AM, 95; PhD, 98. **CAREER** Vis lectr, Harvard Univ; vis lectr, Univ Md; vis asst prof, Ball State Univ; asst prof, James Madison Univ. **HONORS AND AWARDS** Grad Soc Diss Comp Fellow, 97-98; Pirotta Res Fellow, Summer 97; Harvard Univ Cert Distinction Tchg, 94-96; Oscar Schafer Fellow, 96-97; Ctr Euro Stud Travel Grant, 96; John Knowles Paine Travel Fellow, 95; Thorvald Otterstrom Mem Scholar, 92; Alwin M. Pappenheimer Scholar, 92-93, 96-97; High Honors in Hist, Oberlin Col, 92; Charles Martin Hall Awd, Mus Hist, 92; Arion Awd for Mus Excel, 87. **MEMBERSHIPS** Am Musicol Soc; Col Mus Soc; Elgar Soc. **RESEARCH** 19th and 20th century music, focusing on cantatas, oratorios, and the music of Edward Elgar; British Music Education of the 19th and 20th centuries; Wagner and Wagnerism in England and America; aesthetics of music; medieval polyphony; American folk and popular music. **SELECTED PUBLICATIONS** Epic Narration: The Oratorios of Edward Elgar, PhD Thesis, Harvard Univ, 98; Cultural Patronage in Fifteenth-Century England, honors thesis, Oberlin Col, 92. **CONTACT ADDRESS** School of Music, James Madison Univ, Harrisonburg, VA 22807. **EMAIL** mcguirce@jmu.edu

MCGUIRE, DONALD T., JR.
DISCIPLINE CLASSICS **EDUCATION** Brown Univ, BA; Cornell Univ, MA; PhD. **CAREER** Asst prof, Univ Southern CA, 84-92; to dir summer progr Greece, 86-88; asst prof, SUNY Buffalo, 92. **RESEARCH** Latin imperial poetry; epic poetry; Greek and Roman hist and historiography; hist of archit; and mod popular cult and the ancient world. **SELECTED PUBLICATIONS** Auth, Textual Strategies and Political Suicide in Flavian Epic in The Imperial Muse: Ramus Essays on Roman Literature of the Empire, vol 2; History Compressed: The Roman Names of Silius' Cannae Episode, Latomus, 95. **CONTACT ADDRESS** Dept Classics, SUNY, Buffalo, 712 Clemens Hall, Buffalo, NY 14260.

MCGUIRE, PETER
DISCIPLINE AUDIENCE ANALYSIS, DOCUMENTATION DESIGN, AND MULTIMEDIA DESIGN **EDUCATION** Brown Univ, PhD, 75. **CAREER** Prof, Ga Inst of Technol; consult, Europ-Asian Multimedia Commun of Interest. **RESEARCH** The impact of design theory on multimedia. **SELECTED PUBLICATIONS** Coauth, Functional Writing, Readings in Technical Writing; A Guide to Technical Writing. **CONTACT ADDRESS** Sch of Lit, Commun & Cult, Georgia Inst of Tech, Skiles Cla, Atlanta, GA 30332. **EMAIL** peter.mcguire@lcc.gatech.edu

MCGUIRE, PHILIP CARROLL
PERSONAL Born 08/23/1940, Pittsburgh, PA, m, 1989, 2 children **DISCIPLINE** ENGLISH **EDUCATION** LaSalle Col, BA, 62; Stanford Univ, MA, 65, PhD(English), 68. **CAREER** Asst prof, 66-71, assoc prof, 71-82, Prof, English, Mich State Univ, 82- . **MEMBERSHIPS** MLA; Aaup; Renaissance Soc Am; Shakespeare Asn Am. **RESEARCH** English poetry of the Renaissance; Shakespeare; early modern English drama. **SELECTED PUBLICATIONS** Auth, Othello as an assay of reason, Shakespeare Quart, 73; auth, Private prayer and English poetry in the early seventeenth century, Studies English Lit, 74; co-ed, Shakespeare, The Theatrical Dimension, 78; auth, Choreography and language in Richard II, In: Shakespeare: The Theatrical Dimension, 78, AMS Press; auth, Speechless Dialect: Shakespeare's Open Silences, 85; auth, "Shakespeare's Non-Shakespearean Sonnets," Shakespeare Q, 87; auth, Shakespeare: The Jacobean Plays, 94. **CONTACT ADDRESS** Dept of Englishe, Michigan State Univ, East Lansing, MI 48824. **EMAIL** mcguire@pilot.msu.edu

MCHANEY, THOMAS LAFAYETTE
PERSONAL Born 10/17/1936, Paragould, AR, m, 1962, 3 children **DISCIPLINE** AMERICAN LITERATURE **EDUCATION** Miss State Univ, BA, 59; Univ NC, Chapel Hill, MA, 62; Univ SC, PhD(English), 68. **CAREER** Instr English, Univ Miss, 63-65; asst prof, 68-73, assoc prof, 73-78, Prof English, GA State Univ, 78-. **HONORS AND AWARDS** Spec Awd for Fiction, Henry Bellaman Found, 70. **MEMBERSHIPS** MLA; S Atlantic Mod Lang Asn. **RESEARCH** William Faulkner; economics of authorship. **SELECTED PUBLICATIONS** Auth, Sanctuary and Frazer's slain kings, Miss Quart, summer 71; Anderson, Hemingway and Faulkner's The Wild Palms, Pmla, 5/72; William Gilmore Simms, In: The Chief Glory of Every People, Southern Ill Univ, 73; William Faulkner's The Wild Palms, Univ Miss, 76; William Faulkner: A Reference Guide, G K Hall, 76; The prophet, Cimarron Rev, 77; Spell of dry weather, Atlanta Mag, 80; Last of the Civil War orphans, Atlanta New Ploy Proj, 81. **CONTACT ADDRESS** Dept of English, Georgia State Univ, 33 Gilmer St SE, Atlanta, GA 30303.

MCHUGH, SUSAN B.
PERSONAL Born 11/11/1969 **DISCIPLINE** ENGLISH **EDUCATION** Univ Mass, BA, 91; MA, 93; Purdue Univ, PhD, 99. **CAREER** Adj prof, Univ Mass, 93; adj prof, Nichols Col, 93; adj prof, Holyoke Col, 93; instr, Univ Mass, 94; instr, Purdue Univ, 94-97; ed asst, Purdue Univ, 97-99; vis asst prof, Mich State Univ, 99-00; postdoc fel, Georgia Inst Tech, 00-01. **HONORS AND AWARDS** GIT Trav Grnt, 00-01; MSU Trav Grnt, 00; Kneale Awd Lit Crit, Purdue Univ, 99; Virgil Lokke Prize in Lit Theo, Purdue Univ, 99, Hon Men, 98; Purdue Univ Trav Grnt, 97-99; Class of 76 Hum Scholar, Univ Mass, 91; Steinbugler Ess Prize, Univ Mass, 91. **MEMBERSHIPS** MLA; ASA; SCS; ISSNL; SLS; ISA. **RESEARCH** Literary and cultural theory; animal studies; visual media studies; narrative theory; science and literature; genetic aesthetics. **SELECTED PUBLICATIONS** Rev, "Donna Haraway, Modest_Witness_@ Second Millenium.Femaleman¤ Meets Oncomouse: Feminism and Technoscience," Mod Fict Stud 44 (98); rev, "Lauren Berlant, The Queen of America Goes to Washington City: Essays on Sex and Citizenship," Mod Fict Stud 44 (98); auth, "Horses in Blackface: Visualizing Race as Species Difference in Planet of the Apes" S Atl rev 65 (00); auth, "Marrying My Bitch: J. R. Ackerley's Pack Aesthetics" Crit Inqu 27 (00); auth, "Video Dog Star: William Wegman, Aesthetic Agency, and the Animal in Art," in The Representation of Animals, Soc and Anim (forthcoming); auth, "Bitches from Brazil: Cloning and owning through The Missyplicity Project," in Representing Animals at the End of the Century, ed. Nigel Rothfels (Bloomington: IN, UP, forthcoming). **CONTACT ADDRESS** Sch Lit, Comm, Culture, Georgia Inst of Tech, Atlanta, GA 30332-0001. **EMAIL** susan.mchugh@lcc.gatech.edu

MCILVAINE, ROBERT MORTON
PERSONAL Born 12/28/1943, Vernon, TX, m, 1966, 2 children **DISCIPLINE** ENGLISH & AMERICAN LITERATURE **EDUCATION** Davis & Elkins Col, BA, 66; Univ Pa, MA, 67; Temple Univ, PhD, 72. **CAREER** Tchg asst Eng, Temple Univ, 68-72; from Asst Prof to Prof Eng, Slippery Rock Univ, 72-, Chmn Dept, 77-79. **RESEARCH** Am realism and naturalism; Am novel; Victorian lit. **SELECTED PUBLICATIONS** Auth, Robert Herrick and Thorstein Veblen, WA State Univ Res Studies, 6/72; Dos Passo's reading of Thorstein Veblen, Am Lit, 11/72; Edith Wharton's American beauty rose, J Am Studies, 12/73. **CONTACT ADDRESS** Dept of Eng, Slippery Rock Univ of Pennsylvania, SWC Bldg, Slippery Rock, PA 16057-1326. **EMAIL** robert.mcilvaine@sru.edu

MCINNIS, JUDY B.
PERSONAL Born 09/22/1943, Roseau, MN, m, 1967, 3 children **DISCIPLINE** ENGLISH **EDUCATION** Bemidji State Univ, BA, 64; Univ NC, PhD, 74. **CAREER** US Peace Corp, Santiago Chile, 64-66; instr, 71-75; asst prof, 75-82; assoc prof, 82-, Univ Delaware. **HONORS AND AWARDS** Teach of the Year, DCOT; NDEA Schlp; NEH Fel; Folgar Inst Schlp. **MEMBERSHIPS** AATSP; MALLAS; AISA; RSA; AAUP. **RESEARCH** Women in medieval and modern Hispanic literature. **SELECTED PUBLICATIONS** Auth, "Pablo Villamar: Lorca y Dali en el teatro hispano," Rev Interamericana 23 (93): 37-47; auth, "History into Drama: Peter Shaffer and William Prescott," MACLAS: Latin Am Essays 9 (95): 80-97; auth, "Communal Rites: Tea, Wine and Milton in Barbara Pym's Novels," Renascence: Essays on Values in Literature 48 (96): 279-293; auth, "Gabriela Mistral as a Chilean Judith," in Modal idades de representacion del suj eta temenina auto/bio/grafico, ed. Magdalena Maiz, Luis H. Pena (Mexico: Grafo Print Editores, 97); auth, "Martyrs for Love: The Reflections of Sor Juana Ines de la Cruz in/on Lucretia, Julia, Portia, and Thisbe," Hispania 80 (97): 764-774; auth, "Peguena burguesa, artista, feminista?: Edith en 'Domingo' de Rosario Castellanos," MACLAS: Latin Am Essays (98): 111-120; auth, The Cumaean Sibyl: Selected Poetry of Gladys M Ilarrequi, Univ Press South (New Orleans), 99. **CONTACT ADDRESS** Dept English, Univ of Delaware, 42 Amstel Ave, Newark, DE 19716-2799. **EMAIL** jmcinnis@udel.edu

MCINTOSH, ANNE
DISCIPLINE SPEECH COMMUNICATION **EDUCATION** UNC Chapel Hill, BA, 88; Univ of Mont Missoula, MA, 91; Univ of Tex Austin, PhD, 95. **CAREER** Res consult; instr. **HONORS AND AWARDS** Lucia Morgan Scholar, 88; Steve Hodges Awd, 97. **MEMBERSHIPS** Nat Commun Asn; Western States Commun Asn. **RESEARCH** Male-female communication; interpersonal communication; deafness; health communication. **SELECTED PUBLICATIONS** Auth, Getting Back into a Career Again, Hearing Health, 97; Putting ALDs on the Menu, Hearing Health, 97; And Now a Word on Auto Safety.., Hearing Health, 96; Semantic Mapping Across the Curriculum: Helping Students Discover Connections, Perspectives in Ed and Deafness, 95; In Memory of Steve Hodges: An Interview, Hearing Health, 95; Making Science Accessible to Deaf Students, Am Annals of the Deaf, 95; auth, When the Deaf & Hearing Interact: Communication Features Relationships; auth, Disability Issues; auth, Handbook of Communication; auth, People with Disabilities, 00. **CONTACT ADDRESS** PO Box 1961, Davidson, NC 28036-1961. **EMAIL** mcintosh@vnet.net

MCINTOSH, JAMES HENRY
PERSONAL Born 02/04/1934, New York, NY, 1 child **DISCIPLINE** ENGLISH **EDUCATION** Harvard Univ, AB, 55; Yale Univ, PhD, 66. **CAREER** Instr Eng & Ger, 60-61, Scattergood Sch; from instr to asst prof Eng, 62-67, Tufts Univ; from asst prof to assoc prof, 67-75, Yale Univ; dir undergrad stud Am stud, 72-75, assoc prof Eng, 75-, Univ Mich; prof, 88-, actg dir Am stud, 82-, dir, 84-92, Morse Human fel, 71-72, Yale Univ; mem fac, Bread Loaf Sch, 73, 74 & 78; NEH sr fel, 76. **MEMBERSHIPS** Soc Values Higher Educ. **RESEARCH** 19th century American literature; international Romanticism; North & South American literary relations. **SELECTED PUBLICATIONS** Auth, Thoreau as Romantic Naturalist, Cornell Univ, 74; auth, Emerson's Unmoored Self, Yale Rev, 76; auth, Hawthorne's Search for a Wider Public and a Select Society, Forum, Houston, 76; auth, Melville's Use and Abuse of Goethe: The Weaver-Gods in Faust and Moby-Dick, Amerikastudien/ American Studies, 80; ed, Nathaniel Hawthorne's Tales, 87; auth, The Mariner's Multiple Guest, New Essays on Moby Dick, 86; auth, Billy Budd, Sailor, Melville's Last Romance, Critical Essays on Billy Budd, Sailor, 89; auth, Nimble Believing: Dickinson and the Unknown, Univ Mich Press, 00. **CONTACT ADDRESS** Univ of Michigan, Ann Arbor, 505 S State St, Ann Arbor, MI 48109-1003. **EMAIL** jhmci@umich.edu

MCINTYRE, JERILYN S.
DISCIPLINE COMMUNICATION HISTORY **EDUCATION** Univ Wash, PhD, 73; Stanford Univ, AB, 64; MA, 65; Univ of Wash, PhD, 73. **CAREER** Prof. **MEMBERSHIPS** Asn Edu in Jour and Mass Commun; Am Hist Asn; Org Am Hist. **RESEARCH** Communication History, Higher Education Administration. **SELECTED PUBLICATIONS** Auth, Transportation Developments in a Mid-Nineteenth Century Frontier Community, Jour W, 95; Rituals of Disorder: A Dramatistic Interpretation of Radical Dissent, 89; The Avvisi of Venice: Toward an Archaeology of Media Forms, Jour Hist, 87; Repositioning a Landmark: The Hutchins Commission and Freedom of the Press, 87. **CONTACT ADDRESS** Off of Pres, Central Washington Univ, 400 E 8th Ave, Ellenberg, WA 98926. **EMAIL** mcintyrej@cwu.edu

MCIRVIN, MICHAEL D.
PERSONAL Born 08/17/1956, Sidney, NE, d, 2 children **DISCIPLINE** WRITING, LITERATURE **EDUCATION** Univ Wyo, BA, 88; MA, 91. **CAREER** Adj lectr, Colo State Univ, 92-93; lectr, Univ of Wyo, 93-. **HONORS AND AWARDS** Fred Slater Awd for Teaching Excellence; Poets Prize, Acad of Am; Individual Artist Fel, Wyo Arts Coun. **MEMBERSHIPS** Phi Beta Kappa, Phi Kappa phi, Acad of Am Poets, Rocky Mountain MLA. **RESEARCH** Modern and post-modern American literature. **SELECTED PUBLICATIONS** Auth, Love and Myth; auth, Lessons of Radical Finitude; auth, Dog; auth, The Book of Allegory; auth, Whither American Paltry. **CONTACT ADDRESS** Dept English, Univ of Wyoming, PO Box 3353, Laramie, WY 82071-3353.

MCJANNET, LINDA
PERSONAL Born 02/16/1943, Washington, DC, d, 2 children **DISCIPLINE** ENGLISH LITERATURE **EDUCATION** Wellesley Col, BA, 64; Harvard Univ, MA, 66; Harvard Univ, PhD, 71 **CAREER** Asst prof, Cath Univ Amer, 72-75; Expository Writing Prog, Harvard Col, 75-78; assoc Communication, Harvard Grad Sch Bus Admin, 78-81; asst prof, Bentley Col, 81-88; assoc prof, Bentley Col, 88-96; prof English, Bentley Col, 96- **HONORS AND AWARDS** Woodrow Wilson Fel, 64-65; Bentley Col Inst Fel, 90-91; Bentley Col Scholar of Year, 88; Phi Beta Kappa, 63 **MEMBERSHIPS** Mod Lang Assoc; Shakespeare Assoc Amer; **RESEARCH** English Renaissance; Early Modern Drama **SELECTED PUBLICATIONS** Auth, "Genre and Geography: The Eastern Mediterranean in Pericles and The Comedy of Errors." Playing Across the Globe: Genre and Geography in English Renaissance Drama, Fairleigh Dickinson, 98; auth, The Voice of Elizabethan Stage Directions: The Evolution of a Theatrical Code, Univ Delaware, 98; auth, Management Communication, McGraw-Hill, 96 **CONTACT ADDRESS** Bentley Col, MOR 381, Waltham, MA 02452-4705. **EMAIL** lmcjannet@bentley.edu

MCKAY, ALEXANDER G.
PERSONAL Born 12/24/1924, Toronto, ON, Canada **DISCIPLINE** CLASSICS **EDUCATION** Univ Toronto, BA, 46; Yale Univ, MA, 47; Princeton Univ, PhD, 50. **CAREER** Instr, Princeton Univ, 47-49; instr, Wells Col, 49-50; instr, Univ Pa, 50-51; instr, Univ Man, 51-52; asst prof, Mt Allison Univ, 52-53; asst prof, Waterloo Col, 53-55; Dir, Classical Sumer Sch Italy, Vergilian Soc Am, 55-97; asst prof, Univ Man, 55-57; asst prof, 57-59, assoc prof, 59-61, prof, 61-90, Prof Emer Classics, McMaster Univ, 90-, chmn, 62-68, 76-79, dean hum, 68-73; adj prof hum, York Univ, 90-96; vis lectr, Concordia Univ, 92-93. **HONORS AND AWARDS** Off, Order Can; Queen's Silver Jubilee Medal; Centenary Medal, Royal Soc Can; Canada 125 Medal; Woodrow Wilson fel; Killam sr res fel; LLD(hon), Univ Man, 86; LLD(hon), Brock Univ, 90; LLD(hon), Queen's Univ, 91; DLitt (hon), McMaster Univ, 92; DLitt(hon), Waterloo Univ, 93. **MEMBERSHIPS** Acad Hum Soc Sci; Class Asn Can; Vergilian Soc; Int Acad Union **RESEARCH** Ancient Roman architecture and literature. **SELECTED PUBLICATIONS** Auth, Naples and Campania, 62; auth, Victorian Architecture in Hamilton, 67; auth, Vergil's Italy, 70; auth, Ancient Campania, 72; auth, Houses, Villas and Palaces in the Roman World, 75; auth, Vitruvius, Architect and Engineer, 78, 85; auth, Romische Hauser, Villen und Palaste, 80; auth, Roma Antiqua, Latium & Erturia, 86; coauth, Roman Lyric Poetry: Catullus and Horace, 69, 74; coauth, Roman Satire: Horace, Juvenal, Persius et al, 76; coauth, Selections from Vergil's Aeneid, Books I, IV, VI (Dido and Aeneas), 88; coauth, The Two Worlds of the Poet: New Perspectives on Vergil, 92; coauth, Tragedy, Love and Change: Roman Poetic Themes and Variations, 94. **CONTACT ADDRESS** Classics Dept, McMaster Univ, 706 Togo Salmon Hall, Hamilton, ON, Canada L8S 4M2.

MCKEE, PATRICIA
DISCIPLINE ENGLISH LITERATURE **EDUCATION** Brandeis Univ, PhD, 78. **CAREER** Prof, Dartmouth Col. **RESEARCH** Am and Brit lit; the novel; Toni Morrison. **SELECTED PUBLICATIONS** Auth, Public and Private: Gender, Class, and the British Novel (1764-1878), Univ Minn P, 97; Spacing and Placing Experience in Toni Morrison's Sula, Mod Fic Studies, 96; William Faulkner's As I Lay Dying: Experience in Passing, S Atlantic Quart, 91; Heroic Commitment in Richardson, Eliot, and James, Princeton UP, 86. **CONTACT ADDRESS** Dartmouth Col, 3529 N Main St, #207, Hanover, NH 03755.

MCKEEN, WILLIAM
PERSONAL Born 09/16/1954, Indianapolis, IN, d, 3 children **DISCIPLINE** HISTORY; MASS COMMUNICATION; EDUCATION **EDUCATION** Indiana Univ, BA, 74, MA, 77; Univ OK, PhD, 86. **CAREER** Educator, 77-; Prof and ch, jour dept, Univ Florida. **HONORS AND AWARDS** Various teaching Awds **MEMBERSHIPS** Pop culture asn; SO book critics cir; AJHA; asn for edu in journ and mass comm. **RESEARCH** Pop cult; journ hist; music. **SELECTED PUBLICATIONS** Rock and Roll is Here to Stay, 00; Literary Journalism, 00; Tom Wolfe, 95; Bob Dylan: A Bio-Bibliography, 93; Hunter S Thompson, 91; The Beatles: A Bio-Bibliography, 90. **CONTACT ADDRESS** Univ of Florida, 2089 Weimer Hall, Gainesville, FL 32611. **EMAIL** wmckeen@jou.ufl.edu

MCKENDRICK, NORMAN G.
DISCIPLINE ENGLISH COMPOSITION AND LITERATURE **EDUCATION** Loyola Univ, BA, MA; Fordham Univ, PhD; W Baden Pontifical Univ, licentiates. **CAREER** Assoc prof, 62-. **SELECTED PUBLICATIONS** Pub(s), modern poetry, folk singers, and the texts of Greek Fathers. **CONTACT ADDRESS** Dept of Eng, Univ of Detroit Mercy, 4001 W McNichols Rd, PO BOX 19900, Detroit, MI 48219-0900.

MCKENNA, SHEILA
DISCIPLINE ENGLISH AS A SECOND LANGUAGE **EDUCATION** Columbia Univ, PhD. **CAREER** Asst prof, Long Island Univ, C.W. Post Campus. **SELECTED PUBLICATIONS** Auth, English Composition Organizational Patterns

Influenced by Ethnocultural Backgrounds; Orientational Prepositions: Cross-Cultural Misinterpretations; Marge Piercy Poetry & Music. **CONTACT ADDRESS** Long Island Univ, C.W. Post, Brookville, NY 11548-1300.

MCKENZIE, ALAN T.
PERSONAL Born 07/07/1940, Arlington, MA, m, 1962, 2 children **DISCIPLINE** ENGLISH LITERATURE **EDUCATION** Harvard Univ, BA, 62; Univ Pa, MA, 66, PhD(English), 68. **CAREER** Asst prof, 68-73, actg asst head dept, 73-74, asst head dept, 76-79, Assoc Prof English, Purdue Univ, West Lafayette, 73-89; prof, 89-; director Graduate Studies, 89-93; Acting head Dept, 97. **HONORS AND AWARDS** Member, SCR, Pembroke Col, Oxford Univ, 74; Leverhulme fel, Univ Dundee, 81-82; fel, NEH inst, Yale, 85; ASECS-Mellon fel, Clark Lib, UCLA, 89; fel, Center for Humanistic Studies, Purdue, 85, 96. **MEMBERSHIPS** Am Soc 18th Century Studies; MLA; Johnson Soc; Mid-West Am Soc 18th Century Studies. **RESEARCH** Eighteenth century English literature; Samuel Johnson; word processing. **SELECTED PUBLICATIONS** Auth, Thomas Gray: A Reference Guide, G.K. Hall, 82; auth, A Grin on the Interface: Word Processing for the Academic Humanist, MLA, 84; auth, Certain, Lively Episodes: The Ariculation of Passion in Augustan Prose, Georgia, 90; ed, Sent as a Gift: Eight Correspondences from the Eighteenth Century, Georgia, 93; auth, "'I have before me the idea of a dove:' Bringing Motion to Mind in Burke's Enquiry," 1650-1850: Ideas, Aesthetics, and Inquiries in the Early Modern Era, 1, 94; coauth, "'Nature doth everywhere geometrize': Crystals, Crystallization, and Crystallography in the Long Eighteenth Century," SECC 27, ASECS, 98. **CONTACT ADDRESS** Dept of English, Purdue Univ, West Lafayette, 313 Heavilon Hall, West Lafayette, IN 47907-1315. **EMAIL** amck@purdue.edu

MCKENZIE, STANLEY D.
PERSONAL Born Yakima, WA, d, 1 child **DISCIPLINE** LITERATURE **EDUCATION** MIT, BS, 64; Univ Rochester, MA, 67; PhD, 71. **CAREER** Prof to Provost and Vice Pres, Rochester Inst Technol, 74-. **HONORS AND AWARDS** Outstanding Young Teacher Awd, Rochester Inst Technol, 70; NAG Outstanding Service Awd, 86; Fac Awd for Excellence, Office of Student Ombudsman, 96. **MEMBERSHIPS** MLA, AAUP, Phi Kappa Phi, Golden Key. **RESEARCH** Shakespeare. **SELECTED PUBLICATIONS** Auth, "Unshout the noise that banish'd Martius:' Structural Paradox and Dissembling in'Coriolanus," Shakespeare Criticism Vol 9, Gale Research 89; auth, "The Prudence and Kinship of Prince Hal and John of Lancaster in Henry IV Part Two," in Law and Philosophy: the Practice of Theory, Essays in Honor of George Anastaplo, Ohio Univ Press, 92; auth, "I to my selfe am strange: The Competing voices of Drayton's Mistres Shore," in Other voices, Other Views: Expanding the Canon in English Renaissance Studies, 99. **CONTACT ADDRESS** Rochester Inst of Tech, 1 Lomb Memorial Dr, Rochester, NY 14623-5603.

MCKEON, MICHAEL
DISCIPLINE ENLIGHTENMENT, EARLY NOVEL, THEORY OF THE NOVEL, PASTORAL POETRY **EDUCATION** Univ Chicago, BA; Columbia Univ, MA; PhD. **CAREER** Prof Eng, Rutgers, The State Univ NJ, Univ Col-Camden. **RESEARCH** Marvell, Defoe, Swift, pre-history of domestic fiction, and early modern "division of knowledge." **SELECTED PUBLICATIONS** Auth, The Origins of the English Novel. **CONTACT ADDRESS** Dept of English, Rutgers, The State Univ of New Jersey, New Brunswick, Murray Hall 202, New Brunswick, NJ 08903. **EMAIL** complit@rci.rutgers.edu

MCKEOWN, JAMES C.
DISCIPLINE CLASSICAL STUDIES **EDUCATION** Cambridge Univ, PhD, 78. **CAREER** Dept Classics, Wisc Univ **RESEARCH** Latin literature. **SELECTED PUBLICATIONS** Auth, pubs on Latin poetry, and Ovid's Amores. **CONTACT ADDRESS** Dept of Classics, Univ of Wisconsin, Madison, 500 Lincoln Drive, Madison, WI 53706. **EMAIL** jmckeown@macc.wisc.edu

MCKERNAN, JOHN J.
PERSONAL Born 05/11/1942, Omaha, NE, m, 1967, 1 child **DISCIPLINE** ENGLISH **EDUCATION** Univ Omaha, BA, 65; Univ Ark, MA, 67; Columbia Univ, MFA, 71; Boston Univ, PhD, 80. **CAREER** Prof, Marshall Univ, 67-. **HONORS AND AWARDS** Reynolds Outstanding teach, Marshall Univ; NEH Rel, Yale Univ; Univ Fel, Boston Univ. **MEMBERSHIPS** WV writers, Poetry Soc of Am, WV Shakespeare Renaissance Asn. **RESEARCH** Shakespeare's sonnets, Suicide in literature. **SELECTED PUBLICATIONS** Auth, Postcard from Dublin, 99; auth, The Writers Handbook, 91; auth, Walking along the Missouri River, 77. **CONTACT ADDRESS** Dept English, Marshall Univ, 400 Hal Greer Blvd, Huntington, WV 25755-0001. **EMAIL** mckernan@marshall.edu

MCKINLEY, JAMES COURTRIGHT
PERSONAL Born 12/08/1935, Omaha, NE, m, 1959, 4 children **DISCIPLINE** BRITISH & AMERICAN LITERATURE **EDUCATION** Univ Mo-Columbia, BA & BJ, 59, MA, 68, PhD(English), 70. **CAREER** Copy supvr, Procter & Gamble, Inc, 60-64; acct exec, Young & Rubicam Advert, Inc, 64-66; asst prof, 70-77, assoc prof, 77-83, prof and dir, prof writing prog, 89- English, Univ Mo-Kansas City. **HONORS AND AWARDS** Nat Endowment for Humanities fel, 72-73; Fulbright fel, 83, 89, 92; McDowell Colony fel, 84, 89. **MEMBERSHIPS** MLA; PEN; Nat Book Critics Circle; Assoc Writing Progs. **RESEARCH** Twentieth century British poetry. **SELECTED PUBLICATIONS** Auth, Interview with Robert Graves, Playboy, 70; Each New Springtime, Each New Summer, New Lett, 75; Playboy's History of Asassination, Playboy, 76; Child's Play, Choteau Rev, 76; Assassination in America, Harper, 77; Inside Sirhan, Playboy, 78; Foreign Farming, Atlantic Monthly, 78; auth, Act of Love, Baertenbush, 89; auth, The Ficklean Suite and Other Stories, Arkansas, 93. **CONTACT ADDRESS** Univ of Missouri, Kansas City, 510 Rockhill Rd, Kansas City, MO 64110-2499.

MCKOY, SHEILA SMITH
PERSONAL Born 05/27/1958, Raleigh, NC, d, 1 child **DISCIPLINE** AMERICAN LITERATURE, AFRICAN LITERATURE, AFRICAN-AMERICAN LITERATURE **EDUCATION** North Carolina State Univ, BA, 69; Univ of North Carolina, MA, 91; Duke Univ, Ph.D. 94. **CAREER** Instr, St Augustine's Col, 81-93; Instr, Duke Univ, 91-94; Lecturer, North Carolina State Univ, 93-94; Asst Prof, Vanderbilt Univ, 94-; Acting Dir, 98-99. **HONORS AND AWARDS** Acad Achievement Awd, North Carolina State Univ, 88; Minority Presence Fel, Univ of North Carolina, 89; DeWitt-Wallace Fel, Duke Univ, 89-90; Univ Res Grant, Vanderbilt Univ, 95, 96. **MEMBERSHIPS** African Lit. Asn, African Studies Asn, Am Studies Asn, Col Lang Asn, Modern Lang Asn, MELUS, Charles Chesnutt Soc, Toni Morrison Soc. **RESEARCH** South African literature and culture; diaspora oral traditions. **SELECTED PUBLICATIONS** Auth, "Introduction" The Story of the Illinois Federation of Colored Women's Clubs by Elizabeth Lindsay Davis and The History of the Order of the Eastern Star Among Colored People by Mrs. S. Joe Brown for the Africna - American Women Writers, 1910-1940 Seriers, Gen. Ed. Henry Louis Gates, Jr., New York: G.K. Hall & Co., 97; auth, "William Melvin Kelley'" Notable Black American Men, ed. Jessie Carney Smith, Gale Research, 98; auth, "Countoe Cullen," Notable Black American Men, ed. Jessie Carney Smith, Gale Research, 98; auth, "From Behind the Veil: The Dual Legacy of Sexuality in African American Literature," Instructor's Resource Manual - Call and Response: The Riverside Anthology of the African American Literary Tradition, Boston: Houghton Mifflin Co, 98; auth, "Metaphors of Transcendence: Literature, Music, and African American Culture," Instructor's Resource Manual - Call and Response: The Riverside Anthology of the African American Literary Tradition, Boston: Houghton Mifflin Co, 98; auth ,"Responses to Feminism, Womanism, and Beyond: Embracing a Critical Awareness," Instructor's Resource Manual - Call and Response: The Riverside Anthology of the African American Literary Tradition, Boston: Houghton Mifflin Co, 98; auth, "Expanding the Boundaries of Black Masculinity: Writing a Legacy of Empowerment," Instructor's Resource Manual - Call and Response: The Riverside Anthology of the African American Literary Tradition, Boston: Houghton Mifflin Co, 98; auth, "Limbo: Time in the Diaspora Contest," Callaloo: 22.1, 99; auth, "Rescuing the Black Homosexual Lambs: Randall Kenan and the Reconstruction of Southern Gay Masculinity," Black Men's Fiction and Drama, ed. Keith Clark, Champaign: Univ of Ill Pr, forthcoming, 01. **CONTACT ADDRESS** Dept of English, Vanderbilt Univ, Nashville, TN 37235. **EMAIL** sheila.s.mckoy@vanderbilt.edu

MCKUSICK, JAMES C.
PERSONAL Born 04/05/1956, Wilmington, DE, m, 1998 **DISCIPLINE** ENGLISH **EDUCATION** Dartmouth Col, BA, 79; Yale Univ, MA, 80, M Phil, 82; PhD, 84. **CAREER** Asst prof, assoc prof, chmn, Univ Maryland, 84-. **HONORS AND AWARDS** Fletcher Jones Found Fel, 97; Prov Res Fel, U of Maryland, 97; NEH, 90; Andrew W. Mellon Fel, 90; Exxon-Huntington Lib Fel, 86; Sigma Tau Delta; Phi Beta Kappa. **MEMBERSHIPS** ASECS; ASLE; Friends of Coleridge; INSA; John Clare Soc; Keats-Shelley Asn; MLA; NASSR; Wordsworth-Coleridge Asn. **RESEARCH** English romantic poetry; environmental studies; history of science. **SELECTED PUBLICATIONS** Co-ed, Literature and Nature: Four Centuries of Nature Writing, Prentice Hall, 01; auth, Green Writing: Romanticism and Ecology, St. Martin's Press, 00; auth, Coleridge's Philosophy of Language, Yale UP, 86; auth, "A New Poem by Samuel Taylor Coleridge," Mod Philo (87); auth, "'Living Words': Samuel Taylor Coleridge and the Genesis of the OED," Mod Philo (92); auth, "The Politics of Language in Byron's The Island," Eng Lit Hist (92); auth, "John Clare and the Tyranny of Grammar," Stud in Rom (94); auth, "'Wisely forgetful': The Politics of Pantisocracy," in Romanticism and Colonialism: Writing and Empire (Cambridge UP, 98); auth, "Kubla Khan and the Theory of the Earth," in Samuel Taylor Coleridge and the Sciences of Life (Oxford UP, 01); auth, "Coleridge and Symbol," in The Cambridge Companion to Coleridge (Cambridge UP, 01). **CONTACT ADDRESS** Eng Dept., Univ of Maryland, Baltimore, 1000 Hilltop Cir, Baltimore, MD 21250. **EMAIL** mckusick@umbc.edu

MCLAUGHLIN, ANDREE NICOLA
PERSONAL Born 02/12/1948, White Plains, NY **DISCIPLINE** LITERATURE, WOMEN'S STUDIES **EDUCATION** Cornell Univ, BS 70; Univ of MA-Amherst, Med, 71, EdD, 74. **CAREER** Medgar Evers College/CUNY, asst prof/project dir 1974-77, chairperson 1977-79, dean of administration and assoc prof, 79-82, planning coord of Women's Studies Rsch & Develop 1984-89, professor of Humanities, 86-; University of London Institute of Education, distinguished visiting scholar, 86; Hamilton Col, Jane Watson Irwin Visiting Prof of Women's Studies, 89-91; Medgar Evers College/CUNY, prof of literature & language/prof of interdisciplinary studies, 92-, Office of International Women's Affairs, director, 96-. **HONORS AND AWARDS** Natl Endowment for the Humanities Fellow, 1976, 1979, 1984, 1989, 1993; 25 articles published; Amer Council on Educ, Fellow in Acad Admin, 1980-81; Andrew W Mellon Fellow, CUNY Graduate School & Univ Center, 1987; **MEMBERSHIPS** Bd mem, Where We At, Black Women Artists, 1979-87; mem Natl Women's Studies Assoc 1980-84, Amer Assoc of Univ Profs 1982-; founding intl coord, Intl Resource Network of Women of African Descent, 1982-85, founding mem Sisterhood in Support of Sisters in South Africa 1984-; adv bd mem Sisterhood of Black Single Mothers 1984-86; founding intl coordinator, International Cross-Cultural Black Women's Studies Inst, 1987-; chair, Editorial Bd, Network: A Pan African Women's Forum (journal), 1987-91; mem, Policy & Publication Comm, The Feminist Press, CUNY, 1988-99. **SELECTED PUBLICATIONS** Co-editor, Wild Women in the Whirlwind: Afra-American Culture & the Contemporary Literary Renaissance, Rutgers Univ Press, 1990; Author, Double Dutch, poetry, 1989; author, "Black Women's Studies in America," 1989; author, "Urban Politics in the Higher Education of Black Women," 1988; author, "The International Nature of the Southern African Women's Struggles," 1988; author, "Unfinished Business of the Sixties: Black Women on the Front Line," 1990; author, "Black Women, Identity and the Quest for Humanhood and Wholeness," 1990; author, Through the Barrel of Her Consciousness: Contemporary Black Women's Literature and Activism in Cross Cultural Perspective, 1994. Susan Koppelman Book Award for Best Edited Feminist work in Popular/American Culture Studies, 1990; author The Impact of the Black Consciousness and Women's Movements on Black Women's Identity: Intercontinental Empowerment, 1995. **CONTACT ADDRESS** Medgar Evers Col, CUNY, 1650 Bedford Ave, Brooklyn, NY 11225. **EMAIL** mclaughlin@mec.cuny.edu

MCLAUGHLIN, KEVIN P.
PERSONAL Born 08/15/1960, Seattle, WA **DISCIPLINE** MUSIC **EDUCATION** Univ of MN, DAM, 92; Yale Univ, MM, 85; Univ of MI, BM, 83 **CAREER** Inst, 92-95, St Olaf Col; Asst Prof, 95-96, NE MO St Univ **HONORS AND AWARDS** Phi Kappa Phi, 9 1 **MEMBERSHIPS** Am Libr Asn; Asn of Col & Res Librs **RESEARCH** Music hist; Hist of Opera **SELECTED PUBLICATIONS** Auth, The Mirror of Justice, 97; Das Wunderjahr in Jena, 98; The View from the Tower, 98 **CONTACT ADDRESS** Dept of German, Princeton Univ, Princeton, NJ 08544. **EMAIL** tjz@princeton.edu

MCLAUGHLIN, ROBERT
PERSONAL Born 02/20/1957, Rochester, NY, m, 1981 **DISCIPLINE** ENGLISH **EDUCATION** Fordham Univ, BA, 79; MA, 83; PhD, 87. **CAREER** Asst Prof to Assoc Prof, Ill State Univ, 88-. **HONORS AND AWARDS** Res Initiation Awd, Ill State Univ, 94. **MEMBERSHIPS** MLA, Soc for the Study of Narrative Literature, Popular Culture Asn, Sinclair Lewis Soc. **RESEARCH** Postmodern American Fiction; World War II Popular Culture. **SELECTED PUBLICATIONS** Ed, Innovations: An Anthology of Modern and Contemporary Fiction, Dalkey Archive Press, 98; auth, "Theories of Land Tenure and the Charismatic Line in Mason & Dixon," Oklahoma City Univ Law Review, (99): 799-813; auth, "Franz Pokler's anti-Story: Narrative and Self in Gravity's Rainbow," Pynchon Notes, (99): 159-175; auth, "Dream for Us a Different World: Introducing Curtis White," Review of Contemporary Fiction, (98): 7-25; auth, "Mickey Rooney in Gravity's rainbow," Notes on Contemporary Literature, (98): 9-11; auth, "Mark Schorer, Dialogic Discourse, and It Can't Happen her," sinclair Lewis: New Critical Essays, Whitston, 97; auth, "fighting Fire with fire: The Bat bomb in Richard Powers's Prisoner's dilemma," Notes on Contemporary Literature, (97): 3-5; auth, "Oppositional aesthetics/ Oppositional Ideologies: A Brief cultural History of alternative Publishing in the United states," Critique, (96): 171-186; auth, "This is America, too: The discourse of Democracy in assassins," The Sondheim Review, (95): 22-26. **CONTACT ADDRESS** Dept English, Illinois State Univ, Box 4240, Normal, IL 61790-4240. **EMAIL** rmclaugh@ilstu.edu

MCLEAN, ANDREW MILLER
PERSONAL Born 05/25/1941, Brooklyn, NY, 1 child **DISCIPLINE** ENGLISH RENAISSANCE LITERATURE & HISTORY **EDUCATION** St Olaf Col, BA, 63; Brooklyn Col, MA, 67; Univ NC, Chapel Hill, PhD(English), 71. **CAREER** Asst prof, 71-76, Assoc Prof English, 77-82, prof, 82- ,Univ Wis-Parkside; Rev ed, Clio: An Interdisciplinary Jour of Lit, Hist, and Philos of Hist, 71-93; res prof, Catholic Univ Louvain, 75-76. **MEMBERSHIPS** MLA; Soc Studies Midwestern Lit; Renaissance Soc Am; Shakespeare Asn Am. **RESEARCH** Six-

teenth century English literature; Irish literature; interdisciplinary studies; film-Shakespeare. **SELECTED PUBLICATIONS** Auth, Emerson's Brahma, New England Quart, 3/69; James Joyce & A Doblin, Comp Lit, spring 73; English translation of Erasmus, Moreana, 11/74; Castiglione, Cicero & English dialogues, Romance Notes, 75; Barlow, More & the Anglican episcopacy, Moreana, 2/76; contribr, Bibliography on teaching Shakespeare, In: Teaching Shakespeare, Princeton Univ, 77; Barlow & the Lutheran Factions, Renaissance Quart, summer 78; auth, Shakespeare: Annotated Bibliographies and Media Guide for Teachers, MCTE, 80; ed, Work of William Barlowe, Sutton Courtenay press, 81; co-ed, Redefining Shakespeare: Literary Theory and Theater Practice in the German Democratic Republic. Univ Delaware, 98. **CONTACT ADDRESS** Dept of English, Univ of Wisconsin, Parkside, Box 2000, Kenosha, WI 53141-2000. **EMAIL** andrew.mclean@uwp.edu

MCLEAN, KEN

DISCIPLINE ENGLISH LITERATURE **EDUCATION** Waterloo Lutheran Univ, BA; McMaster Univ, MA; York Univ, PhD. **CAREER** Engl, Bishop's Univ. **RESEARCH** Treatment by a number of Irish witers of the traditional pilgrimage to "St. Patrick's Pugatory" in Lough Deg, the response to the "Book of Daniel." **SELECTED PUBLICATIONS** Auth, pubs on John Richardson, William Kirby, Joyce Marshall, Patrick Lane and Margaret Laurence. **CONTACT ADDRESS** English Dept, Bishop's Univ, Lennoxville, QC, Canada JIMIZ 7. **EMAIL** kmclean@ubishops.ca

MCLEOD, ALAN L.

PERSONAL Born 03/13/1928, Sydney, Australia, m, 1954, 2 children **DISCIPLINE** ENGLISH, SPEECH **EDUCATION** Univ Sydney, Australia, BA, 50, MA, 52, Dipl Ed, 51; Univ Melbourne, Australia, BEd, 56; Pa State Univ, PhD, 57. **CAREER** Lectr English & speech, Wagga State Teachers Col, Australia, 52; asst speech, Pa State Univ, 52-53 & 54-56; lectr English & speech, Balmain State Teachers Col, 56-57; from asst prof to assoc prof, State Univ Col Fredonia, 57-62; prof, Dean, Liberal Arts, Lock Haven State Col, 62-66; Prof English & Speech, Rider Univ, 66. **HONORS AND AWARDS** State Univ NY res fel, 62; A.C.L.S. grant 69; NEH grants, 79, 84; Fulbright Prof, India, 83. **RESEARCH** Seventeenth and eighteenth century poetry and drama; commonwealth literature; rhetorical criticism. **SELECTED PUBLICATIONS** Auth, Rex Warner, 60; auth, Commonwealth Pen, 61; auth, Pattern of Aust. Culture, 63; auth, Pattern of N.Z. Culture, 68; ed, Negroes in America, 71; auth, Commonwealth and American Women's Discourse, 96; ed, Li. Of the Indian Diaspora, 00; auth, Wings of the Evening, 01; auth, It So Happen, World Lit Today, vol 0066, 92; South of the West--Postcolonialism and the Narrative Construction of Australia, World Lit Today, vol 0067, 93; One of Bens, a Tribe Transported, World Lit Today, vol 0068, 94; Divina Trace, World Lit Today, vol 0068, 94; Spirits in the Dark, World Lit Today, vol 0069, 95; The 'Longest Memory', World Lit Today, vol 0069, 95; The 'Assistant Professor', World Lit Today, vol 0071, 97; 'How Loud Can the Village Cock Crow' and Other Stories, World Lit Today, vol 0071, 97. **CONTACT ADDRESS** Dept of English, Rider Univ, Lawrenceville, NJ 08648.

MCLEOD, ARCHIBALD

PERSONAL Born 11/05/1906, Edinburg, Scotland, m, 1943, 1 child **DISCIPLINE** DRAMA **EDUCATION** Oberlin Col BA, 33; State Univ Iowa, MA, 34; Cornell Univ, PhD(speech & drama), 42. **CAREER** Instr speech & drama, Kans State Teachers Col, 34-35; assoc prof, Tex State Col Women, 35-39 & 41-43; asst prof, La State Univ, 43-47; chmn dept theatre, 59-75, Prof Speech & Drama, Southern Ill Univ, Carbondale, 47-; Exec Secy, Ill State Theatre CO, 75-, Fulbright lectr dramatic art, Natya Sangh, Madras, India, 62-63. **MEMBERSHIPS** Am Theatre Asn. **RESEARCH** Dramatic literature; theatre audience; aesthetics of the theatre. **SELECTED PUBLICATIONS** Auth, The New Zealand Novels of Langley, Eve, Southerly, vol 0055, 95. **CONTACT ADDRESS** So Illinois Univ, Carbondale, 907 W Schwartz St, Carbondale, IL 62901.

MCLEOD, DOUGLAS M.

DISCIPLINE COMMUNICATIONS **EDUCATION** Univ Wis, BA, 83; Univ Minn, MA, 86; PhD, 89. **CAREER** Res supervr, Univ Minn, 86-89; secy, Intl Commun Assn, 94-96; div hd, Assn Edu in Jour and Mass Commun, 95-96; chair, Assn Edu in Jour and Mass Commun, 95; assoc prof, 89-. **HONORS AND AWARDS** Elliston scholar, Univ Minn, 84-85; Bell and Howell sudent res award, Spec Lib(s) Assn, 87; Casey dissertation award, Univ minn, 88-89; arts and sciences dean's grant, 91, 92; res consult, st paul cable access, 89; co-ed, minn jour, 84. **RESEARCH** Journalism and mass communication. **SELECTED PUBLICATIONS** Co-auth, The Expanding Boundaries of Political Communication Effects, Media Effects: Advances in Theory and Research, Lawrence Erlbaum Assoc(s), 94; Reporters vs Undecided Voters: An Analysis of the Questions Asked During the 92 Presidential Debates, Commun Quart, 94; Direct and Indirect Effects of Socioeconomic Status on Public Affairs Knowledge, Jour Quart, 94; Cultivation in the Newer Media Environment, Commun Res, 94; Gender Stereotypes in MTV Commercials: The Beat Goes On, Jour Broadcasting and Electronic Media, 94; Conflict and Public Opinion: Rallying Effects of the Persian Gulf War, Jour Quart, 94; rev(s), Review of P. Thaler's The Watchful Eye: American Justice in the Age of the Television Trial, Jour Broadcasting and Electronic Media, 39, 95; Review of J. Mueller's, Policy and Opinion in the Gulf War, Amer Jour, 94; A Comparative Analysis of the Use of Corporate Advertising in the United States and Japan, Intl Jour Advt, 94; Actual and Perceived U.S. Public Opinion: The Spiral of Silence During the Persian Gulf War, Intl Jour of Pub Opinion Res, 95; Anarchists Wreak Havoc in Downtown Minneapolis: A Multi-level Study of Media Coverage of Radical Protest, Jour Monogr(s), 95; The Effects of Spokesperson Gender, PSA Appeal, and Involvement on Eevaluations of Safe-sex Public Service Announcements, Health Commun, 96; auth, Communicating Deviance: The Effects of Relevision News Coverage of Social Protest, Jour Broadcasting and Electronic Media, 95. **CONTACT ADDRESS** Dept of Commun, Univ of Delaware, 162 Ctr Mall, Newark, DE 19716. **EMAIL** dmcleod@udel.edu

MCLEOD, GLENDA KAYE W.

PERSONAL Born 08/21/1953, Gainesville, GA, m, 1983 **DISCIPLINE** ENGLISH **EDUCATION** Univ Ga, BA, 75; MA, 85; PhD, 87. **CAREER** Asst prof, Ga S Univ, 87-88; vis prof, Univ Ga, 88-89; asst prof to assoc prof to prof, Gainesville Col, 85-. **MEMBERSHIPS** MLA. **RESEARCH** Medieval women writers. **SELECTED PUBLICATIONS** Auth, Virtue and Venom; auth, Christine's Vision; auth, Visitors to the City. **CONTACT ADDRESS** Humanities Dept, Gainesville Col, PO Box 1358, Danielsville, GA 30503. **EMAIL** gmcleod@gc.peachnet.edu

MCLEOD, STEPHEN G.

DISCIPLINE HIGHER EDUCATION, ENGLISH LITERATURE **EDUCATION** Pensacola Col, AA, 69; Univ W Fla, BA, 71; Vanderbilt Univ, MA, 73; Nova Southeastern Univ, EdD, 92. **CAREER** Adj instr, St Leo Col Military Educ Prog, 84-92; adj instr, Pensacola Jr Col, 91-; grad prog admin, Nova Southeastern Univ, 94-. **HONORS AND AWARDS** Outstanding dissertation, Nova Southeastern Univ; Professional Development Awd (four times), St Leo Col; Chapter 1419 Res Awd, Phi Delta Kappa. **MEMBERSHIPS** Two-year Col English Asn, Nat Coun of Teachers of English, Phi Delta Kappa. **RESEARCH** Writing across the curriculum, assessing writing, the writing process, interdisciplinary connections. **SELECTED PUBLICATIONS** Auth, "A Possible Source of the 'Broken Jaw' Image in T. S. Eliot's 'The Hollow Men,'" Yeats-Eliot Rev 9 (88): 69-71; auth, "The Eve of Rosh Hashanah," TYCA-Southeast J 30.2 (97): 26. **CONTACT ADDRESS** Dept Liberal Arts, Pensacola Junior Col, 5555 W Hwy 98, Pensacola, FL 32507-1015. **EMAIL** mcleod@bellsouth.net

MCLEOD, SUSAN

PERSONAL Born 11/27/1942, Shreveport, LA, m, 1965, 2 children **DISCIPLINE** RHETORIC AND COMPOSITION THEORY **EDUCATION** Wis Univ, PhD. **CAREER** Prof & dept ch, Washington State Univ. **SELECTED PUBLICATIONS** Auth, Dramatic Imagery in the Plays of John Webster, 77 & Notes on the Heart: Affect and the Writing Classroom, 96; ed, Strengthening Programs for Writing Across the Curriculum, 88; sr ed, Writing About the World, text for freshman comp, 91, 2nd ed, 94, & Writing Across the Curriculum: A Guide to Developing Programs, 92; Writing Across the Curriculum for the New Millennium, 00. **CONTACT ADDRESS** Dept of English, Washington State Univ, PO Box 645020, Pullman, WA 99164-5020. **EMAIL** mcleod@wsunix.wsu.edu

MCLUCAS, ANNE DHU

PERSONAL Born 07/26/1941, Denver, CO, d, 1 child **DISCIPLINE** MUSICOLOGY, ETHNOMUSICOLOGY **EDUCATION** Harvard Univ, PhD, 75. **CAREER** Music Dept, Univ Oregon **HONORS AND AWARDS** Dir, NEH-sponsored Summer Inst Col Tchrs, 92; NEH Summer Stipend, Scotland, Brit, 87-88; Am Antiquarian Soc Res Grant, 86-87; NEH Res Grant, 85-86; Clark Fund Res Grant, Harvard Univ, 81-85; Danforth Found Fellow Grad Stud; 65-68; Phi Beta Kappa, Univ Colo, 65; Boettcher Found Scholar, 59; Nat Merit Scholar, 59. **MEMBERSHIPS** Am Musicological Soc; Soc for Ethnomusicology; Col Music Soc; Nat Asn of Schs of Music; Am Folklore Soc, Int Asn for the Study of Popular Music; Int Soc for Traditional Music; Soc for the Study of Traditional Cosmology. **RESEARCH** American Music and its social contexts; British-American folksong; Native-American music; Music of Wilhelm Friedemann Bach. **SELECTED PUBLICATIONS** Ed, Music and Context: Essays for John M. Ward, Cambridge, MA, Harvard Univ, 85; Ed, Charles Dibdin's The Touchstone, or Harlequin Traveller, 1779, 90; ed, Nineteenth Century Melodrama: from A Tale of Mystery to Monte Cristo, Bits and Pieces: Music for Theatre, Harvard Lib Bull, New Series, V 2, n4, 92; ed, Black Sacred Song and the Tune-Family Concept, In Search of New Perspectives in Music: Festschrift Eileen Southern, Warren, MI, Harmonie Pk Press, 92; The Multi-Layered Concept of 'Folk Song' in American Music: The Case of Jean Ritchie's 'The Two Sisters', Themes and Variations: Writings on Music in Honor of Rulan Chao Pian, Cambridge, MA, Harvard Univ Mus Dept, 94, 212-230; Ed, Monte Cristo 1884, Nineteenth-Century Am Mus Theater, NY, Garland Press, 95; From Ballads to Broadway: A Very Brief History of American Musical Theater,1735-1931, Ore Fest of Am Mus Prog Book, 96; On the Importance of Music and Music Education, Tuning up for a Second Century, Portland, OR, Ore Council for the Human, 96; Samuel Preston Bayard: 1908-1997, Folk Mus Jour, 97, 392-393; Louis Moreau Gottschalk and the American Obstacle Course, Ore Festival of Am Mus Prog Book, 97, 12-14; Monodrama, Schetky, Taylor, Pelissier, Tune Families, in The New Grove Dict of Music and Musicians, MacMillan Publ, rev ed, 98; Musical Theater as a Link Between Folk and Popular Traditions, in Vistas of Am Mus: Essays and Compositions in Honor of William K. Kearns, Detroit, Harmonie Pk Press, 98. **CONTACT ADDRESS** Univ of Oregon, 1225 School of Music, Eugene, OR 97403-1225. **EMAIL** amclucas@oregon.uoregon.edu

MCMAHON, ROBERT

DISCIPLINE EPIC, PLATONIST LITERATURE, PHILOSOPHY AND LITERATURE **EDUCATION** Univ Calif, Santa Cruz, PhD, 86. **CAREER** Prof, La State Univ. **HONORS AND AWARDS** Robert L (Doc) Amborski Awd, 87; Phi Kappa Phi Awd, 90; Awd for Excellence in Tchg Freshmen, 94; Alpha Lambda Delta, Nat Freshman Honor Soc; Amoco Awd, 95; Tiger Athletic Found Awd, Honors Col, 96. **RESEARCH** Voegelinian essays; Milton; Dante. **SELECTED PUBLICATIONS** Auth, Homer/Pound's Odysseus and Virgil/Ovid/Dante's Ulysses: Pound's First Canto and the Commedia, Paideuma, 87; Kenneth Burke's Divine Comedy: The Literary Form of The Rhetoric of Religion, PMLA, 89; Augustine's Prayerful Ascent: An Essay on the Literary Form of the Confession, 89; Satan as Infernal Narcissus: Interpretative Translation in the Commedia, in Dante and Ovid: Essays in Intertextuality, 91; 'Coloss. 3.3' as Microcosm, George Herbert J, 93; The Structural Articulation of Boethius' Consolation of Philosophy, Medievalia et Humanistica, 94; The Two Poets of Paradise Lost, 98. **CONTACT ADDRESS** Dept of Eng, Louisiana State Univ and A&M Col, 212K Allen Hall, Baton Rouge, LA 70803.

MCMASTER, JULIET

PERSONAL Born, Kenya **DISCIPLINE** ENGLISH **EDUCATION** Oxford Univ, BA, 59, MA, 62; Univ Alta, MA, 62, PhD, 70. **CAREER** Asst prof, 65-70, assoc prof, 70-76, prof Eng, Univ Alberta, 76-. **HONORS AND AWARDS** Molson Prize Hum Soc Sci, 94. **RESEARCH** 18th and 19th century English novel. **SELECTED PUBLICATIONS** Auth, Thackery: The Major Novels, 71; auth, Trollope's Pallister Novels: Theme and Form, 78; auth, Dickens the Designer, 87; auth, Jane Austen the Novelist: Essays Past and Present, 95; co-ed, The Cambridge Companion to Jane Austen, CUP, 97. **CONTACT ADDRESS** Dept of English, Univ of Alberta, Edmonton, AB, Canada T6G 2E5. **EMAIL** juliet.mcmaster@ualberta.ca

MCMASTER, ROWLAND DOUGLAS

PERSONAL Born 12/05/1928, Sydney, Australia **DISCIPLINE** ENGLISH **EDUCATION** Univ Toronto, BA, 53, MA, 54, PhD(English), 59. **CAREER** Instr, Univ Toronto, 54-56; assoc prof English, Acadia Univ, 57-58; from asst prof to assoc prof, 58-67, Prof English, Univ Alta, 67-. **MEMBERSHIPS** Asn Can Univ Teachers English (pres, 72-74); Int Asn Univ Professors English; MLA; Dickens Soc. **RESEARCH** Victorian novel Dickens; Victorian thought. **SELECTED PUBLICATIONS** Auth, Little Dorrit: experience and design, Queen's Quart, 61; ed, Great Expectations by Charles Dickens, Macmillan, 65; auth, Criticism of civilization in the structure of Sartor Resartus, Univ Toronto Quart, 68; ed, Little Dorrit, Macmillan, 69; Women in the Way We Live Now, English Studies Can, 81; Trollope and the terrible meshes of the law: Mr Scarborough's Family, Nineteenth-Century Fiction, 81; coauth (with Juliet McMaster), The novel from Sterne to James, Macmillan, 81. **CONTACT ADDRESS** Dept of English, Univ of Alberta, Edmonton, AB, Canada T6G 2E5. **EMAIL** rowland.mcmaster@ualberta.ca

MCMILLAN, DOUGLAS J.

PERSONAL Born 07/02/1931, Cleveland, OH, m, 1957, 1 child **DISCIPLINE** ENGLISH LITERATURE **EDUCATION** DePaul Univ, AB, 54; Univ Md, MA, 60; PhD, 63. **CAREER** Instr to assoc prof; Univ of Md, 60-67; assoc prof, Univ of Ark, 67-68; prof, E Carolina Univ, 69-. **HONORS AND AWARDS** Fulbright Fel, Univ Frankfurt, Ger, 54-55. **MEMBERSHIPS** S Atlantic Mod Lang Assoc; Fulbright Assoc; Conf on Christianity and Lit. **RESEARCH** Medieval Liteature, Chaucer, Hoccleue, C.S. Lewis, Religion and Literature. **SELECTED PUBLICATIONS** Auth, "The Phoenix" in Mythical and Fabulous Creatures, ed. Malcolm South (NY:Greenwood, 87) (NY: Peter Bedrick, 88), 59-74; auth, "The Roc" in Mythical and Fabulous Creatures, ed. Malcolm South (NY:Greenwood, 87) (NY: Peter Bedrick, 88), 75-83; auth, "Part One: Materials", Approaches to Teaching Goethe's Faust, Approaches to Teaching World Literature 14, (NY: MLA, 87); auth, "Cistercian Monastic Order is Founded" in Chronology of European History, ed. John Powell (Pasadena: Salem Pr, 97) 1:292-294; auth, "Imprisonment and Death of Boethius" in Chronology of European History, ed. John Powell (Pasadena: Salem Pr, 97), 1:201-202; auth, "Montaigne Publishes His Essays" in Chronology of European History, ed. John Powell (Pasadena: Salem Pr, 97), 2:564-566; coauth, "Rules of Regular Life: Monastic, Canonical, and Mendicant Rules", Documents of Practice Series (Kalamazoo,

MI: The Consortium for Teaching the Middle Ages, Medieval Inst Pub, W Mich Univ, 97); auth, "Discarded and Reclaimed Images, Natives, and Dinosaurs: C.S. Lewis as Teacher and Literary Historian", The Lamp-Post of the S Calif C.S. Lewis Soc: A Lit Rev of Lewis Studies 21 (97):17-25; auth "C.S. Lewis's The Four Loves: A Humanities Synthesis", Humanities in the South No. 80 (98):36-37; auth, "Current Approaches to Selected Medieval and Renaissance Literary Reflections of Religious Culture, rev essay, Relig and the Arts 3.3/4 (99):429-438. **CONTACT ADDRESS** Dept English, East Carolina Univ, 1000 E 5th St, Greenville, NC 27858-2502. **EMAIL** mcmilland@mail.ecu.edu

MCMILLIN, H. SCOTT
PERSONAL Born 06/29/1934, Pittsburgh, PA, m, 1957, 3 children **DISCIPLINE** ENGLISH **EDUCATION** Princeton Univ, BA, 56; Geo Wash Univ, MA, 60; Stanford Univ, PhD, 65. **CAREER** Teach asst, Stanford Univ, 61-63; instr to prof, Cornell Univ, 64-. **HONORS AND AWARDS** Sohmer-Hall Bst Bk Prize; NEH Fel; Clark Dist Teach Awd. **MEMBERSHIPS** SAA; ASTR; MLA. **SELECTED PUBLICATIONS** Auth, The Elizabethan Theatre and the Book of Sir Thomas More, Cornell Univ Press, 87; auth, Shakespeare in Performance: Henry IV Part One, Manchester Univ Press, 91; ed, Wycherley, The Country Wife; Etherege, The Man of Mode; Congreve, The Way of the World; Behn, The Rover; Steele, The Conscious Lovers; and Sheridan, The School for Scandal," in Norton Critical Edition of Restoration and Eighteenth-Century Comedy, WW Norton, 96, 2nd ed; coauth, Queen's Men and Their Plays, 1583-1603, Cambridge Univ Press, 98. **CONTACT ADDRESS** Dept English, Cornell Univ, 252 Goldwin Smith Hall, Ithaca, NY 14853-3201. **EMAIL** hsm3@cornell.edu

MCMULLAN, MARGARET
PERSONAL Born 02/19/1960, Newton, MS, m, 1993, 1 child **DISCIPLINE** ENGLISH **EDUCATION** Grinnell Col, Iowa, BA, 82; Univ Ark, Fayetteville, MFA, 89. **CAREER** Asst prof, Univ Ark, 89-90; fac, Ropewalk Writes Retreat, New Harmony, Ind, June 11-17, 95; vis fac, Harlaxton Col, British Campus of the Univ of Evansville, Grantham, Lincolnshire, England, fall 95; asst prof, Univ of Evansville, 90-96, assoc prof, 96-. **HONORS AND AWARDS** Int Authors and Writers Who's Who; cited in MidAmerica XXIII, 96; Individual Artist Fel, Indiana Arts Comn and NEH, summer 94, 96; Dean's Teacher of the Year Awd, Univ Evansville, 96; First Place in Non-Fiction, The New Press Lit Quart and Lit Soc, NY, fall 93; co-writer and coproducer of film, "Sacred Hearts," selected for competition at the Tenth Annual Ft Lauderdale Int Film Festival, Awded Patrick O'Connor: Winner Special Jury Prize for Best First Feature Film, and Kelly Fritz: Winner Best Feature Film Debut, plus numerous other screenings. **SELECTED PUBLICATIONS** Auth, When Warhol Was Still Alive, Calif: The Crossing Press (94); auth, "When My Friend Died of AIDS," in A Loving Testimony: Remembering Loved Ones Lost to AIDS, ed by Leslea Newman, Calif: The Crossing Press (95): 227-232; auth, "Making Connections," in Tanzania on Tuesday, ed by C. W. Truesdale, Minn: The New Rivers Press (97): 402-406; auth, "To Be Sad Like Ilma," Boulevard, Vol 13, No 1 & 2 (fall 97): 151-160; auth, "The Past is Present in the Pass," Southern Accents, Birmingham, Ala (March/April 97); auth, "Our Mission," Evansville Rev, Vol VII, Evansville, Ind (97); auth, "Why I Took You To the Deathbed of Your Great-Grandmother," Brain, Child, Va (summer 2000); auth, "Love on Wheels," in Shifting Gears: Women and Their Cars, ed by N. Knipe, Papier-Mache Press and Calyx Books (forthcoming); auth, "Driving Home," and "Love on Wheels," in Drive, She Said, ed by Margo Solod, Mass (forthcoming). **CONTACT ADDRESS** Dept English, Univ of Evansville, 1800 Lincoln Ave, Evansville, IN 47714-1506.

MCMULLEN, LORRAINE
PERSONAL Born 07/27/1926, Ottawa, ON, Canada **DISCIPLINE** ENGLISH **EDUCATION** Univ Ottawa, BS, 48, BA, 63, MA, 67, PhD, 70. **CAREER** Asst prof, assoc prof, prof, dept English, Univ Ottawa, 69-92; adj prof, Univ Victoria, 92-; Prof Emer English, Univ Ottawa, 92-. **MEMBERSHIPS** SSHRCC Comt Res Tools, 85-87 **RESEARCH** Canadian literature, images of women in Canadian literature, nineteenth-century Canadian fiction, Fanny Burney, biography. **SELECTED PUBLICATIONS** Auth, Sinclair Ross, G.K. Hall, 79; ed, Ethel Wilson Symposium, Univ of Ottawa Pr, 82; ed, The Race and Other Stories by Sinclair Ross, Univ of Ottawa Pr, 82; auth, An Odd Attempt in a Woman: The Literary Life of Frances Brooke, Univ of BC Pr, 83; auth, Ernest Thompson Seton: the Man and His Works, ECW, 89; ed, Re(Dis)covering our Foremothers: Nineteenth-Century Canadian Women Writers, Univ of Ottawa Pr, 90; coed, New Women: Stories by Canadian Women 1900-1920, Univ of Ottawa Pr, 91; coauth, Silenced Sextet: Six Nineteenth-Century Canadian Women Writers, McGill-Queen's Univ Pr, 93; coed, Aspiring Women: Stories by Canadian Women 1880-1920, Univ of Ottawa Pr, 93; coed, Pioneering Women: Stories by Canadian Women, Beginnings to 1880, Univ of Ottawa Pr, 93. **CONTACT ADDRESS** Dept of English, Univ of Ottawa, 70 Laurier Ave E, Third Floor, PO Box 450, Station A, Ottawa, ON, Canada K1N 6N5. **EMAIL** mcmullen@pop.uvic.ca

MCMULLEN, MARGARET
PERSONAL Born 02/19/1960, Newton, MS, m, 1993, 1 child **DISCIPLINE** ENGLISH **EDUCATION** Grinnell Col, BA, 82; Radcliffe Col, 82; Univ Arkansas, MFA, 89. **CAREER** Assoc Entertainment Ed, Glamour, 82-85; Asst prof English, Univ Arkansas, 89-90; Asst prof English, 90-96, Assoc Prof English, Univ Evansville, 96- ; vis fac, Harlaxton Col, Grantham, Eng, 95; Individual Artist fel, 94 & 96; Dean's Tchr Yr, Univ Evansville, 96. **HONORS AND AWARDS** When Warhol Was Still Alive won award for Best Adult Fiction from the Society of Midland Authors, First Prize Non-Fiction, My Right Breast, New Press Lit Quart & Lit Soc, 93. **MEMBERSHIPS** Auth Guild; Assoc Writing Prog; MLA. **RESEARCH** Creative fiction; Creative nonfiction. **SELECTED PUBLICATIONS** Auth, My Sister's Problem with Food and Me, Eating Our Hearts Out: Women and Food, The Crossing Press, 93; auth, When Warhol Was Still Alive, The Crossing Press, 94; auth, Lifeguarding, Bless Me, Father, Plume/Penguin, 94; Saying Goodbye to Joey, Breaking Up is Hard to Do, The Crossing Press, 94; coauth, Sacred Hearts, Am Mongrel Filmmakers, 95; auth, When My Friend Died of AIDS, A Loving Testimony: Remembering Loved Ones Lost to AIDS, The Crossing Press, 95; ed World Cultures Faculty Handbook, Univ Evansville, 96; auth, To Be Sad Like Ilma, Boulevard, St. Louis Univ, 97; auth, The Past is Present in the Pass, Southern Accents, 97; Our Mission, Evansville Rev, 97. **CONTACT ADDRESS** English Dept, Univ of Evansville, 1800 Lincoln Ave, Evansville, IN 47722. **EMAIL** mm44@evansville.edu

MCMULLEN, WAYNE
PERSONAL Born 12/10/1954, Trenton, NJ **DISCIPLINE** SPEECH **EDUCATION** Temple Univ, BA, 80; Auburn Univ, MA, 82; Pa State Univ, PhD, 89. **CAREER** Instr, Pa State Univ, 82-87; instr to asst prof, West Chester Univ, 88-91; asst to assoc prof, Pa State Univ, 91-. **HONORS AND AWARDS** Outstanding Teacher of the Year, Pa State Univ, 97; George W. Atherton Awd for Excellence in Undergraduate Teaching, 00. **MEMBERSHIPS** Nat Commun Assoc; Org for Res and Women. **RESEARCH** Rhetoric of Film. **SELECTED PUBLICATIONS** Coauth, "Places in the Heart: The Rhetorical Force of an Open Text", Western J of Speech Commun 55, (91): 339-353; coauth, "The Politics of Adaptation: Steven Spielberg's Appropriation of The Color Purple", Text and Performance Quarterly 14, (94): 158-174; auth, "The China Syndrome: Corruption to the Core", Lit/Film Quarterly 23, (95): 55-62; auth, "Mythic Perspectives in Film Criticism", J of the Northwest Commun Assoc 24, (96): 17-30; auth, "Gender and the American Dream in Kramer vs. Kramer", Women's Studies in Commun 19, (96): 29-54; auth, "Reconstruction of the Frontier Myth in Witness", Southern Commun J 62, (96): 31-41; coauth, "Portrayals of Women's Friendships in Thelma and Louise", (forthcoming); auth, "Sleep No More: Issues of Paranoia and conformity in Invasion of the Body Snatchers", (forthcoming). **CONTACT ADDRESS** Dept Speech, Pennsylvania State Univ, Delaware County, 25 Yearsley Mill Rd, Media, PA 19063-5522. **EMAIL** wjm11@psu.edu

MCMUNN, MARADITH T.
PERSONAL Born Shreveport, LA, m, 1966 **DISCIPLINE** ENGLISH **EDUCATION** Ind Univ, BS, 65; MA, 67; Univ Conn, PhD, 78. **CAREER** Prof, RI Col. **HONORS AND AWARDS** Phi Mu; Phi Kappa Phi; Phi Beta Kappa; Dean's List, Ind Univ, 62-65; NEH Grants, 80-81, 87, 89, 92-93, 95, 98-9; Samuel H. Kress Found Grant, 88; RI State Counc for the Arts Grant, 89-90; RI Col Fac Res Grants 84-85, 87, 89, 91-95, 97-99; IREX Grant, 95. **MEMBERSHIPS** Medieval Acad of Am; Anglo-Norman Text Soc; Charles Homer Haskins Soc; Early Book Soc; Int Arthurian Soc; Int Center for the Study of Medieval Art; Int Courtly Lit Assoc; Int Soc of Anglo-Saxonists; Medieval and Renaissance Drama Soc. **RESEARCH** Medieval literature, text and illustration in medieval manuscripts. **SELECTED PUBLICATIONS** Auth, "In Love and War: Images of Warfare in the Illustrated Manuscripts of the Roman de la Rose", Chivalry, Knighthood, and War in the Middle Ages, ed Susan Ridyard, Univ of the South, (Sewanee, TN, 99): 165-193; auth, "A Fragment of an Unknown Manuscript of the Roman de la Rose", Princeton Univ Libr Chronicle 60 (99): 276-303; auth, "Parrots and Poets in Late Medieval Literature", Anthrozoos 12 (99): 68-75; auth, "Reconstructing a Missing Manuscript of the Roman de la Rose: The Jersey Manuscript", Scriptorium 53 (Fall 99): 31-62; auth, "Illustrated Fragments of the Roman de la Rose", Interpreting and Collecting Fragments of Medieval Books, eds Linda Brownrigg and Margaret Smith, Anderson-Lovelace Pr, (Los Altos, 00): 66-81; auth, "The Programs of Illustration in Rose Manuscripts Owned By Patrons and Friends of Christine de Pizan", Acts of the Third Int Christine de Pizan Congress, Univ of Lausanne, Slatkine Pr, (Geneva), 00; auth, "Medieval Manuscripts in South African Libraries", Early Book Soc J, 00; auth, "Illustrating Yseult", Arthurian Women: Studies in Memory of Maureen Fries, eds Fiona Tolhurst and Bonnie Wheeler, 00; auth, "Collins '65-35-3: The Roman de la Rose in the Philadelphia Museum of Art", Leaves of Gold, ed James Tanis, Philadelphia Museum of Art, March 01. **CONTACT ADDRESS** Dept English, Rhode Island Col, 600 Mt Pleasant Ave, Providence, RI 02908-1924. **EMAIL** mmcmunn@ric.edu

MCMURTRY, JOSEPHINE
PERSONAL Born 12/07/1937, Bristol, VA, d, 1 child **DISCIPLINE** ENGLISH LITERATURE **EDUCATION** Tex Woman's Univ, BA, 59; Rice Univ, PhD(English), 69. **CAREER** Asst prof, 69-74, assoc prof, 74-86, Prof English, Univ Richmond, 86-. **MEMBERSHIPS** Shakespeare Asn Am **RESEARCH** Shakespeare; 16th century narrative poetry, 19th century British fiction. **SELECTED PUBLICATIONS** Auth, Victorian Life and Victorian Fiction, Archon Bks, 79; English Language, English Literature, Archon Books, 85; Understanding Shakespeare's England, Archon Books, 89; Shakespeare Films in the Classroom, Archon Books, 94; auth, Julius Caesar: A Guide to the Play, Greenwood Press, 98. **CONTACT ADDRESS** Dept of English, Univ of Richmond, 28 Westhampton Way, Richmond, VA 23173-0002.

MCNAIR, MARCIA
PERSONAL Born 12/17/1957, Summit, NJ, d, 2 children **DISCIPLINE** ENGLISH **EDUCATION** Dartmouth Col, BA, 80; New York Univ, MA, 89. **CAREER** Asst prog coordr, African Studies, New York Univ, 11/84 to 3/87; instr, City Univ of New York, 92-94; prof, Molloy Col, 98-; prof, Nassau Community Col, SUNY, 95-; asst ed, Essence Mag, 10/80 to 11/83; ed, online mag, Intellectual Homegirl. **HONORS AND AWARDS** ABWHE Certificate of Recognition, Long Island Chapter, 95. **MEMBERSHIPS** Sigma Delta Chi, Asn of Black Women in Higher Ed. **RESEARCH** African American literature, African American popular culture. **SELECTED PUBLICATIONS** Auth, "The War on the Poor," Our Times (April 16, 96); auth, "It Takes A Lioness to Raise Young Lions," On the Issues/The Progressive Woman's Quart (fall 98). **CONTACT ADDRESS** Dept english, Nassau Comm Col, 1 Education Dr, Garden City, NY 11530-6719. **EMAIL** mcnairm@sunynassau.edu

MCNAMEE, KATHLEEN
PERSONAL Born 11/27/1949, Cambridge, MA, m, 1986, 2 children **DISCIPLINE** CLASSICS **EDUCATION** Duke Univ, PhD, 77. **CAREER** From instr to prof to ch, Dept Classics, Greek, &Latin, Wayne State Univ, 76-; interim dean, Col Lib Arts, Wayne State Univ, 92-94, chair 94-99. **MEMBERSHIPS** Am Philol Asn. **RESEARCH** Papyrology; Greek literature; Latin poetry. **SELECTED PUBLICATIONS** Auth, Abbreviations in Greek Literary Papyri and Ostraca, 81; auth, Sigla and Select Marginalia in Greek Literary Papyri: Papyrologica Bruxellensia, Aug, 92; auth, Classical Studies Presented to William Hailey Willis, Bulletin of the Am Soc Papyrologists, 85; auth, Another Chapter in the History of Scholia, Class Quart, 98; auth, An Innovation in Annotated Codices on Papyrus, Akten des 21, Internationalen Papyrologenkongresses, Berlin, 1995, 97; auth, Missing Links in the Development of Scholia, Greek, Roman, & Byzantine Studies, July, 96. **CONTACT ADDRESS** Dept of Classics, Greek & Latin, Wayne State Univ, 431 Manoogian Hall, Detroit, MI 48202. **EMAIL** k.mcnamee@wayne.edu

MCNAMEE, MAURICE BASIL
PERSONAL Born 06/05/1909, Montello, WI **DISCIPLINE** ENGLISH **EDUCATION** St Louis Univ, AB, 33, AM, 34, STL, 41, PhD, 45. **CAREER** Instr, 36-37, Creighton Prep Sch; from asst prof to assoc prof Eng, 44-60, prof, 60-77, chmn dept, 56-77, Emer Prof Eng, Art & Art History & Dir, 77-, Cupples House, ST Louis Univ; Fulbright res fel, Belgium, 65-66; Am Philos Soc res grants, 65-66 & 78; Ford Found Jesuit Fac Fund res grant, St Louis Univ, 66-68; dir, Cupples House Mus, 74-77. **HONORS AND AWARDS** Nancy McNeir Ring Outstanding Fac Awd, St Louis Univ, 73. **MEMBERSHIPS** MLA; Col Art Assn Am; Mediaeval Acad Am. **RESEARCH** Symbolism in Flemish painting; mannerism and surrealism in art and literature. **SELECTED PUBLICATIONS** Auth, Literary Decorum in Francis Bacon, St Louis Univ, 50; Reading for Understanding, 68; auth, Honor and the Epic Hero, 59; auth, Literary Types and Themes, Holt, 60; art, Bacon's Inductive Method and Humanistic Grammar, Studies Lit Imag, 71; art, The Origin of the Vested Angel as a Eucharistic Symbol in Flemish Painting, Art Bull, 73; auth, Medieval Latin Liturgical Drama and the Annunciation by the Aix-en-Provence Master, Gaz des Beaux-Arts, 74; art, Good Friday Liturgy and the Hans Memling Antwerp Triptych, J Warburg & Courtauld Insts, 74; auth, Vested Angels, Deeters Loresen, 97. **CONTACT ADDRESS** Dept of Art History, Saint Louis Univ, 221 Grand Ave St, Louis, MO 63103.

MCNARON, TONI ANN HURLEY
PERSONAL Born 04/03/1937, Birmingham, AL **DISCIPLINE** ENGLISH **EDUCATION** Univ Ala, BA, 58; Vanderbilt Univ, MA, 60; Univ Wis, PhD(English), 64. **CAREER** Instr English & geog, All Saint's Episcopal Col, 59-61; asst prof, 64-67, Assoc Prof English, Univ Minn, Minneapolis, 67-. **HONORS AND AWARDS** Distinguished Teacher Awd, Univ Minn, 67, 68, 82, 92; Outstanding Service Awd, Univ Minn, 00. **MEMBERSHIPS** MLA; Nat Women's Studies Asn; NCTE; Aaup; Am Asn Higher Educ. **RESEARCH** Emily Dickinson; Shakespeare's women; lesbian poetry. **SELECTED PUBLICATIONS** Auth, Finding and studying lesbian culture, Radical Teacher, winter 78; co-ed, Voices in the Night: Women's Writings on Incest, Cleis Press, 82; auth, I Dwell in Possibility, Feminist Press, 84; co-ed, New Lesbian Studies: Into the 21st Century, Feminist Press, 97; Poisoned Ivy: Lesbian and Gay Academics Confronting Homophobia, 97. **CONTACT ADDRESS** Dept of English, Univ of Minnesota, Twin Cities, 207 Church St SE, Minneapolis, MN 55455-0156. **EMAIL** mcnar001@tc.umn.edu

MCPEAK, JUDITH L.
PERSONAL Born 01/03/1940, Tampa, FL, m, 1973, 3 children **DISCIPLINE** COMMUNICATION **EDUCATION** Flor State Univ, BS, 87; MS, 89; PhD, 93. **CAREER** Asst prof, Alb State Col, 93-95; assoc prof, prof, 95-, Mob Univ. **HONORS AND AWARDS** Dir Mark Inst Fel. **MEMBERSHIPS** NCA; SSCA; PRCA; Toastmasters Intl. **RESEARCH** Women as persuasive communicators; women in cartoons. **CONTACT ADDRESS** Dept Communication, Univ of Mobile, PO Box 13220, Mobile, AL 36663-0220. **EMAIL** jlmcpeak@hotmail.com

MCPHAIL, MARK L.
DISCIPLINE COMMUNICATION STUDIES **EDUCATION** Univ Mass, PhD, 87. **CAREER** Prof. **RESEARCH** Rhetorical theory and epistemology; language of race relations. **SELECTED PUBLICATIONS** Auth, Zen and the Art of Rhetoric; The Rhetoric of Racism. **CONTACT ADDRESS** Dept of Communication, Univ of Utah, 100 S 1350 E, Salt Lake City, UT 84112.

MCPHAIL, THOMAS LAWRENCE
PERSONAL Born 04/13/1942, Hamilton, Ontario, Canada, m, 1985, 3 children **DISCIPLINE** COMMUNICATION STUDIES **EDUCATION** McMaster Univ, BA; State Univ NYork Buffalo, MA; Purdue Univ, PhD. **SELECTED PUBLICATIONS** Auth, Population Shift Plus Pay-Per-View: The New Dynamics of American TV, Intermedia, 92; Issues and Opportunities for Telecoms in Rural Areas, Telecommunication Rev, 93; co-auth, Communication: The Canadian Experience, Copp Clark Pitman, 90; Teleconferencing in Rural America: Major Obstacles, 91; The Future of Broadcasting: The Effect of Pay-Per-View, Feedback, 92. **CONTACT ADDRESS** Communication Dept, Univ of Missouri, St. Louis, 590 Lucas Hall, Saint Louis, MO 63121. **EMAIL** stlmcph@umsl.edu

MCPHERSON, DAVID
DISCIPLINE RENAISSANCE LITERATURE **EDUCATION** Univ Tex, PhD, 66. **CAREER** Instr, Univ NMex, 72-. **SELECTED PUBLICATIONS** Auth, Shakespeare, Jonson, and the Myth of Venice, 90. **CONTACT ADDRESS** Dept of English, Univ of New Mexico, Albuquerque, Albuquerque, NM 87131. **EMAIL** dmac@unm.edu

MCPHERSON, JAMES ALAN
PERSONAL Born 09/16/1943, Savannah, GA, d, 1 child **DISCIPLINE** LITERATURE, HISTORY, LAW **EDUCATION** Morris Brown Col, BA, 65; Harvard Law School, LLB, 68; Writers Workshop, Univ IA, MFA, 71. **CAREER** Lect, Univ CA at Santa Cruz, 69-71; asst prof, Morgan State Univ, 75-76; assoc prof, Univ VA, 76-81; prof, Univ IA, 81-. **HONORS AND AWARDS** Pulitzer Prize, 78; MacArthur Prize Fellows Award, 81. **MEMBERSHIPS** ACLU; NAACP; Authors Guild; Am Acad of Arts and Scis; fel, Ctr for Advanced Studies, Stanford Univ, 97-98. **RESEARCH** Law. **SELECTED PUBLICATIONS** Auth, Hue and Cry, 69; auth, Railroad, 73; auth, Elbow Room, 77; auth, Crabcakes, 98; Fatherly Daughter, 98. **CONTACT ADDRESS** Dept of English, The Univ of Iowa, Iowa City, IA 52242.

MCQUEENEY, MARY PATRICIA
PERSONAL Born 09/06/1946, Olean, NY **DISCIPLINE** ENGLISH COMPOSITION **EDUCATION** Univ Kans, BSEd, 68; MA, 71; MA, 87; PhD, 95. **CAREER** Teacher, Miss School Dist, 68-76; teacher, Prairie View School Dist, 76-85; GTA to assoc dir, Univ of Kans, 85-99; prof, Johnson County Community Col, 99-. **MEMBERSHIPS** MLA, NCTE, Kans Assoc of Teachers of English, Counc of Writing Program Admin. **RESEARCH** Writing across the curriculum, academic writing, transferability, freshman-sophomore English. **SELECTED PUBLICATIONS** Auth, "Preparing Students for Freshman English. A Question of Critical Literacy," Kans Eng, (92); coauth, "Integrating Writing Skills," Teaching and Directing the Basic Commun Course, (92); coauth, "Writing as a Tool for Teaching Public Speaking: A Campus Application," Basic Commun Course Annual, (94); auth, "Proposing a Writing Center: Experts? Advice?" Writing Center Newsletter, (97); auth, "Cementing Writing: A Writing Partnership with Civil Engineering?" Jour of Lang and Learning Across the Disciplines, (99); auth, "What's in a Name?" Politics of Writing Centers, eds Jane Nelson and Kathy Evertz, (01). **CONTACT ADDRESS** Johnson County Comm Col, 12345 College Blvd, Overland Park, KS 66210. **EMAIL** pmcqueen@jccc.net

MCSHEA, WILLIAM PATRICK
PERSONAL Born 08/16/1930, Pittsburgh, PA, m, 1955, 3 children **DISCIPLINE** HISTORY, LATIN CLASSICS **EDUCATION** St Vincent Col, BA, 52; Duquesne Univ, MA, 54. **CAREER** From instr to assoc prof hist, Mt Mercy Col, 53-70; PROF & CHMN, DEPT HIST, CARLOW COL, 70-, DIR, PEACE STUDIES PROG, 76-, Prof, Comp Communism Consortia, var univs in Pa, 73-; mem adv coun, Int Poetry Forum, 77-. **MEMBERSHIPS** Int Soc Psycho Historians. **RESEARCH** Reformation; psycho history; recent American history. **SELECTED PUBLICATIONS** Coauth, Community of Learners, Pittsburgh Pa Com Press, 70. **CONTACT ADDRESS** Carlow Col, 3333 Fifth Ave, Pittsburgh, PA 15213.

MCTAGGART, WILLIAM
DISCIPLINE WRITING **EDUCATION** Ohio Univ, PhD. **CAREER** Dept ch, 90-95; prof. **HONORS AND AWARDS** Fulbright scholar, Oxford, 68-69; fac adv, rugby. **RESEARCH** Autobiographical writing. **SELECTED PUBLICATIONS** Auth, History of 100 years of Titan football. **CONTACT ADDRESS** Dept of Eng, Westminster Col, Pennsylvania, 6 Gateway Rd., New Wilmington, PA 16142. **EMAIL** bmctagrt@westminister.edu

MCVEIGH, PAUL J.
PERSONAL Born 10/10/1947, Philadelphia, PA, s, 1 child **DISCIPLINE** ENGLISH LITERATURE **EDUCATION** Am Univ, BA, 71; Univ Va, MA, 72; Trinity Col, Dublin, PhD, 84 **CAREER** Chemn, Northern Va Commun Col, 89-. **HONORS AND AWARDS** Chancellor's Common Wealth Prof, 89-91; Excellence Tchg Awd, Northern Va Commun Col Educ Found, 89; dir, inst tchr as learner, state council funds for excellence grant, 94-96. **CONTACT ADDRESS** Humanities Div, No Virginia Comm Col, 3001 N Beauregard St, Alexandria, VA 22311. **EMAIL** nvmcvep@nv.cc.va.us

MCWHORTER, STANLEY B.
PERSONAL Born 06/17/1930, Osco, KY **DISCIPLINE** ENGLISH **EDUCATION** Transylvania Univ, BA, 54; Univ Ky, MA, 61; PhD, 61. **CAREER** Instr, SW Col, 59-60; instr, Morehead State Univ, 60-61; asst prof, E Ky State Univ, 61-63; prof, WVir Wesleyan Col, 63-67; prof, Univ SCar, 67-70; prof, Xavier Univ, 72-75; prof, Univ Dayton, 84-95. **HONORS AND AWARDS** Lindsey Wilson Fel, 48; Transylvania Fel, 53; Univ Ky Fel 60; Hon Leadership Scholar; Folklore Res Grants; Nat Folk Festival Head; Brit-Am Balladry Studies Grant, Wesleyan Univ; Teaching Excellence Grant; Knights Pythias Grant; Res Achievement Scholar. **MEMBERSHIPS** MLA; NCTE; AAUP; CEA; ASDC; Who's Who Midwest; Intl Who's Who; Who's Who in Am; Dict Int Biog; NEA. **RESEARCH** Collect, transcribe, edit, publish and perform the authentic British and American oral ballad and folksong; proposed book-length study of Appalachian and Allegheny Folklore; literary and cultural differences; Appalachian dulcimer; autoharp, guitar and Hohner accordion. **SELECTED PUBLICATIONS** Auth, Annotated Bibliography of William Wordsworth's Writings, Univ Ky, 61; auth, "Impressions of the 49'ers," Kans J (60); auth, Religious Struggle in English Poets, Use of Folk Ballad in English Class, 71; auth, "Superstitions of Appalachia," Ky Folklore Record (75); auth, "What is Life?" Am Sings (80); auth, "Vocabulary of Emotion, "WVir J Teachers English (80); auth, "Poetry About Appalachia," Ann Anthol Co Poetry Lit (80); auth, Johnson and Eliot on the Metaphysicals, AAUP, 82; auth, "Recent Trends in Scholarship: Wordsworth, Coleridge," SCar J Teachers English (85); auth, "The Ballad: Studied and Performed," Ky Folklore Record (89). **CONTACT ADDRESS** English Dept, Univ of Dayton, 300 College Park Ave, Dayton, OH 45469. **EMAIL** mcwhrca@aol.com

MCWILLIAMS, JOHN P.
PERSONAL Born 07/22/1940, Cleveland, OH, m, 1985, 6 children **DISCIPLINE** ENGLISH **EDUCATION** Princeton Univ, AB, 62; Harvard Univ, AM, 63; PhD, 68. **CAREER** Univ CA Berkeley, asst prof 68-74; Univ IL, assoc prof 75-77; prof, Univ of Md, 84-85; prof, Middlebury Col, 78-. **HONORS AND AWARDS** Phi Beta Kappa; 3 NEH fellowships; Woodrow Wilson Nat Fel, 62-63; Univ of Calif Humanities Fel, 71-72. **MEMBERSHIPS** ALA; MLA; ASA. **RESEARCH** Early Am Lit, Cult to 1860. **SELECTED PUBLICATIONS** Auth, Political Justice in a Republic: James Fenimore Cooper's America, Univ of Calif Press, 72; auth, Hawthorne, Melville and the American Character: A Looking Glass Business, Cambridge Univ Press, 84; auth, The Last of the Mohicans: Civil Savagery and Savage Civility, Twayne-Macmillan, 94; ed, James Fenmore Cooper, The Last of the Mohicans, Oxford Univ Press, 90, 2d ed, rev expanded 94, 3d ed 98; The American Epic: Transforming a Genre, Cambridge Univ Press, 89; Indian John and the Northern Tawnies, New Eng Quarterly, 96; Poetry, Columbia Univ Press, 93; The Epic in the Nineteenth Century, Columbia History of America. **CONTACT ADDRESS** Dept of Am Lit, Middlebury Col, Adirondack House, Middlebury, VT 05753. **EMAIL** mcwillia@middlebury.edu

MEADOWS, EDDIE
PERSONAL Born 06/24/1939, LaGrange, TN, m, 1996 **DISCIPLINE** ETHNOMUSICOLOGY, JAZZ STUDIES **EDUCATION** Tenn State Univ, BA; Univ Ill, MS; Mich State Univ, PhD; Univ Calif, postdoc stud; study at Univ of Ghana. **CAREER** Vis prof, Univ Calif, Berkeley; vis prof, Univ Ghana, W Africa; vis prof, UCLA; vis prof, Mich State Univ; prof, grad adv, San Diego State Univ, School of Music and Dance. **HONORS AND AWARDS** Martin Luther King distinguished vis profship, MI State Univ; Meritorious Performance and Prof Promise awards, San Diego State Univ. **MEMBERSHIPS** Jazz Educrs; Soc for Ethnomusicology; African Studies Asn. **RESEARCH** African-American music; Jazz studies. **SELECTED PUBLICATIONS** Auth, Afro-America Music, 76; auth, Theses and Dissertations on Black and American Music, 80; auth, Jazz Reference and Research Materials, 81; auth, Jazz Research and Performance Materials: A Select Annotated Bibliography, 95; coed, California Soul: Music of African Americans in the West, Univ of Calif Press, 98. **CONTACT ADDRESS** Sch Mus and Dance, San Diego State Univ, 5500 Campanile Dr, San Diego, CA 92182. **EMAIL** meadows@mail.sdsu.edu

MEANOR, PATRICK
PERSONAL Born 02/22/1938, Cambridge, OH, s **DISCIPLINE** ENGLISH **EDUCATION** John Carroll Univ, BA, 61; MA, 66; Kent State Univ, PhD, 74. **CAREER** From Instr to Prof, State Univ NYork (SUNY), 74-. **HONORS AND AWARDS** Outstanding Teaching Awd, Kent St Univ, 71; NEH Grant, Univ Calif, 83; Chancellor's Awd for Excellence in Teaching, SUNY, 96; Distinguished Teaching Prof, SUNY, 00. **RESEARCH** Contemporary American short story and classical piano music. **SELECTED PUBLICATIONS** Auth, John Cheever Revisited, Twayne-Macmillan (New York), 95; auth, "The Signing," in Masterplots II: Short Story Suppl (96): 3648-3750; auth, "The Black Cloud," in Magill's Guide to Sci Fiction and Fantasy (Pasadena, CA: Salem Pr, 96), 66-67; auth, "A Conversation with Pianist Jean-Yves Thibaudet," Listener Mag, vol 3, no 3 (97): 60-66; auth, "Making People Come Alive: An Interview with Naumburg winner: Pianist, Anthony Molinaro," Listener Mag, vol 4, no 1 (98): 61-67; auth, "A Conversation with Pianist Sergei Babayan: Patrick Meanor," Listener, vol 5, no 4 (99): 56-58; co-ed, American Short-Story Writers Since World War II: Second Series, vol 218 of The Dict of Lit Biog, 00. **CONTACT ADDRESS** Dept English, SUNY, Col at Oneonta, PO Box 4015, Oneonta, NY 13820-4015.

MEATS, STEPHEN EARL
PERSONAL Born 03/16/1944, LeRoy, KS, m, 1983, 3 children **DISCIPLINE** AMERICAN LITERATURE **EDUCATION** Univ SC, BA, 66, MA, 68, PhD(Am lit), 72. **CAREER** Asst prof English, US Air Force Acad, 68-72; assoc prof, Univ Tampa, 72-74, chp, Humanities Div, 74-79; prof & chp, English Dept, Pittsburg State Univ, 79-, vis res prof, Southern Studies Prog, Univ SC, 75 & 76. **HONORS AND AWARDS** Cert of Commendation, Am Asn State & Local Hist, 77. **MEMBERSHIPS** AWD; Asn Depts English. **RESEARCH** Nineteenth century American literature; William Faulkner; modern Am poetry. **SELECTED PUBLICATIONS** Auth, Who Killed Joanna Burden?, Miss Quart, summer 71; Addenda to Van Winkle: Henry William Herbert (Frank Forester), Publ Bibliog Soc Am, spring 73; Introduction and explanatory notes for Simms' Joscelyn, A Tale of the Revolution, Univ SC Press, 75; co-ed, Revolutionary War Novels of William Gilmore Simms, 8 vols, Reprint Co, 76; auth, Artist vs historian: Simms and the Revolutionary South, In: 18th Century Florida and the Revolutionary South, Univ Presses of Fla, 78; auth & ed, South Carolina Writers in the Spirit of the Times, Gyascutas, Humanities Press, 78; auth, Henry William Herbert (Frank Forester), In: Dict of Literary Biography, Gale Res, 79; ed, Selected Writings of Benjamin F Perry, 3 vols, Reprint Co, 80; auth, "Bald-Head Bill Bauldy: Simms' Unredeemed Captive," Studies in Am Humor, winter 84-85; poetry ed, Midwest Quart, 85-; auth, "Joseph Gault, Unknown Georgia Humorist," Mississippi Quart, fall 98. **CONTACT ADDRESS** English Dept, Pittsburg State Univ, 1701 S Broadway St, Pittsburg, KS 66762-7500. **EMAIL** smeats@pittstate.edu

MEDHURST, MARTIN J.
PERSONAL Born 10/15/1952, Alton, IL, m, 1989, 2 children **DISCIPLINE** SPEECH COMMUNICATION **EDUCATION** Wheaton Col, BA, 74; Northern Ill Univ, MA, 75; Penn State Univ, PhD, 80. **CAREER** Asst prof, 79-85, assoc prof, 85-88, Univ of Calif at Davis; ASSOC PROF, 88-91, PROF, 91-, TEXAS A&M UNIV; coordr, Prog in Presidential Rhetoric, Bush School of Gov and Public Service, 93-. **HONORS AND AWARDS** Nat Commun Asn Golden Anniversary Prize Fund Awd, 82; Religious Speech Commun Asn Pub Awd, 83; Marie Hochmuth Nichols Awd for Outstanding Scholar in Public Address, 95 & 97; Naomi Lews Fac Fel in Liberal Arts, Tex A&M Univ, 93-94 & 94-95; Speech Commun Asn Anniversary Prize Fund Awd, 82; Paul K. Crawford Awd for Outstanding Graduate Student, Northern Ill Univ, 75; found ed, Rhetoric & Public Affais. **MEMBERSHIPS** Nat Commun Asn; Southern Commun Asn; Western Commun Asn; Int Soc for the Hist of Rhetoric; Rhetoric Soc of Am; Soc for Historians of Am Foreign Relations; Coun of Eds of Learned Journs. **RESEARCH** Cold War rhetoric; Presidential rhetoric; rhetoric of film. **SELECTED PUBLICATIONS** Auth, Eisenhower's Atoms for Peace Speech: A Case Study in the Strategic Use of Language, Comm Monos, 54, 87; auth, Truman's Rhetorical Reticence, 1945-1947: An Interpretive Esaay, Q J of Speech 74, 88; co-auth, Cold War Rhetoric: Strategy, Metaphor, and Ideology, Greenwood Pr, 90; ed, Landmark Essays on American Public Address, Erlbaum, 93; auth, Dwight D. Eisenhower: Strategic Communicator, Greenwood Pr, 93; ed, Eisenhower's War of Words: Rhetoric and Leadership, Mich State Univ Pr, 94; auth, Reconceptualizing Rhetorical History: Eisenhower's Farewell Address, Q J of Speech 80, 95; ed, Beyond the Rhetorical Presidency, Tex A&M Unic Pr, 96; auth, Eisenhower and the Cursade for Freedom: The Rhetorical Origins of a Cold War Campaign, Pres Studies Q 27, 97; auth, Writing Speeches for Ronald Reagan: An Interview with Tony Dolan, Rhet & Pub Aff 1, 98; co-ed, Critical Reflections on the Cold War, Tex A&M Univ Pr, 00. **CONTACT ADDRESS** Dept of Speech Commun, Texas A&M Univ, Col Station, College Station, TX 77843. **EMAIL** m-medhurst@tamu.edu

MEDINE, PETER ERNEST
PERSONAL Born 03/30/1941, DeKalb, IL, 1 child **DISCIPLINE** LITERATURE OF THE ENGLISH RENAISSANCE **EDUCATION** Northwestern Univ, Evanston, BA, 63; Univ Wis-Madison, MA, 65, PhD, 70. **CAREER** From instr to asst prof, 69-75, assoc prof 75-94, prof, Univ Ariz, 94-. **HONORS AND AWARDS** Folger Shakespeare Libr fel; Huntington Libr fel. **MEMBERSHIPS** MLA; Renaissance Soc Am; Philol Asn Pac Coast. **RESEARCH** Renaissance poetry, prose and drama. **SELECTED PUBLICATIONS** Ed, Horace His Arte of Poetrie, Scholars' Facsimiles & Reprints, 72; auth, Praise and blame in Renaissance satire, Pac Coast Philol, 72; ed, De Satyrica Graecorum Poesi et Romanorum Satira, Scholars' Facsimiles & Reprints, 73; auth, Object and intention in Jonson's Famous Voyage, Studies English Lit, 75; Casaubon's Prolegomena to the Satires of Persius: An introduction, text & translation, English Lit Renaissance, 76; Martial's Epigrammata and the Poematium: An hypothesis, Pac Coast Philol, 77; auth, Thomas Wilson, Twayne, 86; ed, Thomas Wilson's Art of Rhetoric, Penn State, 94; ed, Soundings of Things Done, Del, 97. **CONTACT ADDRESS** Dept of English, Univ of Arizona, 459 Modern Lang Bldg, PO Box 210067, Tucson, AZ 85721. **EMAIL** medine@u.arizona.edu

MEEK, EDWIN
PERSONAL Born 03/24/1951, Quincy, MA, m, 1985, 1 child **DISCIPLINE** ENGLISH **EDUCATION** Univ Mass, BA, 73; MEA, 76; MA, 98. **CAREER** Sen lecturer, Curry Col, 85-. **MEMBERSHIPS** NCTE, AAUP. **SELECTED PUBLICATIONS** Auth, Pride in Blue, A History of the Milton Police, Quincy MA, 90; auth, "The Question of Audience," New Writers' Magazine, 99; auth, "First-year college students: Remember why you are There," The Learning Section, Boston Globe, 98; auth, "Hunting the Snark," The Connecticut Poetry Review, 98; auth, "Affection," The Christian Science Monitor, 96. **CONTACT ADDRESS** Dept Humanities, Curry Col, 1071 Blue Hill Ave, Milton, MA 02186-2302. **EMAIL** ecmeek@aol.com

MEEKER, JOSEPH W.
DISCIPLINE ENGLISH LITERATURE **EDUCATION** Univ Calif Berkeley, BA; Occidental Col, MA, PhD. **CAREER** Prof. **RESEARCH** Twentieth century literature and philosophy; environmental ethics; human ecology; comedy and tragedy; mythology; systems theory. **SELECTED PUBLICATIONS** Auth, The Comedy of Survival: Studies in Literary Ecology, Guild, 80; Spheres of Life: An Introduction to World Ecology, Charles Scribner's, 75; Ancient Roots of the Modern World, Athabasca Univ, 75. **CONTACT ADDRESS** English Dept, Union Inst, 440 E McMillan St, Cincinnati, OH 45206-1925.

MEEKER, MICHAEL W.
DISCIPLINE MODERN BRITISH AND AMERICAN LITERATURE **EDUCATION** Northern Ill Univ, BA, MA; Univ Wisc, PhD. **CAREER** Tchng Asst, Northern Ill Univ,65-67; Instr, Elgin Community Col, 67-69; Tchng Asst, Univ Wisc, 69-73; Asst prof, Moorhead State Univ, 73-77; Prof, Winona State Univ, 77-. **HONORS AND AWARDS** Acceleration Grant; Grant develop computerized student portfolio system; IDEALS Multimedia Workshop; MSUS Challenge Grant, Hypertext Portfolios; Fac Improvement Grant; Summer Res Grant, Hypercard, WSU; Merit Awd, WSU; Fac Improvement Grant Summer; Release time grant res; Bush Grant release time work Minn Writing Proj; Awd best essay pub Minn Engl Jour; Fac Improvement Grant, NEH Summer Fel; Fac Res Grant; Bush Grant release time work Minn Writing Proj; Bush Grant release time work Great River Writing Proj; Merit Performance Awd, Moorhead State Univ; Awded Tenure, Moorhead State Univ; Promoted Asst Prof, Moorhead State Univ; Fac Improvement Grant, Moorhead State Univ; Fac Improvement Grant, Moorhead State Univ; D.Yale Beach Fel; Excellence Scholarship & Tchng, Univ Wisc. **MEMBERSHIPS** Nat Coun Tchrs Engl; Minn Coun Tchrs Eng; Col Comp & Comm ; Network Cooperative Learning Higher Educ; Asn Writing Ctrs. **RESEARCH** Modern British and American literature, literary theory, composition. **SELECTED PUBLICATIONS** Auth, Readers as Authors in a Hypertext Literature Classroom, Proceedings Conference Comp & Writing, 94; Comp-Mediated Class Jour, An Apple Writer Database Manager,Collegiate. **CONTACT ADDRESS** Winona State Univ, 600 W Franklin Street, Richmond, VA 23220. **EMAIL** meeker@vax2.winona.msus.edu

MEHAFFEY, KAREN RAE
PERSONAL Born 03/16/1959, Ann Arbor, MI, m, 1989 **DISCIPLINE** LIBRARY SCIENCE **EDUCATION** Univ Mich, AB, AMLS. **CAREER** Res coord, Gale Research, 82-84; librn, Univ Mich, 85; librn, St Hedwig High Sch, 86-88; asst librn to libr dir, Sacred Heart Major Sem, 88-. **HONORS AND AWARDS** Appointed to US Civil War Center Panel of Experts, 98. **MEMBERSHIPS** Amer Libr Assoc; Amer Theol Libr Assoc; Mich Libr Assoc; Libr Admin & Mgmt Assoc; Assoc of Col & Res Libr. **RESEARCH** Victorian Amer women 1840-1870; Civil War soc hist; Victorian mourning rituals; nineteenth century temperance movement. **SELECTED PUBLICATIONS** Auth, Victorian American Women, 1840-1880: An Annotated Bibliography, Garland (New York), 92; auth, The After-Life: Mourning and the Mid-Victorians, Laserwriters Publishing (Minn), 93. **CONTACT ADDRESS** Szoka Libr, Sacred Heart Major Sem, 2701 Chicago Blvd, Detroit, MI 48206-1704. **EMAIL** krmehaffey@yahoo.com

MEINERS, ROGER K.
PERSONAL Born 12/05/1932, Forreston, IL, m, 1958, 2 children **DISCIPLINE** ENGLISH **EDUCATION** Wheaton Col, Ill, BA, 54; Univ Denver, MA, 57, PhD, 61. **CAREER** From instr to asst prof English, Ariz State Univ, 59-64; asst prof, Univ Mo-Columbia, 64-65, assoc prof, 66-70, dir grad study, 67-70; assoc prof, 70-71, Prof English, Mich State Univ, 71- **MEMBERSHIPS** MLA. **RESEARCH** Twentieth century American and English literature; literary criticism; 19th and 20th century philosophy, psychology and literature. **SELECTED PUBLICATIONS** Auth Bird Shadows, Centennial Rev, Vol 39, 95; Eikampfs Dialectic, Centennial Rev, Vol 39, 95; Material History, Centennial Rev, Vol 39, 95; Eikampf Singing at the End, Centennial Rev, Vol 39, 95; Dialectics at a Standstill--Orwell, Benjamin and the Difficulties of Poetry, Boundary 2, Int Jour Lit Cult, Vol 20, 93. **CONTACT ADDRESS** Dept of English, Michigan State Univ, 201 Morrill Hall, East Lansing, MI 48824-1036.

MEINKE, PETER
PERSONAL Born 12/29/1932, Brooklyn, NY, m, 1957, 4 children **DISCIPLINE** AMERICAN LITERATURE **EDUCATION** Hamilton Col, AB, 55; Univ of Mich, MA, 61; Univ of Minn, PhD, 65. **CAREER** Asst prof of English, Hamline Univ, 61-66; prof of lit & dir of The Writing Workshop, Eckerd Col, 66-93; WRITER, 93-. **HONORS AND AWARDS** NEA Fel in poetry, 76 & 89; Flannery O'Conner Awd for Short Fiction, 86; Emily Dickinson Awd, Poetry Soc of Am, 92; Sow's Ear Prize, 95. **MEMBERSHIPS** Poetry Soc of Am; Acad of Am Poets. **RESEARCH** Literature. **SELECTED PUBLICATIONS** Auth, The Legend of Larry the Lizard, John Knox Press, 68; auth, Howard Nemerov, Univ of Minn Press, 69; auth, Very Seldom Animals, Possum Press, 70 & 72; auth, Lines from Neuchatel, Konglomerati Press, 74; auth, The Night Train and the Golden Bird, Univ of Pittsburgh Press, 77; auth, The Rat Poems, Bits press, 78; auth, Trying to Surprise God, Univ of Pittsburgh Press, 81; auth, Underneath the Lantern, Heatherstone Press, 86; auth, The Piano Tuner, Univ of Ga Press, 86; auth, Night Watch on the Chesapeake, Univ of Pittsburgh Press, 87; auth, Far From Home, Heatherstone Press, 88; auth, Liquid Paper: New & Selected Poems, Univ of Pittsburgh Press, 91; auth, Camporcorto, Sow's Ear Press, 96; auth, Scars, Univ of Pittsburgh Press, 96; auth, The Shape of Poetry, The Writer, Inc, 99; auth, Zinc Fingers, Univ of Pittsburg Press, 00. **CONTACT ADDRESS** 147 Wildwood Ln, SE, Saint Petersburg, FL 33705-3222. **EMAIL** meinkep@acasun.eckerd.edu

MEISEL, MARTIN
PERSONAL Born 03/22/1931, New York, NY, m, 1957, 3 children **DISCIPLINE** ENGLISH, COMPARATIVE LITERATURE **EDUCATION** Queens Col, NYork, BA, 52; Princeton Univ, MA, 57, PhD(English), 60. **CAREER** Army, 54-56; instr English, Rutgers Univ, 57-58; from instr to assoc prof, Dartmouth Col, 59-65; prof, Univ WI, 65-68; vchm dept, 73-76, prof English, 68-86, chm dept English & comp lit, 80-83, vice pres arts and sciences, 86-87, 89-93, Brander Matthews prof of dramatic lit, Columbia Univ, 87-; Guggenheim fel, 63-64, 87-88; Am Coun Learned our Carribean Poets, Duluth: Poetry Harbor, 96; Lawrence Ferlinghetti, Gregory Corso and Gwendolyn Brooks, in Frank N Magill, ed, Cyclopedia of World Authors, Revised Edition, Pasadena, CA: Salem Press, 97; If Beale Street Could Talk, in Frank N Magill, ed, Masterplots II: Juvenile and Young Adult Literature Series, Supplement, 3 vols, Pasadena, CA: Salem Press, 97; The Wapshot Scandal, The Country Husband, and John Cheever, in David Peck, ed, Identities and Issues in Literature, 3 vols, Pasadena, CA: Salem Press, 97; The Beat Generation: A Bibliographical Teaching Guide, Lanham, MD: Scarecrow Press, 98. **CONTACT ADDRESS** Dept of English, Univ of Wisconsin, Stevens Point, 2100 Main St, Stevens Point, WI 54481-3897.

MEISEL, PERRY H.
PERSONAL Born Shreveport, LA **DISCIPLINE** ENGLISH **EDUCATION** Yale Univ, BA, 70, MPhil, 73, PhD(English), 75. **CAREER** Carnegie teaching fel English, Yale Univ, 70-71, acting instr, 73, teaching fel, 73-74; vis instr, Wesleyan Univ, 74; asst prof, 75-80, assoc prof, 80-87, prof English, NY Univ, 87-, Fel, NY Inst Humanities, 78-81. **MEMBERSHIPS** MLA; PEN; Phi Beta Kappa. **RESEARCH** Modern literature; contemporary literature; theory of fiction and criticism. **SELECTED PUBLICATIONS** Auth, Thomas Hardy: The Return of the Repressed, 72 & The Absent Father, 80, Yale Univ; Freud, Prentice-Hall, 81; Bloomsbury/Freud, Basic, 85; The Myth of the Modern, 87; The Cowby and the Dandy, 98. **CONTACT ADDRESS** Dept of English, New York Univ, 19 University Pl, New York, NY 10003-4556.

MEISER, MARY
PERSONAL Born 01/03/1941, La Crosse, WI, m, 1963, 2 children **DISCIPLINE** ENGLISH **EDUCATION** Harvard Univ, PhD. **CAREER** Comp dir, Acad Skills Ctr, 76-86; dir comp, Eng dept, 86-90. **MEMBERSHIPS** NCTE; WCTE. **RESEARCH** Applied linguistics; composition; English as a second language; English education. **SELECTED PUBLICATIONS** Auth, textbooks dealing with applied linguistics and English education. **CONTACT ADDRESS** Dept of English, Univ of Wisconsin, Eau Claire, Hibbard Hall 358, PO Box 4004, Eau Claire, WI 54702-4004. **EMAIL** meiserm@uwec.edu

MELADA, IVAN
DISCIPLINE VICTORIAN LITERATURE **EDUCATION** Univ Calif, Berkeley, PhD, 67. **CAREER** Instr, Univ NMex, 67-. **SELECTED PUBLICATIONS** Auth, Sheridan Le Fanu, 87. **CONTACT ADDRESS** Dept of English, Univ of New Mexico, Albuquerque, Albuquerque, NM 87131. **EMAIL** melada@unm.edu

MELBOURNE, LUCY
PERSONAL Born 04/20/1948, Philadelphia, PA, d, 1 child **DISCIPLINE** ENGLISH **EDUCATION** George Wash Univ, BA, 70; Cath Univ Am, MA, 72; Univ NCar Chapel Hill, PhD, 84. **CAREER** Grad teaching asst, Cath Univ, 70-73; lectr, George Mason Univ, 80-81; lectr, George Wash Univ, 77-83; lectr to grad teaching asst, Univ NCar Chapel Hill, 73-79, 83-84; assoc prof, St Mary's Col, 84-96; assoc prof, St Aug Col, 96-; vis prof, Meredith Col, 00-; consult, Instl Res Corp, 01-. **HONORS AND AWARDS** Richter-Schonfeld Awd, 70; Pres Fac Fel, 97-98. **MEMBERSHIPS** ACTL; AIS; MLA; SAMLA; SCLA; AGLS. **RESEARCH** Post-colonial studies; contemporary drama and film; the modern novel; interdisciplinary education. **SELECTED PUBLICATIONS** Auth, Double Heart: Explicit and Implicit Texts in Bellow, Camus and Kafta, Peter Lang (NYork), 86; auth, "Plotting the Apple of Knowledge: Tom Stoppard's 'Arcadia' as Iterated Theatrical Algorithm," Mod Dram 41 (98): 557-572. **CONTACT ADDRESS** 414 Fenton St, Raleigh, NC 27604-2111. **EMAIL** llmelbourne@earthlink.net

MELE, ALFRED R.
DISCIPLINE CLASSICS AND PHILOSOPHY **EDUCATION** Wayne State Univ, BA, 73; Univ MI, PhD, 79. **CAREER** Vail Prof Philos, Davidson Col; William H. and Lucyle T. Werkmeister Prof of Philos, Fla State Univ. **RESEARCH** Cognitive philos; hist of ancient philos. **SELECTED PUBLICATIONS** Auth, Irrationality, Oxford Univ Press, 87; auth, Springs of Action, Oxford Univ Press, 92; coed, Mental Causation, Clarendon, 93; auth, Autonomous Agents, Oxford Univ Press, 95; ed, The Philosophy of Action, Oxford Univ Press, 97; auth, Self-Deception Unmasked, Princeton Univ Press, 01. **CONTACT ADDRESS** Dept of Philos, Florida State Univ, 288 Dodd Hall, Tallahassee, FL 32306-1500. **EMAIL** almele@mailer.fsu.edu

MELIA, DANIEL FREDERICK
PERSONAL Born 03/02/1944, Fall River, MA **DISCIPLINE** CELTIC LANGUAGES AND LITERATURE **EDUCATION** Harvard Col, BA, 66, Harvard Univ, MA, 70, PhD(Celtic lang and lit), 72. **CAREER** Asst prof, 72-78, Assoc Prof Rhetoric, Univ Calif, Berkeley, 78-, Assoc Dean, Col Lett and Sci, 81-, Vis asst prof English, Univ Calif, Los Angeles, 73-74; Nat Endowment for Humanities jr res fel Celtic and Regents fac fel humanities, Univ Calif, 75. **MEMBERSHIPS** Celtic Studies Asn (secy treas, 77-79); fel Medieval Acad Ireland; MLA; Medieval Acad Am; Am Folklore Soc. **RESEARCH** Medieval Celtic literature; folklore and mythology; rhetoric and poetics. **SELECTED PUBLICATIONS** Auth, Celtic Languages and Literature See Vol III, The Irish Literary Tradition, Speculum J Medieval Stud, Vol 72, 97; The Irish Tradition in Old English Literature, Speculum J Medieval Stud, Vol 72, 97; From Scythia to Camelot--A Radical Reassessment of the Legends of King Arthur, The Knights of the Round Table, and The Holy Grail, W Folklore, Vol 55, 96. **CONTACT ADDRESS** Dept of Rhetoric, Univ of California, Berkeley, 2125 Dwinelle Hall, Berkeley, CA 94720-2671.

MELL, DONALD CHARLES
PERSONAL Born 05/20/1931, Akron, OH, m, 1957, 2 children **DISCIPLINE** ENGLISH LITERATURE **EDUCATION** Yale Univ, BA, 53, MA, 59; Univ Pa, PhD(English), 61. **CAREER** Instr English, Rutgers Univ, 61-65; asst prof, Middlebury Col, 65-68; asst prof, 68-73, assoc prof, 73-83, prof Eng, Univ Del, 83-. **MEMBERSHIPS** MLA; Am Soc 18th Century Studies. **RESEARCH** Augustan satire; Swift; 18th century literature. **SELECTED PUBLICATIONS** Auth, A poetics of Augustan Elegy, 74; auth, English Poetry 1660-1800, 82; ed, Pope, Swift, and Women Writers, 96; co-ed, Contemporary Studies of Swift's Poetry, 81; auth, Man, God, and Nature in This Enlightenment, 88; auth, Reader Entrapment in 18th Century Literature, Scriblerian Kit Cats, Vol 25, 93. **CONTACT ADDRESS** Dept of English, Univ of Delaware, Newark, DE 19716. **EMAIL** dmell@udel.edu

MELLARD, JAMES MILTON
PERSONAL Born 01/30/1938, West Monroe, LA, m, 1958, 3 children **DISCIPLINE** ENGLISH, AMERICAN LITERATURE **EDUCATION** Lamar Univ, BA, 60; Univ Okla, MA, 61; Univ Tex, PhD(English), 64. **CAREER** Spec instr English, Univ Tex, 63-64; asst prof, Univ Southern Calif, 64-67; from

asst prof to assoc prof, 67-73, dir, Freshman English, 68-72, dir, Grad Studies, 76-78, Prof English, Northern Ill Univ, 73-, Chmn Dept English, 78-84, Acting Dean, Liberal Arts & Sci, 84-85, Athletic Dir (interim), 87; ed, Style, 95-; Presidential teaching prof 99-00; prof emer, 00. **HONORS AND AWARDS** The John Gray Awd, for graduating athlete with highest scholastic average, 60; The Bingman Awd for Outstanding Achievement, 60; Grad Fund Awd, Univ Southern Calif, 65-66, 66-67; NEH Summer Stipend Awd, 68; Dean's Fund Grant, Northern Ill Univ, 72-73; Grad Sch Summer Stipend Awd, 86, 87, 89, 90. **MEMBERSHIPS** MLA; Midwest MLA; Assoc Dept English; Soc Study Southern Lit. **RESEARCH** 20th century American literature; prose fiction/rhetoric of fiction; critical theory; psychoanalytic (particularly Lacanian) theory; William Faulkner. **SELECTED PUBLICATIONS** Auth, Four Modes: A Rhetoric of Modern Fiction, Macmillan, 73; coauth, The Authentic Writer: English Rhetoric and Composition, D.C. Heath, 77; auth, Quaternion: Stories, Poems, Plays, Essays, Scott, Foresman, 78; The Exploded Form: The Modernist Novel in America, Univ Ill Press, 80; Doing Tropology: Analysis of Narrative Discourse, Univ Ill Press, 87; Using Lacan, Reading Fiction, Univ Ill Press, 91; author of over 100 journal articles and reviews. **CONTACT ADDRESS** Dept of English, No Illinois Univ, De Kalb, IL 60115. **EMAIL** jsmellard@aol.com

MELLEN, JOAN

PERSONAL Born 09/07/1941, New York, NY **DISCIPLINE** FILM, LITERATURE **EDUCATION** Hunter Col, BA, 62; City Univ New York, MA, 64, PhD, 68. **CAREER** Assoc prof, 67-77, prof English, Temple Univ, 77-. **MEMBERSHIPS** Soc Cinema Studies; MLA. **RESEARCH** Film criticism; contemporary fiction. **SELECTED PUBLICATIONS** Auth, Natural Tendencies: A Novel, Dial, 81; auth, Privilege: The Enigma of Sasha Bruce, Dial, 82; auth, Bob Knight: His Own Man, 88; auth, Kay Boyle: Author of Herself, 94; auth, Hellman and Hammett, 96. **CONTACT ADDRESS** Dept of English, Temple Univ, 1114 W Berks St, Philadelphia, PA 19122-6029. **EMAIL** joanmellen@aol.com

MELLOR, ANNE KOSTELANETZ

PERSONAL Born 07/15/1941, m, 1969, 1 child **DISCIPLINE** ENGLISH AND COMPARATIVE LITERATURE **EDUCATION** Brown Univ, BA (summa cum laude, English & Philos), 63; Columbia Univ, MA (English & Comparative Lit), 64, PhD (English & Comparative Lit), 68; Courtauld Inst of Art, London, Fulbright-Hays Scholar, 64-65. **CAREER** Asst prof of English, Stanford Univ, 66-73, assoc prof, 73-80, founding dir of Feminist Studies Prog, 82-84, Howard H. and Jessie T. Watkins Univ Prof of English and Feminist Studies, 83-85; vis assoc prof of Humanities, 77, Prof of English, Univ CA, Los Angeles, 84-, Distinguished Prof of English, 96-, dir of Women's Studies Prog, 86-87. **HONORS AND AWARDS** Phi Beta Kappa, 63; Guggenheim fel, 72-73, 83-84; NEH fel for Younger Humanists (declined), 72-73; NEH Summer Stipend, 76; NEH/Huntington Library Fel, 77-78; dir, NEH Summer Seminar for College Teachers, 82, 89, 94; Stanford Univ Deans' Awd for Excellence in Teaching, 82; exec comm, 82-87, Romantics Div, MLA, chair of comm, 86; Howard H. and Jessie T. Watkins Univ Prof of English and Feminist Studies, 83-85; English Lit and Lang Selection Comm, Coun for Int Exchange of Scholars, 87-90, chair of comm, 89-90; Humanities Res Centre fel, Nat Univ of Austalia, Canberra, 90; Rockefeller Found Fel, Bellagio Study Centre (declined), 91; Clark Prof, Clark Library, UCLA, 92. **MEMBERSHIPS** Modern Lang Asn; North Am Soc for the Study of Romanticism; Int Asn of Univ Profs of English; Am Conference on Romanticism; Interdisciplinary Nineteenth Century Studies Asn. **RESEARCH** British Romantic Writing; Women's Studies; 19th Century Art and Lit. **SELECTED PUBLICATIONS** Auth, Blake's Human Form Divine, Univ Calif Pr, 74; auth, English Romantic Irony, Harvard Univ pr, 80; ed, Romanticisim and Feminism, Ind Univ Pr, 88; auth, Mary Shelley, Her Life, Her Fiction, Her Monsters, Routledge, 88; ed, with Audrey Fisch and Esther Schor, The Other Mary Shelley: Beyond Frankenstein, Oxford Univ Press, 93; auth, Romanticism and Gender, Routledge, Chapman & Hall, 93, paperback, 93; ed, with Richard Matlak, British Literature, 1780-1830, Harcourt Brace Pubs, 96; ed, with Maximillian Novak, The Age of Sensibility in a Time of Terror, Univ DE Press, 00; auth, Mothers of the Nation--Women's Political Writing in England, 1780-1830, Ind Univ Press, 00 **CONTACT ADDRESS** 2620 Mandeville Canyon Rd., Los Angeles, CA 90049. **EMAIL** mellor@ucla.edu

MELLOR, RONALD

PERSONAL Born 09/30/1940, New York, NY, m, 1969, 1 child **DISCIPLINE** CLASSICS **EDUCATION** Fordham Col, BA, 62; Princeton Univ, MA, 64, PhD, 68. **CAREER** Stanford Univ, asst prof, 65-75; UCLA, Assoc prof, prof, dept ch, 76-. **HONORS AND AWARDS** NEH fel, ACLS fel, Australian Nat Univ Fel. **MEMBERSHIPS** AHA, APA, AAH, SPRS. **RESEARCH** Roman studies; ancient religion; historiography. **SELECTED PUBLICATIONS** Auth, Thea Rhome: The Worship of the Goddess Roma in the Greek World, Gottingen, 75; auth, From Augustus to Nero: The First Dynasty of Imperial Rome, ed., MSU Pr, 90; auth, Tacitus, Routledge, 93; auth, Tacitus: The Classical Tradition, Garland Books, 95; auth, The Historians of Rome, ed., Routledge, 97; auth, The Roman Historians, Routledge, 99. **CONTACT ADDRESS** Dept of History, Univ of California, Los Angeles, Los Angeles, CA 90095-1473. **EMAIL** mellor@history.ucla.edu

MELLOWN, ELGIN WENDELL

PERSONAL Born 12/29/1931, Selma, AL, m, 1957, 2 children **DISCIPLINE** ENGLISH LITERATURE **EDUCATION** Emory Univ, AB, 54; Univ London, MA, 58, PhD(English), 62. **CAREER** Instr English, Univ Ala, 58-60, asst prof, 62-65; asst prof, 65-68, Assoc Prof English, Duke Univ, 68- **MEMBERSHIPS** MLA. **RESEARCH** Twentieth century British literature. **SELECTED PUBLICATIONS** Auth, Bibliography of the Writings of Edwin Muir, Univ Ala, 64, 2nd ed, Vane, London, 66; The reception of Hopkins' poetry, 1889-1930, In: G M Hopkins, Herder Bk, 69; coauth, A Checklist of Writings about Edwin Muir, Whitston, 71; Character and theme in the novels of Jean Rhys, In: Contemporary Women Novelists, Prentice-Hall, 77; A Descriptive Catalogue of 20th Century British Poets, Novelists and Dramatists, Whitston, 78; Edwin Muir, Twayne, 79; Narrative technique in Tristram Shandy, In: Laurence Sterne, Wissenschaftliche Buchgesellschaft, Darmstadt, 80. **CONTACT ADDRESS** Dept of English, Duke Univ, Durham, NC 27706.

MELNYK, JULIE

PERSONAL Born 04/06/1964, Tampa, FL, m, 1988, 2 children **DISCIPLINE** ENGLISH **EDUCATION** Haverford Col, BA, 86; Oxford Univ, MA, 88; Univ Va, PhD, 93. **CAREER** Grad Instr, Univ of Va, 89-91; Instr, Univ of Mo, 92; Asst/Assoc Prof, Central Methodist Col, 92-. **HONORS AND AWARDS** Phi Beta Kappa, 85; Presidential Fel, Univ of Va, 88-91; Curator's Fac Scholars Grant, 96. **MEMBERSHIPS** MLA, Midwest Victorian Studies Asn, Midwest MLA, Interdisciplinary Nineteenth Century Studies Asn. **RESEARCH** Nineteenth Century Literature, Women's Religious Literature. **SELECTED PUBLICATIONS** Auth, "Emma Jane Worboise and The Christian World Magazine: Christian Publishing and Women's Empowerment," Victorian Periodicals Rev 29.2 (Summer 96): 131-145; auth, "Evangelical Theology and Feminist Polemic: Emma Jane Worboise's Overdale," in Women's Theology in Nineteenth-Century Britain (NY: Garland, 98), 107-121; ed, Women's Theology in Nineteenth-Century Britain: Transfiguring the Faith of Their Fathers, Garland (NY), 98; auth, "Heman's Later Poetry: Religion and the Vatic Poet," in Felicia Hemans: Reimaging Poetry in the Nineteenth-Century(London: Macmillan, forthcoming); co-ed, Felicia Hemans: Reimaging Poetry in the Nineteenth-Century, Macmillan (London), forthcoming. **CONTACT ADDRESS** Dept English and Lang, Central Methodist Col, 411 Central Methodist Sq, Fayette, MO 65248-1129. **EMAIL** jmelnyk@cmc2.cmc.edu

MENDELSON, EDWARD

PERSONAL Born 03/15/1946, New York, NY, m, 1990, 1 child **DISCIPLINE** 19TH-AND 20TH-CENTURY LITERATURE **EDUCATION** Univ Rochester, BA, 66; Johns Hopkins Univ, PhD, 69. **CAREER** Instr, Yale Univ; Harvard Univ, vis prof, 87-88; prof, Colubia Univ, 81-. **HONORS AND AWARDS** Grants & fels: Guggenheim, NEH, Am Coun Learned Socs. **SELECTED PUBLICATIONS** Auth, Early Auden, 81; ed, Complete Works of W.H. Auden, 97; auth, Later Auden, 00; Ed, volume of essays on Pynchon; novels by Hardy, Bennett, Meredith; co-ed, Homer to Brecht: The European Epic and Dramatic Traditions; Romanic Rev; Yale Fr Stud; TLS. **CONTACT ADDRESS** Dept of Eng, Columbia Col, New York, 2960 Broadway, New York, NY 10027-6902. **EMAIL** edward.mendelson@columbia.edu

MENDOZA, LOUIS

DISCIPLINE LITERATURE, CULTURAL STUDIES, GENDER STUDIES **EDUCATION** Univ TX at Austin, MA, PhD. **CAREER** Taught at Univ Houston-Downtown & Brown Univ, asst prof, Univ TX San Antonio. **RESEARCH** Cult studies; contemp lit theory; Chicano/a lit and film; ethnic studies; gender studies; post-colonial lit and theory. **SELECTED PUBLICATIONS** Publ on, computer pedagogy, border lit, poetry of Sara Estela Ramirez and Raul Salinas; ed, East of the Freeway. **CONTACT ADDRESS** Col of Fine Arts and Hum, Dept of English, Univ of Texas, San Antonio, 6900 N Loop 1604 W, San Antonio, TX 78249. **EMAIL** lmendoza@utsa.edu

MENGXIONG, LIU

PERSONAL Born 12/17/1946, Shanghai, China, m, 1973, 1 child **DISCIPLINE** LIBRARY, INFORMATION SCIENCE **EDUCATION** Univ Mich, PhD, 90 **CAREER** Prof, San Jose St Univ, 89-. **HONORS AND AWARDS** Beta Phi Mu Int Honors Soc **MEMBERSHIPS** Amer Libr Assoc **RESEARCH** Digital libr; infor technol; infor seeking behav; svc & technol rsrc. **CONTACT ADDRESS** Clark Libr, San Jose State Univ, One Washington Sq, San Jose, CA 95192. **EMAIL** mliu@email.sjsu.edu

MENIDES, LAURA J.

PERSONAL Born 11/01/1936, New York, NY, m, 1961, 2 children **DISCIPLINE** MODERN AMERICAN LITERATURE, CONTEMPORARY POETRY **EDUCATION** CUNY, Queens Col, BA, 59; Univ Chicago, MA, 64; NY Univ, PhD, 78. **CAREER** Lectr, Univ of Chicago, 63-67; instr, Finch Col, 72-76; instr, Holy Cross Col, 77-78; assoc prof, Worcester Polytechnic Inst. 78-. **MEMBERSHIPS** MLA; ALA; NEMLA; Elizabeth Bishop Soc, Dickens Fel. **RESEARCH** Modern American literature, comtemporary poetry, Elizabeth Bishop, H.D. **SELECTED PUBLICATIONS** Auth, "There, but for the Grace of God, Go I: T.S. Eliot and William Carlos Williams on Poe", Poe and Our Times, ed B.F. Fisher, Poe Soc, (Baltimore, 86): 78-89; auth, "History in American Literature", Dict of Literary Themes and Motifs, ed Jean-Paul Seigneuret, Greenwood Pr, (NY, 88): 601-610; auth, "Elizabeth Bishop: She Made the Casual Perfect", Worcester Magazine, (March 94): 17; auth, "Oliver Wendell Homes", Biographical Dictionary of Transcendentalism, ed Wesley T. Mott (Greenwood, (Westport, London, 96): 145-6; auth, "The Use of the Past in Modern American Poetry: H.D. and Classical Greece", J of Lib Arts 2.2 (June 96): 23-31; auth, "Elizabeth Bishop's Worcester Connections", Worcester Rev 18, (97): 72-84; auth, "H.D." Robert Lowell" and "Charles Olson", An Encyclopaedia of Am Lit, ed Steven Serafin, Continuum Pr, (NY, 99): 285-86, 707-08, 848-49; coed, In Worcester, Massachusetts: Essays on Elizabeth Bishop, Peter Lang, (NY), 99. **CONTACT ADDRESS** Dept Humanities, Worcester Polytech Inst, 100 Institute Rd, Worcester, MA 01609-2247. **EMAIL** lmenides@wpi.edu

MENIKOFF, BARRY

PERSONAL Born 01/02/1939, Brooklyn, NY, 3 children **DISCIPLINE** ENGLISH **EDUCATION** Brooklyn Col, BA, 60; Univ Wis, MS, 62, PhD(English), 66. **CAREER** Asst prof, 65-70, Assoc Prof English, Univ Hawaii, 70-, Fulbright-Hays grant lectr, Univ Santiago, 68-69; vis assoc prof English, Univ Southern Calif, 76-78; Huntington fel, 80; Newberry fel, 81. **MEMBERSHIPS** MLA; Aaup; Am Philos Soc. **RESEARCH** Nineteenth and twentieth century American literature; late Victorian and modern British literature; Henry James and Robert Louis Stevenson. **SELECTED PUBLICATIONS** Coauth, The Short Story: An Introductory Anthology, Little, 69, 75; auth, Punctuation and point of view in the late style of Henry James, Style, 70; The subjective pronoun in the late style of Henry James, English Studies, 71; Oliver Wendell Holmes, In: Fifteen American Authors before 1900, Univ Wis, 71; auth, A house divided: A new reading of The Bostonians, CLA J, 77; contribr, Oliver Wendell Holmes, In: Dictionary of Literary Biography, 78; Robert Louis Stevenson--Letters from Hawaii, Pac Quart, 80. **CONTACT ADDRESS** Dept of English, Univ of Hawaii, Manoa, 1733 Donaghho Rd, Honolulu, HI 96822-2368.

MENTO, JOAN

DISCIPLINE THEATRE, SHAKESPEARE, IRISH DRAMA **EDUCATION** MA, PhD. Dipl, Anglo-Irish Studies, Trinity Col, Dublin. **RESEARCH** Children's theatre, Irish drama. **SELECTED PUBLICATIONS** Rev, plays, Shakespeare Bulletin and NEng Theatre Jour. **CONTACT ADDRESS** Dept of Engl, Westfield State Col, 577 Western Ave., Westfield, MA 01085.

MENTON, SEYMOUR

PERSONAL Born 03/06/1927, New York, NY **DISCIPLINE** SPANISH AMERICAN LITERATURE **EDUCATION** City Col NYork, BA, 48; Nat Univ Mex, MA, 49; NYork Univ, PhD(Span Am lit), 52. **CAREER** Teacher English and hist of Span lang, Inst Recapacitation, Mex, 48-49; teacher, Pub Schs, NY, 49-52; instr Span and Span Am lit, Dartmouth Col, 52-54; from asst prof to prof, Univ Kans, 54-65; chmn dept foreign lang, 65-70, Prof Span and Port, Univ Calif, Irvine, 65-, Ed, Hispania, 63-65. **HONORS AND AWARDS** Judge, Plaza y Jans Colombian Novel Compeetition, 81; judge, Guatemalan Novel Competition, (Concurso Rin), 83; Univ of Calif, Irvine, Ch of Academic Senate, 84-86; Vice-pres of the Asociaci-n Norteamerricana de Colombianistas, 87-89; Pres, 89-93; Pres of the Local Organizing comt for the Meeting at UCI of the Asociaci-n Internacional de Hispanistas, 92; Orden Andr-s Bello, cultural award given by the Venezuelan government, 91; judge, Juan Rulfo International Prize for Literature, Guadalajara, Mexico City, 92, 93; Medal from the Instituto Tecnol-gico y de Estudios Superiores de Monterrey (ITESM) in recognition for contributions to Spanish Am lit, 94; Orden Francisco de Miraanda, cultrual award given by the Venezuelan government, 96; Orden Miguel Angel Asturias, cultural award given by the Guatemalan government, 97. **MEMBERSHIPS** Int Inst Span Am Lit; Am Asn Teachers Span and Port; MLA. **RESEARCH** Cuban prose fiction; Mexican novel; Spanish American short story. **SELECTED PUBLICATIONS** Auth, Saga de Mexico, New York: Appleton-Century-Crofts, 55; auth, Historia cr'tica de la novela guatemalteca, Guatemala City: Universidad de San Carlos Press, 60; auth, El cuento hispanoamericano, Mexico City: Fondo de Cultura Econ-mica, 2 vols., 64; auth, La novela colombiana: planetas y sat-lites, Bogot: Plaza y Jan-s, (78): 394; auth, Magic Realism Rediscovered, 1918-1981, East Brunswick, NJ: Associated Univ Presses and Philadelphia Art Alliance Press, 83; transl, of Alvaro Cepeda Samudio, La casa grande, (Austin: Univ of Texas Press, 91); auth, La narrativa mexicana desde, "Los de abajo," hasta "Noticias del imperio," Tlaxcala: Universidad Aut-noma de Tlaxcala, 91; coord, Critical edition of Mariano Azuela's The Underdogs, Pittsburgh: Univ of Pittsburgh Press, 92; auth, Latin America's New Historical Novel, 1979-1992, Austin: Univ of Texas Press, 93; auth, Historia verdaderra del realismo m-gico, Mexico City: Fondo de Cultura Econ-mica, 98. **CONTACT ADDRESS** Dept of Spanish & Portuguese, Univ of California, Irvine, 2641 Basswood St, Irvine, CA 92697-5275. **EMAIL** smenton@uci.edu

MERITT, LUCY SHOE
PERSONAL Born 08/07/1906, Camden, NJ, w **DISCIPLINE** CLASSICS **EDUCATION** Bryn Mawr Col, AB, 27, MA, 28, PhD, 35; Brown Univ, LHD, 74; Hamilton Col, LHD, 94. **CAREER** Asst prof, 37-41, assoc prof, 41-50, counsellor to chief counsellor of students, Mount Holyoke Col; member of Institue for Advanced Study, 48-49, 50-73, Princeton; ed of publications, 50-72, Amer Sch of Classical Studies at Athens; vis prof, 58, 60, Washington Univ; vis lect, 59, Princeton Univ; prof, 73-74, 75-76, 90, Univ of Texas at Austin, vis scholar, 73- . **HONORS AND AWARDS** Gold Medal of the Archaeological Inst of Amer for Distinguished Archaeological Achievement, 76; Outstanding Woman of Texas Humanities AAUW, 80; Pro Bene Meritis Awd, Univ of Texas at Austin, 97; Centennial med of the Am Acad in Rome, 99. **MEMBERSHIPS** Member of the managing committee of the Amer Sch of Classical Studies at Athens; pres Pathfinders Club Austin, 76-77, 91-92; Thankful Hubbard Chapter DAR, vice-regent 84-86, regent 90-92, honorary regent 92-; Archaeol Inst of Am; Deutsches Archaeol Inst; Soc of Archit Hists. **RESEARCH** Greek, Roman & Etruscan archit. **SELECTED PUBLICATIONS** Auth, Profiles of Greek Mouldings, cambridge, 36; auth, Profiles of Western Greek Mouldings, AAR, 52; auth, Estruscan and Republican Roman Mouldings, AAR, 65; auth, "Geographical Distribution of Greek and Roman Ionic Bases," Hesperia (69); auth, History of the American School of Classical Studies at Athens, 1939-1980, 84; auth, The Athenian Ionic Capital, Eius Virtutis Studiosi, Classical and Post-Classical Studies in Memory of Frank Edward Brown, 1908-1988, Studies in the History of Art, 93; auth, Athenian Ionic Capitals from the Athenian Agora, Hesperia, 96. **CONTACT ADDRESS** Dept Class, Univ of Texas, Austin, Austin, TX 78712.

MERIVALE, PATRICIA
PERSONAL Born 07/19/1934, Derby, England **DISCIPLINE** ENGLISH, COMPARATIVE LITERATURE **EDUCATION** Univ Calif, Berkeley, BA, 55; Oxford Univ, BA, 58, MA, 62; Harvard Univ, PhD(comp lit), 63. **CAREER** From instr to assoc prof, 62-70, Prof English, Univ BC, 70-00, Can Coun fels, 69-70; Prof, emer, Univ BC, 00-. **MEMBERSHIPS** Can Comp Lit Asn (secy-treas, 77-79); MLA; Asn Can Univ Teachers English; Am Comp Lit Asn. **RESEARCH** Artifice and the artist parable; thematics; narrative structure in contemporary fiction. **SELECTED PUBLICATIONS** Auth, Pan the Goat God: His Myth in Modern Times, Patricia Merivale; co-ed, Detecting Texts: The Metaphysical Detective Story from Poe to Postmodernism, Patricia Merivale, Susan Elizabeth Sweeney, 99. **CONTACT ADDRESS** Dept of English, Univ of British Columbia, 397-1873 E Mall, Buchanan Tower, Vancouver, BC, Canada V6T 1Z1. **EMAIL** merivale@interchange.ubc.ca

MERKELY, PAUL B.
DISCIPLINE MUSIC HISTORY **EDUCATION** Harvard Univ, PhD. **CAREER** Prof, Univ Ottawa; dir, Undergraduate Studies, Univ Ottawa. **RESEARCH** Musicology (Medieval Music, Twentieth-Century Music). **SELECTED PUBLICATIONS** Auth, Modal Assignment in Northern Tonaries, Inst of Medieval Mus, 92; Italian Tonaries, Inst Medieval Mus, 88; coauth, The Melodic Tradition of Ambrosian Office Antiphons, Inst Medieval Mus, 90; The Antiphons of the Ambrosian Office, Inst Medieval Mus, 89. **CONTACT ADDRESS** Dept of Music, Univ of Ottawa, 70 Laurier Ave, PO Box 450, Stn A, Ottawa, ON, Canada K1N 6N5. **EMAIL** merkley@aix1.uottawa.ca

MERRIAM, ALLEN H.
PERSONAL Born 07/28/1942, Orange, NJ, m, 1992, 2 children **DISCIPLINE** SPEECH COMMUNICATION **EDUCATION** Drew Univ, BA, 64; Ohio Univ, MA, 70, PhD, 72. **CAREER** Asst prof, The Col of NJ, 72-77; vis asst prof, Univ of Va, 77-78; asst prof, Va Tech, 78-82; assoc prof, Mo S State Col, 82-88; prof, 88-. **HONORS AND AWARDS** Fulbright Study tour in India, 80. **MEMBERSHIPS** Nat Commun Assoc; World Hist Assoc. **RESEARCH** Intercultural rhetoric; history of oratory; third world studies. **SELECTED PUBLICATIONS** Auth, Gandhi vs. Jinnah: The Debate over the Partition of India, 80; auth, People of the Millennium, 00. **CONTACT ADDRESS** 1419 Marzelle Ct, Joplin, MO 64801. **EMAIL** merriam-a@mail.mssc.edu

MERRILL, JEANNE W.
PERSONAL Born 02/03/1947, Gloucester, MA, m, 1969, 2 children **DISCIPLINE** LIBRARY SCIENCE **EDUCATION** Univ Vt, BA, 68; SUNY, Grad Study, 69; Univ Cincinnati, Grad Study, 74; Sch Infor Sci, SUNY, MLS, 00. **CAREER** Libr Tech to Head of Dept, Berkshire Sch, 88-. **HONORS AND AWARDS** Phi Beta Kappa **MEMBERSHIPS** ALA; ACRL; RUSA **RESEARCH** Classical Civilization; Electronic Resource Development and Use; User Education **SELECTED PUBLICATIONS** Auth, "The Internet and Classical Civilization," in The Acquisitions Librarian, (Haworth Press, 00), 97-115; auth, "The Internet and Classical Civilization," in The Internet and Acquisitions: Sources and Resources for Development, (00): 97-115; auth, "In the Blink of an Eye: Developing Trends in Publishing," The Reference Librarian, (00): 3-24; auth, "In the Blink of an Eye: Developing Trends in Publishing," New Technologies and Reference Services, (00): 3-24. **CONTACT ADDRESS** Libr Dir, Berkshire Comm Col, 245 N Undermountain Rd, Sheffield, MA 01257. **EMAIL** tully63@bcn.net

MERRILL, THOMAS F.
PERSONAL Born 01/05/1932, Maplewood, NJ, m, 1957, 4 children **DISCIPLINE** ENGLISH **EDUCATION** Princeton Univ, AB, 54; Univ Nebr, MA, 60; Univ Wis, PhD, 64. **CAREER** Asst prof English, Univ Calif, Los Angeles, 64-66; asst prof English, DePauw Univ, 67-69; Prof English--prof emeritus, Univ Del, 69-. **HONORS AND AWARDS** Fulbright-Hays lectr Am lit, Univ Bordeaux, 66-67; Fulbright-Hays lectr Am lit, Argentina, 82-83. **MEMBERSHIPS** MLA. **RESEARCH** Modern poetry; Renaissance literature; stylistics. **SELECTED PUBLICATIONS** Auth, Yeats Vision Papers, J Irish Lit, Vol 22, 93; Kavanagh, Patrick--A Critical, J Irish Lit, Vol 22, 93. **CONTACT ADDRESS** Dept of English, Univ of Delaware, 103 164 S. College Ave., Newark, DE 19716. **EMAIL** tmerrill@udel.edu

MERRON, JEFFREY L.
DISCIPLINE MASS COMMUNICATION **EDUCATION** Bennington Col, BA, 83; Univ Wis, MA, 85; Univ NC, PhD, 91. **CAREER** Prof. **MEMBERSHIPS** IABC; AEJMC. **SELECTED PUBLICATIONS** Auth, Duke has a wealth of advertising history, 92; Murrow on TV: See It Now, Person to Person, and the Making of a 'Masscult Personality', 88; Undoing Babel: J. Walter Thompson's International Expansion and the Issues of Translation and Pattern Advertising in the 1920s, 92. **CONTACT ADDRESS** State Univ of West Georgia, Carrollton, GA 30118. **EMAIL** jmerron@westga.edu

MESEROLE, HARRISON TALBOT
PERSONAL Born 07/25/1921, Brooklyn, NY, m, 1943 **DISCIPLINE** ENGLISH **EDUCATION** Wilson Col, DC, BS, 42; Univ Md, MA, 54, PhD, 60. **CAREER** Instr English, Univ Md, 56-57; from instr to assoc prof, 57-63, assoc head dept, 72-75, prof to prof emeritus english, PA State Univ, University Park, 63-, head, Am studies prog, 75, Assoc bibliogr, MLA, 63-66, bibliogr-in-chief and ed ann MLA Int Bibliog, 66-75; Coed, Seventeenty-Century News, 69-; Ed, World Shakespeare Bibliog, 75- **MEMBERSHIPS** MLA; Am Studies Asn; Bibliog Soc Am; Malone Soc; Mod Humanities Res Asn. **RESEARCH** American literature of the 17th, 18th and 19th centuries; bibliography. **SELECTED PUBLICATIONS** Auth, World Shakespeare Bibliography 95, Shakespeare Quart, Vol 47, 96. **CONTACT ADDRESS** Dept of English, Pennsylvania State Univ, Univ Park, 119 Burrowes Bldg, University Park, PA 16802.

MESSBARGER, PAUL ROBERT
PERSONAL Born 10/08/1934, Parnell, MO, m, 1959, 6 children **DISCIPLINE** AMERICAN LITERATURE **EDUCATION** St Benedict's Col Kans, BA, 56; Univ Notre Dame, MA, 58; Univ Minn, Minneapolis, PhD, 69. **CAREER** Instr English, St Ambrose Col, 60-61; asst prof, 65-69, dir honors prog, 66-69, Marquette Univ; assoc prof English & chmn dept, St Mary's Col Ind, 69-73; assoc prof English, Loyola Univ Chicago, 73-. **MEMBERSHIPS** Am Studies Assn; Midwest Mod Lang Assn; AAUP. **RESEARCH** American literary history; American religious history. **SELECTED PUBLICATIONS** Auth, Fiction With a Parochial Purpose, Boston Univ, 71. **CONTACT ADDRESS** Dept of English, Loyola Univ, Chicago, 6525 N Sheridan Rd, Chicago, IL 60626-5385. **EMAIL** pmessba@orion.it.luc.edu

MESSENGER, CHRISTIAN KARL
PERSONAL Born 01/16/1943, East Orange, NJ, m, 1968, 3 children **DISCIPLINE** AMERICAN AND MODERN FICTION **EDUCATION** Trinity Col, Conn, BA, 65; Northwestern Univ, PhD(English), 74. **CAREER** Asst prof English, Wittenberg Univ, 74-76; asst prof, 76-82, Assoc Prof English, Univ Ill, Chicago, 82-90, prof English, 90-. **RESEARCH** American fiction; modern and contemporary fiction; popular fiction. **SELECTED PUBLICATIONS** Auth, Football as Narrative--Review Article, A Lit Hist, Vol 7, 95; Sporting with the Gods--The Rhetoric of Play and Game in American Culture, Am Hist Rev, Vol 98, 93. **CONTACT ADDRESS** Dept of English, Univ of Illinois, Chicago, 601 S. Morgan St., Chicago, IL 60607. **EMAIL** chrism1@uic.edu

MESSER, RICHARD
DISCIPLINE ENGLISH **EDUCATION** Univ Colo, MA; Univ Denver, PhD. **CAREER** Prof, Bowling Green State Univ, 75-. **HONORS AND AWARDS** Nancy Dasher Awd, OH Educ Asn, 95. **MEMBERSHIPS** Am Poetry Soc. **RESEARCH** Psychology and Literature. **SELECTED PUBLICATIONS** Auth, Murder in the Family, 94. **CONTACT ADDRESS** Dept English, Bowling Green State Univ, 1001 E Wooster St, Bowling Green, OH 43403-0001. **EMAIL** rmesser@wcnet.org

MESSERE, FRANK
PERSONAL Born 10/07/1948, Syracuse, NY, m, 1982, 1 child **DISCIPLINE** COMMUNICATIONS **EDUCATION** SUNY, BA, 71; MS, 76; Cornell Univ, PhD, 95. **CAREER** Asst to Comnr, FCC, 85-86; Asst to Assoc Prof, SUNY, 99-. **HONORS AND AWARDS** Who's Who in Am; Who's Who in the World; Phi Delta Kappa; Nat Educ Hon Awd; Fac Fel, Annenberg Wash Prog, 93-96; Sr Fel, Annenberg Wash Prog, 93-97. **MEMBERSHIPS** BEA, NCA. **RESEARCH** Broadcast law, telecommunications policy, science and technology policy. **SELECTED PUBLICATIONS** Coauth, Introduction to the Internet for Electronic Media, Wadsworth Publ, 97; coauth, Instructor's Online Resource of Radio and Television Announcing, Wadsworth Publ, 00; coauth, Instructor's Online Resource of Modern Radio Production, Wadsworth Publ, 00; auth, Online Resource Center for Broadcasting, Cable, The Internet and Beyond, McGraw-Hill, 00; coauth, Broadcasting, Cable, The Internet and Beyond, McGraw-Hill, 00. **CONTACT ADDRESS** Dept Commun, SUNY, Oswego, 7060 St Rt 104, Oswego, NY 13126-3560. **EMAIL** messere@oswego.edu

MESTELLER, JEAN C.
DISCIPLINE AMERICAN LITERATURE, AMERICAN STUDIES, WOMEN WRITERS **EDUCATION** Lynchburg Col, BA; Univ Va, MA; Univ Minn, PhD 78. **CAREER** Instr, Univ Minn; Ill State Univ; prof, 78-. **HONORS AND AWARDS** Sally Ann Abshire Awds (3). **RESEARCH** Nineteenth-century popular fiction and the working girl. **SELECTED PUBLICATIONS** Auth, Romancing the Reader: From Laura Jean Libbey to Harlequin Romance and Beyond. **CONTACT ADDRESS** Dept of Eng, Whitman Col, 345 Boyer Ave, Walla Walla, WA 99362-2038. **EMAIL** mastellerj@whitman.edu

METCALF, ALLAN ALBERT
PERSONAL Born 04/18/1940, Clayton, MO, m, 1994, 4 children **DISCIPLINE** ENGLISH, LINGUISTICS **EDUCATION** Cornell Univ, BA, 61; Univ Calif, Berkeley, MA, 64, PhD(English), 66. **CAREER** Asst prof English, Univ Calif, Riverside, 66-73; assoc prof, 73-81, prof English & chmn dept, MacMurray Col, IL, 81-, exec sec, Am Dialect Soc, 81-. **HONORS AND AWARDS** Phi Beta Kappa, Cornell, 61. **MEMBERSHIPS** MLA; Ling Soc Am; Mediaeval Acad Am; Am Dialect Soc; NCTE. **RESEARCH** American English dialects and Lexicography; California dialects; medieval English literature. **SELECTED PUBLICATIONS** Auth, Sir Gawain and you, Chaucer Rev, Winter 71; Riverside English; The Spoken Language of a Southern California Community, Univ Calif, Riverside, 71; Directions of change in Southern California English, J English Ling, 3/72; Poetic Diction in the Old English Meters of Boethius, Mouton, The Hague, 73; Silent Knight: Sum for Cortaysye? Archiv fur das Studium der neueren Sprchen und Literaturen, 76; Chicano English, Ctr Appl Ling, 79; A guide to the California-Nevada field records of the linguistic atlas of the Pacific Coast, Univ Calif, Berkeley, 79; Gawain's number, In: Essays in the Numerical Analysis of Medieval Literature, Bucknell Univ Press, 80; Typography of the Century Dictionary, Dictionaries, v 17, 96; The South in the Dictionary of American Regional English, in: Language Variety in the South Revisited, Univ of Alabama Press, 97; America in So Many Words: Words that Have Shaped America, with David K Barnhart, Houghton Mifflin, 97; The World in So Many Words, Houghton Mifflin, 99; How We Talk: American Regional English Today, Houghton Mifflin, 00. **CONTACT ADDRESS** Dept of English, MacMurray Col, 477 E College Ave, Jacksonville, IL 62650-2510. **EMAIL** aallan@aol.com

METCALF, WILLIAM E.
PERSONAL Born 12/16/1947, East Grand Rapids, MI, m, 1991, 2 children **DISCIPLINE** CLASSIC STUDIES **EDUCATION** Univ Michigan, BA 69, MA 70, PhD 73. **CAREER** The American Numismatic Society, chief curator, curator, assoc curator, asst curator, 73 to 79-00; teaching at Columbia Univ, Princeton Univ, NYU, Bryan Maur College, Universita' di Padova. **HONORS AND AWARDS** NEA Fel; Kraay and Robinson Fel; IAS mem. **MEMBERSHIPS** APA; AIA; RNS; ANS; SPRS. Soc of Antiguaries. **RESEARCH** Roman imperial history and coinage. **SELECTED PUBLICATIONS** Auth, The Silver Coinage of Caesarea in Cappadocia Vespasian to Commodus, NY, Numis Notes and Mono, 96; A Primer of Roman Numismatics, E. J. Brill, 99; Regionalism in the imperial coinage of Asia Minor, in: Region in Asia Minor in the Hellenistic and Roman Periods, Hartford 98; Coins as Primary Evidence, in: Togo Salmon Studies, Ann Arbor, 98; Aurelian's reform at Alexandria, in: studies in Greek Numismatics in memory of Martin Jessop Price, eds, R. H. Ashton, S Hurter, London, 98; Byzantine Imperial Coinage, in: The Glory of Byzantine, art and Cultur of the Middle Byzantine Era A.D. 843-1261, eds, Helen C. Evans, William D. Wixom, New York, 97. **CONTACT ADDRESS** American Numismatic Society, 17 Prescott Ave, Montclair, NJ 07042. **EMAIL** wemetcalf@aol.com

METLITZKI, DOROTHEE
PERSONAL Born Koenigsberg, Germany, 1 child **DISCIPLINE** MIDDLE ENGLISH AND AMERICAN LITERATURE **EDUCATION** Univ London, BA, 36, MA, 38; Yale Univ, PhD(Am studies), 56. **CAREER** Instr English, Hebrew

Univ, Jerusalem, 39-44; lectr, British Coun, Cairo, 45-47; press officer, Ministry Foreign Affairs, Israel, 48-51; secy for affairs of Arab women, Israel Fedn Labor, 51-53; William Coe and Sterling fel Am studies, Yale Univ, 53-57; lectr English, Univ Calif, Berkeley, 57-65, assoc prof, 65-67; sr lectr, 65-76, Prof English, Yale Univ, 76-, Am Coun Learned Soc fel, 63. **MEMBERSHIPS** MLA; Mediaeval Acad Am; Am Orient Soc. **RESEARCH** Arabic material in medieval literature; the study of the Bible in the Middle Ages; American orientalism. **SELECTED PUBLICATIONS** Auth On the Meaning of Hatem in Goethe West Ostlicher Divan, J Am Orient Soc, Vol 0117, 97. **CONTACT ADDRESS** English Dept, Yale Univ, New Haven, CT 06520.

METZ, WALTER C.

PERSONAL Born 11/28/1967, Philadelphia, PA, m, 1990, 2 children **DISCIPLINE** FILM, THEATRE, TELEVISION STUDIES **EDUCATION** Mass Inst Tech, BS, 89; Univ Iowa, MA, 91; Univ Tex Austin, PhD, 96. **CAREER** Lectr, Univ Tex Austin, 96-98; asst prof, Mont State Univ, 98-01. **HONORS AND AWARDS** Univ Tex Austin Fel, 91-92; Col of Commun Teaching Excellence Award, Univ Tex Austin, 97-98. **MEMBERSHIPS** MLA, Soc for Cinema Studies. **SELECTED PUBLICATIONS** Auth, "Pomp(ous) Sirk-umstance: Intertextuality, Adaptation, and All That Heaven Allows,' Jour of Film and Video, (93); auth, "Keep the Coffee Hot, Hugo: Nuclear Trauma in Fritz Lang's The Big Heat," Film Criticism, (97); auth, "Another being we have created called us: Point-of-view, Melancholia, and the Joking Unconscious in the Bridges of Madison County," Velvet Light Trap, (99); auth, "Genre Theory and The Shining," Film Criticism, (99); auth, "Signifying Northing?: Martin Ritt's The Sound and the Fury as Deconstructive Adaptation," Lit/Film Quart, (99); auth, "What Went Wrong?: The American Avant-garde Cinema of the 1960s," The Sixties, (NY: Scribners and Sons, 00). **CONTACT ADDRESS** Dept Media and Theatre Arts, Montana State Univ, Bozeman, Bozeman, MT 59717-3350. **EMAIL** metz@montana.edu

METZGER, DAVID

DISCIPLINE RHETORIC AND COMPOSITION **EDUCATION** Emporia State Univ, BA; Univ Miss, PhD. **CAREER** Assoc prof, Engl, Old Dominion Univ. **HONORS AND AWARDS** Ed, Bien Dire: Jour Lacanian Orientation; Coordr Tchg; Found dir Writing Tutorial Services; English Dept Coun. **RESEARCH** Biblical rhetoric; History of poetics; Psychoanalytical theory; Chaucer. **SELECTED PUBLICATIONS** Ed, "Lacan and the Question of Writing," spec issue Pre/Text, 95; auth, The Lost Cause of Rhetoric, SIUP, 95, auth, "Teaching as a Test of Knowledge, " in Rhetoric in an Antifoundational World, eds Michael Bernard-Donals & Richard Glejzer (Yale Univ Pr, 97); auth, "Kushner's Angels in America and Queer Mysticism," Year's Work in Medievalism Vol IX (97); auth, "Freud's Jewish Science and Lacan's Sinthome," American imago (Summer 97); auth, "The Drives and Sexuation," Umbra (97); ed, "Medievalizm as an Integrated Study," spec issue Year's Work in Medievalism (97); co-ed, Medievalism and the Academy, Boydell and Brewer (Cambridge), 99. **CONTACT ADDRESS** Dept Engl, Old Dominion Univ, BAL 220, Norfolk, VA 23529. **EMAIL** dmetzger@odu.edu

METZGER, LORE

PERSONAL Born 05/08/1925, Frankfurt, Germany **DISCIPLINE** ENGLISH AND COMPARATIVE LITERATURE **EDUCATION** Hunter Col, BA, 46; Columbia Univ, MA, 47, PhD, 56. **CAREER** Instr English, Mt Holyoke Col, 56-59; Am Asn Univ Women fel, 59-60; from instr to asst prof English, Univ Wash, 60-64; assoc prof English and comp lit, Mich State Univ, 64-68; Prof English, Emory Univ, 68-, Huntington Libr res grant, 63; fel consult, Nat Endowment for Humanities, 71-74. **MEMBERSHIPS** MLA; Am Comp Lit Asn; Southern Comp Lit Asn; Northeast Mod Lang Asn. **RESEARCH** Romanticism; literary theory; modern drama. **SELECTED PUBLICATIONS** Auth, Korinth, Studies in Eighteenth Century Culture, Vol 22, 92. **CONTACT ADDRESS** Dept of English, Emory Univ, Atlanta, GA 30322.

MEYER, JOHN

PERSONAL Born 10/11/1964, Tulsa, OK, m, 1991, 1 child **DISCIPLINE** SPEECH COMMUNICATIONS **EDUCATION** Phillips Univ, BS, 86; Univ of Kans, MA, 88; PhD, 91. **CAREER** From asst prof to assoc prof, Univ of Southern Miss, 91-. **MEMBERSHIPS** nat Commun Asn, Southern States Commun Asn, Central States Commun Asn. **RESEARCH** Humor in communication, communication and conflict, organizational cultures. **SELECTED PUBLICATIONS** Auth, "Tell me a story: Eliciting organizational values from narratives," Commun Quart 43 (95): 210-224; auth, "Seeking organizational unity: Building bridges in response to mystery," Southern Commun J 61 (95): 210-219; coauth, "Children and relationship development: Communication strategies in a day care center," Commun Reports 10 (97): 75-85; auth, "Humor in member narratives: Uniting and dividing at work," Western J of Commun 61 (97): 188-208. **CONTACT ADDRESS** Dept Speech Commun, Univ of So Mississippi, 2805 Hardy St, Hattiesburg, MS 39406-0001. **EMAIL** john.meyer@usm.edu

MEYER, KENNETH JOHN

PERSONAL Born 08/24/1930, Manitowoc, WI, m, 1953, 4 children **DISCIPLINE** ENGLISH, AMERICAN STUDIES **EDUCATION** Lawrence Col, BA, 53; Univ Minn, MA, 56, PhD (Am studies), 65. **CAREER** Instr English, Monmouth Col, Ill, 57-61; assoc prof English, 64-67, coordr, Res and Planning Develop Proj, 67-71, Prof English, Huron Col, Sdak, 67-, Chmn Dept, 64- **MEMBERSHIPS** Am Studies Asn; NCTE; Conf Col Compos and Commun; Aaup. **RESEARCH** American literature and cultures, 1800-1900; curriculum in the small liberal arts college; the teaching of composition. **SELECTED PUBLICATIONS CONTACT ADDRESS** 1941 McClellan Dr, Huron, SD 57350.

MEYER, LEONARD B.

PERSONAL Born 01/12/1918, New York, NY, m, 1975, 3 children **DISCIPLINE** MUSIC **EDUCATION** Columbia Univ, AB, 40, AM, 48; Univ Chicago, PhD(hist of cult), 54. **CAREER** From instr to prof music, Univ Chicago, 46-72, chmn dept music, 61-70, Phyllis Fay Horton prof humanities, 72-75; Benjamin Franklin prof to prof emer, Univ Pa, 75-; mem, Nat Humanities Fac, 70-71; Ernest Bloch prof music, Univ Calif, Berkeley, 71; vis prof, School of Music, Univ Mich, 73. **HONORS AND AWARDS** Fel, Ctr Advan Studies, Wesleyan Univ, 60-61; Guggenheim fel, 71-72; sr fel, School of Criticism and Theory, 74-; dhl, grinnell col, 67, loyola univ, chicago, 70 and bard col, 76. **MEMBERSHIPS** Fel Am Acad Arts and Sci; Am Musicol Soc; Am Soc Aesthet; fel AAAS; Soc Music Theory. **RESEARCH** Music theory and analysis; aesthetics; psychology. **CONTACT ADDRESS** Dept of Music, Univ of Pennsylvania, Philadelphia, PA 19174.

MEYER, RUSSELL J.

PERSONAL Born 09/03/1940, Columbus, OH, m, 1966, 2 children **DISCIPLINE** ENGLISH LITERATURE **EDUCATION** Ohio State Univ, BA, MA; Univ Minn, PhD. **CAREER** Asst-assoc prof, Univ Missouri, Columbia, 76-90; vis prof, Universitat des Saarlandes, Saarbrucken, Germany, 82-83; prof, Univ Houston - Downtown, 90-94; chemn, dept English, Emporia State Univ, 94-00; dean, Col of Humanities and Social Sciences, Univ Southern Colorado, 00-. **RESEARCH** Renaissance Literature; rhetoric; computing. **SELECTED PUBLICATIONS** Auth, Edmund Spenser's Faerie Queene: Educating the Reader, 91; pubs on Spenser, Shakespeare; co-auth, Voices and Visions: An Integrated Approach to Reading and Writing, 95. **CONTACT ADDRESS** Col of Humanities and Social Sciences, Univ of So Colorado, Pueblo, CO 81001. **EMAIL** meyerr@uscolo.edu

MEYERING, SHERYL L.

DISCIPLINE ENGLISH **EDUCATION** Michigan State Univ, PhD, 86. **CAREER** Asst Prof, 86-88, Michigan State Univ; Asst Prof, 88-94, Assoc Prof, 94-00, Full Prof, 00-, Southern Illinois Univ Edwardsville **CONTACT ADDRESS** Dept of Eng, So Illinois Univ, Edwardsville, Box 1431, Edwardsville, IL 62026. **EMAIL** meyering@aol.com

MEYERS, MARIAN J.

DISCIPLINE MASS COMMUNICATION **EDUCATION** Univ Wis, Madison, MA; Univ Iowa, PhD, 89; Univ of Massachusetrts--Amherst, BA. **CAREER** Asst prof, Ga State Univ. **RESEARCH** The representation of women and minorities within the news. **SELECTED PUBLICATIONS** Auth, News Coverage of Violence Against Women: Engendering Blame, Sage, 96; ed, Mediated Women: Representations in Popular Cultrue, Hampton Press, 99. **CONTACT ADDRESS** Georgia State Univ, Atlanta, GA 30303. **EMAIL** joumjm@panther.gsu.edu

MEYERS, RONALD J.

PERSONAL Born 03/01/1936, Israel, m, 1959, 2 children **DISCIPLINE** ENGLISH **EDUCATION** Brooklyn Col, BA, 57; Columbia Univ, MA, 59; NYork Univ, PhD, 63. **CAREER** Lectr English, Pratt Inst, 59-60; instr, Brooklyn Col, 60-63; asst prof, Temple Univ, 63-66; assoc prof, 66-70, Prof English, East Stroudsburg State Col, 70-, Lectr, Hunter Col, 62-63; NJIT, 68; Rutgers, 69. **MEMBERSHIPS** The New York Academy of Sciences; Dramatists Guild; Global Awareness Soc. **RESEARCH** Shakespeare; literature and science; literature and sport; cult studies. **SELECTED PUBLICATIONS** Auth, O'Neill's use of the Phedre legand in Desire under the elms, Revue de Lit Comp, 1-3/67; The conflict of generations, Apscuf J, 5-6/70; Is symbiosis between technology and letters possible?, Dialogist, spring 71; Freud and Jung (hist play), 88; Isabella's Duplicity: Discord of Love Marriage and Family in Shakespeare's Problem Plays, Selected papers from West Virginia Shakespeare and Renaissance assoc, 87; auth, "Global Sport," Jrnl of the Global Awareness Soc, 00. **CONTACT ADDRESS** Dept of Eng, East Stroudsburg Univ of Pennsylvania, 200 Prospect St, East Stroudsburg, PA 18301-2999. **EMAIL** meyers@esu.edu

MEYERS, TERRY L.

PERSONAL Born 10/18/1944, Denver, CO, m, 1965, 2 children **DISCIPLINE** ENGLISH **EDUCATION** Lawrence Univ, AB, 67; Univ Chicago, MA, 68, PhD, 73. **CAREER** Instr, 70-73; asst prof, 73-79; assoc prof, 79-94 & prof, 94-, Col William and Mary; assoc dean fac Arts and Sci, 81-84 & ch, Engl Dep, 95-, Col William and Mary. **HONORS AND AWARDS** Ford Found fel; NDEA Title IV fel & Danforth Tutor, Univ Chicago; Alumni fel, 73-74 & Thomas Jefferson Tchg Awd, 80, Col William and Mary; Fac Speaker, Commencement Candlelight Ceremony, 79, 81; Fac Recognition Awd, Swem Libr, 93; VP, 76-78 & pres, 78-80, Victorians Inst; bus ed, Victorians Inst J, 77-79; ACLS grant-in-Aid, est $1100, 75; NEH Summer Stipend, est $3700, 87; NEH Travel To Collections grant, $750, 90 & semester res grant, Col William and Mary, 74 & 90, 01. **MEMBERSHIPS** Victorians Institute **RESEARCH** Victorian Poetry **SELECTED PUBLICATIONS** Auth, Swinburne, Shelley, and Songs before Sunrise, The Whole Music of Passion, Aldershot, England: Scolar Press, 93; Swinburne Shapes His Grand Passion: A Version by 'Ashford Owen, Victorian Poetry 31 1, 93; Two Poems by Swinburne: 'Milton' and On Wagner's Music, Victorian Poetry 31 2, 93; Swinburne's Copyright: Gone Missing, Victorian Poetry 31 2, 93; Found: Swinburne's Copyright, Victorian Poetry, 33 1, 95; Second Thoughts On Rossetti: Tennyson's Revised Letter of October 12, 1882, Tennyson Res Bull, 93; Swinburne and Whitman: Further Evidence, Walt Whitman Quarterly Review, 14 1, 96 & Comments on Amy Clampitt's 'Matoaka, William and Mary Mag, 61 5, 94; ed, The Sexual Tensions of William Sharp: A Study of the Birth of Fiona Macleod, Incorporating Two Lost Works, 'Ariadne in Naxos' and 'Beatrice, NY: Peter Lang Publ, 96; & Vanishing Lives: Style and Self in Tennyson, DG Rossetti, Swinburne and Yeats, Engl Lit in Transition, 32 3, 89; ed., Algenwon Charles Swiwbune, Cambridge Bibliography of English Literature, Cambridge University Press, 00. **CONTACT ADDRESS** Dept of English, Col of William and Mary, PO Box 8795, Williamsburg, VA 23187. **EMAIL** tlmeye@wm.edu

MEYERS, WALTER EARL

PERSONAL Born 07/01/1939, Pittsburgh, PA, m, 1961, 3 children **DISCIPLINE** SCIENCE FICTION, ENGLISH LINGUISTICS **EDUCATION** Duquesne Univ, BA, 64; Univ Fla, PhD(English), 67. **CAREER** From asst prof to assoc prof, 67-78, Prof English, NC State Univ, 78- **HONORS AND AWARDS** SAtlantic Mod Lang Asn Studies Awd, 78. **MEMBERSHIPS** Am Dialect Soc; MLA; Sci Fiction Res Asn. **RESEARCH** Medieval drama; modern English usage. **SELECTED PUBLICATIONS** Auth, Linguistics in TextbooksA 40-Year Comparison, Am Speech, Vol 70, 95;The Work of Aldiss, Brian, W.--An Annotated Bibliography and Guide, Sci Fiction Stu, Vol 20, 93; The Grammarians Desk--Krankor, Sci Fiction Stud, Vol 24, 97. **CONTACT ADDRESS** Dept of English, No Carolina State Univ, Raleigh, NC 27650. **EMAIL** meyers@social.chass.ncsu.edu

MEYLER, JOAN BERNADETTE

PERSONAL Born, NY, m, 1 child **DISCIPLINE** ENGLISH, LAW **EDUCATION** Marymount Col, BA, 65; St John's Univ Law Sch, JD, 75; CUNY Grad Cen, PhD, 98. **CAREER** Adj asst prof, John Jay Col Criminal Justice, 95-. **MEMBERSHIPS** MLA; ABA; BBA. **RESEARCH** Theories of interpretation, metaphor, allegory and meaning; 18th-century; human rights issues. **SELECTED PUBLICATIONS** Auth, "A Matter of (Mis) Interpretation: State Sovereign Immunity, the Eleventh Amendment and the Supreme Court's Reformation of the Constitution in Seminole Tribe and It's Progeny," Howard Law J 44 (forthcoming). **CONTACT ADDRESS** 10 Clinton St, Duplex 11, Brooklyn, NY 11201-2748. **EMAIL** jmeyler@attglobal.net

MEZEY, ROBERT

PERSONAL Born 02/28/1935, Philadelphia, PA, d, 1963, 3 children **DISCIPLINE** AMERICAN & EUROPEAN POETRY **EDUCATION** Univ Iowa, BA, 59. **CAREER** Instr English, Western Reserve Univ, 63-64; vis poet, Beaver Col, 64; asst prof, Franklin & Marshall Col, 65-66; asst prof, Fresno State Univ, 67-68; assoc prof, Univ Utah, 73-76; prof Eng & poet in res, Pomona Col, 76-99. **HONORS AND AWARDS** Ingram-Merrill Found grantee, 73-74, 88-89; Guggenheim fel, 77-78; Lamont Poetry Awd, 60, Poetry Prize, Am Acad of Arts & Letters, 82. **MEMBERSHIPS** N.A.S, A.L.S.C. **RESEARCH** Spanish poetry; Thomas Hardy. **SELECTED PUBLICATIONS** Ed, Selected Poems of Thomas Hardy, Penguin, 98; ed, Selected Poems of E.A. Robinson, Modern Library, 99; auth, Collected Poems, Arkansas, 00. **CONTACT ADDRESS** Dept of English, Pomona Col, 140 W Sixth St, Claremont, CA 91711-6319. **EMAIL** rmezey@pomona.edu

MEZO, RICHARD E.

PERSONAL Born 08/17/1938, Carterville, IL, m, 1983, 1 child **DISCIPLINE** ENGLISH LANGUAGE AND LITERATURE **EDUCATION** San Diego City Col, AA, 69; Calif State Univ, San Diego, BA, 71, MA, 72; Univ NDak, PhD, 78. **CAREER** Various colloges in the US and overseas, 79-89; assoc prof, Univ of Guam, 89-99; lectr, Univ Md, Asian Division, 92-. **MEMBERSHIPS** Am Acad of Am Poets, Asn of Literary Scholars and Critics, Am Asn of Univ Profs, Modern Lang Asn of Am. **RESEARCH** Writing (composition), literature, creative writing. **SELECTED PUBLICATIONS** Auth, A Study of B. Traven's Fiction: The Journey to Solipaz, Edwin Mellon Press (93); contribr, American National Biography, ed John Garraty and Mark Carnes, Oxford Univ Press (99); contribr, Short Stories in the Classroom, ed Carole Hamilton and Peter Kratzke, NCTE (99); several books on writing and literature (including a book on poetry) published by Universal Pubs and Dissertation.com in 99 and 2000. **CONTACT ADDRESS** Dept English, Univ of Guam, 303 University Dr, Mangilao, Guam 96923-1800. **EMAIL** remezo@netpci.com

MIALL, DAVID S.
PERSONAL Born 01/11/1947, Brighton, United Kingdom, m, 1982, 2 children **DISCIPLINE** ENGLISH LITERATURE **EDUCATION** Stirling Univ, BA, 76; Univ Wales, PhD, 80. **CAREER** Tutorial fel, Univ Col, 76-79; lectr, Col of St Paul and St Mary, 79-89; asst prof to prof, Univ Albta, 90-. **MEMBERSHIPS** MLA, Assoc of Can Col and Univ Teachers of English, Int Assoc for the Empirical Study of Lit, Soc for Text and Discourse. **RESEARCH** British Romantic writing, especially Coleridge, Wordswoth and Gothic Fiction, Empirical and theoretical study of literary reading, computing and hypertext in literary studies, teaching of English. **SELECTED PUBLICATIONS** Ed, Metaphor: Problems and Perspectives, Harvester Pr and Humanities Pr, 82; ed, Humanities and the Computer: New Directions, Oxford Univ Pr, 90; auth, "Wordsworth and the Prelude: The Problematics of Feeling," Studies in Romanticism 31, (92): 233-253; coauth, "Foregrounding, Defamiliarization, and Affect: Response to Literary Stories," Poetics 22, (94): 389-407; auth, "Anticipation and Felling in Literary Response: A Neuropsychological Perspective," Poetics 23 (95): 275-298; ed Romanticism: The CD-ROM, Blackwell Publ, 97; auth, "The Hypertextual Moment," English Studies in Can 24, (98): 157-174; coauth, "What is Literariness? Three Components of Literary Reading," Discourse Processes 28, (99): 121-138; auth, "Trivializing or Liberating? The Limitations of Hypertext Theorizing," Mosaic 31, (99): 157-171; auth, "Locating Wordsworth: 'Tintern Abbey' and the Community with Nature," Romanticism on the Net 20, (00). **CONTACT ADDRESS** Dept English, Univ of Alberta, Edmonton, AB, Canada T6G 2E5. **EMAIL** David.Miall@ualberta.ca

MICCICHE, LAURA ROSE
PERSONAL Born Canton, OH **DISCIPLINE** ENGLISH **EDUCATION** Ohio Univ, BA, 91; MA, 94; Univ Wis, PhD, 99. **CAREER** Asst prof, E Car Univ, 99-. **HONORS AND AWARDS** CWPA Res Grant; ECU Summer Teaching Gnt. **MEMBERSHIPS** MLA; NCTE; WPA; ATAC. **RESEARCH** Rhetorical theory; emotion studies; pedagogy. **SELECTED PUBLICATIONS** Auth, " When Class Equals Crass: A Working-Class Students Ways with Words," in Blunderize for a Change: Errors and Expectations in Critical Pedagogy, eds. John Tassoni, Bill Thelin (NH: Boyton/Cook, 00): 24-36; auth, "Contrastive Rhetoric and the Possibility of Feminism," in Contrastive Rhetoric Theory Revisited and Redefined, ed. Clayann Panetta (NJ: Erlbaum, 01): 79-89. **CONTACT ADDRESS** 402 Hillcrest Dr, Greenville, NC 27834-5646. **EMAIL** micciche1@mail.ecu.edu

MICHAEL, JOHN
DISCIPLINE ENGLISH **EDUCATION** Johns Hopkins Univ, PhD. **CAREER** Assoc prof & dir grad stud; taught at, Univ Warsaw Poland, Johns Hopkins Univ & SUNY at Geneseo. **HONORS AND AWARDS** Fulbright Fel, Pres Fel. **RESEARCH** Contemp rel between academic intellectuals and popular polit; problematics of national identity in Am literary romances and films; complex interrelations between the interpretation of lit and the reading of hist. **SELECTED PUBLICATIONS** Auth, Emerson and Skepticism:The Cipher of the World; auth, Emerson, Hawthorne, Poe, neo-pragmatism, the Frankfurt School, Eastern Europe, Stephen Hawking, intellectuals & contemporary cultural politics; auth, Anxious Intellects: Academic Professionals, Public Intellectuals, and Enlightenment Values, Durham, NC: Duke Univ Press, 00. **CONTACT ADDRESS** Dept of Eng, Univ of Rochester, 601 Elmwood Ave, Ste. 656, Rochester, NY 14642. **EMAIL** jnml@troi.cc.rochester.edu

MICHAEL, MARION C.
PERSONAL Born 05/17/1930, Monroe, GA, m, 1957, 2 children **DISCIPLINE** ENGLISH **EDUCATION** Univ Ga, AB, 50, PhD (English), 63; Univ Va, MA, 55. **CAREER** Instr English, Univ Ga, 55-57, 59-61; from asst prof to assoc prof, Southeastern La Col, 61-65; from asst prof to assoc prof, Auburn Univ, 65-71, chmn freshman English, 66-71; prof English and chmn dept, Tex Tech Univ, 71-82; Dean Sch Liberal Arts and Prof Emer English, Auburn Univ, Montgomery, 82-; Assoc Ed, Conradiana, Univ Md, 68-. **MEMBERSHIPS** MLA; SAtlantic Mod Lang Asn; Joseph Conrad Soc. **RESEARCH** Conrad. **CONTACT ADDRESS** Dept of English, Auburn Univ, Montgomery, AL 36124.

MICHAELS, LEONARD
PERSONAL Born 01/02/1933, New York, NY, m, 1965, 3 children **DISCIPLINE** ENGLISH **EDUCATION** NYork Univ, BA, 53; Univ Mich, MA, 56, PhD(English), 67. **CAREER** Asst prof, Univ of Calif-Davis, 66-68; asst prof, Univ of Calif-Berkeley, 69-70; assoc prof, Univ of Calif-Berkeley, 71-76; prof, Univ of Calif-Berkeley, 76-94; prof emer, Univ ofo Calif. **HONORS AND AWARDS** Mass Review Quill Award for Fiction, 64, 66; O Henry Prize Story Collection, 66, 68, 71; Nat Found on the Arts and Humanities Award, 67; Guggenheim Fel, 70; Nominated for National Nook Award, 70; Nominated for Am Book Award and included seversl times in notable books of the year selected by editior of the New York Times Book Review; Am Nat Academy of Arts and Letters award, 72; Distinguished Visiting Prof, Bard Col, 77; Best Am Essays, 90; Best Am Stories, 91; Best Am Essays, 92; Best Am Stories, 97; Anchor Essay Annual, 97; lists Sylvia among Notable Books of the Year, 92. **MEMBERSHIPS** Am Acad Arts and Sci. **RESEARCH** Romantic poetry and prose; modern literature. **SELECTED PUBLICATIONS** Auth, Going Places, Farrar, straus and Giroux, 69; auth, I Would Have Sved Them If I Could, Farrar, Straus and Giroux, 75; auth, The Men's Club, Farrar, Staus and Giroux, 81; auth, The Men's Club, 85; auth, Shuffle, Farrar, straus and Giroux, 90; auth, sylvi, Mercury House, 92; auth, To Feel These Things, Mercury House, 93; auth, A Cat, 95; auth, Time Out of Mind, Riverhead Books, 99; auth, A Girl With A Monkey, Mercury House, 00. **CONTACT ADDRESS** Dept of English, Univ of California, Berkeley, 409 Boynton Ave, Kenington, CA 94707.

MICHAELSON, PAT
DISCIPLINE LITERATURE STUDIES **EDUCATION** Univ Chicago, PhD, 85. **CAREER** Asst prof. **RESEARCH** Comparative studies in literature; 18th century literature and women's studies. **SELECTED PUBLICATIONS** Auth, Women in the Reading Circle, Eighteenth Century Life, 89; Reading Pride and Prejudice, Eighteenth Century Fiction, 90. **CONTACT ADDRESS** Dept of Literature, Univ of Texas, Dallas, Richardson, TX 75083-0688. **EMAIL** pmichael@utdallas.edu

MICHALCZYK, JOHN JOSEPH
PERSONAL Born 06/26/1941, Scranton, PA, m, 3 children **DISCIPLINE** FRENCH LITERATURE, CINEMA **EDUCATION** Boston Col, BA, 66, MA, 67; Harvard Univ, PhD (French lit & cinema), 72; Weston Col, MDiv, 74. **CAREER** Instr & chmn French & cinema, Loyola High Sch, Towson, Md, 67-69; instr, int French through film, Harvard Univ, 71-71; instr, graduate summer program in French, Rivier Col (Nashua, NH), 72-76; asst prof French & cinema, 74-80, assoc prof Fine Arts Dept, Boston Col, 80-, dir of film studies, Boston Col, 84-, prof & chmn Fine Arts Dept, 96-. **HONORS AND AWARDS** 2 New England Emmy Nominations for films: "Of Stars and Shamrocks: Boston's Jews & Irish" and "In the Shadow of the Reich: Nazi Medicine"; Distinguished documentary award from TASH (The Asn for the Severely Handicapped) for "Nazi Medicine"; "Palmes Academiques" from French Government for 25 years of contributions to French culture; Contemporary Authors; Fulbright (Italy); Mellon (Costa-Gavras). **MEMBERSHIPS** Malraux Soc. **RESEARCH** Issues of Social Justice in art, literature, and film; documentary film production. **SELECTED PUBLICATIONS** Auth, Malraux, le cinema, et La Condition humaine, 1/74 & Le cinema polonais en '73, 4/74, Cinema '74; Camus/Malraux: A staged version of Le Temps du mepris, 10/76 & Robbe-Grillet, Michelet and Barthes: From La Sorciere to Glissements progressifs du plaisir, 12/77, Fr Rev; Andre Malraux's Film Espoir: The Propaganda/Art Film and the Spanish Civil War, Romance Monogr, 77; Ingmar Bergman: La, Passion d'etre homme aujourd'hue, Beauchesne, Paris, 77; Recurrent Imagery of the Labyrinth in Robbe-Grillet's Films, Stanford Fr Rev, spring 78; The French Literary Filmmakers, Asn Univ Press, 80; Costa-Gavras: The Political Fiction Film, Arts Alliance Press, 84; Italian Political Filmmakers, Fairleigh Dickinson Univ Press, 86; Medicine, Ethics, and the Third Reich: Historical and Contemporary Issues, Sheed and Ward, 94; The Resisters, the Rescuers, and the Refugees, Sheed and Ward, 97; and articles on film and its relation to literature and the arts in: American Soc Legion of Honor; Annali d'Iliansistica; Cineaste; Cinema (Paris); Cinema and Soc (Paris); Contemporary French Civ; Current Research in Film; French Review; Lit/Film Quart; Magill's Cinema Annual; Melanges Malraux Miscellany; Stanford French Review; Twentieth Century Lit. **CONTACT ADDRESS** Fine Arts Dept, Boston Col, Chestnut Hill, 140 Commonwealth Ave, Chestnut Hill, MA 02167-3800. **EMAIL** john.michalczyk@bc.edu

MICHELINI, ANN NORRIS
PERSONAL Born 03/14/1939, Baltimore, MD, m, 1958, 3 children **DISCIPLINE** CLASSICS **EDUCATION** Radcliff Col, AB, 60; Harvard Univ, PhD, 71. **CAREER** Asst prof, 71-73, Univ Mass Boston; asst prof, 73-78, Harvard Univ; asst, assoc, prof, 78-, Univ of Cincinnati. **MEMBERSHIPS** APA; AAUP; AAUW; Class Asn of Midwest & South. **RESEARCH** Greek tragedy; Plato **SELECTED PUBLICATIONS** Auth, Tradition and Dramatic Form in the Persians of Aeschylus, Cin Class Series 4, sec 1 & sec 2, Brill, 82; auth, Euripides and the Tragic Tradition, Part 1 & Part 2, Wisconsin Univ Press, 87; rev, Black Athena Journal of Womens History, 93; art, The Dance of the Elements Fragment B17 of Empedocles, Power and Spirit, Annalex Univ Turkuensis, 93; art, Political Themes in Euripides Suppliants, Amer Jour Of Phil, 94; rev, Euripides Conformist Deviant or Neoconservative, Arion, 97; art, Alcibiades and Theseus in Euripides Suppliants Colby Quart, 97; art, Rudeness and Irony in Platos Gorgias, Class Phil, 93. **CONTACT ADDRESS** Classics Dept, Univ of Cincinnati, ML 0226, Cincinnati, OH 45221-0226. **EMAIL** ann.michelini@uc.edu

MICHELSON, BRUCE
PERSONAL Born 10/19/1948, Baltimore, MD, m, 1973, 2 children **DISCIPLINE** AMERICAN LITERATURE AND STUDIES, LITERARY THEORY **EDUCATION** Williams Col, AB, 70; Univ of Wash, MA, 74; PhD, 76. **CAREER** Asst prof to prof, Univ of IL, 76-, Dir, Campus Honors Prof, 96-. **HONORS AND AWARDS** Fulbright, Belgium, 83-84; Prokasy Awd for Dist Teaching, 92. **MEMBERSHIPS** MLA, Am Lit Assoc; Mark Twain Circle; Am Homor Studies Assoc; Am Studies Assoc; Richard Wilbury Soc. **RESEARCH** Mark Twain, literary wit, 20th century poetry, literature and technology. **SELECTED PUBLICATIONS** Auth, Wilbur's Poetry, 91; auth, Mark Twain on the Loose, 95; auth, Literary Wit, 00. **CONTACT ADDRESS** Dept English, Univ of Illinois, Urbana-Champaign, 608 s. Wright St., Urbana, IL 61801-3613. **EMAIL** brucem@uiuc.edu

MICHIE, ELSIE B.
DISCIPLINE VICTORIAN NOVEL **EDUCATION** Yale Univ, PhD, 84. **CAREER** Assoc prof, assoc ch, dept Eng, mem, women's and gender stud fac, adj mem, comp lit fac, La State Univ. **RESEARCH** Women, property, and narrative in novels and film; race, class and gender. **SELECTED PUBLICATIONS** Auth, Production Replaces Creation: Market Forces and Frankenstein as a Critique of Romanticism, in 19th-Century Contexts, 89; Frankenstein and Marx's Theories of Alienated Labor, in Approaches to Teaching Frankenstein, 90; From Simianized Irish to Orient Despots: Heathcliff, Rochester, and Racial Difference, Novel, 92; Outside the Pale: Cultural Exclusion, Gender Difference, and the Victorian Woman Writer, 93; White Chimpanzees and Oriental Despots: Racial Stereotyping and Edward Rochester, in Jane Eyre, 96. **CONTACT ADDRESS** Dept of Eng, Louisiana State Univ and A&M Col, 210G Allen Hall, Baton Rouge, LA 70803. **EMAIL** enmich@unix1.sncc.lsu.edu

MICKELSON, SIG
DISCIPLINE MASS COMMUNICATIONS **EDUCATION** Univ Minn, MA, 40; Augustana Col, hon LLD, 87. **CAREER** Distinguished prof, ch, The Manship Sch of Mass Commun, La State Univ; pres, CBS News; hd, Radio Free Europe/Radio Liberty; vpres, CBS, Inc, Time-Life Broadcast Inc, The Encycl Britannica Educ Corp. **SELECTED PUBLICATIONS** Auth, America's Other Voice, the Story of Radio Free Europe and Radio Liberty, Praeger, 83; The First Amendment and the Challenge of New Technology, Praeger, 89; From Whistlestop to Sound Bite: Four Decades of Politics and Television, Praeger, 89; The Northern Pacific Railroad and the Selling of the West: A Case Study of a Nineteenth Century Public Relations Venture, Ctr for Western Stud, 93. **CONTACT ADDRESS** The Manship Sch of Mass Commun, Louisiana State Univ and A&M Col, Baton Rouge, LA 70803.

MIDDENDORF, JOHN HARLAN
PERSONAL Born 03/31/1922, New York, NY, m, 1986, 2 children **DISCIPLINE** ENGLISH **EDUCATION** Dartmouth Col, AB, 43; Columbia Univ, AM, 47, PhD, 53. **CAREER** From instr to assoc prof English, Columbia Univ, 50-65, prof, 65-90, dir grad studies English and comp lit, 71-74, vchmn dept, 76-80. Co-ed, Johnsonian Newslett, 50-78, ed, 78-90; Coun Res in Humanities res grant, 58-59; Am Philos Soc grant, 62; Am Coun Learned Soc grant-in-aid, 62; mem English compos test comt, Col Entrance Exam Bd, 61-67, chmn, 67-69; assoc ed, Yale Ed Works of Samuel Johnson, 62-66, gen ed, 66-; chmn, The Johnsonians, 69 and 79; chmn, Sem Eighteenth Century Cult, Columbia Univ, 73-75, 85-87; Nat Endowment For Humanities Res Grant, 76-88; Prof Emer, 90-. **MEMBERSHIPS** The Johnsonians (secy-treas, 58-68); Grolier Club; MLA; Oxford Bibliog Soc; Am Soc 18th Century Studies. **RESEARCH** Samuel Johnson and his circle; economic theory and attitudes in 18th century English literature; bibliography and editing. **SELECTED PUBLICATIONS** Ed, English Writers of Eighteenth Century, 71. **CONTACT ADDRESS** 404 Riverside Dr, New York, NY 10025.

MIDDLEBROOK, DIANE W.
PERSONAL Born 04/16/1939, Pocatello, ID, m, 1985, 1 child **DISCIPLINE** ENGLISH **EDUCATION** Univ Wash, AB, 61; Yale Univ MA, 62; PhD, 68. **CAREER** Asst prof to prof and chair and assoc dean, Stanford Univ, 66-. **HONORS AND AWARDS** Phi Beta Kappa, 61; Woodrow Wilson Fel, 61; Albert S. Cook Mem Prize, Yale Univ, 62; Fel, Yale Univ, 63-65; Danforth Teaching Fel, Yale Univ, 64-65; Acad of Am Poets Prize, Yale Univ, 65; Theron Rockwell Field Prize, Yale Univ, 68; Fel, Stanford Univ, 75-77; Dean's Award, Stanford, 77; NEH Fel, 82-83; Fel, Radcliffe Col, 82-83; Guggenheim Fel, 88-89; Richard W Lyman Award, Alumnus Asn, 89; Finalist, Nat Book Award, 91; Finalist, Nat Book Critics Circle Award, 92; Bay Area Books Rev Award, 92; Commonwealth Club of Calif Gold Medal, 92; Finalist, Lamba Found Lit Award, 99. **MEMBERSHIPS** MLA; Investigative Reporters and Ed; Calif Class Asn; Intl Asn of Univ Prof; Biographers Club. **RESEARCH** Poetry and Poetics; Biography; Psychoanalysis. **SELECTED PUBLICATIONS** Auth, Anne Sexton, A Biography, Houghton Mifflin, 91; auth, "What Was Confessional Poetry?" in The Columbia History of American Poetry, (Columbia Univ Press, 93), 632-649; auth, "Telling Secrets," in The

Seductions of Biography, (Routledge, 96), 123-129; auth, "Introduction," in The Bell Jar, (Alfred A Knopf, 98), vii-xviii; auth, "In Search of the Autobiography of Ted Hughes," in New Critical Essays on Ted Hughes, (Univ Iowa Press, forthcoming). **CONTACT ADDRESS** Dept English, Stanford Univ, 1101 Green St, San Francisco, CA 94109-2012. **EMAIL** dwm@stanford.edu

MIDDLEBROOK, GEOFFREY C.
PERSONAL Born 12/14/1954, MN, m, 1990 **DISCIPLINE** ENGLISH **EDUCATION** Univ Colo, BA, 87; MA, 89; Univ Haw, PhD, 95. **CAREER** Lectr, Univ of Haw, 88-94; lectr, Calif State Univ, 95-. **HONORS AND AWARDS** Prof of the Year, Calif State Univ, 99-00. **MEMBERSHIPS** Am Lit Assoc, MLA, NCTE. **RESEARCH** 19th and 20th Century American Literature, Teaching the Argument in Critical Writing. **SELECTED PUBLICATIONS** Auth, "Gertrude Simmons 'Bonnin/Zitkala Sa,'" "New Criticism," " William Dean Howells," Facts on File Companion to the Am Short Story, (00).' **CONTACT ADDRESS** Dept English, California State Univ, Los Angeles, 5151 State University Dr, Los Angeles, CA 90032. **EMAIL** gmiddle@calstatela.edu

MIDDLEBROOK, JONATHAN
PERSONAL Born 10/06/1940, New York, NY, m, 1973, 2 children **DISCIPLINE** ENGLISH LITERATURE **EDUCATION** Harvard Univ, BA, 61; Yale Univ, MA, 63, PhD, 65. **CAREER** Asst prof English, Univ Calif, Berkeley, 65-69; lectr, 69-71, assoc prof, 71-76, prof English San Francisco State Univ, 76-, res fel, Univ Reading, UK, 71. **HONORS AND AWARDS** Magna Cum Laude, PBK, Woodrow Wilson Fellow. **MEMBERSHIPS** MLA, American Name Society. **RESEARCH** African-American lit; Shakespeare; 19th century British and American literature. **SELECTED PUBLICATIONS** Ed, Matthew Arnold Dover Beach, C E Merrill, 70; auth, Mailer and the Times of his time, Bay Bks, 76. **CONTACT ADDRESS** Dept of English, San Francisco State Univ, 1600 Holloway Ave, San Francisco, CA 94132-1740. **EMAIL** nonce@sfsu.edu

MIDDLETON, ANNE LOUISE
PERSONAL Born 07/14/1940, Detroit, MI **DISCIPLINE** ENGLISH **EDUCATION** Univ Mich, BA, 62; Harvard Univ, MA, 63, PhD, 66. **CAREER** From Asst Prof to Assoc Prof, 66-80, Prof English, Univ Calif, Berkeley, 81-. **MEMBERSHIPS** MLA; Mediaeval Acad Am; Medieval Asn Pac; New Chaucer Soc. **RESEARCH** Old and Middle English literature. **CONTACT ADDRESS** Dept of English, Univ of California, Berkeley, 322 Wheeler Hall, Berkeley, CA 94720-1030. **EMAIL** medieval@socrates.berkeley.edu

MIDDLETON, JOYCE IRENE
DISCIPLINE ENGLISH **EDUCATION** Univ MD, PhD. **CAREER** Asst prof; taught at, Univ MD at Col Park & Penn State Univ; postdoctoral fel, Univ MD. **RESEARCH** Lit of African Am women writers; Toni Morrison; hist and contemp theories of rhetoric; tchg, orality; literacy; memory. **SELECTED PUBLICATIONS** Articles and rev(s) on, Toni Morrison, Zora Neale Hurston, rhetoric & compos. **CONTACT ADDRESS** Dept of English, St. John Fisher Col, 3690 E. Avenue, Rochester, NY 14618. **EMAIL** middleto@sjfc.edu

MIESZKOWSKI, GRETCHEN
PERSONAL Born 06/13/1938, Plainfield, NJ, m, 1963, 2 children **DISCIPLINE** ENGLISH LITERATURE **EDUCATION** Vassar Col, BA, 60; Yale Univ, MA, 62, PhD, 65. **CAREER** Instr Eng, Univ Chicago, 64-65; from instr to asst prof, Yale Univ, 65-71; asst prof, Queen's Univ, 72-73; assoc prof, 74-79, Prof Lit, Univ Houston Clear Lake, 79-, Am Coun Learned Soc fel, 78-79; Inst Independent Study fel, Radcliffe Col, 78-79; prof listing, Dir of Humanities, 94-. **HONORS AND AWARDS** Piper Awd for Excellence in Tchg, Piper Found, 78. **MEMBERSHIPS** MLA; S Cent Mod Lang Asn; New Chaucer Soc; S Cent Womens Studies Asn **RESEARCH** Medieval lit; Shakespeare; women in lit. **SELECTED PUBLICATIONS** Auth, The Reputation of Criseyde: 1155-1500, Conn Acad Arts & Sci, 71; Pandras in Deschamp's Ballade for Chaucer, Chaucer Rev, 75; R K Gordon and the Troilus and Criseyde Story, Chaucer Rev, 80; Chaucer's Pandarus and Jean Brasdefer's Houdee, Chaucer Rev, 85; No Longer By a Miracle, a Twin: Helen Vendler's Reviews of Adrienne Rich's Recent Poetry, South Central Rev, 88; Chaucer's Much Loved Criseyde, Chaucer Rev, 91; The Prose Lancelot's Galehot, Malory's Lavain, and the Queering of Late Medieval Literature, Arthurian, 95. **CONTACT ADDRESS** Univ of Houston, 2700 Bay Area Blvd, Houston, TX 77058-1025. **EMAIL** mieszkowski@cl.uh.edu

MIGNON, CHARLES WILLIAM
PERSONAL Born 12/11/1933, New York, NY, m, 1959, 2 children **DISCIPLINE** ENGLISH **EDUCATION** Kenyon Col, BA, 56; Univ Conn, MA, 59, PhD(English), 63. **CAREER** Asst prof English, Univ Ill, 63-67; from asst prof to assoc prof, 67-73; actg chmn dept, 77-78, Prof English, Univ Nebr, Lincoln, 73-, Fulbright lectr, Inst English, Warsaw Univ, 72-73. **HONORS AND AWARDS** Annis Chaikin Sorensen Award for distinguished reading in the Humanities, 93; Ralph Emerson Turtchell Award (Historical Society of Nmex); Nicholas E. Powell Award, 97. **RESEARCH** Edward Taylor; American transcendentalists; Ralph W Emersn. **SELECTED PUBLICATIONS** Auth, Design in Puritan American Literature, New England Quart Histl Rev New England Life Letters, Vol 66, 93; ed, "Upon the Types of the Old Testament"; ed, "My Antonia"; ed, "A Lost Lady"; ed, "Death Comes for the Archbishop". **CONTACT ADDRESS** Dept of English, Univ of Nebraska, Lincoln, Lincoln, NE 68508. **EMAIL** cmignon@unlserve.unl.edu

MIKA, JOSEPH JOHN
PERSONAL Born 03/01/1948, MeKees Rocks, PA, m, 3 children **DISCIPLINE** LIBRARY **EDUCATION** **EDUCATION** Univ Pitts, BA, 69, MLS, 71, PhD, 80. **CAREER** Asst librn & instr, Ohio State Univ, 71-73; asst librn & asst prof, Johnson State Col, 73-75; grad asst, tchg fel School Libr & Info Sci, Univ Pitts, 75-77; asst dean, assoc prof libr sci, Univ S Miss, 77-86, dir libr & info sci prog 86-94, Prof, 94- , Wayne State Univ; Co-Ed Jour Educ Libr & Info Sci, 95- . **HONORS AND AWARDS** Served to Col. U.S Army Reserve; Decorated DSM; Army Res Comp Achiev Medal; Meriterious Svc Medal; Army Commendation Medal. **MEMBERSHIPS** Phi Delta Kappa. **SELECTED PUBLICATIONS** Articles to prof jour. **CONTACT ADDRESS** Libr & Info Sci Prog, Wayne State Univ, 106 Kresge Library, Detroit, MI 48202. **EMAIL** aa2500@wayne.edu

MIKELONIS-PARASKOV, VICTORIA M.
DISCIPLINE RHETORIC STUDIES **EDUCATION** Ind Univ Pa, MA, PhD. **CAREER** Prof, Univ Minn. **RESEARCH** Intercultural communication; design of training materials; schema theory. **SELECTED PUBLICATIONS** Auth, "The Role of Models in Technical Writing;" co-auth, "Procedure for Designing and Writing Training Materials." **CONTACT ADDRESS** Rhetoric Dept, Univ of Minnesota, Twin Cities, 64 Classroom Office Bldg, 1994 Buford Ave, Saint Paul, MN 55108. **EMAIL** mikel001@umn.edu

MIKICS, DAVID
PERSONAL Born 05/02/1961, Carteret, NJ, d **DISCIPLINE** ENGLISH LITERATURE **EDUCATION** New York Univ, BA, 83; Yale Univ, MPhil, 86; PhD, 88. **CAREER** Vis asst prof, Trinity Col, 88-89; asst prof to assoc prof, Univ of Houston, 89-. **RESEARCH** English Renaissance, Shakespeare, Milton, Spenser. **SELECTED PUBLICATIONS** Auth, The Limits of Moralizing, Bucknell Univ Press (Lewisburg, PA), 94. **CONTACT ADDRESS** Dept English, Univ of Houston, Houston, TX 77204-0001. **EMAIL** dmikics@uh.edu

MIKO, STEPHEN
DISCIPLINE ENGLISH LITERATURE **EDUCATION** Yale Univ, PhD, 67. **CAREER** Assoc Prof, Eng, Univ Calif, Santa Barbara. **RESEARCH** Modern novel. **SELECTED PUBLICATIONS** Auth, Toward Women in Love, Yale Univ Press, 71; ed, Twentieth-Century Interpretations of Women in Love, Prentice-Hall, 69. **CONTACT ADDRESS** Dept of Eng, Univ of California, Santa Barbara, Santa Barbara, CA 93106-7150.

MILAC, METOD M.
PERSONAL Born 10/02/1924, Prevalje, Slovenia, m, 1951, 3 children **DISCIPLINE** LIBRARIANSHIP; MUSICOLOGY; EMIGRATION STUDIES **EDUCATION** Cleveland Inst Mus, BM, 57; Cleveland Inst Mus, MM, 60; Western Reserve Univ, MSLS, 62; Syracuse Univ, MPh, 87; Syracuse Univ, PhD, 91. **CAREER** Mus Libr, Syracuse Univ Lib, 62-65; Head, Ref Dept, SUL, 65-68; Asst Dir, SUL, 68-73; Actg Dir, SUL, 73-74; Assoc Dir, SUL, 74-92. **HONORS AND AWARDS** Post Std Awd for Excel in Lib Serv, 82; Disting Serv Awd, Syracuse Univ Lib, 89. **MEMBERSHIPS** Am Musicol Soc; Am Assoc Advance of Slavic Stud; Soc Slovene Stud. **RESEARCH** Late 16th century music, composer Jacobus Gallus Carniolus (1550-1591); World War II, Central Europe. **SELECTED PUBLICATIONS** Anno Domini 1574: The Question of Jacobus Gallus and the Imperial Court Chapel, in Gallus Carniolus in Evropska Renesansa (Ljubljana: Slovene Acad of Sci and Arts, 91, 21-48; The War Years, 1941-1945: From My Experiences, Slovene Studies, v16, n2, 94, 31-47; Petje Druzi Nove Priseljence: Ustanovitev in Prva Leta Pevskega Zbora Korotan / Choral Singing Unifies New Immigrants: Founding and First Years of Singing Society Korotan, Dve Domovini/Two Homelands, Migration Studies 8, Ljubljana, Ctr Sci Res of the Slovene Acad Sci and Arts, The Inst for Slovene Emigration Res, 97, 49-70; Porocilo Avstrijskega Centra Za Etnicne Manjsine 1996, Volksgruppen Report/Ethnic Group Report, Zapiski, Chron Am Slovene Congress, Issue III, Autumn 97, 8-13. **CONTACT ADDRESS** 259 Kensington Pl, Syracuse, NY 13210-3307. **EMAIL** mmilac@syr.edu

MILDER, ROBERT
PERSONAL Born 06/03/1945, New York, NY, m, 1970, 2 children **DISCIPLINE** ENGLISH **EDUCATION** Union Col, AB, 67; Harvard Univ, AM, 68; PhD, 72. **CAREER** Asst Prof to Prof, Washington Univ, 72-. **HONORS AND AWARDS** Woodrow Wilson Fel, 67-68; NEH Fel, 80 **MEMBERSHIPS** Mod Lang Asn, Am Lit Asn, Melville Soc, Nathaniel Hawthorne Soc, Emerson Soc, Thoreau soc,. **RESEARCH** Mil-19th Century American literature, especially Melville, Emerson, Hawthorne, Thoreau. **SELECTED PUBLICATIONS** Auth, Reimagining Thoreau, Cambridge Univ Press, 95; ed, Critical Essays on Melville's Billy Budd, Sailor," G.K. Hall, 89; auth, "The Radical Emerson?," in The Cambridge Companion to Emerson, Univ Press, 99; auth, "Hawthorne's Winter Dreams," Nineteenth-Century Literature, (99): 165-201; auth, "Melville and the Avenging Dream," in The Cambridge Companion to Melville, Cambridge Univ press, (98): 250-278; auth, "The American Scholar as Cultural Event," Prospects: An Annual of American Cultural Studies, (91): 119-147; auth, "Herman Melville," in The Columbia Literary History of the United states, Columbia Univ Press, (88): 429-447; auth, "The Scarlet Letter and Its discontents," Nathaniel Hawthorne review, (96): 9-25; auth, "An Arch Between Two Lives: Melville in the Mediterranean, 1856-1857," Arizona Quarterly, (99): 21-47; ed, "Billy Budd, Sailor and Selected Tales, Oxford Univ Press, 95. **CONTACT ADDRESS** Dept English, Washington Univ, 1 Brookings Dr, Saint Louis, MO 63130-4862. **EMAIL** rmilder@artsci.wustl.edu

MILES, DIANA F.
DISCIPLINE ENGLISH **EDUCATION** Ga State Univ, BA, 95; Emory Univ, MA, 98; PhD, 00. **CAREER** Adj prof, Emory Univ, 98-20; adj, Agnes Scott Col, 98-00; res coord, Emory Univ Intl Aff, 01-. **HONORS AND AWARDS** Ga State Univ, Magna Cum Laude, 95; Emory Univ Dean Teaching Fel, 99. **MEMBERSHIPS** MLA; NCTE. **RESEARCH** Modern American culture; ethnic literatures; women's literature. **SELECTED PUBLICATIONS** Auth, Women, Violence, and Testimony in the Works of Zora Neale Hurston, Peter Lang Pub (NYork), 00. **CONTACT ADDRESS** PO Box 430, Lilburn, GA 30048-0430.

MILES, GARY B.
PERSONAL Born 07/21/1940, St. John, NB, Canada, m, 1962, 2 children **DISCIPLINE** CLASSICS **EDUCATION** Colby Col, BA, 62; Harvard Univ, AM, 64; Yale Univ, PhD, 71. **CAREER** Philips Acad, Andover, 64-66; Wesleyan Univ, 68-69; Univ Texas, 70-71; Univ Cal, Santa Cruz, 71-. **HONORS AND AWARDS** Danforth fel, 62-68; NEH fel 86, Excellence Tchg, Univ Cal, 98. **MEMBERSHIPS** AIA/APA; Virgilian Soc; AHA **RESEARCH** Roman literature and cultural history, especially of the Late Republic; Early Empire; Historiography. **SELECTED PUBLICATIONS** Auth, The First Roman Marriage and the Theft of the Sabine Women, Innovations of Antiquity, Routledge, 92; Livy: Reconstructing Early Rome, Cornell Univ Press, 95; auth, The 'Aeneid' as Foundation Story, Reading Vergil's 'Aeneid,' 99. **CONTACT ADDRESS** Cowell Col, Univ of California, Santa Cruz, Santa Cruz, CA 95064. **EMAIL** miles@cats.ucsc.edu

MILES, LIBBY
PERSONAL Born 10/23/1964, Richmond, CA, m, 1994, 1 child **DISCIPLINE** ENGLISH **EDUCATION** Williams Col, BA, 86; Purdue Univ, MA, 95; PhD, 99. **CAREER** Asst Prof, Univ RI, 98-. **HONORS AND AWARDS** James Berlin Mem Outstanding Dissertation Awd, 00. **MEMBERSHIPS** NCTE; CCCC, Writing Prog Admin; Nat Writing Center Asn. **RESEARCH** Rhetoric and composition; Cultural studies; Textbook publishing. **SELECTED PUBLICATIONS** Auth, Cultural Studies and Writing Apprehension, HarperCollins Booklet, 94; auth, "Lingering Questions and Mingling Voices: Ongoing Conversations with Jim Berlin," Works and Days, (96): 239-244; auth, "Globalizing Professional Writing Curricula: Positioning Students and Re-Positioning Textbooks," Technical Communication Quarterly, (97): 179-200; co-auth, "Flexible, Responsive Classroom Practices: What Writing Teachers Need to Know about Their Fair Use Rights," Composition Chronicle, (98): 1-4; co-auth, "Institutional Critique: A Rhetorical Methodology for Change," College Composition and Communication, 00; auth, "Disturbing Practices: Toward Institutional Change in Composition Scholarship and Pedagogy," college English, 00; auth, "Constructing Composition: Reproduction and WPA Agency in Textbook Publishing," WPA: Writing Program Administration, 00. **CONTACT ADDRESS** Dept Eng, Univ of Rhode Island, 60 Upper College Rd, Kingston, RI 02881-2000. **EMAIL** lmiles@uri.edu

MILEUR, JEAN-PIERRE
DISCIPLINE ENGLISH LITERATURE **EDUCATION** Univ Calif-Berkeley, BA; Yale Univ, PhD. **CAREER** Dean, Grad Div, Univ Calif, Riverside. **RESEARCH** Connections between romanticism and critical theory. **SELECTED PUBLICATIONS** Auth, Vision and Revision: Coleridge's Art of Immanence, Univ Calif Press, 82; Literary Revisionism and the Burden of Modernity, Univ Calif Press, 85; The Critical Romance, Univ Wis Press, 90; co-auth, Nietzsche's Case: Philosophy as/and Literature, Routledge, 92. **CONTACT ADDRESS** Dept of Eng, Univ of California, Riverside, 1156 Hinderaker Hall, Riverside, CA 92521-0209.

MILHAM, MARY ELLA
PERSONAL Born 03/22/1922, Waukesha, WI **DISCIPLINE** CLASSICS **EDUCATION** Carroll Col, BA, 43; Univ Wis, MA, 44, PhD(classics, ling), 50. **CAREER** Instr classics and

integrated lib studies, Univ Wis, 50-54; from asst prof to assoc prof, 54-68, Prof Classics, Univ NB, 68-, Can Coun sr res fel, 61-62, leave fel, 68-69; Soc Sci Human Res Coun leave fel, 81-82. **MEMBERSHIPS** Am Philol Asn; Ling Soc Am; Class Asn Can (vpres, 76-78); Humanities Asn Can (secy-treas, 66-68); Renaissance Soc Am. **RESEARCH** Late Latin; Renaissance Latin; textual criticism. **SELECTED PUBLICATIONS** Auth, Editions of Apicius, Feubner, 69, Apatina (MRTS, 98); Phoenix J Classical Assoc Can, Vol 45, 91. **CONTACT ADDRESS** 20900 W Cleveland Ave, New Berlin, WI 53151. **EMAIL** milham@nbnet.nb.ca

MILIC, LOUIS TONKO
PERSONAL Born 09/05/1922, Split, Yugoslavia, m, 3 children **DISCIPLINE** ENGLISH, STYLISTICS **EDUCATION** Columbia Univ, AB, 48, MA, 50, PhD, 63. **CAREER** Instr English, Mont State Col, 52-54; lectr, Columbia Univ, 55-58, from instr to asst prof, 58-67, assoc prof, Teachers Col, 67-69; chmn dept, 69-78, Prof English, Cleveland State Univ, 69-, Rev ed, Comput and Humanities, 66-71; Am Coun Learned Soc/Int Bus Mach fel, 67-68; Gen Ed, New Humanistic Res Ser, Teachers Col; Co-Ed, The Gamut, 79-; Nat Endowment for Humanities fel, summer, 80. **MEMBERSHIPS** Int Asn Univ Professors English; Am Soc 18th Century Studies; Asn Comput in Humanities; Asn Appl Ling. **RESEARCH** Rhetoric; 18th century English literature; computer-assisted literary research. **SELECTED PUBLICATIONS** Auth, Quantitative Aspects of Genre in the Century of Prose Corpus, Style, Vol 28, 94; Words of Ones Own, Some Evidence Against Mens Use of Language as a Tool of Domination, Style, Vol 29, 95 A Comment on Finch, Alison Article, Style, Vol 29, 95; A Comment on Finch, Alison Article, Style, Vol 29, 95. **CONTACT ADDRESS** 3111 Chelsea Dr, Cleveland Heights, OH 44118.

MILLEDGE, LUETTA UPSHUR
PERSONAL Born Savannah, GA **DISCIPLINE** ENGLISH **EDUCATION** Ft Valley State Coll, BA English 1948; Atlanta Univ, MA English 1949; Univ Georgia, PhD English 1971. **CAREER** Savannah State Coll, asst instructor 1949-, assoc prof, prof, chr div humn 1973-80, hd dept English 1972-80, hd dept humnl/fine arts 1980-84, head department of humanities 1984-91, Prof Emerita, 91-. **HONORS AND AWARDS** Regent's Scholarship 1944-48; Ford Found Fellowship 1969-71; George Washington Honor Medal; Freedoms Found Valley Forge Speech Vital Spchs 1973; Phi Kappa Phi, Phi Beta Kappa, Univ of GA; Co-Teacher of the Year School of Humanities 1989. **MEMBERSHIPS** Brd mem GA Endowment for Humanities 1980-83; Elder Butler Presbytery Church; mem Presid Comm Futr Savannah State Coll. **CONTACT ADDRESS** Savannah State Univ, Savannah, GA 31404.

MILLER, ANDREW M.
PERSONAL Born 05/26/1947, CA **DISCIPLINE** CLASSICS **EDUCATION** Univ Calif, BA, anthrop, Greek, 69, MA, 71, PhD, 77, comparative lit. **CAREER** Asst prof classics, 77-83, assoc prof classics, 83-97, prof classics, 97-, Univ Pittsburgh. **HONORS AND AWARDS** NEH Fellowship for Study and Research, 81-82. **MEMBERSHIPS** Amer Philological Assn; Classical Assn Atlantic States. **RESEARCH** Greek and Roman poetry; translation studies. **SELECTED PUBLICATIONS** Auth, From Delos to Delphi: A Literary Study of the Homeric Hymn to Apollo, 86; auth, "Inventa Componere: Rhetorical Process and Poetic Composition in Pinder's Ninth Olympian Ode," Transactions of the American Philological Assn, vol 123, 93; auth, "Pindaric Mimesis: The Associative Mode," Classical Journ, vol 87, 93; auth, Greek Lyric: An Anthology in Translation, 96; auth, "Levels of Argument in Pinder's Second Nemean Ode," Hellas 7, 96. **CONTACT ADDRESS** Dept of Classics, Univ of Pittsburgh, Pittsburgh, PA 15260. **EMAIL** amm2@pitt.edu

MILLER, CAROLYN R.
PERSONAL Born 04/29/1945, Boston, MA, m, 1967 **DISCIPLINE** COMMUNICATION AND RHETORIC **EDUCATION** Rensselaer Polytechnic Inst, PhD, 80. **CAREER** Visiting assoc prof, Dept of Humanities, Mich Tech Univ, spring quarter, 88; visiting assoc prof, Dept of English, Penn State Univ, summer 88; visiting prof, School of Lit, Commun, and Culture, Ga Inst of Tech, winter & spring quarters, 91; INST, DEPT OF ENGLISH, 77-79, ASST PROF, 80-83, ASSOC PROF, 83-90, PROF, NC STATE UNIV, 90-. **HONORS AND AWARDS** Nat Coun of Teachers of English, Best Article in the Philos or Theory of Tech and Sci Commun, 1975-1980, 81, Best Collection of Essays in Sci and Tech Commun, 84; Best Article in Historical Res in Tech or Sci Commun, 99; Outstanding Teacher Awd, NC State Univ, 84; Fel for Col Teachers, Nat Endowment for the Humanities, 92-93; Fel, Asn of Teachers of Tech Writing, 95; Alumni Distinguished Graduate Porf, NC State Univ, 99. **MEMBERSHIPS** Asn of Teachers of Tech Writing; Conf on Col Composition and Commun; Coun for Progs in Tech and Sci Commun; Int Soc for the Hist of Rhetoric; MLA; Nat Commun Asn; Nat Coun of Teachers of English; Rhetoric Soc of Am; Soc for Social Studies of Sci. **RESEARCH** Rhetorical theory; rhetoric of science and technology; rhetoric of professions and disciplines. **SELECTED PUBLICATIONS** Auth, Opportunity, Opportunism, and Progress: Kairos in the Rhetoic of Technology, Argumentation, 94; auth, "Learning from History: World War II and the Culture of High Technology," Journal of Business and Tech Commun, 98; auth, Rhetorical Community: The Cultural Basis of Genre, Genre and the New Rhetoric, Taylor and Francis, 94; auth, Classical Rhetoric without Nostalgia: A Response to Gaonkar, Rhetorical Hermeneutics, SUNY Press, 96; coauth, Reading Darwin, Reading Nature or On the Ethos of Historical Science, Understanding Scientific Prose, Univ of Wis Press, 93, 00; auth, The Low-Level Radioactive Waste Siting Controversy in North Carolina: Toward a Rhetorical Model of Risk Communication, in Green Culture, Univ of Wis, 96; co-ed, Making and Unmaking the Prospects for Rhetoric: Selected papers from the 1996 Rhetoric Society of America Conference, Lawrence Erlbaum, 97; auth, "The Aristoleian Topus: Hunting for Novelty, Rereading Aristotle's Rheteric, Southern Illinois Univ Press, (00). **CONTACT ADDRESS** English Dept, No Carolina State Univ, Box 8105, Raleigh, NC 27695-8105. **EMAIL** crmiller@ncsu.edu

MILLER, CLARENCE HARVEY
PERSONAL Born 08/04/1930, Kansas City, MO, d, 4 children **DISCIPLINE** ENGLISH LITERATURE, HUMANISM **EDUCATION** St Louis Univ, AB, 51; Harvard Univ, MA, 52; PhD(English), 55. **CAREER** From instr to assoc prof, 57-66, Prof English, St Louis Univ, 66-, Fulbright prof English, Univ Wuerzburg, WGer, 60-61; Guggenheim fel, 66-67; guest prof English, Ruhr-Univ, WGer, 76-77; vis prof, Yale Univ, 79-84. **MEMBERSHIPS** MLA; Amici Thomae Mori; Mod Humanities Res Asn; Renaissance Soc Am. **RESEARCH** Renaissance nondramatic English literature; Thomas More; Erasmus. **SELECTED PUBLICATIONS** Trans, "Erasmus, Poems," in Collected Works of Erasmus, Vol 85-86, ed. Harry Vredeveld (Univ of Toronto Press, Buffalo, London, 93); auth, "Style and Meaning in More's Utopia: Hythloday's Sentences and Diction," in Actus Conventus Neo-Latini Hafniensis: Proceedings of the Eight International Congress of Latin Studies, ed. Rhoda Schnur, Ann Moss, Philip Dust, Paul Gerhard Schmidt, Jacques Chomarat, and Francesca Pateo, in Medieval & Renaissance Texts and Studies, Vol 120 (Binghamton, NYork, 94), 675-683; auth, "G.M. Hopkins' 'Spring' as a May-Day Poem," Hopkins Quarterly 21 (96): 23-27; coed, "Thomas More's 'English Poems,' 'Life of Pico,' and 'The Last Thing,'" Vol 1, in The Collected Works of St. Thomas More, (Yale Univ Press, New Haven and London, 97); auth, "Christ as the Philosopher's Stone in George Herbert's 'The Elixir,'" Notes and Queries N.S. 45.1 (Oxford Univ, 98): 39-40; trans, "The First Part of Erasmus' Hyperaspistes Diatribae de Libero Arbitrio," and coed of the commentary, in Collected Works of Erasmus in English, Vol 76 (Univ of Toronto Press, 99); auth, "A Borrowing by Luther from Erasmus' 'Praise of Folly' in 1518," Notes and Queries 245 (NS 47: no. 1) (Oxford, 00): 22-23. **CONTACT ADDRESS** Dept of English, Saint Louis Univ, Saint Louis, MO 63108. **EMAIL** millerp2@slu.edu

MILLER, CLEMENT ALBIN
PERSONAL Born 01/29/1915, Cleveland, OH, m, 1937, 3 children **DISCIPLINE** MUSICOLOGY **EDUCATION** Cleveland Inst Music, BM, 36, MM, 37; Western Reserve Univ, MA, 42; Univ Mich, PhD, 51. **CAREER** Instr music theory, Cleveland Inst Music, 37-65, head, Dept Music Hist, 61-65, Dept Musicol, 55-65, from actg dean to dean fac, 52-65; PROF MUSIC, JOHN CARROLL UNIV, 67-, Instr, Western Reserve Univ, 42-43; Guggenheim Mem Found fel, 74-75. **HONORS AND AWARDS** Outstanding Educator, Outstanding Educators Am, 75. **MEMBERSHIPS** Am Musicol Soc; Music Libr Asn; Royal Music Asn; fel Int Inst Arts and Lett; Renaissance Soc Am. **RESEARCH** Philosophy; literature, particularly medieval and Renaissance; philology. **SELECTED PUBLICATIONS** Auth, The Environmental Imagination, Thoreau, Nature Writing, and the Formation of American Culture, New England Quart Hist Rev New England Life Letters, Vol 69, 96; Musica Enchiriadis and Scolica Enchiriadis,16th Century Jour, Vol 28, 97; The Theory of Music,16th Century Jour, Vol 26, 95; Acts of Discovery, Visions of America in the Lewis and Clark Journals, William Mary Quart, Vol 51, 94. **CONTACT ADDRESS** Apt 411 18975 Van Aken Blvd, Shaker Heights, OH 44122.

MILLER, D. GARY
PERSONAL Born 12/12/1942, Allentown, PA, m, 1967, 2 children **DISCIPLINE** LINGUISTICS CLASSICS **EDUCATION** Moravian Col, AB, 64; Harvard Univ, PhD(ling), 69. **CAREER** Instr ling, Southern Ill Univ, 68-69; asst prof, Univ Ill, Urbana, 69-71 and McGill Univ, 71-72; asst prof ling and classics, 72-76, Assoc Prof Ling and Classics, Uiiv Fla, 76-, Pres, Academics Plus, Inc. **MEMBERSHIPS** Ling Soc Am; Philol Soc. **RESEARCH** Indo-European studies; linguistic theory. **SELECTED PUBLICATIONS** Auth, A Subharmonic Vibratory Pattern in Normal Vocal Folds, JSpeech Hearing Rsch, Vol 39, 96; The Birth of a Journal, Interpretation J Bible Theol, Vol 50, 96; A Structured Approach to Voice Range Profile Phonetogram Analysis, JSpeech Hearing Rsch, Vol 37, 94. **CONTACT ADDRESS** Dept of Classics, Univ of Florida, 3c Arts and Sciences, Gainesville, FL 32611-9500.

MILLER, DAISY SOPHIA
PERSONAL Born 05/29/1968, New York, NY, s, 1968 **DISCIPLINE** ENGLISH **EDUCATION** Hofstra Univ, BA, 90; SUNY Stony Brook, PhD, 00. **CAREER** Adj lectr, Hofstra Univ, 96-00; asst prof, US Mil Acad, 01-. **MEMBERSHIPS** MLA; Phi Beta Kappa; Catherine Marie Sedgewick Soc. **RESEARCH** Shakers; sentimental literature; 19th-century American literature. **CONTACT ADDRESS** 305 W 98th St, Apt 5Fs, New York, NY 10025-5500. **EMAIL** cd4743@usma.edu

MILLER, DAVID G.
PERSONAL Born 03/01/1962, Wellsboro, PA **DISCIPLINE** LITERATURE **EDUCATION** Nyack Col, BA, 84; Baylor Univ, MA, 87; Baylor Univ Waco Texas, PhD, 91. **CAREER** Assoc Prof, Mississippi Col, 91-. **HONORS AND AWARDS** Distinguished Lecturer in Arts and Sciences, Mississippi College, 99; Mississippi Humanities Council Humanities Scholar, Mississippi College, 99. **MEMBERSHIPS** South Central Christianity and Literature Conference; Nineteenth Century Studies Assoc. **RESEARCH** Early Amer Writers; Culture British Romanticism. **SELECTED PUBLICATIONS** Coauth, "Celebrate Advent: Worship and Educational Resources, Smyth & Helwys Press, 99; auth, "The Word Made Flesh Made Word: Failure and Redemption of Metaphor in Edward Taylor's Christographic, Susquehanna VP, 96. **CONTACT ADDRESS** Dept English, Mississippi Col, Clinton, 200 West College St, Clinton, MS 39058. **EMAIL** dmiller@mc.edu

MILLER, DAVID LEE
PERSONAL Born 08/17/1951, Cushing, OK, m, 1984, 3 children **DISCIPLINE** ENGLISH **EDUCATION** Yale Univ, BA, 73; Univ Calif Irvine, MA, 75; PhD, 79. **CAREER** Instr to prof, Univ of Ala, 78-94; prof, Univ of Ky, 94- **HONORS AND AWARDS** Guggenheim Found Fel, 94-95; Mellon Fel, 00-01. **MEMBERSHIPS** MLA, SAMLA, Int Spenser Soc, SE Renaissance Conf, Shakespeare Assoc of Am, Renaissance Soc of Am, Renaissance Eng Text Soc, Soc for the Study of Early Modern Women. **RESEARCH** English Renaissance Literature, Psychoanalysis and Gender Theory. **SELECTED PUBLICATIONS** Auth, "Spenser's Vocation, Spenser's Career," Eng Lit Hist, (83); auth, The Poem's Two Bodies: The Poetics of the 1590 Faerie Queene, Princeton Univ Pr, 88; auth, "The Death of the Modern: Gender and Desire in Marlowe's Hero and Leander," S Atlantic Quart 88.4, (89); coed, The Production of English Renaissance Culture, Cornell Univ Pr, 94; coed, Approaches to Teaching Spenser's Faerie Queene", MLA, 94; auth, "The Earl of Cork's Lute," Spenser's Life and the Subject of Biography, (94). **CONTACT ADDRESS** Dept English, Univ of Kentucky, Lexington, KY 40506-0027. **EMAIL** unique1@pop.uky.edu

MILLER, EDMUND
PERSONAL Born 07/18/1943, Queens, NY, s **DISCIPLINE** LITERATURE, CREATIVE WRITING **EDUCATION** CW Post Campus, Long Island Univ, BA, 65; Ohio State Univ, MA, 69; State Univ of NYork at Stony Brook, PhD, 75. **CAREER** From Asst Prof to Prof, CW Post Campus, Long Island Univ, 80-91; Chairman, 93-. **HONORS AND AWARDS** College English Rhetoric Prize, 69; NEH Summer Seminar, 82; Folger Library Seminar, 86. **MEMBERSHIPS** Modern Language Assoc; Milton Society of America. **RESEARCH** Seventeenth-Century British; Nineteenth-Century British. **SELECTED PUBLICATIONS** Auth, Drudgerie Divine: The Rhetoric of God and Man in George Herbert, Universitat Salzburg (Salzburg), 79; ed, Mount-Orgueil, Divine and Profitable Meditations by William Prynne, Scholars and Facsimiles and Reprints (Delmar) 84; Like Season'd Timber: New Essays on George Herbert, Peter Lang (NY), 87; auth, The Happiness Cure; and Other Poems, Birnham Wood Graphics (Northport NY), 93; auth, George's Herbert Kinship: An Ahnentafel with Annotations, Heritage Press (Bowie, MD), 93; auth, Leavings Birnham Wood Graphics (Northport NY), 95; auth, Nighttimes, Prowler (London), 00; auth, Men of the New York Club Scene: A Celebration in Words and Pictures, Janssen Verlag (Cape Town), 00. **CONTACT ADDRESS** Dept English, Long Island Univ, C.W. Post, 1300 N Blvd., Greenvale, NY 11548-1300. **EMAIL** edmund.miller@liu.edu

MILLER, EDWIN HAVILAND
PERSONAL Born 09/02/1918, Johnstown, PA, m, 1946, 1 child **DISCIPLINE** ENGLISH LITERATURE **EDUCATION** Lehigh Univ, AB, 40; Pa State Col, AM, 42; Harvard Univ, PhD, 51. **CAREER** Instr English, Pa State Col, 40-42 and 45-46; from instr to prof, Simmons Col, 47-61; assoc prof, 61-62, chmn dept, 68-73, Prof English, NY Univ, 62-, Res fel, Folger Shakespeare Libr, 53; Am Coun Learned Soc fel, 59-60; Guggenheim fels, 67-68 and 78-79. **MEMBERSHIPS** MLA; Col English Asn. **RESEARCH** American literature; literature and psychology. **SELECTED PUBLICATIONS** Auth, Symphony New Brunswick--Quartets, Quintets and Full Orchestra, Performing Arts and Entertainment in Canada, Vol 30, 96; Allen, Gay, Wilson, 1903-95, Walt Whitman Quart Rev, Vol 13, 95; Federal Sentencing Guidelines for Organizational Defendants, Vanderbilt Law Rev, Vol 46, 93. **CONTACT ADDRESS** Dept of English, New York Univ, New York, NY 10003.

MILLER, ELIZABETH A.
PERSONAL Born 02/26/1939, St. John's, NF, Canada **DISCIPLINE** LITERATURE **EDUCATION** Memorial Univ Nfld, MA, 75, PhD 88. **CAREER** High sch tchr & prin, 58-68, dir comm, Nfld Tchrs Asn, 68-70, Prof Eng, Memorial Univ N

FLD, 70-. **MEMBERSHIPS** Asn Can Col & Univ Tchrs Eng; Int Asn Fantastic Arts; Int Bram Stoker Soc; British Gothic Soc. **RESEARCH** Dracula/Gothic literature **SELECTED PUBLICATIONS** Auth, The Genesis of Count Dracula, Lumea, 96; auth, "Frankenstein and Dracula: A Question of Influence," Visions of the Fantastic, (96); auth, A Genese do Conde Dracula, Megalon, 97; auth, "Dracula: The History of Myth and the Myth of History," Journal of the Dark No. 9, (97); auth, Blood Offerings for Dracula: Winning Entries for the Count's Ceative Writing Contest, TSD Pub, 97; auth, "The Transylvanian Society of Dracula," Bram Stoker's Dracula: Sucking Through the Century, 97; auth, Reflections on Dracula, White Rock, BC: Transylvania Press, 97; auth, "bats, Vampires and Dracula," Night Flyer: News for the Friends of Florida's Bats vol3, (98), 1-3; auth, Dracula: The Shade and the Shadow, A collection of twenty papers from Dracula 97; Westcliff-on-Sea, Gr Britain: Desert Island Books, 98; auth, Back to the Basics: Re-examining Stoker's Sources for Dracula," Journal of the Fantstic in the Arts, (99), 187-196. **CONTACT ADDRESS** Dept of English, Mem Univ of Newfoundland, Saint John's, NF, Canada A1C 5S7. **EMAIL** emiller@morgan.ucs.mun.ca

MILLER, EUGENE ERNEST
PERSONAL Born 04/18/1930, Akron, OH, m, 1962, 2 children **DISCIPLINE** ENGLISH **EDUCATION** Univ Notre Dame, BA, 55; Ohio Univ, MA, 62; Univ Ill, Urbana, PhD(English), 67. **CAREER** Assoc Prof English, Albion Col, 67-, Nat Endowment for Humanities fel, Howard Univ, 71-72. **MEMBERSHIPS** MLA; Col English Asn. **RESEARCH** English; Afro-American literature; aesthetics. **SELECTED PUBLICATIONS** Auth, Voodoo parallels in Native Son, Col Lang Asn J, 9/72; Some Black thoughts on Don L Lee's Think Black, Col English, 5/73. **CONTACT ADDRESS** Dept of English, Albion Col, Albion, MI 49224.

MILLER, GABRIEL
PERSONAL Born 08/03/1948, Bronx, NY, m, 1974, 2 children **DISCIPLINE** MODERN AMERICAN FICTION, AMERICAN DRAMA & FILM **EDUCATION** Queens Col, BA, 70; Brown Univ, PhD, 75. **CAREER** Asst prof Eng & film, AZ State Univ, 75-76; asst prof Eng, IL State Univ, 77-80; from Asst Prof to Assoc Prof, 80-96, prof eng, Rutgers Univ, Newark, 96, Dept Ch, 92. **MEMBERSHIPS** MLA; ADE. **RESEARCH** Polit and the novel; film hist and theory. **SELECTED PUBLICATIONS** Auth, Hitchcock's wasteland vision: An examination of Frenzy, Film Heritage, spring 76; A laugh gains the upper hand: Woody Allen's Love and Death, Bright Lights, No 7, 78; Daniel Fuchs, Twayne, 79; Screening the Novel, Frederick Ungar, 80; John Irving, Frederick Ungar, 81; auth, introd to Alvah Bessie's Solo Flight & The Serpent Was More Subtil, Chandler & Sharp, 82; Clifford Odets, Continuum, 89; ed, Critical Essays on Clifford Odets, G.K. Hall, 91; auth, Fanfare for the Common Man: The Films of Martin Ritt, Univ Press KY. **CONTACT ADDRESS** Dept of Eng, Rutgers, The State Univ of New Jersey, Newark, 180 University Ave, Newark, NJ 07102-1897. **EMAIL** gamiller@andromeda.rutgers.edu

MILLER, GILL WRIGHT
PERSONAL Born 02/01/1952, Columbus, OH, 4 children **DISCIPLINE** DANCE **EDUCATION** Denison Univ, BFA; Wesleyan Univ, MALS; Laban/Bartenieff Institute of Movement Studies, CMA; NYork Univ, PhD. **CAREER** Assoc prof dance and women's studies, 76-77 and 81-; chr Dance Dept, 81-; instr Eng and adj fac Dance, NY Univ. **HONORS AND AWARDS** Res funds grants, Denison Univ; Robert C Good grant, Denison Univ; Dean's Awd Outstanding Res, NY Univ, 94. **RESEARCH** Performance work; experiential anatomy/kinesiology; Bainbridge Cohen, Olsen/McHose, Juhan, Sweigard/Dowd, and Adler. **SELECTED PUBLICATIONS** Auth, publ(s) in dance criticism, Labanotation theory, women's issues in dance, and women's photography. **CONTACT ADDRESS** Dance Dept, Denison Univ, Granville, OH 43023. **EMAIL** millerg@denison.edu

MILLER, GREG
DISCIPLINE ENGLISH **EDUCATION** Vanderbilt Univ, BA; Stanford Univ, MA; Univ Calif at Berkeley, PhD. **CAREER** Dept ch. **SELECTED PUBLICATIONS** Auth, Iron Wheel, Univ Chicago Press, 98. **CONTACT ADDRESS** Dept of English, Millsaps Col, 1701 N State St, Jackson, MS 39210.

MILLER, JAY
PERSONAL Born 08/21/1959, Seattle, WA, s **DISCIPLINE** ENGLISH **EDUCATION** North Seattle Community Col, AA, 87; Seattle Pacific Univ, BA, 90; Baylor Univ, MA, 93; Wayne State Univ, PhD, 00. **CAREER** Grad TA, Wayne State Univ, 95-00; adj instr, Wayne State Univ, 00-. **HONORS AND AWARDS** Scholar, Seattle Pacific Univ, 89; Thomas C Rumble Grad Fel, 99-00; Diss Fel, Wayne State Univ, 99-00. **MEMBERSHIPS** MLA, Labor and Working Class Hist Assoc. **RESEARCH** American Literature from the Progressive Era, English Literature related to the Industrial Revolution, Labor Studies. **SELECTED PUBLICATIONS** Auth, Days of Roaring Hell: William E. Trautmann and the Rise of the Industrial Workers of the World, forthcoming. **CONTACT ADDRESS** 5855 - 4th St, Apt 22, Detroit, MI 48202-3733. **EMAIL** ad5764@wayne.edu

MILLER, JEANNE-MARIE A.
PERSONAL Born 02/18/1937, Washington, DC, m **DISCIPLINE** ENGLISH **EDUCATION** Howard Univ, BA 1959, MA 1963, PhD 1976. **CAREER** Howard Univ, instr English 1963-76, grad asst prof English 1977-79; Inst for the Arts & the Humanities Howard Univ, asst dir 1973-75, grad assoc prof of English 1979-92; asst for academic planning office of the vice pres for academic affairs 1976-90, grad professor of English, 92-. **HONORS AND AWARDS** Advanced Study Fellowship Ford Found 1970-72; Fellow So Fellowship Fund 1972-74; Grantee Amer Council of Learned Societies; 1978-79; Grantee Natl Endowment for the Humanities 1981-84; Grantee, Howard University Faculty Research Fund, 1994-95, 1996-97; edited book From Realism to Ritual: Form & Style in Black Theatre 1983; Pi Lambda Theta Natl Honor and Professional Assn in Education 1987. **MEMBERSHIPS** Ed Black Theatre Bulletin Amer Theatre Assoc 1977-86; mem exec council Black Theatre Prog Amer Theatre Assoc 1977-86; proposal reviewer Natl Endowment for the Humanities 1979-; adv bd WETA-TV Ed prog on Black Folklore 1976-77; mem Friends of JF Kennedy Ctr for Performing Arts, Amer Assoc of Univ Women, Amer Civil Liberites Union, Amer Film Inst; assoc mem Arena Stage, Washington Performing Arts Soc, Eugene O'Neill Memorial Theatre Ctr, Amer Soc of Business and Exec Women; assoc Art Inst of Chicago, Boston Museum of Fine Arts, Metropolitan Museum of Art, Corcoran Gallery of Art, Smithsonian Inst, Washington Performings Arts Soc, The Washington Opera Guild, World Affairs Council of Washington DC, Drama League of New York, Modern Language Assoc, Amer Studies Assoc, Coll Lang Assoc, Natl Council of Teachers of Engli Amer Assoc for Higher Educ, Natl Assoc for Women Deans Administrators and Counselors, Natl Women's Studies Assoc. **SELECTED PUBLICATIONS** 60 articles in various jrnls & mags **CONTACT ADDRESS** Dept of English, Howard Univ, 2400 6th St NW, Washington, DC 20059.

MILLER, JO ELLEN
PERSONAL Born 12/28/1954, Berkeley, CA, m, 1985, 2 children **DISCIPLINE** LITERATURE **EDUCATION** Univ Ore, BA, 80; Colo State Univ, MA, 84; Univ Ut, PhD, 93. **CAREER** Assoc prof, Grand Valley State Univ, 91-. **MEMBERSHIPS** MLA, Shakespeare Asn of Am, Pacific Northwest Renaissance Soc. **RESEARCH** Shakespeare, Reanaissance Literature. **SELECTED PUBLICATIONS** Auth, "Women and the Market in The Roaring Girl," Renaissance & Reformation 19 (90): 11-23; auth, "Cross-dressing and the Sexual Economy of Beaumont & Fletcher's Philaster," English Lit Renaissance 27 (97): 129-150. **CONTACT ADDRESS** Dept English, Grand Valley State Univ, 1 Campus Dr, Allendale, MI 49401-9401. **EMAIL** millerj@gvsu.edu

MILLER, JOHN F.
PERSONAL Born 02/04/1950, Washington, DC, m, 1972 **DISCIPLINE** CLASSICS **EDUCATION** Xavier Univ, HAB, 72; Univ North Carolina Chapel Hill, MA, 74, PhD, 79. **CAREER** Vis instr, N Carolina State Univ, 77-78; asst prof, Univ Minn, 78-84; asst to assoc prof, Univ Va, 84- . **HONORS AND AWARDS** Alexander von Humboldt-Stiftung fel, Heidelberg, 85-86; ed, Class J, 91-98; ovatio & pres, Class Assoc of Middle West and South, 99. **MEMBERSHIPS** APA; Class Assoc of Middle West and South; Class Assoc of Va; Roman Soc. **RESEARCH** Latin literature; Roman religion; Hellenistic poetry. **SELECTED PUBLICATIONS** Auth, Ovid's Elegiac Festivals: Studies in the Fasti, Studien zur klassischen Philologie 55, NY, 91; auth, Ovidian Allusion and the Vocabulary of Memory, Materiali e discussioni per l'analisi dei testi classici, 93; auth, Virgil, Apollo, and Augustus, in Solomon, ed, Apollo, Origins and Influences, Tucson & London, 94; auth, Apostrophe, Aside and the Didactic Addressee: Poetic Strategies in Ars Amatoria III, Materiali e discussioni per l'analisi dei testi classici, 94; auth, The Memories of Ovid's Pythagoras, Mnemosyne, 94; auth, Lucretian Moments in Ovidian Elegy, Class J, 97. **CONTACT ADDRESS** Dept of Classics, Univ of Virginia, Charlottesville, VA 22903. **EMAIL** JFM4J@virginia.edu

MILLER, JOSHUA L.
PERSONAL Born 06/07/1971, Durham, NC, m, 2000 **DISCIPLINE** US LITERATURE **EDUCATION** Univ Chicago, AB, 93; Columbia Univ, AM, 95; MPhil, 97, PhD, 01. **HONORS AND AWARDS** Mid-East Ctr Travel Grant, 95; Columbia Univ Pres Fel, 95-00; Mrs Giles Whiting Found Diss Fel, 99-00. **MEMBERSHIPS** MLA, ASA, NYMASA, NAPH, AIS. **RESEARCH** US Literature, cultural theory, linguistics, multilingualism, photography. **SELECTED PUBLICATIONS** Auth, "The Discovery of What if Means to be a Witness," James Baldwin Now, ed Dwight McGride, NY Univ Pr, (99); auth," A Striking Addiction to Irreality," Re-Viewing James Baldwin, ed D Quentin Miller, Temple Univ Pr, (00). **CONTACT ADDRESS** Dept Eng and Comp Lit, Columbia Univ, 602 Philosophy Hall, New York, NY 10027. **EMAIL** gnessin@yahoo.com

MILLER, KATHERINE I.
DISCIPLINE COMMUNICATION **EDUCATION** Univ Southern Calif, PhD. **CAREER** Prof, Texas A&M Univ. **SELECTED PUBLICATIONS** Auth, Organizational Communication: Approaches and Processes; contribur, Organizational Communication and Change: Challenges in the NextCentury; Case Studies in Organizational Communication: Perspectives on Contemporary Work Life; Communication and Disenfranchisement: Social Health Issues and Implications; past ed, Mgt Commun Quart. **CONTACT ADDRESS** Dept of Speech Communication, Texas A&M Univ, Col Station, College Station, TX 77843-4234.

MILLER, LAURA
PERSONAL Born 06/01/1951, Atlanta, GA, d **DISCIPLINE** THEATRE **EDUCATION** Tufts Univ, BA, 73; Univ Memphis, MA, 75; Univ Neb, PhD, 93. **CAREER** Dir Theatre, Univ Va, 95-. **MEMBERSHIPS** SE Theatre Conf. **RESEARCH** Political plays. **SELECTED PUBLICATIONS** Auth, Bridges and Burning; auth, Murphy's Law; auth, The Princess of Missouri; auth, The Wayward Child; auth, The Princess Who Wanted the Moon; auth, The Enchanted Swan; auth, A Bad Night on Broadway; auth, The Last Song and Dance. **CONTACT ADDRESS** Dept Visual & Performing Arts, Univ of Virginia, 1 Col Ave, Wise, VA 24293-4400. **EMAIL** lhm3v@virginia.edu

MILLER, MARY JANE
PERSONAL Born 10/09/1941, Beamsville, ON, Canada **DISCIPLINE** FILM STUDIES **EDUCATION** Univ Toronto, BA, 63, MA, 64; Univ Birmingham (UK), PhD, 73. **CAREER** Fac mem, Univ Western Ont, 64-66; fac mem, 68-86, ch 75-78, Prof Film Stud, Dramatic & Visual Arts, Brock Univ, 86-; consult, Nat Arch Can, 79. **HONORS AND AWARDS** Woodrow Wilson fel, 63. **MEMBERSHIPS** Asn Can Theatre Res; Film Stud Asn Can; Asn Can Stud; Asn Commun Stud. **SELECTED PUBLICATIONS** Auth, Turn Up the Contrast: CBC Television Drama Since 1952, 87; auth, Rewind and Search: Conversations with Makers and Decision-Makers of CBC TV Drama, 96. **CONTACT ADDRESS** Dept of Film Studies, Dramatic & Visual Arts, Brock Univ, Saint Catharines, ON, Canada L2S 3A1. **EMAIL** mjmiller@spartan.ac.brocku.ca

MILLER, MARY RUTH
PERSONAL Born 12/22/1926, Bartow, FL **DISCIPLINE** ENGLISH **EDUCATION** Fla State Univ, AB, 48; George Peabody Col, MA, 51; Duke Univ, PhD, 66. **CAREER** Teacher, Fla Public Schs, 48-53; instr, Reinhardt Col, 53-59; asst prof, Fla Southern Col, 62-67; prof, Tenn Wesleyan Col, 67-76; prof, head, N Ga Col, 76-92. **HONORS AND AWARDS** Lewis State Teachers Scholarship, 45-48; Cokesbury Award, Duke, 59-60; Duke Woodrow Wilson Award, 62; Tenn Wesleyan Grant, 68. **MEMBERSHIPS** MLA. **RESEARCH** Fiction writing. **SELECTED PUBLICATIONS** Auth, Thomas Campbell, Twayne Publ, 78; auth, "Five Recently Found Letters by Thomas Campbell," Mod Lang Rev, (88); auth, "Thomas Campbell," Dict of Lit Biog, Vol 93, (90); auth, "Thomas Campbell and General Pepe," Notes and Queries, Vol 243, (98); auth, "Thomas Campbell," Cambridge Bibliog of Eng Lit, Vol 4, (99); auth, Chilhowee, 1st Books Libr, (01). **CONTACT ADDRESS** 2701 Pickett Rd, Apt 4013, Durham, NC 27705. **EMAIL** merrygo@mindspring.com

MILLER, O. VICTOR
PERSONAL Born 07/12/1942, Macon, GA, d, 3 children **DISCIPLINE** ENGLISH **EDUCATION** MA **CAREER** Infor specialist, Armored Sentinel, 68; instr, Tampa Col, 70-71, 72-73; instr, St. Petersburg Junior Col, 71-72; asst prof, Darton Col, 74-. **HONORS AND AWARDS** Ga Outdoor Writers Asn Excellence in Craft. **RESEARCH** Creative writing. **SELECTED PUBLICATIONS** Auth, The Tenderest Touch, 88; auth, One Man's Junk, 94. **CONTACT ADDRESS** Dept Humanities, Darton Col, 2400 Gillionville Rd, Albany, GA 31707-3023. **EMAIL** millerv@mail.dartnet.peachnet.edu

MILLER, PATRICK
DISCIPLINE MUSIC **EDUCATION** Univ Kans, BM, MM; Univ Mich, PhD. **CAREER** Former fac, Pembroke State Univ; Univ Mi; Univ North Texas; Chairperson, Music Theory Department, Hartt, 80-. **MEMBERSHIPS** Musical Heritage Soc. **SELECTED PUBLICATIONS** Auth, College Music Symposium; Perspectives of New Music; Theory & Practice; Gwynn S. McPeek Festschrift. **CONTACT ADDRESS** Hartt Sch Music, Univ of Hartford, 200 Bloomfield Ave, West Hartford, CT 06117.

MILLER, PETER
PERSONAL Born 09/06/1940, Dunkirk, NY, s, 4 children **DISCIPLINE** ENGLISH, RELIGION **EDUCATION** State Univ NY at Fredonia, BA, 66; MS, 70; CAS-SAS, 80; Holy Names Col, MA, 95. **CAREER** High Sch English, 66-89; Principal, 89-90; Trocaire Col, 92-00; Niagara Univ, 99-00. **HONORS AND AWARDS** Listed in Who's Who in College Teachers, 98-00. **MEMBERSHIPS** NCTE, St Luke's Guild, NYSCLA. **RESEARCH** World Religions. **SELECTED PUBLICATIONS** Auth, Right Rites--Right Rituals, Holy Names Col Press (Oakland, CA); auth, The Aurora Experiment, Univ Creation Spirituality Pr (Oakland, CA), forthcoming. **CONTACT ADDRESS** Dept Humanities, Trocaire Col, 360 Choate Ave, Buffalo, NY 14220-2003. **EMAIL** millerpetera@aol.com

MILLER, R. BAXTER
PERSONAL Born 10/11/1948, Rocky Mount, NC, d, 1 child **DISCIPLINE** ENGLISH POETRY **EDUCATION** NC Ctrl Univ, BA, 70; Brown Univ, AM, 72, PhD, 74. **CAREER** Asst prof English, Haverford Col, 74-76; assoc prof English, Univ Tenn, 77-81; prof English & dir Black Lit Prog, 82-92, Lindsay Young prof lib arts & English, 86-87, Prof English & Dir Aft Am Stud, 92- , Univ Georgia; Mellon prof Xavier Univ, 88; lectr, SUNY, 74; Irvine Found vis scholar, Univ San Fran, 91. **HONORS AND AWARDS** Am Book Awd, 91 **MEMBERSHIPS** Langston Hughes Soc; Mod Lang Asn. **RESEARCH** Modern poetry. **SELECTED PUBLICATIONS** Auth, Black American Poets Between Worlds, 1940-1960, 86; The Southern Trace in Black Critical Theory, Xavier Rev, 91; co-ed, Call and Response: African American Tradition in Literature, Houghton Mifflin, 97; coauth, Call and Response: The Riverside Anthology of African-American Literature Houghton Mifflin, 98; ed The Critical Methods of Aftrican Americans: 1865-1988, 99. **CONTACT ADDRESS** African Am Stud, Univ of Georgia, 311 Chandler Hall, Athens, GA 30602-3012. **EMAIL** rbmiller@uga.edu

MILLER, ROBERT H.
PERSONAL Born 08/10/1938, Defiance, OH, m, 1960, 3 children **DISCIPLINE** ENGLISH **EDUCATION** Bowling Green St Univ, BA, 60; MA, 61; Ohio St Univ, PhD, 68. **CAREER** Instr, Mich Tech Univ, 61-64; Prof, Univ Louisville, 65-. **MEMBERSHIPS** Bibliog Soc of Am, AAUP. **RESEARCH** Renaissance literature and culture, the modern novel. **SELECTED PUBLICATIONS** Auth, Understanding Graham Greene, Univ SC Pr (Columbia, SC), 90; auth, Handbook of Literary Research, Scarecrow Pr (Metuchen, NJ), 95; auth, "Hammett's Physical Falcon, or, What Did the Knights Give the Emperor," Studies in Am Cult 21 (98): 46-52; auth, "Graham Greene's Saddest Story," Renascence 51.2 (99): 133-143; **CONTACT ADDRESS** Dept English, Univ of Louisville, 2301 S 3rd St, Louisville, KY 40292-0001. **EMAIL** rhmiller@louisville.edu

MILLER, STEVEN MAX
PERSONAL Born 02/09/1950, Portland, IN, d **DISCIPLINE** ENGLISH **EDUCATION** Col William & Mary, AB, 72; Ind Univ MA, 74; PhD, 85. **CAREER** Asst to Assoc Prof, Millersville Univ, 85-.Asst Prof, Murray State Univ, 89-90. **HONORS AND AWARDS** Who's Who in Am; Who's Who in Teaching; NEH Sem, 90; NEH Workshop, 91. **MEMBERSHIPS** MLA; John Donne Soc of Am; The Spenser Soc; The Bronte Soc. **RESEARCH** 16th and 17th Century British texts, poetry, women writers. **CONTACT ADDRESS** Dept Eng, Millersville Univ of Pennsylvania, PO Box 1002, Millersville, PA 17551-0302. **EMAIL** steven.miller@millersville.edu

MILLER, TICE LEWIS
PERSONAL Born 08/11/1938, Lexington, NE, m, 1963, 2 children **DISCIPLINE** THEATRE HISTORY **EDUCATION** Kearney State Col, BA, 60; Univ Nebr, Lincoln, MA, 61; Univ Ill, Urbana, PhD(Theatre), 68. **CAREER** Instr speech & theatre, Kansas City Jr Col, 61-62; asst prof theatre, Univ WFla, 68-72; assoc prof, 72-79, prof Theatre & Drama, Univ Nebr, Lincoln, 79-, fel, Ctr Great Plains Studies, 78. **HONORS AND AWARDS** Fellow, College of Fellows of American Theatre, JFK Center, Washington, D.C., 92; Sam Davidson Theatre Awd, Lincoln Arts Council, 98. **MEMBERSHIPS** Am Soc Theatre Res; Am Theatre Asn; Univ & Col Theatre Asn; Mid-Am Theatre Conf. **RESEARCH** American theatre; 19th century American theatre; American theatre critics. **SELECTED PUBLICATIONS** Auth, John Ranken Towse: Last of the Victorian critics, Educ Theatre J, 5/70; Towse on Reform in the American Theatre, Cent States Speech Commun J, winter 72; Early Cultural History of Nebraska: The Role of the Opera House, Nebr Speech Commun J, 74; Alan Dale: The Hearst critic, Educ Theatre J, 3/74; From Winter to Nathan: The Critics Influence on the American Theatre, Southern Speech Commun J, winter 76; Identifying the Dramatic Writers for Wilkes's Spirit of the Times, 1859-1902, Theatre Survey, 5/79; Bohemians and Critics: Nineteenth Century Theatre Criticism, Scarecrow Press Inc, 81; Fitz-James O'Brien: Irish Playwright & Critic in New York, 1851-1862, Nineteenth Century Theatre Res, fall 82; co-ed, Cambridge Guide to American Theatre, 93; co-ed, The American Stage, Cambridge, 93; editorial advisory board & major contributor, Cambridge Guide to Theatre, 88, 92, 95; auth, "Plays and Playwrights: Civil War to 1896," The Cambridge History of American Theatre, Vol II, 99. **CONTACT ADDRESS** Dept of Theatre Arts, Univ of Nebraska, Lincoln, PO Box 880201, Lincoln, NE 68588-0201. **EMAIL** tmiller@unlinfo.unl.edu

MILLER, VERNON D.
PERSONAL Born 02/26/1955, Houston, TX, d, 2 children **DISCIPLINE** ORGANIZATIONAL COMMUNICATION **EDUCATION** Baylor Univ, BA, 77, MA, 79; Univ Tx at Austin, PhD, 88. **CAREER** Univ Wis at Milwaukee, 86-90; Mich State Univ, 90-00. **MEMBERSHIPS** Int Commun Asn; Acad of Management; Nat Commun Asn. **RESEARCH** Organizational assimilation; employment interviewing; role leavening; role negotiation. **SELECTED PUBLICATIONS** Coauth, Antecedents to willingness to participate in a planned organizational change, J of Applied Commun, 94; The maternity leave as a role negotiation process: A conceptual framework, J of Managerial Issues, 96; The role of communication in managing reducations in work force, J of Applied Commun Res, 96; Toward a research agenda for the second employment interview, J of Applied Commun Res, 96; The role of a conference in integrating a contractual network of health services organizations, J of Business Commun, 96; An experimental study of newcomers' information seeking behaviors during organizational entry, Commun Studies, 96; Communicating and Connecting: The functions of human communication, Harcourt Brace Col Pub, 96; Testing two contrasting models of innovativeness in a contractual network, Human Commun Res, 97; Survivors' information seeking following a reduction in workforce, Commun Res, 97; Downsizing and structural holes: Their impact on layoff survivors' perceptions of organizational chaos and openess to change, Commun Res, 98; The case of the aggrieved expatriate case analysis: Miller analysis, Management Commun Quart, 98. **CONTACT ADDRESS** Dept of Commun, Michigan State Univ, East Lansing, MI 48824-1212.

MILLER-DAY, MICHELLE
PERSONAL Born 06/12/1960, Wooster, OH, m, 2 children **DISCIPLINE** COMMUNICATION **EDUCATION** Univ S Calif, BA, 82; MFA, 84; Ariz State Univ, PhD, 96 **CAREER** Asst Prof Univ Memphis; Asst Prof, Penn State Univ, 97-. **RESEARCH** Family Communication; Psychodrama; Adolescent drug use. **CONTACT ADDRESS** Sept Speech, Pennsylvania State Univ, Univ Park, 211 Sparks Bldg, University Park, PA 16802-5201. **EMAIL** mam32@psu.edu

MILLICHAP, JOSEPH R.
PERSONAL Born 02/14/1940, Troy, NY **DISCIPLINE** ENGLISH **EDUCATION** St Peters Col, BA, 61; Notre Dame Univ, MA, 62; PhD, 70. **CAREER** From Instr to Asst Prof, Univ Mont, 68-71; From Asst to Assoc Prof, Univ Tulsa, 79-84; From Assoc Prof to Prof, Western Ky Univ, 84- **HONORS AND AWARDS** NDEA Fel, 61-64; Fulbright Fel, 77-78; Wood Res Fel, 96-97. **MEMBERSHIPS** MLA, SAMLA, KPA, SSSL, Robert Penn Warren Circle. **RESEARCH** American literature, film, culture, Southern Renaissance, Robert Penn Warren, landscape, technology, literary culture, railroads. **SELECTED PUBLICATIONS** Auth, "Hamilton Basso," in Twayne U S Authors Ser (Boston: G K Hall, 79); auth, "Lewis Milestone," in Twayne Filmmakers Ser (Boston: G K Hall, 81); auth, "Steinbeck and Film," in Ungar Film Ser (New York: Frederick Ungar, 83); auth, Robert Penn Warren: A Study of the Short Fiction," in Twayne Studies in Short Fiction Ser (Boston: G K Hall, 92). **CONTACT ADDRESS** Dept English, Western Kentucky Univ, 1 Big Red Way St, Bowling Green, KY 42101-5730. **EMAIL** joseph.millichap@wku.edu

MILLIER, BRETT
PERSONAL Born 02/14/1958, Coffeyville, KS, m, 1990, 2 children **DISCIPLINE** LITERATURE **EDUCATION** Yale, BA, 80; Stanford, PhD, 86. **CAREER** Asst Prof, Assoc Prof, Reginald L. Cook Prof, Middlebury Col, 86-. **HONORS AND AWARDS** Mellon Fel, Harvard Univ, 89-90. **MEMBERSHIPS** MLA. **RESEARCH** 20th Century American Poetry and Fiction. **SELECTED PUBLICATIONS** Auth, "Elusive Mastery: The Drafts of Elizabeth Bishop's 'One Art'," New England Rev 13-2 (91): 121-129, in Elizabeth Bishop: the Geography of Gender, ed. May-Lombardi (Univ of Va Press, 93), 233-243, and in The Writer's Home Companion, ed. Joan Bolker, and Henry Holt (97), 101-116; rev, of "Elizabeth Bishop: Questions of Mastery," by Bonnie Costello, and "Elizabeth Bishop: the Biography of a Poetry," Harvard Rev (Spring 92); auth, Elizabeth Bishop: Life and the Memory of It, Univ of Calif Press, 93; co-ed, Columbia History of American Poetry, Columbia Univ Press, 93; auth, "Elizabeth Bishop," and "Louise Bogan," in Dictionary of Literary Biography 169: American Poets Since World War II (Fifth Series) (96), 35-53, and 54-62; rev, of "Searching for Mercy Street: My Journey Back to My Mother, Anne Sexton," by Linda Gray Sexton, New England Rev 17-3 (Summer 95): 182-186; auth, "The Prodigal: Elizabeth Bishop and Alcohol," Contemp Lit 39-1 (Spring 98): 54-76; rev, of "Wait Till Next Year," by Doris Kearns Goodwin, New England Rev 20-1 (Summer 98): 158-161; auth, The Alchemists: American Women Poets and Alcohol, Univ of Calif Press, forthcoming. **CONTACT ADDRESS** Dept Am Lit, Middlebury Col, Middlebury, VT 05753-6200. **EMAIL** millier@middlebury.edu

MILLS, JOHN ARVIN
PERSONAL Born 12/03/1931, Indianapolis, IN, m, 1961 **DISCIPLINE** ENGLISH **EDUCATION** Butler Univ, BA, 53; IN Univ, MA, 59, PhD, 61. **CAREER** Lectr speech & drama, IN Univ, 59-61; assoc prof drama, Univ AZ, 61-66; from asst prof to assoc prof theater, State Univ NY Binghamton, 66-74; Assoc Prof Eng to Assoc Prof Emer, Univ AZ, 74-98. **HONORS AND AWARDS** Found grant-in-aid, 68-69; Guggenheim res fel, London, 72-73. **MEMBERSHIPS** Am Soc Theatre Res. **RESEARCH** Dramatic criticism; mod drama; theatre hist. **SELECTED PUBLICATIONS** Auth, Shaw's Linguistic Satire, Shaw Rev, 1/65; The Comic in Words: Shaw's Cockneys, Drama Surv, summer 66; Language and Laughter: Shaw's Comic Diction, Univ Ariz, 68; Acting is Being: Bernard Shaw on the Art of the Actor, Shaw Rev, 5/70; The Modesty of Nature: Charles Fechter's Hamlet, Theatre Surv, 5/74; What. What-Not!: Absurdity in Saroyan's The Time of Your Life, Midwest Quart, winter 85; Hamlet on Stage: The Great Tradition, Greenwood Press, 85; Old Mr. Picklepin: Simon Gray's Butley, Amer Imago, winter 89. **CONTACT ADDRESS** Dept of English, Univ of Arizona, 470 Modern Lang Bldg, PO Box 210067, Tucson, AZ 85721. **EMAIL** jamills@azstarnet.com

MILLS, SOPHIE J.
PERSONAL Born 06/20/1969, London, England **DISCIPLINE** CLASSICS **EDUCATION** Oxford Univ, BA, 87; MA, 91; DPhil, 92. **CAREER** Randall Maelver Junior Res Fel, Imerulle Col, 91-93; lectr, London Col, 93-94; asst prof, Univ NC at Asheville, 94-. **MEMBERSHIPS** Am Philos Asn, Classical Asn of the Middle W & S, Classical Asn, Hellenic Soc. **RESEARCH** Greek Tragedy, Mythology, History. **SELECTED PUBLICATIONS** Auth, Theseus, Tragedy, & the Athenian Empire, 97. **CONTACT ADDRESS** Dept Classics, Univ of No Carolina, Asheville, 1 University Heights, Asheville, NC 28804-3251. **EMAIL** smills@unca.edu

MILNE, CHRISTOPHER
PERSONAL Born 06/06/1934, Staten Island, NY, m, 1999, 6 children **DISCIPLINE** COMMUNICATION **EDUCATION** Geneva Col, BA, 56; Univ Fla, MA, 85. **CAREER** Teach asst, Univ Fla, 84-85. **MEMBERSHIPS** SPJ; TCA. **RESEARCH** Certification of web pages on the net. **SELECTED PUBLICATIONS** Auth, Ethics for Journalists, forthcoming; auth, Right Time, Right Place, 01; auth, Railroad Stations of Pennsylvania. **CONTACT ADDRESS** Dept Communications, Comm Col of Allegheny County, South, 1750 Clairton Rd, West Mifflin, PA 15122-3029.

MILNER, JOSEPH O'BEIRNE
PERSONAL Born 06/18/1937, m, 1963, 3 children **DISCIPLINE** ENGLISH, EDUCATION **EDUCATION** Davidson Col, AB, 59; Univ NC, Chapel Hill, MA, 65, PhD, 71. **CAREER** Instr Eng, NC State Univ, 65-66; instr, Univ NC, Chapel Hill, 68-69; asst prof, 69-80, Assoc Prof Eng & Educ, Wake Forest Univ, 80, Ed, NC Eng Tchr, 72-; consult, Winston-Salem-Forsyth County Schs, 73. **HONORS AND AWARDS** Chair, English Educators; NCTE. **MEMBERSHIPS** MLA; Aaup; Southeastern Mod Lang Asn. **RESEARCH** Am lit, 1960-1973. **SELECTED PUBLICATIONS** Auth, "Bridging English," Prentice Hall; auth, "Webs and Wardrobes University Press of America; auth, "Developing Teachers University Press of America. **CONTACT ADDRESS** Dept of Eng, Wake Forest Univ, PO Box 7266, Winston-Salem, NC 27109. **EMAIL** milner@wfu.edu

MILOSKY, LINDA M.
DISCIPLINE COMMUNICATION SCIENCES AND DISORDERS **EDUCATION** Univ Wis Madison, PhD, 86. **CAREER** Assoc prof CCC-SLP, Syracuse Univ. **RESEARCH** Lang acquisition and disorders with specific interest in cognitive, linguistic, and soc aspects of discourse processing in normal and clinical populations. **SELECTED PUBLICATIONS** Auth, Addressing Nonliteral Language Abilities: Seeing the Forest for the Trees in Language Learning Disabilities in School-age Children & Adolescents: Some Underlying Principles & Applications, Merrill, 94; Children Listening: the Role of World Knowledge in Discourse Comprehension in Child Talk: Processes in Language Acquisition, Mosby Yearbook, 92. **CONTACT ADDRESS** Syracuse Univ, Syracuse, NY 13244.

MILOWICKI, EDWARD JOHN
PERSONAL Born 03/02/1932, Plains, PA **DISCIPLINE** ENGLISH **EDUCATION** Wilkes Col, BA, 58; Duquesne Univ, MA, 63; Univ Ore, PhD(English), 68. **CAREER** Asst English, Duquesne Univ, 59-61; instr, St Vincent Col, 61-63; instr, Univ Ore, 63-68; dir grad studies, 72-79, assoc prof to prof, English, Mills Col, 68-. **MEMBERSHIPS** MLA; Medieval Asn Pac; Int Courtly Lit Soc; Chaucer Soc. **RESEARCH** Medieval literature, especially Chaucer; classical literature, especially Ovid; character in Western literature. **SELECTED PUBLICATIONS** Auth, Some Medieval Light on Marshall McLukan, Studies in the Literary Imagination, Vol IV, pages 51-59; coauth (with Rawdon Wilson), Character in Paradise Lost: Milton's Literary Formalism, Milton Studies, Vol Xiv, pages 75-94; Characterization in Troilus and Coiseyde: Some Relationships Centered on Hope, Canadian Review of Comparative Lit 11, , 12-24, March 84; Reflections on a Symbolic Heritage: Ovid's Narcissus, Syllecta Classica, 7:155-66, 96; (with Rawdon Wilson) Troilus and Cressida: Voices in the Darkness of Troy, in Reading the Renaissance: Culture, Poetics and Drama, ed Johnathan Hart, New York: Garland, 96; (with Rawdon Wilson), Ovid's Shadow: Character and Characterization in Early Modern Literature, Neohelicon XXII/1, 9-47; (with Rawdon Wilson), Ovid through Shakespeare: The Divided Self, Poetics Today, Vol 12, num 2, 217-252, summer 95. **CONTACT ADDRESS** English Dept., Mills Col, 5000 MacArthur Blvd, Oakland, CA 94613-1000. **EMAIL** milo@ella.mills.edu

MINER, THELMA SMITH
PERSONAL Born 01/15/1915, Ocean City, NJ, m, 1950 **DISCIPLINE** ENGLISH **EDUCATION** Dickinson Col, AB, 35; Univ Pa, AM, 42, PhD(Am civilization), 45. **CAREER** Teacher, Pub Sch, NJ, 35-42; cur, Bibliog Am Lit, Univ Pa, 43-45; instr English, Temple Univ, 45-48; asst prof, Dickinson Col, 48-51; res, France, 51-53; instr, Vassar Col, 53-55 & Univ Kans, 56-57; from asst prof to prof, 57-76, Emer Prof English, Youngstown State Univ, 76- Am Counc Learned Soc scholar, 51-52. Distinguished Prof Award, Youngstown State Univ, 72, 76; Fulbright lectr, Int People's Col, Denmark, 60-61. **MEMBERSHIPS** MLA; Aaup. **RESEARCH** American literature and civilization. **SELECTED PUBLICATIONS** Auth, The Uncollected Poems of James Russell Lowell, Univ Pa, 50; coauth, Transatlantic Migration: The Contemporary American Novel in France, Duke Univ, 55; co-ed, Gold prospecting on Cook Inlet in 1898: The diary of a failure, Pac Northwest Quart, 7/73. **CONTACT ADDRESS** Harborside, ME 04642.

MINER, WARD L.
PERSONAL Born 03/22/1916, Wellman, Iowa, m, 1950 **DISCIPLINE** ENGLISH **EDUCATION** Univ Colo, AB, 38; Univ Chicago, AM, 40; Univ Pa, PhD(Am civilization), 51. **CAREER** Instr English, SDak State Col, 40-42, Colo Sch Mines, 45-46 & Temple Univ, 46-51; asst prof Queens Col, NY, 53-54; assoc prof, 57-63, chmn dept, 63-68, prof Am studies, 63-76, Emer Prof English, Youngstown State Univ, 76- Am Coun Learned Soc fel, 51-52; Am Philos Soc res grant, 55; Fulbright lectr, Turku Univ, Finland, 55-56; vis asst prof, Univ Kans, 56-57; Fulbright lectr, Int People's Col, Elsinore, Denmark, 60-61 & Univ Iceland, 66-67. **MEMBERSHIPS** MLA. **RESEARCH** Colonial printing; 20th century American novel; reception of American literature in Europe. **SELECTED PUBLICATIONS** Auth, The World of William Faulkner, 52, coauth, Transatlantic Migration: The Contemporary American Novel in France, 55 & auth, William Goddard, Newspaperman, 62, Duke Univ Press. **CONTACT ADDRESS** Harborside, ME 04642.

MINK, JOANNA
PERSONAL Born 09/20/1947, Fort Wayne, IN **DISCIPLINE** ENGLISH **EDUCATION** Ill State Univ, BS, 73; MS, 75; PhD, 85. **CAREER** Instr, Ill State Univ, 78-85; Instr, Univ SW La, 85-87; Asst Prof, Barton Col, 87-90; Prof, Minn State Univ, 90-98; Full Prof, Mankato State Univ, 98-. **HONORS AND AWARDS** Intl Authors and Writers Who's Who, 93; Contemporary Authors, 93; Who's Who in Am Educ, 89-90. **MEMBERSHIPS** Midwest Mod Lang Asn, Thomas Hardy Soc (UK), Thomas Hardy Soc, (N Am), Midwest Victorian Studies Asn, The Hypatia Trust. **RESEARCH** Victorian Novel and Culture, Working-Class in 19th and 20th Century Britain, Thomas Hardy, Victorian Women (Britain and America). **SELECTED PUBLICATIONS** Ed, Common Ground: Feminist Collaboration in the Academy, State Univ of NY Press, 98; ed, Communication and Women's Friendships: Parallels and Intersections in Literature and Life, Bowling Green State Univ, Popular Press, 93; ed, The Significance of Sibling Relationships in Literature, Bowling Green State Univ Popular Press, 93; ed, Joinings and Disjoinings: The Significance of Marital Status in Literature, Bowling Green State Univ Popular Press, 91; auth, "Sarah Grand (Frances Elizabeth Clarke McFall)," Nineteenth-Century British Women Writers: A Bio-bibliographical Critical Sourcebook, Greenwood Press, 00; auth, "Emily Jane Bronte," Nineteenth-Century British Women Writers: A Bio-bibliographical Critical Sourcebook, Greenwood Press, 00; auth, "Barbara Hardy," An Encyclopedia of British Women Writers, Rutgers Univ Press, 98; auth, "The Voices of Mary Shelley's Frankenstein, and Lisel Mueller," The Illinois English Bulletin, (97): 72-77; auth, "The Collaborative Term Paper," Ideas for the Working Classroom, NCTE, 93; auth, "Using Journals and Small Groups to Explore Literature," Literature and Life: Making Connections in the Classroom, NCTE, 90; **CONTACT ADDRESS** Dept English, Mankato State Univ, PO Box 8400, Mankato, NM 56002-8400. **EMAIL** joanna.mink@mankato.msus.edu

MINKOFF, HARVEY
PERSONAL Born New York, NY **DISCIPLINE** LINGUISTICS, ENGLISH **EDUCATION** City Col New York, BA, 65, MA, 66, Grad Ctr, PhD, 70. **CAREER** Asst prof English, Iona Col, 67-71; assoc prof English & Ling, 71-90, prof Eng and Ling, Hunter Col, 90-. **MEMBERSHIPS** Ling Soc Am. **RESEARCH** Applications of linguistics to language teaching and learning; theory and practice of literary translation. **SELECTED PUBLICATIONS** Ed, Teaching English Linguistically: Five Experimental Curricula, 71 & auth, The English Verb System, 72; (N)ever write like(?) you talk: Teaching the syntax of reading & composition, English Record, 74; coauth, Mastering Prestige English, Villa Press, 75; auth, Teaching the Transition From Print to Script Analytically, Elementary English, 75; Some Stylistic Consequences of Aelfric's Theory of Translation, Studies in Philol, 76; coauth, Transitions: A key to mature reading and writing, In: Classroom Practices in Teaching English, NCTE, 77; coauth, Complete Course in College Writing, Kendall-Hunt, 84; coauth, Visions and Revisions, Prentice-Hall, 90; ed, Approaches to the Bible, 2 Vols, Bibl Arch Soc, 95; coauth, Exploring America, Harcourt, 95; auth, Mysteries of the Dead Sea Scrolls, Ottenhenmer, 98. **CONTACT ADDRESS** Dept of English, Hunter Col, CUNY, 695 Park Ave, New York, NY 10021-5085.

MINOT, WALTER
PERSONAL Born 04/09/1940, Woonsocket, RI, m, 1963, 1 child **DISCIPLINE** ENGLISH, LITERATURE **EDUCATION** Providence Col, AB, 62; Univ of Nebr, PhD, 70. **CAREER** Instr, Univ of Nebr, 65-66; Dir of Writing Across Curric, Gannon Univ, 89-95; Chair, Dept English, Gannon Univ, 93-98; From Instr to Prof, Gannon Univ, 66-. **HONORS AND AWARDS** NEH Summer Sem, Ohio State Univ, 81. **MEMBERSHIPS** Nat Coun of Teachers of English, Wortsworth-Coleridge Asn. **RESEARCH** Wordsworth, Mary Shelly, Millay, puns, rhetoric. **SELECTED PUBLICATIONS** Auth, Rhetoric: Theory and Practice for Compositon, Winthrop Publ (Cambridge), 81; auth, "Personality and Persona: Developing the Self," Rhet Rev 7 (Spring 89): 352-363; auth, "Response to Richard H. Haswell . . .," CCC 40 (May 89): 226-227; coauth, "Self-Esteem and Writing Apprehension of Basic Writers: Conflicting Evidence," JBW 20 (Fall 91): 116-124; auth, "Blake's 'Infant Joy': An Explanation of Age," Blake: An Illus Quart 25 (Fall 91): 78; auth, "The 'Marriage hearse' in Blake's 'London'," PLL 28 (Winter 92): 89-91; auth, "Keat's ODE TO A NIGHTINGALE, lines 61-62," Explicator 50 (Winter 92): 70-71; auth, "Puns," in Encyclopedia of Romanticism (NY: Garland, 92); rev, of "Eighteenth-Century British and American Rhetorics and Rhetoricicans: Critical Studies and Sources," Rhet Rev 13 (Spring 95): 445-447; rev, of "Presence of Mind: Writing and the Domain Beyond the Cognitive," Compos Chronicle 9 (Mar 96): 14-16. **CONTACT ADDRESS** Dept English, Gannon Univ, 109 Univ Sq, Erie, PA 16541-0002. **EMAIL** minot001@mail1.gannon.edu

MINTER, DAVID LEE
PERSONAL Born 03/20/1935, Midland, TX, m, 1957, 2 children **DISCIPLINE** ENGLISH **EDUCATION** N Texas State, BA, 57, MA, 59; Yale Univ, BD, 61, PhD, 65. **CAREER** Prof, Bruce and Elizabeth Dunlevie prof, Eng, Rice Univ. **HONORS AND AWARDS** Fred Harris Daniels Fel of the Am Antiquarian Soc, 80; George R Brown Awd for Superior Teaching, Rice Univ 74, 76, 77; Am Coun of Learned Socs, Grant-in-Aid, 75; Nat Endowment for Humanties Fel, 69-70; Fulbright Travel Fel, 66. **MEMBERSHIPS** Am Antiquarian Soc; MLA, Am Lit Asn. **RESEARCH** American Literature, 1890-1940. **SELECTED PUBLICATIONS** Auth, The Interpreted Design as a Structural Principle in American Prose, 69; auth, William Faulkner: His Life and Works, 82; auth, A Cultural History of the American Novel: Henry James to William Faulkner, Cambridge Univ Press; auth, biographical essays on Samuel Danforth, James Hammond, Jonathan Mitchell, Thomas Prince, William Stoughton, Patrick Tailfer, and St. George Tucker, in American Writers Before 1800: A Biographical and Critical Dictionary, vols 1-3, Greenwood Press, 83; Faulkner's Questioning Narratives: Fiction of His Major Phase, 1929-42, 01. **CONTACT ADDRESS** Dept of Eng, Rice Univ, Box 1892, Houston, TX 77251. **EMAIL** dcmint@rice.edu

MINTZ, DONALD
PERSONAL Born 05/09/1929, New York, NY, m, 1978, 2 children **DISCIPLINE** MUSIC **EDUCATION** Cornell Univ, BA, 49; Princton Univ, MFA, 51; Cornell Univ, PhD, 60. **CAREER** Ref Asst, Libr Cong, 56-57; instr, Wellesley Col, 57-58; vis asst prof, Cornell Univ, 59-60; Am ed, Int Inventory of Musical Sources, 61-63; staff writer, The Sunday Star, 63-69; vis lectr, Univ Md, 67-68; grad fac, Peabody Conserv Music, 68-72; exec dir, Md Arts Coun, 69-72; dean, Montclair State Col, 72-83; prof, Montclair State Univ, 72-. **HONORS AND AWARDS** Fulbright student grant; Jr Fel, Princeton Univ. **MEMBERSHIPS** Am Musicol Society; Int Musicol Society; Music Libr Asn; Int Music Libr Asn. **RESEARCH** Mendelssohn; Liszt; 19th century concerto. **SELECTED PUBLICATIONS** Transl, Melusine: ein Entwurf Mendelssohns, 82; auth, 1848, Anti-Semitism and the Mendelssohn Reception, Mendelssohn Studies, Cambridge, 92; auth, "Mendelssohn as Performer and Teacher" in The Mendelssohn Companion, ed. Douglass Seaton (Greenwood, 90). **CONTACT ADDRESS** Dept of Music, Montclair State Univ, Montclair, NJ 07043. **EMAIL** dmintz@nac.net

MINTZ, KENNETH A.
PERSONAL Born 03/15/1951, Plattsburgh, NY, d **DISCIPLINE** LIBRARY SCIENCE; ENGLISH **EDUCATION** Univ Redlands, BA, 73; S Ct St Univ, MLS, 78. **CAREER** Asst newsletter ed, First Unitarian Soc New Haven Ct, 79-80; newsletter ed, Unitarian Soc of Rutherford NJ, 84-85; head, Commun Church New York, 93- ; book rev, Libr J 88-93; librn, Bayonne Publ Libr, NJ, 80-88; cataloger, Hoboken Public Libr, 91-. **HONORS AND AWARDS** Guill Poetry Awd, 91; Editor's Choice Awd, 89, 96; Legion of Honor Awd, 98; Decree of Merit, Int Biog Centre, Cambridge England, 97; Outstanding Achievement Diploma Cambridge England, 97; NJ Essay Writer of the Year, 97; Christmas Story Prize, 97; Essay Prize, 94; Bayonne Writers Legion of Honor Awd, 89; Bayonne Writers Special Legion Awd, 96. **MEMBERSHIPS** Acad of Amer Poets; Hoboken Creative Alliance, Bayonne Writers' Group; NY Acad of Sci; Poets' Guild. **RESEARCH** Lit; hist; philos. **SELECTED PUBLICATIONS** Auth, The Holy Ghost (novel), 1980; book revs, Library Jrnl, 88-93, Wilson Lib Bulletin, 89, 90, Am Book Rev, 94,95, Libraries and Culture, 90. **CONTACT ADDRESS** 24 Belviders Ave, Apt 5, Jersey City, NJ 07304-1325. **EMAIL** kmintz351@aol.com

MINTZ, LAWRENCE E.
DISCIPLINE AMERICAN STUDIES, ENGLISH **EDUCATION** Univ SC, BA, 66; MI State Univ, MA, 67, PhD, 69. **CAREER** Am Stud Dept, Univ Md. **RESEARCH** Ethnicity in popular culture and humor; performance comedy (standup comedy, variety theater humor, performance art, humor in magic, juggling, circus, and other performance entertainments). **SELECTED PUBLICATIONS** Auth, "The Standup Comedian as Social and Cultural Mediator," Am Humor, Oxford, 87; ed, Humor in America: A Research Guide to Genres and Topics, Greenwood Press, 88; auth, "Devil and Angel; Philip Roth's Humor" Studies in American Lit 8:2, 89; auth, "Ethos and Pathos in Chaplin's City Lights," in Charles Chaplin: Approaches to Semiotics, (Mouton deGryter, 91); auth, "Humor and Ethic Stereotypes in Vaudeville and Burlesque," MELUS, 96. **CONTACT ADDRESS** Am Stud Dept, Univ of Maryland, Col Park, 10632 Old Barn Rd, New Market, MD 21774. **EMAIL** lm36@umail.umd.edu

MISKELL, JERRY
PERSONAL m, 1987, 1 child **DISCIPLINE** MUSIC **EDUCATION** Univ Akron, BM, 85, MM, 87; Univ SC, DMA, 95. **CAREER** Dept music, Mt Union Col **SELECTED PUBLICATIONS** String quartet & 3 screaming women, Relentless Variations, 94; Auth, Ode to a Painter's Friend, New Mmus Publ, San Rafael, 95; Trio for Flexible Instrumentation; Ode to a Painter's Friend, 95; Piano Quartet, The Winds are Aloft in the Western Reserve, 96; Percussion duo, The Winds are Aloft in the Western Reserve, 96; Violin/Viola duo, Commercial Time Out, 96 Woodwind Quintet; Commissioned by the Tapestry Ensemble, Puzzles and Cannons, 96; compos, Endless Summer Eternity Light and Fireworks, 97; Orchestral Piece, Of Summer and Eternity, 97; auth, Alex Building Send castler Before the Immeasunable Ocean, 99; auth, Multimedia computer work Pieces of Roger, 99; auth, Her Goze Traverser Eternity, 00; auth, The Winds Are Aloft in the Western Reserve, SCI Journal of Scores. **CONTACT ADDRESS** Dept of Music, Mount Union Col, 1972 Clark Ave, Alliance, OH 44601. **EMAIL** miskeljp@muc.edu

MISSEY, JAMES L.
PERSONAL Born 07/09/1935, San Bernardino, CA, 1 child **DISCIPLINE** ENGLISH **EDUCATION** Pomona Col, BA, 57; Univ Pa, MA, 59, PhD(English), 63. **CAREER** Instr English, Beloit Col, 62-64; asst prof, Denison Univ, 64-66; asst prof, 66-68, assoc prof English, Univ Wis-Stevens Point, 68-96, prof English, 96-00, prof emeritus, 00-. **RESEARCH** The fiction of E M Forster. **SELECTED PUBLICATIONS** Auth, Forster's Redemptive Siren, Mod Fiction Studies, winter 64-65; Pacifists and Revolutionary Violence, Win Peace and Freedom through Nonviolent Action 27: 10, Jan 67; The Connected and the Unconnected in Howards End, Wis Studies Lit, 69; A McCullers Influence on Albee's The Zoo Story, Am Notes & Queries, 4/75; The Rhodesian Woman, Wisc Acad Review 28.3: 4-5, 82; Theme and Speakers in Shumway's Song of the Archer, Transactions of the Wisc Acad of Sciences, Arts, and Letters 71, Pt 2: 131-135, 83; Thoreau's Turtledove and Mine, The Christian Science Monitor, 21, Dec 83: 30; Acting in Salinger's Franny and Zooey, Wisc English Journal 25.3: 16-18, 15, 83, cont 26.3: 6, 84; The Eve of Revolution: An Antiwar Memoir, Stevens Point WI: Portage County Hist Soc, 85; The London Theatre: Fall 1985, Wisc Acad Rev 32.3: 9-13, 86; Revisiting the Intensity of the 60's, The Christian Science Monitor, 4 May 90: 16; Hennacy, Ammon, The Book of Ammon, ed Jim Missey and Joan Thomas, 2nd ed, Baltimore: Fortkamp, 94; Ammon Hennacy, Christian Anarchism, and the One-Person Revolution, The Small City and Regional Community 11: 305-310, 95; auth, "An Anarchist Joins the Catholic Churce: Why Ammon Hennacy Became a Catholic," The Small City and Regional Comm 13 (99): 345-350. **CONTACT ADDRESS** Dept of English, Univ of Wisconsin, Stevens Point, 2100 Main St, Stevens Point, WI 54481-3897. **EMAIL** jmissey@uwsp.edu

MITCHELL, ANGELYN
DISCIPLINE ENGLISH LITERATURE **EDUCATION** NC State Univ, BA; NC Central Univ, MA; Howard Univ, PhD. **CAREER** Eng Dept, Georgetown Univ **RESEARCH** American, African American and Caribbean literature; critical theory; cultural studies; women's studies; African American studies. **SELECTED PUBLICATIONS** Auth, pubs on William Wells Brown, Harriet Wilson, Kate Chopin, and Toni Morrison; ed, Within the Circle: An Anthology of African American Literary Criticism from the Harlem Renaissance to the Present, 94. **CONTACT ADDRESS** English Dept, Georgetown Univ, 37th and O St, Washington, DC 20057.

MITCHELL, JUDITH I.
DISCIPLINE ENGLISH LITERATURE **EDUCATION** Univ Saskatchewan, BA, MA; Univ Alberta, PhD. **CAREER** Assoc prof; dir, Hon(s) Prog. **RESEARCH** 19th-century novel; women's poetry; gender studies; feminist theory. **SELECTED PUBLICATIONS** Auth, Hardy's Female Reader, A Sense of Sex: Feminist Perspectives on Hardy, U of Illinois P, 91; Naturalism in George Moore's A Mummer's Wife (1885), The New Nineteenth Century: Feminist Readings of Underread Victorian Fiction, Garland,96; The Stone and the Scorpion: The Female Subject of Desire in the Novels of Charlotte Bronte, George

Eliot and Thomas Hardy, Greenwood Press, 94. **CONTACT ADDRESS** Dept of English, Univ of Victoria, PO Box 3070, Victoria, BC, Canada V8W 3W1. **EMAIL** mitchell@uvic.ca

MITCHELL, KENNETH R.
PERSONAL Born 12/13/1940, Moose Jaw, SK, Canada **DISCIPLINE** ENGLISH **EDUCATION** Univ Sask, BA, 65, MA, 67 **CAREER** English instr, Univ Regina, 67-70; Scott-Can Exchange Fel, 79-80; vis prof, Univ Nanjing, China, 80-81; Prof English, Univ Regina, 84-. **HONORS AND AWARDS** Can Authors Asn Awd Best Can Play, 85; Ottawa Little Theatre Prize Best One Act Play Can Heroes, 71. **MEMBERSHIPS** Playwrights Union Can; Can Asn Univ Tchrs **SELECTED PUBLICATIONS** Auth, Wandering Rafferty, 72; auth, The Meadowlark Connection, 75; auth, The Con Man, 79; auth, Stones of the Dalai Lama, 93; auth, Everybody Gets Something Here, 77; auth, The Shipbuilder, 90; auth, Davin, 79; auth, Gone the Burning Sun, 85; coauth, Cruel Tears, 77; coauth, The Plainsman, 92; coauth, Ken Mitchell Country, 84; coauth, Witches and Idiots, 90; ed, Horizon, Writings of the Canadian Prairie, 77. **CONTACT ADDRESS** Dept of English, Univ of Regina, 3737 Wascana Pkwy, Regina, SK, Canada S4S OA2. **EMAIL** Ken.Mitchell@uregina.ca

MITCHELL, MOZELLA
PERSONAL Born 04/14/1934, Starkville, MS, d, 2 children **DISCIPLINE** ENGLISH **EDUCATION** LeMoyne Col, BA, 59; Univ Mich, MA, 63; Colgate Rochester Divinity School, MA, 73; Emory Univ, PhD, 80. **CAREER** Instr, Alcorn A&M Col, 60-61; instr, Owen Jr Col, 61-65; asst prof, Norfolk State univ, 65-81; prof, Univ of S Fla, 81-. **HONORS AND AWARDS** NEH Summer Stipend, 81; USF Res Awd, 83, 90-91. **MEMBERSHIPS** Am Acad of Relig; Soc for the Study of Black Relig; Phi Kappa Phi; Assoc of Relig and Intellectual Life; Col Theol Soc; Inst for Southern Studies. **RESEARCH** African and African American Religions, Comparative Mysticism, Afro-Caribbean Religions, Wonaist Perspectives in Religion, Contemporary American Religions, Liberation Theology, Women and Religion, Theological Perspectives in Literature, Mahalia Jackson, Howard Thurman. **SELECTED PUBLICATIONS** Auth, "Howard Thurman and Oliver Schreiner: Post-modern Marriage Post Mortem, J of Relig Thought, (81); auth, "The Shaman's Doorway: Techniques of Myth and Ritual in Thurman", Debate and Understanding (83); auth, Spiritual Dynamics of Howard Thurman's Theology, Wyndham Hall Pr, (Bristol, IN), 85; auth, "The Quest for Human Rights: Human Paradox", J of Intergroup Relations XV.1, (87); auth, New Africa in America: The Blending of African and American Religious and Social Practices Among Black People in Meridian, Mississippi and Surrounding counties, Peter Lang Pub, (NY), 94; auth, "Woman at the Well: Mahalia Jackson and the Inner and Outer Spiritual Transformation", Embracing the Spirit: Womanist Perspectives on Hope, Salvation and Transformation, ed Emile M Townes, Orbis Books, (Maryknoll, 97); auth, "Discovering Christian Resources for a Theology of Interfaith Relations from the African Methodist Episcopal Zion Church", Grounds for Understanding Ecumenical Resources for Responses to Religious Pluralism, William b Eerdsman Pub, (Grand Rapids, 98); auth, "Thurman In-to Action", Howard Thurman: A Critical Resources for Ethical Leadership Among Youth and Students, ed Walter Fluker, (forthcoming); auth, "Black Spirituality in Mixed Communions", Spirituality in the Black Church, ed C Eric Lincoln, Thomas Nelson Pub, (forthcoming); auth, "A Risk Well Taken", Active Learning: From Theory to Classroom Application, USF Center for Teaching Enhancement (forthcoming). **CONTACT ADDRESS** Dept Relig Studies, Univ of So Florida, 4202 E Fowler Ave, Tampa, FL 33620-9951. **EMAIL** mmitchel@luna.cas.usf.edu

MITCHELL, SALLY
DISCIPLINE ENGLISH **EDUCATION** Oxford Univ, PhD, 77. **CAREER** Prof, Temple Univ. **HONORS AND AWARDS** Outstanding Ref Work, Am Libr Asn, 88; Outstanding Acad Book, Choice, 96. **RESEARCH** Victorian Literature. **SELECTED PUBLICATIONS** Auth, The Fallen Angel: Chastity, Class and Women's Reading, 1835-1880, Bowling Green Univ Pop Press (Bowling Green, OH)m 81; auth, Dinah Mulock Craik, Twayne's English Authors Series, G.K. Hall (Boston), 83; ed, East Lynne, by Mrs. Henry Wood, Rutgers Univ Press (New Brunswick, NJ), 84; auth, Victorian Britain: An Encyclopedia, Garland Publ (NY), 88; introd, to The Beth Book, by Sarah Grand (Bristol: Thoemmes Press, 94); auth, The New Girl: Girls' Culture in England, 1880-1915, Columbia Univ Press (NY), 95; co-ed, Prose by Victorian Women: An Anthology, Garland Publ (NY), 96; auth, Daily Life in Victorian England, Greenwood (Westport, CT), 96. **CONTACT ADDRESS** Dept English, Temple Univ, 1114 W Berks St, Philadelphia, PA 19122-6007. **EMAIL** smitch@vm.temple.edu

MITCHELL, THOMAS R.
PERSONAL Born 05/08/1950, Monroe, LA, m, 1976, 3 children **DISCIPLINE** ENGLISH **EDUCATION** Northeast La Univ, BA, 71; MA, 73; Tex AM Univ, PhD, 94. **CAREER** Lectr to chmn, Laredo Community Col, 73-98; assoc prof and chmn, Tex AM Univ, 98-. **HONORS AND AWARDS** Arts Humanities Scholar Year Award, 98; Fac Member Year Award, 87. **MEMBERSHIPS** MLA; NHS; MFS; SCMLA; ADE; ADFL; Melville Soc. **RESEARCH** American literary renaissance. **SELECTED PUBLICATIONS** Auth, Hawthorne's Fuller Mystery, Univ Mass Pr, 98. **CONTACT ADDRESS** English Dept, Texas A&M Intl Univ, 5201 University Ave, Laredo, TX 78041. **EMAIL** tmitchell@tamiu.edu

MITCHELL, W. J. THOMAS
PERSONAL Born 03/24/1942, Anaheim, CA, m, 1968, 2 children **DISCIPLINE** LITERATURE **EDUCATION** Mich State Univ, BA, 64; Johns Hopkins Univ, MA, 66, PhD(English), 68. **CAREER** From asst prof to assoc prof English, Ohio State Univ, 68-77; assoc prof, 77-79, prof English, Univ Chicago, 79-89, Gaylord Donnelley Distinguished Service prof, 90-, Humanities res fel, Ohio State Univ, 70-71; Am Philos Soc grant, 70-71, ed consult, Studies Romanticism, 73-; Nat Endowment for Humanities res fel, 78-79; Guggenheim fel, 81-82; ed, Critical Inquiry, 79-. **HONORS AND AWARDS** Outstanding Special Issue of a Scholarly Journal, from CELJ (Conference of Editors of Learned Journals), 80-81; Canterbury Visiting Fellow, Univ of Canterbury, New Zealand, 87; Fairchild Distinguished Scholar, Calicornie Institute of Technology, 94; Charles Rufus Morey Prize in Art History of the College Art Asn, for Picture Theory, 96; Gordon E. Laing Prize for a Chicago Press book by a University of Chicago Author, 97; Franke Institute Fel, 01; Berlin Prize Fel, 02. **MEMBERSHIPS** MLA; Aaup; Am Soc 18th Century Studies. **RESEARCH** Poetry and painting in romantic period; theory of imagery; works of William Blake. **SELECTED PUBLICATIONS** Auth, Poetry and Pictoral Imagination in Blake, Eighteenth Century Studies, fall 69; Blake's Composite Art, In: Blake's Visionary Forms Dramatic, Princeton Univ, 70; Blake's Radical Comedy, In: Blake's Sublime Allegory, Univ Wis, 73; Style as Epistemology, Studies in Romanticism, spring 77; Blake's Composite Art, Princeton Univ, 78; Spatial Form in Literature, Critical Inquiry, winter 79; ed, The Language of Images, 80; On Narrative, 81; The Politics of Interpretation, 82; What is an Image?, New Lit Hist; Iconology, Univ of Chicago Press, 86; Picture Theory, Chicago, 94; auth, Art and The Public Sphere, 93; auth, Landscape and Power, 94; The Last Dinosaur Book, Chicago, 98. **CONTACT ADDRESS** Dept of English, Univ of Chicago, 5540 Greenwood Ave, Chicago, IL 60637-1506. **EMAIL** wjtm@midway.uchicago.edu

MITCHELL-BOYASK, ROBIN N.
PERSONAL Born 05/20/1961, Cambridge, Britain, m, 1990, 2 children **DISCIPLINE** CLASSICS **EDUCATION** Univ Chicago BA, 82; Brown Univ, MA, 85; PhD, 88. **CAREER** Asst prof to assoc prof, Temple Univ, 88-. **HONORS AND AWARDS** Jr Fel, Center for Hellenic Studies, 93-94. **MEMBERSHIPS** Am Philol Asn; Pa Class Asn; Philadelphia Class Soc; Class Asn of the Atlantic States. **RESEARCH** Greek drama; Greek and Roman epic. **SELECTED PUBLICATIONS** Auth, Miasma, Mimesis and Scapegoating in Euripides' Hippolytus, CA, 91; auth, Sine Fine: The Aeneid and Freud's Masterplot, AJP, 96; auth, "Euripides Hippolytus and the Trials of Manhood," Bucknell Rev, 99; auth, Approaches to Teaching the Dramas of Euripides, MLA Press. **CONTACT ADDRESS** Dept Class, Temple Univ, 1114 W Berks St, 353 Anderson Hall, Philadelphia, PA 19122. **EMAIL** robin@astro.temple.edu

MIZEJEWSKI, LINDA
PERSONAL Born 09/08/1952, Pittsburgh, PA, m, 1982 **DISCIPLINE** ENGLISH **EDUCATION** Univ Arkansas, MFA, 78; Univ Pittsburgh, PhD, 89. **CAREER** Prof, Ohio State Univ. **HONORS AND AWARDS** Fulbright Senior Lectureship, 97; ACLS Fel, 94-95. **MEMBERSHIPS** Society for Cinema Studies. **RESEARCH** Culture Studies; Film; Feminist Theory. **SELECTED PUBLICATIONS** Auth, "Ziegfeld Girl: Image and Icon in Cinema & Culture," 99; auth, "Divine Decadence: Fascism, Female Spectacle and the Makings of Sally Bowles", 92. **CONTACT ADDRESS** Dept English, Ohio State Univ, Columbus, 164 West 17th Ave, Columbus, OH 43210-1326. **EMAIL** mizejewski.1@osu.edu

MIZRUCHI, SUSAN L.
PERSONAL Born 07/13/1959, Cortland, NY, m, 1988, 1 child **DISCIPLINE** ENGLISH **EDUCATION** Wash Univ, BA, 81; Princeton Univ, MA, 83; PhD, 85. **CAREER** Lectr, Princeton Univ, 85-86; asst prof to prof, Boston Univ, 86-. **HONORS AND AWARDS** Fel, NEH, 90-91; Fletcher s. Jones Fel, Huntington Libr, 95; Scholar, Chronicle of Higher Educ, 98; Guggenheim Fel, 01-02; Distinguished Teaching Awd, Boston Univ, 01. **MEMBERSHIPS** MLA; Am Studies Asn; Am Lit Asn. **RESEARCH** 19th and 20th Century American literature; Religion and culture; Literary and social theory; Literary history; History of the Social Sciences. **SELECTED PUBLICATIONS** Auth, "Reproducing Women in 'The Awkward Age'," Representations, 92; auth, "Cataloging the Creatures of the Deep, Billy Budd and the Rise of Sociology," in Revisionary Interventions into the Americanist Canon, Duke UP, 94; auth, "Neighbors, Strangers, Corpses: Death and Sympathy in the Early Writings of W.E.B. DuBois," in Centuries Ends, Narrative Means, Stanford UP, 96; auth, The Science of Sacrifice; American Literature and Modern Social Theory, Princeton UP, 98; auth, "The Place of Ritual in Our Time," Am Lit Hist, 00; ed, Religion in an Era of Cultural Studies, Princeton UP , 01; auth, "Getting Religion," Futures of Am Studies, (forthcoming). **CONTACT ADDRESS** Dept English, Boston Univ, 236 Bay State Rd, Boston, MA 02215. **EMAIL** mizruchi@bu.edu

MOCK, MICHELE L.
PERSONAL Born 07/05/1962, Bloomington, IN, d, 2 children **DISCIPLINE** ENGLISH **EDUCATION** Univ Pittsburgh, BA, 91; Ind Univ Pa, 93, PhD, 96. **CAREER** English Teacher, Greater Johnstown Area Vocational Technical Sch, 91-92; adjunct instr, Westmoreland Co Community Col, 94-95; teaching assoc, Indiana Univ of Pa, 94-95, full-time temporary instr, 95-96; asst prof, Univ Pittsburgh, Johnstown, Pa, 96-. **HONORS AND AWARDS** UPJ Scholar Awd, Univ Pittsburgh, 90-91; Univ-wide Doctoral Found Fel, Indiana Univ of Pa, 93-94; Teaching Assoc Awd, Indiana Univ of Pa, 94-95; Fac Scholar Awd, Univ Pittsburgh, 96-97, 99-2000; Instr of the Year, Phi Eta Sigma, Univ Pittsburgh, 98; Student Activities Awd, Univ Pittsburgh, 99; Who's Who Among America's Teachers, 2000; Person of the Year, Nat Org of Women, Johnstown, Pa, 99. **MEMBERSHIPS** Am Studies Asn, Assoc Writing Progs, Emily Dickinson Int Soc, Modern Lang Asn, Nat Women's Studies Asn, Northeast Modern Lang Asn. **RESEARCH** 19th century American women's literature. **SELECTED PUBLICATIONS** Contribr, "Ann Petry's Country Place," in Masterplots II, Salem (94); contribr, "Birthing Death," in New Growth Arts Rev, Indiana Univ of Pa (95); Auth, "Behind the 'barred windows': Imprisonment of Women's Bodies and Minds in Nineteenth-Century America," in WILLA: The J of Women in Lit and Life Assembly, 4 (95): 22-26; auth, "Spitting Out the Seed: Ownership of Mother, Child, Breasts, Milk, and Voice in Toni Morrison's Beloved," in Col Lit23.3 (96): 117-26; auth, "Partnership in Possibility: The Dioalogics of 'his efficient daughter Lavinia and his poetress daughter Emily'," in The Emily Dickinson J, 6 (97): 68-88; contribr, "Rebecca Harding Davis," in Cyclopedia of World Authors, Rev Ed, Salem (97); contribr, "Charlotte Perkins Gilman's Herland," in Masterplots, Salem (97); contribr, "Lavinia Norcross Dickinson," in the Emily Dickinson Encyclopedia, Greenwood (98); contribr, "Lizzie Andrew Borden," in Dictionary of World Biography, Salem (99); auth, " 'An ardor that was human, and a power that was art': Rebecca Harding Davis and the Art of the Periodical," in "Its Only Efficient Instrument": American Women Writers and the Periodical, ed by Aleta Cane and Susan Alves, Univ Iowa Press (forthcoming); auth, " 'A message to be given': The Spiritual Activism of Rebecca Harding Davis," in the NWSA J (forthcoming). **CONTACT ADDRESS** Dept English, Univ of Pittsburgh, Johnstown, 233 Biddle Hall, Johnstown, PA 15905. **EMAIL** mock@pitt.edu

MOEHLMANN, JOHN FREDERICK
PERSONAL Born 12/23/1942, Conover, NC, d, 1965, 2 children **DISCIPLINE** ENGLISH **EDUCATION** Lenoir-Rhyne Col, BA, 65; Appalachian State Univ, MA, 67; Univ Tenn, PhD(English), 74. **CAREER** Instr English, Camp Lejeune Br, E Carolina Univ, 67-69 & Univ SC, Florence, 69-70; Professor of English, High Point Univ, 75-, Lilly scholar English, Duke Univ, 77-78. **HONORS AND AWARDS** Distinguished Teaching-Service Awayd, 81. **MEMBERSHIPS** MLA; S Atlantic Mod Lang Asn; Southeastern Asn 18th Century Studies; AAUP. **RESEARCH** Shakespeare; Restoration and eighteenth century literature. **SELECTED PUBLICATIONS** Auth, A Concordance to the Complete Poems of John Wilmot, Earl of Rochester, Whitston, 79. **CONTACT ADDRESS** High Point Univ, 933 Montlieu Ave, High Point, NC 27262-3598. **EMAIL** jmoehlma@acme.highpoint.edu

MOFFATT, JOHN
DISCIPLINE ENGLISH LITERATURE **EDUCATION** Queen's Univ, PhD. **CAREER** Dept Eng, Queen's Univ **RESEARCH** Theories of oral-traditional narrative in early mediaeval Insular literature; Scottish Gaelic literature; contemporary minority language culture. **SELECTED PUBLICATIONS** Auth, A Commodified Antimodernism: Evangelism, The Gaelic Text, and the Construction of Ethnotourism in Nova Scotia, 97;co-ed, Inside Language: A Canadian Language Reader, Prentice Hall, 98. **CONTACT ADDRESS** English Dept, Queen's Univ at Kingston, Kingston, ON, Canada K7L 3N6. **EMAIL** moffatt-j@rmc.ca

MOGEN, DAVID LEE
PERSONAL Born 09/07/1945, Bremerton, WA, m, 1988 **DISCIPLINE** AMERICAN LITERATURE, SCIENCE FICTION, NATIVE AMERICAN LITERATURE, FRONTIER **EDUCATION** Columbia Univ, BA, 67; Univ Colo, PhD, 77. **CAREER** Tchr Eng, Intermediate Sch, NYork, 68-71; instr, Univ Colo, 71-77; instr, Ga State Univ, 77-79; Asst Prof English, 79-85, assoc prof, 85-90, prof eng, 90-; Asst ed, English Lang Notes, 71-73. **HONORS AND AWARDS** NDEA Fel, City Univ NY, 67-68; Eng Lang Notes fel, 71-76; Univ Fel, Univ CO, 74-75; Fac res grant, CO State Univ, 79-80; NEH Symposium, Univ CA, Berkeley, summer 87; Oliver P Pennock Awd, Distinguished Service, CO State Univ, 94; NEH fac seminar, CSU Am Studies program, 8/97. **MEMBERSHIPS** MLA. **RESEARCH** Am lit; Am frontier mythology; sci fiction. **SELECTED PUBLICATIONS** Auth, Agonies of innocence: The Governess and Maggie Verver, Am Literary Realism, 1870-1910, summer, 76; auth, Owen Wister's Cowboy Heroes, Southwestern Am Lit; auth, "Owen Wister's Cowboy Heroes," The Western: A Collection of Critical Essays, Prentice-Hall, 79; auth, Re-evaluating the John W Campbell Tradition: Elitism, Parochialsim, and Calvinsim, Studies in Popular Culture, spring 80; auth, Frontier Myth and American Gothic, Genre, fall 81;

auth, Wilderness Visions, Past and Future: Science Fiction Westerns, Borgo Press, 81, 2nd ed, 93; auth, Owen Wister, In: Twentieth-Century Western Writers, Gale Research Co, 83; auth, Ray Bradbury, Twayne United States Authors Series, G K Hall and Co, 86; auth, Sex and True West in McMurtry's Fiction, Southwestern Am Lit, spring 89; co-ed, The Frontier Experience and the American Dream, Tex A&M Univ Press, 89; rev, of "Other Destinies and The Heirs of Columbus," Colo Rev, fall 93; co-ed, Frontier Gothic & Book Titles, Assoc Univ Presses, 93; rev, of "Love Medicine," 2nd ed, and "The Bingo Palace," Colo Rev, fall 94; rev, of "Sygo and Justice," Colo Rev, fall 96. **CONTACT ADDRESS** Dept of Eng, Colorado State Univ, Fort Collins, CO 80523-0001. **EMAIL** dmogen@vines.colostate.edu

MOGLEN, HELENE

PERSONAL Born 03/22/1936, New York, NY, m, 1957, 3 children **DISCIPLINE** ENGLISH LITERATURE **EDUCATION** Bryn Mawr Col, BA, 57; Yale Univ, MA, 58, PhD(English lit), 64. **CAREER** From instr to asst prof English lit, NY Univ, 64-71; from assoc prof to prof, State Univ NY Col Purchase, 71-78, actg dean humanities, 76-77; prof English lit, 78-, dean humanities & arts, Univ CA, Santa Cruz, 78-82; fels, Am Coun Learned Soc, 73-74, Am Asn Univ Women, 93-94, & State Univ NY Found, 77. **MEMBERSHIPS** MLA; Pen. **RESEARCH** Victorian literature; English novel; feminist criticism. **SELECTED PUBLICATIONS** Auth, Laurence Sterne and the Contemporary Vision, In: The Winged Skull, Kent State Univ, 71; The Double Vision of Wuthering Heights: A Clarifying View of Female Development, Centennial Rev, 71; Disguise and Development: The Self and Society in Twelfth Night, Lit & Psychol, 73; The Philosophical Irony of Laurence Sterne, Univ FL, 73; Charlotte Bronte: The Self Conceived, Norton, 76; co-ed, with Jim Sleuth and Andrea Lunsford, The Future of Doctoral Studies in English, MLA, 89; co-ed, with Andrea Lunsford and Jim Sleuth, The Rights of Lirtacy, MLA: co-ed, with Elizabeth Abel and Barbara Chrunian, Female Subjects in Black and White, Race, Psychoanalysis, Feminism, Univ CA Press, 97; auth, The Trauma of Gender: A Feminist Theory of the English Novel, Univ of Cal Press, 01. **CONTACT ADDRESS** Kresge Col, Univ of California, Santa Cruz, Santa Cruz, CA 95064-0001. **EMAIL** moglen@cats.ucsc.edu

MOHSEN, RAED

PERSONAL Born 12/15/1959, Lebanon, m, 2000 **DISCIPLINE** INTERPERSONAL COMMUNICATION **EDUCATION** Bowling Green State Univ, BA 83; MA, 84; PhD, 87. **CAREER** Asst prof, assoc prof, Gallaudet Univ, 89-97; assoc prof, Lebanese American Univ, 97-. **HONORS AND AWARDS** Who's Who Among Am Tchrs. **MEMBERSHIPS** NCA; NASW. **RESEARCH** Intimate relationships; commun practices; behav of deaf people. **SELECTED PUBLICATIONS** Auth, Out on Campus: A Challenging Public Speaking Experience, The Speech Comm Teacher, 93; auth, Communicating Like and Dislikes During the Intimate Encounters of Married Couples, FL Comm Jour, 93; Petitioning Governments for Redress of Grievances: A Communication Approach to Terrorism, Speech and Theater Assoc of MO Jour, 93; auth, Communication Issues in deaf/Hearing Intimate Relationships: Toward A Better Future, A Deaf Amer Mono, 93. **CONTACT ADDRESS** Dept of Commun Studies, Lebanese American Univ, 475 Riverside Dr, No 1846, New York, NY 10115-0065. **EMAIL** rmohsen@lau.edu.lb

MOISAN, THOMAS

DISCIPLINE RENAISSANCE LITERATURE **EDUCATION** Harvard Univ, PhD. **CAREER** Prof, St Louis Univ. **SELECTED PUBLICATIONS** Auth, 'Knock Me Here Soundly': Comic Misprision and Class Consciousness in Shakespeare, Shakespeare Quart, 91; Repetition and Interrogation in Othello: 'What needs this Iterance?' or, 'Can anything be made of this?', Fairleigh Dickinson Press, 91; O anything of nothing first create': Gender, Patriarchy, and the Tragedy of Romeo and Juliet, Scarecrow Press, 91; Monsters of the Deep: Social Dissolution in Shakespeare's Tragedies, Shakespeare Quart, 94; Interlinear Trysting and 'Household Stuff': The Latin Lesson and the Domestication of Learning in The Taming of the Shrew , Shakespeare Studies, 95; 'What's that to you?' or, Facing Facts: Anti-Paternalist Chords and Social Discords in The Taming of the Shrew, Renaissance Drama, 97, Antique Fables, Fairy Toys: Elisions, Allusion,and Translation in A Midsummer Night's Dream , Garland, 98; auth, "Now Art Thou What Thou Art'; or, Being Sociable in Verona: Teaching Gender and Desire in Romeo and Juliet, in Approaches to Teaching Romeo and Juliet, Modern Lang Asn (00): 47-58. **CONTACT ADDRESS** Dept of English, Saint Louis Univ, 221 N Grand Blvd, Saint Louis, MO 63103. **EMAIL** moisante@slu.edu

MOLDENHAUER, JOSEPH JOHN

PERSONAL Born 02/09/1934, Rastatt, Germany, m, 1957, 2 children **DISCIPLINE** ENGLISH **EDUCATION** Amherst Col, BA, 56; Columbia Univ, MA, 57, PhD(English), 64. **CAREER** From spec instr to assoc prof, 57-72, prof English, 72-85, M C Boatright Regents Prof, Univ Tx, Austin, 86-, chamn, 79-83; Amherst Col fel, Columbia Univ, 56-57, Southern Fel Fund fac fel, 59-60; Guggenheim fel, 68-69; textual ed, The writings of Henry D Thoreau, 72-. **MEMBERSHIPS** MLA; Bibliographical Soc Am; Thoreau Soc; ALA. **RESEARCH** Nineteenth century American literature; textual editing. **SELECTED PUBLICATIONS** Auth, Unity of Theme and Structure in The Wild Palms, In: William Faulkner: Three Decades of Criticism, MI State Univ, 60; Murder as a Fine Art, Basic Connections Between Poe's Aesthetics, Psychology, and Moral Vision, Pmla, 5/68; Paradox in Walden, In: The Recognition of H D Thoreau, Univ MI, 69; ed, H D Thoreau's The Maine Woods, Princeton Univ, 72; auth, A Descriptive Catalog of .. Poe Manuscripts, Univ TX, Austin, 73; co-ed, H D Thoreau, Early Essays and Miscellanies, Princeton Univ, 75; ed, Poe's The Spectacles: A New Text from Manuscript, In: Studies in the American Renaissance-1977, G K Hall, NY, 78; auth, Bartleby and the Custom-House, Delta No 7, 11/78; ed, H D Thoreau, Cape Cod, Princeton Univ, 88-; auth, Walden and Wordsworth's Guide to the Lake District, in Studies in the American Renaissance--1900, Univ Press VA, 90; Textual Instability in the Riverside Edition of Thoreau, Papers of the Bibligraphical Soc of Am, 12/91; Pym, the Dighton Rock, and the Matter of Vinland, in Poe's Pym: Critical explorations, Duke Univ, 92; The Maine Woods, in Cambridge Companion to Henry David Thoreau, Cambridge Univ, 95. **CONTACT ADDRESS** Dept English, Univ of Texas, Austin, Austin, TX 78712-1164. **EMAIL** eiey567@uts.cc.utexas.edu

MOLETTE, BARBARA J.

PERSONAL Born 01/31/1940, Los Angeles, CA, m, 1960 **DISCIPLINE** THEATRE **EDUCATION** Florida A&M, Tallahasse FL, BA, 1966; Florida State Univ, Tallahassee FL, MFA, 1969; Univ of Missouri, Columbia MO, PhD 1989-. **CAREER** Spelman Coll, Atlanta GA, instructor, 69-75; Texas Southern Univ, Houston TX, asst professor, 75-85; Mayor's Advisory Committee on Arts & Culture, Baltimore MD, dir arts in educ programs, 88-90; Baltimore City Community College, professor, 90-93; Eastern Connecticut State Univ, 93-. **HONORS AND AWARDS** Graduated with Highest Honors from Florida A&M, 1966; Graduate Fellowship, Florida State Univ, 1967-69; Graduate Fellowship, Univ of Missouri, 1986-87; Rosalee Pritchett, performed at Negro Ensemble Company, 1971, published in Black Writers of America; Distinguished Alumna, Univ of Mo, 00. **MEMBERSHIPS** Mem, Dramatist Guild of Amer, 1971-; president, Natl Assn For African-American Theatre, 1989-91; consultant for workshops in theatre and mass communications. **SELECTED PUBLICATIONS** Author of Black Theatre, Wyndham Hall Publishers, 1986; Noahs Ark, published in Center Stage, 1981; Upstage/Downstage, column in Houston Informer, 1977-78; **CONTACT ADDRESS** English Dept, Eastern Connecticut State Univ, Willimantic, CT 06226.

MOLETTE, CARLTON WOODARD, II

PERSONAL Born 08/23/1939, Pine Bluff, AR, m, 1960 **DISCIPLINE** DRAMA **EDUCATION** Morehouse Coll, BA 1959; Univ of KC, graduate study 1959-60; Univ of IA, MA 1962; FL State Univ, PhD 1968. **CAREER** Little Theatre Div of Humanities Tuskegee Inst, asst dir 1960-61; Des Moines Comm Playhouse, designer tech dir 1962-63; Howard Univ Dept of Drama, asst prof of tech production & design 1963-64; FL A&M Univ, asst prof & tech dir 1964-67, assoc prof 1967-69; Spelman Coll, assoc prof of drama, 69-75; Div of Fine Arts, chmn 1974-75; School of Communications TX So Univ, dean 1975-84; Lincoln Univ, dean Col of Arts & Sciences, 85-87; Coppin State Col, vice pres Academic Affairs, 87-91; University of CT, Department of Dramatic Arts, prof, Institute for African-American Studies, senior fellow, 92-; guest dir Univ of MI Feb-Mar 1974. **HONORS AND AWARDS** Graduate fellowship in theatre Univ of KC; Atlanta Univ Center Faculty Rsch Grant 1970-71; Rosalee Pritchett (play) produced by Negro Ensemble Company, 1970; other plays: Dr B S Black (musical), Booji, Noah's Ark; Fortunes of the Moor produced by The Frank Silvera Writers' Workshop, 1995. **MEMBERSHIPS** Mem The Dramatists Guild; National Conference on African American Theatre, past president; Natl Assn of Dramatic & Speech Arts; past editor of "Encore"; mem bd dir Atlanta Arts Festival; vice pres Greater Atlanta Arts Council; chmn bd trustees Neighborhood Arts Center, Miller Theatre Advisory Council; mem, bd dir, Young Audiences of Maryland, 1990-93. **SELECTED PUBLICATIONS** Co-auth, Black Theatre, Premise & Presentation, Wyndham Hall Press, 2nd ed, 1986. **CONTACT ADDRESS** Department of Dramatic Arts, 802 Bolton Rd, Storrs, CT 06268.

MOLINO, MICHAEL R.

PERSONAL Born 09/17/1956, Washington, DC, m, 1987 **DISCIPLINE** ENGLISH **EDUCATION** Univ South Fla, BA, 82; MA, 84; Marquette Univ, PhD, 92. **CAREER** Lectr, Iowa State Univ, 88-92; lectr, Univ of Miss-Rolla, 92-94; lectr, Va Commonwealth Univ, 94-95; asst prof, Bradley Univ, 95-98; asst prof, Southern Ill Univ Carbondale, 98-. **HONORS AND AWARDS** Arthur J. Schmitt Fel, 89-90; Marquette Univ Scholar, 90-91; Fac/Student Res Mentoring Prog, 97; Bradley Summer Res Grant, 97. **MEMBERSHIPS** Modern Lang Asn, Am Conf for Irish Studies, Semiotic Soc of Am. **RESEARCH** Twentieth Century British Literature, Irish Studies, Twentieth Century American Literature. **SELECTED PUBLICATIONS** Auth, "Flying by the Nets of Language and Nationality: Seamus Heaney, the 'English' Language, and Ulster's Troubles," Modern Philol, 91 (Nov 93): 180-201; auth, "Tradition(s) and the Individual Talents: Voices from Within (the Poetry of Auden and Yeats)," in Semiotics 1991, eds, John Deely and Terry Prewitt, Univ Press (93): 272-80; auth, "The Net of Language: Marginalization, Resistance, and Differences in Contemporary Irish Literature," Am J of Semiotics, 11.1-2 (94, pub 96): 157-73; auth, Questioning Tradition, Language, and Myth: The Poetry of Seamus Heaney, Washington, DC: The Cath Univ of Am Press (94); auth, "Charting an Uncertain Flight Path: Irish Writers and the Question of Nation, Identity, and Literature," The Comparatist 20 (May 96): 41-49; ed, Dictionary of Literary Biography, British Novelists of the Twenty-first Century (First Series) (in progress). **CONTACT ADDRESS** Dept English, So Illinois Univ, Carbondale, Mail Code 4503, Carbondale, IL 62901-4503. **EMAIL** MRMolino@aol.com

MOLITIERNO, ARTHUR

PERSONAL Born 06/06/1942, Philadelphia, PA, m, 1969 **DISCIPLINE** ENGLISH **EDUCATION** Villanova, Univ, BA, 64; Univ Dayton, MA, 66; Miami Univ, ABD, 78; Bowling Green, BA, 90; MA, 95. **HONORS AND AWARDS** NEH Fel, Univ of Md, Univ of Pa. **MEMBERSHIPS** MLA; AURCO. **RESEARCH** American literature of the nineteenth century, narcissism. **SELECTED PUBLICATIONS** Auth, "Editor's Desktop: The Real and Virtual World of Paul Glister's Digital Literacy", TEXT Tech 6.2 (97): 78-83; auth, "The Abyss and History: Lukas and the Children of the Holocaust", Midwest Quarterly 39.1, (97): 61-73; auth, "The Authentic Negative Voice of Democracy: Christopher Lasch's Last Will and Testament", Midwest Quarterly, 41.2 (00): 129-144. **CONTACT ADDRESS** Dept English, Wright State Univ, Lake, 7600 State Rte 703, Celina, OH 45822-2921. **EMAIL** arthur.molitierno@wright.edu

MOLLENKOTT, VIRGINIA RAMEY

PERSONAL Born 01/28/1932, Philadelphia, PA, m, 1954, 1 child **DISCIPLINE** ENGLISH, WOMEN'S STUDIES **EDUCATION** Bob Jones Univ, BA, 53; Temple Univ, MA, 55; NYork Univ, PhD, 64. **CAREER** Chmn, Shelton Col, 55-63; chmn, Nyack Col, 63-67; prof to emer, William Paterson Col, 67-97-. **HONORS AND AWARDS** Founder Day Award, 63; Andiron Award, 64. **MEMBERSHIPS** MLA; WIFP; MSA. **RESEARCH** Gender; religion; sexuality. **SELECTED PUBLICATIONS** Auth, Adamant and Stone Chips: A Christian Humanist Approach to Knowledge, 67; auth, In Search of Balance, 69; ed, Women of Faith of Dialogue, 87; auth, Godding: Human Responsibility and the Bible, 87; auth, Speech, Silence, Action: The Cycle of Faith, 87; auth, Women, Men and the Bible, 77, 88; auth, Is the Homosexual My Neighbor? A Positive Christian Response, 78, 94; auth, Sensuous Spirituality: Out from Fundamentalism, 92; auth, The Divine Feminine: Biblical Imagery of God as Female, 83, Ger 85, Fr 90, Ital 93; auth, Omnigender: A Trans-Religious Approach, 01. **CONTACT ADDRESS** 11 Yearling Trl, Hewitt, NJ 07421-2510. **EMAIL** jstvrm@warwick.net

MONACO, PAUL

PERSONAL Born 09/11/1942, Niskayuna, NY, m, 1993 **DISCIPLINE** THEATRE **EDUCATION** Columbia Univ, BS, 65; Brandeis Univ, PhD, 74. **CAREER** From Asst Prof to Assoc Prof, Univ Tex, 75-85; Prof, Mont State Univ, 85-. **HONORS AND AWARDS** Fulbright Awds; Phi Kappa Phi, 99-01. **MEMBERSHIPS** Visual Commun Asn, Univ Film and Video Asn. **RESEARCH** Film, culture, communication, television. **SELECTED PUBLICATIONS** Auth, Ribbons in Time: Movies and Society Since 1945, 87; auth, Understanding Society, Culture and Television, 98; auth, History of American Cinema, 1960-1969, 00. **CONTACT ADDRESS** Dept Theatre, Montana State Univ, Bozeman, W Kagy Ave, Bozeman, MT 59717-0001. **EMAIL** monaco@montana.edu

MONK, DENNIS C.

DISCIPLINE MUSICOLOGY AND MUSIC HISTORY **EDUCATION** San Francisko State Univ, BA, MA; UCLA, PhD. **CAREER** Music Dept, Univ Ala; prof emertitus **HONORS AND AWARDS** Fulbright fel. **SELECTED PUBLICATIONS** Area: Music Hist, Educ, and Administration. **CONTACT ADDRESS** Univ of Alabama, Tuscaloosa, Box 870366, Tuscaloosa, AL 35487-0000. **EMAIL** dmonk@music.ua.edu

MONKMAN, LESLIE G.

DISCIPLINE ENGLISH LITERATURE **EDUCATION** York Univ, PhD. **CAREER** Dept Eng, Queen's Univ **RESEARCH** Canadian and other post-colonial literatures. **SELECTED PUBLICATIONS** Auth, A Native Heritage: Images of the Indian in English-Canadian Literature; pubs on Canadian and other post-colonial literatures in English. **CONTACT ADDRESS** English Dept, Queen's Univ at Kingston, Kingston, ON, Canada K7L 3N6. **EMAIL** monkmanl@post.queensu.ca

MONOSON, S. SARA

DISCIPLINE CLASSICS AND POLITICAL SCIENCE **EDUCATION** Brandeis, BA, 81; London Sch Econ and Polit Sci, MSc, 82; Princeton Univ, PhD, 93. **CAREER** Asst prof, Northwestern Univ, 93-. **RESEARCH** Plato and Athenian democracy. **SELECTED PUBLICATIONS** Auth, Citizen as Erastes: Erotic Imagery and the Idea of Reciprocity in the Periclean Funeral Oration, Polit Theory, 94; Frank Speech, Democracy and Philosophy: Plato's Debt to a Democratic Strategy of Civic Discourse, Athenian Polit Thought and the Reconstruction of Am Democracy, Cornell, 94; auth, Plato's Democratic Entanglements: Athenian Politics and the Practice of Philosophy, Princeton Univ Press, 00. **CONTACT ADDRESS** Dept of Classics, Northwestern Univ, 1801 Hinman, Evanston, IL 60208. **EMAIL** s-monoson@nwu.edu

MONROE, DEBRA
DISCIPLINE ENGLISH **EDUCATION** Univ Wis, BA; KS State Univ, MA; Univ UT, PhD. **CAREER** Southwest Tex State Univ **HONORS AND AWARDS** Flannery O'Connor Awd for Short Fiction. **RESEARCH** Tudor humanists, espec John Colet and Thomas More. **SELECTED PUBLICATIONS** Auth, The Source of Trouble, Univ Ga Press; A Wild, Cold State, Simon & Schuster. **CONTACT ADDRESS** Southwest Texas State Univ, 601 University Dr, San Marcos, TX 78666-4604.

MONTAGNES, IAN
PERSONAL Born 03/11/1932, Toronto, ON, Canada **DISCIPLINE** COMMUNICATIONS **EDUCATION** Univ Toronto, BA, 53, MA, 56. **CAREER** Tchr, Ryerson Inst Tech, 57-59; Info off, Univ Toronto, 59-63; info off, ROM, 63-66; head ed dept, Univ Toronto Press, 72-82; lectr, Fac Lib Sci, Univ Toronto, 89-93. **MEMBERSHIPS** Secy, Asn Can Univ Presses; Asn Am Univ Presses, 75-91; adv bd, Int Fedn Sci Eds, 91-; assoc fel, Massey Col 89-; Arts & Letters, Toronto. **SELECTED PUBLICATIONS** Auth, An Uncommon Fellowship: The Story of Hart House, 69; auth, The University of Toronto: A Souvenir, 84; co-ed, Cold Iron and Lady Godiva: Engineering Education at Toronto, 1920-1972, 72. **CONTACT ADDRESS** 31 Baldwin St, Port Hope, ON, Canada L1A 1S3.

MONTGOMERY, LYNA LEE
DISCIPLINE VICTORIAN LITERATURE **EDUCATION** Univ Ark, PhD. **CAREER** English and Lit, Univ Ark. **HONORS AND AWARDS** Assoc chair. **SELECTED PUBLICATIONS** The Phoenix: Its Use as a Literary Device in English from the 17th Century to the 20th Century, D H Lawrence Rev, 72; co-ed, A Mystery Reader, Scribner's, 75. **CONTACT ADDRESS** Univ of Arkansas, Fayetteville, Fayetteville, AR 72701. **EMAIL** montgo@comp.uark.edu

MONTGOMERY, TONI-MARIE
PERSONAL Born 06/25/1956, Philadelphia, PA, s **DISCIPLINE** MUSIC **EDUCATION** Philadelphia College of Performing Arts, Philadelphia, PA, BM, 1980; University of Michigan, Ann Arbor, MI, MM, 1981, DMA, 1984. **CAREER** Western Michigan University, Kalamazoo, MI, asst director school of music, 85-87; University of Connecticut, Storrs, CT, asst dean, 87-89; Arizona State University, Tempe, AZ, assoc dean/asst professor, 90-96; Arizona State Univ, School of Music, dir, 96-00; dean, School of Fine Arts, Univ of Kans, 00-. **HONORS AND AWARDS** Outstanding Keyboard Performer, American Keyboard Artists, 1988; Black Women's Task Force Arts Awd, 1998. **MEMBERSHIPS** Phoenix Symphony Board, 1998-; member, Tempe Arts Commission, 1991-93; president, Sister Friends: African-American Women, 1990-; member, board of directors, president Faculty Women's Association, 1990-. **CONTACT ADDRESS** Office of the Dean, School of Fine Arts, Univ of Kansas, Lawrence, 1530 Naismith Dr, Bldg 76, 446 Murphy Hall, Lawrence, KS 66045. **EMAIL** tmmontgo@ukans.edu

MOODY, JOYCELYN K.
PERSONAL Born Mobile, AL, 1 child **DISCIPLINE** ENGLISH **EDUCATION** Spring Hill Col, BA, 79; Univ Wis, MA, 81; Univ Kans, PhD, 93. **CAREER** Instr, S Ga Col, 84-85; vis instr to instr, Rockhurst Col, 85-90, asst to assoc prof, Univ of Wash, 91-. **HONORS AND AWARDS** Knight Diss Fel, Kalamazoo Col, 90-91; Women Studies in Religion Assoc, Harvard Divinity School, 96-97; Jane Irwin Watson Chair, Hamilton Col, 01-02. **MEMBERSHIPS** MLA, Am Lit Assoc. **RESEARCH** Autobiography, African American Literature, 19th Century American Literature, Slave Narratives, Women's Literature. **SELECTED PUBLICATIONS** Auth, Sentimental Confessions: Spiritual Narratives of 19th Century African American Women, Univ of Ga Pr, 00. **CONTACT ADDRESS** Univ of Washington, Box 354330, Seattle, WA 98195-4330. **EMAIL** jmoody@u.washington.edu

MOONEY, JACK
DISCIPLINE COMMUNICATION STUDIES **EDUCATION** Univ Ga, MA, 70; Univ Tennessee, PhD, 84. **CAREER** Prof. **SELECTED PUBLICATIONS** Auth, International Printing Pressmen and Assistants' Union of North America, 84; ed, Tennessee's newspapers for the state's bicentennial celebration, 96. **CONTACT ADDRESS** Dept of Communication, East Tennessee State Univ, PO Box 70717, Johnson City, TN 37614-0717.

MOONEY, SUSAN K.
DISCIPLINE ENGLISH, SPANISH **EDUCATION** Queen's Univ, BA, 88; McGill Univ, MA, 91; Univ of Toronto, PhD, 01. **CAREER** Lectr, Nipissing Univ, 99-01; asst prof, Concordia Univ, 01-02. **MEMBERSHIPS** Comp Lit Asn of Can, MLA, Int Comp Lit Asn. **RESEARCH** 19th and 20th Century English, Hispanic, French and Russian Literatures, Literary Theory, Psychoanalytic Approaches to Literature and Theory, Philosophy of Law and Ethics. **SELECTED PUBLICATIONS** Auth, "Bronze by Gold by Bloom: the Aurteur of 'Sirens,'" Bronze by Gold: The Music of Joyce, ed Sebastian DG Knowles, Garland, (NY), 99. **CONTACT ADDRESS** 288 Grosvenor Ave, Westmount, QC, Canada H3Z 2L9. **EMAIL** smooney@chass.utoronto.ca

MOORE, CHARLES B.
PERSONAL Born 12/16/1941, Dyersburg, TN, s **DISCIPLINE** ENGLISH LITERATURE **EDUCATION** Vanderbilt Univ, BA, 63; Princeton Univ, MA, 67; PhD, 73. **CAREER** Instr, Univ Va, 67-70; Instr, Dyers Univ State Commun Col, 70-71; from instr to asst prof, Fairleigh Dickinson Univ, 72-80; asst prof, Christian Brother Col, 81-86; from assoc prof to prof, LeMoyne-Owen Col, 86-. **HONORS AND AWARDS** Phi Beta Kappa; Woodrow Wilson Fel; Fulbright Scholar; NEH Summer Sem, 80, 85, & 93. **MEMBERSHIPS** New Chaucer Soc, Medieval & Renaissance Drama Soc, Medieval Acad of Am. **RESEARCH** Medieval Art History, Chaucer. **SELECTED PUBLICATIONS** Auth, "A Stained Glass Record of York Drama," Studies in Iconography XIII (95). **CONTACT ADDRESS** Dept Humanities, LeMoyne-Owen Col, 807 Walker Ave, Memphis, TN 38126-6510.

MOORE, DON
PERSONAL Born 05/13/1934, Jackson, TN, m, 2 children **DISCIPLINE** SHAKESPEARE, JACOBEAN DRAMA, MODERN DRAMA **EDUCATION** Tulane, PhD, 64. **CAREER** Host; "The Spoken Word", regional public radio; Prof, La State Univ. **HONORS AND AWARDS** Outstanding Tchg award. **MEMBERSHIPS** Exec comt, S Cent Renaissance Soc, 85-89. **RESEARCH** The stagings of Shakespeare. **SELECTED PUBLICATIONS** Auth, John Webster and His Critics; Webster: The Critical Heritage. **CONTACT ADDRESS** Dept of Eng, Louisiana State Univ and A&M Col, 212M Allen Hall, Baton Rouge, LA 70803.

MOORE, JOHN DAVID
PERSONAL Born 08/20/1949, s **DISCIPLINE** NINETEENTH-CENTURY BRITISH LITERATURE **EDUCATION** Univ MT, BA, 73, MA, 77; Univ WA, PhD, 85. **CAREER** Tchg asst, Univ WA, 80-84; Instr, Univ WA, 85; Asst prof, Univ WA , 85-90; Assoc prof, Univ WA, 91-. **HONORS AND AWARDS** Grad Sch Dissertation Fel Univ WA, 83; Ill Hum Coun Mini Grant, 90, 92, 94; EIU Booth Library Fel, 90; Coun Fac Res Grant, EIU, 90. **MEMBERSHIPS** MLA; Midwest Mod Lang Asn; Midwest Victorian Studies Asn; Children's Lit Asn; Col Lang Asn. **SELECTED PUBLICATIONS** Auth, The Vision of the Feminine in William Morris' The Waters of the Wondrous Isles, Pre-Raphaelite Rev, 80; Coleridge and the 'Modern Jacobinical Drama': Osorio, Remorse, and the Development of Coleridge's Critique of the Stage, 1797-1816, Bul Res Hum, 82; Pottering About in the Garden: Kenneth Grahame's Vision of Pastoral in The Wind in the Willows, Jour MMLA, 90; John Masefield's The Box of Delights, Masterplots II: Juvenile and Young Adult Fiction, 91; Angela Brazil's A Fourth Form Friendship, , Masterplots II: Juvenile and Young Adult Fiction, 91; Emphasis and Suppression in Stevenson's Treasure Island: Fabrication of the Self in Jim Hawkins' Narrative, CLA Jour, 91; Richard Peck's Close Enough to Touch, Beacham's Guide Lit For Young Adults, 94; Richard Peck's The Dreadful Future of Blossom Culp, Beacham's Guide Lit For Young Adults, 94; Laurence Yep's Kind Hearts and Gentle Monsters, Beacham's Guide Lit For Young Adults, 94; Donald Barthelme's Paradise, Beacham's Guide Lit For Young Adults, 94; The Indians in Our Cupboards: Images of Native Americans in Books for Children, Ill Eng Bull, 95. **CONTACT ADDRESS** Eastern Illinois Univ, 600 Lincoln Ave, Charleston, IL 61920-3099.

MOORE, JUDITH
PERSONAL Born 05/04/1939, Milwaukee, WI, m, 1987, 2 children **DISCIPLINE** 18TH-CENTURY LITERATURE **EDUCATION** Cornell Univ, PhD. **CAREER** Univ Alaska, Anchorage. **MEMBERSHIPS** Am Soc of 18th Century Studies. **SELECTED PUBLICATIONS** Auth, A Zeal for Responsibility: The Struggle for Professional Nursing in Victorian England, 1868-1883, Univ Ga Press, 88; The Appearance of Truth: The Story of Elizabeth Canning and Eighteenth-Century Narrative, Univ Delaware Press, 94. **CONTACT ADDRESS** Univ of Alaska, Anchorage, 3211 Providence Dr., Anchorage, AK 99508. **EMAIL** afjkm1@uaa.alaska.edu

MOORE, MICHAEL
DISCIPLINE LITERATURE **EDUCATION** Carleton, BA, MA; Queen's, PhD. **CAREER** Prof **HONORS AND AWARDS** WLU Outstanding Tchr Awd, 91; Canada Natl Tchg Awd, 93. **RESEARCH** 19th century lit, Gerard Manley Hopkins, nature lit, theories of writing, literary and discourse theory. **SELECTED PUBLICATIONS** Coauth, A Writer's Handbook of Current English, 83, 88; Coed, Sir Philip Sidney and the Croom Helm, 84; Interpretation of Renaissance Culture; Vital Candle: Victorian and Modern Bearings in Gerard Manley Hopkins, Univ Waterloo Press, 94; Dangerous Beauty: Hopkins and Newman; George Whalley: Remembrances, Quarry Press, 89; Why Hopkins Matters, Hopkins Quart, 98; auth, "Why Hopkins Matters," Hopkins Quarterly 25.1, (98): 14-17; auth, "Genre of Genre: Sidney and Defences of Poetry," Special Festchrift Issue Florilegium Annual 16, (99): 147-54. **CONTACT ADDRESS** Dept of English, Wilfrid Laurier Univ, 75 University Ave W, Waterloo, ON, Canada N2L 3C5. **EMAIL** mmoore@mach1.wlu.cas

MOORE, NATHAN
PERSONAL Born 06/26/1931, Mayaro, Trinidad and Tobago, m, 1967, 2 children **DISCIPLINE** ENGLISH **EDUCATION** Caribbean Union Coll Trinidad, A 1958; Rockford Coll IL, BA 1963; Carleton Univ Ottawa, MA 1965; Univ of British Columbia, PhD 1972. **CAREER** Barbados Secondary Sch, hs tchr 1958-61; Carleton U, sessional lecturer 1964-65, teaching fellow 1963-65; Barrier Sch Dist British Col, hs tchr, 66-67; Walla Walla Coll WA, coll tchr 1967-79; AL State U, professor of English, 79-, chmn dept of Engl 1980-. **HONORS AND AWARDS** Schlrshp Rockford Coll 1961; schlrshp Readers Digest 1962; Carleton Fellow Carleton Univ 1963-65. **MEMBERSHIPS** Mem Modern Lang Assn 1965-; mem Am Soc for 18th Century Studies 1971-; mem South Atlantic MLA 1980-. **CONTACT ADDRESS** Dept of Lang and Lit, Alabama State Univ, S Jackson St, Montgomery, AL 36101. **EMAIL** nmoore@asunet.alasu.edu

MOORE, PATRICK
DISCIPLINE INSTRUMENTAL DISCOURSE **EDUCATION** Univ Minn, PhD. **CAREER** Assoc prof, English and Lit, Univ Ark **RESEARCH** Instrumental discourse; technical communication; world literature. **SELECTED PUBLICATIONS** Auth, Rhetorical versus Instrumental Approaches to Teaching Technical Communication, Technical Comm; Intimidation and Communication, JBTC; When Politeness is Fatal, JBTC; Coauth, Using Gestalt Theory to Teach Document Design and Graphics, TCQ. **CONTACT ADDRESS** Dept of Communication, Univ of Arkansas, Little Rock, 2801 S University Ave., Little Rock, AR 72204-1099. **EMAIL** epmoore@aol.com

MOORE, RAYBURN SABATZKY
PERSONAL Born 05/26/1920, Helena, ARK, m, 1947, 2 children **DISCIPLINE** AMERICAN & SOUTHERN LITERATURE **EDUCATION** Vanderbilt Univ, BA, 42, MA, 47; Duke Univ, PhD(Am Lit), 56. **CAREER** Res asst, Duke Univ, 52, asst, 52-54; from asst prof to prof English, Hendrix Col, 54-59; vis scholar, Duke Univ, 58, 64; assoc prof, 59-65, dir grad studies English, 64-69, Prof English, Univ Ga, 65-, Chmn Am Studies Prog, 68-90, Chmn Div Lang & Lit, 75-90; chmn, executive comt, S Atlantic Grad English Group, 71-72; editing board, Univ Ga Pr, 72-72; Ga Rev, 74-82; chmn, Ga Rev, 80-82. **HONORS AND AWARDS** Blue Key, Phi Beta Kappa; John Hurt Fisher Awd for Distinguished Serv to the Profession, South Assoc of Dept of English, 00. **MEMBERSHIPS** Soc Study Southern Lit; MLA; Am Studies Asn; Southern Hist Asn; S Atlantic Mod Lang Asn; Am Lit Assoc. **RESEARCH** Southern literature since 1820; American literary magazines, 1865-1890; 19th century American realism, especially Henry James. **SELECTED PUBLICATIONS** Auth, Don Joaquin, a forgotten story by George W Cable, Am Lit, 54; Constance Fenimore Woolson, Twayne, 63; The full light of a higher criticism, S Atlantic Quart, winter 64; ed, Major and Selected Short Stores of Constance Fenimore Woolson, CUP, 67; Paul Hamilton Hayne, Twayne, 72; The epistolary James, Sewanee Rev, fall 75; The strange irregular rhythm of life: James's late tales and Constance Woolson, Satlantic Rev, 1976; The literary world gone mad: Hayne on Whitman, Southern Lit J, 1977; ed, A Man of Letters in the 19th Century South: Selected Letters of Paul Hamilton Hayne, La State Univ Press, 82; ed, The History of Southern Lit, La State Univ Pr, 85; ed, Selected Letters of Henry James to Edmund Gosse 1882-1915, La State Univ Pr, 88; ed, The Correspondence of Henry James and the House of MacMillan 1872-1914, MacMillan, 93; auth, Classics Of Civil-War Fiction - Madden,D, Bach,P, Editors, Mississippi Quarterly, Vol 0046, 1993; Meaning In James,Henry - Bell,M, Studies In The Novel, Vol 0027, 1995; Preston,Margaret,Junkin - A Biography - Coulling,Mary, Mississippi Quarterly, Vol 0049, 1996; auth, "Simms's Literary Reputation Since the 1930s," Simms Review, 8 (00); ed, The Letters of Alice James to Anne Ashburner Richards 1873-1878, Resources in Am Literary Study, 00. **CONTACT ADDRESS** Dept of English, Univ of Georgia, Park Hall, Athens, GA 30602-6205.

MOORE, ROBERT HAMILTON
PERSONAL Born 01/03/1913, St. Matthews, KY, m, 1939 **DISCIPLINE** ENGLISH **EDUCATION** Ind Univ, AB, 34, AM, 38; Univ Ill, PhD, 48. **CAREER** Asst English, Ind Univ, 35-38; from asst to instr, Univ Ill, 38-49; from assoc prof to prof, 49-78, chmn compos, 49-77, Emer Prof English, George Wash Univ, 78-. **MEMBERSHIPS** NCTE; Conf Col Compos & Commun. **RESEARCH** Freshman English; linguistics; rhetoric. **SELECTED PUBLICATIONS** Auth, Plan before you

write, 50, Effective writing, 55, 59, 65 & 71, Elements of composition, 60, Handbook of effective writing, 66, 71 & The research paper, 67, Holt. **CONTACT ADDRESS** 314 Van Buren St, Falls Church, VA 22046.

MOORE, ROBERT HENRY
PERSONAL Born 09/16/1940, Madisonville, KY, m, 1964, 2 children **DISCIPLINE** AMERICAN LITERATURE & HISTORY **EDUCATION** Davidson Col, AB, 62; Univ NC, Chapel Hill, MA, 64; Univ Wis-Madison, PhD(English), 70. **CAREER** Instr English, US Mil Acad, 68-70; asst prof, Univ Md, College Park, 70-76, assoc prof, 76-80. Contrib-reader, Dict Am Regional English, 68-; exec secy, Faulkner Concordance Proj, 70-, ed, Faulkner Concordance Newslett, 72-; reviewer, Nat Endowment for Humanities, 72; fel, Inter-Univ Sem Armed Forces & Soc, 73-. **MEMBERSHIPS** MLA; Am Studies Asn; Am Civil Liberties Union. **RESEARCH** twentieth century American language and literature, American studies; armed forces and society. **SELECTED PUBLICATIONS** Coauth, Black puritan, William & Mary Quart, 467; ed, Ellison at West Point, Contempt Lit, spring 74; coauth, School for Soldiers, Oxford Univ, 74; Cameras in state courts, An historical-perspective, judicature, vol 0078, 1994. **CONTACT ADDRESS** 9202 Saybrook Ave Branwell Park, Silver Spring, MD 20901.

MOORE, T. J.
PERSONAL Born 12/11/1959, Bristol, PA **DISCIPLINE** CLASSICS **EDUCATION** Millerville Univ BA 81; Univ North Carolina PhD 86. **CAREER** Univ Texas, assoc and assist prof 91 to 98-; Texas A M Univ, asst prof 86 to 91. **HONORS AND AWARDS** Mellon Fel Harvard, 91; Rome Prize Fel 98; Humboldt Fel, 99. **MEMBERSHIPS** APA; AIA; ACL; TCA; Classical Assoc Middle West and South **RESEARCH** Roman comedy and historiography. **SELECTED PUBLICATIONS** Auth, Artistry and Ideology: Livy's Vocabulary of Virtue, Athenaeum Press, 89; Seats and Social Status in the Plautine Theater, Class Jour 94; Morality, History and Livy's Wronged Woman, Eranos 93; auth, The Theater of Plautus: Playing to the Audience, Univ TX 98; Music and Structure in Roman Comedy, Amer Jour of Philology 98; auth, Facing the Music: Character and Musical Accompaniment in Kemon Comedy, Syllecta Classica 99. **CONTACT ADDRESS** Dept of Classics, Univ of Texas, Austin, Austin, TX 78712-1181. **EMAIL** tfmmoore@utxvms.cc.utexas.edu

MOORE, WILLIAM HAMILTON
PERSONAL Born 06/29/1937, Kansas City, MO, m, 1964, 1 child **DISCIPLINE** ENGLISH **EDUCATION** Southwestern Univ, Tex, BA, 59; Harvard Univ, MA, 60, PhD(English), 63. **CAREER** From instr to asst prof English, Duke Univ, 63-67; from asst prof to assoc prof, 67-76, Prof Humanities, Austin Col, 76- **MEMBERSHIPS** MLA. **RESEARCH** The poetry of Michael Drayton; Elizabethan drama; religion and literature. **SELECTED PUBLICATIONS** Auth, An allusion in 1593 to The Taming of the Shrew, Shakespeare Quart, winter 64; Sources of Drayton's conception of Poly-Olbion, Studies Philol, 10/68. **CONTACT ADDRESS** Dept of English, Austin Col, Sherman, TX 75090. **EMAIL** wmoore@austinc.edu

MOORTI, SUJATA
DISCIPLINE WOMEN'S STUDIES, COMMUNICATION **EDUCATION** Univ Md, PhD, 95. **CAREER** Old Dominion Univ. **SELECTED PUBLICATIONS** Auth, Cathartic Confessions or Emancipatory Texts: Talk Shows and TV Representations of Rape; Desire in a Lost Empire: Constructions of Gendered Identities in The Jewel in the Crown; Newspaper Coverage of Global Climate Change, 1986-1991; Environ Jour, January, 93. **CONTACT ADDRESS** Old Dominion Univ, 436 BAL, College of Arts and Letters, Norfolk, VA 23529. **EMAIL** smoorti@odu.edu

MORACE, ROBERT A.
PERSONAL Born 09/22/1947, Rockville Center, NY, m, 1987, 3 children **DISCIPLINE** ENGLISH **EDUCATION** SUNY at Cortland, BA, 69; MA, 72; Univ SC, PhD, 76. **CAREER** Teach asst, Univ SC, 72-74, 75-76; teach assoc, 76-77; lectr, Warsaw Univ, 85-87; asst prof, to assoc prof, Daemen Col, 77-; dept chemn, 82-85, 98-. **HONORS AND AWARDS** Dist Fac Achie Awd; Fulbright Lectr; Dist Alumni Awd Nom; Burger Prize. **MEMBERSHIPS** MLA; NMLA; ALS; SSNL; John Gardner Soc. **RESEARCH** Contemporary fiction; American literature; narrative theory; bibliography; critical reception; cultural criticism. **SELECTED PUBLICATIONS** Co-ed, John Gardner: Critical Perspectives, Southern Ill UP (Carbondale), 82; auth, John Gardner: An Annotated Secondary Bibliography, Garland (NY), 84; auth, The Dialogic Novels Of Malcolm Bradbury and David Lodge, Southern Ill UP (Carbondale), 89; "Play It Again, Sam," Papers on Lang Lit 29 (93): 246-252; auth, "Dialogues and Dialogics," Modern Lang Studies 23 (93): 73-91; auth, "Tales from the Crypt: A User's Guide to John Cheever's Journals," in The Critical Response to John Cheever. ed. Francis J Bosha (Westport: Greenwood, 94): 224-245; auth, "The Facts in Black and White: Cheever's Falconer and Wideman's Philadelphia Fire," in Powerless Fictions: Ethics Cultural Critique and American Fiction in the Age of Postmodernism ed. Ricardo Miguel-Alfonso (Amsterdam: Rodopi, 96): 85-112; auth, "From Sacred Hoops to Bingo Palaces: Louise Erdrich's Carnivalesque Fiction," in The Chippewa Landscape of Louise Erdrich, ed. Allan Chavkin (Tuscaloosa: U of Alabama P, 99); rev of, The Pathless Forest: John Gardner's Literary Protect, by Bo G. Ekelund, and A Dream of Peace: Art and Death in the Fiction of John Gardner, by Ronald Grant Nutter, "Gardner Studies," Papers on Lang Lit, (99); auth, "W(h)ither Gardner Studies?" Essays on John Gardner, ed. Tim Fessenden, 99. **CONTACT ADDRESS** Dept English, Daemen Col, 4380 Main St, Buffalo, NY 14226-3544. **EMAIL** rmorace@daemen.edu

MORAGNE E SILVA, MICHELE
PERSONAL Born 05/23/1955, White Plains, NY, m, 1983, 2 children **DISCIPLINE** ENGLISH **EDUCATION** Bucknell Univ, BA, 77; Rhode Island Col, MEd, 81; Univ Tex, PhD, 91. **CAREER** Instr, Am Lang Inst, 78-79; Instr, Rhode Island Col, 80-83; Asst Instr, Univ Tex, 84-85; Asst Prof, St Edwards Univ, 85-. **HONORS AND AWARDS** Phi Kappa Phi; Kappa Delta Pi; Family Develop Grant, St Edwards Univ, 86-87, 93-94, 97-99. **MEMBERSHIPS** CCC, TESOL, NCTE. **RESEARCH** Writing processes, second language writing. **SELECTED PUBLICATIONS** Auth, "A Study of Composing in a First and Second Language," Tex Papers in For Lang Educ, vol 1, no 2 (88): 132-151; auth, "First and Second Language Composing Processes Across Tasks," Eric Document, no ed350847 (92). **CONTACT ADDRESS** Dept Humanities, St. Edward's Univ, 3001 S Congress Ave, Austin, TX 78704-6425. **EMAIL** michelem@admin.stedwards.edu

MORAN, BARBARA B.
PERSONAL Born 07/08/1944, Columbus, MS, m, 1965, 2 children **DISCIPLINE** LIBRARY SCIENCE **EDUCATION** Mount Holyoke Col, AB, 66; Emory Univ, M Ln, 73; SUNY, Buffalo, PhD, 82. **CAREER** Grad asst, 72-73, Woodruff Grad Libr, Emory Univ; libr head & dir, audiovisual svc, 74-78, Park Schl Buffalo; intern, 80, office of head Lockwood Mem Libr SUNY, Buffalo; tchng asst, 80-81, Schl of Info & Libr Stud, SUNY; asst prof, 81-87, assoc prof & asst dean, 87-90, dean & prof, 90-98, prof, 99-, Schl of Info & Libr Sci, Univ N C, Chapel Hill. **MEMBERSHIPS** Am Library Assoc, Assoc of Library and Information Sci Edu. **RESEARCH** Organizational leadership, organizational restructuring, career progression patterns **SELECTED PUBLICATIONS** Coauth, Library and Information Center Management, 5th ed, 98; numerous other books and articles. **CONTACT ADDRESS** Sch of Information & Library Sci, Univ of No Carolina, Chapel Hill, CB# 3360, 100 Manning Hall, Chapel Hill, NC 27599-3360. **EMAIL** moran@ils.unc.edu

MORAN, CHARLES
PERSONAL Born 11/06/1936, New York, NY, m, 1964, 2 children **DISCIPLINE** ENGLISH LITERATURE, WRITING **EDUCATION** Princeton Univ, AB, 58; Brown Univ, PhD(English), 67. **CAREER** Co-dir, Western Mass Writing Proj; actg chmn, 78-81, assoc prof English, Univ Mass, Amherst, 67-, dir Writing Prog, 82-, dir, Nat Endowment for the Humanities Inst Teaching Writing, Univ Mass, Amherst, 78-82; vis prof, State Univ NY Albany, 81-82. **HONORS AND AWARDS** Distinguished Teacher Awd, 90; Computers & Composition; Pres, Awd for Public Service, 98; NEATE Outstanding Teacher Awd, 99. **MEMBERSHIPS** MLA; Col English Asn; Nat Coun Teacher English; New England Asn Teachers English. **RESEARCH** The teaching of writing; emerging technologies' implications for the teaching of writing. **SELECTED PUBLICATIONS** Co-ed (with Kathleen Kroll), The letters of Herman White, Mass Rev, Summer 77; auth, Orwell, Jaws and McKuen: A case for good writing, Col English Asn Forum, 2/80; Teaching writing/teaching literature, Col Compos & Commun, 2/80; Hanging out the shingle: The writing tutor, J English Teaching Techniques, Winter 80; Turnpike poem: For Mina, Col Compos & Commun, 10/80; coauth (with Joseph T Skerrett, Jr), English Departments and the in-service training of teachers, Col Eng, 4/81; The secondary-level writing laboratory: A report from the field, In: Tutoring Writing, Scott Foresman, 82; New compos texts: The anatomy of process, Rev & Proc Community Col Humanities Asn, 2/82; co-ed, Writing, Learning, and Teaching in the Disciplines, MLA (New York), 92; Computers and the Teaching of Writing in American Higher Education, 79-94; coauth, Norwood, NJ: Ablex, 96. **CONTACT ADDRESS** Dept of English, Univ of Massachusetts, Amherst, Amherst, MA 01003-0515. **EMAIL** cmoran@english.umass.edu

MORAN, MARY H.
PERSONAL Born 05/01/1947, Boston, MA, m, 1977, 1 child **DISCIPLINE** ENGLISH **EDUCATION** Brown Univ, BA, 69; Univ NMex, MA, 75, PhD, 80. **CAREER** Asst prof, English, Clemson Univ, 82-86; teach to Assoc prof, Univ Ga, 88-. **HONORS AND AWARDS** Best Essay, Carolinas Symp on Brit Stud, 89; NEH Panelist, 98. **MEMBERSHIPS** S Atlantic MLA; Ga/SC Col English Assoc; Nat Asn of Devel Educ. **RESEARCH** Contemporary British Novel; composition & rhetoric; developmental writing. **SELECTED PUBLICATIONS** Auth, Penelope Lively, Twayne, 93; auth, James Burgh, Eighteenth-Century British and American Rhetorics and Rhetoricians, Greenwood Press, 36-41, 94; auth, The Role of Reading Aloud in the Composing Process, Selected Conf Papers from the 20th Ann NADE Conf, 29-30; auth, The Novels of Penelope Lively: A Case for the Continuity of the Experimental Impulse in Postwar British Fiction, S Atl Rev, 1.62, 101-20; auth, Connections Between Reading and Successful Revision, J of Basic Writing, 16.2, 76-89, 97; auth, Mina Shaughnessy, Twentieth-Century Rhetorics and Rhetoricians, Greenwood Press, (in press). **CONTACT ADDRESS** Div Acad Asst, Univ of Georgia, Athens, GA 30602. **EMAIL** mhmoran@arches.uga.edu

MORAN, MICHAEL G.
PERSONAL Born 03/21/1947, Ft. Benning, GA, m, 1977, 1 child **DISCIPLINE** ENGLISH LITERATURE **EDUCATION** City Col NYork, BA, 71; Univ New Mexico, MA, 73, PhD, 78. **CAREER** Asst prof English, Clemson Univ, 80-86; assoc prof English, Univ Rhode Island, 86-88; assoc prof English, Univ Georgia, 88- . **HONORS AND AWARDS** Natl Coun Tchrs of English res award, 86; NEH Summer Inst, 89; Newberry Lib/Columbian Quincentennial Fel, 89; GA-SC Col English Asn res award, 91; GA-SC Col English Asn Teacher/Scholar of the Year, 95. **MEMBERSHIPS** Conf on Col Composition and Commun. **RESEARCH** History of rhetoric and composition; history of technical communication. **SELECTED PUBLICATIONS** Co-ed, Research in Composition and Rhetoric, Greenwood, 84; co-ed, Research in Technical Communication, Greenwood, 85; co-ed, Research in Basic Writing, Greenwood, 90; ed, British and American Rhetorics and Rhetoricians, Greenwood, 94; co-ed, Four Keys to the Past, Ablex, 99. **CONTACT ADDRESS** Dept of English, Univ of Georgia, Athens, GA 30602. **EMAIL** mgmoran@arches.uga.edu

MORANT, MACK BERNARD
PERSONAL Born 10/15/1946, Holly Hill, SC, s **DISCIPLINE** ENGLISH **EDUCATION** Voorhees College, Denmark, SC, BS, business administration, 1968; University of Massachusetts, Amherst, MA, MEd Urban Education, 1972, CAGS, education administration, 1973, EdD, 1976. **CAREER** Belcher Town State School, mental health assistant I, 74-76; University Masachusetts, graduate student, research assistant, 71-74; South Carolina Public School System, history, English, business teacher, 68-71; Dillion-Marion Human Resources Comm, deputy director, 77-81; South Carolina State College, Orangeburg, SC, director small business development ct, 82-85; Virginia State University, Petersburg, VA, placement director, 85-92; Augusta College, assistant professor, teacher, Georgia, 92-96; Voorhees College, student support services program, dir, 97-; Keyboarding and Business Law, Allendale Public School, 99; Computer Tech and Business Law, Barnwell Public School, 00-. **MEMBERSHIPS** Vice-chairman, Virginia State University Assessment Committee, 1986-87; member, Prince Hall Mason, 1986-; member, American Philatelic Society, 1988-; member, Alpha Kappa Psi Fraternity, 1985-. **SELECTED PUBLICATIONS** SPA Articles Include: "Identifying and Evaluation of Black History in Textbooks," The Journal of Secondary School Principals News; "The Gigantic Asylumn," The Carolina Messenger, 1977; "Blues, Jazz, and American Blacks," The Chronicle of Higher Education, 1978; The Insane Nigger, R&M Publishing Co, 1979; Publications include "Demystification of Blackness," Exploration in Education, South Carolina State College, 1983; "Bookselling: Direct Mail Marketing," Interlit, Dec, 1991; Upcoming Book African American on Stamps, McFarland Publishers, 2000. **CONTACT ADDRESS** Publisher, R&M Publishing Co, PO Box 1276, Holly Hill, SC 29059. **EMAIL** mackattack07319@cs.com

MOREHEAD, JOSEPH HYDE
PERSONAL Born 01/30/1931, New York, NY, m, 1966, 1 child **DISCIPLINE** LIBRARY EDUCATION **EDUCATION** Univ Calif-Berkeley, BA, MA, MLS, EdD, 73. **CAREER** Prof, Sch Info Sci & Policy, Univ Albany, 70-. **HONORS AND AWARDS** Phi Beta Kappa, Trinity Col, Hartford, CT, 51; Salutatorian, Honors in English, Trinity Col, 52; Sustained Superior Performance Award, U.S. Civil Service Commission, U.S. Dept of the Air Force, London, 61; Haggin Fel, Univ of KY, 63-64; First recipient, CIS/GODORT/ALA Documents to the People Award, 77; first recipient, Outstanding Alumnus Award, Univ of KY Col of Libr and Information Sciences, 84; Who's Who in the East, 86-87; James Bennet Childs Award, GODORT, Am Libr Asn, 89; Isadore Gilbert Mudge-R.R. Bowker Award, Am Libr Asn, 96. **MEMBERSHIPS** Am Libr Asn. **RESEARCH** Access to governmentt information as a First Right Amendment. **SELECTED PUBLICATIONS** Auth, Theory and Practice in Library Education: The Teaching-Learning Process, Libr Unlimited (Littleton, CO), 80; auth, Introduction to United States Public Documents, 3rd ed, Libr Unlimited, 83; auth, Essays on Public Documents and Government Policies, Haworth Press (NY), 86; auth, Introduction to United States Government Information Sources, 6th ed, Libr Unlimited, 99; more than 170 articles. **CONTACT ADDRESS** Sch Info Sci & Policy, SUNY, Albany, Albany, NY 12222. **EMAIL** jhm@albany.edu

MORELAND, RICHARD
PERSONAL Born 06/14/1953, New Orleans, LA, m, 1976, 2 children **DISCIPLINE** AMERICAN LITERATURE **EDUCATION** Univ Calif, Berkeley, PhD, 87. **CAREER** Assoc prof, dir, grad stud Eng, La State Univ. **HONORS AND AWARDS** Leverhulme Commonwealth/USA vis fel, Univ Wales, Swan-

sea, 91-92. **MEMBERSHIPS** MLA. **RESEARCH** Cross-cultural encounters; critical theory; W. Faulkner. **SELECTED PUBLICATIONS** Auth, Humor, Rage, and Anti-Semitism in Faulkner's Hamlet, Faulkner J, 87; Compulsory and Revisionary Repetition: Faulkner's 'Barn Burning' and the Craft of Writing Difference, in Faulkner and the Craft of Fiction, 89; Faulkner and Modernism: Rereading and Rewriting, 90; 'He Wants to Put His Story Next to Hers': Putting Twain's Story Next to Hers in Toni Morrison's Beloved, Mod Fiction Stud, 93; Teaching Cross-Cultural Encounters and Student Writing with Question- Hypothesis-Questions (QHQs), in Teaching a "New Canon?", 95; Faulkner and Modernism, in Cambridge Companion to Faulkner Studies, 95; coauth, A Continuity in the Southern White Dilemma: Would Huck Finn Vote for David Duke?," in Borderlines: Studies in American Culture, 94; auth, Learning from Difference: Teaching Morrison, Twain, Ellison, and Eliot, 99. **CONTACT ADDRESS** Dept of Eng, Louisiana State Univ, Baton Rouge, LA 70803. **EMAIL** enmore@lsu.edu

MOREY, JAMES
DISCIPLINE ENGLISH LANGUAGE AND LITERATURE **EDUCATION** Hamilton Univ, AB, 83; Cornell Univ, MA, 87; PhD, 90. **CAREER** Fac, Tex Tech Univ; assoc prof/dir undergrad studies, Emory Univ, 94-. **HONORS AND AWARDS** Fulbright scholar, 87-88. **RESEARCH** Old and Middle English, including Chaucer; Old French and Old Norse literature; Renaissance literature with a concentration on religious literature and the vernacular Bible. **SELECTED PUBLICATIONS** Auth, articles in Speculum, JEGP, Studies in Philol, Chaucer Rev, Spenser Studies, and Shakespeare Quart; auth, A Guide to Middle English Biblical Literature, 00. **CONTACT ADDRESS** English Dept, Emory Univ, 1380 Oxford Rd NE, Atlanta, GA 30322-1950. **EMAIL** jmorey@emory.edu

MORGAN, BETSY
DISCIPLINE US LITERATURE **EDUCATION** PhD. **CAREER** Eastern Col **SELECTED PUBLICATIONS** Areas: El Salvador; Justice issues. **CONTACT ADDRESS** Eastern Col, 1300 Eagle Rd, Saint Davids, PA 19087-3696.

MORGAN, EILEEN M.
DISCIPLINE ENGLISH AND IRISH STUDIES **EDUCATION** Colgate Univ, BA, 89; Ind Univ, MA, 92; PhD, 98. **CAREER** Lectr, Univ Mich, 98-00; asst prof, SUNY Onconta, 00-. **HONORS AND AWARDS** James A Work Grad Studies Award, 96; Seed Grant, Univ Mich, 00; Fac Develop Grant, 00; Individual Develop Award, SUNY Onconta, 01. **MEMBERSHIPS** MLA; ACIS. **RESEARCH** Irish radio broadcasting; Edna O'Brien; 20th Century British literature; Irish-American literature (ethnicity studies). **SELECTED PUBLICATIONS** Auth, "Ireland's Lost Action Hero, or, Michael Collins, A Secret History of Irish masculinity," New Hibernia Rev, (98): 26-42; auth, "Mapping Out a Landscape of Female Suffering: Edna O'Brien's Demythologizing Novels," Women's Studies; An Interdisciplinary J, (00): 449-476; auth, "Rethinking the Abbey and the Concept of a National Theatre," in A Century of Irish Drama: Widening the Stage, (Bloomington, 01), xi-xxvii; auth, "Question Time: Radio and the Liberalization of Public Discourse in Ireland after WW2," History Ireland, (forthcoming). **CONTACT ADDRESS** Dept English, SUNY, Col at Oneonta, 85 Spruce St, Oneonta, NY 13820-1549. **EMAIL** morgane@onconta.edu

MORGAN, KATHRYN A.
PERSONAL Born 04/15/1962, Montreal, PQ, Canada, m **DISCIPLINE** CLASSICS **EDUCATION** Univ Calif, Berkeley, PhD, 91. **CAREER** Asst prof classics, Ohio State Univ, 91-95; asst to assoc prof classics, Univ Calif, Los Angeles, 95- . **HONORS AND AWARDS** Jr fel, Ctr for Hellenic Stud, 95-96; Visiting Sr Res Fel, Jesus Col, Oxford, 99-00; George A. and Eliza Gardner Howard Found Fel, 99-00; Univ of Calif President's Res Fel in the Humanities, 99-00. **MEMBERSHIPS** APA. **RESEARCH** Archaic and classical Greek literature; intellectual history; archaeology. **SELECTED PUBLICATIONS** Coauth, A Trophy from the Battle of Chaironeia of 86 BC, Am J of Archaeol, 92; auth, "Pindar the Professional an dthe Rehtoric of the komos," Classical Philology 88, (93): 1-15; auth, Socrates and Gorgias at Delphi and Olympia, Phaedrus 235d6-236b4, Class Q, 94; auth, Apollo's Favorites, Greek, Roman, and Byzantine Stud, 94; coauth, An Athenian Dedication to Herakles at Panopeus, Hesperia, 97; auth, "Designer History: Plato's Atlantis Story and Fourth-Century Ideology," Journal for Hellenic Studies 118, (98): 101-118; auth, Myth and Philosophy form the Presocratics to Plato, Cambridge Univ Press, 00. **CONTACT ADDRESS** Classics Dept, Univ of California, Los Angeles, Dodd 100, 141702, PO Box 951417, Los Angeles, CA 90095-1417. **EMAIL** kmorgan@humnet.ucla.edu

MORGAN, LYLE W., II
PERSONAL Born 04/05/1947, Fremont, NE **DISCIPLINE** ENGLISH EDUCATION **EDUCATION** Doane Col, AB; M. Ed., Fla State Christian Col, MEd; Wayne State Col, MAE, MSE; University Nebr, PhD. **CAREER** Prof. **HONORS AND AWARDS** Fcollp, Col of Teachers, UK. **MEMBERSHIPS** NCTE, CCCC, KATE. **RESEARCH** Late 19th and early 20th Century British fiction, Thomas Haizdn. **SELECTED PUBLICATIONS** Auth, The Homeopathic Treatment of Sports Injuries, 86; Homeopathic Medicine and Emergency Care, 90; Treating Sports Injuries the Natural Way, 84; Homeopathy and Your Child, 92; articles on bk censorship; bk rev(s). **CONTACT ADDRESS** Dept of Eng, Pittsburg State Univ, 1701 S Broadway St, Pittsburg, KS 66762. **EMAIL** lmorgan@pittstate.edu

MORI, AKANE
DISCIPLINE MUSIC **EDUCATION** Toho Gakuen Sch Music, BA; Yale Univ, MA, PhD. **CAREER** Former lectr music theory, Yale Univ; Hartt. 1994-. **SELECTED PUBLICATIONS** Auth, In Theory Only & Jour of Music Theory **CONTACT ADDRESS** Hartt Sch Music, Univ of Hartford, 200 Bloomfield Ave, West Hartford, CT 06117.

MORISON, WILLIAM S.
PERSONAL Born 05/15/1965, Fresno, CA, m, 1997, 1 child **DISCIPLINE** CLASSICS, HISTORY **EDUCATION** Calif State Univ Fresno, BA, 87; MA, 90; BA, 91; Univ Calif Santa Barb, MA, 93; PhD, 98. **CAREER** Vis asst prof, Univ Calif, 98-99; vis asst prof, Utah State Univ, 99-00; vis asst prof, Temple Univ, 00-01; vis asst prof, Grand Val State Univ, 01. **HONORS AND AWARDS** Univ Calif Reg Fel, 91-92, 96-97; John Patrick Sullivan Trav Fel, 93-94; ASCS Fel, 93-94. **MEMBERSHIPS** APA; AAH. **RESEARCH** Classical Athens; critias; epigraphy; philosophy. **SELECTED PUBLICATIONS** Auth, "An Honorary Deme Decree and the Administration of a Palaistra in Kephissia," Zeits fur Papyr Epigr 131 (00); auth, "Attic Gymnasia and Palaistrai: Public or Private?," Ancient World 31 (00); co-auth, "An Encomium on the Life of Saint Theognius, Bishop of Bethelia by Paul of Elusa," Cist Stud Qtly 30 (95); rev, Plutarch: Greek Lives (Oxford, 98) and Plutarch: Roman Lives, trans by R. Waterfield (Oxford, 99) Ploutarchos 17 (00); auth, "Critias," Internet Encycl Philo (00); auth, "Lyceum," Internet Encycl Philo (00). **CONTACT ADDRESS** Dept Hist, Grand Valley State Univ, 1121 Au Sable Hall, Allendale, MI 49010. **EMAIL** wmorison@gvsu.edu

MORLEY, PATRICIA
PERSONAL Born 05/25/1929, Toronto, ON, Canada **DISCIPLINE** ENGLISH **EDUCATION** Univ Toronto, BA, 51; Carleton Univ, MA, 67; Univ Ottawa, PhD, 70; Univ Sudbury, DSLitt, 92. **CAREER** Asst prof, Sir George Williams Univ, 72-75; assoc prof, 75-80, prof Eng & Can Stud, 80-89, Prof Emer, Concordia Univ, 92-; fel, Lonergan Univ Col, 79-84; fel, 79-88, assoc fel, 88-89, lifetime hon fel, Simone de Beauvoir Inst, 89-. **HONORS AND AWARDS** Ottawa Citizen Awd Non-fiction, 87; Ottawa-Carleton Lit Awd, 88, 91; Can Council Non-fiction Awd, 91. **MEMBERSHIPS** Manotick Art Asn; Writers Union Can; Can Asn Commonwealth Lang & Lit Stud. **RESEARCH** Canadian literature **SELECTED PUBLICATIONS** Auth, The Mystery of Unity: Theme and Technique in the Novels of Patrick White, 72; auth, The Immoral Moralists: Hugh MacLennan and Leonard Cohen, 72; auth, Roberston Davies, 76; auth, The Commedians: Hugh Hood and Rudy Wiebe, 77; auth, Morley Callaghen, 78; auth, Margaret Laurence: The Long Journey Home, 91; auth, As Though Life Mattered: Leo Kennedy's Story, 94; ed, Ernest Thompson Seton: Selected Stories, 78. **CONTACT ADDRESS** PO Box 137, Manotick, ON, Canada K4M 1A2.

MORNIN, EDWARD
PERSONAL Born 11/27/1938, Greenock, Scotland, m, 1963, 2 children **DISCIPLINE** MODERN GERMAN LITERATURE **EDUCATION** Univ Glasgow, MA, 61, PhD(Ger), 69. **CAREER** Lectr English, Univ Cologne, Ger, 63-64; instr Ger, 65-68, asst prof, 68-77, Assoc Prof Ger, Univ BC, 77-. **MEMBERSHIPS** Can Asn Univ Teachers Ger; Can Comp Lit Asn; MacKay- Gesellschaft. **RESEARCH** German Romanticism 19th century; JH Mackay, lit, literary anarchism, Scottish - German literary links, literary thematology. **SELECTED PUBLICATIONS** Auth, "National subjects in the works of Achim von Arnim," German Life and Letters, N.S., 2, (71): 316-27; auth, "Some patriotic novels and tales by la Motte Fouque," Seminar, 11, (75): 141-156; transl, Outpourings of an Art-Loving Friar, Wilhelm Heinrich Wackenroder und Ludwig Tieck, Ungar: New York, 75; auth, Die schone Magelone, Ludwig Tieck, Reclam: Stuttgart, 75; Rev, "Taking games seriously, Observations on the German sports novel," Germanic Review, 51, 76; auth, "Art an dalienation in Tieck's Franz Sternbalds Wanderungen," MLN, 94, (79): 510-23; Rev, "Tieck's revision of Franz Sternbalds Wanderungen," Seminar, 15, (79): 79-96; auth, Kunst und Anarchismus: "innere Zusammenhange" in den Schriften John Henry Mackays, Mackay-Gesellschaft: Freiburg, 83; auth, John Henry Mackay, Die gedachte Welt: Ein Roman und drei Geschichten aus dem Nachlab. Peter Lang Verlag: Frankfurt, Bern, New York and Paris, 89. **CONTACT ADDRESS** Dept of Germanic Studies, Univ of British Columbia, 1873 E Mall Buchanan Tower 222, Vancouver, BC, Canada V6T 1Z1. **EMAIL** mornin@interchange.ubc.ca

MORRAL, FRANK R.
PERSONAL Born 04/07/1937, Vanersborg, Sweden, m, 1961, 5 children **DISCIPLINE** ENGLISH **EDUCATION** Whitman Col, AB, 59; Columbia Univ, AM, 60, PhD(English), 65; Col of St Thomas, MA, 80. **CAREER** Instr English, Whitman Col, 62-64; from instr to assoc prof, 64-75, Prof English, Carleton Col, 76-. **RESEARCH** Shakespeare; 16th century literature; James Joyce. **CONTACT ADDRESS** 1 N College St, Northfield, MN 55057-4044.

MORRIS, BERNARD E.
PERSONAL Born 07/25/1935, San Antonio, TX, m, 1998, 1 child **DISCIPLINE** ENGLISH LITERATURE **EDUCATION** Univ Calif, Berkeley, BA, 62; MA, 63; PhD, 73. **CAREER** Assoc prof, Univ of Calif, Berkeley, 65-72. **RESEARCH** Poetry and prose. **CONTACT ADDRESS** Div Lang and Lit, Modesto Junior Col, 435 College Ave, Modesto, CA 95350-5808. **EMAIL** bemsil@pacbell.net

MORRIS, DAVID B.
PERSONAL Born 08/11/1942, New York, NY, m, 1979, 1 child **DISCIPLINE** EIGHTEENTH CENTURY ENGLISH LITERATURE **EDUCATION** Hamilton Col, BA, 64; Univ Minn, PhD, 68. **CAREER** Asst prof, Univ of Va, 69-72; assoc prof, Am Univ, 72-74; prof, Univ of Iowa, 74-82. **HONORS AND AWARDS** Frank Ristine Prize, 63; NDEA Fel, 68; Grant, Am Philos Soc, 71; SAMLA Studies Awd, 72; NEH Fel, 72-73; Guggenheim Fel, 76-77; ACLS Fel, 80-81; NSF/NEH Awd, 82-83, 86, 87; Gottschalk Prize, 85; PEN Spielvogel/Diamonstein Awd, 92; Phi Beta Kappa, 00. **MEMBERSHIPS** Am Pain Soc, Int Assoc for the Study of Pain. **RESEARCH** Alexander Pope; history of criticism; eighteenth century literature. **SELECTED PUBLICATIONS** Auth, The Religious Sublime: Christian Poetry and Critical Tradition in 18th-Century England, 72; auth, Alexander Pope: the Genius of Sense, Harvard Univ Pr, 84; auth, the Culture of Pain, Univ of Calif Pr, 91; auth, Earth Warrior, Fulcrum Publ, 95; auth, Illness and Culture in the Postmodern Age, Univ of Calif Pr, 98. **CONTACT ADDRESS** 4908 Northern Tr NW, Albuquerque, NM 87120-2027. **EMAIL** dbmkirk@aol.com

MORRIS, FRANCIS J.
DISCIPLINE MEDIEVAL BRITISH; MODERN BRITISH; LITERARY **EDUCATION** Saint Joseph's Col, AB, 58, Columbia Univ, MA, 60; Univ PA, PhD, 77. **CAREER** Engl, St. Joseph's Univ. **SELECTED PUBLICATIONS** Auth, Platonic Elements in Chaucer's Parliament of Fowles, PCTE Journal 4, 77; In Critical Survey of Literary Theory, Salem, 88. **CONTACT ADDRESS** Saint Joseph's Univ, 5600 City Ave, Philadelphia, PA 19131. **EMAIL** fmorris@sju.edu

MORRIS, HARRY
PERSONAL Born 08/09/1924, New York, NY, m, 1949, 2 children **DISCIPLINE** ENGLISH **EDUCATION** Univ Miami, AB, 49, AM, 50; Univ Minn, PhD, 57. **CAREER** Teaching fel English, Ind Univ, 52-55; instr, Ohio Univ, 55-56; from instr to asst prof, Tulane Univ, 56-61; from asst prof to assoc prof, 61-67, Prof English, Fla State Univ, 67-, Folger Libr fel, 58. **MEMBERSHIPS** MLA; S Atlantic Mod Lang Asn Res; Renaissance and modern poetry. **RESEARCH** Medieval and renaissance eschatology. **SELECTED PUBLICATIONS** Co-auth, Poetry: A critical and historical introduction, Scott, 62; auth, Richard Barnfield: Colin' child, Fla State Univ; The Snake Hunter, Univ GA, 69; 'Duesenberg, 1929', Poetry, Vol 0165, 1994; 'On The Plight Of Us In The Caravaggio', Kenyon Review, Vol 0016, 1994; 'Sometimes, Late', Antioch Review, Vol 0052, 1994. **CONTACT ADDRESS** Dept of English, Florida State Univ, Tallahassee, FL 32306.

MORRIS, IAN
DISCIPLINE CLASSICS **EDUCATION** BA, 81; Cambridge Univ, PhD, 86. **CAREER** Ch dept class and prof class/hist, Stanford Univ. **RESEARCH** Greek hist; archaeol. **SELECTED PUBLICATIONS** Auth, Death-Ritual and Social Structure in Classical Antiquity, 92; Classical Greece: Ancient History and Modern Archaeologies, 94. **CONTACT ADDRESS** Stanford Univ, Bldg 20, Main Quad, Stanford, CA 94305.

MORRIS, PAUL
PERSONAL Born 09/22/1951, Pomona, CA **DISCIPLINE** COMPUTER-ASSISTED WRITING INSTRUCTION **EDUCATION** Univ Calif Davis, BA; Univ Nev, MA, PhD. **CAREER** Asst prof **RESEARCH** Creative writing, popular culture, American literature; computers and composition. **SELECTED PUBLICATIONS** Auth, The New Literacy: Moving Beyond the 3Rs, 96; two articles about Vietnam; rev, Unforgiven. **CONTACT ADDRESS** Dept of Eng, Pittsburg State Univ, 1701 S Broadway St, Pittsburg, KS 66762. **EMAIL** smorris@pittstate.edu

MORRIS, VIRGINIA BAUMGARTNER
PERSONAL Born 03/28/1942, Ballston Spa, NY, m, 1970, 2 children **DISCIPLINE** ENGLISH & IRISH LITERATURE **EDUCATION** Beaver Col, BA, 64; Columbia Univ, MA, 66, PhD(English), 73. **CAREER** Asst prof, 67-76, Assoc Prof English, John Jay Col Criminal Justice, 76- **MEMBERSHIPS** MLA; Renaissance Soc Am; Acja. **RESEARCH** Sixteenth century English literature; Irish literary Renaissance; Crime and Punishment in literature. **SELECTED PUBLICATIONS** International Perspectives On Social And Policy Issues - Introduction, J Of Arts Management Law And Society, Vol 0026, 1997. **CONTACT ADDRESS** John Jay Col of Criminal Justice, CUNY, 445 W 59th St, New York, NY 10019.

MORRISON, JAMES V.
PERSONAL Born 02/26/1956, New York, NY, m, 1982, 3 children **DISCIPLINE** CLASSICS **EDUCATION** Oberlin Col, BA; Univ Wash, MA; Univ Mich, PhD. **CAREER** Vis fac, Davidson Col; vis fac, Georgetown Univ; fac, Centre Col, 93-; assoc prof, current. **HONORS AND AWARDS** NEH Pres, 00-02. **MEMBERSHIPS** APA; CAMWS. **RESEARCH** Homer and ancient epic; Greek literature and philosophy; late republican and Augustan literature; history and classical tradition in 20th-century literature and culture; Derek Walcott's poetry and drama. **SELECTED PUBLICATIONS** Auth, Homeric Misdirection: False Predictions in the Iliad, Univ Mich Press, 92; contribur, Latomus, Jour Am Cult, Relig Studies Rev. **CONTACT ADDRESS** Centre Col, 600 W Walnut St, Danville, KY 40422. **EMAIL** morrison@centre.edu

MORRISON, ROBERT R.
PERSONAL Born 08/01/1929, Gainesville, FL, m, 1951, 2 children **DISCIPLINE** DRAMA **EDUCATION** George Washington Univ, AB, 50; Middlebury Col, MA, 54; Univ Fla, PhD, 63. **CAREER** Asst to assoc prof, E Car Univ, 58-67; director, NDEA Inst, 65, 67; prof, Southern Adventist Univ, 67-87; assoc prof, Presbyterian Col, 88-94. **MEMBERSHIPS** MLA, SAMLA, AATSP, Comediantes. **RESEARCH** Spanish Golden Age Drama, French 17th Century Drama. **SELECTED PUBLICATIONS** Auth, "Deliberate Choice as One Reason for the Scarcity of Early Castilian Dramatic Texts," Bull of the Comediantes 41, (89): 211-216; auth, "Graciosos con Breviarios: The Comic Element in the 'Comedia de Santos' of Lope de Vega," Critica Hispanica 12, (90): 33-45; auth, Lope de Vega and the Comedia de Santos, Peter Lang, (NY), 00. **CONTACT ADDRESS** PO Box 475, Collegedale, TN 37315-0475.

MORRISON, SIMON
PERSONAL Born 12/30/1964, London, England, m, 1995 **DISCIPLINE** MUSIC HISTORY **EDUCATION** Univ Toronto, BM, 87; McGill Univ, MA, 93; Princeton Univ, MFA, 94, PhD, 97. **CAREER** Asst prof, lectr, Princeton Univ, 97-. **HONORS AND AWARDS** Charlotte Elizabeth Proctor Hon Fel, 95; Am Musicol Soc Diss Fel 96; Alfred Einstein Awd of the Am Musicological Soc, 99. **MEMBERSHIPS** Am Musicol Soc; Col Mus Soc; Am Asn Teachers of Slavic and East Europ Lang; Soc of Dance Hist Scholars. **RESEARCH** Russian 19th and 20th Century Music, French and Russian Symbolism, Neoclassicism, Ballet **SELECTED PUBLICATIONS** Skryabin and the Impossible, Jour Am Musicol Soc 51:2, (98): 201-48; auth, Skryabin and the Impossible, Journal of the Am Musicological Soc, 51:2, (98): 283-330. **CONTACT ADDRESS** Princeton Univ, Woolworth Bldg, Princeton, NJ 08544. **EMAIL** simonm@phoenix.princeton.edu

MORRISON, TONI
PERSONAL Born 02/18/1931, Lorain, OH, d, 2 children **DISCIPLINE** ENGLISH LITERATURE, CREATIVE WRITING **EDUCATION** Howard Univ, BA, 53; Cornell Univ, MA, 55. **CAREER** Tchr, Engl, Texas Southern Univ, 55-57; tchr, Howard Univ, 57-63; assoc ed, Syracuse, 64-66; sr ed, Random House, 67-83; assoc prof English, SUNY Purchase, 71-72; vis lectr, Yale Univ, 76-77; Albert Schweitzer Prof Hum, SUNY Albany, 84- ; Robert F. Goheen Prof, Coun of Hum, Princeton Univ, 87- . **HONORS AND AWARDS** Nobel Prize, Literature; Natl Book Critic's Circle Awd; Am Acad and Inst of Arts and Lett Awd; Natl Coun of the Arts; Pulitzer Prize, 88; auth, the bluest eye, 70; sula, 73; song of solomon, 77; tar baby, 81; dreaming emmett, 86; beloved, 87; jazz, 92; the dancing mind, 97; paradise, 98. **CONTACT ADDRESS** Random House, 201 East 50th St, New York, NY 10022.

MORRISSEY, LEE J.
PERSONAL Born 08/21/1964, Boston, MA **DISCIPLINE** ENGLISH LITERATURE **EDUCATION** Columbia Univ, MA, 88; MA, 90; MPhil, 92; PhD, 95. **CAREER** From asst prof to assoc prof, Clemson Univ, 95-. **HONORS AND AWARDS** Presidential Fel, Columbia Univ, 90-92; Mellon Summer Dissertation Fel, 93. **MEMBERSHIPS** MLA, ASECS. **RESEARCH** Eighteenth-Century British Literature, Literary Theory. **SELECTED PUBLICATIONS** Ed & contribur, The Kitchen Turns Twenty: A Retrospective Anthology, The Kitchen, 92; auth, "Robinson Crusoe and the South Sea Trade: 1710-1720," Money: Lure, Lore, and Literature, Greenwood Press (Westport, CT), 94; auth, "'Affectedly Unaffected': Eighteenth-Century Architectural Follies and Walpole's Castle of Otranto," Postmodern Perspectives on Eighteenth-Century Literature and Culture, Assoc Univ Presses, 98; auth, "Sexuality and Consumer Culture in Early Eighteenth Century England: 'Mutual Love from Pole to Pole' in Lillo's London Merchant," Restoration and Eighteenth-Century Theater Res 13.1 (98): 25-40; auth, "Derrida's 'Nostalgeria': A Post-Colonial Reading of 'Structure, Sign, and Play in the Discourse of the Human Sciences'," Postmodern Culture, (99); auth, From the Temple to the Castle: An Architectural History of English Literature 1660-1760, Univ Press of Va, 99; auth, "'Approach and read the stone': Toward an Archaelogy of Gray's Elegy," The Age of Johnson Vol 9 (forthcoming). **CONTACT ADDRESS** Dept English, Clemson Univ, 801 Strode Tower, PO Box 340523, Clemson, SC 29634-0523. **EMAIL** lmorris@clemson.edu

MORRISSEY, THOMAS J.
DISCIPLINE ENGLISH **EDUCATION** SUNY Binghamton, BA; MA; Rutgers Univ, PhD, 77. **CAREER** Col wrtg dir, Plattsburgh State Univ of NY . **HONORS AND AWARDS** Disting Tchg Prof, Plattsburgh State Univ of NY, 96; NY State Univ Chancellor's Awd Excellence Tchg, 91. **RESEARCH** Sci Fiction; Irish Lit. **SELECTED PUBLICATIONS** Auth, publ-(s) on writing pedag, Irish Lit, and Sci Fiction. **CONTACT ADDRESS** SUNY, Col at Plattsburgh, 101 Broad St, Plattsburgh, NY 12901-2681.

MORRISSON, MARK S.
DISCIPLINE ENGLISH **EDUCATION** Univ Tex, Austin, BA, 88; Univ Chicago, MA, 89, PhD, 96. **CAREER** ASST PROF ENG, PA STATE UNIV, UNIV PK, 96-. **CONTACT ADDRESS** Dept of English, Pennsylvania State Univ, Univ Park, 119 Burrows Bldg, University Park, PA 16802-6200.

MORROW, PATRICK D.
PERSONAL Born 10/01/1940, Inglewood, CA, d, 3 children **DISCIPLINE** LITERATURE **EDUCATION** Calif State Univ, AA, 61; Univ Southern Calif, AB, 63; Univ Wash, MA, 65; PhD, 69. **CAREER** Instr, Univ Wash, 68-69; asst prof, Univ Southern Calif, 69-75; assoc prof, Auburn Univ, 75-; tours for teaching and res, New Zealand, Australia, & Samoa, 81; tours for teaching & res, Fiji, Tonga, Oz, New Zealand, & the Cook Islands, 89. **HONORS AND AWARDS** Teaching & Res Fulbright Grants, 81, 89, & 95; Auburn Res Fel. **MEMBERSHIPS** SAMLA, AAALS, MLA, Fulbright Asn. **RESEARCH** Colonialism and Postcolonialism, particularly in the South Pacific. **SELECTED PUBLICATIONS** Auth, Bret Harte, Literary Critic, 79; auth, Tradition, Undercut, and Discovery: Essays on British Literature from Chaucer to Doris Lessing, 80; ed, Growing Up in North Dakota, 81; auth, The Popular and the Serious in Select Examples of American Fiction, 91; auth, Katherine Mansfield's Fiction, 93; auth, Postcolonial Essays of South Pacific Fiction, 98. **CONTACT ADDRESS** Dept English, Auburn Univ, Auburn, AL 36849-2900.

MORSBERGER, ROBERT E.
PERSONAL Born 09/10/1929, Baltimore, MD, m, 1955, 1 child **DISCIPLINE** ENGLISH **EDUCATION** Johns Hopkins Univ, BA, 50; Univ Iowa, MA, 54, PhD(English), 56. **CAREER** From instr to asst prof English, Miami Univ, 56-59; asst prof, Utah State Univ, 59-61; from asst prof to assoc prof Am Thought & Lang, Mich State Univ, 61-68; prof English, Eastern Ky Univ, 68-69; chmn dept, 74-78, prof English, Calif State Polytech Univ, Pomona, 69-, vis prof & adv, English, Mich State Univ-US Agency for Int Develop team, Univ Nigeria, 64-66; vis assoc prof, NMex State Univ, 67-68; adv Gloveville Proj, Nat Am Studies Fac, 73. **HONORS AND AWARDS** Winner of the Burkhardt Awd for Outstanding Steinbeck Scholarship. **MEMBERSHIPS** Am Studies Asn; Rocky Mountain Mod Lang Asn; Western Literature Asn; John Steinbeck Soc Am; Pen. **RESEARCH** American and African literature; motion pictures; popular culture; Eighteenth Century Studies. **SELECTED PUBLICATIONS** Auth, The language of composition, 65 & coauth, Commonsense grammar and style, 65, rev ed, 72, Crowell; ed, Essays in exposition: an international reader, Univ Nigeria & US Agency for Int Develop, 66; The Wilkes expedition: 1838-1842, Am Hist Illus, 6/72; The Minister's Black Veil: Shrouded in a blackness, ten times black, New Eng Quart, 9/73; ed, John Steinbeck, Viva Zapata!, Viking, 75; coauth, Lew Wallace: Militant Romantic, McGraw-Hill, 80; co-ed, 2 volumes on American Screenwriters in the Dictionary of Literary Biography, et al. **CONTACT ADDRESS** Dept of English and Mod Lang, California State Polytech Univ, Pomona, 3801 W Temple Ave, Pomona, CA 91768-4001. **EMAIL** remorsberger@csupomona.edu

MORSE, CHARLOTTE COOK
PERSONAL Born 10/26/1942, Washington, DC, d **DISCIPLINE** ENGLISH LITERATURE, MEDIEVAL STUDIES **EDUCATION** Brown Univ, AB, 64; Stanford Univ, MA, 68; PhD(English), 70. **CAREER** From instr to asst prof English, Yale Univ, 68-76, assoc prof to prof English, VA Commonwealth Univ, 76-; prog officer div res grants, Nat Endowment for Humanities, 75-76. **HONORS AND AWARDS** Leverhulme fel, 67-68; Morse fel, Yale Univ, 72-73; NEH fel, 82-83, 91-92; VCU Fmaily Res Leave, summer 82, 88, 91-92, summer 00. **MEMBERSHIPS** Early Bk Soc; Mediaeval Acad Am; MLA; Southeastern Medieval Asn; New Chaucer Soc. **RESEARCH** Middle English literature; Medieval intellectual history; Medieval and Renaissance drama. **SELECTED PUBLICATIONS** Auth, "The Image of the Vessel in Cleanness," Univ Toronto Quart 40 (71); auth, "The Pattern of Judgment in the 'Queste del Saint Graal' and 'Cleanness'," Univ Mo, 78; auth, "The Politics of Marriage: Power in Paradise?," Bk Forum 5 (80); auth, "Exemplary Griselda," Studies in the Age of Chaucer 7 (85); auth, "The Value of Editing the Clerk's Tale for the Variorum Chaucer," in Manuscripts and Texts (D.S. Brewer, 87); auth, "Critical Approaches to the 'Clerk's Tale'," in Chaucer's Religious Tales (Boydell and Brewer, 91); coed, contributor, The Uses of Manuscripts in Literary Studies: Essays in Memory of Judson Boyce Allen, Med Inst, 92; auth, "The Manuscripts of The 'Canterbury Tales'," Notes And Queries 40 (93); coed, contributor, Essays on Ricardian Literature in Honour of J.A. Burrow, Clarendon, 97. **CONTACT ADDRESS** Dept of English, Virginia Commonwealth Univ, Box 84, Richmond, VA 23284-2005. **EMAIL** cmorse@vcu.edu

MORSE, JONATHAN
PERSONAL Born 08/29/1940, New York, NY, 1 child **DISCIPLINE** AMERICAN LITERATURE **EDUCATION** Penn State Univ, BS, 62, MS, 65; Ind Univ, PhD, 75. **CAREER** Bacteriologist, Eli Lilly & Co, 64-69; from instr to asst prof English, Wayne State Univ, 73-77; from Asst Prof to Prof English, Univ Hawaii, Manoa, 77-. **MEMBERSHIPS** AAAS; AAUP; MLA; IAPL; Soc Critical Exchange; Emily Dickinson Int Soc. **RESEARCH** Literary history; literary criticism. **SELECTED PUBLICATIONS** Auth, Word by Word: The Language of Memory, Cornell Univ Press, 90; Typical Ashbery, In: The Tribe of John: John Ashbery and Contemporary Poetry, Univ Ala Press, 95; Some of the Things We Mean When We Say "New England", Emily Dickinson J 5.2, 96; Antisemitism as Discourse, H-Net list H-Antisemitism, 1/24/97; Six articles in: An Emily Dickinson Encyclopedia, Greenwood Press, 98; T.S. Eliot Says Jew, Am Lit Hist (in press); author of numerous other articles. **CONTACT ADDRESS** Dept of English, Univ of Hawaii, Manoa, 1733 Donaghho Rd, Honolulu, HI 96822-2368. **EMAIL** morsej001@hawaii.rr.com

MORSE, JOSIAH MITCHELL
PERSONAL Born 01/14/1912, Columbia, SC, m, 1936, 2 children **DISCIPLINE** ENGLISH **EDUCATION** Univ SC, AB, 32, MA, 33; Pa State Univ, PhD(English), 52. **CAREER** Reporter, Columbia Record, SC, 34; news ed, Am Banker, 35- 42; asst ed, The Nation, 43-45; UN correspondent, Free Press India, 46-47; from instr to prof, Pa State Univ, 48-67; prof, 67-79, Emer Prof English, Temple Univ, 79-, Am Coun Learned Soc fel, 51; Mem, Int Fed Mod Lang & Lit; bk rev ed, J Gen Educ, 60- 67; mem ed comt, Pmla, 70-74. **MEMBERSHIPS** MLA; Int Comp Lit Asn; Am Comp Lit Asn. **RESEARCH** James Joyce; comparative literature; problems of teaching English. **SELECTED PUBLICATIONS** Auth, The Sympathetic Alien, NY Univ, 59; Matters of style, Bobbs, 68; The irrelevant English teacher, 72 & Prejudice and Literature, 76, Temple Univ; Popular Science + Response To Johnson,Steven Article On The Vogue Of Chaos Theory Among Teachers Of Liberal-Arts, Lingua Franca, Vol 0006, 1996. **CONTACT ADDRESS** 115 Morris Rd, Ambler, PA 19002.

MORTENSEN, C. DAVID
DISCIPLINE COMMUNICATION **EDUCATION** Bethel Col, BA, 62; Univ Minn, MA, 64; PhD, 67. **CAREER** Acting chemn, Bethel Col, St Paul, 64-67; asst prof, Univ of Washington, 67-70, assoc prof, 70; assoc prof, Univ Wisc, 70-78, Dir, Center for Commun Res, 72-74, Prof, 78-. **HONORS AND AWARDS** Assoc ed, Quart J of Speech, 97-2000. **MEMBERSHIPS** Speech Commun Asn. **SELECTED PUBLICATIONS** Auth, Communication: The Study of Human Interaction, NY: McGraw-Hill Book Co (72); auth, Violence and Communication: Public Reactions to an Attempted Presidential Assassination, Lanham, Md: Univ Press of Am (87); auth, Problematic Communication: The Construction of Invisible Walls, Westport, Ct: Praeger (94); auth, Miscommunication, Thousand Oaks: Sage (97); auth, "The Lingiuistic Construction of Violence, Peace, and Conflict," in L. Kurtz, ed, Encyclopedia of Violence, Peace, and Conflict, Vol 2 , San Diego, CA: Acad Press (99): 333-343; auth, Misunderstanding Other People (forthcoming); auth, The Search for Common Ground (forthcoming). **CONTACT ADDRESS** Commun Arts, Univ of Wisconsin, Madison, 6117 Vilas Hall, Madison, WI 53706-1412.

MORTON, CARLOS
PERSONAL Born 10/15/1947, Chicago, IL, m, 1981, 2 children **DISCIPLINE** ENGLISH DRAMA **EDUCATION** Univ Tex El Paso, BA, eng, 75; Univ Calif San Diego, MFA, drama, 79; Univ Tex Austin, PhD, drama, 87. **CAREER** Instr, speech and drama dept, Laredo Jr Col, 86-88; asst prof, drama, Univ Tex El Paso, 88-89; assoc prof, 90-95, full prof, 96-, theatre, Univ Calif Riverside. **HONORS AND AWARDS** Fulbright lectr, Univ Nat Autonoma de Mex, 89-90; winner, second prize, James Baldwin Playwriting Contest, UMAS, 89; winner, first prize, Nat Latino Playwriting Contest, NY Shakespeare Festival Theatre, NY, 86; Mina Shaughnessy Scholar, FIPSE, Wash, DC, 81. **RESEARCH** U.S. Latino theatre; Chicano theatre; Mexican and Central American theatre. **SELECTED PUBLICATIONS** Play, Cuentos, Una Linda Raza, Fulcrum Publ, 163-172, 98; play, Rancho Hollywood, Great Scenes From Minority Playwrights, Meriwether Publ Ltd, 97-137, 97; play, The Many Deaths of Danny Rosales, Types of Drama, RR Donnelley & Sons, 809-832, 97; auth, At Risk, Players Press, 14, 97; auth, The Drop Out, Players Press, 15, 97; auth, Drug-O, Players Press, 18, 97; auth, Los Fatherless, Players Press, 23, 97; auth, The Fickle Finger of Lady Death and Other Plays, Peter Lang Press, NY, 133, 96. **CONTACT ADDRESS** Theatre Arts Dept., Univ of California, Riverside, Riverside, CA 92525. **EMAIL** carlos.morton@ucr.edu

MORTON, RICHARD E.
PERSONAL Born 11/08/1930, Liverpool, Britain, m, 2 children **DISCIPLINE** ENGLISH **EDUCATION** Univ Wales, BA, 52; Oxford Univ, BLitt, 55. **CAREER** Lectr, Univ Witwa-

tersrand, 55-59; asst prof, Lake Erie Col, 59-62; asst prof to assoc prof to dept chmn to emer, McMaster Univ, 62-. **HONORS AND AWARDS** ACLS Fel, 62; Can Coun Fel, 64, 68, 72. **MEMBERSHIPS** MLA; JF Cooper Soc; Dante Soc. **RESEARCH** 17th and 18th-century literature. **SELECTED PUBLICATIONS** Co-ed, Three Hours After Marriage, by John Gay, Lake Erie Col Pr, 61; ed, Poems, by Anne Killigrew, Scholar's Fac Reprints, 67; ed, Le Lutrin Made English 1682, ARS J (67); co-ed, Women in the Eighteenth Century, Hakkert, 76; auth/co-ed, 1776, Hakkert, 76; auth, The Poems of Sir Aston Cokayne, Cromlech, 77; co-ed, Religion in the Eighteenth Century, Garland, 79; auth, Anne Sexton's Poetry of Redemption, Mellon, 88; auth, "Elizabeth's Elstob's Rudiments of Grammar," Studies 18th Century Cult (90); auth, John Dryden's Aeneas, Univ Victoria Pr, 00. **CONTACT ADDRESS** English Dept, McMaster Univ, Hamilton, ON, Canada L8S 4L9. **EMAIL** mortonre@mcmail.cis.mcmaster.ca

MOSCO, VINCENT
DISCIPLINE COMMUNICATIONS **EDUCATION** Harvard Univ, PhD. **CAREER** Prof, Carleton Univ; supervisor of grad stud. **HONORS AND AWARDS** Ed bd(s), US, Can, Eng, Spain; contrib, ed adv bd of the Intl Encycl of Commun; res positions, US government with the White House Off of Telecommun Policy; Nat Res Coun and the US Congress Off of Tech Assessment; Can with the Fed Dept(s) of Commun, Labour, and Finance; consult, US Gen Accounting Off; the Commun Workers of Amer; Commun Workers of Can; Can Overseas Telecommun Union; pres, Polit Econ Section. **MEMBERSHIPS** Mem, governing coun of the Intl Asn for Mass Commun Res. **RESEARCH** Telecommunication policy, mass media, computers and information technology. **SELECTED PUBLICATIONS** Auth, The Political Economy of Communication: Rethinking and Renewal, London: Sage, 96; **CONTACT ADDRESS** Dept of Commun, Carleton Univ, 1125 Colonel By Dr, Ottawa, ON, Canada K1S 5B6. **EMAIL** vincent_mosco@carleton.ca

MOSELEY, JAMES G.
PERSONAL Born 03/24/1946, Atlanta, GA, m, 1968, 2 children **DISCIPLINE** RELIGION; LITERATURE **EDUCATION** Stanford Univ, BA, 68; Univ Chicago Div Sch, MA, 71, PhD, 73. **CAREER** Cord Amer stud (s) prog, 73-79, Ch Hum div, 79-86, asst, assoc, full prof, 73-86, New Col, Univ S Fla; prof Relig, 86-91, dir honors prog, 89-91, VP acad affairs, Dean fac, 86-89, Chapman Col, Calif; VP, Dean, prof Relig, Transylvania Univ, Ky, 91- . **HONORS AND AWARDS** Fel in res Col tchrs, Natl Endowment Hum, Princeton, 76-77; Ed proj grant, NEH, for curric devel, New Col, 77; summer sem Col tchrs, NEH, 79, Univ Calif, Irvine; summer sem Col tchrs, NEH, 82, Harvard Univ; res and creative scholar awd, Univ S Fla, Summer, 83; Co-dir, summer sem sch tchrs, NEH, 84, New Col; Core Fac, Revisioning Am: Relig and the Life of the Nation, series, Ind Univ, Lilly Endowment, 84-90; Proj Dir, Power and Morality conf for commun leaders and sec sch tchrs, Fla endowment Hum, New Col, 85; dir, summer sem sch tchrs, NEH, New Col, 86; dir, summer sem sch tchrs, NEH, Univ Calif Irvine, 90; dir, summer sem sch tchrs, Transylvania Univ, 92; Core fac, Cultural Diversity and Civic Responsibility, Wye High Sch fac sem, Transylvania Univ, 93; Core Fac, Pub Expressions of Rel in Amer, series, Ind Univ, Lilly Endowment, 92-94. **MEMBERSHIPS** Amer acad Relig; Amer Stud Asn; Org Amer Hist; Amer soc Church Hist; Natl Col honors coun; Amer conf acad Deans; Asn Amer Col Univ; Amer Asn higher educ. **RESEARCH** History of Religion. **SELECTED PUBLICATIONS** Auth, A Complex Inheritance: The Idea of Self-Transcendence in the Theology of Henry James, Sr, and the Novels of Henry James, Amer Acad Relig Diss Series, vol 4, Missoula, MT, AAR and Scholar Press, 75; Conversion through Vision: Puritanism and Transcendentalism in The Ambassadors, Jour Amer Acad Relig, XLIII/3, Sept 75; Religious Ethics and the Social Aspects of Imaginative Literature, Jour Amer Acad Relig, XL vol 3, Sept 77; Religion and Modernity: A Case Granted, Bull of the Couns on the Stud Relig, IX/1, Feb 78; Literature and Ethics: Some Possibilities for Religious Thought, Perspect Relig Stud (s), VI/1, Spring 79; The Social Organization of Religion in America: Then and Now, SEASA '79 Proceedings, Tampa, Fla, Amer Stud (s) Press, 79; Culture, Religion, and Theology, Theol Today, XXXVII/3, Oct 80; auth, A Cultural History of Religion in America, Westport, Conn, Greenwood Press, 81; From Conversion to Self-Transcendence: Religious Experience in American Literature, SEASA '83 Proceedings, Tampa, Fla, Amer Stud (s) Press, 83; Inerrantism as Narcissism: Biblical Authority as a Cultural Problem, Perspectives in Relig Stud (s), Fall 83; An Occasion for Changing One's Mind: A Response to Charles Long, Relig Studs and Theol, vol 3, Sept 85; Winthrop's Journal: Religion, Politics, and Narrative in Early America, in Religion and the Life of the Nation: American Recoveries, Sherrill, Illinois UP, 90, reprinted in Literature Criticism from 1400-1800, LC, vol 31, Bostrom, Detroit, Gale, 95; auth, John Winthrop's World: History as a Story as History, Madison, U of Wisconsin P, 92; Civil Religion Revisited, Relig and Amer Cult: A Jour of Interpretation, 4/1, Winter, 94; rev essay: Jenny Franchot's Roads to Rome: The Antebellum Protestant Encounter with Catholicism, Relig Stud (s) Rev, 23/3, July 97. **CONTACT ADDRESS** Dept of Dean, Transylvania Univ, Lexington, KY 40508. **EMAIL** dean@transy.edu

MOSELEY, MERRITT
PERSONAL Born Dothan, AL, m, 1971, 4 children **DISCIPLINE** ENGLISH LITERATURE AND LANGUAGE **EDUCATION** Huntingdon Col, BA; Univ NC, Chapel Hill, MA, PhD. **CAREER** Prof, dir honors program, Univ NC, Asheville. **RESEARCH** Recent British fiction; Victorian lit; humor. **SELECTED PUBLICATIONS** Auth, Davide Lodge, Borgo Pr, 91; auth, Understanding Kingsley Amis, VSC Pr, 93; auth, Understanding Julian Barnes, Univ SC Press, 97. **CONTACT ADDRESS** Univ of No Carolina, Asheville, Karpen Hall 223, CPO 2130, Asheville, NC 28804-8510. **EMAIL** moseley@unca.edu

MOSER, HAROLD DEAN
PERSONAL Born 10/31/1938, Kannapolis, NC, m, 1964, 2 children **DISCIPLINE** AMERICAN HISTORY, AMERICAN LITERATURE **EDUCATION** Wake Forest Univ, BA, 61, MA, 63; Univ Wis-Madison, PhD(hist), 77. **CAREER** Instr hist, Chowan Col, 63-65; teaching asst, Univ Wis- Madison, 67-69; res asst, State Hist Soc Wis, 68-71; from asst ed to co-ed, Papers of Daniel Webster, Dartmouth Col, 71-78, ed corresp ser, Papers of Daniel Webster, 78-79; Ed & Dir, Papers of Andrew Jackson, Univ Tenn, 79-, Nat Hist Pub Comn fel, Dartmouth Col, 71-72. **HONORS AND AWARDS** Philip M Hamer Awd, Soc Am Archivists, 75. **MEMBERSHIPS** Orgn Am Historians; Southern Hist Asn; AHA. **RESEARCH** Jacksonian America; the Old South; Daniel Webster. **SELECTED PUBLICATIONS** Auth, Reaction in North Carolina to the Emancipation Proclamation, NC Hist Rev, 67; New Hampshire and the ratification of the Twelfth Amendment, Dartmouth Libr Bull; co- ed, The Papers of Daniel Webster: Correspondence Series (Vols 1, 2 & 4), 75-78, ed, Vol 5, 82, Univ Press New Eng; The Papers of Andrew Jackson, Univ Tenn Press, Vol 2 (in prep); Liberty And Power - The Politics Of Jacksonian America - Watson,Hl, Virginia Magazine Of History And Biography, Vol 0101, 1993. **CONTACT ADDRESS** Papers of Andrew Jackson, Univ of Tennessee, Hermitage, Hermitage, TN 37066. **EMAIL** hmoser@utk.edu

MOSER, IRENE
PERSONAL Born 02/28/1943, Middlesboro, KY, m, 1974 **DISCIPLINE** ENGLISH **EDUCATION** Vassar Col, AB, 65; Univ NC, MSLS, 67; Univ Calif, MA, 75; Univ NC, PhD, 92. **CAREER** Public Services Librarian, San Jose Library, 72-77; Instructional Services librarian and Asst Prof, Univ NC, 72-84; Lecturer, Western Carolina Univ, 89-93; Prof, Col W Va, 93-. **HONORS AND AWARDS** Dissertation Fel, UNC-CH, 90; Grad Fel, Univ Calif, Los Angeles, 71; Grants from NC Humanities Council and WV Humanities Council. **MEMBERSHIPS** Am Asn of Univ Women, Am folklore Soc, Appalachian St Studies Conf, Mod Lang Asn of Am, NC Folklore Soc, S Atlantic Mod Lang Asn, WV Asn of Col English Teachers. **RESEARCH** Folklore and Literature--American, British, and World; Native American Literature; Appalachian Literature. **SELECTED PUBLICATIONS** Auth, "Native American Imaginative spaces," American Indian Studies, Peter Lang, (97): 285-297; auth, "Entering the World of American Literature through the discourse of Harmony," in The Canon in the classroom, (95): 193-207. **CONTACT ADDRESS** Dept English, Col of W Va, PO Box A G, Beckley, WV 25802-2800. **EMAIL** imoser@cwv.edu

MOSER, THOMAS COLBORN, SR
PERSONAL Born 11/22/1923, Connellsville, PA, m, 2 children **DISCIPLINE** ENGLISH, AMERICAN LITERATURE **EDUCATION** Harvard Univ, AB, 48; AM, 49; PhD, 55. **CAREER** Instr, Wellesley Col, 52-56; instr to prof emeritus, Stanford Univ, 56-. **HONORS AND AWARDS** ACLS Fel, 63; Guggenheim Fel, 79-80; Phi Beta Kappa. **MEMBERSHIPS** MLA, Joseph Conrad Soc, Ford Madox Ford Soc, Phi Beta Kappa Soc. **RESEARCH** English and American Fiction, Conrad, Ford, Faulkner. **SELECTED PUBLICATIONS** Auth, Joseph Conrad: Achievement and Decline, Harvard, 57; auth, "What is the Matter with Emily Jane? Conflicting Impulses in 'Wuthering Heights,'" Nineteenth-Century Fiction 7.1-19, (62); ed, Wuthering Heights: Text, Sources, Criticism, Harcourt, Brace & world, 62; auth, "Look Homeward Angel," The American Novel, Basic Books, (65); ed, Lord Jim: Norton Critical Edition, 68; auth, The Life in the Fiction of Ford Madox Ford, Princeton, 80; auth, "Ford Madox Ford and 'Under Western Eyes,'" Conradiana 15.3 (83); auth, "An English Context for Conrad's Russian Characters," JML 11.1, (84); ed, Ford Madox Ford: The Good Soldier, Oxford World Classics, 90; auth, "Faulkner's Muse: Speculations on the Genesis of 'The Sound and the Fury,'" Critical Reconstructions, ed RM Polhemus and RP Henkle (Stanford, 94). **CONTACT ADDRESS** 6 Peter Coutts Cir, Stanford, CA 94305-1095. **EMAIL** tmoser@stanford.edu

MOSES, MICHAEL VALDEZ
DISCIPLINE ENGLISH LITERATURE **EDUCATION** VA Univ, PhD, 87. **CAREER** Fac, Duke Univ. **MEMBERSHIPS** MLA; Modern Fiction Studies **RESEARCH** Mod comp and contemp lit, with emphasis on twentieth century Brit, Irish, postcolonial and Third World fiction and theory. **SELECTED PUBLICATIONS** Auth, The Novel and the Globalization of Culture, Oxford, 95; ed, The Writings of J.M. Coetzee, Duke, 94; publ(s) on Hardy; Stoker; Joyce; Beckett; DeLillo; Carpentier; Vargas Llosa; Ngugi; latin Am Lit rev; S Atlantic quart; mod fiction studies. **CONTACT ADDRESS** Eng Dept, Duke Univ, 319 Allen Bldg., Box 90015, Durham, NC 27708. **EMAIL** mmoses@acpub.duke.edu

MOSIER, JOHN
PERSONAL Born 07/09/1944, Bentonville, AR, m, 1986, 3 children **DISCIPLINE** ENGLISH **EDUCATION** Tulane Univ, BA, 64, MA, 66, PhD(English), 68. **CAREER** Instr, Tulane Univ, 66-68; instr 67-68, asst dean, 69-71, exec secy acad aff, 71-74, asst prof, 67-80; assoc dir, Film Inst, 75-85, dir, 85-93; editor, New Orleans, 86-93; chmn, 89-92, prof, Loyola Univ, 86-; contrib editor, Americas Mag, 80-90, contrib editor, New Orleans Art Rev, 92-. **RESEARCH** Flim and history **SELECTED PUBLICATIONS** Auth, Machine intelligence and the arts, New Orleans Rev, 69; coauth, Institute research: A review, Univ Southwestern La, 72; auth, Voando a Brasilia, 1ste e Espectaculo, 76; Depoe, Correio Brasiliense, 76; coauth, Women & men together, Houghton, 77; auth, Latin American film today, Americas, 78; Cineman 77, 1ste e Cinema, 78; The new Brasilian film, New Orleans Rev, 78; contrib auth, Handbook of Popular Culture in Latin America, Greenwood, 85; auth, World Cinema Since 1945, Ungar, 87; auth, Before the Wall Came Down Univ Press Amer, 90; coauth, Cinema polinais Editions du cerf, 89; ed, Artist Under Socialism, nor, 85; ayth Kafkas Ankommen, Kino, 92; auth, On the Edge of the Abyss, Cream City Rev, 89; auth Yankee Hustle, Variety, 80; auth, Sanitizing Stalin, Times Picayune, 97; auth, Surviving Art Films, New Orleans Art Rev, 96; auth, Un Secreto Bien Guardado, Americas, 89. **CONTACT ADDRESS** Loyola Univ, New Orleans, 6363 St Charles Ave, Box 50, New Orleans, LA 70118-6195. **EMAIL** jmosier@loyno.edu

MOSKOVITZ, MARC
DISCIPLINE MUSIC **EDUCATION** NC Sch Arts, BA; IN Univ, MA, PhD. **CAREER** Asst prof, Univ Toledo. **SELECTED PUBLICATIONS** Auth, publ(s) on Berlioz and David Popper. **CONTACT ADDRESS** Dept of Music, Univ of Toledo, Toledo, OH 43606.

MOSS, JOHN E.
PERSONAL Born 02/07/1940, Waterloo County, ON, Canada **DISCIPLINE** ENGLISH **EDUCATION** Univ West Ont, BA, 61, MA, 69; Univ Waterloo, Mphil, 70; Univ NB, PhD, 73. **CAREER** Concordia Univ, 73-76; Univ BC, 77-78; Queen's Univ, 78-80; Prof English (Can Lit) Univ Ottawa 80-; Dobbin ch Can stud, Univ Dublin, 97-98. **MEMBERSHIPS** Asn Can Univ Tchrs Eng; Writers Union Can. **SELECTED PUBLICATIONS** Auth, Arctic Landscape and the Metaphysics of Geography; auth, Sex and Violence in the Canadian Novel; auth, Bellrock; auth, Enduring Dreams: An Exploration of Arctic Landscape; founding ed, J Can Fiction. **CONTACT ADDRESS** 1290 Hilliard St, Peterborough, ON, Canada K9H 5S4. **EMAIL** jmoss@uottawa.ca

MOSS, LAURA
DISCIPLINE ENGLISH LITERATURE **EDUCATION** Univ Toronto, BA; Univ Guelph, MA; Queen's Univ, PhD. **CAREER** Asst prof **RESEARCH** Postcolonial theories and literatures; resistance writing; nationalism; multiculturalism; realisms; intersection of postmodernism and postcolonialism; Southern African and Canadian fiction. **SELECTED PUBLICATIONS** Auth, pub(s) on Chinua Achebe, Ngg, Ian Wedde, Salman Rushdie, and postcolonial theory. **CONTACT ADDRESS** Dept of English, Univ of Manitoba, Winnipeg, MB, Canada R3T 2N2. **EMAIL** mossl@ms.umanitoba.ca

MOSS, S.
PERSONAL Born 02/29/1944, St. Paul, MN, d, 1 child **DISCIPLINE** THEATER, ENGLISH RENAISSANCE DRAMA **EDUCATION** Univ Calif, Los Angeles, BA, 65; Univ S Fla, MA, 93, PhD, 97. **CAREER** Actress, Los Angeles, New York regional theater, 65-90; prof, Univ S Fla, 97-. **MEMBERSHIPS** Shakespeare Asn; Actor's Asn; Marlow Soc. **RESEARCH** Renaissance medicine; performance; philosophy; the occult. **SELECTED PUBLICATIONS** Auth, A Continuing Checklist of Multidisciplinary Scholarship on Aging, J Aging and Identity, 96, 97 ; auth, Biographical entry on Bram Stoker in Dictionary of Literary v 178: British Fantasy and Science-Fiction Writers before World War I, Bruccoli Clark Layman, 97; auth, The Psychiatrist's Couch: Hypnosis, Hysteria, and Proto-Freudian Performance in Dracula, in Sucking Through the Century, 1897-1997, Dundurn, 97; auth, Psychical Research and Psychoanalysis: Bram Stoker and the Early Freudian Investigation into Hysteria, in The Shade and the Shadow: A Critical Anthology, Desert Island Books, 98. **CONTACT ADDRESS** Dept Eng, CPR107, Univ of So Florida, 4202 E Fowler Ave, Tampa, FL 33620. **EMAIL** moss@chuma.cas.usf.edu

MOSS, SIDNEY PHIL
PERSONAL Born 03/27/1917, Liverpool, England, m, 1946, 3 children **DISCIPLINE** ENGLISH **EDUCATION** Univ Ill, BS, 50, MA, 51, PhD, 54. **CAREER** From res asst to asst ed Am Lit, Univ Ill, 50-56; from head res dept to ed, Champaign, Ill, off, Spencer Press, 52-54; from asst prof to prof English, Murray State Univ, 56-64; vis prof, 64, Prof English, Southern

Ill Univ, Carbondale, 65-, Am Philos Soc grants, 66 & 78; Fulbright lectr Am lit, Univ Col, Dublin, 69-70. **RESEARCH** American and English literature, especially of the nineteenth century. **SELECTED PUBLICATIONS** Coauth, Thy Men Shall Fall, Ziff-Davis, 48; auth, Poe's Literary Battles, Duke Univ, 63; Composition by Logic, 66 & Readings for Composition by Logic, 68, Wadsworth; Poe's Major Crisis, Duke Univ, 70; coauth, The New Composition by Logic, Southern Ill Univ, 78; Charles Dickens' Quarrel with America, Whitston, 82; Dickens,Frederick, From Courtship To Courtroom, Dickensian, Vol 0090, 1994. **CONTACT ADDRESS** Dept of English, So Illinois Univ, Carbondale, Carbondale, IL 62901.

MOSSHAMMER, ALDEN ADAMS
PERSONAL Born 03/22/1941, Greenwich, CT, m, 1971 **DISCIPLINE** ANCIENT HISTORY, CLASSICS **EDUCATION** Amherst Col, BA, 62; Brown Univ, PhD(classics), 71. **CAREER** Instr Latin, Laconia High Sch, NH, 62-63; instr classics, Mercersburg Acad, Pa, 63-67, registr, 65-67; instr, Kenyon Col, 70-71; asst prof, Swarthmore Col, 71-72; asst prof, 72-77, Assoc Prof Hist, Univ Calif, San Diego, 77-83; Prof Hist, 83-. **MEMBERSHIPS** Am Philol Asn, North Am Patristic Soc. **RESEARCH** Greek chronography; archaic Greek history; church history. **SELECTED PUBLICATIONS** Auth, The epoch of the seven sages, 76 & Phainias of eresos and chronology, 77, Calif Studies Class Antiq; The Chronicle of Eusebius and Greek Chronographic Tradition, Assoc Univ, 79; The Barberini manuscript of George Syncellus, Greek, Roman, Byzantine Studies, 80; Two fragments of Jerome's chronicle, Rheinisches Mus, 81; Thales' Eclipse, Am Philol Asn, 81; The date of the first pythiad-again, Greek, Roman, Byzantine Studies, 82; auth, "Non-Being and Evil in Gregory of Nyssa," Vigiliae Christianae 44 (90):136-67; ed, Ecolga Chronographiae Georgii Syncelli, Teubner ; Agatharchides Of Cnidos 'On The Erythraean Sea' - Burstein,Sm, J Of The American Oriental Society, Vol 0112, 1992; auth, "Gregory of Nyssa and Christian Hellenism," Studia Patristica 32 (97): 170-195; auth, "Gregory of Nyssa as Homilist," Studia Patristica, 01. **CONTACT ADDRESS** Dept of Hist B-007, Univ of California, San Diego, 9500 Gilman Dr, La Jolla, CA 92093-5003. **EMAIL** amosshammer@ucsd.edu

MOTTO, ANNA LYDIA
PERSONAL Born New York, NY, m, 1959, 2 children **DISCIPLINE** CLASSICS **EDUCATION** Queen's Col, NYork, BA, 46; NYork Univ, MA, 48; Univ NC, PhD, 53. **CAREER** Asst, Univ NC, 49-50, part-time instr, 51-52; asst prof Latin, Greek & Span, Washington Col, 53-57; teacher Latin & French, Northport High Sch, NY, 57-58; asst prof Latin & Greek & chmn dept classics, Alfred Univ, 58-65; assoc prof Latin & Greek & chmn dept, Muhlenberg Col, 65-66; assoc prof, St John's Univ, NY, 66-68; from assoc prof to prof, Drew Univ, 68-73; chmn dept for lang, 74-78, Prof Classics, Univ South Fla, 73-, Fulbright grant, Am Acad Rome & Vergilian Soc, Cumae, 56; vis prof, Univ Mich, 69. **MEMBERSHIPS** Classic Asn Atlantic States (vp, 72-73); Am Philol Asn; Am Classic League; MLA; S Atlantic Mod Lang Asn. **RESEARCH** Seneca the philosopher; Roman Stoicism; Roman satire. **SELECTED PUBLICATIONS CONTACT ADDRESS** Dept of Classics, Univ of So Florida, 4202 Fowler Ave, Tampa, FL 33620-9951.

MOUKHLIS, SALAH M.
PERSONAL m, 1998 **DISCIPLINE** ENGLISH AND COMPARATIVE LITERATURE **EDUCATION** Mohamed V Univ, BA, 86; Keele Univ, MA, 88; SUNY Stony Brook, PhD, 94. **CAREER** Asst prof, Moulay Ismail Univ, 88-00; asst prof, Holyoke Comm Col, 00-. **MEMBERSHIPS** MLA, NEMLA, ALA, Morocco Min Ed. **RESEARCH** Post colonial theory, cultural studies, emerging literatures. **SELECTED PUBLICATIONS** Trans, "In Defense of the Author," by David Hirsch (Maknasat, Univ Moulay Ismail Press, 93), auth, "Spring Cleaning: A Novel by Miloudi Chaghmoum," Offshoot (98); auth, History and Representation in Assia Djebar, Univ Moulay Ismail Press, 99; auth, "Driss Chraibi," ed. John Hawley, Encycl Postcol Stud (forthcoming). **CONTACT ADDRESS** Dept of Eng, Holyoke Comm Col, 303 Homestead Ave, Holyoke, MA 01040. **EMAIL** moukhlis@hotmail.com

MOULTHROP, STUART
DISCIPLINE COMMUNICATIONS **EDUCATION** Yale Univ, PhD. **CAREER** Yale; Univ Tx; Ga Inst Tech; assoc prof, Univ Baltimore. **SELECTED PUBLICATIONS** Auth, Victory Garden; Co-ed, Postmodern Culture On-Line Journal. **CONTACT ADDRESS** Commun Dept, Univ of Baltimore, 1420 N. Charles Street, Baltimore, MD 21201.

MOULTON, JANICE
DISCIPLINE ENGLISH, PHILOSOPHY **EDUCATION** Cornell Univ, BA, 63; Univ Chicago, MA, 68; PhD, 71. **CAREER** Asst prof, Univ Ky, 79-81; prof, Central China Tchrs Univ, 86-87; res fac, Smith Coll, 81-. **HONORS AND AWARDS** Executive Comm, Am Philos Asn, 78; Bd of Dir, Sino-Am Network for Educ Exchange. **MEMBERSHIPS** Am Philos Asn; Sino-Am Network for Educ Exchange; Soc for Women in Philos. **RESEARCH** Philosophy; Methodology; Ethics; Feminism; Philosophy Language; Research Methodology; Fraud. **SELECTED PUBLICATIONS** Auth, Plagiarism; Academic Freedom, Encycl of Ethics, 98; coauth, Scaling the Dragon, 94. **CONTACT ADDRESS** Dept of Philosophy, Smith Col, Northampton, MA 01063. **EMAIL** jmm93@cornell.edu

MOUNT, ERIC, JR.
PERSONAL Born 12/07/1935, Versailles, KY, m, 1958, 4 children **DISCIPLINE** ENGLISH, CHRISTIAN ETHICS AND RELIGION **EDUCATION** Rhodes Col, BA, 57; Union Theol Sem in Va, BD, 60; Yale Divinity Sch, STM, 61; Duke Univ, PhD, 66. **CAREER** Asst prof, 66-70, assoc prof, 70-75, prof, 75-96, Rodes prof, 96-, relig, Centre Col; dir, Centre-in-Europe, 92-93, 00; vpres and dean of students, Centre Col, 83-88; social studies div chair, 80-83, relig prog chair, 84-88, Centre Col; Dir., Centre in Strasburg, 92-93, 00. **HONORS AND AWARDS** BA with distinction; Phi Beta Kappa; Omicron Delta Kappa; NEH summer seminars, 76, 81; BD, second in class; Alsop fel; PhD two univ fel; one Kearns fel; Theologian-in-residence, Amer Church in Paris, 74-75; pres, southeast region, Amer Acad of Relig, 87-88; David Hughes distinguished svc award, Centre Col, 77; Pres, SE, region, Am Acad of Religion, 87-88; Project on the Common Good, Center of Theological Inquiry, 00-03. **MEMBERSHIPS** Soc of Christrian Ethics; Amer Acad of Relig; Soc for Values in Higher Educ; Soc of Bus Ethics; Asn for Practical and Professional Ethics; Assoc of Applied and Prof. Ethics **RESEARCH** Theological ethics; Social ethics; Contemporary theology; Medical ethics; Business ethics; Professional ethics; Christian social ethics **SELECTED PUBLICATIONS** Auth, Covenant, Community, and the Common Good, Pilgrim Pr, 99; Articles, Homing in on Family Values, The Family, Religion and Culture Series, Theol Today, 98; article, European Community and Global Community: A View from Alsace and Beyond, Soundings, 96; article, The Currency of Covenant, Annual of the Soc of Christ Ethics, 96; article, Metaphors, Morals and AIDS, Jour of Ethical Studies, 93; article, Can We Talk? Contexts of Meaning for Interpreting Illness, Jour of Med Humanities, vol 14, no 2, 93; auth, Professional Ethics in Context: Institutions, Images and Empathy, John Knox Press, 90; auth, The Feminine Factor, John Knox Press, 73; auth, Conscience and Responsibility, John Knox Press, 69. **CONTACT ADDRESS** Centre Col, 600 W. Walnut St., Danville, KY 40422. **EMAIL** mounte@centre.edu

MOUNT, NICK JAMES
PERSONAL Born 07/11/1963, Sault Ste Marie, ON, Canada, m, 1990, 1 child **DISCIPLINE** ENGLISH **EDUCATION** Univ Victoria, BA, 93; Dalhousie Univ, MA, 94; PhD, 01. **CAREER** Teaching Fel, Univ of King's Col, 99-01; asst prof, Univ of Toronto, 01-. **HONORS AND AWARDS** SSHRC Fel, 94-98; Killam Scholarship, 94-97. **MEMBERSHIPS** MLA, CAAS. **RESEARCH** Expatriate Canadian literary communities in U.S., 1880s -90s, Transnational literary culture in North America. **SELECTED PUBLICATIONS** Auth, "In Praise of Talking Dogs: The Study and Teaching of Early Canada's Canonless Canon," Essays in Can writing 63, (90): 76-98. **CONTACT ADDRESS** Dept English, Univ of Toronto, 7 King's Col Cir, Toronto, ON, Canada M5S 3K1. **EMAIL** nmount@is2.dal.ca

MOURAO, MANUELA
PERSONAL Born 08/27/1962, Porto, Portugal, m, 1990 **DISCIPLINE** ENGLISH **EDUCATION** Univ Port, BA, 84; Eastern Ill Univ, MA, 85; PhD, 90. **CAREER** Prof, Erasmus Inst, 90-92; vis prof, 94; adj asst prof, Old Dominion Univ, 92-94; vis asst prof, 94-95; vis prof, Univ Fernando, 95, 97; asst prof, Old Dominion, 96-. **HONORS AND AWARDS** Fulbright Grant; Erasmus Fac Sen. **MEMBERSHIPS** MLA; SAMLA; NCSA; INCS; NVSA; Victorians Inst; 18th and 19th Brit Women Writers Asn. **RESEARCH** 18th and 19th Century European literature, esp British and French; world literature; gender studies; critical theory. **SELECTED PUBLICATIONS** Auth, "The Abbess of Crewe: Surveillance, Deception, and the Convent," Actas do XII Encontro da APEAA (91); auth, "Nuns in British Fiction: Study of a Stereotype." Revista da Asn Portuguesa de Estudos Anglo-Americanos (91); auth, "Lettres Portugaises: Passion, Writing and Transgression." Anais UTAD 4 (92); auth, "Delicate Balances: Gender and Power in Anne Thackeray Ritchie's Nonfiction," Women's Writing 4 (97):73-89; auth, "Intertextuality and Feminist Intervention in New Portuguese Letters." in New Reading, of Spiritual Narrative from the Fifteenth to the Twentieth Century: Secular Force and Self-Disclosure, ed. Phebe Davidson (Lewiston: Edwin Mellen Press, 95); auth, The Representation of Female Desire in Early Modern Pornographic Texts: 1660-1745," Sign: J Women Cult 24 (99): 573-602; auth, "Comparative Literature Past and Present" in Comparative Literature Today: Theories and Practice/La Litterature comparee d'aujourd'hui, Theories et realisations, eds. Steven Totosy de Zepetnek, Milan V Dimic (Paris: Honore Champion, 99); auth, "The Compromise of Enlightened Rationalism in Diderot's La Religieuse," Romance Quart (forthcoming); auth, "Religious Communities" in Encyclopedia of Homosexuality, ed. Bonnie Zimmerman (Lesbian Hist Culture, NY: Garland, forthcoming). **CONTACT ADDRESS** Dept English, Old Dominion Univ, Hampton Blvd, Norfolk, VA 23529. **EMAIL** mmourao@odu.edu

MOWLANA, HAMID
PERSONAL Born 02/25/1937, Tabriz, Iran **DISCIPLINE** INTERNATIONAL COMMUNICATION **EDUCATION** Northwestern Univ & Univ Teheran, BA; Northwestern Univ, MS, PhD. **CAREER** Prof, Am Univ, dir, Div of Int Commun. **HONORS AND AWARDS** Pres Int Asn Media Comm Res. **RESEARCH** Cultural and psychological aspects of international relations, and worldwide socio-economic development. **SELECTED PUBLICATIONS** Auth, The Passing of Modernity: Communication and the Transformation of Society, Longman, 90; The Global Media Debate: Its Rise, Fall, and Renewal, Ablex Publications, 93; Global Information and World Communication: New Frontiers in International Relations, Longman, 86; Communication Technology and Development; International Flow of News, UNESCO, 88; Triumph of the Image: The Media's War in the Persian Gulf, Westview, 92 and International Communication in Transition: The End of Diversity? and Invisible Crises: What Conglomerate Control of Media Means for America and the World, Westview, 96 **CONTACT ADDRESS** American Univ, 4400 Massachusetts Ave, Washington, DC 20016. **EMAIL** mowlana@american.edu

MOWRY, HUA-YUAN LI
DISCIPLINE ASIAN AND MIDDLE EASTERN LANGUAGES AND LITERATURES **EDUCATION** Tunghai Univ, BA; Univ Calif Berkeley, MA, PhD. **CAREER** Assoc prof, Dartmouth Col. **HONORS AND AWARDS** EDUCOM Software Awd, 91; proj dir, byrne dictionary; res dir, dartmouth-at-bnu prog, 82, 84, 87, 90, 92, and 94. **SELECTED PUBLICATIONS** Auth, Chinese Love Stories from Ch'ing-shih; Yan-pan Hsi--New Theater in China; Hanzi Assistant; auth, A Multimedia Chinese Reader for Advanced Students. **CONTACT ADDRESS** Dartmouth Col, 3529 N Main St, #207, Hanover, NH 03755. **EMAIL** hua-yuan.l.mowry@dartmouth.edu

MOYER, KERMIT W.
DISCIPLINE CREATIVE WRITING **EDUCATION** Northwestern Univ, PhD. **CAREER** Prof, Am Univ, 70-. **HONORS AND AWARDS** Outstanding Tchr Year. **SELECTED PUBLICATIONS** Auth, Tumbling, Univ Ill Press, 88; articles, F. Scott Fitzgerald, poetry, fiction. **CONTACT ADDRESS** American Univ, 4400 Massachusetts Ave, Washington, DC 20016. **EMAIL** kmoyer@american.edu

MOYER, RONALD L.
PERSONAL Born 07/31/1944, Champaign, IL, m, 1988, 1 child **DISCIPLINE** THEATRE HISTORY, LITERATURE AND ACTING **EDUCATION** Univ IL, BA, 66, MA, 67; Univ Denver, PhD, 74. **CAREER** Prof & dir, Grad Stud; prof, Univ SD, 74-, dept ch, 78-83, 89-91, tenure, 80; dir, Black Hills Playhouse, 76- & assoc mng dir, 79 & 80; tchg fel, Univ Denver, 72-73; instr, Purdue Univ-Calumet, 67-71; grad asst, Univ IL, 66-67; local arrangements ch, SDHSAA One-Act Play Festival, 90 & 85; local arrangements supvr, Irene Ryan Competition, ACTF, Region V North, 89; hon mem, Bd Dir, The Black Hills Playhouse, 92-; second VP & mem, Bd Dir, The Black Hills Playhouse, 83-91; critic, Am Col Theatre Festival Region V N, 84; local arrangements ch, ACTF Region V North Festivention, 83; Univ/Col Theatre Asn Repr, Mid- Am Theatre Conf Coun, 81-83; treasurer, S Dakota Theatre Asn, 78-82, finance comt, 78-82 & nominating comt, 78; co-drafter, Const Rev, 78; local arrangements ch, SDHSAA One-Act Play Festival, 82; mem, Plan Comt, MATC Conv, 80-81; ch, Reg Theatre Auditions, MATC Conv, 81; critic & mem, Reg Screening Team, ACTF Region V North, 80-81; mem, Plan Comt, MATC Conv, 79-80; ch, Reg Theatre Auditions, MATC Conv, 80; local arrangements ch, SDHSAA One-Act Play Festival, 80; univ comt(s), Univ Graphics Rev Comt, 94-95; Grad Coun, 78-83,84-87, 89-; subcomt(s), Univ Senate, 77-78 & Rules and Nominating Comt, 87-89; Presidential-Alumni Scholar Selection Comt, 80, 81; Educ Media Comt, 76-77; Statewide Educ Serv Adv Comt, 75-77. **HONORS AND AWARDS** Sioux Falls Argus Leader, 95; USD Stud Theatre League Fac Appreciation Awd, 92; Courseware develop awd, IBM-Rochester, 91; The Divorce Colony, play won second prize, David Libr of the Am Revolution, 87; USD Stud Theatre League Fac Appreciation Awd, 86; first prize, 2 plays, David Libr Am Revolution nat contest, 76; NDEA Title IV fel, Univ Denver, 71-74; Bush Mini-Grant Prog, 95; USD fac develop prog, 93; vis prof, IBM-Rochester, 92 & 91; USD fac develop prog, 92; Bush Found grant, 89, 88 & 85; SD Arts Coun grant, 82-83. **RESEARCH** Use of the Internet for the study of theatre and drama; Shakespearean performance; methods of playscript analysis. **SELECTED PUBLICATIONS** Auth, American Actors, 1861-1910: An Annotated Bibliography of Books, Troy, NY, Whitston Publ Co, 79; coauth & ed advert brochure, IBM Ultimedia Video Delivery System/400, Rochester, MN, Int Bus Mach Corp, co 92. **CONTACT ADDRESS** Dept of Theatre, Univ of So Dakota, Vermillion, 414 E Clark St, Vermillion, SD 57069. **EMAIL** rmoyer@usd.edu

MUELLER, CLAUS
PERSONAL Born 07/23/1941, Berlin, Germany, m, 1984, 2 children **DISCIPLINE** SOCIOLOGY, MEDIA **EDUCATION** Univ of Cologne, BA (equiv), 64; New Schl for Soc Res, MA, 60, PhD, 70; CEP Inst dEtudes Politiques, Paris, 77. **CAREER**

Sr Part, Media Resource Assoc, 75-85; Pres, Intl Film and TV Exchange Inc, 85-, curator, New York Screening Days, 86-; Adv, 89/95-, Assoc Prof, 76-80, Dir, 85-, Hunter Col, CUNY. **HONORS AND AWARDS** Brd Mem/Off, Intl Film and TV Exchange, NY Film/video Coun; election to Am Council on Germany; Fulbright Scholar, 95. **MEMBERSHIPS** New York Film and Video Coun, Assoc of Independent Video and Film Prof, Carnegie Coun on Intl Relation, New York Film/Video Coun, Intl Radio and TV Soc **RESEARCH** International Communications; information and the class structure; contemporary documentaries. **SELECTED PUBLICATIONS** Auth, The Politics of Communicaiton, Oxford Univ Press, 74, Japanese ed, 76, German ed, 75; auth, Development Communication in the USA, Media Sup and Develop Comm in a World of Change, Bad Honnef: 95; The Refracted Mirror, Intl Jour of Group Tensions, 96; The Cologne Medien Forum, Change Ahead for the Berlinale, Germany's WDR, The Independent, 99, Inside Havana, The Independent, 00; The Ind, 98; US Films at the 2000 Berlinale, Indiwire Third World Television Access to US Media, F Naumann Found, 89. **CONTACT ADDRESS** 420 East 64th W2H, New York, NY 10021. **EMAIL** cmueller@hunter.cuny.edu

MUELLER, MARTIN
DISCIPLINE CLASSICS AND ENGLISH **EDUCATION** Ind Univ, MA, PhD, 66. **CAREER** Prof, Northwestern Univ, 76-. **RESEARCH** Repertorium Homericum, A Relational Database Tool for the Study of Homer. **SELECTED PUBLICATIONS** Auth, Children of Oedipus and Other Essays on the Imitation of Greek Tragedy, 1550-1800, Toronto, 80; The Iliad, London, 84. **CONTACT ADDRESS** Dept of Classics, Northwestern Univ, 1801 Hinman, Evanston, IL 60208. **EMAIL** martinmueller@nwu.edu

MUELLER, ROGER
DISCIPLINE ENGLISH LITERATURE **EDUCATION** Macalester Col, BA, 57; Univ MN, MA, 65, PhD, 68. **CAREER** Prof, Univ Pacific. **HONORS AND AWARDS** UOP, 65-97. **SELECTED PUBLICATIONS** Auth, publ(s) on American Transcendentalism; college writing. **CONTACT ADDRESS** Eng Dept, Univ of the Pacific, Stockton, Pacific Ave, PO Box 3601, Stockton, CA 95211.

MUJCINOVIC, FATIMA
PERSONAL Born Sarajevo, Bosnia **DISCIPLINE** US LITERATURE **EDUCATION** Bluffton Col, BA, 94; Case Western Reserve Univ, MA, 96; Univ Calif Santa Barbara, PhD, 00. **CAREER** TA to instr, Univ Calif Santa Barbara, 96-01; asst prof, Westminster Col, 01-. **HONORS AND AWARDS** Hon Soc Pi Delta; Hon Soc C Henry Smith; George Soros Grant, 94-97; Regents Fel, UC Santa Barbara, 96-97; Chicana Diss Fel, 99-00. **MEMBERSHIPS** MLA, ASA, MELUS, Int Writers and Artists Assoc. **RESEARCH** US ethnic literature, 20th century USA literature, 20th century Latin American literature, Postcolonial literary studies, Women's Studies, Border Studies. **SELECTED PUBLICATIONS** Transl, "Gabriela Mistral's Unpublished Poems," Grand St Magazine, (97); cotransl, "Prologue to Cemetiere Marin, JL Borges," Bull des Etudes Valeryennes, (00); auth, "Multicultural America and Its Resistance to Linguistic Diversity," Santa Barbara Independent, (00); transl, "The Secret of Raspberry Jam," Metamorphoses: Jour for Lit Transl, (01); auth, "Hybrid Latina Identities: Manuevering Between Two Cultures," CENTRO Jour for Puerto Rican Studies, (01). **CONTACT ADDRESS** Dept English, Westminster Col, Pennsylvania, 1840 S 1300 E, Salt Lake City, UT 84105. **EMAIL** fm@umail.ucsb.edu

MUKERJI, CHANDRA
DISCIPLINE COMMUNICATIONS **EDUCATION** Northwestern Univ, PhD, Sociol, 68. **CAREER** Prof, Commun, Univ Calif, San Diego. **RESEARCH** Material aspects of human cult and commun processes. **SELECTED PUBLICATIONS** Auth, From Graven Images: Patterns of Modern Materialism, Columbia, 83; A Fragile Power: Scientists and the State, Princeton, 90; co-auth, Rethinking Popular Culture, Univ Calif, 91. **CONTACT ADDRESS** Dept of Commun, Univ of California, San Diego, 9500 Gilman Dr, La Jolla, CA 92093. **EMAIL** cmukerji@weber.ucsd.edu

MULCAHY, GREGORY
PERSONAL Born St Paul, MN, m, 1983 **DISCIPLINE** ENGLISH **EDUCATION** Univ Minn, BA, 83; Univ Southern Miss, MA, 85. **CAREER** Laborer, 75-89; instr English, Century Commun Col, 89- . **HONORS AND AWARDS** Pulitizer Prize nom, 93. **RESEARCH** Contemporary fiction. **SELECTED PUBLICATIONS** Auth, Out of Work, (93); auth, Constellation, (96); auth, Drinking in Silence, (00). **CONTACT ADDRESS** Dept English, Century Comm and Tech Col, 3401 Century Ave N, Saint Paul, MN 55110-5655. **EMAIL** g.mulcahy@cctc.cc.mn.us

MULCAIRE, TERRY
DISCIPLINE ENGLISH **EDUCATION** UC, Berkeley, PhD. **CAREER** Prof, Northwestern Univ. **RESEARCH** 19th century American literature, cultural studies, popular culture. **SELECTED PUBLICATIONS** Articles on, Stephen Crane & Walt Whitman. **CONTACT ADDRESS** Dept of English, Northwestern Univ, 1801 Hinman, Evanston, IL 60208.

MULFORD, CARLA J.
DISCIPLINE ENGLISH **EDUCATION** Univ Del, BA, 77; MA, 79; PhD, 83. **CAREER** Vis full-time instr, Temple Univ, 82-84; asst prof, Villanova Univ, 84-86; asst prof to assoc prof, Pa State Univ, 86-. **HONORS AND AWARDS** DLB Editor's Awd, 98; richard J. Mccormick Prize in History, New Jersey Historical Commission, 95; Cincinnati History Prize, Society of the Cincinnati in the State of New Jersey, 91. **MEMBERSHIPS** Soc of Early Americanists, Am Hist Asn, Am Soc for Eighteenth-Century Studies, Am Studies Asn, Omohundro Inst of Early Am Hist and Culture, Mod Lang Asn, Org of Am Historians, Penn Hist Asn. **RESEARCH** Early American writings, from European contact to 1830, Early modernism, Women writers in early America, Native American studies, African American studies, The American literary canon, European empire in the Americas, Benjamin Franklin. **SELECTED PUBLICATIONS** Auth, "Joel Barlow and Masonic conspiracy," in Secret Texts: The Literature of Secret Societies, New York, 95; auth, "Huehuetlatolli, Early American Studies, and the Problem of History," with New Directions in Early American Studies, Early American Literature, (95): 154-151; auth, "Benjamin Franklin and the Myths of Nationhood," in Making America/Making American Literature: Franklin to Cooper, Rodopi, (96): 15-58; auth, William Hill Brown's The Power of Sympathy (1789) and Hannah Webster Foster's The Coquette (1797), New York, 96; auth, "Frinklin, Modernity, and Themes of Dissent in the Early Modern Era," Modern Language Studies, (98): 13-27; auth, American Women Prose Writers to 1820, London, 98; auth, "Figuring Benjamin Franklin in American Cultural Memory," New England Quarterly 71, (99): 415-443; auth, "Resisting Colonialism," in Teaching the Literature of Early America, New York, (99): 75-94; auth, "Benjamin Franklin, Native Americans, and European Cultures of Civility," Prospects 24, (99): 49-66; auth, Teaching the Literatures of Early America, New York: Modern Language Asn of Am, 99. **CONTACT ADDRESS** Dept English, Pennsylvania State Univ, Univ Park, 117 Burrowes Bldg, University Park, PA 16802-6200. **EMAIL** cjm5@psu.edu

MULHALLEN, KAREN
PERSONAL Born Woodstock, ON, Canada **DISCIPLINE** ENGLISH **EDUCATION** Waterloo Lutheran Univ, BA, 63; Univ Toronto, MA, 67, PhD, 75. **CAREER** Lectr, 66-70, Prof English, Ryerson Polytech Univ 70-. **HONORS AND AWARDS** Maclean Hunter Arts Journ Fel, 94. **MEMBERSHIPS** Descant Arts & Letters Found; ASECS; CMPA; CSECS; PEN; Writers Union Can. **SELECTED PUBLICATIONS** Auth, Sheba and Solomon, 84; auth, Modern Love Poems 1970-1989, 90; auth, In the Era of Acid Rain, 93; ed, Descant, 73-. **CONTACT ADDRESS** Dept of English, Ryerson Polytech Univ, 350 Victoria St, Toronto, ON, Canada M5B 2K3. **EMAIL** kmulhall@acs.ryerson.ca

MULL, DONALD L.
DISCIPLINE 19TH- AND 20TH-CENTURY AMERICAN LITERATURE **EDUCATION** Yale Univ, PhD. **CAREER** Instr, Rutgers, State Univ NJ, Camden Col of Arts and Sci. **SELECTED PUBLICATIONS** Auth, The Girl in the Black Raincoat, Doell, Sloan, and Pearce, 66; Henry James's Sublime Economy: Money as Symbolic Center in the Fiction, Wesleyan, 73. **CONTACT ADDRESS** Rutgers, The State Univ of New Jersey, New Brunswick, Camden Col of Arts and Sci, New Brunswick, NJ 08903-2101.

MULLEN, EDWARD
PERSONAL Born 07/12/1942, Hackensack, NJ, m, 1971, 2 children **DISCIPLINE** LITERATURE **EDUCATION** West Va Wesleyan, BA, 64; Northwestern, MA, 65, PhD, 68. **CAREER** Asst prof, Purdue Univ, 67-71; from assoc prof to prof, 71-, Univ Mo. **HONORS AND AWARDS** Woodrow Wilson Fel, 64-65; ACLS Grant in Aid, 79; co-ed, the afro-hispanic rev, 87-. **MEMBERSHIPS** MLA; Langston Hughes Soc; Col Lang Asn. **RESEARCH** Afro-Hispanic literature; African-American literature. **SELECTED PUBLICATIONS** Auth, art, Afro-Hispanic and Afro-American Literary Historiography: Comments on Generational Shifts, 95; auth, art, The Teaching Anthology and the Hermaneneutics of Race: The Case of Placido, 95; auth, art, Nicolas Guillen and the Notion of Race in Latin American Literature, 97; auth, Afro-Cuban Literature: Critical Junctures, 98; coauth, El Cuento Hispanico: A Graded Literary Anthology, 99. **CONTACT ADDRESS** Univ of Missouri, Columbia, 143 Arts & Science Bldg, Columbus, MO 65211. **EMAIL** mullene@missouri.edu

MULLEN, KAREN A.
PERSONAL Born 07/05/1941 **DISCIPLINE** ENGLISH, LINGUISTICS **EDUCATION** Grinnell Col, BA, 63; Univ Iowa, MA, 66, PhD(English), 73. **CAREER** Asst rhet, 66-70, asst ling, 70-73, from instr to asst prof ling, 74-75, coord English as foreign lang prog, 75-77, assoc dir, Intensive English Prog, Univ Iowa, 76-78; Assoc Prof & Dir Intensive English, Univ Louisville, 78-, Ed, News lett for spec interest group lang anal & studies humanities, Asn Comput Mach, 71-75; consult ed, Comput & Humanities, 72-75. **MEMBERSHIPS** Asn Teachers English to Speakers Other Lang; Ling Soc Am; MLA; Nat Asn Foreign Student Affairs; Asn Comput Mach. **RESEARCH** Cloze-passage test; relationship between second-language proficiency and intelligence. **SELECTED PUBLICATIONS** Auth, In-core PLI sort and search procedures for lexical data, Siglash Newslett, 73; The Wanderer: Considered again, Neophilologus, 74; Rater reliability and oral proficiency evaluations, Occas Papers Ling, 77; Using rater judgments in the evaluation of writing proficiency for non-native speakers of English, Teaching & Learning English as 2nd Lang: Trends Res & Pract, 77; Direct evaluation of second language proficiency, Lang Learning, 79; More on Cloze tests, Concepts Lang Testing 79; An alternative to the Cloze test, TESOL, 79; Evaluating writing in ESL, chap 15 & Rater reliability and oral proficiency evaluations, chap 8, In: Research in Language Testing, Newbury House, 80; Making Progress In English - Furey,Pr, Menasche,L, Modern Language J, Vol 0077, 1993. **CONTACT ADDRESS** Dept of English, Univ of Louisville, Louisville, KY 40208.

MULLEN, LAURA
DISCIPLINE ENGLISH **EDUCATION** Univ Calif, Berkeley, BA, 84; Univ Iowa, MFA. **CAREER** Vis asst prof, Colby Col, 89-90; asst prof, Univ Miami, 92-94; assoc prof, Colo State Univ (94-). **HONORS AND AWARDS** Nat Endowment for the Arts Fel, 88; Rona Jaffe Awd, 96. **MEMBERSHIPS** Assoc Writing Progs, Modern Lang Asn. **RESEARCH** Poetry. **SELECTED PUBLICATIONS** Auth, The Surface, Univ Ill Press (91); auth, After I Was Dead, Univ Ga Press (99); auth, The Tales of Horror, Kelsey St Press (99). **CONTACT ADDRESS** Dept English 1773, Colorado State Univ, 1 Colorado State, Fort Collins, CO 80523-0001. **EMAIL** Lmullen@vines.colostate.edu

MULLEN, LAWRENCE J.
PERSONAL Born 02/02/1960, Schenectady, NY, m, 1990 **DISCIPLINE** COMMUNICATION STUDIES **EDUCATION** Univ IA, PhD, 92. **CAREER** Asst prof, Augustana Col, Sioux Falls, SD, 92-94; asst prof, UNLV, Las Vegas, NV, 94-. **HONORS AND AWARDS** Outstanding Fac Res Awd, 96; NV Regents Outstanding Fac, 97. **MEMBERSHIPS** Nat Commun Asn; Int Commun Asn; Broadcast Ed Asn; Am Asn of Public Opinion Res. **RESEARCH** Visual literacy; Presidential political commun; mass commun processes and effects. **SELECTED PUBLICATIONS** Auth, An Overview of Political Content Analyses of Magazines, Electronic J of Commun/La Revue Electronique de Communication, 4, 94; with M Pfau, T Diedrich, & K Garrow, Television Viewing and Public Perceptions of Attorneys, Human Commun Res, 21 (3), 95 & the Influence of Television Viewing on Public Perceptions of Physicians, J of Broadcasting and Electronic Media, 39 (4), 95; with E W Rothenbuhler, R DeLaurell, & C R Ryu, Coimmunication, Community Attachment and Involvement, Journalism and Mass Communication Quart, 39 (4), 96; with R DeLaurell, The Audience in Television Production: A Review of 20 Current College Textbooks, Feedback, 37 (3), 96; The President's Visual Image from 1945 to 1974: An Analysis of Spatial Configuration in News Magazine Photographs, Presidential Studies Quart, 27 (4), 97; with R DeLaurell, The Concept of Audience in Radio & Audio Production Textbooks, Feedback, 38 (1), 97; Close-ups of the President: Photojournalistic Distance from 1945 to 1974, Visual Commun Quart, 5 (2), 98; African American Portrayals in Comic Books, Popular Culture Rev, forthcoming, 98; several other articles. **CONTACT ADDRESS** Hank Greenspun School of Commnunication, Univ of Nevada, Las Vegas, 4505 Maryland Pkwy, Las Vegas, NV 89154-5007. **EMAIL** mullen@nevada.edu

MULLEN, RICHARD D.
PERSONAL Born 09/30/1915, Mountain View, MO, m, 1938 **DISCIPLINE** ENGLISH **EDUCATION** Univ Ala, AB, 49; Univ Miss, MA, 50; Univ Chicago, PhD, 55. **CAREER** Instr English, Univ Mass, 50-51, 53-56; from asst prof to assoc prof, 56-68, Prof English, Ind State Univ, Terre Haute, 68-. **MEMBERSHIPS** Sci Fiction Res Asn; MLA. **RESEARCH** English drama to 1642; English literature 1500-1660; science fiction. **SELECTED PUBLICATIONS** Auth, Blish, van Vogt and the uses of Spengler, Riverside Quart, 68; The undisciplined imagination: E R Burroughs and Lowellian Mars, In: Science Fiction: The Other Side of Realism, Bowling Green Popular Press, 71; The prudish prurience of Haggard and Burroughs, Riverside Quart, 73; ed, Science Fiction Studies, Ind State Univ, 73-; The Passage Of The Light, The Recursive Science-Fiction Of Malzberg,Barry,N. - Resnick,M, Lewis,Ar, Science-Fiction Studies, Vol 0021, 1994; A Modern Utopia - Italian - Wells,Hg, Science-Fiction Studies, Vol 0021, 1994; First-Fandom + Organization For Those Active In Science- Fiction Since Before 1938, Science-Fiction Studies, Vol 0023, 1996; Ufos - An Insiders View Of The Official Quest For Evidence - Craig,R, Science-Fiction Studies, Vol 0023, 1996; Outside The Human Aquarium - Masters Of Science-Fiction - Stableford,B, Science-Fiction Studies, Vol 0024, 1997; R.D.-Mullen Reply To Haycock,Christine,E. Criticism Of His Obituary Of Moskowitz,Sam, Science-Fiction Studies, Vol 0024, 1997; Moreau And Plaxy Redivivus + Novels, Science-Fiction, Science-Fiction Studies, Vol 0024, 1997; Wells,H.G. And The Culminating Ape - Kemp,P, Science-Fiction Studies, Vol 0024, 1997; Recent Books From Borgo-Press + Science-Fiction Studies, Science-Fiction Studies, Vol 0024, 1997; Moskowitz,Sam, 1920-1997 + In-Memoriam, Science- Fiction Studies, Vol 0024, 1997; Islands In The Sky - The Space Station Theme In Science-Fiction Literature - Westfahl,G, Science-Fiction Studies, Vol 0024,

1997; Longer Views - Extended Essays - Delany,Sr, James,K, Science-Fiction Studies, Vol 0024, 1997; A Subtler Magick - The Writings And Philosophy Of Lovecraft,H.P. - Joshi,St, Science-Fiction Studies, Vol 0024, 1997. **CONTACT ADDRESS** Dept of English, Indiana State Univ, Terre Haute, IN 47809.

MULLENIX, ELIZABETH REITZ
DISCIPLINE THEATRE ARTS **EDUCATION** Univ Ill, PhD, 95. **CAREER** Assoc dean, asst prof. **MEMBERSHIPS** ATHE, ASTR, MATC. **RESEARCH** Nineteenth-century American theatre history; gender studies and feminist theatre. **SELECTED PUBLICATIONS** Auth, Wearing the Breeches: Gender on the Antebellum Stage; pubs on cross dressing and gender feminist theory. **CONTACT ADDRESS** Dept of Theatre, Illinois State Univ, Normal, IL 61790. **EMAIL** emullen@oratmail.cfu.ilstu.edu

MULLER, ADAM
DISCIPLINE ENGLISH LITERATURE **EDUCATION** Univ Calgary, BA; Univ Alberta, MA; McGill Univ, PhD. **CAREER** Asst prof, Univ of Manitoba. **HONORS AND AWARDS** Vis Scholarship, Aalborg Univ, 97. **RESEARCH** Critical theory; Am modernism; South African lit; narrative film and film theory; literary exile. **SELECTED PUBLICATIONS** Auth, pub(s) on literary theory, cultural studies, and aesthetics. **CONTACT ADDRESS** Dept of English, Univ of Manitoba, Winnipeg, MB, Canada R3T 2N2. **EMAIL** mullera@ms.umanitoba.ca

MULLER, GILBERT HENRY
PERSONAL Born 11/08/1941, Brooklyn, NY, m, 1964, 2 children **DISCIPLINE** AMERICAN LITERATURE **EDUCATION** Stanford Univ, PhD(Eng & Am lit), 67. **CAREER** Tchg asst Eng & Renaissance lit, Stanford Univ, 64-66; asst prof Am & comp lit, Pahlavi Univ, Iran, 67-71; asst prof, 71-73, Assoc Prof AM & Comp Lit, LaGuardia Community Col, City Univ, NY, 73-80, Prof, 80- Nat Endowment for Hum fel, 74-79; Fulbright-Hays exchange scholar, 78-79; fac res award, City Univ NY, 75-77. **MEMBERSHIPS** NEA; Am Studies Asn; MLA; Am Fed Tchrs. **RESEARCH** Interdisciplinary studies; Am studies; rhetoric and compos. **SELECTED PUBLICATIONS** Auth, Flannery O'Conner's Dantean Vision, Ga Rev, 6/69; Revolutionary romanticism, New Republic, 9/72; Nightmares and Visions: Flannery O'Connor and the Catholic Grotesque, Univ Ga, 72; Comparison and Contrast, Harper, 74; Faulkner's Red Leaves and the Garden of the South, Studies Short Fiction, 74; The Basic English Handbook, Harper, 78; The Short Prose Reader, McGraw, Chester Himes, 89, John A. Williams, 84; New Strangers in Paradise: The Immigrant Experience in Contemporary AmLiterature, 99; Bridges: Literature Across Cultures, 94; Ways in Reading and Writing About Literature, 94; Major Modern Essayists, 94; The McGraw Hill Introduction to Literature, 95; The McGraw-Hill Reader, 7e, 00. **CONTACT ADDRESS** 21 Monfort Rd, Port Washington, NY 11050. **EMAIL** gilmr@lagcc.cuny.edu

MULLIN, ANNE
DISCIPLINE ENGLISH LITERATURE **EDUCATION** Univ Mass, PhD, 90. **CAREER** Asst prof emer. **RESEARCH** Composition process; unconscious influences on language use; composition strategies for non-native speakers and for students with disabilities. **CONTACT ADDRESS** Dept of English and Philosophy, Idaho State Univ, Pocatello, ID 83209. **EMAIL** mullanne@isu.edu

MULLIN, MICHAEL A.
PERSONAL Born 11/30/1944, Chicago, IL, s, 4 children **DISCIPLINE** LITERATURE **EDUCATION** Col of the Holy Cross, AB, 66; Yale Univ, MPhil, 70; PhD, 72. **CAREER** From asst prof to prof, Univ of Ill at Urbana-Champaign, 70-. **HONORS AND AWARDS** Hon Member, Golden Key Honor Soc, 85-; Fac Fel, UIUC, 92-93; Fulbright Lectr, Brazil, 95; **MEMBERSHIPS** Am Soc for Theatre Res, Int Shakespeare Asn, Soc for Theatre Res UK, Yale Club NYC, Int Fedn for Theatre Res, Shakespeare Asn of Am, The Players NY, Int Theatre Critics Asn. **RESEARCH** Shakespeare across cultures, theatre history, website development. **SELECTED PUBLICATIONS** Auth, Macbeth Onstage: An Annotated Facsimile of Glen Byam Shaw's 1955 Promptbook, Univ Of Mo Press (Columbia), 76; auth, Theatre at Stratford-upon-Avon: A Catologue-Index to Productions of the Shakespeare Memorial? Royal Shakespeare Theatre, 1879-1978, Greenwood Press (NY and London), 80; auth, Costume and Set Designs by Motley, KaiDib Int (Glendale and London), 88; auth, "Design for Hamlet: Motley's Designs for the 1934, 1939, 1950, and 1958 Productions," Theatre Design and Technol 29 (93): 9-16; ed, Designing and Making Costumes for the Stage, by "Motley," Herbert Press (London), 92; auth, Design by Motley, Univ of Delaware (NY and London), 96. **CONTACT ADDRESS** Dept English, Univ of Illinois, Urbana-Champaign, 608 S Wright St, Urbana, IL 61801-3613. **EMAIL** m-mullin@uiuc.edu

MULLING, SYLVIA S.
PERSONAL Born 12/19/1939, Pittsburgh, PA, d, 2 children **DISCIPLINE** ENGLISH **EDUCATION** Univ Va, BA, 57; Am Univ, MA, 70; NY Univ, PhD, 86. **CAREER** Adj Instr, CUNY, 78; Asst Prof, Bayamon Central Univ, 70-82; Fulbright Prof, Univ Annaba, 82-84; Adj Prof, NYork Univ, 85; Adj Instr, Univ Puerto Rico, 85-86; Foreign Expert, Shanghai Inst, 86-88; Foreign Expert, Shaanxi Teachers Univ, 88-89; Assoc Prof, Kean Univ, 90-. **HONORS AND AWARDS** Model Foreign Expert, Shaanxi; Certificate of Commendation, Shanghai Inst; Teaching Fel, Am Univ, Phi Sigma Iota Nat Romance Lang Honor Soc. **MEMBERSHIPS** TESOL, RCLMS, AAAL, SLFR. **RESEARCH** Reading and vocabulary strategies; Writing; The teaching of research. **SELECTED PUBLICATIONS** Auth, "Use of Morphological Analysis by Spanish LI ESOL Learners," IRAL, forthcoming; auth, "Writing Together: A Project for Team Research, Univ Mich Press, 98; auth, "Vocabulary Recognition in spanish-sp0eaking ESOL Learners," in anthology for Writing Together, Univ Mich Press, 98; auth, "Project LEAD in ESL," in Project LEAD: A plan for the future, Kean College, 95; auth, "In Other Words," in New Ways in Teaching Writing, TESOL, 95. **CONTACT ADDRESS** Dept English, Kean Col of New Jersey, 1000 Morris Ave, Union, NJ 07083-7133.

MULVIHILL, MAUREEN E.
PERSONAL Born Detroit, MI, m, 1983 **DISCIPLINE** LITERATURE, ENGLISH, IRISH **EDUCATION** Univ Wis Madison, PhD, 83. **CAREER** Vis prof, NYU, 92; vis prof, Marymount Col, 92; vis prof, Fordham Univ, 93-95; vis prof, SW Tex State Univ, 96; vis prof, St Joseph's Col, 97; vis prof, Berkeley Col, 00-01. **HONORS AND AWARDS** Princ Res For, 93, 95, 97; Inst Res Hist, 84-89; Univ Wis Mad, Grad Sch Tui Scholar, 75-81; Wayne State Univ, 66-68; Juror, James E. Clifford Awd Comm, Am Soc for 18thC Stud; Frances E. Hutner Awd, Princ Res For, 95, 97; Nom, First Bk Awd, MLA, 92; Small Press Cen, NYC, 93; Guest Speak, Irish Am Hist Soc, 96. **MEMBERSHIPS** PRF; ASAIL; MLA; SHARP; JJSNY; STS; Gluckman Ireland House; BMA; NYPL; NMWA. **RESEARCH** English and Irish literatures, c. 1660-1800; English and Irish women writers, c. 1660-1800; literary manuscripts; multimedia research; rare books. **SELECTED PUBLICATIONS** Ed, "Poems by Ephelia, 1679," Schol Fac and Rep (92), 2nd pr 93; auth, "Casting a Wider Net: The Multimedia Research Initiative," in Standards in 18th-Century Culture 22, Am Soc for 18thC Stud (92); auth, "A Feminist Link in the Old Boys' Network: The Career of Katherine 'Orinda' Philips," in "Curtain Calls: Women & the Theatre," eds. M. A. Schofield and C. Macheski (Ohio State UP, 91); auth, "Butterfly of the Restoration Court: A Preview of Lady Mary Villiers, the New 'Ephelia' Candidate," J Am Notes and Quer (96); auth, Profiles of Irish and English women writers, "Encyclopedia of British Women Writers," eds. Paul and June Schlueter (Rutgers Univ Press, 98); auth, "BookTalk" on "LitPage" website of Robt C. Evans (00); auth, "Essential Stands of Restoration Women Writers, 1912-1986," Restor J (pt 1,87; pt ll, 01); auth, "Thumbprints of Ephelia: The End of an Enigma in Restoration Attribution: Text, Image, Sound" (Re)Soundings website (Millersville, PA, 01); auth, "Irish Women Writers before The Great Hunger" Greenwood Pub Gp (Westport, CT) forthcoming; ed, "Ephelia," in "The Early-Modern Englishwoman: A Facsimile Library," Scolar/Ashgate Pub Co., forthcoming. **CONTACT ADDRESS** Princeton Res Forum, Harrison St., Princeton, NJ 11217. **EMAIL** mulvihill@bway.net

MUMBY, DENNIS K.
DISCIPLINE ORGANIZATIONAL COMMUNICATION, PHILOSOPHY OF COMMUNICATION **EDUCATION** Southern Ill Univ, PhD, 84. **CAREER** Assoc prof, Purdue Univ. **SELECTED PUBLICATIONS** Auth, The Political Function of Narrative in Organizations, Commun Monogr, 87; Communication & Power in Organizations, Ablex, 88; ed, Narrative & Social Control, Sage, 93. **CONTACT ADDRESS** Dept of Commun, Purdue Univ, West Lafayette, 1080 Schleman Hall, West Lafayette, IN 47907-1080. **EMAIL** dmumby@purdue.edu

MUNKER, DONA FELDMAN
PERSONAL Born 03/08/1945, Los Angeles, CA **DISCIPLINE** ENGLISH **EDUCATION** Univ Southern CA, BA (drama), 66; IN Univ, Bloomington, MA (English), 67; New York Univ, PhD (English), 76. **CAREER** Lect or adjunct lect, Hunter Col and Univ of Giessen, Ger, 73-76; asst ed, Little, Brown & Co, 80-85; sr ed, Arbor House Pub Co, consult ed, Time-Life Books, 83-85; self employed, writer, consulting book ed, independent scholar, 85-. **HONORS AND AWARDS** Huntington Library Andrew Mellon Fel, 98-99. **MEMBERSHIPS** CA and Southern CA Hist Socs; The Biography Seminar of NY Univ; The Women Writing Women's Lives Seminar, City Univ Grad Center, NY. **RESEARCH** Biography as a genre; theories of creativity and the psychology of creative development; American and California history in the Progressive Era. **SELECTED PUBLICATIONS** Auth, Swift and the Traditions of Seventeenth Century Poetry, Seventeenth Century News, vol 32, nos 1-2, spring/summer, 75; Men are Only Men: Mary Renault's Theseus, Der historische Roman in England und Amerika, eds R Borgmeier and B Reitz, vol I, Carl Winter Verlag, 86; The Country of the Mind: Notes From a Persian-American Collaboration, Chanteh: A Transcultural J, vol 1, no 1, fall 92; Daughter of Persia: A Woman's Journey from Her Father's Harem through the Islamic Revolution, co-auth with Sattareh Farman-Farmaian, Crown Pubs, 92, Doubleday/Anchor, 93; Enchantment and the Biographical Passion, American Imago: Psycho-Analysis and Culture, vol 54, no 4, winter, 97-98; reviews in The New York Times Book Review, Publisher's Weekly, Chanteh; currently writing book-length study of poet and suffragist Sara Bard Field. **CONTACT ADDRESS** 166 E 61st St, New York, NY 10021-8510.

MUNN, PAUL T.
PERSONAL Born 11/21/1950, Seattle, WA **DISCIPLINE** ENGLISH **EDUCATION** Univ Minn, PhD, 88. **CAREER** Asst Prof, SVSU, 98-91; Assoc Prof, 91-96; Full Prof, 96-. **HONORS AND AWARDS** Visiting Prof, Shikoku Univ, Japan, 95. **MEMBERSHIPS** MLA; NCTE; ALSC. **RESEARCH** Poetry; Milton; Pedagogy. **SELECTED PUBLICATIONS** Auth, "An Interview with John Ashbery," New Orleans Review, 17.2, 90: 59-63; auth, "Vestigial Forms in John Ashbery's A Wave," New Orleans Review 19.1, 92: 19-22; auth, "The Feminist Classroom: A Critique," Journal of the Michigan College English Association 1.1, Fall 95: 103-120; auth, "Are Japanese Proverbs Intelligible to Americans?" With Masa Otagaki and Kazuko Ikumoto, Modern English Teaching January 96: 26-31; auth, "Giroux and Radical Pedagogy: A Humanist's Response," Journal of the Michigan College English Association 3, 97: 87-100. **CONTACT ADDRESS** Dept English, Saginaw Valley State Univ, 7400 Bay Rd., University Center, MI 48710-0001. **EMAIL** ptmunn@svsu.edu

MURDICK, WILLIAM
DISCIPLINE RHETORIC AND LINGUISTICS **EDUCATION** SUNY, Albany, BA; Univ IA, MFA; IN Univ PA, PhD. **CAREER** Instr, CA State Univ PA. **SELECTED PUBLICATIONS** Auth, What English Teachers Need to Know about Grammar, Eng J, Nov 96; coauth, Evolution of a Writing Center, Writing Ctr J, 91; Placing Whole Language in a Workshop Setting, Eng Leadership Quart, Dec 91; Art, Writing, and Politics, Art Educ, Sept 92; Journal Writing and Active Learning, Eng Leadership Quart, Oct 93. **CONTACT ADDRESS** California Univ of Pennsylvania, California, PA 15419s. **EMAIL** murdick@cup.edu

MURDOCK, KATHERINE
DISCIPLINE MUSICOLOGY-COMPOSITION **EDUCATION** Humboldt State Univ, BA; SF State Univ, MA; Eastman Sch Mus, PhD. **CAREER** Instr, Univ Tex-Austin; SF State Univ; Eastman Sch Mus; dir, WSU Contemp Mus Fest; assoc prof. **SELECTED PUBLICATIONS** Publ, Dorn Publ Inc. **CONTACT ADDRESS** Dept of Mus, Wichita State Univ, 1845 Fairmont, Wichita, KS 67260-0062.

MURFIN, ROSS C.
PERSONAL Born 11/14/1948, Richmond, IN, m, 1971, 2 children **DISCIPLINE** ENGLISH **EDUCATION** Princeton Univ, AB, 71; Univ Va, MA, 72; PhD, 74. **CAREER** Asst prof to assoc prof, Yale Univ, 74-82; assoc prof to prof to col dean, Univ Miami, 81-96; prof to provost, vpres, Southern Methodist Univ, 96-. **HONORS AND AWARDS** Va Danforth Fel, 72-74; ACLS Fel, 78-79; NEH Fel, 83; Prof of Year Award, Univ Miami, 85-86; Phi Eta Sigma Honor Soc, 82-83; Honors Student Asn, Univ Miami, 82-83. **MEMBERSHIPS** PMLA. **RESEARCH** 19th and early 20th century literature in English; critical theory; history of criticism; religion and poetry. **SELECTED PUBLICATIONS** Auth, Swineburne, Hardy, Lawrence and the Burden of Belief, Univ Chicago Pr, 78; auth, The Poetry of D. H. Lawrence: Texts and Contexts, Univ Nebr Pr, 83; ed, Conrad Revisited: Essays for the Eighties, Univ Nebr Pr, 85; auth, Sons and Lovers: A Novel of Division and Desire, Twayne, 87; series ed, Case Studies in Contemporary Criticism, Bedford Bks, St Martins Pr, 89-; ed, Heart of Darkness: Case Studies in Contemporary Criticism, Bedford Bks, St Martins Pr, 89; ed, The Scarlet Letter: Case Studies in Contemporary Criticism, Bedford Bks, St Martins Pr, 91; auth, Lord Jim: After the Truth, Twayne, 92; co-auth, The Bedford Glossary of Critical and Literary Terms, Bedford Bks, St Martin's Pr, 97. **CONTACT ADDRESS** English Dept, So Methodist Univ, Rm 219 Perkins Admin Bldg, PO Box 750221, Dallas, TX 75275-0001. **EMAIL** rmurfin@mail.smu.edu

MURGIA, CHARLES EDWARD
PERSONAL Born 02/18/1935, Boston, MA, s **DISCIPLINE** CLASSICS **EDUCATION** Boston Col, AB, 56; Harvard Univ, MA, 60, PhD(Class Philol), 66. **CAREER** Instr Classics, Franklin & Marshall Col, 60-61; vis instr, Dartmouth Col, 64-65; asst prof, 66-72, assoc prof, 72-78, prof Classics, Univ Calif, Berkeley, 78-94, chmn, 80-83, Am Coun Learned Soc grant-in-aid, 68; appointed to edit Vol V of Editio Harvardiana of Servius; Univ Calif Humanities Res Comt res fels, Fall 70; Am Coun Learned Soc fel, 74-75; Nat Endowment for Humanities fel, 78-79; prof Emeritus, 94-; prof grad school, Univ Calif, Berkeley, 95-01. **MEMBERSHIPS** Am Philol Asn; Philol Asn Pac Coast. **RESEARCH** Latin textual criticism; Latin paleography; classical literature. **SELECTED PUBLICATIONS** Auth, Critical notes on the text of Servius' commentary on Aeneid III-V, Harvard Studies Class Philol, 67; Avienus' supposed iambic version of Livy, 70 & More on the Helen episode, 71, The Donatian life of Virgil, DS, and D, 74, Calif Studies Class Antiq; Prolegomena to Servius V--the manuscripts, Vol 11, Class Studies Ser, Univ Calif, 75; The minor works of Tacitus--a study in textual criticism, Class Philol, 77; The length of the

lacuna in Tacitus' Dialogus, Calif Studies Class Antiq, 79; The date of Tacitus' Dialogus, Harvard Studies Class Philol, 80. **CONTACT ADDRESS** Dept of Classics, Univ of California, Berkeley, 7303 Dwinelle Hall, Berkeley, CA 94720-2520. **EMAIL** cem@socrates.berkeley.edu

MURPHEY, KATHLEEN
PERSONAL Born 01/18/1965, Philadelphia, PA, m, 1994, 1 child **DISCIPLINE** DEVELOPMENTAL ENGLISH **EDUCATION** Boston Univ, BA, 84; Univ Pa, MA, 87; MSEd, 92. **CAREER** Lectr, Univ Pa, 94-96; instr, Moore Col of Art and Design, 96-97; instr, West Chester Univ, 98-00; instr, Philadelphia Univ, 93-00; instr, Community Col of Philadelphia, 92-00; asst prof, Camden County Col, 00-. **MEMBERSHIPS** MLA, Am Studies Assoc, Children's Lit Assoc, Col Eng Assoc, Community Col Humanities Assoc, Pa Hist Assoc. **RESEARCH** American Popular Culture, Children's Literature, Loren Corey Eiseley, Computers and Composition. **SELECTED PUBLICATIONS** Auth, "An English Composition Course via the Inernet and E-mail," Proceedings of the Pa Assoc of Two-Year Col, (98); auth, "The Last of the Mohicans: The Novel vs. The 1992 Michael Mann Version," 1999 Film and Hist CD-ROM Annual, (99). **CONTACT ADDRESS** Camden County Col, College Dr, Blackwood, NJ 08012. **EMAIL** kmurphey@camdencc.edu

MURPHY, B. KEITH
PERSONAL Born 09/28/1962, Grayson, KY, m, 1993 **DISCIPLINE** ENGLISH **EDUCATION** Morehead St Univ, BA, 84; Miami Univ, MA, 85; Ohio Univ, PhD, 88. **CAREER** From Asst Prof to Assoc Prof, Ft Valley St Univ, 95-. **HONORS AND AWARDS** Outstanding Student Awd, Ohio Univ, 88; Fac Mem of the Year, Ind Univ - Purdue Univ, 94; Student Serv Awd, Ind Univ - Purdue Univ, 95; Coach of the Year, 95; Annie R Carthon Fac Mentor Awd, Ft Valley St Univ, 96. **MEMBERSHIPS** NFA, GIFA, ARBA. **RESEARCH** Popular culture (comic books, conspiracy theory, computer mediated communication), military communication, history and development of rhetorical theory. **SELECTED PUBLICATIONS** Auth, "Lyman Frank Baum: 1856-1919: U S Writer of Children's Books, Including the Oz Books," Dict of World Biog, Salem Publ (99): 154-156; auth, "Benazir Bhutto," Notable Women in World Govt, Magill Publ (forthcoming); auth, "Communication Systems in North America," Encycl of World Geog, Salem Publ (forthcoming); auth, "Xenophon," Magill's Guide to Military Hist, Magill Publ (forthcoming); auth, "Megiddo, 1918," Magill's Guide to Military Hist, Magill Publ (forthcoming); auth, "Mau Mau Rebellion," Magill's Guide to Military Hist, Magill Publ (forthcoming); auth, "Amin, Idi," Magill's Guide to Military Hist, Magill Publ (forthcoming); auth, "Cryptography," Magill's Guide to Military Hist, Magill Publ (forthcoming). **CONTACT ADDRESS** Dept English & Lang, Fort Valley State Univ, 1005 St University Dr, Ft Valley, GA 31030-4313. **EMAIL** sophist@bigfoot.com

MURPHY, BRENDA C.
PERSONAL Born 05/12/1950, Beverly, MA, m, 1995 **DISCIPLINE** ENGLISH, LITERATURE **EDUCATION** Univ Dayton, AB, 71; Brown Univ, PhD, 75. **CAREER** Asst prof to assoc prof to assoc dean to prof, St Lawrence Univ, 75-89; prof, Univ Conn, 89-. **HONORS AND AWARDS** ACLS Fel, 81-82; NHC Fel, 81-82; NEH Grant, 79, 80, 87, 93; Chancellor Res Fel, 99; Provost Res Fel, 93. **MEMBERSHIPS** MLA; ATHE; ASTR; ASA; ATDS; Eugene O'Neill Soc; Arthur Miller Soc. **RESEARCH** Modern and contemporary Drama; film and television; twentieth-century American literature and culture. **SELECTED PUBLICATIONS** Co-auth, John Hay--Howells Letters: The Correspondence of John Milton Hay and William Dean Howells 1861-1905, Twayne, 80; auth, "American Realism and American Drama, 1880-1940," in Cambridge Studies in American Literature and Culture Series (Cambridge/NYork: Cambridge Univ Pr, 87); auth, Tennessee Williams and Elia Kazan: A Collaboration in the Theatre, Cambridge Univ Pr, 92; auth, Miller: Death of a Salesman, Plays in Production Series, Cambridge Univ Pr, 95; ed, The Cambridge Companion to American Women Playwrights, Cambridge Univ Pr, 99; co-auth, Understanding Death of a Salesman: A Student Casebook to Issues, Sources, Documents, Greenwood, 99; auth, "Plays and Playwrights, 1915-1945," in The Historical Cambridge History of American Theatre Vol 2, eds. Don B. Wilmeth, Christopher Bigsby (Cambridge/NYork: Cambridge Univ Pr, 99): 289-342; auth, Congressional Theatre: Dramatizing McCarthyism on Stage, Film, and Television, Cambridge Univ Pr, 99; auth, O'Neill: Long Day's Journey Into Night. Plays in Production Series, Cambridge Univ Pr, 01. **CONTACT ADDRESS** 59 Woodland Dr, Windham, CT 06280-1040. **EMAIL** brenda.murphy@uconn.edu

MURPHY, BRIAN
PERSONAL Born 05/25/1939, Detroit, MI, m, 1979, 3 children **DISCIPLINE** ENGLISH **EDUCATION** Univ Detroit, BA, 61, MA, 63; Harvard Univ, AM, 65; Univ London, PhD, 74. **CAREER** Instr, eng, 69-73, asst prof, eng, 73-76, assoc prof, eng, 76-96, prof, eng, 96-, dir of honors col and coord of cinema, 85-, Oakland Univ. **HONORS AND AWARDS** Teaching excellence award, 95. **RESEARCH** 19th Century British literature; Shakespeare; Film, Oscar Wilde, G. B. Shaw, C. S. Lewis. **SELECTED PUBLICATIONS** Auth, Critical study of C. S. Lewis, Starmont, 83; auth, The Enigma Variations, Scribner's 81, Blond & Briggs, 82, Het Spectrum, 85-86. **CONTACT ADDRESS** Oakland Univ, 112 Vandenberg Hall, Rochester, MI 48309. **EMAIL** hc@oakland.edu

MURPHY, JOHN J.
PERSONAL Born 04/03/1933, New York, NY, m, 1962, 5 children **DISCIPLINE** ENGLISH **EDUCATION** St John's Univ, BA, 56; MA 61. **CAREER** Instr, Col of St Teresa, 60-65; asst prof to assoc prof, Merrimack Col, 65-84; prof, Brigham Young Univ, 84-. **HONORS AND AWARDS** NEH Fel, 82; NMex Hist Soc R.E. Twitchell Awd, 00. **SELECTED PUBLICATIONS** Auth, My Antonia: The Road Home, 89; ed, Critical Essays on Willa Cather, 84; ed Willa Cather: Family, Community, History, 90; auth, Death Comes for the Archbishop, 99. **CONTACT ADDRESS** Dept English, Brigham Young Univ, 3146 Jkhb, Provo, UT 84602.

MURPHY, PATRICK D.
PERSONAL Born 01/16/1964, Cincinnati, OH, s, 1 child **DISCIPLINE** TELECOMMUNICATION **EDUCATION** Ohio Univ, PhD, 96. **HONORS AND AWARDS** Fulbright-Garcia Robles Fel. **MEMBERSHIPS** ICA; NCA; AEJMC; UDC. **RESEARCH** Transnational media; mass communication theory; cultural studies. **SELECTED PUBLICATIONS** Auth, Contrasting Perspectives: Cultural studies in Latin American and the U.S., a Conversation with Nestor Garcia Canclini, Cultural Studies, 97; Television and Cultural Politics in Mexico: Some notes on Televisa, the state, and transnational culture, Howard J of Commun, 95; coauth, Cultural Identity and Cyberimperialism: Computer Mediated Explorations of Ethnicity, Nation, and Citizenship, Cyberimperialism: Global Relations in the New Electronic Frontier, in press; The Study of Communication and Culture in Latin America: From laggards and the oppressed to resistance and hybrid cultures, The J of Int Commun, 97; auth, Doing audience ethnography: Anarrative accout of establishing ethnographic identity and locating interpretive communities in field work, Qualitative Inquiry, Vol. 5 (4) 479-502, 99; auth, Media cultural studies' uncomfortabel embrace of ethnography, "Journal of Communication Inquiry, Vol. 23 (3) 205-221, 99. **CONTACT ADDRESS** Dept of Mass Communications, So Illinois Univ, Edwardsville, Edwardsville, IL 62026-1775. **EMAIL** pmurphy@siue.edu

MURPHY, PATRICK DENNIS
PERSONAL Born 10/19/1951, Joliet, IL, m, 1982, 1 child **DISCIPLINE** ENGLISH **EDUCATION** Univ Calif Los Angeles, BA, 73; Calif State Univ, MA, 83; Univ Calif Davis, PhD 86. **CAREER** Teaching asst, Calif State Univ, 82-83; teaching asst to lectr, Calif State Univ, 83-87; asst prof to prof, Ind Univ Pa, 87-. **HONORS AND AWARDS** ACLS Intl Travel Grant, 90; SSHE Develop Res Grant, 90; Fulbright Res Scholar, Univ Ryukyus, 97-98; Univ Senate Res Committee Award, 99; Distinguished Fac Award, 99. **MEMBERSHIPS** MLA; Asn for the Study of Lit and Environ; Asn for the Study of Am Indian Lit; Soc for the Study of Multi-Ethnic Lit of the U.S.; W Lit Asn. **RESEARCH** Modern and contemporary American literature, with an emphasis on nature-oriented, women's and multicultural texts, especially poetry; International ecocriticism. **SELECTED PUBLICATIONS** Ed, Critical Essays on Gary Snyder, G.K. Hall, 91; auth, Understanding Gary Snyder, Univ SC press, 92; co-ed, Critical Essays on American Modernism, G.K. Hall, 92; ed, Staging the Impossible: The Fantastic Mode in Modern Drama, Greenwood Press, 92; auth, Literature, Nature, and Other: Ecofeminist Critiques, SUNY Press, 95; co-ed, Essentials of the Theory of Fiction, Duke Univ Press, 96; co-ed, Ecofeminist Literary Criticism and Pedagogy, Univ Ill Press, 98; co-auth, "The Women Are Speaking," in Ecofeminist Literary Criticism and Pedagogy, Univ Ill Press, 98; ed, The Literature of Nature: An International Sourcebook, Fitzroy-Dearborn Pub, 98; auth, A Place for Wayfaring: The Poetry and Prose of Gary Snyder, Ore State Univ Press, 00; auth, Farther Afield in the Study of Nature Oriented Literature, Univ Press of Va, 00. **CONTACT ADDRESS** Dept English, Indiana Univ of Pennsylvania, 110 Leonard Hall, Indiana, PA 15705-0001. **EMAIL** pdmurphy@grove.iup.edu

MURPHY, PETER
DISCIPLINE ENGLISH **EDUCATION** Yale Univ, BA, 81; Johns Hopkins, PhD, 86. **CAREER** Lectr & dean of the Col. **RESEARCH** 18th and 19th century British literature; popular culture; literary culture broadly defined. **SELECTED PUBLICATIONS** Auth, Poetry as an Occupation and an Art in Britain, 1760-1830; Climbing Parnassus, and Falling Off; Scott's Disappointments: Reading The Heart of MidLothian. **CONTACT ADDRESS** Dept of English, Williams Col, Hopkins Hall and Stetson 410, Williamstown, MA 01267. **EMAIL** pmurphy@williams.edu

MURPHY, RICHARD
DISCIPLINE TEACHING OF WRITING, THE STUDY OF FICTION, GRAMMAR, ENGLISH EDUCATION, AND **EDUCATION** Univ Santa Clara, BA, 67; Univ CA, Berkeley, PhD, 77. **CAREER** Prof, Radford Univ, 79-. **HONORS AND AWARDS** Donald N. Dedmon Awd for Prof Excellence, 82. **SELECTED PUBLICATIONS** Auth, The Calculus of Intimacy: A Teaching Life, The Ohio State U P, 94; coauth, Symbiosis: Writing in an Academic Culture, Heinemann, 93. **CONTACT ADDRESS** Dept of English, Curry Col, 1071 Blue Hill Ave, Milton, MA 02186.

MURPHY, RUSSELL E.
PERSONAL Born 05/05/1944, Providence, RI, m, 1980, 8 children **DISCIPLINE** AMERICAN AND BRITISH LITERATURE **EDUCATION** Univ Mass, PhD. **CAREER** English and Lit, Univ Ark, Editor Yeats-Eliot Review. **RESEARCH** W.B. Yeats, T.S. Eliot. **SELECTED PUBLICATIONS** Auth, Structure and Meaning: An introduction to literature; 'It is impossible to say just what I mean': The Wasteland as Transcendent Meaning; The 'Rough Beast' and Historical Necessity: A new consideration of Yeats's 'The Second Coming, Studies Literary Imagination; auth, Cold Rocky Face': W.B. Yeats, The Christ Pantkator, and The Soul's History, Yeats Annual. **CONTACT ADDRESS** Univ of Arkansas, Little Rock, 2801 S University Ave., Little Rock, AR 72204-1099. **EMAIL** remurphy@ualr.edu

MURPHY, SEAN P.
PERSONAL Born 09/01/1970, Rochester, NY, m, 1996 **DISCIPLINE** LITERATURE **EDUCATION** St Bona Univ, BA, 92; SUNY, MA, 94; Kent State Univ, PhD, 99. **CAREER** Asst prof, Col of Lake Cnty, 99-01; asst prof, Cen Mich Univ, 01-. **MEMBERSHIPS** CEA, MLA, Intl James Joyce Found, NATE. **RESEARCH** Modernism and Postmodernism, Irish and British Literature, James Joyce, Critical Theory, Literary Theory, Composition Theory, Psychoanalytic Theory (Lacanian and Freudian). **SELECTED PUBLICATIONS** Auth, "Passing Boldly into that Other World of (W)Holes: Narrativity and Subjectivity," in James Joyce's 'The Dead', Stud in Short Fict (95); auth, "In the Middle of Nowhere: The Interpolative Force of Experimental Narrative Structure in Graham Swift's Waterland, Stud in Human Writ (96); auth, "Identity, Ideology, and Triads in Gertrude Stein's Patriarchal Poetry," Arts and Let (98); auth, "Ida Did Not Go Directly Anywhere: Symbolic Peregrinations, Desire, and Linearity" in Gertrude Stein's Ida, Lit and Psych (01); auth, "Improving Two-Year College Teacher Preparation: Graduate Student Internships," Teach Eng in the Two Yr Col (01); auth, James Joyce and Victims, Fairleigh Dick UP (forthcoming). **CONTACT ADDRESS** Dept of Eng, Central Michigan Univ, Mount Pleasant, MI 48859.

MURRAY, CATHERINE A.
PERSONAL Born Kitchener, ON, Canada **DISCIPLINE** COMMUNICATIONS **EDUCATION** Waterloo, MA; Queen's Univ, PhD, 85. **CAREER** Sr proj dir, Decima Res, 85-89, VP, 89-91; assoc prof, Simon Fraser Univ, 92-. **MEMBERSHIPS** WTN Found; OWL Children's Trust; BC Film. **RESEARCH** Strategic marketing, policy and regulation in telecommunications and broadcasting; political communication and opinion research; social marketing. **SELECTED PUBLICATIONS** Auth, Information Security at Risk?, 93; auth, Privacy Potholes on the Information Highway, 96; coauth, Making Our Voices Heard: The Future of the CBC, NFB and Telefilm. **CONTACT ADDRESS** Dept of Commun, Simon Fraser Univ, 8888 Univ Dr, Vancouver, BC, Canada V5A 1S6. **EMAIL** catherine-murray@sfu.ca

MURRAY, HEATHER
PERSONAL Born Weston, ON, Canada **DISCIPLINE** ENGLISH **EDUCATION** Vic Col, Univ Toronto, BA, 73; York Univ, MA, 77, PhD, 84. **CAREER** Asst prof & postdoc fel, Queen's Univ, 85-87; Assoc Prof Trinty Col, Univ Toronto 87-, dir, Women's Stud Prog, 93-96. **RESEARCH** History of reading and reading cultures, nineteenth-century Ontario cultural history, literary and socialist writngs of Eleanor Marx, spelling reform movements. **SELECTED PUBLICATIONS** Auth, Working in English: History, Institution, Resources, 96; auth, The Toronto Women's Literary Club 1877-1883, Hist Studies in Ed; auth, culture in early Toronto, Essays on Can Writing; auth, Come, bright Improvement! The Literary Societies of Nineteenth-Cnetury Ontario, 00. **CONTACT ADDRESS** Dept of English, Univ of Toronto, Toronto, ON, Canada M5S 1H8. **EMAIL** heather.murray@utoronto.ca

MURRAY, LAURA
DISCIPLINE ENGLISH LITERATURE **EDUCATION** Cornell Univ, PhD. **CAREER** Dept Eng, Queen's Univ **RESEARCH** American literature between the Revolution and the Civil War; contemporary American fiction and autobiography; Native North American literature; cultural theory; theoretical issues arising from scholarly editing; oral cultures in comparison to and in relation with writing-oriented cultures; diaries and correspondences as genres. **SELECTED PUBLICATIONS** Auth, pubs on early Native American writing, Washington Irving's Sketch Book, and phrasebooks for immigrants to America; ed, To Do Good to My Indian Brethren: The Writings of Joseph Johnson 1751-1776, Univ Mass, 98; co-ed, Talking on the Page: Editing Aboriginal Oral Texts, Univ Toronto. **CONTACT ADDRESS** English Dept, Queen's Univ at Kingston, Kingston, ON, Canada K7L 3N6. **EMAIL** lm19@post.QueensU.CA

MURRAY, MICHAEL D.
PERSONAL Born 11/09/1947, St Louis, MO, m **DISCIPLINE** HISTORY, JOURNALISM **EDUCATION** St Louis Univ, BA, 70; MA, 71; Univ Mo, PhD, 74. **CAREER** Asst Proof, Va Tech Univ, 74-76; Assoc. Proof, Univ Louisville, 76-82; Proof, Univ Mo, 82-. **HONORS AND AWARDS** Goldsmith Roes Awd, Harvard Univ, 92; Feel, Stanford Univ, 93. **MEMBERSHIPS** Am Jour Historian's Assoc. **RESEARCH** Journalism and mass communication history. **SELECTED PUBLICATIONS** Auth, The Political Performers, Praeger Pr, 94; ed, Television in America, Iowa State Univ Pr, 98; ed, The Encyclopedia of TV News, Oryx Pr, 99. **CONTACT ADDRESS** Dept Hist, Univ of Missouri, St. Louis, 9870 Cupper Hill Rd, Saint Louis, MO 63124. **EMAIL** murraymd@umsl.edu

MUSGROVE, LAURENCE E.
DISCIPLINE ENGLISH **EDUCATION** Southwestern Univ, BA, 76; Univ of Oregon, Ph.D., 92. **CAREER** Dept of English, Univ of Southern Indiana, 92-98. **MEMBERSHIPS** Ex Bd mem, Ind Tchr(s) Writing, 96-98; Nat Coun Tchr(s) Engl; Sigma Tau Delta, Int Eng Honor Soc. **SELECTED PUBLICATIONS** Ed, COMPONERE: Policies, Resources, Pedagogies, and Perspectives for Composition Teachers at University of Oregon, Eugene, Univ of Oregon, 90; ,ed, The Webfoot Readr, Eugene, Univ of Oregon, 91; "Response to: Beyond Argument in the Feminist Composition by Cathrine Lamb," College Composition and Communication, 91; ed, "Composing Character in Composition." Rhetoric in the Vortex of Cultural Studies: Proceedings of the Fifth Biennial Conference, ed, Arthur Walzer, Minneapolis, Rhetoric Society of American, 93; auth, "Classical Topoi and the Academic Commonplace," ERIC Clearinghouse on Reading and Communication Skills, ED (93): 357-366; auth, "Should I Go or Should I Stay? A Interview with Liam Rector," An Interview, Southern Indiana Review, Vol 4, 97; auth, "Portfolios, Self-Evaluation, and Student Learning," Teaching Matters, Univ of Southern Indiana, 97; auth, "Attitude," English Journal, Vol 87, No 4, (98): 85-86; auth, "Attitude Toward Writing," Journal of the Assembly for Expanded Perspective on Learning, 98,99; auth, Ethics in English. Work-in-Progress. An anthology of classic writing on the intersection of philosophy, literature, and rhetoric. **CONTACT ADDRESS** Dept of Eng and Foreign Lang, Saint Xavier Univ, 3700 W 103rd St, Chicago, IL 60655. **EMAIL** musgrove@sxu.edu

MUSMANN, KLAUS
PERSONAL Born 06/27/1935, Magdeburg, Germany, m, 1986 **DISCIPLINE** LIBRARIANSHIP **EDUCATION** Wayne St Univ, BA, 62; Univ of MI, AMLS, 63, MA, 67; Univ of South CA, PhD, 81 **CAREER** Asst Librn, 65-67, MI St Univ; Asst Librn, 67-68, CA St Poly; Assoc Librn, 84-86, Librn, 86-94, Act Dir, 94-96, Dir, 96-, Univ of Redlands **HONORS AND AWARDS** Res grants **MEMBERSHIPS** ALA; ACRL **RESEARCH** Diffusion of technol innov **SELECTED PUBLICATIONS** Auth, The Ugly Side of Librarianship: Discrimination in Libraries from 1900-1950, Univ of IL, 98; Technological Innovations in Libraries, 1860-1960, Greenwood Press, 93 **CONTACT ADDRESS** Armacost Libr, Univ of Redlands, Redlands, CA 92374. **EMAIL** kmusmann@uor.edu

MUSTAFA, SHAKIR M.
PERSONAL Born 06/15/1952, Baghdad, Iraq, m, 1979, 3 children **DISCIPLINE** ENGLISH **EDUCATION** Baghdad Univ, BA, 74; MA, 77; Ind Univ, PhD, 99. **CAREER** Asst Prof, Mosul Univ, 79-90; Vis Asst Prof, Ind Univ, 99-00; Vis Asst Prof, Boston Univ, 00-. **HONORS AND AWARDS** Res Fel, Ind Univ, 91; Hon Mention, Irish Studies Conf, 97. **MEMBERSHIPS** MLA; S Asn for Comp Lit; Arabic Lit Discussion Group. **RESEARCH** Irish Studies; Arabic Literature; Postcolonial Studies; Translation; Jewish-American Fiction. **SELECTED PUBLICATIONS** Auth, Learning Guide, Ind Univ Press, 96; auth, "Demythologizing Ireland," Can Journal of Irish Studies, 97; auth, "Representations of Natives," Abhath al-Yarmouk, 99; auth, "Book Reviews," Year Book of General and Comparative Lit, 00; co-ed, A Century of Irish Drama, Ind Univ Press. **CONTACT ADDRESS** Dept English, Boston Univ, 718 Commonwealth Ave, Boston, MA 02215. **EMAIL** mustafa@bu.edu

MYERS, DAVID G.
PERSONAL Born 02/27/1952 **DISCIPLINE** ENGLISH, JEWISH STUDIES **EDUCATION** Univ Calif at Santa Cruz, BA, 74; Wash Univ, AM, 77; Northwestern Univ, PhD, 89. **CAREER** From asst prof to assoc prof, Tex A&M Univ, 89-. **MEMBERSHIPS** Asn for Jewish Studies. **RESEARCH** Holocaust literature and reception and their interaction with the history of ideas. **SELECTED PUBLICATIONS** Auth, The Elephants Teach: Creative Writing Since 1880, Prentice Hall, 96; co-ed, Unrelenting Readers: The New Poet-Critics, Story Line Press, forthcoming. **CONTACT ADDRESS** Dept English, Texas A&M Univ, Col Station, College Station, TX 77843-0001. **EMAIL** dgmyers@tamu.edu

MYERS, MARSHALL
PERSONAL Born 12/04/1943, Platteville, WI, m, 1999, 2 children **DISCIPLINE** RHETORIC, COMPOSITION **EDUCATION** Lindsey Wilson Col, AA, Ky Western Col, BA; Eastern Ky Univ, MA, Univ La, PhD. **CAREER** Instr, Elizabethtown Community Col, 66-68; asst prof, Ky Wesleyon, 68-70, 74-75; asst prof, Texas Tech, 93-95; Eastern Ky Univ, 95-. **HONORS AND AWARDS** Excellence in Teaching, Univ of La, Texas Tech Univ. **MEMBERSHIPS** NCTE; Assoc of Teachers of Grammar; Col Composition and Commun. **RESEARCH** Empirical research in technical and business writing. **SELECTED PUBLICATIONS** Auth, "The Pansies by the Porch", My Legacy 20; auth, "The Terror of the Black Flag", Meade County Messenger, (Oct 97); auth, "Pauline Cushman: Scout of the Cumberlands", Ky Civil War J, (Jan 97): 23-24; auth, Barefood: Stories and Sketches, Sunflower Dream Pr, (Galesburg, IL), 98, auth, "Waiting up for Her", My Legacy, 17 (98): 137; auth, "The Wizened Old Woman", Ky Blue 3.1 (98): 15; auth, "Old Pills: General William Tecumseh Sherman at Muldraugh Hill", Cannonade 8.3; (98): 2-3; auth, "Myth and John Hunt Morgan", Cannonade 9.4 (99): 304; auth, "Jim, Constance, and the Clock", Ky Blue 3.3 (99): 35-37; auth, "The Influence of the purpose of a Business Document on its Syntax and Rhetorical Schemes", J of Tech Writing and Composition, (forthcoming). **CONTACT ADDRESS** Dept English, Eastern Kentucky Univ, 521 Lancaster Ave, Richmond, KY 40475-3100. **EMAIL** engmyers@acs.eku.edu

MYERS, MITZI
PERSONAL Born Sulphur Springs, TX, m, 1967 **DISCIPLINE** ENGLISH **EDUCATION** E Tex State Univ, BA, 61, MA, 62; Rice Univ, PhD(English), 69. **CAREER** Asst prof English, Univ Calif, Santa Barbara, 66-73; lectr, Calif State Col, San Bernardino, 74-77; lectr English, Calif State Univ, Fullerton, 76-78, Calif Polytech Inst, 78-80 & Univ Calif, Los Angeles, 80-82; Lectr English, Calif State Univ, Long Beach, 80-, Univ Calif res grant, 69-70. **MEMBERSHIPS** MLA; Philol Asn Pac Coast; Am Soc 18th Century Studies; Western Soc 18th Century Studies; Women's Caucus Mod Lang Asn; Conf British Studies. **SELECTED PUBLICATIONS CONTACT ADDRESS** 2206 Bedford Dr, Fullerton, CA 92631.

MYERS, NORMAN JERALD
PERSONAL Born 06/24/1935, Canton, OH, m, 1959, 2 children **DISCIPLINE** THEATRE **EDUCATION** Hiram Col, AB, 57; Univ Ill, Urbana, MA, 59, PhD, 62. **CAREER** Asst prof speech & drama, Lycoming Col, 59-61; asst prof theatre, Ky Wesleyan Col, 62-63; asst prof, State Univ NY Col Oswego, 63-66; asst prof drama, La State Univ, New Orleans, 66-70; Assoc Prof Theatre, Bowling Green State Univ, 70-91; prof Theatre, Bowling Green State Univ, 91-98; Prof Emeritus, 98; Managing dir, Huron Playhouse, 71-79. **MEMBERSHIPS** Am Theatre Asn. **RESEARCH** American theatre history; British theatre history; dramatic theory and criticism. **SELECTED PUBLICATIONS** Auth, A season at the John Street: From The Theatrical Register, Southern Speech J, winter 68; Early recognition of Gordon Craig in American periodicals, Educ Theatre J, 3/70; Shoestring Shakespeare,Meets the Apocrypha: Arden of Faversham at Bowling Green State University, Proceedings of Wretched Plays and Miserable Fragments, Exploring the Dark Corners of the Shakespeare Canon, Slippery Rock, PA, 95; Proslavery Ideology and the Antebellum/Civil War Theatre, McNeese Review 95-96; Finding a Heap of Jewels in Lesser Shakespeare: The Wars of the Roses and Richard Duke of York, New England Theatre J, 96. **CONTACT ADDRESS** Dept of Theatre, Bowling Green State Univ, 1001 E Wooster St, Bowling Green, OH 43403-0001. **EMAIL** nmyers@bgnet.bgsu.edu

MYERS, SCOTT
PERSONAL Born 08/09/1965, Wichita Falls, TX, s **DISCIPLINE** COMMUNICATIONS **EDUCATION** Ill State Univ, BA, 87; MA, 89; Kent State Univ, PhD, 95. **CAREER** Vis asst prof, Kent State Univ, 95-96; asst prof, McNeese State Univ, 96-98; asst prof, Creighton Univ, 98-. **HONORS AND AWARDS** Teaching Awd, Kent State Univ, 92; distinguished Fac Awd, 98. **MEMBERSHIPS** Nat Comm Asn, Central States comm Asn, Eastern Comm Asn. **RESEARCH** Instructional Communication, Graduate teaching assistant socialization and training, Sibling communication. **SELECTED PUBLICATIONS** Ed, Speak easy: Principles and practices of public speaking, Simon and Schuster: Needham Heights, 97; co-auth, The team trainer: Winning tools and tactics for successful workouts, Irwin Press: Chicago, 96; auth, "Dissertation days," in Completing your thesis or dissertation: Professors share their techniques and strategies, Pyrczak Pub: Los Angeles, (99): 76-77. **CONTACT ADDRESS** Dept comm, Creighton Univ, 2500 Calif Plaza, Omaha, NE 68178-0001. **EMAIL** scotia@creighton.edu

MYERSON, JOEL ARTHUR
PERSONAL Born 09/09/1945, Boston, MA **DISCIPLINE** AMERICAN LITERATURE **EDUCATION** Tulane Univ, AB, 67; Northwestern Univ, Evanston, MA, 68, PhD, 71. **CAREER** Asst prof, 71-76, assoc prof, 76-80, prof English, 80-90, Carolina Prof of Am Lit, 90-96, Carolina Distinguished prof of Am Lit, 96-, Univ SC; assoc ed, Northwestern-Newberry Ed of the Writings of Herman Melville, 70-77; consult, Ctr for Ed Am Authors, 74-76; Am Philos Soc res grantee, 72-73, 84-85; NEH grants, 76, 78-81, 88-92, 94-97, 97-99; ed, Studies in the Am Renaissance, GK Hall, 78-82, Univ Virginia, 83-96; Guggenheim fel, 81-82; ed bd, Pittsburgh Series in Bibl, 78-; consult, Comm on Scholarly Ed, MLA, 78-; consult, Concord Museum, 86-89, 91-97; assoc ed, Am Natl Biog, 89-98; consult Fruitlands Museums, 90-93. **HONORS AND AWARDS** Contemporary Authors, Who's Who in America; Distinguished Service Awd of Asn for Documentary Ed, 86; Children's Lit Asn Book Awd, 90; elected Mass Hist Soc, 94; elected, Am Antiq Soc, 95; Lyman H. Butterfield award, Asn for Documentary Ed, 95; teacher of the year award, 97. **MEMBERSHIPS** Melville Soc; MLA; Bibliog Soc Am; SAtlantic Mod Lang Asn; Asn for Documentary Ed; Northeast MLA; Philol Asn of Carolinas; Soc for Textual Scholarship; Poe Stud Asn; Ralph Waldo Emerson Soc; Margaret fuller Soc. **RESEARCH** New England Transcendentalism; textual and bibliographical studies; R W Emerson. **SELECTED PUBLICATIONS** Coauth, Ralph Waldo Emerson: An Annotated Bibliography of Criticism, 1980-1991, Greenwood, 94; co-ed, Emerson's Antislavery Writings, Yale, 95; ed, The Cambridge Companion to Henry David Thoreau, Cambridge, 95; co-ed, The Professions of Authorship: Essays in Honor of Matthew J. Bruccoli, South Carolina, 96; co-ed, Louisa May Alcott's The Inheritance, Dutton, 97; ed, The Selected Letters of Ralph Waldo Emerson, Columbia, 97; auth, Margaret Fuller: An Annotated Bibliography of Criticism, 1983-1995, Greenwood, 98. **CONTACT ADDRESS** Dept of English, Univ of So Carolina, Columbia, Columbia, SC 29208. **EMAIL** myerson-joel@sc.edu

MYRSIADES, LINDA
PERSONAL Born 08/26/1941, Philadelphia, PA, m, 1965, 2 children **DISCIPLINE** ENGLISH **EDUCATION** Beaver Col, BA, 63; Ind Univ, MA, 65; PhD, 73. **CAREER** Adj fac, Del County Community Col, 71-78; adj fac to asst prof, Widener Univ, 78-89; asst prof to prof, W Chester Univ, 90-. **HONORS AND AWARDS** Fel, NEH; Stipend, Am Philos Soc; Res Grant, Hellenic-Am League; Grant, Pa State Sys of Higher Educ; Col of Arts and Sci Develop Award, W Chester Univ; RAM Award, Asn of Human Resource Management. **MEMBERSHIPS** MLA; NEMLA; ACLA; ALTA; Mod Greek Studies Asn; Soc for the Adv of Management; Asn for Bus Comm. **RESEARCH** Cultural Studies; Greek literature and folklore; Organizational communication. **SELECTED PUBLICATIONS** Auth, Cultural Representation in Historical Resistance; auth, Culture and Comedy; auth, The Karagiozis Heroic Performance; auth, Karagiozis: Three Classic Plays; auth Un-Disciplining Literature; auth, Race-ing Representation; auth, Margins in the Classroom. **CONTACT ADDRESS** Dept English, West Chester Univ of Pennsylvania, 370 N Malin Rd, Newtown Square, PA 19073. **EMAIL** Lmyrsiades@wcupa.edu

N

NA'ALLAH, ABDUL-RASHEED
PERSONAL Born 12/21/1962, Ilorin, Nigeria, m, 1995, 2 children **DISCIPLINE** LITERATURE, FOLKLORE **EDUCATION** BA in English and Education. **CAREER** Teacher, Ilorin School Board--Nigeria, 81-84; lectr, Univ of Ilorin, 89-94; prof, Western Ill univ, 98-. **HONORS AND AWARDS** Gold Key Recognition Awd, Univ of Alberta, 98; Charles Noble Awd, Province of Alberta, 98; Province of Alberta G. Fel, Univ of Alberta, 99. **MEMBERSHIPS** African Lit Asn, African Studies Asn, Int Comparative Lit Asn, Writer's Guild of Alberta. **RESEARCH** Comparative Oral Traditions, Multiculturalism (Africa & New World Societies), African & African American Traditions, Sociolinguistics. **SELECTED PUBLICATIONS** Auth, Introduction To African Oral Literature, 91; auth, Ogoni's Agonies, 98; auth, Almajiri, forthcoming; auth, People's poet, forthcoming. **CONTACT ADDRESS** Dept Afro-American Studies, Western Illinois Univ, 1 University Cir, Macomb, IL 61455-1367. **EMAIL** a-naallah@wiu.edu

NABHOLTZ, JOHN R.
PERSONAL Born 01/06/1931, Cleveland, OH **DISCIPLINE** ENGLISH **EDUCATION** Loyola Univ, Ill, AB, 51; Univ Chicago, MA, 52, PhD(Wordsworth), 61. **CAREER** Instr English, Cornell Univ, 59-63; asst prof, Univ Rochester, 63-69; assoc prof, 69-78, Prof English, Loyola Univ, Chicago, 78- **MEMBERSHIPS** MLA; Byron Soc; Charles Lamb Soc; Wordsworth-Coleridge Asn. **RESEARCH** English romanticism. **SELECTED PUBLICATIONS CONTACT ADDRESS** Dept of English, Loyola Univ, Chicago, Chicago, IL 60626.

NADEL, IRA BRUCE
PERSONAL Born 07/22/1943, Rahway, NJ, m, 1976 **DISCIPLINE** ENGLISH & AMERICAN LITERATURE **EDUCATION** Rutgers Univ, New Brunswick, BA, 65, MA, 67; Cornell Univ, PhD(English), 70. **CAREER** Asst prof English, 70-77, Assoc Prof English, Univ BC, 77-, Leave fels, Can Coun, 75-76 & Soc Sci & Humanities Res Coun Can, 82. **MEMBERSHIPS** MLA Victorian Studies Asn Western Can (pres, 80-82); Asn Can Univ Teachers English. **RESEARCH** Victorian literature and thought; biography. **SELECTED PUBLICATIONS** Auth, Biography: Fiction, Fact and Form, Joyce and the Jews, 84; auth, Varions Positions, A Life of Leonard Cohen, 96; auth, Leonard Cohen: A Life in Art, 94. **CONTACT ADDRESS** Dept of English, Univ of British Columbia, Vancouver, BC, Canada V6T 1Z1. **EMAIL** nadel@atsinterchange.ubc.ca

NAFICY, HAMID
PERSONAL Born 02/02/1944, Isfahan, Iran, m, 1975, 2 children **DISCIPLINE** FILM AND TELEVISION **EDUCATION** Univ Southern Calif, BA, 68; Univ Calif Los Angeles, MFA, 71; PhD, 90. **CAREER** Assoc prof, Free Univ Iran, 73-79; vis assoc prof, Television and Cinema Coll Tehran 74-78; vis asst prof, Univ Southern Calif, 80-81; vis asst prof, Univ Calif Santa Barbara, 90-91; vis asst prof, Univ Southern Calif, 91; asst prof, Rice Univ, 93-95; assoc prof, Rice Univ, 95-. **HONORS AND AWARDS** Numerous Awds from Rice Univ, Univ Calif, Am Film Inst; Rockefeller Fel, 92-93; Doctoral Res Grant, 88; Nat Endowment for Humanities, 85; UNESCO Fel, 76; Chris Awd 33rd Annual Columbus Film festival, 85; Silver Prize Houston Int Film Festival, 85; Second Prize Int Film and TV Fetsival NY, 86. **MEMBERSHIPS** Middle Eastern Studies Asn of N Am; Soc for Cinema Studies; Soc for Iranian Studies; univ Film and Video Asn. **RESEARCH** Cultural studies of film and media, exilic and diasporic culture and cinema, television and media; Iranian cinema and culture, ethnographic and documentary films, ethnicity and media. **SELECTED PUBLICATIONS** Auth, The Making of Exile Cultures: Iranian Television in Los Angeles, 93; ed, Home, Exile, Homeland: Film, Media, and the Politics of Place, 98; co-ed, Otherness and the Media: The Ethnography of the Imagined and the Imaged, 93; auth, An accented Cinema: Exilic and Diasporic Filmaking, 01. **CONTACT ADDRESS** Dept of Art and Art History, Rice Univ, 6100 Main Street, Box 1892, Houston, TX 77005-1892. **EMAIL** naficy@rice.edu

NAGEL, ALAN FREDERICK
PERSONAL Born 03/09/1941, Beverly, MA, m, 1973 **DISCIPLINE** COMPARATIVE LITERATURE, ENGLISH **EDUCATION** Harvard Col, BA, 63; Cornell Univ, MA, 65, PhD(comp lit), 69. **CAREER** Asst prof, 69-72, chmn, Grad Prog, 71-75, assoc prof, 72- 80, Prof English & Comp Lit, Univ Iowa, 80-, Chmn, BA Lett, Univ Iowa, 71-81, chmn, Interdiscipline Prog Lit, Sci & Arts; vis prof, Univ Paul Valery, Montpelier, France, fall, 82. **MEMBERSHIPS** MLA; Am Comp Lit Asn; Midwest Mod Lang Asn. **RESEARCH** Poetics; Renaissance literature, literary theory. **SELECTED PUBLICATIONS** Co-ed, The Three Crowns of Florence: Humanist Assessments of Dante, Petrarca, Boccaccio, Harper, 72; auth, Lies and the limitable inane Contradiction in More's Utopia, Renaissance Quart, 73; Literary and historical context in Ronsard's Sonnets pour Helene, Pub Mod Lang Asn, 79; Rhetoric, value and action in Alberti, Mod Lang Notes, 80; 'Mastro Don Gesualdo', Gender, Dialect, And The Body, Stanford Italian Review, Vol 0011, 1992; Countercurrents - on The Primacy of Texts in Literary-criticism - Prier,ra, Comparative Literature Studies, Vol 0031, 1994. **CONTACT ADDRESS** Dept of Comp Lit, Univ of Iowa, 308 English Phil Bld, Iowa City, IA 52242-1492.

NAGELE, RAINER
PERSONAL Born 08/02/1943, Triesen, Liechtenstein, m, 1971 **DISCIPLINE** GERMAN LITERATURE, LITERARY THEORY **EDUCATION** Univ Calif, Santa Barbara, PhD, 71. **CAREER** Asst prof Ger, Univ Iowa, 71-74; assoc prof Ger lit, Ohio State Univ, 75-77; assoc prof, 77-79; prof, 79-, Johns Hopkins Univ, **MEMBERSHIPS** MLA; Am Asn Teachers Ger. **RESEARCH** German literature of the 20th century; German literature from 1700 to present; literary theory and aesthetics. **SELECTED PUBLICATIONS** Auth, Text, Geschichte und Subjekivitat in Holderlins Dichtung Unebarer Schrift gleich, Metzler (Stuttgart), 85; auth, Reading After Freud. Essays on Goethe, Holderlin, Habermas, Nietzsche, Brecht, Celan, and Freud, Columbia Univ Press (NYork), 87; auth, Theater, Theory, Speculation: Walter Benjamin and the Scenes of Modernity, Johns Hopkins Univ Press (Baltimore), 91; auth, Echoes of Translation. Reading Between Texts, John Hopkins Univ Press (Baltimore), 97; auth, Lesarten der Moderne, Edition Isele (Eggingen), 98. **CONTACT ADDRESS** Dept of Ger, Johns Hopkins Univ, Baltimore, 3400 N Charles St, Baltimore, MD 21218-2680. **EMAIL** nagele@jhn.edu

NAGLE, BETTY ROSE
DISCIPLINE CLASSICAL STUDIES **EDUCATION** Univ Pa, BA, 70; Univ Ind, PhD, 75. **CAREER** Prof, Ind Univ, Bloomington. **SELECTED PUBLICATIONS** Auth, Ovid's Fasti: Roman Holidays, Ind Univ, 95; Ovid: Fasti V, Bryn Mawr, 96. **CONTACT ADDRESS** Dept of Classical Studies, Indiana Univ, Bloomington, 1020 E Kirkwood Ave, 547 Ballantine Hall, Bloomington, IN 47405. **EMAIL** nagle@indiana.edu

NAGLER, MICHAEL NICHOLAS
PERSONAL Born 01/20/1937, New York, NY, m, 1959, 2 children **DISCIPLINE** CLASSICAL LITERATURE AND SOCIETY **EDUCATION** NYork Univ, BA, 60; Univ Calif, Berkeley, MA, 62, PhD(comp lit), 66. **CAREER** Instr foreign lang, San Francisco State Col, 63-65; asst prof, 65-73, humanities res fel, 68-69, Assoc Prof Classics & Comp Lit, Univ Calif, Berkeley, 73-, Am Coun Learned Soc study grant, Sanskrit lang & lit, 71-72. **MEMBERSHIPS** Am Philol Asn; Int Comp Lit Asn. **RESEARCH** Oral poetry, chiefly Homer, Old English and Sanskirt; myth and religion; peace and conflict studies. **SELECTED PUBLICATIONS** Auth, Towards a generative view of the Homeric formula, Trans Am Philol Asn, 67; Oral poetry and the question of originality in literature, Proc Vth Cong Int Comp Lit Asn, 67; Spontaneity and Tradition: A Study of Homer's Oral Art, Univ Calif, 74; Dread goddess endowed with speech, Archaeol News, 77; Mysticism: A hardheaded definition for a romantic age, Study Mystica, 78; Peace as a paradigm shift, Bull Atom Scientists, 81; America Without Violence, Island Press, 82; Epic Singers And Oral Tradition - Lord,ab, Classical J, Vol 0087, 1992; Discourse And Conflict Hesiod - Eris And The Erides, Ramus- critical Studies in Greek And Roman Literature, Vol 0021, 1992; Penelope's Male Hand - Gender And Violence in The Odyssey, Colby Quarterly, Vol 0029, 1993; auth, Is There No Other Way: The Search for a Nonviolent Futere, Berkeley Hills Books, 00. **CONTACT ADDRESS** Peace & Conflict Studies, Univ of California, Berkeley, 101 Stephens Hall, Berkeley, CA 94720. **EMAIL** mnagler@socraates.berkeley.edu

NAGY, GREGORY JOHN
PERSONAL Born 10/22/1942, Budapest, Hungary **DISCIPLINE** CLASSICS, LINGUISTICS **EDUCATION** Ind Univ, AB, 62; Harvard Univ, PhD(classics), 66. **CAREER** Instr classics & ling, Harvard Univ, 66-69, asst prof classics, 69-73; from assoc prof to prof, Johns Hopkins Univ, 73-75; Prof Classics, Harvard Univ, 75- **MEMBERSHIPS** Am Philol Asn; Ling Soc Am. **RESEARCH** Greek literature; Indo-European linguistics; poetics. **SELECTED PUBLICATIONS** Auth, Observations on the sign-grouping and vocabulary of linear A, Am J Archaeol, 65; On dialectal anomalies in Pylian texts, Atti Memorie 1st Cong Int Micenologia, 68; Greek Dialects and the Transformation of an Indo-European Process, Harvard Univ, 70; coauth, Greek: A Survey of Recent Work, Mouton, The Hague: 73; auth, Phaethon, Sappho's Phaon, and the White Rock of Leukas, Harvard Studies Class Philol, 73; Comparative Studies in Greek and Indic Meter, Harvard Univ, 74. **CONTACT ADDRESS** Dept of Classics, Harvard Univ, 204 Boylston Hall, Cambridge, MA 02138-3800. **EMAIL** gnagy@fas.harvard.edu

NAGY, JOSEPH F.
DISCIPLINE ENGLISH **EDUCATION** Harvard Univ, BA, 74; PhD, 78. **CAREER** Prof, UCLA, 78-. **HONORS AND AWARDS** Katharine Briggs Prize, 98; Chicago Folklore Prize, Third Place, 85. **MEMBERSHIPS** Celtic Studies Asn of N Am. **RESEARCH** Celtic folklore and mythology; General folkloristic theory and method; Issues of orality and literacy; Hagiography; Sources of medieval literature. **SELECTED PUBLICATIONS** Auth, Conversing with angels and Ancients: Literary Myths of Medieval Ireland, Cornell Univ Press, 98. **CONTACT ADDRESS** Dept English, Univ of California, Los Angeles, 2225 Rolfe, Box 951530, Los Angeles, CA 90095-1530. **EMAIL** JFNAGY@HUMNET.UCLA.EDU

NAHRGANG, WILBUR LEE
PERSONAL Born 06/06/1939, Iowa Park, TX, m, 1964 **DISCIPLINE** MODERN GERMAN LITERATURE **EDUCATION** Texas Christian Univ, BA, 60; Univ Kans, MA, 63, PhD, 66. **CAREER** From instr to assoc prof, 65-69, Assoc Prof Ger, North Tex State Univ, 69-, Co-ed, Schatzkammer, 77-. **MEMBERSHIPS** Am Asn Teachers Ger; Am Coun Teaching Foreign Lang; MLA Western Asn Ger Studies. **RESEARCH** Heinrich Boll and his works; German novels of World War II. **SELECTED PUBLICATIONS** Heinrich Boll's war books: A study in changing literary purpose, Mod Lang Notes, 10/73. **CONTACT ADDRESS** Dept of Foreign Lang & Lit, Univ of No Texas, P O Box 311127, Denton, TX 76203-1127. **EMAIL** nahrgang@unt.edu

NAIDITCH, P. G.
PERSONAL Born Los Angeles, CA, s **DISCIPLINE** CLASSICS **EDUCATION** SMCC, AA 69; Univ Southern Calif, BA, 71; Univ London, MA, 76; Ind Univ, MLS, 80. **CAREER** Publ ed, Dept Spec Collections, 87-; classics bibliogr 91-; Curator of Medieval and Renaissance Manuscripts, 00-; Charles E. Young Res Libr, UCLA. **MEMBERSHIPS** Am Philo Asn; Bibliog Soc. **RESEARCH** A.E. Housman; history of classical scholarship; history of the book. **SELECTED PUBLICATIONS** Auth, A.E. Housman at University College, London, 88; coauth, Philodemus and Greek Papyri, 94; auth, Problems in the Life and Writings of A.E. Housman, 95. **CONTACT ADDRESS** Special Collections, Charles E. Young Research Lib, Univ of California, Los Angeles, Box 951575, Los Angeles, CA 90095-1575. **EMAIL** naiditch@library.ucla.edu

NAIR, SUPRYIA M.
DISCIPLINE POSTCOLONIAL LITERATURE AND THEORY, AFRICAN AND DIASPORA STUDIES **EDUCATION** St Joseph's Col, Vizag, India, BA, 82; Univ Hyderabad, India, MA, 84; Baylor Univ, MA, 86; Univ TX at Austin, PhD, 92. **CAREER** Assoc prof, 92, Tulane Univ. **HONORS AND AWARDS** Tex Excellence Teaching Award, Univ of Tex, 91; Tulane Univ Excellence in Undergraduate Teaching Award, 98. **RESEARCH** Caribbean Literatures, cultural studies, feminist theory, postcolonial theory. **SELECTED PUBLICATIONS** Auth, Melancholic Women: The Intellectual Hysteric(s) in Nervous Conditions, Res African Lit 26.2, 95; auth, Caliban's Curse: George Lamming and the Revisioning of History, Univ of Michi Press, 96; auth, "Postmodern Utopias and Expressive Countercultures: A Caribbean Context," Res in African Lit 27.4, (96), 71-87; auth, "Homing Instincts: Immigrant Nostalgia and Genbder Politics in Representation, The Univ Press of Virgina, 99; auth, "Creolization, Orality and Nation Language in the Caribbean," A Companion to Postcolonial studies, (00), 236-251. **CONTACT ADDRESS** Dept of Eng, Tulane Univ, 6823 St Charles Ave, New Orleans, LA 70118. **EMAIL** supriya@tulane.edu

NAKADATE, NEIL EDWARD
PERSONAL Born 09/01/1943, East Chicago, IN, d, 3 children **DISCIPLINE** AMERICAN LITERATURE, RHETORIC & COMPOSITION **EDUCATION** Stanford Univ, AB, 65; Ind Univ, Bloomington, MA, 68 PhD(English), 72. **CAREER** Asst instr English, Ind Univ, 67-70; asst prof, Univ Tex, Austin, 70-77; asst prof, 77-80, Assoc Prof English, Iowa State Univ, 80-85; prof english, Iowa State Univ, 85- . **HONORS AND AWARDS** IA State Univ Fnd Awd for Career Achievement in Tchg; Golden Key NHS; **MEMBERSHIPS** Conf Col Compos & Commun; Soc Study Southern Lit; MLA; National Japanese Am Historical Society. **RESEARCH** Twentieth Century American literature; contemporary fiction. **SELECTED PUBLICATIONS** Auth, Robert Penn Warren and the confessional novel, Genre, 12/69; The function of colloquy in Robert Penn Warren's Brother to Dragons, Tenn Studies Lit, 76; ed, Robert Penn Warren: A Reference Guide, G K Hall, 77; ed, Robert Penn Warren: Critical Perspectives, Univ Press Ky, 81; auth, Identity, dream, and exploration: Warren's later fiction, in Robert Penn Warren: Critical Perspectives, 81; coauth, Writing in the Liberal Arts Tradition: A Rhetoric with Readings, Harper & Row, 85, 2nd ed, 90; coed, A Rhetoric of Doing: Essays on Written Discourse in Honor of James L. Kinneavy, S Illinois Univ, 92; auth, Understanding Jane Smiley, Univ SC, 99. **CONTACT ADDRESS** Dept of English, Iowa State Univ of Science and Tech, Ames, IA 50011-1201. **EMAIL** neiln@iastate.edu

NAKELL, MARTIN E.
PERSONAL Born 06/23/1945, Alpena, MI, m, 2000 **DISCIPLINE** ENGLISH **EDUCATION** Calif State Univ Northridge, BA, 71; San Francisco State Univ, MA, 74; SUNY Albany, Dr Arts, 83. **CAREER** Prof, Chapman Univ, 83-. **HONORS AND AWARDS** Fel, Fine Arts Work Ctr; Fel, Nat Endowment for Arts; Gertrude Stein Awd; Fel, Blue Mt Ctr; Fel, Gell Found. **MEMBERSHIPS** Encycl of Twentieth Cent Fiction Panel; Educ Art Found; Los Angeles Exp Poets Soc. **RESEARCH** Modernist/Post-Modernist Literature. **SELECTED PUBLICATIONS** Auth, Ramon, Jahbone Pr, 89; auth, The Myth of Creation, Parentheses Writing Series, 93; auth, The Library of Thomas Rivka, Sun & Moon Pr, 98; auth, Two Fields That Face and Mirror Each Other, Green Integer Series, 00. **CONTACT ADDRESS** Dept English, Chapman Univ, 333 N Glassell St, Orange, CA 92866-1011.

NALBANTIAN, SUZANNE
DISCIPLINE COMPARATIVE LITERATURE, CRITICAL THEORY **EDUCATION** Columbia Univ, PhD. **CAREER** Prof, Long Island Univ, C.W. Post Campus. **SELECTED PUBLICATIONS** Auth, Aesthetic Autobiography; The Symbol of the Soul from Holderlin to Yeats: A Study in Metonymy; Seeds of Decadence in the Late Nineteenth-Century Novel. **CONTACT ADDRESS** Long Island Univ, C.W. Post, Brookville, NY 11548-1300.

NAPIERALSKI, EDMUND ANTHONY
PERSONAL Born 11/06/1937, Buffalo, NY, m, 1964, 3 children **DISCIPLINE** LITERATURE **EDUCATION** Canisius Col, BA, 61; Loyola Univ, Chicago, PhD(English), 67. **CAREER** From instr to asst prof English, Georgetown Univ, 64-71; asst prof, 71-80, Prof English, King's Col, Pa, 80-, Dir honors prog, Ctr Independent Learning; Coordr of the Core Curriculum Assessment. **MEMBERSHIPS** Asn Lit Schol and Critics; Multi-Ethnic Lit of the U.S.; Asn for the Study of Am Indian Lit. **RESEARCH** Tragedy; dramatic form; comparative literature. **SELECTED PUBLICATIONS** Auth, Restoration and 18th Century Theatre Research Bibliography, Restoration & 18th Century Theatre Res, 61-73; contribr, Restoration and Eighteenth Century Theatre Research: A Bibliographical Guide, 1900-1968, Southern Ill Univ, 71; auth, The tragic knot: Paradox in the experience of tragedy, J Aesthet & Art Criticism, 73; Tennessee Williams' The Glass Menagerie: The dramatic metaphor, Southern Quart, 10/77; Miss Julie: Strindberg's Tragic Fairy Tale, Mod Drama, 9/83, reprinted in Twentieth Century Lit Criticism, 47, 93; Thomas's A Refusal to Mourn the Death, by Fire, of a Child in London, The Explicator, Spring 92; Morrison's The Bluest Eye, The Explicator, Winter 94; coauth, Assessing Learning in Programs, In: Handbook of the Undergraduate Curriculum, Jossey-Bass Publ, 97. **CONTACT ADDRESS** Dept of English, King's Col, 133 N River St, Wilkes-Barre, PA 18711-0801. **EMAIL** eanapier@kings.edu

NAPPA, CHRISTOPHER
DISCIPLINE CLASSICAL STUDIES **EDUCATION** Univ Tex, BA, 90; Univ Va, MA, 92, PhD, 96. **CAREER** Instr. **SELECTED PUBLICATIONS** Auth, Agamemnon 717-36: The Parable of the Lion Cub, 94; Catullan Provocations (rev), Univ Ca, 93; Virgil, New Haven, 91. **CONTACT ADDRESS** Dept of Classics, Knoxville, TN 37996.

NARDO, ANNA
DISCIPLINE RENAISSANCE AND 17TH CENTURY BRITISH LITERATURE, JOHN MILTON, GEORGE ELIOT **EDUCATION** Emory Univ, PhD, 74. **CAREER** Alumni Prof, La State Univ. **HONORS AND AWARDS** Fel, Nat Hum Ctr, 81; HM "Hub" Cotton Fac Excellence Awd, 88; James Holly Hanford Awd, 91; Nicholson Awd, 93; Alumni Professorship, 98. **MEMBERSHIPS** MLA; John Donne Soc; Milton Soc of Am. **RESEARCH** John Milton; George Eliot. **SELECTED PUBLICATIONS** Auth, Academic Interludes in Paradise Lost, Milton Stud, 91; The Ludic Self in Seventeenth-Century English Literature, 91; Milton and the Academic Sonnet, in Milton in Italy, 91; The Education of Milton's Good Angels,' Arenas of Conflict, 97; auth, "Romola and Milton: A Cultural History of Rewriting," Nineteenth-Century Literature (98): 328-63; auth, "John Milton, Object of the Erotic Gaze?" Living Texts: Interpreting Milton eds. Charles W. Durham and Kristin A Pruitt (Selinsgrove: Susquehanna Univ Press, 00), 57-79; auth, "A Space for Academic Recreation: Milton's Proposal in The Reason of Church-government," Literary Circles and Cultural Communities in Renaissance England, eds. Ted-Larry Pebworth and Claude Summers (Columbia: Univ of Missouri Press, 00), 128-47. **CONTACT ADDRESS** Dept of Eng, Louisiana State Univ and A&M Col, 229F Allen Hall, Baton Rouge, LA 70803. **EMAIL** anardo@lsu.edu

NAREMORE, JAMES
PERSONAL Born 04/04/1941, Shreveport, LA, m, 1981, 1 child **DISCIPLINE** ENGLISH **EDUCATION** Univ Wis, PhD, 70. **CAREER** From Asst Prof to Prof, Ind Univ, 70- **HONORS AND AWARDS** Tracy Sonneborn Prize for Res and Teaching, Ind Univ, 94; Nat Gallery of Art Fel, 94; Guggenheim Fel, 95. **MEMBERSHIPS** Soc for Cinema Studies, Mod Lang Assoc. **RESEARCH** Film, modern literature. **SELECTED PUBLICATIONS** Auth, The Filmguide to Psycho, Ind Univ Pr (Bloomington, IN), 73; auth, The World Without a Self: Virginia Woolfe and the Novel, Yale Univ Pr (New Haven, CT), 73; auth, The Magic World of Orson Welles, Oxford Univ Pr (New York, NY), 78; auth, Acting in the Cinema, Univ Calif Pr (Berkeley, CA), 88; auth, The Films of Vincente Minnelli, Cambridge Univ Pr (New York, NY), 93; auth, More Than Night: Film Noir in its Concepts, Univ Calif Pr (Berkeley, CA), 98. **CONTACT ADDRESS** Dept English, Indiana Univ, Bloomington, 809 E 7th, Bloomington, IN 47405. **EMAIL** naremor@indiana.edu

NASH, ELIZABETH
PERSONAL Born 07/13/1934, New Rochelle, NY, s **DISCIPLINE** THEATRE ARTS, MUSIC **EDUCATION** Columbia Univ, BFA, 57: MA, 71; Indiana Univ, PhD, 75; Harvard Univ, Arts Management Cert, 78. **CAREER** Leading Coloratura Soprano, Pfalztheater, Kaiserslautern, 61-62; Theater am Domhof, Osnabruck, 62-63, Landestheater, Detmold, 63-64; Hessisches Staatstheater, Kassel, 64-67; guest artist, Salzburg, Amiens, Nancy, Strasbourg, Bruges, Ghent, Luxembourg, Lugano, 68-70; singer/actress, Children's Theater Co, Minn, 79-80; assoc instr to assoc prof, Indiana Univ, 71-; lectr, Am theatre Assoc, 79; Assoc for Theatre in Higher Ed, 87, 89, 93; Christian Science Monitor World Radio, 89; Univ of Tex, 91, 92; Theaterhochschule Hans Otto, Ger, 89, 92; Opera N, 97. **HONORS AND AWARDS** Fulbright Grant, Germany, 59-61; Christian Science Monitor World Radio Interviews, 89; Int Who's who in Music and Musicians Dir, 90, 92; Contemp Auth, 94; The Writers Dir, 95-97, 98-00; Who's Who of Am Women, 79-80, 99-00. **MEMBERSHIPS** Nat Assoc Teachers of Singing; Voice and Speech Trainers Assoc; German Equity. **RESEARCH** Actresses, Opera Prime Donne, African-American Classical Singers. **SELECTED PUBLICATIONS** Auth, Always First Class: The Career of Geraldine Farrar, 81; auth, The Luminous Ones: A History of the Great Actresses, 91; auth, "Geraldine Farrar", International Dictionary of Opera, 93; auth, Pieces of Rainbow, 94; auth, "Geraldine Farrar", The St. James Opera Encyclopedia: A Guide to People and Works, 97; auth, "Singing Acting", The Vocal Vision: Views on Voice by 24 Leading Teachers, Coaches and Directors, 97; auth, "The Master Singer: An Interview with Todd Duncan", American Legacy, 98. **CONTACT ADDRESS** Theatre Arts, Univ of Minnesota, Edina, 4504 Oak Dr, Edina, MN 55424. **EMAIL** nashx001@tc.umn.edu

NASS, CLIFFORD I.
PERSONAL Born 04/03/1958, Jersey City, NJ, m, 1989, 1 child **DISCIPLINE** COMMUNICATIONS **EDUCATION** Princeton Univ, BA, 81; PhD 86. **CAREER** Prof/dir Interface Lab, Center for the Study of Language and information (CSLI) Stanford Univ. **MEMBERSHIPS** Am Sociol Asn, Int Commun Asn; Am Statist Asn; Am Psychol Soc. **RESEARCH** Human-computer interaction; social responses to communications technology; statistical methods; organization theory. **SELECTED PUBLICATIONS** Auth, 50 publ on tech and statistical methodology; coauth, The Media Equation: How People Treat Computers, Television, Cambridge UP; auth, New Media Like Real People and Places, Cambridge UP. **CONTACT ADDRESS** Dept of Commun, Stanford Univ, McClatchy Hall Rm. 300D, Stanford, CA 94305. **EMAIL** nass@leland.stanford.edu

NASSAR, EUGENE PAUL
PERSONAL Born 06/20/1935, Utica, NY, m, 1969, 3 children **DISCIPLINE** ENGLISH, CRITICISM **EDUCATION** Kenyon Col, BA, 57; Oxford Univ, MA, 60; Cornell Univ, PhD(English), 62. **CAREER** Instr English, Hamilton Col, 62-64; from asst prof to assoc prof, 64-71, Prof English, Utica Col, 71-, Nat Found Arts & Humanities fel, 73-74; Rhodes scholar; Woodrow Wilson fel. **RESEARCH** Literary criticism. **SELECTED PUBLICATIONS** Auth, Wallace Stevens: An Anatomy of Figuration, Univ Pa, 65; The Rape of Cinderella: Essays in Literary Continuity, Ind Univ, 70; The Cantos of Ezra Pound: The Lyric Mode, Johns Hopkins Univ, 75; Essays: Critical and Metacritical, Fairleigh Dickinson Univ Press, 82; Illustrations to Dante's Inferno, Fairleigh Dickinson Univ Press, 94; auth, A Walk Around the Block, Syracuse Univ Press, 99. **CONTACT ADDRESS** Dept of English, Utica Col of Syracuse Univ, 1600 Burrstone Rd, Utica, NY 13502-4892. **EMAIL** pnassar@dreamscape.com

NATHANSON, LEONARD
PERSONAL Born 09/22/1933, New York, NY **DISCIPLINE** ENGLISH LITERATURE **EDUCATION** Brooklyn Col, BA, 54; Duke Univ, MA, 55; Univ Wis, PhD, 59. **CAREER** Instr Eng, Northwestern Univ, 59-60; asst prof, Univ Cincinnati, 60-66; Assoc Prof Eng, Vanderbilt Univ, 66-98, Prof Emer Eng, Vanderbilt Univ, 98-; Taft Mem Fund res grant, 62; mem exec comt, Milton Soc Am, 72-75. **MEMBERSHIPS** MLA; Mod Hum Res Asn; Renaissance Soc Am; S Atlantic MLA; Milton Soc Am. **RESEARCH** Seventeenth century lit; Milton. **SELECTED PUBLICATIONS** Auth, The Strategy of Truth: A Study of Sir Thomas Browne, Univ Chicago, 67; ed, Shakespeare, The Tempest, W C Brown, 69; ed & contribr, A Milton Encyclopedia (9 vols), Bucknell Univ, Vol Viii, 78-81. **CONTACT ADDRESS** Dept of English, Vanderbilt Univ, Nashville, TN 37235.

NATOV, RONI
DISCIPLINE ENGLISH LITERATURE **EDUCATION** City Univ NYork, BA, MA, PhD. **CAREER** Prof. **RESEARCH** Literature and psychology; women's studies; children's studies and fantasy; fairy tales and myths. **SELECTED PUBLICATIONS** Auth, Leon Garfield, Twayne/Macmillan, 94; Mothers and Daughters: Jamaica Kincaid's Pre-Oedipal Narrative, Children's Lit, 90; The Child Hero: Internal and External Journeys, Children's Lit Edu, 89; Living in Two Cultures: Bette Bao Lord's Stories of Chinese-American Experience, Lion Unicorn, 87; The Truth of Ordinary Lives: Autobiographical Fiction for Children, Children's Lit Edu, 86; Stories We Need to Hear, Or the Reader and the Tale, Lion Unicorn, 86; The Power of the Tale, Children's Lit, 85. **CONTACT ADDRESS** English Dept, Union Inst, 440 E McMillan St, Cincinnati, OH 45206-1925.

NATUNEWICZ, MARY ANN T.
PERSONAL Born 12/16/1937, NJ, m, 1966, 2 children **DISCIPLINE** CLASSICS **EDUCATION** Wellesley Col, BA, 58; Univ Wis, MA, 61; Univ Wis, PhD, 70. **CAREER** Wells Col, 64-67; Houston Independent School District, 86-. **MEMBERSHIPS** Am Philol Assoc; J Classical League **RESEARCH** Cicero; Homer **SELECTED PUBLICATIONS** Auth, Thucydides and Euripides: Changing Civic and Moral Values, Houston Teachers Inst, 99; auth, Foundation Myths of Rome, Univ at Houston Teachers Inst, 00. **CONTACT ADDRESS** 2107 Teague Rd, Houston, TX 77088. **EMAIL** cmanatun@gateway.net

NE JAME, ADELE
PERSONAL Born, NJ, d, 1 child **DISCIPLINE** ENGLISH, LITERATURE, CREATIVE WRITING **EDUCATION** Univ Hawaii, BA, 85; Univ Hawaii, MA, 87. **CAREER** Instr, Univ Hawaii, 87-89; Prof, Univ Wis, 89-90; Prof, Hawaii Pac Univ, 90-. **HONORS AND AWARDS** Nat Endowment Arts/Poetry; Pablo Neurada Prize for Poetry; Madison creative Writing Fel, Univ Wis. **RESEARCH** Poetry, traul, Middle East, deserts, South Pacific. **SELECTED PUBLICATIONS** Auth, Inheritance, Ridgeway Pr, 89; auth, Field Work, Petronium Pr, 90. **CONTACT ADDRESS** Dept English, Hawaii Pacific Univ, 1188 Ft Street Mall, Ste 430, Honolulu, HI 96813-2713. **EMAIL** nejame@hpu.edu

NEAMAN, JUDITH S.
PERSONAL Born 09/20/1936, m, 1964, 1 child **DISCIPLINE** LITERATURE **EDUCATION** Univ Mich, BA, 58; Columbia Univ, MA, 60; PhD, 68. **CAREER** Adj instr, Lehman Col, 63-68; asst prof, Hoftra Univ, 68-74; med writer, 68-74; adj assoc prof, Hunter Col, 74-76; adj assoc prof, Touro Col, 77-80; adj assoc prof to prof, Yeshiva Univ, 82-. **HONORS AND AWARDS** NEH Fel, 63. **MEMBERSHIPS** Medieval Acad of Am, MLA, AVISTA, Int Center for Medieval Art, Medieval Club of NY, Columbia Medieval Seminar, Soc for the Study of NeoPlatonic Philos, NY Hagiographic Soc. **RESEARCH** Optics in medieval science, art and religion, medieval literature, art and science. **SELECTED PUBLICATIONS** Coauth, The American Vision, Scott Foresman, 73; auth, Suggestion of the Devil: Insanity in the Middle Ages, Doubleday Anchor, Farrar Straus, 76/76; coauth, "Kind Words: A thesaurus of Euphemisms," Facts on File, (Avon, Wordsworth, 83); auth, "Allusion, Image, and Associative Pattern: the Answers in Mansfield's 'Bliss,'" Twentieth Century Lit 32.2 (86): 242-254; auth, "The Harlot Bride, from Biblical Cod to Mystical Topos," Vox Benedictiana 4.4 (87); coauth, Thesaurus of Euphemisms, Revised and Expanded Edition, Avon, Wordsworth, 90; auth, "Magnification As Metaphor," English in the Thirteenth Century, ed Mark Ormrod, (Stamford, Eng: Paul Watkins, 91): 277-332; auth, "The Mystery of the Ghent Bird and the Invention of Spectacles," Viator 24, (93): 189-214. **CONTACT ADDRESS** Yeshiva Univ, 215 Lexington Ave, New York, NY 10016.

NEELD, ELIZABETH HARPER
PERSONAL Born 12/25/1940, Brooks, GA, m, 1983 **DISCIPLINE** ENGLISH **EDUCATION** Univ Chattanooga, MS, MS; Univ Tenn, Knoxville, PhD. **CAREER** Head, Hum Div, Cleveland State Commun Col, 67-73; dir, Eng Prog, MLA, 73-76; prof, Eng, Texas A&M Univ, 76-83; independent scholar, and auth, 83-00. **HONORS AND AWARDS** Listed, Contemporary Authors, Who's Who in America, Who's Who in the World. **RESEARCH** Eighteenth century; prayer; literature; change. **SELECTED PUBLICATIONS** Auth, Writing, 3 eds; auth, Writing Brief, 3 eds; auth, Readings for Writing; auth, The Way a Writer Reads; auth, Options for the Teaching of English: The Undergraduate Curriculum; auth, Either Way Will Hurt & Other Essays on English; auth, Harper & Row Studies in Language and Literature; auth, Fairy Tales of the Sea; auth, From the Plow to the Pulpit; auth, Seven Choices, 3d ed; auth, Sacred Primer. **CONTACT ADDRESS** 6706 Beauford Dr, Austin, TX 78750. **EMAIL** cppaustin@aol.com

NEELY, CAROL THOMAS
PERSONAL Born 05/16/1939, Philadelphia, PA, m, 1965, 3 children **DISCIPLINE** ENGLISH LITERATURE **EDUCATION** Smith Col, BA, 61; Yale Univ, MA, 63, PhD(English), 69. **CAREER** From instr to asst prof English, Univ Ill, Urbana Champaign, 65-73; instr, 75-76, Assoc Prof English, Ill State Univ, 80-. **MEMBERSHIPS** MLA; Shakespeare Asn Am. **RESEARCH** Shakespeare; poetry of the English Renaissance; feminist criticism. **SELECTED PUBLICATIONS** Auth, The Winter's Tale: The Triumph of Speech, Studies English Lit, 75; Detachment and Engagement in Shakespeare's Sonnets: 94, 116, 129, Pmla, 77; Women and Men in Othello, Shakespeare Studies, 77; The Structure of English Renaissance Sonnet Sequences, J English Lit Hist, 78; Women and issue in The Winter's Tale, Philol Quart, 78; co-ed (with Carolyn Lenz & Gayle Greene), The Woman's Part: Feminist Criticism of Shakespeare, Univ Ill Press, 80; auth, Feminist Modes of Shakespearean Criticism: Compensatory, Justificatory, Transformational, Women's Studies, 81. **CONTACT ADDRESS** 708 Arlington Ct, Champaign, IL 61820.

NEFF, JOYCE
DISCIPLINE MANAGEMENT WRITING **EDUCATION** Western Md Col, BA; Univ Md, MA; Univ Pa, PhD. **CAREER** Engl, Old Dominion Univ. **MEMBERSHIPS** Univ Interdisciplinary Studies Comt; Arts & Letters Practicum (CAP) Comt; Dept Curr & Instruction Comt. **SELECTED PUBLICATIONS** Coauth, Professional Writing in Context: Lessons from Teaching and Consulting in Worlds of Work, Lawrence Erlbaum; Literacy among Undergraduates: How We Represent Students as Writers and What It Means When We Don't, in Rhetoric, Cultural Studies, and Literacy. Earlbaum, 95; "Rhetoric in a Bureaucracy: Government Evaluators as Report Writers" in Studies in Technical Communication. Univ N Tex, 96. **CONTACT ADDRESS** Old Dominion Univ, 4100 Powhatan Ave, Norfolk, VA 23058. **EMAIL** JNeff@odu.edu

NEIVA, EDUARDO
PERSONAL Born 08/31/1950, Brazil, m, 1993, 2 children **DISCIPLINE** COMMUNICATION **EDUCATION** Pontificia Universidade Catolica do Rio de Janeiro, BA, 79; Universidade Federal do Rio de Janeiro, MA, 83, PhD, 89. **CAREER** Assoc prof, Universidade Federal Fluminense, 75-93; assoc prof, St Univ of Rio de Janeiro, 89-93; chair, Catholic Univ of Rio de Janeiro, 87-89; vis prof, Universidade Fernando Pessoa, Oporto, Portugal, 95; vis prof, Ind Univ Bloomington, 90; asst prof to assoc prof to dir, Univ Al Birmingham, 93-. **HONORS AND AWARDS** Travel grant, Int Conf on Word & Image Stud, 96; Fulbright Scholar, Ind Univ, 90; Conselho Nacional de Pesquisa grant, 91-93. **MEMBERSHIPS** Assoc for Semiotic Res; Int Commun Assoc. **RESEARCH** Image & visual culture; semiotics; commun theory. **SELECTED PUBLICATIONS** Auth O que aprender com antigas catastrofes, Sao Paulo, Atica, 96; Comunicacao na era pos-moderna, Rio de Janeiro, Vozes, 97; O racionalismo critico de Karl Popper, Sao Paulo, Francisco Alves, 98; Mythologies of vision, Peter Lang, 99; Ideology, in Encyclopaedic Dictionary of Semiotics, Berlin, Mouton de Gruyter, 94. **CONTACT ADDRESS** Dept of Commun, Univ of Alabama, Birmingham, UAB Station, Birmingham, AL 35294. **EMAIL** neiva@uab.edu

NELIHAUS, TOBIN
DISCIPLINE LIBRARY SCIENCE, THEATER **EDUCATION** Univ Mich, BA, 77; Univ Iowa, MA, 80; Northwestern Univ, PhD, 91; Simmons Col, MLS, 00. **CAREER** Lectr, Ohio State Univ, 92-94; vis scholar, Univ of Wash, 95; vis lectr, Tufts Univ, 96; libr, Yale Univ, 00-. **HONORS AND AWARDS**

ACLS Fel, 96-97; Fulbright Lect, 97-98. **MEMBERSHIPS** MLA; Am Libr Assoc; Am Soc for Theatre Res, Theater Libr Assoc, Assoc for Computers in the Humanities. **RESEARCH** Performance Theory, theater history, social and cultural theory. **SELECTED PUBLICATIONS** Auth, "Literacy, Tyranny, and the Invention of Greek Tragedy," Jour of Dramatic Theory and Criticism 3.2 (89): 53-71; auth, "Mementos of Things to Come: Orality, Literacy, and Typology in the Biblia pauperum," Printing the Written Word: The Social History of Books, c 1450-1520, ed Sandra Hindman, Cornell Univ Pr, (NY, 91): 292-321; auth, "Self-Possessed Jonson: Reason, Will, Ownership, Power," Jour of Dramatic Theory and Criticism 8.1, (93): 5-17; auth, "Science, History, Theater: Theorizing in Two Alternatives to Positivism," Theatre Jour 45, (93): 505-27; auth, "Performance, Hegemony, and Communication Practices: Toward a Cultural Materialist Analysis," Theatre Annual 49, (96): 3-14; auth, "Signs, Social Ontology, and Critical Realism," Jour for the Theory of Soc Behav 28.1, (98): 1-24; auth, "Social Ontology and (Meta)theatricality: Reflexions on Performance and Communication in History," Jour of Dramatic Theory and Criticism 14.2 (00): 3-39; coed, Performing Democracy: International Perspectives on Urban Community-Based Performance, Univ of Mich Pr, (Ann Arbor) forthcoming. **CONTACT ADDRESS** Sterling Mem Libr, Yale Univ, 120 Wall St, PO Box 208240, New Haven, CT 06520-8240. **EMAIL** tobin.nelhaus@yale.edu

NELLES, WILLIAM

PERSONAL Born 09/26/1953, Evanston, IL, m, 1986, 2 children **DISCIPLINE** ENGLISH, LITERATURE **EDUCATION** Northern Ill Univ, BA, 79; MA, 81; Diploma, Univ de Nante, France, 86; Norther Ill Univ, PhD, 87. **CAREER** Asst prof, Northwestern State Univ, 88-95; from Asst to Assoc Prof, Univ of Mass Dartmouth, 95-. **MEMBERSHIPS** New Chaucer Soc, Soc for the Study of Narrative Lit. **RESEARCH** Literary theory, medieval literature. **SELECTED PUBLICATIONS** Coauth, "Index to Volumes 1-21 of the "Mark Twain Journal, 1936-1983," Mark Twain J (Charleston, SC), 85; auth, "Stories Within Stories: Narrative Levels and Embedded Narrative," Studies in Literary Imagination 25.1 (92): 61-74; auth, "Historical and Implied Authors and Readers," Comp Lit 45.1 (93): 22-46; auth, "A Bibliography of Bibliographies Appearing in 'Style', 1967-1994," Style 28.4 (94): 485-497; auth, "Myth and Symbol in 'Madame Bovary'" in Approaches to Teaching 'Madame Bovary', ed. Laurence M. Porter and Eugene F. Gray (NY: MLA,95), 55-60; auth, "Michael Riffaterre: A Checklist of Writings through 1996," Style 30.4 (96): 572-583; auth, Frameworks: Narrative Levels and Embedded Narrative, Peter Lang (NY, NY), 97; ed, "Chaucerian Poetics," spec issue of Style 31.3 (97): 369-568; auth "Beowulf's 'sorbfullne sid' with Breca," Neophilogus 83.2 (99): 299-312; auth, "Edna Pontellier's Revolt Against Nature," Am Lit Realism 1870-1910 32.1 (99): 43-50. **CONTACT ADDRESS** Dept of English, Univ of Massachusetts, Dartmouth, 285 Old Westport Rd, North Dartmouth, MA 02747-2356. **EMAIL** wnelles@umassd.edu

NELSEN, ROBERT

PERSONAL Born 01/21/1952, Brigham City, UT, m, 1975, 1 child **DISCIPLINE** LITERATURE STUDIES **EDUCATION** Univ Chicago, PhD, 89. **CAREER** Assoc prof; director of Creative Writing. **HONORS AND AWARDS** Exec ed, "Best Journal in Humanities, Social Studies, and Social Sciences, 1993," Common Knowledge; exec ed, The Am Asn of publishers, 94 "Ten Best Journals," Common Knowledge, 93; Library Journal: The Pushcart Prize Best of the Small Presses: Distinguished Stories Awd, 91; ed, common knowledge. **MEMBERSHIPS** AWP; ALTA; TCFS; FAC; TACWT; GCAWT. **RESEARCH** Southern Literature; Contemporary Literature; Creative Writing. **SELECTED PUBLICATIONS** Auth, Spirits Colliding, Descant, 00; auth, "The Sun, The Moon, The Star," Southwest Review (96): 538-544; auth, Miles Away From Home, TriQuart, 95; auth, They Fly Up and Drop, Quart W, 94; auth, We Bums Are Not Homeless, Chariton Rev, 93; auth, Everybody Needs a Fine Dancer, SW Rev, 92; auth, Something Big, Northwestern Univ, 90; auth, The Story of a Mighty and Ferocious Warrior, Other Voices, 89. **CONTACT ADDRESS** Arts and Humanities, Univ of Texas, Dallas, Box 830688 JO3.1, Richardson, TX 75083-0688. **EMAIL** nelsen@utdallas.edu

NELSON, ARDIS L.

PERSONAL Born 08/14/1942, Auburn, NY **DISCIPLINE** HISPANIC CINEMA, CUBAN AND CENTRAL AMERICAN LITERATURE **EDUCATION** Oberlin Col, Ba, 65; Middlebury Col, Madrid, MA, 72; IN Univ, Bloomington, PhD, 80 **CAREER** Prof, 94-99, E TN St Univ; Assoc Prof, 85-94, Asst prof, 81-85, FL St Univ; Inst, 79-81, Dickinson Col; Lect, 77-78, Gettysburg Col; Assoc Inst, 72-77, IN Univ; Second Sch Tchr, 65-71, Rochester, NY **MEMBERSHIPS** Modern Language Assoc, Instituto Internacional de Literatura Iberoamericana, Am Asn of Tchrs of Spanish and portugese. **RESEARCH** Juan felyre Toruino, Carmen Naranjo. **SELECTED PUBLICATIONS** Auth, Cabrera Infante in the Menippean Tradition, Newark, Delaware: Juan de la Cuesta Hispanic monographs, 83; ed, Guillermo Cabrera Infante: Assays, Essays, and other Arts, Twayne Publishers, 99. **CONTACT ADDRESS** Dept of Foreign Lang, East Tennessee State Univ, Johnson City, TN 37614-0312. **EMAIL** nelsona@etsu.edu

NELSON, BARBARA J.

PERSONAL Born 04/20/1947, Bellevue, IA, m, 1971, 1 child **DISCIPLINE** ENGLISH **EDUCATION** Sul Ross State Univ, BS, 71; MA, 90; Univ Nev Reno, PhD, 97. **CAREER** Lectr, Sull ross State Univ, 90-94; grad fel, Univ of Nev Reno, 94-96; instr to asst prof, Sul Ross State Univ, 96-. **HONORS AND AWARDS** Who's Who Among Am Teachers, 96, 98; Big Bend Hall of Fame, 98. **MEMBERSHIPS** W Am Lit Assoc; Assoc for the Study of Lit and Environ; Rural Women Studies Assoc; Mayflower Soc; Cormac McCarthy Soc; Mary Hunter Austin Soc; Austin Writer's League; Phi Kappa Phi Interdisciplinary Acad Honor Soc. **RESEARCH** Mary Austin, Ecocriticism, representation of animals in literature. **SELECTED PUBLICATIONS** Auth, The Last Campfire: The Life Story of Ted Gray, a West Texas Rancher, Texas A & M Pr, 84; auth, "W.D. Smithers: Big Bend Photographer", Jof Big Bend Studies 4 (93): 89-96; auth, "Edward Abbey's Cow", in Coyote in the Maze: Critical Essays on Edward Abbey, ed Peter Quigley, Univ of Utah Pr, (Salt Lake City, 98), 206-225; auth, "An Ecocritical Sense of Time and Place in Mary Austin, Gretel Ehrlich, and Linda Hasselstrom", N Dak Quart (Winter, 99); auth, "The Flock: An Ecocritical Look at Mary Austin's Sheep and John Muir's Hoofed Locusts", in Exploring the Lost Borders: Critical Essays on Mary Austin, ed Melody Graulich and Betsy Klimasmith, Univ of Nev Pr, (Reno, 99), 221-242; auth, "Gretel Ehrlich", Dict of Lit Biography: Twentieth-Century Am Western Writers, ed Richard H. Cracroft, Bruccoli Clark Layman (Columbia, SC), 44-51; auth, "Rustling Thoreau's Cattle: Wilderness and Domesticity in Walking", Thoreau's Sense of Place: New Essays in Am Environ Writing, ed Richard Schneider (forthcoming); auth, The Wild and the Domestic: Animal Representation, Ecocriticism and Western American Literature (forthcoming). **CONTACT ADDRESS** Dept Lang and Lit, Sul Ross State Univ, 400 N Harrison St, Alpine, TX 79832-8300. **EMAIL** bnelson@sulross.edu

NELSON, CARY ROBERT

PERSONAL Born 05/15/1946, Philadelphia, PA **DISCIPLINE** ENGLISH & AMERICAN LITERATURE **EDUCATION** Antioch Col, BA, 67; Univ Rochester, PhD(English), 70. **CAREER** From asst to assoc prof, English, 70-82, Prof English & Criticism & Interpretive Theory, 82- ; Jubilee Prof of Liberal Arts and Sci, 91- ,Univ Ill, Urbana; Vis prof, State Univ NY Col Buffalo, 77; coordr, Fac Criticism Sem, Univ Ill, Urbana, 77-, assoc fel, Ctr Advan Studies, 78, dir, Unit for Criticism & Interpretive Theory, 81- **MEMBERSHIPS** MLA; AAUP; Midwest MLA; Tchrs for a Democratic Culture; Kenneth Burke Soc; Ernest Hemingway Soc; Natl Counc Tchrs English. **RESEARCH** Modern English and American literature; critical theory. **SELECTED PUBLICATIONS** Auth, The Incarnate Word: Literature as Verbal Space, Illinois, 73; auth, Our Last First Poets: Vision and History in Contemporary American Poetry, Illinois, 81; auth, Repression and Recovery: Modern American Poetry and the Politics of Cultural Memory, 1910-1945, Wisconsin, 89; auth, Shouts from the Wall: Posters and Photographs Brought Back from the Spanish Civil War by American Volunteers, Illinois, 96; auth, Manifesto of a Tenured Radical, New York Univ, 97; coauth, Academic Keywords: A Devil's Dictionary for Higher Education, Routledge, 99. **CONTACT ADDRESS** Dept of English, Univ of Illinois, Urbana-Champaign, 608 S Wright St, Urbana, IL 61801.

NELSON, CLAUDIA B.

PERSONAL Born 11/02/1960, Fort Belvoir, VA, 1 child **DISCIPLINE** ENGLISH **EDUCATION** Bryn Mawr Col, AB, 80; Indiana Univ, PhD, 89. **CAREER** Fac to assoc prof, English, Southwest Texas State Univ, 93- . **HONORS AND AWARDS** Pres Awd for Excellence in Scholarly/Creative Activity; SWT; NEH Fel, 99; memb, bd of dir, children's lit asn. **MEMBERSHIPS** Children's Lit Asn; MLA. **RESEARCH** Victorian literature and culture; children's studies; history of the family. **SELECTED PUBLICATIONS** Auth, Boys Will Be Girls: The Feminine Ethic and British Children's Fiction, 1857-1917, Rutgers, 91; co-ed, with Vallone, The Girl's Own: Cultural Histories of the Anglo-American Girl, 1830-1915, Univ Georgia, 94; auth, Invisible Men: Fatherhood in Victorian Periodicals, 1850-1910, Univ Georgia, 95; co-ed, with Holmes, Maternal Instincts: Visions of Motherhood and Sexuality in Britain, 1875-1925, Macmillan, 97; auth, "Mixed Messages: Authoring and Authority in British Boys Magazines," The Lion and the Unicorn, 97; auth, "Art for Man's Sake: Frances Browne's Magic and Victorian Social Aesthetics," Bookbird, 98; auth, "David and Jonathan--and Saul--Revisited: Homodomestic Patterns in British Boys Magazine Fiction, 1880-1915," ChLA Quarterly, 98; auth, "Growing Up," in A Companion to Victorian Literature and Culture, ed. Herbert F. Tucker, Blackwell, 99; auth, "Playing Patients: The Medico-Moral Context of The Heavenly Twins," 'Journal of Contemporary Thought, 99. **CONTACT ADDRESS** Dept of English, Southwest Texas State Univ, 601 Univ Dr, San Marcos, TX 78666. **EMAIL** cho2@swt.edu

NELSON, DANA D.

DISCIPLINE ENGLISH LITERATURE **EDUCATION** MI State Univ, PhD. **CAREER** Vis prof, 98-99. **RESEARCH** Colonial to nineteenth century Am lit; promotional, travel and frontier lit; early national and early US Novel; multi ethnic US lit; women's lit and gender studies; femnist and gender theory; cult and race theory. **SELECTED PUBLICATIONS** Auth, The Word in Black and White: Reading Race in American Literature. **CONTACT ADDRESS** Eng Dept, Duke Univ, Durham, NC 27706.

NELSON, DAVID C.

DISCIPLINE COMMUNICATIONS **EDUCATION** Purdue Univ, BA, MA, PhD. **CAREER** Ed, Col Media Rev, 88-93; Assoc ed, College Media Rev, 93-; Assoc ed, Newspaper Res Jour, 92-. **SELECTED PUBLICATIONS** Rev ed, Writing the News, Wadsworth Publ, 93; Understanding Grammar, Brown & Benchmark, 93, State of the Art: Issues in Contemporary Communication, St Martins Press, 92; A Handbook for Reporters, Allyn & Bacon, 92; Coauth, Viability and the Mass Communication Curriculum , 93; Designing client services for academic organizations , 92. **CONTACT ADDRESS** Southwest Texas State Univ, 601 University Dr, San Marcos, TX 78666-4604.

NELSON, HARLAND S.

PERSONAL Born 08/11/1925, Hawley, MN, m, 1954, 3 children **DISCIPLINE** ENGLISH **EDUCATION** Concordia Col, Minn, BA, 49; Wash State Univ, MA, 51; Univ Minn, PhD, 59. **CAREER** Instr English, Univ Mo, 51-53, Univ Conn, 59-62; Asst Prof English 62; Assoc 67; Prof 67-92, Prof Emeritus 92-; Consortium Agr and World Hungerr 81-86, Luther Col, IA. **HONORS AND AWARDS** Fulbright Lectr, Univ Bergen, Norway, 67-68, Univ Innsbruck, Austria, 72-73; Phi Kappa Phi, Phi Beta Kappa. **MEMBERSHIPS** AAUP, MLA, Col English Asn, Soc Values Higher Educ, Asn for Religion in Intellectual Life, Norwegian-American Historical Asn. **RESEARCH** Victorian literature; Dickens; modern and contemporary fiction. **SELECTED PUBLICATIONS** Auth, Dickens' plots: The Ways of Providence or the influence of Collins?, Victorian Newslett, spring 61; Stephen Crane's achievement as a poet, Tex Studies Lit & Lang, winter 63; Dickens' Our Mutual Friend and Henry Mayhew's London Labour and the London Poor, 19th-Century Fiction, 1265; Steinbeck's politics then and now, Antioch Rev, spring 67; contribr, Shonfield and Forster's India: A controversial exchange, Encounter, 668; auth, Theology and the films of Ingmar Bergman, Dialog, summer 71; Staggs's Gardens: The railway through Dickens' World, Dickens' Studies Annual, 74; "Charles Dickens," Twayne, 81; Dickens Studies Annual - Essays on Victorian Fiction, Vol 23 - Timko,m, Kaplan,f, Guiliano,e, Dickens Quarterly, Vol 0013, 1996; Charles Dickens, Twayne, 81; Dickens, Religion, And Nubile Girls, Dickens Quarterly, Vol 0014, 1997; "Recent Dickens Studies: 1998," Dickens Studies Annual, Vol 29, 00. **CONTACT ADDRESS** Dept of English, Luther Col, Decorah, IA 52101. **EMAIL** nelsonhs@lurher-edu

NELSON, JAMES GRAHAM

PERSONAL Born 12/20/1929, Covington, KY **DISCIPLINE** ENGLISH LITERATURE **EDUCATION** Univ Ky, BA, 52; Columbia Univ, MA, 55, PhD, 61. **CAREER** Lectr English, Columbia Univ, 58-61; from instr to assoc prof, 61-69, Prof English, Univ Wis-Madison, 69-, Guggenheim fel, 65-66. **MEMBERSHIPS** MLA; Milton Soc Am. **RESEARCH** Romantic and Victorian literature; Pubishing history; John Milton. **SELECTED PUBLICATIONS** Auth, The Sublime Puritan: Milton and the Victorians, Univ Wis, 63; Sir William Watson, Twayne, 67; The Early Nineties: A View From the Bodley Head, Harvard Univ, 71. **CONTACT ADDRESS** Dept of English, Univ of Wisconsin, Madison, Madison, WI 53706.

NELSON, MALCOLM A.

PERSONAL Born 05/29/1934, Carbondale, IL, m, 1993, 5 children **DISCIPLINE** ENGLISH **EDUCATION** Williams Col, BA, 55; Northwestern Univ, MA, 57, PhD, 61 **CAREER** Asst, Northwestern Univ, 56-59; from instr to asst prof English, Miami Univ, 59-65; asst prof, Grinnell Col, 65-68; assoc prof, 68-73, prof, 73-83, Distinguisher Teaching Prof, State Univ NY Col Fredonia, 83-; State Univ NY Res Found grant, 69 & 71; Am Philos Soc grant, 71. **HONORS AND AWARDS** Chancellor's Awd for Excellence in Teaching, State Univ NY, 75; distinguished teaching prof of Eng, 83. **MEMBERSHIPS** Catch Soc Am (exec secy, 68-); Am Fedn Teachers; Am Culture Assoc. **RESEARCH** Shakespeare; 16th-18th century poetry and music--catches, canons and glees; American gravestone poetry and art; Mari Sandoz and the American West, American Indians. **SELECTED PUBLICATIONS** Auth, The Poet and the Goddess, Nous, 3/67; co-ed, A Collection of Catches, Canons and Glees, 1762-1793 (4 vols), Mellifont, 70; auth, Catches, glees and chaces: Cantici bibendi et alii, Lyric & Song, 6/71; The Robin Hood Tradition in the English Renaissance, Univ Salzburg, 73; coauth, Resurrecting the epitaph, Markers, Vol I, 80; auth, See an account by Sir G Esterling, 1598, Shakespeare Quart, Vol 31, No 1; coauth, Grinning skulls, smiling cherubs, bitter words, J Popular Cult, Vol 15, No 4; Epitaph and Icon: A Field Guide to the Old Burying Grounds of Cape Cod, Martha's Vineyard, and Nantucket, Parnassus, 83; Hamlet the Fool, In: Fools and Jesters in Literature, Art and History, Greenwood Press, 98; auth "Images of Nebraska Sandhills Pioneer Women," Proceedings of Soc for Interdis Study of Social Imagery, (97); co-ed, American Indian Studies series, Peter Lang Publishing. **CONTACT ADDRESS** Dept of English, SUNY, Col at Fredonia, SUNY at Fredonia, Fredonia, NY 14063-1143. **EMAIL** nelson@fredonia.edu

NELSON, MARIE
PERSONAL Born 09/13/1928, Des Moines, IA, w, 2 children **DISCIPLINE** ENGLISH **EDUCATION** Iowa State Teacher's Col, BA, 50; Univ N Iowa, MA, 67; Univ Ore, PhD, 73. **CAREER** Instr, Univ N Iowa, 67-69; instr, Univ Ore, 73-74; asst prof to prof, Univ Fla, 74-. **HONORS AND AWARDS** Kappa Delta Pi. **MEMBERSHIPS** medieval Acad; SE Medieval Asn. **RESEARCH** Old English literature; Stylistics approach to literary and non-literary texts. **SELECTED PUBLICATIONS** Auth, Structures of Opposition in Old English Poetry; auth, Judith, Juliana, and Elene: Three Fighting Saints. **CONTACT ADDRESS** Dept English, Univ of Florida, 3525 NW 50th Ave, Gainesville, FL 32605-1067. **EMAIL** mnelson@english.ufl.edu

NELSON, MARILYN
PERSONAL Born 04/26/1946, Cleveland, OH, s, 2 children **DISCIPLINE** ENGLISH **EDUCATION** Univ Calif Davis, BA, 68; Univ Penn, MA, 70, Univ Minn, PhD, 79. **HONORS AND AWARDS** Annisfield-Wolf Awd; Poets' Prize; Contemplative Practices Fel; Fulbright Fel. **MEMBERSHIPS** AAUP; AWP. **RESEARCH** Poetry; Aframerican Literature. **SELECTED PUBLICATIONS** Auth, The Fields of Praise: New and Selected Poems, LSU Pr; auth, The Homeplace, LSU Pr. **CONTACT ADDRESS** Dept English, Univ of Connecticut, Storrs, 337 Mansfield Rd, U-25, Storrs, CT 06269-1025. **EMAIL** marilyn.nelson@uconn.edu

NELSON, NICOLAS HARDING
PERSONAL Born 07/07/1940, Nebraska City, NE, m, 1965, 2 children **DISCIPLINE** ENGLISH LITERATURE **EDUCATION** Stanford Univ, BA, 62; Univ Wis, Madison, MA, 65, PhD(English), 71. **CAREER** Lectr English, 69-71, asst prof, 71-76, Assoc Prof English, Ind Univ, Kokomo, 76-, Chmn Div Humanities, 71-. **MEMBERSHIPS** MLA; Am Soc 18th Century Studies; Johnson Soc Cent Region; Augustan Reprint Soc. **RESEARCH** Samuel Butler; Hudibras; 18th century English satire. **SELECTED PUBLICATIONS** Auth, Astrology, Hudibras, and the Puritans, J Hist Ideas, 7-976; Narrative Transformations, Prior Art of The Tale, Studies in Philology, Vol 0090, 1993; Narrative Transformations, Prior Art of The Tale, Studies in Philology, Vol 0090, 1993. **CONTACT ADDRESS** Div of Humanities, Indiana Univ, Kokomo, 2300 S Washington St, Kokomo, IN 46902.

NELSON, RANDY FRANKLIN
PERSONAL Born 05/20/1948, Charlotte, NC, m, 1968, 1 child **DISCIPLINE** AMERICAN LITERATURE **EDUCATION** NC State Univ, BA, 70, MA, 72; Princeton Univ, MA, 75, PhD(English), 76. **CAREER** Asst prof English, Univ Louisville, 76-77; Asst Prof English, Davidson Col, 77-, Ed, Textual Res, Writings of Henry David Thoreau, 76-. **MEMBERSHIPS** MLA; Thoreau Soc; Mark Twain Soc; Southern Writers Conf; Poe Soc. **RESEARCH** H D Thoreau; Mark Twain; Southern literature. **SELECTED PUBLICATIONS** Slave Ship', African American Review, Vol 0030, 1996. **CONTACT ADDRESS** Dept of English, Davidson Col, Davidson, NC 28036. **EMAIL** ranelson@davidson.edu

NELSON, RICHARD ALAN
DISCIPLINE MASS COMMUNICATIONS **EDUCATION** Fla State Univ, PhD, 80. **CAREER** Assoc dean, grad stud and res, La State Univ; Instr, assoc dir, Int Telecommun Res Inst, Univ Houston; hd, PR, Kans State Univ; Accredited PR Prof, PR Soc of Am. **MEMBERSHIPS** Pres, Int Acad of Bus Disciplines, 97-99. **SELECTED PUBLICATIONS** Auth, Lights! Camera! Florida! Ninety Years of Moviemaking and Television Production in the Sunshine State, Fla Endowment for the Hum, 87; Bias Versus Fairness: The Social Utility of Issues Management, in PR Rev 16,1, 90; Activist Groups and New Technologies: Influencing the Public Affairs Agenda, in Lloyd B. Dennis, ed, Practical Public Affairs in an Era of Change: A Communications Guide for Business, Government, and College, PR Soc of Am/UP of Am, 95; A Chronology and Glossary of Propaganda in the United States, Greenwood Press, 96; coauth, Issues Management: Corporate Public Policymaking in an Information Society, Sage Publ, 89. **CONTACT ADDRESS** The Manship Sch of Mass Commun, Louisiana State Univ and A&M Col, Baton Rouge, LA 70803. **EMAIL** rnelson@unix1.sncc.lsu.edu

NELSON, ROY RAY
PERSONAL Born 07/27/1929, Pittsburgh, PA, m, 1954, 2 children **DISCIPLINE** LITERATURE, FRENCH **EDUCATION** Univ Pitts, AB; 51; Middlebury Col, MA, 52; Univ Ill, PhD, 58. **CAREER** Instr to asst prof to assoc prof to emer, Univ Mich, 57-. **HONORS AND AWARDS** Emeritus Fr Lit. **MEMBERSHIPS** AATF; MLA. **RESEARCH** Modern French prose fiction. **SELECTED PUBLICATIONS** Auth, Peguy, Poete du Sacre, L'Amitie Charles Peguy (Paris), 60; auth, "Reflections in a Broken Mirror: Varda's Cleo de 5 a 7," Fr Rev 5 (83): 735-743; auth, Causality and Narrative in French Fiction from Zola to Robber Grilet, Ohio State UP, 89; auth, "Joris-Karl Huysmans," Dict Lit Biog 123 (93): 138-157. **CONTACT ADDRESS** 8730 Midnight Pass Rd, Apt 304A, Sarasota, FL 34242-2894. **EMAIL** rnelson01@home.com

NEMANIC, MARY LOU
PERSONAL Born 09/17/1950, Minneapolis, MN, m, 1988 **DISCIPLINE** MEDIA STUDIES **EDUCATION** Univ Minn, BA (Summa cum Laude), 75; Univ Minn, MA, 77; PhD, 96. **CAREER** Adj instr, Univ Minn, 75-77 & 92-97; adj instr, Metropolitan State Univ, 84-98; asst prof, Western State Col, 98-. **HONORS AND AWARDS** Phi Beta Kappa; Kappa Tau Alpha; Turpie-Bowron Fel, 92 & 95. **MEMBERSHIPS** Orgn of Am Historians, Am Studies Asn. **RESEARCH** American Popular Culture, American Cultural History, Media Studies, the Digital Revolution, Visual Media. **SELECTED PUBLICATIONS** Contribur, The St James Encyclopedia of Popular Culture, Full Circle Pr, 00. **CONTACT ADDRESS** Dept Commun Arts, Western State Col of Colorado, 600 N Adams St, Gunnison, CO 81231-7000. **EMAIL** mnemanic@western.edu

NEMETH, NEIL
DISCIPLINE COMMUNICATION **EDUCATION** Ohio Univ, BS; Ohio State Univ, MA; Ind Univ, PhD. **CAREER** Asst prof, 94-. **RESEARCH** Reporting, editing, mass communication law, mass communication ethics. **SELECTED PUBLICATIONS** Publ, Newspaper Res Jour, Southwestern Mass Commun Jour **CONTACT ADDRESS** Dept of Commun, Pittsburg State Univ, 1701 S Broadway St, Pittsburg, KS 66762.

NERONE, JOHN
DISCIPLINE COMMUNICATIONS **EDUCATION** Xavier, HAB, 78; Univ Notre Dame, BA, 80, PhD, 82. **CAREER** Assoc prof, Inst Comm Res, PROF, UNIV ILL **MEMBERSHIPS** Am Antiquarian Soc **RESEARCH** US Newspapers **SELECTED PUBLICATIONS** Auth, Lessons from American History, in Journalists in Peril, Media Studies Rev, Fall 96; coauth, News Photography and the New Long Journalism," in Visual Representation and History; auth, The Culture of the Press in the Early Republic: Cincinnati, 1793-1848; auth, Violence Against the Press: Policing the Public Sphere in U.S. History; ed, Last Right: Revisiting Four Theories of the Press. **CONTACT ADDRESS** 505 E Armory Ave, Champaign, IL 61820. **EMAIL** j-nerone@uiuc.edu

NERSESSIAN, NANCY
DISCIPLINE COGNITIVE SCIENCES **EDUCATION** Case Western Reserve Univ, PhD. **CAREER** Prof, Ga Inst of Technol; ser ed, Sci and Philos bk ser, Kluwer Acad Publ. **MEMBERSHIPS** Gov bd, Philos of Sci Asn. **RESEARCH** The role of imagery, analogy, and thought experimenting in conceptual change. **SELECTED PUBLICATIONS** Auth, Faraday to Einstein: Constructing Meaning in Scientific Theories, Kluwer Acad Publ, 84, 90; How do scientists think? Capturing the dynamics of conceptual change in science, in Cognitive Models of Science, R Giere, ed, Minn Stud in Philos of Sci 15, Univ Minn Press,91; Constructing and Instructing: The role of 'abstraction techniques' in developing and teaching scientific theories, in Philosophy of Science, Cognitive Science, and Educational Theory and Practice, R Duschl & R Hamilton, eds, SUNY Press, 92; In the theoretician's laboratory: thought experimenting as mental modeling, PSA 92, Vol 2, D Hull, M Forbes, K Okruhlik, eds, 93. **CONTACT ADDRESS** Sch of Lit, Commun, & Cult, Georgia Inst of Tech, Skiles Cla, Atlanta, GA 30332. **EMAIL** nancyn@cc.gatech.edu

NESANOVICH, STELLA
DISCIPLINE ENGLISH **EDUCATION** La State Univ, BA, 66; MA, 68; PhD, 79. **CAREER** Instr, Univ New Orleans, 68-71; Teaching Asst to Instr, La State Univ, 71-79; Instr, Winthrop Col, 79-82; Asst Prof to Prof, McNeese State Univ, 82-. **HONORS AND AWARDS** Fel, La Division of the Arts, 99-00; Finalist , Foley Prize, America Magazine, 91; Fel Va Ctr for the Creative Arts, 86, 87; English speaking Union Scholarship, Univ London, 68. **MEMBERSHIPS** Conf on Christianity and Literature, S Central Mod Lang Asn. **RESEARCH** 20th Century American (especially Southern) literature; Women's Studies. **SELECTED PUBLICATIONS** Auth, A Brightness that mad my should Tremble: Poems on the Life of Hildegard of Bingen, Blue Heron Press, 96; auth, "The Early Novels of Anne Tyler: A Reconsideration," in Anne Tyler as Novelist, Univ Iowa Press, 94; auth, "The Individual in the Family: Anne Tyler's Searching for Calleb and Earthly Possessions," in Critical Essays on Anne Tyler, G.K. Hall, 92; auth, "The Pearl," in something in Common: Contemporary Louisiana Stories, La State Univ Press, 90. **CONTACT ADDRESS** Dept Lang, McNeese State Univ, PO Box 92655, Lake Charles, LA 70609.

NESBITT, JOHN D.
PERSONAL Born 12/14/1948, Lompoc, CA, m, 1 child **DISCIPLINE** ENGLISH, SPANISH **EDUCATION** Univ Calif, Los Angeles, BA, 71; Univ Calif, Davis, MA, 74; PhD, 80. **CAREER** Instr, Eastern Wyo Col, 81-. **HONORS AND AWARDS** Phi Beta Kappa, 71; Fel, Wyo Counc for the Humanities, 88; Fel, Wyo Counc on the Arts, 1988, NISOD Excellence in Tea;ching Awd, 94; Arizola Magnenat Awd, 99; Fiction Awd, Wyo Hist Soc. 99. **MEMBERSHIPS** Western Lit Assoc; Western Writers of Am; Wyo Poets. **RESEARCH** History of prose fiction, Western American literature, popular fiction, Wyoming in general, Mexican fiction. **SELECTED PUBLICATIONS** Auth, "Lesser Known Works of Wyoming Fiction", Eastern Wyo col, 90; auth, One Foot in the Stirrup: Western Stories, Thorndike Pr, (Thorndike, Maine), 95; auth, Blue Book of Basic Writing, Endeavor Books, (Casper), 96; auth, Adventures of the Ramrod Rider: Gripping Tales, Augmented and Revised by the Author, Endeavor books, (Casper), 99; auth, A Good Man to Have in Camp, Endeavor Books (Casper), 99; auth, Coyote Trail, Leisure Books (NY), 00; auth, Writing for Real, Endeavor Books, (forthcoming); auth, North of Cheyenne Leisure Books, (forthcoming), auth, Man from Wolf River, Leisure Books (forthcoming). **CONTACT ADDRESS** Dept Humanities and Soc Sci, Eastern Wyoming Col, 3200 West C St, Torrington, WY 82240-1603.

NESS, ARTHUR J.
PERSONAL Born 01/27/1936, Chicago, IL, m, 1984 **DISCIPLINE** MUSIC **EDUCATION** Univ S Cal, BM Music Theory, 58; Harvard Univ, AM, 63; New York Univ, PhD, 84. **CAREER** Univ S Cal, asst prof, 63-76; Daemen Col, assoc prof, dept chair, 76-84; SUNY/Buffalo, adjunct prof music, 83-85. **HONORS AND AWARDS** Charles Healey Awd, Outstanding Diss in Humanities; Fulbright Fel Univ Munich **MEMBERSHIPS** Am Musicol Soc; Int Musicol Soc; Lute Soc, UK; Nederlandse Luitvereniging Int; Asn of Music Libraries. **RESEARCH** Music for LuteWind; Music of Mozart & Contemporaries. **SELECTED PUBLICATIONS** The Lute Music of Francesco Canova da Milano, 1497-1543, Harvard Univ Press, 70. **CONTACT ADDRESS** 2039 Commonwealth Ave, Ste 10, Boston, MA 02135. **EMAIL** 71162.751@Compuserve.com

NESSET, KIRK
DISCIPLINE ENGLISH **CAREER** Assoc prof Eng, Allegheny Col. **HONORS AND AWARDS** Pushcart Prize, 99. **MEMBERSHIPS** MLA; AWP. **RESEARCH** Fiction writing; Poetry; Native Am Lit. **SELECTED PUBLICATIONS** Auth, "The Final Stitch: Raymond Carver and Metaphor," Profils Americains, Paris, 94; rev, "Gates to Buddhist Practice," Mountain Record, 95; auth, The Stories of Raymond Carver: A Critical Study, 95, Ohio Univ Press; auth, "The Noise That Wants To Be Joy," Witness, 96; auth, "Snakes having Babies," Indiana Review, 96; auth, "Behind the Wheel," South Carolina review, 97; auth, "It Me," New Letters, 99; auth, Heartland," 99; auth, "The Cage," Storyquarterly, 99; auth, "American Magic and Dread: Don DeLillo's Dialogue With Culture," Am Lit, (forthcoming, 01). **CONTACT ADDRESS** Dept of English, Allegheny Col, Meadville, PA 16335. **EMAIL** knesset@alleg.edu

NETHERCUT, WILLIAM ROBERT
PERSONAL Born 01/11/1936, Rockford, IL **DISCIPLINE** CLASSICS **EDUCATION** Harvard Univ, AB, 58; Columbia Univ, MA, 60, PhD(Classics), 63. **CAREER** From instr to asst prof Greek & Latin, Columbia Univ, 61-67; from assoc prof to prof Classics, Univ Ga, 67-75; prof Classics, Univ Tex, Austin, 75-, Lawrence Chamberlain fel, Columbia Univ, 67; lectr, First Int Conf on Ovid, Constanta, Romania, 72, Int Soc Homeric Studies, Athens, 73, 74, Int Congr Cypriot Studies, 74 & Int Congr SE Europ Studies, 74. **MEMBERSHIPS** Am Philol Asn; Class Asn Mid W & S; Archaeol Inst Am; Vergilian Soc Am; Petronian Soc. **RESEARCH** Propertius; Vergil; Greek poetry. **SELECTED PUBLICATIONS** Auth, The conclusion of Lucretius' fifth book, Class J, 12/67; Notes on the structure of Propertius, book IV, Am J Philol, 10/68; Apuleius' literary art, Class J, 69; The ironic priest: Propertius' Roman elegies, Am J Philol, 10/70; Propertius, 3/11, Trans Am Philol Asn, 71; The imagery of the Aeneid, Class J, 71-72; Vergil's De Return Natura, 73 & The epic journey of Achilles, 76, Ramus; Recent Scholarship on Propertius, Aufstieg und Noedergang cler Romischer Welt, 83. **CONTACT ADDRESS** Dept of Classics, Univ of Texas, Austin, 123 Waggener Hall, Austin, TX 78712-1026. **EMAIL** nethercut@mail.utexas.edu

NETTELS, ELSA
PERSONAL Born 05/25/1931, Madison, WI **DISCIPLINE** ENGLISH, AMERICAN LITERATURE **EDUCATION** Cornell Univ, AB, 53; Univ Wis, MA, 55, PhD(Eng), 60. **CAREER** Instr Eng, Mt Holyoke Col, 59-62, asst prof, 63-67; from asst prof to assoc prof, 67-75, Prof Eng, Col William & Mary, 75-, Prof Emeritus, 97. **HONORS AND AWARDS** S Atlantic MLA Studies Awd, 75; NEH fel for col Tchrs, 83-84. **MEMBERSHIPS** MLA; NE MLA, S Atlantic MLA; Henry James Soc; Edith Wharton Soc, Am Stud Asn. **RESEARCH** Am lit; mod fiction. **SELECTED PUBLICATIONS** Auth, The ambassadors and the sense of the past, Mod Lang Quart, 6/70; Action and point of view in Roderick Hudson, English Studies, summer 72; James and Conrad on the art of fiction, Tex Studies Lit & Lang, fall 72; Heart of darkness and the creative process, Conradiana, summer 73; The scapegoats and martyrs of Henry James, Colby Libr Quart, 9/74; The grotesque in Conrad's fiction: Nineteenth-Century Fiction, 11/74; James and Conrad, Univ Ga, 77; William Dean Howells and the American language, New Eng Quart, fall 80; Language, Race, and Social Class in Howells's America, Univ Press of Ky, 88; Language and Gender in American Fiction: Howells, James, Wharton, and Cather, Macmillan, 97. **CONTACT ADDRESS** Dept of English, Col of William and Mary, Williamsburg, VA 23185. **EMAIL** eynett@wm.edu

NETTL, BRUNO
PERSONAL Born 03/14/1930, Prague, Czechoslovakia, m, 1952, 2 children **DISCIPLINE** MUSICOLOGY **EDUCATION** Indiana Univ, AB, 50, PhD, 53; Univ of Mich, MA, 60. **CAREER** Instr, asst prof and music libn, Wayne State Univ, 53-56; lectr, Univ of Kiel, Germany, 56-58; from assoc prof to prof, Univ of Ill, 64-92; prof emer, Univ of Ill, 92-. **HONORS AND AWARDS** Distinguished Alumni Serv Awd, Ind Univ, 86; Hon Doctorate, Univ of Chicago, 93; Koizumi Prize for Ethnomusicology, Japan, 94; Hon mem, Am Musicological Soc, 95; Hon Doctorate, Univ of Ill, 96; Fel, Am Acad of Arts and Scis, 97. **MEMBERSHIPS** Soc for Ethnomusicology; Am Musicological Soc; Sonneck Soc; Soc for Asian Music; Int Coun for Traditional Music. **RESEARCH** Ethnomusicology; musical cultures of Iran; Native American music; intellectual history of ethnomusicology. **SELECTED PUBLICATIONS** Auth, North American Indian Musical Styles, 54; Music in Primitive Culture, 56; An Introduction to Folk Music in the United States, 60; Cheremis Musical Styles, 60; Theory and Method in Ethnomusicology, 64; Folk and Traditional Music of the Western Continents, 65; The Study of Ethnomusicology: 29 Issues and Concepts, 83; The Western Impact on World Music, 85; The Radif of Persian Music: Studies of Structure and Cultural Context, 87; Blackfoot Musical Thought: Comparative Perspectives, 89; Heartland Excursions: Ethnomusicological Reflections on Schs of Music, 95; coauth, Folk Music in the United States, 3rd ed of Introd to Folk Music in the United States, 76; Daramad of Chahargah, 72; Contemporary Music and Music Cultures, 73; Excursions in World Music, 92; ed, Reference Materials in Ethnomusicology, 61; Eight Urban Musical Cultures, 78; coed, Comparative Musicology and Anthropology of Music: Essays on the History of Ethnomusicology, 91; Community of Music: An Ethnographic Seminar in Champaign-Urbana, 93; In the Course of Performance: Studies in the World of Musical Improvisation, 98. **CONTACT ADDRESS** Sch of Music, Univ of Illinois, Urbana-Champaign, 1114 West Nevada, Urbana, IL 61801. **EMAIL** b-nettl@uiuc.edu

NEUENDORF, KIMBERLY A.
DISCIPLINE MASS COM THEORY, FILM **EDUCATION** MI State Univ, BA, MA, PhD. **CAREER** Comm, Cleveland St Univ. **SELECTED PUBLICATIONS** Arms Co-auth, TV Entertainment, News, and Racial Perceptions of College Students, Jour Commun, 92; Exposure Effects and Affective Responses to Music, Commun Monogr, 94. **CONTACT ADDRESS** Commun Dept, Cleveland State Univ, 83 E 24th St, Cleveland, OH 44115. **EMAIL** k.neuendorf@csuohio.edu

NEUFELD, JAMES EDWARD
PERSONAL Born 12/09/1944, Niagara, ON, Canada, m, 1974, 2 children **DISCIPLINE** ENGLISH DRAMA, CANADIAN LITERATURE **EDUCATION** Univ Toronto, BA, 67; Univ Chicago, AM, 69, PhD(comp lit), 74. **CAREER** Asst Prof, Trent Univ, 72-79; assoc prof, Trent Univ, 79-89; vis assoc prof, Univ of Victoria (B.C.), 82; full prof, Trent Univ, 89; principal of catharine parr trail colege, Trent Univ, 82-97; vice pres, Univ Services, Trent Univ, 90-94; acting vice pres, admin and Univ Services, Trent Univ, 94-95. **HONORS AND AWARDS** Woodrow Wilson fel, 67; Univ of Chic fel, 68; Canada Counc Doctoral fel, 69-72; Social sci and hum res counc of Canada leave fel, 79; Social scci and hum res counc of Canada res Grant, 87; Social sci and Humanities res counc of Canada res Grant, 89; Canadian Federation for the hum, Aid to Scholarly publications program, 96; Trent Univ: SSHRC com on res, 97. **MEMBERSHIPS** Asn Can Univ Teacher English. **RESEARCH** Seventeenth century English comedy: Ben Jonson and the restoration; connections between English literature and other art forms; Canadian literature. **SELECTED PUBLICATIONS** Auth, "Literary Derivatives: the Ballet in 1985-86," Journal of Canadian Studies, XXI, 3, (fall 86): 164-172; auth, "Keepers of the Flame: the National Ballet in 1986-87," Journal of Canadian Studies, XXII, 3, (fall 87), 127-133; auth, "Progency: the Ballet in 1987-88," Journal of Canadian Studies, XXII, 3, (fall 88): 130-138; auth, "Shaping the Legacy: the Ballet in 1988-89," Journal of Canadian Studies, XXIV, 3, (fall 89), 129-139; auth, "Music Matters: the Ballet in 1989-90," Journal of Canadian Studies, XXV, 3, (fall 90), 160-166; auth, "Contexts: the Ballet in 1990-91," Journal of Canadian Studies, XXVI, 3, (fall 91): 163-168; auth, "Scorecard: the Ballety in 1991-92," Journal of Canadian Studies, XXVI. 3 (fall, 92): 128-134; auth, Entries on "Celia Franca" and "The National Ballet of Canada," for The International Dictionary of Ballet, (Detroit, London, Washington DC: St. James Press), 93; auth, "The Expanded Moment," published in Following Sir Fred's Steps: Ashton's Legacy, Proceedings of the Ashton Conference, Roehampton Institute, London, 12-13 November, 94, edited by Stephanie Jordan and Andree Grau, London: Dance Books, 96, 22-28; auth, "Power to Rise: The Story of the National Ballet of Canada," Toronto, Buffalo, London: University of Toronto Press, 96, pp.368. **CONTACT ADDRESS** Dept of English Lit, Trent Univ, Peterborough, ON, Canada K9J7B8. **EMAIL** jneufeld@trentu.ca

NEUFELDT, LEONARD N.
PERSONAL Born 11/03/1937, Yarrow, BC, Canada, m, 1961, 3 children **DISCIPLINE** ENGLISH **EDUCATION** Waterloo Univ Col, BA, 61; Univ Ill, AM, 62, PhD, 66. **CAREER** Asst prof English, Univ Wash, 66-72; assoc prof Am lit, Univ Tex of the Permian Basin, 73-78; prof Am lit, Purdue Univ, 78-, Fulbright prof Am studies, Univ Erlangen, 72-73; Am Coun Learned Soc grants, 75 & 77; Am Philos Soc grant, 77. **MEMBERSHIPS** MLA. **RESEARCH** American transcendentalism; unitarianism; poetry. **SELECTED PUBLICATIONS** Auth, The Vital Mind: Emerson's Epistemology, in Philol Quart, 4/71; Time and Man's Possibilities in Light in August, in Ga Rev, spring 71; Emerson and the Civil War, in J English & Ger Philol, 10/72; A Way of Walking, Univ NB, 72; ed, Ralph Waldo Emerson: New Appraisals, Transcendental Bks, 73; The Science of Power, in J Hist Ideas, 4/77; The House of Emerson, Univ Nebr, 82; Journal Vol II of H D Thoreau, Princeton, 87; The Economist: Henry Thoreau and Enterprise, Oxford, 89; Raspberrying, Black Moss, 91; Journal Vol IV of H.D. Thoreau, Princeton, 92; Yarrow, Black Moss, 93; Car Failure North of Nimes, 94; Trees Partly of Wood, (in press). **CONTACT ADDRESS** 9722 Harborview Pl, Big Harbor, WA 98332. **EMAIL** neufeldt@gte.net

NEUFELDT, VICTOR A.
DISCIPLINE 19TH-CENTURY BRITISH LITERATURE **EDUCATION** Univ Brit Col, BA; Univ Ill, PhD. **CAREER** Adj prof. **HONORS AND AWARDS** Canada Council Leave fel, 74-75; Canada Council res grant, 72-73; SSHRCC grants, 80-81, 81-82, 88-90, 90-91, 91-92, 92-95, 97-99; vis fel, Clare Hall, Univ Cambridge, 95-96; pres, victorian stud assn of w can. **MEMBERSHIPS** Ed bd, Eng Lit Stud Monogr and The Victorian Rev. **SELECTED PUBLICATIONS** Auth, George Eliot's Middlemarch Notebooks, U of California P, 79; The Poems of Charlotte Bronte, Garland, 85; The Poems of Patrick Branwell Bronte, Garland, 90; A Bibliography of the Manuscripts of Patrick Branwell Bronte, Garland, 93; The Works of Patrick Branwell Bronte, vol 1, Garland, 97. **CONTACT ADDRESS** Dept of English, Univ of Victoria, PO Box 3070, Victoria, BC, Canada V8W 3W1.

NEUMAN, SHIRLEY C.
PERSONAL Born 10/10/1946, Edmonton, AB, Canada **DISCIPLINE** CANADIAN AND WOMEN'S LITERATURE **EDUCATION** Univ Alta, BA, 68, MA, 69, PhD, 76. **CAREER** Lectr, 76-77, asst prof, 77-81, assoc prof, 81-86, Prof Eng, Univ Alta, 86-, chair, Women's Stud, 87-89, McCalla Res Prof, 89-90, dept chair, 92-95; Dean of Arts, Univ British Columbia, 96-. **HONORS AND AWARDS** Gabriel Roy Crit Essay Awd, Asn Can & Que Lit, 84 **MEMBERSHIPS** Acad Hum & Soc Sci, Royal Soc Can (pres 94-96); Can Assoc Chairs Eng (pres, 93-94); Asn Can Univ Tchrs Eng (pres, 90-92). **SELECTED PUBLICATIONS** Auth, Gertrude Stein: Autobiography and the Problem of Narration, 79; auth, Some One Myth: Yeats' Autobiographical Prose, 82; coauth, Labyrinths of Voice: Conversations with Robert Kroetsch, 82; co-ed, A Mazing Space: Writing Canadian Women Writing, 86; co-ed, ReImagining Women, 94. **CONTACT ADDRESS** Faculty of Arts, Univ of British Columbia, 1866 Main Mall, B130, Vancouver, BC, Canada V6T 1Z1. **EMAIL** shirley.neuman@ubc.ca

NEUMANN, FREDERICK
PERSONAL Born 12/15/1907, Czechoslovakia, m, 1957, 1 child **DISCIPLINE** MUSIC HISTORY **EDUCATION** Univ Berlin, PhD(polit sci), 34; Columbia Univ, MA, 47, PhD, 52. **CAREER** Prof violin & music lit, Univ Miami, 48-51; prof music hist, strings & orchestra, Univ Richmond, 55-78. Am Philos Soc grant-in-aid, 64; Am Coun Learned Soc grants-in-aid, 65, 66 & 71; Guggenheim Mem Found fel, 67-68 & 74-76; vis prof music & sr fel, Coun Humanities, Princeton Univ, 70-71; Nat Endowment for Humanities fel, 77-78. **MEMBERSHIPS** Am Musicol Soc; Fr Musicol Soc; Am String Teachers Asn; New Bach Soc; Int Musicol Soc. **RESEARCH** Economics; violin technique; historical performance. **SELECTED PUBLICATIONS** Auth, The French Inegales, Quantz, and Bach, J Am Musicol Soc, fall 65; La note pointee, Rev Musicol, 65; External evidence and uneven notes, Musical Quart, 66; The use of Barogue Treatises on musical performance, Music & Lett, 1067; Couperin and the Downbeat Doctrine for appoggiatures, Acta Musicol, 71; The question of rhythm in Bach's French Overture, BWV 831, In: Studies in Renaissance and Barogue Music in Honor of Arthur Mendel, Barenreiter, 74; Facts and fiction about overdotting, Musical Quart, 77; Ornamentation in Barague and Post Barogue Music, Princeton Univ, 78; Improper Appoggiaturas in The 'Neue Mozart Ausgabe' + The Cataloging And Presentation of Musical Texts, J of Musicology, Vol 0010, 1992; Performance-practice in Mozart, Music & Letters, Vol 0074, 1993; Performance-practice in Mozart + Response to Maunder,richard on The Unwritten Appoggiaturas, Music & Letters, Vol 0075, 1994. **CONTACT ADDRESS** 4102 W Franklin St, Richmond, VA 23221.

NEUMEYER, PETER F.
PERSONAL Born 08/04/1929, Munich, Germany, m, 1952, 3 children **DISCIPLINE** ENGLISH **EDUCATION** Univ Calif, Berkeley, BA, 51, MA, 54, PhD, 63. **CAREER** Teacher pub schs, Calif, 57-58, 60-61; assoc supvr dept educ, Univ Calif, Berkeley, 61-62, actg instr English, 62-63; asst prof educ & tutor English, Grad Sch, Harvard Univ, 63-69; assoc prof English, State Univ NY Stony Brook, 69-75, dir freshman English, 73-75; chmn dept & prof English, W VA Univ, 75-78; prof English & Comp Lit & dir Freshman English, San Diego State Univ, 78-95; prof emeritus, San Diego State Univ, 95-. **HONORS AND AWARDS** NEH; Int Youth Libr, Munich; Dorothy C. McKenzie Awd for distinguished contributions to chidlren's lit. **RESEARCH** German-English literary relations; freshman English; children's literature. **SELECTED PUBLICATIONS** Auth, Franz Kafka and England, Ger Quart, 67; A structural approach to the teaching of literature to children, Elem English, 67; Donald and the .., Addison-Wesley, 69; The Faithful Fish, Young-Scott, 71; co-ed, Elements of Fiction, Wm C Brown, 74; auth, Thomas Mann, Max Brod and New York Pubic Library, Mod Lang Notes, 75; The art of the world, English J, 577; What makes a good children's book? The structure of Charlotte's Web, S Atlantic Bull, 79; Charlotte, Arachnida + 'Annotated Charlottes Web' - The Scientific Sources, Lion And The Unicorn, Vol 0019, 1995; 'We Are All in The Dumps With Jack And Guy' - 2 Nursery Rhymes With Pictures by Sendak,maurice, Childrens Literature in Education, Vol 0025, 1994. **CONTACT ADDRESS** Dept of English & Comp Lit, San Diego State Univ, San Diego, CA 92182.

NEUSSENDORFER, MARGARET R.
DISCIPLINE LITERATURE & AMERICAN STUDIES **EDUCATION** Coll St Scholastica, BA, 55; St. Louis, MA, 63; Yale Univ, MPhil, 71, PhD, 75. **CAREER** Assoc prof, lit & Am stud, Texas Permian Basin; IND SCHOLAR. **MEMBERSHIPS** Am Antiquarian Soc **RESEARCH** Elizabeth Palmer Peabody **SELECTED PUBLICATIONS** Auth, Elizabeth Peabody Writes to Wordswoth, Stud in Am Renaissance, 84. **CONTACT ADDRESS** 23 Minthorne St, Worcester, MA 01603.

NEVILLE, DON
DISCIPLINE MUSIC **EDUCATION** Cambridge Univ, PhD, 86. **CAREER** Assoc prof, Univ of Western Ontario. **HONORS AND AWARDS** Vis fel, Oxford, 96; dir, Metastasio. **RESEARCH** History of opera; history of the American musical theatre; 18th century opera. **SELECTED PUBLICATIONS** Auth, "Cartesian Principles in Mozart's La clemenza di Tito," in Music and Drama, vol. 2 of Studies in the History of Music, (New York: Bruode Bros., 88): 97-123; auth, "Metastasio's Reinterpretation of Aristotle," Musica antiqua 9/1: Acta Musicologica Bydgoszcz, (91): 21-23; auth, "Mazzola, Caterina," "Metastasio," "Rondo," in The New Grove Dictionary of Opera, ((London: Macmillan, 92); auth, "From Myth to Libretto," in W.A. Mozart: Idomeneo, ed. Julian Rushton, (Cambridge: Cambridge Univ Press, 93): 72-82; auth, "Semiramide in Vienna: beyond Metastasian Metastasis," Studien zur Musikwissenschaft 44, (95): 113-29; auth, "The rondo in Mozart's Late Operas," Mozart Jahbuch 1994, Salzburg: Internationale StiftungMozarteum, (95): 141-55; auth, "From Simplicity to Complexity in La clemenza di Tito," in Wolfgang Amade Mozart: Essays on his Life and Music, ed. Stanley Sadie, (Oxford: Oxford Univ Press, 95): 483-96; auth, "Metastasio: Beyond the Stage in Vienna," Studies in Music from the Univ of Western Ontario 16, (97): 87-109. **CONTACT ADDRESS** Dept of Music, Univ of Western Ontario, London, ON, Canada N6A 5B8. **EMAIL** dneville@julian.uwo.ca

NEVILLE, MARY EILEEN
PERSONAL Born 07/11/1930, York, NE **DISCIPLINE** ENGLISH **EDUCATION** Mt Marty Col, SDak, AB, 53; St Louis Univ, MA, 56, PhD, 58. **CAREER** Instr English, 57-68, chmn dept, 65-69, Prof English, Mt Marty Col, SDak, 68-, Dir Intercult Educ, 73-80; Vis prof English & educ, Univ Nebr, 69-70, fel, 69-70. **MEMBERSHIPS** NCTE; Conf Col Compos & Commun; Conf English Educ. **RESEARCH** Native American literature and culture; Afro-American literature; priorities in American values. **CONTACT ADDRESS** Mount Marty Col, Yankton, 1100 W Eighth St, Yankton, SD 57078. **EMAIL** eneville@rs6.mtmc.edu

NEVIN, THOMAS R.
PERSONAL Born 10/27/1944, m, 1977, 4 children **DISCIPLINE** CLASSICAL STUDIES **EDUCATION** Univ of Colo, BA, 66; Univ of Wisc, MA, 68; PhD, 73 **CAREER** Asst Prof, 80-88, Assoc Prof, 88-95, Prof, 95-, John Carroll Univ **HONORS AND AWARDS** Phi Beta Kappa; Woodrow Wilson Fel **MEMBERSHIPS** Am Philol Asn; Dante Soc of Am **RESEARCH** Dante; Catholicism. **SELECTED PUBLICATIONS** Auth, Ernst Junger and Germany: Into the Abyss, 1914-1945, Duke Univ Press, 96, London: Constable, 97; Simone Weil: Portrait of a Self-Exiled Jew, Chapel Hill, Univ of NC Press, 91 **CONTACT ADDRESS** Class & Mod Langs & Cultures Dept, John Carroll Univ, 20700 N Park Blvd, University Heights, OH 44118. **EMAIL** tnevin@jcu.edu

NEW, MELVYN
PERSONAL Born 10/08/1938, New York, NY, m, 1959, 2 children **DISCIPLINE** ENGLISH **EDUCATION** Columbia Univ, BA, 59; Vanderbilt Univ, MA, 62, PhD, 66. **CAREER** Instr English, Univ Tenn, Martin, 62-63 & Vanderbilt Univ, 65-66; from asst prof to assoc prof, 66-76, prof English, Univ Fla, 76-, chmn, 79-88, Nat Endowment Humanities younger scholar fel, 73-74; Am Philos Soc grants, 68, 71 & 76; Nat Endowment for Humanities fel, 80-81, 94-95. **MEMBERSHIPS** Am Soc 18th Century Studies. **RESEARCH** Restoration and 18th century English literature; satire. **SELECTED PUBLICATIONS** Auth, Laurence Sterne as Satirist: A Reading of Tristram Shan-

dy, Univ Fla, 69; co-ed, The Works of Laurence Sterne: Tristram Shandy: The Text (2 vols), Univ Fla, 78; The Commentary, 1 Vol, Univ Fla, 84; ed, ed, Sterne-Smollett, The Scriblerian, 86; advisory ed, The Shandeam, 89-; ed, Approaches to Teaching Sterne's Tristram Shandy, MLA, 89; ed, New Casebook on Tristram Shandy, Macmillan and St. Martin's, 92; Telling New Lies: Essays in Fiction, Past and Present, Univ Fl, 92; The Complete Novels and Selected Writings of Amy Levy, Univ Fl, 93; Tristram Shandy: A Book for Free Spirits, Twayne-Macmillan, 94; The Sermons: The Text (1 vol.), Univ Fl, 96; The Commentary (1 vol.), Univ Fl, 96; ed, Life and Opinions of Tristram Shandy, Penguin, 97; Critical Essays on Lawrence Sterne, G.K. Hall, 98. **CONTACT ADDRESS** Dept of English, Univ of Florida, P O Box 117310, Gainesville, FL 32611-7310. **EMAIL** melnew@nervm.nerdc.ufl.edu

NEW, WILLIAM H.
PERSONAL Born 03/28/1938, Vancouver, BC, Canada **DISCIPLINE** CANADIAN LITERATURE **EDUCATION** Univ BC, BEd, 61, MA, 63; Univ Leeds, PhD, 66. **CAREER** Prof English, Univ British Columbia, 65-, asst dean, grad stud, 75-77, Brenda & David McLean Chair Can Stud, 95-97. **HONORS AND AWARDS** Killam Res Prize, 88; Gabrielle Roy Awd, 88; Jacob Biely Prize, 95; Killam Tchg Prize, 96. **MEMBERSHIPS** Royal Soc Can **SELECTED PUBLICATIONS** Auth, Malcolm Lowry, 71; auth, Articulating West, 72; auth, Among Worlds, 75; auth, Critical Writings on Commonwealth Literature, 75; auth, Malcolm Lowry: A Reference Guide, 78; auth, Dreams of Speech and Violence, 87; auth, A History of Canadian Literature, 89; auth, Science Lessons, 96; auth, Land Sliding, 97; ed, Four Hemispheres, 71; ed, Dramatists in Canada, 72; ed, Modern Canadian Essays, 76; ed, Margaret Laurence, 77; ed, A Political Art, 78; ed, Canadian Writers in 1984, 84; ed, Canadian Short Fiction, 86, 2nd ed, 97; ed, Canadian Writers since 1960, 2 vols, 86, 87; ed, Canadian Writers, 1920-1959, 1st series 88, 2nd series 89; ed, Canadian Writers, 1890-1920, 90; ed, Canadian Writers Before 1890, 90; ed, Literary History of Canada, vol IV, 90; ed, Native Writers and Canadian Writing, 90; ed, Inside the Poem, 92; co-ed, Voice and Vision, 72; co-ed, Modern Stories in English, 75, 2nd ed, 86, 3rd ed, 91; co-ed, Active Voice, 80, 2nd ed 86, 3rd ed 91; co-ed, A 20th Century Anthology, 84; co-ed, Literature in English, 93. **CONTACT ADDRESS** Dept of English, Univ of British Columbia, 397-1873 E Mall, BuTo, Vancouver, BC, Canada V6T1Z1. **EMAIL** wnew@interchange.ubc.ca

NEWBERRY, FREDERICK
PERSONAL Born 10/15/1941, Detroit, MI, m, 1982, 2 children **DISCIPLINE** ENGLISH **EDUCATION** Univ Redlands, AB, 69; Wash State Univ, PhD, 76. **CAREER** Lect, Univ Calif, Los Angeles, 76-77; Asst Prof, Univ Ore, 77-85; Asst Prof, Duquesne Univ, 87-89; Assoc Prof, Duquesne Univ, 89-94; Prof, Duquesne Univ, 94-. **HONORS AND AWARDS** Fulbright Scholar, 83. **MEMBERSHIPS** Mod Lang Assoc, Western Lit Assoc, Nathaniel Hawthorne Soc. **RESEARCH** Colonial and 19th-Century American literature, western American literature. **SELECTED PUBLICATIONS** Auth, "Tradition and Disinheritance in 'The Scarlet Letter'," ESQ: J of the Am Renaissance 23 (77): 1-26; Auth, "Tradition and Disinheritance in 'The Scarlet Letter'," in Norton Critical Ed of The Scarlet Lett, 3rd ed (NY: Norton, 87), 231-248; auth, "A Red-Hot A and a Lusting Divine: Sources for 'The Scarlet Letter'," New Eng Quart 60 (87): 256-264; auth, Hawthorne's Divided Loyalties: England and America in His Works, Dickinson Univ Pr (Rutherford, NJ), 87; auth, "The Biblical Veil: Sources and Typology in Hawthorne's 'The Minister's Black Veil'," Tex Studies in Lit and Lang 31 (89): 169-195; auth, "Hawthorne," in Am Lit Scholar 1988-1991 (Durham, NC: Duke Univ Pr, 90-93); auth, "Fantasy, Reality and Audience in Hawthorne's 'Drowne's Wooden Image'," Studies in the Novel 23 (91): 28-45; auth, "'The Artist of the Beautiful': Crossing the Transcendent Divide in Hawthorne's Fiction," Nineteenth-Century Lit 50 (95): 78-96; auth, "Male Doctors and Female Invalidism in American Women's Fiction, 1850-1900: Valid or Invalid?" in Separate Spheres No More (Univ Ala Pr, 00). **CONTACT ADDRESS** Dept English, Duquesne Univ, 600 Forbes Ave, Pittsburgh, PA 15282-0001. **EMAIL** newberryf@duq.edu

NEWBERRY, RUTH E.
PERSONAL Born 01/30/1958, Elko, NV, m, 1982, 2 children **DISCIPLINE** ENGLISH **EDUCATION** Univ Oreg, BA, 81; MA, 87. **CAREER** Teacher, Springfield High Sch, 84-87; instr, La Roche Col, 90-91; instr, Robert Morris Col, 91-95; lectr, Duquesne Univ, 92-. **HONORS AND AWARDS** Duquesne Univ Award, 97, 97-98; Hunkele Grant, 97-98; Patron Saint Teaching Award, 98, 99. **MEMBERSHIPS** MLA, NCTE, Col Comp and Commun, Asn for Study of Lit and Environ, W Am Lit Asn, Soc for the Study of Am Women Writers, Am Lit Asn, Nat Writing Centers Asn, Sierra Club. **RESEARCH** Western American Literature and History, Environmental History, 20th Century American Writers of the West, Adult Education, Educational Technologies. **CONTACT ADDRESS** Duquesne Univ, 600 Forbes Ave, Pittsburgh, PA 15282. **EMAIL** newberryr@duq.edu

NEWFIELD, CRISTOPHER
DISCIPLINE NINETEENTH- AND TWENTIETH-CENTURY AMERICAN LITERATURE **EDUCATION** Cornell Univ, PhD, 88. **CAREER** Assoc Prof, Eng, Univ Calif, Santa Barbara. **RESEARCH** Lit and soc theory; Gender, sexuality, and race. **SELECTED PUBLICATIONS** Auth, "Corporate Pleasures for a Corporate Planet," Social Text, 95; "White Philosophy," Critical Inquiry, 94; Te Emerson Effect: Individualism and Submission in America, Univ Chicago Press, 95; co-ed, After Political Correctness: The Humanities and Society in the 1990s, Westview, 95; Mapping Multiculturalism, Univ Minn Press, 95. **CONTACT ADDRESS** Dept of Eng, Univ of California, Santa Barbara, Santa Barbara, CA 93106-7150. **EMAIL** cnewf@humanitas.ucsb.edu

NEWKIRK, GLEN A.
PERSONAL Born 08/23/1931, Strawn, KS, m, 1957, 3 children **DISCIPLINE** ENGLISH LITERATURE **EDUCATION** Kans State Col, AB, 53, MA, 56; Univ Denver, PhD(English), 66. **CAREER** Asst ed, Emporia Times, Kans, 53-54; instr English, Kans State Col, 55-57, Colo State Univ, 57-58 & Southwest Mo State Col, 58-60; dir Pubicity, Southwestern Col, Kans, 60-61; instr commun, Univ Denver, 61-63; from asst prof to assoc prof, 63-67, acting chmn dept, 68, grad coordr, 69-72, Prof English, Univ Nebr, Omha, 67- **MEMBERSHIPS** Renaissance Soc Am; MLA. **RESEARCH** Renaissance courtesy books, Shakespeare; Elizabethan drama. **SELECTED PUBLICATIONS** Ed, Contemporary Issues & auth, Instructors Manual, Scott, 71; Anaya Archetypal Women in 'Bless Me, Ultima', South Dakota Review, Vol 0031, 1993. **CONTACT ADDRESS** Dept of English, Univ of Nebraska, Omaha, Omaha, NE 68101.

NEWMAN, ARNOLD E.
PERSONAL Born 06/20/1934, New York, NY, m, 1959, 5 children **DISCIPLINE** ENGLISH **EDUCATION** State Univ NY at Albany, BA, 56; MA, 57; Univ Wis, PhD, 65. **CAREER** Teacher, Whitney Point Central School, 59-60; TA, Univ of Wis, 60-64; asst prof, Calif State Univ Col, 64-67; prof, Kutztown Univ, 67-. **HONORS AND AWARDS** Distinguished Service Awd, PA State System Universities, 97; First Annual Friend of the Keystone Newspaper Awd, 98. **MEMBERSHIPS** Nat Council of Teachers of English; English Assoc of the PA State System Univ. **RESEARCH** American realism and naturalism, Jewish-American immigrant literature. **SELECTED PUBLICATIONS** Auth, The Rise of David Levinsky and the Rise of David Schearl: Literary Artistry in the American-Jewish Immigrant Novel, 93; auth, Mary Antin and Anzia Yezierska: Immigrant Chronicler Versus Literary Artist, 96; auth, Urban Nightmare in the Novels of Samuel Ornitz: Confession and Revelation, 97. **CONTACT ADDRESS** Dept English, Kutztown Univ of Pennsylvania, PO Box 730, Kutztown, PA 19530-0730. **EMAIL** newman@kutztown.edu

NEWMAN, BARBARA J.
PERSONAL Born 08/14/1953, Chicago, IL, m, 1986 **DISCIPLINE** ENGLISH, LITERATURE, RELIGION **EDUCATION** Oberlin Col, BA, 75; Univ of Chicago Divinity School, MA, 76; Yale Univ, Phd, 81. **CAREER** Prof of English & Religion, Northwestern Univ, 92-; Asst Prof, 81-87; Assoc Prof, 87-92; Prof, 92-. **HONORS AND AWARDS** Guggenheim Fellow, 00-01; ACLS Fellow, 87-88; Fellow of the Medieval Academy, elected 99; Distinguished Teaching Awd, 91; Outstanding Academic Book Awd, 87. **MEMBERSHIPS** Medieval Academy of America; Modern Lang Assn; Amer Society of Church History; AAVP **RESEARCH** Medieval Religion and literature; History of Spirituality; Women Mystics. **SELECTED PUBLICATIONS** Auth, Sister of Wisdom: St. Hildegard's Theology of the Feminine, Berkeley: Univ of Calif Press, 87; auth, Symphonia Armoni Celestium Revelationum, Ithaca; Cornell Univ Presss, 88; auth, From Virile Woman to Woman Christ: Studies in Medieval Religion and Literature, Philadelphia: Univ of Pennsylvania Press, 95; auth, Voice of the Living Light: Hildegard of Bingen and Her World, Berkeley: U of California Press, 98. **CONTACT ADDRESS** Dept English, Northwestern Univ, University Hall 215, 1897 Sheridan Rd, Evanston, IL 60208-2240. **EMAIL** bjnewman@northwestern.edu

NEWMAN, GEOFFREY W.
PERSONAL Born 08/29/1946, Oberlin, OH, s **DISCIPLINE** DRAMA **EDUCATION** Howard Univ, Washington DC, BFA, 1968; Wayne State Univ, Detroit MI, MA, 1970; Howard Univ, Washington DC, PhD, 1978. **CAREER** Actor, educator, consultant, theorist and director in theatre; Howard Univ, Wabash College, Drama Dept, chmn; Montclair State Coll, dean of School of the Arts, 88-. **HONORS AND AWARDS** Directed world premiere of Owen Dodson's Sound of Soul and European premiere of Robert Nemiroff's Raisin; received Amoco Awd for Theatrical Excellence, by John F Kennedy Center for the Permorming Arts in conjunction with Amer Theatre Assn; received special commendations from Mayor Marion Barry Jr, Washington DC, Mayor Pat Screen, Baton Rouge LA, and Gov Harry Hughes, State of Maryland; published articles in professional journals; served as nominator for Washington DC Awds Society's Helen Hayes Awds. **MEMBERSHIPS** Mem, grant screening panels, District of Columbia Commn on the Arts and Humanities, Pennsylvania State Council for the Arts, and Illinois State Arts Council; artistic dir and cofounder, Takoma Players, Takoma Theatre, Washington DC; artistic dir, Ira Aldridge Theatre, Howard Univ, Washington DC; artistic dir, Park Place Productions, Washington DC; artistic dir, Young Audiences of District of Columbia. **CONTACT ADDRESS** Dean, School of the Arts, Montclair State Univ, 1 Normal Ave, Montclair, NJ 07043-1624. **EMAIL** newmang@mail.montclair.edu

NEWMAN, LEA BERTANI VOZAR
PERSONAL Born 08/03/1926, Chicago, IL, m, 1976, 5 children **DISCIPLINE** AMERICAN LITERATURE **EDUCATION** Chicago Teachers Col, BA, 47; Wayne State Univ, Detroit, MA, 66; Univ Mass, Amherst, PhD(English), 79. **CAREER** Instr compos, Macomb Community Col, 65-66; instr compos & lit, Pa State Univ, Schuylkill, 66-68; instr, 68-73, asst prof, 73-79, assoc prof, 79-81, Prof Compos & Lit, 81-92, Prof Emer, 92- , Mass Col Lib Arts (N Adams State Col). **HONORS AND AWARDS** Fulbright Univ Bologna, 73-74; Dir NEH pilot grant, 81-82; pres, Hawthorne Soc, 89-90; Mass State Col Asn Sen Fac award, 93; pres, Melville Soc 96. **MEMBERSHIPS** Nathaniel Hawthorne Soc; MLA; Melville Soc. **RESEARCH** Nathaniel Hawthorne's fiction; Herman Melville's life and works; interdisciplinary approaches to teaching literature; Dante's influence on Hawthorne and Melville; Robert Frost's poetry of New England. **SELECTED PUBLICATIONS** Auth, Yeats, Swift, Irish Patriotism and rationalistic anti-intellectualism, Mass Studies English, III: 108-16; A Reader's Guide to the Short Stories of Nathaniel Hawthorne, G K Hall, 79; auth, A Readers Guide to the Short Stories of Herman Melville, G K Hall, 86; auth, Melville's Copy of Dante, Studies in the American Renaissance, Va Univ Press, 93; auth, Hawthorne's Summer in Florence, Poetics of Place: Florence Imagined, Olschki, 00; auth, Robert Frost: The Places, People and Stories Behind His New England Poetry, New England Press, 00. **CONTACT ADDRESS** 120 Imperial Ave, Bennington, VT 05201. **EMAIL** chick@sover.net

NEWMAN, MARCY J. KNOPF
PERSONAL Born 03/21/1969, Los Angeles, CA **DISCIPLINE** ENGLISH **EDUCATION** Univ Cincinnati, BA, 92; Miami Univ, PhD, 01. **CAREER** Asst prof, Boise State Univ, 01-. **HONORS AND AWARDS** Outstanding Grad Student Teacher Awd, 98; Sinclair Diss Awd, 00-01. **MEMBERSHIPS** MLA, Am Studies Assoc. **RESEARCH** Queer Studies, American Studies, Public Sphere Theory, Politics and Literature. **SELECTED PUBLICATIONS** Ed, The Sleeper Wakes: Harlem Renaissance Stories by Women, Rutgers Univ Pr, (New Brunswick), 93; ed, Jessie Fauset, The Chinaberry Tree and Selected Writings, Northeastern Univ Pr, (Boston), 95; auth, "Bi-nary Bi-sexuality: Third Spaces, Queer Places in Jane Bowles Two Serious Ladies," Representing Bisexual Subjects: Cultures of Fluid Desire, ed Donald E. Hall and Maria Pramaggione, NY Univ Pr, (NY, 96). **CONTACT ADDRESS** Dept English, Boise State Univ, 1910 University Dr, Boise, ID 83725-1525. **EMAIL** mjk_newman@yahoo.com

NEWMAN, ROBERT P.
PERSONAL Born 01/26/1922, Hannibal, MO, d, 3 children **DISCIPLINE** COMMUNICATION STUDIES **EDUCATION** Univ Redlands, BA 43; Oxford Univ BA 49; Univ Conn, PhD 56. **CAREER** Smith Col, inst 49-50; Univ Conn, inst 50-52; Univ Pitts, asst, assoc, prof, 52-95; Univ Iowa, Adj prof, 95-. **HONORS AND AWARDS** Pulitzer Nomination; Nat Book Awd nom; LA Times Bk Prize runner up; Import Bk on Civil Liberties; Diamond Ann Bk Awd; Dist Res Awd. **MEMBERSHIPS** AHA; SHAR; SMH; NCA; HESS; OAH **RESEARCH** US China Policy; Cold War; Amer Inquisition; Holocaust; Japanese Surrender **SELECTED PUBLICATIONS** Auth, Framing the Enola Gay Debate: Identity Ethnicity Obscurantism, in: Rhetoric and Public Memory, eds, Stephen Browne David Henry, Sage, in press; NSC National Insecurity 68: Nitze's Second Hallucination, in: Public Disclosure in Cold War America, eds, H. W. Brands Martin Medhurst, TX A&M, in press; Sinners in the Hands of an Angry Goldhagen: A Narrative of Guilt and Redemption, Rhetoric and Pub Affs, 98; Hiroshima and the Trashing of Henry Stimson, NEQ, 98; On the Enola Gay Symposium, letter to the editor, Jour of Amer Hist, 96; Roosevelt and Unconditional Surrender: An Analogy That Held, in: Argumentation and Values, ed Sally Jackson, SCA, 95; Truman and the Hiroshima Cult, MSUP, 95, ten known revs, Diamond Jub Book Awd, NCA 97; Ending the War with Japan: Paul Nitze's , Early Surrender Counterfactual, PHR, 95. **CONTACT ADDRESS** Dept of Communications, The Univ of Iowa, 105 Becker Communication Bldg, Iowa City, IA 52242. **EMAIL** robert-newman@uiowa.edu

NEWMYER, STEPHEN THOMAS
PERSONAL Born 07/10/1948, Pittsburgh, PA, w, 1978 **DISCIPLINE** CLASSICS **EDUCATION** Duquesne Univ, BA, 70; Univ NC, Chapel Hill, PhD(classics), 76. **CAREER** Asst prof, 76-80, Assoc Prof Classics, 80-84, Prof Classics, 84-, Duquesne Univ, Fel, Inst Teaching Post-Bibl Found Western Civilization, Jewish Theol Sem Am, 78. **MEMBERSHIPS** Am Philol Asn; Vergilian Soc; Class Asn Middle West & South; Class Asn Atlantic States. **RESEARCH** Roman epic poetry; classical influence on later literature; medicine. **SELECTED PUBLICA-**

TIONS Auth, Pessimistic Prometheus: A Comparison of Aeschylus and Robert Lowell, Helios, fall-winter 78-79, The Silvae of Statius: Structure and Theme, Brill, Leiden, 79; Ancient and Talmudic Medicine: A Course Description, Helios, winter-spring 79-80; Talmudic medicine: A Classicist's perspective, Judaism, 29: 360- 367; Robert Lowell and the weeping philosopher, Class and Mod Lit, winter 80; Talmudic medicine, Jewish Digest, 81; Charles Anthon: Knickerbocker scholar, Class Outlook, 12-181-82; Statius, 'Thebaid Ix' - English And Latin - Dewar,m, Editor- translator, American J of Philology, Vol 0113, 1992. **CONTACT ADDRESS** 119 S 21st St, Pittsburgh, PA 15203. **EMAIL** newmyer@duq.edu

NEWSOM, DOUGLAS ANN
PERSONAL Born 01/16/1934, Dallas, TX, w, 1993, 4 children **DISCIPLINE** PUBLIC RELATIONS **EDUCATION** Univ Texas, BJ, 54; Univ Texas, BFA, 55; Univ Texas, MJ, 56; Univ Texas, PhD, 78. **CAREER** Instr, Univ Texas, 61-62; visiting prof, Univ Okla, 79; Fulbright lectr, Osmania Univ, 88. **HONORS AND AWARDS** Kappa Tau Alpha; Phi Kappa Phi; Phi Beta Delta; Fine Arts Commun nominee for Chancellor's Award for Res & Creativity, 95; Named Scholarship, Public Relations Students, created by TCU PRSSA chapt, 93; First 25 Named to Public Relations Women Pioneers, 93; Public Relations Soc Amer Col of Fellows, 90; Fulbright Scholar to India, 88; Fulbright Scholar to Singapore, 98; **MEMBERSHIPS** Pub Rel Soc Amer; Comn Pub Rel Educ; Col of Fel; Center Pub Rel Task Force, 91-91; Friends of PRSSA; Assoc for Educ Jour and Mass Commun; Vanguard Found Board; Intl Commun Assoc; Intl Pub Rel Assoc; Fulbright Assoc; Amer Assoc Univ Women; Soc Prof Journalist; World Commun Assoc **RESEARCH** Public Relations; Women's Studies; Consumerism. **SELECTED PUBLICATIONS** Co-ed, Silent Voices, Univ Press Amer, 95; coauth, This is PR: The Realities of Public Relations, Wadsworth, 96; coauth, Public Relations Writing: Form & Style, Wadsworth, 98. **CONTACT ADDRESS** Texas Christian Univ, TCU 298060, Fort Worth, TX 76129. **EMAIL** d.newsom@TCU.edu

NEWSOM, ROBERT
PERSONAL Born 10/18/1944, New York, NY, m, 1973, 2 children **DISCIPLINE** LITERATURE **EDUCATION** Columbia Col, BA, 66; Cambridge Univ, BA, 68; MA, 72; Columbia Univ, PhD, 72. **CAREER** Asst prof, Columbia Univ, 72-75; lectr, Univ of Calif at Irvine, 77-78; lectr, Univ of Calif at Riverside, 78-79; from asst prof to prof, Univ of Calif at Irvine, 79-. **HONORS AND AWARDS** Magna Cum Laude; Phi Beta Kappa; Euretta J. Kellett Fel, Cambridge Univ; Columbia Council for Res in the Humanities Fel, 73; Irvine Fac Res Grant, 90; Resident Fel, Rockefeller Study Ctr, 96. **MEMBERSHIPS** MLA, Dickens Soc, The Dickens Project. **RESEARCH** Victorian Literature, British Novel, Theory of Fiction. **SELECTED PUBLICATIONS** Auth, A Likely Story: Probability and Play in Fiction, Rutgers Univ Press, 88; auth, "Pickwick in the Utilitarian Sense," Dickens Studies Annual 23 (94): 49-72; auth, "Walks of Life: Administrative," A Companion to Victorian Literature, Blackwell, 99; auth, Charles Dickens Revisited, Twayne Pub, 00; auth, "Fictions of Childhood," The Cambridge Companion to Kickens, Cambridge Univ Press, forthcoming. **CONTACT ADDRESS** Dept English, Univ of California, Irvine, Irvine, CA 92697. **EMAIL** rnewsom@uci.edu

NEWTON, ADAM ZACHARY
PERSONAL Born 03/23/1957, New York, NY, s **DISCIPLINE** ENGLISH **EDUCATION** Harvard Univ, 92; San Francisco State Univ, 89; Hartford Col, 80. **CAREER** Univ Texas, prof. **HONORS AND AWARDS** Thomas Wilson Prize; NS Perkins Prize. **MEMBERSHIPS** MLA; AJS; SSNL. **RESEARCH** Narrative Theory, Diaspore Studies, 19th Century British Lit; 20th Century Amer lit; Modern Jewish Thought, lit, ethnicity; Eastern and Central European lit. **SELECTED PUBLICATIONS** Auth, The Fence and A Neighbor: Levinas Leibowitz and Israel Among the Nations, forthcoming; Facing Black and Jew: Literature as Public Space, 20th C Amer, Cambridge U Press, 99; auth, Narrative Ethics, Harvard U Press, 95. **CONTACT ADDRESS** Dept of English, Univ of Texas, Austin, Austin, TX 78712. **EMAIL** adam.zach@mail.utexas.edu

NEY, JAMES WALTER
PERSONAL Born 07/28/1932, Nakuru, Kenya, m, 1954, 3 children **DISCIPLINE** ENGLISH, LINGUISTICS **EDUCATION** Wheaton Col, Ill, AB, 55, AM, 58; Univ Mich, EdD(English), 63. **CAREER** English specialist, Dade County Pub Schs, Fla, 61-62 & Univ Ryukyus, 62-64; asst prof, Mich State Univ, 65-69; assoc prof, 69-75, Prof English, Ariz State Univ, 75-98, Res grant, NCTE, 76, chmn comt to evaluate ling, 77-80; Prof Emer, 98. **MEMBERSHIPS** Can Ling Soc; Nat Asn Foreign Student Affairs; Teaching English to Speakers Other Lang; Ling Soc Am; MLA. **RESEARCH** Teaching English as a second language; teaching of written composition to native speakers of English. Coauth, Readings on American Society, 69, Readings from Samuel Clemens, 69, Blaisdell; Adventures in English, Laidlaw Bros, 72; Marckwardt, 72; Two apparent fallacies in current grammatical thought, Gen Ling, 74; Linguistics, Language Teaching and Composition in the Grades, Mouton, The Hague, 75; The modals in English: A floating Semantic feature analysis, JEnglish Ling, 76; Sexism in the English language: A biased view in a biased society, ETC, 76; Semantic Structures, Mouton, The Hague, 81; Generativity, The History of a Notion That Never Was, Historiographia Linguistica, Vol 0020, 1993; Letters - Resource Books For Teachers - Burbidge,n, Gray,p, Levy,s, Rinvolucri,m, Modern Language J, Vol 0081, 1997. **CONTACT ADDRESS** Dept of English, Arizona State Univ, Tempe, AZ 85281. **EMAIL** james.ney@asu.edu

NGUYEN, DINH-HOA
PERSONAL Born 01/17/1924, Hanoi, Vietnam, m, 1952, 4 children **DISCIPLINE** LINGUISTICS, LITERATURE **EDUCATION** Union Col, BA, 50; NYork Univ, MA, 52, PhD(English educ), 56. **CAREER** Lectr Vietnamese, Columbia Univ, 53-57; from asst prof to prof English & ling, Univ Saigon, 57-65, dean fac lett, 57-58, chmn dept, 57-65; Prof Ling & Foreign Lang to Prof emer, Southern Ill Univ, Carbondale & Dir Ctr Vietnamese Studies, 69-, Dir cult affairs, Ministry of Educ, Saigon, Vietnam, 62-65; secy-gen, Vietnam Nat Comm, Unesco, 62-65; vis prof, Univ Wash, 65-66; cult counr, Embassy of Vietnam, Washington, DC, 66-69. **HONORS AND AWARDS** Fulbright prof ling & English, Rabat, Morocco, 81-82; two res grants, Nat Endowment for Humanities, 77-82; Fulbright grant ling, Morocco, 81-82. **MEMBERSHIPS** Ling Soc Am; Am Orient Soc; Asn Asian Studies; Dict Soc NAm; Am Coun Teachers Uncommonly-Taught Asian Lang (pres, 76-77 & 77-78). **RESEARCH** Students' review grammar of Vietnamese; English-Vietnamese dictionary; outline of Vietnamese culture. **SELECTED PUBLICATIONS** Auth, Read Vietnamese, 66 & Hoa's Vietnamese-English Dictionary, 66 Tuttle; Vietnamese-English Student Dictionary, 71 & Colloquial Vietnamese, 74, Southern Ill Univ; Beginning English for Vietnamese Speakers & Intermediate English for Vietnamese Speakers, Tuttle, 76; 201 Vietnamese Verbs, Barron's 79; Language in Vietnamese Society, 80 & Essential English- Vietnamese Dictionary, 80, Asia Bks; 'Nuoc Chay Qua Cau' - Tran,tbg, World Literature Today, Vol 0067, 1993; Ca Lon' - Dao- khanh, World Literature Today, Vol 0067, 1993; 'Dam Khuya' - Hoang,tdt, World Literature Today, Vol 0067, 1993; Les 'Enfants De Thai Binh,' Vol 1, 'Nostalgies Provinciales' - Duyen-anh, World Literature Today, Vol 0068, 1994; Tuyen-tap Van-tho Van But Nam Hoa-ky' - Nguyen,vs, World Literature Today, Vol 0069, 1995; Bao-ninh The 'Sorrow of War' - a Novel of North-vietnam - Palmos,f, Hao,pt, World Literature Today, Vol 0069, 1995; 'Two Shores Deux Rives' - English, French - Vuongriddick,t, World Literature Today, Vol 0070, 1996; The 'Stone Boy' And Other Stories - Thich,nh, World Literature Today, Vol 0071, 1997; The 'Other Side of Heaven' - Postwar Fiction by Vietnamese And American Writers - Karlin,w, World Literature Today, Vol 0071, 1997; 'Hoa Dia-nguc' - The 'Flowers of Hell' - English, Vietnamese - Nguyen,ct, Nguyen,nb, World Literature Today, Vol 0071, 1997; an Anthology of Vietnamese Poems - From The 11th Through The 20th Centuries - Huynh,st, World Literature Today, Vol 0071, 1997; b Vietnam - a Travelers Literary Companion - Balaban,j, Nguyen,qd, World Literature Today, Vol 0071, 1997. **CONTACT ADDRESS** Dept of Ling, So Illinois Univ, Carbondale, Carbondale, IL 62901.

NIANG, SADA
DISCIPLINE AFRICAN; CARIBBEAN LITERATURES **EDUCATION** Univ York, PhD. **RESEARCH** African cinema. **SELECTED PUBLICATIONS** Coauth, Elsewhere in Africa, Hatier, Paris,78; African Continuities/L'heritage africain, erebi, Toronto, 89; auth, Litterature et cinema en Afrique francophone, L'Harmattan, Paris, 96. **CONTACT ADDRESS** Dept of French, Univ of Victoria, PO Box 3045 STN CSC, Victoria, BC, Canada V8W 3P4. **EMAIL** sniang@uvic.ca

NICHOLL, JAMES ROBERT
PERSONAL Born 12/11/1938, Plainview, TX, m, 1967, 2 children **DISCIPLINE** ENGLISH LITERATURE **EDUCATION** Univ Tex, Austin, BA, 61, PhD(English), 70; post-doctoral studies: Columbia Univ, 90, Univ Va, 94, 96, The Shakespeare Centre, Stratford upon Avon, 96. **CAREER** Asst prof English, 70-77, dir freshman composition, 76-80, assoc prof, 77-82, Prof English, Western Carolina Univ, 82-, Dept Head, 83-90; exec secy, NC English Teachers Asn, 81-84; co-dir, Mountain Area Writing Project, 84-90. **HONORS AND AWARDS** Nat Endowment for Humanities summer sem, Huntington Lib, 78; Col Arts and Sci Superior Teaching Awd, 94. **MEMBERSHIPS** Shakespeare Asn Am; NCTE; Conf Col Compos & Commun; Western Lit Asn; Nat Coun Teachers of English. **RESEARCH** Shakespearean drama, rhetoric and composition; history and literature of the American West. **SELECTED PUBLICATIONS** Auth, Community resources and the teaching of literature, NC English Teacher, spring 75; More Captivates America: The popular success of A Man for All Seasons, Moreana, 9/76; Shakespeare course for non-English majors, CEA Forum, 12/76; The case for local lore and literary magazines, or, Teaching without seeming to, In: Action Learning: English Language Arts, K-12, State Dept Pub Instr, 77; coauth, Rhetorical Models for Effective Writing, Winthrop, 78, 3rd ed, Little, Brown, 78, 81, & 85; auth, The in-class journal, College Composition and Communication, 10/79; Another time, another place: Imagination and Shakespearean drama, Exercise Exchange, spring 80; Walt Whitman's visit to Missouri, Kansas, and Colorado, Heritage of the Great Plains, winter 81; Computers in English Instruction: The Dream and the Reality, In: Micro to Main Frame: Computers in English Education, NCTE, 83; A Dedication to the Memory of Philip Ashton Rollins, 1869-1950, Ariz and the West, 84; The First Mexican American Fictional Hero, Res in Educ, 12/92; coauth, Effective Argument: A Writer's Guide with Readings, Allyn & Bacon, 2nd ed, 91, 98; Models for Effective Writing, Allyn & Bacon, 2nd ed, 94, 00. **CONTACT ADDRESS** Dept of English, Western Carolina Univ, Cullowhee, NC 28723. **EMAIL** jnicholl@wcu.edu

NICHOLS, ASHTON
PERSONAL Born 07/07/1953, Washington, DC, m, 1975, 4 children **DISCIPLINE** ENGLISH **EDUCATION** Univ Va, BA, 75; MA, 79; PhD, 84. **CAREER** Asst Prof, Auburn Univ, 84-88; Asst Prof, Dickinson Col, 88-92; Vis Lect, Univ of E Anglia, 94-95; Assoc Prof, Dickinson Col, 92-98; Prof, Dickinson Col, 98-. **HONORS AND AWARDS** Phi Beta Kappa, 75; Ganoe Awd for Inspirational Teaching, 94; Lindback Awd for Distinguished Teaching, 93. **MEMBERSHIPS** MLA. **RESEARCH** Romantic natural history, nineteenth-century literature, nature writing. **SELECTED PUBLICATIONS** Auth, "Browning's Modernism: The Infinite Moment as Epiphany," Browning Inst Studies, 11 (83): 81-99; auth, "'Will Sprawl' in the 'Ugly Actual': The Positive Grotesque in Browning," Victorian Poetry, 21 (83): 157-171; auth, "Towards 'Spots of Time': Visionary Dreariness in 'An Evening Walk'," The Wordsworth Circle, 14 (83): 233-237; auth, "Ecology, Gender and Revolution in 'News from Nowhere'," in William Morris: A Celebration of World Citizenship 1896-1996, Actas do Cologuio (Braga: Universidade do Minho, 96), 15-30; auth, "Mumbo Jumbo: Mungo Park and the Rhetoric of Romantic Africa," in Romanticism, Race and Imp Cult 1780-1834 (Bloomington: Ind Univ Pr, 96), 93-113; auth, "Electronic Resources for Nineteenth-Century Studies: A Provisional Appraisal," Nineteenth-Century Studies, 11 (97): 203-214; auth, "The Anxiety of Species: Toward a Romantic Natural History," The Wordsworth Circle, spec issue on Romantic Ecol, 128:3 (97): 130-136; auth, "Cognitive and Pragmatic Linguistic Moments: Literary Epiphany in Thomas Pynchon and Seamus Heaney," in Moments of Moment: Aspects of the Literary Epiphany (Amsterdam, Atlanta: Rodopi, 99), 467-481; Auth, The Poetics of Epiphany: Nineteenth-Century Origins of the Modern Literary Moment, Univ Ala Pr (Tuscaloosa, AL), 87; auth, The Revolutionary "I": Wordsworth and the Politics of Self-Presentation, Macmillan, St. Martin's (London, UK, New York, NY), 98. **CONTACT ADDRESS** Dept English, Dickinson Col, 1 Dickenson Col, Carlisle, PA 17013-2846. **EMAIL** micholsa@dickinson.edu

NICHOLS, JAMES
DISCIPLINE LITERATURE **EDUCATION** Univ Miss, BA; Univ Birmingham, MA; Univ Wash, PhD, 64. **CAREER** Prof, 68-; **HONORS AND AWARDS** Chairperson dept English, 68-93. **SELECTED PUBLICATIONS** Area: satire and a novel **CONTACT ADDRESS** Winona State Univ, PO Box 5838, Winona, MN 55987-5838.

NICHOLS, KATHLEEN L.
DISCIPLINE AMERICAN LITERATURE AND DRAMA **EDUCATION** Augustana Col, BA; Univ Nebr, MA, PhD. **CAREER** Prof. **RESEARCH** Minority women writers, women's studies. **SELECTED PUBLICATIONS** Publ, articles on Hemingway, Cather, Sexton, Susanna Rowson, Agnes Smedley, women dramatists; bk rev(s). **CONTACT ADDRESS** Dept of Eng, Pittsburg State Univ, 1701 S Broadway St, Pittsburg, KS 66762. **EMAIL** knichols@pittstate.edu

NICHOLS, MARIAM F.
PERSONAL Born Vancouver, BC, Canada, d **DISCIPLINE** ENGLISH **EDUCATION** Simon Fraser Univ, BA, 80; MA, 82; York Univ, PhD, 87. **CAREER** Instr, Medicine Hat Col, 87-88; adj prof, Simon Fraser Univ, 88-94; prof, Univ Col of the Fraser Valley, 94-. **HONORS AND AWARDS** Fel, SSHRC, 82-86. **MEMBERSHIPS** MLA, IAPL, ACCUTE. **RESEARCH** Contemporary poetics (post-1950), American and Canadian. **SELECTED PUBLICATIONS** Auth, "The Poetry of Hell: Jack Spicer, Robin, Blaser, Robert Duncan," Line 12, (99): 14-41; auth, "Robin Blaser's Poetics of Relation: Thinking Without Bannisters," Sagetrieb 9.1&2, (90): 121-145; auth, "Writing Writing in the 70s and 80s," Behind the Sign, (Vancouver: Artspeak Gallery, 93); auth, "Three for Public: Steve McCaffery, Nicole Brossard, and Robin Blasard," Public 12, (95): 98-111; auth, "Robin Blaser," Dict of Lit Biog, ed Joseph Conte, (Detroit: Gale Res/Bruccoli Clark Layman, 96): 57-68; auth, "Tensing the Difference: Daphne Marlatt, Karen MacCormack, and Susan Howe," Tessera 27, (99): 39-54; auth, "Subjects of Experience: Post-cognitive Subjectivity in the work of bpNichol and Daphne Marlatt," SCL/ELC 25.2 (00): 108-130; auth, "Radical Affections: Charles Olson's 'Maximus,'" Open Letter 11.1, (01): 72-82; auth, "A/Politics of Contemporary Anglo-Canadian Poetries: The Toronto Research Group and Kootenay School of Writing," Assembling Alternatives, ed Romana Huk, (Wesleyan UP, forthcoming); ed, Even on Sunday: Essays, Readings and Archival Materials on the Poetry and Poetics of Robin Blaser, Nat Poetry Found (Orono, ME), forthcoming. **CONTACT ADDRESS** Dept English, Univ Col of Fraser Valley, 33844 King Rd, Abbotsford, BC, Canada V2S 7M8. **EMAIL** nicholsm@ucfv.bc.ca

NICHOLS, PATRICIA CAUSEY
PERSONAL Born 12/29/1938, Conway, SC, m, 1959, 2 children **DISCIPLINE** ENGLISH, LINGUISTICS **EDUCATION** Winthrop Col, BA, 58; Univ Minn, MA, 66; San Jose State Univ, MA, 72; Stanford Univ, PhD(ling), 76. **CAREER** Teacher, Hampton Pub Schs, Va, 58-60; Lectr English, Ling & Educ, San Jose State Univ, 76-, Co-ed, Women & Lang News, 76; vis asst prof English, Univ SC, 80-81; vis instr, Univ Calif, Santa Barbara, 82. **MEMBERSHIPS** MLA; Ling Soc Am; Am Dialect Soc. **RESEARCH** Gullah; gender and sex differences in speech; American dialects. **SELECTED PUBLICATIONS** Auth, A sociolinguistic perspective on reading and black children, Lang Arts, 54: 150-157; Ethnic consciousness in the British Isles, Lang Problems & Lang Planning, 1: 10-31; Black women in the rural south: Conservative and innovative, Int J Sociol Lang, Vol 17, 78; Planning for language change, San Jose Studies, 6: 18-25; Variation among Gullah speakers in rural South Carolina, In: Language Use and the Uses of Language, Georgetown Univ Press, 80; Women in their speech communities, In: Women and Language In Literature and Society, Praeger Publ, 80; Creoles in the USA, In: Language in the USA, Cambridge Univ Press, 81; Linguistic options and choices for black women in the rural South, In: Language, Gender and Society, Newbury House Publ (in press). **CONTACT ADDRESS** 1430 Westmont Ave, Campbell, CA 95008.

NICHOLSON, JOHN H.
PERSONAL Born 01/11/1958, Atlanta, GA **DISCIPLINE** CLASSICS **EDUCATION** Univ South, BA, 80; Univ Ga, MA, 86; Univ NC, PhD, 91. **CAREER** Asst prof, Univ Del, 91-98; instr, Univ Ga, 98-. **HONORS AND AWARDS** Fourmy Classical Scholar, 86-89. **MEMBERSHIPS** Am Philol Asn **RESEARCH** Latin literature **SELECTED PUBLICATIONS** Auth, Cicero's Return from Exile, 92; auth, The Delivery and Confidentiality of Cicero's Letters, 94; auth, Goats and Gout in Catullus 71, 97; auth, The Survival of Cicero's Letters, 98; auth, Catullus 84: In vino veritas?, 99; auth, Chiasmus in Catullus 85, 00. **CONTACT ADDRESS** Dept of Classics, Univ of Georgia, Park Hall, Athens, GA 30602. **EMAIL** jhn@arches.uga.edu

NICHOLSON, NIGEL
PERSONAL Born 10/30/1968, Aldershot, United Kingdom, m, 1996, 1 child **DISCIPLINE** CLASSICS **EDUCATION** Oxford Univ, BA, 90; Univ Penn, MA, PhD, 94. **CAREER** Asst prof, Wellesley Col, 94-95; asst prof, Reed Col, 95- . **HONORS AND AWARDS** Sunderland Prize, 90; first class honors, 90; William Penn Fel, 90-93; Dean's Scholar, 91; Andrew W. Mellon Diss Fel, 93-94. **MEMBERSHIPS** Am Philol Asn; Class Asn of the Pacific Northwest. **RESEARCH** Archaic Greek lyric poetry. **SELECTED PUBLICATIONS** Auth, The Truth of Pederasty: A Supplement to Foucault's Genealogy of the Relation between Truth and Desire in Ancient Greece, Intertexts, 98; auth, Bodies Without Names, Names Without Bodies: Propertius 1.21-22, Class J, 98/99; auth, Pederastic Poets and Adult Patrons, Class W, 00; auth, Victory without Defeat? Carnival Laughter and its Appropriation in Pindar's Victory Odes, in Barta; ed, Carnivalizing Difference: Bakhtin and the Other, Harwood, forthcoming; auth, Pindar NE, 4.57-58, Arethusa, forthcoming; auth, Polysemy and Ideology in Pindar, Pythian T, Phoenix, Az, forthcoming. **CONTACT ADDRESS** Classics Dept, Reed Col, 3203 SE Woodstock Blvd, Portland, OR 97202. **EMAIL** nigel.nicholson@reed.edu

NICHOLSON, PETER C.
PERSONAL Born 06/16/1948, New York, NY **DISCIPLINE** ENGLISH **EDUCATION** Univ Conn, BA, 69; Univ Penn, MA, 70; PhD, 73. **CAREER** Asst to Full Prof, Univ Hawaii, 74-. **RESEARCH** Medieval English Literature **SELECTED PUBLICATIONS** Auth, An Annotated Index to the Commentary on Gower's Confessio Amautis, Binghamton, 89; auth, Gower's Confessio Amautis: A Critical Anthology, Cambridge, 91. **CONTACT ADDRESS** Dept English, Univ of Hawaii, Honolulu Comm Col, 1733 Donagho Rd, Honolulu, HI 96822-2315. **EMAIL** nicholso@hawaii.edu

NICKELS, CAMERON C.
PERSONAL Born 08/20/1941, Sabetha, KS, 2 children **DISCIPLINE** LITERATURE **EDUCATION** Ft Hays State Univ, BA, 62; Southern IL Univ, MA, 64; Univ MN, PhD, 71. **CAREER** Instr Eng, Cent MO State Univ, 64-67; assoc prof, 71-82; prof, James Madison Univ, 82. **HONORS AND AWARDS** Nat Endowment for Hum, summer sem, 79; Fulbright lectr, 95; pres, Am Humor Studies Asn, 96-97. **MEMBERSHIPS** MLA; Am Studies Asn; SAtlantic Mod Lang Asn; Am Humor Studies Asn. **RESEARCH** American humor; early American literature; nineteenth-century American culture. **SELECTED PUBLICATIONS** Auth, "Seba Smith embattled," Maine Hist Soc Quart, 73; contribr, The Oldest Revolutionary: Essays on Benjamin Franklin, Univ Pa, 76; ed, An Early Version of The Tar Baby Story, J Am Folklore, 81; auth, The Idology of Early New England Humor, Early Am Lit, 82; auth, New England Humor, From the Revolutionary War to the Civil War, 93; ed, To Wit, newsltr, 91. **CONTACT ADDRESS** Dept of Eng, James Madison Univ, 800 S Main St, Harrisonburg, VA 22807-0002. **EMAIL** nickelcc@jmu.edu

NICKERSON, CATHERINE ROSS
DISCIPLINE ENGLISH LANGUAGE AND LITERATURE **EDUCATION** Yale Univ, PhD, 91. **CAREER** Dir undergrad studies/assoc prof Grad Inst Lib Arts/dept Engl, Emory Univ. **RESEARCH** Detective fiction; Lizzie Borden; narrative and the representation of mystery, crime, and violence; Asian American literature. **SELECTED PUBLICATIONS** Auth, "Serial Detection and Serial Killers in Twin Peaks," Literature/Film Quarterly 21, (93): 271-76; auth, "Murder as Social Criticism, Am Literary Hist, vol. 9, no. 4, 97. **CONTACT ADDRESS** Grad Inst Lib Arts, Emory Univ, 1380 Oxford Rd NE, Atlanta, GA 30322-1950. **EMAIL** cnicker@emory.edu

NICKS, JOAN P.
PERSONAL Born Cudworth, SK, Canada **DISCIPLINE** COMMUNICATIONS **EDUCATION** Brock Univ, BA, 79; Carlton Univ, MA, 84. **CAREER** Lectr, 78-84, asst prof, fine arts, 81-84, Assoc Prof Film Studs, Dramatic & Visual Arts, Brock Univ, 93-. **HONORS AND AWARDS** Brock Univ Alumni Association's Excellence in Teaching Awd, 94; Brock Univ Student's Union Teaching Excellence Awd, 94. **MEMBERSHIPS** Film Studs Asn Can. **RESEARCH** Film history; Canadian, women's, and post-colonial cinemas; Visual and print media; structures/codes/ideologies; Performing body discourses in popular culture. **SELECTED PUBLICATIONS** Auth, Aesthetic Memory in Mourir a tue-tete: Fragments from Screens of Silence in Responses, 92; auth, Sex, Lies and Landscape: Meditations on vertical tableaux in Joyce Wieland's The Far Shore and Jean Beaudin's J. A. Martin, Photographe in Can J Film Studs 1,2-3, 93; auth, "The Documentary of Displaced Persona: Michael Rubbo's Daisy: The Story of a Facelift," in Documenting the Documentary, eds. Barry Grant, Jeannette Slonioweki, (Detroit: Wayne State Univ Press, 302-317; auth, "Fragmenting the Feminine: Aesthetic Memory in Anne Claire Poirier's Cinema," in Gendering the Nation: Canadina Women's Cinema, eds. Kass Banning, Kay Armatage, Brenda Longfellow, Janine Marchessault, (Toronto: Univ of Toronto Press, 99): 225-243. **CONTACT ADDRESS** Dept of Film Studies, Dramatic and Visual Arts, Brock Univ, 500 Glenridge Ave, Saint Catherines, ON, Canada L2S 3A1. **EMAIL** jpnicks@spartan.ac.brocku.ca

NICOL, CHARLES DAVID
PERSONAL Born 12/21/1940, St. Louis, MO, 2 children **DISCIPLINE** AMERICAN & CONTEMPORARY LITERATURE **EDUCATION** Univ KS, BA, 62, MA, 66; Bowling Green State Univ, PhD, 70. **CAREER** From instr to asst prof, 66-73, assoc prof, 73-79, Prof English & Humanities, IN State Univ, 79-; Vladimir Nabokov Soc, Pres 79-81, board 79-; Assoc ed, Sci-Fiction Studies, 74-78, board 88-; Nabokovian , Annot ed, 80-95; Para-doxa, ed board 95-. **HONORS AND AWARDS** Fulbright Sr Lecturer, Tbilisi, 84. **MEMBERSHIPS** MLA; Sci Fiction Res Asn; Melville Soc; Nabokov Soc. **RESEARCH** Vladimir Nabokov; contemporary fiction; Am Renaissance. **SELECTED PUBLICATIONS** Auth, Don Juan Out of Hell, Atlantic Monthly, 6/69; Pnin's History, Novel, summer 71; A Study in Counterfeit, NY Times Book Rev, 7/77; Poets Grilled and Served, Chronicle Higher Educ, 1/78; ed Nabokov's Fifth Arc, Univ TX, 83; reprt Critical Essays on Vladimir Nabokov, ed Roth, G K Hall, 84; One Hundred Years on a Raft, Harper's, 7/86; ed, A Small Alpine Form, Garland, 93. **CONTACT ADDRESS** Dept of English, Indiana State Univ, 210 N 7th St, Terre Haute, IN 47809-0002. **EMAIL** ejnicol@root.indstate.edu

NIEDZWIECKI, CHARISSA K.
PERSONAL Born Omaha, NE, m **DISCIPLINE** COMMUNICATION STUDIES **EDUCATION** Univ Nebr-Lincoln, PhD, 96. **CAREER** Asst prof, Univ Wis-La Crosse, 94-. **HONORS AND AWARDS** Most Accessible Instructor Awd, by Students Advocating Potential Ability, 97; recipient of numerous grants. **MEMBERSHIPS** Nat Commun Asn; Int Listening Asn; Central States Commun Asn. **RESEARCH** Family communication; gender; intercultural. **SELECTED PUBLICATIONS** Auth, Listen and You Will be Heard, Criss Cross Currents, 80; auth, Listening Comprehension Exercises, in International Listening Association's Teaching Ideas in Listening, 96, 97, 98; auth, Intercultural Interview, The Nat Commun Asn J Ideas, Res and Strategies for Learning, Summer 98; auth, A Multicultural Shakespeare, In: Culture Shock in the Classroom: Stories from America's Schools (forthcoming); auth, "Symbolic Representations of Cultural Tensions in Education: A Rhetorical Explanation of Fair Cinematic Portrayals of the Teacher," Jrnl of the WI Comm Assn, Wol XXXI, (00). **CONTACT ADDRESS** 1725 State St, La Crosse, WI 54601. **EMAIL** niedzwie.char@uulax.edu

NIELSEN, MICHAEL
DISCIPLINE COMMUNICATIONS **EDUCATION** Univ IL, BS, 72, PhD, 85. **CAREER** Tchg asst, Univ IL, 80-82, 84; asst prof, FL Atlantic Univ, 84-89; prof, dept hd, 89-. **HONORS AND AWARDS** Tenure, 95; Kappa Tau Alpha; Phi Kappa Phi. **RESEARCH** A cult studies critique of derivative copyright works. **SELECTED PUBLICATIONS** Auth, Labor's Stake in the Electronic Cinema Revolution, Jump Cut, Rev Contemp Media, 90; The struggles of progressive union members in reforming the motion picture workers' union (IATSE) in the period 1937-1950, Hollywood's Other Blacklist, Brit Film Inst, London, 96; co-auth, Bright Lights, Low Wages, S Exposure, 92. **CONTACT ADDRESS** Dept of Media Arts, Wesley Col, Delaware, 120 N State St, Dover, DE 19901-3875. **EMAIL** mike.nielsen@dol.net

NIEMI, ROBERT
PERSONAL Born 04/17/1955, Fitchburg, MA, m, 1994, 1 child **DISCIPLINE** ENGLISH **EDUCATION** Univ Massachusettes, BA, 77; MA, 88; PhD, 90; Columbia Univ, MS, 78. **CAREER** Res asst, Univ Massachusettes, 87-90; teach asst, 84-89; assoc prof, St Michaels' Col, 90-. **HONORS AND AWARDS** NEH; Univ Fel; Charles A Peters Prize. **RESEARCH** American realism, naturalism, and romanticism; Anglo-American modernism and post-modernism; literary theory and criticism; contemporary American working class fiction; film and cultural studies. **SELECTED PUBLICATIONS** Coauth, The Bibliography of Weldon Kees, Parrish House (Jackson, MS) 97; auth, Russell Banks, Simon and Schuster (NY), 97; Auth, "The Poetry of Langston Hughes," in Masterpieces of African-American Literature, ed. Salem Press (Harper Collins, 92): 340-343; auth, "JFK as Jesus: The Politics of Myth in Phil Ochs' 'Crucifixion',"' J Am Cult 16 (93): 35-40; auth, 'John, A Portrait," Ver Lit Rev 1 (94): 28-36; auth, "The Trouble With Gump," Ver Times (94): 18; auth, "Voice Recorder Blues," Strabotomy 1 (95); auth, "Rule–of the Bone," in Magill's Lit Ann (Pasadena, CA: Salem Press, 95): 668-671; auth, "Noam Chomsky: A Life of Dissent," in Magill's Lit Ann (Pasadena, CA: Salem Press, 98): 598-602; auth, "They Shoot Horses, Don 't They?," in Magill's Masterplots II: Am Fic (Pasadena, CA: Salem Press, forthcoming); auth, "Cloudsplitter," in Magill's Lit Ann (Salem Press: Pasadena, CA, forthcoming). **CONTACT ADDRESS** Dept English, Saint Michael's Col, 1 Winooski Park, Colchester, VT 05439-0002. **EMAIL** niemi@smcvt.edu

NIGG, JOSEPH EUGENE
PERSONAL Born 10/27/1938, Davenport, IA, m, 1989, 2 children **DISCIPLINE** ENGLISH, CREATIVE WRITING **EDUCATION** Kent State Univ, BA, 60; MFA Writer's Workshop, State Univ Iowa, 63; Univ Denver, PhD, 75. **CAREER** Teacher, Nunda Central Sch NY, 63-65; Instr to Asst Prof, Western State Col of Colo, 65-70; Teach Fel and Instr, Univ of Denver, 70-75; Honorarium Instr, Univ of Colo at Denver, Metropolitan State Col, Arapaho Jr Col, 75-80. **HONORS AND AWARDS** Mary Chase Author of the Year, 85; Colorado's Author's League Top Hand Awd for Non-fiction Book of the Year, 83, 85, 89; Colorado's Author's League Top Hand Awd for Short Story of the Year, 96. **MEMBERSHIPS** Colorado's Author's. **RESEARCH** Mythology, folklore and legend, specifically mythical animals. **SELECTED PUBLICATIONS** Auth, The Book of Gryphons, Apple-wood Books, 82; auth, Gryphons; The Strength of Lions and Flight of Eagles, Green Tiger Press, 82; auth, "The Moonship," Short Story Int, Seeling Ser; auth, "The Master of Mythology," and interview with Joseph Campbell, Bloomsbury Rev (Apr/May 84), and Living in Words; auth, A Guide to the Imaginary Birds of the World, Apple-Wood Books, 84; auth, Winegold, Wayland Press, 85; auth, The Great Balloon Festival, Free Flight Press, 89; auth, Wonder Beasts, Libr Unlimited, 95; auth, The Books of fabulous Beasts, Oxford Univ Press, 98. **CONTACT ADDRESS** RE/MAX Int, PO Box 3907, Englewood, CO 80155-3907. **EMAIL** jegryphon@aol.com

NIGHTINGALE, ANDREA WILSON
DISCIPLINE CLASSICS **EDUCATION** BA, 81; Oxford Univ, MA, 84; Univ CA Berkeley, MA, 85; PhD, 89. **CAREER** Assoc prof, Stanford Univ. **RESEARCH** Ancient philos, Greek and Latin lit, lit and philos of ecology. **SELECTED PUBLICATIONS** Auth, Writing/Reading a Sacred Text: A Literary Interpretation of Plato's Laws, Class Philol, 93; Towards an Ecological Eschatology: Plato and Bakhtin on Other Worlds and Times in Bakhtin and the Classics, Northwestern UP, 97; Aristotle on the 'Liberal' and 'Illiberal' Arts, Proceedings Boston Area Colloq Ancient Philos, 97; Genres in Dialogue: Plato and the Construct of Philosophy, Cambridge, 95; auth, "Plato on the Origins of Evil: The Statesman Myth Reconsidered," Ancient Philosophy 88 (96): 65-91; auth, "Historiography and Cosmology in Plato's Laws," Ancietn Philosophy 19 (99): 1-28; auth, "Sages, Sophists, and Philosophers: Greek Wisdom Literature," in Literature in the Greek and Roman Worlds: A New Perspective, ed. Oliver Taplin (Oxford Univ Press, 00), 156-191; auth, "Distant Views: Realistic and Fantastic Mimesis in Plato," in New Approaches to Plato and Socrates, ed. J. Annas and C. Rowe (Harvard Univ Press, 01). **CONTACT ADDRESS** Dept of Classics, Stanford Univ, Bldg 20, Main Quad, Stanford, CA 94305. **EMAIL** andrean@leland.stanford.edu

NIGRO, AUGUST JOHN
PERSONAL Born 12/11/1934, Jersey City, NJ, m, 1967, 3 children **DISCIPLINE** ENGLISH **EDUCATION** Fairleigh Dickinson Univ, BA, 58; Univ Miami, MA, 60; Univ Md, PhD, 63. **CAREER** Asst English, Univ Miami, 58-60 & Univ Md, 60-63; lectr, Univ Md, Europe, 63-65; asst prof, Niagara Univ, 65-67; Prof English, Kutztown Univ Pa, 67-. **HONORS AND AWARDS** NEH Summer Seminar, 74, 81; NEH Fel-in-Residence, 76-77; NEH secondary school summer seminar di-

rectorship (88-91); USIA Summer Inst For Educ Directorship, 93. **RESEARCH** Modern poetry and American fiction; myth and psychological criticism. **SELECTED PUBLICATIONS** Auth, The long march: Expansive hero in closed world, Critique, winter 67-68; coauth, William Styron: A configuration, Minard, Rev Lett Mod, Paris, 68; The Diagonal Line: Separation and Reparation in American Literaturte, Susquehanna Univ Press, 84. **CONTACT ADDRESS** Dept of English, Kutztown Univ of Pennsylvania, Kutztown, PA 19530. **EMAIL** nigro@kutztown.edu

NIKOLOVA, IRENA N.
PERSONAL Born 01/31/1962, Sofia, Bulgaria **DISCIPLINE** LITERATURE, COMPOSITION **EDUCATION** Sofia Univ, MA, 86; Eastern Ill Univ Charleston, MA, 93; Univ Western Ont, PhD, 97. **CAREER** Lectr, Univ Western Ont, 97-; lectr, Univ Ottawa, 99-00. **HONORS AND AWARDS** Univ Western Ont Fel, 96-97; Ont Grad Scholar, 96-97; Grant, Univ Ottawa, 00. **MEMBERSHIPS** MLA, NASSR. **RESEARCH** English, German and Comparative Literature of the Romantic Period, Romantic Aesthetics, Romantic Theory of Representation, Gothic Literature. **SELECTED PUBLICATIONS** Auth, "Yeat's Revision of the Quest in At the Hawk's Well," Can Jour of Irish Studies, (97); auth, "Unwritten/Written/Rewritten Histories: The Glory of the Khan and Boris I as Alternative Historical Narratives in Bulgarian Cinema," Can Slavonic Papers, (00); auth, "The European Romantic Epic and the History of a Genre," Benjamins, (forthcoming); auth, Complementary Modes of Representation in Keats, Novalis, and Shelley, Peter Lang Publ, (NY, forthcoming). **CONTACT ADDRESS** 141 Lyon Crt, Apt 104, Toronto, ON, Canada M6B 3H2. **EMAIL** lebed_2000@yahoo.com

NILES, LYNDREY ARNAUD
PERSONAL Born 05/09/1936, m **DISCIPLINE** SPEECH **EDUCATION** Columbia Union Coll, BA 1963; Univ of MD, mA 1965; Temple U, phD 1973. **CAREER** School of Communications Howard Univ, chmn Comm Arts & Sci Dept 1979-; Howard Univ, prof & asso dean 1975-79; Univ of MD, lectr 1971-75; Univ of DC, asst prof 1968-74, instr 1965-68; Columbia Union Coll, lectr 1964-65; Leadership Resources Inc, mgmt consult 1974-75; Lecturer **MEMBERSHIPS** Mem Speech Commn Assn/InternatrA Commn Assn/Am Soc for Training & Devel/NAACP; pres Met Wash Commn Assn 1974-75; . **RESEARCH** Stylistic features in African American Preaching **SELECTED PUBLICATIONS** "Listening & Note Taking Methods" 1965; "Black Rhetoric five yrs of growth, Encoder 1974; "Communication in Dental Office", article in Encoder 1979 **CONTACT ADDRESS** Dept of Communication, Univ of Maryland, Col Park, 2130 Skinner Bldg., College Park, MD 20742-7635.

NIMS, JOHN FREDERICK
PERSONAL Born 11/20/1913, Muskegon, MI, m, 1947, 3 children **DISCIPLINE** ENGLISH LITERATURE **EDUCATION** Univ Notre Dame, AB, 37, AM, 39; Univ Chicago, PhD, 45. **CAREER** Asst prof, Univ Toronto, 45-46; assoc prof English, Univ Notre Dame, 39-45, 46-55, prof, 55-61; vis writer in residence, Univ Ill, Urbana, 61-62, prof English, 62-65; prof, Univ Ill, Chicago Circle, 65-73 & Univ Fla, 73-76; Prof English to Prof Emer, Univ Ill, Chicago, 76-, Fulbright lectr, Univ Milan, 52-53 & Univ Florence, 53-54; vis prof, Univ Madrid, 58-60; vis ed, Poetry, Chicago, 60-61, ed, 78-; vis prof, Harvard Univ, 64 & 68-69; Nat Found on Arts & Humanities sabbatical grant, 67-68; Nat Inst Arts & Lett grant, 68; Creative Arts Citation in Poetry, Brandeis Univ, 74; Phi Beta Kappa poet, Harvard Univ, 78. **RESEARCH** Creative writing; Elizabethan and Jacobean drama; comparative literature. **SELECTED PUBLICATIONS** Auth, Knowledge of the Evening, Rutgers Univ, 60; ed, Arthur Golding's transl of Ovid's Metamorphoses, Macmillan, 65; auth, Of Flesh and Bone, 67 & Sappho to Valery: Poems in Translation, 71, Rutgers Univ & Princeton Univ Press, 80; Western Wind: An Introduction to Poetry, Random, 74; The Harper Anthology of Poetry, Harper & Row, 81; The Kiss: A J Ambalaya, Houghton Mifflin, 82; Selected Poems, Univ Chicago, 82. **CONTACT ADDRESS** Dept English, Univ of Illinois, Chicago, 601 S Morgan St, M/C 162, Chicago, IL 60607-7120.

NISHIMURA-JENSEN, JULIE M.
PERSONAL Born 07/26/1965, Berkeley, CA, m, 1993, 1 child **DISCIPLINE** CLASSICS **EDUCATION** Univ Wis, Madison, PhD, 96. **CAREER** Asst prof of Classical Languages, AZ State Univ, 97-. **HONORS AND AWARDS** Col of Liberal Arts and Sciences Undergraduate Teaching Development Grant, ASU, 97-98; fac grant-in-aid of res, ASU, 97. **MEMBERSHIPS** Am Philol Asn; Classical Asn of the Middle West and South; Women's Classical Caucus. **RESEARCH** Hellenistic poetry; genre studies. **SELECTED PUBLICATIONS** Auth, The Poetics of Aethalides: Silence and Poikilia in Apollonius' Argonautica, Classical Quart, 98. **CONTACT ADDRESS** Dept of Classics, Univ of Pennsylvania, 3451 Walnut, Philadelphia, PA 19104. **EMAIL** julienj@sas.upenn.edu

NITSCHE, RICHARD
PERSONAL Born 09/28/1939, Cleveland, OH, d, 1 child **DISCIPLINE** ENGLISH, ENGLISH AS A SECOND LANGUAGE, CHINESE **EDUCATION** Oh State Univ, BA, 66; PhD, 77; Nat Taiwan Univ, MA. **CAREER** Instr, Youngstown State Univ, 69-75; asst prof, prog dir, Monterey Inst Intl Stud, 77-80; lectr, Tianjin Univ, China, 80-81; instr, Monterey Peninsula Univ, 81-. **HONORS AND AWARDS** Rockefeller Gnt; Geraldine R Dodge Found Gnt; Fulbright Gnt. **MEMBERSHIPS** CLTA; CFLP. **SELECTED PUBLICATIONS** Auth, Situational Exercises in Cross-Cultural Awareness, Chas Merrill Pub (77); auth, Becoming Fluent in English, Kendall/Hunt pub, (73). **CONTACT ADDRESS** Dept Humanities, Monterey Peninsula Col, 980 Fremont St, Monterey, CA 93940. **EMAIL** rnitsche@hotmail.com

NIXON, ROB
DISCIPLINE AFRICAN AND BRITISH LITERATURES **EDUCATION** Rhodes Univ, S Africa, BA, 77; Univ Iowa, MA, 82; Columbia Univ, PhD, 89. **CAREER** Assoc prof. **SELECTED PUBLICATIONS** Auth, London Calling: VS Naipaul, Post-Colonial Mandarin, Oxford UP, 92; Homelands, Harlem, Hollywood: South African Culture and the World Beyond, Routledge, 94; auth, ninety essays and rev, New Yorker; Critical Inquiry; NY Times; TLS; London Rev of Bks; The Village Voice; S Atlantic Quart; Grand St; Nat; Black Renaissance/Renaissance Noire; Transition; The Independent. **CONTACT ADDRESS** Dept of Eng, Columbia Col, New York, 2960 Broadway, New York, NY 10027-6902.

NOBLE, MARIANNE K.
DISCIPLINE AMERICAN LITERATURE **EDUCATION** Columbia Univ, PhD. **CAREER** Asst prof, Am Univ. **RESEARCH** American literature, culture and studies; construction of sexuality in 19th century American Women's literature. **SELECTED PUBLICATIONS** Articles, Gothic and sentimental literature. **CONTACT ADDRESS** American Univ, 4400 Massachusetts Ave, Washington, DC 20016. **EMAIL** mnoble@american.edu

NOHRNBERG, JAMES CARSON
PERSONAL Born 03/19/1941, Berkeley, CA, m, 1964, 2 children **DISCIPLINE** RENAISSANCE & MEDIEVAL LITERATURE, BIBLE STUDIES **EDUCATION** Harvard Col, BA, 62; Univ Toronto, PhD, 70. **CAREER** Tch fel Eng, Univ Toronto, 63-64; Jr fel, Soc of Fel, Harvard Univ, 65-68; adj Eng, Harvard Univ, 67-68; Actg instr Eng, Yale Univ, 68-69, lectr, 69-70, asst prof, 70-75; Prof English, Univ VA, 75-; lectr, 74-00, Yale, Princeton, MLA, Columbia, Hopkins, Kenyon, NEH Seminars, Cornell, Univ VA, Georgetown, Emory, Univ Calif Irvine, Ind Univ, Newberry Libr, Loyola Balitmore, Univ South. **HONORS AND AWARDS** Robert Frost Poetry Prize, Kenyon Col 60; Acad of Am Poets Prize, harvard Col, 62; Woodrow Wilson Fel, Univ of Toronto, 62-63; Queen Elizabeth II Ontario Scholarship, 64-65; Soc of Fels, Harvard Univ, 65-68; Morse Fel, Yale Univ, 74-75; Center for Advanced Studies, Univ of VA, 75-78; Guggenheim Fel, 81-82; Gaus Seminar lectures, Princeton Univ, 87; Institute for Advanced Study, Indiana Univ, 91. **MEMBERSHIPS** MLA; Spenser Society, ACLA, PBK. **RESEARCH** Bible, Dante, Spenser, Shakespeare, Milton, allegory. **SELECTED PUBLICATIONS** Auth, Allegories of scripture, Shofar, winter 93; Like unto Moses: The Constituting of an Interruption, Ind Univ, 95; The Descent of Geryon: the Moral System of Inferno XVI-XXXI, Dante Studies, 98; Allegory De-Veiled: A New Theory for Construing Allegory's Two Bodies, Modern Philol, 11/98; Fortune and romance: Boiardo in America, In: Orlando's Opportunity: Chance, Luck, Fortune, Occasion, Boats, and Blows in Boiardo's Orlando Innamorato, Ariz State Univ, 98; Lectura Dantis, Inferno, In: Inferno XVIII: Introduction to Malebolge, Univ CA, 98; auth, Earthly Love, Spiritual Love, Love of Saints, The Love That Moves the Sun and Other Stars in Inferno XVIII, Univ Souht, 99; auth, Health, Sickness, and Death in the Middle Ages, Dante's Adam's Dropsy: A Case-Study in the Literary Etiology of the Sickness of Sin, Univ South, 99; Sparks and Seeds: Medieval Literature and Its Afterlife: Essays Honor of John Freccero, The Love That Moves the Sun and Other Stars in Dante's Hell, Brepol, 00. **CONTACT ADDRESS** Dept of Eng, Univ of Virginia, 219 Bryan Hall, Charlottesville, VA 22903. **EMAIL** jnc@virginia.edu

NOLAN, BARBARA
PERSONAL Born 01/26/1941, Indianapolis, IN **DISCIPLINE** ENGLISH **EDUCATION** Trinity Col, DC, BA, 62; Univ Wis, Madison, MA, 63, PhD(English), 67. **CAREER** Teaching asst, Univ Wis, Madison, 62-65; from instr to asst prof English, 66-72, fac fel, 67-68, assoc prof English, Wash Univ, 72-78; Prof English, Univ Va, 78-. **HONORS AND AWARDS** Fulbright Scholar, 65-66; NEH Summer Grants, 68, 78; Guggenheim Fel, 78. **MEMBERSHIPS** MLA; Mediaeval Acad Am; Dante Soc. **RESEARCH** Thirteenth and fourteenth century religious poetry and art; Beowulf and Old English poetry; medieval romance. **SELECTED PUBLICATIONS** Auth, "Chaucer's Tales of Trnascendence: Rhyme Royal and Christian Prayer in the Canterbury Tales," in Chaucer's Religious Tales, eds. C.D. Benson and E. Robertson, 90; auth, Chaucer and the Tradition of the Roman Antique, Cambridge UP, 92; auth, "Sir Thomas Malory's Tale of Sir Lancelot and Tale of Sir Gareth," in A Campanion to Malory Studies, (D.S. Brewer, 96); auth, "Turning over the Leaves of Medieval Fabliau-Anthologies: The Case of Bibliotheque Ntionale ms francais 2173," Medieval Perspectives 8, (98): 1-31; auth, "Promiscuos Fictions: Medieval bawdy Tales and their Textual Liaisons," in The Body and the Soul in Medieval Literature, eds. Piero Boitani and Anna Torti, (Woodridge, Suffolk: Boydell and Brewer, 99): 79-105; **CONTACT ADDRESS** Dept of English, Univ of Virginia, 219 Bryan Hall, PO Box 400121, Charlottesville, VA 22904-4121. **EMAIL** bn9a@virginia.edu

NOLAN, EDWARD FRANCIS
PERSONAL Born 03/30/1915, Fernandina, FL **DISCIPLINE** ENGLISH **EDUCATION** Univ Fla, Bae, 37, AM, 38; Princeton Univ, PhD, 41. **CAREER** Head dept English, Presby Jr Col, 41-42; instr, Presby Col, 42-44, assoc prof, 46-47; adJprof, 47-48, assoc prof, 48-63, Prof English, Univ Sc, 63- **MEMBERSHIPS** Southeast Renaissance Conf; Southern Atlantic Mod Lang Asn. **RESEARCH** Old English; Renaissance. **SELECTED PUBLICATIONS** Auth, Shakespeare's Sonnet Lxxiii; Verdi's Macbeth; The death of Bryan Lyndon; Barron's Simplified Approach to Shakespeare: Romeo and Juliet, 67, Barron's Simplified Approach to Shakespeare: Othello, 67, coauth, Barron's Simplified Approach to Shakespeare: King Lear, 68 & auth, A Simplified Approach to Shakespeare: The Merchant of Venice, 71, Barron's; Browning 'Rabbi Ben Ezra', Lines 124-5, Explicator, Vol 0051, 1993. **CONTACT ADDRESS** Dept of English, Univ of So Carolina, Columbia, Columbia, SC 29208.

NOLLER, DAVID K.
DISCIPLINE DEVELOPMENT OF CRITICAL AND CREATIVE THINKING **EDUCATION** PhD. **CAREER** Univ Albany - SUNY **SELECTED PUBLICATIONS** Articles, Inklings. **CONTACT ADDRESS** SUNY, Albany, 1400 Washington Ave, Albany, NY 12222. **EMAIL** noller@cnsunix.albany.edu

NOLLETTI, ARTHUR E., JR.
PERSONAL Born 05/17/1941, Wooster, OH, m, 1970, 1 child **DISCIPLINE** ENGLISH **EDUCATION** Ohio Univ, AB, 63; Univ of Wisconsin, MA, 65; PhD, 70. **CAREER** Univ of Wisconsin, Teaching Fellowship, 65-70; Cleveland State Univ, 70-71; Framingham State College, 71-. **HONORS AND AWARDS** Graduated cum laude, Ohio Univ, 63; National Endowment for the Humanities Fellowship, NEH Summer Stipend, Asian Cultural Council, Northeast Asian Society Grant. **MEMBERSHIPS** PMLA, Society for Cinema Studies. **RESEARCH** American and International Film. **SELECTED PUBLICATIONS** Ed, Reframing Japanese Cinema, with David Desser (Indiana UP, 92); ed, The films of Fred Zinnemann, (SUNY Press, 99). **CONTACT ADDRESS** Dept English, Framingham State Col, 100 State St, Framingham, MA 01702-2460.

NOONAN, JAMES S.
PERSONAL Born 08/26/1933, Ottawa, ON, Canada **DISCIPLINE** LITERATURE **EDUCATION** St. Patrick's (Ottawa), BA, 54; Univ Ottawa, BTh, 59, STL, 60; Cambridge Univ, MA, 71; Jules & Gabrielle Leger Fel, 86. **CAREER** Prof English, Carleton Univ, 67- **MEMBERSHIPS** Oblates of Mary Immaculate, 54-84. **SELECTED PUBLICATIONS** Contribur, Supplement to the Oxford Companion to Canadian History and Literature, 73; contribur, The Oxford Companion to Canadian Literature, 83, 2nd ed, (updated) 97; contribur, The Oxford Companion to Canadian Theatre, 89; ed, Biography and Autobiography: Essays on Irish and Canadian History and Literature, 93; bk rev ed, Theatre History in Canada, 83-94; bk rev ed, English Studies in Canada, 89-95. **CONTACT ADDRESS** Dept of English, Carleton Univ, 1125 Colonel By Dr, Ottawa, ON, Canada K1S 5B6. **EMAIL** james_noonan@carleton.ca

NOONE, PAT
DISCIPLINE MODERN LITERATURE **EDUCATION** New Rochelle, BA, 60, Hunter Col, MA, 64; Univ NYork, PhD, 71. **CAREER** Engl, Col Mt. St. Vincent **HONORS AND AWARDS** Adv, Fonthill Dial; Hum rep Undergrad Comt. **SELECTED PUBLICATIONS** Auth, 'Six Ways of Looking at a City': Literature and New York of the Late Nineteenth Century, Turn of the Century, 96. **CONTACT ADDRESS** Col of Mount Saint Vincent, 6301 Riverdale Ave, Riverdale, NY 10471. **EMAIL** pnoone@cmsv.edu

NORBERG, PETER
DISCIPLINE AMERICAN ROMANTICISM **EDUCATION** Boston Col, BA, 90, Rice Univ, MA, 94, PhD, 97. **CAREER** Engl, St. Joseph's Univ. **SELECTED PUBLICATIONS** Auth, Post-Colonial Theory and the Problem of American Pluralism, Boston Univ, 97. **CONTACT ADDRESS** Saint Joseph's Univ, 5600 City Ave, Philadelphia, PA 19131. **EMAIL** norberg@sju.edu

NORD, DAVID P.
PERSONAL Born 03/04/1947, Beech Grove, IN, m, 1970, 3 children **DISCIPLINE** JOURNALISM AND HISTORY **EDUCATION** Valparaiso, BA, 69; Univ of Minn, MA, 72; Univ Wis, PhD, 79. **CAREER** Assoc prof, jour, PROF, JOUR & AM STUD, IND UNIV BLOOMINGTON Am stud. **HONORS**

AND AWARDS Catherine Covert Award, 90 **MEMBERSHIPS** Am Antiquarian Soc **SELECTED PUBLICATIONS** Auth, "The Evangelical Origins of Mass Media in America, 1815-1835," Journ Monographs 88, 84; auth, "Working Class Readers: Family, Community and Reading in Late 19th- Century America," Comm Res 11, 86; auth, "A Republican Literature: A Study of Magazine Reading and Readers in Late Eighteenth-Century New York," Am Quart 40, 88; auth, "Theology and News: The Religious Roots of American Journalism, 1630-1730, Jour of Am Hist 77, 90; auth, "Systematic Benevolence: Religious Publishing and the Marketplace in Early Nineteenth-Century America," in Communications and Change in American Religious History, Eerdmans, 93; auth, "Reading the Newspaper: Strategies and Politics of Reader Response, Chicago, 1912-1917," Jour of Comm 45, Summer 95; auth, "Religious Reading and Readers in Antebellum America," Jour of the Early Rep 15, Summer 95; auth, "Readership as Citizenship in Late 18th-Century Philadelphia," in A Melancholy Scene of Devastation: The Public Response to the 1793 Yellow Fever Epidemic, Coll of Physicians of Phil; auth, "Free Books, Free Grace, Free Riders: The Economics of Religious Publishing in Early Nineteenth-Century America, " Procs of the AAS. **CONTACT ADDRESS** Sch of Jour, Indiana Univ, Bloomington, Bloomington, IN 47405. **EMAIL** nord@indiana.edu

NORDLING, JOHN G.
PERSONAL Born 03/17/1957, Portland, OR, m, 1985 **DISCIPLINE** CLASSICS AND LATIN LITERATURE **EDUCATION** Concordia Col, AA, 77; Valparaiso, BA, 80; Concordia Sem, M.Div, 85; Washington Univ, MA, 85; Univ of Wis-Madison, Ph.D, 91. **CAREER** Asst prof, dept foreign lang & lit, Valparaiso Univ, 94-. **MEMBERSHIPS** Amer Philol Asn; Soc of Bibl Lit; Archaeol Inst of Amer. **RESEARCH** Ancient epistelography; Paul - life and theology; Ancient slavery. **SELECTED PUBLICATIONS** Auth, "Onesimus Fugitivus: a Defense of the Runaway Slave Hypothesis in Philemon" Journal for the Study of the New Testament 41 (91): 97-119; auth, "The Ph.D. in the Parish", Logia 4 (950: 88-91; auth, "The Pastoral Office is Not an Option", Journal of English District Pastors 8 (96): 4-7; auth, New Testament Backgrounds, ed, C.E. Evans and S.E. Porter, Sheffield (97): 263-283; "Valparaiso Goes to Rome," Cresset 61 (97): 15-19; auth, "Christ Leavens Culture: St. Paul on Slavery," Concordia Journal 24 (98): 43-52; auth, "The Prayer that Jesus Gave," For the Life of the World 3 (99): 6-7; auth, "Christians in Context: The Four 'House Church' Passages," Spade and Stole: Festschrift in Honor of Professor Horace Hummel (forthcoming). **CONTACT ADDRESS** Dept of Classics, Baylor Univ, Waco, 303 Old Main, PO Box 97352, Waco, TX 76798. **EMAIL** john_nordling@baylor.edu

NORDLOH, DAVID JOSEPH
PERSONAL Born 05/03/1942, Cincinnati, OH, m, 1968, 2 children **DISCIPLINE** AMERICAN LITERATURE, AMERICAN STUDIES, BIBLIOGRAPHY **EDUCATION** Holy Cross Col, AB, 64; Ind Univ, PhD(English), 69. **CAREER** From instr to asst prof English, 68-75, assoc prof, 75-81, Prof English, Ind Univ, Bloomington, 81-, Textual ed, A selected edition of W D Howells, Ind Univ, 68-73, gen ed, 74-; textual expert, Ctr Eds Am Auth, MLA, 68-76; vis prof English, Univ Va, 78; ed, Twayne's United States Authors Series, 78-; chmn comt Scholarly Ed, MLA, 79-82; Fulbright Senior Prof, U of Heidelberg, Germany, 82-83; co-ed, American Literary Scholarship: An Annual, 91--. **MEMBERSHIPS** Soc Textual Scholar Am Lit Assoc. **RESEARCH** Nineteenth century American literature; bibliography and textual editing; W D Howells. **SELECTED PUBLICATIONS** W D Howells at Kittery Point, Harvard Lib Bull, 80; gen ed, Selected Howells Letters I-VI, 79-83; 19th Century American Literature, American Literary Scholarship, 85-87, 89-90; auth, American Literary Scholarship, 88-89, 93-94, 96, 98, 00; Setting Pages and Fixing Words - Bal and Critical Editing of American Literature, Papers of the Bibliographical Society of America, 92; co-ed, Selected Lit Crit, 3 vol., Selected ed. W.D. Howells, 93; Creating a Natl Agenda--and Abandoning It, Text, 94. **CONTACT ADDRESS** Dept of English, Indiana Univ, Bloomington, Bloomington, IN 47405. **EMAIL** nordloh@indiana.edu

NORDQUIST, RICHARD
PERSONAL Born New York, NY **DISCIPLINE** ENGLISH & RHETORIC **EDUCATION** SUNY at Geneseo, BA; Univ of Leicester, MA; Univ of Ga, PhD, 91. **CAREER** Instr of English for European Div of the Univ of Md, 76-80; vis prof, Tallinn Pedagogical Univ, 98; Prof of English & Rhetoric, 80-, Dir of Composition, 88-93, Dir of Writing Center, 82-88, Dir of General Studies, 97-, Dir of British Studies Prog, 96-, Asst Dean of Academic Services & Dir of Nontraditional Learning, Armstrong Atlantic State Univ, 93-98. **HONORS AND AWARDS** Armstrong Alumni Asn Outstanding Fac Awd, 94; Armstrong Student Govt Svc Awd, 96. **MEMBERSHIPS** MLA. **RESEARCH** Twentieth-century lit and lit nonfiction. **SELECTED PUBLICATIONS** Auth, Passages: A Writer's Guide, 4th edition, St. Martin's Press, 00; articles on the American essay, Encyclopedia of Am Lit, 99; Forms of Imposture in the Essays of E.B. White, Critical Essays on E.B. White, G.K. Hall, 95. **CONTACT ADDRESS** Dept of Lang & Lit, Armstrong Atlantic State Univ, Savannah, GA 31419. **EMAIL** richard_nordquist@mailgate.armstrong.edu

NORGAARD, ROLF
PERSONAL Born 03/22/1952, Galion, OH, m, 1991, 2 children **DISCIPLINE** LITERATURE, WRITING **EDUCATION** Wesleyan Univ, BA, 74; Stanford Univ, AM, 79; PhD, 82. **CAREER** Prof & Sen Instr, Univ Colo, 87-. **HONORS AND AWARDS** Nat Endowment Humanities Fel, Univ Colo, 87-89; Fac Fel, Univ Colo, 97-98; Ctr for the Humanities and the Arts Fel, Univ Colo, 98-. **MEMBERSHIPS** RJA, NCTE, CCCC. **RESEARCH** Rhetorical theory history and criticism, analytic and argumentative writing, writing across the curriculum and writing in the disciplines, the rhetoric of inquiry, genre theory and analysis, curriculum design. **SELECTED PUBLICATIONS** Auth, Ideas in Action: A Guide to Critical Thinking and Writing, Longman (New York, NY), 94; auth, "The Rhetoric of Writing Requirements," Rhet, Cult Studies and Literacy (95): 153-160; auth, "The Prospect of Rhetoric in Writing Across the Curriculum," Making and Unmaking the Prospects for Rhet, (97): 149-156; auth, "The Rhetoric of Civility and the Fate of Argument," Rhet, the Polis and the Global Village, Lawrence Erlbaum Publ (99): 247-253; auth, "Negotiating Expertise in Disciplinary 'Contact Zones'," Lang and Learning Across the Disciplines, 3.2 (99): 44-63; auth, "The Curricular Physics of Rhetoric Education," The Realms of Rhet: A Multidisciplinary Inquiry into the Prospects of Rhet Educ, St Univ NY (SUNY) Pr (forthcoming); auth, Composing Knowledge: Literacy. Community. Inquiry," Bedford/St Martin's Pr (New York, NY), forthcoming. **CONTACT ADDRESS** Dept Lit, Univ of Colorado, Boulder, PO Box 359, Boulder, CO 80309-0359. **EMAIL** rolf.norgaard@colorado.edu

NORLAND, HOWARD BERNETT
PERSONAL Born 03/01/1932, Palo Alto Co, IA **DISCIPLINE** ENGLISH **EDUCATION** St Olaf Col, BA, 54; Univ Wis, MS, 58, PhD(English), 62. **CAREER** Instr English, Univ Kans, 61-63; from asst prof to assoc prof, 63-71, Prof English to Prof Emer, Univ Nebr, Lincoln, 71-. **HONORS AND AWARDS** Folger Shakespeare Libr fel, 67; ed bd, Genre, 67-; Frank H Woods fel humanities, 74. **MEMBERSHIPS** MLA; Renaissance Soc Am; Int Asn Neo-Latin Studies. **RESEARCH** Renaissance drama and critical theory; modern drama. **SELECTED PUBLICATIONS** Auth, The text of The Maid's Tragedy, Papers Bibliog Soc Am, 67; ed, Critical Edition of Beaumont and Fletcher's The Maid's Tragedy, 68 & Study of Ben Jonson, 69, Univ Nebr; auth, The design of Ben Jonson's Catiline, Sixteenth Century J, 78; Vives critical view of drama, Humanistica Lovaniensia, J Neo- Latin Studies, 81; The role of drama in More's literary career, 16th Century J, 82; The role of drama in Erasmus' literary thought, Bologna Acta: Selected Papers Int Cong Neo-Latin Studies. **CONTACT ADDRESS** Dept of English, Univ of Nebraska, Lincoln, 202 Andrews Hall, Lincoln, NE 68588-0333. **EMAIL** hnorland2@unl.edu

NORMAN, JOANNE S.
DISCIPLINE ENGLISH LITERATURE **EDUCATION** Univ Calgary, BA; Univ Toronto, MA; Univ Ottawa, PhD. **CAREER** Engl, Bishop's Univ. **SELECTED PUBLICATIONS** Auth, pubs on medieval Scottish poetry, medieval manuscripts, and word and image studies. **CONTACT ADDRESS** English Dept, Bishop's Univ, Lennoxville, QC, Canada JIMIZ 7. **EMAIL** jnorman@ubishops.ca

NORMAN, PARALEE FRANCES
PERSONAL Born 01/02/1932, Lubbock, TX, s **DISCIPLINE** ENGLISH **EDUCATION** Univ Mo, BA, 54; Drake Univ, MA, 59; Univ Iowa, PhD, 78. **CAREER** Asst prof, W Va Wesleyan Univ, 67-69; asst prof, Marycrest Col, 70-72; prof, Northwestern State Univ, 79-. **HONORS AND AWARDS** Fac Fel, England, 90; Cert of appreciation for Patriotic Civilian Serv, Dept of the Army, 86. **MEMBERSHIPS** NCTE; LCTE; MLA; Victorious Inst. **RESEARCH** English; American literature. **SELECTED PUBLICATIONS** Auth, "The Island of Higgledy-Piggledy: Marmion Savage's 'My Uncle the Curate', 1849,' Eire-Ireland: A Journal of Irish Studies, (90): 93-110; rev, of "Making Progress from Paragraphs to Essays," by Ellen Andrews Knodt, in Teaching English in The Two-Year College, (Nat Coun of Teachers of English, 92), 313-314; rev, of "James Clarence Mangan, Edward Walsh and Nineteenth Century Irish Literature in English," by Anne MacCarthy, Mellen Press, 00; auth, Marmion Wilme Savage1804-1872: Dublin's Victorian Satirist, Edwin Mellen Press, 00; auth, "Marmion W. Savage," in Irish Writers, ca. 1500-1890: a Biocritical Sourcebook, Greenwood, 00; auth, "Marmion W. Savage," in New Dictionary of National Biography, Oxford Univ Press, (forthcoming). **CONTACT ADDRESS** Dept Lang and Comm, Northwestern State Univ of Louisiana, 3329 University Pkwy, Leesville, LA 71446-9041. **EMAIL** normanp@alpha.nsula.edu

NORRIS, ETHEL MAUREEN
PERSONAL Born 03/03/1956, Petersburg, VA, s **DISCIPLINE** MUSIC **EDUCATION** East Carolina Univ, B Mus 1977; OH State Univ, MA 1978; summer study, Westminster Choir Coll 1985-86; Ohio State Univ, doctoral study in music history 1987-; Ohio State Univ, PhD, 1994. **CAREER** St Pauls Coll, instructor of music; Virginia State Univ, asst prof of music, currently. **HONORS AND AWARDS** Finalist Natl Achievement Scholarship Program for Outstanding Negro Students 1973; One-Year Minority Fellowship OH State Univ 1977-78; Graduate Teaching Assistantship OH State Univ 1987-88; Grant, UNCF, 1987-88; Grant, National Endowment for the Humanities, 1989-90; OSU Presidential Fellowship, 1993-94. **MEMBERSHIPS** Instr Piano Lessons 1979-; mem Sigma Alpha Iota, Coll Music Soc, Amer Guild of Organists, Phi Kappa Phi; Sonneck Society. **CONTACT ADDRESS** Dept of Music, Virginia State Univ, 1 Hayden Dr., Petersburg, VA 23806-0001.

NORSTEDT, JOHANN A.
PERSONAL Born 07/09/1937, Kulpmont, PA, m, 1965 **DISCIPLINE** ENGLISH **EDUCATION** Univ Pa, AB, 59; AM, 61; Univ Col, Dublin, PhD, 72. **CAREER** Inst, Temple Univ, 62-64; Instr, Am Univ of Beirut, 64-67; asst prof to assoc prof, Va Tech, 79-. **MEMBERSHIPS** Am Conf for Irish Studies. **RESEARCH** Anglo-Irish literature **SELECTED PUBLICATIONS** Auth, Thomas MacDonagh: A Critical Biography, Univ Pr of Va, 79; auth, "The Gift of Reputation: Yeats and MacDonagh," in EIRE-IRELAND (84). **CONTACT ADDRESS** Dept English, Virginia Polytech Inst and State Univ, 100 Virgina Tech, Blacksburg, VA 24061-0001. **EMAIL** jnorsted@vt.edu

NORTH, HELEN FLORENCE
PERSONAL Born 01/31/1921, Utica, NY **DISCIPLINE** CLASSICAL LITERATURE, RHETORIC **EDUCATION** Cornell Univ, AB, 42, AM, 43, PhD(classics), 45. **CAREER** Sibley fel, 45-46; instr class lang, Rosary Col, 46-48; asst prof Greek & Latin, 48-53, assoc prof, 53-62, William J Kenan prof, 73-78, Prof Classics, Swarthmore Col, 62-, Chmn Dept, 59-, Centennial Prof, 78-91, Ford & Fulbright fels, Rome, 53-54; vis assoc prof, Barnard Col, Columbia Univ, 54-55; Guggenheim fel, Rome, 58-59; secy adv coun, Sch Class Studies, Am Acad Rome, 60-62 & 64, mem bd trustees, 72-75 & 77-91; Asn Univ Women res fel, Rome, 62-63; Nat Endowment for Hum sr fel, Rome, 67-68; chmn, Cath Comn on Intellectual & Cult Affairs, 68-69; mem bd dir, King's Col, Pa, 69-71 & 73-75; Am Coun Learned Soc fel, Rome, 71-72; Martin class lectr, Oberlin Col, 72; mem bd trustees, La Salle Col, 73-; Guggenheim fel, 75-76; Nat Endowment for the Humanities Fel for College Teachers, 83-84; Amer Coun Learned Soc fel, Rome, 87-88. **HONORS AND AWARDS** Harbison Tchg Prize, Danforth Found, 69; Charles A Goodwin Awd for Sophrosyne, Am Philol Asn, 69. **MEMBERSHIPS** Am Philol Asn (2nd vpres, 74, pres, 76); Class Asn Atlantic States; Class Soc Am Acad Rome (pres, 60-61); AAAS, 75; Am Philos Soc, 91; Centennial Medal, Am Acad in Rome, 95; Am Philos Asn Medal for Distinguished Service, 96. **RESEARCH** Concept of Sophrosyne in Greek lit; Plato's rhetoric; Roman rhetoric. **SELECTED PUBLICATIONS** Trans Milton's Second Defence of the English people, In: Vol IV, Complete Prose Works of John Milton, Yale Univ, 66; Sophrosyne: Self-Knowledge and Self-Restraint in Greek Literature, 66 & coed, Of Eloquence; Studies in Ancient and Mediaeval Rhetoric, Cornell Univ, 70; auth, Ancient Salt: The New Rhetoric and the Old, J Hist Ideas, 74; ed, Interpretations of Plato: A Swarthmore Symposium, Brill, 77; auth, The Yoke of necessity: Aulis and beyond, Class World, 77; From Myth to Icon, Cornell Univ, 79; auth, Opening Socrates, Ill Class Stud, 94; auth, The Dacian Walls Speak, Festschrift for Paul MacKendrick, 98; coauth, The West of Ireland: A Megalithic Primer, 99. **CONTACT ADDRESS** 604 Ogden Ave, Swarthmore, PA 19081.

NORTHROP, DOUGLAS A.
PERSONAL Born 04/12/1935, Ontario, NY, m, 1956, 4 children **DISCIPLINE** ENGLISH **EDUCATION** Wesleyan Univ, BA, 56; Univ Chicago, MA, 57; PhD, 66. **CAREER** From prof to prof emeritus, Ripon Col, 74-; vpres and dean, Ripon Col, 77-94; Helen Swift Neilson Prof of Cultural Studies, Ripon Col, 98-00. **HONORS AND AWARDS** Severy and Uhrig Awds for Teaching Excellence, 65-66 & 70-71; NEH fac fel in residence, 75-76. **MEMBERSHIPS** Renaissance Soc of Am. **RESEARCH** Renaissance literature (English), Courtesy literature. **SELECTED PUBLICATIONS** Auth, "Spenser's Defense of Elizabeth," UTQ 38 (69): 277-294; auth, "Mercilla's Court as Parliament," HLQ 36 (73): 153-158; auth, "The Double Structure of Paradise Lost," Milton Studies 12 (78): 75-90. **CONTACT ADDRESS** Dept English, Ripon Col, PO Box 248, Ripon, WI 54971-0248. **EMAIL** northropd@ripon.edu

NORTON, CAMILLE
DISCIPLINE ENGLISH LITERATURE **EDUCATION** Univ MA, BA, 83; Harvard Univ, MA, 87, PhD, 92. **CAREER** Assoc prof, Univ Pacific. **HONORS AND AWARDS** Grolier Prize, 81; Derek Bk Awd, 92; Eberhart Teacher Scholar, 98. **SELECTED PUBLICATIONS** Co-ed, Resurgent: New Writing by Women, Univ IL, 92. **CONTACT ADDRESS** Eng Dept, Univ of the Pacific, Stockton, Pacific Ave, PO Box 3601, Stockton, CA 95211. **EMAIL** cnorton@nop.edu

NORTON, KAY
DISCIPLINE MUSIC HISTORY **EDUCATION** Univ Colo, PhD. **CAREER** Asst prof, Brenau Women's Col; assoc prof, Univ Mo, Kansas City; sen lect, Arizona State Univ, 99-. **MEMBERSHIPS** The Am Musicological Soc; The Col Music Soc; The Hymn Soc; The Soc for Am Music. **RESEARCH** Art music traditions of the 19th and 20th centuries. **SELECTED**

PUBLICATIONS Auth, Normand Lockwood: His Life and Music, Scarecrow Press, 93; auth, "Musical Emissary in America: Nadia Boulanger, Normand Lockwood, and American Musical Pedagogy," in Vistas of American Music: Essays in Honor of William K. Kearns (Harmonie Park Press, 98); auth, "Normand Lockwood," in New Grove Dictionary, 2nd ed (forthcoming); auth, Mercer's Cluster: Baptist Offspring and Southern Midwife, College Music Society. **CONTACT ADDRESS** School of Music, Arizona State Univ, P.O.Box 870405, Tempe, AZ 85287-0405. **EMAIL** Kay.Norton@asu.edu

NORWOOD, JAMES
DISCIPLINE THEATRE ARTS **EDUCATION** Univ Calif Berkeley, PhD. **CAREER** Assoc prof **SELECTED PUBLICATIONS** Auth, pubs on Shakespeare, modern French theatre, and film criticism. **CONTACT ADDRESS** Theatre Arts and Dance Dept, Univ of Minnesota, Twin Cities, 106 Norris Hall, 172 Pillsbury Dr SE, Minneapolis, MN 55455. **EMAIL** nowo001@maroon.tc.umn.edu

NOURIE, ALAN RAYMOND
PERSONAL Born 12/30/1942, Kankakee, IL, m, 1969, 1 child **DISCIPLINE** ENGLISH, LIBRARY SCIENCE **EDUCATION** Southern Ill Univ, Carbondale, BA, MA, PhD; Univ of Ill, Champaign-Urbana, MS. **CAREER** Instr & asst prof, Southeast Mo State Univ, 78-81; librarian III, head of Humanities dept, Auburn Univ, 81-85; ASSOC PROF TO PROF, SOCIAL SCI LIBRARIAN, ILL STATE UNIV, 85-. **MEMBERSHIPS** ACRL; T.S. Eliot Soc. **SELECTED PUBLICATIONS** Compiler, A Concordance to the Collected Poems of T.S. Eliot, 84; T.S. Eliot's Criterion Miscellany: A Lost Series, Serials Librarian, spring 87; co-ed, American Mass Market Magazines, 91; auth, Twentieth Century Literature in English, Guide to Infor Access: A Complete Res Handbook and Directory, Am Libr Asn/Random House, 94. **CONTACT ADDRESS** Milner Library, Illinois State Univ, Normal, IL 61761. **EMAIL** alan@mhsgate.mlb.ilstu.edu

NOVAK, MAXIMILLIAN E.
PERSONAL Born 03/26/1930, New York, NY, m, 1966, 3 children **DISCIPLINE** ENGLISH LITERATURE **EDUCATION** Univ Calif, Los Angeles, BA, 52, MA, 54, PhD, 58; St John's Col, Oxford, DPhil, 61. **CAREER** Asst prof, Univ Mich, 58-62; from asst prof to prof, Univ Calif, Los Angeles, 62- . **HONORS AND AWARDS** Fulbright fel, 55-57; Guggenheim fel, 65-66, 85-86; NEH fel, 80-81; Clark Lib prof, 77-78; pres fel, UCLA, 91-92; pres, johnson soc of southern calif; pres, western soc for eighteenth cent stud. **MEMBERSHIPS** MLA; ASECS. **RESEARCH** Eighteenth century and Restoration English literature; Jewish American literature. **SELECTED PUBLICATIONS** Auth, Realism, Myth, and History in Defoe's Fiction, Nebraska, 83; auth, Eighteenth-Century English Literature, Schocken, 84; ed, The California Edition of the Works of John Dryden, v. 10, 13, California, 70, 84; co-ed, The Stoke Newington Edition of Daniel Defoe, v.1, 2, AMS Press, 99, 00. **CONTACT ADDRESS** English Dept, Univ of California, Los Angeles, PO Box 90095-1530, Los Angeles, CA 90095-1530. **EMAIL** novak@humnet.ucla.edu

NOVELLI, CORNELIUS
PERSONAL Born 05/07/1930, Dunkirk, NY, d, 8 children **DISCIPLINE** DRAMA **EDUCATION** State Univ NY at Fredonia, BS, 52; Ohio Univ, MA, 55; Univ Notre Dame, PhD, 63. **CAREER** Prof, Le Moyne Col, 58-; chair of dept of English, Le Moyne Col, 63-65 & 71-77; drama critic, Syracuse Newspapers, 88-. **MEMBERSHIPS** Asn for Theatre in Higher Educ, AAUP, Northeast MLA, Medieval and Renaissance Drama Soc. **RESEARCH** Literature and drama--ancient through modern. **SELECTED PUBLICATIONS** Auth, "Francis Phelan and the Hands of Heracles: Hero and City in William Kennedy's Ironweed," Classical and Modern Lit 12 (92): 199-126; auth, "Sin, Sight, and Sactity in the Miller's Tale: Why Chaucer's Blacksmith Works at Night," Chaucer Rev 33 (98): 168-175; auth, "Feste," in Fools and Jesters in Literature, Art, and History, ed. Vicki K. Janik (Greenwood Press, 98). **CONTACT ADDRESS** Dept English, Le Moyne Col, 1419 Salt Springs Rd, Syracuse, NY 13214-1302.

NOVERR, DOUGLAS ARTHUR
PERSONAL Born 05/13/1942, Battle Creek, MI, m, 1968 **DISCIPLINE** AMERICAN LITERATURE & STUDIES **EDUCATION** Cent Mich Univ, BA, 65, MA, 66; Miami Univ, PhD(English), 72. **CAREER** Instr English, Cent Mich Univ, 66-67 & Miami Univ Ohio, 67- 69; from instr to asst prof, 70-78, Assoc Prof English, Mich State Univ, 78-, Nat Endowment Humanities fel English, Miami Univ Ohio, 68-69; sr Fulbright lectr Am lit, Marie Curie Sklodowska Univ, Poland, 76-77. **MEMBERSHIPS** MLA; Am Studies Asn; Popular Cult Asn; Thoreau Soc; Soc Am Baseball Res. **RESEARCH** Nineteenth century American literature; American painting and literature; American sports history. **SELECTED PUBLICATIONS** Auth, Emily Dickinson and the art of despair, Emily Dickinson Bull, 73; Bryant and Cole in the Catskills, Bull NY Pub Libr, 75; Midwestern travel literature in the nineteenth century: Romance and reality, MidAmerica, 77; coauth, The athletic revolution reconsidered, Sport Sociol Bull, fall 77; The Relationship of Painting and Literature: A Guide to Information Sources, Gale Res, 78; Midwester Regionalist Painting and the Origins of Midwestern Popular Culture, Mid Am, 80; coauth, Violence in American sports, In: Sports in Modern America, River City Publ Ltd, 81; Sports in the twenties, In: The Evolution of Mass Culture in America, Forum Press, 82. **CONTACT ADDRESS** Dept of Lang, Michigan State Univ, 229 Bessey Hall, East Lansing, MI 48824-1033.

NOWLIN, MICHAEL E.
PERSONAL Born 12/19/1962, Lethbridge, AB, Canada, 2 children **DISCIPLINE** LITERATURE **EDUCATION** Univ Western Ont, BA, 84; Univ Toronto, MA, 85; Univ Calif Los Angeles, PhD, 91. **CAREER** Asst prof, Univ Victoria, 99-. **MEMBERSHIPS** MLA; MSA. **RESEARCH** Modern American literature. **SELECTED PUBLICATIONS** Auth, "Toni Morrison's 'Jazz' and the Racial Dreams of the American Writer," Am Lit (99); auth, "F. Scott Fitzgerald's Elite Syncopations: The Racial Makeup of the Entertainer," Studies of Can (01). **CONTACT ADDRESS** English Dept, Univ of Victoria, Stn Csc, PO Box 3070, Victoria, BC, Canada V8W 3W1. **EMAIL** mnowlin@uvic.ca

NOYES, MARTHA
PERSONAL Born 12/23/1949, San Francisco, CA, d **DISCIPLINE** COMMUNICATIONS **EDUCATION** Haw Loa Col, Kane'ohe, BA, 75; Univ Haw at Manoa, Honolulu, MA, 78. **CAREER** Workshop Leader, Leeward Community Col, 92, 93, 98; Instr, Leeward Community Col, 92-93; Lectr, Haw Pac Univ, 95-. **HONORS AND AWARDS** Kahili Awd, First Place in Boardcast Media, 94; Chris Awd, Columbus Int Film Festival, 96; Best Shirt Film, Toronto Worldwide Film Festival, 97; Cone Golden Eagle, 97; Bronze Awd, USA Film Festival, 97; Kahili Awd, First Place in Print Media, 98; Pa'I Awd, Third Place, Haw Publ Asn, 00. **RESEARCH** Multicultural literature, Myths and legends, Hawaiian history, Hawaiian traditions, practices, cultures, Native American peoples, cultures, traditions, Writing in a multicultural society. **SELECTED PUBLICATIONS** Auth, "Land of Gods," and "We Will Eat Stones," ed. Bob Dye (Univ of Haw Press, 96), and Haw Chronicles; Illusr, coauth, Hawaiian Healing herbs, Ka'Imi Pono Press (Honolulu, HI), 97; auth, "Ryuzo Yanagimachi: Islander or the Year," Honolulu Magazine (Jan 99); auth, "Leilehua," SPSM&H 28; auth, "The Ala Wai: Waikiki's Grand Canal," Spirit of Aloha Magazine (June 99); auth, "Lana'I," Spirit of Aloha Magazine (Aug 99); auth, "When Hula Fell from Grace and Rose Again," Spirit of Aloha Magazine (Apr 00); auth, "Hawaiian Songs of Places," Spirit of Aloha Magazine (June 00); Illusr, coauth, Medicinal Plants of Hawai'I, Bess Press (Honolulu, HI), forthcoming 00; coauth, Once There Were Many, Ka'Imi Pono Press (Honolulu, HI), forthcoming 00. **CONTACT ADDRESS** Dept Arts and Sci, Hawaii Pacific Univ, 1188 Fort St mall Ste 430, Honolulu, HI 96813-2713. **EMAIL** 74543.1751@compuserve.com

NUERNBERG, SUSAN M.
PERSONAL Born 09/05/1946, Milwaukee, WI, 2 children **DISCIPLINE** ENGLISH **EDUCATION** Miami Univ, BA, 68; Univ Mass, MA, 78, PhD, 90; Univ Dijon, France, 85. **CAREER** Asst prof, 90-96; assoc prof Eng, 96-, Univ Wis, Oshkosh. **HONORS AND AWARDS** Mention Bien for Diplome d'Etudes Approfondies, Univ of Dijon, France, 84; High Pass for defence of Doctoral dissertation, U Mass, 89; Regents Teaching Excellence Award, Univ of Wis-Oshkosh, 92; Jack London woman of the Year award, 95. **MEMBERSHIPS** Jack London Soc; Jack London Found; Popular Culture Asn; Am Lit Asn. **RESEARCH** Late 19th & early 20th century Am lit. **SELECTED PUBLICATIONS** Auth, "The Rhetoric of Race," in The Stowe Debate: Rhetorical Strategies in Uncle Tom's Cabin, U of Mass P, 94; ed, The Critical Response to Jack London, Greenwood, 95; ed, The Letters of Rus Kingman, David Rejl, 99; auth, "Stowe, the Abolition Movement, and Prevailing Theories of Race in Nineteenth-Century America," in Teaching Uncle Toms Cabin, MLA, 00. **CONTACT ADDRESS** English Dept, Univ of Wisconsin, Oshkosh, Oshkosh, WI 54901. **EMAIL** nuernber@uwosh.edu

NULL, ELISABETH M.
PERSONAL Born 12/01/1942, Worcester, MA, 2 children **DISCIPLINE** FOLKLORE, HISTORY, LIBRARY SCIENCE **EDUCATION** Sarah Lawrence Col, BA; MA; Yale Univ 85; MPhil, 89; Univ of Pa, MA, 86; Cath Univ of Am, MLIS, 95. **CAREER** Librarian, ed, digital content provider, Lib of Congress, 95-98; guest lectr, Georgetown Univ, 91-98; writer, cybrarian, Rural Sch Community Trust, 99-; co-chair, Washington Folk Festival, 99-00. **MEMBERSHIPS** Am Folklore Soc. **RESEARCH** American musical life and cultural history. **SELECTED PUBLICATIONS** Reviews in Journal of Am Folklore, New York Folklore Quarterly, New England Quarterly; produced ethnographic recordings, Green Linnet Records; edited digitized historical collections, Lib of Congress. **CONTACT ADDRESS** 706 Bonifant Street, Silver Spring, MD 20910-5534. **EMAIL** elisabeth.null@tcs.wap.org

NUNES, ZITA
DISCIPLINE AFRICAN-AMERICAN LITERATURE **EDUCATION** B.A., Brown, 83; M.A., Berkeley, 86; PhD, Berkeley, 93. **CAREER** Asst prof. **HONORS AND AWARDS** Fel, Soc Sci Res Coun; fel, Fulbright. **RESEARCH** Brazil on the modernist period. **SELECTED PUBLICATIONS** Auth, pubs on Brazilian modernism, racial theory, and the relationship between lit and anthrop. **CONTACT ADDRESS** Dept of Eng, Columbia Col, New York, 2960 Broadway, New York, NY 10027-6902.

NUNNALLY, THOMAS E.
PERSONAL Born 06/10/1950, Tuscaloosa, AL, m, 1972, 2 children **DISCIPLINE** ENGLISH, LINGUISTICS **EDUCATION** Univ Ala, BA, 72; Univ Georgia, MA, 74; PhD, 85. **CAREER** Instr, asst prof, assoc prof, Auburn Univ, 84-. **HONORS AND AWARDS** Fulbright Lectr, Res, 88, 01-02; NEH, 95; Phi Kappa Phi, Nat Hon Soc. **MEMBERSHIPS** ADS; DSNA; LSA; LSN; SAMLA; SCL. **RESEARCH** Linguistics change in English grammar and lexis; development of world Englishes; language uses attitudes; linguistic studies of literature. **SELECTED PUBLICATIONS** Co-ed, From the Gulf States and Beyond: The Legacy of Lee Pedersen and LAGS, Univ Ala Press, 98; auth, co-ed, Language Variety in the South Revisited, Univ Ala Press, 97; auth, "Glossing the Folk: A Review of Selected Lexical Research into American Slang and Americanisms," Am Speech 66 (01); auth, "Word Up, Word Down: The Social Vicissitudes of 'Blop' and 'Bleeper,''' Nat Forum 75 (95): 36-39; auth, "Man's Son/Son of Man: Translation, Textual Conditioning, and the History of the English Genitive," in History of Englishes: New Methods and Interpretations in Historical Linguistics, ed. Matti Rissanen, Ossi Ihalainen, Terttu Nevalainen, Irma Taavitsainen (Berlin and NY: de Gruyter, 92): 359-72; auth, "The Possessive with Gerunds: What the Handbooks Say and What They Should Say," Am Speech 66 (91): 359-370; auth, "Morphology and Word Order Within the Old English Noun-Phrase: Grammatical Efficiency," Neuphilol Mitteil 92 (91): 421-431; auth, "An Evaluative Taxonomy of Diachronic Corpora," SECOL Rev 15 (91): 21-36. **CONTACT ADDRESS** Eng Dept, Auburn Univ, Auburn, AL 36849-0002. **EMAIL** nunnath@auburn.edu

NUSSBAUM, FELICITY
PERSONAL Born 08/12/1944, Dayton, OH, d, 2 children **DISCIPLINE** ENGLISH **EDUCATION** Austia Col, BA, 65; IN Univ, MA, 67, PhD, 70. **CAREER** PROF OF ENGLISH, UCLA; advisory bd, Auto/biography Studies, 90-; ed bds, Studies in English Lit 1500-1900, 94-, 18th Century Studies, 90-93; advisory committee, PMLA, 97-2000; advisor ed, 18th Century Studies, 95-98. **HONORS AND AWARDS** NEH summer grant, 81; Rockefeller Humanist-in-Residence fel, 87; Co-recipient, Louis Gottschalk Prize, Am Soc for 18th Century Studies, for Autobiographical Subject, 89; Marta Sutton Weds fel, Stanford Humanities Center, 91-92; John Simon Guggenheim Memorial Found fel, 93; Andrew Mellon Short-term fel, Huntington Library, 97-98; NEH fel, 98; William Andrew Clara Library Prof, 99-2000. **MEMBERSHIPS** PMLA; ASECS. **RESEARCH** 18th century British lit; women's studies; critical theory; autobiography. **SELECTED PUBLICATIONS** Auth, The Plays of David Mallet (1705?-1765), facsimile ed with critical intro, Garland Press, 80; The Brink of All We Hate: English Satires on Women, 1660-1750, Univ Press KY, 84; The New Eighteenth Century: Theory/Politics/English Literature, co-ed with Laura Brown, Methuen, 87; The Politics of Difference, special issue of Eighteenth-Century Studies, ed and intro, 23.4, summer 90; The Autobiographical Subject: Gender and Ideology in Eighteenth-Century England, Johns Hopkins Univ Press, 89, paperback, 95; Torrid Zones: Maternity, Sexuality and Empire in Eighteenth-Century English Narrative, Johns Hopkins Univ Press, 95; Defects: Engendering the Modern Body, co-ed with Helen Deutsch, lead vol in Corporealities series, Univ MI Press, 00; author of numerous essays. **CONTACT ADDRESS** Dept of English, Univ of California, Los Angeles, Box 951530, Los Angeles, CA 90095. **EMAIL** nussbaum@humnet.ucla.edu

NYCE, BENJAMIN M.
PERSONAL Born 04/25/1932, Buffalo, NY, m, 1967 **DISCIPLINE** ENGLISH **EDUCATION** Princeton Univ, AB, 54; Claremont Grad Sch, PhD(English), 67. **CAREER** Lectr English, Scripps Col, 61-63; instr, Univ Calif, Riverside, 63-64; asst prof, Calif State Polytech Col, 64-67; asst prof, 67-77, assoc prof, 77-80, prof English, Univ San Diego, 80-, Fulbright-Hays prof Am studies, Univ Mohammed V, Morocco, 69-70 & Univ Nairobi, 72-73. **MEMBERSHIPS** MLA. **RESEARCH** English and American novel, late 19th and 20th century; political fiction; African Literature and Film. **SELECTED PUBLICATIONS** Auth, Ignazio Silone's Political Trilogy, New Orleans Rev, 68; Joyce Cary's Political Trilogy: The Atmosphere of Power, Mod Lang Quart, 3/71; Joseph Conrad's Nostromo, Recovering Lit, spring 72; Satyajit Ray: A Study of his Films, Praeger, 89. **CONTACT ADDRESS** Dept of English, Univ of San Diego, 5998 Alcala Park, San Diego, CA 92110-2492. **EMAIL** agardner@cts.com

O

O'BARR, WILLIAM M.
DISCIPLINE ENGLISH LITERATURE **EDUCATION** Northwestern Univ, PhD, 69. **CAREER** Prof, Duke Univ. **SE-**

LECTED PUBLICATIONS Auth, Culture and the Ad: Representations of Otherness in the World of Advertising, Westview, 94; Language and Politics, 76; Language and Power, 84; Rules Versus Relationships: The Ethnography of Legal Discourse, 90; pubs on lang and commun domains law and polit. **CONTACT ADDRESS** Dept of Cult Anthrop, Duke Univ, Durham, NC 27706.

O'BRIEN, CHARLES
DISCIPLINE FILM STUDIES **EDUCATION** Univ Iowa, PhD, 92. **CAREER** Dept Art & Cult, Carleton Univ, 94. **HONORS AND AWARDS** Chateaubriand FEL,a Soc Sci and Hum Res Coun; res fel, Camargo Found in Cassis, Fr. **RESEARCH** Analysis of the French reception of Japanese films. **SELECTED PUBLICATIONS** Auth, articles and bk chapters on silent films of the 1920s, film noir in Paris, French films of the German occupation, Jean Renoir's American films, and French colonial films; transl, Francesco Casetti's Within the Gaze, Univ Ind Press. **CONTACT ADDRESS** Dept of Art and Cult, Carleton Univ, 1125 Colonel By Dr, Ottawa, ON, Canada K1S 5B6. **EMAIL** charles_obrien@carleton.ca

O'BRIEN, GEORGE
PERSONAL m, 2 children **DISCIPLINE** ENGLISH **EDUCATION** St Augustine's Col, Ireland; Ruskin Col, Eng; Univ Warwick, Eng, BA, PhD. **CAREER** Lect, Eng, Univ warwick, 76-80; vis asst prof, Vassar Coll, 80-84; asst prof, Georgetown Univ, 84-90; assoc prof, Georgetown Univ, 90-97; Prof, Georgetown Univ, 97-. **SELECTED PUBLICATIONS** The Village of Longing/Dancehall Days, Viking, 90; Dancehall Days, Blackstaff, 94; Out of Our Minds, Blackstaff, 94; co-edr, The Ireland Anthology, St. Martin's Press, 98. **CONTACT ADDRESS** Dept Eng, Georgetown Univ, Washington, DC 20057. **EMAIL** obriengl@georgetown.edu

O'BRIEN, KEVIN
PERSONAL m, 1963, 3 children **DISCIPLINE** LITERATURE STUDIES **EDUCATION** St Francis, BA, 61; Univ Notre Dame, MA, 66; PhD, 72. **CAREER** Eng Prof, Xavier Univ, 66. **RESEARCH** Biography of literary figures. **SELECTED PUBLICATIONS** Auth, Oscar Wilde 1854-1900; Robert Harborough Sherard 1861-1943; Irene Osgood 1869-1922. **CONTACT ADDRESS** St. Francis Xavier Univ, Antigonish, NS, Canada B2G 2W5. **EMAIL** kobrien@stfx.ca

O'BRIEN, SUSIE
DISCIPLINE ENGLISH LITERATURE **EDUCATION** Queen's Univ, BA, PhD; Queensland Univ, MA. **RESEARCH** Post colonial theory; Eco-criticism; Canadian literature; theory of popular culture. **CONTACT ADDRESS** English Dept, McMaster Univ, 1280 Main St W, Hamilton, ON, Canada L8S 4L9. **EMAIL** obriensu@mcmaster.ca

O'BRIEN-O'KEEFFE, KATHERINE
DISCIPLINE OLD ENGLISH LITERATURE **EDUCATION** Univ Pa, PhD. **CAREER** Prof, Univ Notre Dame. **HONORS AND AWARDS** Nat Hum Ctr fel; Distinguished Achievement Awd in Tchg, Tex A&M Univ; Guggenheim Fel. **RESEARCH** The intellectual milieu which produced the Old English Solomon and Saturn poems. **SELECTED PUBLICATIONS** Auth, Visible Song. **CONTACT ADDRESS** Dept of English, Univ of Notre Dame, 356 O'Shaughnessy Hall, Notre Dame, IN 46556. **EMAIL** Katherine.O.O'Keeffe.4@nd.edu

O'CONELL, ROBERT J.
DISCIPLINE CLASSICS **EDUCATION** Sorbonne, PhD. **CAREER** Prof emer, Fordham Univ. **SELECTED PUBLICATIONS** Auth, Augustine's Early Theory of Man, 68; St Augustine's Confessions: The Odyssey of Soul, 69; Soundings in St Augustine's Imagination, 94. **CONTACT ADDRESS** Dept of Class Lang and Lit, Fordham Univ, 113 W 60th St, New York, NY 10023.

O'CONNELL, BARRY
DISCIPLINE ENGLISH **EDUCATION** Harvard Univ, BA, 66; MA, 72; PhD, 76. **CAREER** Prof, Amherst Col. **MEMBERSHIPS** AM Antiquarian Soc. **SELECTED PUBLICATIONS** Auth, On Our Own Ground: The Complete Works of William Apess, Univ Mass Press, (A Pequot), 92. **CONTACT ADDRESS** Amherst Col, Box 2234, Amherst, MA 01002-5000. **EMAIL** boconnell@amherst.edu

O'CONNELL, MICHAEL
PERSONAL Born 11/11/1943, Seattle, WA, m, 1982, 4 children **DISCIPLINE** ENGLISH **EDUCATION** Univ San Francisco, AB, 66; Yale Univ, MA, 69; PhD, 71. **CAREER** From Asst Prof to Prof, Univ of Calif Santa Barbara, 70-; Dir, Univ of Calif Educ Abroad Prog for UK and Ireland, London, 92-94. **HONORS AND AWARDS** Woodrow Wilson Fel, 66; NEH Fel in Humanities, 73-74; Am Philos Soc Res Travel Grant, 76; Univ of Calif Res Grants, 76, 78, 80, 84, 86, 88, 93, 98; UCSB Interdisciplinary Humanities Ctr Fel, 88; UC President's Fel in the Humanities, 88; Resident Scholar, Centro Teatro Ateneo, Universita di Roma, 88; NEH Summer Fel, 91. **MEMBERSHIPS** MLA, Renaissance Soc of Am, Medieval and Renaissance Drama Soc, Societe Interationale pour l'Etude du theatre Medieveal, Spenser Soc. **RESEARCH** Renaissance Literature, Medieval and Renaissance Drama, Spenser, Shakespeare, Milton. **SELECTED PUBLICATIONS** Auth, Mirror and Veil: The Historical Dimension of Spenser's Faerie Queene, Univ of NC (Chapel Hill), 77; auth, The Elisaeis of William Alabaster, Studies in Philology, 79; auth, "The Idolatrous Eye: Iconoclasm, Anti-theatricalism, and the Image of the Elizabethan Theater," ELH 52 (85): 279-310; auth, Robert Burton, G.K. Hall (Boston), 86; auth, "Epic and Romance," in Literature and Criticism: a New Century Guide (London: Croom Helm, 90), 177-187; auth, "Milton and the Art of Italy: a Revisionist View," in Milton and Italy: Context, Images, Contradictions, ed. Mario de Cesare (SUNY Univ Press, 90), 215-236; auth, "God's Body: Incarnation, Physical Embodiment, and the Legacy of Biblical Theater in the Sixteenth Century," in Subjects on the World's Stage, ed. David Allen and Robert White (Del Univ Press, 95); auth, "The Civic Theater of Suffering: Hans Memling's Passion and Late Medieval Drama," in European Iconography East and West, Symbola et Emblemata series, ed. Gyorgy Szonyi (Leiden: E.J. Brill, 96), 22-34; auth, "Vital Cultural Practices: Shakespeare and the Mysteries," J of Medieval and Early Mod Studies 29 (99): 149-168; auth, The Idolatrous Eye: Iconoclasm and Theater in Renaissance England," Oxford Univ Press, 00. **CONTACT ADDRESS** Dept English, Univ of California, Santa Barbara, 552 Univ Rd, Santa Barbara, CA 93106-0002. **EMAIL** oconnell@humanitas.ucsb.edu

O'CONNELL, SHAUN V.
PERSONAL Born 12/29/1934, Natick, MA, m, 1958, 3 children **DISCIPLINE** ENGLISH **EDUCATION** Univ Mass, BA, 57; MA, 65; PhD, 70. **CAREER** Prof, Univ Mass Boston, 65-. **MEMBERSHIPS** MLA; ACIS. **RESEARCH** Post Civil War American literature. **SELECTED PUBLICATIONS** Auth, Imaging Boston: A Literary Landscape, Beacon Pr, 90; auth, Remarkable, Unspeakable New York: A Literary History, Beacon Pr, 95. **CONTACT ADDRESS** English Dept, Univ of Massachusetts, Boston, Boston, MA 02125. **EMAIL** shauno@mediaone.net

O'CONNOR, EUGENE
PERSONAL Born 09/03/1948, Buffalo, NY **DISCIPLINE** CLASSICS **EDUCATION** Univ Cal Santa Barbara, PhD 84. **CAREER** Prometheus Book, editor 89-; Univ Montana, vis asst prof 88-89; The Col of Wooster, vis asst prof 87-88; Univ Cal Irvine, vis lect 85-87; Univ Cal Santa Barbara, vis lectr 84-85. **HONORS AND AWARDS** BA Cum Laude **MEMBERSHIPS** APA **RESEARCH** Greek and Roman satire and epigram; neo latin; gay studies. **SELECTED PUBLICATIONS** Auth, Martial the Moral Jester: Priapic Motifs and the Restoration of Order in the Epigrams, in: Martial, ed, F. Grewing, N. Holzberg, Stuttgart: Franz Syeiner Verlag, 98; Panormita's Reply to His Critics: The Hermaphroditus and the Literary Defense, Renaissance Quart, 97; Hell's Pit and Heaven's Rose: The Typology of Female Sights and Smells in Panormita's Hermaphroditus, Medievalia et Humanistica, 96; The Essential Epicurus: Letters, Principal Doctrines, Vatican Sayings and Fragments, translated with an introduction by Eugene O'Connor, Amherst NY, Prometheus Books, 93. **CONTACT ADDRESS** Prometheus Books, Apt B30, Buffalo, NY 14201. **EMAIL** pontano@aol.com

O'CONNOR, LEO F.
PERSONAL Born 07/24/1936, Jersey City, NJ, m, 1976, 6 children **DISCIPLINE** ENGLISH, AMERICAN STUDIES **EDUCATION** St Peter's Col, BS, 58; New York Univ, MA, 62, PhD, 72. **CAREER** Instr/asst prof, NYork Inst of Technol, 62-65; asst prof, Fairfield Univ, 65-75, assoc prof and dir of Am Studies, 76-86, prof and dir of Undergrad and Grad Am Studies progs, 86-. **HONORS AND AWARDS** Founders Day Awd, New York Univ, 72; Teacher of the Year, Fairfield Univ, 82; Distinguished Fac Awd, Fairfield Univ, 86; initiated and directed the Honors Prog at Fairfield Univ; initiated and directed the Am Studies prog which was the first interdisciplinary major in the Col of Arts and Scis; initiated and directed the first grad prog (MA in Am Studies). **MEMBERSHIPS** Am Studies Prog, Asn of Lit Scholars and Critics. **RESEARCH** Religion in American literature, film and literature. **SELECTED PUBLICATIONS** Auth, Religion in the American Novel: The Search for Belief (84); major contrib to The Dictionary of Contemporary Catholic Writers (88); auth, The Protestant Sensibility in the American Novel: A Critical Guide (91). **CONTACT ADDRESS** Dept English, Fairfield Univ, 1073 N Benson Rd, Fairfield, CT 06430-5171.

O'CONNOR, MARY E.
DISCIPLINE ENGLISH LITERATURE **EDUCATION** McGill Univ, BA; Univ Toronto, MA; PhD. **RESEARCH** Feminist theory; African-American women writers; Victorian and mod Brit lit. **SELECTED PUBLICATIONS** Auth, John Davidson, 87. **CONTACT ADDRESS** English Dept, McMaster Univ, 1280 Main St W, Hamilton, ON, Canada L8S 4L9. **EMAIL** moconnor@mmaster.ca

O'CONNOR, MICHAEL P.
PERSONAL Born 04/07/1950, Lackawanna, NY, s **DISCIPLINE** LITERATURE **EDUCATION** Notre Dame, BA, 70; Univ British Columbia, MA, 72; Univ Mich, AM, 74; PhD, 75. **CAREER** Asst prof, Univ St Thomas Minn, 92-95; assoc prof, Union Theol Sem NYork City, 92-97; Catholic Univ, 97-. **RESEARCH** Ancient Semitic languages and literature. **SELECTED PUBLICATIONS** Auth, Hebrew Verse Structure, Eisenbrauns (Winona Lake, IN), 80, 2nd printing with afterword, 97; coauth, An Introduction to Biblical Hebrew Syntax, Eisenbrauns (Winona Lake, IN), 90, 6th printing 97; coed, The Word of the Lord Shall Go Forth: Essays in Honor of David Noel Freedman in Celebration of His Sixtieth Birthday, for American Schools of Oriental Research, Eisenbrauns (Winona Lake, IN), 83; coed, The Bible and Its Traditions, Mich Qtly Rev, (Ann Arbor, MI), 83; coed, Backgrounds for the Bible, Eisenbrauns (Winona Lake, IN), 87; coed, Non-fluent Aphasia in a Multilingual World, John Benjamins (Amsterdam), 95; ed, Jerome D Quinn, The Early Church: Two Studies, with a Bibliography of His Writings, Univ St Thomas (St Paul), 96. **CONTACT ADDRESS** Dept Semitic Egypt Lang Lit, Catholic Univ of America, 620 Michigan Ave NE, Washington, DC 20064-0001. **EMAIL** oconnorm@cua.edu

O'CONNOR, PATRICIA E.
DISCIPLINE ENGLISH LITERATURE **EDUCATION** Marshall Univ, BA; Georgetown Univ, MA, PhD. **CAREER** Eng Dept, Georgetown Univ **RESEARCH** Functions of story; Appalachian narratives; teaching writing; prison teaching; literacy struggles. **SELECTED PUBLICATIONS** Auth, pubs on narrative strategies, discourses of violence, and service learning; co-auth, Literacy Behind Prison Walls, 94. **CONTACT ADDRESS** English Dept, Georgetown Univ, 37th and O St, Washington, DC 20057.

O'DEA, SHANE
PERSONAL Born 07/06/1945, St. John's, NF, Canada **DISCIPLINE** ENGLISH **EDUCATION** Memorial Univ, BA, 66, MA, 74. **CAREER** Lectr, 70-75, asst prof, 75-80, assoc prof, 80-89, Prof English, Memorial Univ Nfld, 89-; Chair Bd Govs, Heritage Can. **HONORS AND AWARDS** Southcott Awd, 88; Heritage Can Comm Serv Awd, 78; Lt-Gov Awd, 90; Memorial Univ Distinguished Tchr Awd, 88; Can 125 Medal, 92. **MEMBERSHIPS** Life mem, Nfld Hist Trust, 73; vice-ch, St John's Heritage Adv Comt, 77-91; pres, Nfld Hist Soc, 81-83; ch, Heritage Found Nfld & Lab, 89-92; Gov Heritage Can, 95-. **SELECTED PUBLICATIONS** Auth, The Domestic Architecture of Old St. John's, 74; coauth, A Gift of Heritage, 75; co-ed, Ten Historic Towns, 78; co-ed, Dimensions in Canadian Architecture, 83. **CONTACT ADDRESS** Dept of English, Mem Univ of Newfoundland, Saint John's, NF, Canada A1C 5S7. **EMAIL** sodea@morgan.ucs.mun.ca

O'DELL, LESLIE
DISCIPLINE PERFORMANCE THEORY **EDUCATION** Queen's, BA; Toronto, MA, PhD. **CAREER** Assoc Prof **RESEARCH** Performance theory, Canadian theatre hist and criticissm, theatre for social change, dramatic lit, experimental theatre. **SELECTED PUBLICATIONS** Auth, Private Scenes in Public Places, or Friday Night at the Mall, 97; auth, "Garrison Theatre," in The History of Theatre in Ontario, vol. 1, ed. Ann Saddlemyer. **CONTACT ADDRESS** Dept of English, Wilfrid Laurier Univ, 75 University Ave W, Waterloo, ON, Canada N2L 3C5. **EMAIL** lodell@mach1.wlu.ca

O'DONNELL, ANNE M.
PERSONAL Born 12/03/1939, Baltimore, MD, s **DISCIPLINE** ENGLISH **EDUCATION** Trinity Col, BA, 62; Stanford Univ, MA, 63; Yale Univ, PhD, 72. **CAREER** Instr, Trinity Col, 65-67, asst prof to prof, Catholic Univ of Am, 73-. **MEMBERSHIPS** MLA; Neo-Latin Assoc; Am Assoc of Univ Women; Amici Thomae Mori; Renaissance Soc of Am; Erasmus Soc; Renaissance English Text Soc; Sixteenth Century Studies; Soc for the Study of Early Modern Women; Tyndale Soc. **RESEARCH** Erasmus, More, Tyndale. **SELECTED PUBLICATIONS** Auth, "Enchiridion Militis Christiani: An English Version", Early English Text Soc 282, Oxford Univ Pr, 81; auth, "Cicero, Gregory the Great and Thomas More: Three Dialogues of Comfort", in Miscellanea Moreana: Essays for Germain Marc'hadour, ed Clare M. Murphy, Medieval & Renaissance Texts & Studies, (Binghamton, NY, 89): 169-97; auth, "Editing the Independent Works of William Tyndale", in Editing Texts From the Age of Erasmus, ed Erika Rummel, Univ of Toronto Pr, (96): 49-70; coed, Word, Church and State: Tyndale Quincentenary Essays, Catholic Univ of Am Pr, (Washington, DC), 98; coed, An Answere Vnto Sir Thomas Mores Dialoge, Catholic Univ of Am Pr, (forthcoming). **CONTACT ADDRESS** Dept English, Catholic Univ of America, 620 Michigan Ave NE, Washington, DC 20064-0001. **EMAIL** odonnell@cua.edu

O'DONNELL, JAMES J.
PERSONAL Born 02/26/1950, Germany **DISCIPLINE** CLASSICAL STUDIES **EDUCATION** Princeton Univ, AB, 72; Yale Univ, PhD, 75. **CAREER** Lectr to prof, classics, Bryn Mawr, 75-76; Catholic Univ, 76-77; Cornell Univ, 77-81; Univ Pa, 81-; vice prov, 96-. **HONORS AND AWARDS** Guggenheim Fel; NEH Fel. **RESEARCH** Late antiquity, esp, Augustine. **SELECTED PUBLICATIONS** Auth, Cassiodorus, Univ Cal Press (Berkeley and LA), 79; auth, Boethius, Consolatio

Philosophiae: Text and Commentary, Bryn Mawr Commentaries, 84; auth, Augustine, Twayne Pub (Boston), 85; auth, Augustine, Confessions: Text and Commentary, Clarendon Press (Oxford), 92; co-ed, Scholarly Journals at the Crossroads: A Subversive Proposal for Electronic Publishing, Asn Res Libraries (Washington), 95; auth, Avatars of the Word, Harvard Univ Press (Cambridge, MA), 98. **CONTACT ADDRESS** Dept Classical Studies, Univ of Pennsylvania, 255 S 36th St, Philadelphia, PA 19104-3805. **EMAIL** jod@sas.upenn.edu

O'DONNELL, MABRY MILLER
PERSONAL Born 07/18/1945, Huntsville, AL, m, 1972, 3 children **DISCIPLINE** SPEECH COMMUNICATION, GENDER STUDIES **EDUCATION** La State Univ, BA, 67; Univ Ala, MA, 69; Bowling Green State Univ, PhD(interpersonal and public commun), 77. **CAREER** Instr to assoc prof, 69-88, Prof Speech, Mairetta Col, 88-, Forensics Coach, 69-; dir of forensics, 95-. **HONORS AND AWARDS** Outstanding Fac Awd, 88, 97; Alpha Lambda Delta Fac Awd, 89, 90; Outstanding Fac Mem in Continuing Educ, 91; Harness Fel, 92-95, 99-02; McCoy Prof, 94-98; Speech Commun Asn of Ohio's 1994 Col Teacher of the Year; William R. and Marie Adamson Flescher Prof of Humanities, 95-99; Pi Kappa Delta Coaches Hon Roll, 95, 97; E.R. Nichols Awd, Outstanding Forensics Instr in the Nation, presented by Pi Kappa Delta, 96. **MEMBERSHIPS** Nat Commun Asn; Ohio Acad of Hist; Ohio Forensic Asn; Alpha Epsilon Rho; Alpha Lambda Delta; Delta Gamma; Omicron Delta Kappa; Order of Omega; Phi Alpha Theta; Pi Kappa Delta. **RESEARCH** Frances Wright; forensics; public address. **SELECTED PUBLICATIONS** Auth, Effective Interviewing or How to Get Your Client to Tell You What You Need to Know, Proc of Small Bus Inst Dir Asn, 2/94; Interpersonal Communication, In: Ready for the Real World. **CONTACT ADDRESS** 215 5th St., Marietta, OH 45750-4025. **EMAIL** odonnelm@marietta.edu

O'DONNELL, THOMAS G.
DISCIPLINE ENGLISH **EDUCATION** Col Charleston, BA, 86; Fla State Univ, MA, PhD, 96. **CAREER** Asst prof. **RESEARCH** Contemporary theories of composition; classical rhetoric; history of rhetoric; philosophy and rhetoric. **SELECTED PUBLICATIONS** Auth, Politics and Ordinary Language: A Defense of Expressivist Rhetorics, Col Engl, 96; Putting Correctness in its Place: Justifications for Teaching and Learning Alternate Grammars in Elements of Alternate Style: Essays on Writing and Revision; Speech-Acts, Conventions, and Voice: Challenges to a Davidsonian Conception of Writing, J Advan(d) Composition, 94. **CONTACT ADDRESS** Dept of English, Loyola Univ, Chicago, 6525 N Sheridan Rd, Crown Ctr for the Humanities, Chicago, IL 60626. **EMAIL** todonne@orion.it.luc.edu

O'DONNELL, VICTORIA
PERSONAL Born 02/12/1938, Greensburg, PA, m, 1993, 2 children **DISCIPLINE** SPEECH COMMUNICATION **EDUCATION** Pa State Univ, BA 59; MA, 61; PhD, 68. **CAREER** Asst prof to prof, Dept of Commun/Pub Address, Univ of N Tex, 67-89; Dept Ch, 81-89, Dept of Commun/Pub Address, Univ of N Tex; Dept Ch, Dept of Speech Commun, Ore State Univ, 89-91; Prof, Dept of Speech Commun, Mont State Univ, 91-93; Dir, Univ Honors Prog, Mont State Univ, 93-. **HONORS AND AWARDS** Honors prof, Univ of N Tex, 76; Mortar Board Top Prof, 79, 86; Mo State Univ Alum Assoc & Bozeman Chamber of Com Excellence Awd, 97. **MEMBERSHIPS** Nat Commun Assoc; Int Commun Assoc; Western States Commun Assoc; Nat Col Honors Coun. **RESEARCH** Television criticism; propaganda & persuasion; env commun; documentary filmmaker. **SELECTED PUBLICATIONS** Auth, British Public Address, Persuasion, Random House, 82; coauth, Persuasion and Propaganda, Sage, 86, 92, 93, 99; Dir/Auth, Women, War, and Work, PBS film, (94, 99); Auth, Introduction to Public Communication, Kendall-Hunt, 92, 93; auth, Collective Memory and the End of the Cold War, The National Honors Report, 95. **CONTACT ADDRESS** Univ Honors Prog, Montana State Univ, Bozeman, PO Box 172140, Bozeman, MT 59717-2140. **EMAIL** vodonnel@montana.edu

O'GRADY, GENEVIEVE J.
PERSONAL Born 07/30/1938, Winona, MN, m, 1961, 6 children **DISCIPLINE** ENGLISH **EDUCATION** Col St Teresa, BA; Winona State Univ, MS; Walden Univ, PhD, 93. **CAREER** Director, Elementary and Secondary School, Riverhaven; Instructor, Univ Wisc, 84-. **HONORS AND AWARDS** Bush Fel. **MEMBERSHIPS** NCTE. **RESEARCH** Education, Composition. **CONTACT ADDRESS** Dept English, Univ of Wisconsin, La Crosse, 1725 State St, La Crosse, WI 54601. **EMAIL** mgogrady@rconnect.com

O'GRADY, JEAN
DISCIPLINE ENGLISH **EDUCATION** Yale Univ, MA, 65; Univ Toronto, BA, 64, PhD, 78. **CAREER** Lectr, York Univ, 65-66; lectr, Univ Toronto, 67-69; lectr, Ryerson Polytechnic, 80; postdoc fel, Collected Works of John Stuart Mill, 81-90; res assoc, Collected Works of Northrop Frye, 94-. **HONORS AND AWARDS** Gov General's Gold Medal in Eng, 64; Yale Univ Fel; Woodrow Wilson Fel; Can Coun Doctoral Awd, 78. **MEMBERSHIPS** Victorian Studs Asn Ont. **SELECTED PUBLICATIONS** Auth, Special Writer: an Annotated Bibliography of the Writings of R.E. Knowles in the Toronto Daily Star and Star Weekly, 93; auth, A Pocket Guide to the Peerage in Newsl of the Victorian Studs Asn, 88; contribur, Oxford Companion to Canadian Literature; contribur, Canadian Encyclopedia; contribur, Victorian Britain: an Encyclopedia. **CONTACT ADDRESS** Victoria Col, Univ of Toronto, 73 Queen's Park Cres, Toronto, ON, Canada M5S 1K7. **EMAIL** jean.ogrady@utoronto.ca

O'HARA, JAMES J.
DISCIPLINE AUGUSTAN POETRY **EDUCATION** Col Holy Cross, AB; Univ Mich, PhD. **CAREER** Vis asst prof, 86-87; asst prof, 87-92; assoc prof, 92-97; Professor, 97-. **HONORS AND AWARDS** Holy Cross, Nat Merit Scholar; Henry Bean four-year full-tuition Classics Sch; Philip A. Conniff Clas Prize; Valedictorian Mich: Sci & Arts First-year Fel; dept Clas Studies, Dissertatoion fel, Horace H. Rackham Predoctoral Fel. **SELECTED PUBLICATIONS** Auth, Death and the Optimistic Prophecy in Vergil's Aeneid, Princeton, 90; auth, "True Names: Vergil and the Alexandrian Tradition of Etymological Wordplay, Ann Arbor, 96. **CONTACT ADDRESS** Wesleyan Univ, Middletown, CT 06459. **EMAIL** johara@wesleyan.edu

O'HARA, MICHAEL M.
PERSONAL Born 10/10/1959, Princeton, NJ, d **DISCIPLINE** PERFORMING ARTS **EDUCATION** Fordham Univ, BA, 82; Univ Md, MA, 90, PhD, 97. **CAREER** Adj lectr, Mary Washington Col, 94; lectr, Univ Md, 95;, artist dir, Old Dominion Opry, 96; adj lectr, Univ Md, 97; consult, Theatre Resoure Productions, 94-; asst prof, Ball State Univ, 97-. **HONORS AND AWARDS** Pi Kappa Delta, 83, Honorary Forensics Fraternity; Omicron Delta Kappa, 90, Nat Honorary Leadership Fraternity; Nat 1st Place Winner, 92, NCI/ACTF; Who's Who Among Students, Am Univ Col, 92; Cert Recognition Outstanding Contrib to Students, 92, UMCP; nominee, Outstanding Teacher Year, 92, UMCP; Cert Teaching Excellence, 95, 96, UMCP; Univ excellence in Teaching Awd, Office of the Provost, BSU, 99; Outstanding Prof, Delta Rho chap of Alpha Phi, BSU, 00. **MEMBERSHIPS** Nat Commun Asn; Am Theatre in Higher Educ; Am Society Theatre Res; Am Theatre and Drama Soc; Bernard Shaw Soc. **RESEARCH** Shaw and American Theatre; theatrical pedagogy and technology. **SELECTED PUBLICATIONS** Auth, On the Rocks and the Federal Theatre Project, 92; auth, Class of 29 and the American Dream, 93; auth, Arms and the Man and Federal Theatre: Love and War in Troubled Times, 94; auth, Federal Theatre's Androcles & The Lion, 99; auth, "John Howard Lawson," Dictionary of Literary Biography: Modern Am Dramatists, Vol. 228, Christopher Wheatley, ed., Detroit: Gale Publishers, (00): 171-178. **CONTACT ADDRESS** Dept of Theatre and Dance, Ball State Univ, Muncie, IN 47306. **EMAIL** mohara@bsu.edu

O'HEARN, CAROLYN
DISCIPLINE ENGLISH LINGUISTICS AND LITERATURE **EDUCATION** Univ Mo, BS; Ariz State Univ, MA, PhD; **CAREER** Assoc prof. **RESEARCH** Medieval literature, technical writing. **SELECTED PUBLICATIONS** Auth, Writing, Grammar and Usage, 89; articles on ling and lit. **CONTACT ADDRESS** Dept of Eng, Pittsburg State Univ, 1701 S Broadway St, Pittsburg, KS 66762. **EMAIL** cohearn@pittstate.edu

O'KELL, ROBERT P.
DISCIPLINE ENGLISH LITERATURE **EDUCATION** Carleton Univ, BA; Univ Ind, MA; PhD. **CAREER** Prof **RESEARCH** Cultural studies, relation between lit and social hist. **SELECTED PUBLICATIONS** Political career of Benjamin Disraeli. **CONTACT ADDRESS** Dept of English, Univ of Manitoba, Winnipeg, MB, Canada R3T 2N2. **EMAIL** robert_okell@umanitoba.ca

O'LEARY, BRIAN EUGENE
PERSONAL Born 03/11/1942, Minneapolis, MN, s **DISCIPLINE** FILM STUDIES **EDUCATION** Univ Houston, BA, 60; Univ N Tex, MA, 94; Univ Tex Dallas, PhD, 99. **CAREER** Asst prof, Univ Penn, 99-00; lectr, Penn State Univ Erie, 00-. **MEMBERSHIPS** MLA; SCS; UFVA. **RESEARCH** Film studies. **CONTACT ADDRESS** 140 Glencoe Rd, Erie, PA 16509-5410.

O'MALLEY, SUSAN GUSHEE
PERSONAL Born 11/19/1942, Boston, MA, d, 2 children **DISCIPLINE** WOMEN'S STUDIES, ENGLISH LITERATURE **EDUCATION** Smith Col, AB, 64; Tulane Univ, MA, 65, PhD, 73. **CAREER** Asst Prof to Prof, Kingsborough Community Col, 74-. **HONORS AND AWARDS** Fulbright Scholar; Mellon Fel; CUNY Collaborative Grant; Huntington Library Fel; Folger Seminar Fel; NEH Travel Grants; NEH Summer Seminar. **MEMBERSHIPS** MLA; NCTE; Soc for the Study of Women in the Renaissance; Shakespeare Asn of Am. **RESEARCH** English early modern pamphlets on women, Women's Studies. **SELECTED PUBLICATIONS** Auth, Defences of Women: Jane Anger, Constantia munda, Ester Sowernam, Rachel Speght, The Printed Writings of Renaissance Englishwomen 1500-1640, Scolar Press, 96; A Critical Old-Spelling Edition of Thomas Goffe's The Courageous Turk 1618, Garland Pub, 79; coauth, Moving the Mountian: Women and Social Change, Femonist Press, 80; coauth, Disabled, Female, and Proud, Bergin-Garvery, 90; "Single Parent Maneuvers in Academia," in The Family Track, Univ of Ill Press, 98; "The Pamphlet Controversy about Women: Class and Gender," Attending to Women in Early Modern England, Univ of Delaware Press, 94; coauth, Politics of Education, SUNY Press, 90. **CONTACT ADDRESS** English Dept, Kingsborough Comm Col, CUNY, 2001 Oriental Blvd, Brooklyn, NY 11235. **EMAIL** gushee271@aol.com

O'MEALLY, ROBERT
DISCIPLINE AFRICAN AMERICAN LITERATURE **EDUCATION** Stanford Univ, BA, 70; Harvard Univ, PhD, 75. **CAREER** Zora Neale Hurston prof. **HONORS AND AWARDS** Co-ed, Norton Anthology of African Amer Lit. **SELECTED PUBLICATIONS** Auth, The Craft of Ralph Ellison, Harvard, 80; Seeing Jazz, Smithsonian, 97; ed, New Essays on Invisible Man Cambridge, 89; Tales of the Congaree, Univ NC, 90; The Jazz Cadence of American Culture, Columbia, 98; co-ed, History and Memory in African American Culture, Oxford, 94. **CONTACT ADDRESS** Dept of Eng, Columbia Col, New York, 2960 Broadway, New York, NY 10027-6902.

O'NEILL, JOHN H.
PERSONAL Born 12/04/1941, Madison, WI, m, 1966, 2 children **DISCIPLINE** ENGLISH **EDUCATION** Wis State Col, BS, 63; Univ Minn, MA, 68; PhD, 72. **CAREER** Instr, Univ of Minn, 64-72; asst prof to prof, Hamilton Col 72-; Leavenworth prof, Hamilton Col, 97-. **HONORS AND AWARDS** NEH Summer Stipend, 73. **MEMBERSHIPS** MLA; Am Soc for 18th Century Studies. **RESEARCH** Restoration and 18th Century English literature and culture. **SELECTED PUBLICATIONS** Auth, "Oldham's 'Sardanapalus': A Restoration Mock-Encomium and Its Topical Implications", Clio 5 (76): 193-210; auth, "Essential Studies of Restoration Libertine Court Poetry", Restoration 1 (77): 4-5; auth, "An Unpublished 'Imperfect Enjoyment' Poem", Papers on Lang and Lit 13, (77): 197-202; auth, "Rochester's 'Imperfect Enjoyment': 'The True Veine of Satyre' in Sexual Poetry", Tenn Studies in Lit 25, (80): 57-71; auth, "The Experience of Error: Ironic Entrapment in Augustan Narrative Satire", Papers on Lang and Lit 28, (82): 278-290; auth, "Edward Hyde, Heneage Finch, and the Duke of Buckingham's Commonplace Book", Mod Philogy 83, (85): 51-54; auth, George Villiers, Second Duke of Buckingham, Twayne Pub Div, G.K. Hall (Boston), 84; auth, "George Villiers, Second Duke of Buckingham", Restoration and Eighteen-Century Dramatists, ed Paula r. Backscheider, (89): 245-262, 89; coauth, "Composite Authorship: Katherine Philips and an Antimarital Satire", Papers of the Bibliog Soc of Am 87.4, (93): 487-502; auth, "Samuel Pepys: The War of Will and Pleasure" Restoration 19.2 (95): 88-94. **CONTACT ADDRESS** Dept English, Hamilton Col, New York, 198 College Hill Rd, Clinton, NY 13323-1218. **EMAIL** joneill@hamilton.edu

O'NEILL, KERILL
PERSONAL Born 06/30/1965, Dublin, Ireland **DISCIPLINE** CLASSICS **EDUCATION** Trinity Col, BA, 87; Cornell Univ, PhD, 95. **CAREER** Vis asst prof, 94-99; Colby Col. **MEMBERSHIPS** APA; CAMWS. **RESEARCH** Latin love elegy; Greek tragedy, intertextuality. **SELECTED PUBLICATIONS** Auth, "Neolithic Chipped Stone," "Excavations at Halai, 1990-1991," Hesperia 61, 92, 265-289; auth, "Propertius 4.4: Tarpeia and the Burden of Aetiology," Hermathena 158, 95, 53-60; auth, "Propertius 4.5 The Classical Journal 94.1, 98, 49-80; auth, "Aeschylus, Homer, and the Serpent at the Breast," Phoenix 52, 98, 216-229; auth, "The Shadow of Clytemnestra in Louisa Siefert's Jalousie: Maternity, Sexuality, and a Woman's Poetic Voice," Classical and Modern Literature, 99, 257-277; auth, "Ovid and Propertius: Reflexive Annotation in Amores 1.8," Mnemosyne 99, 286-307; auth, "Second Preliminary Report on Neolithic Chipped Stone Artifacts from Halai," an appendix to John E. Coleman, "Halai, 92-94" Hesperia 68.3, 99; auth, "Slumming with Vertumnus," American Journal of Philology, 00 **CONTACT ADDRESS** Dept of Classics, Colby Col, 4161 Mayflower Hill, Waterville, ME 04901. **EMAIL** knoneill@colby.edu

O'NEILL, MEGAN
DISCIPLINE RHETORIC AND COMPOSITION **EDUCATION** Eastern WA Univ, BA, 90, MA, 92; Univ NM, PhD, 96. **CAREER** Adj asst prof; dir, Compos Rhet & Compos. **SELECTED PUBLICATIONS** Auth, The Listserv in the Networked Writing Classroom: Building Community, ACE J, 1:1, 97; Bibliog essay on Helen MacInnes, Dictionary Lit Biog 96, 98; regular rev(s), Star Trek novels, TV Zone, publ in UK; rev, essays of Romanticism scholar on New Bk(s)in 19th Century Stud Rev essay of Michael Macovski's Dialogue & Lit 94, Readerly/Writerly Texts 1:2, 94; textbk rev(s) & eval for, Addison-Wesley-Longman, Mayfield, Prentice-Hall, Houghton-Mifflin & McGraw-Hill. **CONTACT ADDRESS** Dept of Eng, Creighton Univ, 2500 CA Plaza, CA 306A, Omaha, NE 68178. **EMAIL** moneill@creighton.edu

O'SHEA, EDWARD
PERSONAL Born 01/30/1943, Chicago, IL, m, 2 children **DISCIPLINE** ENGLISH LITERATURE **EDUCATION** Northwestern Univ, PhD, 75. **CAREER** Prof, SUNY Oswego, 80-. **HONORS AND AWARDS** Dir, NEH Sems, 92, 95, 98; ch, fac assbly, suny oswego. **MEMBERSHIPS** MLA; New York Yeats Soc. **RESEARCH** Modern British and Irish literature; Literary criticism and theory. **SELECTED PUBLICATIONS** Auth, Descriptive Catalogue of W.B. Yeats's Library; auth, Yeats as Editor; essays on Yeats, Shakespeare, pedagogical issues in Eng educ. **CONTACT ADDRESS** SUNY, Oswego, 207C Swetman, Oswego, NY 13126. **EMAIL** edoshea@Oswego.edu

O'SHEA, MICHAEL J.
PERSONAL Born 06/13/1955, Atlanta, GA **DISCIPLINE** ENGLISH **EDUCATION** Emory Univ, BA, 77; Univ Del, MA, 81; PhD, 84. **CAREER** Instr, Univ Del, 79-82; asst prof to assoc prof, Drexel Univ, 84-91; prof to dept chmn to ed, Newberry Col, 92-. **HONORS AND AWARDS** Univ Del Fel, 82-8; Nat Merit Scholar, 73-77; Westinghouse Scholar, 73-74; Sypherd Award, 84; Prof of Year Award, Newberry Col, 97. **MEMBERSHIPS** MLA; NCTE; ACIS; IACI; AAUP; CELJ; James Joyce Found. **RESEARCH** Literature; Irish studies; heraldry. **SELECTED PUBLICATIONS** Auth, James Joyce and Heraldry, SUNY Pr, 86; ed, Studies in Short Fiction, Newberry Col, 90; co-auth, 50 Secrets of Highly Successful Cats, Dell, 94; co-auth, Schnurrende Tyrannen, Dromer-Knaur, 96. **CONTACT ADDRESS** English Dept, Newberry Col, 2100 College St, Newberry, SC 29108. **EMAIL** moshea@newberry.edu

O'SULLIVAN, MICHAEL K.
PERSONAL Born 05/31/1950, St. Louis, MO, m, 1977, 1 child **DISCIPLINE** LIBRARY AND INFORMATION SCIENCE **EDUCATION** Univ MO, Columbia, BJ, 72; Univ Northern IA, Cedar Falls, MA (Communications Media), MA, 76; Univ IA, Iowa City, MA (Library and Information Science), 96. **CAREER** Instructional Media Coordinator, Rosemount High School, Rosemount, MN, 96-; Reference Librarian, Hanline Univ, St. Paul, MN, 97-. **HONORS AND AWARDS** Outstanding Young Man of America, 75, 85; Iowa Volunteer of the Year Awd, 94. **MEMBERSHIPS** ALA; ACRL. **RESEARCH** Information literacy; internet evaluation. **CONTACT ADDRESS** 4533 149th Ct., Apple Valley, MN 55124. **EMAIL** mosullivan@gw.hamline.edu

O'TOOLE, TESS
DISCIPLINE VICTORIAN STUDIES **EDUCATION** Harvard Col, AB, 84; Univ Chicago, MA, 86; Harvard Univ, PhD, 92. **CAREER** Vis asst prof, UCLA, 92-93; asst prof, SUNY Oneonta, 93-94; asst to assoc prof, McGill Univ, 94-. **HONORS AND AWARDS** Lars Dudek Awd for Excellence in Teaching. **RESEARCH** Family and the novel in 19th-centry Britain. **SELECTED PUBLICATIONS** Auth, Genealogy and Fiction in Hardy: Family Lineage and Narrative Lines, Macmillan, 97; auth, "Siblings and Suitors in the Narrative Architecture of The Tenant of Wildfell Hall," SEL 39.4, (99); auth," Adoption and the 'Improvement of the Estate' in Trollope and Craik," Imaging Adoption: Essays on Literature and Culture, Univ Mich Pr, (01). **CONTACT ADDRESS** Dept English, McGill Univ, 853 Sherbrooke St W, Montreal, QC, Canada H3A 2T6.

OAKES, ELISABETH
PERSONAL m, 3 children **DISCIPLINE** SHAKESPEARE AND AMERICAN WOMEN POETS **EDUCATION** Vanderbilt Univ, PhD, 91. **CAREER** Assoc prof, Western Ky Univ. **RESEARCH** Shakespeare and early modern widows; Shakespere pedagogy, women's literature. **SELECTED PUBLICATIONS** Auth, Polonius, the Man behind the Arras: A Jungian Study, New Essays on Hamlet, AMS Press, 94; Enacting Shakespeare's Language, Teaching Shakespeare Today: Practical Approaches and Productive Strategies, NCTE, 93. **CONTACT ADDRESS** Western Kentucky Univ, 1526 Big Red Way Street, Bowling Green, KY 42101.

OAKS, HAROLD RASMUS
PERSONAL Born 06/20/1936, Provo, UT, m, 1960, 5 children **DISCIPLINE** THEATRE **EDUCATION** Brigham Young Univ, BA, 60, MA, 62; Univ Minn, PhD(Speech, Theatre Arts), 64. **CAREER** Instr Speech & Theatre Arts, Univ Minn, 62-64, admin asst Off Adv Drama res, 63-64; asst prof Speech & Drama, Frostburg State Univ, 64-66; assoc prof & dir Theatre, Univ Nebraska-Kearney, 66-68; assoc prof Dramatic Arts, Colo State Univ, 68-70; prof Theatre & Media Arts, 70-; chmn, 80-93; assoc prof Dramatic Arts & coord Child Drama, Bringham Young Univ, 70-, US Off Econ Humanities & Soc Sci Develop Prog grant-in-aid, 66-68; consult Integrated Arts Prog, Provo City Schs, 76-77. **HONORS AND AWARDS** Gold Medallion of Excellence, Am Col Theatre Festival, Amoco Oil Co, 78; Presidential Citation, Am Alliance for Theatre & Ed, 93. **MEMBERSHIPS** Am Theatre Asn (treas, 72-73); Rocky Mountain Theatre Asn (pres, 70-71); US Inst Theatre Technol; Children's Theatre Asn; Int Asn Theater for Children and Youth. **RESEARCH** Theatre administration: improvisation and child drama; puppetry as a teaching tool; US & int theatre for young audiences. **SELECTED PUBLICATIONS** Auth, Theatre management and administration training in American colleges and universities, US Inst Theatre Technol, 9/67; Introduction to the Theatre, Brigham Young Univ, 71; coauth, An evening of historical vignettes, Ensign, 10/72; auth, Puppets, Patterns, and Plays, Brigham Young Univ, 76, rev, 81; Puppets as a Teaching Tool, Welfare Serv, Latter-day Saints Church, 77; Using puppets in health teaching, Health & Elem Teaching, Appendix B, 77; Mormon Montage (play), produced at Brigham Young Univ, 3 & 8/78; Outstanding Plays for Young Audiences International Bibliography, vol IV, ed, ASSITEJ/USA, Provo, Utah, Brigham Young University Press, 93; What's Happening in Theatre for Young Audiences?, TYA Today, vol 9, no 2, March, 95; Vigilance Against Violence, the Ensign, vol 27, no 8, August, 97. **CONTACT ADDRESS** Dept of Theatre & Cinematic Arts, Brigham Young Univ, 581 Hfac, Provo, UT 84602-0002. **EMAIL** harold_oaks@byu.edu

OBY, JASON B.
PERSONAL Born 08/13/1963, Baton Rouge, LA, s **DISCIPLINE** MUSIC **EDUCATION** Manhattan Sch of Music, BM, 88, MM, 90; FL St Univ, DM, 96 **CAREER** Asst prof, Ala State Univ, 91-93; asst prof, Eastern Ky Univ, 94-95; asst prof, Tex Southern Univ, 96-. **HONORS AND AWARDS** Artist-scholar, 94; Phi Kappa Phi; Univ Fel at FSU; Fels to Aspen Music Fest. **MEMBERSHIPS** Nat Asn of Teachers **SELECTED PUBLICATIONS** Auth, Equity in Operatio Casting as Perceived by African American Male Singers, Edwin Mellan Press, 98 **CONTACT ADDRESS** Dept of Fine Arts, Texas So Univ, 3100 Cleburne Ave, Houston, TX 77004. **EMAIL** jbo813@aol.com

OCZKOWICZ, EDYTA KATARZYNA
PERSONAL Born 08/30/1964, Krakow, Poland, s **DISCIPLINE** LITERATURE **EDUCATION** Albright Col, BA, 88; Lehigh Univ, MA, 90; PhD, 94. **CAREER** Asst prof to assoc prof, Salem Col, 94-. **HONORS AND AWARDS** Who's Who Am/Am Women; Sigma Tau Delta Int English Hon Soc; Teaching Fel, 91-94; Phi Beta Delta Hon Soc; Grad Asstshp; Acad Scholar; Soc Jacob Albright Scholar. **MEMBERSHIPS** MLA; NCTE; CWWSA; SSML. **RESEARCH** 20th-century ethnic literatures in the U.S.; ethnic and immigrant women writers; Anglophone Caribbean women writers; multi-cultural literature; cognition; culture; contemporary literary theory. **SELECTED PUBLICATIONS** Auth, "Jamaica Kincaid's Lucy: Cultural Translation as Creative Exploration of the Past," MELUS 21 (96); rev of, "Peasants, Princes, and Other Polish Selves: Ethnicity in America," by Thomas Gladsky, MELUS 21 (96); ed, Wladimir de Terlikowski: His Life and Art, by Bernard B. Perlman, Blue Ridge Printing (Asheville, NCar), 98; auth, "Triadic Empowerment: Invention of the Female Identity in Erna Brodber's Myal and Louisiana," MaComere 1 (98). **CONTACT ADDRESS** English Dept, Salem Col, PO Box 10548, Winston-Salem, NC 27108-0548. **EMAIL** edyta@salem.edu

ODEN, GLORIA
PERSONAL Born 10/30/1923, Yonkers, NY, m **DISCIPLINE** ENGLISH **EDUCATION** Howard Univ, BA 1944, JD 1948; NYork Univ, grad study. **CAREER** Amer Inst of Physics, editor 1961-66; Inst of Electric & Electronic Engrs, sr editor 1966-67; Appleton-Century-Crofts, supr 1967-68; Holt Rinehart & Winston, proj dir for science and language arts books 1968-71; Univ of MD Baltimore County, assistant prof, assoc prof, prof of English. **HONORS AND AWARDS** Creative Writing Fellowships John Hay Whitney Found 1955-57; Fellowship to Yaddo Saratoga Springs NY 1956; Breadloaf Writers Scholarship Middlebury College 1960; interviewed for Black Oral History Prog Fisk Univ Library 1973; Living Black American Authors 1973; Black Writers Past & Present 1975; Distinguished Black Women's Awd, Towson University, 1984; William H Hastie Symposium Awd, 1981; numerous others. **MEMBERSHIPS** PEN; The Poetry Soc of Amer; The Society for the Study of the Multi-Ethnic Literature of the United States. **CONTACT ADDRESS** English Dept, Univ of Maryland, Baltimore County, Baltimore, MD 21228.

OGASAPIAN, JOHN
PERSONAL Born 10/01/1940, Worcester, MA, m, 1967, 1 child **DISCIPLINE** MUSICOLOGY **EDUCATION** Boston Univ, B. Mus, 62, M.Mus 64, PhD, 77. **CAREER** Lowell State Col, Instr, 65-69, asst prof, 69-76; Univ of Lowell, asst prof, 76-79; Univ of MA, prof, 79; Lowell ch, acad studies dept, Col of Fine Arts, 77-80, 92-96 ed. **HONORS AND AWARDS** Organ Hist Soc, Distinguished Ser Awd, 94. **MEMBERSHIPS** Organ Hist Soc Am Musicological Soc Sonneck Soc for Am Music Am Guild of Organists. **RESEARCH** 19th-century Am organ building, organ music and urban church music. **CONTACT ADDRESS** Univ of Massachusetts, Lowell, 217 Durgin Hall, Lowell, MA 01854. **EMAIL** john_ogasapian@uml.edu

OGDEN, DUNBAR HUNT
PERSONAL Born 03/01/1935, Portsmouth, OH, m, 1957, 2 children **DISCIPLINE** DRAMATIC ART **EDUCATION** Davidson Col, AB, 55; Duke Univ, MA, 56; Yale Univ, PhD, 62. **CAREER** Instr English, Univ Md Overseas Prog, 58; instr Ger, Southern Conn State Col, 60-62; asst prof, 62-70, chmn Grad Studies, 69-79, dramatic art, 70-89, prof dramatic art, 89-, Univ Cal, Berkeley; Humanities Res Prog fel, Univ Calif, 67-68; Am Coun Learned Soc fel, 68-69; vis prof, Inst Dramatic Art, Univ Amsterdam, 74-75, 88; dramaturg, Berkeley Shakespeare Festival, 78-80; Humanities Res Prog fel, Univ Calif, 82; Assoc Prof, 89-94, Resident, Netherlands Inst for Advanced Study, 91-92; Prof Emeritus, 94-; Fulbright Prof, Univ Amsterdam, 88-89; Stage Dir, Amesterdam Schola Cantorum, 94-96. **MEMBERSHIPS** Int Fed Theatre Res; Am Theatre Asn; Am Soc Theatre Res; Theatre Lib Asoc. **RESEARCH** Classical, Medieval, and Renaissance theater and drama; German and Dutch theater and drama of the 20th century to present; Italian Baroque scene design. **SELECTED PUBLICATIONS** Auth, The Staging of Drama in the Medieval Church, Assoc Univ Press, 00; auth, The Italian Baroque Stage, 78; auth, Actor Training and Audience Response, 84; auth, Performance Dynamics and the Amsterdam Werkteater, 87; auth, Das Werkteater von Amsterdam, 93; ed The Theatre and Drama of Greece and Rome, James Butler, 72; ed, Theatre West: Image and Impact, 90; ed, The International Theatre Exhibition: Amsterdam, 1922, 92; ed, The Play of Daniel: Critical Essays, 97. **CONTACT ADDRESS** Dept of Dramatic Art, Univ of California, Berkeley, 101 Dwinelle Anx, Berkeley, CA 94720-2560.

OGDEN, JOHN T.
DISCIPLINE ENGLISH LITERATURE **EDUCATION** Princeton Univ, BA; Johns Hopkins Univ, MA; Univ Ill, PhD. **CAREER** Assoc prof, Univ of Manitoba. **RESEARCH** Poetry. **SELECTED PUBLICATIONS** Auth, pub(s) on Wordsworth, Coleridge, and 18th century aesthetic theory. **CONTACT ADDRESS** Dept of English, Univ of Manitoba, Winnipeg, MB, Canada R3T 2N2. **EMAIL** ogden@cc.umanitoba.ca

OGEDE, ODE S.
PERSONAL Born 09/16/1958, Uchenyim, Ibilla-Igede, m, 1986, 3 children **DISCIPLINE** LITERATURE **EDUCATION** Ahmadu Bello Univ, BA, 79; MA, 82; PhD, 87. **CAREER** Sr lectr, Ahmadu Bello Univ, 80-94; vis prof, Univ of Pa, 94-95; vis prof, Lincoln Univ, 95-96; prof, NC Central Univ, 96-. **HONORS AND AWARDS** Andrew Mellon post-Doctoral Fel, Univ of Pa, 94-95. **MEMBERSHIPS** MLA of Nigeria, African Lit Asn of Am, MLA of America, Nigerian Folklore Soc. **RESEARCH** African Oral Tradition, The African Novel, Modern African Poetry. **SELECTED PUBLICATIONS** Auth, Art, Society, and Performance: Igede Praise Poetry, 97; auth, Ahi Kwei Armah, Radical Iconoclast: Atting Imaginary Worlds Against the Actual, Ohio Univ Press, 00; auth, Achebe and the Politics of Representation, Africa World Press, 00. **CONTACT ADDRESS** Dept English, No Carolina Central Univ, 1801 Fayetteville St, Durham, NC 27707-3129.

OGLES, ROBERT M.
DISCIPLINE SOCIAL PSYCHOLOGICAL EFFECTS OF MASS COMMUNICATION CONTENT, HISTORY OF MASS **EDUCATION** Univ Wis, PhD, 87. **CAREER** Assoc prof, Purdue Univ. **RESEARCH** History of mass communications. **SELECTED PUBLICATIONS** Auth, Getting Research Out of the Classroom and Into the Newspaper, Col Media Rev, 91; MTV: Music Television in R.G. Picard (ed), The Cable Network Handbk, 93; coauth, Question Specificity in Studies of Television's Contributions to Viewers' Fear and Perceived Probability of Criminal Victimization", Mass Commun Rev, 93. **CONTACT ADDRESS** Dept of Commun, Purdue Univ, West Lafayette, 1080 Schleman Hall, West Lafayette, IN 47907-1080. **EMAIL** rogles@sla.purdue.edu

OHLGREN, THOMAS HAROLD
PERSONAL Born 11/08/1941, Minneapolis, MN, m, 1962, 2 children **DISCIPLINE** MEDIEVAL ENGLISH LITERATURE **EDUCATION** Univ Mich, BA, 63, MA, 65, PhD(English), 69. **CAREER** Asst prof, 69-75, asst dean interdisciplinary prog, chmn humanities, soc sci & educ, 78-82, Assoc Prof English, Purdue Univ, West Lafayette, 75-89, assoc head, 92-96; prof, 94-. **HONORS AND AWARDS** NEH Younger Humanist Fel, 73-74; NEH Travel to Collections Grant, 84; Lilly Endowment Fac Fel, 87-88; Getty Ctr for the Hist of Art and the Humanities, proj dir, 87-91. **MEMBERSHIPS** Mediaeval Acad Am; Int Robin Hood Soc. **RESEARCH** Old and Middle English language & literature; medieval iconography; medieval outlaw tales. **SELECTED PUBLICATIONS** Co-ed, The New Languages: A Rhetorical Approach to the Mass Media and Popular Culture, Englewood Cliffs, NJ: Prentice-Hall, 77; auth, Illuminated Manuscripts: An Index to Selected Bodleian Library Color Reproductions, Garland Publishing (New York & London), 77; auth, Illuminated Manuscripts and Books in the Bodleian Library: A Supplemental Index, Garland Publishing (New York & London), 78; auth, Insular and Anglo-Saxon Illuminated Manuscripts: An Iconographic Catalogue, Garland Publishing (New York & London), 86; auth, Anglo-Saxon Textual Illustration: Photographs of Sixteen Manuscripts with Descriptions and Index Medieval Institute Publications (Kalamazoo), 92; co-ed, Robin Hood and Other Outlaw Tales, Medieval Institute Publications (Kalamazoo), 97; auth, Medieval Outlaws: Ten Tales in Modern English, Stroud: Sutton Publishing, 98; **CONTACT ADDRESS** Dept of English, Purdue Univ, West Lafayette, West Lafayette, IN 47907-1968. **EMAIL** tohlgren@purdue.edu

OHLHAUSER, JON B.
PERSONAL Born 02/06/1966, Calgary, AB, Canada, m, 1991, 4 children **DISCIPLINE** COMMUNICATION **EDUCATION** Regent Univ, PhD, 97. **CAREER** Gov mem res, 90-93, Legisl Assembly of Alberta; asst prof, 96-, Atlantic Baptist Univ. **MEMBERSHIPS** Nat Commun Asn. **RESEARCH** Parlimentary debate; spirituality & commun. **SELECTED PUBLICATIONS** Auth, Human Rhetoric: Accounting for Spiritual Intervention, Howard J of Commun, 7, 96. **CONTACT ADDRESS** Dept of Arts and Scis, Atlantic Baptist Univ, PO Box 6004, Moncton, NB, Canada E1C 9L7. **EMAIL** johlhauser@abu.nb.ca

OKAFOR, DUBEM
DISCIPLINE ENGLISH **EDUCATION** Univ Nigeria, BA, 73; Univ Sussex, MA, 76; Univ Minn, PhD, 94. **CAREER** Assoc prof, State Univ NYork Rockland Col, 95; asst prof, Kutztown Univ, 95-. **RESEARCH** Literatures of the non-Western World. **SELECTED PUBLICATIONS** Auth, The Dance of Death: Nigerian History and the poetry of Chris Okigbo; auth, Garlands of Anguish. **CONTACT ADDRESS** Dept English, Kutztown Univ of Pennsylvania, Kutztown, PA 19530.

OKECHUKWU, CHINWE C.
PERSONAL Born 04/01/1958, Ouidi, Nigeria, w, 3 children **DISCIPLINE** ENGLISH **EDUCATION** Univ Nigeria, BA, 84; MA, 87; Univ Exeter, MEd, 91; Catholic Univ Am, PhD, 98. **CAREER** Prof, Montgomery Col. **HONORS AND AWARDS** For and Commonwealth Office Awd, Britain; Hornby Trust Awd, British Coun. **MEMBERSHIPS** Asn of Literary Schoars & Critics; African Lit Asn; Intl Asn for the Hist of Rhetric; Afircan Studies Asn. **CONTACT ADDRESS** Dept For Lang, Montgomery Col, Rockville, 51 Mannakee St, Rockville, MD 20850-1101. **EMAIL** cokechuk@mc.cc.md.us

OKHAMAFE, IMAFEDIA
PERSONAL s **DISCIPLINE** PHILOSOPHY,. ENGLISH **EDUCATION** Purdue Univ, PhD, Philosophy and English, 1984. **CAREER** Univ of NE at Omaha, prof of philosophy & English 1993-. **MEMBERSHIPS** Modern Language Association of America; American Philosophical Association. **SELECTED PUBLICATIONS** Articles have appeared in periodicals such as Black Scholar, Journal of the British Soc for Phenomenology, UMOJA, Intl Journal of Social Educ, Auslegung, Rsch in African Literatures, Soundings, Philosophy Today, and Africa Today. **CONTACT ADDRESS** Prof of Philosophy & English, Univ of Nebraska, Omaha, Annex 39, Omaha, NE 68182-0208.

OKKER, PATRICIA ANN
DISCIPLINE AMERICAN LITERATURE **EDUCATION** Allegheny Col, BA, 82; Univ Ga, MA, 85; Univ Ill Urbana-Champaign, PhD, 90. **CAREER** Asst prof to assoc prof, Univ Mo Columbia, 90=. **RESEARCH** 19th Century American Literature, American Periodicals, Women's Literature. **SELECTED PUBLICATIONS** Auth, Our Sister Editors: Sarah J Hole and the Tradition of Nineteenth-Century American Women Editors, (Ga), 95. **CONTACT ADDRESS** Dept English, Univ of Missouri, Columbia, 101 Tate, Columbia, MO 65211-0001.

OKOAMPA-AHOOFE, KWAME, JR
PERSONAL Born 04/08/1963, Ghana, s, 1 child **DISCIPLINE** ENGLISH, AFRICAN LITERATURE **EDUCATION** City Col, NY, BA, 90; Te,mple Univ, MA, 93, PhD, 98. **CAREER** Instr, Ind Univ, 94-95; Instr, Nassau Community Col, 97-. **HONORS AND AWARDS** Ford Found Undergrad Fel, City Col, 87-90; Nat Dean's List honoree; Best Essay Awd, Nassau Rev, SUNY-Nassau, 99. **MEMBERSHIPS** African Studies Asn, NCTE, MLA, AHSA. **RESEARCH** Anglophone and traditional African literatures, holocaust and genocide studies. **SELECTED PUBLICATIONS** Auth, "When Human Dignity is Besieged-An Afrocentric Critique of 'The Diary of Anne Frank,' " Nassau Rev, 99; reviews in the Western J of Black Studies; over 200 book revs in The NY Amsterdam News. **CONTACT ADDRESS** Dept English, Nassau Comm Col, 1 Ed Dr, Garden City, NY 11530-6719.

OLASKY, MARVIN N.
PERSONAL Born 06/12/1950, Malden, MA, m, 1976, 4 children **DISCIPLINE** JOURNALISM, HISTORY **EDUCATION** Yale Univ, BA, 71; Univ Mich, MA, 74; Univ Mich, PhD, 76. **CAREER** From Asst Prof to Prof, Univ Tex, 83-. **HONORS AND AWARDS** Progress and Freedom Sen Fel, Acton Inst. **MEMBERSHIPS** NAS, Am United for Life. **RESEARCH** Poverty-fighting, religion, Christian journalism. **SELECTED PUBLICATIONS** Auth, Prodigal Press, 88; auth, Central Ideas in the Development of American Journalism, 90; auth, The Tragedy of American Compassion, 92; auth, Abortion Rites, 92; auth, Fighting for Liberty and Virtue, 95; auth, Renewing American Compassion, 96; auth, The American Leadership Tradition, 99; auth, Compassionate Conservatism, 00. **CONTACT ADDRESS** Dept Jour & Hist, Univ of Texas, Austin, Austin, TX 78712-1013. **EMAIL** molasky@aol.com

OLBRICHT, THOMAS H.
PERSONAL Born 11/03/1929, Thayer, MO, m, 1951, 5 children **DISCIPLINE** BIBLICAL THEOLOGY, RHETORIC **EDUCATION** Northern IL, BS, 51; Univ IA, MA 53, PhD, 59; Harvard Divinity School, STB, 62. **CAREER** Chair speech, Univ Dubuque, 55-59; assoc prof speech and humanities, Pa State, 62-67; prof biblical theol, Abilene Christian Univ, 67-86; dean, Col of Liberal and Fine Arts, Abilene Christian Univ, 81-85; chair, relig div, Pepperdine Univ, 86-96; from distinguished prof relig to distinguished prof emeritus, Pepperdine Univ, 94-. **MEMBERSHIPS** Soc of Biblical lit; Nat Commun Asn; Am Academy Relig. **RESEARCH** Rhetorical analysis of scripture; history of Biblical interpretation. **SELECTED PUBLICATIONS** Co-auth, with Stanley E Porter, Rhetoric and the New Testament 1991 Heidelberg Conference, Sheffield Academic Press, 93; auth, Hearing God's Voice: My Life with Scriptures in Churches of Christ, ACU Press, 96; co-auth, with Stanley E Porter, Rhetoric, Theology and the Scriptures, Pretoria Conf, Sheffield Academic Press, 96; with Stanley E Porter, The Rhetorical Analysis of Scripture: Essays from the 1995 London Conference, Univ of Sheffield, 97. **CONTACT ADDRESS** 14 Beaver Dam Rd, South Berwick, ME 03908-1818. **EMAIL** Tolbrich@gw1.net

OLDANI, LOUIS JOSEPH
PERSONAL Born 03/01/1933, St. Louis, MO, s **DISCIPLINE** AMERICAN & ENGLISH LITERATURE **EDUCATION** St Louis Univ, AB, 57, PhL, 59, MA, 62, STB, 66; Penn, PhD(English), 72. **CAREER** From instr to asst prof, 71-77, from assoc prof to prof English, Rockhurst Col, 77-85, Lilly grant fac develop, Eli Lilly Found, 75 & 77; Mellon sr fel, Univ Kans, 79; ed, Jesuit Drama Series, Inst Jesuit Sources. **HONORS AND AWARDS** Alpha Sigma Nu Distinguished Teaching Awd, 95; AAUP, pres Rockhurst Chap. **MEMBERSHIPS** MLA; Am Lit Sec. **RESEARCH** Dreiser, descriptive and textual bibliography; the novel; Jesuit drama. **SELECTED PUBLICATIONS** Auth, Muriel Spark's delightful and savage heroes, Current Rev Catholicism, summer 64; Bibliographical description of Dreiser's The Genius, Libr Chronicle, winter 73; Dreiser and paperbacks: An unpublished letter, Dreiser Newsletter, fall 75; The lively state of Dreiser bibliography, Res Studies, 12/76; Two unpublished Pound letters: Pound's aid to Dreiser, Libr Chronicle, spring 77; Literary language and postmodern theories of semiotics, In: Semiotic Themes, Univ Kans Humanistic Studies, Vol 53, 81; ed, An introduction to the Jesuit theater & Jesuit Theater Englished, 89; Inst Jesuit Sources; Dreiser's Genius in the Making, Studies in Bibliography, 94; Jesuit Theater in Italy: A Bibliography, AHSI, 97; Jesuit Theater in Italy: Its Entrances and Exit, Italica, 99. **CONTACT ADDRESS** Dept of English, Rockhurst Col, 1100 Rockhurst Rd, Kansas City, MO 64110-2561. **EMAIL** oldani@vaxl.rockhurst.edu

OLIKER, MICHAEL A.
PERSONAL Born 01/09/1946, Philadelphia, PA, m, 1982 **DISCIPLINE** PHILOSOPHY OF EDUCATION, LIBRARY AND INFORMATION SCIENCE, ENGLISH **EDUCATION** Kutztown Univ of Pa, BA, 67; Temple Univ, EdM, 69; Univ Ill-Urbana, PhD, 76; Drexel Univ, MS, 80. **CAREER** Tchg asst, Syracuse Univ, 69-70; adj fac, Phila Commun Col, 70; vis fac, 70-71, adj fac, 83-84, Glassboro State Col; adj fac, Bloomsburg State Col, 74; tchg asst, 71-72, 73-75, adj fac, 76, Univ Ill-Urbana; vis fac, 76-77, adj fac, 80, 89-91, Loyola Univ Chicago; adj fac, 80 & 83, Temple Univ; adj fac, Ill State Univ, 84; asst prof, E Ill Univ, 95-97; adj fac, NE Ill Univ, 97-. **MEMBERSHIPS** Midwest Philos Educ Soc; Am Educ Stud Asn; Am Libr Asn; Am Philos Asn; Mod Lang Asn; Philos Educ Soc; Popular Cult Asn. **RESEARCH** Applied critical thinking to: (1) Popular culture, (2) Educational administration and policy; Douglas McGregors 'Theory Y' approach to administration; Philosophy of Plato and John Dewey; History of American educational thought. **SELECTED PUBLICATIONS** Auth On the Images of Education in Popular Film, Educ Horizons, 93; Analytical Philosophy and the Discourse of Institutional Democracy, Proceedings of the Midwest Philosophy of Education Society 1991-92, The Society, 93; Popular Film as Educational Ideology: A Framework for Critical Analysis, Proceedings of the Midwest Philosophy of Education Society 1993-94, The Society, 95; Educational Policy and Administration, 96; Censorship, in Philosophy of Education, Garland, 96; Superman, Adolescents, and the Metaphysics of Popular Culture, 97; The Language of Educational Policy and Administration, Proceedings of the Midwest Philosophy of Education Society, The Society, 97; Toward an Intellectual Understanding of Anti-Intellectual Popular Culture, Jour of Thought, 98. **CONTACT ADDRESS** 5006 W Grace St, Chicago, IL 60641. **EMAIL** moliker@sprynet.com

OLIN-AMMENTORP, JULIE
PERSONAL Born 01/07/1959, Duluth, MN, m, 1982, 2 children **DISCIPLINE** ENGLISH **EDUCATION** Middlebury Col, AB, 81; Univ Mich, PhD, 87. **CAREER** Asst prof to prof, Le Moyne Col, 88-. **HONORS AND AWARDS** Phi Beta Kappa; Scholar, Bread Loaf Writers Conf, 81; Fel, Univ of Mich, 82-83; Matteo Ricci Awd, Le Moyne Col, 99. **MEMBERSHIPS** Edith Wharton Soc; MLA. **RESEARCH** Edith Wharton, 20th Century American Literature. **SELECTED PUBLICATIONS** Auth, "Edith Wharton's Negative Hero Revisited", Edith Wharton Rev, 89; auth, "Adrienne Rich: The Limitations of Poetry", Rackham Jour of Arts and Humanities, 90; auth, "Edith Wharton, Margaret Aubyn and the Woman Novelist", Women's Studies, 20.2, 91; auth, "Wharton's View of Women in French Ways and Their Meaning:, Edith Wharton Rev, IX.2, (92):15-18; auth, "Wharton through a Kristevan Lens: The Maternality of the Gods Arrive", in Wretched Exotic: Essays on Edith Wharton in Europe, ed Katherine Joslin and Alan Price (NY: Peter Lang, 93), 295-312; auth, "A Circle of Petticoats': The Feminization of Merton Densher", Henry James Rev, 15.1 (94):38-54; auth, "Martin Boyne and the 'Warm Animal Life' of The Children", Edith Wharton Rev, 12.1 (95):15-19; auth, "Not Precisely War Stories': Edith Wharton's Short Fiction from the Great War", Studies in Am Fiction, 23.2 (95):153-172; auth, "Edith Wharton, the War, and French Churches", Lit and Belief, 18.2 (98):22-32; auth, "Female Models and Male Mentors in Wharton's Early Fiction", in Am Lit Mentors, ed Irene C. Goldman-Price and Melissa McFarland Pennell (Gainesville: Univ Pr of Fla, 99), 84-95; coauth, "Undine Spragg and the Transcendental 'I'", (forthcoming). **CONTACT ADDRESS** Dept English, Le Moyne Col, 1419 Salt Springs Rd, Syracuse, NY 13214-1399. **EMAIL** olinamme@maple.lemoyne.edu

OLIN-HITT, MICHAEL
PERSONAL Born 07/30/1964, Dayton, OH, m, 2 children **DISCIPLINE** ENGLISH **EDUCATION** Otterbein Col, BA, 86; Oh State Univ, MA, 89; PhD, 93. **CAREER** Assoc Prof, Mount Union Col, 93-. **MEMBERSHIPS** MLA; Asn Writers Programs; Virginia Woolf Soc. **RESEARCH** Native American Literature; american Literature; Virginia Woolf. **SELECTED PUBLICATIONS** Auth, "Confronting Fascism in the 'Home of Freedom': Virginia Woolf's Outsiders' Society as Foucauldian Resistance," The Virginia Woolf Miscellany, 94; auth, "Desire, Death, and Plot: The Subversive Play of Orlando," Women's Studies: An Interdisciplinary Journal, (95): 483-496; auth, "Power, Discipline, and Individuality: Subversive Characterization in Jacob's Room," in Virginia Woolf: Texts and Contexts, (Pace Univ Press, 96), 128-133; auth, "Fishing," The Georgetown Review, (97): 132-149; auth, "Saying Grace," The Nebraska Review, 00; auth, "Simple Comforts," The Nebraska Review, forthcoming. **CONTACT ADDRESS** Dept Eng, Mount Union Col, 1972 Clark Ave, Alliance, OH 44601. **EMAIL** olinhim@muc.edu

OLIPHANT, DAVE
PERSONAL Born 07/18/1939, Fort Worth, TX, m, 1967, 2 children **DISCIPLINE** ENGLISH **EDUCATION** Lamar Univ, BA, 63; Univ Tex, MA, 66; Northern Ill Univ, PhD, 75. **CAREER** Prof, Univ Tex, 76-. **MEMBERSHIPS** Tex Inst of Letters. **RESEARCH** Poetry, jazz, Latin American literature. **SELECTED PUBLICATIONS** Auth, Texas Jazz, Univ Tex Pr, 96; auth, Figures of Speech, Poems of Enrique Lihn, Translations, 99. **CONTACT ADDRESS** Dept English, Univ of Texas, Austin, Main 201, Austin, TX 78712-1013. **EMAIL** doliphant@mail.utexas.edu

OLIVER, EILEEN
DISCIPLINE ENGLISH LITERATURE **EDUCATION** Univ Tex at Austin, PhD. **CAREER** Assoc prof, Washington State Univ; assoc dean, Col od Ed, Cal St Univ San Marcos. **RESEARCH** Influence of assignment on the writing quality of nonmainstream students. **SELECTED PUBLICATIONS** Auth, Crossing the Mainstream: Multicultural Perspectives in Teaching Literature, 94. **CONTACT ADDRESS** California State Univ, San Marcos, 333 S. Twin Oaks Valley Rd., San Marcos, CA 92096. **EMAIL** eoliver@mailhost1.csusm.edu

OLIVER, ELIZABETH L.
PERSONAL Born 12/13/1951, Frankfurt, Germany, s **DISCIPLINE** ENGLISH **EDUCATION** Smith Col, BA, 73; Harvard Univ, ALM, 86; PhD, 95. **CAREER** Lecturer, Northeastern Univ, 94-96; Lecturer, Harvard Univ, 95-96; Asst Prof, La State Univ, 96-. **HONORS AND AWARDS** Nat Opera Inst Directing Grant, 77; soc activist Awd, DDR, 78; Whiting Fel Dissertation Grant, 94; Teaching Awds, Harvard Univ, 89-93; English Grad student Awd, LSU, 97; Phi Beta Kappa Awd, LSU, 99. **MEMBERSHIPS** Intl Soc of Anglo-Saxonists, Medieval Acad of Am, Linguistic Soc of am, Celtic Studies Asn of N Am, Medieval Linguistic Soc, DNRC. **RESEARCH** Early Medieval Law and Linguistics. **SELECTED PUBLICATIONS** Co-ed, Writings in Honor of Calvert Watkins, 98; ed, Selected Writings of Calvert Watkins, 95; auth, "Cyninges fedesl: The feeding of the King in Oethelbert ch.12," Anglo-Saxon England, 98; auth, "Towards freeing a slave in Germanic Law," in Writings in honor of Calvert Watkins, 98; auth, "Irish influence on early Kentish orthographic prachico," in Nowele, 98; auth, "spilled Wine and Lost resonance in Cretiens Percival," Neophilogische Mitteilwingen, 95. **CONTACT ADDRESS** Dept English, La State Univ, Baton Rouge, LA 70803-0104. **EMAIL** lolive1@unix1.sncc.lsu.edu

OLIVER, MARY BETH
DISCIPLINE COMMUNICATIONS **EDUCATION** VA Polytech Inst & State Univ, BA, 86; Univ Wis, MA, 88, PhD, 91. **CAREER** Asst Prof, Va Polytech Inst & State Univ, 91-96; assoc prof, Pa State Univ, 96-. **HONORS AND AWARDS** Second-ranked student paper, Interpersonal div, Int Comm Asn,

89; Outstanding Grad Student Tchr Awd, 90; Grad Student Tchg Excellence, 90; Top student paper, Mass Comm, Int Comm Asn, 90; Elizabeth Warner Risser fel, 90; Top Three paper in the Mass Comm Div, Speech Comm Asn, 95; Certificate Tchg Excellence Awd, Va, Tech, 95; Alumni Tchg Awd, 96; Mem, Acad Tchg Excellence, 96; Member, Acad Tchg, VA Tech, 96-; COTA Fel, 96-. **MEMBERSHIPS** Adv, 45 Undergraduates each semester; Fac dir, Supervisor, Fac Adv; Mem, VA Small Grants Comt, Scholar Comt, Comm studies search comt, Comm studies grad comt; Freshman Fac Conversation gp; Comput liaison; VA Tech; Mem, Women's hist month comt. **SELECTED PUBLICATIONS** Auth, Review On television: The violence factor, Jour Hist, 98; Rev Measuring psychol responses media], Jour Broadcasting & Electronic Media, 98. **CONTACT ADDRESS** Col of Commun, Pennsylvania State Univ, Univ Park, 210 Carnegie, University Park, PA 16802. **EMAIL** mbo@psu.edu

OLIVERA, OTTO H.
PERSONAL Born 04/20/1919, Cuba, m, 1950, 3 children **DISCIPLINE** LITERATURE, SPANISH **EDUCATION** Univ de la Habana, Doc Filo, 45; La State Univ, MA, 47; Tulane Univ, PhD, 53. **CAREER** Asst prof to assoc prof to prof, Syracuse Univ, 54-65; prof to dept chmn to emer, Tulane Univ, 65-. **MEMBERSHIPS** MLA; AAUL; AATSP; IILI. **RESEARCH** Spanish American literature; Colonial 19th-century; modernismo; literature of Spanish Antilles. **SELECTED PUBLICATIONS** Auth, Breve Historia de la Literatura Antillana, 57; auth, Cuba en su Poesia, 65; co-auth, La Prosa Mondernista en Hispano-American, 71; auth, La Literatura en Publicaciones Periodicas de Guatemala, 74; auth, La Literatura en Periodicos y Revista de Puerto Rico, 86. **CONTACT ADDRESS** 3801 St Charles Ave, Apt 203, New Orleans, LA 70115-7107.

OLMSTED, JANE
PERSONAL 3 children **DISCIPLINE** AMERICAN LITERATURE, WOMEN'S STUDIES **EDUCATION** Bowling Green State Univ, BFA; Univ Louisville, MA; Univ Minn, PhD. **CAREER** Prof **RESEARCH** Women Writers. **SELECTED PUBLICATIONS** Auth, The Pull to Memory and the Language of Place in Paule Marshall's The Chosen Place, The Timeless People, and Praisesong for the Widow, African Am Rev, 97; auth, "The Uses of Blood in Leslie Maronon Silko's 'Almanac of the Dead,'" Contemporary Literature, fall 99; auth, "Black Moves, White Ways, Every Body's Blues: Langston Hughes' The Way of White Folks," in Black Orpheus (NY: Garland, 99). **CONTACT ADDRESS** Western Kentucky Univ, 1 Big Red Way, Bowling Green, KY 42101. **EMAIL** jane.olmsted@wku.edu

OLNEY, JAMES
DISCIPLINE NARRATIVE THEORY, AUTOBIOGRAPHY, MODERN POETRY, AFRICAN LITERATURE **EDUCATION** Columbia Univ, PhD, 63. **CAREER** LSU Found Henry J. Voorhies Prof Eng, La State Univ; coed, Southern Review. **SELECTED PUBLICATIONS** Auth, Tell Me Africa, 73; ed, Behind the Scenes; or Thirty Years a Slave and Four Years in the White House by Elizabeth Keckley, 88; auth, The Rhizome and the Flower: The Perennial Philosophy-Yeats and Jung, 80; ed, Studies in Autobiography, 88; ed, T.S. Eliot: Essays from the "Southern Review," 88; auth, The Language(s) of Poetry: Walt Whitman, Emily Dickinson, Gerard Manley Hopkins, 93; auth, Memory and Narrative: The Weave of Life-Witing, 99. **CONTACT ADDRESS** Dept of Fr Grad Stud, Louisiana State Univ and A&M Col, Baton Rouge, LA 70803. **EMAIL** jolney@lsu.edu

OLSEN, ALEXANDRA
PERSONAL Born 05/01/1948, Polson, MT, m, 1967 **DISCIPLINE** ENGLISH **EDUCATION** Univ of Calif at Berkeley, BA, 70; MA, 73; PhD, 77. **CAREER** Asst prof, Univ of Colo, 78-80; from asst prof to prof, Univ of Denver, 80-. **HONORS AND AWARDS** Phi Beta Kappa; Methodist Scholar/Teacher Awd. **MEMBERSHIPS** MLA, Medieval Acad, PAMLA, RMMLA, RMMRH, ISAS. **RESEARCH** Old & Middle English, Old Norse, Hagiography. **SELECTED PUBLICATIONS** Auth, "The Rise of the Middle Class in Middle English Literature," Geardagum 17 (96): 51-57; auth, "Gender Roles," in A Beowulf Handbook, ed. Robert E. Bjork and John D. Niles (NE: Univ of Nebr, 97), 311-324; auth, "Re-Vision: A Comparison of A Canticle for Leibowitz and the Novellas Originally Published," Extrapolation 38.2 (97): 135-149; auth, "The Homiletic Tradition in Old English," Geardagum 18 (97):1-13; coauth, Poems and Prose from the Old English, Yale Univ Press, 98; auth, "Texts with Roots in Oral Tradition: Beowulf," in Teaching Oral Tradition, ed. John M. Foley (NY: The Modern Lang Asn, 98): 351-358. **CONTACT ADDRESS** Dept English, Univ of Denver, 2140 S Race St, Denver, CO 80210-4639. **EMAIL** aolsen@du.edu

OLSEN, LANCE
PERSONAL Born 10/14/1956, Englewood, NJ, m, 1981 **DISCIPLINE** FICTION, FICTION WRITING **EDUCATION** Univ Wisc, BA, 78; Univ Iowa, MFA, 80; Univ Va, MA, 82; PhD, 85. **CAREER** Instr, Univ of Iowa, 79-80; instr, Univ of Va, 81-85; asst prof to prof, Univ of Idaho, 85-. **HONORS AND AWARDS** Idaho Writer-In-Residence, 96-98; Pushcart Prize, 98; Fulbright, Finland, 00. **MEMBERSHIPS** Assoc Writing Programs; Nat Book Critics Circle. **RESEARCH** Postmodern theory and fiction, pop culture, science fiction, Vladimir Nabokov, Cyberpunk, Avant-pop. **SELECTED PUBLICATIONS** Auth, Ellipse of Uncertainty; An Introduction to Postmodern Fantasy, 87; auth, Circus of the Mind in Motion: Postmodernism and the Comic Vision, 90; auth, William Gibson, 92; auth, Lolita: A Janus Text, 95. **CONTACT ADDRESS** Dept English, Univ of Idaho, 375 S Line St, Moscow, ID 83844-0001. **EMAIL** lolsen@uidaho.edu

OLSEN, LESTER C.
PERSONAL Born 05/17/1955, Kensol, ND, s **DISCIPLINE** COMMUNICATION **EDUCATION** Moorhead State Univ, BA, 77; Pa State Univ, MA, 79; Univ Wis-Madison, PhD, 84. **CAREER** Vis asst prof, Univ of Calif, Davis, 88; asst prof, Univ of Pittsburgh, 84-90, assoc prof, 90-, Dir of Grad Studies, 91-92 and 94-96. **HONORS AND AWARDS** Phi Eta Sigma, 74; Phi Kappa Phi, 78; Donald H. Ecroyd Emerging Scholar Awd, Speech Commun Asn of Pa, 86; Karl Wallace Awd, Speech Commun Asn, 86; John Bowman Awd, Int Exchange Prog, Univ of Pittsburgh, 87; NEH Travel Grant, 87; Am Coun of Learned Socs Travel Grant, 87; Discretionary Fund Awd, Univ of Pittsburgh, 90; James A. Winans-Herbert A. Wichelns Memorial Awd, Speech Commun Asn, 92; Packard Humanities Inst Grant, 94; Chancellor's Distinguished Teacher Awd, Univ of Pittsburgh, 96. **SELECTED PUBLICATIONS** Auth, Emblems of American Community in the Revolutionary Ear: A Study in Rhetorical Iconology, Washington, DC, Smithsonian Inst Press (91); auth, "The American Colonies Portrayed as an Indian: Race and Gender in Eighteenth-Century British Caricatures," Imprint: J of the Am Hist Print Collectors Soc, 17 (92): 2-13; coauth with Trudy Bayer, "Lucretia Mott (1793-1880), Religious Reformer and Advocate of the Oppressed: A Case Study in the Rhetoric of the Women's Movement," Women Public Speakers in the United States: A Bio0-Critical Sourcebook, ed Karlyn Kohrs Campbell, Westport, Conn: Greenwood (93): 125-142; auth, "On the Margins of Rhetoric: Audre Lorde Transforming Silence into Language and Action," Quart J of Speech, 83 (97): 49-70; auth, "Liabilities of Language: Audre Lorde Reclaiming Difference," Quart J of Speech, 84 (98): 448-470; auth, "The Personal, the Political, and Others: Audre Lorde Denouncing 'The Second Sex Conference'," Philos and Rhetoric, vol 33.3 (fall 2000); auth, "A Reply to Jessica Benjamin," Philos and Rhetoric, Vol 33.3 (fall 2000); auth, Benjamin Franklin's Vision of America: Images of the Emerging Nation, 1754-1784, Univ Press (under review); auth, Informant' Privilege: Representing Sexualized Aggression (forthcoming). **CONTACT ADDRESS** Dept Commun, Univ of Pittsburgh, 1117 Cathedral of Learning, Pittsburgh, PA 15260-6299. **EMAIL** olson+@pitt.edu

OLSEN, RICHARD K.
PERSONAL Born 03/27/1964, Bristol, VA, m, 1994, 1 child **DISCIPLINE** COMMUNICATIONS **EDUCATION** Regent Univ, PhD, 98; Pa State Univ, MA, 89; Univ North Carolina at Wilmington, BA, 87. **CAREER** Asst Prof, Univ of North Carolina at Wilmington, 98-; Teaching Fellow, Regent Univ, 98-95; Instr, Radford Univ, 95-98. **HONORS AND AWARDS** Committee's Choice: Top Four Papers in Am Studies for Drafting a new Am dream: TV Logic and the 1995 NBA Draft, 96; Teacher of the Year, Radford Univ Student Government Assoc, 94; Top Communication and Avoidance Published Article, for the Effects of Interactive Video Instruction in Coping With Speech Anxiety, 94; Winner of Sony/T.H.E. Journal, Innovations in Multi Media, Education Division, 92. **MEMBERSHIPS** National Communication Assoc; Southern States Communication Assoc; Religious Speech Communication Assoc; Popular Culture Assoc of the South; Carolinas Communication Assoc. **RESEARCH** Critical Examinations of popular cultural (Historical/Rhetorical and Cultural Studies); Communication Ethics; Rhetorical Methodology; Communication Education. **SELECTED PUBLICATIONS** Auth, "The effects of interactive video instruction in coping with speech fright," by Cronin, M., Grice, G., & Olsen, R., Communication Education, 43, 94: 42-53; auth, "Making sense of the Statue of Liberty: Using the Statue of Liberty to teach research methods," by Olsen, R., The Speech Communication Teacher, 13, 4, 99: 13-13; auth, "The Role of questioning in the basic text," by Olsen, R. and Bollinger, D., Communication Education, 99. **CONTACT ADDRESS** Dept of Communication Studies, Univ of No Carolina, Wilmington, 601 South College Road, Wilmington, NC 28403-3297. **EMAIL** olsenr@uncwil.edu

OLSON, PAUL A.
PERSONAL Born 07/07/1932, Washburn, WI, w, 1952, 3 children **DISCIPLINE** ENGLISH **EDUCATION** Betlong, BA, 51; Univ Nebr, MA, 53; PhD, 57. **CAREER** Asst prof to prof, Regents Prof, Kate Foster Prof, Univ of Nebr Lincoln. **HONORS AND AWARDS** Fulbright, 53-54; Guggenheim, 62-63; Fel, Inst for Adv Studies, Edinburgh, 87, 97. **MEMBERSHIPS** MLA, Medieval Acad. **RESEARCH** Medieval literature and education, Chaucer, Shakespeare, Native American literature, educational policy. **SELECTED PUBLICATIONS** Auth, Uses of Myth: Teacher Education in the United States; auth, The Canterbury Tales and the Good Society; auth, The Struggle for the Land; auth, The Journey to Wisdom; auth, The Book of the Omaba; auth, A Few Great Pawnee Stories; auth, A Curriculum for English.auth, Human Empire, forthcoming. **CONTACT ADDRESS** 2535 A St, Lincoln, NE 68502-1840. **EMAIL** polson@unlserve.unl.edu

OLSON, STEVEN
PERSONAL Born 09/07/1950, Morris, MN, m, 1972, 2 children **DISCIPLINE** ENGLISH **EDUCATION** Moorhead State Col, BA, 72; Univ of Tex El Paso, MA, 78; Univ of Ill Urbana-Champaign, PhD, 86. **CAREER** Asst prof of English, Northern Montana Col, 86-89; prof of English, Central Wash Univ, 89-. **RESEARCH** 19th Century American literature; William Faulkner. **SELECTED PUBLICATIONS** Auth, The Prairie in Nineteenth-Century American Poetry, Univ of Ok Press, 94; Now the wild prairie to the view Appears': Nineteenth-century Ill Poets of the Prairies, Western Ill Regional Studies, 88; A Perverted Poetics: Bryant's and Emerson's Concern for a Developing American Literature, Am Transcendental Quart, 86; William Cullen Bryant's View of Prairie America's Conflicting Values, NDak Quart, 85; Coming Home, SDak Rev, 82; several entries in The Walt Whitman Encyclopedia, forthcoming. **CONTACT ADDRESS** English Dept, Central Washington Univ, 400 E 8th Ave, Ellensburg, WA 98926-7558. **EMAIL** olsons@cwu.edu

OMANCHONU, JOHN
PERSONAL Born 12/28/1949, Kano, Nigeria, m, 1976, 4 children **DISCIPLINE** MASS COMMUNICATIONS **EDUCATION** Diploma in Broadcasting Conn School Broadcasting, 76; Howard Univ, MA, 85; PhD, 90; BS, 91. **CAREER** Asst prof, Bethune-Cookman Col, 91-93; consult, ARI, 92-93; asst prof, Fla A&M Univ, 93-96; Chair, asst prof, Fort Valley State Univ, 96-. **HONORS AND AWARDS** Freedom Forum Found Fel, 92, 97; Fel, Poynter Inst, 92; Who's Who in Commun, 98-99; Hoover Pres Res, 97-98. **MEMBERSHIPS** ICA; AEJMC; BCCA. **RESEARCH** Global communications, communications ethics, technology, history and regulations. **SELECTED PUBLICATIONS** Auth, "Media Management in the Age of Convergence: A theoretical synthesis", Feedback 36.1 (95): 24-27; auth, WFVS AM 530 Radio Policy and Training Manual, 97. **CONTACT ADDRESS** Dept Mass Commun, Fort Valley State Univ, 1005 State University Dr, Fort Valley, GA 31030-4313. **EMAIL** omachonj@mail.fvsu.edu

OMOSUPE, EKUA RASHIDA
PERSONAL Born 08/29/1951, Yazoo, MI, m, 1999, 3 children **DISCIPLINE** ENGLISH, WOMEN'S STUDIES **EDUCATION** Univ Colo Colorado Springs, BA, 85; Univ Calif Santa Cruz, MA, 89; PhD, 97. **CAREER** prof, Cabriello Col, 92-. **HONORS AND AWARDS** Cert of Honor, Univ of Calif, Santa Cruz, 97; Who's Who Among am Col Teachers, 98; Santa Cruz County Ethnic Arts Awd, 00; Teacher, Friend, Mentor Awd, Aptos, CA, 00. **MEMBERSHIPS** MLA, Santa Clara Alliance of Black Educators. **RESEARCH** Gay and Lesbian Studies, Cultural Studies, Gender Studies, African American Literature. **SELECTED PUBLICATIONS** Auth, "Differences," Jour of Feminist cult Studies 3.2, (Providence, RI: Brown, 91; auth, From Wedded Wife to Lesbian Lives, Spinsters Aunt Lute Books, (Oakland, CA), 95; auth, Legacy, 97; auth, Quarry West, Collected Poetry Publ, Univ of Calif Santa Cruz, 97. **CONTACT ADDRESS** 21 San Tomas Way, Watsonville, CA 95076. **EMAIL** makua@cruzio.com

ONG, RORY J.
DISCIPLINE ASIAN AMERICAN LITERATURE, RHETORIC AND COMPOSITION **EDUCATION** Miami, PhD. **CAREER** Asst prof, Washington State Univ. **RESEARCH** Ethnic studies, cultural studies, discourse theory. **CONTACT ADDRESS** Dept of English, Washington State Univ, 1 SE Stadium Way, PO Box 645020, Pullman, WA 99164-5020. **EMAIL** rjong@wsuvm1.csc.wsu.edu

ONWUEME, TESS O.
PERSONAL Born 08/09/1955, Ogwashi-Uku, Nigeria, m, 1998, 5 children **DISCIPLINE** ENGLISH **EDUCATION** Univ Ife, BA, 79; MA, 82; Univ Benin, PhD, 87. **CAREER** Assoc Prof, Imo St Univ, 87-89; Assoc Prof, Wayne St Univ, 89; Assoc Prof, Montclair St Univ, 90-93; Vis Prof, Vassar Col, 92-93; Prof, Univ Wis, 94-. **HONORS AND AWARDS** Excellence and Role Model Awd, 93; Nigerian Eagle Awd, 93; Achiever's Awd in Lit, 94; Awd of Excellence, Univ Wis, 95; Drama Prize, Asn of Nigerian Authors, Wayne St Univ, 95; Distinguished Writer-in-Residence Awd, S Ill Univ, 96. **MEMBERSHIPS** PEN, WPI, OWWA. **RESEARCH** Cultural studies, global women studies, African women studies, African drama, culture and folklore/folkways. **SELECTED PUBLICATIONS** Auth, Go Tell It To Women, 1st Ed, Heinemann Educ Books (Ibadan), 92; auth, Three Plays: An Anthology of Three Plays by Tess Onwueme, Wayne St UP (Detroit, MI), 93; auth, Riot in Heaven, Africana Legacy Pr (New York), 96; auth, The Missing Face, Africana Legacy Pr (New York), 97; auth, Tell It To Women, Rev Ed, Wayne St UP (Detroit, MI), 97. **CONTACT ADDRESS** Dept English, Univ of Wisconsin, Eau Claire, PO Box 4004, Eau Claire, WI 54702-4004. **EMAIL** onwuemto@uwec.edu

ONWUMECHILI, CHUKWUKA
PERSONAL Born 07/14/1960, Nigeria, m, 1997, 2 children **DISCIPLINE** COMMUNICATIONS **EDUCATION** Northwestern Univ, MSA, 85; Howard Univ, PhD, 90. **CAREER** Asst prof, Bowie State Univ, 90-92; Grad Prof Coordinator, Bowie State Univ, 92-. **HONORS AND AWARDS** Top GPA Awd, Howard Univ, 90. **MEMBERSHIPS** ICA; ECA; NCA; ACCE. **RESEARCH** Telcom Policy, International Comm, Dev Comm, Intercul Comm. **SELECTED PUBLICATIONS** Auth, "Organizations: New directions for dev comm", Africa Media Review 9.1 (95):53-69; coed, Commun and Transformation of Society, UPA, 95; auth, "Privatization of the electronic media in Nigeria", Howard Jour of Commun 7.4 (96):365-372; auth, "Org Cul in Nigeria", Commun Res Reports 13.2 (96):239-249; auth, African Democratization and Military Coups, Praeger, 98. **CONTACT ADDRESS** Dept Communications, Bowie State Univ, 14000 Jericho Park Rd, Bowie, MD 20715-3319. **EMAIL** conwumechili@bowiestate.edu

ONYSHKEVYCH, LARISSA M. L. Z.
PERSONAL Born Stryi, Ukraine, m, 1961, 3 children **DISCIPLINE** DRAMA & LITERATURE **EDUCATION** Univ Toronto, BA, 62; Univ Pa, MA, 66; PhD, 73. **CAREER** Vis lectr, Rutgers Univ, 74-78, 90; acad res, Princeton, 81-82; literary ed, Suchastinst Monthly, 83-85, 88-94; director, PRF, 87-97; prof, Lviv Univ, Ukraine, 97-98; pres, Shevchenko Sci Soc, 00-. **HONORS AND AWARDS** NDEA IV; Fel, Univ of Pa; NJ Comm for the Humanities; IREX Travel Grant; IREX Joint Project Grant; Fulbright Grant; ACLS Grant. **MEMBERSHIPS** MLA, AAASS, Am Assoc Ukranian Studies, Am Assoc Teachers Slavic and E Europ, Shevchenko Sci Soc. **RESEARCH** Contemporary Ukranian Drama, Postmodernist Drama and Literature, Literary Translations. **SELECTED PUBLICATIONS** Auth, ""Echoes of Glasnost: Chornobyl in Soviet Ukrainian Literature," Echoes of Glasnost in Soviet Ukraine, ed Romana M. Bahry; auth, "Ingenuity versus Modernization: Kulish and Kostetzky," Slavic Drama: The Question of Innovation, ed Andrew Donslov; auth, "Ukrainian Theater," Ethnic Theater in America, ed M Schwartz Seller, (83); coed, The Worlds of Taras Shevchenko, NY, v.1 (91), v.II, (01); auth, "Ukrainian Poetry," Shifting Borders: East European Poetries of the Eighties, ed W Cummings, (93); ed, Borys Antonenko-Davydovych: Knight of Non-Absurdist Ideas: Reminiscences, Letters and a Play, 94; auth, "An Anthology of Literary Critical Thought of the 20th Century," ed M Zubrytska and J Fizer, (96); ed, Essays on Ukrainian Orthography and Language, 97; auth, The Twins Shall Meet Again: An Anthology of Ukrainian Drama in the Diaspora, 97; ed, Modern Ukrainian Drama: An Anthology, v.1, 98. **CONTACT ADDRESS** 9 Dogwood Dr, Lawrenceville, NJ 08648-3259. **EMAIL** larissa@onyshkievych.com

OPPENHEIMER, PAUL
PERSONAL Born 05/01/1939, New York, NY, d, 2 children **DISCIPLINE** ENGLISH **EDUCATION** Princeton Univ, BA, 61; Columbia Univ, MA, 63; PhD, 70. **CAREER** Prof, CUNY City Col. **HONORS AND AWARDS** Woodrow Wilson Fel, 61-62; Alfred Hodder Fel, 69-70; Fulbright Sr Scholar, 93-94; Eisner Awd, 98Phi Beta Kappa. **MEMBERSHIPS** Dante Soc of Am. **RESEARCH** Comparative medieval literature, Baroque art, German literature and politics, history of science, modern poetry. **SELECTED PUBLICATIONS** Auth, Before a Battle and Other Poems, Harcourt, Brace, 67; auth, A Pleasant Vintage of Till Eulenspiegel, Wesleyan Univ Pr, 72; auth, Beyond the Furies, Editions Faust, (Paris/NY), 85; auth, The Birth of the Modern Mind: Self, Consciousness, and the Invention of the Sonnet, Oxford Univ Pr, 89; auth, Till Eulenspiegel: His Adventures, Garland 91; auth, Evil and the Demonic: A New Theory of Monstrous Behavior, NY Univ Pr, 96; auth, An Intelligent Person's Guide to Modern Guilt, Duckworth, 97; auth, Rubens, A Portrait: Beauty and the Angelic, Duckworth, Nov, 99; auth, Rilke, Freud, Einstein and the Orpheus Mystery, Ger Inst, (forthcoming). **CONTACT ADDRESS** Dept English, City Col, CUNY, 160 Convent Ave, New York, NY 10031-9101.

ORAVEC, CHRISTINE
DISCIPLINE COMMUNICATIONS **EDUCATION** Lawrence, BA, 71; Univ Wis at Madison, MA, 72, PhD, 79. **CAREER** Asst prof, to PROF, DEPT COMM, UNIV UTAH **MEMBERSHIPS** Am Antiquarian Soc **SELECTED PUBLICATIONS** Auth, "Conservatism vs. Preservationism in the Controversy over the Hetch Hetchy Dam," Quart Jour of Speech 70, 84; auth, "The Democratic Critics: An Alternative American Rhetorical Tradition of the Nineteenth Century," Rhetorica 4, 86; auth, "William Leggett: A Benthamite Rhetorical Critic," in Visions of Rhetoric: History, Theory, and Criticism, Rhetoric Soc Am, 87; coauth, "A Prairie Home Companion and the Fabrication of Community," CSMC 4, 87, repr in Rhetorical Dimensions in Media: A Critical Casebook, Kendall Hunt, 91; auth, "The Sublimation of Mass Consciousness in the Rhetorical Criticism of Jacksonian America," Comm 11, 90; auth, "To Stand Outside of Oneself: The Sublime in the Discourse of Natural Scenery," in The Symbolic Earth: Discourse and Our Creation of the Environment, Univ Press Ky, 96. **CONTACT ADDRESS** Dept of Comm, Univ of Utah, Salt Lake City, UT 84112. **EMAIL** c.oravec@m.cc.utah.edu

ORCHARD, LEE F.
DISCIPLINE THEATRE ARTS **EDUCATION** Concordia Univ, BA, BE; Northwestern Univ, MA; Univ OR, PhD. **CAREER** Act pedag;assoc prof, 91-, Truman State Univ. **HONORS AND AWARDS** Adjudicator, Am Col Theatre Fest, 88. **RESEARCH** Performance pedag, directing, theatre and cult, musical theatre. **SELECTED PUBLICATIONS** Auth, Acting: Onstage and Off **CONTACT ADDRESS** Theatre Dept, Truman State Univ, 100 E Normal St, Kirksville, MO 63501-4221.

ORDOWER, HENRY M.
PERSONAL Born Chicago, IL, 3 children **DISCIPLINE** TAXATION LAW, MEDIEVAL LITERATURE **EDUCATION** Washington Univ, St Louis, AB, 67; Univ Chicago, MA, 70, JD, 75. **CAREER** Instr law, Univ Chicago Law Sch, 75-76; assoc atty, Sonnenschein, Calin, Nath & Rosenthal, 75-77; asst prof, 77-80, assoc prof Law, St Louis Univ Law Sch, 80-83. **MEMBERSHIPS** Soc Advan Scand Studies. **RESEARCH** United States taxation of income, estates and gifts; the Icelandic family saga. **SELECTED PUBLICATIONS** Art, Separating Statutory Frameworks: Incompatibility of the Complete Liquidation & Reorganization Provisions of the Internal Revenue Code, St Louis Univ Law J, 81; auth, Tax Act Offers New Choices: Planning the Large Estate, Trusts & Estates, 82. **CONTACT ADDRESS** Law School, Saint Louis Univ, 3700 Lindell Blvd, Saint Louis, MO 63108-3412. **EMAIL** ordoweh@slu.edu

OREL, HAROLD
PERSONAL Born 03/31/1926, Boston, MA, m, 1951, 2 children **DISCIPLINE** ENGLISH LANGUAGE AND LIT **EDUCATION** UNH, BA, 48; Univ Mich, MA, 49, PhD, 52. **CAREER** Instr, Univ MD, Col Pk, 52-56; Info Spec, GE, Evendale OH, 56-57; Assoc prof, Univ Kansas, 57-62, prof, 63-74, dist prof, 74-. **HONORS AND AWARDS** Orator Poets Corner Westminster Abbey, 78, 86; Am Comm on Irish Stud, Pres, 70-72; Thomas Hardy Soc, Eng, VP, 68-; Royal Soc Lit, Eng, fel, 86-; Higuchi Res Achmt Awd, 90. **RESEARCH** 19th and 20th C, Brit and Am Lit. **SELECTED PUBLICATIONS** The Brontes: Interviews and Recollections, ed, London, Macmillan, Iowa, Univ Iowa press, 97; The Historical Novel from Scott to Sabatini, London, Macmillan, 95; Critical Essays on Thomas Hardy's Poetry, ed, NY, G K Hall, 95; Critical Essays on Sir Arthur Conan Doyle, NY, G K Hall, 92; numerous other books and articles. **CONTACT ADDRESS** Dept English, Univ of Kansas, Lawrence, Lawrence, KS 66045-2115.

ORIARD, MICHAEL
PERSONAL Born 05/26/1948, Spokane, WA, m, 1971, 2 children **DISCIPLINE** AMERICAN LITERATURE **EDUCATION** Univ Notre Dame, BA, 70; Stanford Univ, PhD, 76. **CAREER** Engl, Oregon St Univ. **HONORS AND AWARDS** Phi Beta Kappa, 70; Danforth Fellowship, 70; NEH fellowships, (1984-85, 1998-99), named Distinguished Professor, 98. **MEMBERSHIPS** Am Studies Assoc, North Am Society for Sport; History; Sport Lit Assoc **RESEARCH** Am sport and sport lit; Am lit and culture **SELECTED PUBLICATIONS** Auth, Dreaming of Heroes: American Sports Fiction, 1868-1980, Nelson-Hall, 82; The End of Autumn: Reflections on My Life in Football, Doubleday, 82; Sporting With the Gods: The Rhetoric of Play and Game in American Culture, Cambridge Univ Press, 91; Reading Football: How the Popular Press Created an American Spectacle, Univ N Carolina Press, 93; auth, King Football: Sport and Spectacle in the Golden Age of Radio and Newsreels, Movies and Magazines, the Weekly and the Daily Press, University of North Carolina Press, 01. **CONTACT ADDRESS** Dept of English, Oregon State Univ, Corvallis, OR 97331. **EMAIL** moriard@orst.edu

ORLIK, PETER B.
PERSONAL Born 09/30/1944, Hancock, MI, m, 1967, 2 children **DISCIPLINE** MASS COMMUNICATION **EDUCATION** Wayne St Univ, BA, 65, MA, 66, PhD, 68. **CAREER** Instr, Wayne St Univ, 66-69; founder, prog head to prior learning coordr to chair, Broadcast and Cinematic Arts, Cent Mich Univ, 69- . **HONORS AND AWARDS** Bd of gov Scholar, Wayne St Univ, 62-65; Wayne St Univ Symphony Orchestra Scholar, 62-65; Acad Excellence Awd, Wayne St Univ, 65; Univ Achievement Awd, Cent Mich Univ, 74; Outstanding Young Men of Amer, 79; Who's Who, 80-99; Outstanding People of the Twentieth Century, 99. **MEMBERSHIPS** Alpha Epsilon Rho/Nat Broadcasting Soc; Assoc for Educ in J & Mass Commun; Broadcast Educ Assoc; Nat Assoc of Television Prog Exec; Phi Kappa Phi Honor Soc. **RESEARCH** Media writing; criticism; hist & prog. **SELECTED PUBLICATIONS** Auth, Mass Media Description and Performance, National Textbook, 79; auth, Critiquing Radio and Television Content, Allyn & Bacon, 88; auth, The Electronic Media: An Introduction to the Profession, Allyn & Bacon, 92, Iowa St Univ Press, 97; Broadcast/Cable Copywriting, Allyn & Bacon, 78, 82, 86, 90, 94, 98; Electronic Media Criticism: Applied Perspectives, Focal Press, 94, 2nd ed, Lawrence Erlbaum, 00; Two Hockey Inaugurals: A Ritual comparison of Senators and Ducks, Mid-Atlantic Almanack, 96. **CONTACT ADDRESS** 613 Kane St, Mount Pleasant, MI 48858. **EMAIL** Peter.B.Orlik@cmich.edu

ORMAND, KIRK
PERSONAL Born 11/05/1962, Traverse City, MI, m, 1989, 2 children **DISCIPLINE** CLASSICAL STUDIES **EDUCATION** Stanford Univ, PhD, 92. **CAREER** Vis Asst Prof, Oberlin Col, 92-93; Asst Prof, Loyola Univ Chicago, 93-97. **HONORS AND AWARDS** John J. Winkler Memorial Prize, 91; Gildersleeve Prize, Am J Philol, 96; Solmsen Fel, Inst Res Humanities, 98-99. **MEMBERSHIPS** Am Philol Asn; Women's Classical Caucus; Lesbian Gay and Bisexual Classical Caucus. **RESEARCH** Ancient Greek literature and culture; modern critical theory. **SELECTED PUBLICATIONS** Auth, Trachiniae 1055ff: More Wedding Imagery, Mnemosyne 67, 93; Lucan's auctor vix fidelis, Classical Antiquity, 94; Silent by Convention? Sophocles' Tekmessa, AJP, 96; Exchange and the Maiden: Marriage in Sophoclean Tragedy, Univ Tex Press (forthcoming 99). **CONTACT ADDRESS** 2 Haverhill Circle, Madison, WI 53717. **EMAIL** kormand@facstaff.wisc.edu

OROZCO, S. LUZ MARIA
PERSONAL Born 11/03/1933, Mexico City, Mexico, s **DISCIPLINE** LITERATURE **EDUCATION** Marycrest Col, BA, 56; Marquette Univ, MA, 58; Univ Minn, PhD, 73. **CAREER** Assoc prof to prof to chmn, Marycrest Col, 60-; vis prof, St Gerome, 79; vis prof, Yale Univ, 86-89. **HONORS AND AWARDS** Danforth Grant, 67-69; Fulbright Fel, 70-72; Excellence Teaching Awd, 90. **MEMBERSHIPS** MLA. **RESEARCH** 18th-century (Pope, Swift, Novel); Chaucer; Middle Ages; Shakespeare. **SELECTED PUBLICATIONS** Author for 41 yrs of articles, in journals and mags. **CONTACT ADDRESS** Humanities Dept, Marycrest Intl Univ, Davenport, IA 52804. **EMAIL** lmorozco@ad.com

ORR, LEONARD
DISCIPLINE ENGLISH **EDUCATION** Ohio State Univ, PhD. **CAREER** Coord, Liberal Arts, prof, english, Wash State Univ. **MEMBERSHIPS** MLA, Am Comp Lit Asn, Asn for the Study of Lit and the Environ. **RESEARCH** Modern British and American literature, narrative theory, psychoanalytic criticism, history of criticism, representations of the Holocaust. **SELECTED PUBLICATIONS** Auth, Problems and Poetics of the Nonaristotelian Novel; Yeats and Postmodernism; The Dictionary of Critical Theory, 91 & Critical Essays on Samuel Taylor Coleridge, 92; auth, A Joseph Conrad Companion, 99. **CONTACT ADDRESS** Dept of English, Washington State Univ, 2710 Univ Dr, Richland, WA 99352-1671. **EMAIL** orr@beta.tricity.wsu.edu

ORR, MARILYN
DISCIPLINE ENGLISH LITERATURE **EDUCATION** Univ Ottawa, PhD. **RESEARCH** Early nineteenth century British novel; women's writing. **SELECTED PUBLICATIONS** Auth, Almost Under the Immediate Eye: Framing Displacement, 93; auth, The Return of the Different: Rereading in Scott and Calvino, Dalhousie Rev, 92; auth, Real and Narrative Time: Waverley and the Education of Memory, 91; auth, Repetition, Reversal, and the Gothic: The Pirate and St. Ronan's Well, 90. **CONTACT ADDRESS** English Dept, Laurentian Univ, 935 Ramsey Lake Rd, Sudbury, ON, Canada P3E 2C6. **EMAIL** morr@nickel.laurentian.ca

ORR, N. LEE
DISCIPLINE MUSIC HISTORY AND LITERATURE **EDUCATION** Univ NC, Chapel Hill, PhD. **CAREER** Prof, Ga State Univ; ed bd, th-Century Stud J; ed bd, Organ Hist Soc Press. **RESEARCH** American church music of the 19th century. **SELECTED PUBLICATIONS** Auth, Church Music Handbook, Abingdon Press, 91; Alfredo Barili and the Rise of Classical Music in Atlanta, Scholars Press-Emory Univ, 96; coed, the stage works of John Hill Hewitt, Garland Press. **CONTACT ADDRESS** Georgia State Univ, Atlanta, GA 30303.

ORTIZ, RICARDO
DISCIPLINE ENGLISH LITERATURE **EDUCATION** UCLA, PhD, 92. **CAREER** Asst prof, Dartmouth Col. **RESEARCH** Lit theory and criticism. **SELECTED PUBLICATIONS** Auth, John Rechy and the Grammar of Ostentation in Cruising the Performative: Interventions into the Representation of Ethnicity, Nationality, and Sexuality, Ind UP, 95; Rechy, Isherwood and the Numbers Game in El Poder Hispano: Actas del V Congreso de Culturas Hispanas de los Estados Unidos, Servisio de Publicaciones y Centro de Estudios Norteamericanos de la Universidad de Alcala, 94; Fielding's 'Orientalist' Moment: Historical Fiction and Historical Knowledge in Tom Jones, Studies Eng Lit 1500-00, 93. **CONTACT ADDRESS** Dept English, Georgetown Univ, PO Box 571131, Washington, DC 20057-1131.

ORVELL, MILES
PERSONAL Born 01/09/1944, New York, NY, m, 1987, 2 children **DISCIPLINE** AMERICAN LITERATURE, AMERICAN STUDIES **EDUCATION** Columbia Univ, BA, 64; Harvard Univ, MA, 65; PhD, 70. **CAREER** Prof, Temple Univ, 69-; dir of Am Studies, Temple Univ, 75-80; vis prof, Univ Pa, 86-87; Fulbright Prof in Am Studies, Univ Copenhagen, 88. **HONORS AND AWARDS** Woodrow Wilson Fac Development Grant, 82; Reva and David Logan Grant, 85; Fulbright

Awd, Univ Coppenhagen, 88; John Hope Franklin Publication Prize, Am Studies Asn, 90; NEH Summer Sem Dir, 91, 93, 94, 95, & 99. **MEMBERSHIPS** Am Studies Asn. **RESEARCH** American Cultural Studies, American Literature, Photography, Visual Studies. **SELECTED PUBLICATIONS** Auth, Invisible Parade: The Fiction of Flannery O'Connor, Temple Univ Press, 72 (reprinted at Flannery O'Connor: An Introduction, Univ Press Miss, 91); auth, The Real Thing: Imitation and Authenticity in American Culture, 1880-1940, Univ NC Press, 89; auth, After the Machine: Visual Arts and the Erasing of Cultural Boundaries, Univ Press of Miss, 95; co-ed, Inventing America: Readings in Identity and Culture, St. Martin's Press, 95. **CONTACT ADDRESS** Dept English, Temple Univ, Philadelphia, PA 19122. **EMAIL** orvell@astro.ocis.temple.edu

OSBERG, RICHARD H.
PERSONAL Born 01/25/1947, Boston, MA, m, 1969, 1 child **DISCIPLINE** ENGLISH, MEDIEVAL STUDIES **EDUCATION** Dartmouth Col, BA, 69; Claremont Grad Sch, MA, 70; PhD, 74. **CAREER** Asst Prof, Barat Col, 75-78; Asst Prof, Hamilton Col, 78-82; From Asst Prof to Prof, Santa Clara Univ, 82-. **HONORS AND AWARDS** NEH Fel, 82. **MEMBERSHIPS** MLA, MAP, MAA. **RESEARCH** Chaucer, alliterative poetry, Medievalism. **SELECTED PUBLICATIONS** Auth, "Pages Torn From the Book: Narrative Disintegration in Terry Gilliam's 'The Fisher King'," Studies in Medievalism 8 (95): 194-224; auth, "A Voice for the Prioress: The Context of English Devotional Prose," Studies in the Age of Chaucer 18 (96): 25-54; auth, "The Prosody of Middle English 'Pearl' and the Alliterative Lyric Tradition," in English Hist Metrics (Cambridge: Cambridge Univ Pr, 96), 150-174; auth, "The Maimed King, the Wasteland, and the Vanished Grail in Iris Murdoch's 'The Green Knight'," in The Year's Work in Medievalism X (Holland, MI: 98), 21-32; auth, "Humanist Allusions and Medieval Themes: The 'Receyving' of Queen Anne, London 1533," in Medievalism in the Mod World: Essays in Hon of Leslie Workman (Brepols: Turnhout, 98), 27-41; auth, "Rewriting Romance: From 'Sir Gawain' to 'The Green Knight'," in The Future of the Middle Ages and the Renaissance: Problems, Trends and Opportunities for Research (Brepols: Turnhout, 98), 93-108; coauth, "Language Then and Language Now in Arthurian Film," in King Arthur on Film: New Essays on Arthurian Cinema (Jefferson, NC: McFarland & Co, 99), 39-66. **CONTACT ADDRESS** Dept English, Santa Clara Univ, 500 El Camino Real, St Joseph's 223, Santa Clara, CA 95053-0001. **EMAIL** rosberg@scu.edu

OSBORNE, CAROL D.
PERSONAL Born 07/25/1955, Greensboro, NC **DISCIPLINE** ENGLISH **EDUCATION** Univ NCar Chapel Hill, BA, 76; MAT, 78; Univ Va, MA, 90; PhD, 98. **CAREER** Asst prof, Murray State Univ, 98-. **HONORS AND AWARDS** Scholar-in-Residence, Univ Va, 89; Teaching Awd, Univ Va, 97. **MEMBERSHIPS** MLA, PCA, NCTE, AAUW. **RESEARCH** Contemporary Literature and Popular Culture, English Education. **SELECTED PUBLICATIONS** Auth, "A Teacher of Parody," Ariz Eng Bull 25.3, (83); auth, "Constructing the Self through Memory: Cat's Eye as a Novel of Female Development," Frontiers: A Jour of Women Studies 14.3, (94); auth, "From Primals to Inner Children: Atwood's Reflections on Therapy," LIT: Lit Interpretation Theory 6.3-4, (95); auth, "Fashioning an Identity: Battles over the Zoot," Popular Cult Rev 7.1, (96). **CONTACT ADDRESS** Eng and Philos, Murray State Univ, 7C-20 Faculty Hall, Murray, KY 42071. **EMAIL** carol.osborne@murraystate.edu

OSEGUERA, A. ANTHONY
PERSONAL Born 09/09/1939, Bingham Canyon, UT, m, 1994, 2 children **DISCIPLINE** COMMUNICATION **EDUCATION** Univ Missouri, BS, 70; St Louis Univ, MA, 73; Univ Missouri, Columbia, PhD, 76. **CAREER** Asst prof, 76-80, Valdosta St Univ, GA; prof, mass comm, 80-, E Illinios Univ. **HONORS AND AWARDS** Paul Harris Fel; NCA, La Raza Caucus & Div, Cert of Recognition; A Better Place, Outstanding United Way Film, Lowndes County GA, 79. **MEMBERSHIPS** NCA, SCAPR, ICA **RESEARCH** Intl broadcasting; political communication; and media criticism. **SELECTED PUBLICATIONS** Art, The Theory, Research, and Practice of Communication in Spain, ERIC's RIE, 87; art, Nicaragua: Political-Economy as Communication and Media Influence, ERIC's RIE, 88; art, Internationalizing the College and University Campus: Four Paradigms, Intlng Curricula, IL St Univ Publ, 88; art, Internationalizing the US College and University Curricula through the International Mass Communication Minor, ERIC's RIE, 90; art, Historicity, The Television Critic, and the third World Scholar, ERIC's RIE, 91; art, Classical Theatre and the TV Critic, formerly: A Critical View of Television Through the Eyes of Classical Drama, ERIC's RIE, 91. **CONTACT ADDRESS** Eastern Illinois Univ, 114 E Coleman Hall, Charleston, IL 61920. **EMAIL** cfaao@eiu.edu

OSINUBI, OLUMIDE
DISCIPLINE ENGLISH LITERATURE **EDUCATION** Univ Lancaster, PhD. **CAREER** Asst prof. **RESEARCH** Language and literature, dialectology, psycholinguistics, critical linguistics, and statistical linguistics. **SELECTED PUBLICATIONS** Auth, African American Writers and the Use of Dialect in Literature: The Foregrounding of Ethnicity, Jour Commonwealth and Postcolonial Studies, 96. **CONTACT ADDRESS** Clark Atlanta Univ, 223 James P Brawley Dr, SW, Atlanta, GA 30314.

OSTER, JUDITH
DISCIPLINE COMPOSITION AND ENGLISH AS A SECOND LANGUAGE TEACHING **EDUCATION** Case Western Reserve Univ, BA, MA, PhD. **CAREER** English, Case Western Reserve Univ. **HONORS AND AWARDS** Dir, Writing Ctr. **SELECTED PUBLICATIONS** Auth or ed, Toward Robert Frost: The Reader and the Poet; From Reading to Writing: A Rhetoric and Reader. **CONTACT ADDRESS** Case Western Reserve Univ, 10900 Euclid Ave, Cleveland, OH 44106.

OSTERMEIER, TERRY H.
PERSONAL Born 04/15/1937, New London, WI, m, 1964, 2 children **DISCIPLINE** COMMUNICATION **EDUCATION** Wis State Univ, BS, 59; Marquette Univ, MA, 61; Mich State Univ, PhD, 66. **CAREER** Instr, State Univ of NY, 63-66; Commun Dept ch, Univ of Wis Whitewater, 68-88; from asst prof to assoc prof to prof, Univ of Wis Whitewater, 68- . **HONORS AND AWARDS** Kappa Delta Phi, 59; Disting. Alumnus Awd Pi Kappa Delta, 73; Phi Kappa Phi, 83; Wis Col Tchr of the Year, 95; Dean's Col Awd, 97; Outstanding Col Res Awd, 98. **MEMBERSHIPS** Int Listening Asn; World Commun Asn; Int Asn for Intercult Commun Studies; Nat Commun Asn; Wis Commun Asn; Central States Commun Asn. **RESEARCH** Intercult listening; Nonverbal commun; Intercult commun. **SELECTED PUBLICATIONS** Auth, Sprechnormen - Internationale Vergleiche, Sprechkultur im Medienzeitalter, ed Freyr Varwig, 86; Auditory Illusions and Confusions, Experimental Listening: Tools for Teachers and Trainers, ed C. Coakley and A. Wolvin, 89; Perceptions of Cultural Values and Communicating Interculturally: A Simulation Experience, World Commun, vol 18, 89; Auditory Illusions and Confusions: Impact on Listening, Int Listening Jour, vol 3, 89; To Communicate in a Culturally Diverse World: A Curricular Approach to Gain Competency for the 1990s, Jour of the Wis Commun Asn, vol XXII, 91; Fast Talkers and Speeding Listeners: Television/Radio Commercials, Int Listening Jour, vol 5, 91; Listening as a Theme of a Corporation Annual report, Jour of the Wis Commun Asn, vol XXIV, 93; Perception of Nonverbal Cues in Dialogic Listening in an Intercult Interview, Int Listening Jour, spec issue, 93; Meaning Differences for Nonverbal Cues: Easier or More Difficult for the Intercult Listener, Intercult Commun Studies, vol V:1, 95; A Short History of Speech at a Wisconsin Public University: The First 65 Years, Jour of the Wis Commun Asn, vol XXIX, 98. **CONTACT ADDRESS** 11258 E. State Rd 59, Whitewater, WI 53190-3320. **EMAIL** Ostermet@uwwvax.uww.edu

OSTOVICH, HELEN
DISCIPLINE ENGLISH LITERATURE **EDUCATION** Univ Toronto, BA, MA, PhD. **RESEARCH** Renaissance drama; Ben Johnson; eighteenth century novel; detective fiction. **SELECTED PUBLICATIONS** Auth, "Reader as Hobby-horse in Tristram Shandy," Philological Quarterly 68 (89): 325-42; auth, "Manfrede?: Reconstruction of a Misprint in Jonson's Every Man Out of his Humour (1600)," Notes and Queries (89): 330-1; auth, "Two Jonsonian Neologisms," Cahiers elisabethians 38 (90):65-7; auth, "Our views must now be different: Imprisonment and Friendship in Clarissa," Modern Language Quarterly 52 (91): 41-57; auth, "So Sudden and Strange a Cure: A Rudimentary Masque in Every Man Out of his Humour," English Literary Renaissance 22.3 (92): 315-332; auth, "Reader as Hobby-horse in Tristram Shandy," in Melvyn New, ed., New Casebooks: Tristram Shandy (London: MacMillan, 92), 155-73; auth, "The Appropriation of Pleasure in The Magnetic Lady," Studies in English Literature, (94): 425-42; auth, "Teach you our princess English?: Equivocal Translation of the French in Henry V," in Genering Rhetorics: Postures of Dominance and Submission in History, ed, Richard Trexler (Binghamton, NY: Medieval & Renaissance Texts & Studies , 94), 147-162; auth, "Mistress and Maid: Women's Friendship in The New Inn," Ben Jonson Journal 4 (97); auth, Ben Jonson: Four Comedies, 97. **CONTACT ADDRESS** English Dept, McMaster Univ, 1280 Main St W, Hamilton, ON, Canada L8S 4L9. **EMAIL** ostovich@mcmaster.ca

OSTRIKER, ALICIA
PERSONAL Born New York, NY, m, 1958, 3 children **DISCIPLINE** ENGLISH LANGUAGE AND LITERATURE **EDUCATION** Brandeis, BA; Univ Wis, PhD. **CAREER** Prof Eng, Ctr for the Stud of Jewish Life, Rutgers, The State Univ NJ. **HONORS AND AWARDS** National Endowment for the Arts Awd, 76; New Jersey Arts Council Awd in Poetry, 77; Rockefeller Foundation Fel, 82; Guggenheim Foundation Fel, 84-85; Strousse Poetry Prize, Prairie Schooner, 86; Poetry Society of America William Carlos Williams Prize, 86; New Jersey Arts Council Awd, 92; Anna Rosenberg Poetry Awd, Judah Magnes Museum, 94; National Book Awd Finalist, 96; Poem in Best American Poetry, 96; Poem in Yearbook of American Poetry, 96; Paterson Poetry Prize, 97; San Francisco State Poetry Center Awd, 98; Reader's Choice Awd, Prairie Schooner, 98; National Book Awd Finalist, 98; Finalist , Lenore Marshall Awd, Academy of American Poets, 99. **MEMBERSHIPS** PEN, MLA **RESEARCH** Poetry; feminism; religion. **SELECTED PUBLICATIONS** Auth, Vision and Verse in William Blake; auth, Writing Like a Woman; auth, The Little Space: Poems Selected and New; auth, Dancing at the Devils Party: Essays on Poetry, Politics and the Erotic; auth, Stealing the Language: the Emergence of Women's Poetry in America; The Nakedness of the Fathers: Biblical Visions and Revisions; The Mother/Child Papers; The Imaginary Lover; Green Age, The Crack in Everything. **CONTACT ADDRESS** Dept of Lit in Eng, Rutgers, The State Univ of New Jersey, New Brunswick, Murray Hall 203B, New Brunswick, NJ 08903. **EMAIL** ostriker@rci.rutgers.edu

OSTROM, HANS
PERSONAL Born 01/29/1954, Grass Valley, CA, m, 1983, 1 child **DISCIPLINE** ENGLISH AND AMERICAN LITERATURE; CREATIVE WRITING **EDUCATION** Univ Calif, Davis, BA, 75; Univ Calif, Davis, MA, 79; Univ Calif, Davis, PhD, 82. **CAREER** Prof, Univ Puget Sound, 77-80 & 81-83; vis lectr, Johannes Gutenberg Univ, Ger, 80-81; prof, Univ Puget Sound, 83-; Fulbright sr lectr, Uppsala Univ, Sweden, 94. **HONORS AND AWARDS** Martin Nelson sabbatical fel, 78; Burlington Northern Fac Achievement Awd, Univ Puget Sound, 86 & 89; Alumni Asn's Citation for Excellence, Univ Calif, Davis, 89; Fulbright Fel, 94; John Lantz fel, Univ Puget Sound, 96-97; Distinguished Prof, Univ Puget Sound, 00-. **MEMBERSHIPS** Am Asn of Univ Prof; Conf on Col Compos and Commun; MLA; Nat Book Critics Circle; Nat Coun Tchr Eng; Alumni Asn, Univ of Calif, Davis. **RESEARCH** African Am Poetry, Langston Hughes; Composition Studies; Leigh Hunt. **SELECTED PUBLICATIONS** Auth, William Everson's Earth Poetry and the Progress Toward Feminism, in Essays in Honor of William Everson, Castle Peak Ed, 93; Langston Hughes: A Study of the Short Fiction, Twayne/Macmillan, 93; coauth, Water's Night: Poetry Chapbook, Mariposite Press, 94; coed, Colors of a Different Horse, Nat Counc Tchr Eng, 94; co-ed, Genre and Writing: Issues Arguments, Alternatives, with Bishop, Heinemann/Boynton Cook, 98; auth, Subjects Apprehended: Poems, Pudding House Press, 00; coauth, Metro: Journeys in Writing Creatively, with Bishop and Haake, Addison, Wesley, Longman, 01; auth, A Langston Hughes Encyclopedia, Greenwood Publishers, 01. **CONTACT ADDRESS** Dept of Eng, Univ of Puget Sound, 1500 North Warner, Tacoma, WA 98416. **EMAIL** ostrom@ups.edu

OSTROWSKI, CARL
DISCIPLINE AMERICAN LITERATURE **EDUCATION** Wayne State Univ, BA, 90; Univ Tenn, MA, 92; Univ SC, PhD, 97. **CAREER** Teach assoc, 91, teach asst, 91-92, Univ Tenn; adj instr, Midlands Tech Col, 96-97; teach asst, Univ SC, 93-97; asst prof, Cameron Univ, 97-99; asst prof, Middle Tenn State Univ, 99- . **SELECTED PUBLICATIONS** Auth, "'I Stand Upon Their Ashes in Thy Beam': William Cullen Bryant's Literary Removals," American Transcendental Q 9.4 (95): 299-312; auth, "'The Minister's Grievous Affliction': Diagnosing Hawthorne's Parson Hooper," Literature and Medicine 17.2 (98): 197-211; auth, "James Alfred Pearce and the Question of a National Library in Antebellum America," Libraries & Culture 35.2 (00): 255-77 **CONTACT ADDRESS** Dept of English, Middle Tennessee State Univ, Univ Honors Col, 1301 E Main St, Murfreesboro, TN 37132-0001. **EMAIL** costrows@frank.mtsu.edu

OSUMARE, HALIFU
PERSONAL Born 11/27/1946, Galveston, TX, m, 1978 **DISCIPLINE** AMERICAN STUDIES, DANCE **EDUCATION** Univ Without Walls, Berkeley, BA, 75; San Francisco State Univ, MA, 93; Univ Haw, PhD, 99. **CAREER** Lectr, Stanford Univ, 81-93; vis asst prof, Univ Calif Riverside, 99; vis lectr, Univ Calif Berkeley, 00; asst prof, Bowling Green State Univ, 00-. **HONORS AND AWARDS** HCH, Res Grant; Hon Men Gabriel Diss Prize; Brown-Denny Awd. **MEMBERSHIPS** DASA. **RESEARCH** My research focus encompasses the fields of Cultural Studies and African American Studies, with an emphasis on how African American performance has historically utilized resistance, complicity, and play in relation to social structures of power. **SELECTED PUBLICATIONS** Auth, "Aesthetic of the Cool Revisited: The Ancestral Dance Link in the African Diaspora," UCLA J Dan Ethnol 17 (93); auth, "Viewing African Women Through Dance," SAGE 2 (94); auth, "Phat Beats, Dope Rhymes, and Def Moves: Hip Hop's African Aesthetics as Signifying Intertext," in Cultural Patrimony: Africa, New World Connections, and Identities, ed. Niyi Afolabi (forthcoming); auth, "Beat Streets in the Global Hood: Connective Marginalities of the Hip Hop Globe," J Am Cult (forthcoming). **CONTACT ADDRESS** Sch Human Movement, Bowling Green State Univ, Bowling Green, OH 43403-0001. **EMAIL** hosuamre@aol.com

OTT, BRIAN L.
PERSONAL Born 03/22/1969, Erie, PA **DISCIPLINE** SPEECH COMMUNICATION **EDUCATION** PA State Univ, PhD, 97. **CAREER** Asst prof of Media Studies, CO State Univ, 98-. **HONORS AND AWARDS** Col of Liberal Arts Outstanding Teaching Awd, PA State, 96. **MEMBERSHIPS** Nat Commun Asn; Int Commun Asn. **RESEARCH** Critical media studies; television criticism; cultural studies. **SELECTED PUBLICATIONS** Auth, Memorializing the Holocaust:

Schindler's List and Public Memory, The Rev of Ed/Pedagogy/ Cultural Studies, 18, 96. **CONTACT ADDRESS** Dept of Speech Commun, Colorado State Univ, 202 Eddy Hall, Fort Collins, CO 80523. **EMAIL** Bott@vines.colostate.edu

OTTEN, TERRY RALPH
PERSONAL Born 04/15/1938, Dayton, KY, m, 1960, 2 children **DISCIPLINE** ENGLISH **EDUCATION** Geoergetown Coll, BA, 59; Univ KY, MA, 61; Ohio Univ, PhD, 66; Georgetown Coll, DLTT, 97. **CAREER** Instr, Western KY State Univ, 61-63; instr, Ohio Univ, 65-66; PROF, WITTENBERG UNIV, 66-. **MEMBERSHIPS** Mod Lang Asn; Midwest MLA; Toni Morrison Soc; Arthur Miller Soc; Wordsworth and His Circle; North Am Soc Study Romanticism. **SELECTED PUBLICATIONS** "Arthur Miller and the Temptation of Innocence," The Achievement of Arthur Miller, Contemp Res Press, 95; "Morrison on Morrison," Modern Lang Asn, 97; Transfiguring the Narrative-Beloved from Slave Narrative to Tragedy," Critical Essays on Toni Morrison's Beloved, GK Hall, 98; "Tar Baby and the Fall Myth," in Toni Morrison: Contemporary Critical Essays, MacMillan, 98; "Historical Drama and the Dimensions of Tragedy: A Man for All Seasons and The Crucible," Am Drama, 96. **CONTACT ADDRESS** Eng Dept, Wittenberg Univ, Springfield, OH 45501. **EMAIL** totten@wittenberg.edu

OTTENHOFF, JOHN
DISCIPLINE RHETORIC, LINGUISTICS AND BRITISH LITERATURE **EDUCATION** Univ Chicago, PhD. **CAREER** Prof, adv, Sigma Tau Delta, Alma Col. **HONORS AND AWARDS** Outstanding Fac Mem in Hum Awd. **RESEARCH** Shakespeare; Shakespeare on film. **SELECTED PUBLICATIONS** Publications in his specialty, Renaissance devotional poetry. **CONTACT ADDRESS** Alma Col, Alma, MI 48801.

OTTER, MONIKA
DISCIPLINE ENGLISH LITERATURE **EDUCATION** Columbia Univ, PhD, 91. **CAREER** Assoc prof, Dartmouth Col. **RESEARCH** Brit and Medieval lit. **SELECTED PUBLICATIONS** Auth, Inventiones: Fiction and Referentiality in Twelfth-Century English Historical Writing, NC UP, 96; New Werke: St. Erkenwald, St. Albans, and the Medieval Sense of the Past, Jour Med and Ren Studies, 94. **CONTACT ADDRESS** Dartmouth Col, 3529 N Main St, #207, Hanover, NH 03755.

OUTKA, PAUL HAROLD
PERSONAL Born 05/24/1964, New haven, CT, m, 1998 **DISCIPLINE** AMERICAN LITERATURE **EDUCATION** Yale Univ, BA, 86; Univ Va, MA, 95; PhD, 00. **CAREER** Vis asst prof, New Col of Fla, 99-01; asst prof, Univ Maine Farmington, 01-. **HONORS AND AWARDS** Grad Sch Dissertation Fel, 99-00; Dept English Dissertations Fel, 96; Teaching Award, Univ Va, 94-95. **MEMBERSHIPS** MLA **RESEARCH** American Literature; Ecocriticism; The Sublime; Romanticism; Cultural Theory. **SELECTED PUBLICATIONS** Auth, "Publish or Perish: Food, Hunger and the Imagination in Kingston's The Woman Warrior," Contemporary Literature, 97; auth, "Whitmanian Cybernetics," Mickle Street Rev, 01; auth, "Whitman and Race (He's queer, he's unclean, get used to it.)," J of Am Studies, (forthcoming). **CONTACT ADDRESS** Dept Humanities, Univ of Maine, Farmington, 722 Indian Beach Ln, Sarasota, FL 34234-5745. **EMAIL** outka@sar.usf.edu

OWENS, SUZANNE
DISCIPLINE ENGLISH, AMERICAN STUDIES **EDUCATION** Miami Univ, BA, 76; Col Will Mary, MA, 77; Ohio State Univ, PhD, 82. **CAREER** Instr, Winthrop Univ, 79-80; instr, Univ Fla, 81-82; lectr, Ohio State Univ, 83-85; assoc prof, Ursuline Col, 85-88; prof, Lorain CC Col, 88-. **HONORS AND AWARDS** Post doc fel, 83; Who's Who Am Teachers, 96-00; Phi Beta Kappa. **MEMBERSHIPS** ASA; NCTE; CCCC; MMLA; CEA; WHGC. **RESEARCH** American studies: regional art, architectural and cultural history. **SELECTED PUBLICATIONS** Auth, "Home, House and Solitude: Journals and Diaries of May Sarton," in May Sarton: Woman and Poet, ed. Constance Hunting (Nat Poet Found, 82); auth, "Circles of Power: Domestic Authority in Novels of Marilynne Robinson and Joan Chase," Wom Study Rev (84); auth, "Charlotte Perkins Gilman and a Feminist Ghost Story," in Haunting the Houses of Fiction, eds. Lynette Carpenter, Wendy Kolmar (Univ Tenn Pr, 91). **CONTACT ADDRESS** Arts Humanities Div, Lorain County Comm Col, 1005 N Abbe Rd, Elyria, OH 44035. **EMAIL** sowens@loraincc.edu

OWENS, WILLIAM M.
DISCIPLINE CLASSICS **EDUCATION** Cornell Univ, BA, 76; Yale Univ, PhD, 86. **RESEARCH** Social hist; anc slavery; Roman comedy; the Greek novel. **CONTACT ADDRESS** Dept of Classics, Ohio Univ, Athens, OH 45701. **EMAIL** owensb@ohio.edu

OWER, JOHN
PERSONAL Born 01/17/1942, Palmerston North, New Zealand, m, 1986, 2 children **DISCIPLINE** ENGLISH **EDUCATION** Univ Alberta, BA, 63, MA, 66, PhD, 72. **CAREER** Asst Prof, Univ Tenn, 70-72; Lecturer, Univ Waikato, 72-73; Asst Prof, Univ SC, 73-78; Assoc Prof, Univ SC, 78-96; ret, 96. **HONORS AND AWARDS** Woodrow Wilson Fellow; Canada Counc Post-Doctoral Res Fellow; SC Arts Commision Individual Artist Fellow; Winthrop Col Awd for Excellence in Writing in Poetry; Univ of SC Eng Dept Tchng Awd. **RESEARCH** Romantic poetry; modernist literature; science fiction; Canadian literature. **SELECTED PUBLICATIONS** Auth, Edith Sitwell: Metaphysical Medium and Metaphysical Message, 20th Cent Lit, 16:4, 253-267, 10/70; auth, Sociology, Psychology, and Satire in The Apprenticeship of Duddy Kravitz, Mod Fiction Stud, 22:3, 413-428, 76; auth, The Aesthetic Hero: His Innocence, Fall, and Redemption, Bucknell Rev, 23:2, 96-115, 77; auth, Legendary Acts, Univ Ga Press, 77; auth, The Death-Fires, the Fire-Flags, and the Corposant in The Rime of the Ancient Mariner, Philol Quart, 70:2, 199-218, 91. **CONTACT ADDRESS** 142 Stafford Dr, Athens, GA 30605-3718.

OWOMOYELA, OYEKAN
PERSONAL Born 04/22/1938, Ifon, Nigeria, m, 1975 **DISCIPLINE** AFRICAN LITERATURE **EDUCATION** Univ London, BA, 63; Univ Calif, Los Angeles, MFA, 66, PhD(theater hist), 70. **CAREER** Lectr audio visuals, Univ Ibadan, Nigeria, 68-71; asst prof, 72-75, assoc prof, 75-81, Prof Lit & Drama, Univ Nebr- Lincoln, 81-, Sr consult, Ctr Mgt Develop, Nigerian, 75. **MEMBERSHIPS** African Studies Asn; African Lit Asn; Am Folklore Soc. **RESEARCH** Sociology of African literature; Yoruba folklore and society. **SELECTED PUBLICATIONS** Auth, Folklore and Yoruba theater, Res in African Lit, fall 71; The Sociology of sex and crudity in Yorbua Proverbs, Proverbium: Bull d'information sur les recherches paremiologiques, 20: 751-758; coauth (with Bernth Lindfors), Yoruba Proverbs: Translations and Annotations, Ohio Univ Ctr Int Studies, 73; auth, Western humanism and African usage: A critical survey of non-African responses to African literature, Issue: A Quart J Opinion IV, winter 74; African Literatures: An Introduction, Crossroads Press, 79; Obotunde Ijimere, the phantom of Nigerian theater, 4/79 & Dissidence and the African writer: Commitment or dependency, 3/81, Studies Rev; The pragmatic humanism of Yoruba culture, J African Studies, fall 81. **CONTACT ADDRESS** Dept of English, Univ of Nebraska, Lincoln, P O Box 880333, Lincoln, NE 68588-0333.

OZSVATH, ZSUZSANNA
PERSONAL Born 07/02/1934, Subotica, Yugoslavia, m, 1954, 2 children **DISCIPLINE** LITERATURE STUDIES **EDUCATION** Univ Tex, PhD, 68. **CAREER** Prof. **RESEARCH** 19th and 20th century European literature and history; Holocaust studies. **SELECTED PUBLICATIONS** Co-transl, Foamy Sky: The Major Poems of Milkos Radnoti, Princeton, 92; pubs in Partisan Review, Poetry, The Webster Rev, Judaism, The Canadian-American Rev of Hungarian Studies, Lit Rev, Ger Studies Rev, Res Studies; co-transl, The Iron - Blue Vault, Major Poems of Attila Jozsef, Bloodaxe, 99. **CONTACT ADDRESS** Dept of Literature, Univ of Texas, Dallas, PO Box 830688, Richardson, TX 75083-0688. **EMAIL** zozsvath@utdallas.edu

P

PAANANEN, VICTOR N.
PERSONAL Born 01/31/1938, Ashtabula, OH, m, 1964, 2 children **DISCIPLINE** ENGLISH **EDUCATION** Harvard Univ, AB, 60; Univ Wis Madison, MA, 64; PhD, 67. **CAREER** Instr, Wofford Col, 62-63; asst prof, Williams Col, 66-68; asst prof to assoc prof to prof to dept chmn, Mich State Univ, 68-. **HONORS AND AWARDS** Harvard Nat Scholar, 56-60; Phi Beta Kappa; Roehampton Inst Hon Fel, 92. **MEMBERSHIPS** MLA. **RESEARCH** 19th and 20th century British literature; romanticism; Marxism. **SELECTED PUBLICATIONS** Auth, "Dylan Thomas as Social Writer," Nature Soc Thought (90); auth, William Blake, 96; auth, British Marxist Criticism, 00. **CONTACT ADDRESS** English Dept, Michigan State Univ, 201 Morrill Hall, East Lansing, MI 48824. **EMAIL** paananen@msu.edu

PACE, KAY ROBERTINE
PERSONAL Born Mobile, AL **DISCIPLINE** MUSIC **EDUCATION** Xavier Univ LA, BA 1968; Southern IL Univ Carbondale, MM 1970; Peabody Conservatory of Johns Hopkins Univ Baltimore, DMA 1984. **CAREER** Southern IL Univ, instr music & coord of accompanying 1970-73; AL State Univ, asst prof of piano. **HONORS AND AWARDS** Elected mem Phi Kappa Phi Natl Honor Soc 1969, Pi Kappa Lambda Music Honor Soc 1970; Solo piano concerts throughout US 1970-; 1st Place Winner IL State Music Teachers Young Artist Comp 1972, St Louis Artist Presentation Comp 1973; Spec Study Grant Van Cliburn Intl Piano Comp 1977; Otto Ortmann Theory Awd Peabody Conserv of Music 1978; Fellowship Ford Foundation for Doctoral Study 1978-81; SE Reg Winner Natl Black Music Comp 1979; A Portrait of Kay Pace AL Public TV 30 min spec 1979. **MEMBERSHIPS** Coord Univ Piano Guild 1975-; mem Delta Omicron Music Frat for Women 1976-; coord of keyboard AL State Univ 1979-; pres & founder Soc of Friends of Music Montgomery 1979; mem AL Theory Teachers Assoc 1981-; chairperson Dean Selection Comm Music ASU 1982-83; mem Delta Sigma Theta Sor 1983. **CONTACT ADDRESS** Alabama State Univ, 915 S Jackson St, Montgomery, AL 36195.

PACKER, BARBARA LEE
DISCIPLINE ENGLISH, LITERATURE **EDUCATION** Stanford Univ, BA, 68; Yale Univ, MPhil, 71; PhD, 73. **CAREER** Asst prof, Yale Univ, 73-78; asst prof to assoc prof to prof, Univ Calif Los Angeles, 78-. **HONORS AND AWARDS** Rockwell Prize, 74; Luckman Distinguished Teaching Award, 94; Eby Award, 94. **MEMBERSHIPS** Ralph Waldo Emerson Soc; ALA. **RESEARCH** American literature. **SELECTED PUBLICATIONS** Auth, Emerson's Fall, (NYork), 82; auth, "The Transcendentalists," in Cambridge History of American Literature (NYork, 94). **CONTACT ADDRESS** 2850 Woodwardia Dr, Los Angeles, CA 90077-2123. **EMAIL** PACKER@HUMNET.UCLA.EDU

PACKER, JAMES
DISCIPLINE CLASSICS **EDUCATION** UC Berkeley, BA, 59, MA, 60, PhD, 64. **CAREER** Prof, Northwestern Univ, 66-. **RESEARCH** The Temple of the Divine Trajan, Rome; The Theatre of Pompey, Rome. **SELECTED PUBLICATIONS** Auth, The West Library of the Forum of Trajan: the Problems and Some Solutions, Nat Gallery Art, 92; The Forum of Trajan: A Study of the Monuments, Calif, 97. **CONTACT ADDRESS** Dept of Classics, Northwestern Univ, 1859 Sheridan Rd, Kresge 12, Evanston, IL 60208-2200. **EMAIL** j.packer@nwu.edu

PADDEN, CAROL
PERSONAL Born 06/08/1938, Fergus Falls, MN, m, 1963, 3 children **DISCIPLINE** COMMUNICATIONS **EDUCATION** Univ Calif, San Diego, PhD, Ling, 83. **CAREER** Assoc Prof, Commun, Univ Calif, San Diego. **HONORS AND AWARDS** Fulbright Scholar, Nat Chengchi Univ, Taiwan, 97-98. **MEMBERSHIPS** Asn for Edu in Journ and Mass Commun. **RESEARCH** Symbolic develop in young children, Interplay of child develop and cult inst, Communication history and law, journalistic writing. **SELECTED PUBLICATIONS** Co-auth, Deaf in America: Voices from a Culture, Harvard, 88; auth, "Lessons To Be Learned from Young Deaf Orthographers," Ling and Edu, Vol 5, 93; "Folk Explanation in Language Survival," Collective Remembering, Sage, 90. **CONTACT ADDRESS** Sch of Journalism, So Illinois Univ, Carbondale, 117 Archelle Dr, Carbondale, IL 62901-1943. **EMAIL** cpadden@weber.ucsd.edu

PADDON, ANNA R.
DISCIPLINE COMMUNICATIONS **EDUCATION** Wheaton Col, BA, 91; Columbia Univ, MS, 63; Univ Tenn, PhD, 85. **CAREER** Instr, Univ Tenn, 73-88; head journ dept, Benedict Col, 85- 88; PROF, SOUTHERN ILL UNIV, 88-. **CONTACT ADDRESS** Sch Journalism, So Illinois Univ, Carbondale, 102-C North Violet Ln, Carbondale, IL 62901-1943. **EMAIL** paddona@siu.edu

PADILLA, MARK
DISCIPLINE CLASSICS **EDUCATION** Princeton, PhD, 87. **CAREER** Asst prof, 85-92, assoc prof, 93-present, Assoc Prof, 93-99; Prof, Bucknell Univ, 99-. **HONORS AND AWARDS** Summer NEH Fel **MEMBERSHIPS** Amer Philogical Assn **RESEARCH** Greek drama; Greek myth. **CONTACT ADDRESS** Classics Dept, Bucknell Univ, Lewisburg, PA 17837.

PAGE, JUDITH W.
PERSONAL Born New Orleans, LA, m, 1973, 2 children **DISCIPLINE** ENGLISH **EDUCATION** Newcomb Col; Univ Chicago, PhD. **CAREER** Teaches in Engl dept & assoc dean, div arts and letters. **HONORS AND AWARDS** 2 NEH grants. **SELECTED PUBLICATIONS** Auth, Wordsworth and the Cultivation of Women, Univ Calif Press, 94. **CONTACT ADDRESS** Dept of English, Univ of Florida, Gainesville, FL 32611. **EMAIL** jwp@english.ufl.edu

PAGEN, MICHELE A.
PERSONAL Born 05/02/1968, Uniontown, PA, s **DISCIPLINE** THEATRE **EDUCATION** Calif Univ of Pa, BA, Theatre, 5/90, MA, 8/91; Bowling Green State Univ, Dr of Philos in Theatre, 9/94. **CAREER** Asst prof of theatre, Univ of Findlay, 94-95; asst prof of theatre, Calif Univ of Pa, 95-; admin dir, Cal Rep Pa, 96-. **HONORS AND AWARDS** Grad res grant, 94; Outstanding Young Alumni, Calif Univ of Pa, 95; Irene O'Brien Res Grant, 98; alpha psi omega, nat theatre honorary, 90. **MEMBERSHIPS** Nat Commun Assoc (secy, theatre div); Assoc for Theatre in Higher Educ; Am Col Theatre Fest; East Coast Theatre Conf; Theatre Commun Grp. **RESEARCH** Pedagogy in higher education. **SELECTED PUBLICATIONS** Auth, Life as a Performer: Ethnographic Qualities in the Performance of Self, ERIC Higher Educ Doc ED 368 030, 10/94. **CONTACT ADDRESS** Theatre Dept, California Univ of Pennsylvania, 250 Univ Dr, California, PA 15419. **EMAIL** pagen@cup.edu

PAGLIA, CAMILLE
PERSONAL Born 04/02/1947, Endicott, NY **DISCIPLINE** MEDIA STUDIES **EDUCATION** SUNY, Binghamton, BA, 68; Yale Univ, MA, 71, PhD, 74. **CAREER** Univ of the Arts; Prof, 91-00; Univ Prof of Humanities and Media Studies, 00; Columnist, Salon Com, 95. **HONORS AND AWARDS** Fac, Bennington Col, 72-80; Vis Lecturer, Wesleyan Univ, 80; Yale Univ, 80-84; Univ of the AArts, Asst Prof, Hum, 84-87, Assoc Prof, 87-91, Prof, 91. **SELECTED PUBLICATIONS** Auth, Sexual Personae: Art and Decadence from Nefertiti to Emily Dickinson, Yale Univ Press, 90; auth, Sex Art, and American Culture, Vintage Books, 92; auth, Vamps and Tramps: New Essays, Vintage Books, 94; auth, Alfred Hitchcock's The Birds, Brit Film Inst, 98. **CONTACT ADDRESS** Univ of the Arts, College of Media and Communication, 320 S Broad St, Philadelphia, PA 19102.

PAHL, DENNIS A.
PERSONAL Born 04/09/1951, New York, NY, m, 1997, 0 child **DISCIPLINE** ENGLISH **EDUCATION** SUNY, Buffalo, PhD, 86. **CAREER** Assoc prof, Long Island Univ, CW Post Camp, 90-. **HONORS AND AWARDS** NEH, Univ Arizona, 88; Fulbright Fel, Haifa Uni v, Israel, 94. **MEMBERSHIPS** MLA. **RESEARCH** Nineteenth-century American literature and culture; Poe; Melville; Henry James. **SELECTED PUBLICATIONS** Auth, Architects of the Abyss: The Indeterminate Fictions of Poe, Hawthorne and Melville; Poe/Script: The Death of the Author in The Narrative of Arthur Gordon Pym; Rediscovering Byron: Poe's The Assignation; Framing Poe: Fictions of Self and Self-Containment; Godard's Alphaville: A Journey through Film Space; articles pub in TSLL, Criticism, Studies in short fiction; auth, The Gaze of History in Beuito Cereuo, Decomposing Poe's "Philosophy". **CONTACT ADDRESS** Dept English, Long Island Univ, C.W. Post, 720 Northern Blvd, Greenvale, NY 11548-1319. **EMAIL** dapahl@earthlink.net

PAILLIOTET, ANN WATTS
PERSONAL Born 10/10/1955, Long Beach, CA, s **DISCIPLINE** EDUCATION, ENGLISH **EDUCATION** Col Santa Fe, BS; Syracuse Univ, MS, 92, PhD, 95. **CAREER** Asst prof of Educ, Whitman Col, Wall Walla, Wash, 95-. **HONORS AND AWARDS** Grad Doctoral Fel, Syracuse Univ, 3 year Awd; Nat Reading Conf Grad Res Awd; Grad Convocation Speaker, Sch of Educ, Syracuse Univ; Masters Thesis Awd, Syracuse Univ Gad Sch; Syracuse Univ Sch of Educ Res Apprenticeship Awd; Whitman Col 1999 Ball Advising Awd; Nat Sci Found Grant; Col Composition and Commun Citation for Outstanding Classroom Practice. **MEMBERSHIPS** Am Educ Res Asn, Assembly on Media Arts, Asn of Teacher Educators, Nat Coun of Teachers of English, Nat Media Educators, Phi Delta Kappa, American Mensa Ltd, Nat Alliance for Media Arts and culture, WORD (Washington Int Reading Asn). **RESEARCH** Media literacy, technology, preservice teacher education. **SELECTED PUBLICATIONS** Auth, "Deep Viewing: Intermediality in Teacher Education," in Intermediatality: The Teachers' Handbook of Critical Media Literacy, L. Semali and A. Watts Pailliotet, eds, Westview/Harper Collins (98): 31-51; co-ed with L. Semali, Intermediatality: The Teachers' Handbook of Critical Media Literacy, L. Semali and A. Watts Pailliotet, eds, Westview/Harper Collins (98); coauth, "Preparing the Post-Formalist Practitioner: Pitfalls and Promises," in J. Kincheloe & S. Steinberg, eds, Prethinking Intelligence: Confronting psychological assumptions about teaching and learning, Routledge (99): 165-88; coauth, "Standards of Complexity in Preservice education," in The Encyclopedia of Educational Standards, Joe L. Kincheloe, Shirley R. Steinberg, and Dan Weil, eds, Garland (forthcoming); coauth, "Intermediality: Path to Critical Media Literacy," The Reading Teacher (forthcoming); coauth, "Recommended Print and Electronic Resources for Teaching about Media and Technology in the K-12 Classroom," Reconceptualizing Literacy in the Media Age, JAI/ABLEX/Elsevier Press (forthcoming); auth, "Reconceptulaizing Literacy in the Media Age: The 4 I's of Media Literacy," Reconceptualizing Literacy in the Media Age, JAI/Ablex/Elsevier Press (forthcoming); co-ed, Reconceptualizing Literacy in the Media Age, JAI/Ablex/Elsevier Press (forthcoming); invited section ed, Reading On-Line: "New Literacies," 99-2002. **CONTACT ADDRESS** Dept Educ, Whitman Col, 122 Maxey Hall, Walla Walla, WA 99362. **EMAIL** pailliaw@whitman.edu

PALEY, SAMUEL M.
PERSONAL Born 10/15/1941, Manchester, NH, M, 3 children **DISCIPLINE** CLASSICS **EDUCATION** Columbia Univ, PhD, 74. **CAREER** Fac, 77; prof, present, The Univ at Buffalo, SUNY; Asst dir Alishar Hoyuk Res Proj, Sorgun, Turkey; dir Emeq Hefer Proj, Israel. **HONORS AND AWARDS** Asst dir Alishar Hoyuk Res Proj, Sorgun, Turkey; dir Emeq Hefer Proj, Univ Buffalo. **MEMBERSHIPS** AIA, ASOR, BSAI, IES, AOS. **RESEARCH** The ancient Near East and Egypt, Judaism, Semitic Languages. **SELECTED PUBLICATIONS** Auth, King of the World: Ashurnasirpal II of Assyria (833-859 B.C.), Brooklyn Mus, 76; coauth, The Reconstruction of the Relief Representations and Their Positions in the Northwest Palace of Kalhu (Nimrud), vols II/III, Philipp von Zabern, 87 and 92. **CONTACT ADDRESS** Dept Classics, SUNY, Buffalo, 338 Millard Fillmore Acad Core, Buffalo, NY 14261. **EMAIL** clapaley@acsu.buffalo.edu

PALISCA, CLAUDE VICTOR
PERSONAL Born 11/24/1921, Fiume, Italy, m, 1960, 2 children **DISCIPLINE** MUSIC **EDUCATION** Queens Col, BA, 43; Harvard Univ, MA, 48, PhD(music), 54. **CAREER** From instr to asst prof music, Univ Ill, 53-59; assoc prof hist of music, 59-64, chmn dept music, 69-75, dir grad studies music, 67-70, chmn & dir grad studies Renaissance studies, 77- 80, prof hist of music, 64-80, Henry L & Lucy G Moses Prof Music, Yale Univ, 80-, Guggenheim fel, 60 & 80; vis assoc prof & sr fel, Princeton Univ, 61; dir sem on music educ, US Off Educ, 63, consult, 63-; sr fac fel, Yale Univ, 66-67; consult, Nat Endowment for Humanities, 67-, sr fel, 72-73. **HONORS AND AWARDS** MA, Yale Univ, 64. **MEMBERSHIPS** Am Musicol Soc (1st vp, 65-67, pres, 70-72); Renaissance Soc Am; Col Music Soc; fel Am Coun Arts in Educ (pres, 67-69); Int Musicol Soc (vp, 77-82). **RESEARCH** Musicology, history of Renaissance and baroque music; history of music theory. **SELECTED PUBLICATIONS** Auth, Baroque Music, Prentice-Hall, 68, 2nd ed, 81; co- transl, G Zarlino, the Art of Counterpoint, Yale Univ, 68; The Artusi-Monteverdi controversy, In: The Monteverdi Companion, Faber & Faber, 68; The Alterati of Florence, pioneers in the theory of dramatic music, In: New Looks at Italian Opera, Cornell Univ, 68; auth, Ut oratoria musica: The rhetorical basis of musical mannerism, In: The Meaning of Mannerism, Univ New England, 72; ed & auth of introd, Hucbald, Guido and John on Music: Three Medieval Treatises, Yale Univ, 78; coauth, History of Western Music, 80 & ed, Norton Anthology of Western Music, 80, Norton; The Court Musicians in Florence During The Principate of The Medici, With a Reconstruction of The Artistic Establishment - Kirkendale,w, Notes, Vol 0051, 1995; Doni,giovanni,battista Interpretation of The Greek Modal System, J of Musicology, Vol 0015, 1997. **CONTACT ADDRESS** 68 Spring Rock Rd Pine, Orchard Branford, CT 06405. **EMAIL** claude.palisca@yale.edu

PALMA, RONALD B.
PERSONAL Born 11/18/1946, Suffern, NY **DISCIPLINE** CLASSICS **EDUCATION** Cornell Univ, BA, 68; Univ Cincinnati, MA, 72, and work completed to PhD. **CAREER** Tchr, classics, Dept of Lang, Holland Hall Sch, Tulsa, Okla, 73- . **HONORS AND AWARDS** Merit Scholar, Cornell Univ, 64-68; Semple fel, Univ Cincinnati, 68-73; Fulbright fel, 81; Rockefeller Found fel, 87; tchr of the year, 82; citation, Comt on Pres Scholars, 83; Col Bd Advanced Placement Special Recognition Awd, 91; APA/ACL Excellence in PreCollegiate Teaching Awd, 99. **MEMBERSHIPS** Am Philol Asn; Am Class League; Vergilian Soc. **RESEARCH** The connection between high school and college teaching in Classics and establishing national standards in teaching Latin and Greek. **SELECTED PUBLICATIONS** Coauth, Ecce Romani: A Latin Reading Program, Addison-Wesley, 84, 95; ed, Review and Test Preparation Guide for the Beginning Student, Addison-Wesley, 95; ed, Review and Test Preparation Guide for the Intermediate Student, Addison-Wesley, 95; articles in The Class Outlook, The New England Class Newsl, The Longman Latin Newsl; ACL Newsl. **CONTACT ADDRESS** Holland Hall School, 5666 E 81st St., Tulsa, OK 74137. **EMAIL** ronpalma@iamerica.net

PALMER, BARTON
DISCIPLINE ENGLISH LITERATURE **EDUCATION** NYork Univ, PhD, 89. **CAREER** Dept Eng, Clemson Univ **RESEARCH** Medieval literature; film studies. **SELECTED PUBLICATIONS** Auth, Hollywood's Dark Cinema: The American Film Noir, Twayne, 94; Perspectives on Film Noir, G.K. Hall, 95; trans, Guiollaume de Machaut: Comfort d'ami, Garland, 92; co-trans and ed, Guiollaume de Machaut: Le Livre dou Voir Dit, Garlan, 92. **CONTACT ADDRESS** Clemson Univ, 802 Strode, Clemson, SC 29634. **EMAIL** ppalmer@clemson.edu

PALMER, WILLIAM
PERSONAL Born 03/31/1952, Detroit, m, 3 children **DISCIPLINE** RHETORIC, CREATIVE WRITING **EDUCATION** Mich State Univ, PhD. **CAREER** Prof, Alma Col. **HONORS AND AWARDS** Charles A Dana Prof Eng, 93. **SELECTED PUBLICATIONS** Published essays and poetry in Eng J, Col Compos and Commun and Chicago Tribune Mag. **CONTACT ADDRESS** Alma Col, Alma, MI 48801. **EMAIL** palmer@alma.edu

PALMERI, FRANK
PERSONAL Born 08/06/1952, Denver, CO, m, 1990 **DISCIPLINE** ENGLISH **EDUCATION** Columbia Univ, BA, 74, MA, 75, PhD, 81. **CAREER** Vis asst prof, 82-83, Univ of Anhim, People's Rep of China; instr, adj asst prof, 83-84, Univ Denver, CO; asst prof, 84-90, assoc prof, 90-, Univ Miami. **RESEARCH** 18th & 19th century narrative; comparative lit. **CONTACT ADDRESS** Dept of English, Univ of Miami, Coral Gables, FL 33124. **EMAIL** fpalmeri@miami.edu

PALMQUIST, MIKE
PERSONAL Born 10/01/1957, Minneapolis, MN, m, 1985, 2 children **DISCIPLINE** RHETORIC AND COMPOSITION **EDUCATION** St Olaf Col, BA; Carnegie Mellon Univ, PhD. **CAREER** Assoc prof; prof, Univ Distinguished Teaching Scholar. **HONORS AND AWARDS** Oliver P. Pennock Distinguished Service Award, 98; Kairos Best Webtext Award, 98; N. Preston Davis Award for Instrutional Innovation, 99. **MEMBERSHIPS** Am Educational Res Asn, Asn of Teachers of Advanced Composition, Conference on College Composition and Commun, Coun of Writing Program Administrators, Nat Coun of Teachers of English, Phi Beta Kappa. **RESEARCH** Writing across the curriculum; the effects of computer and network technologies on writing instruction; the use of hypertext, hypermedia in instructional settings. **SELECTED PUBLICATIONS** Auth, pubs in Computers and Compositions; Written Communication; IEEE Transaction on Professional Communication; IEEE Transaction on Professional Communication; Engineering Education; Social Forces. **CONTACT ADDRESS** Dept of English, Colorado State Univ, Fort Collins, CO 80523. **EMAIL** mike.palmquist@colostate.edu

PANCRAZIO, JAMES
DISCIPLINE SPANISH AMERICAN LITERATURE **EDUCATION** Ill State Univ, BA, 87; Univ Ill, MA, 91, PhD, 95. **CAREER** Asst prof, The Univ of Ark at Little Rock, 95-97; asst prof, Ill State Univ, 97-. **HONORS AND AWARDS** Tinker Res Grant, 94; Univ Res Grant, 99; Univ Res Grant to travel, 00. **MEMBERSHIPS** Latin Am Studies Asn; AATSP; Midwest Modern Lang Asn. **RESEARCH** Cuban and Caribbean Culture; (Neo)Baroque and Post-Modern culture in Cuba and the Caribbean; Cuban Narrative; The Baroque in Colonial Latin America. **SELECTED PUBLICATIONS** Auth, "Etica y estetica: el cuerpo en Songoroo cosongo y otros poemas tempranos de Nicolas Guillen," Memorias de la conferencia international sobre la obra de Nicolas Guillen, Havana: La Fundacion Nicolas Guillen, 94; auth, "Rethinking Carpentier's Baroque," Monographic Rev/Revista monografica, X, (94): 82-91; auth, "El terreno corporal: las fronteras de identidad en Songoro cosongo de Nicolas Guillen," Marges 18, (97): 237-249; auth, "Bodily Terrain and the Borders of Identity in Latin America," Diaspora 6.6, (97): 48-65; auth, "We're all Guilty: Lo Cubano in the Confession," Imagination Beyond Nation: Latin American Popular Culture, Pittsburgh: Univ of Pittsburgh Press, (98): 129-41; auth, La lepra creadora: El barroco como discurso poscolonial, Hojas universitarias 48, (99): 132-40; auth, Maceo's Corps(e): The Paradox of Black and Cuban, Caribe 2.2, (99): 83-99. **CONTACT ADDRESS** Dept of Foreign Languages, Illinois State Univ, 243 Stevenson Hall, Normal, IL 61790-4300. **EMAIL** jjpancr@ilstu.edu

PANEK, JENNIFER MARIE
DISCIPLINE ENGLISH **EDUCATION** Univ Man, BA, 92; Dalhousie Univ, MA, 93; Univ Toronto, PhD, 99. **CAREER** Lectr, Mass Inst of Tech, 99; lectr, Univ Mass, 99-00; fel, Harvard Univ, 00-01; asst prof, Univ Ottawa, 01-. **HONORS AND AWARDS** Fel, SSHRC, 94-98, 00-01; Killam Grad Fel, 92-93; Clifford Leech Dissertation Prize, 99. **MEMBERSHIPS** MLA; Shakespeare Asn of Am. **RESEARCH** Early modern drama, especially non-Shakespearean. **CONTACT ADDRESS** Dept English, Univ of Ottawa, Dept English, Ottawa, ON, Canada K1N 6N5. **EMAIL** jenpanek@yahoo.com

PANNAPACKER, WILLIAM ALBERT
PERSONAL Born 04/25/1968, Camden, NJ, m, 1992, 1 child **DISCIPLINE** ENGLISH **EDUCATION** St Joseph's Univ, BA, 90; Univ Miami, MA, 93; Harvard Univ, MA, 97, PhD, 99. **CAREER** Teaching fel to lectr, Harvard Univ, 95-00; asst prof, Hope Col, 00-. **HONORS AND AWARDS** Crimson and Gray Prize, Saint Joseph's Univ, 89; Bowdoin Prize, Harvard Univ, 94, 99; Helen Choate Bell Prize, Harvard, 95, 98; Phillip Hofer Prize, Harvard Univ, 96; William Harris and Gertrude Weld Arnold Prize, Harvard Univ, 98; Pres Scholar, Saint Joseph's Univ, 86-90; Fel, Harvard Univ, 93-95; Whiting Found Fel, 98-99. **MEMBERSHIPS** MLA; Am Lit Asn; Am Studies Asn. **RESEARCH** American literature and culture. **SELECTED PUBLICATIONS** Auth, "A Question of Character: Visual Images and the Nineteenth-Century Construction of Edgar Allan Poe," Harvard Libr Bulletin, (96): 9-24; auth, "Edward Carpenter, Walt Whitman, and Working-Class Comradeship," in mapping male Sexuality: Nineteenth-Century England, (Fairleigh Dickinson Univ Press, 00), 277-298; auth, "Emerson's Anti-Slavery Lecture," in Against Slavery: An Abolitionist Reader, (Penguin Books, 00), 301-312; auth, "Ralph Waldo Emerson," in A House Divided: The Antebellum Slavery, Princeton Univ Press, 01; auth, "Walt Whitman," in A House Divided: The Antebellum Slavery, Princeton Univ Press, 01. **CONTACT ADDRESS** Dept English, Hope Col, Hope C, Holland, MI 49422. **EMAIL** pannapacker@hope.edu

PAOLETTI, JO
DISCIPLINE AMERICAN CULTURE **EDUCATION** Syracuse Univ, BS, 71; Univ RI, MS, 76; Univ MD, PhD, 80. **CAREER** Am Stud Dept, Univ Md **RESEARCH** 1970s unisex trends, on-line exhibition and publ. **SELECTED PUBLICATIONS** Co-auth, Conclusion" in Men and Women: Dressing the Part, Smithsonian Inst Press, 89; The Children's Department,Men and Women: Dressing the Part, Smithsonian Inst Press, 89; auth, Little Lord Fauntleroy and His Dad, Hope and Glory, 91; The Value of Conversation in Teaching and Learning, Essays on Teaching, Univ Md IBM-TQ Project, 97; The Gendering of Infants' and Toddlers' Clothing in America, The Material Culture of Gender/The Gender of Material Culture,

Winterthur Mus, 97. **CONTACT ADDRESS** Am Stud Dept, Univ of Maryland, Col Park, 4210 Underrwood St, University Park, MD 20782. **EMAIL** jp4@umail.umd.edu

PAPAZIAN, MARY A.
PERSONAL Born 02/25/1959, Santa Monica, CA, m, 1991, 2 children **DISCIPLINE** RENAISSANCE LITERATURE **EDUCATION** Univ Calif, BA, 81; MA, 83; PhD, 88. **CAREER** Asst prof to assoc dean, Oakland Univ, 88-. **HONORS AND AWARDS** Phi Beta Kappa; Lily Bess Campbell Diss Fel, 86-87; Oakland Univ Fac Res Fel, 90; Dept of English Merit Awd, 91; Distinguished Publication in Donne Studies, John Donne Soc, 91. **MEMBERSHIPS** John Donne Soc; MLA; Milton Soc of Am; Renaissance Soc of Am; Sixteenth Century Studies Assoc; S Central Renaissance Conf. **RESEARCH** John Donne, John Milton, Religion and Literature, Literature and Politics, 17th-Century Poetry, Devotional Literature. **SELECTED PUBLICATIONS** Auth, "The Latin Stationes in John Donne's Devotions Upon Emergent Occasions", Mod Philology 89.2, (91): 196-210; auth, "The Politics of John Donne's Devotions Upon Emergent Occasions Reconsidered", Renaissance and Reformation 15.3 (91): 233-248; auth, "Richard Corbett", Seventeenth-Century British Non-Dramatic Poetcs, ed M Thomas Hester, Bruccoli, Clark Layman, (Detroit/London, 92): 59-67; auth, "Donne, Election and the Devotions Upon Emergent Occasions", Huntington Libr Quarterly 55.4 (92); 603-612; auth, "The Lazarus Motif in Donne and Rembrandt: Some Religious and Artistic Parallels", Low Countries and Beyond, ed robert Kirsner, Univ Pr of Am, (Lanham, 93); 269-279; auth, "Literary Things Indifferent: The Shared Augustinianism of Donne's Devotions and Bunyan's Grace Abounding", John Donne's Religious Imagination Essays in Honor of John T Shawcross, eds Raymond-Jean Frontain and Frances Malpezzi, Univ of Central Ark Pr, (95): 324-349; auth, "The Fiery Call of the Soul: A Reading of Artem Haroutiunian's Letter to Noah and Other Poems", J for the Soc of Armenian Studies 8, (95): 53-73; auth, "Critical Commentary on Donne criticism in the 1940s, Donne Variorum Project", Songs & Sonets, Ind Univ Pr, 95; auth, "John Donne" and "Lucy, Countess of Bedford", Ben Jonson Encyclopedia, ed Robert Evans, 98; rev of "Gender and the Sacred Self", by Elizabeth Hodgson, Sixteenth Century J XXX.1 (00): 285-286; auth, John Donne and the Thirty Year's War, (forthcoming). **CONTACT ADDRESS** Dept English, Oakland Univ, 207 Varner Hall, Rochester, MI 48309-4401. **EMAIL** papazian@oakland.edu

PAPPANO, MARGARET
DISCIPLINE LATE MEDIEVAL ENGLISH LITERATURE **EDUCATION** Dartmouth Col, AB, 87; Sussex Univ, MA, 89; Columbia Univ, MA, 90; Columbia Univ, PhD, 98. **CAREER** English and Lit, Columbia Univ **SELECTED PUBLICATIONS** Auth, The Priest's Body: Literature and Popular Piety in Late Medieval England. **CONTACT ADDRESS** Columbia Univ, 2960 Broadway, New York, NY 10027-6902.

PARINS, MARYLYN
DISCIPLINE ARTHURIAN LITERATURE **EDUCATION** Univ Mich, PhD. **CAREER** English and Lit, Univ Ark **SELECTED PUBLICATIONS** Auth, Malory: The critical heritage; Looking for Arthur: Theories of origin and historicity; King Arthur; Scholarship, Modern Arthurian, The New Arthurian Encyclopedia; Malory's Expurgations, Arthurian Tradition: Essays in Convergence. **CONTACT ADDRESS** Univ of Arkansas, Little Rock, 2801 S University Ave., Little Rock, AR 72204-1099. **EMAIL** mjparins@ualr.edu

PARIS, BERNARD J.
PERSONAL Born 08/19/1931, Baltimore, MD, m, 1949, 2 children **DISCIPLINE** ENGLISH **EDUCATION** Johns Jopkins Univ, BA, 52; PhD, 59. **CAREER** Instr, Lehigh Univ, 56-60; asst, assoc and prof, Michigan State Univ, 60-81; prof, Univ Fl, 81-96; dir, Inst for Psychol Study of the Arts, 85-92; prof emer, 96- . **HONORS AND AWARDS** Phi Beta Kappa, 52; fel, NEH, 69-70; fel, Guggenheim Found, 74-75. **MEMBERSHIPS** MLA; Asn for Advanc of Psychoanalysis; Am Acad of Psychoanalysis; Int Karen Horney Soc. **RESEARCH** Literature and psychology; fiction; Shakespeare; Karen Horney; history of psychoanalysis. **SELECTED PUBLICATIONS** Auth, Experiments in Life: George Eliot's Quest for Values, Wayne State Univ, 65; auth, A Psychological Approach to Fiction: Studies in Thackeray, Stendhal, George Eliot, Dostoevsky, and Conrad, Indiana, 74; auth, Character and Conflict in Jane Austen's Novels: A Psychological Approach, Wayne State, 78; auth, Bargains with Fate: Psychological Crises and Conflicts in Shakespeare and His Plays, Plenum, 91; auth, Character as a Subversive Force in Shakespeare: The History and the Roman Plays, Fairleigh Dickinson, 91; auth, Karen Horney: A Psychoanalyst's Search for Self-Understanding, Yale, 94; auth, Imagined Human Beings: A Psychological Approach to Character and Conflict in Literature, NY Univ, 97; ed, The Therapeutic Process: Essays and Lectures, Yale, 99; ed, The Unknown Karen Horney: Essays on Gender, Culture, and Psychoanalysis, Yale, 00. **CONTACT ADDRESS** 1430 NW 94th St, Gainesville, FL 32606. **EMAIL** bjparis@ufl.edu

PARISH, CHARLES
PERSONAL Born 05/11/1927, Shreveport, LA, m, 1965, 3 children **DISCIPLINE** ENGLISH, LINGUISTICS **EDUCATION** Brooklyn Col, BA, 52; Univ NM, MA, 55, PhD (English ling), 58. **CAREER** Instr English, Univ Wichita, 56-57, asst prof, 58-59; asst prof English & ling, Southern Ill Univ, Alton, 59-63; assoc prof, 65-71, Prof Ling to Prof Emer, Southern Ill Univ, Carbondale, 71-. **HONORS AND AWARDS** Fulbright lectr, Univ Mandalay, 61-62 & Univ Rome, 62-64, 68-69; Coun Am Study Rome, 63-65; consult, Univ Rome, 79. **MEMBERSHIPS** Ling Soc Am; MLA; Teachers English to Speakers Other Lang. **RESEARCH** English as a foreign language teacher-training; second- language acquisition. **SELECTED PUBLICATIONS** Ed, Corso d'Inglese Parlato, Vol 3, 65 & coauth, Vol 4, 68, Harcourt; auth, Some phonetic problems for Burmese speakers of English, Lang Learning, 64; Tristram Shandy Notes, Cliff's Notes, 68; Agenbite of Agendath Netaim, James Joyce Quart, spring 69; The Shandy Bull vindicated, Mod Lang Quart, 370; ESL practice-teaching utilizing videotape, 76 & A practical philosophy of pronunciation, 77, TESOL Quart. **CONTACT ADDRESS** Dept of Ling, So Illinois Univ, Carbondale, Carbondale, IL 62901. **EMAIL** cparish@siu.edu

PARISI, BARBARA
PERSONAL Born 03/31/1954, Brooklyn, NY, m, 1995 **DISCIPLINE** THEATRE PERFORMANCE STUDIES **EDUCATION** New York Univ, PhD 91. **CAREER** chemn, Long Island Univ Bklyn. **HONORS AND AWARDS** Shubert Archive Fel. **MEMBERSHIPS** NYSSCA; NCA; ATHE; Art NY. **RESEARCH** Women's Theatre; Musical Theater. **SELECTED PUBLICATIONS** Auth, Empowerment Through Communication, Kendall Hunt, Culture Inst of Brooklyn, BAM BCBD St Ann's as Performing Arts Culture Inst, Scarecrow Press. **CONTACT ADDRESS** Long Island Univ, Brooklyn, 35 Brighton 8th Pl, Brooklyn, NY 11235-6366. **EMAIL** ryanrep@juno.com

PARISI, PETER
DISCIPLINE JOURNALISTIC WRITING AND PRESS CRITICISM, THEORY AND HISTORY **EDUCATION** Ind Univ, PhD, 74. **CAREER** Fac, Penn State Harrisburg, CW Post Campus of Long Island Univ & Hunter univ; taught Engl comp & lit at, Bucknell Univ and Rutgers Univ; 6 yrs, reporter, reviewer & ed; past ed, division's newsl, 2 yrs. **RESEARCH** Language and ideology in the press and the problem of expanding the scope of journalistic discourse. **SELECTED PUBLICATIONS** Publ on, journalism & popular culture; in, J Popular Cult, Jour Educator, Chronicle Higher Educ, Col Engl & Urban Geog; ed, Artist of the Actual: Essays on Paul Goodman, Scarecrow Press, 86. **CONTACT ADDRESS** Dept of Film and Media Studies, Hunter Col, CUNY, 695 Park Ave, New York, NY 10021.

PARK, CLARA C.
PERSONAL Born 08/19/1923, Tarrytown, NY, m, 1945, 4 children **DISCIPLINE** ENGLISH **EDUCATION** Radcliffe Col, AB, 44; Univ Mich, AM, 48. **CAREER** Faculty Member in English, Berkshire Community Col, 60-72; Lecturer, Williams Col, 72; 76-97. **HONORS AND AWARDS** Award, National Asn for Mental Health, 69, Honorary Degrees, Williams College, 76, North Adams State College, 83, Distinguished Alumna Awd, Radcliffe College, 76, National Magazine Editor's Awd, 99, **MEMBERSHIPS** Editorial Board, The Hudson Review, 97-. **SELECTED PUBLICATIONS** Auth, The Siege: The First Eight Years of an Autistic Child, New York: Harcourt, Brace and World, 67; auth, You Are Not Alone: Understanding and Dealing with Mental Illness, with Leon N. Shapiro, M.D., Boston: Little, Brown, 76; auth, "Growing Out of Autism," in E. Schopler and G. Mesibov, eds., Autism in Adolescents and Adults (New York: Plenum, 83); auth, "A Reconsideration: Werner Jaeger's Paideia," Modern Age, 84; rev, "Faith, Grace, and Love," Hudson Review, 85; auth, "Social Growth in Autism: A Parent's Perspective," in E. Schopler and G. Mesibov, eds., Social Behavior in Autism (New York: Plenum, 86); rev, "First Fight, Then Fiddle," The Nation, 87; rev, "From New Delhi: Letter to a Graduate Student,: Southwest Review, 87; rev, "Coping with the D-Word," Hudson Review, 91; auth, "Readers, Pre-and Postlapsarian: A Voice from the Margin," ADE Bulletin, 91. **CONTACT ADDRESS** Dept English, Williams Col, 880 Main St, Williamstown, MA 01267-2600.

PARK-FULLER, LINDA M.
PERSONAL Born 08/18/1948, Minot, ND, m, 1975 **DISCIPLINE** SPEECH; THEATRE **EDUCATION** Univ of Ndak, BA, 70; Univ of Mo, MA, 71; Univ of Tex, PhD, 80. **CAREER** Instr, St Cloud State Univ, 71-81; prof, Mo State Univ, 81-; asst prof, Arizona State Univ. **HONORS AND AWARDS** Phi Beta Kappa; Phi Kappa Phi, 99-; Leslie Irene Coger Awd for Distinguished Perfomance. **MEMBERSHIPS** Nat Commun Asn; Asn for Theatre in Higher Educ; Speech and Theatre Asn of Mo; Nat Wellness Asn. **RESEARCH** Performance Studies; Interactive Theatre; Theatre and Social and Health Issues; Playback Theatre, Narrative lit in performance. **SELECTED PUBLICATIONS** Auth, Understanding What We Know: A Production Record of Tillie Olsen's Yonnondio: From the Thirties, Lit in Performance, 4, 83; Voices: Bakhtin's Heteroglossia and Polyphony, and the Performance of Narrative Literature, Lit in Performance, 7, 86; Performance as Praxis: The Intercollegiate Performance Festival, Text and Performance Quart, 14, 94; Narration and Narratization in a Cancer Story: Composing and Performing A Clean Breast of It, Text and Performance Quart, 15, 95; Towards and Interdisciplinary Performance Course: Process and Politics, in Performance Studies in the Next Millenium, Improvising Disciplines: Performance Studies and Theatre, in Teaching Performance Studies; Re-Valuing the Oral Tradition in Higher Education: Playback Theatre in the Academy, in the Proceedings of the First Int Symposium on Playback Theatre; coauth, Minding the Stops: Performance and Affective Stylistics, Text and Performance Quart, 10, 90; Charting Alternative Performance and Evaluative Practices, Commun Educ, 44, 95. **CONTACT ADDRESS** Dept of Human Communication, Arizona State Univ, Tempe, AZ 85287. **EMAIL** linda.park-fuller@asu.edu

PARKER, DOUGLAS
DISCIPLINE ENGLISH LITERATURE **EDUCATION** Univ Birmingham, PhD. **RESEARCH** Renaissance drama; Reformation lit; children's lit. **SELECTED PUBLICATIONS** Auth, From Reading to Writing: A Reader, Rhetoric and Handbook, 89;auth, The Third Suitor in King Lear, English Studies, 91; art, Bilingual Students: A Challenge for Canadian Universities, Can Modern Lang Rev, 87; art, Common Concerns in Marian Engel's Children's Stories and her Adult Fiction, Can Children's Lit, 86; co-auth, Rede me and be nott wrothe 1528, 92. **CONTACT ADDRESS** English Dept, Laurentian Univ, 935 Ramsey Lake Rd, Sudbury, ON, Canada P3E 2C6.

PARKER, HOLT
DISCIPLINE CLASSICS **EDUCATION** Tulane Univ, BA, 78; Yale Univ, MA, 80, MPhil, 82, PhD, 86. **CAREER** Assoc prof, Univ Cincinnati. **HONORS AND AWARDS** 5-Star Teaching Awd, 86; Provost's Teaching Improvement Awd, 87; Res Grant, 88; NEH Summer Stipend, Univ of Ariz, 89; Phi Beta Kappa, Judah Touro Medal in Classics, Phi Delta Kappa (German), German Dept Book Prize, Univ Col London: Platt Prize in Greek; NEH Fel, 90-91; Women's Classical Caucus Prize, 92; Rome Prize, Fel of Am Academy in Rome, NEH Fel, 96; Nomination: A B Cohen Teaching Awd, Univ of Cinnati, 96. **MEMBERSHIPS** Am Philol Asn; Soc Ancient Med; Women's Classical Caucus; Screen Actor's Guild. **RESEARCH** Gender studies; Augustan poetry; Greek lyric poetry; Roman comedy; linguistics; literary theory; ancient medicine. **SELECTED PUBLICATIONS** Auth, Crucially Funny or Tranio on the Couch, TAPA, 89; auth, Another Go at the Text of Philaenis, ZPE, 89; auth, The Bones: Propertius 1.21.9-10, Clas Philol, 91; auth, In the Mood: Prop. 2. 26. 1-3, Mnemosyne, 92; auth, The Fertile Fields of Umbria: Propertius 1. 22. 10, Mnemosyne, 92; auth, Love 's Body Anatomized: The Ancient Erotic Manuals and the Rhetoric of Sexuality, Oxford Univ Press, 92; auth, Fish in Trees and Tie-Dyed Sheep: A Function of the Surreal in Roman Poetry, Arethusa, 92; auth, Other Remarks on the Other Sulpicia, CW, 92; auth, Sappho Schoolmistress, TAPA, 93; auth, Sulpicia, the Auctor de Sulpicia and the Authorship of 3.9 and 3.11 of the Corpus Tibullianum, Helios, 94; auth, Innocent on the Face of it: An Overlooked Obscenity in Martial, Mnemosyne, 94; auth, A Curiously Persistent Error: Satyricon 43.4, Clas Philol, 94; auth, Heterosexuality, Oxford Univ Press, 96; auth, Women Physicians in Greece, Rome, and the Byzantine Empire, Univ Press Ky, 97; auth, Latin and Greek Poetry by Five Renaissance Italian Women Humanists, SUNY Press, 97; auth, Plautus vs. Terence: Audience and Popularity Re-examined, AJP, 96; auth, The Teratogenic Grid, Princeton Univ Press, 97. **CONTACT ADDRESS** Dept of Classics, Univ of Cincinnati, PO Box 210226, Cincinnati, OH 45210-0226. **EMAIL** parkerhn@email.us.edu

PARKER, JO ALYSON
PERSONAL Born 01/08/1954, CA, m, 1 child **DISCIPLINE** EIGHTEENTH-CENTURY NOVEL **EDUCATION** Univ CA, BA, 81; MA, 84; PhD, 89. **CAREER** Engl, St. Joseph's Univ. **HONORS AND AWARDS** Phi Beta Kappa, 81. **SELECTED PUBLICATIONS** Auth, The Author's Inheritance: Henry Fielding, Jane Austen, and the Establishment of the Novel, Northern Ill UP (DeKalb), 98; auth, "Pride and Predjudice: Jane Austen's Double Inheritance Plot," Real 7, 90; a uth, Complicating a Simple Story: Inchbald's Two Versions of Female Power, Eighteenth-Century Studies 30, 97; Spiraling Down 'the Gutter of Time': Tristram Shandy and the Strange Attractor of Death, Weber Studies 14, 97; Strange Attractors in Absalom, Absalom!" in Reading Matters: Narrative in the New Media Ecology, Cornell Univ Press, 97; Gendering the Robot: Stanislaw Lem's 'The Mask,' Science-Fiction Studies 19, 92. **CONTACT ADDRESS** Saint Joseph's Univ, 5600 City Ave, Philadelphia, PA 19131. **EMAIL** jparker@sju.edu

PARKER, MARK M.
PERSONAL Born 08/14/1952, Royal Oak, MI, m, 1980, 3 children **DISCIPLINE** MUSIC THEORY **EDUCATION** Bob Jones Univ, BA, 74; Univ Rochester, MA, 76; Univ N Tex, PhD, 88. **CAREER** Bob Jones Univ, 76-86, 85-. **MEMBERSHIPS** Soc for Mus Theory, Mus Theory Southeast, Tech Inst Mus Educators. **RESEARCH** Hist mus theory, Schenkerian analysis, mus tech. **SELECTED PUBLICATIONS** various **CONTACT ADDRESS** Bob Jones Univ, Box 34441, Greenville, SC 29614. **EMAIL** mparker@bju.edu

PARKER, MARY
PERSONAL Born, Columbia, M, 1971 **DISCIPLINE** LITERATURE **EDUCATION** Hunter Col, BA, 70; MA, 74; CUNY Grad Ctr, MPhil, 79; PhD, 86. **CAREER** P/T lectr, Hunter Col, 74-79; p/t instr, Boston Univ, Boston Col, 80-85. **HONORS AND AWARDS** Pres Distinction Award Nomination; Doctoral Fel Award; Woodrow Wilson Fel Nomination; NSHA Award; Hunter Col CCAH Dept Student Rep. **MEMBERSHIPS** MLA; AAUP; AISO. **RESEARCH** How and why writings of American authors project more than their specific world vision; Heteropias and the 21st century; biography and political writings as history or literary creation; elements that determine literary form in our particular space and time; life and the intellect; the pros/cons of a practical approach to education and/or or dominant ideologies and the biases injected in curricula at all levels. **SELECTED PUBLICATIONS** Auth, "Santas Reinas, Martires y Contesanas, La Mujer en el Teatro de Juan Bautista Diamante," in Spanish Dramatists of the Golden Age: A Bio-Bibliographical Sourcebook, ed. Mary Parker (Conn: Greenwood Pr, 98); auth, "Fr. J. Bautista Diamante: A Bibliography of Primary Sources," Bull Bibliog 49 (92). **CONTACT ADDRESS** 710 Park Ave, New York, NY 10021. **EMAIL** sparker@msn.com

PARKER, PATRICIA L.
DISCIPLINE ENGLISH **EDUCATION** Western Maryland Col, BA, 63; Univ Chicago, MA, 64; New York Univ, PhD, 81. **CAREER** Visiting Lectr, Osaka Jogakuin, Japan, 86-87; Visiting Lectr, Hiroshima Shudo Univ, Japan, 91-92 and 93-94; Asst Prof, 73-82, Assoc Prof, 82-88, Prof, 88-, Salem State Col. **SELECTED PUBLICATIONS** Auth, Inescapable Romance, a Study of Romance from Ariosto to Wallace Stevens; Literary Fat Ladies: Rhetoric, Gender, Property; Shakespeare from the Margins; co-ed, Shakespeare and the Question of Theory and Women; Race and Writing in the Early Modern Period. **CONTACT ADDRESS** English Dept, Salem State Col, Salem, MA 01970. **EMAIL** pparker@salem.mass.edu

PARKER, RICHARD W.
DISCIPLINE CLASSICS **EDUCATION** Univ of Calif at Santa Barbara, BA, 74; MA, 78; Univ of British Columbia, PhD, 86. **CAREER** Lect, Univ of Saskatchewan, 84-85, 86-87; lect, Brock Univ, 85-86; asst prof, Univ Western Ontario, 87-88; asst prof, 88-96, Assoc Prof, 96-, Dept Chair, Brock Univ, 93-98. **HONORS AND AWARDS** Am School of Classical Studies in Athens, 80-81. **MEMBERSHIPS** Archaeological Inst of Am, brd of governors (AIA-Canada); Can Archaeological Inst in Athens; Am Philol Asn; Classical Asn Can; Asn Internationale d'Epigraphie Grec et Latine. **RESEARCH** Greek hist; Greek epigraphy; Greek lit. **SELECTED PUBLICATIONS** Auth, A Greek Inscription from Honoring a Julio-Claudian, Zeitschrift fur Papyrologie und Epigraphik 75, 88; Potamon of Mytilene and His Family, Zeitschrift fur Papyrologie und Epigraphik 85, 91; with E. H. Williams, A Fragment of a Diocletianic Tax Assessment from Mytilene, Echos du Monde Classique XXXIX, New Series 14, 95. **CONTACT ADDRESS** Dept of Classics, Brock Univ, 500 Glenridge Ave, Saint Catherines, ON, Canada L2S 3A1. **EMAIL** rparker@spartan.ac.brocku.ca

PARKER-STARBUCK, JENNIFER
PERSONAL Born 04/28/1962, Montpelier, VT, 1 child **DISCIPLINE** THEATRE **EDUCATION** NYork Univ, BFA, 85; Univ Ariz, MA, 93. **CAREER** Adj prof, CUNY Baruch Col, 98-. **HONORS AND AWARDS** Jewish Found Educ Women, 01; Vera Roberts Dissertation Award, 01. **MEMBERSHIPS** ATHE; ASTR; SDHS; MLA. **RESEARCH** Contemporary and avant-garde theater; multimedia theater; technology; cyborg studies; disability studies. **SELECTED PUBLICATIONS** Auth, "Triangulated Nation, George Coates Performance Works and Lizard Monitors, Cathy Weis at Dizon Place," Theater J (99); auth, "The Far Side of the Moon, by Robert Lepage," Theater J (00). **CONTACT ADDRESS** Fine/Performing Arts Dept, Baruch Col, CUNY, 17 Lexington Ave, A-1209, New York, NY 10010. **EMAIL** zstarbuck@aol.com

PARKES, ADAM
PERSONAL Born 02/25/1966, Wolver Hampton, Britain, m, 2000, 1 child **DISCIPLINE** ENGLISH **EDUCATION** Cambridge Univ, BA, MA, 85-88; Univ Rochester, PhD, 93. **CAREER** Asst prof to assoc prof, Univ Ga, 93-. **HONORS AND AWARDS** Charlotte W Newcombe Fel, 92-93; Res Grant, Univ Ga, 01-02. **MEMBERSHIPS** MLA; IJJF. **RESEARCH** Modern British and American literature; Victorian literature; literary impressionism. **SELECTED PUBLICATIONS** Auth, Modernism and the Theater of Censorship, Oxford Univ Pr, 96; auth, "Ezra Pound: Poet as Censor," Centennial Rev (99); auth, "Moore, Snow, and 'The Dead,'" English Lit Transition (99); auth, "A Sense of Justice: Whistler, Ruskin, James, Impressionism," Victorian Studies (00); auth, "Kazuo Ishiguro's' The Remains of the Day:' A Reader's Guide," Contiuum (01). **CONTACT ADDRESS** English Dept, Univ of Georgia, Athens, GA 30602-6205. **EMAIL** aparkes@arches.uga.edu

PARKS, SHERI L.
DISCIPLINE COMMUNICATION **EDUCATION** Univ NC-Chapel Hill, BA, 78; Univ MA-Amherst, MA, 83, PhD, 85. **CAREER** Assoc dean in undergrad stud. **RESEARCH** Revolve around popular American aesthetics with a special focus on culture, family, and gender. In particular she is interested in the aesthetics of everyday esperiences, including mass media na dother popular culture artifacts. **SELECTED PUBLICATIONS** Auth, Feminism in the Lives of Ordinary Women, Barnard Col Papers, 90; In My Mother's House: Traditional Black Feminism in the PBS Production Underlying 'A Raisin in the Sun, Feminism and Theater, Fairleigh Dickinson UP, 94. **CONTACT ADDRESS** Am Stud Dept, Univ of Maryland, Col Park, Taliaferro Hall, Rm 2131, College Park, MD 20742-8821. **EMAIL** sp10@umail.umd.edu

PARKS, STEPHEN ROBERT
PERSONAL Born 07/18/1940, Columbus, OH **DISCIPLINE** ENGLISH LITERATURE, BIBLIOGRAPHY **EDUCATION** Yale, BA, 61; Cambridge, England (King's Col), PhD, 65. **CAREER** Assoc curator, then curator, James M and Marie Louise Osborn Collection, Beinecke Rare Book and Manuscript Library, Yale Univ, 67-; librarian, Elizabethan Club of Yale Univ, 72-. **SELECTED PUBLICATIONS** Ed with intro, Sale catalogues of Libraries and Eminent Persons, gen ed, A N L Munby, vol 5: Poets and Men of Letters, London, 72; ed with bibliographical notes, The English Book Trade 1660-1853; Titles Relating to the Early History of English Publishing, Bookselling, the Struggle for Copyright and the Freedom of the Press, 38 vols, New York, 75-76; auth, John Dunton and the English Book Trade; A Study of His Career with a Checklist of His Publications, New York, 75; The Bibliographical Society of America 1904-1979; A Retrospective Collection, compiled by Stephen Parks for the Bibliographical Soc of Am, Charlottesville, 80; Literary Autographs, papers read ata a Clark Library Seminar by Parks and P J Croft, Stephen Parks, Charles Cotton and the Derby Manuscript, Los Angeles, 83; auth, The Elizabethan Club of Yale University and Its Library, Yale Univ Press, 86; auth, The Luttrell File: Narcissus Luttrell's Inscriptions of Dates of Publication on Contemporary Pamphlets, 1679-1720, supp to the Yale Univ Lib Gazette, winter 96-97; author of numerous articles. **CONTACT ADDRESS** Beinecke Library, Yale Univ, P O Box 208240, New Haven, CT 06520. **EMAIL** stephen.parks@yale.edu

PAROTTI, PHILLIP
PERSONAL Born 05/18/1941, Silver City, NM, m, 1964, 2 children **DISCIPLINE** ENGLISH **EDUCATION** United Sts Naval Academy, BS, 63; Univ New Mexico, MA, 69; PhD, 72. **CAREER** Midshipman to Lieutenant Commander, United States Navy, 59-67; Prof of English, Sam Houston State Univ, 72-00. **HONORS AND AWARDS** Sam Houston State Univ 87; Excellence in Teaching Awd. **RESEARCH** The English Renaissance; Military History. **SELECTED PUBLICATIONS** Auth, The Greek Generals Talk, Univ of Illinois Press, 86; auth, The Trojan Generals Talk, Univ of Illinois Press, 88; auth, Fires in the Sky, Ticknor & Fields, 90. **CONTACT ADDRESS** Dept English, Sam Houston State Univ, PO Box 2146, Huntsville, TX 77341-2146. **EMAIL** eng_pxp@shsu.edu

PARRY, HUGH
PERSONAL Born 07/11/1934, Liverpool, England, m, 1931, 2 children **DISCIPLINE** CLASSICS **EDUCATION** Cambridge Univ, BA, 56; Univ Calif Berkeley, 63. **CAREER** Lectr to prof and div chair, York Univ, 63-. **HONORS AND AWARDS** Scholar, Cambridge Univ, 53-56; Fulbright Travel Grant, 59-64; Can Coun Leave Fel, 78; Outstanding Teaching Awd, York Univ, 91. **MEMBERSHIPS** APA; CAMWS; Class Asn of Ont. **RESEARCH** Greek drama and religion; Magic in ancient and modern fiction. **SELECTED PUBLICATIONS** Auth, Thelxis: Magic and Imagination in Greek Myth and Poetry, Lanham, 92; auth, "The Apologos of Odysseus: Lies, All Lies?," Phoenix (94): 1-20; auth, Visions of Enchantment: Essays on Magic in Fiction, Lanham, 01. **CONTACT ADDRESS** Div Humanities, York Univ, 4700 Keele St, 262 Vanier Col,, Toronto, ON, Canada M3J 1P3. **EMAIL** hparryhm@yorku.ca

PARRY, JOSEPH D.
PERSONAL Born 12/02/1960, Salt Lake City, UT, m, 1989, 1 child **DISCIPLINE** ENGLISH **EDUCATION** Brigham Young Univ, BA, 85, MA, 87; Univ Utah, PhD, 95. **CAREER** Lectr, 87-88, Asst Prof, 93-, Grad Coord, 95-, Brigham Young Univ. **HONORS AND AWARDS** Clark-Harris Outstanding Grad Stud Awd, 87; Allan D Breck Awd, Rocky Mountain Medieval and Renaissance Asn, 95; Col Hum Res, Travel Grants, Brigham Young Univ, 94-99; grad student instr, brigham young univ, 85-87; teaching fel, univ utah, 88-93. **MEMBERSHIPS** Renaissance Soc Am; Medieval Acad Am; Rocky Mtn Medieval, Renaissance Asn. **RESEARCH** Medieval and Renaissance literary and visual narratives, espec Lawman, Chaucer, Malory and Spenser. **SELECTED PUBLICATIONS** Auth, "Margery Kempe's Inarticulate Narration," Magistra 1.2, 95; "Dorigen, Narration and Coming Home in the Franklin's Tale," Chaucer Rev 30, 96; "Narration and Quattrocento Annunciation Paintings," JRMMRA 17, 96; "Following Malory out of Arthur's World," Mod Philol 95, 97; "Exploring the Middle Ages with the Medieval May," Interdisciplinary Humanities, 15.1, 98; "Narrators, Messengers and Lawman's Brut," Arthuriana 8.3, 98; **CONTACT ADDRESS** Dept of Hum, Classics and Comp Lit, Brigham Young Univ, Provo, UT 84602. **EMAIL** joseph_parry@byu.edu

PARRY-GILES, TREVOR
DISCIPLINE COMMUNICATION **EDUCATION** Ripon Col, BA, 85; Univ Nmex, 87; Indiana Univ, PhD, 92. **CAREER** Asst prof, St Ambrose Univ, 91-97; asst prof, West Ill Univ, 97-98; sr Writer, Campaign Performance Group, 98-; vis asst prof, Univ of Maryland. **MEMBERSHIPS** Nat Commun Asn. **RESEARCH** Investigate the relationship that exist between rhetoric, politics, law, and the mass media. **SELECTED PUBLICATIONS** Auth, "Ideological Anxiety and the Censored Test: Real Lives-At the Edge of the Union," Critical Stud in Mass Commun, 94; auth, "Property Rights, Human Rights, and American Jurisprudence: The Rejection of John J. Parker's Nomination to the Supreme Court," South Commun Jour, 94; auth, "Idealogy and Poetics in Public Issue Construction: Thatcherism, Civil Liberties, and Terrorism' in Northern Ireland," Commun Q, 95; auth, "Character, the Constitution, and the Ideological Embodiment of Civil Rights' in the 1967 Nomination of Thurgood Marshall to the Supreme Court," Q Jour Speech, 96; coauth, "Gendered Politics and the Presidential Image Construction: A Reassessment of the 'Feminine Style,'", Commun Monogr, 96; coauth, "Political Scopophilia, Presidential Campaigning, and the Intimacy of American Politics," Commun Stud, 96; coauth, "'A Stranger to Its Laws': Freedom, Civil Rights, and the Legal Ambiguity of Romer vs. Evans," Argumentation & Advocacy, 97; coauth, "Meta-Imaging, The War Room, and the Hyperreality of U.S. Politics," Journal of Communication 49, (99): 28-45; auth, "For the Soul of the Supreme Court: Porgressivism, Ethics, and Social Justice in the 1916 Trail of Louis D. Brandeis, Rhetoric & Publilc Affairs 2, (99): 83-106; auth, "Speechwriting," in The Manship School Guide to Political Communication, Baton Rouge: Louisiana State Univ Press, 99. **CONTACT ADDRESS** Dept of Communication, Univ of Maryland, Col Park, 2130 Skinner Building, College Park, MD 20742-7635. **EMAIL** tp54@umail.umd.edu

PARSONS, JAMES
DISCIPLINE MUSICOLOGY **EDUCATION** Fla State Univ, BachMus, 78; Univ N Texas, PhD Musicol, 92. **CAREER** Vis asst prof, Univ Mo, 92-95; ASSC PROF, COORD MUSIC HIST, SOUTHWEST MO STATE UNIV, 99-. **HONORS AND AWARDS** German Acad Exchange Study Visit Grant for res in Berlin, Germany, Summer 00. **MEMBERSHIPS** Am Musicological Soc **RESEARCH** Ger Art song; Beethoven music and aesthetics. **SELECTED PUBLICATIONS** Auth, "Annalecta Husserliana," vol 61, 00; auth, Cambridge Companion to the Lied, Cambridge University Press, 02; auth, "Bethoven Forum," vol 9, 02. **CONTACT ADDRESS** 4355 S National Ave, #1209, Springfield, MO 1209. **EMAIL** jap614f@mail.smsu.edu

PARSONS, JEDEDIAH DAVID
PERSONAL Born 02/02/1971, New York, NY, m, 1997 **DISCIPLINE** CLASSICS **EDUCATION** Harvard Univ, BA, 93; Univ Calif Berk, MA, 95, PhD, 00. **RESEARCH** Roman comedy; Latin literature. **SELECTED PUBLICATIONS** Auth, A New Approach to the Saturnian Verse, Trans of the APA, forthcoming. **CONTACT ADDRESS** Dept of Classics, Univ of California, Berkeley, 7233 Dwinelle Hall No 2520, Berkeley, CA 94720-2520. **EMAIL** jed@socrates.berkeley.edu

PASCAL, PAUL
PERSONAL Born 03/26/1925, New York, NY, m, 1948, 2 children **DISCIPLINE** CLASSICS, MEDIEVAL LATIN **EDUCATION** Univ VT, BA, 48; Univ NC, PHD(classics), 53. **CAREER** Prof Classics, Univ Wash, 53-. **MEMBERSHIPS** Am Philol Asn. **RESEARCH** Mediaeval Latin literature. **SELECTED PUBLICATIONS** Coauth, The Institutionum Disciplinae of Isidore of Seville, Traditio, 57; Notes on Missus Sum in Vineam of Walter of Chatillon, Studies in Honor of B L Ullman, Rome, 64; The Conclusion of the Pervigilium Veneris, Neophilologus, 65; The Julius Exclusus of Erasmus, Ind Univ, 68. **CONTACT ADDRESS** Dept of Classics, Univ of Washington, Seattle, WA 98105.

PASLER, JANN C.
PERSONAL Born 07/06/1951, Milwaukee, WI **DISCIPLINE** MUSIC **EDUCATION** Vanderbilt Univ, BA, 73; Univ Chicago, MA, 74, PhD, 81. **CAREER** Actg asst prof, Univ Va, 78-80; prof, Univ Cincinnati, 81; prof, Univ Calif, San Diego, 81-. **HONORS AND AWARDS** Magna Cum Laude, 73; NEH grant, 82; NEH fel, 85, 88-89; Univ Calif Pres Fel, 88-89; Stanford fel, 93-94; Univ Calif Hum Res Inst, co-dir res residency, 94. **SELECTED PUBLICATIONS** Auth, Debussy, Stravinsky and the Ballets Russes: The Emergence of a New Musical Logic, Univ of Chicago, 81; auth, Confronting Straviinsky: Man, Musician, and Modernist, Univ of Calif Pr, 86; auth, "India and its Music in the French Imagination before 1913," Journal of the Indian Musicological Society Baroda, India (96): 27-51; auth, "Directions in Musicology," Acta Musicological Journal of the International Musicological Society, Basel, Switzerland (97): 15-20; auth, "The Ironies of Gender, or Virility and Politics in the Music of Augusta Holmes, Women and Music 2 (98): 1-25; auth, "Timbre, Voice-leading and the Musical Arabesque in Debussy's Piano Music," Debussy in Performance, ed James Briscoe, Yale Univ Pr, 00); auth, "Magnus Synnestvedt: A Scandinavian Musical Amateur in Paris, 1902-1908, in France in Nordic Music, ed. Anders Edling, London:

Gordon and Breach, 00); auth, "Building a public for orchestral music: Les Concerts Colonne," in Concert et public: mutation de la vie musicale en Europe de 1780 a 1914, Paris: Edition de la Maison des Sciences Humaines, 00; auth, "Race, Orientalism, and Distinction in the Wake of the Yellow Peril," Western Music and its Others, ed. Gerogina Born, Univ of Calif Pr, 00. **CONTACT ADDRESS** Univ of California, San Diego, La Jolla, CA 92093. **EMAIL** jpasler@ucsd.edu

PASSAMANECK, STEPHEN MAURICE
PERSONAL Born 12/07/1933, Pittsburgh, PA, m, 1988, 3 children **DISCIPLINE** RABBINIC LITERATURE **EDUCATION** Univ Pittsburgh, BA, 55; Hebrew Union Col, MA, 60, PhD, 64; Oxford Univ, dipl law, 63. **CAREER** From instr to assoc prof, 63-72, Prof Rabbinics, Hebrew Union Col, Calif, 72-. **MEMBERSHIPS** Cent Conf Am Rabbis; International Conference of Police Chaplains, Jewish Law Association. **RESEARCH** Rabbinic law; Criminal justice & Law enforcement; rabbinic jurisprudence. **SELECTED PUBLICATIONS** Auth, Caravan custom in early rabbinic sources, Tijdschrift voor Rechtsgeschiedenis, 68; A case of piracy, Hebrew Union Col Ann, 70; Two aspects of rabbinic maritime law, J Jewish Studies, 71; Insurance in Rabbinic Law, Edinburgh Univ, 74; ed, Jewish Law and Jewish Life, Union Am Hebrew Congregations, 77; ed, Intro to the History & Sources of Jewish Law, Oxford, 96. **CONTACT ADDRESS** Hebrew Union Col-Jewish Inst of Religion, California, 3077 University Mall, Los Angeles, CA 90007. **EMAIL** spassamaneck@huc.edu

PASTERNACK, CAROL BRAUN
PERSONAL 1 child **DISCIPLINE** ENGLISH LITERATURE AND MEDIEVAL STUDIES **EDUCATION** UCLA, PhD, 83. **CAREER** Assoc Prof, Eng, Univ Calif, Santa Barbara. **RESEARCH** Hist of Eng lang; Gender in the middle ages information technology. **SELECTED PUBLICATIONS** Auth, Stylistic Disjunctions in The Dream of the Rood in Anglo-Saxon England, 84; Textuality in Old English Poetry, Cambridge Univ Press, 95; "Anonymous Polyphony and the Textuality of the Wanderer," Anglo-Saxon Eng, 91; co-ed, Vox intexta: Orality and Textuality in the Middle Ages, Univ Wis Press, 91; auth, "Post-structuralist Theories: The Subject and the Text, Reading Old English Texts, ed, K. O'Brien O'Keeffe, Cambridge Univ Press, 97. **CONTACT ADDRESS** Dept of Eng, Univ of California, Santa Barbara, Santa Barbara, CA 93106-7150. **EMAIL** cpaster@humanitas.ucsb.edu

PATERSON, DOUGLAS L.
PERSONAL Born 10/26/1945, Omaha, NE **DISCIPLINE** THEATRE **EDUCATION** Yankton Col, Yankton, SD, BA, 68; Cornell Univ, MA, 70, PhD, 72. **CAREER** Asst prof, 72-75, Yankton Col; asst prof, 75-79, Willamette Univ; co-member, 79-81, The Dakota Theatre Caravan; assoc prof, prof, chair, 81-, Univ Neb Omaha; bd, 82-88, Alliance for Cultural Democracy; vice-pres, 90-92, Assoc for Theatre in Higher Educ; vice-pres, 94-96, ATHE; chair, 94-97, Pedagogy of the Oppressed Conf. **HONORS AND AWARDS** Ford Found Fel, 68-70; Teacher of the Year, 74; Isaacson Endowed Chair, 98; us leading practitioner/theorist of theatre techniques develop by brazilian dir augusto boal. **MEMBERSHIPS** Assoc Theatre in Higher Educ; Pedagogy & Theatre of the Oppressed. **RESEARCH** Theatre of the oppressed; techniques of Augusto Boal; theatre & soc change; post-moderism; cultural materialism; new historicism. **SELECTED PUBLICATIONS** Auth, A Role to Play for the Theatre of the Oppressed, Drama Rev, 94; coauth, We Are All Theatre: An Interview with Augusto Boal, High Performance, 96; auth, foreward, Hope is Vital, Heineman, 98; auth, The Embodiment of Embodied Pedagogy, Embodied Pedagogy, 99. **CONTACT ADDRESS** Dept of Theatre, Univ of Nebraska, Omaha, Fine Arts Bldg, Omaha, NE 68182. **EMAIL** paterson@unomaha.edu

PATEY, DOUGLAS L.
PERSONAL Born 05/20/1951, New York, NY, s, 1 child **DISCIPLINE** ENGLISH **EDUCATION** Hamilton Col, AB, 72; Univ Va, MA, 73; MA, 77; PhD, 79. **CAREER** Prof, Smith Col, 79-. **HONORS AND AWARDS** Guggenheim Found Fel; NEH Fel. **MEMBERSHIPS** Am Soc for Eighteenth-Century Studies, Hist of Sci Soc. **SELECTED PUBLICATIONS** Auth, "Aesthetics' and the Rise of Lyric in the Eighteenth Century," Studies in English Literature 33.3 (93): 587-608; auth, "Anne Finch, John Dyer, and the Georgic Syntax of Nature," in Augustan Subjects: Essays in Honor of Martin Battestin, ed. Albert J. Rivero (DE: Univ Del Press, 97), 29-46; auth, "The Institution of Criticism in the Eighteenth Century," and "Ancients and Moderns," in Cambridge History of Literary Criticism Vol 4: The Eighteenth Century (Cambridge Univ Press, 97), 3-71 & 798-809; auth, Evelyn Waugh: A Critical Biography, Blackwell, 98. **CONTACT ADDRESS** Dept English, Smith Col, 98 Green St, Northampton, MA 01063-1000. **EMAIL** dpatsy@hotmail.com

PATRAKA, VIVIAN
DISCIPLINE THEATER **EDUCATION** Brooklyn Col, BA; Univ Michigan, MA, PhD. **CAREER** Prof English & dir, Inst for the Study of Culture and Soc, Bowling Green State Univ. **HONORS AND AWARDS** Cum laude, BA; pres, Women and Theatre Program; vice-pres, Res and Publs, and mem, Bd of Governors, Asn for Theatre in Higher Educ; Am Soc for Theatre Res program comm, 96. **SELECTED PUBLICATIONS** Contribur, Making a Spectacle: Feminist Essays on Contemporary Women's Theatre, Michigan; contribur, Performing Feminism: The Critical Act, Johns Hopkins; contirbur, Critical Theory and Performance, Michigan; contribur, Acting Out: Feminist Performances, Michigan; contribur, Performance and Cultural Politics, Routledge; contribur, Jews and Other Differences, Minnesota; auth, Spectacles of Suffering: Theatre, Fascism and the Holocaust, Indiana Univ, 99. **CONTACT ADDRESS** Institute for the Study of Culture and Society, Bowling Green State Univ, College Park Office Bldg, Bowling Green, OH 43403-0023. **EMAIL** vpatrak@bgnet.bgsu.edu

PATRICK, BARBARA
DISCIPLINE AMERICAN LITERATURE AND AMERICAN ENGLISH GRAMMAR **EDUCATION** Univ NC, Chapel Hill, PhD, 91. **CAREER** Instr, Rowan Col of NJ. **SELECTED PUBLICATIONS** Works on the dramatic poetry of W.H. Auden; on collaborative writing in the classroom; Publications on Ghost Stories by American Women of the 19th Century. **CONTACT ADDRESS** Rowan Univ, Glassboro, NJ 08028-1701. **EMAIL** patrick@rowan.edu

PATTEN, ROBERT LOWRY
PERSONAL Born 04/26/1939, Oklahoma City, OK, d, 2 children **DISCIPLINE** ENGLISH **EDUCATION** Swarthmore Col, BA, 60; Princeton Univ, MA, 62, PhD, 65. **CAREER** Lect, asst prof, 64-69, Bryn Mawr Col; asst prof, prof, 69-, Rice Univ; Lynette S Autrey Prof in Humanities, 96-. **HONORS AND AWARDS** Woodrow Wilson Fel, 60-61; Fulbright Scholarship, Univ of London, 63-64; NEH Fel 68-69, 77-78, 87-88; Guggenheim Fel, 80-81; Nat Humanities Center Fel, 87-88; Assoc Center for Advanced Study in the Visual Arts, Nat Gal of Art, 88-89; NEH Proj Grant Dir and PI, 87-90; George R Brown Awd for Sup Tchng, Rice Univ, 88, 89, 91; Grad Stud Assoc Outstanding Serv Awd, 94; Robert Lowry Patten Grad Stud Serv Awds est in honor, 96; Grad Stud Assoc Mentor Awd, 00; Rice U Hudspeth Service Awd, 00. **MEMBERSHIPS** Modern Language Assoc; Beta of TX Chapt, Phi Beta Kappa, Pres; Phi Beta Kappa Alumni of Gr Houston, Dir; The Dickens Proj, Univ of CA Santa Cruz, Dir; AAUP; Soc for History of Authorship Reading and Pub. Dir. **RESEARCH** Charles Dickens; George Cruikshank; British and European fiction to 1900; the illustrated book; the history of the book 19th cent British lit and art. **SELECTED PUBLICATIONS** Auth, George Cruikshanks Life Time and Art, New Brunswick Rutgers Univ Press, London, Lutterworth Press, 96; co ed, Literature in the Marketplace Nineteenth Century British Publishing and Reading Practices, Cambridge Univ Press, 95; coauth, Introduction Publishing History as Hypertext, Lit in the Marketplace; auth, Serialized Retrospection in the Pickwick Papers, ch 6, Lit in the Marketplace; art, When Is a Book Not a Book, Biblion the Bulletin of the NY Pub Lib 4, 96. **CONTACT ADDRESS** Dept of English MS 30, Rice Univ, 6100 Main St, PO Box 1892, Houston, TX 77251-1892. **EMAIL** patten@rice.edu

PATTERSON, ANITA
PERSONAL Born 04/08/1961, New York, NY, m, 1995 **DISCIPLINE** ENGLISH **EDUCATION** Harvard Col, BA, 83; Harvard Univ, MA, 87; PhD, 92. **HONORS AND AWARDS** Fac Fel, Univ Ill, 93; Teaching Recognition Awd, Univ Ill, 97; Jr Fel, Boston Univ, 00. **MEMBERSHIPS** MLA: Modernist Studies Asn; Am Studies Asn. **RESEARCH** Modern American poetry; African-American poetry; Caribbean poetry; American Romanticism. **SELECTED PUBLICATIONS** Auth, "American Philosophy as Praxis: From Emerson and Thoreau to Martin Luther King," Salmagundi, (95): 181-207; auth, "Comparative Identities: Exile in the Writings of Frantz Fanon and W.E.B. DuBois," in Borders, Boundaries, and Frames, (Routledge, 95), 107-132; auth, From Emerson to King: Democracy, Race, and the Politics of Protest, Oxford Univ Press, 97; auth, "Jazz, Realism, and the Modernist Lyric: The Poetry of Langston Hughes," Mod Lang Quart, (00): 651-682; auth, "Contingencies of Pleasure and Shame: Jamaican Women's Poetry," in Feminist Consequences: Theory for the New Century, (Columbia Univ Press, 00), 254-282. **CONTACT ADDRESS** Dept English, Boston Univ, 236 Bay State Rd, Boston, MA 02215. **EMAIL** apatters@bu.edu

PATTERSON, BOB E.
PERSONAL Born 08/29/1931, Kings Mountain, NC, m, 1953, 2 children **DISCIPLINE** LITERATURE AND THEOLOGY **EDUCATION** Gardner-Webb Univ, AA, 50; Baylor Univ, BA, 52, MA, 57; Southern Baptist Theol Seminary, Mdiv, 56, PhD, 60. **CAREER** Distinguished Prof of Rel, Dept of Rel, 61-, Baylor Univ. **HONORS AND AWARDS** Alpha Chi Scholastic Fraternity; Outstanding Educ Of Amer; Outstanding Faculty Member; Permanent Distinguished Prof of Rel; Regional Pres of AAR; Natl Pres of N.A.B.P.R. **MEMBERSHIPS** AAR, A. A.U.D., NABPR. **RESEARCH** Theology, Faith and Science, Biblical Studies, Philosophy of Religion. **SELECTED PUBLICATIONS** Auth, Science, Faith and Revelation; Perspectives on Theology; Discovering Ezekiel and Daniel; Discovering Matthew; Discovering Revelation; Theologians, Carl F. H. Henry, Reinhold Niebuhr; Who is Jesus Christ?, ed, 18 vol series, Makers of Modern Theological Mind. **CONTACT ADDRESS** Dept of Religion, Baylor Univ, Waco, Waco, TX 76798. **EMAIL** Bob_Patterson@baylor.edu

PATTERSON, CELIA
DISCIPLINE TECHNICAL WRITING **EDUCATION** E Tex State Univ-Texarkana, BS, MS; Univ Tulsa, PhD. **CAREER** Asst prof. **RESEARCH** Modern American fiction, Anglo American WW1 literature. **SELECTED PUBLICATIONS** Publ, articles on tech wrtg, Chopin and Faulkner; bk rev(s). **CONTACT ADDRESS** Dept of Eng, Pittsburg State Univ, 1701 S Broadway St, Pittsburg, KS 66762. **EMAIL** cpatters@pittstate.edu

PATTERSON, WARD L.
PERSONAL Born 12/26/1933, Killbuck, OH, s **DISCIPLINE** COMMUNICATION **EDUCATION** PhD, Ind Univ. **CAREER** Campus Minister, Ind Univ, 72-90; Prof, Cincinnati Bible Col & Seminary, 91-00. **HONORS AND AWARDS** Rotary Student Exchange Fellow for Study in Australia. **RESEARCH** Church & culture; public speaking; humor; intercultural communication. **CONTACT ADDRESS** 2852 McKinley Ave, Cincinnati, OH 45211. **EMAIL** wardlamont@netzero.net

PATTERSON, WILLIS CHARLES
PERSONAL Born 11/27/1930, Ann Arbor, MI, m, 1958, 4 children **DISCIPLINE** MUSIC **EDUCATION** University of Michigan, MusB, M Mus; PhD, Higher Education. **CAREER** Southern Univ, Baton Rouge, LA, 59-61; Virginia State Col, associate professor, 62-68; Univ of Michigan, professor, 77; Univ of Michigan, School of Music, associate dean, 79; Major, Our Own Thing Inc, performer; Univ of Michigan School of Music, associate dean/prof of voice; Emer. **HONORS AND AWARDS** Compiled "Anthology of Art Songs by Black Amer Composers", Edward B Marks Music Corp, 1977; Recorded with: RCA Victor, Philips Records, NBC, BBC. **MEMBERSHIPS** National Opera Assn; National Assn Teachers Singing; Alpha Phi Alpha; NAACP; Natl Assn of Negro Musicians; Natl Black Music Caucus. **RESEARCH** African Am Music. **SELECTED PUBLICATIONS** Auth, Anthology of Art Songs by Black American Composers. **CONTACT ADDRESS** Univ of Michigan, Ann Arbor, 3028 Moore - Music Bldg, Ann Arbor, MI 48109-2085. **EMAIL** wcp@umich.edu

PATTISON, EUGENE H.
PERSONAL Born 01/08/1935, Pontiac, MI **DISCIPLINE** ENGLISH **EDUCATION** Alma Col, BA, 56; Univ Mich, MA, 57, PhD, 63; Harvard Univ, STB, 64. **CAREER** From asst prof to assoc prof to prof to chemn 64-98, prof 98-00, prof emeritus, 00; Alma Col; ordained min, Presbyterian Church, 64- . **HONORS AND AWARDS** State Col Scholar; Presbyterian Grad Fel, 62-63; Dist Prof Year, 73, 81, Alma Col; NEH, 81; Grand Prytanis Key Ldr Awd; Tau Kappa Epsilon, 75; Order of Omega; Phi Beta Kappa; Coolidge Res Fel, 95; Chapter Advisory Hall of Fame, Tau Kappa Epsilon, 99; Posey Awd for Faculty Excellence, Alma College, 99. **MEMBERSHIPS** Am Asn Univ Prof; Asn Relig Intellectual Life; Conf Col Compos Commun; Modern Lang Asn; Society Stud Midwestern Lit Culture. **RESEARCH** American literature, 1865-1920, Annie Dillard; Robinson Jeffers; Gene Stratton Porter; Booth Tarkington; Midwestern literature. **SELECTED PUBLICATIONS** Auth, art, A Century of Alma College Leadership, 86; auth, art, The Great Lakes Childhood: The Experience of William Dean Howells and Annie Dillard, 88-89; auth, art, Who is Blennerhassett: Three Twentiheth Century Novels Give Answer, 89; auth, art, The Landscape and the Sense of the Past in William Dean Howells, 93; auth, art, The Limberlost, Tinker Creek Science and Society: Gene Stratton-Porter and Annie Dillard, 94-95; ed, Wm. Dean Howells, The Leatherwood God, Indiana Univ Press, 76; auth, art. God and Humanity at Continent's Western Edge: Robinson Jeffers and Annie Dillard, 95; auth, entries on Wm. Dean Howells, Wm. Henry Venable, and Bruce Catton, Dic of Midwest Lit, 01. **CONTACT ADDRESS** Alma Col, Alma, MI 48801-1599. **EMAIL** pattison@alma.edu

PATTON, MARILYN D.
PERSONAL Born, China, m, 2 children **DISCIPLINE** ENGLISH **EDUCATION** Stanford Univ, BA, 70; Univ Calif Santa Cruz, MA, 83; PhD, 89. **CAREER** Lectr, Stanford Univ, 88-89; vis asst prof, Univ Calif Santa Cruz, 89-91; prof, De Anza Col, 91-. **HONORS AND AWARDS** NEH Travel Grant. **MEMBERSHIPS** MLA; Poe Studies Asn; Margaret Atwood Soc; Melville Soc. **RESEARCH** Literary cannibalism; Melville; Postcolonialism; Women's fiction. **SELECTED PUBLICATIONS** Auth, "Lady Oracle: Politics of the Body," ANEL, 91; auth, "Tourists and Terrorists: The Creation of Bodily Harm," PLL, 92. **CONTACT ADDRESS** Dept English, De Anza Col, 131 Dake Ave, Santa Cruz, CA 95062-1501. **EMAIL** mdpatton@aol.com

PATTON, VENETRIA
DISCIPLINE LITERATURE **EDUCATION** Univ LaVerne; BA; 90; Univ Calif-Riverside, MA, 92; PhD, 96. **CAREER** Asst prof, English & African Am & African Student, 96-, coordr, African Am & African Student. 98-, Univ Nebr-Lincoln. **HONORS AND AWARDS** Hum Rights and Hum Diversity Summer Fac Fel; Teaching Coun Summer Vac Fel; Fac Summer Res Fel. **MEMBERSHIPS** MLA, ASA,MELUS, NCBS,NAES. **RESEARCH** Black women writers, Motherhood, Racial markers. **SELECTED PUBLICATIONS** Auth, Women in Chains: The Legacy of Slavery in Black Women's

Fiction, NY: SUNY, 2000. **CONTACT ADDRESS** Dept English, Univ of Nebraska, Lincoln, 202 Andrews, PO Box 880333, Lincoln, NE 68588-0333. **EMAIL** vpatton1@unl.edu

PAUL, GEORGE MACKAY
PERSONAL Born 07/16/1927, Glasgow, Scotland, m, 1956, 3 children **DISCIPLINE** CLASSICS, ANCIENT HISTORY **EDUCATION** Oxford Univ, BA & MA, 54; Univ London, PHD(classics), 63. **CAREER** From asst lectr to lectr classics, Univ W Indies, 55-64; from asst prof to assoc prof, 64-70, chmn dept, 73-76, Prof Classics, McMaster Univ, 70, Mem, Comt Coord Acad Libr Serv Ont Univs, 66-67; Can Coun leave fel, 71-72. **MEMBERSHIPS** Class Asn Can (treas, 67-69); Am Philol Asn; Soc Prom Roman Studies; Asn Ancient Historians; Soc Prom Hellenic Studies. **RESEARCH** Greek and Roman historiography; Roman history. **SELECTED PUBLICATIONS** Ed, Roman Coins and Public Life under the Empire: E. Togo Salmon Papers II, Univ Mich Press, (Ann Arbor, Mi), 99. **CONTACT ADDRESS** Dept of Classics, McMaster Univ, 1280 Main St W, Hamilton, ON, Canada L8S 4M2. **EMAIL** gepaul@mcmaster.ca

PAULEY, JOHN L.
PERSONAL Born 06/01/1951, Prescott, AZ, m, 1975, 2 children **DISCIPLINE** COMMUNICATION, SPEECH **EDUCATION** Southwestern Col, BA, 73; Denver Conservative Baptist Sem, MDiv, 77; Univ Tex, MA, 89; Univ Tex, PhD, 91. **CAREER** From Asst Prof to Assoc Prof, St Mary's Col, 92-. **HONORS AND AWARDS** Fel, Ctr for Acad Innovation, St Mary's Col. **MEMBERSHIPS** Nat Commun Asn, Relig Commun Asn. **RESEARCH** Religious rhetoric, religion and media, history of preaching, Louis Farrakhan, women's rhetoric. **SELECTED PUBLICATIONS** Auth, "Metaphors in Reformation Era Hermeneutic and Homiletic Theory: Common Rusts, Different Extensions," J of Commun and Relig, 17 (94): 53-70; auth, "Reshaping Public Persona and the Prophetic Ethos: Louis Farrakhan at the Million Man March," Western J of Commun 62 (98): 512-536. **CONTACT ADDRESS** Dept Commun, Saint Mary's Col, Indiana, 105 Moreau Hall, Notre Dame, IN 46556. **EMAIL** jpauley@saintmarys.edu

PAULY, THOMAS HARRY
PERSONAL Born 03/06/1940, Missoula, MT, m, 1988, 1 child **DISCIPLINE** LITERATURE **EDUCATION** Harvard Col, BA, 62; Univ Calif Berkeley, MA, 65, PhD, 70. **CAREER** Asst prof, 70, assoc prof, 77, prof, 84, Univ Del. **RESEARCH** American literature. **SELECTED PUBLICATIONS** Auth, Maurine Watkins, Chicago and her Chicago Tribune articles, 98; article, The Criminal as Culture, Amer Lit Hist, 9, 776-85, Winter, 97; article, Murder Will Out, and It Did in Chicago, NY Times, sec 7, 5, 22 Dec, 96; article, Gatsby as Gangster, Studies in Amer Fiction, 21, 225-36, Autumn, 93; article, Man for Two Seasons: Bill Reid Jr., Harvard Mag, 67-72, Nov-Dec, 91; article, Black Images and White Culture During the Decade Before the Civil Rights Movement, Amer Studies, 31, 101-119, Fall, 90; book rev, Picture Book, Amer Quart, 41, 558-62, Sept, 89; article, American Art and Labor: The Case of Anshutz's The Ironworkers Noontime, Amer Quart, 40, 333-50, Sept, 88; auth, Maxwell Anderson Truckline Cafe, 85; auth, An American Odyssey: Elia Kazan and American Culture, Temple Univ Press, 83. **CONTACT ADDRESS** Univ of Delaware, Memorial Hall, Newark, DE 19716. **EMAIL** t.pauly@udel.edu

PAVEL, THOMAS
PERSONAL Born 04/04/1941, Bucharest, Romania, m, 3 children **DISCIPLINE** ENGLISH **EDUCATION** Ecole Haute Etudes Scis Soc, Paris, doctorate, 71 **CAREER** Prof, Univ Ottawa, 70-80; prof, Univ Quebec, Montreal, 80- 86; prof, Univ Calif, Santa Cruz, 86-90; prof, Princeton Univ, 90-98; prof, Univ Chicago, 98-, dept chair, 01-. **HONORS AND AWARDS** Rene Weller prize for best book in literary theory, 92; Am Comparative Lit Asn fel. **MEMBERSHIPS** MLA, ALCS **RESEARCH** 17th-century French literature, 20th-century French literature and intellectual history, poetics and history of fiction, interactions between literary criticism, linguistics and philosophy. **SELECTED PUBLICATIONS** Co-auth, De Barthes a Balzac, Albin Michel, 98; auth, L'Art de l'eloignement. Essai sur l'imagination classique, Gallimard, 96; auth, The Feud of Language, Blackwell, 89, paperback 90, Fr ed, 88, Port trans, 90, Romanian trans, 94; auth, Fictional Worlds, Harvard Univ Press, 86, paperback ed, spring 89, Fr ed, 88, It trans, 92, Romanian trans, 94; Span trans, 96. **CONTACT ADDRESS** Dept of Romance Lang and Lit, Univ of Chicago, 1050 E 59th St, Chicago, IL 60637. **EMAIL** t-pavel@uchicago.edu

PAVITT, CHARLES
DISCIPLINE COMMUNICATION THEORY **EDUCATION** Queens Col-CUNY, BA, 76; Univ Wis, MA, 79; PhD, 83. **CAREER** Tchg asst, Univ Wis, 76-82; instr, George Mason Univ, 84; lectr, Howard Univ, 86; lectr, George Wash Univ, 86-87; asst prof, 87-94; assoc prof, 94-. **HONORS AND AWARDS** Univ Del Grant, 87, 89, 90; paper reviewer, commun res, 87; human commun res, 87, 88, 89; commun theory, 89, 91; jour soc and personal relships, 90. **MEMBERSHIPS** Mem, Intl Commun Assn; E Commun Assn. **RESEARCH** The Role of Belief Structures and Decision Processes in Face-to-face Interaction. **SELECTED PUBLICATIONS** Auth, A Controlled Rest of Some Complicating Factors Relevant to the Inferential Model for Evaluations of Communicative Competence, W Jour Speech Commun, 90; An Analysis of Artificial Intelligence Based Models for Describing Communicative Choice, Commun Theory, 91; co-auth, Implicit Theories of Marriage and Evaluations of Marriages on Television, Human Commun Res, 90; Implicit Theories of Leadership and Judgments of Leadership Among Group Members, Small Gp Res, 91. **CONTACT ADDRESS** Dept of Commun, Univ of Delaware, 162 Ctr Mall, Newark, DE 19716.

PAXMAN, DAVID B.
PERSONAL Born 12/31/1946, Salt Lake City, UT, m, 1996, 10 children **DISCIPLINE** ENGLISH LITERATURE **EDUCATION** Univ Chicago, PhD 82, MA 72; Brigham Young Univ, BA 71. **CAREER** Brigham Young Univ, assoc prof, 88-; Brigham Young Univ HI, asst prof, assoc prof, 76-88. **MEMBERSHIPS** ASECS; WSECS. **RESEARCH** Eighteenth-century British Literature; Intellectual History. **SELECTED PUBLICATIONS** Auth, Samuel Johnson Life's Incompleteness and the Limits of Representation, Lit and Belief, 98; auth, Failure as Authority: Poetic Voices and the Muse of Grace in William Cowper's The Task, 1650-1850, Ideas Aesthetics and Inquiries in the Early Modern Era, 98; auth, Writing about the Arts and Humanities, coauth, Needham Hts MA, Pearson, Custom, 00; auth, Adam in a Strange Country: Locke's Language Theory and Travel Literature, Modern Philology, 95; auth, Oral and Literate Discourse in Aphra Behn's Oroonoko, Restoration: Studies in English Literary Culture, 1600-1700, 94; auth, A Newcomer's Guide to Hawaii, Honolulu, Mutual Pub, 93; auth, Aesthetics as Epistemdogy, or Knowledge Without Certainty, Eighteenth-Century Studies, 93; auth, Language and Difference: The Problem of Abstraction, Journal of the History of Ideas, 93; auth, The Genius of English, Philological Quarterly, 90. **CONTACT ADDRESS** Dept of Literature, Brigham Young Univ, 3136 JKHB, Provo, UT 84602. **EMAIL** david_paxman@byu.edu

PAXTON, MARK
PERSONAL Born Logan, WV, m, 1997, 1 child **DISCIPLINE** NEWSWRITING AND REPORTING **EDUCATION** Univ TN, PhD, 95. **CAREER** Southwest Mo State Univ **MEMBERSHIPS** AESMC. **RESEARCH** Media law. **SELECTED PUBLICATIONS** Articles: Charleston Daily Mail; Nashville Banner; The Associated Press; College Media Rev; Journalism and Mass Communication Editor. **CONTACT ADDRESS** Southwest Missouri State Univ, Springfield, 901 S. National, Ste. 50, Springfield, MO 65804-0094. **EMAIL** mop944f@mail.smsu.edu

PAYANT, KATHERINE B.
PERSONAL Born 08/25/1943, Marinette, WI, m, 1991, 2 children **DISCIPLINE** ENGLISH **EDUCATION** Univ Mich, BA, 65; Univ Mich, MA, 66; Northern Mich Univ, MA, 68; Univ Mich, DA, 75. **CAREER** Prof, Northern Mich Univ, 68-. **HONORS AND AWARDS** Mich Asn of Governing Boards Distinguished Fac Awd, 93; Distinguished Fac Awd, Northern Mich Univ, 94. **MEMBERSHIPS** Popular Cult Assoc, MELUS, AAUP. **RESEARCH** Women's literature, multicultural literature, popular culture. **SELECTED PUBLICATIONS** Auth, Becoming and Bonding: Contemporary Feminism and Popular Fiction by American Women Writers, Greenwood Pr, 93; coauth, The Immigrant Experience in North American Literature: Carving Out a Niche, Greenwood Pr, 99; auth, "From Alienation to Reconciliation in the Novels of Cristina Garcia," MELUS: The J for the Multi-Ethnic Lit of the US (forthcoming). **CONTACT ADDRESS** Dept English, No Michigan Univ, 1401 Presque Isle Ave, Marquette, MI 49855. **EMAIL** kpayant@nmu,edu

PAYNE, F. ANNE
PERSONAL Born 08/28/1932, Harrisonburg, VA, s **DISCIPLINE** ENGLISH EUROPEAN MEDIEVAL LIT **EDUCATION** Shorter col, BA, BMUS, piano, 53; Yale Univ, MA, 54, PhD, 60. **CAREER** Instr, Conn Col, 56; Instr, Univ Buff, 58-60, lectr, 60; asst prof, SUNY, Buff, 60-67; assoc prof, SUNY, Buff, 67-75, prof, 75-; Adj Fel St Anne's Col, 66-. **HONORS AND AWARDS** AAUW Fellowshp to Oxford, 66-67; SUNY, C S Fellowshp, 67, 68, 71, 72; Julian Park Pub Awd, SUNY, 99; Who's Who Am Women; Who's Who in Am. **MEMBERSHIPS** Medieval Acad; ISAS; New Chaucer Soc; Pi Kappa Lambda. **RESEARCH** Medieval late classical lit and satire. **SELECTED PUBLICATIONS** King Alfred and Boethius, WI Univ Press, 67; Chaucer and Menippean Satire, WI Univ Press, 81; 3 Aspects of Wyrd in Beowulf, Pope Festschrift. **CONTACT ADDRESS** SUNY, Buffalo, Dept Eng, Clemens hall, Buffalo, NY 14260. **EMAIL** fapayne@acsu.buffalo.edu

PAYNE, J. GREGORY
PERSONAL Born 09/18/1949, McLeansboro, Jamaica, s **DISCIPLINE** COMMUNICATIONS **EDUCATION** Univ Ill, BA, 71; MA, 72; Harvard Univ, MPA, 84; Univ Ill, PhD, 77. **CAREER** Grad Asst, Univ Ill, 72-75; Instr, Univ Southern Calif, 76-83; Asst Prof, Calif Lutheran Col, 76-77; Asst Prof, Occidental Col, 77-83; Chair of Comm studies, Emerson Col, 88-98; Co-director, Center for Ethics, Emerson Col, 96-; Director, Global Marketing Brussels Center, 97-98; Assoc Prof, Tufts Univ, 97-; Assoc Prof, Emerson Col, 83-. **HONORS AND AWARDS** Phi Kappa Phi; Phi Bet Kappa; Outstanding Alumni Awd, Univ Ill, 97; Awd for Leadership in Friends of the Emerson Majestic, Emerson Col, 93; Robert F Kennedy Awd, Emerson Col, 90; Emerson Polit News Study Group Grant; Loftsgordon Awd for Outstanding Teaching, Occidental Col, 82; Annenberg Washington Prog Fel, 85; Rockefeller Foundation Focus Group Designate; NEH Summer Fel, 83. **MEMBERSHIPS** ACIUM, AAUP, Intl Comm Asn, Eastern Comm Asn, Nat Comm Asn, Delta sigma Rho-Tau Kappa alpha, Eastern States Comm Asn, Univ Ill Alumni Asn, Univ Ill LAS Alumni committee, Harvard Univ Kennedy School Alumni, Outstanding Young Men of America. **RESEARCH** Political communication; Negotiation; Health communication; Professional communication. **SELECTED PUBLICATIONS** Auth, Mayday: Kent State, Kendall Hunt, 81; auth, "Critical analysis of Newspaper Coverage of the Mad Cow Crisis," in Health and the Public Good, London, 97; auth, "AIDS: A Plan for the 21st Century-Thinking globally, Acting Locally: AIDS Action 2000 Plan," in AIDS: Effective Health communication for the 90s, London, 93; auth, "Crisis in communication: coverage of Magic Johnson AIDS Disclosure," in AIDS: Effective Health communication for the 90s, London, 93; auth, "Introduction," American Behavioral Scientist, 97; auth, "Status and scope of Health communication," Journal of Health communication, 96; auth, "Effective health message Design: The America Responds to AIDS Campaign," American Behavioral Scientist, 94; auth, "The Selling of princess Monica," Media ethics, 99; auth, "Princess Diana: The Press and the Public, One Year Later," Media Ethics, 98; auth, "Kent State: Why the Shroud of silence?'" Task Force Newsletter, 90. **CONTACT ADDRESS** Dept Comm, Emerson Col, 100 Beacon St, Boston, MA 02116-1501. **EMAIL** gpayne@emerson.edu

PAYNE, MICHAEL
PERSONAL Born 01/17/1941, Dallas, TX, 4 children **DISCIPLINE** ENGLISH LITERATURE **EDUCATION** South Ore Univ, BA, 62; Univ Ore, PhD, 69. **CAREER** Asst prof to prof, Bucknell Univ, 69-86; JOHN P. CROZER PROF, ENG LIT, BUCKNELL UNI, 86-; Chair of the Faculty, Bucknell Univ, 00. **HONORS AND AWARDS** Lindback Awd for Distinguished Teaching, 76; Bucknell Class of 1956 Lectureship for Inspirational Teaching, 76; Presidential Prof, 82; James Miller Prize for Distinguished Services to The College English Assoc, 88; Professional Achievement Awd, College English Assoc, 93. **MEMBERSHIPS** Inst Romance Stud, Coll Eng Asn, MLA **RESEARCH** Shakespeare; Renaissance Literature; Literature & Cultural Theory. **SELECTED PUBLICATIONS** Reading Theory: An Introduction to Lacan, Derrida, and Kristeva, Blackwell Publ, 93; co-edr, The Bucknell Lectures in Literary Theory, Blackwell Publ, 90-94; The Dictionary of Cultural and Critical Theory, Blackwell Publ, 96; Reading Knowledge: An Introduction to Barthes, Foucault, and Althusser, Blackwell Publ, 97. **CONTACT ADDRESS** Dept Eng, Bucknell Univ, Lewisburg, PA 17837. **EMAIL** payne@bucknell.edu

PAZDERNIK, CHARLES
PERSONAL Born 07/03/1968, Breckenridge, MN, m, 1996 **DISCIPLINE** CLASSICS **EDUCATION** Cornell Univ, BA summa cum laude 90; Oxford Univ, Mphil 92; Princeton Univ, MA 95, PhD 97. **CAREER** NY Univ Law Sch, Samuel I. Golieb Fel, 97-98; Brooklyn College, adj asst prof, 98; Emory Univ Law Sch, Mellon post doc fel, 98-. **HONORS AND AWARDS** Phi Beta Kappa; Telluride Sch; Stanley Seeger Fel; Princeton Grad Fel. **MEMBERSHIPS** APA. **RESEARCH** Ancient law; classical historiography; late antiquity; epic poetry; Greco-Roman legal and political history. **SELECTED PUBLICATIONS** Auth, Justinian's Novels and the law of succession, in: The Transformation in Law and Society in Late Antiquity Proceedings of Shifting Frontiers II, ed, R. Mathisen, forthcoming; Odysseus and his audience: Odyssey 9.30-40 and its formulatic resonance's, The Amer Jour of Philology, 95; Our most pious consort given us by God: Dissident reactions to the partnership of Justinian and Theodora AD 525-48, Classical Antiquity, 94; auth, "Procopius and Thucydides on the Labors of War: Belisarius and Brasdas in the Field," Transactions of the Am Philol Asn 130 (00). **CONTACT ADDRESS** Dept of Classics, Emory Univ, N404G Callaway Ct, Atlanta, GA 30322. **EMAIL** cpazder@emory.edu

PEARCE, JAMES
DISCIPLINE GREEK AND LATIN LANGUAGE AND LITERATURE **EDUCATION** Baylor Univ, BA; Univ TX-Austin, MA, PhD. **CAREER** Prof,68-, Trinity Univ. **RESEARCH** Pastoral poetry. **SELECTED PUBLICATIONS** Auth, The Eclogues of Calpurnius Siculus, 90; The Eclogues of Nemesian and the Einsiedeln Manuscript, 92. **CONTACT ADDRESS** Dept of Class, Trinity Univ, 715 Stadium Dr, San Antonio, TX 78212.

PEARCE, RICHARD
DISCIPLINE MODERN FICTION, MODERN DRAMA **EDUCATION** Hobart Col, BA; Columbia Univ, MA, PhD. **CAREER** Engl, Wheaton Col. **SELECTED PUBLICATIONS** Publ, The Politics of Narration: James Joyce, William Faulkner, and Virginia Woolf; The Novel in Motion: An Approach to Modern Fiction; Stages of the Clown: Perspectives on Modern

Fiction from Dostoyevsky to Beckett; William Styron; ed, James Joyce and Thomas Pynchon; A Forum on Fiction. **CONTACT ADDRESS** Dept of Eng, Wheaton Col, Massachusetts, 26 East Main St, Norton, MA 02766. **EMAIL** Richard_Pearce@wheatonma.edu

PEARSALL, DEREK A.
PERSONAL Born 08/28/1931, Birmingham, England, m, 1952, 5 children **DISCIPLINE** ENGLISH **EDUCATION** Univ of Birmingham, UK, BA, 51, MA, 52. **CAREER** King's Col, London, 59-65; Univ of York, 65-85; Harvard Univ, 85-2000. **HONORS AND AWARDS** Fel, AAAS; fel, Medieval Acad. **MEMBERSHIPS** New Chaucer Soc; Medieval Acad; IAUPE; Early Eng Text Soc. **RESEARCH** Medieval English literature. **SELECTED PUBLICATIONS** Auth, The Canterbury Tales, Allen & Unwin, 85; auth, The Life of Geoffrey Chaucer, Blackwell, 92; auth, Chaucer to Spenser: Writings in English, 1375-1575, Blackwell, 98. **CONTACT ADDRESS** 4 Clifton Dale, York Y030 6LJ. **EMAIL** dpearsal@fas.harvard.edu

PEARSON, JOHN H.
DISCIPLINE AMERICAN LITERATURE **EDUCATION** Eckerd Col, BA; Boston Univ, PhD. **CAREER** Eng Dept, Stetson Univ **RESEARCH** Nineteenth and early twentieth century fiction; autobiography; literary theory and criticism. **SELECTED PUBLICATIONS** Auth, Framing the Modern Reader: The Prefaces of Henry James, Penn State; pubs on frame theory in literature and the other arts, American colonial literature, and Henry James. **CONTACT ADDRESS** English Dept, Stetson Univ, De Land, Unit 8378, DeLand, FL 32720-3771.

PEARSON, JUDY C.
PERSONAL Born 09/02/1946, Pipestone, MN, m, 1977, 6 children **DISCIPLINE** COMMUNICATION **EDUCATION** St. Cloud State Univ, BA, 68; Ind Univ, MA, 73, PhD, 75. **CAREER** Asst prof & basic course dir, Ind Univ, 76-81; vis prof, Mich State Univ, 81; from assoc prof to prof & dir grad studies, Ohio Univ, 81-95; dir, N Va Ctr & assoc dean grad sch & prof, Va Tech, 95-; assoc dean of Arts, Humanities & Social Sciences & dir doctoral program & prof comm, North Dakota State Univ. **HONORS AND AWARDS** Outstanding Women of Achievement, 76; Cent States Speech Asn Outstanding Young Tchr Awd, 77; Distinguished Alumni Awd, St. Cloud State Univ, 87; Honorary alumnus, Ohio Univ, 91; Scholar of the Year, Cent States Commun Asn, 95. **MEMBERSHIPS** Speech Commun Asn; Int Commun Asn; Am Educ Res Asn; Cent States Speech Asn; Ind Speech Asn; Ill Speech & Theater Asn; Am Asn Univ Prof; Iowa Commun Asn; Am Inst Parliamentarians; E Commun Asn; Speech Commun Asn Ohio; World Commun Asn; Commun Asn Japan; Counc Grad Sch; Nat Commun Asn; Nat Asn State Univ & Land Grant Col. **RESEARCH** Relational maintenance; higher education; the changing PhD; women in education. **SELECTED PUBLICATIONS** Coauth, Let's Go Krogering: Children's Compliance Gaining and Adults' Compliance Resistance in a Naturalistic Setting, Speech Commun Annual, 93; coauth, Sweet Pea and Pussy Cat: An Examination of Idiom Use and Marital Satisfaction Over the Life Cycle, Jour Soc & Personal Relationships, 93; coauth, Antecedent and Consequent Conditions of Student Questioning: An Analysis of Classroom Discourse Across the University, Comm Educ, 94; coauth, Children's Perspectives of the Family: A Phenomenological Inquiry, Human Studies, 94; coauth, Interpersonal Rituals in Marriage and Adult Friendship, Commun Monogr, 97; coauth, Confidence in Public Speaking, 93; auth, Communication and the Family: Seeking Satisfaction in Changing Times, 93; coauth, Understanding and Sharing: An Introduction to Speech Communication, 94; coauth, Understanding and Sharing: Audio Companion, 94; coauth, Gender and Communication, 95; auth, Marriage After Mourning: The Secrets of Surviving Couples, 95; coauth, Confidence in Public Speaking, 95; coauth, Understanding and Sharing, 97. **CONTACT ADDRESS** College of Arts, Humanities & Social Sciences, No Dakota State Univ, Box 5075, Fargo, ND 58105-5075. **EMAIL** judy_pearson@ndsu.nodak.edu

PEARSON, MICHAEL
DISCIPLINE CREATIVE WRITING (NON-FICTION) **EDUCATION** Fordham Univ, BA;Univ SF, MA; Pa State Univ. **CAREER** Engl, Old Dominion Univ. **RESEARCH** Literary non-fiction ; memoirs. **CONTACT ADDRESS** Old Dominion Univ, 4100 Powhatan Ave, Norfolk, VA 23058. **EMAIL** MPearson@odu.edu

PEASE, DONALD E.
DISCIPLINE ENGLISH LITERATURE **EDUCATION** Univ Chicago, PhD, 73. **CAREER** Avalon Prof Hum and Prof English, MALS chair, Dartmouth Col. **RESEARCH** Am drama, fiction, and criticism. **SELECTED PUBLICATIONS** Auth, Regulating Multi-adhoccerists, Fish('s) Rules, Crit Inquiry, 97; Negative interpellations: From Oklahoma City to the Trilling-Matthiessen Transmission, Boundary, 96; Visionary Compacts: American Renaissance Writings in Cultural Context, Univ Wis, 87; ed, National Identities and Post-Americanist Narratives, Duke UP, 94; New Americanists: Revisionist Interventions into the Canon, boundary 2, 89; co-ed, Cultures of United States Imperialism, Duke UP, 93; The American Renaissance Reconsidered: Selected Papers of the English Institute, Johns Hopkins UP, 85. **CONTACT ADDRESS** Dept of English, Dartmouth Col, 6032 Sanborn House, Hanover, NH 03755. **EMAIL** Donald.E.Pease.Jr@dartmouth.edu

PEASE, TED
PERSONAL m **DISCIPLINE** COMMUNICATION STUDIES **EDUCATION** Univ New Hampshire, BA, 78; Univ Minn, MA, 81; Univ Ohio, PhD, 91. **CAREER** taught at Univ of Minn; Univ of Dayton; Ohio Univ and St. Michael's Col in Vermont **RESEARCH** On minorities and the media, gender, and various aspects of media criticism **SELECTED PUBLICATIONS** Auth, The Newsroom Barometer: Job Satisfaction and the Impact of Racial Diversity on U.S. Daily Newspapers, 91; No Train, No Gain: Continuing Education in Newspaper Newsrooms, 93; co-auth, The Forgotten Medium, Transaction, 95; coed, Publishing Books, 97; coed, The Media in Black and White, 96; coed, Children and the Media, 96; coed, Radio-The Forgotten Medium, 95, 97. **CONTACT ADDRESS** Dept of Communication, Utah State Univ, 3580 S Highway 91, Logan, UT 84321. **EMAIL** tpease@cc.usu.edu

PECK, RUSSELL A.
DISCIPLINE ENGLISH **EDUCATION** IN Univ, PhD. **CAREER** John Hall Deane prof; taught at IN Univ, Univ Hull Yorkshire, Col St Thomas & Colgate Univ; bibliogr, Stud in the Age of Chaucer & MLA; Mercer Brugler prof of Humanities, 82-85. **HONORS AND AWARDS** Edward Peck Curtis prize, 72; E. Harris Harbison awd, 72; Students' Asn awd, 82; Prof of the Yr, Coun for the Advancement and Support Educ, 85; Guggenheim fel; Danforth Assoc fel & NEH sem dir, Bd of the Conf on Christianity and Lit MLA; founder & gen ed, middle eng text ser; founding dir, medieval house. **MEMBERSHIPS** Assoc ed Mediaevalia ed bd, Grad Record Examination; ch ed bd, TEAMS; dir, Drama House. **RESEARCH** Eng and Scottish lit of the 13th through the 15th centuries and var facets of medieval cultural studies. **SELECTED PUBLICATIONS** Auth, Kingship and Common Profit in Gower's Confessio Amantis; Chaucer's Lyrics and Anelida and Arcite: An Annotated Bibliography; Chaucer's Boece, Romaunt, Astrolabe, Equatorie, Lost Works and the Chaucer Apocrypha: An Annotated Bibliography, ed, Gower's Confessio Amantis; Heroic Women from The Old Testament in Middle English; Religious Typology in Recent Cinema. **CONTACT ADDRESS** Dept of English, Univ of Rochester, 500 Wilson Blvd, RC Box 270451, Rochester, NY 14627-0451. **EMAIL** rpec@mail.cc.rochester.edu

PECKHAM, JOEL
PERSONAL Born 08/31/1970, Newton, MA, m, 1997, 1 child **DISCIPLINE** ENGLISH **EDUCATION** Micklebury Col, BA, 92; Baylor Univ, MA, 94; Univ Nebr, PhD. **CAREER** Lecturer, Hope Col, 97-00; vis asst prof, Hope Col, 00-01. **HONORS AND AWARDS** Wilson Fel, UNL, 98; McDonald Fel, UNL, 97; Reichenback Fel, 97. **MEMBERSHIPS** AWP, MLA. **RESEARCH** Southern literature, Regional literature. **SELECTED PUBLICATIONS** Auth, "Jean Toomer's Cane: Self as Montage and the drive Toward Integration," American Literature, (forthcoming); auth, "Segregation/Integration: Narrative in the American South," The Southern Quarterly, (forthcoming); auth, "James Dickey and the Narrative Mode of Transmission: The Sheep Child's Other Realm," Mississippi Quarterly, (99): 239-258; auth, "Eudora Welty's The Gold Apples: Abjection and the Maternal South," Texas Studies in Literature and Language, (forthcoming). **CONTACT ADDRESS** Dept English, Hope Col, 137 E 12th St, Holland, MI 49423-3607. **EMAIL** peckham@hope.edu

PECORA, VINCENT P.
PERSONAL Born 09/07/1953, Baltimore, MD, m, 1992, 2 children **DISCIPLINE** ENGLISH **EDUCATION** Brown Univ, BA, 75; Columbia Univ, MA, 78, PhD, 83. **CAREER** Asst prof, Univ AR, 84-85; asst prof, 85-90, assoc prof, 90-95, Prof, Univ CA, Los Angeles, 95-. **HONORS AND AWARDS** NEH Summer Stipend, 85; fel, Univ CA Humanities Res Inst, Univ CA, Irvine, 89; Nominated for Distinguished Teaching Awd, Mortar Board Soc, UCLA, 92; Excellence in Academia Awd, Young President's Organization, 99; fel, NEH, 01-02; dir, center for modern and contemporary studies, ucla, 96-; dir, humanities consortium and mellon postdoctoral fellowship prog, ucla, 97-. **MEMBERSHIPS** Western Humanities Alliance (Bd of Dirs); Modern Lang Asn. **RESEARCH** Modern British and comparative lit; intellectual hist; literary theory. **SELECTED PUBLICATIONS** Auth, Self and Form in Modern Narrative, Johns Hopkins Univ Press, 89; auth, Households of the Soul, Johns Hopkins Univ Press, 97; ed, Nations and Identities: Classic Readings, Blackwell Publishers, 01. **CONTACT ADDRESS** Dept of English, Univ of California, Los Angeles, Los Angeles, CA 90095-1530. **EMAIL** pecora@humnet.ucla.edu

PEDERSON, LEE
DISCIPLINE ENGLISH LANGUAGE AND LITERATURE **EDUCATION** Univ Chicago, PhD, 64. **CAREER** Charles Howard Candler Prof. **RESEARCH** Linguistics. **SELECTED PUBLICATIONS** Auth, East Tennessee Folk Speech; An Annotated Bibliography of Southern Speech; Pronunciation of English in Metropolitan Chicago; co-auth, A Manual for Dialect Research in the Southern States; ed, The Linguistic Atlas of the Gulf States, (v 1-4). **CONTACT ADDRESS** English Dept, Emory Univ, 1380 Oxford Rd NE, Atlanta, GA 30322-1950. **EMAIL** lpeders@emory.edu

PEEL, ELLEN S.
DISCIPLINE ENGLISH **EDUCATION** Harvard Univ, AB, 73; Yale Univ, MPhil, 79; PhD, 82. **CAREER** Asst Prof to Assoc Prof, Univ Cincinnati, 83-89; Asst Prof to Full Prof, San Francisco State Univ, 90-. **HONORS AND AWARDS** Bain Res Group, Univ Calif, 95; Affirmative Action Fac Development Awd, San Francisco State Univ, 92; Nominated for Boyce Teaching Awd, Univ Cincinnati, 84, 85, 89; Phi Beta Kappa, 73. **MEMBERSHIPS** Mod Lang Asn, Intl Comparative Literature Asn, Am Comparative Literature Asn, Women's Caucus in the Mod Lang, Pacific Ancient and Mod Lang Asn, Doris Lessing Soc, Soc for Critical Exchange, Calif Humanities Asn, Phi Sigma Iota. **RESEARCH** 18th and 19th Century fiction (French, English); 20th Century fiction (English, US); Literary theory and criticism (especially narrative, feminist, psychoanalytic, reader response); Women's literature; Modern drama; Surveys of Western and world literature. **SELECTED PUBLICATIONS** Auth, "The emergence of Galatea: Rewritings of a Myth," Proceedings of the 1999 International Conference - Feminist Literature: Global Outlook on Gender Issues, forthcoming; co-auth, "Corinne and the Woman as Poet in England: Hemans, Jewsbury, and Barrett Browning," in The Novel's Seductions: Stael's Corinne in Critical Inquiry, London, 99; auth, "He Reads, she speaks: How Narrative Form conveys conflicting Values in Corinne, or Italy," in Reader: Essays in reader-Oriented Theory, Criticism, and Pedagogy, 98; auth, "I baci PC di 'Star Trek': politicamente corretti o piuttosto conservatori?', ("Star Trek's PC Kisses: Politically Correct or Pretty conservative?"), Lindau, 98; auth, "Black and White and Read All Over: The Semiotics of Difference and Chiaroscuro in Le Guin's Left Hand of Darkness," Semiotics around the World: Synthesis in Diversity--Proceedings of the Fifth Congress of the International Association for Semiotic studies, Berkeley, 94; auth, "Reading Piebald patterns in Le Guin's The Left Hand of Darkness," women of Other Worlds: Excursions through Science Fiction and Feminism, 99; auth, "Beyond Utopia: Pragmatic Feminism, Persuasion, and Narrative, forthcoming. **CONTACT ADDRESS** Dept English, San Francisco State Univ, 1600 Holloway Ave, San Francisco, CA 94132. **EMAIL** epeel@sfsu.edu

PEEMOELLER, HELEN C.
PERSONAL Born 01/24/1939, Wilmington, DE, m, 1973 **DISCIPLINE** ENGLISH **EDUCATION** Bryn Mawr Coll, AB, 60; Univ Wis, MA, 61; Univ Pa, 61-67. **CAREER** Inst Moore Col Art, 65-66; inst Northampton County Area Community Col, 67-70; PROF, CHAIR HUM, READING AREA COMMUNITY COL, 71-. **HONORS AND AWARDS** NEH scholar **MEMBERSHIPS** MLA **RESEARCH** Film, writing, medieval & Renaissance **SELECTED PUBLICATIONS** various **CONTACT ADDRESS** Reading Area Comm Col, PO Box 1706, Reading, PA 19603. **EMAIL** hpeemoeller@email.racc.cc.pa.us

PEIRCE, KATE L.
DISCIPLINE COMMUNICATIONS **EDUCATION** FL State Univ, BA, MS, Univ TX, PhD. **CAREER** Comm Dept, Southwest Tex State Univ **HONORS AND AWARDS** Ed, The Forim. **SELECTED PUBLICATIONS** Auth, A Feminist Theoretical Perspective on the Socialization Messages in Seventeen magazine, Sex Roles, 90; Forces That Inhibit Transformation to a Feminist Future, gender & Comm, 92; The Changing Portrayal of Suicide in the Media, Mid-South Sociol Asn, 92; Socialization of Teenage Girls Through Teen-magazine Fiction: The Making of a New Woman or an Old Lady?, Sex Roles, 93; Socialization Messages in Teen and Seventeen Magazines in Women and Media, Wadsworth Publ, 94; YM in Women's Periodicals in the United States, Greenwood Press, 94; Seventeen in Women's Periodicals in the United States, Greenwood Press, 94. **CONTACT ADDRESS** Southwest Texas State Univ, 601 University Dr, San Marcos, TX 78666-4604.

PELTO, WILLIAM
DISCIPLINE MUSIC THEORY **EDUCATION** Yale Univ, BA; San Francisco State Univ, MA; Univ Tex, PhD. **CAREER** Assoc prof; assoc dean, School of Music Ithaca Col, 01. **MEMBERSHIPS** Col Music Soc; Soc Music Theory. **SELECTED PUBLICATIONS** Auth, pubs on musical analysis and music theory pedagogy. **CONTACT ADDRESS** Dept of Music History, Theory and Composition, Ithaca Col, 3322 Whalen Center for Music, Ithaca, NY 14850. **EMAIL** pelto@ithaca.edu

PELZER, LINDA C.
PERSONAL Born 03/31/1952, South Bend, IN, w, 1974 **DISCIPLINE** ENGLISH **EDUCATION** Ball State Univ, BA, 74; Univ Notre Dame, MA, 76; PhD, 84. **CAREER** Admin Asst, Ball State Univ London Centre, 82-83; Asst Prof, Ball State Univ, 80-82, 83-86, 86-88; From Assoc Prof to Prof, Wesley Col, 88-. **HONORS AND AWARDS** Fulbright Collab Res Grant, Gr Brit 86; Del Humanities Forum Res Grant, 89. **MEMBERSHIPS** MLA, NEMLA. **RESEARCH** Women fiction writers. **SELECTED PUBLICATIONS** Auth, Critical Companion to Mary Higgins Clark, 95; auth, Critical Companion to Erich Segal, 97; auth, Student Companion to F. Scott Fitzgerald, 00. **CONTACT ADDRESS** Dept Lib Arts, Wesley Col, Delaware, 120 N State St, Dover, DE 19901-3835.

PENA, JUAN A.
PERSONAL Born 12/16/1962, Bilbao, Spain, m, 1990, 0 child **DISCIPLINE** BUSINESS COMMUNICATION **EDUCATION** Univ Deusto, BA, 87; Univ Mass Amherst, PhD, 94. **CAREER** Asst prof, Western Ky Univ, 92-95; asst prof, InterAm Univ PR, 95-98; asst prof, Univ PR, 97-. **MEMBERSHIPS** Am Manage Asn; Mod Lang Asn; Am Bus Comm; Am Asn of Teach of Span and Port. **RESEARCH** Technology as a tool for business communication; social dimension of language; e-resumes. **SELECTED PUBLICATIONS** TA, El e-mail @ su alcance, (Pub Puertorriquenas), 00; rev, "Lexicon of Intentionally Ambiguous Recommendations," Forum (00); auth, "Una economia global con estilos comunicativos," Acts (4th Intl Conf on Lang for Specific Purposes, 01). **CONTACT ADDRESS** Comunicacion Empresarial, Univ of Puerto Rico, Rio Piedras, Facultad Administracion Empresas, Rio Piedras, PR 00939. **EMAIL** jpena@prw.net

PENCEAL, BERNADETTE WHITLEY
PERSONAL Born 12/16/1944, Lenoir, NC, m, 1967 **DISCIPLINE** ENGLISH **EDUCATION** Syracuse Univ, Syracuse NYork, BS, 1966; The City Coll, New York NYork, MA, 1973, Letter of Completion, 1974; Fordham Univ, New York NYork, PhD, 1989. **CAREER** Fashion Inst of Technology, New York NY, instructor of English, 73-74; Green Haven Maximum Security Prison, Stormville NY, instructor of English, 74-76; Malcolm-King Coll, New York NY, instructor of English, 74-78; Hunter Coll, New York NY, instructor of reading, 74-79; Coll of New Rochelle, New Rochelle NY, instructor of English, 77-89; New York Univ, New York NY, mentor of English, 80-. **HONORS AND AWARDS** "Bernadette Penceal Day," Office of the President of the Borough of Manhattan, City of New York, 1987. **MEMBERSHIPS** Mem, Assn of Black Faculty & Admin, New York Univ, 1981-, Phi Delta Kappa, 1981-; pres, Assn of Black Women in Higher Educ Inc, 1985-87, J & B Whitley's Inc, 1985-; bd mem, Urban Women's Shelter, 1985-87; mem, New York Urban League, 1987-, Amer Assn of Univ Women, 1989-. **SELECTED PUBLICATIONS** "Non-Intellective Factors as Predictions of Academic Performance of Non-Traditional Adult College Freshmen," 1989. **CONTACT ADDRESS** English Mentor, New York Univ, 239 Green St, 8th Floor, New York, NY 10039.

PENDELL, SUE D.
DISCIPLINE COMMUNICATION STUDIES **EDUCATION** Fla State Univ, BS; Auburn Univ, MA; Univ Utah, PhD. **CAREER** Prof. **RESEARCH** Interpersonal communication; intercultural communication; nonverbal communication; group communication; communication theory. **SELECTED PUBLICATIONS** Auth, Deviance and Conflict in Small Group Decision Making, Small Group Res, 90; co-auth, The Myth of Viewer-Listener Disagreement in the First Kennedy-Nixon Debate, Central States Speech J, 87; An Introduction to Speech Communication; Winning Presidential Debates: An Analysis of Criteria Influencing Audience Response, W J Speech Commun, 87. **CONTACT ADDRESS** Speech Communication Dept, Colorado State Univ, Fort Collins, CO 80523-1783. **EMAIL** spendell@lamar.colostate.edu

PENDERGRAFT, MARY L.
PERSONAL Born 02/14/1953, Charlotte, NC, m, 1975, 3 children **DISCIPLINE** CLASSICS **EDUCATION** Univ NC at Chapel Hill, AB, 75; PhD, 82. **CAREER** Vis asst prof, Univ of NC at Greensboro, 84, 86; vis asst prof, Duke Univ, 87-88; from vis asst prof to assoc prof, Wake Forest Univ, 83-. **HONORS AND AWARDS** Nat Merit Scholar; Phi Beta Kappa; Eben Alexander Prize in Greek; Albert Suskin Prize in Latin; Univ Fel, 76-77. **MEMBERSHIPS** Am Philol Asn, Classical Asn of the Middle W and S, Archaeol Inst of Am, NC Classical Asn, Am Asn of Univ Professors, Vergilian Soc, Am Classical League, For Lang Asn of NC. **RESEARCH** Greek and Latin Literature. **SELECTED PUBLICATIONS** Auth, "Aratean Echoes in Theocritus," Quaderni Urbinati di Cultura classica, 24.3 (86): 47-54; auth, "On the Nature of the constellations: Aratus, Ph. 367-85," Eranos 88 (90): 99-106; auth, "Eros at Play: Arg. 3.132-41," Materiali e discussioni per l'analisi dei testi classici 26 (91): 95-102; auth, "Thou Shalt Not Eat the Hyena: A Note on "Barnabas' Epistle 10.7," Vigiliae Christianae 46 (92): 75-79; coauth, "Naming the Figures: A Controversial Stele in the Sparta Museum," Maia 46 (94): 283-289; auth, "Euphony and Etymology: Aratus' Phaenomena," Syllecta Classica 6 (95): 43-57. **CONTACT ADDRESS** Dept Classical Lang, Wake Forest Univ, PO Box 7343, Winston-Salem, NC 27109-7343. **EMAIL** pender@wfu.edu

PENELLA, ROBERT J.
PERSONAL Born 02/16/1947, Boston, MA, m, 1968, 1 child **DISCIPLINE** CLASSICS **EDUCATION** Boston Col, AB, 67; Harvard Univ, MA, 69, PhD, 71. **CAREER** Asst prof, Fordham Univ, 71-78, assoc prof, 78-91, prof, 91-, chemn, Classics, 77-83. **HONORS AND AWARDS** Boston Col, AB, summa cum laude, 67; Woodrow Wilson Fel, 67-68; Am Coun of Learned Socs grant-in-aid, 84; NEH Fel for Univ Teachers, 93. **MEMBERSHIPS** Am Philol Asn, Classical Asn of Atlantic States. **RESEARCH** Late Antiquity, Imperial Greek prose, Roman historiography. **SELECTED PUBLICATIONS** Auth, The Letters of Apollonius of Tyana: A Critical Text with Prolegomena, Translation and Commentary, Leiden: E. J. Brill (79); auth, Greek Philosophers and Sophists in the Fourth Century A.D.: Studies in Eunapius of Sardis, Leeds: Francis Cairns (90); auth, The Private Orations of Themistius, Berkeley: Univ of Calif Press (90). **CONTACT ADDRESS** Dept Classics, Fordham Univ, 441 E Fordham Rd, Bronx, NY 10458-5149. **EMAIL** rpenella@fordham.edu

PENNISTON, JOYCE K.
PERSONAL Born 12/22/1939, Buffalo, NY, m, 1960, 2 children **DISCIPLINE** CLASSICS **EDUCATION** Radcliffe, BA, 61; Harvard Grad Sch of Educ, MAT, 62; Univ NC Chapel Hill, MA, 76; Univ Mn, PhD, 83. **CAREER** Instr, St. Olaf Col, 79-81; instr, Mn Bible Col, 81- ; instr, St. Mary's Univ Mn, 93-. **HONORS AND AWARDS** Summer stud, Amer Sch for Classical Stud, Athens, Greece, 81, Rome, Italy, 78; NEH Summer Sem, Harvard with Gregory Nagy, 84. **MEMBERSHIPS** Amer Philol Assoc; Classical Assoc of the Midwest & South; Vergilian Soc; Classical Assoc of Mn. **RESEARCH** Ancient comedy. **SELECTED PUBLICATIONS** Auth, Quot Homines Tot Sententiae: Off-Stage Acquaintances in Ancient Comedy, Classical J, 91; Pragma and process in Greek and Roman Comedy, Syllecta Classica, 96; Commentary on the Acts of the Apostles in Study Bible for Women, Baker books, Grand Rapids, Mich, 96; Translation of Cicero's De Finibus, Hackett, 00-01; Translation of Latin passages in Anatomy of Radical Prostatectomy as defined by Magnetic Resonance Imaging, The J of Urology, 98. **CONTACT ADDRESS** 835 10 1/2 St SW, Rochester, MN 55902. **EMAIL** joyce.penniston@prodigy.net

PENROD, DIANE
PERSONAL Born 10/27/1958, Buffalo, NY, m, 1986 **DISCIPLINE** COMPOSITION, RHETORIC **EDUCATION** Medaille Col, BS, 80; SUNY Oswego, MEd, 89; Syracuse Univ, MA, 92; PhD, 95. **CAREER** Instr, SUNY Oswego, 93; instr, Syracuse Univ, 89-94; asst to assoc prof, Rowan Univ, 94-. **HONORS AND AWARDS** Who's Who in Am Women, 98-00; Who's Who in the Millenium; Who's Who in Am, 01; CASE US Prof of the Year Nominee, 96, 00, 01. **MEMBERSHIPS** MLA, NCTE. **RESEARCH** Postmodernism, media ethics, media literacy, social writing assessment. **SELECTED PUBLICATIONS** Coauth, "Co-Authoring the World," Written Commun, (96); auth, "To Rise Above One's Station," Political Moments in the Classroom, Heinemann, (96); auth, Miss Grundy Doesn't Teach Here Anymore, Heinemann, 97; auth, "Linguistics" and "Logcentrism," Encycl of Postmodernism, Routledge, (01); auth, "Can't We All Just Get Along?" Professing in the Contact Zones, NCTE, forthcoming; auth, "A Dream Deferred," Desperately Seeking Ethics, Scarecrow Pr, forthcoming. **CONTACT ADDRESS** Rowan Univ, Hawthorn Hall, Glassboro, NJ 08028. **EMAIL** penrod@rowan.edu

PERADOTTO, JOHN JOSEPH
PERSONAL Born 05/11/1933, Ottawa, IL, m, 1959, 4 children **DISCIPLINE** GREEK & LATIN LANGUAGES & LITERATURE **EDUCATION** St Louis Univ, AB, 57, MA, 58; Northwestern Univ, PhD(Greek & Latin), 63. **CAREER** Instr Greek, Latin & English, Western Wash State Col, 60-61; from instr to asst prof Greek & Latin, Georgetown Univ, 61-66; from asst prof to assoc prof classics, State Univ NY Buffalo, 66-73; prof & chmn dept, Univ Tex, Austin, 73-74; chmn dept, 74-77, Prof Classics, State Univ NY Buffalo, 74-, Dean, 78-, Nat Endowment for Humanities fel, Ctr Hellenic Studies, 72-73; ed-in-chief, Arethusa, 75-; distinguished teaching prof emer. **HONORS AND AWARDS** Chancellor's Awd for Excellence in Teaching, State Univ NY, 75. **MEMBERSHIPS** Am Philol Asn; Class Asn Atlantic States. **RESEARCH** Greek literature; Greek mythology and religion; narrative analysis. **SELECTED PUBLICATIONS** Auth, The omen of the eagles and the ethos of Agamemnon, Phoenix, 69; Classical Mythology, Am Philol Asn, 73; Odyssey 8 564-671: Verisimilitude, narrative analysis, and bricolage, Tex Studies Lit & Lang, 74; co-ed, Population Policy in Plato and Aristotle, 75; ed, Classical Literature and Contemporary Literary Theory, 77, Women in the Ancient World, 78, co-ed, Virgil 2000 Years, 81 & Semiotics and Classical Studies, 83, Arethusa; Rethinking the Classical Canon, 94; ed, Horace: 2000 Years, 95; co-ed, The NewSimonides, 96; The Iliad and its Contexts, 97, Arethusa; co-ed, Modern Theoretical Approaches to Homer," in Barry Powell and Ian Morris eds., A New Companion to Homer, (Leiden 97): 380-95. **CONTACT ADDRESS** Dept of Classics, SUNY, Buffalo, 346 Milard Fillmore Academic Ctr, Buffalo, NY 14260-4650. **EMAIL** peradott@acsu.buffalo.edu

PERAINO, JUDITH A.
DISCIPLINE MUSIC **EDUCATION** Univ Chicago, BA, 87; Univ Calif at Berkeley, MA, 90, PhD, 95. **CAREER** Asst prof **MEMBERSHIPS** Amer Musicol Soc; Soc for Ethnomusicol. **RESEARCH** 13th-century French secular music; music and queer identity; Rock music. **SELECTED PUBLICATIONS** Auth, Et pui conmencha a canter: Refrains, Motes, and Melody in the Thirteenth-century Narritive Renart le nouvel, Plainsong and Medieval Music, 97; PJ Harvey's 'Man-size Sextet' and the Inaccessible, Inescapable Gender," Women and Music: A Journal of Gender and Culture, Spring, 98; Courtly Obsessions: Music and Masculine Identity in Gottfried von Strassburg's Tristan, Repercussions 4:2 95; I am an Opera: Identifying with Henry Purcell's Dido and Aeneas, En Travesti: Women, Gender Subversion, Opera, NY: Columbia UP, 95. **CONTACT ADDRESS** Dept of Music, Cornell Univ, 104 Lincoln Hall, Ithaca, NY 14853. **EMAIL** jap28@cornell.edu

PERDICOYIANUI-PALEOLOGOU, HELENE
PERSONAL Born 02/12/1959, Greece **DISCIPLINE** CLASSICS **EDUCATION** Sorbonne Univ, PhD, 92. **CAREER** From vis prof to lectr, Hellenic Col, 96-; vis scholar, Harvard Univ, 98; guest vis scholar, Harvard Divinity Sch, 97-01, vis scholar, Brown Univ, 97-01. **MEMBERSHIPS** Can Asn Univ Tchrs; Int Asn Papyrology; Int Asn Greek & Latin Epigraphy; Asn Linguistics Paris; Grammatical Info; Asn Guillaume Bude; Am Philol Asn; Chronicle High Educ; VITA LATINA; Int Soc Class Tradition; Am Soc Papyrologists; Ling Soc Am. **RESEARCH** Greek and Latin Philology and Linguistics. **SELECTED PUBLICATIONS** Auth, Etude Lexicologique des Familles de Daenai, de Didaskein et de Paideuein d'Homere a Hippocrate, 94; auth, L'enonciation dans l'Hecube d'Euripide, Miscellanea Linguistica Graeco-latina, 93; auth, Le vocabulaire de l'education d'Homere a Euripide. Etude lexicologique: les familles de daenai de didaskein et de paideuein d'Homere a Euripide, IG, 93; auth, Le Vocabulaire de la douleur dans l'Hecube et les Troyennes d'Euripide, LEC, 93; auth, Le vocabulaire de l'habitation chez Euripide, LEC, 96; auth, Philos chez Euripide, RB Ph. H, 96. **CONTACT ADDRESS** Dept of Classics, Hellenic Col, 50 Goddard Ave., Brookline, MA 02146. **EMAIL** hperpal@hotmail.com

PEREIRA, MALIN
PERSONAL Born Washington, DC **DISCIPLINE** ENGLISH **EDUCATION** Univ Wisc Madison, BA, 84; MA, 86; PhD, 92. **CAREER** Lectr, Univ Wis Madison, 92; asst prof to assoc prof, Univ NC Charlotte, 92-. **HONORS AND AWARDS** Excellence in Teaching Awd, Univ Wisc Madison, 89; Outstanding Mentor, Ronald E. McNair Achievement Prog, 95, 97; NEH Summer Stipend, 00. **MEMBERSHIPS** MLA; Toni Morrison Soc; George Moses Thorton Soc for the Study of African Am Poetry; Gwendolyn Brooks Center. **RESEARCH** 20th Century African American literature, especially Black Women Writers and Poetry. **SELECTED PUBLICATIONS** Auth, "And All the Interests Are Vested: Canon-Building in Recent Morrison Criticism", Modern Fiction Studies 39.3&4, (93): 781-794; auth, "Toni Morrison's Tar Baby: Re-Figuring the Colonizer's Aesthetics", Cross-Cultural Performances: Differences in Women's Re-Visions of Shakespeare, ed Marianne Novy, Univ of IL Pr, (Chicago, 93): 137-149; auth, "Re-Writing Native Son: Gwendolyn Brooks' Domestic Aesthetic in Maud Martha", Tulsa Studies in Women's Lit 13.1 (94): 143-145; auth, "Be(e)-ing and Truth: Toni Morrison's Signifying on Sylvia Plath's Bee Poems", Twentieth Century Lit 42.4 (96): 526-534; auth, "Works by and About Pauline Hopskins", The Unruly Voice: Rediscovering Pauline Elizabeth Hopkins, ed John Cullen Greaser, Univ of IL Pr, (Chicago, 96): 221-230; auth, "Periodizing Toni Morrison's Work from the Bluest Eye to Jazz: The Importance of Tar Baby", MELUS 22.3 (97): 71-82; auth, "Rita Dove, African American Poetry, and the Cultural Mulatto: The Spray Paint King as Kunstlerroman", Painting With Words and Music: the Poetry of Rita Dove, Yusef, Komunyakaa, and Margaret Walker, ed Trudier Harris, Univ of NC Pr, (Chapel Hill), 00; auth, Embodying Beauty: Twentieth-Century American Women Writers; Aesthetics, Lit Criticism and Cultural Theory: The Interaction of Text and Society series, Garland, 00; auth, Rita Dove: The Cultural Mulatto and the New Black Aesthetic, (forthcoming). **CONTACT ADDRESS** Dept English, Univ of No Carolina, Charlotte, 2901 University City Blvd, Charlotte, NC 28223-0001.

PERELMAN, BOB
PERSONAL Born 12/02/1947, Youngstown, OH **DISCIPLINE** ENGLISH **EDUCATION** Univ Mich, BA, 69; MA, 70; Univ Iowa, MFA, 71; Univ Calif Berkeley, PhD, 90. **CAREER** Prof, Univ Pa, 90-; vis poet, Univ Iowa, 96. **MEMBERSHIPS** MLA; MSA. **RESEARCH** Poetics; modernism. **SELECTED PUBLICATIONS** Auth, The Trouble With Genius, Calif Univ Pr, 94; auth, The Marginalization of Poetry: Language Writing and Literary History, Princeton Univ Pr, 96; auth, The Future of Memory, Roof Bks, 98; auth, Ten to One: Selected Poems, Wesleyan Univ Pr, 99. **CONTACT ADDRESS** English Dept, Univ of Pennsylvania, 34th Walnut St, Philadelphia, PA 19104. **EMAIL** perelmen@english.upenn.edu

PEREZ, FRANK E.
DISCIPLINE ENGLISH **EDUCATION** Univ La, BA, 91; MA, 97; Tex Christ Univ, PhD. **CAREER** Adj instr, Tarrant C Col. **HONORS AND AWARDS** Webb Awd, Outstanding New Grad, 96; 3rd Place Poetry Prize; Chancellor Round Table Member. **MEMBERSHIPS** MLA; NCTE; CCCC; CCTET. **RESEARCH** Rhetoric; poetics; modernism. **SELECTED PUBLICATIONS** Auth, "Let's Get Medieval on McVeigh," Nat Writing Project E-J (97); auth, "The Song of Angels," SW Rev (97); auth, "Between the Beach and the Boys," Image (98); auth, "A Formulist Analysis of E. A. Robinson's Richard Cory," in Writing Literature Criticism, ed. Ann Dobie (forthcoming); auth, "Chavais Clerk of Oxford: Prototype for Prufrock?" Yeat's Ell Rev (forthcoming); "Re-Reading Langston Hughes:

Rhetorical Pedagogy in Theme for English 13," in New Voices on Harlem Renaissance, eds. Australia Tarver, Paula Barnes (Fairleigh Dick, forthcoming). **CONTACT ADDRESS** 5908 Beverly Dr W, Apt 1214, Fort Worth, TX 76132-5827.

PEREZ-TORRES, RAFAEL
DISCIPLINE ENGLISH **EDUCATION** Loyola-Marymount Univ, BA, 82, MA, 84; Stanford Univ, 89. **CAREER** Asst prof, Univ Wis, Madison, 89-92; asst prof, Univ Pa, 92- 94; asst prof, 94-96, assoc prof, 96-97, dept Chicano stud, Univ Calif, Santa Barbara; ASSOC PROF, DEPT ENG, UNIV CALIF, LOS ANGELES, 98-. **HONORS AND AWARDS** Univ Calif, Santa Barbara, Regent's Hum Fac fel, 96; Univ Wis System Inst Race and Ethnicity res grant, 91, 92. **MEMBERSHIPS** Mod Lang Asn; Am Stud Asn; Lat Am Stud Asn. **RESEARCH** Postmodern theory and cult; Chicano cult stid; Chicano poetry; postcolonial stud; race and Chicano cult; multicult lit; contemp Am lit. **SELECTED PUBLICATIONS** Auth, Movements in Chicano Poetry-Against Myths, Against Margins, Cambridge Univ Press, 95; auth, Chicano Ethnicity, Cultural Hybridity, the Mestizo Voice, Am Lit 70.1, Spring 98; auth, Knitting and Knotting the Narrative Thread - Beloved as Postmodern Novel, reprint Reading Toni Morrison: Theoretical and Critical Approaches, Johns Hopkins Press, 98; Refiguring Aztlan, Aztlan: A J Chicano Stud 22.2, Fall 97; auth, Nomads and Migrants - Negotiating a Multicultural Postmodernism, Latinos and Education: A Critical Reader, Routledge, 97; auth, Tracing and Erasing: Race and Pedagogy in The Bluest Eye. Approaches to Teaching the Novels of Toni Morrison, Mod Lang Asn Pubs, 97; auth, Chicano/a Cultural Discourse: Coyotes at the Border, Am Lit 67, Dec 95; auth, Feathering the Serpent: Chicano Mythic Memory, in Memory and Cultural Politics: New Approaches to American Ethnic Literatures, Northeastern Univ Press, 96; Nomads and Migrants - Negotiating a Multicultural Postmodernism, Cultural Critique 26, Winter93/94; auth, The Ambiguous Outlaw: John Rechy and Complicitous Homotextuality, in The Fiction of Masculinity: Crossing Cultures, Crossing Sexualities, NY Univ Press, 94; auth, Chicano Literature entry in Encyclopedia of English Studies and Language Arts, Scholastic, 94. **CONTACT ADDRESS** Dept of English, Univ of California, Los Angeles, 2319 Rolfe Hall, Los Angeles, CA 90095. **EMAIL** perezt@humnet.ucla.edu

PERITZ, JANICE H.
PERSONAL Born 12/06/1948, Edmonton, AB, Canada, M, 1979, 2 children **DISCIPLINE** ENGLISH **EDUCATION** Univ Pa, BA, 70; Stanford Univ, MA, 74; PhD, 78. **CAREER** Asst prof, Univ Tex Austin, 77-81; assoc prof, chair, Beaver Col 81-89; assoc prof, CUNY Queens Col, 89-. **HONORS AND AWARDS** Stanford Univ Fel, 72-76; Whiting Found Fel, 76-77; CUNY Grant, 90-91, 97, 98. **MEMBERSHIPS** MLA, NCTE, CCC, NASSR, ACR. **RESEARCH** Literacies, Rhetoric, Feminisms, British Literature and Culture, 1750-1850. **SELECTED PUBLICATIONS** Auth, "Shadow-Hunting: Romantic Irony, Sartor Resartus, and Victorian Romanticism," Studies in Romanticism, (78); auth, "In Quest of Mistaken Beauties: Allegorical Interdeterminacy in Collins' Poetry," ELH, (81); auth, "Monumental Feminism and Literature's Ancestral House: Another Look at The Yellow Wallpaper," Women's Studies, (85); auth, "Refraining from the Romantic Image: Yeats' Deformation of Metaphysical Aestheticism," Studies in Romanticism, (86); auth, "Engendering the Exemplary Daugher: The Deployment of Sexuality in Richardson's Clarissa," Daughters and Fathers, (Johns Hopkins Univ Pr, 89); coauth, The Practice of Writing 4e, St Martin's 94; auth, "Sexual Politics and the Subject of Nutting: Ideology, Rhetoric, Fantasy," Studies in Romanticism, (99); coauth, The Practice of Writing 5e, Bedford, St Martin's, (forthcoming); coauth, The College Writer, McGraw-Hill, (forthcoming). **CONTACT ADDRESS** Dept English, Queens Col, CUNY, 65-30 Kissena Blvd, Flushing, NY 11367. **EMAIL** jlhperitz@aol.com

PERKINS, BARBARA M.
PERSONAL Born 07/09/1933, St. Benedict, PA, m, 1964, 3 children **DISCIPLINE** AMERICAN LITERATURE **EDUCATION** Baldwin-Wallace Col, BA, 56; Kent State Univ, MA, 59; Univ Pa, PhD, 72. **CAREER** Teacher, Cleveland, OH Public Schools, 56-58; lectr to asst prof, Baldwin Wallace Col, 58-63; asst prof, Fairleigh-Dickinson Univ, 64-66; Dir, E Mich Univ, 76-78; Managing Ed, Jour of Narrative Technique, E Mich, Univ, 77-92; adj prof, Univ of Toledo, 92-98; assoc ed, Narrative, Ohio State Univ, 93-. **HONORS AND AWARDS** Fel, Univ of Pa, 63-64; Danforth Teaching Fel, Nat Libr of Scotland, 67-67. **MEMBERSHIPS** MLA, Soc for the Study of Narrative Lit. **RESEARCH** American literature, 19th Century women novelists. **SELECTED PUBLICATIONS** Coauth, Benet's Readers Encyclopedia of American Literature, 87; coauth, Kaleidoscope, 93, coauth, Women's Work, 94; coauth, Harper Handbook to Literature, 97; coauth, The American Tradition in Literature, 9th Ed, 99; coauth, The American Tradition in Literature, forthcoming. **CONTACT ADDRESS** 1316 King George Blvd, Ann Arbor, MI 48108. **EMAIL** eng-perkins@online.emich.edu

PERKINS, DAVID
PERSONAL Born 10/25/1928, Philadelphia, PA, s **DISCIPLINE** ENGLISH **EDUCATION** Harvard Univ, AB, 51, AM, 52, PhD, 55. **CAREER** Instr to Assoc Prof, 57-64, Prof English, Harvard Univ, 64-95, Chair, Dept English, 76-81, Chair, Dept Lit, 87-89; Vis Prof English, Gttingen Univ, 68-69; Vis Prof, Univ Calif-Irvine, 96-97,00. **HONORS AND AWARDS** Guggenheim Fel, 62, 73; ACLS Fel, 77; Fulbright Fel to Ger, 68-69; Walter Channing Cabot Awd for Distinguished Achievement in the Humanities, 87; Distinguished Schol Awd, Keats-Shelley Asn, 90. **MEMBERSHIPS** Keats-Shelley Asn; Byron Soc; Ed Bd, The Wordsworth Circle; Ed Bd, Mod Lang Quart. **RESEARCH** English Romanticism; Modern and Contemporary English; American Poetry. **SELECTED PUBLICATIONS** Auth, The Quest for Permanence: The Symbolism of Wordsworth, Shelley, and Keats, 59; Wordsworth and the Poetry of Sincerity, 64; English Romantic Writers, 67, 2nd ed, 94; A History of Modern Poetry, Vol I: From the 1890s to the High Modernist Mode, 76; Vol II, Modernism and After, 87; Is Literary History Possible?, 92; author of numerous other publications and articles. **CONTACT ADDRESS** English Dept, Harvard Univ, 12 Quincy St., Cambridge, MA 02138.

PERKINS, GEORGE
PERSONAL Born 08/16/1930, Lowell, MA, m, 1964, 3 children **DISCIPLINE** ENGLISH **EDUCATION** Tufts Col, AB, 53; Duke Univ, MA, 54; Cornell Univ, PhD, 60. **CAREER** Prof, Eastern Mich Univ. **HONORS AND AWARDS** Duke Univ Fel; Cornell Univ Fel; Sen Fulbright Fel, Australia. **MEMBERSHIPS** Soc for the Study of Narrative Lit, MLA. **RESEARCH** American Literature. **SELECTED PUBLICATIONS** Auth, The American Tradition in Literature, McGraw-Hill, 99; auth, Benet's Readers Encyclopedia of American Literature, HarperCollins, 91; auth, Women's Work, Oxford, 94; auth, The Harper Handbook to Literature, 2nd ed, Longman, 97. **CONTACT ADDRESS** Dept English, Eastern Michigan Univ, 612 Pray Harrold Hall, Ypsilanti, MI 48197-2210. **EMAIL** eng_perkins@online.emich.edu

PERKINS, JAMES ASHBROOK
PERSONAL Born 02/07/1941, Covington, KY, m, 1963, 2 children **DISCIPLINE** ENGLISH AMERICAN LIT **EDUCATION** Centre Col, BA 63; Miami Univ, MA 65; Univ Tenn, PhD 72. **CAREER** Memphis Univ, instr, 65-67; Univ Tenn, instr 67-72; Westminster Col, prof 73-. **HONORS AND AWARDS** Fulbright; NEH sem Prin, Yale, NYU; NEH Inst, NYU, Princ. **MEMBERSHIPS** MLA; SAMLA; Robert Penn Warren Circle. **RESEARCH** Robert Drake; Robert Penn Warren; Southern Lit. **SELECTED PUBLICATIONS** Robert Penn Warren's All the Kings Men: Three stage Vers, with James A Grimshaw Jr, Athens, Univ GA Press, 99; Southern Writers at Century's End, with Jeffery Folks, Lexington, Univ Press KY, 97. **CONTACT ADDRESS** Dept Eng, Westminster Col, Pennsylvania, Box 62, New Wilmington, PA 16142. **EMAIL** jperkins@westminster.edu

PERKINS, LEEMAN LLOYD
PERSONAL Born 03/27/1932, Salina, UT, m, 1957, 4 children **DISCIPLINE** MUSICOLOGY **EDUCATION** Univ Utah, BFA, Phi Beta Kappa, 54; Yale Univ, PhD, 65. **CAREER** From instr to asst prof musicol, Yale Univ, 64-71; assoc prof, Univ Tex, Austin, 71-76; PROF MUSICOL, COLUMBIA UNIV, 76-, Morse fel, Yale Univ, 67-68; Am Coun Learned Socs fel & grant, Univ Res Inst, Univ Tex, Austin, 73-74; Nat Endowment for Humanities fel, 79. **HONORS AND AWARDS** Otto Kinkeldey Awd, Am Musicol Soc, 80; La Medaille de la Ville de Tours, 97. **MEMBERSHIPS** Am Musicol Soc; Int Musicol Soc; Renaissance Soc Am; Amici Thomae Mori. **RESEARCH** The history of the music of the Renaissance, the 15th and 16th centuries, with special interest in primary sources, musical institutions, and the development of musical style. **SELECTED PUBLICATIONS** Ed, Johannis Lheritier Opera Ominia, Am Inst Musicol 69; auth, Notes bibliographiques au sujet de l'ancien fond musical de l'eglise de St Louis des Francais a Rome, Fontes Artis Musicae, 69; Mode and structure in the masses of Josquin, J Am Musicol Soc, 73; contribr, Grove's Dict of Music and Musicians; co-ed, The Mellon Chansonnier, Yale Univ, 79; gen ed, Masters and Monuments of the Renaissance, Broude Bros Ltd, Music in the Age of Renaissance, W W Norton and Co, 98. **CONTACT ADDRESS** Dept Music, Columbia Univ, 2960 Broadway, New York, NY 10027-6900. **EMAIL** LLPI@columbia.edu

PERLIS, VIVIAN
PERSONAL Born 04/26/1928, Brooklyn, NY, w, 1949, 3 children **DISCIPLINE** MUSIC LITERATURE, HISTORY **EDUCATION** Univ Mich, BA, 49, MA, 52; Columbia Univ, PhD, 65-67. **CAREER** Vis lectr, USC, Eastman, Duke, Smith, Cornell, Wesleyan; sr res assoc, lectr, Dir Oral History & Am Music, Yale School Music & Library, 73-. **HONORS AND AWARDS** Am Inst Acad Arts & Lectrs Ines Awd, 71; Kinkeldey Awds, 75; ASCAP Book Awd, 85; Sovneck Soc Book Awd, 89. **MEMBERSHIPS** Am Musicol Soc; Sovneck Soc; Oral Hist Asn. **RESEARCH** Contemporary composition; 20th Century music history. **SELECTED PUBLICATIONS** Auth Charles Ives, Remembered, 74; coed An Ives Celebration, 75; Copeland 1900-'942, 84; Copeland since 1943, 89. **CONTACT ADDRESS** School of Music and Library, Yale Univ, 425 College St, New Haven, CT 06520. **EMAIL** vivian.perlis@yale.edu

PERLMUTTER, DAVID
DISCIPLINE MASS COMMUNICATIONS **EDUCATION** Univ Pa, MA; Univ Minn, PhD, 95. **CAREER** Assoc prof, La State Univ, 95-. **RESEARCH** Political communication, public opinion, film, photography, history of visual representation of war. **SELECTED PUBLICATIONS** Auth, Photojournalism and Foreign Policy: Framing Icons of Outrage in International Crises, Greenwood (Westport, CT), 98; ed, The Manship School Guide to Political Communication, Louisiana State Univ Press (Baton Rouge), 99; auth, Visions of War: Picturing Warfare from the Stone Age to the Cyberage, St. Martin's (NYork), 99; auth, Policing the Media: Televisual Reality and Cop Work, Sage (Beverly Hills), 00. **CONTACT ADDRESS** The Manship Sch of Mass Commun, Louisiana State Univ and A&M Col, Baton Rouge, LA 70803. **EMAIL** dperlmu@lsu.edu

PERLOFF, MARJORIE GABRIELLE
PERSONAL Born 09/28/1931, Vienna, Austria, m, 1953, 2 children **DISCIPLINE** ENGLISH LITERATURE **EDUCATION** Oberlin Col, 48-52; Barnard Col, AB, 53; Cath Univ Am, MA, 56, PhD, 65. **CAREER** Florence Scott prof, Eng and Comparative Lit, Univ South Calif, 76-85; prof, Eng & Compar Lit, Stanford Univ, 86-90; Prof, Hum, Emerita, Stanford Univ, 00-. **HONORS AND AWARDS** Guggenheim Fel, NEH for the Humanities Sr. Fel, Phi Beta Kappa; Visiting Professorship. **MEMBERSHIPS** Mod Lang Asn; Am Compar Lit Asn; Stanford Hum Inst; Elected to Am Academy of Arts and Sciences, 97-; **RESEARCH** Modernism; Postmodernism; 20th century poetry. **SELECTED PUBLICATIONS** Radical Artifice: Writing Poetry in the Age of Media, Univ Chicago Press, 94; The Dance of the Intellect: Studies in the Poetry of the Pound Tradition, Cambridge Univ Press, 96; Wittgenstein's Ladder: Poetic Language and the Strangeness of the Ordinary, Univ Chicago Press, 96; In Preparation: Poetry On & Off the Page: Essays for Emergent Occasions, Northwestern Univ Press, 98. **CONTACT ADDRESS** Dept Eng, Stanford Univ, Stanford, CA 94305. **EMAIL** mperloff@earthlink.net

PERLOFF, RICHARD M.
DISCIPLINE POLITICAL COM, JOURNALISM, PERSUASUION **EDUCATION** PhD, Univ of Wis, MA, Univ of Pittsburgh, BA, Univ of MI. **CAREER** Comm, Cleveland St Univ. **SELECTED PUBLICATIONS** Auth, Political Communication: Politics, Press, and Public in America, Lawrence Erlbaum Assoc, 97; Perceptions and Conceptions of Political Media Impact: The Third-person Effect and Beyond, The Psychology of Political Communication, Univ MI Press, 96; The Dynamics of Persuasion, Lawrence Erlbaum Assoc, 93. **CONTACT ADDRESS** Commun Dept, Cleveland State Univ, 83 E 24th St, Cleveland, OH 44115. **EMAIL** r.perloff@csuohio.edu

PERRAKIS, PHYLLIS J.
PERSONAL Born 07/10/1941, Washington, DC, m, 1969, 2 children **DISCIPLINE** ENGLISH LITERATURE **EDUCATION** Univ of Rochester, BA, 63; Univ Calif Berkeley, MA, 67; PhD, 75. **CAREER** Replacement prof, Univ of Ottawa, 78-. **HONORS AND AWARDS** Phi Beta Kappa, 63. **MEMBERSHIPS** Doris Lessing Soc, Margaret Atwood Soc. **RESEARCH** Doris Lessing, Margaret Atwood, DH Lawrence, women writers and spirituality, women writers and psychological intersubjectivity. **SELECTED PUBLICATIONS** Auth, "The Portrait of the Artist as a Young Girl: Alice Munro's 'Lives of Girls and Women,'" Atlantis 7, (81); auth, "Doris Lessing's 'The Golden Notebook:' Separation and Symbiosis," Am Imago 38.4, (81); auth, "The Marriage of Inner and Outer Space in Lessing's 'Shikasts,'" Sci Fiction Studies 17.2, (90); auth, "Sufism, Jung and the Myth of Kore: Revisionist Politics in Lessing's 'Marriages,'" Mosaic 25.3, (92); rev of "Touring Lessing's Fictional World," Sci Fiction Studies 19.1, (92); auth, "Touring Lessing's Fictional World," Sci Fiction Studies 19.1 (92); auth, "The Female Gothic and the (M)other in Atwood and Lessing," Doris Lessing Newsletter 17.1, (95); coed, DH Lawrence: The Cosmic Adventure, Borealis Pr, 96; ed, Spiritual Exploration in the Works of Doris Lessing, Greenwood, 99; auth, "Spiritual Oppression in 'Frankenstein,'" Jour of Baha'i Studies 9.4, (99); **CONTACT ADDRESS** Dept English, Univ of Ottawa, Ottawa, ON, Canada K1N 6N5. **EMAIL** pperrak@uottawa.ca

PERRICONE, JACK
PERSONAL Born 03/19/1940, New Haven, CT, m, 1987, 2 children **DISCIPLINE** MUSIC **EDUCATION** Haitt Col Music, PM, 61; Ind Univ, MM, 68. **CAREER** Writer, pop, country, R & B songs; teacher, chair, founder, Songwriting Dept, Berklee Col Music. **HONORS AND AWARDS** ASCAP awards; songwriters guild **MEMBERSHIPS** ASCAP **SELECTED PUBLICATIONS** Auth, Melody In Songwriting: A Study of its Components and Relationship to Harmony, Berklee Press. **CONTACT ADDRESS** Berklee Col of Music, 1140 Boylston St, Boston, MA 02215. **EMAIL** JPerricon@berklee.edu

PERRY, JOHN
PERSONAL Born 11/12/1937, Kingston, NY, s **DISCIPLINE** SPEECH COMMUNICATION, WRITING **EDUCATION** Syracuse Univ, BS, 60; MA, 64; Southern Ill Univ, PhD, 71. **CAREER** Special Doctoral Asst, Southern Ill Univ, 66-68; div

chemn of fine arts, Blue Mountain Col, 72-74; lectr, Univ of Tex at San Antonio, 87-88; coord of speech & assoc prof, Univ of the Incarnate Word, 88-00. **HONORS AND AWARDS** NDEA Grant to Bradloaf Sch of English at Middlebury Col; listed in Who's Who Among Am Teachers. **MEMBERSHIPS** Speech Commun Asn. **RESEARCH** Nonverbal Communication. **SELECTED PUBLICATIONS** Auth, Jack London: An American Myth, Nelson Hall (Chicago, IL); auth, James A. Heine: The American Ibsen, Nelson Hall (Chicago, IL). **CONTACT ADDRESS** Dept Humanities & Fine Arts, Univ of the Incarnate Word, 4301 Broadway, San Antonio, TX 78209-6318. **EMAIL** perry@universe.uiwtx.edu

PERRY, PATSY BREWINGTON
PERSONAL Born 07/17/1933, Greensboro, NC, m, 1955, 1 child **DISCIPLINE** ENGLISH **EDUCATION** North Carolina Coll, Durham, NC, BA (magna cum laude), 1950-54; North Carolina Coll, Durham, NC, MA, 1954-55; Univ of North Carolina, Chapel Hill, NC, PhD, 1968-72. **CAREER** Georgetown High School, Jacksonville, NC, teacher, 55-56; Duke University, visiting professor, 75; North Carolina Central Univ, Durham, NC, reserve book librarian, 56-58, instructor, 59-63, asst prof, 64-71, assoc prof, 72-74, prof, 74-, English dept chmn, 79-90, special asst to the chancellor, Univ Honors Program Dir, 93-95; Provost/Vice Chancellor for Academic Affairs, 95-98. **HONORS AND AWARDS** Alpha Kappa Mu Honorary Soc, 1953; Danforth Scholarship Grant, Summer, 1967; Career Teaching Fellowship, Univ of North Carolina, 1968-69; Faculty Fellow, North Carolina Central Univ, 1968-71; nominee, ACE Fellow Program in Academic Admin, Amer Council on Educ, 1977; Ford Foundation Writing Fellow, Recognition for Excellence in Teaching Writing, 1989; Silver Medallion Awd for Excellence in Education, YWCA of Durham, 1991; Research Awd, North Carolina Central University, 1991. **MEMBERSHIPS** Mem, YWCA, 1976-; mem The Links Inc, 1976-; life mem, Coll Language Assn; mem, senator 1986-, Philological Assn of the Carolinas; mem, South Atlantic Modern Language Assn; mem, Assn of Departments of English; mem, The Langston Hughes Soc; reader, College Board English Composition Test (ETS), 1985-; board member, Women in Action for the Prevention of Violence, 1990-. **SELECTED PUBLICATIONS** Author of "The Literary Content of Frederick Douglass' Paper Through 1860," CLA Journal 1973, "One Day When I Was Lost: Baldwin's Unfulfilled Obligation," chapter in James Baldwin: A Critical Evaluation, edited by Therman B O'Daniel, Howard Univ Press 1977, and biographical essays in Southern Writers-Biographical Dictionary, Louisiana State Univ Press 1979, The Dictionary of Literary Biography, 1986; Notable BlackAmerican Women, edited by Jessie Smith, 1991, Southern Writers of the Second Renascence--Poets, Dramatists, Essayists, and Others, edited by Joseph Flora and Robert Bain, 1992. **CONTACT ADDRESS** No Carolina Central Univ, Durham, NC 27707.

PERSE, ELIZABETH M.
DISCIPLINE TELECOMMUNICATIONS, MASS COMMUNICATION **EDUCATION** Northwestern Univ, BA, 71; Kent State Univ, MA, 85, PhD, 87. **CAREER** Rev, criticism asst, Jour of Broadcasting, 83-84; ed asst, Jour Broadcasting & Electronic Media, 84-86; secy, Speech Commun Assn, 87-88; act ch, 93; ch, Speech Commun Assn, 93-94; pres, Arts and Sci Col Senate, 93-94; ch, dept search comm. 91-92, 93-94; ch, Speech Commun Assn, 93-94; assoc prof, 87-. **HONORS AND AWARDS** David B Smith fel, Kent State Univ, 86; grad stud senate res award, Kent State Univ, 86; Univ fel, Kent State Univ, 86-87; doc hon(s) fel, Speech Commun Assn, 87; grad stud senate dissertation award, Kent State Univ, 87; grant, 88, 91, 94; top paper award, Assn Edu in Jour and Mass Commun, 92; rev and criticism ed, jour broadcasting & electronic media, 94-97. **MEMBERSHIPS** Mem, Assn Edu in Jour and Mass Commun; Broadcast Edu Assn; E Commun Assn; Intl Commun Assn; Speech Commun Assn; Amer Acad Advt. **SELECTED PUBLICATIONS** Auth, Uses of Erotica and Acceptance of Rape Myths, Commun Res, 94; Sensation Seeking the Use of Television for Arousal, Commun Rpt, 96; co-auth, Gratifications From Newer Television Technologies, Jour Quart, 94, repr, Ablex, 97; Direct and Indirect Effects of Socioeconomic Status on Public Affairs Knowledge, Jour Quart, 94;Cultivation in the Newer Media Environment, Commun Res, 94; Measures of Mass Communications, Commun Research Measures: A sourcebook, Guilford, 94; Sports and Media Events Orientations to the 92 Winter Olympics, Jour Intl Commun, 95; The stability of College Students' Implicit Theories of Marriage as Measured by the Relational Dimensions Instrument, Commun Quart, 95; Women in Communications, Greenwood, 96; The Effects of Spokesperson Gender, PSA Appeal, and Involvement on Evaluations of Safe-sex Public Service Announcements, Health Commun, 96; News Coverage of Abortion Between Roe and Webster: Public Opinion and Real-world Events, Commun Res Rpt 14, 97; Uses of Interpersonal Communication Motives and Humor by Elders, Commun Res Rpt 14, 97; Gender Differences in Television Use: An Exploration of the Instrumental-expressive Dichotomy, Commun Res Rpt 14, 97; Communicate Oonline, Mountain View, Mayfield, 98; The Mayfield Quick Guide to the Internet for Communnications Students, Mountain View, Mayfield, 98; rev(s), Review and Criticism Editor's Note, Jour Broadcasting & Electronic Media, 95, 96. **CONTACT ADDRESS** Dept of Commun, Univ of Delaware, 162 Ctr Mall, Newark, DE 19716. **EMAIL** eperse@udel.edu

PERSON, LELAND S.
DISCIPLINE 19TH-CENTURY AMERICAN LITERATURE **EDUCATION** IN, PhD, 77. **CAREER** Univ Ala **HONORS AND AWARDS** Pres, Henry James Soc. **SELECTED PUBLICATIONS** Auth, Aesthetic Headaches: Women and a Masculine Poetics in Poe, Melville, and Hawthorne, 88. **CONTACT ADDRESS** Univ of Alabama, Birmingham, 1400 University Blvd, Birmingham, AL 35294-1150.

PETERFREUND, STUART S.
PERSONAL Born 06/30/1945, Brooklyn, NY, d, 1 child **DISCIPLINE** CREATIVE WRITING, ENGLISH LITERATURE **EDUCATION** Cornell Univ, BA, 66; Unif of Calif at Irvine, MFA, 68; Univ of Wash, PhD, 74. **CAREER** Asst prof, Univ of Ark at Little Rock, 75-78; from asst prof to prof, Northeastern Univ, 78-; chemn, Northeastern Univ, 91-. **HONORS AND AWARDS** School of Criticism and Theory Fel, 77; Southern Arts Agencies Fel, 77; 4 NEH summer seminars, 79, 83, 88, & 90-91; Dibner Fel, 95. **MEMBERSHIPS** MLA; ASECS; AWP; SLS; Wordsworth-Coleridge Asn; Keats-Shelley Soc; Byron Soc; HSS. **RESEARCH** Eighteenth and Nineteenth-century English literature; literature and science; social history of science. **SELECTED PUBLICATIONS** Auth, Literature and Science: Theory and Practice, 90; William Blake in a Newtonian World, 98; numerous essays published in JHI, Configurations, Criticism, ELH, TWC, Eighteenth-Century Life, and others. **CONTACT ADDRESS** English Dept, Northeastern Univ, 360 Huntington Ave, Boston, MA 02115-5096. **EMAIL** speterfr@lynx.neu.edu

PETERS, ERSKINE ALVIN
PERSONAL Born 03/16/1948, Augusta, GA, s **DISCIPLINE** ENGLISH **EDUCATION** Yale Univ, summer study 1968; Paine Coll, BA English 1969; Oberlin Coll, Post-baccalaureate study 1969-70; Princeton Univ, PhD English 1976; Sorbonne Paris, summer study 1984. **CAREER** Morristown Coll, tutor 1970-72; Univ of CA Berkeley, assoc prof of Afro-Amer Literature; Univ of Notre Dame, prof of English, currently. **HONORS AND AWARDS** First Recipient of Frank J Henry Awd, Univ of GA 1968; Rockefeller Fellowship in Afro-Amer Studies 1972-76. **MEMBERSHIPS** Advisor Oakland Scholar Achiever Program 1980-82; discussion leader SATE Program at San Quentin Prison 1980-83. **SELECTED PUBLICATIONS** Auth, William Faulkner, The Yoknapatawpha World and Black Being 1983, African Openings to the Tree of Life 1983, Fundamentals of Essay Writing 1983. **CONTACT ADDRESS** Professor of English, Univ of Notre Dame, Notre Dame, IN 46556.

PETERS, FRANCIS EDWARD
PERSONAL Born 06/23/1927, New York, NY, m, 1957, 1 child **DISCIPLINE** CLASSICS, ISLAMIC STUDIES **EDUCATION** St Louis Univ, AB, 50, MA, 52; Princeton Univ, PhD(Orient studies), 61. **CAREER** Instr English, Latin & Greek, Canisius High Sch, Buffalo, NY, 52-54; instr English, Scarborough Country Day Sch, NY, 55- 56; from asst prof to assoc prof classics, 61-69, Prof Hist & Near Eastern Lang & Lit & Chmn Dept Near Eastern Lang & Lit, New York Univ, 70-. **MEMBERSHIPS** Am Orient Soc; Mid E Studies Asn. **RESEARCH** Social and intellectual history of Late Antiquity and Early Islam; Near Eastern urbanism. **SELECTED PUBLICATIONS** Auth, Greek Philosophical Terms, 67 & Aristotle and the Arabs, 68, New York Univ; Aristoteles Arabus, Brill, 68; The Harvest of Hellenism, 71 & Allah's Commonwealth, 74, Simon & Schuster; Ours, R Mareck, 81; The Children of Abraham: Judaism, Christianity, Islam, Princeton Univ Press, 82. **CONTACT ADDRESS** Dept of Near Eastern Lang & Lit, New York Univ, New York, NY 10003.

PETERS, JOHN U.
PERSONAL Born Snohomish, WA, s **DISCIPLINE** ENGLISH **EDUCATION** UCLA, BA, 67; Johns Hopkins Univ, MA, 70; Univ Wisc, PhD, 73. **CAREER** Jr Instructor, Johns Hopkins Univ, 69-70; Lecturer, Los Angeles Community Col, 72-; Lecturer, Calif State Univ, 77-. **HONORS AND AWARDS** Teaching Fel, Johns Hopkins Univ, 69-79. **MEMBERSHIPS** MLA. **RESEARCH** 19th and 20th Century British and American literature; Literary criticism and reading theory. **SELECTED PUBLICATIONS** Auth, The Elements of Critical Reading, Macmillan, 91; auth, "Five Ways of Interpreting a Text," in The Allyn and Bacon Sourcebook for College Writing Teachers, Allyn and Bacon, 96; auth, "Ruskin and the Languages of Art," Journal of the Theory and Criticism of the Visual Arts, (82): 35-45; auth, "My Sister's Sleep: Rossetti's Midnight Mass," Victorian Poetry, (79): 265-268. **CONTACT ADDRESS** Dept English, California State Univ, Northridge, 18111 Nordhoff St, Northridge, CA 91330-0001. **EMAIL** john.u.peters@csun.edu

PETERS, JULIE
DISCIPLINE DRAMA AND THEATRE HISTORY **EDUCATION** Yale Univ, AB, 81; Princeton Univ, PhD, 87. **CAREER** Asoc prof. **HONORS AND AWARDS** Fel, Fulbright found; fel, Folger Library; fel, Amer Coun Learned Soc; fel, Humboldt found. **RESEARCH** Law and literature. **SELECTED PUBLICATIONS** Auth, Congreve, the Drama, and the Printed Word, Stanford, 90; co-ed, Women's Rights, Human Rights: International Feminist Perspectives, Routledge, 95. **CONTACT ADDRESS** Dept of Eng, Columbia Col, New York, 2960 Broadway, New York, NY 10027-6902.

PETERSEN, MEG
PERSONAL Born 10/08/1956, Peterborough, NH, d, 3 children **DISCIPLINE** ENGLISH **EDUCATION** Univ NH, PhD, 91. **CAREER** Assoc Prof, Plymouth State Col. **HONORS AND AWARDS** New Eng Poet of the Year, 97. **MEMBERSHIPS** NCTE, NH Writer's Proj. **SELECTED PUBLICATIONS** Auth, "The Cutting," and "Seeing Anna," in Everyday Epiphanies: An Anthology of Teachers' Writing (97); auth, "Angels and Demons," in Lessons Learned: An Anthology of Teachers' Writing (98); auth, "Writing Alongside Our Students: Student as Apprentice in the Writing Workshop," The Leaflet, vol 98, no 1 (99); auth, "Letter to a Student Teacher," The Leaflet, vol 98 nos 2&3 (99); auth, "Waters Will Recede," and "The Atomic Weight of Oxygen," in Shifts of Vision: An Anthology of Teachers' Writing (99); auth, "Before Lift Off," and "At the Recycling Center," in MCTE: The J of the Miss Coun of Teachers of English, vol 20, no 2 (99); auth, "Red Hair," and "At Your Mother's Gravesite," in Voices from the Ctr, vol 4 (99); auth, "Walk With Children," and "Not One Small Change," in Ala English (forthcoming). **CONTACT ADDRESS** Dept English, Plymouth State Col of the Univ System of New Hampshire, 17 High St, Plymouth, NH 03264-1595.

PETERSON, CARLA L.
PERSONAL Born 09/04/1941, New York, NY, m, 1968, 2 children **DISCIPLINE** ENGLISH **EDUCATION** Radcliffe Col, BA, 65; Yale Univ, PhD, 76. **CAREER** Asst prof to prof, Univ of Md, 77-. **HONORS AND AWARDS** Fel, Nat Res Counc for Minorities, 81-82; fel, Ctr for Advan Study in Behav Sci, 87-88; fel, Am Asn of Univ Women, 91-92; fel, Am Counc of Learned Soc, 91-92. **MEMBERSHIPS** MLA; Am Studies Assoc. **RESEARCH** Nineteenth Century African-American literary culture with a focus on fictional and non-fictional narrative, intersections of race and gender, and minority discourse. **SELECTED PUBLICATIONS** Auth, The Determined Reader: Gender and Culture in the Novel from Napoleon to Victoria, Rutgers Univ Pr, 86; coauth, "We Hold These Truths to be Self-Evident" The Rhetoric of Frederick Douglass Journalism", Critical Essays on Frederick Douglass, ed Eric Sundquist, Cambridge Univ Pr, 90; auth, " Capitalism, Black (Under)development, and the Production of the African-American Novel in the 1850s", Am Lit Hist 4 (92); auth, "Unsettled Frontiers: Race, History, and Romance in Pauline Hopkin's Contending Forces", Famous Last Words: Women Against Novelistic Endings, ed Alison booth, Univ of Va Pr, 93; auth, "Further Liftings of the Veil: Gender, Class, and Labor in Frances Harper's Iola Leroy", Listening to Silences: New Essays in Feminist Criticism, Ed Shelly Fisher Fishkin and Elaine Hedges, Oxford Univ Pr, 94; auth, Doers of the Word: African-American Women speakers and Writers in the North (1830-1880), Oxford Univ Pr, 95; auth, "The Remaking of Americans: Gertrude Stein's Melanchta and African-American Musical Traditions", Criticism and the color Line: Race and Revisionism in American Literary Studies, ed Harry Wonham, Rutgers, 96; auth, "Le surnaturel dans Moi, Tituba sorciere..Noire de Salem de Maryse Conde et Beloved de Toni Morrison", L'Oeuvre de Maryse Conde. Actes Du Colloque sur l'oeuvre de Maryse Conde, L'Hartmattan, (Paris), 96; coauth, "the Color of Memory: Interpreting Twentieth-Century U.S. Social Policy from a Nineteenth-Century Perspective", Feminist Studies, 98; auth, "Reconstructing the Nation: Frances Harper, Charlotte Forten, and the Racial politics of Periodical Publication", Proceedings of the Am Antiquarian Soc, (forthcoming). **CONTACT ADDRESS** Comp Lit Prog, Univ of Maryland, Col Park, 2107 Susquehanna Hall, College Park, MD 20742-8800. **EMAIL** cp10@umail.umd.edu

PETERSON, DALE E.
PERSONAL Born 11/10/1966, Bridgewater, MA, m, 1966, 2 children **DISCIPLINE** ENGLISH, RUSSIAN **EDUCATION** Harvard Col, BA, 63; Yale Univ, MA, 65; PhD, 70. **CAREER** Instr to prof, Amherst Col, 68-. **HONORS AND AWARDS** Trustee Fac Fel, Amherst, 74-75; Fac Res Fel, Amherst, 97-00. **MEMBERSHIPS** MLA, Assoc of Teachers of Slavic and E Europ Lang, Am Assoc for the Advan of Slavic Studies, Nabokov Soc. **RESEARCH** Comparative American and Russian Literature and intellectual history. **SELECTED PUBLICATIONS** Auth, The Clement Vision: Poetic Realism in Turgenev and James, Kennikat Pr,/Nat Univ Pr, 75; auth, "Solzhenitsyn's Image of America: The Survival of a Slavophile Idea," Mass Rev, (78); auth, "Nabokov's Invitation: Literature as Execution," PMLA, (81); auth, "Maiakovskii's Lenin: The Fabrication of a Bolshevik bylina," Slavic Rev, (82); auth, "Russian Gothic: The Deathless Paradoxes of Bunin's Dry Valley," Slavic and E Europ Jour, (87); auth, "Nabokov and the Poe-etics of Composition," Slavic and E Europ Jour, (89); auth, "Response and Call: The African American Dialogue with Bakhtin," Am Lit, (93); auth, "Richard Wright's Long Journey from Gorky to Dostoevsky," African Am Lit, (94); auth, Up From Bondage: The Literatures of Russian and African American Soul, Duke Univ Pr, 00. **CONTACT ADDRESS** Amherst Col, Campus Box 2234, Amherst, MA 01002-5000. **EMAIL** depeterson@amherst.edu

PETERSON, ERIC E.
DISCIPLINE COMMUNICATIONS **EDUCATION** Southern IL Univ, PhD, 80. **CAREER** Assoc prof, ch, dept Commun and Jour, Univ ME. **RESEARCH** The integration of media consumption; interpersonal play. **SELECTED PUBLICATIONS** Auth, Media consumption and girls who want to have fun, Critical Stud in Mass Commun, 4, 87; The technology of media consumption, Am Behavioral Sci, 32, 88; Moving toward a gender balanced curriculum in basic speech communication courses, Commun Educ, 40, 91; Diversity and Franco-American identity politics, Maine Hist Soc Quart, 34, 94; Nonsexist language reform and "political correctness," Women and Lang, 17, No.2, 94. **CONTACT ADDRESS** Univ of Maine, Orono, ME 04469-5752. **EMAIL** peterson@maine.edu

PETERSON, LARRY
PERSONAL Born 12/10/1941, Wichita, KS, m, 1965, 2 children **DISCIPLINE** MUSICOLOGY **EDUCATION** Texas Christian Univ, BM, 64, MM, 69; Univ NC-Chapel Hill, PhD, 73. **CAREER** Inst mus, Jersey State Col, 73-75; assoc prof music, 75-77, dir, Sch Mus, 78-80, George Peabody Col; Chair, Dept Mus, 80-85, prof mus, 85- , Univ Del. **HONORS AND AWARDS** Masters of Innovation Awd, 2nd pl, Zenith Data Systems Nat Compet, 91; EDUCOM's Joe Wyatt Challenge Awd, 91; Nat Endow Human Summer Sem, Mus and Tech, 87; Gold CINDY Awd; Univ Nebr Merit award, 86; Nat Endow Human grant, 82-84; Woodrow Wilson Fellow, 71. **MEMBERSHIPS** Am Guild of Organists; Am Musicol Soc; Assoc Develop of Computer-based Inst Syst; Asn Tech Mus Instr; Col Mus Soc; Comp Mus Asn; Int Soc Tech Ed; Mus Ed Nat Conf; Phi Mu Alpha Sinfonia. **RESEARCH** Music and Poetry of Olivier Messiaen; Uses of new technologies to teach music; The lament tradition. **SELECTED PUBLICATIONS** The Complete Organ Works of Simon Lohet, Am Inst Musicol, 75; Handel's 'He Was Despised:' The Tradition of Laments, Nats Bulletin, Spr, 89; The Information Highway: Computer Networking for Choral Musicians, The Choral Jour, April 94; Music Literature Instruction and Multimedia: A Delaware Perspective, in Musicus: Computer Applications in Music Education, v4, June 95; Messiaen and Surrealism: A Study of His Poetry, in Messiaesn's Language of Mystical Love, Siglind Bruhn, ed., Garland Publ, 98; **CONTACT ADDRESS** Univ of Delaware, Dept of Music, Newark, DE 19711. **EMAIL** peterson@udel.edu

PETERSON, LINDA H.
PERSONAL Born 10/11/1948, Saginaw, MI **DISCIPLINE** ENGLISH **EDUCATION** Wheaton Col, BA, 69; Univ Rhode Island, MA, 73; Brown Univ, PhD, 78. **CAREER** Lectr, 77-78, asst prof, 78-85, assoc prof, 85-92, dir undergrad study in English, 90-94, Prof, 92- , chr Dept of English, 94-00, Yale Univ, 77- ; Dir Bass Writing prog, Yale Col, 79-89 & 90-. **HONORS AND AWARDS** Morse fel, 81-82; Mellon fel, 84-85 & 97-98; NEH fel, 89-90; Life fel, Clare Hall, Cambridge, 98. **MEMBERSHIPS** MLA; NCTE; WPA; RSVP. **RESEARCH** 19th Century British literature. **SELECTED PUBLICATIONS** Auth, Victorian Autobiography: The Tradition of Self-Interpretation, Yale Univ Press, 86; coauth, Writing Prose, Yale Col, 89; ed, Wuthering Heights: A Case Study in Contemporary Criticism, St Martin's Press, 92; coauth, A Struggle for Fame: Victorian Woman Artists and Authors, Yale Ctr Brit Art, 94; auth, Traditions of Victorian Women's Autobiography: The Poetics and Poetics of Life Writing,, Univ Press Va, 99; ed The Norton Reader, & Instructors Guide to the Norton Reader, W W Norton, 00. **CONTACT ADDRESS** English Dept, Yale Univ, PO Box 208302, New Haven, CT 06520-8302.

PETERSON, LORNA INGRID
PERSONAL Born 07/22/1956, Buffalo, NY **DISCIPLINE** LIBRARY SCIENCE **EDUCATION** Dickinson College, Carlisle, PA, BA, 1977; Case Western Reserve Univ, Cleveland, OH, MS library science, 1980; Iowa State University, PhD, 1992. **CAREER** Wright State University, Dayton, OH, humanities reference librarian/special college cataloger, 80-81; Ohio Univ, Athens, OH, special college cataloger, 82-82; Iowa State Univ, Ames, IA, cataloger, 83-85, bibliographic instructor, 85-91; SUNY-Buffalo, NY, assistant professor, Assoc Prof, currently. **MEMBERSHIPS** Board member, Ames, ISU YWCA, 1984-89; chair communications committee, Iowa Library Assn/ACRL, 1984-86; chair membership committee, Iowa Library Assn/ACRL, 1987-88; representative to ALA/RTSD Org & Bylaws, American Library Assn, 1984-86; member, Black Caucus of ALA, 1980, 1988-; African American Librarian Assn of Western New York, 1990-; ALA-Lirt Research Committee, 1994-96; ALA-ACRL/BIS, Education for Bibliographic Instruction, 1994-96; ALA-RASD/MOPSS, Catalog Use Committee, 1992-96; Committee on Accreditation, 1997-2001. **CONTACT ADDRESS** Sch of Info & Library Studies, SUNY, Buffalo, 534 Baldy Hall, Buffalo, NY 14260.

PETERSON, R. G.
PERSONAL Born 01/09/1936, Chicago, IL **DISCIPLINE** ENGLISH LITERATURE **EDUCATION** Univ Minn, BA, 56, PhD, 63; Northwestern Univ, MA, 58. **CAREER** Instr Eng, Univ Minn, 60-62; from asst prof to assoc prof, 63-76, Prof Eng & Classics, St Olaf Col, 76-96, prof emer, 96- ; book rev ed, Eighteenth-Century Studies, 79-83; exec secy, Am Soc for Eighteenth-Century Stud, 83-89; exec comt, Int Soc for Eighteenth-Century Stud, 83-94. **HONORS AND AWARDS** William Riley Parker Prize, MLA, 75-76. **MEMBERSHIPS** MLA; Am Soc 18th Century Stud; Johnson Soc Cent Region; Class Asn Midwest & South. **RESEARCH** The classics in the Restoration and eighteenth century; Latin literature, especially poetry and history; literary structure. **SELECTED PUBLICATIONS** Auth, Larger Manners and Events: Sallust and Virgil in Absolom and Achitophel, PMLA, 67; auth, The Unity of Horace Epistle 17, Class J, 68; auth, The Unavailing Gift: Dryden's Roman Farewell to Mr. Oldham, Mod Philol, 69; auth, The Unknown Self in the Fourth Satire of Persius, Class J, 73; auth, Renaissance Classicism in Pope's Duncaid, Studies Eng Lit, 75; auth, Samuel Johnson at War with the Classics, 18th Century Stud, 75; auth, Critical Calculations: Measure and Symmetry in Literature, PMLA, 76. **CONTACT ADDRESS** 1158 Fifth Ave, 12-A, New York, NY 10029-6917. **EMAIL** Petersor@idt.net

PETERSON, RICHARD SCOT
PERSONAL Born 07/14/1938, Ayr, Scotland, m, 1965, 1 child **DISCIPLINE** ENGLISH **EDUCATION** Princeton Univ, BA, 60; Univ Calif Berkeley, MA, 63; PhD, 69. **CAREER** Instr to asst prof, Princeton Univ, 66-72; lectr, Univ Va, 72-76; asst prof, Yale Univ, 76-80; assoc prof to prof, Univ of Conn, 80-. **HONORS AND AWARDS** Phi Beta Kappa; Fulbright Scholar, Oxford, 60-61; Woodrow Wilson Fel, 61-62; NEH-Newberry Fel, 76; Am Philos Soc Fel, 76; NEH Summer Stipend 84; ACLS Fel 84-85; Bibliog Soc of Am Fel, 86. **MEMBERSHIPS** MLA; John Donne Soc; Spenser Soc; Ren Soc of Am. **RESEARCH** Renaissance English Literature, European Renaissance Literature, Classical Backgrounds, Music, Art. **SELECTED PUBLICATIONS** Auth, Imitation and Praise in the Poems of Ben Johnson, Yale Univ Pr, 81; ed, Essays on Literature and the Visual Arts, John Donne Soc, 86; auth, "Envies Scourge, and Vertues Honour, PULC 47.1 (96): 155-74; auth, "In from the Cold: An English at Rome 1595", ANQ 5.2-3 (92): 115-21; auth, "Spurting Froth Upon Courtiers", TLS 4911 (97): 14-15; auth, "Laurel Crown and Ape's Tail: New Light on Spenser's Career from Sir Thomas Tresham", Spenser Studies 12, (98): 1-35; coauth, "Rereading Colin's Broken Pipe: Spenser and the Problem of Patronage", Spenser Studies 14, (00): 233-72. **CONTACT ADDRESS** Dept English, Univ of Connecticut, Storrs, 337 Mansfield Rd, Unit U-25, Storrs, CT 06269-1025. **EMAIL** rpeters@uconnvm.uconn.edu

PETHICA, JAMES
DISCIPLINE ENGLISH **EDUCATION** Oxford Univ, BA, 80; DPhil, 87. **CAREER** Vis asst prof. **RESEARCH** Modern British literature; Irish studies; modern drama; contemporary Irish poetry; modernist and experimental fiction. **SELECTED PUBLICATIONS** Auth, WB Yeats: Last Poems, Manuscript Materials, Editor Lady Gregory's Diaries 1892-1902. **CONTACT ADDRESS** Dept of English, Williams Col, Statson d-18, Williamstown, MA 01267. **EMAIL** james.l.pethica@williams.edu

PETIT, SUSAN
PERSONAL Born 08/25/1945, OH, m, 1984 **DISCIPLINE** FRENCH, ENGLISH **EDUCATION** Knox Col, BA, 66; Purdue Univ, MA, 68; Notre Dame Col, MA, 83. **CAREER** Prof, Col San Mateo, 68-. **HONORS AND AWARDS** Phi Beta Kappa. **MEMBERSHIPS** AATF; ALSC; CCCFLC; CLTA; Christianity and Literature; CCHA; CIEF; FSFS; FLANC; FLASC; MLA; PAMLA; Simone de Beauvoir Soc; Women in Fr. **RESEARCH** 20th-century French novel. **SELECTED PUBLICATIONS** Auth, "Joachim de Fiore, the Holy Spirit, and Michel Tournier's Les Maeores," Modern Lang Studies 16 (86): 88-100; auth, "Fugal Structure, Nestonanism, and St. Christopher in Michel Tournier's Le Roi des Aulnes," Novel 19 (86): 232-45; auth, "Psychological, Sensual, and Religious Initiation in Tournier's Pierrot ou les Secrets de la Nuit," Children's Lit 18 (90): 87-100; auth, "Michel Tournier's Metaphysical Fictions," in Monographs in Romance Languages 37 (91); auth, "Michel Tournier and Victor Hugo: A Case of Literary Parricide," Fr Rev 68 (94): 251-60; auth, "Michel Tournier," in The Contemporary Novel in France, ed. William Thompson (FL: UP of Florida, 95): 248-63; auth, "The Meaning of Food and the Body in Mallet-Jons's Divine," Lit Interpretations Theory 8 (97): 105-22; auth, "La Critique Religieuse de L'oeuvre de Tournier," Euvres et Critiques 23 (98): 40-51; auth, Francoise Mallet-Joris, Rodopi (Amsterdam/Atlanta) 01; auth, "Mallet-Joris's Divine: A Twentieth-Century Mystic," in Divine Aporia: Postmodern Conversations about the Other, ed. John C. Hawley (PA: Bucknell UP, 01): 190-207. **CONTACT ADDRESS** Fr Dept, Col of San Mateo, San Mateo, CA 94402. **EMAIL** petits@pacbell.net

PETITJEAN, THOMAS D., JR
PERSONAL Born 11/15/1956, Rayne, LA, s **DISCIPLINE** ENGLISH **EDUCATION** La State Univ, BA, 79; MA, 92; PhD, 95. **CAREER** Adj Instructor, Univ La, 91-; Adj Instructor, La State Univ, 95-; Teacher, Rayne High School, 95-. **HONORS AND AWARDS** Grad Teacher of the Year, Univ La, 91; High School Teacher of the Year, Rayne High School, 96. **MEMBERSHIPS** SECOL, NEA, LAE, Soc of Linguists, ASCD, NASSP, Phi Kappa Phi, Sigma Tau Delta. **RESEARCH** Gay Literature, The Vampire in Literature, Romantic British Writers, The American Novel (especially Henry James and Edith Wharton). **SELECTED PUBLICATIONS** Auth, "Introduction to Gay Literature," in American Diversity, American Identity; auth, "James's The Europeans," The Explicator. **CONTACT ADDRESS** Dept English, Univ of Southwestern Louisiana, Box 44691, Lafayette, LA 70504-0001. **EMAIL** jedpeck@aol.com

PETRAGLIA-BAHRI, DEEPIKA
DISCIPLINE ENGLISH LANGUAGE AND LITERATURE **EDUCATION** Bowling Green Univ, PhD, 92. **CAREER** Fac, Ga Inst Tech, 94; fac, Bowling Green Univ, 92-94; asst prof, Emory Univ, 95. **RESEARCH** Postcolonial lit and theory; technology, culture, and postcolonialism. **SELECTED PUBLICATIONS** Auth, "Boethius and Sir Thomas Browne: The Common Ground," Mythes, Croyances et Religion dans le monde Anglo-Saxon 10, (92): 43-53; auth, "Disembodying the Corpus: Postcolonial Pathology in tsitsi Dangarembga's Nervous Conditions," Postmodern Culture: An electronic Journal of Interdisciplinary Criticism 5.1, (94): 1-59; auth, "Once more with Feeling: What is Postcolonialism?" ARIEL: A Review of International English Literature 26.1, (95): 51-82; ed and contrib, Between the Lines: South Asians and Postcoloniality, Temple UP, 96; auth, "Marginaly Off-Center: Postcolonialism in the Teaching Machine," College English 59.3, (97): 277-98; auth, "Swallowing for Twenty Years/ the American Mind and Body": An Interview with G.S. Sharat Chandra," Journal of Commonwealth and Postcolonial Studies 5.1, (97): 9-17; auth, "Terms of Engagement: Postcolonialism, Transnationalism, and Compositiono Studies," Exploring Borderlands: Postcolonial and Composition Studies, JAC: A Journal of Composition Theory, 18.1, (98): 29-44; auth, "Always Becoming: Narratives of Nation and Self in Bharati Mukherjee's Jasmine," Women, America, and Movement: Narratives of Relocation, ed. Susan roberson, (Columbia: U of MO Press, 98): 137-54; auth, "With Kaleidoscope Eyes: The Potential (Dangers) of Identitarian Coalitions," A Part, Yet Apart: South Asian Americans in Asian America, ed. Lavina Dhingra Shanker & Rajini Srikanth, (Temple UP, 98): 25-48; co-ed, "While Calcutta Burns: Narratives of and Imprisoned Self," (in press), Keepers of the Flame: Power, Myth, and Cultural Consciousness in Ethnic Female Identity, ed. Sondra Neale and Cynthia Tompkins, (Wayne State UP, 99). **CONTACT ADDRESS** English Dept, Emory Univ, 201 N Callaway, Atlanta, GA 30322. **EMAIL** dpetrag@emory.edu

PETRAGLIA-BAHRI, JOSEPH
DISCIPLINE RHETORIC AND COGNITIVE SCIENCE **EDUCATION** Carnegie Mellon Univ, PhD, 91. **CAREER** Asst prof, Ga Inst of Technol. **RESEARCH** The rhetoric of inquiry. **SELECTED PUBLICATIONS** Ed, Reconceiving Writing, Rethinking Writing Instruction, Lawrence Erlbaum, 95. **CONTACT ADDRESS** Sch of Lit, Commun, & Cult, Georgia Inst of Tech, Skiles Cla, Atlanta, GA 30332. **EMAIL** joseph.petraglia@lcc.gatech.edu

PETRESS, KENNETH C.
PERSONAL Born 11/01/1939, Chicago, IL **DISCIPLINE** SPEECH COMMUNICATION **EDUCATION** Northern IL Univ, BS Ed, 77, MA, 79, CAS, 80; LA State Univ, PhD, 88. **CAREER** Instr, Northern IL Univ, 80-83; vis prof, Xi Dian Univ, Xian, China, 83-84; lect, Empora State Univ, 84-86; prof, Univ ME at Presque Isle, 88-. **MEMBERSHIPS** Nat Commun Asn; Int'l Common Asn; Southern States Commun Asn; Yale-China Asn. **RESEARCH** Rhetoriaty of political symbols. **SELECTED PUBLICATIONS** Auth, Coping with a New Educational Environment: Chinese Students' Imagined Interactions Before Beginning Studies in the US, J of Instr Psychol, 22 (1), 95; A Partial Solution to the University Journal Subscription Problem, J of Instr Psychol, 22 (3), 95; Questions of Obligation, Cost Effectiveness, and Efficiency: University Remedial Programs, Education, 116 (1), 95; The Multiple Roles of An Undergraduate's Academic Advisor, Education, 117 (1), 96; The Dilema of University Undergraduate Student Attendance Policies: To Require Class Attendance or Not, Col Student J 30 (3), 96; Broasdcasting in China, in Alan Wells, ed, World Broadcasting: A Comparative View, Ablex, 96; with Kurt O Hofmann, The Community Review Board Offers Students Fairness in Administrative Decision Appeals, Education, 118 (1), 97; auth, Listening: A Vital Skill, Journal of Instructional Psychology, 26, 4, 99; 261-262; auth, Letters of Recommendation: Their Motive and Content, College Student Journal, 33, 4, 00; 485-487; auth, In-class tutoring provides vital assistance to in-need students, Education, 120, 2: 247-248. **CONTACT ADDRESS** 181 Main St, Presque Isle, ME 04769-2888. **EMAIL** petress@polaris.umpi.maine.edu

PETRIE, NEIL
DISCIPLINE ENGLISH LITERATURE **EDUCATION** Univ Nothern Colo, BA; Kent State Univ, PhD. **CAREER** Assoc prof. **SELECTED PUBLICATIONS** Auth, pubs on drama and fiction writers. **CONTACT ADDRESS** Dept of English, Colorado State Univ, Fort Collins, CO 80523. **EMAIL** npetrie@vines.colostate.edu

PETRONELLA, VINCENT F.
PERSONAL Born 01/10/1935, New York, NY, m, 1965 **DISCIPLINE** ENGLISH **EDUCATION** City Col of NYork, BA, 62; Univ of Oregon, MA, 64; Univ of Mass at Amherst, PhD, 69. **CAREER** Tchg asst, Univ of Ore, 62-64; instr, Univ of Mass, 64-66; asst prof, 66-67, assoc prof, Boston State Col, 67-70; Prof of English, Univ of Mass, 70-. **HONORS AND AWARDS** Tchg Svc Awd, Boston State Col, Univ of Mass, 80; Healey Pub Svc Awd, Univ of Mass, 96. **MEMBERSHIPS** Boston Browning Soc, 93-98; Int Shakespear Asn; MLA. **RESEARCH** Shakespeare; The English Renaissance; the impact of the age of Shakespeare on the Nineteenth Century; Robert Browning; George Bernard Shaw. **SELECTED PUBLICATIONS** Auth, Shakespeare's Dramatic Chambers, Festschrift for G. Blakemore Evans, Fairleigh Dickinson Univ Press, 99; Shakespeare's The Comedy of Errors, Shakespearean Criticism 34, Gale Research, 97; William Archer and Bernard Shaw, British Playwrights 1880-1956: A Research and Production Sourcebooks, Greenwood Press, 96; Robert Browning and Julia Wedgwood: The Intellectual and Emotional Relationship, Ars Ceramica 14, 98. **CONTACT ADDRESS** Dept of English, Univ of Massachusetts, Boston, 100 Morrissey Blvd, Boston, MA 02125-3393.

PETRULIONIS, SANDRA H.
DISCIPLINE ENGLISH **EDUCATION** Armstrong State Col, BA, 83; Ga State Univ, MA, 90; PhD, 96. **CAREER** Teaching Asst, Ga State Univ, 91-96; Asst Prof, Pa State Univ, 96-. **HONORS AND AWARDS** Fel, GA State Univ, 91-92, 95. **MEMBERSHIPS** Melville Soc; Thoreau Soc; Soc for the study of Am Women Writers; Asn for documentary Editing; Soc for Hist of the Early Am Republic. **SELECTED PUBLICATIONS** Auth, "By the Light of Her Mother's Lamp: Woman's Work Versus Man's Philosophy in Louisa May Alcott's 'Transcendental Wild Oats'," in Studies in the American Renaissance, (Univ Press VA, 95), 69-81; auth, "Elizabeth Drew Stoddard," in Nineteenth Century American Women Writers: A Bio-Bibliographical Critical Sourcebook, (Greenwood Press, 97), 397-405; auth, "Re-Reading 'Bachelors' and Maids': Melville as Feminist?," Melville Soc Extracts, (97): 1, 5-10; auth, "Bathsheba Bowers," in American Women Prose Writers to 1820. Dictionary of Literary Biography, (Bruccoli Clark Layman, 98), 62-66; auth, "Selective Sympathy: The Public and Private Mary Merrick Brooks," Thoreau Society Bulletin, (99): 1-3, 5; auth, "William Henry Channing," in The American Renaissance in New England. Dictionary of Literary Biography, Vol I, (Bruccoli Clark Layman, 00); auth, "Profile: Jessie Benton Fremont," Legacy: A Journal of American Women Writers, forthcoming. **CONTACT ADDRESS** Dept Eng, Pennsylvania State Univ, Altoona, 3000 Ivyside Park, Altoona, PA 16601-3760. **EMAIL** shp2@psu.edu

PETRUZZI, ANTHONY
DISCIPLINE RHETORIC AND COMPOSITION **EDUCATION** Franconia Col, BA; Middlebury Col, MA; Univ Conn, PhD. **CAREER** Instr, dir, Compos, Univ Nebr, Kearney; asst prof, English, Bentley Col, 98- . **HONORS AND AWARDS** Grad Stud Tchg Awd, Univ Conn. **CONTACT ADDRESS** Dept of English, Bentley Col, 175 Forest St, Waltham, MA 02452-4705. **EMAIL** petruzzia@platte.unk.edu

PETRY, ALICE HALL
PERSONAL Born 07/08/1951, Hartford, CN, m, 1997, 1 child **DISCIPLINE** ENGLISH **EDUCATION** Univ Conn, BS, 73; Conn Col, MA, 76; Brown Univ, PhD, 79. **CAREER** Asst prof to prof, chair, RI School of Design, 80-85; vis prof, Univ of Colo, 87; Lectr, Arts America, Japan, 91; prof, chair, S Il Univ Edwardsville, 95-01. **HONORS AND AWARDS** Fel, Am coun of Learned Soc, 87-88. **RESEARCH** Southern fiction, American women writers, American short story. **CONTACT ADDRESS** Dept English, So Illinois Univ, Edwardsville, PO Box 1431, Edwardsville, IL 62026-1431. **EMAIL** apetry@siue.edu

PETTEY, GARY R.
DISCIPLINE MASS COM THEORY, METHODS, JOURNALISM **EDUCATION** Univ Wis, BA, MA, PhD. **CAREER** Comm, Cleveland St Univ. **SELECTED PUBLICATIONS** Co-auth, The Relationship of Perceived Physician Communicator Style to Patient Satisfaction, Commun Rep(s); Designing a commun campaign to teach intravenous drug users and sex partners about AIDS, Publ Health Rep(s), 91. **CONTACT ADDRESS** Commun Dept, Cleveland State Univ, 83 E 24th St, Cleveland, OH 44115. **EMAIL** g.pettey@csuohio.edu

PETTIS, JOYCE
PERSONAL Born, NC, m **DISCIPLINE** AFRICAN AMERICAN LITERATURE **EDUCATION** Winston Salem State Univ, BS, 68; East Carolina Univ, MA, 74; Univ N Carolina, Chapel Hill, PhD, 83. **CAREER** Pitt Commun Col, 72-74; East Carolina Univ, 74-85; assoc prof, Eng, North Carolina State Univ, 85- ; vis assoc prof, Univ Ala, 94-96. **HONORS AND AWARDS** College Lang Asn For Scholarship Awd, 95; 1997 nominee for Provost's African-American Prof Dev Awd. **MEMBERSHIPS** Col Lang Asn; Charles Chesnutt Soc; MLA; George Moses Horton Soc. **RESEARCH** Festivity and celebration in fiction. **SELECTED PUBLICATIONS** Auth, Legacies of Community and History in Paule Marshall's Daughters, Stud in the Lit Imagination, 93; auth, The Marrow of Tradition: Charles Chesnutt's Novel of the South, No Carolina Lit Rev, 94; auth, Toward Wholeness in Paule Marshall's Fiction, Univ Virginia, 95; auth, An Interview with Gerald Barrax, Callaloo, 97; auth, Read Ann Petry's The Narrows into Black Literary Tradition, in Hubbard, ed, Recovered Writers/Recovered Texts, Univ Tenn, 97. **CONTACT ADDRESS** English Dept, No Carolina State Univ, PO Box 8105, Raleigh, NC 27695. **EMAIL** jopettis@aol.com

PETTIT, RHONDA S.
PERSONAL Born 06/02/1955, Covington, KY, m, 1993 **DISCIPLINE** ENGLISH **EDUCATION** Univ Ky, BA, 77; MA, 90; Univ Cincinnati, PhD, 96. **CAREER** Journalist, Ky, 77-79; tech ed, Univ Ky, 79-88; teaching asst, Univ Ky, 88-90; teaching asst, Univ Cincinnati, 90-96; adj prof and instr, N Ky Univ, asst prof, Univ Cincinnati, 98-. **HONORS AND AWARDS** Al Smith Fel Grant, Ky Arts Coun, 97; Taft Mem Fund Dissertation Fel, Univ Cincinnati, 93-94; Acad of Am Poets Col and Univ Prize, Univ Ky, 89; Creative Writing Fel, Ky Found for Women, 88. **MEMBERSHIPS** MLA; Midwest MLA; Nat Coun of Teachers of English; Teachers and Writers Collaborative; Acad of Am Poets. **RESEARCH** Poetry; Dorothy Parker. **SELECTED PUBLICATIONS** Auth, "Interview with Poet David Lehman," Passages North, (97): 28-39; auth, "Material Girls in the Jazz Age: Dorothy Parker's Big Blonde as an Answer to Anita Loos's Gentlemen Prefer Blondes," Ky Philol Rev, (97): 48-54; auth, "A Perilous Balance: Seamus Heaney's Poet of Redress in 'Mycenae Lookout," Working Papers in Irish Studies, 98; auth, "Three Moments in Paris (by Mina Loy)," in Masterplots II: Poetry Series Supplement, Salem Press, 98; auth, "The Waltz (by Dorothy Parker)," in Beacham's Encyclopedia of Popular Fiction, Beacham Pub Co, 98; auth, Joy Harjo, Boise State Univ Press, 98; auth, "Mina Loy", in American Women Writers 1900-1945: A Bio-Bibliographical Critical Sourcebook, Greenwood Pub, 00; auth, A Gendered Collision: Sentimentalism and Modernism in Dorothy Parker's Poetry and Fiction, Fairleigh Dickinson Univ Press, 00; auth, "Adrienne Rich," in Encyclopedia of American Poetry: The Twentieth Century, Fitzroy Dearborn, 01. **CONTACT ADDRESS** Dept English, Univ of Cincinnati, 3312 Elizabeth St, Erlanger, KY 41018-2202. **EMAIL** Rhonda.Pettit@uc.edu

PFAFF, DANIEL W.
PERSONAL Born 05/19/1940, Nampa, ID, m, 1966, 2 children **DISCIPLINE** JOURNALISM, MASS COMMUNICATION **EDUCATION** Univ OR, BS, 62; Penn State Univ, MA, 68; Univ MN, PhD, 72. **CAREER** Penn State Univ, Asst to Prof Journalism, 71-98; Col Communications, Assoc Dean, 90-94. **HONORS AND AWARDS** Frank Luther Mott-Kappa Tau Alpha Research Awd **MEMBERSHIPS** Am Journalism Hist Asn **RESEARCH** Am Hist and Biogr, 19 and 20th cent. **SELECTED PUBLICATIONS** Joseph Pulitzer II and the Post Dispatch: A Newspaperman's Life, Um¤inv Pk, PA, Penn State Press, 91; Essays for Oxford Univ Press on Joseph Pulitzer, Joseph Pulitzer II, George Jones and John Wien Forney for American National Biography; Essays for Onyx Press on Spiro Agnew's Anti Press Campaign, Edward P Morgan and Howard K Smith for the Encyclopedia of Television News, ed by Michael D Murray. **CONTACT ADDRESS** Pennsylvania State Univ, Univ Park, 260 Homan Av, State College, PA 16801-6332. **EMAIL** dwp1@psu.edu

PFAU, MICHAEL
PERSONAL Born 03/14/1945, Washington, DC, m, 1968, 2 children **DISCIPLINE** COMMUNICATION, JOURNALISM **EDUCATION** Univ of NH, BA, 1970, MA, 1971; Uniz of Ariz, PhD, 87. **CAREER** Alexander Ramsey High Sch, Dept of Social Studs, Instructor, 71-75; Augustana Col, Dept of Commun & Theatre, asst prof, 75-81, dir of forensics, 75-84, assoc prof & dept head, 81-88, prof/dept head, 88-93; Univ of Ariz, Teaching Assoc, 84-86; Univ of Wisc-Madison, prof, 93-, Dir of Grad Studs, 95-. **HONORS AND AWARDS** Finalists, Nat Debate Tournament, 76, 80, 83; Top 3 Paper, Hlth Commun Div, Speech Commun Assoc, Int Commun Assoc, 87; finalist, dissertation award, Speech Commun Assoc, 88; Burlington North Found Fac Achievement Awd, 90; Augustana Res and Artists's Fund grant, 84, 87-93; Golden Anniversary Awd, Speech Commun Assoc, 91; Vilas Assoc App, 96-97; Top Four Paper, Info Sys Div, Int Commun Assoc, 98; summa cum laude grad, univ of nh. **MEMBERSHIPS** Assoc for Educ in J & Mass Commun; Broadcast Educ Assoc; Cent States Commun Assoc; Int Commun Assoc (sec, 95-97, membership ch, 97-99); Pub Relations Soc of Am; Nat Comun Assoc; Am Forensic Assoc; Speech Commun Assoc. **RESEARCH** Media influence. **SELECTED PUBLICATIONS** Co-auth, Persuasive Communication Campaigns, Allyn & Bacon, 93; co-auth, With Malice toward All? The Media and Public Confidence in Democratic Institutions, Praeger Pubs, (in press); co-auth, Communication and Public Opinion, Sage, (in progress); co-auth, Relational and Competence Perceptions of Presidential Candidates during Primary Election Campaigns, J of Broadcasting & Elec Media, vol 37, 275-292. 93; co-auth, The persistence of Inoculation in Conferring Resistance to Smoking Initiation among Adolescents: The Second Year, Hum Commun Res, vol 20, 413-430, 94; co-auth, Effectiveness of Adwatch Formats in Deflecting Targeted Political Attack Ads, Commun Res, vol 21, 325-341, 94; auth, Impact of Product Involvement, Message Format, and Receiver Sex of the Efficacy of Comparative Advertising Messages, Commun Quart, vol 42, 244-258, 94; co-auth, Television Viewing and Public Perceptions of Attorneys, Hum Commun Res, vol 21, 307-330, 95; co-auth, Influence of Communication Modalities on Voters' Perceptions of Candidates during Presidential Primary Campaigns, J of Commun, vol 45, 122-133, 95; co-auth, An Innoculation Theory Explanation for the Effects of Corporate Issue/Advocacy Advertising Campaigns, Commun Res, vol 22, 485-505, 95; co-auth, The Influence of Television Viewing on Public Perceptions of Physicians, J of Broadcasting & Elec Media, vol 39, 441-458, 95; co-auth, Television Viewing and Perception of Social Reality among Native American Adolescents, Intercultural Commun Studs, vol 1, 1-7, 96; co-auth, Influence of Traditional and Non-Traditional News Media in the 1992 Election Campaign, West J of Commun, vol 60, 214-232, 96; co-auth, Enriching the Inoculation Construct: The Role of Critical Components in the Process of Resistance, Hum Commun Res, vol 24, 187-215, 97; co-auth, Influence of Communication During the Distant Phase of the 1996 Republican Presidential Primary Campaign, J of Commun, vol 47, 6-26, 97; co-auth, Nuances in Inoculation: The Role of Inoculation Approach, Ego-Involvement, and Message Processing Disposition in Resistance, Commun Quart, vol 45, 461-481, 97; co-auth, The Influence of Individual Communication Media on Public Confidence in Democratic Institutions, The South Commun J, vol 63, 91-112, 98; co-auth, Use of Political Talk Radio versus Other Media and Public Confidence in Democratic Institutions, J & Mass Commun Quart, (in press); co-auth, Media Use Public Confidence in Democratic Institutions, J of Broadcasting & Elec Media, (in press). **CONTACT ADDRESS** Sch of J & Mass Commun, Univ of Wisconsin, Madison, 17 Rye Cir, Madison, WI 53717. **EMAIL** mwpfau@facstaff.wic.edu

PFAU, THOMAS
DISCIPLINE ENGLISH LITERATURE **EDUCATION** SUNY Buffalo, PhD, 89. **CAREER** Assoc prof, Duke Univ. **RESEARCH** 18th and 19th century intellectual and lit hist, with an emphasis on Eng Romanticism and on continental aesthetic and epistemological theory. **SELECTED PUBLICATIONS** Auth, Wordsworth's Profession: Form, Class, and The Logic of Early Romantic Cultural Production, Stanford UP, 97; ed, Friedrich Holderlin: Essays and Letters on Theory, SUNY, 87; Idealism and the Endgame of Theory: Three Essays (rev), SUNY, 94; co-ed, Rhetorical and Cultural Dissolution in Romanticism, a special issue of South Atlantic Quarterly, 96; coed, Lessons of Romanticism: A Critical Companion, Duke UP, 98. **CONTACT ADDRESS** Eng Dept, Duke Univ, Durham, NC 27706. **EMAIL** tpfau@sprintmail.com

PFEFFERLE, W. T.
PERSONAL Born 02/27/1962, Winnipeg, MB, Canada, m, 1984 **DISCIPLINE** WRITING **EDUCATION** Ariz State, BA, 83; Am Univ, MFA, 84; Univ S Miss, PhD, 90. **CAREER** Instr, McLennan Col, 89-92; asst prof, Texas Wesleyan Univ, 92-98; assoc prof, Nova Southeastern Univ, 99-00; director, Johns Hopkins Univ, 00-. **MEMBERSHIPS** MLA, NCTE, CCCC. **RESEARCH** Writing, teaching of writing. **SELECTED PUBLICATIONS** Auth, "Meetings," Ohio Rev, (93); coauth, Plug In, Prentice Hall, 96; auth, Writing that Matters, Prentice Hall, 99; auth, "A Former Adjunct Professor Comes (Mostly) Clean," Chronicle of Higher Educ, (99); auth, "The Sorry Plight of the Successful Job Candidate," Chronicle of Higher Educ, (00). **CONTACT ADDRESS** Johns Hopkins Univ, Baltimore, 3400 N Charles St, Owen House, Baltimore, MD 21218. **EMAIL** wt@jhu.edu

PFEIFFER, JOHN R.
PERSONAL Born 06/11/1938, Detroit, MI, 7 children **DISCIPLINE** ENGLISH **EDUCATION** Univ Detroit, BA, 61; MA, 63; Univ Ky, PhD, 69. **CAREER** Teaching fel, Univ Detroit, 61-63; teaching fel, Univ Ky, 63-67; asst prof, USAF Acad, 67-71; prof, Central Mich Univ, 71-. **MEMBERSHIPS** NY Shaw Soc, London Shaw Soc. **RESEARCH** British Literature and Culture (1800-1950), Bernard Shaw, Biography, Cultural History. **SELECTED PUBLICATIONS** Auth, "Richard Francis Burton (19 March 1821-20 October 1890)," in British Travel Writers, 1837-1875: The Dictionary of Literary Biography Volume 166, eds. Barbara Brothers and Julia Gergits, (SC: Bruccoli Clark Layman, Inc., 96), 98-119; auth, "A Continuing Checklist of Shaviana," in SHAW: Unpublished Shaw: The Annual of Bernard Shaw Studies Volume 16, eds. Dan H. Laurence and Margot Peters (PA: Penn State Univ Press, 96), 233-245; auth, "Ray Bradbury's Bernard Shaw," in Shaw and Science Fiction: SHAW: The Annual of Bernard Shaw Studies XVII, ed. Milton Wolf (PA: Penn State Univ Press, 97), 119-131; auth, "A Continuing Checklist of Shaviana," SHAW: The Annual of BernardShaw Studies: XVII (PA: Penn State Univ Press, 98), 221-224; auth, "Octavia Butler Writes the Bible," in Festschrift for Stanley Weintraub, ed. Susan Rusinko (NJ: Sesquehanna Univ Press, 98), 140-152; auth, "Octavia Butler," in Science Fiction Writers: Critical Studies of the Major Authors from the Early Nineteenth Century to the Present Day, ed. Richard Bleiler (NY: Charles Scribner's Sons, 99), 147-158; auth, "A Continuing Checklist of Shaviana," SHAW: The Annual of Bernard Shaw Studies Volume 19, ed. Fred D. Crawford (PA: Penn State Univ Press, 99), 187-219. **CONTACT ADDRESS** Dept English, Central Michigan Univ, 100 W Preston Rd, Mount Pleasant, MI 48859-0001. **EMAIL** pfeif1jr@mail.cmich.edu

PFEIFFER, WILLIAM S.
PERSONAL Born 07/29/1947, Akron, OH, m, 1976, 2 children **DISCIPLINE** TECHNICAL COMMUNICATION, INTERNATIONAL COMMUNICATION, JAPANESE CULTURE **EDUCATION** Amherst Col, BA, 69; Kent State Univ, MA, 73; PhD, 75. **CAREER** Asst Prof, Southwest Tex State Univ, 75-76; Asst Prof, Univ Houston, 76-80; Prof, Southern Polytech State Univ, 80-. **HONORS AND AWARDS** Asian Studies Develop Prog, 92; Japan Found Fel, 94; Japan Studies Inst, 96; Fulbright Summer Fel, 98. **MEMBERSHIPS** JSA, Soc for Tech Commun. **RESEARCH** International Communication, Japanese culture, technical communication. **SELECTED PUBLICATIONS** Auth, Technical Writing: A Practical Approach 4th ed, Prentice Hall Publ, 00; auth, Proposal Writing: The Art of Friendly and Winning Persuasion, Prentice Hall Publ, 00; auth, Pocket Guide to Technical Writing, 2nd ed, Prentice Hall, forthcoming. **CONTACT ADDRESS** Dept Humanities & Soc Sci, So Polytech State Univ, 1100 S Marietta Pkwy, Marietta, GA 30060-2855. **EMAIL** pfeiffer@spsu.edu

PFORDRESHER, JOHN P.
DISCIPLINE ENGLISH LITERATURE **EDUCATION** Georgetown Col, BA; Univ Minn, PhD. **CAREER** Eng Dept, Georgetown Univ **RESEARCH** Victorian literature; relationship of painting to literature in 19th century; Catholic studies. **SELECTED PUBLICATIONS** Auth, England in Literature, 89; Classics in World Literature, 89; Variorum Edition: Tennyson's Idylls of the King, 73. **CONTACT ADDRESS** English Dept, Georgetown Univ, 37th and O St, Washington, DC 20057.

PHEGLEY, JENNIFER J.
PERSONAL Born 07/13/1970 **DISCIPLINE** ENGLISH **EDUCATION** SW Tex Univ, BA, 92; Ohio State Univ, MA, 95, PhD, 99. **CAREER** Asst prof, Univ Miss/Kansas, 99-. **HONORS AND AWARDS** Fac Res Grnt, Univ Miss/Kansas, 01; Muste Awd Dis of the Yr Hon Mention, Ohio St, 00; Gee Awd Res on Women, Ohio St, 99; Estrich Dis Fel , 99. **MEMBERSHIPS** MLA, MVSA, ASA, Res Soc Vict Period. **RESEARCH** Victorian periodical literature; 19th cen woman readers. **SELECTED PUBLICATIONS** Co-ed, Writing Lives: Exploring Literacy and Community, St Martins Press (NY), 96; co-auth, "Considering Research Methods in Rhetoric and Composition," in Ethics and Representation in Qualitive Studies of Literacy, eds, Gesa Kirsch and Peter Mortensen (Urbana: Nat Coun Teach of Eng, 96); co-auth, "Writing Writing Lives: The Collaborative Production of a Composition Text in a Large First-Year Writing Program," in College Composition Textbooks at the Turn of the Century: Theory, Pedagogy, and Praxis, eds. Frederick and Xin Liu Gale (Albany: SUNY Press, 99); auth, "Clearing Away 'The Briars and Brambles': The Education and Professionalization of the Cornhill Magazine's Women Readers, 1860-65," Vict Per Rev 33 (00): 22-43; auth, "Girls and Reading in America" in Girlhood in America: An Encyclopedia, ed. Miriam Formanek-Brunell (ABC-CLIO, 01). **CONTACT ADDRESS** Eng Dept, Univ of Missouri, Kansas City, 5100 Rockhill Rd, Cockefair Hall, Kansas City, MO 64110. **EMAIL** phegley@umkc.edu

PHELAN, JAMES PIUS X.
PERSONAL Born 01/25/1951, New York, NY, m, 1972, 2 children **DISCIPLINE** ENGLISH LITERATURE **EDUCATION** Boston Coll, BA, Eng Lit, 72; Univ Chicago, MA, Eng Lang & Lit, 73, PhD, 77. **CAREER** Instr, Sch Art Inst Chicago, Lib Arts, 75-77; asst prof, Ohio State Univ, 77-83; assoc prof, Ohio State Univ, 83-89; PROF, OHIO STATE UNIV, ENG, 89-; Ch, Eng Dept, Ohio State Univ, 94-. **MEMBERSHIPS** Soc Study Narr Lit; MLA, NCTE, Midwest MLA **RESEARCH** Narrative theory; Critical theory; English & American novel. **SELECTED PUBLICATIONS** Auth, Worlds from Words, Univ of Chicago Press, 81; auth, Reading People, Reading Plots, Univ of Chicago Press, 89; auth, Beyond the Tenure Track, Ohio State Univ Press, 91; Narrative as Rhetoric: Technique, Audiences, Ethics, Ideology, Ohio State Univ Press, 96; co-edr, Understanding Narrative, Ohio State Univ Press, 94; coedr, Adventures of Huckleberry Finn: A Case Study in Critical Controversy, Bedford Books, 95; "Now I Lay Me: Nick's Strange Monologue, Hemingway's Powerful Lyric, and the Reader's Disconcerting Experience," New Essays on the Short Stories of Ernest Hemingway, Cambridge Univ Press, 98; "Before Reading in its Own Terms," Before Reading: Narrative Conventions and the Politics of Interpretation, Ohio State Univ Press, 98; "Narrative as Rhetoric: Reading the Spells of Porter's Magic'," The Critical Tradition, Bedford Books, 98; co-ed, The Tempest: A Case Study in Critical Controversy, Bedford Books, 00. **CONTACT ADDRESS** Dept Eng, Ohio State Univ, Columbus, 164 W. 17th Ave, Columbus, OH 43210-1370. **EMAIL** phelan.1@osu.edu

PHILIPON, DANIEL J.
PERSONAL Born 05/16/1969, Syracuse, NY, m, 2000 **DISCIPLINE** ENGLISH, RHETORIC **EDUCATION** Georgetown Univ, BA, 91; Univ Va, MA, 93; PhD, 98. **CAREER** Asst prof rhet, Univ Minn, 98- . **HONORS AND AWARDS** Sci & Relig Course Awd, 99. **MEMBERSHIPS** Am Soc Environ Hist; Am Student Asn; Asn Student Lit & Environ; Mod Lang Asn. **RESEARCH** Environmental rhetoric, history, and ethics, Nature writing, Science and religion, American cultural studies, Regionalism and place studies. **SELECTED PUBLICATIONS** Co-ed, The Height of Our Mountains, Johns Hopkins Univ Press, 98; ed, The Friendship of Nature, Johns Hopkins Univ Press, 99. **CONTACT ADDRESS** Rhetoric, Univ of Minnesota, Twin Cities, 1994 Buffered Ave, Saint Paul, MN 55108-6038. **EMAIL** danp@tc.umn.edu

PHILIPPIDES, DIA M.
DISCIPLINE CLASSICS **EDUCATION** Radcliffe Col, BA, 70; Boston Col, MA, 72; MA, 74; Princeton Univ, MA, 76; PhD, 78. **CAREER** Lecturer, Harvard Univ, 78-84; Asst to Full Prof, Boston Col, 84-. **HONORS AND AWARDS** Fulbright Program, Greece, 85, 90, 98; Literary Awd, Acad of Athens Greece, 88; Res grant, Jasper and Marion Whiting foundation, 91; Summer stipend, NEH, 94; Visiting Bye-Fel, Univ Cambridge, 94; Awd for res, Alexander S Onassis Public Benefit foundation, 96. **MEMBERSHIPS** Am Philol Asn, Mod Greek Studies Asn, Asn for Literary and Linguistic Computing. **RESEARCH** Modern Greek literature (Cretan Renaissance); Literary and linguistic analysis by computer; ancient Greek tragedy (especially meter). **SELECTED PUBLICATIONS** Auth, The Iambic Trimiter of Euripides: Selected Plays, Arno Press, 81; auth, The Sacrifice of Abraham on the Computer, Hermes Press, 86; auth, Census of Modern Greek Literature: Check-list of English-Language Sources useful in the Study of Modern Greek Literature (1824-1987), Modern Greek Studies Association, 90; auth, As the Wheel Turns: Electronic Analysis of the Erotokritos, Hermes Pub, 96. **CONTACT ADDRESS** Dept classical Studies, Boston Col, Chestnut Hill, 140 Commonwealth Ave, Chestnut Hill, MA 02467-3800. **EMAIL** dia.philippides@bc.edu

PHILLIPS, C. ROBERT, III
DISCIPLINE ANCIENT HISTORY AND LITERATURE **EDUCATION** PhD, Brown Univ. **CAREER** Prof, Lehigh Univ **RESEARCH** Social history and Greco-Roman religion. **SELECTED PUBLICATIONS** Areas: Roman religion, early christianity, and magic. **CONTACT ADDRESS** Lehigh Univ, Bethlehem, PA 18015.

PHILLIPS, DENNY
DISCIPLINE COMMUNICATION STUDIES **EDUCATION** Hiram Col, BA; Univ Ohio, MA, PhD. **CAREER** Prof. **RESEARCH** Communication and popular culture; organizational communication; media programming and management. **SELECTED PUBLICATIONS** Auth, Meddling in Metal Music, Studies Social Sci, 92; The Organization Communication Perspective, Speech Tchr, 91; Communication Investments, Broadcast Cable Financial J, 91; co-auth, Strip Mining for Gold and Platinum: Record Sales and Chart Performance Pre- and Post-MTV, Popular Music Soc, 92; Influence in the Workplace: Maximizing Personal Empowerment; MTV and the New Artist: Bullet, Breaker or Bust?, Popular Music Soc, 92. **CONTACT ADDRESS** Speech Communication Dept, Colorado State Univ, Fort Collins, CO 80523. **EMAIL** dphillips@vines.colostate.edu

PHILLIPS, ELIZABETH
PERSONAL Born 01/29/1919, Spruce Pine, NC, s **DISCIPLINE** ENGLISH **EDUCATION** Univ NCar, BA, 39; Univ Iowa, MA, 45; Univ Pa, PhD, 57. **CAREER** Instr, Lees-McRae Jr Col, 45-46; instr, Butler Univ, 46-48; asst prof, Milwaukee-Downer Col, 49-54, asst prof to prof emerita, Wake Forest Col, 57-. **HONORS AND AWARDS** Phi Beta Kappa; Medallion of Merit, Wake Forest Univ; Smith-Mundt Prof, Seould Nat Univ, 60-61; Fulbright Prof, Seoul Nat Univ, 62-63 **MEMBERSHIPS** MLA, Emily Dickinson Int Soc. **RESEARCH** Texts and Pre-Texts, The relations between poetry and painting. **SELECTED PUBLICATIONS** Auth, Edgar Allan Poe: An American Imagination, 79; auth, Marianne Moore, 82; auth, Emily Dickinson: Personae and Performance, 88; auth, "Marianne Moore," Dict of Lit Biog vol 45, (86); auth, "Poe's Poems: 1824-1835," A Companion to Poe Studies, 96. **CONTACT ADDRESS** 2170 Royall Dr, Winston-Salem, NC 27106-5241.

PHILLIPS, GENE D.
DISCIPLINE ENGLISH **EDUCATION** Loyola Univ Chicago, AB, 57; Loyola Univ Chicago, MA, 59; Fordham Univ NYork, PhD, 70. **CAREER** Assist Prof, Loyola Univ, 70-74; Assoc Prof, Loyola Univ, 75-80; Prof, Loyola Univ Chicago, 81-. **MEMBERSHIPS** Jury Mem, Student Acad Awards; Acad of Motion Picture Arts and Sciences, 96-; Founding Mem, Ed Bd of Literature/Film Quarterly, 73-; Founding Mem, Ed Bd of The Tennessee Williams Journal, 89-. **RESEARCH** Modern novel, British & American; adaptation of literature to film; film history, British & American. **SELECTED PUBLICATIONS** Auth, Hemingway and Film, Ungar, 80; Fiction, Film, and F. Scott Fitzgerald, Loyola UP, 86; Fiction, Film, and Faulkner: The Art of Adaptation, Univ Tenn Press, 88; Conrad and Cinema: The Art of Adaptation, Lang, 97; Auth, Exiles in Paradise: Major European Film Directors in America, Assoc Univ Presses, 98; **CONTACT ADDRESS** Dept of English, Loyola Univ, Chicago, Crown Center for the Humanities, 6525 N Sheridan Rd, Chicago, IL 60626. **EMAIL** gphilli@wpo.it.luc.edu

PHILLIPS, JANE ELLEN
PERSONAL Born 09/27/1943, Philadelphia, PA **DISCIPLINE** CLASSICS **EDUCATION** Millersville State Col, BA, 65; Univ NC, Chapel Hill, PhD(classics), 69. **CAREER** Asst prof classics, Univ NC, Chapel Hill, 69-71; adj instr, Dickinson Col, 71-72; adj instr, Franklin & Marshall Col, 71-72, vis asst prof, 72-73; asst prof, 73-80, Assoc Prof Classics, Univ KY, 80-91, ; Visiting Assoc Prof, Univ of Toronto, 90-91; Full Prof, 91-. **HONORS AND AWARDS** Fel in residence for col teachers, Nat Endowment for Humanities, 75-76. **MEMBERSHIPS** Am Philol Asn; Class Asn Midwest & South, Archaeol Inst Am, Am Class League, Vergilian Soc, Renaissance Soc of Am, Erasmus of Rotterdam Soc. **RESEARCH** Latin historiography and Latin poetry, Erasmus' biblical scholarship. **SELECTED PUBLICATIONS** Auth, Verbs compounded with trans in Livy's triumph reports, 74 & Form and language in Livy's triumph notices, 74, Class Philol; The pattern of images in Catullus, Am J Philol, 76; Juno in Aeneid, Vergilius, 77; Roman mothers and the lives of their adult daughters, Helios, 78; Livy and the beginning of a new society, Class Bull, 79; Lucretian echoes in Shelley's Mont Blanc, Class & Mod Lit, 82; auth, "The Gospel, the Clergy, and the Laity in Erasmus' Paraphrase on the Gospel of John, " Erasmus of Rotterdam Society Yearbook 10 (90): 85-100; transl and annot, "Collected Works of Erasmus, Vol 46 Paraphrase on the Gospel of John, Toronto, 91; auth, "Food and Drink in Erasmus' Gospel Paraphrase," Erasmus of Rotterdam Society Yearbook 14 (94): 24-25; Roman Marriage - Iusti-coniuges from the Time of Cicero to the Time of Ulpian - Treggiari,s/, Classical World, Vol 0087, 94 **CONTACT ADDRESS** Dept of Classics, Univ of Kentucky, 500 S Limestone St, Lexington, KY 40506-0027. **EMAIL** claphil@pop.uky.edu

PHILLIPS, KENDALL R.
PERSONAL Born 05/12/1969, San Antonio, TX, m, 1994 **DISCIPLINE** SPEECH COMMUNICATION **EDUCATION** Southwest Baptist Univ, BS, 90; Cent Mo State Univ, MA, 92; Pa State Univ, PhD, 95. **CAREER** Asst prof, Cent Mo State Univ, 95-. **HONORS AND AWARDS** Kathryn DeBoer Distinguished Teaching award; Top Paper, Rhetoric & Pub addres, E Commun Assoc. **MEMBERSHIPS** Nat Commun Assoc; Rhet Soc of Am; Am Forensics Assoc. **RESEARCH** Rhetorical theory/criticism; continental philosophy. **SELECTED PUBLICATIONS** Co-auth, Self-monitoring and argumentativeness: Using argument as impression management, Argument in Controversy, Speech Commun Assoc, 193-196, 91; co-auth, Impact and implications of parliamentary debate format on American debate, Advanced debate: Readings in theory, practice, and teaching, Net Textbook Co, 94-104, 92; co-auth, Cyberphobia and Education, Commun Law & Policy Newsletter, vol 7, no 1, 3, 96; auth, The spaces of public dissension: Reconsidering the public sphere, Commun monographs, vol 63, 231-248, 96; auth, Interpretive controversy and The Silence of the Lambs, Rhet Soc Quart, vol, 28, 33-47, 98; auth, Rhetoric, resistance and criticism: A response to Sloop and Ono, Philos & Rhet, (in press); auth, Tactical apologies: The American Nursing Association and assisted suicide, South Commun J, (in press). **CONTACT ADDRESS** Dept of Speech Commun, Syracuse Univ, Syracuse, NY 13244. **EMAIL** kphillip@syr.edu

PHILLIPS, LOUIS
PERSONAL Born 06/15/1942, Lowell, MA, m, 1973, 2 children **DISCIPLINE** ENGLISH, COMPARATIVE LITERATURE **EDUCATION** Stetson Univ, BA, 64; Univ NC, MA, 65; City Univ New York, MA, 67. **CAREER** Sch of Visual Arts, New York City, 75-. **HONORS AND AWARDS** NEA in Playwriting; Regents Fel in Playwriting at the Univ of Calif at San Diego. **MEMBERSHIPS** Dramatists Guild, Soc of Am Magicians. **RESEARCH** Theater history, the films of Alfred Hitchcock, American humor. **SELECTED PUBLICATIONS** Auth, Alligator Wrestling and You (juvenile), New York: Avon Books (92); auth, A Dream of Countries Where No One Dare Live (short stories), SMU Press (94); auth, Savage Steps to the House of Meaning (poetry), New York: Prologue Press (95); ed, The Random House Treasury of Humorous Verse, Random House (95); auth, Plays (comic one-acts), Broadway Play Pubs (95); auth, Hot Corner: Baseball Stories, Livingston Press (96); auth, The Ballroom in St Patriock's Cathedral (full length play), Louisville: Aran Press (96); auth, Ask Me Anything About Monsters (nonfiction), New York: Avon Books (97); auth, 16 Points on a Hurricane's Compass (full length play), Louisville: Aran Press (97); auth, The Krazy Kat Rag (poetry), Chicago: Light Reprints 999). **CONTACT ADDRESS** Dept Humanities and Scis, Sch of Visual Arts, New York, 209 E 23rd St, New York, NY 10010-3901.

PHILLIPS, ROBERT
PERSONAL Born 02/02/1938, Milford, DE, m, 1963, 1 child **DISCIPLINE** ENGLISH, COMMUNICATIONS **EDUCATION** Syracuse Univ, BA (English), 60, BA (Communications), 60, MA (English), 62. **CAREER** Prof of English and Dir of Creative Writing Program, 91-96; Moores Univ Scholar, Univ Houston, 98-; poetry rev ed, Modern Poetry Studies, 69-73; poetry reviewer, The Houston Post, 92-95; poetry rev, The Houston Chronicle, 95-. **HONORS AND AWARDS** Awd in Lit, Am Academy of Arts and Letters; CAPS Awd in Poetry. **MEMBERSHIPS** PEN; Poetry Soc of Am; Poets' House; ASCAP. **RESEARCH** 20th century Am poetry and fiction. **SE-**

LECTED PUBLICATIONS Auth, Triumph of the Night, Carroll & Graf, 89, reissued as The Omnibus of 20th-Century Ghost Stories, Robison, 90, Italian, German, and Russian eds, 91, Carroll & Graf paperback, 92; Shenandoah and Other Verse Plays, BOA Eds, 92; Public Landing Revisited, Story Line Press, 92; Delmore Schwatz & James Laughlin: Selected Letters, W W Norton, 93 (Chosen as a Notable Book of the Year by the New York Times Book Review); Face to Face (poetry), Wings Press, 93; Breakdown Lane, Johns Hopkins Univ Press, 94 (Chosen as a Notable Book of the Year by the New York Times Book Review); William Goyen: Selected Letters from a Writer's Life, Univ TX Press, 95, with an afterword by Sir Stephen Spender; New Selected Poems by Marya Zaturenska, Syracuse Univ Press, 01; The Madness of Art: Literary Interviews, Syracuse Univ Press, 01; Fiction's Forms (textbook), forthcoming; numerous other publications. **CONTACT ADDRESS** Dept of English, Univ of Houston, Creative Writing Prog, Houston, TX 77204-3012.

PHILLIPS, ROMEO ELDRIDGE
PERSONAL Born 03/11/1928, Chicago, IL, m **DISCIPLINE** MUSIC EDUCATION **EDUCATION** Chicago Conservatory Coll, MusB 1949; Chicago Musical Coll, MusM 1951; Eastern MI Univ, MA 1963; Wayne State Univ, PhD 1966. **CAREER** Chicago IL Public Schools, teacher 1949-55; Detroit MI Public Schools, teacher 1955-57; Inkster MI Public Schools, teacher 1957-66; Kalamazoo Coll, chmn dept of educ 1974-86, tenured prof of educ/music 1968-93, prof emeritus, 93-; Portage MI, city councilman, 91-. **HONORS AND AWARDS** Invited by the govt of the Republic of Nigeria West Africa to be a guest to the World Festival of Black and African Art 1977; Omega Psi Phi Leadership Awd 1982; Committee of Scholars for the Accreditation of MI Colls 1982-84; Kalamazoo NAACP Appreciation Awd 1982; Fulbright Scholar to Liberia West Africa 1984-85; **MEMBERSHIPS** Mem Amer Assoc of Coll for Teacher Educ, Music Educators Natl Conf, MI Sch Vocal Assoc, Assoc for Supervison & Curriculum Develop, MI Assoc for Supervision & Curriculum Develop, MI Assoc for Improvement of Sch Legislation, Natl Alliance of Black School Educators, Natl Assoc of Negro Musicians, Phi Delta Kappa, Kappa Alpha Psi; conductor AfraAmerican Chorale. **SELECTED PUBLICATIONS** article; 2 book reviews; chapters contributed to or credit given in 6 books. **CONTACT ADDRESS** Prof Emeritus, Kalamazoo Col, 1200 Academy, Kalamazoo, MI 49006.

PHILPOTT, JEFFREY S.
DISCIPLINE SPEECH COMMUNICATIONS, RHETORIC **EDUCATION** Lewis and Clark Col, BA, 80; Univ NE Lincoln, MA, 83; Univ WA, PhD, 95. **CAREER** Comm, Seattle Univ. **MEMBERSHIPS** Nat Commun Asn; Western States Commun Asn; Pacific and Asian Commun Asn. **SELECTED PUBLICATIONS** Auth, Recurrent Form, Time, and Situation: Common Rhetorical Responses to Public Crisis as Synchronic Genre, Paper presented at the 2nd Int Symp on Genre, Simon Fraser Univ, Vancouver, BC, 98; Turning Tragedy into Triumph: Rhetorical Transformation and the Explosion of the Space Shuttle Challenger, Paper presented at the Western Speech Commun Asn Conv, Monterey, Calif, 97; Eternal Questions, Evolving Answers: Fifty Years of Seattle University Mission Statements, Gaffney Lect, Seattle Univ, 96; From 'Major Malfunction' to 'Bold Pioneers': Public Rhetoric in the Aftermath of the Challenger Disaster, Sharon James Mem Lect, Seattle Univ, 96; Edmund Burke, Thomas Paine, and the Motive for Political Action, Paper presented at the Northwest Conf on Brit Stud, Vancouver, Wash, 93; Defense Spending and the New World Order: Scenic Placement in Post-Cold War Military Rhetoric, Paper presented at Western Speech Commun Asn annual conv, Boise, 92; King George: Metaphoric Constructions of President Bush in Patrick Buchanan's 1992 Presidential Campaign, Presentation at the Western Speech Commun Asn annual conv, Boise, 92. **CONTACT ADDRESS** Dept of Commun, Seattle Univ, 900 Broadway, Seattle, WA 98122-4460. **EMAIL** jphilpot@seattleu.edu

PIACENTINO, EDWARD J.
PERSONAL Born 02/06/1945, Marion, OH, m, 1998, 2 children **DISCIPLINE** ENGLISH **EDUCATION** Univ NC, Chapel Hill, BA, 67; PhD, 73; Appalachian State Univ, MA, 68. **CAREER** Instr, Southeastern Community Col, 68-70; prof, High Point Univ, 73-. **HONORS AND AWARDS** Meredith Clark Slone Distinguished Teaching Service Awd, High Point Univ, 86. **MEMBERSHIPS** Am Lit Section of MLA, Soc for the Study of Southern Lit, A, Honor Studies Asn, South Atlantic MLA, Popular Culture Asn of the South, William Gilmore Simms Soc. **RESEARCH** Southern American literature, American humor, 19th century American literature. **SELECTED PUBLICATIONS** Auth of intro and ed, Doesticks: What He Says, by Mortimer N. Thompson (86); auth of intro and ed, Birthright, by T.S. Stribling 987); auth, T.S. Stribling: Pioneer Realist in Modern Southern Literature (88); co-ed with M. Thomas Inge, The Humor of the Old South: Critical Perspectives, Univ Ky Press (forthcoming 2001); contribur, essays and revs in Miss Quart, Am Lit, Southern Lit J, South Atlantic Rev, Studies in Am Humor, Poe Studies, Studies in Short Fiction, Studies in Am Culture; contribur, articles in Sinclair Lewis at 100: Papers Presented at the Centennial Conf (85); American Humor Magazines and Comic Periodicals (87); Encyclopedia of American Humorists (88); Major Literary Characters: Antonia (91); Encyclopedia of United States Popular Culture (98); Dictionary of Literary Biog 202: Nineteenth Century American Fiction Writers (99); The Encyclopedia of American Literature (99), and A Companion to Southern Literature: Themes, Genres, Places, Movements, and Motifs (2000). **CONTACT ADDRESS** Dept English, High Point Univ, University Station, Montlieu Ave, High Point, NC 27262-3598. **EMAIL** epiacent@acme.highpoint.edu

PIAN, RULAN CHAO
PERSONAL Born 04/20/1922, Cambridge, MA, m, 1945, 1 child **DISCIPLINE** ETHNO-MUSICOLOGY **EDUCATION** Radcliffe Col, BA, 44, MA, 46, PhD, 60. **CAREER** Tchng asst Chinese, 47-58, instr, 59-61, lectr, 61-74, prof East Asian lang, civilizations, and of music, 74-92, Harvard Univ; Yenching Inst grant travel & res Orient music in Japan, Hong Kong, Taiwan & Korea, 58-59; Am Coun Learned Socs-J D Rockefeller III Fund travel & res grant Peking opera, US, Asia & Europe, 65-66; NEH grant res abroad, 78-79; vis prof, music, 75, 78-79, 82, 94, Chinese Univ Hong Kong; vis prof, 90-, Inst Lit Natl Tsing Hua Univ Taiwan; vis prof, 92-, Schl Human Natl Central Univ Taiwan. **HONORS AND AWARDS** Caroline I Wilby Prize, Radcliffe Col, 60; Otto Kinkeldey Awd, Am Musicol Soc, 68; Radcliffe Grad Soc Medal, 80; Academician, Acad Sinica Taiwan ROC, 90. **MEMBERSHIPS** Am Musicol Soc; Soc Ethnomusicol; Intl Musicol Soc; Soc for Asian Music; Assn for Asian Stud; Int Coun for Trad Music; Chinese Lang Tchrs Assn; Assn for Chinese Music Res. **RESEARCH** Chinese modern language; Chinese music history; interpretation of Sonq dynasty musical sources; present day Chinese musical dramatic and narrative arts. **SELECTED PUBLICATIONS** Auth, A Syllabus for the Mandarin Primer, 61; auth, Sonq Dynasty Musical Sources and Their Interpretation, Harvard Univ, 67; auth, The Function of Rhythm in the Peking Opera, The Musics of Asia, Nat Music Coun Philippines-UNESCO Nat Comn Philippines, 71; auth, Aria Structural Patterns in the Peking Opera, 71; auth, Text Setting with the Shipyi Animated Aria, Words and Music, the Scholar's View: A Medley of Problems and Solutions, Harvard Univ, 72; auth, Modes, Transposed Scales, Melody Types and Tune Types, Proc 12th Cong Int Musicol Soc; auth, Transcription and Study of the Medley Song, The Courtesan's Jewel Box, Chinoperl Papers, Vol 9, No 10, Cornell Univ. **CONTACT ADDRESS** Dept of East Asian Lang & Civilizations, Harvard Univ, 2 Divinity Ave, Cambridge, MA 02138. **EMAIL** thhpian@aol.com

PICHASKE, DAVID
PERSONAL Born 09/02/1943, Kenmore, NY, m, 1991, 2 children **DISCIPLINE** ENGLISH LITERATURE **EDUCATION** Wittenberg Univ, BA, 65; Ohio Univ, PhD, 69. **CAREER** Bradley Polytech Inst, 69-80; Southwest State Univ, 80-, chair, 86-89. **HONORS AND AWARDS** Sr Fulbright Lectr, Poland, 89-91, Latvia, 97-98. **RESEARCH** Medieval English/Chaucer, Popular Culture - Music, Midwest Literature, Rural Literature. **SELECTED PUBLICATIONS** Auth, Writing Sense: A Handbook of Composition, Free Pr, 75; auth, Chaucer's Literary Pilgrimage: Movement in the Canterbury Tales, Norwood, 77; auth, A Generation in Motion: Popular Music and Culture in the Sixties, Schirmier Books, 79; auth, Beowulf to Beatles and Beyond: the Varieties of Poetry, Macmillan, 81; auth, Visiting the Father and Other Poems, Dakotah Territory Pr, 87; auth, Poland in Transition, 1989-91, Ellis Pr, 91; auth, "When Students Make Sexual Advances", Chronicles of Higher Educ XLI.24, (95): B1-2; auth, "Junkbonding the Canon", Polish-American Literary Confrontations, eds Joanna Durczak and Jerzy Durczak, Maria Curie-Sklodowska Univ Pr, (95): 91-111; auth, Southwest Minnesota: The Land and the People, Crossings Pr, 00; auth, "Dave Etter: Fishing for Our Lost American Souls", J of Mod Lit, (forthcoming). **CONTACT ADDRESS** Dept English, Southwest State Univ, 1501 State St, Marshall, MN 56258-3306. **EMAIL** pichaske@ssu.southwest.musus.edu

PICKENS, ERNESTINE W. MCCOY
PERSONAL Born 12/21/1936, Braden, TN, m, 1977 **DISCIPLINE** ENGLISH **EDUCATION** Tennessee State University, BS, 1958; Atlanta University, MA, 1975; Emory University, PhD, 1986. **CAREER** Shelby County Board of Education, Barret's Chapel High School, teacher, 58-60; Cassopolis High School, teacher, 61-62; Weaver High School, teacher, 64-71; John Overton High School, teacher, 71-73; Atlanta University, communications skills instructor, 73; Clark College, asst prof of English, 75-86; Clark-Atlanta Univ, Prof of English, 87-. **HONORS AND AWARDS** United Negro College Fund, Lilly Grant, 1982, Dana Awd, 1981; US Labor Department, Appreciation Awd, 1992; National Council of Teacher's of English, Appreciation Awd, 1990; Clark College, Outstanding Teacher Awd, 1978. **MEMBERSHIPS** College Language Association Standing Committee: English Curriculum; American Studies Association; National Council of Teachers of English; Toni Morrison Society; Langston Hughes Society. **SELECTED PUBLICATIONS** Author: Charles W Chesnutt and the Progressive Movement, 1994; Charles W Chesnutt's "The Conjure Woman," Masterpieces African-American Literature, Harper and Collins Publishing, 1992; Charles W Chesnutt's "The House Behind the Cedars in Master Plots," Salem Press, 1993; Scholar in Residence, New York Univ, 1996; founding pres, Charles Waddell Chessnutt Assn. **CONTACT ADDRESS** English, Clark Atlanta Univ, James P Brawley Dr & Fair St, Atlanta, GA 30314.

PICKENS, WILLIAM GARFIELD
PERSONAL Born 12/27/1927, Atlanta, GA, m, 1950 **DISCIPLINE** ENGLISH **EDUCATION** Morehouse College, BA (magna cum laude), 1948; Atlanta University, MA, 1950; University of Hartford, 1953-54, 1964-65; Trinity College, Summers, 1954-59; University of Connecticut, PhD, 1969. **CAREER** Hillside High School, Durham NC, teacher, 50; Chandler Evans, W Hartford CT, clerk, 52-54; Hartford Board of Education, Hartford CT, teacher & dept head, 54-70; US Post Office, Hartford CT, clerk, 54-56; Pickens Realty, Hartford CT, pres, 56-71; Morehouse College, Atlanta GA, professor/dept chmn, 70-84; prof, 70-; Emory Univ, Atlanta, visiting prof of humanities, 92-93. **HONORS AND AWARDS** Service plaque, Realty Bd of Greater Hartford, 1964; Author, Trends in Southern Sociolinguistics, 1975; Benj E Mays & Margaret Mitchell, A Unique Legacy in Medicine, 1996; Phi Beta Kappa, Delta of Georgia, 1984; Distinguished Faculty Scholar, UNCF, 1984-85; Dana Faculty Fellowship, Dana Foundation, 1992-93. **MEMBERSHIPS** College Language Assn, 1970-; Natl Council of Teachers of English, 1971-; Conference of College Composition & Communication, 1972-; American Dialect Society, 1975-; Friendship Baptist Church, 1977-; Peyton Woods Chalet Community Organization, 1978-; Langston Hughes Society, 1983-; Toni Morrison Society, 1992-; Phi Beta Kappa. **SELECTED PUBLICATIONS** Social Dialectology in Chesnutt's House behind Cedars, 1987; **CONTACT ADDRESS** Dept of English, Morehouse Col, 830 Westview Dr SW, Brawley Hall 224, Atlanta, GA 30314.

PICKER, JOHN
PERSONAL Born 05/12/1970, New Brunswick, NJ, s **DISCIPLINE** ENGLISH **EDUCATION** Swarthmore Coll, BA, 92; Univ Va, MA, 95, PhD (expected) **CAREER** Instr, Univ Va, 95-00; Asst Prof, Harvard Univ, 00-. **HONORS AND AWARDS** DuPont Fel, 95-97; Arts and Sci Dissertation Year Fel, 98-99; Thomas J. Griffis Prize, 99-00. **MEMBERSHIPS** MLA **RESEARCH** 19th and 20th century lit **SELECTED PUBLICATIONS** Auth, Judaism, Shylock and the Struggle for Closure, 94; Walt Whitman Quarterly Review, The Union of Music and Text in Whitman's Drum-Taps and Higginson's Army Life in a Black Regiment, 95; Journal of Theatre and Drama, Shakespeare Divided: Revision and Transformation in Marowitz's Variations on The Merchant of Venice and Wesker's Shylock, 96; English Literary History, Disturbing Surfaces: Representations of the Fragment in The School for Scandal, 98; auth, Victorian Studies, The Soundproof Study: Victorian Professionals, Work Space, and Urban Noise, 00. **CONTACT ADDRESS** 3069 Chimey Ridge, Charlottesville, VA 22911. **EMAIL** jmp7u@virginia.edu

PICKER, MARTIN
PERSONAL Born 04/03/1929, Chicago, IL, m, 1956, 3 children **DISCIPLINE** MUSICOLOGY **EDUCATION** Univ of Chicago, PhB, 74, MA, 51; Univ of Calif, PhD, 60. **CAREER** Instr, Univ of Ill, 59-61; from asst prof to prof, Rutgers Univ, 61-, prof emer, 97-. **HONORS AND AWARDS** Harvard Univ, I Tatti Fel, 66-67; NEH Sen Fel, 72-73. **MEMBERSHIPS** Am Musicological Soc; Int Musicological Soc; Royal Soc for Dutch Music Hist **RESEARCH** Renaissance Music **SELECTED PUBLICATIONS** Auth, Johannes Ockeghem and Jacob Obrecht, A Guide to Research, 88; The Habsburg Courts in the Netherlands and Austria, in The Renaissance: From the 1470s to the End of the 16th Century, 90; Henricus Isaac, A Guide to Research, 91; The Career of Marbriano de Orto, in Collectanea II, Studien zur Geschichte der Paepstlichen Kapelle, 94; Isaac in Flanders: The Early Works of Henricus Isaac, in From Ciconia to Sweelinck, donum natalicium Willem Elders, 94; ed, The Chanson Albums of Marguerite of Austria, 65; Fors Seulement: Thirty Compositions, 81; The Motet Books of Andrea Antico, 87; auth, "Reflections on Ockeghem and Mi-mi," in Johannes Ockeghem (Actes, 98); auth, "Liber selectarum cantionum," in Die Entstehung einer musikalischen Quelle im 15, und 16, (Jahrhundert, 98); auth, "Henricus Isaac and Fortuna desperata," in Antoine Busnoys (99); ed, New Josquin Edition 16, 00. **CONTACT ADDRESS** 3069 Chimney Ridge, Charlottesville, VA 22911. **EMAIL** mpicker@cfw.com

PICKLESIMER, DORMAN
DISCIPLINE COMMUNICATION, HISTORY **EDUCATION** Morehead State Univ, AB, 60; Bowling Green State Univ, MA, 65; Ind Univ, PhD, 69. **CAREER** Prof, Boston Col, 69-. **HONORS AND AWARDS** Phi Kappa Delta; Gold Key Honor Soc. **MEMBERSHIPS** Nat Communication Asn; Eastern Communication Asn; World Communication Asn. **RESEARCH** History of American public address; classical rhetoric. **CONTACT ADDRESS** Dept of Communcations, Boston Col, Chestnut Hill, Lyons Hall 215, Chestnut Hill, MA 02167. **EMAIL** picklesi@bC.edu

PICOT, JOCELYNE
DISCIPLINE COMMUNICATION STUDIES **EDUCATION** Univ Montreal, BA; Univ Concordia, MA; Simon Fraser Univ, PhD. **CAREER** Adj prof, McGill Univ. **HONORS AND AWARDS** Canadian Univ Fel, McGill Univ, 96; Medal of

Quebec Minister of ed, 69. **RESEARCH** Communications technologies; evaluation and needs analysis; telehealth, telemedicine, tele-learning and telework; policy studies relevant to the information highway. **SELECTED PUBLICATIONS** Auth, Report of the Focus Group on Office Technology in Federal Government Establishments, Public Works Can, 90; auth, "The Politics of Inter-institutional Cooperation: A Case study and some New Perspectives," Ed Technology and Training Int, 91; auth, Is There a Telehealth Industry in Canada? Informationa Technology and Community Health (ITCH), Univ of Victoria, 96; auth, The Telehealth Industry-Part 1: Overveiw and Prospects, Industry Can, 98; auth, "Telemedicine and Telehealth in Canada: Forty Years of Change in the Use of Information and Communicaitons Technologies in a Publicly Administerded Health Care System," Telemedicine J, vol 4, (98), 199-206; auth, "Towards a Methdology for Developing and Implementing Best Practices in Telehealth and Telemedicine," in The Impact of Telemedicine on Health Care Management, IOS Press vol 64, 99. **CONTACT ADDRESS** Dept Communications, McGill Univ, 845 Sherbrooke St, Montreal, QC, Canada H3A 2T5.

PIEPHO, LEE
PERSONAL Born 10/01/1942, Detroit, MI, m, 1964 **DISCIPLINE** ENGLISH **EDUCATION** Kenyon Col, BA; Columbia Univ, MA; Univ VA, PhD. **CAREER** Sara Shallenberger Prof Eng. **HONORS AND AWARDS** Folger Shakespear Library Senior Fellowship, 89-90; Stu Govt Assn Excellence Tchg Awd, Sweet Briar Col, 91, 00; Medrick Fellowship, 96. **MEMBERSHIPS** Renaissance Society of Am, Modern Language Asn of Am, Int Asn for Neo-Latin Studies. **RESEARCH** Italian humanism in 16th-century Eng cult. **SELECTED PUBLICATIONS** Auth, transl and commentary of Mantuan's Eclogues; articles on Renaissance poetry. **CONTACT ADDRESS** English Dept, Sweet Briar Col, Sweet Briar, VA 24595. **EMAIL** lpiepho@sbcedu

PIERCE, JOHN
DISCIPLINE ENGLISH LITERATURE **EDUCATION** Univ Toronto, PhD **CAREER** Dept Eng, Queen's Univ **HONORS AND AWARDS** ASUS Tchg Awd. **RESEARCH** Romantic poetry; late 18th and early 19th century fiction. **SELECTED PUBLICATIONS** Auth, Flexible Design: Blake's Writing of Vala or The Four Zoas, McGill-Queen's Univ, 98. **CONTACT ADDRESS** English Dept, Queen's Univ at Kingston, Kingston, ON, Canada K7L 3N6. **EMAIL** piercej@qsilver.queensu.ca

PIERSON, JEFFERY A.
PERSONAL Born Atlantic City, NJ **DISCIPLINE** ENGLISH **EDUCATION** North Carolina State Univ, BA, 86; Temple Univ, MA. 88; Rutgers Univ, PhD, 94. **CAREER** Teach asst, Temple Univ, 86-88; adj fac, Mercer Cnty Comm Col, 88-91; adj fac, Col New Jersey, 89-92; teach asst, Rutgers Univ, 88-92; instr, Bridgewater Col, 92-94; asst prof, 94-98; assoc prof, 98-. **MEMBERSHIPS** NCA; ICA; ECA; ADA; AFA; NFA; NEDA; CFA. **SELECTED PUBLICATIONS** Coauth, "Instructional Methods for infusing AIDS into the Communication Course," in Communicating About Communicable Diseases, eds. Linda K Fuller, Lillie McPherson Shilling (Hum Res Dev Press, 95); asst ed, Information and Behavior, eds. B Ruben, J Schement (New Brunswick, NJ: Transaction Press, 93); coauth, Instructors Manual for Communication and Human Behavior, Prentice Hall (Englewood Cliffs, NJ, 92); assoc ed, Speaker & Gavel, Nat J DSR-TKA, HFS, 95-; contrib, Tocqueville in the Classroom: Exploring Democracy in America: An Educator's Resource, C-SPAN TV Network (97); coauth, Integrating HIV/AIDS Education into Communication Courses, Speech Comm Asn, 97. **CONTACT ADDRESS** Dept English, Bridgewater Col, 402 E College St, Bridgewater, VA 22812-1511.

PIERSON, STEVEN J.
PERSONAL Born 02/05/1950, IL, m, 1979, 2 children **DISCIPLINE** EDUCATION, MUSIC **EDUCATION** Univ Ill, BA, 72; MS, 74; Wheaton Col, MA, 83; Trinity Int Univ, PhD, 98. **CAREER** Acad Dean, Nordiska Bibelinstitutet, 77-92; Wheaton Col, Col Du Page, Trinity Int Univ, 96-. **HONORS AND AWARDS** Wedell Awd for Scholar in Educ, Trinity Int Univ. **MEMBERSHIPS** Asn for the Advanc of Baltic Studies, N Am Asn for Prof of Christian Educ. **RESEARCH** Baltic Singing Culture. **SELECTED PUBLICATIONS** Auth, "De Vanligaste Fragorna och Studierktorns Svar," ("The Most Common Questions and Answers from the Academic Dean"), Nymark (Winter 91): 3; auth, "NMI och des Profil," ("Nordiska Bibelinstitutet and Its Profile"), Nymark (Summer 91): 4; auth, "Cures for Performance Nerves," The Instrumentalist (Mar 98): 62-68; auth, "Laulsime End Vabaks: Muusikaline Tegevus Ja Selle Areng Eesti Kristlaste Seas," ("We Sang Ourselves Free: Musical Experience and Development among Estonian Christians"), Teater Muusika Kino (Dec 98): 23-28; auth, "Misjoniajaloo Iuhiulevaade," ("Missions History"), Oleviste (Aug/Sep 94): 7; auth, "Sweden," "Ansgar," "The Baltics," "Latvia," "Lithuanian," "Dialogue," "Sociology of Music," in The Evangelical Dictionary of Missions, ed. Scott Moreau (Grand Rapids, MI: Baker Book House, 99); auth, "A Nation Than Sang Itself Free," Christianity Today (Oct 25, 99): 99. **CONTACT ADDRESS** Dept Humanities and Fine Arts, Col of DuPage, 425 22nd St, Glen Ellyn, IL 60137-6784. **EMAIL** Pierstevj@aol.com

PIFER, ELLEN
PERSONAL Born 06/26/1942, New York, NY, m, 1962, 1 child **DISCIPLINE** ENGLISH AND COMPARATIVE LITERATURE **EDUCATION** Mills Col, Oakland, CA; Univ CA, Berkeley, BA (English, with Distinction), MA, PhD (Comparative Lit, English, Russian, French), 76. **CAREER** Asst prof, dept of English, Univ DE, 77-81; asoc prof, English and Comparative Lit, dept of English, Univ DE, 81-89; vis prof, Comparative Lit, Univ CA, Berkeley, spring 90; Distinguished Vis Prof of Am Lit, Universite Jean Moulin, Lyon III, France, spring 92; prof of English and Comparative Lit, Dept of English, Univ DE, 89-. **HONORS AND AWARDS** Nominated for Excellence in Teaching Awd, Univ DE, 86, 88, 97; General Univ Res grant, Univ DE, 78, 81, 86, 90; DE Humanities Forum Res fel, 87-88; DE Arts Coun Individual Artists fel (Non-Fiction Prose), 89-90; Nat Endowment for the Humanities summer stipend for res, 91; Outstanding Academic Book Awd (for Saul Bellow Against the Grain), Choice Magazine, 90-91; Distinguished Vis Prof of Am Lit, Univ Lyon III, France, 92; Fulbright Scholar, France, 92; Rector's Distinguished Vis Prof in Am Lit, Univ Helsinki, Finland, March 28-April 8, 93; Center for Advanced Studies fel, Univ DE, 93-94; listed in Who's Who in the World, Who's Who in Ed, The International Authors and Writers Who's Who, Dictionary of Am Scholars, etc. **MEMBERSHIPS** Modern Language Asn; Am Lit Asn; Int Vladimir Nabokov Soc (pres, 98-2000, vice-pres, 96-98, member, bd of dirs). **RESEARCH** Modern and contemporary lit; the novel; the image of childhood in contemporary writing and culture. **SELECTED PUBLICATIONS** Auth, Nabokov and the Novel, Harvard Univ Press, 80, 81; ed and intro, Critical Essays on John Fowles, G K Hall, 86; auth, Saul Bellow Against the Grain, Univ PA Press, 90; Lolita, The Garland Companion to Vladimir Nabokov, ed Vladimir E Alexandrov, Garland, 95; Birds of a Different Feather: Nabokov's Lolita and Kosinski's Boy, Cycnos 12, 2, 95; Nabokov's Discovery of America: From Russia to Lolita, in The American Columbiad: Discovering America, Inventing the United States, eds Mario Materassi and Maria I Ramalho de Sousa Santos, VU Univ Press, 96; Winners and Losers: Bellow's Dim View of Success, in Saul Bellow and the Struggle at the Center, ed Eugene Hollahan, AMS Press, 96; The River and Its Current: Literary and Collective Memory in Toni Morrison's Beloved, Sounding the Depths: Water as Metaphor in North American Literatures, eds Gayle Wurst and Christine Raguet-Bouvart, Univ of Liege Press, 98; The Children: Wharton's Creative Ambivalence to Self, Society and the New World, in Edith Wharton: A Forward Glance, eds Clare Colquitt, Susan Goodman and Candace Waid, Univ DE Press, 99; Her Monster, His Nymphet: Nabokov and Mary Shelley, in Nabokov and His Fiction: New Perspectives, ed Julian W Connolly, Cambridge Univ Press, 99; auth, Demon or Doll: Images of the Child in Contemporary Writing and Culture, Univ Pr Va, 00; 'Did she have a precursor?': 'Lolita' and Wharton's 'The Children,' ed. Jane Grayson, Arnold McMillin & Priscilla Meyer, MacMillan/St. Martin's Pr, forthcoming. **CONTACT ADDRESS** English Dept, Univ of Delaware, Memorial Hall, Newark, DE 19716. **EMAIL** epifer@udel.edu

PIKE, DAVID
DISCIPLINE MODERNISM, DANTE, AND FILM **EDUCATION** Columbia Univ, PhD. **CAREER** Asst prof, Am Univ. **HONORS AND AWARDS** Gustave O. Arlt Awd, 97; mellon doc fel, columbia univ, 93-95. **RESEARCH** Changing images of underground London and Paris. **SELECTED PUBLICATIONS** Auth, Passage through Hell: Modernist Descents, Medieval Underworlds Cornell Univ Press. **CONTACT ADDRESS** American Univ, 4400 Massachusetts Ave, Washington, DC 20016. **EMAIL** dpike@american.edu

PINCHIN, JANE LAGOUDIS
PERSONAL Born 06/21/1942, New York City, NY, m, 1969, 3 children **DISCIPLINE** WOMEN IN LITERATURE **EDUCATION** Harpur Col, SUNY, BA, 64; MA, Columbia Univ, MA, 65, PhD,73. **CAREER** Instr, Brooklyn Col, 66-67, prof-(pt-time), 69; dir, div univ studies, 87-91; div hum, 91-94; dean, 94-; Provost and Dean of Faculty, Colgate Univ. **HONORS AND AWARDS** W.W. Fellow, 64. **RESEARCH** EM Forster and Virginia Woolf. **SELECTED PUBLICATIONS** Auth, Alexandria Still: Forster, Durrell and Cavafy, Princeton UP, 77, Am Univ Cairo Press, 89; Lawrence and Gerald Durrell, Blood Brothers: Siblings as Writers, 83; publ, Twentieth Century Lit Criticism, Mod Fiction Studies, Critical Essays on Lawrence Durrell, 87. **CONTACT ADDRESS** Dept of Eng, Colgate Univ, Office of the Provost & Dean of Faculty, 13 Oak Dr, Hamilton, NY 13346. **EMAIL** jpinchin@mail.colgate.edu

PINEDO, ISABEL
DISCIPLINE MEDIA **EDUCATION** Univ Chicago, MA; CUNY Grad Ctr, PhD. **CAREER** Dept Ed, Hunter Col City Univ NY **RESEARCH** Relation between Media and Society. **SELECTED PUBLICATIONS** Auth, Recreational Terror: Women and The Pleasures of Horror Film Viewing, Albany: SUNY Press, 97; Recreational Terror: Postmodern Elements of the Contemporary Horror Film, J Film Video, vol 48, 96 & And Then She Killed Him: Women and Violence in the Slasher Film, in Mediated Women: Representations in Popular Culture, Cresskill, NJ: Hampton Press, 97. **CONTACT ADDRESS** Dept of Education, Hunter Col, CUNY, 695 Park Ave, New York, NY 10021.

PINKA, PATRICIA G.
PERSONAL Born 02/27/1935, Pittsburgh, PA, m, 1999, 1 child **DISCIPLINE** ENGLISH **EDUCATION** Univ Pittsburgh, BA 56; San Francisco State Univ, MA 64; Univ Pittsburgh, PhD 69. **CAREER** Agnes Scott College, asst prof, assoc prof, prof, 69-; Point Park College, inst, 66-67. **HONORS AND AWARDS** Mellon Fel; 2 NEH Fel; Outstanding Tchr; Who's Who Among Amer Tchrs. **MEMBERSHIPS** MLA; AAUP; MS; JDS. **RESEARCH** 17th century poetry; feminist lit and theory. **SELECTED PUBLICATIONS** Auth, John Donne, Micropedia, Encycl Britannica, 14th ed, 94, revised 98; Donne Idios and the Somerset Epithalamion, Studies in Philosophy, 93; Timely Timelessness in Two Nativity Odes, in: Bright Shoots of Everlastingness, eds TL Pebworth Claude Summers, CO, UMP, 87; This Dialogue of One: The Songs and Sonnets of John Donne, Tuscaloosa, UAP, 82; The Autobiographical Narrator in the songs and Sonnets, That Subtle Wreath, ed MW Pepperdene, Decatur GA, 74; auth, "I'm still at Agnes Scott," 69-. **CONTACT ADDRESS** Dept of English, Agnes Scott Col, 141 E College Ave, Decatur, GA 30030. **EMAIL** ppinka@agnesscott.edu

PINKETT, HAROLD THOMAS
PERSONAL Born 04/07/1914, Salisbury, MD, m, 1943 **DISCIPLINE** ARCHIVES, HISTORY **EDUCATION** Morgan Col, AB, 35; Univ Pa, AM, 38; Am Univ, PhD, 53. **CAREER** Teacher, High Sch, Md, 36-38; prof hist, Livingstone Col, 38-39 & 41-42; archivist, Nat Archs, 42-79; consult archivist & historian, 80-, Coun Libr Resources fel, 72-73; lectr hist & archival admin, Howard Univ, 70-76; lectr, Am Univ, Washington, DC, 76-77. **HONORS AND AWARDS** Bancroft Hist Prize, 47 & 48; book award, agric hist soc, 68. **MEMBERSHIPS** Fel Soc Am Archivists; AHA; Orgn Am Historians; Forest Hist Soc (pres, 76-78); Agr Hist Soc (pres, 82-83); SAA established Harold T. Pinkett Minority Student Award, 88. **RESEARCH** Archival administration, history and use; American conservation history; progressive era. **SELECTED PUBLICATIONS** Art, American Archival Theory: The State of the Art, American Archivist, summer 81, and other articles on M. H. Review, J. of Am. Histroy, Agric. History, and J. of Forest History; auth, National Church of Zion Methodism, 89; auth, Conservationists at the Cosmos Club, 90. **CONTACT ADDRESS** 5741 27th Street NW, Washington, DC 20015.

PINNELL, RICHARD
PERSONAL Born 01/09/1942, Whittier, CA, m, 1966, 3 children **DISCIPLINE** MUSIC HISTORY, GUITAR **EDUCATION** Univ Utah, BA; BYU, MA; UCLA, PhD, 76. **CAREER** Dept Music, Wisc Univ **HONORS AND AWARDS** Senior Res Fulbright to Argentina and Uruguay, 88-89. **RESEARCH** Women's music; jazz; Latin American music. **SELECTED PUBLICATIONS** Auth, Francesco Corbetta and the Baroque Guitar, UMI Res, 80; The Rioplatense Guitar, Bold Strummer, 93. **CONTACT ADDRESS** Dept of Music, Univ of Wisconsin, La Crosse, 1725 State St, La Crosse, WI 54601. **EMAIL** pinnell.rich@uwlax.edu

PINSKER, SANFORD S.
PERSONAL Born 09/28/1941, Washington, PA, m, 1968, 2 children **DISCIPLINE** ENGLISH **EDUCATION** Washington & Jefferson Col, BA, 63; Univ of Wash, PhD, 67. **CAREER** Teaching Asst, Univ of Wash, 63-67; From Asst Prof to Shade Humanities Prof, Franklin and Marshall Col, 67-; Vis Prof, UC Riverside, 73, 75; **HONORS AND AWARDS** Grad Inst of Mod Letters Fel, 68; NEH Young Humanist, 70-71; NEH Sem in Am Humor, 78-79; Fulbright Sr Lectr, Belgium, 84-85; Pa Humanist, 85-87, 96-97; Fulbright Sr Lectr, Spain, 90-91; Simon Rocker Awd, 98, 99. **SELECTED PUBLICATIONS** Auth, The Uncompromising Fictions of Cynthia Azoic, Univ of Mo Press, 87; auth, Bearing the Bad News: Contemporary American Literature and Culture, Univ of Iowa Press, 90; auth, Understanding Joseph Heeler, Univ of SC Press (Columbia, SC), 91; co-ed, Jewish-American Literature and Culture: An Encyclopedia, Garland Publ (NY), 92; auth, Jewish-American Fiction, 1917-1987, Twayne (NY), 92; auth, Sketches of Spain, Plowman Press, 92; auth, The Catcher in the Rye: Innocence under Pressure, Twayne (NY), 93; auth, Oedipus Meets the Press and Other Trago-Comedies of Our Time, Mellon Poetry Press (Lewisburg, NY), 96; auth, Worrying About Race, 1985-1995: Reflections During a Troubled Time, Whitston Publ (Troy, NY), 96; auth, The Catcher in the Rye: A Casebook, Greenwood Publ (Westport, CN), 99. **CONTACT ADDRESS** Dept English, Franklin and Marshall Col, PO Box 3003, Lancaster, PA 17604-3003. **EMAIL** S_PINSKER@FandM.edu

PINSKY, ROBERT
PERSONAL Born 10/20/1940, Long Branch, NJ, m, 3 children **DISCIPLINE** ENGLISH **EDUCATION** Rutgers Univ, BA 62; Stanford Univ, MA 65, PhD 66. **CAREER** Univ Chicago, asst prof 66-67; Wellesley Col, prof 67-80; Harvard Univ, vis lect 80; Univ Cal Berk, prof 80-89; Boston Univ, prof 88-; The New Republic, poetry ed 78-87; Slate, poetry ed 96-. **HONORS AND AWARDS** Woodrow Wilson fel; Fulbright fel; Guggenheim fel; Stegner fel; NEH; NEA; Shelly Mem Awd; Poet Laureate of the US; Lenore Marshall Prize; Oscar Blumenthal Prize; Nominated for 1995 Pulitzer Prize in Poetry; Ambassador Book Awd; Wm Carlos Williams Awd; Saxifrage Prize;

Landon Translation Prize. **SELECTED PUBLICATIONS** Auth, The Handbook of Heartbreak, Wm Morrow and Co, 98; The Sounds of Poetry, Farrar Straus Giroux, 98; The Figured Wheel: New and Collected poems 1966-1996, FS&G, 95; The Inferno of Dante, Farrar Straus Giroux, 95; The Want Bone, The Ecco Press, 90; Mindwheel, interactive fiction for computer, with Stephen Hales and William Mataga programmers, pub by Broderbund Software. **CONTACT ADDRESS** Dept of English, Boston Univ, 236 Bat State Rd, Boston, MA 02215.

PINSON, HERMINE DOLOREZ
PERSONAL Born 07/20/1953, Beaumont, TX, m, 1976 **DISCIPLINE** ENGLISH **EDUCATION** Fisk University,, BA, 1975; Southern Methodist University, MA, 1979; Rice University, PhD, 1991. **CAREER** Houston, Community Coll, 77-79; Texas Southern Universitys, asst prof, 79-92; College of William & Mary, Assoc Prof of English, 92-. **HONORS AND AWARDS** Vermont Studio Ctr, fellowship, 1997; Macdowell Colony, fellow, 1996; Yaddo Colony, fellow, 1996; Ford Postdoctoral, fellow, 1991; National Endowment for the Humanities fellow, 1988. **MEMBERSHIPS** Modern Language Assn; Southern Conference on African-American Studies, Inc; American Literature Assn; Southern Modern Language Assn. **SELECTED PUBLICATIONS** Author: "Ashe," collection of poems, 1992; Mama Yetta and Other Poems, 1988; work published in anthologies: Common Bonds, 1986; Loss of Ground Note, Callaloo and African-American Review, 1989. **CONTACT ADDRESS** Dept of English, Col of William and Mary, PO Box 8795, Williamsburg, VA 23187-8795. **EMAIL** hdpins@facstaff.wm.edu

PINTI, DANIEL J.
PERSONAL Born 10/06/1963, Warren, OH, m, 1988, 3 children **DISCIPLINE** LITERATURE **EDUCATION** Kent State Univ, BA, 86; Ohio State Univ, MA, 88; PhD, 92. **CAREER** Asst to assoc prof, NMex State Univ, 92-01; assoc prof, Niagara Univ, 01-. **HONORS AND AWARDS** NEH Fel, 98-99; Am Philos Soc Fel, 98-99. **MEMBERSHIPS** Dante Soc of Am, New Chaucer Soc, Medieval Acad of Am, MLA, Am Ital Hist Assoc. **RESEARCH** Medieval literature, especially Dante and Chaucer, Italian American literature. **SELECTED PUBLICATIONS** Auth, "Alter Maro, Alter Maphaeus: Gavin Douglas's Negotiation of Authority in Eneados 13," JMRS, (93); auth, "The Vernacular Gloss(ed) in Gavin Douglas's Eneados," Exemplaria (95); auth, "Court, King and Community in the Taill of Rauf Coilyear," Chaucer Yearbook (96); auth, "Governing the Cook's Tale in Bodley 686," Chaucer Rev, (96); ed, Writing After Chaucer: Essential Readings on Chaucer and the Fifteenth Century, Garland, 98; auth, "Commentary and Comedic Reception: Dante and the Subject of Reading in the Parliament of fowls," Studies in the Age of Chaucer, (00); auth, "The Comedy of the Monk's Tale: Chaucer's Hugelyn and Early Commentary on Dante's Ugolino," Comp Lit Studies (00); auth, "The Power of Ovidio: Figuring the Poet in Pascal D'Angelo's Son of Italy," VIA: Voices in Ital Am, (01). **CONTACT ADDRESS** Dept English, Niagara Univ, Niagara Univ, NY 14109. **EMAIL** dpinti@niagara.edu

PIRRAGLIA, ELVIRA
PERSONAL Born Buenos Aires, Argentina, m, 1988, 2 children **DISCIPLINE** LITERATURE **EDUCATION** Univ de Dijon, Troisieme degre, 79; Lehman Col, BA, 80; Facolta di Lettere e Filosofia, Naples, Italy, Dottorato in letterature hispaniche, 87; City Univ NYork Grad Center, MPhil, 93; PhD, 97. **CAREER** Adjunct lectr, Herbert H. Lehman Col, 97, asst prof, 98-; vis prof, City Col, CUNY, 99-2000. **HONORS AND AWARDS** George N. Schuster Fel, Lehman Col, 98, 99. **MEMBERSHIPS** GRECMU, Modern Lang Asn, Am Asn of Teachers of Spanish and Portuguese, NEMLA, CARLA. **SELECTED PUBLICATIONS** Auth, La donna-microcosmo nelle poesie di Antonio Machado, Montevideo: Ed Latina (94); auth, Tres ensayos: literatura y la mujer, Montevideo: Ed Latina (96); auth, "Valle-Inclan y su sabotaje a los generos literarios," submitted for publication, Revista de literatura, Madrid (98); auth, "El esperpento, una tecnica estructuradora," submitted for publication Modern Lang Studies (June 98); auth, "El discurso ironico e intertextual en al macrotexto valleinclaniano," submitted for publication, Academia Argentina de Letras (Sept 98). **CONTACT ADDRESS** Dept Lang & Lit, Lehman Col, CUNY, 250 Bedford Park Blvd W, Bronx, NY 10468-1527.

PISANI, MICHAEL
DISCIPLINE MUSIC HISTORY **EDUCATION** Univ Rochester, PhD. **CAREER** Asst prof. **HONORS AND AWARDS** Conductor & cast preparation for Houston Grand Opera, Seattle Opera, and Opera Company of Boston; asst, Leonard Bernstein, 85, 86 on Europ productions of his opera, A Quiet Place at La Scala, Vienna State Opera. **RESEARCH** Opera, theater and film music, musical exoticism. **SELECTED PUBLICATIONS** Cintrubu, The Exotic in Western Music, Northeast Univ Pres, 98. **CONTACT ADDRESS** Classic Dept, Vassar Col, 124 Raymond Ave., Poughkeepsie, NY 12604. **EMAIL** mipisani@vassar.edu

PITCHFORD, NICOLA
DISCIPLINE ENGLISH **EDUCATION** Univ Wis, PhD. **CAREER** Asst prof, Fordham Univ. **SELECTED PUBLICATIONS** Auth, Reading Feminism's Pornography Conflict: Implications for Postmodernist Reading Strategies, Genders, 96. **CONTACT ADDRESS** Dept of Eng, Fordham Univ, 441 E Fordham Rd, Bronx, NY 10458.

PITMAN, GROVER A.
DISCIPLINE MUSICOLOGY **EDUCATION** Univ Tex, Austin, BM, MM; The Catholic Univ Am, PhD; Postdoc, Monastery of Solesmes, France, Biblioteque Nationale in Paris, the Brit Mus, London, Old Sarum, Eng. **CAREER** Instr, Muskingum Col, Winthrop Col; prof, 78-. **MEMBERSHIPS** Mem, Mus Edu Nat Conf; Westminister Commun People. **RESEARCH** French horn; Gregorian chant. **SELECTED PUBLICATIONS** Co-Auth, Philosophy and Purposes, Undergrad Bulletin. **CONTACT ADDRESS** Dept of Mus, Westminster Col, Pennsylvania, New Wilmington, PA 16172-0001. **EMAIL** pitmanga@westminster.edu

PITT, DAVID G.
PERSONAL Born 12/12/1921, Musgravetown, NF, Canada **DISCIPLINE** LITERATURE **EDUCATION** Mt Allison Univ, BA, 46, LLD, 89; Univ Toronto, MA 48, PhD, 60. **CAREER** Assoc prof, 49-61, prof, 61-82, dept head 70-82, Prof Emer English, Memorial, Univ Nfld, 82-. **HONORS AND AWARDS** Hum Res Coun Fel, 56; Can Coun Sr Fel, 69; Univ BC Medal Can Biog, 85; City Toronto Bk Awd Finalist, 85; Nfld & Labrador Arts Coun Artist of the Yr Awd, 89; Memorial Univ Eaton Honor Soc, 95. **MEMBERSHIPS** Hum Asn Can; Nfld Geneal Soc. **SELECTED PUBLICATIONS** Auth, Elements of Literacy, 65; auth, Windows of Agates, 66, 2nd ed, rev & enlarged, 90; auth, E.J. Pratt: The Truant Years 1882-1927, 84; auth, E.J. Pratt: The Master Years 1927-1964, 87; auth, Towards the First Spike: The Evolution of a Poet, 87; auth, Tales from the Outer Fringe: Five Stories and a Novella, 90; coauth, Goodly Heritage, 84; ed, Here the Tides Flow (E.J. Pratt), 62; ed, Critical Views on Canadian Writers: E.J. Pratt, 69; contribur, The Encyclopedia of Newfoundland and Labrador; contribur, The Canadian Encyclopedia; contribur, The Dictionary of Newfoundland and Labrador Biography; contribur, Encyclopedia of Post-Colonial Literatures in English. **CONTACT ADDRESS** Dept of English Lang and Lit, Mem Univ of Newfoundland, Saint John's, NF, Canada A1C 5S7.

PIZER, DONALD
PERSONAL Born 04/05/1929, New York, NY, m, 1966, 3 children **DISCIPLINE** ENGLISH **EDUCATION** Univ Calif LA, BA, 51; MA, 52; PhD, 55. **CAREER** From Asst Prof to Prof, Tulane Univ, 57-. **HONORS AND AWARDS** Guggenheim Fel, 62-63; Fel, Am Coun of Learned Soc, 71-72; Fel, Nat Endowment for the Humanities, 78-79. **MEMBERSHIPS** Mod Lang Asn, Am Lit Asn. **SELECTED PUBLICATIONS** Auth, Twentieth-Century American Literary Naturalism: An Interpretation, Southern Ill UP (Carbondale, IL), 82; auth, Dos Passos' "U.S.A": A Critical Study, UP of Va (Charlottesville), 88; coauth, Theodore Dreiser: A Primary Bibliography and Reference Guide, 2nd Ed, GK Hall (Boston, MA), 91; auth, The Theory and Practice of American Literary Naturalism: Selected Essays and Reviews, Southern Ill UP (Carbondale, IL), 93; auth, American Expatriate Writing and the Paris Moment: Modernism and Place, La St UP (Baton Rouge, LA), 96. **CONTACT ADDRESS** Dept English, Tulane Univ, 6823 St Charles Ave, New Orleans, LA 70118-5665. **EMAIL** dpizer@mailhost.tcs.tulane.edu

PIZZATO, MARK
DISCIPLINE THEATRE, PLAYWRIGHTING; FILM STUDIES **EDUCATION** Univ Notre Dame, BA, 82; Cath Univ Am, MFA, 84; Univ Wis, Milwaukee, PhD, 92. **CAREER** Prof, Univ NC, Charlotte. **SELECTED PUBLICATIONS** Publ articles on ritual in mod drama, on the edges of perception in stage and screen structures, and on violence in the mass media; his plays are available through Aran Press; auth, Edges of Loss: From Modern Drama to Postmodern Theory, Michigan, 98. **CONTACT ADDRESS** Univ of No Carolina, Charlotte, Charlotte, NC 28223-0001. **EMAIL** mpizzato@atsemail.uncc.edu

PIZZO, JOSEPH S.
DISCIPLINE ENGLISH **EDUCATION** Trenton State Col, BA, 73, MA, 75. **CAREER** Eng teacher, Middlesex Pub Schs, 74-75; teac SAT prep, Bound Brook Comm Jointure Adult Sch, 77-81; ed, Morris County Counc Ed Asns, 82-83; TEACH, CHESTER TWP PUB SCHS, 75-; ADJ PROF, BUS, COMMUN, ENG, CENTENARY COL, 92-; adj teach trainer, Middlesex County Col, 95; FOUNDER, PRES, WORK SMART INC, 95-; ADJ PROF ENG, UNION COUNTY COL, 97-. **CONTACT ADDRESS** English Dept, Union County Col, 1033 Springfield Ave, Cranford, NJ 07016-1599.

PLANK, STEVEN E.
DISCIPLINE MUSICOLOGY **EDUCATION** Univ Louisville, BM, 73, MM, 74; Wash Univ, PhD, 80. **CAREER** Visiting ass, prof, Univ Mass, 75; tchg asst, Wash Univ, 77-79; affil tchr, St Louis Univ, 78-79; prof, Oberlin Coll, 80-. **MEMBERSHIPS** Mem, Hist Perf Prog; fac mem: Louisville Orchestra, 70-76; Early Mus Ensemble of St. Louis, 78-79 **RESEARCH** Early music performance, 17th century music. **SELECTED PUBLICATIONS** co-transl, Edward Tarr's TheTrumpet, 88; author, The Way to Heaven's Doors: An Introduction to Liturgical Process and Musical Style, 94; assoc ed, Historical Brass Soc Jour; contrib, Early Music, Musical Times, Music and Letters, Rel Stud. Rev. **CONTACT ADDRESS** Dept of Mus, Oberlin Col, Oberlin, OH 44074.

PLATH, JAMES
PERSONAL Born 10/29/1950, Chicago, IL, m, 1995, 5 children **DISCIPLINE** ENGLISH **EDUCATION** Cal State Univ, Chico, BA, 80; Univ Wis, Milwaukee, MA, 82, PhD, 88. **CAREER** Asst prof Ill Wesleyan Univ, 88-93, ASSOC PROF ENGLISH, 93-98; Prof English, 99-. **HONORS AND AWARDS** Fulbright Scholar, Caribbean Regional Lect Prog, Univ W Indies, 95-96; Graduate of Last Decade Awd, UWN Alumni Asn, 92; Editor's Awd Council of Lit Mag & Presses, 90. **MEMBERSHIPS** Acad Am Poets; Coun Lit Mag & Presses; Fitzgerald Soc; Fulbright Asn; Hemingway Soc; Soc of Midland Auths. **RESEARCH** John Updike, Ernest Hemingway, Raymond Carver, modernism and minimalism. **SELECTED PUBLICATIONS** Auth, "Shadow Rider: The Hemingway Hero as Western Archetype," in Hemingway and the Natural World, 99, Univ Idaho Press; auth, "Verbal Vermeer: Updike's Middle-Class Protraiture," in Rabbit Tales: Poetry and Politics in John Updike's 'Rabbit Novels, 98, Univ Ala Press; auth, "The Sun Also Rises as 'A Greater Gatsby': 'Isn't it Pretty to Think So?'" in French Connections: Hemingway and Fitzgerald Abroad, 98, St. Martin's; auth, "Le Torero and 'The Undefeated': Hemingway's Foray into Analytical Cubism," in Hemingway Repossessed, 94, Praeger, and Studies in Short Fiction, Summer 93; coauth, Remembering Ernest Hemingway, 99, Ketch & Yawl Press; auth, Conversations with John Updike, 94, Univ Press of Miss; auth, "Santiago at the Plate: Baseball in The Old Man and the Sea," The Hemingway Rev, Fall 96; auth, Fishing for Tension: The Dynamics of Hemingway's 'Big Two- Hearted River'," North Dakota Quarterly, Spring 94-95; auth, "After the Storm and After the Denim: Raymond Carver Comes to Terms with the Hemngway Influence," The Hemingway Rev, Spring 94. **CONTACT ADDRESS** Dept of English, Illinois Wesleyan Univ, Bloomington, IL 61702-2900. **EMAIL** jplath@titan.iwu.edu

PLOEGER, KATHERINE
PERSONAL Born 06/12/1955, San Francisco, CA, s **DISCIPLINE** ENGLISH, WRITING **EDUCATION** San Diego State Univ, BA, 78; San Francisco State Univ, MA, 94; Calif State Univ, MA. **CAREER** Adj instr, San Joaquin Delta Col, 94; adj instr, Valley Comm Col, 95; adj instr, Modesto Jr Col, 94-98; lectr, Calif State univ, 95-; lectr, Chapman Univ, 95-. **RESEARCH** Genre analysis. **SELECTED PUBLICATIONS** Auth, Character Workshop, CBI/In-depth Collection, Children's Book Insider, 94; auth, Plot Workshop, CBI/In-depth Collection, Children's Book Insider, 94; auth, Brainstorming Workshop, CBI/In-depth Collection, Children's Book Insider, 95; auth, "Brainstorm with Freewriting", Children's Book Insider, Aug 95; auth, "Exercises for Defining Your Characters", Children's book Insider Feb 96; auth, "English Composition", Model Curriculum for Telecommun, eds Jackie Ireland and Joan Stanley, VATEA, 96; auth, Simplified Paragraph Skills, NTC/ Contemporary Pub, (Lincolnwood, IL), July 99; auth, Simplified Essay Skills, NCT/Contemporary Pub, (Lincolnwood, IL), (forthcoming). **CONTACT ADDRESS** Dept English, California State Univ, Stanislaus, 801 W Monte Vista Ave, Turlock, CA 95382-0256. **EMAIL** kploeger@ainet.com

PLUMMER, JOHN F.
DISCIPLINE MEDIEVAL LITERATURE, TEXTUAL CRITICISM **EDUCATION** Univ Wash, PhD. **CAREER** Instr, Vanderbilt Univ. **RESEARCH** Signs and identity in the medieval romance. **SELECTED PUBLICATIONS** Auth, articles on Middle English Drama, ChrQtien de Troyes, Malory and Sir Gawain and the Green Knight; ed, Variorum Chaucer edition of The Summoner's Tale. **CONTACT ADDRESS** Vanderbilt Univ, Nashville, TN 37203-1727.

PLUMSTEAD, WILLIAM
PERSONAL m, 3 children **DISCIPLINE** ENGLISH **EDUCATION** Western Univ, BA; Univ Rochester, MA, PhD. **CAREER** Asst prof, Nipissing Univ. **MEMBERSHIPS** Past ch steering comt, Nipissing's third annual Visions/Voices conf. **RESEARCH** American Renaissance literature. **SELECTED PUBLICATIONS** Auth, Loon, 92; Freddy Dimwhistle's, Northcountry Sketchbook, 97. **CONTACT ADDRESS** Dept of English, Nipissing Univ, 100 College Dr, Box 5002, North Bay, ON, Canada P1B 8L7. **EMAIL** williamp@einstien.unipissing.ca

POAGUE, LELAND A.
PERSONAL Born 12/15/1948, San Francisco, CA, m, 1969, 2 children **DISCIPLINE** ENGLISH **EDUCATION** San Jose State Col, BA, 70; Univ Ore, PhD, 73. **CAREER** Instr, State Univ NYork (SUNY), 73-74; Vis Asst Prof, Univ Rochester, 77; Asst Prof, State Univ NY, 74-78; From Asst Prof to Prof, Iowa State Univ, 78-. **HONORS AND AWARDS** NDEA Fel. **MEMBERSHIPS** MLA, Soc for Cinema Studies. **SELECTED PUBLICATIONS** Auth, Howard Hawks, Twayne (Boston,

MA), 82; coauth, Film Criticism: A Counter theory, Iowa St UP (Ames, IA), 82; co-ed, A Hitchcock Reader, Iowa St UP (Ames, IA), 86; auth, Another Frank Capra, Cambridge UP (Cambridge), 94; co-ed, Conversations with Susan Sontag, UP of Miss (Jackson, MI), 95; coauth, Susan Sontag: An Annotated Bibliography 1948-1992, Garland Publ (New York), forthcoming. **CONTACT ADDRESS** Dept English, Iowa State Univ, Ames, IA 50011-2010.

PODIS, JOANNE
DISCIPLINE ENGLISH LITERATURE **EDUCATION** Case Western Reserve Univ, PhD, 94. **CAREER** Prof. **RESEARCH** 19th century British literature. **SELECTED PUBLICATIONS** Auth, pubs on aspects of the student writing process; coauth, Writing: Invention, Style, and Form, 84; Rethinking Writing, 96. **CONTACT ADDRESS** Dept of English, Ursuline Col, 2550 Lander Road, Pepper Pike, OH 44124. **EMAIL** jpodis@ursuline.edu

POE, ELIZABETH
PERSONAL Born, CA **DISCIPLINE** CHILDREN'S AND YOUNG ADULT LITERATURE AND READER RESPONSE THEORY **EDUCATION** Pitzer Col, BA; CO State Univ, MA; Univ CO, PhD. **CAREER** Instr, Univ WI prof, Radford Univ; ed, SIGNAL (J of Int Reading Asn). **SELECTED PUBLICATIONS** Auth, Focus on Sexuality, 90; Focus on Relationships, 93. **CONTACT ADDRESS** Radford Univ, Radford, VA 24142. **EMAIL** eapoe@runet.edu

POGEMILLER, LEROY
PERSONAL Born 01/03/1932, Morning Sun, IO, m, 1955, 2 children **DISCIPLINE** MUSIC HISTORY **EDUCATION** Conserv Mus, Kansas City, Bachelor of Mus, 57, Master of Mus, 57; Univ Mo, Kansas City, Doctor of Mus Arts, 67. **CAREER** Asst prof, 59-61, tchg assoc, 64-67, assoc prof, 67-70, prof, 70-, prin grad adv, 77-84, 87-, actg assoc dean, grad stud, 88-90, assoc dean, grad stud, 90-97, interim dean, 93-94, Prof Emer, Univ Mo, Kansas City, 97-; pvt piano tchr, New Rochelle, NY, 61-62; vocal mus tchr, Pub Sch, East Liverpool, Ohio, 62-64. **HONORS AND AWARDS** AMOCO Good Tchg Awd, 78, 84; Conserv Bd of Trustees Good Tchg Awd, 87; Weldon Spg Presidential Outstanding Tchg Awd, 91; UKC Bd of Trustees Tchg Awd, 91. **MEMBERSHIPS** UMKC Alumni Asn; UMKC Retirees Asn. **RESEARCH** A computer software program to analyze figured bass progressions. **SELECTED PUBLICATIONS** Auth, Some Observations on College T eaching Vacancies, Newsl, Col Mus Soc, Mar, 91; College Teaching Jobs and the Marketplace, Am Mus Tchr, Dec/Jan, 91/92. **CONTACT ADDRESS** Univ of Missouri, Kansas City, Kansas City, MO 64110-2499. **EMAIL** lpogemiller@cctr.umkc.edu

POGUE, SAMUEL FRANKLIN
PERSONAL Born 04/11/1919, Cincinnati, OH, 1 child **DISCIPLINE** MUSICOLOGY **EDUCATION** Princeton Univ, AB, 41, MFA, 63, PhD(music), 68. **CAREER** From asst prof to assoc prof, 68-77, Prof Music, Col Conserv Music, Univ Cincinnati, 77-. **HONORS AND AWARDS** LLD, Edgecliff Col, 73. **MEMBERSHIPS** Am Musicol Soc; Int Musicol Soc; New Bach Soc. **RESEARCH** Early music printing. **SELECTED PUBLICATIONS** Auth, Jacques Moderne, Lyons Music Printer of the Sixteenth Century, Editions Droz, Geneva, 69; contribr, articles, In: Grove's Dictionary of Music and Musicians, 74-75; Further notes on Jacques Moderne, Bibliotheque D'Humanisme et Renaissance, 75; A sixteenth century editor at work: Gardana and Moderne, J of Musicol, 82; Catalog of Editions of Music Pubished in Louvain by Phalese,Pierre and His Sons 1545-1578 - French - Vanhulst,H, Notes, Vol 0049, 1993. **CONTACT ADDRESS** Col Conserv of Music, Univ of Cincinnati, Cincinnati, OH 45221.

POHLSANDER, HANS ACHIM
PERSONAL Born 10/10/1927, Celle, Germany, m, 1956, 3 children **DISCIPLINE** CLASSICS **EDUCATION** Univ Utah, BA, 54; Univ Calif, Berkeley, MA, 55; Univ Mich, PhD, 61. **CAREER** Teacher Latin & Ger, Carmel High Sch, Calif, 56-58; asst prof Classics, Wash Univ, 61-62; asst prof to prof Classics, 62-95, prof Relig Studies, 91-95, emeritus 95-, State Univ NY Albany; vis assoc prof classics & cult studies, Am Univ Beirut, 68-69; vis prof Classics, Ohio State Univ, Columbus, 83-83. **HONORS AND AWARDS** Am Coun Learned Soc grant-in-aid, 62; Ger Acad Exchange Serv study grant, 82; Am Philos Soc res grants, 83, 88; NEH res grant, 86. **MEMBERSHIPS** Am Philol Asn; Archaeol Inst Am; Hagiographic soc. **RESEARCH** Later Roman Empire; early Christianity; Trier. **SELECTED PUBLICATIONS** Auth, Metrical Studies in the Lyrics of Sophocles, Brill, Leiden, 64; Helena: Empress and Saint, Ares, Chicago, 95; The Emperor Constantine, Routledge, London, 96; Maximinus und Paulinus: Two Bishops of Trier in the Fourth Century, Trierer Zeitschrift, 96; Die Anfunge des Christentums in der Stadt Trier, Trierer Zeitschrift, 97. **CONTACT ADDRESS** Dept of Classics, SUNY, Albany, 1400 Washington Ave., Albany, NY 12222-1000. **EMAIL** pohlsander@global2000.net

POIRIER, RICHARD
PERSONAL Born 09/09/1925, Gloucester, MA, s **DISCIPLINE** AMERICAN AND ENGLISH LITERATURE **EDUCATION** Amherst Coll, BA, 49; Yale Univ, MA, 51; Cambridge Univ, Fulbright Scholar, 52-53; Harvard Univ, PhD, 60. **CAREER** Instr, 50-52, Williams Coll; teach Fel, 53-60, Instr, 60-61, Asst Prof, 61-63, Harvard; Prof & Chmn Rutgers Coll Eng Dept, 63-66, Disting Prof & Chmn Eng dept, 66-68, Disting Prof & chmn, New Brunswick Eng dept, 68-73, Disting Prof & Dir Eng Grad Studies, 73-77, Dir Eng Grad Studies, 77-81, Rutgers Univ; Beckman Prof, 76, Univ Cal Berkeley; Marius Bewley Prof of Amer & Eng Lit, 77-98, Prof Emeritus 98-; editor, 62-71, Partisan Review; editor, 81-, Raritan Qtly Review; co-founder, 83, Chmn of board, 84-, VP, 89-, Library of America. **HONORS AND AWARDS** Fulbright Scholar, Guggenheim Found Grant, NEH Fel, LLD Amherst Coll, Lindback Awd Rutgers Univ, AAAS Fel, AAIA&L, Achievement Awd, Pushcart Prize, NYIH Fel, J B Hubbell Awd. **MEMBERSHIPS** AAA&S, AAUP, MLA, PEN, Lit Class of US, NBCC, PMLA, Amer Acad Arts and Letters. **SELECTED PUBLICATIONS** Auth, A World Elsewhere, The Place of Style in American Literature, NY Oxford UP 66, reissued Madison Wis UP, 85; Norman Mailer, Modern Masters Series, NY, Viking, 72; Robert Frost, The Work of Knowing, NY, Oxford UP, 77; The Renewal of Literature, Emersonian Reflections, NY Random House, 87; Poetry and Pragmatism, Cambridge Harvard UP, 92; Trying It Out in America, Literary and Other Performances, Farrar Straus & Giroux, 99. **CONTACT ADDRESS** Raritan Quarterly, 104 West 70th St., H 9B, New York, NY 10023.

POLAND, TIM
PERSONAL Born Findlay, OH **DISCIPLINE** AMERICAN LITERATURE **EDUCATION** OH Univ, BA; GA state Univ, MA, PhD. **CAREER** Prof, Radford Univ. **RESEARCH** Western Am lit; Native Am lit; fiction writing. **SELECTED PUBLICATIONS** Auth, "Escapee," Beloit Fict J (Spring 97); auth, Escapee, Am House, forthcoming. **CONTACT ADDRESS** Dept of English, Radford Univ, Radford, VA 24142. **EMAIL** tpoland@radford.edu

POLHEMUS, ROBERT M.
PERSONAL Born 12/12/1935, San Francisco, CA, 4 children **DISCIPLINE** ENGLISH **EDUCATION** Univ of Calif at Berkeley, BA, 57, MA, 59, PhD, 63. **CAREER** Prof of English, 63-98, Howard and Jesse Watkins Univ Prof, Stanford Univ, 92-. **HONORS AND AWARDS** Guggenheim Fel; Dean's Teaching Awd, Stanford Univ. **MEMBERSHIPS** MLA. **RESEARCH** Victorian and 19th century literature; film; psychology & art; cultural studies. **SELECTED PUBLICATIONS** Auth, Erotic Faith, 90; Comic Faith, 80; The Changing World of Anthony Trollope; Critical Reconstructions, 95; The Lot Complex, Rereading Texts, Rethinking Critical Presuppositions, 97. **CONTACT ADDRESS** Dept of English, Stanford Univ, MC 2087, Stanford, CA 94305-2087. **EMAIL** polhemus@leland.stanford.edu

POLK, NOEL E.
PERSONAL Born 02/23/1943, Picayune, MS, d, 2 children **DISCIPLINE** ENGLISH **EDUCATION** Mississippi College, BA, 65, MA, 66; Univ SC, PhD, 70. **CAREER** Univ Texas at Arlington, 70-74; Univ S Carolina, S Studies Prog, 74-76; Professeur Associe, 80-81, Univ Strasbourg; vis Prof, 96, Univ Rennes; Prof, Univ Southern Miss. **MEMBERSHIPS** MLA **RESEARCH** Bibliography, Am Novel, Faulkner, Welty. **SELECTED PUBLICATIONS** Auth, Outside the Southern Myth, UP Miss, 96; Children of the Dark House, UP Miss, 95; Eudora Welty: A Bibliography of her work, UP Miss, 93. **CONTACT ADDRESS** English Dept, Univ of So Mississippi, Hattiesburg, MS 39406. **EMAIL** noel.polk@usm.edu

POLLARD, TANYA LOUISE
DISCIPLINE ENGLISH **EDUCATION** Yale Univ, BA, 90; Magdalen Col, MA, 92; Yale Univ, PhD. **CAREER** Asst prof, Macalester Col, 99-. **HONORS AND AWARDS** Rhodes Scholar; Mellon Fel; Whiting Fel; Frances Yates Fel. **MEMBERSHIPS** MLA; SAA; RSA. **RESEARCH** Shakespeare and renaissance drama; medicine and theater; genre; gender. **SELECTED PUBLICATIONS** Auth, "Beauty's Poisonous Properties," Shakespeare's Studies 27 (99). **CONTACT ADDRESS** 111 Kellogg Blvd E, Apt 2909, Saint Paul, MN 551101-1237. **EMAIL** pollard@macalester

POLLOCK, DELLA
DISCIPLINE COMMUNICATION STUDIES **EDUCATION** Northwestern Univ, BS, 80; MA, 81; PhD, 86. **CAREER** Asst prof, Univ NC, 86-92, assoc prof, 92-99, prof, 99-, Dir, Univ Prog in Cultural Studies, 95-. **HONORS AND AWARDS** Ford Found Grant, 96-97; Tanner Awd for Excellence in Undergrad Teaching, Univ NC, 96; North Carolina Humanities Coun Major Grant, 96-97; Edith L. Bernstein Fel, Inst for the Arts and Humanities, Univ North Carolina, 98; Univ Res Coun Grant, 98; Lilla A. Heston Awd for Performance Scholarship, Nat Commun Asn, 98; Academy of Distinguished Teaching Scholars, UNC, Chapel Hill, 2000. **MEMBERSHIPS** Asn for Theatre in Higher Educ, Int Commun Asn, Nat Commun Asn, Oral Hist Asn, Performance Studies Int, Southern Speech Commun Asn. **RESEARCH** Performance studies; cultural studies. **SELECTED PUBLICATIONS** Auth, "(Un)Becoming Voices: Representing Sexual Harassment in Performance," Conceptualizing Sexual Harassment as Discourse, ed Shereen Bingham, Praeger (94); auth, "Performativity," Oxford Companion to Women's Writing, ed Linda Wagner-Martin and Cathy N. Davidson, Oxford Univ Press (94): 657-658; auth, "Origins in Absence: Performing Birth Stories," TDR: The Drama Rev 41.1 (97): 11-42; auth, "Beyond Performativity?," The Future of Performance Studies, ed Sheron Dailey, Nat Commun Asn (98): 37-46; auth, "Performance, Feminist Subjects, Cultural Studies," At the Helm in Communication Studies, ed Judith Trent, Allyn and Bacon (98): 396-403; auth, "Performing Writing," The Ends of Performance, ed Peggy Phelan and Jill Lane, New York Univ Press (98): 73-103; auth, "Making History Go," Exceptional Spaces: Essays in Performance and History, ed Della Pollock, Univ NC Press (98): 1-45; ed, Exceptional Spaces: Essays in Performance and History, Univ NC Press (98); auth, Telling Bodies Performing Birth, Columbia Univ Press (99). **CONTACT ADDRESS** Dept Commun Studies, Univ of No Carolina, Chapel Hill, Chapel Hill, NC 27599-3285.

POLLOCK, JAMES
PERSONAL Born 04/08/1968, Sudbury, ON, Canada **DISCIPLINE** ENGLISH **EDUCATION** York Univ, BA, 91; Univ of Houston, MA, 94; PhD, 01. **CAREER** Writer in residence, Writers in the Schs, 94-95; TA, Univ Houston, 91-97; lectr, Univ Houston Downtown, 97-01. **HONORS AND AWARDS** Cullen Educ Trust Fel, 91; Stella Ehrhart Mem Fel, 91; C Glenn Cambor/Inprint Fel, 91; Inprint Diss Fel, 00. **MEMBERSHIPS** MLA, Associated Writing Prog, Asn of Lit Sch and Critics. **RESEARCH** Creative Writing (Poetry, Literary Non-Fiction), Poetry, Romanticism, Modern European Literature, Canadian Culture. **SELECTED PUBLICATIONS** Auth, "A Widow Phones Her Sister," Gulf Coast, (92); auth, "The Christmas Flood," Western Humanities Rev, (94); auth, "Memorandum," Tex Rev, (01); auth, "Map of the Interior," Grain, (01); auth, "Invocation," Journal, (01); auth, "Northwest Passage," Paris Rev, (01); auth, "Scholarly Notes," Complete Poems and Selected Letters of John Keats, (Random House, 01). **CONTACT ADDRESS** Dept English, Univ of Houston, 1 Main St, Houston, TX 77002-1001. **EMAIL** pjpollock@yahoo.com

POLLOCK, JOHN
PERSONAL Born 01/14/1945, New York, NY, m, 1969, 1 child **DISCIPLINE** LITERATURE **EDUCATION** Univ Calif-Davis, BA, 67; MA, 69; PhD, 71. **CAREER** From asst prof to prof, San Jose State Univ, 71-. **HONORS AND AWARDS** Phi Beta Kappa; Phi Kappa Phi; NDEA Grad Fel; Kraft Awd. **MEMBERSHIPS** AAUP, MLA. **RESEARCH** Renaissance literature **SELECTED PUBLICATIONS** Ed, The Blackfeet of the Peacock: The Color Concept "Black" from the Greeks through the Renaissance. **CONTACT ADDRESS** Dept English, San Jose State Univ, 1 Washington Sq, San Jose, CA 95192-0001.

POOLE, JOHN R.
DISCIPLINE THEATRE ARTS **EDUCATION** Univ Ga, PhD, 95. **CAREER** Asst prof. **RESEARCH** Early twentieth century protest drama of the Depression era; southern regional minority drama. **SELECTED PUBLICATIONS** Auth, pubs in Theatre Studies Jour, Theatre Jour. **CONTACT ADDRESS** Dept of Theatre, Illinois State Univ, Normal, IL 61761.

POOLE, MARSHALL SCOTT
DISCIPLINE COMMUNICATION **EDUCATION** Univ Wis, PhD. **CAREER** Prof, Texas A&M Univ. **HONORS AND AWARDS** Golden Anniversary Monograph Awd, Speech Commun Asn. **MEMBERSHIPS** Acad of Management, INFORMS, Asn for Information Systems, Nat Communication Asn, International Communication Asn. **RESEARCH** Organizational communication, small group communication, communication technology. **SELECTED PUBLICATIONS** Coauth and co-ed, Research on the Management of Innovation; Communication and Group Decision-Making & Working Through Conflict; contribur, to Organizations and Communication Technology; Communication Perspectives on Negotiation; Communication and Organizations; auth, Organizational Change and Innovation Processes: Theological Methods for Research. **CONTACT ADDRESS** Dept of Speech Communication, Texas A&M Univ, Col Station, College Station, TX 77843-4234. **EMAIL** mspoole@tamu.edu

POPE, DEBORAH
PERSONAL Born Cincinnati, OH, 2 children **DISCIPLINE** BRITISH & AMERICAN LITERATURE **EDUCATION** Univ Wisc, PhD, 79. **CAREER** Prof, Duke Univ. **HONORS AND AWARDS** Phi Beta Kappa; Richard K. Lublin Univ Tchg Awd, Duke Univ. **RESEARCH** Women's lit; poetry; feminist crit. **SELECTED PUBLICATIONS** Auth, A Separate Vision: Isolation in Contemporary Women s Poetry, LSU, 84; auth, Ties That Bind: Essays on Mothering and Patriarchy, Univ Chicago, 89; auth, Fanatic Heart, LSU, 92; auth, Mortal World, LSU, 95; auth, Falling Out of the Sky, 99. **CONTACT ADDRESS** Eng Dept, Duke Univ, PO Box 90015, Durham, NC 27708-0015. **EMAIL** dpope@acpub.duke.edu

POPE, REBECCA A.
DISCIPLINE ENGLISH LITERATURE **EDUCATION** Barat Col, BA; Oxford Univ, M.Phil; Univ Chicago, MA, PhD. **CAREER** Eng Dept, Georgetown Univ **MEMBERSHIPS** MLA **RESEARCH** 19th century British literature; history and theory of gender and sexuality; the relations between illness, medicine, and culture. **SELECTED PUBLICATIONS** Auth, pubs on 19th century British writers, gothic fiction, detective fiction, opera and performance art, AIDS; co-auth, The Diva's Mouth: Body, Voice, Prima Donna Politics, 96. **CONTACT ADDRESS** English Dept, Georgetown Univ, 37th and O St, Washington, DC 20057. **EMAIL** poper@gunet.georgetown.edu

POPPITI, KIM
PERSONAL Born 07/20/1968, Long Island, NY, m, 1999 **DISCIPLINE** THEATRE **EDUCATION** Suffolk Cmty Col, AA, 88; Stony Brook Univ, BA, 91; MFA, 94. **CAREER** Adj Lecturer to Instructor, Dowling Col, 94-. **HONORS AND AWARDS** Winner, SUNY Playwriting Competition, 92; Winner, SUNY Playwriting Competition, 93; John Gassner Awd, MFA, 94. **CONTACT ADDRESS** Dept Humanities, Dowling Col, 150 Idle Hour Blvd, Oakdale, NY 11769-1906. **EMAIL** poppiti@aol.com

PORTALES, MARCO
PERSONAL Born 10/22/1948, Edinburgh, TX, m, 1972, 2 children **DISCIPLINE** ENGLISH, LITERATURE **EDUCATION** Univ Tex Austin, BA, 70; SUNY Buffalo, PhD, 74. **CAREER** Univ of Calif Berkeley, 74-79; Dean, Tex Southmost Col, 86-88; Univ of Houston, 79-86, 88-91; prof, Tex A&M Univ, 91-00. **HONORS AND AWARDS** Teaching Fel, SUNY, 70-74. **MEMBERSHIPS** MELUS; Soc for the Study of Multi-Ethnic Lit of the US. **RESEARCH** Chicano literature, life and culture. **SELECTED PUBLICATIONS** Auth, Crowding Out Latinos: Mexican Americans in the Public Consciousness, Temple Univ Pr, 00. **CONTACT ADDRESS** Dept English, Texas A&M Univ, Col Station, 1 Tex A & M Univ, College Station, TX 77843-0001. **EMAIL** mportales@tamu.edu

PORTER, DAVID H.
PERSONAL Born 10/29/1935, New York, NY, m, 1987, 4 children **DISCIPLINE** CLASSICS; MUSIC. **EDUCATION** Swarthmore College, BA, 58; Princeton Univ, PhD, 62; Philadelphia Conserv Music, 55-62. **CAREER** Instr, Carleton Col 62-63; from asst prof to prof, Skidmore Col, 63-; pres, Skidmore Col, 74-99; vis prof, Williams Col, 99-. **HONORS AND AWARDS** NEH fel, 69-70, 83-84; ACLS fel, 76-77; hon doctor of letters, Skidmore Col, 98. **MEMBERSHIPS** Am Philol Asoc; Classical Asoc of the Atalantic States. **RESEARCH** Greek tragedy; Latin poetry, especially Horace; contemporary music. **SELECTED PUBLICATIONS** Auth, Horace's Poetic Journey: A Reading of Odes 1-3, 87; auth, Only Connect: Three Studies in Greek Tragedy, 87; auth, A Note on Aeschylus, Agamemnon 332, Classical Philol, 88; auth, The Structure of Beethoven's Diabellil Variations, op. 120-Again, Music Rev, 93; auth, Quo, quo scelesti ruitis: The Downward Momentum of Horace's Epodes, Ill Classical Studies, 95. **CONTACT ADDRESS** Skidmore Col, 5 Birch Run Drive, Saratoga Springs, NY 12866. **EMAIL** ddodger@skidmore.edu

PORTER, ELLEN-JANE LORENZ
DISCIPLINE HISTORY OF MUSIC **EDUCATION** Wellesley, BA, 29; Wittenberg, MSM, 71; Union Grad Sch, PhD, 78. **CAREER** IND LECT, AUTHOR, COMPOSER. **MEMBERSHIPS** Am Antiquarian Soc **RESEARCH** Spirituals **SELECTED PUBLICATIONS** Auth, Folk Hymns for Handbells, 75; auth, Music Our Forefathers Sang, 78; auth, articles on Am mus; comp, for choruses, chamber groups; auth, Glory Hallelujah: The Story of the Campmeeting Spiritual, 80; comp, anthem arr of Am folk hymns, The Hymn 41; auth, "The Hymnody of the Evangelical United Brethren Church," Jour of Theol 91, 87. **CONTACT ADDRESS** 6369 Pebble Court, Dayton, OH 45459.

PORTER, J. I.
DISCIPLINE CLASSICAL STUDIES AND COMPARATIVE LITERATURE **EDUCATION** Univ CA, Berkeley, PhD, 86. **CAREER** Asst and assoc prof, Dept of Classical Studies and Prog in Comparative Lit, Univ MI, 86-. **HONORS AND AWARDS** NEH, 89; fel, Stanford Humanities Center, 95, 96; Humboldt fel, 97, 98. **MEMBERSHIPS** APA. **RESEARCH** Cultural and literary history. **SELECTED PUBLICATIONS** Auth, Nietzsche and the Philosophy of the Future, Stanford, 00; The Invention of Dionysus, Stanford, forthcoming; ed, Construction of the Classical Body, Univ MI press, 99; articles on Greek philos and poetics. **CONTACT ADDRESS** Dept of Classical Studies, Univ of Michigan, Ann Arbor, Ann Arbor, MI 48109. **EMAIL** jport@umich.edu

PORTER, JOSEPH A.
DISCIPLINE ENGLISH LITERATURE **EDUCATION** Univ CA Berkeley, PhD, 72. **CAREER** Prof, Duke Univ. **HONORS AND AWARDS** NEH/Fulger Inst Fel, 87; Andrew W Mellon Leave Fel, 85. **MEMBERSHIPS** MLA; SAMLA; SRC; SAA; ISC; AAUP. **RESEARCH** Shakespeare, Ren. Drama; Pragmatics; Consciousness Studies. **SELECTED PUBLICATIONS** Auth, Shakespeare's Mercutio: His History and Drama, UNC, 89; ed, Critical Essays on Shakespeare's Romeo and Juliet, GK Hall, 97; pubs on criticism; fiction; auth, The Drama of Speech Acts, Univ Calif, 99. **CONTACT ADDRESS** Eng Dept, Duke Univ, Durham, NC 27706. **EMAIL** japorter@duke.edu

PORTER, JOYCE K.
PERSONAL Born 12/21/1949, Chicago, IL, m, 1980, 1 child **DISCIPLINE** THEATER, FILM **EDUCATION** Univ Ill, BA, 71; Nor Wes Univ, MA, 72. **CAREER** Adj fac, Columbia Col, 80-82; prof, Mor Val Com Col, 72-. **HONORS AND AWARDS** Who's Who in Am, Am Women, Midwest, World. **MEMBERSHIPS** ITA; CCHA; Bd Dir Fest Thea. **RESEARCH** Field based teaching techniques. **SELECTED PUBLICATIONS** Auth, Humanities On the Go, Kendall Hunt; auth, Experience the Arts, Kendall Hunt, forthcoming. **CONTACT ADDRESS** Dept Fine Arts, Humanities, Moraine Valley Comm Col, 10900 South 88th St, Palos Hills, IL 60465-2175. **EMAIL** porter@moraine.cc.il.us

PORTER, MICHAEL LEROY
PERSONAL Born 11/23/1947, Newport News, VA, s **DISCIPLINE** LITERATURE, HISTORY **EDUCATION** VA State Univ, BA, (hon) sociology 1969; Atlanta Univ, MA, hist 1972; Leonardo DaVinci Acad, Rome, Italy, MCP Contem 1983-84; Emory Univ, PhD hist/Amer studies 1974; Sorbonne Univ, postdoct, hist, Paris France, 1979; Thomas Nelson Community Coll, cert crim justice 1981; US Armed Forces Staff Coll, Norfolk VA, US Pres Appt, 1987. **CAREER** WA State Univ, asst prof of history, black studies prog 1974-75; Mohegan Comm Coll, Dept History lectr 1975-76; Newport News VA, asst education coord, education comp, target proj prog 1977; Hampton Univ, asst prof history 1977-80; NC Mutual Ins Co, life ins underwriter 1980-81; Mullins Prot Serv VA Bch, private investigator, 81-83; Amer Biographical Inst Raleigh, media freelancer 1984-85, publications dir/deputy governor 1985-; Old Dominion Univ, Norfolk VA, consultant 1985; Michael Porter Enterprises International, president, founder, 85-88; INTL Biographical Ctr, Cambridge England, Deputy Dir Gen, 86-. **HONORS AND AWARDS** 1st Black Concert Pianist to play Carnegie Hall, 1963; Lyon Dissertation Prize, 1974; Ebony Magazine, Eligible Bachelor, 1975; Outstanding Black, 1992; Hero, 1992; International Honors Cup, 1992; Abira Genius Grant, 1992; World Greetings, 1992; Pioneer Awd, 1992; Great American, 1991; World Intellectual, 1993; Golden Academy Awd, 1991; One of 500 Leaders of Influence in the 20th Century; Intl Hall of Leaders, Amer Biographical Inst, 1988; participant (exhibit), DuSable Museum of Black History, 1988; honoree, Intl Exhibit, Singapore, Malaysia, 1988; Outstanding Man of the World, Ormiston Palace, Tasmania, Australia, 1989; Exhibit, Intl Music Museum, London, ENG, 1989; Poetry Reading, Royal Palace, Lisbon, Portugal, 1998; Michael Porter Poetry Exhibit, Internet Intl Poetry Hall of Fame, 1997-2002; Lecture, Oxford Univ, Oxford, ENG, 1997; Famous Quote, Leningrad, Russia, 1998; 20th Century Awd for Achievement, 1990; Black History Maker, 1992; International Man of the Year, 1992; Most Admired Person of the Decade, 1990-99; Recipient, Grant For Exceptionally Gifted Poets, 1998; US Congress, Certificate of Appreciation, 1991; Honorary US Congressman, 1993; Hampton History Center, Historical Marker, 1992; Appearances before US President's Council of Economic Advisors & Senate Finance Committee, 1992; Honorary Knighthood, 1997; US Presidential Medal of Freedom, 1993; Outstanding People of the 20th Century. **MEMBERSHIPS** Life patron World Inst of Achievement 1985; curator "Michael L Porter Historical & Literary Collection"; World Literary Acad 1984-85; World Biographical Hall of Fame 1985; Federal Braintrust, 1990; Intl Advisory Council, 1989-; African American Hall of Fame, 1994; Elite International, 1992; bd of governors, Amer Biog Inst, 1986; Phi Beta Kappa; Intl Academy of Intellectuals, 1993; Famous Poet's Society, 1996; chairman, US Selective Service Bd #32, 1986-92; chief delegate, Intl Congress on Arts & Communications, Nairobi, Kenya, 1990. **SELECTED PUBLICATIONS** Auth, "Black Atlanta: The Formation of a Black Community, 1905-1930," Journal of Ethnic Studies (78); auth, "Atlanta's Black Constructed Buildings: Expressions of the Black Experience," Journal of Ethnic Studies (78); Television Programs: Cited On World News Tonight; Hard Copy; 60 Minutes; Current Affairs; Entertainment Tonight; CBS Evening News; The Remarkable Journey; Journey of African American Athelete, 1995; Eve's Bayou, 1997; 4 Little Girls; NBC Nightly News; Film: The Making of Black Atlanta, 1974; 1st Black Elected to Intl Academy of Intellectuals, Paris, France, 1993; Radio: Empire State Bldg Broadcasting Ctr, WRIN, 1997; Publications: Ebony, Jet, Intl, Digest, Talent; Contemporary Authors, Outstanding Scholars of the 20th Century. **CONTACT ADDRESS** Archives Administrator, 3 Adrian Circle, Hampton, VA 23669-3814.

POSFAY, EVA
DISCIPLINE LITERATURE OF THE SEVENTEENTH CENTURY **EDUCATION** Princeton, PhD. **CAREER** Literature, Carleton Col. **SELECTED PUBLICATIONS** Auth, L'architecture du pouvoir feminin dans La Princesse de Cleves, Papers French Seventeenth Century Lit. **CONTACT ADDRESS** Carleton Col, 100 S College St., Northfield, MN 55057-4016.

POST, JONATHAN F. S.
PERSONAL Born 05/11/1947, Rochester, NY, m, 1975, 2 children **DISCIPLINE** ENGLISH LITERATURE **EDUCATION** Amherst Col, AB, 70; Univ Rochester, PhD. **CAREER** Asst prof, Yale Univ, 75-79; assoc to full prof, 79- , Dept Chr, 90-93, UCLA, 79-. **HONORS AND AWARDS** NEH fel, 79-80; Guggenheim fel, 84-85. **MEMBERSHIPS** Renaissance Soc Am; Milton Soc Am. **RESEARCH** Renaissance-17th century English literature; modern poetry. **SELECTED PUBLICATIONS** Auth, Henry Vaughn: The Unfolding Vision, Princeton, 82; Sir Thomas Browne, G K Hall, 87; auth, English Lyric Poetry: The Early Seventeenth Century, Routledge, 99; ed George Herbert in the Nineties: Reflections and Reassessments, George Herbert Monogr, 95. **CONTACT ADDRESS** English Dept, Univ of California, Los Angeles, Los Angeles, CA 90095-1530. **EMAIL** Post@humnet.UCLA.edu

POST, ROBERT M.
PERSONAL Born Buckhannon, WV **DISCIPLINE** DRAMATIC ARTS AND SPEECH **EDUCATION** West Virginia Wesleyan Col, BA, 56; Ohio Univ, MA, 58, PhD, 61. **CAREER** From Instr to assistant and assoc prof, Univ of Washington, 60- . **HONORS AND AWARDS** Phi Kappa Phi; Rose Lefcowitz Prize, 92-93. **MEMBERSHIPS** Northwest Commun Asn; Western States Commun Asn; National Commun Asn. **RESEARCH** Performance; literature. **SELECTED PUBLICATIONS** Auth, Politics, Prison, and Poetry: South Africa's Breyten Breytenbach, Poet Lore, 92-93; auth, Salvation or Damnation? Death in the Plays of Edward Albee, Am Drama, 93; auth, Victims in the Writing of Athol Fugard, in Draper, ed, Contemporary Literary Criticism, v.80, Gale, 94; auth, An Audience is an Audience: Gertrude Stein Addresses the Five Hundred, Kentucky Rev, 96. **CONTACT ADDRESS** Dept of Speech Communications, Univ of Washington, PO Box 353415, Seattle, WA 98195. **EMAIL** bobpost@u.washington.edu

POSTER, CAROL
PERSONAL Born 08/05/1956, New York, NY **DISCIPLINE** ENGLISH **EDUCATION** Univ Missouri, PhD 94; E Wash Univ, MFA 92; Hollins College, BA cum laude, 77. **CAREER** Vis fel, 99, Univ Iowa; Assoc Prof, 97-, Montana State Univ; Asst Prof, Assoc Prof, 94 to 98-, Univ N Iowa; Instr, 92-94, Univ Missouri; teach Asst, 90-92, E Wash Univ; Pres, 84-89, Amaryllis Software. **HONORS AND AWARDS** Gildersleeve Prize; MCB Outstanding Contr Auth Recog Awd; George Blocker Pace Awd; G Ellsworth Huggins Doct Schshp; Phi Kappa Phi Hon Soc; Dan Walden Awd; Tanner Humanities Center, Fellow, 00-01. **MEMBERSHIPS** MLA; Rocky Mtn MLA; RSA; ISHR; ASHR; NCA; APA; CAMW&S; CAPNW; ISSN. **RESEARCH** History of Rhetoric, Classical Philosophy, Classical tradition. **SELECTED PUBLICATIONS** Auth, "Ideas of Order in Plato's Dialogues", Phoenix , 99; transl, Aristophanzs' Clands, in D. Slavitt & P. bovie, eds, Aristophanzs 3, Univ of Pennsylvania Press, 99; coed, Letter Writing Manuals from Antiquity to the Present, U S Carolina Press, forthcoming; auth, Phila Epideictic Rhetoric and Epistolary Theory in Late Antiquity, in: coed, Letter Writing Manuals form Antiquity to the Present, Columbia SC, U of S Carolina Press, forthcoming; Re-Positioning Pedagogy: A Feminist Historiography of Aristotle's Rhetorica, Feminist Interpretations of Aristotle, ed, Cynthia Freeland, Univ Pk PA, Penn State U Press, simultaneous hrdcv and pbk editions, 98; auth, Being Time and Definition: Towards a Semiotics of Figural Rhetoric, Philo and Rhetoric, 00; Silence as a Rhetorical Strategy for Neoplatonic Mysticism, Mystics Qtly, 98; Canonicity and the Campus Bookstore: Teaching Victorian Women Writers, Feminist Teach, 97; Aristotle's rhetoric against Rhetoric: Unitarian Reading and Esoteric Hermeneutics, Amer J of Philology, 97; Being and Becoming: Rhetorical Ontology in Early Greek Thought, Philo and Rhetoric, 96; rev, Christopher Lyle Johnston, ed, Theory Text Context, Rhetoric Soc Qtly, 98; Skiing: Faceplants Eggbeaters and Snowsnakes: A Guide to the Ski Bum Lifestyle, Merrillville IN, ICS Books, 95; The Basic Essentials of Alpine Skiing, Merrillville IN, ICS books, 93; Auth poetry, Surrounded by Dangerous Things, CT, Singular Speech Press, 95; auth, Plautus' Stichus in D. Slavitt & Palmer Bovie, eds, Plautus 4, Johns Hopkins UP, 95. **CONTACT ADDRESS** English Dept, Montana State Univ, Bozeman, Bozeman, MT 59717-0230. **EMAIL** poster@english.montana.edu

POSTON, LAWRENCE S.
PERSONAL Born 10/29/1938, Louisville, KY, m, 1966, 2 children **DISCIPLINE** ENGLISH **EDUCATION** Univ Okla, BA, 60; Prince Univ, MA, 62; PhD, 63. **CAREER** Instr, Univ Neb, 63-64; asst prof, 64-67; assoc prof, 67-72; prof, 72-76; assoc sec, AAUP, 69-71; ed, AAUP, 70-75; vis prof, Univ Tulsa, 75-76; prof, Univ Ill, 76-; assoc vice chan, 83-87; sr assoc dean, 96-. **MEMBERSHIPS** MLA; MVSA. **RESEARCH** Victorian literature. **SELECTED PUBLICATIONS** Auth, "Browning's Political Skepticism: Sordello and the Plays," PMLA (73); auth, "The Commercial Motif of the Waverley Novels," ELH (75); auth, "Browning and the Altered Romantic Landscape," in Nature and the Victorian Imagination, eds. U C Knoepflmacher, G B Tennyson (Univ Cal Press, 77); auth, "Three Versions of Victorian Pastoral," Genre (80); auth, "Millites and Millenarians: The Context of Carlyle's 'Signs of the Times,"' Vict Stud (; auth, "'Worlds Not Realized': Words-

worthian Poetry in the 1830's," Tex Stud Lang Lit (86); auth, "Poetry as Pure Act: A Coleridgean Ideal in Early Victorian England," Mod Philo (86); auth, "Beyond the Occult: The Godwinian Nexus of Bulwer's Zanoni," Stud Roman (98); auth, "History in Focus: 1832," in A Companion to Victorian Literature and Culture, ed. Herbert F Tucker (Blackwell, 99). **CONTACT ADDRESS** Dept English, Univ of Illinois, Chicago, 601 South Morgan St, Chicago, IL 60607-7100.

POTEE, NANETTE
DISCIPLINE SPEECH COMMUNICATION **EDUCATION** S Il Univ Carbondale, BS, 84; MS, 91; PhD, 98. **CAREER** TA, S Il Univ, 90-95; vis asst prof, S.I.U., Japan, 95-97; asst prof, NE IL Univ, 98-. **HONORS AND AWARDS** PEW Charitable Trust Awd for Excell in Teaching, 91, 92. **MEMBERSHIPS** Nat Commun Assoc; Int commun Assoc. **RESEARCH** Instructional communication, Intercultural communication, organizational communication, communication education, service learning. **SELECTED PUBLICATIONS** Auth, "Graduate Teaching Assistant (GTA) Concerns and Multiple Role Conflicts: A Longitudinal Study in Teaching Graduate Students to Teach: Engaging the Discipline, ed. T.A. Heenan and K.F. Jerich, Univ of Il, 95. **CONTACT ADDRESS** Dept Speech, Northeastern Illinois Univ, 5500 N Saint Louis Ave, Chicago, IL 60625-4679. **EMAIL** n-potee@neiu.edu

POTHECARY, SARAH
PERSONAL Born 05/10/1958, Trinidad and Tobago, m, 1986, 1 child **DISCIPLINE** CLASSICS **EDUCATION** St Anne's Col, Oxford Univ, BA, 81; Univ Toronto, MA, 89, PhD, 95. **CAREER** Author **RESEARCH** Shrabo; ancient geography. **CONTACT ADDRESS** 117 Lytton Blvd, Toronto, ON, Canada M4R 1L5. **EMAIL** spothecary@aol.com

POTKAY, ADAM S.
PERSONAL Born 01/11/1961, Trenton, NJ, m, 1991, 1 child **DISCIPLINE** ENGLISH **EDUCATION** Cornell Univ, BA, 82; Johns Hopkins Univ, MA, 86; Rutgers Univ, PhD, 90. **CAREER** Teaching Asst, Johns Hopkins Univ, 84-85; Lecturer, Rutgers Univ, 86-88; Vis Lecturer, Univ Aberdeen, 97; Asst prof to Assoc prof, Col of William & Mary, 90-. **HONORS AND AWARDS** Phi Beta Kappa , Va, 97; Alumni Fel Awd, Col of William and Mary, 96; Dissertation Awd, Northeastern Asn of Grad Schools, 93. **MEMBERSHIPS** Am Soc of 18th Century Studies, Hume Soc, AAUP. **RESEARCH** 18th and 19th Century literature and philosophy. **SELECTED PUBLICATIONS** Auth, "Whatever Happened to Happiness?," Philosophy Now, forthcoming; auth, "The Structure of His Sentences is French: Johnson and Hume in the History of English," Language Science, forthcoming; auth, "David Hume: Moral Painter," Studies in Early Modern Philosophy, forthcoming; auth, "Leaving Box Hill: Emma and Theatricality," Romantic Praxis, forthcoming; auth, The Passion for Happiness: Samuel Johnson and David Hume, Cornell Univ Press, 00; auth, An Education of the Delaware: St. Mary's Hall/Doane Academy, 1837-1999, Burlington County Historical Society, 00; auth, The Fate of eloquence in the Age of Hume, Cornell Univ press, 94; ed Black Atlantic Writers of the Eighteenth Century: Living the New Exodus in England and the Americas, St Martin's press, 95; ed, Manners of Reading: Essays in Honor of Thomas R Edwards, Johns Hopkins Univ Press, 92. **CONTACT ADDRESS** Dept English, Col of William and Mary, PO Box 8795, Williamsburg, VA 23187-8795.

POTTER, ROBERT ALONZO
PERSONAL Born 12/28/1934, New York, NY, d, 5 children **DISCIPLINE** DRAMATIC ART **EDUCATION** Pomona College, BA, 56; Clavermont Grad Sch, MA, 63, PhD, 65. **CAREER** Asst Prof, Lectr, Assoc Prof, 66-81, Prof dramatic art, 81-, Univ California Santa Barbara; Instr, 65, Harvey Mudd College. **HONORS AND AWARDS** Fulbright Fel; Harold J Pious Awd; Vis Prof, Univ Kent at Canterbury. **MEMBERSHIPS** Dramatists Guild; SITM; MRDS; MLA; ATHE. **RESEARCH** Medieval and Renaissance drama; Playwriting. **SELECTED PUBLICATIONS** Auth, The Holy Spectacles of Hildegard of Bingen, Euro Medieval Drama, 98; Auth, The Auto da Fe as Medieval Drama, in: Festive Drama, ed Meg Twycross, Cambridge, DS Brewer, 96; EEn Esbattement van s'Menshen Sin en Verganckelijcke Schoonheit, Man's Desire and Fleeting Beauty, ed, Elsa Strietman, co translated, Leeds Medieval Studies, Leeds, Cen for Med Stud, 95; 24 original plays and stage adaptations including, Saint Barbara in the Flesh 95; La Celestina 90; The Lady in the Labyrinth 89; Just Across the Border 82; The Vision of Children 80. **CONTACT ADDRESS** Dept of Dramatic Art, Univ of California, Santa Barbara, Santa Barbara, CA 93106. **EMAIL** potter@humanitas.ucsb.edu

POTTER, TIFFANY
PERSONAL Born Victoria, BC, Canada **DISCIPLINE** ENGLISH **EDUCATION** Univ Victoria, BA, 89; Queen's Univ, MA, 90; PhD, 96. **CAREER** Post-Doc Fel, Univ Alta, 96-98; Lectr, Univ Calgary, 98-99; Lectr, Univ BC, 99-. **HONORS AND AWARDS** SSHRC Post Doc Fel, Univ Alta, 96-98; ASECS-McMaster Fel, Am Soc for 18th Cent Studies, 98; Clark Fel, UCLA, 00; Standard Res Grant, Soc Sci and Humanities Res Coun of Can, 00-03. **MEMBERSHIPS** CSECS; RMMLA; Asn of Can Col and Univ Teachers of English. **RESEARCH** Eighteenth century British and American literature; Libertinism; Gender studies; Henry Fielding; Eliza Haywood; Mary Davys; Elizabeth Cooper; British constructions of indigenous femininity in North America, 1682-1763; (cultural and literary studies). **SELECTED PUBLICATIONS** Auth, "A low but very feeling tone: The Lesbian Continuum and Power Relations in Jane Austen's Emma," in English Studies in Canada, (94): 187-203; auth, "Strategies of Assimilation and Resistance in Witi Ihimaera's 'Dear Miss Mansfield'," World Literature Written in English, (95): 58-74; auth, "A Colonial Source for Cannibalistic Breeding in Swift's 'A Modest Proposal'," Notes and Queries, (99): 347-348; auth, "Glory in the Triumph: The Female Libertine," in TransAtlantic Crossings: Sexuality and Textuality in the Eighteenth Century, (St John's Mem UP, 99), 75-88; auth, "A Certain Sign that he is One of Us: Clarissa's Other Libertines," Eighteenth Century Fiction, (99): 403-420; auth, Honest Sins: Georgian Libertinism and the Plays and Novels of Henry Fielding, McGill-Queen's UP, 99; auth, "Decorous Disruption: The Cultural Voice of Mary Davys," Wigheenth-Century Women,)01): 63-93; auth, "A God-like Sublimity of Passion: Eliza Haywoods Libertine Consistency," in The Eighteenth Century Novel, in press; auth, "The Language of Sexualized Femininity: Gendered Voice in Eliza Haywood's 'Love in Excess' and 'Fantomina'," in Women's Writing, forthcoming. **CONTACT ADDRESS** Dept English, Univ of British Columbia, 397-1873 E Mall, Vancouver, BC, Canada V6T 1Z1. **EMAIL** tiffany_potter@hotmail.com

POTVIN, GILLES E. J.
PERSONAL Born 10/23/1923, Montreal, PQ, Canada **DISCIPLINE** MUSIC, HISTORY **CAREER** Journalist, Le Canada, 46-48; librn, 48-50, public relations, 50-53, radio/TV producer 54-58, dir casting, CBC, 62-65; instr, McGill opera stud, 57; critic, Nouveau Journal, 61; critic, Le Devoir, 61-66; critic, La Presse, 66-70; instr, Can music, Ecole Normale de Musique, 70-71; critic, Le Devoir, 73-89. **HONORS AND AWARDS** Canada 125 Medal; mem, Royal Soc Can; Order Can. **MEMBERSHIPS** CMC Coun (bd mem), 68-77; Jeunesses Musicales (pres, 76-80); Asn des retraites de Radio-Can. **SELECTED PUBLICATIONS** Ed, Canada Music Book, 70-76; Fr ed, Encyclopedia of Music in Canada, 81. **CONTACT ADDRESS** 208 Bloomfield Rd, Outremont, QC, Canada H2V 3R4.

POWELL, BARRY
PERSONAL Born 04/30/1942, Sacramento, CA, m, 1967, 2 children **DISCIPLINE** CLASSICS **EDUCATION** Berkeley Univ, BA, 63, PhD, 70; Harvard, MA, 65. **CAREER** Asst Prof, 69-73, Northern Arizona Univ; Asst, Assoc to Full Prof, 73-. **HONORS AND AWARDS** Woodrow Wilson Nat Fel. **MEMBERSHIPS** Am Philos Asn, Archaeological Institute of Am, Phi Beta Kappa. **RESEARCH** Homer; Mythology; Writing; Egyptology. **SELECTED PUBLICATIONS** Auth, Classical Myth, 2nd ed, 97; A New Companion to Homer, 97; Homer and the Origin of the Greek Alphabet; auth, Classical Myth, 3rd ed, 00. **CONTACT ADDRESS** Dept Classics, Univ of Wisconsin, Madison, 1220 Linden Dr, Madison, WI 53706. **EMAIL** BBPowell@facstaff.wisc.edu

POWELL, JOSEPH E.
PERSONAL Born 01/22/1952, Ellensburg, WA, m, 1988, 1 child **DISCIPLINE** CREATIVE WRITING, AMERICAN POETRY **EDUCATION** Univ Wash, BA, 75; Cen Wash Univ, MA, 78; Univ Ariz, MFA, 81. **CAREER** Asst prof to prof, Cen Wash Univ, 90-. **HONORS AND AWARDS** Quart Rev Bk Awd, 86, 97. **MEMBERSHIPS** AWP. **RESEARCH** Modern Greek Poetry. **SELECTED PUBLICATIONS** Auth, Counting the Change, QRL, 86; auth, Winter Insomnia, Arrowood Books, 93; auth, Getting There, QRL, 97; auth, "Aegean Dialogs," March Street Press (98). **CONTACT ADDRESS** Dept English, Central Washington Univ, 400 East 8th Ave, Ellensburg, WA 98926. **EMAIL** powellj@cwu.edu

POWELL, MICHAEL
PERSONAL Born 02/24/1958, Portsmouth, OH, m, 1988, 1 child **DISCIPLINE** ENGLISH **EDUCATION** Shawnee State Univ, BA, 97; Ohio Univ, MA, 99. **CAREER** Adj Fac to Sen Instructor, Southern State Cmty Col, 99-. **HONORS AND AWARDS** Awarded T.A., Ohio State Univ, 00-01. **MEMBERSHIPS** Shawnee State Univ Paralegal Asn, Credit Committee Chair. **RESEARCH** Communication patterns among blue-colored Appalachians. **CONTACT ADDRESS** Dept Humanities & Fine Arts, Shawnee State Univ, 940 2nd St, Portsmouth, OH 45662-4303. **EMAIL** michaelp@zoomnet.net

POWELL, RONALD R.
PERSONAL Born 05/24/1944, Columbia, MO, m, 1967, 2 children **DISCIPLINE** LIBRARY SCIENCE **EDUCATION** Univ Mo, Columbia, AB, 62-67; Western Mich Univ, Kalamazoo, MS, 67-68; Univ Ill, PhD, 71-76. **CAREER** Libr dir, Univ Charleston, 76-79; asst prof, Univ Mich, 79-86; assoc prof, Univ Mo Columbia, 86-92; dir grad studies, Univ Mo Columbia, 87-90; chemn of libr sci, Univ Mo Columbia, 90-92; prof, Wayne State Univ, 93-; interim dir, Wayne State Univ, 99. **HONORS AND AWARDS** Beta Phi Mu; Who's Who Libry & infor Sciences, 82; Sen Fel, UCLA, 82; Contemporary Authors, 85; Who's Who Midwest, 95-96, 96-97. **MEMBERSHIPS** Am Libry Asn; Asn Col Res Librys; Asn Libry Infor Science Educ Mich Libry Asn. **RESEARCH** Measurement and evaluation of library and information resources and services; education for library and information science; research methods; academic libraries. **SELECTED PUBLICATIONS** Coauth, Basic Reference Sources, a Self-Study Manual, 85; coauth, Success in Answering Reference Questions: Two Studies, 87; auth, art, Report on Russia Project-Moscow, 1996, 97; auth, art, Development of Research Abilities for PhD Students in Library and Information Science, 97; auth, Basic Research Methods for Librarians, 97. **CONTACT ADDRESS** Library and Information Science Program, Wayne State Univ, 106 Kresge Library, Detroit, MI 48202. **EMAIL** ad5328@wayne.edu

POWER, MARY
DISCIPLINE IRISH AND WOMEN'S LITERATURE **EDUCATION** Univ Wis, PhD, 67. **CAREER** Instr, Univ NMex, 67-. **RESEARCH** James Joyce. **SELECTED PUBLICATIONS** Auth, Molly Bloom and Mary Anderson: The Inside Story, Europ Joyce Stud, 90. **CONTACT ADDRESS** Univ of New Mexico, Albuquerque, Albuquerque, NM 87131. **EMAIL** rejoyce@unm.edu

POWERS, ALAN W.
PERSONAL Born 11/15/1944, Springfield, MA, m, 1966, 2 children **DISCIPLINE** ENGLISH LITERATURE **EDUCATION** Amherst Col, BA, 66; Univ Minn, MA, 71; PhD, 76. **CAREER** Teaching asst, Univ of Minn, 66-71; Berkshire Community Col, 71-73; asst to assoc prof, 74-88, prof of English, Bristol Community Col, 88-, chair, 88-92. **HONORS AND AWARDS** Postdoctoral Fel in Renaissance Italian Hist, 79-80; Consultant and onscreen in two poetry films, one Oscar-nominated, Keats and His Nightingale (86); NEMLA bd; Mass Found for Humanities, bd; NEMLA Summer Fel, 96; Whiting Found Fel, 96. **MEMBERSHIPS** Shakespeare Asn of Am, NEMLA, ALSC, ASCAP. **RESEARCH** Shakespeare (law, medicine, social history); Giordano Bruno; Renaissance Italian literature and culture. **SELECTED PUBLICATIONS** Auth, "When the Punishment is a Crime: Arrests of Women in Fall River, 18920-1922," in ed Ryckebusch, Proceedings of the Lizzie Borden Conf, Portland, Me: King Phillip Pub (93); auth, Westport Soundings: Poems and Translations, Westport, Mass (94); auth, "Gallia and Gaul, French and Welsh: Comic Ethnic Slander in Henry the Fifth," in Acting Funny: Comic Theory and Practice in Shakespeare's Plays, ed Frances Teague, London and Toronto: Assoc Univ Presses (94); auth, "Rip Van Angelo Awakens from the Late Elizabethan Sleep to Law Reform, 1604," Open Submission Winning Paper, Shakespeare Asn of Am, 94 Meeting, Albuquerque, Upstart Crow, vol 15 (96): 35-47; transl of Giordano Bruno's Candelaio (under review). **CONTACT ADDRESS** Dept Humanities & Fine Arts, Bristol Comm Col, 777 Elsbree St, Fall River, MA 02720-7307.

POWERS, DORIS BOSWORTH
PERSONAL Born 09/17/1938, Seattle, WA, m, 2 children **DISCIPLINE** MUSICOLOGY **EDUCATION** Univ Wash, BA; Kans State Univ, MM; Univ NC--Chapel Hill, MA, PhD. **CAREER** Inst, mus hist, violin, Sterling Col, 80-83, 74-78; adj prof, Hutchinson Comm Jr Col, 76-78; tchr, mus supvr, Amherst Pub Schs, 62-63. **HONORS AND AWARDS** Phi Beta Kappa **MEMBERSHIPS** Am Musicol Soc; Col Mus Soc; Am String Tchr Asn. **RESEARCH** Late 18th Century: C.P.E. Bach, Johann Nikolaus Forkel **SELECTED PUBLICATIONS** Review of John Christian Bach: Mozart's Friend and Mentor, by Heinz Gartner, Notes 53/1, 96, 70-71; A Bow and A Beautiful Art in the Late Eighteenth Century, Continuo 15/5, 91, 12-14. **CONTACT ADDRESS** 301 Hickory Dr., Chapel Hill, NC 27514. **EMAIL** dbpowers@juno.com

POWNALL, FRANCES SKOCZYLAS
PERSONAL Born 10/17/1963, Sarnia, ON, Canada, m, 1994, 1 child **DISCIPLINE** CLASSICS **EDUCATION** McGill, BA, 85; Univ British Columbia, MA, 87; Univ Toronto, PhD, 93. **CAREER** Lectr, Memorial Univ, Newfoundland, 92-93; asst prof, Univ Alberta, 93- . **HONORS AND AWARDS** Summer scholar, Center for Hellenic Stud, 94. **MEMBERSHIPS** APA; Class Asn of Can; Class Asn of the Can West; Class Asn of the Middle West and South; Vergilian Soc. **RESEARCH** Greek history and historiography; Greek religion; Greek oratory. **SELECTED PUBLICATIONS** Auth, Presbeis Autokratores: Andocides' De Pace, Phoenix, 95; auth, Condemnation of the Impious in Xenophon's Hellenica, Harvard Theol Rev, 98; auth, What Makes A War A Sacred War, Class Views, 98; auth, Shifting Viewpoints in Xenophon's Helenica: The Arginusae Episode, Athenaeum, forthcoming. **CONTACT ADDRESS** Dept of History and Classics, Univ of Alberta, 2-28 Tory, Edmonton, AB, Canada T6G 2H4. **EMAIL** fskoczl@gpu.srv.ualberta.ca

PRAHLAD, SW. ANAND
DISCIPLINE POETRY AND FOLKLORE **EDUCATION** UCLA, PhD, 91. **CAREER** Assoc prof; adj fac, anthropology dept and Black Studies Prog. **HONORS AND AWARDS** Grants to work on the production of multimedia packages for classroom instr. **MEMBERSHIPS** Inst for African Diasporan Literatures and Languages. **SELECTED PUBLICATIONS**

Auth, Hear My Story and Other Poems, Berkeley Poets Workshop, 82; Under His Own Vine and Fig Tree: A Theory of Contextual Meaning in African-American Proverb Speech Acts, Univ Miss Ptes, 96; auth, African-American Proverbs in Context, UP of Miss, 96. **CONTACT ADDRESS** Dept of English, Univ of Missouri, Columbia, 306 Tate Hall, Columbia, MO 65211. **EMAIL** FollyD@missouri.edu

PRATT, JOHN CLARK
PERSONAL Born 08/19/1932, St Albans, VT, m, 1968, 6 children **DISCIPLINE** ENGLISH **EDUCATION** Univ Calif at Berkeley, BA, 54; Columbia Univ, MA, 60; Princeton Univ, PhD, 65. **CAREER** Instr to prof, USAF Acad, 60-74; English Dept Chemn, Colo State Univ, 74-80; prof, Colo State Univ, 80-. **HONORS AND AWARDS** George McClean Harper Fel, Princeton Univ, 63-65; Fulbright Lectureship, Univ Lisbon, 74-75; Fulbright Lectureship, State Univ of Leningrad, 80; Colo Sem Awd, 85; Oliver C. Pennock Awd for Distinguished Services, CSU, 89; Honors Prof Awd, CSU, 89; Golden Apple Awd, CSU, 95; Excellence in the Arts Awd, Vietnam Veterans of Am, 95; John M. Stern Distinguished Prof Awd, CSU, 00; CSU Alumni Distinguished Fac Awd, 00. **MEMBERSHIPS** Vietnam Veterans of Am. **RESEARCH** Vietnam War Literature. **SELECTED PUBLICATIONS** Ed, Ken Kesey's One Flew Over the Cuckoo's Nest, Viking Critical Libr, 73 & Penguin, 96; auth, The Royal Lao Air Force: 1959-70, George W. Dalley, Inc., 95; ed, Graham Greene's The Quiet American, Penguin, 96; auth "Tim O'Brien's Reimagination of Reality: an Exercise in Metafiction," War, Literature, and the Arts (96); auth, "Project Checo," "Poetry," "Film," and "Drama," in The Vietnam Encyclopedia, ed. Spencer Tucker (ABC-Clio, 98); auth, Vietnam Voices: Perspectives on the War Years, Viking Penguin, 84 & Univ Ga Press, 98; ed, Gunning for Ho, Univ Nev Press, 99; auth, "To a God Unknown," and "Journal of a Novel," in The Steinbeck Encyclopedia, ed. Brian Railsback (Greenwood Press, 00). **CONTACT ADDRESS** Dept English, Colorado State Univ, Fort Collins, CO 80523-0001. **EMAIL** jcpratt@lamar.colostate.edu

PRATT, L.
PERSONAL Born 11/24/1960, New York, NY, m, 1988, 2 children **DISCIPLINE** CLASSICAL STUDIES **EDUCATION** Williams Col, BA 82; Univ Michigan, AM 84, PhD 88. **CAREER** Bowdoin Col, vis asst prof, 88-89; Emory Univ, asst prof, assoc prof, 89 to 95-. **HONORS AND AWARDS** BK **MEMBERSHIPS** APA; CA of Midwest and S; WCC; GCA; ACL. **RESEARCH** Ancient Greek and Roman Lang; Literature and Culture. **SELECTED PUBLICATIONS** Auth, Lying and Poetry for Homer to Pindar: Falsehood and Deception in Archaic Greek Poetics, Univ Mich Press, 93; auth, Odyssey: On the Interpretations of Dreams and Signs in Homer, Classical Philos, 94; auth, The Seal of Theognis Writing and the Oral Poetry, Amer Jour of Philo, 95. **CONTACT ADDRESS** Dept of Classics, Emory Univ, 404 D Callaway Cen North, Atlanta, GA 30322. **EMAIL** lpratt@emory.edu

PRATT, LINDA RAY
PERSONAL Born 02/03/1943, New Orleans, LA, m, 1969 **DISCIPLINE** ENGLISH **EDUCATION** Florida Southern Col, BA, 65; MA, 66, PhD, 71, Emory Univ. **CAREER** Asst Prof to Prof, 68-, Univ Nebraska-Lincoln; Dept Chair, 92-00; Interm Dean of Arts and Science, 00. **HONORS AND AWARDS** Distinguished Teaching Award, 88; National Pres of AAUP, 92-94; Fl Southern Col Alumni Award, 95; Emory Univ Alumni Award, 00; Ed Board of Profession, 00-; Exec Comt of Asn of Depts of English (ADE), 00-02. **MEMBERSHIPS** Modern Languages Asn, ADE, AAUP. **RESEARCH** Victorian and Modern Poetry, higher education. **SELECTED PUBLICATIONS** Auth, Matthew Arnold Revisited, 00; essays in Higher Education Under Fire; Will Teach for Food; Victorian Studies, Victorian Poetry; Academe. **CONTACT ADDRESS** Dept of English, Univ of Nebraska, Lincoln, Lincoln, NE 68588. **EMAIL** lpratt@unlserve.unl.edu

PRATT, LOUIS HILL
PERSONAL Born 08/11/1937, Savannah, GA, m **DISCIPLINE** ENGLISH **EDUCATION** Savannah State College, BS (cum Laude), 1958; Columbia Univ Teacher Coll, MA, 1967; Florida State University, Tallahassee, PhD, 1974. **CAREER** Public School State of Georgia, teacher, 58-62, 64-69; US Army Air Def Command, operations assistant, 62-64; Florida A&M University, Language Dept, instr, 69-74; Florida A&M University, Freshman Comp Dept of Language & Lit, asst professor & director, 74-75; Florida A&M University, Department of English, Prof of English, 75-. **HONORS AND AWARDS** Recipient NDEA Fellowship, Florida State University, 1972-74; J Russell Reaver Awd, Florida State University, best creative scholarship in American Literature in dissertation, 1974-75; National Endowment for the Humanities Stipend to attend Afro-Amer Culture Inst, Univ of Iowa, 1977; Man of the Year Awd, Alpha Phi Alpha, 1979; Presidential Medallion, Excellence from the Savannah State Univ Natl Alumni Assn, 1990; Teacher of the Year, 1994; Advanced Teacher of the Year, Florida A&M University, 1995. **MEMBERSHIPS** Life member, College Language Association; Alpha Phi Alpha; pres, Middle Atlantic Writers Assn, 1994-96; charter member, Seven Hills Toastmasters Club. **CONTACT ADDRESS** English Dept, Florida A&M Univ, Rm 414, Tucker Hall, Tallahassee, FL 32307-4800.

PRATT, MINNIE BRUCE
DISCIPLINE ENGLISH LITERATURE **EDUCATION** Univ Ala, BA, 68; Univ NCar, PhD, 79 **CAREER** Asst prof, Shaw Univ, 80-82; adj lectr, George Wash Univ, 84-88; vis asst prof, Univ Md, 85-86; adj asst prof, Vermont Col, 85-86; adj prof, Univ Md, 86-87; writer-in-res, Community Writers' Proj, 88; vis asst prof, Univ Md, 89-90; writer-in-res, The Lit Fest at St Mary's Col, 99; fac, The Grad Sch of the Union Inst, 90- . **HONORS AND AWARDS** Gay and Lesbian Bk Awd, 91, 00; Simpson Arnow Prize Poetry. **RESEARCH** Women's studies; intersections of race, class, and gender; Renaissance and seventeenth century literature. **SELECTED PUBLICATIONS** Auth, The Sound of One Fork, 81; co-auth, Yours in Struggle: Three Feminist Perspectives on Anti-Semitism and Racism, 84; auth, We Say We Love Each Other, 85; auth, Crime Against Nature, 90; auth, Rebellion: Essays 1980-1991, 92; auth, S/HE, 95; auth, Walking Back Up Depot Street, 99. **CONTACT ADDRESS** English Dept, Union Inst, 440 E McMillan St, Cincinnati, OH 45206-1925. **EMAIL** mbpratt@tui.edu

PRELOCK, PATRICIA A.
PERSONAL Born 05/31/1954, Youngstown, OH, 1 child **DISCIPLINE** SPEECH-LANGUAGE PATHOLOGY **EDUCATION** Kent State Univ, BS, 76, MA, 77; Univ of Pittsburgh, PhD, 83. **CAREER** Grad, res and teaching asst, Kent State Univ, 76-79; speech-lang pathologist, 76-79; instr, Univ of Pittsburgh, 81-82; transdisciplinary team mem/lang consult, Children's Hosp of Pittsburgh, 82-83; dir of clinical assessment and vpres of res & assessment serv, Transact Health Systems, Monroeville, Penn, 84-85; clinical supvr/researcher, Univ of Pittsburgh, 85-86; asst prof, Col of St Rose, 86-87; transdisciplinary team mem/lang consult, Cincinatti Ctr for Developmental Disorders, 88-90; adj, vis and res asst prof, Univ of Cincinnati, 88-94; assoc prof, Univ of Vermont, 94-; Full Prof, Univ of VT. **HONORS AND AWARDS** Alpha Lambda Delta, Kent State Univ, 73; City of Akron Panhellic Scholar, 74; Who's Who in Cols and Univs, 74-76; Mortar Bd, Kent State Univ, 75; Pierce Mem Award for Speech, Kent State Univ, 75; Magna Cum Laude, Kent State Univ, 76; Doctoral Fel, Univ of Pittsburgh, 80-82; Delta Epsilon Sigma, Col of St Rose, 87; ASHA Award for Continuing Educ, 88, 94; 97, 99; Who's Who Among Human Service Professionals, 88-89; Nat Distinguished Serv Registry: Speech, Lang & Hearing, 90; SWOSHA Honors of the Asn, 94; Who's Who Among Educ Professionals, 94-96; Friends Award, Vermont Parent Infor Ctr, 98. **MEMBERSHIPS** Autism Soc of Am; Austin Soc of VT, Coun of Supvrs in Speech-Lang Pathology & Audiology; Vermont Asn for Supv & Curric Develop; Nat Asn for Supv & Curric Develop; Vermont Speech & Hearing Asn; VT Austin Task Force, Coun for Exceptional Children; Int Clinical Phonetics & Ling Asn; Am Speech, Lang and Hearing Asn. **RESEARCH** Child language, especially assessment and intervention; phonological intervention; efficacy of service delivery models; autism. **SELECTED PUBLICATIONS** Auth, A proactive approach for managing the language/learning needs of the communication-impaired preScher, in Clinics in Commun Disorders 3, 93; Communication Science Resource Manual, 94; Rethinking collaboration: A speech-language pathology perspective, in J of Educational and Psychological Consultation 6, 95; Assessment of young children: Making connections for families, in HEARSAY 10, 96; Language-based curriculum analysis: A collaborative assessment and intervention process, in J of Childhood Commun Disorders 19, 97; Where are associations going as the millennium approaches?, in ASHA Spec Interest Div 1 Lang, Learning & Educ Newsletter 5, 98; coauth, Metapragmatic awareness of explanation adequacy: Developing skills for academic success from a collaborative communications skills unit, in Lang, Speech, Hearing Servs in Schs 25, 94; Teacher Perceptions of Communication-Impaired Students, in Lang, Speech, Hearing Servs in Schs 25, 94; Collaboration in supervision: The First Year, in J of Childhood Commun Disorders 16, 95; Language regression in children with autism, in J of Autism 25, 95; Effects of collaboration on language performance, in J of Childhood Commun Disorders 17, 95; Collaborative partnerships in a language in the classroom program, in Lang, Speech, Hearing Servs in Schs 26, 95; Prosodic analysis of child speech, in Topics in Lang Disorders 17, 97; Foreword, in Topics in Lang Disorders 17, 97; Maintenance of Metapragmatic Awareness of Explanation Adequacy Six Months Following Intervention, in Lang, Speech Hearing Servs in Schs 28, 97; rev, Communication skills in children with Down Syndrome: A book review, in Down Syndrome Quart 2, 97; ed, Special Interest Division 1 Newsletter, Language Learning & Education, 96, 97, 98, 99; coed, Topics in Language Disorders, 97; Speech and Language Development in rev course for OESPA, 95; Language, Speech, Hearing Services in Schs, 98-01; ed, Role of Related Services Personnel in Inclusive Schools; auth, A Model for family-centered Interdisciplinary Practice, Topics in Language Disorders, 99; chapter in, Restructuring for effective and caring education, 00. **CONTACT ADDRESS** Dept of Communication Sciences, Univ of Vermont, 489 Main St, 407 Pomeroy Hall, Burlington, VT 05405-0024. **EMAIL** pprelock@zoo.uvm.edu

PRENSHAW, PEGGY
DISCIPLINE SOUTHERN LITERATURE, AMERICAN LITERATURE **EDUCATION** Univ of Tex, Austin, PhD, 70. **CAREER** Fred C. Frey Prof, La State Univ; Ed, 73-91, adv ed, Southern Quart, 92-; gen ed, Lit Conversations series, 84-; secy-treas, Conf of Eds of Learned J, 84-87; ch, Miss Hum Coun, 86-87; adv ed, J of Fla Lit, 89-; Pres, Soc for the Stud of Southern Lit, 90-92; bd of LEH, 92-95; exec comt, SCMLA, 93-95. **HONORS AND AWARDS** NEH grant, 86; outstanding spec issue prize (Southern Quart), CELJ, 86; guest lectr, Gorky Inst, Moscow, 90; Charles Frankel prize, NEH, 94. **MEMBERSHIPS** Pres, Soc for the Stud of Southern Lit, 90-92; pres, Eudora Welty Soc, 93-95. **RESEARCH** Autobiographical writings of Southern women; Eudora Welty. **SELECTED PUBLICATIONS** Auth, Sex and Wreckage in the Parlor: Welty's'Bye-Bye Brevoort,' Southern Quart, 95; The True Happenings of My Life: Reading Southern Women Autobiographers, in Haunted Bodies: Rethinking the South through Gender, 97; The Construction of Confluence: The Female South and Eudora Welty's Art, in The Late Novels of Eudora Welty, 97; ed, More Conversations with Eudora Welty, 96. **CONTACT ADDRESS** Dept of Eng, Louisiana State Univ and A&M Col, 237C Allen Hall, Baton Rouge, LA 70803. **EMAIL** enpren@unix1.sncc.lsu.edu

PRESCOTT, ANNE L.
PERSONAL Born 01/19/1936, New York, NY, m, 1957, 2 children **DISCIPLINE** ENGLISH **EDUCATION** Barnard Col, BA, 59; Columbia Univ, MA, 61; PhD, 67. **CAREER** Asst prof to prof, Barnard Col, 67-; Helen Goodhart Altschul Prof, 98-. **HONORS AND AWARDS** Phi Beta Kappa. **MEMBERSHIPS** Renaissance Soc of Am; Spenser Soc. **RESEARCH** Spenser, Renaissance Satire, Anglo-French relations, psalms, early modern women. **SELECTED PUBLICATIONS** Auth, French Poets and the Renaissance, Yale, 78; coed, The Norton Critical Edition of Spenser, Norton, 93; coed, Spenser Studies: A Renaissance Poetry Annual, AMS Pr; auth, Imagining Robelais in Renaissance England, Yale 98; coed, Female and Male Voices in Early Modern England, Columbia, 00; coed, Approaches to Teaching Shorter Elizabethan Poetry, MLA, 00; auth, "The Evolution of Tudor Satire", The Cambridge Companion to English Literature 1500-1600, ed Arthur Kinney, Cambridge, 00; auth, "Foreign Policy in Fairyland", Spencer Studies 14, 00. **CONTACT ADDRESS** Dept English, Columbia Univ, 3009 Broadway, New York, NY 10027-6501.

PRESTON, CATHY L.
PERSONAL Born 05/18/1952, CO, m, 1978, 2 children **DISCIPLINE** ENGLISH **EDUCATION** Univ Colo at Boulder, BA, PhD. **CAREER** Instr, Univ of Colo Boulder, 86-. **MEMBERSHIPS** Am Folklore Soc; MLA. **RESEARCH** Women's Literature, American Folklore, 18th and 19th Century Brit Literature, Women's Vernacular Culture. **SELECTED PUBLICATIONS** Auth, The Other Print Tradition, Garland, 95; auth, Folklore, Literature, and Cultural Theory, Garlane, 95. **CONTACT ADDRESS** Dept English, Univ of Colorado, Boulder, PO Box 226, Boulder, CO 80309-0226. **EMAIL** prestonc@stripe.colorado.edu

PRESTON, JOAN M.
DISCIPLINE COMMUNICATIONS **EDUCATION** Univ W Ontario, PhD. **CAREER** Prof, Brock Univ. **RESEARCH** Virtual reality, multimedia, media reality and fantasy, television. **SELECTED PUBLICATIONS** Auth, TV reality: The truth and nothing but?, Intl Commun Assn Conf, 95; co-auth, Selective viewing: Cognition, personality and TV genres, Brit Jour Soc Psychol, 94; Integration in personal constructions of television, Intl Jour Personal Construct Psychol, 90. **CONTACT ADDRESS** Dept of Communications Studies, Brock Univ, 500 Glenridge Ave, Saint Catharines, ON, Canada L2S 3A1. **EMAIL** jpreston@spartan.ac.brocku.ca

PRESTON, KATHERINE K.
PERSONAL Born 12/07/1950, Hamilton, OH, m, 1 child **DISCIPLINE** HISTORY OF MUSIC **EDUCATION** Evergreen State Col, BA, 71; Univ Maryland, MM, 81; CUNY, PhD, 89. **CAREER** ASSOC PROF, MUS, COLL WM & MARY **HONORS AND AWARDS** Various Fellowships. **MEMBERSHIPS** Am Antiquarian Soc, Soc for Am Music, Am Musicological Soc, College Music Soc. **RESEARCH** History of Music in the United States Emp 19th century, Music & Theatre in U.S. **SELECTED PUBLICATIONS** Auth, articles for New Grove Dictionary of American Music; auth, "Popular Music in the Gilded Age," Popular Music: A Year Book, 85; auth, Music for Hire: The Working Journeyman Musicians in Washington, DC 1875-1900, Pendragon Press, 92; auth, Opera on the Road: Traveling Opera Troupes in the United States, 1820-1860, Univ Ill Press, 93; consult ed/auth on itinerant opera companies for New Grove Dictionary of Opera, Macmillan Press, 93; auth, "Antebellum Concert-Giving and Opera-Singing: The Triumphant 1838-1840 American Tour by Jane Shereff and John Umlson, British Vocal Stars," in American Musical Life in Context and Practice to 1865, Garland, 94; coauth, The Mulligan Guard Ball and Reilly and the 400, in Nineteenth- Century : American Musical Theater, Garland, 94; auth, bibliog entries, American National Biography, Oxford Univ Press; auth, "The Development of Art Music in the United States, 1800-1865," in The Cambridge History of American Music, Cambridge Univ Press. **CONTACT ADDRESS** Dept of Music, Col of William and Mary, Williamsburg, VA 23185. **EMAIL** kkpres@wm.edu

PRETTIMAN, C. A.
PERSONAL Born 08/09/1968, Greensburg, PA, m, 1998 **DISCIPLINE** LITERATURE **EDUCATION** Pa State Univ, BA, 89, MA, 90; Princeton Univ, PhD, 95 **CAREER** Teaching asst, 89-90, Pa St Univ; asst, 90-94, Princeton Univ; asst prof, 94-96, Cedar Crest Col; vis asst prof, 95, 96, Muhlenberg Col & Allentown Col of St Francis de Sales; asst prof, chair, asst dir, 96-, Cedar Crest Col; assoc prof, 00-; Exec Comt ch. **HONORS AND AWARDS** Univ Scholar Prog, 87-90; Samuel P Bayard Award for Excellence in Camparative Lit; Phi Beta Kappa, 89; Mary Cross Fel, 90; Andrew W Mellon Found Grant, 95-97; Culpeper Found Grant, 98; Culpeper Found Grant, 99, 00. **MEMBERSHIPS** Modern Lang Asn; Am Comparative Lit Asn; Renaissance Soc Am; Asn Literary Scholars & Critics; Discussion Group for the Study of Celtic Languages and Literatures. **RESEARCH** European Baroque era; Celtic lang & lit; modernism. **SELECTED PUBLICATIONS** Auth, John Dryden's Dramatic Theory and Its Debts to the Spanish Comedia; Renaissance Soc Amer, 96; art, The English Segismundo: Aphra Behn's The Young King, Amer Comparative Lit Assoc; 97; art, The Laws of Hywel Dda and the Portrayal of Women in Medieval Welsh Literature, Modern Lang Assoc, 97; art, The Influence of the Commedia dell'arte on the Early plays of Lope de Vega, Renaissance Soc Amer, 98; art, Micheal O Coileain, Sewanee Review, 98; auth, Literature that Changed the World: Designing an Undergraduate World Literature Course," 00; Annual conference of the North American Association for the Study of Welsh Culture and History, Bryn Mawr Univ, 00; auth, "Dryden, Behn, Wycherly and the Politics of Plagiarism in English Drama, 1660-1680," 00; auth, "Literature thaat Changed the World: Designing an Undergraduate World Literature Course," 00; auth, "Fernan Perez de Guzman," and "The Picaresque Novel," in The Encyclopedia of Life Writing, Margaretta Jolly, ed., (London: Fitzroy Dearborn Publishers, 01). **CONTACT ADDRESS** 100 College Dr, Allentown, PA 18104. **EMAIL** CPrettiman@aol.com

PREUSSNER, ARNOLD
PERSONAL Born 07/21/1945, Chicago, IL, m, 1973, 1 child **DISCIPLINE** ENGLISH **EDUCATION** Luther Col, BA, 67; Univ Colo, Boulder, MA, 69; PhD, 77. **CAREER** Asst/Assoc Prof, Yonkton Col, 78-84; Instr, Asst Prof, Univ of Kans, 85-88; Assoc Prof to Prof, Truman State Univ, 88-. **HONORS AND AWARDS** NDEA Fel, Univ of Colo Boulder, 67-69, 71-72; NEH Fel, Brown Univ, 81-82; Lit Prize, Univ of Southern Calif, 87; Sixteenth Century Studies Conf, 98. **MEMBERSHIPS** MLA, Shakespeare Asn of Am, Sixteenth Century Studies Conf, Nat Coun of Teachers of English, Am Asn of Univ Prof. **RESEARCH** Brit Renaissance Drama, Shakespeare, Film and Stage Comedy. **SELECTED PUBLICATIONS** Auth, "Language and Society in Jonson's 'Epicoene'," Thoth 15,2 (75): 9-20; auth, "Chapman's Anti-festive Comedy: Generic Subversion and Classical Allusion in 'The Widow's tears'," Iowa State J of Res 59 (85): 263-272; auth, "Woody Allen's 'The Purple Rose of Cairo' and the Genres of Comedy," Lit/Film Quart 16,1 (88): 39-43; auth, "Waiting in 'Hamlet' and 'Twelfth Night'," Hamlet Studies 10, 1-2 (88): 95-103; auth, "Countergenre and Performance: 'Twelfth Night'," in A Humanist's Legacy: Essays in Honor of John C. Bale, ed. Dennis M. Jones (Decorah: Luther Col, 90), 16-25; auth, "The Actaeon Myth in Ovid, Petrarch, Wyatt, and Sidney," Bestia 5 (93): 95-108; auth, "Re-Staging Jonson's 'The New Inn'," PMPA: Publ of Mo Philol Asn 18 (93): 1-7; auth, "Reading the Hunting/Temptation Sequence in 'Sir Gawain and the Green Knight'," Bestia 6 (94): 27-39; auth, "Tourneur's 'The Atheist's Tragedy' in Performance," PMPA: Publ of Mo Philol Asn 21 (96): 69-76; auth, "Shakespearean Criticism and the Uses of Theory," Sixteenth Century J 27 (96): 135-144. **CONTACT ADDRESS** Dept Lang and Lit, Truman State Univ, 100 E Normal St, Kirksville, MO 63501-4200. **EMAIL** LLGI@truman.edu

PREVOTS, NAIMA
PERSONAL Born 05/27/1935, NY, m, 1979, 2 children **DISCIPLINE** DANCE **EDUCATION** Brooklyn Coll, BA 55; Univ Wis, MA 60; Univ S CA, PhD 83. **CAREER** Performer, Choreographer, Tchr, free lance, 55-67; Am Univ, 67-83; Hollywood Museum Dir 83-88; Am Univ, ch 88. **HONORS AND AWARDS** Fulbright fellow; NEH; Phi Beta Kappa. **MEMBERSHIPS** Phi Delta Kappa; CORD; SDHS; NDE. **RESEARCH** 20th Century cult hist, mainly Am. **SELECTED PUBLICATIONS** Dance for Export: Cultural Diplomacy and the Cold War, Univ Press New Eng, 98; American Pageantry: A Movement for Art and Democracy, UMI Press, 90; Dancing in the Sun; Hollywood Choreographers 1915-1937, UMI Press, 87; Benjamin Zemach, Ballet Rev, 98. **CONTACT ADDRESS** Dept of Performing Arts, American Univ, 4400 Massachusetts Ave NW, Washington, DC 20016. **EMAIL** prevots@american.edu

PRICE, ALAN
PERSONAL Born 05/11/1943, Rushville, IN, m, 1998 **DISCIPLINE** ENGLISH, AMERICAN LITERATURE **EDUCATION** Earlham Col, BA, 65; Penn State Univ, MA, 66; Univ of Rochester, PhD, 76. **CAREER** INSTR, 66-76, ASST PROF OF ENGLISH, 76-88, ASSOC PROF OF ENGLISH, 88-97, PROF OF ENGLISH, 97-, PENN STATE UNIV. **HONORS AND AWARDS** NEH Summer Seminar fels, 80 & 87; NEH Travel to Collections grants, 85 & 91; twice elected Hazleton Campus Teacher of the Year, Penn State; George W. Atherton Awd for Excellence in Teaching, Penn State, 91; profiled in Who's Who in the World and Who's Who in the East; listed in Who's Who in America. **MEMBERSHIPS** MLA; Am Studies Asn; Nat Coun of Teachers of English; Col English Asn; Edith Whaton Soc; Am Lit Soc. **RESEARCH** American Literature; Edith Wharton; World War I. **SELECTED PUBLICATIONS** Auth, The End of the Age of Innocence: Edith Wharton and the First World War, St Martin's Press, 96; auth, Far More Than They Know: Current Wharton Studies, Review, Univ of Va Press, 97; auth, Frank Tuohy, British Short-Fiction Writers 1945-1980, The Dictionary of Literary Biography Vol 139, Gale Research Inc, Bruccoli Clark Layman, 94; auth, Dorothy Canfield Fisher, The Oxford Companion to Women's Writing in the United States, Oxford Univ Press, 94; auth, Literature, The Artworld and Its Audience: Art as Kaleidoscope, Haven Press, 93; co-ed & contribur, Wretched Exotic: Essays on Edith Wharton in Europe. **CONTACT ADDRESS** Pennsylvania State Univ, Hazleton, Hazleton, PA 18201. **EMAIL** pym@psu.edu

PRICE, BERNADETTE B.
PERSONAL Born 03/07/1959, White Plains, NY **DISCIPLINE** AMERICAN LITERATURE **EDUCATION** Manhatlunville Col , M Liberal Arts. **CAREER** Sr Mngr, Orbis Books, NY. **HONORS AND AWARDS** Cath Press Asn Awd of Merit; Special Promotion. **MEMBERSHIPS** Cath Book Publishers Asn; Asn Theol Booksllers. **RESEARCH** 19th Century American Short Stories. **CONTACT ADDRESS** Orbis Books, Box 308, Maryknoll, NY 10545-0308. **EMAIL** bpnce@maryknoll.org

PRICE, DANIELLE E.
PERSONAL Born 04/05/1966, Baudette, MN, m, 1998, 1 child **DISCIPLINE** BRITISH LITERATURE **EDUCATION** Univ Ottawa, BA, 88; MA, 89; Univ Calif Los Angeles, PhD, 96. **CAREER** Vis asst prof, Col of the Holy Cross, 97-00. **MEMBERSHIPS** MLA. **RESEARCH** Nineteenth-Century British Literature and Culture, Childhood Studies. **SELECTED PUBLICATIONS** Auth, "Cultivating Mary: The Victorian Secret Garden," Children's Lit Assoc Quart, (01). **CONTACT ADDRESS** 929 Princeton Rd, Berkley, MI 48072. **EMAIL** deprice22@hotmail.com

PRICE, DAVID C.
DISCIPLINE COMMUNICATION STUDIES **EDUCATION** ID State Univ, BA, 87, MA, 88;Univ UT, PhD, 97. **CAREER** Asst prof commun studies, Doane Col, 93-. **HONORS AND AWARDS** Robert F. Kennedy Minority News Awd. **MEMBERSHIPS** Nat Commun Asn; Western States Commun Asn; Soc Prof Jour; Nebr Col Media Asn. **RESEARCH** Commun in Crises; Rhetorical Commun in the News Media; Organizational Commun in Newsrooms; Commun Silence. **SELECTED PUBLICATIONS** Auth, The Death of Partisanship in Idaho? A Rhetorical Analysis of the 1986 Gubernatorial Election, Idaho State Univ, 88. **CONTACT ADDRESS** Commun Studies Dept, Doane Col, Boswell Ave, PO Box 1014, Crete, NE 68333. **EMAIL** dprice@doane.edu

PRIDGEN, ALLEN
PERSONAL Born 10/16/1943, Portsmouth, VA, m, 1972, 1 child **DISCIPLINE** ENGLISH **EDUCATION** Univ NC, Chapel Hill, AB, 65; E Carolina Univ, MA, 68; Fla State Univ, PhD, 75. **CAREER** Asst prof, William and Mary, 71-77; prof, Chowan Col, 79-87; prof, chair, Va Intermong Col, 87-. **HONORS AND AWARDS** Vis Scholar, Univ NC Chapel Hill, 98. **MEMBERSHIPS** S Atlantic Mod Lang Assoc; Soc for the Study of S Lit; Christianity and Lit Assoc. **RESEARCH** Literature of the American South. **SELECTED PUBLICATIONS** Auth, "Going Home: James Dickey's South", Studies in Popular Cult 1 (77):16-25; rev, of "The Habit of Being: Letters of Flannery O'Connor" in The News and Observer, May 79; rev, of "Alnilam" by James Dickey, Virginian-Pilot, June 87; rev, of "The Edge of the Swamp: A Study in the Literature and Society of the Old South" by Louis Rubin, Virginian-Pilot, June 89; rev, of "The House of Percy", by Bertram Wyatt-Brown, Virginian-Pilot, Dec 94; auth, "Up in His Head: Orbit and Sacrament in Walker Percy's The Thanatos Syndrome", S quarterly 34.1 (Fall 95):32-38; auth, "The Brownian Leaves: Sacramental Presence in Walker Percy's The Last Gentleman", Renascence 48.2 (Summer 96):297-308; auth, "Nature as Sacrament in Walker Percy's The Second Coming", Miss Quarterly 51.1 (Winter 97-98):3-13; auth, Walker Percy's Sacramental Landscapes: The Search in the Desert, Susquehanna Univ Pr, 00. **CONTACT ADDRESS** Dept Arts and Sci, Virginia Intermont Col, 1013 Moore St, Bristol, VA 24201-4225. **EMAIL** apridgen@vic.edu

PRIEBE, RICHARD K.
PERSONAL Born 10/10/1942, Philadelphia, PA, m, 1969, 1 child **DISCIPLINE** ENGLISH **EDUCATION** Franklin and Marshall Col, BA, 64; Univ Mich, Ann Arbor, MA, 68; Univ Tex, PhD, 73; Va Commonwealth Univ, BA,00. **CAREER** Asst prof to prof, Va Commonwealth Univ, 73-. **HONORS AND AWARDS** Grant, Soc Sci Research Coun and Am Coun of Learned Soc, 87. **MEMBERSHIPS** African Lit Assoc; MLA; African Studies Assoc; Am Folklore Soc. **RESEARCH** West African literature, folklore and popular culture. **SELECTED PUBLICATIONS** Coed, The Teaching of African Literature, Univ of Texas Pr, 77; coed, Artist and Audience: African Literature as Shared Experience, Three Continents Pr, (Washington, DC), 79; auth, Ghanaian Literature, Greenwood Pr, (Westport, CT), 88; auth, Myth, Realism, and the West African Writer, Africa World Pr, (Trenton, NJ), 88. **CONTACT ADDRESS** Dept English, Virginia Commonwealth Univ, PO Box 842005, Richmond, VA 23284-2005. **EMAIL** rpriebe@vcu.edu

PRIEVE, BETH A.
DISCIPLINE COMMUNICATION SCIENCES AND DISORDERS **EDUCATION** Univ OH, PhD, 89. **CAREER** Asst prof CCC-A, Syracuse Univ. **RESEARCH** Physiological auditory functions and their clinical applications; evoked otoacoustic emissions, electrocochleography and auditory brainstem responses; diagnostic audiology; identification of hearing loss in infants and children. **SELECTED PUBLICATIONS** Auth, COAEs and SSOAEs in Adults with Increased Age, Ear and Hearing, 95;. Otoacoustic Emissions in Infants and Children: Basic Characteristics and Clinical Applications, Sem Hearing, 92; coauth, Analysis of Transient-evoked Otoacoustic Emissions in Normal-hearing and Hearing-impaired Ears, Jour Acoustical Soc Am, 93. **CONTACT ADDRESS** Syracuse Univ, Syracuse, NY 13244.

PRINCE, SUSAN
PERSONAL Born 06/26/1964, Wilmington, DE, m, 1999 **DISCIPLINE** CLASSICS **EDUCATION** Yale Univ, BA, 86; Oxford Univ, BA, 89; Univ of Mich, PhD, 97. **CAREER** Vis asst prof, Mich State Univ, 97-98; asst prof, Univ of Colo, 98. **HONORS AND AWARDS** Distinguished Diss Awd, Univ of Mich, 97. **MEMBERSHIPS** Am Philolol Assoc; Class Assoc of the Middle West and South; Women Class Caucas; Soc of Ancient Greek Philos. **RESEARCH** Intellectual history, philosophy, rhetoric, fiction. **SELECTED PUBLICATIONS** Auth, "Ajax, Odysseus, and the Act of Self-Representation", Ancient Philos 19, (99): 55-64. **CONTACT ADDRESS** Dept Classics, Univ of Colorado, Boulder, Boulder, CO 80309. **EMAIL** susan.prince@colorado.edu

PRINEAS, MATTHEW L.
DISCIPLINE ENGLISH LITERATURE **EDUCATION** Univ Rochester, PhD, 95. **CAREER** Asst prof, Idaho State Univ. **RESEARCH** Textual criticism; history and theory of rhetoric; Bible; Renaissance prosody. **SELECTED PUBLICATIONS** Auth, pubs on Henry Vaughan, Anna Trapnel, Andrew Marvell. **CONTACT ADDRESS** Dept of English and Philosophy, Idaho State Univ, Pocatello, ID 83209. **EMAIL** prinmatt@isu.edu

PRIOLI, CARMEN A.
PERSONAL Born 01/04/1946, Boston, MA, m, 1978, 2 children **DISCIPLINE** ENGLISH **EDUCATION** Suffolk Univ, BA, 68; Boston Col, MA, 71; SUNY Stony Brook, PhD, 75. **CAREER** Vis asst prof, SUNY Stony Brook, 75-76; lect, Boston Univ, Tufts Univ, 76; asst, assoc, prof, NCSU, 77-. **HONORS AND AWARDS** Outstand Ex Ser Awd, NCSU; Outstand Teach Awd, NCSU. **MEMBERSHIPS** SAMLA; SEA. **RESEARCH** American literature; history; popular culture; folkways. **SELECTED PUBLICATIONS** Auth, The Poems of Gen George S Patton, Jr, 92; auth, Hope for a Good Season: The Ca'e Bankers of Harkers Island, 98. **CONTACT ADDRESS** Dept English, No Carolina State Univ, Box 8105, Raleigh, NC 27695-0001.

PRIOR, SANDRA PIERSON
DISCIPLINE MEDIEVAL LITERATURE **EDUCATION** Wellesley Col, BA, 62; Columbia Univ, MA, 77, PhD, 83. **CAREER** Dir, compos; instr, NYU; Queens Col; prof, 77-. **HONORS AND AWARDS** Ed, Envoi. **RESEARCH** Guide for teaching logic and rhetoric. **SELECTED PUBLICATIONS** Auth, articles, Jour of Medieval and Renaissance Stud; Mod Philol; Jour Eng and Ger Philol; monogr, Twayne Authors Series; The Fayre Formez of the Pearl Poet, Mich State UP. **CONTACT ADDRESS** Dept of Eng, Columbia Col, New York, 2960 Broadway, New York, NY 10027-6902.

PRITCHARD, SUSAN V.
PERSONAL Born 09/12/1943, Appleton, WI, m, 1994, 4 children **DISCIPLINE** LIBRARY SCIENCE **EDUCATION** Univ Ariz, MLS, 89; Ariz State Univ, BA, 95. **CAREER** Dir, Devry Inst of Technol, 89-. **HONORS AND AWARDS** ASU Acad Scholar; 1st recipient of $5000 scholar to obtain MLS. **MEMBERSHIPS** ALA; SLA; Ariz State Library Asn; Central Ariz Library Cooperative. **CONTACT ADDRESS** Devry Inst of Tech, 2149 W Dunlap Ave, Phoenix, AZ 85021. **EMAIL** spritchard@devry-phx.edu

PRITCHARD, WILLIAM H.
PERSONAL Born 11/12/1932, Binghamton, NY, m, 1957, 3 children **DISCIPLINE** ENGLISH **EDUCATION** Amherst Col, BA, 53; Columbia Univ, 54; Harvard Univ, MA, 56; PhD, 60. **CAREER** Henry Clay Folger prof, Amherst Col, 58- .

HONORS AND AWARDS Phi Beta Kappa; Guggenheim fel, 73-74; ACLS fel, 63-64, 77-78; NEH fel, 77-78, 86; script writer for "Robert Frost: A Question of Place" (NPR), 78; Under Critcism: Essays for William H. Pritchard, 98. **MEMBERSHIPS** Asoc of Lit Scholars and Critics. **RESEARCH** English and American poetry, fiction, criticism--especially 20th century. **SELECTED PUBLICATIONS** Auth, Randall Darrell: A Literary Life, 90; auth, Playing It by Ear: Literary Essays and Reviews, 94; auth, English Papers: A Teaching Life, 95; auth, Talking Back to Emily Dickinson, and Other Essays, 98; ed, Mountain Interval and New Hampshire, 99. **CONTACT ADDRESS** English Dept, Amherst Col, Amherst, MA 01002.

PROEHL, GEOFFREY
PERSONAL Born 05/10/1950, Portland, OR, m, 1971, 2 children **DISCIPLINE** THEATER **EDUCATION** George Fox Col, BA, 73; Wayne State Univ, MFA, 77; Stanford Univ, PhD, 88. **CAREER** Asst prof, 88-94, chmn, grad stud prog, Villanova Univ; assoc prof, Univ Puget Sound, 94-. **HONORS AND AWARDS** Teaching Excellence Award, Univ of Puget Sound, 00. **MEMBERSHIPS** Asn for Theater in Higher Education; Literary Managers and Dramaturgs of the Americas. **RESEARCH** Dramaturgy and theatricality; Am drama. **SELECTED PUBLICATIONS** Auth, Coming Home Again: American Family Drama and the Figure of the Prodigal, Fairleigh Dickinson Univ Press, 97; co-ed, Dramaturgy in American Theater: A Source Book, Harcourt Brace Jovanovich, 97. **CONTACT ADDRESS** Dept of Commun and Theatre Arts, Univ of Puget Sound, 1500 North Warner, Tacoma, WA 98416. **EMAIL** gproehl@ups.edu

PRUFER, KEVIN D.
PERSONAL Born 10/22/1969, Cleveland, OH, s **DISCIPLINE** CREATIVE WRITING, CONTEMPORARY POETRY **EDUCATION** Wesleyan Univ, BA, 92; Hollins Univ, MA, 94; Washington Univ, MFA, 96. **CAREER** Assoc prof, Central Mo State Univ, 96-; ed, Pleiades: A J of New Writing, 96-. **HONORS AND AWARDS** Fac Achievement Awd, Central Mo State Univ, 98; Winthrop Poetry Series Awd, 96. **MEMBERSHIPS** Assoc Writing Programs **RESEARCH** Contemporary Poetry. **SELECTED PUBLICATIONS** Auth, Strange Wood, 96; auth, The New Young American Poets, Southern Ill Univ Press, 00. **CONTACT ADDRESS** Dept English, Central Missouri State Univ, Warrensburg, MO 64093. **EMAIL** kdp8106@cmsu2.cmsu.edu

PRUITT, VIRGINIA D.
PERSONAL Born 05/08/1943, Rochester, MN, d **DISCIPLINE** ENGLISH **EDUCATION** St. Olaf Col, BA, 65; Univ NC at Chapel Hill, 66; Univ Va, PhD, 74. **CAREER** Instr, Memphis State Univ, 68-71; prof, Washburn Univ, 74-. **HONORS AND AWARDS** Phi Beta Kappa, 65; Mayo Found Scholar Awd, 71-74. **MEMBERSHIPS** MLA; popular Culture Asn. **RESEARCH** Doris Lessing; Alice Munro; W.B. Yeats. **SELECTED PUBLICATIONS** Auth, The Selected Correspondence of Karl A. Menninger: 1919-1945, 95; co-ed, The Selected Correspondence of Karl A. Menninger: 1946-1965, 95; co-ed, Dear Dr. Menninger: Women's Voices From the Thirties, 97. **CONTACT ADDRESS** Washburn Univ of Topeka, Topeka, KS 66621.

PUCCI, PIETRO
PERSONAL Born 11/27/1927, Modena, Italy, m, 1984, 2 children **DISCIPLINE** CLASSICS **EDUCATION** Liceo Muratori, BA (Classics), 45; Univ Pisa, PhD (Classics), 49; Univ Florence, Libera Docenza (Classics), 60. **CAREER** Asst prof, Classics, Univ Florence, 51-52; asst prof, Classics, Univ Ottawa; asst prof, Classics, Univ KS, 61-62; vis prof, Classics, Santa Cruz Univ, 69; vis prof, Classics, Univ Florence, 70; Directeur d'Etudes, Ecole des Hautes Etudes Paris, 84, 89; asst prof, 62-67, assoc prof, 67-72, prof, dept of Classics, 72-91, chmn, 83-87, 90-91, 92-93, Golwin Smith prof of Classics, Cornell Univ, 91-. **HONORS AND AWARDS** Fel of the French govt, 55-57; fel of the German govt, 57-58; Jr fel at the Center for Hellenic Studies, Washington, 70; fel of the ACLS, 72; fel of the Guggenheim Memorial Found, 80-81; fel of the NEH, 89; resident of the Am Academy in Rome, 96. **SELECTED PUBLICATIONS** Auth, "Hesiod and the Language of Poetry," Baltimore: Johns Hopkins Univ Press, 77; auth, "The Violence of Pity in Euripides," Media, Ithaca: Cornell University Press, 80; auth, Oedipus and the Fabrication of the Father, Johns Hopkins Univ Press, 92; Human Sacrifice in the Oresteia, in Innovations in Antiquity, Ralph Hexter and Daniel Seldon, eds, Routledge, 92; Io e l'altro nel racconto di Odisseo sui Ciclopi, SIFC XI, 93; Antiphonal Lament between Achilles and Briseis in Colby Quart, XXXIX, 93; God's Intervention and Epiphany in Sophocles, AJP 115, 94; Persuasione nell' Orestea di Eschilo, Museum Criticum, XXXIX, 94; Ulysse Polytropos, French trans of Odysseus Polytropos, Septentrion, Presses Univ, Lille, 95; Enigma Segreto Oracolo, Instituto Editoriale: Roma, 96; L'Apologie d'Apollon, METIS, 96; Auteur et Destinataires dans le Travaux d'Hesiode, in Le Metier du Mythe, Lectures d'Hesiode, Septentrion, Presses Univ, Lille, 96; The Song of the Sirens and Other Essays, a book of old and new Homeric essays, Rowman & Littlefield, 97; numerous other publications. **CONTACT ADDRESS** Dept of Classics, Cornell Univ, 125 Goldwin Smith Hall, Ithaca, NY 14853. **EMAIL** pp26@cornell.edu

PUCHEK, PETER A.
PERSONAL Born 04/28/1956, Philadelphia, PA, s **DISCIPLINE** ENGLISH **EDUCATION** Haverford Col, BA, 79; Kutztown Univ, MA, 92; Lehigh Univ, PhD, 99. **CAREER** Teaching Fel, Lehigh Univ, 94-97; lectr, DeSales Univ, 97-; instr, W Chester Univ, 99-01. **HONORS AND AWARDS** Tuition Scholar, Haverford Col, 74-78; Grad Asst, Kutztown Univ, 92-93; T.S. Eliot Soc Young Scholar Award, 95; E.W. Fairchild Fel, Lehigh Univ, 95-96 **MEMBERSHIPS** MLA; T.S. Eliot Soc. **RESEARCH** American Modernisms; The Beats; British Romanticism; Poetry; Myth; Film; Gender studies; Cultural politics. **SELECTED PUBLICATIONS** Co-ed, The History of England. By Jane Austen, Juvenilia Press, 95; auth, "Faulkner's Light in August: Epiphany, Eternity, and Time," S Quart, (97): 25-36; auth, "The Tenuous Christianity of Eliot's 'Gerontion': History as Pagan Whirlwind," Yeats Eliot Rev, (97): 10-17; auth, "From Revolution to Creation: Beat Desire and Body Poetics in Anne Waldman's Poetry," in Beat Women and Beat Writing, (Rutgers Univ Press, forthcoming0; auth, Rewriting Creation: Myth, Gender, and History in Ponge, Williams, Bly and Waldman, (Peter Lang Press, forthcoming). **CONTACT ADDRESS** Dept English, West Chester Univ of Pennsylvania, 7304 Sharpless Rd, Elkins Park, PA 19027-3041.

PUGH, CHRISTIAN A.
DISCIPLINE CREATIVE WRITING, LITERATURE **EDUCATION** Wesleyan Univ, BA, 88; Harvard Univ, PhD, 98; Emerson Col, MFA, 01. **CAREER** Lectr, Harvard Univ, 98-01; adj prof, Emerson Col, 99-01; asst prof, CUNY Staten Island, 01-. **HONORS AND AWARDS** Outstanding Col Students of Am, 88; Phi Beta Kappa, 88; Whiting Fel for the Humanities, 97-98; INTRO Awd in Poetry, 00; Grolier Poetry Prize, 00; Ruth Lilly Poetry Prize, 00; Who's Who in Am, 01. **MEMBERSHIPS** MLA, Am Comp Lit Assoc, Int Assoc for Philos and Lit. **SELECTED PUBLICATIONS** Auth, "Film and the Lyric: The Generic Project of Kiewslowski's 'Bleu,'" Annual of Foreign Films and Lit 4, (98): 97-103; auth, "Cherry Mary," Tar River Poetry 39.2, (00): 6; auth, "Picasso's Blue," Ekphrasis 2.2, (00): 26; auth, "Enceinte," "Savior," "Crown", Grolier Poetry Prize Annual 17, (00):13-14, 12, 10-11; auth, "Rotary," Hayden's Ferry Rev 27, (00): 122-123; auth, "On Paternity," "First in Flight," Smartish Pace 4, (01): 21-22; auth, "Non-Pictorial Mimesis in the Ekphrastic Lyric: Louise Bogan's 'After the Persian,'" Interrogating Images, ed Stephen Barker, Northwestern Univ Pr, forthcoming. **CONTACT ADDRESS** 32 Pearson Rd, Apt 2, Somerville, MA 02144-1314. **EMAIL** cpugh@gis.net

PULHAM, CAROL ANN
PERSONAL 2 children **DISCIPLINE** MEDIEVAL PERIOD **EDUCATION** Cedar Crest Col, BA, Lehigh Univ, MA, PhD. **CAREER** English Lit, Cedar Crest Col; Chair of Humanities Dept. **SELECTED PUBLICATIONS** Auth, Promises, Promises: Dorigen's Dilemma Revisited, Chaucer Rev. **CONTACT ADDRESS** Cedar Crest Col, 100 College Drive, Allentown, PA 18104. **EMAIL** capulham@cedarcrest.edu

PULLIN, NICOLAS G.
PERSONAL Born 03/08/1963, Coventry, Britain, m, 1989 **DISCIPLINE** THEATRE **EDUCATION** Guildford Sch Acting, Diploma, 86; Cambridge Univ, BA, 85; MA, 90; Loyola Univ, MA, 97; PhD, 99. **CAREER** Adj fac, DePaul Univ Theater Sch, 94-; fight dir, Lyric Opera, 99-; teach fel to adj fac, Loyola Univ, 99-. **HONORS AND AWARDS** Loyola Teaching Fel, 99-00; Nat Jesuit Honors Soc, 99; Stanley Clayes Mem Essay Winner, 97, 98; Grad Asstshp, 95-99. **MEMBERSHIPS** MLA; AEA; AFTRA; Soc Am Fight Dir. **RESEARCH** Shakespeare in performance; audience analysis; cultural semiotics; modern British drama. **SELECTED PUBLICATIONS** Auth, "Ben Johnson's 'On My First Son;'" Masterplots II (01), 2nd ed; auth, "Death By Genre: Heywood's A Woman Killed with Kindness," Text/Presentation (00) **CONTACT ADDRESS** 2114 W Morse Ave, Chicago, IL 60645-4974. **EMAIL** npullin@wpo.it.luc.edu

PURCELL, WILLIAM
PERSONAL Born 01/29/1955, Ford Ord, CA, m, 1988, 1 child **DISCIPLINE** COMMUNICATION **EDUCATION** Auburn Univ, BA, 76; Univ Ala, MA, 83; Indiana Univ, PhD, 86. **CAREER** Asst prof, Augustana Col, 86-88, Univ Wash, 88-95; assoc prof, Seattle Pac Univ, 95- . **HONORS AND AWARDS** Outstanding Grad Teaching Asst, Univ Ala, 83. **MEMBERSHIPS** Int Soc Hist Rhet. **RESEARCH** History of rehtorical theory, American public address, Argumentation. **SELECTED PUBLICATIONS** Auth, Avs Poetriae: Rhetorical and Grammatical Invention at the Margin of Literacy, Univ S. Carolina Press, (96). **CONTACT ADDRESS** Dept Hum, Seattle Pacific Univ, 3307 3 Ave W, Seattle, WA 98119-1940. **EMAIL** purcell@spu.edu

PURINTON, JEFFREY S.
PERSONAL Born 05/08/1960, Wilmington, DE **DISCIPLINE** CLASSICS **EDUCATION** Princeton Univ, PhD, 92. **CAREER** Vis asst prof philos, Univ Okla, 93- . **MEMBERSHIPS** APA. **RESEARCH** Epicureanism. **SELECTED PUBLICATIONS** Auth, Epicurus on the Telos, Phronesis, 93; auth, Magnifying Epicurean Minima, Ancient Philos, 94; auth, Aristotle's Definition of Happiness, Oxford Stud in Ancient Philos, 98. **CONTACT ADDRESS** Dept of Philosophy, Univ of Oklahoma, Dale Hall Tower 622, Norman, OK 73019. **EMAIL** Jeffrey.S.Purinton_1@ou.edu

PURINTON, MARJEAN D.
DISCIPLINE ENGLISH LITERATURE **EDUCATION** TX A & M Univ, PhD, 91. **CAREER** Asst prof, TX Tech Univ. **MEMBERSHIPS** Pres, S Cent Women's Stud Asn. **RESEARCH** Brit romantic period. **SELECTED PUBLICATIONS** Auth, Romantic Ideology Unmasked: The Mentally Constructed Tyrannies in Dramas of William Wordsworth, Lord Byron, Percy Shelley, and Joanna Baillie, Delaware UP, 94. **CONTACT ADDRESS** Texas Tech Univ, Lubbock, TX 79409-5015. **EMAIL** cbmdp@ttacs.ttu.edu

PUTNAM, LINDA L.
PERSONAL Born Frederick, OK, m, 1970, 1 child **DISCIPLINE** COMMUNICATION **EDUCATION** Univ Minn, PhD. **CAREER** Prof, Texas A&M Univ. **HONORS AND AWARDS** Amoco Found Awd for Distinguished Tchg; Speech Commun Association's Charles H. Woolbert Res Awd; ICA Fel, Int Commun Asn; gov bd, Acad Mgt & pres elect, Int Commun Asn, Distinguished Scholar Awd; mem ed bd 8 scholarly jour, quart j speech; mgt commun quart & commun theory. **RESEARCH** Organizational communication, gender & communication, negotiation & conflict management. **SELECTED PUBLICATIONS** Co-ed, Communication and Negotiation; Handbook of Organizational Communication & Communication and Organization: An Interpretive Approach. **CONTACT ADDRESS** Dept of Speech Communication, Texas A&M Univ, Col Station, TAMU 4234, College Station, TX 77843-4234. **EMAIL** 1putnam@tamu.edu

PUTNAM, MICHAEL C. J.
PERSONAL Born 09/20/1933, Sprinfield, MA **DISCIPLINE** CLASSICS **EDUCATION** Harvard Univ, AB, 54; MA, 56; PhD, 59; Lawrence Univ, LlD (hon), 85. **CAREER** Instructor, Smith Col, 59-60; Instructor to Prof, Brown Univ, 60-. **HONORS AND AWARDS** Goodwin Awd of Merit, Am Philol Asn, 71; Fel, Guggenheim Memorial Foundation, 66-67; Sen Fel, NEH, 73-74; Fel, Am Coun of Learned Soc, 83-84. **MEMBERSHIPS** Am Acad in Rome; Am Philol Asn; Am Acad of Arts and Sci; Am Philos Soc; Classical Asn of N Eng; Medieval Acad of Am; Asn of Literary Scholars and Critics. **RESEARCH** Greek and Latin Literature, expecially the poetry of the Roman Republic and Empire. **SELECTED PUBLICATIONS** Ed, Virgil: 2000 Years, Arethusa, 81; auth, Essays on Latin Lyric, Elegy, and Epic, Princeton Univ Press, 82; auth, Artifices of Eternity: Horace's Fourth book of Odes, Cornell Univ Press, 86; auth, Virgil's Epic Designs: Ekphrasis in the Aeneid, Yale Univ Press, 98. **CONTACT ADDRESS** Dept Classics, Brown Univ, Providence, RI 02912-1856. **EMAIL** michael_putnam@brown.edu

PYE, CHRISTOPHER
PERSONAL Born 06/09/1953, Princeton, NJ, s, 1 child **DISCIPLINE** ENGLISH LITERATURE **EDUCATION** Oberlin Col, BA, 74; Univ Col London, MPhil, 76; Cornell Univ, PhD, 84. **CAREER** Prof, Williams Col, 84-. **HONORS AND AWARDS** Clark Teaching Prize, Cornell Univ; Herbert A Lehman Fel, Williams Col; Class of 1924 Prof of Eng, Williams Col, 01-; Fel, Cornell Soc for the Humanities. **MEMBERSHIPS** MLA. **RESEARCH** Renaissance Literature and Culture, Literary and Psychoanalytic Theory. **SELECTED PUBLICATIONS** Auth, The Regal Phantasm: Shakespear and the Politics of Spectacle, Routledge, 90; auth, The Vanishing: Shakespeare, the Subject, and Early Modern Culture, Duke Univ Pr, 00. **CONTACT ADDRESS** 1119 N Hoosac Rd, Williamstown, MA 01267-2333. **EMAIL** christopher.pye@williams.edu

Q

QI, SHOUHUA
PERSONAL Born 02/01/1957, Nanjing, China, m, 1982, 1 child **DISCIPLINE** COMMUNICATIONS ARTS & SCIENCES **EDUCATION** Nanjing Teachers Univ, BA, 81; Nanjing Teachers Univ, MA, 85; Ill State Univ, PhD, 93. **CAREER** Adj Prof, Pa State Univ, 97-; From Asst Prof to Prof, Harrisburg Area Community Col, 93-. **HONORS AND AWARDS** Teaching Excellence Awd, 85-86; Teaching Excellence and Innovation Awd, 98-99; Who's Who in Am, 2000/Millennium Ed, 00; **MEMBERSHIPS** MLA, NCTE. **RESEARCH** Rhetoric/composition, modern English, American and Chinese literatures, cross-cultural issues. **SELECTED PUBLICATIONS** Transl, A Pair of Blue Eyes by Thomas Hardy, Transl Pr, 94; transl, The Well-Beloved by Thomas Hardy, Transl Pr, 98; auth, Bridging the Pacific: Searching for Cross-Cultural Understanding Between the United States and China, China Books, 00; auth, Success in Advanced English Writing: A Comprehensive Guide, Shanghai For Lang Educ Pr, 00; auth, An Introduction to Western Rhetoric: Theories, Pedagogies and Practices,

Shanghai For Lang Educ Pr, forthcoming; auth, The New Century Guide in Practical English Communication, Shanghai For Lang Educ Pr, forthcoming. **CONTACT ADDRESS** Dept Commun, Harrisburg Area Comm Col, 1 Hacc Dr, Harrisburg, PA 17110-2903. **EMAIL** s9qi@hacc.edu

QIAN, ZHAOMING
PERSONAL Born 07/25/1944, Shanghai, China, m, 1969, 2 children **DISCIPLINE** ENGLISH, COMPARATIVE LITERATURE **EDUCATION** Beijing For Studies Univ, BA, 67; MA, 80; Tulane Univ, PhD, 91. **CAREER** Instr, Tulane Univ, 88-91; from asst prof to assoc prof, Univ of New Orleans, 91-. **HONORS AND AWARDS** Beinecke Fel, Yale Univ, 92-93; NEH Fel, 98-99. **MEMBERSHIPS** MLA, Ezra Pound Soc, William Carlos Williams Soc, Wallace Stevens Soc. **RESEARCH** Chinese influence in modern American poetry. **SELECTED PUBLICATIONS** Ed & contribur, Annotated Shakespeare: The Sonnets, Commecid Press, 91; auth, Orientalism and Modernism: The Legacy of China in Pound and Williams, Duke Univ Press, 95. **CONTACT ADDRESS** Dept English, Univ of New Orleans, 2000 Lakeshore Dr, New Orleans, LA 70148-0001.

QUALLS, BARRY V.
PERSONAL Born 05/13/1945, Paintsville, KY, s **DISCIPLINE** ENGLISH LANGUAGE AND LITERATURE **EDUCATION** Fla State Univ, BA; Northwestern Univ, MA; PhD. **CAREER** FAS Dean of Humanities, Rutgers Univ. **HONORS AND AWARDS** Susman Awd for Outstanding Teaching; FAS Awd for Distinguished Contribution to Undergraduate Educ; Phi Beta Kappa. **RESEARCH** Victorian literature; Biblical literature; poetry. **SELECTED PUBLICATIONS** Auth, The Secular Pilgrims of Victorian Fiction: the Novel as Book of Life. **CONTACT ADDRESS** Dept of English, Rutgers, The State Univ of New Jersey, New Brunswick, 510 George St, Murray Hall, New Brunswick, NJ 08901-1167. **EMAIL** qualls@fas-admin.rutgers.edu

QUANTIC, DINE D.
PERSONAL Born 09/11/1941, Kansas City, MO, m, 1966, 2 children **DISCIPLINE** ENGLISH **EDUCATION** Kans State Univ, BA, 62; MA, 66; PhD, 71. **CAREER** Instr, Univ N Colo, 70-72; asst prof to prof and prog dir, Wichita State Univ, 73-. **HONORS AND AWARDS** Soc of Midland Authors Nonfiction Award, 95; Fulbright Sr Lectr, Bulgaria, 86-87. **MEMBERSHIPS** W Lit Asn; MLA; Nat Coun of Teachers of English; Kans Asn for Teacher of English; Mari Sandez Heritage Soc. **RESEARCH** Great Plains literature, history, ecology. **SELECTED PUBLICATIONS** Auth, William Allen White, Boise State Univ Press, 93; auth, The Nature of the Place: A Study of Great Plains Fiction, Univ Nebr Press, 95; auth, A Great Plains Reader: Stories, Poems, Essays, Univ Nebr Press, (forthcoming). **CONTACT ADDRESS** Dept English, Wichita State Univ, PO Box 14, Wichita, KS 67260-0001. **EMAIL** diane.quantic@wichita.edu

QUEMA, ANNE
PERSONAL Born 01/26/1960, France **DISCIPLINE** ENGLISH **EDUCATION** Univ Savoie, Lic, 82; Carleton Univ, MA, 86; MA, 87; Univ London, PhD, 91. **CAREER** Lectr to adj prof, Carleton Univ, 92-00; asst prof, Acadia Univ, 00-. **MEMBERSHIPS** ACCUTE; MLA; Gothic Studies. **RESEARCH** 20th century British fiction and poetry; 20th century Gothic fiction and culture; theories of art and literature; visual arts; Canadian fiction and poetry. **SELECTED PUBLICATIONS** Auth, "A Genealogy of Impersonality," Philos/Lit (94); auth, The Agon of Modernism: Wyndham Lewis's Allegories, Aesthetics, and Politics, Assoc Univ Pr/Bucknell Univ Pr, 99. **CONTACT ADDRESS** English Dept, Acadia Univ, Wolfville, NS, Canada B0P 1X0. **EMAIL** aquema@acadia.ca

QUIGLEY, AUSTIN E.
DISCIPLINE ENGLISH LITERATURE **EDUCATION** Univ Nottingham; BA, 67, MA, 69; Univ Calif, Santa Cruz, PhD, 71. **CAREER** Instr, Univ Nottingham; Univ Geneva; Univ Konstanz; Univ Mass; dept ch, Univ Va; H. Gordon Garbedian prof, 90; dean, Columbia Col, 95-. **HONORS AND AWARDS** Fel, Danforth; fel, NEH; assocship, Univ Va; former ch, mla drama div exec comm; ch, columbia's docl subcomm on theatre and film; interdept comm on drama and theatre arts; ed bd, new lit hist; mod drama; the pinter rev. **SELECTED PUBLICATIONS** Auth, The Pinter Problem and The Modern Stage and Other Worlds; auth, pub, articles on mod drama and lit theory **CONTACT ADDRESS** Dept of Eng, Columbia Col, New York, 2960 Broadway, New York, NY 10027-6902.

QUIGLEY, AUSTIN F.
DISCIPLINE DRAMA, MODERN LITERATURE **EDUCATION** Univ Nottingham, BA, 67; Univ Birmingham, MA, 69; Univ Calif, PhD, 67. **CAREER** English and Lit, Columbia Univ **HONORS AND AWARDS** Dean, Columbia Col, 95-; Danforth fel, NEH fel. **SELECTED PUBLICATIONS** Auth, The Pinter Problem; The Modern Stage and Other Worlds. **CONTACT ADDRESS** Columbia Univ, 2960 Broadway, New York, NY 10027-6902.

QUILLEN, RITA S.
PERSONAL Born 09/08/1954, Kingsport, TN, m, 1973, 2 children **DISCIPLINE** ENGLISH **EDUCATION** Mountain Empire Cmty Col, AS, 78; E Tenn State Univ, BS, 80; MA, 85. **CAREER** Assoc Prof, Neb State Tech Cmty Col, 87-99; Instructor, Mountain Empire Cmty Col, 99-. **HONORS AND AWARDS** Outstanding Fac Awd, NSTCC, 91; Outstanding Alumni, AACJC, 99; Who's Who Among Am Teachers, 98, 99. **RESEARCH** Appalachian literature and history; Women's literature. **SELECTED PUBLICATIONS** Auth, Counting the Sums. New and collected poems, Sow's Ear Press, 96; auth, "A User's Guide to 'Go Tell in on the Mountain': Appalachian Women Writers," Radio Series, WMMT Radio, 97; auth, "Counting the Sums," in Bloodroot: Essays on Place by Appalachian Women Writers, Univ KY Press, 98. **CONTACT ADDRESS** Dept Arts & Sci, Mountain Empire Comm Col, PO Box 700, Big Stone Gap, VA 24219-0700. **EMAIL** rquillen@me.cc.va.us

QUIN, CAROLYN L.
PERSONAL Born 10/12/1947, Yazoo City, MS **DISCIPLINE** MUSICOLOGY, MUSIC HISTORY AND LITERATURE **EDUCATION** Millsaps Col, Jackson, Miss, BA, 70; Univ Ark, MM, 74; Univ Ky, PhD, 81. **CAREER** Ch, Div of Liberal Stud, 79-92; ch, Dept of Music, Winthrop Univ, Rockhill, SC, 92-96; assoc prof Music, Riverside Community Col, Riverside, CA, 96-. **HONORS AND AWARDS** Grants for res and travel from: Andrew W. Mellon Found; United Negro Col Fund; NEH; US Dept of Education; Jeannie E Lane Awd for Teaching Excellence (Lane Col); Outstanding Teaching asn (Univ Kentucky); sabbatical leave to complete a book, Winthrop Univ; Stover Fel for Excellence in Teaching, 00, Riverside Community Col. **MEMBERSHIPS** Col Music Soc; Am Musicol Soc; Music Asn Cal Comm Col. **RESEARCH** William Grant Still, 1895-1978, African American class composer, Fanny Mendelssohn Hensel, 1805-1847, German composer; women composers, piano & harpsichord performance, online teaching for music appreciation. **SELECTED PUBLICATIONS** Co-author, William Grant Still: A Bio-Bibliography, Greenwood Press, 96; Fusion of Cultures in the Piano Music of William Grant Still, in William Grant Still and the Fusion of Cult in Am Mus, Master-Player Library, 95, Classical Music Trivia, Lisa Huffman (musicol consult to author), Master-Player Library, 97; Fanny Mendelssohn Hensel: Her Contributions to Nineteenth-Century Musical Life, UMI, 81; Online Study Guide to accompany The Enjoyment of Music, with Kristine Forneg, pub in WebCT format on the Internet. **CONTACT ADDRESS** Riverside Comm Col, 4800 Magnolia Ave, Riverside, CA 92506. **EMAIL** cquin@rccd.cc.ca.us

QUINLAN, KIERAN
PERSONAL Born 09/01/1945, Dublin, Ireland, m, 1991, 2 children **DISCIPLINE** MODERN AMERICAN AND IRISH LITERATURE **EDUCATION** Vanderbilt Univ, PhD, 84. **CAREER** Univ Ala **SELECTED PUBLICATIONS** Auth, John Crowe Ransom's Secular Faith, LSU Press, 89; Walker Percy, The Last Catholic Novelist, LSU Press, 96. **CONTACT ADDRESS** Univ of Alabama, Birmingham, 1400 University Blvd, Birmingham, AL 35294-1150. **EMAIL** kquinlan@uab.edu

QUINN, WILLIAM A.
DISCIPLINE MEDIEVAL LITERATURE **EDUCATION** Ohio State Univ, PhD. **CAREER** English and Lit, Univ Ark. **HONORS AND AWARDS** Dir, Grad studies. **SELECTED PUBLICATIONS** Auth, Jongleur: A Modified Theory of Oral Improvisation and its Effects on the Performability and Transmission of Middle English Romance, Univ Press Am, 82; Chaucer's Rehersynges: The Performability of the "Legend of Good Women", Catholic Univ Press, 94. **CONTACT ADDRESS** Univ of Arkansas, Fayetteville, Fayetteville, AR 72701.

QUINSEY, KATHERINE M.
DISCIPLINE ENGLISH LANGUAGE; LITERATURE **EDUCATION** Trent, BA; London, PhD, 89. **CAREER** Assoc prof **HONORS AND AWARDS** SSHRCC grant, 93-96. **RESEARCH** Pope, Dryden, print culture; seventeenth-century and Restoration rhetoric and linguistic philosophy; feminism 1600-1800. **SELECTED PUBLICATIONS** Ed, Broken Boundaries: Women and Feminism in Restoration Drama, 96. **CONTACT ADDRESS** Dept of English Language and Literature, Univ of Windsor, 401 Sunset Ave, Windsor, ON, Canada N9B 3P4. **EMAIL** kateq@uwindsor.ca

QUINTERO, RUBEN
PERSONAL Born 05/05/1949, Montebello, CA, m, 1973, 4 children **DISCIPLINE** ENGLISH; AMERICAN LITERATURE; LANGUAGE **EDUCATION** CSULA, BA, 78, 80; Harvard Univ, AM, 83, PhD, 88. **CAREER** Assoc Prof, CSULA; Phi Kappa Phi. **HONORS AND AWARDS** Univ DE Press Manuscript Awd 18th Century Studies, 90. **MEMBERSHIPS** ASECS; ASLSC; Int Soc Hist Rhet **RESEARCH** Restoration and eighteenth-century British literature. **SELECTED PUBLICATIONS** Literate Culture: Pope's Rhetorical Art, 82. **CONTACT ADDRESS** Dept of English, California State Univ, Los Angeles, 5151 State Univ Dr, Los Angeles, CA 90032-8537. **EMAIL** rquinte@calstatela.edu

QUIRK, RUTHMARIE
PERSONAL Born 06/12/1955, MA, s, 1 child **DISCIPLINE** LIBRARY SCIENCE **EDUCATION** Ba, 79; MLS, 81. **CAREER** Head librarian, Univ Hawaii,95-. **MEMBERSHIPS** ALA; HLA; SDG; IDL; HAAL. **RESEARCH** Sacred Dance in Asia Pacific. **CONTACT ADDRESS** 7253 Nohili St, Honolulu, HI 96825-2249. **EMAIL** rmq@hawaii.edu

QUIRK, THOMAS VAUGHAN
PERSONAL Born 12/28/1946, Houston, TX, m, 1986, 3 children **DISCIPLINE** ENGLISH **EDUCATION** AZ State Univ, BA, 70; Univ NM, MA, 72, PhD, 77. **CAREER** Asst prof, 78-79, New Mexio-Gallup; asst prof, prof, 79-88, Univ MO-Columbia. **MEMBERSHIPS** Melville Soc; Mark Twain Cir; Amer Lit Assn. **RESEARCH** 19th and early 20th Amer literature and culture **SELECTED PUBLICATIONS** Auth, Melville's Confidence-Man: From Knave to Knight (82); Bergson in American Culture: the Worlds of Willa Cather and Wallace Stevens (90); Coming to Grips with 'Huckleberry Finn' (93); Mark Twain: A Study of the Short Fiction. (97); Mark Twain, American Literary Scholarship, 94,95, 96; Ed, Selected Tales, Essays, Speeches, and Sketches of Mark Twain (94); Tales of Soldiers and Civilians and Other Stories by Ambrose Bierce (2000); Coed, Romanticism: Critical Essays in American Literature (86); Writing the American Classics (90); American Realism and the Canon: A Collection of Essays (94); Biographies of Books: The Backgrounds, Genesis, and Composition of Notable American Writings (96); Viking Portable American Realism Reader, 1865-1918 (97). **CONTACT ADDRESS** Dept of Eng, Univ of Missouri, Columbia, 107 Tate Hall, Columbia, MO 65211. **EMAIL** quirkt@missouri.edu

R

RAAFLAUB, KURT A.
PERSONAL Born 02/15/1941, Buea, Cameroon, m, 1978 **DISCIPLINE** CLASSICS **EDUCATION** Univ of Bard, PhD, 70. **CAREER** Asst prof, 72-78, Freic Univ, Berlin; asst, assoc, prof, 78-, Brown Univ; joint dir, 92-00, Ctrs for Hellenic Stud, Wash, DC. **RESEARCH** Social political and intellectual hist of archaic and classical Greece and of the Roman Rep **CONTACT ADDRESS** Dept of Classics, Brown Univ, Providence, RI 02912-1856. **EMAIL** kurt_raaflaub@brown.edu

RABILLARD, SHEILA M.
DISCIPLINE MODERN LITERATURE; DRAMA **EDUCATION** Queen's Univ, BA, MA; Univ W Ontario, Bed; Princeton Univ, PhD. **CAREER** Assoc prof. **RESEARCH** Theories of drama and performance; gender studies. **SELECTED PUBLICATIONS** Auth, Shepard's Challenge to the Modernist Myths of Origin and Originality: Angel City and True West, Rereading Shepard, Macmillan, 93; essays reprinted in Theatre Criticism Vol V, Gale, 95, Theatre Criticism Vol VI, Gale, 95; ed, Essays on Caryl Churchill: Contemporary Re-Presentations, Blizzard, 98; auth, Negotiating a Welcome: The Coast Salish Nation, Elizabeth II, and Circulations of Power at the Fifteenth Commonwealth Games, " Post, Colonial Stages, ed., Helen Gilbert, Dangaroo, 99. **CONTACT ADDRESS** Dept of English, Univ of Victoria, PO Box 3070, Victoria, BC, Canada V8W 3W1. **EMAIL** rabillar@uvic.ca

RABKIN, ERIC S.
PERSONAL Born 03/08/1946, Queens, NY, m, 1967, 2 children **DISCIPLINE** ENGLISH **EDUCATION** Cornell Univ, AB, 67; Univ Iowa, PhD, 70. **CAREER** Assoc prof to prof, Univ of Mich, 70-. **HONORS AND AWARDS** Horace H. Rackham Fac Res Grant, 73; ACLS Fel, 73; Univ of Mich Teaching Awd 90-91; Arthur F. Thurnau Professorship, 90-93; Am Philos Soc Res Grant, 91; Univ of Mich Res Partnership, 91-92. **RESEARCH** Fantasy, Science Fiction, Academic Computing, Pedagogy, Composition. **SELECTED PUBLICATIONS** Auth, "The Composite Novel in Science Fiction", Foundation (96): 93-100; auth, "Eat and Grow Strong: The Super-natural Power of Forbidden Fruit", Food of the Gods, (96): 21-38; auth, "The Joke's On Us", Inside (96): 33-41; auth, "A Grandfather's Thunderstorms" Record-Eagle (Traverse City, MI), 24 Jul 97, 31; coauth, "E-Comp: A Few Words About Teaching Writing With Computers", T.H.E. J, (Sept 97): 66-67; auth, "Science-Fiction Novel, Encyclopedia of the Novel, ed Paul Schellinger, Fitzroy Dearborn (Chicago, 98): 1188-1194; auth, "Infant Joys" The Pleasures of Disempowerment in Fantasy and Science Fiction", Nursery Realms" Children in the Worlds of Science Fiction, Fantasy and Horror, eds Gary Westfahl and George Slusser, Univ of Ga Pr, (Athens, 99): 3-19; auth, "Astounding Tales That Might come True!", Business Week (23-30 Aug 99): 116; auth, "Immortality: The Self-Defeating Fantasy", Il Fantastico, ed Romolo Runcini, Mondadori(Rome) (forthcoming); auth, "The Fantastic and the Pretty", Aspects of Fantasy, eds George Slusser and Jean-Pierre Barricelli, Borgo Pr, (forthcoming). **CONTACT ADDRESS** Dept English, Univ of Michigan, Ann Arbor, 505 S State St, Ann Arbor, MI 48109-1045. **EMAIL** esrabkin@umich.edu

RACE, WILLIAM H.
PERSONAL Born 03/24/1943, Wooster, OH, m, 1969, 2 children **DISCIPLINE** CLASSICS **EDUCATION** Univ Mich, BA, 65; Stanford Univ, MA, 72, PhD, 73. **CAREER** Tchr Latin & English, Detroit Country Day Sch, 68-69; asst prof Classics, Univ Calif Berkeley, 73-76; from asst prof to assoc prof to prof Classics, Vanderbilt Univ, 76-96; George L. Paddison prof Classics, Univ NC Chapel Hill, 96-. **HONORS AND AWARDS** Nat Endowment Hum grant, 85, 91; Outstanding Grad Tchr Awd, Vanderbilt Univ, 92. **MEMBERSHIPS** Phi Beta Kappa; Am Philological Asn; Class Asn Mid W & S; Am Inst Archeol; Am Class League; Vergilian Soc; Int Soc Class Trad; Int Plutarch Soc; ed bd, Am Jour Philol. **RESEARCH** Classical Greek poetry; Augustan Poetry; rhetoric; classical tradition. **SELECTED PUBLICATIONS** Auth, The Classical Priamel from Homer to Boethius, 82; auth, Pindar, Twayne World Auth Ser, 86; auth, Classical Genres and English Poetry, 88; auth, Style and Rhetoric in Pindar's Odes, 90; auth, Pindar, Loeb Class Libr, 97. **CONTACT ADDRESS** Dept of Classics, Univ of No Carolina, Chapel Hill, CB 3145, Chapel Hill, NC 27599-3145. **EMAIL** whrace@email.unc.edu

RADDEN, VIKI
PERSONAL Born, Germany **DISCIPLINE** ENGLISH **EDUCATION** Univ Ariz, BA, 83; San Francisco State Univ, MA, 88. **HONORS AND AWARDS** NEH Fel, 93-94. **MEMBERSHIPS** Phi Kappa Phi Nat Honor Soc; CA Teachers Asn. **RESEARCH** African diaspora; Japanese culture and literature; Career change. **SELECTED PUBLICATIONS** Auth, "Riding the Wheel of Fortune," Anthology: Sisterfire, Harper Collins, 94; auth, "Preparing the Corn," Palo Alto Review, 95; auth, "Snow Peaches," Palo Alto Review, 95; auth, "Shalanda the Reading Girl," Bless me, Father: Stories of Catholic Childhood, Plume Press, 95; auth, "Trapped Behind Glass," California State Poetry Soc Quarterly, 95; auth, "Pearl Necklace," California State Poetry Soc Quarterly, 96; auth, "Japan in my Dreams," You Go, Girl: Travel Writing by Black Women, Eighth Mountain Press, 97; auth, "Mr. Robert," The Broken Bridge: Fiction From Expatriates in Literary Japan, Stone Bridge Press, 97; auth, "A Thing About Italy," A Line of Cutting Women, CALYX Press, 99. **CONTACT ADDRESS** Dept Eng, Dominican Col of San Rafael, 50 Acacia Ave, San Rafael, CA 94901-2230. **EMAIL** rviki10@hotmail.com

RADEL, NICHOLAS F.
PERSONAL Born 04/06/1955, Cincinnati, OH **DISCIPLINE** ENGLISH, AMERICAN LITERATURE **EDUCATION** Univ Cincinnati, BA, 76; Ind Univ, MA, 78; PhD. 82. **CAREER** Asst instr, Ind Univ, 78-82; vis asst prof, Hamilton Col, 83-84; vis asst prof, St Lawrence Univ, 84-86; asst prof to prof, Furman Univ, 86-; vis prof, Agnes Scott Col, 96-. **HONORS AND AWARDS** Fulbright, 99. **MEMBERSHIPS** Shakespeare Assoc of Am, Nordic Assoc of Am Studies, MLA. **RESEARCH** English Renaissance Literature, American Drama, Sexuality Theory, Gay and Lesbian Studies. **SELECTED PUBLICATIONS** Auth, "Then thus I Turne My Language to You: the Transformation of Theatrical language in Philaster," Medieval and Renaissance Drama in England III (86): 129-147; coauth, "Linguistic Subversion and the Artifice of Rhetoric in The Two Noble Kinsmen," Shakespeare quart 38, (87): 405-425; auth, "Provincetown Plays: Women Writers and O'Neill's American Intertext," Essays in Theatre 9.1 (90): 31-43; auth, "Self as Other: Identity Politics in the Works of Edmund White," Queer Words Queer Images, NY Univ Pr, (93); auth, "Reading as a Feminist: Measure for Measure," Theory in Practice: Measure for Measure, (96); auth, "Homoeroticism, Discursive Change, and Politics: Readings Revolution in Seventeenth-Century English TragiComedy," Medieval and Renaissance Drama in England IX, (96); auth, "The Transnational Ga(y)ze: Two Essays on Gay Film and Drama after the Fall of the Wall," Cinema Jour, (01). **CONTACT ADDRESS** Furman Univ, 206 Oregon St, Greenville, SC 29605. **EMAIL** nick.radel@furman.edu

RADFORD, GARY P.
DISCIPLINE COMMUNICATION **EDUCATION** Sheffield Hallam Univ, Engl, BA, 83; Southern Ill Univ, Carbondale, MS, 84; State Univ NJ, PhD, 91. **CAREER** Assoc prof, 97-; asst prof, William Paterson Univ NJ, 90-97; instr, William Paterson Univ NJ, 89-90; grad tchg asst, State Univ NJ, 86-89; instr, State Univ NJ, 84-86; grad tchg asst, Sheffield Hallam Univ, Engl, 83-84; Southern Ill Univ Carbondale. **SELECTED PUBLICATIONS** Auth, Foucault inserted: Philosophy, struggle, and transgression, Transgressing discourses: Communication and the voice of other, Albany, NY: SUNY Press, 97; Science, the voice of other, and Kant's foggy island of truth, Transgressing discourses: Communication and the voice of other, Albany, NY: SUNY Press, 97; Characterizing the Mod library experience: Rationality or fantasia, Continuity and Transformation: The Promise of Confluence, Proceedings of the 7th Nat Conf of the Asn of Col and Res Libr(s), Chicago, IL: Amer Libr Asn, 95; A Foucauldian perspective of the relationship between communication and information, Between Communication and Information, Information and Behavior, 93; coauth, Transgressing discourses: Communication and the voice of other,Albany, NY: SUNY Press, 97; Instructor's manual: Communication and human behavior, 2nd ed, NY: Macmillan, 88; We do need a philosophy of Library and Information Science, we're not confused enough: A response to Zwadlo, Libr Quart, 97; Power, knowledge, and fear: Feminism, Foucault, and the stereotype of the female librarian, Libr Quart, 97; The impact of four conferencing formats on the efficiency and quality of small group decision making in a laboratory experiment setting, Telematics and Informatics, 94. **CONTACT ADDRESS** Dept of Communication, William Paterson Col of New Jersey, Hobart Hall, Room 211, Wayne, NJ 07470. **EMAIL** radfordg@nebula.wilpaterson.edu

RADICE, MARK A.
PERSONAL Born 07/17/1951, Passail, NJ, m, 4 children **DISCIPLINE** MUSIC HISTORY; COMPOSER **EDUCATION** Boston Univ, BM; Univ Cincinnati, MM; Eastman Sch Music, PhD. **CAREER** Assoc prof. **SELECTED PUBLICATIONS** Auth, "History of Opera Staging, Music Research Techniques," Original Compositions, editions of music. **CONTACT ADDRESS** Dept of Music History, Theory and Composition, Ithaca Col, Center for Music/ 953 Dansy Rd., Ithaca, NY 14850. **EMAIL** mradice@ithaca.edu

RADNER, HILARY A.
DISCIPLINE COMMUNICATIONS, THEATRE **EDUCATION** Univ Calif at Berkeley, BA, 76; MA, 80; Univ Tex at Austin, PhD, 88. **CAREER** Asst prof, Univ of Pittsburgh, 87-88; from asst prof to assoc prof, Univ of Notre Dame, 88-; vis scholar, Univ of Ariz at Tucson, 96 & 97; vis lectr, Univ of Tex at Austin, 97-98; vis scholar, La Sorbonne Nouvelle, 98. **MEMBERSHIPS** Soc for Cinema Studies. **RESEARCH** Film, Television, Popular Culture. **SELECTED PUBLICATIONS** Co-ed, Film Theory Goes to the Movies, Routledge (New York), 95; auth, Shopping Around: Feminine Culture and the Pursuit of Pleasure, Routledge, 95; co-ed, Constructing the New Consumer Society, Macmillan, 97; co-ed, Swinging Single: Representing Sexuality the 1960s, Univ of Minn Press (Minneapolis, MN), 99. **CONTACT ADDRESS** Dept Commun & Theatre, Univ of Notre Dame, 320 O Shaugnessy Hall, Notre Dame, IN 46556-5639.

RADWAY, JANICE
PERSONAL Born 01/02/1949, NJ, 1 child **DISCIPLINE** AMERICAN LITERATURE **EDUCATION** MI State Univ, PhD, 77. **CAREER** Prof, Duke Univ. **HONORS AND AWARDS** Phi Beta Kappa; Guggenheim Fellowship; National edowment for the Humanities Fellowship: Christian & Navy Lindback Teaching Awd. **RESEARCH** Cult studies; feminist theory. **SELECTED PUBLICATIONS** Auth, Reading the Romance and A Feeling for Books: The Book-of-the-Month Club; Literary Taste; Middle Class Desire. **CONTACT ADDRESS** Program in Literature, Duke Univ, Durham, NC 27706.

RAE, PATRICIA
DISCIPLINE ENGLISH LITERATURE **EDUCATION** Oxford Univ, DPhil. **CAREER** Dept Eng, Queen's Univ **RESEARCH** Modern British and American poetry and fiction; early twentieth century philosophy and psychology; classical pragmatism and neopragmatism; modern literature and the visual arts; Imagism and Vorticism; literature and politics in the 1930s. **SELECTED PUBLICATIONS** Auth, The Practical Muse: Pragmatist Poetics in Hulme, Pound, and Stevens, 97; Mr. Charrington's Junk Shop: T.S. Eliot and Modernist Poetics in Nineteen Eighty-Four, 97; Cannon Aspirin: Wallace Stevens' Defense of Pleasure, 97; From Mystical Gaze to Pragmatic Game: Representations of Truth in Vorticist Art, 89; T.E. Hulme's French Sources: A Reconsideration, 89. **CONTACT ADDRESS** English Dept, Queen's Univ at Kingston, Kingston, ON, Canada K7L 3N6. **EMAIL** pmr1@qsilver.queensu.ca

RAEBURN, JOHN H.
PERSONAL Born 07/18/1941, IN, m, 1986, 2 children **DISCIPLINE** AMERICAN STUDIES, ENGLISH **EDUCATION** Ind Univ, BA, 63; Univ Pa, MA, 64; PhD, 69. **CAREER** Asst prof, Univ Mich, 67-74; vis lectr, Univ Iowa, 75; assoc prof, Univ Louisville, 75-76; from assoc prof to prof, Univ Iowa, 76-; chemn, Univ Iowa English Dept, 85-91; chemn, Univ Iowa American Studies Dept, 83-85 & 94-00. **MEMBERSHIPS** ASA, OAH. **RESEARCH** Photography as a cultural practice. **SELECTED PUBLICATIONS** Auth, Fame Because of Him: Hemingway as Public Writer, Ind Univ Pr, 84. **CONTACT ADDRESS** Dept Am Studies, The Univ of Iowa, 202 E Jefferson St, Iowa City, IA 52245-2135. **EMAIL** john-raeburn@uiowa.edu

RAFAEL, VICENTE
DISCIPLINE COMMUNICATIONS **EDUCATION** Cornell Univ, PhD, Hist, 84. **CAREER** Assoc Prof, Commun, Univ Calif, San Diego. **RESEARCH** Compar colonial discourses; Polit and cult of nationalisms. **SELECTED PUBLICATIONS** Auth, Contracting Colonialism: Translation and Christian Conversion in Tagalog Society Under Early Spanish Rule, Duke, 93; "White Love: Surveillance and Nationalist Resistance in the U.S. Colonization of the Philippines," Cultures of U S Imperialism, Duke, 93; auth, White Love and Other Events in Filipino History, Duke Univ Press, 00; ed, Figures of Criminality in Indonesia, the Philipines, and Colonial Vietnam, Cornell (Ithaca), 99. **CONTACT ADDRESS** Dept of Commun, Univ of California, San Diego, 9500 Gilman Dr, La Jolla, CA 92093. **EMAIL** vrafael@ucsd.edu

RAFFEL, BURTON
PERSONAL Born 04/27/1928, New York, NY, m, 1974, 5 children **DISCIPLINE** ENGLISH **EDUCATION** BA, Brooklyn Coll, 48; MA, OH State Univ, 49; JD, Yale Univ, 58. **CAREER** Distinguished Prof of Hum, Prof of Enf, Univ of LA, 89-; Dir, The Adirondack Mtn Found, 87-89; Prof of Eng, Univ of Denver, 75-87; Vis Prof, Eng, Emory Univ, 74; Vis Prof of Hum, York Univ(Toronto), 72-75; Sr Tutor, (Dean)Ontario Coll of Art(Toronto),71-72; Assoc Prof of Eng, State Univ of NY, Buffalo, 66-68; Inst of Eng, State Univ of NY, Stony Brood, 64-65; Attorney Milbank, Tweed, Hadley and McCloy, NY, 58-60. **SELECTED PUBLICATIONS** The Development of Modern Indonesian Poetry, State Univ of NY Press, 67; The Art of Translating Prose, Penn State Univ Press, 94; American Victorians: Explotations in Emotional History, Archon Books, 84; Politicians, Poets and Con Men, Archon Books, 86; The Annotated Milton: The Complete English Poems with annotations lexical, syntactical, prosodic, and referential, Bantam Books, 99; Lyrics From the Old English, with Robert P.Creed, Folkways LP No FL, 9858; Metrical Dramaturgy in Shakespeares Early Plays, The CEA Critic, 95; A Lost Poem by Chairil Anwar, Indonesia Circle, 95; Translation and Creativity, Western Humanities Review, 96; Who Heard the Rhymes and How: Shakespeares Dramaturgical Signals, Oral Tradition, 98; Mark Twain's View of Huck Finn, Ball State U Forum, 83(XXIV:3). **CONTACT ADDRESS** Dept Eng, Univ of Louisiana, Lafayette, Lafayette, LA 70504-4691. **EMAIL** bnraffel@netconnect.net

RAGEN, BRIAN A.
PERSONAL Born 10/23/1958, San Diego, CA, s **DISCIPLINE** ENGLISH **EDUCATION** Pomona Col, BA, 80; Princeton Univ, MA, 82; PhD, 87. **CAREER** Lectr, Princeton Univ, 84-88; from asst prof to prof, S Ill Univ, 88-. **MEMBERSHIPS** MLA, Am Studies Assoc, Popular Culture Assoc, Conf on Christianity and Lit. **RESEARCH** Flannery O'Connor, Tom Wolfe, W.H. Auden, Rudyard Kipling, religion and literature, hymnody, heraldry. **SELECTED PUBLICATIONS** Auth, A Wreck on the Road to Damascus: Innocence, Guilt, and Conversion in Flannery O'Connor, Loyola UP, 89; auth, An Uncanonical Classic: The Politics of the Norton Anthology; auth, A Wretch Like Who?, on rev of traditional hymns; auth, Semiotics and Heraldry; auth, "Another Woman and Another Room: Men, Women and Flannery O'Connor," J of Contemporary Thought. **CONTACT ADDRESS** Dept English, So Illinois Univ, Edwardsville, PO Box 1431, Edwardsville, IL 62026-1431. **EMAIL** abelragen@aol.com

RAGSDALE, J. DONALD
DISCIPLINE COMMUNICATION THEORY, INTERPERSONAL COMMUNICATION, FILM **EDUCATION** Samford Univ, BA, 61; Univ Ill, MA, PhD. **CAREER** Prof, La State Univ. **MEMBERSHIPS** Pres, Southern States Commun Asn. **RESEARCH** Marital communication. **SELECTED PUBLICATIONS** Author of numerous scholarly articles and book chapters in communication theory, interpersonal communication, film, and marital communication. **CONTACT ADDRESS** Dept of Speech Commun, Louisiana State Univ and A&M Col, Baton Rouge, LA 70803.

RAGUSSIS, MICHAEL
DISCIPLINE ENGLISH LITERATURE **EDUCATION** City Col NYork, BA; Columbia Univ, MA; Johns Hopkins Univ, PhD. **CAREER** Eng Dept, Georgetown Univ **RESEARCH** Eighteenth and nineteenth centuries, with focus on fiction and drama; literary theory; Anglo Jewish studies; cultural studies. **SELECTED PUBLICATIONS** Auth, The Subterfuge of Art: Language and the Romantic Tradition, Johns Hopkins Univ, 78; Acts of Naming: The Family Plot in Fiction, Oxford, 86; Figures of Conversion: "The Jewish Question" and English National Identity, Duke, 95. **CONTACT ADDRESS** English Dept, Georgetown Univ, 37th and O St, Washington, DC 20057.

RAHMAN, SHAFIQUR
PERSONAL Born 12/14/1946, Bangladesh, m **DISCIPLINE** COMMUNICATION **EDUCATION** Dhaka Univ, Bangladesh, BA, 67, MA, 68, 73; Simon Fraser Univ, Vancouver, BC, Canada; PhD, 87. **CAREER** Asst prof, Chittagong Univ, 81-83; Instructor, Louisiana State Univ, 87; Asst prof, 88-90; Acting chair, 93-94; Prof, 94-01. **HONORS AND AWARDS** Am Pr Inst, Journalism Educators Fel Awd, 91; Fac Development Mini-Grant, 92; The Freedom Forum Technol Seminar Participation Awd, 94; Poynter Inst Journalism Educators Workshop Awd, 95; Freedom Forum J Educ Admin Workshop, San Francisco, Calif, 97; Amer Press Inst Critical Mgmt Skills Sem, Reston, Va, 98; Int Who's Who's of Professionals, 99. **MEMBERSHIPS** Asn for Educ in Journalism and Mass Commun, Asn for Schs of Journalism and Mass Commun, Black Col Commun Asn, Broadcasting Educators Asn, Asn of Commun Admin, Public Broadcasting Management Asn, BBC and VOA Commentator on Nat and Int Socio-political and Media issues, Committee for Undergraduate Communs Curriculum Seminar, Am Pr Inst, Int Commun Asn, The Freedom Forum Journal Educ Admin Seminar, The Poynter Inst Journal Educators Seminar, Intercultural Commun Conference, Asian Studies Asn, Canadian Economic Asn, Nat Commun Policy and Project Planning Conference, Bangladesh Federation of Film Societies, Dhaka

Theater Group, Simn Praser Univ Speakers Bureau. **RESEARCH** Mass media analysis, media & the minorities, political-economy of org & bureaucracy, int, intercultural commun, third world commun, educ & develop, Asian media syst, Freedom of the press. **SELECTED PUBLICATIONS** Auth, Bureaucratic Organizational Communication: Implication of Definition-Building Roles of Bureaucracies in Development Programs, Dhaka Univ, Bangladesh, 90; The role of Selective Perception in Creating and Communicating Definitions of Development in Organizations, Univ Wi Oshkosh, 91; Comparative Content Analysis of Selected Mississippi Newspapers: Coverage of News About Afro-American People and Issues, Alcorn St. Univ, Ms, 92-95; Reactions of Bangladesh Television Viewers Towards Foreign News and Dubbed Foreign English Satellite Programs, Dhaka, Bangledesh, 98; auth, State, Mass Media and Bangladesh Television: How Free Is the Medium?, Thikana, New York, 99; auth, Interactive Media and Radio and Television in Bangladesh, Thikana, New York, 00. **CONTACT ADDRESS** Dept of Commun, Alcorn State Univ, 1000 ASU Dr, #269, Lorman, MS 39096-9402. **EMAIL** srahman@lorman.alcorn.edu

RAILTON, BENJAMIN A.
PERSONAL Born 08/15/1977, Charlottesville, VA, s **DISCIPLINE** COMPOSITION **EDUCATION** Harvard Univ, BA, 00. **CAREER** TA, Temple Univ, 00-. **HONORS AND AWARDS** Harvard Hoopes Prize; Temple Presidential Fel, 00-04. **MEMBERSHIPS** MLA. **RESEARCH** American history and historical literature, Southern literature, Literature of the early republic, 19th Century definitions of America and American identity. **CONTACT ADDRESS** 2101 Chestnut St, Apt 420, Philadelphia, PA 19103-3108. **EMAIL** barailton@hotmail.com

RAILY, KEVIN
PERSONAL Born 10/28/1954, Brooklyn, NY, m, 1998, 1 child **DISCIPLINE** ENGLISH **EDUCATION** SUNY Albany, BA, 77; SUNY Stony Creek, MA, 85; PhD, 90. **CAREER** Vis asst prof, Skidmore Col, 89-91; asst prof to assoc prof to prof to chmn, SUNY Buffalo, 91-. **HONORS AND AWARDS** Carnegie Scholar Teaching Awd. **MEMBERSHIPS** MLA; NCTE; The Faulkner Soc. **RESEARCH** William Faulkner; teaching and social justice; ethnic American literature; masculinity. **SELECTED PUBLICATIONS** Auth, Natural Aristocracy: History, Ideology and the Production of William Faulkner. **CONTACT ADDRESS** English Dept, SUNY, Buffalo, 1300 Elmwood Ave, Buffalo, NY 14222-1004. **EMAIL** raileyk@bscmail.buffalostate.edu

RAINEY, KENNETH T.
DISCIPLINE COMMUNICATION STUDIES **EDUCATION** OH State Univ, PhD. **CAREER** Prof tech commun, Southern Polytech State Univ. **HONORS AND AWARDS** Outstanding Faculty Awd, 92. **MEMBERSHIPS** STC; Asn Tchr Tech Writing; Soc Tech Commun; Nat Council Tchr Eng. **SELECTED PUBLICATIONS** Auth, articles on compos and rhet; Am cult; tech commun. **CONTACT ADDRESS** Hum and Tech Commun Dept, So Polytech State Univ, S Marietta Pkwy, PO Box 1100, Marietta, GA 30060. **EMAIL** krainey@spsu.edu

RAINEY, PENELOPE
PERSONAL Born 12/06/1940, New York, NY, m, 1986, 2 children **DISCIPLINE** CLASSICS **EDUCATION** Harvard, BA, 62; Columbia, MA, PhD, 72 **CAREER** Germantown Friends Sch, 74-present. **HONORS AND AWARDS** Phi Beta Kappa, NEH Research grant **MEMBERSHIPS** APA, ALA, Vergehan Soc **RESEARCH** Medieval Latin poetry; classical Latin poetry; Plato **SELECTED PUBLICATIONS** Plato Laches Bryan Manor Commentaries, Medieval Latin Verse **CONTACT ADDRESS** 20 W. Willow Grove Ave., Philadelphia, PA 19118. **EMAIL** pennyr@gfsnet.org

RAINWATER, CATHERINE
PERSONAL Born 05/31/1953, Corpus Christi, TX, s **DISCIPLINE** LITERATURE **EDUCATION** Del Mar Col, AA, 72; Univ Tex Austin, BA, 74; PhD, 82; Univ Calif, MA, 76. **CAREER** Asst instr, lectr, Univ of Tex, 76-85; adj prof to prof, St Edward's Univ, 85-. **HONORS AND AWARDS** Phi Kappa Phi; Foerster Prize, MLA, 90; Choice Awd, 99. **MEMBERSHIPS** MLA; Ellen Glasgow Soc; ALA; ASAIL; SCMLA. **RESEARCH** 19th and 20th Century Literature, Native American Literature. **SELECTED PUBLICATIONS** Auth, "Planes, Lines, Shapes, and Shadows: N Scott Momaday's Iconological Imagination", Tex Studies in Lit and Lang 37, (95): 376-393; auth, "Indian Captivity Narrative", Encycl of Am Lit, ed Steven R Serafin, Continuum, (NY, 99): 565-567; auth, "Intertextual Twins and Their Relations: Linda Hogan's Mean Spirit and Solar Storms", Mod Fiction Studies 45 (99): 1-21; auth, "The Way to Rainy Mountain", The Sixties in America, ed Rowena Wildin, Salem Pr, (Pasadena, 99); auth, Dreams of Fiery Stars: The Transformation of Native American Fiction, Univ of Pa Pr, (Philadelphia), 99; auth, "Leslie Marmon Silko", Contemp Am Women Fiction Writers: A Bio-bibliographical Critical Sourcebook, eds Laurie Champion and Rhonda Austin, Greenwood, (Westport, 00). **CONTACT ADDRESS** Dept Humanities, St. Edward's Univ, 3001 S Congress Ave, Austin, TX 78704-6425. **EMAIL** cathernr@admin.stedwards.edu

RAISOR, PHILIP
DISCIPLINE 20TH CENTURY AMERICAN, BRITISH, AND WORLD POETRY, FICTION, DRAMA **EDUCATION** La State Univ, BA, MA; Kent State Univ, PhD. **CAREER** Engl, Old Dominion Univ. **HONORS AND AWARDS** Fac Rep, ODU Board Visitors; Chair Fac Form; Chair & Dir Grad Studies Eng; Pres New Virginia Rev; Mem Assoc Writing ProgBoard Dir; President ODU chapter Phi Kappa Phi. **RESEARCH** Poetry. **SELECTED PUBLICATIONS** Tuned and Under Tension: The Recent Poetry of W. D. Snodgrass. **CONTACT ADDRESS** Old Dominion Univ, 4100 Powhatan Ave, Norfolk, VA 23058. **EMAIL** PRaisor@odu.edu

RAJAGOPAL, ARVIND
DISCIPLINE CULTURAL STUDIES, MASS MEDIA, POSTCOLONIAL STUDIES **EDUCATION** Madras, BF, 81; Univ of Ky, MA, 84; Univ of Calif, Berkeley, PhD, 92. **CAREER** Asst prof, Purdue Univ. **HONORS AND AWARDS** Eli Sagan Awd, Univ of Calif, 90; Univ of Calif, Berkeley, Departmental Fel, 90-91; Rockefeller Fel, Univ of Chicago, 93; Amer Inst of Indian Studs Sr Fel, 93-94, 96-97; Macarthur Found Fel for Res and Writing on Peace and Int Coop, 96-97; Sawyer Fel, Int Inst, Univ of Mich, 96-97; NYork Univ challenge Grant, 99-00. **RESEARCH** Political economy of culture, social theory, contemporary South Asia, globalization. **SELECTED PUBLICATIONS** Auth, "Communalism and the Consuming Subject," Econ & Polit Weekly Vol 31, No 6 (96): 341-348; auth, "Mediating Modernity: Theorizing Reception in a Non-Western society," Commun Rev Vol 1, no 4 (96): 441-469; auth, "Hindu Immigrants in the US: Imagining Different Communities?" Bulletin of Concerned Asian Scholars (97): 51-65; auth, "Advertising, Politics and the Sentimental Education of the Indian Consumer," Visual Anthrop Rev Vol 14, No 2 (98/99): 14-31; auth, "Communities Imagined and Unimagined: Contemporary Indian Variations on the Public Sphere," Discourse: J for the Theoret Study of Media & Cult Vol 21, No 2 (99): 48-84; auth, "Thinking through emerging markets: brand logics and the cultural forms of political society in India," Social Text 60 (Fall 99): 131-149; auth, "Hindu Nationalism in the US: Changing Configurations of Political Practice," Ethnic & Racial Studies Vol 23, No 3 (00), 67-96. **CONTACT ADDRESS** Dept of Cult & Commun, New York Univ, Sch of Education, East Bldg 7th Fl, 239 Greene St, New York, NY 10003. **EMAIL** arvind.rajagopal@nyu.edu

RAJAN, BALACHANDRA
PERSONAL Born 03/24/1920, Tounsoo, Myanmar, m, 1946, 1 child **DISCIPLINE** ENGLISH **EDUCATION** Cambridge Univ, BA, 41; MA, 42; PhD, 46. **CAREER** Dir of Studies, Trinity Col Cambridge, 45-48; Member, Indian For Serv, 48-61; prof to dept head and dean, Delhi Univ, 61-64; vis prof, Univ Wisc, 64-65; prof, Univ Windsor, 65-66; prof to prof emeritus, Univ W Ont, 66-. **HONORS AND AWARDS** Fel, Trinity Col Cambridge, 44-48; Honored Scholar, Milton Soc of Am, 79; Fel and Medallist, Royal Soc of Can, 75, 81. **MEMBERSHIPS** MLA **RESEARCH** 17th Century; Romantic and 20th Century poetry; India in English literature; Imperialisms **SELECTED PUBLICATIONS** Auth, The Form of the Unfinished, Princeton Univ Press, 85; auth, Under Western Eyes. India from Milton to Macaulay, Duke Univ Press, 99; co-ed, Milton and the Imperial Vision, Duquesne Univ Press, 99. **CONTACT ADDRESS** Dept English, Univ W Ont, 478 Regent St, London, ON, Canada N5Y 4H4.

RAJAN, TILOTTAMA
PERSONAL Born, NY **DISCIPLINE** ENGLISH, CRITICISM **EDUCATION** Univ Toronto, BA, 72, MA, 73, PhD, 77. **CAREER** Asst prof, Univ Western Ont, 77-80; asst prof, 80-83, assoc prof, Queen's Univ, 83-85; prof, Univ Wisconsin, Madison, 85-90; prof Eng/Ctr Theory & Criticism, Univ Western Ont, 90-. **HONORS AND AWARDS** John Simon Guggenheim Fel, 87-88; Res Fel, SSHRCC, 90-94. **MEMBERSHIPS** MLA; North Am Soc Stud Romanticism; Fel, Royal Society Can. **RESEARCH** Romantic literature and its connections to contemporary and nineteenth-century theory; Nineteenth-Century Philosophy, Aesthitics and Theory; Contemporary theory and continental philosophy. **SELECTED PUBLICATIONS** Auth, The Supplement of Reading: Figures of Understanding in Romantic Theory and Practice, Ithaca: Cornell Univ Press, (90): 361; co-ed, Intersections: Nineteenth-Century Philosophy and Contemporary Theory, Albany: State Univ of New York Press, (95): 386; co-ed, "Radical Phenomenology: Hegel and the Dis(place)ment of Art," Toronto: Univ of Toronto Press, (95): 23-43; ed, "Phenomenology and Romantic Theory: Hegel and the Subversion of Aesthetics," Baltimore: Johns Hopkins Univ Press, (95): 155-78, 298-300, co-ed, "Promethean Narrative: Overdetermined Form in Shelley's Gothic Fiction," Baltimore: Johns Hopkins Univ Press, (95): 240-52, 308-9; auth, "Coleridge, Wordsworth, and the Textual Abject,' in Rhetorical and Cultural Dissolution in Romanticism, ed. Thomas Pfau and Rhonda Ray Kercsmar, South Atlantic Quarterly, 95:33, (96): 797-820; auth, "(Dis)figuring the System: Vision, History, and Trauma in Blake's Lambeth Books," in William Blake: Images and Texts, ed. Essick, Viscomi, (San Marino: Huntington Library, 97): 107-36; coauth, "Introduction," Cambridge: Cambridge Univ Press, (97): 1-18; auth, "Keats, Poetry, and The Absence of the Work," 95:3, (98): 334-51; co-ed, Romanticism, History and the Possibilities of Genre, Cambridge: Cambridge Univ Press, (98): 292. **CONTACT ADDRESS** English Dept, Univ of Western Ontario, University College, London, ON, Canada NGA3K7. **EMAIL** trajan@julian.uwo.ca

RALSTON, STEVEN
DISCIPLINE COMMUNICATION STUDIES **EDUCATION** Old Domnion Univ, BA; Univ Tennessee, MA; Ind Univ, PhD. **CAREER** Assoc prof. **MEMBERSHIPS** Am Soc Training Develop; , Med Off Managers Asn, Int Auditors Asn; Asn Bus Commun; Int Commun Asn; Speech Commun Asn. **SELECTED PUBLICATIONS** Auth, pubs on business and professional communication, applied organizational communication, interviewing, and communication education. **CONTACT ADDRESS** Dept of Communication, East Tennessee State Univ, PO Box 70717, Johnson City, TN 37614-0717.

RAMAZANI, JAHAN
PERSONAL Born 02/17/1960, Charlottesville, VA, m, 1995, 1 child **DISCIPLINE** ENGLISH **EDUCATION** Univ Virginia, BA, 81; Oxford, MA, 83; Yale, MA 85, PhD, 88. **CAREER** Asst prof, 88-94, Univ VA, prof, 94-present,. **HONORS AND AWARDS** NEH Fellowship, 92-93; Nominated, Natl Book Critics Circle, 95; William Riley Parker Award, MLA, 97; Guggenhein Fellowship, 00-01. **MEMBERSHIPS** MLA **RESEARCH** Modern poetry, post colonial literature **SELECTED PUBLICATIONS** Auth, The Hybrid Muse: Postcolonial Poetry in English, Chicago, 01; Poetry of Mourning, Chicago, 94; Yeats and the Poetry of Death, Yale, 90. **CONTACT ADDRESS** Dept of English, Univ of Virginia, Bryan Hall, P O Box 400121, Charlottesville, VA 22903. **EMAIL** ramazani@virginia.edu

RAMBUSS, RICHARD
PERSONAL Born Buffalo, NY **DISCIPLINE** RENAISSANCE LITERATURE, CULTURAL STUDIES **EDUCATION** Amherst Col, BA, 83; Johns Hopkins Univ, MA, 86, PhD, 90. **CAREER** Asst prof, Kenyon Col, 90-92; asst prof, Tulane Univ, 92-96; assoc prof, Emory Univ, 96-2000, prof, 2000-. **HONORS AND AWARDS** Amherst Col, BA, summa cum laude, 83; Isabel MacCaffrey Prize, 93. **MEMBERSHIPS** MLA, SAA, RSA. **RESEARCH** Renaissance literature and culture; the metaphysical poets; Milton; Spenser; Shakespeare; film. **SELECTED PUBLICATIONS** Auth, Closet Devotions, Duke UP, 98; Spenser's Secret Career, Cambrigge UP, 93; Spenser's Lives, Spenser's Careers in Spenser and the Subject of Biography, U Mass P, 97; Devotion and Defilement: The Haigiographics of Chaucer's 'Prioress' Tale' in Textual Bodies, SUNY P, 97; Homodevotion in Cruising the Performative, Indiana UP, 95; and Christ's Ganymede, Yale Jour Law Hum, 95. **CONTACT ADDRESS** Dept English, Emory Univ, Atlanta, GA 30322-1061'. **EMAIL** rrambus@emory.edu

RAMET, CARLOS
PERSONAL Born 03/30/1955, London, England, m, 1990 **DISCIPLINE** ENGLISH **EDUCATION** Univ Southern Calif, BA, 77; San Francisco State Univ, MA, 80; Univ IL Chicago, PhD, 88. **CAREER** Asst prof, Ind Univ in Malaysia, 88-90; asst prof to prof, Saginaw Valley State Univ, 91-. **HONORS AND AWARDS** Phi Beta Kappa; UIC Campus Serv Awd, 87; SVSU Fac Grants, 91-94; 96; Creative Writers in the Schools, 94-96; Univ of Mysore (India) Fac Exchange Prof, 96. **MEMBERSHIPS** Mich Acad of Letters, Arts and Sci; Popular Cult Assoc; Phi Beta Kappa. **RESEARCH** Creative Writing Theory and Practice, Film Theory and Interpretation, Late 19th and Early 20th Century British Popular Fiction. **SELECTED PUBLICATIONS** Auth, "Apostle's Creed", Kola 4.3 (91); 25-30; auth, "Chalk Drawings", RAFALE: Revue Lit 6.2 (92); 2; coauth, "An Investigation into Pronunciation Patterns of Malaysian Students of English: An Evaluation Approach", J of the Mysore Univ 50.2, (95); 30-42; auth, "Shadow Love", Critic, (95): 108-113; auth, "Two for Tea", Bilingual Rev 21.1 (96): 68-71; auth, "Reinvigorating the Thriller: Ken Follett's Eye of the Needle as Literature", Mich Acad 30.4, (98): 387-397; auth, "Ken Follett and the Mystery of Early Success", Clues: A J of Detection 19.2 (98): 159-169; auth, Ken Follett: The Transformation of a Writer, Bowling Green, 99; auth, "Following the Eagle", Chiricu 8.2 (99): 35-46. **CONTACT ADDRESS** Dept English, Saginaw Valley State Univ, 7400 Bay Rd, University Center, MI 48710-0001. **EMAIL** ramet@svsu.edu

RAMPERSAD, ARNOLD
PERSONAL Born 11/13/1941, Port of Spain, Trinidad and Tobago, m **DISCIPLINE** ENGLISH **EDUCATION** Bowling Green State Univ, Bowling Green, OH, BA, 1967, MA, 1968; Harvard Univ, Cambridge, MA, 1969, PhD, 1973. **CAREER** Univ of VA, Charlotteville, VA, asst prof, 73-74; Stanford Univ, Stanford, CA, prof, 74-83; Rutgers Univ, New Brunswick, NJ, prof, 83-88; Columbia Univ, New York, NY, prof, 88-90; Princeton Univ, Princeton, NJ, Woodrow Wilson prof of literature, 90-, dir, Program in Afro-American Studies, 94-. **MEMBERSHIPS** Dir, Program in American Studies, Princeton Univ, 1990-95. **SELECTED PUBLICATIONS** The Collected Poems of Langston Hughes, editor, 1994; Jackie Robinson: A Biography, author, Knopf, 1998; Art & Imagination of W E B DuBois, Harvard Univ Press, 1976; Life of Langston Hughes (2 Vols), Oxford Univ Press, 1986, 1988. **CONTACT ADDRESS** Professor, Princeton Univ, McCosh 22, Princeton, NJ 08544.

RAMSEY, C. EARL
DISCIPLINE EIGHTEENTH CENTURY LITERATURE **EDUCATION** Univ Fla, PhD. **CAREER** English and Lit, Univ Ark **HONORS AND AWARDS** Dir, Donaghey Scholars Prog. **SELECTED PUBLICATIONS** Auth, A Midsummer Night's Dream, Homer to Brecht; Ed, No More Elegies. **CONTACT ADDRESS** Univ of Arkansas, Little Rock, 2801 S University Ave., Little Rock, AR 72204-1099. **EMAIL** ceramsey@ualr.edu

RAMSEY, JAROLD
PERSONAL Born 09/01/1937, Bend, OR, m, 1959, 3 children **DISCIPLINE** ENGLISH **EDUCATION** Univ OR, BA honors 59; Univ WA, PhD 66. **CAREER** Univ Rochester, asst, assoc, prof eng, 66-98, prof emeritus 98-; Univ Victoria, BC, vis prof 74-76; Univ WA, instr 63-65. **HONORS AND AWARDS** Lilian Fairchild Awd; Don Walker Awd; NEH Fell; Ingram Merrill writ Grant; QRL Intl Poetry Prize. **MEMBERSHIPS** MLA; AFS; Assn Studies of Amer Indian Lits. **RESEARCH** Shakespeare; Amer Indian Lit; Environmental Lit; Mod Poetry. **SELECTED PUBLICATIONS** The Stories We Tell: An Anthology Of Oregon Folk Literature, Ore St Press, 94; Nehalem Tillamook Tales, Ore St Press, 90; Reading the Fire: Essays in the Traditional Indian Literatures of the Far West, Univ Neb Press, revised and expanded edition forthcoming form Univ Wash Press, 99; Hand Shadows, Qtly Rev Press, 89; Coyote Goes Up River: A cycle for Story Theater and Mime, Georgia Rev, 81. **CONTACT ADDRESS** Eng Dept, Univ of Rochester, Rochester, NY 14627. **EMAIL** ramsey@macmail.

RAMSEY, JOHN T.
PERSONAL Born 07/13/1946, Auburn, NY, m, 1976, 1 child **DISCIPLINE** CLASSICS **EDUCATION** Harvard Col, AB, 68; Balliol Col, BA, 70, MA, 80; Harvard Univ, PhD, 75. **CAREER** Vis assoc prof, Univ Chicago, 82; from asst prof to assoc prof to prof, UIC, 75-. **HONORS AND AWARDS** Phi Beta Kappa, 68; Phi Kappa Phi, 93; NEH Fel, 93-94; AB, summa cum laude; chemn, uic, 97-2000. **MEMBERSHIPS** Am Philological Asn; Asn Ancient Historians; Classical Asn Canada. **RESEARCH** Roman republican history; Roman prose authors; ancient astronomy. **SELECTED PUBLICATIONS** Auth, Studies in Asconius, 76; auth, The Prosecution of C. Manilius in 66 B.C. and Cicero's pro Manilio, 80; auth, Sallusts BELLUM CATILINAE, 84; auth, Cicero & Sallust on the Conspiracy of Catiline, 88; coauth, The Comet of 44 B.C. and Caesar's Funeral Games, 97. **CONTACT ADDRESS** Dept of Classics, Univ of Illinois, Chicago, 601 S Morgan, Chicago, IL 60607-7112. **EMAIL** j-ramsey@uic.edu

RAMSEY, MARY K.
PERSONAL Born 05/27/1962, Okla City, OK, s **DISCIPLINE** ENGLISH **EDUCATION** Okla Baptist Univ, BA, 84; Univ St. Andrews, MPhil, 89; Univ Okla, MA, 93; Yale Univ, PhD, 98. **CAREER** ASST PROF ENG, GA STATE UNIV, 98- **MEMBERSHIPS** Int Soc Anglo-Saxonists; Medieval Acad Am; Southeastern Medieval Asn; S Atlantic Mod Lang Asn. **RESEARCH** Old Eng lang, lit, cult; Dante stud; rel, lit. **SELECTED PUBLICATIONS** various **CONTACT ADDRESS** Dept English, Georgia State Univ, Atlanta, GA 30303-2083. **EMAIL** mkramsey@gsu.edu

RAMSEY, RENEE R.
PERSONAL Born 09/12/1952, Newburgh, NY, m, 1999 **DISCIPLINE** ENGLISH LITERATURE, ARTS **EDUCATION** Univ Ky, BA; MA; PhD. **CAREER** Admin fel, Off Provost; vpres Acad Aff, 98-; assoc prof, Ind State Univ. **HONORS AND AWARDS** Post doc fel; Williams Andrew Clark Mem Lib. **MEMBERSHIPS** John Donne Soc; SCRC; NAWE. **RESEARCH** 17th-Century literature; the metaphysical poets; literature and the arts. **SELECTED PUBLICATIONS** Auth, "The Poet as Art Critic: Identity and Representation Marvell's 'The Gallery'," Studies in Iconography; auth, "Self Presentation in Larew's 'To A.L. Persuasions to Love'," Lit and Culture, 1400-1800. **CONTACT ADDRESS** Dept English, Indiana State Univ, 210 N 7th St, Terre Haute, IN 47809-0001. **EMAIL** aafrenee@isugw.indstate.edu

RANDALL, DALE B. J.
DISCIPLINE ENGLISH, DRAMA **EDUCATION** Western Reserve Univ, BA, 51; Rutgers Univ, MA, 53; Univ of Pa, PhD, 58. **CAREER** Instr, 57-60; asst prof, 60-65; assoc prof, 65-70; full prof, 70-99; prof, dramatic lit, 91-94; prof, practice of drama, 94-99; prof emertius, 99. **HONORS AND AWARDS** Harrison fel, 55-56; Duke fac res fel, 64-65; Duke Endow fel, 70-71; Guggenheim Memorial found fel,, 70-71; NEH Senior fel, 78; senior fel, Folger Shakespeare libr, 86; Am Philos soc, 86; NEH pub award, Winter Fruit, 95; Randall Scholarship for Outstanding Academic Achievement, Alpha Sigma Delta Corp., 96; Randall Awd for Outstanding Undergraduate essay, Duke Univ, 99; harrison fel, 55-56; duke fac res fel, 64-65; duke endow fel, 70-71; guggenheim memorial found fel, 70-71; neh senior fel, 78; senior fel, folger shakespeare libr, 86. **MEMBERSHIPS** Asn of Lit Sch and Critics; Gypsy Lore Soc; Int Shakespeare Asn; Malone Soc; Marlowe Soc; Medieval and Renaissance Drama Soc; MLA; Shakespeare Asn of Am; Southeastern Renaissance Conference. **RESEARCH** Sixteenth and seventeenth-century English prose, poetry, and drama; early twentieth-century American history. **SELECTED PUBLICATIONS** Auth, The Golden Tapestry: A Critical Survey of Non-Chivalric Spanish Fiction in English Translation, 63; auth, Joseph Conrad and Warrington Dawson: The Record of a Friendship, 68; auth, Jonson's "Gypsies Unmasked": Background and Theme of "The Gypsies Metamorphos'd," 75; coed, Studies in Continental Background of Renaissance English Literature, 77; auth, Gentle Flame: The Life and Verse of Dudley, Fourth Lord North, 83; auth, Renaissance Papers, 84-90; auth, "Theatres of Greatness": A Revisionary View of Ford's "Pekin Warbeck," 86; auth, Winter Fruit: English Drama 1642-1660, 95; auth, Soliloquy of a Farmer's Wife: The Diary of Annie Luella Perrin, 99; auth, "Image-making and Image-breaking: Seeing 'The Minister's Black Veil' Through a Miltonic Glass Darkly" in Resources for Am Lit Study, 97. **CONTACT ADDRESS** Dept of English, Duke Univ, Box 90015, Durham, NC 27708. **EMAIL** DBJANDPR@ACPUB.DUKE.EDU

RANES, BARBARA
DISCIPLINE VICTORIAN LITERATURE **EDUCATION** Univ IA, BA, 61, MA, 65, PhD, 70; TESL Cert, Univ Wis, 84. **CAREER** Instr, Univ IA; UW-Oshkosh; UW-Milwaukee; UW-Waukesha; MATC-Madison; Loyola; DePaul; Vis lectr, 95-. **SELECTED PUBLICATIONS** Auth, Psyche: Contemporary Women Poets, 73; From Baba to Tovarishch: The Bolshevik Revolution and Women's Struggle for Liberation, 94. **CONTACT ADDRESS** Dept of Lib Arts, Sch of the Art Inst of Chicago, 37 S Wabash Ave, Chicago, IL 60603.

RANK, HUGH
PERSONAL Born 11/03/1932, Chicago, IL, d, 1958, 4 children **DISCIPLINE** ENGLISH **EDUCATION** Notre Dame, BA, 54, MA, 56, PhD, 69. **CAREER** Ariz State, 59; Fel, Notre Dame, 60-61; St Joseph's, 62-67; Sacred Heart Univ, 68-72; prof, Governors State Univ, 72-99, prof emeritus, 2000-. **HONORS AND AWARDS** Notre Dame Fel; Notre Dame Scholarship; Fulbright Prof; Orwell Awd; Prof of the Year, Governors State Univ. **MEMBERSHIPS** NCTE. **RESEARCH** Persuasian analysis. **SELECTED PUBLICATIONS** Auth, The Pitch; auth, The Pepe Talk; auth, Persuasian Analysis; auth, Language and Public Policy. **CONTACT ADDRESS** 109 W. Mason #2, Santa Barbara, CA 93101. **EMAIL** hughrank@aol.com

RANSOME, CORA
PERSONAL Born 03/08/1944, Northampton Co., VA, m, 1972 **DISCIPLINE** ENGLISH **EDUCATION** Va State Univ, BA, 69; Bowie State Univ, Med, 98; Columbia Pac Univ, PhD, 97. **CAREER** Teacher, Public Sch Syst Northampton Co Va, 67-72; teacher, Public Sch Syst, Charles Co Md, 72-90; teacher, Public Sch Syst DC, 90-91; Prof, Bowie State Univ, Dir of the Comput-Assisted Writing Center, 91-. **HONORS AND AWARDS** Cert of Appreciation for serving as NAACA act-so judge. **MEMBERSHIPS** MAWA, CEA-Mag, Asn for Supv and Curric Develop. **RESEARCH** The impact of technology on teaching and learning. **SELECTED PUBLICATIONS** Auth, African-American Presence in American History Textbooks, Univ Manuscripts Int, 99; auth, African-American Presence in American History Textbooks, forthcoming. **CONTACT ADDRESS** Dept English and Lang, Bowie State Univ, 14000 Jericho Pk Rd, Bowie, MD 20715-3319. **EMAIL** Upshurransome@aol.com

RANTA, RICHARD R.
PERSONAL Born, MN **DISCIPLINE** FILM, COMMUNICATIONS **EDUCATION** Univ Minn, Duluth, BA, 65; Cornell Univ, MA; Univ Iowa, PhD, 74. **CAREER** Instr, Univ Va, 69-72; Dir of Commun Studies, Interim Dean, Univ Col, Asst VP of Acad Affairs, Univ of Memphis, 72-; General Manager, High Water Records; Vice Chemn, Gilliam Commun, Inc. **HONORS AND AWARDS** Who's Who in Am. **MEMBERSHIPS** Memphis Shelby County Film and Tape Comn; Crossroads Music Expo; Tenn Film; Entertainment and Music Comn Advisory Board; Concerts Int; Libertyland/Mid-South Fair; Inst of Egyptian Art and Archaeol; Asn for Commun Admin Bulletin Ed Board; Citizens Law Enforcement Rev Comt; Crime Stoppers; Southern Arts Fed Folk Arts Advisory Board; Delta Sailing Asn; Southern States Commun Asn; Nat Acad of Recording Arts & Sci. **CONTACT ADDRESS** Col of Commun & Fine Arts, Univ of Memphis, Campus Box 526546, Memphis, TN 38152-6546.

RAO, NAGESH
DISCIPLINE INTERCULTURAL COMMUNICATION **EDUCATION** Univ of Southern Miss, MS; Mich State Univ, PhD, 94. **CAREER** Asst prof, Univ Md; asst prof, Oh Univ . **HONORS AND AWARDS** Outstanding Teacher Award, Univ of Md; Outstanding Teacher of the Year Award, Univ of NMex; Pew Teaching Leadership Award; Excellence in Teaching Award, Int Commun Asn. **RESEARCH** Intercultural communication, health communication, role of emotion in creating attitude and behavior change, entertainment-education. **SELECTED PUBLICATIONS** Coauth, "Communication and Community in a City Under Seige: The AIDS Epidemic in San Francisco," Commun Res 22 (95). **CONTACT ADDRESS** School of Interpersonal Commun, Ohio Univ, Athens, OH 45701. **EMAIL** rao@ohio.edu

RAO, RAMESH N.
PERSONAL Born 11/18/1956, Ramanagara, m, 2000 **DISCIPLINE** INTERPERSONAL, INTERCULTURAL, AND MASS COMMUNICATION **EDUCATION** Bangalore Univ, India, BA, 77; Univ S MS, MS, 87; MI State Univ, PhD, 92. **CAREER** Assoc prof, 91-, Truman State Univ. **HONORS AND AWARDS** Kulapati award, Bharatiya Vidya Bhavan, India, 85; grad stud award for tchg excellence, Intl Commun Assn, 91. **MEMBERSHIPS** Mem, Nat Commun Assn; Consult Comm on Indic Traditions and Conflict Mgt, Columbia Univ. **RESEARCH** Asian Indians in the US, and hostage negotiations. **SELECTED PUBLICATIONS** Pub(s), Commun Res; Intl Jourf Gp Tensions; Media Devel; Jour Intl Commun. **CONTACT ADDRESS** Dept of Commun, Truman State Univ, 100 E Normal St, Kirksville, MO 63501-4221. **EMAIL** LL88@Truman.edu

RAO, SANDHYA
DISCIPLINE COMMUNICATIONS **EDUCATION** Banglore Univ, BS, BA, MS; Bowling Green State Univ, PhD. **CAREER** Comm Dept, Southwest Tex State Univ **SELECTED PUBLICATIONS** Auth, International Communication: History, Conflict and Control of the G Metropoliy, Wadsworth Publ, 93; Towards the Development of Computer Attitude Scales for Developing Countries, Int Comm Asn Conf, 94; Role of attitudes and perceptions of users in the implementation of NICNET, in Karnataka State, India, an example, Gazette, 94. **CONTACT ADDRESS** Southwest Texas State Univ, 601 University Dr, San Marcos, TX 78666-4604.

RAPER, JULIUS R.
PERSONAL Born 03/12/1938, Raleigh, NC, m, 1993, 2 children **DISCIPLINE** ENGLISH AND AMERICAN LITERATURE **EDUCATION** Univ NC, BA, 60; Duke Univ, MA, 62; Northwestern Univ, PhD, 66. **CAREER** TA, Northwestern Univ, 63-64; asst prof to prof, Univ of NC, 66-00, **HONORS AND AWARDS** Brooks Scholar, UNC, 56-60; Phi Beta Kappa; Wood Wilson Scholar, 60; Fulbright Scholar, Greence, 72-74, 79-81; Fel of Coun S Univ, 60-63. **MEMBERSHIPS** Soc for Study of S Lit; SAMLA; MLA, Int Lawrence Durrell Soc; Thomas Wolfe Soc; St George Tucker Soc. **RESEARCH** Literature of the American South, especially Glasgow, Wolfe, Faulkner, Barth, Styron, Percy and Contemporary Brit and American fiction, especially Durrell, Barth, Fowles, Bellow, Pynchon. **SELECTED PUBLICATIONS** Auth, Without Shelter: The Early Career of Ellen Glasgow, 71; auth, From the Sunken Garden: The Fiction of Ellen Glasgow, 1916-1945, 80; ed, Ellen Glasgow's Reasonable Doubts: A Collection of her Writing, 88; auth, Narcissus from Rubble: Competing Models of Character in Contemporary Brit and American Fiction, 92; coed, Lawrence Durrell: Comprehending the Whole, 95. **CONTACT ADDRESS** Dept English, Univ of No Carolina, Chapel Hill, Campus Box 3520, Chapel Hill, NC 27599-3520. **EMAIL** jrraper@email.unc.edu

RAPP, M. H. KRIS
DISCIPLINE ENGLISH **EDUCATION** Southwest Mo State univ, BS, 57; Univ Tulsa, MA, 75. **CAREER** ESL, Univ of Tulsa, 75-78; adv to asst prof, Tulsa Community Col, 78-79. **HONORS AND AWARDS** Outstanding Teachers in Am. **MEMBERSHIPS** MLA, NCTE, TETYC. **RESEARCH** Rhetoric, Freshman Writing, Literature (American emphasized). **SELECTED PUBLICATIONS** Auth, The Little Blue Book: 56 Most Frequently Made Errors, McGraw Hill. **CONTACT ADDRESS** 4226 E 52nd St, Tulsa, OK 74135-3907. **EMAIL** krisrap@webzone.net

RASCHKE, DEBRA
DISCIPLINE ENGLISH **EDUCATION** Colo State Univ, BA, 74; MA, 79; Univ Mass, PhD, 91. **CAREER** Vis Asst Prof, Va Commonwealth Univ, 92-94; , Vis Asst Prof, Col of William & Mary, 96-97; From Asst Prof to Prof, Southeast Mo State Univ, 95-. **HONORS AND AWARDS** Kent Libr Endowment Grant, 99; Grad Sch Res Grant, 99; Spec Libr Allocation Grant, 97, 00; Who's Who of Am Teachers, 00; Who's Who in Am Women, 00; Who's Who in Am, 00. **MEMBERSHIPS** MLA, Margaret Atwood Soc, Doris Lessing Soc, Int Virginia Woolf Soc, Iris Murdock Soc, Soc for the Study of Narrative, Modernist Studies Asn. **RESEARCH** Twentieth-Century British literature, modern and contemporary, post-colonial literature, contemporary critical theory, post-colonial theory, gender studies. **SELECTED PUBLICATIONS** Auth, Penelope Lively's 'Moon Tiger': Re-Envisioning the 'History of the World'," Ariel, 26 (95): 115-132; auth, "Margaret Atwood's 'The Handmaid's Tale': False Borders and Subtle Subversions," Lit Interpretation Theory, 6 (95): 257-268; auth, "Rescuing the Concrete and Other Things Physical from the Dung Heap: Eavan Boland's 'Outside History' and 'In a Time of Violence'," Colby Quart, 32 (96): 135-142; auth, "Re-Envisioning Plato's Cave: Forter's 'Passage to India'," The Comparatist, 21 (97): 10-24; auth, "Breaking the Engagement with Philosophy: Re-Envisioning Hetero/Homo Relations in 'Maurice'," in Queer Forster (Chicago: Univ Chicago Pr, 97), 151-165; auth, "'To the Lighthouse' 'Through the Looking Glass': Woolf's Revisionary Metaphysics," in Virginia Woolf and her Influences (New York: Pace UP, 98), 288-293; auth, "Cabalistic Gardens: Doris Lessing's 'Memoirs of a Survivor'," in Spiritual Exploration in

the Works of Doris Lessing (Westport, CT: Greenwood Pr, 99), 43-54. **CONTACT ADDRESS** Dept English, Southeast Missouri State Univ, 1 University Plaza, Cape Girardeau, MO 63701-4710.

RASKIN, JONAH
PERSONAL Born 01/03/1942, Brooklyn, NY **DISCIPLINE** COMMUNICATIONS **EDUCATION** Columbia Col, BA, 63; Columbia Univ, MA, 64; Univ Manchester, PhD, 67. **CAREER** Prof, chemn, Commun Stud Dept. **HONORS AND AWARDS** Fulbright prof, Belgium, 86-87. **SELECTED PUBLICATIONS** Auth, For the Hell of It: The Life and Times of Abbie Hoffman, 96. **CONTACT ADDRESS** 1801 E Cotati Ave, Rohnert Park, CA 94928. **EMAIL** jonah.raskin@sonoma.edu

RASULA, JED
DISCIPLINE ENGLISH LITERATURE **EDUCATION** Univ Calif Santa Cruz, PhD. **CAREER** Dept Eng, Queen's Univ **HONORS AND AWARDS** Frank Knox Awd. **RESEARCH** Modernism; modern poetry and poetics; literary sociology; critical theory; cultural studies and history of ideas; jazz; film; architecture; literature and science. **SELECTED PUBLICATIONS** Auth, The American Poetry Wax Museum: Reality Effects 1940-1990, NCTE, 95; ed, Imagining Language, MIT, 96. **CONTACT ADDRESS** English Dept, Queen's Univ at Kingston, Kingston, ON, Canada K7L 3N6. **EMAIL** rasulaj@post.QueensU.CA

RATCLIFFE, STEPHEN
PERSONAL Born Boston, MA, d, 1975, 1 child **DISCIPLINE** ENGLISH **EDUCATION** Univ Calif at Berkeley, BA, MA, PhD. **CAREER** Asst prof; Mills Col, 84-. **RESEARCH** Creative writing; Shakespeare; Renaissance Poetry; English Romantic poetry; contemporary poetry and poetics. **SELECTED PUBLICATIONS** Writing [Echoes] Writing, Santa Barbara Rev, Vol 2, 94; Dahlen's Reading, Raddle Moon 13, Vol 6, 94; Preface to Mallarme: poem in prose, Poetic Briefs, 94; Untitled, range/landscape, 94; Correspondences, Santa Barbara Rev, Vol 3, 95; Michael Gregory, Catalogue for Gail Severn Gallery, 95; Conceal me what I am: Reading Act 1, Scene 2 of Twelfth Night, Univ Miss Stud in Engl, New Ser 11-12, 95; 'Shakespeare' and 'I., Exemplaria: A J Theory in Medieval and Renaissance Stud, Vol 8, 96; Grenier's Scrawl, Witz: A J Contemp Poetics, 96; auth, Words and Music: Campion and the Madrigal Ayre Tradition, Approaches to Teaching Shorter Elizabethan Poetry, MLA Approaches to Teaching World Lit Ser, 97; What Doesn't Happen in Hamlet: The Queen's Speech, Exemplaria: A J Theory in Medieval and Renaissance Stud, 97; Eigner's Scores, Witz, 97; Auth, Listening to Reading, Suny Press, 00. **CONTACT ADDRESS** Dept of English, Mills Col, 5000 MacArthur Blvd, Oakland, CA 94613-1301. **EMAIL** sratclif@mills.edu

RATHBURN, PAUL A.
DISCIPLINE LITERATURE **EDUCATION** Univ Wis, PhD. **CAREER** Prof emer, Univ Notre Dame. **HONORS AND AWARDS** Hesburgh Lectr. **RESEARCH** Performance theory, interconnections between medieval and English Renaissance drama, teaching Shakespeare through performance. **SELECTED PUBLICATIONS** Publishes essays in Shakespeare-on-Film, and lectures on Shakespearean tragedy in the Notre Dame Great Teachers Series, Golden Dome Productions, 92. **CONTACT ADDRESS** Dept of English, Univ of Notre Dame, 202 Decio Fac Hall, Notre Dame, IN 46556. **EMAIL** paul.a.rathburn.1@nd.edu

RATLIFF, GERALD LEE
PERSONAL Born 10/23/1944, Middletown, OH **DISCIPLINE** ENGLISH; COMMUNICATION **EDUCATION** Georgetown Col, BA, 67; Univ Cincinnati, MA, 70; Bowling Green St Univ, PhD, 75. **HONORS AND AWARDS** Medallion of Honor, Theta Alpha Phi, 89; Silver Medal of Honor, Int Biog Centere, 98; Teaching Fel, East Commun Assoc, 98; Man of Year, Amer Biog Inst, 998; Deputy Gen Dir Int Biog Centre, 99; theta alpha phi nat theatre honorary, 90; fulbright scholar, 90; fel, int schools of theatre assoc, 91; us delegate john f. kennedy center for perf arts, int scholar exchange prog, 91; outstanding graduate alumni award, bowling green st univ, 94; fel, nat **MEMBERSHIPS** E Commun Assoc; Nat Commun Assoc, NY Col English Assoc; Fulbright Assoc. **RESEARCH** Dramatic imagery in Mamet & O'Neill; Reader's Theatre approaches to visualization; literary themes in contemporary drama & poetry **SELECTED PUBLICATIONS** Coauth, An Introduction to Theatre, Rosen Press, 88; auth, The Politics of Machiavelli's The Prince, Barron's Publ Ltd, 86; A Sourcebook for Playing Scenes, Meriwether Publ Ltd, 93; Contemporary Scene Study, Meriwether Publ Ltd, 96; The Theatre Handbook, Meriwether Publ Ltd, 98. **CONTACT ADDRESS** Office of Provost, SUNY, Col at Potsdam, 44 Pierrepont Ave, Potsdam, NY 13676-2200. **EMAIL** ratlifgl@potsdam.edu

RATLIFF, PEGGY S.
PERSONAL Born 07/26/1958, Orangeburg, SC, m, 1993 **DISCIPLINE** ENGLISH **EDUCATION** SC State Univ, BA; SC State Univ, M.Ed; Howard Univ, PhD, 90. **CAREER** From grad asst to instr, Howard Univ; from assoc to prof, Claflin Col; adjunct prof, SC State Univ. **HONORS AND AWARDS** SC Electric and Gas Company Fel, SC State Col, 74; Dick Horne's Found Fel, SC State Col, 74; United Negro College Fund Fel, 81-83, 85-88; NEH Fel, 85; Dorothy C. Danforth Fel, 89; Lilly Found Dissertation Scholar, 89; Who's Who of Am Women, 92; named Outstanding Young Woman of Am, 91; grant, Office of Congressman James Clyburn, 95; Hunters Awd for Excellence in Teaching, 97; **MEMBERSHIPS** Nat Coun of Teachers of English, Alpha Kappa Alpha, Good Hope AME Church, Nat Asn for the Advancement of Colored People, Col Lang Assoc, SC Curriculum Congress, Am Asn of Col for Teacher Educ, SC Asn of Departments of English, George Moses Horton Soc, SC Humanities Coun Board of Dir. **RESEARCH** Women writers, African American and Caribbean women writers, mythology and Shakespeare. **SELECTED PUBLICATIONS** Auth, "The Black Athlete and His Education," CORT (80); auth, "Wit and Alexander Pope's The Rape of the Lock," CORT (81); auth, "African-American Women, Conflicts of Gender," Encyclopedia of Multiculturalism (94); contributing ed, "American Civilization and Culture Vol 1, Am Heritage Custom Pub Group, 94; contributing ed, American Civilization and Culture Vol 2, Am Heritage Custom Pub Group, 95; auth, "Not a Bastions of PhD's at Historical Black Colleges, University Faculty Vocie (97); "Ed Bullins," Contemporary African-American Novelist: A Bio-Bibliographical Critical Sourcebook, Greenwood Press (New York), 98; auth, "Marcus Garvey," African-American Authors, 1745-1945. A Bio-Bibliographical Critical Sourcebook, Greenwood Press (New York), 99. **CONTACT ADDRESS** Dept Commun, Claflin Col, 400 College St, Orangeburg, SC 29115-4472. **EMAIL** pratliff@claflin.edu

RAVITZ, A.
DISCIPLINE LITERATURE **EDUCATION** CCNY, BA, 49; NYU, MA, 50; PhD, 55. **CAREER** Asst prof, Pa State Univ, 53-58; prof, Hiram Col, 58-66; prof, emeritus prof, & chemn of english dept, Calif State Univ at Dominguez Hills, 66-. **HONORS AND AWARDS** Outstanding Prof, 70. **RESEARCH** American Literature 1865-1930. **SELECTED PUBLICATIONS** Auth, Rex Beach, Boise State Univ Press, 92; auth, Thunder on the Left: Leane Zugsmith's Prose, Int Pub, 94; auth, Imitations of Life: Fannie Hurst's Gaslight Sonatas, SIU Press, 97. **CONTACT ADDRESS** Dept English, California State Univ, Dominguez Hills, 1000 E Victoria St, Carson, CA 90747-0001.

RAVITZ, ABE C.
PERSONAL Born 05/20/1927, New York, NY, m, 1989, 4 children **DISCIPLINE** AMERICAN LITERATURE **EDUCATION** CCNY, BA, 49; NYork Univ, MA, 50, PhD, 55. **CAREER** Asst Prof, Pa State Univ, 53-58; Assoc Prof to Prof English, Hiram Col, 58-66; Prof English, 66-86, Dept Chair, 66-86, Calif State Univ - Dominguez Hills, Emeritus Prof English, 86-. **MEMBERSHIPS** MLA; ASA **RESEARCH** American literature; American popular culture. **SELECTED PUBLICATIONS** Auth, Alfred Henry Lewis, Boise State Univ Press, 86; Rex Beach, Boise State Univ Press, 95; Thunder on the Left: Leane Zugsmith's Prose, Int Publ, 95; Imitations of Life: Fannie Hurst's Gaslight Sonatas, Southern Ill Univ Press, 97. **CONTACT ADDRESS** English Dept, California State Univ, Dominguez Hills, Dominguez Hills, CA 90747.

RAWLINGS, WENDY MAI
PERSONAL Born 02/14/1967, Washington, DC, s **DISCIPLINE** ENGLISH **EDUCATION** Trinity Colo, BA, 88; Colo State Univ, MFA, 96; Univ Ut, PhD, 00. **CAREER** Asst prof, Univ Ala, 00-. **HONORS AND AWARDS** Sandstone Prize, Ohio State Univ Press, 00; Steffensen Cannon Scholar, Univ Ut; Lauren Husted Scholar, Bread Loaf Writer's Conf; Patricia Highsmith-Plangman Residency Recipient, Yaddo. **MEMBERSHIPS** Assoc Writing Prog. **RESEARCH** Short fiction by women; The comic novel. **SELECTED PUBLICATIONS** Auth, "Come Back Irish," The Atlantic Monthly, 98; auth, "Heteroworld," Colo Rev, 99; auth, "Batcatching," The Bellingham Rev, 00; auth, "I'm from Ballymullet," The Atlantic Monthly, 00; auth, Come Back Irish, Ohio State Univ Press, (forthcoming). **CONTACT ADDRESS** Dept English, Univ of Alabama, Tuscaloosa, Box 870244, Tuscaloosa, AL 35487-0244. **EMAIL** wraling@bama.ua.edu

RAWLINS, WILLIAM K.
DISCIPLINE INTERPERSONAL COMMUNICATION AND COMMUNICATION THEORY **EDUCATION** Temple Univ, PhD, 81. **CAREER** Prof, dir, grad stud, Purdue Univ. **RESEARCH** The communicative achievement; management of friendship across the life course. **SELECTED PUBLICATIONS** Auth, A Dialectic Analysis of the Tensions, Functions, and Strategic Challenges of Communication in Young Adult Friendships, Commun Yearbk, 12, 89; Friendship Matters: Communication, Dialectics, and the Life Course, Aldine de Gruyter, 92. **CONTACT ADDRESS** Dept of Commun, Purdue Univ, West Lafayette, 2130 LAEB, West Lafayette, IN 47907-1080. **EMAIL** wrawlins@purdue.edu

RAY, EILEEN BERLIN
DISCIPLINE ORGANIZATIONAL COMMUNICATION, HEALTH COMMUNICATION **EDUCATION** Univ SC, BA, MEd; MI State Univ, MA; Iniv Wash, PhD. **CAREER** Undergrad prog dir, Cleveland State Univ. **SELECTED PUBLICATIONS** Auth, Communication and Disenfranchisement: Social Health Issues and Implications, Lawrence Erlbaum & Assoc, 96; Case studies in communication and disenfranchisement: Applications to social health issues, Lawrence Erlbaum & Assoc, 96; Case Studies in Health Communication, Lawrence Erlbaum & Assoc, 93. **CONTACT ADDRESS** Commun Dept, Cleveland State Univ, 83 E 24th St, Cleveland, OH 44115. **EMAIL** e.berlinray@csuohio.edu

RAY, GEORGE B.
DISCIPLINE COMMUNICATION & CULTURE, LANGUAGE & COMMUNICATION, INTERPERSONAL COMMUNUNICATION **EDUCATION** Bowling Green State Univ, BA; Cornell Univ, MPS; Univ WA, PhD. **CAREER** Comm, Cleveland St Univ. **SELECTED PUBLICATIONS** Co-auth, Shyness, Self-confidence and Social Interaction, Soc Psychol Quart, 93; auth, Identities in Crisis: Individualism, Disenfranchisement and the Self-help Culture, Communication and Disenfranchisement: Social Health Issues and Implications, Lawrence Erlbaum, 96. **CONTACT ADDRESS** Commun Dept, Cleveland State Univ, 83 E 24th St, Cleveland, OH 44115. **EMAIL** g.ray@csuohio.edu

RAY, ROBERT H.
PERSONAL Born 04/29/1940, San Saba, TX, m, 1962, 2 children **DISCIPLINE** ENGLISH **EDUCATION** Univ of Tex at Austin, BA, 63, PhD, 67. **CAREER** From asst prof to prof, Baylor Univ, 67- . **HONORS AND AWARDS** Phi Beta Kappa. **MEMBERSHIPS** MLA; Asn of Lit Scholars and Critics; John Donne Soc. **RESEARCH** Donne; Herbert; Marvell; Shakespeare; Hooker. **SELECTED PUBLICATIONS** Auth, The Herbert Allusion Book: Allusions to George Herbert in the Seventeenth Century, Studies in Philol 83:4, 86; Approaches to Teaching Shakespeare's King Lear, 86; A John Donne Companion, 90; A George Herbert Companion, 95; An Andrew Marvell Companion, 98. **CONTACT ADDRESS** Dept of English, Baylor Univ, Waco, PO Box 97406, Waco, TX 76798. **EMAIL** robert_ray@baylor.edu

RAYOR, DIANE J.
PERSONAL Born 04/18/1958, Cheyenne, WY, m, 1986, 1 child **DISCIPLINE** CLASSICAL LITERATURE **EDUCATION** Univ CA, Santa Cruz, PhD, 87. **CAREER** Vis asst prof, , 88-91, Northwestern Univ; assoc prof, 91-, Grand Valley St Univ. **MEMBERSHIPS** APA; Women's Classical Caucus. **RESEARCH** Translation; Greek poetry (Archaic & Hellenistic); women in antiquity. **SELECTED PUBLICATIONS** ed., Latin Lyric and Elegiaic Poetry, Garland, 95; auth, Sappho's Lyre, 91-; coauth, Callimachus, Johns Hopkins, 88. **CONTACT ADDRESS** Dept of Classics, Grand Valley State Univ, 1 Campus Dr, Allendale, MI 49401. **EMAIL** rayord@gvsu.edu

REAL, MICHAEL
PERSONAL m, 1 child **DISCIPLINE** TELECOMMUNICATIONS **EDUCATION** St Paul Sem, BA; St Thomas Col, MA; Univ IL, PhD. **CAREER** Instr, Univ IL; prof, Univ CA; dept ch, 86-91; prof-, Fordham Univ. **RESEARCH** Media, cult, and soc responsibility. **SELECTED PUBLICATIONS** Auth, Mass Mediated Culture, Prentice Hall, 77; Global Ritual: Olympic Media Coverage and International Understanding, UNESCO, 86; Super Media: A Cultural Studies Approach, Sage, 89. **CONTACT ADDRESS** Dept of Commun, San Diego State Univ, 5500 Campanile Dr, San Diego, CA 92182. **EMAIL** mreal@sciences.sdsu.edu

REARDON, COLLEEN
DISCIPLINE MUSIC HISTORY **EDUCATION** UCLA, AB; MA; PhD. **CAREER** Assoc prof and dir undergrad studies, 93. **HONORS AND AWARDS** NEH Summer Stipend; Fulbright Fellow. **RESEARCH** Music in seventeenth-century Siena; convent music. **SELECTED PUBLICATIONS** Auth, Musica franca: Essays in Honor of Frank A. D'Accone, Pendragon, 96; Agostino Agazzari and Music at Siena Cathedral 1597-1641, Oxford UP, 93; Music as Leitmotif in Louisa May Alcott's Little Women, Children's Literature, 96; Insegniar la zolfa ai gittatelli: Music and Teaching at Santa Maria della Scala, Siena, during the Late Sixteenth and Early Seventeenth Centuries in Musica franca: Essays in Honor of Frank A. D'Accone, Pendragon, 96;, Music and Musicians at Santa Maria di Provenzano, Siena, 1595-1640, Jour Musicol, 93; Two Parody Magnificats on Palestrina's Vestiva i colli, Studi musicali, 86. **CONTACT ADDRESS** Dept Music, SUNY, Binghamton, PO Box 6000, Binghamton, NY 13902-6000.

REBHOLTZ, RONALD A.
PERSONAL Born 05/28/1932, St. Louis, MO **DISCIPLINE** ENGLISH **EDUCATION** St Louis Univ, BA, 53; Oxford Univ, BA, 58; MA, 61; PhD, 65. **CAREER** Instr, asst prof, assoc prof, prof, prof emeritus, Stanford Univ, 61-. **HONORS AND AWARDS** Woodrow Wilson Fel, 53-54; Danforth Fel, 53-61; Rhodes Scholar, 56-59; Dinkelspiel Awd, 81; Dean's Awd for Excel in Teach, 86; Richard W. Lyman Awd for Univ Ser, 93. **MEMBERSHIPS** MLA; RSA. **RESEARCH** Renaissance literature with a current emphasis on the history plays of Shakespeare; opera; baseball. **SELECTED PUBLICATIONS**

Auth, The Life of Fulke Greville, First Lord Brooke (Oxford: Clarendon Press, 71); ed, The Complete Poems of Sir Thomas Wyatt (Hadmondsworth: Penguin Books, 78); auth, "Love's Newfangleness: A Comparison of Greville and Wyatt," Stud in Lit Imagin (78); auth, "Fulke Greville," in Tudor England: An Encyclopedia (Hamden, CT: Garland Pub, 01). **CONTACT ADDRESS** Eng Dept, Stanford Univ, Stanford, CA 94305. **EMAIL** rebholtz@stanford.edu

RECK, DAVID
PERSONAL Born 01/12/1935, Rising Star, TX, m, 1968, 2 children **DISCIPLINE** ETHNOMUSICOLGY; COMPOSITION **EDUCATION** Univ of Houston, BM, 58; Univ of Texas, MM, 59; Wesleyan Univ, PhD, 84. **CAREER** Prof, Amherst Col, 74-. **HONORS AND AWARDS** Guggenheim fel. **RESEARCH** Music of South India **SELECTED PUBLICATIONS** Coauth, Worlds of Music, 97; auth, Music of the Whole Earth, 97. **CONTACT ADDRESS** Dept of Music, Amherst Col, Amherst, MA 01002. **EMAIL** dbreck@amherst.edu

REDDICK, ROBERT J.
PERSONAL Born Minneapolis, MN, m, 1967, 2 children **DISCIPLINE** ENGLISH **EDUCATION** Univ MN, BS, 66, MA, 69, PhD, 75. **CAREER** Assoc prof; assoc ed, Harold Frederic Edition, 78-85; ed, Market-Place, 81, Damnation of Theron Ware or Illumination, 85 & Gloria Mundi, 86; asst ed, Allegorica, 78-87; UTA Adv Bd, Pre/Text, 83-. **HONORS AND AWARDS** 1,642 Summer stipend, Univ TX, Arlington, 78. **MEMBERSHIPS** Int Soc Anglo-Saxonists; Ling Soc Am, 70-95; MLA; Tex Medieval Asn. **SELECTED PUBLICATIONS** Auth, On the Underlying Order of Early West Saxon, J Ling 18, 82; Old English unlaed: A Note on Andreas, Engl Lang Notes 22, 85 The Grammar of Logic, Pre/Text 6, 85; Textlinguistics, Text Theory, and Language Users, Word 37, 86; rev, Techniques of Translation: Chaucer's Boece, Allegorica 9, 87-88; Clause-Bound Grammar and Old English Syntax, Stud Philol 87, 90; English Expository Discourse, Language in Context: Essays for Robert E. Longacre, Dallas, Summer Inst Ling, 92; Heavy Noun Phrases in Pre-900 Prose, Engl Stud 74, 93. **CONTACT ADDRESS** Dept of Eng, Univ of Texas, Arlington, 203 Carlisle Hall, PO Box 19035, Arlington, TX 76019-0595. **EMAIL** breddick@exchange.uta.edu

REDDY, MAUREEN T.
PERSONAL Born 03/20/1955, Boston, MA, m, 1979, 2 children **DISCIPLINE** ENGLISH **EDUCATION** BA, 76, MA, 78, Boston Col; PhD, 85 Univ Minnesota. **CAREER** Asst Prof, 85-87, Haverford Col; Prof, 87-, Rhode Island Col. **HONORS AND AWARDS** Pioneer and Trailblazer Award, Rhode Island Commission on Women, 95; Koppelman Award for Excellence in Feminist Studies of Popular Culture and American Culture, 95; Minnesota Book Award for Mother Journeys, 95. **MEMBERSHIPS** Southern New England Consortium on Race and Ethnicity; Natl Women's Studies Assoc; Northeast Victorian Studies Assoc; Modern Lang Assoc. **RESEARCH** Race and interracial relationships in genre fiction **SELECTED PUBLICATIONS** Auth, Crossing the Color Line: Race, Parenting, and Culture, 94; Coauth, Mother Journey's: Feminists Write About Mothering, 94; ed, Everyday Acts Against Racism, 96; Auth, Elizabeth Cleghorn Gaskell, Dictionary of Literary Biography, 95; Racism, The Reader's Companion to US Women's History, 97; Invisibility/Hypervisibility: The Paradox of Normative Whiteness, Tranformations, 98; auth, The Female Detective in Mystery & Suspense Writers, ed, Robin Winks, Scribners, 99. **CONTACT ADDRESS** Dept of English, Rhode Island Col, 600 Mt. Pleasant Ave., Providence, RI 02908. **EMAIL** mreddy@ric.edu

REDFIELD, JAMES M.
PERSONAL Born Chicago, IL, m, 4 children **DISCIPLINE** CLASSICAL LANGUAGE AND LITERATURE **EDUCATION** Univ Chicago, BA, 54, PhD, 61. **CAREER** Instr, Comt Soc Thought, 60-62; Asst prof, 62-65; Assoc prof, 65-75; Prof, Univ Chicago, 76-. **HONORS AND AWARDS** Woodrow Wilson Fel; NEH Younger Sch; Am Coun Learned Socs; Martha Sutton Weeks Fel; NEH Grant. **MEMBERSHIPS** APA. **SELECTED PUBLICATIONS** Auth, Anthropology and the Classics, Arion, 91; auth, The Politics of Immortality, Recherches et Rencontres, 91; auth, The Sexes in Hesiod, Reinterpreting the Classics, 93; auth, Homo Domesticus, the Greeks, Univ Chicago Press, 94; auth, "Nature and Culture in the Iliad: The Tragedy of Hector," 2nd ed, Duke Univ Press, 94. **CONTACT ADDRESS** Univ of Chicago, 1126 E 59th St, SS Box 94, Chicago, IL 60637. **EMAIL** jmredfie@midway.uchicago.edu

REDFIELD, MARC
PERSONAL Born 10/06/1958, New York, NY, m, 1 child **DISCIPLINE** ENGLISH **EDUCATION** Yale Univ, BA, 80; Cornell Univ, PhD, 90. **CAREER** Asst prof, Universite de Geneve, 86-90; asst prof to assoc prof, Claremont Grad Univ, 90-. **HONORS AND AWARDS** MLA Prize for First Book, 97. **MEMBERSHIPS** MLA; NASSR; ACLA. **RESEARCH** Romanticism, Literary Theory. **SELECTED PUBLICATIONS** Auth, Phantom Foundations: Aesthetic Ideology and the Buildings Roman, Cornell Univ Pr, 96. **CONTACT ADDRESS** Dept English, Claremont Graduate Sch, 170 East 10th St, Claremont, CA 91711-5909. **EMAIL** marc.redfield@cgu.edu

REDFORD, BRUCE
PERSONAL Born 08/09/1953, Djakarta, Indonesia **DISCIPLINE** ENGLISH LITERATURE **EDUCATION** Brown Univ, BA, 75; King's Col, BA, 77; Princeton Univ, PhD, 81. **CAREER** Asst prof, 81-86, assoc prof, 86-91, prof, 91-98, Univ Chicago; prof, 98-, Boston Univ. **HONORS AND AWARDS** Guggenheim Fel; Kress Fel; Nat Gallery Art; Vis Fel, All St's Coll, Oxford. **MEMBERSHIPS** ALSC. **RESEARCH** 17th and 18th century English literature; the classical tradition. **SELECTED PUBLICATIONS** Auth, "Frederick Albert Pottle," Yale Univ Lib Gazz 66 (91): 64-69; auth, "Venice Mythologized," Apollo 140 (94): 13-16; auth, "Johnson Ventrilo quens," Transactions of the Johnson Soc (95):1-11; co-ed, Essays in Honor of J D Fleeman, Studies in Bibliography 48 (95); auth, "Frisch weht der Wind': Reynolds und das parodistische Portraet," in Edgar Wind: Kunstizistoriker und Philosoph, ed. Horst Bredekamp et al. (Akademie Verlag, 98), 13-31; auth, Boswell's Life of Johnson: An Edition of the Original Manuscript, Volume II, Yale Univ Press and Edinburgh Univ Press (98); auth, Taming Savage Johnson," in Lit Imagination I (99), 85-10. **CONTACT ADDRESS** University Professors, Boston Univ, 745 Commonwealth Ave, Boston, MA 02215. **EMAIL** bredford@bu.edu

REDMAN, TIM
DISCIPLINE LITERATURE STUDIES **EDUCATION** Univ Chicago, PhD, 87. **CAREER** Assoc prof. **RESEARCH** American and British modernism; American studies; medieval and renaissance Italian literature. **SELECTED PUBLICATIONS** Auth, Ezra Pound and Italian Fascism, Cambridge, 91; Louis Zukofsky, Charles Scribner's Sons, 91; ed, Offical Rules of Chess, 87. **CONTACT ADDRESS** Dept of Literature, Univ of Texas, Dallas, Richardson, TX 75083-0688. **EMAIL** redman@utdallas.edu

REECE, DEBRA J.
PERSONAL Born 04/10/1958, Denver, CO, m, 1994 **DISCIPLINE** COMMUNICATION **EDUCATION** Regent Univ, Va Bch, Va, MA, 90; Univ Ky, Lexington, PhD, 96. **CAREER** Asst prof, Bethel Col, St Paul, Minn, 96-. **MEMBERSHIPS** Nat Commun Assoc **RESEARCH** Media uses & gratifications within cross-cultural contexts; reception analysis of news programming. **SELECTED PUBLICATIONS** Auth, review of Mind Media Industry in Europe, J Quart, vol 72, 475-476, 95; auth, Covering and communication: The symbolism of dress among Muslim women, Howard J of Commun, vol 7, 35-52, 96; auth, The Gendering of Prayer: An Ethnographic Study of Muslim Women in the United States, J of Commun & Relig, vol 20, 37-47, 97. **CONTACT ADDRESS** Bethel Col, Minnesota, 3900 Bethel Dr, Saint Paul, MN 55112. **EMAIL** debra-reece@bethel.edu

REECE, STEVE
DISCIPLINE GREEK AND ROMAN EPIC **EDUCATION** Univ HI, BA, 82, MA, 84; UCLA, PhD, 90. **CAREER** Assoc Prof, classics, St Olaf Col. **HONORS AND AWARDS** Phi Beta Kappa, 82-; Am sch of Classical Studies at Athens, Lord Fel, 88; Univ of Missouri, NEH Fel, 92; Am Acad in Rome, Fulbright Fel, 94; Eta Sigma Phi, Honorary Mem, 95-; Center for Hellwnic studies, Washington DC, Grant, 00. **MEMBERSHIPS** Am Philological Assoc, classical Assoc of the middle west and south, classical assoc of Minnesota, Am sch of Classical Studies in athens, am Acad in Rome, Am soc of paprologists, Nat endowment for the Huanities, Am assoc of Unvi Prof, Nat assoc of storytelling. **RESEARCH** Homeric studies, especially all aspects of oral-formulaic theory, but including Indo-European philology, Linear B, dialectology, metriccs, archaelogy, textural transmission and criticim, scholia, comparative epic. **SELECTED PUBLICATIONS** Auth, "Homeric Influence in stesichorus Nostoi," Bulletin of the Am Soc of Papyrologists, vol 25, (88), 1-8, auth, The Stanger's Welcome: Oral theory and the easthetics of the Homeric Hospitality Scene, Ann Arbor: Univ of MI Press, (93), 264; auth, "The Cretan Odyssey: a Lie Truer than Truth," Am J of Philology, vol 115, (94), 157-173; auth, "The Three Circuits of the Suitors: A Ring compositon in Odyssey, (95), 207-229; auth, "A Figura Etymologica in the Homneric Hym to Hermes," Classical j, (97), 29-39; auth, "Teaching Koine Greek in a Classics Department," Calssical J, (98), 417-429; auth, "Some Homeric Etymologies in the Light of Oral-formulaic Theory," calssical world, (99), 185-199; auth, "Sokos Erioumios Hermes Iliad 20.72: the Modification of a traditional formula," Glotta: Zeitschrift fur griechische und lateinische sprache, (99-00), 259-280; auth, "The Cypriot Syllabaries," Encyclopedia of Greece and the Hellenic Tradition, (London: Fitzroy dearborn pub, 00), 1587-1588; auth, "the Epithet Eridromos in Nonnus dionysaca," Philologus: Zeitschrift fur antike Literatru und ihre Rezeption , forthcoming. **CONTACT ADDRESS** St. Olaf Col, 1520 St Olaf Ave, Northfield, MN 55057. **EMAIL** reece@stolaf.edu

REED, BILL
DISCIPLINE COMMUNICATION STUDIES **EDUCATION** Univ Memphis, BA; Univ Mich, MA, PhD. **CAREER** Asst prof. **RESEARCH** Argumentation and debate; business communication; early American political and religious rhetorical discourse. **SELECTED PUBLICATIONS** Co-auth, Speech Communication in a Democratic Society. **CONTACT ADDRESS** Dept of Communication, SUNY, Col at Brockport, Brockport, NY 14420. **EMAIL** breed@po.brockport.edu

REED, JOHN R.
PERSONAL Born 01/24/1938, Duluth, MN, w, 1971 **DISCIPLINE** ENGLISH LITERATURE **EDUCATION** Univ of Minn at Duluth, double BA, 59; Univ of Rochester, PhD, 63. **CAREER** Instr, Univ of Cincinnati, 62-64; asst prof, Univ of Conn, 64-65; vis fel & lectr, Univ of Warwick, 66-67; asst prof, 65-68, assoc prof, 68-71, prof, Wayne State Univ, 71-. **HONORS AND AWARDS** Guggenheim Fel, 70-71 & 83-84; distinguished prof, Wayne State Univ, 90. **MEMBERSHIPS** MLA; AAUP; Dickens Soc; H.G. Wells Soc; Midwest Victorian Studies Asn; Victorians Inst. **RESEARCH** Nineteenth- and Twentieth-century British literature and culture. **SELECTED PUBLICATIONS** Auth, Old School Ties: The Public Schools in British Literature, Syracuse Univ Press, 64; Perception and Design in Tennyson's Idylls of the King, Ohio Univ Press, 70; Victorian Conventions, Ohio Univ Press, 75; The Natural History of H.G. Wells, Ohio Univ Press, 82; Decadent Style, Ohio Univ Press, 85; Victorian Will, Ohio Univ Press, 89; Dickens and Thackeray: Punishment and Forgiveness, Ohio Univ Press, 95; Hercules, Fiddlehead Poetry Books, 73; A Gallery of Spiders, Ontario Rev Press, 80; Stations of the Cross, Ridgeway Press, 92; Great Lake, Ridgeway Press, 95; Life Sentences, Wayne State Univ Press, 96. **CONTACT ADDRESS** English Dept, Wayne State Univ, 51 W. Warren, Detroit, MI 48202. **EMAIL** john.reed@wayne.edu

REED, PETER J.
PERSONAL Born 05/14/1935, London, England, m, 1961 **DISCIPLINE** ENGLISH **EDUCATION** Univ Idaho, BA, 60; Univ Wash, MA, 62, PhD, 65; Harvard Univ, 62-63. **CAREER** Tchg asst, Univ Wash, 60-63; asst prof, San Diego State Col, 67-68; asst prof, 65-67 & 68-72, assoc prof, 72-79, PROF, 79-, Assoc Dean Col Language Arts, 91-96, Univ Minn; Phi Beta Kappa; Phi Delta Kappa; Sigma Delta Chi; Phi Kappa Phi; Alpha Delta. **HONORS AND AWARDS** CLA Distinguished Tchr, 86; grad sch grant-in-aid, Vonnegut Study, 96-97; Univ Col Outstanding Team Awd, 96. **MEMBERSHIPS** Soc Fantastic Arts; Int Air Hist Soc. **RESEARCH** 20th Century British novel; 20th Century British poetry & drama; 20th century Am Fict; Kurt Vonnegut **SELECTED PUBLICATIONS** Coauth Kurt Vonnegut: A Checklist, 1985-92, Bulletin of Bibliog, 93; Kurt Vonnegut, Dictionary of Lit Biog 152, American Novelists Since World War II, Bruccoli Clark Layman, 95; auth The Responsive Shaman: Kurt Vonnegut and His World, The Vonnegut Chronicles, Greenwood Publ, 96, Lonersome Once More: The Family Theme in Kurt Vonnegut's Slapstick, The Vonnegut Chronicles, Greenwood Publ, 96; The Graphics of Kurt Vonnegut, The Vonnegut Chronicles, Greenwood Publ, 96; Kurt Vonnegut: A Selected Bibliography 1985-1994, The Vonnegut Chronicles, Greenwood Publ, 96; A Portrait of the Writer as a Busy Man, Star Tribune of the Twin Cities, 96; The Vonnegut Chronicles: Interviews and Essays, Greenwood Publ, 96; The Short Fiction of Kurt Vonnegut, Greenwood Press, 97; Collecting Kurt Vonnegut, Firsts: The Book Collectors Magazine, 98. **CONTACT ADDRESS** Dept of English, Univ of Minnesota, Twin Cities, 203 Johnston Hall, Minneapolis, MN 55455. **EMAIL** reedx001@umn.edu

REED, RON S.
PERSONAL Born 10/17/1948, Louisville, KY, m, 1971, 3 children **DISCIPLINE** ENGLISH **EDUCATION** Berea Col, BA, 70; Univ Dayton, MST, 83; MA, 85; Univ Kentucky, PhD, 87. **CAREER** Instr, asst prof, assoc prof, prof, Hazard Comm Col, 87-. **HONORS AND AWARDS** NEH, 94; UK Stud Grnt, 91; HCC Fac Mem of the Year, 90; Nat Inst for Staff and Org Dev Teach Awd, 90; NISOD Mast Teach, 92; UK C Col Sys Ldshp Acad, 91; HCC Fac Co-Chair, 91-93; Bd of Ed KY Philo Rev, 91. **MEMBERSHIPS** MLA, SAMLA, KPA, Country Dance and Song Soc. **RESEARCH** Arthurian legend; Courtoise; Jane Austen. **SELECTED PUBLICATIONS** Auth, The Venture System, ERIC (91); co-auth, Institutional Cohesiveness, ERIC (91); auth, Problematic Abstraction of Time for Dickens and Twain, KY Philo Rev (90); auth, An Old Story, Kudzu (95). **CONTACT ADDRESS** Eng Dept., Hazard Comm Col, Hwy 15 South, Hazard, KY 41701. **EMAIL** ron.reed@kctcs.net

REED, T. V.
DISCIPLINE CULTURAL THEORY, CONTEMPORARY AMERICAN FICTION, AND THE 1960S **EDUCATION** Univ Calif, Santa Cruz, PhD. **CAREER** Assoc prof & dir Amer Stud, Washington State Univ. **RESEARCH** Various art forms as they have helped to shape social movement cultures from the Civil Rights era to the 1990s. **SELECTED PUBLICATIONS** Auth, Fifteen Jugglers, Five Believers: Literary Politics and the Poetics of American Social Movements, 92. **CONTACT ADDRESS** Dept of English, Washington State Univ, 1 SE Stadium Way, PO Box 645020, Pullman, WA 99164-5020. **EMAIL** reedtv@wsu.edu

REED, WALTER
PERSONAL Born 02/09/1943, New York, NY, m, 1964, 3 children **DISCIPLINE** ENGLISH AND COMPARATIVE LITERATURE **EDUCATION** Yale, BA, 65; Yale, PhD, 69; Univ of Texas a Austin; Emery Univ, English and Comparative Literature. **CAREER** Fac, Yale Univ; fac, Univ Tex Austin; prof/chemn dept, Emery Univ, 87-. **HONORS AND**

AWARDS Guggenheim Fel, 77-78; NEH, 95; Univ Scholar/ Teacher Awd, Emery, 00; co-dir, neh summer sem col tchrs, 95. **MEMBERSHIPS** MLA, SAMLA, IATS. **RESEARCH** Romanticism, History and Theory of the Novel, Bible as literature. **SELECTED PUBLICATIONS** auth, Meditations on the Hero, 74; auth, An Exemplary History of the Novel, 81; auth, Dialogues of the Word, 93. **CONTACT ADDRESS** English Dept, Emory Univ, 1380 Oxford Rd NE, Atlanta, GA 30322-1950. **EMAIL** wlreed@emory.edu

REEDER, HEIDI M.
DISCIPLINE INTERPERSONAL COMMUNICATION, RELATIONAL COMMUNICATION **EDUCATION** Univ OR, BS, summa cum laude, 91; Stanford Univ, MA, 93; AZ State Univ, PhD, 96. **CAREER** Dept Comm, Univ NC **RESEARCH** Interpersonal commun; male-female relationships. **SELECTED PUBLICATIONS** Auth, The subjective experience of love through adult life, Int J of Aging and Human Develop, 43, 96; coauth, Unwanted escalation of sexual intimacy: Male and female perceptions of connotations and relational consequences of resistance messages, Commun Monogr, 62, 95; Disclosure of sexual abuse by children and adolescents, J of Appl Commun, 24, 96. **CONTACT ADDRESS** Dept of Commun Stud, Univ of No Carolina, Greensboro, 102 Fergus, Greensboro, NC 27412-5001. **EMAIL** hmreeder@hamlet.uncg.edu

REESMAN, J. C.
PERSONAL Born 09/19/1955, Shreveport, LA, m, 1982, 1 child **DISCIPLINE** ENGLISH **EDUCATION** Centenary College, BA 77; Baylor Univ, MA 79; Univ Penn, PhD 84. **CAREER** Univ Texas SA, asst prof, assoc prof, prof, dir div eng, interim dean, 86 to 98-; Univ Penn, tchg asst 79-84, vis asst prof, 85-96; Univ Hawaii, asst prof, 84-85; Baylor Univ, teach asst, 77-79; Interim Dean of Graduate Studies, University of Texas at San Antonio, 98-; Dir, Division of English, Classics, Philosophy, and Communication Univ of Texas at San Antonio, 94-98; Prof of Englis, Univ of Texas at San Antonio, 95-; Assoc Prof of English, Univ of Texas at San Antonio, 92-95; Asst Prof of English, Univ of Texas at San Antonio, 86-92; Univ of Hawaii, 84-86; Teaching Fellow, Lecturer, and vis assist prof of English, Univ of Penn 79-84, 85-86; Teaching Asst, Baylor Univ, 77-79. **HONORS AND AWARDS** Fac Dev Awd; Golden Key Hon Soc Mem; Jack London Woman of the Year Awd; Presidents Dist Ser Awd; Robt A Miller Awd; Who's Who In Amer; Omicron Delta Kappa; Sigma Tau Delta Awd; Mabel Campbell awd. **MEMBERSHIPS** MLA; SCMLA; ALS/MLA; ALA; Henry James Soc; Faulkner Soc; Jack London Soc. **RESEARCH** Jack London; Henry James; William Faulkner; Amer Women Writers; Amer Lit; 19th and 20th Century Amer Novel; Narrative Theory; American Literature; Nineteenth- and Twentieth-Century American Novel; Narrative Theory; Naturalism; Feminism; Jack London; Henry James; William Faulkner; American Women Writers. **SELECTED PUBLICATIONS** auth, Jack London: A Study of the Short Fiction, NY, Twayne, 99; Speaking the Other Self: American Women Writers, Athens, U of GA Press, 97; Rereading Jack London, co-ed, Stanford, Stanford Univ Press, 96; Jack London Revised Edition, coauth, NY, Twayne, 94; A Handbook of Critical Approaches to Literature, 3rd, 4th ed, coauth, Oxford, Oxford Univ Press, 92,98; Fiction 1900-1930, Amer Lit Schshp, Duke Univ Press, 97 and 98; Never Travel Alone: Naturalism Jack London and the White Silence, Amer Lit Realism, 97; Women Language and the Grotesque in Flannery O'Connor and Eudora Welty in: Flannery O'Connor: New Approaches, eds Sura Rath, Mary Neff Shaw, Athens, Univ GA Press, 96; auth, American Designs : The Late Novels in James and Faulkner, Phila Univ of Pennsylvania Press, 90; auth, No. Mentor But Myself: Jack London in Writers and Writing, coed Stanford UP, 99; auth, In the House of Pride: Jack London and Race, Book manuscript in progress; auth, Jack London: One Hundred Years a Writer, Ed. Jeanne Campbell Reesman and Sara S. Hodson, In progress; auth, French editions of John Barleycorn and Tales of the Fish Patrol by Jack London, Ed. Noel Mauberret and Jeanne Campbell Reesman, Introd. Jeanne Campbell Reesman, Trans. Francois Postif and Noel Mauberret, Paris: Editions Phebus, Forthcoming, 00; auth, French edition of The Star Rover by Jack London, Ed. Noel Mauberret and Jeanne Campbell Reesman, Introd, Francis Lacassin, Trans, Francois Postif and Noel Mauberret, Paris: Editions Phebus, Forthcoming 00; auth, Trickster Lives: Culture and Myth in American Fiction, Ed. Jeanne Campbell Reesman, Forthcoming 00, from the University of Georgia Press. **CONTACT ADDRESS** Dept of English, Univ of Texas, San Antonio, Office of Graduate Studies, San Antonio, TX 78249. **EMAIL** jreesman@utsa.edu

REEVE, F. D.
PERSONAL Born Philadelphia, PA, m **DISCIPLINE** ENGLISH **EDUCATION** Columbia Univ, PhD, 58. **CAREER** Lecturer to Asst Prof, Columbia Univ, 53-61; Assoc Prof to Prof, Wesleyan Univ, 62-; Visiting Prof, Moscow, 61; Visiting Prof, Oxford Univ, 64; Visiting Prof, Columbia Univ, 88; Visiting Prof, Yale Univ, 74-86. **HONORS AND AWARDS** Literature Awd, Am Acad of Arts and Letters; Golden Rose, New England Poetry Soc. **SELECTED PUBLICATIONS** Auth, The White Monk: an Essay on Dostoevsky and Melville, Vanderbilt; auth, A Few Rounds of Old Maid and Other Stories; auth, The Moon and Other Failures, Michigan State Univ Press. **CONTACT ADDRESS** Dept Letters, Wesleyan Univ, Middletown, CT 06459-3139. **EMAIL** freeve@wesleyan.edu

REEVES, BYRON
DISCIPLINE COMMUNICATIONS **EDUCATION** Southern Methodist Univ, BA; MI State Univ, PhD. **CAREER** Dir grad studies/assoc chr Mass Comm Res Ctr, Univ Wis; fac, Stanford Univ, 85-; to Paul C. Edwards Prof, present. **RESEARCH** Psychological processing of television with emphasis on processes of attention, memory and emotion. **SELECTED PUBLICATIONS** Auth, publ in bks of collected studies and jour(s) such as Human Communication Research, Journal of Social Issues, Journal of Broadcasting, and Journalism Quarterly. **CONTACT ADDRESS** Dept Commun, Stanford Univ, McClatchy Hall Rm 300A, Stanford, CA 94305. **EMAIL** reeves@leland.stanford.edu

REGE, JOSNA E.
DISCIPLINE ENGLISH LITERATURE **EDUCATION** Univ Ma Amherst, PhD, 95. **CAREER** Asst prof, Dartmouth Col. **RESEARCH** Am and Brit lit. **SELECTED PUBLICATIONS** Auth, Indian Literature in English in The Encyclopedia of English Studies and Language Arts, Scholas and NCTE, 94. **CONTACT ADDRESS** Dartmouth Col, 3529 N Main St, #207, Hanover, NH 03755.

REGELSKI, THOMAS ADAM
PERSONAL Born 05/04/1941, Goshen, NY, m, 1993 **DISCIPLINE** MUSIC EDUCATION **EDUCATION** State Univ Col, Fredonia, BM (Music Ed), 58; Columbia Univ, MA (Choral and Vocal Music), 63; State Univ Col, Fredonia graduate studies, 63-64; OH Univ, Athens, PhD (Comparative Arts), 70. **CAREER** Public schools, New York City, 62-63; central schools, Bemus Point, NY, 63-65; public schools, Middletown, NY, 65-66; School of Music, State Univ Col, Fredonia, 66-68; OH Univ at Athens and Zanesville, 68-70; School of Music, State Univ Col, Fredonia, NY, 70-; vis prof, Aichi Univ, Nagoya, Japan, 84-85; assoc in ed, Harvard Univ, fall 91. **HONORS AND AWARDS** Kappa Delta Pi, SUNY Fredonia, 62; cum laude, SUNY Fredonia, 62; Dean Earl C Siegfred Awd, OH Univ, 70; Phi Kappa Phi, OH State Univ, 70; Outstanding Educators of Am, 73-74; Distinguished Prof Awd and rank, SUNY Board of Trustees, 83; vis teaching and res scholar, Aichi Univ , Nagoya, Japan, 84-85; vis scholar, Philos of Ed Res Center, Harvard Graduate School of Ed, fall 91; Kasling Awd for Senior res, SUNY Fredonia 99; Fulbright Awd as lecturer, Sibelius academy of Music, Helsinki Finland, 00. **RESEARCH** Philos of music; philos of ed; sociol of music; sociol of ed. **SELECTED PUBLICATIONS** Auth, Action Research and Critical Theory: Empowering Music Teachers to Professionalize Praxis, Bul of the Coun for Res in Music Ed, no 123, winter 94-95; Scientism in Experimantal Music Research, Philos of Music Ed Rec, vol 4, no 1, spring 96; Taking the Art of Music for Granted: A Critical Sociology of the Aesthetic Philosophy of Music, in Critical Reflections on Music Education, ed L R Bartel and D J Elliott, Univ of Toronto, Can Music Ed Res Center, 96; Action for Change in Music Education-Guiding Ideals of the MayDay Group, with J T Gates, Univ Buffalo, postion paper of the MayDay Group, fall 96 (www.members.aol.com/jtgates/maydaygroup/); Critical Theory as a Basis for Critical Thinking in Music Education, in Studies in Music from the Univ of Western Ontario, vol 17, 98; A Prolegomenon to a Praxial Theory of Music and Music Education, Finnish J of Music Ed, vol 1 no 1, fall, 96, reprinted and expanded in Can Music Educator, vol 38, no 3, spring 97; A Critical Pagmatism of Creativity for General Music, General Music Today, vol 10, no 3, spring 97; Action Learning: Curriculum as and for Praxis, Proceedings of the Charles Fowler Conference on Arts Education, Univ MD, College Park, May 97; Critical Theory and Praxis: Professionalizing Music Education, MayDay Group, web page(see above); The Aristotelian Bases of Music and Music Education, The Philos of Music Ed Rev, spring 98; numerous other publications. **CONTACT ADDRESS** School of Music, SUNY, Col at Fredonia, Mason Hall, Fredonia, NY 14063. **EMAIL** regelski@cecomet.net

REGINALD, ALLEN
DISCIPLINE CLASSICS **EDUCATION** Haverford, AB, 53; Yale Univ, MA, 55; St Andrews, BPhil, 57; Yale Univ, PhD, 58. **CAREER** Prof, Northwestern Univ, 78-. **RESEARCH** Socratic Ethics; Plato's Ion; Hippias Minor; Laches; Protagoras; Lysias. **SELECTED PUBLICATIONS** Auth, Collected Dialogues of Plato, v.II, Yale, 91; ed, R. E. Allen, Plato's Parmineds, trans and analysis, Univ Minn. **CONTACT ADDRESS** Dept of Classics, Northwestern Univ, Kresge 15, Evanston, IL 60201-2200. **EMAIL** r-allen2@nwu.edu

REGNEY, GABRIELLE
PERSONAL Born 09/09/1966, Burlington, VT, s **DISCIPLINE** COMPOSITION, GENDER STUDIES **EDUCATION** Univ Conn Storrs, BA, 89; Hunter Col, MA, 92; CUNY, PhD, 00. **CAREER** Asst prof, Mercer County Community Col, 96-00; asst prof, Bronx Community Col, 00-. **HONORS AND AWARDS** Honors Scholar, Univ Conn, 89. **MEMBERSHIPS** CLAGS, Acad of Am Poets, MLA, Col Eng Assoc, Nat Assoc of Women's Studies. **RESEARCH** Semiotics, modern poetry, pre-Christian culture, biography, gender, feminist theory, American Literature. **SELECTED PUBLICATIONS** Auth, "Asphodel Out of the Grave - HD's Novel Trilogy," Jour of Imagism, 01. **CONTACT ADDRESS** 1755 Highview Lane, Upper Black Eddy, PA 18972. **EMAIL** gregney@ptd.net

REHM, RUSH
DISCIPLINE CLASSICS; DRAMA **EDUCATION** BA, 73; MA, 75; Stanford Univ, PhD, 85. **CAREER** Assoc prof, Stanford Univ. **RESEARCH** Greek tragedy. **SELECTED PUBLICATIONS** Auth, The Oresteia: A Theatre Version, 78; auth, Greek Tragic Theatre, 92; Marriage to Death: The Conflation of Marriage and Funeral Rituals in Greek Tragedy, 94; auth, The Play of Space: Spatial Transformations in Greek Tragedy, 01. **CONTACT ADDRESS** Stanford Univ, 551 Serra Mall, Stanford, CA 94305-5010. **EMAIL** mrehm@stanford.edu

REICH, ROBERT D.
PERSONAL Born 04/25/1951, Miami, FL **DISCIPLINE** MASS MEDIA & COMMUNICATION; MEDIA STUDIES **EDUCATION** New School for Social Res, MA, 82; Temple Univ, PhD, 95. **CAREER** Advertising copywriter, Tech Graphics, 89; Rusiald & Assocs, 90-92; Wyeth-Ayerst Pharmaceuticals, 92-94; ASST PROF, MARY BALDWIN COL. **MEMBERSHIPS** Int Commun Asn; Am Advertising Asn; Nat Commun Asn. **RESEARCH** Psychology of advertising; advertising to children. **CONTACT ADDRESS** Dept of Communication, Mary Baldwin Col, Staunton, VA 24401. **EMAIL** rreich@cit.mbc.edu

REICHARDT, MARY R.
DISCIPLINE AMERICAN LITERATURE **EDUCATION** Aquinas Col, BA, 78; Univ Ill, MA, 80; Univ Wis, PhD, 87. **CAREER** From asst prof to prof, Univ St Thomas, 88-. **HONORS AND AWARDS** Harry Hayden Clark Awd in Am Lit, 86; Teaching Asst Excellence Awd, Univ Wis, 87; Univ Scholars Grant Awd, Univ St Thomas, 00. **MEMBERSHIPS** MMLA, ALA. **RESEARCH** American Writers, American Women Authors, Catholic Studies, the Short Story, Autobiography. **SELECTED PUBLICATIONS** Auth, A Web of Relationship: Women in the short Stories of Mary Wilkins Freeman, Univ Press of Miss, 92; auth, The Uncollected Short Stories of Mary Wilkins Freen, Univ Press of Miss, 92; auth, A Mary Wilkins Freeman Reader, Univ Nebr Press, 97; auth, Mary Wilkins Freeman: A Study of the Short Fiction, Twayne, 97; auth, Catholic Women Writers: A bio-Bibliographic Sourcebook, Greenwood, forthcoming. **CONTACT ADDRESS** Dept English & Catholic Studies, Univ of St. Thomas, Minnesota, 2115 Summit Ave, Saint Paul, MN 55105-1048.

REID, LOREN
PERSONAL Born 08/26/1905, Gilman City, MO, m, 1930, 4 children **DISCIPLINE** COMMUNICATION **EDUCATION** BA, Grinnell Col, 27; PhD, Univ of Iowa, 32. **CAREER** Univ of Mo, 35-39; Syracuse Univ, 39-44; Univ of Mo, 44-75; Vis prof, Univ S Calif, 47, 54; Vis prof, Univ Utah, 52; Vis prof, Univ of Md, overseas, 52-53, 60-61; Vis prof, Univ Mich, 57; Vis prof, Univ of Ha, 57; Vis prof, Univ of Iowa, 58; Ret, 75-. **HONORS AND AWARDS** Distinguished Res or Serv, Grinnell Col, Univ of Mo, Ohio Univ, Speech & Theatre Asn of Mo, NY State Comm Asn, Cent States Comm Asn (pres, 42-40); Sesquicentennial prof, Univ of Mo; Fellowship, Roy Hist Soc. **MEMBERSHIPS** Cent States Comm Asn; Natl Comm Asn (exec sec 45-52, pres 57); Amer Comm Asn Univ Profs; Royal Hist Soc. **RESEARCH** British political speaking; Missouri social history. **SELECTED PUBLICATIONS** Auth, Charles James Fox, Longmans, 79; auth, Hurry Home Wednesday, Univ Mo Pres, 79; auth, Finally It's Friday, Univ Mo Press, 81, Jap ed (sels), 86; auth, Professor on the Loose, Mortgage Ln Press, 92; Reflections, Mortgage Ln Press, 98. **CONTACT ADDRESS** 200 E Brandon Rd, Columbia, MO 65203. **EMAIL** commreid@showme.missouri.edu

REID, LOUANN
DISCIPLINE ENGLISH LITERATURE **EDUCATION** Linfield Col, BA; Wash State Univ, MA; NYork Univ, PhD. **CAREER** Asst prof. **SELECTED PUBLICATIONS** Auth, pubs on interactive classroom; teachers as researchers; teaching of critical thinking in response to literature. **CONTACT ADDRESS** Dept of English, Colorado State Univ, Fort Collins, CO 80523. **EMAIL** lreid@vines.colostate.edu

REID, PANTHEA
PERSONAL Born 09/11/1940, Birmington, AL, m, 1976, 2 children **DISCIPLINE** AMERICAN LITERATURE, NOVEL **EDUCATION** Univ Ala, BA, 62, MA, 63, Univ NC, PhD(English), 71. **CAREER** Instr English, Univ Ala, 64-65, Montreat-Anderson Col, 65-66; from instr to asst prof, Va Polytech inst & State Univ, 67-74; vis asst prof, 74-75; assoc prof, 75-80, Prof English, LA State Univ, 80-, Sr Fulbright lectr, Portugal, 76; exec bd, Soc Study Southern Lit. **HONORS AND AWARDS** NEH Fel for Univ Teachers, 99-00; SCMLA's Best Bk Award, "Art and Affection: A Life of Virginia Woolf," 96; NEH Travel to Collections grant, 85; CIES Res Grant-in-Aid to the United Kingdom, 83; NEH Summer Res Grant, 83; Senior Fulbright Lecturer, Univ of Porto, Portugal, 76; Phi Beta Kappa. **MEMBERSHIPS** MLA; Soc Study Southern Lit; Am Soc 18th Century Studies; South Cent Mod Lang Asn; Women's Caucus Mod Lang. **RESEARCH** Literary biography; The modern novel; Interartisic studies; William Faulkner; Virginia Woolf; Tillie Olsen. **SELECTED PUBLICATIONS** Auth, William Faulkner, The Abstract and the Actual, 74; ed, The Art of Walker Percy: Strategems for Being, 79; auth,

"Troublesomeness and Guilt: New Evidence from 1895," The Virginia Woolf Miscellany (97); auth, Art and Affection: A Life of Virginia Woolf, 97; auth, "Archives and Art and Affection," Viriginia Woolf & Her Influences (98); auth, "On My Redating," The Virginia Woolf Miscellany (98); auth, "Ellen Douglas and Truth: Invention and Truth," Virginia Quarterly Review (99); auth, "Virginia Stephen Woolf, Julia Margaret Cameron, and the Prince of Abbysinia: An Inqury into Certain Colonialist Representations," Biography (99). **CONTACT ADDRESS** Dept of English, Louisiana State Univ and A&M Col, Baton Rouge, LA 70803. **EMAIL** preid@lsu.edu

REID, PETER L. D.
PERSONAL Born 01/30/1937, Edinburgh, Scotland, m, 1995, 2 children **DISCIPLINE** CLASSICS **EDUCATION** Cambridge Univ, BA, 60, MA, 64; UCLA, PhD, 74. **CAREER** Tchr, 60-70; Sec Sch in Scotland, NZ, USA; Asst Prof, Assoc Prof, Prof, 73-, Class, Tufts Univ. **HONORS AND AWARDS** NEH Inst for Tchr. **MEMBERSHIPS** APA. **RESEARCH** Medieval Latin **SELECTED PUBLICATIONS** Auth, Ratherii Veronensis: Opera Minora, Brepols, Corpus Christianorum, Cont Mediaevalis XLVI, 76; Tenth Century Latinity, Undena, 81; Ratherii Veronensis: Opera Maiora, Brepols, Corpus Christianorum, Cont Med XLVIA, 84; Rather of Verona: Complete Works in Translation, CEMERS, Binghamton, 91; Reviewed in; Church History, 95; Speculum, 94; Manuscripta, 92; Ecclesiastical History, 93. **CONTACT ADDRESS** Dept of the Classics, Tufts Univ, Medford, Medford, MA 02155. **EMAIL** preid@infonet.tufts.edu

REID, ROBERT L.
PERSONAL Born 10/11/1943, Charlotte, NC, m, 1968, 2 children **DISCIPLINE** ENGLISH **EDUCATION** Yale Univ, BA, 66; Univ VA, PhD, 71. **CAREER** English dept, VA Intermont Col, 71-81; English Dept, Emory & Henry Col, 81-, chair, 86-, Henry Carter Stuart prof English, 91-. **HONORS AND AWARDS** Yale English Honors prog, grad with high honors; Yale Honors Thesis ("H D & Imagism"), won Richard Schoenberg Awd, 66; Teaching Excellence Awd, 81, 99; VA Shakespeare Lect (appointed by VA Found for Humanities), 89. **MEMBERSHIPS** MLA; SAMLA; Southeastern Renaissance Conf; Spenser Soc; Carolina Symposium of British Studies. **RESEARCH** Spenser's Fairie Queene; Shakespeare; Renaissance physiology & psychol; Renaissance dramaturgical structure & epic narrative structure. **SELECTED PUBLICATIONS** Auth, "Man, Woman, Child or Servant: Family Hierarchy as a Figure of Tripartite Psychology in 'The Faerie Queene,'" Studies in Philol 79, 81; auth, "Alma's Castle and the Symbolization of Reason in 'The Faerie Queen,'"J of English and Germanic Philol 80, 81; auth, "Spenserian Psychology & the Structure of Allegory in Books I and II of The Faerie Queene, '"Modern Philol 79, 82; auth, "Eratic Interruptions: First Year in the Chair," ADE Bul, fall 88; auth, "Platonic Psychology, Soul, House of Holiness," in The Spenser Encyclopedia, Univ Toronto, 90; auth, MacBeth's Three Murders: Shakespearean Psychology and Tragic Form, Renaissance Papers, 91; auth, "'The Faerie Queene': Gloriana or Titania?, "The Upstart Crow 13, 93; auth, Lear's Three Shamings: Shakespearean Psychology and Tragic Form, Renaissance Papers, 96; auth, "Humoral Psychology in Shakespeare's Henriad," Comparative Drama, 30, 96-97; auth, "Epiphanal Encounters in Shakespearean Dramaturgy," Comparative Drama, 32, 98-99; auth, Shakespeare's Tragic Form: Spirit in the Wheel, Univ Delaware Pr (Newark), 00. **CONTACT ADDRESS** English Dept, Emory & Henry Col, Emory, VA 24327. **EMAIL** rlreid@ehc.edu

REID, RONALD F.
PERSONAL Born 07/24/1928, Herington, KS, w, 1953, 2 children **DISCIPLINE** SPEECH; RHETORIC **EDUCATION** George Pepperdine Univ, BA, 50; Univ of NMex, MA, 51; Purdue Univ, PhD, 54. **CAREER** From instr to asst prof, Wash Univ, 54-59; from asst prof to assoc prof, Purdue Univ, 59-66; prof, Univ of Mass, 66-91, dept head, 66-70. **HONORS AND AWARDS** Winans/Wichelms Awd for Disting. Scholarship, 76; SCA Monograph Awd, 83; Relig Speech Commun Awd for Outstanding Publ, 96. **MEMBERSHIPS** Am Soc for the Hist of Rhet: Int Soc for the Hist of Rhet; Int Soc for the Class Tradition; Nat Commun Asn. **RESEARCH** Hist of Am Polit Rhet; Hist of Am Rhet Theory. **SELECTED PUBLICATIONS** The Boylston Professorship of Rhetoric and Oratory, 1806-1904, Quart Jour of Speech, 45, 59; Newspaper Response to the Gettysburg Addresses, Quart Jour of Speech, 53, 67; New England Rhetoric and the French War, 1754-1760: A Case Study in the Rhetoric of War, Commun Monographs, 43, 76; The American Revolution and the Rhetoric of History, 78; Prophecy in New England Victory Sermons, ca. 1760: A Study in American Concepts of Historic Mission, 80; Apocalypticism and Typology: Rhetorical Dimensions of a Symbolic Reality, Quart Jour of Speech, 69, 83; Three Centuries of American Rhetorical Discourse: An Anthology and a Review, 88, 2nd ed, 95; Edward Everett: Unionist Orator, 90; Edward Everett and Neoclassical Oratory in Genteel America, Oratorical Culture in Nineteenth-Century America: Transformations in the Theory and Practice of Rhetoric, eds G. Clark and S. M. Halloran, 93; Disputes Over Preaching Method, The Second Awakening, and Ebenezer Porter's Teaching of Sacred Rhetoric, Jour of Commun and Relig, 18, 95; Walter Edward Williams (1936-), Professor, Editorialist, African-American Orators: A Bio-Critical Sourcebook, ed R. W. Leeman, 96. **CONTACT ADDRESS** PO Box 209, Northfield, MA 01360-0209.

REID, STEPHEN
DISCIPLINE ENGLISH LITERATURE **EDUCATION** Grinnell Col, BA; Univ Mo, MA; Univ Kans, PhD. **CAREER** Prof. **SELECTED PUBLICATIONS** Auth, The Prentice Hall Guide for College Writers, 95; Purpose and Process: A Reader for Writers, 94. **CONTACT ADDRESS** Dept of English, Colorado State Univ, Fort Collins, CO 80523. **EMAIL** sreid@vines.colostate.edu

REIFF, RAYCHEL A.
PERSONAL Born 01/09/1945, Pelican Rapids, MN, m, 1973, 4 children **DISCIPLINE** ENGLISH **EDUCATION** Concordia Col, BA, 67; Univ Ut, MA, 69; PhD, 71. **CAREER** Instr to asst prof, Tex A & I Univ, 70-75; asst prof, Univ Wis River Falls, 76-77; lectr, Col of St Scholastica, 90-92; from lectr to assoc prof, Univ Wis Superior, 90-. **HONORS AND AWARDS** NDEA Fel, Univ Ut, 67-70; Outstanding Young Women of Am, 74; listed in World Who's Who of Women in Educ, 77; Fac Development Grant, Univ Wis Superior, 94, 95, & 99; listed in Who's Who Among Am Teachers, 98 & 00. **MEMBERSHIPS** Nat Coun of Teachers of English, Asn of Univ of Wis Professionals. **RESEARCH** Literature: Chaucer, Ole E. Rolvaag, Ralph Waldo Emerson, Teaching Activities. **SELECTED PUBLICATIONS** Auth, "Making Poems Come Alive," Statement: J of the Colo Lang Arts Soc of the Nat Coun of Teachers of English 34.1 (97): 8-9; auth, "My Christmas Story," Lutheran Woman Today 11.10 (98): 32; auth, "Almost Like a Fairy Tale: The Ecstasy and the Agony of Norwegian Immigrants' Lives as Seen in O.E. Rolvaag's Giants in the Earth," NDak Quart 65.4 (98): 58-79; auth, "Teaching an Appreciation of Poetry: Tennyson's The Lotos-Eaters," The English Record 49.3 (99): 44-48; auth, "Helping Students Document Sources," statement: The J of the Colo Lang Arts Soc 36.1 (99): 58-59; auth, "Chaucer's The Pardoner's Tale, 855-58," The Explicator 57.4 (99): 195-197. **CONTACT ADDRESS** Dept Lang & Lit, Univ of Wisconsin, Superior, PO Box 2000, Superior, WI 54880-4500. **EMAIL** rreiff@staff.uwsuper.edu

REIGELMAN, MILTON M.
PERSONAL Born 04/28/1942, Washington D.C., m, 1965, 3 children **DISCIPLINE** ENGLISH LITERATURE **EDUCATION** Col William and Mary, BA; Univ Pa, MA; Univ Iowa, MA; PhD. **CAREER** Fac, 71; vice pres planning and resources, 91-96; J. Rice Cowan Prof Eng, present; acting pres, 97-98; director of Int progs & special asst to the pres, 98-. **HONORS AND AWARDS** Rookie of Yr Awd, Centre Col; David Hughes Outstanding Prof Awd, Centre, Col; Fulbright lectr; senior Fulbright Lectr to Poland, 78; to USSR, 87; pub and co-found, danville quart, 74-77; dean, governor's scholars prog, centre col. **RESEARCH** American literature and culture; Melville. **SELECTED PUBLICATIONS** Auth, The Midland: A Venture in Literary Regionalism, Univ Iowa P. **CONTACT ADDRESS** Centre Col, 600 W Walnut St, Danville, KY 40422. **EMAIL** reigelma@centre.edu

REILLY, JOHN M.
PERSONAL Born 02/18/1933, Pittsburgh, PA, m, 1995, 3 children **DISCIPLINE** AMERICAN & AFRICAN AMERICAN LITERATURE **EDUCATION** W Va Univ, BA, 54; Washington Univ St Louis, MA, 63; PhD, 67. **CAREER** Instr, Washington Univ, 59-60; asst prof, Univ Puerto Rico, 61-63; asst prof to prof, SUNY Albany, 63-94; prof, Howard Univ, 95-. **HONORS AND AWARDS** Woodrow Wilson Fel, 54-55; Danford Found Fel, 66-67; NEH Fel, 70-71; Edgar Allan Poe Awd, 80; MELUS Awd, 88; George Dove Awd, 89; Johnetta G Davis Awd; Howard Univ Provost Fund, 97, 99. **MEMBERSHIPS** MLA, Col Lang Asn, am Studies Asn, Mystery Writers of Am, MELUS, Charles W Chestnut Soc, George Moses Horton Soc, Phi Beta Kappa. **RESEARCH** African American prose genres and adaptations of history, function of conventions of popular fiction. **SELECTED PUBLICATIONS** Ed, Richard Wright: The Critical Reception, Burt Franklin, 78; auth, "Reconstruction of Genre as Entry into Conscious History," Black Am Lit Forum, 79; ed, Twentieth Century Crime and Mystery Writers, St Martin's, 80; auth, "The Testament of Ralph Ellison," Speaking for You, ed K Benston, (87); auth, "Giving Bigger a Voice," New Essays on Native Son, (Cambridge Univ Pr, 90); auth, "Richard Wright and the Art of Non-Fiction," Criticism of Richard Wright, eds Gates and Appiah, (93); auth, Tony Hillerman: A Critical Companion, Greenwood, 96; auth, "History of the Genre," Oxford Companion to Crime and Mystery Writing, (99); coed, Oxford Companion to Crime and Mystery Writing, Oxford Univ Pr, 99; auth, Larry McMurtry: A Critical Companion, Greenwood, (00). **CONTACT ADDRESS** Howard Univ, 2400 6th St NW, Washington, DC 20059. **EMAIL** jreilly@fac.howard.edu

REILLY, LINDA
DISCIPLINE CLASSICAL STUDIES **EDUCATION** Vassar Col, AB, 65; Johns Hopkins Univ, MA, 66, PhD, 69. **CAREER** Assoc prof, 74-; ch, 92-95; asst prof, 69-74; assoc provest, 81-86 & dean Undergrad Progr and asst VP for Acad Aff, Col William and Mary; Abby Leach fel, low, Amer Sch Class Stud, Athens, Greece, 66-67; Ctr Hellenistic Stud, Wash, 74-75; sr res assoc, Amer Sch Class Stud, Athens, Greece, 86-87 & 95-96. **RESEARCH** Ancient dogs; Ancient city; Neoclassical traditions in North America. **SELECTED PUBLICATIONS** Auth, Slaves in Ancient Greece, Ares Publishers, 78, repr, 84; The Dogs from the Hunting Frieze at Vergina, J Hellenic Stud, Vol 113, 93; A Greek Inscription at Williamsburg, Amer J Archaeol, 74; New Inscriptions from Echinos, Amer J Philol, 71; Who Stole the Sphinx's Nose, Mediter Soc Am, Richmond, 96; participant and guest lecturer, La State Semr for High Sch Humanities Teachers, Northwestern State Univ, Natchidoches, 93; A Protogemometric Naiskos From Crete CAMWS, Boulder, 97; Neo-Classical Achitecture in Williamsburg, VA, CAMWS-SS, Richmond, 92; Kerberos and Orthos: Two Monstrous Brothers, given at CAMWS in Austin, 92; Rumpus: One of A Kind, Dog World, 86 & Rumpus: A Full Life for a Deaf Corgi, Dog World, 90. **CONTACT ADDRESS** Dept of Classical Studies, Col of William and Mary, Morton Hall, Williamsburg, VA 23187-8795. **EMAIL** lcreil@morton.wm.edu

REINHEIMER, DAVID
PERSONAL Born 03/16/1967, Clifton Springs, NY, s **DISCIPLINE** RHETORIC; COMPOSITION **EDUCATION** Univ Dallas, BA, 89, MA, 89; Univ CA, MA, 91, PhD, 95. **CAREER** Instr, 90-91; Assoc prof, 91-92; tchg asst, 93-94; adj prof, 94-95; adj lectr, Univ CA, 95-96; instr, Sacramento City Col, 95-96; asst prof, SE MO State Univ, 97-; dir, Writing Assessment Prog, SE MO State Univ, 00-. **MEMBERSHIPS** MLA; Sixteenth Century Studies Asn; South-Central Renaissance Conf; Midwest Mod Lang Asn; Southeast Missouri English Teachers Asn; Nat Coun of Teachers of English; Conf on Col Composition and Communication; Am Asn of Univ Professors. **SELECTED PUBLICATIONS** Auth, The Roman Actor, Censorship, and Dramatic Autonomy,98; The N-Town Play: Cotton MS Vespasian D.8.(rev), 96; The Renaissance Bible: Scholarship, Subjectivity, and Sacrifice (rev) 96; The English Faust Book (rev), 96; Ethical and Ontological Allusion: Shakespeare in The Next Generation, 95; Drama and the Market in the Age of Shakespeare (rev), 94; Last Things and Last Plays: Shakespearean Eschatology (rev), 93; auth, This Stage-Play World: Texts and Contexts, 1580-1625, 98; auth, English Drama 1586-1642: The Age of Shakespeare, 98; auth, "Chaucer's Mystery: Cycle Plays and Unity in the Canterbury Tales," (99); auth, From Sources to Purpose: A Guide to Researched Writing, 00. **CONTACT ADDRESS** Eng Dept, Southeast Missouri State Univ, MS4600, 1 University Plz, Cape Girardeau, MO 63701. **EMAIL** dreinheimer@sermovm.semo.edu

REIS, RAUL
PERSONAL Born 04/23/1964, Belem, Brazil, s **DISCIPLINE** COMMUNICATION, JOURNALISM **EDUCATION** Kans State Univ, MS, 94; Univ Oregon, PhD, 98. **CAREER** Multi-year lectr, Calif State Univ, Monterey Bay, 97-2000; asst prof, Calif State Univ, Long Beach, 2000-. **HONORS AND AWARDS** Rotary Int Scholar, 92-93; Reader's Digest Res Grant, 94; Doctorate Scholar, CAPES, 94, 97; Grad Teaching Fel, Univ Oregon, 94, 97; Doctoral Res Travel Grant, 96; Best 1997-1998 Doctoral Diss Awd, Univ Oregon, 98; Best 1997-1998 Int/Intercultural Diss Awd, 99; Fieldwork Res Grant, 2000. **RESEARCH** Social/cultural impact of media on traditional communities; Brazilian media; international journalism. **SELECTED PUBLICATIONS** Coauth, "Public Journalism: What Difference Does It Make to Editorial Content?," in Assessing Public Journalism, ed by Ed Lambeth, Phil Meyer, and Esther Thorson, Univ Miss Press (97); auth, "The Impact of Television Viewing in the Brazilian Amazon," Human Organization, J of the Soc for Applied Anthol, Vol 57, 3 (98); auth, "What Prevents Cable TV from Taking off in Brazil?," J of Broadcasting and Electronic Media, Vol 43, 3 (99); auth, "Environmental News: Coverage of the Earth Summit by Brazilian Newspapers," Sci Commun, Vol 21, 2 (99); coauth, "Teaching Journalism at Distance: The Oregon Experiment," HJ and Mass Commun Educ, Vol 55, 1 (2000); auth, "Love It and The It: Brazilians' Ambiguous Relationship with Disney," in Dazzled by Disney: Communication Across Cultures, ed by Janet Wasko, Eileen Meehan, and Mark Philip, Univ of Leicester Press (forthcoming); auth, "A Gente se Fala depois da Novela: The Impact of Television on Traditional Cultures of the Amazon--The Case of Sao Joao de Pirabas," Museu Paraense Emilio Goeldi-Colecao Eduardo Galvao, Belem, Brazil (forthcoming). **CONTACT ADDRESS** Dept Arts, Calif State Univ Monterey Bay, 100 Campus Center, Seaside, CA 93955-8000. **EMAIL** raul_reis@hotmail.com

REISMAN, ROSEMARY C.
PERSONAL Born 11/18/1927, Des Moines, IO, w, 4 children **DISCIPLINE** ENGLISH **EDUCATION** Univ Minn, BA, 49, MA, 52; La State Univ, PhD, 71. **CAREER** TA, Univ of Minn, 49-52; instr, La State Univ, 61-69; asst prof to prof, Troy State Univ, 71-94; adj prof, Charleston Southern Univ, 96-99. **HONORS AND AWARDS** NDEA Fel, 69-71. **MEMBERSHIPS** AEA; NEA; Assoc of Col English Teachers of Ala; SAMLA; Low Country Phi Beta Kappa Assoc. **RESEARCH** Southern literature, women's literature, 18th century studies. **SELECTED PUBLICATIONS** Ed, Perspectives: The Alabama Heritage, Troy State Univ Pr, 78; auth, "Introduction", Trial Balance, by William March, Univ of Ala Pr, (Tuscaloosa), 87; auth, "A Clergyman-Poet and the Church in Change", Studies on Voltaire and the Eighteenth Century 263 (89): 398-399; coauth,

Contemporary Southern Women Fiction Writers, Scarecrow Pr, (Metuchen, NJ), 94; auth, "Introduction", Great Women Writers, ed Frank N. Magill, Henry Holt, (NY) 94; auth, "The Presence of the Past: American identities in the South", American Diversity, American Identity, ed John K. Roth, Henry Holt, (NY), 95; coauth, Contemporary Southern Men Fiction Writers, Scarecrow Pr, (Lanham, MD), 98; auth, Alabama Women Writers, Univ of Ala Pr, (forthcoming). **CONTACT ADDRESS** Dept English, Charleston So Univ, PO Box 118087, Charleston, SC 29423-8087.

REISS, BENJAMIN D.
PERSONAL Born 10/26/1964, Boston, MA, m, 1998, 1 child **DISCIPLINE** ENGLISH **EDUCATION** Oberlin Col, BA, 86; Univ Calif Berkeley, MA, 95; PhD, 97. **CAREER** Lectr, Univ Calif Berkeley, 98; asst prof, Tulane Univ, 98-. **HONORS AND AWARDS** Mellon Fel, 89-90, 90-91, 93-94; Univ Calif Diss Grant, 95-96, 96-97; Am Antiquarian Soc/NEH Fel, 01-02. **MEMBERSHIPS** MLA, Am Studies Assoc, Interdisciplinary 19th Century Studies Assoc. **RESEARCH** 19th Century American Literature and Culture, Slavery and US Culture, History of US Popular Culture, Literature and Psychiatry. **SELECTED PUBLICATIONS** Auth, "Madness and Mastery in Melville's 'Benito Cereno,'" Criticism, (96); auth, "PT Barnum, Joice Heth, and Antebellum Spectacles of Race," Am Quart, (99); auth, The Showman and the Slave: Race, Death and Memory in Barnum's American, Harvard Univ Pr, 01. **CONTACT ADDRESS** Dept English, Tulane Univ, 7115 Camp St, New Orleans, LA 70118. **EMAIL** breiss@tulane.edu

REISS, JOHN
PERSONAL Born 05/12/1935, Milwaukee, WI, m, 1956, 7 children **DISCIPLINE** AMERICAN LITERATURE **EDUCATION** Univ Wis, PhD. **CAREER** Eng, St. Michaels Col. **HONORS AND AWARDS** NEH Fel, Yale, 77; Rathges Teaching Award, 98. **MEMBERSHIPS** ALSC **RESEARCH** 19th and 20th american lit. **CONTACT ADDRESS** Saint Michael's Col, Winooski Park, Colchester, VT 05439.

RELIHAN, JOEL C.
DISCIPLINE CLASSICS **EDUCATION** Univ Ill, BA, 76; Univ Wis, MA, PhD,85. **CAREER** Class, Wheaton Col. **RESEARCH** Augustine; Boethius; myth; Egyptian lang & cult; ancient ecology; **SELECTED PUBLICATIONS** Auth, Ancient Menippean Satire, Johns Hopkins UP, 93. **CONTACT ADDRESS** Dept of Class, Wheaton Col, Massachusetts, 26 East Main St, Norton, MA 02766. **EMAIL** Joel_Relihan@wheatonma.edu

REMPEL, GERHARD
PERSONAL Born, Soviet Union, m, 2 children **DISCIPLINE** ENGLISH LITERATURE **EDUCATION** Wheaton Col, BA, 59; Northwestern Univ, MA, 61; Univ Wis, PhD, 71. **CAREER** Admin tchg asst, Univ Wis, 67-69; asst prof, WNEC, 69-75; ch, fac personnel comm, 72-73; vis asst prof, Univ Md, 72-73; ch, fac devel comm, 74-76; ch, faculty senate, 75-76; assoc prof, WNEC, 75-81; ch, dept hist, govt, econ, 79-82; dir, cult prog, 78-90; prof, WNEC, 81-. **HONORS AND AWARDS** Non-Resident scholarship, Univ Wis, 66-68; spec summer fel, Univ Wis, 67-69; Ford res fel, 68-69; travel grant, Univ Wis, 68; summer res grant, WNEC, 91, 92; res grant, DAAD, 92. **SELECTED PUBLICATIONS** Auth, Hitler's Children: The Hitler Youth and the SS, Univ NC Press, 89; Gottlob Berger and Waffen-SS Recruitment, 33-45, Militaergeschichtliche Mitteilungen, 80; Training Teenage Spies and Policeboys: The Hitler-Jugend Streifendienst, The Citadel Devel Found, 82. **CONTACT ADDRESS** Dept of Eng, Western New England Col, 1215 Wilbraham Rd., Springfield, MA 01119-2654. **EMAIL** grempel@wnec.edu

REMPEL, JOHN W.
DISCIPLINE ENGLISH LITERATURE **EDUCATION** Univ British Columbia, BA; Univ Tex Austin, MA; PhD. **CAREER** Assoc prof **RESEARCH** 18th century women writers; musical literary relations; bibliography; restoration comedy; book collecting. **SELECTED PUBLICATIONS** Auth, pub(s) on Shakespeare and Nahum Tate, Dryden, Swift, 18th and 20th century wine, 17th and 18th century poetry, Georgian silver, American, Victorian and continental 19th century music; auth, "Scrolls, Codices and Contemporary Technologies: Writing the Book," Descant. **CONTACT ADDRESS** Dept of English, Univ of Manitoba, Winnipeg, MB, Canada R3T 2N2. **EMAIL** jrempel@cc.umanitoba.ca

RENFRO, PAULA C.
DISCIPLINE COMMUNICATIONS **EDUCATION** Baylor Univ, BA, MA, Univ TX, PhD. **CAREER** Comm Dept, Southwest Tex State Univ **HONORS AND AWARDS** Ast Chair, Dept Mass Comm; Ed, Leadtime. **MEMBERSHIPS** AJHA; NAJA. **SELECTED PUBLICATIONS** Auth, Expectations of Change in the High School Press after Hazelwood, Southwestern Mass Comm Jour, 88; Coauth, Rupert Murdoch's Style: The New York Post, Newspaper Res, 88; Jour Post-Hazelwood: Survey Results Indicate Little Change, Hooray for High School Journalism, 89; Southwestern Art in Regional Magazines of the United States, Greenwood Press, 91; TV Guide Under Murdoch: Less Serious Analysis, More Entertainment, Southwestern Mass Comm Jour, 92; Chronicle of Higher Education, Greenwood Press, 94; Folio, Greenwood Press, 94; Southwestern Art in Regional Magazines of the United States, Southern Mag; coauth, An Appraisal of Murdock and the U.S. Daily Press, Newspaper Res, 99. **CONTACT ADDRESS** Southwest Texas State Univ, 601 University Dr, San Marcos, TX 78666-4604. **EMAIL** prol@swt.edu

RENFRO, R. BRUCE
DISCIPLINE COMMUNICATIONS **EDUCATION** Univ TX, BA, MA, PhD. **CAREER** Comm Dept, Southwest Tex State Univ **SELECTED PUBLICATIONS** Coauth, A Bibliometric Analysis of Public Relations Research, Jour Public Relations Res, 92; Auth, Public Relations Writing and Media Techniques, Harper/Collins Publ, 93; How to Get the Most Out of Press Releases, Tex Intercollegiate Press Asn/Southwest Journalism Congress Convention, 94. **CONTACT ADDRESS** Southwest Texas State Univ, 601 University Dr, San Marcos, TX 78666-4604.

RENNIE, MAIRI C.
PERSONAL Born 10/17/1937, Oxford, England, d, 2 children **DISCIPLINE** LITERATURE **EDUCATION** Univ St Andrews, MA; Univ Southhampton, PhD. **CAREER** English fac, Highbury Col, 69-87; principal, Kensington Park/Dixon Wolfe Tutorial Col, 87-93; dir, Armstrong Browning Libr at Baylor Univ, 96-. **MEMBERSHIPS** MLA, Browning Soc. **RESEARCH** Poetry/Biography of Robert Browning and Elizabeth Barrett Browning. **SELECTED PUBLICATIONS** Auth, Robert Browning's London, 89. **CONTACT ADDRESS** Dept English, Baylor Univ, Waco, PO Box 97404, Waco, TX 76798-7404. **EMAIL** mairi_rennie@baylor.edu

RENO, J. DAVID
PERSONAL Born 02/03/1949, Bethlehem, PA, m, 1995, 1 child **DISCIPLINE** COMMUNICATION STUDIES **EDUCATION** Emerson Col, BS, SP, 73, MA, 95. **CAREER** Alliance Independent Sch, Bd Dir, 93-95; Nat Alliance HUD Tenants, BD Dir, 95-97; Assoc Former Intelligence Officers, Bd Dir, 95-. **HONORS AND AWARDS** Awd Appreciation, AFIO. **MEMBERSHIPS** AIS; IRE; NCIS; CAJ; NWU; PEN; AFIO; IRE. **RESEARCH** Amer History; Investigative Reporting as Schshp; Literary Landmarks of Amer. **SELECTED PUBLICATIONS** Auth, The Magic of Accounting, IRE Jour, 85; auth, Yellowstone and the Presidency, Christian Sci Monitor, 89; auth, White Collar Crime, The Journalist's Guide to its Literature, IRE Jour, 86; auth, Secret New England, AFIO, 91; auth, To Protect Serve National Security, Investigative Reporters and Editors Jour, 90; auth, Erle Stanley Gardner and the Court of Last Resort, Mystery Writers of Amer, NY, The Players Club 95. **CONTACT ADDRESS** The Piano Factory, 791 Tremont St W-113, Boston, MA 02118-1062. **EMAIL** renod.gpd@ci.boston.ma.us

RENZA, LOUIS A.
DISCIPLINE ENGLISH LITERATURE **EDUCATION** Univ CA Irvine, PhD, 72. **CAREER** Prof, Dartmouth Col. **RESEARCH** Am lit; Edgar Allen Poe; lit criticism. **SELECTED PUBLICATIONS** Auth, 'Ut Pictura Poe': Poetic Politics in 'The Island of the Fay' and 'Morning on the Wissahicon' in The American Face of Edgar Allan Poe, Johns Hopkins UP, 95; Poe's Masque of Mass Culture: Or, Other-Wise: A Review Essay, Poe Studies: Dark Romanticism: Hist, Theory, Interp, 95; Influence in Critical Terms for Literary Study, Univ Chicago P, 90; A White Heron and the Question of Minor Literature, Univ Wis P, 84; coauth, The Irish Stories of Sarah Orne Jewett; S Ill UP, 96. **CONTACT ADDRESS** Dept of English, Dartmouth Col, 6032 Sanborn House, Hanover, NH 03755. **EMAIL** Louis.A.Renza@dartmouth.edu

RESINSKI, REBECCA
PERSONAL Born 11/19/1968, Johnstown, PA **DISCIPLINE** CLASSICS **EDUCATION** Bucknell Univ, BA, 90; Univ CA, Los Angeles, MA, 93, PhD, 98. **CAREER** Asst prof Classics, Dept of Relig and Classics, Univ Rochester, 98-. **HONORS AND AWARDS** William Bucknell Prize, 90; A D White fel at Cornell Univ, 90-92; Chancellor's fel at UCLA, 92-93; Luckman Awd for Distinguished Teaching, UCLA, 97. **MEMBERSHIPS** Am Philol Asn; Women's Classical Caucus. **RESEARCH** Ancient poetry; ancient social thought; representations of women in antiquity; the classical tradition in 20th century lit. **SELECTED PUBLICATIONS** Auth, Cosmos and Cosmetics: Constituting an Adorned Female Body in Ancient Greek Literature, UCLA dissertation, 98. **CONTACT ADDRESS** Hendrix Col, Department of Foreign Languages, Conway, AR 72032. **EMAIL** beci@troi.cc.rochester.edu

REUSHER, JAY
DISCIPLINE CLASSICS **EDUCATION** Fordham Univ, PhD, 69. **CAREER** Assoc prof, 69-, Georgetown Univ. **RESEARCH** Kant. **CONTACT ADDRESS** 900 10th St NE, Washington, DC 20002-3718. **EMAIL** reushej@garnet.georgetown.edu

REVELL, DONALD
PERSONAL Born 06/12/1954, Bronx, NY, m, 1992, 1 child **DISCIPLINE** ENGLISH **EDUCATION** SUNY, Buffalo, PhD (English), 80. **CAREER** Asst prof, English, Ripon Col, 82-85; asst prof to assoc prof, English, Univ Denver, 85-94; prof English, Univ UT, 94-. **HONORS AND AWARDS** NEA fel in Poetry, 88, 95; Guggenheim fel in Poetry, 92. **MEMBERSHIPS** Nat Book Critics Circle. **RESEARCH** Poetics. **SELECTED PUBLICATIONS** Auth, Erasures, Wesleyan/UPNE, 92; Beautiful Shirt, Wesleyan/UPNE, 94; Alcools, Wesleyan/UPNE, 95; auth, There Are Three, Wesleyan, 98. **CONTACT ADDRESS** English Dept, Univ of Utah, Salt Lake City, UT 84112. **EMAIL** donald.revell@m.cc.utah.edu

REVERAND, CEDRIC D.
PERSONAL Born 12/03/1941, Brooklyn, NY, m, 1965 **DISCIPLINE** ENGLISH LITERATURE **EDUCATION** Yale Univ, BA, 63; Columbia Univ, MA, 64; Cornell Univ, PhD, 72. **CAREER** Lect, St. John's Univ, 66-67; inst, 71-72, asst prof, 72-77, assoc prof, 77-82, Prof, 82-, Dir Cultural Progs, Univ Wyo, 78-. **HONORS AND AWARDS** Phi Beta Kappa; Ford fel, Cornell; hon fel, Clare Hall, Cambridge; Univ Wyo for outstanding teaching, Andrew Mellow fel, Univ Calif Los Angeles, Yale. **MEMBERSHIPS** Mod Lang Asn; Am Soc for 18th cent Stud, Western Arts Alliance **RESEARCH** Dryden; Pope; Restoration & 18th cent poetry; fine arts. **SELECTED PUBLICATIONS** various **CONTACT ADDRESS** Univ of Wyoming, Box 3353 Univ Sta, Laramie, WY 82071. **EMAIL** reverand@uwyo.edu

REYDAMS-SCHILS, GRETCHEN
PERSONAL m, 3 children **DISCIPLINE** CLASSICS; ANCIENT PHILOSOPHY **EDUCATION** Katholieke Universiteit Leuven, Belgium, AB (classics, magna cum laude), 87; Univ Cincinnati, MA, 89; KU Leuven, Belgium, Inst of Philos, res, 91-92; Univ CA, Berkeley, Candidate Philos, 91, PhD, 94. **CAREER** Prog dir, Int House, Berkeley, 89-91; teaching asst, Univ Cincinnati, 88-89; press & info office, European Parliament, Brussels, summer 90; post-graduate sem moderator, KU Leuven, Inst for Philos, 91-92; grad student instr, Univ CA, Berkeley, 92-93; press office Brussels, Council of the European Communities, spring 94; asst prof, Prog Liberal Studies, Univ Notre Dame, 94-; vis prof, Spiritan Missionary Sem, Arusha, Tanzania, spring 98 (sabbatical); assoc prof, Univ of Notre Dame, 00-. **HONORS AND AWARDS** Fulbright fel, 87-92; Louise Semple-Taft fel, Univ Cincinnati, 87-89; Sather Assist, Univ CA, Berkeley, 89-91; Louise McKay Prize in Latin Prose Composition, Univ CA, Berkeley, 91; Mellon Dissertation Res grant, 91; fel, Center of Western European Studies, spring 93; Chancellor's Dissertation Year fel, Univ CA, Berkeley, 93-94; Scientific Council of the Found Hardt, Geneva, 96; Belgian Univ Found pub grant, 96; Fac Res Grant, Univ of Notre Dame, 99; Erasmus Institute Fac Workshop, Theol and Fiction, 99; Paul M. and Barbara Henkels Vis Scholars Series, Univ of Notre Dame, 99-00; Jr Fel at the Center for Hellenci Studies, Washington D.C., 00-01. **SELECTED PUBLICATIONS** Auth, Solon and the Hektemoroi, Ancient Soc 22, Leuven, 91; Plato's Myth of Er: the Light and the Spindle, l'Antiquite Classique 62, 93; Stoicized Readings of Plato's Timaeus in Philo of Alexandria, Soc Bib Lit, sem papers 94, Studia Philonica Annual 7, 95; The European Union and Cultural Policy, European Intergration and American Federalism: A Comparative Perspective, Richard Herr and Steven Weber, eds, Berkeley, 96; Plato's World Soul: Grasping Sensibles without Sense-Perception, Interpreting the Timaeus-Critias: Proceedings of the IV Symposium Platonicum, selected papers, Int Plato Studies 9, ed L. Brisson and T. Calvo, Sankt Augustin, 97; Posidonius and Plato's Timaeus: Off to Rhodes and Back to Plato?, Classical Quart 47, 97; Romand and Stoic, the Self as a Mediator, Dionysius, New Series 16, (98): 35-62; Demiurge and Providence, Stoic and Platonist Readings of Plato's Timaeus, Monotheismes et Philosophie, (Brepols Publishers: Turnhout, Belgium, 99); contrib, Socrates Request: Tim, 19B-20C in the Tradition of Platonism, forthcoming in The Ancient World, Conference Papers, 98; An Anthology of Snakebites, (Philosophy/Gender Studies, Seven Bridges Press, 01); ed, Plato's Timeus as Cultural Icon. **CONTACT ADDRESS** Prog Liberal Studies, Univ of Notre Dame, Notre Dame, IN 46556. **EMAIL** gretchen.j.reydams-schils.1@nd.edu

REYNOLDS, DAVID S.
PERSONAL Born 08/30/1948, Providence, RI, m, 1983, 1 child **DISCIPLINE** ENGLISH; AMERICAN LITERATURE **EDUCATION** Amherst Col, BA, 70; Univ Calif Berkeley, PhD, 79 **CAREER** Asst prof, Northwestern Univ, 80-83; assoc prof, Rutgers Univ, 86-89; prof, Baruch Col, 89-95; distinguished prof, Baruch Col, 96- **HONORS AND AWARDS** Bancroft Prize; Ambassador Book Awd; Finalist, Ntl Book Critics Circle Awd; Christian Gauss Awd **MEMBERSHIPS** Modern Lang Assoc; Amer Antiquarian Soc; Amer Studies Assoc **RESEARCH** American Literature and Culture; American Renaissance; American History **SELECTED PUBLICATIONS** Co-ed, The Serpent in the Cup: Temperance and American Literature, Univ Mass, 97; auth, Walt Whitman's America: A Cultural Biography, Vintage, 96; auth, Beneath the American Renaissance: The Subversive Imagination in the Age of Emerson and Melville, Knopf, 88 **CONTACT ADDRESS** 16 Linden Ln, Old Westbury, NY 11568. **EMAIL** reyno45@ibm.net

REYNOLDS, MARK
PERSONAL Born Tuscaloosa, AL, m, 1 child **DISCIPLINE** ENGLISH **EDUCATION** Univ Alabama, BA, 67; MA, 70; Carnegie Mellon Univ, DA, 81. **CAREER** Prof of English, Chair Division of Humanities, Jefferson Davis Community Col, Brewton, AL 69-; **HONORS AND AWARDS** Teaching Excellence Awd, Jefferson Davis Community College, 93; NISOD Excellence Awd, Community College Leadership, Univ Texas, 93; Pickett Service Awd, National Two-Year College English Assoc., 00. **MEMBERSHIPS** National Council of Teacher of English; Conference on College Composition and Communication; Modern Language Assoc; National Two-Year College English Assoc; College English Assoc; TYCA Southeast; SAMLA Rhetoric Society of America; WPA; NEA. **RESEARCH** Composition; British Romantics. **SELECTED PUBLICATIONS** Auth, "Two-Year College English: Essays for a New Century," Book, NCTE; auth, "Creating a Profession: Teaching Two-Year College English," Book, NCTB. **CONTACT ADDRESS** Dept Humanities, Jefferson Davis Comm Col, PO Box 958, Brewton, AL 36427-0958. **EMAIL** mreynolds@acet.net

REYNOLDS, RICHARD CLAY
PERSONAL Born 09/28/1949, Quanah, TX, m, 1972, 2 children **DISCIPLINE** AMERICAN LITERATURE **EDUCATION** Univ TX Austin, BA, 71; Trinity Univ, MA, 74; Univ Tulsa, PhD, 79. **CAREER** Grad Tchng Fel, 74-77, Univ of Tulsa; instr, English, 77-78, Tulsa Junior Col; instr, English, 77-78 Claremore Col; assoc prof, 78-88 Lamar Univ Beaumont TX; Prof, novelist in res, 88-92, Univ of N TX; vis prof, writer in res, Spring 94, Villanova Univ; vis prof, writer, Summer Ses, 95, West TX A&M Univ; vis writer, consult, Fall 95, Univ of South Dakota; vis lect, Sept 96, Univ of TX at Austin; adj prof, Fall 96, TX Womans Univ; vis lect, Fall 97, Summer 98, Univ of TX Dallas; freelance writer, 92-; assoc prof, 98- Univ of TX Dallas. **HONORS AND AWARDS** Deans List, Univ of TX, 70; Grad Tchng Fel, 74-77, Comm intern, 76, Grad Res Intern, 77, Faculty Res Grant, 78, Univ of Tulsa; Beaumont Art Museum Scholarship for US Landscape Sem, 82; Top Prof Volunteer KVLU Lamar Univ, 81-82; Amer Biographical Inst Adv Board, 82-88; Dir of Amer School, 82-87; Col of Arts & Sciences Deans Merit Awd, 82-87; Univ Mini Grant, Lamar Univ, 83; Sum Dev Leave, Lamar Univ, 83; Regents Merit Awd, 86; Oppie Awd for the Vigil, 87; Dev Leave Lamar Univ, 87; Col of Arts & Sciences Excellence in res Awd, Lamar Univ, 88; TX Inst of Letters, 88; Western Writers of Amer, 89; The National Faculty, 90; WWA Spur Awd, Finalist Best Western Short Fiction, 92; Key to the City of Fort Worth Friends of the Library Awd, 92; Violet Crown Fiction Awd, 92; ALE Awd for Short Fiction, 93; Pulitzer Prize Entrant for Fiction, 92; WWA Spur Awd Finalist Best Novel of the West, 93; Fel National Endowment for the Arts, 94; PEN Texas Awds for Essay and Fiction, 97; Texas Coun for the Arts/Austin Writers League Literature Grant, 97; Council on National Literatures Fiction Awd, 98. **MEMBERSHIPS** The National Faculty; PEN West; Western Writers of Amer; TX Inst of Letters; Modern Lang Asn; South Central Modern Lang Asn; Western Amer Lit Asn; TX Asn of Creative Writing Tchrs; Asn Writing Programs. **RESEARCH** Amer West, Amer lit, Amer history. **SELECTED PUBLICATIONS** Auth, The Vigil, NY St Martins Press/Richard Marek, 86; auth, Agatite, NY St Martins Press, 86; ed, Taking Stock A Larry McMurtry Casebook, SMU Press 89; auth, Franklins Crossing, NY Signet, 92; auth, "The Texas Blacklands," in Where the West Begins or Where the South Ends, Texas Blackland Prairie Land History Culture, Baylor Univ Press, 93; auth, Mexico, That's What I Like About the South and Other Stories for the Nineties, Univ of South Carolina Press, 93; auth, Summer Seeds, Careless Weeds, SMU Press, 93; auth, Fist Fight, Texas Short Fiction A World in Itself, ALE Pub 93; auth, Ettas Pond, Higher Elevations Stories from the West, Ohio Univ Press, 93; auth, Shechem, Cimarron Review, 93; auth, Andrew Hudgins 1951-, Oxford Companion to Twentieth Century Poetry in English, Oxford Univ Press, 94; auth, Early Innings, ie Magazine, 94; auth, Dogstar, Sulphur River Review, 94; auth, Forward, Coffee, How the Cimarron River Got Its Name and Other Stories about Coffee, Rep of TX Press, 95; auth, One Hundred Years of Heroes The Southwestern Exposition and Livestock Show, Fort Worth, TCU Press, 95; auth, Right Field Blues, Rev Texas Short Fiction a World in Itself II, ALE Pub, 95; ed, Sound Warehouse A Memoir The Early Years of an American Retailer, Privately Pub, 95; auth, Nickleby, South Dakota Review, 96; auth, The First Tour, Texas Rev, 96; auth, Goodnight Sweetheart, Texas Short Stories, Browder Springs Press, 97; auth, The Last Wolf, Potpourri, 97; auth, Players, NY Carroll and Graf, 97; auth, The State of Publishing, Dict of Lit Biography Yearbook 1997, TX Review, Layman Press, 98; auth, Twenty Questions Answers for the Aspiring Writer, Browder Springs Press, 98; auth, Of Snakes and Sex and Playing in the Rain, Best Texas Writing, Rancho Loco Press, 98; auth, A Trilogy Blue Coach & The Player, Suddenly Prose Poetry and Sudden Fiction, Martin House, 98; auth, Screenplay, Players, The Vigil and Daydream, Daydream Entertain, 98; auth, "A Trilogy: 'Blue,' 'Coach,' & 'The Player,'" in Suddenly: Prose Poetry and Sudden Fiction, ed. Jackie Pelham (Houston: Martin House, 98), 49-54; coauth, Let Us Prey, Genesis Pr (Columbus, Miss), 99; auth, Monumnets, Texas Tech Univ Pr (Lubbock), 00; auth, "Sex on the Beach," in Texas Short Stories 2, ed. Billy Bob Hill and Laurie Champion (Dallas: Browder Springs Pr, 00), 263-285. **CONTACT ADDRESS** 909 Hilton Pl, Denton, TX 76201. **EMAIL** RclayR@aol.com.

RHODE, ROBERT T.
PERSONAL Born 07/25/1954, IN, s **DISCIPLINE** ENGLISH **EDUCATION** Ind Univ, BS, 76; MA, 78; PhD, 81. **CAREER** Asst prof to prof, N Ky Univ, 81-. **HONORS AND AWARDS** Lieber Awd for Distinguished Teaching, Ind Univ; Strongest Influence Awd, N Ky Univ. **MEMBERSHIPS** Poe Studies Assoc. **RESEARCH** Early American literature in general, Edgar Allan Poe, Walt Whitman, the steam power era. **SELECTED PUBLICATIONS** Coauth, Speak No Evil! A Grammar Guide, McGraw-Hill (NY), 95; auth, Your Personal Writing Workout, McGraw-Hill (NY), 96; coauth, "Voices from the Margins: What Students Want to Hear from Instructor Comments", The Teaching Prof, 10.9 (96): 5; auth, "When Steam Was King. . . And Cincinnati Was Queen", Queen city Heritage 55.1 (97): 36-48; auth, "The Road-Building Ruebels of Cincinnati", Queen City Heritage 56.2 (98): 29-35; coauth, Your Personal Writing Workout, 2nd Ed, McGraw_Hill, (NY), 98; auth, "The Disenchanted Generation", Nat Honors Report 20.4 (99): 27-28; coauth, "Notes on 'Invocation' by Ogden Nash", Notes and Queries 46.4 (99): 497-500; auth, "William Dean Howells: Hamiltonian, bostonian, or New Yorker?", Ky Philog Rev 14, (99): 32-39. **CONTACT ADDRESS** Dept Lang and Lit, No Kentucky Univ, Highland Heights, KY 41099. **EMAIL** rhode@nku.edu

RHODES, CHIP
PERSONAL Born 05/09/1965, Boston, MA, m, 1996, 1 child **DISCIPLINE** ENGLISH **EDUCATION** Trinity Col, BA; State Univ NY at Stony Brook, PhD. **CAREER** Vis Asst Prof, Univ Nev, Las Vegas, 94-96; Asst Prof, Colo State Univ, 96-. **HONORS AND AWARDS** Best Dissertation Awd, 99. **MEMBERSHIPS** MLA, AMA. **RESEARCH** American Studies, African-American Literature, Marxist Theory, Hollywood Novel. **SELECTED PUBLICATIONS** Auth, Structures of the Jazz Age: Mass Culture and Buckil Disclosures in American Modernism, Verso, 98; articles in Am Lit, Mod Fiction Studies, MLN, J of Am Studies. **CONTACT ADDRESS** Dept English, Colorado State Univ, Fort Collins, CO 80523-0001. **EMAIL** wrhodes@vines.colostate.edu

RHULE, IMOGENE G.
PERSONAL Born 04/17/1941, Akron, OH, m, 1972 **DISCIPLINE** ENGLISH **EDUCATION** Anderson Univ, BA, 69; Ball State Univ, MA, 76; ABD. **CAREER** Teacher, Pendleton High School, 69-81; Asst Prof, Anderson Univ, 84-. **HONORS AND AWARDS** Who's Who in Am Educ; Who's Who Among Am Teachers. **MEMBERSHIPS** NCTC, CCC, ITW, ICEA, ICTE, AAK. **RESEARCH** Basic writing; Rhetoric. **CONTACT ADDRESS** Dept English, Anderson Univ, 1100 E 5th St, Anderson, IN 46012-3462. **EMAIL** itrhule@anderson.edu

RIBEIRO, ALVARO
PERSONAL Born 09/17/1947, Hong Kong **DISCIPLINE** ENGLISH LITERATURE **EDUCATION** Univ Hong Kong, BA; Weston Sch Theol, Mdiv, STL; Oxford Univ, DPhil. **CAREER** Eng Dept, Georgetown Univ **HONORS AND AWARDS** NEH, 99 **RESEARCH** 17th and 18th century British literature and culture; analytical bibliography and textual criticism; music history; theology and literature. **SELECTED PUBLICATIONS** Ed, Tradition in Transition: Women Writers, Marginal Texts, and the Eighteenth-Century Canon, Oxford, 96; The Letters of Dr Charles Burney, Volume I: 1751-1784, Oxford, 91; co-ed, Evidence in Literary Scholarship, Oxford, 79. **CONTACT ADDRESS** English Dept, Georgetown Univ, 37th and O St, Washington, DC 20057-1131. **EMAIL** ribeiroa@georgetown.edu

RICCIARDI, CYNTHIA BOOTH
PERSONAL Born Raynham, MA, m **DISCIPLINE** ENGLISH **EDUCATION** Bridgewater State Col, BA, 81; Boston col, MA, 83; Brandeis Univ, PhD, candidate. **CAREER** Vis lecturer, Bridgewater State Col, 84-; instr, Newbury Col, 84-89; adj instr, Bristol Cmty Cl, 90-91. **MEMBERSHIPS** NCTE. **RESEARCH** Elizabeth Griffith and 18th century women of letters; Uses of pop culture in composition classroom. **SELECTED PUBLICATIONS** Ed, Griffith, Elizabeth, The Delicate Distress, Kentucky Press, 97. **CONTACT ADDRESS** Dept English, Bridgewater State Col, 131 Summer St, Bridgewater, MA 02325-0001. **EMAIL** cricciardi@bridgew.edu

RICCIO, TOM
PERSONAL Born 03/01/1955, Cleveland, OH, m, 1998 **DISCIPLINE** THEATRE **EDUCATION** Cleveland State Univ, BA, 78; Boston Univ, MFA, 82. **CAREER** Artistic dir, Organic Theatre, Chicago, 84-88; Cleveland Playhouse, 85-86; vis prof, Univ of Dan Es Salaam, 89; Korean Nat Univ of the Arts, 96; Univ Alaska, 88-. **HONORS AND AWARDS** APPEX-Asian Pacific Performance Exchange (Univ Calif, Los Angeles, Ford Found), Fel; NEH fel; Alaska State Coun on the Arts; ATT Directing grant; Cleveland Critics Awd; Mellon Found; British Coun. **MEMBERSHIPS** ATHE (Am Theatre in Higher Ed), Asian Theatre Asn, Advisory bds: Edwards Albee Theatre Conf, Outworth Theatre, Bod, Fairbanks Drama Asn. **RESEARCH** Indigenous and ritual performance and theatre, Alaska Native/American Native peformance, alternative and experimental theatre. **SELECTED PUBLICATIONS** Theatre forum, "Performing the Spirits in Zambia,"; theatre forum, "People Come Out of Here, Making a New Story with there Bushman,"; auth, "Politics, Slapstick and Zulu on Town," The Drama Rev; auth, "Gift from the Eagles' Mother," The Drama Rev. **CONTACT ADDRESS** Dept Theatre, Univ of Alaska, Fairbanks, PO Box 755700, Fairbanks, AK 99775-5700. **EMAIL** FFTPR@aurora.alaska.edu

RICE, ALBERT R.
PERSONAL Born 06/09/1951, Pasadena, CA, m, 1987, 2 children **DISCIPLINE** MUSICOLOGY; LIBRARY SCIENCE **EDUCATION** Calif State Univ-Fullerton, BA, 74; Claremont Grad Univ, MA, 77, PhD, 87; San Jose Univ, MLS, 94. **CAREER** Curator, Kenneth G. Fiske Mus of Musical Instruments at Claremont Col, 86-; Libn, Los Angelas Public Lib, 98-. **HONORS AND AWARDS** NEA Travel to Collections res grant, 90-91; refereee on the Music Hist panel for the Travel to Collections Grants, 92-93. **MEMBERSHIPS** Am Mus Instrument Soc; Galpin Soc; Am Lib Asn. **RESEARCH** 18th & 19th century clarinets, flutes, and pianos; 18th & 19th century musical literature for the clarinet. **SELECTED PUBLICATIONS** Auth, The Clarinet d'amour: A request for additional information, FoMHRI Quart, no 70, 17-17, 1/93; auth, The earliest clarinet concertos: Johann Valentin Rathgeber's Chelys Sonora (1728), The Clarinet, vol XX, no 4, 24-28, 93; auth, Some Performance Practice Aspects of American Sheet Music, 1793-1830, Music in Performance and Society: Essays in Honor of Roland Jackson, Harmonie Pk Press, 229-247, 97. **CONTACT ADDRESS** 495 St Augustine Ave, Claremont, CA 91711. **EMAIL** al_rice@cucmail.claremont.edu

RICE, GRANTLAND S.
DISCIPLINE ENGLISH **EDUCATION** Colby, BA, 86; Univ Penn, MA, 87; Brandeis, MA, 91, PhD, 94. **CAREER** Asst prof, eng, Ohio State Univ, 94-98; sen consultant, Taylor Group, Greenwich, CT, 98-99; assoc dir, Tufts Univ, 99-. **HONORS AND AWARDS** Fulbright fel; Am Coun of Learned Soc, fel; Stanford Hum Ctr, fel; Just for US study at Univ of London, fel; NEH fel. **MEMBERSHIPS** Am Antiquarian Soc **SELECTED PUBLICATIONS** Auth, H.S. Crevecoeur and the Politics of Authorship in Republican America," Early Am Lit 28; 93; auth, H. H. Brackenbridge and the Resistance to Textual Authority," Am Lit, 95; auth, The Transformation of Authorship in America, Univ Chicago Press, 97. **CONTACT ADDRESS** Tufts Univ, Medford, Packard Hall, 1st Floor, Medford, MA 02155. **EMAIL** grantland.rice@tufts.edu

RICE, JULIAN
PERSONAL Born 01/17/1940, Milwaukee, WI, m, 1973, 1 child **DISCIPLINE** ENGLISH **EDUCATION** Univ Wisc, BA, 61; CUNY, MA, 64; Univ Calif Los Angeles, PhD, 68. **CAREER** Asst prof, Calif State Univ, 68-71; asst to prof, Fla Atlantic Univ, 72-97. **HONORS AND AWARDS** Outstanding Acad Book, CHOIC, 92. **MEMBERSHIPS** MLA; Asn for the Study of Am Indian Lit. **RESEARCH** American Indian Literature; Spiritual Traditions of the Plains Indians; Artistic Creation and Religion. **SELECTED PUBLICATIONS** Auth, Black Elk's Story, Univ NMex Press, 91; auth, Deer Women and Elk Man: The Dakota narratives of Elk Deloria, Univ NMex Press, 92; auth, Elk Deloria's Iron Hawk, Univ NMex Press, 93; auth, Ella Deloria's The Buffalo People, Univ NMex Press, 94; auth, Before the Great Spirit: The Many Faces of Sioux Spirituality, Univ NMex Press, 98. **CONTACT ADDRESS** Dept English, Florida Atlantic Univ, 5033 NW 3rd Ter, Boca Raton, FL 33431-4703. **EMAIL** julianrice@sprintmail.com

RICE, LOUISE ALLEN
PERSONAL Born Augusta, GA, m, 1965, 2 children **DISCIPLINE** ENGLISH **EDUCATION** Tuskegee Univ, BS 1963; Columbia Univ Teachers Coll, MA 1969; Univ of GA, PhD 1979. **CAREER** Washington High Sch, English teacher 1963-66; Lucy Laney High School, English Teacher 1966-68; Paine Coll, instructor/reading specialist 1968-71; Lansing School Dist, instructor/reading specialist 1971-72; Paine Coll, assoc prof/asst academic dean 1972-77, 79-81; Lamar Elem Sch, instructional lead teacher 1981-84; Augusta Coll, assoc dir of admissions 1984-88, asst prof of educ and reading 1988-, assoc prof of learning support reading 1989-. **HONORS AND AWARDS** Black Womanhood Speaker's Awd Paine Coll 1983; Distinguished Serv Awd Augusta Pan-Hellenic Council 1984; Urban Builders Awd Augusta Black History Comm 1985; Outstanding Comm Svcs, Leadership and Achievement Certificate Amer Assoc of Univ Women 1986, Educ of the Year, Lincoln League, Augusta, 1988; Distinguished Leadership Awd United Negro College Fund 1990; Woman of the Year Augusta Alumnae Ch Delta Sigma Theta Sorority 1991; National Secretary, Delta Sigma Theta Sorority, Inc., 1992-. **MEMBERSHIPS** Adv bd Richmond Co Bd of Educ 1982-; bd dirs CSRA Economic Opportunity Authority Inc 1984-; dir Southern Region Delta Sigma Theta Sor Inc 1986-91; Educ Comm Augusta Human Relations Comm, 1989-90. **CONTACT ADDRESS** Department of Learning Support, Augusta State Univ, 2500 Walton Way, Augusta, GA 30904-2200. **EMAIL** lrice@aug.edu

RICE, PEGGY S.
PERSONAL Born 02/17/1959, Carrollton, IL, m, 1991, 1 child **DISCIPLINE** ENGLISH **EDUCATION** W Ill Univ, BA, 80; Univ Tex, MEd, 91; La State Univ, PhD, 98. **CAREER** Teacher, Blessed Sacrament Sch, 84-85; Teacher, El Paso Independent Sch Dist, 85-91; Teach, La State Univ Laboratory Sch, 92-94; Teacher, Austin Independent Sch Dist, 94-95; Grad Asst, La State Univ, 95-98; Asst Prof, Ball State Univ, 98-. **HONORS AND AWARDS** Who's Who of Am Women; Gift Honoree, Am Asn of Univ Women, 99; Teacher of the Year, Houston Tex, 87; Who's Who in Am Educ; Who's Who Among Young Am Professionals. **MEMBERSHIPS** Nat Coun of Teachers of English; Nat Reading Conf; Intl Reading Asn; Asn of Teacher Educr; Am Educ Res Asn; am Asn of Univ Women; Kappa Delta Pi; Phi Delta Kappa. **RESEARCH** Issues pertaining to children's literature, such as gender, race and the elderly as well as preadolescent literacy. **SELECTED PUBLICATIONS** Auth, "Gendered Readings of a Traditional 'Feminist' Folktale by Sixth-Grade Boys and Girls," J of Literacy Res, 00; auth, "Critical Issues Response: Revisiting Gendered Readings," J of Literacy Res, 00. **CONTACT ADDRESS** Dept English, Ball State Univ, Robert Bell Bldg, Room 297, Muncie, IN 47306. **EMAIL** psrice@bsu.edu

RICE, WILLIAM
PERSONAL Born 08/07/1952, Montgomery, AL, m, 1978, 2 children **DISCIPLINE** AMERICAN LITERATURE, RHETORIC **EDUCATION** Huntingdon Col, BA, 74; Auburn Univ, MA, 78; Univ Ga, PhD, 93. **CAREER** Instr, Andrew Col, 83-86; asst prof to assoc prof, Shorter Col, 86-; chair, div of general educ, Shorter Col, 96-. **HONORS AND AWARDS** Teacher of the Year, Andrew Col, 84 & 85. **MEMBERSHIPS** S Atlantic MLA. **RESEARCH** African American literature, the American west, business writing. **SELECTED PUBLICATIONS** Auth, "An Incomplete Circle: Images in Part Two of Cane," Col Lang Asn J 29 (86): 442-461; auth, "The Singers in Cane," Markham Rev 15 (85-86): 17-19; auth, "Two Work Songs in Cane," Black Am Lit Forum 23 (89): 593-599; auth, "Computers in Freshman English," Teaching English in the Two-Year Col 16 (89): 29-33; auth, Politics and Precision: Teaching the Art of the Memo," Business Commun Quart 58 (95): 31-34; auth, "Those Who Are Sick," Ind Rev 18 (95): 151-159; auth, Toni Morrison and the American Tradition: A Rhetorical Reading, Peter Lang (New York, NY) 96 & 98; auth, "Searching for Jean Toomer," Am Legacy (97); auth, "Derrida Meets IBM: Using Deconstruction to Teach Business Writing," ERIC online database of articles concerning commun (97); auth, "Using a Web Page to Teach Business Communication," Educ 119 (98): 91-98. **CONTACT ADDRESS** Dept Humanities, Shorter Col, Georgia, PO Box 2016, Rome, GA 30165-4267. **EMAIL** wrice@shorter.edu

RICHARD, RON
DISCIPLINE DEVELOPMENTAL DRAMA **EDUCATION** Concordia Univ, MA, 92; McGill Univ, PhD, 94. **CAREER** Prof; actor; dir; playwright. **RESEARCH** Theatre for young audiences and drama for special populations. **SELECTED PUBLICATIONS** Pub(s), in Creating a Theatre in Your Classroom. **CONTACT ADDRESS** Dept Art Hist, Concordia Univ, Montreal, 1455 de Maisonneuve W, Montreal, QC, Canada H3G 1M8. **EMAIL** ronrich@alcor.concordia.ca

RICHARD, THELMA SHINN
PERSONAL Born 09/10/1942, Flint, MI, 5 children **DISCIPLINE** ENGLISH **EDUCATION** Cent Conn State Col, BA, 65; Purdue Univ, MA, 67, PhD(English), 72. **CAREER** Instr English, Col of Our Lady of the Elms, 71-73; asst prof, Westfield State Col, 73-75; vis lectr, 75-76, dir women's studies, 77-80, ASSOC PROF ENGLISH, ARIZ STATE UNIV, 76-. **MEMBERSHIPS** MLA; AAUP; Am Asn Univ Women; Women's Caucus Mod Lang. **RESEARCH** Contemporary novel, 19th and 20th century women and Am ethnic writers, Am drama, and mythological backgrounds of women's lit. **SELECTED PUBLICATIONS** Auth, Whats In A Word, Possessing A.S. Byatt's, Meronymic Novel/, Papers On Lang And Lit, Vol 0031, 1995; auth, "Gender Images and Patterns from Novel to Film," In Gender, Ideology: essays on theory, fiction and film, (Amsterdam: Rodopi B.V., 96): 451-59; co-ed, "Is Hope A Fiction? Women and the Meronymic Novel," In Daughters of Restlessness: Womens Literature at the End of the Millennium, eds. Sabine Coelsch-Foisner, Hanna Wallinger, and Gerhild Reisner, (Heidelberg: Universitatsverlag C. Winter, 98): 129-39; ed, "ReCreating Memory in the American West," in Communities in the American West, Navada Humanities Committee, Reno, NV: Halcyon, (99): 31-55. **CONTACT ADDRESS** Dept of English, Arizona State Univ, Tempe, AZ 85287. **EMAIL** tjrichard@asu.edu

RICHARDS, CONSTANCE S.
PERSONAL Born 09/18/1948, Columbus, OH, s **DISCIPLINE** ENGLISH, WOMEN'S STUDIES, BLACK STUDIES **EDUCATION** Ohio State Univ, BA, 90; MA, 92; PhD, 96. **CAREER** Lectr, Ohio State Univ, 96-; adj asst prof, Ohio Wesleyan Univ, 97-. **MEMBERSHIPS** Nat Womens Studies Assoc, Mod For Lang Assoc. **RESEARCH** Global/TransNational Women's Literature. **SELECTED PUBLICATIONS** Auth, On the Winds and Waves of Imagination: Transnational Feminism and Literature, (Garland, NY), 00. **CONTACT ADDRESS** Ohio Wesleyan Univ, 3550 Olentangy Blvd, Columbus, OH 43214-4023. **EMAIL** richards.5@osu.edu

RICHARDS, JEFFREY H.
PERSONAL Born 12/04/1948, Libertyville, IL, m, 1978, 2 children **DISCIPLINE** ENGLISH **EDUCATION** Yale Univ, BA, 71; Univ North Carolina, PhD, 82. **CAREER** Asst dir, Dowling Col, 71-72; tchg asst to instr, 74-79, vis assoc prof, 86-87, Univ North Carolina; instr to asst prof to assoc prof, 79-87, dir, 80-83, chair, 83-87, Lakeland Col; vis foreign prof, Beijing Normal Univ, 84-85; vis lect, 87-92, asst dir, 88-92, North Carolina Univ; vis asst prof, Duke Univ, 92; asst prof, 92-95, assoc prof, 95-, chair, 95-, Old Diminion Univ. **HONORS AND AWARDS** Aurelian Honor Society, 70-71, Yale Univ; Outstanding Tchr, 82-83, Lakeland Col; Most Inspiring Fac Awd, 96-00, Old Dominion Univ; Phi Kappa Phi Honor Society, 97, Old Dominion Chapter. **MEMBERSHIPS** Mod Lang Asn; Am Stud Asn; South Atlantic Mod Lang Asn; Society Early Am; Am Lit Asn. **RESEARCH** Early American literature; American drama; 19th century American literature. **SELECTED PUBLICATIONS** Auth, Theatre Enough: American Culture and the Metaphor of the World Stage, 1607-1789, 91; auth, Merch Otis Warren, 95; auth, Early American Drama, 97; auth, "Joseph Dennie," American National Biography, Oxford UP, 99; auth, "Decorous Violence; Manners, Class, and Abuse in Rebecca Rush's Kelroy," Over the Threshold: Intimate Violence in Early America, ed. Christine Daniels and Michael V. Kennedy, New York; Routledge, 99; auth, "Brogue Irish Take the American Stage, 1767-1808," New Hibernia Review: A Quarterly Record of Irish Studies, 99; auth, "Early American Drama and Theater," In Teaching the Literatures of Early America, ed. Carla Mulford, New York: Modern Language Asn, 99; auth, " Samuel Davies and Calvinist Poetic Ecology," Early American Literature 35.1, 00; auth, Mimic Life, by Anna Cora Mowatt. Acton, Mass: Copley, forthcoming, 00; auth, The Early Plays of Eugene O'Neill, New York: Penguin, forthcoming, 01. **CONTACT ADDRESS** Dept of English, Old Dominion Univ, Norfolk, VA 23529. **EMAIL** jhrichar@odu.edu

RICHARDS, LEON
PERSONAL Born 06/07/1945, Montgomery, AL, m, 1969, 2 children **DISCIPLINE** INTERNATIONAL RELATIONS, POLITICAL SCIENCE, ENGLISH **EDUCATION** Alabama State Univ, BS (summa cum laude), 1968; University of Hawaii-Manoa, MA, 1970, PhD, 1974, MA, 00. **CAREER** East-West Center, Univ of Hawaii, Honolulu, HI, res assistant, 70-71, 74-75; Leeward Community Col, Pearl City, HI, staff dev specialist, 75-77; Kapiolani Community Col, Honolulu, HI, asst dean of instruction, 77-81, acting provost, 83-84, dean of instruction, 83-. **HONORS AND AWARDS** Alpha Kappa Mu Scholastic Honorary Society, 1966-68; Sigma Rho Sigma Scholastic Honorary Soc for History Majors, 1966-68; Am Council on Education Fellow in Academic Administratiion, 1981-82; Summer In-Residence Fel at Nat Center for Res in Vocational Education, 1979; East-West Ctr Fellows, 1993-97; Field Study Fellows to Peking Univ; Fulbright Study Abroad, Korea Foundation, for Field Study in China and Korea; Field Study Fellow to Peking Univ, East - West Center, Fulbright study abroad to Vietnam, 99. **MEMBERSHIPS** Vice president, Hawaii Asn of Staff, Program & Organizational Development, 1978-90; member, Nat Committee of Black Political Scientist, 1979-; member, Nat Council of Resource Dev, 1980-. **CONTACT ADDRESS** Dean of Instruction, Univ of Hawaii, Manoa, 4303 Diamond Head Road, Honolulu, HI 96816.

RICHARDS, PHILLIP M.
DISCIPLINE AFRO-AMERICAN LITERATURE **EDUCATION** Yale Univ, BA, 72; Univ Chicago MA, 74, PhD, 87. **CAREER** Instr, Howard Univ; Ar State Univ; assoc prof, 87-. **RESEARCH** Early Am lit. **SELECTED PUBLICATIONS** Auth, Nationalist Themes in the Preaching of Jupiter Hammon, Early Am Lit; ed, Julian Mayfield's The Hit and The Long Night. **CONTACT ADDRESS** Dept of Eng, Colgate Univ, 13 Oak Drive, Hamilton, NY 13346.

RICHARDSON, ANNE
PERSONAL Born 12/22/1942, Berkeley, CA, d **DISCIPLINE** ENGLISH; LIBRARY SCIENCE **EDUCATION** Univ Calif Berkeley, BA, 65; Yale Univ, PhD, 76; Univ Calif Berkeley, Sch of Libr and Info Studies, MLS, 78. **CAREER** Instr, eng, Yale Univ,. 69; instr, eng, Albertus Magnus Col, 69-70; instr, eng, George Washington Univ, 71-74; instr, eng, Anna Head-Josiah Royce Sch, 76; asst reference libr, Univ Kans Libr, 78-79. **HONORS AND AWARDS** Phi Beta Kappa; Woodrow Wilson fel; Univ Calif Berkeley regents' fel. **MEMBERSHIPS** William Tyndale Proj; Renaissance Eng Text Soc; Hagiography Soc; Mod Lang Asn; Inst for Hist Study. **RESEARCH** William Tyndale; Early modern period. **SELECTED PUBLICATIONS** Auth, On Representing Tyndale's English, New Ways of Looking at Old Texts II: Papers of the Renaissance English Text Society, 1992-1996, Medieval & Renaissance Texts & Studies, 98; book rev, William Tyndale: A Biography, Moreana, 122, 99-109, Jun 95; co-ed, William Tyndale and the Law, William Tyndale and the Bill of Rights, Sixteenth Century Jour Publ, 94; auth, Tyndale's Quarrel with Erasmus: A Chapter in the History of the English Reformation, Fides et Hist, XXXV, 3, 46-65, Fall, 93; film rev, Hamlet, The Sixteenth Century Jour, 22, 862-64, Winter, 91; auth, Scripture as Evidence, The Obedience of a Christian Man, Moreana, 28, 106-107, 83-104, Jul, 91; auth, The Assault on Access: a Public Scholar attends the AHA, The Independent Scholar, 5, 2, 5-6, Spring, 91; film rev, Henry V, The Sixteenth Century Jour, 21, 500, Fall, 90; film rev, God's Outlaw: The Story of William Tyndale, The Sixteenth Century Jour, 733-34, Winter, 89; auth, The Evidence Against an English First Edition of Tyndale's Obedience, Moreana, 52, 47-52, 76. **CONTACT ADDRESS** 543 Vincente Ave., Berkeley, CA 94702.

RICHARDSON, BETTY
PERSONAL Born 02/14/1935, Louisville, KY, d, 1 child **DISCIPLINE** ENGLISH **EDUCATION** Univ of Louisville, BA, 57; Univ of Nebr, MA, 63, PhD, 68. **CAREER** Tchg asst and instr, Univ of Nebr, 63-68; from asst prof to prof, Southern Ill Univ, 68- . **HONORS AND AWARDS** SIUE Tchg Excellence Awd, 91; various local recognitions. **MEMBERSHIPS** Int Soc for Humor Studies; Nat Writers Club; Auths Guild; Popular Cult Asn. **RESEARCH** Popular fiction and cult hist; Detective fiction; Women's fiction; 19th and 20th century social and intellectual hist. **SELECTED PUBLICATIONS** Auth, Victoria, Queen of England, The 1890s: An Encycl of Brit Lit, ed G.A. Cevasco, 93; Leslie Ford, Great Women Mystery Writers, ed K. Gregory Klein, 94; Gladys Mitchell, Great Women Mystery Writers, ed K. Gregory Klein, 94; W. Somerset Maugham, Encycl of Brit Humorists, ed S. Gale, 96; Samuel Butler, Encycl of Brit Humorists, ed S. Gale, 96; George Bernard Shaw, Encycl of Brit Humorists, ed S. Gale, 96; G.K. Chesterton, Encycl of Brit Humorists, ed S. Gale, 96; Moll Cutpurse: Mirror of Majesty, Popular Cult Asn Conv, 97; Ladies Unleashed, or The Daughter Also Rises, Popular Cult Asn Conv, 97; Highlights of Film Censorship, 5000-word filmography, Censorship, 97; Highlights of Film Propaganda, 5000-word filmography, Encycl of Propaganda, 97. **CONTACT ADDRESS** Dept of English, So Illinois Univ, Edwardsville, Edwardsville, IL 62025. **EMAIL** brichar@siue.edu

RICHARDSON, CHARLES R.
PERSONAL Born 09/19/1935, Gorman, TX, m, 1964, 2 children **DISCIPLINE** COMMUNICATIONS **EDUCATION** Howard Payne Univ, BS, 58; Hardin-Simmons Univ, MA, 70; Tex A & M, MS, 77. **CAREER** Adj Prof, Hardin-Simmons Univ, 66-67, 79-. **HONORS AND AWARDS** Staff Member of the Year, Hardin-Simmons Univ, 94; Hall of Fame, Tex Baptist Public Rel Asn, 90; Paul Harris Fel, Rotary Intl. **MEMBERSHIPS** Pub Rel Soc of Am, Baptist Comm Asn, Relig Pub Rel Coun, Coun for the Advancement and Support of Education. **RESEARCH** University presidents; Religion; Religious journalism. **SELECTED PUBLICATIONS** Auth, True Servant Leader: James H Landes, Hardin-Simmons Univ, 00; co-ed, Civil War Memories of A.M. Curry, 88; co-ed, "A History of the William Oscar and Cynthia Effie Loyd Family," 77. **CONTACT ADDRESS** Dept Comm, Hardin-Simmons Univ, Abilene, TX 79698. **EMAIL** crichard@hsutx.edu

RICHARDSON, DAVID A.
PERSONAL Born 10/01/1943, Greenville, SC, m, 1968, 2 children **DISCIPLINE** ENGLISH **EDUCATION** Kans State Univ, BA, 65; Univ NC, MA, 67; PhD, 72. **CAREER** Instructor, Univ NC, 69; Asst Prof, Case Western Reserve Univ, 70; Adj Asst Prof to Prof, Cleveland State Univ, 73-. **HONORS AND AWARDS** NEH/Folger Inst Grant, 91, 95; Ohio Bd. of Regents Res Challenge Awd, 86, 87; NEH Interpretive Res Awd, 86, 87; IREX Travel Grant, 84, 85; NEH Res Tools Grant, 80-87; SE Inst of Medieval & Ren Studies Fel, 79; NEH Summer Stipend, 76, 92; Woodrow Wilson Dissertation Fel, 69; NDEA Grad Fel, 65-68; Woodrow Wilson Grad Fel, 65. **MEMBERSHIPS** Spenser Soc of N Am. **RESEARCH** Spenser; Biography; Shakespeare authorship issue. **SELECTED PUBLICATIONS** Co-ed, Spenser and the Subject of Biography, eBooks, 00; auth, "Fair Allurements to Learning: The Legacy of a Professing Teacher," in Classical, Renaissance, and Postmodernist Acts of the Imagination, Arthur F Kinney, 96; ed, Sixteenth-Century British Nondramatic Writers, 4 Series: Vols 132, 136, 167, 172 of Dictionary of Literary Biography, 93-96; ed, The Spenser Encyclopedia, 90. **CONTACT ADDRESS** Dept English, Cleveland State Univ, 1983 E 24th St, Cleveland, OH 44115-2403. **EMAIL** d.richardson@csuohio.edu

RICHARDSON, DON
PERSONAL Born 08/07/1938, Malta, OH, m, 3 children **DISCIPLINE** COMMUNICATION **EDUCATION** Auburn Univ, BA, 61; OH Univ, MA, 63, PhD, 64. **CAREER** Asst Prof, Univ GA, 64-66; Prof, Assoc Dean of grad school, Chair, div of Arts and Sciences, Chair, Dept of Communications, Auburn Univ, 66-91; Chair, Dept of Public Communication, Sam Houston State Univ, 91-. **MEMBERSHIPS** Speech Communication Asn; Southern States Communication Asn. **SELECTED PUBLICATIONS** Auth, with others, The Multidimensionality of Presbycusis: Hearing Losses on the Content and Relational Dimensions of Speech, Jour of Int Listening Asn, VII, 93; Presbycusis and Conversation: Elderly Interactants Adjusting to Multiple Hearing Losses, with others, Res on Lang and Social Interaction, 39, 97; book chapter, The Production of Listening, Working Memory, and Hemispheric Lateralization, in TR5: An

Introduction to Research Writing, Simon & Schuster Custom Pub, 98; ed, Conversations with Carter, Lynne Rienner Pubs, 98. **CONTACT ADDRESS** Dept of Public Communication, Sam Houston State Univ, Huntsville, TX 77341. **EMAIL** scm_drr@shsu.edu

RICHARDSON, DON
PERSONAL Born 07/22/1942, Correctionville, IA, m, 1987, 2 children **DISCIPLINE** ENGLISH **EDUCATION** Fort hays Kans State Univ, BA, 67; MA, 71; Ariz State Univ, Tempe, PhD, 85. **CAREER** Prof, Phoenix Col. **HONORS AND AWARDS** Guest Prof, Univ of Heidelberg, 87-88; Vis Prof, Wuyi Univ, Jiagmen City, China, 87; Vis Prof, Univ in la Communidad, Guadalajara, Mex, 99; Phi Kappa Phi. **MEMBERSHIPS** AAUP. **RESEARCH** Howard R. Bernard, Pioneer Kans Educator. **SELECTED PUBLICATIONS** Auth, "Late Registration . . .", Teaching in the Community College, 95; coauth, "Articulation & Transfer . . . ," (96); coauth, "MCCCD Proposed Statewide Criteria for College Course Level," (97). **CONTACT ADDRESS** Dept English, Phoenix Col, 1202 W Thomas Rd, Phoenix, AZ 85013-4208. **EMAIL** don.richardson@pcmail.maricopa.edu

RICHARDSON, DONALD
DISCIPLINE GREEK AND ROMAN CLASSICS, WORLD CLASSICS **EDUCATION** Univ Minn, PhD; post-doc work, Stanford Univ; Univ Oslo. **CAREER** Ex dept ch; prof. **SELECTED PUBLICATIONS** Transl, Euripides' Iphigenia At Aulis; auth, Great Zeus And All His Children; Eyewitnesses; Stories of the Greeks and Romans. **CONTACT ADDRESS** Dept of Eng, Univ of Evansville, 1800 Lincoln Ave, Evansville, IN 47714. **EMAIL** dr26@evansville.edu.

RICHARDSON, GARY A.
PERSONAL Born 07/11/1949, Shreveport, LA, m, 1980, 2 children **DISCIPLINE** ENGLISH **EDUCATION** Univ La Monroe, BA, 71; MA, 75; Univ Ill Urbana-Champaign, PhD, 83. **CAREER** Asst prof to prof, Mercer Univ, 83-. **HONORS AND AWARDS** Fel, UIUC Grad Col, 79-80; Mellon Found Fel, 86; William Andrews Clark Libr Fel, 87; Fulbright Lectr, 87; Fel, Irish Am Cult Inst, 91; NEH, 01. **MEMBERSHIPS** MLA, SAMLA, Am Conf for Irish Studies, Am Soc for 18th Century Studies, SE Am Soc for 18th Century Studies, Am Soc for Theater Res, Am Theatre and Drama Soc, Eugene O'Neill Soc, David Mament Soc, Am Studies Asn. **RESEARCH** English, American, and Irish Drama and Theatre. **SELECTED PUBLICATIONS** Auth, American Drama from the Colonial Period through World War I: A Critical History, Twayne, 93; coauth, America Drama: Colonial to Contemporary, Harcourt Brace, 95. **CONTACT ADDRESS** Dept English, Mercer Univ, Macon, 1400 Coleman Ave, Macon, GA 31207. **EMAIL** richardson_g@mercer.edu

RICHARDSON, GRANETTA L.
DISCIPLINE LITERATURE **EDUCATION** Univ Akron, BA; Ohio State Univ, MA; Univ Tenn, Knoxville, PhD. **CAREER** Asst prof, Univ NC, Wilmington. **RESEARCH** Film theory and film criticism; Vietnam War literature. **SELECTED PUBLICATIONS** Wrote on topics as diverse as Puritan influences on Vietnam poetry to the Barbie doll. **CONTACT ADDRESS** Univ of No Carolina, Wilmington, Morton Hall, Wilmington, NC 28403-3297. **EMAIL** richardsongr@uncwil.edu

RICHARDSON, MALCOLM
PERSONAL Born 02/04/1947, Oak Ridge, TN, m **DISCIPLINE** ENGLISH **EDUCATION** Univ Tenn, BA, 69; UNLV, MA, 74; Univ Tenn, PhD, 78. **CAREER** Texas, AM Univ, 77-83; Univ AL, 83-86; LA State Univ, 86-. **HONORS AND AWARDS** NEH; ACLS Gnts. **MEMBERSHIPS** MLA; ATTW; ISHR; RSA. **RESEARCH** Medieval language, literature and rhetoric; professional communications. **SELECTED PUBLICATIONS** Coauth, An Anthology of Chauncery English, Univ Tenn Press, 84; auth, The English Chauncery under Henry V (List index Soc, HMSO, 99); auth, "Early Equity Judges: Keepers of the Rolls in Chauncery, 1415-1447, Am J Legal Hist 36 (92): 441-465; coauth, "Power Relations, Technical Writing Theory, and Workplace Writing, J Bus Tech Write 7 (93): 112-137; auth, "Women Commercial Writers of Late Medieval England," Disputatio: A Trans J Medieval Stud 1 (96): 123-146; auth, "Women, Commerce, and Rhetoric in Late Medieval England," in Listening to their Voices: Essays on the Rhetorical Activities of Hist Women, ed. Molly Mejier Wertheimer (Columbia, SC, Univ SC Press, 97). **CONTACT ADDRESS** Dept English, Louisiana State Univ Baton Rouge, Baton Rouge, LA 70803-0104. **EMAIL** enmric@lsu.edu

RICHARDSON, STEPHANIE A.
DISCIPLINE BRITISH LITERATURE **EDUCATION** Univ Akron, BA; Ohio State Univ, MA; PhD. **CAREER** Tchg asst, Ohio State Univ; asst prof, Univ NC, Wilmington. **HONORS AND AWARDS** Univ-wide tchg award, Ohio State Univ. **RESEARCH** Classical rhetoric; modern British literature. **SELECTED PUBLICATIONS** Write in the following areas: classical rhetoric; modern British literature; literary criticism; film studies; popular culture; Biblical studies. **CONTACT ADDRESS** Univ of No Carolina, Wilmington, Morton Hall, Wilmington, NC 28403-3297. **EMAIL** richardsons@uncwil.edu

RICHETTI, JOHN J.
PERSONAL Born 11/14/1938, NY, NY, m, 1960, 2 children **DISCIPLINE** ENGLISH LITERATURE **EDUCATION** St Francis Col, BA, 60; Columbia Univ, MA, 61; PhD, 68. **CAREER** Asst prof, Columbia Univ, 67-70; assoc prof to prof, Rutgers Univ, 67-89; prof, Univ Pa, 89-. **HONORS AND AWARDS** Danforth Fel, 65-67; Fulbright Fel, 65-67; Guggenheim Fel, 71-72; ACLS, Fel, 76-77; Lindback Teaching Award, 82; NEH Fel 89-90. **MEMBERSHIPS** MLA, Am Soc for 18th Century Studies, Asn of Lit Schol and Critics. **RESEARCH** The British Novel, 18th Century Literature and Culture. **SELECTED PUBLICATIONS** Auth, Popular Fiction Before Richardson: Narrative Patterns 1700-1739, Oxford Univ Pr, 69; auth, Defoe's Narratives: Situations and Structures, Oxford Univ Pr, 75; auth, "Philosophical Writing: Locke, Berkeley, Hume," Harvard Univ Pr, 83; ed, Columbia History of the British Novel, Columbia Univ Pr, 93; ed, Cambridge Companion to the 18th Century Novel, Cambridge Univ Pr, 96; auth, The English Novel in History: 1680-1781, Routledge, (00). **CONTACT ADDRESS** English Dept, Univ of Pennsylvania, Bennett Hall, Philadelphia, PA 19104. **EMAIL** jrichett@english.upenn.edu

RICHLIN, AMY
DISCIPLINE CLASSICS AND THE STUDY OF WOMEN AND MEN IN SOCIETY **EDUCATION** Yale Univ, PhD. **CAREER** Prof, Univ Southern Calif. **RESEARCH** Construction of masculinity in the Roman rhetorical schools. **SELECTED PUBLICATIONS** Auth, The Garden of Priapus: Sexuality and Aggression in Roman Humor, 83, rev 92; ed, Pornography & Representation in Greece & Rome, 92 & Feminist Theory & the Classics, co-edited with Nancy Sorkin Rabinowitz, 93. **CONTACT ADDRESS** Col Letters, Arts & Sciences, Univ of So California, University Park Campus, Los Angeles, CA 90089. **EMAIL** richlin@.usc.edu

RICHMAN, GERALD I.
PERSONAL Born 04/01/1948 **DISCIPLINE** ENGLISH **EDUCATION** Univ Mass, Amherst, BA, 70; Brasenose Col, Oxford Univ, BA, 72; Yale Univ, PhD, 77. **CAREER** Asst Prof, Mankato State Univ, 79-82; Asst to Full Prof, Suffolk Univ, 82-. **RESEARCH** Old and Middle English Literature, Renaissance Literature,. 17th Century Literature, Boston. **SELECTED PUBLICATIONS** Auth, "Speaker and Speech Boundaries in 'The Wanderer'," JEGP 82 (82): 469-79; auth, "A New Version of Malory's 'Le Morte Darthur': A Book Review," Avalon to Camelot 1, 1-9 (83):11; auth, "Artful Slipping in Old English," Neophilologus 70 (86): 279-291; auth, "Idea Combining," in Creativity and Liberal Learning, ed. David G. Tuerck (Norwwod, NJ: Ablex, 87), 76-89; auth, "Rape and Desire in 'The Wife of Bath's Tale'," Studia Neophilologica 61 (89): 161-165; auth, Speaker and Speech Boundaries in 'The Wanderer'," in Basic Readings in Anglo-Saxon England: Old English Shorter Poems, ed. Katherine O'Brien O'Keefee (Garland, 93); auth, "Thucydides and 'The Battle of Maldon'," In Geardagum XX (99): 111-123; auth, "Poet and Scop in 'Beowulf'," In Geardagum XXI (00, forthcoming); auth, "A Possible Source for Dryden's Bee and Drone Image in the 'Prologue to Amphitryon'," English lang Notes (forthcoming). **CONTACT ADDRESS** Dept English, Suffolk Univ, 8 Ashburton Place, Boston, MA 02108-2701. **EMAIL** grichman@acad.suffolk.edu

RICHMOND, HUGH M.
PERSONAL Born 03/20/1932, Burton-upon-Trent, England, m, 1958, 2 children **DISCIPLINE** LITERATURE **EDUCATION** Cambridge Univ, BA, 54; Oxford Univ, DPhil, 57. **CAREER** Lieutenant, Royal Artillery, 51-52; Youth Camp Warden, 54; Asst d'anglais, Lcee J. Perrin, Lyon, France, 54-55; Instr to Prof, 57-94, Prof Emeritus English, Univ Calif - Berkeley, 94- (recalled, 94-96), Dir, Shakespeare Prog, 73-, Dir Shakespeare Program, 80-95, Chancellor's Adviser, Educ Development, 83-86; Dir, Educ Div, Shakespeare Globe Ctr, 95-98. **HONORS AND AWARDS** UK State Schol, 48; Open Schol, Emmanuel Col, Cambridge, 49; Tripos Prize, 54; ACLS Fel, 64-65; UC Res Prof, 68, 75; UC Humanities Inst Awds, 73, 76, 87; UC Regents Teaching Grants, 73, 74, 76-78; UCB Teaching Grants, 75, 79, 83, 85, 95; NEH Educ Grants, 76-78, 84-86; NEH Res Fel, 77, 88; UCB Campus Awd for Distinguished Teaching, 79; UCB Humanities Ctr Grant, 93; British Airways Travel Fel, 95, 96. **MEMBERSHIPS** MLA, Shakespeare Assn. **RESEARCH** Video Documentaries: Shakespeare and the Globe, Films for Humanities, 86 and Shakespeare Globe Restored, TMW, 98. **SELECTED PUBLICATIONS** Auth, The School of Love, Princeton, 64; Shakespeare's Political Plays, Random House, 67, Peter Smith, 77; Shakespeare's Sexual Comedy, Bobbs-Merrill, 71; Renaissance Landscapes, Mouton, 73; The Christian Revolutionary: John Milton, UC Press, 74; Puritans & Libertines, UC Press, 81; Shakespeare in Performance: King Richard III, Manchester Univ Press, 90; Shakespeare in Performance: King Henry VIII, Manchester Univ Press, 94; author of numerous journal articles. **CONTACT ADDRESS** Univ of California, Berkeley, Berkeley, CA 94720. **EMAIL** hmr@uclink4.berkeley.edu

RICHMOND, M. TEMPLE
PERSONAL Born 12/08/1951, Texarkana, AR, d **DISCIPLINE** ENGLISH AND WRITING **EDUCATION** Univ Ar., Little Rock, BA, Eng, 84. **CAREER** Consulting astrologer, 81-; found and dir, Sch of Esoteric Astrology, 97-. **HONORS AND AWARDS** Phi Kappa Phi, Univ Ar., Little Rock. **MEMBERSHIPS** Amer Fed Astrols; Amer Acad Relig. **RESEARCH** The roots of esoteric philosophy in ancient sacred traditions. **SELECTED PUBLICATIONS** Auth, Sirius, Source Publ, 97. **CONTACT ADDRESS** 7224 Stonecliff Dr., Apt 3, Raleigh, NC 27615-4332. **EMAIL** blueray@msn.com

RICHMOND, VELMA BOURGEOIS
PERSONAL Born 03/12/1931, New Orleans, LA, m, 1958, 2 children **DISCIPLINE** ENGLISH LITERATURE; MEDIEVAL STUDIES **EDUCATION** La State Univ, BA, 51, MA, 52; Oxford Univ, BLitt, 57; Univ NC, PhD, 59. **CAREER** Instr, La State Univ, 57-58; Instr to Prof, 58-96, Prof Emeritus English, Holy Names Col, 96-, Chmn English, 70-76, Dean Acad Affairs, 80-85. **HONORS AND AWARDS** Fulbright Schol, Oxford Univ, 55-57; ACLS Fel, 76; Project Dir, NEH Implementation Grant for Core Prog in Humanities Studies, 81-84; Conf on Christianity & Lit Bk Awd, 00. **MEMBERSHIPS** Medieval Acad; New Chaucer Soc; Medieval Asn Pac; Mod Lang Asn; Mod Humanities Res Asn; Christianity and Lit; Int Arthurian Soc. **RESEARCH** Chaucer; medieval romance; Shakespeare; children's literature; contemporary Catholic fiction. **SELECTED PUBLICATIONS** Auth, Laments for the Dead in Medieval Narrative, Duquesne Univ Press, 66; The Popularity of Middle English Romance, Bowling Green State Univ Press, 75; Muriel Spark, Frederick Ungar Publ Co, 84; Geoffrey Chaucer, Continuum, 92; The Legend of Guy of Warwick, Garland, 96; author of numerous articles and reviews; auth, Shakespeare, Catholicism, and Romance, Continuum, 00. **CONTACT ADDRESS** 1280 Grizzly Peak Blvd., Berkeley, CA 94708.

RICHTER, DAVID H.
PERSONAL Born 10/01/1945, Chicago, IL, m, 1983, 2 children **DISCIPLINE** ENGLISH **EDUCATION** Univ Chicago, BA, 65; MA, 66; PhD, 71. **CAREER** From Asst Prof to Prof, Queens Col, 71-; Prof, City Univ NYork (CUNY), 95-. **HONORS AND AWARDS** NEH Fel, 86-87. **MEMBERSHIPS** MLA, ASECS, NS. **RESEARCH** Eighteenth-Century literature, literary theory, biblical narrative. **SELECTED PUBLICATIONS** Auth, "Midrash and Mashal: Difficulty in the Blessing of Esau," Narrative 5 (96): 253-264; auth, "A Name by Any Other Rose: Umberto Eco and the Semiotics of Detection," in Reading Eco (Bloomington, IN: Ind Univ Pr, 96), 227-247; auth, Narrative / Theory, Longman (White Plains, NY), 96; auth, The Progress of Romance: Literary Historiography and the Gothic Novel, Ohio St UP (Columbus, OH), 96; auth, Ideology and Form in Eighteenth-Century Literature, Tex Tech UP (Lubbock, TX), 99; auth, "Farewell My Concubine: The Difficult, the Stubborn and the Outrage of Gibeah," in Agendas for Midrash Study in the 21st Century (Williamsburg, VA: William & Mary Pr, 99), 101-122; auth, Form and Ideology in True Crime Fiction, forthcoming; auth, The Robe of Samuel: Difficulty in Biblical Narrative, forthcoming; auth, "Narrativity and Stasis in Martin Rowson's 'Tristram Shandy'," The Shandean (forthcoming). **CONTACT ADDRESS** Dept English, City Col, CUNY, 6530 Kissena Blvd, Flushing, NY 11367-1575. **EMAIL** david_richter@qc.edu

RICKE, JOSEPH M.
DISCIPLINE ENGLISH **EDUCATION** Rice Univ, PhD. **CAREER** Dept Eng, Hunter Col, City Univ NY **MEMBERSHIPS** MLA; Medieval and Renaissance Drama Soc & Conf Christianity and Lit. **SELECTED PUBLICATIONS** Publ on, from Shakespeare's Taming of the Shrew to the value of lit study in Christian higher educ. **CONTACT ADDRESS** Dept of English, Hunter Col, CUNY, 695 Park Ave, New York, NY 10021. **EMAIL** jricke@huntington.edu

RICKLY, REBECCA
DISCIPLINE RHETORIC AND COMPOSITION **EDUCATION** Ball State Univ, PhD, 95. **CAREER** Instr, Univ MI; vis asst prof, TX Tech Univ. **MEMBERSHIPS** Ch, NCTE's Instruct Technol Comt. **RESEARCH** The influence of tech on pedag; research methodology. **SELECTED PUBLICATIONS** Auth, Reflection and Responsibility in (Cyber)Tutor Training: Seeing Ourselves Clearly On and Off the Screen, in Wiring the Writing Center, ed Eric H. Hobson; Promotion, Tenure, and Technology: Do We Get What We Deserve?, in Electronic Networks: Crossing Boundaries/Creating Communities, eds, Tharon Howard, Dixie Goswami, Rocky Gooch; The Gender Gap in Computers and Composition Research: Must Boys Be Boys?, Comput and Compos. **CONTACT ADDRESS** Texas Tech Univ, Lubbock, TX 79409-5015. **EMAIL** R.Rickly@ttu.edu

RIDDELL, RICHARD
DISCIPLINE ENGLISH LITERATURE **EDUCATION** Stanford Univ, PhD, 78. **CAREER** Mary D. B. T. and James H. Semans prof pract drama; dir drama prog. **HONORS AND AWARDS** Tony Awd; Drama Desk Awd; Maharam Awd. **SELECTED PUBLICATIONS** Auth, publ(s) on educ; Europ theater. **CONTACT ADDRESS** Eng Dept, Duke Univ, Durham, NC 27706.

RIDDLE, RITA SIZEMORE
PERSONAL Born Coeburn, VA **DISCIPLINE** SHAKESPEARE, THE ESSAY, AND POETRY **EDUCATION** Hiwassee Col, AA, 62; E TN State Univ, BS, 63, MA, 63; Univ TN, Knoxville, PhD, 71. **CAREER** Grad tchg asst, E TN State Univ, 65-66; grad tchg asst, Univ TN, 68-71; prof, Radford Univ, 71-. **HONORS AND AWARDS** Irene Leach Mem Awd, 92; fac prof develop grant, Ctr for Acad Excellence, 95; James Still Awd for Poetry, Appalachian Writers Asn, 95; prof leave, Radford Univ, 97; **SELECTED PUBLICATIONS** Auth, Chicken Hymns from Pipestem, Newsl of the Ctr for Acad Excellence, Vol IV, No 2, 94; Soot and Sunshine, Radford Univ Arts and Sci Occas Publ Comt, 94; Early Ripes, Story Stitches Vol II, No 1, 94; Pieces for Emma, Radford Univ Arts and Sci Occas Publ Comt, 94; Communication, Gingerbread Man, Asheville Poetry Rev, 95; Creation, Asheville Poetry Rev, 95; Aluminum Balloons and Other Poems, Pocahontas Press, 96; Still Lives, Asheville Poetry Rev, 97. **CONTACT ADDRESS** Radford Univ, Radford, VA 24142. **EMAIL** rriddle@runet.edu

RIDLAND, JOHN
PERSONAL Born 07/04/1933, m, 1957, 2 children **DISCIPLINE** ENGLISH LITERATURE **EDUCATION** Claremont Grad Sch, PhD, 64. **CAREER** Prof, Eng, Univ Calif, Santa Barbara. **RESEARCH** Poetry; Creative writing; Robert Frost; Lit of Australia and New Zealand. **SELECTED PUBLICATIONS** Auth, Ode on Violence, 69; And Say What He Is, 75; In the Shadowless Light, 78; Elegy for my Aunt, 81; Palms, 93; auth, John the valiant, 99; auth, Life with Unki'e, 99. **CONTACT ADDRESS** Dept of Eng, Univ of California, Santa Barbara, Santa Barbara, CA 93106-7150. **EMAIL** jridland@silcon.com

RIEBLING, BARBARA
PERSONAL Born 11/13/1949, Columbus, OH, s **DISCIPLINE** ENGLISH LITERATURE **EDUCATION** Univ Pennsylvania, PhD, 93 **CAREER** Pierce Col, 75-87; visiting asst prof, Swarthmore Col, 91-92; assoc prof, Univ Toledo, 93-98 **MEMBERSHIPS** MLA; SAA; RSA **RESEARCH** Early Modern English Literature; History of Political Thought; Literary Theory **SELECTED PUBLICATIONS** Auth, "Milton on Machiavelli: Representations of the State in Paradise Lost," Renaissance Quart, 96; auth, "England Deflowered and Unmanned: The Sexual Image of Politics in Marvell's Last Instructions," SEL: Studies in English Lit, 1500-1900, 95; coauth, After Poststructuralism: Interdisciplinarity and Literary Theory, Northwestern, 93 **CONTACT ADDRESS** Dept of English Lang and Lit, Univ of Toledo, Toledo, OH 43606.

RIECKMANN, JENS
DISCIPLINE TWENTIETH-CENTURY LITERATURE **EDUCATION** Harvard Univ, PhD, 75. **CAREER** Asst prof, Univ Va, 75-81; asst prof to prof, Univ Wash, 81-92; prof, UC Irvine, 92-. **HONORS AND AWARDS** Mellon fac fel, Harvard Univ, 80-81; res grant, ACLS, 83-84; Guggenheim fel, 88-89. **RESEARCH** Critical biography of the young Hofmannsthal. **SELECTED PUBLICATIONS** Auth, Der Zauberberg: Eine geistige Autobiographie Thomas Manns, Stuttgart: Akademischer Verlag Heinz, 77, 79; Aufbruch in die Moderne: Die Anfange des Jungen Wien, osterreichische Literatur und Kritik im Fin de Siecle, Konigstein, Ts: Athenaum, 85, 86; Leopold von Andrian, osterreichische Tagebuchschriftsteller, Wien: Edition Atelier, 94. **CONTACT ADDRESS** Ger dept, Univ of California, Irvine, Irvine, CA 92697. **EMAIL** jrieckma@uci.edu

RIEGLE, ROSALIE G.
PERSONAL Born 02/19/1937, Flint, MI, 4 children **DISCIPLINE** ENGLISH **EDUCATION** St Mary's Col, BA, 59; Wayne State Univ, MA, 71; Univ Mich, DA, 83. **CAREER** Lectr to prof, Saginaw Valley State Univ, 69-. **HONORS AND AWARDS** NEH, 85; Landee Award for Excellence in Teaching; Rush Distinguished Lectureship; FA Scholar Award; Women's Advocacy Award; Saginaw NOW Women's Equity Award. **MEMBERSHIPS** MLA, NCTE, Conf on Comp and Commun, Mich Womens Studies Asn, Mich Oral Hist Asn, Oral Hist Asn, Mich Acad. **RESEARCH** Catholic Worker movement, Dorothy Day, oral history, African-American Women Writers, mothers and daughters in literature, memoir and autobiography. **SELECTED PUBLICATIONS** Ed, Historic Women of Michigan, Mich Women's Studies Asn, 88; ed, Voices from the Catholic Worker, Temple Univ Pr, 93; auth, Memory Matters: Reflections on Autobiography and Identity, Saginaw Valley State Univ, 01; auth, Dorothy Stories: Memories of Dorothy Day From Those Who Knew Her, Orbis Pr, (forthcoming). **CONTACT ADDRESS** Saginaw Valley State Univ, 7400 Bay Rd, Univesity Center, MI 48710. **EMAIL** riegle@svsu.edu

RIEHL, JOSEPH E.
DISCIPLINE ENGLISH **EDUCATION** Univ Minn, BA, 69; Tulane, MA, 71; Univ Denver, PhD, 80. **CAREER** Prof, Univ of La-Lafayette, 75-. **HONORS AND AWARDS** Distinguished Prof, 81. **RESEARCH** British Romantics; Charles Lamb. **SELECTED PUBLICATIONS** Auth, Charles Lambs Children's Literature, Salzburg, 81; auth, That Dangerous Figure: Charles Lamb and the Critics, Boydell & Brewer, 98. **CONTACT ADDRESS** Dept English, Univ of Southwestern Louisiana, PO Box 44691, Lafayette, LA 70504-0001. **EMAIL** real@louisiana.edu

RIELLY, EDWARD J.
PERSONAL Born 12/22/1943, Darlington, WI, m, 1969, 2 children **DISCIPLINE** ENGLISH **EDUCATION** Lora Col, BA, 66; Univ of Notre Dame, MA, 68; PhD, 74. **CAREER** Instr, St Ambrose Col, 69-70; instr, St Francis Col, 77-78; prof, St Joseph's Col, 78-. **HONORS AND AWARDS** Hemingway Found Grant, 89; Distinguished Teaching Awds, 88, 90, 92; NEH Grant, 94; Greater Portland Alliance Grant, 98. **MEMBERSHIPS** MLA; Hemingway Soc; F Scott Fitzgerald Soc. **RESEARCH** English literature, popular culture, Vietnam war, Hemingway and Fitzgerald. **SELECTED PUBLICATIONS** Auth, Approaches to Teaching Swift's Gulliver's Travels, MLA, 88; auth, My Struggling Soil, Plowman Pr, 94; auth, Anniversary Haiku, Brooks Books, 97; auth, How Sky Holds the Sun, AHA, 98; auth, "John Wayne", Dictionary of World Biography, Salem Pr, 99; auth, Abandoned Farmhouse and Other Haiku, Press Here Pr, 00; auth, Baseball: A Dictionary of Popular Culture, ABC-Clio (forthcoming); auth, The 1960s, Greenwood, (forthcoming); auth, "Ellis Peters: Brother Cadfael", Detectives as Historians, Popular Pr, (forthcoming); auth, "Dark Angel: Vietnam War Poetry by American Women Veterans", A Soldier and a Woman: Women in the Military Since 1945, Addison Wesley Longman (forthcoming). **CONTACT ADDRESS** Dept English, Saint Joseph's Col, Maine, 278 Whites Bridge Rd, Standish, ME 04084-5236. **EMAIL** erielly@sjcme.edu

RIELY, JOHN CABELL
PERSONAL Born 08/27/1945, Philadelphia, PA, m, 1969, 2 children **DISCIPLINE** ENGLISH LITERATURE; ART HISTORY **EDUCATION** Harvard Col, AB, Cum laude, 67; Univ Pa, MA, 68, PhD, 71. **CAREER** Assoc res ed, Yale Edition Horace Walpole's Correspondence, 71-79; lectr, Yale Univ, 73-79; asst prof, Columbia Univ, 79-80; vis prof, Univ Minn, 80-81; from asst to assoc prof, Boston Univ, 81-. **HONORS AND AWARDS** Huntington Lib Fel, 73; ACLS Grant, 72; Vis Fel, 82-83, Yale Ctr for British Art; NEH Senior Fel, 88-89, Boston Public Libr Fel, 95-96; Fel Soc Antiquanes London and Royal Soc Arts. **MEMBERSHIPS** ASECS, NEASECS, Asn Lit Scholar Critics, Col Art Asn, Walpole Soc, The Johnsonians (USA), Johnson Club (UK). **RESEARCH** Late 17th thru early 19th early literature and art history; Johnson and his circle; Sir Joshua Reynolds; Horace Walpole; Alex Pope; Biography and Portraiture; caricature and comic art, esq Thomas Rowlandson; English country house and landscape garden, The history of taste and connoisseurship. **SELECTED PUBLICATIONS** Auth, Rowlandson Drawings from the Paul Mellon Collection, 77; auth, The Age of Horace Walpole in Caricature 73, 90; ed, Horace Walpole's Miscellaneous Correspondence, 80; coauth, "Gainsborough and Rowlandson, 90. **CONTACT ADDRESS** Dept of English, Boston Univ, 236 Bay State Rd, Boston, MA 02215. **EMAIL** johnriely@aol.com

RIETZ, JOHN
PERSONAL Born 04/01/1960, Akron, OH, m, 1998 **DISCIPLINE** ENGLISH **EDUCATION** Kent State Univ, BA, 82; MA, 84; Univ Mich, PhD, 92. **CAREER** instr, Kent State Univ, 82-87; instr, Univ Akron, 84-87; instr, Univ Mich, 87-93; instr, Hen Ford Com Col, 93-. **HONORS AND AWARDS** Mellon Diss Fel; Valedic, KSU, 82. **MEMBERSHIPS** MLA. **RESEARCH** American renaissance writers; generation X. **SELECTED PUBLICATIONS** Auth, "Criminal Ms. - Representation: Moll Flanders and Female Criminal Biography," Stud Fic (91). **CONTACT ADDRESS** Dept English, Henry Ford Comm Col, 5101 Evergreen Rd, Dearborn, MI 48128-2407. **EMAIL** jrietz@hfcc.net

RIFE, JERRY E.
DISCIPLINE MUSIC HISTORY **EDUCATION** Kans State Univ, BS, MM; Mich State Univ, PhD. **CAREER** Ch, Rider Univ; contrib writer, The Saxophone Jour, 89;assoc producer, dir, If You Knew Sousa, doc film, 92-; conductor, Rider Univ Concert Band, 92; instr, Rider Univ, 84-; Westminister, 92-. **HONORS AND AWARDS** Hon, NJ State Senate, 93; cert appreciation, Somerset County, 93; Lindback award, 93. **MEMBERSHIPS** Am Musicol Soc. **RESEARCH** Life and music of Florent Schmitt, Igor Stravinsky, John Philip Sousa, Carl Nielsen, improvisation, single reed acoustics. **SELECTED PUBLICATIONS** Publ, numerous articles on Florent Schmitt, Sousa. **CONTACT ADDRESS** Dept of Theory and Mus Hist, Westfield State Col, 577 Western Ave., Westfield, MA 01085.

RIGG, ARTHUR GEORGE
PERSONAL Born 02/17/1937, Wigan, England, m, 1964 **DISCIPLINE** MEDIEVAL ENGLISH & LATIN **EDUCATION** Oxford Univ, BA, 59, MA, 62, DPhil. **CAREER** Lectr English, Merton Col, Oxford Univ, 61-63, Merton & Balliol Cols, 63-66 & Oxford Univ, 65-66; vis asst prof, Stanford Univ, 66-68; assoc prof, 68-76, actg dir ctr, 76-78; Prof English & Medieval Latin, Ctr Medieval Studies, Univ Toronto, 76- **MEMBERSHIPS** Mediaeval Acad Am. **SELECTED PUBLICATIONS** Auth, Medieval Ltin: an Introduction and Bibliographical Guide, F.A.C. Mantello, 96; auth, Serlo of Wilton: biographical notes', Medium Aevum 65, 96; auth, Latin poem on St. Hilda and Whitby Abbey', Journal of Medieval Latin 6, 96; auth, Anglo-Latin literature in the Ricardian Age', in Essays on Ricardian Literature in honour of J.A. Burrow, 97; transl, Lawrence of Durham: Dialogue and Easter Posem, A Verse translation'', Journal of Medieval Latin 7, (97): 42-126; auth, Calchas, renegade and traitor: Dares Phrygius and Joseph of Exeter', Notes and Queries 243, 98; auth, 'Walter Map, the Shaggy Dog story, and the Quaestio Disputata' in Roma magistra mundi, (98): 723-35; auth, 'Coincidence, convention, or copycat crime,' Florilegium 16, 99; auth, 'Propaganda of the Hundred Years War, Poems on the battles of Crecy and Durham (1346): a critical edition,' vol 54, 169-211, Traditio, 99; auth, A Book of British Kings 1200 BC to 1399 AD, 00. **CONTACT ADDRESS** Ctr for Medieval Studies, Univ of Toronto, 39 Queen's Park Crescent E, Toronto, ON, Canada M5S 2C3.

RIGGS, ROBERT
PERSONAL Born 10/27/1946, Mexico, MO, m, 1 child **DISCIPLINE** MUSIC HISTORY **EDUCATION** Harvard Univ, PhD. **CAREER** Instr, 87-, actg ch, dept Mus, Univ MS, 96-; vis assoc prof, Univ UT, 94-96. **SELECTED PUBLICATIONS** Wrote numerous articles on the music of Mozart, Haydn, and Beethoven. **CONTACT ADDRESS** Univ of Mississippi, University, MS 38677. **EMAIL** muriggs@olemiss.edu

RIGGS, WILLIAM G.
PERSONAL Born 05/24/1938, Wellsville, NY, m, 1965, 3 children **DISCIPLINE** ENGLISH **EDUCATION** Univ Rochester, AB, 60; Univ Calif Berkeley, MA, 62; PhD, 68. **CAREER** Prof, Boston Univ, 67-. **HONORS AND AWARDS** ACLS Study Fel. **MEMBERSHIPS** Renaissance Soc of Am. **RESEARCH** Milton; 17th Century English Literature. **SELECTED PUBLICATIONS** Auth, "Poetry and Method in Milton's 'Of Education'," Studies in Philol, 92; auth, "The Temptation of Milton's Eve", JEGP, 95. **CONTACT ADDRESS** Dept English, Boston Univ, 236 Bay State Rd, Boston, MA 02215. **EMAIL** wriggs@bu.edu

RIGNEY, BARBARA
PERSONAL Born 10/18/1938, NJ, m, 1964, 1 child **DISCIPLINE** ENGLISH **EDUCATION** Ohio State Univ, BA, 60; Ohio State Univ, MA, 64; Ohio State Univ, PhD, 77. **CAREER** Instr, Escuela Normal Superior de Cajamarca, 66-69; From Instr to Prof, Ohio State Univ, 70-. **HONORS AND AWARDS** Alumni Awd for Distinguished Teaching, Ohio State Univ , 74; Arts and Sci Teaching Awd, 89; Col of Humanities Travel Grant, 94. **SELECTED PUBLICATIONS** Rev, "Africa Wo/ Man Palava: The Nigerian Novel by Women," Res in African Lit (97); rev "Against Amnesia: Contemporary North American Women Writers and the Crisis in Historical Memory," by Nancy Peterson, OSLI Pr, 97; auth "Hagar's Mirror: Self and Identity in Morrison's Fiction," in Toni Morrison: Contemp Critical Essays (London: Macmillan Pr, 98); co-ed, Exile: A Memoir of 1939, Ohio St Univ Pr (Columbus, OH), 98; auth, "'Breaking the Back of Words': Language, Silence and the Politics of Identity in 'Beloved'," in Toni Morris Beloved (New York: Prentice-Hall, forthcoming); auth, "Alias Grace: Narrative Games and Gender Politics," in Toni Morrison: Contemp Critical Essays (Columbia, SC: Camden House/Boydell & Brewer, forthcoming). **CONTACT ADDRESS** Dept English, Ohio State Univ, Columbus, 164 W 17th Ave, Columbus, OH 43210-1326.

RIGOLOT, FRANCOIS
PERSONAL Born 05/21/1939, France, m, 1970, 2 children **DISCIPLINE** LITERATURE **EDUCATION** Ecole Des Hautes Etudes Commerciales, BA, 61; Northwestern Univ, MA, 63; Univ Wis, PhD, 69. **CAREER** Asst prof, Univ Mich, 69-74; from asst prof to assoc prof to prof, 74-, Princeton Univ. **HONORS AND AWARDS** NEH Fel, 80; Guggenheim Fel, 83; Gilbert Chinard Literary Prize, 84; Chevalier Des Palmes Academiques, 87; James Russell Lowell Prize, 90; Behrman Awd for Distinguished Achievment, Hum, 93; chair, 84-91, 96-99, meredith howland pyne prof, 81-, princeton univ. **MEMBERSHIPS** AATF; AIEF; RHR; MLA; RSA; SPFA; SAM; SARD; RHLF; SFS **RESEARCH** Renaissance studies; French literature; poetics; stylistics; history of rhetoric. **SELECTED PUBLICATIONS** Auth, Les Langages de Rabelais, 72; auth, Poetique et Onomastique, 79; auth, Le Texte de la Renaissance, 82; auth, Les Metamorphoses de Montaigne, 88; auth, Louise Labe Lyonnaise, ou la Renaissance au feminin, 98. **CONTACT ADDRESS** Romance Languages Dept, Princeton Univ, 201 E Pyne, Princeton, NJ 08544-5264. **EMAIL** rigolot@princeton.edu

RIGSBY, ENRIQUE D.
DISCIPLINE RHETORICAL THEORY **EDUCATION** Univ Ore, PhD. **CAREER** Prof, Texas A&M Univ. **HONORS AND AWARDS** Outstanding New Teacher Awd, Southern States Commun Asn; Col of Liberal Arts Distinguished Teaching Awd, Asn Former Students at Texas A&M Univ & Univ-Wide Distinguished Achievement Awd in Tchg, Asn of Former Students and Texas A&M Univ. **RESEARCH** Rhetorical theory & criticism, civil rights rhetoric, media studies. **SELECTED PUBLICATIONS** Contribur, African American Orators & Television Criticism. **CONTACT ADDRESS** Dept of Speech Communication, Texas A&M Univ, Col Station, College Station, TX 77843-4234.

RILEY, SAM G.
PERSONAL Born 10/08/1939, Raleigh, NC, d, 2 children **DISCIPLINE** COMMUNICATIONS, JOURNALISM **EDUCATION** Davidson Coll, BA, 61; Univ NC-Chapel Hill, MBA, 62, PhD, 70. **CAREER** Asst prof, Jour, Temple Univ, 70-74; assoc prof, Jour, Georgia South Univ, 74-81; dept head, Va Tech, Jour, 81-85; PROF, VA TECH, COMMUN STUD, 81-. **MEMBERSHIPS** Asn educ Jour & Mass Commun; Am Jour Hist Asn; Res Soc Am Periodicals; Kappa Tau Alpha; Nat Soc Newspaper Column **RESEARCH** Mass media history; Journal writing. **SELECTED PUBLICATIONS** Consumer Magazines of the British Isles, Greenwood Press, 93; The Best of the Rest: Non-Syndicated Newspaper Columnists Select Their Best Work, Greenwood Press, 93; Dictionary of Literary Biography: American Magazine Journalists, 1900-1960, Gale Res, 94; Biographical Dictionary of American Newspaper Columnists, Greenwood Press, 88, 89, 90, 95; The American Newspaper Columnist, Praeger, 98. **CONTACT ADDRESS** Virginia Polytech Inst and State Univ, Blacksburg, VA 24061. **EMAIL** sriley@vt.edu

RIMAL, RAJIV NATH
DISCIPLINE COMMUNICATION **EDUCATION** Bhopal Univ, BE, 88; Southern Ill Univ, MA, 91; Stanford Univ, PhD, 95. **CAREER** Asst prof, Tex A & M Univ, 91-95. **HONORS AND AWARDS** Fel, Am Heart Asn; Top Paper, Int Commun Asn. **MEMBERSHIPS** Int commun Asn, Nat Commun Asn. **RESEARCH** Health Communication, Public Health, Technology and Communication. **SELECTED PUBLICATIONS** Auth, Human Communication Research; auth, Communication Research; auth, Health Communication. **CONTACT ADDRESS** Dept Speech & Theatre, Texas A&M Univ, Col Station, College Station, TX 77843-0001. **EMAIL** rrimal@aol.com

RINEHART, JOHN
DISCIPLINE MUSIC **EDUCATION** Kent State Univ, AB; Cleveland Inst of Mus, MM; OH State Univ, PhD. **CAREER** Prof, Antioch Col; Composer. **HONORS AND AWARDS** ASCAP Ernest Bloch Awd in compos, 60; grant, Am Mus Ctr, Nat Endowment for Arts, NY Coun of Arts, Margaret Jory Fund, Jerome Found, Bascom Little Found; Founding mem, Res Musica Am; Premier of Chaconne for Wind Quintet by Prague Quintet at Prague Acad of Music, 00. **MEMBERSHIPS** Nat Coun of Am Soc of Univ Composers; Am Composers Alliance, NY. **SELECTED PUBLICATIONS** Publ research in collaboration with behaviorist Carl Charnetski and geneticist Lester Turoczi on the effect of music on the production of immunoglobulin A (IgA) in hum(s); Compositions by American Composers Edition. **CONTACT ADDRESS** Antioch Col, Yellow Springs, OH 45387. **EMAIL** jrinehart@antioch-college.edu

RINEHART, LUCY
DISCIPLINE ENGLISH **EDUCATION** Barnard Col, BA, 84; Columbia MA, 85, MPhil, 88, PhD, 94. **CAREER** ASST PROF, ENG, DEPAUL UNIV **MEMBERSHIPS** Am Antiquarian Soc **SELECTED PUBLICATIONS** Assoc ed & contr auth, The Cambridge Handbook of American Literature, Cambridge Univ Press, 86; auth, "A Nation's Noble Spectacle: Royall Tyler's The Contrast as Metatheatrical Commentary," American Drama, Spring 94; auth, "George Henry Boker," "James Kirke Paulding," in The Garland Companion to American Nineteenth-Century Verse, 95. **CONTACT ADDRESS** Dept of Eng, DePaul Univ, 802 W Belden, Chicago, IL 60614. **EMAIL** lrinehar@wppost.depaul.edu

RINGER, ALEXANDER
DISCIPLINE MUSIC **EDUCATION** New Sch Soc Res, MA; Columbia Univ, PhD. **CAREER** Prof emer, 58-, Univ IL Urbana Champaign. **RESEARCH** Medieval organum; music of the French Revolution; nineteenth-century music; and contemp Am compos(s); Middle Eastern music; Hebrew music; aesthetics and sociology of music; and music in educ. **SELECTED PUBLICATIONS** Auth, Arnold Schoenberg The Composer as Jew,90; The Early Romantic Era Between Revolutions: 1789 and 1848, 90; Musik als Geschichte,93; co-auth, Beethoven Interpretationen seiner Werke, 94. **CONTACT ADDRESS** Dept of Music, Univ of Illinois, Urbana-Champaign, E Gregory Dr, PO Box 52, Champaign, IL 61820. **EMAIL** a-ringer@staff.uiuc.edu

RINGER, MARINELLE
PERSONAL Born 10/28/1953, Little Rock, AR, m, 1999 **DISCIPLINE** ENGLISH **EDUCATION** Rhodes Col, BA, 76; Univ Windsor, MA, 77; Okla State Univ, PhD, 87. **CAREER** Grad asst, Univ of Windsor, 76-77; part-time instr, Univ of Central Ark, 79; part-time lectr, Univ of Ark, 82; grad assoc, Okla State Univ, 83-87; part-time lectr, Univ of Ark, 87-88; instr, Univ of Tenn, 88-93; asst prof, philander Smith Col; adjunct fac, Pulaski Tech Col, 95-; adjunct fac, Philander Smith Mgt Inst, 97-; assoc prof, chair dept of lang and letters, Philander Smith Col, 99-. **HONORS AND AWARDS** First place, Poets' Roundtable of Ark Col Poetry Contest, 73; scholar, Rhodes Col, 75; distinguished service Awds, Univ of Tenn, 91-93; outstanding educ service Awd, Philander Smith Col, 94; exemplary work Awd, Univ of Ark at Little Rock, 96-97. **MEMBERSHIPS** MLA, Phi Beta Kappa. **RESEARCH** Letters of Samuel Taylor Coleridge. **SELECTED PUBLICATIONS** Auth, "and no end," "the rich and the poor," "when it gets too close," "prom dresses and discharge papers," and "On every rule of thumb, " San Fernando Poetry J, 95; auth, "Safe," Little Rock Free press (96); auth, "Cardinal" and "This Junebug Bombardment," Reflections (97); auth, "Le Grand Menton," First Intensity, forthcoming; auth, "When All Else Fails," First Intensity, forthcoming; auth, "Letter to Greg Johnson," excerpted in Invisible Writer: A Biography of Joyce Carol Oates, Dutton (NY), 98; coauth, No Man's Land is Ours, 00. **CONTACT ADDRESS** Dept Humanities, Philander Smith Col, 812 W 13th St, Little Rock, AR 72202-3718. **EMAIL** MRMgrcls2@aol.com

RINGER, MARK
PERSONAL Born 12/08/1959, Los Angeles, CA, m, 1995 **DISCIPLINE** GREEK THEATRE, DRAMA **EDUCATION** Univ Calif, BA, 82; Univ Calif, MFA, 84; Univ Calif, PhD, 93. **CAREER** Asst Prof, Denison Univ, 94-97; Asst Prof, Marymount Manhattan Col, 97-. **MEMBERSHIPS** ATHE, ASTR, APA. **RESEARCH** Ancient Greek theater, Shakespeare, opera. **SELECTED PUBLICATIONS** Auth, "A Piece on Seamus Heaney's 'The Cure at Troy,' A Modern Adaptation of Sophocles' 'Philoctetes'," The NY Times (98); auth, Electra and the Empty Urn: Metatheatre and Role Playing in Sophocles, Univ NC Pr (Chapel Hill, NC), 98 auth, The Diotima: The Dramaturgy of Monteverdi's Operas (forthcoming). **CONTACT ADDRESS** Dept Humanities, Marymount Manhattan Col, 221 E 71st St, New York, NY 10021-4501.

RINGLER, RICHARD N.
PERSONAL Born 01/21/1934, Milwaukee, WI, m, 1959, 2 children **DISCIPLINE** ENGLISH **EDUCATION** Harvard Col, AB, 55; Univ Wisconsin, MA, 56; Harvard Univ, PhD, 61. **CAREER** Instr; Asst Prof; Assoc Prof; Prof; Univ of Wisconsin, 71-. **HONORS AND AWARDS** ACLS Study Fellowships, 65-66, and 71-72. **MEMBERSHIPS** Society for the Advancement of Scandinavian Study; International Society of Anglo-Saxonists. **RESEARCH** Anglo-Saxan England and Viking-Mgt Scandanavia: history; languages; literatures. **SELECTED PUBLICATIONS** Auth, "Brigut's Old english Grammar and Reader," 3rd ed. New York, 71, with Frederic G. Cassidy; auth, "Jonas Hallgrimsson: Selected Poetry and Prose," Madison, WI, 97. **CONTACT ADDRESS** Dept English, Univ of Wisconsin, Madison, 600 North Park St, 7187 Helen White Hall, Madison, WI 53706-1403. **EMAIL** rringler@factstuff.wisc.edu

RINKEVICH, THOMAS E.
DISCIPLINE CLASSICS **EDUCATION** Xavier Univ, BA, 64; Ohio State Univ, MA, 66, PhD, 73. **CAREER** Instr, 67-73, asst prof, 73-96, assoc prof, 96-, actg ch, Classics, Univ Nebr, Lincoln. **MEMBERSHIPS** APA, (CAMWS, ACL, CML); MAM. **RESEARCH** Greek & Latin languages; Greek poetry; Latin poetry; Egyptian language; ancient near-eastern literature. **SELECTED PUBLICATIONS** Auth, A KWIC Concordance to Lucretius, De Rerum Natura. **CONTACT ADDRESS** Dept of Classics, Univ of Nebraska, Lincoln, 234 Andrews, Lincoln, NE 68588-0337. **EMAIL** trinkevich1@unl.edu

RISING, CATHARINE C.
PERSONAL Born Berkeley, CA, m **DISCIPLINE** ENGLISH **EDUCATION** Univ Calif Berkeley, BS, 50; San Francisco State Univ, MA, 79; Univ Calif Berkeley, PhD, 87. **CAREER** Indep Scholar. **MEMBERSHIPS** MLA **RESEARCH** 19th and 20th Century literature; Psychological approaches to literature. **SELECTED PUBLICATIONS** Auth, Darkness at Heart: Fathers and Sons in Conrad, Greenwood Press, 90; auth, "The Complex Death of Kayerts," Conradiana, (91): 157-169; auth, Outside the Arch: Kohut and Five Modern Writers, Univ Press of Am, 99. **CONTACT ADDRESS** PO Box 1541, Lucerne, CA 95458-1541.

RISSER, JAMES V.
DISCIPLINE COMMUNICATIONS **EDUCATION** Univ NE, BA; Univ San Francisco Sch Law, JD. **CAREER** WA Bureau Chief, Des Moines Register, 76-85; prof and dir grad prog, Stanford Univ, 85; vis lctr, Wells Col, Mills Col, Drew Univ, and Bowdoin; res ed, Univ NE Sch Jour. **HONORS AND AWARDS** Pulitzer Prize,76 and 79; Raymond Clapper Mem Awd, 76 and 78; Thomas L. Stokes Awd, 71 and 78; dir john s. knight fel prog, standford univ. **MEMBERSHIPS** Pulitzer Prize bd, Soc Prof Jour; Investigative Rptrs Eds; Gridiron Club Washington; Ed Adv Bd Reuter Found London. **SELECTED PUBLICATIONS** Auth, articles and editorials for Des Moines Register. **CONTACT ADDRESS** Dept Commun, Stanford Univ, McClatchy Hall, Stanford, CA 94305.

RITTER, KURT
PERSONAL Born 06/18/1944, San Mateo, CA, m, 1966, 1 child **DISCIPLINE** SPEECH COMMUNICATION **EDUCATION** Ind Univ, PhD. **CAREER** Prof, Texas A&M Univ. **HONORS AND AWARDS** Amoco Found Awd ,Distinguished Tchg; Winans-Wichelns Awd , Distinguished Scholarship in Rhetoric and Public Address; National Commun Association's Karl R.Wallace Mem Res Awd & annual Aubrey Fisher Awd for the outstanding article in the Western J Commun. **RESEARCH** Political Rhetoric, American Public Address. **SELECTED PUBLICATIONS** Coauth, Ronald Reagan: The Great Communicator & The American Idealogy: Reflections of the Revolution in American Rhetoric; Contribur, The Clinton Presidency: Images; Issues,and Communication Strategies, African American Orators; The Modern Presidency and Crisis Rhetoric; US Presidents as Orators; Inaugural Addresses of 20th Century American Presidents; Contemporary American Public Discourse; Rhetorical Studies of National Political Debates. **CONTACT ADDRESS** Dept of Speech Communication, Texas A&M Univ, Col Station, 4234 TAMU, College Station, TX 77843-4234. **EMAIL** ritter@acs.tamu.edu

RITVO, HARRIET
DISCIPLINE HISTORY; ENGLISH **EDUCATION** Harvard Univ, AB, 68, PhD, 75. **CAREER** Arthur J. Conner Prof of Hist, MIT. **HONORS AND AWARDS** Guggenheim Fel; Nat Endowment for the Humanities Fel; Whiting Writers Prize. **MEMBERSHIPS** AHA; SHNH; PEN; HSS. **RESEARCH** British cultural history; history of biology/natural history; human-animal relations. **SELECTED PUBLICATIONS** Auth, The Platypus and the Mermaid and Other Figments of Classifying Imagination, Harvard Univ Press, 97; The Animal Estate: The English and Other Creatures in the Victorian Age, Harvard Univ Press, 87, Penguin Books, 90; The Sincerest Form of Flattery, Dead or Alive: Animal Captives of Human Cultures, Princeton Univ Press, 99; The Roast Beef of Old England, Mad Cows and Modernity: Cross-disciplinary Reflections on the Crisis of Creutzfeldt-Jacob Disease, Humanities Res Centre, 98; Introduction, The Variation of Animals and Plants under Domestication, Johns Hopkins Univ Press, 98; Zoological Nomenclature and the Empire of Victorian Science, Contexts of Victorian Science, Univ of Chicago Press, 97; co-ed, The Macropolitics of Nineteenth-Century Literature: Nationalism, Imperialism, Exoticism, Univ of Pa Press, 91, Duke Univ Press, 95. **CONTACT ADDRESS** Massachusetts Inst of Tech, 77 Massachusetts Ave., E51-285, Cambridge, MA 02139. **EMAIL** hnritvo@mit.edu

RIVERO, ALBERT J.
PERSONAL Born 08/02/1953, m, 1989, 1 child **DISCIPLINE** ENGLISH **EDUCATION** Princeton Univ, AB, 75; Univ Va, MA, 77; PhD, 82. **CAREER** Asst Prof to Full Prof, Marquette Univ, 82-. **HONORS AND AWARDS** NEH Sen Fel, 00-01; Fel, Am Philos Soc, 96; Post-doctoral Fel, Clark Library, 86; Fel, Newberry Library, 85; Fel, ACLS, 85; Fulbright Scholarship, Univ London, 75-76. **MEMBERSHIPS** Am Soc for Eighteenth Century Studies, Johnson Soc, Mod Lang Asn. **RESEARCH** Restoration and Eighteenth Century British literature/Novel; Textual Studies/Editing; Samuel Richardson's correspondence. **SELECTED PUBLICATIONS** Ed, Critical Essays on Henry Fielding, G.K.Hall, 98; ed, Augustan Subjects: Essays in Honor of Martin C. Battestin, Univ Del Press, 97; ed, New Essays on Samuel Richardson, St Martin's Press, 96; auth, The plays of Henry Fielding: A Critical Study of His Dramatic Career, Univ Press of Va, 89; auth, "Response: Whose Work is it Anyway? Or, How We Learned to Stop Worrying about the author and Love the Text," in Textual Studies and the Common Reader: Essays on Editing Novels and Novelists, Univ of Ga Press, 00; auth, "Aphra Behn's Oroonoko and the blank spaces of colonial Fictions," Studies in English Literature 1500-1900, (99): 443-462; auth, "Hieroglifick'd' History in Aphra Behn's Love Letters between a Nobleman and His sister," Studies in the Novel, (98): 126-138. **CONTACT ADDRESS** Dept English, Marquette Univ, PO Box 1881, Milwaukee, WI 53201-1881.

RIVERS, LOUIS
PERSONAL Born 09/18/1922, Savannah, GA, m **DISCIPLINE** SPEECH **EDUCATION** Savannah State Coll, BS 1946; New York Univ, MA 1951; Fordham Univ, PhD 1975. **CAREER** WV State Coll, instructor 1951-52; Southern Univ, instructor 1952-53; Tougaloo Coll, asst prof 1953-58; New York City Tech Coll, professor 1970-. **HONORS AND AWARDS** John Hay Whitney Theater 1957; Outstanding Teacher Plaque from Kappa Delta Pi 1983; Andrew Mellon Creative Writing Fellowship 1984. **MEMBERSHIPS** Mem Natl Writers Club, Dramatist Guild, Speech Communication Assn, College Language Assn, Phi Delta Kappa, Kappa Delta Pi. **CONTACT ADDRESS** Professor of Writing/Speech, New York City Tech Col, CUNY, 300 Jay St, Brooklyn, NY 11201.

RIVERS, WILGA MARIE
PERSONAL Born Melbourne, Australia **DISCIPLINE** FRENCH, ENGLISH **EDUCATION** Univ Melbourne, dipl educ, BA, 40, MA, 48; Univ Lille, dipl French studies, 50; Univs Lille & Montpellier, Lic es Lett, 52; Univ Ill, Urbana-Champaign, PhD(educ & French), 62. **CAREER** Sr teacher French & English, Australian high & prep schs, 40-59; asst prof French, Northern Ill Univ, 62-64; from lectr to assoc prof, Monash Univ, Australia, 64-69; vis prof, Teachers Col, Columbia Univ, 70-71; prof, Univ Ill, Urbana-Champaign, 71-74; Prof Romance Lang & Lang Coordr, Harvard Univ, 74-, Teacher English Lycee Jeune Filles, Douai, & Norm Sch, Montpellier, 49-52; participant, Can UNESCO sem biling, 67; vis scholar, French govt, 68; consult, Rockefeller Found English teaching proj, Bangkok, 71; prof ling, Mid East Ling Inst, Cairo, 74 & Ling Soc Am, Ling Inst, Oswego, NY, 76; consult, Nat Endow-

ment for Humanities, 75-76; JACET sem, Tokyo, 79. **HONORS AND AWARDS** Florence Steiner Awd, Am Coun Teachers Foreign Lang, 77. **MEMBERSHIPS** Am Asn Appl Ling (pres, 77-78); Ling Soc Am; Am Coun Teaching Foreign Lang; Am Asn Teachers Fr; Teachers English to Speakers Other Lang. **RESEARCH** Language teaching; psycholinguistics; college curriculum. **SELECTED PUBLICATIONS** Auth, The Psychologist and the Foreign Language Teacher, 64 & Teaching Foreign Language Skills, 68 & 81, Univ Chicago; Speaking in Many Tongues, 72, 76 & co-ed, Changing Patterns in Foreign Language Programs, 72, Newbury House; auth, Practical Guide to the Teaching of French, 75, coauth, Practical Guide to the Teaching of German, 75, Practical Guide to the Teaching of Spanish, 76 & Practical Guide to the Teaching of English SL, 78, Oxford Univ; Cultures, Languages And The International Smorgasbord--Musings For A New Millennium, Canadian Modern Language Review-Revue Canadienne Des Langues Vivantes, Vol 50, 93. **CONTACT ADDRESS** Dept of Romance Lang & Lit, Harvard Univ, 206 Boylston Hall, Cambridge, MA 02138.

RIVEST, JOHANNE
PERSONAL Born 01/25/1956, Ormstown, PQ, Canada, s **DISCIPLINE** MUSICOLOGY **EDUCATION** Univ Montreal, CA, BM 80, Mmus 87, PhD 96. **CAREER** Univ IL, Urbana, vis schol 98-2000; Can Univ Music Soc, secre 97-99; Indepen Sch 96-98; Univ Montreal, guest lectr 95; Les Cahiers de la Soc PQ de res music, ed 93-98; Univ Montreal, teach asst 92-93; Univ of Quebec, Montreal, res asst 89-91. **HONORS AND AWARDS** Hum post doct Gnt; doct Gnt Univ MT; Human Schlshp; George Proctor Prize. **MEMBERSHIPS** AMS; Sonneck Soc Am Mus; CMS; CUMS; SQRM. **RESEARCH** 20th century music; am music; John Cage; can music **SELECTED PUBLICATIONS** John Cage's Concert for Piano and Orchestra: Essays in Amer Music, ed James R Heintze Michael Saffle, Hamden CT, Garland Pub, 98; Atlas Eclipticalis, commande montrealaise, Circuit revue nor-americaine de musique du Xxe siecle, 97; Marie-Therese Lefebvre, Jean Vallerand et la vie musicale du Quebec, 1915-1994, Review, Can Univ Music Review, 97. **CONTACT ADDRESS** Univ of Illinois, Urbana-Champaign, 404 South New St, Champaign, IL 61820. **EMAIL** rivestjo@dsuper.net

ROBARDS, BROOKS
PERSONAL Born 08/21/1942, Mount Kisco, NY, m, 1988, 3 children **DISCIPLINE** COMMUNICATION **EDUCATION** Bryn Mawr, AB, 64; Hartford Univ, MA, 70; Univ Mass/Amherst, PhD, 82. **CAREER** Prof, Westfield St Col, 79-00. **HONORS AND AWARDS** Fulbright, Beijing, 93-94. **MEMBERSHIPS** Natl Comm Assn; Intl Comm Assn; Popular Cult Assn; Soc for Prof Journalists. **RESEARCH** Film; TV journalism; women's studies. **SELECTED PUBLICATIONS** Auth, Arnold Schwarzenegger, Brompton, 92; auth, Sweet & Sour: One Women's Chinese Adventure; One Man's Chinese Torture, Summerset, 94; auth, The Medieval Knight at War, Barnes & Noble, 97; auth, A Magical Place: Poems, Paintings & Photographs of Martha's Vineyard, Summerset, 98. **CONTACT ADDRESS** Dept of Communication, Westfield State Col, Westfield, MA 01086.

ROBB, MICHAEL P.
DISCIPLINE COMMUNICATION SCIENCES **EDUCATION** Western Mich Univ, BS, 79; Syracuse Univ, MS, 83, PhD, 88. **CAREER** Assoc prof, Univ Conn; instr, Univ Hawaii. **RESEARCH** Acoustic and phonetic characteristics of vocal development among infants and toddlers. **SELECTED PUBLICATIONS** Coauth, Formant Frequency Fluctuation in Stutterers and Nonstutterers, J Fluency Disorders 23, 98; How Steady are Vowel Steady-States, Clinical Ling and Phonetics 12, 98; A Note on Vowel Centralization in Stuttering and Nonstuttering Individuals, J Speech, Lang, and Hearing Res 41, 98; Vocal Tract Resonance Characteristics of Adults Wth Obstructive Sleep apnea, Acta Otolaryngologica 117, 97; Formant Frequency and Bandwidth Development in Infants and Toddlers, Folia Phoniatrica 49, 97; Formant Frequency Development: 15-36 months, J Voice 11, 97; An Acoustic Template of Normal Newborn Cry, Folia Phoniatrica 49, 97; An Acoustic Template of Normal and At-Risk Infant Crying, Biology of the Neonate 71, 97; Analysis of F2 Transitions in the Speech of Stutterers and Nonstutterers, J Fluency Disorders 22, 97; An Acoustic Examination of Naturalistic Modal and Falsetto Voice Registers, Logopedics, Phoniatrics and Vocology 22, 97; A Note on Prespeech Early Speech Coarticulation, Logopedics, Phoniatrics and Vocology 22, 97. **CONTACT ADDRESS** Dept of Communication Sci, Univ of Connecticut, Storrs, 850 Bolton Rd, Storrs, CT 06269-1085. **EMAIL** mrobb@uconnvm.uconn.edu

ROBB, STEPHEN
DISCIPLINE CONTEMPORARY PUBLIC ADDRESS, MASS COMMUNICATION **EDUCATION** Ind Univ, PhD, 67. **CAREER** Assoc prof, Purdue Univ. **RESEARCH** Advertising as goal-directed persuasion involving identification of demographic and psychographic groups; persuasion as a focus for understanding recent history as related to politics and art. **SELECTED PUBLICATIONS** Auth, The Voice of Black Rhetoric: Selections, 71; Fundamentals of Evidence and Argument, 76; Psychographics and the Liquor Industry, 83; coauth, Crisis Management and the Paradigm Case, in E. Toth and R. Heath (eds), Rhetorical and Critical Approaches to Public Relations, Erlbaum, 92. **CONTACT ADDRESS** Dept of Commun, Purdue Univ, West Lafayette, 1080 Schleman Hall, West Lafayette, IN 47907-1080. **EMAIL** srobb@purdue.edu

ROBBINS, BRUCE
PERSONAL Born 12/14/1949, New York, NY, m, 2 children **DISCIPLINE** MARXIST THEORY, POSTCOLONIAL THEORY, THEORY OF PROFESSIONAL FORMATION, CULT **EDUCATION** Harvard Univ, BA, MA, PhD. **CAREER** Prof Eng, Rutgers, The State Univ NJ, New Brunswick; coed, Soc Text. **RESEARCH** 19th & 20th century literature; Marxist theory. **SELECTED PUBLICATIONS** Auth, The Servant's Hand: English Fiction from Below; Secular Vocations: Intellectuals, Professionalism, Culture. **CONTACT ADDRESS** Dept of Lit in Eng, Rutgers, The State Univ of New Jersey, New Brunswick, Murray Hall 041, New Brunswick, NJ 08903. **EMAIL** brobbins@interport.net

ROBBINS, HELEN W.
DISCIPLINE ENGLISH **EDUCATION** Smith Col, AB; Duke Univ, MA, PhD. **CAREER** Assoc prof, Lyon Col. **RESEARCH** Victorian lit; feminist theory; film. **SELECTED PUBLICATIONS** Auth, More Human Than I Am Alone: Womb Envy in The Fly and Dead Ringers in Screening the Male. **CONTACT ADDRESS** Dept of Eng, Lyon Col, 300 Highland Rd, PO Box 2317, Batesville, AR 72503.

ROBBINS, KENNETH
PERSONAL Born 01/07/1944, Douglasville, GA, m, 1989, 2 children **DISCIPLINE** THEATRE; PLAYWRITING **EDUCATION** Univ Ga, MFA, 69; S Ill Univ-Carbondale, PhD, 82. **CAREER** Prof, Dept Theatre, Univ S. Dakota, 85-98; dir, sch of perf arts, LA Tech Univ, 98-. **HONORS AND AWARDS** Japan Found Artists fel; S Dakota Sr Artist fel, Asoc Writing Prog Novel Awd; Toni Morrison Awd Fiction; SETC New Play Awd. **MEMBERSHIPS** Dramatists Guild; PLaywrights Ctr; Asn Theatre in Higher Educ. **RESEARCH** Theatre of the Middle East. **SELECTED PUBLICATIONS** Auth, Calling the Cows, N Dakota Quart, 92; Leaving Prosperity, Briar Cliff Rev, 93; A Conversation with William Kloefkorn, S Dakota Rev, 94; The Hunger Feast, Palmetto Play Serv, 95; A Selection from The Baptism of Howie Cobb, Heritage of the Great Plains, 96; Atomic Field, S Theatre, 96; Mollys Rock, Palmetto Play Serv, 96; Vestiges of Power: Censorship in Contemporary Egyptian Theatre and Society, New Theatre Vistas, Garland Press, 96; The Closed Door Policy, S Quart, 96; Planespotting, S Quart, 97. **CONTACT ADDRESS** School of Perf Arts, Louisiana Tech Univ, Ruston, LA 71272. **EMAIL** if45128@latech.edu

ROBERSON, SUSAN L.
PERSONAL Born 07/18/1950, Carlsbad, NM, m, 1985, 2 children **DISCIPLINE** ENGLISH **EDUCATION** Baylor Univ, BA, 72; Tex A&M, MA, 80; PhD, 87. **CAREER** Instr, Lamar Univ, 86-88; instr, Auburn Univ, 88-99; asst prof, Ala State Univ, 99-. **HONORS AND AWARDS** Phi Kappa Phi; NEH Grants, 92, 94, 96; Fel, Nat Ctr for the Study of Civil Rights and African-Am Culture, 00. **MEMBERSHIPS** MLA, Am Lit Assoc, Emerson Soc, Margaret Fuller Soc, Am Travel Lit Soc. **RESEARCH** Ralph Waldo Emerson, Theories of Travel, Women's Travel narratives, 19th-Century Antebellum Literature. **SELECTED PUBLICATIONS** Auth, "The Private Voice Behind the Public Text: Two Emerson Sermons," ESQ, (86); auth, "Young Emerson and the Mantle of Biography," Am Transcendental Quart, (91); ed and auth, "Degenerate effeminacy and the making of A Masculine Spirituality in the Sermons of Ralph Waldo Emerson," Muscular Christianity: Embodying the Victorian Age, (94); ed and auth, "Stowe's Matriarchy and The Rhetoric of Domesticity," The Stowe Debate: Rhetorics in Uncle Tom's Cabin, (94); auth, Emerson in His Sermons: A Man-Made Self, Univ of Miss, 95; auth, "Translocations and Transformations: Place and Self in N. Scott Momaday's 'The Ancient Child,'" Am Indian Quart, (98); auth, "Ellen Montgomery's Other Friend: Race Relations in an Expunged Episode of Susan Warner's 'The Wide, Wide World,'" ESQ, (99); ed, Reform and the Interior Landscape: Mapping Emerson's Political Sermons, Univ of Ga, 00; ed, Defining Travel: Diverse Visions, Univ Pr of Miss, forthcoming. **CONTACT ADDRESS** Alabama State Univ, 901 Tacoma Dr, Auburn, IL 36830. **EMAIL** slroberson@mindspring.com

ROBERT, LUCIE
PERSONAL Born 05/22/1954, Jonquiere, PQ, Canada **DISCIPLINE** LITERATURE **EDUCATION** Laval Univ, BA, 76, MA, 80, PhD, 87. **CAREER** Res assoc, Dictionnaire des oeuvres litteraires du Quebec, Univ Laval, 78-86; Prof Literary Studies, Univ Quebec at Montreal, 86-. **HONORS AND AWARDS** Prix Edmond-de-Nevers, 80-91; Can Fedn Hum Best Bk Fre, 90-91. **MEMBERSHIPS** Ctr de Recherche en Litterature Quebecoise, Univ Laval **RESEARCH** Quebec literature **SELECTED PUBLICATIONS** Auth, Le Manuel de Mgr. Camille Roy, 82; auth, L'Institution du litteraire au Quebec, 89; coauth, Dictionnaire des oeuvres litteraires du Quebec, 78-87; coauth, La Vie litteraire au Quebec 1764-1914, 6 vols, 91-99; coauth, Litterature et societe Anthologie, 94; coauth, Litterature du Quebec, 94; contribur, Jeu; contribur, Poetics Today; contribur, Recherches Sociographiques; contribur, Etudes francaises; contribur, Etudes litteraires; contribur, Spirale; contribur, Lettres quebecoises; contribur, Voix & Images/Litterature quebecoise. **CONTACT ADDRESS** Dept Literary Stud, Univ of Quebec, Montreal, Box 8888, Station Centre-Ville, Montreal, QC, Canada H3C 3P8. **EMAIL** robert.lucie@uqam.ca

ROBERTO, ANTHONY J.
DISCIPLINE COMMUNICATION **EDUCATION** Mich State Univ, PhD, 95. **CAREER** Violence prevention scientist, Mich Public Health Inst, 95-; Adj Asst Prof, Dept of Commun, Mich State Univ, 96-. **HONORS AND AWARDS** Outstanding Article Awd, 98; Bronze Telly Awd, 98; Awd of Merit, 98; Top-four Paper, 96; Garrison Mem Awd for Outstanding Scholar, 92. **MEMBERSHIPS** Am Pub Health Asn; Eastern Commun Asn; Int Asn of Conflict Mgt; Int Commun Asn; Nat Commun Asn. **RESEARCH** Health Communication; Conflict Management; Violence prevention; Persuasion/social influence. **SELECTED PUBLICATIONS** Coauth, "Relational Development as Negotiated Order in Hostage Negotiation," Human Commun Res, 93; coauth, "Revisiting mediator issue intervention strategies," Mediation Q, 94; coauth, "An Empirical Examination of Three Models of Integrative and Distributive Bargaining," Internatl J of Conflict Management, 96; coauth, "The Assessment of Argumentativeness and Verbal Aggressiveness in Adolescent Populations," Commun Q, 97; coauth, "The Firearm Injury Reduction Education (FIRE)Program: Formative Evaluation Insights and Implications," Social Marketing Q, 98. **CONTACT ADDRESS** Michigan Public Health Inst, 2438 Woodlake Cir, Ste. 240, Okemos, MI 48864.

ROBERTS, BRIAN
DISCIPLINE ENGLISH **EDUCATION** Calif State Univ at Sacramento, BA, 86; MA, 89; Rutgers Univ, PhD, 95. **CAREER** ASST PROF, ENG, RUTGERS UNIV **MEMBERSHIPS** Am Antiquarian Soc **SELECTED PUBLICATIONS** Mus from the Colonial era through the Civil War **CONTACT ADDRESS** Dept of Hist, Rutgers, The State Univ of New Jersey, New Brunswick, New Brunswick, NJ 08903-5059.

ROBERTS, CHARLES
PERSONAL 2 children **DISCIPLINE** COMMUNICATION STUDIES **EDUCATION** Davidson Col, BA; Temple Univ, MA, PhD. **CAREER** Prof, 90-. **MEMBERSHIPS** Int Listening Asn; Eastern Commun Asn; Southern Speech Commun Asn. **SELECTED PUBLICATIONS** Auth, A First Look At Communication Theory; co-auth, Intrapersonal Communication Processes; Intrapersonal Communication Processes: Original Essays. **CONTACT ADDRESS** Dept of Communication, East Tennessee State Univ, PO Box 70667, Johnson City, TN 37614-0667. **EMAIL** robertsc@etsu.edu

ROBERTS, DONALD F.
PERSONAL Born Seattle, WA, M, 1983, 4 children **DISCIPLINE** COMMUNICATIONS **EDUCATION** Columbia Univ, AB, 61; Univ CA Berkeley, MA, 63; Stanford Univ, PhD, 68. **CAREER** Fac, 68-; to dir Inst Comm Res, 85-90; to chr dept comm, 90-96; to Thomas More Storke Prof, 96-. **HONORS AND AWARDS** DIC, ABC, KIDS WB!; Fox Kids, ICA, APA, AEJMC; consult, filmation, disney, mgm animation, jp kids; planner/panelist, conf families and media. **RESEARCH** Children and adolescent use of and response to media. **SELECTED PUBLICATIONS** Auth, chaps in The Handbook of Communication, Learning from Television: Psychological and Education Research, International Encyclopedia of Communications; revs on effects of mass communication for the Annual Review of Psychology and Handbook of Social Psychology;coauth, chapter on public opinion processes in the Handbook of Communication Science; Television and Human Behavior; Its Not Only Rock and Roll: Popular Music in the Lives of Adolescents; co-ed, The Process and Effects of Mass Communication. **CONTACT ADDRESS** Dept Commun, Stanford Univ, McClatchy Hall, Stanford, CA 94305. **EMAIL** droberts@leland.stanford.edu

ROBERTS, JOHN
PERSONAL Born 03/07/1934, IN, m, 1955, 6 children **DISCIPLINE** ENGLISH **EDUCATION** Ind State Univ, BA, 55; Univ of Ill, MA, 57; PhD, 62. **CAREER** Instr to asst prof, Univ of Wis at Madison, 62-66; assoc prof, Univ of Detroit, 66-68; assoc prof to prof emeritus, Univ of Mo, 68-00. **HONORS AND AWARDS** Special Awd, John Donne Soc; Byler Distinguished Prof Awd; NEH fel, Saint Edmund's Col. **MEMBERSHIPS** Milton Soc of Am, John Donne Soc. **RESEARCH** 17th-Century English poetry and prose, specifically John Donne, George Herbert, and Richard Crasaw, recusant literature. **SELECTED PUBLICATIONS** Rev, Cambridge Companion to Poetry--Donne to Marvell, SCN 52 (94): 43-44; auth, "John T. Shawcross: Critic of John Donne," John Donne's Religious Imagination: Essays in Honor of John T. Shawcross, UCA Press (Conway, AR), 95; ed of commentary, The Variorum Edition of the Poetry of John Donne: Vol 6: The Anniversaries and the Epicedes and the Obsequies, Ind Univ Press (Bloomington and Indianapolis, IN), 95; ed of commentary, The Variorum Edition of the Poetry of John Donne: Vol 8: The Epigrams, Epithalamions, Epitaphs, Inscriptions, and Miscella-

neous Poems, Ind Univ Press (Boomington and Indianapolis, IN), 95; auth, "George Herbert," The Cambridge Bibliogr of English Lit 3rd edition, forthcoming; auth, commentary on Donne's Elegies, Variorum edition vol 2, Indiana Univ Press, forthcoming. **CONTACT ADDRESS** Dept English, Univ of Missouri, Columbia, 107 Tate Hall, Columbia, MO 65211-1500. **EMAIL** robertsjr@missouri.edu

ROBERTS, JULIE
DISCIPLINE COMMUNCATION SCIENCES **EDUCATION** Univ Pa, PhD, 94. **CAREER** Dept Comm, Vermont Univ **MEMBERSHIPS** Ling Soc Am; Am Dialect Soc; Int Asn Study Child Lang; Am Speech Lang Hearing Asn. **SELECTED PUBLICATIONS** Auth, Learning to talk Philadelphian; Acquisition of shot a by preschool children, 95; Late talkers at two: Outcome at age three, Jour Speech Hearing Res, 97. **CONTACT ADDRESS** Dept of Communication Sciences, Univ of Vermont, 360 Waterman Bldg, Burlington, VT 05405. **EMAIL** jroberts@polyglot.uvm.edu

ROBERTS, KENNETH C., JR.
PERSONAL Born, PA **DISCIPLINE** MUSIC **EDUCATION** Univ Mich, Ann Arbor, Bmus, Mmus, PhD. **CAREER** A Barton Hepburn prof, Williams Col, 62-; past fac, Univ Mich; consult, Amer symphony orchestras. **HONORS AND AWARDS** Ger govt DAAD Awd, 62; founded, williams col choral soc and chamber singers & conducted them for 25 years; founding pianist, williams trio, 70. **SELECTED PUBLICATIONS** Auth, a book on choral music; contribur to, New Grove Dictionary of Music; rev(s) for, Notes, Mus Libr Asn jour. **CONTACT ADDRESS** Music Dept, Williams Col, 54 Chapin Hall Dr., Williamstown, MA 01267.

ROBERTS, MICHAEL
PERSONAL Born 09/16/1947, Eccles, United Kingdom, m, 1970, 1 child **DISCIPLINE** CLASSICS **EDUCATION** Cambridge Univ BA, 69, MA, 73; Univ IL Urbana-Champaign, MA, 74, PhD, 78. **CAREER** Vis lectr, Univ WI-Milwaukee, 78-80; asst prof, 80-86, assoc prof, 86-91, prof, 91-, Robert Rich Prof of Lat, 92-, Wesleyan Univ. **HONORS AND AWARDS** NEH summer sem fel, 82 & 86; ACLS fel, 87; NEH fel, Jan-June, 92. **MEMBERSHIPS** Am Philol Asn; Am Inst Archaeol; Medieval Acad of Am; N Am Patristic Societe; Medieval Lat Asn N Am. **RESEARCH** Late antiquity; Latin literature; rhetoric. **SELECTED PUBLICATIONS** Auth, Poetry and the Cult of the Martyrs, Michigan, 93; St. Martin and the Leper, Jour of Medieval Lat, 94; The Description of Landscape in the Poetry of Venantius Fortunatus, Traditio, 94; Martin Meets Maximus, Rev des etudes augustiniennes, 95. **CONTACT ADDRESS** Dept of Classical Studies, Wesleyan Univ, Middletown, CT 06459-0146. **EMAIL** mroberts@wesleyan.edu

ROBERTS, NANCY L.
PERSONAL Born 02/12/1954, Utica, NY, s **DISCIPLINE** SCHOOL OF JOURNALISM AND MASS COMMUNICATION **EDUCATION** Brown Univ, MA; Univ Minn, MA, PhD. **CAREER** Prof. **HONORS AND AWARDS** Pax Christi Book Awd, 96. **MEMBERSHIPS** Asn for Education in Journalism and Mass Comm, Am Studies Asn, Orgn of American Historians, American Journalism Historians Asn, Society of Professional Journalist, Am Asn for Univ Professors. **RESEARCH** History of U.S. Journalism. **SELECTED PUBLICATIONS** Auth, American Peace Writers, Editors, and Periodicals: A Dictionary, 90; Dorothy Day and the 'Catholic Worker', 84; coauth, As Ever, Gene: The Letters of Eugene O'Neill to George Jean Nathan, 87; coauth, American Catholic Pacifism: The Influence of Dorothy Day and the Catholic Worker Movement, 96; coauth, The Press and America: An Interpretive History of the Mass Media, 9th ed, 00. **CONTACT ADDRESS** Mass Communication Dept, Univ of Minnesota, Twin Cities, 111 Murphy Hall, 206 Church St SE, Minneapolis, MN 55455. **EMAIL** rober003@tc.umn.edu

ROBERTS, THOMAS J.
PERSONAL Born 06/10/1925, Omaha, NE, d, 3 children **DISCIPLINE** ENGLISH; AMERICAN LITERATURE **EDUCATION** Univ of Minn, BA, 48, MA, 52, PhD, 58. **CAREER** Instr, Univ of Kansas, 52-55; Univ of Minn, 55-58; from asst prof to assoc prof, Am Univ of Cairo, 58-63; assoc prof, Univ of Alaska, 60-61; from asst prof to prof, Univ of Conn, 63- . **HONORS AND AWARDS** Consult, Nat Survey of Undergrad Progs in Eng; Nat Endowment for the Hum fel for Independent Study and Res, 81-82. **RESEARCH** Lit Theory; Vernacular Lit; Graphic Novel. **SELECTED PUBLICATIONS** Auth, When Is Something Fiction, 72; The Network of Literary Identifications, New Lit Hist, 5(1), 73; An Aesthetics of Junk Fiction, 90; Gold Bullet Sport: A Dime Novel by Buffalo Bill; or, A Record of an Expedition into the Great American Literary Desert, Tex Studies in Lit and Language, 33, 91; Popular Fiction Under the Old Dispensation and The New, LIT 4, 93. **CONTACT ADDRESS** Dept of English, Storrs, CT 06269. **EMAIL** roberts@uconn.edu

ROBERTSON, PATRICIA C.
PERSONAL Born 03/30/1954, Newark, NJ, m, 1987 **DISCIPLINE** MUSIC **EDUCATION** Univ Ma, BS, 77, Ball St Univ, MA, 89; PhD, 98; Univ ME, BS, 77 **CAREER** Instr, Ball St Univ, 90-91; adj prof, Anderson Univ, 91-98; adj prof to asst prof, Taylor Univ, 91-99; Asst Prof, Taylor Univ, 99-01. **HONORS AND AWARDS** Doctoral recital-lecture entitled Selected Lieder of Fanny Mendelssohn Hensel, 1805-1847, first place, Mu Phi Epsilon Int Res Competition, 90. **MEMBERSHIPS** NATS; Pi Kappa Lambda; Mu Phi Epsilon. **RESEARCH** Vocal literature; the Art Song and other related topics. **SELECTED PUBLICATIONS** Auth, Fanny Mendelssohn Hensel, Junior Keynotes, 91; The Artsong: A Practical Investigation of Artsong Literature, Composers and Musico-poetic Structure for the Collegiate Singer Accompanied by a Performance-based Interpretation workbook, Doctor of Arts dissertation, 98. **CONTACT ADDRESS** 1512 Lynnwood Dr, Anderson, IN 46012. **EMAIL** ptrobertson@tayloru.edu

ROBERTSON-GUTIERREZ, NOEL D.
PERSONAL Born 07/20/1952, San Francisco, CA, m, 1994, 2 children **DISCIPLINE** LITERATURE, ENGLISH, CREATIVE WRITING **EDUCATION** Univ Calif Berkeley, BA, 91; MA, 92. **CAREER** Instr, Los Medanos Univ, 93-94; instr, Dominican Univ, 94-; instr, Col Marin, 93-. **HONORS AND AWARDS** Grad Opportunity Fel; Phi Beta Kappa; Dean's Honor List; Student Life Achievement Award; Alpha Gamma Sigma; Dr. Harry Hensler Scholar. **MEMBERSHIPS** MLA; PEN. **RESEARCH** American ethnic literature; history and American autobiography. **SELECTED PUBLICATIONS** Auth, "Roachville Redemption," Tuxedo (97); auth, "The Troll and the Trashman," Tuxedo (98). **CONTACT ADDRESS** English Dept, Col of Marin, 835 College Ave, Kentfield, CA 94904. **EMAIL** noel@marin.cc.ca.us

ROBEY, DAVID H.
DISCIPLINE SPEECH COMMUNICATION **EDUCATION** Pillsbury Col, BA, 70; Bob Jones Univ, MA, 72; Union Inst, PhD. **CAREER** Prof, Tennessee Temple Univ, 72-81; Prof, Cedarville Col, 81-. **SELECTED PUBLICATIONS** Auth, Two for Missions, Lillenas Publ Co, Kansas City, Miss, 88. **CONTACT ADDRESS** Cedarville Col, PO Box 601, Cedarville, OH 45314.

ROBINSON, AMY
DISCIPLINE ENGLISH LITERATURE **EDUCATION** Oberlin Col, Univ Pa, MA, PhD. **CAREER** Eng Dept, Georgetown Univ **RESEARCH** Cultural studies; performance studies; African American literature and culture; gay and lesbian studies; feminist and literary theories; 19th and 20th century American literature. **SELECTED PUBLICATIONS** Auth, Authority and the Public Display of Identity: Wonderful Adventures of Mrs. Seacole in Many Lands, Feminist Studies, 94; It Takes One to Know One: Passing and Communities of Common Interest, Critical Inquiry, 94; Is She or Isn't She: Madonna and the Erotics of Appropriation, 93; The Trouble of Passing, 93. **CONTACT ADDRESS** English Dept, Georgetown Univ, 37th and O St, Washington, DC 20057.

ROBINSON, CHRISTINE A.
PERSONAL Born 10/08/1949, New York, NY, m, 1984, 2 children **DISCIPLINE** ENGLISH **EDUCATION** Univ Miami, BA, 70; MA, 72; Fla Atlantic Univ, EdS, 75; EdD, 76. **CAREER** Prof, Miami Dade Community Col, Kendall Campus, 75-. **MEMBERSHIPS** Am Mensa. **RESEARCH** The Internet as an educational vehicle. **SELECTED PUBLICATIONS** Auth, Say It With Style; auth, The collegiate Reader; auth, Power Paragraphs; auth, Good Grief: Grammar; auth, Internet for Free. **CONTACT ADDRESS** Dept English, Miami-Dade Comm Col, 11011 SW 104th St, Miami, FL 33176-3330. **EMAIL** crobinso@mdcc.edu

ROBINSON, DAVID
PERSONAL Born 12/01/1947, Odessa, TX, m, 1970, 2 children **DISCIPLINE** ENGLISH **EDUCATION** Univ Tex, BA, 70; Harvard Divinity Sch, MTS, 72; Univ Wis, MA, 73; PhD, 76. **CAREER** From Asst Prof to Prof, Ore St Univ, 76-. **HONORS AND AWARDS** NEH Fel, 79-80; ACLS Fel, 83-84; Fac Excellence Awd for Teaching, Ore St Board of Higher Educ, 84; Fulbright Fel, Univ Heidelberg, 84-85; Nat Endowment Humanities Fel, 87, 89-94, 96, 98. **MEMBERSHIPS** ACLS, Unitarian Universalist Asn. **SELECTED PUBLICATIONS** Auth, The Unitarians and the Universalists, Greenwood Pr, 85; auth, "Poetry, Personality and the Divinity School Address," Harvard Theol Rev, 82 (89): 185-199; auth, Emerson and the Conduct of Life, Cambridge UP, 93; auth, World of Relations: The Achievement of Peter Taylor, Ky UP, 98; auth, "Transendentalism and Its Times," The Cambridge Companion to Ralph Waldo Emerson, Cambridge UP (99): 13-29; auth, "Wilderness and the Agrarian Principle," ISLE: Interdisciplinary Studies in Lit and Environ, 6 (99): 15-27; auth, "Emerson and Religion," Hist Guide to Ralph Waldo Emerson, Oxford UP (00): 151-177. **CONTACT ADDRESS** Dept English, Oregon State Univ, 238 Moreland Hall, Corvallis, OR 97331-5302. **EMAIL** drobinson@orst.edu

ROBINSON, EDWARD A.
PERSONAL Born 06/13/1935, Gary, IN, m **DISCIPLINE** ENGLISH **EDUCATION** Howard University, BA, 1959; University of Chicago, MAT, 1970; Northwestern University, PhD, 1974. **CAREER** Northeastern Illinois University, assistant professor; Lake Forest Col, IL, English instructor, 70-72; Chicago Board of Education, HS English consultant, 70-72; Wendell Phillips & Summer HS, Chicago, instructor, 61-64; English Department, Harlan HS, Chicago, instructor & chairman, 60-69; Carver HS, Chicago, instructor, 59-60; Emmy Award Winning TV Prog, "The Giants", "The Common Men", narrator, 67; "Like It Was the black man in America", teacher/host, 69; Midwest Modern Language Association convention, presented paper, 73; NDEA Institute, University of Chicago, summer participant, 65. **HONORS AND AWARDS** Recipient, Experienced Teacher Fellowship, University of Chicago, 1969-70; Ford Foundation Fellowship for Black Americans, 1973-74. **MEMBERSHIPS** South Shore Valley Community Organization, 1969-74; Faulkner School Association, 1974-75; Faulkner School Father's Club, 1974-75; National Urban League, 1968-74; Operation PUSH, 1972. **SELECTED PUBLICATIONS** numerous publications **CONTACT ADDRESS** Ciriculum & Instruction, Northeastern Illinois Univ, 550 N St Louis Avenue, Chicago, IL 60625-4625.

ROBINSON, ELLA S.
PERSONAL Born 04/16/1943, Wedowee, AL, d, 1980, 1 child **DISCIPLINE** ENGLISH, HISTORY **EDUCATION** Ala St Univ, BS, 65; Univ of Nebr, MA, 70; PhD, 76. **CAREER** Asst Prof, Univ of Nebraska, 81-91; Assoc Prof, Tuskegee Univ, 94-00; Asst Prof, Univ of Illinois, 75-77; Asst Prof, Atlanta Univ, 77-79. **HONORS AND AWARDS** Who's Who of American Women; Who's Who in the South and Southwest; Who's Who Among Black Americans. **MEMBERSHIPS** Modern Language Assoc (MLA); African Lit Assoc (ALA); Lincoln Nebraska Chaparral Poets (LCNP); National Council of Teachers of English (NCTE). **RESEARCH** African American; Women's Lit; Poetry and Crititcism. **SELECTED PUBLICATIONS** Auth, "The Tragic Life of Bessie Head: Lit in South Africa;" auth, "Myth as Regeneration in Aime Cesaire's Poetry." **CONTACT ADDRESS** Dept English and Reading, Tuskegee Univ, 1 Tuskegee Univ, Tuskegee Institute, AL 36088-1600. **EMAIL** e-robin@acd.tusk.edu

ROBINSON, FRED
PERSONAL Born 09/27/1942, Park Ridge, IL, m, 1990, 4 children **DISCIPLINE** ENGLISH **EDUCATION** Univ Redlands, BA, 64; Univ Wash, MA, 66; PhD, 72. **CAREER** Instr to prof, Univ of Mass, 70-91; prof, chair, Univ of San Diego, 91-. **HONORS AND AWARDS** Distinguished Teaching Awd, Univ of Mass, 87; NEH Seminar Director, 97; University Professorship, Univ of San Diego, 97-98. **MEMBERSHIPS** MLA. **RESEARCH** Comedy, Cultural Studies, Modern Literature, Narratology. **SELECTED PUBLICATIONS** Auth, The Comedy of Language: Studies in Modern Comic Literature, Univ of Mass Pr, (Amherst), 80; ed, Comedy, Mass Rev, Winter 81; auth, "Strategies of Smallness: Wallace Stevens and Emily Dickinson", Wallace Stevens J 10, (86); auth, "The Wizard Proprieties of Poe and Magritte", Word & Image 3 (87): 156-61; coed, A Good Deal: Selected Stories from the Massachusetts Review, Univ of Mass Pr, (Amherst), 88; auth, "Tray Bong! Godot and Music Hall", Approaches to Teaching Beckett's Waiting for Godot, ed June Schleuter and Enoch Brater, MLA, (ny, 91): 64-70; auth, "Pennsylvania", TriQuarterly 73, (88): 31-44; auth, Comic Moments, Univ of Ga Pr, (Athens, GA), 92; auth, The Man in the Bowler Hat: His History and Iconography, Univ of NC Pr, (Chapel Hill), 93. **CONTACT ADDRESS** Dept English, Univ of San Diego, 5998 Alcala Pk, San Diego, CA 92110-2429. **EMAIL** fredr@bcusd.edu

ROBINSON, FRED C.
PERSONAL Born 09/23/1930, Birmingham, AL, m, 1959, 2 children **DISCIPLINE** ENGLISH, PHILOLOGY **EDUCATION** Birmingham Southern Col, BA, 53; MA, 54, PhD, 61, Univ N Carolina; Williams Col, DLit (honorary), 85; Yale Univ, MA (honorary), 89. **CAREER** Instr and Asst Prof, 60-65, Assoc Prof/Prof, 67-72, Stanford Univ; Asst and Assoc Prof, Cornell Univ, 65-67; Visiting Prof, Harvard Univ, 82; Prof, 72-83, Douglas Tracy Smith Prof, 83-, Yale Univ. **HONORS AND AWARDS** Rector's Medal, Univ of helsinki, 84; Haskins Medal of the Medieval Acad of Am, 84; Sir Israel Gollancz Prize of the British Acad, 97; Wlliam Clyde DeVane Medal of Phi Beta Kappa at Yale, 99; fel, Am Acad of Arts and Sci, 76-; Fel, Medieval Acad of Am, 79-; Corresponding fel, British Acad, 94-; Corresponding fel, Meddeleuse Verenigung van Suidelike Afrika, 75-; Foreign mem, Finnish Acad of Sci and letters, 99-; Res fel, Japan Soc for the Promotion of Sci, 89; Ireland Distinguished Vis Scholar Awd, Univ of Alabama, 99; Professore solo per ricerca, La Sapienza, Univ of Rome, 00; Hon mem of Int Soc of Anglo-Saxonists, 99; Hon d.Littt., Williams col, 85; hon M.A., Yale Univ, 89. **MEMBERSHIPS** Early English Text Soc; Henry Bradshaw Soc; Medieval Acad of Am (pres 83-84); New England Medieval Confernece (pres 82-83). **RESEARCH** Old English language and literature; English philology of all periods. **SELECTED PUBLICATIONS** Auth, Old English Literature: A Select Bibliography (Toronto), 70; coauth, A Bibliography of Publications on Old English Literature (Toronto), 80; auth, Beowulf and the Appositive Style (Knoxville), 85; coauth, Old English Verse Texts from Many Sources: A Comprehensive Collection (Copenhagen), 91; auth, The Tomb of Beowulf (Oxford), 93; auth, The Editing of Old

English (Oxford), 94; coauth, Beowulf: An Edition with Relevant Shorter Texts (Oxford), 98; coauth, A Guide to Old English, 6th ed. (Oxford), 00. **CONTACT ADDRESS** Dept of English, Yale Univ, PO Box 208302, New Haven, CT 06520-8302.

ROBINSON, GABRIELLE S.
PERSONAL Born 10/17/1942, Berlin, Germany, m, 1 child **DISCIPLINE** ENGLISH **EDUCATION** Univ Illinois, BA, 64; Columbia Univ, MA, 65; Univ London, PhD, 68. **CAREER** Asst Prof, Univ of Illinois, Urbana, 68-70; Asst Prof, Indiana Univ, South Bend, 78-81; Assoc Prof, 81-86; Full Prof, 86-. **HONORS AND AWARDS** Woodrow Wilson Fel, 64-65; Phi Beta Kappa, 64; Lilly Fac Fel, 91-92; Ryan Awd for Distinguished Contributions to International Studies, 98. **RESEARCH** Modern Drama; Popular Culture; Detective Fiction. **SELECTED PUBLICATIONS** Auth, "A Private Mythology," Buckerell VP, 88. **CONTACT ADDRESS** Dept English, Indiana Univ, South Bend, PO Box 7111, South Bend, IN 46634-7111. **EMAIL** grobinso@iusb.edu

ROBINSON, GERTRUDE JOCH
DISCIPLINE COMMUNICATION STUDIES **EDUCATION** Swarthmore Col, BA; Univ Chicago, MA; Univ Ill, PhD. **CAREER** Prof. **HONORS AND AWARDS** Gannett Ctr for Media Studies Sr Fel, Columbia Univ; ed, can j commun **RESEARCH** History/theory of communication; media industries and globalization; media and gender; comparative broadcast regulation; high/low culture; audiencing behavior. **SELECTED PUBLICATIONS** Auth, "Here be Dragons: Problems in Charting the History of Mass Communication Studies in the United States," Communications, 13:3, (88), 97-119; ed, "Dieta Sixt, Women and Power: Canadian and German Experiences," Montreal: McGill Studies in Communication/Goethe Institut, (90), 127-64; auth, "Women Politicians and their Media Coverage: A Generational Approach," in Women in Canadian Politics: Toward Equity, Vol. 6 , Research Studies, Royal Commission on Electoral Reform, ed. Cathy Megyvery, (Toronto: Dundee Press, 92), 127-64; auth, "West Germany: The End of Public Service Broadcasting as we Know It," in Public Service Broadcasting in a Multi-Channel Environment, ed. Robert K. Avery, (NY: Longman, 93), 53-74; auth, "The Study of Women and Journalism: From Positivist to Feminist Approaches," in Cees Hamelink et.al., Mass Communication Research: On Problems and Policies, Ablex, (94), 191-203; auth, "East Germany" in Glasnost and After, ed. David Paletz Creskill, (N.J. Hampton Press, 94), 169-93. **CONTACT ADDRESS** Dept of Philos, McGill Univ, 855 Sherbrooke St W, Leacock Bldg, Montreal, QC, Canada H3A 2T7. **EMAIL** cxro@musica.mcgill.ca

ROBINSON, JEFFREY CANE
PERSONAL Born 02/06/1943, Durham, NC, m, 1989, 3 children **DISCIPLINE** LITERATURE **EDUCATION** Harvard Univ, AB, 64; Univ Chicago, MA, 65; Brandeis Univ, PhD, 72. **CAREER** Instr, Lake Forest Col, 66-69; asst prof to prof, Univ Colo, 71-. **HONORS AND AWARDS** Guggenheim Fel, 93; Fel, Univ Colo, 77, 80, 86, 00; Book Award, Univ Colo, 91; Res and Creative Work Award, Univ Colo, 96. **MEMBERSHIPS** MLA; NASSR. **RESEARCH** British Romanticism and Poetics; The Lyric Poem; Writing Poetry. **SELECTED PUBLICATIONS** Auth, The Current of Romantic Passion, 91; auth, Romantic Presences, 95; auth, Spliced Romanticism, 97; auth, Reception and Poetics in Keats, 98; ed, The Walker's Literary Companion, 00; ed, The Quotable Walker, 00. **CONTACT ADDRESS** Dept Lit, Univ of Colorado, Boulder, 1065 10th St, Boulder, CO 80302-7203. **EMAIL** jjrobins@stripe.colorado.edu

ROBINSON, KELLY A.
DISCIPLINE ACQUIRED NEUROGENIC DISORDERS OF COMMUNICATION **EDUCATION** SUNY, BA, MA; Emerson Col, PhD. **CAREER** Emerson Col. **SELECTED PUBLICATIONS** Area: affect acquired brain injury has on attention, memory, and lang(s). **CONTACT ADDRESS** Emerson Col, 100 Beacon Street, Boston, MA 02116-1596.

ROBINSON, LAURA
DISCIPLINE ENGLISH LITERATURE **EDUCATION** Queen's Univ, PhD. **CAREER** Dept Eng, Queen's Univ **RESEARCH** Women writers; feminist theory. **SELECTED PUBLICATIONS** Auth, pubs on L.M. Montgomery. **CONTACT ADDRESS** English Dept, Queen's Univ at Kingston, Kingston, ON, Canada K7L 3N6. **EMAIL** 3lmr5@qlink.queensu.ca

ROBINSON, ROCHELLE
PERSONAL Born 04/16/1969, Chicago, IL, s **DISCIPLINE** ENGLISH **EDUCATION** Bradley Univ, BA, 91; DePaul Univ, MA, 93. **CAREER** Adj prof, DeVry Inst, 93-96; asst prof, Olia Harvey Col, 96-. **HONORS AND AWARDS** Nominee, Preferred prof, 96-97. **MEMBERSHIPS** MLA. **RESEARCH** African American Literature; American Literature; The Romantics. **SELECTED PUBLICATIONS** Auth, "Mardi Gras 1999: A Hiatus in the Festivities," African Am Rev; auth, "Just a White God," African Am Rev; auth, "The Cry of the Wild Child," in In Other Words. **CONTACT ADDRESS** 5512 S Woodlawn Ave, Chicago, IL 60637-1637. **EMAIL** rrobinson@cu.edu

ROBINSON, SOLVEIG C.
PERSONAL Born 11/16/1962, Minneapolis, MN, m, 1996 **DISCIPLINE** ENGLISH **EDUCATION** Gustavus Adolphus Col, BA, 83; Univ Chicago, MA, 87; PhD, 94. **CAREER** Asst prof, Univ Puget Sound, 94-98; asst prof, Mary Wash Col, 00-01; asst prof, Pac Lutheran Univ, 01-. **HONORS AND AWARDS** Phi Beta Kappa; Mellon Fel; Fel, Am Coun of Learned Soc. **MEMBERSHIPS** MLA; SHARP; RSVP. **RESEARCH** Victorian Women Critics; Publishing History. **SELECTED PUBLICATIONS** Auth, "Editing Belgravia. M.E. Braddon's Defense of Light Literature," Victorian Per Rev, 95; auth, "Amazed at Our Success: The Laughan Place Editors and the Emergence of a Feminist Critical Tradition," Victorian Per Rev, 96; auth, "Of Haymakers and City Artisans: The Chartist Poetics of Eliza Cook's Songs of Labor," Victorian Poetry, forthcoming; auth, Critical Prose by Victorian Women, Broadview, forthcoming. **CONTACT ADDRESS** Dept English, Pacific Lutheran Univ, Pac Lutheran Univ, Tacoma, WA 98447. **EMAIL** solveig_robinson@hotmail.com

ROBINSON, WILLIAM HENRY
PERSONAL Born 10/24/1922, Newport, RI, m, 1948 **DISCIPLINE** ENGLISH **EDUCATION** New York Univ, BA, 1951; Boston Univ, MA, 1957; Harvard Univ, PhD, 1964. **CAREER** Prairie View Agr & Mech Coll, Prairie View TX, English instructor, 51-53; NC Agr & Tech State Univ, Greensboro, mem of English faculty, 56-61, 64-66; Boston Univ, MA, assoc prof of English & humanities, 66-68; Howard Univ, Washington DC, prof of English, 68-70; Rhode Is Coll, Providence, prof of English and dir black studies, 70-85; vis prof of Amer & English lit, Brown Univ, 87--. **MEMBERSHIPS** Bd mem, RI Commn on the Humanities; Bd mem, RI Black Heritage Soc; Intl Lecture Platform Assn; mem, NSLCAH; Nat Com on Black Studies; NAACP; Urban League; Coll Language Arts Assn; Assn for Study of Negro Life & Culture. **SELECTED PUBLICATIONS** Editor of Early Black American Poets, W.C. Brown, 1969, Early Black American Prose, W.C. Brown, 1970, Nommo: An Anthol of Modern Black African & Black American Lit, Macmillan, 1972, Critical Essays on Phillis Wheatley, G.K. Hall, 1982; author of Phillis Wheatly in the Black American Beginnings, Broadside, 1975, Phillis Wheatley: A Bio-ibliography, G.K. Hall, 1981, Phillis Wheatley and Her Writings, Garland, 1984; also autho of num TV, stage, radio scripts; contr to journals. **CONTACT ADDRESS** English Dept, Rhode Island Col, 600 Mt Pleasant Ave, Providence, RI 02908.

ROBINSON, ZAN
PERSONAL Born 07/15/1935, Abington, PA, m, 1973, 5 children **DISCIPLINE** ENGLISH **EDUCATION** SUNY, PhD, 90. **CAREER** Assoc Prof, Erie Cmty Col, 80-; Adj Prof, Buffalo State Col. **HONORS AND AWARDS** Chancellor's Awd for Excellence in Teaching, SUNY, 97; President's Awd, Erie Cmty Col, 96; Distinguished Alumnus Awd, Buffalo State Col, 00. **MEMBERSHIPS** United Univ Prof. **RESEARCH** Linguistics and Literature. **SELECTED PUBLICATIONS** Auth, Effective Writing: As Easy as 1,2,3, Connors Pub Co, 00; auth, Practical Writing Techniques, Eighth Ed., Pearson Custom Press, 00; auth, Practical Writing Techniques, Seventh Ed, Schuster Custom Press, 98; auth, Fundamentals of Writing, Connors Pub Co, 97; auth, Practical Writing Techniques, Sixth Ed, Simon & Schuster Custom Press, 96; auth, The Spirit of November, Simon & Schuster Custom Press, 96; auth, Practical Writing Techniques, Fifth Ed, Simon & Schuster Custom Press, 95; auth, Ferdie the Fay Meets Flutterby the Butterfly: A Forest Fable of Fear and Courage, E.W. Connors Pub Co, 95; auth, practical Writing Techniques, Fourth Ed, Ginn Press, 94; auth, Robinson's Resource Guide for Writing Resumes and Cover letters, Connors Pub Co, 93. **CONTACT ADDRESS** Dept English, Buffalo State Col, 1300 Elmwood Ave, Buffalo, NY 14222-1004. **EMAIL** robinsz@juno.com

ROCHELLE, WARREN GARY
PERSONAL Born 11/21/1954, Durham, NC, s **DISCIPLINE** ENGLISH **EDUCATION** UNC Chapel Hill, BA, 77; Columbia Univ, MS, 78; UNC Greensboro, MFA, 91; PhD, 97. **CAREER** Lectr, UNC Greensboro, 97-98; asst prof, Limestone Col, 98-00; asst prof, Mary Washington Col, 00-. **HONORS AND AWARDS** Fullerton Mem Teaching Awd, Limestone Col, 99-00. **MEMBERSHIPS** NCTE, SAMLA, Sci Fiction and Fantasy Writers of Am, Sci Fiction Res Assoc. **RESEARCH** Science fiction, Utopia, myths, Ursula LeGuin, Composition Theory, Pedagogy. **SELECTED PUBLICATIONS** Auth, Communities of the Heart: The Rhetoric of Myth in the Fiction of Ursula K LeGuin, Liverpool Univ Pr, 01; auth, The Wild Boy, Golden Gryphon Pr, 01. **CONTACT ADDRESS** 2111 Cowan Blvd, No 16C, Fredericksburg, VA 22401-1076.

ROCKS, JAMES E.
PERSONAL Born 05/26/1939, Cleveland, OH, m, 1973 **DISCIPLINE** ENGLISH **EDUCATION** Duke Univ, PhD. **CAREER** Assoc prof; sr assoc dean, Grad Sch. **RESEARCH** American literature and Southern literature. **SELECTED PUBLICATIONS** Auth, Whittier's Snow-Bound: The circle of our hearth and the Discourse on Domesticity, in Stud in the Am Renaissance 17, UP Va, 93. **CONTACT ADDRESS** Dept of English, Loyola Univ, Chicago, 6525 N Sheridan Rd, Chicago, IL 60626. **EMAIL** jrocks@wpo.it.luc.edu

ROCKWELL, SUSAN L.
PERSONAL Born 09/01/1957, Canton, OH, s **DISCIPLINE** LITERATURE **EDUCATION** Univ Ala Birmingham, BA, 90; MA, 93; Ariz State Univ, PhD, 01. **CAREER** Admin asst, Univ Ala, 81-93; dir, Nat Asn for Ethnic Studies, 94-00; fac assoc, Ariz State Univ, 96-; prof, Cook Col and Theol Sch, 00-. **HONORS AND AWARDS** Grad Res Support Prog Grant, Ariz State Univ, 98; Wassaja Summer Res Grant, Ariz State Univ, 97. **MEMBERSHIPS** Asn for Study of Am Indian Lit; MLA. **RESEARCH** Native American autobiography; Native American literature; Teaching Native American students. **SELECTED PUBLICATIONS** Auth, "Writing the Oral Tradition: Leslie Marmon Silko's Storyteller," Explorations in Ethnic Studies, (94): 195-206; auth, "The Delivery of Power: Reading American Indian Childbirth Narratives," Am Indian Culture and Res J, (95): 71-85; auth, "Indian Child Welfare Act," in Handbook of American Women's History, 2nd ed, Sage Pub, 99; auth, "Louise Erdrich," in Handbook of American Women's History, 2nd ed, Sage Pub, 99; auth, "Anna Moore Shaw," in Handbook of American Women's History, 2nd ed, Sage Pub, 99. **CONTACT ADDRESS** Sch of Theol, Arizona State Univ, 708 S Lincoln Ln, PO Box Ccts D7, Tempe, AZ 85281-3221. **EMAIL** susikati2@aol.com

RODERICK, JOHN M.
DISCIPLINE ENGLISH LITERATURE **EDUCATION** Providence Col, BA; Rhode Island Col, MA; Brown Univ, PhD. **CAREER** Prof, Hartford Univ. **HONORS AND AWARDS** Larsen Awd, 96. **SELECTED PUBLICATIONS** Auth, The Welder; Clotheslines and Baseball, Alembic Magazine, 97. **CONTACT ADDRESS** English Dept, Univ of Hartford, 200 Bloomfield Ave, West Hartford, CT 06117.

RODOWICK, DAVID N.
DISCIPLINE ENGLISH **EDUCATION** Univ IA, PhD. **CAREER** Prof & dir Film Stud Prog; taught at, Univ IA & Yale Univ. **HONORS AND AWARDS** Created & administered, Yale Film Stud Prog, Yale Univ. **RESEARCH** Film theory of Gilles Deleuze; philos implications of new commun technol. **SELECTED PUBLICATIONS** Auth, The Difficulty of Difference: Psychoanalysis, Sexual Difference, and Film Theory & The Crisis of Political Modernism: Criticism and Ideology in Contemporary Film Theory; articles on, film theory & cult criticism. **CONTACT ADDRESS** Dept of Eng, Univ of Rochester, 601 Elmwood Ave, Ste. 656, Rochester, NY 14642. **EMAIL** rdwk@troi.cc.rochester.edu

RODRIGUEZ, BARBARA R.
PERSONAL Born 09/21/1965, Socorro, TX, m, 1999 **DISCIPLINE** AFRICAN AMERICAN LITERATURE **EDUCATION** Univ Notre Dame, BA, 86; Harvard Univ, MA, 87; PhD, 93. **CAREER** Asst prof, Col of the Holy Cross, 93-94; asst prof, Northeastern Univ, 94-98; asst prof, Tufts Univ, 98-. **HONORS AND AWARDS** Dean's List, Univ Notre Dame, 83-86; Mellon Found Fel, 86-93, 00; Harvard Grad Prize, Fel, 86-93; NEH Grant, 95-96; Ford Found Fel, 98; WEB DuBois Inst Fel, 98-99; Woodrow Wilson Fel, 01. **MEMBERSHIPS** MLA. **RESEARCH** African-American Literature: prose and poetry since 1760, African-American cultural studies, African-American literary criticism and theory, American Writers of Color, American literature, American Autobiography: genre theory. **SELECTED PUBLICATIONS** Auth, Autobiographical Inscriptions: Form, and Personhood and the American Woman Writer of Color, Oxford Univ Pr, 99; auth, "The American Slave Narrative: Slavery and the Persistence of Form," Series on Autobiography, ed William Andrews, (Univ Wis Pr, forthcoming). **CONTACT ADDRESS** Dept English, Tufts Univ, Medford, Medford, MA 02155. **EMAIL** barbara.rodriguez@tufts.edu

RODRIGUEZ, CLEMENCIA
DISCIPLINE COMMUNICATIONS **EDUCATION** Univ Javeriana, Bogota, BA, 84; OH Univ, Athens, MA, 90, PhD, 94. **CAREER** Asst prof, Univ TX at San Antonio, 94-; instr, OH Univ, 93; vis prof, Univ Centroamericana, 91-92; educ material evaluator, UNICEF/Radio Neth, , Managua, 91; grad asoc, OH Univ, 89-90; dir Educ Commun Prog, Univ Javarima, Bogota, 88; Commun Proj Coordr, CINEP, Bogota, 84-88; prof, Univ Javarima, Bogota, 84-88; res asst, ACICS, Bogota, 83-84 & Univ Javarima, 88. **HONORS AND AWARDS** Fac Res Awd, Univ TX at San Antonio, 95-96; Nat Coun Churches Christ in US, Dissertation grant, 93; John Houk Memorial Grant, OH Univ, 93; Certificate of Achievement, Commun & Develop Stud Prog, OH Univ, 90; rad Associateship, Sch Telecommun, OH Univ, 89. **MEMBERSHIPS** Int Commun Asn; Union Democratic Commun; San Antonio Hisp Res Network. **SELECTED PUBLICATIONS** Auth, Shedding Useless Notions of Alternative Media, Peace Rev 8 1, 96; The Rise and Fall of the Popular Correspondents' Movement in Revolutionary Nicaragua, 1982-1990, Media Cult and Soc 16 3, 94; A Process of Identity Deconstruction: Latin American Women Producing Video Stories, Women in Grassroots Communication, Furthering Social Change, Thousand Oaks, Sage, 94; De Cristal a Sassa Mutema: la Trayectoria del Melodrama Televisivo, From Cristal to Sassa Mutema: the Historic Evolution of Television Melodrama, Suplemento Gente, Barricada, 91; "Media for Participation and Social Change: Local Television in Catalonia, Comm

Dev News, 91; Cuando la C mara se Convirtio en Espejo Electronico. Cronicas del Video Participativo, When the Camera Transmutes into an Electronic Mirror, Tales of Participatory Video, Cinep Informa, 2 5, 90; coauth, La Telenovela en Colombia: Mucho m s que Amor y L grimas, Colombian Telenovelas: Much more than Love and Tears, Coleccion Controversia, #155, Bogota, CINEP, 89; Information Technology, Culture, and National Development in Latin America, Political Communication Research: Approaches, Studies, Assessments, Vol II, Norwood, Ablex Publ Co, 96; Propuesta para una Nueva Agenda de Investigacion sobre Comunicacion Internacional, Dialogos de la Comun, Colombia, 42, 95; Propuesta para una Nueva Agenda de Investigacion sobre Comunicacion Internacional, Comun y Sociedad, Mexico 24, 95; ed, Contando Historias, Tejiendo Identidades, Telling Stories, Weaving Identities, Bogota, CINEP, 87; **CONTACT ADDRESS** Col of Fine Arts and Hum, Univ of Texas, San Antonio, 6900 N Loop 1604 W, San Antonio, TX 78249.

RODRIGUEZ, LYDIA H.
PERSONAL Born 03/13/1967, Eureka, CA, s **DISCIPLINE** CLASSICS, LANGUAGE, LITERATURE **EDUCATION** Col Redwoods, AA, 91; Humboldt State Univ, BA, 92; Calif State Univ, MA, 94; Univ Cinci, PhD, 99. **CAREER** Instr, Pizer Col, Cinci State Col, 96-98; teaching asst to adj instr, Univ Cinci, 94-00; asst prof, Ind State Univ, 00-. **HONORS AND AWARDS** Grad Min Scholar; Cert Achievement Awd; Tuition Grant; Hon Soc Sigma Delta Pi. **MEMBERSHIPS** MLA; Sigma Delta Pi; CRR. **RESEARCH** Latin American female authors and literature; Chicana literature. **SELECTED PUBLICATIONS** Auth, "Teenagers of Peru," article (forthcoming); auth, The Mestizuje of the Canon represented in the Works of Helena Maria Vitamontes, bk, (forthcoming). **CONTACT ADDRESS** 131 Dolores Cir, Apt 4, Indiana, PA 15701-3323. **EMAIL** rodriglh@grove.iup.edu

ROEDER, BEA
PERSONAL Born 11/08/1941, Pasadena, CA, m, 1966, 2 children **DISCIPLINE** LITERATURE, FOLKLORE, MYTHOLOGY **EDUCATION** Univ Calif Santa Barb, BA, 63; Univ Calif Berk, MA, 65; Univ Calif LA, PhD, 84. **CAREER** Part time fac, Univ Colo, Univ Denver, Colo Col, Pike Peak Comm Col, 75-98; state folklorist, CCA, 79-. **HONORS AND AWARDS** NEA, NEH, 88, 90-91, 93, 96, 97, 00; IAC and UCLA Grants, 79, 80; UCLA Res Asstshp, 78-79; Berkeley TA, 64-65; Woodrow Wilson Fel, 63. **MEMBERSHIPS** AFS; AWSF. **RESEARCH** Coloradan folklore; Southwestern cultures; Lakota and Latino studies; folk medicine and narrative; dance. **SELECTED PUBLICATIONS** Auth, Chicano Folk Medicine from the Greater Los Angeles Area, Univ Calif Pr, Berkeley, 88; co-auth, "Los Dias," Mono Hisp New Year's Tradition, 95; co-auth, Ties that Bind: Coloradan Folk Arts in the Classroom, 97. **CONTACT ADDRESS** 10 Ridge Rd, Colorado Springs, CO 80904-1145. **EMAIL** bearoeder@yahoo.com

ROEMER, KENNETH M.
PERSONAL Born 06/06/1945, East Rockaway, NY, m, 1968, 2 children **DISCIPLINE** AMERICAN LITERATURE, AMERICAN STUDIES **EDUCATION** Harvard Univ, BA, 67; Univ Pa, MA, 68; PhD, 71. **CAREER** From asst prof to prof, Univ Tex at Arlington, 71-; vis prof, Shimane Univ, 82-83; vis prof, Int Christian Univ, 88. **HONORS AND AWARDS** Grant, Exxon Educ Found, 78; Grant, ACLS, 86; Chancellor's Outstanding Teaching Awd, 88; Sr Scientist Fel, Japan Soc for the Promotion of Sci, 88; Director Grants, NEH Summer Sem, 92, 94, 96, & 98; Acad of Distinguished Teachers Awd, 98; Writer of the Year, Wordcraft Circle of Native Am Writers & Storytellers, 98. **MEMBERSHIPS** MLA; Soc for Utopia Studies; Asn for the Study of Am Indian Lit; ASA; Melville Soc. **RESEARCH** American Indian Literatures, Utopian Literature. **SELECTED PUBLICATIONS** Auth, The Obsolete Necessity: American in Utopian Writings, 1888-1900, Kent State Univ Pr, 76; auth, "The Nightway Questions American Literature," Am Lit 66 (94): 817-829; auth, "Indian Lives: The Defining, the Telling," Am Quart 46 (94): 81-91; auth, "Contemporary American Indian Literature: The Centrality of Canons at the Margins," Am Lit Hist 6 (94): 583-599; ed, Native American Writers of the united States Volume 175, The Gale Group (Detroit, MI), 97; auth, "Silko's Arroyos as Mainstream," Modern Fiction Studies 45.1 (99): 10-37. **CONTACT ADDRESS** Dept English, Univ of Texas, Arlington, PO Box 19035, Arlington, TX 76019. **EMAIL** roemer@uta.edu

ROEN, DUANE
PERSONAL Born 02/19/1949, River Falls, WI, m, 1978, 2 children **DISCIPLINE** RHETORIC, COMPOSITION **EDUCATION** Univ Wisc, BS, 71; MS, 74; Univ Minn, PhD, 81. **CAREER** Asst prof, Univ of Nebr Lincoln 81-82; asst to assoc prof, Univ of Ariz, 82-88; prof, Syracuse Univ, 93-95; prof, Ariz State Univ, 95-. **HONORS AND AWARDS** Who's Who in Am Educ, 90; Grant, Indian Studies Summer Com, 90; Awd for Excellence in Teaching 93; President's Awd for Innovation, 97; Service Awd, 99. **MEMBERSHIPS** Ariz English Teachers Assoc; NY State English Counc; Assoc of Depts of English, 91; RMMLA; Rhetoric Soc of Am; TESOL; Assoc of Teachers of Advan Composition; Writing Prog Admin; MLA; Nat Counc of Teachers of English. **RESEARCH** Composition Theory, Rhetorical Theory, Composition Pedagogy, Collaboration, Teaching Portfolios. **SELECTED PUBLICATIONS** Coauth, Wisconsin Authors, Wis Counc of Teachers of English, 78; coed Richness in Writing: Empowering ESL Students, Longman (NY), 89; coauth, Becoming Expert: Writing and Learning Across the Disciplines, Kendall-Hunt, (Dubuque, IA), 90; coauth, A Sense of Audience in Written Discourse, Sage, (Newbury Park, CA), 90; coauth, The Writer's Toolbox", Allyn and Bacon, (Boston), 96; coauth, "Louise Rosenblatt", Encyclop of Rhetoric and Composition: Communication from Ancient Times to the Information Age, ed Theresa Enos, Garland, (NY, 96): 643-44; coauth, Audience and the Evaluation of Writing", The Role of Teachers' Knowledge, eds Charles Cooper and Lee Odell, NCTE, (Urbana, IL, 99): 53-71; auth, "The Education of a Wisconsin Farm Boy", Composing Our Lives in Rhetoric and Composition: Stories About the Growth of a Discipline, eds, Duane H. Roen, Theresa Enos and Stuart Brown, Lawrence Erlbaum, (Mahwah, NY, 99): 123-127; coauth, "The Story of One Family's Journal", Centerspace (forthcoming). **CONTACT ADDRESS** Dept English, Arizona State Univ, PO Box 870302, Tempe, AZ 85287-0302. **EMAIL** duane.roen@asu.edu

ROESKE, PAULETTE
PERSONAL m, 1 child **DISCIPLINE** ENGLISH, CREATIVE WRITING **EDUCATION** Univ Iowa, BA, 67; Northwestern Univ, MA, 68; Warren Wilson Col, MFA, 82. **CAREER** Prof of English and Creative Writing, ed of Willow Rev, Dir of the Reading Series, Col of Lake County, Grayslake, Il, 69-. **HONORS AND AWARDS** Carl Sandburg Book Awd for Poetry (for Divine Attention); Teaching Excellence Awd from the Nat Inst for Staff and Org Develop; Ill Arts Coun Individual Artist Fel; Ill Arts Coun Literary Awds in three different years. **MEMBERSHIPS** Acad of Am Poets, Assoc Writing Progs, Modern Poetry Asn, Poetry Soc of Am, Poets and Writers. **RESEARCH** Twentieth Century American poetry. **SELECTED PUBLICATIONS** Auth, "Breathing Under Water," Stormline Press (88); auth, "Divine Attention," LSU (95); auth, "Unmasked: Responding to the Photographs of Diane Arbus," in Great Ideas Today (97); auth, "The Hard Fact," Glimmer Train (summer 98); auth, "In the Absence of Heroines: A Response to Gerda Lerner's Why History Matters," in The Great Ideas Today, ed John Van Doren, Encyclopedia Britannica, Inc: Chicago, Ill (98); auth, "Anvil, Clock, and Last," La State Univ Press (2001); auth, "Preparing the Dead," and "Trust," in Illinois Voices: An Anthology of Twentieth-Century Poetry from Illinois, eds Kevin Stein and G. E. Murray, Univ Ill Press forthcoming); auth, "The Body Can Ascend No Higher," in The Yellow Shoe Poets: A Millennium Anthology, ed George Garrett, La State Univ Press (forthcoming); auth, "In Sympathy, My Daughter Sleeps Beside Me," Essential Love: Parent and Child, ed Ginny Connors, Poetworks, a div of Grayson Books (forthcoming); auth, "The Body Can Ascend No Higher," in Knowing Stones: Poems of Exotic Places, ed Maureen Flannery (forthcoming). **CONTACT ADDRESS** Dept Humanities & Fine Arts, Col of Lake County, 19351 W Washington St, Grayslake, IL 60030-1148. **EMAIL** rreid@usi.edu

ROGERS, DEBORAH D.
DISCIPLINE ENGLISH **EDUCATION** Rutgers Univ, BA; Univ Calif, MA; Columbia Univ, MPhil; PhD. **CAREER** Prof, Univ Maine, 96-. **RESEARCH** Eighteenth-Century literature, cultural studies, women's studies. **SELECTED PUBLICATIONS** Auth, "Bookseller as Rogue: John Almon and the Politics of Eighteenth-Century Publishing," in Univ Studies Ser IV, English Lang and Lit, vol 28 (NY: Peter Lang, 86); auth, The Critical Response to Ann Radcliffe, Greenwood Press (Westport, CT), 94; auth, Afterward in Rob Roy (NY: Signet Classics, 95); Ed and Introd, Two Gothic Classics by Women: The Italian and Northanger Abbey (NY: Signet Classics, 95); auth, Ann Radcliffe: A Bio-Bibliography, Greenwood Pr (Westport, CT), 96. **CONTACT ADDRESS** Dept English, Univ of Maine, 5752 Neville Hall, Orono, ME 04469-5752.

ROGERS, FRANKLIN R.
DISCIPLINE LITERATURE **EDUCATION** Fresno State Col, BA, 50; MA, 52; Univ Calif Berkeley, PhD, 58. **CAREER** Asst prof, Univ Wis, 58-63; asst prof, Univ Calif Davis, 63-64; assoc prof, San Jose State Univ, 64-86; vis prof, Univ Lyon, 69-71; vis prof, Univ Paris Sorbonne, 75-76. **HONORS AND AWARDS** Fulbright Prof, France, 66-67; Sem Lectr, France, 76; Japan, 86. **MEMBERSHIPS** MLA. **RESEARCH** The American novel and Mark Twain; the aesthetics of the literary work; the characteristics of the literary language. **SELECTED PUBLICATIONS** Auth, "The Tale of Gamelyn and the Editing of the Canterbury Tales," J English Germ Philo18 (59): 49-59; auth, Mark Twain's Burlesque Patterns, S Methodist UP, 60; auth, The Pattern for Mark Twain's Roughing It, Univ Calif Pr (Berkeley), 61; ed, "Simon Wheeler, Detective by Mark Twain," New York Pub Lib, 63; auth, "The Road to Reality: Burlesque Travel Literature and Mark Twain's Roughing It," Bull NY Pub Lib 67 (63): 155-168; auth, "Mark Twain and Alphonse Daudet: A Tramp Abroad and Tartarin sur les Alpes," Comp Lit 16 (64): 254-263; ed, "Mark Twain's Satires and Burlesques," Vol 1, The Mark Twain Papers, (Univ Calif Pr, Cambridge UP, 67); ed, "Roughing It," Vol 11, The Works of Mark Twain, (Univ Calif Pr, Cambridge UP, 72); auth, Painting and Poetry: Form, Metaphor, and the Language of Literature, Bucknell UP (Lewisburg), 85; auth, Occidental Ideographs: Image, Sequence, and Literary History, Bucknell UP (Lewisburg), 91. **CONTACT ADDRESS** 206 Woodland Rd, Los Gatos, CA 95033-7810. **EMAIL** frrogers@email.sjsu.edu

ROGERS, JACK E.
PERSONAL Born 12/13/1957, Stillwater, OK, m, 1991, 4 children **DISCIPLINE** SPEECH COMMUNICATION, SOCIOLOGY **EDUCATION** La State Univ, PhD, 94. **CAREER** Assoc prof, Southern Univ, 86-95; Asst Prof, Univ of TX at Tyler, 96-. **HONORS AND AWARDS** Pres, Int Debat Asn. **MEMBERSHIPS** NCA, SSCA, CEDA, IPDA. **RESEARCH** Debate; forensics. **SELECTED PUBLICATIONS** Auth, A Community of Unequals: An Analysis of Dominant and Subdominant Culturally Linked Perceptions of Participation and Success within Intercollegiate Competitive Debate, Contemporary Argumentations & Debate: The J of the Cross-Examination Debate Asn, 97; A Critique of the Lexis/Nexis Debate: What's Missing Here?, The Southern J of Forensics, 96; Interrogating the Myth of Multiculturalism: Toward Significant Membership and Participation of Afrian Americans in Forensics, The Forensic of Pi Kappa Delta, 95; The Minority Perspective: Toward the Future Forensics Participation of Historically Black College and Universities, Proceedings from the Pi Kappa Delta Development Conf, 95; Constructing the Deconstruction: Toward the Empowerment of Women and Minorities in Forensics, Pi Kappa Delta Nat Development Conf, 95; What do they have that I haven't got? Comparison Survey Data of the Resources and Support Systems of Top CEDA Programs and Directors, CEDA Yearbook, 91. **CONTACT ADDRESS** Univ of Texas, Tyler, 3900 University Blvd, Tyler, TX 75799.

ROGERS, JIMMIE N.
DISCIPLINE POLITICAL AND CULTURAL COMMUNICATION **EDUCATION** Fla State Univ, PhD. **CAREER** Comm Stu, Univ Ark. **SELECTED PUBLICATIONS** Auth, The Country Music Message Revisited, Univ Ark Press, 89. **CONTACT ADDRESS** Univ of Arkansas, Fayetteville, AR 72701.

ROGERS, KATHARINE MUNZER
PERSONAL Born 06/06/1932, New York, NY, m, 1956, 3 children **DISCIPLINE** ENGLISH LITERATURE **EDUCATION** Barnard Col, BA, 52; Columbia Univ, PhD, 57. **CAREER** Prof, Brooklyn Coll CUNY, 58-88; Prof Emer, Brooklyn Coll CUYN, 88-. **RESEARCH** Animals in literature; L Frank Baum's life 7 works; women writers; Women in literature **SELECTED PUBLICATIONS** edr, Meridian Anthology of Restoration and Eighteenth-Century Plays by Women, Penguin USA, 94; auth, The Cat and the Human Imagination: Feline Images from Bast to Garfield, Univ Mich Press, 98. **CONTACT ADDRESS** Dept Eng, Brooklyn Col, CUNY, Brooklyn, NY 11210.

ROGERS, LYNNE
DISCIPLINE MUSIC THEORY **EDUCATION** Pomona Col, BA, 76; Univ of Wash, MA, 80; Princeton Univ, MFA, 83, PhD, 89. **CAREER** Fac, Univ Tex, Austin, 87-94; asst prof, Oberlin Coll, 94-; Visiting lectr, University of Wis, 84. **HONORS AND AWARDS** Fel, Pach Sacher Found, Switzerland, 97; Univ Res Inst Summer Res Awd, Univ Tex, 91. **SELECTED PUBLICATIONS** Contribu, Intl Jour of Musicol and Jour Musicol. **CONTACT ADDRESS** Dept of Mus, Oberlin Col, Oberlin, OH 44074.

ROGERS, PHIL
DISCIPLINE ENGLISH LITERATURE **EDUCATION** Harvard Univ, PhD. **CAREER** Dept Eng, Queen's Univ **RESEARCH** Medieval literature; comparative literature. **SELECTED PUBLICATIONS** Auth, pubs on medieval and modern literature and language. **CONTACT ADDRESS** English Dept, Queen's Univ at Kingston, Kingston, ON, Canada K7L 3N6. **EMAIL** rogersp@qsilver.queensu.ca

ROGERS, RICHARD A.
PERSONAL Born 09/24/1965, Fairfield, CA, s **DISCIPLINE** COMMUNICATION **EDUCATION** Humboldt State Univ, BS, 88; Univ Utah, MS, 90; PhD, 94. **CAREER** Instr to asst prof, N Ariz Univ, 95-. **HONORS AND AWARDS** Who's Who Among Am Teachers, 98. **MEMBERSHIPS** Nat Commun Assoc; Western Commun Assoc; Orgn for Res on Women and Commun. **RESEARCH** Intercultural communication, media criticism, critical and cultural theory, gender and communication. **SELECTED PUBLICATIONS** Auth, "1984 to Brazil: From the Pessimism of Reality to the Hope of Dreams", Text and Performance Quarterly 10 (90):34-46; auth, "Pleasure, Power and Consent: The Interplay of Race and Gender in New Jack City", Women's Studies in Commun, (93):62-85; coauth, "Particularities and Possibilities: Reconceptualizing Knowledge and Power in Sexual Harassment Research, Conceptualizing Sexual Harassment as Discursive Practice, Praeger Pub, (94):159-172; auth, "Rhythm and the Performance of Organization", Text and Performance Quarterly, (94):222-237; auth, "A Dialogics of Rhythm: Dance and the Performance of Cultural Conflict", Howard Jour of Commun, (98):5-27; auth, "Overcoming the Objectification of Nature in Constitutive Theories: Toward a Transhuman, Materialist Theory of Communication,

W Jour of Commun, (98):244-272; auth, "Is this a Great Time or What?: Information Technology and the Erasure of Difference, World Commun Jour, 00. **CONTACT ADDRESS** School of Commun, No Arizona Univ, PO Box 5619, Flagstaff, AZ 86011-0001.

ROGERS, WILLIAM E.
PERSONAL Born 12/12/1944, Greenville, SC, m, 1969, 2 children **DISCIPLINE** ENGLISH **EDUCATION** Yale Univ, BA, 66; Univ NCar, 70, PhD. **CAREER** Asst prof, US Military Acad, 70-72; asst prof, Ga State Univ, 72-74; prof, Furman Univ, 74-. **HONORS AND AWARDS** NEH Fel, 77-78; Dana Found, 89-90; Phi Beta Kappa. **MEMBERSHIPS** AAUP. **RESEARCH** Middle English literature, Charles Sanders Peirce. **SELECTED PUBLICATIONS** Auth, Image and Abstraction: Six Middle English Religious Lyrics, Rosenkilde and Bagger, 72; auth, The Three Genres and the Interpretation of Lyric, Princeton, 83; auth, Upon the Ways: The Structure of the Canterbury Tales, Univ of Victoria, 86; auth, Interpreting Interpretation: Textual Hermeneutics as an Ascetic Discipline, Pa State Univ, 94; auth, Interpretation in Piers Plowman, Catholic Univ of Am, forthcoming. **CONTACT ADDRESS** Dept English, Furman Univ, 3300 Poinsett Hwy, Greenville, SC 29613. **EMAIL** bill.rogers@furman.edu

ROHMAN, CHAD
PERSONAL Born 07/03/1963, East Lansing, MI, m, 1993, 2 children **DISCIPLINE** ENGLISH **EDUCATION** Mich State Univ, BA, 86; Bowling Green State Univ, 88; Mich State Univ, MA, 88. **CAREER** English Instr, Indian Hills Comm Col, 90-95; Graduate Fellow, Bowling Green State Univ, 95-98; Asst Prof of English, Dominican Univ, 98-. **HONORS AND AWARDS** Charles E. Shanklin Awd for Research Excellence, 98; The Quarry Farm Fellowsip at The Ctr for Mark Twain Studies, 98. **MEMBERSHIPS** Modern Language Assoc; Western Literature; Amer Literature Assoc; Mark Twain Circle of Amer. **RESEARCH** Mark Twain; The Amer Novel; Amer Women Regional Writers; Western Amer Literature. **SELECTED PUBLICATIONS** Auth, "Searching for the Fructifying dew of Truth: Negative Evidence and Epistemological Uncertainty in Mark Twain's No. 44, the Mysterious Stranger," In American Literary Realism, 31.2, 99: 72-88; auth, "What Is Man? Mark Twain's unresolved Attempt to Know," Forthcoming article in Nineteenth Century Studies, 00-01; auth, "Mark Twain, Epistemologist: Philosophical and Literary Dimensions of a Skeptical Mind," Forthcoming book, Northern Illinois Univ Press, 01-02. **CONTACT ADDRESS** Dept English, Dominican Univ, 7900 Division St, River Forest, IL 60305-1066. **EMAIL** crohman@mail.dom.edu

ROISMAN, HANNA M.
PERSONAL Born Wroclaw, Poland, m, 1971, 2 children **DISCIPLINE** CLASSICS **EDUCATION** Tel Aviv Univ, BA, 72, MA, 76; Univ Wash, PhD, 81. **CAREER** Lect, Tel Aviv Univ, 81-89; Assoc prof, Colby Col, 90-94, full prof, 94-. **HONORS AND AWARDS** Fel, Center Hellenic Studies **MEMBERSHIPS** APA **RESEARCH** Early Greek epic and tragedy; Classics and Film. **SELECTED PUBLICATIONS** Auth, Nothing Is As It Seems: The Tragedy of the Implicit in Euripedes, 98; co-auth, The Odyssey Re-Formed, 96; auth, Loyalty in Early Greek Epic and Tragedy, 84. **CONTACT ADDRESS** Dept of Classics, Colby Col, Waterville, ME 04901. **EMAIL** h_roisma@colby.edu

ROLLER, MATTHEW B.
PERSONAL Born 07/27/1966, Denver, CO **DISCIPLINE** CLASSICS, ROMAN STUDIES **EDUCATION** Stanford Univ, BA, 88; Univ Cal-Berkeley, MA, 90; PhD, 94. **CAREER** Asst prof of Classics, Johns Hopkins Univ, 94-00, assoc prof Classics, Johns Hopkins Univ, 00-; Mellon fel Hum, 88-90 and 93; Mellon Diss fel, 92 & 94. **HONORS AND AWARDS** Am Coun of Learned Societies Jun Fel, 00-01; Solmsen Fel, Inst for Res in the Humanities, Univ of Wisc-Madison, 00-01. **MEMBERSHIPS** Am Philol Asn; Archaeol Inst Am; Class Asn Atlantic Stud. **RESEARCH** Latin literature; Roman social and cultural history; Graeco-Roman philosophy. **SELECTED PUBLICATIONS** Auth Ethical Contradiction and the Fractured Community in Lucan's Bellum Civile, Class Antiquity, 96; Color-blindness: Cicero's death, declamation, and the production of history, Class Philol, 97; Pliny's Catullus: the politics of literary appropriation, Transactions of the Am Philol Asn; 98; auth, Constructing Autocracy: Aristocrats and Emperors in Julio-Claudian Rome, Princeton Univ Press, 01. **CONTACT ADDRESS** Dept of Classics, Johns Hopkins Univ, Baltimore, 3400 N Charles St, Baltimore, MD 21218-2690. **EMAIL** mroller@jhu.edu

ROLLIN, LUCY
DISCIPLINE ENGLISH LITERATURE **EDUCATION** Emory Univ, PhD, 89. **CAREER** Dept Eng, Clemson Univ **RESEARCH** Children's literature. **SELECTED PUBLICATIONS** Auth, The Antic Art: Enhancing Children's Literary Experiences with Film and Video, Highsmith Press, 94; Arthur Rackham, Dictionary of Literary Biography,94; Dreaming in Public: The Psychology of Nursery Rhyme Illustration, Children's Lit Asn Quart, 94; ed, Mark Twain's The Prince and the Pauper, Oxford Univ Press, 96. **CONTACT ADDRESS** Clemson Univ, 314 Strode, Clemson, SC 29634. **EMAIL** rlucy@clemson.edu

ROLLINS, PETER
PERSONAL Born Boston, MA, m, 1992 **DISCIPLINE** AMERICAN FILM STUDIES **EDUCATION** Harvard, PhD, 72. **CAREER** Comm Stu, Okla St Univ; Univ Prof, 72. **HONORS AND AWARDS** Peter C. Rollin Awd, SW/TXPCA/ACA; Peter C. Rollins and Susan Rollins Awd, national PCA/ACA; Distinguished Service Awd, national PCA/ACA. **MEMBERSHIPS** Popular Culture Asn, Am Culture Film and History League, Am Legion, Military Order of the World Wars. **RESEARCH** Film and History; film and society; Am Studies; Popular Culture; War and Culture. **SELECTED PUBLICATIONS** Auth, Hollywood's World War I, Popular Press; Hollywood's Indian, UP Ky; Hollywood as Historian, UP Ky; auth, Will Rogers: A aaBiobibliography (Greenwood, 83); auth, Hollywood as Historians 2nd ed. (UP of Kentucky, 98); auth, Hollywood's Indian (KY, 98); Hollywood's World War I (Popular Press, 98); Television Histories, (KY, 001); auth, The Columbia UP Guide to American History on Film, 01. . **CONTACT ADDRESS** Oklahoma State Univ, Stillwater, Popular Culture Center, RR 3, PO Box 80, Cleveland, OK 74020. **EMAIL** rollinspc@aol.com

ROLLYSON, CARL E., JR.
PERSONAL Born 03/02/1948, Miami, FL, m, 1981, 1 child **DISCIPLINE** ENGLISH **EDUCATION** Mich State Univ, BA, 69; Univ Toronto, MA, 70, PhD, 75. **CAREER** Prof eng, Prof art, 87 to 95-, CUNY Baruch; Asst Prof, Assoc Prof, Prof, 76-87, Wayne State Univ. **HONORS AND AWARDS** Phi Beta Kappa; NEH Fel; ACLS Gnt; APS Gnt. **MEMBERSHIPS** Authors Guild. **RESEARCH** Biography **SELECTED PUBLICATIONS** Auth, Marilyn Monroe: A Life of the Actress, 86; auth, Lillian Hellman: Her Legend and Her Legacy, 88; auth, Nothing Ever Happens to the Brave: The Story of Martha Geilhorn, 90; auth, The Many Lives of Norman Mailer, 91; coauth, Rebecca West: A Life, 96; auth, Susan Sontag: The Making of an Icon, 00. **CONTACT ADDRESS** Baruch Col, CUNY, 17 Lexington Ave, Box 6-0732, New York, NY 10010. **EMAIL** crlp@bellatlantic.net

ROMA-DEELEY, LOIS
PERSONAL Born 03/05/1952, Long Island, NY, m, 1970, 2 children **DISCIPLINE** ENGLISH **EDUCATION** Ariz State Univ, BA; MA; PhD, 00. **CAREER** Instr, Paradise Valley Community Col, 96-. **HONORS AND AWARDS** 3 Grants, Paradise Valley Community Col, 96-97; Lodestar Grant, 96-97. **MEMBERSHIPS** PVCC, AWW. **SELECTED PUBLICATIONS** Auth, "Angelina's Place," la bella figura: A Choice, malafemmina pr (93); auth, "The Mime's Box," The Best New Voices in Poetry, New Voices (93); auth, "Near the Gate Called Collina," Class Antiquity, Pig Iron Pr (94); auth, "The Anxiety of Righteous Being," Confluence (94); auth, "And, Or and Not," Pinyon Rev (96); auth, "Any Other Place But Here, Any Other Time But Now," Faultline (96). **CONTACT ADDRESS** Dept Humanities, Paradise Valley Comm Col, 18401 N 32nd St, Phoenix, AZ 85032. **EMAIL** lois.roma-deeley@pvmail.maricopa.edu

ROMAN, CAMILLE
PERSONAL Born 02/18/1948, LaPlatta, MD, m, 1975 **DISCIPLINE** ENGLISH **EDUCATION** Univ Mich, BA, 70; Boston Coll, MA, 85; Brown Univ, PhD, 90. **CAREER** Instr, Aquinas Coll, 78-85; adj prof, Brown Univ, 90-92; asst prof, assoc prof, Wash St Univ, 92-. **HONORS AND AWARDS** Jean Untermeyer Poetry Prize; Founding Co-editor Twayne's Music Series. **MEMBERSHIPS** MLA; ASA; EBS; RFS; DLS. **RESEARCH** American Poetry; 20th century literature and cultural studies; women's studies and literature. **SELECTED PUBLICATIONS** Auth, Elizabeth Bishop's WWII-Cold War View, St Martin's Press (00); ed, The Women and Language Debate, Rutgers UP (92); co-ed, Lester Young, The Beatles, Black Women Composers, Claude Debussy, Sonny Rollins, Downhome Blues Lyrics, in Twaynes Music Series: Twayne Pub. **CONTACT ADDRESS** Dept English, Washington State Univ, PO Box 645020, Pullman, WA 99164-5020. **EMAIL** roman@wsu.edu

ROMAN-MENDOZA, ESPERANZA
PERSONAL Born 06/20/1965, Madrid, Spain, m, 1996 **DISCIPLINE** CLASSICS **EDUCATION** Univ Complutense, Spain, lic, 89; transl dip, 92; Univ Nat de Edu a Dist, Spain, PhD, 97. **CAREER** Res assoc, Univ Nat de Edu a Dist, Spain, 92-96; instr, Univ Pont Com, Spain, 95-96; vis asst prof, George Mason Univ, 96-97; asst prof, 97-. **HONORS AND AWARDS** Extr Doct Awd, Spain, 97; Fel, Nat Plan Res, Spain, 92-95. **MEMBERSHIPS** MLA; AATSP; CALICO; FLAVA. **RESEARCH** Computer-assisted language learning; computer-assisted translation; Spanish sociolinguistics. **SELECTED PUBLICATIONS** Auth, "Eurodicautom: La base de datos terminol6gica de la Comunidad Europea" in Traducci6ny ensenanza de lenguas con ordenadores, ed. G. Ruiperez (Madrid: Ediciones Pedag6gicas, 95); auth, "Pasado, presente y flituro de Ia aplicaci6n de Ia informatica en Ia ensenanza de lenguas extranjeras." Puertas a Ia lectura 6/7 (99): 69-73; auth, "Adaptation of Video-based Language Learning Materials for the WWW" in Theory and Practice of Multimedia CALL, ed. K. Cameron (Exeter: Elm Bank Publications, 98); auth, "La World Wide Web y Ia enseiLanza del espanol como lengua extranjera: el ejemplo de Estados Unidos." Actas del VIII Congreso Internacional de la ASELE (Alcala' de Henares, Uuiversidad de Mcala, 97); auth, "Aplicaciones practicas de los recursos telematicos a la traducci6n de acro'nios y abreviaturas" in La Palabra Vertida. investigaciones en torno a la Traducci6n, eds.MA Vega, R Martin-Gaitero (Madrid, Univ Complutense, 97); coauth, "Aplicaci6n de Intemet en la difusi6n de la infonnaci6n sobre Terminologia" in La Palabra Vertida, eds. MA Vega, R Martin-Gaitero, Investigaciones en torno a Ia Traduccion (Madrid, Universidad Cornplutense, 97); coauth, "Erfahnmgen rnit Multirnedia-Software fur den DaFUnterricht mit Sprachausgabe und -eingabe" in Thesenband der X, Internationalen Deutschlehrertagung (Leipzig), 93. **CONTACT ADDRESS** Dept Modern and Classical Lang, George Mason Univ, Fairfax, 4400 University Dr, Fairfax, VA 22030-4422.

ROMAN-MORALES, BELEN
PERSONAL Born 01/17/1953, Puerto Rico, d, 3 children **DISCIPLINE** SPANISH AMERICAN LITERATURE **EDUCATION** Univ Puerto Rico, BA; MA, 85; Fla State Univ, PhD, 91. **CAREER** Teacher, Puerto Rico; prof, St Cloud State Univ, 1991-. **HONORS AND AWARDS** Teaching Asst Awd, Fla State Univ. **MEMBERSHIPS** ALFAL; AATSP. **RESEARCH** Spanish Linguistic, Poetry written by women. **SELECTED PUBLICATIONS** Auth, La Poetia de Julia de Burgess. **CONTACT ADDRESS** Dept Foreign Lang, St. Cloud State Univ, PO Box 64, Saint Cloud, MN 56302. **EMAIL** belen@stcloudstate.edu

ROMANO, SUSAN
PERSONAL m, 4 children **DISCIPLINE** COMPOSITION, RHETORIC **EDUCATION** Univ TX at Austin, MA, PhD. **CAREER** Asst prof, U of New Mexico, Albaquerque. **HONORS AND AWARDS** Ellen Nold awd, 93. **MEMBERSHIPS** MLA, NCTE **RESEARCH** Composition, rhetoric, electronic media, history of education, Mexico and Southeast US, professional writing. **SELECTED PUBLICATIONS** Publishes on Social identies, ethinicity, gender, writing program administration, literary, and electronic media. **CONTACT ADDRESS** Col of Fine Arts and Hum, Univ of Texas, San Antonio, 6900 N Loop 1604 W, San Antonio, TX 78249. **EMAIL** sromano@unm.edu

ROMANOWSKI, WILLIAM D.
PERSONAL Born 08/02/1954, m, 1977, 2 children **DISCIPLINE** AMERICAN CULTURE STUDIES **EDUCATION** Ind Univ Pa, BA, 76; Youngstown State Univ, MA, 81; Bow Gr State Univ, PhD, 90. **CAREER** Min, CCO, 76-88; grad asst, Bowling Green State Univ, 86-88; vis fac fel, Calvin Col, 88-89; assoc prof, 92-96; prof, 96-. **HONORS AND AWARDS** Thomas F Staley Dist Schl, 91-; Peter J Steen Awd, 88; CCCS Res Fel, 88; Christ Today Crit Choic Awd; CC Alum Res Gnt; CC Res Fel, 93, 98, 00; Billy Graham Res Gnt; Who's Who in Midwest; CCA Res Gnt, 94, 95; CCC Schl Gnt, 00. **RESEARCH** American pop culture; film; religion. **SELECTED PUBLICATIONS** Auth, Pop Culture Wars: Religion and the Role of Entertainment in American Life, InterVar Press (Downers Grove, IL), 96; coauth, Dancing in the Dark: Youth, Popular Culture and the Electronic Media, Eerdmans Pub (Grand Rapids, Mich), 91; coauth, Risky Business: Rock in Film, Trans Bks (New Brunswick), 91; auth, Evan gelicals and Popular Music: The Contemporary Christian Music Industry," in Religion and Popular Culture in America, eds. Jeffrey H Mahan, Bruce Forbes (LA: Univ Cal Press, 00): 105-24; auth, "Boycotts, Baptists, and NYPD Blue," Theol News Notes (97): 14-17; " 'Take Your Girlie to the Movies': Dating and Entertainment in Twentieth-Century America," in Religion, Feminism and the Family, eds. Ann Cair, Mary Stewart Van Leeuwen (The Family, Religion, and Culture, eds. Don S Browning, Ian S Evison, Philadelphia: Westminster John Knox Press, 96); auth, "'You Talkin' to Me?': The Christian Liberal Arts Tradition and the Challenge of Popular Culture," in Keeping Faith: Embracing the Tensions in Christian Higher Education (Grand Rapids, MI: Eerdmans, 96); auth, "John Calvin Meets the Creature from the Black Lagoon: The Christian Reformed Church and the Movies 1928-1966," Christ Schol Rev 25 (95): 47-62; auth, "The Joys Are Simply Told: Calvin Seerveld's Contribution to the Study of Popular Culture," in Pledges of Jubilee: Essays on the Arts and Culture in Honor of Calvin G Seerveld, eds. Lainbert Zuidervart, Henry Luttikhuizen (Grand Rapids, Mich: Eerdmans, 95). **CONTACT ADDRESS** Dept Communication Arts Sciences, Calvin Col, 3201 Burton St S, Grand Rapids, MI 49546-4301. **EMAIL** romw@calvin.edu

ROMBES, NICHOLAS
DISCIPLINE EARLY AMERICAN LITERATURE **EDUCATION** Bowling Green State Univ, BS; Pa State Univ, MA, PhD. **CAREER** Asst prof, 95-. **HONORS AND AWARDS** Contrib, Heath Anthology of Amer Lit. **RESEARCH** Terrors of the enlightenment in early American fiction. **SELECTED PUBLICATIONS** Pub(s), articles on The Federalist Papers, Thomas Jefferson, Robert Frost, Salman Rushdie, and numerous early American authors; co-ed, intl peer-reviewed jour, Post Identity. **CONTACT ADDRESS** Dept of Eng, Univ of Detroit Mercy, 4001 W McNichols Rd, PO BOX 19900, Detroit, MI 48219-0900. **EMAIL** nick@libarts.udmercy.edu

ROMER, F. E.
PERSONAL Born 02/24/1946, Brooklyn, NY, s **DISCIPLINE** CLASSICS **EDUCATION** NYork Univ, BA, 68; Stanford Univ, MA, 71, PhD, 74. **CAREER** Asst prof, Univ Vt, Sept 74-jun 75; asst prof, Oh State Univ, Sept 77-jun 78; asst prof, Johns Hopkins Univ, Jul 78-jun 86; book rev ed, The Amer Jour of Philol, Jan 82-dec 86; assoc prof, Hobart and William Smith Col, Jul 86-jun 91; assoc prof, Univ Ariz, Aug 91-. **HONORS AND AWARDS** Sch of Hist Studies, Inst for Adv Study, Princeton, Aug 86-jun 87; jr fel, Ctr for Hellenic Studies, Sept 84-jun 85; Stanford Univ dissertation prize in humanities, Jun 74; NY Univ Maitland prize in classics, may 68. **MEMBERSHIPS** Amer Philol Asn; Archaeol Inst of Amer; Asn of Ancient Hist; Class Asn of the Midwest and South. **RESEARCH** Ancient geography; Greek and Roman intellectual history, literature, and religion; Historical analysis for archaeological excavations at Chianciano Terme and Lugnano, Italy. **SELECTED PUBLICATIONS** Auth, Pomponius Mela's Description of the World, Univ Mich Press, 98; article, Good Intentions and the .., The City As Comedy: Society and Representation in Athenian Comedy, Univ NC Press, 51-74, 97; article, Diagoras the Melian, CW, 89, 393-401, 95/96; article, Atheism, Impiety, and the Limos Melios at Aristoph, Birds, 186, AJP, 115, 351-365, 94; article, Pliny, Vesuvius, and the Troublesome Wind, CW, 78, 587-591, 85; article, A Case of Client-Kingship, AJP, 106, 75-100, 85; article, When is a Bird Not a Bird?, TAPA, 113, 135-142, 83; article, The Aesymneteia: A Problem in Aristotle's Historical Method, AJP, 103, 25-46, 82; article, Gaius Caesar's Military Diplomacy in the East, TAPA, 109, 199-214, 79; article, A Numismatic Date for the Departure of C. Caesar?, TAPA, 108, 187-202, 78; auth, "Explaining Suetonius (Tib. 16.1): Tiberius' Tribunicia Potestas in A.D.4, Eranos 95 (97): 89-98; auth, "Famine, Pestilence, and Brigandage in Italy in the Fifth Century A.D.," in D. and N. Soren, eds, A Roman Villa and Late Roman Infant Cemetery (Bretschneider, 99), 465-475; auth, "Okheia and Mules in a Prometheus Play: Amending LSJ and Unemending Aesch. 189a R," TAPA 130 (00): 67-87. **CONTACT ADDRESS** Dept. of Classics - ML 371, Univ of Arizona, Tucson, AZ 85721-0067. **EMAIL** feromer@u.arizona.edu

ROMM, JAMES S.
DISCIPLINE GREEK HISTORIOGRAPHY, GREEK PROSE LITERATURE **EDUCATION** Princeton, PhD. **CAREER** Vis assoc prof, Fordham Univ. **SELECTED PUBLICATIONS** Auth, The Edges of the Earth in Ancient Thought: Geography, Exploration, and Fiction, Princeton, 92; Strabo, Greek Authors, Dictionary of Lit Biog, 97. **CONTACT ADDRESS** Dept of Class Lang and Lit, Fordham Univ, 113 W 60th St, New York, NY 10023.

ROMPKEY, RONALD G.
PERSONAL Born 02/10/1943, St John's, NF, Canada **DISCIPLINE** ENGLISH LITERATURE **EDUCATION** Memorial Univ, BA, 64; BEd, 66; MA, 68; Univ of London, Kings Col, PhD, 72. **CAREER** Prof to univ res prof, Memorial Univ, 93-. **MEMBERSHIPS** Royal Hist Soc, MLA, ACCUTE, Asn for Can Studies, Can Soc for the Hist of Med, Am Soc for 18th Century Studies, Can Soc for 18th Cent Studies. **RESEARCH** 18th-Century English literature, biography, autobiography, travel literature, Newfoundland and Labrador. **SELECTED PUBLICATIONS** Auth, Expeditions of Honour, Univ Del Pr, 82; auth, Soame Jenyns, BK Hall, 84; auth, Grenfell of Labrador, Univ of Toronto Pr, 91; auth, Labrador Odyssey, McGill-Queens Univ Pr, 96; auth, Jessie Luther at the Grenfell Mission, McGill-Queens Univ Pr, 01. **CONTACT ADDRESS** Dept English, Memorial Univ, Saint John's, NF, Canada A1C 5S7. **EMAIL** rrompkey@mun.ca

RONALD, ANN
DISCIPLINE ENGLISH **EDUCATION** Northwestern Univ, PhD 70; Univ Colorado, MA 66; Whitman Col, BA 61. **CAREER** Western Lit Assoc, exec sec, pres exec coun, 78-81, 83-84; Western Amer Lit, Studies in Short Fiction, ISLE: ed board. **CONTACT ADDRESS** Dept of English, Univ of Nevada, Reno, Reno, NV 89557. **EMAIL** ronald@unr.edu

RONAN, CLIFFORD J.
PERSONAL Born 07/22/1935, Boston, MA, m, 1960, 2 children **DISCIPLINE** ENGLISH LITERATURE **EDUCATION** Amherst Col, AB, 57; Univ Calif, Berkeley, MA, 60, PhD, 71. **CAREER** Asst prof, instr, Univ Tex, Austin, 65-72; Asst prof to Prof, Southwest Tex State Univ, 72-; Sr Fulbright Lectr, British and Am Inst, Univ of Silesia-Katowice, Poland, 95-96. **HONORS AND AWARDS** NEH Summer Seminar, Univ Calif, Berkeley, 75; Commemorative Medal of the Univ of Silesia, 94; Fulbright Sr Lectr, Univ of Silesia, 95-96; SWT Presidential Seminar Awd, Southwest Tex State Univ, 97. **MEMBERSHIPS** Shakespeare Asn of Am, Renaissance Asn of Am, South-Central Renaissance Conf. **RESEARCH** Shakespeare, Tudor-Stuart drama and Renaissance high-culture, American literature. **SELECTED PUBLICATIONS** Auth, "Homo Multiplex and the 'Man' Equivocation in 'Hamlet'," Hamlet Studies, 4 (82): 33-53; auth, "Daniel, Rainolde, Demosthenes, and the Degree Speech of Shakespeare's Ulysses," Renaissance and Reformation, 9, (85): 111-18; auth, "Sallust, Beasts That 'Sleep and Feed,' and Hamlet 5.2," Hamlet Studies, 8 (85): 72-80; auth, "Snakes in Catiline," Medieval and Renaissance Drama in England, 3 (86): 149-63; auth, "Eliot's Polypheman Pastoral," Yeats Eliot Rev, 8 (86): 109-18; auth, "Caesar's Revenge and the Roman Thoughts in Anthony and Cleopatra," Shakespeare Studies, 19 (87): 171-82; auth, "The Onomastics of Shakespeare's Plays with Classical Settings," in Names in Literature: Essays from Literary Onomastics Studies, ed Grace Alvarez-Altman and Frederick M. Burelbach, Lanham, Md: Univ Press of Am (87): 53-68; auth, "The Lucanic Omens in Julius Caesar," Comparative Drama, 22 (summer 88): 138-44; auth, "Lucan and the Self-Incised Voids of Julius Caesar," in Drama and the Classical Heritage: Comparative and Critical Essays, ed Clifford Davidson, Rand Johnson, and John H. Stroupe, AMS Ser, in Ancient and Classical Cultures, No 1, New York: AMS (93): 132-43; auth, 'Antike roman': Power symbology and the Roman Play in Early Modern England, 1585-1635, Athens and London: Univ Ga Press (95). **CONTACT ADDRESS** Dept English, Southwest Texas State Univ, 601 Univ Dr, San Marcos, TX 78666-4685. **EMAIL** cr06@swt.edu

RONAN, JOHN J.
PERSONAL Born 06/18/1944, San Diego, CA, m, 1987, 2 children **DISCIPLINE** MEDIA AND COMMUNICATIONS **EDUCATION** Loyola Univ, Chicago, BA, 67; Univ IL, Chicago, MA, 69. **CAREER** Prof, Chair, Media and Communications, North Shore Community College, Danvers, MA. **HONORS AND AWARDS** UCROSS Fellow, 94; NEA Fellow in Poetry, 99. **MEMBERSHIPS** Poetry Soc of Am; Academy of Am Poetry. **RESEARCH** Contemporary French poetry. **SELECTED PUBLICATIONS** Auth, The Catching Self, Foley Cove, 96; auth, The Curable Corpse, Foley Cove, 99; John Ronan's Greatest Hits, Pudding House, 00. **CONTACT ADDRESS** Box 5524, Gloucester, MA 01930. **EMAIL** jronan@nscc.mass.edu

RONDA, BRUCE
PERSONAL Born 08/06/1947, Oak Park, IL **DISCIPLINE** ENGLISH LITERATURE **EDUCATION** Hope Col, BA; Yale Univ, PhD. **CAREER** Prof. **MEMBERSHIPS** MLA; ASA; Children's Lit Asn. **RESEARCH** Antebellum literature and culture. **SELECTED PUBLICATIONS** Auth, Intellect and Spirit: The Life and Work of Robert Coles, 89; ed, The Letters of Elizabeth Palmer Peabody, American Renaissance Woman, 84; auth, Elizabeth Palmer Peabody. A Reformer on her own terms, 99. **CONTACT ADDRESS** Dept of English, Colorado State Univ, Fort Collins, CO 80523. **EMAIL** bronda@lamar.colostate.edu

RONNICK, MICHELE VALERIE
DISCIPLINE CLASSICS, GREEK, LATIN **EDUCATION** Boston Univ, PhD, 90. **CAREER** Assoc Prof, Dept of Classics, Wayne State Univ; Classical Asn of the Middle West and South Award for Outstanding Projects for the Comm for the Promotion of Latin, 99 and 00. **HONORS AND AWARDS** Awd For Teaching Excellence, APA, 97; Awd for Outstanding State VP, Classical Asn of the Middle West and South, 96; Awd for the Most Significant Project, 96; Incentive Awd for Younger Scholars, Classical and Modern Literature, 94. **MEMBERSHIPS** Int Soc for the Classical Tradition; APA; Classical Asn of the Middle West and South; Classical Asn of the Atlantic States; Am Asn for Neo-Latin Studies; National Committee for Latin and Greek. **RESEARCH** Latin literature; Classical tradition; Classical studies & people of African descent. **SELECTED PUBLICATIONS** Auth, Substructural Elements of Architectonic Rhetoric and Philosophical Thought in Fronto's Epistles, Roman Persuasion, 97; Aratus, Dictionary of Literary Biography: Ancient Greek Authors, Gale Research Co, 97; Cicero's Paradoxa Stoicorum: A Commentary, an Interpretation, and a Study of Its Influence, 91; Frankfurt Bos, Fur, Sus, atque Sacerdotes: Additional Light on Kaiser's Solution of a Minor Mystery, Proceedings of the Mass Hist Sco, 95; Concerning the Dramatic Elements in Milton's Defensiones: Theater Without a Stage, Classical and Modern Lit, 95; Seneca's Medea and Ultima Thule in Poe's Dream-land, Poe Studies/Dark Romanticism, 94; David Paul Brown's Sertorius or The Roman Patriot (1830): Another Influence on John Wilkes Booth, J of Am Culture, 96; Seneca's Epistle 12 and Emerson's Circles, Emerson Soc Papers, 96; Further Evidence Concerning the Origin of Cromwell's Title Lord Protector: Milton's Pro Se Defensio, Cromwelliana, 97; After Lefkowitz and Bernal: Research Opportunities in Classica Africana, The Negro Hist Bull, 97; auth, "Horace's Ep. 1.24 and Hannibal's Escape from one Ager Falernus," Scholia (00). **CONTACT ADDRESS** Dept of Classics, Wayne State Univ, 431 Manoogian Hall, Detroit, MI 48202. **EMAIL** mronnic@wayne.edu

ROOKE, CONSTANCE M.
PERSONAL Born 11/14/1942, New York, NY **DISCIPLINE** ENGLISH **EDUCATION** Smith Col, BA, 64; Tulane Univ, MA, 66; Univ NC, PhD, 73. **CAREER** Lectr, 69, asst prof, 73, assoc prof, 81, ch Women's Stud Prog, 79, dir, Learning & Teaching Centre, 81-83, Univ Victoria; prof English, 88-, dept ch, 88-93, Associate Vice-Pres Academic, Univ Guelph, 94-. **MEMBERSHIPS** Mem, Can Per Publs Asn; dir, Asn Can Univ Tchrs Eng; Can Res Inst Advan Women; exec, Can Fed Hum; bd dir, PEN Int, Can Ctr. **SELECTED PUBLICATIONS** Auth, Reynolds Price, 83; auth, Fear of the Open Heart, 89; ed, Night Light: Stories of Aging, 86; ed, Writing Away: The PEN-Canada Travel Anthology, 97. **CONTACT ADDRESS** Dept of English Speech and Theatre on Agri Col, Univ of Guelph, Guelph, ON, Canada N1G 2W1. **EMAIL** connier@exec.admin.uoguelph.ca

ROOME, DOROTHY M.
PERSONAL Born Johannesburg, South Africa, m, 3 children **DISCIPLINE** WOMEN'S STUDIES, MEDIA STUDIES **EDUCATION** Univ Ariz, MA, 94; Univ Natal, Durban, PhD, 98. **CAREER** Managing ed, Critical Arts: A J of Cultural Studies, 95-98; lectr/consult, Varsity Col, Durban, 97-98; lectr, Univ Natal, Durban, South Africa, 95-98; adjunct fac/instr, Essex Community Col, Baltimore, Md, fall 98; adjunct fac/instr, Univ Md Baltimore County, spring 99, fall 99; adjunct fac/instr, Univ Ariz, summer 99; adjunct fac/instr, Towson Univ, Baltimore, Md, 98-2000. **HONORS AND AWARDS** Mem, Gender Studies Initiative to establish a department at Univ Natal campus, 95-96; mem, Development Support Commun, a res group involved in formulating commun policy within a multicultural context in South Africa, sponsored by the Human Services Res Coun, 96-97; Centre for Sci Development Scholar, PhD, 96, 97; mem, Ed Bd for Critical Arts: A J of Cultural Studies, 99. **MEMBERSHIPS** Nat Commun Asn, African Coun for Commun Ed, Int Asn Media & Commun Res, Comn on the Status of Women (Univ Ariz), Univ Ariz Child Care Steering Comt. **RESEARCH** Reception analysis for "Homicide, Life Everlasting "(2000), made-for-tv film; women's issues discussed during reception analysis. **SELECTED PUBLICATIONS** Auth, Introduction to "Culture and Media" in Critical Arts: A J for Cultural Studies, 2, 1 (95): auth, "Transformation ands Cultural Reconciliation: 'Simunye', a Flexible Model," in Critical Arts: A J of Cultural Studies, 11, 1 (97); co-theme ed with Ruth Teer-Tomaselli, for "Identity and Popular Culture," in Critical Arts, 11, 1 (97); auth, "Global versus Local: Audience-as-public in South African Situation Comedy," in the Int J for Cultural Studies, 2, 3 (Dec 99); auth, "Humour as 'Cultural Reconciliation' in South African Situation Comedy: Suburban Bliss and Multicultural Viewers," in the J for Film and Video (April 2000). **CONTACT ADDRESS** Dept Women's Studies & Electronic Media & Film, Towson State Univ, 8000 York Rd, Baltimore, MD 21252-0001.

ROORBACH, BILL F.
PERSONAL Born 08/18/1953, Chicago, IL, m, 1990 **DISCIPLINE** ENGLISH **EDUCATION** Ithaca Col, Ba, 76; Columbai Univ, MFA, 90. **CAREER** Assoc Prof, Univ Minn, 91-95; Assoc Prof, Oh State Univ, 95-. **HONORS AND AWARDS** Flannery O'Connor Awd, 99; OH Arts Coun Awd, 99. **MEMBERSHIPS** MLA; AWP; Maine Writers & Pub Alliance. **RESEARCH** Nature Writing; Memoir; Fiction; Journalism. **SELECTED PUBLICATIONS** Auth, Big Band, forthcoming; auth, Writing Life, 98; auth, Summer with Juliet, Houghton, 92. **CONTACT ADDRESS** Dept Eng, Ohio State Univ, Columbus, 164 W 17th Ave, Columbus, OH 43210-1326. **EMAIL** roorbach.1@osu.edu

ROOT, DEANE LESLIE
PERSONAL Born 08/09/1947, Wausau, WI, m, 1972, 2 children **DISCIPLINE** MUSIC, MUSICOLOGY **EDUCATION** Univ IL, Urbana, PhD, 77, M mus, 71; New Col, Sarasota, FL, BA, 68. **CAREER** Prof, Music, Univ Pittsburgh, 98-; Curator, Foster Hall Collection, 82-; Instr, Lake City Comm Col, FL, 81-82; Research Assoc, Univ IL, 76-80; ed, New Grove Dict Music Musicians, 74-76; Lectr, Univ WI, 73. **HONORS AND AWARDS** Woodrow Wilson Fellow, 68; Hon Pi Kappa Lambda, 72; Music Lib Asn Awd, 81; Am Lib Asn, Choice Awd, 91-92; Distinguished Service Citation, Soc Am Music, 00. **MEMBERSHIPS** Am Musicological Soc; Soc Am Music; Music Lib Asn; Am Studies Asn. **RESEARCH** Am Music; Am Musical Theater; Music Bibliography; Am Pop Culture. **SELECTED PUBLICATIONS** The Music of Florida Historic Sites, Tallahassee: The FL State Univ Sch of Music, 83; Resources of American Music History: A Diary of Source Materials from Colonial Times to WW II, gen ed, co auth, with D W Krummel, Jean Geil, Doris J Dyen, Urbana, Chicago, London, Univ Press, 81; American Pop Stage Music, 1860- 1880, Ann Arbor, MI, UMI Res Press, 81, ppbk, 83; The Sketchbook of Stephen Collins Foster, in progress; Nineteen Cent American Musical Theater, gen ed, 16 vols, NY, London, Garland Pub, 94; The Music of Stephen C Foster: A Critical Edition, ed with Steven Saunders, 2 vols, WA, London, Smithsonian Inst Press, 90; "Music Research in Nineteen Cent Theater or the Case of a Burlesquer a Baker and a Pantomime Maker," in Vistas of American Music, Essays and Compositions in Honor of William Kearns, ed Susan L Porter & John Graziano, ch 13, 179-194, Warren, MI, Harmonie Pk Press, 99; Rev of The Voices that are Gone: Themes in Nineteen Cen American Pop Song, by Jon W Finson, J Am Musicological Soc, XLIX/3, 96; "The Stephen Foster-Antonin Dvorak Connection," in Dvorak in America, 1892-1895, ed by John C Tibbets, ch 18, 243-54, Portland OR, Amadeus Press, 93; "The Mythstory of Stephen C Foster, Why His True Story Remains Untold," the Am Music Research Cen J I, 91; "The Pan American Association of Composers, 1928-34," Yearbook for Inter-American Music Research VIII, 72. **CONTACT ADDRESS** Univ of Pittsburgh, Center for Am Music, Pittsburgh, PA 15260. **EMAIL** dlr@pitt.edu

ROOT, ROBERT L., JR.
PERSONAL Born 11/16/1942, Lockport, NY, m, 1983, 3 children **DISCIPLINE** ENGLISH **EDUCATION** State Univ Col at Geneseo, NY, 66; Univ Iowa, MA, 71; Univ Iowa, Phd, 75. **CAREER** English Teacher, Wilson High School, Wilson, NY, 66-70; Asst Prof, Department of English, Central Michigan Univ, 76-80; Assoc Prof, CMU, 80-85; Prof, CMU, 85-. **HONORS AND AWARDS** Charles Carpenter Fries Awd for Distinguished Service to the Profession, 88. **MEMBERSHIPS** National Council of Teachers of English; Conference on College Composition and Communication; Associated Writing Programs; Michigan Council of Teachers of English. **RESEARCH** Composition and rhetoric; Creative nonfiction; English education. **SELECTED PUBLICATIONS** Auth, "Thomas Southerne," Twayne English Authors Series, Boston: G.K. Hall, 81; auth, "The Rhetorics of Popular Culture: Advertising, Advocacy, Entertainment," Contributions to the Study of Popular Culture, Westport, CT: Greenwood Press, 87; auth, "Working at Writing: Columnists and Critics Composing," Carbondale, IL: Southern Illinois University Press, 91; auth, "Teaching Wordsmithery: A Guide for Instructors," New York: Macmillan, 94; 2nd Edition, New York: Allyn & Bacon, 98; auth, "Wordsmithery: A Guide to Working at Writing," New York: Macmillan, 94,2nd Edition, New York: Allyn & Bacon, 98; auth, "Critical Essays on E.B. White, New York: G.K. Hall, 94; auth, "Those Who Do, Can: Teachers Writing, Writers Teaching, with Michael Steinberg, Urbana: NCTE, 96; auth, "The Fourth Genre: Contemporary Writers of/on Creative Nonfiction," with Michael Steinberg, New York: Allyn & Bacon, 98; auth, "Time By Moments Steals Away: The 1848 Journal of Ruth Douglas," Detroit: Wayne State University Press, 98; auth, E.B. White: The Emergence of an Essayist," Iowa City: University of Iowa Press, 99; auth, "The Island Within Us," co-edited with Jill Burkland, Houghton: Isle Royale Natural History Association, 00. **CONTACT ADDRESS** Dept English, Central Michigan Univ, 100 W Preston Rd, Mount Pleasant, MI 48859-0001. **EMAIL** robert.root@cmich.edu

ROPER, ALAN
PERSONAL Born 07/17/1933, Bridgend, Wales, m, 1957, 1 child **DISCIPLINE** ENGLISH **EDUCATION** Cambridge Univ, BA, 57, MA, 61; Dalhousie Univ, MA, 59; Johns Hopkins Univ, PhD (English), 61. **CAREER** Instr, English, Harvard Univ, 61-62; supervisor, English, Queens' Col, Cambridge, 62-65; asst prof, 65-68, assoc prof, 68-71, prof, 71-94, Prof Emeritus, Univ CA, Los Angeles, 94-. **HONORS AND AWARDS** Res fel, Queens' Col, Cambridge, 62-65; Guggenheim fel, 69-70; assoc gen ed, works of John Dryden, 75-78, gen ed, 78-89; assoc investigator, NEH, 76-78, principal investigator, 78-85, 87-89; Clark Library Prof, 79-80. **MEMBERSHIPS** MLA. **RESEARCH** Dryden and seventeenth-century political poetry. **SELECTED PUBLICATIONS** Auth, Dryden's Poetic Kingdoms, Routledge & KP, 65; Arnold's Poetic Landscapes, Johns Hopkins Univ Press, 69; Drawing Parallels and Making Applications in Restoration Literature, in Politics as Reflected in Literature, Clark Library, 89; Dryden, Sunderland, and the Metamorphoses of a Trimmer, Huntington Library Quart, 91; How Much Did Farquhar's Beaux Spend in London? Studies in Bibliography, 92; co-ed, The Works of John Dryden, Vol XVIII, Univ CA Press, 74, Vol XI, 78, Vol XIX, 79, Vol XIII, 84, Vols V & VI, 87, Vol XX, 89, Vol XIV, 92. **CONTACT ADDRESS** Dept of English, Univ of California, Los Angeles, Los Angeles, CA 90095-1530. **EMAIL** roper@humnet.ucla.edu

ROSA, ALFRED
PERSONAL Born 02/07/1942, Waterbury, CT, m, 1967, 1 child **DISCIPLINE** ENGLISH **EDUCATION** Univ Conn, BA, 64; Univ Mass, MA, 66, PhD, 71. **CAREER** Prof Eng, Univ Vt; Fulbright lectr, Univ Sassari, Sardinia, 73-74; found & pres, New England Press, 78- . **HONORS AND AWARDS** Found, Mass Stud in Eng, Univ Mass, 67; trustee, Dick Raymond Found; trustee, Vt Commons Sch; pres, Vt chap, Fulbright Asn. **MEMBERSHIPS** NCTE, Authors Guild. **RESEARCH** Composition, Italian American Lit. **SELECTED PUBLICATIONS** Co-ed, Language Awareness, St Martin's; co-ed, Language: Introductory Readings, St Martin's; co-ed, Subject and Strategy, St Martin's; co-ed, Models for Writers, St Martin's; co-ed, Outlooks and Insights, St Martin's; co-ed, Themes for Writers, St Martin's; co-ed, Controversies: Contemporary Arguments for College Writers, Allyn & Bacon; coauth, The Writer's Brief Handbook, Allyn & Bacon; coauth, The Writer's Pocket Handbook, Allyn & Bacon; ed, The Old Century and The New: Essays in Honor of Charles Angoff; auth, Salem, Transcendentalism, and Hawthorne. **CONTACT ADDRESS** Dept of English, Univ of Vermont, 304 Old Mill, Burlington, VT 05405-4030. **EMAIL** arosa@zoo.uvm.edu

ROSALES, ELISA
PERSONAL Born 08/20/1961, La Coruna, Spain, s **DISCIPLINE** LITERATURE **EDUCATION** Univ Autonoma de Madrid, Licenciatura, 85; Syracuse Univ, PhD, 90. **CAREER** Vis asst prof, Utica Col, 92-93; asst prof, Univ of N Iowa, 93-98; asst prof, N Ariz Univ, 98-. **HONORS AND AWARDS** NHE Inst, SUNY at Binghamton, 93. **MEMBERSHIPS** MLA, Am Asn of Teachers of Spanish & Portugese **RESEARCH** 20th century Spanish Peninsular literature, poetry. **SELECTED PUBLICATIONS** Auth, Comportamiento Etico de la Poesia de Antonio Machado, Juan de la Cuesta (Delaware), 98. **CONTACT ADDRESS** Dept Mod Lang, No Arizona Univ, CB 6004, PO Box Nau, Flagstaff, AZ 86011-0001. **EMAIL** elisa.rosales@nau.edu

ROSE, ELLEN CRONAN
PERSONAL Born 06/03/1938, Greenville, SC, d, 3 children **DISCIPLINE** ENGLISH **EDUCATION** Univ Mass Amherst, PhD, 74. **CAREER** Dir, Women's Studies Program, Univ Nev Las Vegas; Prof, Univ Nev Las Vegas. **SELECTED PUBLICATIONS** Auth, pubs on Contemporary Women Writers, particularly Doris Lessing and Margaret Drabble. **CONTACT ADDRESS** Women's Studies Program, Univ of Nevada, Las Vegas, 4505 Md Pky, Las Vegas, NV 89154-5055. **EMAIL** ecrose@nevada.edu

ROSE, JUDITH
PERSONAL Born 11/01/1947, Philadelphia, PA, m, 1969, 3 children **DISCIPLINE** ENGLISH **EDUCATION** Marlboro Col, BA, 72; Ind Univ, MLS, 77; Univ Calif Davis, MA, 90; PhD, 98. **CAREER** Instr, Solano Comm Col, 96-97; lectr, Univ of Calif Davis, 98-99; Vis asst prof, Allegheny Col, 99-. **HONORS AND AWARDS** UC Regents Diss Fel; UC Davis Humanities Res Awd. **MEMBERSHIPS** MLA; Shakespeare Assoc of Am; AAUP. **RESEARCH** Early Modern Women Writers, Feminist Theory. **SELECTED PUBLICATIONS** Auth, "The Child's Ear", Shock's Bridge, 88; auth, Monkey Dreams", Blind Date 4, 88; auth, "Against Angels", Whiskey Island, 90; auth, "In the Specimen Room", Carbuncle 2, 90; auth, "Pray 4 Me", Iowa Rev 20.3 (90); auth, "Woodworms, Christ's Tears", Va Quarterly Rev 67.2 (91); auth, "The Blue Fire", Carbuncle 3, 92; auth, "Down North Bradford Street", Equinox II.1 93; auth, "gift", Prairie Schooner 68.2 94; auth, "Arabesque", Ind Rev 17.1, 94; auth, "Mirrors of Language, Mirrors of Self: the conceptualization of Artistic Identity in Gaspara Stampa and Sofonisba Anguissola", in Mothers and Others: Caregiver Figures in the Early Modern Period, eds Naomi J. Miller and Naomi Yavneh, Ashgate, London (forthcoming). **CONTACT ADDRESS** Dept English, Allegheny Col, 520 N Main St, Meadville, PA 16335-3903. **EMAIL** jrose@alleg.edu

ROSE, PETER WIRES
PERSONAL Born 05/13/1936, Paterson, NJ, m, 1997, 2 children **DISCIPLINE** CLASSICS **EDUCATION** Williams Col, BA, 57; Harvard Univ, MA, 58; PhD, 67. **CAREER** Lectr, 63-66, Yale Univ; asst prof, 71-74, Univ Texas Austin; vis assoc prof, 74, Haverford Col; fac mem, 77-80, prof and chmn, classics dept, 75-83, prof, 75-, Miami Univ. **HONORS AND AWARDS** Phi Beta Kappa, 56; Woodrow Wilson Fel, 57-58; Frank Knox fel, Harvard, 61; Fulbright Fel, Rome, 61-62; Billings fel, Wale, Summer, 67; Morse fel, Yale, 68-69; appointed fel at the Ctr for Hellenic Studies in Washington D.C., 75-76; Nat Endowment for the Humanities fel, 79-80. **RESEARCH** Homer Greek tragedy; Pindar and Greek lyric poetry. **SELECTED PUBLICATIONS** Auth, "Teaching Greek Myth and Confronting Contemporary Myths," in Classics and Cinema, ed. Martin M. Winkler (Bucknell Univ Press, London and Toronto, 91), 17-39; auth, Sons of the Gods, Children of Earth: Ideology and Literary Form in Ancient Greece, Cornell Univ Press (Ithaca, NY), 92; auth, "The Case for Not Ignoring Marx in the Study of Women in Antiquity," in Feminist Theory and Classics, ed. Nancy Rabinowitz and Amy Richlin (Routledge, 93); auth, "Historicizing Sophocles' Ajax," in History, Tragedy, Theory, ed. Barbara Goff (Univ of Tex Press, 94); auth, "Cicero and the Rhetoric of Imperialism: Putting Politics Back into Political Rhetoric," Rhetorica 13.4 (95): 359-399; auth, "The Politics of the Trilogy Form: Lucia, the Oresteia, and the Godfather," Film-Historia 5.2-3 (95): 93-116; auth, "Ideology in the Illiad: Polis, Basileus, Theoi" Arethusa 30 (97): 151-199; auth, "Theorizing Athenian Imperialism and the Athenian State," in Contextualizing Classics: Ideology, Performance, Dialogue. Essays in Honor of John J. Peradotto, ed. Thomas M. Falkner, Nancy Felson, and David Konstan (Rowman and Littlefield, 99). **CONTACT ADDRESS** Dept of Classics, Miami Univ, Oxford, OH 45056. **EMAIL** rosepw@muohio.edu

ROSE, PHYLLIS DAVIDOFF
PERSONAL Born 10/26/1942, New York, NY, 1 child **DISCIPLINE** ENGLISH LITERATURE **EDUCATION** Radcliffe Col, BA, 64; Yale Univ, MA, 65; Harvard Univ, PhD(English), 70. **CAREER** Asst prof, 69-76, assoc prof, 76-81, Prof English, Wesleyan Univ, 81- ; vis prof, Univ Calif, Berkeley, 81-82. **HONORS AND AWARDS** Nat Endowment for Humanities grant, 73-74 **RESEARCH** Nineteenth and 20th century English literature; biography. **SELECTED PUBLICATIONS** Auth, Woman of Letters: A Life of Virginia Woolf, Oxford Univ, 78; auth, Parallel Lives, Knopf, 83; auth, Writing of Women, Wesleyan, 85; auth, Jazz Cleopatra: Josephine Baker in He Time, 89; ed, The Norton Book of Women's Lives, Norton, 93; auth, The Year of Reading Proust, Scribner, 97. **CONTACT ADDRESS** Dept of English, Wesleyan Univ, Middletown, CT 06457.

ROSE, TOBY
PERSONAL Born 02/09/1941, Chicago, IL, s, 3 children **DISCIPLINE** ENGLISH **EDUCATION** Ohio State Univ, BA; UT, Med, 74; MA, 88; Univ Toledo, PhD, 77. **CAREER** Prof, N Mich Univ, 77- . **HONORS AND AWARDS** Fulbright Schol Lect, 92. **RESEARCH** Literary lives abroad (Immigrant literature), Caribbean literature/post-Colonial, Grammar teaching. **SELECTED PUBLICATIONS** Auth, The Immigrant Experience in North American Literature, Greenwood Press, (99); co-auth, Carving out a Niche. **CONTACT ADDRESS** Dept English, No Michigan Univ, 1401 Presque Isle Ave, Marquette, MI 49855-5305. **EMAIL** trose@nmu.edu

ROSEN, DAVID
PERSONAL Born 09/21/1938, San Francisco, CA, m, 1960 **DISCIPLINE** MUSIC **EDUCATION** Reed Col, BA, 60; Univ Calif at Berkeley, MA, 64, PhD, 76. **CAREER** Prof **HONORS AND AWARDS** Amer Coun Learned Societies, Grant-in-Aid, 85; Nat Endowment for the Humanities felp for Independent Study and Res, 79; Amer Philos Soc Grant-in-Aid, 77; Martha Baird Rockefeller Found Grant-in-Aid, 68-69; Woodrow Wilson fel, 60-61. **MEMBERSHIPS** Exec bd, Amer Inst Verdi Stud; Fondo Ruggero Leoncavallo, Consiglio scientifico; Amer Musicol Soc. **RESEARCH** Verdi; music in 19th-century Italy; opera theory and criticism; Mozart. **SELECTED PUBLICATIONS** Auth, Verdi: Requiem, Cambridge Music Handbooks, Cambridge: Cambridge UP, 95; Critical edition of Verdi's Messa da Requiem, in The Works of Giuseppe Verdi, ser III, v 1, Chicago and London; Milan: Univ Chicago Press and Ricordi, 90; Meter, Character, and Tinta in Verdi's Operas, in Verdi's Middle Period: Source Studies, Analysis, and Performance Practice 1849-1859, Chicago and London: Univ Chicago Press, 97; 'Unexpectedness' and 'Inevitability' in Mozart's Piano Concertos, in Mozart's Piano Concertos: Text, Context, Interpretation, Ann Arbor: Univ Mich Press, 96; Reprise as Resolution in Verdi's Requiem, Theory and Practice 19, 94; Cone's and Kivy's 'World of Opera', Cambridge Opera J 4, 92; How Verdi's Serious Operas End, in Atti del XIV Congresso della Societa internazionale di musicologia, Turin: EDT, 90; co-ed, Verdi's Macbeth: A Sourcebook, NY: Norton, 84; Coauth, "La disposizione scenica per 'Un ballo in maschera': Studio critico," in Un ballo in maschera di Giuseppe Verdi, Ricordi (Milan), 00; ed, The Verdi Forum, Jrnl of Amer Inst Verdi Stud. **CONTACT ADDRESS** Dept of Music, Cornell Univ, 104 Lincoln Hall, Ithaca, NY 14853. **EMAIL** dbr2@cornell.edu

ROSEN, KENNETH MARK
PERSONAL Born 03/07/1938, New York, NY, 2 children **DISCIPLINE** AMERICAN LITERATURE **EDUCATION** Cornell Univ, BA, 59; San Francisco State Univ, MA, 64; Univ NM, PhD, 69. **CAREER** Asst prof, 69-73, Assoc Prof Eng, 73-80, prof eng, Dickinson Col, 80-, Ford Found hum grants, 70-71 & 72; ed, Hemingway Notes, 71-74; sr Fulbright lectr Am lit, Univ Thessaloniki, Greece, 75-76, Beijing Univ, China, 80-81, Mada Univ, Gadjah Yogyakarta, Indonesia, 90-91. **MEMBERSHIPS** Assn Studies Am Indian Lit; MLA; Am Studies Asn; AAUP. **RESEARCH** The Am novel; Am Indian lit; Hemingway. **SELECTED PUBLICATIONS** Auth, O'Neill's Brown and Wilde's Gray, Mod Drama, 2/71; Kate Chopin's The Awakening: Ambiguity as art, J Am Studies, 8/71; Ten eulogies: Hemingway's Spanish death, Bull NY Pub Libr, 74; The Man to Send Rain Clouds, 74 & Voices of the Rainbow, 75, Viking; Heminway Repossessed, Praeger, 94. **CONTACT ADDRESS** Dept of Eng, Dickinson Col, 1 Dickinson Col, Carlisle, PA 17013-2897.

ROSEN, NINA
PERSONAL Born Los Angeles, CA, m, 1983, 3 children **DISCIPLINE** ENGLISH **EDUCATION** San Diego State Univ, BA, 71; Univ S Calif, MA, 84. **CAREER** Asst Prof, Glendale Cmty Col, 991-97; Instructor, Santa Rosa Jr Col, 97-. **HONORS AND AWARDS** Outstanding Teacher, USC, 83; Outstanding Publications, SRJC, 00. **RESEARCH** Second Language Reading Fluency. **SELECTED PUBLICATIONS** Auth, My New School; auth, Mi Nueva Escuela; auth, Javier, A Young Man Arrives in the US; auth, Changing Generations. **CONTACT ADDRESS** Dept Eng, Santa Rosa Junior Col, 1501 Mendocio Ave, Santa Rosa, CA 95401-4332. **EMAIL** Rsrndr@aol.com

ROSEN, ROBERT CHARLES
PERSONAL Born 12/29/1947, Brooklyn, NY, d, 1992, 1 child **DISCIPLINE** ENGLISH **EDUCATION** MIT, BS, Math, 70; Rutgers Univ, MA, PhD, Eng, 78. **CAREER** Prof, Eng, William Paterson Univ, 78-. **RESEARCH** American literature; politics and literature **SELECTED PUBLICATIONS** auth, John Dos passos: Politics and the Writer, Univ of Nebr, 81; coed, Politics of Education: Essays from "Radical Teacher", SUNY Press, 90; coauth, Literature and Society: An Introduction to Fiction, Poetry, Drama, Nonfiction, Prentice-Hall, 90; coauth, Against the Current: Readings for Writers, Prentice Hall, 98. **CONTACT ADDRESS** Dept of English, William Paterson Univ of New Jersey, 300 Pompton Rd, Wayne, NY 07470. **EMAIL** rosenr@wpunj.edu

ROSENBERG, BETH C.
DISCIPLINE 20TH CENTURY BRITISH LITERATURE **EDUCATION** PhD, 92. **CAREER** Instr, Univ Nev, Las Vegas. **RESEARCH** Virginia Woolf. **SELECTED PUBLICATIONS** Auth, How Should One Write a Memoir?: Virginia Woolfs 'A Sketch of the Past', in Re:Reading, Re:Writing. Re:

Teaching Virginia Woolf, eds, Eileen Barrett and Patricia Cramer, Pace UP, 95; Virginia Woolf and Samuel Johnson: Common Readers, St Martin's Press and Macmillan Publ, 95; Virginia Woolf, in The St James Guide to Feminist Writers,St James Press, 96; Sandra Gilbert and Susan Gubar, in The St. James Guide to Feminist Writers, St James Press, 96; '..in the wake of the matrons': Virginia Woolf's Rewriting of Fanny Burney, in Virginia Woolf: Texts and Contexts, eds, Beth Rigel Daugherty and Eileen Barrett, Pace UP, 96; coed, Virginia Woolf and the Essay, St Martin's Press and Macmillan Publ, 97. **CONTACT ADDRESS** Dept of Eng, Univ of Nevada, Las Vegas, 4505 Maryland Pkwy, PO Box 455011, Las Vegas, NV 89154. **EMAIL** drbeth@nevada.edu

ROSENBERG, BRUCE
PERSONAL Born 07/27/1934, New York, NY, m, 1981, 4 children **DISCIPLINE** ENGLISH; FOLKLORE **EDUCATION** Hofstra Univ, BA, 55; Pa State Univ, MA, 62; Ohio State Univ, PhD, 65. **CAREER** Instr English, Univ Wis-Milwaukee, 62; asst prof, Univ Calif, Santa Barbara, 65-67 & Univ Va, 67-69; prof English & comp lit, Pa State Univ, 69-77; prof to prof emer English lit & American Civilization, Brown Univ, 77-. **HONORS AND AWARDS** Am Coun Learned Soc fel, 67-68; James Russell Lowell Prize, 70; Nat Endowment for Humanities fel, 72-73; Guggenheim fel, 82-83. **MEMBERSHIPS** MLA; Folklore Fel Int; Am Folklore Soc. **RESEARCH** Middle English literature; folklore; comparative literature. **SELECTED PUBLICATIONS** Auth, Annus Mirabilis distilled, PMLA, 6/64; Wandering Angus & Celtic renaissance, Philol Quart, fall 67; Lord of the fire Flies, Centennial Rev, winter 67; ed, The Folksongs of Virginia, Univ Va, 69; auth, The Art of the American Folk Preacher, Oxford Univ, 70; co-ed, Medieval Literature and Folklore Studies, Rutgers Univ, 71; auth, Custer and the Epic of Defeat, Penn State, 75; The Code of the West, Ind Univ, 82; The Neutral Ground, 94. **CONTACT ADDRESS** Dept English, Brown Univ, Box 1892, Providence, RI 02912-1892. **EMAIL** bruce_rosenberg@brown.edu

ROSENBERG, EDGAR
PERSONAL Born 09/21/1925, Germany, d **DISCIPLINE** ENGLISH **EDUCATION** Cornell Univ, BA, 49, MA, 50; Stanford Univ, PhD, 58. **CAREER** Instr to asst prof, Harvard Univ, 57-65; assoc prof to prof, Cornell Univ, 65-. **HONORS AND AWARDS** Stanford Fel, 51-52; Bread Loaf Writing Fel, 52; Res Grant, Cornell, 69, 70; Guggenheim Fel, 73-74; Fulbright Fel, Haifa Univ, 88; Clark Distinguished Teaching Awd, 93. **RESEARCH** Nineteenth and Twentieth Century English and Continental Fiction, Dickens, History of the Nazi Period, German Judaica. **SELECTED PUBLICATIONS** Auth, From Shylock to Svengali: Jewish Stereotypes in English Fiction, Stanford Univ Pr, 60; auth, "The Jew in Western Drama", Bull of The NY Pub Libr 72, (68): 442-91; auth, "A Preface to Great Expectations", Dickens Studies Annual 2, (72): 294-335; auth, "Restoration in Cloisterham" Dickens Studies Newsletter 5 (74): 70-84; auth, "Last Words on 'Great Expectations': A Textual Brief on the Six Endings", Dickens Studies Annual 9, (81): 87-115; auth, "Vanish Acts", Commentary 73, (May 82): 50-62; ed, Charles Dickens, Great Expectations, W.W. Norton, (NY, 99); auth, "Hitler Over My Head", Judaism 48 (99): 313-333. **CONTACT ADDRESS** Dept English, Cornell Univ, 250 Goldwin Smith Hall, Ithaca, NY 14853-3201. **EMAIL** er31@cornell.edu

ROSENBERG, JOHN D.
PERSONAL Born 04/17/1929, Brooklyn, NY, m, 1972, 1 child **DISCIPLINE** ENGLISH LITERATURE **EDUCATION** Columbia Univ, BA, 50, MA, 51; Clare Col, BA, 53; Cambridge Univ, MA, 58; Columbia Univ, PhD, 60. **CAREER** Instr, Harvard Univ; Princeton Univ; Univ Brit Columbia; William Peterfield Trent prof, 62. **HONORS AND AWARDS** Kellett award; award for distinguished serv, Columbia Col Core Curriculum; Amer Coun of Learned Soc; fel, Guggenheim; fel, NEH; ch, hum prog; ed bd, victorian stud; nineteenth-century lit; exec comm, mla victorian div; adv bd, victorians inst jour; the carlyle annual. **MEMBERSHIPS** Modern Lang Asn. **RESEARCH** John Ruskin. **SELECTED PUBLICATIONS** Ed, works by Ruskin, Mayhew, Swinburne, and Tennyson; auth, The Darkening Glass, 61; The Fall of Camelot, 73; Carlyle and the Burden of History, 85. **CONTACT ADDRESS** Dept of Eng, Columbia Col, New York, 2960 Broadway, New York, NY 10027-6902. **EMAIL** jdr2@columbia.edu

ROSENBERG, JUDITH
PERSONAL Born 01/26/1947, Washington, DC, m, 1968, 2 children **DISCIPLINE** ENGLISH **EDUCATION** Univ Ill at Urbana, BA; MA; PhD. **CAREER** Instr, Ind Univ, 73-78; instr, Univ Ill, 68-72; assoc dean, Col of Lake Cnty, 86-90; prof, 81-00. **HONORS AND AWARDS** Univ Fel; Teach Asstshp; Res Asstshp; Bk of Hons; Dean's List. **MEMBERSHIPS** STC; NCTE; DH Lawrence Soc. **RESEARCH** DH Lawrence; SY Agnon; Isak Dinesen; modern British literature; technical communication; online education. **SELECTED PUBLICATIONS** auth, "Assessing Online Student Learning via Dante's Test," Virtual Univ J (00); auth, "Dreaming of Skates," Kaleidoscope (97); auth, "Isak Dinesen's 'Blue Jar'," in Reference Guide to Short Fiction (St James Press, 94); auth, "SY Agnon's 'The Kerchief'," in Reference Guide to Short Fiction (St James Press, 94). **CONTACT ADDRESS** Dept Humanities, Col of Lake County, 19351 West Washington St, Grayslake, IL 60030-1148. **EMAIL** jrosenb@clc.cc.il.us

ROSENBERG, MARVIN
PERSONAL Born Fresno, CA, 1 child **DISCIPLINE** DRAMATIC ART **EDUCATION** Univ CA, AB, MA, PhD(English). **CAREER** Ed, Off War Inform, 43-45; chief Thailand sect, int broadcasting div, US Dept State, 45-47; prof emer, dramatic art, Univ Ca, Berkeley, 48-. **HONORS AND AWARDS** Guggenheim fel, Falger Library-British Academy fel; NEH fel. **MEMBERSHIPS** Shakespeare Asn Am; MLA; Int Fed Theatres Res; Int Shakespeare Asn. **RESEARCH** Literature and criticism of drama; Shakespeare; theatre history. **SELECTED PUBLICATIONS** Auth, The Masks of Othello, 61, The Masks of King Lear, 72 & The Masks of Macbeth, 78, Univ CA; The Masks of Hamlet, 92; The Adventures of a Shakespeare Scholar, 97. **CONTACT ADDRESS** Dept Dramatic Art, Univ of California, Berkeley, Berkeley, CA 94720-2560.

ROSENBERG, TEYA
PERSONAL Born 11/10/1962, Martinsville, IN **DISCIPLINE** ENGLISH **EDUCATION** Memorial Univ Nfld, BA, 85; Carleton Univ, MA, 88; Univ Alta, PhD, 94. **CAREER** Sessional Instr, Univ of Alta, 88-96; Asst Prof, Southwest Tex State Univ, 96-00. **HONORS AND AWARDS** English Dept Outstanding Sessional Instr, Univ of Alta, 93. **MEMBERSHIPS** MLA, Asn of Can Col and Univ Teachers of English, C's Lit Asn. **RESEARCH** Children's and Young Adult fantasy, Magical realism, Picture books. **SELECTED PUBLICATIONS** Auth, "Romanticism and Archetypes in Ruth Nichol's 'Song of the Pearl'," in Literature and the Child: Romantic Continuations, Postmodern Contestations, ed. James H. McGavran (Univ of Iowa Press, 99), 233-255. **CONTACT ADDRESS** Dept English, Southwest Texas State Univ, 601 Univ Dr, San Macros, TX 78666-4685. **EMAIL** tr11@swt.edu

ROSENBLATT, JASON PHILIP
PERSONAL Born 07/03/1941, Baltimore, MD, m, 1964, 2 children **DISCIPLINE** ENGLISH LITERATURE **EDUCATION** Yeshiva Univ, BA, 63; Brown Univ, MA, 66, PhD, 68. **CAREER** Asst prof English, Univ PA, 68-74; asst prof, 74-76, assoc prof eng, Georgetown Univ, 76-83, prof of English, 83-; Vis lectr, Swarthmore Col, 72-73, Univ MD, spring, 80; Guggenheim Mem Found fel, 77. **HONORS AND AWARDS** Nat Endowment for Hum Fel, 84, 90-91; Milton Soc Amer Hanford Awd, 88; Milton Soc Am, vice pres, 98, pres 99; Editorial board, Milton Studies, 92; Folger Shakespeare libr/NEH Fel, 99-00; Adjunct Fel, Ctr for Advanced Judaic Studies, Univ of Pennsylvania, 99-00. **MEMBERSHIPS** Milton Soc Am; Modern language Assoc (MLA); Renaissance Society of America. **RESEARCH** The works of John Milton; 17th century Eng relig poetry. **SELECTED PUBLICATIONS** Auth, Celestial entertainment in Eden: Book V of Paradise Lost, Harvard Theol Rev, 10/69; Structural unity and temporal concordance: The war in heaven in Paradise Lost, PMLA, 1/72; Adam's pisgah vision, J English Lit Hist, 3/72; The mosaic voice in Paradise Lost, In: Eyes Fast Fixt, Univ Pittsburgh, 75; Audacious Neighborhood: Idolatry in Paradise Lost, Book I, Philol Quart, summer 75; Aspects of incest in Hamlet, Shakespeare Quart, 78; Sir Edward Dering's Milton, Mod Philol, 5/82; Angelic tact: Raphael on creation, In: Milton and the Middle Ages, Bucknell Univ Press, 82; co-ed, Not in Heaven: Coherence and Complexity in Biblical Narrative, IN Univ Press, 91; auth, Torah and Law in Paradise Lost, Princeton Univ Press, 94. **CONTACT ADDRESS** Dept of Eng, Georgetown Univ, PO Box 571131, Washington, DC 20057-1131. **EMAIL** rosenblj@gunet.georgetown.edu

ROSENBLUM, JOSEPH
PERSONAL Born 12/19/1947, Waterburg, CT, m, 1975, 1 child **DISCIPLINE** ENGLISH **EDUCATION** Univ Connecticut, BA, 69; Univ North Carolina at Chapel Hill, M.L.S., 76; Duke Univ, PhD, 75. **CAREER** Lecturer, Univ of North Carolina at Greensboro, 80. **HONORS AND AWARDS** Phi Beta Kappa, 68; Best Article, Southeastern Librarian, 82; Second Prize, Oxford Univ Press, English Detective Story Contest, 90. **MEMBERSHIPS** Trollope Society; Alcuin Society. **RESEARCH** British Literature; History of the Book. **SELECTED PUBLICATIONS** Auth, "A Bibliographic History of the Book: An Annotated Guide to the Literature, Lanham, MD: Scarecrow, 95; auth "Thomas Holcroft; Literature and Politics in England in the Age of the French Revolution, Lewiston, NY: Edwin Mellen, 95; ed, Shakespeare, Pasadena, CA: Salem Press, 98; ed, "Sir Walter Wilson Greg: A Selection of His Writings, Lanham, MD: Scarecrow, 98; auth, "The Prince of Forgers, New Castle, DE: Oak Knoll Press, 98; auth, "Practice to Deceive, New Castle, DE: Oak Knoll Press, 00. **CONTACT ADDRESS** Dept English, Univ of No Carolina, Greensboro, 1000 Spring Garden, Greensboro, NC 27412-0001.

ROSENHEIM, SHAWN
DISCIPLINE ENGLISH **EDUCATION** Oberlin, BA, 84; Yale Univ, PhD, 92. **CAREER** Assoc prof. **RESEARCH** Nonfiction film; technology and culture, Hollywood film. **SELECTED PUBLICATIONS** Auth, The Cryptographic Imagination: Secret Writing from Edgar Poe to the Internet; co-ed, The American Face of Edgar Allan Poe; essays on literature and film in, Persistence of Hist, Film Quart, NY Times **CONTACT ADDRESS** Dept of English, Williams Col, Statson d-24, Williamstown, MA 01267. **EMAIL** srosenheim@williams.edu

ROSENTHAL, JUDITH ANN
PERSONAL Born 08/22/1945, Syracuse, NY, m, 1980 **DISCIPLINE** ENGLISH LITERATURE **EDUCATION** State Univ NYork Binghamton, BA, 66; Univ Pittsburgh, MA, 67, PhD(English), 70. **CAREER** Asst instr English, Univ Pittsburgh, 70-71; asst prof, 71-77, assoc prof, 77-79, Prof, Calif State Univ, Fresno, 79-, Ed, Anonymous: A Journal for the Woman Writer, 73-75. **HONORS AND AWARDS** NEH seminar, 96. **MEMBERSHIPS** MLA **RESEARCH** Women in literature; medieval drama; Renaissance literature. **SELECTED PUBLICATIONS** Coauth, Norman Mailer: Prisoner of Sexism, Lilith, 4/71; auth, Anaisnin: Beyond race, culture, Calif Advocate, 5/74; auth, Margery Kempe and Medieval Anti-Judaic Ideology, Medieval Encounters, 99. **CONTACT ADDRESS** Dept of English, California State Univ, Fresno, 5245 N Backer, Fresno, CA 93740-8001. **EMAIL** judithr@csufresno.edu

ROSENTHAL, MARGARET F.
DISCIPLINE ITALIAN RENAISSANCE ITALIAN LITERATURE **EDUCATION** Yale Univ, PhD. **CAREER** Asso prof, Univ Southern Calif. **RESEARCH** Women writers in early-modern Venice; social, cultural, political forces in Venice in the 16th century. **SELECTED PUBLICATIONS** Auth, The Honest Courtesan, Veronica Franco, Citizen and Writer in Sixteenth-Century Venice, 92. **CONTACT ADDRESS** Col Letters, Arts & Sciences, Univ of So California, University Park Campus, Los Angeles, CA 90089.

ROSENTHAL, MICHAEL
PERSONAL Born 04/27/1937, m, 3 children **DISCIPLINE** BRITISH LITERATURE AND CULTURE **EDUCATION** Harvard Univ, BA, 58; Univ Wis, MA, 59; Columbia Univ, PhD, 67. **CAREER** Roberto William Campbell Professor in the Humanities, 00-. **HONORS AND AWARDS** Rockefeller Humanities Fel, 78-79; Guggenheim Fel, 94-95; Spencer Found Fel, 94-95. **SELECTED PUBLICATIONS** Auth, Virginia Woolf and The Character Factory: Baden-Powell's Boy Scouts and the Imperatives of Empire. **CONTACT ADDRESS** Dept of Eng, Columbia Col, New York, 2960 Broadway, New York, NY 10027-6902.

ROSENTHAL, PEGGY
PERSONAL Born 02/23/1944, Baltimore, MD **DISCIPLINE** LITERATURE **EDUCATION** Brown Univ, BA, 64; Rutgers Univ, PhD, 71. **CAREER** Asst prof, Wheaton Col, 71-74; independent scholar, 75-; co-director, Poetry Retreats, 99-. **HONORS AND AWARDS** Hon Mention, Book of the Year, Oxford Univ Pr, 00. **MEMBERSHIPS** MLA, Nat Coalition of Independent Scholars. **RESEARCH** Poetry and Spirituality. **SELECTED PUBLICATIONS** Auth, Words and Value, Oxford Univ Pr, 84; auth, "The Nuclear Mushroom Chore as Cultured Image," Am Lit Hist, (91); coed, Divine Inspiration: The Life of Jesus in World Poetry, Oxford Univ Pr, 98; auth, The Poets' Jesus, Oxford Univ Pr, 00. **CONTACT ADDRESS** 537 Harvard St, Rochester, NY 14607-3325. **EMAIL** pegrosenthal@yahoo.com

ROSENWALD, JOHN
PERSONAL Born 06/25/1943, IL, m, 1976, 1 child **DISCIPLINE** AMERICAN POETICS **EDUCATION** Univ Ill, BA, 64; MA, 65; Duke Univ, PhD, 69. **CAREER** Asst prof, Assumption Col, 69-75; asst to assoc prof, Beloit Col, 76-. **HONORS AND AWARDS** Fulbright Scholar, 65-66, 96-97, 01-02; Underkofler Awd for Teaching Excellence, 96. **MEMBERSHIPS** MLA. **RESEARCH** Rilke's Late Work, Victorian culture, Contemporary American Poetry, Contemporary Chinese Poetry. **SELECTED PUBLICATIONS** Auth, Smoking People: Encountering the New Chinese Poetry, 88; coed, Fissures, 00. **CONTACT ADDRESS** Granite Rose Farm, Box 389, South Andover, ME 04216. **EMAIL** rosey@beloit.edu

ROSENWALD, LAWRENCE A.
DISCIPLINE ENGLISH **EDUCATION** Columbia Col, BA, 70; Columbia, MA, 71, PhD, 79. **CAREER** PROF, ENG, WELLESLEY COLL **MEMBERSHIPS** Am Antiquarian Soc **SELECTED PUBLICATIONS** Auth, "Cotton Mather as Diarist," Prospects 8; auth, "Sewall's Diary and the Margins of Puritan Literature," Am Lit, 86; auth, Emerson and the Art of the Diary, Oxford, 88; auth, Theory, Texted Music, Performance," Jour of Musicol, Winter 93; ed & trans, Martin Buber and Franz Rosenzweig, Scripture and Translation, Ind Univ Press, 94. **CONTACT ADDRESS** Dept of Eng, Wellesley Col, Wellesley, MA 02181. **EMAIL** lrosenwald@wellesley.edu

ROSIVACH, VINCENT JOHN
PERSONAL Born 05/08/1940, Jersey City, NJ **DISCIPLINE** CLASSICAL STUDIES **EDUCATION** Fordham Univ, AB, 61, MA, 64, PhD(classics), 66. **CAREER** Adj instr Latin, Sch Educ, Fordham Univ, 63-64; from instr to assoc prof, 65-76, Prof Classics, Fairfield Univ, 76-. **MEMBERSHIPS** Am Philol Asn; Class Asn New Eng; Asn of Ancient Hist. **RESEARCH**

Greek and Roman drama; Greek history. **SELECTED PUBLICATIONS** Auth, Plautine stage settings, Trans & Proc Am Philol Soc, 70; Manuscripts of Matthias Corvinus in the Barberini Collection, Manuscripta, 71; Terence, Adelphoe 155-9, Class Quart, 73; Terence, Adelphoe 60-63, Class Philol, 75; The first stasimon of the Hecuba, Am J Philol, 75; Sophocles' Ajax, Class J, 76; Hector in the Rhesus, Hermes, 77; Earthborns and Olympians: The parodos of the Ion, Class Quart, 77; The System of Public Sacrifice in Fourth Century Athens, Scholars Press, 94; When a Young Man Falls in Love: The Sexual Exploitation of Women in New Comedy, Routledge, 98. **CONTACT ADDRESS** Greek and Roman Studies, Fairfield Univ, 1073 N Benson Rd, Fairfield, CT 06430-5195. **EMAIL** Rosivach@fair1.fairfield.edu

ROSOWSKI, SUSAN JEAN
PERSONAL Born 01/02/1942, Topeka, KS, m, 1963, 2 children **DISCIPLINE** AMERICAN LITERATURE **EDUCATION** Whittier Col, BA, 64; Univ Ariz, MA, 67, PhD, 74. **CAREER** Instr, 71-76, Univ NE, Lincoln, Asst prof Brit romantics and women's studies, Univ NE, Omaha, 76-78, assoc prof, Univ NE, Omaha, 78-82, Univ NE, Lincoln, 82-86, Prof, Univ NE, Lincoln, 86-91, Adele Hall Prof, 91-97, Adele Hall distinguished prof, Univ NE, Lincoln, 97; Danforth Found Assoc, 80; Berdahl-Rolvaag lectr, Augustana Col, 86; vis scholar, Willamette Univ, 89; Lectr Eng Scholar series, Univ CA Davis, 89; vis scholar, St Lawrence Univ, 90; script consult, Singing Cather's Song: A Portrait of Mildred R Bennett, 89-90, and O Pioneers, 89-91. **HONORS AND AWARDS** Dir, Int Sems on Willa Cather, 83, 85, 87, 90, 00; Great Tchr Awd, Univ Neb-Omaha, 84; Annis Chaikin Sorensen Awd for Dist Tchg in the Human, Univ Neb-Lincoln, 86; pres, Western Lit Asn, 86-87; NEH funding for Willa Cather Schlrly Ed, 94, 97, 99; NEH Grant, 99-00; Thomas J Lyon Awd for Outstanding Bk in Am Lit Crit, 00. **MEMBERSHIPS** Counc Edof Learned Jour; MLA; Am Lit Asn; Western Lit Asn; Willa Cather Pioneer Mem and Educ Found; AAUP; Margaret Fuller Soc; Ellen Glasgow Soc; Soc for Textual Editing; Nebra Center for the Bk; Asn for the Study of Lit & the Environ; Soc for the Study of Am Women Writers. **RESEARCH** Willa Cather; Am lit; Western and Plains lit; Women's studies; environ lit. **SELECTED PUBLICATIONS** Auth, The Voyage Perilous: Willa Cather's Romanticism, Univ Neb Pr (Lincoln, NE), 86; ed & contrib, Approaches to Teaching Cather's 'My Antonia,' MLA (New York, NY), 89; guest ed, Cather in the Classroom, Neb Engl J (Fall, 91); auth, "Prospects for the Study of Willa Cather," Res's for Am Lit Study 22:2 (96): 147-165; auth, "The Western Hero as Logos, or, Unmaking Meaning," Western Am Lit 32.2 (November 97): 269-292; sr sec ed, Updating the Literary West, Tex Christian Pr, 97; auth, The Place of Literature and the Cultural Phenomenon of Willa Cather, Univ Neb Dist Prof Lect Series, 98; auth, Birthing a Nation: Gender, Creativity, and the Significance of the West in American Literature, univ Neb Pr, 99; guest ed, American Literary Realism: A Special Cather Issue, 00; co-auth, "The Issue of Authority in a Scholarly Edition: Editing Cather," in Textual Studies and the Common Reader, ed Alex Pettit (Univ Ga Pr, 00). **CONTACT ADDRESS** Eng Dept, Univ of Nebraska, Lincoln, PO Box 880333, Lincoln, NE 68588-0333. **EMAIL** srosowski2@unl.edu

ROSS, BILLY I.
DISCIPLINE COMPUTER-ASSISTED REPORTING, EMERGING MEDIA TECHNOLOGIES **EDUCATION** Southern Ill Univ, PhD, 64. **CAREER** Distinguished vis prof, La State Univ; Dir, Jour sch, Tex Tech Univ. **MEMBERSHIPS** Mem, Accrediting Coun in Jour and Mass Commun; pres, Am Soc of Jour Sch Adminr, Am Acad of Advert. **SELECTED PUBLICATIONS** Auth, The Case Approach to Problem Situations, Advert Educ Works, 89; The Status of Advertising Education, Advert Educ Works, 91; coauth, Where Shall I Go To Study Advertising and Public Relations?, Advert Educ Works, 65; ed, Seventy-Five Years of Journalism and Mass Communication Leadership, Asn of Sch of Jour and Mass Commun, 93. **CONTACT ADDRESS** The Manship Sch of Mass Commun, Louisiana State Univ and A&M Col, Baton Rouge, LA 70803. **EMAIL** bilross@lsu.edu

ROSS, CATHERINE S.
PERSONAL Born 11/04/1945, London, ON, Canada **DISCIPLINE** COMMUNICATIONS **EDUCATION** Univ Toronto, MA, 68; Univ W Ont, BA, 67, PhD, 76. **CAREER** Fac mem, 73-, assoc dean, grad stud, 95-96, acting dean, Communications Open Learning, 96-97, prof, Univ Western Ontario. **HONORS AND AWARDS** Sci Writers Can Awd, 97. **MEMBERSHIPS** Ont Lib Asn. **RESEARCH** Reading and the reading experience; the reference transaction; information seeking and use. **SELECTED PUBLICATIONS** Auth, Readers' Advisory Service: New Directions, RQ 30, (91): 503-518; auth, A Double Life: A Biography of Alice Munro, Toronto: Toronto: ECW Press, 92; auth, Triangles: Shapes in Math, Science and Nature, Toronto: Kids Can Press, 94; contrib, Harvesting Thistles: The Textual Garden of L.M. Montgomery, Guelph: Canadian Children's Lit Press, 23-35; coauth, "Flying a light aircraft: Reference service evaluation from a user's viewpoint, RQ, 34, (94): 217-230; coauth, Best Practices: an analysis of the best (and worst) in 52 public library reference transactions, Public Libraries, (94): 261-266; auth, "If they read Nancy Drew, so what?: Series book readers talk back," Library and Information Science Res, 17, (95): 201-236; auth, "Reading series books: what readers say about it," School Library Media Quarterly, (96): 165-171; auth, Squares: Shapes in Math, Science and Nature, Toronto: Kids Can Press, 96; coauth, Communicationg Professionally, New York: Neal-Schuman, 98. **CONTACT ADDRESS** Elborn College, Univ of Western Ontario, London, ON, Canada N6A 5B8. **EMAIL** ross@julian.uwo.ca

ROSS, DANIEL W.
PERSONAL Born 05/29/1952, Atlanta, GA, m, 1976, 2 children **DISCIPLINE** ENGLISH **EDUCATION** Univ of Ga, ABJ, 77; MA, 77; Purdue Univ, PhD, 84. **CAREER** Asst prof, Allentown Col of St. Francis de Sales, 85-90; asst prof, Columbia Col, 90-95; Chair, Columbia State Univ, 95-. **HONORS AND AWARDS** Sasaka Fel, Japan Studies Inst, 99. **MEMBERSHIPS** MLA. **RESEARCH** Psychoanalysis and Literature, S Literature. **SELECTED PUBLICATIONS** Auth, "Celie in the Looking Glass: The Desire for Selfhood in 'The Color Purple'", Mod Fiction Studies 34, (88): 69-84; auth, "Seeking a Way Home: The Uncanny in Wordsworth's 'Immortality Ode'", SEL, (92): 625-43; auth, The Critical Response to William Styron, Greenwood Pr, 95. **CONTACT ADDRESS** Dept Lang and Lit, Columbus State Univ, 4225 University Ave, Columbia, GA 31907-5679. **EMAIL** ross_daniels@colstate.edu

ROSS, DAVID
DISCIPLINE MUSIC **EDUCATION** Oberlin Conservatory Music, PhD. **CAREER** Prof, Univ Tex at El Paso. **MEMBERSHIPS** Int Clarinet Soc. **SELECTED PUBLICATIONS** Auth, pubs on eighteenth century clarinet and its literature. **CONTACT ADDRESS** Dept of Music, Univ of Texas, El Paso, El Paso, TX 79968. **EMAIL** dross@utep.edu

ROSS, DEBORAH
PERSONAL Born 02/22/1954, Utica, NY, d, 2 children **DISCIPLINE** ENGLISH, LITERATURE **EDUCATION** Kirkland Col, BA, 75; Univ Rochester, PhD, 80. **CAREER** Asst prof, Univ Haw, 80-85; from assoc prof to prof, Haw Pacific Univ, 95-. **HONORS AND AWARDS** Trustees' Awd for Excellence in Teaching, Haw Pacific Univ, 92. **MEMBERSHIPS** MLA, Northeast Am Soc for Eighteenth-century Scholars, Nat Coun of Teachers of English, Haw Coun of Teachers of English, Children's Lit Haw, Popular Culture Asn of the Pacific. **RESEARCH** Women and narrative in literature and in the popular media. **SELECTED PUBLICATIONS** Auth, "The Excellence of Falsefod: Romance, Realism, and Women's Contribution to the Novel, Univ Pr of Ky, 92; auth, "Home by Tea-Time: Fear of Imagination in Disney's Alice in Wonderland," in Film/Fiction Annual, 00. **CONTACT ADDRESS** Dept Arts & Sci, Hawaii Pacific Univ, 1188 Fort St Mall, Ste 430, Honolulu, HI 96813-2713. **EMAIL** dross@hpu.edu

ROSS, DONALD
PERSONAL Born 10/18/1941, New York, NY, m, 3 children **DISCIPLINE** ENGLISH **EDUCATION** Lehigh Univ, AB, 63; MA, 64; Univ Mich, PhD, 67. **CAREER** Grad asst, Lehigh Univ, 63-64; teach fel, Univ Mich, 64-67; asst prof, Univ Pa, 68-71; asst prof, 71-76, Univ Minn; assoc prof, 76-83; prof, 83-. **HONORS AND AWARDS** Phi Kappa Phi; NSF; ACLS; FIPSE; Diss Teach Awd, Univ Minn. **MEMBERSHIPS** MLA; ACH; NCTE. **RESEARCH** Nineteenth century American literature; travel writing; computers; the humanities. **SELECTED PUBLICATIONS** Coauth, Revising Mythologies: The Composition of Thoreau's Major Works (Univ Press Vir); co-ed, American Travel Writers, 1776-1864 (Diction Lit Biog, 88); co-ed, American Travel Writers, 1850-1915 (Diction Lit Biog, 88); auth American History and Culture from First Contact to Cable TV (Peter Lang, forthcoming). **CONTACT ADDRESS** Dept English, Univ of Minnesota, Twin Cities, 207 Church St SE, Minneapolis, MN 55455-0134. **EMAIL** rossj001@tc.umn.edu

ROSS, MARILYN J.
DISCIPLINE ENGLISH **EDUCATION** BA, 69; MA, 72; PhD, 95. **CAREER** Asst Prof to Prof and Div Coordinator, Fla Memorial Col, 71-. **HONORS AND AWARDS** Service Awd, Black Archives Hist and Res Foundation of S Fla; chairperson's Awd, Fla Memorial Col, 87; Div of Humanities Awd, Fla Memorial Col, 86; Epsilon Tau Lambda; Kappa Delta Pi; Phi Lambda Pi; Delta Theta Mu; Phi Kappa Phi; Phi alpha Theta. **MEMBERSHIPS** Mod Lang Asn, Nat Coun of Teachers of English, am Asn of Univ women, Asn of Educ Leadership. **RESEARCH** Ethnic Studies. **SELECTED PUBLICATIONS** Auth, Success Factors of Young African American Males at a Historically Black College, Greenwood, 98; auth, Success Factors of Young African American Women at a Historically Black College, (forthcoming). **CONTACT ADDRESS** Dept Humanities & Educ, Florida Mem Col, 15800 NW 42 Ave, Opa Locka, FL 33054-6155. **EMAIL** mjulia@bellsouth.net

ROSS, THEOPHIL
PERSONAL Born 02/11/1948, Belleville, IL, d, 1 child **DISCIPLINE** THEATRE, COMMUNICATION **EDUCATION** Clarion Univ, BS, 70; Bradley Univ, MA, 72; MA, 74; Univ Mo, PhD, 81. **CAREER** Teacher, Camden Central High Sch, 70-71; instr, Bradley Univ, 73-74; Dept Theatre, Northwest Mo State Univ, 78-95; prof & chair of Dept of Commun and Theatre Arts, Northwest Mo State Univ, 96-. **MEMBERSHIPS** Nat Commun Asn, Asn for Theatre in H. E., Asn for Commun Admin, Am Soc for Theatre Res. **CONTACT ADDRESS** Dept Commun, Northwest Missouri State Univ, 800 University Dr, Maryville, MO 64468-6015. **EMAIL** ross@mail.nwmissouri.edu

ROSS, THOMAS W.
PERSONAL Born 04/16/1923, Colorado Springs, CO, m, 1943, 2 children **DISCIPLINE** ENGLISH **EDUCATION** Colo Col, AB, 46; AM, 47; Univ Mich, PhD, 51. **CAREER** Interpreter, U.S. Army, 43-36; prof to asst dean, Colo Col, 51-; vis prof, Mass Inst of Technol, 55; asst dir, Salzburg Sem, 56-58; NATO prof, Univ Regensburg, 67. **HONORS AND AWARDS** Phi Beta Kappa; Phi Kappa Psi; Am Philos Soc. **MEMBERSHIPS** MLA; Medieval Acad of Am; Soc Dantesca; New Chaucer Soc. **RESEARCH** Chaucer; Shakespeare; Medieval Latin; Middle English. **SELECTED PUBLICATIONS** Auth, "Five Fifteenth-Century Emblem Verses," Brit Mus Addit; auth, On the Evil Times of Edward II; auth, Claudius Plays at Shove-Groat (on Hamlet); ed, Thomas Kyd's Spanish Tragedy; auth, Chaucer's Bawdy; ed, A Book of Elizabethan Magic; auth, Thomas Hill's Natural and Artificial Conclusions (1570); auth, An Approach to Teaching Chaucer's Language. **CONTACT ADDRESS** 1709 N Tejon St, Colorado Springs, CO 80907-7442. **EMAIL** tross50@excite.com

ROSS, TREVOR T.
PERSONAL Born 08/18/1961, Ottawa, ON, Canada **DISCIPLINE** ENGLISH, LITERATURE **EDUCATION** Carleton Univ, BA, 83; MA, 84; Univ Toronto, PhD, 88. **CAREER** Asst prof, Univ Toronto, 88-92; asst prof to assoc prof, Carleton Univ, 92-. **HONORS AND AWARDS** SSHRCC Fel, 87-88; ASECS James L. Clifford Prize, 93; HSSFC Grant, 96; SSHRCC Res Grant, 01-04. **MEMBERSHIPS** MLA; ASECS; NASECS. **RESEARCH** 18th century English literature; history of criticism and critical theory; Canon formation; law and literature. **SELECTED PUBLICATIONS** Auth, "Just When Did the 'British Bards Begin t'Immortalitize?'" in Studies in Eighteenth-Century Culture, eds. Leslie Ellen Brown, Patricia B. Craddock (Colleagues Pr, 89); auth, "Copyright and the Invention of Tradition," Eighteenth-Century Studies 26 (92); auth, "The Emergence of Literature: Making and Reading the English Canon in the Eighteenth-Century," ELH 63 (96); auth, "'Pure Poetry:' Cultural Capital and the Rejection of Classicism," MLA Quart 58 (97); auth, The Making of the English Literary Canon: From the Middle Ages to the Late Eighteenth-Century, McGill/Queen's Univ Pr, 98; auth, "The Rules of the Game, or Why Neoclassicism Was Never an Ideology," in Ideology and Form Eighteenth-Century Literature, ed. David H. Richter (Tex Tech Univ Pr, 99); auth, "Translation and the Caonical Text," Studies Lit Imagination 33 (00). **CONTACT ADDRESS** English Dept, Dalhousie Univ, 6135 University Ave, Halifax, NS, Canada B3H 3J8. **EMAIL** Trevor.ross@dal.ca

ROSSIGNOL, ROSALYN
PERSONAL Born 03/17/1959, Lenoir Co., NC, m, 1989, 3 children **DISCIPLINE** ENGLISH LITERATURE **EDUCATION** Augusta Col, BA, 82; Univ NC Chapel Hill MA, 86; PhD, 92. **CAREER** Asst prof, Loras Col, 95-. **MEMBERSHIPS** MLA, International Arthurian Asn. **RESEARCH** Chaucer, Arthurian literature. **SELECTED PUBLICATIONS** Auth, Chaucer A-Z: The comple Reference to His Life and Works, Facts On File Pub, (New York), 99. **CONTACT ADDRESS** Dept English, Loras Col, 1450 Alta Vista St, Dubuque, IA 52001-4327.

ROSSMAN, CHARLES R.
PERSONAL Born 02/13/1938, Brookings, SD, m, 1963, 2 children **DISCIPLINE** ENGLISH **EDUCATION** Calif State Col Los Angeles, BA, 62; Univ Southern Calif, MA, 65, PhD(-English), 68. **CAREER** Teacher English, Colegio Abelardo Moncayo, Ecuador, 62-63; assoc, Univ Calif, Los Angeles, 67-68; asst prof, 68-75, Assoc Prof English, Univ Tes, Austin, 75-90, Dir Plan II Honors Prog, 77-, Fulbright prof, Nat Univ, Mex, 72-73, Fulbright Prof, Paul Valery Univ, Montpelier France, 82; Prof English, 90-; Distinguished Teaching Prof, 96-. **MEMBERSHIPS** MLA **RESEARCH** Modern Latin American fiction; 20th century British literature. **SELECTED PUBLICATIONS** Auth, The Gospel According to D H Lawrence, spring 70, Lawrence on the Critic's Couch, summer 70 & Four Versions of Lawrence, spring 73, D H Lawrence Rev; auth, Stephen Dedalus's Villanelle, James Joyce Quart, spring 75; Art and Life in Joyce's Portrait, In: Forms of Modern British Fiction, Univ Tex, 75; Myth and Misunderstanding D H Lawrence, Bucknell Rev, 77; ed, Mario Vargas Llosa: A Collection of Critical Essays, Univ Tex, 78; ed, D H Lawrence Rev, 96. **CONTACT ADDRESS** Dept English, Univ of Texas, Austin, Austin, TX 78712-1026. **EMAIL** rossman@mail.utexas.edu

ROSTECK, H. THOMAS
DISCIPLINE COMMUNICATION AND CULTURE AND RHETORICAL STUDIES **EDUCATION** Univ Wisc, PhD. **CAREER** Comm, Univ Ark **HONORS AND AWARDS** Dir, Depts Undergrad Honors Prog; Emerging Scholar, 89; Nichols Awd in Public Address, 99. **MEMBERSHIPS** Nat Commun

Asn. **RESEARCH** Documentary television, culture and communication. **SELECTED PUBLICATIONS** Auth, See It Now Confront McCarthyism: Television Documentary and the Politics of Representation, Univ Alab Press; ed, At the Intersection: Cultural Studies and Rhetorical Studies, Guilford 00. **CONTACT ADDRESS** Univ of Arkansas, Fayetteville, Fayetteville, AR 72701.

ROSTON, MURRAY
PERSONAL Born 12/10/1928, London, England, m, 1956, 3 children **DISCIPLINE** ENGLISH **EDUCATION** Cambridge Univ, BA, 52; Univ London, MA, 56; Univ London, PhD, 61. **CAREER** prof to dept chair and prof emeritus, Bar Ilan Univ, 69-; adj prof, UCLA, 99-. **HONORS AND AWARDS** Fel, Nat Humanities Center, 85-86. **RESEARCH** Relationship between literature and the visual arts (painting, architecture and sculpture); The Bible in English literature; The search for identity in modern literature. **SELECTED PUBLICATIONS** Auth, Changing Perspectives: in literature and the visual arts, 1650-1820, Princeton Univ Press, 90; auth, Victorian Contexts: literature and the visual arts, Macmillan Press, 97; auth, Modernist Patterns: in literature and the visual arts, Macmillan Press, 00; auth, The Search for Selfhood in Modern Literature, Palgrave Press, (forthcoming). **CONTACT ADDRESS** Dept English, Univ of California, Los Angeles, 2225 Rolfe, PO Box 951530, Los Angeles, CA 90095-1530. **EMAIL** rostom@mail.biu.ac.il

ROTA, C. DAVID
PERSONAL m **DISCIPLINE** ENGLISH **EDUCATION** Univ Minn, MA, 79; Southern Ill Univ, MA, 83; PhD, 92. **CAREER** Reference librn, McKendric Col, 79-81; instr, Southern Ill Univ at Edwardsville, 82-83; sr lectr, Univ of Mo at St. Louis, 83-00. **RESEARCH** American Literature, Religious Studies, Biblical Studies. **SELECTED PUBLICATIONS** Auth, Literature of the Old Testament, Center for Independent Study at the Univ of Mo, 94; auth, American Literary Masterpieces, Center for Independent Study at the Univ of Mo, 97; auth, Literature of the New Testament, Center for Independent Study at the Univ of Mo, 00. **CONTACT ADDRESS** Dept English, Univ of Missouri, St. Louis, 8001 Natural Bridge Rd, Saint Louis, MO 63121-4401.

ROTH, LANE
PERSONAL Born 00/00/1943, New York, NY **DISCIPLINE** CINEMA, COMMUNICATIONS **EDUCATION** NYork Univ, BA, 64; Fla State Univ, MA, 74, PhD, 76. **CAREER** Asst prof, Univ Evansville, 76-78; assoc prof, 78-82; Assoc Prof, Commun, Lamar Univ, 82-. **HONORS AND AWARDS** National German Honors, 64; Regents' Merit Awd for Teaching Excellence, Lamar Univ, 80. **MEMBERSHIPS** Intl Asn for the Fantastic in Arts, Bd, Mental Health Asn Jefferson Cty; pres of the bd, 1997- **RESEARCH** Jungian psychol, literary criticism, philos. **SELECTED PUBLICATIONS** Auth, Humanity, Technology and Comedy in Microbi, a Hungarian Animated Science Fiction Television Series, World Communication, 93; Co-auth, G. M. Broncho Billy" Anderson: The First Movie Cowboy Hero, in Back in the Saddle: Essays on Western Film and Television Actors, McFarland Publ, 98. **CONTACT ADDRESS** Communications Dept, Lamar Univ, Beaumont, PO Box 10050, Beaumont, TX 77710-0050.

ROTH, LORNA
PERSONAL Born Montreal, PQ, Canada **DISCIPLINE** COMMUNICATION STUDIES **EDUCATION** McGill Univ, Cert Educ, 67, MA, 83; Concordia Univ, BA, 72, PhD, 94. **CAREER** Tchr, 68-73; cross-cultural Commun & Educ Consult, private sector, 77-93; lectr, 92-94, Asst Prof Commun Studs, Concordia Univ, 94-. **MEMBERSHIPS** Ctr Res/Action Race Relations; Can Commun Asn; Asn Can Univs Northern Studs; Fel, Commun Studs & Public Affairs; Can Asn Journalists. **SELECTED PUBLICATIONS** Auth, Election Broadcasting in Canada, Vol 21, 91; auth, Mohawk Airwaves and Cultural Challenges: Some Reflections on the Politics of Recognition and Cultural Appropriation After the Summer of 1990, in Can J Commun, Vol 18, 93; auth, Seeing Ourselves: Media Power and Policy in Canada, 96. **CONTACT ADDRESS** Dept of Commun Studies, Concordia Univ, Montreal, 7141 Sherbrooke W, Montreal, QC, Canada H4B 1R6. **EMAIL** roth@microtec.net

ROTH, PHYLLIS ANN
PERSONAL Born 01/06/1945, New York, NY, d, 1 child **DISCIPLINE** ENGLISH LITERATURE **EDUCATION** Clark Univ, AB, 66; Univ Conn, MA, 67, PhD(English), 72. **CAREER** Instr, Univ Conn, 67; from instr to asst prof, Northeastern Univ, 69-76; asst prof, 76-78, from assoc prof English, Skidmore Col, 78-85; dept chmn, 85-89; dean fac, 90-00; act pres, 92; interim pres, 99. **MEMBERSHIPS** AAUP; MLA; NCTE. **RESEARCH** Literary theory; fiction. **SELECTED PUBLICATIONS** Auth, In search of aesthetic bliss: A rereading of Lolita, Col Lit, winter 75; The psychology of the double in Nabakov's Pale Fire, Essays in Lit, Fall 75; Suddenly sexual women in Bram Stoker's Dracula, Lit & Psychol, Fall 77; Nabokov: The man behind the mystification, In: Nabokov's Fifth Arc, 82; Bram Stoker, 82; G K Hall, Critical Essays on Vladimir Nahokov, ed, G K Hall, 84. **CONTACT ADDRESS** Dept of English, Skidmore Col, 815 N Broadway, Saratoga Springs, NY 12866-1698. **EMAIL** paroth@skidmore.edu

ROTHENBUSCH, ESTHER H.
DISCIPLINE CHURCH MUSIC **EDUCATION** Baldwin-Wallace Col, BM; Univ Mich, MA, PhD. **CAREER** Instr, Univ Mich, Adrian Col, Bowling Green State Univ; asst prof, S Baptist Theol Univ, 94-. **SELECTED PUBLICATIONS** Auth, The Joyful Sound: Women in the Nineteenth-Century United States Hymnody Tradition; Hallelujah! Handel Meets the Megachurch. **CONTACT ADDRESS** Sch Church Mus and Worship, So Baptist Theol Sem, 2825 Lexington Rd, Louisville, KY 40280. **EMAIL** erothenbusch@sbts.edu

ROTHFELD, ANNE
PERSONAL Born 01/12/1967, MD, s, 1 child **DISCIPLINE** ARCHIVES HISTORY **EDUCATION** Catholic Univ Am, MSLS, 98. **CAREER** Archives Techn, US Holocaust Memorial Museum, 93-98; Infor spec, Univ Md, 98-99; Archivist/Historians, 99-. **MEMBERSHIPS** Am History Asn; Orgn of Am History; Am Libr Asn; Special Libr Asn; Am Asn State and Local Hist; Society Hist Progressive and Gilded Age. **RESEARCH** Local and public history; late 19th/early 20th century American and German history; archives and special collections. **SELECTED PUBLICATIONS** Auth, rev, Economics of Digital Information: Collection, Storage, and Delivery, 99; auth, rev, Louis Shores: Defining Educational Librarianship, 99; auth, rev, More Than the Facts: The Research Division of the National Education Association, 1922-1997; auth, "A Source of Holocaust Research: The United Restitution Organization," Perspectives, 00; auth, "Electronic Reference Desk," The History Highway 2000: A guide to internet resources, 00. **CONTACT ADDRESS** 3806 Stepping Stone Ln, Burtonsville, MD 20866. **EMAIL** arothfeld@usmint.treas.gov

ROTHMAN, IRVING N.
PERSONAL Born 04/10/1935, Pittsburgh, PA, m, 1962, 2 children **DISCIPLINE** ENGLISH LITERATURE **EDUCATION** Univ Pittsburgh, BA, 57; Univ Pittsburgh, MA, 59; Univ Pittsburgh, PhD, 67. **CAREER** Asst prof, Univ Houston, 67-73; mem grad fac, Univ Houston, 71; assoc prof, Univ Houston, 73-80; prof, Univ Houston, 80-. **CONTACT ADDRESS** Department of English, Univ of Houston, Houston, TX 77204-3012. **EMAIL** irothman@uh.edu

ROTHSTEIN, WILLIAM
DISCIPLINE MUSIC **EDUCATION** Northwestern Univ, BM, 74; Yale Univ, MPhil, 78, PhD, 81; Postgrad study, New England Conserv, 74-76. **CAREER** Fac mem, Amherst Coll, Univ of Mich; Assoc prof, Oberlin Col, 92-; Guest lectr, Britten-Pears Sch for Advanced Mus Studies, Eng, 93. **HONORS AND AWARDS** ASCAP-Deems Taylor Awd, 90. **SELECTED PUBLICATIONS** Auth, Phrase Rhythm in Tonal Music, Schirmer Bk(s). **CONTACT ADDRESS** Dept of Mus, Oberlin Col, Oberlin, OH 44074.

ROTHWELL, KENNETH S.
PERSONAL Born 03/27/1955, Rochester, NY, m, 1989, 2 children **DISCIPLINE** CLASSICS **EDUCATION** Univ Vt, BA, 77; Columbia Univ, PhD, 85. **CAREER** Asst prof, Holy Cross Coll, 84-91; asst prof, Wellesley Coll, 91-92; asst prof, Boston Coll, 92-94; asst prof, Univ Mass Boston, 95-; Assoc Prof, 99-. **MEMBERSHIPS** APA; CANE. **RESEARCH** Greek Comedy. **SELECTED PUBLICATIONS** Auth, Politics and Persuasion in Aristophanes' Ecclesiazusae, 90. **CONTACT ADDRESS** Univ of Massachusetts, Boston, 100 Morrissey Blvd, Boston, MA 02125. **EMAIL** kenneth.rothwell@umb.edu

ROTHWELL, KENNETH SPRAGUE
PERSONAL Born 05/26/1921, Bay Shore, NY, m, 1954, 4 children **DISCIPLINE** ENGLISH **EDUCATION** Univ NC, BA, 48; Columbia Univ, Ma, 49, PhD(English), 56. **CAREER** Instr English, Univ Kans, 49-50, Univ Rochester, 52-55 & Univ Cincinnati, 55-57; asst prof, Univ Kans, 57-62, from assoc prof to prof 62-70; chmn dept, 70-76, Prof English, Univ VT, 76-, Am Philos Soc grant-in-aid, 63 & 68; co-ed, Shakespeare on Film Newsletter, 76- **HONORS AND AWARDS** Kroepch-Maurice Outstanding Teacher; Dean's Lecturer, Univ of VT; Keynote speaker Shakespeare on Film Conpereuce, Univ of Malaga, Spain, 99. **MEMBERSHIPS** Malone Soc; Renaissance Soc Am; MLA; Cent Renaissance Conf (pres, 69); Shakespeare Asn Am. **RESEARCH** Shakespeare and the Elizabethans; Shakespeare and film. **SELECTED PUBLICATIONS** Auth, Questions of Rhetoric and Usage, Little, 70; A Mirror for Shakespeare, IDC, 80; auth, Shakespeare on Screen: An International Filmography and Videography, 90; A History of Shakespeare on Screen, 99. **CONTACT ADDRESS** Dept of English, Univ of Vermont, Burlington, VT 05405. **EMAIL** krothwell@zoo.uvm.edu

ROUILLARD, ZELDA JEANNE
PERSONAL Born 06/06/1929, Kearney, NE, m, 1959, 1 child **DISCIPLINE** ENGLISH **EDUCATION** Univ Nebr, AB, 51; Univ Wyo, MA, 53; Univ Colo, PhD, 59. **CAREER** Instr, Univ Boulder, 59-60; instr, Univ Wyo, 53-54; teacher, Colo, 60-69; prof, Western State Col, 69-. **HONORS AND AWARDS** Fulbright Scholar; AAUW Rock Mtn Fel. **MEMBERSHIPS** NCTE; MLA; WLA; RMMLA; CCCC; AFS; Western Folklore. **RESEARCH** Folklore; literature. **CONTACT ADDRESS** 121 Roundtree Rd, Gunnison, CO 81230-4125. **EMAIL** zrouillard@western.edu

ROUMAN, JOHN CHRIST
PERSONAL Born 05/01/1916, Tomahawk, WI **DISCIPLINE** CLASSICS, LINGUISTICS **EDUCATION** Carleton Col, BA, 50; Columbia Univ, MA, 51; Univ Wis-Madison, PhD, 65. **CAREER** Tchr, Seton Hall Prep Sch, NJ, 54-56 & Malverne High Sch, NY, 57-59; res asst Greek epigraphy, Inst Advan Study, Princeton Univ, 62-63; asst prof, 65-71, chmn dept Span & class, 72-76, assoc prof, 71-91, prof class, Univ NH, 91-, Chair classics, 87-98, Coord classics, 98-; Pres, Strafford Cty Greco-Roman Found, Bd mem, Phi Kappa Theta Nat Found. **HONORS AND AWARDS** Noyse Prize for Greek, Carleton Col, 50; Fulbright Scholar, Univ Kiel, WGer, 56-57; UNH Alumni Asn, Distinguished Tchg Awd, 85; Barlow-Beach Awd for Serv, Cause of Class, Class Asn of New Engl, 91; Am Philol Asn Nat Awd for Excellence in Tchg, Class, 91; AHEPA and Daughters of Penelope, Pericles Awd, 93. **MEMBERSHIPS** Am Philol Asn; Medieval Acad Am; Mod Greek Studies Asn; Class Asn New Engl. **RESEARCH** Class philol, espec Pindar and Homer; mod Greek studies; Byzantine hist. **SELECTED PUBLICATIONS** Auth, Nominal-Compound Epithets in Pindar: A Linguistic Analysis, Univ Microfilms, 67; coauth, More still on the Trojan Horse, Class J, 4-5/72. **CONTACT ADDRESS** Dept of Langs, Lit and Cult, Univ of New Hampshire, Durham, 209 Murkland Hall, PO Box 54, Durham, NH 03824-4724. **EMAIL** jcrouman@christa.unh.edu

ROUSSELOW, JESSICA
DISCIPLINE COMMUNICATION ARTS **EDUCATION** Univ MN, PhD. **CAREER** Prof, 67-, assoc dean, Div Fine and Appl Arts, Taylor Univ. **SELECTED PUBLICATIONS** Coauth, God's Ordinary People, No Ordinary Heritage. **CONTACT ADDRESS** Taylor Univ, Upland, Upland, IN 46989.

ROUZIE, ALBERT
PERSONAL Born 07/07/1952, New Orleans, LA, m, 1993 **DISCIPLINE** ENGLISH **EDUCATION** Portland State Univ, BA; MA; Univ Texas, PhD, 97. **CAREER** Asst Prof, Ohio Univ, 96-. **MEMBERSHIPS** NCTE, CCCC, AAUP. **RESEARCH** The Play Element in Computer communication; Computers and composition pedagogy. **SELECTED PUBLICATIONS** Auth, "The Composition of Dramatic Experience: Play as Symbolic Action in Student Electronic Projects," Computers and Compositions, 00; auth, "The Dialectic of Work and Play: Serio-ludic play in Composition Studies," JAC, 00. **CONTACT ADDRESS** Dept English, Ohio Univ, 1 Ohio Univ, Athens, OH 45701-2942. **EMAIL** rouzie@ohiou.edu

ROWAN, KATHERINE E.
PERSONAL Born 02/17/1954, Alexandra, VA **DISCIPLINE** COMMUNICATIONS **EDUCATION** George Mason Univ, Fairfax, VA, BA (English Lit), 75; Univ IL, Urbana-Champaign, MA (Speech Commun), 78; Purdue Univ, PhD (English), 85. **CAREER** Teaching asst, Dept of Speech Commun, Univ IL, Urbana, 76-79; lect, English div, Parkland Col, Champaign, Il, 78-79; lect, Dept of Rhetoric & Commun, SUNY, Albany, 79-81; lect, Master's in Managrment Prog, Col of St Rose, Albany, NY, 80; lect, Dept of English (evening div), Russell Sage Col, Troy, NY, 80-81; teaching asst, Dept of English, Purdue Univ, 82-84; graduate instr, 84-85, asst prof, 85-91, assoc prof, 91-95, prof, Dept of Commun, Purdue Univ, West Lafayette, IN, 96-. **HONORS AND AWARDS** Graduated magna cum laude, George Mason Univ, 75; listed, Who's Who Among American Colleges and Universities; Phi Kappa Phi, Purdue Univ, 83; David Ross Summer res fel, Dept of English, Purdue Univ, 84; Gannett Foun Teaching fel, IN Univ, Bloomington, 87; Poynter Inst Teaching fel, Poynter Inst for Media Studies, St Petersburg, FL, 88; X-L Summer res grant, Purdue Univ, 86, 90; Outstanding Young Teacher Awd, Central States Commun Asn, 90; Purdue Univ School of Liberal Arts Educational Excellence Awd, 91; Top 3 Paper, Public Relations Interest Group, Int Commun Asn, 92; directed two master's theses which won the Outstanding Master's Thesis Awd, Health Commun Div of the Nat Commun Asn and Int Commun Asn (Rose G Campbell, 94, and Susan L Smith, 96). **MEMBERSHIPS** Asn for Ed in Journalism and Mass Commun; Int Commun Asn; Nat Commun Asn; Nat Coun of Teachers of English; Phi Kappa Phi; Soc of Professional Journalists. **SELECTED PUBLICATIONS** Auth, review of Psycholinguistics of Readable Writing, by Alice S Horning, Commun Theory, 4, 94; Why Rules for Risk Communication Fail: A Problem-Solving Approach to Risk Communication, Risk Analysis, 14, 94; The Technical and Democratic Approaches to Risk Situations: Their Appeal, Limitations, and Rhetorical Alternative, Argumentation, 8, 94; Expository Writing, in A C Purves, ed, Encyclopedia of English Studies and Language Arts, vol 1, Scholastic, Inc, 94; with M R Dennis, R A Feinberg, R Widdows, and R E Crable, Corporate Civil Disobedience in the Consumer Interest: The Case of Kellogg's Catalytic Defiance of FDA Health Claim Laws, Advancing the Consumer Interest, 6, 94; with D M Hoover, Communicating Risk to Patients: Detecting, Diagnosing, and Overcoming Lay Theories, Communicating Risk to Patients, US Pharmacopeial Convention, 94; What Risk Communicators Need to Know: An Agenda for Research, in B R Burleson, ed, Communication Yearbook, 18, Sage, 95; A New Pedagogy for Explanatory Speaking: Why Arrangement Should Not Substitute for Invention, Conmmunication Education, 44, 95; Exposition, in T Enos, ed, Encyclopedia of Rhetoric and Composition: Communication from Ancient Times to the Infor-

mation Age, Garland Pub, 96; numerous other publications. **CONTACT ADDRESS** Dept of Commun, George Mason Univ, Fairfax, MS 3D6, Fairfax, VA 22030-4444. **EMAIL** krowan@gmu.edu

ROWAN, STEPHEN C.
DISCIPLINE ENGLISH LITERATURE **EDUCATION** Fairfield Univ, BA, 66; St Mary's Sem and Univ, STB, 68; Univ Brit Columbia, MA, 75, Doctorate, 85. **CAREER** Instr, Seattle Univ. **MEMBERSHIPS** Shakespeare Asn of Am; Pacific Northwest Renaissance Soc; Conf on Christianity and Lit; MLA. **SELECTED PUBLICATIONS** Auth, 'Religiously the Ask A Sacrifice': The Strategy and the Theme of the Scapegoat in Titus Androicus, Symp, Seattle Univ, 87; Words From the Cross, Twenty Third Publ, 88; The Nicene Creed: Poetic Words for a Prosaic World, Stu in Formative Spirituality, Duquesne Univ, 89; The Nicene Creed: Poetic words for a Prosaic World, Twenty third Publ, 90; Much Have I Travelled in the Realms of Gold, Spiritual Life, 94; The Parables of Calvary: Reflections on the Last Words of Jesus, Twenty Third Publ, 94. **CONTACT ADDRESS** Seattle Univ, Seattle, WA 98122-4460. **EMAIL** srowan@seattleu.edu

ROWE, ANNE ERVIN
PERSONAL Born 09/05/1945, Gainesville, FL, m, 1963, 3 children **DISCIPLINE** AMERICAN LITERATURE **EDUCATION** Fla State Univ, BA, 67; Univ NC, Chapel Hill, MA, 69, PhD, 73. **CAREER** Vis Asst Prof, 72-73, from Asst Prof to Assoc Prof, 73-84, prof English, Fla State Univ, 84-; Assoc Dean, College of Arts and Sciences, 97-. **MEMBERSHIPS** MLA; South Atlantic Mod Lang Asn; Col English Asn. **SELECTED PUBLICATIONS** Auth, The Enchanted Country: Northern Writers in the South, 1865-1910, 78 & Lefcadio Hearn, In: A Bibliographical Guide to Southern Literature, 79, La State Univ Press; The Idea of Florida in the American Literary Imagination, La State Univ Press, 86. **CONTACT ADDRESS** Dept of English, Florida State Univ, 600 W College Ave, Tallahassee, FL 32306-1096. **EMAIL** arowe@garnet.acns.fsu.edu

ROWE, JOHN CARLOS
PERSONAL Born 12/11/1945, Los Angeles, CA, m, 1968, 3 children **DISCIPLINE** ENGLISH **EDUCATION** Johns Hopkins Univ, BA, 67; State Univ NY, Buffalo, PhD, 72. **CAREER** Asst prof, Univ of Md, 71-75; vis prof, Emory Univ, 74; asst prof to prof, Univ of Calif Irvine, 75-. **HONORS AND AWARDS** Fulbright Lectr, W Ger, 74-75; UCI Alumni Asn Distinguished Teaching Awd, 81; Rockefeller Found Fel, 82-83; NEH Summer Sem, 86; Fac Senate Lectr for Distinguished Teaching, 88-89, NEH Grant, 94-96; Outstanding Prof in the School of Humanities, 00. **RESEARCH** Nineteenth and Twenthieth Century U.S. Literature and Cultures, Critical Theory. **SELECTED PUBLICATIONS** Auth, The Theoretical Dimensions of Henry James, Univ of Wis Pr, 84; coed, "American Representations of Vietnam", Cult Critique * (86); coed, "The Vietnam War and American Culture, Columbia Univ Pr, 91; ed, New Essays on the Education of Henry Adams, Cambridge Univ Pr, (NY), 96; auth, At Emerson's Tomb: The Politics of Classic American Literature, Columbia Univ Pr, 97; auth, The Other Henry James, Duke Univ Pr, 98; ed, Culture and the Problem of the Disciplines, The Critical Theory Inst Series, Columbia Univ Pr, (NY), 98; ed, Post-Nationalist American Studies, Univ of Calif Pr, (Berkeley), 00; auth, Literary Culture and U.S. Imperialism: From the American Revolution to World War II, Oxford Univ Pr, 00; auth, A Future for American Studies, Univ of MN Pr, (forthcoming). **CONTACT ADDRESS** Dept English, Univ of California, Irvine, Irvine, CA 92697. **EMAIL** jcrowe@uci.edu

ROWE, JOYCE A.
DISCIPLINE 19TH CENTURY AMERICAN LITERATURE AND CULTURE **EDUCATION** Columbia, PhD. **CAREER** Assoc prof; dept ch, Fordham Univ. **HONORS AND AWARDS** Fordham Fac Fellow, 94 & 99. **MEMBERSHIPS** MLA; ASA; Columbia Univ Seminar in American Civilization. **SELECTED PUBLICATIONS** Auth, Equivocal Endings in Classic American Novels Cambridge UP, 88; Social History and the Politics of Manhood in Melville's Redburn, Mosaic 26, 93; auth, Murder, What a lovely voice!: Sex, Speech and the Public/Private Problem in the Bostonians, Texas Studies in Literature and Language, 98; auth, Holden Caulfield and American Professor, New Essays on J. D. Salinger's The Cathcher in the Rye, Cambridge UP, 91, rpt, J.D. Salinger's The Catcher in the Rye, Chelsea House, 99. **CONTACT ADDRESS** Dept of Eng Lang and Lit, Fordham Univ, Dealy Hall, Bronx, NY 10458. **EMAIL** rowe@fordham.edu

ROWE, KAREN E.
PERSONAL Born 07/26/1945, Philadelphia, PA **DISCIPLINE** ENGLISH **EDUCATION** Mount Holyoke Col, AB (with Great Distinction, Magna Cum Laude), 67; IN Univ, MA, 67, PhD, 71. **CAREER** Assoc instr, IN Univ, 69-70; asst prof, English, 71-79, assoc prof, 79-97, Prof of English, UCLA, 97-, Dir, UCLA Center for the Study of Women, 84-88. **HONORS AND AWARDS** Woodrow Wilson Dissertation Year fel, 70-71; NEH fel for Independent Study and Res, 77-78; fel, Radcliffe Inst for Independent study, 77-78; fel, Univ CA Mgt Inst, 81; Bryn Mawr/HERS Mid-Am Inst for Women in Higher Ed Admin, 86; City of Los Angeles, Cert of Appreciation, 88; Outstanding Citizenship and Community Betterment; County of Los Angeles, Cert of Appreciation, Los Angeles County Commission for Women, 88; Calif Senate, Resolution and Commendation, 88; Calif Legis, Assembly Resolution and Commendation, 88; sarah williston scholar, phi beta kappa, 65. **RESEARCH** Early Am lit to 1800; women's lit (17th-20th Am and British); English Renaissance and seventeenth-century lit; English poetry; French and British fairy tales and folklore; curriculum and institutional multiculturalism. **SELECTED PUBLICATIONS** Auth, Sacred or Profane?: Edward Taylor's Meditations on Canticles, Modern Philol 72, 74; Feminism and Fairy Tales, Women's Studies: An Interdisciplinary J, 6, 79, numerous reprints; Fairy-born and Human-bred: Jane Eyre's Education in Romance, in The Voyage In: Fictions of Female Development, ed Elizabeth Abel, Marianne Hirsch, and Elizabeth Langland, Univ Press, New England, 83; Prophetic Visions: Typology and Colonial American Poetry, in Puritan Poets and Poetics: Seventeenth-Century American Poetry in Theory and Practice, ed Peter White, PA State Univ Press, 85; Saint and Singer: Edward Taylor's Typology and the Poetics of Meditation, Cambridge Univ Press, 86, To Spin a Yarn: The Female Voice in Folklore and Fairy Tale, in Fairy Tales and Society: Illusion, Allusion, and Paradigm, ed Ruth B. Bottigheimer, Univ PA Press, 86; Shifting Models, Creating Visions: Process and Pedagogy for Curriculum Transformation, in Women of Color and the Multicultural Curriculum: Transforming the College Classroom, ed Liza Fiol-Matta and Mariam K. Chamberlain, The Feminist Press, 94; Multiculturalism and the Humanities Core: From Policy to Pedagogy, in Selected Papers from the Texas Seminar on the Core Curriculum, 1993, 1994, 1995, ed Shirley D. Ezell and Cay Smith Osmon, Univ Houston and NEH, 95; The Rise of Women's Education in the United States and Korea: A Struggle for Educational and Occupational Equality, co-auth with Byong-Suh Kim, Asian J of Women's Studies 3, 97; In The Heath Anthology of American Literature, ed Paul Lauter, Richard Yarborough, et al, 3rd ed, 2 vols, Houghton Mifflin, 98; numerous other publications. **CONTACT ADDRESS** Dept of English, Univ of California, Los Angeles, Box 90095-1530, Los Angeles, CA 90095-1530. **EMAIL** rowe@hornnet.ucla.edu

ROWE, PATSY BAXTER
PERSONAL Born Philadelphia, PA, m, 2 children **DISCIPLINE** MUSIC **EDUCATION** Philadelphia Musical Acad, BM & BME; Temple Univ, MM & PhD. **CAREER** Asst Prof, Community Col of Philadelphia., 76-90; Dir of Arts Sch, Freedom Theatre, 86-87; Interim Dean of Women, Lincoln Univ, 95-96; Assoc Prof, Lincoln Univ, 95-00; Chair, Music Dept, Lincoln Univ, 98-00. **HONORS AND AWARDS** Woman Achiever of the Year Awd, Zeta Phi Beta Sorority; Four year doctoral Fel. **MEMBERSHIPS** Nat Assoc of Schs of Music; Nat Coalition of 100 Black Women. **RESEARCH** Music pschology; healing power of music; African-American creative process. **SELECTED PUBLICATIONS** Auth, "An Investigation of the Ability of Fourth Grade Student to Master The Rhythmnic Intricacies of Traditional African -Derived Music," Bull of Res in Music Educ, vol 21, 95-96. **CONTACT ADDRESS** Music Dept, Lincoln Univ, Pennsylvania, PO Box 179, Lincoln University, PA 19352. **EMAIL** rowepb@lincoln.edu

ROWLAND, BERYL
PERSONAL Born, Scotland **DISCIPLINE** ENGLISH **EDUCATION** Univ London, BA, 80; Univ Alta, MA, 58; Univ BC, PhD, 62. **CAREER** Asst prof, 62-68, assoc prof, 68-71, prof, 71-83, Distinguished Prof Emer English, York Univ, 83-; DLitt (hon), Mt St Vincent Univ, 82. **HONORS AND AWARDS** Alta Golden Jubilee Drama Awd, 55; Am Univ Presses Bk Awd, 74; Huntington Fel, Int Asn Univ Profs Eng, 76; Canada 125 Medal, 93. **MEMBERSHIPS** Asn Can Univ Tchrs Eng; Hum Asn; Eng Asn; MLA; New Chaucer Soc. **SELECTED PUBLICATIONS** Auth, Blind Beasts: Chaucer's Animal World, 71; auth, Animals with Human Faces, 73; auth, Birds with Human Souls, 78; auth, Earl Birney: Chaucerian Irony, 85; auth, Chaucer's Working Wyf: The Unraveling of a Yarn Spinner, in Chaucer in the Eighties, 96. **CONTACT ADDRESS** Dept of English, York Univ, North York, ON, Canada V8W 2Y2.

ROWLAND, GORDON
DISCIPLINE COMMUNICATION STUDIES **EDUCATION** Univ Ind, PhD. **CAREER** Assoc prof. **SELECTED PUBLICATIONS** Auth, pubs on include design, learning systems, and design education. **CONTACT ADDRESS** Dept of Communication, Ithaca Col, 100 Job Hall, Ithaca, NY 14850.

ROWLEY, HAZEL JOAN
PERSONAL Born 11/16/1951, London, UK, s **DISCIPLINE** LITERARY STUDIES **EDUCATION** S Australia Univ, PhD, 82 **CAREER** Sen lectr, Deekin Univ Melbourne, 84-96; professional writer, 97-. **HONORS AND AWARDS** Bunting Fel, Radcliffe Inst, 99-00; Rockefeller Fel, Univ Iowa, 97; Beinecke Libr Fel, 97. **MEMBERSHIPS** NWU; PEN; Amnesty **RESEARCH** 20th Century African American history and culture; The cold war and its effects on writers; Expatriatism and writing. **SELECTED PUBLICATIONS** Auth, Christina Stead: A Biography, Heinemann, 93; auth, Richard Wright: The Life and Times, Henry Holt, 01. **CONTACT ADDRESS** 46 Highland Ave, Apt 2R, Cambridge, MA 02139-1042. **EMAIL** hrowley@wans.net

ROWLINSON, MATTHEW C.
DISCIPLINE ENGLISH LITERATURE **EDUCATION** Cornell Univ, PhD, 86. **CAREER** Assoc prof, Dartmouth Col. **RESEARCH** Romantic and Victorian Brit lit; Tennyson. **SELECTED PUBLICATIONS** The Skipping Muse: Repetition and Difference in Two Early Poems of Tennyson, Victorian Poetry, 84, auth, "The Ideological Moment of Tennyson's Ulysses," Victorian Poetry 30 (92): 265-76, Reprinted in Tennyson, R. Stoff, ed. Longmans, (96); rptd in Critical Essays on Alfred Lord Tennyson, G.K. Hall, 93; auth, Tennyson's Fixations: Psychoanalysis and the Topics of the Early Poetry, UP Va, 94; auth, "Reading Capital with Little Nell," Yale J of Criticism 9 (96): 347-380; auth, "The Scott Hate Gold: Nation, Identity, and Paper Money," Nation-States and Money: The Past, Present and Future of National Currencies, (99); auth, "Victorian Lyric," in the Blackwell's Companion to Victorian Poetry, forthcoming. **CONTACT ADDRESS** Dept of English, Dartmouth Col, 6032 Sanborn House, Hanover, NH 03755. **EMAIL** Matthew.C.Rowlinson@dartmouth.edu

ROY, ABHIK
PERSONAL Born 01/26/1954, Calcutta, India, m, 1991 **DISCIPLINE** COMMUNICATIONS **EDUCATION** St Xavier's Col, BS, 72; Univ of Calcutta, LLB, 75; Univ of Kansas, MS, 85, PhD, 96. **CAREER** Acct exec, Phoenix Advert Ltd, 75-79; sen acct exec, Kenyon & Eckhardt, 79-81; Phoenix Advert Ltd, 81-82; asst prof, Mankato State Univ, 88-91; commun consult, 91-93; asst prof, Metrop State Univ, 93- . **HONORS AND AWARDS** Kappa Tau Alpha. **MEMBERSHIPS** Nat Commun Asn, Int Commun Asn. **RESEARCH** Media globalization and local resistance; Media representation of race, gender, ethnicity and age. **SELECTED PUBLICATIONS** Coauth, Underrepresented, positively portrayed: Older adults in television commercials, Jour of Applied Commun Res, 25, 97; auth, Marion Barry's road to redemption: A textual analysis of ABC's news story aired on 14 September 1994, The Howard Jour of Commun, 7, 96; Images of domesticity and motherhood in Indian television commercials: A critical study, Jour of Popular Cult, forthcom.; Images of women in Indian television commercials: A critical study, forthcom.; Indian press response to international satellite television: A textual analysis, Television in Asia, eds M. Richards & D. French, forthcom. **CONTACT ADDRESS** Howard Univ, 2400 Sixth St, NW, Washington, DC 20059. **EMAIL** royab001@metvax.metro.msus.edu

ROY, ALICE M.
PERSONAL Born, PA **DISCIPLINE** ENGLISH **EDUCATION** Univ Mich, BA, 59; Univ Md, MA, 63; Univ Mich, MA, 73; PhD, 78. **CAREER** Prof, Calif State Univ, 84-. **HONORS AND AWARDS** Mellon Fel, Univ S Calf, 82-83. **MEMBERSHIPS** Nat Coun of Teachers of English, Conf on Col Composition and Comm, Writing Prog Admin. **RESEARCH** Language and Literacy. **SELECTED PUBLICATIONS** Co-ed, Perspectives on Plagiarism and Intellectual property in a Postmodern World, SUNY Press, 99; auth, "Multiple Languages, Multiple Literacies," in Situated Stories: Valuing Diversity in Composition Research, Cook Pub, 98; auth, "The Grammar and rhetoric of Inclusion," College English, (95): 182-195; auth, "The English Only Movement," The Writing Instructor, (87): 39-46. **CONTACT ADDRESS** Dept English, California State Univ, Los Angeles, 5151 State Univ Dr, Los Angeles, CA 90032-4226. **EMAIL** aroy@calstatela.edu

ROY, EMIL L.
PERSONAL Born 06/18/1933, Fremont, NE **DISCIPLINE** ENGLISH **EDUCATION** Univ Redlands, BA, 55; Univ Calif, Berkeley, MA, 56; Univ Southern Calif, PhD(English), 61. **CAREER** Instr English, Fullerton Jr Col, 57-59 & Cerritos Col, 60-61; from instr to asst prof, Univ Southern Calif, 61-66; assoc prof, Northern Ill Univ, 66-68; Purdue Univ, West Lafayette, 68-73 & Univ PR, Mayaguez, 73-74; prof English & chm dept, Univ Tenn, Martin, 74-75; prof English & Acad Dean, Univ Sc, Aiken, 75-, Fulbright prof, Univ Kiel, Ger, 64-65. **MEMBERSHIPS** MLA **SELECTED PUBLICATIONS** Coauth, Studies in Fiction, Harper, 65; auth, King Lear and Desire Under the Elms, Die Neueren Sprachen, 1/66; Studies in Drama, Harper, 68; Christopher Fry, 68 & British Drama Since Shaw, 72, Southern Ill Univ, War and Manliness in TrC, Comp Drama, 72; coauth, Literary Spectrum, Allyn & Bacon, 74; Literature I, Macmillan, 76. **CONTACT ADDRESS** Univ of So Carolina, Aiken, 171 University Pky., Aiken, SC 29801-6309. **EMAIL** Emilroy@hotmail.com

ROY, G(EORGE) ROSS
PERSONAL Born 08/20/1924, Montreal, PQ, Canada, m, 1954, 1 child **DISCIPLINE** ENGLISH, COMPARATIVE LITERATURE **EDUCATION** Concordia Univ, BA, 50; Univ Montreal, MA, 51, PhD(English), 59; Univ Strasbourg, dipl, 54; Univ Paris, DUniv(comp lit), 58. **CAREER** Lectr English, Royal Mil Col, St Jean, 54-56; asst prof, Univ Ala, 58-61; from asst prof to assoc prof, Univ Montreal, 61-63; prof, Tex Technol Univ, 63-65; prof English & Comp Lit, Univ SC, 65-90; Hun-

tington Libr grant, 62; Can Coun & Am Philos Soc grant, 63; founding mem bd gov & chmn libr comt, Am-Scottish Found, NY, 66-; founding ed, Studies in Scottish Lit, 63- ; gen ed, Scottish Poetry Reprints, Quarto Press, London & Dept English Bibliog Ser, Univ SC. **HONORS AND AWARDS** Founding vice-pres, Asn for Scottish Lit Stud; fel, Soc of Antiq of Scotland; hon life pres, Robert Burns Federation; Robert Bruce Award, Old Dominion Univ; distinguished prof Univ S Carolina, 89. **MEMBERSHIPS** Int Comp Lit Asn; Am Comp Lit Asn; MLA; S Atlantic MLA; Edinburgh Bibl Soc; Thomas Carlyle Soc; James Boswell Soc. **RESEARCH** Comparative literature; Scottish literature; Robert Burns. **SELECTED PUBLICATIONS** ed & trans, Twelve Modern French-Canadian Poets, Toronto, 58; auth, Le sentiment de la nature dans la poesie canadienne anglaise 1867-1918, Paris, 61; auth, French Translations/Critics of Robert Burns to 1893, Revue de Litterature Comparee, 63-4; auth, French Stage Adaptations of Tom Jones, Revue de Litterature Comparee, 70; ed, Scottish section, New Cambridge Bibliography of English Literature, 1660-1800, Cambridge, 71; auth, The French Reputation of Thomas Carlyle in the Nineteenth Century, in Drescher, ed, Thomas Carlyle 1981, Frankfurt am Main, 83; ed, The Letters of Robert Burns, 2 vols, Oxford, 85; auth, Scottish Poets and the French Revolution, Etudes Ecossaises, 92; auth, Editing Burns' Letters in the Twentieth Century, in Carnie, ed, Robert Burns: Some Twentieth Century Perspectives, Calgary, 93; auth, Editing Robert Burns in the Nineteenth Century, in Simpson, Burns Now, Edinburgh, 94. **CONTACT ADDRESS** Dept of English, Univ of So Carolina, Columbia, Columbia, SC 29208.

ROY, PARAMA
DISCIPLINE ENGLISH LITERATURE **EDUCATION** Univ Delhi, BA; Univ Rochester, MA, PhD. **CAREER** Prof, Univ Calif, Riverside. **RESEARCH** Analysis of colonial discourse and postcolonial theory and literatures. **SELECTED PUBLICATIONS** Auth, The Victorians Inst Jour, 89; Studies in English Literature 1500-1900, 89; Indian Traffic: Identities in Question in Colonial and Postcolonial India, Univ Calif Press, 99. **CONTACT ADDRESS** Dept of Eng, Univ of California, Riverside, 1156 Hinderaker Hall, Riverside, CA 92521-0209. **EMAIL** proy@ucrac1.ucr.edu.

ROZAKIS, LAURIE
PERSONAL Born 07/20/1952, New York, NY, m, 1974, 2 children **DISCIPLINE** ENGLISH **EDUCATION** Hofstra Univ , BA, 73, MA, 75; SUNY Stony Brook, PhD, 84. **CAREER** Teacher, Commack UFSD #10, 73-84; adjunct asst prof, Hofstra Univ, 79-86; summer writing instr, Center for Talented Youth, Johns Hopkins Univ, 93-; assoc prof, SUNY Farmingdale, 86-. **HONORS AND AWARDS** Farmingdale Col Found Fac Merit Awd, 91; included in "Something About the Author," 94; SUNY Chancellor's Awd for Excellence in Teaching, 94; founding member, WILLA: The Women's Issues in Literature and Life Assembly, Nat Coun of Teachers of English, 91. **MEMBERSHIPS** Women in Lit and Life Assembly, Int Soc of Humor Studies, United Univ Profs, Laura Ingalls Wilder Mem Soc; Mass Hist Soc, Am Asn Univ Women, Nat Ed Asn, Nat Coun of Teachers of English. **SELECTED PUBLICATIONS** Auth, "A Placement Writing Program," Exercise Exchange, Utah State Univ (88); auth, "To Change the Things That Can be Changed," Mo English Bull (88); auth, "My Personal Reflections on Enhancing Student Success," Proceedings of the 3rd Annual Farmingdale Fac Conf (89); auth, "Holistic Evaluation of Writing: A Grading Practicum," Proceedings of the SUNY Coun on Writing 3rd Annual Conf (89); auth, "Puritan Punishment for Adulterous Conduct," The Nathanial Hawthorne Rev, vol XV, no 2 (90); auth, Merriam-Webster's Guide to Parlimentary Procedure, Merriam-Webster, Mass (94); auth, University Books: British Literature and University Books: American Literature, Random House, NY (94); auth, The Dictionary of American Biography, Charles Schribner's Sons, NY (94); auth, "Grouping for Success: Teaching to Varied Ability Levels in the Language Arts Classroom," and "What is Assessment?," Prentice-Hall Teacher Desk Ref (95). **CONTACT ADDRESS** Dept English, SUNY, Col of Tech at Farmingdale, 1250 Melville Rd, Farmingdale, NY 11735-1313.

ROZBICKI, MICHAL J.
PERSONAL Born 06/24/1946, Gdynia, m, 1991, 1 child **DISCIPLINE** ENGLISH LITERATURE, HISTORY **EDUCATION** Warsaw Univ, Poland, MA, 70, PhD, 84; Maria Curie-Sklodowska Univ, Poland, 75. **CAREER** Asst prof to assoc prof, 76-92, Warsaw Univ; asst prof to assoc prof, 92-, St Louis Univ. **HONORS AND AWARDS** Free Univ Berlin Fel, 82, 89; Oxford Univ Fel, 84; Rockefeller Found Fel, 90; John Carter Brown Libr Fel, 86; Huntington Libr Fel, 91; Amer Coun of Learned Soc Fel, 79-80. **MEMBERSHIPS** AAUP; Org Amer Hist. **RESEARCH** Cultural hist of colonial British Amer **SELECTED PUBLICATIONS** Auth, Transformation of English Cultural Ethos in Colonial America: Maryland 1634-1720, Univ Press Amer, 88; auth, The Birth of a Nation: History of the United States of America to 1860, Interim Publ House, Warsaw, 91; art, Between East-Central Europe and Britain: Reformation, Science, and the Emergence of Intellectual Networks in Mid-Seventeenth Century, E Europe Quart, 96; art, The Curse of Provincialism: Negative Perceptions of Colonial American Plantation Gentry, J S Hist, 97; auth, A Bridge to a Barrier to American Identity? The Uses of European Taste among Eighteenth-Century Plantation Gentry in British America, Amerikastudien, Heidelberg, 98; auth, The Complete Colonial Gentleman: Cultural Legitimacy in Plantation America, Univ Press Va, 98. **CONTACT ADDRESS** Dept of History, Saint Louis Univ, 3800 Lindell Blvd, PO Box 56907, Saint Louis, MO 63156-0907. **EMAIL** rozbicmj@slu.edu

ROZEMA, HAZEL J.
PERSONAL Born 10/16/1953, Grand Rapids, MI, m, 1988 **DISCIPLINE** COMMUNICATION **EDUCATION** Calvin Col, BA, 75; Mich State Univ, MA, 76; Univ Kans, PhD, 81. **CAREER** Asst prof, Western Mich Univ, 81-83; Asst prof, Univ Ark, at Little Rock, 83-88; assoc prof & ch, commun dept, Millikin Univ, 88-95; prof & ch, Mankato State Univ, 95-97; asst prof, commun dept, Univ Ill ar Springfield, 97-. **HONORS AND AWARDS** Outstanding Teacher Awd, Univ Kans, Millikin Univ; Faculty Scholar Awd, Univ Ark. **MEMBERSHIPS** Nat Commun Assoc; CSSA; PCA. **RESEARCH** Interpersonal & organizational communication; diversity & gender communication; sex education. **SELECTED PUBLICATIONS** Var articles in Family Relations, The Speech Communication Teacher. **CONTACT ADDRESS** 11 Baker Lane, Decatur, IL 62526. **EMAIL** rozema.hazel@uis.edu

ROZGA, MARGARET
PERSONAL Born 07/06/1945, Milwaukee, WI, w, 3 children **DISCIPLINE** ENGLISH **EDUCATION** Alverno Col, BA, 67; Univ Wisc, MA, 71; PhD, 77. **HONORS AND AWARDS** Arthur Kaplan Teaching Awd, Univ Wisc, 98. **MEMBERSHIPS** Mod Lang Asn, Midwest Mod Lang Asn, Soc for the Study of Midwestern Literature, Nat Coun of Teachers of English. **RESEARCH** Native American Literature; Midwestern Literature; Poetry; Joyce Carol Oates. **CONTACT ADDRESS** Dept English, Univ of Wisconsin, Waukesha, 1500 N Univ Dr, Waukesha, WI 53188-2720. **EMAIL** mrozga@uwc.edu

RUBEN, BRENT DAVID
PERSONAL Born 10/17/1944, Cedar Rapids, IA, m, 1967, 2 children **DISCIPLINE** COMMUNICATION **EDUCATION** Univ Iowa, BA, 66, MA 68, PhD, 70. **CAREER** Inst of Mass Commun, 68-70; asst prof of Mass Commun, Univ of Iowa, 70-71; asst prof of Commun, 71-74, assoc prof of Commun, 74-80; asst chairperson, Dept of Commun, 76-80; prof of Commun, 80-87, fel, Douglass Col, 87-; chmn, Dept of Commun, 80-84; dir, PhD prog, school of Commun, Infor, and Libr Studies, 84-93; EXEC DIR, UNIV PROG FOR ORGANIZATIONAL QUALITY AND COMMUN IMPROVEMENT, 93-; DISTINGUISHED PROF OF COMMUN, 87-; exec dir, Rutgers Univ, 93-; Joint Fac Member, Grad School of Applied and Professional Psychology, Rutgers Univ, 97-. **HONORS AND AWARDS** Recipient of Daniel Gorestein Award for Outstanding Scholarship and Distinguished Service, Rutgers Univ, 70; ch, Exec Coun, Nat Consortium for Continous Improvement in Higher Eudcation, 00-01; Distinguished Service Award, School of Commun, Infor, and Libr Studies, 93 94; Distinguished Service Award, Rutgers Univ, 93-94; Distinguished Teaching Award, School of Commun, Infor, and Libr Studies, Rutgers Univ, 92-93; Excellence in Teaching Award, Dept of Commun, Rutgers Univ, 92-93; Distinguished Service Award, Coalition of Digestive Disease Orgns, 84. **MEMBERSHIPS** Inst for Health, Rutgers Univ; Quality New Jersey; Nat Inst of Sci and Tech; Nat Higher Ed Quality Coun; Speech Commun Asn; Am Asn for Higher Ed; Int Commun Asn; Am Asn for Higher Ed; Eastern Commun Asn; Nat/Speech Commun Asn; Acad for Intercultural Studies; Am Soc for Infor Sci; Kappa Tau Alpha; Alpha Kappa Psi. **RESEARCH** Commun and Human Interaction, health and medical commun, organizational commun, higher education, interpersonal relationships. **SELECTED PUBLICATIONS** Auth, Excellence in Higher Education: A Baldrige-Based Guide to Assessment, Planning and Improvement, Wash, DC: Nat Asn of Col and Univ Business Officers, 00; coauth, Communication and Human Behavior, Fourth Edition, Allyn-Bacon, 98; auth, Organizational Communication and Systems Theory, Commun Theory: A Reader, 98; Quality in Higher Education, Transaction Books, 95; coauth, Excellence in Higher Education: A Guidebook for Self-Assessment, Strategic Planning and Improvement in Higher Education, Kendall-Hunt, 97; coauth, Excellence in Higher Education: A Workbook for Self-Assessment, Strategic Planning and Improvement in Higher Education, Kendall-Hunt, 97; coauth, Process Improvement in Higher Education, Kendall-Hunt, 97; auth, The Face of Higher Education: An Introduction to Service Excellence and Quality on the Front Line, Kendall-Hunt, 96; auth, Tradition of Excellence: Higher Education Quality Self-Assessment Guide, Kendall-Hunt, 94; coauth, The New Jersey Shore Cleanup Initiative: A Case of Quality Practice, Proceedings, Ocean Community Conference, Marine Tech Soc, Inc, 98; auth, The Quality Approach in Higher Education: Concepts and Context for Change, in Quality in Higher Ed, Transaction Books, 95; auth, Defining and Assessing Quality in Higher Education: Beyond TQM, in Quality in Higher Ed, Transaction Books, 95; auth, What Students Remember: Teaching, Learning and Human Communication, Quality in Higher Ed, Transaction Books, 95. **CONTACT ADDRESS** Ctr for Organizational Dev and Leadership, Rutgers, The State Univ of New Jersey, New Brunswick, 4 Huntington St, New Brunswick, NJ 08901-1071. **EMAIL** ruben@odl.rutgers.edu

RUBENSTEIN, ROBERTA
PERSONAL Born 11/05/1944, Milford, DE, m, 1971, 2 children **DISCIPLINE** ENGLISH LITERATURE **EDUCATION** Univ CO, BA (magna cum laude), 66; Univ London, PhD, 69. **CAREER** Instr, 69-70, asst prof, 70-74, assoc prof, 74-80, full prof, Dept of Lit, American Univ, Washington, DC, 80-, acting chair, 76-77, dir of women's studies prog, 82-88. **HONORS AND AWARDS** American Univ: Outstanding Teacher Awd, Col of Arts and Sciences, 74, 79; Sr Scholar Awd, CAS, 87; Univ Fac Awd for Outstanding Contrib to Academic Development, 89; Am Univ Scholar/Teacher of the Year Awd, 94. **MEMBERSHIPS** Modern Lang Assn; Phi Beta Kappa (Zeta chapter). **RESEARCH** Modern and contemporary fiction; women's lit and feminist theory; psychological approaches to lit. **SELECTED PUBLICATIONS** Auth, The Novelistic Vision of Doris Lessing: Breaking the Form of Consciousness, Univ IL Press, 79; Boundaries of the Self: Gender, Culture, Fiction, Univ IL Press, 87; Worlds of Fiction, co-ed, with Charles R Larson, Macmillan, 93; Fragmented Bodies/Selves/Narratives: Margaret Drabble's Postmodern Turn, Contemporary Lit 35-1, 94; Fixing the Past: Yearning and Nostalgia in Woolf and Lessing, in Woolf and Lessing: Breaking the Mold, ed Ruth Saxton and Jean Tobin, St Martin's Press, Homeric Resonances: Longing and Belonging in Barbara Kingsolver's Animal Dreams, in Homemaking: Women Writers and the Politics and Poetics of Home, ed Catherine Wiley and Fiona R Barnes, Garland, 96; House Mothers and Haunted Daughters: Shirley Jackson and Female Gothic, Tulsa Studies in Women's Literature, 15-2, 96; History and Story, Sign and Design: Faulknerian and Postmodern Voice in Toni Morrison's Jazz, in Unflinching Gaze: Morrison and Faulkner Re-Envisioned, ed Carol A Kolmerten, Stephen M Ross, and Judith Bryant Wittenberg, Univ Press MS, 97; Singing the Blues/Reclaiming Jazz: Toni Morrison and Cultural Mourning, Mosaic: The Interarts Project, Part II: Cultural Agendas 31-2, 98; over ninety book reviews and review-essays published between 1970-2000 in the following scholarly journals and newspapers: J of Modern Lit, Modern Fiction Studies, Woolf Studies Annual, Doris Lessing Newsletter, Belles Lettres, The Women's Rev of Books, Books Abroad, The New Republic, The Progressive, Res in African Lits, World Lit Written in English, The Nat Observer, Chicago Tribune Book World, Washington Post Book World, The Detroit News, The World and I, Worldview. **CONTACT ADDRESS** Dept of Lit, American Univ, Gray Hall 214, Washington, DC 20016. **EMAIL** rubenst@american.edu

RUBIN, ANDREW M.
PERSONAL Born 01/30/1969, Pittsburgh, PA **DISCIPLINE** ENGLISH LITERATURE **EDUCATION** Brown Univ, BA, 92; Univ Sussex, MA, 93; Columbia Univ, MA, 96; M Phil, 99; PhD, 02. **CAREER** Instr, Columbia Univ, 97-00; adj prof, Barnard Col, 01-. **HONORS AND AWARDS** Pres Fel, Stern Fel, Magna Cum Laude, Brown Univ. **MEMBERSHIPS** MLA, ACLA. **RESEARCH** Nineteenth and twentieth-century English literature; modernism; literary criticism and post colonial criticism; Frankfurt School. **SELECTED PUBLICATIONS** Ed, The Edward Said Reader, Vintage, 00; ed, Adorno: A Critical Reader, Blackwell, 01. **CONTACT ADDRESS** Eng Dept., Columbia Univ, New York, NY 10027. **EMAIL** anr5@columbia.edu

RUBIN, L.
PERSONAL Born 11/25/1942, Pittsburgh, PA, m, 1964, 2 children **DISCIPLINE** ENGLISH **EDUCATION** Carnegie Mellon Univ, PhD, 84. **CAREER** Instr to assoc prof, Pa State Univ. **MEMBERSHIPS** Nat Counc of Teachers of English; Pa Col English Assoc. **RESEARCH** Composition pedagogy, Jewish women writers. **SELECTED PUBLICATIONS** Auth, "Catching the Ephemeral: A Teacher Studies Classroom Talk", Teaching English in the Two Year College 22 (May 95): 89-101; coauth, "Model for Active Learning: Collaborative Peer Teaching", College Teacher 46.1 (98): 25-31; auth, "Nessa Rapoports Preparing for Sabbath: A Jewish Coming of Age", Studies in Am Jewish Lit 17, (98): 25-31; auth, "Two Jewish Girls Come of Age: Gender and Ethnicity in Allegra Maud Goldman and Leaving Brooklyn", Mod Jewish Studies Vol II, (99): 70-85. **CONTACT ADDRESS** Dept English, Pennsylvania State Univ, New Kensington, 3550 7th St Rd, New Kensington, PA 15068-1765. **EMAIL** lxr5@psu.edu

RUBIN, REBECCA B.
PERSONAL Born 12/11/1948, York, PA, m **DISCIPLINE** SPEECH COMMUNICATION **EDUCATION** Penn St Univ, BA, 70, MA, 71; Univ IL UC, PhD, 75 **CAREER** Instr, Messiah Col PA, 71-72; tchng/res asst, Dept of Speech and Drama, 72-75, Univ of IL; part-time instr, Georgia Southern Col, 75-76; instr, Dept of Drama & Speech, Univ of NC, 76-77; asst prof, Communication Discipline, Univ WI, 77-81; asst prof, Dept of Communication, Cleveland St Univ, 81-82; from assoc prof, School of Speech Comm, to prof, School for Communication Stud, Kent St Univ, 88-. **HONORS AND AWARDS** Who's Who in the Media and Communications; Women in Communication a Biographical Sourcebook; Outstanding Merit Awd Speech Comm Asn, 95; Kent St Univ Pres Honor Roll, 92; Phi Beta Delta Honor Soc for Intl Scholars, 92. **MEMBERSHIPS** Natl Comm Asn; Intl Comm Asn. **RESEARCH** Interpersonal communication; communication competence. **SELECTED PUBLICATIONS** Coauth, Test of a Self-Efficacy Model of In-

terpersonal Communication Competence, Comm Quart 41, 93; coauth, The Role of Self-Disclosure and Self-Awareness in Affinity-Seeking Competence, Comm Res Reports 10, 93; auth, Communication Competency Assessment Instrument High School Edition, Spectra Inc, 94; auth, Communication Competency Assessment Instrument, Spectra, 94; coauth, Development of a Communication Flexibility Measure, South Comm Jour 59, 94; coauth, Development of a Measure of Interpersonal Communication Competence, Comm Res Reports 11, 94; auth, SCA Summer Conference Proceedings and Prepared Remarks, Speech Comm Asn, 94; co-ed, Communication Research Measures: A Sourcebook, Guilford, 94; coauth, Organizational Entry: An Investigation of Newcomer Communication Behavior and Uncertainty, Comm Res 22, 95; coauth, A New Measure of Cognitive Flexibility, Psychol Reports 76, 95; coauth, Performance Based Assessment of High School Speech Instruction, Comm Ed 44, 95; coauth, Media Education Assessment Handbook, Erlbaum, 97; coauth, Preparing Competent College Graduates Setting New and Higher Expectations for Student Learning, 97; coauth, Effects of Instruction on Communication Apprehension and Communication Competence, Comm Ed 46, 97; coauth, Communication and Personality Trait perspectives, Hampton Press, 98; coauth, Affinity-Seeking in Initial Interactions, South Jour of Comm, 98; coauth, Communication Research Strategies and Sources, Wadsworth, 5th ed, 00. **CONTACT ADDRESS** Kent State Univ, PO Box 5190, Kent, OH 44242-0001. **EMAIL** rrubin@kent.edu

RUBIN, STEVEN J.
PERSONAL Born New York, NY **DISCIPLINE** ENGLISH **EDUCATION** Univ Mich, PhD. **CAREER** Prof and Dept Chair, Univ S Fla. **MEMBERSHIPS** MLA, SAMLA **RESEARCH** Jewish Studies; American Literature. **SELECTED PUBLICATIONS** Auth, Telling and Remembering: A Century of American Jewish Poetry, Beacon Press, 97; auth, Writing Our Lives: autobiographies of American Jews, Jewish Pub Soc, 92. **CONTACT ADDRESS** Dept English, Univ of So Florida, 4202 E Fowler Ave, Tampa, FL 33620-9951. **EMAIL** rubin@chuma1.cas.usf.edu

RUBIO, MARY H.
PERSONAL Born 10/02/1939, Mattoon, IL **DISCIPLINE** LITERATURE **EDUCATION** DePauw Univ, BA, 61; Univ Illinois, MA, 65; McMaster Univ, PhD, 82. **CAREER** Prof Eng, Univ Guelph, 67-; co-founder & current co-ed, CCL: Canadian Children's Literature/Litterature canadienne pour la jeunesse, 75. **MEMBERSHIPS** ISRCL; ACUTE; ChLA. **RESEARCH** 19th and early 20th century Canadian literature; children's literature; women's life-writing; popular fiction. **SELECTED PUBLICATIONS** Auth, Kanata: An Anthology of Canadian Children's Literature, Methuen, 76; auth, The Genesis of Grove's The Adventure of Leonard Broadus: A Text and Commentary, CCP, 83; coed, The Selected Journals of L.M. Montgomery, vols 1, 2, 3, Oxford Univ Press, 85, 87, 92; ed, Harvesting Thistles: The Textual Garden of L.M. Montgomery, Essays on Her Novels and Journals, CCP, 94; coauth, Writing a Life: L.M. Montgomery, ECW Press, 95. **CONTACT ADDRESS** Dept of English, Univ of Guelph, Guelph, ON, Canada N1G 2W1. **EMAIL** mrubio@uoguelph.ca

RUDD, JILL
DISCIPLINE INTERPERSONAL COMMUNICATION, GROUP COMMUNICATION **EDUCATION** Kent State Univ, BA, MA, PhD. **CAREER** Comm, Cleveland St Univ. **SELECTED PUBLICATIONS** Auth, Divorce Mediation: One Step Forward Two Steps Back?, Communication and the Disenfranchised,L. Erlbaum Assoc, 96. **CONTACT ADDRESS** Commun Dept, Cleveland State Univ, 83 E 24th St, Cleveland, OH 44115. **EMAIL** j.rudd@csuohio.edu

RUDE, CAROLYN D.
DISCIPLINE TECHNICAL COMMUNICATION **EDUCATION** Univ IL, PhD, 75. **CAREER** Prof Eng, 81-, dir, Tech Commun, TX Tech Univ. **HONORS AND AWARDS** Soc for Technical Commun, Fel; Best Article on philos or theory of Technical or Scientific Communication, 96; J.R. Gould Award for Teaching, 98. **MEMBERSHIPS** assoc of teachers of Technical Writing . **RESEARCH** Decision making. **SELECTED PUBLICATIONS** Auth, Technical Editing, 2nd ed, 98; coauth, Technical Communication, 2nd ed, 00. **CONTACT ADDRESS** Texas Tech Univ, Lubbock, TX 79409-3091. **EMAIL** carolyn.rude@ttu.edu

RUDE, DONALD W.
PERSONAL Born 12/01/1936, Great Bend, KS, m, 1968 **DISCIPLINE** ENGLISH LITERATURE **EDUCATION** Univ IL, PhD, 71. **CAREER** Prof, dir, grad stud, TX Tech Univ. **MEMBERSHIPS** Joseph Conrad Soc of Am. **SELECTED PUBLICATIONS** Auth, A Critical Edition of Sir Thomas Elyot's The Boke Named The Governour; articles on Joseph Conrad, Sir Thomas Elyot, T.S. Eliot, William Shakespeare, and John Donne; original poetry. **CONTACT ADDRESS** Texas Tech Univ, Lubbock, TX 79409-3019. **EMAIL** don.rude@ttu.edu

RUDE, ROBERTA N.
DISCIPLINE THEATRE **EDUCATION** Wichita State Univ, BA, 65; London Acad Music & Dramatic Art, post-graduate profession certificate, 69; Trinity Univ, MA, 70. **CAREER** Asst prof, Oberlin Col, 80-85; asst prof & producer, St Mary's Col, 85-92; assoc prof & chair Dept of Theatre, Univ SDak, 92-. **MEMBERSHIPS** Actors Equity Asn, Screen Actors Guild, Asn for Theatre in Higher Educ, Popular Culture Asn, Nat Asn of Schs of Theatre Comn on Accreditation. **RESEARCH** Applications of the Alexander Technique to the Acting Process, Directing Shakespeare. **CONTACT ADDRESS** Dept Theatre, Univ of So Dakota, Vermillion, 414 E Clark St, Vermillion, SD 57069-2307. **EMAIL** rrude@usd.edu

RUDERMAN, JUDITH
DISCIPLINE ENGLISH LITERATURE **EDUCATION** Duke Univ, PhD, 77. **CAREER** Prof, Duke Univ. **MEMBERSHIPS** DH Lawrence Soc N Am. **SELECTED PUBLICATIONS** Auth, D. H. Lawrence and the Devouring Mother, Duke, 84; William Styron, Ungar, 87; Joseph Heller, Ungar, 91. **CONTACT ADDRESS** Eng Dept, Duke Univ, Durham, NC 27706.

RUDOLPH, ROBERT SAMUEL
PERSONAL Born 10/05/1937, Philadelphia, PA, m, 1960, 1 child **DISCIPLINE** ENGLISH **EDUCATION** Temple Univ, BA, 59; Univ Wis, MA, 61, PhD(English), 66. **CAREER** Asst prof English, 65-69, from assoc prof to prof English Lang & Lit, Univ Toledo, 69-81. **MEMBERSHIPS** NCTE. **RESEARCH** Diachronic linguistics; Medieval English literature. **CONTACT ADDRESS** 2801 W Bancroft St, Toledo, OH 43606-3390.

RUFFIN, PAUL
DISCIPLINE NINETEENTH-CENTURY LITERATURE **EDUCATION** MS State Univ, BS, 64, MA, 68; Univ Southern MS, PhD, 74. **CAREER** EngDept, Sam Houston State Univ **HONORS AND AWARDS** Dir, Eng Writing Option; Found & Dir, TX Rev Press; Fac adv, Sam Houston State Rev. **MEMBERSHIPS** TX Inst Letters; MS Inst Arts & Letters; S-Central Mod Lang Asn; Conf Col Tchrs Eng; Conf Eds Learned Jours; TX Asn Creative Writing Tchrs; Gulf Coast Asn Creative Writing Tchrs. **SELECTED PUBLICATIONS** Auth, Mississippi Poets, 76; The Texas Anthology, 79; Lighting the Furnace Pilot, 82; Our Women, 85; Contemporary New England Poetry: A Sampler, 86-87; The Storm Cellar, 87; To Come Up Grinning: A Tribute to George Garrett, 89; Contemporary Southern Short Fiction: A Sampler, 91; Images of Texas in the Nation, 91; That's What I Like (About the South): Southern Fiction fbr the 1990's, Univ S Carolina Press, 93; The Man Who Would Be God, Southern Methodist Univ Press, 93; After The Grapes of Wrath: Essays on John Steinbeck, Ohio Univ Press, 95; Circling, Browder Springs Press, 96; A Goyen Companion: Appreciations of a Writers Writer, Univ Tex Press, 97. **CONTACT ADDRESS** Sam Houston State Univ, Huntsville, TX 77341.

RUGGLES, MYLES A.
DISCIPLINE INSTITUTIONAL CONTEXT OF SOCIAL COMMUNICATION PROCESSES **EDUCATION** Simon Fraser, MA, PhD. **CAREER** Fac, Univ Windsor, 94-. **RESEARCH** Institutional context of social communication processes; aspects of the trajectories of development of communication technologies and institutions, and of the relationship between tacit and explicit forms of knowledge and rationality in the determination of social order. **SELECTED PUBLICATIONS** Auth, "Personal Information Flows and Boundaries in the Intelligent Network," CIRCIT Policy Res Paper Series No. 28, Melbourne: Centre fo International Reseach on Communication and Information Technologies, (92), 70; auth, "Balance and Freedom of Speech: The Challenge for Canadian Broadcasting," Paper in Can J of Commun, (92), 17, 37-59; auth, "Mixed Signals: Pesonal Data Control in the Intelligent Network," Paper in Media Infor Australia, 67, (93), 28-40; auth, "The Audience Reflected in the Medium of Law," Ablex Publishers: Nowood, New Jersey: Ablex Communication and Information Science Series, (94), 185; auth, "What kind of global culture? Mass Communication in a Changing Context," Can J of Commun, 98. **CONTACT ADDRESS** Dept of Communication Studies, Univ of Windsor, 401 Sunset Ave, Windsor, ON, Canada N9B 3P4. **EMAIL** ruggles@uwindsor.ca

RUGOFF, MILTON
PERSONAL Born 03/06/1913, New York, NY, m, 1937, 1 child **DISCIPLINE** HISTORY, ENGLISH **EDUCATION** Columbia Col, BA, 33; Columbia Univ, MA, 34, PhD, 40. **CAREER** Ed, Alfred E Knopf, Inc, 42-47; assoc ed, 47-48, Mag of the Year; ed, 53, Readers Subscription Bk Club; ed, vice pres, 48-93, Chanticleer Press, Inc, NY. **HONORS AND AWARDS** Literary Lion medal, NY Pub Lib, 90; Ohioana Bk Awd, 82. **MEMBERSHIPS** Soc Amer Hist; Authors' Guild. **RESEARCH** American Biography; Elizabethan literature; history of traveland exploration. **SELECTED PUBLICATIONS** Auth, The Penguin Book of World Folk Tales, Viking, 49; ed & intro, The Great Travelers, S and S, 61; auth, Donne's Imagery: A Study in Creative Sources, Atheneum, 62; auth, Marco Polo's Adventures in China, Caravel Bks, 64; auth, Prudery and Passion: Sexuality in Victorian America, Putnam, 71; ed, Britannica Encycl of American Art, Simon, 73; auth, The Beechers: An American Family in the Nineteenth Century, Harper & Row, 81; auth, America's Gilded Age: Intimate Portraits from an Era of Extravagance and Change, Holt & Co, 89. **CONTACT ADDRESS** 18 Ox Ridge Rd, Elmsford, NY 10523.

RULAND, RICHARD
DISCIPLINE ENGLISH **EDUCATION** Univ of Western Ont, BA, 53; Univ of Detroit, MA, 55; Univ of Mich, PhD, 60. **CAREER** Instr to asst prof, Yale Univ, 60-68; Prof, Washington Univ, 67-; member, St Louis Science Center Steering Committee, 88-. **HONORS AND AWARDS** Bruern Fel, 64; Morse Fel, 66; Fulbright Fel, 75, 78; ACSL Travel Grant, 81; Guggenheim Res Fel, 82. **RESEARCH** Literary History, tradition and a canon formation, cultural nationalism, British-American cultural relations, the history, theory and method of literary study in the United States. **SELECTED PUBLICATIONS** Auth, "A View from Back Home: Kafka's Amerika", Am Quarterly XIII (61): 33-41; auth, "The American Plays of Bertolt Brecht", Am Quarterly XV (63): 371-398; auth, The Rediscovery of American Literature: Premises of Critical Taste, 1900-1940, Harvard Univ Pr, 67; ed, Walden: A Collection of Critical Essays, Prentice Hall, 67; ed The Native Muse: Theories of American Literature, Vol I: From Bradford to Whitman, EP Dutton, 72; coed, Sacred Texts and Usable Pasts: What is Literary History?, Anglo-American Romanticisms; auth, America in Modern European Literature: From Image to Metaphor, NY Univ Pr, 76; auth, "Kate Chopin and The Awakening", Essays on English and American Literature, ed J Barker, JA Verlun and Jvd Vriesenaerde, Rodopi (Amsterdam, 87): 119-130; auth, From Puritanism to Postmodernism: A History of American Literature, Routledge, (London), 91; auth, "Literary History and the Legacy of Pragmatism", Am Lit Hist 6, (94): 354-370. **CONTACT ADDRESS** Dept English, Washington Univ, 505 Westgate, Saint Louis, MO 63130. **EMAIL** rruland@artsei.wustl.edu

RUMOLD, RAINER
PERSONAL Born 10/29/1941, Elbig, Germany, m, 2 children **DISCIPLINE** LITERATURE **EDUCATION** Stanford, PhD, 71 **CAREER** Vis asst prof, Stanford Univ, 73-76, assoc prof, Northwestern Univ. **MEMBERSHIPS** MLA **RESEARCH** 20th century lit & thought; modernism & avant-garde stud. **SELECTED PUBLICATIONS** Auth, Sprachliches Experiment und literarische Tradition, Stanford German Stud, 75; Gottfried Benn und der Expressionismus, Skriptor/Athenaeum, 82; ed, The Ideological Crisis of Expressionism, Camden House 90; Man from Babel, Yale Univ Press, 98, gen ed, Series in the Study of the Avant-Garde and Modernism, Northwestern Univ Press, 93-; The Janus Face of the German Avant-garde, Northwestern Univ. Press, 2001. **CONTACT ADDRESS** Dept of German Lit & Critical Thought, Northwestern Univ, 1427 Noyes St, Evanston, IL 60201. **EMAIL** r-rumold@nwu.edu

RUNGE, LAURA
PERSONAL Born 05/04/1966, Yonkers, NY **DISCIPLINE** ENGLISH **EDUCATION** Univer of Rochester, BA, 88; Emory Univ, MA, 91, PhD 93. **CAREER** Assoc prof, 93-, Univ of South Florida. **HONORS AND AWARDS** Phi Beta Kappa, 87; Undergraduate teach award, 95-96; USF Research & Creative Scholarship grant 98. **MEMBERSHIPS** MLA; ASECS; Aphra Behn Soc (exec secretary); AAUW **RESEARCH** Women's Literature; 18th century British literature, aesthetics **SELECTED PUBLICATIONS** Auth, Gender and Language in British Literary Critcism, 1660-1780, Cambridge Univ Press, 97. **CONTACT ADDRESS** Dept of English, Univ of So Florida, 4202 E. Fowler Ave., Tampa, FL 33620. **EMAIL** runge@chuma.cas.usf.edu

RUNYAN, WILLIAM RONALD
PERSONAL Born 07/18/1940, Steubenville, OH, 1 child **DISCIPLINE** EIGHTEENTH CENTURY ENGLISH LITERATURE, RHETORIC **EDUCATION** Wayne State Univ, BA, 63, MA, 65; Princeton Univ, PhD(English), 75. **CAREER** Grad asst English, Wayne State Univ, 63-65; instr, Wright State Univ, 65-69; instr humanities, Morgan State Col, 69-71; grad asst English, Princeton Univ, 74-75; vis lectr, Univ Wis, Parkside, 69-71; asst prof, 76-80, assoc prof English, Salem Col, 80-82, full prof, Salem-Teikyo Univ, 83-; Salem International Univ, 00-. **MEMBERSHIPS** MLA; AAUP **RESEARCH** The satirical element in English romantic poetry; rhetorical theory and classical translations; contemporary continental rhetorical theory. **SELECTED PUBLICATIONS** Auth, Bob Southey's diabolical doggerel: source and authorship, Wordsworth Circle, winter 76. **CONTACT ADDRESS** Dept of Liberal Studies, Salem-Teikyo Univ, Salem, WV 26426.

RUPP, RICHARD
PERSONAL Born 11/16/1934, Indianapolis, IN, m, 1963, 5 children **DISCIPLINE** ENGLISH **EDUCATION** Univ of Notre Dame, BA, 56; MA, 57; Ind Univ, PhD, 64. **CAREER** Asst prof, Georgetown Univ, 61-68; asst prof, Univ of Miami, 68-72; assoc prof, Brooklyn Col of CUNY, 72-74; grad dean, Appalachian State Univ, 75-79; prof, Appalachian State Univ, 79-. **HONORS AND AWARDS** Allstate Scholar, Indiana, 60; Bobbs Merrill Traveling Fel, 68; Georgetown Summer Res Fel, 68; Appalachian Res & Travel Grant, 95. **MEMBERSHIPS** Am Inst of Irish Studies, Popular Culture Asn. **RESEARCH**

Anglo-Irish literature, writing fiction. **SELECTED PUBLICATIONS** Auth, Celebration in Post War American Fiction 1945-1967, Univ of Miami Press, 70; auth, Critics on Whitman, Univ of Miami Press, 72; Critics on Emily Dickinson, Univ of Miami Press, 72; auth, Getting Through College, Paulist Press, 84; auth, Unity, 1st Books, 99. **CONTACT ADDRESS** Dept English, Appalachian State Univ, Boone, NC 28608-0001. **EMAIL** rupprh@appstate.edu

RUPPERSBURG, HUGH
PERSONAL Born 03/01/1950, Atlanta, GA, m, 1978, 3 children **DISCIPLINE** ENGLISH **EDUCATION** Univ Ga, AB, 72; Univ SC, MA, 74; Univ SC, PhD, 78. **CAREER** From Instr to Prof, Univ Ga, 77-. **HONORS AND AWARDS** Outstanding Honors Prof, 83, 87; Sandy Beaver Teaching Awd, Franklin Col, 89; Ga Author of the Year, Asn Ga Col Bookstores, 92. **MEMBERSHIPS** S Atlantic Mod Lang Asn, Mod Land Asn, Soc for the Study of Southern Lit, Robert Penn Warren Circle, Coun for Cols of Arts and Sci. **SELECTED PUBLICATIONS** Auth, Robert Penn Warren and the American Imagination, Univ Ga Pr (Athens, GA), 90; ed, Georgia Voices I: Fiction, Univ Ga Pr (Athens, GA), 92; ed, Georgia Voices II: Non-Fiction, Univ Ga Pr (Athens, GA), 94; auth, Reading Faulkner: Light in August, UP of Miss (Jackson, MI), 94; co-ed, Georgia Voices III: Poetry, Univ Ga Pr (Athens, GA), 00; co-ed, Critical Essays on Don Delillo, GK Hall (New York, NY), forthcoming. **CONTACT ADDRESS** Dept English, Univ of Georgia, 310F New College, Athens, GA 30602-0002. **EMAIL** hruppers@uga.edu

RUSHING, JANICE H.
DISCIPLINE RHETORICAL AND MASS MEDIA CRITICISM **EDUCATION** Univ S Calif, PhD. **CAREER** Comm Stu, Univ Ark **SELECTED PUBLICATIONS** Articles, Critical Studies in Mass Comm, Western Jour Comm, Quart Jour Speech, Southern Comm Journal, Comm Education, Comm Monographs, Comm Studies. **CONTACT ADDRESS** Univ of Arkansas, Fayetteville, Fayetteville, AR 72701.

RUSSELL, ANNE
DISCIPLINE EARLY MODERN DRAMA; POETRY **EDUCATION** Trent, BA; York, MA, PhD. **CAREER** Assoc prof. **RESEARCH** Renaissance drama and poetry, 17th century women writers, Aphra Behn. **SELECTED PUBLICATIONS** Auth, A Critical Edition of Aphra Behn's "The Rover," Peterborough: Broaadview Press, 94; co-ed, Enacting Gender on the English Renaissnce Stage, Univ of Illinois Press, 98. **CONTACT ADDRESS** Dept of English, Wilfrid Laurier Univ, 75 University Ave W, Waterloo, ON, Canada N2L 3C5. **EMAIL** arussell@wlu.ca

RUSSELL, CHARLES G.
DISCIPLINE COMMUNICATION STUDIES **EDUCATION** Southern IL Univ, BS, 59, MS, 65, PhD, 71. **CAREER** Asst prof, Eastern IL Univ, 65-71; asst prof, WV Univ, 71-75; assoc prof, 75-76; prof, Univ Toledo, 85-99; pres, Int Soc for Gen Semantics, 99- . **SELECTED PUBLICATIONS** Auth, The Interpersonal Process, Burgess Int Group, 96; Instructor's Guide for The Interpersonal Process, Burgess Int Group, 96; Language and Behavior, Burgess Int Group, 93; Interpersonal is Between, Burgess Int Group, 93. **CONTACT ADDRESS** Int Soc for Gen Semantics, Box 2469, San Francisco, CA 94126.

RUSSELL, DAVID L.
PERSONAL Born 05/25/1946, Wauseon, OH, m, 1978, 3 children **DISCIPLINE** ENGLISH **EDUCATION** Bowling Green State Univ, BA, 68; MA, 71; PhD, 78. **CAREER** Instr, Bowling Green State Univ, 71-80; prof, Ferris State Univ, 80-. **HONORS AND AWARDS** Mich Asn of Governing Boards Distinguished Fac Awd; Acad Excellence Awd, Ferris Univ. **MEMBERSHIPS** Intl Children's Lit Asn. **RESEARCH** Children's Lit, Adolescent Lit. **SELECTED PUBLICATIONS** Auth, Patricia Maclachlan, Twayne, 97; auth, Scott O'Dell, Twayne, 99; auth, Literature for Children, 4th ed, Longman, 00. **CONTACT ADDRESS** Dept Lang & Lit, Ferris State Univ, 901 South State St, Big Rapids, MI 49307-2251.

RUSSELL, TILDEN A.
DISCIPLINE MUSIC **EDUCATION** Univ NC, PhD, 83. **CAREER** Asst prof, 86-92; assoc prof, 92-, Southern Conn State Univ. **SELECTED PUBLICATIONS** Auth, publ(s) on Baroque; Classic; Romantic Eras; Beethoven; chamber music; historical musicology. **CONTACT ADDRESS** Music Dept, So Connecticut State Univ, 501 Crescent St, New Haven, CT 06515-1355. **EMAIL** Russell_T@scsu.ctstateu.edu

RUSSO, JOHN PAUL
PERSONAL Born 05/31/1944, Boston, MA, s **DISCIPLINE** ENGLISH **EDUCATION** Harvard Univ, AB, 65, MA, 66, PhD, 69. **CAREER** Asst prof, 69-73, Harvard Univ; assoc prof, 77-78, prof, 80-82, Rutgers Univ Camden; prof, 82-, Univ Miami; vis prof, Univ of Palermo, 80-81; Rome, 87; Genoa, 90 **RESEARCH** history of criticism, representations of Italy. **SELECTED PUBLICATIONS** Auth, Alexander Pope: Tradition and Identity; I. A. Richards: His Life and Work; ed, Italian Americana **CONTACT ADDRESS** Dept of English, Univ of Miami, Coral Gables, FL 33124. **EMAIL** jprusso@umiami.edu

RUSSO, JOSEPH ANTHONY
PERSONAL Born 04/14/1937, Brooklyn, NY, m, 1960, 2 children **DISCIPLINE** CLASSICS **EDUCATION** Brooklyn Col, BA, 58; Yale Univ, MA, 60, PhD, 62. **CAREER** From instr to assoc prof classics, Yale Univ, 62-70; assoc prof, 70-76, prof classics, Haverford Col, 76-, chmn dept, 80-, fel, Ctr Hellenic Studies, Wash, DC, 65-66; Nat Endowment for Humanities younger humanist fel, 73-74; Am Coun Learned Soc grant-in-aid, 74; Nat Endowment Hum Summer Stipend, 82 & 90; vis prof class studies, Univ Mich, 77-78; Univ Ca Berkley, 83. **HONORS AND AWARDS** Distinguished Alumni Awd, Brooklyn Col, 82. **MEMBERSHIPS** Class Asn Atlantic States; Am Philol Asn. **RESEARCH** Greek literature and metrics; Homeric poetry; oral literature and folklore. **SELECTED PUBLICATIONS** Auth, A Closer Look at Homeric Formulas, Trans Am Philol Asn, 64; The Structural Formula of Homeric Verse, Yale Class Studies, 66; coauth, Homeric Psychology and the Oral Epic Tradition, J Hist Ideas, 68; Homer Against his Tradition, Arion, 68; The Inner Man in Archilochus and the Odyssey, Greek, Roman & Byzantine Studies, 74; Reading the Greek Lyric Poets, Arion, 75; How, and what, does Homer communicate, Class J, 76; contribr, Is Aural or oral composition the cause of Homer's formulaic style?, Oral Literature and the Formula, Univ Mich, 76; co-auth, A Commentary on Homer's Odyssey, Oxford Univ, 92; auth, Omero, Odissea V, Libri XVII-XX, Mondadori, Roma, 92. **CONTACT ADDRESS** Dept of Classics, Haverford Col, 370 Lancaster Ave, Haverford, PA 19041-1392. **EMAIL** jrusso@haverford.edu

RUSSO, MARY
DISCIPLINE LITERATURE AND CRITICAL THEORY **EDUCATION** Cornell Univ, PhD. **CAREER** Prof Lit and Critical Theory, dean, Sch of Hum, Arts and Cult Stud, Hampshire Col. **SELECTED PUBLICATIONS** Auth, Female Grotesque: Risk, Excess and Modernity, Routledge; coed, Nationalism and Sexualities, Routledge; Design in Italy: Italy in Europe, Africa, Asia and the Americas, Univ MN Press. **CONTACT ADDRESS** Hampshire Col, Amherst, MA 01002.

RUST, EZRA GARDNER
DISCIPLINE MUSIC **EDUCATION** UCLA, BA; UCB, MA, PhD. **CAREER** Prof; campus coordr, Interdisciplinary Stud Prog; past ch, Mus Dept; Sonoma State Univ, 68-. **RESEARCH** World music; World religious music and dance; Voice. **SELECTED PUBLICATIONS** Music and Dance of the World's Religions: A Comprehensive, Annotated Bibliography of Materials in the English Language, Greenwood Press, 96. **CONTACT ADDRESS** Dept of Music, Sonoma State Univ, 1801 E. Cotati Ave., Rohnert Park, CA 94928-3609. **EMAIL** gardner.rust@sonoma.edu

RUST, RICHARD DILWORTH
PERSONAL Born 09/04/1937, Provo, UT, m, 1960, 3 children **DISCIPLINE** ENGLISH **EDUCATION** Brigham Young Univ, BS, 61; Univ Wis, MS, 62, PhD(English), 66. **CAREER** From asst prof to assoc prof, 66-77, Prof English, Univ NC, Chapel Hill, 77-, Sr Fulbright lectr, Univ Heidelberg, 71-72 & 77-78; gen ed, Complete Works of Washington Irving, 77-. **HONORS AND AWARDS** Outstanding Work of Literary Criticism, Asn for Mormon Letters, for book "Feasting on the Word," 97; Outstanding Fac Awd, UNC's Senior Class, 98. **MEMBERSHIPS** SAtlantic Mod Lang Asn; Nathaniel Hawthorne Soc; Melville Soc; Mark Twain Circle; Poe Studies Asn; James Fenimore Cooper Asn. **RESEARCH** Nineteenth century American literature, especially writers of the American Renaissance period; the Book of Mormon as lit. **SELECTED PUBLICATIONS** Auth, "On the Trail of a Craftsman: The Art of 'The Pathfinder,'" in James Fenimore Cooper: New Historical and Literary Contexts, ed. W. M. Verhoeven (Amsterdam, Atlanta: Rodopi, 93), 177-184; auth, "Ancient and Modern in the Writings of Washington Irving," in Making Am/Making Am Lit, ed. A. Robert Lee and W. M. Verhoeven (Amsterdam, Atlanta: Rodopi, 96), 183-198; auth, Feasting on the Word: The Literary Testimony of the Book of Mormon, Deseret Book Company (Salt Lake City), 97; auth, "'I Love All Men Who Dive': Herman Melville and Joseph Smith," BYU Studies 38.1 (99): 151-169. **CONTACT ADDRESS** Dept of English, Univ of No Carolina, Chapel Hill, Chapel Hill, NC 27599-3520 27599-3520. **EMAIL** rust@email.unc.edu

RUSZKIEWICZ, JOHN JOSEPH
PERSONAL Born 05/28/1950, Cleveland, OH **DISCIPLINE** RHETORIC AND COMPOSITION **EDUCATION** St Vincent Col, BA, 72; Ohio State Univ, MA, 73, PhD, 77. **CAREER** From Asst Prof to Assoc Prof, 77-95, prof English, Univ Tex, Austin, 95-. **MEMBERSHIPS** Rhet Soc Am; NCTE; Conf Col Teachers English. **RESEARCH** Renaissance drama; rhetoric and composition. **SELECTED PUBLICATIONS** Auth, Liberality, Friendship and Timon of Athens, Thoth, 75-76; Parody and pedagogy: Explorations in imitative literature, Col English, 40: 693-701; Well-Bound Words: A Rhetoric, Scott, Foresman, 81; The Scott, Foresman Handbook for Writers, Scott, Foresman, 91; The Presence of Others, St Martin's, 94; Everything's an Argument, Bedford/St Martin's, 99; Bookmarks, Longman 00. **CONTACT ADDRESS** Div Rhetoric and Comp, Univ of Texas, Austin, Austin, TX 78712-1026. **EMAIL** ruszkiewicz@mail.utexas.edu

RUTHERFORD, CHARLES SHEPARD
PERSONAL Born 09/10/1940, Chicago, IL, m, 1962, 2 children **DISCIPLINE** MEDIEVAL LITERATURE **EDUCATION** Carleton Col, BA, 62; Ind Univ, Bloomington, MA, 66, PhD(English), 70. **CAREER** Lectr, 68-70, Asst Prof English, Univ Md, College Park, 70-, Assoc Dean, Arts and Humanities, 80-. **HONORS AND AWARDS** Am Coun on Educ fel, 77-78. **MEMBERSHIPS** MLA; SAtlantic Mod Lang Asn; Medieval Acad Am. **RESEARCH** Chaucer; Middle English poetry; Old English poetry. **SELECTED PUBLICATIONS** Auth, Pandarus as a lover: A joly wo or loves shotes keene, Annuale Mędaevale, 72; A new dog with an old trick: Archetypal patterns in Sounder, J Popular Film, spring 73; The Boke of Cupide reopened, Neuphilologische Mitteilungen, 77. **CONTACT ADDRESS** Col of Arts and Humanities, Univ of Maryland, Col Park, College Park, MD 20742-0001. **EMAIL** cruther@deans.umd.edu

RUTHERFORD, PAUL F. W.
PERSONAL Born 02/22/1944, Middlesex, England **DISCIPLINE** HISTORY, MEDIA STUDIES **EDUCATION** Carleton Univ, BA, 65; Univ Toronto, MA, 66, PhD, 73. **CAREER** Lectr, 69-73, asst prof, 73-75, assoc prof, 75-82, chmn, 82-87, Prof History, Univ Toronto, 82-. **HONORS AND AWARDS** SSHRC res grant, 90-91; SSHRC res grant, 93-96; SSHRC res grant, 99-02. **RESEARCH** Cultural history, canadian history, and the study of twentieth century popular culture. **SELECTED PUBLICATIONS** Auth, The Making of the Canadian Media, 78; auth, A Victorian Authority: The Daily Press in Late Nineteenth Century Canada, 82; auth, When Television Was Young: Primetime Canada 1952-1967, 90; auth, The New Icons? The Art of Television Advertising, 94; ed, Saving the Canadian City: The First Phase 1880-1920, 74. **CONTACT ADDRESS** Dept of History, Univ of Toronto, Toronto, ON, Canada M5S 1A1. **EMAIL** prutherf@chass.utoronto.ca

RUTLEDGE, HARRY CARRACI
PERSONAL Born 01/23/1932, Chillicothe, OH **DISCIPLINE** CLASSICS **EDUCATION** OH State Univ, BScEd, 54, MA, 57, PhD, 60. **CAREER** From asst prof to assoc prof classics, Univ GA, 60-68; assoc prof, head Romance lang, 72-79, Prof Class, Univ TN, Knoxville, 69-96, Prof Emer, 96-, Head Dept, 68-91, Secy adv coun, Am Acad Rome, 71-75. **MEMBERSHIPS** Am Philol Asn; Archaeol Inst Am; Vergilian Soc(pres , 77-79); Southern Comp Lit Asn (pres, 78-79); Class Asn Mid West & South (pres, 79-80); Am Class League (pres, 90-94). **RESEARCH** Lit of the Augustan Age; Vergil; class tradition in the 20th century. **SELECTED PUBLICATIONS** Auth, Propertius' Tarpeia: The poem itself, Class J, 11/64; Eliot and Vergil: Parallels in the Sixth Aeneid and Four Quartets, Vergilius, 66; Classical Latin poetry: An art for our time, In: The Endless Fountain, Ohio State Univ, 72; Contest and possession: Classical imagery in Henry James' The Golden Bowl, Comparatist, 5/77; Vergil's Dido in modern literature, Class & Mod Lit, summer 81; The Guernica Bull: Studies in the Classical Tradition in the Twentieth Century, Univ Ga Press, 89. **CONTACT ADDRESS** Dept of Class, Univ of Tennessee, Knoxville, 1101 McClung Tower, Knoxville, TN 37996-0471.

RUTLEDGE, STEVEN H.
PERSONAL Born 06/28/1963, Fresno, CA, m, 1985 **DISCIPLINE** CLASSICS **EDUCATION** Univ Mass - Boston, BA, 89; Brown Univ, PhD, 96. **CAREER** Asst Prof, Univ Md - College Park, 96-. **HONORS AND AWARDS** Grad Res Bd Fel, Univ Md, 97; Grad Res Board, Fel, 99. **MEMBERSHIPS** APA; CAAS; CAMWS. **RESEARCH** Roman social history; Roman literature of the Early Empire. **SELECTED PUBLICATIONS** Auth, Trajan and Tacitus Audience: reader Reception of Annales 1-2, Ramus vol 27, (98), 141-159; auth, Delatores and the Tradition of Violence in Roman Oratory," Am J of Philology 120, (99), 555-573; auth, "Plato, tacitus, and the dialogus de oratoribus," Latomus 254, (00), 345-357; auth, Tacitus in Tartan: Textual colonization and Expansionist Discourse in tacitus Agricol," gelios 27, (00), 75-95; auth, Imperial Inquisitions: Prosecutors and Informants from Tiberius to Domittian, 01. **CONTACT ADDRESS** Classics Dept, Univ of Maryland, Col Park, 2407 Marie Mount Hall, College Park, MD 20742. **EMAIL** srutled@deans.umd.edu

RUTTER, JEREMY B.
PERSONAL Born 06/23/1946, Boston, MA, m, 1970, 2 children **DISCIPLINE** CLASSICS **EDUCATION** Haverford Col, BA, 67; Univ Pa, PhD, 74. **CAREER** Vis asst prof, Univ Calif, Los Angeles, 75-76; from asst prof to assoc prof to prof to chairmn, 76-, Dartmouth Col. **HONORS AND AWARDS** Phi Beta Kappa, 67; Woodrow Wilson Fel, 67; Olivia James Travelling Fel, 75; NEH Res Grant, 79-81; ACLS Travel Grant, 82. **MEMBERSHIPS** Archaeol Inst Am; Am Sch Classical Stud, Athens; British Sch Archaeol, Athens; Classical Asn, New England. **RESEARCH** Aegean Prehistory; Ceramic Production and Exchange; Greco-Roman Athletics. **SELECTED PUBLICATIONS** Auth, The Transition to Mycenaean, 76; auth, Ceramic Change in the Aegean Early Bronze Age, 79; auth, Review of Aegean Prehistory II: The Pre-Palatial Bronze Age of the Southern and Central Greek Mainland, 93; auth, Lerna III: The Pottery of Lerna IV, 95; **CONTACT ADDRESS** Dept of Classics, Dartmouth Col, Hanover, NH 03755. **EMAIL** jeremy.rutter@dartmouth.edu

RUUD, JAY
PERSONAL Born 11/03/1950, Racine, WI, d, 2 children **DISCIPLINE** ENGLISH **EDUCATION** Univ Wis, BA, 72; MA, 74; PhD, 81. **CAREER** Instr, Univ Wis Park, 77-83; instr, Univ Wis Mara, 84-85; prof, N State Univ, 85-98; dean, CAS, N State Univ, 98-. **HONORS AND AWARDS** Outstand Fac Mem, NSU, 89; Burlington North Fac Ach Awd, 89. **MEMBERSHIPS** New Chaucer Soc; MAM; CCAS. **RESEARCH** Chaucer; Julian of Norwich; medieval literature. **SELECTED PUBLICATIONS** Auth, " 'My Spirit Hath His Fostryng in the Bible': The Summoner's Tale and the Holy Spirit," in Rebels and Rivals: The Contestive Spirit in the Canterbury Tales, ed. Susanna Greer Fein, David Raybin, Peter Braeger (Kalamazoo: Medieval Inst Pub, 91), 125-48; auth, "Teaching the 'Hoole' Tradition through Parallel Passages," in Approaches to Teaching Arthurian Tradition, ed. Maureen Fries, Jeanie Watson (NY: MLA, 92), 73-76; auth, "Nature and Grace in Julian of Norwich," Mystics Quart 19 (93): 71-81; auth, "Language of the Self in Julian of Norwich," Auto/Bio Stud 9 (94): 231-45; auth, "Julian of Norwich and the Nominalist Questions," in Literary Nominalism and the Theory of Rereading Late Medieval Texts, ed. Richard Utz (Lewiston: Edwin Mellen, 95), 31-50; auth, "Images of the Self and Self Image in Julian of Norwich." Studia Mystica 16 (95): 82-105; auth, Many a Song and Many a Lecherous Lay, Garland Press (NY), 92; auth, "'I Wolde for Thy Love Die': Julian, Romance Discourse, and the Masculine," in Julian of Norwich: A Casebook, ed. Sandra McEntire (NY: Garland, 99), 183-206. **CONTACT ADDRESS** Dept English, No State Univ, 1200 S Jay St, Aberdeen, SD 57401-7155. **EMAIL** ruudj@northern.edu

RYALS, CLYDE DE L.
PERSONAL Born 12/19/1928, Atlanta, GA, m, 1971 **DISCIPLINE** ENGLISH **EDUCATION** Emory Univ, AB, 47, MA, 49; Univ Pa, PhD, 57. **CAREER** Instr English, Univ Md, 56-67; from instr to prof, Univ Pa, 57-73, grad chmn, 69-72; chmn dept, 79-82, Prof English, Duke Univ, 73-, Guggenheim fel, 72-73. **MEMBERSHIPS** MLA; Am Soc Aesthet; NCTE. **RESEARCH** Nineteenth century literature. **SELECTED PUBLICATIONS CONTACT ADDRESS** 1620 University Dr, Durham, NC 27707.

RYAN, LAWRENCE VINCENT
PERSONAL Born 06/22/1923, St. Paul, MN, m, 1945, 4 children **DISCIPLINE** ENGLISH **EDUCATION** Col St Thomas, BA, 44; Northwestern Univ, MA, 46, PhD(English), 52. **CAREER** Instr English, Col St Thomas, 46-52; from instr to prof 52-77, dir grad prog humanities, 58-67, assoc dean sch humanities & sci, 67-70, actg dean, 74, chmn adv bd, 74-75, Joseph S Atha Prof Humanities, Stanford Univ, 77-88, Chmn Humanities Spec Prog, 73-83; Huntington Libr grants-in-aid, 53, 56 & 72; Am Philos Soc grant-in-aid, 57; co-ed, Neo Latin News, 57-97; Guggenheim fel, 58; assoc Harvard Renaissance Ctr, Florence, 64; Am Coun Learned Soc grant-in-aid, 71.Prof Emeritus, 88-. **MEMBERSHIPS** Dante Soc Am; Int Asn Neo-Latin Studies; MLA; Renaissance Soc Am; Conf Brit Studies. **RESEARCH** Literature of the English Renaissance; modern Latin literature; literature of the Italian Renaissance. **SELECTED PUBLICATIONS** Auth, The Renaissance Dialog - Literary Dialog In Its Soc And Political Contexts, Castiglione To Galileo - Cox,V/, Moreana, Vol 0030, 1993; Medievalia-Et-Humanistica - Studies In Medieval And Renaissance Cult - Clogan,Pm/, Moreana, Vol 0033, 1996; More,Thomas - Complete Epigrams - Italian - Firpo,L, Paglialunga,L, Translators/, Moreana, Vol 0033, 1996; Virgil In Medieval Eng, Figuring The 'Aeneid' From The 12th-Century To Chaucer - Baswell,C/, Albion, Vol 0028, 1996. **CONTACT ADDRESS** Dept of English, Stanford Univ, Stanford, CA 94305.

RYAN, ROBERT M.
DISCIPLINE BRITISH ROMANTICISM, RELIGION IN LITERATURE **EDUCATION** Columbia Univ, PhD. **CAREER** Instr, Rutgers, State Univ NJ, Camden Col of Arts and Sci. **MEMBERSHIPS** Bd dir, Keats-Shelley Asn of Am, 19th-Century Stud Asn. **SELECTED PUBLICATIONS** Auth, Keats: The Religious Sense, Princeton Univ Press, 76; contribu, Mod Philol, keats-Shelley Jour, Wordsworth Circle, Jour of Rel. **CONTACT ADDRESS** Rutgers, The State Univ of New Jersey, New Brunswick, Camden Col of Arts and Sci, New Brunswick, NJ 08903-2101. **EMAIL** rmryan@camden.rutgers.edu

RYCKEBUSCH, JULES
PERSONAL Born 02/12/1940, Boston, MA, w, 1969, 2 children **DISCIPLINE** ENGLISH **EDUCATION** Holyoke Jr Col, AA, 59; Am Int Col, BA, 62; Univ Mass, MA, 65. **MEMBERSHIPS** Acad of Am Poets. **RESEARCH** Lizzie Borden **SELECTED PUBLICATIONS** Ed, Proceedings of the Lizzie Borden Conf, King Philip, 93. **CONTACT ADDRESS** Dept Humanities & Fine Arts, Bristol Comm Col, 777 Elsbree St, Fall River, MA 02720-7307.

RYE, MARILYN
DISCIPLINE ENGLISH LITERATURE **EDUCATION** Rutgers Univ, PhD. **CAREER** Dir Freshman Wrtg, Fairleigh Dickinson Univ. **RESEARCH** Writing; native Am writers; detective fiction. **SELECTED PUBLICATIONS** Auth, Making Cultural Connections, Bedford Bks; essays and reviews in Murder is Academic, Oxford Dict Mystery and Crime Wrtg, Crit Survey Mystery and Detective Fic. **CONTACT ADDRESS** Fairleigh Dickinson Univ, Teaneck-Hackensack, 1000 River Rd, Teaneck, NJ 07666.

RYKEN, LELAND
PERSONAL Born 05/17/1942, Pella, IA, m, 1964, 3 children **DISCIPLINE** ENGLISH **EDUCATION** Central Col, BA; Univ OR, PhD. **CAREER** Wheaton Col, IL, prof eng, 68-. **MEMBERSHIPS** Modern Lang Asn; Milton Soc Am; Conf on Christianity and Lit; Evangelical Theological Soc. **RESEARCH** Milton; Shakespeare; Christianity and Lit; The Bible as Lit; Puritanism. **SELECTED PUBLICATIONS** A Dictionary of Biblical Imagery, co ed, Inter Varsity, 98; Redeeming the Time: A Christian Approach to Work and Leisure, Baker 95; The Discerning Reader: Christian Perspectives on Literature and Theory, co ed, Inter-Varsity/Baker, 95; A Complete Literary Guide to the Bible, co ed, Zondervan, 93; numerous more books. **CONTACT ADDRESS** Dept Eng, Wheaton Col, Illinois, Wheaton, IL 60187. **EMAIL** leland.ryken@wheaton.edu

S

SABINO, OSVALDO R.
PERSONAL Born 12/26/1950, Caseros, Argentina **DISCIPLINE** ENGLISH **EDUCATION** Univ del Museo Social Argentine, BA, 73; Univ Calif, MA, 86; Boston Univ, PhD, 92. **CAREER** Asst prof, Marygrove Col, 92-94; vis prof, Mich State Univ, 94-95; vis prof, Wayne County community Col, 97; vis prof, Oakland Univ, 96-99; lectr, Wayne State Univ, 97-. **HONORS AND AWARDS** Fulbright Scholar, 93; Dist Prof Awd, Univ de la republica Uruguay, 94; Fel, Fundacion Valparaiso, Spain, 98; Grant, Wayne State Univ, 99, 00. **MEMBERSHIPS** Am Lit Transl Assoc; Assoc Argentina de Estudios Norteamericanos; Assoc de Lit Femenina Hispanica; Am Judaic Studies Assoc; MLA; Phi Sigma Iota. **RESEARCH** Latin American literature/Gay and Lesbian Studies/Women's Studies/Creative Writing. **SELECTED PUBLICATIONS** Auth, Borges: Una imagen del amor y de la muerte, Ediciones Corregidor, Argentina, 87; auth, Mujeres solas, Ediciones Corregidor, Argentina, 90; auth, Revolucion y redencion: La isla de los organilleros de Luisa Mercedes Levinson, Ediciones Corregidor, Argentina, 93; auth, The Lights of Sunset, Marygrove Univ Pub, (Detroit, MI), 94; auth, Atlantida, Editorial Graffiti, Uruguay, 94; auth, Senales para hallar ese extrano lugar en el que habito, Editorial Betania, 95; auth, Borges: Una nueva vision de Ulrica, Huega y Fierro, Spain, 99; auth, El Juguete erotico y otros cuentos, Editorial Odisea, Spain 99; auth, La historia de las panteras y de algunos de los animales conversos, Editorial Huerga 7 Fierro, Spain 99; auth, Nadando en el volcan, Editorial Huerga & Fierro, Spain, (forthcoming). **CONTACT ADDRESS** Dept English, Wayne State Univ, 51 W Warren Ave, Detroit, MI 48201-1305.

SABISTON, ELIZABETH
PERSONAL Born 08/19/1937, New York, NY, s **DISCIPLINE** ENGLISH **EDUCATION** NY Univ, BA, 59; Ind Univ, MA, 60; Cornell Univ, PhD, 69. **CAREER** Instr to asst prof, Well Col, 64-72; lectr, York Univ, 74-75; vis lectr, Univ Toronto, 76-79, 85-86; asst prof to assoc prof, York Univ, 79-. **HONORS AND AWARDS** Phi Beta Kappa; Sigma Delta Omicron; Pi Delta Phi; Alumnae Club Award; Fel, Ind Univ, 59-60; Fel, Cornell Univ, 60-61; Res Grant, Cornell Univ, 64. **MEMBERSHIPS** MLA; ACCUTE; JASNA; Victorian Studies Asn of Ont; Willa Cather Pioneer Memorial and Educ Found. **RESEARCH** Women in literature; 19th Century fiction (British, American, French); Victorian studies; American literature. **SELECTED PUBLICATIONS** Auth, The Prison of Womanhood: Four Provincial Heroines in Nineteenth Century Fiction, New York, 87; auth, "Anglo-American Connections: Elizabeth Gaskell, Harriet Beecher Stowe and the 'Iron of Slavery'," in The Discourse of Slavery, Routledge, 94; auth, "Bouraoui's The Critical Strategy: or, A New Trend in Canadian Criticism," in Hedi Bouraoui: I!! Conoclaste et Chantre du Transculturel, Ottawa, 96. **CONTACT ADDRESS** Dept English, York Univ, 4700 Keele St, 208 Stong Col, Toronto, ON, Canada M3J 1P3. **EMAIL** sabiston@yorku.ca

SACCIO, PETER
DISCIPLINE ENGLISH LITERATURE **EDUCATION** Princeton Univ, PhD, 68. **CAREER** Leon D. Black Prof Shakespearean Studies and Prof Eng, Dartmouth. **RESEARCH** Shakespearean drama; mod Brit drama; gay male lit. **SELECTED PUBLICATIONS** Shakespeare's English Kings: History, Chronicle and Drama, Oxford UP, 77; Modern British Drama (vid lecs) in Superstar Tchrs Series, Teaching Co, 94; auth, Shakespeare: The Word and the Action (vid lecs) in Superstar Tchrs Series, Teaching Co, 95; **CONTACT ADDRESS** Dept of English, Dartmouth Col, 6032 Sanborn House, Hanover, NH 03755. **EMAIL** Peter.C.Saccio@dartmouth.edu

SACHSMAN, DAVID B.
PERSONAL Born 08/16/1945, New York, NY, m, 1967, 2 children **DISCIPLINE** COMMUNICATION **EDUCATION** Univ of Pa, BA, English, 67; Stanford Univ, AM, Commun, 68; Stanford Univ, PhD, Pub Aff Commun, 73. **CAREER** Teaching asst, Dept of Commun, Stanford Univ, 70; asst prof, Calif State Univ, Hayward, 69-71; asst prof, Rutgers Univ, 71-76; Sr Fulbright-Hays Schol, Univ of Nigeria, Nsukka, 78-79; assoc prof, Rutgers Univ, 76-88; assoc mem, grad faculty, Rutgers Grad Sch, 86-88; Adjunct assoc prof, Univ of Med & Dent of NJ-Robert Wood Johnson Med Ctr, 87-89; prof of commun, Calif State Univ, Fullerton, 88-91; prof of commun, UTC, 91-; adjunct prof, Univ Tenn, Knoxville, 96-. **HONORS AND AWARDS** Special award for Res about J and Journalistic Media, 84, 86, 88, 89; ch of excellence in commun & public aff. **MEMBERSHIPS** Assoc for Educ in J and Mass Commun; Int Commun Assoc; Nat Commun Assoc; Soc of Env J; Invest Reporters and Eds; Radio-Television News Dirs Assoc; Chattanooga Press Assoc. **RESEARCH** Env jour; risk commun; mass commun & soc. **SELECTED PUBLICATIONS** Mass Communication Education: Moving Toward Diversity, Mass Comm Rev, vol 20, no 3 & 4, 180-91, 93; Communication Between Scientists and the Media: Introducing the Concepts of Risk, Risk Analysis, and Risk Communication to Journalists, Hazardous Waste and Pub Hlth: int Congress on the Health Effects of Hazardous Waste, Princeton Scientific Publishing Co., Inc, 945-52, 94; The Mass Media Discover the Environment: Influences on Environmental Reporting in the First Twenty Years, The Symbolic Earth: Discourse, and Our Creation of the Environment, Univ Press of Ky, 241-56, 96; Reporting Risks and Setting the Environmental Agenda, Environmental Education for the 21st Century: International and Interdisciplinary Perspectives, Peter Lang Publ, 129-141, 97; Co-auth, Proceedings of the Conference on Communication and Our Environment, Univ of Tenn at Chattanooga Graphic Svcs, 97; auth, "Commentary: Should reportes Use risk as a Dererminant of Environmental Coverage," Scie Communication, vol 21, (99), 88-95; coauth, The Civil War and the Press, New Brunswick, NJ: Transction Pub, 00; auth, auth, The Role of Mass Media in Shaping Perceptions and Awarness of Environmental Issues," Climate Change Commun: Proceedings of an Int Conf, Univ of Waterloo and Environment Canada, 00. **CONTACT ADDRESS** West Ch of Commun, Univ of Tennessee, Chattanooga, 615 McCallie Ave, Chattanooga, TN 37403-2504. **EMAIL** david-sachsman@utc.edu

SADDLEMYER, ANN
PERSONAL Born 11/28/1932, Prince Albert, BC, Canada **DISCIPLINE** ENGLISH, DRAMA **EDUCATION** Univ Sask, BA, 53; Queen's Univ, MA, 55; Univ London, PhD, 61; Univ Sask, D Litt, 91. **CAREER** Asst prof to assoc prof to prof, Univ Vic, 60-71; cen dir to act dir, Univ Toronto, 71-86; vis prof, NYork Univ, 75; sr fel to mst fel to mst emer, Univ Tor Massey Col, 75-95-; adj prof to prof to emer, Univ Toronto, 71-95-; adj prof, Univ Victoria, 95-. **HONORS AND AWARDS** IODE War Memorial Scholar, 57; Can Council Doct Fel, 58, 59; Guggenheim Fel, 65, 77; Can Council Leave Fel, 68; Fel Royal Soc Can, 76; JP Soc Prom Sci Exchange Fel, 84; Ontario Distinguished Ser Awd, 85; Connaught Sr Res Fel, 86-87'; British Acad Rose Mary Crawshay Awd, 86; Fel Royal Soc Arts, 87; Creation of Ann Saddlemyer Book Prize, Can Theatre Hist, by Asn for Can Theater Res, 89; Alum Awd Univ Tor, 91; Woman Distinguished Awd, YWCA; App Officer of Order of Canada, 95; Rosenthal Awd, Yeats Soc NYork, 01; Hon D Litt, Univ Vic, 89, McGill Univ, 89, Univ Windsor, 90, Univ Toronto, 99; Hon LLD, Queen's Univ, 77, Concordia Univ, 00. **MEMBERSHIPS** FRSC; FRSA; ACTR; IASIL; CAIS; ACIS; ACCUTE; MLA. **RESEARCH** English literature; Anglo Irish literature; biography; Canadian theater and drama. **SELECTED PUBLICATIONS** Co-auth, The World of W.B. Yeats: Essays in Perspective, Univ Wash Pr, 67; auth, The Plays of J.M. Synqe: Books One and Two. Volumes III and IV of the Oxford Synge, Oxford Univ Pr (Oxford), 68; auth, The Plays of Lady Gregory, Books 1,2,3,4. Vols. V, VI, VII, VIII of the Coole Ed, Colin Smythe, 70; excerpted, In Defense of Lady Gregory, Playwright, in 20th Century Literary Criticism, Gale Res, 77; auth, Theatre Business, The Letters of the First Abbey Theatre Directors (W.B. Yeats, Lady Gregory and J.M. Synge). Univ Penn State Pr, 82; auth, The Collected Letters of John Millington Synge, Clarendon Pr, 83; 84; co- ed, Lady Gregory Fifty Years After, Colin Smythe, 87; auth, Early Stages: Theatre in Ontario 1800 to 1914, Toronto Univ Pr, 90; auth, J. M. Synge The Playboy of the Western World and Other Plays, Oxford Univ Pr (London/NYork), 95; Co-auth, Later Stages: Essays on Ontario Theatre from World War I to the 1970s, Toronto Univ Pr, 97. **CONTACT ADDRESS** 10876 Madrona Dr, Sidney, BC, Canada V8L 5N9. **EMAIL** saddlemy@uvic.ca

SADOCK, GEOFFREY
PERSONAL Born 09/30/1942, New York, NY, m, 1971, 1 child **DISCIPLINE** ENGLISH **EDUCATION** Brooklyn Col, BA, 64; Tufts Univ, MA, 66; Brown Univ, PhD, 73. **CAREER** Instructor, Brown Extension Div, 68-71; Instructor, Fairleigh-Dickinson, 71-72; Prof, Bergen Cmty Col, 72-. **HONORS AND AWARDS** Mid-Career Fel, Princeton, 94; Post-Doc Fel, CUNY, 91; Who's Who Among Am Teachers, 94, 99. **MEMBERSHIPS** NJCE; Victorian Soc; English First; US Eng; NALS. **RESEARCH** Victorian Literature; Psychology. **CON-**

TACT ADDRESS Dept Eng, Bergen Comm Col, 400 Paramus Rd, Paramus, NJ 07652-1508.

SAENGER, MICHAEL B.
PERSONAL Born 10/30/1969, Minneapolis, MN, m, 1997 **DISCIPLINE** ENGLISH **EDUCATION** Univ Calif Berkeley, BA, 91; Univ Toronto, MA, 94; PhD, 99. **CAREER** Instr, Univ Western Ont, 99-00; vis asst prof, Cornell Col, 00-01; asst prof, Southwestern Univ, 01-. **HONORS AND AWARDS** Univ Toronto Fel. **MEMBERSHIPS** MLA; AAUP; SCSC; SAA. **RESEARCH** Early modern interaction between physical books and ideas of literature; interactions between non-dramatic and dramatic texts. **SELECTED PUBLICATIONS** Auth, "The Costumes of Caliban and Ariel qua Sea-Nymph," Notes/Queries (95); auth, "Will Stephen Wrest Bombast from Falstaff?" James Joyce Quart (97); auth, "A Reference to Ovid in Coriolanus," English Lang Notes (97); auth, "Nashe, Moth and the Date of Love's Labor's Lost," Notes/Queries (98); auth, "Did Sidney Revise Astrophil and Stella?" Studies Philos (99); auth, "Ah Ain't Heard Whut de Tex' Wuz:' The (Il)legitimate Textuality of Old English and Black English," Oral Tradition (99); auth, "Pericles and the Burlesque of Romance," in Pericles: Critical Essays, ed. David Skeele (00); auth, "The Birth of Advertising," in Parenting and Printing in Early Modern England, ed. Douglas Brooks (forthcoming). **CONTACT ADDRESS** English Dept, Southwestern Univ, 1001 East University Ave, Georgetown, TX 78626. **EMAIL** saengerm@southwestern.edu

SAFER, ELAINE BERKMAN
PERSONAL Born 09/18/1937, Brooklyn, NY, d, 3 children **DISCIPLINE** ENGLISH **EDUCATION** Brooklyn Col, BA, 58; Univ Wis, MS, 59; Case Western Reserve Univ, MA, 61, PhD, 67. **CAREER** Instr, Northwestern Univ, 63-66; from asst prof to prof English, 67-. **HONORS AND AWARDS** Teaching fel English, Case Western Reserve Univ, 61-63; Summer fac fel, Univ Del, 71, 78, 81, 92; NEH summer stipend, 83; Fulbright scholar, 90; Distinguished prof Univ Jean-Moulin Lyon III, 90, 92, 93, 94, 95, 96; Univ Del Excellence Tchg Awd, 93; fel Ctr Advan Stud, Univ Del, 97-98. **MEMBERSHIPS** MLA; Milton Soc; Renaissance Soc Am; AAUP; Int Soc Humor Studies; Am Lit Sect MLA; Am Lit Asn; Am Humor Stud Asn, pres 97-98; Pres Saul Bellow Soc Am Lit Asn, 92-95. **RESEARCH** Twenteith Century American literature; The Novel; John Milton. **SELECTED PUBLICATIONS** Coed John Milton: L'Allegro and Il Penseroso, Charles Merrill, 70; auth, The Contemporary Am Comic Epic: The Nvoels of Barth, Pynchon, Gaddis, and Kesey, Wayne State Univ Pr, 88; auth, "William Gass," in The Columbia Companion to the 20th Century Am Short Story, ed. Blanche Gelfant; auth, "Pynchon's World and Its Legendary Past: Humor and the Absurd in a Twentieth-Century 'Vineland,'" Critique 32 (90): 107-125; auth, "Degrees of Comic Irony in 'A Theft' and 'The Bellarosa Connection,'" Saul Bellow J 9 (90): 1-19; auth, "Metamorphoses and the River in John Barth's 'Tidewater Tales,'" in Le Fleuve Et Ses Metamorphoses, ed. Francois Piquet (Paris: Dideir Erudition, 93); auth, "Comic Irony in Saul Bellow's 'More Die of Heartbreak," Critique: Studies in Contemporary Fiction 34 (93): 203-219; auth, "'High-Tech Paranoia' and the Jamesonian Sublime: An Approach to Pynchon's Postmodernism," in Tradition, Voices and Dreams, ed. Siegel and Friedman (Newark: Univ Deleware Pr, 95): 279-297; auth, "The Double, Comic Irony, and Postmodernism in Philip Roth's 'Operation Shylock," Melus 21 (96): 157-172; auth, "Response to Roundtable on Political Correctness and Humor," Humor , Int J of Humor Res, 10 (97): 507-509; auth, "The Tragi-Comic and Metafiction in Philip Roth's 'Sabbath Theater,' in Am Literary Dimensions: Poems and Essays in Honor of Melvin Friedman, ed. Jay Halio and Ben Siegel (Univ Deleware Pre, 99), 168-179; **CONTACT ADDRESS** Dept of English, Univ of Delaware, Newark, DE 19711. **EMAIL** safer@udel.edu

SAFFIRE, PAULA REINER
PERSONAL Born 09/05/1943, NJ, s, 2 children **DISCIPLINE** CLASSICS AND PHILOSOPHY **EDUCATION** Mount Holyoke Col, BA, 65; Harvard, PhD, 76. **CAREER** Assoc Prof, Butler Univ, 89-. **HONORS AND AWARDS** Writing Across the Curriculum Awd, Butler Univ; Creative Tchr Awd; Indiana Classical Conference. **MEMBERSHIPS** APA, ICC **RESEARCH** Sappho; tragedy; mythology; pedagogy; performance. **SELECTED PUBLICATIONS** Auth, Aristotle on Personality and Some Implications for Friendship, in: Ancient Phil, 91; auth, Ancient Greek Alive, Aldine Press, 92; Coauth, Deduke men a Selanna: The Pleiades Mid-Sky, Mnemosyne, 93; coauth, Ancient Greek Alive, Univ of North Carolina Press, Performer of Songs of Sappho, 93-; auth, Whip, Whipped and Doctors: Homers Iliad and Camus the Plague, Interpretations, 94. **CONTACT ADDRESS** Dept of Classics, Butler Univ, 4600 Sunset Ave, Indianapolis, IN 46208. **EMAIL** psaffire@butler.edu

SAFFLE, MICHAEL
PERSONAL Born 12/03/1946, Salt Lake City, UT, m, 1977, 1 child **DISCIPLINE** MUSICOLOGY, INTERDISCIPLINARY STUDIES **EDUCATION** Univ of Utah, BA (honors), Bmus (honors), 68; Boston Univ, AM, 70; Harvard Univ Divinity School, STM, 71; Stanford Univ, PhD, 77. **CAREER** Instr, Stanford Univ, 77-78; asst prof, 78-83, assoc prof, 83-93, prof, 93-, Va Tech. **HONORS AND AWARDS** Phi Beta Kappa, 68; Francis Booth Prize in Choral Composition, Harvard Univ, 69; DAAD Fel, Univ of Bonn, 74-75; Alexander von Humboldt-Stiftung Fel, 84-86 & 93; Senior Fulbright Res Fel, 89-90; Bicentennial Prof, Univ of Helsinki, 00-01. **MEMBERSHIPS** Am Musicological Soc; Int Musicological Soc; Soc for Am Music; Va Humanities Conf. **RESEARCH** Liszt; Wagner; Am music of the 19th and early 20th centuries; interdisciplinary studies in the arts. **SELECTED PUBLICATIONS** Auth, Liszt in Germany: 1840-1845: A Study in Sources, Documents, and the History of Reception, Franz Liszt Studies Series, Pendragon Press, 94; auth, Franz Liszt: A Guide to Research, Garland Composers Resource Guide, Garland Pub, 91; general ed, Franz Liszt Studies Series, Pendragon Press, 91-; general ed, Perspectives in Music Criticism and Theory, Garland Pub, 93-; co-ed, Essays in American Music, Garland Pub, 94-99; biographical entries for the revised edition of Die Musik in Geschichte und Gegenwart, Barenreiter, 94-; ed, Journal of the American Liszt Society, 87-91; auth, book chapters and conference papers published in the Proceedings of the XIV, XV, & XVI Int Musicological Soc Congresses and other publications. **CONTACT ADDRESS** Virginia Polytech Inst and State Univ, Blacksburg, VA 24061-0227. **EMAIL** msaffle@vt.edu

SAGE, MICHAEL
PERSONAL Born 12/04/1944, New York, NY, m, 2 children **DISCIPLINE** ROMAN HISTORY & CLASSICS **EDUCATION** Univ Mich, BA, MA (hist); Univ Toronto, MA (classics), PhD. **CAREER** Univ Waterloo, asst prof (hist), 74-75; Univ Cincinnati, asst prof (classics), 75-81, assoc prof, 81-90, prof, 90-. **HONORS AND AWARDS** Canada Coun, Province of Ontario, Semple Fel. **MEMBERSHIPS** Am Philological Asn; Soc Promotion Roman Studies. **RESEARCH** Late Roman hist; Christianity; ancient mil hist. **SELECTED PUBLICATIONS** Ancient Greek Warfare, London, 96. **CONTACT ADDRESS** Univ of Cincinnati, 407 Blegen Libr, Cincinnati, OH 45221. **EMAIL** Michael.Sage@uc.edu

SAHA, PROSANTA KUMAR
PERSONAL Born 12/04/1932, Calcutta, India, m, 1958, 2 children **DISCIPLINE** ENGLISH, LINGUISTICS **EDUCATION** Univ Calcutta, BA, 56; Oberlin Col, MA 57; Western Reserve Univ, PhD(English), 66. **CAREER** Teacher, Hawken Sch, 57-62; instr English, 62-64, asst prof English & ling, 66-72, Assoc Prof English & Ling & Chmn Ling & Undergrad Humanities Prog, Case Western Reserve Univ, 72- **HONORS AND AWARDS** Carl F Wittke Awd, Case Western Reserve Univ, 71. **MEMBERSHIPS** Ling Soc Am. **RESEARCH** English literature and linguistics; computer analysis of literature, especially stylistics; Bengali literature and linguistics. **SELECTED PUBLICATIONS** Auth, Reflexive Revisited + English Pronouns/, Am Speech, Vol 0068, 1993. **CONTACT ADDRESS** Dept of English, Case Western Reserve Univ, Clark Hall Rm 103 Case, Cleveland, OH 44106.

SAHNI, CHAMAN LALL
PERSONAL Born 06/10/1933, Thatta, India, m, 1960, 2 children **DISCIPLINE** ENGLISH, FAR EASTERN LITERATURE **EDUCATION** Agra Univ, India, BA, 54; Lucknow Univ, India, MA, 56; Univ RI, MA, 68; Wayne State Univ, PhD, 74. **CAREER** Lectr Eng, Bareilly Col, India, 56-59; head dept, Seth Motilal Col, 59-60; lectr, S D Col, India, 60-62 & Kurukshetra Univ, 62-67; from instr to asst prof, Wayne State Univ, 71-75; asst prof, 75-78, assoc prof, 78-81, prof eng, 81, dept chair, Boise State Univ, 94-00. **MEMBERSHIPS** MLA; SAsian Lit Asn **RESEARCH** Mod Brit fiction. **SELECTED PUBLICATIONS** Ed with introd & notes, Chaucer: The Prologue, 66 & Milton's Samson Agonistes, 67, Kitab Ghar, India; auth, The Marabar Caves in the light of Indian thought, In: Focus on Forster's A Passage to India, Humanities, 76; ed with introd & notes, Shelley's Adonais, 7th ed, 93, coauth, Advanced Literary Essays, 16th ed, 94 & auth, Principles and History of Literary Criticism, 3rd ed, 77, Bareilly U P, India; Forster's A Passage to India: The Religious Dimension, Arnold-Heinemann, India, 81, and Humanities Press 81; Gandhi and Tagore, SAsian Rev, 7/81; E M Forster's A Passage to India: The Islamic Dimension, South Asian Rev, 83, and Cahiers Victoriens & Edouardiens, 83; Indian Writers of English Fiction, Advanced Lit Essays, Prakash Book Depot, India, 85; Indian Poetry in English, Advanced Lit Essays, Prakash Book Depot, India, 85; The Images of Mahatma Gandhi in Indo-English Fiction, Advanced Lit Essays, Prakash Book Depot, India, 85; Rabindranath Tagore: Sidelights, Contemporary Authors, Gale Res Co, 87; Steppenwolf and Indian Thought, South Asian Rev, 88; Raja Rao: The Serpent and the Rope, Kamala Markandaya: Nectar in a Sieve, and Anita Desai: Fire on the Mountain, In: Cyclopedia of Literary Characters II, Salem Press, 90; R K Narayan, E M Forster, and Bharati Mukherjee, In: Critical Survey of Short Fiction, rev ed, Salem Press, 93; Sasthi Brata, In: Writers of the Indian Diaspora: A Bio-Bibliographical Source Book, Greenwood Press, 93; Donald Duk by Frank Chin, and Jasmine by Bharati Mukherjee, In: Masterplots II: American Fiction, supplement, Salem Press, 94; Krishna Janamashtami, Lala Hardayal, Gayatri Chakravorti Spivak, and Bharati Mukherjee, In: Asian American Encyclopedia, Marshall Cavendish, 95; Wife by Bharati Mukherjee, In: Masterplots II: Women's Literature, Marshall Cavendish, 95; Anita Desai, In: Magill's Survey of World Literature, Supplement, Salem Press, 95; Siddhartha by Hermann Hesse, In: Masterplots: Revised Second Edition, Salem Press; 96; Jasmine by Bharati Mukherjee, In: Masterplots II: Short Story, Supplement, Salem Press, 96; Kamala Markandaya and Anita Desai, In: Cyclopedia of World Authors, rev ed, Salem Press, 97. **CONTACT ADDRESS** Dept of Eng, Boise State Univ, 1910 University Dr, Boise, ID 83725-0399. **EMAIL** csahni@boisestate.edu

SAID, EDWARD
DISCIPLINE ENGLISH **EDUCATION** Princeton Univ, AB, 57; Harvard Univ, AM, 60, PhD, 64. **CAREER** Instr, Harvard Univ; Johns Hopkins Univ; Yale Univ; Univ Chicago; ch, comp lit; prof 63-. **HONORS AND AWARDS** Fel, Stanford Ctr Advan Stud in Behavioral Sci; Columbia's Trilling award; Wellek prize, Amer Comp Lit Assn; dir, neh sem on lit criticism, 78; lect, gauss sem, princeton, 77; eliot memorial lectures, kent univ, 85; messenger lectures, cornell univ, 86; frye lectures, univ toronto, 86; davie academic freedom lecture, univ cape town, 91; camp lectures, stanford u **MEMBERSHIPS** Mem, For Rel Coun; sr fel, Sch of Criticism and Theory. **SELECTED PUBLICATIONS** Auth, Beginnings; Orientalism; The Question of Palestine; Covering Islam; The World, the Text and the Critic; After the Last Sky; Blaming the Victims; Culture and Imperialism; The Politics of Dispossession; Wellek and Reith Lectures, Musical Elaborations and Representations of the Intellectual.Peace and Its Discontents, 96. **CONTACT ADDRESS** Dept of Eng, Columbia Col, New York, 2960 Broadway, New York, NY 10027-6902.

SAILLANT, JOHN D.
PERSONAL Born 07/25/1957, Providence, RI, m, 3 children **DISCIPLINE** EARLY AMERICAN LITERATURE; HISTORY **EDUCATION** Brown Univ, BA, 79; MA, 81; DPhil, 89. **CAREER** Assoc prof, English, W Mich Univ. **HONORS AND AWARDS** NEHGrant, 97; Ames Fel, Univ Mass, 97; Am Acad Relig Grant, 96; The Huntington & British Acad Grant; RI Comt Hum Grant, 96; Va Hist Soc Mellon Res Grant, 94, 96; Am Counc Learned Socs Fel, 92-93; **MEMBERSHIPS** Am Acad Relig; Am Hist Asn; Am Soc Eighteenth-Century Studies; Am Studies Asn; Forum Eu Expansion & Global Interaction; Great Lakes Am Studies Asn; New England Hist Asn; Soc of Early Amists; Soc Historians Early Republic. **SELECTED PUBLICATIONS** Auth, The Black Body Erotic and the Republican Body Politic, 1790-1820, Jour Hist Sexuality, 95; Slavery and Divine Providence in New England Calvinism: The New Divinity and a Black Protest, New England Quart, 95; Explaining Syncretism in African American Views of Death: An Eighteenth-Century Example, Cult & Tradition, 95; Hymnody in Sierra Leone and the Persistence of an African American Faith, The Hymn, 97; The American Enlightenment in Africa: Jefferson's Colonizationism and Black Virginians' Migration to Liberia, 1776-1840, Eighteenth-Century Studies, 98. **CONTACT ADDRESS** Dept of Engl, Western Michigan Univ, Sprau Tower, Kalamazoo, MI 49008-5092. **EMAIL** john.saillant@wmich.edu

SAJDAK, BRUCE T.
PERSONAL Born 11/22/1945, Chicago, IL, m, 1979, 1 child **DISCIPLINE** ENGLISH, LIBRARY SCIENCE **EDUCATION** Loras Col, AB, 66; Univ of Mich, MA, 67, PhD, 74, AMLS, 75. **CAREER** Humanities libr, Univ of Houston, Victoria Campus, 75-77; reference libr, Univ of Md, Col Park, 77-80; reference libr, Smith Col, 80-. **MEMBERSHIPS** Modern Humanities Res Asn; Asn of Col & Res Librs, New England. **RESEARCH** Bibliography; Shakespeare. **SELECTED PUBLICATIONS** PhD dissertation: Silence on the Shakespearean Stage, Univ of Mich, 74; contribur, World Shakespeare Bibliography, Shakespeare Quarterly, 92-; auth, Shakespeare Index, Kravs, 92; assoc am ed, Annual Bibliography of English Language & Literature, 96-. **CONTACT ADDRESS** Smith Col, 79 South St., Northampton, MA 01060. **EMAIL** bsajdak@smith.edu

SALAMON, LINDA B.
PERSONAL Born 11/20/1941, Elmira, NY, d, 2 children **DISCIPLINE** ENGLISH **EDUCATION** Radcliffe Col, BA, 63; Bryn Mawr, AM, 64; PhD, 71. **CAREER** Lectr, Univ Pa, 77-79; assoc prof, dean Col Arts Sci, Washington Univ, 79-92; dean Columbian Sch Arts Sci, Geo Wash Univ, 92-95; prof, 92-. **HONORS AND AWARDS** DHL; Chemn Bd Dir, AAC; Morton Bender Awd; Folger Lib Fel. **MEMBERSHIPS** Phi Beta Kappa; MLA; Cosmos Club. **RESEARCH** Shakespeare; cultural studies in early modern Europe; 20th Century British literature. **SELECTED PUBLICATIONS** Coauth, Nicholas Hilliard's Art of Limning, Northeastern UP, 83; auth, "Reading the Sea and Sky," The World and I (97): 58-67; auth, :looking for Richard in History: Postmodern Villainy in Richard III and Scareface," J Pop Film TV (00); auth, "Theory avant la lettre: An Excavation in Early Modern England," in Writing Theory, Figuring History, ed. Michael O'Driscoll, Tilottama Rajan (Univ Toronto Press, 00). **CONTACT ADDRESS** Dept English, The George Washington Univ, 2035 H St, Washington, DC 20052-0001. **EMAIL** lbs@gwu.edu

SALAZAR, ABRAN J.
DISCIPLINE COMMUNICATION **EDUCATION** Univ Iowa, PhD. **CAREER** Assoc prof, Texas A&M Univ. **HONORS AND AWARDS** Southern States Commun Association's annual awd for the best article in the Southern Commun J; Col Liberal Arts Distinguished Tchg Awd from the Former Students Asn Texas A&M Univ. **RESEARCH** Group organizational communication, interpersonal communication & health. **SELECTED PUBLICATIONS** Publ in, Health Commun; Human Commun Res, Southern Commun J; Small Gp Res. **CONTACT ADDRESS** Dept of Speech Communication, Texas A&M Univ, Col Station, College Station, TX 77843-4234.

SALDIVAR, TONI
PERSONAL Born 08/15/1940, Jacksonville, FL, m, 1964, 2 children **DISCIPLINE** ENGLISH **EDUCATION** Fl State Univ, BA, 63; SUNY, MA, 75; NYork Univ, PhD, 90. **CAREER** Assoc Prof and Div Chair, Mount Saint Mary Col. **HONORS AND AWARDS** Phi Beta Kappa; Phi Kappa Phi; Sigma Tau Delta. **MEMBERSHIPS** MLA; NEMLA. **RESEARCH** Modern British and american Literature. **SELECTED PUBLICATIONS** Auth, "Sylvia Plath; The Wound and the Cure of Words," Southern Humanities Review, (92): 182-184; auth, "Shelley's Goddess: Maternity, Language, Subjectivity," Southern Humanities Review, (94): 190-193; auth, "Voice Lesson: On Becoming a (Woman) Writer," Southern Humanities Review, (95): 384-387; auth, "Ordinary Time: Cycles in Marriage, Faith and Renewal," Southern Humanities Review, (95): 382-384; auth, "The art of John Updike's 'A & P'," Studies in Short Fiction, (97): 215. **CONTACT ADDRESS** Dept Arts, Mount Saint Mary Col, 330 Powell Ave, Newburgh, NY 12550-3412. **EMAIL** saldivar@msmc.edu

SALE, MARY
PERSONAL Born 11/27/1929, New Haven, CT, m, 1991, 3 children **DISCIPLINE** PHILOSOPHY; CLASSICS **EDUCATION** BA, 51, MA, 54, PhD, 58, Cornell Univ. **CAREER** Instr, Yale Univ, 57-58; Instr, 58-59, Asst Prof, 59-64, Assoc Prof, 64-75, Prof, 75-, Washington Univ. **MEMBERSHIPS** London Inst of Classical Studies; Honorary Fel, Univ Wales, Univ College Cardiff. **RESEARCH** Philosophy; Classics **SELECTED PUBLICATIONS** Auth, Homer, Iliad, Odyssey, Reader's Guide to World Literature, 93; Homer and the Roland: the Shared Formulary Technique, Oral Tradition, 93; The Government of Troy: Politics in the Illiad, Greek, Roman and Byzantine Studies, 94; Homer and Avdo: Investigating Orality through External Consistency, Voice into Text, 96; In Defense of Milman Parry, Oral Tradition, 96; Virgil's Formularity and Pius Aeneas, Epos and Logos, 98. **CONTACT ADDRESS** 2342 Albion Pl, Saint Louis, MO 63104. **EMAIL** Aperkins@midwest.net

SALEM, PHILIP
PERSONAL Born 08/07/1945, Sioux City, IA, d, 1 child **DISCIPLINE** COMMUNICATION STUDIES; SPEECH COMMUNICATION **EDUCATION** Northern State Col, BS, 68; Univ S Dakota, 80; Univ Denver, MA, 72; Univ Denver, PhD, 74 **CAREER** Radio Announcer, KABR Aberdeen, S Dak, 66-69; TV Newsman, KXAB Aberdeen S Dak, 68; Teacher, Webster Independent School District, S Dak, 69-71; Radio Announcer, KADX, 71-74; Graduate Teaching Asst, Univ Denver, 73-74; prof, Southwest Tex St Univ, 74- **HONORS AND AWARDS** Dir, "Organizational Communication and Change: Challenges in the Next Century," 96; President's Awd Res, nominee to the SWTSU President, 84, 85, 88, 92, 95, 97; President's Awd Teaching, nominee to the SWTSU President, 84, 95; Southwest Bus Syposium Awd, 94; Fund for Improvement of Postsecondary Education Grant, 94 **MEMBERSHIPS** Tex Speech Comm Assoc; Western States Comm Assoc; Conflict Resolution Education Network; Acad Management; Ntl Comm Assoc; ;Int Comm Assoc **RESEARCH** Communication Theory; Organizational Communication; Interpersonal Communication; Information Systems; Communication and Technology; Communication and Conflict Management **SELECTED PUBLICATIONS** Ed, Organizational communication and change, Hampton Pr, forthcoming; Institutional factors influencing the success of Drug Abuse Education and Prevention Programs, US Dept Education, 91; Organizational communication and higher education, Amer Assoc Education, 81 **CONTACT ADDRESS** Dept Speech Comm, Southwest Texas State Univ, San Marcos, TX 78666. **EMAIL** ps05@swt.edu

SALIEN, JEAN
DISCIPLINE LINGUISTICS, LITERATURE **EDUCATION** Univ de Montreal, BA, 67; Columbia Univ, MA, 71; Univ de Strasbourg, MA, 75; Univ Kans, PhD, 77. **CAREER** Prof, Fort Hays State Univ, 77-. **HONORS AND AWARDS** NEH Summer Scholar for Col Teachers, 82 & 85. **MEMBERSHIPS** Am Asn of Teachers of French **RESEARCH** Eighteenth century French literature, pre-romantic era, Pere Dumas, francophone literatures. **SELECTED PUBLICATIONS** Auth, "Passions et raison dans la pensee de Jean-Jacques Rousseau," Int Studies in Philos (81); auth, "Negritude et lutte des classes..," Presence Francophone (82); auth, "Francophonie et sous-developpement.., Contemporary French Civilization (81); auth, "Syncretisme religieux et theatre aux Antilles francophones," Etudes Francophones de Louisiane (87); auth, "Quebec french: Attitudes and pedagogical Perspectives," Modern Lang J (98); auth, "Appropriation et publics du discours antillais," Mots Pluriels (98). **CONTACT ADDRESS** Dept Modern Lang, Fort Hays State Univ, 600 Park St, Hays, KS 67601-4009. **EMAIL** jsalien@fhsu.edu

SALOMAN, ORA FRISHBERG
PERSONAL Born 11/14/1938, New York, NY, m, 1968 **DISCIPLINE** MUSICOLOGY **EDUCATION** Barnard College, AB 59; Columbia Univ, MA 63, PhD 70. **CAREER** City Univ NY Baruch Col, asst assoc prof 72-81, chair 78-84, prof 82-; Grad Center, prof, 96-. **HONORS AND AWARDS** NEH; Fulbright fel; Vis sch Queens Univ Kingston ON. **MEMBERSHIPS** AMS; SAM; ABS; CMS; FAA; Columbia Univ Grad Sch Alum Assoc. **RESEARCH** Music; reception history of Beethoven, Gluck, Le Sueur, and Berlioz; hist of opera and of music criticism; 19th century genre theories of symphony and opera; Euro-Amer connections in aesthetics, social hist and concert life. **SELECTED PUBLICATIONS** Auth, French Revolution perspectives on Chabonon's Dela musique of 1785, in: Music and the French Revolution, ed. Malcolm Boyd, Cambridge, Cambridge Univ Press, 92; Continental and English Foundations of J. S. Dwight's Early American Criticism of Beethoven's Ninth Symphony, Jour of Royal Musical Assoc, 94; auth, Beethoven's Symphonies and J. S. Dwight: The Birth of American Music Criticism, Boston, Northeastern Univ Press, 95; Origins Performances and Reception History of Beethoven's Late Quartets, rev of, Beethoven: Naissance et Reniassance des Derniers Quatuors, by Ivan Mahaim, Paris Desclee De Brouwer 64, Music Quart, 96; auth, "Chretien Urhan and Beethoven's Ninth Symphony in Paris 1838," in Mainzer Studien zur Musikwissenschaft: Festschrift Walter Wiora, eds, Christoph-Hellmut Mahling, Ruth Seiberts, Tutzing, Hans Schneider, 97. **CONTACT ADDRESS** Dept of Music, Baruch Col, CUNY, 17 Lexington Ave., Box A-1209, New York, NY 10010. **EMAIL** ora_saloman@baruch.cuny.edu

SALOMON, DAVID A.
PERSONAL Born 11/08/1963, Bronx, NY, m, 1993 **DISCIPLINE** ENGLISH, PHILOSOPHY, RELIGION **EDUCATION** Fairleigh Dickinson Univ, BA, 87; Herbert Lehman Col, CUNY, MA, 88; Univ Conn, PhD, 99. **CAREER** Adj lectr, Univ of Conn, 90-99; asst prof, Lyme Acad of Fine Arts, 97-99; asst prof, Black Hills State Univ, 99- **MEMBERSHIPS** Am Acad of Relig, Soc for Bibl Lit, MLA. **RESEARCH** Mysticism, Spirituality, Religion and Literature, Recusancy. **SELECTED PUBLICATIONS** Auth, "Forging a New Identity: Narcissism and Imagination in the Mysticism of Ignatius Loyola," Christianity and Literature, (98). **CONTACT ADDRESS** Black Hills State Univ, 1200 University, Unit 9063, Spearfish, SD 57799. **EMAIL** davidsalomon@bhsu.edu

SALOMON, HERMAN PRINS
PERSONAL Born 03/01/1930, Amsterdam, Netherlands **DISCIPLINE** LITERATURE **EDUCATION** NYork Univ, Am, 52, PhD(French), 61. **CAREER** From instr to asst prof French, Rutgers Univ, 61-65; asst prof French, Queens Col, NY, 65-68; asst prof French, 68-76, Assoc Prof Romance Lang, State Univ NY, Albany, 76- **MEMBERSHIPS** Am Asn Teachers Fr; MLA; Ned Ver Leraren in Levende Talen; Int Asn Fr Studies. **RESEARCH** Seventeenth century French literature; literature of the Netherlands; history of Spanish and Portuguese Judaism. **SELECTED PUBLICATIONS** Auth, Hist Of The Jews In The Netherlands - Dutch - Blom,Jch, Fuksmansfeld,Rg, Schoffer,I/, Studia Rosenthaliana, Vol 0030, 1996; Congregation-Shearith-Israel First Language + Uniting The Sephardim And Ashkenazim Congregation As A Linguistic Subculture Within New-York Dutch Society - Port/, Tradition-A J Of Orthodox Jewish Thought, Vol 0030, 1995; Another Lost Book Found - The Melo Haggadah, Amsterdam, 1622/, Studia Rosenthaliana, Vol 0029, 1995. **CONTACT ADDRESS** Dept of Romance Lang, SUNY, Albany, Albany, NY 12203. **EMAIL** hs138@albany.edu

SALOMON, ROGER B.
DISCIPLINE AMERICAN AND MODERN ENGLISH LITERATURE **EDUCATION** Harvard Univ, BA, Univ Calif, MA, PhD. **CAREER** English, Case Western Reserve Univ. **HONORS AND AWARDS** Dir, Writing Ctr. **SELECTED PUBLICATIONS** Auth or ed, Twain and the Image of History; Desperate Storytelling: Post-Romantic Elaborations of the Mock-Heroic Mode. **CONTACT ADDRESS** Case Western Reserve Univ, 10900 Euclid Ave, Cleveland, OH 44106.

SALTZMAN, ARTHUR MICHAEL
PERSONAL Born 08/10/1953, Chicago, IL, d, 1 child **DISCIPLINE** ENGLISH & AMERICAN LITERATURE **EDUCATION** Univ Ill, AB, 75, AM, 76, PhD, 79. **CAREER** Prof English, Mo Southern State Col, 92-; from asst prof to assoc prof, 81-92. **HONORS AND AWARDS** Outstanding Teacher, MSSC Found, 92; 1st Annual Roy T. Ames Memorial Essay Awd, 98; First Series Creative Nonfiction Awd, Mid-List Press, 99. **MEMBERSHIPS** MLA. **RESEARCH** Contemporary fiction; 20th century literature. **SELECTED PUBLICATIONS** Auth, The Fiction of William Gass: The Consolation of Language, Southern Ill, 86; Understanding Raymond Carver, SC, 88; Designs of Darkness in Contemporary American Fiction, Penn, 90; The Novel in the Balance, SC, 93; Objects and Empathy, in Ohio Rev, 97; From the Letters to Gamma Man, in Evansville Rev, 98; Once More Upon a Time Again, in Contemp Educ, 98; The Girl in the Moon, in Literal Latte, 98; The Nightmare of Relation in William Gass' The Tunnel, in Into the Tunnel, Del, 98; Incipience and Other Alibis, in Gettysburg Rev, 99; Understanding Nicholson Baker, SC, 99; Avid Monsters: The Look of Agony in Contemporary Fiction, in Twentieth Century Lit, 99; auth, Living Spaces, Iowa Rev., 99; auth, Gimme Kilter, Santa Clara Rev, 99; auth, Offerings Cream City Review, 00; author of numerous other journal articles and book reviews; auth, This Mad Instead: Governing Metaphors in Contemporary American Fiction, SC, 00; auth, Action Figures, Florida Rev, 00; auth, Awful Symmetric in Don Delillos Underworld in Critical Essays on Don DeLillo, 00; auth, Futility and Robert Frost, in Midwest Quality, 00. **CONTACT ADDRESS** Dept of English, Missouri So State Col, 3950 Newman Rd, Joplin, MO 64801-1595. **EMAIL** saltzman-a@mail.mssc.edu

SALWAK, DALE F.
PERSONAL Born 02/07/1947, Greenfield, MA, m, 1985, 1 child **DISCIPLINE** ENGLISH **EDUCATION** Purdue Univ, BA, 69; Univ Southern Calif, MA, 70, PhD, 74. **CAREER** Asst Ed, Dept Agricultural Info, 66-69; Instr, Univ Southern Calif, 72-73; Prof English, Citrus Col, 73-. **HONORS AND AWARDS** Paul A. Sidwell Awd for Novel-in-Progress, Purdue, 69; NDEA Title IV Fel, Univ Southern Calif, 69-72; Teacher of the Year, Citrus Col, 76-77, 78-79, 82-83; NEH grant, 85; Res Fel, Citrus Col Found, 86; Distinguished Alumni Awd, Purdue Univ, 87; Best Essay 96-97, Inside English. **RESEARCH** Bible; modern British literature; detective novel; biography; philosophy. **SELECTED PUBLICATIONS** Auth, The Wonders of Solitude, New World Libr, 95; ed, The Literary Biography: Problems and Solutions, Univ Iowa Press, 96; auth, The Words of Christ, New World Libr, 96; The Wisdom of Judaism, New World Libr, 97; ed, A Passion for Books, Macmillan/St. Martin's Press, 98; The Power of Prayer, New World Libr, 98; auth, In Defense of the Bible (forthcoming); author of numerous other publications. **CONTACT ADDRESS** Citrus Col, 1000 W Foothill Blvd., Glendora, CA 91741. **EMAIL** dsalwak@citrus.cc.ca.us

SALYER, GREGORY
DISCIPLINE LITERATURE, RELIGION **EDUCATION** King Col, BA; West Ky Univ, MA; Emory Univ, PhD, 92. **CAREER** Asst prof Humanities, Huntingdon Col, 93-. **HONORS AND AWARDS** Lilly Tchg Fel. **MEMBERSHIPS** AAR; MLA; SHC. **RESEARCH** Native American literature and culture. **SELECTED PUBLICATIONS** Co-ed, Literature and Theology at Century's End, 95; auth, Leslie Marmon Silko, 97. **CONTACT ADDRESS** Dept of Humanities, Huntingdon Col, 1500 E Fairview Ave, Montgomery, AL 36106. **EMAIL** gsalyer@huntingdon.edu

SALZBERG, JOEL
PERSONAL Born 05/31/1934, Brooklyn, NY **DISCIPLINE** AMERICAN LITERATURE **EDUCATION** City Col New York, BA, 56; Ind Univ, MA, 60; Univ Okla, PhD(English), 67. **CAREER** Asst prof English, Univ Northern Iowa, 65-68; asst prof, 68-72, Assoc Prof English, Univ Colo, Denver Ctr, 72-. **MEMBERSHIPS** MLA **RESEARCH** American Romanticism; psychology and literary criticism; 19th century realism. **SELECTED PUBLICATIONS CONTACT ADDRESS** Dept of English, Univ of Colorado, Boulder, Denver, CO 80210.

SAMMONS, MARTHA CRAGOE
PERSONAL Born 11/27/1949, Philadelphia, PA, m, 1973, 3 children **DISCIPLINE** ENGLISH **EDUCATION** Wheaton Col, BA, 71; Univ NC, Chapel Hill, PhD(English), 74. **CAREER** Teaching asst chem & grad asst English, Univ NC, 73-74; lectr, Duke Univ, 74; instr, Univ NC, 75; from asst prof to assoc prof, 75-87, Prof English, Wright State Univ, 87-. **RESEARCH** Technical writing; online documentation; writing for the Web. **SELECTED PUBLICATIONS** Auth, A Guide Through Narnia, Shaw Publ, 79, Brendow, 98; A Guide Through C S Lewis' Space Trilogy, Cornerstone Bks, 80; A Better Country: The Worlds of Religious Fantasy and Science Fiction, Greenwood Press, 88; Multimedia Presentations on the Go: An Introduction and Buyer's Guide, Libr Unlimited, 96; The Internet Writer's Handbook, Allyn & Bacon, 99; auth, "A Far-Off Country,": A Guide to C.S. Lewis Fantasy Fiction, Univ Press of Am, 00. **CONTACT ADDRESS** Dept of English, Wright State Univ, Dayton, Dayton, OH 45435-0002. **EMAIL** martha.sammons@wright.edu

SAMPLE, MAXINE J.
PERSONAL Born Port Norris, NJ **DISCIPLINE** ENGLISH, PHILOSPHY **EDUCATION** Col NJ, BA, 72; Clark Atlanta Univ, MA, 77; Emory Univ, PhD, 90. **CAREER** Instr, Atlanta Public Schs; Assoc Prof, Dekalb Col; Assoc Prof, State Univ W Ga. **HONORS AND AWARDS** NISOD Excellence in Teaching Awd, 91, 94; Cole Fel, Dekalb Col, 94; CASE Prof of the Year, 94; Fulbright Fel, 95. **MEMBERSHIPS** MLA, NEA, Ga Asn Educ, Toni Morrison Soc, Nat Coun Black Studies, African Lit Asn. **RESEARCH** African women writers, African-American literature, women's studies. **SELECTED**

PUBLICATIONS Co-ed, The Polishing Cloth, Kendall Hunt (Dubuque), 95; auth, "Behind the Gated Fence (from a Kenyan Journal)," Chattahoochee Rev 16.3 (96): 130-133; auth, "The Bridal 8:4:4: Graduation Day at the University of Nairobi (from a Kenyan Journal)," Chattahoochee Rev 17.2 (97): 100-104; auth, "Richard Bruce Nugent," African-American Authors 1745-1945: A Bio-Bibliog Critical Sourcebook, Greenwood Pr (Westport, CT), 00; rev, "Alice Walker's 'Possessing the Secret of Joy'," The Explicator (forthcoming); ed, Critical Essays on Bessie Head, Greenwood Pr (Westport, CT), forthcoming. **CONTACT ADDRESS** Dept English & Philos, State Univ of West Georgia, 1601 Maple St, Carollton, GA 30117-4116. **EMAIL** msample@westga.edu

SAMPSON, EDWARD C.
PERSONAL Born 12/20/1920, Ithaca, NY, m, 1968, 2 children **DISCIPLINE** ENGLISH **EDUCATION** Cornell Univ, BA, 42, PhD, 57; Columbia Univ, MA, 48. **CAREER** Instr Eng, Hofstra Univ, 46-49; fel, Cornell Univ, 49-52; from instr to prof lib studies, Clarkson Col Technol, 52-66, prof hum, 66-69; Prof English, State Univ NY Col Oneonta, 69-, Fulbright lectr, Univ Panjab, Pakistan, 59-60. **MEMBERSHIPS** MLA; Nathaniel Hawthorne Soc. **RESEARCH** Hawthorne; E B White; Thomas Hardy. **SELECTED PUBLICATIONS** Auth, Motivation in The Scarlet Letter, Am Lit, 1/57; Afterword, The House of the Seven Gables, Signet, 61; Three unpublished letters by Hawthorne to Epes Sargeant, Am Lit, 3/62; Critical study of E B White, Vol 232, In: Twayne United States Authors Series, Twayne; Thomas Hardy: Justice of the peace, Colby Libr Quart, 12/77, E.B.White, Dictionary of Literary Biography, vol ii, American Humorists, part 2, Gale Research, 82. **CONTACT ADDRESS** 89 Hemlock Dr, Killingworth, CT 06419. **EMAIL** ecsampson@snet.net

SAMRA, RIS¤ JANA
PERSONAL Born 03/19/1952, Green Bay, WI, s **DISCIPLINE** PROFESSOR, COMMUNICATION STUDIES **EDUCATION** Univ Arizona, PhD, 85. **CAREER** Author **MEMBERSHIPS** Nat Communication Assoc; Southern States Communication Assoc; Florida Communication Assoc; Int Soc of Bus Disciplines. **RESEARCH** Mideast Peace Process and the US Healthcare system. **CONTACT ADDRESS** Dept of Communication, Barry Univ, 4001 S Ocean Dr # 5L, Miami, FL 33161. **EMAIL** rsamra@mail.barry.edu

SAMSON, DONALD
PERSONAL Born, NY **DISCIPLINE** TECHNICAL WRITING AND EDITING, BRITISH AND AMERICAN LITERATURE **EDUCATION** Cornell Univ, BA; Univ NC, MA, PhD. **CAREER** Prof, Radford Univ; tech writer/ed, Lockheed Martin Corp. **SELECTED PUBLICATIONS** Auth, Editing Technical Writing, Oxford, 93; coauth, Professional Writing in Context: Lessons from Teaching and Consulting in Worlds of Work, Erlbaum, 95. **CONTACT ADDRESS** Radford Univ, Radford, VA 24142. **EMAIL** dsamson@runet.edu

SAMSON, JOHN W.
DISCIPLINE AMERICAN LITERATURE **EDUCATION** Cornell Univ, PhD, 80. **CAREER** Assoc prof, TX Tech Univ; ed, The 18th Century: Theory and Interpretation. **HONORS AND AWARDS** Co-founder, Soc for 18th-Century Am Stud. **MEMBERSHIPS** Pres, Soc for 18th-Century Am Stud. **RESEARCH** The hist and theoretical study of Am novels and narratives. **SELECTED PUBLICATIONS** Auth, White Lies: Melville's Narratives of Facts, 89. **CONTACT ADDRESS** Texas Tech Univ, Lubbock, TX 79409-5015. **EMAIL** ditjs@ttacs.ttu.edu

SAMTER, WENDY
DISCIPLINE INTERPERSONAL COMMUNICATION **EDUCATION** LaSalle Univ, BA, 81; Purdue Univ, MA, 83; PhD, 89. **CAREER** Tchg asst, Purdue Univ, 81-88; res asst, Purdue Univ; asst dir, Purdue Univ, 83-86; asst prof, 89-. **HONORS AND AWARDS** Univ fel, Purdue Univ, 81-82; David Ross Found summer dissertation res grant, Purdue Univ, 84; Intl Commun Assn award for outstanding grad stud tchr, 85; Bruce Kendall Awd for excellence in tchg, Purdue Univ, 85; David Ross res fel, Purdue Univ, 84-85; Alan H Monroe scholar, Purdue Univ, 88-89; intl travel grant, 90; supplemental funds grant, 90, 91; award for distinguished achievement field of commun, Commun Dept, Lasalle Univ, 93; pres, tri-state commun assn, 1993 **MEMBERSHIPS** Mem, Intl Commun Assn; Speech Commun Assn; Tri-State Commun Assn. **RESEARCH** Individual differences in social cognition. **SELECTED PUBLICATIONS** Co-auth, Cognitive and Motivational Influences on Spontaneous Comforting Behavior, Brown & Benchmark, 93; A Social Skills Analysis of Relationship Maintenance: How Individual Differences in Communication Skills Affect the Achievement of Relationship Ffunctions, Communication and Relational Maintenance, Acad Press, 94; auth, Unsupportive Relationships: Deficiencies in the Support-giving Skills of the Lonely Pperson's Friends, Communication of Social Support: Messages, Interactions, Relationships, and Community, Sage, 94. **CONTACT ADDRESS** Dept of Commun, Univ of Delaware, 162 Ctr Mall, Newark, DE 19716.

SAMUELS, MARILYN S.
DISCIPLINE TECHNICAL COMMUNICATIONS **EDUCATION** Hunter Col, BA, MA; Univ NYork, PhD. **CAREER** English, Case Western Reserve Univ. **HONORS AND AWARDS** Dir, Technical Writing. **SELECTED PUBLICATIONS** Auth or ed, The Technical Writing Process; Writing the Research Paper. **CONTACT ADDRESS** Case Western Reserve Univ, 10900 Euclid Ave, Cleveland, OH 44106.

SAMUELS, SHIRLEY
PERSONAL Born 08/28/1957, Chicago, IL, d, 1981, 2 children **DISCIPLINE** ENGLISH **EDUCATION** Univ Calif at Berkeley, BA, 77, MA, 81, PhD, 86. **CAREER** Prof & Dir, Won's Stud, Cornell Univ. **MEMBERSHIPS** Am Antiquarian Soc; MLA; ASA. **SELECTED PUBLICATIONS** Auth, "Plague and Politics in 1793: Arthur Mervyn," Criticism, 85; auth, "The Family, the State, and the Novel in the Early Republic," Am Quart, 86; auth, "Infidelity and Contagion: The Rhetoric of Revolution," Early Am Lit, 87; auth, "Wieland: Alien and Infidel," Early Am Lit, 90; auth, "Generation through Violence," in New Essays on Last of the Mohicans, 92; auth, "The Identity of Slavery," in The Culture of Sentiment: Race, Gender and Sentimentality in 19th-Century America, Oxford Univ Press, 92, repr in Romances of the Republic: Women, the Family and Violence in the Literature of the Early American Nation, Oxford Univ Press, 96; auth, "Miscegenated America," Am Lit Hist, Fall 97. **CONTACT ADDRESS** Eng Dept, Cornell Univ, Goldwin Smith Hall, Ithaca, NY 14853. **EMAIL** srs8@cornell.edu

SAMUELS, WILFRED D.
PERSONAL Born 02/07/1947, Puerto Limon, Costa Rica, m, 1980 **DISCIPLINE** ENGLISH **EDUCATION** Univ of California, Riverside, CA, BA, 1971; University of Iowa, Iowa City, IA, MA, PhD, 1971-77. **CAREER** Univ of Colorado, Boulder, CO, asst prof, 78-85; Benjamin Banneker Honors Coll, Prairie View AM, TX, assoc prof, 85-87; Univ of Utah, Salt Lake City, UT, assoc prof, 87-. **HONORS AND AWARDS** Ford Foundation Post Doctoral Fellow, Ford, 1984, 1985; CAAS UCLA, Postdoctoral Fellow, 1982, 1983; NEH Symposium Grants, 1980, 1984, 1989; Outstanding Teacher Awd, several, 1978-84; Ramona Cannon Awd for teaching Excellence in the Humanities, 1992; Student's Choice Awd, 1993; The University of Utah, Distinguished Teaching Awd, 1994. **MEMBERSHIPS** Popular Culture; MLA; Am Literature Assn. **CONTACT ADDRESS** Professor, Department of English, Univ of Utah, 3407 LNCO, Salt Lake City, UT 84112.

SAMUELSON, DAVID N.
PERSONAL Born 02/05/1939, New York, NY, m, 1966, 1 child **DISCIPLINE** ENGLISH, LITERATURE **EDUCATION** Drew Univ, BA, 62; Univ S Calif, PhD, 69. **CAREER** From Instr to Prof, Calif State Univ Long Beach, 66-. **HONORS AND AWARDS** Proctor and Gamble, MIT, 56-57; Nat Defense Educ Awd, 62-66; Floariah Fel, 65-66. **MEMBERSHIPS** MLA, Pac Ancient and Mod Lang Asn, Sci Fiction Res Asn, Soc for Utopian Studies, Soc for Tech Commun, Coun for Prog in tech and Sci Commun, Soc for Lit and Sci. **RESEARCH** Science Fiction, Fantasy and Utopian Literature, 20th Century English Literature, Technical Communication, Science and Literature. **SELECTED PUBLICATIONS** Auth, Visions of Tomorrow, 74; auth, Arthur C. Clarke, 84; auth, "Hard Science Fiction," special issue of Sci Fiction Studies (93). **CONTACT ADDRESS** Dept English, California State Univ, Long Beach, 11250 N Bellflower Rd, Mhb 419, Long Beach, CA 90840-0006. **EMAIL** dnsmlsn@csulb.edu

SAMWAY, PATRICK H.
PERSONAL Born 05/12/1939, New York, NY **DISCIPLINE** AMERICAN LITERATURE **EDUCATION** Fordham Univ, BA, 63; PhL, 65; MA, 65; Woodstock Theol Sem, MDiv, 69; Univ NCar, PhD, 72. **CAREER** Assoc prof, LeMoyne Col, 72-83; vis assoc prof, Boston Col, 83-84; literary ed, Am Mag, 84-99, prof, St Peter's Col, 99-01; prof, St Joseph's Univ, 01-. **HONORS AND AWARDS** Fulbright Lectr, 75-76, 79-80. **MEMBERSHIPS** MLA, Soc for the Study of Southern Lit. **RESEARCH** American South. **SELECTED PUBLICATIONS** Coed, Stories of the Modern South, Penguin, 77; auth, Faulkner's Intruder in the Dust: A Critical Study of the Typescripts, Whitston Publ, 80; coed, Faulkner and Idealism: Perspectives From Paris, Univ Pr of Miss, 83; coed, A Modern Southern Reader, Peachtree Pr, 86; coed, Stories of the Old South, Penguin, 89; coed, A New Reader of the Old South, Peachtree Pr, 90; ed, Signposts in a Strange Land, Farrar, Straus 7 Giroux, 91; ed, A Thief of Peirce: The Letters of Kenneth Laine Ketner and Walker Percy, Univ Pr of Miss, 95; auth, Walker Percy: A Life, Farrar, Straus & Giroux, 97. **CONTACT ADDRESS** 5600 City Ave, Philadelphia, PA 19131. **EMAIL** psamwaysj@aol.com

SANCHEZ-EPPLER, KAREN
PERSONAL Born 02/04/1959, NY, m, 1984, 2 children **DISCIPLINE** AMERICAN LITERATURE **EDUCATION** Williams Col, BA; Cambridge Univ, BA; Johns Hopkins Univ, PhD. **CAREER** Prof, Amherst Col. **MEMBERSHIPS** ALA, ASA. **RESEARCH** Imagining rel(s) between lit, soc structures, and soc change. **SELECTED PUBLICATIONS** Auth, Touching Liberty: Abolition, Feminism and the Politics of the Body, 93. **CONTACT ADDRESS** Amherst Col, Amherst, MA 01002-5000. **EMAIL** kjsanchezepp@amherst.edu

SAND, R. H.
PERSONAL Born 12/30/1936, New York, NY, m, 1964, 2 children **DISCIPLINE** ENGLISH **EDUCATION** Harvard Col, BA 58; Harvard Law Sch, JD 61. **CAREER** Kaye Scholer Fierman Hays and Handler, 65-70; Allied Signal Inc, 70-. **MEMBERSHIPS** Assoc of the Bar NYC **RESEARCH** Legal developments in occupational safety and health. **SELECTED PUBLICATIONS** Employee Relations Law Journal, columnist on Safety and Health. **CONTACT ADDRESS** Honeywell Int Inc, 101 Columbia Rd, Morristown, NJ 07962.

SANDBERG, STEPHANIE L.
PERSONAL Born 01/31/1971, Salt Lake City, UT, m, 1992, 2 children **DISCIPLINE** THEATRE **EDUCATION** BA, Westmont Col, 92; UCSB, MA, 94; PhD, 98. **CAREER** Asst Prof, Calvin Col, 96-. **HONORS AND AWARDS** Excellence in Teaching Awd, UCSB. **MEMBERSHIPS** Asn for Theatre in Higher Educ, Am Soc for Theatre Res. **RESEARCH** Irish Theatre, 19th Century European Theatre, Religion and Theatre. **CONTACT ADDRESS** Dept Comm Arts & Sci, Calvin Col, 3201 Burton St SE, Grand Rapids, MI 49546-4301. **EMAIL** ssandber@calvin.edu

SANDERS, IVAN
PERSONAL Born 01/24/1944, Budapest, Hungary, m, 1968, 2 children **DISCIPLINE** COMPARATIVE LITERATURE, EAST EUROPEAN FICTION **EDUCATION** Brooklyn Col, BA, 65, MA, 67; NYork Univ, PhD(comp lit), 72. **CAREER** Prof English, Suffolk County Community Col, 68-, vis assoc prof, Sch Continuing Educ, Columbia Univ, 78-79. **HONORS AND AWARDS** Irex fel, Hungarian Acad Sci, Inst Lit Res, Budapest, 79; sr fel, Inst ECent Europe, Columbia Univ, 82; Fulbright fel, 89. **MEMBERSHIPS** MLA; Am Hungarian Educ Asn; Am Fed Teachers. **RESEARCH** Contemporary American fiction; contemporary East European fiction and film; Hungarian literature. **SELECTED PUBLICATIONS** Auth, Engaol'd tongue?: Notes on the Language of Hungarian Americans, Valosag, Budapest, Vol XVI, No 5; The Gifts of Strangeness: Alienation and Creation in Jerzy Kosinski's Fiction, Polish Rev, Vol XIX, No 3-4; Human Dialogues are Born, Nation, 4/23/77; trans, George Konrad's The City Builder, Harcourt Brace Jovanavich, 77; auth, Simple Elements and Violent Combinations: Reflections on the Fiction of Amos Oz, Judaism, Vol XXVII, No 1; The Possibilities of Fiction: On Recent American Novels, Valosag, Vol XXI, No 1, 78; trans, George Konrad's The Loser, Harcourt Brace Jovanavich, 82; co-ed, Essays on World War I: Total War and Peacemaking, A Case Study on Trianon, Columbia Univ Press, 82; auth, The Other Europeans, The Nation, 87; trans, Milan Fust, The Story of My Wife, PAJ, 87; auth, Budapest Letter: New Themes, New Writers, NY Times Book Rev, 88; co-trans, Peter Nadas, A Book of Memories, Farrar STraus & Giroux, 97. **CONTACT ADDRESS** 4 Coed Ln, Stony Brook, NY 11790. **EMAIL** sanderi@sunysuffolk.edu

SANDERS, LIONEL
PERSONAL Born 05/21/1942, Hitchin, United Kingdom, d, 1 child **DISCIPLINE** HISTORY; CLASSICS **EDUCATION** McMaster, PHD **CAREER** Lect, 70-71, Univ Kingston, Ont; Asst Prof, 72-74, Loyola Col, Montreal; Assoc Prof, 76-96, Concordia Univ, Montreal; Full Prof, 96-pres, Concordia Univ **MEMBERSHIPS** Hellenic Soc; Canadian Class Assoc; Am Philol Assoc **RESEARCH** History and Historiography of Greek Sicily **SELECTED PUBLICATIONS** Auth, "Plato's First Visit to Sicily," Kokalos, 79, 207-19; auth, "Dionysius I of Syracuse and the Validity of the Hostile Tradition," SCI, 79, 64-84; auth, "Diodorus Siculus and Dionysius I of Syracuse," Historia, 81, 394-411. **CONTACT ADDRESS** Dept. Of Classics Modern Langs, Concordia Univ, Montreal, 1435 De Maisonneuve Blvd W, Montreal, QC, Canada H3G 1M8. **EMAIL** sanders@alcor.concordia.ca

SANDERS, MARK
DISCIPLINE ENGLISH LANGUAGE AND LITERATURE **EDUCATION** Brown Univ, PhD, 92. **CAREER** Assoc prof **RESEARCH** African-American literature; 20th-century American literature. **SELECTED PUBLICATIONS** Ed, A Son's Return: Selected Essays of Sterling A. Brown. **CONTACT ADDRESS** English Dept, Emory Univ, 1380 Oxford Rd NE, Atlanta, GA 30322-1950. **EMAIL** msander@emory.edu

SANDERS, ROBERT E.
DISCIPLINE INTERPERSONAL COMMUNICATION **EDUCATION** PhD. **CAREER** Univ Albany - SUNY **HONORS AND AWARDS** SCA Spotlight on Scholarship Honoree, 97; SCA Dissertation Awd, 71 **RESEARCH** Talk and behavior in social interaction **SELECTED PUBLICATIONS** Auth, Cognitive Foundations of Calculated Speech, 87; The role of mass communication processes in the social upheavals in the Soviet Union, Eastern Europe, and China, SUNY Press, 92; Cognition, computation, and conversation, Human Comm Res, 92; Culture, communication, and preferences for directness in the ex-

pression of directives, Comm Theory, 94; A retrospective essay on the consequentiality of communication, Lawrence Erlbaum, 95; A neo-rhetorical perspective: The enactment of role-identities as interactive and strategic, Lawrence Erlbaum, 95; The sequential-inferential theories of Sanders and Gottman, SUNY Press, 95; An impersonal basis for shared interpretations of messages in context, Context Press , 97; The production of symbolic objects as components of larger wholes , Lawrence Erlbaum, 97; Children's neo-rhetorical participation in peer interactions, Falmer , 97; Find your partner and do-si-do: The formation of personal relationships between social beings, Jour Soc & Personal Relationships, 97. **CONTACT ADDRESS** Communication Dept, SUNY, Albany, 1400 Washington Ave, Albany, NY 12222. **EMAIL** r.sanders@albany.edu

SANDERS, SCOTT P.
DISCIPLINE PROFESSIONAL WRITING AND EDITING **EDUCATION** Univ Colo, PhD, 80. **CAREER** Instr, Univ NMex, 84-; past ed, IEEE Transactions on Prof Commun. **HONORS AND AWARDS** NCTE Awd for Best Article, 89. **RESEARCH** Technical communication. **SELECTED PUBLICATIONS** Coauth, The Physics of Skiing, Am Inst of Physics Press, 96; coed, Frontier Gothic, 93; Weber Studies, spec issue on Nat Am Lit; IEEETransPC issue on ethics and prof commun. **CONTACT ADDRESS** Univ of New Mexico, Albuquerque, Albuquerque, NM 87131. **EMAIL** ssanders@unm.edu

SANDIFORD, KEITH
PERSONAL Born Barbados, WI **DISCIPLINE** EIGHTEENTH CENTURY BRITISH LITERATURE, THE NOVEL, CULTURAL STUDIES **EDUCATION** Univ Ill, Urbana-Champaign, PhD, 79. **CAREER** Prof, La State Univ. **HONORS AND AWARDS** NEH Research Fel, 87; LSU Col of Arts and Sciences Manship Summer Grant for Faculty Research, 93; LSU Research Grand, summer 86. **MEMBERSHIPS** Am Soc for Eighteenth Century Studies, South Central Soc for Eighteenth Century Studies, Group for Early Modern Cultural Studies. **RESEARCH** Slavery, Anti-Slavery, Sugar and Colonial Commodities, Hybridity, Genre and Colonial Text Formation. **SELECTED PUBLICATIONS** Auth, "Paule Marshall's Praisesong for the Widow: The Reluctant Heiress, Or Whose Life is it Anyway?," Black American Literature Forum, 86;auth, ' Images of the African in his Literature from Renaissance to Enlightenment," essay in Daniel Droixhe and Klaus H. Keifer, Images de L African de l Antiquite au Xxe Siecle,(Frankfurt: Verlag Peter Lanf, 87); auth, Measuring the Moment: Strategies of Protest in Eighteenth-Century Afro-English Writing, 88; auth, " Inkle and Yarico: The Construction of Alterity from History to Literature," Nieuwe West-Indische Gids, 90; auth, Gothic and Intertextual Constructions in Gloria Naylor's Linden Hills, Arizona Quaterly, 91; auth, "Rochefort's History: The Poetics of Collusion in a Colonizing Narrative," Papers in Language and Literature, 93; auth, " Our Caribs are not Savages: The Use of Colloquy in Rochefort's Natural and Moral History of the Carribby-Islands, " Studies in Western Civilization, 93; auth, Monk Lewis and the Slavery Sublime: The Agon of Romantic Desire in the Journal" Essays in Literature 23:1, (96): 84-98; auth, " Sugar Slaves and Machines: An Economy of Bodies in Colonizing Narratives," Synthesis, 98; auth,The Cultural Politics of Sugar, Cambridge Univ Press,00. **CONTACT ADDRESS** Dept of Eng, Louisiana State Univ and A&M Col, 212V Allen Hall, Baton Rouge, LA 70803. **EMAIL** ksandif@lsu.edu

SANDNER, DAVID M.
PERSONAL Born 06/04/1966, San Francisco, CA, m, 2001 **DISCIPLINE** ENGLISH **EDUCATION** Univ Calif Santa Cruz, BA, 88; San Francisco State Univ, MA, 95; Univ Ore, PhD, 00. **CAREER** Asst prof, Grinnell Col, 00-. **HONORS AND AWARDS** Everett D. Monte Award, Univ Ore, 99-00; Grad Student Award, 00. **MEMBERSHIPS** Intl Asn of the Fantastic in the Arts; N Am Soc for the Study of Romanticism. **RESEARCH** Romanticism; The Sublime; The Fantastic. **SELECTED PUBLICATIONS** Auth, The Fantastic Sublime: Romanticism and Transcendence in 19th Century Children's Fantasy Literature, Greenwood, 96; auth, The Treasury of the Fantastic: Romanticism to Early Twentieth Century Literature, N Atlantic, 01. **CONTACT ADDRESS** Dept English, Grinnell Col, 304 4th Ave W, Apt 10, Grinnell, IA 50112-1847. **EMAIL** sandnerd@grinnell.edu

SANDS, HELEN R.
DISCIPLINE COMMUNICATION **EDUCATION** Univ VT, BA; Southern IL Univ, MA, PhD. **CAREER** Prof & Coordr, Interpersonal-Orgn Commun; fac, Univ Southern IN, 69-; fac sponsor, Commun Arts Club & USI's chap Alpha Chi. **HONORS AND AWARDS** Alumni Teach of the Yr, 81; Order of Omega Teach of the Yr, 97. **MEMBERSHIPS** Speech Commun Assoc. **RESEARCH** Interpersonal communication; public address. **SELECTED PUBLICATIONS** Coauth, textbk, Public Conversations. **CONTACT ADDRESS** Dept of Commun, Univ of So Indiana, 8600 University Blvd, Evansville, IN 47712. **EMAIL** hsands.ucs@smtp.usi.edu

SANDY, STEPHEN
PERSONAL Born 08/02/1934, Minneapolis, MN, m, 2 children **DISCIPLINE** ENGLISH **EDUCATION** Yale Univ, BA, 55; Harvard Univ, AB, 60; PhD, 63. **CAREER** Vis Prof, Brown Univ, 68-69; Prof, Bennington Col, 69-. **HONORS AND AWARDS** Co-winner Mudfish Poetry Prize, 98; Reader's digest Residency for distinguished Writers, 97; Chubb LifeAmerica Fel, Mac Dowel colony, 93; NEH Creative Writing Fel, 88; NEA Poet in Residence, Philadelphia, 85; Huber Foundation Grant, 73; Fulbright Vis Lectureship, Japan, 67-68; Acad of am Poets prize, 55; Pulitzer Prize nominee, 71, 88. **RESEARCH** American poetry; English fiction, 1780-1820. **SELECTED PUBLICATIONS** Auth, The Raveling of the Novel, Studies in Romantic Fiction from Walpole to Scott, Arno Press, 80; auth, "Seeing Things: The Visionary Ardor of Seamus Heaney," Walcott and Heaney: Readings of Nobel laureates, 98; auth, "Auden at Bennington in 1946," The W.H. Auden Society Newsletter, (97): 7-11; auth, "William Gass, An Introduction," Bennington Chapbooks in Literature, 96; auth, "From Chinoiserie to Chinese Hills and the Slag Tombs, Notes on the Villanelle," Poetry Pilot, 95; auth, "Writing As A Career: an Early Auden Lecture in the States," The W.H. Auden Society Newsletter, (93): 3-8; auth, "Seeing Things: The Visionary Ardor of Seamus Heaney," Salmagundi, (93): 207-225; auth, "An Enlarging Pleasure," The Day I was Older, on the Poetry of Donald Hall, Story Line Press, 89; auth, "James Merrill," Dictionary of Literary Biography, Yearbook 1985, Gale Research, 86; auth, "Japanese Literature in Chinese: Poetry and Prose in Chinese by Japanese Writers of the later period, Vol 2," Journal of Asian and African Studies, 80. **CONTACT ADDRESS** Dept Lang & Lit, Bennington Col, Bennington, VT 05201. **EMAIL** sandys@bennington.edu

SANSONE, DAVID
PERSONAL Born 09/23/1946, New York, NY, m, 1969, 2 children **DISCIPLINE** CLASSICS **EDUCATION** Hamilton Col, AB, 68; Univ Wis, MA, 69, PhD, 72. **CAREER** Asst prof, Univ HI, 72-74; from asst prof to prof, Univ Ill, 74-; chair, classics dept, 96-. **MEMBERSHIPS** Am Philol Asn; Soc for the Promotion of Hellenic Studies; Cambridge Philol Soc; Int Plutarch Soc. **RESEARCH** Greek tragedy; ancient biography; Greek and Roman sport. **SELECTED PUBLICATIONS** Auth, Aeschylean Metaphors for Intellectual Activity (Hermes Einzelschriften 35), F. Steiner Verlag, Wiesbaden, 75; Euripides, Iphigenia in Tauris, B. G. Teubner Verlag, Leipzig, 81; Greek Athletics and the Genesis of Sport, Univ CA Press, Berkeley, 88; Plutarch: Lives of Aristeides and Cato, Aris & Phillips, Warminster, 89; Towards a New Doctrine of the Article in Greek: Some Observations on the Definite Article in Plato, Classical Philol 88, 93; Plato and Euripides, IL Classical Studies 21, 96. **CONTACT ADDRESS** Dept of Classics 4090 For Lang, Univ of Illinois, Urbana-Champaign, 707 S Mathews Ave., Urbana, IL 61801. **EMAIL** dsansone@uiuc.edu

SANTAVICCA, EDMUND F.
PERSONAL Born 01/04/1947, Detroit, MI, s **DISCIPLINE** LIBRARY SCIENCE **EDUCATION** Wayne State Univ, BA, 68; Univ Mich, AMLS, 71; Wayne State Univ, MA, 72; Univ Mich, PhD, 77. **CAREER** Asst Prof, Northern Ill Univ, 76-77; Asst Prof, Atlanta Univ, 77-78; Asst Prof, Vanderbilt Univ, 79-81; Prof, Estrella Mt Community Col, 94-. **HONORS AND AWARDS** First Prize, Grad Div, Govt of France, 69; President's Prog Awd, Libr Admin and Management Assoc, 86. **MEMBERSHIPS** Am Libr Assoc, Assoc Col & Res Librs. **RESEARCH** Cyber-based information seeking behavior, humanities interdisciplinarities, information literacy and critical thinking, management of information literacy technology services. **SELECTED PUBLICATIONS** Auth, "A Case Study of Bibliographic Instruction in France," Res Strategies, 8 (90); auth, "Art and Museum Libraries of Nice," Special Librs, 82 (91); auth, "Integrating AIDS Into the Academic Curriculum," Urban Acad Librn, 8 (91-92); auth, "Internet as a Reference and Research Tool: A Model for Educators," in Librns on the Internet (94). **CONTACT ADDRESS** Dept Lib Arts, Estrella Mt Community Col, 3000 N Dysart Rd, Avondale, AZ 85323. **EMAIL** ed.santavicca@ememail.maricopa.edu

SANTOS, JOSE ANDRE
PERSONAL Born 09/12/1956, Provins, France, s **DISCIPLINE** CLASSICS, LINGUISTICS **EDUCATION** Univ Paris, Lic de Let, 79; Univ Vir, MA, 85; CUNY Grad Sch, PhD, 91. **CAREER** Vis asst prof, Bard Col, 91-92; asst prof, Russell Sage Col, 92-99; asst prof, Tex Tech Univ, 99-. **MEMBERSHIPS** MLA; AATF. **RESEARCH** 19th C French literature; Francophone literature. **SELECTED PUBLICATIONS** Auth, L'Art du Recit Court Chez Jean Lorrain, Nizet (Paris), 95; auth, "Actualite de Jean Lorrain," Asn Jean Lorr (00); auth, "Les Revers de la Fraternite: Le Cas de Jean et Taos Amrouche," La Mag Let (forthcoming); auth, entry on 'Fadhma Amrouche,' in Who's Who in Contemporary Women Writers (NY: Routledge, 00). **CONTACT ADDRESS** Classics Dept, Texas Tech Univ, Lubbock, TX 79409. **EMAIL** jose.santos@ttu.edu

SANTOS, SHEROD
PERSONAL Born 09/09/1948, Greenville, SC, m, 1975, 2 children **DISCIPLINE** ENGLISH, PHILOSOPHY **EDUCATION** San Diego State Univ, BA, 71; MA, 74;, MFA, 78; Univ Utah, PhD, 82. **CAREER** Asst prof, Calif State Univ San Bernardino, 82-83; asst prof, Univ Mo Columbia, 83-86; vis prof, Univ Calif Irvine, 89-90; assoc prof, Univ Mo Columbia, 86-92; prof, Univ MO Columbia, 93-. **HONORS AND AWARDS** Utah Arts Coun Awd in Lit, 80; Discovery The Nat award, 78; Pushcart Prize in Poetry, 80; Oscar Blumenthal Prize, 81; Nat Poetry Series Selection, 82; Meralmikjen Fel in Poetry, Bread Loaf Writers' Conf, 82; Ingram Merrill Found Grant, 82; The Robert Frost Poet, 84; Mo Arts Coun Awd in Lit, 87; Fel to the Yaddo Center fort he Arts, 87; NBC Today Show Appearance, 87; Nat Endowment for the Arts Grant, 87; Weldon Springs Res Grant, Univ Mo, 91-92; Chancellor's Awd for Outstanding Fac Res, Univ Mo, 93; Pushcart Prize in the Essay, 94; British Arts Coun Int Travel Grant, 95; Appointed Mem, Nat Endowment for the Arts Lit Panel, 95; BF Conners Awd in Poetry, 98; Finalist, New Yorker Book Awd in Poetry, 99; Finalist, Nat Book Awd in Poetry, 99; Acad Awd in Literature, Am Acad of Arts & Letters, 99; Presidents Awd for Outstanding Res and Creativity Acitivity, Univ of Missouri, 99; The Poetry Society of Am Lyric Poetry Prize, 99. **MEMBERSHIPS** Acad Am Poets; Poetry Soc of Am; PEN Am Center; Robinson Jeffers Soc; Poets and Writers; Associated Writing Programs. **RESEARCH** Poetry and Poetics. **SELECTED PUBLICATIONS** Auth, The City of Women, 93; The Pilot Star Elegies, 99; auth, "A Poetry of Two Minds," (a collection of literary essays), 00. **CONTACT ADDRESS** Dept of English, Univ of Missouri, Columbia, 107 Tate Hall, Columbia, MO 65211. **EMAIL** santoss@missouri.edu

SANTOSUOSSO, ALMA
DISCIPLINE MUSIC HISTORY **EDUCATION** British Columbia, Bmus, MMus; Univ Ill, PhD. **CAREER** Teaching music history, Univ of Illinois, Dartmouth Col. **RESEARCH** Medieval music. **SELECTED PUBLICATIONS** Auth, Letter Notations in the Middle Ages; Analysis, Inventory and Text. **CONTACT ADDRESS** Dept of Music, Wilfrid Laurier Univ, 75 University Ave W, Waterloo, ON, Canada N2L 3C5. **EMAIL** asantosu@wlu.ca

SAPERSTEIN, JEFF
DISCIPLINE COMPOSITION, AMERICAN LITERATURE, SHAKESPEARE, AND FILM **EDUCATION** SUNY, Albany, BA; Northeastern Univ, MA; Univ NH, PhD. **CAREER** Prof, Radford Univ. **RESEARCH** Compos theory/pedag; gender studies; film theory; ethnic studies; Shakespeare. **SELECTED PUBLICATIONS** Publ articles in film studies, on films of Woody Allen, on Roth, Thoreau, Morrison, and Atwood. **CONTACT ADDRESS** Radford Univ, Radford, VA 24142. **EMAIL** jsaperst@runet.edu

SARGENT, STUART H.
PERSONAL Born Portland, OR **DISCIPLINE** CHINESE LITERATURE **EDUCATION** Stanford Univ, PhD. **CAREER** Assoc prof. **RESEARCH** Chinese poetry of the late 11th century. **SELECTED PUBLICATIONS** Auth, pubs on literary theory and poetry. **CONTACT ADDRESS** Foreign Languages and Literature Dept, Colorado State Univ, Fort Collins, CO 80523. **EMAIL** stuart.sargent@colostate.edu

SARKODIE-MENSAH, KWASI
PERSONAL Born 06/13/1955, Ejisu, Ashanti, Ghana, m, 1980, 3 children **DISCIPLINE** LIBRARY SCIENCE **EDUCATION** Universidad Complutense, diploma, 1978; University of Ghana, BA (w/honors), 1979; Clarion University, MSLS, 1983; University of Illinois, PhD, 1988. **CAREER** Ahmadiyya Secondary School, teacher, 79-80; Origbo Community High School, teacher, 80-82; Clarion University, graduate asst, 82-83; University of Illinois, graduate asst, 84-86; Xavier University of Louisiana, head of public services, 86-89; Northeastern University, library instruction coordinator, 89-92; Boston Col, chief reference librarian, 92-95; Commonwealth of Massachusetts, court interpreter, 92-; US Attorney General's Office, Boston, consultant, African languages; Col of Advancing Studies, Boston Col, faculty, 96-; Boston Col Libraries, manager of instructional services, 95-. **HONORS AND AWARDS** University of Illinois, Fellow, 1986-87; Research Strategies, Top 20 Articles in Library Instruction, 1986; Origbo Community High School, Best Teacher, 1981, 1982; Spanish Government, Scholarship to study abroad, 1978; University of Ghana, Scholarship, 1975-79. **MEMBERSHIPS** American Library Assn, 1984-; Massachusetts Faculty Development Consortium, advsry bd mbr, 1992-; ACRL/IS Diverse Committee, chair, 1993-95; Northeastern University Committee to Improve College Teaching, 1989-92; Multicultural Network, 1992-; Boston College, Martin Luther King Committee, 1993-; ACRL/IS Committee on Education for Library Instructors, ACRL/IS Award Committee; African Pastoral Center, Archdiocese of Boston, bd mem. **SELECTED PUBLICATIONS** Auth, works include: Making Term Paper Counseling More Meaningful, 1989; Writing in a Language You Don't Know, 1990; The Intl Ta: A Beat from a Foreign Drummer, 1991; Dealing with Intl Students in a Multicultural Era, 1992; Paraprofessionals in Reference Services: An Untapped Mine, 1993; editor: Library Instruction Roundtable Newsletter, 1991-92; consultant: Northeastern Univ Project on the History of Black Writing, 1990-; The International Student in the US Academic Library: Bldg Bridges to Better Bibliographic Instruction; Nigerian Americans, 1995; Human

Aspect of Reference in the Era of Technology, 1997; Using Humor for Effective Library Instruction, 1998; International Students US Trends, Cultural Adjustments, 1998; Reference Services for the Adult Learner, 1999; auth, Research in the Electronic Age, 99; auth, The Difficult Patron Issue, 00; auth, Reference Services for the Adult Learner, 00; auth, The International Student on Campus, 00. **CONTACT ADDRESS** Manager, Instructional Services, Boston College, 307 O'Neill Library, Chestnut Hill, MA 02167. **EMAIL** sarkodik@bc.edu

SARLOS, ROBERT KAROLY
PERSONAL Born 06/06/1931, Budapest, Hungary, m, 1962, 2 children **DISCIPLINE** THEATRE HISTORY **EDUCATION** Occidental Col, BA, 59; Yale Univ, PhD(hist of theatre), 65. **CAREER** Instr English, Mitchell Col, 62-63; from lectr to acting asst prof, 63-65, asst prof, 66-70, assoc prof, 70-79, Prof Dramatic Art, Univ Calif, Davis, 79-, Vpres, Woodland Opera House Inc, 80- **MEMBERSHIPS** Int Fed Theatre Res; Am Soc Theatre Res. **RESEARCH** Elizabethan, Baroque and American theatre. **SELECTED PUBLICATIONS** Auth, Development and operation of the first Blackfriars theatre, In: Studies in the Elizabethan Theatre, 61; Two outdoor productions of Giuseppe Galli Bibiena, Theatre Surv, 5/64; coauth, The Woodland Opera House: The end of an era in California theatre, Calif Hist Soc Quart, 12/69; auth, Jig Cook and the Provincetown Players: Theatre in Ferment, Univ Mass Press, 82. **CONTACT ADDRESS** Dept of Dramatic Art, Univ of California, Davis, Davis, CA 95616.

SASSO, MICHAEL J.
PERSONAL Born 12/30/1955, Yonkers, NY, m, 1978, 3 children **DISCIPLINE** ENGLISH **EDUCATION** SUNY, BS, 98; Ohio State Univ, MA, 00. **CAREER** Pastor to prin, Calvary Chapel, 85-96, instr, Twin Peaks Bible Col, 90-95; prog admin to lectr, Ohio State Univ, 98-. **HONORS AND AWARDS** Award, SUNY, 96; Morgan Fel, SUNY, 97; Sigma Tau Delta, 97; Alpha Chi Fel, 98; Ohio Eng Scholars Awd, 00. **MEMBERSHIPS** MLA, NCTE, Rhetoric Soc of Amer, Soc for Disability Studies, Writing Prog Admin Assoc, Assoc for Bus Commun, Nat Assoc of Sec Sch Prin, Assoc of Prof Commun Cons. **RESEARCH** Writing and Disability, Disability Studies, Rhetoric of the Body, Ohio Deaf-Write Project. **SELECTED PUBLICATIONS** Auth, Composition Pedagogy: First Year Students and Access to the University, Ohio State Univ Pr, (Columbus, OH), 99; ed, Starting Places: Beginning Your Teaching Career, Ohio State Univ Pr, (Columbus, OH), 99; ed, The First Year Writing Program Handbook, Ohio State Univ Pr, (Columbus, OH), 99; ed, Writing Lives: Reading Communities, Pearson (Boston, MA), 00; ed, Writing in Multicultural Settings: The Bedford Bibliography of Basic Writing, (Bedford, NY), 01. **CONTACT ADDRESS** 1593 Waterstone Cr, Columbus, OH 43235-1936. **EMAIL** sasso1@osu.edu

SASSON, SARAH DIANE HYDE
PERSONAL Born 08/27/1946, Asheville, NC, m, 1969, 3 children **DISCIPLINE** AMERICAN LITERATURE & HISTORY **EDUCATION** Univ NC, BA, 68, PhD(Eng), 80; Univ IL, Urbana, MA, 71. **CAREER** Instr Eng, 80-81, lectr Am studies, 81-82, Dir, Master of Arts in Lib Studies Prog, Duke Univ, 87-; Dir, Univ MAT Prog, Duke Univ, 91-95; Assoc of Graduate Lib Studies, Pres, 94-96. **HONORS AND AWARDS** Am Coun Learned Soc Fel. **MEMBERSHIPS** Am Folklore Soc; Am Studies Asn; MLA. **RESEARCH** Shaker lit; Am autobiography; Am relig lit. **SELECTED PUBLICATIONS** Auth, The Shaker Personal Narrative, Univ TN Press (in prep). **CONTACT ADDRESS** Duke Univ, Box 90095, Durham, NC 27708.

SASSON, VICTOR
PERSONAL Born 12/20/1937, Baghdad, Iraq, d, 1 child **DISCIPLINE** RELIGION; ENGLISH LITERATURE **EDUCATION** Univ London, BA honors, 73; New York Univ, PhD, 79. **CAREER** Univ S Africa, sr lectr, 81-85; Long Island Univ, asst prof, 90-91; Touro Col NY, asst prof, 90-96. **HONORS AND AWARDS** Thayer fel; AAR. **MEMBERSHIPS** Colum Univ Sem Hebrew Bible and Shakespeare; SOTS. **RESEARCH** Text and language of Hebrew bible; N W Semitic Epigraphy; tense and aspect in Biblical Hebrew and old Aramaic; ancient near east. **SELECTED PUBLICATIONS** Auth, The Literary and Theological Function of Job's Wife in the Book of Job, Biblica, 98; Some Observations on the Use and Original Purpose of the Waw Consecutive in Old Aramaic and Biblical Hebrew, VT, 97; The Inscription of Achish Governor of Eqron and Philistine Dialect, Cult and Culture, UF, 97; The Old Aramaic Inscription for Tell Dan: Philological Literary and Historical Aspects, JSS, 95; The Book of Oraccular Visions of Balaam from Deir Alla, UF, 86. **CONTACT ADDRESS** PO Box 971, Brooklyn, NY 11235.

SAUCERMAN, JAMES RAY
PERSONAL Born 11/14/1931, Colorado Springs, CO, m, 1951, 1 child **DISCIPLINE** ENGLISH **EDUCATION** Univ Northern Colo, Greeley, BA, 57, MA, 58; Univ Mo-Columbia, PhD(English), 77. **CAREER** Teacher English & French, Scottsbluff High Sch, Nebr, 58-62; from instr to asst prof English, 62-75, assoc prof, 77-80, Prof English, Northwest MO State Univ, 80- **MEMBERSHIPS** MLA; Midwest Mod Lang Asn; Thoreau Soc; Poe Studies Asn; Western Lit Asn. **RESEARCH** Nineteenth century American literature; twentieth century American literature; Western American literature. **SELECTED PUBLICATIONS** Auth, Henry David Thoreau's Small Town, 2/75, Thoreau's geologic sand image as symbol, 8/76 & Dissolving coherence in the tales of Edgar Allan Poe, 8/76, Northwest Mo State Univ Studies; Mark Twain's pistol characterizations in Roughing It, Mark Twain J, winter 77-78; A Critical Approach to Plains Poetry, Western Am Lit, summer 80. **CONTACT ADDRESS** Dept of English, Northwest Missouri State Univ, 800 University Dr, Maryville, MO 64468-6015.

SAUER, DAVID K.
PERSONAL Born 01/27/1944, Oak Park, IL, m, 1967, 3 children **DISCIPLINE** ENGLISH, THEATRE **EDUCATION** Univ Notre Dame, AB, 66; Indiana Univ, 72,77, PhD. **CAREER** Prof, Spring Hill Col, 72-. **HONORS AND AWARDS** NEH Summer Inst, 81; Teacher of the Year Spring Hill Col; NEH Summer Sem, 92; NEH Institute, 92-93; Danforth Asn for Outstanding Teachers 78-92; Teacher of the Year, Spring Hill Col, 79-80, 87-88; NEH Grant, 95. **MEMBERSHIPS** MLA; Am Soc for theatre Res, Ala Co lEnglish Teachers Assoc; Theatre Commun Group. **SELECTED PUBLICATIONS** Auth, "Apart from Etherege: Stage Directions in the Man of Mode", Restoration and Eighteenth Century Theatre Res, Second Series, 8.2 (93):29-48; auth, "English Faculty and the Postmodern Library; Or, Is there Any There There?", College and Undergraduate Libraries 1.2 (94):127-39; auth, "George S. Kaufman's Exploitation of Women (Characters): Dramaturgy and Feminism, American Drama 4.2 (95):55-81; auth, "Only a Woman in Arms and the Man", Shaw: Annual of Bernard Shaw Studies 15 (95):151-69; auth, "Speak the Speech, I Pray You; or Suiting the Method to the Moment: A Theory of Classroom Performance of Shakespeare", Shakespeare Quarterly 46.2 (95):173-83; auth, "Performance Reviews: The Interview and No One will Be Immune, The David Mamet Review 2 (95):8-9; auth, "The Marxian Child's Play of Mamet's Tough Guys and Churchill's Top Girls", Glengarry Glen Ross: Text and Performance, ed. Leslie Kane (NY and London: Garland, 96), 131-57; auth, "Suiting the Word to the Action: Kenneth Branagh's Interpolations in Hamlet", Shakespeare Yearbook 8 (97):325-49; coauth, "The Theory and Practice of Shakespeare in Performance", Teaching Shakespeare through Performance", ed. Milla Riggio (NY:MLA, 99) 33-47. **CONTACT ADDRESS** Dept English, Spring Hill Col, 4401 The Cedars, Mobile, AL 36608. **EMAIL** sauer@shc.edu

SAUER, ELIZABETH
PERSONAL Born Kitchener, ON, Canada **DISCIPLINE** ENGLISH **EDUCATION** Wilfred Laurier Univ, HBA, 86; Univ Western Ont, MA, 87, PhD, 91. **CAREER** Res asst, transl, Wilfred Lauier Univ, 82-86; tchg asst, 86-90, res asst, 90-91, Univ Western Ont; asst prof, 92-95, Assoc Prof, Brock Univ 95-. **HONORS AND AWARDS** Can Fedn Hum Grant, 94-97; SSHRC Doc Fel, Univ Western Ont, 88-91; Gold Medal Eng, Wilfred Laurier Univ, 86. **MEMBERSHIPS** Milton Soc Am; Can Soc Renaissance Studs; Asn Can Col Univ Tchrs Eng; Renaissance Soc Am; Ctr Reformation Renaissance Studs. **RESEARCH** Early modern English literature, politics, gender relations, reading and censorship practices, colonialism, and postmodern representations of creative contestation. **SELECTED PUBLICATIONS** Auth, Barbarous Dissonance and Images of Voice in Milton's Epics, McGill-Queen's UP, 96; coauth, Agonistics: Arenas of Creative Contest, SUNY P, 97; coauth, Milton and the Imperial Vision, Duquesne UP, 99; auth, A Cultural History of Reading in Early Modern England, Univ of Pa Press, 01. **CONTACT ADDRESS** Dept of English, Brock Univ, 500 Glenridge Ave, Saint Catherines, ON, Canada L2S 3A1. **EMAIL** emsauer@spartan.ac.brocku.ca

SAUNDERS, T. CLARK
PERSONAL Born 05/06/1955, Newburgh, NY, m, 1979, 3 children **DISCIPLINE** MUSIC **EDUCATION** State Univ NYork, Buffalo, BFA, MFA; Temple Univ, PhD. **CAREER** Asst prof, Lebanon Valley Col; asst prof, Univ of Maryland; ch, Graduate Music Ed; prof, Hartt School Music. **MEMBERSHIPS** MENC, OAKE. **RESEARCH** Music assessment, music perception and cognition. **SELECTED PUBLICATIONS** Auth, pubs in J Research in Music Ed, Bulletin of the Council for Res in Music Ed, The Quarterly Update & Music Educators J. **CONTACT ADDRESS** Hartt Sch Music, Univ of Hartford, 200 Bloomfield Ave, West Hartford, CT 06117.

SAUNDERS, WILLIAM
PERSONAL Born 11/05/1946, Port Chester, NY, m, 1977, 2 children **DISCIPLINE** ENGLISH **EDUCATION** Denison Univ, BA summa cum laude 68; Univ Iowa, MA 73, PhD 75; Harvard Univ, postdoc 79-80. **CAREER** Harvard Univ Grad Sch Design, editor, 94-, various responsibilities 82-93, program adv 80-82; Tchr at Harvard, Tufts, Boston and Wittenburg Univs 72-82. **HONORS AND AWARDS** Phi Beta Kappa; Environmentalist of the Year. **MEMBERSHIPS** AIA **RESEARCH** Architecture and the arts; criticism; cultural studies. **SELECTED PUBLICATIONS** Auth, Orthodoxies of the Anti-Orthodox: A Review of the Critical Landscape, Design Bk Rev, 00; auth, From Photograph to Place: Disappointment or Delight, Harv Design Mag, 98; The Early Work of Daniel Urban Kiley, ed, Princeton Archi Press, 99; auth, Richard Haag: Bloedel Reserve and Gas Works Park, ed, NY, Princeton Archi Press, 97; auth, Poetic Perception and Gnomic Fantasy in the Writing of Rem Koolhaas, Jour of Archi Edu, 97; auth, A Skeptic's Approach to Prayer, The World, 97; auth, Durability and Emphemerality: From the Editor, Harvard Design Mag, 97; auth, Recognizing Neglected Design: Harvard Design Mag, 97; auth, Changing Cities and New Urbanism: Harvard Design Mag, 97; auth, Reflections on Architectural Practices in the Nineties, ed, NY, Princeton Archi Press, 96; auth, Historic Auburndale, ed, 2nd rev exp edition, Auburndale Assoc Press, 96; auth, State of Design Publishing: GSD News, 96; auth, Architecture Teaching and Research: From the Editor, GSD News, 96; auth, Modern Architecture: Photography of Stolber, Abrams, 90, 99. **CONTACT ADDRESS** Harvard Univ, 48 Quincy St., Cambridge, MA 02138. **EMAIL** saunders2@mediaone.net

SAUPE, KAREN E.
PERSONAL Born 03/03/1959, Dayton, OH, s **DISCIPLINE** ENGLISH **EDUCATION** Univ Rochester, PhD, 96; Wright State Univ, MA, 87; Wittenberg Univ, BA, 81. **CAREER** Asst Prof, Calvin Col, 94-97; Assoc Prof, Calvin Col, 97-. **MEMBERSHIPS** MLA; TEAMS; NCTE. **RESEARCH** Medieval English Lyric; Chaucer; Shakespeare; Medieval Christianity; Lucy Boston. **SELECTED PUBLICATIONS** Auth, "Middle English Marian Lyrics," Medieval Institute Publications, 98. **CONTACT ADDRESS** Dept English, Calvin Col, 3201 Burton St SE, Grand Rapids, MI 49546-4301. **EMAIL** ksaupe@calvin.edu

SAUR, PAMELA S.
PERSONAL Born New York, NY, m, 1969, 2 children **DISCIPLINE** LITERATURE **EDUCATION** Univ Iowa, BA 70, MA 72, PhD 82; Univ Mass, MEd 84. **CAREER** Auburn Univ, asst prof 84-88; Lamar Univ, asst prof to assoc prof, 89-. **HONORS AND AWARDS** Schtzkammer Ch Ed; TFLAB Ed. **RESEARCH** Modern Austrian Literature; Lang and Lit; Pedagogy; Comparative Lit. **SELECTED PUBLICATIONS** Auth, The Place of Asian Literature in Translation, in Amer Univ's, CLA Jour, 98; Barbara Frischumth's Use of Mythology in Her Demeter Triology, Out from the shadows: Essays on Contemporary Aust Women Writers and Filmmakers, Margarette Lamb-Faffelbeger, ed, Riverside CA, Ariadne Press, 97; Real and Imaginary Journeys In Barbara Frischmuth's Writings, Ger Notes and Rev, 97; Amer Lit and Aust Lit, Two Histories, Geschichte der osterreichischen Lit, Teil I, Donald G. Daviau, Herbert Arlt, eds, St Ingbert, Rohrig Univ, 96; Regional dramas of Karl Schonherr and the Nazi Stigma, Ger Notes and Rev, 96; Property Wealth and the Amer Dream, in: Barn Burning, Teaching Faulkner, Cen for Faulkner Stud, MO State U, 95; Captain Anthony Forthcoming; Lucas: An Austrian Pioneer, Austrian Info, 95. **CONTACT ADDRESS** Dept of English and Foreign Languages, Lamar Univ, Beaumont, PO Box 10023, Beaumont, TX 77710. **EMAIL** saurps@hal.lamar.edu

SAUTER, KEVIN O.
PERSONAL Born 03/29/1952, Minneapolis, MN, m, 1981, 3 children **DISCIPLINE** COMMUNICATION **EDUCATION** Moorhead State Univ, BA, 74; Miami Univ, MA, 76; Penn State Univ, PhD, 84. **CAREER** Instr, James Madison Univ, 79-82; Assoc Prof, Univ St. Thomas, 82-; reviewer, Houton Mifflin Publ, 92-93; reviewer, McGraw Hill Publ, 92. **HONORS AND AWARDS** Mem, Media Schol Roundtable, Central States Commun Asn Convention, 4/97; First place award in Original Arts Production category, for:: Stained Glass, Minn Community Television Awds, 93. **MEMBERSHIPS** Nat Commun Asn; Broadcast Educr Asn; Central States Commun Asn; Minn Commun & Theater Asn; Screenwriters Workshop. **RESEARCH** Television criticism; politics and TV; Presidential public address. **SELECTED PUBLICATIONS** Auth, The 1976 Mondale-Dole Debate, Thetorical Studies of National Political Debates, Praeger Press, 89, 93; Local Television, Lighting in a Tube: The Television Industry in America, Allyn and Bacon, 96; Martha's Magic, 91; Stained Glass, 93; A Couple of Blaguards, 93; Producer, Date of Birth, 98; producer of numerous other video/audio productions. **CONTACT ADDRESS** 2205 Dellwood St. N., Roseville, MN 55113-4308. **EMAIL** kosauter@stthomas.edu

SAVAGE, ANNE
DISCIPLINE ENGLISH LITERATURE **EDUCATION** Calgary Univ, BA; Univ London, PhD. **RESEARCH** Old and Middle English lit and language; medieval allegory; semiotic theory. **SELECTED PUBLICATIONS** Trans, The Anglo-Saxon Chronicles, 82; trans, Anchoritic Spirituality, 91. **CONTACT ADDRESS** English Dept, McMaster Univ, 1280 Main St W, Hamilton, ON, Canada L8S 4L9. **EMAIL** savage@mcmaster.ca

SAVAGE, ELIZABETH
PERSONAL Born 10/23/1939, Buffalo, NY **DISCIPLINE** ENGLISH **EDUCATION** Medaille Col, BA, 61; St Louis Univ, PhD(English), 71. **CAREER** From instr to asst prof, 71-75, chmn, Div Humanities, 74-81, assoc prof English, Medaille Col, 75-; coord general Education, 97-. **MEMBERSHIPS** MLA **RESEARCH** Renaissance literature. **SELECTED PUB-**

LICATIONS Ed, John Donne's Devotions upon Emergent Occasions: A Critical Edition with Introduction and Commentary, Inst English Speech & Lit, Salzburg, 75; compiler (with Walter Lehrman & Dolores Sarafinski), The Plays of Ben Jonson: A Reference Guide, G K Hall, 80. **CONTACT ADDRESS** Dept of English, Medaille Col, 18 Agassiz Circle, Buffalo, NY 14214-2695.

SAVARD, JEANNINE
PERSONAL Born 09/04/1950, Glen Falls, NY, m, 1999 **DISCIPLINE** ENGLISH **EDUCATION** SUNY Plattsburgh, BS, 73; Univ NH, MA, 80. **CAREER** Assoc prof, Ariz State Univ, 92-. **HONORS AND AWARDS** Jerome Shestack Prize, Am Poetry Rev. **MEMBERSHIPS** Assoc Writing Programs. **RESEARCH** Buddhist Dohas (songs). **SELECTED PUBLICATIONS** Auth, Snow Water Cove, Univ of Utah Pr, 88; auth, Trumpeter, Carnegie Mellon Univ Pr, 93. **CONTACT ADDRESS** Dept English, Arizona State Univ, PO Box 870302, Tempe, AZ 85287-0302. **EMAIL** jsavard@asu.edu

SAVERS, ANN C.
PERSONAL Born Springfield, MA, m, 2000 **DISCIPLINE** ENGLISH **EDUCATION** Notre Dame Col, BA; Midwestern State Col, MEd; MA; Univ Calif Riverside, PhD. **CAREER** Teaching asst, Midwestern State Univ, 78-79; teaching assoc, Univ Calif Riverside, 80-82; lectr, Univ Tex San Antonio, 83-85; asst prof, Univ Haw, 85-88; ed vpres, Chadwyck-Healey, 89-95; asst prof, Notre Dame Col, 98-. **HONORS AND AWARDS** Sigma Tau Delta. **MEMBERSHIPS** RAA; SCRC; RCSC; SCSC; SSEMW; MLA; SAMLA; NMLA **RESEARCH** British renaissance; renaissance romance; the pastoral; early modern women. **SELECTED PUBLICATIONS** Auth, "River," Voices (79); rev, "New Ways of Looking at Old Texts: Papers of the Renaissance Text Society 1985-1991," Anal Enumerative Bibliog (94), auth, "Earth Touch," Touchstone (98); rev, "New Ways of Looking at Old Texts: Papers of the Renaissance Text Society 1991-1996," Anal Enumerative Bibliog (00); rev, "Editing Women," Anal Enumerative Bibliog (forthcoming). **CONTACT ADDRESS** English Dept, Notre Dame Col, 2321 Elm St, Manchester, NH 03104. **EMAIL** asavers@notredame.edu

SAVVAS, MINAS
PERSONAL Born 04/02/1939, Athens, Greece, M, 2 children **DISCIPLINE** COMPARATIVE LITERATURE, CREATIVE WRITING **EDUCATION** Univ Ill, BA, 64, MA, 65; Univ Calif, Santa Barbara, PhD(English), 71. **CAREER** Asst prof English, Univ Calif, Santa Barbara, 65-68; assoc prof, 68-74, Prof English, San Diego State Univ, 74- **HONORS AND AWARDS** Best Review Awd, Books Abroad, 71; NEH Fellowship, 87; Golden Poet Awd, 89; MPPP Professional Merit Awd, 89; Alexandrian Awd, Hellenic Cultural Society, 93. **MEMBERSHIPS** MLA; Mod Greek Studies Asn; Hellenic Cult Soc. **RESEARCH** Modern Greek literature; continental novel; translation. **SELECTED PUBLICATIONS** Auth, Scars and Smiles, Diegenes Press, Athens, 75; auth, Chronicle of Exile, verse translations of Y. Ritsos, WirePress, San Francisco, 77; auth, The Subterranean Herses, Ohio Univ Press, 81; Auth, Remembering Ritsos,Yannis + Poet/, Literary Review, Vol 0036, 93; The 'Fourth Dimension' - Ritsos,Y, Green,P, Translator, Bardsley,B, Translator/, World Lit Today, Vol 0068, 94; The Oldest Dead White Europ Males And Other Reflections On The Classics - Knox,B/, J Of Modern Greek Studies, Vol 0012, 94; 'Vreghmeno Rouho' - Bramos,G/, World Lit Today, Vol 0068, 94; 'Mavra Litharia' - Ganas,M/, World Lit Today, Vol 0068, 94; I 'Mihani Ton Mistikon' - Siotis,D/, World Lit Today, Vol 0068, 94; The Poetry And Poetics Of Cavafy,Constantine,P - Aesthetic Visions Of Sensual Reality - Anton,Jp/, World Lit Today, Vol 0070, 96; 'Oudheteri Zoni' - Greek - Kariotis,M/, World Lit Today, Vol 0070, 96; To 'Taxidi 1963-1992' - Greek - Tsaloumas,D/, World Lit Today, Vol 0070, 96. **CONTACT ADDRESS** Dept of English & Comparative Lit, San Diego State Univ, San Diego, CA 92115.

SAWAYA, FRANCESCA
DISCIPLINE AMERICAN LITERATURE **EDUCATION** Univ Calif, BA, 84; Univ York, Eng, MA, 86; Cornell Univ, MA, 88, PhD, 92. **CAREER** Asst prof, 95-. **SELECTED PUBLICATIONS** Auth, The Problem of the South: Economic Determination, Gender Determination, and the Politics of Genre in Glasgow's Virginia, Ellen Glasgow: New Perspectives, Tennessee Univ Press; Domesticity, Cultivation, and Vocation in Jane Addams and Sarah Orne Jewett, Nineteenth-Century Lit 48, 94; Between Revolution and Racism: Colonialism and the American Indian, The Prairie, James Finimore Cooper: His Country and His Art, The Bicentennial Papers, SUNY Oneonta, 91. **CONTACT ADDRESS** Dept of Eng, Portland State Univ, PO Box 751, Portland, OR 97207-0751. **EMAIL** sawaya@nhl.nh.pdx.edu

SAWYER-LAUCANNO, CHRISTOPHER
PERSONAL Born 01/04/1951, San Mateo, CA, m, 1987, 2 children **DISCIPLINE** LITERATURE **EDUCATION** Univ Calif, Santa Barbara, BA, 71; Brandeis Univ, MA, 75, PhD, 82. **CAREER** Lecturer, Mass Inst of Tech, 82-90; Writer-in-residence, Mass Inst of Tech, Prog in Writing & Humanistic Stud, 90-. **HONORS AND AWARDS** NEA Translation Fellow, 91. **RESEARCH** Contemporary comparative lit; translation theory & practice; biography; ethnography. **SELECTED PUBLICATIONS** Transl, Destruction of the Jauar: Poems form the Books of Chilm Balam, City Lights, 87; auth, An Invisible Sepctator: A Biography of Paul Bowles, Weidenfeld & Nicholson, 89; trans, Frederico Garcia Lorca, Barbarous Nights, City Lights, 90; auth, The Continual Pilgrimage: American writers in Paris 1944-1960, Grove Pr, 92; auth, The World's Words: A Semiotic Reading of Joyce and Rabelais, Alyscamps, 93; trans, Rafael Alberti, Concerning the Angels, City Lights, Alyscamps, 93; trans, Demons & Spirits: Contemporary Chol Mayan Chants & Incantations, Alyscamps; auth, An Invisible Spectator: A Biograhy of Paul Bowles, Weidenfeld & Nicholson, 89; rpt Grove Press, 99; auth, The Continual Pligrimage: American Writers in Paris 1944-1960, Grove Press, 92; rpt, City Lights, 99. **CONTACT ADDRESS** Prog in Writing & Humanistic Stud, Massachusetts Inst of Tech, Cambridge, MA 02139. **EMAIL** csl@mit.edu

SAXON, ARTHUR HARTLEY
PERSONAL Born 03/24/1935, Pittsburgh, Pa, m, 1957, 2 children **DISCIPLINE** HISTORY OF THE THEATRE **EDUCATION** Univ Pittsburgh, BA, 56; Columbia Univ, MA, 61; Yale Univ, PhD(hist of theatre), 66. **CAREER** Asst prof speech, theatre & English, Univ Pittsburgh, 66-69; assoc prof theatre, Univ Conn, 69-7; City Col New York & Grad Sch, City Univ New York, 71-76; Temple Univ, 78-81; gen ed, Archon Bks on Popular Entertainments, Shoe String Press, Inc, 77-80, Auth, Ed & Lectr, 76-, Am ed, Theatre Res/Rech Theatrales, 70-73; Guggenheim fel, 71-72, 82-83; Am Coun Learned Socs fel, 77-78; vis prof Am studies, Yale Univ, 81; mem bd Barnum Mus, 80-**HONORS AND AWARDS** Medal Barnum Festival Soc, 80; Membre d'Honneur, Club du Cirque, 80; "Key to the City" of Bridgeport, CT, 83; Barnard Hewitt Awd for "P.T. Barnum: The Legend and the Man," 90. **MEMBERSHIPS** Club du Crique. **RESEARCH** History of the circus and popular entertainments. **SELECTED PUBLICATIONS** Auth, A brief history of the Claque, Theatre Surv, 64; Enter Foot and Horse: A History of Hippodrama in England and France, Yale Univ, 68; contribr, Le Grand Livre du Cirque, Edito-Serv, 78; auth, The Life and Art of Andrew Ducrow & The Romantic Age of the English Circus, 78 & ed, The Autobiography of Mrs Tom Thumb, 79, Archon; Selected Letters of P. T. Barnum, Columbia Univ, 83; trans, As Barnum par Lui-Meme, Editions de la Gardine, 86; auth, P.T. Barnum: The Legend and the Man, Columbia Univ, 89; auth, Letters I Wish P.T. Barnum Had Written, Jumbo's Press, 94; auth, Barnumiana: A Select, Annotated Bibliog of Works By or Relating to P.T. Barnum, Jumbo's Press, 95; auth, Circus Language: A Glossary of Circus Terms, Jumbo's Press, 00. **CONTACT ADDRESS** 166 Orchard Hill Dr., Fairfield, CT 06430.

SAYERS, KARI
PERSONAL Born, Norway, m, 3 children **DISCIPLINE** ENGLISH **EDUCATION** CSU Long Beach, BA; MA. **CAREER** Asst prof, Marymount Col, 86-. **MEMBERSHIPS** NCTE **RESEARCH** Drama, short stories **SELECTED PUBLICATIONS** Auth, Views and Values, Wadsworth, 96 **CONTACT ADDRESS** Dept English, Marymount Col, Palos Verdes, California, 30800 Palos Verdes Dr E, Rancho Palos Verdes, CA 90275-6273. **EMAIL** ksayers@marymountpv.edu

SAYRE, ROBERT F.
PERSONAL Born 11/06/1933, Columbus, OH, m, 1988, 5 children **DISCIPLINE** ENGLISH **EDUCATION** Wesleyan Univ, BA, 55; Yale Univ, MA, 58, PhD(English), 62. **CAREER** Vis instr English, Wesleyan Univ, 60; from instr to asst prof, Univ Ill, 61-65; from asst prof to assoc prof, 65-72, Prof English, Univ Iowa, 72-, Prof., 98-; lectr Am lit, Lund Univ, Sweden, 63-64, res fel, 64-65; Guggenheim fel, 73-74; Visiting prof., Montpellier France, 84; Copenhagen 88-89. **MEMBERSHIPS** American Landscape. **RESEARCH** American autobiography; American Indian literature; American Landscape. **SELECTED PUBLICATIONS** Auth, "The Examined Self: Benjamin Franklin, Henry Adams, Henry James," Princeton, N.J.: Princeton University Press, 64, Republished, Univ of Wisconsin Press, 88; auth, "Introduction to Vachel Lindsay: Adventures, Rhymes, and Designs," New York: Eakins Press, 68, Paperback title, Earthman and Star-Thrower; auth, "Thoreau and the American Indians," Princeton, N.J.: Princeton University Press, 77; 86; ed, "A Week on the Concord and Merrimack Rivers, Walden, The Maine Woods, & Cape Cod, by H. D. Thoreau, New York: The Library of America, 85; ed, "Take This Exit: Re-Discovering the Iowa Landscape," Ames: Iowa State Univ Press, 89; ed, "New Essays on Walden," New York: Cambridge Univ Press, 92; ed., "American Lives: An Anthology of Autobiographical Writing," Madison: Univ. of Wisconsin Press, 94; ed., "To Recover a Continent: New Prospects of the American Prairie, Madison: Univ of Wisconsin Press, 99; ed., "Take the Next Exit: New Views of the Iowa Landscape, Ames: Iowa State Univ Press, 00. **CONTACT ADDRESS** 416 Hutchinson Ave., Iowa City, IA 52246. **EMAIL** bob-sayre@uiowa.edu

SAYRE, SHAY
PERSONAL Born 09/21/1942, oh, s, 2 children **DISCIPLINE** COMMUNICATIONS **EDUCATION** Oh State Univ, BA, 64; BSEduc, 64; Univ San Diego, MEd, 82; EdD, 86. **CAREER** Assoc Prof, San Jose State Univ, 86; Visiting Prof, Francisco State Univ, 88; Prof, Calif State Univ, 92-. **HONORS AND AWARDS** Fulbright-Hays, 90. **MEMBERSHIPS** Asn for Educ in Journalism and Mass Comm; Intl Advertising Asn; Popular Culture Asn; Semiotic Soc of Am; Soc for Consumer Psychol; Asn Consumer Res; Am Acad of Advertising. **RESEARCH** Qualitative inquiry into Consumer Behaviors; Disaster research. **SELECTED PUBLICATIONS** Auth, "T-Shirt Messaes: Fortune or Folly for Advertisers?," in Advertising and Popular Culture, (Popular Press, 92), 73-82; co-auth, "A Comparison of Reader Response with Informed Author/Viewer Analysis," in Semiotics 1991, (Univ Press of Am, 93), 127-132; co-auth, "Technology and Art: A Postmodern Reading of Orwell as Advertising," in Art, Science and Visual Literacy: Selected Readings, (Blackburg VA, 93), 22-34; auth, "Teaching Symbloic communication: An Exercise in Reading Material Culture," Journalism Educator 47, (93): 13-19; auth, "Images of Freedom and Equality: A Values Analysis of Hungarian Political Commercials," Journal of Advertising 23, (94): 97-110; co-auth, "Penetrating the Cultural Curtain: Apple's 1984 Commercial Goes to Russia," World Communication 52, (96): 2; co-auth, Earth, Wind, Fire and Water: Perspectives on Natural Disaster, Open Door Pub, 96; auth, Ad Campaign Planner, SW Col Pub, 98; auth, "Using Self-Narrative to Analyze Consumption: A Case of Plastic Surgery," Consumption, Markets and Culture, (00): 99-127; co-auth, "Self-Disclosure and Technology: The Viability of Video-elicitation for Consumer Research," in Research in Consumer Behavior, 00. **CONTACT ADDRESS** Dept Comm, California State Univ, Fullerton, 800 N State Col Blvd, Fullerton, CA 92384-6846. **EMAIL** ssayre@fullerton.edu

SCAGLIONE, ALDO
PERSONAL Born 01/10/1925, Torino, Italy, m, 1992 **DISCIPLINE** LITERATURE **EDUCATION** Univ Torino, Dottre in Lettere Moderne, 48. **CAREER** Instr, Univ of Toulouse, France and Univ of Chicago, 51-52; instr, Univ of Calif at Berkeley, 52-54, asst prof, assoc prof, full prof, 55-68; W. R. Kenen Prof of Comparative Lit, Univ NC at Chapel Hill, 68-87; E.M. Remargue Prof of Lit, New York Univ, 87-. **HONORS AND AWARDS** J. S.Guggenheim Fel; Fulbright Fel; Rockefeller Found Fel; Sr Res Fel, Univ of Wisc; Knighted to the Order of M.Hu Pres of the Republic of Italy. **RESEARCH** Medieval literature, Renaissance humanism, study of linguistics. **SELECTED PUBLICATIONS** Auth, Nature and Love in the Late Middle Ages: An Essay on the Cultural Context of the Decameron, Berkeley-Los Angeles: Univ Calif Press, Cambridge, England: Cambridge Univ Press (63), Westport, Ct: Greenwood Press (76); auth, The Classical Theory of Composition from Its Origins to the Present: A Historical Survey, Chapel Hill: Univ NC Press, "U. N. C. Studies in Comparative Literature, 53," (72); auth, The Theory of German Word Order, from the Renaissance to the Present, Minneapolis: Univ of Minn Press (81); auth, The Liberal Arts and the Jesuit College System, Amsterdam: John Benjamins (86); auth, Knights at Court: Courtliness, Chivalry, and Courtesy from Ottonian Germany to the Italian Renaissance, Berkeley-Los Angeles: Univ of Calif Press (91); auth, Essays on the Arts of Discourse: Linguistics, Rhetoric, Poetics, ed by P. Cherchi, A. Mandelbaum, S. Murphy, and G. Velli, Frankfurt, London, New York: Peter Lang (97). **CONTACT ADDRESS** Dept of Italian, New York Univ, 24 W 12th St, New York, NY 10011-8604. **EMAIL** aldo.scaglione@nyu.edu

SCALABRINI, MASSIMO
PERSONAL Born 05/20/1964, Toano, Italy **DISCIPLINE** ENGLISH, LITERATURE, SPANISH, FRENCH **EDUCATION** Univ di Balogna, Laur Let, 90; Yale Univ, PhD, 98. **CAREER** Teach asst, Yale Univ, 92-95; lectr, Princeton Univ, 95-98; asst prof, Univ Wash Seattle, 98-00; asst prof, Ind Univ, 00-. **HONORS AND AWARDS** Baltz-Seronde Fel, 92-94; Sterling Prize Fel, 92-94; Grad Student Exchange Award, 91-92; Erasmus Scholar, 89. **MEMBERSHIPS** AATI; AAIS; MLA; RSA. **RESEARCH** Renaissance and early modern literature and culture; lyric poetry; heroic and mock-heroic poetry; comic literature; humanism. **SELECTED PUBLICATIONS** Auth, "Il Cigno Senz'ali" L'idea di Dante Nell 'Orlando Furioso," Schede Umanistiche (94); auth, "La Schiatta di Mastro Iachelino: Una Proposta per Il Negromante," Lingua e Stile (96); auth, "Cingar 'Salsa Diabli' e La Strategia del Comico Folenghiano," Quaderni Folenghiani (97); auth, "Umanesimo e Anti-Umanesimo in Giovanni Della Casa," Schede Umanistiche (99); auth, "Un Edito Travestimento Secentesco del Baldus," Rivista di Let Ital (01); auth, "Nascita e Infanzia Dell'eroe Macaronia, " Quaderni Folenghiani (01). **CONTACT ADDRESS** For Lang Dept, Indiana Univ, Bloomington, Bloomington, IN 47405. **EMAIL** mscalabr@indiana.edu

SCAMMELL, MICHAEL
PERSONAL Born 01/16/1935, Lyndhurst, United Kingdom, m, 4 children **DISCIPLINE** CREATIVE WRITING **EDUCATION** Univ Nottingham, BA, 58; Univ Columbia, PhD, 85. **CAREER** Instr, Hunter Col; Freelance transl; Lang Sup, BBC, London, UK; Ed, "Index on Censorship," London, UK; Freelance Writer; Prof, Russ Lit, Cornell Univ; Prof, Creative Writing, Columbia Univ. **HONORS AND AWARDS** Los Angeles Times Bk Awd, 84; English PEN Ctr Awd, 85. **MEMBER-**

SHIPS Int PEN; Am Acad of Poets. **RESEARCH** Arthur Koestler. **SELECTED PUBLICATIONS** Auth, Solzhenitsyn, a Biography; ed, The Solzhenitsyn File, Unofficial Art from the Soviet Union and Russia's Other Writers; transl, Cities and Years, by Fedin; transl, The Gift, by Nabokov; transl, The Defense, by Nabokov; transl, Crime and Punishment, by Dostoevsky; transl, Childhood, Boyhood and Youth, by Tolstoy; transl, My Testimony, by Marchenko; transl, To Build a Castle, by Bukovsky. **CONTACT ADDRESS** Sch of Arts, Columbia Col, New York, 2960 Broadway, New York, NY 10027-6902. **EMAIL** ms474@columbia.edu

SCANLAN, J. T.
DISCIPLINE EIGHTEENTH-CENTURY ENGLISH LITERATURE, LEGAL HISTORY **EDUCATION** Rutgers Col, A.B.; Univ Mich, A.M.; PhD. **CAREER** Vis asst prof, Vassar Col; assoc prof Eng, Providence Col. **RESEARCH** Eighteenth-century writing; legal history, contemporary non-fiction. **SELECTED PUBLICATIONS** Writes on eighteenth-century English literature, legal history, and contemporary non-fiction. **CONTACT ADDRESS** Dept of Eng, Providence Col, Providence, RI 02918-0001. **EMAIL** hambone@providence.edu

SCANLAN, RICHARD T.
PERSONAL Born 05/30/1928, St. Paul, MN, m, 1951, 5 children **DISCIPLINE** CLASSICS **EDUCATION** Univ Minn, BS, 51, MA, 52. **CAREER** Teacher Latin, Edina High Sch, Minn, 55-67; assoc prof, 67-80, prof Classics, Univ Ill, Urbana, 80-, mem Latin Achievement Test Comt, Col Entrance Exam Bd, 60-65, chmn Latin Advan Placement Exam Comt, 67-72, chief examr, Classics Prog, 73-77. **MEMBERSHIPS** Am Philol Asn; Am Class League; Class Asn midwest & S; Am Coun Teaching Foreign Lang; Archives Asn Am. **RESEARCH** The teaching of Latin; computer applications to the teaching of Latin; teaching of classical humanities. **SELECTED PUBLICATIONS** Auth, A survey of Latin textbooks, Class J, 76; A computer-assisted instruction course in vocabulary building, Foreign Lang Ann, 76; Suggestions for a course in ancient and modern tragedy, Class Outlook, 77; Beginning Latin, 77, Word Power, 77 & Latin Composition, 77, Control Data Co; Some criteria for the evaluation of Latin textbooks, 78 & The grading of the 1977 advanced placement examination, 78, Class J. **CONTACT ADDRESS** Dept of Classic, Univ of Illinois, Urbana-Champaign, 707 S Mathews Ave, Urbana, IL 61801-3625. **EMAIL** rscanlon@uiuc.edu

SCANLAN, THOMAS
DISCIPLINE RHETORIC STUDIES **EDUCATION** Cornell Univ, MA, Univ Minn, PhD. **RESEARCH** Landscape as index to cultural values; family and literature in America; technology and control of nature. **SELECTED PUBLICATIONS** Auth, Family, Drama, and American Dreams; The Prairie Eye. **CONTACT ADDRESS** Rhetoric Dept, Univ of Minnesota, Twin Cities, 64 Classroom Office Bldg, 1994 Buford Ave, Saint Paul, MN 55108. **EMAIL** scanl001@maroon.tc.umn.edu

SCATTERDAY, MARK DAVIS
DISCIPLINE MUSIC **EDUCATION** Univ Akron, BM, 81; Univ Mich, MM, 83; Eastman Sch Music, DMA, 89. **CAREER** Prof. **HONORS AND AWARDS** Martha Holden Jennings Tchg Scholar; Conductor, New York State Music Educators Wind Ensemble, 96; Guest Clinician, Duke Univ Wind Ensemble Symp, 94; Guest Clinician, Col Band Director's Nat Asn, Eastern Div Conf, Wash DC, 94. **MEMBERSHIPS** Sec and treasCol Band Director's Nat Asn, Eastern Div; Conductor's Guild; Music Educator's Nat Conf; World Asn Symphonic Bands and Wind Ensembles; Nat Fed Musicians Union Local 132-314. **RESEARCH** Contemporary Music; Renaissance Instrumental Music; Conducting; Wind Ensembles, Chamber Orchestras. **SELECTED PUBLICATIONS** Auth, "Solutions to Gabrieli's Instrumental Works, Windworks," Husa's Smetana Fanfare, CBDNA J;auth, Karel Husa's Music for Prague 1968, Band Director's Guide, 92; Karel Husa's Apotheosis of this Earth, Band Director's Guide, 93; assoc ed, WindWorks, Warner Brothers Publ, 97. **CONTACT ADDRESS** Dept of Music, Cornell Univ, 104 Lincoln Hall, Ithaca, NY 14853. **EMAIL** mds27@cornell.edu

SCHAAFSMA, DAVID
PERSONAL Born 01/06/1953, Grand Rapids, MI, m, 1994, 1 child **DISCIPLINE** ENGLISH **EDUCATION** Calvin Col, BA, 75; Univ of Mich, MA, 82, PhD, 90; Western Mich Univ, MFA, 84. **CAREER** English teacher, Holland Christian High School, 76-77; English teacher, Hudsonville Unity Christian High School, 77-81; English instr, Grand Valley State Univ, 81-85; English ed, Univ of Mich, 85-90; English ed, Univ of Wis-Madison, 90-95; English Ed, Teachers Col, Columbia Univ, 95-99; Univ of Ill at Chicago, 99-00. **HONORS AND AWARDS** NCTE Richard A. Meade Awd, 94. **MEMBERSHIPS** NCTE; MLA; AERA. **RESEARCH** Narrative inquiry; English education; community-based writing projects; teaching of writing. **SELECTED PUBLICATIONS** Auth, Eating on the Street: Teaching Literacy in a Multicultural Society, Pittsburgh Press, 93; coauth, Language and Reflection, MacMillan, 92; co-ed, Literacy and Democracy, NCTE, 98. **CONTACT ADDRESS** Teachers Col, Columbia Univ, 525 W 120th St., New York, NY 10027. **EMAIL** schaaf1@uic.edu

SCHABER, BENNET
DISCIPLINE ENGLISH LITERATURE **EDUCATION** Brown Univ, PhD, 87. **CAREER** Asst prof, SUNY Oswego. **RESEARCH** Theory; lit and the visual arts; earlier Eng lit. **SELECTED PUBLICATIONS** Auth, Postmodernism Across the Ages, Syracuse UP, 94; Vision Procured: Psychoanalysis and the Social History of Art in Vision and Textuality, Duke UP, 96; essays on Film, Freud, Chaucer, Boccaccio, Lacan. **CONTACT ADDRESS** SUNY, Oswego, 213C Swetman, Oswego, NY 13126. **EMAIL** schaber@Oswego.edu

SCHACHTERLE, LANCE E.
DISCIPLINE ENGLISH **EDUCATION** Haverford, BA, 66; Univ Penn, PhD, 70. **CAREER** Asst prof, to prof, Eng, and provost, Worcester Polytech Inst **MEMBERSHIPS** Am Antiquarian Soc **RESEARCH** James Fenimore Cooper **SELECTED PUBLICATIONS** Auth, "The Three 1823 Editions of Cooper's The Pioneers," Procs of the AAS 84, 74; ed, Cooper's The Deerslayer, 84; ed, Cooper's 'The Spy', 85; co-ed, James Fenimore Cooper, The Pioneers, SUNY Press, 80, Lib Am, 85, Viking-Penguin, 87; coauth, "Fenimore Cooper's Literary Defenses: Twain and the Text of The Deerslayer," Stud in the Am Renaissance, 88; auth, "Bandwith as Metaphor for Consciousness in Pynchon's Gravity's Rainbow," Stud in the Lit Imagination 22, Spring 89; co-ed, The Meritorious Price of Our Redemption by William Pynchon; auth, "Cooper's Spy and the Possibility of American Fiction," Stud in the Hum, 91; auth, "Cooper and Wordsworth," Univ of Miss Stud in Eng, 92. **CONTACT ADDRESS** 32 Massachusetts Ave, Worcester, MA 01602-2123.

SCHACTLER, CAROLYN
PERSONAL Born 01/23/1927, Logan, UT, m, 1948, 6 children **DISCIPLINE** APPAREL DESIGN, FASHION, PATTERN DEVELOPMENT **EDUCATION** Wash State Univ, BA, 49; CWU, BS, 75; MA, 76. **CAREER** Private bus, 20 yrs; prof, Cent Wash Univ, 76-. **HONORS AND AWARDS** Nom Dist Prof, CWU; Tech Merit Awd; Most Visu Dyn Piece Awd, ITAA; Best of Show, ITAA; Best Fun Awd, ITAA; Dist Prof Year, CWU; Res Year, Wash Asn Fam Con Sci. **MEMBERSHIPS** ITAA; AAFCS; WSAFCS. **RESEARCH** Apparel design; ethnic costume research. **SELECTED PUBLICATIONS** Auth, Basic Pattern Drafting and Pattern Development, Burgess Pub, 81; auth, Tailoring That Really Works, Burgess Pub, 91. **CONTACT ADDRESS** Dept Home Economics, Central Washington Univ, 400 E 8th St, Ellensburg, WA 98926. **EMAIL** schactler@aol.com

SCHAEFER, JOSEPHINE O'BRIEN
PERSONAL Born 11/28/1929, New York, NY, d, 2 children **DISCIPLINE** ENGLISH LITERATURE **EDUCATION** Hunter Col, BA, 52; Smith Col, MA, 53; Stanford Univ, PhD, 62. **CAREER** Instr English, Univ Nebr, 53-55; lectr, Ind Univ, 60-61; asst prof, Western Col, Ohio, 61-65; assoc prof, Trinity Col, 67-70 & Western Col, 70-74; prof English, Univ Pittsburgh, 74-92. **HONORS AND AWARDS** Phi Beta Kappa, 52; Fulbright, 60, 65, 87; NEH, 69; Distinguished Teaching Awd, 91. **MEMBERSHIPS** MLA; Northeast Mod Lang Asn. **RESEARCH** Modern British fiction; Virginia Woolf; James Joyce. **SELECTED PUBLICATIONS** Auth, The Three Fold Nature of Reality in the Novels of Virginia Wolf, Mouton, 65; Art, Vision in Virginia Woolf's biographies, Virginia Woolf Quart, 76; art, Sterne's A Sentimental Journey and Woolf's Jacob's Room, Mod Fiction Studies, summer 77; auth, The Great War and This Late Age of World's Experience in Cather and Woolf, Virginia Woolf: The Fiction, The Reality, and The Myth of War, Syracuse, 91. **CONTACT ADDRESS** 1790 West Crestline Dr, Littleton, CO 80120.

SCHAEFER, RICHARD J.
PERSONAL Born 09/29/1951, Jamaica, NY, m, 1975, 1 child **DISCIPLINE** COMMUNICATION, JOURNALISM **EDUCATION** Univ Notre Dame, BA, 73; Univ Ut, MS, 87; PhD, 92. **CAREER** Teaching fel, Univ Ut, 87-90; asst prof, Tex A & M Univ, 91-96; assoc prof & assoc chair of dept of commun & journalism, Univ NMex, 96-. **MEMBERSHIPS** Asn for Educ in Journalism and Mass Commun, Broadcast Educ Asn, Int Commun Asn, NMex Broadcasters Asn, Nat Commun Asn. **RESEARCH** Broadcast Journalism Production Techniques and Telecommunication Policy. **SELECTED PUBLICATIONS** Coauth, "Audience Conceptualizations of Late Night with David Letterman," J of Broadcasting & Electronic Media 37.3 (93): 253-273; auth, "A Theoretical and Normative Approach to National Information Infrastructure Policy," Internet Res: Electronic Networking Applications and Policy 5.2 (95): 4-13; auth, "Editing Strategies in Television News Documentaries," J of Commun 47.4 (97): 69-88; auth, "The Development of CBS News Guidelines During the Salant Years," J of Broadcasting and Electronic Media 42.1 (98): 1-20. **CONTACT ADDRESS** Dept Commun, Univ of New Mexico, Albuquerque, Communication & Journalism Bldg, Rm 235 W, Albuquerque, NM 87131-0001. **EMAIL** schaefer@unm.edu

SCHAEFFER, PETER MORITZ-FRIEDRICH
PERSONAL Born 05/14/1930, Breslau, Germany, m, 1968 **DISCIPLINE** GERMANIC STUDIES, CLASSICS, RELIGIOUS STUDIES. **EDUCATION** Univ Ottawa, Lic Theol, 59; Princeton Univ, PhD(Germanic studies), 71. **CAREER** From lectr to asst prof Germanic studies, Princeton Univ, 70-74; vis lectr Ger & comp lit, Univ CA, Berkeley, 74-76; Assoc Prof to Prof Ger, Univ CA, Davis, 76-. **HONORS AND AWARDS** Outstanding Advisor, 86; Outstanding Mentor of the Year, 93. **MEMBERSHIPS** ALSC; Renaissance Soc Am; Erasmus Soc; Tyndale Soc. **RESEARCH** Renaissance; Neo-Latin literature; Classical tradition. **SELECTED PUBLICATIONS** Auth, Joachim Vadianus, De poetica, Text, Translation & Commentary, Wilhelm Fink, Munich, 73; Hoffmannswaldau, De curriculo studiorum, Peter Lang, Bern, 91; Sapidus Consolator, Annuaire de Selestat, 96. **CONTACT ADDRESS** German Dept, Univ of California, Davis, One Shields Ave, Davis, CA 95616-5200. **EMAIL** pmschaeffer@ucdavis.edu

SCHAFER, WILLIAM JOHN
PERSONAL Born 09/18/1937, Richmond, IN, m, 1958, 2 children **DISCIPLINE** ENGLISH **EDUCATION** Earlham Col, AB, 59; Univ Minn, MA, 64, PhD(English & art hist), 67. **CAREER** Instr, 64-73, assoc prof, 73-74, PROF ENGLISH & HUMANITIES, BEREA COL, 74-, Nat Endowment for Humanities younger humanist fel, 71-72; traveling humanist, Ky Coun for Humanities, 78-79. **HONORS AND AWARDS** Chester Tripp Chair in Humanities, 1984-. **MEMBERSHIPS** AAUP **RESEARCH** Black music and its influence on American popular culture; contemporary American and British fiction; history of ideas in American culture. **SELECTED PUBLICATIONS** Auth, 'Kentucky Straight' - Offutt,C/, Appalachian J, Vol 0021, 1993; The 'Same River Twice' - Offutt,C/, Appalachian J, Vol 0021, 1993; 'Gains And Losses'/, South Dakota Rev, Vol 0031, 1993; Appalachia Inside-Out, Vol 1, Conflict And Change, Vol 2, Cult And Custom - Higgs,Rj, Manning,An, Miller,Jw/, Appalachian J, Vol 0022, 1995; The Bridges Of Johnson,Fenton/, Appalachian J, Vol 0022, 1995; 'Sharpshooter' - A Novel Of The Civil-War - Madden,D/, Appalachian J, Vol 0024, 1997. **CONTACT ADDRESS** 101 Chestnut St, Berea, KY 40404-0003.

SCHALLER, KRISTI
DISCIPLINE COMMUNICATION **EDUCATION** Ill State Univ, BA, MA; Ohio Univ, PhD, 93. **CAREER** Asst prof, Ga State Univ. **HONORS AND AWARDS** Tchg award, Ohio Univ; tchg award, Int Commun Asn. **RESEARCH** Teacher-student communication. **SELECTED PUBLICATIONS** Published articles in Commun Rpt, Early Child Develop & Care, and J of Grad Tchg Asst Develop. **CONTACT ADDRESS** Georgia State Univ, Atlanta, GA 30303. **EMAIL** kschaller@gsu.edu

SCHAMBERGER, J. EDWARD
DISCIPLINE AMERICAN LITERATURE **EDUCATION** Colo State Univ, BS; Univ Colo, MA; Univ Pa, PhD. **CAREER** Assoc prof. **SELECTED PUBLICATIONS** Auth, pubs on American literature; American authors. **CONTACT ADDRESS** Dept of English, Colorado State Univ, Fort Collins, CO 80523. **EMAIL** schamberger@colostate.edu

SCHAPIRO, BARBARA
PERSONAL Born 03/04/1952, St. Louis, MO, m, 1979, 2 children **DISCIPLINE** ENGLISH **EDUCATION** MA, PhD, Tafts Univ; BA, Univ Mich. **CAREER** Prof English, Rhode Island Col, 87-. **HONORS AND AWARDS** Phi Beta Kappa. **MEMBERSHIPS** MLA; Mass Assoc for Psychoanalytic Psychol. **RESEARCH** Psychoanalysis and Lit; Modern & Contemporary Ficton. **SELECTED PUBLICATIONS** D H Lawrence and the Paradoxes of Psychic Life, SUNY Press, Forthcoming, 99; Literature and The Relational Self, NYU Press, 94; Narcissism and the Text: Studies in Literature and the Psychology of Self, co-ed, NYU Press, 86; The Romantic Mother: Narcissistic Patterns in Romantic Poetry, John Hopkins Univ Press, 83. **CONTACT ADDRESS** Dept English, Rhode Island Col, 60 Mount Pleasant Ave, Providence, RI 02908. **EMAIL** busric@aol.com

SCHARFFENBERGER, ELIZABETH WATSON
PERSONAL Born 09/14/1957, Wheeling, WV, s **DISCIPLINE** THEATRE **EDUCATION** Univ Chicago, AB, 77; Columbia Univ, MA, 80, MPhil, 83, PhD, 88. **CAREER** Instr, 85-86, Clarkson Univ; instr, 86-88, NY Univ; asst prof, 88-94, Wash Univ; lectr, 95, 96, 98, 99, Columbia Univ; adj asst prof, 96, Barnard Col; vis asst prof, adj assoc prof, 96-98, Columbia Univ; lectr, 97-, NY Univ, Gallatin Schl; vis asst prof, 99, Yale Univ. **RESEARCH** Athenian Drama & Theatre; Comic Lit; Influence of Classics in renaissance & modern times. **CONTACT ADDRESS** 380 Riverside Dr, New York, NY 10025.

SCHECHNER, RICHARD
PERSONAL Born 08/23/1934, Newark, NJ, m, 1987, 2 children **DISCIPLINE** PERFORMANCE STUDIES **EDUCATION** Cornell Univ, BA, 56; State Univ Iowa, MA, 58; Tulane Univ, PhD, 62. **CAREER** Asst to assoc prof Theatre, Tulane Univ, 62-67; prof drama, NY Univ, 67-79; prof perf stud, NY Univ,80-; univ prof 1992; ed, Tulane Drama Rev, 62-67; ed. The Drama Rev, 67-69, 85-; co-dir, Free South Theatre, 64-66; co-fndr, dir, New Orleans Grp, 65-67; fndr, dir, The Performance Grp, NY, 67-80; fnde, dir, E Coast Artists, 92-; Univ

Prof, 92-. **HONORS AND AWARDS** Guggenheim fel, Fulbright Comn, Indo-Am fel, Hoffman Eminent Schol, NEH Sr fel, Asian Cult Coun, Whitney Halstead Schol, Emmens Prof, Hum fel, Old Dominion fel, Am Inst, Indian Stu Sr fel, Montgomery fel; Andrew H. White, Professor at Large, Cornell Univ; Mondello Prize, Honorary Prof, Shanghai Theatre Acad; Honorary Prof Institute of Fine Arts, Havana, Cuba; Special Awds; Andrew H. White, Prof at large, Cornell Univ. **MEMBERSHIPS** Performance Studies International; Am Soc for Theatre. **RESEARCH** Performance studies, relationship of ritual, play, aesthetics, performance in everyday life; American Society for theatre research, Asian theatre asn. **SELECTED PUBLICATIONS** Auth, Public Domain, Bobbs, 68; co-ed, The Free Southern Theatre, Bobbs, 69; ed, Dionysus in 69; Farrar, Straus, and Giroux, 70; auth, Environmental Theatre, Hawthorn, 73, Reprint Applause, 94; co-ed, Ritual, Play, and Performance, Seabury, 76; coauth, Theatres, Spaces, and Environments, 77; auth, Essays on Performance Theory, 77; Drama Bk Specialists, expanded as Performance Theory, Routledge, 88; auth, The End of Humanism, Perf Arts J, 82; auth, Performative Circumstances, Seagull, 83; auth, Between Theater and Anthropology, Univ of Pa, 85; co-ed, By Means of Performance, Cambridge Univ, 90; ed, Worlds of Performance Series, Routledge, 94; auth, The Future of Ritual, Routlaedge, 93; coed, The Grotowski Sourcebook, Routledge, 97. **CONTACT ADDRESS** Dept of Performance Studies, New York Univ, 721 Broadway, New York, NY 10003. **EMAIL** rs4@nyu.edu

SCHECHTER, JOEL
PERSONAL Born 06/21/1947, Washington, DC, m **DISCIPLINE** THEATRE ARTS **EDUCATION** Antioch Col, BA, 69; Yale Sch Drama, MFA, DFA, 72,73. **CAREER** Lit Adv, Am Place Theatre, 73-77; lectr, New Sch Social Res, 74; asst prof, SUNY, 74-77; ed chief, Theatre Magazine, 77-92; dramaturg, Yale Repertory Theatre, 77-92; prof, Yale Sch Drama, 77-92; prof, chemn, San Francisco State Univ, 92-. **HONORS AND AWARDS** Danforth Fel; John Gassner Prize Criticism; Fox Fellow Moscow Univ; **MEMBERSHIPS** Brecht Soc **RESEARCH** Political satire; circus history, popular theatre. **SELECTED PUBLICATIONS** Auth, Durov's Pig: Clowns, Politics and Theatre, 85; auth, Satiric Impersonations: From Aristophanes to the Guerilla Girls, 94; auth, The Congress of Clowns and Other Russian Circus Acts, 98. **CONTACT ADDRESS** Dept of Theatre Arts, San Francisco State Univ, 1600 Holloway Ave, San Francisco, CA 94116.

SCHECKTER, JOHN
DISCIPLINE AUSTRALIAN LITERATURE, AMERICAN LITERATURE **EDUCATION** Iowa, PhD. **CAREER** Assoc prof, Long Island Univ, C.W. Post Campus. **SELECTED PUBLICATIONS** Auth, The Australian Novel 1830-1980: A Thematic Introduction; The Lost Child in Australian Fiction; Australia Lost and Founded: Versions of the First Settlement in Two Modern Novels; Now That the (Water) Buffalo's Gone: James Welch and the Transcultural Novel; History, Possibility, and Romance in The Pioneers. **CONTACT ADDRESS** Long Island Univ, C.W. Post, Brookville, NY 11548-1300.

SCHEDLER, GILBERT W.
PERSONAL Born 03/11/1935, Vancouver, BC, Canada, m, 1975, 3 children **DISCIPLINE** LITERATURE **EDUCATION** Concordia Col, BA, 57; Concordia Sem, BD, 60; Washington Univ, MA, 63; Univ Chicago, PhD(lit & relig), 70. **CAREER** Instr Humanities, Wittenberg Univ, 63-64; asst prof, 67-71, assoc prof, 71-79, assoc prof relig, 79-81, PROF RELIG & ENGLISH, UNIV PAC, 81-, Guest lectr, Univ Bangalore, India, 69-70; dep dir, Callison Col, Overseas Ctr, India, 69-70. **RESEARCH** Contemporary religious thought; recent American poetry; Taoism and Eastern religions. **SELECTED PUBLICATIONS** Auth, College Study Guide in American Literature, Am Sch, 66; Southern California Has Never Been Christian (poem), Epos, spring-summer 74; Urban Man (poem), Contemp Quart, spring 77; Waking Before Dawn, Wampeter Press, 78; Extended Family (poem), In: Celebration: Best Poems of the 70's, Calif State Poetry Quart, spring 80; A Spring Day on Campus (poem), In: Anthology of Magazine Verse and Yearbook of American Poetry, 80; Sermons (poem), Christian Century, 9/81; Till Death Do Us Part (poem), Calif State Poetry Quart, winter 82. **CONTACT ADDRESS** English Dept, Univ of the Pacific, Stockton, 3601 Pacific Ave, Stockton, CA 95211-0197. **EMAIL** gschedle@uop.edu

SCHEEDER, LOUIS
DISCIPLINE DRAMA **EDUCATION** Georgetown Univ, BA, 68; NYork Univ, MA, 95, PhD candidate. **CAREER** Vis consult, Univ Md, 83-91; teacher, Sarah Lawrence Col, 91-97; teacher, Columbia Univ, Hammerstein Center, 91-92; full-time fac, NY Univ/Tisch Sch of the Arts, 89-. **HONORS AND AWARDS** Dixon Medal, Georgetown Univ, 68; Mayor's Art Awd, Washington, DC, 82; Awd for Academic Excellence, 95; Distinction, Area Exams in Performance Studies, Movement and Modernism, Minstrelsy & Am Popular Culture, 98. **MEMBERSHIPS** Soc of Dance Hist Scholars, Popular Culture Asn/Am Culture Asn. **SELECTED PUBLICATIONS** Rev of "Bodies of the Text: Dance as Theory, Literature as Drama," eds Goellner & Murphy, New England Theatre J, Vol 7 (96); rev of "Moving Toward Life: Five Decades of Transformational Dance," Anna Halprin, TDR (winter 98); auth, "Let's Twist Again," Mid-Atlantic Almanak (fall 99); coauth, All the Words on Stage: How to Say all the words in all the plays (in prep). **CONTACT ADDRESS** Dept Drama, New York Univ, 721 Broadway, New York, NY 10003-6807. **EMAIL** Louis.Scheeder@nyu.edu

SCHEELE, HENRY ZAEGEL
PERSONAL Born 08/27/1933, Sheboygan, WI, m, 1956, 2 children **DISCIPLINE** SPEECH, COMMUNICATION **EDUCATION** Lake Forest Col, BA, 56; Purdue Univ, MS, 58, PhD-(speech), 62. **CAREER** Asst prof, 62-72, assoc prof speech, Purdue Univ, West Lafayette, 72-, res grant, Purdue Univ, 64. **HONORS AND AWARDS** Excellence in Teaching Awd, 79, 94. **MEMBERSHIPS** National Commun Asn; Cent States Speech Commun Asn; Center for the Study of the Presidency. **RESEARCH** Political communication. **SELECTED PUBLICATIONS** Auth, Ronald Reagan's 1980 Acceptance Address: A Focus on American Values, The Western Journal of Speech Communication, 84; The 1956 Nomination of Dwight D. Eisenhower: Maintaining the Hero Image, Presidential Studies Quart, 86; Response to the Kennedy Administration: The Joint Senate-House Republican Leadership Press conferences, Presidential Studies Quart, 89; President Dwight D. Eisenhower and U.S. House Leader Charles A. Halleck: An Examination of an Executive-Legislative Relationship, Presidential Studies Quart, 93; and Prelude to the Presidency: An Examination of the Gerald R. Ford-Charles A. Halleck House Minority Leadership Contest, Presidential Studies Quart, 95. **CONTACT ADDRESS** Dept of Commun, Purdue Univ, West Lafayette, West Lafayette, IN 47907-1998. **EMAIL** hscheele@sla.purdue.edu

SCHEELE, ROY M.
PERSONAL Born 01/10/1942, Houston, TX, m, 1965, 2 children **DISCIPLINE** ENGLISH **EDUCATION** Univ Nebr, BA, 65; MA, 71. **CAREER** Instr, Univ of Tenn at Martin, 66-68; Instr, Theodor Heuss Gymnasium, Waltrop, Ger, 74-75; Lectr, Creighton Univ, 77-79; Vis Instr, Univ of Nebr-Lincoln, 80-81; Instr, Doane Col, 82-90; Poet in Residence, Doane Col, 90-. **HONORS AND AWARDS** Winner, John G. Neihardt Found nationwide poetry competition, 83; Individual Artist Fel, Nebr Arts Coun, 93. **RESEARCH** Modern and contemporary poetry, Robert Frost, Gerard Manley Hopkins. **SELECTED PUBLICATIONS** Auth, "The Laborious Dream: Frost's 'After Apple-Picking'," Gone into If Not Explained: Essays on Poems by Robert Frost, Pebble 14 & 15 (July 76): 145-153; auth, "Sensible Confusion in Frost's 'The Subverted Flower'," The SC Rev 10-1 (Nov 77): 89-98, cited in American Literary Scholarship: An Annual/1977 (Duke Univ Press, 79), 357, and in American and British Poetry: A Guide to Criticism, 1925-1978 (Swallow, 84); auth, "Source and Resource: A Stylistic Note on Frost's 'Spring Pools'," Papers on Lang & Lit 15-3 (Summer 79): 316-319, cited in The Year's Work in English Studies (The English Asn, Vol 60, 79), 436; auth, "Edward Thomas," in Modern British Essayists: First Series, Dictionary of Literary Biography vol 98 (90), 302-313; auth, "The Poems of W.R. Moses," afterward to Moses' collection of poems Edges (Juniper Press, 94), 59-63; auth, "William Carlos Williams's 'The Red Wheelbarrow'," in Teaching Composition with Literature: 101 Writing Assignments from College Instructors, ed. Dana Gioia and Patricia Wagner (Longman, 99), 249-250; auth, "'The Slate, the Stone, the Moss': A Consideration of Place in Poetry," Platte Valley Rev 28-1 (Winter 00): 100-106; auth, "'Another That Came to Nothing': An Unpublished Fragment by Robert Frost," Robert Frost Rev (forthcoming). **CONTACT ADDRESS** Dept Humanities and Fine Arts, Doane Col, 1014 Boswell Col, Crete, NE 68333-2421. **EMAIL** rscheele@doane.edu

SCHEICK, WILLIAM J.
PERSONAL Born 07/15/1941, Newark, NJ **DISCIPLINE** AMERICAN LITERATURE **EDUCATION** Montclair State Col, BA, 63; Univ Ill, Urbana, MA, 65; PhD, 68. **CAREER** Asst prof, 69-74; assoc prof, 74-79; prof, 79-86; J R Milligan Cent Prof, 86-, Univ Tex, Austin; ed, Tex Stud Lit Lang, 75-92; ed, Soc Early Am NL, 89-; ed, Native Plant Soc, Tex News, 00-. **HONORS AND AWARDS** Choice Awd, Outstand Acad Bk, 78; Pushcart Prize, 91. **MEMBERSHIPS** ALA; SEA; SCMLA; SCRS; HSS. **SELECTED PUBLICATIONS** Auth, Fictional Structure and Ethics: The Turn-of-the-Century English Novel (90); auth, Design in Puritan American Literature (92); auth, Paine, Scriptures, and Authority (94); auth, The Ethos of Romance at the Turn of the Century (94); auth, Authority and Female Authorships in Colonial America (98). **CONTACT ADDRESS** Dept English, Univ of Texas, Austin, Austin, TX 78712-1164. **EMAIL** scheick@mail.utexas.edu

SCHEIDE, FRANK MILO
PERSONAL Born 04/01/1949, Redwing, MN, m, 1993 **DISCIPLINE** FILM HISTORY AND MASS MEDIA CRITICISM **EDUCATION** Univ Wisc, BS, 71, MA, 72, PhD, 90. **CAREER** Lect, Univ Wisc, 73; Tchg asst, Univ Wisc, 73-75; Instr, Univ Wisc, 75-76; Asst prof, Ball State Univ, 76-77; Instr, Univ Ark, 77-83; 84-91; Asst prof, Univ Ark, 91-. **RESEARCH** Silent Film, Cherokee History and Culture. **SELECTED PUBLICATIONS** Auth, Introductory Film Criticism: A Historical Perspective, Kendall/Hunt Publ Co, 94; **CONTACT ADDRESS** KH 417 Dept Comm, Univ of Arkansas, Fayetteville, Fayetteville, AR 72701. **EMAIL** fscheide@comp.uark.edu

SCHEIFFELE, EBERHARD
PERSONAL Born 09/10/1959, Wehr, Germany, s **DISCIPLINE** PSYCHOLOGY, THEATRE ARTS **EDUCATION** Universitat Freiburg, Germany, 82; Univ TX, Austin, MA, 85; Univ Calif, Grad cert, 91, PhD, 95. **CAREER** Tchng asst, 82-83, Univ Freiburg; tchng asst, 84-85, Univ TX; tchng asst, 84-85, Univ Mich; tchng asst, 85-87, 89-90, 92, 95, grad stud instr, logic, 87-88, knowledge & its limits, 89, Univ Calif, Berkeley; tchng asst, 91, Univ Calif, Santa Cruz; tchng asst, guest presenter, Psychodrama/role playing for Hum Int, guest presenter, Dynamic Med for Psychol of Conscious, 98-, West Chester Univ; Adjunct Prof of Psychol, West Chester, Pa, 00-. **HONORS AND AWARDS** Myrtle L. Judkins Mem Schol, 93-94; Wheeler Fel, 85-86; UC Berkeley; German Exchan Fel, Univ TX, Austin **MEMBERSHIPS** Amer Sc of Group Psychotherapy & Psychodrama; Assn for Theatre in Higher Ed; Intl Fed for Theare Res; Amer Soc Theatre Res; Natl Assn for Drama Therapy; Amer Phil Assn; Amer Psychol Assn; Natl Ed Assn. **RESEARCH** Psychodrama, spontaneity & improvisation; theatrical theories & influences of Jacob Levy Moreno. **SELECTED PUBLICATIONS** Coauth, Proof by Mathematical Induction, Discov Geometry Tchrs Res Book, Key Curr Press, 77; auth, Writing a Logic Puzzle, Discov Geometry Tchrs Res Book, Key Curr Press, 97; art, The Theatre of Truth, Res in Drama Ed, 97; art, Therapeutic Theatre and Spontaneity: Goethe and Moreno, J of Group Psychotherapy, Psychodrama & Sociometry, 96. **CONTACT ADDRESS** Group in Logic and Methodology of Sci, Univ of California, Berkeley, Berkeley, CA 94720. **EMAIL** scheiffe@math.berkeley.edu

SCHEINBERG, CYNTHIA
PERSONAL m, 1999, 1 child **DISCIPLINE** ENGLISH **EDUCATION** Harvard-Radcliffe Col, BA, 85; Rutgers Univ, PhD, 92. **CAREER** Assoc prof; Mills Col, 92-. **HONORS AND AWARDS** Res Associate: Harvard Divinity School Program in Women's Stud and Relig, 96-7; Northern Calif Phi Beta Kappa Teaching Award, 98; Skirball Fel, Oxford Centre for Hebrew and Jewish Stud, 01; Carnegie Found CASTL Fel, 00-01. **RESEARCH** Victorian Lit, emphasis poetry; Anglo-Jewish lit and hist; women's studies; relig and literature; feminist theory; genre studies; cinema studies; composition and pedagogy; community service/service learning curriculum dev. **SELECTED PUBLICATIONS** Auth, "Victorian Poetry and Religious Diversity," in Cambridge Companion to Victorian Poetry, Joe Bristow, ed., (Cambridge UP, 01); auth, Recasting Sympathy and Judgment: Amy Levy, Women Writers, and the Victorian Dramatic Monologue, Victorian Poetry, 97; Measure to yourself a prophet's place': Biblical Heroines, Jewish Difference, and Victorian Women's Poetry, in Women's Poetry late Romantic to late Victorian, Gender and Genre 1930-1900, London: Macmillan Press, 97 & Canonizing the Jew: Amy Levy's Challenge to Victorian Poetic Identity, Victorian Stud 39 2, 96; rev, The Complete Novels and Selected Poetry of Amy Levy, 1861-1889, Victorian Poetry, 95; Elizabeth Barrett Browning's Hebraic Conversions: Gender and Typology in Aurora Leigh, Victorian Lit and Cult, 95 & Rethinking Diversity, Creating Community: The Presence of Others' in the College Writing Classroom, Notes in the Margins, Stanford Univ, 95. **CONTACT ADDRESS** Dept of English, Mills Col, 5000 MacArthur Blvd, Oakland, CA 94613-1301. **EMAIL** cyns@mills.edu

SCHELL, RICHARD
DISCIPLINE ENGLISH LITERATURE **EDUCATION** York Univ, PhD. **SELECTED PUBLICATIONS** coauth, Shorter Poems of Edmund Spenser, 89; auth, "J.B. Priestley" and "Leonard Woolf," Dictionary of Literary Biography: Modern British Essayists, 90; co-auth, Leonard Woolf, Yale Ed of Short Poems of Edmund Spenser, 90; auth, The Dictionary of Biblical Tradition in English Literature, 92. **CONTACT ADDRESS** English Dept, Laurentian Univ, 935 Ramsey Lake Rd, Sudbury, ON, Canada P3E 2C6. **EMAIL** rdschell@nickel.laurentian.ca

SCHEPONIK, PETER C.
PERSONAL Born 08/09/1952, Philadelphia, PA, m, 1973, 2 children **DISCIPLINE** ENGLISH **EDUCATION** Villanova Univ, MA, 85. **CAREER** Instructor and Facilitator of the Dev Studies Lab, Montgomery Cty Cmty Col, 91-. **HONORS AND AWARDS** Awd of Merit, WordArt Competition, 98; Outstanding Adj Fac Awd; Awd for Developing Paragraph Writing Software Program. **MEMBERSHIPS** IDEA **RESEARCH** Contemporary American poetry with an emphasis on the analysis, explication, and impact of the poetry of Sharon Olds; The development, implementation, and impact of computer mediation in college academics. **SELECTED PUBLICATIONS** Auth, "A Focus on Assignments: Exemplification," Connect News, 96; auth, "The Cut Rose," Black Bear review, 97; auth, "There Were Days," WordArt, 98; auth, "Olds' 'My Father Speaks to Me from the Dead'," The Explicator, 98; auth, "A Technology Educator's View from the Trenches," Education Digest, 99; auth, "Must Have Management Skills to Master Technology," Teaching For success, 99; auth, "Psalms to Padre Pio," Nat Centre for padre Pio, 99; auth, "When Matter Dreams: the Transcendent in Sharon Olds' Poetry," One Trick Pony, 00; auth, "Birth," blue Ink Press, 00; auth, "Review of Sharon Olds' Blood, Tin, Straw," The Thirteenth Warrior Review, 00. **CONTACT ADDRESS** Dept Humanities, Montgomery County Comm Col, 340 Dekalb Pike, PO Box 400, Blue Bell, PA 19422-0796. **EMAIL** pschepon@mc3.edu

SCHEPS, WALTER
PERSONAL Born 06/19/1939, New York, NY, m, 1963, 2 children **DISCIPLINE** ENGLISH **EDUCATION** City Col New York, BA, 63; Univ Ore, PhD(English), 66. **CAREER** Asst prof English, Case Western Reserve Univ, 66-69; from asst prof to assoc prof, Ohio State Univ, 69-75; ASSOC PROF ENGLISH, STATE UNIV NY STONY BROOK, 75-, Reader, Chaucer Rev, 72- **MEMBERSHIPS** MLA; Mediaeval Acad Am. **RESEARCH** Chaucer; 15th century literature; popular literature in the Middle Ages. **SELECTED PUBLICATIONS** Chaucer's anti-fable; Reductio ad absurdum in the Nun's Priest's Tale, Leeds Studies English, 70; Chaucerian synthesis: The art of The Kingis Quair, Studies Scottish Lit, 71; Chaucer's Man of Law and the Tale of Constance, PMLA, 74; Historicity and oral narrative in Njals Saga, Scandinavian Studies, 74; The Goldyn Targe: Dunbar's comic psychomachia, Papers on Lang & Lit, 75; Up roos oure Hoost, and was oure aller cok: Harry Bailly's tale-telling competition, Chaucer Rev, 75; Chaucer's Theseus & the knight's tale, Leeds Studies English, 77; Chaucer's Mumismatic Pardoner and the Personification of Avarice, Am Community Theatre Asn, 77. **CONTACT ADDRESS** Dept of English, SUNY, Stony Brook, 100 Nicolls Rd, Stony Brook, NY 11794-0002.

SCHERB, VICTOR I.
PERSONAL Born 11/10/1957, Bakersfield, CA, s **DISCIPLINE** ENGLISH **EDUCATION** BA, Univ Calif at Los Angeles, 80; MA, 82; PhD, 89. **CAREER** Post-doctoral fel, Ariz State Univ, 89-91; Univ of Tex at Tyler, 91-. **HONORS AND AWARDS** Res grants, Univ of Tex at Tyler, 92-93, 97-98, & 98-99; Outstanding Fac Member Awd, Alpha Chi Omega, 98-99. **MEMBERSHIPS** MLA, Medieval Acad of Am, Tex medieval Asn, Medieval and Renaissance Drama Soc. **RESEARCH** Medieval Drama, Social Spectacle, Early Sixteenth-Century British Literature. **SELECTED PUBLICATIONS** Auth, "Violence and the Social Body in the Croxton Play of the Sacrament," in Violence and the Drama (Themes in Drama 13), ed. James Redmond (Cambridge: Cambridge Univ Press, 91), 69-78; auth, "The Tournament of Power: Public Combat and Social Inferiority in Late Medieval England," Studies in Medieval and Renaissance Hist 12 (91): 105-128; auth, "Worldly and Sacred messengers in the Digby Mary Magdalene," English Studies 12 (91): 105-128; auth, "Frame Structure in the Conversion of Saint Paul," Comparative Drama 26 (92): 1-9; auth, "Conception, Flies, and Heresy in Skelton's 'Replycacyon'," Medium Aevum 62 (93): 51-60; auth, "Ritual and Community in N-Town Passion Play I," Comparative Drama 29 (95-96): 478-493; auth, The Idol of the Other: Iconoclasm in the Execution of Friar Forest," in Formes Teatrals de la Tradicio Medieval: Actes del VII Col-loqui de la Societe Internationale Pour L'Etude due Theatre Medieval, ed. Fransec Massip (Barcelona: Inst del Teatre, 96), 469-475; auth, "Setting and Memory in Part II of Beowulf," English Studies 79 (98): 109-119; auth, "Blasphemy and the Grotesque in the Digby Mary Magdalene," Studies in Philol 96 (99): 225-240; auth, "Skelton's 'Agenst Garnesche': Poetic Territorialism at the Court of Henry VIII," Quidditas: J of the Rocky Mountain Medieval and Renaissance Asn, (forthcoming). **CONTACT ADDRESS** Dept Humanities, Univ of Texas, Tyler, 3900 University Blvd, Tyler, TX 75799-0001. **EMAIL** vscherb@mail.uttyl.edu

SCHERZINGER, M.
DISCIPLINE MUSIC THEORY; MUSICOLOGY **EDUCATION** Columbia Univ, MPhil 97, MA 93; Wits Univ SA, BMus 87-91, BA 84-86. **CAREER** Asst prof, dept music, Columbia Univ. **HONORS AND AWARDS** Pres Fel; Young Sch Awd; Herbert L Hutner Fel; Mellon Fel; FCA Intl Schsp for Music; Ntl Postgrad Schshp; Merit Awds for Best Student; Abraham and Olga Lipman Schshp; Tongaat Hullet Merit Schshp. **MEMBERSHIPS** SAMRO; MUNY; MSUW; ICTM; PNM. **RESEARCH** Music theory, musicology, ethnomusicology, African studies, German romanticism, philosophy, literary theory, cultural studies. **CONTACT ADDRESS** Dept of Music, Columbia Univ, 100 Morningside Dr # 5H, New York, NY 10027. **EMAIL** mrs22@columbia.edu

SCHEYE, THOMAS EDWARD
PERSONAL Born 07/02/1942, Savannah, GA, m, 1972 **DISCIPLINE** ENGLISH, DRAMA **EDUCATION** Georgetown Univ, AB, 63; Yale Univ, MA, 65; Univ Pa, PhD(English), 70. **CAREER** Asst prof, Essex Community Col, 65-67 & Towson State Univ, 65-70; assoc prof English & Acad vpres, Loyola Col, MD, 70-, theater critic, Baltimore News-Am, 65-77; host/writer, Survey of English Lit, Md Ctr Pub Broadcasting, 72-75. **HONORS AND AWARDS** Distinguished Teacher Awd, Loyola Col, 74. **MEMBERSHIPS** MLA; SAtlantic Mod Lang Asn; Milton Soc Am. **RESEARCH** Shakespeare; modern drama; Renaissance. **SELECTED PUBLICATIONS** Auth, Two gentlemen of Milan, Shakespeare Studies, 75; The Glass Menagerie: It's no tragedy, Freckles, In: Tennessee Williams: A Tribute, 77. **CONTACT ADDRESS** Loyola Col, 4501 N Charles St, Baltimore, MD 21210-2694. **EMAIL** scheye@loyola.edu

SCHIERLING, STEPHEN P.
DISCIPLINE ANCIENT GREEK AND LATIN LANGUAGE, GREEK AND ROMAN COMEDY **EDUCATION** St Louis Univ, PhD, 80. **CAREER** Assoc prof Lat and Ancient Greek, coordr, undergrad Lat instr, 80-88; sec hd, Class, 86-89; Arts and Sci fac senate, 87-91, 95-97; pres, Arts and Sci fac senate, 90-91; Prescott Hall comp network admin, 92-, La State Univ. **RESEARCH** Greek and Latin paleography; textual criticism; computer applications to textual criticism. **SELECTED PUBLICATIONS** Auth, Vaticanus Graecus 2203 in the Manuscript Tradition of Thucydides, in Rev d'Hist des Texts, 11, 81; Rossi 508 and the Text of Sallust, in Manuscripts, XXIX, 85; New Evidence for Diomedes in Two Passages of Sallust, in Hermes, 113, 2, 85; Bellum Jugurthinum 113.3: A Restoration of the Text, in Manuscripta, XXXI. 87; SPSS/PC As a Useful Tool in Determining the Text of Sallust's Jugurtha: A Text Critic's Point of View, in The Class Bull, 65, nos 1 & 2, 89; The Jugurtha Epitaphs: The Texts and Tradition, in Manuscripta, 93. **CONTACT ADDRESS** Dept of For Lang, La State Univ, Baton Rouge, Baton Rouge, LA 70803-0001. **EMAIL** sschierl@homer.forlang.lsu.edu

SCHIFF, FREDERICK
PERSONAL s **DISCIPLINE** SOCIOLOGY AND COMMUNICATION **EDUCATION** Reed College, BA, 64; UCLA, MA, 65, PhD, 70. **CAREER** Assoc Prof comm, 89-, Univ Houston; Asst Prof, 86-89, Univ Dayton; Asst Prof, 70-75, Wash Univ. **HONORS AND AWARDS** NIMH; NSF; Nat Science Found, 00-02; Am Newspaper Publishers: Ideological Management and Class Bias in the News; One of 21 grants in sociology in 00. **MEMBERSHIPS** ASA; AEJMC; NSA; ICA; MESA. **RESEARCH** Media Corp; News Content; Ideology. **SELECTED PUBLICATIONS** Auth, "The Lebanese Prince: The Aftermath of the Continuing Civil War: Journal of South Asian and Middle Eastern Studies, 12:3, (89): 7-36; auth, "Brazilian Film and Military Censorship: Cinema Novo, 1964-1974," Historical Journal of Film, Radio and Television, 12:4, (93): 487-512; auth, "Deconstructing Attitude Structure in Public Opinion Studies," Critical Studies in Mass Communication, 11:3, (94): 287-297; auth, "Ethical Problems in Advising Theses and Dissertations," Journalism and Mass Communication Educator, 51:1, (96): 23-35; auth, "The Dominant Ideology and Brazilian Tabloids: News Content in Class-Targeted Newspapers," Sociological Perspectives 39:1, (96): 175-206; auth, The Associated Press: Its Worldwide Staff and American Interests," International Communication Bulletin, 31:3-4, (96): 3-9; auth, "How Public Opinion is Perceived and Produced by U.S. Newspaper Publishers," Javnost, The Public: Journal of the European Institute for Communication and Culture, 4:2, (97): 71-90; auth, "Nude Dancing: Scenes of Sexual Celebration in a Contested Culture," Journal of Am Culture, 2:4, (99): 9-16. **CONTACT ADDRESS** 701 Welch St, Houston, TX 77006-1307. **EMAIL** fschiff@uh.edu

SCHIFF, JAMES A.
PERSONAL Born 12/06/1958, Cincinnati, OH, m, 1989, 3 children **DISCIPLINE** ENGLISH, AMERICAN LITERATURE **EDUCATION** Duke Univ, BA, 81; New York Univ, MA, 85; PhD, 90. **CAREER** Vis instr to asst prof, Univ Cincinnati, 89-. **MEMBERSHIPS** MLA. **RESEARCH** Contemporary American Fiction. **SELECTED PUBLICATIONS** Auth, John Updike Revisited, Twayne, 98; ed, Critical Essays on Reynolds Price, GK Hall, 98; auth, Understanding Reynolds Price, South Carolina, 96; auth, Updike's Version: Rewriting 'The Scarlet Letter', 92. **CONTACT ADDRESS** Dept English, Univ of Cincinnati, PO Box 210069, Cincinnati, OH 45221-0069. **EMAIL** james.schiff@uc.edu

SCHIFFER, JAMES M.
PERSONAL Born 11/26/1948, Philadelphia, PA, m, 1970, 2 children **DISCIPLINE** ENGLISH **EDUCATION** Univ Penn, BA, 73; Univ Chicago, MA, 74; PhD, 80. **CAREER** Vis asst prof, Lawrence Univ, 78-80; asst prof, Blackburn Col, 80-85; asst prof to assoc prof to dept chmn to prog dir to chmn to prof, Hampden-Sydney College, 85-00; prof to head, N Mich Univ, 00-. **HONORS AND AWARDS** Schaff Awd, Univ Penn, 73; Phi Beta Kappa; Snowday Prize, Univ Chicago, 76; Whiting Fel, 77-78; Mettauer Res Awd, Hampden-Sydney Col, 94; Crawley Ser Awd, 97; NEH, 83, 88, 99. **MEMBERSHIPS** SAA; MLA; RSA; RMMLA; SRC. **RESEARCH** Shakespeare's poetry and plays; English Renaissance drama, especially Marlowe and Jonson. **SELECTED PUBLICATIONS** Co-auth, Foul Deeds, St Martin's, 89; auth, Richard Stern, Twane/Macmillan, 93; ed, Shakespeare's Sonnets: Critical Essays, Garland, 99; ppbk, Routledge/Garland, 00; auth, Videotape: Sonnet Variations: A Performance of Selected Sonnets by Shakespeare, produced by Hampden-Sydney Col, distrib Films for the Human Sci, 00. **CONTACT ADDRESS** English Dept, No Michigan Univ, 1401 Presque Isle Ave, Marquette, MI 49855-5301. **EMAIL** jschiffe@nmu.edu

SCHIFFHORST, GERALD JOSEPH
PERSONAL Born 10/13/1940, St. Louis, MO, m, 1987 **DISCIPLINE** ENGLISH, ART HISTORY **EDUCATION** St Louis Univ, BS, 62, MA, 63; Wash Univ, PhD(English), 73. **CAREER** Instr English, Univ Mo-St Louis, 66-67; asst prof to prof English, Univ Cent Fla, 70-, Nat Endowment for Humanities fel art hist, Southeastern Inst Medieval & Renaissance Studies, Duke Univ, 74; . **MEMBERSHIPS** MLA; Shakespeare Asn Am; Milton Soc Am; SAtlantic Mod Lang Asn. **RESEARCH** Milton; Renaissance iconography of patience; teaching English composition. **SELECTED PUBLICATIONS** Ed & coauth, The Triumph of Patience: Medieval and Renaissance Studies, Fla Univ, 78; coauth, Short English Handbook, Scott, 79, 2nd ed, 82, 3rd ed, 86; auth, Patience & the Humbly Exalted Heroism of Milton's Messiah (art), Milton Studies, XVI, 82; auth, John Milton, 90; Short Handbook for Writers, McGraw Hill, 91, 97; co-ed, The Witness of Times, Duquesne Univ Press, 93; assoc ed, Seventeenth-Century News, 96-99. **CONTACT ADDRESS** Dept of English, Univ of Central Florida, PO Box 161346, Orlando, FL 32816-1346. **EMAIL** schiffhg@mail.ucf.edu

SCHIFFMAN, JOSEPH
PERSONAL Born 06/13/1914, New York, NY, m, 1942, 2 children **DISCIPLINE** ENGLISH, AMERICAN STUDIES **EDUCATION** LI Univ, BA, 37; Columbia Univ, MA, 47; NYork Univ, PhD, 51. **CAREER** From instr to assoc prof English, LI Univ, 45-58, coordr grad prog Am studies, 56-58; chmn dept English, 59-68, prof English, 58-68, James Hope Caldwell prof Am studies, 68-79, EMER PROF ENGLISH & PROF CONTINUING EDUC, DICKINSON COL, 79-86, 90-96; Acting ed, Am Quart, 60; head Am lit, Int Bibliog Comt, 61-64; founding dir, Am Studies Res Ctr, India, 64; vis Fulbright prof, Univ Bordeaux, France, 65-66; vis prof, Univ South Fla, 81; Fulbright-Hays vis prof, Univ of Indonesia, 81-82. **HONORS AND AWARDS** Lindback Found Distinguished Teaching Awd, 62. **MEMBERSHIPS** MLA; Am Studies Asn. **RESEARCH** American literature and civilization. **SELECTED PUBLICATIONS** Auth, Introduction to Lindsay Swift's Brook Farm, Corinth, 61; ed, Three Shorter Novels of Herman Melville, Harper, 62; Edward Bellamy's Duke of Stockbridge, Harvard Univ, 62; coauth, A critical history of American literature: from its beginning to the present, In: Cassell's Encyclopedia of World Literature, 73. **CONTACT ADDRESS** Dickinson Col, Carlisle, PA 17013.

SCHILLER, ANITA R.
PERSONAL Born 06/16/1926, New York, NY, m, 1946, 2 children **DISCIPLINE** LIBRARY SCIENCE **EDUCATION** NYork Univ, BA, 49; Pratt Inst, MLS, 59. **CAREER** Res assoc, asst prof, 64-70, Univ Il; ref bibliog, 70-90, Univ Calif San Diego; Ralph R Shaw vis scholar, 78, Rutgers Univ; Librn Emeritus, 91-, Univ Calif San Diego. **HONORS AND AWARDS** Coun Libr Res Fel, 76-77; PEN Awd for Magazine Writing, 82; Amer Libr Assoc Equality Awd, 85. **MEMBERSHIPS** Amer Libr Assoc, Amer Soc for Infor Sci; Assoc of Col & Res Libr; Libr & Infor Tech assoc. **RESEARCH** Infor policy; intellectual property; women in librarianship. **SELECTED PUBLICATIONS** Auth, Women in Librarianship, in Advances in Librarianship, IV, Academic Press, 74; art, Shifting Boundaries in Information, Libr J, 81; auth, Information as a Commodity: There's No Such Thing as a Free Hunch, Technicalities, 82; coauth, The Privatizing of Information: Who Can Own What America Knows?, The Nation, 82; auth, The Age of Information and the Year of the Reader, On Reading: In the Year of the Reader, Calif St Libr Found, 87. **CONTACT ADDRESS** 7109 Monte Vista, La Jolla, CA 92037-5326. **EMAIL** aschiller@ucsd.edu

SCHIRMEISTER, PAMELA J.
DISCIPLINE ENGLISH **EDUCATION** Yale Univ, BA, 80; PhD, 88; Johns Hopkins Univ, MA, 81. **CAREER** ASST PROF, ENG, NY UNIV **MEMBERSHIPS** Am Antiquarian Soc **SELECTED PUBLICATIONS** Auth, The Consolations of Space: The Place of Romance in Hawthorne, Melville, and James, Stanford Univ Press, 90; ed and introd, Representative Man by Ralph Waldo Emerson, Marsilio, 96; auth, "Taking Precautions: Gender Identification as Masquerade in James Fenimore Cooper," Stud in Biog, vol 3, AMS Press, 97; coauth, biography of James Fenimore Cooper, Addison Wesley; coauth, "James Fenimore Cooper: Entrepreneur of the Self," Procs of the AAS. **CONTACT ADDRESS** 19 University Pl, No. 200, New York, NY 10003.

SCHLACHTER, GAIL ANN
PERSONAL Born 04/07/1943, Detroit, MI, m, 1986, 2 children **DISCIPLINE** LIBRARY SCIENCE **EDUCATION** Univ Calif at Berkeley, BA, 64; Univ Wis, joint MA, 66; Univ Southern Calif, MPA, 76; Univ Minn, PhD, 71. **CAREER** Assist Prof, Library School, Univ S Calif, 71-74; Head Librn, Dept Soc Sci, Calif State Univ, 74-76; Assist Univ Librn, Public Services, Univ Calif Davis, 76-81; Dir, Serials, ABC-CLIO, 81-82; Vice Pres, Books, ABC-CLIO, 82-83; Vice Pres/Mgr, ABC-CLIO, 83-85; Adj Prof, School of Library and Information Science, San Jose, 91-; Pres, Reference Service Press, 85-. **HONORS AND AWARDS** Title II-B Fel, Higher Ed Act, Univ Minn, 68-71; Beta Phi Mu, 71; Outstanding Libr Sci Prof, Univ Southern Calif, 73; Outstanding Reference Book, Choic, 78 & 97; Awd for Lib Lit, Knowledge Industry Pub, 85; Best Professional Book, RQ, 86; Best of the Best Reference Book, Nat Ed and Infor Center, 88; Best Reference Book of the Year, School Libr J, 89; Best Reference Book, NY Public Libr, 89; Best Reference Book of the Year, Libr J, 90; Isador Gilbert Mudge Awd, 92, Louis Shores-Oryx Press Awd, Am Libr Asn, 97. **MEMBERSHIPS** Am Libr Asn; Calif Libr Asn. **SELECTED PUBLICATIONS** Coauth, RSP Funding for Nursing Students and

Nurses, Reference Service Press, 98-; Financial Aid for African Americans, Reference Service Press, 97-; Financial Aid for Asian Americans, Reference Service Press, 97-; Financial Aid for Hispanic Americans, Reference Service Press, 97-; Financial Aid for Native Americans, Reference Service Press, 97-; The Back-to-School Money Book: A Financial Guide for Midlife and Older Women, 2nd Edition, Am Asn of Retired Persons, 96; Money for Graduate Students in the Humanities, Reference Service Press, 96-; Money for Graduate Students in the Sciences, Reference Service Press, 96-; Money of Graduate Students in the Social Sciences, Reference Service Press, 96-; College Student's Guide to Merit and Other No-Need Funding, Reference Service Press, 96; High School Senior's Guide to Merit and Other No-Need Funding, Reference Service Press, 96. **CONTACT ADDRESS** Reference Service Press, 5000 Windplay Dr, Ste 4, El Dorado Hills, CA 95762. **EMAIL** findaid@aol.com

SCHLAM, CARL C.
PERSONAL Born 10/23/1936, New York, NY, m, 1967 **DISCIPLINE** CLASSICS **EDUCATION** Columbia Univ, BA, 56, MA, 58, PhD(Greek & Latin), 68. **CAREER** Instr classics, Rutgers Univ, 64-66; preceptor Greek & Latin, Columbia Col, 66-67; asst prof, 67-73, Assoc Prof Classics, Ohio State Univ, 73- **MEMBERSHIPS** Am Philol Asn. **RESEARCH** Ancient literature; neo-Latin; paleography. **SELECTED PUBLICATIONS** **CONTACT ADDRESS** Dept of Classics, Ohio State Univ, Columbus, Columbus, OH 43210.

SCHLEICHER, ANTONIA YETUNDE FAELARIN
DISCIPLINE AFRICAN LITERATURE **EDUCATION** Univ Kans, PhD. **CAREER** Dept African Lang, Wisc Univ **MEMBERSHIPS** African Lang Tchr Asn. **RESEARCH** Interface between phonology and morphology; experimental phonetics; foreign language learning and teaching; Yoruba culture. **SELECTED PUBLICATIONS** Auth, Je K'A Sae Yoruba, Yale, 93. **CONTACT ADDRESS** Dept of African Languages and Literature, Univ of Wisconsin, Madison, 500 Lincoln Drive, Madison, WI 53706. **EMAIL** ayschlei@facstaff.wisc.edu

SCHLEINER, WINFRIED H.
PERSONAL Born 10/19/1938, Mannheim, Germany, w, 1968, 3 children **DISCIPLINE** ENGLISH & COMPARITIVE LITERATURE **EDUCATION** Univ Kiel, Staatsexamen, 64; Brown Univ, MA, 65, PhD, 68. **CAREER** Asst master & schoolmaster Eng & French, Max-Planck-Schule, Kiel, Ger, 68-70; asst prof Eng, RI Col, 70-73; asst prof, 73-75, assoc prof, prof eng, Univ CA, Davis; Full Prof, 85-. **HONORS AND AWARDS** UC Pres Fel Hum; NEH; Foreign Lib; Wolfenbuttel Biblothek fel. **MEMBERSHIPS** MLA; 16th Century Conf; Renaissance Soc Am; Am soc Hist of Med. **RESEARCH** Renaissance lit; comp lit; linguistics; hist med; gender studies. **SELECTED PUBLICATIONS** Auth, The Imagery of John Donne's Sermons, Brown Univ, 70; Aeneas' flight from Troy, Comp Lit, 75; Franklin and the infant Hercules, 18th Century Studies, 76-77; coauth, New material from the Grimm-Emerson correspondence, Harvard Libr Bull, 77; The Imagery of John Donnes Sermons, Brown Univ Press, 70; Melancholy Genius and Utopia in the Renaissance, Harrassowitz, 91; Medical Ethics in the Renaissance, Georgetown Univ Press, 95; A plot to his mose and cares cutt of: Schoppe as seen by the Archbishop of Canterbury, Renaissance and Reformation, 95; Cross-Dressing, Gender Errors and Sexual Taboos in Renaissance Literature in: Gender Reversals and Gender Cultures, London, 96; auth, John Selden's Letter to Ben Jonson on Cross-Dressing and Bisexual Gods, English Literary Renaissance, 99; auth, Early Modern Controversies about the One-Sex Model, Renaissance, 00. **CONTACT ADDRESS** Dept of Eng, Univ of California, Davis, Davis, CA 95616-5200. **EMAIL** whschleiner@ucdavis.edu

SCHLICK, YAEL
DISCIPLINE ENGLISH LITERATURE **EDUCATION** Duke Univ, PhD. **CAREER** Dept Eng, Queen's Univ **RESEARCH** Travel writing; autobiography; literary theory. **SELECTED PUBLICATIONS** Auth, pubs on colonial literature, nineteenth-century women writers, and French-Canadian Fiction. **CONTACT ADDRESS** English Dept, Queen's Univ at Kingston, Kingston, ON, Canada K7L 3N6. **EMAIL** ys2@post.queensu.ca

SCHLISSEL, LILLIAN
PERSONAL Born 02/22/1930, New York, NY, d, 2 children **DISCIPLINE** ENGLISH **EDUCATION** Brooklyn Col, BA, 51; Yale Univ, PhD, 57. **CAREER** Vis prof, Univ Santa Clara, 70; vis prof, Univ N Mex, 79,81,92,95; prof to prof emeritus, CUNY, 93-98. **SELECTED PUBLICATIONS** Auth, Bawdy Women: Becoming Imperfect, forthcoming; auth, Western Women's Reader, Harper, 00; ed, Three Plays by May West, New York, 97; auth, Black Frontiers (for young readers), New York, 97; auth, Women's Diaries of the Westward Journey, New York, 82; auth, Diary of Amelia Stewart Knight, New York, 92; auth, Far from Home: Families of the Westward Journey, New York, 89; ed, Western Women: Their Land, Their Lives, 88; ed, Washington Irving, Journals and Notebooks, Boston, 81; ed, Conscience in America, New York, 70; ed, World of Randolph Bourne, New York, 65. **CONTACT ADDRESS** Dept English, Brooklyn Col, CUNY, 2901 Bedford Ave, Brooklyn, NY 11210-2813.

SCHLOBIN, ROGER CLARK
PERSONAL Born 06/22/1944, Brooklyn, NY, m, 1970 **DISCIPLINE** MEDIEVAL LITERATURE **EDUCATION** C W Post Col, BA, 66; Univ Wis-Madison, MA, 68; Ohio State Univ, PhD (English), 71. **CAREER** Teaching asst English & asst dir, Ctr Medieval & Renaissance Studies, Ohio State Univ, 69-71; asst prof, 71-78, assoc prof to prof English, 78-00, prof emer, Purdue Univ, NCent Campus, 00- ; instr English, Upward Bound Prog, Ohio Dominican Col, 68-71; consult, Michigan City Pub Libr, 72-; consult ed, Proceedings of the Int Conf on the Fantastic, 81. **MEMBERSHIPS** Int Arthurian Soc; Early English Text Soc; Midwest Mod Lang Asn; Sci Fiction Res Asn; Mediaeval Acad Am. **RESEARCH** Arthurian literature; Chaucer; fantasy. **SELECTED PUBLICATIONS** Co-ed, The Year's Scholarship in Science Fiction and Fantasy: 1974, Extrapolation, 12/76; coauth, The Research Guide to Science Fiction Studies, Garland, 77; auth, A Bibliography of the Works of Andre Norton, G K Hall; An Annotated Bibliography of Fantasy Fiction, CEA Critic, 1/78; co-ed, The Year's Scholarship in Science Fiction and Fantasy: 1975, Extrapolation, 5/78; The Year's Scholarship in Science Fiction and Fantasy: 1972-1975, Kent State Univ, 78; auth, Women Science Fiction Writers, In: Fantastic Females, Bowling Green Popular, 78; ed, Starment Reader's Guides to Contemporary Science Fiction and Fantasy Author, 79; The Aesthetics of Fantasy Literature and Art, 82; ed, J of the Fantastic in the Arts, 88-. **CONTACT ADDRESS** Dept of English, Purdue Univ, No Central, 1402 S U S Hwy 421, Westville, IN 46391-9542. **EMAIL** dragon@greenvillenc.com

SCHLOSSMAN, DAVID A.
PERSONAL Born 12/20/1966, Beaufort, SC **DISCIPLINE** THEATRE **EDUCATION** Pomona, Col, BA, 89; Northwestern Univ, MA, 94; PhD, 96. **CAREER** Instr, Columbia Col Chicago, 96-98; lectr, Loyola Univ Chicago, 98; lectr, Univ Md College Park, 01. **HONORS AND AWARDS** Phi Beta Kappa, 89; Mellon Fel, 89; Woodrow Wilson Fel, 89. **MEMBERSHIPS** MLA, Theatre Commun Group. **RESEARCH** Theatre and society, theatre and social change, performance studies, world drama, symbolic interaction sociology, the politics of representation and cultural studies. **SELECTED PUBLICATIONS** Auth, Actors and Activists: Performance, Politics, and Exchange Among Social Worlds, Routledge/Garland, 01. **CONTACT ADDRESS** 430 6th St NE, Washington, DC 20002. **EMAIL** dswithjm@megsinet.net

SCHMEMANN, S.
PERSONAL Born 04/12/1945, Paris, France, m, 1970, 3 children **DISCIPLINE** ENGLISH **EDUCATION** Harvard, BA, 67; Columbia Univ, MA, 71. **CAREER** Reporter, 71-80, Associated Press; Bureau Chief, Moscow, 80-, 90-94, Bonn Germany, 86-90, Jerusalem, 95-98, NY Times. **HONORS AND AWARDS** 1991 Pulitzer Prize Intl Reporting; DLitt (HC) Middlebury Col, 92; Martha Albrand Awd, 98. **RESEARCH** Russian History **SELECTED PUBLICATIONS** Auth, Echoes of a Native Land Two Centuries of A Russian Village, Knopf, 97. **CONTACT ADDRESS** New York Times, 229 W 43 St, New York, NY 10036. **EMAIL** schmemann@compuserve.com

SCHMIDT, BARBARA QUINN
PERSONAL Born Chicago, IL, m, 1966, 2 children **DISCIPLINE** LITERATURE **EDUCATION** Univ Chicago, BA, 59; Creighton Univ, MA, 63; St Louis Univ, PhD, 80. **CAREER** Assoc prof English, Southern Ill Univ, 64-. **MEMBERSHIPS** Res Soc Victorian Periodicals. **RESEARCH** The Cornhill magazine; Smith Elder Publishers; Victorian literature; African-American literature; women's studies. **SELECTED PUBLICATIONS** Auth, Pearson's Magazine, British Lit Mag, 1890s Encyclopedia, Greenwood Press, Windsor Magazine, Coverbill Magazine. **CONTACT ADDRESS** English Dept, So Illinois Univ, Edwardsville, Box 1431, Edwardsville, IL 62026-1431. **EMAIL** rschmid@siue.edu

SCHMIDT, JACK
DISCIPLINE MUSIC, MUSICOLOGY **EDUCATION** Wheaton Col, BA; DePaul Univ, MA; Northwestern Univ, PhD. **CAREER** Fac, Delaware Valley Col, Towson Univ, Northwestern Univ, Elgin Comm Col, present. **HONORS AND AWARDS** Conductor,Oregon Bach Festival, 96; coord cult affairs progs, Delaware Valley Col; band/chorale conductor, Delaware Valley Col. **RESEARCH** Musicology; Ger Baroque Music; Choral Music. **SELECTED PUBLICATIONS** Auth, articles about Ger baroque music for the Am Musicol Soc, Am Choral Dirs Asn; recs, Polygram and Liturgical Press. **CONTACT ADDRESS** Delaware Valley Col, 700 E Butler Ave, Doylestown, PA 18901-2697. **EMAIL** SchmidtJ@devalcol.edu

SCHMIDT, MARK
PERSONAL Born 11/17/1953, Dallas, TX, m, 1981, 6 children **DISCIPLINE** ENGLISH, LITERATURE, PHILOSOPHY **EDUCATION** Dallas Bible Col, BS, 76; Univ Tex at Dallas, MA, 80; Univ Tex at Arlington, PhD, 90. **CAREER** Asst prof, Univ of Ark at Monticello, 92-. **RESEARCH** The idea of human nature. **SELECTED PUBLICATIONS** Auth, Human Nature: Opposing Viewpoints, Greenhaven Press, 99; auth, The 1970s: American Decades, Greenhaven Press, 00. **CONTACT ADDRESS** Division Arts & Lang, Univ of Arkansas, Monticello, PO Box 3460, Monticello, AR 71656-3460. **EMAIL** schmidt@uamont.edu

SCHMIDT, PATRICIA LOIS
PERSONAL Born 11/08/1942, York, PA **DISCIPLINE** RHETORICAL THEORY & CRITICISM **EDUCATION** PA State Univ, BA, 64, MA, 68, PhD, 73. **CAREER** Instr debate & dir, Speech Commun, Univ DE, 68-71; asst prof behav studies, 73-76, assoc prof & chmn, 76-78, assoc prof Eng, 78-79, asst dean, Res Rhet Criticism, 79-80, Assoc Deam, Res Rhet Criticism, Univ FLA, 81-86, Assoc Vice Chancellor for Acad Prog, FL Board of Regents, 87-88; Actg Vice Chancellor for Acad Prog, FL Board of Regents, 88-89; PROF ENGL 89-; Referee, Quart J Speech, 78-; expert witness, Pub Doc Law, FL House Rep, 81; ed, Fla Patent Newslett, 82. **HONORS AND AWARDS** Sigma Tau Delta, 63; Delta Sigma Rho-Tau Kappa Alpha, 64; Phi Kappa Phi, 72; Sparks Diss Fel, PA State Univ, 72-73; Pres Scholar, Univ FL, 75-76; Speech Commun Asn of Am, 77; Winans-Wichelns Awd nominee, Outstanding Article in Rhetorical Theory and Criticism; Golden Key Hon Fac Inductee, 78; Outstanding Young Women of Am, 79; Univ of FL, Col of Lib Arts & Sci Tchr of the Year Awd, 95; Nat Press Club's Author's Night invitee, 96; Nominee, Joan Kelly Memorial Prize in Women's Hist, John H. Dunning Prize in US Hist, AHA, 97; MLA prize for First Book nominee, 97. **MEMBERSHIPS** Int Soc Hist Rhet; Eastern Forensic Asn; Speech Commun Asn Am; Nat Coun Univ Res Adminr; MLA; AHA; Southern Speech Commun Soc. **RESEARCH** The role of moral force in soc change; private morality and its rel to the public sphere; Brit public address. **SELECTED PUBLICATIONS** Auth, Lord Ashley: The role of moral force in social change, Quart J Speech, 2/77; The rhetoric of factory reform: The campaign for the ten hour bill, J President's Scholars, fall 80; The First Year Experience: A View from Florida, In: Proceedings of the Fourth Int Conf of the First Year Experience: An Int Phenomenon, Univ of Edinburgh, 89; A View from Mt. Olympus: Quality vs. Control, In: New Perspectives for the 1990's: The Role of the Graduate Dean, Proceedings of the Nineteenth Annual Meeting of Southern Graduate Schools, 90; Margaret Chase Smith: Beyond Convention, Univ of Maine Press, 96; Beyond Convention, and Epilogue, In: What Can I Do for You: People Remember Margaret Chase Smith, Central Maine Publ, 97; Rethinking Gender and Power at the Century's Mid-Point: Margaret Chase Smith and Her Times, In: A History of Women in Maine, Univ or Maine Press, 98. **CONTACT ADDRESS** Eng Dept, Univ of Florida, PO Box 117310, Gainesville, FL 32611-7310. **EMAIL** pats@english.ufl.edu

SCHMIDT, PETER JARRETT
PERSONAL Born 12/23/1951, IL **DISCIPLINE** AMERICAN LITERATURE **EDUCATION** Oberlin Col, AB, 75; Univ Va, PhD, 80. **CAREER** From asst prof Am lit to prof English, Swarthmore Col, 80-. **HONORS AND AWARDS** Nat Endowment for Hum grant, 82; C Hugh Holman Awd, 92. **MEMBERSHIPS** MLA **RESEARCH** Mod 20th century lit; contemp poetry; 19th-century Am lit; Southern US lit. **SELECTED PUBLICATIONS** Auth, "Paterson and Epic Tradition," in Critical Essays on William Carlos Williams, ed. Stephen Gould Axelrod and Helen Deese, (NYork: G. K. Hall, 95); auth, "Welty: Reviews and Criticism," Mississippi Quart 49.4 (fall 96): 833-841; auth, "Notes on Charles Simic's New 'White', 1997," The Harvard Rev, 13 (fall 97): 138-148; auth, "On Optimist's Sons and Daughters: Eudora Welty's 'The Optimist's Daughter' and Peter Taylor's 'A Summons to Memphis,'" Missisippi Quart 50.4 (fall 97): 689-714; co-ed, Postcolonial Theory and the US: Race, Ethnicity, and Lit, Univ Pr of Mississippi (Jackson), fall 00. **CONTACT ADDRESS** Dept of Eng, Swarthmore Col, 500 College Ave, Swarthmore, PA 19081-1306. **EMAIL** pschmid1@swarthmore.edu

SCHMIDT, ROGER
DISCIPLINE ENGLISH LITERATURE **EDUCATION** Univ Wash, PhD, 89. **CAREER** Assoc prof. **RESEARCH** Jacobitism in the Eighteenth Century. **SELECTED PUBLICATIONS** Auth, pubs in Eighteenth Century Studies, The Proceedings of the Northwest Society of Eighteenth Century Studies. **CONTACT ADDRESS** Dept of English and Philosophy, Idaho State Univ, Pocatello, ID 83209. **EMAIL** schmroge@isu.edu

SCHMIDT, STEVEN J.
PERSONAL Born 04/01/1953, Indianapolis, IN, m, 1976, 3 children **DISCIPLINE** LIBRARY SCIENCE **EDUCATION** Butler Univ, BA, 75; IN Univ, MLS, 83. **CAREER** Team leader, IUPUI Univ Libr, 84-. **HONORS AND AWARDS** Outstanding Librarian, 92, IN Library Fed; Pres, IN Libr Fed. **MEMBERSHIPS** ALA; ILF **RESEARCH** History of printing and bookmaking; librarian in the cinema. **SELECTED PUBLICATIONS** Auth, "Do Hoosiers Sell Best?," IN Libraries, 90; Indiana Telefax Directory, S Butler Press, 90; coauth, "Monitor Talk," Diabetes Forecast, 91; auth, "The Depiction of Libraries, Librarians and the Book Arts in Film and Television," IN Libraries, 96. **CONTACT ADDRESS** 755 W Michigan St, Indianapolis, IN 46202. **EMAIL** schmidt@iupus.edu

SCHMIDTBERGER, LOREN F.
PERSONAL Born 10/10/1928, Victoria, KS, m, 1958, 6 children **DISCIPLINE** ENGLISH LITERATURE **EDUCATION** Ft Hays Ks State Col, AB, 51; Fordham Univ, MA, 57, PhD, 65. **CAREER** From instr to assoc prof, 55-76, chmn dept, 71-

78, prof English, St Peters Col, 76-, chmn English dept, 81-. **MEMBERSHIPS** MLA; Col English Asn; AAUP; Asn Depts English. **RESEARCH** Medieval and American literature. **SELECTED PUBLICATIONS** Ed, Dreiser's An American Tragedy, 66 & Faulkner's Absalom, Absalom, 66, Simon & Schuster. **CONTACT ADDRESS** Dept English, Saint Peter's Col, 2641 Kennedy Blvd, Jersey City, NJ 07306-5997. **EMAIL** lorenfs@juno.com

SCHMITZ-BURGARD, SYLVIA
DISCIPLINE 19TH-CENTURY LITERATURE **EDUCATION** Univ Cologne & Univ Va, MA & PhD, 91-97. **HONORS AND AWARDS** Cert of Distinct in Tchg, 00. **RESEARCH** 18th to 20th century German and Austrian literature; French and English lieterature of the 18th century. **SELECTED PUBLICATIONS** Auth, Das Schreiben des anderen Geschlechts: Richardson, Rousseau und Goethe, 98; essays include stud of, Wolf, Jelinek, Laplanche, Freud, Droste-Hnlshoff & exam of the aesthetics and politics of gender in Ger lit. **CONTACT ADDRESS** Dept of Germanic Languages and Literature, Harvard Univ, 12 Quincy St, Barker Ctr 365, Cambridge, MA 02138. **EMAIL** schmitz@fas.harvard.edu

SCHNEIDAU, HERBERT N.
PERSONAL Born 08/26/1935, New Orleans, LA, m, 1961, 2 children **DISCIPLINE** ENGLISH **EDUCATION** Dartmouth Col, BA, 57; Princeton Univ, MA, 60, PhD(English), 63. **CAREER** Instr English, Duke Univ, 61-63; from asst prof to assoc prof, State Univ NY Buffalo, 63-70; assoc prof English, Univ Calif, Santa Barbara, 70-75, prof, 75-80; prof to prof emer English, Univ Ariz, 80-, Andrew Mellon vis prof, Rice Univ, 78. **RESEARCH** Modern literature; Bible and literature. **SELECTED PUBLICATIONS** Auth, Ezra Pound: The Image and the Real, La State Univ, 69; Sacred Discontent, La State Univ & Univ Calif, 76; Ezra Pound/Letters/John Theobald, ed with D Pearce, Black Swan, 84; Waking Giants, Oxford, 91. **CONTACT ADDRESS** Dept of English, Univ of Arizona, 445 Modern Languages Bldg, PO Box 210067, Tucson, AZ 85721.

SCHNEIDER, BARBARA J.
PERSONAL Born 12/20/1954, Richland, WA **DISCIPLINE** ENGLISH **EDUCATION** Gonzaga Univ, BA, 77; Wayne State Univ, MA 97; PhD, 00. **CAREER** Asst prof, Univ of Toledo, 00-. **HONORS AND AWARDS** Thomas C Rumble Res Fel; Excellence in Teaching. **MEMBERSHIPS** CCCC, NCTE, MLA. **RESEARCH** Rhetoric, Feminisms, Composition Studies. **SELECTED PUBLICATIONS** Auth, Reading Maternity Materially: The Case of Demi Moore, ed Sharon Crowley and Jack Selzer, Univ of Wis Press (Madison), 99. **CONTACT ADDRESS** Univ of Toledo, 15467 Ellen Dr, Livonia, MI 48154-2319. **EMAIL** barbara-schneider@utoledo.edu

SCHNEIDER, CHRISTIAN IMMO
PERSONAL Born 01/27/1935, Dresden, Germany, m, 1964, 1 child **DISCIPLINE** MODERN GERMAN LITERATURE **EDUCATION** Univ Calif, Santa Barbara, PhD, 68; Cent Wash Univ, MA, 78. **CAREER** Asst Ger, Antioch Univ, 64-65; assoc, Univ Calif, Santa Barbara, 65-68; from Asst Prof to Prof Ger, 68-91, CWU Distinguished Prof, Cent Wash Univ, 91-. **RESEARCH** German literature of the 20th century; Hermann Hesse research, concert organist and composer. **SELECTED PUBLICATIONS** Auth, Das Todesproblem bei Hermann Hesse, NG Elwert, Marburg, 73; Hermann Hesse (monography), C.H. Beck, Munich 91; Twelve Short Organ Pieces, Augsburg Fortress, 91. **CONTACT ADDRESS** Dept of Foreign Lang, Central Washington Univ, Ellensburg, WA 98926-7502. **EMAIL** schneidc@cwu.edu

SCHNEIDER, DUANE
PERSONAL Born 11/15/1937, South Bend, IN, m, 4 children **DISCIPLINE** ENGLISH **EDUCATION** Miami Univ, BA, 58; Kent State Univ, MA, 60; Univ Colo, PhD(English lit), 65. **CAREER** Instr English in engineering, Univ Colo, 60-65; from asst prof to assoc prof, 65-75, PROF ENGLISH, OHIO UNIV, 75- **MEMBERSHIPS** MLA; Charles Lamb Soc; Soc Study Southern Lit. **RESEARCH** Romantic movement in English literature; Thomas Wolfe; Anais Nin. **SELECTED PUBLICATIONS** Auth, Thomas Wolfe and the quest for language, Ohio Univ Rev, 69; The art of Anais Nin, Southern Rev, spring 70; The Lucas edition of Lamb's letters: Corrections and notes, Notes & Queries, 5/74; Thomas Wolfe 1900-1938, In: First Printings of American Authors, Gale Res Co, 77; Anais Nin in the Diary: The creation and development of a persona, Mosaic, winter 78; coauth, Anais Nin: An Introduction, Ohio Univ, 79. **CONTACT ADDRESS** Dept of English, Ohio Univ, Athens, OH 45701-2979.

SCHNEIDER, KAREN
PERSONAL Born 08/01/1948, Chicago, IL, m **DISCIPLINE** WOMEN'S FICTION, MODERN BRITISH LITERATURE, FILM, SCIENCE FICTION **EDUCATION** Univ Tex, BA; Colo State Univ, Ma; Ind Univ, PhD. **CAREER** Assoc prof, Western KY Univ. **HONORS AND AWARDS** Outstanding Teacher Awd, 99-00; Univ Teaching Awd, 99-00. **RESEARCH** Film and contemporary women's fiction. **SELECTED PUBLICATIONS** Auth, Loving Arms: British Women Writing the Second World War. **CONTACT ADDRESS** Western Kentucky Univ, Cherry Hall, Bowling Green, KY 42101. **EMAIL** karen.schneider@wku.edu

SCHNEIDER, MATTHEW T.
DISCIPLINE ENGLISH AND COMPARATIVE LITERATURE **EDUCATION** Univ CA, Berkeley, BA, 80; Univ Chicago, MA, 82; UCLA, PhD, 91. **CAREER** Lect, Conspiracy Cult Conf, King Alfred's Col, Engl, Jl 98; Interdisciplinary 19th-century Stud Ann Conf, New Orleans, La, Apr 98; UCLA Ctr Stud Rel, Los Angeles, CA, Apr 97; Int Conf on Representations Despair and Desire, Atlanta, GA, Oct 96; Chapman Univy Fac Develop Workshop, Mar 96; Northeast Mod Lang Asn Ann Conv, Boston, MA, Apr 95; Chapman Univ Engl Grad Colloquium, Mar 95; referee, PMLA, Mosaic; ed bd, Anthropoetics. **HONORS AND AWARDS** Fac excellence, Chapman Univ Awd, 97; fac Summer res grant, Chapman Univ, 94; Valerie Scudder Awd, Chapman Univ, 94; fac Summer res grant, Chapman Univ; 93; best essay awd, UCLA grad stud asn, 91; HT Swedenberg dissertation fel, UCLA, 90; grad high Hon & distinction, Univ CA, Berkeley, 80. **MEMBERSHIPS** Colloquium on Violence and Rel; MLA; NAm Soc for the Stud Romanticism; Pac Ancient & Mod Lang Asn; Wordsworth-Coleridge Asn. **SELECTED PUBLICATIONS** Auth, The Sign, The Thing, and Titanic, Chronicles of Love and Resentment 132, Apr, 98; Violent Delights and Violent Ends: Abjection in Oliver Twist, J Asn Interdisciplinary Stud of the Arts 3:1, 97; Writing in the Dust: Irony and Lynch-Law in the Gospel of John, Anthropoetics III,97; Wrung by sweet enforcement: Druid Stones and the Problem of Sacrifice in British Romanticism, Anthropoetics II, 97; Mimetic Polemicism: Rene Girard and Harold Bloom contra the School of Resentment, Anthropoetics II, 96; Romantic Bards and English Composers: The Case of Keats and Holst, Europ Romantic Rev 6, 95; Original Ambivalence: Violence and Autobiography in Thomas De Quincey, Peter Lang Publ, Inc, 95; Sacred Ambivalence: Mimetology in Aristotle, Horace, and Longinus, Anthropoetics I, 95. **CONTACT ADDRESS** Dept of Eng and Comp Lit, Chapman Univ, Orange, CA 92866. **EMAIL** schneide@chapman.edu

SCHNEIDER, VALERIE LOIS
PERSONAL Born 02/12/1941, Chicago, IL **DISCIPLINE** SPEECH & COMMUNICATION **EDUCATION** Carrol l Col, BA, 63; Univ Wis, Madison, MA, 66; Univ FL, PhD(speech), 69; Appalachian State Univ, cert, 81. **CAREER** Interim asst prof speech, Univ FL, 69-70; asst prof, Edinboro State Col, 70-71; assoc prof, 71-75, prof speech, 75-97, prof emeritus, speech & commun, E TN State Univ, 98-; Danforth assoc, 77. **HONORS AND AWARDS** Best Article Awd, Relig Speech Commun Asn, 76; Finalist, Money Magazine Best Personal Finance Manager in America contest, 94. **MEMBERSHIPS** Speech Commun Asn; Southern Speech Commun Asn; Relig Speech Commun Asn. **RESEARCH** Persuasion; rhetorical criticism; study skills. **SELECTED PUBLICATIONS** Auth, Informal Persuasion Analysis, Speech Teacher, 1/71; Hugh Blair's Theories of Style and Taste, NC J Speech, 12/71; Role-playing and your Local Newspaper, Speech Teacher, 9/71; Parker's Assessment of Webster: Argumentative Synthesis through the Tragic Metaphor, Quart J Speech, 10/78; Mainlining the Handicapped: An Analysis of Butterflies are Free, J Humanics, 12/78; A Process for Self-mastery for Study Habits, J Develop & Remedial Educ, winter 79; Experimental Course Formats, Nat Asn Pub Continuing & Adult Educ Exchange, winter 80; Two Courses for the Price of One: A Study Skills Component for a Speech Communications Course, J Develop & Remedial Educ, spring 82; and various other articles in Speech Communication Teacher, 88-94; writer of Video Visions column, Kingsport Times-News, 84-86; ed, ETSU Evening and Off-Campus newsletter, 86-93. **CONTACT ADDRESS** East Tennessee State Univ, PO Box 23098, Johnson City, TN 37614-0001.

SCHNEIDERMAN, DAVIS A.
DISCIPLINE ENGLISH **EDUCATION** Penn State Univ, BA, 96; Binghamton Univ, MA, 98; PhD, 01. **CAREER** Asst prof, Lake Forest Col, 01-. **HONORS AND AWARDS** Grad Studies Awd Teaching Excel; Bing Univ, 00; Dis Yr Fel; 00-01; Constance Saltonstall Found Arts Fel, NYork, 00. **MEMBERSHIPS** MLA; MSA. **RESEARCH** Creative writing; American literature; postmodernism; experimental and avant-garde literature; William S. Burroughs; cultural studies; multicultural literatures; jazz; composition and rhetoric. **SELECTED PUBLICATIONS** Auth, "Review of The Novel: Language and Lit From Cervantes to Calvino," Studies Novel 32 (00): 519-521; auth, "Send in the Clowns, They're Already Here," Iowa Rev 29 (99); auth, "Review of Reading Lessons: The Debate Over Literacy," Rad Teaching 56 (99); auth, "Rinse, Repeat, Sanitize and a Propaedeutic Sight Gag," Little Mag 22 (00); auth, "The Making of Amalgams: Sampling the 'Narrative' of Word Virus: The William S. Burroughs Reader," Rev Canaria de Estudies Ing 39 (00): 61-78; auth, "On the Origin of the Specious," Neotrope: Progressive Fiction 2 (01): auth, "Sound and (Re:)Vision," Neotrope: Progressive Fiction 2 (01); auth, "Forecast Calls For More of the Same," Qtr After Eight. 7 (01): 116-134; co-auth, "Fex During the Occupation of France," Happy (forthcoming). **CONTACT ADDRESS** English Dept, Lake Forest Col, 555 North Sheridan Rd, Lake Forest, IL 60045.

SCHNELL, JAMES
PERSONAL Born 08/03/1955, Columbus, OH, m, 1995, 1 child **DISCIPLINE** COMMUNICATION **EDUCATION** Capital Univ, BA, 77; State Univ of NYork, MA, 79; Ohio Univ, PhD, 82. **CAREER** Instr, Ohio Univ, 82-83; asst prof, Miami Univ, 83-84; asst prof, Univ of Cinn, 84-89; prof, Ohio Dominican Col, 89-. **HONORS AND AWARDS** Who's Who in Media and Commun; Vis Fel, E W Center, Hawaii. **MEMBERSHIPS** Nat Commun Assoc; Lieutenant Colonel, US Air Force Res. **RESEARCH** Cross-cultural communication; U.S. - China relations. **SELECTED PUBLICATIONS** Auth, Interpersonal Communication: Understanding and Being Understood, 96; auth, S.T.E.P.S. Toward Effective Public Speaking, 98; auth, Perspectives on Communication in the People's Republic of China, 99; Qualitative Research Methods in Communication Studies, 00. **CONTACT ADDRESS** Dept Fine and Commun Arts, Ohio Dominican Col, 1216 Sunbury Rd, Columbus, OH 43219-2086. **EMAIL** schnellj@odc.edu

SCHNELLER, BEVERLY
PERSONAL Born 02/05/1958, Fort Worth, TX, m, 1985 **DISCIPLINE** PROFESSIONAL WRITING, COMPOSITION, 18TH AND 19TH CENTURY BRITISH LITERATURE **EDUCATION** Cath Univ Am, PhD, 87. **CAREER** Tenured assoc prof; Millersville Univ, 89-; postdr, Univ Va, 95 & Amer Antiquarian Soc, 95; Ch, Univ Promotion and Tenure comt 97-98; Enrollment Mgt Taskforce co-ch 96-97 Acad Theme; sec, Fac Sen;ch, Evaluation Comt; ch, Comp Comt; ch, Search Comt; ch, ad hoc Senate Policies Rev Comt; auth/creator, Admissions, Advisement, Stud Aff Comt, EC-ASECS 22nd Annual Meeting, ch; ch, Women's Film Evening; asst dir, Marist Col Writing Prog, 85-89. **HONORS AND AWARDS** NEH Summer Sem, 93; Folger Inst, 92; Folger Weekend Workshop,92 & NEH Summer Inst, 90. **MEMBERSHIPS** MLA; ASECS; Mod Poetry Assn.; Vergilian Soc Amer; BSA; SHARP; NASSR; NAmer Conf Bri Stud; Oxford Bibliog Soc; Am Asn of Lit Scholars and Critics. **RESEARCH** 18th and 19th Century Irish Literature; Textual Criticism; Canadian Literature; 18th Century British Book Trade; 20th-century Am poetry. **SELECTED PUBLICATIONS** Auth, British Women Writers, Critical Reference Guide, Continuum, 87; auth, Writing About Science, Oxford UP, 91; British Romantic Novelists, Gale, 92; British Literary Publishing Houses, 2 vols, Gale, 92; Encyclopedia of Romanticism, Greenwood, 92; Magazines of the British Isles, Greenwood, 93; Writers, Books, and Trade, An 18th-century Miscellany for William B. Todd, AMS, 94; Teaching Composition from Literature, Harper Collins, 94; auth, Writing About Business and Industry, Oxford UP, 95; Feminist Literary Theory, A Dictionary, Garland, 96; Masterplots, Salem Press, 96; Encyclopedia of World Auth, rev ed, Salem Press, 96; contrib, Poetry Masterplots II, 98; contrib, Shakespeare and Irish Nationalism, Macmillan, 97; contrib, Critical Survey of Long Fiction, Salem, 00; The New DNB, Oxford at Clarendon from 96-00, forthcoming; essays published in McNeese Rev, Eire-Ireland, J of Newspaper and Periodical Hist. **CONTACT ADDRESS** Dept of English, Millersville Univ of Pennsylvania, PO Box 1002, Millersville, PA 17551-0302. **EMAIL** bschnell@marauder.millersv.edu

SCHNITZER, DEBORAH
PERSONAL Born Sault Ste. Marie, ON, Canada **DISCIPLINE** ENGLISH **EDUCATION** Univ Western Ont, BA, 72; Univ Calgary, MA, 73; Univ Man, PhD, 86. **CAREER** Tchr, Dept Northern Affairs, Koostatak, Man, 75-77; lectr, Eng, Univ Man, 77-79, 84-86; dir, Writing Ctr, 88-91, asst prof, 91-94, Assoc Prof English, Univ Winnipeg, 94-. **HONORS AND AWARDS** Gold Medal English & Philos, Univ Western Ont, 72; Univ Man Grad Fel, 77-81; SSHRC Doctoral Fel, 83-84; Merit Awd, Univ Winnipeg, 90; Red River Valley Educ Awd, 91; Clifford J. Robson Awd Excellence Tchg, 93. **MEMBERSHIPS** Asn Can Col & Univ Tchrs; Man Tchrs Eng; Hadassah Wizo Bk Club. **SELECTED PUBLICATIONS** Auth, The Pictorial in Modernist Fiction from Stephen Crane to Earnest Hemingway, 88; auth, English 300: A Community-Based University Entrance Curriculum, 89; auth, Tricks: Artful Photographs and Letters in Carol Shields' Stone Diaries and Anita Brookner's Hotel du Lac, in Prairie Fire, 95. **CONTACT ADDRESS** Dept of English, Univ of Winnipeg, Winnipeg, ON, Canada R3M 2E9. **EMAIL** d.schnitzer@uwinnipeg.ca

SCHOEN, CAROL BRONSTON
PERSONAL Born 05/14/1926, Plainfield, NJ, d, 2 children **DISCIPLINE** AMERICAN LITERATURE **EDUCATION** Radcliffe, BA, 48; Columbia, MA, 63; PhD, 68. **CAREER** Assoc prof, CUNY Lehman, 67-91. **HONORS AND AWARDS** Who's Who. **MEMBERSHIPS** MLA. **SELECTED PUBLICATIONS** Auth, Anzia Yesierska; auth, Sara Teasdale. **CONTACT ADDRESS** 70 E 10th St, Apt 2V, New York, NY 10003-5102. **EMAIL** cbschoen@aol.com

SCHOENBACH, PETER J.
PERSONAL Born 03/11/1941, Philadelphia, PA, m, 1981, 2 children **DISCIPLINE** MUSIC **EDUCATION** Swarthmore Univ, BA, 62; Columbia Univ, MA, 64; Rutgers Univ, PhD, 73. **CAREER** DIR, SCH MUSIC, CHAUTAUQUA INST, 97-; DIR, SCH MUSIC, SUNY, FREDONIA, 93-; chair, dept mus, Wayne State Univ, 84-92; dir, Sch Mus, Boston Univ, 82-84; assoc dean, New England Conserv, 78-82; dean Curtis Inst Mus, 73-77; Univ Minn; Temple Univ. **RESEARCH** Portuguese and Latin Am Music. **CONTACT ADDRESS** Sch Music, SUNY, Col at Fredonia, Fredonia, NY 14063. **EMAIL** schoenbach@fredonia.edu

SCHOENECKE, MICHAEL KEITH
PERSONAL Born 03/17/1949, Oklahoma City, OK, m, 1971, 2 children **DISCIPLINE** FILM, AMERICAN LITERATURE **EDUCATION** Cent State Univ, Okla, BA, 71, MA, 74; Okla State Univ, PhD(Am studies), 79. **CAREER** Teacher hist, Edinburg Consolidated Sch Dist, 71-73; asst prof film & lit, Bellevue Col, 79-81; assoc prof film, Tex Tech Univ, 81- **MEMBERSHIPS** Popular Cult Asn; Am Cult Asn; SCent Mod Lang Asn; Univ Film Asn. **RESEARCH** American studies, film, and sports. **SELECTED PUBLICATIONS** Ed, Proceedings of the First Texas Southwest Popular Culture Association, Okla Hist Soc, 79; auth, Jack London's beauty ranch: A world view, J Regional Cult, 81. **CONTACT ADDRESS** English Dept, Texas Tech Univ, Lubbock, TX 79409-0001. **EMAIL** cbmks@ttacs.ttu.edu

SCHOENFIELD, MARK
DISCIPLINE BRITISH ROMANTICISM **EDUCATION** Univ Southern Calif, PhD. **CAREER** Instr, Vanderbilt Univ. **RESEARCH** The relation of law, economics, and disciplinarity to literary studies. **SELECTED PUBLICATIONS** Auth, Voices Together: Lamb, Hazlitt, and the London, SIR; Professional Wordsworth: Law, Labor and the Poet's Contract, 96. **CONTACT ADDRESS** Vanderbilt Univ, Nashville, TN 37203-1727.

SCHOLES, ROBERT
PERSONAL Born 05/19/1929, Brooklyn, NY **DISCIPLINE** ENGLISH, COMPARATIVE LITERATURE **EDUCATION** Yale Univ, AB, 50; Cornell Univ, MA, 56, PhD, 59. **CAREER** From instr to asst prof English, Univ Va, 59-63; from assoc prof to prof, Univ Iowa, 64-70; Prof English, Brown Univ, 70-; Jr fel, Inst Res Humanities, Univ Wis, 63-64; Guggenheim Found fel, 77-78. **HONORS AND AWARDS** Am Acad Arts & Sci, 98. **MEMBERSHIPS** MLA; NCTE; PEN; Acad Lit Studies; Science Fiction Res Asn. **RESEARCH** Semiotics; composition; modern literature. **SELECTED PUBLICATIONS** Coauth, The Nature of Narrative, 66 & auth, The Fabulators, 67, Oxford Univ; auth, Structuralism in Literature, Yale Univ, 74; coauth, Science Fiction: History, Science, Vision, 77 & Elements of Literature, 78, Oxford Univ; auth, Fabulation and Metafiction, Univ Ill, 79; coauth, The Practice of Writing, St Martin's, 81; auth, Semiotics and Interpretation, Yale Univ, 82; auth, Textual Power, Yale Univ, 85; auth, Protocols of Reading, Yale Univ, 89; co-auth, Hemingway's Genders, Yale Univ, 94; auth, The Rise and Fall of English, Yale Univ, 98. **CONTACT ADDRESS** ENGLISH, Brown Univ, MCM Box 1957, Providence, RI 02912-9127. **EMAIL** Robert_Scholes@brown.edu

SCHOLNICK, ROBERT JAMES
PERSONAL Born 06/22/1941, Boston, MA, m, 1964, 1 child **DISCIPLINE** AMERICAN LITERATURE & STUDIES **EDUCATION** Univ Pa, AB, 62; Brandeis Univ, MA, 64, PhD(English & Am lit), 69. **CAREER** Asst prof, 67-72, assoc prof, 73-80, PROF ENGLISH, COL WILLIAM & MARY, 80- **MEMBERSHIPS** MLA **RESEARCH** American literature; American poetry; Walt Whitman. **SELECTED PUBLICATIONS** Auth, The Original Eye, Whitman, Schelling And The Return To Origins/, Walt Whitman Quart Rev, Vol 0011, 1994; Cult Or Democracy - Whitman, Benson,Eugene, And The Galaxy/, Walt Whitman Quart Rev, Vol 0013, 1996. **CONTACT ADDRESS** Dept of English, Col of William and Mary, Williamsburg, VA 23185.

SCHONHORN, MANUEL
PERSONAL Born 01/29/1930, Brooklyn, NY, m, 1958, 2 children **DISCIPLINE** ENGLISH **EDUCATION** Brooklyn Col, BA, 55; Univ Pa, MA, 59, PhD(English), 63. **CAREER** From instr to asst prof English, Univ Kans, 62-66; asst prof, State Univ NY, Binghamton, 66-68; assoc prof, 68-73, PROF ENGLISH, SOUTHERN ILL UNIV, 73-, Newberry Libr fel, 74, exchange fel, Brit Acad, 76-77. **MEMBERSHIPS** MLA; Am Soc 18th Century Studies. **RESEARCH** Daniel Defoe and Alexander Pope; 18th century history of ideas; literature and politics. **SELECTED PUBLICATIONS** Auth, Sterne 'Tristram Shandy' - New,M/, Scriblerian And The Kit-Cats, Vol 0027, 1995; 'Tristram Shandy' - A Book For Free Spirits - New,M/, Scriblerian And The Kit-Cats, Vol 0027, 1995. **CONTACT ADDRESS** Dept of English, So Illinois Univ, Carbondale, Carbondale, IL 62901. **EMAIL** mannys@siu.edu

SCHOR, ESTHER
PERSONAL Born Tallahassee, FL **DISCIPLINE** BRITISH ROMANTICISM **EDUCATION** Yale Univ, BA, 78, MPhil, 92, PhD, 95, **CAREER** Tchg asst, Yale Univ, 90; Instr, Yale Univ, 92-95; Assoc prof, Princeton Univ, 95-. **RESEARCH** Poetry; theory and criticism; British Romanticism. **SELECTED PUBLICATIONS** Bearing the Dead: The British Culture of Moving From the Enlightenment to Romanticism; Co-ed, The Other Mary Shelley: Beyond Frankenstein; Women's Voices: Visions and Perspectives. **CONTACT ADDRESS** Dept of English, Princeton Univ, 1 Nassau Hall, Princeton, NJ 08544.

SCHOR, HILARY
DISCIPLINE ENGLISH **EDUCATION** Stanford Univ, PhD. **CAREER** Assoc prof, Univ Southern Calif. **RESEARCH** Contemporary fiction; feminist theory and representations of women in Victorian literature. **SELECTED PUBLICATIONS** Auth, Scheherezade in the Marketplace: Elizabeth Gaskell & the Victorian Novel, 92. **CONTACT ADDRESS** Col Letters, Arts & Sciences, Univ of So California, University Park Campus, Los Angeles, CA 90089.

SCHOTCH, PETER K.
PERSONAL Born 07/26/1946 **DISCIPLINE** PHILOSOPHY IN LITERATURE, INTERMEDIATE LOGIC, STOICISM. **EDUCATION** Waterloo Univ, PhD, 73. **CAREER** Prof, 84-. **RESEARCH** Formal logic and its applications, philosophy of Descartes, the early Stoa. **SELECTED PUBLICATIONS** Auth, Paraconsistent Logic: The View from the Right, PSA 92; Remarks on Copenhagen Semantics, Essays in Honour of R.E. Jennings, Simon Fraser Univ, 93; Hyperdeontic Logic: An Overview, Social Rules, Westview Press, Boulder, 96; co-auth, Logic on the Track of Social Change, Oxford, Clarenden, 95. **CONTACT ADDRESS** Dept of Philos, Dalhousie Univ, Halifax, NS, Canada B3H 3J5. **EMAIL** peter.schotch@dal.ca

SCHRADER, RICHARD J.
PERSONAL Born 08/24/1941, Canton, OH, s **DISCIPLINE** ENGLISH **EDUCATION** Univ Notre Dame, BA, 63; Ohio State Univ, MA, 65; PhD, 68. **CAREER** Asst prof, Princeton Univ, 68-75; asst prof to prof, Boston Col, 75-. **HONORS AND AWARDS** John Witherspoon Bicentennial Preceptor, Princeton, 72-75; Mellon Grants, 80-81; NEH Summer Stipend, 95. **MEMBERSHIPS** Medieval Acad, Mencken Soc, New Chaucer Soc, Asn of Literary Scholars and Critics. **RESEARCH** Medieval literature, Bibliography and textual criticism, Modern Arthurian literature, H.L. Mencken. **SELECTED PUBLICATIONS** Auth, H.L. Mencken: A Documentary Volume, Gale: Detroit, 00; auth, H.L. Mencken: A Descriptive Bibliography, Univ Pittsburgh Press: Pittsburgh, 98; auth, "Old English Poetry and the genealogy of Events," Medieval Texts and Studies 12, 93; auth, Arator's On the Acts of the Apostles, Scholars Press: Atlanta, 87; auth, God's Handiwork: Images of Women in Early Germanic Literature, Greenwood Press: Westport, 83; auth, The Reminiscences of Alexander Dycel, Ohio State Univ: Columbus, 72. **CONTACT ADDRESS** Dept English, Boston Col, Chestnut Hill, 140 Commonwealth Ave, Chestnut Hill, MA 02467-3800. **EMAIL** richard.schrader.1@bc.edu

SCHROEDER, CHRISTOPHER L.
PERSONAL Born 07/24/1970, St Louis, MO, m, 2 children **DISCIPLINE** ENGLISH **EDUCATION** S Ill Univ, BA, 92; Univ Mo, MA, 94; Univ La, PhD. **CAREER** Asst prof, Flagler Col, 99-00; asst prof, Long Island Univ, 00-. **RESEARCH** Postmodern literacies, academic institutions and cultures. **SELECTED PUBLICATIONS** Auth, Reinventing the Universities Literacues and Legitimacy in the Postmodern Academy. **CONTACT ADDRESS** 22 Firwood Road, First Fl, Port Washington, NY 11050-1510. **EMAIL** christopher.schroeder@liu.edu

SCHROEDER, FREDERIC M.
PERSONAL Born 12/19/1937, Ottawa, ON, Canada, m, 1984 **DISCIPLINE** CLASSICS **EDUCATION** Univ Toronto, BA, 61; MA, 64; PhD, 70. **CAREER** Lectr to prof, Queen's Univ, 66-. **HONORS AND AWARDS** Res Grant, German Acad Exchange Serv, 82; Can Coun Leave Fel, 74-75. **MEMBERSHIPS** Class Asn of Can; Ont Class Asn; Can Soc for Neoplatonic Studies; Am Soc for Neoplatonic Studies; Soc Aristotelica Jannone. **RESEARCH** Ancient Philosophy; Neoplatonism; Late Aristotelianism. **SELECTED PUBLICATIONS** Coauth, Two Greek Aristotelian Commentators on the Intellect, Toronto, 90; auth, Form and Transformation. A Study in the Philosophy of Plotinus, Queen's Press, 92; auth, "Plotinus and Language", in Cambridge Companion to Plotinus, (Cambridge Univ Press, 96), 336-355; auth, "Prophecy and Remembrance in Plotinus," Colloquium, (96): 1-22; auth, "Plotinus and Aristotle on the good Life," in The Perennial Tradition of Neoplatonism, (Leuven Univ Press, 97), 207-220; **CONTACT ADDRESS** Dept Class, Queen's Univ at Kingston, 99 University Ave, Kingston, ON, Canada K7L 3N6. **EMAIL** schroedr@post.queensu.ca

SCHRUM, STEPHEN
PERSONAL Born 06/25/1957, PA, m, 1989 **DISCIPLINE** THEATRE **EDUCATION** Temple Univ, BA, 81; Univ Calif, MA, 93; PhD, 96. **CAREER** Lecturer, Pa State Univ, 91-98; adj prof, Univ Charleston, 98-. **MEMBERSHIPS** Asn for Theatre in Higher Educ. **RESEARCH** Goethe's Faust, Elizabethan Drama, Use of Technology in Teaching and Performance. **SELECTED PUBLICATIONS** Auth, "Going Digital: Computers in Theatre Class," Teaching Theatre, 99; auth, "The Living Biology Laboratory Manual: Learning About Life via Interactive Software", Molecular Biology of the Cell, 93; auth, Tennessee Williams and Elia Kazan: A Collaboration in Theatre, 94; auth, Directing for the Stage: A Workshop Guide of Creative Exercises and Projects, 98; ed, Theatre in Cyberspace: Issues of Teaching, Acting and directing, 99. **CONTACT ADDRESS** Dept Humanities, West Virginia Univ, Charleston, 2300 Maccorkle Ave Southeast, Charleston, WV 25304-1045.

SCHUCHARD, W. RONALD
DISCIPLINE ENGLISH LANGUAGE AND LITERATURE **EDUCATION** Univ Tex Austin, PhD, 69. **CAREER** Fac, 69; dir Emory Univ Brit Studies Prog Univ Col, Oxford Univ, present; Goodrich C. White Prof, concurrent. **RESEARCH** Modern British and Irish literature; T. S. Eliot and W. B. Yeats. **SELECTED PUBLICATIONS** Ed, T. S. Eliot's Clark and Turnbull Lectures, The Varieties of Metaphysical Poetry, Faber, 93; rptd Harcourt, 94; rptd Harvest, 96; co-ed, The Collected Letters of W. B. Yeats (v 3), Oxford UP, 94; auth, Eliot's Dark Angel, Oxford Univ Press, 99. **CONTACT ADDRESS** English Dept, Emory Univ, 1380 Oxford Rd NE, Atlanta, GA 30322-1950. **EMAIL** engrs@emory.edu

SCHULER, ROBERT
PERSONAL Born 06/25/1939, San Mateo, CA, m, 1963, 3 children **DISCIPLINE** ENGLISH **EDUCATION** Stanford Univ, BA,61; Univ Calif, Berkeley, MA in Comparative. **CAREER** Instr, English, Menlo Col, 65-67; Faculty Member, Humanities Area, Shimer Col 67-77; Prof, Univ Wisconsin-Stout, 78-. **HONORS AND AWARDS** Univ of Wisconsin, Stout Researcher of the Year; Chancellor's Outstanding Teacher's Awd, 88; Wisconsin Arts Board Fellowship in Literature, 97-98. **MEMBERSHIPS** Phi Kappa Phi Honors Society. **RESEARCH** Art History; Religion; Music; American History; Novels; Poems; Ecology; Wildlife. **SELECTED PUBLICATIONS** Auth, "Journeys Toward The Original Mind: The Long Poems of Gary Snyder," New York, Bern, Berlin: Peter Lang Publishing, 95; auth, "Putting Myself in my Place," Imaging Home: Writing Home: Writing From the Midwest, EDS. Mark Vinz and Thom Tammaro, Minneapolis, London: Univ of Minnesota Press, 95. **CONTACT ADDRESS** Dept of English & Philosophy, Univ of Wisconsin, Stout, PO Box 790, Menomonie, WI 54751-0790. **EMAIL** schulerr@uwstovt.edu

SCHULER, ROBERT M.
DISCIPLINE RENAISSANCE LITERATURE **EDUCATION** Bellarmine Col, BA; Univ Colo, MA, PhD. **CAREER** Prof, Univ of Victoria. **HONORS AND AWARDS** Ed, Eng Lit Stud Monogr Series. **RESEARCH** Shakespeare; relations between literature and science; textual criticism. **SELECTED PUBLICATIONS** Auth, Three Renaissance Scientific Poems, 78; English Magical and Scientific Poetry to 1700: An Annotated Bibliography, 79; Francis Bacon and Scientific Poetry, 92; Alchemical Poetry 1575-1700, 95. **CONTACT ADDRESS** Dept of English, Univ of Victoria, C313 Clearihue Bldg, PO Box 3070 STN CSC, Victoria, BC, Canada V8W 3W1.

SCHULTE, RAINER
DISCIPLINE LITERATURE STUDIES **EDUCATION** Univ Mich, PhD, 65. **CAREER** Prof. **HONORS AND AWARDS** Dir, Center Translation Studies; ed, Translation Rev. **RESEARCH** Translation studies; 20th century Latin American and European literature; literature and the arts; poetry writing. **SELECTED PUBLICATIONS** Auth, The Craft of Translation, Univ Chicago, 89; Theories of Translation: From Dryden to Derrida, Univ Chicago, 91; Giant Talk: An Anthology of Third World Writing, Random House, 75; Contemporary Short Stories: The Modern Tradition, W.W. Norton, 68; Suicide at the Piano, book of poems, 70; The Other Side of the Word, 78. **CONTACT ADDRESS** Dept of Literature, Univ of Texas, Dallas, Richardson, TX 75083-0688. **EMAIL** schulte@utdallas.edu

SCHULTZ, HEIDI M.
PERSONAL m, 1998 **DISCIPLINE** ENGLISH **EDUCATION** Lenoir-Rhyne Coll, BA, 80; Univ N Carol at Charlotte, MA, 89; Univ of N Carol at Chapel Hill, PhD, 97. **CAREER** Adj asst prof, Kenan Flagler Business Sch, Univ NC Chapel Hill **MEMBERSHIPS** CCC, ABC. **SELECTED PUBLICATIONS** Auth, "Edgar Allan Poe Submits The Bells": Resources for American Literary Study, Nov 96; "The Editor's Desk at Sartain's Magazine," Am Per vol 6, 96; auth, Elements of Electronic Communication, Allan and Bacon, 00. **CONTACT ADDRESS** Kenan-Flagler Business Sch, Univ of No Carolina, Chapel Hill, McColl, CB 3490, Chapel Hill, NC 27599-3490. **EMAIL** heidi_schultz@unc.edu

SCHULTZ, R.
PERSONAL Born 09/20/1951, Fort Dodge, IA, m, 1975, 2 children **DISCIPLINE** ENGLISH; AMERICAN LITERATURE; CREATIVE WRITING **EDUCATION** Luther Col, BA 74; Cornell Univ, MFA 76, MA 78, PhD 81. **CAREER** Lectr, Univ Va, 82-85; lectr, Cornell Univ, 79-8; from asst prof to prof, Luther Col, 85-; vis prof, Univ Virginia, 93-94. **HONORS AND AWARDS** NEA fel; Corson Bishop Poetry Prize; Emily Clark Balch Prize; Danforth fel; VFH and Pub Pol Res fel; Yale Younger Poets Prize Finalist; Walt Whitman Awd Finalist. **RESEARCH** Contemporary Lit; Literary Modernism; Ezra Pound; Film. **SELECTED PUBLICATIONS** Auth, The Madhouse Nudes, Simon & Schuster, 97; Winter in Eden, Loess Hills Books, 97; Vein Along the Fault, The Laueroc Press, 79; Numerous essays, poems, short stories reviews. **CONTACT ADDRESS** Dept of English, Luther Col, 700 College Dr., Decorah, IA 52101. **EMAIL** schultbo@luther.edu

SCHULTZ, WILLIAM J.
PERSONAL Born 10/05/1936, Dodge City, KS, m, 1960, 4 children **DISCIPLINE** AMERICAN LITERATURE **EDUCATION** Hastings Col, BA, 58; Univ Ark, Fayetteville, MA, 64; Kans State Univ, PhD(English), 68. **CAREER** Instr English, Sterling Col, 61-64; ASST PROF ENGLISH, MUSKINGUM COL, 68- **MEMBERSHIPS** AAUP; MLA **RESEARCH** William Faulkner; American literature before 1860. **SELECTED PUBLICATIONS CONTACT ADDRESS** Dept of English, Muskingum Col, New Concord, OH 43762.

SCHULTZE, QUENTIN J.
DISCIPLINE COMMUNICATION **EDUCATION** Univ of Ill, BS, 74, MS, 76, PhD, 78. **CAREER** Prof of mass commun, Drake Univ, 78-82; prof of commun, Calvin Col, 82-. **RESEARCH** Commun and culture, espec religion. **SELECTED PUBLICATIONS** Redeeming Television; American Evangelicals and the Mass Media; Televangelism and American Culture; Dancing in the Dark: Youth, Popular Culture and the Electronic Media. **CONTACT ADDRESS** Dept of Commun Arts and Sciences, Calvin Col, 3201 Burton St SE, Grand Rapids, MI 49546. **EMAIL** schul@calvin.edu

SCHULZ, GERALYN
PERSONAL Born 03/22/1957, Chicago, IL **DISCIPLINE** COMMUNICATION SCIENCES AND DISORDERS **EDUCATION** Univ Wis at Green Bay, BA, 79; State Univ NY at Buffalo, MA, 81; Univ Md, PhD, 94. **CAREER** Teaching asst, State Univ of NYork at Buffalo, 80-82; teaching asst, Univ of Md, 83-94; Res Speech Pathologist, NIDCD, NIH, 82-94; Res Speech Pathologist and Acting Chief in Chief's absence, NIDCD, NIH, 94-95; asst prof, Univ of Fla, 95-. **HONORS AND AWARDS** Scholar, Ling Soc of Am at Univ of Md, 82; Ten Year Length of Service Awd, United States Govt, 93; Special Achievement Awd, US Dept of Health and Human Services, 95; Sustained High Quality Work Performance, US Dept of Health and Human Services, 91, 93, & 95; Awd of Merit, Nat Inst of Health, 95. **MEMBERSHIPS** Am Speech-Language-Hearing Asn, Fla Speech-Language-hearing Asn, Am Asn of Univ Women, Women in Neuroscience, Women's Fac Asn at the Univ of Fla. **RESEARCH** Speech Motor Control, Speech Motor Learning/relearning, Neurophysiological Bases of Speech, Voice, Language. **SELECTED PUBLICATIONS** Coauth, "Altered patterns of cerebral activity during speech and language production in developmental stuttering. An H215O positron emission topography study," Brain 120 (97): 761-784; auth, "Speech production impairments following right vs. left hemisphere stroke," NeuroRehabilitation 9 (97): 89-102; coauth, "Voice and Speech Characteristics in Individuals with Parkinson's Disease Pre- and Post Pallidotomy Surgery: Preliminary Findings," J of Speech Lang and Hearing Res 42 (99): 1176-1194; coauth, "Speech and oral motor learning in individuals with cerebellar atrophy," J of Speech Lang and Hearing Res 42 (99): 1157-1175; coauth, "The effects of Parkinson's treatments on speech: A review of the literature," J of Commun Disorders 33 (00): 59-88; coauth, "Changes in vocal intensity in Parkinson's disease following pallidotomy surgery," J of Voice (in press). **CONTACT ADDRESS** Dept Commun Disorders, Univ of Florida, 33 Dauer Hall, Gainesville, FL 32611.

SCHURMAN, LYDIA CUSHMAN
DISCIPLINE ENGLISH **EDUCATION** Cornell Univ, BA, 50; Harvard, MAT, 54; George Mason Col, MA, 76; Univ of Maryland, PhD, 84. **CAREER** Prof, to PROF EMER, ENG, N VIRGINIA COMM COLL **MEMBERSHIPS** Am Antiquarian Soc **SELECTED PUBLICATIONS** Auth, "The Sensational Stories and Dime Novel Writing Days of Louisa May Alcott, Horatio Alger, Theodore Dreiser, and Upton Sinclair," Dime Novel Round-Up, Dec 88; auth, "Anthony Comstock's Lifelong Crusade Against 'Vampire Literature,'" Dime Novel Round-Up, Dec 89; auth, "Those Famous American Periodicals The Bible, The Odyssey and Paradise Lost-Or, The Great Second-Class Mail Swindle," Publ Hist XL, 96; co-ed, Pioneers, Passionate Ladies, and Private Eyes: Dime Novels, Service Books, and Paperbacks, 97. **CONTACT ADDRESS** 3215 N 22nd St, Arlington, VA 22201. **EMAIL** nvschul@nv.cc.va.us

SCHUSTER-CRAIG, JOHN
PERSONAL Born 01/13/1949, St. Louis, MO, m, 1980, 2 children **DISCIPLINE** MUSIC THEORY **EDUCATION** Univ Louisville, BM, 71; Univ No Carolina, MA, 76; Univ Kentucky, PhD, 87. **CAREER** Vis asst prof, musicology, Indiana Univ, 89, 90; asst prof, Music Theory, 88-93, Univ Louisville; assoc & chair prof, Webster Univ, 93-96; assoc prof, head, Dept of Music, Clayton Col & State Univ, 96- . **HONORS AND AWARDS** Andrew W. Mellon res fel, Harry Ransom Hum Res Ctr, Univ Texas. **MEMBERSHIPS** Am Musicological Soc; Soc for Music Theory; Col Music Soc. **RESEARCH** Twentieth century music. **SELECTED PUBLICATIONS** Auth, Contrasting Collections in Scriabin's Etudes, Op. 65, Theoretically Speaking, 92; auth, Compositional Process in Clermont Pepin's Quasars, SONUS, 92; auth, Bizarre Harmony and the So-Called Newest Style: The Harmonic Language of Rimsky-Korsakov's Le Coq d'or, J of the Am Liszt Soc, 98; auth, Stravinsky's Scenes de ballet and Billy Rose's The Seven Lively Arts: The Abravanel Account, in Parisi, ed, Music in the Theater, Church, and Villa; Essays in Honor of Robert Lamar Weaver and Norma Wright Weaver, Harmonie Park Press, forthcoming. **CONTACT ADDRESS** 100 Waldrop Way, Fayetteville, GA 30215. **EMAIL** rimsky@mail.clayton.edu

SCHWAB, ALLEN
PERSONAL Born 11/07/1942, Chicago, IL, m, 1967, 1 child **DISCIPLINE** ENGLISH **EDUCATION** Univ Ill, AB, 64; Univ Washington, MA, 66; Tufts Univ, PhD. **CAREER** Instructor to Teaching Asst, Univ Washington, 64-68; Teaching Fel, Tufts Univ, 67-69; Visiting Asst Prof, Northwestern Univ, 72-73; Lecturer, Colgate Univ, 73-83; Assoc Prof, Lindenwood Col, 83-89; Visiting Fac Member, St Louis Univ, 89-90; Visiting Fac Member, Maryville Univ, 96-97; Prof, Washington Univ, 90-96; Assoc Prof, NW Mo State Univ, 97-99; Prof, Eureka Col, 99-. **HONORS AND AWARDS** Teaching Excellence, Washington Univ; Leadership Awd, Lindenwood Col; Presidential Service Awd, Nat Asn of Acad Affairs Admin; Leah F Trelease Creative Writing Awd, Univ Ill. **MEMBERSHIPS** Am Asn of Univ Prof, Am Asn of Higher Educ, Am Studies Asn, Herman Melville Soc, Elijah Lovejoy Soc, Gustav Mahler. Soc. **RESEARCH** Inter-relationships of literature, music, visual arts; American culture history of ideas. **SELECTED PUBLICATIONS** Auth, Dexter Morrill, Broadcast Music Inc, in press; auth, "Aaron Feuerstein, Polartec, Malden Mills, and the Loss of One's Life Work," Ballwin, 98; auth, "All a Poet Can do Today is Warn': the War Requiem of Benjamin Britten," Mo Theatre, 98; auth, "The Life and art of Felix Mendelssohn," Mo Theatre, 98; auth, "The Bridges We Must Cross to Link In and Out of Classroom Learning," Mo State Univ, 97; auth, "Bowling alone and our ambivalent search for Community," Ballwin Mo, 97. **CONTACT ADDRESS** Div Humanities, Eureka Col, 508 W Burton Ave, Eureka, IL 61530-1310.

SCHWARTZ, DEBORA B.
PERSONAL Born 03/31/1960, Cleveland, OH, m, 1 child **DISCIPLINE** MEDIEVAL LITERATURE **EDUCATION** Bryn Mawr Col, BA, 82; Princeton Univ, MA, 86; PhD, 94. **CAREER** Assistarte, Lycee Marie Curie, 83-84; lectr, Princeton Univ, 90-91; asst prof, Ariz State Univ, 91-95; vis prof, Inst d'Etudes francaises D'Avignon, 95; asst prof, Calif Polytec State Univ, 96-. **HONORS AND AWARDS** Nat Meric Scholar, 78; Fulbright Fel, 83-84; Princeton Univ Grad Fel, 84-89; DAAD Fel, 87-88; Teacher of the Year, Calif Polytech State Univ, 97-98. **MEMBERSHIPS** MLA, Medieval Acad of Am, Medieval Assoc of the Pacific, Int Arthurian Soc, Int Courtly Lit Soc, Tristan, Soc, Rocky Mountain Medieval and Renaissance Assoc. **RESEARCH** Medieval literature (French, English, German), Arthurian literature (medieval to modern). **SELECTED PUBLICATIONS** Auth, Translatio Studii: Essays in Honor of Karl D. Vitti. **CONTACT ADDRESS** Dept English, California Polytech State Univ, San Luis Obispo, 1 Grand Ave, San Luis Obispo, CA 93407-9000. **EMAIL** dschwart@calpoly.edu

SCHWARTZ, DONA B.
DISCIPLINE MASS COMMUNICATION STUDIES **EDUCATION** Univ Pa, MA, PhD. **CAREER** Assoc prof **SELECTED PUBLICATIONS** Auth, Picturing Rural Change: Community Life in Waucoma Iowa, 92; Visual Ethnography: Using Photography in Qualitative Research, Qualitative Sociology, 89. **CONTACT ADDRESS** Mass Communication Dept, Univ of Minnesota, Twin Cities, 111 Murphy Hall, 206 Church St SE, Minneapolis, MN 55455. **EMAIL** dona@tc.umn.edu

SCHWARTZ, HENRY J.
DISCIPLINE ENGLISH LITERATURE **EDUCATION** McGill Univ, BA; Rutgers Univ, MA; Duke Univ, PhD. **CAREER** Eng Dept, Georgetown Univ **RESEARCH** Literary theory and cultural studies; theory of history; South Asian literature; film. **SELECTED PUBLICATIONS** Auth, Writing Cultural History in Colonial and Postcolonial India, 97; Reading the Shape of the World: Toward an International Cultural Studies, Westview, 96. **CONTACT ADDRESS** English Dept, Georgetown Univ, 37th and O St, Washington, DC 20057.

SCHWARTZ, HOWARD
DISCIPLINE ENGLISH LITERATURE **CAREER** Prof, Univ Mo, St Louis. **HONORS AND AWARDS** 1st Place Awd, Acad of Am Poets poetry contest, Wash Univ, 69; Poetry fel, St Louis Arts and Hum Comn, 81; Am Bk Awd, Before Columbus Found, 84; Sydney Taylor Bk Awd, 92; Hon Doctorate, Spertus Inst Jewish Stud, 96; Nat Jewish Bk Awd, Hebrew Un Col, NY, 96; Aesop Prize, Am Folklore Soc, 97. **SELECTED PUBLICATIONS** Auth, Rooms of the Soul, Rossel Books (NY), 84; auth, Sleepwalking Beneath the Stars, BkMk Pr (Kansas City), 92; auth, Adam's Soul: The Collected Tales of Howard Schwartz Jason Aronson (Northvale, NJ), 93; ed, Gabriel's Palace: Jewish Mystical Tales, Oxford Univ Pr (New York & Oxford), 93; ed, First Harvest: Jewish Writing in St Louis: 1991-1996, The Brodsky Lib Pr (St Louis), 97; auth, Reimagining the Bible: The Story telling of the Rabbis, Oxford Univ Pr (New York & Oxford), 98; auth, The Four Who Entered Paradis, Jason Aronson (Northvale, NJ), 00; auth, A Journey to Paradise & Other Jewish Tales, Pitspopany Pr (Jerusalem), 00; auth The Day the Rabbi Disappeared: Jewish Holiday Tales of Magic, Viking (New York), 00; auth, Invisible Kingdoms: Jewish tales of Angels, Spirits and Demons, HarperCollins (New York), forthcoming. **CONTACT ADDRESS** Dept of English, Univ of Missouri, St. Louis, 8001 Natural Bridge Rd, Saint Louis, MO 63121. **EMAIL** hschwartz@umsl.edu

SCHWARTZ, JEFF L.
PERSONAL Born 02/18/1968, Culver City, CA **DISCIPLINE** LITERATURE **EDUCATION** Univ Calif Santa Cruz, BA, 90; Bowling Green St Univ, MA, 92; Univ Tx Austin, MLIS, 99. **CAREER** Teaching Fellow, Bowling Green St. Univ, 91-2, 93-97; Library Staff, Bowling Green State Univ, 97-98; Library Staff, Univ TX Austin 98-99; Reference Library, Fresno Public library, 99-00; Reference Librarian, Santa Monica Public Library, 00-. **HONORS AND AWARDS** Amer Stud Prog Essay Prize, Bowling Green St Univ, 97; Acad Competitive Scholar, Univ Tx Austin, 98-99. **MEMBERSHIPS** MLA; ASA; ALA; ACRL. **RESEARCH** Jazz & popular musics; critical theory; polit & avant-garde art. **SELECTED PUBLICATIONS** Auth, Postmodernity, History, and the Assassination of JFK, Bowling Green St Univ, 92; Writing Jimi: Rock Guitar Pedagogy as Postmodern Folkloric Practice, Popular Music, 93; Sister Ray: Some Pleasures of a Musical Text, in The Velvet Underground Companion, Schirmer, 97; It's Only rock and Roll?, review of The Sex Revolts: New Black Music: Amiri Baraka and Archie Shepp, dissertation, Bowling Green St Univ, forthcoming. **CONTACT ADDRESS** 10751 Rose Ave., No. 101, Los Angeles, CA 90034. **EMAIL** jeff_1968@excite.com

SCHWARTZ, LLOYD
PERSONAL Born 11/29/1941, Brooklyn, NY **DISCIPLINE** ENGLISH **EDUCATION** Harvard Univ, PhD, 76. **CAREER** University Mass Boston. **HONORS AND AWARDS** Pulitzer Prize for criticism; NEA Creative Writing Grant for poetry; 3 ASCAP Deems Taylor Awds for Music Criticism. **MEMBERSHIPS** PEN. **RESEARCH** Elizabeth Bishop. **SELECTED PUBLICATIONS** Auth, These People, 81; Goodnight, Gracie, 92; ed, Elizabeth Bishop and Her Art, 83; auth, Cairo Traffic, 00. **CONTACT ADDRESS** Dept of English, Univ of Massachusetts, Boston, Boston, MA 02125. **EMAIL** lloyd.schwartz@umb.edu

SCHWARTZ, MIMI J.
PERSONAL Born 06/01/1940, New York, NY, m, 2 children **DISCIPLINE** ENGLISH **EDUCATION** NYork Univ, BA, 61; UCLA, MA, 62; Rutgers Univ, EdD, 80. **CAREER** Prof, Richard Stockton Col, 80-. **HONORS AND AWARDS** Editor's Awd, FL, 99; Writer's Digest Awd, 98. **RESEARCH** Creative nonfiction--role of memory and imagination; Issues of ethics; Relation of fact to fiction. **SELECTED PUBLICATIONS** Co-ed, Under Age, An Anthology of Children's Poetry, Arts Coun Pub, 89; ed, Writer's Craft, Teacher's Art: Teaching what we know, Heinemann, Boynton, Cook, 91; auth, "Journeys through the Writing Process," in Landmark Essays on the Writing Process, Hermagoras Press, 94; auth, "If and When," in How to Write Creative Nonfiction, Chicago Rev Press, 96; auth, "Memoir, Fiction, Where's the Line?," Creative Nonfiction, 98; ed, Our Stories, Our Selves. An Anthology of student and faculty autobiography, Richard Stockton Col Press, 99; auth, "From Memory to Memoir," Writer's Digest, 99; auth, "Why I Teach Autobiography," Writing on the Edge, 99; auth, "The Ethics of Creative Nonfiction," AWP Chronicle, 99 **CONTACT ADDRESS** Dept Writing Prog, Richard Stockton Col, PO Box 195, Pomona, NJ 08240-0195. **EMAIL** schwartm@stockton.edu

SCHWARTZ, REGINA
DISCIPLINE ENGLISH **EDUCATION** Univ Va, PhD. **CAREER** Prof, Northwestern Univ. **HONORS AND AWARDS** Milton Society prize. **RESEARCH** 17th century literature, psychoanalytic and postmodern theory. **SELECTED PUBLICATIONS** Auth, Remembering and Repeating: Biblical Creation in Paradise Lost,88; The Book and the Text: The Bible and Literary Theory, 90; Desire in the Renaissance: Psychoanalysis and Literature, 94; The Postmodern Bible, 95; The Curse of Cain: The Violent Legacy of Monotheism; An interview with Regina M. Schwartz, Univ Chicago Press; Remembering and Repeating: Biblical Creation in Paradise Lost. **CONTACT ADDRESS** Dept of English, Northwestern Univ, 1801 Hinman, Evanston, IL 60208. **EMAIL** regina-s@northwestern.edu

SCHWARTZ, RICHARD A.
PERSONAL Born 02/03/1951, Miami, FL, m **DISCIPLINE** ENGLISH, LIBERAL STUDIES **EDUCATION** Univ South Fla, BA, 72; Univ Chicago, MA, 74, PhD, 77. **CAREER** Asst prof, 79-85, assoc prof, 85-97, prof, Fla Int Univ, 97-. **HONORS AND AWARDS** Excellence in Teaching Awd, Fla Int Univ, 92; Cold War Reference Guide named an Outstanding Academic Book by Choice Mag, 97. **RESEARCH** 20Tth century American film and fiction; Cold War-related literature, film, fine arts, and popular culture; film studies. **SELECTED PUBLICATIONS** Auth, "Yeats's High Modernism and Disney's Postmodernism: A Contrast in Ideal Worlds," The J of Aesthetic Educ, vol 29, no 1 (spring 95): 79-84; coauth with Kemp Williams, "Metaphors We Teach By," The J of Aesthetic Educ, vol 29, no 2 (summer 95): 103-110; auth, "Frederick Wiseman's Modernist Vision: Central Park," Literature/Film Quart, vol 23, no 3 (95): 223-228; auth, "The Tragic Vision of Thelma and Louise," J of Evolutionary Psychol, vol 17, no 1 and 2 (March 96): 101-107; auth, Cold War Reference Guide:

A General History and Annotated Chronology, with Selected Biographies, Jefferson, NC: McFarland & Co (97); auth, Encyclopedia of the Persian Gulf War, Jefferson, NC: McFarland & Co (98); auth, Cold War Culture, New York: Facts on File (98, paperback, 2000; auth, :How the Film and Television Blacklists Worked," Film & Hist Annual for 1999, CD ROM; auth, Woody, From Antz to Zelig: Reference Guide to Woody Allen's Creative Work, 1964-1998, Westport, CT: Greenwood Press (2000). **CONTACT ADDRESS** Dept English, Florida Intl Univ, Miami, FL 33199-0001. **EMAIL** schwartz@fiu.edu

SCHWARTZ, RICHARD B.
DISCIPLINE ENGLISH LITERATURE **EDUCATION** Univ Notre Dame, BA; Univ Ill, MA, PhD. **CAREER** Eng Dept, Georgetown Univ **RESEARCH** Eighteenth century intellectual and social history; contemporary American fiction and culture; creative writing. **SELECTED PUBLICATIONS** Auth, Samuel Johnson and the New Science, 71; Samuel Johnson and the Problem of Evil, 75; Boswell's Johnson: A Preface to the LIFE, 78; Daily Life in Johnson's London, 83; After the Death of Literature, 97; Frozen Stare, 89; ed, The Plays of Arthur Murphy, 79; Theory and Tradition in Eighteenth Century Studies, 90. **CONTACT ADDRESS** English Dept, Georgetown Univ, 37th and O St, Washington, DC 20057.

SCHWARTZ, ROBERT BARNETT
PERSONAL Born 03/20/1950, New York, NY **DISCIPLINE** RENAISSANCE LITERATURE **EDUCATION** Tulane Univ, BA, 72; Univ Va, PhD, 78. **CAREER** Instr English, Univ Va, 74-78; from Asst Prof to Assoc Prof, 78-91, Prof English, Ore State Univ, 91-, Chair of English, 94-. **MEMBERSHIPS** Philol Asn Pacific Coast; Rocky Mt Mod Lang Asn. **RESEARCH** Shakespeare; Renaissance; folklore. **SELECTED PUBLICATIONS** Ed, Shakespeare and the Popular Tradition in the Theater, Johns Hopkins Univ Press, 78; auth, Birons Wortspieleriches'Spiel Aus Kinderzeit', Shakespeare Jahrbuch, 78; The social character of May games, Zeitschrift fur Anglistik und Amerikanistik, 79; Speaking the unspeakable: The meaning of form in Christabel, Lang Quart, 80; Approaching the sonnets: Shakespeare's Parted Eye, Wascana Rev, 82; Coming apart at the Seems: More on the complexity of Hamlet, Pac Coast Philol, 82; Shakespeare's Parted Eye: Perception, Knowledge and Meaning in the Sonnets and Plays, Peter Lang, 90. **CONTACT ADDRESS** Dept of English, Oregon State Univ, 238 Moreland Hall, Corvallis, OR 97331-5302. **EMAIL** rschwartz@orst.edu

SCHWARZ, DANIEL R.
PERSONAL Born 05/12/1941, Rockville Center, NY, m, 1998, 2 children **DISCIPLINE** ENGLISH **EDUCATION** Union Col, BA, 63; Brown Univ, MA, 65; PhD, 68. **CAREER** Asst prof, Cornell Univ, 68-74; assoc prof, 74-80; prof, 80-; Stephen H Weiss Presidential Fel, 99-. **HONORS AND AWARDS** Phi Beta Kappa; Stephen and Marjory Russell Dist Teach Awd. **MEMBERSHIPS** MLA; SSNL. **RESEARCH** The British novel; 19th and 20th Century; literary theory; twentieth Century modernism, American and European fiction; Victorian and modern poetry; Holocaust studies; modern art. **SELECTED PUBLICATIONS** Auth, The Transformation of the English Novel, 1890-1930: Studies in Hardy, Conrad, Joyce, Lawrence, Forster, and Woolf, St. Martin's Press (London: Macmillan; NY: St Martin's Press), 89, rev 2nd ed, 95; auth, The Case for a Humanistic Poetics, Univ Penn Press (London: Macmillan; Philadelphia), 91; auth, Narrative and Representation in the Poetry of Wallace Stevens, St. Martin's Press (London: Macmillan; NY), 93; auth, Reconfiguring Modernism: Explorations In the Relationship Between Modern Art and Literature, St Martin's Press (NY and London: Macmillan), 97; auth, Imagining the Holocaust, St. Martin's Press (NY, London: Macmillan), 99; auth, James Joyce's 'The Dead': A Case Study of Contemporary Criticism, St Martin's Press (NY), 94; coauth, Narrative and Culture, Univ Georgia Press (Athens), 94; auth, Joseph Conrad's 'The Secret Sharer': A Case Study in Contemporary Criticism, St Martin's Press (NY), 97. **CONTACT ADDRESS** Dept English, Cornell Univ, 304 Rockefeller Hall, Ithaca, NY 14853-3201. **EMAIL** drs6@cornell.edu

SCHWARZ, KATHRYN
DISCIPLINE RENAISSANCE LITERATURE AND CULTURE, SHAKESPEARE **EDUCATION** Harvard Univ, PhD. **CAREER** Instr, Vanderbilt Univ. **RESEARCH** Renaissance representations of gender, violence, and the body. **SELECTED PUBLICATIONS** Auth, Amazon Encounters in the Jacobean Queen's Masque; Missing the Breast. **CONTACT ADDRESS** Vanderbilt Univ, Nashville, TN 37203-1727.

SCHWARZ, MAY L.
PERSONAL Born 10/04/1945, Sandusky, OH, d, 2 children **DISCIPLINE** CHURCH MUSIC **EDUCATION** Oberlin Col, BM, 67; Ohio State Univ, MM, 68; Trinity Lutheran Sem, MTS, 89. **CAREER** Asst prof to prof, Trinity Lutheran Sem 89-. **HONORS AND AWARDS** Pi Kappa Lambda. **MEMBERSHIPS** ALCM; AGO; ACDA; Hymn Soc in Am and Can. **RESEARCH** Psalmody, including music, texts, performance practices in use in today's churches, Building Parish Music Programs, including the role and partnership of clergy and musicians, Organ chorale preludes of J.S. Bach compared to those of contemporary composers. **SELECTED PUBLICATIONS** Auth, "The Prelude: A Foretaste of the Feast to Come", Sursum Corda, Jan 89; auth, "The Psalms in Worship: Strategies for Congregational Use", Sursum Corda, Dec 89; auth, "Music During Distribution", Sursum Corda, July 91; auth, "Church Music at Trinity Seminary", Grace Notes, VII.2 (April 92); auth, "Partnership of Clergy and Musician", The Guilder, January 94. **CONTACT ADDRESS** Dept Pastoral Ministry, Trinity Lutheran Sem, 2199 E Main St, Columbus, OH 43209-3913. **EMAIL** mschwarz@trinity.capital.edu

SCHWARZBACH, FREDRIC S.
PERSONAL Born New York, NY **DISCIPLINE** ENGLISH LITERATURE, URBAN STUDIES **EDUCATION** Columbia Univ, AB, 71, MA, 72; London Univ, PhD(English), 76. **CAREER** Res asst English, Univ Col London, 74-77; ASST PROF ENGLISH, WASH UNIV, ST LOUIS, 77-, Am Coun Learned Soc fel, 80. **MEMBERSHIPS** MLA **RESEARCH** Nineteenth century literature; social context of literature; literature and the city. **SELECTED PUBLICATIONS** Auth, Dickens And The 1830s - Chittick,K/, Victorian Studies, Vol 0036, 1992. **CONTACT ADDRESS** Dept of English, Washington Univ, Saint Louis, MO 63130. **EMAIL** fschwarz@kent.edu

SCHWARZLOSE, RICHARD A.
PERSONAL Born 03/18/1937, Chicago, m, 1963, 2 children **DISCIPLINE** JOURNALISM **EDUCATION** Univ Ill, BA, 59, MA, 60, PhD, 65. **CAREER** Prof, Jour, Northwestern Univ **MEMBERSHIPS** Assoc for Education in Journalism and Mass Communication; Assoc for Practical and Prof Ethics. **RESEARCH** Journalism history, journalism ethics, journalism law. **SELECTED PUBLICATIONS** Auth, American Wire Services: A Study of Their Development as a Social Institution, 79; auth, Newspapers: A Reference Guide, Greenwood Press, 87; auth, The Nation's Newsbrokers: Vol 1: The Formative Years, from Pretelegraph to 1865, Northwestern, 88; auth, The Nation's Newsbrokers, Vol 2: The Rush to Institution, from 1865 to 1920, Northwestern, 89. **CONTACT ADDRESS** Medill School of Jour, Northwestern Univ, 1845 Sheridan Rd, Evanston, IL 60208. **EMAIL** r-schwarzlose@northwestern.edu

SCHWEDA, DONALD NORMAN
PERSONAL Born 04/18/1937, Chicago, IL, m, 1957, 1 child **DISCIPLINE** AMERICAN & ENGLISH LITERATURE **EDUCATION** Ill Inst Technol, BS, 62; Univ Fla, AM, 63; Loyola Univ Chicago, PhD(English), 73. **CAREER** Teacher English, Kelvyn Park High Sch, Chicago, 62 & Mount Prospect High Sch, 64; instr, 64-66, assoc prof, 68-76, prof English, Quincy Col, 76-99, chemn dept, 68-96, Evaluator, Clearing House Reading & Commun Skills, Educ Resources Info Ctr, 74-. **HONORS AND AWARDS** NEH Summer Seminars, CUNY, 77; CUNY, 81; Yale, 89; Yale, 94. **MEMBERSHIPS** NCTE; Midwest Mod Lang Asn. **RESEARCH** American poetry; 19th century American literature; Robert Frost. **SELECTED PUBLICATIONS** Auth, Emersonian ideas and Whitman's Song of Myself, J Loyola Hist Soc, fall 67; A History of Newness (A Review), riverword, 78; Poetry, riverrun, 86, 83, 81; Arts Quincy, 85; consulting advisor, Norton Anthology of African American Literature, 97. **CONTACT ADDRESS** Dept of English, Quincy Univ, 1800 College Ave, Quincy, IL 62301-2670. **EMAIL** schweda@quincy.edu

SCHWEICKART, PATROCINIO PAGADUAN
PERSONAL Born 08/07/1942, Manilla, Philippines, m, 1966, 2 children **DISCIPLINE** ENGLISH **EDUCATION** Univ Philippines, BChem Eng, 63; Univ Va, MChE, 65, MA, 69; Ohio State Univ, PhD, 80. **CAREER** Lectr math, Loyola Univ, Chicago, 76-77, lectr English, 77-78; Asst Prof English, Univ NH, 79-, Consult, NH Coun for Humanities, 81-82; ed, New Eng Women's Studies Newslett, 81-; scholar, Sch Criticism & Theory, Northwestern Univ, 81-; prof English and Women's Studies, Purdue Univ. **MEMBERSHIPS** MLA; Nat Women's Studies Asn. **RESEARCH** Women's studies; science and literature; literary criticism and theory. **SELECTED PUBLICATIONS** Auth, Reading Feminisms, College English, 97. **CONTACT ADDRESS** Dept English, Purdue Univ, 1356 Heavilon Hall, West Lafayette, IN 47907. **EMAIL** pschweic@sla.purdue.edu

SCHWEIK, ROBERT CHARLES
PERSONAL Born 08/05/1927, Chicago, IL, m, 1954, 2 children **DISCIPLINE** ENGLISH **EDUCATION** Loyola Univ, Ill, BA, 51; Univ Notre Dame, PhD, 58. **CAREER** Instr English, Marquette Univ, 53-58, from asst prof to assoc prof, 59-69; prof, 69-80, DISTINGUISHED TEACHING PROF, STATE UNIV NY COL FREDONIA, 80-, Mem Victorian bibliog comt, MLA, 68-72; vis prof, Univ Trier, Ger, 72-73. **MEMBERSHIPS** MLA; Int Asn Univ Prof English; Thomas Hardy Soc. **RESEARCH** Victorian novel; bibliography; nineteenth-century prose non-fiction. **SELECTED PUBLICATIONS** Auth, The ethical structure of Hardy's The Woodlanders, Archiv, 74; Rhetorical art and literary form in Mill's The Subjection of Women, Quart J Speech, 75; contribr, Hardy: The Tragic Novels, Macmillan, 75; auth, English and American literature: Recent developments in enumerative bibliography and indexing, Lit Res Newslett, 76; contribr, Budmouth Essays on Thomas Hardy, Thomas Hardy Soc, 76; coauth, Reference Sources in English and American Literature, Norton, 77; auth, Fictions in the criticism of Hardy's fiction, English Lit Transition, 77; contribr, Thomas Hardy, Macmillan, 78. **CONTACT ADDRESS** Dept of English, SUNY, Col at Fredonia, Fredonia, NY 14063.

SCHWEITZER, IVY
DISCIPLINE ENGLISH LITERATURE **EDUCATION** Brandeis Univ, PhD, 83. **CAREER** Assoc prof, Dartmouth Col. **RESEARCH** Am lit and poetics; women's studies. **SELECTED PUBLICATIONS** Auth, The Work of Self-Representation: Lyric Poetry in Colonial New England, Univ NC P, 91; Maternal Discourse and the Romance of Self-Possession in Kate Chopin's The Awakening, boundary, 90, rptd in Revisionary Interventions into the Americanist Canon, Duke UP, 94. **CONTACT ADDRESS** Dept of English, Dartmouth Col, 6032 Sanborn House, Hanover, NH 03755. **EMAIL** Ivy.T.Schweitzer@dartmouth.edu

SCHWENINGER, LEE
DISCIPLINE LITERATURE **EDUCATION** Univ of NC, PhD, 84; Univ of CT, MA, 80; Univ of CO, BA, 76 **CAREER** Prof, Univ of NC **HONORS AND AWARDS** Resig interdisc minor in Native Am studies **MEMBERSHIPS** Asn for the study of lit and the environ **RESEARCH** Early Am lit **SELECTED PUBLICATIONS** Auth, The Writings of Celia parker Woolley (1848-1918), Literary Activist, Lewiston: Edwin Mellen Press, 98; John Winthrop, Boston: Twayne Pub, 90 **CONTACT ADDRESS** Dept of English, Univ of No Carolina, Wilmington, Wilmington, NC 28403. **EMAIL** schweningerl@uncwil.edu

SCHWOCH, JAMES J.
PERSONAL Born 05/08/1955, Milwaukee, WI **DISCIPLINE** INTENATIONAL AND COMMUNICATION STUDIES **EDUCATION** Univ Wis, BA, 76; Northwestern Univ, MA, 80, PhD, 85. **CAREER** Instr, 82-83, vis asst prof to assoc prof, 89-, Northwestern Univ; asst prof, Marquette Univ, 86-89. **HONORS AND AWARDS** NEH Grants, 86, 87; Ford found Grant, 96-99; Fulbright Scholar, 97; Libr of Am Broadcasting Acad Advisory Board, 97; Leonard Marks Fel, 97-98; Ameritech Found Grant, 99. **RESEARCH** Media history and American Foreign policy, telecommunications policy, international studies, research methodologies. **SELECTED PUBLICATIONS** Auth, The American Radio Industry and Its Latin American Activities, 1900-1939, Univ of IL Pr, (Urbana), 90; coauth, Media Knowledge: Readings in Popular Culture, Pedagogy, and Critical Citizenship, SUNY, (Albany), 92; auth, "Race, Television, and the Prime Time News Program", Common culture: Reading and Writing about American Popular Culture, eds Michael F. Petracca and Madeline Sorapure, Prentice-Hall, (NY), 95; auth, "Television, Chechnya, and the National Identity After the Cold War: Whose Imagined Community?", Writing Media Histories: Nordic Views, Eds Raimo Salokangas, James Schwoch, and Kalle Virtapohja, Univ of Jyvaskyla Pr, (97): 69-107; coed, Writing Media Histories: Nordic Views, Univ of Jyvaskyla Pr, 97; auth, "Satellites, Rocketry, Security, and Space Policy: A Comparative History", Hist J of Film, Radio and Television 18.2 (98): 295-299; auth, "Origins, Paradigms, and Topographies: Methodological Considerations Regarding Area Studies and Broadcast Histories", Am Journalism 99; coed, Cultural Studies and the Questions of Methodology, Blackwell (forthcoming); auth, "auth, "Adieu to Static (History): Telecommunications Policy, the Global Dialogue, and the Paradigmatic Shift to Complexity", Convergences (forthcoming). **CONTACT ADDRESS** Dept Commun Studies, Northwestern Univ, 1815 Chicago Ave, Evanston, IL 60208-0865. **EMAIL** j-schwoch@northwestern.edu

SCOBIE, STEPHEN A. C.
PERSONAL Born 12/31/1943, Carnoustie, Scotland **DISCIPLINE** ENGLISH **EDUCATION** Univ St Andrews, MA, 65; Univ BC, PhD, 69. **CAREER** Fac mem, 69-81, prof, Eng, Univ Alta, 80-81; prof Eng, Univ Victoria, 81-; guest prof, Christian-Albrechts-Univ, Ger, 90. **HONORS AND AWARDS** Gov Gen Awd Poetry, 80; fel, Royal Soc Can, 95. **MEMBERSHIPS** League Can Poets (vice pres, 72-74, 86-88); Victoria Lit Arts Festival Soc, 92-96. **RESEARCH** Canadian literature. **SELECTED PUBLICATIONS** Auth, Leonrad Cohen, 78; auth, Nichol: What History Teaches, 84; auth, Signature Event Cantext, 89; coauth, The Pirates of Pen's Chance, 81; co-ed, The Maple Laugh Forever: An Anthology of Canadian Comic Poetry, 81; auth, Alias Bob Dylan, 91; auth, Ghosts: A Glossary of the Intertext, Wolsak and Wynn, 90; auth, Gospel, Red Deer Col Press, 94; auth, Taking the Gate: a journey through Scotland, Red Deer Col Press, 96; auth, Earthquakes and Explorations: Language and Painting from Cubism to Concrete Poetry, 97; auth, And Forget My Name, Ekstasis, 99. **CONTACT ADDRESS** English Dept, Univ of Victoria, Victoria, BC, Canada V8W 3W1. **EMAIL** sscobie@uvic.ca

SCOTT, BONNIE KIME
PERSONAL Born 12/28/1944, Philadelphia, PA, m, 1967, 3 children **DISCIPLINE** ENGLISH, WOMEN'S STUDIES **EDUCATION** Wellesley Col, BA, 67; Univ NC, Chapel Hill, MA, 69, PhD(Eng), 73. **CAREER** Asst prof, 75-80, assoc, 80-86, prof Eng, Univ DE, 86-; dir grad stud in Eng; Fac res grants

Eng, Univ DE, 76, 81, 87, 95, 00. **HONORS AND AWARDS** DE Outstanding young woman, Outstanding Young Women Am, 77. **MEMBERSHIPS** MLA; Am Conf Irish Studies; James Joyce Found; VA Wolf Soc; Soc for the Study of Narrative Lit. **RESEARCH** Women's studies; modernism; James Joyce; Irish lit. **SELECTED PUBLICATIONS** Auth, Joyce and Feminism. Indiana, 84; auth, James Joyce, Humanities, 87; ed and contribur, New Alliances in Joyce Studies: "Whan it's Aped to Foul a Delfian," Delaware, 88; ed and contribur, The Gender of Modernism, Indiana, 90; auth, Refiguring Modernism, 2v, Indiana, 95; co-ed, Images of Joyce: Papers of the 12th International James Joyce Symposium, 2v, Colin Smyth, 98; ed and contribur, The Selected Letters of Rebecca West, Yale, 00. **CONTACT ADDRESS** Dept of English, Univ of Delaware, Newark, DE 19716. **EMAIL** bscott@udel.edu

SCOTT, JAMES F.

DISCIPLINE VICTORIAN LITERATURE **EDUCATION** Univ KS, PhD. **CAREER** Dorothy McBridge Orthwein Prof of English Lit, St. Louis Univ **SELECTED PUBLICATIONS** Auth, Film: the Medium and the Maker, Holt, Rinehard, and Winston, 75; auth, "New Terms for Order: Network Style and Individual Experiment in American Documentary Film," in Ideas of Order in Literature and Film, (Tallahassie: Florida State Univ Press, 81), 59-72; videos: Doing Business in Hungary, 91; Worlds of Bright Glass: The Ravenna Mosaics Company, 92; Inland Voyages: The Poetry of John Knoepfle, 95; Articulate Space: the Architectural Heritage of St. Louis, 98; auth, "Cleansing the Valleys: Joh Knoepfle's Vision of the American Heartland," ATE: Illinois English Bulletin 84 (97): 36-42 **CONTACT ADDRESS** English Dept, Saint Louis Univ, 221 N Grand Blvd, Saint Louis, MO 63103.

SCOTT, JAMES FRAZIER

PERSONAL Born 07/09/1934, Atchison, KS, m, 1961, 2 children **DISCIPLINE** ENGLISH, CINEMA, TELEVISION **EDUCATION** Rockhurst Col, BS, 55; Univ Kans, MA, 57; PhD, 60. **CAREER** Instr English, Univ Ky, 60-62; from asst prof to assoc prof, 62-72, prof English, St Louis Univ, 72-. **MEMBERSHIPS** MLA. **RESEARCH** Nineteenth century fiction; the aesthetics of cinema. **SELECTED PUBLICATIONS** Auth, Film: The Medium and the Maker, Holt, 75; auth, "New Terms for Order: Network Style and Individual Experiment in American Documentary Film," in Ideas of Order in Literature and Film (Tallahassie, Florida State Univ, 81), 59-72; producer, director, Inland Voyages: The Poetry of John Knoepfle, 95; auth, "Cleansing the Valleys: John Knoepfle's Vision of the American Heartland," IATE: Illinois English Bulletin 84 (97): 36-42; producer, director, Articulate Space: the Architectural Heritage of St. Louis, 98. **CONTACT ADDRESS** Dept of English, Saint Louis Univ, 221 N Grand Blvd, Saint Louis, MO 63103. **EMAIL** scotJF@slu.edu

SCOTT, MARY JANE W.

PERSONAL Born 05/18/1949, Washington, DC, m, 1973, 2 children **DISCIPLINE** SCOTTISH & ENGLISH LITERATURE **EDUCATION** Emory Univ, BA, 71; Univ Edinburgh, 72, PhD, 79; Midlands Tech Col, criminal just, 98. **CAREER** Tutor Scottish lit, 75-76, Univ Edinburgh; instr Eng, 78, Col Gen Studies, Univ SC; asst prof, 79-80, res & writing, 81-, reader & consult, Studies Scottish Lit, 76- Columbia Col; adj instr, writing tutor, 85-90, 95-98, Midlands Tech Col; campus min, 90-91, St Thomas More Ctr, Univ SC; hum svcs, 92-95, Central SC Habitat for Hum; victim advoc, 98-, Forest Acres, SC Police Dept. **MEMBERSHIPS** Assn Scottish Lit Studies; Soc Antiquaries (Scotland). **RESEARCH** The poetry of James Thomson 1700-1748; 18th-20th century Anglo-Scottish poetry; the poetry of Norman MacCaig. **SELECTED PUBLICATIONS** Art, Neoclassical MacCaig, Studies Scottish Lit, 1/73; art, Robert Ayton: Scottish metaphysical, Scottish Lit J, 75; The Identity of MisJohn: A Footnote to James Thomson, The Bibl, Vol 8, 76; art, Alexander Smith: Poet of Victorian Scotland, Studies Scottish Lit, Vol XIV, 76; art, Hugh Blair on Campus in America, Univ Edinburgh J, Vol XXIX, 80; auth, Scottish Language in the Poetry of James Thomson, Neuphilol Mitt, Vol LXXXII, No 4; coauth, The Manuscript of James Thomson's Scot's Elegy, Studies Scottish Lit, Vol XVII; auth, James Thomson, Anglo-Scot, Univ Georgia Press, 88; auth, James Thomson and the Anglo-Scots, Hist of Scottish Lit, Hook, 87. **CONTACT ADDRESS** 1703 Belmont Dr, Columbia, SC 29206.

SCOTT, PATRICK G.

PERSONAL Born 02/20/1945, Grimsby Lines, United Kingdom, m, 1973, 2 children **DISCIPLINE** ENGLISH LITERATURE **EDUCATION** Merton Col, BA, 66; MA, 70; Leicester Univ, MA, 69; Edinburgh Univ, PhD, 76. **CAREER** Lectr, Edinburgh Univ, 70-76; from assoc prof to prof, Univ SC, 76-; assoc Univ librn for special collections, Thomas Cooper Libr, 96-. **HONORS AND AWARDS** NEH Summer Res Grant, 91; Leat Awd, Am Libr Asn, 99. **RESEARCH** Victorian and Scottish Literature, History of the Book. **SELECTED PUBLICATIONS** Auth, Tennyson's Enoch Arden, 70; auth, Victorian Poetry 1830-1870, 71; ed, The Bothie, 76; ed, Culture and Education in Victorian England, 90. **CONTACT ADDRESS** Dept English, Univ of So Carolina, Columbia, Columbia, SC 29225. **EMAIL** scottp@gwm.sc.edu

SCOTT, PETER DALE

PERSONAL Born 01/11/1929, Montreal, PQ, Canada, m, 1956, 3 children **DISCIPLINE** ENGLISH, POLITICAL SCIENCE **EDUCATION** McGill Univ, BA, 49, PhD(polit sci), 55. **CAREER** Lectr polit sci, McGill Univ, 55-56; foreign serv off, Can Foreign Serv, 56-61; lectr speech, 61-62, acting asst prof, 62-63, asst prof, 63-66, asst prof, 66-68, assoc prof, 68-80, PROF ENGLISH, UNIV CALIF, BERKELEY, 80-, Humanities res fel, Univ Calif, Berkeley, 68; Guggenheim fel, 69-70. **RESEARCH** Covert Politics; medieval Latin poetry; literature and politics. **SELECTED PUBLICATIONS** Auth, Mcnamara And Vietnam - Reply/, New York Rev Of Books, Vol 0042, 1995. **CONTACT ADDRESS** 2823 Ashby Ave, Berkeley, CA 94705.

SCOTT, ROBERT LEE

PERSONAL Born 04/19/1928, Fairbury, NE, m, 1947, 3 children **DISCIPLINE** SPEECH **EDUCATION** Univ N Colo, BA, 50; Univ Nebr, MA, 51; Univ Ill, PhD, 55. **CAREER** Asst prof speech, Univ Houston, 53-57; from asst prof to assoc prof, 57-64, prof speech, Univ Minn, Minneapolis, 64-; ed, Quart J Speech, 72-74. **HONORS AND AWARDS** Winans Res Awd, Nat Commun Asn, 69; Woolbert Res Awd, NCA, 81; Distinguished Teaching Awd, Col of Lib Arts, Univ of Minn, 81; Ehninger Res Awd, NCA, 89; Distinguished Scholar of the Asn, NCA, 92. **MEMBERSHIPS** Speech Commun Asn; NCTE. **RESEARCH** Criticism of contemporary public address; contemporary rhetorical theory. **SELECTED PUBLICATIONS** Coauth, Thinking and Speaking: A Guide to Intelligent Oral Communication, Macmillan, 62, 68, 73 & 78; auth, On Viewing Rhetoric as Epistemic, Cent States Speech J, 2/67; coauth, The Rhetoric of Black Power, Harper, 69; Moments in the Rhetoric of the Cold War, Random, 72; auth, On not defining rhetoric, Philos & Rhet, spring 73; The Conservative Voice in Radical Rhetoric, Speech Monogr, 6/73. **CONTACT ADDRESS** Univ of Minnesota, Twin Cities, 224 Church St SE, 225 Ford Hall, Minneapolis, MN 55455. **EMAIL** Scott033@tc.umn.edu

SCOTT, WILLIAM CLYDE

PERSONAL Born 09/14/1937, Oklahoma City, OK, m, 1964, 3 children **DISCIPLINE** CLASSICS **EDUCATION** Princeton Univ, AB, 59, MA, 62, PhD(classics), 64. **CAREER** Instr classics, Phillips Acad, Andover, 59-60; asst prof, Haverford Col, 64-66; asst prof classics, 66-70, assoc prof classics & drama, 70-75, assoc dean fac, 70-72, chemn dept, 70-76, prof classics & drama, 75-, humanities res prof, 88-, Dartmouth prof of classics, Dartmouth Col, 94-, Dartmouth fac fel, 67-68; mem managing comt, Am Sch Class Studies Athens. **HONORS AND AWARDS** Goodwin Awd of Merit, Am Philol Asn, 86. **MEMBERSHIPS** Am Philol Asn; Am Inst Archaeol. **RESEARCH** Greek epic; Greek drama; Roman lyric. **SELECTED PUBLICATIONS** Auth, The confused chorus (Agamemnon 975-1034), Phoenix, 69; Catullus and Caesar (c 29), Class Philol, 71; A repeated episode at Odyssey 1 125-48, TAPha, 71; The Oral Nature of the Homeric Simile, Leiden, 74; Lines for Clytemnestra (Ag 489-502), 78 & Non-Strophic Elements in the Oresteia, 82, TAPhA; Musical Design in Aeschylean Theater, 84; Plato's The Republic, 85; Musical Design in Sophoclean Theater, 96. **CONTACT ADDRESS** Dept of Classics, Dartmouth Col, 6086 Reed Hall, Hanover, NH 03755-3506. **EMAIL** william.c.scott@dartmouth.edu

SCOTT, WILLIAM O.

PERSONAL Born 02/19/1932, Berlin Township, MI, d, 2 children **DISCIPLINE** ENGLISH **EDUCATION** Univ Chicago, BA, 52; Univ Mich, BA, 54; Duke Univ, MA, 55; Princeton Univ, PHD, 59. **CAREER** Instr, 58-61, asst prof, 61-65, assoc prof, 65-79, PROF, ENG, UNIV KANS, 79-. **MEMBERSHIPS** Shakespeare Assoc Am., Am. Assoc Univ Prof. **RESEARCH** Shakespeare; law and literature; economics and literature; philosophy and literature. **SELECTED PUBLICATIONS** auth, Landholding, Leasing, and Inheritance in Richard II. Forthcoming 02 in Studies Eng Lit; Reading History, Reading Power, Reading Plays: Graham Holderness on Shakespeare's History Plays, in Contextualizing the Renaissance, ed. Triconic, 99; auth, The Liar Paradox or Self-Modeary: Hamlet's Postmodern Cogito, in Mosaic, 90. **CONTACT ADDRESS** English Dept, Univ of Kansas, Lawrence, Wescoe Hall, Lawrence, KS 66045-2115. **EMAIL** wscott@ukans.edu

SCRIVENER, MICHAEL HENRY

PERSONAL Born 10/30/1948, Washington, DC, m, 1976, 2 children **DISCIPLINE** ENGLISH **EDUCATION** State Univ NYork, Binghamton, MA, 72; State Univ NYork, Buffalo, PhD, 76. **CAREER** Prof eng, Wayne State Univ, 76. **MEMBERSHIPS** MLA; AAUP. **RESEARCH** Romantic poetry; 19th century Brit lit; sociological criticism. **SELECTED PUBLICATIONS** Auth, Radical Shelley, Princeton, 82; Poetry and Reform, Wayne State, 92. **CONTACT ADDRESS** Dept of Eng, Wayne State Univ, 51 West Warren, Detroit, MI 48202-1308. **EMAIL** aa1973@wayne.edu

SCULLION, SCOTT

DISCIPLINE CLASSICS **EDUCATION** Univ Toronto, BA, 82; Harvard Univ, PhD, 90. **MEMBERSHIPS** Am Philol Asn. **RESEARCH** Greek religion; Greek literature, especially drama. **SELECTED PUBLICATIONS** Auth, Three Studies in Athenian Dramaturgy, Teubner, 94; auth, Olympian and Chthonian, Class Antiquity, 94; auth, Dionysos and Katharsis in Antigone, Class Antiquity, forthcoming; auth, Three Notes on Attic Sacrificial Calendars, Zeitschrift fur Papyrologie und Epigraphik, forthcoming; auth, Saviours of the Father's Hearth: Olympian and Chthonian in the Oresteia, in Hagg, ed, Greek Sacrificial Ritual, Olympian and Chthonian, Stockholm, Paul Astroms Forlag, forthcoming. **CONTACT ADDRESS** Dept of Classics, Union Col, New York, Schenectady, NY 12308.

SCULLY, STEPHEN P.

PERSONAL Born 06/04/1947, m, 3 children **DISCIPLINE** CLASSICAL STUDIES **EDUCATION** NYork Univ, BA, 71; U NC Chapel Hill, MA, 75; Brown Univ, PhD, 78. **CAREER** Mellen Fellow, 78-80, John Hopkins Univ; Assoc Prof, 80-, Boston Univ. **HONORS AND AWARDS** NEH Summer Stipend; Jasper Whiting Fellowship; Honor and the Sacred City; Best Acad Books, Choice. **MEMBERSHIPS** Amer Philos Assoc; New England Class Assoc. **RESEARCH** Epic; Tragedy; Near Eastern Lit; Renaissance Stud. **SELECTED PUBLICATIONS** Coauth, Arion, 3rd Series, 3.1 and 4.1, Special Issue, The Chorus in Greek Tragedy and Culture, 96 & 96; auth, Homer and The Sacred City, Ithaca, NY, Cornell Univ, 90; coauth, Euripides Suppliant Women, Oxford, Oxford Univ Press, 95. **CONTACT ADDRESS** Dept Classics, Boston Univ, 745 Commonwealth Ave, Boston, MA 02215. **EMAIL** sscully@bu.edu

SEABURY, MARCIA

DISCIPLINE ENGLISH LITERATURE, COMPOSITION, INTERDISCIPLINARY STUDIES **EDUCATION** Wooster Col, BA; Univ Ill, AM; PhD. **CAREER** Assoc prof, Univ of Hartford. **SELECTED PUBLICATIONS** Ed, Interdisciplinary General Education: Questioning Outside the Lines, College Board, 99. **CONTACT ADDRESS** English Dept, Univ of Hartford, 200 Bloomfield Ave, West Hartford, CT 06117. **EMAIL** seabury@mail.hartford.edu

SEADLE, MICHAEL S.

DISCIPLINE HISTORY; LIBRARY SCIENCE **EDUCATION** Earlham Col, BA, 72; Univ Mich, MS, 97; Univ Chicago, MA, 73, PhD, 77. **CAREER** Asst dir, Acad Computing Svcs, E Mich Univ, 87-89; online oper mgr, asst dir, Libr Tech Dept, Cornell Univ, 89-92; pres, Seadle Consult, 92-96; digital info assoc, Univ Mich, 96-97; DIGITAL SVCS LIBRN, MICH STATE UNIV, 98-. **SELECTED PUBLICATIONS** Ed, Library Hi Tech, 97-. **CONTACT ADDRESS** Michigan State Univ, 100 Library, East Lansing, MI 48224-1048. **EMAIL** seadle@mail.lib.msu.edu

SEAMAN, JOHN

DISCIPLINE ENGLISH LITERATURE **EDUCATION** Princeton Univ, BA, 54; Stanford Univ, MA, 59, PhD, 62. **CAREER** Prof, Univ Pacific. **HONORS AND AWARDS** Lit Awd Jury. **SELECTED PUBLICATIONS** Auth, The Moral Paradox of Paradise Lost, Mouton, 71; pubs on Shakespeare, Milton, and lang and style. **CONTACT ADDRESS** Eng Dept, Univ of the Pacific, Stockton, Pacific Ave, PO Box 3601, Stockton, CA 95211.

SEARL, STANFORD J.

DISCIPLINE ENGLISH LITERATURE **EDUCATION** Syracuse Univ, BA; PhD; State Univ NYork Buffalo, MA. **CAREER** Prof. **SELECTED PUBLICATIONS** Auth, Portraits in Black and White: Photographic Essay about Mental Retardation Institutions, 85; Education Reporter, 83; co-auth, The Disabled in America, 87; Achieving the Complete School, 85. **CONTACT ADDRESS** English Dept, Union Inst, 440 E McMillan St, Cincinnati, OH 45206-1925.

SEARLES, GEORGE J.

PERSONAL Born 11/10/1944, Bayonne, NJ **DISCIPLINE** PROFESSIONAL WRITING **EDUCATION** Marist Col, BA, 68; SUNY New Paltz, MA, 71; Binghamton Univ, PhD, 79. **CAREER** Adj instr, 76, NY Inst of Tech; adj instr, Utica Col, 80-81, Syracuse Univ; adj instr, 91-92, SUNY Inst of Technology; adj grad faculty, 91-92, New Sch for Soc Res; prof, 76-, Mohawk Valley Commun Col. **HONORS AND AWARDS** St Univ NY Chancellor's Medal for Excellence in Teaching, 85; Mohawk Valley Commun Col Awd for Excellence in Svc, 85; keynote address, SUNY Librns, Assoc Convention, 91; listed in poets & writers, inc's dir of amer poets & fiction writers; selected for inclusion in ny coun for the humanities speakers prog, 90-92; chosen poet to read at 83 ne modern lang assoc conv. **MEMBERSHIPS** MLA; NE Modern Lang Assoc; Classical Assoc of Empire St; NCTE. **RESEARCH** Contemporary poetry & fiction; popular culture; tech writing. **SELECTED PUBLICATIONS** Ed, A Casebook on Ken Kesey's One Flew Over the Cuckoo's Nest, Univ NM Press, 92; auth, Conversations With Philip Roth, Univ Press Miss, 92; auth, Workplace Communications: The Basics, Allyn & Bacon, 99; auth, "Fictionof Philip roth and John Updike," So. Illinois Univ Press, 95. **CONTACT ADDRESS** Humanities Dept, Mohawk Valley Comm Col, 1101 Sherman Dr, Utica, NY 13501.

SEARS, PRISCILLA F.
DISCIPLINE ENGLISH LITERATURE **EDUCATION** Tufts Univ, PhD, 75. **CAREER** Sr Lctr Eng and Women's Studies. **RESEARCH** Lit, compos, women's studies. **SELECTED PUBLICATIONS** 'Suspended in Language:' Revisioning Knowledge and the Cirruculum; Feminist Perspectives, Mich State Univ, 90; auth, All Purpose Valentine, Am Stage Festival, 92; Sasquatch, Plymouth Rec, 91; auth, Cradling Your Mother, Mothers and Daughters, York Univ Press, 97; auth, Women and Peace, Sanski Most, 98; auth, Choose Life, Kazarac, 99; auth, The Phoenix, Sanski Most, 00; auth, Deep Democracy, Konjic, 00; auth, What is Difficult Can Be Done at Once, Politics in the Women's Movement. **CONTACT ADDRESS** Dept of English, Dartmouth Col, 6032 Sanborn House, Hanover, NH 03755. **EMAIL** Priscilla.F.Sears@dartmouth.edu

SEATON, DOUGLASS
PERSONAL Born 06/08/1950, Baltimore, MD, m, 1972 **DISCIPLINE** HISTORICAL MUSICOLOGY **EDUCATION** Columbia Univ, PhD, 77. **CAREER** Fla State Univ, 78- . **MEMBERSHIPS** Am Musicol Soc; The Col Mus Soc; 19th Cent Stud Asn; Lyrica Soc Word-Music Rel. **RESEARCH** Felix Mendelssohn Bartholdy, song, criticism. **SELECTED PUBLICATIONS** The Art Song: A Research and Information Guide, 87; Ideas and Styles in the Western Musical Tradition, 91. **CONTACT ADDRESS** School of Music, Florida State Univ, Tallahassee, FL 32306-1180. **EMAIL** seaton_d@cmr.fsu.edu

SEAVEY, WILLIAM
DISCIPLINE CLASSICS **EDUCATION** Univ NC, PhD, 93. **CAREER** Vis asst prof, E Carolina Univ, 94-00. **HONORS AND AWARDS** Outstanding hist prof, E Carolina Univ, 97. **MEMBERSHIPS** APA, CAMWS, Ploutarchos. **RESEARCH** Roman War law; Greek and Roman intellectual history. **CONTACT ADDRESS** Dept of History, East Carolina Univ, Brewster A-305, Greenville, NC 27858-4353. **EMAIL** seaveyw@mail.ecu.edu

SEBESTA, JUDITH LYNN
PERSONAL Born Chicago, IL **DISCIPLINE** CLASSICAL LANGUAGES AND LITERATURE, ANCIENT HISTORY, WOMEN IN ANTIQUITY **EDUCATION** Univ Chicago, AB, 68; Stanford Univ, PhD, 72. **CAREER** From instr to asst prof, 72-77, Assoc Prof Classics, Univ S Dak, 77-, Dir, Integrated Humanities Prof, Univ SDak, 81, Dir Classics, 81, Chair, Dept Hist, 97-. **HONORS AND AWARDS** Phi Beta Kappa, 67; Harrington Lectr, Col Arts & Sci, 94. **MEMBERSHIPS** Am Philol Asn; Class Asn Midwest & South; Am Classical League. **RESEARCH** The Roman army; provinces of the Roman empire; classical philology. **SELECTED PUBLICATIONS** Auth, Carl Orff Carmina Burana, Bolchazy-Carducci Publ, 84, 96; Mantles of the Gods and Catullus 64, Syllectu Classica 5, 93; coauth, The World of Roman Costume, Univ Wis Press, 94; auth, Women's Costume and Feminine Civic Morality in Augustan Rome, Gender & Hist 9, 97; Aliquid Sem per Novi: New Challenges & New Approaches, in Latin for the 21st Century, Addison-Wesley, 97. **CONTACT ADDRESS** Dept of Hist, Univ of So Dakota, Vermillion, 414 E Clark St, Vermillion, SD 57069-2390. **EMAIL** jsebesta@sunbird.usd.edu

SEBOUHIAN, GEORGE
PERSONAL Born 11/29/1931, New York, NY, m, 1965, 3 children **DISCIPLINE** LITERATURE **EDUCATION** OH State Univ, PhD, 73. **CAREER** Tchr Eng, Pub Schs, FL & OH, 60-65; instr, Miami Univ, 65-68; asst prof, 72-80, assoc prof eng, State Univ NY Col Fredonia, 80, prof, 87, Fulbright-Hays lectr, Poland, 76-77; japan, 92-93. **HONORS AND AWARDS** Woodrow Wilson fel, 59-60. **MEMBERSHIPS** MLA **RESEARCH** Am Puritans; Am transcendentalists; Ralph Waldo Emerson; jaoanese aestetics. **SELECTED PUBLICATIONS** Auth, Emerson's experience: An approach to content and method, Emerson Soc Quart, 67; The transcendental imagination to Merton Densher, Mod Lang Studies, 75; Thomas A Kempis and Emerson's first crisis, Am Transcendental Quart, 76; Henry James's transcendental imagination, Essays Lit, 76; The marginalia in James Pierrepont Greaves in Emerson's library, Papers Bibliog Soc Am, 78. **CONTACT ADDRESS** Dept of Eng, SUNY, Col at Fredonia, Fredonia, NY 14063-1143. **EMAIL** sebouhian@fredonia.edu

SECOR, ROBERT ARNOLD
PERSONAL Born 06/29/1938, Brooklyn, NY, m, 1965, 2 children **DISCIPLINE** ENGLISH & AMERICAN LITERATURE **EDUCATION** Syracuse Univ, BA, 60; Brown Univ, MA, 63, PhD(English), 69. **CAREER** Instr English, Northwestern Univ, 66-69; asst prof, 69-72, assoc prof English, Pa State Univ, 72-86; prof English, 86; dept head, 90-95; Vice Provost for Academic Affairs, 95-. **MEMBERSHIPS** MLA **RESEARCH** Nineteenth century English and American literature, especially Ruskin; the Pre-Raphaelites; Henry James. **SELECTED PUBLICATIONS** Auth, The Rhetoric of Shifting Perspectives: Conrad's Victory, Pa State Univ, 71; American Literature I (Colonial Period to 1890), Simon & Schuster, 71; Christopher Newman: How Innocent is James's American?, Studies Am Fiction, autumn 73; ed, Pennsylvania 1776, Pa State Univ, 75; coauth, Violet Hunt's Tales of the Uneasy, Women & Lit, spring 78; Pre-Raphaelites and Aesthetes: Oscar Wilde and the Sweetest Violet in England, Tex Studies Lit & Lang, fall 79; Robert Browning and the Hunts of South Kensington, Browning Institute Studies: An Annual in Victorian Literary and Cultural History, Vol 7, 79; John Ruskin and Alfred Hunt: New Letters and the Record of a Friendship, Univ of Victoria, 82. **CONTACT ADDRESS** Office of the President, Pennsylvania State Univ, Univ Park, 201 Old Main, University Park, PA 16802. **EMAIL** r52@psu.edu

SECREAST, DONALD
DISCIPLINE CREATIVE FICTION WRITING AND MODERN BRITISH LITERATURE **EDUCATION** Univ IA, PhD. **CAREER** Prof, Radford Univ. **SELECTED PUBLICATIONS** Auth, The Rat Becomes Light, 90; White Trash, Red Velvet, 93; coauth, Adventuring in the Andes, 85. **CONTACT ADDRESS** Radford Univ, Radford, VA 24142. **EMAIL** dsecreas@runet.edu

SEELIG, HARRY E.
PERSONAL Born 03/13/1937, New York, NY, m, 1967, 2 children **DISCIPLINE** GERMAN LITERATURE, MUSIC **EDUCATION** Oberlin Col, AB, 59, Conserv, BM, 61; Univ Kans, MA, 64, PhD(German), 69. **CAREER** Instr, Univ Kans, 66-67; instr, 67-69, asst prof, 69-80, assoc prof German, Univ Mass, 80-, vis lectr, Univ Kent, 78-79; res dir, UMass Baden-Wuerttemberg Exchange Prog, 85-86m 86-97. **HONORS AND AWARDS** NDEA Fell, 961-65; German Govt Grant, Dankstipendium, 63-64; Newberry Library Grant in Aid, 67; Pi Kappa Lambola; Delta Phi Alpha. **MEMBERSHIPS** MLA; Am Asn Teachers German. **RESEARCH** German literature since Goethe; poetry and music; translation of contemporary German poetry. **SELECTED PUBLICATIONS** Transl, Rolf Bongs, Insel-Ile-Island, Guido Hildebrandt Verlag Duisburg, WGermany, 73; Rolf Bongs, Aufstieg zum Kilimandscharo, The Literary Rev, 74; auth, Schuberts Beitrag zu besserem Verstadnis' von Goethes Suleika-Gestalt: Eine literarischmuskalische studie der Suleika-Lieder, Beitrage zur Musikwissenschaft, 75; transl, Rolf Bongs, Oberwelt, 76 & Ralph Glockler's, Ich Sehe Dichnoch und andere lyrik, 76, Dimension; The Literary Context: Goethe as Source and Catalyst, in: German Lieder of the Nineteenth Century, New York: Macmillan, G Schirmer Books, 96. **CONTACT ADDRESS** German Dept, Univ of Massachusetts, Amherst, Herter Hall, Amherst, MA 01003-0002. **EMAIL** seelig@german.umass.edu

SEELIG, SHARON CADMAN
PERSONAL Born 01/08/1941, Mountain Lake, MN, m, 1967, 2 children **DISCIPLINE** ENGLISH LITERATURE **EDUCATION** Carleton Col, BA, 62; Columbia Univ, MA, 64, PhD, 69. **CAREER** Instr English, Wellesley Col, 67-69; instr, Northfield Sch, 69-70; from lectr to assoc prof, Mt Holyoke Col, 70-80; from lectr to full prof, Smith Col, 80-; Regional assoc, Am Lit Manuscripts Census, 70-74. **HONORS AND AWARDS** Woodrow Wilson Fel, 62-63; Fulbright Fel, Freie Universität Berlin, 63-64; President's Fel, Columbia Univ, 64-65; Lizette Fisher Fel, Columbia Univ, 65-66; Newberry Library Junior Fel, 66-67; Picker Fel, Smith Col, 93-94, 94-95. **MEMBERSHIPS** MLA; AAUP **RESEARCH** Seventeenth-century English literature; Shakespeare. **SELECTED PUBLICATIONS** Auth, "The Origins of Ecstasy: Traherne's 'Select Meditations'," English Lit Renaissance 9 (79): 419-431; auth, The Shadow of Eternity: Belief and Structure in Herbert, Vaughan, and Traherne, Univ Ky Press (Lexington, KY), 81; auth, "Our General Mother: The Pattern for Mankind," Quart Rev 1 (81): 71-83; auth, "Sir Thomas Browne and Stanley Fish: A Case of Malpractice," Prose Studies 11 (88): 72-84; auth, "In Sickness and in Health: Donne's 'Devotions upon Emergent Occasions'," John Donne J 8 (89): 103-113; auth, "'My Curious Hand or Eye': The Wit of Richard Lovelace," in The Wit of Seventeenth-Century Poetry, ed. Claude J. Summers and Ted-Larry Pebworth (Columbia: Univ of Mo Press, 95), 151-170; auth, "Loyal Fathers and Treacherous Sons: Familial Politics in 'Richard II'," J of English and Germanic Philol 94 (95): 347-364. **CONTACT ADDRESS** Dept of English, Smith Col, Northampton, MA 01063. **EMAIL** sseelig@smith.edu

SEERY, CAROL H.
PERSONAL Born 12/24/1958, Champaign, IL, m, 1999 **DISCIPLINE** SPEECH-LANGUAGE PATHOLOGY **EDUCATION** Univ Ill, BS, 81; MS, 82; Univ Wash, Seattle, 92. **CAREER** Unit speech clinician, Farmer City-Mansfield Pub Sch, 82-84; speech-language pathologist, Burnham Hosp, 84-86; teaching assoc/res asst, Univ Wash, Seattle, 86-92; res assoc, Univ Ill, 93; Asst Prof, Univ Wis-Milwaukee, 93-99, assoc prof, Univ Wis-Milw, 99- . **RESEARCH** Fluency; stuttering; psycholinguistics. **SELECTED PUBLICATIONS** auth with D. Prins, Syllabic Stress and the Occurrence of Stuttering, Jour of Speech and Hearing Res, 91; with D. Prins, Constancy of Interstress Intervals in the Fluent Speech of People Who Stutter During Adaptation Trials, Jour of Speech and Hearing Res, 92; with D. Prins, Word Familiarity, Syllabic Stress Pattern, and Stuttering. Jour of Speech and Hearing Res, 94; Reliability of Judgments of Stuttering and Disfluency in Young Children's Speech. Jour of Commun Disorders, 98; Stuttering, Stressed Syllables, and Word Onsets. Jour of Speech, Language, and Hearing Res, 98. **CONTACT ADDRESS** Dept Comm Sci and Disorders, Univ of Wisconsin, Milwaukee, PO Box 413, Milwaukee, WI 53201. **EMAIL** cseery@sahp.uwm.edu

SEGAL, CHARLES P.
PERSONAL Born 03/19/1936, Boston, MA, m, 1988, 3 children **DISCIPLINE** CLASSICS **EDUCATION** Harvard Col, AB, 57; Harvard Univ, PhD, 61. **CAREER** Teaching Fel to Instructor, Harvard Univ, 59-64; Asst Prof to Assoc Prof, Univ Pa, 64-67; Assoc Prof to Prof, Brown Univ, 68-86; Prof, Princeton Univ, 87-90; Prof, Harvard Univ, 90-. **HONORS AND AWARDS** Detur Prize, Harvard Col, 54-55; Bowdoin Prize, Harvard Col, 55-57; Richardson Prize, Harvard, 57; Fulbright Fel, Athens, 57-58; Fel, Guggenheim, 81-82; Fel, NEH, 85-86; Fel, Ctr for Adv Study in the Beh Sci, 89-90; Fel, Am Acad of Arts and Sci, 92-. **MEMBERSHIPS** Am Philol Asn; classical Asn of N Eng; Virgilian Soc; Alumni Asn of the Am Sch of Classical Studies in Athens; Alumni Asn of Am Acad in Rome; Women's Classical Caucus. **SELECTED PUBLICATIONS** Auth, Lucretius on Death and Anxiety: Poetry and Philosophy in De Rerum Natura, Princeton Univ Press, 90; auth, Singers, Heroes, and Gods in the Odyssey, Cornell Univ Press, 94; auth, Sophocles' Tragic World: Divinity, Nature, and Society, Harvard Univ Press, 95; auth, Aglaia: The Poetry of Alcman, Sappho, Pindar, Bacchylides, and Corinna, Rowman and Littlefield, 98; auth, Sophocles' Oedipus Tyrannus: Tragic Heroism and the Limits of Knowledge, Oxford Univ Press, 00; auth, Euripides' Bakkhai, Oxford Univ Press, 00. **CONTACT ADDRESS** Dept Classics, Harvard Univ, 319 Boylston Hall, Cambridge, MA 02138. **EMAIL** cpsegal@fas.harvard.edu

SEIDEL, MICHAEL ALAN
PERSONAL Born 08/24/1943, New York, NY, 4 children **DISCIPLINE** ENGLISH LITERATURE **EDUCATION** Univ Calif, Los Angeles, BA, 66, PhD(English), 70. **CAREER** From asst prof to assoc prof English, Yale Univ, 70-77; assoc prof, 77-80, prof English, Columbia Univ, 80-, Siegal Prof of Humanities, 00. **HONORS AND AWARDS** NEH Fel, 74-75. **MEMBERSHIPS** MLA; Am Soc 18th Century Studies. **RESEARCH** Satire; 17th and 18th century English literature and 18th century narrative; James Joyce Baseball history. **SELECTED PUBLICATIONS** Auth, Epic Geography: James Joyce's Ulysses, Princeton Univ, 76; Homer to Brecht, Yale Univ, 77; Satiric Plots of Gravity's Rainbow, In: Twentieth-Century Views, Englewood Cliffs, 77; Satiric Inheritance, Rabelais to Sterne, Princeton Univ, 79; Crusoe's Exile, Publ Mod Lang Asn Am, 81; Exile and the Narrative Imagination, 86; Streak: Joe DiMaggio and the Summer of 1941, Ted Williams: A Baseball Life, 90; Robinson Crusoe: Island Myths and the Novel, 90; The Works of Daniel Defoe, 98. **CONTACT ADDRESS** Dept of English, Columbia Univ, 2960 Broadway, New York, NY 10027-6900. **EMAIL** mas8@columbia.edu

SEIDEN, MORTON IRVING
PERSONAL Born 07/29/1921, New York, NY **DISCIPLINE** ENGLISH, COMPARATIVE LITERATURE **EDUCATION** NYork Univ, BS, 43; Columbia Univ, MA, 44, PhD, 52. **CAREER** Instr English, City Col New York, 45-46, NY Univ, 46-49, Smith Col, 49-52 & Queens Col, NY, 52-53; from instr to assoc prof, 53-70, Prof English, Brooklyn Col, 70-; Lectr, Columbia Univ Grad Sch, 48-49. **HONORS AND AWARDS** Brooklyn Col Excellence in Teaching Awd, 67. **MEMBERSHIPS** MLA; Mod Humanities Res Asn; English Inst. **RESEARCH** Nineteenth and Twentieth Century English literature; English, Irish Renaissance; Comparative Literature. **SELECTED PUBLICATIONS** Auth, A psychoanalytical essay on William Butler Yeats, Accent, spring 46; Myth in the Poetry of William Butler Yeats, Am Imago, 12/48; W B Yeats as a playwright, Western Humanities Rev, winter 49; William Butler Yeats: The Poet as a Mythmaker-- 1865-19339, Mich State Univ, 62; The Paradox of Hate: A Study in Ritual Murder, Yoseloff, 68; coauth, Ivan Goncharov's Oblomov: A study of the anti-Faust as a Christian saint, Can Slavic Studies, spring 69. **CONTACT ADDRESS** Dept of English, Brooklyn Col, CUNY, 2901 Bedford Ave, Brooklyn, NY 11210-2813.

SEIDMAN, STEVEN A.
DISCIPLINE COMMUNICATION STUDIES **EDUCATION** Univ Ind, PhD. **CAREER** Assoc prof. **SELECTED PUBLICATIONS** Auth, pubs on sex-role stereotyping, burnout in the workplace, media utilization, music soundtracks, and instructional development. **CONTACT ADDRESS** Dept of Communication, Ithaca Col, 100 Job Hall, Ithaca, NY 14850.

SEIGNEURIE, KENNETH E.
PERSONAL Born 09/03/1958, Yale, MI, m **DISCIPLINE** ENGLISH **EDUCATION** Mich State Univ, BS, 82; BA, 82; Univ Mich Ann Arbor, MA, 91; PhD, 95. **CAREER** Asst prof, Univ of Balamand, Lebanon, 96-99; asst prof, Lebanese Am Univ, Lebanon, 99-. **MEMBERSHIPS** MLA, Am Comp Lit Assoc, Middle East Studies Assoc, Soc for the Study of Narrative Lit, Lawrence Durrell, Soc. **RESEARCH** 20th Century British Literature, Contemporary Arabic Novel, Narrative Theory, Marxist Approaches to Culture. **CONTACT ADDRESS** Lebanese Am Univ, PO Box 13-5053, Chouran, Beirut, Lebanon 1102-2801. **EMAIL** kseigneurie@lau.edu.lb

SEILER, WILLIAM JOHN
PERSONAL Born 10/17/1942, Milwaukee, WI, m, 1966, 2 children **DISCIPLINE** SPEECH COMMUNICATION **EDUCATION** Univ Wis, Whitewater, BEd, 65; Kans State Univ,

MA, 67; Purdue Univ, West Lafayette, PhD(speech), 71. **CAREER** Asst prof speech, Purdue Univ, Calumet Campus, 70-72; assoc prof speech commun, Univ Nebr, Lincoln, 75-83, prof, 84-, dept chmn, 90-, dir undergrad studies, 82-86, Courtesy Appt-Teachers College 3/10/80. **HONORS AND AWARDS** Outstanding Young Alumni, Univ of Wisc-Whitewater, 74; Outstanding Young Col Teacher, Nebr Speech Commun Asn, 75; Outstanding Educators of America, 76; International Who's Who in Education, 77; Distinguished Alumni Awd, Univ of Wisc-Whitewater, 89; UNL Parent's Recognition Awd, 90. **MEMBERSHIPS** Am Educ Res Asn; Nat Commun Asn; Int Commun Asn; Cent States Commun Asn. **RESEARCH** Classroom communication; organizational communication; communication apprehension. **SELECTED PUBLICATIONS** Auth, Audiovisual Materials in Classroom Instruction: A Theoretical Approach, 72 & coauth, Performance-Based Teacher Education Program in Speech and Drama, 75, Speech Teacher; The Effects of Talking Apprehension on Student Academic Achievement: Three Empirical Investigations in Communication-Restricted and Traditional Laboratory Classes in the Life Sciences, Int Commun Yearbk I, 77; Communication Apprehension and Teaching Assistants, J Chem Educ, 78; Effects of Communication Apprehension on Student Learning in College Science Classes, J Col Sci Teaching, 78; Learners Cognitive Style and Levels of Learning in TV & Print Instruction for Use in Open Learning: An Exploratory Study, Int & Nat J Instr Media, 81; Communications in Business & Professional Organizations, Addison-Wesley, 82; auth, PSI: An Attractive Alternative for the Basic Speech Communication Course, Commun Educ, Jan 83; Developing the Personalized System of Instruction for the Basic Speech Communication Course, with Marilyn Fuss-Reincki, Commm Ed, April 86; The Temporal Organization of Classrooms as an Interactional Accomplishment, with Drew McGukin, Journal of Thought, winter 87; The Comparative Effectiveness of Systematic Desensitation and Visualization Therapy Treatments in Treating Public Speaking Anxiety, with Ana Rossi, Imagination, Cognition, and Personality, 89; What We Know About the Basic Course: What has the Research Told Us?, with Drew McGukin, Basic Course Annual, 89; An Investigation Into the Communication Needs and Concerns of asian Students in Speech Performance Classes, with Ester Yook, Basic Course Annual, 90; The Nebraska Department of Communication Story: There are Happy Endings that Go Beyond Football and a Good Crop Year. JACA, 95; Learning Style Preferences and Academic Achievement within the Basic Communication Course, with Chuck Lubbers, Basic Course Annual, 98; and many publications, textbooks, and other materials. **CONTACT ADDRESS** Dept of Commun Studies, Univ of Nebraska, Lincoln, PO Box 880329, Lincoln, NE 68588-0329. **EMAIL** bseiler@unl.edu

SEITZ, JAMES E.
PERSONAL Born 09/20/1958, Oahu, HI, m, 1991, 1 child **DISCIPLINE** ENGLISH **EDUCATION** Univ Calif, Santa Barbara, BA, 80; Univ N Mex, MA, 85; NYork Univ, PhD, 90. **CAREER** Asst prof, 88-92, dir of writing, 91-92, Long Island Univ; asst prof, 92-, Univ Pittsburgh **RESEARCH** Writing, rhetoric, metaphor, tchng, curriculum reform. **CONTACT ADDRESS** Dept of English, Univ of Pittsburgh, Pittsburgh, PA 15260.

SELF, CHARLES C.
PERSONAL m, 4 children **DISCIPLINE** JOURNALISM **EDUCATION** Andrews Univ, BA, 66; Univ Mo, MA, 71; Univ Iowa, PhD, 74. **CAREER** Prof, assoc dean Col of Lib Arts, Tex A&M Univ. **HONORS AND AWARDS** Phi Beta Delta Honor Soc for Int Scholars, 93; UA Dept Jour Outstanding Leadership Awd, 90; Omnichron Delta Kappa Leadership Hon, 87; Kappa Tau Alpha Commitment to Tchg Awd, 86. **RESEARCH** Alliances between practitioner organizations and journalism and mass communication schools and departments. **SELECTED PUBLICATIONS** Auth, News editing text: On Line Editing, Vision Press, 94. **CONTACT ADDRESS** Dept of Journalism, Texas A&M Univ, Col Station, 601 Blocker Bldg, College Station, TX 77843-4111. **EMAIL** c-self6@tamu.edu

SELF, ROBERT THOMAS
PERSONAL Born 03/01/1941, Portsmouth, VA, m, 1969, 1 child **DISCIPLINE** FILM STUDIES, AMERICAN LITERATURE **EDUCATION** FL State Univ, BA, 63; Univ Chicago, MA, 65; Univ NC, PhD, 70. **CAREER** Tchg asst Eng, Univ NC, 65-68; instr, Duke Univ, 68-69; asst prof, 69-77, assoc prof, Northern IL Univ, 78-86; prof, 86-. **HONORS AND AWARDS** Nat Sci Foundation: Summer Inst for Humanistic; NIU Dean's Fund Res Grants, 71, 72, 73; Excellence in Teaching Awd, 71, 72, 73; Nat Endowment for the Humanities: Summer Inst In Narrative Film, Univ of Wis, 78; NIU Graduate Sch Grant, 80; Film/Video Panel (Juror), Illinois Arts Council, 80-82; Committee for the Improvement of Undergraduate Educ Grant, 81, 84, 90; Macintosh Computer Laboratory: Grant form Apple Computer, 89; NIU Assessment Grant, Assessing Freshman English, 90, 91, 92, 93; Sr Fulbright Scholar, 93; United States Information Service Conference and Library Acquisitions Grant, 93; Illinois Humanities Coun Grant, 93-94; Sigma Tau Delta, Pi Delta Phi. **MEMBERSHIPS** MLA, Midwest Mod Lang Asn, Am Fedn Tchr(s), Modern Lang Asn; Am Federation of Teachers, Nat Coun of Teachers of English, Soc for Cinema Studies. **RESEARCH** Am lit hist; lit and film; film theory and criticism. **SELECTED PUBLICATIONS** Auth, Barrett Wendell, Twayne American Author Series, G.K. Hall & Co., 75; auth, Literature, Society and Politics: Selected Essays of Barret Wendell, edited with critical introduction, John Colet Archive of American Literature, John Colet Pr, 77; auth, "The Perfect Couple: 'Two are Halves of One' in the Films of Robert Altman," Wide Angle 5, 83; auth, "Film and Literature: Current Theory and Practice," Film Studies, 83; auth, "Robert Altamn and the Theory of Authorship," Cinema Journal, 85; auth, "Dialogue with Leland Pogue," Cinema Journal, 86; auth, "Film and Literature: Parameters of a Discipline," Literature/Film, 87; auth, "Author, Text, and Self in Robert Atltman's Buffalo Bill and the Indians,: in Ambiguity in Literature and Film, ed. Hans Braendlin, Univ Pr of Florida, 89; auth, "The Sound of MASH," in Close Viewings: Understanding Film, ed. Peter Lehman, Univ Pr of Florida, 90; auth, "Redressing the Law in Kathryn Bigelow's Blue Steel," Journal of Film and Video, 94. **CONTACT ADDRESS** Dept of Eng, No Illinois Univ, 1425 W Lincoln Hwy, De Kalb, IL 60115-2825. **EMAIL** rself@niu.edu

SELFE, RICHARD J.
PERSONAL Born 04/22/1951, Des Moines, IA, m **DISCIPLINE** RHETORIC AND TECHNICAL COMMUNICATION **EDUCATION** Mich Tech Univ, PhD, 1997 **CAREER** Mich Tech Univ, Tech Comm Spec, 75-87, ADJUNCT PROF RHETORIC & TECH COMMUN, 97-. **HONORS AND AWARDS** Ellen Nold Awd, Best Article in Comput and Compos Studies, 95. **MEMBERSHIPS** AAHE, NCTE **RESEARCH** Critical and tech literacy studies. **SELECTED PUBLICATIONS** Co-ed, Electronic Communnunication Across the Cirrculum, 98, NCTE; "What are we Doing to and for Ourselves?" in New Words, New Worlds: Exploring Pathways for Writing about and in Electronic Environments, J. Barber & D. Grigar, eds, forthcoming, MIT Press; Coauth, "Examining the Relevance of Technology Use in English Studies: Using Technology-Rich Communication Facilities as Sites of Teaching, Learning, Action, and Response" in The Relevance of English, R. P. Yagelski & S. A. Leonard, eds, forthcoming; Coauth "Traveling the Virtual Terrain: Practical Strategies for Survival in the Electronic Classroom," in The On-line Writing Classroom, R. Rickly, S. Harrington, & M. Day, eds, forthcoming, Hampton Press; Coauth, "Forces of Conservatism and Change in Computer- Supported Communication Facilities: Programmatic and Institutional Responses to Change," in Computers and Technical Communication: Pedagogical and Programmatic Perspectives, Stuart Selber, ed, 97, Ablex; Coauth, "Writing as Democratic Social Action in a Technological World: Politicizing and Inhabiting Virtual Landscapes," in Multidisciplinary Research in Nonacademic Writing, A. Duin and C. Hansen, eds, 96, Lawrence Erlbaum Asoc. **CONTACT ADDRESS** 1400 Townsend Dr, Houghton, MI 49930. **EMAIL** rselfe@mtu.edu

SELFRIDGE-FIELD, ELEANOR
DISCIPLINE MUSIC; JOURNALISM; MUSIC HISTORY **EDUCATION** Drew Univ, BA, 62; Columbia Univ, MS, 63; Oxford Univ, PhD, 69. **CAREER** Consulting prof, Stanford Univ, admin, Center for Computer Asst Research in the Hum; lectr, writer, tchr and music technologist. **HONORS AND AWARDS** Am Council of Learned Societies fel, 76-77; Gladys Krieble Delmas Found fel, 94, 83, 77; Aston Magna Found fel, 80-81; Am Academy in Rome, 98, 96. **MEMBERSHIPS** IMS, AMS,SMT, IEEE CS. **RESEARCH** Music, instrumental music and opera, Venetian culture form 1585 to 1825, theories of computer applications, reception hist of recording. **SELECTED PUBLICATIONS** Auth, Pallade Venta: Writings on Music in Venetian Society, 1650-1750, 85; auth, The Works of Benedetto an dAlesandro Marcello, 90; auth, Beyond MIDI: The Handbook of Musical Codes, 97; auth, Venetian Insturmental Music form Gabrieli to Vivaldi, 75, 80, 94; auth, Antonio Vivaldi, The Concertos Op. 8, 95. **CONTACT ADDRESS** Music Dept, Stanford Univ, Braun 129, Stanford, CA 94305-3076. **EMAIL** esf@ccrma.stanford.edu

SELIG, ROBERT L.
PERSONAL Born 06/24/1932, New York, NY **DISCIPLINE** ENGLISH **EDUCATION** Univ NC, BA, 54; Columbia Univ, MA, 58, PhD(English), 65. **CAREER** Instr English, Queens Col, NY, 61-67; asst prof, 67-71, assoc prof, 71-81, PROF ENGLISH, PURDUE UNIV, CALUMET, 81- **MEMBERSHIPS** MLA **SELECTED PUBLICATIONS** Auth, The Collected Letters Of Gissing,George, Vol 2, 1881-1885 - Mattheisen,Pf, Young,Ac, Coustillas,P, Eds/, Nineteenth Century Prose, Vol 0020, 1993; Vol 0022, 1995. **CONTACT ADDRESS** Dept of English, Purdue Univ, Calumet, 2233 171st St, Hammond, IN 46323-2094.

SELLERY, J'NAN MORSE
PERSONAL Born 01/03/1928, Oakland, CA, m, 1947, 4 children **DISCIPLINE** ENGLISH **EDUCATION** Univ Calif, BA, 65; MA, 67; PhD, 70. **CAREER** Asst Prof to Prof and Dept Chair, Harvey Mudd Col, 70-. **HONORS AND AWARDS** Res Grant, Walter Lantz Foundation, 99; Fulbright Sen Scholar, Calgary Inst for the Humanities, 98-99; ACLS Travel Grant, 96; Visiting Res Fel, Calgary Inst for the Humanities, 92; Calif Humanities Coun Grant, Claremont Col, 90; Mellon Curriculum Grant, 89; Res Grant, Harvey Mudd Col, 71-90; Sloan Foundation Curriculum Awd, 73-74; Shell Assist Fund, Harvey Mudd Col, 73; NDEA Fel, Univ Calif, 67-70. **MEMBERSHIPS** MLA, Soc Cinema Studies, ACSWS, Margaret Atwood Soc, Margaret Laurence Soc, AAUW, CYJung Inst, Virginia Wolf Soc, Am Film Studio Asn. **RESEARCH** Film Studies, Canadian Studies, 20th Century Literature, Women's Studies. **SELECTED PUBLICATIONS** Auth, Elizabeth Bowen: A Bibliography, Humanities Research Grant, 81; auth, The Scapegoat: Some literary Permutations, Houghton Mifflin, 72; auth, "Western Frontiers and Evolving Gender Identity in Aritha van Herk's the Tent Peg," Conference Proceedings: Defining the Prairies, 99; auth, "Decolonizing Gender and Racial Boundaries in Women's West African and Caribbean Film," West Virginia University Philological Papers, (99): 138-146; auth, "Women and the Doctor/Patient Relationship: Control, Promotion or Partnership," New Zealand Family Physician, (97): 33-38; auth, "Gender: Crossing Mental Barriers and Cultural Boundaries," Psychological Perspectives, 90; auth, "The necessity for symbol and Myth: A Literary amplification," Archetypal Process: Self and Divine in Whitehead, Jung, and Hillman, 89; auth, "Elizabeth Bowen," in Cyclopedia of World Authors II, Salem Press, 89; auth, "Women Writers: Breaking the Tics that Bind," Psychological Perspectives, 86; auth, "Women's Voices," Psychological Perspectives, 86. **CONTACT ADDRESS** Dept Humanities & Soc Sci, Harvey Mudd Col, 301 E 12th St, Claremont, CA 91711-5901. **EMAIL** jnan_sellery@hmc.edu

SELLIN, PAUL R.
PERSONAL Born 11/14/1930, Everett, WA, m, 1957, 3 children **DISCIPLINE** ENGLISH LITERATURE **EDUCATION** Washington State Univ, Pullman, BA, 52; Univ Chicago, MA, 55, PhD, 63. **CAREER** From instr to asst prof & asst to the Dean for Honors, Roosevelt Univ, 58-66; from asst to full prof, prof emeritus, Univ Calif, Los Angeles, 66- ; Prof Ordinarius English Lit after 1500, Free Univ of Amsterdam, Netherlands, 81-87; Eng Dept, Univ Stockholm, Sweden, 93-94. **HONORS AND AWARDS** Van Loon fel, Netherlands, 59-60; Roosevelt Univ fel, 63-64; Grants-in-aid, Am Philos Soc; NEH grants; ACLS grants; Adv Bd, Am Assoc for Netherlandic Study; vchemn, chemn, Netherlandic Study Prog, 76-93; chemn, Dept English, Free Univ of Amsterdam, 84-86; consulting ed with responsibility for the Netherlands forthcoming Oxford Companion to the Recaussance, Oxford University Press; adv bd, am asn for netherlandic stud; vchemn, chemn, netherlandic stud prog, 76-93; chemn, dept english, free univ of amsterdam, 84-86; consulting ed who responsibility for re neh awards, for oxford companion to me renaissance, oxford univ press . **MEMBERSHIPS** MLA; John Donne Soc of Am; Milton Soc of Am; Int Asn for Neo-Latin Stud; Am Asn for Netherlandic Stud; Am Asn of Neo-Latin Stud. **RESEARCH** Renaissance criticism; Donne; Milton; Neo-Latin criticism; Anglo-Dutch relations; Sixteenth and Seventeenth centuries; Swedish-Anglo-Dutch relations. **SELECTED PUBLICATIONS** Auth, Daniel Heinsius and Stuart England, Oxford, 68; auth, John Donne and Calvinist Views of Grace, Amsterdam, 83; auth, So Doth, So Is Religion: John Donne and Diplomatic Contexts in The Reformed Netherlands, 1619-1620, Columbia, 88; auth, John Milton's Paradise Lost and De doctrina christiana on Predestination, Milton Stud, 96; auth, The Reference to John Milton's Tetrachordon in De doctrina christiana, Stud in Eng Lit, 97; auth, Michel Le Blon and England, 1632-1649: With Observations on Van Dyck, Donne, and Vondel, Dutch Crossing, 98. **CONTACT ADDRESS** Dept of English, Univ of California, Los Angeles, Los Angeles, CA 90095-1980. **EMAIL** psellin@ucla.edu

SELMON, MICHAEL
DISCIPLINE RHETORIC, DRAMA AND BRITISH LITERATURE **EDUCATION** Univ Md, PhD. **CAREER** Assoc prof, Alma Col. **RESEARCH** The way literature and drama reflect broader cultural concerns. **SELECTED PUBLICATIONS** Published articles in Mod Drama, Ling and Old Northwest, exploring works by Eugene O'Neill, T. S. Eliot and Caryl Churchill, as well as broader topics like language theory and theatre history. **CONTACT ADDRESS** Alma Col, Alma, MI 48801.

SEMEIKS, JONNA GORMELY
DISCIPLINE MODERN BRITISH LITERATURE **EDUCATION** Rutgers, PhD. **CAREER** Assoc prof, Long Island Univ, C.W. Post Campus. **SELECTED PUBLICATIONS** Auth, Visions of Solitude: D. H, Lawrence's Sun, St. Mawr, and The Man Who Loved Islands; Writing in Response to Reading in the Freshman Composition Course; coauth, The Goblin Child: Folktale Symbolism in Popular Art; Leather-Stocking in 'Nam: Rambo, Platoon, and the American Frontier Myth; coed, Discoveries: Fifty Stories of the Quest and Patterns in Popular Culture. **CONTACT ADDRESS** Long Island Univ, C.W. Post, Brookville, NY 11548-1300.

SEMINARA, GLORIA
PERSONAL Born 12/12/1934, New York, NY, m, 1958, 3 children **DISCIPLINE** SPEECH LANGUAGE PATHOLOGY, SPEECH COMMUNICATION **EDUCATION** Brooklyn Col, BA, MA; Columbia Univ, MPhil, PhD. **CAREER** Assoc prof, past chair, division of Humanities, St. John's Col, St. John's Univ; private practice in SLP. **HONORS AND AWARDS** Summa Cum Laude; Phi Beta Kappa; Certificate of Scholastic Distinction; Recip of several St. John's Univ Merit

awds for productivity of research and publication, and of Univ research grants; Outstanding Fac Awd, St John's Univ. **RESEARCH** Aphasia and other communication disorders; higher education issues in SLP-A; oral communication. **CONTACT ADDRESS** St. John's Univ, 300 Howard Ave, Staten Island, NY 10301. **EMAIL** Seminarg@stjohns.edu

SEMMENS, RICHARD
DISCIPLINE MUSIC **EDUCATION** Stanford Univ, PhD, 80. **CAREER** Assoc prof, Univ of Western Ontario. **RESEARCH** Theory and practice of French baroque music; baroque dance and dance music; 17th century music and science; history of woodwind instruments; history of theory. **SELECTED PUBLICATIONS** Auth, "Music and Poetry in a Chanson by Gilles Binchois," in Beyond the Moon: Festschrift Luther Dittmer, eds. B. Gillingham and P. Merkley, (Ottawa: Institute of Medieval Music, 90): 307-322; auth, "Joseph Sauveur and the Absolute Frequency of Pitch," Theoria 5, (91): 1-41; auth, "Such Sweet Harmonie: Mozart's Chamber Music for Wind Instruments," Studies in Music from the Univ of Western Ontario 14, (93): 131-154; auth, "Dancing and Dance Music in Purcell's Operas," in Performing the Music of Henry Purcell, ed. Michael Burden, (Oxford: Oxford Univ Press, 96): 180-96; auth, "La Furstenberg," and "St Martin's Lane,": Purcell's French Odyssey, Music and Letters, 7, (97): 337-48. **CONTACT ADDRESS** Dept of Music, Univ of Western Ontario, London, ON, Canada N6A 5B8. **EMAIL** musrts@julian.uwo.ca

SENA, JOHN F.
PERSONAL Born 06/26/1940, Summit, NJ, m, 1966, 2 children **DISCIPLINE** ENGLISH LITERATURE **EDUCATION** Seton Hall Univ, BA, 62; Princeton Univ, MA, 65, PhD(English), 67. **CAREER** Asst prof, 67-71, ASSOC PROF ENGLISH, OHIO STATE UNIV, 71-, Am Philos Soc grant, 68; Ohio State Univ grant, 69. **MEMBERSHIPS** MLA; Am Soc 18th Century Sudies; Am Soc Hist Med. **RESEARCH** Eighteenth century English literature; history of medicine; satiric theory. **SELECTED PUBLICATIONS CONTACT ADDRESS** Dept of English, Ohio State Univ, Columbus, Columbus, OH 43210.

SENDRY, JOSEPH M.
PERSONAL Born 10/22/1935, Cleveland, OH **DISCIPLINE** ENGLISH **EDUCATION** Cath Univ Am, BA, 57; Univ MI, MA, 58; Harvard Univ, PhD, 63. **CAREER** Asst prof, 63-66, Assoc Prof Eng, Cath Univ Am, 66-90, Chmn Dept, 78-93, prof eng, Cath Univ Am, 90-, Vis fel, St Edmund's Col, Cambridge Univ, 71, 83-84. **MEMBERSHIPS** MLA; ALSC; Victorians Inst; Amer Conf for Irish Stud; Am Conf on Christianity & Lit. **RESEARCH** Victorian poetry; Tennyson; mod Irish lit; Joyce. **SELECTED PUBLICATIONS** Auth, The In Memoriam manuscripts: Some solutions to the problems, 4/73 & In Memoriam: The minor manuscripts, 1/79, Harvard Lib Bull; Guide to the year's work in Victorian poetry: Tennyson, Victorian Poetry, fall 76-90; The Wreck of the Deutschland: the elegy as heroic poem, Thought, 12/90; The poet as interpreter: Richard Murphy's The Mirror Wall, In: Snow Path: Track 10, 94; In Memoriam as Apocalypse, In: Sense and Transcendence, 95. **CONTACT ADDRESS** Dept of Eng, Catholic Univ of America, 620 Michigan Ave NE, Washington, DC 20064-0002.

SENSIBAR, JUDITH L.
PERSONAL Born Washington, DC, m, 2 children **DISCIPLINE** LITERATURE **EDUCATION** Vassar Col, BA, 63; Univ Chicago, MA, 72, PhD, 82. **CAREER** Asst Teacher, The Bruno Bettelheim Orthogenic Sch, Univ Chicago, 72; Lectr, Chicago Inst Psychoanalysis, Fall 82; Lectr, Univ Chicago Extension Prog, 82, 84; Vis Asst Prof, Univ Ill - Chicago, 84; Asst Prof, 85-88, Assoc Prof, Ariz State Univ, 88-99; prof, Ariz State Univ, 99-. **HONORS AND AWARDS** Jane Addams Fel, Am Asn Univ Women, 80-81; Departmental Late Awds Grant, Univ Chicago, 81-82; ACLS Fel for Recent Recipients of the PhD, 83-84; Women's Studies Fel, ASU, 87; Am Coun Learned Soc Fel, 87-88;Women's Studies Fel - WS Fac Development Prog, 91; Rockefeller Regional Schol Fel, 92; NEH Travel Grant, 92; Va Found Humanities and Public Policy Fel, 93; NEH Sr. Fel Univ Teachers, 93-94; ASU Grad Students of English Asn Awd for Outstanding Mentor to Grad Students in English, 98. **MEMBERSHIPS** Edith Wharton Soc; MLA; SMLA; MLA Women's Caucus; Faulkner & Wharton Soc; AAUW; ALA; ASA; NE-MLA; SSSL. **RESEARCH** Faulkner; modernism; literary cultural biography; American studies; feminist and psychoanalytic theory. **SELECTED PUBLICATIONS** Ed, Vision in Spring, Univ Tex Press, 84; auth, The Origins of Faulkner's Art, Univ Tex Press, 84; Faulkner's Poetry: A Bibliographical Guide to Texts and Criticism, Univ Mich Res Press, 88; author of numerous articles, chapters, and reviews. **CONTACT ADDRESS** Dept of English, Arizona State Univ, MC 0302, Tempe, AZ 85287. **EMAIL** judith.sensibar@asu.edu

SERIO, JOHN N.
PERSONAL Born 10/08/1943, Buffalo, NY, m, 1972, 3 children **DISCIPLINE** LITERATURE **EDUCATION** State Univ NYork, Buffalo, BS, 65; Northwestern Univ, MA, 66; Univ Notre Dame, PhD, 74. **CAREER** Instr, Univ of Notre Dame, 73-74, Asst Prof to Prof, Clarkson Univ, 74-. **HONORS AND AWARDS** Outstanding J Article Awd, Soc for Tech Commun, 89; Phoenix Awd for Significant Ed Achievement, Coun of Ed of Learned J, 90; NEH Summer Stipend, 91; Sr Fulbright Lectr Awd to Greece, Aristotle Univ of Thessaloniki, 93; Nat Parents Bd, Syracuse Univ, 94-98; Sr Fulbright Lect Awd to Belgium, Instelling Univ of Antwerp, 98. **MEMBERSHIPS** MLA, Wallace Stevens Soc. **RESEARCH** Wallace Stevens, American Poetry. **SELECTED PUBLICATIONS** Auth, "Poetry Scansion in Ventura," Ventura Prof (July 91): 19-21, Editor's Notes 11.1 (Spring 92): 51-54; auth, Wallace Stevens: An Annotated Secondary Bibliography, Univ of Pittsburgh Press (Pittsburgh), 94; coauth, ed, Teaching Wallace Stevens: Practical Essays, Tenn Studies in Lit Vol 35, Univ of Tenn Press (Knoxville), 94; ed, A Morning Pose, The Wallace Stevens Soc Inc (Potsdam, NY), 94; ed, Inhabited World: New and Selected Poems 1970-1995, by John Allman, The Wallace Stevens Soc Inc (Potsdam, NY), 95; ed and publ, Dear Home: The 1901 and 1902 Diaries of Mabel Lila Wait, ed. Susan Ward, Friends of Owen D. Young Libr, St. Lawrence Univ Press (Canton, NY), 96; ed, Hiking Tropical Australia: Queensland and Northern New South Wales, by Lewis Hinchman, Grass Tree Press (Potsdam, NY), 99; ed, Make it Happen: The Inspiring Story of NCAA Wrestling Champion, by Mitch Clark and Scott Conroe, White Pillars Press (Canton, NY), 99; auth, "Frost's 'Fire and Ice' and Dante's 'Inferno'," The Explicator 57-4 (Summer 99): 218-221; auth, "The Wallace Stevens Society," in Dictionary of Literary Biography Yearbook 1999 (forthcoming). **CONTACT ADDRESS** Dept Lib Arts, Clarkson Univ, 1 Clarkson Ave., Potsdam, NY 13676-1409. **EMAIL** serio@clarkson.edu

SERUM, ROBERT W.
PERSONAL Born 09/06/1941, Grand Rapids, MI, m, 1967, 2 children **DISCIPLINE** ENGLISH LANGUAGE & LITERATURE **EDUCATION** Hope Col, AB, 63; Univ Ala, MA, 72, PhD(English), 74. **CAREER** Teacher, Hudsonville Mich Publ High Schs, 63-69; grad teaching asst English, Univ Ala, 69-72; asst prof, 74-75, assoc prof & head dept English, 75-80, assoc dir, Univ Col, 75-80, acad dean, 80-891 dean, Univ Col, 89-; dean, grad stu, 91-; VP of Acad and dean of int prgm, 93-. **MEMBERSHIPS** Soc Advan Scand Studies; NCTE; MLA; AAUP; Int Soc Gen Semantics. **RESEARCH** Ibsen; poetry (English & American); semantics. **CONTACT ADDRESS** 4000 Whiting Dr, Midland, MI 48640-2398. **EMAIL** serum@northwood.edu

SESSIONS, WILLIAM ALFRED
PERSONAL Born 08/04/1938, Conway, SC, m, 1961, 2 children **DISCIPLINE** ENGLISH **EDUCATION** Univ NC, Chapel Hill, AB, 57; Columbia Univ, MA, 59, PhD(English, Comp Lit), 66. **CAREER** Asst prof English, State Univ W Ga, 59-60; asst prof, Spring Hill Col, 60-62; asst prof, St John's Univ, 62-66; assoc prof, 66-72, dir grad sch, dept English, 69-75, prof, 72-93, REGENTS' PROF ENGLISH, GA STATE UNIV, 93-. **HONORS AND AWARDS** Nikos Kazantzakis Medal, Greece, 78. **MEMBERSHIPS** MLA; Renaissance Soc Am; Southeastern Renaissance Soc; Medieval Inst; Am Lit Asn; Inst Hist Res. **RESEARCH** Early Modern English; Henry Howard, the Poet Earl of Surrey; Francis Bacon; Spenser; Milton: Flannery O'Connor; Walker Percy; modern poetic theory. **SELECTED PUBLICATIONS** Auth, Henry Howard, the POet Earl of Surrey, A Life: Enough Survives, Oxford Univ Press, 99; auth, Francis Bacon Revisited, Twayne English Authors series, Simon and Schuster, 96; auth, Francis Bacon's Legacy of Texts: The Art of Discovery Grows with Discovery, AMS Press, 90; auth, Henry Howard, The Poet Early of Surrey 1517-1547, G. K. Hall & Co, 86; auth, How to Ready Flannery O'Connor: Passing by the Dragon, in Flannery O'Connor and the Christian Mystery, Literature and Belief 17, 97; auth, Surrey's Waytt: The New Poet in Autumn 1542, in Rethinking the Henrician Age, Univ Ill Press, 94; auth, Milton and the Dance, in Milton and the Fine Arts, Pa State Univ Press, 89; auth, Where Does a Poet Come From? The Southern Review 34:1, Winter 98; auth, Teaching Where Three Interstates Meet, Profession 93, 12; Jan 94. **CONTACT ADDRESS** Dept of Eng, Georgia State Univ, Rm 974, Gen Classroom Bldg, Atlanta, GA 30303. **EMAIL** wsessions@gsu.edu

SETHI, ROBBIE CLIPPER
PERSONAL Born 08/13/1951, Camden, NJ, m, 1975, 1 child **DISCIPLINE** ENGLISH **EDUCATION** Indiana Univ, Bloomington, BA, 73; Univ Calif, Berkeley, MA, 75, PhD, 81. **CAREER** Asst prof, Rider Univ, Lawrenceville, NJ, 86-92, assoc prof, 92-95, prof, 95-, chair, English Dept, 2000-. **HONORS AND AWARDS** Phi Beta Kappa, Nat Defense Scholarship; Nat Endowment for the Arts; NJ State Coun on the Arts fels in prose. **MEMBERSHIPS** Assoc Writing Progs. **RESEARCH** Fiction. **SELECTED PUBLICATIONS** Auth, "Faith Healers," Passaic County Community Col Poetry Center Anthology (87); auth, "A Lesson for Novelists: or, The Dramatic Structure of Eugene Onegin, Russian Literature XIV (83), Nineteenth-Century Lit Criticism, Gale Res Inc (90); auth, "The Pilgrimage," (short story), Mass Rev (winter 92-93); auth, The Bride Wore Red, Bridge Works (96), Picador (97); auth, "Doctor Doktor," (short story), Menaka (Marathi trans) (March 97); auth, "Siamese, if you Please," (short story) Philadelphia Inquirer Mag (08/24/97); auth, "Fast Friend," (short story) US1 Worksheets (spring 98); auth, "A Marriage of Cultures," in India Today, New Delhi, India (08/16/99); auth, "Three Sisters," (short story) Other Voices (Nov 99); auth, "Fifty Fifty," (short story) Screaming Monkeys (in press). **CONTACT ADDRESS** Dept English, Rider Univ, 2083 Lawrenceville Rd, Trenton, NJ 08648-3001. **EMAIL** nsrcs@aol.com

SETTLE, PETER
DISCIPLINE ORGANIZATIONAL AND INTERPERSONAL COMMUNICATION **EDUCATION** Marquette Univ, MA; Bowling Green Univ, PhD. **CAREER** Mgt. Communs. **HONORS AND AWARDS** Andrew T. Weaver Awd; Alumnus Awd -- Wisconsin Gamma of Pi Kappa Delta, Louis and Norman Alheiger, Execellence in Teaching, **RESEARCH** Human Resources, Mgt. Communs. **SELECTED PUBLICATIONS** Articles, Asn Comm Administration Jour, Wis Comm Asn Jour. **CONTACT ADDRESS** Carroll Col, Wisconsin, 100 N East Ave, Waukesha, WI 53186. **EMAIL** psettle@cc.edu

SEXTON, JAMES P.
DISCIPLINE ENGLISH, LITERATURE **EDUCATION** Univ Brit Colum, BA, 69; Univ Ore, DA, 80; Univ Victoria, PhD, 97. **CAREER** Inst, 71-, dept chmn, 81-83, 91-93, Camosun Col. **HONORS AND AWARDS** SSHRC Fel, 93-98; Elect Cur Aldous Huxley Soc, Univ Munster. **MEMBERSHIPS** MLA; Aldous Huxley Soc; Utopian Study Soc. **RESEARCH** Modern British; Aldous Huxley; utopian/dystopian. **SELECTED PUBLICATIONS** Auth, "Four Quartets and the Christian Calendar," Am Lit 43 (71); ed, Aldous Huxley's Hearst Essays, Garland, 94; auth, "Now More Than Ever: Huxley's Lost Play," in Aldous Huxley Centenary Symposium 94, ed. Nugel (Peter Lang, 95); auth, "Brave New World and the Rationalization of Industry," in Critical Essays on Aldous Huxley, ed. Meckier (GK Hall, 96); co-ed, Complete Essays of Aldous Huxley, 01; auth, Now More Than Ever, Univ Tex Pr, 01; auth, "Aldous Huxley's Utopias, Positive and Negative," Aldous Huxley Ann (01). **CONTACT ADDRESS** English Dept, Camosun Col, 3100 Foul Bay Rd, Landsdown Campus, Victoria, BC, Canada V8P 5J2. **EMAIL** sexton@camosun.bc.ca

SEYMOUR, DEBORAH M.
PERSONAL Born 10/02/1961, Baltimore, MD, m, 1994, 2 children **DISCIPLINE** ENGLISH **EDUCATION** Hunter Col, BA, 82; City Univ New York; M Phil, 92; PhD, 95. **CAREER** Adj asst prof, Queens Col, 95-97; adj asst prof, Hunter Col, 95-. **MEMBERSHIPS** Phi Beta Kappa. **RESEARCH** Theoretical linguistics; rhetoric and composition; philosophy of language. **SELECTED PUBLICATIONS** Co-ed, The Language Reader, Harcourt Coll Pub, forthcoming. **CONTACT ADDRESS** Dept English, Hunter Col, CUNY, 695 Park Ave, New York, NY 10021-5024.

SEYMOUR, VICTOR
PERSONAL Born 05/17/1929, Brooklyn, NY, m, 1965, 1 child **DISCIPLINE** SPEECH, THEATRE **EDUCATION** Univ Utah, BS, 54; Columbia Univ, MA, 58; Univ Wis, PhD(-Theatre), 65. **CAREER** Instr speech, Bates Col, 58-60; lectr, Hunter Col in the Bronx, 62-65; asst prof Speech & Theatre, NY Inst Technol, 65-68; from asst prof to assoc prof, 68-77, prof speech & theatre, Queensborough Community Col, NY, 77-, Off observer, Actors Studio Dir Univ, NYC, 60-; dir theatre, NY Inst Technol, 65-68. **MEMBERSHIPS** Speech Commun Asn. **SELECTED PUBLICATIONS** Auth, Director's workshop: Six years' activity of the Actors Studio Directors Unit, 3/66 & Theatre Keeps pace in secondary education, 10/68, Educ Theatre J. **CONTACT ADDRESS** Dept of Speech & Drama, Queensborough Comm Col, CUNY, 22205 56th Ave, Flushing, NY 11364-1432.

SHA, RICHARD
PERSONAL Born 12/25/1963, New York, NY, m, 1989, 2 children **DISCIPLINE** LITERATURE **EDUCATION** Univ Pa, BA, 85; Univ Tex, MA, 88; PhD, 92. **HONORS AND AWARDS** Andrew Mellon Fel, 92, 99; Giles and Elise Mead Fel, 99. **MEMBERSHIPS** MLA, Ctr for Advanced Study in Visual Arts, Wordsworth-Coleridge Soc. **RESEARCH** British romanticism. **SELECTED PUBLICATIONS** Auth, The Visual and Verbal Sketch in British Romanticism, Penn Pr, 98. **CONTACT ADDRESS** Dept Lit, American Univ, 4400 Mass Ave NW, Washington, DC 20016. **EMAIL** rcsha@american.edu

SHADDOCK, JENNIFER
DISCIPLINE ENGLISH LITERATURE **EDUCATION** Univ Colo Boulder, PhD. **CAREER** Fac, 93-. **RESEARCH** 19th and 20th Century British literature; cultural studies and criticism; composition. **SELECTED PUBLICATIONS** Auth, Narrative Enactments: Surviving Oppression through Story in Tracks and Ceremony in Feminist Nightmares: Women at Odds; Cultural Studies and Classroom Practice: An Introduction, Wis Eng Jour. **CONTACT ADDRESS** Dept of English, Univ of Wisconsin, Eau Claire, Hibbard Hall 618, PO Box 4004, Eau Claire, WI 54702-4004. **EMAIL** shaddoj@uwec.edu

SHAFER, GREGORY
PERSONAL Born 11/16/1959, Muskegon, MI, m, 1992 **DISCIPLINE** ENGLISH **EDUCATION** Mich State Univ, BA, 82, MS, 84; Univ Mich, PhD, 92. **CAREER** Teach asst, Univ

Mich, 89-92; Inst, Kellog Community Col, 93-97; INSTR ENG, MOTT COMMUNITY COL, 97-. **HONORS AND AWARDS** Kellogg Fdn Exc in Educ Awd, 94, 95, 96, 96; Phi Kappa Phi; Golden Key; Kappa Delta Pi. **MEMBERSHIPS** Nat Counc Teachers Eng; Mich Counc Teachers Eng' Mich Reading Asn. **RESEARCH** Composition; reading; Eng educ; literacy stud; postmodernism. **SELECTED PUBLICATIONS** Auth, On the Importance of Writing with Students, Lang Arts J Mich, Fall 96; auth, School Reform and the High School Proficiency Test, Eng J, Sep 97; auth, Reader Response Makes History, Eng J, Nov 97; auth, Revision, Reflection, and Conferencing: An Alternative to Traditional Grading, Ariz Eng Bull, Fall 97; auth, Nostalgia and Back to Basics, bull J, Sep 97; auth, Conferences, Compassion, and Composition: A Modest Proposal for Inspiring the Alienated Student, lang Arts J Mich, Spring 97; auth, Facilitating Meaningful Parent/Teacher Conferences, Sec Educ Today, Fall 97; auth, From Prescriptive Grammar to Problem Psing; An Alternative to Traditional Grammar Instruction, Calif Eng, Spring 98; auth, Whole Language: Origins and Practice, Lang Arts J Mich, Spring 98; Some Basic Truths about Back to Basics, The Humanist, Nov/Dec 98; auth, The Myth of Competition and the Case Against School Choice, The Humanist, March/April 99; auth, What I Learned from Reading the Everglades, Mich Reading Teach, Spring 99; auth, Watching Three Sovereigns for Sarah, Eng J, forthcoming; auth, The Importance of Voice and Audience in the Writing Center, Teach Eng in the Two Year Coll, forthcoming. **CONTACT ADDRESS** 974 Touraine Ave, East Lansing, MI 48823. **EMAIL** gshafer@email.mcc.edu

SHAFER, RONALD G.
PERSONAL Born 01/30/1946, Kittanning, PA, m, 1968, 2 children **DISCIPLINE** ENGLISH & AMERICAN LITERATURE **EDUCATION** Indiana Univ, Pa, BS, 68, MA, 70; Duquesne Univ, PhD(English), 75. **CAREER** Teacher, Ford City High Sch, 68-70; from asst prof to assoc prof, 70-76, PROF ENGLISH, INDIANA UNIV, PA, 76-, Asst ed, Shakespeare Newslett, 77-78; Fulbright-Hays vis prof, 78-79; dir, Int Milton Symposia, 81 & 83. **HONORS AND AWARDS** Indiana Univ, Pa, Excellence in Teaching Awd, 77; award, American Assoc of Univ Prof, 86; Fulbright Commission, 78-79; Presidents Medal of Distinction, 85; Distinguished Univ Prof, 96; National Endowment for the Humanities, 86-87; president- pennsylvania col english assoc, 84; board of dir, national col english assoc, 95-97; pres, exe dir, of two documentary films, robert rusku: our premier bet scholar99; donald hall & jane kenyou, " keeping you safe beside me" , 99' **MEMBERSHIPS** Friends of Milton's Cottage (pres, 77-); MLA; Friends of Bemerton; Milton Cottage Trust; Japan Milton Society. **RESEARCH** Drama of William Shakespeare; poetry of George Herbert; poetry of John Donne. **SELECTED PUBLICATIONS** Auth, Updike,John Talks About Writing, His Life, And His Works + Discussions From The Writing Workshop Held At Indiana-Univ-Of-Penn On March-30,1992 .2./, Cea Critic, Vol 0057, 1995; Vol 0057, 1995. **CONTACT ADDRESS** Dept of English, Indiana Univ of Pennsylvania, Leonard Hall, North Walk, Indiana, PA 15705-1094. **EMAIL** rshafer@grove.iup.edu

SHAFFER, BRIAN W.
DISCIPLINE ENGLISH **EDUCATION** Wash Univ, AB, 83; Univ Iowa, PhD, 89. **CAREER** Tutor, Oxford Univ, 97; From Asst Prof to Assoc Prof, Rhodes Col, 90-. **HONORS AND AWARDS** Phi Beta Kappa, 83; Fel, Univ Iowa, 84-88; NEH Fel, Univ NC, 89-90; NEH Fel, Univ Calif, 93; Clarence Day Dean's Awd, 95. **SELECTED PUBLICATIONS** Auth, "Civilization in Bloomsbury: Woolf's 'Mrs Dalloway' and Bell's 'Theory of Civilization'," J of Mod Lit, 19 (95): 73-87; auth, "'The Commerce of Shady Wares': Politics and Pornography in Conrad's 'The Secret Agent'," ELH, 62 (95): 443-466; auth, "Nationalism at the Bar: Anti-Semitism in 'Ulysses' and 'Under the Volcano'," Joyce/Lowry: Critical Perspectives, UP Ky (97): 84-95; auth, Understanding Kazuo Ishiguro, Univ SC Pr, 98; auth, "Joseph Conrad's 'The Nigger of the Narcissus'," A Joseph Conrad Companion, Greenwood Pr (99): 49-64; auth, Approaches to Teaching Conrad's "Heart of Darkness" and "The Secret Sharer," MLA, forthcoming. **CONTACT ADDRESS** Dept English, Rhodes Col, 2000 N Parkway, Memphis, TN 38112-1624.

SHAHEEN, NASEEB
PERSONAL Born 06/24/1931, Chicago, IL, s **DISCIPLINE** SHAKESPEARE; RENAISSANCE ENGLISH LITERATURE **EDUCATION** Am Univ Beirut, BA, 62; Univ Calif, Los Angeles, MA, 66, PhD(English), 69. **CAREER** Asst prof English lit, 69-77, assoc prof, 77-82, prof 83-, English,Univ of Memphis **MEMBERSHIPS** MLA **RESEARCH** Artistic use of the Bible in English literature; Shakespeare. **SELECTED PUBLICATIONS** Auth, The use of scripture in Cymbeline, Shakespeare Studies, 68; auth, Of Oreb, or of Sinai, English Language Notes 9, 25-28, 71; auth, Spenser and the New Testament, American Notes and Queries 10, 4-5, 71; The 1590 and 1596 texts of The Faerie Queene, Papers Bibliog Soc Am, 74; Biblical References in The Faerie Queene, Memphis State Univ, 76; The Siloam end of Hezekiah's tunnel, Palestine Explor Quart, London, 77; Like the base Judean, Shakespeare Quart, 80; auth, Ramallah: Its History and Its Genealogies, Birzeit Univ, 82; auth, Biblical References in Shakespeare's Tragedies, Univ Del, 87; auth, Biblical References in Shakespeare's Comedies, Univ Del, 93; auth, A Pictoral History of Ramallah, Arab Inst for Res, 92; auth, Biblical References in Shakespeare's History Plays, Univ Del, 93; auth, Biblical References in Shakespeare's Plays, Univ Del, 99. **CONTACT ADDRESS** Dept of English, Univ of Memphis, 3706 Alumni St, Memphis, TN 38152-0001.

SHAHID, IRFAN ARIF
PERSONAL Born 01/15/1926, Nazareth, Palestine, m, 1976 **DISCIPLINE** HISTORY, LITERATURE **EDUCATION** Oxford Univ, BA, 51; Princeton Univ, PhD, 54. **CAREER** Jr fel Arab-Byzantine rel, Ctr Byzantine Studies, 59-60; assoc prof, Ind Univ, Bloomington, 60-62; assoc prof, 62-66, prof Arabic, Georgetown Univ, 66-, Fulbright-Hays fel Arabic-Am lit, US Off Educ, 68-69; vis fel, Inst Advan Studies, Princeton, 76; Sultanate of Oman prof Arabic & Islamic lit, Georgetow Univ, 81- **HONORS AND AWARDS** Andrew W Mellon Fund Distinguished Lectureship in Lang & Ling, Sch Lang & Ling, Georgetown Univ, 77-79. **MEMBERSHIPS** Am Orient Soc; Mediaeval Acad Am; Mid East Studies Asn NAm; Mid East Inst; Am Asn Tchr(s) Arabic; Life mem, Clare Hall, Cambridge Univ, Engl, 89. **RESEARCH** Arab hist; Arab-Byzantine rel; Arabic lit. **SELECTED PUBLICATIONS** Auth, The martyrs of Najran: new documents, In: Subsidia Hagiographica, 71; Epistula de re publica genereda, In: Themistii Orationes, Vol III, Teubner Class Ser, 74; Rome and the Arabs, 84, Byzantium and the Arabs in the Fourth Century, 84, Byzantium and the Arabs in the Fifth Century, 89, Byzantium and the Arabs in the Sixth Century, 95, Dumbarton Oaks. **CONTACT ADDRESS** Dept of Arab Lang, Lit & Ling, Georgetown Univ, Washington, DC 20057-1046. **EMAIL** shahidi@gunet.georgetown.edu

SHAILOR, JONATHAN G.
DISCIPLINE COMMUNICATION **EDUCATION** Univ MA-Amherst, BA, MA, PhD. **CAREER** Assoc prof; dir, Prog in Conflict Analysis and Resolution; coordr, Dispute Resolution Ctr Theatre of Empowerment. **RESEARCH** Conflict resolution; narrative commun; intercultural commun; Asian Am commun; theatre of empowerment. **SELECTED PUBLICATIONS** Auth, Empowerment in Dispute Mediation: A Critical Analysis of Communication, Praeger, 94. **CONTACT ADDRESS** Commun Dept, Univ of Wisconsin, Parkside, 900 Wood Rd, CART 210, PO Box 2000, Kenosha, WI 53141-2000. **EMAIL** jonathan.shailor@uwp.edu

SHAKINOVSKY, LYNN
DISCIPLINE 19TH- AND 20TH-CENTURY AMERICAN; BRITISH WOMEN WRITERS **EDUCATION** Witwatersrand, BA; Toronto, MA, PhD. **CAREER** Assoc Prof **RESEARCH** 19th and 20th century Am and British women writers, Emily Dickinson, feminist literary theory, psychoanalysis. **SELECTED PUBLICATIONS** Auth, The Return of the Repressed: Illiteracy and the Death of the Narrative in Hawthorne's The Birthmark; No Frame of Reference: The Absence of Context in Emily Dickinson's Poems; Hidden Listeners: Dialogism in the Poetry of Emily Dickinson; Emily Dickinson's Poem 293. **CONTACT ADDRESS** Dept of English, Wilfrid Laurier Univ, 75 University Ave W, Waterloo, ON, Canada N2L 3C5. **EMAIL** lshakino@wlu.ca

SHALE, RICK
DISCIPLINE FILM STUDY; POPULAR CULTURE **EDUCATION** Ohio esleyan Univ, BA, 69; Univ Mich, MA, 72, PhD, 76. **CAREER** Fac member, Youngstown State Univ, 76-. **HONORS AND AWARDS** Phi Beta Kappa; Phi Kappa Phi. **MEMBERSHIPS** Univ Film & Video Assoc; Popular Culture Asn; Col Eng Asn. **RESEARCH** Film study; screwball comedy; Hitchcock; screenwriting. **SELECTED PUBLICATIONS** Auth, Academy Awards: The Complete Categorical and Chronological Record, Greenwood Press, 93. **CONTACT ADDRESS** Dept of English, Youngstown State Univ, Youngstown, OH 44555-3415.

SHAND, ROSA
PERSONAL Born 05/08/1937, Wilmington, NC, d, 3 children **DISCIPLINE** ENGLISH **EDUCATION** Randoph-Macon Women's Col, BA, 59; Univ Tex, MA, 81; PhD, 83. **CAREER** Instr, Bishop Tucker Col, 62-69; Instr, Episcopal Sem of the Southwest, 74-77; Instr, Iona Col, 82-83; Instr, Univ Tex, 84-85; Prof, Converse Col, 85-. **HONORS AND AWARDS** Phi Beta Kappa; Phi Kappa Phi; SC Fel in Fiction; NEA Fel; Katherine Anne Porter Fiction Awd. **MEMBERSHIPS** Authors' Guild, AWP. **SELECTED PUBLICATIONS** 30 stories in Lit J's; auth, New Southern Harmonies: Four Emerging Fiction Writers, Hub City Writers Proj, 98; auth, The Gravity of Sunlight, Soho Pr, 00. **CONTACT ADDRESS** Dept English, Converse Col, 580 E Main St, Spartanburg, SC 29302-1931. **EMAIL** rosashand@mindspring.com

SHANER, JAYE L.
DISCIPLINE COMMUNICATION **EDUCATION** Miami Univ (Ohio), BA, 90; Univ of Kans, MA, 93, PhD, 96. **CAREER** Asst prof, Ga State Univ, 96-. **MEMBERSHIPS** Nat Commun Assoc; Gerontological Soc of Am; Int Commun Assoc; Ga Alzheimer's Res Consortium. **RESEARCH** Intergenerational commun; commun & sterotypes of older adults; mass media messages about aging. **SELECTED PUBLICATIONS** Co-auth, Patronizing speech to the elderly as a function of stereotyping, Communication Studies, vol 45, 145-158, 95; co-auth, Steroetypes of the elderly held by young, middle-aged, and elderly adults, Journal of Gerontology: Psychological Sciences, vol 49, 240-249, 94; co-auth, Judgements about sterotypes of the elderly: Attitudes, age associations, and typicality ratings of young, middle-aged and elderly adults, Research on Aging, vol 17, 168-189, 95; co-auth, Beliefs about language performance: Adults' perceptions about self and elderly targets, Journal of Language and Social Psychology, vol 14, 235-259, 95; co-auth, Cognitive processes affecting communication with older adults, Handbook of communication and aging research, Lawrence Erlbaum Associates, 105-131, 95; co-auth, Sterotyping of older adults, Psychology and Aging, vol 12, 107-114, 97; co-auth, Social skills of older people: Conversations in same and mixed age dyads, Discourse Processes, (in press); co-auth, Communication with older adults: The influence of age sterotypes, context, and communicator age, Human Communication Research, (in press); coauth, Sterotyping of Older Adults: The Role of Target Facial Cues and Receiver Characteristics, Psychology & Aging vol 12, 107-114, 97; coauth, Communication with Older Adults: The Influence of Age Stereotypes, Context, and Communication age, Human Communication Research, vol 25, 124-151, 98; coauth, Social Skills of Older People: Conversations in Same and Mixed age, Discover Processes, vol 27, 55-76, 99. **CONTACT ADDRESS** Dept of Commun, Georgia State Univ, 1 Park Pl S, Atlanta, GA 30303-2911. **EMAIL** jshaner@gsu.edu

SHANKLE, NANCY
PERSONAL Born 03/30/1956, Phoenix, AZ, m, 1973, 2 children **DISCIPLINE** ENGLISH **EDUCATION** Tex A & M Univ, BA, 77; MA, 79; PhD, 90. **CAREER** Grad Asst, East Tex State Univ, 78-79; Lecturer to Grad Asst, Tex A & M Univ, 79-90; Asst Prof to Prof and Chair, Abilene Christian Univ, 90-. **HONORS AND AWARDS** Cullen Res Grant, Abilene Christian Univ, 99; NEH Travel to Collections Grant, 91. **RESEARCH** Colonial American literature; Women's Studies. **SELECTED PUBLICATIONS** Auth, "Mary Roberts Rinehart," in Bibliography of American Fiction: 1866-1918, New York: Facts on File, 93; rev, of "The Divine Dramatist: George Whitefield and the rise of Modern Evangelicalism," by Harry S. Stout, Restoration Quarterly, (92): 184; auth, "Have You Told Her You Love Her?," Up Reach, (91): 26-27. **CONTACT ADDRESS** Dept English, Abilene Christian Univ, Acu box 28252, Abilene, TX 79699-0001. **EMAIL** shanklen@acu.edu

SHANKS, HERSHEL
PERSONAL Born 03/08/1930, Sharon, PA, m, 1966, 2 children **DISCIPLINE** ENGLISH LITERATURE; SOCIOLOGY; LAW **EDUCATION** Haverford Col, BA, 52; Colombia Univ, MA, 56; Harvard Law Sch, LLB, 56. **CAREER** Founder and ed, Bibl Archaeol Rev, 74-; ed, Bible Rev, Archaeol Odyssey, and Moment. **MEMBERSHIPS** ASOR; SBL; AOS; NEAS; ABA. **RESEARCH** Archaeol; Bible; Judaism. **SELECTED PUBLICATIONS** Ed, Understanding the Dead Sea Scrolls, Random Hse, 92; co-auth, The Rise of Ancient Israel, Biblical Archaeol Soc, 92; ed, Christianity and Rabbinic Judaism: A Parallel History of Their Origins and Early Development, Biblical Archaeol Soc, 92; auth, Jerusalem: An Archaeological Biography, Random Hse, 95; auth, The Mystery and Meaning of the Dead Sea Scrolls, Random Hse, 98. **CONTACT ADDRESS** Biblical Archael Soc, 5208 38th St, NW, Washington, DC 20015. **EMAIL** shanks@clark.net

SHANNON, LAURIE
DISCIPLINE ENGLISH LITERATURE **EDUCATION** Harvard Univ, JD, 89; Univ of Chicago, PhD, 96. **CAREER** Asst prof, Duke Univ. **HONORS AND AWARDS** ACLS; NEH; Phi Beta Kappa. **MEMBERSHIPS** MLA; Shakespeare Assoc of Am. **RESEARCH** Sixteenth and early seventeenth century Eng lit. **SELECTED PUBLICATIONS** Auth, publ(s) on rhet of friendship; gender; conditions of personage in Renaissance imaginings of commonwealth. **CONTACT ADDRESS** Eng Dept, Duke Univ, Durham, NC 27708.

SHAPIRO, ANN
PERSONAL Born 02/28/1937, Brooklyn, NY, d, 3 children **DISCIPLINE** ENGLISH **EDUCATION** Radcliffe Col, AB, 58; Harvard Sch Ed, AMT, 60; NYork Univ, PhD, 85. **CAREER** Instructor, Rider Col, 62-65; Instructor, Suffolk Cty Cmty Col, 66-67; Prof, SUNY Farmingdale, 74-. **HONORS AND AWARDS** NEH Summer Sem, Univ IL, 90; NEH Summer Sem, Yale, 94; Judaica Ref Book Awd, Asn of Jewish Libraries, 95. **MEMBERSHIPS** MLA: AJS: MELUS: CEWHC. **RESEARCH** Jewish American Women Writers; Am Lit (19th and 20th Cent). **SELECTED PUBLICATIONS** Auth, "The Novels of E. M. Broner: A Study in Secular Feminism and Feminist Judaism," Studies in American Jewish Literature, 91; ed, Jewish American Women Writers: A Bio-Bibliographical and Critical Sourcebook, Greenwood, 94; auth, "The Ultimate Shaygets and the Fiction of Anzia Yezierska," MELUS, 96; auth, "Edna Ferber," Historical Encyclopedia of Chicago Women, IN Univ Press, forthcoming; auth, "Edna Ferber: A Jewish American Success Story," Shofar, forthcoming. **CONTACT ADDRESS** Dept Eng, SUNY, Col of Tech at Farmingdale, 1250 Melville Rd, Farmingdale, NY 11735-1313. **EMAIL** shapirar@aol.com

SHAPIRO, JAMES S.
PERSONAL Born 09/11/1955, New York City, NY, m, 1992, 1 child **DISCIPLINE** ENGLISH **EDUCATION** Columbia Univ, BA, 77; Univ Chicago, Phd, 82. **CAREER** Prof. **HONORS AND AWARDS** Bainton Prize, best bk on sixteenth-century lit; awards, NEH; Huntington Library; Memorial Found for Jewish Cult; co-ed, columbia anthology of brit poetry; assoc ed, columbia hist brit poetry; fulbright lectr, bar ilan and tel aviv univ. **SELECTED PUBLICATIONS** Auth, Rival Playwrights: Marlowe, Jonson, Shakespeare, 91; Shakespeare and the Jews, 95; auth, Oberammergau: The Troubling Story of the World's Most Famous Passion Play, 00. **CONTACT ADDRESS** Dept of Eng, Columbia Col, New York, 2960 Broadway, New York, NY 10027-6902. **EMAIL** js73@columbia.edu

SHAPIRO, MICHAEL
PERSONAL Born 03/31/1938, Rochester, NY, m, 1961, 4 children **DISCIPLINE** ENGLISH **EDUCATION** Univ Rochester, BA, 59; Columbia Univ, MA, 60, PhD, 67. **CAREER** Lectr, City Col NY, 61-65; instr, NY Inst Technol, 66-67; from Asst Prof to Assoc Prof, 67-93, prof eng, Univ IL, Urbana, 93, Dir, Drobny Prog in Jewish Cult and Soc, 98-; Lectr Eng, Pace Col, 61-62; vis assoc prof, Cornell Univ, 75 & Reading Univ, Engl, 78-79; vis prof, Tamkaug Univ, Taiwan, 93. **MEMBERSHIPS** MLA; Renaissance Soc Am; Shakespeare Asn Am. **RESEARCH** Elizabethan drama; Renaissance lit; Am-Jewish writers. **SELECTED PUBLICATIONS** Auth, Children of the Revels: The Boy Companies of Shakespeare's Time and Their Plays, Columbia Univ, 77; Gender in Play on the Shakespeare Stage, Univ MI Press, 94. **CONTACT ADDRESS** Dept of Eng, Univ of Illinois, Urbana-Champaign, 608 S Wright St, Urbana, IL 61801-3613. **EMAIL** mshapir@uiuc.edu

SHAPIRO, SUSAN
DISCIPLINE ENGLISH LITERATURE **EDUCATION** Bryn Mawr Univ, PhD. **CAREER** Fac, Fairleigh Dickinson Univ. **RESEARCH** Shakespeare; drama; ESL. **SELECTED PUBLICATIONS** Auth, essays in Rev Eng Studies, CEA Critic, Atlantis, 17th-Century News, Hist Today. **CONTACT ADDRESS** Fairleigh Dickinson Univ, Teaneck-Hackensack, 1000 River Rd, Teaneck, NJ 07666.

SHARF, BARBARA F.
PERSONAL Born 03/27/1948, Philadelphia, PA, m, 1988 **DISCIPLINE** HEALTH COMMUNICATION, RHETORICAL ANALYSIS **EDUCATION** Univ Minn, PhD. **CAREER** Prof, Texas A&M Univ. **CONTACT ADDRESS** Dept of Speech Communication, Texas A&M Univ, Col Station, College Station, TX 77843-4234. **EMAIL** bsharf@tamu.edu

SHARMA, R. N.
PERSONAL Born 10/22/1944, Punjab, India, m, 1972, 2 children **DISCIPLINE** LIBRARY AND INFORMATION SCIENCE; HIGHER EDUCATION; HISTORY **EDUCATION** Univ Delhi, BA, 63, MA, 66; N TX State Univ, MLS, 70; SUNY, Buffalo, PhD, 82. **CAREER** Asst librn, Col Ozarks, 70-71; ref librn, Colgate Univ, 71-81; head librn, Penn State Univ, Beaver Campus, 81-85; asst dir, Univ WI, 85-89; dir, Univ Evansville, 89-95; dir, WV State Col, 96-. **HONORS AND AWARDS** Who's Who Among Asian Am, 92-94; advisory bd, 94-98, Asian Lit; Humprhy/OCLC/Forest Press Awd, 97, ALA; chair, Am Librns Delegation to Palestine, 97; Am Librns Delegation to Northern Ireland, 97; Benjamin Franklin Awd, 98, Publishers Marketing Asn; Editor-in-Chief, Library Times International 84; President, Asian/American Libraries Association, 93-94. **MEMBERSHIPS** Am Libr Asn; Asn Col Res Libr; Int Relations Round Table; Indian Libr Asn; Asian/Pacific Am Librn Asn. **RESEARCH** International librarianship; history of libraries; library administration; reference services. **SELECTED PUBLICATIONS** Auth, "Indian Librarianship: Perspectives and Prospects," Kalayni 81; auth, Indian Academic Libraries and Dr. S. R. Ranganathan: A Critical Study, Sterling, 86; Ranganathan and the West, Sterling, 92; Research and Academic Librarians: A Global View, Resources in Education, 92; Changing Dimensions: Managing Library and Information Services for the 1990's: A Global Perspective, Ed Resources Infor Center, 94; Linking Asian/Pacific Collections to America, Educational Resources Infor Center, 95; auth, "Libraries and Education in Palestine, Near East and South Asia," Subcommittee/Internetional Relations/ALA, 99. **CONTACT ADDRESS** Drain-Jordan Library, West Virginia State Col, PO Box 1002, Institute, WV 25112-1002. **EMAIL** sharmarn@mail.wvsc.edu

SHARMA, VISHNU
PERSONAL Born 10/26/1933, Patti, Amritsar, India, m, 1954, 3 children **DISCIPLINE** ENGLISH **EDUCATION** Punjab Univ, MA, 62; MA, 65; PhD, 74. **CAREER** Assoc prof, Guru Nanak Dev Univ, 65-88; asst prof, CUNY, 92-; asst prof, Hostos Community Col, 89-98. **MEMBERSHIPS** Soc of Indian Acad in Am. **RESEARCH** Writing, adapting and translating scripts for the stage, radio and TV in Hindi, Urdu and Punjabi languages used in India. **CONTACT ADDRESS** Dept Asian Studies, City Col, CUNY, 138 Convent Ave, New York, NY 10031-9101. **EMAIL** vsharmajyo@aol.com

SHARP, RONALD ALAN
PERSONAL Born 10/19/1945, Cleveland, OH, m, 1968, 1 child **DISCIPLINE** ENGLISH **EDUCATION** Kalamazoo Col, BA, 67; Univ Mich, MA, 68; Univ Va, PhD, 74. **CAREER** Instr English, Western Mich Univ, 68-70; instr of Eng, 70-72, asst prof, 74-78, assoc prof, Eng, Kenyon Col, 78-, co-ed, Kenyon Rev, 78-; prof, 85-90. **HONORS AND AWARDS** Nat Endowment for Humanities fel, 81-82, 84-87, 93, 94, 96, 98; Nat Humanities Ctr fel, 81-82, 86-87. **MEMBERSHIPS** MLA; Wordsworth-Coleridge Assn; Keats-Shelley Assn. **RESEARCH** Romanticism; contemporary poetry; the epic. **SELECTED PUBLICATIONS** Auth, Keats, Skepticism, and the Religion of Beauty, Univ of Georgia Press, 79; auth, Friendship and Literature: Spirit and Form, Duke Univ Press, 86; coauth, The Norton Book of Friendship, Norton, 91; coauth, Reading George Steiner, Johns Hipkins Univ Press, 94; auth, "Steiner's Ficiton and the Hermeneutics of Transcendence," in Reading George Steiner, ed. Nathan A. Scoot, Jr., and Ronald A. Sharp, Johns Hopkins Univ Press, 94; auth, "Celebrating Keat's Bicenteninial," Keats-Shelley Journal, 95; auth, "Friendship: Fast and Fleeting," The Philadelphia Inquirer, reprinted in The Washington Tiems, 96; coauth, The Persistence of Poetry: Bicentennial Essays on John Keats, Univ of Mass Press, 98; auth, "Keats and Friendship," in The Persistence of Poetry: Bicentennial Essays on John Keats, ed. Robert M. Ryan and Ronald A. Sharp, Univ of Mass Press, 98; auth, "Interview with George Steinier," The Paris Review, reprinted in The Winter Chapbook, Newton Library, 99. **CONTACT ADDRESS** Kenyon Col, Office of Provost, Gambier, OH 43022-9623. **EMAIL** sharp@kenyon.edu

SHARPE, JENNY
PERSONAL Born, Britain, m, 2 children **DISCIPLINE** ENGLISH **EDUCATION** Univ Tex Austin, BA, 81; PhD, 87. **CAREER** Asst prof, Boston Col, 87-93; asst prof, UCLA, 93-. **HONORS AND AWARDS** UC Pres Res Fel, 98-99; Fel, Univ Calif Irvine, 95; Fel, Brown Univ, 87-88. **MEMBERSHIPS** MLA. **RESEARCH** Colonial/postcolonial studies of India and the Caribbean; Critical theory; Gender studies. **SELECTED PUBLICATIONS** Auth, "The Unspeakable Limits of Rape: Colonial Violence and Counter-Insurgency," Genders, (91): 25-46; auth, "The Violence of Light in the Land of Desire: or, How William Jones Discovered India," Boundary, (92): 26-46; auth, Allegories of Empire: The Figure of Woman in the Colonial Text, Univ Minn Press, 93; auth, "The Original Paradise: Grenada Ten Years After the U.S. Invasion," Transition, (93): 48-57; auth, "Is the United States Postcolonial? Transnationalism, Immigration, and Race," Diaspora, (95): 181-199; auth, "The Limits of What is Possible: Reimagining sharam in Salman Rushdie's 'Shame'," Jouvert, 96; auth, "Something Akin to Freedom: The Case of Mary Prince," Differences, (96): 31-56; auth, "Postcolonial Studies in the House of US Multiculturalism," in Blackwell's Companion to Postcolonial Studies, (London, 99), 112-125; auth, The Haunting of History: A Literary Archeology of Slave Women's Lives, Univ Minn Press, (forthcoming). **CONTACT ADDRESS** Dept English, Univ of California, Los Angeles, 2225 Rolfe, PO Box 951530, Los Angeles, CA 90095-1530.

SHARY, TIMOTHY
PERSONAL Born 08/17/1967, Cheverly, MD, s **DISCIPLINE** FILM HISTORY **EDUCATION** Hampshire Col, BA, 91; Ohio Univ, MA, 93; Univ of Mass, PhD, 98. **CAREER** Lectr, Univ Mass Amherst; Vis Lectr, Clark Univ, 97-. **HONORS AND AWARDS** Phi Kappa Phi. **MEMBERSHIPS** Soc for Cinema Studies; Univ Film & Video Asn. **RESEARCH** Contemporary American cinema and media; East European cinema; the phenomenology of film and video; new media technology; Films of Alfred Hitchcok, Ingmar Bergman, and Atom Egoyan. **SELECTED PUBLICATIONS** Auth, Reification and Loss in Postmodern Puberty: The Cultural Logic of Fredric Jameson and Young Adult Movies, Postmodernism in the Cinema, Berghahn Books, 98; The Teen Film and its Methods of Study, J of Popular Film and Television, 97; The Only Place To Go Is Inside: Confusions of Sexuality and Class in Clueless and Kids, Pictures of a Generation on Hold: Youth in Film and Television of the 90s, Media Studies Working Group, 96; Exotica: Atom Egoyan's Neurotic Thriller, Point of View, 95; Video as Accessible Artifact and Artificial Access: The Early Films of Atom Egoyan, Film Criticism, 95; Viewing Experience: Structures of Subjectivity in East and West European Films, Echoes and Mirrors, 94; Present Personal Truths: The Alternative Phenomenology of Video in I've Heard the Mermaids Singing, Wide Angle, 93. **CONTACT ADDRESS** Dept of Visual & Performing Arts, Clark Univ, 950 Main St., Worcester, MA 01610. **EMAIL** tshary@clarku.edu

SHATSKY, JOEL
PERSONAL Born 11/30/1943, Vancouver, WA, m, 1967, 2 children **DISCIPLINE** ENGLISH **EDUCATION** Queens Col, CUNY, 64; Univ Chigago, MA, 65; NYork Univ, PhD, 70. **CAREER** Prof, SUNY Cortland, 68- **HONORS AND AWARDS** Phi Kappa Phi; Phi Eta Sigma; faculty exchange scholar, 84-85; coordinator, honor's prog, 90-95. **RESEARCH** Jewish-American lit; modern drama. **SELECTED PUBLICATIONS** Ed, Theresienstadt: Hitler's Gift to the Jews, Univ NC Chapel Hill, 91; coed, Contemporary Jewish-American Novelists; A Bio-bibliographical Sourcebook, Greenwood Press, 97; Contemporary Jewish-American Dramatists and Poets: A Bio-bibliographical Sourceboo **CONTACT ADDRESS** Dept of English, SUNY, Col at Cortland, Box 2000, Cortland, NY 13045. **EMAIL** shatzkj@snycorva.cortland.edu

SHATTUCK, ROGER
PERSONAL Born 08/20/1923, New York, NY, m, 1949, 4 children **DISCIPLINE** LITERATURE **EDUCATION** Yale Univ, BA, 1947. **CAREER** Info officer, film sect, UNESCO, Paris, Fr, 47-48; asst trade ed, Harcourt, Brace & Co, 49-50; instr, fr, Harvard Univ, 53-56; asst prof to prof, fr and eng, Univ Tex Austin, 56-71; Commonwealth prof, Fr, Univ Va, 74-88; prof and prof emer, mod foreign lang, Boston Univ, 86-97. **HONORS AND AWARDS** Jr fel, soc fel, Harvard Univ, 50-53; Nat Book Awd, 75; Fulbright prof, Amer lit, Univ Dakar, Senegal, 84-85; Doctorate honoris causa, Univ Orleans (France), 90; fel, Am Acad Arts and Sciences, 90. **MEMBERSHIPS** Asn Lit Scholars & Critics. **RESEARCH** Literature; A public morality; The fine arts. **SELECTED PUBLICATIONS** Auth, Proust's Binoculars, 63; auth, Half Tame, 64; auth, The Banquet Years, 58; auth, Marcel Proust, 74; auth, The Forbidden Experiment: the Story of the Wild Boy of Aveyron, 80; auth, The Innocent Eye: On Modern Literature and the Arts, 84; auth, Forbidden Knowledge: From Prometheus to Pornography, 96; auth, Candor and Perversion: Lit, Education, and the Arts, 99; auth, Proust's Way: A Field Guide to 'The Search of Lost Time,' 00. **CONTACT ADDRESS** 231 Forge Hill Rd., Lincoln, VT 05443.

SHAUGHNESSY, EDWARD
PERSONAL Born 06/14/1932, Indianapolis, IN, m, 1957, 4 children **DISCIPLINE** ENGLISH **EDUCATION** Butler Univ, AB, 58; MA, 63; Ind Univ, PhD, 72. **CAREER** Lectr, prof, Edna R. Cooper prof emeritus, 65-. **HONORS AND AWARDS** Butler Univ Grants, 83, 84, 85; Edward L. Shaughnessy Prize In Irish Lit, est 93; Hibernian Res Awd, 94; Hiberniean Publ Awd, 96; Butler Univ Serv Medal, 01. **MEMBERSHIPS** MLA, Eugene O'Neill Soc, Am Irish Hist Soc, Am Conf on Irish Studies, Santayana, Soc. **RESEARCH** Modern Irish and Modern American Drama, American Poetry, 1900-1975. **SELECTED PUBLICATIONS** Auth, "Oliver Alden and Studs Lonigan: Heirs to Spiritual Poverty," Markham Rev, (74); auth, "Santayana: Latter-Day Janus," Jour of Aesthetics and Art Criticism, (75); auth, "Santayana on Athletics," Jour of Am Studies, Cambridge Univ Pr, (76); auth, Eugene O'Neill in Ireland: The Critical Reception, Greenwood Pr, 88; auth, "Ella, James and Jamie O'Neill; My Name is Might-Have-Been," Eugene O'Neill Rev, (91); auth, Down the Nights and Down the Days: Eugene O'Neill's Catholic Sensibility, Univ of Notre Dame Pr, 96; auth, "Ella O'Neill and the Imprint of Faith," Eugene O'Neill Rev, (98); auth, "Eugene O'Neill," Encycl of the Irish in Am, ed Michael Glazier, Univ of Notre Dame Pr, (99); auth, A Brief History of the Benedictine Oblates of Saint Meinrad Archabbey: 1877-1977, Abbey Pr, (St Meinrad, IN), 00. **CONTACT ADDRESS** Butler Univ, 1410 Northbrook Dr, Indianapolis, IN 46260. **EMAIL** eshaughn@butler.edu

SHAW, DONALD LEWIS
PERSONAL Born 10/27/1936, Raleigh, NC, m, 1960, 4 children **DISCIPLINE** MASS COMMUNICATIONS HISTORY **EDUCATION** Univ NC, Chapel Hill, AB, 59, MA, 60; Univ Wis, PhD(mass commun), 66. **CAREER** From asst prof to assoc prof, 66-76, prof jour, 76- , Kenan Prof, 92- , Univ NC, Chapel Hill. **MEMBERSHIPS** Asn Educ in Jour; AJHA; AAPOR; WAPOR. **RESEARCH** Relationship among technology, mass communication and culture. **SELECTED PUBLICATIONS** Coauth, The Agenda-Selling Function of Mass Media, Publ Opinion Quart, summer 72; coauth (with McCombs), The Emergence of American Political Issues: The Agenda-Setting Function of the Press, West Pub Co, 77; coauth, Communication and Democracy. **CONTACT ADDRESS** Sch of Journalism, Univ of No Carolina, Chapel Hill, Chapel Hill, NC 27514.

SHAW, HARRY EDMUND
PERSONAL Born 05/01/1946, Norristown, PA, m, 1982, 2 children **DISCIPLINE** ENGLISH LITERATURE **EDUCATION** Harvard Col, AB, 69; Univ Calif, Berkeley, MA, 74, PhD, 78. **CAREER** Prof English, Cornell Univ, 78-. **RESEARCH** 18th and 19th century British novel; Historical fiction. **SELECTED PUBLICATIONS** Auth, The Forms of Historical Fiction: Scott and his Successors, Cornell Univ Press, 83; Narratives of Reality: Austen, Scott, Eliot, Cornell Univ Press, 99. **CONTACT ADDRESS** Dept of English, Cornell Univ, Rockefeller Ha, Ithaca, NY 14853-0001. **EMAIL** HES3@Cornell.edu

SHAW, MICHAEL
DISCIPLINE CLASSICS **EDUCATION** Univ TX, PhD, 71. **CAREER** Assoc prof, Univ KS. **HONORS AND AWARDS** Mem, Ad hoc Comm for Women's Stud, 72-77. **RESEARCH** Greek and Roman lit. **SELECTED PUBLICATIONS** Auth, The Female Intruder: Women in Fifth-century Drama, Class Philol 70, 75; The ethos of Theseus in The Suppliant Women, Hermes 110, 82. **CONTACT ADDRESS** Dept of Class, Univ of Kansas, Lawrence, Admin Building, Lawrence, KS 66045. **EMAIL** gorgo@kuhub.cc.ukans.edu

SHAW, PATRICK W.
DISCIPLINE AMERICAN LITERATURE **EDUCATION** La State Univ, PhD, 71. **CAREER** Prof, TX Tech Univ. **RESEARCH** The mod Am novel. **SELECTED PUBLICATIONS** Auth, Willa Cather and the Art of Conflict: Re-Visioning Her Creative Imagination; his essays have been reproduced in such collections as Major Literary Characters: Antonia, The Viking Critical Edition of John Steinbeck's The Grapes of Wrath, and A New Study Guide to Steinbeck's Major Works. **CONTACT ADDRESS** Texas Tech Univ, Lubbock, TX 79409-5015. **EMAIL** ditps@ttacs.ttu.edu

SHAW, WAYNE EUGENE
PERSONAL Born 05/23/1932, Covington, IN, m, 1957, 3 children **DISCIPLINE** HOMILETICS, SPEECH **EDUCATION** Lincoln Christian Col, AB, 54; Christian Theol Sem, BD, 60; Butler Univ, MS, 63; Ind Univ, PhD, 69. **CAREER** Prof preaching, Lincoln Christian Sem, 66-, acad dean, 74-, Mem chaplaincy endorsement comn, Christian Churches & Churches of Christ, 74-; academic dean, 74-00; Pres, North Am Christian Convention, 99. **MEMBERSHIPS** Acad Homiletics. **RESEARCH** Preaching; communication; Biblical studies. **SELECTED PUBLICATIONS** Auth, The historian's treatment of the Cane Ridge Revival, Filson Quart, 62; contribr, The Seer, The Savior, The Saved, Col Press, 63; coauth, Birth of a Revolution: How the Church Can Change the World, Standard, 74; auth, Designing the Sermon, Bicentennial Comt, 75; Love in the midst of crises, Christian Standard, 77; auth, Pastoral Epistles: Blueprint for 28 Messages Built on God's Word, 99; auth, "The Plymouth Pulpit: Henry Ward Beecher's Auction Block". **CONTACT ADDRESS** 100 Campus View Dr, Lincoln, IL 62656-2111. **EMAIL** shaw@lccs.edu

SHAWCROSS, JOHN THOMAS
PERSONAL Born 02/10/1924, Hillside, NJ **DISCIPLINE** ENGLISH **EDUCATION** NJ State Col, Montclair, AB, 48; NYork Univ, AM, 50, PhD, 58. **CAREER** From instr to prof English, Newark Col Eng, 48-63; prof English, Douglass Col, Rutgers Univ, 63-67; prof, Univ Wis, Madison, 67-70; distinguished prof, Col Staten Island & Grad Ctr, City Univ New York, 70-79; PROF ENGLISH, UNIV KY, 79-, Lectr, City Col New York, 58-63; vis prof, NY Univ, 62 & 65, C W Post Col, Long Island Univ, 63, Univ Del, 65-66 & State Univ NY, Stony Brook, 74. **HONORS AND AWARDS** LittD, Montclair State Col, NJ, 75. **MEMBERSHIPS** Milton Soc (treas, 62-72, vpres, 73, pres, 74-75); Col English Asn; Renaissance Soc Am; Bibliog Soc Am; MLA. **RESEARCH** Milton; 17th century; modern poetry. **SELECTED PUBLICATIONS** Auth, Introduction + Issue On Cross-Gender Writing/, Cea Critic, Vol 0056, 1993; The Political And Liturgical Subtext Of Milton 'On The Death Of A Fair Infant Dying Of A Cough'/, Anq-A Quart J Of Short Articles Notes And Revs, Vol 0007, 1994; Catalog Of The Kohler Collection Of 550 Different Editions Of The Writings Of Milton,John Published Between 1641 And 1914 - Milton,J/, Anq-A Quart J Of Short Articles Notes And Revs, Vol 0008, 1995; The New-Eng Milton, Literary Reception And Cult Authority In The Early Republic - Vananglen,Kp/, Anq-A Quart J Of Short Articles Notes And Revs, Vol 0008, 1995; A Note On 'Paradise Lost' Book-2, Milton Quart, Vol 0029, 1995; The Christ-Figure In Some Literary-Texts - Images And Theme, Cithara-Essays In The Judeo-Christian Tradition, Vol 0035, 1996; Soc Visions - Wilding,M/, Anq-A Quart J Of Short Articles Notes And Revs, Vol 0009, 1996. **CONTACT ADDRESS** Dept of English, Univ of Kentucky, Lexington, KY 40506.

SHAY, ROBERT
DISCIPLINE MUSIC HISTORY, CHORAL MUSIC **EDUCATION** Wheaton Col, BMus; NEngl Conserv Mus, MMus; Univ NC, Chapel Hill, MA, PhD. **CAREER** Assoc prof, Lyon Col. **SELECTED PUBLICATIONS** Auth, Henry Purcell: The Early Manuscript Sources, Cambridge UP. **CONTACT ADDRESS** Dept of Music, Lyon Col, 300 Highland Rd, PO Box 2317, Batesville, AR 72503. **EMAIL** shay@lyon.edu

SHEA, ANN MARIE
PERSONAL Born 12/17/1939, Worcester, MA **DISCIPLINE** PERFORMING ARTS **EDUCATION** Anna Maria Col, BA, 61; The Catholic Univ of Am, MA, 64; New York Univ, PhD, 84. **CAREER** Instr of Theatre, Col Misericordia, 66-68; Prof of Theatre, Worcester State Col, 68-. **HONORS AND AWARDS** Moss Hart Memorial Awd, New England Theatre Conf, 90; Zonta Club Scholar, 61; Anna Maria Col Scholar, 57-61. **MEMBERSHIPS** New England Theatre Conf; Asn for Theatre in Higher Ed; Kennedy Center/Am Col Theatre Festival. **SELECTED PUBLICATIONS** Auth, Mythic Realities in Miller's All My Sons, Worcester Forum Theatre, 92; St. Genesius, The New Catholic Encycl, 64; Winter Glory, Worcester Children's Theatre, 79; coauth, The Powwow of the Thunderbird American Indian Dancers, The Drama Rev, 82. **CONTACT ADDRESS** Dept of Visual and Performing Arts, Worcester State Col, 486 Chandler St, Worcester, MA 06102. **EMAIL** ashed@worcester.edu

SHEA, DANIEL B.
PERSONAL Born 10/29/1936, Minneapolis, MN, m, 1978, 5 children **DISCIPLINE** EARLY AMERICAN LITERATURE **EDUCATION** Univ of St. Thomas, BA (summa cum laude), 58; Stanford Univ, MA, 62, PhD, 66. **CAREER** Inst to Prof, 62-, Dept Chair, Wash Univ, 78-84 & 95-98; fulbright lectr, Univ of Caen, 68-69; vis fel, Clare Hall, Cambirdge, 84-85. **HONORS AND AWARDS** Richard Beale Davis Prize, MLA, 88; tchg awds, Wash Univ, 89 & 90; Woodrow Wilson Fel, 58; Fulbright-Hays Sr Lectureship, 68; NEH Summer Grant, 61; distinguished fac awd, Washington Univ, 85; Phi Beta Kappa. **MEMBERSHIPS** MLA; AFTRA; Equity. **RESEARCH** Early American Lit; American women's fiction to 1900. **SELECTED PUBLICATIONS** Auth, Spiritual Autobiography in Early America, Wisconsin, 88; section ed, Columbia Literary History of the United States, Columbia, 88; ed, Some Account of the Fore Part of the Life of Elizabeth Ashbridge, Wisconsin, 90. **CONTACT ADDRESS** Dept of English, Washington Univ, Saint Louis, MO 63130. **EMAIL** dbshea@artsci.wustl.edu

SHEA, JOHN STEPHEN
PERSONAL Born 07/18/1933, New York, NY, m, 3 children **DISCIPLINE** ENGLISH **EDUCATION** Iona Col, AB, 54; Marquette Univ, AM, 56; Univ MN, PhD, 67. **CAREER** From instr to asst prof Eng, WA Univ, 64-69, chmn freshman Eng, 65-68; asst prof, 69-72, asst chmn dept, 73-76, assoc prof eng, Loyola Univ Chicago, 72-, chmn dept, 76-84, Director, Writing Across the Curriculum, 86-96, Prof Emeritus, 98-; Reader advan placement exam, Col Entrance Exam Bd, 68-73; ed, Restoration & 17th Century Theatre Res, 72-79; Mellon res grant, Mellon Found & Loyola Univ, 75. **MEMBERSHIPS** MLA; Am Soc 18th Century Studies. **RESEARCH** Restoration and 18th century Eng lit; literary criticism. **SELECTED PUBLICATIONS** Coauth, Themes and Exercises, Dept Eng, Univ MN, 60, 61 & 62; ed, Mandeville's Aesop Dress'd, Augustan Reprint Soc, 66; co-ed, Studies in Criticism and Aesthetics, 1660-1800, Univ MN, 67. **CONTACT ADDRESS** Dept Eng, Loyola Univ, Chicago, 6525 N Sheridan Rd, Chicago, IL 60626-5385.

SHEARON, FORREST BEDFORD
PERSONAL Born 09/07/1934, Bolivar, TN, m, 1981, 2 children **DISCIPLINE** ENGLISH, BRITISH LITERATURE **EDUCATION** Union Univ, Tenn, AB, 56; Univ Louisville, MA, 65, PhD, 73. **CAREER** Teacher English, Halls High Sch, Tenn, 56-58, Pleasure Ridge Park High Sch, Ky, 58-62, 63-65; asst prof English, Ky Southern Col, Louisville, 65-68; instr., Univ Louisville, 69-73; from asst prof to prof Humanites, 73-98, Prof Emeritus, Eastern Ky Univ, 98-. **HONORS AND AWARDS** Outstanding Graduating Male, Union Univ, Summer 56; Phi Kappa Phi, Univ Louisville, 66; Outstanding Graduating Senior, Grad Sch, Univ Louisville, 74; John Hay Fel in the humanities, Northwestern Univ, 62-63; NEH Summer Seminar, Univ Va, 79; Fulbright/Hayes Fel travel/study tour of India, Summer 87. **MEMBERSHIPS** MLA; Southern Humanities Coun; SAtlantic Mod Lang Asn; Ky Philol Asn. **RESEARCH** Ethics, evolution, and the arts. **SELECTED PUBLICATIONS** Auth, The South from a distance, Tri-Quart, spring 63; The prince introduces Imlac to general semantics, Etc: A Review of General Semantics 30, 3/73; Visual Imagery and Internal Awareness in Pirsig's Zen and the Art of Motorcycle Maintenance, KPA Bull, 84; Article Reprinted in Guidebook to Zen and the Art of Motorcycle Maintenance, William Morrow, 90; Taxi Ride from Jaipur to Delhi, Int Mag 9, Eastern Ky Univ, 88; Random Reflections on Teaching Humanities, Accent Marks 2, Eastern Ky Univ, Spring 98. **CONTACT ADDRESS** 610 Benjamin Drive, Richmond, KY 40475-3051. **EMAIL** fshearon@kyblue.com

SHEASBY, R.
PERSONAL Born 11/03/1932, Chicago, IL, s **DISCIPLINE** ENGLISH **EDUCATION** Univ Ill, Chicago, AB, 69; Depaul Univ, MA, 71; Northern Ill Univ, PhD, 97. **CAREER** Inst, Chicago State Univ, 72-74; inst, City Col of Chicago, 76-80; asst prof, Loyola Univ of Chicago, 98-. **HONORS AND AWARDS** TA, NIU, 71, RA, NIU, 71; TA, NIU, 91-93. **MEMBERSHIPS** College Language Asn **RESEARCH** American Literature **SELECTED PUBLICATIONS** Auth, "Dual Reality: Echoes of Burke's Tiger in Cullen's Heritage," CLA J 39 (95): 2. **CONTACT ADDRESS** Dept English, Loyola Univ, Chicago, 6525 N Sheridan Rd, Chicago, IL 60626-5344. **EMAIL** rsheasb@luc.edu

SHEATS, PAUL DOUGLAS
PERSONAL Born 06/17/1932, Albany, NY, m, 1964, 2 children **DISCIPLINE** ENGLISH **EDUCATION** Harvard Univ, BA, 54, MA, 63, PhD(English), 66; Oxford Univ, AB, 57. **CAREER** Instr English, Haverford Col, 58-60; teaching fel, Harvard Univ, 63-66; from asst prof to assoc prof, 66-78, vchmn dept, 76-78, PROF ENGLISH & CHMN DEPT, UNIV CALIF, LOS ANGELES, 78- **MEMBERSHIPS** MLA **RESEARCH** Wordsworth; Romantic poetry. **SELECTED PUBLICATIONS** Auth, The making of Wordsworth's poetry, 1785-1798, Harvard Univ, 73; rev ed, The Poetical Works of Keats, Houghton Mifflin, 75; Wordsworth's Retrogrades and the Shaping of The Prelude, J English & Ger Philol, 72; The Poetical Works of Wordsworth, Houghton Mifflin, 82. **CONTACT ADDRESS** Univ of California, Los Angeles, 2225 Humanities Bldg, Los Angeles, CA 90024.

SHEDLETSKY, LEONARD JERALD
PERSONAL Born 04/04/1944, m, 1979, 2 children **DISCIPLINE** COMMUNICATION STUDIES **EDUCATION** Brooklyn Col, BA, 65; San Francisco State Col, MA, 68; Univ Ill, PhD, 74. **CAREER** Asst prof, Univ Conn, 74-79; asst prof, 79-84; assoc prof, 84-91; prof, 91-. **HONORS AND AWARDS** Asst ed, Nat Commun Asn. **MEMBERSHIPS** Speech Commun Asn; Int Commun Asn; Eastern Commun Asn; Western States Commun Asn; Int Listening Asn; Northeastern Edu Res Asn. **RESEARCH** Intrapersonal Communication **SELECTED PUBLICATIONS** Auth, Meaning & Mind: An Intrapersonal Approach to Human Communication, 89; Teaching with computer-mediated communication, 95; Where do we locate intrapersonal communication within the cognitive domain?, 95; coauth, Intrapersonal Communication Processes, 95; Teaching as experiential learning, 96; auth, A lot of teachers who can, don't, 97; Communication technology: Using e-mail and the World Wide Webin the communication course, 97. **CONTACT ADDRESS** Dept of Communication, 98 Bedford St., Portland, ME 04103. **EMAIL** lenny@maine.edu

SHEEHAN, DONALD
DISCIPLINE ENGLISH LITERATURE **EDUCATION** Univ Wis, PhD, 69. **CAREER** Sr Lctr Eng and Classics. **RESEARCH** Lit and compos. **SELECTED PUBLICATIONS** Auth, The Seeds of Iconography: Notes on Beginning the Practice, Orthodox New England, 88; Mary de Rachewiltz in Ital Transl of Pound's Cantos I-XXX: A Prosodic Note, Paideuma, 83. **CONTACT ADDRESS** Dept of English, Dartmouth Col, 6032 Sanborn House, Hanover, NH 03755. **EMAIL** Donald.Sheehan@dartmouth.edu

SHEFFEY, RUTHE G.
PERSONAL Born Essex County, VA, m, 1950, 2 children **DISCIPLINE** ENGLISH **EDUCATION** Morgan State Univ, BA 1947; Howard Univ, MA 1949; Univ of PA, PhD 1959. **CAREER** Howard Univ, graduate asst in English, 47-48; Claflin Coll, instructor, English, French, 48-49; Morgan State Coll, asst prof, 59-64, assoc prof, 64-70; chairperson, English dept, 70-74, prof, dept of English, 75-. **HONORS AND AWARDS** Coll Language Assn Creative Achievement Awd, 1974; United Fund Awd for Community Serv, 1975; Community Serv Awd, Jack & Jill of Amer, 1979; Distinguished Alumni Citation, Natl Assn for Equal Opportunity, 1980; Faculty Rsch Grants for studies in Shakespearean Production, 1983; Achievement Awd for Preservation of Higher Educ Standards & Contributions to African-American History & Culture, 1984; Morgan State Univ Women Awd, 1985; Citations for Outstanding Service to Scholarly and Literary Communities, 1985-93; Maryland Assn for Higher Education, Faculty Member of the Year Awd, 1994; Howard Univ, Baltimore Chapter, Alumna of the Year, 1987; Towson State Univ, Distinguished Black Woman of America, 1984; numerous other citations and awards; Morgan State Univ, Hall of Fame, 1998. **MEMBERSHIPS** Coll English Assn; Coll Language Assn; Modern Language Assn; Natl Cncl of the Teachers of English; Eighteenth Century Studies Assn; Middle Atlantic Writers Assn; Langston Hughes Soc; founder, pres, Zora Neale Hurston Soc; editor, Zora Neale Hurston Forum; Assn for the Study of Afro-American Life & Culture; Kings Kids Mentor, Heritage United Church of Christ; Mayor's Cncl on Women's Rights; delegate, White House Conf on Women as Economic Equals; Morgan State, Howard Univ, & the Univ of PA Alumni Assns; communications comm, United Fund of MD, 1972-74; commnr & vice chair, Baltimore Co Human Relations Commn; MD state delegate, Paula Hollinger's Scholarship Award Panel; Maryland Council for the Humanities, 1990-96. **SELECTED PUBLICATIONS** Author of numerous books, articles, and reviews. **CONTACT ADDRESS** Professor of English, Morgan State Univ, Coldspring & Hillen Rds, Baltimore, MD 21239. **EMAIL** rsheffey@moac.morgan.edu

SHEIDLEY, WILLIAM E.
PERSONAL Born 05/29/1940, Kansas City, MO, m, 1962, 2 children **DISCIPLINE** ENGLISH **EDUCATION** Stanford Univ, AB, 62, AM, 66, PhD, 68. **CAREER** Teach asst, Standord Univ, 63-65; asst prof, 66-72, assoc prof, 72-81, prof Eng, 81-94, Univ Conn; vis lectr, 92-93, assoc prof, 94-95, PROF ENG, 95-, CHAIR DEPT ENG, FOR LANG, 95-, UNIV S COLO; asst prof Eng, US Air Force Acad, 93-94. **HONORS AND AWARDS** Phi Beta Kappa; Sigma Tau Delta; cofounder, dir, conn writing project, 82-87. **RESEARCH** English Renaissance lit; the Hamlet tradition. **SELECTED PUBLICATIONS** Auth, Barnabe Googe, G. K. Hall, 81; auth, George Gascoigne and The Spoyle of Antwerpe (1576), War, Literature, and the Arts 8.1, 96; auth, The Play(s) within the Film: Tom Stoppard's Rosencrantz & Guildenstern Are Dead, Screen Shakespeare, Univ Aarhus Press, 94; auth, Making Hamlet Pirouette: The 1816 Pantomime Tragique by Louis Henry (and trans), Hamlet Studies 15, 93; auth, Born in Imitation of Someone Else: Reading Turgenev's Hamlet of the Shchigrovsky District as a Version of Hamlet, Studies in Short Fiction 27, 90; auth, Hamlet as a Vision of Renewal, Hamlet Studies 12, 90; auth, The Autor Penneth, Wherof He Hath No Proofe: The Early Elizabethan Dream Poem as a Defense of Poetic Fiction, Studies in Philol 81, 84; auth, "Hamlets and Hierarchy," Peace Review 11.2, 99. **CONTACT ADDRESS** Dept of English & For Langs, Univ of So Colorado, 2200 Bonforte Blvd, Pueblo, CO 81001-4901. **EMAIL** sheidley@uscolo.edu

SHELBURNE, D. AUDELL
PERSONAL Born 05/10/1965, Phoenix, AZ, m, 1988, 5 children **DISCIPLINE** ENGLISH **EDUCATION** Univ Dallas, BA, 87; Univ Houston, MA, 91; Tex Tech Univ, PhD, 97. **CAREER** Vis asst prof, Tex Tech Univ, 97-98; asst prof, Univ of Mary Hardin Baylor, 98-. **HONORS AND AWARDS** Eldon Durrett Mem Scholarship, 83-87; Helen Hodges Educ Trust Awd, 93, 94; Phi Kappa Phi, 94; William Byran Gates Fel, 93, 95; George T Prigmore Awd, Texas Tech Univ, 94; Sigma Tau Delta, 00; Who's Who of Am Teachers, 00. **MEMBERSHIPS** MLA, John Donne Soc. **RESEARCH** John Donne, Ben Jonson, the connection between Classical Roman and Elizabethan literature. **SELECTED PUBLICATIONS** Auth, "The Textual Problem of 'Twicknam Garden,'" John Donne Jour, Vol 17, (98). **CONTACT ADDRESS** Univ of Mary Hardin-Baylor, 900 College St, Box 8008, Belton, TX 76513. **EMAIL** ashelburne@umhb.edu

SHELDON, TED P.
PERSONAL Born Oak Park, IL, m, 1965, 2 children **DISCIPLINE** LIBRARY **EDUCATION** Elmhurst Col, BA, 64; Ind Univ, MA, 65, PhD, 76; Univ Ill, Champaign-Urbana, MALS, 77. **CAREER** Instr, 66-68, Elmhurst Col; asst prof, 70-76, Millikin Univ; ref libr/hist bibl, 77-79, head, collect develop, 78-80, Univ Kansas Libraries; ass dir of libr, 80-83, SUNY, Binghamton; assoc dir of libr, 83-85, adj prof, hist, 88-, dir of libr, 85-, Univ Missouri-Kansas City; adj prof libr sci, 89-94, Univ Missouri-Columbia, **RESEARCH** Management of special collections and archives; audio archiving; standards for audio preservation; management issues in libraries. **CONTACT ADDRESS** Univ of Missouri, Kansas City, 5100 Rockhill Rd, Kansas City, MO 64110-2499. **EMAIL** sheldont@umkc.edu

SHELL, MARC
DISCIPLINE ENGLISH **EDUCATION** Stanford Univ, BA, 68; Trinity Col, Cambridge, BA, 70; Yale Univ, MA, 72, PhD, 75. **CAREER** Assoc, prof, Eng, State Univ NY Buffalo; HARVARD UNIV. **MEMBERSHIPS** Am Antiquarian Soc **SELECTED PUBLICATIONS** Auth, Money, Language, and Thought: Literary and Philosophical Economies from the Medieval to the Modern Era, Univ Calif Press, 82; auth, The End of Kinship: "Measure for Measure," Incest, and the Idea of Universal Siblinghood, Stanford Univ Press, 88; auth, "Babel in America; or, The Politics of Language Diversity in the United States," Critical Inquiry 20, 93. **CONTACT ADDRESS** Dept of Eng and Am Lit and Language, Harvard Univ, 11 Prescott St, Cambridge, MA 02138.

SHELLEY, BRYAN
PERSONAL Born 02/25/1949, Williston, ND, s **DISCIPLINE** ENGLISH; ROMANTIC STUDIES **EDUCATION** Bryan Col, BA, 71; Appalachian State Univ, MA, 73; Middlebury Col, MLit, 81; Oxford Univ, DPh, 86. **CAREER** Tchg asst, Appalachian State Univ, 71-73; sports ed, Laurens Cty Advert, 73-75; instr english, Bryan Col, 75-76; vis asst prof, Wheaton Col, 89; assoc prof, Campbell Univ, 89- . **HONORS AND AWARDS** Who's Who in the S & SW, 99. **MEMBERSHIPS** Mod Lang Asn; Wordsworth Dove Cottage Trust; Nat Asn Schol; Oxford C.S. Lewis Soc; Keats-Shelley Asn. **RESEARCH** Romantic poets, Gnosticism (ancient and modern), Biblical influence on literature. **SELECTED PUBLICATIONS** Auth, "The Synthetic Imagination: Shelley and Associationism" Wordsworth Circle, (83); auth, "The Interpreting Angel in 'The Triumph of Life'", Rev English Stud, (88); auth, Shelley and Scripture: The Interpreting Angel, Oxford Univ Press, (94). **CONTACT ADDRESS** Dept English, Campbell Univ, 20 Country Rd, Hendersonville, NC 28791. **EMAIL** bkshelley@cytechcis.net

SHELMERDINE, CYNTHIA WRIGHT
PERSONAL Born 01/07/1949, Boston, MA **DISCIPLINE** CLASSICS; CLASSICAL ARCHAEOLOGY **EDUCATION** Bryn Mawr Col, AB, 70; Cambridge Univ, BA, 72, MA, 80; Harvard Univ, AM, 76, PhD, 77. **CAREER** Asst prof Classics, Univ Tex, Austin, 77-84; assoc prof, 84-97; prof, 97-; chair, 98-. **HONORS AND AWARDS** Marshall scholar, 70-72; Ctr. for Hellenic Studies, jr fel, 81-82; Pres assocs tchg award, Univ of Texas, 88. **MEMBERSHIPS** Archaeol Inst Am; Am Philol Asn; Am Sch Class Studies Athens Alumni Asn; Class Asn Middle West & South. **RESEARCH** Mycenaean Greek; Bronze Age Archaeology. **SELECTED PUBLICATIONS** Auth, The Pylos Ma tables reconsidered, Am Jour Archaeol, 73; contribur, Excavations at Nichoria (vol II), Univ Minn, (in press); Nichoria in context, Am Jour Archeol, 81; coauth, The Pylos Regional Archaeological Project. Part1: Overview and the Archaeological Survey, Hesperia 66, 97; auth, Review of Aegean Prehistory VI: The Palatial Bronze Age of the Central and Southern Greek Mainland, Am Jour of Archeol 101, 97; contribur, Sandy Pylos. From Nestor to Navarino, Univ Texas, 98. **CONTACT ADDRESS** Dept of Classics, Univ of Texas, Austin, Austin, TX 78712-1181. **EMAIL** cwshelm@mail.utexas.edu

SHELMERDINE, SUSAN C.
PERSONAL Born 04/21/1954, Boston, MA, s **DISCIPLINE** CLASSICAL STUDIES **EDUCATION** Smith Col, BA, 76; Univ Mich, MA, 77, PhD, 81. **CAREER** Lect, Univ N Carolina, 81-82, ast prof, 82-88; vis asoc prof, Univ Mich, 88-89; asoc prof, Univ N Carolina, 88- , dept head, 89-92, asoc dean, 92-95. **HONORS AND AWARDS** Jr fel, Ctr Hellenic Stud, Washington DC, 95-86; NEH Fel, 96-97. **MEMBERSHIPS** APA; Class Asn Middle West & South. **RESEARCH** Greek poetry; language pedagogy. **SELECTED PUBLICATIONS** Co-auth, Greek for Reading, Univ Mich, 94; auth, The Homeric Hymns, Focus Information Grp, 95; contribur, HarperCollins Dictionary of Religion, HarperCollins, 95; auth, "Greek Studies Today," Class Jrnl, 96 **CONTACT ADDRESS** Dept of Classical Studies, Univ of No Carolina, Greensboro, PO Box 26170, Greensboro, NC 27402-6170. **EMAIL** shelmerd@uncg.edu

SHELTON, LEWIS E.
PERSONAL Born 10/12/1941, Roll, IN, m, 1990 **DISCIPLINE** THEATRE **EDUCATION** Taylor Univ, BA, 63; Indiana Univ, Bloomington, MA, 65; Univ Wisc, Madison, MA, 68, PhD, 71. **CAREER** Asst prof, Calif State Univ, Hayward, 71-73; assoc prof, Kans State Univ, 73-. **MEMBERSHIPS** Asn for Theatre in Higher Ed, The Am Theatre and Drama Soc. **RESEARCH** American stage directors. **SELECTED PUBLICATIONS** Auth, "David Storey and The Invisible Event," Midwest Quart (summer 81); auth, "Ben Teal: America's Abusive Director," The J of Am Drama and Theatre (spring 90); auth, "Alan Schneider's Direction of 'Who's Afraid of Virginia Woolf?" The J of Am Drama and Theatre (fall 91); auth, "David Belasco and the Scientific Perspective of Directing," The J of Am Drama and Theatre (winter 98); auth, "Arthur Hopkins and the Neo-Romantic Perspective of Directing," The J of Am Drama and Theatre (winter 99); auth, "George Abbott and the Theatrical Perspective of Directing," The J of Am Drama and Theatre (winter 2000). **CONTACT ADDRESS** Speech, Theatre & Dance, Kansas State Univ, 129 Nichols Hall, Manhattan, KS 66506-2300. **EMAIL** shelton@ksu.edu

SHELTON, RICHARD WILLIAM
PERSONAL Born 06/24/1933, Boise, ID, m, 1956, 1 child **DISCIPLINE** ENGLISH, CREATIVE WRITING **EDUCATION** Abilene Christian Col, BA, 58; Univ Ariz, MA, 61. **CAREER** Asst prof, 70-74, assoc prof, 74-78, dir, Creative Writing prog, 79-81, prof English, Univ Az, 78-, dir, Univ Ariz Poetry Ctr, 64-65; consult, Ariz Comn Arts & Humanities, 74-; dir, Writer's Workshop, Ariz State Prison, 74-; Regents prof, 91-. **HONORS AND AWARDS** US Awd, Int Poetry Forum, 70; Az Governor's Awd, 91; Western States Awd for Creative Nonfiction, 92; 2 NEA Writer's Fellowships. **MEMBERSHIPS** Pen Club; Poetry Soc Am. **RESEARCH** Surrealism, post-symbolist French poetry; translation of contemporary Mexican poets; contemporary American poetry. **SELECTED PUBLICATIONS** Auth, Journal of Return, Kayak, 69; The Tattooed Desert, Univ Pittsburgh, 71; Calendar, Baleen, 72; Of All the Dirty Words, Univ Pittsburgh, 72; Among the Stones, Monument Press, 73; You Can't Have Everything, Univ Pittsburgh, 75; Chosen Plance, Best Cellar Press, 75; The Bus to Veracruz, 78 & Selected Poems: 1969-81, 82, Univ Pittsburgh; A Kind of Glory, Copper Canyon Press, 82; Hohokam, Confluence Press, 86; Going Back to Bisbee, Univ of Az Press, 92. **CONTACT ADDRESS** Dept of English, Univ of Arizona, 1 University of Az, Tucson, AZ 85721-0001. **EMAIL** rshelton@u.arizona.edu

SHEN, FUYUAN
DISCIPLINE ADVERTISING **EDUCATION** Univ NC-Chapel Hill, PhD. **CAREER** Asst prof; fac, Univ SD, 97-. **MEMBERSHIPS** Am Acad Advert; Asn Educ in Jour & Mass Commun; Am Marketing Asn: Newspaper Asn Am. **SELECTED PUBLICATIONS** Auth, Characteristics of online consumers: A diffusion of innovation approach, Southern Asn of Public Opinion Res Annual Conf, Raleigh, 95; coauth, Assessment of television's anti-violence messages, In Nat TV Violence Study, Vol 1, Thousand Oaks, Sage Publ, 97; Audience reaction to commercial advertising in China in the 1980s, Int J of Advert, 14, 95; Position of TV advertisement in a natural pod, A preliminary analysis of concepts, measurements and effects, Proceedings of the 95 Annual Conf Amer Acad Advert, 95; Exploratory analysis of the effectiveness of television industry†¤s antiviolence public service announcements, Asn Educ Jour and Mass Commun Annual Conf, Anaheim, 96. **CONTACT ADDRESS** Dept of Mass Commun, Univ of So Dakota, Vermillion, 414 E Clark St, Vermillion, SD 57069. **EMAIL** fshen@usd.edu

SHEPARD, ALAN
DISCIPLINE ENGLISH **EDUCATION** St. Olaf Col, BA, 83; Univ Va, PhD, 90. **CAREER** Writing Ctr Tutor, St. Olaf Col, 81-83; Tutor, 84-90, Instr, 87-89, Grad Instr, Univ Va, 86-90; Asst Prof, 90-96, Assoc Prof , Tex Christian Univ, 96-. **HONORS AND AWARDS** George Weida Spohn Prize, St. Olaf Col, 82; Phi Beta Kappa; recipient of numerous grants from The Folger Libr, Tex Christian Univ, and others; recipient of numerous fellowships. **MEMBERSHIPS** Mod Lang Asn; Renaissance Soc Am; Group for Early Mod Cult Studies; Soc Lit & Sci; Renaissance Early Text Soc. **SELECTED PUBLICATIONS** Auth, Endless Sacks: Soldiers' Desire in Tamburlaine, Renaissance Quart, 93; The Literature of a Medical Hoax: The Case of Mary Toft, The Pretended Rabbet-Breeder, Eighteenth-Century Life 2, 95; Aborted Rage in Beth Henley's Women, repr, States of Rage: Emotional Eruption, Violence, and Social Change, NY Univ Press, 96; Thou art no soldier; Thou art a merchant: The Mentality of War in Malta, In: Marlowe, History, and Sexuality: New Critical Essays on Christopher Marlowe, AMS Press, 98; co-ed, Coming to Class: Pedagogy and the Social Class of Teachers, Heinemann Boynton/Cook, 98; auth, Marlowe's soldieres, London: Ashgate, 01. **CONTACT ADDRESS** English Dept, Texas Christian Univ, Box 297270, Fort Worth, TX 76129. **EMAIL** a.shepard@tcu.edu

SHEPHERD, JOHN
DISCIPLINE HISTORY OF POPULAR MUSIC **EDUCATION** Carleton Univ, BA, BM; Royal Col of Mus, ARCM; Univ York, UK, DPhil. **CAREER** Prof; ch of Editorial Bd and managing ed, the Encyclopedia of Popular Music of the World, Cassell. **HONORS AND AWARDS** Davidson Dunton res lectrship, 92; adj res prof, grad prog in musicology, york univ; dept of mus, univ ottawa. **RESEARCH** Sociology and aesthetics of music, popular music stud, theory and method in musicology, cultural stud, and the sociology of music education. **SELECTED PUBLICATIONS** Auth, Music as Social Text, Polity Press, 91; co-auth, Rock and Popular Music: Politics, Policies, Institutions, Routledge, 93; Music and Cultural Theory, Polity Press of Cambridge, 97; Popular Music Studies: A Select International Bibliography, 97; co-ed, Relocating Cultural Studies: Developments in Theory and Research, Routledge, 93. **CONTACT ADDRESS** Carleton Univ, 1125 Colonel By Dr, Ottawa, ON, Canada K1S 5B6.

SHEPHERD, REGINALD
PERSONAL Born 04/10/1963, New York, NY **DISCIPLINE** ENGLISH **EDUCATION** Bennington Col, BA, 88; Brown Univ, MFA, 91; Univ Iowa, MFA, 93. **CAREER** Asst prof, North Ill Univ, 95-99; asst prof, Cornell Univ, 99-. **HONORS AND AWARDS** Constance Saltonstall Found, 00; Ill Arts Coun, 98; NEA, 95; Amy Lowell Poet Trav Fel, 94; Pushcart Prize, 99; Merit Awd, George A. and Eliza Gardner Howard Found, 98; George Kent Prize,94; Paumanok Poet Awd, 93; Asn Writ Prog Awd in Poet, 93; "Discovery"/The Nation Awd, 93. **MEMBERSHIPS** PSA, MLA, AWP. **RESEARCH** Creative writing; modern and contemporary poetry; gay and lesbian studies. **SELECTED PUBLICATIONS** Auth, Wrong, UPP, 96; auth, Angel Interrupted, UPP, 99; auth, Some Are Drowning, UPP, 00; auth, Otherhood, UPP, forthcoming. **CONTACT ADDRESS** Eng Dept., Cornell Univ, Ithaca, NY 14853. **EMAIL** rsheperd@worldnet.att.net

SHERARD, TRACEY
PERSONAL Born 07/17/1966, Fresno, CA **DISCIPLINE** ENGLISH **EDUCATION** Calif State Univ, BA, 88; San Francisco State Univ, MA, 93; Washington State Univ, PhD, 98. **CAREER** Teaching Asst to Instructor, Washington State Univ, 94-. **HONORS AND AWARDS** Blackburn Postdoc Fel, Washington State Univ, 98-99. **MEMBERSHIPS** Mod Lang Asn, Virginia Woolf Soc, Asn of Fac Women. **RESEARCH** Narrative Theory; Gender Theory; The 20th Century Novel; Virginia Woolf. **SELECTED PUBLICATIONS** Auth, "Women's classic Blues in Toni Morrison's Jazz: Cultural Artifact as Narrator," GENDERS, 00; auth, "Parcival in the forest of Gender: Wagner, Homosexuality, and The Waves," Virginia Woolf: Turning the Centuries, Pace Univ Press, 00; auth, "Sonny's Bebop: Baldwin's 'Blues Text' as Intracultural Critique," African American Review, (98): 691-705; auth, "Voyage Through the Waves: Woolf's Kaleidoscope of the Unpresentable," Virginia Woolf & The Arts, Pace Univ Pres, 97; auth, "The Birth of the Female Subject in The Crying of Lot 49," Pynchon Notes, (93): 60-74. **CONTACT ADDRESS** Dept English, Washington State Univ, PO Box 645020, Pullman, WA 99164-5020. **EMAIL** shertra@aol.com

SHERIDAN, JENNIFER A.
PERSONAL Born 04/01/1962, Englewood, NJ **DISCIPLINE** CLASSICS **EDUCATION** Montclair State Col, BA, 84; Columbia Univ, MA, 85, PhD, 90. **CAREER** Asst prof, St Joseph's Univ, 90-95; Asst prof, Wayne State Univ, 95-. **MEMBERSHIPS** APA, ANS, ASP, AIP, DCA, MCC, CAMWS **RESEARCH** Papyrology; Women in the ancient world. **SELECTED PUBLICATIONS** co-auth, Greek and Latin Documents from 'Abu Sha'ar, 1990-1991, Jour Amer Res Ctr In Egypt 31, 94; Greek and Latin Documents from 'Abu Sha'ar, 1992-1993, Bull Amer Soc Papyrologists 31, 94; auth, Women without Guardians: An Updated List, Bull Amer Soc Papyrologists 33, 96; Papyri numbers 257, 259, 286, Columbia Papyri X, 96; Not at a Loss for Words: The Economic Power of Literate Women in Late Antique Egypt, Transactions of Amer Philol Asn, 98; Columbia Papyri IX: The Vestis Militaris Codex, 98. **CONTACT ADDRESS** Dept of Classics, Wayne State Univ, 431 Manoogian Hall, Detroit, MI 48202. **EMAIL** aa2191@wayne.edu

SHERK, ROBERT K.
DISCIPLINE CLASSICS **EDUCATION** Johns Hopkins Univ, PhD, 50. **CAREER** Fac, 62; to prof emer, present, SUNY Buffalo. **RESEARCH** Hellenistic and Roman hist; epigraphy; ancient biog; Roman empire from Augustus to Hadrian. **SELECTED PUBLICATIONS** Auth, Roman Documents from the Greek East, Johns Hopkins, 69; Municipal Decrees of the Roman West, Buffalo, 70; The Roman Empire from Augustus to Hadrian, Cambridge, 88; articles on Hellenistic and Roman

history; co-ed, Translated Documents of Greece and Rome, Cambridge, 177-85. **CONTACT ADDRESS** Dept Classics, SUNY, Buffalo, 712 Clemens Hall, Buffalo, NY 14260.

SHERMAN, SANDRA
DISCIPLINE RESTORATION AND EIGHTEENTH-CENTURY LITERATURE **EDUCATION** Univ Pa, PhD. **CAREER** English and Lit, Univ Ark. **SELECTED PUBLICATIONS** Auth, Printing the Mind: The Economics of Authorship in Areopagitica, ELH, 93; Trembling Texts: Margaret Cavendish and the Dialectic of Authorship, eng Literary Renaissance, 94; Servants and Semiotics: Reversible Signs, Capital Instability, and Defoe's Logic of the Market, ELH, 95; Instructing the 'Empire of Beauty': Lady Mary Wortley Montagu and the Politics of Female Rationality, S Atlantic Rev, 95; Promises, Promises: Credit as a Contested Metaphor in Early Capitalist Discourse, Modern Philol, 96; Finance and Fictionality in the Early Eighteenth Century, Cambridge, 96.s **CONTACT ADDRESS** Univ of Arkansas, Fayetteville, Fayetteville, AR 72701.

SHERMAN, STUART
DISCIPLINE RESTORATION AND EIGHTEENTH-CENTURY LITERATURE **EDUCATION** Columbia Univ, PhD. **CAREER** Art, Washington Univ. **SELECTED PUBLICATIONS** Ed, Johnsonian News Letter. **CONTACT ADDRESS** Washington Univ, 1 Brookings Dr, Saint Louis, MO 63130.

SHERMAN, THEODORE
PERSONAL Born 01/19/1962, San Jose, CA, m, 1985, 3 children **DISCIPLINE** ENGLISH **EDUCATION** Covenant Col, BA, 87; Univ Central Fla, MA, 88; Univ Southern Miss, PhD, 93. **CAREER** Assoc prof, Middle Tenn State Univ, 93-. **MEMBERSHIPS** John Donne Soc, Intl Soc of Anlo-Saxonist, Early English Text Soc, Christianity and Literature. **RESEARCH** Beowulf, John Donn, Medieval and renaissance manuscript studies, Bibliography, C.S. Lewis, J.R.R. Tolkien, Charles Wiliams and mythopoeic literature. **SELECTED PUBLICATIONS** Ed, The Holy Sonnets, in The Variorum Edition of the Poetry of John Donne, (forthcoming); ed, Mythlore: A Journal of J.R.R. Tolkien, C.S. Lewis, Charles Williams, and Mythopoeic Literature; auth, The Wetmoreland Manuscript of John donne's Poetry and Prose: The Facsimile edition, (forthcoming). **CONTACT ADDRESS** Dept English, Middle Tennessee State Univ, 1301 E Main St, Murfreesboro, TN 37132-0001. **EMAIL** tsherman@mtsu.edu

SHERMAN, WILLIAM H.
PERSONAL Born 01/26/1966, MN, m, 1998 **DISCIPLINE** ENGLISH **EDUCATION** Columbia Univ, BA, 88; Cambridge Univ, MPhil, 89, PhD, 92. **CAREER** Asst prof, Univ MD, 93-99, assoc prof, 99-, dir, English Honors Prog, 98-; vis prof fel, Queen Mary & Westfield Col, Univ London,95-96. **HONORS AND AWARDS** Phi Beta Kappa, 88; Jr CAIRD Fel, Nat Maritime Mus, 92-93; res awards from the Huntington Library, the Folger Shakespeare Library, the Mellon Found, the British Acad, and the Bibliographical Soc. **MEMBERSHIPS** MLA, Renaissance Soc, Hakluyt Soc, SHARP. **RESEARCH** English renaissance culture, the literature of travel, the history of the book. **SELECTED PUBLICATIONS** Auth, "Thomas Dekker's 'Old Fortunatus' and England's Golden Age," Medieval & Renaissance Drama in England, 6, 85-102 (93); auth, "Thomas Digges," "Thomas Harriot," and "Maurice Kyffin," in Dictionary of Literary Biography, vol 136: Sixteenth-Century Non-Dramatic Authors, Columbia: Bruccoli Clark Layman (94); coauth with Lisa Jardine, "Pragmatic readers: knowledge transactions and scholarly services in late Elizabethan England," in Anthony Fletcher and Peter Roberts, eds, Religion, culture and society in early modern Britain: essays in honor of Patrick Collinson, Cambridge: Cambridge Univ Press (94); auth, John Dee: The Politics of reading and Writing in the English Renaissance, Amherst: Univ MA Press (95, paperback, 97); auth, "Anatomizing the Commonwealth: Language, Politics, and the Elizabethan Social Order," in Elizabeth Fowler and Roland Greene, eds, The Project of Prose in Early Modern Europe and the New World, Cambridge: Cambridge Univ Press (77); auth, "Putting the British Seas on the Map: John Dee's Imperial Cartography," in James Akerman, ed, Çartography, Statecraft, and Political Culture, Cartographica, 35:3/4, 1-10 (98); auth, "'The Book thus put in every vulgar hand', Marking Readers in Early English Printed Bibles," in Kimberly Van Kampen and Paul Saenger, eds, The Bible as Book: The First Printed Editions, London: The British Library (99); coed, Peter Hulme, The Tempest and its Travels, London: Reaktion Books (2000), **CONTACT ADDRESS** Dept English, Univ of Maryland, Col Park, 3101 Susquehanna Hall, College Park, MD 20742-8800. **EMAIL** ws76@umail.umd.edu

SHERR, RICHARD JONATHAN
PERSONAL Born 03/25/1947, New York, NY, S **DISCIPLINE** MUSIC HISTORY **EDUCATION** Columbia Univ, BA, 69; Princeton Univ, MFA, 71, PhD(Musicol), 75. **CAREER** Lectr music, Univ Calif, Los Angeles, 73-74; vis lectr, Univ Wis-Madison, 74-75; asst prof 75-80, assoc prof, 80-86; prof, 86-, music, Smith Col. **MEMBERSHIPS** Am Musicol Soc; Renaissance Soc Am; Int Musicol Soc. **RESEARCH** Music and musicians in Rome in the late 15th and early 16th centuries; music in Mantua in the late 16th century; Arthur Sullivan and popular music of the 19th century. **SELECTED PUBLICATIONS** Auth, New archival data concerning the Chapel of Clement VII, J Am Musicol Soc, 76; contribr, Josquin des Prez: Proc Int Josquin Festival-Cong, 76; auth, Notes on two Roman manuscripts of the early sixteenth century, Musical Quart, 77; The publications of Guglielmo Gonzaga, J Am Musicol Soc, 78; From the diary of a 16th century papal singer, Current Musicol, 78; ed, Bertrandi Vaqueras: Opera Omnia, Hanssler Verlag, 79; auth, Guglielmo Gonzaga and the Castrati, Renaissance Quart, 80; Schubert, Sullivan and Grove, Musical Times, 80; auth, Papal Music Manuscripts in Late Fifteenth and Early Sixteenth Century Rome, Hanssler Verlag, 96; music and musicians in Renaissance Rome and other Courts, Ashgate, 99; ed, Papal Music and Musicians in Late Medieval and Renaissance Rome, Oxford Univ Press, 98. **CONTACT ADDRESS** Dept of Music, Smith Col, Northampton, MA 01063-0001. **EMAIL** rsherr@smith.edu

SHERRILL, CATHERINE ANNE
PERSONAL Born 02/26/1938, Houston, TX **DISCIPLINE** ENGLISH; EDUCATION **EDUCATION** Univ Texas, Austin, BA, 60, MA, 69; Univ Iowa, PhD, 81. **CAREER** Instr, 60-66, Houston Independent Sch Dist; teacher, 69-78, Col of Mainland; instr, prof English, E Tenn St Univ. **HONORS AND AWARDS** Fac mem of the Year from Panhellenic Asn, E Tenn State Univ, 89. **MEMBERSHIPS** Nat Coun of Teachers of English. **RESEARCH** Young people's literature; composition and rhetoric. **SELECTED PUBLICATIONS** Auth, Carlson, G.R. and Anne Sherrill, Varies of Readers: How We Come to Love Books, NCTE, 88; auth, Literature Is: Collected Essays of G. Robert Carlsen, U of Iowa Foundation, Auburn Univ East Tennessee State Univ, 94, articles and essays in books and professional journals. **CONTACT ADDRESS** Dept of English, East Tennessee State Univ, Johnson City, TN 37614. **EMAIL** sherrill@etsu.edu

SHERRY, LEE F.
PERSONAL Born 08/22/1954, Marietta, OH, m, 1992 **DISCIPLINE** CLASSICS **EDUCATION** Univ Texas, Austin, BA, 79; Columbia Univ, MA, 82, MPhil, 84; PhD, 91. **CAREER** Instr, Columbia Univ, 82-89; instr, NY Univ, 86-87; lectr, Queens Col, 88; tchr Latin, Trinity School, 87-91; lectr, Catholic Univ, 92-96; res assoc, Dumbarton Oaks, 91-96; tchr Latin, Kent Place School, Summit NJ, 96- . **HONORS AND AWARDS** Phi Kappa Phi, 78; Phi Beta Kappa, 79; Summa Cum Laude, 79; ETS approved scorer of AP Latin examination essays, 98-03; Cum Laude Soc, Kent Place Sch Chapter, 99; fac consultant to the AP 2000 Latin Reading, 00. **MEMBERSHIPS** APA; Am Class League; Class Asn of the Atlantic States; NJ Class Asn. **RESEARCH** Greek language and literature; Latin language and literature; Medieval and Byzantine studies; patristics; computers and the humanities. **SELECTED PUBLICATIONS** Coauth, Dumbarton Oaks Hagiography Database of the Ninth Century, 95; cotrans, The Poem of Maria Komnene Palaiologina to the Virgin and Mother of God, the Chorine, Cahiers Archeologiques, 95; coauth, Thesaurus Pseudo-Nonni quondam Panopolitani, Paraphrasis Evangelii S. Ioannis, Corpus Christianorum, 95; coauth, The Dumbarton Oaks Byzantine Hagiography Database Project, Medieval Prosopography, 96; trans, Vita of Athanasia of Aegina, in Talbot, ed, Byzantine Saints' Lives in Translation Series, Dumbarton Oaks, 96; auth, The Paraphrase of St. John Attributed to Nonnus, Byzantion, 96; coauth, The Tale of a Happy Fool: The Vita of St. Philaretos the Merciful, Byzantion, 96; coauth, "Anonymous Miracles of St. Artemios," in AETOE: Studies in honour of Cyril Mango, ed. I. Sevcenko & I. Hutter (Teubner, 98), 200-209; coauth, History of Byzantine Lit, Vol I, Lit from 650 to 850, Inst for Byzantine Res/The Nat Hellenic Res Foundations (Athens), 99; transl, "Sappho 1," in The Classical Outlook, 77 (00): 2. **CONTACT ADDRESS** Kent Place Sch, 42 Norwood, Summit, NJ 07902-0308. **EMAIL** sherryl@kentplace.summit.nj.edu

SHERWOOD, STEVEN E.
PERSONAL Born 06/22/1955, Wichita, KS, d, 2 children **DISCIPLINE** ENGLISH **EDUCATION** Univ Colo, BS, 77; Univ Mont, MFA, 87. **CAREER** Lectr, Mont State Univ, 87-88; coord, Tex Christ Univ, 88-96; interim dir, 96-97; assoc dir, 97-99; instr, 99-. **HONORS AND AWARDS** AP Citation; Masquer Theater Play Writing Contest Winner; NWCA Outstand Scholarshp Awd; PEN Writing Prize. **MEMBERSHIPS** CCCC; NCTE; NWCA; SCWCA. **RESEARCH** Classical rhetoric; contemporary composition and rhetoric; creative writing; writing centers; theories of humor. **SELECTED PUBLICATIONS** Coauth, Writing Centers: An Annotated Bibliography, Greenwood (Westport), 96; coauth, The St Martin's Sourcebook for Writing Tutors, St Martin's (NY), 95; "Computers and the Writing Center: An Annotated Bibliography," in Wiring the Writing Center, ed. Eric Hobson., (Logan: Utah St UP, 98): 216-30; auth, "Philosophies, Ethics, and Methods," in Nat Writing Cen Asn Handbook, ed. Bobbie Silk (NWCA Press, 98): 1-8; auth, "The Dark Side of the Helping Personality: Student Dependency and the Potential for Tutor Burnout," in Writing Center Perspectives, ed. Byron L. Stay, Christina Murphy, Eric Hobson (Emmitsburg: NWCA Press, 95): 63-70; auth, "Cage" in New Texas '99: A Center for Texas Studies Book, eds. Donna Walker-Nixon, James Ward Lee (Belton, TX: U of Mary Hardin-Baylor P, 99): 209-14; auth, "Censoring Students, Censoring Ourselves: Constraining Conversations in the Writing Center," Writing Cen J 20 (99): 51-60; auth, "Ethics and Improvisation." Writing Lab NL 22 (97): 1-5; auth, "Understanding the Role of Co-discovery in the Writing Conference," Dialogue: A J Writing Specialists 3 (97): 41-52; auth, "Apprenticed to Failure: Learning from the Students We Can't Help," Writing Cen J 17 (96): 49-57; auth, "The Bright Side," Riversedge 9 (95): 77-82; auth, "Tutoring and the Writer's 'Felt Sense': Developing and Safeguarding the Mind's Ear," Writing Lab NL 19 (95): 10-14. **CONTACT ADDRESS** Dept English, Texas Christian Univ, Fort Worth, TX 76129. **EMAIL** s.sherwood@tcu.edu

SHERWOOD, TERRY G.
DISCIPLINE RENAISSANCE LITERATURE **EDUCATION** Univ Oregon, BA; Univ Calif, Berkeley, MA, PhD. **CAREER** Ch, 988-92; assoc VP Acad, 96; prof. **HONORS AND AWARDS** Post dr fel(s), Univ Toronto, Univ Victoria. **RESEARCH** Religion and literature; Spenser, Shakespeare; Donne, Jonson; Herbert, Milton. **SELECTED PUBLICATIONS** Auth, Fulfilling the Circle: A Study of John Donne's Thought, U of Toronto P, 84; Herbert's Prayerful Art, U of Toronto P, 89. **CONTACT ADDRESS** Dept of English, Univ of Victoria, PO Box 3070, Victoria, BC, Canada V8W 3W1. **EMAIL** sherwood@uvvm.uvic.ca

SHESGREEN, SEAN NICHOLAS
PERSONAL Born 12/05/1939, Derry City, Ireland, d, 2 children **DISCIPLINE** ENGLISH LITERATURE, ART HISTORY **EDUCATION** Loyola Univ Chicago, BA, 62, MA, 66; Northwestern Univ, PhD(English), 70. **CAREER** Teaching asst English, Northwestern Univ, 68-69; asst prof, 69-74, assoc prof, 74-82, Prof English, Northern IL Univ, 82-, Presidential Res Prof, 90-95; Vis fac mem, Univ CA, Riverside, 74-75; Am Philos Soc grant-in-aid, 76; exchange prof English, Xian Foreign Lang Inst, People's Repub China, 81-82. **HONORS AND AWARDS** Huntington Library Summer fel, 98; Yale Univ Center for Art fel, 90; Ball Brothers Found fel, Lilly Library , IN Univ, Bloomington; NEH Newberry Library Sr fel, 98-99; Houghton Lib Fel, 95. **MEMBERSHIPS** MLA; Am Soc 18th Century Studies. **RESEARCH** Eighteenth century novel with emphasis on Henry Fielding; 18th century graphic art with emphasis on William Hogarth; cries of London. **SELECTED PUBLICATIONS** Auth, Literary Portraits in the Novels of Henry Fielding, Northern Ill Univ, 72; ed, Engravings by Hogarth, Dover, 73; auth, A Harlot's Progress and the Question of Hogarth's Didacticisms, 18th Century Life, 75; Hogarth's Industry and Idleness, 18th Century Studies, 76; Hogarth and the Times-of-the-Day Tradition, Cornell Univ Press, 82; Marcellus Laroon's Cryer of the City of London, Studies Bibliog, 82; The Crier and Hawkers of London, Stanford Univ Press, 90. **CONTACT ADDRESS** No Illinois Univ, 1425 W Lincoln Hwy, De Kalb, IL 60115-2825. **EMAIL** shesgreen@niu.edu

SHEY, HOWARD JAMES
PERSONAL Born 07/21/1935, m, 1962, 2 children **DISCIPLINE** CLASSICS **EDUCATION** Creighton Univ, BA, 62; Ind Univ, Bloomington, MA, 63, Univ Iowa, PhD(classics), 68. **CAREER** From instr to asst prof classics, 66-72, Assoc Prof Classics, Univ Wis-Milwaukee, 72-, Bk rev ed, Class J, 68-73. **MEMBERSHIPS** Am Philol Asn; Class Asn Mid W & S. **RESEARCH** Latin and Greek lyric poetry; Latin epic. **SELECTED PUBLICATIONS** Auth, Petronius and Plato's Gorgias, Class Bull, 5/71; The poet's progress: Horace Ode 1 1,9/71 & Tyrtaeus and the art of propaganda, 5/76, Arethusa; Petrarch's Secretum, 89. **CONTACT ADDRESS** Dept of Classics, Univ of Wisconsin, Milwaukee, PO Box 413, Milwaukee, WI 53201-0413.

SHIAU, WENDY
PERSONAL Born 07/29/1958, Taiwan, China, m, 1988, 1 child **DISCIPLINE** ACCOUSTICS & AUDIOLOGY **EDUCATION** Taipie Med Col, BS, 82; Univ Cincinnati, MA, 90; PhD, 94. **CAREER** Assoc prof, Chiu Normal Col ROC, 94-95; asst prof, Southeastern La Univ, 96-97; asst prof, Univ of Ala, 97-. **HONORS AND AWARDS** Scholar, Univ of Cinc, 88-93. **MEMBERSHIPS** ASHA, Am Acad of Audiology, ASA **RESEARCH** Signal processing, noise and human efficiency, computer modeling in acoustics. **SELECTED PUBLICATIONS** Coauth, "Genetics of age-related hearing loss in mice: III. Susceptibility of inbred and F1 hybrid strains to noise-induced hearing loss," hearing Res 93 (96): 181-197; auth, Introduction to Audiology, Wu-Nang Publ Co (Taiwan, ROC), 97; coauth, "UA experts say watch for winter ear trouble that could delay speech," Univ of Ala News (97); coauth, "Frequent ear infections may cause child to lose hearing," Tuscaloosa News (98); coauth, "A pilot correlational study of TTS and PTS for inbred mice," HEARSAY 13(2) (00): 21-25. **CONTACT ADDRESS** Common Disorders, Univ of Alabama, Tuscaloosa, PO Box 870242, Tuscaloosa, AL 35487-0154. **EMAIL** wshiau@woodsquad.as.ua.edu

SHIELDS, BRUCE E.
PERSONAL Born 08/09/1937, PA, m, 1957, 3 children **DISCIPLINE** NEW TESTAMENT AND HOMILETICS **EDUCATION** Milligan Col, BA, 59; Princeton Theol Sem, BD, 65;

Eberhard-Karls Universitaet zu Tubingen, D Theol, 81. **CAREER** Prof, 77-83, Lincoln Christian Sem; prof , 83-, Emmanuel Sch Relig. **HONORS AND AWARDS** NEH sum grant, 91. **MEMBERSHIPS** Soc of Bibl Lit; Acad of Homiletics; Societas Homiletica. **RESEARCH** Preaching in the early church. **SELECTED PUBLICATIONS** Auth, Romans, Cincinnati: Standard Pub Co, 88; auth, Campbell on Language and Revelation and Modern Approaches to Language, Building Up the Church: Scripture, Hist, & Growth, A Festschrift in Honor of Henry E. Webb, Milligan Col, 93, TN; rev, Dale B. Martin, Slavery as Salvation: The Metaphor of Slavery in Pauline Christianity, Yale Univ Press, 90, Restor Quart vol 35, 93; rev, Sidney Greidanus, The Modern Preacher and the Ancient Text: Interpreting and Preaching Biblical Literature, Eerdmans Pub Co, 88, J for Christian Stud, 93; auth, The Areopagus Sermon as a Model for Apologetic Preaching, Faith in Pract: Stud in Bk of Acts, A Festschrift in Honor of Earl and Ottie Mearl Stuckenbruck, European Evangel Soc, 95; auth, John Henry Jowett, Concise Encycl of Preaching, Westminster/John Knox Press, 95; rev, Jeffrey T. Myers, Unfinished Errand into the Wilderness: Tendenzen und Schwerpunkte der Homilitic in den USA 1960-1985, doct diss, Johannes Gutenburg Univ, Mainz, Germany, in Homiletic, XXI/1, 96; rev, H. David Schuringa, Hearing the Word in a Visual Age in Encounter, 97; auth, Integrating Ministry and Theology: One Seminary's Story, Theological Ed, vol 33, no 2, 97; auth, Preaching and Culture, Homiletic vol XXII no 2, 97; auth, Readers Guide: Literary Resources for Worship, Leaven vol 6, no 1, 98. **CONTACT ADDRESS** Emmanuel Sch of Religion, One Walker Dr, Johnson City, TN 37601-9438. **EMAIL** shieldsb@esr.edu

SHIELDS, CAROL
PERSONAL Born Oak Park, IL **DISCIPLINE** ENGLISH **EDUCATION** Univ Exeter, Eng, exchange student, 55-56; Hanover Col, Ind, 57; Univ Ottawa, MA, 75. **CAREER** Author, Prof Univ Manitoba, 80-. **HONORS AND AWARDS** Best Novel, Can Authors' Asn, 76; First Prize, CBC Drama Awd, 83; First Prize, Nat Mag Awd, 85; Arthur Ellis Awd best Can crime novel, 87; Marian Engle Awd, 90; Gov Gen Awd, 93; Can Booksellers Awd, 94; Nat Critics Circle Awd, US, 95; Pulitzer Prize Lit, 95. **MEMBERSHIPS** TWUC; PUC; PEN; Can Coun. **SELECTED PUBLICATIONS** Auth, Small Ceremonies, 76; auth, The Box Garden, 77; auth, Happenstance, 80; auth, Swan, 87; auth, The Republic of Love, 92; auth, The Stone Diaries, 93. **CONTACT ADDRESS** Chancellor, Univ of Winnipeg, Fletcher Avenue Building, Winnipeg, MB, Canada R3T 5V5. **EMAIL** carol.shields@uwinnipeg.ca

SHIELDS, DAVID S.
DISCIPLINE ENGLISH **EDUCATION** Coll Wm & Mary, BA, 73; Univ Chicago, MA, 75, PhD, 82. **CAREER** Asst prof, 84-88, assoc prof, 88-93, prof, Eng, 93-, The Citadel. **HONORS AND AWARDS** Citadel Development Found Res Fel, 93-96; Citadel Fac Teaching Award, 90; Am Philos Soc Res grant, 89; NEH summer res grant, 87. **MEMBERSHIPS** Am Antiquarian Soc; Soc of Early Americanists; MLA. **SELECTED PUBLICATIONS** Auth, "Then Religion to America Shall Flee: New World Exegetes of Herbert's Prophecy of America's Rising Glory," in Like Season'd Timber: New Essays on George Herbert, ed. Robert DiYanni (NYork, Peter Lang, 87); auth, Oracles of Empire: Poetry, Politics, and Commerce in British America, 1690-1750, Univ Chicago Press, 90; coauth, The Cambridge History of American Literature, Vol 1, 1590-1820, ed. Sacvan Bercovitch (Cambridge Univ Press, 93); auth, "Cosmopolitan and the Anglo-Jewish Elite in British America," in A Mixed Race: Ethnicity in Early America, ed. Frank Shuffelton (NYork, Oxford Univ Press, 93); auth, "Reading the Landscape of Federal America," Everyday Life in Federal America, Proceedings of the Winterthur Conference (Wilmington, Del, Winterthur Mus, 95); auth, Civil Tongues and Polite Letters in British America, Univ of North Carolina (Chapel Hill), 97; contributer, The History of the Book in America, Vol 1; From European Settlement to Independence, ed. David Hall and Hugh Amory (Cambridge Univ press, 98). **CONTACT ADDRESS** The Citadel, The Military Col of So Carolina, 171 Moultrie St., Charleston, SC 29409. **EMAIL** shieldsd@citadel.edu

SHIELDS, DONALD C.
PERSONAL Born 12/14/1944, Kansas City, MO, m **DISCIPLINE** COMMUNICATION STUDIES **EDUCATION** Univ Mo Kans City, BA, MA; Univ Minn, PhD. **SELECTED PUBLICATIONS** Symbolic Theories in Applied Communication Research: Bormann, Burke, and Fischer, Hampton, 95; An Expansion of the Rhetorical Vision Component of the Symbolic Convergence Theory: The Cold War Paradigm Case, Commun Monographs, 96; coauth, Understanding Communication Theory: The Communicative Forces for Human Action, 98; "Explicating the Saga Component of Symbolic Convergence Theory: The Case of Arbin's Radio B92 in Cyberspace," Critical Studies in Mass Commun, 00. **CONTACT ADDRESS** Communication Dept, Univ of Missouri, St. Louis, 590 Lucas Hall, Saint Louis, MO 63121. **EMAIL** shieldsd@msx.umsl.edu

SHIELDS, DONALD J.
PERSONAL Born 10/28/1937, Paris, IL, m, 1962, 2 children **DISCIPLINE** COMMUNICATION, POLITICAL SCIENCE **EDUCATION** Eastern IL Univ, BS, 59; Purdue Univ, MS, 61, PhD, 64. **CAREER** Staff asst speech, IN State Democratic Comt, 62; asst prof, Cornell Univ, 64-65; asst prof, 65-71, assoc prof, 71-79, prof speech, IN State Univ, Terre Haute, 79. **MEMBERSHIPS** Speech Commun Asn; Nat Soc Studies Commun; Am Forensic Asn; Am Asn Univ Prof. **RESEARCH** Polit persuasion and commun networks. **CONTACT ADDRESS** Dept of Speech, Indiana State Univ, 210 N 7th St, Terre Haute, IN 47809-0002. **EMAIL** cmshield@ruby.indstate.edu

SHIELDS, JOHN CHARLES
PERSONAL Born 10/29/1944, Phoenix, AZ, s **DISCIPLINE** AMERICAN & CLASSICAL LITERATURES, COMPARATIVE LITERATURE **EDUCATION** Univ Tenn, Knoxville, BA, 67, MACT, 79, PhD(English), 78; George Peabody Col Teachers, EdS, 75. **CAREER** Teacher English & art hist, Sevier County High Sch, Sevierville, Tenn, 67-68; head dept English & teacher Latin, Battle Ground Acad, Franklin, Tenn, 67-68; dir acad, Brentwood Acad, Tenn, 71-73; Instr English, Columbia State Community Col, 75-76; assoc prof english, Ill State Univ, 86-93; prof, 93-; Instr English & dir writing lab, Univ Tenn, Nashville, 71-74; fac res grant, Ill State Univ, summers 80 & 81. **HONORS AND AWARDS** Nat Endowment for the Humanities Summer Seminar, 89, 93; Principal Project director of "Phillis Wheatley: An Aesthetic Appreciation on the Bicentennial of Her Death," funded by Nat Endowment for the Humanities, 84; Fel of the Soc for the Humanities at Cornell Univ, 84-85; Nat Endowment for the Humanties Summer Stipend, 83; The John C. Hodges Awd for teaching Excellence at the Univ of Tenn; Ford Found Fel. **MEMBERSHIPS** MLA; Medieval Acad Am; Soc Cinema Studies; Melville Soc; Am Studies Asn; Int Soc for Eighteenth-century Studies. **SELECTED PUBLICATIONS** Ed, The Collected Works of Phillis Wheatley, Oxford Up, 88; guest ed, African American Poetics: Style 26(3), 93; auth, Wheatley,Phillis Subversive Pastoral/, Eighteenth-Century Studies, Vol 0027, 1994; advisory ed and contrib, Oxford Companion to African American Literature, 97; advisory ed and contrib, American Naional Biography, 99; auth, The American Aeneas: Classical Origins of the American Self (forthcoming). **CONTACT ADDRESS** English Dept, Illinois State Univ, Normal, IL 61761.

SHIELDS, KENNETH
PERSONAL Born 12/08/1951, Phillipsburg, PA, m, 3 children **DISCIPLINE** ENGLISH **EDUCATION** Penn State Univ, BA, MA, PhD. **CAREER** Prof & dept ch, Millersville Univ Penn **HONORS AND AWARDS** Phi Beta Kappa; Phi Kappa Phi; Penn Academy for the Prof of Teaching, Salute to Teaching Awd. **RESEARCH** Historical Indo-European linguistics; language change; dialects of American English. **SELECTED PUBLICATIONS** Auth, A History of Indo-European Verb Morphology, Amsterdam: John Benjamin's, 92; Indo-European Noun Inflection: A Developmental History, Univ Park: Penn State Press, 82; Comments about IE oi-'1', J Indo-Europ Stud 22, 94; Germanic Locative Adverbs in on-, Amer J Ger Ling and Lit 7, 95; Gothic 1st Pl Pret -um, Historische Sprachforschung 107, 94; On the Origin of Hittite Accusative Plural Suffix - us, Hethitica 12, 94; Rattleband(ing)'Shivaree': Another Pennsylvania Variant, Amer Speech 68, 93; The Indo-European Genitive Marker *-r: Evidence from Germanic and other Dialects, Nowele 25, 95; The Origin of the IE r-/n-Stems: An Alternative Proposal, Folia Ling Historica 15, 94; The Role of Deictic Particles in the Indo-European Personal Pronoun System, Word 45, 94; Typological Inconsistencies in the Indo-European Color Lexicon: A Cosmic Connection, Indoger Forschungen 101, 96; A Proposal Regarding the Etymology of the Word God, Leuvense Bijdragen 85, 96. **CONTACT ADDRESS** Dept of English, Millersville Univ of Pennsylvania, PO Box 1002, Millersville, PA 17551-0302. **EMAIL** kshields@marauder.millersv.edu

SHIFLETT, ORVIN LEE
PERSONAL Born 08/01/1947, Melbourne, FL, m, 1990, 2 children **DISCIPLINE** LIBRARY SCIENCE **EDUCATION** Univ FL, BA, 69; Rutgers Univ, MLS, 71; FL State Univ, PhD, 79. **CAREER** LA State Univ, prof 94, assoc prof 83-94, asst prof 79-83. **MEMBERSHIPS** ALA; Assn Lib Info Sci Edu; Louisiana Library Asn. **RESEARCH** History of the library; history of the book. **SELECTED PUBLICATIONS** Auth, Origins of American Academic Librarianship, Ablex Publishing Corporation, 81; auth, "The American Library Association's Quest for a Black Library School," Jour Of Edu for Lib and Info Sci 35 (94): 68-72; coauth, "Hampton, Fisk, and Atlanta: The Foundations, the American Library Association, and Library Education for Blacks, 1925-1941," Libs And Culture 31 (96): 299-325; auth, Louis Shores: Defining Educational Librarianship, Scarecrow Press, 96; auth, "The American Library History Round Table: The First Quarter Century," Library History Round Table Newsletter: New Series 4 (00): 5-10; auth, "Louis Shores and Library History," Libraries and Culture 35 (00): 35-40; auth, "Sense-Making and Library History," Jour of Education for Library and Information Science 41 (00): 86-90. **CONTACT ADDRESS** Sch of Libr and Info Sci, Louisiana State Univ and A&M Col, Baton Rouge, LA 70803. **EMAIL** lsshif@lsu.edu

SHILLER, DANA
DISCIPLINE VICTORIAN LITERATURE **EDUCATION** Univ Wash, PhD. **CAREER** Prof; dir, Wrtg; Women's Stud Prog. . **SELECTED PUBLICATIONS** Auth, article on uses of the past in contemporary historical fiction, in Studies in the Novel. **CONTACT ADDRESS** Dept of Eng, Univ of Evansville, 1800 Lincoln Ave, Evansville, IN 47714. **EMAIL** ds2@evansville.edu.

SHILLINGSBURG, PETER LEROY
PERSONAL Born 03/24/1943, Colombia, m, 1967, 5 children **DISCIPLINE** ENGLISH LITERATURE **EDUCATION** Univ SC, BA, 66, MA, 67, PhD, 70. **CAREER** Archivist, SC Archives Dept, 68-69; asst prof, 70-73, assoc prof, 73-78, prof English, Ms State Univ, 78-97; coordr CSE, MLA, 76-77; assoc dir grad stud, Lamar Univ, 97; prof, Univ N Tex. **HONORS AND AWARDS** Guggenheim fel, 82; Robert W Harrigan, III, Distinguished Fac Mem, 95; Wm L Giles, Distinguished Prof, 97; Outstanding Honors Faculty Member, 92; Burlington Norther Acievement Awd for Teaching, 91; NEH, Editing Grant, 77-96. **MEMBERSHIPS** MLA; SCent MLA; SAtlantic MLA. **RESEARCH** Nineteenth and twentieth-century fiction; nineteenth-century publishing and book production history; theory and practice of textual criticism and scholarly editing; literary theory, communication theory; computer applications to editing and publishing; the electronic book. **SELECTED PUBLICATIONS** Auth, The first edition of Thackeray's Pendennis, Papers Bibliog Soc Am, 72; Thackeray texts: a guide to inexpensive editions, Costerus, 74; Thackeray's Pendennis: a rejected page of manuscript, Huntington Libr Quart, 75; Critical editing and the Center for Scholarly Editions, Scholarly Pub, 77; articles in Editing Nineteenth Century Fiction, 78, Review, 80, The Book Collector, 80, Etudes Anglaise, 81, Studies in the Novel, 81, Studies in Bibliography, 81, Institute Studies, 81; Pegasus in Harness, UP Va, 92; Scholarly Editing in the Computer Age, Univ Mi, 96; Resisting Texts, Univ Mi, 98. **CONTACT ADDRESS** Dept of English, Univ of No Texas, Denton, TX 76203. **EMAIL** psl1@unt.edu

SHILSTONE, FREDERICK WILLIAM
DISCIPLINE ENGLISH LITERATURE **EDUCATION** Ind Univ, PhD, 74. **CAREER** Dept Eng, Clemson Univ **RESEARCH** British Romantic literature. **SELECTED PUBLICATIONS** Ed, MLA Approaches to Teaching Byron's Poetry. **CONTACT ADDRESS** Clemson Univ, 807 Strode, Clemson, SC 29634. **EMAIL** sfreder@clemson.edu

SHIN, ANDREW
PERSONAL Born, Korea, s **DISCIPLINE** ENGLISH, LITERATURE **EDUCATION** Univ Toronto, BA, 84; Univ Va, PhD, 96. **CAREER** Vis asst prof, Brown Univ, 96-99; vis lectr, Univ Minn, 97-98; asst prof, Calif State Univ, 99-. **HONORS AND AWARDS** Inn Instr Awd, 00-01. **MEMBERSHIPS** MLA; AAAS. **RESEARCH** 20th century American literature; critical theory; gender and sexuality; postcolonial literature; children's literature. **SELECTED PUBLICATIONS** Co-auth, "Beneath the Black Aesthetic: James Baldwin's Primer of Black American Masculinity," African Am Rev 32 (98): 247-62. **CONTACT ADDRESS** 475 S Oakland Ave, Apt 5, Pasadena, CA 91101-3357. **EMAIL** ashin@calstatela.edu

SHINAGEL, MICHAEL
PERSONAL Born 04/21/1934, Vienna, Austria, m, 2 children **DISCIPLINE** ENGLISH LITERATURE **EDUCATION** Oberlin Col, AB, 57; Harvard Univ, MA, 59, PhD, 64. **CAREER** Tutor English, Harvard Univ, 58-64; from instr to asst prof, Cornell Univ, 64-67; mem regional selection comt, Woodrow Wilson Nat Fel Found, 66-68; from assoc prof to prof, Union Col, NY, 67-75, chmn dept, Union Col, NYork, 67-73; dean, continuing educ & dir, Univ Exten, Harvard Univ, 75-, sr lectr English, 83-. **HONORS AND AWARDS** Phi Beta Kappa; NEH grant, 66-67; Doctor Honris Causa, International Univ Ecuador, 97. **MEMBERSHIPS** The Johnsonians, Mass Hist Soc, Saturday Club. **RESEARCH** English literature of the 18th century; satire; novel. **SELECTED PUBLICATIONS** Coauth, Handbook on Summer Institutes in English, Col Bd, 65; auth, The maternal theme in Moll Flanders: Craft and character, Cornell Libr J, winter 68; Daniel Defoe and Middle-Class Gentility, Harvard Univ, 68; Concordance to Poems of Jonathan Swift, Cornell Univ, 72; Memoirs of a woman of pleasure: Pornography and the mid-18th century English novel, In: Studies in Change and Revolution, Scholar, 72; Robinson Crusoe, Norton, 75, rev 93; co-ed, Harvard Scholars in English (1890-1990), 91. **CONTACT ADDRESS** Harvard Univ, 51 Brattle St, Cambridge, MA 02138-3701. **EMAIL** shinagel@hudce.harvard.edu

SHINE, THEODIS
PERSONAL Born 04/26/1931, Baton Rouge, LA, s **DISCIPLINE** DRAMA, ENGLISH **EDUCATION** Howard University, Washington, DC, BA, 1953; University of Iowa, 1958; University of California, Santa Barbara, CA, PhD, 1973. **CAREER** Dillard University, New Orleans, LA, instructor in drama and English, 60-61; Howard University, Washington, DC, assistant professor of drama, 61-67; Prairie View A & M University, Prairie View, TX, professor and head of department of drama, 67-. **HONORS AND AWARDS** Brooks-Hines Awd for Playwriting, Howard University. **MEMBERSHIPS** Nation-

al Theatre Conference, National Conference of African American Theatres; Southwest Theatre Conference; Texas Educational Theatre Association; Texas Non-Profit Theatres, board member. **SELECTED PUBLICATIONS** Author of "Plantation," contribution, "The Woman Who Was Tampered with in Youth," "Shoes", " Three Fat Batchelors"; Delta Sigma Theta Award-teacher; Beanie Award-Teaching; author of over sixty television scripts for series "Our Street." **CONTACT ADDRESS** P O Box 2082, Prairie View, TX 77446-0519.

SHIPPEY, T. A.
DISCIPLINE MEDIEVAL LITERATURE **EDUCATION** Cambridge Univ, PhD. **CAREER** Eng Dept, St. Edward's Univ **HONORS AND AWARDS** Ch, Hum dept . **SELECTED PUBLICATIONS** Auth, Poems of Wisdom and Learning in Old English, D.S. Brewer, 76, 77; The Road to Middle-earth, Allen & Unwin, 82, 83, 93; Beowulf, Chelseas House, 78, 88; Old English Verse, Hutchinson's, 72; Ed, The Oxford Book of Fantasy Stories, Oxford Univ Press, 94; Consult ed, Magills Guide to Science Fiction and Fantasy Literature, Salem Press, 96; coed, The Critical Heritage: Beowulf, Routledge, 98; coed, Medievalism in the Modern World: Essays in Honour of Leslie Workman, Turnbout, 98; auth, J.R.R. Tolkien: Author of the Century, Harper Collins, 00. **CONTACT ADDRESS** Dept of English, Saint Louis Univ, 221 N Grand Blvd, Saint Louis, MO 63103. **EMAIL** shippey@slu.edu

SHIPPS, ANTHONY WIMBERLY
PERSONAL Born 08/26/1926, Tryon, NC, m, 1949, 1 child **DISCIPLINE** ENGLISH, LIBRARY SCIENCE **EDUCATION** Mercer Univ, AB, 49; Northwestern Univ, MA, 51; PhD, 59; Univ Mich, AMLS, 60. **CAREER** Instr English, Wayne State Univ, 54-59; asst librn, Utah State Univ, 60-61; circulation librn, Univ Colo Libr, 61-62, humanities librn, 62-64, head ref dept, 64-67; librn english, Ind Univ libr, Bloomington, 67-. **MEMBERSHIPS** MLA; Am Libr Asn. **RESEARCH** Literary quotations; English Renaissance. **SELECTED PUBLICATIONS** Auth, Webster,Daniel - Reply, Notes And Queries, 93; Quotations And References In Hardy - Reply, Notes And Queries, 93; Epigraph Of 'Blindness And Insight' - Reply, Notes And Queries, 94; Poem Of World War II - Reply, Notes And Queries, 94; Sources Wanted - Reply, Notes And Queries, 95. **CONTACT ADDRESS** Univ Library, Indiana Univ, Bloomington, 107 S. Indiana Ave., Bloomington, IN 47405-7000. **EMAIL** ashipps@indiana.edu

SHIRES, LINDA M.
PERSONAL Born 07/29/1950, Providence, RI, m, 1988, 4 children **DISCIPLINE** ENGLISH **EDUCATION** Wheaton Col, BA, 72; Brown Univ, MA, 73; Oxford Univ, BA, 77; Princeton Univ, MA, 79; PhD, 81. **CAREER** Asst prof, Syracuse Univ, 81-88; assoc prof, 88-96; prof, 96-; vis prof, Princeton Univ, 90-92; vis prof, New York Univ, 97. **HONORS AND AWARDS** Phi Beta Kappa; Dodds Dist Fel; Guggenheim Fel; NEH Dir Sum Sem, 93, 95; **MEMBERSHIPS** MLA; NVA. **RESEARCH** 19th Century literature and culture; gender studies; narrative theory; Jewish studies. **SELECTED PUBLICATIONS** Ed, The Trumpet-Major, by Thomas Hardy, Penguin Press (London and NY), 97; contrib and ed, Rewriting the Victorians: History, Theory, and the Politics of Gender, Routledge Press (London and NY), 92; coauth, Telling Stories: A Theoretical Analysis of Narrative Fiction, Routledge Press (London and NY), New Accents Series, 88, 2nd ed, 91; 3rd ed, 93; 4th ed, 96; trans Korean 97; to Chinese 98, Chapter 1 reprinted in The Communications Theory Reader, ed. Paul Cobley (NY: Routledge, 96); auth, British Poetry of the Second World War, Macmillan Press and St. Martin's Press (London and NY), 85; ed, "The Dramatic 'I' Poem" Spec Iss Victorian Poetry 22 (84); auth, "The Aesthetics of the Victorian Novel: Structure, Subjectivity, Politics," in Cambridge Companion to the Victorian Novel, ed. Deirdre David (Cambridge and NY: Cambridge Univ Press, forthcoming); auth, "Victorian Studies and Culture Studies: A Call for Critical Realism," in "Forum," ed. Carolyn Williams, Victorian Lit Culture 27 (99): 481-87; auth, "The Radical Aesthetic of Tess of the d'Urbervilles," in Cambridge Companion, ed. Dale Kramer (Cambridge and NY: Cambridge Univ Press, 99), 145-64; auth, Death, Literary Careers, and the Body Politics of David Copperfield," Am-British essay collection by John Schad (Manchester: Manchester Univ Press, 96), 117-35. **CONTACT ADDRESS** Dept English, Syracuse Univ, 401 Hall of Languages, Syracuse, NY 13244-1170. **EMAIL** lmshires@aol.com

SHIRLEY, FRANCES A.
PERSONAL Born 06/11/1931, Altoona, PA, s **DISCIPLINE** DRAMA & LITERATURE **EDUCATION** Bryn Mawr, AB, 53; MA, 54; PhD, 60. **CAREER** Instr, Johns Hopkins Univ, 55-56; instr to prof, Wheaton Col, 60-. **HONORS AND AWARDS** Bryn Mawr Scholar; Johns Hopkins Pres Scholar; Meneely Professorship, Wheaton Col. **MEMBERSHIPS** Shakespeare Assoc of Am, Int Shakespeare Assoc, Soc for Theatre Res, Am Soc for Theatre Res. **RESEARCH** Shakespeare, Elizabethan Drama, Musical Theatre. **SELECTED PUBLICATIONS** Auth, Shakespeare's Use of Off-Stage Sounds; auth, Swearing and Perjuring in Shakespeare's Plays; auth, John Webster's Devil's Law-Case; auth, King John and Henry VIII - Critical Essays. **CONTACT ADDRESS** Wheaton C, Norton, MA 02766. **EMAIL** fshirley@wheatonma.edu

SHOAF, R. ALLEN
PERSONAL Born 03/25/1948, Lexington, NC, m, 1975, 2 children **DISCIPLINE** ENGLISH **EDUCATION** Wake Forest Univ, BA, 70; Univ E Anglia, BA, 72; Cornell Univ, MA, 75; PhD, 77. **CAREER** Asst prof to assoc prof, Yale Univ, 71-85; prof to alumni prof, Univ of Fla, 86-. **HONORS AND AWARDS** NEH fel, 82-83 & 99-00; Awded Univ sabbatical, 94; Teaching Incentive Prog Awd, 94 & 98; Special Summer Stipend, Office of Res, Technol, and Grad Educ, 95; listed in Who's Who in the World, 96; Prof Excellence Prog Awd, Univ of Fla, 96. **MEMBERSHIPS** Acad of Am Poets, Dante Soc of Am, S Atlantic MLA, Medieval Acad of Am, New Chaucer Soc, John Gower Soc, Milton Soc of Am, Am Asn for Italian Studies, L'AISLII, Omicron Delta Kappa, Phi Beta Kappa. **RESEARCH** Medieval and Renaissance poetry (English, Italian, French, Latin), literary theory, poetry writing. **SELECTED PUBLICATIONS** Auth, Dante, Chaucer, and the Currency of the Word: Money, Images, and Reference in Late Medieval Poetry, Pilgrim Books (Norman, OK), 83; auth, The Poem as Green Girdle: "Commercium" in "Sir Gawain and the Green Knight," Humanities Monographs Series of Univ of Fla 55, Univ Presses of Fla (Gainesville, FL), 84; auth, Milton, Poet of Duality: A Study of Semiosis in the Poetry and the Prose, Yale Univ Press (New Haven, CT), 85 and Univ Press of Fla, 93; ed, Chaucer Rev 21, 2 (86); auth, Chaucer's Troilus and Criseyde--"Subgit to alle poesye": Essays in Criticism, Pegasus Press (Binghamton), 92. **CONTACT ADDRESS** Dept English, Univ of Florida, PO Box 117310, Gainesville, FL 32611-7310. **EMAIL** ras@ufl.edu

SHOEMAKER, MELVIN H.
PERSONAL Born 02/11/1940, Jay County, IN, m, 1961, 3 children **DISCIPLINE** NEW TESTAMENT BIBLICAL LITERATURE; BIBLICAL THEOLOGY **EDUCATION** Indiana Wesleyan University, AB, 62; Hebrew Seminar in Israel, Univ of Wisconsin, Graduate Studies, 66; Asbury Theological Seminary, MDiv, 67; Drew Univ, MPhil, 88; Fuller theological seminary, Pasadena, CA, D Min, 97. **CAREER** Instr, Indiana Wesleyan Univ, 66-67; prof, Bartlesville Wesleyan Col, 79-84; prof, CP Haggard Sch of Theology, 86-, dir, honors program, Azusa Pacific Univ, 95-. **HONORS AND AWARDS** Biographical listings in Dictionary of International Biography, 79; Who's Who in Religion, 92; Alphi Chi Teacher of the Year at Azusa Pacific Univ, 93; Who's Who in the West, 97; Who's Who in America, 99. **MEMBERSHIPS** Wesleyan Theological Soc, 80-82, 91-present; APU Honors Program Council, 91-present; APU Education Council, 94-present; Soc of Biblical Lit, 87-present; International Soc of Theta Phi; Advisory Council for the Oxford Honors Semester of the Coalition for Christian Colleges & Universities, 97-2003; International Education Committee of the National Collegiate Honors Council 97-2003; Small College Honors Programs Committee of the National Collegiate Honors Council, 97-2003. **RESEARCH** NT Biblical Literature and theology; gospels. **SELECTED PUBLICATIONS** Auth, Good News to the Poor in Luke's Gospel, Connection, 94; King, Christ as, Lamb, Lamb of God, Life, Priest, Christ as, Baker BookHouse, 96; Discipling Generation X, Fuller Theological Seminary, 97; The Frusit that Jesus Seeks, Decision, Nov 98. **CONTACT ADDRESS** Azusa Pacific Univ, 901 E Alosta, Azusa, CA 91702-7000. **EMAIL** mshoemaker@apu.edu

SHOEMAKER, PAMELA J.
PERSONAL Born 10/25/1950, Chillicothe, OH, d, 1 child **DISCIPLINE** MASS COMMUNICATIONS **EDUCATION** Ohio Univ, BS, 72, MS, 72; Univ of Wis-Madison, PhD, 82. **CAREER** Dept grad adviser, dept of journalism, 84-87, asst prof, 82-87, assoc prof 87-91, Univ of Tex at Austin; prof & dir of journalism, school of journalism, Ohio State Univ, 91-94; JOHN BEN SNOW PROF, SINEWHOUSE SCHOOL OF PUBLIC COMMUN, SYRACUSE UNIV, 94-. **HONORS AND AWARDS** Fel to the John A. Beul Centennial Prof in Commun, summer 84, fel to the Amon G. Carter Jr. Centennial Prof in Commmun, Univ of Tex, Austin, 86-87; Krieghbaum Under-40 Awd, Assoc for Ed in Journalism and Mass Commun, 90. **MEMBERSHIPS** Coun of Commun Asns; Coun of Presidents of Nat Journalism Orgs; ICC; SCA; AAPOR; IAMGR; APSA; Midwest Asn for Public Opinion Res. **RESEARCH** Mass Communications; gatekeeping; media sociology; political communications; media public opinion. **SELECTED PUBLICATIONS** Coauth, Korean-language edition of Mediating the Message: Theories of Influences on Mass Media Content, NANAM Pub House, 97; coauth, Mediating the Message: Theories of Influences on Mass Media Content, Longman, 91 & 96; coauth, La Mediatizacion del Mensaje: Teorias de Las Influencias en el Contenido de los Medios de Comunicacion, Editorial Diana, 94; auth, Hard-wired for News: Using Biological and Cultural Evolution to Explain the News, J of Commun, 96; coauth, Communication in Crisis: Theory, Curricula and Power, J of Commun, 93; auth, Critical Thinking for Mass Communication Students, Critical Studies in Mass Commun, 93; auth, Reconsidering the Role of Scholarship, ASJMC Insights, 93. **CONTACT ADDRESS** Newhouse School of Public Commun, Syracuse Univ, Syracuse, NY 13244-2100. **EMAIL** snowshoe@syr.edu

SHOKOFF, JAMES
PERSONAL Born 08/18/1935, Teaneck, NJ, m, 1962, 2 children **DISCIPLINE** ENGLISH LITERATURE, FILM **EDUCATION** Rutgers Univ, BA, 60; Columbia Univ, MA, 65; Univ Ill, Urbana PhD(English), 70. **CAREER** Teacher English, Benjamin Franklin High Sch, New York, 62-66; teaching asst, Univ Ill, Urbana, 66-68, instr, 68-70; asst prof, 70-73, ASSOC PROF ENGLISH, STATE UNIV NY COL FREDONIA, 73-, Managing ed, Drama & Theatre, 71-75; Prof, English, 83-; Sr Ed, Almanack, 98-. **HONORS AND AWARDS** Woodrow Wilson Fellow, 60. **MEMBERSHIPS** Popular Culture Assn; Wordsworth-Coleridge Assn; Mid Atlantic Popular/American Culture Assoc. **RESEARCH** English Romantic literature; film study. **SELECTED PUBLICATIONS** Auth, Wordsworth Duty As A Poet In 'We Are Seven' And 'Surprised By Joy'/, J Of English And Ger Philol, Vol 0093, 1994. **CONTACT ADDRESS** Dept of English, SUNY, Col at Fredonia, 1 Suny at Fredonia, Fredonia, NY 14063-1143. **EMAIL** shokoff@fredonia.edu

SHORES, DAVID LEE
PERSONAL Born 01/28/1933, Tangier, VA, m, 1956, 2 children **DISCIPLINE** ENGLISH, LINGUISTICS **EDUCATION** Randolph-Macon Col, BA, 55; George Peabody Col, MA, 56, EdS, 64, PhD(English), 66. **CAREER** Instr English & Ger, Richard Bland Col, Col William & Mary, 61-62; from asst prof to assoc prof, 66-70, dir freshman English, 70-73, grad prog dir English, 73-75, chmn dept, 75-80, PROF ENGLISH, OLD DOMINION UNIV, 70-, Instr & assoc dir, US Off Educ Inst Col English Instr Black Cols, 70-73; consult, Nat Teachers Exam, Educ Testing Serv, 72-73. **MEMBERSHIPS** MLA; SAtlantic Mod Lang Asn; NCTE; Am Dialect Soc; Southeast Conf Ling. **RESEARCH** Old and Middle English language and literature; Chaucer; English linguistics. **SELECTED PUBLICATIONS** Auth, More On Porchmouth + Va Tidewater Pronunciation/, Am Speech, Vol 0069, 1994. **CONTACT ADDRESS** Dept of English, Old Dominion Univ, Norfolk, VA 23508.

SHORTER, ROBERT NEWLAND
PERSONAL Born 05/11/1931, Canton, OH, m, 1985, 1 child **DISCIPLINE** ENGLISH **EDUCATION** Union Col, NYork, AB; Duke Univ, MA, 58, PhD, 64. **CAREER** From instr to assoc prof, 58-77, prof English, 77-, chemn English dept, 75-, assoc dean grad sch, 95, Wake Forest Univ, 77-. **MEMBERSHIPS** MLA **RESEARCH** Chaucer; medieval drama. **SELECTED PUBLICATIONS** Auth, Becket as Job: T S Eliot's Murder in the Cathedral, SAtlantic Quart, fall 68. **CONTACT ADDRESS** Dept English, Wake Forest Univ, 1853 Waycross Dr, Winston-Salem, NC 27106. **EMAIL** shorterr@wfu.edu

SHOSTAK, DEBRA
PERSONAL Born 06/17/1953 **DISCIPLINE** ENGLISH **EDUCATION** Carleton Col, BA, 75; Univ Wisc, Madison, MA, 77, PhD, 85. **CAREER** Managing ed, Contemporary Lit, 82-87; vis asst prof, The Col of Wooster, 87-90, asst prof, 90-94, assoc prof, 94-. **HONORS AND AWARDS** Vilas Fel, Univ Wisc, Madison, 81-82; research leaves, The Col of Wooster, 90-91, 96-97. **MEMBERSHIPS** Modern Lang Asn, Soc for the Study of Narrative Lit. **RESEARCH** Contemporary American fiction; narrative theory. **SELECTED PUBLICATIONS** Auth, " 'This obsessive reinvention of the real': Speculative Narrative in Philip Roth's The Counterlife," Modern Fiction Studies 37.2 (summer 91); auth, "The Family Romances of John Irving," Essays in Lit 21.1 (spring 94): 129-45; auth, "Maxine Hong Kingston's Fake Books," in Memory, Narrative, and Identity: New Essays in Ethnic American Literatures, ed Amritjit Singh, Joseph Skerret, and Robert Hogan, Boston: Northeastern Univ Press (94); auth, "Plot as Repetition: John Irving's Narrative Experiments," Critique: Studies in Contemporary Fiction, 37.1 (fall 95): 51-70; auth, "Philip Roth," "Goodbye, Columbus," and "Portnoy's Complaint," Issues and Identities in Literature, Pasadena: Salem Press (96); auth, "The Diaspora Jew and the 'instinct for impersonation': Philip Roth's Operation Shylock," Contemporary Lit, 38.4 (winter 97): 726-54; auth, "Roth/CounterRoth: Postmodernism, the Masculine Subject, and Sabbath's Theater," Ariz Quart, 54.3 (autumn 98): 119-42; auth, "Return to The Breast: The Body, the Masculine Subject, and Philip Roth," Twentieth Century Lit, 45.3 (fall 99): 317-35; auth, "Philip Roth's Fictions of Self-Exposure," Shofar (forthcoming). **CONTACT ADDRESS** Dept English, The Col of Wooster, 1189 Beall Ave, Wooster, OH 44691-2393. **EMAIL** dshostak@acs.wooster.edu

SHOTWELL, CLAYTON M.
PERSONAL Born 07/27/1946, Libby, MT, m, 1974, 2 children **DISCIPLINE** MUSIC **EDUCATION** Hastings Col, BA, 70; Univ Minn, MA, 74, PhD, 87. **CAREER** Asst Dean, asst prof, Univ of the Pacific, 89-94; assoc prof, chemn of dept, Augusta State Univ, 94-99. **MEMBERSHIPS** Col Music Soc; Soc for Ethnomusicology; Africah Stud Asn; Int Asn for the Study of Popular Music. **RESEARCH** Music in West Africa; Latin America; Chicano music; technology. **SELECTED PUBLICATIONS** Auth, Ethnic Enclaves in America: Teaching Resources on Native American and Mexican Music and Culture, in, Teaching World Music; Proceedings of the Second International Symposium on Teaching Musics of the World, Basel, 93; auth, Corridos, Mariachi Music, in, Encyclopedia of the Latino

Experience, Salem Press, 95. **CONTACT ADDRESS** Dept of Fine Arts, Augusta State Univ, Augusta, GA 30904-2200. **EMAIL** cshotwel@aug.edu

SHOUT, JOHN
DISCIPLINE ENGLISH **EDUCATION** Oberlin Col, BA; Univ MI, MA; PhD, 74. **CAREER** Eng Dept, Plattsburgh State Univ **RESEARCH** Drama and theater hist; musical theater. **SELECTED PUBLICATIONS** Auth, publ(s) about drama and theater hist. **CONTACT ADDRESS** SUNY, Col at Plattsburgh, 101 Broad St, Plattsburgh, NY 12901-2681.

SHOWALTER, ELAINE
DISCIPLINE 19TH AND 20TH CENTURY FICTION **EDUCATION** UC Davis, PhD, 70. **CAREER** Author **RESEARCH** Feminist criticism; history of psychiatry; popular history. **SELECTED PUBLICATIONS** Auth, A Literature of Their Own: British Women; Novelists from Bronte to Lessing; The Female Malady: Women Madness, and Society 1830-1980; Sexual Anarchy; Sister's Choice: Tradition and Change in American Women's Writing; Hystories, Inventing Herself. **CONTACT ADDRESS** 45 Mc Cosh Hall, Princeton, NJ 08544. **EMAIL** ecshowalter@cs.com

SHUCARD, ALAN ROBERT
PERSONAL Born 12/02/1935, Brooklyn, NY, m, 1962, 1 child **DISCIPLINE** AMERICAN & ENGLISH LITERATURE **EDUCATION** Union Col, NYork, AB, 57; Univ Conn, MA, 63; Univ Ariz, PhD, 71. **CAREER** Instr II English, Univ BC, 65-70; from Asst Prof to Assoc Prof, 70-86, prof English, Univ of Wis Parkside, 86-; Prof emer, Univ of Wis-Parkside, 98-. **HONORS AND AWARDS** Wis Alumni Res Found grant, 72; Fulbright Fel, 80-81; SE Wis Educ Hall of Fame, 98. **MEMBERSHIPS** MLA; Soc Values Higher Educ; Am Studies Asn. **RESEARCH** Modern poetry; Afro-American literature; American literature. **SELECTED PUBLICATIONS** Auth, The Gorgon Bag, 70 & The Louse on the Head of a Yawning Lord, 72, Ladysmith, Que; Mari Evans, Kenneth Leslie & Stanley Moss, in Contemporary Poets, 2nd ed, St James, London, 74; Tantalus, Sysyphus, and Kafka, Chronicle Higher Educ, 12/76; A J Cronin & Alec Waugh, in Contemp Novelists, 77; The contribution of faculty development to the humanities, Lib Educ, 12/77; Gwendolyn Brooks, Walter Van Tilburg Clark & Paul Laurence Dunbar, in Writers in English, 78; Countee Cullen, 84; American Poetry Puritans Through Walt Whitman, 90; Modern American Poetry, 1865-1950, 89. **CONTACT ADDRESS** Div of Humanities, Univ of Wisconsin, Parkside, Box 2000, Kenosha, WI 53141-2000. **EMAIL** shucard@aol.com

SHUFFELTON, FRANK
PERSONAL Born 03/10/1940, St. Mary's, OH, m, 1963, 2 children **DISCIPLINE** ENGLISH **EDUCATION** Harvard, BA, 62; Stanford Univ, MA, 68; PhD, 72. **CAREER** Instr, Stanford Univ, 66-68; instr to full prof, Univ Rochester, 69-. **HONORS AND AWARDS** Mellon Fel; NEH Sen Fel. **MEMBERSHIPS** MLA, ASECS, ALA Emerson, Soc, Melville Soc. **RESEARCH** Thomas Jefferson, Early American literature and history. **SELECTED PUBLICATIONS** Ed, Notes on the State of Virginia by Thomas Jefferson, New York, 99; auth, "The American Enlightenment and Endless Emancipation," in Teaching Early American Literature, New York, (99): 155-169; auth, "Power, Desire, and American Cultural Studies," Early American Literature, (99): 94-101; auth, "Emerson's Politics of Biography and History," in Emersonian Circles: Essays in Honor of Joel Myerson, (96):53-66; auth, "Ties That Bind? Authority, the Family, and the Public Sphere in Jefferson's correspondence," in Thomas Jefferson and Education of a Citizen, (99); 28-47; auth, "Phillis Wheatley, the Aesthetic, and the Form of Life," Studies in Eighteenth-Century Culture, (98): 73-85 ed, The American Enlightenment, Univ Rochester, 93; ed, A Mixed Race: Ethnicity in Early America, New York, 93; auth, Thomas Jefferson, 1981-1990: A Comprehensive Critical Bibliography, New York, 92; auth, Thomas Jefferson: A Comprehensive Annotated bibliography of Writings About Him, 1826-1980, New York, 83; auth, Thomas Hooker, 1586-1647, Princeton Univ Press, 77. **CONTACT ADDRESS** Dept English, Univ of Rochester, PO Box 270451, Rochester, NY 14627-0451. **EMAIL** fcsh@troi.cc.rochester.edu

SHUGER, DEBORA
PERSONAL Born 12/15/1953, New York, NY, m, 1973, 1 child **DISCIPLINE** ENGLISH LITERATURE **EDUCATION** Vanderbilt Univ, BA, 75, MA, 78, MAT, 78; Stanford Univ, PhD, 83. **CAREER** Asst prof, Univ Mich, 82-88; assoc prof, Univ Arkansas, 88-89; prof, Univ Calif, Los Angeles, 89- . **HONORS AND AWARDS** Rocekfeller Fel, Natl Hum Ctr, 87-88; Guggenheim fel, 91-92; UCLA Pres Fel, 91-92; NEH fel 97-98. **MEMBERSHIPS** MLA; RSA. **RESEARCH** Tudor-Stuart literature and culture; early modern religion, politics, and law. **SELECTED PUBLICATIONS** Auth, Sacred Rhetoric: The Christian Graud Style in the English Renaissance, Princeton, 88; auth, The Renaissance Bible: Scholarship, Subjectivity, and Sacrifice, California, 94; auth, Subversive Fathers and Suffering Subjects: Shakespeare and Christianity, in Strier, ed, Religion, Literature, and Politics in Post-Reformation England, 1540-1688, Cambridge, 95; co-ed and contribur, Religion and Culture in Early Modern England, Cambridge, 97; auth, Irishmen, Aristocrats, and Other White Barbarians, Renaissance Q, 97; auth, Habits of Thought in the English Renaissance: Religion, Politics, and the Dominant Culture, California, 90, reprint, Toronto, 97; auth, Castigating Livy: The Rape of Lucretia and the Old Arcadia, Renaissance Q, 98; auth, Civility and Censorship in Early Modern England, in Post, ed, Censorship and Silencing, Getty Research Inst, 98; auth, Gums of Glutinous Heat and the Stream of Consciousness: The Theology of Milton's Maske, Representations, 98. **CONTACT ADDRESS** Dept of English, Univ of California, Los Angeles, 405 Hilgard Ave, Los Angeles, CA 90095-1530. **EMAIL** shuger@humnet.ucla.edu

SHUGRUE, MICHAEL F.
PERSONAL Born 07/28/1924, Chicago, IL, s **DISCIPLINE** ENGLISH **EDUCATION** Univ Nebr, AB, 56; Duke Univ, MA, 57; PhD, 60. **CAREER** Dir, MLA, 64-74; prof and dean, Col of Staten Island CUNY, 74-99. **MEMBERSHIPS** MLA; NCTE; CEA. **RESEARCH** The Novel; 18th Century English Literature; The Teaching of English. **SELECTED PUBLICATIONS** Auth, English in a Decade of Change; auth, Foundation of the Novel. **CONTACT ADDRESS** 300 Mercer St, Apt 28K, New York, NY 10003-6724.

SHULMAN, JEFFREY
DISCIPLINE ENGLISH LITERATURE **EDUCATION** Univ Md, BA; Univ Wis, MA, PhD. **CAREER** Eng Dept, Georgetown Univ **RESEARCH** Renaissance literature; Elizabethan and Jacobean drama; Restoration comedy. **SELECTED PUBLICATIONS** Auth, pubs in English Lit Hist; Studies English Lit; Classical Jour. **CONTACT ADDRESS** English Dept, Georgetown Univ, 37th and O St, Washington, DC 20057.

SHULMAN, ROBERT P.
PERSONAL Born 05/11/1930, Syracuse, NY, m, 1952, 2 children **DISCIPLINE** ENGLISH **EDUCATION** Syracuse Univ, BA, 52; Ohio State Univ, MA, 54; PhD, 59. **CAREER** Grad Asst, Ohio State Univ, 52-57; Instr, Ohio State Univ, 58-59; Instr, Univ Wis, 59-61; From Asst Prof to Prof, Univ Wash, 61-. **HONORS AND AWARDS** APS Philos Grant; Fulbright Res Grant; Royalty Res Great, Univ Wash, Teaching Commendation. **MEMBERSHIPS** Am Studies Asn, Arthur Miller Soc. **RESEARCH** Intersection of literature, politics and history, radical writers in cold war America. **SELECTED PUBLICATIONS** Auth, Social Criticism and Nineteenth-Century American Fictions, Univ Mo Pr (Columbia), 87; co-ed and "Introduction," The Yellow-Wall Paper and Other Stories, Oxford World's Classics (95); auth, "American Writers, the Welfare State and the Opportunity Society 1932-1995," in Soc and Secure: Polit and Cult of the Welfare St (Amsterdam: VU Univ Pr, 96), 183-194; co-ed and "Introduction," The Virginian, Oxford World's Classics (98); auth, "Violence and American Fiction," Violence in Am: An Encycl, Scribner's (00); auth, The Power of Political Art: The 1930s Literary Left Reconsidered, Univ NC Pr (Chapel Hill, NC), 00. **CONTACT ADDRESS** Dept English, Univ of Washington, PO Box 354330, Seattle, WA 98195-4330. **EMAIL** rshulman@u.washington.edu

SHULTIS, CHRISTOPHER
DISCIPLINE MUSIC HISTORY **EDUCATION** Univ NMex, PhD. **CAREER** Prof, Univ N Mex, 80-. **HONORS AND AWARDS** Deems Taylor Awd, 96. **SELECTED PUBLICATIONS** Auth, Silencing the Sounded Self: John Cage and the Intentionality of Non-Intention, Musical Quarterly, 95; Cage in Retrospect: A Review Essay, J Musicol, 96. **CONTACT ADDRESS** Music Dept, Univ of New Mexico, Albuquerque, 1805 Roma NE, Albuquerque, NM 87131. **EMAIL** cshultis@unm.edu

SHUMAN, R. BAIRD
PERSONAL Born 06/20/1929, Paterson, NJ **DISCIPLINE** ENGLISH, EDUCATION **EDUCATION** Lehigh Univ, AB, 51; Temple Univ, EdM, 53; Univ Vienna, cert, 54; Univ Pa, PhD, 61. **CAREER** Asst instr English, Univ Pa, 55-57; instr humanities, Drexel Inst Technol, 57-59: asst prof English, San Jose State Col, 59-62; from asst prof to prof educ, Duke Univ, 62-77; prof to prof emeritus englist & dir english educ, Univ Ill, Urbana-Champaign, 77-, dir freshman rhetoric, 79-, Lectr Am lit, Linz Sem Austrian Teachers, Austria, 53; univ scholar, Univ Pa, 56; vis lectr English, Moore Inst Art, 58; vis prof humanities, Philadelphia Conserv Music, 58-59, King Faisal Univ, Saudi Arabia, 78, 81, East Tenn State Univ, 80, Bread Loaf Sch English, Middlebury Col, 80; consult, Am Col Testing Prog & NC Dept Pub Instr, 75-, Kans State Col, Pittsburg, 80, Univ Ark, Little Rock, 80, Nat Univ Singapore, 81; exec ed, The Clearing House, 75-; contribr ed, Reading Horizons, 75-80; consult ed, Poet Lore, 76-, Cygnus, 78-, J Aethetic Ed, 78-82; ed, Speaking out column, The Clearing House, 76- **MEMBERSHIPS** MLA; NCTE; Int Asn Univ Prof English; Conf English Educ; Conf Col Comp & Commun. **RESEARCH** The teaching of writing and the teaching of reading; humanities education; educational drama. **SELECTED PUBLICATIONS** Auth, Signifying As A Scaffold For Literary Interpretation - The Pedagogical Implications Of An African-Am Discourse Genre, African Am Rev, 95. **CONTACT ADDRESS** Bos 27647, Las Vegas, NV 89126-1647. **EMAIL** rbaird@vegasnet.net

SHUMWAY, DAVID R.
PERSONAL Born 03/25/1952, Fremont, OH, m, 2001 **DISCIPLINE** LITERATURE **EDUCATION** Indiana Univ, Phd. **CAREER** Prof of English and Literarary and Cultural Studies, Carnegie Mellon Univ. **HONORS AND AWARDS** Fellowships Ctr for the Humanities, Oregon SU; Ctr for the Humanities Wesleyan Univ (Conn). **MEMBERSHIPS** Mod Lang Assoc; Soc for Cinema Studies; Int Asn for the Study of Popular Music; Nat Coun at Teacher of English. **RESEARCH** Cultural Studies; History of English Studies. **SELECTED PUBLICATIONS** Auth, Michel Foucault; auth, Creating American Civilization. **CONTACT ADDRESS** Carnegie Mellon Univ, 5000 Forbes Ave, Pittsburgh, PA 15213. **EMAIL** shumway@andrew.cmu.edu

SHUMWAY, ERIC BRANDON
PERSONAL Born 11/08/1939, Holbrook, AZ, m, 1963, 7 children **DISCIPLINE** ENGLISH LITERATURE & POLYNESIAN LANGUAGES **EDUCATION** Brigham Young Univ, BA, 64, MA, 66; Univ VA, PhD, 73. **CAREER** From instr to assoc prof, 66-78, prof eng, Brigham Young Univ, HI, 78. **RESEARCH** Browning's love poetry; love in 19th century lit; the Tongan oral tradition. **SELECTED PUBLICATIONS** Auth, Intensive Course in Tongan, Univ HI, 71, rev, Inst of Polynesian Studies, with tapes, 88; Coe Ta'ane: A Royal Marriage (video doc), fall 76 & The Punake of Tonga (video doc), fall 77, Brigham Young Univ-HI; The eulogistic function of the Tongan poet, Pac Studies, fall 77; Tonga Saints: Legacy of Fartl, Inst for Polynesian Studies, 91; Koe Fakapangai: In the Circle of the Sovereign, 93 (video doc). **CONTACT ADDRESS** 55-220 Kulanui St, Laie, HI 96762-1294. **EMAIL** shumwaye@byuh.edu

SHUMWAY, LARRY V.
PERSONAL Born 11/25/1934, Winslow, AZ, m, 1971, 6 children **DISCIPLINE** ETHNOMUSICOLOGY **EDUCATION** Brigham Young Univ, BA, 60; Seton Hall Univ, MA, 64; Univ Washington, PhD. **CAREER** Assoc Prof, Brigham Young Univ, 75-. **MEMBERSHIPS** Soc for Ethnomusicology; Natl Assoc for Humanities Education **RESEARCH** Music of Japan, Tonga, traditional USA **SELECTED PUBLICATIONS** Auth, Non-Western Humanities in the Undergraduate Curriculum: Developing an International Perspective, Interdisciplinary Humanities, 97; auth, Dancing the Buckles of Their Shoes in Pioneer Utah (bundled with CD recording including 7 of Mr. Shumway's fiddle tunes), BYU Studies, 97-98; auth, "Foundations of the Tradition: During Among the Mormon Pioneers," in Craig R. Miller, Social Dance in the Mormon West, with Craig R. Miller, (Salt Lake City: Utah Arts Coun, 00); auth, An Old-Time Utah Dance Party: Sheet Music and Dance Steps, Salt Lake City: Utah Arts Counc, 00. **CONTACT ADDRESS** Brigham Young Univ, JKHB 2007B, Provo, UT 84602. **EMAIL** larry_shumway@byu.edu

SHUMWAY, NICOLAS
PERSONAL Born 09/22/1945, AZ, s **DISCIPLINE** LITERATURE, SPANISH **EDUCATION** BYU, BA, 69; UCLA, MA, 71; PhD, 76. **CAREER** Prof, Yale Univ, 92; prof to dir, Univ Tex, 93-. **HONORS AND AWARDS** Fulbright Prof, 00; Tomas Rivera Regents Prof, 93. **MEMBERSHIPS** MLA; LASA. **RESEARCH** Nationalism issues through literature. **SELECTED PUBLICATIONS** Auth, Invention of Argentina, Univ Calif Pr, 91; auth, Espanol en Espanol, Holt, Rinehart and Winston, 96, 4th ed. **CONTACT ADDRESS** Inst Latin Am Studies, Univ of Texas, Austin, Austin, TX 78712. **EMAIL** shumway@mail.utexas.edu

SHURR, WILLIAM HOWARD
PERSONAL Born 08/29/1932, Evanstan, IL, m, 1968, 1 child **DISCIPLINE** AMERICAN LITERATURE **EDUCATION** Loyola Univ Chicago, AB, 55, PhL, 58, MA, 59, STL, 64; Univ NC, Chapel Hill, PhD(English), 68. **CAREER** Asst prof English, Univ Tenn, 68-72; assoc prof, Wash State Univ, 72-75, prof, 75-81; PROF ENGLISH, UNIV TENN, KNOXVILLE, 81-, Reader, Publ Mod Lang Asn Am, 71- **HONORS AND AWARDS** SAtlantic Mod Lang Asn Prize Manuscript, 72. **MEMBERSHIPS** MLA; Melville Soc; Hopkins Soc; Am Studies Asn (regional pres, 79-81). **RESEARCH** American literature; general world literature; history of theology. **SELECTED PUBLICATIONS** Auth, The Mystery of Iniquity; auth, The Marriage of Emily Dickinson; auth, New Poems of Emily Dickinson; auth, Rappaccini's Children. **CONTACT ADDRESS** Dept of English, Univ of Tennessee, Knoxville, 558 Fearrington Post, Pittsboro, NC 27312. **EMAIL** wshurr@email.unc.edu

SHUTER, BILL
DISCIPLINE THE ROMANTIC REBELLION IN BRITAIN **EDUCATION** PhD. **CAREER** E Mich Univ **SELECTED PUBLICATIONS** Auth, Rereading Walter Pater, Cambridge Univ Press. **CONTACT ADDRESS** Eastern Michigan Univ, Ypsilanti, MI 48197. **EMAIL** ENG_Shuter@online.emich.edu

SHUTTLEWORTH, JACK M.
PERSONAL Born 10/24/1935, Covington, OH, m, 1956, 3 children **DISCIPLINE** ENGLISH LITERATURE; AMERI-

CAN LITERATURE **EDUCATION** Ohio Wesleyan Univ, BA, 57; Stanford Univ, MA, 64; Univ Denver, PhD(English lit), 68. **CAREER** Instr English, Prep Sch, 64-65, from asst prof to assoc prof, 67-77, PROF ENGLISH & HEAD DEPT, US AIR FORCE ACAD, 77-, Chmn, Humanities Div, 96-; Lectr English, Univ Colo, Colorado Springs, 68-71; contrib ed, Ann Bibliog English Lang & Lit, Mod Humanities Res Asn, 68-. **MEMBERSHIPS** Mod Humanities Res Asn; Shakespeare Oxford Soc. **RESEARCH** Seventeenth century drama; Herbert of Cherbury; 20th century novel; Shakespeare authorship question. **SELECTED PUBLICATIONS** Co-ed, Satire: Aesop to Buchwald, Odyssey, 71; ed, The Life of Lord Herbert of Cherbury, Oxford Univ, 74; coauth, Practical College Writing, 78 & Writing Research Papers, 80, Holt. **CONTACT ADDRESS** Dept of English, United States Air Force Academy, CO 80840. **EMAIL** shuttleworthjm.offeng@usafa.edu

SHYLES, LEONARD C.
PERSONAL Born 12/24/1948, Brooklyn, NY, m, 1977, 2 children **DISCIPLINE** MAN COMMUNICATION, MEDIA TECHNOLOGY **EDUCATION** Brooklyn Col, BA, 71; MS, 75; Ohio State Univ, PhD, 81. **CAREER** Instr, Ill State Univ, 80-81; asst prof, Purdue Univ, 81-83; asst prof, Univ Maryland, 83-89; assoc prof, Villanova Univ, 89-. **MEMBERSHIPS** SCA; ICA. **RESEARCH** Man communication; media communication; political communication. **SELECTED PUBLICATIONS** Auth, Video Production Handbook, Houghton Mifflin (Boston, MA), 98; auth, Instructor's Resource Manual and Test Items, Houghton Mifflin (Boston, MA), 98; coauth, "On ethnocentric truth and pragmatic justice," in Recovering pragmatism's voice: the classical tradition, Rorty, and the philosopher of communication, eds. Smith, Langsdorf (Univ NY Press: NY, 95); co-ed, The 1000 hour war: communication in the gulf, Greenwood Press (Westport, CT, 94); auth, "Issue content and legitimacy in 1988 televised political advertising: hubris and synecdoche in promoting presidential candidates," in Television and political advertising, ed. Frank Biocca (Lawrence Erlbaum Associates: Hillside, NJ, 91); coauth, " Arab vs. Israeli news coverage in the New York Times 1976 and 1984," in Current issues in international communication, eds. John L Martin, Ray Hiebert (Longman Press: NY, 90); coauth, "The Army's "Be all you can be" Campaign," Armed Forces Soc 16 (90): 162-166. **CONTACT ADDRESS** Dept Communication, Villanova Univ, 800 E Lancaster Ave, Villanova, PA 19085-1603. **EMAIL** leonard.shyles@villanova.edu

SICARI, STEPHEN
PERSONAL Born 07/03/1957, New York, NY, m, 1980, 4 children **DISCIPLINE** ENGLISH **EDUCATION** Manhattan Col, BA, 79; Cornell Univ, MA, 83, PhD, 86. **CAREER** Asst prof to assoc prof, Adelphi Univ, 86-96; assoc prof, St John's Univ, 96-, Dir, Doctor of Arts Prog in English, 96-, chair, Dept of English, 97-. **HONORS AND AWARDS** Phi Beta Kappa, Manhattan Col, 79; Medals for highest achievement in the Liberal Arts, in Lit, and in Philos, Awded by the Manhattan Col, 79; Sage Grad Fel, Cornell Univ, 80-81; The Martin Sampson Teaching Fel, Cornell Univ, 84; Merit Awd, Adelphi Univ, summer 89; nominated as Teacher of the year by the Student Govt Asn, May 96; English Prof of the Year, Awded by Sigma Tau Delta, 97. **MEMBERSHIPS** Modern Lang Asn, Ezra Pound Soc, James Joyce Soc. **RESEARCH** Literary modernism, history of novel, the epic. **SELECTED PUBLICATIONS** Auth, "Poetry and Politics in Pound and Yeats," Paideuma, Vol 19, No 3 (winter 90): 65-78; auth, Pound's Epic Ambition: Dante and the Modern World, State Univ of New York Press, Albany, NY (91); auth, "Rereading Ulysses: 'Ithaca' and Modernist Allegory," Twentieth Century Lit (fall 97); auth, "Pound's Modernist Allegory," in Dante e Pound, a collection of essays pub by the Opera di Dante, Ravenna, Italy (98); auth, Joyce's Modernist Allegory: Ulysses and the History of the Novel, Univ SC Press (fall 2000); auth, "The Fifth Decad of Cantos," The Ezra Pound Encyclopedia, Greenwood Press (fall 2000); auth, "Reconstructing Nature: Pound as Archaeologist," Paideuma (forthcoming). **CONTACT ADDRESS** Dept English, St. John's Univ, 8150 Utopia Pkwy, Jamaica, NY 11439-0001. **EMAIL** sicaris@stjohns.edu

SICK, DAVID
PERSONAL Born 01/24/1966, Lancaster, PA, s **DISCIPLINE** CLASSICS **EDUCATION** Univ MN, PhD, 96. **CAREER** Instr, Macalester Col, 96-97; Asst Prof, Rhodes Col, 97-. **MEMBERSHIPS** Amer Philol Assoc; Amer Academy Relig; Soc Biblical Lit. **RESEARCH** Graeco-Roman relig; comparative myth. **SELECTED PUBLICATIONS** Auth, Cattle-Theft and the Birth of Mithras, JIES 24, 96. **CONTACT ADDRESS** Greek and Roman Studies, Rhodes Col, 2000 North Parkway, Memphis, TN 38112-1690. **EMAIL** sick@rhodes.edu

SICKER, PHILIP
DISCIPLINE 20TH CENTURY BRITISH AND EUROPEAN FICTION **EDUCATION** Univ VA, PhD. **CAREER** Dir, grad stud; assoc prof, Fordham Univ. **SELECTED PUBLICATIONS** Auth, Pale Fire and Lyrical Ballads: The Dynamics of Collaboration, Papers on Language and Literature 28, 92; Lawrence's Auto da Fe: The Grand Inquisition in The Plumed Serpent, Comp Lit Stud 29, 92. **CONTACT ADDRESS** Dept of Eng Lang and Lit, Fordham Univ, 113 W 60th St, New York, NY 10023.

SIDER, JOHN W.
DISCIPLINE ENGLISH **EDUCATION** Univ Notre Dame, PhD, 71. **CAREER** Adj prof, Santa Barbara City Col, 73-74; adj prof, Jesuit Novitate, 78; asst prof, Bethel Col, 66-68, 70-72; prof, Westmont Col, 72-. **HONORS AND AWARDS** Fac res award, 85. **RESEARCH** Brit & Am lit. **SELECTED PUBLICATIONS** Auth, Interpreting the Parables: A Hermeneutical Guide to Their Meaning, Zondervan, 95; One Man in His Time Plays Many Parts, Authorial Theatrics of Doubling in Early Renaissance Drama, Stud in Philol, 95; The Parables, The Complete Literary Guide to the Bible, Zondervan, 93. **CONTACT ADDRESS** Dept of English, Westmont Col, 955 La Paz Rd, Santa Barbara, CA 93108-1099.

SIEBENSCHUH, WILLIAM R.
PERSONAL Born 08/27/1942, Chicago, IL, m, 1965, 2 children **DISCIPLINE** ENGLISH LITERATURE, COMPOSITION **EDUCATION** Grinnell Col, BA, 64; Univ Calif, MA, 66; PhD, 70. **CAREER** Asst prof English, Fordham Univ, 71-78; asst prof, 78-80, prof Eng, Case Western Reserve Univ, 80-, dir compos & writing ctr, 80-. **RESEARCH** Biography-autobiography; Johnson and Boswell; the novel. **SELECTED PUBLICATIONS** Coauth, The Struggle for Modern Tibert: The Autobiography of Tasli Tsering, M.E. Sharpe, 97. **CONTACT ADDRESS** Case Western Reserve Univ, 10900 Euclid Ave, Cleveland, OH 44106-4901. **EMAIL** wrs2@p.o.cwru.edu.

SIEBER, JOHN HAROLD
PERSONAL Born 09/19/1935, Janesville, WI, m, 1960, 2 children **DISCIPLINE** RELIGION, CLASSICS **EDUCATION** Luther Col, BA, 58; Luther Theol Sem, BD, 62; Claremont Grad Sch, PhD(relig), 66. **CAREER** Asst prof classics, 65-67, asst prof relig, 67-72, assoc prof, 72-78, Prof to Prof Emer Relig & Classics, Luther Col, 78-. **HONORS AND AWARDS** Am Philos Soc res grant, 72. **MEMBERSHIPS** Soc Bibl Lit. **RESEARCH** Theology of Rudolf Bultman; Gnostic library from Nag-Hammdi, Egypt. **SELECTED PUBLICATIONS** Auth, An introduction to the Tractate Zostrianos from Nag Hammadi, Novum Testamentum, 7/73. **CONTACT ADDRESS** Dept of Relig, Luther Col, 700 College Dr, Decorah, IA 52101-1045. **EMAIL** sieberjo@luther.edu

SIEBERT, HILARY
DISCIPLINE TEACHING WRITING, TEACHER TRAINING, THE SHORT STORY, AND AMERICAN LITERATUR **EDUCATION** Univ IA, BA, PhD; Middlebury Col, MA. **CAREER** Prof, Radford Univ. **SELECTED PUBLICATIONS** Publ articles on tchg writing and lit and on the short story, partic the stories of Raymond Carver. **CONTACT ADDRESS** Radford Univ, Radford, VA 24142. **EMAIL** hsiebert@runet.edu

SIEGEL, ADRIENNE
PERSONAL Born 06/10/1936, New York, NY, m, 1972 **DISCIPLINE** AMERICAN HISTORY, POPULAR LITERATURE **EDUCATION** Univ Pa, BS, 57; Columbia Univ, MA, 59; New York Univ, PhD(hist), 73. **CAREER** Teacher, James Madison High Sch, 62-82; asst prof hist, Long Island Univ, 77-93: Fel, New York Univ, 71-72; assoc, Danforth Found, 72-82; Fulbright fel India, 78; fel, Inst Res in Hist, 81-82; Asst Prof, City Univ NY, Col Staten Island, 93-. **HONORS AND AWARDS** Phi Delta Kappa Scholarship, 90; Phi Delta Kappa Chapter Editor & Fdn Rep, 88-93; Phi Delta Kappa Cert Rec, 89; NY Univ Alumnae Awd, 74; Bronx Educ Endowment Fund Board 84-93. **MEMBERSHIPS** Orgn Am Historians; Popular Cult Asn. **RESEARCH** History of the American city. **SELECTED PUBLICATIONS** Auth, When Cities Were Fun, J Popular Cult and in Twentieth Cent Lit Crit, 75; Philadelphia: A Chronological and Documentary History, Oceana, 75; Brothels, Bets and Bars, NDak Quart, 76; The Image of the American City in Popular Literature, Kennikat, 81; auth, The Marshall Court, Associated Faculty Press, 87; auth, Visions for the Reconstruction of the NYC School System, in Urban Education, Jan 86; auth, Incubator of Dreams: Directing College Guidance at America's Most Elite Minority High School, Education, Winter 89; auth, A Case for Colaboratives: Turning Around Bronx Public Schools, Urban Review, 88; auth, Mission Possible: The Rescue of Bronx Public Schools, Phi Delta Kappa Fastback, 88; auth, Don't Wait, Communicate: Helping Teachers to Talk Shop, The Effective School Report, 87; auth, Collective Dreams or Urban Realities: Psychohistory, Persons & Communities, 83; auth, The Myth of Mobility in the Media of Another Century, in The Many Faces of Psychohistory, Intl. Psychohistorical Assn, 84. **CONTACT ADDRESS** 330 W Jersey St, Elizabeth, NJ 07202. **EMAIL** siegel@postbox.csi.cuny.edu

SIEGEL, GERALD
PERSONAL Born 04/22/1941, Jersey City, NJ, M, 1984, 2 children **DISCIPLINE** LITERATURE **EDUCATION** Western Md Col, BA; Texas Christian Univ, MA; George Washington Univ, PhD. **HONORS AND AWARDS** Fulbright lect, Macedonia, Belguim; **MEMBERSHIPS** MLA, NCTE, CEA. **RESEARCH** Middle-European tales of terror, popular culture. **SELECTED PUBLICATIONS** auth, Directory of Writing Prog; auth Business and Professional Writing: A Guide to The Process; auth, The Tale of Terror. **CONTACT ADDRESS** York Col, Pennsylvania, 441 Country Club Road, York, PA 17403. **EMAIL** gsiegel@ycp.edu

SIEGEL, JOEL E.
DISCIPLINE ENGLISH LITERATURE **EDUCATION** Cornell Univ, BA; Northwestern Univ, Mam PhD. **CAREER** Eng Dept, Georgetown Univ **HONORS AND AWARDS** Fiction Awd, 63; Washington Dateline Awd, 89; Grammy Awd, 93. **MEMBERSHIPS** Am Soc Composers; Artists and Publishers; Nat Soc Recording Arts and Sci. **SELECTED PUBLICATIONS** Auth, Val Lewton: The Reality of Terror, Viking, 73; pubs in City Paper, Film Heritage, December, American Film Institute Magazine, Premiere, Bright Lights, Washingtonian Magazine. **CONTACT ADDRESS** English Dept, Georgetown Univ, 37th and O St, Washington, DC 20057.

SIEGEL, KRISTI
PERSONAL Born 01/02/1951, Breckenridge, MN, m, 1978, 4 children **DISCIPLINE** ENGLISH **EDUCATION** Univ Wis, BA, 79; Univ Wis, MA, 87; Univ Wis, PhD, 91. **CAREER** From Teaching Asst to Lectr, Univ Wis, 89-91; From Lectr to Asst Prof, Mt Mary Col, 92-. **HONORS AND AWARDS** Sigma Tau Delta, 79. **MEMBERSHIPS** MLA, Autobiographical Soc, Simone de Beauvoir Soc. **RESEARCH** Theory - literary and cultural, autobiography, travel writing and theory, genre studies, postmodern literature, medicine and technology. **SELECTED PUBLICATIONS** Auth, Word 97 Intermediate/Advanced for the Workplace, Mt Mary Col Pr, 99; auth, Excel 97 Fundamentals/Intermediate and Powerpoint 97 for the Workplace, Mt Mary Col Pr, 99; auth, "Criticism, Theory and Life-Writing: 20th-Century Movements in 1950s," Encycl of Life-Writing, Fitzroy-Dearborn (forthcoming); auth, Women's Autobiographies, Culture, Feminism, Peter Lang Publ (New York, NY), forthcoming; auth, "Annie Dillard," Encycl of Life-Writing (forthcoming). **CONTACT ADDRESS** Dept English, Mount Mary Col, 2900 N Menomonee River Pkwy, Milwaukee, WI 53222-4545. **EMAIL** siegelkr@mtmary.edu

SIEGEL, PAUL N.
PERSONAL Born 06/24/1916, Paterson, NJ, w, 1948, 1 child **DISCIPLINE** ENGLISH LITERATURE **EDUCATION** City Col NYork, BS, 36; Harvard Univ, AM, 39, PhD, 41. **CAREER** Instr, Univ Conn, 46; instr, City Col NY, 46-49; from assoc prof to prof English, Ripon Col, 49-56; chmn dept, 56-71, prof, 56-78, EMER PROF ENGLISH, LONG ISLAND UNIV, 78-, Ford Found Fund Advan Educ fel, 52-53; ed consult, PMLA, 63-; consult mem, World Ctr Shakespeare Studies, London, 72; mem adv bd, World Ctr Shakespeare Studies, US, 72-; Columbia Univ Sem in the Renaissance. **MEMBERSHIPS** MLA **RESEARCH** Shakespeare; Marxist literary criticism; 20th century novel. **SELECTED PUBLICATIONS** Auth, Shakespearean Tragedy and the Elizabethan Compromise, NY Univ, 57; ed, His Infinite Variety, Lippincott, 63; contribr, Reader's Encycl of Shakespeare, Crowell, 66; auth, Shakespeare in His Time and Ours, Univ Notre Dame, 68; contribr, The Achievement of Isaac Bashevis Singer, Southern Ill Univ, 69; ed, Leon Trotsky on Literature and Art, 70 & Revolution and the 20th-Century Novel, 79, Pathfinder; contribr, Shakespearean Comedy, NY Lit Forum, 80; auth, Shakespeare's English and Roman History Plays, Fairleigh Dickinson Univ, 86; reprinted as The Gathering Storm, Redwords, 92; auth, The Meek and the Militant: Religion and Power Across the World, Zed, 86; auth, The Great Reversal: Politics and Art in Solzhenitsyn, Walnut, 91. **CONTACT ADDRESS** 101 W 85th St, New York, NY 10024.

SIEMENS, RAYMOND G.
DISCIPLINE ENGLISH **EDUCATION** Univ Waterloo, BA, 89; Univ Albta, MA, 91; Univ Brit Colum, PhD, 97. **CAREER** Postdoc fel, Univ Albta, 97-99; asst prof, Malaspina Univ Col, 99-. **HONORS AND AWARDS** SSHRC, 95-96, 99-00, 00-03; UGF, 96-97; Simcoe, 91-92; Killam PDF, 97-99. **RESEARCH** Renaissance English literature; **SELECTED PUBLICATIONS** Auth, "Robert Cawdrey's A Table Alphabeticall," Renaissance Electronic Texts (94); auth, auth, "Tottel's Miscellany," in Using Tact with Electronic Texts: A Guide to Text Analysis Computing Tools, eds. Ian Lancashire, et al (NYork: MLA, 96); auth, "Technologising the Humanities/Humanitising the Technologies," Text Tech Computing (98); auth, "Milton's Works and Life: Select Studies and Resources," in The Cambridge Companion to Milton, ed. Dennis Danielson (Cambridge: Cambridge Univ Pr, 99); auth, "Renaissance Literary Studies and Humanities Computing," Early Mod Lit Studies (00); auth, "Wrestling With God: Literature and Theology in the English Renaissance," Early Mod Lit Studies (01); auth, "Henry VIII and Poetry of Politics," in Reading Monarchs Writing: The Poetry of Henry VIII, Mary Stuart, Elizabeth I, and James VI/I, ed. Peter Herman (Medieval Renaissance Texts and Studies, 01); auth, "The Lyrics of the Henry VIII Manuscript," (forthcoming); auth, "The Credibility of Electronic Publishing: A Report of the Humanities and Social," Text Tech (forthcoming); auth, "Shakespearean Apparatus? Explicit Textual Structures and the Implicit Navigation of Accumulated Knowledge," Text (02). **CONTACT ADDRESS** English Dept, Malaspina Univ Col, Nanaimo, BC, Canada V9R 5S5. **EMAIL** siemensr@mala.bc.ca

SIEMON, JAMES RALPH
PERSONAL Born 11/14/1948, St. Louis, MO, m, 1972, 4 children **DISCIPLINE** ENGLISH LITERATURE **EDUCATION**

Washington Univ, AB, 70; State Univ NYork Buffalo, MA, 76, PhD(English), 77. **CAREER** Asst prof English, Boston Univ, 77-94, prof English, 95-, vis asst prof, Harvard Univ, 81. **MEMBERSHIPS** Shakespeare Asn Am; Int Shakespeare Asn; MLA. **RESEARCH** Shakespeare; Bakhtin, Literary Theory. **SELECTED PUBLICATIONS** Auth, Poetic Contradiction in Resolution and Independence, In: On Contradiction, 74 & Turn our Impressed Lances in Our Eyes: Iconoclasm in King Lear, In: Literature and Iconoclasm: Shakespeare, 76, State Univ NY Press; Shakespearean Iconoclasm, Berkely: Univ of California Press, 85; Nay, that's not next: Othello, V.ii. in Performance, 1760-1900, Shakespeare Quart 37, 86; Dialogial Formalism: Word, Action, and Object in The Spanish Tragedy, Medieval and Renaissance Drama 5, 90; Subjected thus: Utterance, Character, and Richard II, Shakespeare Jahrbuch (DDR) 126, 90; Landlord Not King: Agrarian Change and Inarticulation, in Richard Burt and John Michael Archer, eds, Enclosure Acts: Discourses of Sexuality, Property, and Culture in Early Modern England, Ithaca: Cornell UP, 94; The Word Itself Against the Word: Close Reading After Voloshinov, in Russ McDonald, ed, Shakespeare Reread, Ithaca: Cornell UP, 94; Sporting Kyd, English Literary Renaissance 24, 94; Perplexed beyond Self-explication: Cymbeline and Early Modern/Post-modern Europe, in Derek Roper and Michael Hattaway, eds, Shakespeare in the New Europe, Sheffield: Sheffield UP, 94; ed, Christopher Marlowe, The Jew of Malta, London: A & C Black, 94; auth, Sign, Cause or General Habit: Toward an 'Historicist Ontology' of Character on the Early Modern Stage, in Hugo Keiper, ed, Nominalism and Literary Discourse: New Perspectives, Rodopi Press, 98. **CONTACT ADDRESS** Dept of English, Boston Univ, 236 Bay State Rd, Boston, MA 02215-1403. **EMAIL** jsiemon@bu.edu

SIGMAN, STUART J.
PERSONAL Born 01/29/1955, Brooklyn, NY **DISCIPLINE** COMMUNICATION **EDUCATION** Univ PA, PhD, 82. **CAREER** Dean, School of Communication, Management and Public Policy, Emerson Col, 98-. **HONORS AND AWARDS** Development grant, State Ed Dept, New York State, 93-94; Eastern Commun Asn Scholar, 93-94; res grant, The Union Inst, Cincinnati, OH, 98-99. **MEMBERSHIPS** Int Commun Asn; Nat Commun Asn. **RESEARCH** Sociolinguistics; ethnography; social theory. **SELECTED PUBLICATIONS** Auth, A Perspective on Social Communication, Lexington Books, 87(Chapter 1 excerpted and reprinted as Social Communication, in John Corner and Jeremy Hawthorne, eds, Communication Studies: An Introductory Reader, 3rd ed, Edward Arnold, 89); Toward an Intergration of Diverse Communication Contexts: Commentary on the Chapter by Fry, Alexander, and Fry, in James A Anderson, ed, Communication Yearbook 13, Sage, 90; Descriptive Respnsibility and Cultural Critique, in, Res on Lang and Social Interaction, vol 23, 90; Handling the Discontinuous Aspects of Continuous Social Relationships: Toward Research on the Persistance of Social Forms, Commun Theory, vol 1, no 2, 91; Do Social Approaches To Interpersonal Communication Constitute a Contribution to Communication Theory?, Commun Theory, vol 2, no 4, 92; Regles de Communication, in Lucien Sfez, ed, Dictionnaire Critique de la Communication, vol 2, Presses Universitaires de France, 93; Question: Evidence of What? Answer: Communication, Western J of Commun, 95; Order and Continuity in Human Relationships: A Social Communication Approach to Defining 'Relationship,' in Wendy Leeds-Hurwitz, ed, Social Approaches to Communication, Guilford Press, 95; The Consequentiality of Communication, Lawrence Erlbaum Assocs, 95; with Adam Kendon, Ray L Birdwhistell (1918-1994), Semiotica, vol 112, nos 1-2, 96. **CONTACT ADDRESS** School of Commun, Mgmt, Pub Policy, Emerson Col, 120 Boylston St, Boston, MA 02116. **EMAIL** stuart_sigman@emerson.edu

SIGNORIELLI, NANCY
PERSONAL Born 07/29/1943, New York, NY, m, 1980, 2 children **DISCIPLINE** COMMUNICATION **EDUCATION** Wilson Col, BA, 65; Queens Col, MA, 67; Univ Pa, PhD, 75. **CAREER** Res Adminr, Annenberg School for Commun, Univ of Pa, 75-87; assoc prof, 87-89, Prof, Univ Delaware, 89-. **MEMBERSHIPS** Int Commun Asn; Nat Commun Asn; Broadcast Ed Asn; Asn for Ed in Journalism & Mass Commun. **RESEARCH** Television images and relationship to people's conceptions about social reality. **SELECTED PUBLICATIONS** Auth, Women in Communication: A Bibliographic Sourcebook, Greenwood Press, 96; Mass Media Images and Impact on Health, Greenwood Press, 93; Health Images on Television, Commun in Medical Ethics, Greenwood Press, 98; coauth, Television and Children's Conceptions of Nutrition, Health Commun, 97; Cultivation Analysis-Research and Practice, An Integrated Approach to Commun Theory and Res, 96; Violence on Television: The Cultural Indicators Project, J of Broadcasting & Electronic Media, 94; auth, "Television's Contribution to Stereotyping: Past, present, future," Handbook of Children and the Media, 00; auth, "Recognition and respect: a content analysis of prime-time television characters across 3 decades," Sex Roles, 99. **CONTACT ADDRESS** Commun Dept, Univ of Delaware, Newark, DE 19716. **EMAIL** nancys@udel.edu

SILBIGER, ALEXANDER
PERSONAL Born 05/14/1935, Rotterdam, Netherlands, m, 1977 **DISCIPLINE** MUSIC **EDUCATION** Brandeis Univ, PhD. **CAREER** Musicol prof, Duke Univ. **RESEARCH** Hist and performance of early keyboard music. **SELECTED PUBLICATIONS** Auth, publ(s) on Renaissance and Baroque music. **CONTACT ADDRESS** Dept of Music, Duke Univ, Mary Duke Biddle Music Bldg, Durham, NC 27708-0665. **EMAIL** alexander.silbiger@duke.edu

SILCOX, MARY
DISCIPLINE ENGLISH LITERATURE **EDUCATION** Univ Western Ontario, BA; Queen's Univ, MA, PhD. **RESEARCH** 16th and 17th century lit; emblem studies. **SELECTED PUBLICATIONS** Auth, English Emblem Tradition II, 93; co-auth, The Modern Critical Reception of the English Emblem, 91; co-auth, The English Emblem: Bibliography of Secondary Literature, 90. **CONTACT ADDRESS** English Dept, McMaster Univ, 1280 Main St W, Hamilton, ON, Canada L8S 4L9. **EMAIL** silcox@mcmaster.ca

SILET, C. LORING
PERSONAL Born 04/25/1942, Chicago, IL, m, 1976, 4 children **DISCIPLINE** ENGLISH **EDUCATION** Butler Univ, BA, 64; Ind Univ, MA, 66; PhD, 73. **CAREER** Assoc Instructor, Ind Univ, 69-70, 71-73; Istructor to Assoc Prof, Iowa State Univ, 73-86; Visiting Prof, Univ Glasgow, 89; Prof, Iowa State Univ, 85-. **HONORS AND AWARDS** Distinguished Teaching Awd, Iowa State Univ, 98. **MEMBERSHIPS** Soc for Cinema Studies, Mod Lang Asn, Am Studies Asn. **RESEARCH** Film; Contemporary Literature and Culture. **SELECTED PUBLICATIONS** Auth, The films of Steven Spielberg, forthcoming; auth, Oliver Stone: Interviews, 00; co-auth, The World Between Two rivers: Perspectives on American Indians in Iowa, 00; auth, The Critical Response to Chester Himes, 99; auth, Talking Murder: Interviews with 20 Mystery Writers, 99; auth, Images of American Indians on film: an annotated Bibliography, 85; auth, The Critical Reception of Hamlin Garland, 1891-1978, 85. **CONTACT ADDRESS** Dept English, Iowa State Univ, Ames, IA 50011-2010. **EMAIL** csilet@iastate.edu

SILL, GEOFFREY M.
PERSONAL Born 10/05/1944, Cleveland, OH, 2 children **DISCIPLINE** ENGLISH LITERATURE **EDUCATION** Pa State Univ, PhD, 74. **CAREER** Assoc prof, Rutgers Univ, 74-; chair, dept of Eng, 99- . **MEMBERSHIPS** Am Soc for 18th Century Studies **RESEARCH** 18th century Brit novel; Daniel Defoe; Med and lit. **SELECTED PUBLICATIONS** Auth, Defoe and the Idea of Fiction, 83; The Authorship of An Impartial History of Michael Servetus, PBSA 87, 93; Crusoe in the Cave: Defoe and the Semiotics of Desire, Eighteenth-Century Fiction 6, 94; Swift's As Sure as God's in Gloc'ster and the Assurance of the Moderns, Notes and Queries 240, 95; Neurology and the Novel: Alexander Monro, Robinson Crusoe, and the Problem of Sensibility, Literatue and Medicine 16, 97; The Source of Robinson Crusoe's Sudden Joys, Notes and Queries 243, 98; auth, "Roxana's Susan: Whose Daughter is She Anyway?" Stud in Eighteent-Cent Cult 29 (00); coed, Walt Whitman and the Visual Arts, 92; The Witlings and The Woman-Hater, 97; ed, Walt Whitman of Mickle Street: A Centennnial Collection, 94. **CONTACT ADDRESS** Dept of English, Rutgers, The State Univ of New Jersey, Camden, 311 N 5th St., Camden, NJ 08102. **EMAIL** sill@crab.rutgers.edu

SILLARS, MALCOLM O.
PERSONAL Born 02/12/1928, Union City, NJ, m, 1948, 3 children **DISCIPLINE** SPEECH **EDUCATION** Univ Redlands, BA, 48, MA, 49; State Univ IA, PhD, 55. **CAREER** Instr speech, IA State Univ, 49-54; instr, Los Angeles State Col, 54-56; from asst prof to assoc prof speech, San Fernando Valley State Col, 56-61, prof, 62-71, chmn dept, 56-63 & 66-68, assoc dean sch lett & sci, 63-66, actg dean, 69-70, actg pres, 69; prof commun, Univ Mass, Amherst, 71-74; dean, Col Humanities, 74-81, prof commun, Univ UT, 74-98, Res assoc, Univ IL, 61-62; assoc ed, Quart J Speech, 63-66; chmn educ policies bd, National Commun Asn, 70-71, chmn awards comt, 72, mem finance bd, 74-76, vis prof, Univ UT, 71. **MEMBERSHIPS** Speech Commun Asn (pres, 79-80); Am Forensic Asn (secy-treas, 55-57); Western Speech Commun Asn, pres, 90-91. **RESEARCH** Am public address; contemp rhetorical theory. **SELECTED PUBLICATIONS** Auth, Robert Penn Warren's All the Kings Men, a study in populism, Am Quart, 56; The 1960 Democratic Convention, Quart J Speech, 60; The rhetoric of the petition in Boots, Speech Monogr, 6/72; coauth, Argumentation and the Decision-Making Process, Longman, 01; Speech: Content and Communication, Waveland, 91; Messages Meaning and Culture, Waveland, 01. **CONTACT ADDRESS** 3508 E Oaks Dr, Salt Lake City, UT 84124.

SILVA, J. DONALD
PERSONAL Born 01/19/1935, Lowell, MA, m, 1957, 4 children **DISCIPLINE** ENGLISH **EDUCATION** Univ NHamp, BA, 57; MA, 65. **CAREER** Prof, Thompson Sch, 63-. **HONORS AND AWARDS** Teaching Excellence Awd, 73. **MEMBERSHIPS** AAUP; NCTE; CCC. **RESEARCH** English Composition; Maderian culture; Modern Portugal. **SELECTED PUBLICATIONS** Ed, Bibliography of the Maderia Islands, 87. **CONTACT ADDRESS** Thompson Sch, Univ of New Hampshire, Durham, 115 Mast Rd, Durham, NH 03824-4724. **EMAIL** jdsilva@nh.ultranet.com

SILVA, JOHN O.
PERSONAL Born Newark, NJ, m, 1978, 3 children **DISCIPLINE** ENGLISH **EDUCATION** City Univ New York: Graduate School, PhD, 77. **CAREER** Prof of English, The City Univ of New York: LaGuardia Community Col, 89-. **HONORS AND AWARDS** PSC CUNY Research Awd, 00, PSC CUNY Researc Awd, 98, PSC CUNY Research Awd, 96; PSC CUNY Research Awd, 91, National Endowment for the Humanities Summer Stipend, 90, National Endowment for the Humanities Summer Seminar Fel, Doctoral Orals. **MEMBERSHIPS** The Renaissance Society of America, The North-East Modern Language Assoc of America, The Society of the Classical Guitar. **SELECTED PUBLICATIONS** Auth, "Shakespeare and Portugal: A Synopsis." The Shakespeare Newsletter XXV, 75; auth, "Naming and the Literary Context. "Literary Onomastic Studies VII (80): 139-48; auth, "Sir Philip Sidney and the Castilina Tongue." Comparative Literature XXXIX (82): 130-45; auth, "Recurrent Onomastic Textures in the Diana of Jorge de Montemayor and the Arcadia of Sir Philip Sidney." Studies in Philogy LXXIX (82): 30-40; auth, "Plainness and Truth: A Reading of the Secular and Spiritual Sonnets of Henry Constable," Univ of Hartford Studies in Literature XV, #3 and XVI, #1 (84): 33-42:, auth, "Portuguese Pastoral before Montemayor: Crisfal and the Eclogues of Sa de Miranda," Portuguese Studies IX (93): 116-27; auth, "Structures and Restructures in Montemayor's Diana," Bulletin of Hispanic Studies, LXXII (55): 165-73; auth, "Reinventing the Nation: Luis de Camoes's Epic Burden," Mediterranean Studies: IX (01), pagination is forthcoming; auth, "Exile under Fire: Reassessing the Poetics and Practice of Camoes's First Editor, Manuel de Faria e Sousa" in the Global Impact of Portuguese Literature and Culture, New Brunswick: Transaction Press, publication date is forthcoming; auth, "Moving the Monarch': The Rhetoric of Perusasion in Camoes's Lusiadas," Renaissance Quarterly: issue number and publication date forthcoming. **CONTACT ADDRESS** Dept English, LaGuardia Comm Col, 3110 Thomson Ave, Long Island City, NY 11101-3007.

SILVER, BRENDA R.
DISCIPLINE ENGLISH LITERATURE **EDUCATION** Harvard Univ, PhD, 73. **CAREER** Prof, Dartmouth Col. **RESEARCH** Brit, postmodern, and feminist lit; Virginia Woolf. **SELECTED PUBLICATIONS** Virginia Woolf's Reading Notebooks, Princeton UP, 83; co-ed, Rape and Representation, Columbia UP, 91; Textual Criticism as Feminist Practice: Or, Who's Afraid of Virginia Woolf Part II in Representing Modernist Texts: Editing as Interpretation, U of Michigan P, 91; Mis-fits: The Monstrous Union of Virginia Woolf and Marilyn Monroe, Discourse, 93; auth, Periphrasis, Power, and Rape in A Passage to India in E. M. Forster, St Martin's, 95; auth, Virginia Woolf Icon, Univ of Chicago Press, 99. **CONTACT ADDRESS** Dept of English, Dartmouth Col, 6032 Sanborn House, Hanover, NH 03755. **EMAIL** Brenda.R.Silver@dartmouth.edu

SILVER, CAROLE GRETA
PERSONAL Born 06/06/1937, New York, NY, m, 1991 **DISCIPLINE** VICTORIAN LITERATURE **EDUCATION** Alfred Univ, BA, 58; Univ Mich, MA, 59; Columbia Univ, PhD(English, comp lit), 67 **CAREER** Instr English, Vassar Col, 66 & Hunter Col, 67-68; asst prof, 68-74, assoc prof, 74-88, Prof English, Stern Col, Yeshiva Univ, 88-, Chair, Humanities Div, 93-. **MEMBERSHIPS** Northeast Victorian Studies Asn (vpres, 77); NAm William Morris Soc; MLA **RESEARCH** William Morris; pre-Raphaelite poetry and art; myth and folklore in Victorian literature. **SELECTED PUBLICATIONS** Auth, The defense of Guenevere: A further interpretation, Studies in English Lit, 69; The earthly paradise: Lost, Victorian Poetry, 75; co-ed, Studies in the Late Romances of William Morris, 76 & auth, Myth and ritual in the last romances of William Morris, 76, William Morris Soc; The Romance of William Morris, 82; co-auth, Kind Words: A Thesaurus of Euphemism, 83, 90, 95; co-ed, Socialism..and William Morris, 91; auth, Strange and Secret People: Fairies and Victorian Consciousness, 98. **CONTACT ADDRESS** Yeshiva Univ, 245 Lexington Ave, New York, NY 10016-4699. **EMAIL** csilver@ymail.yu.edu

SILVERBERG, CAROL
PERSONAL Born 06/27/1967, New York, NY, s **DISCIPLINE** ENGLISH **EDUCATION** Pace Univ, BA, 89; SUNY, MA, 95; PhD, 02. **CAREER** Adjunct Lect, State Univ NYork (SUNY), 95-97; Instr, State Univ NYork (SUNY), 98-. **RESEARCH** Composition studies, dramatic literature, theatre. **SELECTED PUBLICATIONS** Auth, Contemporary Theatre and Academic Programs, State Univ NY Pr (Binghamton, NY), 94. **CONTACT ADDRESS** Dept English, SUNY, Binghamton, PO Box 6000, Binghamton, NY 13902-6000. **EMAIL** bc21568@binghamton.edu

SILVERBERG, MARK A.
PERSONAL Born 05/20/1965, Toronto, ON, Canada, m, 1998, 1 child **DISCIPLINE** ENGLISH AND AMERICAN LITERATURE **EDUCATION** York Univ, BA, 89; Univ of Toronto, BEd, 90; Dalhousie Univ, MA, 96; PhD, 00. **CAREER** Teach-

er, Int Community Sch, Ethiopia, 90-92; teacher, Taylor's Col, Malaysia, 92-94; vis prof, St Mary's Univ, Gambia, 98; adj prof, Dalhousie Univ, 00-. **HONORS AND AWARDS** Lucille Herbert Mem Award, 89; Joseph Howe Poetry Competition, First Prize, 95; Dalhousie Univ Fel, 94-98; Izaak Walton Killam Mem Scholar, 98-99. **MEMBERSHIPS** MLA, ACCUTE. **RESEARCH** New York School Poetry and Painting, Abstract Expressionism, Pop Art, Outsider Art, Response Theory, Adolescent Readers, and Formative Literature, Kenneth Patchen. **SELECTED PUBLICATIONS** Rev, "Personality and Poetics, Review of Frank Lentricchia's Modernist Quartet," Henry St 5.2, (95): 102-106; auth, "A Bouquet of Empty Brackets: Author-Function and the Search for JD Salinger," Dalhousie Rev 75.2, (95): 222-246; auth, "George Oppen," Scribner Encycl of Am Lives, ed Kenneth T Jackson, (NY: Scribner's, 98): 613-614; auth, "A Readership of None: The Later Poetry of WS Graham," English Studies in Can 24.2, (98): 39-55; auth, "Reading the New York School," Henry St 8.2, (99): 81-102; auth, "James Schuyler," Scribner Encycl of Am Lives, ed Kenneth T Jackson, (NY: Scribner's 00); auth, "The Can(adi)onization of Al Purdy," Essays on Can Writing 70 (00): 226-51; auth, "Where There's a Will, There Are Always Two Ways: Doubling in World of Wonders," Robertson Davies: A Reappraisal, ed Camille La Bossiere, (Univ of Ottawa Pr, forthcoming). **CONTACT ADDRESS** 5537 Macara St, Halifax, NS, Canada B3K 1W1. **EMAIL** msilv@is2.dal.ca

SILVERMAN, FRANKLIN H.

PERSONAL Born 08/16/1933, Providence, RI, m, 1983, 1 child **DISCIPLINE** SPEECH PATHOLOGY **EDUCATION** Emerson Col, BS, 60; Northwestern Univ, MA, 61; Univ Iowa, PhD, 66. **CAREER** Res assoc, Univ Iowa, 65-68; asst prof, Univ Ill, Urbana-Champaign, 68-71; assoc prof, Marquette Univ, 71-77, prof, 77-; clinical prof at Rehabilitation Med, Med Col of Wisc, 78-. **HONORS AND AWARDS** Fac Awd for Teaching Excellence, Marquette Univ, 89; Alumni Achievement Awd, Emerson Col, 97; Disabled Children Asn of Saudi Arabia Awd for Res on Rehabilitation, 98; Text and Academic Asn Keedy Awd for Service to Academic Authors, 99. **MEMBERSHIPS** Am Speech-Language-Hearing Asn, Text and Academic Authors Asn. **RESEARCH** Speech disorders, academic authoring. **SELECTED PUBLICATIONS** Auth, Stuttering and Other Fluency Disorders, 2nd ed, Needham, Ma: Allyn & Bacon (96); auth, Computer Applications for Augmenting the Management of Speech, Language, and Hearing Disorders, Needham, Ma: Allyn & Bacon (97); auth, Research Design and Evaluation in Speech-Language Pathology and Audiology, 4th ed, Needham, Ma: Allyn & Bacon (98); auth, Authoring Books and Materials for Students, Academics, and Professionals, Westport, Ct: Praeger Pubs (98); auth, Fundamentals of Electronics for Speech-Language Pathologists and Audiologists, Needham, Ma: Allyn & Bacon (99); auth, Professional Issues in Speech-Language Pathology and Audiology, Ma: Allyn & Bacon (99); auth, The Telecommunication Relay Service (TRS) Handbook, Middletown, RI: Aegis Pub Group (99); auth, Publishing for Tenure and Beyond, Westport, Ct: Praeger Pubs (99); auth, Self-Publishing Books and Materials for Students, Academics, and Professionals, Greendale, WI: CODI Pubs (2000); auth, Second Thoughts About Stuttering, Greendale, WI: CODI Pubs (2000). **CONTACT ADDRESS** Dept Speech Path & Audiol, Marquette Univ, PO Box 1881, Milwaukee, WI 53201-1881. **EMAIL** franklin.silverman@marquette.edu

SILVERMAN, JAY R.

PERSONAL Born 11/01/1947, New York, NY, m, 1984, 2 children **DISCIPLINE** ENGLISH **EDUCATION** Amherst Col, AB, 63; Univ VA, PhD, 77. **CAREER** Assoc prof, VA Highlands Comm Col, 71-80; prof, Nassau Comm Col, 80-. **HONORS AND AWARDS** Fulbright Fel, Cameroon, 79-80. **SELECTED PUBLICATIONS** Auth, Rules of Thumb: A Guide for Writers, McGraw Hill, 4th ed, 00. **CONTACT ADDRESS** Dept English, Nassau Comm Col, 1 Education Dr, Garden City, NY 11530-6719.

SILVERMAN, KENNETH EUGENE

PERSONAL Born 02/05/1936, New York, NY, 2 children **DISCIPLINE** ENGLISH, AMERICAN STUDIES **EDUCATION** Columbia Univ, BA, 56, MA, 58, PhD(English), 64. **CAREER** Instr English, Univ WY, 58-59; preceptor, Columbia Col, 62-64; PROF ENGLISH, NY UNIV, 64-, Danforth assoc, 68-71; Nat Endowment for Humanities Bicentennial grant, 72-74; Am Coun Learned Soc grant-in-aid, 86; Am Philos Soc grant, 86. **HONORS AND AWARDS** Ambassador of Honor Book Awd, 84; Bancroft Prize in Am Hist, 85; Pulitzer Prize for Biography, 85; John Simon Guggenheim Memorial Found fel, 89-90; Edgar Awd, The Mystery Writers of America, 92; Christopher Literary Awd, Soc of Am Magicians, 97. **MEMBERSHIPS** Fel, Am Antiqn Soc; The Authors' Guild; fel, Soc Am Hist; The Century Asn; Soc Am Magicians. **RESEARCH** American culture. **SELECTED PUBLICATIONS** Ed, Colonial American Poetry, Hafner, 68; auth, Timothy Dwight, Twayne, 69; ed, Literature in America I: The Founding of a Nation, Free Press, 71; Selected Letters of Cotton Mather, La State Univ, 71; auth, A Cultural History of the American Revolution, Crowell, 76; A Cultural History of the American Revolution, Thomas Y. Crowell, 76; co-ed, Adventures in American Literature, Harcourt Brace Jovanovich, 80, rev eds, 85, 89; auth, The Life and Times of Cotton Mather, Harper & Row, 84; Edgar A. Poe. Mournful and Never-ending Remembrance, HarperCollins, 91; ed, New Essays on Poe's Major Tales, Cambridge Univ Press,93, with intro; HOUDINI!!! The Career of Ehrich Weiss, HarperCollins, 96. **CONTACT ADDRESS** Dept of English, New York Univ, 19 University Pl, New York, NY 10003-4556. **EMAIL** ks2@is2.nyu.edu

SIMMONS, DIANE

DISCIPLINE ENGLISH **EDUCATION** Univ Ore, BA, 70; CUNY, MA; PhD. **CAREER** Asst prof, Boro Manhattan Comm Col. **HONORS AND AWARDS** Melvin Dixon Awd, Bst Diss; HL Davis Awd; Dejur Awd; Wolfe Awd; CUNY Teach Fel; Idaho Press Club Awd; Listed in Dir Am Poets and Writers. **MEMBERSHIPS** NMLA; ASA; ACS. **RESEARCH** Literature of Empire; postcolonial literature. **SELECTED PUBLICATIONS** Auth, Dreams Like Thunder, Story Line Press (Brownsville, OR), 92, ppbk, 95; auth, Jamaica Kincaid, Twayne/Macmillan (NY), 94, CD ROM, 95; auth, Maxine Hong Kingston, Twayne/Macmillan (NY), 99; auth, Coming of Age in the Snare of History: Jamaica Kincaid's The Autobiography of My Mother," in The Girl: Constructions of the Girl in Contemporary Fiction by Women, ed. Ruth O Saxton (NY: St Martin's Press, 99), 107-118; "Loving Too Much: Jamaica Kincaid and the Dilemma of Constructing a Postcolonial Identity," in Postcolonialism and Autobiography, eds. Alfred Hornung, Ernstpeter Ruhe (Amsterdam: Rodopi, 99); auth, "Pig in a Poke: An Interview with Maxine Hong Kingston," in A Pool of Readings (Boston: Bedford/St Martin's, 00); auth, "Fatima Shaik: An Interview," Xavier Rev 18 (98): 13-27; auth, "An Interview with Maxine Hong Kingston," Crab Orch Rev (98): 96-118; auth, "In Dialogue with the Canon: John Milton, Charlotte Bront, and Jamaica Kincaid," MELUS (98); auth, "Fareast Logistics," Green Mountains Rev 7 (94): 48-60. **CONTACT ADDRESS** Dept English, Borough of Manhattan Comm Col, CUNY, 199 Chambers St, New York, NY 10007-1044. **EMAIL** dianesimmons@erols.com

SIMMONS, DONALD B.

DISCIPLINE PUBLIC ADDRESS; COMMUNICATION. **EDUCATION** Ohio Univ, PhD, 81. **CAREER** Prof Commun Asbury Col, 81-. **HONORS AND AWARDS** Mem Advisory Coun Documentary Channel, 98. **MEMBERSHIPS** Nat Commun Asn. **RESEARCH** Public speaking; speech criticism. **SELECTED PUBLICATIONS** Auth, The Golden Rule Philosophy of Samuel M. Jones, Proceedings of the Ky Commun Asn, 9/98. **CONTACT ADDRESS** Communication Arts Dept, Asbury Col, 1 Macklem Dr., Wilmore, KY 40390. **EMAIL** don.simmons@asbury.edu

SIMMONS, JOSEPH LARRY

PERSONAL Born 12/09/1935, Tylertown, MS, d, 3 children **DISCIPLINE** ENGLISH **EDUCATION** Fla State Univ, BMus, 56; NYork Univ, BA, 62; Univ Va, PhD(English), 67. **CAREER** Instr English, NTex State Univ, 62-64; from asst prof to assoc prof, 67-74, Grant Huntington, 69; chmn dept, 77-80, PROF ENGLISH, TULANE UNIV, 74-, Nat Endowment for Humanities Younger Humanists fel, 73-74; Am Coun Learned Soc grant-in-aid, 76-77; Grant Folger, 70, 72. **MEMBERSHIPS** MLA; Shakespeare Asn Am. **RESEARCH** Shakespearean and Renaissance drama; 17th century poetry. **SELECTED PUBLICATIONS** Auth, Coming Out In Shakespeare The 'Two Gentlemen Of Verona'/, Elh-English Lit Hist, Vol 0060, 1993; Masculine Negotiations In Shakespeare History-Plays - Hal, Hotspur, And The-Foolish-Mortimer/, Shakespeare Quart, Vol 0044, 1993. **CONTACT ADDRESS** Dept of English, Tulane Univ, 6823 St Charles Ave, New Orleans, LA 70118-5698. **EMAIL** jlsimm@tulane.edu

SIMON, JAMES

PERSONAL Born 11/27/1952, Clifton, NJ, m, 1977, 1 child **DISCIPLINE** ENGLISH **EDUCATION** Rutgers Univ, BA, 74; Ariz State Univ, MA, 92; PhD, 93. **CAREER** Adj Prof, Rutgers Univ, 77-79; Asst Prof, Univ Pacific, 94-97; Asst Prof, Fairfield Univ, 97-. **HONORS AND AWARDS** Fel, Inst for Journalism Excellence, 00; Grant, Fairfield Univ, 00; Scholar in Res, Univ TN, 94. **MEMBERSHIPS** Soc of Environmental Journalists; Asn for Educ in Journalism and Mass Comm; Col Media Advisers; Am Asn of Univ Prof, 98. **RESEARCH** News reporting, writing and editing; Environmental journalism; Political communication/public opinion; Political socialization, especially role of news media. **SELECTED PUBLICATIONS** Co-auth, "Revisiting media choice and election turnout," Southwestern Mass Comm Journal, (93): 106-115; co-auth, "Boosting turnout: The Kids Voting program," Journal of Social Studies Res, (94): 3-7; co-auth, "Telling the truth: Respondent accuracy in mass media polling," Southwestern Mass Comm Journal, (96): 3-12; auth, "Media use and voter turnout in a presidential election," Newspaper Res Journal, (97): 25-34; co-auth, "Elitism revisited: Efforts to increase diversity on college forensics teams," Nat Forensics Journal, (96): 1-22; co-auth, "Nurturing democracy, citizenship and civic virt6ue: The Kids Voting program revisited," Journal of Soc Studies Res, (98): 19-27; co-auth, "Political socialization in the classroom revisited: the Kids voting program," The Soc Sci Journal, (98): 29-42. **CONTACT ADDRESS** Dept Eng, Fairfield Univ, 1073 N Benson Rd, Fairfield, CT 06430-5171.

SIMON, LINDA

PERSONAL Born 12/12/1946, New York, NY, m, 1992, 1 child **DISCIPLINE** ENGLISH **EDUCATION** Brandeis Univ, PhD, 83. **CAREER** Instr, Emory Univ, 82-83; lectr, Harvard Univ, 83-97; assoc prof, Skidmore Col, 97-. **MEMBERSHIPS** MLA; Nat Coun of Teachers of English; Assoc for the Study of Lit and the Environ. **RESEARCH** Late 19th Century American Literature and Culture. **SELECTED PUBLICATIONS** Auth, The Biography of Alice B. Toklas, Doubleday, 77; auth, Thornton Wilder: His World, Doubleday, 79; auth, Of Virtue Rare: Margaret Beaufort, Matriarch of the House of Tudor, Houghton Mifflin, 82; auth, Genuine Reality: A Life of William James, Harcourt Brace, 98. **CONTACT ADDRESS** Dept English, Skidmore Col, 815 N Broadway, Saratoga Springs, NY 12866-1631. **EMAIL** lsimon@skidmore.edu

SIMONSON, HAROLD PETER

PERSONAL Born 12/27/1926, Tacoma, WA, m, 1951, 3 children **DISCIPLINE** ENGLISH & AMERICAN LITERATURE **EDUCATION** Univ Puget Sound, BA, 50, BEd, 51; Northwestern Univ, MA, 51, PhD, 58; Univ St Andrews, BPhil, 72. **CAREER** Instr English, Thessalonika Agr & Indust Inst, Greece, 53-54; from instr to prof Am lit, Univ Puget Sound, 55-68; PROF AM LIT, UNIV WASH, 68-, Fulbright grant, 53. **MEMBERSHIPS** MLA Am Studies Asn; Melville Soc Am. **RESEARCH** American Middle West realism; Frederick Jackson Turner's frontier thesis; literature and theology. **SELECTED PUBLICATIONS** Coauth, Salinger: Clamor and Criticism, Heath, 63; Writing Essays, Harper, 66; Francis Grierson, Twayne, 66; American Perspectives, McGraw, 68; auth, The Closed Frontier, 70 & Strategies in Criticism, 71, Holt; co-ed, Dimensions of Man, Harper, 73; auth, Rolvaag and Kierkegaard, Scand Studies, winter 77; The tempered romanticism of John Muir, Western Am Lit, 12/78. **CONTACT ADDRESS** Dept of English, Univ of Washington, Seattle, WA 98195.

SIMPSON, HASSELL ALGERNON

PERSONAL Born 05/08/1930, Barksdale, SC, m, 1953, 3 children **DISCIPLINE** ENGLISH & AMERICAN LITERATURE **EDUCATION** Clemson Univ, BS, 52; Fla State Univ, MA, 57, PhD(English), 62. **CAREER** Instr English, Fla State Univ, 58-59; instr, Auburn Univ, 59-62; assoc prof, 62-65, chm dept, 68-76, chm div humanities, 70-73, prof English, 65-95, PROF EMER, 95- , HAMPDEN-SYDNEY COL. **RESEARCH** Modern fiction; American literature; Shakespeare. **SELECTED PUBLICATIONS** Auth, Rumer Godden, Twayne, 73. **CONTACT ADDRESS** Dept of English, Hampden-Sydney Col, Hampden-Sydney, VA 23943. **EMAIL** hsimpson@hsc.edu

SIMPSON, MEGAN B.

DISCIPLINE ENGLISH **EDUCATION** Univ Calif at Santa Cruz, BA, 83; San Francisco State Univ, MA, 87; Univ NMex, PhD, 95. **CAREER** Lectr, San Francisco State Univ, 87-90; grad asst & adj, Univ NMex, 91-97; asst prof, Univ Tex of the Permian Basin, 97-00; asst prof, Pa State Univ, 00-. **RESEARCH** Poetry, Contemporary American Literature, Women & Minority Authors, Gender, Experimental Writing. **SELECTED PUBLICATIONS** Auth, Poetic Epistemologies: Gender and Knowing in Women's Language-Oriented Writing, State Univ NY Press, 00. **CONTACT ADDRESS** Dept Humanities & Fine Arts, Univ of Texas of the Permian Basin, 4901 E University Blvd, Odessa, TX 79762-8122.

SIMPSON, MICHAEL

DISCIPLINE CLASSICAL STUDIES **EDUCATION** Yale Univ, PhD, 64. **CAREER** Prof. **SELECTED PUBLICATIONS** Auth, Gods and Heroes of the Greeks: The Library of Apollodorus, Univ Mass, 95; Manners as Morals: Hospitality in the Odyssey, Art Inst, 92; Artistry in Mood: Iliad 3.204-224, Class Jour, 88; Cosmologies and Myths, Charles Scribner's Sons, 88. **CONTACT ADDRESS** Dept of Classics, Univ of Texas, Dallas, Richardson, TX 75083-0688. **EMAIL** msimpson@utdallas.edu

SIMPSON, PETER P.

PERSONAL Born, England **DISCIPLINE** CLASSICS, PHILOSOPHY **EDUCATION** Victoria Univ Manchester, UK, PhD **CAREER** Asst prof, Univ Col Dublin, Ireland, 82-84; asst prof, Catholic Univ Am, DC, 84-88; Full prof, City Univ NY, 88- . **HONORS AND AWARDS** Earhart found fel, 95; Jr fel, Ctr Hellenic stud, 92. **MEMBERSHIPS** APA; ACPA; APSA; SAGP; APPA. **RESEARCH** Ancient and medieval philosophy; moral and political philosophy. **SELECTED PUBLICATIONS** Auth, The Politics of Aristotle, U of North Carolina P, 97; A Philosophical Commentary on the Politics of Aristotle, U of North Carolina P, 98. **CONTACT ADDRESS** Dept of Philosophy, Col of Staten Island, CUNY, 2800 Victory Blvd, 2N, Staten Island, NY 10314. **EMAIL** simpson@postbox.csi.cuny.edu

SIMS, JAMES HYLBERT

PERSONAL Born 10/29/1924, Orlando, FL, m, 1944, 5 children **DISCIPLINE** ENGLISH LITERATURE **EDUCATION** Univ Fla, BA, 49, MA, 50, PhD, 59 **CAREER** Asst, 49-50, Univ Fla; instr, 50-51, Tenn Temple Col; Tri-St Baptist Col, 51-54, & Univ Fla, 55-59; prof, chmn dept, 59-61, Tift Col; prof, chmn dept, 61-66, Austin Peay St Univ; prof, 66-76, Univ Okla; prof, dean, col of lib arts, 76-82, Univ S Miss; vice pres, Acad Affairs, 82-89; dist prof, 89-95; consult, choice, 64-; fel, 65 & 66, Southeastern Inst Medieval & Renaissance Stud; assoc ed, 68-, 17th Century News; Huntington Libr fel, 73; Natl Endowment for Humanities fel, 78-79, Huntington Libr & Art Gallery; dir, 79-81, pres, 88-90, Conf Christianity & Lit. **MEMBERSHIPS** S Cent Renaissance Conf; Milton Soc Am; MLA; Southeastern Renaissance Conf; Conf Christianity & Lit. **RESEARCH** Biblical lit; Renaissance lit, esp Milton. **SELECTED PUBLICATIONS** Auth, The Bible in Milton's Epics, Univ Fla, 62; auth, Dramatic Use of Biblical Allusions in Marlowe and Shakespeare, Univ Fla, 66; auth, Paradise Lost: Aria Document of Christian Poem? Etudes Anglaises, 67; auth, Christened Classicism in Paradise Lost and the Lusiads, Comp Lit, 72; auth, The Fortunate Fall of Sir Gawayne in Sir Gawayne and the Grene Knight, Orbis Literarum, 75; auth, The Narrator's Mortal Voice in Camoes and Milton, Rev Lit Comp 77; auth, Milton and the Bible as Literature and Literature as a Bible, Milton Tercentenary Essays, Univ Wisc, 78; contrib, Milton Encycl Bucknell, 78; auth, The Major Literary Prophecy of the Old Testament, Dalhousie Rev, 82; auth, Milton and Scriptural Tradition, Univ Mo,. 84; auth, Comparative Literary Study of Daniel and Revelation, Mellen 95; auth, Essays in Milton Studies, 95; Comparative Literature, 97. **CONTACT ADDRESS** Dept of English, Univ of So Mississippi, PO Box 5037, Hattiesburg, MS 39401. **EMAIL** j.sims@usm.edu

SINCLAIR, GAIL
PERSONAL Born 08/27/1956, Lancaster, WI, m, 1977, 2 children **DISCIPLINE** ENGLISH **EDUCATION** Univ Mo, BA, 77; MA, 83; Univ S Fla, PhD, 97. **CAREER** Adj prof, Univ Cen Fla, 98-99; vis asst prof, Univ Cen Fla, 01; vis asst prof, Rollins Col, 01-. **HONORS AND AWARDS** Fac Intl Travel Grant; Alice Hearne Awd, Outstanding Doctoral Candidate, 98; Who's Who Am Teacher, 96, 97; English Speak Union Studies Grant, 97. **MEMBERSHIPS** MLA; SSSL; SAMLA; F. Scott Fitz Ger Soc; Ernest Hemingway Soc. **RESEARCH** Twentieth-century literature; American literature; women's literature. **SELECTED PUBLICATIONS** Auth, "Revisiting the Code: Female Foundations and 'The Undiscovered Country,' in For Whom the Bell Tolls," in Hemingway and Women: Female Critics and the Female Critics, Univ Ala Pr, (forthcoming); auth, "The Great Hollow Phrase?: Fitzgerald and the Play of Language in 'The Great Gatsby," in Approaches to Teaching Fitzgerald's 'The Great Gatsby,' MLA Series (forthcoming). **CONTACT ADDRESS** 320 Seneca Tr, Maitland, FL 32751-4951.

SINEATH, TIMOTHY W.
PERSONAL Born 05/21/1940, Jacksonville, FL, m, 1962, 2 children **DISCIPLINE** LIBRARY AND INFORMATION SCIENCE **EDUCATION** Florida State Univ, BS, 62, MS, 63; Univ Illinois, PhD, 70. **CAREER** Dean and Prof, School of Library and Infor Sci, Univ of Kentucky. **HONORS AND AWARDS** NEA federal fel, Lib and Infor Sci, Univ Ill; service award, Asn for Lib and Infor Sci Educ. **MEMBERSHIPS** ASIS; Asn for Lib and Infor Sci Educ; ALA. **RESEARCH** Management of nonprofits; organizational development; planning. **SELECTED PUBLICATIONS** Auth, Library Personnel and Training, Encyclopedia Americana, Grolier, 93; ed, Library and Information Science Education Statistical Report 1993, ALISE, 93; auth, Faculty, in, Library and Information Science Education Statistical Report 1998, ALISE, 98; auth, Managing the Information Organization: Creating and Maintaining a Learning Organization, ABLEX, 99. **CONTACT ADDRESS** School of Library and Information Science, Univ of Kentucky, 502 M.I. King South, Lexington, KY 40506-0039. **EMAIL** tsineath@pop.uky.edu

SINGH, AMRITJIT
PERSONAL Born 10/20/1946, Rawalpindi, British India, m, 1968, 2 children **DISCIPLINE** ENGLISH **EDUCATION** Panjab Univ, BA, 63; Kurukshetra Univ, MA, 65; New York Univ, AM, 70; PhD, 73. **CAREER** Lectr, Univ Delhi, 65-68; lectr, asst prof, Lehman Col, CUNY, 71-72, 73-74; instr, NYork Univ, 71-72; res assoc, ASRC, vis lectr, Osmania Univ, 77-78; vis prof, Univ Peradeniya, 81; prof, dept ch, Univ Rajasthan, 81-82; vis lectr, Wesleyan Univ, 84-85; adj prof, NYork Univ, 85-86; assoc prof, Hofstra Univ, 84-86; assoc prof, RI Col, 86-89; dir, AAAS, 90-91; dist prof, 91-92; dist lectr, Col Holy Cross, 93; vis prof, Univ Cal, 94; prof, RI Col, 89-. **HONORS AND AWARDS** Fulbright-Smith Mundt Awd; ACLS Fel; NEH Fel; Ford Found Fel; Rockefeller Found Awd; Killam Res Fel; Can Stud Fac Awd. **RESEARCH** African-American studies; post Colonial literature; American literature; 19th and 20th Centuries. **SELECTED PUBLICATIONS** Co-ed, New Perspectives in Indian Literature in English: Essays in Honor of MK Naik, Sterling (New Delhi), 95; co-ed, Conversations With Ishmael Reed, Univ Press MS (Jackson), 95; auth, " African Americans and New Immigrants," in Between the Lines: South Asians and Postcolonialty, eds. Deepika Bahri, Mary Vasudeva (Phil: Temple Univ Press, 96), reprint, in MultiAmerica, ed. Ishmael Reed (NY: Viking Press, 97); auth, "Harlem Renaissance," in Oxford Companion to American History, ed. Paul Boyer NY: Oxford Univ Press, 00); co-transl of "Gurcharan Rampuri: A Portrait," and "Massacre," "Phoenix," "Faith," "Spring," "Song of the Stream," by Gurcharan Rampuri, Toronto Rev Contemp Writing Abroad 18 (99): 37-45; co-ed, Conversations with Ralph Ellison, Univ Press MS (Jackson), 95; co-ed, Memory and Cultural Politics: New Approaches to American Ethnic Literatures, North eastern Univ Press (Boston), 96; co-ed, Postcolonial Theory and the United States: Race, Ethnicity and Literature, Univ Press MS (Jackson), 00. **CONTACT ADDRESS** Dept English, Rhode Island Col, 600 Mount Pleasant Ave, Providence, RI 02908-1924. **EMAIL** asingh@ric.edu

SINGLEY, CAROL J.
PERSONAL Born Philadelphia, PA, m, 1972, 2 children **DISCIPLINE** ENGLISH **EDUCATION** Penn State Univ, BA, 72, MA, 75; Brown Univ, PhD, 86. **CAREER** ASSOC PROF, ENG, RUTGERS UNIV **HONORS AND AWARDS** Provost's Teaching Excellence, 96. **MEMBERSHIPS** MLA; Northeast MLA; Soc for Study of Narrative Lit; Am Studies Assoc; Assoc for Research in Mothering. **RESEARCH** American Lit and Culturel; Feminist Theory. **SELECTED PUBLICATIONS** Co-ed, Anxious Power: Reading, Writing, and Ambivalence in Narrative by Women, Albany: State Univ of New York Press, 93; auth, Edith Wharton: Matters of Mind and Spirit, NY: Cambridge Univ Press, 95; ed, The Calvinist Roots of the Modern Era: Essays on Fiction, Drama and Poetry, Hanover: Univ Press of New England, 97; ed, The Age of Innocence, Houghton Mifflin, forthcoming; ed, An Historical Guide to Edith Wharton, Oxford Univ Press, forthcoming. **CONTACT ADDRESS** Dept of Eng, Rutgers, The State Univ of New Jersey, Newark, Camden, NJ 08102. **EMAIL** singley@crab.rutgers.edu

SINOS, REBECCA H.
PERSONAL Born 12/13/1954, Baltimore, MD, m, 1991 **DISCIPLINE** CLASSICS **EDUCATION** Col William and Mary, AB, 76; Johns Hopkins Univ, MA; PhD, 80. **CAREER** Asst Prof to Prof, Amherst Col, 80-. **HONORS AND AWARDS** Fel, Am Coun of Learned Soc, 82; Fel, NEH, 86; Phi Beta Kappa. **MEMBERSHIPS** Am Philol Asn; Archaeol Inst of Am; Am Sch of Class Studies at Athens. **RESEARCH** Ancient Greek literature; Archaeology; Religion. **SELECTED PUBLICATIONS** Co-auth, The Wedding in Ancient Athens, Univ Wis Press, 93. **CONTACT ADDRESS** Dept Class, Amherst Col, Amherst, MA 01002. **EMAIL** rhsinos@amherst.edu

SIPAHIGIL, TEOMAN
PERSONAL Born 02/13/1939, Istanbul, Turkey **DISCIPLINE** ENGLISH LITERATURE, RHETORIC **EDUCATION** Earlham Col, BA, 61; Miami Univ, MA, 63; Univ Calif, Los Angeles, PhD, 70. **CAREER** Asst prof, 70-75, assoc prof, Univ Id, 75-. **MEMBERSHIPS** NCTE **RESEARCH** Shakespeare. **CONTACT ADDRESS** Dept of English, Univ of Idaho, Moscow, ID 83843. **EMAIL** tsipahi@uidaho.edu

SIPORIN, STEVE
DISCIPLINE ENGLISH; HISTORY **EDUCATION** Stanford Univ, BA, 69; Univ Ore, MA, 74; Ind Univ, PhD, 82. **CAREER** Lectr, Ind Univ, 76; folklore consult to Iowa Arts Coun, 77-78; folk arts coordr, Ore Arts Comn, 80-81; folk arts coordr, Idaho Comn on the Arts, 82-86; from asst prof to assoc prof, Utah State Univ, 90-. **HONORS AND AWARDS** Conference Fel, Institute of the Am West, 83; Res Fel, Memorial Found for the Jewish Culture, 84-85; Res Fel, Hebrew Univ of Jerusalem, 85; Travel Fel, 85; Fac Res Fel, Utah State Univ, 88-89; Fund for the Translation of Jewish Lit Grant, 88; Fulbright Lectureship, 92-93; Honorable Mention, Giuseppe Pitre International Folklore Prize, 93; Humanist of the Year, Utah State Univ, 94; Res Fel, Memorial Found for the Jewish Culture, 99-00. **MEMBERSHIPS** Int Soc for Folk Narrative Res; Am Folklore Soc; Folklore Soc Utah; Int Conf Group on Portugal. **SELECTED PUBLICATIONS** Public Folklore: A Bibliographic Introduction, Public Folklore, Wash., D.C.: Smithsonian Inst. Press, 92; Folklife and Survival: The Italian- Americans of Carbon County, Utah, Old Ties, New Attachments: Italian-American Folklife in the West, Wash., D.C.: Libr. Of Congress, 92; American Folk Masters: The National Heritage Fellows, 92; The Sephardim: Field Report From Portugal, Jewish Folklore and Ethnology Review 15, 93; Memories of Jewish Life, New Horizons in Sephardic Studies, Albany: State Univ of NY Press, 93; From Kashrut to Cucina Ebraica: The Recasting of Italian Jewish Foodways, Jour of Am Folklore 107, 94; Halloween Pranks: Just a Little Inconvenience, Halloween and Other Festivals of Death and Life, Knoxville: Univ of Tenn. Press, 94; National Heritage Fellows, Am Folklore: An Encyclopedia, New York: Garland, 96; auth, " County Football Scholarships," Foaftale News: Newsletter of The International Society for Contemporary Legend Research 45 (99): 2-4; auth, "On Scapegoating Public Folklore," Journal of American Folklore, 00; auth, "Tall Tales and Sales," in Worldview and the American West: The Life of the Place Itself, (Utah State Univ Press, 00); auth, Introduction to Worldview and American West: The Life of Place Itself, Utah State Univ Pr, 00. **CONTACT ADDRESS** Dept of English, Utah State Univ, Logan, UT 84322-3200. **EMAIL** siporin@cc.usu.edu

SITKO, BARBARA
DISCIPLINE CONTEMPORARY RHETORICAL THEORY **EDUCATION** Carnegie Mellon, PhD. **CAREER** Assoc prof, Washington State Univ. **RESEARCH** Studies of audience adaptation, instructional uses of computers, culturally sensitive writing instruction. **CONTACT ADDRESS** Dept of English, Washington State Univ, 1 SE Stadium Way, PO Box 645020, Pullman, WA 99164-5020. **EMAIL** sitko@wsu.edu

SITTER, JOHN
DISCIPLINE ENGLISH LANGUAGE AND LITERATURE **EDUCATION** Harvard Univ, BA, 66; Univ Minn, PhD, 69. **CAREER** Fac, Univ Mass Amherst; fac, Univ Kent Canterbury; fac, Emory Univ, 80-; Charles Howard Candler Prof, present. **HONORS AND AWARDS** Nat Humanities Center Fel; Gottschalk Prize; NEH Seminar Dir. **RESEARCH** 18th-century literature; satire and poetry; literary criticism; Restoration literature; contemporary poetry. **SELECTED PUBLICATIONS** Auth, The Poetry of Pope's "Dunciad"; Literary Loneliness in Mid-Eighteenth-Century England; Arguments of Augustan Wit; Eighteenth-Century British Poets; articles on Restoration and 18th-century literature and on contemporary poetry. **CONTACT ADDRESS** English Dept, Emory Univ, Atlanta, GA 30322-1950. **EMAIL** engjs@emory.edu

SITTERSON, JOSEPH
DISCIPLINE ENGLISH LITERATURE **EDUCATION** Univ NC, BA, PhD. **CAREER** Eng Dept, Georgetown Univ **RESEARCH** British Romantic literature; literary theory; epic; biblical interpretation. **SELECTED PUBLICATIONS** Auth, pubs on Wordsworth, Coleridge, Keats, psychoanalytic and literary theory, Ariosto, and biblical interpretation. **CONTACT ADDRESS** English Dept, Georgetown Univ, 37th and O St, Washington, DC 20057.

SIVELL, JOHN
DISCIPLINE ENGLISH LITERATURE **EDUCATION** Univ Toronto, BA; Univ Cambridge, dipl; Univ Wales Inst Sci and Tech, Med; Univ East Anglia, Eng, PhD. **CAREER** Instr, 83; prof; dean. **RESEARCH** Celestin Freinet. **SELECTED PUBLICATIONS** Auth, classroom ESL Reading textbooks, From Near and Far, Full Blast Productions, 92; Jigsaw Activities for Reading and Writing, Full Blast Productions, 93; Canada from Eh to Zed: People, 95; pub(s), ELT Jour; The Mod Eng Tchr; TESL Can Jour; McGill Jour Edu; Eng Tchg Forum. **CONTACT ADDRESS** Humanities, Brock Univ, 500 Glenridge Ave, Saint Catharines, ON, Canada L2S 3A1. **EMAIL** jsivell@spartan.ac.BrockU.CA

SIVIER, EVELYN M.
PERSONAL Born 05/15/1916, Milwaukee, WI, w, 1959, 1 child **DISCIPLINE** THEATRE **EDUCATION** San Jose St Univ, BA, 51; Stanford Univ, MA, 52; Wayne St Univ, PhD, 61. **CAREER** Instr, Stanford Univ, 51-52; instr, Wayne State Univ 52-57; asst prof, Humboldt State Univ, 57-59; assoc prof, Wayne State Univ, 63-81, assoc prof emer, 81- . **HONORS AND AWARDS** AAUW Honors Awd; Woman Student of the Year; first PhD candidate chosen (speech), Wayne St Univ. **MEMBERSHIPS** Nat Speech Asn; Am Assoc Univ Women. **RESEARCH** Change and professionalism; teaching of speech and theater; concern over present day performance standards. **SELECTED PUBLICATIONS** Auth, English Poets, Teachers, and Festivals in a Golden Age of Poetry Speaking, 1920-1950,in Perfromance of Literature in Historical Perspectives, Univ Pr of Am, 83; auth, Penny Readings: Popular Elocution in Late Nineteenth Century England, in Performance of Literature in Historical Perspectives, Univ Pr of Am, 83; auth, Shaw and the Theatre, Calvin Acad of Lifelong Learning (Grand Rapids, MI), 99; auth, The Play's the Thing, Hamlet, Patience, Gilbert and Sullivan; Calvin Acad of Lifelong Learning (Grand Rapids, MI), 00. **CONTACT ADDRESS** 4185 Nature Trl Dr SE, Apt #11, Kentwood, MI 49512.

SIZEMORE, CHRISTINE WICK
PERSONAL Born 11/17/1945, Washington, DC, m, 1968, 2 children **DISCIPLINE** ENGLISH RENAISSANCE & 20TH CENTURY LITERATURE **EDUCATION** Carnegie Inst Technol, BA, 67; Univ PA, MA, 68, PhD(English), 72. **CAREER** Asst prof, GA State Univ, 72-78; asst prof, 78-84, assoc prof, 84-92, PROF ENGLISH, SPELMAN COL, 92-. **MEMBERSHIPS** Southeastern Renaissance Soc; MLA; SAtlantic Mod Lang Asn. **RESEARCH** Contemporary British and post-Colonial novel; urban literature. **SELECTED PUBLICATIONS** Auth, The Author of the Mystery of Rhetoric Unveiled, Papers of the Bibliog Soc Am, winter 75; Seventeenth Century Advice Books: The Female Viewpoint, SAtlantic Bull, 1/76; Anxiety in Kafka: A Function of Cognitive Dissonance, J Mod Lit, fall 77; The Small Cardboard Box: A Symbol of the City and Winnie Verlac in Conrad's Secret Agent, Mod Fiction Studies, spring 78; Structural Repetition in John Bunyan's Holy War, Tenn Studies Lit, 79; Cognitive Dissonance and the Anxiety Response to Kafka's The Castle, Comparatist, 80; Attitudes to Ward the Education and Roles of Women: Sixteenth-century Humanista and Seventeenth Century Advice Books, Univ Dayton Rev, spring 81; Ridgway's Militant Weekly and the Serial Version of Conrad's Secret Agent, Anal & Enumerative Bibilog, spring 82; Reading the City as Palimpseat: The Experiential Perception of the City in Doris Lessing's Four-Gaited City, Women Writers and the City, ed Susan Squier, Univ TN Press, 84; A Female Vision of the City: London in the Novels of Five British Women, Univ TN Press, 89; Masculine and Feminine Cities: Marge Piercy's Going Down Fast and Fly Away Home,

Frontiers: a Journal of Women Studies, 13.1, spring 92; The Outsider Within: Virginia Woolf and Doris Lessing as Urban Novelists, Woolf and Lessing: Breaking the Mold, eds Ruth Saxton and Jean Tobin, St Martin's Press, 94; The London Novels of Buchi Emecheta, Emerging Perspectives on Buchi Emecheta, ed Marie Umek, African World Press, 96; Virginia Woolf as Modernist Foremother in Maureen Duffey's A Nightingale in Bloomsberry Square, Unmanning Modernism: Gendered Rereadings, eds E. J. Harrison and Shirley Peterson, Univ TN Press, 97; Negotiating between Ideologies: the Search for Identity in Tsitsi Dangarembga's Nrevous Conditions and Margaret Atwood's Cat's Eye, Teaching African Literature, a Special Edition, eds, Tuzyline Allan and Florence Howe, Women's Studies Quart, 25, nos 3 & 4, fall/winter 97; Doris Lessing, Postcolonial African Writers: a Bio-Bibliographical Critical Sourcebook, eds Pushpa N. Parekh and Siga F. Jagne, Greenwood Press, 98. **CONTACT ADDRESS** Spelman Col, Box 273, Atlanta, GA 30314.

SKAGGS, MERRILL MAGUIRE

PERSONAL Born 10/01/1937, Florala, AL, d, 1960, 2 children **DISCIPLINE** AMERICAN LITERATURE **EDUCATION** Stetson Univ, BA, 58; Duke Univ, MA, 60, PhD, 65; Stetson Univ, PhD, 88. **CAREER** Tutor English, Duke Univ, 61-62; vis instr, Fairleigh Dickinson Univ, 62-63; lectr, Brooklyn Col, 65; assoc ed sch dept, Macmillan Co, 66-67; instr lit & lang, Columbia Teachers Col, 70-75; from Adj Assoc Prof to Assoc Prof Am Lit, 76-82, Dean, Grad Sch, 86-92, Baldwin Prof of the Humanities, Drew Univ, 92-; consult lit, Norton Anthology Am Lit, 81; grant consult, Am Coun Learned Soc, 82. **HONORS AND AWARDS** Ed Winfield Parks Awd, Soc Study Southern Lit, 73; Bks of the Year Awd, Am J Nursing, 75; Alumni Initiate, Phi Beta Kappa, 88. **MEMBERSHIPS** MLA; Soc Study Southern Lit. **RESEARCH** Nineteenth century Am lit; Southern lit; early Am lit, Willa Cather. **SELECTED PUBLICATIONS** Auth, The Folk of Southern Fiction, Univ Ga, 72; coauth, The Mother Person, Bobbs Merrill, 75; auth, After the World Broke in Two: The Later Novels of Willa Cather, Univ Press Va, 90; ed, Willa Cather's New York, FDU Press, 00. **CONTACT ADDRESS** Drew Univ, 36 Madison Ave, Madison, NJ 07940-1493. **EMAIL** mskaggs@drew.edu

SKARBARNICKI, ANNE

DISCIPLINE BRITISH LITERATURE **EDUCATION** Toronto, BA, 71; Yale, Mphil, 73, PhD, 75. **CAREER** Assoc prof, Royal Military Col of Canada. **HONORS AND AWARDS** Assoc ed, Carlyle Newsl. **RESEARCH** Anglo-saxon and medieval language and literature. **SELECTED PUBLICATIONS** Ed, Jane Welsh Carlyle; Carlyle Encyclopedia. **CONTACT ADDRESS** Dept of English, Royal Military Col, 315 Massey Bldg, PO Box 17000, Kingston, ON, Canada K7K 7B4. **EMAIL** skarbarnicki-a@rmc.ca

SKARDA, PATRICIA LYN

PERSONAL Born 03/31/1946, Clovis, NM **DISCIPLINE** BRITISH LITERATURE **EDUCATION** Sweet Briar Col, 68; Tex Tech Univ, BA, 69; Univ Tex, Austin, PhD, 73. **CAREER** Teaching asst, Univ Tex, Austin, 69-70, 72-73; asst prof, 73-88, Assoc Prof English, Smith Col, 88-; Dir, NMex Girls State, 73; govt suprv, Girls Nation, 73; secy fac, Smith Col, 76-78, Danforth assoc, 77-83; fel, Am Coun Educ, 78-79. **HONORS AND AWARDS** Phi Beta Kappa, 67; Sr fac teaching award, 86. **MEMBERSHIPS** MLA; NASSR **RESEARCH** Romantic and Victorian literature; Gerard Manley Hopkins; Gothic fiction. **SELECTED PUBLICATIONS** Auth, Smith writers, Smith Alumnae Quart, fall 75; Juvenilia of the family of Gerard Manley Hopkins, Hopkins Quart, summer 77; Expressions of form and formlessness, Smith Alumnae Quart, summer 77; The Evil Image: Two Centuries of Gothic Short Fiction & Poetry, New Am Libr, 81; Teaching Essays on Tintern Abbey, Christabel and Kubla Khan, in approaches to Teaching Wordsworth and Coleridge, 85 & 90; Vampirism and plaigarism: Byron's influence and Polidori's practice, Studies in Romanticism, summer 89; Samuel Rogers, in Dictionary of Literary Biography: Romantic Poets, 1st series, 89; Smith Voices: Selected Works by Smith College Women, 90, 99; Thomas Moore, in Dictionary of Literary Biography: Romantic Poets, 2nd series, 90; William Hazlitt, in Dictionary of Liteary Biography: Romantic Prose, 91; For Yearbooks of Dictionary of Literary Biography, Robert Ludlum, 83, Alfred Coppel, 84, Peter Straub, 85, Susan Alba Toth, 86; auth, Smith Voices; Selected Words by Smith College Alumnae, 99; auth, A Celebratrion of Ada Comstock Scholars at Smith College, 00. **CONTACT ADDRESS** Dept of English, Smith Col, 98 Green St, Northampton, MA 01063-0001. **EMAIL** pskarda@smith.edu

SKAU, MICHAEL WALTER

PERSONAL Born 01/06/1944, Chicago, IL **DISCIPLINE** LITERATURE **EDUCATION** Univ of Ill, Urbana-Champaign, BA, 65, MA, 67, PhD(English), 73. **CAREER** Asst prof to prof English, Univ Nebr, Omaha, 73-. **HONORS AND AWARDS** Jefferis Chair in English, 97-. **MEMBERSHIPS** MLA; AAUP. **RESEARCH** Modern and contemporary British and American literature. **SELECTED PUBLICATIONS** Auth, Flimnap, Lilliput's Acrobatic Treasurer, Am Notes & Queries, 70; coauth, Joyce's Araby, Explicator, 76; auth, Jack Kerouac--Visions of America, Periodical Art Nebr, 77; Toward Underivative Creation: Lawrence Ferlinghetti's Her, Critique, 78; Toward a Third Stream Theatre: Lawrence Ferlinghetti's Plays, Mod Drama, 79; American ethos: Richard Brautigan's Trout Fishing in America, Portland Rev, 81; The Central Verbal System: The prose of William S Burroughs, Style (in prep); coauth, A modern bestiary: Jerzy Kosinski's The Painted Bird, Polish Rev, 82; auth, The Poetas Poem: Ferlinghetti's Songs of Myself, Concerning Poetry, 87; Constantly Risking Absurdity: The Writings of Lawrence Ferlinghetti, Whitston, 89; To Dream, Perchance To Be: Gregory Corso and Imagination, Univ Daytona Rev, 89; Elegiac Feelings American: Gregory Corso and America, McNeese Rev, 89; auth, "A Clownina Grave:" Complexities and Tensions in the Works of Gregory Corso," Southern Illinois UP, 00. **CONTACT ADDRESS** Dept of English, Univ of Nebraska, Omaha, 6001 Dodge St, Omaha, NE 68182-0002. **EMAIL** michael_skau@unomaha.edu

SKELLINGS, EDMUND

DISCIPLINE POETRY **EDUCATION** Univ of Mass, BA, 57; Univ of Iowa, PhD, 62. **CAREER** Dir & prof, State Univ Sywtem of Fla, 68-98. **HONORS AND AWARDS** Honorary doctor of fine arts, Int Col of Fine Arts; Poet Laureate of Fla. **MEMBERSHIPS** Acad of Am Poets. **RESEARCH** Poetry and supercomputing animation. **SELECTED PUBLICATIONS** Auth, Collected Poems, 1958-1998, Univ Press of Fla; Selected Poems: Compact Disk, Univ Press of Fla. **CONTACT ADDRESS** 600 NE Second Pl., Dania, FL 33004. **EMAIL** poet1@laureate.cec.fau.edu

SKELNAR, ROBERT JOHN

PERSONAL Born 04/20/1963, Detroit, MI **DISCIPLINE** CLASSICS **EDUCATION** Univ Mich, BA, 85; Princeton Univ, MA, 88; Univ Mich, JD, 91, PhD, 96. **CAREER** Asst Inst, Princeton Univ, 87-88; tchg asst, 91-95; lect Class Studs, 96-97, Univ Mich; inst, Latin, The Emerson Sch, 96-97; Mellon postdoc fel, vis asst prof Classics, Swarthmore Col. **HONORS AND AWARDS** Phi Beta Kappa; Mellon Fellow Humanities; Mellon Diss Grant. **MEMBERSHIPS** Amer Philol Asn; Class Asn Middle West and South. **RESEARCH** Greek and Roman civilization, Greek Mythology. **SELECTED PUBLICATIONS** Auth, The Death of Priam: Aeneid 2.506-558, Hermes 118, 90, 67-75; Horace, Odes 1, 3, AC 60, 91, 266-269; Multiple Structural Divisions in Horace, Odes 1.38, pp 46, 91, 444-448; Rullus' Colonies: Cicero, De Lege Agraria 1.16-17 and 2. 73-75, Eos 80, 92, 81-82; Recusatio and Praeteritio in American Judicial Rhetoric, Acta Univ Carolinae, 38, 92, 97-114; Charles Baudelaire: Meditation, The Formalist, 3,1,92; SEG XXXII 1243, 13-15, RhM 136, 93, 93-94; Rainer Maria Rilke: Autumn Day, The Formalist, 4,1, 93; Papinian on the Interdict unde vi, RiDA 41, 94, 379-389; Catullus 36: Beyond Literary Polemics, RBPh 74, 96, 57-59; The Centrality of the Civic Image in Droste's Mondesaufgang, Droste-Jahrbuch 3, 97, 127-134. **CONTACT ADDRESS** Dept of Classics, Swarthmore Col, Swarthmore, PA 19081. **EMAIL** rsklenal@swarthmore.edu

SKERPAN-WHEELER, ELIZABETH P.

PERSONAL Born 10/11/1955, Ravenna, OH, m, 1997 **DISCIPLINE** ENGLISH LITERATURE **EDUCATION** Miami Univ, AB, 76; Univ Wisc-Madison, MA, 77, PhD, 83. **CAREER** Asst Prof, 83-89, Assoc Prof, 89-97, Prof of English, 97-, SW Tex State Univ. **HONORS AND AWARDS** Short-term Res Fellow, William Clark Memorial Library, 94; Phi Beta Kappa; Phi Kappa Phi. **MEMBERSHIPS** Modern Lang Asn; Renaissance Soc of Am; Milton Soc of Am; Tex Fac Asn. **RESEARCH** Milton; 17th century poetry & prose; history of rhetoric. **SELECTED PUBLICATIONS** Auth, The Rhetoric of Politics in the English Revolution, 1642-1660, Univ Mo Press, 92; auth, Sir John Denham, Dictionary of Leterary Biography, vol 126 2nd series, Bruccoli Clark Layman, 97-108, 93; auth, The Eikon Basilike, Dictionary of Literary Biography, vol 151, 143-48, 95; auth, Eikon Basilike and the Rhetoric of Self-Representation, The Royal Image: Representations of Charles I, Cambridge Univ Press, 99; auth, Sir Francis Bacon, Dict of Lit Biog, vol 236, 12-39, 01; auth, Life Writings, 2 vols, The Early Modern Englishwoman: A Facsimile Library of Essential Works, 1500-1750, series II, Scolar/Ashgate, in press. **CONTACT ADDRESS** Dept of English, Southwest Texas State Univ, 601 Univ Dr, San Marcos, TX 78666. **EMAIL** es10@swt.edu

SKILLMAN, JUDITH

PERSONAL Born 05/04/1954, Syracuse, NY, m, 1976, 3 children **DISCIPLINE** ENGLISH LITERATURE, COMPARATIVE LITERATURE **EDUCATION** Univ Md, BA, 76, MA, 83. **CAREER** TA, Univ of Md, 76-77; instr, Bellevue Community Col, 87-90; tutor, Educ Tutoring and Consulting Inc, 89-92; adj fac mem, City Univ, 90-. **HONORS AND AWARDS** William Stafford Awd, 83; King County Arts Comm Publ Prize, 87; Wash State Arts Comm Writer's Fel, 91; King County Pub Arts Project, 94-97; Centrum Found, 96, 98; Eric Mathieu King Awd, 98. **MEMBERSHIPS** ALTA, MLA, AWP. **SELECTED PUBLICATIONS** Auth, Worship of the Visible Spectrum, Breitenbush Books, 88; auth, Beethoven and the Birds, Blue Begonia Pr, 96; auth, Storm, Blue Begonia Pr, 98; auth, Red Town, Silverfish Rev Pr, 01; Sweetbrier, Blue Begonia Pr, 01. **CONTACT ADDRESS** 14206 SE 45th Pl, Bellevue, WA 98006. **EMAIL** jskillman@halcyon.com

SKINNER, EWART C.

PERSONAL Born 01/02/1949, s **DISCIPLINE** COMMUNICATIONS **EDUCATION** Univ of Hartford, Hartford, CT, 1967-69; Tarkio Coll, Tarkio, MO, BA, 1971; American Univ in Cairo, Cairo, Egypt, MA, 1974; MI State Univ, East Lansing, MI, PhD, 1984. **CAREER** Self-employed media consultant, Trinidad and Tobago, 75-79; UNESCO, Trinidad and Tobago, West Indies, 87; MI State Univ, East Lansing, MI, instructor, 83-84; Purdue Univ, West Lafayette, IN, asst prof, 84-. **HONORS AND AWARDS** Specialist in Caribbean Mass Media Systems and Intl Media; Poet. **MEMBERSHIPS** Intl Assn for Mass Communications Research; Intl Communication Assn; Intl Peace Research Assn; Semiotics Society of America; Assn for Education in Journalism ans Mass Communication; Caribbean Studies Assn. **CONTACT ADDRESS** Department of Communication, Purdue Univ, West Lafayette, 1366 Heavilon Hall 304, West Lafayette, IN 47907-1366.

SKINNER, KNUTE R.

PERSONAL Born 04/25/1929, St. Louis, MO, m, 1978, 3 children **DISCIPLINE** ENGLISH **EDUCATION** Univ NColo, BA, 51; Middlebury Col, MA, 54; Univ of Iowa, PhD, 58. **CAREER** Teacher English, Boise Sr High Sch, 51-54; instr, State Univ Iowa, 54-55, 56-57, 60-61; asst prof, Okla Col Women, 61-62; asst prof, 62-63, lectr, 64-71, assoc prof, 71-73, Prof English, Western Wash Univ, 73-97, Prof Emer, 97-; Fel creative writing, Nat Endowment for Arts, 75; co-ed & publ, Bellingham Rev, 77-95. **HONORS AND AWARDS** Include a Nat Endowment for the Arts fel, a Governonis invitational writers' day certificate of recognition, Washington State, and residencies awarded by the Huntington Hartford Found, The Millay Colony for the Arts, and Fundacion Valparaiso. **MEMBERSHIPS** Wash Poets Asn; Am Comt Irish Studies. **RESEARCH** Poetry; creative writing. **SELECTED PUBLICATIONS** Auth, A Close Sky Over Killaspuglonane, Dolmen, 68, 2nd ed, Burton Int, 75; In Dinosaur Country, Pierian, 69; The Sorcerers: A Laotian Tale, Goliards, 72; Hearing of the Hard Times, Northwoods Press, 81; The Flame Room, Folley Press, 83; Selected Poems, Aquila Press, 85; Learning to Spell Zucchini, Salmon Publ, 88; the Bears and Other Poems, Salmon Publ, 91; What Trudy Knows and Other Poems, Salmon Publ, 94; The Cold Irish Earth: Selected Poems of Ireland, 1965-95, Salmon Publ, 96; An Afternoon Quiet and Other Poems, Pudding House, 98 **CONTACT ADDRESS** M/S 9055, Bellingham, WA 98225-5996. **EMAIL** kielskin@eircom.net

SKINNER, ROBERT EARLE

PERSONAL Born 06/25/1948, Alexandria, VA, d, 3 children **DISCIPLINE** AMERICAN LITERATURE **EDUCATION** Old Dominion Univ, Norfolk, Va, BA, 70; Ind Univ, Bloomington, IN, MA, 77; Univ New Orleans, MFA cand, 91-93. **CAREER** Asst prof, La St Univ, 79-84; sr consult, Robert L. Siegel & Assoc, 85-87; librn, Xavier Univ La, New Orleans, 87-. **HONORS AND AWARDS** Who's Who, 93-94, 99,00; Anthony Boucher Awd nominee, 98. **MEMBERSHIPS** Mystery Writer of Amer; Amer Libr Assoc. **RESEARCH** Mystery & suspense lit; career of Chester Himes; western novelists. **SELECTED PUBLICATIONS** Auth, Chester Himes: An Annotated Primary and Secondary Bibliography, Greenwood Press, 92; coed, Plan B Univ Press Ms, 93; Conversations with Chester Himes, Univ Press Ms, 95; auth, The New Hard-Boiled Dicks: Heroes for a New Urban Mythology, Borgo Press, 95; auth, Two Guns from Harlem: The Detective Fiction of Chester Himes, Bowling Green Popular Press, 89; auth, " Elmore Leonard" in Firsts, 96; auth, " Stretching Limits of Form/Douglas C. Jones" Firsts, 95; "A. B Guthrie, Jr" Firsts 96; auth," Paperback Original/Donald Hamilton" Firsts, 97; coauth; Elmore Leonard, in Mystery and Suspense Writers: The Literature of Crime, Detections, and Espionage, Charles Scriber's Sons, 98; auth, " Donald Hamilton" Gorman, et al, ed The Big Book of Noir", Carroll & Graf, 98; auth, 'Streets of Fear" Fine, ed, Los Angeles Fiction," Uof New Mexico, 95; auth, Skin Deep, Blood Red, Kensington ,97; auth, Cat-Eyed Trouble, Kensington, 98; auth, Daddy's Gone a-Hunting, Poisoned Pen, 99; auth, Blood to Drink, Poisoned Pen, 00. **CONTACT ADDRESS** Xavier Univ, Louisiana, 1 Drexel Drive, New Orleans, LA 70125-1098. **EMAIL** rskinnerj@xula.edu

SKLOOT, ROBERT

PERSONAL Born 07/27/1942, Brooklyn, NY **DISCIPLINE** THEATRE, DRAMA, JEWISH STUDIES **EDUCATION** Union Col, NYork, AB, 63; Cornell Univ, MA, 65; Univ Minn, Minneapolis, PhD, 68. **CAREER** Prof theatre & drama & Jewish studies, Univ of Wis-Madison, 68-, Assoc Vice-Chancellor Acad Affairs, 96-, Dir Ctr Jewish Studies, 99-; Fulbright prof theatre, Hebrew Univ, Jerusalem, Israel, 80-81, Univ Austria, Vienna, 88, Cath Univ Valparaiso, Chile, 96. **RESEARCH** Holocaust drama; British, classical and American drama; directing. **SELECTED PUBLICATIONS** Ed, The Theatre of the Holocaust: Four Plays, Univ Wis Press, 82, vol 2, 99; auth, The Darkness We Carry: The Drama of the Holocaust, Univ Wis Press, 88. **CONTACT ADDRESS** Dept of Theatre & Drama, Univ of Wisconsin, Madison, 821 University Ave, Madison, WI 53706-1497. **EMAIL** rskloot@facstaff.wisc.edu

SKURA, MEREDITH ANNE
PERSONAL Born 05/11/1944, Brooklyn, NY, m, 1981, 2 children **DISCIPLINE** RENAISSANCE LITERATURE **EDUCATION** Swarthmore Col, BA, 65; Yale Univ, PhD(English), 71. **CAREER** Instr, Univ Bridgeport, 68-71, asst prof, 71-73; asst prof, Yale Univ, 73-78; asst prof, 78-80, ASSOC PROF ENGLISH, RICE UNIV, 80-, Fel, Am Coun Learned Soc, 81 & Guggenheim, 82. **HONORS AND AWARDS** NEH 89; MELLON, 97. **MEMBERSHIPS** MLA; Shakespeare Asn Am; Medieval & Renaissance Drama Soc. **RESEARCH** Autobiography; Renaissance drama; Renaissance literature. **SELECTED PUBLICATIONS** Auth, The Literary Use of the Psyhoanalytic Process, 81, auth, Shakespeare The Actor and The Purposes of Playing, 93. **CONTACT ADDRESS** English Dept, Rice Univ, 6100 S Main St, Houston, TX 77005-1892. **EMAIL** skura@rice.edu

SLABEY, ROBERT M.
PERSONAL Born 08/21/1931, Hamden, CT **DISCIPLINE** AMERICAN LITERATURE **EDUCATION** Fairfield Univ, BSS, 53; Univ Notre Dame, MA, 55, PhD(English), 61. **CAREER** Teaching fel, Univ Notre Dame, 54-57, instr English, 57-58; instr, Pa State Univ, 58-60; asst prof, Villanova Univ, 60-63; Andrew Mellon fel, Univ Pittsburgh, 63-64; asst prof, 64-67, assoc prof English, Univ Notre Dame, 67-96, prof emer, 96-; Fulbright prof, Univ Oslo, 68-69. **HONORS AND AWARDS** Skaggs Found, 92-93; Indiana Humanities Council, 93. **MEMBERSHIPS** Am Studies Asn; MLA. **RESEARCH** Modern American fiction; Southern literary tradition; Literature and films of the Vietnam war. **SELECTED PUBLICATIONS** Auth, Henry James and The Most Impressive Convention in All History, Am Lit, 58; Myth and Ritual in Light in August, Tex Studies Lit & Lang, 60; The Structure of Hemingway's In Our Time, Moderna Sprak, 66; The Swimming of America, Crit Essays on John Cheever, ed R.G. Collins, G.K. Hall, 83; The United States and Vietnam: From War to Peace, McFarland, 96. **CONTACT ADDRESS** Dept of English, Univ of Notre Dame, 356 O'Shaugnessy Hall, Notre Dame, IN 46556.

SLADE, CAROLE
PERSONAL Born, CA **DISCIPLINE** COMPARATIVE LITERATURE, ENGLISH **EDUCATION** Pomona Col, BA, 65; Univ Wis, MA, 66; New York Univ, PhD(comp lit), 73. **CAREER** Lectr English, Bronx Community Col, City Univ New York, 71-74, asst prof, 74-78; asst prof, Baylor Univ, 78-80; Asst Prof English & Comp Lit, Columbia Univ, 80- **MEMBERSHIPS** MLA; Northeast Mod Lang Asn; Am Comp Lit Asn; Dante Soc Am; NCTE. **SELECTED PUBLICATIONS** **CONTACT ADDRESS** Dept of English, Columbia Univ, New York, NY 10027.

SLAGLE, JUDITH BAILY
PERSONAL Born 11/20/1949, Kingsport, TN, m, 1969 **DISCIPLINE** CLASSICAL LITERATURE **EDUCATION** East Tenn State Univ, MA, 85; Univ Tenn, PhD, 91. **CAREER** Asst Prof, Middle Tenn State Univ, 93-97; Chr Humanities, Roane State Col, 97-99; Chr of English, East Tenn State Univ, 99-. **HONORS AND AWARDS** Honorary Research Fel, Univ of Edinburgh Inst for Advanced Studies in the Humanities, 96. **MEMBERSHIPS** Amer Soc for Eighteenth Century Studies; Eighteenth Century Scottish Studies Soc. **RESEARCH** Thomas Shadwell (Restoration Dramatist); Joanna Baillie (Scottish playwright) **SELECTED PUBLICATIONS** Auth, The Collected Letters of Joanna Baillie, 99. **CONTACT ADDRESS** East Tennessee State University, Box 70683, Johnson City, TN 37614. **EMAIL** slagle@etsu.edu

SLAKEY, ROGER L.
DISCIPLINE ENGLISH LITERATURE **EDUCATION** Univ Ca, BA; Univ Mich, MA; Johns Hopkins Univ, PhD. **CAREER** Eng Dept, Georgetown Univ **RESEARCH** Victorian history; poetry; rhetoric; relations between religion and ethics and literature. **SELECTED PUBLICATIONS** Auth, pubs on Milton, Wordsworth, Frost and diverse Victorian writers. **CONTACT ADDRESS** English Dept, Georgetown Univ, 37th and O St, Washington, DC 20057.

SLANE, ANDREA
DISCIPLINE FILM HISTORY **EDUCATION** Rutgers Univ, BA; Univ Calif, PhD. **CAREER** Engl, Old Dominion Univ. **RESEARCH** Video and Multimedia. **SELECTED PUBLICATIONS** Area: Kinks in the System: Six Shorts About People Left to their own Devices; Six short videos on the human processing of information received by machines; Irresistible Impulse (feature length video); Research on images of fascism. **CONTACT ADDRESS** Old Dominion Univ, 4100 Powhatan Ave, Norfolk, VA 23058. **EMAIL** ASlane@odu.edu

SLATE, JOSEPH EVANS
PERSONAL Born 12/31/1927, Lubbock, TX, m, 1972, 3 children **DISCIPLINE** ENGLISH **EDUCATION** Univ Ok, BA, 49, MA, 52; Univ Wi, PhD, 57. **CAREER** Instr English, McMicken Col, Univ Cincinnati, 54-57; assoc prof, Austin Col, 57-59; instr, 59-62, asst prof, 62-66, assoc prof English, Univ Tx, Austin, 66-, Dir, Inst Advan Studies English, 66-68; guest prof Am lit & film, Univ Vienna, 72-73; Montpellier III, 92-93. **RESEARCH** Social history of authorship, reading, & publishing; film & literature **SELECTED PUBLICATIONS** Auth, W C Williams and the modern short story, Southern Rev, summer 68; Dahlberg's moral book of erotic beasts, Edward Dahlberg, American Ishmael, 68; Kora in opacity: Williams' improvisation, J Mod Lit, 5/71; Keaton and What No Beer, New Orleans Rev, spring 81. **CONTACT ADDRESS** Dept English, Univ of Texas, Austin, Austin, TX 78712-1026. **EMAIL** jeslate@mail.utexas.edu

SLATER, JOHN W.
DISCIPLINE SPEECH **EDUCATION** DePauw Univ, BA, 60; Univ NC, MA, 71; PhD, 93. **CAREER** Asst Prof, Queens Col, 86-89; Assoc Prof, Wingate Col, 93-94; From Asst Prof to Assoc Prof, Western Carolina Univ, 94-. **MEMBERSHIPS** Asn for Educ in Jour and Mass Commun, Am Jour Historians Assn, N Am Soc for Sport Hist. **RESEARCH** The history of the relationship between mass media and the olympic games, the history of media technology. **SELECTED PUBLICATIONS** Coauth, "The Role of Communication in Achieving Shared Agenda Under New Organizational Leadership," J of Public Relations Res, vol 10, no 4 (98): 219-235; auth, "Changing Partners: The Relationship Between the Mass Media and the Olympic Games," in Global and Cult Critique: Problematizing the Olympic Games (London, Ontario: Int Ctr for Olympic Studies, 98), 49-68; auth, "The Technology of News Gathering and Transmission," in Hist of Am Jour (Vision Pr, forthcoming). **CONTACT ADDRESS** Dept Speech, Western Carolina Univ, 1 University Dr, Cullowhee, NC 28723-9646. **EMAIL** slater@wcu.edu

SLATER, THOMAS J.
PERSONAL Born 12/16/1955, Kalamazoo, MI, m, 1981, 2 children **DISCIPLINE** ENGLISH **EDUCATION** Mich St Univ, BA, 78; Univ Maryland, MA, 81; Okla State Univ, PhD, 85. **CAREER** Lectr, NW Missouri State Univ, 85-86; lectr Missouri W State Col/Univ Missouri-KC, 86-87; asst prof, Ill State Univ, 87-90; asst prof to Assoc Prof, Indiana Univ of Penn, 90-. **HONORS AND AWARDS** Contemp Am Auth Gale Res, 93. **MEMBERSHIPS** Soc Cinema Stud; Univ Film Video Asn; NE Mod Lang Asn. **RESEARCH** Women screenwriters and directors in American silent film. **SELECTED PUBLICATIONS** auth Milos Forman: A Bio-Bibliography, Greenwood Press, 87; Teaching Vietnam: The Politics of Documentary, Inventing Vietnam: The War in Film and Television, Temple Univ Press, 91; A Handbook of Soviet and East European Film and Filmmakers, Greenwood Press, 91; June Mathis: A Woman Who Spoke Through Silents, Griffithiana: A Journal of Film History, 95; Olivier, Godard, and the Violence of Creation: Considering the Relationship of Theater and Film in a (Post-) Apocalypitic Age, Interdisciplinary Humanities, 97; June Mathis's Classified: One Woman's Response to Modernism, Journal of Film and Video, 98; Transcending Boundaries: Lois Weber and the Discourse Over Women's Roles in the Teens and Twenties, Quarterly Review of Film and Video, 01; co-ed, A Slightly Different Light: Exploring Marginalized Issues and Forces in American Silent Film, Southern IL UP, 02. **CONTACT ADDRESS** Dept of English, Indiana Univ of Pennsylvania, 110 Leonard Hall, Indiana, PA 15705-1094. **EMAIL** tslater@grove.iup.edu

SLAUGHTER, BEVERLEY
PERSONAL Born New Orleans, LA, m **DISCIPLINE** COMMUNICATIONS **EDUCATION** Univ Cent Fla, BA, 75; MA, 76. **CAREER** Assoc prof, Brevard Comm Col, 76-; campus coord, 94-; prog dir, 99-. **HONORS AND AWARDS** Who's Who Am Teach; Freshman Adv; Dist Educator. **MEMBERSHIPS** FACC; NCTE. **RESEARCH** Southern literature; elements contributing to students success; use of technology in teaching and learning. **SELECTED PUBLICATIONS** Coauth, The Rinehart Reader, vol 1,2,3. **CONTACT ADDRESS** Dept Lib Arts, Brevard Comm Col, 3865 North Wickham Rd, Melbourne, FL 32935-2310. **EMAIL** slaughterb@brevard.cc.fl.us

SLAVIN, ARTHUR J.
PERSONAL Born 02/15/1933, Brooklyn, NY, m, 1968, 5 children **DISCIPLINE** ENGLISH LITERATURE, HISTORY **EDUCATION** La State Univ, BA, 58; Univ NC, PhD, 61. **CAREER** Asst prof hist, Bucknell Univ, 61-65; from asst prof to prof, Univ Calif, Los Angeles, 65-73; prof & chmn dept, Univ Calif, Irvine, 73-74; dean col arts & sci, Univ Louisville, 74-77, Justus Bier Distinguished Prof Humanities & prof hist, Univ Louisville, 77-98, Emeritus, 98-; mem, Bd Consults, Nat Endowment Humanities, 76-; Clark lectr, William A Clark Libr, 77-78; distinguished lectr hist, Brigham Young Univ, 80; distinguished lectr, NC Asn Col Universities, 82. **HONORS AND AWARDS** Guggenheim fel, 67-68; fel, Royal Hist Soc of Great Britain, 69; sr res fel, Fogler Libr, 70-71; Henry Huntington Libr res fel, 75; Nat Endowment for Humanities fel, 80-81. **MEMBERSHIPS** AHA; Conf Brit Studies; Medieval Acad Am; Am Soc Reformation Res; Renaissance Soc Am. **RESEARCH** Tudor England; The Holocaust and imaginative literature; literature, politics and modern culture. **SELECTED PUBLICATIONS** Auth, Politics and Profit, Cambridge Univ Pr, 66; auth, Henry VII and the English Reformation, 68; auth, Thomas Cromwell on Reform and Reformation, 69; auth, Tudor Men and Institutions, 72; auth, The Precarious Balance, 73; auth, The Ways fo the West, 3 vols, 73-75; auth, The Tudor Age and Beyond, 86; auth, Politics and Ideology in the Sixteenth Century, 94; auth, State Sovereigns and Society, 98. **CONTACT ADDRESS** 502 Club Lane, Louisville, KY 40207. **EMAIL** ajslav01@athena-louisville.edu

SLAWEK, STEPHEN
PERSONAL Born 05/01/1949, W. Chester, PA, m, 2 children **DISCIPLINE** MUSIC AND ASIAN STUDIES **EDUCATION** Univ IL at Urbana-Champaign, PhD. **CAREER** Prof; Univ TX at Austin, 83-. **RESEARCH** Musical traditions of South Asia. **SELECTED PUBLICATIONS** Auth, Sitar Technique in Nibaddh Forms, Delhi, Motilal Banarsidass, 87; coauth, Musical Instruments of North India: Eighteenth century Portraits by Baltazard Solvyns, Delhi, Manohar Publ, 97. **CONTACT ADDRESS** School of Music, Univ of Texas, Austin, 2613 Wichita St, Austin, TX 78705. **EMAIL** slawek@mail.utexuas.edu

SLEVIN, JAMES
DISCIPLINE ENGLISH LITERATURE **EDUCATION** Providence Col, BA; Univ Va, MA, PhD. **CAREER** Eng Dept, Georgetown Univ **RESEARCH** Rhetoric and composition; rhetorical theory; literary theory; theories of literacy; 18th century literature. **SELECTED PUBLICATIONS** Auth, Critical Theory and the Teaching of Literature: Politics, Curriculum, Pedagogy, 95; Making Faculty Work Visible: Reinterpreting Professional Service, Teaching, and Research in the Fields of Language and Literature, 96; The Next Generation: Preparing Graduate Students for the Professional Responsibilities of College Teachers, 93; co-ed, The Future of Doctoral Studies in English, 89; The Right to Literacy, 90. **CONTACT ADDRESS** English Dept, Georgetown Univ, 37th and O St, Washington, DC 20057.

SLIGH, GARY LEE
PERSONAL Born 05/09/1958, Roanoke, VA, m, 1990, 3 children **DISCIPLINE** LITERATURE **EDUCATION** Univ Va, BA, 80; Am Univ, MA, 84; Wesley Theol Sem, MDiv, 84; Ind Univ Pa, PhD, 98. **CAREER** Adj instr, Commonwealth Col, 92-93; adj instr, Old Dominion Univ, 94-97; adj instr, Tidewater Community Col, 94-99; adj instr, Averett Col, 98-99; instr, Lake-Sumter Community Col, 99-. **HONORS AND AWARDS** Outstanding Adj, Tidewater Community Col, 95. **MEMBERSHIPS** MLA, Soc for the Study of Multi-Ethnic Lit of the United States. **RESEARCH** Native American Literature, Ethnic Literature, Novel, Regional Studies. **CONTACT ADDRESS** Dept Arts & Sci, Lake-Sumter Comm Col, 9501 US Hwy 441, Leesburg, FL 34788-3950. **EMAIL** gsligh@lscc.cc.fl.us

SLOANE, DAVID EDWARD EDISON
PERSONAL Born 01/19/1943, West Orange, NJ, 4 children **DISCIPLINE** AMERICAN LITERATURE **EDUCATION** Wesleyan Univ, BA, 64; Duke Univ, MA, 66, PhD, 70. **CAREER** Instr, Lafayette Col, 68-70, asst prof, 70-74; dir, Writing Ctr, Livingston Col, Rutgers Univ, 73-74; instr writing, Fashion Inst Technol, 74-75; asst chmn div acad develop, Medgar Evers Col, 75-76; assoc prof, 76-82, prof English, Univ New Haven, 82-. **HONORS AND AWARDS** Winchester Fel for Grad Study, Wesleyan Univ, 64; Yale-Mellon Vis Conn Fac Fel, 80-81; USIA lectr on American humor to the Asn Brazillian Prof of English annual convention, 88; First Henry Nash Smith Fel, Ctr for Mark Twain Studies, 89; Keynote Speaker, "Interpreting Edison," Edison Nat Hist Site, Edison Sesquicentennial Conf, 6/97. **MEMBERSHIPS** MLA; Am Humor Studies Asn (pres 89); ALA; Mark Twain Circle (pres 92-94); NEMLA. **RESEARCH** American literature, 1860-1910, remedial writing. **SELECTED PUBLICATIONS** Auth, Mark Twain as a Literary Comedian, La State Univ Press, 79, 82; The Literary Humor of the Urban Northeast, 1830-1890, La State Univ Press, 83; American Humor Magazines and Comic Periodicals, Greenwood, 87; Writing for Tax Professionals, KPMG-Peat Marwick, Rptd, 88; Adventures of Huckleberry Finn: American Comic Vision, G.K. Hall-Twayne, 88; Sister Carrie: Theodore Dreiser's Sociological Tragedy, Macmillan, 92; Mark Twain's Humor: Critical Essays, Garland Publ, 93; American Humor: New Studies, New Directions, Univ Ala Press, 98; author of numerous journal articles. **CONTACT ADDRESS** 300 Orange Ave, West Haven, CT 06516-1999.

SLOANE, THOMAS O.
PERSONAL Born 07/12/1929, West Frankfort, IL, m, 1952, 3 children **DISCIPLINE** RHETORIC **EDUCATION** Southern Ill Univ, BA, 51, MA, 52; Northwestern Univ, PhD, 60. **CAREER** Lectr speech, Southern Ill Univ, 56; asst interpretation, Northwestern Univ, 57-58; instr English Washington & Lee Univ, 58-60; asst prof speech, Univ Ill, Urbana, 60-65, assoc prof, 65-70, fac fel, 64, instr develop award, 65, asst dean lib arts & sci, 66-67, assoc head dept speech, 67-68; vis assoc prof, 68-69, chmn dept, 72-76, PROF RHET, UNIV CALIF, BERKELEY, 70-92, Guggenheim fel, 81-82; prof emer, 93-. **HONORS AND AWARDS** Huntington Libr Res Awd, 67; Humanities Res Awd, Univ Calif Berkeley, 74. **MEMBERSHIPS** MLA; Renaissance Soc Am. **RESEARCH** Rhetoric and poetry in the English Renaissance; History of Rhetoric. **SELECTED**

PUBLICATIONS Auth, Donne, Milton, and the End of Humanist Rhetoric, 85; auth, On the Contrary, 97. **CONTACT ADDRESS** Dept of Rhet, Univ of California, Berkeley, Berkeley, CA 94720. **EMAIL** tos@uclink.berkeley.edu

SLONIOWSKI, JEANNETTE
DISCIPLINE COMMUNICATIONS **EDUCATION** Univ Toronto, BA, PhD; Brock Univ, BA; State Univ NY, MA. **CAREER** Prof, Brock Univ. **HONORS AND AWARDS** Ed bd, Can Jour Commun. **RESEARCH** Television, docudrama, documentary, the grotesque, theories of transgression; ideology. **SELECTED PUBLICATIONS** Auth, "Violations: The Boys of St. Vincent," Canadian Journal of Communications 21, (96): 365-379; auth, "A Cross-Border Study of the Teen Genre: The Case of John N. Smith," Journal of Popular Film and Television 25, (97): 130-137; auth, "It was an Atrocious Film, George Franju's Le Sang des betes," in Documenting the Documentary; coauth, Documenting the Documentary, Wayne State Univ Press, 96; auth, Canadian Communications: Issues in Contemporary Media and Culture, Scarborough: Prentice Hall Allyn and Bacon, 98; auth, "Las Hurdes and the Political Efficacy of the Grotesque," Canadian Journal of Film Studies, vol. 7, no. 2, (98): 30-48; **CONTACT ADDRESS** Dept of Film Stud, Dramatic and Visual Arts, Brock Univ, 500 Glenridge Ave, Saint Catharines, ON, Canada L2S 3A1. **EMAIL** jeanette@spartan.ac.BrockU.CA

SLOTKIN, ALAN
PERSONAL Born 11/07/1943, Brooklyn, NY, s **DISCIPLINE** ENGLISH **EDUCATION** Univ Miami, AB, 65; Univ SC, MA, 69; PhD, 70. **CAREER** Asst prof, Technol Univ, 70-76, assoc prof, English, 76-83, prof 83-. **HONORS AND AWARDS** NOEA Fel , 65; NSF Fel, 70. **MEMBERSHIPS** Robert Penn Women Circle, Am Dialect Soc, Ling Soc of Am, Ling Asn of Can and the US, SE Conference on Ling, Int Asn for World Englishes; Ling Asn of Can and the US; Robert Penn Warren Circle. **RESEARCH** American dialects; American dialect literature; neologisms. **SELECTED PUBLICATIONS** auth, "Bungstarter, Mightish Well, and Cultural Confusion," Am Speech, LIV (79): 69-71; auth, "Dialect Manipulation in An Experiment in Misery," Am Literary Realism, XIV (81): 273-6; auth, "Hawkes's The Cannibal," The Explicator 40 (82): 57-9; auth, "Stella Snow and Her Carriage Ride: A Point of Historical Focus in John Hawkes The Cannibal," Notes on Contemporary Lit, XIII (83): 8-11; auth, "Faulkner's Use of the Interplay of External and Internal Dictional Modes for Jason Compson: Speech as an Adjunct of Narrative Technique in The Sound and the Fury," Lang and Lit (85): 37-49; auth, "Absent Without: Adjective, Participate, or Preposition," Am Speech (85): 222-7; auth, "The Language of Social Interactions: The Idiolect of Willie Stark in Robert Penn Warren's All the King's Men," CLA Journal (87): 294-307; auth, "Response: Prepositional absent: An Afterword," Am Speech (89): 167-8; auth, "To Go Missing 'To Disappear': Another British Syntactic Intrusion?", Am Speech (90): 196; auth, "Adjectival-less and -free: A Case of Shifting Institutional Currency," Am Speech, (90): 33-49; auth, "You as a Multi-leveled Dictional Device in Stephen Crane's Representation of Bowery Dialect in Maggie: A Girl of the Street," Special Issue: Linguistics and Literature, South Central Review (90): 40-53; auth, "Improvography: A Contradiction in Terms," Am Speech (93): 437-438; auth, The Language of Stephen Crane's Bowery Tales: Growing Mastery of Character Diction, (New York): Garland Publishing Co., 93; auth, "A Back (-to-the-Future)-formation," Am Speech (93): 323-327; auth, "Two New Obscenities: The Acceptability of Taboo Words," Am Speech, (94): 220-224; auth, "Absent without: A New American Engish Preposition," Centennial Usage Studies (94): 194-202; auth, "The Ecological Newspeak of Kim Stanley Robinson," Am Speech (97): 240-243; auth, "Free Again: A Poential Functional Shift," Am Speech, (98), 112. **CONTACT ADDRESS** Dept English, Tennessee Tech Univ, 1999 N Dixie Ave, Cookeville, TN 38505-0001. **EMAIL** aslotkin@tntech.edu

SMALL, JUDY JO
PERSONAL Born 09/01/1943, Bristol, VA, m, 1966, 2 children **DISCIPLINE** ENGLISH **EDUCATION** Duke Univ, AB, 65; Univ Pa, MA, 66; Univ NCar Chapel Hill, PhD, 86. **CAREER** Instr, Wake Forest Univ, 66-70; instr, Meredith Col, 79-81; lectr to prof, NCar State Univ, 86-. **HONORS AND AWARDS** Phi Beta Kappa; C Hugh Holman Fel; Outstanding Acad Book Awd, Choice Magazine; Outstanding Teacher Awd, NCar State Univ. **MEMBERSHIPS** MLA, Am Lang Assoc, Emily Dickinson Int Soc, Sherwood Anderson Soc, Phi Beta Kappa. **RESEARCH** American poetry, prosodic technique, American nature writing. **SELECTED PUBLICATIONS** Auth, "Robert Beverley and the New World Garden," Am Lit 55, (93): 525-40; coauth, "Hemingway v Anderson: The Final Rounds," Hemingway Rev 14, (95): 1-17; auth, A Reader's Guide to The Short Stories of Sherwood Anderson, GK Hall, 94; auth, Positive As Sound: Emily Dicksinson's Rhyme. **CONTACT ADDRESS** Dept English, No Carolina State Univ, Box 8105, Raleigh, NC 27695-8105. **EMAIL** jtsmall@gateway.net

SMALL, RAY
PERSONAL Born 08/02/1915, Winters, TX, m, 1998, 2 children **DISCIPLINE** ENGLISH **EDUCATION** West Tex State Univ, BA, 37; Univ Tex, Austin, MA, 41, PhD(English), 58. **CAREER** From instr to prof English, Amarillo Col, 46-61; asst to pres, 61-63, dean arts & sci, 63-67, dean col lib arts, 67-79, prof English, Univ Tex, El Paso, 61-, emer dean Col Lib Arts, 80-, emer prof English, 84-, emer prof Communication, 93-. **RESEARCH** William Butler Yeats; Cardinal Newman and the Oxford movement. **SELECTED PUBLICATIONS** Auth, Pursuit of Diamond after Grainne, (Univ microfilm). **CONTACT ADDRESS** Dept of English, Univ of Texas, El Paso, 500 W University Ave, El Paso, TX 79968-0001.

SMALLENBURG, HARRY RUSSELL
PERSONAL Born 07/17/1942, Burbank, CA, 2 children **DISCIPLINE** ENGLISH LITERATURE **EDUCATION** Univ Calif, Santa Barbara, BA, 65; Univ Calif, Berkeley, MA, 66, PhD (English), 70; Cranbrook Art Acad, MFA, 78. **CAREER** Asst prof, Wayne State Univ, 70-; Chmn Dept Gen Studies, Ctr Creative Stu, 77-86; assoc prof, Pasadena City Col, 89-. **RESEARCH** Creative writing; 20th century literature, humanities, music/composition. **SELECTED PUBLICATIONS** Auth, Milton's cosmic sentences, Lang & Style, 72; Government of the spirit: Style, structure and theme in Treatise of civil power, In: Achievements of the Left Hand: Essays on the Prose of John Milton, Univ Mass, 74. **CONTACT ADDRESS** Dept of Eng and For Lang, Pasadena City Col, 1570 E Colorado Blvd, Pasadena, CA 91106. **EMAIL** hrsmallenburg@paccd.cc.ca.us

SMARR, JANET L.
PERSONAL Born 05/20/1949, Chicago, IL, m, 1973, 2 children **DISCIPLINE** DRAMA, LITERATURE, ITALIAN STUDIES **EDUCATION** Brown Univ, BA, 70; Princeton Univ, PhD, 75. **CAREER** Instr, Princeton Univ, 75-76; instr, Univ of Mass, 76-77; asst prof, Yale Univ, 79-80; asst prof to prof, Univ of Ill, 80-00; prof, Univ of CA San Diego, 00- **HONORS AND AWARDS** AAUW Fel, 74-75; SE Inst of Medieval and Renaissance Studies, 76; Mellon Fel, 77-78, Fel, Univ of Ill, 86, 99; Awd, Am Asn of Ital Studies, 84; ALTHE Awd, 96. **MEMBERSHIPS** MLA, Renaissance Soc of Am, Am Assoc of Ital Studies, Am Soc for Theatre Res, Am Boccaccio Assoc. **RESEARCH** Renaissance, Italian and Comparative Literature, Renaissance Women writers. **SELECTED PUBLICATIONS** Auth, "Petrarch: A Vergil Without a Rome," Rome in the Renaissance, the City and the Myth, (82); ed and transl, Italian Renaissance Tales, Solaris Pr, 83; auth, Boccaccio and Fiammetta: the Narrator as Lover, Univ of Ill Pr, 86; transl, Boccaccio's Eclogues, Garland Publ, 87; auth, "Poets of Love and Exile," Dante and Ovid: Essays in Intertextuality, (91); auth, "Boccaccio and Renaissance Women Writers," Studi sul Boccaccio, (91-92); ed, Historical Criticism and the Challenge of Theory, Univ of Ill Pr, 93; auth, "A dialogue of dialogues: Tullia d-Aragona and sperone Speroni," MLN, (98); auth, Other Races, Other Spaces: Boccaccio's Representation of non-Christian People and Places in the Decameron, Studi sul Boccaccio, 99; auth, Substituting for Laura: Objects of Desire for Renaissance Women Poets, Comp Lit Studies, 00. **CONTACT ADDRESS** Dept Theatre and Dance, Univ of California, San Diego, La Jolla, CA 92093-0344. **EMAIL** jsmarr@ucsd.edu

SMART, PATRICIA
PERSONAL Born 02/03/1940, Toronto, ON, Canada **DISCIPLINE** LITERATURE **EDUCATION** Univ Toronto, BA, 61; Laval Univ, MA, 63; Queen's Univ, PhD, 77. **CAREER** Fac mem, 71-86, Prof French, Carleton Univ, 86-, Marston Lafrance Leave Fel, 86-87, dir, Inst Can Stud, 87-88. **HONORS AND AWARDS** Gov Gen Awd Non-fiction (Fr lang); Gabrielle Roy Awd. **MEMBERSHIPS** Royal Soc Can; Asn Can & Que Lit; Asn Can Stud. **SELECTED PUBLICATIONS** Auth, Hubert Aquin, Agent Double, 73; auth, Ecrire dans la maison du Pere: l'emergence du feminin dans la tradition litteraire du Quebec, 88; auth & transl, Writing in the Father's House: the Emergence of the Feminine in the Quebec Literary Tradition, 91; ed & transl, The Diary of Andre Laurendeau 1964-67, 91; auth, Langues, cultrues et valeurs au Canada a l'aube du XXIe siecle, sous la direction de A. Lapierre, P.Smart et P. Savard, Ottawa: Carleton Univ Press, 96; auth, Les Femmes du Refus global, Montreal, Editions du Boreal, 98. **CONTACT ADDRESS** French Dept, Carleton Univ, bureau 1623 Dunton Tower, Ottawa, ON, Canada K1S 5B6. **EMAIL** pat_smart@carleton.ca

SMEDICK, LOIS KATHERINE
DISCIPLINE ENGLISH LANGUAGE; LITERATURE **EDUCATION** Wilson, BA; Toronto, MSL; Bryn Mawr, PhD,-63. **CAREER** Prof **RESEARCH** Chaucer and his contemporaries; chivalric romance; and Middle English prose style. **SELECTED PUBLICATIONS** Pub (s), medieval devotional prose; Form of Living of Richard Rolle; Latin stylistic device, the cursus. **CONTACT ADDRESS** Dept of English Language and Literature, Univ of Windsor, 401 Sunset Ave, Windsor, ON, Canada N9B 3P4. **EMAIL** smedick@uwindsor.ca

SMETHURST, MAE J.
PERSONAL Born 05/28/1935, Houghton, MI, m, 1956 **DISCIPLINE** CLASSICS **EDUCATION** Dickinson Col, BA, 57; Univ Mich, MA, 60, PhD(classics), 68. **CAREER** Instr classics, Univ Mich, 66-67; from instr to asst prof, 67-76, Assoc Prof Classics, Univ Pittsburgh, 76- **MEMBERSHIPS** Am Philol Asn. **RESEARCH** Aeschylus; tragedy; Oresteia. **SELECTED PUBLICATIONS** Auth, The Appeal Of A Plotless Tragedy + Aeschylus And Zeami, A Comparative-Study Of Greek Tragedy And No/, Coll Lit, Vol 0023, 1996. **CONTACT ADDRESS** Dept of Classic, Univ of Pittsburgh, 207 Hillman Libr, Pittsburgh, PA 15260-0001.

SMITH, BARBARA
PERSONAL Born New York, NY, m, 2 children **DISCIPLINE** WRITING, GENDER STUDIES **EDUCATION** Southern CT State Col, BS; SUNY, MA, 86, PhD, 92. **CAREER** Engl, Col Mt. St. Vincent **HONORS AND AWARDS** Hum rep Undergrad Comt. **SELECTED PUBLICATIONS** Auth, A Case Study of Myself as a Writer. A Community of Writers: A Workshop Course in Writing, Random House, 89; The Women of Ben Jonson's Poetry: Female Representations in the Non-Dramatic Verse, Aldershot: Scolar Press, 95; Teaching in the 21st Century: Adapting Writing Pedagogies to Discipline- Specific Classrooms, Garland Press In, 99; auth, Early Modern Women Poets and Cultural Constraints, Ashgate Publishing, 00. **CONTACT ADDRESS** Col of Mount Saint Vincent, 6301 Riverdale Ave, Riverdale, NY 10471. **EMAIL** barbsmith9@aol.com

SMITH, BARBARA H.
DISCIPLINE ENGLISH **EDUCATION** Brandeis Univ, BA, 54; PhD, 65. **CAREER** From Fac to Asst Prof, Bennington Col, 61-73; Vis Lectr and Prof, Univ Pa, 73-87; Prof, Duke Univ, 87-. **HONORS AND AWARDS** Christian Gauss Awd, 68; Fel, Stanford Univ, 85-89. **MEMBERSHIPS** Hist of Sci Soc, Int Asn for Philos and Lit, Int Comp Lit Asn, Soc for Soc Studies of Sci, Mod Lang Asn of Am. **RESEARCH** History of criticism and literary theory, Twentieth-Century theories of language and communication, contemporary accounts of knowledge, science and cognition. **SELECTED PUBLICATIONS** Auth, Poetic Closure: A Study of How Poems End, Univ Chicago Pr, 68; auth, On The Margins of Discourse: The Relation of Literature to Language, Univ Chicago Pr, 78; auth, Contingencies of Value: Alternative Perspectives for Critical Theory, Harvard UP, 88; auth, Belief and Resistance: Dynamics of Contemporary Intellectual Controversy, Harvard UP, 97. **CONTACT ADDRESS** Dept English, Duke Univ, PO Box 90015, Durham, NC 27708-0015. **EMAIL** bhsmith@duke.edu

SMITH, BRENDA AUSTIN
DISCIPLINE ENGLISH LITERATURE **EDUCATION** Acadia Univ, BA; Victoria Univ, MA; Univ Manitoba, PhD. **CAREER** Asst prof **HONORS AND AWARDS** Ed, Can Dimension. **RESEARCH** Narration and rhetoric in fiction and film; representation of subjectivity in fiction and film; point of view; film and effect; 'women's' films; film theory; Henry James; critical theory. **SELECTED PUBLICATIONS** Auth, pubs on Patricia Rozema and Canadian film. **CONTACT ADDRESS** Dept of English, Univ of Manitoba, Winnipeg, MB, Canada R3T 2N2. **EMAIL** basmith@ms.umanitoba.ca

SMITH, BRUCE RAY
PERSONAL Born 03/21/1946, Jackson, MS **DISCIPLINE** ENGLISH LITERATURE **EDUCATION** Tulane Univ, BA, 68; Univ Rochester, MA, 71, PhD(English), 73. **CAREER** From asst prof to prof English, Georgetown Univ, 72-; dir, grad program in English, Georgetown Univ, 87-91; dir, undergrad studies in English, Georgetown Univ, 92-95; ed board, Shakespeare Quart, 94-; ed board, PMLA, 00-03. **HONORS AND AWARDS** Folger Inst fel English, 78; Am Coun Learned Soc fel, 78-79; NEH fel, Folger Lib, 87-88; Virginia Foundation for Humanities fel, 89; Mellon fel, Huntington Lib, 96; Folger Institute fel, 96; Int Globe Fellowship, Shakespeare's Globe, London, 97; NEH summer fel, 99. **MEMBERSHIPS** Southeastern Renaissance Conf; Medieval & Renaissance Drama Soc; Shakespeare Asn Am; Modern Language Asn of Am; Committee for Gay and Lesbian History; Renaissance Soc Am; Soc for Study of Early Modern Woman. **RESEARCH** Renaissance drama; Shakespeare; 17th century literature; acoustics. **SELECTED PUBLICATIONS** Auth, Ben Jonson's Epigrammes: Portrait-Gallery, Theater, Commonwealth, Studies English Lit, 74; Sir Amorous Knight and the Indecorous Romans: Plautus and Terence Play Court in the Renaissance, 75, Landscape with Figures: The Three Realms of Queen Elizabeth's Country House Revels, 78 & Towards the Rediscovery of Tragedy: Seneca's Plays on the English Renaissance Stage, 79, Renaissance Drama; The Contest of Apollo and Marsyas: Ideas About Music in the Middle Ages, In: By Things Seen: Reference and Recognition in Medieval Thought, 79; On Reading the Shepheardes Calender, Spenser Studies, 80; Pageant's into Play: Shakespeare's Three Perspectives on Idea and Image, in David m. Bergeron, ed, Pageantry in the Shakespearean Theater, Athens: Univ of Ga Press, 85; Sermons in Stones: Shakespeare and Renaissance Sculpture, Shakespeare Studies 17, 85; Ancient Scripts and Modern Experience on the English Stage, 1500-1700, Princeton Univ Press, 88; Parolles' Recitations: Oral and Literate Structures in Shakespeare's Plays, Renaissance Papers 1989, Southeastern Renaissance Conference, 89; Homosexual Desire in Shakespeare's England: A Cultural Poetics, Univ of Chicago Press, 91, paperback, 94; Reading Lists of

Plays in Early Modern England, Shakespeare Quart 42, 91; Makimg a Difference: Male/Male Desire in Tragedy, Comedy, and Tragi/Comedy, in Erotic Politics: The Dynamics of Desire on the English Renaissance Stage, ed Susan Zimmerman. London: Routledge, 92; Roasting the Swan of Avon: Shakespeare's Redoubtable Enemies and Dubious Friends Washington, D.C.: Folger Shakespeare Lib, and Seattle: Univ of Washington Press, 94; Prickly Characters, in Reading and Writing in Shakespeare, ed David M. Bergeron, Newark: Univ of Delaware Press, 96; Rape, Rap, Rupture, Rapture: R-Rated Futures On the Global Market, Textual Practice 9, 95; Locating the Sexual Subject, in Alternative Shakespeares, vol 2, ed Terry Hawkes, London: Routledge, 96; "A Night of Errors and the Dawn of Empire: Male Enterprise in the Comedy of Errors," in Shakespeare's Sweet Thunder, ed Michael Collins, Newark: Univ of Delaware Press, 97; "I, You, He, She, and We: On the Sexual Politics of Shakespeare's Sonnets," in Shakespeare's Sonnets: Critical Essays, ed James Schiffer, Garland Reference Lib of the Humanities (New York: Garland, 98); The Acoustic World of Early Modern England, Chicago: Univ of Chicago Press, 99; auth, Shakespeare and Masculinity, Oxford Univ Pr, 00; William Shakespeare, Twelfth Night: Texts and Contexts, Bedford Books, forthcoming. **CONTACT ADDRESS** Dept of English, Georgetown Univ, P O Box 571131, Washington, DC 20057-1131. **EMAIL** smithb@georgetown.edu

SMITH, CAROL HERTZIG
PERSONAL Born 08/17/1929, Pittsburgh, PA, d, 1953, 1 child **DISCIPLINE** ENGLISH **EDUCATION** OH Wesleyan Univ, BA, 52; Univ MI, MA, 55, PhD, 62. **CAREER** From instr to assoc prof English, 59-70, Prof English, Rutgers Univ, 70-, chmn dept, 80-86, Dir of Graduate Studies, 98-. **MEMBERSHIPS** MLA **RESEARCH** Modern literature, especially drama, novel and poetry; women writers of modernism. **SELECTED PUBLICATIONS** Auth, T S Eliot's Dramatic Theory and Practice: From Sweeney Agonistes to The Elder Statesman, Princeton, 63, T S Eliot: The Poet as Playwright, Nation, 10/66; other critical articles on modernism. **CONTACT ADDRESS** Dept of English, Rutgers, The State Univ of New Jersey, New Brunswick, 510 George St, New Brunswick, NJ 08903-1167. **EMAIL** chs@rci.rutgers.edu

SMITH, DANIEL L.
DISCIPLINE LAW, LIBRARY SCIENCE, COMPARATIVE LITERATURE **EDUCATION** Univ Iowa, BS (biochemistry), 80, BA (Russian), 89, MFA (Comp lit), 93, JD, 93, MA (Libr, Info Sci), 94. **CAREER** Publisher, Canonymous Pr, 92-; ref librn, curator, Cornell Law Libr, 97-00; asst ed, Exchanges: A J of Translations, Univ Iowa, 89-93. **SELECTED PUBLICATIONS** Auth, "Postmodern [Sic]ness: Ecritique of Anesthetic Judgement," Ecritique 1 (92); auth, Minims, 93; auth, "Self-Determination in Tibet: The Politics of Remedies," Ecritique, 2 (96); auth, "The Legacy of Nuremberg: Sustaining Human Rights," Cornell Law Forum, 25 (99). **CONTACT ADDRESS** Canonymous Pr, P. O. Box 6613, Ithaca, NY 14851-6613. **EMAIL** smith@canonymous.com

SMITH, DAVID J.
PERSONAL Born 12/19/1942, Portsmouth, VA, m, 1966, 3 children **DISCIPLINE** ENGLISH **EDUCATION** Ohio Univ, PhD, 76. **CAREER** Teacher, Poquoson High School, 65; TA, S IL Univ, 67-69; USAF, 69-73; TA, Ohio Univ, 72-73; instr, Western Mich Univ, 73-74; asst prof, Cottey Col, 74-75; TA, Ohio Univ, 75-76; asst prof to assoc prof, Univ of Utah, 76-81; assoc prof, Univ of Fla, 81-82; prof, Va Commonwealth Univ, 82-90; prof, La State Univ, 90-. **HONORS AND AWARDS** Guggenheim Fel; Pushcart Prize; Am Acad and Inst of Arts and Letters, Awd; NEA Fel; Distinguished Univ Scholar, VCU; Fel of Southern Writers. **MEMBERSHIPS** Fel of Southern Writers; AWP; MLA; SAMLA; Am Acad of Poets; Poetry Soc of Am. **RESEARCH** American Literature, Poetry. **SELECTED PUBLICATIONS** Auth, Gray Soldiers, Stuart Wright (Winston-Salem, NC), 84; coed, The Morrow Anthology of Younger American Poets, William Morrow & co, (NY), 85; auth, Local Assays: On Contemporary American Poetry, Univ of IL Pr, (Urbana, IL), 85; auth, the Roundhouse Voices: Selected and New Poems, Harper and Row (NY), 85; auth, Cuba Night, William Morrow, (NY), 90; auth, The Essential Poe, ECCO Pr, 91; auth, Night Pleasures: New and Selected Poems, Bloodaxe Books, (Newcastle, England), 92; auth Fate's Kite: Poems 1991-1995, La State Univ Pr, (Baton Rouge, LA), 95; auth, Floating On Solitude: three Books of Poems Univ of IL Pr, (Urbana, IL), 96; auth, Tremble, The Black Warrior Review Chapbook Series (Tuscalloosa, AL), 96; auth, The Wick of Memory: New and Selected Poems 1970-2000, La State Univ Pr, (Baton Rouge, LA), 00. **CONTACT ADDRESS** Dept English, La State Univ Baton Rouge, Baton Rouge, LA 70803-0104. **EMAIL** davidjsmith2@compuserve.com

SMITH, DAVID LEE
PERSONAL Born 06/29/1944, Portsmouth, VA, m, 1985, 4 children **DISCIPLINE** ENGLISH **EDUCATION** Old Dominion Univ, BA, 66, MA, 70; Univ NC, Chapel Hill, PhD(English), 75. **CAREER** Instr English, Univ NC, Chapel Hill, 75-76; asst prof to prof English, Cent Mo State Univ, 76-; chair, dept English and Philos, 93-. **MEMBERSHIPS** MLA **RESEARCH** Victorian literature; prose fiction. **CONTACT ADDRESS** Dept of English and Philosophy, Central Missouri State Univ, Warrensburg, MO 64093-8888. **EMAIL** dls4426@cmsu2.cmsu.edu

SMITH, DAVID QUINTIN
PERSONAL Born 11/30/1938, Tiffin, OH, m, 1960, 2 children **DISCIPLINE** ENGLISH LITERATURE **EDUCATION** Columbia Univ, AB, 60; NYork Univ, MA, 63; Univ Ill, Urbana, PhD(English), 68. **CAREER** Asst prof, 67-73, ASSOC PROF ENGLISH, UNIV TOLEDO, 73- **MEMBERSHIPS** MLA; AAUP **RESEARCH** English Romanticism; Wordsworth; Blake. **SELECTED PUBLICATIONS** Auth, The wanderer's silence: A strange reticence in Book IX of The Excursion, Wordsworth Circle, spring 78. **CONTACT ADDRESS** Dept of English, Univ of Toledo, 2801 W Bancroft St, Toledo, OH 43606-3390.

SMITH, DAVID RICHARD
PERSONAL Born 04/24/1942, Jersey City, NJ, m, 1989, 5 children **DISCIPLINE** CLASSICAL STUDIES **EDUCATION** David Lipscomb Col, BA, 64; Vanderbilt Univ, MA, 66; Univ PA, PhD(class studies), 68. **CAREER** Asst prof classics, Univ CA, Riverside, 68-70; asst prof, 70-75, assoc prof, 75-80, prof hist, CA State Polytech Univ Pomona, 80-; assoc ed, Helios J Class Asn Southwest, 75-77. **MEMBERSHIPS** Class Asn Southwest; Am Philol Asn; AHA; WHA. **RESEARCH** Greek history, religion and philosophy of history; world history and teaching methodologies. **SELECTED PUBLICATIONS** Auth, Hieropoioi and Hierothytai on Rhodes, L'Antiquite Classique, 72; The Hieropoioi on Kos, Numen, 73; The Coan Festival of Zeus Polieus, Class J, 10/73; Review of G S Kirk, Myth: Its Meaning and Function in Ancient and Other Cultures, Helios, 5/76; The Poetic Focus in Horace, Odes 3.13, Latomus, 76; Teaching Religion in the Medieval Period, World Hist Bull, 90-91; Teaching and Assessing the Doing World History Method in the World History Survey, Aspen World Hist Handbook, vol 2, 97; Technology in the World History Survey, Aspen World Hist Handbook, vol 2, 97. **CONTACT ADDRESS** Dept Hist, California State Polytech Univ, Pomona, 3801 W Temple Ave, Pomona, CA 91768-4001. **EMAIL** drsmith2@csupomona.edu

SMITH, DIANE E.
PERSONAL Born 02/27/1959, Grand Rapids, MI, m, 1981, 4 children **DISCIPLINE** CLASSICS, LATIN **EDUCATION** Villanova Univ, MA 86; Univ of Michigan, BA, 80; Richmond Col, 76-77; Intercollegiate Center for Classical Stud, Rome, 79-80; Amer School of Classical Stud, Athens, 82. **CAREER** Tchr, 86-88, School of the Holy Child, Rye NY; Scholar and Typesetter, in Greek, Latin, Linguistics and Modern Lang, 88-, Teacher, 87-, Waco Christian Sem, Waco, TX. **HONORS AND AWARDS** Graduate Fellowship, Villanova Univ. **MEMBERSHIPS** Classical Assoc of Midwest and South; Amer Classical League. **SELECTED PUBLICATIONS** Typesetting in the following; Bolchazy-Carducci, Schemling, Gareth and Jon D. Mikalson, eds, Qui Miscuit Utile Dulci, Festschrift Essays for Paul Lachlan MacKendrick, 98; L & L Enterprises/Bolchazy-Carducci, DuBose, Gaylan, Farrago, 97; Franz Steiner Verlag, Linderski, J., Ed, Imperium Sine Fine, Festschrift for T.R.S. Broughton, Historia-Einzelschrift, 105, 96; Rowmand and Littlefield, Edmunds, Lowell, Oedipus at Colonus, 96; Oxford University Press, Battye, Adriand and Ian Roberts, eds, Clause Structure and Language Change, 95; Longman Publishing Group, Davis, Sally, Review and Test Preparation Guide for the beginning Latin Student, 94. **CONTACT ADDRESS** 5801 Fairview Dr, Waco, TX 76710.

SMITH, DIANE M.
PERSONAL Born 03/22/1953, Lawrence, MA, m, 1995 **DISCIPLINE** EDUCATION, ENGLISH **EDUCATION** Univ of MA, MA, 98; Univ of So CA, BA, 81 **CAREER** Pub Svc libr, 93-, Bunker Hill Cmnty Col Lib; **MEMBERSHIPS** ALA; ACRL **RESEARCH** Infor Literacy **CONTACT ADDRESS** Library, Bunker Hill Comm Col, Boston, MA 02129-2925. **EMAIL** smith@noblenet.org

SMITH, DUANE
DISCIPLINE SEVENTEENTH AND 18TH CENTURY BRITISH LITERATURE **EDUCATION** Auburn Univ, PhD. **CAREER** Eng Dept, St. Louis Univ. **SELECTED PUBLICATIONS** Auth, England, My England as Fragmentary Novel, D.H. Lawrence Rev, 92; Repetitive Patterns in Samuel Johnson's Rasselas, Studies Eng Lit, 96; auth, "Richard Lewis" in American National Biography, Oxford Univ Press, forthcoming. **CONTACT ADDRESS** Dept of English, Saint Louis Univ, 221 N Grand Blvd, Saint Louis, MO 63103. **EMAIL** smithdh@slu.edu

SMITH, ELTON EDWARD
DISCIPLINE LITERATURE, RELIGIOUS STUDIES **EDUCATION** NYU, BS, 37; Andover Newton Theol Sch, MST, 40; Syracuse Univ, PhD, 56. **CAREER** Pastor in churches, Mass, Ore, NYork, Fla, 40-56; dist prof, Univ S Fla, 61-. **HONORS AND AWARDS** Distinguished Prof Brit Lit and Bible; Dr Div, Linfield Col; Fulbright Lectureships, Univ Algiers, Mod V Univ, Univ Paris, Univ London; Grad Tuition, Cambridge Univ. **MEMBERSHIPS** MLA; SAMLA; AAUP. **SELECTED PUBLICATIONS** Auth, Charles Reade; co-auth, William Godwin; auth, My Son, My Son, Pentland Pr; auth, Angry Young Men of the Thirties; auth, auth, The Two Voices: A Tennyson Study, Univ Nebr Pr, 64; Tennyson's 'Epic Drama', up Am (Lanham, Md), 97; co-ed, The Haunted Mind: The Supernatural in Victorian Literature (Lanham, Md: Scarecrow Pr, 99). **CONTACT ADDRESS** 14714 Oak Vine Dr, Lutz, FL 33549-3229.

SMITH, EVANS L.
PERSONAL Born 08/23/1950, Baltimore, MD, m, 1984, 3 children **DISCIPLINE** ENGLISH, COMPARATIVE LITERATURE **EDUCATION** Williams Col, BA, 73; Antioch Int, MA, 76; Claremont Graduate Univ, MA; PhD, 86. **CAREER** Adj instr, Harvey Mudd Col, 80-86; adj instr, Mt San Antonio Community Col, 83-86; adj instr, Pitzer Col, 84-86; instr, Franklin Col, 86-88; instr, Anne Arundel Community Col, 88-90; prof, Midwestern State Univ, 90-. **MEMBERSHIPS** MLA. **RESEARCH** Modernist Literature, Painting, and Film, Manhattan and London in the 18th and 19th Centuries. **SELECTED PUBLICATIONS** Auth, The Descent to the Underworld: Jung and His Brothers, Princeton Univ Pr, 90; auth, "Perinatal Imagery in Hamlet," Explicatory, (94); auth, Ricorso and Revelation; An Archetypal Poetics of Modernism, Camden House, 95; auth, "The Golem and the Garland of Letters," Jour of the Fantastic in the Arts, (96); auth, Figuring Poesis: A Muthical Geometry of Postmodernism, Peter Lang, 97; auth, The Hero Journey in Literature: Parables of Poesis, Univ Pr of Am, 97; auth, "The Lyrical Nekyia: Metaphors of Poesis in Wallace Stevens," Jour of Mod Lit, (98); auth, "Amazing Underworlds: Yourcenar and Nabokov," Yearbook of Comp and Gen Lit, (98); auth, "Postmodernist Revisionings of the Grail," Mythosphere, (99); auth, The Descent to the Underworld in Modernist Literature, Film, and Painting, 01. **CONTACT ADDRESS** Midwestern State univ, 3410 Taft Blvd, Wichita Falls, TX 76308. **EMAIL** lansing.smith@nexus.mesu.edu

SMITH, F. LESLIE
PERSONAL Born 01/19/1939, Orlando, FL, m, 1961, 1 child **DISCIPLINE** MASS COMMUNICATIONS **EDUCATION** Univ FL, BS, 61; OH Univ, MA, 64; FL State Univ, PhD, 72. **CAREER** Instr radio-TV, St Petersburg Jr Col, 64-67; asst prof commun arts, Univ WFL, 67-70; asst prof radio-TV-film, NTX State Univ, 72-75, prof, 75-82; PROF Telecommunications, Univ FL, 82, Ch Telecommunication, Univ Fla 96-, Danforth assoc, 81. **HONORS AND AWARDS** Broadcast Preceptor Awd, San Francisco State Univ, 81. **MEMBERSHIPS** Asn for Educ in Journalism & Mass Comm; Am Journalism Historians Asn; Broadcast Educ Asn. **RESEARCH** Hist of radio and TV; station management and programming; broadcast law and regulation. **SELECTED PUBLICATIONS** Auth, Education for broadcasting: 1929-1963, J Broadcasting, 11/64; The selling of the Pentagon: Case study of a controversy, In: Mass News, Prentice-Hall, 73; coauth, Perceived ethicality of some TV new production techniques by a sample of Florida legislators, Speech Monogr, 11/73; auth, Hunger in America controversy: Another view, J Broadcasting, winter 74; coauth, The cigarette commercial ban: A pattern for change, Quart J Speech, 12/74; auth, Selling of the Pentagon and the First Amendment, Jounalism Hist, spring 75; The Charlie Walker case, J Broadcasting, spring 79; Quelling radio's quacks: the FCC's first programming campaign, Jour Quart, autumn 94; Electronic media and government: regulation of wireless and wired communication, Longman, 95; Perspectives on Radio and Television: An Introduction to Telecommunication in the United States, 4th ed, Laurence Erlbaum Assoc, 98. **CONTACT ADDRESS** Univ of Florida, PO Box 118400, Gainesville, FL 32611-8400. **EMAIL** lesmith@ufl.edu

SMITH, FRANCIS J.
PERSONAL Born 05/22/1920, Lorain, OH **DISCIPLINE** LITERARY CRITICISM **EDUCATION** Xavier Univ, Ohio, Litt B, 42; Loyola Univ, Ill, MA, 46; WBaden Col, STL, 53; Oxford Univ, AM, 60. **CAREER** Instr English & Latin, High Sch, Univ Detroit, 46-49; instr English, Univ, 58-60; asst prof, Colombiere Col, 60-63; from asst prof to assoc prof, 63-72, prof Eng, John Carroll Univ, 72-. **MEMBERSHIPS** MLA; Col English Assn. **RESEARCH** T S Eliot; Chaucer; modern fiction. **SELECTED PUBLICATIONS** Auth, First Prelude, Loyola Univ Press, winter 81; auth, All Is A Prize, The Pterodactyl Press, 89; auth, Haiku Yearbook, The Cobham & Hatherton Press, 91. **CONTACT ADDRESS** Dept of English, John Carroll Univ, 20700 N Park Blvd, Cleveland, OH 44118-4581.

SMITH, GAIL K.
DISCIPLINE ENGLISH **EDUCATION** Yale Univ, BA, 85; Univ Virginia, PhD, 93. **CAREER** ASST PROF, ENG, MARQUETTE UNIV **MEMBERSHIPS** Am Antiquarian Soc **SELECTED PUBLICATIONS** Auth, "Reading with the Other: Hermeneutics and the Politics of Difference in Stowe's Dred," Am Lit, June 97; auth, "From the Seminary to the Parlor: The Popularization of Hermeneutics in The Gates Ajar," Ariz Quart, 98. **CONTACT ADDRESS** Dept of Humanities, Mississippi Univ for Women, Columbus, MS 39701. **EMAIL** gsmith@muw.edu

SMITH, GAYLE LEPPIN
PERSONAL Born 07/05/1946, New York, NY **DISCIPLINE** AMERICAN LITERATURE, STYLISTICS **EDUCATION** Univ Denver, BA, 68; Univ Mass, MA, 72, PhD(English), 77. **CAREER** Teaching asst compos, Univ Mass, 68-70, instr Am lit, 72 & 73; instr lang & lit, Holyoke Community Col, 75; ASST PROF ENGLISH, PA STATE UNIV, 77- **MEMBERSHIPS** MLA; NCTE; Conf Col Compos & Commun; Northeast Mod Lang Asn. **RESEARCH** Emerson studies; style studies; composition and rhetoric. **SELECTED PUBLICATIONS** Auth, Transformational theory and developmental compositon, Exercise Exchange, spring 80; When students grade themselves: What we teach and what we learn, Pa Coun Teachers English Bull, 5/81; Style and vision in Emerson's experience, ESQ: J Am Renaissance, spring 81; The language of transcendence in S O Jewett's A White Heron, Colby Libr Quart (in prep); From graveyard to classroom: Thinking about data, Teaching English Two-Yr Col; contribr, Revising: New Essays for Writing Teachers, NCTE; Reading Song Of Myself--Assuming What Whitman Assumes, Am Transcendental Quart, Vol 06, 92. **CONTACT ADDRESS** Dept of English, Pennsylvania State Univ, Worthington Scranton, 120 Ridgeview Dr, Dunmore, PA 18512-1602.

SMITH, GRANT WILLIAM
PERSONAL Born 07/26/1937, Bellingham, WA, m, 1961, 2 children **DISCIPLINE** ENGLISH **EDUCATION** Reed Col, BA, 64; Univ Nev, Reno, MA, 67; Univ Del, PhD(English lit), 75. **CAREER** Fac Pres, 76-77, asst prof, 68-72, assoc prof, 72-81, Prof English, Eastern Wash Univ, 81-, Chm Dept, 78-84; Coordr Humanities, 84-. **MEMBERSHIPS** Spokane Area Coun English Teachers; Am Asn Univ Prof; Am Dialect Soc (reg secy, 81-98); Archaeol Inst Am; Am Name Soc; Am Soc Geolinguistics; Brit Studies Asn; Can Soc for the Study of Names; Int Coun on Onomastic Sci; Mod Lang Asn; NW Conf on Brit Studies; Philol Asn of the Pacific Coast; Rocky Mountain Mod Lang Asn (prog ch, 87-95); Societe Internationale de Dialectologie et Geolinguistique; Western States Conf on Geographic Names. **RESEARCH** Onomastics; Shakespeare. **SELECTED PUBLICATIONS** Auth, Density Variations in Indian Placenames: A Comparison Between British Columbia & Washington State, Onomastica Canadiana, 71.4, 89; coauth, Computer Fields & the Classification of Toponymic Data, 90; auth, Shakespeare's Use of Feminine Names, Georgetown Univ, 90; Plans for the U.S. Survey of Geographic Names, Proceedings of the XVIIth Intl. Congress of Onomastic Sciences, Univ Helsinki Press, 91; A Comparison of Hispanic Names in Washington State and British Columbia, Onomastica Canadiana, 12/94; Amerindian Place Names: A Typology Based on Meaning and Form, Onomastica Canadiana, 12/96 (this article has been adopted as the basis for a national study of Amerindian Place Names to be published by Univ of Okla Press and involving leading specialists in all Amerindian language groups). Numerous other articles for NAMES and other journals. **CONTACT ADDRESS** Dept of English, Eastern Washington Univ, M/S 25, Cheney, WA 99004-2496. **EMAIL** gsmith@ewu.edu

SMITH, HERB J.
PERSONAL Born 11/05/1945, Providence, RI **DISCIPLINE** ENGLISH, COMMUNICATIONS **EDUCATION** Northeastern Univ, BA, 68; MA, 70; Kent State Univ, PhD, 80. **CAREER** Asst Prof, Clarkson Univ, 80-87; Asst Prof, Southern Col of Tech, 87-92; Assoc Prof, Southern Polytech State Univ, 92-. **HONORS AND AWARDS** Personal computer Curriculum Development Awd, Clarkson Univ, 87; Fel, Prof Inst for Direct Mail Marketing, New York, 83; Pringle Fel, Kent State Univ, 78; Sen Fel, Kent State Univ, 80. **MEMBERSHIPS** Soc for Tech Comm; Asn of Teachers of Tech Writing; Coun for Programs in Tech and Sci Comm **RESEARCH** Technical communication in Germany; Portfolios and technical communication; Irish-American fiction. **SELECTED PUBLICATIONS** Co-auth, "Text and Other Resources for Training in Technical and Scientific communication," IEEE Transactions on Professional communication, (90): 205-219; auth, "The Company Profile Case Study: A Multipurpose Assignment with an Industrial Slant," The Technical Writing Teacher, (90): 119-123; auth, "Technical communications and the Law: Product Liability and Safety Labels," Journal of Technical Writing and Communication, (90): 307-319; co-auth, "Textbooks in Technical and Scientific communication: An Update," IEEE Transactions on Professional Communication, (91): 186-187; auth, "Technical communication: Preparing for the Twenty-first Century," CPTSC Proceedings 1993, 87-89; auth, "Using Videotaping to Teach Writing and Revising," Strategies for Technical Communication: A collection of Teaching Tips," Society for Technical Communication, (94): 82-83; auth, "Analysis Tools: Their Place in Business communications," in Communication: Today and Tomorrow, Asn for Bus comm, 94; auth, "Restructuring Our Undergraduate Programs: Internationalizing Our Curricula," CPTSC Proceedings 1997, 117-118. **CONTACT ADDRESS** Dept Humanities & Soc Sci, So Polytech State Univ, 1100 S Marietta Pkwy SE, Marietta, GA 30060-2855. **EMAIL** hsmith@spsu.edu

SMITH, JEFFREY A.
PERSONAL Born 01/25/1958, Valparaiso, IN **DISCIPLINE** ENGLISH, AMERICAN STUDIES **EDUCATION** Valparaiso Univ, BA, English/Humanities, 80; Univ Chicago, MA, English, 81; Univ Calif, Los Angeles, MFA, film/theater/television, 93. **CAREER** Lectr, English, Univ Illinois-Chicago, 81-82; instructor, Dept of Popular Culture, Bowling Green State Univ, 86-87; lecturer, writing programs, Univ Calif-Los Angeles, 87-99; lectr, Marshall School of Business, Univ Southern Calif, 99-. **HONORS AND AWARDS** Fulbright Fellowship to Great Britain, 84-86; honorable mention, Danforth Graduate Fellowship, 80. **MEMBERSHIPS** Natl Coun of Teachers of English, Conf on Coll Composition and Commun; Modern Language Assn. **RESEARCH** Writing; commun and pedagogy; Amer culture; politics; popular arts and media. **SELECTED PUBLICATIONS** Auth, "Students' Goals, Gatekeeping, and Some Questions of Ethics," College English, Mar 97; "The L.A. Riots: A Case Study of Debate Across the Political Spectrum," in Writing and Reading Across the Curriculum, 97; "Why College," College English, Mar 96; "Against 'Illegeracy': Toward a New Pedagogy of Civic Understanding," College Composition and Commun, May 94; coauth, "In Search of Lost Pedagogical Synthesis," College English, Nov 93. **CONTACT ADDRESS** 8533 Cashio St., 5, Los Angeles, CA 90035-3650. **EMAIL** smith@humnet.ucla.edu

SMITH, JOHN KARES
PERSONAL Born 06/29/1942, Oak Park, IL, m, 1968, 2 children **DISCIPLINE** COMMUNICATION STUDIES **EDUCATION** Northwestern Univ, BS, 64, MA, 65; Oxford Univ, postgraduate study, 71; Northwestern Univ, PhD, 74. **CAREER** Instr, speech, Benedictine Univ, 65-66, asst prof, 67-69; asst prof, 74-76, assoc prof, 77-85, prof, Communication Studies, State Univ of New York-Oswego, 86-. **HONORS AND AWARDS** IL State Scholar, 60-64; Oxford Univ, Univ College Scholar, 71; Northwestern Univ Graduate Assistantships, 69-71; Northwestern Univ fel, 71-72; Distinguished Humanities Scholar: A Learning Odyssey, NY Conference on Library Programming for Young Adults, 89; State of New York and United Univ Professions Excellence Awd for Professional Service, 91; Chancellor's Awd for Excellence in Teaching, SUNY, 93. **MEMBERSHIPS** Nat Commun Asn; Eastern Commun Asn; New York State Commun Asn; Oswego Opera Theatre, Inc. **RESEARCH** Presidential and political rhetoric; social movements theory; application of Internet resources in commun classrooms; infusing a Languages Across the Curriculum program into commun study, sponsored by the Languages Across the Curriculum Project. **SELECTED PUBLICATIONS** Auth, Upton Sinclair and the Celestial Crown: the Rhetoric of The Dead Hand Series, dissertation, Univ Microfilms, 74; Scarred Hopes Outworn: Unton Sinclair and the Decline of the Muckraking Movement, in Dieter Herms ed, Upton Sinclair: Literature and Social Reform, Peter Lang, 90; Why Shouldn't We Believe That? We Are Americans: Rhetorical Myths and Fantasies in the Reagan Inaugurals, in Ronald Reagan's America, vol II, ed by Eric Schmertz, Natalie Datlof and Alexej Ugrinsky, Greenwood Press, 97; Interdependence, Interaction and Influence: LAC in Communication 240: Group Interaction and Discussion, in Using Languages Across the Curriculum, ed by Virginia M Fichera and H Stephen Straight, Center for Research in Translation of State Univ of New York at Binghamton, 97; Once More Unto the Breach, Dear Friends: War in the Persian Gulf as a Rhetorical System, in George Bush, the Forty-First President, ed by William F Levantrosser and Rosanna Perotti, Greenwood Pub Co, 2000. **CONTACT ADDRESS** SUNY, Oswego, 3 Lanigan Hall, Oswego, NY 13126. **EMAIL** smith@oswego.edu

SMITH, JONATHAN
PERSONAL Born 11/05/1963, Alexandria, VA, m, 1988 **DISCIPLINE** ENGLISH **EDUCATION** Yale Univ, BA, 85; Univ Va, MA, 89; MEd, 89; PhD, 94. **CAREER** Vis Lecturer, Univ Wisc, 94-95; Vis Lecturer, Carroll Col, 94-95; Asst Prof, Miss State Univ, 95-. **HONORS AND AWARDS** Best Grad Instructor, Univ Va, 93; Recognition Awd, Miss State Univ, 97; Humanities & Arts Res Program Awd, Miss State Univ, 97. **MEMBERSHIPS** Mod Lang Asn, Am Lit Asn, Am Studies Asn, Nat Coun of Teachers of English, Conf on Col Composition and Comm, Soc for the Study of Southern Lit, Asn for the Study of Lit and the Environment, Am Soc for Environmental Hist, S Atlantic Mod Lang Asn. **RESEARCH** American Literature, US Southern Literature, Literature and the Environment, Inter-American Literature. **SELECTED PUBLICATIONS** Auth, "John Das Passos, Anglo-Saxon," Modern Fiction Studies, (98): 282-305; auth, "Faulkner, Galsworthy and the Bourgeois Apocalypse," The Faulkner Journal, (98): 131-145; auth, "The Wetly Boom!," Contemporary Literature, (95): 553-569. **CONTACT ADDRESS** Dept English, Mississippi State Univ, PO Box E, Mississippi State, MS 39762-5505. **EMAIL** jon@ra.msstate.edu

SMITH, JULIAN
PERSONAL Born 12/14/1937, New Orleans, LA, m, 1964, 3 children **DISCIPLINE** FILM STUDIES, AMERICAN LITERATURE **EDUCATION** Tulane Univ, BA, 59, MA, 62. **CAREER** Instr Eng, Spring Hill Col, 62-63; instr, Georgetown Univ, 63-65; instr Univ NH, 65-69; asst prof, Ithaca Col, 69-73; hon fel, Univ NH, 73-75; vis fac, San Diego State Univ, 75-76; Assoc Prof, 77-85, prof film studies, Univ FL, 85-. **HONORS AND AWARDS** Res grants, Nat Endowment for Hum, 70 & Am Coun Learned Soc, 79. **RESEARCH** Am film. **SELECTED PUBLICATIONS** Auth, Coming of age in America: Young Ben Franklin and Robin Molineux, Am Quart, 65; Hawthorne's Legends of the Province House, 19th Century Fiction, 69; Hemingway and the thing left out, J Mod Lit, 70; Looking Away: Hollywood and Vietnam, Scribner's, 75; Nevil Shute, In: Twayne English Authors Series, 76; The automobile in the American film, Mich Quart Rev, 80-81; Chaplin, Twayne Filmmakers Series, 84. **CONTACT ADDRESS** Dept of Eng, Univ of Florida, PO Box 117310, Gainesville, FL 32611-7310. **EMAIL** smithj@english.ufl.edu

SMITH, KAREN A.
PERSONAL Born 11/30/1965, Brooklyn, NY, s **DISCIPLINE** SPEECH COMMUNICATION **EDUCATION** CUNY, BA, 89; SUNY, MA, 92; S IL Univ, Carbondale, 96 **CAREER** Lect, 96-97, SIU-Carbondale; Asst Prof, 97-, Col of St Rose **MEMBERSHIPS** Nat Commun Asn **RESEARCH** Methods, Critical Pedagogy; mediated experience and everyday experience; television/media literacy and pedagogy; and popular culture influences. **CONTACT ADDRESS** Dept of Public Communications, Col of Saint Rose, 432 Western Ave., Albany, NY 12203. **EMAIL** ksmith@rosnet.strose.edu

SMITH, KIM A.
PERSONAL Born 01/15/1951, London, England, d, 2 children **DISCIPLINE** JOURNALISM, MASS COMMUNICATION **EDUCATION** Univ Wisc Madison, BA, 74; MA, 76; PhD, 78. **CAREER** Asst prof, Univ of Louisville, 77-80, 82-83; asst prof, E Carolina Univ, 83-86; assoc prof, Bowling Green State Univ, 86-89; assoc prof to prof, Iowa State Univ, 89-. **HONORS AND AWARDS** Master Teacher Nominee, Bowling Green State Univ, 87; Outstanding Teaching, Bowling Green State Univ, 87-88; Who's Who in the Midwest 99-; Who's Who in the US, 99-. **MEMBERSHIPS** Assoc for Educ in Jour and Mass Commun. **RESEARCH** Poltical communication, political socialization, media effects. **SELECTED PUBLICATIONS** Coauth, "Partisan Orientations and Use of Political Television", Jour Quarterly 67, (90): 864-874; auth, "Teaching the Undergraduate Research Methods Course", Teaching Mass Communication, ed Michael D. Murray, Praeger, 92; auth, "Children's Television Programming", Encyclopedia of Media History, ed Margaret Blanchard, Fitzroy Dearborn 98; auth, "Reactions to People with Disabilities: Personal Contact versus Viewing of Specific Media Portrayals", Jour Quarterly 76, (99): 659-672; auth, "Dick Cavett" and "Mike Wallce", Encycl of Television News, ed Michael Murray, Oryx, 99; auth, "Family Communication Patterns", "Voter Need for Orientation" and "Political Persuaders", Historical Dictionary of Political Communication in the United States, eds Guido Stempel and Jacqueline Nash Gifford, Greenwood, 99. **CONTACT ADDRESS** Greenlee Sch of Jour and Commun, Iowa State Univ, 122 Hamilton Hall, Ames, IA 50011. **EMAIL** kimsmith@iastate.edu

SMITH, L. RIPLEY
PERSONAL Born 06/04/1964, Thermopolis, WY, m, 1986, 4 children **DISCIPLINE** COMMUNICATION STUDIES **EDUCATION** Univ Dubuque, BA, 86; Univ Minn, MA, 90, PhD, 96. **CAREER** Grad teaching asst, Univ Minn, 89-92; adjunct prof, Concordia Col, St Paul, 90-93; assoc prof, chair, Northwestern Col, 92-. **HONORS AND AWARDS** Grad Teaching Awd, Univ of Minn. **MEMBERSHIPS** Int Commun Asn, Nat Commun Asn, Int Network of Social Network Analysts. **RESEARCH** Intercultural communication, refugee social networks and cultural adjustment, international networks and media influence. **SELECTED PUBLICATIONS** Auth, "Media-Networking: An Intercultural Communication Model for Global Management of Socio-Cultural Change," Int and Intercultural Commun Annual, 16 (92); auth, "Sending Management Technology Abroad: Crucial Communication Dimensions of Effecting a Management Technology Transfer to China," Commun and Theater Asn of Minn J, 19 (92); auth, "Kinesics in the Multicultural Classroom: An Analysis of Hispanics and Anglos," Ariz Commun Asn J, 19 (93); auth, "The Utility and Promise of a Socio-structural Approach to Acculturation," Int J of Intercultural Relations, 23, 4 (99); auth, "Foundations of Communication: An Instructor Curriculum Guide," Northwestern Pathway Prog, Assoc of Arts (2000); auth, "The Social Architecture of Communicative Competence: A Methodology For Social Network Research," Int J of the Sociol of Lang (in press). **CONTACT ADDRESS** Dept Commun, Northwestern Col, Minnesota, 3003 Snelling Ave N, Saint Paul, MN 55113-1501.

SMITH, LARRY
PERSONAL Born 02/11/1943, Stenbenu, OH, m, 1965, 3 children **DISCIPLINE** ENGLISH **EDUCATION** Muskingum Col, BA, 65; Kent State Univ, MA, 69; PhD, 74. **CAREER** Assoc prof to prof, Firelands Col, Bowling Green Univ, 78-. **HONORS AND AWARDS** NEH Summer Fel, 76; Fulbright Lectr, Italy, 80-81; Fel, Ohio Arts Coun, 97-98; Ohioana Poetry Awd, 99. **MEMBERSHIPS** Thoreau Soc; Am Studies Assoc. **RESEARCH** Working-Class Literature and Film, The Beat Movement, American Transcendental Movement. **SELECTED PUBLICATIONS** Auth, Kenneth Patchen, GK Hall Pub, (Twayne), 74; auth, Lawrence Ferlinghetti: Poet-At-Large, Southern IL Univ Pr, 83; auth, Beyond Rust, 96; auth, Working It Out, 99; auth, Kenneth Patchen: Rebel Poet in America, 00. **CONTACT ADDRESS** Dept Humanities, Firelands Col, 1 University Dr, Huron, OH 44839-9719. **EMAIL** lsmithdog@aol.com

SMITH, LARRY D.
DISCIPLINE COMMUNICATIONS **EDUCATION** Ohio State Univ, PhD, 86. **CAREER** Assoc prof, Purdue Univ. **RESEARCH** Presidential nominating conventions; television advertising; popular media. **SELECTED PUBLICATIONS** Auth, Reagan's Strategic Defense Initiative as Political Innovation, Polit Commun Rev, 90; Party Platforms as Institutional Discourse, Presidential Stud Quart, 92; coauth, Cordial Concurrence: Orchestrating National Party Conventions in the Telepolitical Age, Praeger, 91. **CONTACT ADDRESS** Dept of Commun, Purdue Univ, West Lafayette, 1080 Schleman Hall, West Lafayette, IN 47907-1080.

SMITH, LORRIE
PERSONAL Born 07/29/1953, Orange, NJ, m, 3 children **DISCIPLINE** AMERICAN POETRY **EDUCATION** Brown Univ, PhD. **CAREER** St. Michaels Col. **SELECTED PUBLICATIONS** Auth, Area: Literature of the Vietnam War. **CONTACT ADDRESS** Saint Michael's Col, Winooski Park, Colchester, VT 05439. **EMAIL** lsmith@smcvt.edu

SMITH, LOUISE
PERSONAL Born 05/24/1942, Grand Rapids, MI, m, 1965, 2 children **DISCIPLINE** ENGLISH **EDUCATION** Univ Mich, BA, 64; Univ Calif, MA, 66; Univ Va, PhD, 74. **CAREER** Editor-in-Chief, Col English, 92-99; Fulbright Sen Scholar, Institute fur anglistik, 97; Prof, Univ Mass, 74-. **HONORS AND AWARDS** Distinguished scholarship, Nat Coun of Teachers of English, 99; Outstanding Achievement Awd, Univ Mass, 99; Outstanding Achievement in Scholarship, Univ Mass, 86; Woodrow Wilson Foundation Fac Development Grant, 80; NEH summer stipend, 75; Woodrow Wilson Fel, Univ of Calif, 64; Regents' Scholar, Univ Mich, 60-64. **MEMBERSHIPS** Mod Lang Asn, Conf on Col Composition and Comm, Nat Coun of Teachers of English. **RESEARCH** 19th Century British literature; 20th Century American essay; Rhetoric and composition. **SELECTED PUBLICATIONS** Auth, "Make Me a Letter: Personal Criticism and The Epistolary Symposium," The Personal Narrative: Writing Ourselves as Teachers and Scholars, Calendar Islands Press, 99; auth, "Anonymous Review and the Boundaries of 'Intrinsic Merit,'", Journal of Information Ethics, (98): 54-67; auth, "Prosaic Rhetoric in Still Life and Personal Essays," Mosaic: A Journal for the Interdisciplinary Study of Literature, (98): 125-142; auth, "Homeless in the Golden Land: Joan Didion's Regionalism," Conversations: Rethinking American Literature, Nat Council of Teachers of English, 97; auth, "Beyond the 'Imaginary Museum': Interested Readings, Interesting Tropes," Reconceptualizing American Literary and Cultural Studies: Rhetoric, History, and Politics in the Humanities, Garland Pub, 96. **CONTACT ADDRESS** Dept English, Univ of Massachusetts, Boston, 100 Morrissey Blvd, Dorchester, MA 02125-3300. **EMAIL** louise.smith@umb.edu

SMITH, MADELINE C.
PERSONAL Born 10/09/1948, Middletown, NY **DISCIPLINE** ENGLISH **EDUCATION** Mount St Mary Col, BA, 71; SUNY NY, MA, 73; W Va Univ, PhD, 82. **CAREER** Fraud investigator, NY Dept of Soc Serv, 73-76; reporter, Port Jervis Union Gazette, 78-79; vis asst prof, W Va Univ, 84-85; asst prof, Christopher Newport Univ, 85-90; asst to prof, Calif Univ of Pa, 90-. **HONORS AND AWARDS** Christopher Newport Univ, 85, 88; Calif Univ of Pa, 95, 96, 99, 00. **MEMBERSHIPS** MLA, Eugene O'Neill sock, NEMLA, W Va Assoc of Col Eng Teachers, Am Conf of Irish Studies, Int Soc for the Study of Europ Ideas. **RESEARCH** Eugene O'Neill, American Drama. **SELECTED PUBLICATIONS** Auth, "Four Letters by Eurgene O'Neill," Eurene O'Neill Newsletter, (87); auth, Eugene O'Neill: An Annotated Bibliography, 1973-1985, Garland Publ, 88; auth, "Anna Christie's Baptism," Recorder, (89); auth, "More Roads to Xanadu," Eurgene O'Neill Rev, (91); auth, "The O'Neill-Komroff Connection," Eugene O'Neill Rev, (93); auth, "The Truth About Hogan," Eugene O'Neill Rev, (94); auth, "Beatrice Ashe and Eugene O'Neill," Philol Papers, (98); auth, "Con-Fusion: Con Melody's Identity Crisis," S Car Rev, (99); auth, Eugene O'Neill: An Annotated International Bibliography, 1973-1999, McFarland Publ, 01. **CONTACT ADDRESS** English Dept, California Univ of Pennsylvania, 229 Park St, Morgantown, WV 26501. **EMAIL** smith_mc@cup.edu

SMITH, MATTHEW
PERSONAL Born 01/31/1971, Wheeling, WV, s **DISCIPLINE** ARTS, COMMUNICATION **EDUCATION** W Liberty State Col, BA, 93; Ohio Univ, MA, 95; PhD, 98. **CAREER** Grad Teaching Assoc, Ohio Univ, 93-98; Vis Asst Prof, Miami Univ, 98-99; Asst Prof, Ind Univ, 99-. **HONORS AND AWARDS** Claude E Kantner Res Fel, 97-98. **MEMBERSHIPS** Nat Commun Asn, Eastern Commun Asn, Popular Cult Asn. **RESEARCH** Computer-mediated communication, popular culture, rhetorical discourse. **SELECTED PUBLICATIONS** Auth, "Publishing Online: Challenging standards of Hiring, Promotion and Tenure," Am Commun J; auth, "Stands in the Web: Community-Building Strategies in Online Franzines," J of Popular Cult (98); auth, Exploring Human Communication, Roxbury (Los Angeles, CA), 99; **CONTACT ADDRESS** Dept Arts, Indiana Univ, South Bend, PO Box 7111, South Bend, IN 46634-7111. **EMAIL** msmith4@ivsb.edu

SMITH, MICHAEL W.
PERSONAL Born 12/04/1963, Wheeling, WV, m, 2001 **DISCIPLINE** ENGLISH **EDUCATION** Va Tech, BS, 87; MA, 89; Fla State Univ, PhD, 95. **CAREER** Vis instr, Fla State Univ, 95; adj prof, Marshall Univ Grad Col, 97-; assoc prof, Bluefield State Col, Univ Pr of Va, (forthcoming). **HONORS AND AWARDS** Fac Achievement Award, Bluefield State Col, 99. **MEMBERSHIPS** MLA. **RESEARCH** Literary Theory. **SELECTED PUBLICATIONS** Auth, Reading Simulaera, SUNY, 01; auth, Fishing the New River Valley, Univ Pr Va, forthcoming. **CONTACT ADDRESS** 5738 Floyd Hwy S, Willis, VA 24380-4002. **EMAIL** msmith@swva.net

SMITH, NELSON C.
DISCIPLINE AMERICAN; CANADIAN LITERATURE **EDUCATION** Princeton Univ, AB; Oberlin Col, MAT; Univ Wash, PhD. **CAREER** Assoc prof; dir, Lit Prog. **HONORS AND AWARDS** Can Coun Leave fel, 73-74. **RESEARCH** 19th-century British fiction; mystery fiction; the novel. **SELECTED PUBLICATIONS** Pub(s), articles and rev(s), Col Composition and Commun, Melville Soc Newsl, SEL, ESC, Prairie Forum, Supernatural Fiction Writers, Sci Fiction Writers, Pop Fiction in Am, Dictionary of Lit Biogr, A Trollope Companion, Encycl of Can Lit; coauth, Language BC, 76; The Art of Gothic, 80; James Hogg, 80; co-ed, Wilkie Collins to the Forefront, 95. **CONTACT ADDRESS** Dept of English, Univ of Victoria, PO Box 3070, Victoria, BC, Canada V8W 3W1. **EMAIL** ncsmith@uvic.ca

SMITH, PAT CLARK
DISCIPLINE CREATIVE WRITING, POETRY, AMERICAN LITERATURE, AND WORLD LITERATURE **EDUCATION** Yale Univ, PhD, 70. **CAREER** Instr to prof, Univ NMex, 70-. **SELECTED PUBLICATIONS** Auth, Changing Your Story, 91; coed, Western Literature in a World Context, 95. **CONTACT ADDRESS** Dept of English, Lang and Lit, Univ of New Mexico, Albuquerque, 217 Humanities Bldg, Albuquerque, NM 87131.

SMITH, PATRICK J.
PERSONAL Born 09/07/1931, Menominee, MI, m, 1954, 7 children **DISCIPLINE** ENGLISH, FILM **EDUCATION** Marquette Univ, BS, 53, MA, 59; Univ Calif, Davis, PhD(English), 66. **CAREER** Assoc, Univ Calif, Davis, 62-64, assoc English, 64-66; PROF ENGLISH, UNIV SAN FRANCISCO, 66-, CHMN 78-, Publ, Pancake Press, 75-; assoc ed, Contemp Quart, 76; exec ed, San Francisco Rev Bks, 76-80. **RESEARCH** Modern English and American literature; film study and filmmaking; linguistics. **SELECTED PUBLICATIONS CONTACT ADDRESS** Dept of English, Univ of San Francisco, San Francisco, CA 94117.

SMITH, RALPH R.
DISCIPLINE PUBLIC RELATIONS **EDUCATION** Columbia Univ, PhD, 73. **CAREER** City Univ of Nyork, Mo State Univ **RESEARCH** Gender rhetoric; sexual orientation rhetoric. **CONTACT ADDRESS** Southwest Missouri State Univ, Springfield, 901 S. National, Ste. 50, Springfield, MO 65804-0094. **EMAIL** rrs953f@smsu.edu

SMITH, REBEKAH M.
DISCIPLINE CLASSICS **EDUCATION** Univ S, BA, 82; Univ NC, Chapel Hill, PhD, 91. **CAREER** Lectr, Univ NC, Chapel Hill. **HONORS AND AWARDS** Phi Beta Kappa, 80-82; tchg fel, Univ S, 80-82; Wilkins scholar, 80-81; Salutatorian, Class of 82; Green Latin Medal, 82. **SELECTED PUBLICATIONS** Auth, Photius on the Ten Attic Orators, Greek, Roman and Byzantine Stud 33, 92; Two Fragments of 'Longinus' in Photius, Class Quart 44, 94; A Hitherto Unrecognized Fragment of Caecilius, Am J of Philol 115, 4, 94; A New Look at the Canon of the Ten Attic Orators, Mnemosyne 48, 95. **CONTACT ADDRESS** Univ of No Carolina, Chapel Hill, Chapel Hill, NC 27599.

SMITH, RILEY BLAKE
PERSONAL Born 07/07/1930, Mexico, MO **DISCIPLINE** ENGLISH, LINGUISTICS **EDUCATION** Univ Tex, Austin, BA, 58, PhD, 73. **CAREER** Asst prof English, Tex A&M Univ, 68-70; actg asst prof, Univ Calif, Los Angeles, 70-72; lectr Anglistics, Univ Duisburg, Ger, 74-76 & Univ Wuppertal, Ger, 76-77; asst prof, 77-81, Assoc Prof English, Bloomsburg Univ, 81-; Fulbright lectr, Leningrad Polytech Inst, USSR, 81. **HONORS AND AWARDS** Nat Endowment for Humanities fel, summer sem, Univ Pa, 80; Fulbright Grantee, USSR, 81. **MEMBERSHIPS** Ling Soc Am; Am Dialect Soc; Teachers English to Speakers Other Lang; Ling Asn Can & US; Int Sociol Asn. **RESEARCH** American dialects; language attitudes; language policy. **SELECTED PUBLICATIONS** Auth, Interrelatedness of certain deviant grammatical structures of Negro nonstandard dialects, 3/69 & Hyperformation and basilect reconstruction, 3/74, J English Ling; Black English: Books for English education, English educ, 4-5/75; Research perspectives on American Black English: A brief historical sketch, Am Speech, 76; Interference in phonological research in nonstandard dialects: its implication for teaching, In: Soziolinguistik, Hochschulverlag, Stuttgart, 78; coauth, Standard and disparate varieties of English in the United States: Educational and sociopolitical implications, Int J Sociol Lang, 79. **CONTACT ADDRESS** Dept of English, Bloomsburg Univ of Pennsylvania, 400 E 2nd St, Bloomsburg, PA 17815-1399.

SMITH, ROBERT E.
DISCIPLINE LITERATURE AND COMMUNICATIONS **EDUCATION** Univ Mo, PhD, 69. **CAREER** Assoc prof; dir, basic crse, Purdue Univ. **RESEARCH** Writing of literature; performance of literature. **SELECTED PUBLICATIONS** Auth, Fundamentals of Oral Interpretation, 78; Principles of Human Communication, Kendall-Hunt, 91; The Outstanding Senior Award: A Realistic Small Group Decision-Making Exercise, The Speech Commun Tchr, 93. **CONTACT ADDRESS** Dept of Commun, Purdue Univ, West Lafayette, 1080 Schleman Hall, West Lafayette, IN 47907-1080. **EMAIL** resmith@sla.purdue.edu

SMITH, ROBERT MARK
PERSONAL Born 04/23/1960, Tulsa, OK, m, 1985, 2 children **DISCIPLINE** ENGLISH **EDUCATION** NE La Univ, BA, 82; Univ SW La, MA, 87; PhD, 92. **CAREER** Asst to assoc prof, Valdosta State Univ, 93-. **MEMBERSHIPS** MLA, Conf of Col Comp and Commun, Col English Asn, Soc of Tech Commun. **CONTACT ADDRESS** Dept English, Valdosta State Univ, Valdosta, GA 31698. **EMAIL** marksmit@valedosta.edu

SMITH, RONALD E.
DISCIPLINE COMPOSITION, DEVELOPMENTAL WRITING, TECHNICAL WRITING **EDUCATION** Mich State Univ, BA, 76, MA, 77; Ind Univ Pa, PhD, 88. **CAREER** Instr, Lansing Commun Col, 77-79; instr, Mary Holmes Col, 79-80; assoc prof Eng, Univ N Ala, 80-. **MEMBERSHIPS** NCTE; Conf on Col Compos and Commun; Asn of Tchr of Tech Writing; Asn of Col Eng Tchr of Ala. **SELECTED PUBLICATIONS** Auth, War Stories, N Am Rev, Jl/Aug, 92; auth, Secretaries as Producers of Text, Bull of Asn for Bus Commun, Dec, 92; auth, Yasunari Kawabata, Magill's Surv of World Lit, 93; auth, Community and Self in First Year Composition, ERIC Clearinghouse on Reading, Writing and Commun, Mar 95; auth, "Nick Adams and Post-Traumatic Stress Disorder," War, Literature, and the Arts (97). **CONTACT ADDRESS** Dept of English, Univ of No Alabama, Willingham Hall, UNA Box 5050, Florence, AL 35632-0001. **EMAIL** rsmith@unanov.una.edu

SMITH, ROWLAND
DISCIPLINE 20TH-CENTURY BRITISH LITERATURE **EDUCATION** Natal, BA; Oxon, MA; Natal, PhD. **CAREER** Prof. **RESEARCH** 20th-century British, Canadian, and post-colonial lit. **SELECTED PUBLICATIONS** Auth, "The Voyage Out: Exile, Escape and Obligation in Nadine Gordimer's Fiction," Voyages and Explorations: Southern African Writing, MATATU 11, (94): 51-7; auth, "Interview [Isabel Santolalla]: Pre-Fixing Colonialism, An Unfinished Business," Links and Letters 4, 97. **CONTACT ADDRESS** Dept of English, Wilfrid Laurier Univ, 75 University Ave W, Waterloo, ON, Canada N2L 3C5. **EMAIL** rsmith@mach2.wlu.ca

SMITH, SARAH
PERSONAL Born 12/09/1947, Boston, MA, m, 1979, 2 children **DISCIPLINE** ENGLISH **EDUCATION** Radcliffe Col, Harvard Univ, BA, 68; Slade Film School, London, 68-69; Harvard Grad School of Arts and Sciences, PhD, 75. **CAREER** Asst Prof, 76-82, Northeastern Univ, Tufts Univ & Boston Univ; Dept Mgr, 82-90, Computer Firms; Novelist, Consultant, 90-. **HONORS AND AWARDS** NY Times Notable Book of The Year-The Knowledge of Water, 96, The Vanished Child, 92; Woman of the Year Col Club of Boston, 97; Mellon Fel, Tufts Univ, 77; Bowdoin Prize, Harvard Univ, 75; Frank Know Fellow, Harvard, 72-73; Harvard Grad Prize Fel, 69-74; Fulbright Fel, 68-69; Phi Beta Kappa; member of contracts com; science ficton and fantasy writers of amer; reg bd mem; website dev; mystery writers of amer, 92. **MEMBERSHIPS** Science Fiction and Fantasy Writers of Amer, 88; Mystery Writers of Amer, 92; Sisters in Crime, 92; Cambridge Speculative Fiction Workshop, 86, Signet Soc, 74, Amnesty Intl, PEN/New England. **RESEARCH** 1890-1920, esp Feminism, socialism, the origins of WWI; hypermedia and non-paper based media. **SELECTED PUBLICATIONS** Auth, King of Space, Eastgate, 91; auth, The Vanished Child, Ballantine, 92; auth, Christmas at the Edge, Christmas Forever, Tor Books, 93; CoAuth Future Boston, Tor Books, 93; auth, Touched by the Bomb, Fantasy & Science Fict, 93; auth, When the Red Storm Comes or the History of a Young Womans Awakening to her Nature, in: Shudder Again, 93; auth, The Knowledge of Water, Ballantine Books, 96; auth, Doll Street, Tribune Media Svcs, 96; auth, Riders, Tribune Media Svcs, 97, auth, Fearful, Crime Through Time II, Berkley, 98; A Citizen of the Country, Ballantine, 00. **CONTACT ADDRESS** 32 Bowker St, Brookline, MA 02445-6955. **EMAIL** swrs@world.std.com

SMITH, SHAWN M.
DISCIPLINE AMERICAN LITERATURE **EDUCATION** Univ Calif San Diego, PhD **CAREER** Asst prof, Washington State Univ. **RESEARCH** American cultural studies,visual culture. **CONTACT ADDRESS** Dept of English, Washington State Univ, 1 SE Stadium Way, PO Box 645020, Pullman, WA 99164-5020. **EMAIL** smsmith@wsu.edu

SMITH, STEPHANIE A.
PERSONAL Born 04/30/1959, Oceanside, NY **DISCIPLINE** ENGLISH LITERATURE **EDUCATION** Boston Univ, BA, 81; Univ Calif, PhD, 90. **CAREER** Asst ed, W Imprints, 82-85; tchg asst, Univ Calif, 87-89; tchg assoc, Univ Calif, 89; asst prof, Univ of Fla, 90-95; assoc prof, Univ of Fla, 95-. **HONORS AND AWARDS** Phi Beta Kappa, Boston Univ, 79; Draper fel, Boston Univ, 81; outstanding tchg asst award, Univ Calif, 90; tchg improvement award excellence in tchg, 95-96; summer res grant, 91, 92, 97; NEH, 98; Einstein Forum in Potsdam, Germany, 99. **SELECTED PUBLICATIONS** Auth, Morphing, Materialism and the Marketing of Xenogenesis, Genders, 93; The Tender of Memory: Restructuring Value in Harriet Jacobs's Incidents in the Life of a Slave Girl, Harriet Jacobs and Incidents in the Life of a Slave Girl: New Critical Essays, Cambridge Univ Press, 95; Other Nature, St Martin's/TOR, 95; rev, Of The Culture of Sentiment, Women's Rev of Bk(s), Oxford, 93; auth, Conceived By Liberty: Maternal Figures and Nineteenth-Century American Literature, Cornell Univ Press, 94; auth, "Bombshell," in Body Politics and the Fictional Double, (Indiana UP, 00); co-ed, "Bloomers" in The Cambridge Guide to 19th Century American Women's Writing, ed. Dale Bauer and Philip Gould, (01); auth, "Suckers", in differences, special issue "Eating and Disorder", (Vol. 10, No. 1); auth, "Cyber (genetics)," in Genealogie und Genetik, series Einstein-Bucher, Akademie Verlag, Berlin, Germany, (01). **CONTACT ADDRESS** Dept of Eng, Univ of Florida, 4008 Turlington Hall, Gainesville, FL 32611. **EMAIL** ssmith@english.ufl.edu

SMITH, STEPHEN A.
DISCIPLINE METHODOLOGY OF COMMUNICATION RESEARCH **EDUCATION** Northwestern Univ, PhD. **CAREER** Comm Stu, Univ Ark. **HONORS AND AWARDS** Received the Fulbright Col Master Teacher Awd, 86; Lambda Pi Eta Nat Awd for Teaching Excellence, 98; Chancellor's Lectr, 93; awarded the SCA Golden Anniversary Monograph Awd; SCA Wichelns Awd for Communication and Law; SCA Haiman Awd for Scholarship in Freedom of Expression; SCA William O. Douglas Prize; SSCA Madison Prize; Arkansas Library Association's Arkansiana Awd; Fulbright Res Prize in Commun Studies; vis fel,univ wisc's la follette inst public affairs; vis fel, princeton univ; vis scholar, stanford law sch; andrew mellon fel, univ pa; vis fel wolfson coll, fac law, univ cambridge; vis scholar, st. benet' s hall; vis fel manchester col, univ oxford, vi **SELECTED PUBLICATIONS** Auth, Myth, Media and the Southern Mind, 85; Clinton on Stump, State and Stage: The Rhetorical Road to the White House, 94; Preface to the Presidency: The Speeches of Bill Clinton, 1974-1992, 96; auth, The Star Chamber, 98. **CONTACT ADDRESS** Dept of Commun, Univ of Arkansas, Fayetteville, 340 Rollston Ave, Fayetteville, AR 72701. **EMAIL** liberrtas@comp.uark.edu

SMITH, VONCILE MARSHALL
PERSONAL Born 03/17/1931, Ft Myers, FL, m, 1951, 5 children **DISCIPLINE** SPEECH COMMUNICATION, COMMUNICATION THEORY **EDUCATION** Univ Fla, BAEd, 60, MA, 64, PhD(speech), 66. **CAREER** Asst prof speech, 60-70, assoc prof, 70-78, prof Commun, Fla Atlantic Univ, 78-, Chm Dept Commun, 73-82, 94-98, ed, Fla Speech Commun J, 78-81; ed, J Int Listening Asn, 86-88. **HONORS AND AWARDS** Phi Kappa Phi. **MEMBERSHIPS** Nat Commun Asn; Southern States Commun Asn; Asn for Commun Admin; Fla Commun Asn. **RESEARCH** Studies in listening; interpersonal communication; communication theory. **SELECTED PUBLICATIONS** Coauth, Communication for Health Professionals, Lippincott, 79. **CONTACT ADDRESS** Dept of Commun, Col of Arts and Letters, Florida Atlantic Univ, PO Box 3091, Boca Raton, FL 33431-0991. **EMAIL** vsmith@acc.fau.edu

SMITHER, HOWARD ELBERT
PERSONAL Born 11/15/1925, Pittsburg, KS, m, 1946, 2 children **DISCIPLINE** HISTORICAL MUSICOLOGY **EDUCATION** Hamline Univ, AB, 50; Cornell Univ, MA, 52, PhD(musicol), 60. **CAREER** From instr to asst prof music, Oberlin Col, 55-60; asst prof, Univ Kans, 60-63; assoc prof, Tulane Univ, 63-68; assoc prof, 68-71, prof music, 71-79, dir grad studies music, 77-79, HANES PROF OF HUMANITIES IN MUSIC, UNIV NC, CHAPEL HILL, 79-, Fulbright res grant, Italy, 65-66; Nat Endowment for Humanities sr res fel, Italy, 72-73 & England, 79-80, Prof Emeritus, 91. **HONORS AND AWARDS** Deems Taylor Awd, Am Soc Composers, Authors & Publ, 78. **MEMBERSHIPS** Am Musicol Soc (pres, 80-82); Libr Asn; Int Musicol Soc. **RESEARCH** History of the oratorio; music in the Italian baroque; rhythmic techniques in 20th century music.; jazz history and performance. **SELECTED PUBLICATIONS** Auth, The rhythmic analysis of twentieth century music, J Music Theory, 64; The Latin dramatic dialogue, J Am Musicol Soc, 67; Narrative and dramatic elements in the Laude Filippine, 1563-1600, Acta Musicologica, 69; Domenico Alaleona's Studi su la storia dell'oratorio, Notes, 75; Carissimi's Latin oratorios, Analecta Musicologica, 76; The baroque oratorio: A report on research, Acta Musicologica, 76; A History of the Oratorio (vols 1 & 2), Univ NC, 77, vol 3, 87, vol 4, 00; Oratorio and sacred opera, 1700-1825, Proc Royal Musicol Asn, 79-80; Il-Tempio-Armonico--Music From The Oratorio-Dei-Filippini Of Rome: 1575-1705, Music & Letters, Vol 74, 93. **CONTACT ADDRESS** Dept of Music, Univ of No Carolina, Chapel Hill, Chapel Hill, NC 27514. **EMAIL** hes@email.unc.edu

SMITTEN, JEFFREY
PERSONAL Born 07/08/1941, Oakland, CA, m, 1988, 2 children **DISCIPLINE** ENGLISH **EDUCATION** Univ Calif, Berkeley, BA, 63; MA, 66; Univ Wis, Madison, PhD. **CAREER** Lectr, Humboldt State Col, 66-67; asst prof to prof, Texas Tech Univ, 72-90; Chair, Texas Tech Univ, 86-90, prof to Head, Utah State Univ, 90-. **HONORS AND AWARDS** Wis Res Studentship, Oxford; NEH Summer Fel; NEH Grant; Spencer A. Wells Fac Awd. **MEMBERSHIPS** Am Soc for Eighteenth-Centur Studies; MLA; Eighteenth Century Scottish Studies Soc; N Am Conf on British Studies. **RESEARCH** Eighteenth-century British literature; Scottish Enlightenment. **SELECTED PUBLICATIONS** Auth, "The Shaping of Moderation: William Robertson and Arminianism", Studies in Eighteen-Century Culture 22 (92):281-300; auth, "Hume's Dialogues Concerning Natural Religion as Social Discourse" in Sociability and Society in Eighteenth-Century Scotland, ed. John Dwyer and Richard B. Sher, (Edinburgh: Mercat, 93); coed, works of William Robertson, Thoemmes-Routledge, 96; ed, Dugald Stewart's Account of the Life and Writings of William Robertson, Thoemmes Pr, (Bristol), 97. **CONTACT ADDRESS** Dept English, Utah State Univ, 3200 Univ Blvd, Logan, UT 84322-3200. **EMAIL** jsmitten@english.usu.edu

SMOOT, JEANNE
PERSONAL Born 06/10/1943, Spartanburg, SC, m, 1965, 4 children **DISCIPLINE** LITERATURE **EDUCATION** Eckerd Col, BA, 64; Univ NC Chapel Hill, PhD, 68. **CAREER** Vis to Emeritus Prof, NC State Univ, 68-00; Dir, Office of Cand Prog, US Information Agency, Wash DC, 83-88. **HONORS AND AWARDS** N Am Treas - Int Comp Lit Asn Foler Fel, 98-00; Woodrow Wilson Fel; Woodrow Wilson Career Teaching Scholar; Fulbright Scholar, NEH Young Humanist Fel. **MEMBERSHIPS** Asn of Lit Scholars of Critics, Int Am and Southern Comp Lit Asn, Asn for Core Text and Core Courses. **RESEARCH** Literary relations in French, Spanish and British American literature, especially use of classical themes, motifs, and techniques in the drama, Educational Policy, International Exchange. **SELECTED PUBLICATIONS** Auth, The Poets and Time! A Comparison of Plays by John Millington Synge and Federico Garcia Lorca, Porrua, 78; auth, "What a College Professor Wishes Her Students Had Read," in What's At State in the K-12 Standard Wars, ed. Sandra Stotsky (Peter Lang Publ, 00). **CONTACT ADDRESS** Dept English, No Carolina State Univ, Box 8105, Raleigh, NC 27695-0001. **EMAIL** smoot@bellsouth.net

SNARE, GERALD
DISCIPLINE RENAISSANCE LITERATURE **EDUCATION** Univ CA at Santa Barbara, BA, 63; UCLA, PhD, 68. **CAREER** Instr, 88, Tulane Univ. **SELECTED PUBLICATIONS** Auth, The Countess of Pembroke's Ivychurch, Calif State UP, 75; The Mystification of George Chapman, Duke UP, 90; Grammatical Heresy and the Hermeneutics of Martin Luther, Renaissance Papers, 94; Glossing in Late Antiquity and the Renaissance, SP, 95. **CONTACT ADDRESS** Dept of Eng, Tulane Univ, 6823 St Charles Ave, New Orleans, LA 70118.

SNOW, HELENA
DISCIPLINE ENGLISH LITERATURE **EDUCATION** Univ Birmingham, Eng, graduated; Shakespearean Inst, PhD. **CAREER** Sr mem, Brit fac, Harlaxton Col; vis prof, 97. **RESEARCH** Shakespeare, particularly on the roles of his fools. **SELECTED PUBLICATIONS** Asst ed, Shakespeare Survey. **CONTACT ADDRESS** Dept of Eng, Univ of Evansville, 1800 Lincoln Ave, Evansville, IN 47714. **EMAIL** hsnow@harlaxton.edu.

SNYDER, DAVID W.
PERSONAL Born 03/21/1961, IN **DISCIPLINE** MUSIC EDUCATION **EDUCATION** Doctorate of music EDU , 96. **CAREER** Illinois state Univ, asst prof, 95-. **HONORS AND AWARDS** Teaching, Res, Ser Initiative Awds. **MEMBERSHIPS** CMS; MENC **RESEARCH** Teacher EDU ; pre-student teaching experience; classroom management. **CONTACT ADDRESS** Dept of Music, Illinois State Univ, Campus Box 5660, Normal, IL 61790. **EMAIL** dsnyder@ilstu.edu

SNYDER, EMERY
PERSONAL Born 08/04/1960, Bethlehem, PA **DISCIPLINE** LINGUISTICS & LITERATURE **EDUCATION** Princeton Univ, AB, 82; Harvard Univ, AM, 86; PhD, 92. **CAREER** Asst prof, Princeton Univ, 92-99; asst prof, Rutgers Univ, 99-00; info archit, igicom inc, 00-. **HONORS AND AWARDS** Harvard GSAS, 88; Whiting Found, 91-92; DAAD, 93; Harv Teach Awd. **MEMBERSHIPS** Asn Comput Mach. **RESEARCH** Early modern European literature; pragmatics; rhetoric; linguistics and literature; letters as a literary form. **SELECTED PUBLICATIONS** Auth, "Sketches of Johnson and Johnson's 'Skizze,,'" in Barock: Neue Sichtweisen (Wien: Bohlau, 94); auth, "Is Freud's model of the mind autopoietic?," Germ Rev 74 (99); auth, "Eine Problemstellung der Barocken Semiotik," Uwe-Johnson Jahrbuch (01). **CONTACT ADDRESS** igicom, 580 Broadway, Ste. 601, New York, NY 10012.

SNYDER, ROBERT LANCE
PERSONAL 3 children **DISCIPLINE** ENGLISH **EDUCATION** Univ Mich, BA, 67; Northwest Univ, MA, 68; PhD, 79. **CAREER** Instr, West Lib State Col, 68-71; grad teach asst, Northwest Univ, 71-74; instr, Wake For Univ, 74-78; asst prof, Geor Inst Tech, 79-84; assoc prof, Seat Pac Univ, 84-92; prof, State Univ West Geor, 92-. **HONORS AND AWARDS** Phi Kappa Phi,; Who's Who Hum, 92; NEH, 85; Phoenix Awd J Revit Coun of ELJ, Hon men, 90. **MEMBERSHIPS** MLA, SAMLA, CELJ, CCL, AAUP. **RESEARCH** Twentieth-century British literature; British romantic poetry and prose; philosophy, religion and literature; literary, theory and criticism. **SELECTED PUBLICATIONS** Auth, "Malory and 'Historical' Adaptation," Ess Lit (74); auth, "Apocalypse and Indeterminacy in Mary Shelley's The Last Man," Stud Roman (78); auth, "The Epistolary Melancholy of Thomas Gray," Biog, Int Qtly (79); auth, "Byron's Ontology of the Creating Self in Childe Harold," Buck Rev (80); auth, "Klosterheim: De Quincey's Gothic Masque," Res Stud (81); ed, Thomas de Quincy: Bicentenary Studies, Univ OK Press, 85; auth, "'The Loom of Palingenesis': De Quincey's Cosmology in 'System of the Heavens,'" Thomas de Quincy: Bicen Stud (85); auth, "De Quincey's Literature of Power: A Mythic Paradigm" Stud Eng Lit, 1500-1900 (86); auth, "De Quincey's Liminal Interspaces: 'On Murder Considered as one of the Fine Arts'" Nineteenth Cen Prose (01). **CONTACT ADDRESS** Eng Dept., State Univ of West Georgia, Carrollton, GA 30118-2200. **EMAIL** rsnyder@westga.edu

SNYDER, STEPHEN W.
DISCIPLINE ENGLISH LITERATURE **EDUCATION** Univ Idaho, BA; MA; Univ Fla, PhD. **CAREER** Assoc prof **RESEARCH** Italian cinema; contemporary literary criticism; 19th century American Literature; modern painting; cinematography. **SELECTED PUBLICATIONS** Auth, pub(s) on Vittorio De Sica. **CONTACT ADDRESS** Dept of English, Univ of Manitoba, Winnipeg, MB, Canada R3T 2N2. **EMAIL** wsnyder@cc.umanitoba.ca

SNYDER, SUSAN BROOKE
PERSONAL Born 07/12/1934, Yonkers, NY **DISCIPLINE** ENGLISH **EDUCATION** Hunter Col, AB, 55; Columbia Univ, MA, 58, PhD(Eng), 63. **CAREER** Lectr Eng, Queens Col, NY, 61-63; from instr to assoc prof, 63-75, chmn dept Eng, 75-80, Prof Eng, Swarthmore Col, 75-93, Eugene M. Lang res prof, 82-86; Gil and Frank Mustin Prof, 90-93; Nat Endowment for Hum fel, 67-68; Folger Shakespeare Libr sr fel, 72-73; Guggenheim fel, 80-81 Emer prof, 93-; Scholar in Residence, Folger Shakespeare Library 94-. **MEMBERSHIPS** Renaissance Soc Am, Council 79-81; Shakespeare Asn Am, Trustee 80-83; Ed Bd, Skaespeare Quarterly, 73-. **RESEARCH** Shakespeare; Spenser; Renaissance poetry. **SELECTED PUBLICATIONS** Ed, Sylvester's DuBartas, Oxford Univ, 79; The Comic Matrix of Shakespeare's Tragedies, Princeton Univ, 79; Othello: Critical Essays, Garland, 88; ed, All's Well That Ends Well, Oxford, 93; Pastoral Process, Stanford Univ, 98. **CONTACT ADDRESS** Folger Shakespeare Libr, 201 E Capitol St SE, Washington, DC 20008. **EMAIL** sbsnyder@worldnet.att.net

SOBRER, JOSEP MIQUEL
PERSONAL Born 09/01/1944, Barcelona, Spain, m, 1994, 3 children **DISCIPLINE** LITERATURE, LINGUISTICS **EDUCATION** Univ Barcelona, Lic, 66; Univ Ore, MA, 69; PhD, 72. **CAREER** Asst prof, Univ Puget Sound, 74-75; asst prof, Univ Mich, 75-81; asst prof to assoc prof to chmn to dir grad studies to prof, Univ Ind, 85-. **HONORS AND AWARDS** ACLS Fel, 79-80; NEH, 89; NACS Pres, 95-98. **MEMBERSHIPS** MLA; NACS. **RESEARCH** Current projects: A study of machismo in modern Spanish literature. A translation into English of Merce Rodoreda's Mirall trencat. **SELECTED PUBLICATIONS** Auth, La Doble Soledat d'Ausias March, Edicions dels Quadrens Crema (87); auth, Catalonia, a Self-Portrait, Ind UP, 92; auth, "Ironic Allegory in Terenci Moix's El Sexe dels Angels," Bulletin Hisp Studies 75 (98): 339-356; auth, "Man and Beast: the Nietzschean Heroics of Angel Guimera's Terra Baixa," Romance Quart 46 (99): 196-203. **CONTACT ADDRESS** Dept Foreign Lang, Indiana Univ, Bloomington, Bloomington, IN 47405. **EMAIL** sobrer@indiana.edu

SODERLIND, SYLVIA
DISCIPLINE ENGLISH LITERATURE **EDUCATION** Univ Toronto, PhD. **CAREER** Dept Eng, Queen's Univ **RESEARCH** Comparative postmodern fiction; modern Canadian and American literature; semiotics and literary theory; postcolonial literature. **SELECTED PUBLICATIONS** Auth, Margin/Alias: Language and Colonization in Canadian and Quebecois Fiction; pubs on postmodernism, Canadian, Quebecois and American fiction. **CONTACT ADDRESS** English Dept, Queen's Univ at Kingston, Kingston, ON, Canada K7L 3N6. **EMAIL** ss8@qsilver.queensu.ca

SOENS, A. L., JR.
DISCIPLINE LITERATURE **EDUCATION** Harvard Univ, PhD. **CAREER** Prof emer, Univ Notre Dame. **RESEARCH** The history of fencing and arms. **SELECTED PUBLICATIONS** Wrote on Shakespeare and other dramatists and edited Sidney's Defense of Poetry. **CONTACT ADDRESS** Dept of English, Univ of Notre Dame, Notre Dame, IN 46556.

SOFER, ANDREW
DISCIPLINE ENGLISH **EDUCATION** Hebrew Univ, BA, 87; Boston Univ, MFA, 90; Univ Mich, PhD, 98. **CAREER** Asst prof, Boston Col, 99-. **HONORS AND AWARDS** Univ Mich Fel, 97-98; Mellon Found Fel, 96; Hebrew Univ Fel, 87-88; Moscow Prize, 98; Heberle Essay Prize, Univ Mich. **MEMBERSHIPS** ASTR; ATDS; MLA; ATHE; SAA; TCG. **RESEARCH** Modern and contemporary drama; renaissance drama; performance and dramatic theory. **SELECTED PUBLICATIONS** Auth, "Self Consuming Artifacts: Power, Performance and the Body in Tennessee William's 'Suddenly Last Summer,'" Mod Drama 38 (95): 336-47; auth, "Felt Absences: The Stage Properties of Othello's Handkerchief," Comp Drama 31 (97): 367-93; auth, "The Skull on the Renaissance Stage: Imagination and the Erotic Life of Props," English Lit Renaissance 28 (98): 47-74; auth, "Absorbing Interests: Kyd's Bloody Handkerchief as Palimpsest," Comp Drama 34 (00): 127-53; auth, "From Technology to Trope: The Archbishop's Ceiling and Arthur Miller's Prismatic Drama," in Arthur Miller's America: Theater and Culture in a Century of Change, ed. Enoch Brater (Univ Mich Pr, forthcoming). **CONTACT ADDRESS** English Dept, Boston Col, Chestnut Hill, 438 Carney Hall, Chestnut Hill, MA 02467. **EMAIL** sofer@bc.edu

SOL, ADAM
PERSONAL Born 12/25/1969, New York, NY, m, 1 child **DISCIPLINE** ENGLISH **EDUCATION** Tufts Univ, BA, 91; Ind Univ, MFA, 95; Univ Cincinnati, PhD, 00. **HONORS AND AWARDS** Tennessee Williams Scholarship, 97; Midlist Pr First Series Awd, 99; Jacob Rader Marcus Ctr Fel, 00-01; Can Counc Grant for Writers, 01. **MEMBERSHIPS** MLA, AJHS. **RESEARCH** Jewish American Literature, Creative Writing, Contemporary Ethnic Literature, American Poetry. **SELECTED PUBLICATIONS** Auth, "Searching for Middle Ground in Abraham Cahan's 'The Rise of David Levinsky' and Sidney Nyburg's 'The Chosen People,'" Studies in Am Jewish lit 16, (97); auth, "The Story As It's Told: Prodigious Revisions in Leslie Marmon Silko's 'Almanac of the Dead,'" Am Indian Quart 23.3&4, (99); auth, Jonah's Promise, Midlist Pr, 00; auth, "Mark Richard," Dict of Lit Biog 234, Am Short-Story Writers Since World War II, ed Patrick Meanor, (Boston: Gale Publ, 00); auth, " American Jewish Poetry," Reader's Guide to Judaism, ed Michael Terry, (Chicago: Fitzroy Dearborn, 00). **CONTACT ADDRESS** 65 Lawrence Ave, Toronto, ON, Canada M4N 1S5. **EMAIL** adamyael@interlog.com

SOLDATI, JOSEPH ARTHUR
PERSONAL Born 09/27/1939, Rochester, NH, d **DISCIPLINE** AMERICAN & EUROPEAN LITERATURE **EDUCATION** Oglethorpe Univ, BA, 61; Univ Calif, Santa Barbara, MA, 68; Wash State Univ, PhD(English), 72. **CAREER** Teaching asst, Wash State Univ, 68-71, asst prof, 71-72; asst prof English, 72-76, assoc prof, 76-80, Prof Humanities, Western Ore Univ, 80-97; prof emer, 97-. **HONORS AND AWARDS** NEH Summiner Seminar, 79 & 82; Fulbright fel, Mansoura Univ, Egypt, 83-84, Cote d'Ivoire, West Africa, 89-90; Salzburg fel, Salzburg, Austria, 10/84; Teacher of the Year, Western Ore Univ, 93-94; Icarus Int Poetry Awd, 00. **MEMBERSHIPS** Phi Kappa Phi; Asn Literary Scholars & Critics; Mountian Writers (Portland, Ore); Friends of William Stafford. **RESEARCH** American Romantic Movement; Afro-American poetry, Modern poetry, Comparative religion. **SELECTED PUBLICATIONS** Auth, The Americanization of Faust: A study of Brockden Brown's Wieland, Emerson Soc Quart, 1/74; Cosmic instability and modern man, Kronos: J Interdisciplinary Synthesis, summer 75; Functions of color in poetry, Essays in Lit, spring 77; Configurations of Faust: Three Studies in the Gothic 1798-1820, Arno Press, 80; Talking like gods: New voices of authority, In: Pagan and Christian Anxiety: A Response to E R Dodds, Univ Press Am, 84; Making My Name (poems), Mellen Poetry Press, 92; co-auth, O Poetry! Oh Poesia! Poems of Oregon and Peru, Western Ore Univ & Cuardernos Trimestrales de Poesia, Trujillo, Peru, 97; auth, "Homer's Self-Portraits: Phemius and Demodocus in the 'Odyssey,'" Arcturus (00); auth, "The Sound of Bone on Wood: Captain Ahab's Funeral March in 'Moby Dick,'" Arcturus (00); auth, "Lessons of the Loon: Henry David Thoreau's 'Walden,'" The Larcom Rev (01). **CONTACT ADDRESS** 710 NW Naito Pkwy, C-20, Portland, OR 97209-3779. **EMAIL** joesol@aol.com

SOLEY, LAWRENCE C.
PERSONAL Born 11/01/1949, Minneapolis, MN, m, 1984, 3 children **DISCIPLINE** MASS COMMUNICATION **EDUCATION** Cal St Univ, BA, 74; MA, 76; Mich St Univ, PhD, 81. **CAREER** Asst prof, Penn St Univ, 81-82; asst prof, Univ Geo, 82-83; asst prof to assoc prof, Baruch Coll, 83-87; assoc prof to prof, Univ Minn, 97-92; prof, Marq Univ, 92-. **HONORS AND AWARDS** Sigma Delta Chi Awd; AAA Bst Art Awd; Proj Cen Awd. **MEMBERSHIPS** NCA. **RESEARCH** Propaganda; underground media; private restrictions on public discourse. **SELECTED PUBLICATIONS** Auth, Clandestine Radio Broadcasting, Praeger, 87; auth, Radio Warfare, Praeger, 89; auth, The News Shapers, Praeger, 92; auth, Leasing the Ivory Tower, South End, 95; auth, Free Radio, Westview, 98. **CONTACT ADDRESS** Dept Journalism, Marquette Univ, PO Box 1881, Milwaukee, WI 53201-1881. **EMAIL** soleyl@marquette.edu

SOLLORS, WERNER
PERSONAL m, 2 children **DISCIPLINE** ENGLISH; AMERICAN STUDIES **EDUCATION** Freie Universitaet Berlin, Germany, PhD, 75. **CAREER** Asst prof, Berlin, 75-78; Columbia Univ, 78-82; assoc prof, Columbia Univ, 82-83; prof, Harvard Univ, 83- . **HONORS AND AWARDS** Guggenheim fel; Andrew W. Mellon fel; Constance Rouske Prize. **MEMBERSHIPS** MLA; ASA; OAH; ACLA. **RESEARCH** Am Studies; Comp Lit. **SELECTED PUBLICATIONS** Auth, Beyond Ethnicity: Consent and Descent in American Culture, 86; The Return of Thematic Criticism, 93; Theories of Ethnicity: A Classical Reader, 96; Neither Black Nor White Yet Both: Thematic Explorations of Interracial Literature, 97; Multilingual America: Transnationalism, Ethnicity, and the Languages of American Literature, 98; The Multilingual Anthology of American Literature: A Reader of Original Texts with English Translations, 00; Interracialism: Black-White Inter marriage il American History, Literature, and Law, 00. **CONTACT ADDRESS** Barker Center, Harvard Univ, 12 Quincy Ave, Cambridge, MA 02138. **EMAIL** amciv@fas.harvard.edu

SOLODOW, JOSEPH B.
PERSONAL Born 11/13/1946, Brooklyn, NY, m, 1967 **DISCIPLINE** CLASSICS **EDUCATION** Columbia Univ, AB, 67; Harvard Univ, MA, 69; PhD, 71. **CAREER** Instr, Univ Mass, 70-71; asst prof, Columbia Univ, 71-77; assoc prof, Bard col, 77-83; adj assoc prof, Boston col, 83-84; vis assoc prof, Columbia Univ, 84-85; vis res scholar, Yale Univ, 85-88; vis assoc prof, Univ Calif, 88-89; vis assoc prof, Stanford Univ, 88; vis assoc prof, Univ Calif, 89-90; vis assoc prof, State Univ New York, 90-92; asst to full prof, Southern Conn State Univ, 92-99; vis prof, Yale Univ, 00-. **HONORS AND AWARDS** Phi Beta Kappa, 67; Rome Prize, Am Acad in Rome, 80-81; Scaglione Translation Prize, Mod Lang Asn, 95. **MEMBERSHIPS** AAUR, Am Philol Asn. **RESEARCH** Latin literature and philology, Spanish-American literature. **SELECTED PUBLICATIONS** Auth, " Ars Poetica," New England Classical Newsletter, (91): 42-45; auth, "Persistence of Virgilian Memories," Liverpool Classical Monthly (89): 119-121; auth, "Forms of Literary Criticism in Catullus: Polymetric vs. Epigram," Classical Philology, (89): 312-319; auth, "The Canon of Texts for a Latin Data Bank," Favoniu, (87): 21-24; auth, "On Catullus 95," Classical Philology, (87): 141-145; auth, "Ravcae, Tva Cvra, Palvmbes: Study of a Poetic Word Order," Studies in Classical Philology, (86): 129-153; auth, "Livy and the Story of Horatius, 1.24-26," Transactions of the Philological Associations, (79): 251-268; auth, The Latin Particle Quidem, American Classical Studies, American Philological Asn: Boulder, 78; auth, The World of Ovid's Metamorphoses, Univ NC: Chapel Hill, 88; auth, "Poeta Impotens: the Last Three Eclogues," Latomus 36 (77): 757-771. **CONTACT ADDRESS** Dept For Lang, So Connecticut State Univ, 501 Crescent St, New Haven, CT 06515-1330. **EMAIL** solodow@southernet.edu

SOLOMON, ANDREW JOSEPH
PERSONAL Born 11/15/1944, New York, NY, d, 1 child **DISCIPLINE** ENGLISH LITERATURE, CREATIVE WRITING **EDUCATION** Univ Pittsburgh, BA, 66, MA, 70, PhD, 74. **CAREER** Asst prof, 75-80, dir creative writing prog, 75-, assoc prof to prof, Eng, Univ Tampa, 80-92. **MEMBERSHIPS** MLA; Shakespeare Assn Am; Natl Book Critics Circle **RESEARCH** The writing of fiction; Shakespeare. **SELECTED PUBLICATIONS** Art, Jim and Huck: Magnificent misfits, Mark Twain J, winter 72; auth, A reading of The Tempest, In: Shakespeare's Late Plays, Ohio Univ, 75; art, Oh His Kindness (poetry), Atlantic Monthly, 12/77; art, Use of Progress Intensive journal in creative writing courses, Fla English J, 4/82. **CONTACT ADDRESS** Dept of English, Univ of Tampa, 401 W Kennedy Blvd, Tampa, FL 33606-1490.

SOLOMON, BARBARA HOCHSTER
PERSONAL Born 09/25/1936, Brooklyn, NY, m, 1958, 2 children **DISCIPLINE** AMERICAN LITERATURE, WOMEN'S STUDIES **EDUCATION** Brooklyn Col, BA, 58; Univ Kans, MA, 60; Univ Pittsburgh, PhD(English), 68. **CAREER** Instr English, Doane Col, 60-62; adv to undergrads, Univ Pittsburgh, 63-65; instr, Temple Univ, 65-67; asst prof, 69-73, assoc prof, 73-80, PROF ENGLISH, IONA COL, 80- **MEMBERSHIPS** MLA **RESEARCH** The American heroine in nineteenth and twentieth century American literature. **SELECTED PUBLICATIONS** Ed, Short Fiction of Sarah Orne Jewett and Mary Wilkins Freeman, New Am Lib, 79; ed, Ain't We Got Fun: Essays, Lyrics and Stories of the Twenties, New Am Lib, 80; co-ed with Paula Berggren, A Mary Wllstonecraft Reader, New Am Lib, 83; ed, American Wives: Thirty Stories by Women, New Am Lib, 86; ed, American Families, New Am Lib, 89; ed, Other Voices, Other Vistas: Twenty-Five Non-Western Stories, New Am Lib, 92; ed, Herland and Selected Stories of Charlotte Perkins Gilman, New Am Lib, 92; ed, Rediscoveries: American Short Sotries by Women, 1832-1916, New Am Lib, 94; ed, Bernice Bobs Her Hair and Other Stories of F. Scott Fitzgerald, Dutton/Signet, 96; ed, Critical Essays on Toni Morrison's Beloved, Twayne, 98. **CONTACT ADDRESS** Dept of English, Iona Col, 715 North Ave, New Rochelle, NY 10801-1890.

SOLOMON, H. ERIC
PERSONAL Born 10/08/1928, Boston, MA, m, 1954, 2 children **DISCIPLINE** ENGLISH **EDUCATION** Harvard Univ, BA, 50, MA, 52, PhD, 58. **CAREER** Teaching fel English, Harvard Univ, 51-53 & 55-58; from instr to asst prof, OH State Univ, 58-64; assoc prof, 64-68, Prof English, San Francisco State Univ, 68-; Am Philos Soc travel grant, 61-62. **MEMBERSHIPS** Am Studies Asn; MLA. **RESEARCH** Am literature; 19th century fiction. **SELECTED PUBLICATIONS** Auth, The Faded Banners: An Anthology of 19th Century Civil War Fiction, Yoseloff, 58; The incest theme in Wuthering Heights, 19th Century Fiction, 6/59; Huckleberry Finn once more, 12/60 & Jane Eyre: Fire and water, 12/63, Col English; Stephen Crane in England, Ohio State Univ, 64; Stephen Crane: From Parody to Realism, Harvard Univ, 66. **CONTACT ADDRESS** Dept of English, San Francisco State Univ, 1600 Holloway Ave, San Francisco, CA 94132-1740.

SOLOMON, JACK
DISCIPLINE ENGLISH **EDUCATION** Brandeis Univ, BA, 76; Harvard Univ, MA, 78; PhD, 81. **CAREER** Asst prof, Univ Calif, Los Angeles, 81-90; asst prof to prof, Cal State Univ Northridge, 91-. **HONORS AND AWARDS** Phi Beta Kappa, 76. **RESEARCH** Semiotics, popular culture, cultural studies. **SELECTED PUBLICATIONS** Auth, Discourse and Reference in the Nuclear Age, 85; auth, The Signs of Our Time: the Secret Meanings of Everyday Life, 90; coauth, California Dreams and Realities: Readings for Critical Thinkers and Writers, 99; coauth, Signs of Life in the USA: Readings on Popular Culture for Writers, 00. **CONTACT ADDRESS** Dept English, California State Univ, Northridge, 18111 Nordhoff St, Northridge, CA 91330-0001. **EMAIL** james.solomon@csun.edu

SOLOMON, JULIE R.
PERSONAL Born 02/25/1955, Washington, DC, m, 1988 **DISCIPLINE** ENGLISH LITERATURE **EDUCATION** Univ Md, BA, 77; Univ Pa, MA, 82; PhD, 87. **CAREER** Asst prof, Ohio State Univ, 87-88; asst to assoc prof, Am Univ, 88-. **HONORS AND AWARDS** NEH Newberry Libr Fel, 90-91; ACLS Fel, 97-98. **MEMBERSHIPS** MLA, Shakespeare Soc of Am, Renaissance Soc of Am. **RESEARCH** Renaissance literature and addiction. **SELECTED PUBLICATIONS** Auth, Objectivity in the Making: Francis Bacon and the Politics of Inquiry, Johns Hopkins Univ Pr, 98. **CONTACT ADDRESS** American Univ, 4400 Massachusetts Ave NW, Washington, DC 20016. **EMAIL** jsolomo@american.edu

SOLOMON, STANLEY J.
PERSONAL Born 01/03/1937, New York, NY, m, 1958, 2 children **DISCIPLINE** ENGLISH **EDUCATION** Brooklyn Col, BA, 57; Univ Kans, MA, 60; Temple Univ, PhD, 68. **CAREER** Instr, Doane Col, 60-62 & Chatham Col, 62-64; asst prof, Temple Univ, 67-68; from instr to assoc prof, 68-72, chmn, Dept English, 71-74, Dir Film Stud, 71-72, Dir Mass Commun, 73-76; prof emeritus, Iona Col, 72-, Chmn, New Rochelle Coun Arts, 76; Dir, Multi-Image Ctr, 79-90. **MEMBERSHIPS** MLA; AAUP. **RESEARCH** Samuel Johnson; Film studies; Multi-media production. **SELECTED PUBLICATIONS** Auth, The Film Idea, 72 & ed, The Classic Cinema, 73, Harcourt; Beyond Formula: American Film Genres, Harcourt, 76; Film Genres, Writing and Film Genres, 82; Aristotle in twilight, Studies in the Literary Imagination, 83; Subverting propriety, Literature Criticism from 1400-1800, 85; Detective as moralist, A Short Guide to Writing about Literature, 85; They Know Where I Live, Alfred Hitchcock Mystery Mag, 92; Gift Givers, Alfred Hitchcock, Mystery Mag,93; Barterers, Raconteur Mag, 96; Columnist, Casino Mag, 94-96; Corresponding effects, artless writing in the age of e-mail, Mod Age, 98. **CONTACT ADDRESS** English Dept, Iona Col, 715 North Ave, New Rochelle, NY 10801-1890. **EMAIL** ssolomon@iona.edu

SOLOSKI, JOHN
PERSONAL Born 11/18/1952, New York, NY, m, 1974, 2 children **DISCIPLINE** JOURNALISM & MASS COMMUNICATION **EDUCATION** Boston Col, AB, 74; Univ Iowa, MA, 76, PhD(Mass Commun), 78. **CAREER** From instr to assoc prof, 77-92, prof jour & mass commun, Univ Iowa, 92-, dir, Sch Jour & Mass Commun, 96-, head, grad studies, 85-95; vis fac mem, Univ Technology, Sydney, Australia, Prof/Dir, Daniel and Amy Starch, 00. **HONORS AND AWARDS** Fel, Open Soc Inst; Distinguished Service Awd for Research About Journalism, for Libel and the Press (book), Soc Professional Jour, Sigma Delta Chi, 87. **MEMBERSHIPS** Asn Educ Jour & Mass Commun; Int Commun Asn. **RESEARCH** Media law; media economics. **SELECTED PUBLICATIONS** Coauth, Libel and the Press: Myth and Reality, The Free Press, 87; co-ed, Reforming Libel Law, Guilford Publ, 92; coauth, On Defining the Nature of Graduate Education, Jour Educ, Summer 94; coauth, Sullivan's Paradox: The Emergence of Judicial Standards for Journalism, NC Law Rev 73, 94; auth, The United States Libel System, Medialine, Summer 96/97; coauth, The New Media Lords: Why Institutional Investors Call the Shots, Columbia Jour Rev, Sept-Oct/96. **CONTACT ADDRESS** Sch Jour & Mass Commun, Univ of Iowa, Iowa City, IA 52242. **EMAIL** john-soloski@uiowa.edu

SOMMER, DORIS
PERSONAL Born 01/15/1947, Germany, m, 1975, 2 children **DISCIPLINE** LITERATURE **EDUCATION** Douglass Col, BA, 68; Hebrew Univ Jerusalem, MA, 70; Rutgers Univ, PhD, 77. **CAREER** Asst prof, Rutgers Univ, 77-80; prof, Amherst Col, 80-91; prof, Harvard Univ, 91- . **HONORS AND AWARDS** NEH Fel, 83-84; Guggenheim Fel, ACLS Fel, 93-94. **MEMBERSHIPS** LASA; MLA. **RESEARCH** Ethnic literature of the Americas; national and gender constructions in literature. **SELECTED PUBLICATIONS** Auth, Foundational Fictions: The National Romances of Latin America, Univ of Cal Pr, 93; auth, Proceed with Caution when Engaged by Minority Literatures of the Americas, Harvard Univ Pr, 99. **CONTACT ADDRESS** 50 S School St, Portsmouth, NH 03801. **EMAIL** dsommer@fas.harvard.edu

SOMMERS, LAURIE.
PERSONAL Born 01/18/1955, Lansing, MI, m, 1995 **DISCIPLINE** WORLD MUSIC, FOLK AND ETHNIC MUSIC **EDUCATION** Univ Mich, BA; Ind Univ, MA, PhD. **CAREER** Adj prof, Valdosta State Univ; pub sector folklorist, ethnomusicologist, Ind Div of State Parks, Bur of Fla Folklife, Smithsonian Inst; folklife spec, cur, Mich State Univ Mus, 87-95; dir, S Ga folklife proj. **HONORS AND AWARDS** Society for Ethnomusicology; Am Folklore Society. **RESEARCH** Musics of the Americas; regional and ethnic music traditions of North America. **SELECTED PUBLICATIONS** Auth, Beaver Island House Party; Fiesta, Fe, y Cultura: Celebrations of Faith and Culture in Detroit's Colonia Mexicana; Anatomy of a Folklife Festival: Michigan on the Mall. **CONTACT ADDRESS** South Georgia Folklife Project, Valdosta State Univ, 1500 N. Patterson St, Valdosta, GA 31698. **EMAIL** lsommers@valdosta.edu

SONKOWSKY, ROBERT PAUL
PERSONAL Born 09/16/1931, Appleton, WI, m, 1956, 3 children **DISCIPLINE** CLASSICS **EDUCATION** Lawrence Col, AB, 54; Univ NC, PhD, 58. **CAREER** Teaching asst, Univ NC, 55-56, teaching fel, 57-58; from instr to asst prof classics, Univ Tex, 58-61; assoc prof, Univ Mo, 62-63; chmn dept, 64-78, assoc prof Classics, Speech & Theatre Arts, Univ Minn, Minneapolis, 63-, Johnson fel, Inst Res Humanities, 61-62; vis prof, Univ of Colo, 68; selection juror, Am Acad Rome Fels, 70; distinguished Marbook vis prof, Macalester Col, 89. **HONORS AND AWARDS** U of Minn Distance Education Awd: Interactive TV. **MEMBERSHIPS** Am Philol Asn: Class Asn Mid W & S; Int Soc Chronobiol; Classical Asn of Atlantic States; Soc for the Oral Reading of Greek and Latin Lit. **RESEARCH** Ancient rhetoric and drama; Latin lit; oral performance. **SELECTED PUBLICATIONS** Auth, An Aspect of Delivery in Ancient Rhetorical Theory, Trans & Proc Am Philol Asn, 59; Scholarship and Showmanship, 61 & Greek Euphony and Oral Performance, 67, Arion; A Fifteenth Century Rhetorical Opusculum, Class Medieval & Renaissance Studies for B L Ullman, 69; Euphantastik Memory and Delivery in the Classical Rhetorical Tradition, Rhetoric, Brown & Steinmann, 79; Recordings: selections from Cicero, Vergil, Cattullus, Horace, Ovid, Jeffrey Norton, In: Oedipus in Oedipus Rex, Digital Excellence, Inc. **CONTACT ADDRESS** Dept of Classical and near Eastern Studies, Univ of Minnesota, Twin Cities, 9 Pleasant St S E, Minneapolis, MN 55455-0194. **EMAIL** sonko001@tc.umn.edu

SORKIN, ADAM J.
PERSONAL Born 08/09/1943, New York, NY, m, 1964, 2 children **DISCIPLINE** AMERICAN LITERATURE PROSE FICTION, TRANSLATION OF CONTEMPORARY ROMANIAN LITERATURE **EDUCATION** Cornell Univ, AB, 64, MA, 65; Univ NC, PhD, 72. **CAREER** Instr Eng, Univ IL, Chicago Circle, 65-66; instr Eng & Am lit, Univ NC, Chapel Hill, 70-71; instr, Stockton State Col, 71-73; instr, Drexel Univ & Community Col Philadelphia, 73; asst prof Eng & Am lit, Bluefield State Col, 74-78; from Asst Prof to Prof Eng, PA State Univ, 78-; Fulbright lectr, Univ Bucharest, Romania, 80-81. **HONORS AND AWARDS** NEH Summer Seminar, 75; IREX Fel, 91; Rockefeller Found Residency, Study and Conf Ctr, Italy, 95; Recommended Transl, Poetry Bk Soc, for The Sky Behind the Forest, 97; The Sky Behind the Forest shortlisted for Weidenfeld Prize for Translation, 97; Crossing Boundaries Translation Awd, Int Quart, for The Europ Mechanism, Fall 97; Story Short Short Competition winner, 14th place, for The Telephone, 97; Kenneth Rexroth Memorial Translation Prize, for Marta Petrey translations, 99. **MEMBERSHIPS** Am Lit Translr(s) Asn. **RESEARCH** Am lit; Romanian lit; mod lit. **SELECTED PUBLICATIONS** Ed, Politics and the Muse: Studies in the Politics of Recent American Literature, Bowling Green State Univ Popular Press, 89; Conversations with Joseph Heller, Literary Conversations Series, Univ Press MS, 93; auth, Marin Sorescu: Comedian of Antiheroic Resistance, Romanian Civilization, Summer 92; Half in Flight Half in Chains: The Paradoxical Vision of Iona Ieronim's Poetry, Conn Rev, Fall 95; Petre Stoica's Tiananmen Square II: Anger, Protest, and an Angel with a Crow's Wings, Romanian Civilization, Winter 95-96; Liliana Ursu's Poetry, Delos: A J Transl & World Lit 18, 96; The Forbidden World and Hidden Words: Steadfast Illumination in Marin Sorescu's Poems Selected by Censorship, Romanian Civilization, Fall 96; Postmodernism in Romanian Poetry: The Abnormally Normal, Romania & Western Civilization / Romania si civilizatia occidentala, Iasi: The Ctr for Romanian Studies, 97; On The Circle by Martin Sorescu, Two Lines: A J of Transl, Spring 97; I Was of Three Minds: Some Notes on Translating, Metamorphoses, April 98; author of numerous other articles, translator of short stories and hundreds of poems in 13 books and in 200 literary magazines. **CONTACT ADDRESS** Eng Dept, Pennsylvania State Univ, Delaware County, 25 Yearsley Mill Rd, Media, PA 19063-5596. **EMAIL** ajs2@psu.edu

SORUM, CHRISTINA ELLIOTT
DISCIPLINE CLASSICS **EDUCATION** Wellesley Col, BA, 67; Brown Univ, PhD, 75. **CAREER** Asst prof, for lang and lit, North Carolina State Univ, 75-82; chemn, 82-91, assoc prof, 82-86, Frank Bailey Assoc Prof, 86-92, Frank Bailey Prof, Classics, 92- , Dean of Arts and Sci, Union Col,94-99; Dean of Faculty and VP for Acad Affairs, 99-. **HONORS AND AWARDS** Outstanding Teacher Award, 82; Fac Merit Service Award, 94. **MEMBERSHIPS** Am Philol Asn; Class Asn of the Atlantic States; Class Asn of the Middle W and S; Class Asn of the Empire State; Asn of Am Col and Univ; Asn of General and Liberal Studies; AAUW. **RESEARCH** Greek and Latin language and literature; Greek and Latin drama and epic in translation; classical mythology. **SELECTED PUBLICATIONS** Auth, Monsters and the Family: The Exodos of Sophocles' Trachiniae, Greek, Roman and Byzantine Stud, 78; auth, The Family in Sophocles' Antigone and Electra, the Classical World, 82; auth, The Authorship of the Agesilaus, La Parola del Passato, 84; auth, Sophocles' Ajax in Context, The Classical World, 86; auth, Myth, Choice, and Meaning in Euripides: Iphigenia at Aulis, Am J of Philology, 92; auth, Euripides' Judgment: Literary Creation in Andromache, Am J of Philology, 95; auth, "Vortex, Clouds, and Tongue: New Problems in the Humanities?," J of the Acad of Arts and Sciences, (99). **CONTACT ADDRESS** Dept of Classics, Union Col, New York, Feigenbaum Hall, Schenectady, NY 12308. **EMAIL** sorumc@union.edu

SOSNOSKI, JAMES JOSEPH
PERSONAL Born 06/18/1938, Dickson City, PA, m, 1965, 1 child **DISCIPLINE** ENGLISH **EDUCATION** Loyola Univ, Ill, AB, 60, MA, 65; Pa State Univ, PhD(English), 67. **CAREER** Asst prof, 67-72, ASSOC PROF ENGLISH, MIAMI UNIV, 72- **MEMBERSHIPS** MLA; Col English Asn; Mediaeval Acad Am; Early English Text Soc. **RESEARCH** Literary criticism; Medieval literature. **SELECTED PUBLICATIONS** Auth, Craft and intention in James Agee's A Death in the Family, J Gen Educ, 68. **CONTACT ADDRESS** Dept of English, Miami Univ, Oxford, OH 45056.

SOSOWER, MARK L.
PERSONAL Born 04/26/1949, Teaneck, NJ, m, 2000, 2 children **DISCIPLINE** CLASSICS **EDUCATION** Univ Rochester, BA, 71; MA, 72; MA, 75; NYU, PhD, 81. **CAREER** Asst prof, assoc prof, prof, NYU, 92-. **HONORS AND AWARDS** NEH, 91, 98; Andrew W. Mellon Trav Grnt, 91; A. Bartlett Giamatti Fel, Ren Stud, 90; APS Trav Grnt, 90; NEH Sum Sem, 89; NCar State Alumni Outs Ext Awd, 91. **MEMBERSHIPS** APA; USNCB; AFVL; CAMWS; NCCA; Richard Stanhope Pullen Soc; Sigma Iota Rho Hon Soc. **RESEARCH** Greek Paleography and codicology; history of early humanistic libraries. **SELECTED PUBLICATIONS** Auth, Palatinus Graecus 88 and the Manuscript Tradition of Lysias, Adolf Hakkert, 87; co-auth, Learning from the Greeks: An Exhibition commemorating the 500th Anniversary of the Founding of the Aldine Press, Yale UP, 94; co-auth, Librorum graecorum Bibliothecae Vaticanae index a Nicolao de Maioranis compositus a Fausto Saboeo collatus anno 1533, Vatican Lib, 98; auth, "Palla Strozzi's Greek Manuscripts," Stud Itali de fiolo Class 3 (86): 140-51; auth, "Marcus Musurus and a Codex of Lysias," Greek Roman Byz Stud 23 (82): 377-92; auth, "Seven Manuscripts Palla Strozzi Gave to the S. Giustina Library," J Warburg Court Inst 47 (84): 190-91; auth, "A Greek Codex of Sir Thomas Phillips Once in the Clermont Library," Syllecta Class 2 (90): 95-102; auth, "Antonio's Eparchos and a Codex of Archimedes in the Bodmer Library," Museum Helvet 50 (93): 144-57; auth, "A Forger Revisited: Andreas Darmarios and Beinecke," Jahrb der Oster Byzan 43 (93): 289-306; auth, "A Manuscript of Guillaume Pellicier," (d. 1567) in the Beinecke Library, Scriptorium 52 (98): 372-80. **CONTACT ADDRESS** Dept of Classics, No Carolina State Univ, PO Box 8106, Raleigh, NC 27695. **EMAIL** mlsfll@unity.ncsu.edu

SOSSAMAN, STEPHEN
DISCIPLINE CREATIVE WRITING, WORLD LITERATURE, MODERN AMERICAN LITERATURE **EDUCATION** Columbia Univ, BA; State Univ NYork, MA; NYork Univ, PhD. **CAREER** Bus wrtg consult. **SELECTED PUBLICATIONS** Publ, Paris Rev, Centennial Rev, Southern Hum Rev. **CONTACT ADDRESS** Dept of Engl, Westfield State Col, 577 Western Ave., Westfield, MA 01085.

SOTO, GILBERTO D.
PERSONAL Born 05/09/1961, Torreon, Mexico, m, 1986, 2 children **DISCIPLINE** MUSIC **EDUCATION** Universidad Antonoma del Noneste, BA, 83; Abilene Christian Univ, BA, 86; Univ Southern Ms, MM, 88, PhD, 98. **CAREER** Instr, 86-90, Ms Gulf Coast Commun Col; instr, 90-, Laredo Commun Col. **HONORS AND AWARDS** Tepsichorean Award, 93; Nisod Teaching Excellence Award, 95; LU Presidential Award, 98; performed at the white house, washington, dc, 92. **MEMBERSHIPS** TMEA; MENC; TAMS. **RESEARCH** Music education for young children. **CONTACT ADDRESS** West End Washington St., Laredo, TX 78040.

SOUKUP, PAUL A.
PERSONAL Born 08/15/1950, Burbank, CA, s **DISCIPLINE** COMMUNICATION **EDUCATION** Saint Louis Univ, AB, 73; Jesuit School Theology, MDiv, 78; STM, 80; Univ Tex Austin, PhD, 85. **CAREER** Teacher, Loyola High School, 73-76; assoc pastor, St Theresa's Parish, 80-85; asst to assoc prof, Santa Clara Univ, 85-. **HONORS AND AWARDS** Fel, Univ of Tex Austin, 80-83. **MEMBERSHIPS** Nat Commun Assoc; Int Commun Assoc; Int Assoc for Mass Commun Res; Unda; Western Commun Assoc. **RESEARCH** Communication and theology, orality and literacy studies, communication technology. **SELECTED PUBLICATIONS** Auth, Communication and Theology: Introduction and Review of the Literature, World Assoc for Christian Commun, (London), 83; auth, Christian Communication: A Bibliographical Survey, Greenwood, (Westport, CN), 89; coed, Media, Consciousness, and Culture: Explorations of Walter Ong's Thought, Sage (Beverly Hills), 91; coed, Ong, Walter, J Faith and Contexts, 4 vols, Scholars Pr, (Atlanta), 92, 95, 99; coed, Lonergan and Communication: Common Ground for Forging the New Age, Sheed and Ward, (Kansas City), 93; coed, Mass Media and the Moral Imagination, Sheed and Ward, (Kansas City), 94; ed, Media, Culture, and Catholicism, Sheed and Ward, (Kansas City), 96; coed, From One Medium to Another, Sheed and Ward, (Kansas City), 97; coed, Fidelity and Translation: Communicating the Bible in New Media, Sheed and Ward (Chicago), 99. **CONTACT ADDRESS** Dept Commun, Santa Clara Univ, 500 El Camino Real, Santa Clara, CA 95053-0001. **EMAIL** psoukup@scu.edu

SOULE, GEORGE
PERSONAL Born 03/03/1930, Fargo, ND, m, 1961, 1 child **DISCIPLINE** ENGLISH LITERATURE **EDUCATION** Carleton Col, BA, 51; Yale Univ, MA, 56, PhD, 60. **CAREER** Instr English, Oberlin Col, 58-60; asst prof, Univ Wis, 60-62; from asst prof to assoc prof, 62-71, chmn English dept, 78, PROF ENGLISH, CARLETON COL, 71-95, Prof English Emeritus, 95-; CHMN ENGLISH DEPT, 80-83, Consult, US Dept Health, Educ & Welfare, 65-66; dir centennial celebration, Carleton Col, 65-67 & NDEA Summer English Inst, 65; dir, Carleton London prog, 74 & 79, 84, 92 & dir, Carleton summer writing prog, 80-85. **HONORS AND AWARDS** Rotary International fellowship for advanced study at Cambridge, England, 1952-53. **MEMBERSHIPS** Johnson Soc Lichfield; Boswell Soc Auchinleck; MLA. **RESEARCH** Shakespeare; Boswell and Johnson; Wordsworth, Iris Murdoch, Anita Brockner. **SELECTED PUBLICATIONS** Ed, The Theatre of The Mind, Prentice-Hall, 75; Spots of Earth in the Excursion, Charles Lamb Bulleting, January, 94; True And False Princesses In The Excursion, Wordsworth Circle, Vol 26, 95; Annotated & Critical Secondary Bibliography, Scarecrow, 98; Murdoch's Gift: The Narrator in The Book and the Brotherhood, 00; New Visions for Old: Three Recent Novels by Anita Brookner, 00. **CONTACT ADDRESS** Dept of English, Carleton Col, Northfield, MN 55057. **EMAIL** gsoule@carleton.edu

SOURIAN, PETER
PERSONAL Born 04/07/1933, Boston, MA, m, 1971, 2 children **DISCIPLINE** ENGLISH, MEDIA **EDUCATION** Harvard Univ, BA, 55. **CAREER** From instr to assoc prof, 65-75, Prof English, Bard Col, 75-, TV critic, The Nation Mag, 75-80; Chair, Div Languages and Literature, 84-86, 90-94. **HONORS AND AWARDS** Bardian Awd, 00. **MEMBERSHIPS** MLA; AAUP; Nat Bk Critics Circle; Pen. **RESEARCH** The novel; television. **SELECTED PUBLICATIONS** Auth, Miri, Pantheon, 57; The Best & Worst of Times, Doubleday, 61; The Gate, Harcourt, 65; Open admissions: A Pilgrim's Progress, Nation, 4/73; Eric Rohmer, Transatlantic Rev, winter 73-74; Television, Nation, 11/79; At the French Embassy In Sofia, 92. **CONTACT ADDRESS** Dept of Eng, Bard Col, PO Box 5000, Annandale, NY 12504-5000.

SOUTHALL, GENEVA H.
PERSONAL Born 12/05/1925, New Orleans, LA, d **DISCIPLINE** MUSIC **EDUCATION** Dillard University, BA, 1945; National Guild Pianist, Artist Diploma, 1954; American Conservatory of Music, MusM, 1956; University of Iowa, PhD, 1966. **CAREER** University of Minnesota, professor Afro-American Music Culture in New World, 70-; Grambling College, professor, 66-70; South Carolina State College, associate professor, 62-64; Knoxville College, assistant music professor, 59-61; United States Information Service, chamber pianist, 55. **MEMBERSHIPS** American Student Faculty Assembly, University of Minnesota; Womens Student Assembly, University of Minnesota; Field Research Activ, Haiti & Jamaica; graduate faculty, Music Department, University of Minnesota; African Studies Council, University of Minnesota; music editor, Howard University Press; board directors, Urban League; NAACP; board of directors, Urban Coalition of Minneapolis; life member, board directors, Association for the Study of Afro-American Life & History; Metropolitan Cultural Arts Center;

admissions board, Park Avenue Unit Methodist Church; board directors, National Women Helping Offenders; Society for Ethnomusicology; American Musicol Society; Crusade Scholar, Methodist Church, 1961-62; Pi Kappa Lamda, National Honors Music Society. **SELECTED PUBLICATIONS** Published in "Reflections in Afro-American Music", "Black Perspectives in Music". **CONTACT ADDRESS** Afro-American Studies, Univ of Minnesota, Twin Cities, 808 Social Science, Minneapolis, MN 55455.

SOUTHERN, EILEEN JACKSON
PERSONAL Born 02/19/1920, Minneapolis, MN, m **DISCIPLINE** MUSIC **EDUCATION** Univ of Chicago, BA 1940, MA 1941; New York Univ, PhD 1961. **CAREER** Prairie View State Coll, lecturer, 41-42; Southern Univ, asst prof 1943-45, 49-51; Alcorn Coll, asst prof 1945-46; Claflin Univ, asst prof 1947-49; City Univ of New York, asst to full prof 1960-75; Harvard Univ, full prof 1975-87, prof emeritus. **HONORS AND AWARDS** Alumni Achievement Awd, Univ of Chicago 1971; Achievement Awd, Natl Assn Negro Musicians 1971; Citation Voice of Amer, 1971; Deems Taylor Awrd ASCAP 1973; Bd of Dir, Amer Musicological Soc, 1974-76; Honorary MA, Harvard Univ 1976; Honorary Phi Beta Kappa Radcliffe/Harvard Chapter 1982. **MEMBERSHIPS** Concert pianist Touring in USA, Haiti 1942-54; co-founder/editor, The Black Perspective in Music scholarly journal 1973-; mem, Assn for Study of Afro-Amer Life & History; mem, Alpha Kappa Alpha; bd, New York City YWCA, 1950; leader, Girl Scouts of Amer, 1950-1960; American Musicological Society; Sonneck Society for American Music, International Musicological Society. **SELECTED PUBLICATIONS** Readings in Black American Music WW Norton 1971, revised 1983; The Buxheim Organ Book (Brooklyn, NY) 1963; The Music of Black Amer (New York) 1971, 2nd Ed 1983, 3rd ed, 1997; Anonymous Pieces in the Ms El Escorial IVa24 Basel, Switzerland 1981; author, Biographical Dictionary of Afro-Amer & African Musicians (Westport) 1982; author of articles in The New Grove Dictionary of Music and Musicians (Macmillan) 1980 and The New Grove Dictionary of American Music (Macmillan), 1986; Honorary DA Columbia College, Chicago,1; bd of dirs Sonneck Soc of Ame Music 1986-88; co-editor, African-American Traditions: An Annotated Bibliography, Westport: Greenwood Press, 1990; Peabody Medal, Johns Hopkins Univ, 1991; African-American Musical Theater, Nineteenth Century, 1994. **CONTACT ADDRESS** PO Drawer I, Cambria Heights, NY 11411.

SOUZA, M.
PERSONAL Born 12/11/1966, Bolivia, m, 1989 **DISCIPLINE** LITERATURE **EDUCATION** UMSA Bolivia, BA, 92; Boston Col, MA, 95; PhD, 98. **CAREER** Asst prof, St Louis Univ, 98-. **HONORS AND AWARDS** Excellence in Teaching Awd, Boston Col, 95. **MEMBERSHIPS** MLA, AATSP **RESEARCH** Latin American poetry, 19th-century American literature, film and theory. **SELECTED PUBLICATIONS** Auth, "Augusto Monterroso: 'Que tienen las moscas que no tengamos nosotros'," Textos e Ideas (97): 5-7; auth, "El triangulo del lago: El nuevo cine antropologico," Cultura La Razon (99): 3; auth, "Teoria de la metafora en Ortega y Gasset: Que quiere decir el poeta cuando dice que el 'cipres es una llama muerta'?" Con-textos 23 (99): 19-32; auth, "La figura del archivo en la narrativa de Ricardo Piglia," Cincinnati Romance Review 20 (00). **CONTACT ADDRESS** Dept Mod & Class Lang, St. Louis Univ, 221 N Grand Blvd, Saint Louis, MO 63103-2006. **EMAIL** souzamm@slu.edu

SOVEN, MARGOT
PERSONAL Born 10/18/1940, New York, NY, m, 1961, 3 children **DISCIPLINE** ENGLISH EDUCATION **EDUCATION** Univ Penn, PhD, 80. **CAREER** Prof, English dept, 81-, LaSalle Univ. **HONORS AND AWARDS** Instl Summer Grants; NEH Summer Seminar Grant **MEMBERSHIPS** MLA; NCTE **RESEARCH** The teaching of writing; Amer lit. **SELECTED PUBLICATIONS** Coauth, Writings from the Workplace Documents Models Cases, 96; auth, Write to Learn: A Guide to Writing Across the Curriculum, 96; auth, The Teaching of Writing in Middle & Secondary Schools, 98. **CONTACT ADDRESS** La Salle Univ, 1900 W Olney Ave, Philadelphia, PA 19141. **EMAIL** Soven@lasalle.edu

SOWARDS, STEVEN W.
DISCIPLINE HISTORY, LIBRARY SCIENCE **EDUCATION** Stanford Univ, BA, 73; Ind Univ, MA, 76, PhD, 81, MLS, 86. **CAREER** Ref librn, Hanover Col, 86-88; hum librn, Swarthmore Col, 88-96; soc scis & hum ref, 96-98, head, main libr ref, Mich State Univ librs, 98-. **HONORS AND AWARDS** Fulbright res fel, Vienna, 77-78 **MEMBERSHIPS** ALA, Libr Hist Round Table, MLA. **RESEARCH** Mod Balkan hist; hist libr; web-based ref tools. **SELECTED PUBLICATIONS** Auth, Austria's Policy of Macedonian Reform, East European Monographs, 89; auth, Historical Fabrications in Library Collections, Collection Management 10/3- 4, 88; auth, Save the Time of the Surfer: Evaluating Web Sites for Users, Library Hi Tech 15/3-4, 97; auth, A Typology for Ready Reference Web Sites in Libraries, First Monday: Peer-Reviewed J on the Internet 3/5. May 98; auth, "Novas, Niches and Icebergs: Practical Lessons for Small-Scale Web Publishers," in JEP: The J of Electronic Publishing, vol 5, 99. **CONTACT ADDRESS** Libraries, Michigan State Univ, 100 Library, East Lansing, MI 48224. **EMAIL** sowards@msu.edu

SPAETH, BARBETTE S.
PERSONAL Born 03/26/1956, Chicago, IL, s **DISCIPLINE** GREEK AND ROMAN RELIGION, MYTHOLOGY, LATIN LITERATURE **EDUCATION** John Hopkins Univ, PhD, 87. **CAREER** Class, Tulane Univ. **HONORS AND AWARDS** Phi Beta Kappa, 76; Lord fel,Amer Sch Class Stud at Athens, 83; Robinson travel fel, John Hopkins Univ, 86; fel, Am Sch Class Stud at Athens, 86-87; Broneer fel, Am Acad, Rome, 90-91. **MEMBERSHIPS** Am Philol Asn; Arch Inst. **RESEARCH** Witchcraft in antiquity, women's cults in antiquity, instructional technology in classics. **SELECTED PUBLICATIONS** Auth, The Goddess Ceres and the Death of Tiberius Gracchus, Hist, 90; Athenians and Eleusinians in the West Pediment of the Parthenon, Hesperia, 91; The Goddess Ceres and Roman Women, Newcomb Ctr for Res on Women Newsletter, 93; The Goddess Ceres in the Ara Pacis Augustae and the Carthage Relief, Amer Jour Archaeol 98, 94; auth, The Roman Goddess Ceres, Univ of TX Pr, Austin, 96; auth, The Pompeii Project and Issues in Multimedia Devleopment, Classical World, 91.6, 98, 503-512. **CONTACT ADDRESS** Dept of Class, Tulane Univ, 6823 St Charles Ave, New Orleans, LA 70118. **EMAIL** spaeth@mailhost.tcs.tulane.edu

SPANCER, JANET
PERSONAL Born San Antonio, TX, M, 2 children **DISCIPLINE** ENGLISH LITERATURE **EDUCATION** University of Texas-San Antonio, B.A., M.A.University of Pennsylvania, Ph.D **CAREER** Assoc prof. **HONORS AND AWARDS** Fel, Charlotte Newcombe, NEH. **MEMBERSHIPS** MLA, SAA. **RESEARCH** Renaissance literature, Shakespeare's historical plays. **SELECTED PUBLICATIONS** Auth, articles on Shakespeare's plays. **CONTACT ADDRESS** Dept of Eng, Wingate Univ, Campus Box 3076, Wingate, NC 28174. **EMAIL** jspencer@wingate.edu

SPANOS, WILLIAM
PERSONAL Born 01/01/1925, Newport, NH, d, 1954, 4 children **DISCIPLINE** ENGLISH, POSTMODERN THEORY **EDUCATION** Wesleyan Univ, BA, 50; Columbia Univ, MA, 54; Univ Wis, PhD (Eng), 64. **CAREER** Master Eng, Mt Hermon Sch, 51-53; asst ed, Encycl Americana, Grolier, 54-56; instr Eng, Univ KY, 60-62; asst prof, Knox Col, 62-66; Asst Prof Eng & Comp Lit, State Univ NY Binghamton, 66-, Fulbright prof Am lit, Nat Univ Athens, 69-70; founder & ed, boundary 2, 72-. **HONORS AND AWARDS** Hon degree, Univ of Athens, 87. **MEMBERSHIPS** MLA; Col Eng Asn; Mod Greek Studies Asn. **RESEARCH** Contemporary theory, postmodernism. **SELECTED PUBLICATIONS** Ed, A Casebook on Existentialism, Crowell, 66; auth, The Christian Tradition in Modern British Verse Drama: The Poetic of Sacramental Time, Rutgers Univ, 67; Modern drama and the Aristotelian tradition: The formal imperatives of absurd time, Contemp Lit, summer 71; The detective and the boundary: Some notes on the postmodern literary imagination, fall 72, Heidegger, Kierkegaard and the Hermenentic circle: Toward a postmodern theory of interpretation as dis-closure, winter 76 & Breaking the circle: Hermenentics as dis-closure, winter 77, boundary 2; ed, Existentialism 2, Random House, 77; Repititions: the Postmodern Occasion in Literature and Culture, Louisiana State Univ Press, 87; Heidegger and Criticism: Retrieving The Politics of Destruction, Univ of MN Press, 93, The End of Education, Univ of MN Press, 93; The Errant Art of Moby Dick: The Canon, the Cold War and the Struggle for American Studies, Duke Univ, 95; auth, America's Shadow: An Anatomy of Empire, Univ Minn Press, 00. **CONTACT ADDRESS** Dept of English, SUNY, Binghamton, Binghamton, NY 13901. **EMAIL** wspanos@binghamton.edu

SPARKS, ELISA KAY
DISCIPLINE ENGLISH LITERATURE **EDUCATION** Bryn Mawr Magna Cum Laude with Honors, BA, 73; Ind Univ, PhD, 79. **CAREER** Dept Eng, Clemson Univ. **HONORS AND AWARDS** Herman Strauss Memorial Fel, IU, 73; Gentry Awd for Excellence in Humanities Teaching, Clemson U, 00. **MEMBERSHIPS** Va Woolf Soc. **RESEARCH** Literary criticism; women's studies; science fiction, web-based pedagogy. **SELECTED PUBLICATIONS** Ed, "Old Father Nile: T.S. Eliot and Harold Bloom on the Creative Process as Spontaneous Generation," in Engendering the Word: Feminist Essays in Psychosexual Politics, eds. Temma F. Berg, Anna Shannon Elfenbein, Jeanne Larsen, and Elisa Kay Sparks, Illinois Univ Press, 89; auth, Virginia O'Keeffe has an exhibit of drawings at 291: Paradoxes of Feminist Pin-Ups in Re: Reading, Re: Writing, Re: Teaching Virginia Woolf: Selected Papers from the Fourth Annual Conference on Virginia Woolf, Pace Univ Press, 95; Marge Piercy, Great Lives from History: American Women, Salem, 95; Woman on the Edge of Time by Marge Piercy, Masterplots II: Women's Literature Series, Salem, 95; A Match Burning in a Crocus: Modernism, Feminism, and Feminine Experience in Virginia Woolf and Georgia O'Keeffe in Virginia Woolf: Themes and Variations: Selected Papers from the Third Annual Conference on Virginia Woolf, Pace Univ Press, 94; Exhibition of ten prints--silkscreen, photo-intaglio, and computer generated--on Virginia Woolf and Georgia O'Keeffe at the Seventh Annual Conference on Virginia Woolf, 97; ed, "Webbing the Universe of Science Fiction," Electronic Networks: Crossing Boundaries and Creating Communities, ed. Dixie Goswami, Tharon Howard, and Chris Benson, Heineman, 99; auth, "The Dial as Matrix: Periodical Community between Virginia Woolf and Georgia O'Keeffe," Virginia Woolf & Communities: Selected Papers from the Eight Annual Conference on Virginia Woolf, ed. Jeanette McVicker and Laura Davis, Pace Univ Press, 00. **CONTACT ADDRESS** Clemson Univ, Clemson, SC 29634. **EMAIL** sparks@clemson.edu

SPARKS, GLENN G.
PERSONAL Born 08/21/1953, Baltimore, MD, m, 1975, 3 children **DISCIPLINE** MEDIA EFFECTS **EDUCATION** Wheaton Col, BA, 75; Northern Ill Univ, MA, 76; Univ Wis, Madison, PhD, 83. **CAREER** Asst prof, Cleveland State Univ, 83-86; asst prof, 86-90, assoc prof, 90-95, prof, Purdue Univ, 95-. **HONORS AND AWARDS** Eight Top Paper Awds, Int Competition Serv; interviewed or quoted on media effects research by ap press, nbc-tv, cnn radio, cbs-tv, national public radio, newsweek magazine, time magazine, the cleveland plain dealer, the boston globe, the washington post, the chicago tribune, the indianapolis star, **RESEARCH** Cognitive and emotional responses to various types of content, including frightening programs and movies, violence, and depictions of paranormal events. **SELECTED PUBLICATIONS** Auth, The Role of Preferred Coping Style and Emotional Forewarning in Predicting Emotional Reactions to a Suspenseful Film, Commun Rpt, 94; Media Impact on Fright Reactions and Belief in UFOs: The Potential Role of Mental Imagery, Commun Res, 95; The Relationship Between Exposure to Televised Messages About Paranormal Phenomena and Paranormal Beliefs, J of Broadcasting & Electronic Media, 97. **CONTACT ADDRESS** Dept of Commun, Purdue Univ, West Lafayette, 1366 Lib Arts & Educ Bldg 2114, West Lafayette, IN 47907-1080. **EMAIL** gsparks@purdue.edu

SPARKS, SHERRY L.
PERSONAL Born 04/10/1958, Tell City, IN, m, 1983, 1 child **DISCIPLINE** COMMUNICATIONS **EDUCATION** Ind State Univ, Terre Haute, BS, 80; SIU-C, MS, 93. **CAREER** Intern United Way of Am, 80-82; asst dir, UW of Adams Co, 82-85; sales corresp, Knapheit Mfg, 85-89; Ill Dept of Emp security, 89-94; promotions development dir, Quincy YMCA, 95-97; Nat trainer, YMCA of the Arts & Humanities training, 98-; dir of commun ed, John Wood Community Col, 99-. **HONORS AND AWARDS** BS, Ind State Univ, cum laude, 80; YWCA Women of Achievement Maggie Thomas Commun Awd; local and district Jr Women's Club Service Winner; Ill Cluster Spirit Awd, YMCA, 98; Nat 4-H Scholarship/project Awds; numerous writing/speech contest Awds. **MEMBERSHIPS** ICCET, FTCHY, NCCET. **SELECTED PUBLICATIONS** Auth, Seasons of Love (poetry, 99); columnist, "It's About Time." **CONTACT ADDRESS** Dir Commun Ed, John Wood Comm Col, 150 S 48th St, Quincy, IL 62301.

SPEAREY, SUSAN
DISCIPLINE EARLY VICTORIAN LITERATURE **EDUCATION** Leeds Univ, PhD, 93. **CAREER** Assoc prof **RESEARCH** Mmigrant/diaspora literature from Southeast Asia, literature of the British Empire. **SELECTED PUBLICATIONS** Auth, Mapping and Masking: The Migrant Experience in Michael Ondaatje's In the Skin of a Lion, Borderblur: Poetry and Poetics, Contemp Can Lit, Quadriga, 96, Jour of Commonwealth Lit, 94; "Cultural Crossings: The Shifting Subjectivities And Stylistics of Michael Ondaatje's Running In The Family and In The Skin Of A Lion," Brit Jour Can Stud, 96; rev(s), Canadian Canons: Essays in Literary Value, Univ Toronto Press, 91; Canadian Storytellers, Red Kite Press, 91; Can Lit, 93; Fawzia Afzal-Khan, Cultural Imperialism and the Indo-English Novel: Genre and Ideology, Univ Pa Press, 93, The Yearbook of Eng Stud 26, 96. **CONTACT ADDRESS** Department of English, Brock Univ, 500 Glenridge Ave, Saint Catharines, ON, Canada L2S 3A1. **EMAIL** sspearey@spartan.ac.brocku.ca

SPEARS, LEE A.
DISCIPLINE TECHNICAL ND BUSINESS WRITING **EDUCATION** Western Ky Univ, Ma; Univ Ky, PhD. **CAREER** Assoc Prof, Western Ky Univ. **RESEARCH** Professional writing with a particular focus on pedagogy. **SELECTED PUBLICATIONS** Articles, Writing Inst; Bull Asn Bus Comm. **CONTACT ADDRESS** Western Kentucky Univ, 1526 Big Red Way Street, Bowling Green, KY 42101. **EMAIL** lee.spears@wku.edu

SPECTOR, ROBERT DONALD
DISCIPLINE ENGLISH **EDUCATION** Long Island Univ, BA, 48; NY Univ, MA, 49; Columbia Univ, PhD, 62. **CAREER** Instr to prof, LIU, 48-. **HONORS AND AWARDS** Fel, Huntingfon Libr, 74; Fel, Folger Libr, 75; Fel, Newberry Libr, 76; Trustee Awd, LIU, 78; Tristram Walker Alumnus of the Year, 81; DHL, Long Island Univ, 94. **MEMBERSHIPS** PEN, MLA. **RESEARCH** Eighteenth Century Literature. **SELECTED PUBLICATIONS** Auth, English Literary Periodicals, 66; auth, Tibius George Snollett, 68; auth, Per Lagerkuist, 73; auth, Arthur Murphy, 79; auth, Tobias Smoffett: A Reference Guide, 80; auth, The English Gothic, 83; auth, Background Restoration and 18th Century Literature, 89; auth, Political Continiums, 92; auth, Smoffett's women, 94; auth, Samuel Johnson and the Essay, 97. **CONTACT ADDRESS** 1761 E 26th St, Brooklyn, NY 11229-2405.

SPEER, DONALD R.
DISCIPLINE MUSIC - PIANO; PIANO PEDAGOGY **EDUCATION** Louisiana Col, BM, 1983; Southern Ill Univ-Edwardsville, MM, 85; Lousiana State Univ, PhD, 91. **CAREER** Assoc Prof, Western KY Univ, 91- . **MEMBERSHIPS** Ky Music Teachers Asn; Music Teachers Nat Asn; Music Educators Nat Conference. **RESEARCH** Piano pedagogy. **SELECTED PUBLICATIONS** Auth with C. Yarbrough and S. Parker, Perception and Performance of Dynamics and Articulation among Young Pianists, Bull of the Coun for Res in Music Educ, 93; auth, An Analysis of Sequential Patterns of Instruction in Piano Lessons, Jour of Res in Music Educ, 94. **CONTACT ADDRESS** Dept of Music, Western Kentucky Univ, Bowling Green, KY 42101. **EMAIL** donald.speer@wku.edu

SPEIRS, LOGAN
DISCIPLINE ENGLISH LITERATURE **EDUCATION** Cambridge Univ, PhD, 65. **CAREER** Asspc Prof, Eng, Univ Calif, Santa Barbara. **RESEARCH** Poetry and drama. **SELECTED PUBLICATIONS** Auth, Tolstoy and Chekhov, Cambridge, 71. **CONTACT ADDRESS** Dept of Eng, Univ of California, Santa Barbara, Santa Barbara, CA 93106-7150. **EMAIL** lspeirs@humanitas.ucsb.edu

SPENCER, DARRELL W.
PERSONAL Born 07/23/1971, IN, s **DISCIPLINE** THEATRE, COMMUNICATION **EDUCATION** Franklin Col, BA, 93; Ind State Univ, MA, 96. **CAREER** TA, Ind State Univ, 94-96; Dir, Ind Theatre Assoc, 97-99; fac, Butler Univ, 97-98; fac, Marian Col, 97-; fac, Franklin Col, 00-. **HONORS AND AWARDS** Fel, Ind State Univ; Key Theatre Awd, Franklin Col; Teaching Excellence Awd, Ind State Univ. **MEMBERSHIPS** Ind Theatre Assoc; Lambda Chi Alpha; Theta Alpha Phi. **RESEARCH** Group communication, group process, creative process. **CONTACT ADDRESS** Dept Performing Arts, Marian Col, 3200 Cold Spring Rd, Indianapolis, IN 46222-1960.

SPENCER, GREGORY H.
DISCIPLINE RHETORIC AND COMMUNICATION **EDUCATION** Univ Oregon, PhD, 85. **CAREER** Instr, McKenzie Stud Ctr, 80-87; sem instr, Antioch Univ, 92, 94; assoc prof, Westmont Col, 87-. **HONORS AND AWARDS** Tchr yr, 90. **RESEARCH** Media ethics; rhetorical theory criticism. **SELECTED PUBLICATIONS** Auth, The Rhetoric of Malcolm Muggeridge's Gradual Christian Conversion, Jour of Commun and Rel, 95; A Heart For Truth: Taking Your Faith to College, Baker Bk House, 92; Unethical Ethos? Flannery O'Connor's 'Wise Blood' in Word and Image, Rhetoric of Film, Kendall/Hunt, 94; Response to John E Phelan, Jr's Theology and Life: Expressing Our Faith Today, Covenant Comp, 92. **CONTACT ADDRESS** Dept of Commun, Westmont Col, 955 La Paz Rd, Santa Barbara, CA 93108-1099.

SPENGEMANN, WILLIAM C.
DISCIPLINE ENGLISH LITERATURE **EDUCATION** Stanford Univ, PhD, 61. **CAREER** Patricia F. and William B. Hale '44 Prof Arts and Sci and Prof Eng. **RESEARCH** Am fiction and poetry. **SELECTED PUBLICATIONS** Auth, A New World of Words: Redefining Early American Literature, Yale UP, 94; ed, Herman Melville's Pierre or The Ambiguities, Penguin, 96; Herman Melville: Pierre, Penguin, 95; co-ed, 19th-century American Poetry, Penguin, 96. **CONTACT ADDRESS** Dept of English, Dartmouth Col, 6032 Sanborn House, Hanover, NH 03755. **EMAIL** William.C.Spengemann@dartmouth.edu

SPERRY, STUART M.
PERSONAL Born 02/22/1929, New York, NY **DISCIPLINE** ENGLISH **EDUCATION** Princeton Univ, AB, 51; Harvard Univ, AM, 55, PhD, 59. **CAREER** Lectr, 58-59, from instr to assoc prof, 59-70, PROF ENGLISH, IND UNIV, BLOOMINGTON, 70-, Vis assoc prof, Univ Calif, Riverside, 68-69. **HONORS AND AWARDS** Wordsworth Bicentenary Colloquium Competition Prize Essay, The Wordsworth Circle & Dept English, Temple Univ, 70. **MEMBERSHIPS** MLA **RESEARCH** Romantic period. **SELECTED PUBLICATIONS** Auth, Richard Woodhouse's interleaved and annotated copy of Keats's Poems (1817), Lit Monogr, 67; Keats the Poet, Princeton Univ, 73; Toward a definition of romantic irony in English literature, In: Romantic and Modern: Revaluations of Literary Tradition, Univ Pittsburgh, 77; Necessity and the role of the hero in Shelley's Prometheus Unbound, Publ Mod Lang Asn Am, 81; Oracles And Hierophants--Constructions Of Romantic Authority, J Of English And Germanic Philology, Vol 92, 93. **CONTACT ADDRESS** Dept of English, Indiana Univ, Bloomington, Bloomington, IN 47401.

SPIEGELMAN, WILLARD LESTER
PERSONAL Born 12/29/1944, St. Joseph, MO **DISCIPLINE** ENGLISH LITERATURE **EDUCATION** Williams Col, AB, 66; Harvard Univ, AM, 67, PhD, 71. **CAREER** Asst prof, 71-77, assoc prof, 77-86, prof eng, Southern Methodist Univ, 86, chmn, 91-94, Hughes Prof Engl, 93-; Vis prof, Williams Col, 87-88; Ed, Southwest Rev, 84-, Columnist, Wall Street Jour, 88. **HONORS AND AWARDS** Perrine Prize, Phi Beta Kappa, 81., NEH Summer Grant, 83 & 89, and year long stipend, 90-91; Rockefeller Found, Scholar-in-Residence, Poetry Center, 85-86; Guggenheim Fel, 94-95. **MEMBERSHIPS** MLA; Wordsworth-Coleridge Soc; Asn Literary Scholars & Critics. **RESEARCH** Eng romantic poetry; contemp poetry; class. **SELECTED PUBLICATIONS** Auth, Wordsworth's Aeneid, Comp Lit, 74; Landscape and knowledge: The poetry of Elizabeth Bishop, Mod Poetry Studies, 75; Ben Belitt's places, Mod Poetry Studies, 76; Elizabeth Bishop's Natural Heroism, Centennial Rev, 78; The Rake's Progress: An operatic version of pastoral, Southwest Rev, 78; The rituals of perception, Parnassus, 78; Alphabeting the void, Salmagundi, 78; Breaking the mirror: Interruption in the trilogy, In: James Merrill: Essays in Criticism, Cornell Univ Press, 82; Some Lucretian Elements in Wordsworth, Compartative Lit, 84; Wordsworth's Heroes, Univ Calif Press, 85; Peter Grimes: The development of a hero, Studies in Romanticism, 85; The Didactic Muse: Scenes of Instruction in Contemporary American Poetry, Princeton Univ Press, 89; Majestic Indolence: English Romantic Poetry and the Work of Art, Oxford Univ Press, 95. **CONTACT ADDRESS** Dept of Eng, So Methodist Univ, PO Box 750001, Dallas, TX 75275-0001. **EMAIL** wspiegel@mail.smu.edu

SPILKA, MARK
PERSONAL Born 08/06/1925, Cleveland, OH, m, 7 children **DISCIPLINE** ENGLISH, COMPARATIVE LITERATURE **EDUCATION** Brown Univ, BA, 49; Ind Univ, MA, 53, PhD(comp lit), 56. **CAREER** Ed asst, Am Mercury, 49-51; instr English lit, Univ Mich, 54-58, asst prof, English, 58-63; assoc prof, 63-67, chmn, Dept English, 68-73, PROF ENGLISH LIT, BROWN UNIV, 67-, Fel, Ind Sch Lett, 61; managing ed, Novel: A Forum on Fiction, Brown Univ, 67-77, ed, 78-; Guggenheim fel, 67-68; Nat Endowment for Humanitites fel independent study & res, 78-79; vis prof, Ind Univ, summer, 76. **MEMBERSHIPS** MLA **RESEARCH** English and American novel, especially 19th and 20th centuries; comparative literature; modern literary criticism. **SELECTED PUBLICATIONS** Auth, Love Ethic of D H Lawrence, 55 & Dickens and Kafka: A Mutual Interpretation, 63, Ind Univ; ed, D H Lawrence: A Collection of Critical Essays, Prentice-Hall, 63; Towards a Poetics of Fiction, Ind Univ, 77; auth, Virginia Woolf's Quarrel with Grieving, Univ Nebr Press, 80; auth, Renewing the Normative D. H. Lawrence: A Personal Progress, Missouri, 92; auth, Eight Lessons in Love: A Domestic Violence Reader, Missouri, 97. **CONTACT ADDRESS** 294 Doyle Ave, Providence, RI 02906. **EMAIL** mark.spilka@brown.edu

SPINELLI, DONALD C.
PERSONAL Born 12/09/1942, Rochester, NY, m, 1971, 1 child **DISCIPLINE** LITERATURE **EDUCATION** SUNY, BA, 64, MA, 66; Ohio State Univ, PhD, 71. **CAREER** From asst prof to prof to assoc dean, 72-, Wayne State Univ. **HONORS AND AWARDS** NEH editor's grant, 92-94; Florence Gould Found Grant, 92-94. **MEMBERSHIPS** AATF; MLA. **RESEARCH** 18TH century French literature. **SELECTED PUBLICATIONS** Coauth, Beaumarchais. Correspondance, 78; auth, art, A Concordance to Marivaux's Comedies in Prose, 79; coauth, Beaumarchais: A Bibliography, 88; coauth, French Language and Literature: An Annotated Bibligraphy, 89; auth, art, L'Inventaire apres deces de Beaumarchais, 97. **CONTACT ADDRESS** Wayne State Univ, 2226 FAB, Detroit, MI 48202. **EMAIL** d.spinelli@wayne.edu

SPINELLI, EMILY L.
PERSONAL Born 04/27/1942, Bucyrus, OH, m, 1971, 1 child **DISCIPLINE** LITERATURE **EDUCATION** Ind Univ, BA, 64; Ohio State Univ, MA, 67; PhD, 71. **CAREER** Asst prof to prof, Univ of Mich, 82-. **HONORS AND AWARDS** Stephan A. Freeman Awd, 88; Founders Awd. **MEMBERSHIPS** Phi Beta Kappa, Am Coun on the Teaching of For Lang, Am Asn of Teachers of Span & Portuguese. **RESEARCH** Spanish Language, Literature, Culture. **SELECTED PUBLICATIONS** Auth, Encuentros 3rd ed, Holt, Rinehart & Winston, 97; auth, Interacciones 3rd ed, Holt Rinehart & Winston, 98. **CONTACT ADDRESS** Dept Humanities, Univ of Michigan, Dearborn, 4901 Evergreen Rd, Dearborn, MI 48128-2406. **EMAIL** espinell@umich.edu

SPINKS, C. WILLIAM
PERSONAL Born 06/26/1942, Whiteright, TX, m, 2 children **DISCIPLINE** ENGLISH **EDUCATION** Wayland Baptist Univ, BA, 64; Univ Nebr, MA, 65; PhD, 70. **CAREER** Teaching Asst, Univ Nebr, 64-66; Instr, Univ Nebr, 66-70; Asst Prof, Trinity Univ, 70-76; Vis Prof, Univ Tex, 77; From Assoc Prof to Prof, Trinity Univ, 76-. **HONORS AND AWARDS** NEH Fel, 76; Outstanding Young Men in Am Entry, 75; Acad Awds for Res, 78, 87, 96; Summer Progs and Awds, 85, 94, 98; Trinity Univ Summer Awd for Res, 77, 79, 81, 83, 91, 98, 00. **MEMBERSHIPS** Semiotic Soc of Am, Int Asn for the Study of Semiotics, Int Asn for the Fantastic in the Arts, Asn for the Anthrop Study of Play. **RESEARCH** Semiotics, myth, trickster, science fiction and Nineteenth-Century British literature. **SELECTED PUBLICATIONS** Auth, Peirce and Triadomania: A Walk in the Semiotic Wilderness, Mouton de Gruyter (Berlin, Germany), 91; auth, Semiotics, Marginal Signs and Trickster: A Dagger of the Mind, Macmillan (London, UK), 91; auth, "Myth, Semiosis and Virtual Reality: Or Something Virtual Comes This Way," in Semiotics 1993, 95; auth, "Peirce's Lake and Coleridge's River: Water and Metaphors of the Mind," in Semiotics 1995: Proceedings of the Semiotic Soc of Am (NY: Peter Lang Publ, 96); co-ed, Semiotics 1996: Proceedings of the Semiotic Society of America, Peter Lang Publ (New York, NY), 97; co-ed, Semiotics 1997: Proceedings of the Semiotic Society of America, Peter Lang Publ (New York, NY), 98; guest ed, Trickster: Boundaries, Ambivalence and Semiosis, special issue of Am J of Semiotics, 99; ed, co-ed, Semiotics 1998: Proceedings of the Semiotic Society of America, Peter Lang Publ (New York, NY), 99 **CONTACT ADDRESS** Dept English, Trinity Univ, 715 Stadium Dr, San Antonio, TX 78212-3104. **EMAIL** cspinks@trinity.edu

SPIRES, JEFFREY
DISCIPLINE NINETEENTH-CENTURY FRENCH LITERATURE, FRENCH CULTURAL STUDIES **EDUCATION** Univ KS, BA, 86; Princeton Univ, MA, 91; PhD, 97. **CAREER** Engl, Colgate Univ. **HONORS AND AWARDS** Fulbright tchg asst, France, 86-1988; Armstrong fel, Princeton Univ, 88-92; McMahon grant, Princeton Univ, 90, 91. **SELECTED PUBLICATIONS** Auth, Revolutionary Grimace: Carnival in Victor Hugo's Notre-Dame de Paris, Nineteenth-Century Fr Stud, 97. **CONTACT ADDRESS** Dept of Romance Lang, Colgate Univ, 13 Oak Drive, Hamilton, NY 13346.

SPITZBERG, BRIAN H.
DISCIPLINE COMMUNICATION **EDUCATION** Univ TX, BA, 78; Univ S CA, MA, PhD, 81. **CAREER** Vis asst prof, Univ WI-Madison; prof, Univ N TX; prof, San Diego State Univ. **HONORS AND AWARDS** Grad dir, Interaction Stud, Intl and Intercult Stud and Applied Commun Stud. **RESEARCH** Stalking, conflict management, courtship violence, sexual commun. **SELECTED PUBLICATIONS** Auth, co-auth, over 50 scholarly articles and chapters, four scholarly bk(s); co-auth, The Dark Side of Close Relationships, The Dark Side of Interpersonal Communication. **CONTACT ADDRESS** School of Commun, San Diego State Univ, 5500 Campanile Dr, San Diego, CA 92182. **EMAIL** spitz@mail.sdsu.edu

SPITZER, JOHN
DISCIPLINE MUSIC HISTORY **EDUCATION** Harvard Univ, BA; Cornell Univ, PhD. **CAREER** Prof, John Hopkins Univ. **MEMBERSHIPS** Am Musicol Soc. **SELECTED PUBLICATIONS** Auth, pubs in Journal of Musicology; Early Music; Harvard Dictionary of Music. **CONTACT ADDRESS** Dept of Musicology, Johns Hopkins Univ, Baltimore, 1 E Mt Vernon Pl, Baltimore, MD 21202-2397. **EMAIL** spitzer@peabody.jhu.edu

SPIVACK, CHARLOTTE K.
PERSONAL Born 07/23/1926, Schoharie, NY, w, 1956, 2 children **DISCIPLINE** ENGLISH **EDUCATION** SUNY Albany, BA, 47; Cornell Univ, MA, 48; Univ Mo, PhD, 54. **CAREER** Rich Prof Inst, 54-56; assoc prof, Fick Univ, 56-64; prof, Univ Mass, 64-. **HONORS AND AWARDS** AAUW Fel; Distinguished Teaching Awd. **MEMBERSHIPS** MLA; NEMLA; Pop Cult 15th-Century Studies. **RESEARCH** Medieval and renaissance English drama; fantasy fiction; Arthurian literature. **SELECTED PUBLICATIONS** Auth, Early English Drama, 66; auth, George Chapman, 67; auth, The Comedy of Evil on Shakespeare's Stage, 78; auth, Ursula LeGuin, 84; auth, Merlin's Daughters: Contemporary Women Fantasy Writers, 87; Merlin vs. Faust, 92; auth, The Company of Camelot, 94; auth, Merlin: A Thousand Heroes With One Face, 94. **CONTACT ADDRESS** English Dept, Univ of Massachusetts, Amherst, PO Box 30515, Amherst, MA 01003.

SPIVAK, GAYATRI CHAKRAVORTY
DISCIPLINE ENGLISH LITERATURE **EDUCATION** Univ Calcutta, BA, 59; Cornell Univ, MA, 62, PhD, 67. **CAREER** Instr, Brown Col; Univ Tex-Austin; Univ Calif-Santa Cruz; Jawaharlal Nehru Univ; Stanford Univ; Univ Brit Columbia; Goethe Univ, Frankfurt; Riyadh Univ; Emory Univ; Andrew W Mellon prof, Pittsburgh Univ; prof, 91-. **HONORS AND AWARDS** Fel, Nat Hum Inst; Ctr Hum, Wesleyan Col; Hum Res Ctr, Australian Nat Univ; Ctr Stud Soc Sci, Calcutta; Davis Ctr Hist Stud, Princeton; Rockefeller found, Bellagio; Kent fel; Guggenheim fel; distinguished fac fel, Tagore, Maharaja Sayajirao, Univ Baroda, India; transl prize, Sahitya Akademi, India, 97; lect, davie memorial lect, cape town; ed bd, cultl critique; new formations; diaspora; ariel; re-thinking marxism; pub cult; parallax; interventions; year's work in critical & cult theory. **MEMBERSHIPS** Mem, Subaltern Studies Collective **RESEARCH** Works of Mahasweta Devi. **SELECTED PUBLICATIONS** Transl, Of Grammatology; Imaginary Maps and Breast. **CONTACT ADDRESS** Dept of Eng, Columbia Col, New York, 2960 Broadway, New York, NY 10027-6902.

SPIVEY, TED RAY
PERSONAL Born 07/01/1927, Ft. Pierce, FL, m, 1962, 2 children **DISCIPLINE** ENGLISH LITERATURE **EDUCATION** Emory Univ, AB, 49; Univ Minn, MA, 51, PhD(English), 54. **CAREER** Instr, Emory Univ, 54-56; from asst prof to assoc prof English, 56-64, PROF ENGLISH, GA STATE UNIV, 64-, PROF URBAN LIFE, 70- **HONORS AND AWARDS** GSU

Alumni distinguished prof; listed, Who's Who in America. **MEMBERSHIPS** SAtlantic Mod Lang Asn; MLA; AAUP. **RESEARCH** Modern poetry and modern British fiction; Southern literature. **SELECTED PUBLICATIONS** Auth, Revival: Southern Writers in the Modern City, Univ Press Fla, 86; auth, The Writer as Shaman: The Pilgrimages of Conrad Aiken and Walker Percy, Mercer Univ, 86; auth, Beyond Modernism: Toward A New Myth Criticism, Univ Press of America, 88; auth, Conrad Aiken: A Priest of Consciousness, AMS, 89; auth, Flannery O'Connor: The Woman, The Thinker, The Visionary, Mercer, 95; auth, Time's Stop in Savannah: Conrad Aiken's Inner Journey, Mercer, 97. **CONTACT ADDRESS** Dept of English, Georgia State Univ, University Plaza, Atlanta, GA 30303.

SPLITTER, RANDOLPH N.

DISCIPLINE ENGLISH **EDUCATION** Hamilton Col, BA, 68; Univ Calif Berkeley, PhD, 74; Univ Calif Samta Cruz, BA Comput and Infor Sci, BA, 82. **CAREER** Asst Prof, Calif Inst of Technology, 75-82; Instr, De Anza Col, 89-; Chair of English Dept, De Anza Col, 98-. **HONORS AND AWARDS** NEH Summery Study Grant. **RESEARCH** American literature and culture - representation of violence and gender in American literature, film, and popular culture. **SELECTED PUBLICATIONS** Auth, "Proust's 'Recheroche': A Psychoanalytic Interpretation, Routledge & Kegan Paul, 81; auth, Body and Soul, Creative Arts Book Co, 99. **CONTACT ADDRESS** Lang Arts Div, De Anza Col, 21250 Stevens Creek Blvd, Cupertino, CA 95014-5702. **EMAIL** rsplitter@earthlink.net

SPONBERG, ARVID FREDERIC

PERSONAL Born 11/08/1944, Minneapolis, MN, m, 1972, 2 children **DISCIPLINE** AMERICAN DRAMA **EDUCATION** Augustana Col, BA, 66; Univ Chicago, MA, 67; Univ Mich, PhD(English), 73. **CAREER** Instr, Henry Ford Community Col, 70-71; asst prof, 72-78, ASSOC PROF ENGLISH, VALPARAISO UNIV, 78-, Actg ed, The Cresset, 75-76; reader, Advan Placement Exams, Educ Test Serv, 77, 80 & 82; dir, Cambridge Overseas Study Ctr, Valparaiso Univ, 77-79 & chmn English Dept, 80-83. **HONORS AND AWARDS** Lily Endowment Fel, 83-84; Valpariaiso Univ Alumni Assoc Grant, 87; Valparaiso Univ Expense Grant. **MEMBERSHIPS** MLA; National Council of Teachers of English: American Society for Theatre Research; American Theatre and Drama Society. **RESEARCH** The profession of playwright in the United States; rhetoric, especially the structure of argument and metaphor in literature and science. **SELECTED PUBLICATIONS** Auth, "Can Theater Thrive in America? Performink: Chicago's Biweekly Theatre News Journal, (91): p 12; auth, "Acting in the 21st Century," Performink, (91): p 15; auth, Broadway Talks: What Professional Think About Commerical Theater in America, Greenwood Press, 91; auth, "A R Gurney: An Interview," The Playright's Art, Rutgers Univ Press, 94; auth, "Foreword," A R Gurney: Collected Plays, Vol 1, Smith & Kraus, 95; auth, " Neil Simon, Menander, and the Tradition of Gentle Comedy," Neil Simon: A Casebook, Garland Press, 97; Rev, The Actor Speaks: Actors Discuss Their Experiences and Their Careers, Westport, CT: Greenwood Press in Theatre Research International, 97; auth, "James Dearn," American National Biography, Oxford Univ Press, 99; auth, "Five Books About the Masters Golf Tournament," Aethlon: The Journal of Sport Literature, 99. **CONTACT ADDRESS** Dept English, Valparaiso Univ, 651 College Ave, Valparaiso, IN 46383-6493. **EMAIL** arvid.sponberg@valpo.edu

SPRICH, ROBERT

PERSONAL Born 06/15/1938, St. Louis, MO, m, 1961, 2 children **DISCIPLINE** ENGLISH LITERATURE **EDUCATION** Mass Inst Technol, BS, 61; Brandeis Univ, MA, 63; Tufts Univ, PhD, 71. **CAREER** From asst prof to assoc prof, 66-77, Prof English Bentley Col, 77-, Lectr, Grad Div Northeastern Univ, 66-68; lectr English, Exp Col, Tufts Univ, 69-71; adj instr, Boston Psychoanalytic Inst, 91-99. **HONORS AND AWARDS** Fel, Ctr for Psychol Study Arts, State Univ NY, Buffalo, spring, 76; vis scholar, Univ Va Film Festival, 94-98. **MEMBERSHIPS** Popular Culture Asn; Am Film Inst; Board of Dir, Boston Musical Theater, 86-00. **RESEARCH** Film studies, comic sensibility; applications of psychoanalysis to literary criticism. **SELECTED PUBLICATIONS** Coauth, Hell, Encycl Britannica, 64; auth, Theme and structure in T S Eliot's The Hippopotamus, CEA Critic, 4/69; Pressed flowers, fresh flowers: New directions in psychoanalytic criticism, Colby Libr Quart, 3/77; co-ed, The Whispered Meanings, Univ Mass, 77; auth, The appeal of Star Wars, Am Imago, summer 81; Essays on William Faulkner and Katherine Anne Porter, Literature and Psychoanalysis, Lisbon, 97, 98. **CONTACT ADDRESS** Dept of English, Bentley Col, 175 Forest St, Waltham, MA 02452-4705. **EMAIL** rsprich@bentley.edu

SPRING, HOWARD

PERSONAL Born 11/20/1947, Toronto, ON, Canada, m, 1977, 2 children **DISCIPLINE** MUSICOLOGY **EDUCATION** York Univ, Toronto, BA, 76; York Univ, Toronto, MFA, 83; Univ of Ill at Urbana-Champaign, PhD, 93. **CAREER** Asst prof, Univ Guelph, 92-. **MEMBERSHIPS** Soc for Ethnomusicology; Am Musicological Soc; Ctr for Black Music Res. **SELECTED PUBLICATIONS** Auth, "The Use of Formulas in the Improvisation of Charlie Christian", in Jazzforschung 22, 90; auth, "Swing and the Lindy Hop: Dance, Venue, Media, and Tradition", in American Music 15, 97. **CONTACT ADDRESS** School of Fine Art and Music, Univ of Guelph, Guelph, ON, Canada N1G 2W1. **EMAIL** hspring@arts.uoguelph.ca

SPRINGER, CARL P. E.

PERSONAL Born 11/28/1954, San Diego, CA, m, 1980, 4 children **DISCIPLINE** CLASSICS **EDUCATION** Univ of Wis Madison, PhD, 84. **CAREER** Asst prof, Ill State Univ, 84-90; assoc prof, Ill State Univ, 91-96; prof and chair dept of Foreign Lang, Ill State Univ, 96- ; assoc dean, Southern Illinois Univ Edwardsville. **HONORS AND AWARDS** Fulbright res Grant, 90; Alexander von Humboldt Fel, 93-94. **MEMBERSHIPS** Am Philos Asn; N Am Patristic Soc. **RESEARCH** Late Antiquity; Latin Epic; Biblical Poetry. **SELECTED PUBLICATIONS** Auth, Fannius and Scaevola in Cicero's De Amicitia, Studies in Latin Lit and Roman Hist VII, 94; The Concinnity of Ambrose's Illuminans Altissimus, Panchaia, Festschrift fur Professor Klaus Thraede, 95; The Manuscripts of Sedulius, A Provisional Handlist, 95; rev, early Christian Poetry, J of Early Christian Studies, 96. **CONTACT ADDRESS** College of Arts and Sciences, Campus Box 1608, Illinois State Univ, Peck Hall 3432 Southern Illinois University Edwardsville, Edwardsville, IL 62026. **EMAIL** cpsproner@stu.edu

SPRINGER, HASKELL SAUL

PERSONAL Born 11/18/1939, New York, NY, m, 1993, 2 children **DISCIPLINE** AMERICAN LITERATURE & STUDIES **EDUCATION** Queens Col, NYork, BA, 61; Ind Univ, MA, 65, PhD, 68. **CAREER** Instr, Univ Va, 66-68; from asst prof to assoc prof, 68-78, prof Eng, 78-, Univ Kans; Fulbright prof Am lit, Universidade Catolica & Universidade Fed, Rio de Janeiro, Brazil, 75-76; vis prof, amer lit, Sorbonne, Paris, 85-86. **MEMBERSHIPS** MLA; AAUP; Melville Soc; Amer Cult Assn. **RESEARCH** Classic American literature; hypertext literature; textual scholarship. **SELECTED PUBLICATIONS** Ed, America and the Sea: A Literary History, University of Georgia, 95; auth, The Captain's Wife at Sea, Iron Men, Wooden Women: Gender and Seafaring in the Atlantic World, 1700-1920, Johns Hopkins, 96. **CONTACT ADDRESS** Dept of English, Univ of Kansas, Lawrence, Lawrence, KS 66045-0001. **EMAIL** springer@ukans.edu

SPRINKER, MICHAEL

PERSONAL Born 02/08/1950, m **DISCIPLINE** ENGLISH AND COMPARATIVE LITERATURE **EDUCATION** Northwestern Univ, BA, 72; Princeton Univ, MA, 74; PhD, 75. **CAREER** Prof, 88-. **SELECTED PUBLICATIONS** Auth, Counterpoint of Dissonance: The Aesthetics and Poetry of Gerard Manley Hopkins, Johns Hopkins Univ, 80; Imaginary Relations: Aesthetics and Ideology in the Theory of Historical Materialism, 87; History and Ideology in Proust: 'A la recherche du temps perdu' and the Third French Republic, Cambridge, 94; The Mughal Empire (rev), Radical History Rev, 94; co-ed, Late Imperial Culture, 95. **CONTACT ADDRESS** English Dept, SUNY, Stony Brook, Stony Brook, NY 11794.

SPROW, RICHARD

DISCIPLINE ENGLISH **EDUCATION** Purdue University, PhD. **CAREER** Prof; dept ch. **HONORS AND AWARDS** NEH fel. **RESEARCH** Shakespeare; modern drama; modern lit; film; interdisciplinary studies; popular culture. **SELECTED PUBLICATIONS** Co-auth, Write This Way. **CONTACT ADDRESS** Dept of Eng, Westminster Col, Pennsylvania, New Wilmington, PA 16172-0001.

SPRUNGER, DAVID A.

DISCIPLINE ENGLISH LITERATURE **EDUCATION** Bethel Col, BA, 82; Univ Kans, MA, 85; Univ Ill Urbana-Champaign, PhD, 92. **CAREER** Asst prof, 92-98, assoc prof, Concordia Col, 98-. **MEMBERSHIPS** Am Folklore Soc; Int Arthurian Asn; Medieval Acad Am; Medieval Asn Midwest; MLA. **SELECTED PUBLICATIONS** Auth, Parodic Animal Physicians from the Margins of Medieval Manuscripts, Garland, 96. **CONTACT ADDRESS** English Dept, Concordia Col, Minnesota, 901 8th St S, Moorhead, MN 56562. **EMAIL** sprunger@cord.edu

SPURGEON, DICKIE A.

PERSONAL Born 03/04/1936, Van Duser, MO, m, 1958, 3 children **DISCIPLINE** ENGLISH **EDUCATION** S IL Univ Edwardsville, BA, 61; S IL Univ Edwardsville, MA, 62; S IL Univ Edwardsville, PhD, 67. **CAREER** Asst prof, Univ Md, 67-71; prof, S IL Univ Edwardsville, 71-. **HONORS AND AWARDS** Alumni Great Teachers, SIUE, 76. **MEMBERSHIPS** NEA. **RESEARCH** Renaissance Literature; Bibliography; Editing; Periodicals. **SELECTED PUBLICATIONS** Auth, Three Tudor Dialogues, 78; auth, Tudor Translations of the Colloquies of Erasmus, 82. **CONTACT ADDRESS** Dept English, So Illinois Univ, Edwardsville, PO Box 1431, Edwardsville, IL 62026-1431. **EMAIL** dspurge@siue.edu

SPURLOCK, JOHN HOWARD

PERSONAL Born 10/22/1939, Huntington, WV, m, 1962, 1 child **DISCIPLINE** LINGUISTICS, AMERICAN LITERATURE **EDUCATION** WVa Univ, BA, 62; Univ Louisville, MA, 64, PhD, 86. **CAREER** Instr English, Western Ky Univ, 64-69 & Louisville Country Day Sch, 69-70; assoc prof, 71-86, prof English, Western Ky Univ, 86-. **HONORS AND AWARDS** Awd for Editorial Excellence, Jesse Stuart Found, 96. **MEMBERSHIPS** Appalachian Writers Asn; Jesse Stuart Found (ed and mem bd dir); Ky Speakers' Bureau. **RESEARCH** Sociolinguistics; Appalachian literature; Kentucky literature. **SELECTED PUBLICATIONS** Auth, He Sings For Us--A Sociolinguistic Analysis of the Appalachian Subculture and of Jesse Stuart as a Major American Author, Univ Press of Am, 80 & 82; Appalachian--Appalachia/strange man--strange land, In: Speechways of American Subcultures, Univ Press of Ky, 82; ed, Jesse Stuart's Daughter of the Legend, Jesse Stuart Found, 94; Jesse Stuart's Beyond Dark Hills, Jesse Stuart Found, 96. **CONTACT ADDRESS** 1 Big Red Way St, Box 495, Bowling Green, KY 42101-3576. **EMAIL** john.spurlock@wku.edu

ST PIERRE, PAUL MATTHEW

PERSONAL Born 08/02/1953, Winnipeg, MB, Canada, s **DISCIPLINE** ENGLISH **EDUCATION** Univ Brit Colum, BA, 75; Queen's Univ, MA, 76; Univ Sydney, PhD, 82. **CAREER** Lectr, Univ Brit Colum, 81-83, 85-89; vis asst prof, Univ of Victoria, 83-85; instr to asst prof, Simon Fraser Univ, 87-. **HONORS AND AWARDS** Can Res Fel, 89-92. **MEMBERSHIPS** MLA, SSNL, NACBS. **RESEARCH** Barry Humphries, Commonwealth literature, British Music Hall, British Cinema. **SELECTED PUBLICATIONS** Auth, "The Architectonics of Deconstructivism: Vancouver Skylines and Storylines," Vancouver: Representing the Postmodern City, ed Paul Delaney (Vancouver: Arsenal Pulp Pr, 94): 162-78; auth, "De-Burking Johnny Burke, an Excluded Canadian Troubadour," Can Poetry 36, (95): 114-19; auth, "Marguerite Bourgeoys and Abbe Henri-Raymond Casgrain, Founders of Canadian Historical Letters," Brit Jour of Can Studies 11.1, (96): 42-52; auth, "Quelle heur est-il, Monsieur ricouer? A Semiotic Narratology of Duration, Term, Tempo, and Rec(oe)urrence, Tol(le)d from the Criticism of Paul Riceur," Semiotica 114.1/2, (97): 21-30. **CONTACT ADDRESS** Dept English, Simon Fraser Univ, Burnaby, BC, Canada V5A 1S6. **EMAIL** stpierr@sfu.ca

ST. AMANT, KIRK R.

DISCIPLINE RHETORIC, SCIENTIFIC, TECHNICAL, COMMUNICATION **EDUCATION** Bowdoin Col, BA, 93; James Madison Univ, MA, 98. **CAREER** Instr, Blue Ridge CC, 97-98; teaching asst, James Madison Univ, 97-98; dir to ed-in-chief to asst coord to grad teaching asst, Univ Minn, 99-. **HONORS AND AWARDS** COGS Leadership Award; Pres Ser Award; Student Leadership Award, Indst Tech Univ Minn; STS Sigma Tau Chi Honor Soc; Outstanding Tech Sci Commun Grad Student. **MEMBERSHIPS** STC; IEEE; RSA. **RESEARCH** International and intercultural communication; online communication; Internet commerce and online business. **SELECTED PUBLICATIONS** Auth, "International Integers and Intercultural Expectations," Intercom (99); auth, "When Culture and Rhetoric Contrast: Examining English as the International Language of Technical Communication," IEEE (99); co-auth, "Mutual Intercultural Perception: How Does it Affect Technical Communication," Tech Commun (00); auth, "Resources and Strategies for Successful International Communication," Intercom (00); auth, "Expanding Translation Use to Improve the Quality of Technical Communication," IEEE (00); auth, "Success in the International Virtual Office," in Telecommuting and Virtual Offices, ed. Nancy Johnson (00); auth, "Aspects of International Online Marketing Communication," Impact (01); auth, "Identity and International Online Communication," Intercom (01); auth, "Humor, Credibility and International Exchanges," Intercom (01); auth, "Organizational and Intercultural Communication: An Annotated Bibliography," Tech Commun Quart (01). **CONTACT ADDRESS** Rhetoric Dept, Univ of Minnesota, Twin Cities, 1994 Buford Ave, 64 Classroom, Saint Paul, MN 55108. **EMAIL** stam0032@umn.edu

ST. CLAIR, GLORIANA

PERSONAL Born 12/13/1939, Tonkawa, OK **DISCIPLINE** MANAGEMENT; LITERATURE **EDUCATION** Univ Okla, BA, 62, PhD, 70; Univ Calif, Berkeley, MLS, 63; Univ Tex, San Antonio, MBA, 80. **CAREER** Res asst, 62-63, asst librn, 63-65, Univ Calif, Berkely; cat, Univ Okla, 65-68; asst prof, Western Carolina Univ, 69-71; asst prof, Col Charleston, 71-76; vis lectr, Medical Univ, SC, 75; adj full prof, Walsh Col, 76-77; tchg assoc, Univ Tex, San Antonio, 79-81; sup librn, San Antonio Public Libr, 80-84; div head, 84-87, bibliogr, 85, Tex A&M Univ Libry; asst dir, Ore State Univ, 87-90; from int assoc dean to int dean, 96-97, assoc dean, 97-98, Pattee Libry, Pa State Univ; librn, Carnegie Mellon Univ, 98-. **HONORS AND AWARDS** Tex Libry Asn Resolution of Thanks, 86; Charles W. Plum Dist Service Awd, 86; Partnership for Excellence, 93, Pa State Univ, Pa Quality Leadership Awds Examiner Training, 94; Pa Quality Leadership Found, 94; Who's Who Am Women, 97-98; Who's Who World, 97-98; The World Who's Who Women, 97-98. **MEMBERSHIPS** Ore Chapter Asn Col Res

Librys; OR Libry Asn; Tex Libry Asn; Ore State Univ Fac Women's Network; Mythopoeic Soc; Libry Res Round Table; Libry, Information Technol Asn; Asn Col Res Librys; Nat Digital Libry Fed Board; Asn Res Librys, Inst Representative. **RESEARCH** Copyright law; digital libraries **SELECTED PUBLICATIONS** Auth, art, Steps Toward Writing a Sure Thing, 97; auth, art, Third-Party Payer System Explored, 97; coauth, art, Changing Copyright Legislation: Two Views, 97; coauth, art, Active and Collaborative Learning in Online Courses: Penn State's Project Vision, 97; auth, art, Assessment: How & Why, 99. **CONTACT ADDRESS** Univ Libraries, Carnegie Mellon Univ, 4909 Frew St, Pittsburgh, PA 15213. **EMAIL** gstclair@andrew.cmu.edu

ST. OMER, GARTH
DISCIPLINE AMERICAN AND CARIBBEAN LITERATURE **EDUCATION** Princeton Univ, PhD, 75. **CAREER** Prpf, Eng, Univ Calif, Santa Barbara. **RESEARCH** Fiction; creat writing. **SELECTED PUBLICATIONS** Auth, A Room on the Hill, Faber and Faber, 68; Shades of Grey, Faber and Faber, 68; Nor Any Country, Faber and Faber, 69; Black Bam and the Masqueraders, Faber and Faber, 72. **CONTACT ADDRESS** Dept of Eng, Univ of California, Santa Barbara, Santa Barbara, CA 93106-7150.

STAAL, ARIE
PERSONAL Born 09/27/1933, Grand Rapids, MI, m, 1963, 2 children **DISCIPLINE** AMERICAN & NETHERLANDIC LITERATURE **EDUCATION** Calvin Col, BA, 63; Univ Mich, MA, 64, PhD(English), 70. **CAREER** Instr, Calvin Col, 64-65 & Eastern Mich Univ, 68-70; lectr, Univ Helsinki, 70-71; asst prof, 71-76, assoc prof, 76-82, PROF ENGLISH, EASTERN MICH UNIV, 82-, Lectr, Bur of Sch Serv, Univ Mich, 68-70; Fulbright lectr, US Govt, 70. **MEMBERSHIPS** Can Asn Advan Netherlandic Studies; AAUP; Fine Arts Soc; Conf Christianity & Lit. **RESEARCH** Narrative techiques in traditional American fiction; narrative techniques in twentieth-century Netherlandic fiction; experimentation in twentieth-century Netherlandic poetry. **SELECTED PUBLICATIONS** Auth, Hawthorne's Narrative Art, The Revisionist Press, 77; Social norms, morality & conflict in The Scarlet Letter, Notes on Teaching English, 77; I met Adam, Christianity & Lit, 80; ed, Wantij Neap-Tide, The Netherlandic Press, 81; auth, Technical writing & the freshman composition program, Notes on Teaching English, 81; contribr, Life signs and death signals, World Lit Today, 82; Under Dutch skies, Can J of Netherlandic Studies, 82; auth, Whodunit first: Poe or Hawthorne, Unicorn, 82. **CONTACT ADDRESS** English Dept, Eastern Michigan Univ, 612 Pray Harrold, Ypsilanti, MI 48197-2201.

STACK, RICHARD
DISCIPLINE PUBLIC RELATIONS **EDUCATION** Ind Univ, BA; Univ Mo, JD. **CAREER** Asst prof, Am Univ. **HONORS AND AWARDS** Founder & pres, RAS Consulting. **RESEARCH** Legal communication and public service/public relations. **SELECTED PUBLICATIONS** Coauth, Litigation in Public Relations; contribur, Wash Post, LA Times, St. Louis Dispatch, WCA Agenda, Comm & Law, The Champion, Jour Mo bar. **CONTACT ADDRESS** American Univ, 4400 Massachusetts Ave, Washington, DC 20016.

STADE, GEORGE
PERSONAL Born 11/25/1933, New York, NY, m, 1956, 4 children **DISCIPLINE** ENGLISH **EDUCATION** St Lawrence Univ, BA, 55; Columbia Univ, MA, 58, PhD, 65. **CAREER** Instr Eng, Rutgers Univ, 60-61; asst prof, 62-69, PROF ENGLISH, COLUMBIA UNIV, 69-, Coun Res Hum grant, 67-68; ed-in-chief, Columbia Essays on Mod Writers; ed-in-chief, Europ Writers, Scribner's. **MEMBERSHIPS** PEN Club; Nat Bk Critics Circle. **RESEARCH** Mod lit; popular fiction; theory of lit. **SELECTED PUBLICATIONS** Auth, Robert Graves, Columbia Univ, 67; coauth, Selected Letters of E E Commings, Harcourt, 68; contribr, A Closer Look at Ariel, Harper's Mag Press, 72; ed, Six Modern British Novelists, 74 & Six Contemporary British Novelists, 76, Columbia Univ; Confessions of a Lady-Killer, Norton, 79; over 150 reviews, articles and introductions. **CONTACT ADDRESS** Columbia Univ, 2960 Broadway, New York, NY 10027-6900. **EMAIL** ggs3@columbia.edu

STADLER, EVA MARIA
PERSONAL Born 03/28/1931, Prague, Czechoslovakia, m, 1957 **DISCIPLINE** COMPARATIVE LITERATURE, FILM STUDIES **EDUCATION** Barnard Col, AB, 52; Columbia Univ, PhD(French), 67. **CAREER** Lectr French, Columbia Univ, 53-57; instr French & Ger, Wash Col, 57-58; instr French, Douglass Col, Rutgers Univ, 58-64; asst prof French & Ger, 65-67, assoc prof, Manhattan Community Col, 67-68; assoc prof Comp Lit, French & Film Studies, 68-95, chair Humanities div, 73-79, dir Media Studies, 88-95, Assoc Prof English Commun & Media Studies, Fordham Univ, Lincoln Center, 95-. **MEMBERSHIPS** MLA; ACLA; Soc 18th Century Studies; ACLA Nat Cmt on Undergraduate prog, 71-75 & 78-82; Colloquium fel in Comp Lit, NYU, 72-92; Juror, Am Film Festival 80 & 81 **RESEARCH** History and theory of the novel; fiction and film; French film and film theory; 18th Century literature. **SELECTED PUBLICATIONS** Coauth, Premiers textes litteraires, Blaisdell, 66, Wiley, 75; auth, Rameau's Nephew by Diderot: Un film de Michael Snow, In: Interpeter Diderot Au-jourd'hui, Le Sycomore, 84; Espace acoustique et cinema moderne: l'exemple de Rovert Bresson, In: Bulletin de la SPFFA, 86-87; The Red Dress of Oriane de Guermantes, In: Reading Proust Now, Lang, 90; Diderot et le cinema: Les paradoxes de l'adaptation, Francographies, 92; Defining the Female Body within Social Space; The Function of Clothes in Some 18th Century Novels, Proceedings of the XIIth Congress of the ICLA, 90; Francophonie et cinema: l'exemple de deux cineastes senegalais, Francographies, 93; Addressing Social Boundaries: Dressing the Female Body in Early Realist Fiction, In: Reconfigured Spheres: Feminist Explorations of Literary Space, Univ Mass Press, 94; Une femme douce de Robert Bresson: Le cinema et ses pre-textes, Francographies, 95 **CONTACT ADDRESS** Dept of English, Fordham Univ, 441 E Fordham Rd, Bronx, NY 10458. **EMAIL** evastadler@aol.com

STADTER, PHILIP AUSTIN
PERSONAL Born 11/29/1936, Cleveland, OH, m, 1963, 3 children **DISCIPLINE** CLASSICAL LITERATURE **EDUCATION** Princeton Univ, AB, 58; Harvard Univ, MA, 59, PhD, 63. **CAREER** From instr to assoc prof, 62-71, prof Classics, 71- , Eugene Falk prof of Humanities, 91- , Univ NC, Chapel Hill, 71-; Chmn Dept, 76-86, Guggenheim fel, 67-68; Nat Endowment for Humanities sr fel, 74-75; Am Coun-Learned Soc fel, 82-83; Nat Hum Ctr fel, 89-90. **MEMBERSHIPS** Am Philol Asn; Class Asn Midwest & South; Asn Ancient Historians. **RESEARCH** Plutarch, Arrian, Greek in Renaissance; Greek historiograph **SELECTED PUBLICATIONS** Auth, Plutarch's Historical Methods, Harvard Univ, 65; Flavius Arrianus: The new Xenophon, Greek, Roman & Byzantine Studies, 67; The structure of Livy's history, Historia, 72; coauth, The Public Library of Renaissance Florence, Antenore, Italy, 72; ed, The Speeches of Thucydides, Univ NC, 73; auth, Pace, Planudes, and Plutarch, Ital Medioevale e Umanistica, 73; Arrianus, Flavius, In: Catalogus Translationum et Commentariorum, Vol III, Cath Univ Am, 76; Arrian of Nicomedia, Univ NC, 80; A Commentary on Plutarch's Pericles, Univ NC, 89; ed Plutarch and the Historical Tradition, Routledge, Eng, 92; auth, "Socialisor, Liberalisor & Martisor," in Modern Japanese Thought, ed. Bob T. Wakabayashi, (Cambridge U Press, 98). **CONTACT ADDRESS** Dept of Classics, Univ of No Carolina, Chapel Hill, CB 3145, Murphey Hall, Chapel Hill, NC 27599-3145. **EMAIL** stadter@unc.edu

STAGG, LOUIS CHARLES
PERSONAL Born 01/03/1933, New Orleans, LA, m, 1959, 2 children **DISCIPLINE** ENGLISH **EDUCATION** La Col, BA, 55; Univ Ark, MA, 57, PhD, 63. **CAREER** Asst English, Univ Ark, 55-59; asst prof, William Jewell Col, 59-60; instr, Stephen F Austin State Col, 60-62; from asst prof to prof emeritus English, Univ Memphis, 62-; dir English Drama Players, Memphis State Univ, 68-88; consult, State Based Progs, Nat Endowment for Humanities, 75-78; circulation mgr, Interpretations, 76-80; assoc ed, SCent Bull, SCent Mod Lang Asn, 82-84. **HONORS AND AWARDS** Phi Beta Kappa, 57; fac res grants, Memphis State Univ, 69-71; Pres, Memphis Alumni Asn, Phi Beta Kappa, 85-88. **MEMBERSHIPS** MLA; Southern Humanities Coun (secy-treas, 74-76, Council Chair, 93-94); SCent Mod Lang Asn; SCent Renaissance Conf; Acad Exchange Quart Advisory Board, 97-; Shakespeare Asn Am; Renaissance Soc of Am; Col English Asn; Eugene O'Neill Soc; Soc for the Study of Harold Pinter (treas & mem Exec Comt, 94-98; Am Asn of Univ Prof; The Stratford Festival; Conf on Christianity and Lit; Int Shakespeare Asn; Am Asn for Theatre Res; Int Soc for Theatre Res; Marlowe Soc of Am (Reviewer of Books, 83-93); Samuel Beckett Soc; originator of the Alliance for Creative Theatre, Educ, and Res at the Univ Memphis in 1986 (Chair of Schedules and mem Steering Comt, 86, 89, 90, 92, 94, 96, and consultant, 98); Int Conf on Patristic, Medieval, and Renaissance Studies; Am Theatre Asn. **RESEARCH** Renaissance drama; development of English drama from the medieval beginnings through the Renaissance and on to existentialism and modern rock opera; world drama, tragedy. **SELECTED PUBLICATIONS** Coauth, An Index to Poe's Critical Vocabulary, Transcendental Bks, 66; auth, Figurative imagery in revenge tragedies by three seventeenth century contemporaries of Shakespeare, SCent Bull, winter 66; coauth, Special collections on Southern culture in college and university libraries, Humanities in the south, spring 67; auth, An index to the figurative language of John Webster's, Ben Jonson's, Thomas Heywood's, George Chapman's, John Marston's, Cyril Tourneur's, and Thomas Middleton's tragedies, Bibliog Soc, Univ Va, 67-70; Characterization through nature imagery in the tragedies of George Chapman, Ball State Univ Forum, winter 68; George Bernard Shaw and the existentialist-absurdist theatre, Tenn Philol Bull, 7/77; Index to the Figurative Language of the Tragedies of Shakespeare's Chief 17th Century Contemporaries: Chapman, Heywood, Jonson, Marston, Webster, Tourneur, Middleton, Memphis State Univ, 77, 3rd ed, Garland Publ Inc, 82; Critical essays on Thomas Heywood, Nicholas Rowe, William H Gillette, Lord Dunsany and Christopher Fry, In: Major Writers of the English Language, Vol III, St Martin's Press, 79 & Macmillan, UK, 79; Index to the Tragedies of Shakespeare's Chief 16th Century Contemporaries, Garland Publ, 84; Essays on William Gillette, Death of a Salesman, and Long Day's Journey Into Night, In: Reference Guide to American Literature, St. James Press, 2nd ed, 87. **CONTACT ADDRESS** 5219 Mason Rd, Memphis, TN 38117-2104.

STAHL, JOHN D.
PERSONAL Born 04/03/1952, Mt Pleasant, PA, m, 1994, 2 children **DISCIPLINE** ENGLISH **EDUCATION** Goshen Col, BA, 73; Univ Pittsburgh, MA, 76; Univ Conn, PhD, 82. **CAREER** From asst prof to assoc prof, Va Tech, 82-. **HONORS AND AWARDS** Certificate of Teaching Excellence; Alumni Teaching Awd. **MEMBERSHIPS** MLA, Children's Literature Asn. **RESEARCH** Comparative Literature, World Literature, Mark Twain, Children's Literature, Literature and Film, German Literature. **SELECTED PUBLICATIONS** Auth, Mark Twain, Culture and Gender: Envisioning America Through Europe, Univ Ga Press (Athens, GA & London), 94; auth, "'Lasting Obligations:' The Friendship of Samuel Clemens and Mary Mason Fairbanks," Mark Twain J 34.2 (96): 7-16; auth, "Mark Twain's 'Slovenly Peter' in the Context of Twain and German Culture," The Lion and the Unicorn 20.2 (96): 166-180; auth, "A Secure World of Childhood: The Artistry of Elizabeth Enright," The Hollins Critic 35.2 (98): 1-17; auth, "Mark Twain and Leadership," The Five Owls 14.2 (99): 36-37. **CONTACT ADDRESS** Dept English, Virginia Polytech Inst and State Univ, 100 Virginia Tech, Blacksburg, VA 24061-0112. **EMAIL** stahl@vt.edu

STAINES, DAVID
PERSONAL Born 08/08/1946, Toronto, ON, Canada, s **DISCIPLINE** ENGLISH **EDUCATION** Univ Toronto, BA, 67; Harvard Univ, AM, 68; PhD, 73. **CAREER** Asst prof, Harvard Univ, 77-78; hon res fel, Univ Col London, 78-85; assoc prof, Univ Ottawa, 82-84; five col prof, Smith Col, 85-; prof to fac dean, Univ Ottawa, 95-. **HONORS AND AWARDS** Lorne Pierce Medal, 98; SSHRCC Fel, 86; NEH Fel, 77. **MEMBERSHIPS** MAA; MLA; IAS; ACCUTE. **RESEARCH** Medieval literature and culture; Canadian literature and culture. **SELECTED PUBLICATIONS** Ed, The Canadian Imagination: Dimensions of a Literary Cultures, 77; auth, Tennyson's Camelot: The Idylls of the King and It's Medieval Sources, 82; auth, The Forty-ninth and Other Parallels: Contemporary Canadian Perspectives, 86; auth, The Complete Romances of Chretien de Troyes, 90; auth, Stephen Leacock: My Financial Career and Other Follies, 93; auth, Beyond the Provinces: Literary Canada at Century's End, 95; auth, Margaret Laurence: Critical Reflections, 01. **CONTACT ADDRESS** English Dept, Univ of Ottawa, Ottawa, ON, Canada K1N 6N5. **EMAIL** dstaines@uottawa.ca

STALEY, GREGORY A.
PERSONAL Born 08/12/1948, Hagerstown, MD, m, 1979, 1 child **DISCIPLINE** CLASSICS **EDUCATION** Dickinson Col, AB, 70; Princeton Univ, MA, 73, PhD, 75. **CAREER** Instr, Dickinson Col, 74-75; Asst Prof, Fordham Univ at Lincoln Center, 75-76; Sessional Lectr, Univ Alberta, 76-78; Asst Prof, Dickinson Col, 78-79; Asst Prof to Assoc Prof Classics, Univ Md, 79-. **HONORS AND AWARDS** NEH Grants, Div Educ, 80, 89; Rome Prize Fel, Am Acad Rome, 83-84. **MEMBERSHIPS** Am Philol Asn; Am Classical League; Int Soc Classical Tradition. **RESEARCH** Classical tradition in America; Latin literature; mythology. **SELECTED PUBLICATIONS** Auth, But Ancient Violence Longs to Breed: Robinson Jeffers' The Bloody Sire and Aeschylus' Orestia, Classical & Mod Lit, 83; The Literary Ancestry of Sophocles' Ode to Man, The Classical World, 85; Aeneas' First Act, The Classical World, 90. **CONTACT ADDRESS** Classics Dept, Univ of Maryland, Col Park, 2407 Marie Mount Hall, College Park, MD 20742-4811. **EMAIL** gs32@umail.umd.edu

STALEY, LYNN
PERSONAL Born 12/24/1947, Madisonville, KY **DISCIPLINE** CHAUCER, MEDIEVAL LITERATURE AND CULTURE, SPENSER, EARLY RENAISSANCE LITERA **EDUCATION** Univ KY, AB, 69; Princeton Univ, MA, PhD, 73; **CAREER** Colgate Univ, Asst Prof, 74; Assoc Prof, 81; Prof, 86; Harrington and Shirley Drake, prof in the Humanities, 95. **HONORS AND AWARDS** Book Review Editor, Speculum, 00-03. **MEMBERSHIPS** Modern Language Association; Medieval Academy of America; New Chaucer Society; Spenser Society. **RESEARCH** Medieval women writers; Chaucer; Medieval English history and politics; Medieval devotional writing. **SELECTED PUBLICATIONS** Auth, "The Voice of the Gawain-Poet," Madison: Wis., 84; auth, "The Shepheardes Calender: An Introduction," University Park: Pa, 90; auth, "The Pearl Dreamer and the Eleventh Hour," Text and Matter, a New Critical Perspective of the Pearl-Poet, 91; rev(s), Am Notes and Queries, Mediaevalia et Humanistica, Renaissance Quart, Spenser Newsletter, Speculu; auth, "Margery Kempe's Dissenting Fictions," University Park: Pa., 94; ed., "The Book of Margery Kempe," Medieval Inst Publ, 96; co-auth, "The Powers of the Holy. Religion, Politics, and Gender in Late Medieval English Literautre," Univ Park: Pa, 96; auth, "HM 140 and the Politics of Re-Telling," in Retelling Tales. Essays in Honor of Russell Peck, 97; auth, "Pearl and the Contingencies of Love and Piety," in Medieval Literature and Historical Inquiry," 00; **CONTACT ADDRESS** Dept of Eng, Colgate Univ, 13 Oak Drive, Hamilton, NY 13346. **EMAIL** lstaley@mail.colgate.edu

STALEY, THOMAS F.
DISCIPLINE BRITISH LITERATURE **CAREER** Teaching fel, Univ of Pittsburgh, 58-60; asst prof, Rollins Col, 61-62; from asst prof to prof, Univ of Tulsa, 62-88; dean, Grad Sch, Univ of Tulsa, 69-76; acting vpres for acad affairs, Univ of Tulsa, 77; chmn, Grad FacS of Modern Letters, Univ of Tulsa, 79-81; dean, Col of Arts and Scis, Univ of Tulsa, 81-83; provost and vpres for acad affairs, Univ of Tulsa, 83-88; Chancellor's Coun Centennial prof in the Book Arts, Univ of Tex, 88-92; dir, Harry Ransom Hums Res Ctr and prof, Univ of Tex, 88-. **HONORS AND AWARDS** Fulbright Res Prof, Trieste, Italy, 66-67, 71; Pres of James Joyce Found 1969-73; Am Coun of Learned Socs Grant, 69, ACLS Grant-in-Aid, 80, 82; Harry Huntt Ransom Chr in Lib Arts, 1992-. **MEMBERSHIPS** Soc for Textual Scholar; MLA; Int Asn for the Study of Anglo-Irish Lit; Am Comt for Irish Studies; James Joyce Found; English Inst; Int Asn for Univ Profs of English; English Speaking Union; Tex Philos Soc. **SELECTED PUBLICATIONS** Auth, James Joyce's Portrait of the Artist, 68; Dorothy Richardson, 76; Jean Rhys: A Critical Study, 79; An Annotated Critical Bibliography of James Joyce, 89; The Marginality of the Humanities, in The Center for the Book, 90; Literary Canons, Literary Studies and Library Collections: A Retrospective on Collecting Twentieth Century Writers, in Rare Books and Manuscripts Librarianship, 90; Selections from the Paris Diary of Stuart Gilbert, in Joyce Studies Annual I, 90; Religious Elements and Thomistic Encounters: Noon on Joyce and Aquinas, in Re-Viewing Classics of Joyce Criticism, 91; On the Selling of Literary Archives, in The Author, vol. CIV, no 1, 93; Perspectives on the Rare Book Library at the End of the Century, in Rare Book and Manuscript Libraries at the End of the Century, 93; ed, James Joyce Today: Essays on the Major Works, 66; Italo Svevo: Essays on His Work, 69; Ulysses: Fifty Years, 74; Twentieth Century Women Novelists, 82; Joyce Studies: An Annual, 89-; Studies in Modern Literature, book series, 90-; coed, James Joyce Quarterly, 1963-89; coed, Literature and Theology, 69; Dubliners: A Critical Handbook, 69; The Shapeless God: Essays on the Modern Novel, 68; Approaches to Ulysses: Ten Essays, 70; Approaches to Joyce's Portrait: Ten Essays, 76; Dorothy Richardson, 76; Jean Rhys: A Critical Study, 80; Reflections on James Joyce, 93; Writing the Lives of Writers, 98. **CONTACT ADDRESS** Harry Ransom Humanities Research Center, Univ of Texas, Austin, PO Drawer 7219, Austin, TX 78713-7219. **EMAIL** tfs@mail.utexas.edu

STALLWORTH, FRANCES H.
PERSONAL Born 08/22/1935, Midway, FL, m, 1958, 3 children **DISCIPLINE** ENGLISH **EDUCATION** Fla A & M Univ, BS, 53; MS, 68; Fla State Univ, PhD, 82. **CAREER** Teacher, Howard Acad, 57-63; Teacher, Middle School, 63-69; Teacher, Rickards High School, 69-89; Fla A & M Univ, 89-92; Albany State Univ, 92-93; Fla A & M Univ, 93-. **HONORS AND AWARDS** Teacher of the Year, 95; Teacher Incentive Awd, 95; Exchange Teacher in China, 97-98; Woman of the Month, 00. **MEMBERSHIPS** Nat Coun of Teachers of English, Fla Coun of Teachers of English, Col Lang Asn. **SELECTED PUBLICATIONS** Auth, "Indispensable Punctuation," Florida English Journal, 98; auth, "Ebonics Debate Continues," Florida English Journal, 97; auth, "To Write or Not to Write is Not an Option," The Florida Journal, 96. **CONTACT ADDRESS** Dept Lang & Lit, Florida A&M Univ, 1500 Wahnish Way, Tallahassee, FL 32307-3100.

STAMBOVSKY, PHILLIP
PERSONAL Born 09/02/1952, Springfield, MA, m, 1978, 1 child **DISCIPLINE** ENGLISH **EDUCATION** Univ Mass, AMherst, BA, 77, MA, 79, PhD, 87. **CAREER** Prof, 87-88, dept chair, 88-98, Albertus Magnus Coll; independent scholar, 99-. **HONORS AND AWARDS** NEH vis scholar, Emory Univ, 93; NEH vis scholar, Univ Mo, 98; Univ Mass grad sch fel, 86-87; Yale Mellow vis fac fel, 90- 91. **MEMBERSHIPS** Asn Lit Scholars, Critics **RESEARCH** Emily Dickinson; myth theory; metaphor theory; philos approaches to lit. **SELECTED PUBLICATIONS** Auth, Louis, National Poetry Competition Winners, Chester H. Jones Fdn, 95; auth, Myth and the Limits of Reason, Rodopi, 96; auth, Poetic Work of Emily Dickinson: A Readers' Text, 96; auth, The Psychosocial Construction of Character in The Ambassadors, in Henry James ou le fluide sacre de la fiction, L'Harmattan, 98; auth, Hortense Calisher, George P Elliott, John O'Hara, and Delmore Schwartz in The Columbia Companion to the 20th Century American Short Story, Columbia Univ Press, forthcoming; auth, The Depictive Image: Metaphor and Literary Experience, Massachusetts, 88. **CONTACT ADDRESS** 9 Birch Dr, New Haven, CT 06515.

STANFORD, DONALD ELWIN
PERSONAL Born 02/07/1913, Amherst, MA, m, 1953 **DISCIPLINE** ENGLISH **EDUCATION** Stanford Univ, BA, 33, PhD, 53; Harvard Univ, MA, 34. **CAREER** Instr English, Colo State Col, 35-37, Dartmouth Col, 37-41 & Univ Nebr, 41-42; from instr to assoc prof, 49-59, prof, 59-80, ALUMNI PROF ENGLISH, LA STATE UNIV, BATON ROUGE, 80-, CO-ED, SOUTHERN REV, 63-, Guggenheim fel, 59-60; vis assoc prof, Duke Univ, 61-62; ed, Humanities Ser, Univ Press, La State Univ, Baton Rouge, 62-68; La State Univ Found distinguished fac fel, 73-74. **MEMBERSHIPS** MLA; SCent Mod Lang Asn; PEN Club; SAtlantic Mod Lang Asn. **RESEARCH** The poetry of Edward Taylor; 17th century New England theology and literature; contemporary British and American poetry. **SELECTED PUBLICATIONS** Auth, New England Earth (poems), Colt, 41; The Traveler (poems), Cummington, 55; ed, The Poems of Edward Taylor, Yale Univ, 60; auth, Edward Taylor, Univ Minn, 62; ed, Edward Taylor's Metrical History of Christianity, Xerox, 62; Selected Poems of S Foster Damon, Abattoir Ed, 74; Selected Poems of Robert Bridges, Carcanet, 74; auth, In the Classic Mode: The Achievement of Robert Bridges, Univ Del, 78; As Far As Light Remains, Sewanee Rev, Vol 104, 96; Elizabeth Bishop--Life And The Memory Of It, Sewanee Rev, Vol 102, 94. **CONTACT ADDRESS** Dept of English, Louisiana State Univ and A&M Col, Baton Rouge, LA 70803.

STANLEY, DONALD
DISCIPLINE ENGLISH LITERATURE **EDUCATION** Univ British Columbia, BA; PhD; NY State Univ, MA. **CAREER** Senior tutor. **SELECTED PUBLICATIONS** Auth, pubs on English literature. **CONTACT ADDRESS** English Dept, Open Learning Agency, 4355 Mathissi Place, Burnaby, BC, Canada V5G 4S8. **EMAIL** ouocweb@ola.bc.ca

STANLEY, WILLIAM CHAD
PERSONAL Born 03/24/1968, Hartford, CT, s **DISCIPLINE** ENGLISH **EDUCATION** Syracuse Univ, BA, 92; Univ Conn, MA, 95. **CAREER** Teaching Asst, Univ Conn, 94-; **MEMBERSHIPS** AAUP. **RESEARCH** Shakespeare, Joyce, Fay Weldon, Don DeLillo and Cold War Fiction. **SELECTED PUBLICATIONS** Auth, "Swift's 'The Day of Judgment'," The Explicator, (95): 73-75. **CONTACT ADDRESS** Dept English, Univ of Connecticut, Hartford, 85 Lawler Rd, West Hartford, CT 06117-2620.

STANTON, DON
DISCIPLINE POLITICAL COMMUNICATION **EDUCATION** OH State Univ, PhD, 72. **CAREER** Southwest Tex State Univ **SELECTED PUBLICATIONS** Area: hist of polit commun. **CONTACT ADDRESS** Southwest Missouri State Univ, Springfield, 901 S. National, Ste. 50, Springfield, MO 65804-0094.

STANTON, ROBERT J.
PERSONAL Born 07/07/1942, New York, NY, m, 1959, 2 children **DISCIPLINE** ENGLISH **EDUCATION** Hofstra Univ, BA, 70; Univ Mass, MA, 72; completed doctoral exam, 93. **CAREER** Teaching asst, Univ of Mass, 74-77; **HONORS AND AWARDS** Teacher of the Year, Duval County Public Schools, 87; listed in Who's Who Among America's Teachers, 96 & 00; listed in Who's Who in America, 98-; listed in Who's Who in the World, 98-. **MEMBERSHIPS** Mark Twain Soc, MLA, Fla Asn of Departments of English, Paradoxist Lit Movement Soc, Int Biog Asn, Am Biographian **RESEARCH** Contemporary Writing and Writers (Gore Vidal, Truman Capote, C. P.Snow), American Poetry and Fiction, Group fiction Writing. **SELECTED PUBLICATIONS** Auth, A Bibliography of Modern British Novelists (2 vols), 78; auth, Gore Vidal, 78; auth, Truman Capote, 80; auth, Views From a Window: Conversations with Gore Vidal, 80; contribur, The Devil's Road, 99; auth, Collected Word Paintings, 00; auth, Gore Vidal: A Menippean Satirist, 00. **CONTACT ADDRESS** Dept Humanities, Jacksonville Univ, 2800 University Blvd N, Jacksonville, FL 32211.

STANWOOD, PAUL G.
PERSONAL Born 04/25/1933, Des Moines, IA, m, 1964, 2 children **DISCIPLINE** ENGLISH **EDUCATION** Iowa State Teachers Col, BA, 54; Univ Mich, MA, 56; PhD, 61. **CAREER** Teacher, Des Moines, 54-55; Teaching Fel, Univ Mich, 56-61; Instr to Asst Prof, Tufts Univ, 61-65; Asst Prof to Prof Emeritus, Univ BC, 65-; Vis Assoc Prof, Univ Alta, 72; Vis Prof, Univ of York, 93-94; Vis Prof, Univ Wuerzburg, 99. **HONORS AND AWARDS** Fel, Weil Inst, 64; Fel, Can Coun, 68-69, 74-75; Fel, Folger Shakespeare Libr, 72; Fel, Soc Sci and Humanities Res Coun of Can, 79-80, 84-85; Fel, Can Fed for the Humanities, 89; Fel, Centre for Reformation and Renaissance Studies, 92; Alumni Asn Fac Citation Awd, Univ BC, 98. **MEMBERSHIPS** MLA; Renaissance Soc of Am; Can Soc for Renaissance Studies; Renaissance English Text Soc; Milton Soc of Am; John Doone Soc of Am; Spenser Soc; Conf on Christianity and Lit; Intl Asn of Univ Prof of English. **RESEARCH** English Renaissance and Reformation; Earlier seventeenth-century non-dramatic English literature; Devotional writing; Spenser, Donne, and Milton; Textual bibliography and criticism. **SELECTED PUBLICATIONS** Auth, The Sempiternal Season: Studies in Seventeenth-Century Devotional Writing, Peter Lang, 92; ed, Of Poetry and Politics: New Essays on Milton and His World, 95; auth, Izaak Walton: 1593-1683, Twayne, 98; co-ed, Selected Prose of Christina Rossetti, St Martin's Press, 98; ed, Variorum Edition of the Poetry of John Donne: Holy Sonnets, Ind Univ Press, 01. **CONTACT ADDRESS** Dept English, Univ of British Columbia, 397-1873 E Mall, Vancouver, BC, Canada V6T 1Z1. **EMAIL** stap@home.com

STARGARDT, UTE
DISCIPLINE RHETORIC, ENGLISH AND AMERICAN LITERATURE, CHAUCER **EDUCATION** Univ Tenn,PhD. **CAREER** Prof, Alma Col. **RESEARCH** Medieval literatures and languages. **SELECTED PUBLICATIONS** Her articles have appeared in the US, Argentina and Germany. **CONTACT ADDRESS** Alma Col, Alma, MI 48801.

STARK, JAMES A.
DISCIPLINE MUSIC **EDUCATION** Univ Minn, BA; Univ Toronto, MA, PhD. **CAREER** Prof. **HONORS AND AWARDS** Assoc ed, Jour Res Singing. **CONTACT ADDRESS** Mount Allison Univ, 63D York St, Sackville, NB, Canada E4L 1E4. **EMAIL** jstark@mta.ca

STAROSTA, WILLIAM J.
PERSONAL Born 05/23/1946, Oconomowoc, WI, m, 1967, 1 child **DISCIPLINE** INTERCULTURAL COMMUNICATION **EDUCATION** Indiana Univ, AM, 70, PhD, 73. **CAREER** Univ of Va, asst prof, 72-78; Howard Univ, grad prof, 78-. **HONORS AND AWARDS** Fulbright diss. fel; Am Inst of Indian Studies fel; Wis-Berkeley Year-in-India scholar; held professional office in regional and national socs. **MEMBERSHIPS** Nat Commun Asn; Eastern Commun Asn; World Commun Asn; Intl. Commun Asn. **RESEARCH** Ethnic conflict; Third Culture; Multiculturalism; Interethnic and intercultural communication; Culture and rhetoric. **SELECTED PUBLICATIONS** Coauth, Foundations of Intercultural Communication; ed, The Howard Jour of Communs; co-ed, comm in Global Society **CONTACT ADDRESS** Dept of Human Communication Studies, Howard Univ, 3015 Rosemoor Ln., Fairfax, VA 22031. **EMAIL** wstarosta@howard.edu

STARR, LARRY
PERSONAL Born 04/17/1946, Brooklyn, NY, m, 1968, 3 children **DISCIPLINE** MUSIC HISTORY **EDUCATION** BA, Queens Col, CUNY, 67, PhD, Univ of CA at Berkeley. **CAREER** Asst prof, SUNY, Stony Brook, 70-77; at Univ of WA 77, full prof 93. **RESEARCH** Am music, espec in the 20th century. **SELECTED PUBLICATIONS** A Union of Diversities: Style in the Music of Charles Ives, 92. **CONTACT ADDRESS** Univ of Washington, Box 353450, Seattle, WA 98195. **EMAIL** lstarr@u.washington.edu

STATHOPOULOS, E. T.
PERSONAL Born 04/27/1949, Milwaukee, WI, m, 2 children **DISCIPLINE** COMMUNICATION **EDUCATION** Indiana Univ, PhD 80; Univ Wisconsin Mad, MS 73; Univ Wisconsin Milw, BSc 71. **CAREER** SUNY Buff, prof 79-; Univ Colorado, vis sen res 95-96; Univ Arizona, vis res sc 88-89; Indiana Univ, assoc inst 76-79. **HONORS AND AWARDS** ASHA PSI; Yng Res Awd; SUNY Res fel. **MEMBERSHIPS** ASLHA; ASA; NYS SLHA **RESEARCH** Normal speech production; development and aging of the speech system. **SELECTED PUBLICATIONS** Auth, Effects of a circumferentially-vented pneumotachograph mask on respiratory kinematic and volumetric measures, coauth, in: Jour of SLH Res, 98; Approximations of open and speech quotient from glottal airflow and electroglottographic waveforms: Effects of measurement criteria and sound pressure level, coauth, in: Jour of Voice, 98; Effects of varied intensity on ventilatory responses, coath, in: Jour SLH Res, 98; Expiratory muscle conditioning in hypotonic children with low vocal intensity levels, coauth, in: Jour of Med SL Pathology, 97; Developmental changes in laryngeal and respiratory function with variations in sound pressure level, coauth, in: Jour of SH Res, 97; Speech breathing during reading in women with vocal nodules, coauth, in: Jour of Voice, 97; Speech tasks effects on acoustic and aerodynamic measures of women with vocal nodules, coauth, in: Jour of Voice, 95; Glottal airflow - what can it tell us about a voice disorder? Coauth, In: Topicos em Fonoaudiologia, 96. **CONTACT ADDRESS** Dept of Commun Sci and Disorders, SUNY, Buffalo, North Campus, Buffalo, NY 14260. **EMAIL** stathop@buffalo.edu

STAUFFER, GEORGE B.
PERSONAL Born 02/18/1947, Hershey, PA, m, 1986, 1 child **DISCIPLINE** MUSIC HISTORY, LITERATURE, PERFORMANCE **EDUCATION** Columbia Univ, PhD. **CAREER** Prof & dean ch; gen ed, Monuments Western Mus ser at Macmillan. **HONORS AND AWARDS** Guggenheim, Fulbright, ACLS, and IREX fellowships. **MEMBERSHIPS** Pres, Amer Bach Soc. **RESEARCH** Baroque music; works and life of J.S. Bach in particular. **SELECTED PUBLICATIONS** Auth, J.S. Bach as Organist; Bach Perspectives 2 & Bach: The Mass in B Minor; articles in, Early Mus, Mus Quart, J Musicol, Bach-Jahrbuch. **CONTACT ADDRESS** Rutgers, The State Univ of New Jersey, New Brunswick, Mason Gross School of the Arts, 33 Livingston Ave, New Brunswick, NJ 08901-1959. **EMAIL** stauffer@rci.rutgers.edu

STAUFFER, HELEN WINTER
PERSONAL Born 01/04/1922, Mitchell, SD, m, 1944, 4 children **DISCIPLINE** ENGLISH **EDUCATION** Kearney State Col, BA, 64, MA, 68; Univ Nebr, PhD(English), 74. **CAREER** Teacher English, Giltner High Sch, 64, Grand Island High Sch, 64-67; from instr to assoc prof, 68-75, PROF ENGLISH, KEARNEY STATE COL, 75- **MEMBERSHIPS** MLA; Western Lit Asn (pres, 80); Soc Study Midwestern Lit; Willa Cather Found; NEA. **RESEARCH** American literature; modern West-

ern regional literature. **SELECTED PUBLICATIONS** Auth, Mari Sandoz and Western Biography, In: Women, Women Writers and the West, Whitston, 80; Two authors and a hero: Neihardt, Sandoz and Crazy Horse, Great Plains Quart, 1/81; Mari Sandoz and the university, Prairie Schooner, spring 81; Mari Sandoz, Story Catcher of the Plains, Univ Nebr Press, 82; co-ed (with Susan J Rosowski), Women in Western American Literature, Whitston, 82; auth, Mari Sandoz, In: Fifty Western American Writers, Greenwood, 82; Mari Sandoz, Boise State Univ; Neihardt's The River and I: The Beginning of an Epic, Neihardt Centennial Commemorative Collection; Mari Sandoz, Portrait Of An Artists Youth, Great Plains Quart, Vol 16, 96; Robert Henri Nebraska Years, Great Plains Quart, Vol 16, 96. **CONTACT ADDRESS** Dept of English, Univ of Nebraska, Kearney, Kearney, NE 68847.

STAVES, SUSAN
PERSONAL Born 10/05/1942, New York, NY, s **DISCIPLINE** ENGLISH **EDUCATION** Univ Chicago, AB, 63; Univ Va, MA, 64, PhD(English), 67. **CAREER** Woodrow Wilson Intern English, Bennett Col, Greensboro, NC, 66-67; vis assoc prof English, Univ Md, Baltimore, 74-75; asst prof, 64-76, ASSOC PROF ENGLISH, BRANDEIS UNIV, 76- **MEMBERSHIPS** MLA; Am Soc Eighteenth Century Studies; English Inst; AAUP; fel Am Coun Learned Soc. **RESEARCH** Restoration and 18th century British literature; legal history; social history. **SELECTED PUBLICATIONS** Auth, " The Man of Mode and the Secrets of Genteel Identity, " Studies in 18th Century Culture, 89; auth, "' The Liberty of a She-Subject of England': Rights Rhetoric and the Female Thucydides," Cardozo Studies in Law and Literature, 89; auth, Married Women's Separate Property in England, 1660-1833, Harvard Univ, 90; auth, " French Fire, English Asbestos: Ninon de Lenclos and Elizabeth Griffith, " Studies on Voltaire and the 18th-Century, 93; auth, " English Chattel Property Rules and the Construction of Personal and National Identity, " Law and History Review, 94; auth, " Fielding and the Comedy of Attempted Rape, in History, Gender and the 18th-Century Literature, Univ of GA, 94; auth, " The Construction of the Public Interest in the Debates over Fox's India Bills," Prose Studies, 95;coed, Early Modern Conceptions of Property in England, 1660-1833, Routledge, 95; coed, Elizabeth Griffith's Delicate Distress, U of KY, 97; auth, " Investments, Votes, and 'Bribes'": Women as Shareholders in the Chartered National Companies," in Women Writers and the Early Modern British Political Tradition, Cambridge,99. **CONTACT ADDRESS** Dept of English, Brandeis Univ, MS 023, Waltham, MA 02254-9110.

STECKLINE, C. TURNER
PERSONAL Born 12/28/1954, Sanborn, NY **DISCIPLINE** SPEECH COMMUNICATION, DRAMTIC ARTS, PERFORMANCE STUDIES **EDUCATION** Univ of Northern Colo, BA, 75; Univ of Iowa, MA, 78; Southern Ill Univ at Carbondale, PhD, 97. **CAREER** Chair, dept of speech commun, Univ of Dubuque, 79-82; asst prof of speech commun, Loras Col, 82-87; instr/asst dir of forensics, Iowa State Univ, 88-89; dir of forensics, 89-91, asst prof, 91-95, Univ of Wis-Platteville; ASST PROF OF SPEECH COMMUN AND THEATRE ARTS, NORTHEAST LA UNIV, 97-. **HONORS AND AWARDS** Marion Kleinau Theatre Awd, Southern Ill Univ, 95; Kleinau Theatre Production Assistantship, 95 & 96; Graduate Teaching Assistantship, Southern Ill Unive, 92-95, 97; initiating honors sequence: Vision, Language & Reality, Univ of Wis-Platteville, 91-92; adjunct fac appointment, 80-82, teaching Excellence, Loras Col, 86; grad teaching asst, The Rhetoric Prog, Univ of Iowa, 76-79. **MEMBERSHIPS** Nat Commun Asn; Southern States Commun Asn; La Commun Asn; Nat Coun for Teachers of English; Nat Women's Studies Asn; Nat Storytelling Asn. **RESEARCH** Whistleblowing/ethical resistances; diffusion; response theory & bearing witness; disability and family communication; performance of ethnography/ethnography of performance. **SELECTED PUBLICATIONS** Auth, Ideas and Images of Performed Witnessing: A Cross-Genre Analysis, Southern Ill Univ at Carbondale, 97; auth, Books in Review: Ecological Feminism, Ecological Literary Criticism: Romantic Imagining and the Biology of the Mind, Text and Performance Quarterly, 96. **CONTACT ADDRESS** Dept of Speech Commun & Theatre, Univ of Louisiana, Monroe, Monroe, LA 71203. **EMAIL** coyote@hc3.com

STEEL, DAVID WARREN
DISCIPLINE MUSIC HISTORY **EDUCATION** Harvard Univ, AB, 68; Univ Mich, AM, 76, PhD, 82. **CAREER** ASSOC PROF, MUS & SOUTHERN CULT, UNIV MISS **MEMBERSHIPS** Am Antiquarian Soc **SELECTED PUBLICATIONS** Auth, "Truman S. Wetmore and His Republican Harmony," Conn Hist Soc Bull 45, 80; auth, "L.L. Jones and The Southern Minstrel (1849)," Am Mus 6, 88; auth, "John Wyeth and the Development of Southern Folk Hymnody," in Music from the Middle Ages through the 20th Century, Gordon & Breach, 88; auth, Stephen Jenks, in New Grove Dict of Am Music; ed, Stephen Jenks: Collected Works, A-R Editions, 95. **CONTACT ADDRESS** Dept of Music, Univ of Mississippi, Meek Hall, University, MS 38677. **EMAIL** mudws@olemiss.edu

STEEN, SARA JAYNE
PERSONAL Born 12/09/1949, Toledo, OH, m, 3 children **DISCIPLINE** ENGLISH RENAISSANCE STUDIES **EDUCATION** Bowling Green State Univ, BS, 70, PhD(English), 78; Ohio State Univ, MA, 74. **CAREER** Prof English, Mont State Univ, 78-. **MEMBERSHIPS** MLA; Renaissance Soc Am. **RESEARCH** Shakespeare; women writers. **SELECTED PUBLICATIONS** Auth, The Letters of Lady Arbella Stuart. Women Writers in English 1350-1850; Oxford Univ Press, 94; Ambrosia in an Earthern Vessel: Three Centuries of Audience and Reader Response to the Works of Thomas Middleton, AMS Press, 93; also auth., Thomas Middleton: A Reference Guide, G K Hall, 84; coauth, Intersections: The Elements of Fiction in Science Fiction, The Popular Press, 78; guest co-ed, Shakespear Quarterly, 47, 4, 96. **CONTACT ADDRESS** Dept of English, Montana State Univ, Bozeman, Bozeman, MT 59717-2300. **EMAIL** steen@english.montana.edu

STEENSMA, ROBERT CHARLES
PERSONAL Born 11/24/1930, Sioux Falls, SD, m, 1964, 5 children **DISCIPLINE** ENGLISH LANGUAGE & LITERATURE **EDUCATION** Augustana Col, SDak, BA, 52; Univ SDak, MA, 55; Univ Ky, PhD, 61. **CAREER** Instr English, Augustana Col, SDak, 55-57; asst prof, Univ SDak, 59-62 & Utah State Univ, 62-66; assoc prof & asst chmn, 66-70, dir advan placement, 68-76, PROF ENGLISH, UNIV UTAH, 70-, Res grant, Utah State Univ, 63-64; Fulbright lectr, Finland, 72-73; David Gardner fac res fel, Univ Utah, 79; Outstanding Prof for Teaching, English Dept, Univ of Utah, 90. **HONORS AND AWARDS** Navy Commendation Medal, 83. **MEMBERSHIPS** Us Naval Inst; VFW; Western Lit Asn. **RESEARCH** Jonathan Swift; 18th century English literature; Graham Greene, Jane Austen, Wallace Stegner. **SELECTED PUBLICATIONS** Ed, Sir William Temple's Essay Upon the Origin and Nature of Government, Augustan Reprint Soc, 64; Sir William Temple, Twayne, 70; Dr. John Arbuthnot, Twayne, 79; auth, Drifting to an Unknown Future, Center for Western Studies, Augustana Col, 00. **CONTACT ADDRESS** Dept of English, Univ of Utah, Orson Spencer Hall, Salt Lake City, UT 84112-8916. **EMAIL** rsteensma@earthlink.net

STEER, HELEN V.
PERSONAL Born 05/20/1926, Manchester, England, s **DISCIPLINE** SPEECH, THEATRE **EDUCATION** LSU, BA, 54, MA, 58, PhD, 67. **CAREER** Theatre dir & spch tchr, Howard Col, 56-59; Teaching asst, LSU, 60-63; Assoc prof, East Carolina Univ, 63-88; Dialect coach, The Lost Colony, 88. **HONORS AND AWARDS** Pres, NC Speech & Drama Assoc, 71. **MEMBERSHIPS** Nat Commun Assoc; Southern Speech Commun Assoc; Phi Kappa Phi. **RESEARCH** Dialects, especially stage use. **SELECTED PUBLICATIONS** Ed, co-auth, Your Speech, 3rd ed, 96. **CONTACT ADDRESS** 2306 E 3rd St, Greenville, NC 27858.

STEFFEL, SUSAN B.
PERSONAL Born 02/09/1951, Muskegon, MI, m, 1975 **DISCIPLINE** ENGLISH **EDUCATION** Hope Col, BA, 73; Mich State Univ, MA, 78; PhD, 93. **CAREER** Teacher, Maple Valley HS, 73-91; from instr to assoc prof, Cent Mich Univ, 91-. **HONORS AND AWARDS** Excellence in Teaching Awd, CMU, 96; Outstanding teacher Awd, Sigma Tau Delta, 97; Edwin Towle Prof, 98. **MEMBERSHIPS** Phi Delta Kappa, Golden Key Nat Honor Soc, Phi Kappa Phi Int Honor Soc, AAUW, AERA, ASCD, ALAN, Nat Council of Teachers of English, Women in Lit & Life Assembly Conf on English Educ. **RESEARCH** Young adult literature, reading theory, composition theory, English education, literacy and learning. **SELECTED PUBLICATIONS** Auth, "Discipline through Community," rev of "Beyond Discipline: From Compliance to Community," Land Arts J Mich 13.1 (97); auth, "Han Nolan," "Linda Crew," "Randy Powell," and "Gary Paulsen," St. James Guide to Young Adult Writers 2nd Ed; auth, "You've Got Mail: Extending Literary Responses Through Email Dialogues," Lang Arts J of Mich 15.1 (99). **CONTACT ADDRESS** Dept English, Central Michigan Univ, 215 Anspach, Mount Pleasant, MI 48859-0001.

STEHLE, CHERYL F.
PERSONAL Born 07/15/1946, Latrolie, PA, m **DISCIPLINE** ENGLISH **EDUCATION** SUNY, BA, 69; MA, 73; EdAdmin, 79; Univ Rochester, PhD, 81. **CAREER** Adj Prof, Univ SC, 86-; Adj Prof, Grad Regional Studies Univ SC, 86-. **HONORS AND AWARDS** Prof of the Year, Univ SC, 94. **MEMBERSHIPS** Intl Alliance for Invitational Educ. **RESEARCH** Affective learning, self-concept development, Invitational learning, English, Language arts, Curriculum, counseling, Gifted/talented education, Career education, Humanistic learning, Leadership, and Administration. **SELECTED PUBLICATIONS** Auth, Invitational Learning for counseling and development, ERIC, 90. **CONTACT ADDRESS** Dept English, Univ of So Carolina, Beaufort, 1 Col Center Dr, Hilton Head, SC 29928.

STEIN, ARNOLD
PERSONAL Born 04/27/1915, Brockton, MA, m, 1942, 2 children **DISCIPLINE** ENGLISH LITERATURE **EDUCATION** Yale Univ, AB, 36; Harvard Univ, AM, 38, PhD, 42. **CAREER** Instr, Univ Minn, 40-46; asst prof, Ohio State Univ, 46-48; from assoc prof to prof English lit, Univ Wash, 48-71; prof English, Johns Hopkins Univ, 71-74, Sir William Osler prof, 74-80; PROF ENGLISH, UNIV ILL, URBANA, 80-, Ford Found Advan Educ fel, 53-54; Guggenheim fel, 59-60; sr ed, J English Lit Hist, 74-80. **MEMBERSHIPS** Renaissance Soc Am; MLA; Milton Soc Am; Acad Lit Studies. **RESEARCH** Criticism; 17th century and contemporary literature. **SELECTED PUBLICATIONS** Auth, Answerable Style 53, Heroic Knowledge, 57 & John Donne's Lyrics: The Eloquence of Action, 62, Univ Minn; ed, Theodore Roethke: Essays on the Poetry, Univ Wash, 65; auth, George Herbert's Lyrics, Johns Hopkins Univ, 68; ed, On Milton's Poetry, Fawcett, 69; auth, The Art of Presence, Univ Calif, 77; Imagining Death, The Ways Of Milton, Milton Studies, Vol 29, 92. **CONTACT ADDRESS** Dept of English, Univ of Illinois, Urbana-Champaign, Urbana, IL 61801.

STEIN, KAREN F.
PERSONAL Born 07/01/1941, Brooklyn, NY, d, 2 children **DISCIPLINE** ENGLISH, WOMEN'S STUDIES **EDUCATION** Brooklyn Col, BA, 62; Pa State Univ, MA, 66; Univ Conn, PhD, 82. **CAREER** Prof of English and Women's Studies, Univ of Rhode Island, 68-. **HONORS AND AWARDS** Graduated cum laude, Brooklyn Col, 62; Phi Beta Kappa; Woman of the Year, Asn of Academic and Prof Women, URI, 93; Can Govt Fac Enrichment Grant, 94; URI Found Summer Res Grant, 97; Champlin Found Grant; "Women, Science and Engineering Curricular Project," Am Asn of Cols and Univs, Second Tier Team Member; Development of "Women and the Natural Sciences," participant in FIPSE grant to bridge the humanities and science. **MEMBERSHIPS** AAUP, PBK, Margaret Atwood Soc, Toni Morrison Soc. **RESEARCH** Margaret Atwood, the Gothic, contemporary American poetry. **SELECTED PUBLICATIONS** Auth, "Speaking in Tongues: Margaret Laurence's A Jest of God as Gothic narrative," Studies in Can Lit, 20.2 (winter 95): 74-95; auth, "The Handmaid's Tale: Margaret Atwood's Modest Proposal," Can Lit, 148 (spring 96): 57-73; auth, Margaret Atwood Revisited, Twayne (99); auth, "Films of the Frankenstein Myth: Children of an Angry God," for Gary Harmon, ed, Film and Gender: Myth, Power and Change (with W. Brownell), Popular Press (forthcoming). **CONTACT ADDRESS** Dept English, Univ of Rhode Island, 60 Upper Col Rd, Kingston, RI 02881-2000. **EMAIL** karen_s@uri.edu

STEIN, KEVIN J.
PERSONAL Born 01/01/1954, Anderson, IN, m, 1979, 2 children **DISCIPLINE** ENGLISH **EDUCATION** Ball State Univ, BS, 76; MA, 78; Ind Univ, MA, 82; PhD, 84. **CAREER** Prof, Bradley Univ, 84-. **HONORS AND AWARDS** Frederick Bock Prize, 87; Nat Endow for the Arts Fel, 91; Devins Awd, 92; Indiana Rev Poetry Prize, 98. **MEMBERSHIPS** AWP; Soc of Midland Authors. **RESEARCH** Contemporary American Poetry and Poetics, Poetry of James Wright. **SELECTED PUBLICATIONS** Auth, James Wright: The Poetry of a Grown Man, Ohio Univ Pr, 89; auth, A Circus of Want: Poems, Univ of Mo, 92; auth, Private Poets, World Acts, Ohio Univ, 96; AUTH, Bruised Paradise: Poems, Univ of IL, 96; auth, Chance Ransom: Poems, Univ of IL, 00. **CONTACT ADDRESS** Dept English, Bradley Univ, 1501 W Bradley Ave, Peoria, IL 61625-0001. **EMAIL** kstein@bradley.edu

STEIN, ROBERT DAVID
PERSONAL Born 10/09/1937, Chicago, IL, m, 1960, 3 children **DISCIPLINE** ENGLISH **EDUCATION** Brown Univ, AB, 59; Northwestern Univ, MA, 61, PhD(English), 68. **CAREER** Lectr, Northwestern Univ, 64-65; from instr to asst prof, Univ Chicago, 65-73; prof English & chmn dept, Washburn Univ, Topeka, 73-; dean, Univ Honors Prog, 82-. **MEMBERSHIPS** MLA; Am Bus Commun Asn. **RESEARCH** Literature, science and religion in the 19th century; critical theory; the arts of Victorian prose. **CONTACT ADDRESS** Dept of English, Washburn Univ of Topeka, 1700 SW College Ave, Topeka, KS 66621-0001. **EMAIL** zzstei@washburn.edu

STEINBERG, ERWIN RAY
PERSONAL Born 11/15/1920, New Rochelle, NY, m, 1954, 2 children **DISCIPLINE** ENGLISH **EDUCATION** State Univ NYork Albany, BS, 41, MS, 42; NYork Univ, PhD, 56. **CAREER** From instr to assoc prof, 46-61, head dept gen studies, 56-60, dean, Margaret Morrison Carnegie Col, 60-73, dean div humanities & soc sci, 65-68, dean, Col Humanities & Soc Sci, 68-75; Prof English, 61-75, Prof, 75-80, Thomas S. Baker Prof English & Interdisciplinary Studies, 81-92, Prof English & Rhetoric, Carnegie-Mellon Univ, 93-, Vice-Provost for Educ, 91-96; Commun consult; coordr, Prof English, US Off Educ, 63-64; vis scholar, Ctr Advan Studies Behav Sci, 70-71; mem comn scholars, Bd Higher Educ, State Ill, 74-. **HONORS AND AWARDS** Carnegie Teaching Awd, 56; Distinguished Alumnus, State Univ NY-Albany, 69; Alumnus of the Year, State Univ of NY Col-Plattsburgh, 71; Phi Beta Kappa; Phi Kappa Phi; Phi Delta Kappa; Kappa Delta Pi; Robert Doherty Prize for substantial and sustained contributions to excellence in education, 90. **MEMBERSHIPS** NCTE; MLA. **RESEARCH** The modern novel; myth in modern literature; communication in business and industry. **SELECTED PUBLICATIONS** Coauth, Communication in Business and Industry, Holt, 60; auth, Needed Research in the Teaching of English, US Govt

Printing Off, 63; gen ed, Insight Series (14 vols), 68-73 & co-ed, English Education Today, 70, Noble; English Then and Now, Random, 70; auth, The Stream of Consciousness and Beyond in Joyce's Ulysses, Univ Pittsburgh, 73; ed, The Stream-of-Consciousness Technique in the Modern Novel, Kennikat, 79; co-ed, Approaches to Teaching Joyce's Ulysses, Mod Lang Asn, 92; co-auth, Ulysses on Montmarte, Carnegie Mellon Univ, Pr, 02. **CONTACT ADDRESS** Col of Humanities & Soc Sci, Carnegie Mellon Univ, 5000 Forbes Ave, Pittsburgh, PA 15213-3890. **EMAIL** es2t@andrew.cmu.edu

STEINBERG, THEODORE LOUIS
PERSONAL Born 01/08/1947, Baltimore, MD, m, 3 children **DISCIPLINE** MEDIEVAL ENGLISH; JEWISH LITERATURE **EDUCATION** Johns Hopkins Univ, BA, 68; Univ Ill, AM, 69, PhD(English), 71. **CAREER** Asst prof, 71-75, assoc prof, 75-79, prof English, State Univ NY Col Fredonia, 79-**HONORS AND AWARDS** Chancellor's Awd for Excellence in Teaching, 96; **MEMBERSHIPS** Medieval Acad Am; Am Asn Prof Yiddish; Spenser Soc. **RESEARCH** Medieval and Renaissance literature; Jewish literature. **SELECTED PUBLICATIONS** Auth, Spenser's Shepherdes Calender and EK's, Mod Lang Studies, winter 73; The schoolmaster: Teaching sixteenth century literature, English Rec, 73; I B Singer: Responses to catastrophe, Yiddish, 75; The anatomy of Euphues, Studies English Lit, 77; Mendele Mocher Seforim, G K Hall, 77; The humanities and the Holocaust, Humanist Educators, 80; Poetry and the perpendicular style, J Aesthet & Art Criticism, 81; Piers Plowman and Prophecy, Garland, 91. **CONTACT ADDRESS** Dept of English, SUNY, Col at Fredonia, Fredonia, NY 14063. **EMAIL** theodore.steinberg@fredonia.edu

STEINBRINK, JEFFREY
PERSONAL Born 08/29/1945, Erie, PA **DISCIPLINE** ENGLISH **EDUCATION** Allegheny Col, BA, 67; Univ NC, Chapel Hill, MA, 68, PhD(English), 74. **CAREER** Instr English, Behrend Campus, Pa State Univ, 68-71; instr, Univ NC, Chapel Hill, 74-75; vis asst prof, 75-77, asst prof, 77-80, assoc prof, 80-91, prof English, 91- , chemn, 89-92, Franklin & Marshall Col. **HONORS AND AWARDS** NEH summer stipend, 76, 83; fel, Penn-Lilly Prog, 79; USIS AmPart lectr, Republic of Philippines, 85; NEH fel, 85-86; Natl Adv Bc, Elmira Col Ctr for mark Twain Stud, 86- . **MEMBERSHIPS** AAUP; MLA; Northeast Mod Lang Asn; Popular Cult Asn. **RESEARCH** Relationship between history and American literature; the American novel; Mark Twain. **SELECTED PUBLICATIONS** Auth, Why the Innocents Went Abroad: Mark Twain and American Tourism in the Late Nineteenth Century, Am Lit Realism, 83; auth, mark Twain and Hunter Thompson: Continuity and Change in American Outlaw Journalism, Stud in Am Humor, 83-84; auth, Who Wrote Huckleberry Finn: mark Twain's Control of the Early Manuscript, in Sattelmeyer, ed, One Hundred Years of Huckleberry Finn: The Boy, His Book, and American Culture, Missouri, 84; auth, Getting To Be Mark Twain,Univ Calif, 91. **CONTACT ADDRESS** Dept of English, Franklin and Marshall Col, PO Box 3003, Lancaster, PA 17604-3003. **EMAIL** j_steinbrink@acad.fandm.edu

STEINER, JOAN ELIZABETH
PERSONAL Born 02/16/1933, Oberlin, OH **DISCIPLINE** ENGLISH & AMERICAN LITERATURE **EDUCATION** Oberlin Col, AB, 55; Univ Mich, Ann Arbor, MA, 56, PhD, 71. **CAREER** Teacher English, Grosse Pointe Pub Schs, Mich, 56-59; staff mem, Second Cong Dist Off, US House Rep, 65-67; from instr to asst prof, 68-76, assoc prof, 76-83, Prof English, Drew Univ, 83-98, Prof Emer, 98-, chmn, English dept, 86-90. **HONORS AND AWARDS** Phi Beta Kappa, Phi Kappa Phi. **MEMBERSHIPS** MLA; AAUP. **RESEARCH** Twentieth century British and American fiction; history of the novel; Afro-American literature. **SELECTED PUBLICATIONS** Auth, Conrad's The Secret Sharer; Complexities of the doubling relationship, Conradiana, Vol 12, 80; Modern pharisees and false apostles: Ironic New Testament parallels in Conrad's Heart of Darkness, 19th Century Fiction, Vol 37, 82. **CONTACT ADDRESS** Dept of English, Drew Univ, 36 Madison Ave, Madison, NJ 07940-1493. **EMAIL** jsteiner@drew.edu

STEINER, THOMAS ROBERT
PERSONAL Born 08/18/1934, Budapest, Hungary, m, 1991, 2 children **DISCIPLINE** ENGLISH, COMPARATIVE LITERATURE **EDUCATION** Cornell Univ, BA, 55; Columbia Univ, MA, 60 PhD, 67. **CAREER** Lectr, Hunter Col, City Univ NYork, 61-64; lectr, Brooklyn Col, City Univ NYork, 64-66; vis assoc prof, Univ Ill, Urbana-Champaign, 74-74; from asst prof to full prof, Univ Calif, Santa Barbara, 66-94; prof emeritus, Univ Calif, Santa Barbara, 94-; adj prof, Univ S Calif, 96, 98-99. **HONORS AND AWARDS** Calif Humanities Inst Fel, 69; Nathanael West Essay Contest Prize, Southern Rev, 70; Univ Calif, Santa Barbara, Instruct Dev Awd, 83-84. **RESEARCH** Eighteenth century English literature; detective fiction; literary theory. **SELECTED PUBLICATIONS** Auth, "Precursors to Dryden: Seventeenth-Century French and English Theories of Translation," CLS 7 (70): 50-81; auth, "West's Lemuel and the American Dream," S Rev 7 (71): 994-1006; auth, English Translation Theory, 1650-1800, Van Gorcum, 75; auth, "Homer's Ape: Teaching Pope," ECL 5 (79): 46-53; auth, "Stanislaw Lem's Detective Stories," MFS 29 (83): 451-462; auth, "The Mind of the Hard-boiled: Ross Macdonald and the Roles of Criticism," SDak Rev 24 (86): 29-53; auth, "The Origin of Raymond Chandler's 'Mean Streets,'" ANQ 7 (94): 225-227; auth, "Richard Gwinnett and His 'Virtuous Lover,' Elizabeth Thomas: A Literary Romance of Eighteenth-Century Gloucestershire," Ga Hist Quart 78 (94): 794-809. **CONTACT ADDRESS** Dept of English, Univ of California, Santa Barbara, Santa Barbara, CA 93106. **EMAIL** tsteiner@humanities.ucsb.edu

STEINER, WENDY LOIS
PERSONAL Born 03/20/1949, Winnipeg, MB, Canada, 2 children **DISCIPLINE** ENGLISH LITERATURE **EDUCATION** McGill Univ, BA, 70; Yale Univ, MPhil, 72, PhD(English), 74. **CAREER** Asst prof English, Yale Univ, 75-76; asst prof, Univ Mich, Ann Arbor, 76-79; from Asst Prof to Prof, 79-93, Richard L. Fisher Prof English, Univ Pa, 93-; Dir, Penn Humanities Forum, 98-. **HONORS AND AWARDS** Nat Endowment for Humanities summer grant, 80; Guggenheim fel, 82-83. **MEMBERSHIPS** MLA. **RESEARCH** Modern literature; modern critical theory; relation of painting to literature. **SELECTED PUBLICATIONS** Auth, Exact Resemblance to Exact Resemblance: The Literary Portraiture of Gertrude Stein, Yale Univ, 78; auth, The Colors of Rhetoric: Problems in the Relation between Modern Painting and Literature, Chicago Univ, 82; Pictures of Romance, Chicago Univ, 88; The Scandal of Pleasure, Chicago Univ, 95; auth, Postmodern Fictions, 1970-1990 In: The Cambridge History of American Literature, 99. **CONTACT ADDRESS** Dept of English, Univ of Pennsylvania, 3340 Walnut St, Philadelphia, PA 19104-6203. **EMAIL** wsteiner@english.upenn.edu

STEINMAN, LISA M.
PERSONAL Born 04/08/1950, Willimantic, CT, m, 1984 **DISCIPLINE** ENGLISH **EDUCATION** Cornell Univ, BA,71, MFA, 73, PhD, 76 **CAREER** Teaching asst, Cornell Univ, 70-76; asst prof to assoc prof to prof to Kenan Prof, Reed Col, 76-, dir NEH Summer Seminar for School Teachers, 86, 88, 90, 92, 99. **HONORS AND AWARDS** Rockefeller Fel, 87; Burlington Northern Awd, 87; Pablo Neruda Awd, 87; elect to PEN, 89; Vollum Awd, 90; Oregon Book Awd, 93; Nat Endow for Humanities Fel, 96. **MEMBERSHIPS** AWP; ASA; MLA; ALA. **RESEARCH** Poetry **SELECTED PUBLICATIONS** Auth, Made In America: Science, Technology, and American Modernist Poets, Yale Univ Press, 87, 89; All that Comes to Light, Arrowood Books Inc, 89; A Book of Other Days, Arrowood Books Inc, 93; Ordinary Songs 26 books, 96; Masters of Repetition: Poetry, Culture, and Work, St. Martin's Press, 98. **CONTACT ADDRESS** Dept of English, Reed Col, 3203 SE Woodstock Blvd, Portland, OR 97202. **EMAIL** lisa.steinman@reed.edu

STELZIG, EUGENE LOUIS
PERSONAL Born 08/18/1943, Bischofshofen, Austria, m, 1968 **DISCIPLINE** ENGLISH & AMERICAN LITERATURE **EDUCATION** Univ Pa, BA, 66; Cambridge Univ, BA, 68, MA, 72; Harvard Univ, MA, 69, PhD(English), 72. **CAREER** Asst prof, 72-79, assoc prof English, State Univ NY Col Genesco, 78-79, Nat Endowment for Humanities fel, 78-79; prof, 84-90; SUNY disting teaching prof, 96-; chair, English dept, State Univ NY Col Genesco, 97-. **HONORS AND AWARDS** NEH Fel, 78-79, 85-86; SUNY Chancellor's Awd for Excellence in Teaching, 85. **MEMBERSHIPS** MLA **RESEARCH** British and American and European romanticism; autobiography and confession. **SELECTED PUBLICATIONS** Auth, The Romantic Subject in Autobiography: Rousseau and Goethe, Univ of Virginia UP, 00; auth, All Shades of Consciousness: Wordsworth's Poetry and the Self in Time, Mouton, 75; Herman Hesse's Fictions of the Self: Autobiography and the Confessional Imagination, Princeton UP, 1988. **CONTACT ADDRESS** Dept of English, SUNY, Col at Geneseo, 1 College Cir, Geneseo, NY 14454-1401. **EMAIL** stelzig@geneseo.edu

STEN, CHRISTOPHER W.
PERSONAL Born 01/03/1944, Minneapolis, MN, m, 1969, 2 children **DISCIPLINE** ENGLISH **EDUCATION** Carleton Col, BA, 66; Ind Univ, MA, 68; PhD, 71. **CAREER** Instr, George Wash Univ, 70; asst prof, 71-78; assoc prof, 78-88; Prof, 88-. **HONORS AND AWARDS** Sr Fulbright Lectr, Germany, 75-76. **MEMBERSHIPS** MLA; Fulbright Asn. **RESEARCH** Melville, Cather, ethnicity, the novel, the city. **SELECTED PUBLICATIONS** Auth, "The Dialogue of Crisis in The Confidence-Man: Melville's 'New Novel'," Studies in the Novel 6 (74): 65-85; auth, "Bartleby the Transcendentalist: Melville's Dead Letter to Emerson," Mod Lang Quart 35 (74): 30-44; ed, Savage Eye: Melville and the Visual Arts, Kent State Univ Press (Kent, OH), 92; auth, The Weaver-God, He Weaves: Melville and the Poetics of the Novel, Kent State Univ Press (Kent, OH), 96; auth, Sounding the Whale: Moby-Dick as epic novel, Kent State Univ Press (Kent, OH), 96; **CONTACT ADDRESS** Dept English, The George Washington Univ, 2035 H Street Northwest, Washington, DC 20052-0001. **EMAIL** csten@gwu.edu

STEPHENS, CHARLES RALPH
PERSONAL Born 01/14/1943, Nashville, TN, m, 1986 **DISCIPLINE** AMERICAN LITERATURE **EDUCATION** Univ Md, PhD, 85. **CAREER** Prof English & Dean of Humanities & Arts, Essex Commun Col. **MEMBERSHIPS** Col Eng Assoc; Soc Study S Lit; MLA; SMLA **RESEARCH** Southern American literature. **SELECTED PUBLICATIONS** auth The Craft of Peter Taylor, Univ Alabama Press; The Fiction of Anne Tyler, The Correspondence of Flannery O'Connor and the Brainard Cheneys, Univ Press Miss. **CONTACT ADDRESS** Humanities & Arts, Comm Col of Baltimore County-Essex Campus, Baltimore, MD 21237. **EMAIL** rstephens@ccbc.cc.md.us

STEPHENS, JESSICA
PERSONAL Born 09/26/1963, Versailles, KY **DISCIPLINE** ENGLISH **EDUCATION** Ky State Univ, BA, 85; Univ Ky, MA, 88; DEd, 96. **CAREER** Instr, Univ of Ky, 86-89; instr, Highland Bus Col, 89-90; instr, Operation Read, 90-91; instr, Eastern Ky Univ, 91-95; dir, Student Lit Centre, Univ of Ky, 95-96; asst prof, Univ of Ky, 97-00; asst prof, Eastern Ky Univ, 96-. **HONORS AND AWARDS** Univ English Awd, 85; Presidential Scholar, 81-84; Minority Fel, 85-87; English Dept Fel, 85-87; Lyman t. Johnson Fel, 94-96. **MEMBERSHIPS** NADE; KYTESOL; NSSE; AERA; Phi Delta Kappa; KADE; KCTE. **RESEARCH** Multiculturalism, literacy student persistence. **SELECTED PUBLICATIONS** Coauth, "Family diversity: Perceptions of university students relative to gender and college major: Urban Educ 31, (96): 91-106; coauth, "From minority to majority: The student faculty of tomorrow", Sch Bus Affairs 63.4 (97): 13-18; coauth, "Forty years after Brown: The impact of immigration policy on desegregation", Educ and Urban Soc 29, (97): 182-190; coauth, "Self-concept, racial identity, and academic achievement among African Americans in higher education", Negro Educ Rev 48, (97): 131-140; auth, "Wanted: Minority educators for U.S. schools", Sch Bus Affairs 65, (99): 37-42. **CONTACT ADDRESS** Dept English, Eastern Kentucky Univ, 521 Lancaster Ave, Richmond, KY 40475-3100. **EMAIL** engsteph@acs.eku.edu

STEPHENS, MARGARET HOLLER
PERSONAL Born 03/29/1948, St Louis, MO, s **DISCIPLINE** ENGLISH **EDUCATION** Univ Mo Columbia, BJ, 70; Univ Mo Kansas City, MA, 86; Auburn Univ, PhD, 97. **CAREER** Adj instr, Univ of Mo Kansas City, 85-89; TA to instr, Auburn Univ, 89-98; asst prof, Ala State Univ, 98-. **HONORS AND AWARDS** Phi Kappa Phi. **MEMBERSHIPS** Am Soc for Eighteenth Century Studies; Col Lang Assoc; NCTE; AFT; Ala Writers Forum; Ala Folklife Assoc; Delta Kappa Gamma; Phi Kappa Phi; Langston Hughes Soc; Charles Waddell Chestnutt Assoc. **RESEARCH** Alexander Pope; Robert Walpole, 18th Century Journalism and Letters, Hermeneutics, Trans-Atlantic slave trade - British involvement. **CONTACT ADDRESS** Dept of Humanities, Alabama State Univ, PO Box 271, Montgomery, AL 36101-0271.

STEPHENS, MARTHA THOMAS
PERSONAL Born, GA, m, 3 children **DISCIPLINE** ENGLISH **EDUCATION** Indiana Univ, PhD. **CAREER** Univ Cincinnati, prof english emerita. **RESEARCH** Literature of the South; Lit and Society; Lit and Medicine. **SELECTED PUBLICATIONS** Auth, Children of the World, SMU Press, 94; Cast a Wistful Eye, Macmillan, 77, condensed in Redbook; The Question of Flannery, O'Connor, LSU Press, 73. **CONTACT ADDRESS** Univ of Cincinnati, 2600 Clifton Ave, Cincinnati, OH 45220-2872. **EMAIL** stephem@email.uc.edu

STEPHENS, ROBERT OREN
PERSONAL Born 10/02/1928, Corpus Christi, TX, m, 1956, 3 children **DISCIPLINE** ENGLISH **EDUCATION** TX Col Arts & Indust, BA, 49; Univ TX, MA, 51, PhD(Eng), 58. **CAREER** Tchr high sch, Shiner, TX, 49-50; spec instr, Univ TX, 57-58, instr, 58-61; from asst prof to assoc prof, 61-66, dir grad studies Eng, 67-81, Prof Eng, Univ NC, Greensboro, 68-94, Head Dept Eng, 81-88; Duke Univ-Univ NC coop prog in hum fel, 65-66; Danforth assoc, 67. **MEMBERSHIPS** MLA; Am Studies Asn; S Atlantic Mod Lang Asn; NCTE. **RESEARCH** Contemp Am lit; Southern Am lit; Am Renaissance. **SELECTED PUBLICATIONS** Auth, Hemingway's Nonfiction: The Public Voice, Univ NC, 68; Language magic and reality in For Whom the Bell Tolls, Criticism, 72; Hemingway and Stendhal: The Matrix of A Farewell to Arms, PMLA, 73; Ernest Hemingway: The Critical Reception, Burt Franklin, 77; Cable's The Grandissimes and the Comedy of Manners, Am Lit, 80; The Family Saga in the South, La State Univ, 95. **CONTACT ADDRESS** 1706 Sylvan Rd, Greensboro, NC 27403. **EMAIL** vjstep@aol.com

STEPHENS, SUSAN A.
DISCIPLINE CLASSICS **EDUCATION** BA, 65; Columbia Univ, MA, 67; Stanford Univ, PhD, 72. **CAREER** Prof, Stanford Univ. **RESEARCH** Ancient novel; attic prose; Greek prose compos; papyrology. **SELECTED PUBLICATIONS** Auth, Yale Papyri in the Beinecke Library II, 85; Who Reads Ancient Novels? in Search for the Ancient Novel, 94; coauth, Ancient Greek Novels--the Fragments, 95. **CONTACT ADDRESS** Stanford Univ, Bldg 20, Main Quad, Stanford, CA 94305.

STEPTO, ROBERT BURNS
PERSONAL Born 10/28/1945, Chicago, IL, m, 1967, 2 children **DISCIPLINE** ENGLISH **EDUCATION** Trinity College, Hartford CT, BA (cum laude), English, 1966; Stanford University, Stanford, CA, MA, 1968, PhD, 1974. **CAREER** Williams College, Williamstown, MA, assistant professor, 71-74; Yale University, New Haven, CT, assistant professor, 74-79, associate professor, 79-84, professor, 84-. **HONORS AND AWARDS** Woodrow Wilson Fellowship, Woodrow Wilson Foundation, 1966-67; Morse Fellowship, Yale University, 1977-78. **MEMBERSHIPS** Chair, MLA Commn on the Literatures & Languages of America, 1977-78; Connecticut Humanities Council, 1980-82; trustee, Trinity College, 1982-92; associate editor, Callaloo, 1984-88; advisor, Yale-New Haven Teachers Institute, 1985-, Anson Phelps Stokes Institute, 1985-; board of editors, American Literature, 1987-88; advisor, Southern Connecticut Library Council, 1987; advisory editor, Callaloo, 1988-. **SELECTED PUBLICATIONS** From Behind the Veil: A Study of Afro-Amer Narrative, 1979; Edited with M Harper, Chant of Saints: Afro-Amer Literature, Art, Scholarship, 1979; Edited with D Fisher, Afro-Amer Literature: The Reconstruction of Instinction, 1979; Senior Fellowship, National Endowment for the Humanities, 1981-82; Alumni Medal, Trinity College, 1986; Editor, The Selected Poems of Jay Wright, 1987; Contributor to the Columbia Literary History of the United States, 1987; Robert Frost Professor, Bread Loaf School of English, 1995; Co-Editor of The Harper American Literature since 1992; auth, Blue as the Lake: A Personal Geography, 98. **CONTACT ADDRESS** Professor, English American Studies, African-American Studies, Yale Univ, PO Box 203388, New Haven, CT 06520-3388.

STERN, JULIA
PERSONAL Born 04/22/1959, Chicago, IL, m, 1982, 1 child **DISCIPLINE** ENGLISH **EDUCATION** Wellesley Coll, BA; 81; Columbia Univ, MA, 83; PhD, 91. **CAREER** Asst prof, Northwestern Univ, 91-97; assoc prof, 98-. **HONORS AND AWARDS** Phi Beta Kappa; Summa cum Laude; NEH Fel; Human Cen Fel, NWU; Stud Govt Teach Prize; PHO Teach Recog. **MEMBERSHIPS** MLA; ASA; ASECS; SEA. **RESEARCH** 18th and 19th C American literature. **SELECTED PUBLICATIONS** Auth, The Plight of Feeling: Sympathy and Dissent in the Early American Novel, UCP (Chicago), 97. **CONTACT ADDRESS** Dept English, Northwestern Univ, 215 University Hall, Evanston, IL 60208-001. **EMAIL** j-stern3@nwu.edu

STERN, MILTON R.
PERSONAL Born 08/22/1928, Boston, MA, m, 1949, 2 children **DISCIPLINE** ENGLISH **EDUCATION** Northeastern Univ, AB, 49; Univ Conn, MA, 51; Mich State Univ, PhD(English), 55. **CAREER** Instr, Univ Conn, 49-51; from instr to asst prof, Univ Ill, 54-58; from asst prof to assoc prof, 58-63, PROF ENGLISH, UNIV CONN, 63-, Am Coun Learned Soc grant, 62; vis prof, Coe Inst Am Studies, Univ Wyo, 64; Fulbright prof Am lit, Univ Warsaw, 64-65; Guggenheim fel, 71-72; Nat Humanities Inst fel, Yale Univ, 77-78. **MEMBERSHIPS** MLA; Melville Soc. **RESEARCH** American literature; the politics of American literature; Hawthorne. **SELECTED PUBLICATIONS** Auth, Discussions of Moby Dick, Heath, 60; coauth, The Viking Portable American Literature Survey (4 vols), Viking, 62, 68 & 75; auth, Herman Melville, In: Patterns of Commitment in American Literature, Univ Toronto, 67; Millennium, Moby Dick and politics, Emerson Soc Quart, fall 68; The Golden Moment: Novels of F S Fitzgerald, Univ Ill, 70; ed, Billy Budd, Bobbs-Merrill, 74; auth, American Values and Romantic Fiction in American Fiction, Northeastern Univ & Twayne, 77; ed, House of the Seven Gables, Penguin, 81; F. Scott Fitzgerald--A Biography, Am Lit, Vol 67, 95. **CONTACT ADDRESS** Dept of English, Univ of Connecticut, Storrs, Storrs, CT 06268.

STERN, RICHARD G.
PERSONAL Born 02/25/1928, New York, NY, m, 1985, 4 children **DISCIPLINE** ENGLISH **EDUCATION** Univ NC, BA, 47; Harvard Univ, MA, 49; State Univ Iowa, PhD, 54. **CAREER** Fulbright asst, Jules Ferry Col, Versailles, France, 49-50; asst, Univ Heidelberg, 50-51; part-time instr English, Coe Col, 52-53; instr, State Univ Iowa, 53-54; instr, Conn Col, 54-55; from instr to assoc prof, 55-65, prof Eng, Univ Chigao, 65-; vis lectr, Univ Venice, 62-63; vis prof, State Univ NY Buffalo, 67; prof, Harvard, 69; prof, Nice, 71; prof, Urbine, 73; Guggenheim fel, 73-74; prof, Helen A Regenstein prof, 90. **HONORS AND AWARDS** Longwood Award, 61; Friends of Lit Award, 63; Rockefeller Award, 65; Nat Found Arts & Sci Award, 67-68; Nat Instr Arts & Lett Award, 68; Sandbury Award, 78; Medal of Merit for the Novel, American Academy of Arts & Sciences, 85; Heartland Award, Best Work of Non-Fiction, 85; Sun-Times Award, Best Fiction, 90. **MEMBERSHIPS** Am Acad of Arts & Sci; Quadrangle Club. **RESEARCH** Prose fiction. **SELECTED PUBLICATIONS** Auth, Noble Rot, Stories 1949-88, Grove, 90; auth, Shares and Other Fictions, Delphinium, 92; auth, One Person and Another, On Writers and Writing, Baskerville, 93; auth, A Sistermony, Donald I. Fine, 95. **CONTACT ADDRESS** 5845 Ellis Ave, Chicago, IL 60637-1476. **EMAIL** rstern@midway.uchicago.edu

STERNBERG, JOEL
DISCIPLINE MASS COMMUNICATIONS **EDUCATION** Northwestern Univ, PhD. **CAREER** St Xavier Univ **SELECTED PUBLICATIONS** Chapters and biog essays, Dictionary Litery Biography, Encyclopedia Television, Encyclopedia Historic Chicago Women; Articles: Res Strategies, Nine, Chicago Hist, Screen, Chicago Film & Video; Sound & Commun. **CONTACT ADDRESS** Saint Xavier Univ, 3700 W 103rd Street, Chicago, IL 60655.

STERNLICHT, SANFORD
PERSONAL Born 09/20/1931, New York, NY, w, 2 children **DISCIPLINE** ENGLISH **EDUCATION** SUNY, BS; Colgate Univ, MA; Syracuse Univ, PhD. **CAREER** Prof and Chair, SUNY, 59-86; Prof, Syracuse Univ, 86-. **HONORS AND AWARDS** Chancellor's Excellence in Teaching, State Univ of New York, 74; Res Fel, SUNY, 63, 64, 65, 69, 70; Teacher of the Year, Syracuse Univ, 86, Who's Who in Am, Who's Who in Contemporary Authors. **MEMBERSHIPS** Mod Lang Asn, Intl Shakespeare Asn, Am conference for Irish Studies, Canadian Asn for Irish Studies, World Congress of the Intl Fed for Theatre Res, Shakespeare Asn of Am, MLA, NEMLA. **SELECTED PUBLICATIONS** Auth, R.F. Delderfield, 88; ed, Selected Poems of Padraic Colum, 89; auth, Stevie Smith, 90; ed, In Search of Stevie Smith, 91; auth, Stephen Spender, 92; auth, Siegfried Sassoon, 93; auth, All Things Herriot: James Herriot and His Peaceable Kingdom, 95; co-ed, New Plays from the Abbey Theatre 1993-1995, 96; auth, Jean Rhys, 97; auth, A Reader's Guide to Modern Irish Drama, 98; auth, C.S. Forester and the Hornblower Saga, 99. **CONTACT ADDRESS** Dept English, Syracuse Univ, Syracuse, NY 13244-1170.

STETZ, MARGARET
DISCIPLINE ENGLISH LITERATURE **EDUCATION** Queens Col, BA; Sussex Univ, MA; Harvard Univ, PhD. **CAREER** Eng Dept, Georgetown Univ **RESEARCH** Women's studies; comedy; Victorian fiction; modernism; women's war literature. **SELECTED PUBLICATIONS** Auth, England in the 1890s: Literary Publishing at the Bodley Head, 90; England in the 1880s: Old Guard and Avant-Garde, 89; pubs on Victorian history, poetry of E. Nesbit, and female authorship in the 1890s. **CONTACT ADDRESS** English Dept, Georgetown Univ, 37th and O St, Washington, DC 20057.

STEVEN, LAURENCE
DISCIPLINE ENGLISH LITERATURE **EDUCATION** McMaster Univ, PhD. **RESEARCH** Mod lit in English; rhetoric composition. **SELECTED PUBLICATIONS** Auth, "Who says the real world is out there: a response to Wayne Lucey," Inkshed, 9 (91): 14-19; auth, "The grain of sand in the oyster: Competency testing as a catalyst for attitude change at the university," Textual Studies in Canada, 1, (91): 115-144; auth, "The woman who rode away: D.H. Lawrence's cul-de-sac," in D.H. Lawrence: critical assessments, (Bromley, EN: Christopher Helm Publishers Limited, 92; co-ed, Contextual literacy: writing across the curriculum, Winnipeg, MB: Inkshed Publications, 94; co-ed, Towards writing across the curriculum/Vers langue integree aux programmes, vol. 1, Sudbury, ON: Laurentian Univ, (94): 231; auth, "Beyond the cure-all/scapegoat axis: the English Department and WAC," in Contextual literacy: writing across the curriculum, ed. by C.F. Schryer and L.D. Steven, (Winnipeg, MB: Inkshed Publications, 94): 117-127; auth, "The grain of sand in the oyste: competency testing as a catalyst for attitude change at the University," in Towards writing across the curriculum/Vers langueintegree aux programmes, vol. 1, ed. by C.F. Schryer, L.D. Steven and R. Corbeil, (Sudbury, ON: Laurentian Univ/Universite Laurentienne, (94): 51-78; auth, "A rich atmosphere for writing: not an oxygen tent," Inkshed, 13, (94): 4-6; auth, "North Country Spring: a book of verse for children, by Elizabeth Kouhi, ill. by Judi Pennanen", in Canadian Book Review Annual 93, (94): 6201; auth, "Best bedtime stories, in Canadian Book Review Annual 93, (94): 6200; **CONTACT ADDRESS** English Dept, Laurentian Univ, 935 Ramsey Lake Rd, Sudbury, ON, Canada P3E 2C6. **EMAIL** lsteven@nickel.laurentian.ca

STEVENS, EARL EUGENE
PERSONAL Born 04/06/1925, Chicago, IL, m, 1952 **DISCIPLINE** ENGLISH **EDUCATION** Ind Univ, AB, 49; Univ Mich, MA, 51; Univ NC, PhD, 63. **CAREER** Instr, Univ NC, 52-55 & 57-58; assoc prof English, WTex State Col, 56-57; asst prof, Pfeiffer Col, 58-63, chmn, Div Fine Arts, 61-62; assoc prof English, Trinity Univ, 63-64; from assoc prof to prof, Wis State Univ, Stevens Point, 64-68; PROF ENGLISH, RI COL, 68- **MEMBERSHIPS** MLA **RESEARCH** Victorian literature; the novel; criticism. **SELECTED PUBLICATIONS** Auth, The Tyrian trader in Mathew Arnold's The Scholar Gypsy, Victorian Newslett, 63; contribr, Joseph Conrad: An Annotated Secondary Bibliography, Northern Ill Univ, 71; auth, John Galsworthy, In: British Winners of the Nobel Literary Prize, Univ Okla, 73; co-ed, Annotated Secondary Bibliography of the Writings of John Galsworthy, Northern Ill Univ, 78; Pound, Thayer, Watson And The Dial--A Story In Letters, English Lit In Transition 1880-1920, Vol 39, 96; Waking Giants--The Presence Of The Past In Modernism, English Lit In Transition 1880-1920, Vol 36, 93. **CONTACT ADDRESS** Dept of English, Rhode Island Col, Providence, RI 02908.

STEVENS, JOHN A.
PERSONAL Born 09/11/1963, Elmhurst, IL, m, 1988, 2 children **DISCIPLINE** CLASSICS **EDUCATION** Univ Iowa, BA, 86, MA, 88; Duke Univ, PhD, 92. **CAREER** Vis asst prof, NY Univ, 92-93; vis asst prof, E Carolina Univ, 93-94; from asst prof to assoc prof, E Carolina Univ, 94-. **MEMBERSHIPS** Soc Ancient Greek Philos; Am Philol Asn; Classical Asn Middle W & S; Vergilian Soc. **RESEARCH** Latin literature; ancient philosophy; lyric poetry. **SELECTED PUBLICATIONS** Auth, Posidonian Polemic and Academic Dialectic: The Impact of Carneades Upon Posidonius, GRBS, 95; Friendship and Profit in Xenophon's Oeconomicus in The Socratic Movement, 94. **CONTACT ADDRESS** Classical Studies Dept FLL, East Carolina Univ, General Classroom Bldg., Greenville, NC 27858-4353. **EMAIL** stevensj@mail.ecu.edu

STEVENS, LIZBETH JANE
PERSONAL Born 10/31/1949, Angola, IN, m, 1968, 3 children **DISCIPLINE** SPEECH PATHOLOGY **EDUCATION** Univ of Mich, BA, 74, MS, 76; Wayne St Univ, PhD, 92. **CAREER** Tchr of speech and lang impaired, 78-98, Warren Woods School District; adj instr, 97-98, Wayne St Univ; asst prof, 98-, Eastern Mich Univ. **HONORS AND AWARDS** Awds for Cont Ed, Amer Speech-Lang-Hearing Assoc, 98, 96, 93, 90, 87, 83; Clara B. Stoddard, Wayne St Univ, 86; James B Angell Scholar, 75. **MEMBERSHIPS** Amer Speech-Lang-Hearing Assoc; MI Speech-Lang-Hearing Assoc; Macomb/St Clair Speech-Lang-Hearing Assoc; ISAAC; Us Soc for AAC. **RESEARCH** Augmentative/alternative comm, child language **SELECTED PUBLICATIONS** Cauth, , Conflict Resolution Abilities of Children with Specific Language Impairment and Normal Language, J of Speech and Hearing Res, 95; art, Comparison of Two Measures of Receptive Vocabulary, Mich Speech-Lang-Hearing Assoc J, 87. **CONTACT ADDRESS** Dept of Scpecial Ed, Eastern Michigan Univ, 126 Porter, Ypsilanti, MI 48197. **EMAIL** Lizbeth.Stevens@emich.edu

STEVENS, MARK
PERSONAL 2 children **DISCIPLINE** COMMUNICATION STUDIES **EDUCATION** FL State Univ, PhD. **CAREER** Tchr lit, Southern Polytech State Univ. **SELECTED PUBLICATIONS** Auth, publ(s) on compos; Brit lit; music appreciation. **CONTACT ADDRESS** Hum and Tech Commun Dept, So Polytech State Univ, S Marietta Pkwy, PO Box 1100, Marietta, GA 30060. **EMAIL** mstevens@spsu.edu

STEVENS, PAUL
DISCIPLINE ENGLISH LITERATURE **EDUCATION** Univ Toronto, PhD. **CAREER** Dept Eng, Queen's Univ **HONORS AND AWARDS** Milton Soc Am Hanford Awd; pres, can asn chairs english, 98-99. **RESEARCH** Milton and Renaissance literature; the rhetoric of early modern colonialism; literary theory and history. **SELECTED PUBLICATIONS** Auth, Imagination and the Presence of Shakespeare in "Paradise Lost", Univ Wis, 85; co-ed, Discontinuities: New Essays on Renaissance Literature and Criticism, U of Toronto Press, (forthcoming). **CONTACT ADDRESS** English Dept, Queen's Univ at Kingston, Kingston, ON, Canada K7L 3N6. **EMAIL** stevensp@atsqsilver.queensu.ca

STEVENS, PETER S.
PERSONAL Born 11/17/1927, Manchester, England **DISCIPLINE** LITERATURE **EDUCATION** Univ Nottingham, BA, Cert Educ, 51; McMaster Univ, MA, 63; Univ Sask, PhD, 68. **CAREER** Tchr, Eng schs, 51-57; tchr, Hillfield-Strathallan Col (Hamilton, Ont), 57-64, head Eng, 61-64; lectr, McMaster Univ, 61-64; lectr to asst prof, Univ Sask, 64-69; assoc prof, 69, prof, 76, Prof Emer, Univ Windsor. **RESEARCH** Poetry **SELECTED PUBLICATIONS** Auth, Modern English-Canadian Poetry, 78; auth, Coming Back, 81; auth, Revenge of the Mistresses, 82; auth, Out of the Willow Trees, 86; auth, Swimming in the Afternoon: New & Selected Poems, 92; auth, Dorothy Livesay: Patterns in a Poetic Life, 92; auth, Rip Rap: Yorkshire Ripper Poems, 95; auth, Thinking into the Dark, 97; auth, Attending to this World, 98; ed, The McGill Movement, 69; poetry ed, Can Forum, 68-73; poetry ed, Lit Rev Can, 94-. **CONTACT ADDRESS** 2055 Richmond St, Windsor, ON, Canada N8Y 1L3.

STEVENSON, CATHERINE BARNES
PERSONAL Born 05/23/1947, Chicago, IL, m, 1970 **DISCIPLINE** VICTORIAN LITERATURE, WOMEN'S STUDIES **EDUCATION** Manhattanville Col, BA, 68; NYork Univ, MA, 69, PhD(English), 73. **CAREER** Asst prof, Bryant Col, 75-77; ASST PROF ENGLISH, UNIV HARTFORD, 78-, Ed, Victorian Studies Bull, 78- **MEMBERSHIPS** Northeast Victorian Studies Asn; MLA; Tennyson Soc. **RESEARCH** Victorian poetry; women's travel writing; 19th century novel. **SELECTED PUBLICATIONS** Auth, The aesthetic function of the weird seizures in Tennyson's The Princess, Victorian Newsletter, 74; Tennyson's mutability canto: Time, memory, and art in The Princess, Victorian Poetry, 75; Druids, Bards, and Tennyson's Merlin, Victorian Newsletter, 79; Tennyson's Dying Swan: Mythology and the definition of the poet's role, Studies in English Lit, 80; Swinburne and Tennyson's Tristram, Victorian Poetry, 81; How it struck a contemporary: Tennyson's Lancelot and Elaine and Pre-Raphaelite art, Victorian Newsletter, 81;

The shade of Homer exorcises the ghost of De Quincey: Tennyson's The Lotos-Eaters, Browning Inst Studies, 82; Victorian Women Travellers to Africa, G K Hall, 82; *Pub What Must Not Be Said, North And South And The Problem Of Womens Work, Victorian Lit And Culture, Vol 19, 91. **CONTACT ADDRESS** Dept of Literature, Univ of Hartford, 380 W Mountain Rd, West Simsbury, CT 06092. **EMAIL** stevenson@mail.hartford.edu

STEVENSON, JOHN A.
PERSONAL Born 11/06/1952, Clinton, SC, m **DISCIPLINE** ENGLISH AND HISTORY **EDUCATION** Duke Univ, BA, 75; Univ Va, PhD, 83. **CAREER** Asst prof, 82-90, assoc prof, 90-, chair, 96-, Eng, Univ Colo. **HONORS AND AWARDS** Nat Merit Scholar; AB Duke Scholar; Phi Beta Kappa; Boulder Facul Teaching Awd, 90. **MEMBERSHIPS** MLA. **RESEARCH** 18th century British literature. **SELECTED PUBLICATIONS** Auth, Tom Jones and the Stuarts, ELH, 94; auth, The British Novel, Defoe to Austen, 90; auth, A Vampire in the Mirror, PMLA, 88; auth, Clarissa and the Harlowes Once More, ELH, 81. **CONTACT ADDRESS** Dept. of English, Univ of Colorado, Boulder, Box 226, Boulder, CO 80309. **EMAIL** john.stevenson@colorado.edu

STEVENSON, JOHN WEAMER
PERSONAL Born 07/24/1918, Pittsburgh, PA, m, 1941, 1 child **DISCIPLINE** ENGLISH **EDUCATION** Wofford Col, AB, 48; Vanderbilt Univ, MA, 49, PhD(English), 54. **CAREER** From instr to assoc prof, Presby Col, SC, 50-57, prof & chmn dept, 58-62; assoc prof, Millsaps Col, 57-58; prof, 62-75, chmn dept, 62-80, CHARLES A DANA PROF ENGLISH, CONVERSE COL, 75-, HEAD DIV LANG & LIT, 71-, Coop Prog in Humanities fel, Duke Univ & Univ NC, 66-67; assoc ed, Humanities in South, 71-82; Lilly vis scholar, Duke Univ, 78-79. **MEMBERSHIPS** SAtlantic Mod Lang Asn; SAtlantic Asn Dept Eng (pres, 73-74). **RESEARCH** Nineteenth century; modern poetry. **SELECTED PUBLICATIONS** Auth, The pastoral setting in the poetry of A E Housman, SAtlantic Quart; Arcadia re-settled: Pastoral poetry and romantic theory, Studies English Lit, fall 67; The ceremony of Housman's style, Victorian Poetry, spring 72; Wordsworth's Modern Vision, Va Quart Rev, winter 77; Walker Percy: The novelist as poet, Southern Rev, winter 81; Poetry As Prescription For The Worlds Body, Va Quart Rev, Vol 69, 93. **CONTACT ADDRESS** Dept of English, Converse Col, Spartanburg, SC 29301.

STEWART, CHARLES J.
DISCIPLINE COMMUNICATION **EDUCATION** Univ Ill, PhD, 63. **CAREER** Prof, Purdue Univ. **SELECTED PUBLICATIONS** Auth, Explorations in Rhetorical Criticism, Pa State Univ, 73; Persuasion and Social Movements, Waveland, 94; Interviewing: Principles and Practices, McGraw-Hill, 00. **CONTACT ADDRESS** Dept of Commun, Purdue Univ, West Lafayette, 1366 Liberal Arts and Educ Bldg, West Lafayette, IN 47907-1366. **EMAIL** cstewart@sla.purdue.edu

STEWART, E. KATE
DISCIPLINE ENGLISH **EDUCATION** Univ Miss, BA, MA, PhD. **CAREER** Univ Miss, 75-82; Worcester Polytechnic Inst, 84-87; Univ Ark, Prof, 88-. **HONORS AND AWARDS** Alpha Chi Tchr Year, 91; Sigma Tau Delta Service Awd, 97. **MEMBERSHIPS** Board of Trustees, Ers Kine Col, 98-02. **SELECTED PUBLICATIONS** Auth, Arthur Sherburne Hardy: Man of American Letters, Scripta Humanistica, 86; auth, 'The Raven' and 'The Bracelets': Another Source for Poe's Poem, Edgar Allan Poe Soc, 90; auth, Essays on Russell Baker and Sarah Kemble Knight in Encyclopedia of American Humorists, Garland, 88; auth, Essays on Cincinnati Mirror and Baltimore Mounument in American Humor Magazines and Comic Newspapers, Greenwood, 86; auth, Biographical Dictionary of Transcendentalism, Dictionary of Transcendentalism and Encyclopedia of American Literature. **CONTACT ADDRESS** Univ of Arkansas, Monticello, BOX 3460, Monticello, AR 71656. **EMAIL** stewar@uamont.edu

STEWART, HENRY R., JR.
PERSONAL Born 04/16/1944, Wilmington, DE, m, 1977, 1 child **DISCIPLINE** LIBRARY SCIENCE **EDUCATION** Cornell Col, BA, 66; Univ Denver, MA, 67; Ind Univ, PhD, 72. **CAREER** Ref Libr, 67-69, Cornell Col; assoc prof, 72-77, Univ Alabama; assoc dir, manage & pub svc, 77-84, Old Dominion Univ; dir, libr svcs, 84-96, Emporia St Univ; dean, libr svc, 96-, Troy St Univ. **HONORS AND AWARDS** Beta Phi Ma, USOE Title II B Fellowship. **RESEARCH** Library management; distance education. **CONTACT ADDRESS** 405 Wilson Dr., Troy, AL 36079. **EMAIL** hstewart@trojan.troyst.edu

STEWART, JOHN OTHNEIL
PERSONAL Born 01/24/1933, m **DISCIPLINE** ENGLISH **EDUCATION** CA State Univ, Los Angeles, CA, BA, 1960; Stanford Univ, MA 1965; Univ of IA, MFA 1966; Univ of CA LA, PhD 1973. **CAREER** Univ of IA, English instr; CA State Univ, prof of Engl; Univ of IL, prof of anthrop/writer; OH State Univ, prof English 1984-91; UC Davis, prof of African Studies, currently. **HONORS AND AWARDS** Fellow, Amer Anthropology Assn; Winifred Holtby Prize for Novel Royal Soc of Lit London 1972. **MEMBERSHIPS** Mem Inst for Advanced Study Princeton 1979-80. **CONTACT ADDRESS** African American & African Studies, Univ of California, Davis, 2143 Hart Hall, Davis, CA 95616.

STEWART, LARRY
DISCIPLINE ENGLISH LITERATURE **EDUCATION** Simpson Col, BA, 63; Case W Reserve, MA, 64, PhD, 71. **CAREER** Prof. **SELECTED PUBLICATIONS** Auth, A Guide To Literary Criticism and Research. **CONTACT ADDRESS** Dept of Eng, The Col of Wooster, Wooster, OH 44691.

STEWART, MAAJA AGUR
PERSONAL Born 06/27/1938, Estonia, m, 1959, 1 child **DISCIPLINE** ENGLISH **EDUCATION** Oberlin Col, AB, 60; Univ Mich, MA, 61, PhD(English), 66. **CAREER** ASST PROF ENGLISH, NEWCOMB COL, TULANE UNIV, 65- **MEMBERSHIPS** MLA **RESEARCH** Theory of Comedy; English novel; 18th century English literature. **SELECTED PUBLICATIONS CONTACT ADDRESS** Dept of English, Tulane Univ, 6823 St Charles Ave, New Orleans, LA 70118-5698.

STEWART, STANLEY N.
DISCIPLINE ENGLISH LITERATURE **EDUCATION** UCLA, BA, MA, PhD. **CAREER** Prof, Univ Calif, Riverside. **HONORS AND AWARDS** Fel(s), Mellon; Guggenheim. **MEMBERSHIPS** Asn of Literary Scholars and Critics; 16th Century Studies Conf. **RESEARCH** Wittgenstein and Renaissance criticism. **SELECTED PUBLICATIONS** Auth, The Enclosed Garden: The Tradition and the Image, 17th-Century Poetry, Univ Wis Press, 66; The Expanded Voice: The Art of Thomas Traherne, Huntington Lib, 70; George Herbert, G.K. Hall, 76; 'Renaissance' Talk: Ordinary Language and the Mystique of Critical Problems, Duquesne, 97; co-auth, Nietzsche's Case: Philosophy as/and Literature, Routledge, 92; Evidence and Historical Criticism, Duquesne Univ Press, 95; co-ed, The Ben Jonson Journal: Literary Contexts in the Age of Elizabeth, James, and Charles, Univ Nev Press; auth, The Cambridge Companion to Ben Johnson, Cambridge, 00. **CONTACT ADDRESS** Dept of English, Univ of California, Riverside, 1156 Hinderaker Hall, Riverside, CA 92521-0209. **EMAIL** stanley.stewart@ucr.edu

STEWART, THOMAS D.
PERSONAL Born 12/29/1955, East Liverpool, OH, m, 1981, 2 children **DISCIPLINE** COMMUNICATION **EDUCATION** Slippery Rock Univ, BA, 80; Univ Iowa, MA, 82; PhD, 89. **CAREER** Instr, Univ Wis, 84-85; Asst Prof, Slippery Rock Univ, 85-. **MEMBERSHIPS** Nat Commun Asn, Broadcast Educ Asn. **RESEARCH** Application of research methodologies, media use and disabled audiences. **SELECTED PUBLICATIONS** Coauth, Principles of Research in Communication, 1st Ed, forthcoming. **CONTACT ADDRESS** Dept Commun, Slippery Rock Univ of Pennsylvania, 14 Maltby Dr, Slippery Rock, PA 16057-1303. **EMAIL** thomas.stewart@sru.edu

STHELE, EVA
DISCIPLINE GREEK AND ROMAN LITERATURE **EDUCATION** Univ Cincinnati, PhD. **CAREER** Instr, Wheaton Col; prof-. **HONORS AND AWARDS** Coord, dept's Latin Day. **RESEARCH** Ancient relig(s). **SELECTED PUBLICATIONS** Auth, Performance and Gender in Ancient Greece: Nondramatic Poetry in its Setting, Princeton UP, 96; Women Looking at Women: Women's Ritual and Temple Sculpture, Sexuality in Ancient Art, Cambridge UP, 96; Help Me to Sing, Muse, of Plataia, The New Simonides, Arethusa 29, 96. **CONTACT ADDRESS** Dept of Class, Univ of Maryland, Col Park, 4229 Art-Sociology Building, College Park, MD 20742-1335. **EMAIL** es39@umail.umd.edu

STILLINGER, JACK
PERSONAL Born 02/16/1931, Chicago, IL, m, 1971, 4 children **DISCIPLINE** ENGLISH **EDUCATION** Univ Tex, BA, 53; Northwestern Univ, MA, 54; Harvard Univ, PhD, 58. **CAREER** From asst prof to assoc prof, 58-64, prof English, Univ Ill, Urbana, 64-, ed, J English & Ger Philol, 61-73; Guggenheim Mem Found fel, 64-65; permanent mem, Univ Ill Ctr Advan Study. **HONORS AND AWARDS** Natl Woodrow wilson fel, 53-54; Guggenheim Mem Found fel, 64-65; Keats-Shelley Asn Dist Scholar award, 86; fel Am Acad Arts & Sciences, 93. **MEMBERSHIPS** MLA; Keats-Shelley Asn Am; Wordsworth-Coleridge Asn; Byron Soc; Natl Council of Teachers of English; Soc for Textual Scholarship. **RESEARCH** English romantic movement; textual and literary theory. **SELECTED PUBLICATIONS** Ed, The Early Draft of John Stuart Mill's Autobiography, Univ Ill, 61; Anthony Munday's Zelauto: The Fountaine of Fame, Southern Ill Univ, 63; Wordsworth: Selected Poems and Prefaces, Houghton, 65; The Letters of Charles Armitage Brown, Harvard Univ, 66; Twentieth Century Interpretations of Keats's Odes, Prentice-Hall, 68; John Stuart Mill: Autobiography and Other writings, Houghton, 69. Auth, The Hoodwinking of Madeline and Other Essays on Keats's Poems, Univ Ill, 71; The Texts of Keats's Poems, 74 & ed, The Poems of John Keats, 78, Harvard Univ. Ed, Collected Works of John Stuart Mill, vol 1, Univ Toronto, 81; John Keats: Complete Poems, Harvard Univ, 82; The Norton Anthology of English Literature, Norton, 86, 93, 00; John Keats: Poetry Manuscripts at Harvard, Harvard Univ, 90. Auth, Multiple Authorship and the Myth of Solitary Genius, Oxford Univ, 91; Coleridge and Textual Instability: The Multiple Versions of the Major Poems, Oxford Univ, 94; Reading The Eve of St Agnes: The Multiples of Complex Literary Transaction, Oxford Univ, 99. **CONTACT ADDRESS** Univ of Illinois, Urbana-Champaign, 608 S Wright St, Urbana, IL 61801-3613. **EMAIL** jstill@uiuc.edu

STIMPSON, CATHARINE R.
PERSONAL Born 06/04/1936, Bellingham, WA **DISCIPLINE** CONTEMPORARY LITERATURE, WOMEN'S STUDIES **EDUCATION** Bryn Mawr Col, AB, 58; Cambridge Univ, BA, 60, MA, 65; Columbia Univ, PhD(English), 67. **CAREER** From instr to asst prof, 63-73, assoc prof, Columbia Univ, 73-80; prof English, Rutgers Univ, 80-, mem, Nat Emergency Civil Liberties Comt; ed, SIGNS: J Women in Cult & Soc, 74-80; Nat Humanities Inst fel, 75-76; consult, Nat Inst Educ, 78-80; dir, Rutgers Inst for Res Women; chemn, Mass Bd Scholarship, Res & Educ. **MEMBERSHIPS** MLA; PEN. **RESEARCH** Post-modern literature; women and literature; relationship of revolution to literature. **SELECTED PUBLICATIONS** Auth, J R R Tolkien, Columbia Univ, 69; ed, Women and the Equal Rights Amendment, 72 & Discrimination Against Women, 73, Bowker; Class Notes, Times Bks, 78 & Avon, 79. **CONTACT ADDRESS** GSAS Dean's Office, New York Univ, 6 Washington Square N, Rm 12, New York, NY 10003-6668. **EMAIL** catharine.stimpson@nyu.edu

STINSON, JOHN JEROME
PERSONAL Born 09/30/1940, Brooklyn, NY, m, 1969, 2 children **DISCIPLINE** MODERN BRITISH LITERATURE **EDUCATION** St John's Univ, NYork, BA, 62, MA, 63; NYork Univ, PhD, 71. **CAREER** From instr to asst prof, 65-74, assoc prof, 74-78, prof English, State Univ NY Col Fredonia 78-, Res award, 73. **MEMBERSHIPS** MLA **RESEARCH** Modern British literature especially contemporary novels and short stories. **SELECTED PUBLICATIONS** Auth, The Christian symbolism in After the Fall, Mod Drama, 12/67; Trying to exorcise the beast: The grotesque in the fiction of William Golding, Cithara, 11/71; Anthony Burgess: Novelist on the margin, J Pop Cult, summer 73; Graham Greene's The Destructors: Fable for a world far east of Eden, Am Benedictine Rev, 12/73; The Manichee world of Anthony Burgess, Renascence, Autumn, 73; Nothing Like the Sun: The faces in Bella Cohen's mirror, J Mod Lit, 2/76; Dualism and paradox in the Puritan Plays of David Storey, Mod Drama, 6/77; Better to be hot or cold: 1985 and the dynamic of the manichean duoverse, Mod Fiction Studies, autumn, 81; Anthony Burgess Revisited, Twayne Publ, 91; V.S. Pritchett: A Study of the Short Fiction, Twayne-Macmillan, 92. **CONTACT ADDRESS** Dept of English, SUNY, Col at Fredonia, 1 Suny at Fredonia, Fredonia, NY 14063. **EMAIL** stinson@fredonia.edu

STINSON, ROBERT WILLIAM
PERSONAL Born 09/12/1941, Elmhurst, IL, m, 1966, 2 children **DISCIPLINE** AMERICAN HISTORY, HISTORIOGRAPHY, FILM HISTORY, MUSICOLOGY **EDUCATION** Allegheny Col, BA, 64; Ind Univ, MA, 66, PhD(hist), 71. **CAREER** From Asst Prof to Assoc Prof, 70-88, PROF HIST, MORAVIAN COL, 88-. **HONORS AND AWARDS** Lindback Awd for Distinguished Teaching, Christian and Mary Lindback Found, 72. **RESEARCH** United States, 1865 to the present; history of journalism; history of film; historiography. **SELECTED PUBLICATIONS** Auth, S S McClure's My autobiography: The progressive as self-made man, Am Quart, summer 70; McClure's road to McClure's: How revolutionary were the 1890's magazines?, Jour Quart, summer 70; Ida Tarbell and the ambiguities of feminism, Pa Mag Hist & Biog, 4/77; Lincoln Steffens' Shame of the Cities reconsidered, New Republic, 7/77; How they kept the trust: Ida Tarbell's John D Rockefeller, Nation, 11/77; On the death of a baby, Atlantic Monthly, 7/79; Lincoln Steffens, Ungar, 79; The Long Dying of Baby Andrew, Little, Brown, 83; The Faces of Clio, Nelson-Hall, 87. **CONTACT ADDRESS** Dept of History, Moravian Col, 1200 Main St, Bethlehem, PA 18018-6650. **EMAIL** merws01@moravian.edu

STINSON, RUSSELL
DISCIPLINE MUSIC **EDUCATION** Stetson Univ, Bmus; Univ Chicago, MA, PhD. **CAREER** Assoc prof & Col organist, Lyon Col. **RESEARCH** Music hist; theory; performance. **SELECTED PUBLICATIONS** Auth, The Bach Manuscripts of Johann Peter Kellner and His Circle, Duke UP, 90. **CONTACT ADDRESS** Dept of Music, Lyon Col, 300 Highland Rd, PO Box 2317, Batesville, AR 72503.

STITT, J. MICHAEL
DISCIPLINE FOLKLORE, MEDIEVAL LITERATURE **EDUCATION** Pa State Univ, BA, 73; Ind Univ, MA, 75, cert, 78, PhD, 81. **CAREER** Instr, Ind Univ-Purdue Univ, 79-81; asst prof, 81-91, assoc prof, 91-, interim dir, freshman compos, 91-92, Univ Nev, Las Vegas; ed bd, J Medieval Folklore. **HONORS AND AWARDS** Grant, Nevada Humanities Council, 82; University Research council grant, 83, 86, 88; sr Fulbright lectr, Univ Sofia, 97. **MEMBERSHIPS** Nev State Bd Geog Names. **RESEARCH** Bulgarian folk music and dance. **SELECTED**

PUBLICATIONS Auth, Conversational Genres at a Las Vegas '21' Table, Western Folklore 45, 86; Beowulf and The Bear's Son. Epic, Saga, and Fairytale in the Northern Germanic Area, Albert B Lord Monogr Ser, Garland, 92; coauth, A Type and Motif Index of Early American Almanac Narrative, Greenwood, 91. **CONTACT ADDRESS** Dept of Eng, Univ of Nevada, Las Vegas, 4505 Maryland Pky, PO Box 455011, Las Vegas, NV 89154. **EMAIL** stitt@nevada.edu

STITZEL, JUDITH GOLD

PERSONAL Born 03/23/1941, New York, NY, m, 1961, 1 child **DISCIPLINE** ENGLISH, WOMEN'S STUDIES **EDUCATION** Barnard Col, BA, 61; Univ Wis, MA, 62; Univ MN, PhD, 68. **CAREER** Asst prof, 68-72; dir writing laboratory, 69-73; assoc prof, 72-79, coor and dir Center for Women's Stud 80-92, prof eng and women's studies, WVA Univ, 92-98, Assoc, Danforth Found, 75-82; WVA deleg NCent Women's Studies Asn, 79. **HONORS AND AWARDS** Phi Beta Kappa; Case Silver Medalist; National Prof of the Year. **MEMBERSHIPS** Nat Women's Studies Asn. **RESEARCH** Lit criticism; pedag; women's studies; Creative non-fiction. **SELECTED PUBLICATIONS** Auth, The uses of humor, Doris Lessing Newslett, 77; Morning cycle, Colo Quart, autumn, 79; Humor and survival in the works of Doris Lessing, Regionalism and the Female Imagination, 4: 61-69; Reading Doris Lessing, Col English, 40: 498-504; Toward the new year, Trellis, summer 79; Challenging curricular assumptions: Teaching, learning women's literature from a regional perspective, She who laughs firt, Stepping Off the Pedetal-Academic Women in the South, MLA, 82; auth, Reshaping the Introductory womens studies course: Dealing Upfront with Anger, Resistance and Reality (wit Ardeth Dery), Feminist Teacher, 6, 1 (Summer 91), 29-33. **CONTACT ADDRESS** 449 Devon Rd, Morgantown, WV 26505. **EMAIL** jstitzel@wvu.edu

STOCK, ROBERT DOUGLAS

PERSONAL Born 12/02/1941, Akron, OH, m, 1 child **DISCIPLINE** ENGLISH **EDUCATION** Kent State Univ, BA, 63; Princeton Univ, MA, 65, PhD(English), 67. **CAREER** From asst prof to assoc prof, 67-77, Prof English, Univ Nebr-Lincoln, 77- **HONORS AND AWARDS** BA summa cum laude, 63; Wilson Fel and Dissertation Fel, 63, 66; Phi Beta Kappa, 95; teaching awards, 93, 94, 96, 98. **MEMBERSHIPS** Soc 18th Century Studies; Asn Lit Scholars & Critics; Nat Scholars Asn. **RESEARCH** Eighteenth-century literature; literary expression of religious experience; silent film. **SELECTED PUBLICATIONS** Auth, Samuel Johnson and Neoclassical Dramatic Theory, 73 & Samuel Johnson's Literary Criticism, 74, Univ Nebr; Prosser Hall Frye: Conservative humanist, Mod Age, 75; Agents of evil and justice in the novels of Sayers, In: As Her Whimsy Took Her, Kent State, 79; The New Humanists in Nebraska, Univ Nebr, 79; The Tao and the objective room: A pattern in C S Lewis's novels, Christian Scholar's Rev, 80; The Holy and the Daemonic from Sir Thomas Browne to William Blake, Princeton Univ, 82; The Flutes of Dionysus: Daemonic Enthrallment in Literature, Univ Nebr, 89; Salem Witchcraft and Spiritual Evil, Christianity and Lit, 92. **CONTACT ADDRESS** Dept of English, Univ of Nebraska, Lincoln, PO Box 880333, Lincoln, NE 68588-0333. **EMAIL** rstock2@unl.edu

STOCKMAN, IDA J.

PERSONAL Born 09/06/1942, Sumner, MS, m, 1969 **DISCIPLINE** AUDIOLOGY AND SPEECH SCIENCES **EDUCATION** Jackson State Univ, Jackson, MS, BS, 1962; University of Iowa, Iowa City, IA, MA, 1965; Pennsylvania State Univ, State College, PA, PhD, 1971. **CAREER** Jackson State University, Jackson, MS, instructor, 65-66; Rehabilitation Center, Binghamton, NY, speech/language pathologist, 66-67; Kantonsspital St Gallen, St Gallen, Switzerland, research assoc, 72-76 summers; Howard University, Washington, DC, asst/prof assoc, 71-79; Center for Applied Linguistic, Washington, DC, research assoc, 80-82; Michigan State University, East Lansing, MI, assoc prof, 82-. **HONORS AND AWARDS** Information Exchange Scholar, World Rehabilitation Fund Inc, 1985; Research Grant Awd, National Science Foundation, 1985; Research Grant Awd, National Institute of Education, 1980; Outstanding Woman Achiever, Michigan State University, 1986; Phi Delta Kappa Professional Honor Society, 1981. **MEMBERSHIPS** Board of directors, National Association Black Speech, Language & Hearing, 1989-; board of directors, Michigan Association-Deaf, Speech and Hearing Services, 1989-; editorial board, Howard Journal of Communication; Howard University, Washington, DC, 1988-; editorial board, Journal of Linguistics and Education, 1988-; educational standards board, The American Speech, Language, Hearing Association, 1990-. **CONTACT ADDRESS** Dept of Audiology and Speech Sciences, Michigan State Univ, 371 Communication Arts & Sciences Bldg, East Lansing, MI 48824.

STOCKWELL, ROBERT PAUL

PERSONAL Born 06/12/1925, OK, m, 1946, 1 child **DISCIPLINE** ENGLISH LANGUAGE & LINGUISTICS **EDUCATION** Univ VA, BA, 46, MA, 49, PhD(English philol & ling), 52. **CAREER** Instr English, Univ Okla City, 46-48; dir English for foreigners proj Nashville Auto-Diesel Col, 52; from instr to assoc prof ling, Foreign Serv Inst, US Dept State, 52-56, chmn Latin-Am lang & area prog, 53-56; asst prof English, 56-58, from assoc prof to prof, 58-62, chmn dept, 66-73, Prof Ling, Univ Calif, Los Angeles, 66-, Chmn Dept, 80-85, Vis prof, Philippines, 59 & 60, vis prof, Univ Tex, 61; Am Coun Learned Soc fel, 63-64; vis prof, Univ Mich, 65; Dir Lim Inst, UCLA, 83. **HONORS AND AWARDS** Distinguished Teaching Awd, Univ Calif, Los Angeles, 68; Fel of the ACLS, 63-64. **MEMBERSHIPS** MLA; Ling Soc Am; Philol Soc, England. **RESEARCH** English and Spanish language; history of English phonology and syntax; general linguistic theory. **SELECTED PUBLICATIONS** Coauth, Patterns of Spanish Pronunciation, 60, Sounds of English and Spanish, 65 & Grammatical Structure of English and Spanish, 65, Univ Chicago; co-ed, Linguistic Change and Generative Theory, Ind Univ 72; coauth, Major Syntactic Structures of English, Holt, 73; auth, Foundations of Syntactic Theory, Prentice-Hall, 77; A History of Old-English Meter, Language, Vol 71, 95; Dwight,L Bolinger, Language, Vol 69, 93; The Cambridge Hist of the English-Language, Vol 2 1066-1476, J Of Linguistics, Vol 30, 94; coauth, Structure and History of English Words, Cambridge Univ Press, 01. **CONTACT ADDRESS** Dept of Ling, Univ of California, Los Angeles, Los Angeles, CA 90024. **EMAIL** stockwel@ucla.edu

STODOLA, ZABELLE

PERSONAL Born 06/22/1949, London, England, m, 1989 **DISCIPLINE** EARLY AMERICAN LITERATURE **EDUCATION** Penn State Univ., PhD. **CAREER** English and Lit, Univ Ark **HONORS AND AWARDS** NEH Summer Stipend; Faculty Excellence Awd for Research, UALR. **SELECTED PUBLICATIONS** Coauth, The Indian Captivity Narrative; Ed, Early American Literature and Culture, Jour & Occasional Writings of Sarah Wister; Auth, Puritan Orthodoxy and the 'Survivor Syndrome' in Mary Rowlandson's Indian Captivity Narrative; The Indian Captivity Narratives of Mary Rowlandson and Olive Oatman; Ed., Women's Indian Captivity Narratives, Penguin 98. **CONTACT ADDRESS** Univ of Arkansas, Little Rock, 2801 S University Ave., Little Rock, AR 72204-1099. **EMAIL** kzstodola@ualr.edu

STOHL, CYNTHIA B.

DISCIPLINE ORGANIZATIONAL COMMUNICATION, SOCIAL NETWORKS **EDUCATION** Univ Purdue, PhD, 82. **CAREER** Prof, Purdue Univ. **RESEARCH** Participatory processes in multicultural/international organizations. **SELECTED PUBLICATIONS** Auth, European Managers Interpretations of Participation: a semantic network analysis, Human Commun Res, 93; Participating and Participation, Commun Monogr, 93; Organizational Communication: Connectedness in Action, Sage, 95; Paradoxes of Participation, Orgn and Commun, 95. **CONTACT ADDRESS** Dept of Commun, Purdue Univ, West Lafayette, 1080 Schleman Hall, West Lafayette, IN 47907-1080. **EMAIL** cstohl@purdue.edu

STOKES, JAMES

PERSONAL Born 08/08/1943, Conrad, MT, m, 1967, 2 children **DISCIPLINE** ENGLISH LITERATURE **EDUCATION** San Francisco State Univ, BA, 68; MA, 69; Wash State Univ, PhD, 79. **CAREER** Instr, Univ Hawaii, 69-71; Instr, Col of Great Falls, 71-73; From Teaching Asst to Prof, Univ Wis, 74-. **HONORS AND AWARDS** System Fel, Univ Wis, 86-88; Hon Fel, Univ Wis, 90; Fel, Inaugural Friends of the Univ Wis, 91-92; Hon Fel, Univ Wis, 92; Guggenheim Found Grant, 92; Distinguished Achievement Awd, Univ Wis, 94; System Fel, Inst for Res in the Humanities, Univ Wis, 97-98; Eugene Katz Distinguished Fac Member, Univ Wis, 99; Letter and Sci Teacher/Scholar Awd, 99. **MEMBERSHIPS** MLA, Medieval and Renaissance Drama Soc, Somerset Archaeol Soc, Inter-Soc for the Study of Medieval Drama. **RESEARCH** Medieval and Renaissance drama, culture and history. **SELECTED PUBLICATIONS** Auth, Somerset (2 volumes): Records of Early English Drama, Univ Toronto Pr (Toronto), 96; auth, "The Waits of Lincolnshire," Early Theatre 1 (98): 75-111; auth, "The Processional Elements in Parish Drama," in The Semiotics of Performance (99); coauth, "The Donington Cast List: Innovation and Tradition in Parish Guilds in Early Elizabethan Lincolnshire," Early Theatre 2 (99); auth, Lincolnshire: Records of Early English Drama, Univ Toronto Pr (Toronto), forthcoming; auth, The Effects of the Reformation on Traditional Culture in Somerset 1532-1642, forthcoming. **CONTACT ADDRESS** Dept English, Univ of Wisconsin, Stevens Point, 2100 Main St, Stevens Point, WI 54481-3871. **EMAIL** jstokes@uwsp.edu

STONE, DONALD DAVID

PERSONAL Born 01/17/1942, Los Angeles, CA **DISCIPLINE** ENGLISH LITERATURE **EDUCATION** Univ Calif, Berkeley, BA, 63; Harvard Univ, MA, 64, PhD(English), 68. **CAREER** Dexter traveling fel, 68; asst prof, 68-72, assoc prof, 72-80, prof, English, Queens Col, NY, 80- . **HONORS AND AWARDS** John Simon Guggenheim Memorial Fellowship, 77. **MEMBERSHIPS** IAUPE. **RESEARCH** Victorian literature; history of the novel; art and literature. **SELECTED PUBLICATIONS** Auth, Novelists in a Changing World, 72; auth, The Romantic Impulse in Victorian Fiction, 80; co-ed, Nineteenth-Century Lives, 89; auth, Communications with the Future: Matthew Arnold in Dialogue, 97; auth, Thackeray, The Newcomer, Nineteenth-Century Lit, vol. 53, 98; auth, Delacroix and Turner, Sewanee Review, vol 107, 99. **CONTACT ADDRESS** Dept of English, Queens Col, CUNY, 6530 Kissena Blvd, Flushing, NY 11367.

STONE, GREGORY

DISCIPLINE MEDIEVAL AND RENAISSANCE LITERATURE, LITERARY THEORY AND CRITICISM **EDUCATION** Bowdoin Col, BA, 78-83; Yale Univ, PhD, 89. **CAREER** Asst prof, 89-94; assoc prof, 94-99; prof, 99-, dept of French and Italian, La State Univ. **SELECTED PUBLICATIONS** Auth, The Death of the Troubadour, 94; auth, Dante's Averoistic Hermeneutics, in Dante Stud, 94; auth, The Philosophical Beast: On Boccaccio's Tale of Cimone, Animal Acts, 96. **CONTACT ADDRESS** Dept of Fr Grad Stud, Louisiana State Univ and A&M Col, Baton Rouge, LA 70803. **EMAIL** stone@lsu.edu

STONE-BLACKBURN, SUSAN

PERSONAL Born, WI **DISCIPLINE** ENGLISH **EDUCATION** Lawrence Col, BA, 63; Univ Colorado, MA, 67, PhD, 70. **CAREER** Asst prof, 73-79, assoc prof, 79-86, assoc dean hum, 85-89, Prof, Univ Calgary, 86-. **MEMBERSHIPS** Sci Fiction Res Asn; Asn Can Theatre Res; Maenad Theatre Prods. **SELECTED PUBLICATIONS** Auth, Robertson Davies, Playwright: A Search for the Self on the Canadian Stage, 85; auth, Consciousness Evolution and Early Telepathic Tales, in Sci Fiction Studs, 20, 2, 93; auth, Feminist Nurturers and Psychic Healers, in Imaginative Futures, 95. **CONTACT ADDRESS** Dept of English, Univ of Calgary, Calgary, AB, Canada T2N 1N4. **EMAIL** sstonebl@acs.ucalgary.ca

STONUM, GARY LEE

PERSONAL Born 07/10/1947, Sacramento, CA, m, 1970, 1 child **DISCIPLINE** ENGLISH **EDUCATION** Reed Col, BA, 69; Johns Hopkins Univ, MA, 71, PhD(English), 73. **CAREER** Asst prof, 73-80, assoc prof English, Case Westerm Reserve Univ, 80-90; vis asst prof Criticism & Theory, Univ Calif, Irvine, 76-77; oveatt prof of english, 99-. **MEMBERSHIPS** MLA; Emily Dickerson International Soc; ALA, Medernist Studies Asn. **RESEARCH** Emily Dickinson Int Soc; literary theory; the novel. **SELECTED PUBLICATIONS** Auth, A prophet of desire, Diacritics, 77; For a cybernetics of reading, MLN, 77; Faulkner's Career, Cornell Univ, 78; The Dickenson Sublime, U of Wisconsin, 90; ed, Emily Dickerson Journal, 99-. **CONTACT ADDRESS** Dept of English, Case Western Reserve Univ, 10900 Euclid Ave, Cleveland, OH 44106-4901. **EMAIL** gxs11@po.cwtu.edu

STORY, KENNETH ERVIN

PERSONAL Born 07/09/1941, Albemarle, NC **DISCIPLINE** ENGLISH, NINETEENTH CENTURY BRITISH LITERATURE **EDUCATION** Pfeiffer Col, AB, 63; Univ Tenn, MA, 65, PhD, 67. **CAREER** Asst prof English, Va Polytech Inst, 67-69; asst prof, Ohio Wesleyan Univ, 69-72; prof Eng, 72-, Chmn Dept, 80-83, 95-98, Head Humanities Area, 81-, Hendrix Col. **HONORS AND AWARDS** Nat Endowment for Humanities fel, Princeton Univ, summer, 77. **MEMBERSHIPS** MLA; Mod Lang Assn; S Atlantic Mod Lang Assn. **RESEARCH** Fiction of Flannery O'Connor; poetry of Tennyson. **SELECTED PUBLICATIONS** Auth, Theme and image in The Princess, Tenn Studies Lit, 75; coauth, Browning's Soliloquy of the Spanish Cloister, Explicator, spring 80; auth, Throwing a Spotlight on the Past: Narrative Method in Ann Beatties's Jacklighting, Studies in Short Fiction, 92. **CONTACT ADDRESS** Dept of English, Hendrix Col, 1600 Washington Ave, Conway, AR 72032-3080.

STOTT, WILLIAM MERRELL

PERSONAL Born 06/02/1940, New York, NY, d, 2 children **DISCIPLINE** AMERICAN STUDIES, ENGLISH **EDUCATION** Yale Univ, AB, 62; MPh, 70; PhD, 72. **CAREER** Foreign serv officer, US Info Agency, 64-68; asst prof, 71-74; assoc dean, Div Gen & Comp Studies, 75-77; assoc prof, 74-80; prof, Univ Tex, Austin, 80-01; dir, Am Studies Prog, 81-84; Guggenheim Mem Found Fel, 78; Fulbright lectr, Polytechnic of Cent London, 80-81; Univ of Leiden, 86-87. **MEMBERSHIPS** Am Studies Asn. **RESEARCH** Journalism; mass culture; autobiography. **SELECTED PUBLICATIONS** Auth, Documentary Expression and Thirties America, Oxford Univ, 73, Chicago UP, 86; coauth, On Broadway, Univ Tex, 78; auth, Write to the Point, Columbia UP, 90; auth, Facing the Fire: Experiencing and Expressing Anger Appropriately, Doubleday, 93. **CONTACT ADDRESS** Dept of Am Studies, Univ of Texas, Austin, GAR 303, B7100, Austin, TX 78712-1026. **EMAIL** wstott@mail.utexas.edu

STOWE, WILLIAM

PERSONAL Born 12/07/1946, New Haven, CT, m, 1976 **DISCIPLINE** ENGLISH **EDUCATION** Princeton Univ, BA, 68; Yale Univ, MPhil, 77; PhD, 78. **CAREER** Asst Prof, Wesleyan Univ, 78-84; Assoc Prof, 84-90; Prof, 90-; Benjamin L. Waite, Professor of English, 98-; Chair, Dept of English, 92-95, 00. **HONORS AND AWARDS** Woodrow Wilson Fellow; Fulbright Fellowship; PBK; Yale Univ Fellowship, 73-77; Spend Edgar Allen Poe Awd for The Poetics of March, 84; Faculty Fellow; Wesleyan Center for the Humanities, 84, 97. **MEMBERSHIPS** MLA; ASLE. **RESEARCH** 19 US Literature; Literature & Environment; Literature of Travel. **SELECTED PUBLICATIONS** Auth, "The Poetics of Murder," edited by Glenn W. Most and William W. Stowe, Harcourt Brace Jovanovich, 1983; auth, "Balzac, James, and the Realistic

Novel," Princeton Univ Press, 83, paperback, 86; auth, "Going Abroad: European Travel in Nineteenth-Century American Cutlure, Princeton Univ Press, 94; auth, "Jame's Elusive Wings," in Jonathan Freedman, ed., The Cambridge Companion to Henry James, Cambridge Univ Press, 98; auth, "Doing History on Vacation: Thoreau's 'Ktaadn' and Jewett's The Country of the Pointed Firs," New England Quarterly, June 98. **CONTACT ADDRESS** Dept English, Wesleyan Univ, 285 Court St., Middletown, CT 06457-3330. **EMAIL** wstowe@wesleyan.edu

STRAIN, ELLEN
DISCIPLINE MULTIMEDIA DESIGN AND VIDEO PRODUCTION **EDUCATION** Univ Southern Calif, PhD, 96. **CAREER** Asst prof, Ga Inst of Technol. **RESEARCH** The theorization of cross-cultural spectatorship in popular culture. **SELECTED PUBLICATIONS** Published articles on stereoscopic depictions of the building of the Panama Canal, the development of popular anthropology in the late 19th century, and the implications of cross-cultural filmic depictions for the Greek political situation. **CONTACT ADDRESS** Sch of Lit, Commun, & Cult, Georgia Inst of Tech, Skiles Cla, Atlanta, GA 30332. **EMAIL** ellen.strain@lcc.gatech.edu

STRAITON, T. HARMON, JR.
PERSONAL Born 06/28/1941, Selma, AL, s **DISCIPLINE** LIBRARY SCIENCE **EDUCATION** Auburn Univ, BS, 63; Univ Alabama, MLS, 79. **CAREER** Head, Mathematics and science dept, Tallassee (Ala) City Schools, 66-79; Head, microforms and documents dept, 80-98, Asst Dean for Information Services, 98-, Auburn Univ. **HONORS AND AWARDS** Beta Phi Mu; Alpha Zeta. **MEMBERSHIPS** ALA. Lib. Assoc; Southeastern Library Assoc; Amer Lib Assoc. **RESEARCH** Technology; Info. Sci; Lib. Sci; Reference. **SELECTED PUBLICATIONS** Auth, Reference Services and Media/Merrill, Martha, New York: Haworth Information Press, (99), 176, ill. 22cm (chapter one); auth, Electronic Resources for Alabama State & Local Government Publications/compiled by T. Harmon Straiton, Jr. for the State Publications Task Force, Alabama Public Library Service, Government Documents Round Table of the Alabama Library Association, The Task Force, 99; auth, Health Data on the Internet: An Annotated Bibliography and Guide/compiled by Robert H. Schrimsher and T. Harmon Straiton, Jr. Series: MLA BibKit, Publication Information: Chicago: Medical Library Association, (99), 29, 28 cm. + 3 3/4X3 1/2 in. computer diskette; auth, Information Services in the Year 2000 and Beyond, Reference Librarian, No. 65, (99), 3-14; auth, Electronic Resources for Federal Publications, Presentation, 1999 Alabama Educational Technology Conference, Birmingham, Alabama; auth, Web Resources for Academic Libraries, Presentation, Alabama Library Assoc Conference 2000, Birmingham, Alabama, 00; auth, Internet Resources for Academic Libraries, Web site; auth, Leadership for the New Millenium, Presenter and panelist, Alabama Library Assoc preconference, workshop sponsored by eLibrary, Inc., Birmingham, Alabama, 00. **CONTACT ADDRESS** PO Box 132, Auburn, AL 36831. **EMAIL** straith@auburn.edu

STRANBERG, VICTOR H.
PERSONAL Born 05/16/1935, Deerfield, NH, m, 1961, 2 children **DISCIPLINE** ENGLISH **EDUCATION** Clark Univ, AB, 57; Brown Univ, BA, 59; PhD, 62. **CAREER** Asst Prof, Univ of Vt, 62-66; From Asst Prof to Prof, Duke Univ, 66-. **HONORS AND AWARDS** Fulbright Prof in Sweden, Belgium, Ger, Czech Republic. **MEMBERSHIPS** ASCL, ALA, MLA, SAMLA, SSSL, Robert Penn Warren Circle. **RESEARCH** 19th and 20th century American literature. **SELECTED PUBLICATIONS** Auth, The Poetic Vision of Robert Warren; auth, A Faulkner Overview: Sin Perspectives; auth, Religious Psychology in American Literature: A Study in the Reference of William James; auth, Greek Mind, Jewish Soul: The Conflicted Art of Cynthia Ayick. **CONTACT ADDRESS** Dept English, Duke Univ, PO Box 90015, Durham, NC 27708-0015. **EMAIL** vhs@duke.edu

STRAND, DANA
DISCIPLINE LITERATURE **EDUCATION** Vanderbilt Univ, PhD. **CAREER** Literature, Carleton Col. **HONORS AND AWARDS** Chair, Romance Lang & Lit. **SELECTED PUBLICATIONS** Auth, Colette: A Study of the Short Fiction, Macmillan. **CONTACT ADDRESS** Carleton Col, 100 S College St., Northfield, MN 55057-4016.

STRATE, LANCE
PERSONAL Born 09/17/1957, New York, NY, m, 1991, 2 children **DISCIPLINE** COMMUNICATION, MEDIA STUDIES **EDUCATION** Cornell Univ, BS, 78; CUNY, MA, 81; NY Univ, PhD, 91. **CAREER** Adj lectr, Adelphi Univ, 84-87; adj lectr, Univ of Conn, 85-88; instr, William Paterson Col of NJ, 88-89; adj asst prof, NYork Univ, 91-94; instr to assoc prof, chair, Fordham Univ, 89-. **HONORS AND AWARDS** Kappa Delta Pi, 82; Fordham Univ Grants, 93-94, 97-98; Mellon Fund Res Grant, 96-97; John F. Wilson Fel Awd, NY State Commun Assoc, 98; Can Consulate Grant, 98-. **MEMBERSHIPS** Nat Commun Assoc; Int Commun Assoc; Am Commun Assoc; Eastern Commun Assoc; Lambda Pi Eta; Int Soc for General Semantics. **RESEARCH** Media ecology, communication theory, popular culture, technology studies. **SELECTED PUBLICATIONS** Coauth, Myths, Men, and Beer: An Analysis of Beer Commercials on Broadcast Television, 1987, AAA Found for Traffic Safety, (Falls Church, VA), 87; auth, "Cybertime", Communication and Cyberspace, (351-377); coed, Communication and Cyberspace: Social Interaction in an Electronic Environment, Hampton Pr, (Cresskill, NJ); auth, "Understanding MEA", In Media Res (Fall 99): 1-2; auth, "The Varieties of Cyberspace: Problems in Definition and Delimitation", W J of Commun 63.3 (99): 382-412; auth, "Narcissism and Echolalia: Sense and the Struggle for Self", Speech commun Annual 14 (forthcoming); coed, Critical Studies in Media Commercialism, Oxford Univ Pr, (forthcoming); auth, "Baseball as Medium", Baseball and the Meaning of Life, eds Gary Gumpert and Susan Drucker, Hampton Pr, (forthcoming); coed, Cybertheory and the Ecology of Digital Media, Hampton Pr, (forthcoming). **CONTACT ADDRESS** Dept Commun & Media Studies, Fordham Univ, 441 E Fordham Rd, Bronx, NY 10458-5149. **EMAIL** strate@fordham.edu

STRATTON, CHARLES R.
DISCIPLINE ENGLISH LITERATURE **EDUCATION** Carroll Col, BS, 60; Rensselaer Polytech Inst, MA, 68; Univ Wis Madison, PhD, 71. **CAREER** Prof. Hartford Univ. **SELECTED PUBLICATIONS** Auth, Technical Writing: Process and Product, Holt, Rinehart and Winston, 84; Operation and Maintenance Manual, Rupert, 80. **CONTACT ADDRESS** English Dept, Univ of Idaho, 415 W 6th St, Moscow, ID 83844.

STRATTON, SUSAN B.
PERSONAL Born 10/06/1941 **DISCIPLINE** ENGLISH **EDUCATION** Lawrence Univ, BA, 63; Univ Colo, MA, 67, PhD 70. **CAREER** Asst to assoc prof, 73-86, assoc dean hum, 85-89, prof Eng, Univ Calgary, 86-, assoc dean grad stud, 93-98; bd dir, Maenad Theatre Prod, 91-93. **MEMBERSHIPS** Sci Fiction Res Asn; Soc Utopian Stud; Asn Stud Lit Environ; Asn Can Col Univ Tchrs Eng. **RESEARCH** Canadian theatre. **SELECTED PUBLICATIONS** Auth, Robertson Davies, Playwright: A Search for the Self on the Canadian Stage, Vancouver: Univ of British Columbia Press, 85; auth, Consciousness Evolution and Early Telepathic Tales," Science-Fiction Studies 20:2, (93): 241-250; auth, "Aphra Behn and Contemporary Canadian Women Playwrights," Woman as Artist: Papers in Honour of Marsha Hanen, eds., Christine Sutherland and Beverly Rasporich, (U of Calgary Press, 93): 89-108; co-ed, "Feminists, Nurturers and Psychic Healers," Imaginative Futures, Milton Wolf and Daryl Mallett, eds., SFRA Press, 94; auth, "Recent Plays on Women's Playwriting," Essays in Theatre 14:1, (95): 37-48; auth, "Science and Sprituality in Back to Methuselah and Last and First Men," SHAW 17: Shaw and Speculative Fiction, (97): 183-96. **CONTACT ADDRESS** Dept of English, Univ of Calgary, Social Sciences Tower, 11 Fl, 2500 Univ Dr, Calgary, AB, Canada T2N 1N4. **EMAIL** stratton@acs.ucalgary.ca

STRAUB, KRISTINA
DISCIPLINE EIGHTEENTH-CENTURY BRITISH LITERATURE **EDUCATION** Emory Univ, PhD. **CAREER** Lit, Carnegie Mellon Univ. **SELECTED PUBLICATIONS** Area: eighteenth century & feminist theory. **CONTACT ADDRESS** Carnegie Mellon Univ, 5000 Forbes Ave, Pittsburgh, PA 15213.

STRAUBEL, LINDA HELEN
PERSONAL Born 12/14/1949, Worcester, MA, d **DISCIPLINE** ENGLISH **EDUCATION** SUNY Utica, BA, 80; Univ Wis Milwaukee, MA, 92; PhD, 98. **CAREER** TA, Univ Wis Milwaukee, 94-98; adj prof, lakeland Col, 94-98; lectr, Univ Wis Rock County, 98-. **HONORS AND AWARDS** Second Chance Scholar Essay Winner, 78; Meritorious Rating, Univ Wis, 99-01; TAFA Grant, 99; Hybrid Project Grant, 00. **MEMBERSHIPS** MLA, Soc for Study of the Short Story, Col Pr. **RESEARCH** Modern American Novels, e-Learning, Web Enhanced Efficiency and its efficacy. **SELECTED PUBLICATIONS** Auth, Eng Comp II Web Sites, 00; auth, "Margaret Eleanor Atwood: From Descartes to Dancing Girls", A Reader's Companion to the Short Story in English, 01; auth, "E-Learning iw Work(ing)," Teaching With Technology Today, 01. **CONTACT ADDRESS** 12040 Six Corners E, Whitewater, WI 53091. **EMAIL** lstraube@uwc.edu

STRAUS, BARRIE RUTH
DISCIPLINE ENGLISH LANGUAGE; LITERATURE **EDUCATION** Oregon Univ, BA; Iowa Univ, MA, PhD, 90. **CAREER** Prof **RESEARCH** Medieval literature; contemporary critical theory; women's studies; modern narrative. **SELECTED PUBLICATIONS** Auth, Catholic Church & Skirting the Texts. **CONTACT ADDRESS** Dept of English Language and Literature, Univ of Windsor, 401 Sunset Ave, Windsor, ON, Canada N9B 3P4. **EMAIL** straus@uwindsor.ca

STRAUSS, ALBRECHT BENNO
PERSONAL Born 05/17/1921, Berlin, Germany, m, 1978, 3 children **DISCIPLINE** ENGLISH **EDUCATION** Oberlin Col, BA, 42; Tulane Univ, MA, 48; Harvard Univ, PhD(English), 56. **CAREER** Instr English, Tulane Univ, 48-49; instr, Brandeis Univ, 51-52; instr, Yale Univ, 55-59; asst prof, Univ Okla, 59-60; from asst prof to assoc prof, 60-70, dir grad studies, 67-68, PROF ENGLISH, UNIV NC, CHAPEL HILL, 70-, Ed, Studies Philol, 74-80. **MEMBERSHIPS** MLA; SAtlantic Mod Lang Asn; Am Soc 18th Century Studies; Col English Asn; Southeastern Am Soc 18th Century Studies (pres, 80-81). **RESEARCH** Eighteenth century English literature; English novel; stylistics. **SELECTED PUBLICATIONS** Auth, On Smollett's Language, In: English Institute Essays, 1958, Columbia Univ, 59; The dull duty of an editor: On editing the text of Johnson's Rambler, Bookmark, 6/65; co-ed, Essays in English Literature of the Classical Period Presented to Dougald MacMillan, Univ NC, 67; co-ed, The Rambler, Vols III, IV & V, In: The Yale Edition of the Works of Samuel Johnson, Yale Univ, 69; You-Cant-Go-Home-Again, Thomas Wolfe And I, Southern Lit J, Vol 27, 95, Thomas Wolfe and Samuel Johnson: An Unlikely Pair, Southern Lit J, Vol 31, 99. **CONTACT ADDRESS** Dept English, Univ of No Carolina, Chapel Hill, Chapel Hill, NC 27599-3520. **EMAIL** strausshaus@mindspring.com

STRAW, WILLIAM O.
DISCIPLINE COMMUNICATION STUDIES **EDUCATION** Carleton Univ, BA, 78; McGill Univ, MA, 80; PhD, 91. **CAREER** Asst prof, Carleton Univ, 84-93; assoc prof, McGill Univ, 93-. **HONORS AND AWARDS** Fac of Arts Tchg Awd, Carleton Univ, 88. **SELECTED PUBLICATIONS** Auth, "Getting Down To Business: Cultural Politics and Policies in Canada," in Benjamin D. Singer, ed. Communivations in Canadian Society, Toronto: Nelson Canada, (95): 332-356; auth, "Bewitched, Bothered and Bewildered," in Will Straw, Jody Berland and Dave Tomas, ed., Theory Rules: Art as Theory, Theory and Art, Toronto: Univ of Toronto Press/YYZ, 96; auth, "Sound Recording," In Michael Dorland, ed., The Cultural Industries in Canada, Toronto: James Lorimer nad Ocmpany, (96): 95-117; auth, "Scenes and Communities in Popular Music," in Ken Gelder and Sarah Thornton, eds., The Subcultures Reader, London: Routledge, 96; auth, "Urban Confidential: The Lurid City o fthe 1950s," In David B. Clarke, ed. The Cinematic City, London: Routledge, (97): 110-128; auth, "Organized Disorder: The Changing Space of the Record Shop," In Steve Redhead, Derek Synne and Justin O'Connor, eds., The Clubcultures Reader: Readings in Popular Cltural Studies, Oxford: Blackwell Publishers Ltd., (97): 57-65; auth, "Sizing Up Record Collections: Gender and Connoisseurship in Rock Music Cultrue," In Sheila Whiteley, ed. Sexing the Groove: Popular Musec and Gender, London: Routledge, (97): 3-16; auth, "Canadian Cinema," In John Hill, Pamela Church Givson, eds., The Oxford Guide to Film Studies, Oxford: Oxford Univ Press, (98): 23-26; auth, "Ornament, Entrance nad the Theme Song," In Philip Broophy, ed. Cinesonic: The World of Sound in Film, North Ryde, NSW: Australian Film Television and Radio School, (99): 213-228; auth, "Authorship," In Burce Horner and Thomas Swiss, eds. Key Terms in Popular Music and Culture, Malden, Mass. and Oxford: Blackwell publishers, (99): 199-208. **CONTACT ADDRESS** Dept Communications, McGill Univ, 845 Sherbrooke St, Montreal, QC, Canada H3A 2T5. **EMAIL** cxws@musica.mcgill.ca

STRAZNICKY, MARTA
DISCIPLINE ENGLISH LITERATURE **EDUCATION** Univ Ottawa, PhD. **CAREER** Dept Eng, Queen's Univ **RESEARCH** Early modern women writers; theatre history; Renaissance drama; feminist and reception theory. **SELECTED PUBLICATIONS** Auth, pubs on Renaissance comedy and seventeenth-century women dramatists. **CONTACT ADDRESS** English Dept, Queen's Univ at Kingston, Kingston, ON, Canada K7L 3N6. **EMAIL** straznic@qsilver.queensu.ca

STRECKER, JUDY
PERSONAL Born 11/16/1942, Amarillo, TX, m, 1990 **DISCIPLINE** MUSIC **EDUCATION** Eastman School Music, MA, 71; Univ Colo, DMA, 79. **CAREER** Dept Chair, Dicarnate Word Col, 71-76; Dept Chair, St Mary's of the Plains Col, 87-90; Dept Chair, Frank Phillips Col, 92-. **HONORS AND AWARDS** Outstanding Teacher of the Year Awd, NISOD, 99; Who's Who among am Teachers, 97-99. **MEMBERSHIPS** TMEA, MENC, TCDA, Am Col of Musicians. **RESEARCH** Performance related. **CONTACT ADDRESS** Dept Lib Arts, Frank Phillips Col, Box 5118, Borger, TX 79008.

STREET, JACK DAVID
PERSONAL Born 04/17/1929, Lafayette, AL, m, 1955, 2 children **DISCIPLINE** FRENCH, ENGLISH **EDUCATION** Jacksonville State Col, AB & BS, 50; Univ Ala, MA, 52; State Univ Iowa, PhD(French), 64 Univ of Florence, dipl(Ital lang, lit & cult), 75; Scuola Dante Alighieri, dipl(Ital lang, lit & cult), 77. **CAREER** Teacher French & English, Tuscaloosa High Sch, 51-52; asst prof mod lang, NCent Col, 58-61; from asst prof to assoc prof, 61-72, prof mod lang, 72-97, chmn dept of mod lang & lit, 75-97, Harry C Moore Prof Mod Lang, Beloit Col, 97-. **MEMBERSHIPS** Am Asn Teachers Fr; Am Coun Teaching Foreign Lang; AAUP **RESEARCH** Marcel Proust; Chateaubriand; Montherlant; French in the Valley d'Aosta, Italy. **SELECTED PUBLICATIONS** Auth, Seminar in France, 1959: An appraisal, 2/60 & A statistical study of the vocabulary of Les aventures du dernier Abencerage by Chateaubriand, 10/68, Fr Rev; 8 articles on French in the Valley d'Aosta, Italy, in: Contemporary French Civilization and French Rev. **CONTACT ADDRESS** Dept of Mod Lang, Beloit Col, 700 College St, Beloit, WI 53511-5595. **EMAIL** streetj@beloit.edu

STREET, RICHARD L., JR.
DISCIPLINE HEALTH COMMUNICATION **EDUCATION** Univ Tex, PhD. **CAREER** Prof, Texas A&M Univ; res prof, Col Med, Texas A&M Univ. **HONORS AND AWARDS** Col Liberal Arts Distinguished Tchg Awd, Former Students Asn Texas A&M Univ. **SELECTED PUBLICATIONS** Co-ed, Health Promotion and Interactive Technology; contribur, Talk of the Clinic: Explorations in the Analysis of Medical and Therapeutic Discourse; Communication and Health Outcomes; Handbook of Interpersonal Communication; Applied CommunicationTheory and Research. **CONTACT ADDRESS** Dept of Speech Communication, Texas A&M Univ, Col Station, College Station, TX 77843-4234. **EMAIL** r-street@tamu.edu

STREETER, DONALD
PERSONAL Born 04/24/1911, Huron, SD, d, 2 children **DISCIPLINE** ENGLISH, SPEECH **EDUCATION** Univ of Minn, BEd, 33; Univ of Iowa, MA, 38, PhD, 48. **CAREER** High school instr, 33-38; teaching fel, Univ of Iowa, 38-41 & 46-48; prof & chair, Univ of Memphis, 48-57; prof & chair emeritus, Univ of Houston, 57-76; adjunct, Tx A&M, Alvin Col, & Galveston Col, 76-96. **HONORS AND AWARDS** Outstanding Achievement, Galveston Col, 96; Educator of the Year, Rotary Int, 97. **MEMBERSHIPS** Tx Speech Commun; Speech Asn of Am. **SELECTED PUBLICATIONS** Auth, 50 Years of the Texas Speech Association; major public addreses of LQC Lamar, autobiography. **CONTACT ADDRESS** 6210 Sea Isle, Galveston, TX 77554-9600.

STREIGHT, IRWIN
DISCIPLINE ENGLISH LITERATURE **EDUCATION** Queen's Univ, PhD. **CAREER** Dept Eng, Queen's Univ **RESEARCH** Christianity and literature; semiotic theory; postmodernity; sociolinguistics. **SELECTED PUBLICATIONS** Auth, A Good Hypogram is Not Hard to Find, Lit Belief, 97; Is There a Text in this Man?: A Semiotic Reading of 'Parker's Back', Flannery O'Connor Bull, 94. **CONTACT ADDRESS** English Dept, Queen's Univ at Kingston, Kingston, ON, Canada K7L 3N6. **EMAIL** ihs@post.queensu.ca

STRELKA, JOSEPH PETER
PERSONAL Born 05/03/1927, Wiener Neustadt, Austria, m, 1963, 1 child **DISCIPLINE** GERMAN LITERATURE, THEORY OF LITERATURE **EDUCATION** Univ Vienna, PhD(Ger lit), 50. **CAREER** Assoc prof Ger lit, Univ Southern Calif, 64, dir Vienna prog, Univ Vienna, 65; prof Ger, Pa State Univ, University Park, 66-71; Prof Ger & Comp Lit, State Univ NY Albany, 71-, Theodor Koerner Found award, 55-57; City of Vienna award, 58; Austrian Govt res fel, Austrian Inst Cult Affairs Paris, 58-59; ed, Yearbook of Comparative Criticism Ser, 68 & Penn State Series in German literature, 71-; exchange scholar, State Univ NY, 75; Inst Humanistic Studies fel, 77; New Yorker Beitrage zur Vergleichenden Literaturwissenschaft, 82-; New Yorker Studien zur Neueren Deutschen Literaturgeschichte, 82- **HONORS AND AWARDS** Austrian Cross of Honor for the Arts and Sci First Class, Republic of Austria, 78. **MEMBERSHIPS** Pen Club; Int Asn Ger Studies, Int Comp Lit Asn; MLA; Humboldt-Gesellschaft. **RESEARCH** LIterary theory; literature of the Renaissance; German literature of the 20th century. **SELECTED PUBLICATIONS** Brucke u vielen Ufern, Europa, Vienna, Frankfurt, Zurich, 66; Vergleichende Literaturkritik, Francke, Bern, 70; Die gelenkten Musen, Europa, Vienna, Frankfurt, Zurich, 71; Auf der Suche nach dem verlorenen Selbst, Francke, Bern, 77; Werk, Werkverstandnin, Wertung, Francke, Bern, 78; Methodologie der Literaturwissenschaft, Nimeyer, Tubingen, 78; Esoterik bei Goethe, Niemeyer Tubingen, 80; Stefan Zweig, Osterreichischer Bundesverlag, Vienna, 81. **CONTACT ADDRESS** Dept of Ger, SUNY, Albany, Albany, NY 12222.

STRICKLAND, JOHNYE
DISCIPLINE WOMEN WRITERS **EDUCATION** Univ Ark, PhD. **CAREER** English and Lit, Univ Ark **SELECTED PUBLICATIONS** Auth, Vietnamese Refugees in America: Expectations and Realities, SW Asian Soc Newsl; Huy Luc and Phan Tung Mai: Prize Winning Vietnamese Writers, S Central Mod Lang Asn Bull; Oral History in the College Classroom, Oral Hist Rev; The Position of Women--Teachers and Students, Col Comm & Composition; Two Hundred Years of Law and Liberty, Ark Lawyer. **CONTACT ADDRESS** Univ of Arkansas, Little Rock, 2801 S University Ave., Little Rock, AR 72204-1099. **EMAIL** jestrickland@ualr.edu

STRIER, RICHARD
PERSONAL Born 08/21/1945, Baltimore, MD, m, 1990 **DISCIPLINE** ENGLISH **EDUCATION** Harvard Univ, PhD, 78. **CAREER** From Instr to Prof, Univ Chicago, 73-. **HONORS AND AWARDS** Frank L. Sulzberger Professorship. **MEMBERSHIPS** MLA, ASA, SAA. **RESEARCH** Sixteenth-Century literature, religion, politics. **SELECTED PUBLICATIONS** Auth, "Radical Donne: Satire III," ELH 60 (93): 283-322; auth, "Martin Luther and the Real Presence in Nature," Graven Images 1 (94): 52-72; co-ed, The Theatrical City: Culture, Theatre and Politics in London, 1576-1649, Cambridge Univ Pr, 95; co-ed, Religion, Literature and Politics in Post-Reformation England, 1540-1688, Cambridge Univ Pr, 96; auth, Resistant Structures: Particularity, Radicalism and Renaissance Texts, Univ Calif Pr, 97; auth, "Milton Against Humility," in Relig and Cult in the English Renaissance (Cambridge Univ Pr, 97), 258-286. **CONTACT ADDRESS** Dept English, Univ of Chicago, 1050 E 59th St, Chicago, IL 60637.

STRIPLING, LUTHER
PERSONAL Born 08/25/1935, Tingnall, GA, m, 1997, 2 children **DISCIPLINE** VOCAL PEDAGOGY, PERFORMANCE **EDUCATION** Clark Coll, AB 1957; Atlanta Univ, attended 1960-65; Univ KY, MMus 1968; Univ CO, DMus 1971. **CAREER** Hamilton HS, teacher 1957-66, chmn music dept 1960-66; GA Interscholastic Assn, chmn vocal div 1964-66; Univ KY, instructor 1966-68; Univ CO, 70-71; Macalester Coll, coordinator vocal activities 71-83; So IL Univ at Edwardsville, assoc prof of music/dir of opera workshop; Tarrant County Jr Coll NE Campus, 84-95; prof of vocal music/dir; Bel Canto Women's Chorus, currently. **MEMBERSHIPS** Pres MN chapter Natl Opera Assn Inc; general dir Macalester Coll Opera Workshop; assn general dir Assoc Coll of the Twin Cities Opera Workshop; minister of music Pilgrim Baptist Church; pres St Louis Dist Chapter of Natl Assn of Teachers of Singing 1980-82; numerous performances orchestral appearances directing papers in field; mem, bd of governors, NE Trinity Arts Council, 1989-91. **SELECTED PUBLICATIONS** Contributor Burkhart Charles Anthology for Musical Analysis 3rd Ed NY Holt Rinehart & Winston 1978. **CONTACT ADDRESS** Professor of Music, Tarrant County Junior Col, 828 Harwood Rd, FAB 147, Hurst, TX 76053. **EMAIL** lstrip@tccd.net

STRIPLING, MAHALA YATES
PERSONAL Born 06/04/1944, Eau Claire, WI, m, 1979, 2 children **DISCIPLINE** ENGLISH, RHETORIC **EDUCATION** Texas Christian Univ, BA, 75, MLA, 86, MA, 93, PhD, 97. **CAREER** Schl, Lectr, 98-, Yale Med Sch; Univ Texas Med Br; Texas Wesleyan Univ, et al; Asst editor, writing consul, 96-97, WM L Adams Writing Cen. **HONORS AND AWARDS** TCU creative writing Awds; Best Grad Essay, Poetry, News Story; Pres Vol Action Awd nom; Governor's Awd Outstanding Vol. **MEMBERSHIPS** NCIS; SHHV; MLAA; SCMLA; RRAA; et al. **RESEARCH** Rhetorical engendering of violence against women; Doctor-Patient Relationship; Richard Selzer, biography, literary criticism, and bibliography. **SELECTED PUBLICATIONS** Auth, Searching for Father, Med Humanities Rev, 98; Richard Selzer: Poet of the Body, Yale Med Sch's Humanities J, 98; Reclaiming Rhetorica: A Class Action, JAC, A J Composition Theory, 97; auth, The Tending Act-An Interview with Richard Slezer, J Med Humanities and Comp Studies, 96; A Dialogic/Rhetorical Analysis of Richard Selzer's, Smoking from Mortal Lessons, Readerly/Writerly, Texts, 96; The Ultimate Case History: A Doctor Describes His Own Coma, and Death, Med Humanities Rev, 94; Richard Slezer b 1928: A Checklist, Bulletin of Bibliography, 90. **CONTACT ADDRESS** 3301 Rogers Ave, Fort Worth, TX 76109. **EMAIL** DrRhetoric@aol.com

STROFFOLINO, CHRIS
PERSONAL Born 03/26/1963, Reading, PA, s **DISCIPLINE** ENGLISH **EDUCATION** Albright Col, BA, 86; Temple Univ, MA, 88; State Univ NY (SUNY), PhD, 00. **CAREER** Instr, State Univ NYork (SUNY), 94-95; Instr, Rutgers Univ, 97-. **HONORS AND AWARDS** Wash Rev Prize, 98; Pusncart Prize, 00. **MEMBERSHIPS** Shakespeare Asn of Am, Poetry Soc of Am, MLA. **RESEARCH** Contemporary poetry, Shakespeare, Laura Jackson. **SELECTED PUBLICATIONS** Auth, Light as a Feather, Situations (New York, NY), 97; auth, "One Last Leopard of Love for You," Proliferation #4 (97); auth, "18 1/2 Minute Gap," The Baffler #10 (98); auth, Stealer's Wheel, Hard Pr (West Stockbridge, MA), 99; rev, "Gender Bending: Review of John Yau's 'My Symptoms'," Am Book Rev, vol 21, no 1 (99): 28; auth, "Organizational Propaganda: Towards a Harrymanian Reading of Shakespeare," Assembling Alternatives, (Wesleyan UP, forthcoming). **CONTACT ADDRESS** Dept English, Rutgers, The State Univ of New Jersey, New Brunswick, PO Box 5454, New Brunswick, NJ 08903.

STROHKIRCH, CAROLYN
PERSONAL Born 08/11/1952, Gladwin, MI, s **DISCIPLINE** SPEECH COMMUNICATION **EDUCATION** Univ Mich, BA, 74; Central Mich Univ, MA, 80; Univ Wash, PhD, 88. **CAREER** Teacher & speech coach, Jesus & Mary High Sch, 76-78; lectr & dir of forensics, Univ of Tex at El Paso, 80-82; instr & dir of forensics, McMurry Univ, 82-84; grad teaching asst, Univ of Wash, 84-87; asst prof, Ill State Univ, 87-94; dept supervisor for student teachers, Ill State Univ, 87-93; basic course dir & dept supervisor of student teachers in dept of commun, Fort Hays State Univ, 94-; asst prof, Fort Hays State Univ, 94-98; area dir for general commun of dept of commun, Fort Hays State Univ, 97-. **MEMBERSHIPS** Nat Commun Asn, Central States Commun Asn, Ill Speech & Theater Asn, Tex Speech Asn, Kans Speech Asn, Commun Educ Asn. **RESEARCH** Communication Apprehension, Academic Attributions, Sex Differences. **SELECTED PUBLICATIONS** Coauth, Fundamentals of Oral Communication: Theory and Practice, McGraw Hill, 95; coauth, "General and context dependent relationships between communication apprehension and gender role orientations," J of the Ill Speech and Theater Asn 47 (96): 59-72; coauth, "Technological answers to student instructional needs: Issues and impacts of using a multimedia approach to course delivery," Proceedings of the Fourteenth Annual Conference Academic Chairpersons: Changing Answers to Recurring Questions 47 (96): 59-72; auth, "Using debate and argumentation to develop students' voices and audience awareness," Kans Speech J 56 (97): 32-38; coauth, Fundamentals of Oral Communication: Theory and Practice 2nd ed, McGraw-Hill, 97; coauth, "Influence methods and innovators: Technocrats and champions," The J of Leadership Studies 4.2 (97): 43-54; coauth, "Cognitive differentiation and organizational influence tactics: Findings and implications for leaders as agents of influence," The J of Leadership Studies 4.3 (97): 152-161; auth, Competent communicators: K-12 speaking, listening, and media literacy standards and competency statements, Nat Commun Asn (Annandale, VA), 98; rev, of "Cognitive Styles and Classroom Learning," Personal Relationship Issues 6 (99): 19-21. **CONTACT ADDRESS** Dept Commun, Fort Hays State Univ, 600 Park St, Hays, KS 67601-4009. **EMAIL** sstrohki@fhsu.edu

STROHMAIER, MAHLA
DISCIPLINE COMMUNICATION **EDUCATION** Purdue Univ, PhD, 97. **CAREER** Lectr, Speech Commun, 89, instr of Commun, Univ Alaska, Fairbanks, 89-95; Adjunct Fac, Tanana Valley Campus, Univ Alaska, 95-. **HONORS AND AWARDS** Cavett Robert Scholar, Nat Speakers Asn, 97; Alan H. Monroe Scholar, Purdue Univ, 97. **MEMBERSHIPS** Nat Commun Asn. **RESEARCH** Cross-cultural Commun; human-computer interaction; distance education. **SELECTED PUBLICATIONS** Coauth, Ethical Information Security in a Cross-cultural Environment, Infor Security-the Next Decade, 95; End-user Perception and Software Quality Assessment, J of Int Infor Management, 97; Implementing Speaking Across the Curriculum: A Case Study, 92; Faculty Development and Distance Education Proceedings of the International ED-MEDIA/ED-Telecom '98 Conference; The Global Community and Cultural Diversity, Proceedings of the Soc for Infor Tech and Teacher Ed 8th Int Conf, 97; Ethical Accountability in the Cyberspace, Proceedings of the ACM Ethics in the Computer Age Conference, 94; auth, The SynCon Project: Communicating Potential Health Effects of Contaminants to Circumpolar Arctic Communities, Arctic Research of the United States, in press; auth, Effective Distance Education Via Interactive Video, Proceedings of the 1999 Conference on Educational Multimedia, Hypermedia & Telecommunications ED-MEDIA/ED-Telecom '99 conference proceedings, 99; auth, Effective Distance Education, Proceedings of the American Society of Business and Behavioral Sciences: Information Systems, 99; auth, Computer-Mediated Communication as a Facilitator for Student Teacher Communication, Proceedings of the 10th International Conference of the Society for Information Technology & Teacher Education, 99. **CONTACT ADDRESS** PO Box 80484, Fairbanks, AK 99708-0484. **EMAIL** ffms@uaf.edu

STROM, WILLIAM O.
PERSONAL Born 06/12/1958, Baton Rouge, LA, m, 1988, 3 children **DISCIPLINE** COMMUNICATION **EDUCATION** Wheaton Col, BA, 80; Northern Ill Univ, MA, 83; Univ of Iowa, PhD, 88. **CAREER** Asst To Assoc Prof Of Commun, Chemn of Commun Dept, Trinity Western Univ, 87-. **HONORS AND AWARDS** Paul K. Crawford Awd for Outstanding Grad Study, Commun Studies Dept, Northern Ill Univ, 83. **MEMBERSHIPS** Nat Commun Asn; Religious Commun Asn. **RESEARCH** Religion and Communication; interpersonal communication; intercultural communication. **SELECTED PUBLICATIONS** Auth, Personal and cultural identity in cross-cultural relationships on the university campus, Mass Journal of Commun, 92; auth, The Effects of a Conversational Partners Program on ESL and University Students, The Howard Journal of Commun, 93; auth, More Than Talk: Communication Studies and the Christian Faith, Kendall/Hunt Pub Company, 98. **CONTACT ADDRESS** Dept of Communication, Trinity Western Univ, 7600 Glover Rd, Langley, BC, Canada V2Y 1Y1. **EMAIL** strom@twu.ca

STROUD, RONALD SIDNEY
PERSONAL Born 07/08/1933, Toronto, ON, Canada, m, 1963, 2 children **DISCIPLINE** CLASSICS **EDUCATION** Univ Toronto, BA, 57; Univ Calif, Berkeley, PhD(classics), 65. **CAREER** Secy, Am Sch Class Studies Athens, 60-63; from asst prof to assoc prof, 65-72, Prof Classics, Univ Calif, Berkeley, 72-, Am Philos Soc, Am Coun Learned Socs & Guggenheim fels, 77-78; Mellon Prof, Classical Studies, Am Sch Class Studies Athens, 96-99. **RESEARCH** Greek history; Greek epigraphy; classical archaeology. **SELECTED PUBLICATIONS** Auth, Drakon's Law on Homicide, Univ Calif, 68; An Ancient Fort on Mt Oneion, 71 & Inscriptions from the North Slope of the Acropolis, 71 & 72, Hesperia; Thucydides and the Battle of Solygeia, Calif Studies Class Antiq, 71; An Athenian Law on Silver Coinage, Hesperia, 74; The Axones and Kyrbeis of Drakon and Solon, Univ Calif, 79; Athenian Economy And Society--A Banking Perspective, Mnemosyne, Vol 49, 96; auth, The Athenian Grain-Tax Law of 374/3 B.C., Hesperia, Suppl, 29 (98); co-ed, Supplementum Epigraphieum Graecum, Vol 26, 79, 47 (00). **CONTACT ADDRESS** Dept Classics, Univ of California, Berkeley, Berkeley, CA 94720. **EMAIL** rsstroud@socrates.berkeley.edu

STROUD, THEODORE ALBERT
PERSONAL Born 01/25/1914, Marcella, AR, m, 1939 **DISCIPLINE** ENGLISH **EDUCATION** Ark Col, AB, 32; Univ Ark, AM, 37; Univ Chicago, PhD, 47. **CAREER** Instr, Univ Ark, 37-38; instr, Univ Chicago, 43-46; asst prof, Univ Fla, 46-47; assoc prof, 47-51, interim chmn dept, 57-58, PROF ENGLISH, DRAKE UNIV, 51-, Ford fel, 54-55. **MEMBERSHIPS** MLA; Mid West Mod Lang Asn; NCTE. **RESEARCH** Middle English; the Fi manuscript of Chaucer's Canterbury Tales. **SELECTED PUBLICATIONS** Co-ed, The Literature of Comedy, Ginn, 68; Lucio And The Balanced Structure Of Measure For Measure, English Studies, Vol 74, 93. **CONTACT ADDRESS** Dept of English, Drake Univ, Des Moines, IA 50311.

STROUP, SARAH CULPEPPER
PERSONAL Born 11/10/1967, Honolulu, HI **DISCIPLINE** CLASSICS **EDUCATION** Univ Wash, BA, 92; Univ Calif Berkeley, MA, 95; PhD, 00. **CAREER** Acting asst prof to prof, Univ Wash, 00-. **HONORS AND AWARDS** Lulu J. Blumberg Fel, 93-94; Chancellor's Humanities Fel, 95; Outstanding Grad Student Instr Award, 98; Mellon Dissertation Fel, 98; Women's Class Caucus Paper Award, 99. **MEMBERSHIPS** Am Philol Asn; Archaeol Inst of Am; Women's Class Caucus. **RESEARCH** Roman Prose, especially rhetoric, philosophy, and epistolography; Greek and Roman Drama; Greek and Roman Art and Archaeology; Literary and Cultural Criticisms. **SELECTED PUBLICATIONS** Rev, of "Changing Bodies, Changing Meanings," by Dominic Montserrat, Bryn Mawr Class Rev, (98): 7-20; co-auth, "Phthonos d'Apesto: The Translation of Transgression in Aiskhylos' Agamemnon," Class Antiquity, (99): 153-182; auth, Political Muse: Cicero, Catullus, and Textual Culture in the Late Republic, (forthcoming); auth, By Fire of By Sword: The Catilinarian Conspiracy through the Eyes of Cicero, Sallust, Appian and Dio, Focus Pub, (forthcoming); auth, "Designing Women: Aristophanes' Lysistrata and the 'Hetairization' of the Greek Wife," (forthcoming). **CONTACT ADDRESS** Dept Class, Univ of Washington, PO Box 353110, Seattle, WA 98195-3110. **EMAIL** scstroup@u.washington.edu

STRYCHACZ, THOMAS
DISCIPLINE ENGLISH **EDUCATION** Warwick Univ, England, BA, 81; Princeton Univ,MA, 83 PhD, 86. **CAREER** Assoc prof; Mills Col, 88-. **RESEARCH** American literature; mass culture; political and cultural approaches to literature; science fiction. **SELECTED PUBLICATIONS** Auth, Modernism, Mass Culture, and Professionalism. Cambridge UP, 93; American Sports Writers and 'Unruly Rooters': The Significance of Orderly Spectating, J Amer Stud, 94; coauth, Beyond Mainstream: An Interdisciplinary Study of Music and the Written Word, J Lang and Learning Across the Disciplines, 96; contrib with, Soccer and Rock Climbing/Sport Climbing, in the Encycl US Popular Cult, 95. **CONTACT ADDRESS** Dept of English, Mills Col, 5000 MacArthur Blvd, Oakland, CA 94613-1301. **EMAIL** toms@mills.edu

STUART, DABNEY
PERSONAL Born 11/04/1937, Richmond, VA, m, 1983, 3 children **DISCIPLINE** MODERN FICTION, POETRY **EDUCATION** Davidson Col, AB, 60; Harvard Univ, AM, 62. **CAREER** Instr English, Col William & Mary, 61-65; from instr to assoc prof, 65-71, prof English, Washington & Lee Univ, 72-, Poetry ed, Shenandoah, 66-76, editor-in-chief, 88-95; vis asst prof English, Middlebury Col, 68-69; poet-in-schs, Richmond Intercult Ctr for Humanities, Va, 71-72, 77 & 81 & Albemarle County Dept Educ, Va, 72-73; NEA creative writing fel, 75 & 82; Guggenheim fel in poetry, 87-88; Individual Artist fel, 96; adv ed, Poets in South, 76; poet-in-residence, Trinity Col, Hartford, spring, 78; lectr in writing, Univ Va, fall, 81; poet-in-residence, Univ Va, 82-83. **HONORS AND AWARDS** First Governor's Award for the Arts, Va, 79; S Blount Mason Jr Prof, 98; Residency at Rockefeller Study and Conference Ctrs (Bellagio), 00. **MEMBERSHIPS** Auth Guild. **RESEARCH** Fiction of Vladimir Nabokov; modern and contemp poetry. **SELECTED PUBLICATIONS** Auth, The Diving Bell, 66 & A Particular Place, 69, Knopf; The Other Hand, La State Univ Press, 74; Friends of Yours, Friends of Mine, Rainmaker, 74; Round and Round, 77 & Nabokov: The Dimensions of Parody, 78, La State Univ Press; Rockbridge Poems, Iron Mountain, 81; Common Ground, La State Univ Press, 82; Don't Look Back, La State Univ Press, 87; Narcissus Dreaming, La State Univ Press, 90; Sweet Lucy Wine, La State Univ Press, 92; Light Years: New and Selected Poems, La State Univ Press, 94; Long Gone, La State Univ Press, 96; Second Sight: Poems for Paintings By Carroll Cloar, Univ of Mo Press, 96; The Way to Cobbs Creek, Univ Mo Press, 97; auth, Settlers, LSU Pr, 99; auth, Strains of the Old Man, Sow's Ear Pr, 99. **CONTACT ADDRESS** Dept of English, Washington and Lee Univ, Lexington, VA 24450-2504. **EMAIL** stuartd@wlu.edu

STUBBS, JOHN C.
PERSONAL Born 08/05/1936, Philadelphia, PA, m, 1959, 1 child **DISCIPLINE** ENGLISH **EDUCATION** Yale Univ, AB, 58; Princeton Univ, PhD, 63. **CAREER** Instr, Univ Wis, 62-64; asst prof to assoc prof, Univ Ill, 64-89; prof, Vir Poly Inst, 89-. **HONORS AND AWARDS** Fulbright Prof to Denmark, 70-71; Fulbright to Italy, 77; Vis Scholar, Am Acad, Rome, 97, 00. **MEMBERSHIPS** MLSA; SCS. **RESEARCH** Modern American literature. **SELECTED PUBLICATIONS** Auth, "Hawthorne's Scarlet Letter: Theory of the Romance," PMLA 88 (68): 1439-47; auth, The Pursuit of Form: Hawthorne and the Romance, UP Ill, 70; auth, Fedrico Fellini: References and Resources, G. K. Hall, 78; auth, "John Hawkes and the Dream-Work of The Lime Twig and Second Skin," Lit Psych 21 (71): 149-60; auth, "Ernest Hemingway and Role-Playing in Farewell to Arms," Fitzgerald/Hemingway Annual (73): 271-84; trans, ed, Two Fellini Screenplays: Moraldo in the City and A Journey with Anita (UP Ill, 1983); auth, "The Evolution of Orson Wells's Touch of Evil from Novel to Film," Cincinnati J 24 (85): 19-39. **CONTACT ADDRESS** English Dept, Virginia Polytech Inst and State Univ, 214 Williams Hall, Blacksburg, VA 24061. **EMAIL** jcstubbs@vt.edu

STUBER, FLORIAN
PERSONAL Born 03/01/1947, Buffalo, NY **DISCIPLINE** ENGLISH LITERATURE, THE NOVEL **EDUCATION** Columbia Univ, BA, 68, MA, 69, PhD(English), 80. **CAREER** Preceptor English, Columbia Col, Columbia Univ, 70-72, instr, 72-75; LECTR ENGLISH, BARNARD COL, COLUMBIA UNIV, 79-, Admin coordr, Conf Humanities & Pub Policy Issues, Columbia Univ, 74-76; consult, King-Hitzig Prod, 77; adj instr English, Fashion Inst Tech, 77-; consult, Citibank, New York City, 81 & Collectors Guild & Am Express, 82. **MEMBERSHIPS** MLA; Northeast Am Soc 18th Century Studies. **RESEARCH** Samuel Richardson; Charles Dickens; James Joyce. **SELECTED PUBLICATIONS** Co-ed & contribr, Small Comforts for Hard Times: Humanists on Public Policy, Columbia Univ Press, 77; Los humanistas y la politica, Fondo Cult Econ, Mexico City, 81; Clarissa, A Religious Novel, Studies In The Literary Imagination, Vol 28, 95. **CONTACT ADDRESS** 134 W 93rd St 3B, New York, NY 10025.

STULL, WILLIAM L.
PERSONAL Born 05/18/1948, Los Angeles, CA, m, 1987 **DISCIPLINE** ENGLISH **EDUCATION** Calif State Univ, BA, 69; Univ NMex, MA, 74; Univ Calif, PhD, 78. **CAREER** Asst prof to prof, Univ of Hartford, 79-. **MEMBERSHIPS** MLA. **RESEARCH** Contemporary American Literature, specializing in the work of Raymond Carver and Tess Gallagher. **SELECTED PUBLICATIONS** Auth, "Raymond Carver, 1938-1988", Dictionary of Literary Biography Yearbook, Gale Research, (Detroit, 89): 199-213; coed, Conversations with Raymond Carver, Univ Pr of Miss, (Jackson), 90; coed, Remembering Ray: A Composite Biography of Raymond Carver, Capra Pr, 93; auth, "Prose as Architecture: Two Interviews with Raymond Carver", Clockwatch Rev 10.1-2, (95-96): 8-18; ed, Il Mestiere Di Scrivere, Einaudi, (Turin), 97; ed, All of Us: The Collected Poems, Knopf, (NY), 98; coauth, "Two Darings", Philos and Lit 22.2 (98): 468-77; auth, "Raymond Carver", Am Nat Biography, Oxford Univ Pr, (NY), 99; ed, Raymond Carver, Call if You Need Me: the Uncollected Prose and Fiction, Harvill Pr, (London), 00. **CONTACT ADDRESS** Dept English, Univ of Hartford, 200 Bloomfield Ave, West Hartford, CT 06117-1545. **EMAIL** stull@mail.hartford.edu

STYAN, JOHN LOUIS
PERSONAL Born 07/06/1923, London, England, m, 1945, 4 children **DISCIPLINE** ENGLISH, DRAMA **EDUCATION** Cambridge Univ, MA, 47. **CAREER** Asst master grammar sch, Eng, 48-50; staff tutor lit & drama, Dept Adult Educ, Univ Hull, 50-62, sr staff tutor, 62-65; prof English, Univ Mich, Ann Arbor, 65-74, chmn dept, 73-74; Andrew W Mellon prof English, Univ Pittsburgh, 74-77; Franklin Bliss Snyder Prof English Lit, Northwestern Univ, 77-87, Mem, Univs Coun Adult Educ Broadcasting Subcomt, Gt Brit, 62-65, adult educ liaison comt, Brit Broadcasting Corp, 62-65, adult educ adv comt, Independent TV Authority, 62-65 & adv bd, World Ctr Shakespeare Studies, 72-; Nat Endowment for Humanities fel, 78-79; chmn, Int Shakespeare Globe Theatre Ctr Acad Adv Coun NAm, 81- **HONORS AND AWARDS** Res fel NEH, 78-79; Guggenheim Found fel, 83; Robert Lewis Medal for Lifetime Achievement in theatre res, Kent S.U., 95. **MEMBERSHIPS** MLA; Guild Drama Adjudicators, Gt Brit; Brit Drama League; Shakespeare Asn Am; Royal Overseas League. **RESEARCH** Contemporary drama; Shakespeare; dramatic theory. **SELECTED PUBLICATIONS** Auth, The Elements of Drama, 60, The Dark Comedy, 62, The Dramatic Experience, 65, Shakespeare's Stagecraft, 67 & Chekhov in Performance, 71, Cambridge Univ; ed, The Challenge of the Theatre, Dickenson, 72; auth, Drama, Stage and Audience, 75, The Shakespeare Revolution: Criticism and Performance in the Twentieth Century, 77 & Modern Drama in Theory and Practice (3 Vols), 81. Cambridge Univ; auth, Max Reinhardt, 82; Shakespeare in Performance: All's Well That Ends Well, 84; auth, The State of Drama Study, 84; auth, Restoration Comedy in Performance, 86; The Play Of Personality In The Restoration Theater, Albion, Vol 25, 93; auth, The English Stage, 96; auth, Perspectives on Shakespeare in Performance, 00; auth, Drama: A Guide to the Study of Plays, 00. **CONTACT ADDRESS** Dept of English, Northwestern Univ, Evanston, IL 60201. **EMAIL** johnlstyan@ukgateway.net

SUBLETTE, WALTER
PERSONAL Born 09/06/1940, Chicago, IL, m, 1974, 3 children **DISCIPLINE** ENGLISH **EDUCATION** Univ Ill, BA; MA; Northern Ill Univ, PhD. **CAREER** Prof, Aurora Univ, 17 years. **HONORS AND AWARDS** ISOP Awd; Marcus Taumball Awd. **MEMBERSHIPS** PSA; ASJA. **RESEARCH** Contemporary poets and poetry. **SELECTED PUBLICATIONS** Auth, The Resurrection on Friday Nights; auth, Naked Exile; auth, Go Now In Darkness. **CONTACT ADDRESS** Dept Humanities, Aurora Univ, 347 S Gladstone Ave, Aurora, IL 60506-4877.

SUBRAMANIAN, JANE M.
PERSONAL Born 03/07/1950, Schenectady, NY, m, 1973, 2 children **DISCIPLINE** LIBRARY SCIENCE **EDUCATION** SUNY Potsdam, BM, 72, MS, 74; Univ at Albany, MLS, 95. **CAREER** Lib tech asst, 74-87, staff assoc, 87-98, assoc librn, 98- , SUNY Potsdam. **MEMBERSHIPS** ALA; Asn for Lib Collections and Tech Serv; ACRL; SUNY Librns Asn; Eastern NY chap, ACRL; Music Lib Asn; NY/Ontario chap Music Lib Asn; Nat Flute Asn; Soc of Am Archivists; Mid Atlantic Regional Archives Conf; New England Archivists. **RESEARCH** American women's history; history of local musical community groups; reference service. **SELECTED PUBLICATIONS** Auth, Laura Ingalls Wilder: An Annotated Bibliography of Critical, Biographical, and Teaching Studies, Greenwood, 97; auth, Patron Attitudes Toward Computerized and Print Resources: Discussion and Considerations for Reference Service, Reference Librn, 98. **CONTACT ADDRESS** 63 Bay St, Potsdam, NY 13676. **EMAIL** subramjm@potsdam.edu

SUBRYAN, CARMEN
PERSONAL Born 12/30/1944, Linden, Guyana, d **DISCIPLINE** ENGLISH **EDUCATION** Howard University, Washingtn DC, BA, 1971, MA, 1973, PhD, 1983. **CAREER** University of the District of Columbia, Washington DC, academic support, 73-74; Howard University, Washington DC, instructor, program coordinator, 74-. **HONORS AND AWARDS** Phi Beta Kappa, Howard University, 1971; Magna Cum Laude, Howard University, 1971; Reprise, a book of poetry, 1984. **MEMBERSHIPS** National Council of Teachers of English, 1980-84, College Language Association, 1981-86, National Association of Developmental Education, 1985-87, GUYAID, 1985-. **SELECTED PUBLICATIONS** "Walter Dean Myers," article in Dictionary of Literary Biography, 1984; "A B Spellman," article in Dictionary of Literary Biography, 1985; Woman's Survival, booklet, 1989; Black-Water Women, a novel, 1997. **CONTACT ADDRESS** Howard Univ, 2400 6th St, NW, Washington, VT 20059.

SUCHY, PATRICIA
DISCIPLINE PERFORMANCE STUDIES **EDUCATION** Northwestern Univ, MFA, PhD. **CAREER** Asst prof, La State Univ. **RESEARCH** The narrative and cultural theory of Mikhall Bakhtin; 19th century Russion literature; post-war American fiction; contemporary experimental theatre and performance art. **SELECTED PUBLICATIONS** Writes about the nature of authorship in performance contexts. **CONTACT ADDRESS** Dept of Speech Commun, Louisiana State Univ and A&M Col, Baton Rouge, LA 70803. **EMAIL** psuchy@lsu.edu

SUDERBURG, ROBERT
DISCIPLINE MUSIC **EDUCATION** Univ Minnesota, BA; Yale Sch Mus, MM; Univ Pa, PhD. **CAREER** Prof; composer-in-residence; dir, Group for 20th century Mus, Nat Young Composers Competition, Williams Col; taught at, Bryn Mawr, Univ Pa, Philadelphia Mus Acad; co-dir, Contemp Mus Group, Univ Wash; chancellor, NC Sch of the Arts; pres, Cornish Inst; Williams Col 85-; NEA, Composers Panel, 75-81. **HONORS AND AWARDS** Guggenheim fel (2); NEA prizes (2); awd(s) & commissions, BMI, ASCAP, Rockefeller Found, Amer Mus Ctr, Hindemith Found, Seattle Symphony, Washington State Arts Commn, ITG (2); bio appeared, amer grove dictionary of mus. **SELECTED PUBLICATIONS** Comp, Chamber Musics I-XI; SIX MOMENTS for solo piano; rec(s), Concerto, within the mirror of time, for piano and orchestra, Columbia; Chamber Music II, Concerto, voyage de nuit d'apres Baudelaire, for voice and chamber orchestra, Vox-Turnabout; Chamber Musics III, Night Set IV, V Steven son, for voice, string quartet and tape, Amer Rec Soc; Chamber Music VII, Rituals, for trumpet and piano, 4 rec(s) Vox, ITG, Coronet & Okla; Chamber Music VIII, 3 rec(s), Vox, Coronet & Okla; Chamber Music XI, Strophes of Night and the Dawn, Fla & Coronet. **CONTACT ADDRESS** Music Dept, Williams Col, 54 Chapin Hall Dr., Williamstown, MA 01267.

SUDOL, RONALD A.
PERSONAL Born 06/16/1943, New London, CT, m, 1973 **DISCIPLINE** RHETORIC **EDUCATION** St Michael's Col, BA, 65; Brown Univ, MA, 67; SUNY, Stony Brook, PhD, 76. **CAREER** Asst prof, 77-83, assoc prof, 83-91, prof of Rhetoric, Oakland Univ, 91-. **HONORS AND AWARDS** NEH summer seminar, 78; NEH summer stipend, 81; Danforth Found Assoc, 81-86; Oakland Univ Res Fel, 90. **MEMBERSHIPS** NCTE; CCCC. **RESEARCH** Writing and rhetoric; television criticism; rhetoric and public address. **SELECTED PUBLICATIONS** Auth, Textfiles: A Rhetoric for Word Processing, Harcourt

Brace Jovanovich, 87; The Accumulative Rhetoric of Word Processing, College English, Dec 91; Writers, Computers, and Personality, Most Excellent Differences: Essays on Using Type Theory in the English Classroom, ed Thomas Thompson, Consulting Psychologists Press, 96; Self-Represention and Personality Type in Letter From Birmingham Jail, Understanding Literacy: Personality Preference in Rhetorical and Psycholinguistic Contexts, Hampton Press, 96; ed with Alice Horning, Understanding Literacy: Personality Preference in Rhetorical and Psycholinguistic Contexts, Hampton Press, 96; ed with Alice Horning, The Literary Connection, Hampton Press, 98. **CONTACT ADDRESS** Rhet, Commun & Journalism Dept, Oakland Univ, Rochester, MI 48309. **EMAIL** sudol@oakland.edu

SUGANO, DOUGLAS
PERSONAL m, 2 children **DISCIPLINE** ENGLISH LITERATURE, ASIAN AMERICAN LITERATURE **EDUCATION** UC Berkeley, BA; UCLA, MA, PhD. **CAREER** Asst Prof, 88-93; Assoc, 93-00; Full Prof, 00-. **HONORS AND AWARDS** Outstanding Prof, 92. **RESEARCH** Early British literature, Shakespeare, Asian American Literature. **SELECTED PUBLICATIONS** Publ, articles on medieval English drama; ed, Midlands Ministeries. **CONTACT ADDRESS** Dept of Eng, Whitworth Col, 300 West Hawthorne Rd, Spokane, WA 99251-2901. **EMAIL** dsugano@whitworth.edu

SUGG, RICHARD PETER
PERSONAL Born St. Louis, MO, 1 child **DISCIPLINE** AMERICAN LITERATURE FILM **EDUCATION** Univ Notre Dame, BA, 63; Univ Fla, MA, 67, PhD(Am Lit), 69. **CAREER** Asst prof Humanities, Univ Fla, 69-70; asst prof English, Ark State Univ, 71-73; asst prof, Univ Ky, 73-77; dir Humanities, 77-79, from assoc prof to prof English, Fla Int Univ, 79-85, Fulbright sr lectr, Czechoslovakia, 79-80. **HONORS AND AWARDS** Dir, NEH Summer Seminar, FI U, 96; Teacher Incentive Awd, FIU, 96. **MEMBERSHIPS** MLA; Am Film Inst. **RESEARCH** Modern American literature; film. **SELECTED PUBLICATIONS** Auth, Appreciating Poetry, Houghton, 75; The Bridge: A Description of its Life, Univ Ala, 76; Jungian Literary Criticism, Northwestern, 92. **CONTACT ADDRESS** Dept of English, Florida Intl Univ, 3000 NE 151 St, Miami, FL 33181-3000. **EMAIL** suggrp@cs.com

SUGNET, CHARLES JOSEPH
PERSONAL Born 06/20/1944, Port Huron, MI, 3 children **DISCIPLINE** ENGLISH & AMERICAN LITERATURE **EDUCATION** Boston Col, BA, 66; Univ Va, MA, 67, PhD(English), 70. **CAREER** Assoc prof English, Univ Minn, 70- ; dir Program in Creative and Professional Writing, 86-89, 94; dir College in the Schools Literature Program, 84-94. **HONORS AND AWARDS** Loft Creative Nonfiction Awd, 88; Bush Found grant, 90-91; Fulbright lectr and res fel, Senegal, 95-96; Morse-Alumni Awd, 95; CLA Distinguished Teaching Awd, 98. **MEMBERSHIPS** MLA; Midwest Mod Lang Asn. **RESEARCH** Postcolonial literature, especially fiction and film of the African diaspora; creative nonfiction writing; the contemporary novel; multi-cultural instruction in the high schools. **SELECTED PUBLICATIONS** Coauth, The Imagination on Trial: A Study of the Working Methods of Eleven Contemporary British and American Novelists, Schocken, 81; auth, Vile Bodies, Vile Places; Travel Writing and Neocolonialism in Granta, Transition, 91; auth, Nervous Conditions: Tsitsi Dangarembga's Feminist Reinvention of Fanon, in Nnaemeka, ed, Politics of Mothering: Epistemology, Ontology, and the Problematic of Womanhood in African Literature, Routledge, 96; **CONTACT ADDRESS** Univ of Minnesota, Twin Cities, 207 Church St. SE, 207 Lind Hall, Minneapolis, MN 55455. **EMAIL** sugne001@tc.umn.edu

SUKENICK, RONALD
PERSONAL Born 07/14/1932, Brooklyn, NY, m **DISCIPLINE** ENGLISH & AMERICAN LIT **EDUCATION** Cornell Univ, BA, 55; Brandeis Univ, PhD, 62. **CAREER** Sarah Lawrence, Cornell Univ, Univ Cal, Irvine, Writer in Res; Univ Colorado, Boulder, Full Prof since, 75. **HONORS AND AWARDS** Guggenheim fel; Nat Endow Arts; Fulbright fel; Univ Colorado Faculty fel. **MEMBERSHIPS** Authors Guild; PEN; MLA; Nat Book Critics Circ. **RESEARCH** Contemp Am; writers theory; creative writing. **SELECTED PUBLICATIONS** Down & In; Doggy Bag; 98.6; Mosaic Man; Narralogues. **CONTACT ADDRESS** Univ of Colorado, Boulder, Dept Eng, Box 226, Boulder, CO 80309.

SUKHOLUTSKAYA, MARA
PERSONAL Born 09/04/1950, Karaganda, Kazhastan, d, 2 children **DISCIPLINE** ENGLISH, SECOND LANGUAGE ACQUISITION **EDUCATION** Kiev State Univ Linguistics, Ukraine, BA, MA, 72, EdD, 87. **CAREER** Teacher, Secondary Sch No 80, Kiev, Ukraine, 72-84; asst prof, Kiev State Univ of Linguistics, 87-91, head, laboratory of Primary Foreign Langs Educ; asst prof of Foreign Langs and Lit, East Central Univ, Ada, Okla, 96-. **HONORS AND AWARDS** Ada Rotary Educator of the Month, May 96; Who's Who in the South and Southwest, 97; George Platt Awd, Outstanding Teacher of Russian in Okla, 98; Proj coordr, "Leadership in Languages," U.S. Dept of Educ and State Dept of educ, 96-99; Pres, Okla Coun of Teachers of Russian,96-; Bd of Dirs, Okla Foreign Lang Asn, 96-; Bd of Dirs, Southwest Conf on Language Teaching, 98-2001; founder and chair, Central Asn of Russian Teachers of Am, 98-. **MEMBERSHIPS** Okla Coun of Teachers of Russian, Okla Foreign Lang Asn, Southwest Conf on Language Teaching, Central Asn of Russian Teachers of Am. **RESEARCH** Second language acquisition and Russian culture. **SELECTED PUBLICATIONS** Auth, Method Guide for Teaching English, German and Spanish at Special Foreign Language Schools, Kiev: Radyanska Shkola (90); auth, Method Guide for Initial Teaching of English to Junior Graders, Kiev (90); auth, "Music in English Classes in the First Grade," Pochatkova Shkola, No 2 (91); auth, "Humanizing Role of Puppets in Teaching Foreign Languages," Pochatkova Shkola, No 9-10 (92); auth, Speak and Read Essential Ukranian I, Heinle & Heinle Enterprises, Inc, Concord, Mass (93); rev of E. Daum and W. Schenk, A Dictionary of Russian Verbs, NY: Hippocrene (95), in Modern Lang J, Vol 80, No 1 (spring 96): 124; rev of Thomas Karras, A Concise English-Russian Phrase Book, Columbus, Ohio: Slavica (95), in Modern Lang J, Vol 80, No 4 (winter96): 557-558; rev of Emily Tall and Valentina Vlasikova, Let's Talk About Life: A Integrated Approach to Russian Conversation, NY: Wiley (96), in Modern Lang J, Vol 81, No 1 (spring 97): 140-141; rev of Lidija Iordanskaja and Slava Paperno, A Russian-English Collocational Dictionary of the Human Body, Columbus, Ohio: Slavica (96), in Modern Lang J, Vol 81, No 3 (fall 97): 434; rev of Derrek Offord, Using Russian: A Guide to Contemporary Usage, NY: Cambridge Univ Press (96), in Modern Lang J (forthcoming). **CONTACT ADDRESS** Dept English & Langs, East Central Univ, 1100 E 14th St, Ada, OK 74820-6915. **EMAIL** msukholu@mailclerk.ecok.edu

SULLIVAN, BRAD
PERSONAL Born 09/07/1961, Richmond, VA, m, 1994, 2 children **DISCIPLINE** ENGLISH LITERATURE, RHETORIC, COMPOSITION **EDUCATION** Univ Virginia, BA, 83; Ball State Univ, MA, 93; PhD, 97. **CAREER** Instr, Ball state Univ, 94-96; instr, Florida Gulf Coast Univ, 96-97; asst prof, 97-. **HONORS AND AWARDS** Carol Ann Kendrick Diss Schl; Univ Grad Fel, Ball state. **MEMBERSHIPS** MLA; NASSK; NCTE. **RESEARCH** Romantic ecology; romantic rhetoric; Wordsworth; literature and science. **SELECTED PUBLICATIONS** Auth, " 'Education By Poetry' in Robert Frost's Masques," Papers Lang Lit 22 (86): 312-21; auth, " 'Grown Sick With Hope Deferred' : Christina Rosetti's Darker Musings, " Papers Lang Lit 32 (96): 227-44; auth, Wordsworth and the Composition of Knowledge: Refiguring Relationships Among Minds, Worlds, and Words (Peter Lang, 00). **CONTACT ADDRESS** Dept Arts & Sciences, Florida Gulf Coast Univ, 10501 Florida Gulf Coast Univ Blvd, Fort Myers, FL 33965-6565. **EMAIL** bsulliva@fgcu.edu

SULLIVAN, C. W., III
PERSONAL Born 06/07/1944, Kingsport, TN, m, 1966, 2 children **DISCIPLINE** ENGLISH **EDUCATION** SUNY Albany, BA, 66; MA, 69; Univ Ore, DA, 75; PhD, 76. **CAREER** Instr, SUNY Albany, 68-71; grad asst to instr, Univ of Ore, 72-77; prof, E Car Univ, 77-. **HONORS AND AWARDS** Centennial Awd, Am Folklore Soc, 89; Phi Beta Delta; Member, Welsh Soc; Awd, E Car Univ, 97; Res Awd, Ambassador of Ireland, 98; Distinguished Prof for Teaching, Univ of NCar, 00; Phi Kappa Phi, 01; Distinguished Prof for Res, 01. **MEMBERSHIPS** Am Folklore Soc, Celtic Studies Assoc of N Am, Children's Folklore Section (AFS), Int Assoc for the Fantastic in the Arts, Irish Am Cult Inst, MLA, Welsh Acad, Sci Fiction Res Assoc. **RESEARCH** Medieval Welsh Celtic Mythology and Legend, 19th Century Fenian Diaries and Other Writings, Fantasy and Science Fiction Literature. **SELECTED PUBLICATIONS** Auth, Welsh Celtic Myth in Modern Fantasy, Greenwood, 89; auth, "Cultural Worldview: Marginalizing the Fantastic in the Seventheenth Century," Para*doxa: Studies in World Literary Genres 1.3, (95): 287-300; auth, The Mabinogi: A Book of Essays, Garland, 96; auth, "Inheritance and Lordship in Math," The Mabinogi: A Book of Essays, (Garland, 96): 347-366; auth, Fenian Diary: Denis B Cashman on Board the Hougoumont, 1867-1868, Wolfhound, 01. **CONTACT ADDRESS** Dept English, East Carolina Univ, Greenville, NC 27834. **EMAIL** sullivanc@mail.ecu.edu

SULLIVAN, CLAUDIA N.
PERSONAL Born 08/07/1950, Fort Worth, TX, s **DISCIPLINE** THEATER **EDUCATION** Butler Univ, BA; Trinity Univ, Dallas Th Cen, MFA; Univ CO, PhD. **CAREER** Schreiner Col, 77-. **MEMBERSHIPS** ATHE; Soc Movement Specialists. **RESEARCH** Theater movement; acting and actor training. **SELECTED PUBLICATIONS** Auth, The Actor Alone, McFarland Pub; auth, Summer Come, Summer Go, Nortex Press; auth, The Actor Moves, McFarland Pub. **CONTACT ADDRESS** Dept Liberal Arts, Schreiner Col, 2100 Memorial Blvd, Kerrville, TX 78028-5611. **EMAIL** claudia@hctc.net

SULLIVAN, D.
PERSONAL Born 11/05/1960, Urbana, IL, d **DISCIPLINE** ENGLISH **EDUCATION** Univ Chicago, BA, 84; Univ Calif at Irvine, PhD, 93. **CAREER** Prof, Cabrillo Community Col, 95-. **HONORS AND AWARDS** Grant to Study Major Film Proposal, 99-00; Second Place Prize, Quarry West Poetry, 00. **MEMBERSHIPS** MLA. **RESEARCH** Modern Literature (British, Irish, & American), James Joyce, Emily Dickinson, Film. **SELECTED PUBLICATIONS** Auth, "Listening to Joyce's Portrait," James Joyce J (97); auth, "Sueing Sue: Emily Dickinson Writing'Susan Gilbert,'" Emily Dickinson Rev (98); ed, Porter Gulch Literary Rev, 00. **CONTACT ADDRESS** Dept English & Film, Cabrillo Col, 6500 Soquel Dr, Aptos, CA 95003-3119. **EMAIL** dasulliv@cabrillo.cc.ca.us

SULLIVAN, DALE L.
PERSONAL Born 01/16/1951, Holyoke, CO, m, 1971, 4 children **DISCIPLINE** RHETORIC & COMMUNICATION **EDUCATION** Rensselaer Polytechnic Inst, PhD, 88. **CAREER** Teaching asst, Wichita State Univ, 77-79; asst prof, Kansas Tech Inst, 80-85; teaching asst, Rensselaer Polytechnic Inst, 85-87; dir of writing, Gordon Col, 87-88; asst prof of Rhetoric, Mich Tech Univ, 88-91; asst prof to assoc prof, Univ of Neb at Kearney, 91-94; assoc prof of English, Northern Ill Univ, 94-97; ASSOC PROF OF RHETORIC & TECH COMMUN, MICH TECH UNIV, 97-. **MEMBERSHIPS** Nat Commun Asn; Am Soc for the Hist of Rhetoric; Conf on Col Composition & Commun. **RESEARCH** Rhetoric of science; rhetoric of religion. **SELECTED PUBLICATIONS** Auth, Two-Year College Programs, Ed in Sci and Tech Commun: Acad Progs the Work, Soc for Tech Commun, 97; auth, Displaying Disciplinarity, Written Commun, 96; auth, Migrating Across Disciplinary Boundaries: The Case of David Raup's and John Sepkoski's Periodicity Paper, Social Epistemology, 95, Sci & Tech Commun, 97; auth, Galileo's Apparent Orthodoxy in The Letter to the Grand Duchess Christina, Rhetorica, 94; auth, Exclusionary Epideictic: NOVA's Narrative Excommunication of Fleischmann and Pons, Sci Tech & Human Values, 94; auth, A Closer Look at Education as Epideictic Rhetoric, Rhetoric Soc Quarterly, 93; auth, The Ethos of Epideictic Encounter, Philos and Rhetoric, 93; auth, The Epideictic Character of Rhetorical Criticism, Rhetoric Review, 93. **CONTACT ADDRESS** Humanities Dept, Michigan Tech Univ, Houghton, MI 49931. **EMAIL** dsulliva@mtu.edu

SULLIVAN, JACK R.
PERSONAL Born 11/26/1946, Greenville, SC, m, 1985, 2 children **DISCIPLINE** ENGLISH, LITERATURE **EDUCATION** Furman Univ, BA, 69; Columbia Univ, MA, 70; MPhil, 74; PhD, 76. **CAREER** Adjunct assoc prof, NYork Univ; prof, Rider Univ, 84-; Dir Am Studies, Rider Univ, 92-. **HONORS AND AWARDS** Woodrow Wilson Fellow, Columbia Univ Fellow, Rider Univ Fellow, creation of numerous interdisciplinary courses in literature, music, film, and popular culture. **RESEARCH** Music in relation to literature, American literature, film, Gothicism. **SELECTED PUBLICATIONS** Auth, Elegant Nightmares: The English Ghost Story from Le Fanu to Blackwood, Ohio Univ press (78); auth, Lost Souls: A Colllection of English Ghost Stories, Ohio Univ Press, 83; auth, The Penguin Encyclopedia of Horror and the Supernatural, Viking (86); auth, Words on Music, Ohio Univ Press (90); auth, New World Symphonies: How American Culture Changed European Music, Yale Univ Press (spring 99); about 175 essays and reviews in the NY Times Book Rev, Washington Post Book Rev, New Grove, The New Republic, Newsday, the Chicago Tribune, the Int Herald Tribune, Keynote, Sat Rev, The Am Record Guide, Harper's, USA Today, The Am Organist, Literature, Interpretation, Theory, Colliers Encycl, and in volumes for Schribners, Chelsea House Library of Literary Criticism, R. R. Bowker, Prentice-Hall, Reader's Digest Books. **CONTACT ADDRESS** Dept English and Am Studies, Rider Univ, 2083 Lawrenceville Rd, Trenton, NJ 08648-3001. **EMAIL** sullivanja@earthlink.net

SULLIVAN, JAMES
PERSONAL Born 08/05/1960, Seattle, WA, m, 1993, 2 children **DISCIPLINE** ENGLISH **EDUCATION** Loyola Univ Chicago, BA, 82; Univ Illinois at Urbana Champaign, AM, 85; Univ Illinois at Urbana-Champaign, PhD, 91. **CAREER** Instr, Bradley Univ, 91-95; Instr, Illinois Central C, 93-98; Instr, Lincoln C, 98-. **HONORS AND AWARDS** Dissertation Fel, Univ of Illinois, 90; Fac Who Made a Difference, Illinois Central College, 98. **MEMBERSHIPS** MLA; Midwest MLA; NCTE; AAUP. **RESEARCH** 20th Century Poetry; Literature and Visual Art; Amer Literature. **SELECTED PUBLICATIONS** Auth, "On the Walls and in the Streets: American Poetry Broadsides from the 1960s, U of ILP, 97. **CONTACT ADDRESS** Dept Humanities, Lincoln Col, 300 Keokuk St, Lincoln, IL 62656-1630.

SULLIVAN, JOHN P.
PERSONAL Born 07/13/1930, Liverpool, England **DISCIPLINE** CLASSICAL LANGUAGES AND LITERATURE **EDUCATION** Cambridge Univ, BA, 53, MA, 57; Ozford Univ, MA, 57. **CAREER** Teacher classics, Clare & Magdalene Cols, Cambridge Univ, 52-53; teacher philos & classics, Hertford & Lincoln Cols, Oxford Univ & Queens' Col, Cambridge Univ, 53-55; fel & tutor classics, Lincoln Col, Oxford Univ, 55-62, dean, 60-61; vis prof class lang, Univ Tex, Austin, 61-62, assoc prof, 62-63, prof class lang, 63-69, actg chmn dept classics, 62-63, chmn dept, 63-65, Univ Res Inst grants, 61, 62, Bromberg award, 62; provost, State Univ NY, Buffalo, 72-75,

fac profarts & lett, 69-78; Prof Classics, Univ Calif, Santa Barbara, 78-, Lectr, Oxford Univ, 56-60; co-ed, Arion, 61-69; Am Coun Learned Soc grant, 63; Nat Endowment Humanities sr fel, 67-68; ed, Arethusa, 71-; vis fel classics, Clare Hall, Cambridge Univ, 75-76; Martin lectr Neronian lit, Oberlin Col, 76; vis prof classics, Univ Hawaii, Manoa, 77; Gray lectr Martial, Cambridge Univ, 78; vis fel, Wolfson Col, Oxford Univ, 81; vis Hill prof, Univ Minn, 82. **MEMBERSHIPS** Am Philol Asn; Hellenic Soc. **RESEARCH** Latin literature; comparative literature. **SELECTED PUBLICATIONS CONTACT ADDRESS** Classics Dept, Univ of California, Santa Barbara, Santa Barbara, CA 93010.

SULLIVAN, MARY C., RSM
PERSONAL Born 06/15/1931, Rochester, NY **DISCIPLINE** LITERATURE, RELIGION **EDUCATION** Nazareth Col Rochester, BA, 54; Univ Notre Dame, MA, 61, PhD(English), 64; Univ London, MTh, 88. **CAREER** Asst prof English, Catherine McAuley Col, 63-65, pres, 65-68; asst prof, Marymount Col, NY, 67-69; assoc prof lang & lit, 69-81, Prof Lang & Lit, Rochester Inst Technol, 81-, dean col liberal arts, 77-87, chair, acad senate, 96-99; Consult & evaluator, Comn Higher Educ, Mid States Asn, 68-90. **MEMBERSHIPS** MLA; Mercy Higher Ed Colloquium; Mercy Asn in Scripture and Theol. **RESEARCH** Nineteenth and 20th century English and American literature; religion and literature; biography. **SELECTED PUBLICATIONS** Auth, The function of setting in Howells' The Landlord at Lion's Head, Am Lit, 63; Moby Dick, CXXIX: The cabin, Nineteenth Century Fiction, 65; Caroline Gordon: A Reference Guide, G K Hall, 77; Conrad's Paralipsis in the narration of Lord Jim, Conradiana, 78; Catherine McAuley and the Tradition of Mercy, Univ Notre Dame Press, 95; auth, The Friendship of Florence Nightingale and Mary Clare Moore, Univ Pa Press, 99. **CONTACT ADDRESS** Col of Lib Arts, Rochester Inst of Tech, 1 Lomb Memorial Dr, Rochester, NY 14623-5603. **EMAIL** mxsgsl@atsrit.edu

SULLIVAN, PAULA
PERSONAL Born 11/16/1942, Brighton, MA, m, 1966, 3 children **DISCIPLINE** ENGLISH COMPOSITION AND LITERATURE **EDUCATION** Univ St Thomas, Houston, Tex, BA; Univ Tulsa, MA. **CAREER** Asst prof of English, Tulsa Community Col, 84-. **MEMBERSHIPS** Nat Coun of Teachers of English **RESEARCH** British literature since 1800, autobiography, creative nonfiction. **SELECTED PUBLICATIONS** Auth, The Mystery of Mystory, Paulist Press, Mahwah, NJ, 91. **CONTACT ADDRESS** Commun Div, Tulsa Comm Col, 10300 E 81st St, Tulsa, OK 74133-4500.

SULLIVAN, ROSEMARY
PERSONAL Born Montreal, PQ, Canada **DISCIPLINE** ENGLISH **EDUCATION** McGill Univ, BA, 68; Univ Conn, MA, 69; Univ Sussex, PhD, 72. **CAREER** Asst-associe, Univ Dijon, 72; asst associe, Univ Bordeaux, 73; asst prof, Univ Victoria, 74-77; asst prof, 77-80, assoc prof, 80-90, Prof, Univ Toronto, 90-. **HONORS AND AWARDS** Gerald Lampert Prize Poetry, League Can Poets, 86; Silver Medal Nat Mag Awds, 86; Guggenheim Fel, 92; Gov Gen Awd Non-Fiction, 95; Can Authors Awd Non-Fiction, 95; Medal Biog, Univ BC, 95. **MEMBERSHIPS** Writers' Union Can; Can PEN. **RESEARCH** Canadian biography; poetry. **SELECTED PUBLICATIONS** Auth, The Garden Master: Style and Identity in the Poetry of Theodore Roethke, 75; auth, The Space A Name Makes, 86; ed, More Stories by Candian Women, 87; ed, Poetry by Canadian Women, 89; auth, Blue Panic, 91; auth, By Heart: Elizabeth Smart/A Life, 91; auth, Shadow Maker: The Life of Gwendolyn MacEwen, 95; auth, The Red Shoes: Margaret Atwood Starting Out, 98; ed, The Oxford Book of Stories by Canadian Women, 99; auth, The Bone Ladder: New and Selected Poems, 00. **CONTACT ADDRESS** Dept of English, Univ of Toronto, Toronto, ON, Canada M5S 1A1. **EMAIL** rsulliva@credit.erin.utoronto.ca

SULLIVAN, SALLY A.
DISCIPLINE ENGLISH ROMANTICISM, NORTH CAROLINA LITERATURE, CREATIVE WRITING **EDUCATION** Univ NC, Greensboro, BA, MA, PhD. **CAREER** Assoc prof, Univ NC, Wilmington. **RESEARCH** English romanticism; North Carolina literature. **SELECTED PUBLICATIONS** Author of three books, the most recent two a composition text and a book of essays by fiction writers and poets on their writing. **CONTACT ADDRESS** Univ of No Carolina, Wilmington, Morton Hall, Wilmington, NC 28403-3297. **EMAIL** sullivans@uncwil.edu

SULLIVAN, SHEILA J.
PERSONAL Born 09/21/1952, Wells, MN, m, 1977, 2 children **DISCIPLINE** COMMUNICATION **EDUCATION** SUNY at Geneseo, BA (Comparative lit & English, magna cum laude), 75; SUNY at Buffalo, MA (Communication), 85, PhD (Commun), 90. **CAREER** Instr, Army Corps of Engineers, Buffalo, NY, June 86; instr, Fulbright Three-week Pre-Academic Orientation Prog, SUNY at Buffalo, summer 86; instr, Millard Fillmore Col at SUNY at Buffalo, 85-87, teaching asst, Dept of Commun, 83-87, co-dir, Com 101-Interpersonal Communication, 84-87; vis lect, Div of Humanities & Social Sciences, Penn State/Behrend Col, 88-89; asst prof of Commun, Dept of Commun, MS State Univ, 89-90; lect, Dept of Commun, SUNY at Buffalo, 93; asst prof of Commun, Communication Studies, Canisius Col, 93-94; asst prof of Commun, Dept of Commun, Miss State Univ, 96-00; asst prof, Middle Tenn State Univ, 00-. **HONORS AND AWARDS** Special Merit Assistantships at SUNY at Buffalo, 84-85, 85-86, & 86-87; Honorable Mention: Excellence in Teaching Awd, SUNY at Buffalo, 86, 87. **RESEARCH** Communication theory; family relationships. **SELECTED PUBLICATIONS** Coauth, Conversation Data Aquisition and Analysis in C Tardy, ed, Methods and Instruments of Communication Research: A Handbook for the Study of Human Interaction, Ablex, 87; auth, Why Do Women Do Such Womenly Things?: The Genre and Socio-Historical Analogs of Basket Parties, in Women's Studies in Communication, 91; Why Do Women Do Such Womenly Things?: The Genre and Socio-Historical Analogs of Home Parties, in S J Sigman, ed, Introduction to Communication: Behavior, Codes and Social Action, Ginn Press, 92; co-auth with W Leeds-Hurwitz and S J Sigman, Social Communication Theory: Communication Structures and Performed Innovations: A Revision of Scheflen's Notion of Programs, in S J Sigman, ed, The Consequentiality of Communication, A Volume in LEAS Communication Series, 95. **CONTACT ADDRESS** Dept of Speech and Theatre, Middle Tennessee State Univ, 1301 E Main St, Box 43, Murfreesboro, TN 37123. **EMAIL** ssulliva@mtsu.edu

SULLIVAN, SHERRY A.
DISCIPLINE ENGLISH **EDUCATION** Univ Oregon, Ba, 68; Saskatchewan, MA, 71; Univ Toronto, PhD, 79. **CAREER** ASST PROF, ENG, UNIV ALA, BIRMINGHAM **MEMBERSHIPS** Am Antiquarian Soc **SELECTED PUBLICATIONS** Auth, "The Literary Debate over the Indians in the 19th Century," Am Indian Cult and Res Jour, 85; auth, "Indians in American Fiction: An Ethnohistorical Perspective, 1820-50," Clio, 86; auth, "The Indianization of Heroes and Heroines in 19th-Century American Fiction," JMMLA, 87. **CONTACT ADDRESS** 1459 Milner Crescent, Birmingham, AL 35205.

SULLIVAN, WALTER L.
PERSONAL Born 01/04/1924, Nashville, TN, m, 1947, 3 children **DISCIPLINE** ENGLISH **EDUCATION** Vanderbilt Univ, BA, 47; State Univ Iowa, MFA, 49. **CAREER** From instr to assoc prof, 49-63, PROF ENGLISH, VANDERBILT UNIV, 63-, Ford Found fel, 51-52; Sewanee Rev fel, 55; lectr, WDCN-TV, Nashville, Tenn, 72-73. **HONORS AND AWARDS** O Henry Awd, 80; founding member, Fellowship of Southern Writers, 87; elected alumni member, Phi Beta Kappa, 90; Literary achievement award from Southern Heritage Soc, 96; Vice Chancellor, Fel of Southern Writers, 97; littd, episcopal theol sem, ky, 73. **MEMBERSHIPS** SAtlantic Mod Lang Asn; MLA. **RESEARCH** Fiction writing; contemporary British and American theological themes in modern literature. **SELECTED PUBLICATIONS** Auth, Sojourn of a Stranger, 57 & The Long, Long Love, 59, Henry Holt; Death by Melancoly, La State Univ, 72; A Requiem for the Renascence, Univ Ga, 76; ed, A Band of Prophets, La State Univ, 82; Writing from the Inside, W W Norton, 83; In Praise of Blood Sports, LSU Press, 90; A Time to Dance, LSU Press, 95; The War the Women Lived, J.S. Sanders & Co, 96. **CONTACT ADDRESS** Dept of English, Vanderbilt Univ, 2201 W End Ave, Nashville, TN 37240-0001. **EMAIL** sullivwl@ctrvax.vanderbilt.edu

SULLIVAN, ZOHREH TAWAKULI
PERSONAL Born 12/18/1941, Tehran, Iran, d, 2 children **DISCIPLINE** ENGLISH LITERATURE **EDUCATION** Western Col, BA, 62; Univ IL, Urbana, MA & PhD, 71. **CAREER** Instr Eng lit, Webster Col, 69-70; prof, Damavand Col, Teheran, Iran, 70-72; from assoc prof to prof eng lit, Univ IL, Urbana-Champaign, 78-. **HONORS AND AWARDS** Sch Hum Tchg Excellence Awd, 78; Prog Study of Cult Values & Ethics Fel, 92-93; All Campus Luckman Awd in Undergraduate Tchg, 94; Hum Awd in Undergrad Tchg, 94. **MEMBERSHIPS** MLA. **RESEARCH** Mod novel; colonial and postcolonial lit; the middle-east ethnography. **SELECTED PUBLICATIONS** Auth, Approaches to Teaching Achebe's Thnis Fall Apart, MLA, 91; auth, Narratives of Empire: the Fictions of Rudyard Kipling, Cambridge Univ Press, 93; auth, Servants and Gender in Talat Abbasi's Fiction, Commonwealth and American Women's Discourse, Sterling, 96; Eluding the Feminist, Overthrowing the Modern: Transformations in 20th Century Iran, Remaking Women: Feminism and Modernity in the Middle-East, Princeton Univ Press, 98; auth, Norton Critical Editon of 'Kim,' forthcoming; auth, Exiled Memories: Stories of Iranian Diaspora, Temple Univ Pr, forthcoming; numerous articles in Mod Fict Studies, Jour Narrative Techniques, Col English, Ariz Quart, Centennial Rev. **CONTACT ADDRESS** Dept of Eng, Univ of Illinois, Urbana-Champaign, 608 S Wright St, Urbana, IL 61801-3613. **EMAIL** zsulliva@uiuc.edu

SULLOWAY, ALISON G.
PERSONAL Born 07/31/1917, New York, NY, w, 3 children **DISCIPLINE** ENGLISH **EDUCATION** Columbia Univ, MA, 58, PhD(English lit), 68. **CAREER** Lectr English, Columbia Univ, 58-59 & Barnard Col, Columbia Univ, 61-62; instr, Beloit Col, 65-68; asst prof, Cedar Crest Col, 68-75, assoc prof, 72-75; ASSOC PROF ENGLISH, VA POLYTECH INST & STATE UNIV, 75-, sr fel, Nat Endowment for Humanites, 70-80. **HONORS AND AWARDS** Ansley Publ Awd, Columbia Univ, 68. **MEMBERSHIPS** MLA; Int Hopkins Asn. **RESEARCH** Hopkins' poetry; Jane Austen's novels; Victorian literature. **SELECTED PUBLICATIONS** Auth, Gerald Manley Hopkins and the Victorian Temper, Columbia Univ, 72 & Routledge & Kegan Paul, 72; St Ignatius Loyola and the Victorian Temper: Hopkins Windhover as diabolic gravity, Hopkins Quart, 74; Intimations of myth and tragedy in The Wreck of the Deutschland, Readings of The Wreck, Loyola Univ, 76; Emma Woodhouse and A Vindication of The Rights of Woman, Wordsworth Circle, 76; Hopkinsian biography and the grounds of our being: A study of representative biographical materials, priorities and techniques, Hopkins Quart, 77; Jane Austen--Real And Imaginary Worlds, Wordsworth Circle, Vol 25, 94; Jane Austen Sense And Sensibility, Wordsworth Circle, Vol 25, 94; Jane Austen Novels--The Art Of Clarity, Wordsworth Circle, Vol 25, 94. **CONTACT ADDRESS** Dept of English, Virginia Polytech Inst and State Univ, Blacksburg, VA 24061.

SULTAN, STANLEY
PERSONAL Born 07/17/1928, Brooklyn, NY, m, 1966, 2 children **DISCIPLINE** ENGLISH **EDUCATION** Yale Univ, PhD, 55. **CAREER** Instr, Smith Col, 55-59; asst prof to prof, Clark Univ, 59-. **MEMBERSHIPS** AAUP; PEN; Malone Soc; James Joyce Soc. **RESEARCH** Literary history, literary theory, modernist English literature. **SELECTED PUBLICATIONS** Auth, The Argument of Ulysses, Ohio State Univ, (Columbus), 65; auth, Eliot, Joyce and Company, Oxford Univ Pr, (NY), 87; auth, "The Strand (Bloom)", Critical Essays on James Joyce's Ulysses, ed B. Benstock G.K. Hall (Boston, 89); auth, "Was Modernism Reactionary?", J of Mod Lit, (94); auth, "Rabbi: A Tale of the Waning Year", Shepardic-American Voices: Two Hundred Years of a Literary Legacy, ed Diane Matza, Univ Pr of New England, (Hanover), 96; auth, "The Country Mouse: Con-Text, Para-Text, Contra-Text", In Worcester, Massachusetts: Essays from the 1997 Elizabeth Bishop Conf, ed Laura Menides and Angela Dorenkamp, Peter Lang, (NY), 99; auth, "Lawrence of the Anti-Autobiographer", J of Mod Lit, (00); auth, "Joycesday", Joyce Studies Annual 2000, ed Thomas Staley, Univ of Tex Pr, (Austin), (forthcoming); auth, Joyce's Becoming, Univ of Fla Pr, (Gainesville), (forthcoming). **CONTACT ADDRESS** Dept English, Clark Univ, 950 Main St, Worcester, MA 01610-1400.

SUMMERS, CLAUDE JOSEPH
PERSONAL Born 12/06/1944, Galvez, LA, s **DISCIPLINE** ENGLISH LITERATURE **EDUCATION** La State Univ, BA, 66; Univ Chicago, MA, 67, PhD, 70. **CAREER** From Asst Prof to Prof Eng, 70-89, William E. Stirton Professor in the Hum, Univ MI-Dearborn 89; Assoc ed, Seventeenth Century News, 73. **HONORS AND AWARDS** Crompton-Noll Awd, 82; Fac Res Awd, 86; Outstanding Acad Bk Awd for "Gay Fictions..", Choice, 91-92; Donne Soc Publ Awd, 92; Distinguished Tchg Awd, 95; Lambda Literary Awd, 96; Distinguished Fac Awd, MI Asn Governing Bds, 97. **MEMBERSHIPS** MLA; Milton Soc Am; Renaissance Soc Am; John Donne Soc. **RESEARCH** Seventeenth century poetry; Renaissance drama; mod lit; gay studies. **SELECTED PUBLICATIONS** Auth, Gay Fictions / Wilde to Stonewall: Studies in a Male Homosexual Literary Tradition, Continuum, 90; E.M. Foster: A Guide to Research, Garland, 91; co-ed, On the Celebrated and Neglected Poems of Andrew Marvell, Univ Mo Press, 92; ed, Homosexuality in Renaissance and Enlightenment England: Literary Representations in Historical Context, special double issue of J Homosexuality, Haworth Press, 92; co-ed, Renaissance Discourses of Desire, Univ Mo Press, 93; The Wit of Seventeenth-Century Poetry, Univ Mo Press, 95; Selected Poems of Ben Jonson, Pegasus Books, Medieval and Renaissance Texts and Studies, 95; ed, The Gay and Lesbian Literary Heritage: A Companion to the Writers and Their Works from Antiquity to the Present, Henry Holt, 95; co-ed, Representing Women in Renaissance England, Univ MO Press, 97; author and editor of numerous other publ. **CONTACT ADDRESS** Dept of Hum, Univ of Michigan, Dearborn, 4901 Evergreen Rd, Dearborn, MI 48128-1491. **EMAIL** csummers@umich.edu

SUNDSTROM, ROY ALFRED
PERSONAL Born 02/24/1934, Mineola, NY, m, 1963, 2 children **DISCIPLINE** ENGLISH & EARLY MODERN EUROPEAN HISTORY **EDUCATION** Univ Mass, Amherst, AB, 56; Western Mich Univ, MA, 66; Kent State Univ, PhD(Hist), 72. **CAREER** Asst prof, 69-73, assoc prof, 73-79, prof Hist, Humboldt State Univ, 79-, Am Philos Soc res grant, 74 & 75. **MEMBERSHIPS** AHA; Conf Brit Historians; Huguenot Soc London. **RESEARCH** Late Stuart England; biography of Sidney Godolphin, 1645-1712. **SELECTED PUBLICATIONS** Auth, Some original sources relating to Huguenot refugees in England, 1680-1727, Brit Studies Monitor, Summer 76; The French Huguenots and the Civil List, 1696-1727: A study of alien assimilation in England, Albion, Fall 76; Sidney Godolphin: Servant of the State, Univ of Delaware, Press, 92. **CONTACT ADDRESS** Dept of History, Humboldt State Univ, 1 Harps St, Arcata, CA 95521-8299.

SUNUNU, ANDREA
PERSONAL Born 06/20/1947, New York, NY, s **DISCIPLINE** ENGLISH LITERATURE **EDUCATION** Mount Hol-

yoke Col, AB, 69; Brown Univ, AM, 71; PhD, 74. **CAREER** TA, Brown Univ, 72-73; instr to assoc prof, Mount Holyoke Col, 73-83; assoc prof, Swarthmore Col, 83-84; assoc prof, Univ of NH, 84-85; assoc prof, Oberlin Col, 85-86; assoc prof, Univ of NH, 86-87; assoc prof, Swarthmore Col, 87-89; assoc prof, Univ of NH, 89-90; assoc prof to prof, DePauw Univ, 90-. **HONORS AND AWARDS** Exemplary Teaching Awd, 93; DePauw Distinguished Professorship, 99-00. **MEMBERSHIPS** MLA; SAA. **RESEARCH** Katherine Philips, 17th century poetry. **SELECTED PUBLICATIONS** Coauth, "New Manuscript Texts of Katherine Philips, The Matchless Orinda", English Manuscript Studies 4 (93): 174-219; coauth, "Further Manuscript Texts of Katherine Philips, The Matchless Orinda", EMS 5 (95): 127-169. **CONTACT ADDRESS** Dept English, DePauw Univ, Greencastle, IN 46135-0037. **EMAIL** asununu@depauw.edu

SUNYOGER, MARY ANN
PERSONAL m **DISCIPLINE** ENGLISH COMPOSITION **EDUCATION** Franciscan Univ Steubenville, BA; Kent State Univ, MA; PhD. **CAREER** Teach & Dept Chair, Catholic Cent High School, 70-80; instr, Jefferson Comm Col, 80-88; prof, Univ Steubenville, 88-. **MEMBERSHIPS** MLA, NCJE, Kappa Delta Phi, Sigma Lau Delta, Phi Delta Kappa. **RESEARCH** Influence of computers on writing. **CONTACT ADDRESS** Dept English, Franciscan Univ of Steubenville, 1235 University Blvd, Steubenville, OH 43952-1763. **EMAIL** drsuny@1st.net

SUPER, ROBERT HENRY
PERSONAL Born 06/13/1914, Wilkes-Barre, PA, m, 1953, 2 children **DISCIPLINE** ENGLISH LITERATURE **EDUCATION** Princeton Univ, AB, 35, PhD, 41; Oxford Univ, BLitt, 37. **CAREER** Instr English, Princeton Univ, 38-42; asst prof, Mich State Norm Col, 42-47; lectr, 47, from asst prof to assoc prof, 47-60, PROF ENGLISH, UNIV MICH, ANN ARBOR, 60-, Fulbright res grant, UK, 49-50; Am Coun Learned Socs fel, 59-60; Guggenheim fels, 62-63 & 70-71; vis prof, Rice Univ, 65-66; Nat Endowment for Humanities fel, 78-79. **MEMBERSHIPS** MLA **RESEARCH** English literature of the 19th century; Matthew Arnold; Anthony Trollope. **SELECTED PUBLICATIONS** Auth, Publication of Landor's Works, Bibliog Soc, London, 54; Walter Savage Landor: A Biography, NY Univ, 54; ed, Matthew Arnold's Complete Prose Works, 11 vols, 60-77, auth, The Time-Spirit of Matthew Arnold, 70, Trollope in the Post Office, 81 & ed, Anthony Trollope's Marion Fay, 82, Univ Mich; Truth And Fiction In Trollope Autobiography, Nineteenth-Century Lit, Vol 48, 93. **CONTACT ADDRESS** 1221 Baldwin Ave, Ann Arbor, MI 48104.

SURACE, PETER C.
DISCIPLINE ENGLISH **EDUCATION** Cuyahoga Cmty Col, AA, 69; Kent State Univ, BA, 70; MA, 72; Case Western Reserve Univ, PhD, 96. **CAREER** Prof, Cuyahoga Cmty Col. **HONORS AND AWARDS** Teaching Fel, Kent State Univ, Case Western Reserve Univ. **MEMBERSHIPS** AAUP, USCF. **RESEARCH** Literature and Culture of the 1950s. **SELECTED PUBLICATIONS** Auth, Round Trip Journeys,96. **CONTACT ADDRESS** Dept of Humanities & Fine Art, Cuyahoga Comm Col, Western, 11000 West Pleasant Valley Rd, Cleveland, OH 44130-5114. **EMAIL** peter.surace@tri-c.cc.oh.us

SURRIDGE, LISA A.
DISCIPLINE ENGLISH LITERATURE **EDUCATION** Queen's Univ, BA, 86; Univ Toronto, MA, 87, PhD, 92. **CAREER** Asst prof, Univ of Victoria **RESEARCH** Victorian fiction; sensation fiction; domestic violence in 19th century literature; 19th century women novelists. **SELECTED PUBLICATIONS** Auth, Dogs' /Bodies, Women's Bodies: Wives as Pets in Mid-Nineteenth-Century Narratives of Domestic Violence, Victorian Rev 20, 94; Representing the Latent Vashti: Theatricality in Charlotte Bronte's Villette, Victorian Newsletter 87, 95; Madame de Stael Meets Mrs Ellis: Geraldine Jewsbury's The Half Sisters, Carlyle Stud Annual 15, 95; Unspeakable Histories: Hester Dethridge and the Narration of Domestic Violence in Man and Wife, Victorian Rev 22, 96; Domestic Violence, Female Self-Mutilation, and the Healing of the Male in Dombey and Son, Victorians Inst Jour 25, 97; auth, "John rokesmith's Secret: Detection, Sensation, and the Policing of the Feminine in Our Mutual Firend, (Dickens Studies Annual 26, 98), 265-84; auth, "Animals and Violence in Wutheing Heights," Bonte Society Transactions 24:2, (99), 161-73. **CONTACT ADDRESS** Dept of English, Univ of Victoria, PO Box 3070, Victoria, BC, Canada V8W 3W1. **EMAIL** lsurridg@uvic.ca

SUSSMAN, HERBERT
PERSONAL Born 01/20/1937, New York, NY, m, 1960, 2 children **DISCIPLINE** ENGLISH **EDUCATION** Princeton Univ, BA, 58; Harvard Univ, MA, 59, PhD, 63. **CAREER** Asst prof English, Univ Berkeley, 63-71; assoc prof, 71-80, Prof English, Norhteastern Univ, 80-. **RESEARCH** Victorian literature. **SELECTED PUBLICATIONS** Auth, Victorians and the Machine, Harvard Univ, 68; Fact into Figure, Ohio State, 81. **CONTACT ADDRESS** Dept of English, Northeastern Univ, 360 Huntington Ave, Boston, MA 02115-5000.

SUSSMAN, LEWIS ARTHUR
PERSONAL Born 06/26/1941, New York, NY, m, 1965 **DISCIPLINE** CLASSICS **EDUCATION** Princeton Univ, AB, 64; Univ NC, Chapel Hill, PhD(classics), 69. **CAREER** Asst prof classics, Univ CA, Irvine, 69-76, chm dept, 72-75; assoc prof classics, 76-94, prof, Univ FL, 94-,chm dept, 93-00; Univ FL Humanities Coun grant, 77; Nat Endowment for Humanities summer sem, Rome, 79. **MEMBERSHIPS** Am Philol Asn; Class Asn Mid West & South (secy-treas, 77-78). **RESEARCH** Ancient rhetoric; Ovid; Roman literature of the Augustan Age. **SELECTED PUBLICATIONS** Auth, Early imperial declamation: A Translation of the Elder Seneca's Prefaces, Speech Monogr, 6/70; The Artistic Unity of the Elder Seneca's First Preface & Controversiae as a Whole, Am J Philol, 4/71; The Elder Seneca's Discussion of the Decline of Roman Eloquence, CA Studies Class Antiq, 72; The Elder Seneca, E J Brill, 78; Latin and Basic Skills, Class J, 78; Arellius Fuscus and the Unity of Seneca's Suasoriae, Rheinisches Mus, 78; The Major Declamations Ascribed to Quintilian, Peter Lang, 87; The Declamations of Calpurnius Flaccus, E J Brill, 94. **CONTACT ADDRESS** Dept Classics, Univ of Florida, 3c Daver Hall, Gainesville, FL 32611-7435. **EMAIL** sussman@ufl.edu

SUTHERLAND, ELIZABETH H.
PERSONAL Born 07/05/1963, Princeton, NJ, m, 2000 **DISCIPLINE** CLASSICS **EDUCATION** Univ of Calif Berk, PhD, 94. **CAREER** Univ Calif Santa Cruz, lectr, 95; Univ Calif Irvine, lectr, 95-96; Univ Tenn Knoxville, asst prof, 96-. **MEMBERSHIPS** APA; CAMWS; TFLTA; TCA. **RESEARCH** Augustan poetry; feminist theory **SELECTED PUBLICATIONS** Auth, Visions and Desire in Horace's Carm 2.5, Helios, 97; auth, Audience Manipulation and Emotional Experience in Horace's Pyrrha Ode, AJP, 95; auth, Literary Women in Horace's Odes 2.11 and 2.12, forthcoming in Festschrift for WS Anderson. **CONTACT ADDRESS** Dept of Classics, Univ of Tennessee, Knoxville, 1101 McClung Tower, Knoxville, TN 37996. **EMAIL** ehsuther@utk.edu

SUTHERLAND, WILLIAM OWEN SHEPPARD
PERSONAL Born 01/19/1921, Wilmington, NC, m, 1947, 4 children **DISCIPLINE** ENGLISH LITERATURE **EDUCATION** Univ NC, AB, 42, AM, 47, PhD, 50. **CAREER** Part-time instr English, Univ NC, 46-50, instr, 50-51; instr, Northwestern Univ, 51-54; from asst prof to assoc prof, 54-65; prof English, Univ Tex, Austin, 65-, assoc Dean of the Graduate Sch, 70-73; dir Prog in Humanities, 80-83; chair of the Dept of English, 83-89; R.A. Law and Thos. L.Law Centennial Prof of Humanities, 86-; consultant to Office of Education, 62-72; mem then chair Col Bd AP Comt, 65-68; consultant to Educational Testing Serv; consultant and panel mem NEH; served on exec comt and other committees of NCTE, CCCC, SCMLA; prof of english, emer, 98; Robt. A. Law and Thos. L. Law Centennial Prof of humanities, emer, 98. **HONORS AND AWARDS** Scarborough Excellence in Teaching Awd, 59; President's Associates Awd for Excellence in Teaching, 82; Liberal Arts Pro Bene Meritis Awd, 96. **MEMBERSHIPS** MLA; SCent Mod Lang Asn; NCTE; Conf Col Compos & Commun. **RESEARCH** Elizabethan drama; 18th century English literature, especially periodicals and drama; 18th century novel; website history of ghost town Buena Vista, MN, wwwvms.utexas.edu/~wos/index.html. **SELECTED PUBLICATIONS** Auth, Popular imagery in The Medal, Univ Tex Studies English, 56; Essay forms in Aaron Hill's Prompter, In: Studies in the Early English Periodical, Univ NC, 57; Art of the Satirist, Univ Tex, 65. **CONTACT ADDRESS** Dept of English, Univ of Texas, Austin, Univ of Texas, Austin, TX 78712-1026. **EMAIL** woss@utxvms.cc.utexas.edu

SUTTON, DANA FERRIN
DISCIPLINE CLASSICS **EDUCATION** The New Sch for Soc Res, BA, 65; The Univ Wis, MA, 66, PhD, 70; postdoc, sr mem, Darwin Col, The Univ Cambridge, Eng, 72-74; postdoc res fel, The Univ Auckland, New Zealand, 74-75. **CAREER** Instr, Univ Minn, 67-68; tchg asst, Univ Wis, 68-69; lectr, Herbert Lehman Col, City Univ NY, 69-72; asst prof, Univ Ill, 75-79; asst prof, 79-81; assoc prof, 81-88; Prof, Univ Calif, Irvine, 88-. **HONORS AND AWARDS** Fel, John Simon Guggenheim Memorial Found, 75-76; Adele Mellen prize, Edwin Mellen Press, 96; grad prog dir, 80-83, 85-86, 94-96; ch, sch hum grants and travel comm, 84-85; act ch, dept classics, 85; dept ch, 86-94; sr admin off, s calif classics res sharing consortium, 90-92; ch, acad sen, 94. **MEMBERSHIPS** Am Philological Assn; Am Neo-Latin Assn; Calif Renaissance Soc; Calif Classics Assn. **RESEARCH** Greek and Latin poetry and drama; Anglo-Latin literature. **SELECTED PUBLICATIONS** Auth, Self and Society in ARitsophanes, Univ Press Am, 80; auth, The Dramaturgy of the Octavia, in Beitrage zur klassischen Philologie, Verlag Anton Hain, Konigstein/Taunus, 83; auth, The Lost Sophocles, Univ Press Am, 84; auth, The Satyr Play, in Cambridge History of Classical Literature I, 85; auth, Seneca on the Stage, in Mnemosyne, E. J. Brill, 86; auth, The Greek Dithyrambographers, Georg Olms Verlag, 89; auth, Thomas Legge: The Complete Plays, Peter Lang Verlag, 93; auth, Ancient Comedy: The Conflict of the Generations, in Twaynes' Literary Genres and Themes Series, Macmillan, 93; auth, The Catharsis of Comedy, in Greek Studies: Interdisciplinary Approaches, Rowman and Littlefield, 94; auth, William Gager: The Complete Works, Garland Press, 94; auth, Oxford Poetry by Richard Eedes and George Peele, Garland Press, 95; auth, The Complete Works of Thomas Watson (1556-1592), Edwin Mellen Press, 96; auth, The Complete Latin Poetry of William Savage Landor, Edwin Mellen Press, forthcoming. **CONTACT ADDRESS** Dept of Classics, Univ of California, Irvine, 120 HOB II, Irvine, CA 92697. **EMAIL** danas64562@aol.com

SUTTON, JANE
PERSONAL Born 07/10/1952, Bessemer, AL, m, 1994 **DISCIPLINE** COMMUNICATION, RHETORIC **EDUCATION** Western State Col, Gunnison, Co, BA, 74, MA, 80; Univ Colo, Boulder, PhD, 84. **CAREER** Assoc prof, Pa State Univ, 92-, member of Grad Fac, 92-. **HONORS AND AWARDS** "Best Article Awd," Second Place, Southern Commun J, Vols 56-58,"The Taming of Polos/Polis: Rhetoric As an Achievement Without Woman." **MEMBERSHIPS** Int Soc for the Hist of Rhetoric, Am Soc for the Hist of Rhetoric, Can Soc for the Hist of Rhetoric, Rhetoric Soc of Am, Nat Commun Asn, Eastern Commun Asn, Speech Commun Asn of Pa. **RESEARCH** Tropology and rhetoric, rhetoric of antiquity, history of rhetoric, feminism(s) and rhetoric(s). **SELECTED PUBLICATIONS** Auth, "The Death of Rhetoric and its Rebirth in Philosophy," Rhetorica, 4 (86): 203-26; auth, "Antiphon's 'On the Chorus Boy': The Practice of Practical Truth," PreText: A J of Rhetorical Theory, 10 (89): 100-106; auth, "Rereading Sophistical Arguments: A Political Intervention," Argumentation, 5 (91): 141-157; auth, "The Marginalization of Sophistical Rhetoric and the Loss of History," in Rethinking the History of Rhetoric: Multidisciplinary Essays on the Rhetorical Tradition," Takis Poulakos, ed, Boulder, Co: Westview Press (93): 75-90; auth, "Structuring the Narrative for the Canon of Rhetoric: The Principles of Traditional Rhetorical Historiography (an essay) with the Dead's Differend (a collage)," in Writing Histories of Rhetoric, Victor Vitanza, ed, Carbondale, Ill: Southern Ill Univ Press (94): 156-179; auth, "Rhetoric and the Peacock: an Antiphonic Spectacle of Preconceptual Linguistic Equipment for an Art of Rhetoric," The Can J of Rhetorical Studies/La Revue Canadienne D'Etudes Rhetoriques, 4 (94): 123-42; auth, "The Taming of the Polos/Polis: Rhetoric As an Achievement Without Woman," in Contemporary Rhetorical Theory: A Reader, John Louis Lucaites, Celeste Michelle Condit, and Sally Caudill, eds, New York: Guilford Press (99): 101-126. **CONTACT ADDRESS** Dept of Speech Commun, Pennsylvania State Univ, York, 1031 Edgecomb Ave, York, PA 17404. **EMAIL** jss@psu.edu

SUTTON, MAX K.
PERSONAL Born 06/03/1937, Huntsville, AK, m, 1960, 3 children **DISCIPLINE** ENGLISH **EDUCATION** Univ of Ark, BA, 59; Duke Univ, MA, 60; PhD, 64. **CAREER** Univ of Kans, 64-. **RESEARCH** Victorian Literature, Framed Narratives. **SELECTED PUBLICATIONS** Auth, W.S. Gilbert, Twayne, 75; auth, R.D. Blackmore, Twayne, 79; auth, The Drama of Storytelling in T.E. Brown's Manx Yars, Delaware, 91; auth, Fo'c'sle Yarns: An Uncensored Edition of Four Manx Narratives in Verse, Univ Pr of Am, 98. **CONTACT ADDRESS** Dept English, Univ of Kansas, Lawrence, Lawrence, KS 66045-0001. **EMAIL** msutton@eagle.cc.ukans.edu

SUTTON, SHARYN
DISCIPLINE PUBLIC RELATIONS **EDUCATION** Univ Toledo, BS; Univ Md, MS, PhD. **CAREER** Asst prof, Am Univ. **HONORS AND AWARDS** Golden Screen Awd, Blue Pencil Awd, Communication Excellence for Black Audiences award; dir, nutrition, mkt & educ, u.s. dept agriculture; branch chief, infor proj , natl inst health. **SELECTED PUBLICATIONS** Auth, Strategic Questions forConsumer Based Health Communications. **CONTACT ADDRESS** American Univ, 4400 Massachusetts Ave, Washington, DC 20016.

SUZUKI, MIHOKO
PERSONAL Born 12/16/1953, Kobe, Japan, m, 1990 **DISCIPLINE** ENGLISH **EDUCATION** Cornell Univ, AB, 75; Yale Univ, M Phil, 78, PhD, 82. **CAREER** Vis asst prof, 83-89, Dartmouth Col; asst prof, 92-94 assoc prof, 89,, Univ Miami. **RESEARCH** Renaissance lit and culture women's studies. **CONTACT ADDRESS** Dept of English, Univ of Miami, Coral Gables, FL 33124. **EMAIL** msuzuki@miami.edu

SWAIM, KATHLEEN MACKENZIE
PERSONAL Born 01/23/1936, Carlisle, PA **DISCIPLINE** ENGLISH **EDUCATION** Gettysburg Col, BA, 57; Pa State Univ, MA, 58; Middlebury Col, MA, 63; Univ Pa, PhD(English), 66. **CAREER** Instr, Dickinson Col, 58-60; from instr to asst prof, Univ Pa, 64-67; from asst prof to assoc prof, 67-76, actg assoc head dept English, 73, dir grad studies English, 76-78, PROF ENGLISH, UNIV MASS, AMHERST, 76-, Vis prof, Brown Univ, 78; managing ed, Lit Renaissance, 78-79. **MEMBERSHIPS** MLA; NCTE; Milton Soc Am. **RESEARCH** Milton; Swift; allegory. **SELECTED PUBLICATIONS** Coauth, A Concordance to Milton's English Poetry, Clarendon, Oxford, 72; auth, A Reading of Gulliver's Travels, Mouton, The Hague, 72; The art of the maze in Book IX of Paradise Lost, Studies English Lit, 72; Lycidas and the Dolphins of Apollo, J English & Ger Philol, 73; Cycle and circle: Time and structure in L'Allegro and Il Penseroso, Tex Studies Lang & Lit, 76; Structural Parallelism in Paradise Lost, Milton Studies, 77; Hercules,

Anaaeus, and Prometheus: A study of the climactic epic similes in Paradise Regained, Studies English Lit, 78; Allegorical Poetry in Milton's Ludlow Mark, Milton Studies, Vol XVI, 83; The Tudor And Stuart Monarchs And Monarchical Transition In The English Renaissance--Preface, English Literary Renaissance, Vol 26, 96. **CONTACT ADDRESS** Dept of English, Univ of Massachusetts, Amherst, Amherst, MA 01002.

SWAIN, JOSEPH

PERSONAL Born 05/19/1955, Malden, MA, m, 3 children **DISCIPLINE** MUSIC **EDUCATION** Dartmouth Col, AB, 77; Harvard Univ, AM, 80; Harvard Univ, PhD, 83. **CAREER** Assoc Prof Mus, Colgate Univ. **MEMBERSHIPS** Am Musicol Soc; Soc Mus Percept and Cognition; Am Bach Soc. **RESEARCH** Music criticism and critical theory. **SELECTED PUBLICATIONS** Sound Judgment: Basic Ideas About Music, San Francisco Press, 87; The Broadway Musical: A Critical Survey, NY, Oxford Univ Press, 90; Leonard Meyer's New Theory of Style, Mus Anal, 11, (2-3), Jul-Oct 92, 335-354; The Practicality of Chant in Modern Liturgy, The Diapason, Jul 92; How They Do It in Venice, Italy, Past Mus 16:3, 15-17; What is Meant by 'Musical Structure', Crit Mus, 2:1-2, Summer 94, 20-44; Musical Communities and Music Perception, Mus Percep, 11(3), Spring 94, 307-320; Operatic Conventions and the American Musical, in Opera and the Golden West: The Past, Present, and Future of Opera in the USA, London, Assoc Univ Press, 94, 296-301; The Concept of Musical Syntax, Mus Quart, 77:2, Summer 95, 285-308; The Range of Musical Semantics, The Jour Aesthet and Art Crit, 54.2, Spring 96, 135-152; Missalettes: Wrong Idea, Mod Liturgy, Oct 96, 6-7; Musical Languages, NY, WW Norton, 97; Bowdlerizing the Liturgy, Am, Aug 16-23; Musical Disguises in Mozart's Late Comedies, The Opera Quart 13.4, 97, 47-58; Liturgy as Artwork, Celebration 27.6, 1998, 285-287; Dimensions of Harmonic Rhythm, Music Theory Spectrum 20.1, 98,48-71; Finding a Way to Cure Sing-Song Syndrome, Pastoral Mus, Feb-Mar 98, 16-17. **CONTACT ADDRESS** Music Dept., Colgate Univ, 13 Oak Dr, Hamilton, NY 13346-1298. **EMAIL** jswain@mail.colgate.edu

SWANGER, DAVID

PERSONAL Born 08/01/1940, Newark, NJ, m, 1970, 3 children **DISCIPLINE** PHILOSOPHY, CREATIVE WRITING **EDUCATION** Swarthore Col, BA, 63; Harvard Univ, MAT, 64; EdD, 70. **CAREER** Prof, Univ Calif-Santa Crux, 87-. **HONORS AND AWARDS** NEA Poetry Fel; 'Golden Apple' UCSC Teaching Awd. **MEMBERSHIPS** Phi Delta Kappa, Philos of Educ Soc, Poets & Writers. **RESEARCH** Educational philosophy, poetry. **SELECTED PUBLICATIONS** Auth, Essays in Aesthetic Education, Mellen, 91; auth, This Waking Unafraid, Univ of Mo, 95. **CONTACT ADDRESS** Dept Educ, Univ of California, Santa Cruz, 1156 High St, Santa Cruz, CA 95064-1077. **EMAIL** dswanger@cats.ucsc.edu

SWANN, BRIAN

PERSONAL Born 08/13/1940, Wallsend **DISCIPLINE** ENGLISH **EDUCATION** Queens Col, BA, 62; Cambridge Univ, MA, 64; Princeton Univ, PhD(English), 70. **CAREER** Instr English, Princeton Univ, 65-66 & Rutgers Univ, 66-67; asst prof, Princeton Univ, 70-72; asst prof, 72-75, assoc prof, 75-80, PROF ENGLISH, COOPER UNION, 80-, Nat Endowment for Arts creative writing fel, 78. **HONORS AND AWARDS** John Florio Prize, 77. **MEMBERSHIPS** MLA; Asn Study Am Indian Lit. **RESEARCH** Nineteenth century English novel; modern-contemporary, British-American poetry; 20th century Italian poetry. **SELECTED PUBLICATIONS** Auth, Middlemarch: Realism and symbolic form, J English Lit Hist, 6/72; co-ed & co-transl, The Collected Poems of Lucio Piccolo, Princeton Univ, 73; The Mill on the Floss and tragedy, English Miscellany, spring 74; Daniel Deronda: Jewishness, Ecumenicism and the novel, Novel, spring 74; co-ed & co-transl, Selected Poetry of Andrea Zanzotto, 75 & Selected Poems of Tudor Arghezi, 76, Princeton Univ; ed, Smoothing the Ground: Essays on Native American Oral Literature, Am Indian Studies Ctr, Univ Calif, Los Angeles, 82. **CONTACT ADDRESS** Dept of Humanities, Cooper Union for the Advancement of Science and Art, 41 Cooper Square, New York, NY 10003-7136.

SWANSON, DONALD ROLAND

PERSONAL Born 11/20/1927, Pittsburgh, PA, m, 1955 **DISCIPLINE** ENGLISH **EDUCATION** Washington & Jefferson Col, BA, 53, Univ CT, MA, 55; Rutgers Univ, PhD, 65. **CAREER** From instr to assoc prof, Upsala Col, 55-71; prof eng, Wright State Univ, 71-98, Coordr, Orange Opportunity Corp, 66; Upsala Col fac res fel, 69; dir, Col Eng Asn, 74-77; ed, Univ Monogr, 77-82; dir, grad studies in Eng, 92-98; prof Emeritus, 98. **MEMBERSHIPS** MLA; Eng Inst; Col Eng Asn (treas, 71-73). **RESEARCH** Mod Brit lit. **SELECTED PUBLICATIONS** Auth, Three Conquerors, Mouton, 69; Far and fair within: a walk to Wachusett, ESQ, 3rd quarter 69; The exercise of irony in Benito Cereno, Am Transcendental Quart, summer 70; The growth of a poem: Coleridge's Dejection, BSU Forum, fall 71; The uses of tradition: King Arthur in the Modern World, CEA Critic, 3/74; The observer observed: Notes on the narrator of Under Western Eyes, Renaissance & Mod, 76; The Transmutations of To One in Paradise, CEA Forum, 7/76; W.S Gilbert and Evelyn Waugh in Encyclopedia of British Humorists, NY Garland pub, 96; D.H Lawrence, in British Travel Writers, 1910-1939, Detroit, Gale Research, 98. **CONTACT ADDRESS** 1550 Benson Dr, Dayton, OH 45406-4514.

SWARDSON, HAROLD ROLAND

PERSONAL Born 09/16/1925, Chicago, IL, m, 1949, 3 children **DISCIPLINE** ENGLISH **EDUCATION** Tulane Univ, BA, 47, MA, 48; Univ Minn, PhD, 56. **CAREER** Instr English, Univ Cincinnati, 48-49; from instr to assoc prof, 54-69, Prof Engl, Oh Univ, 69-97; Prof Emer, 97. **RESEARCH** Literary criticism; seventeenth century literature; philosophy. **SELECTED PUBLICATIONS** Auth, Poetry and the Fountain of Light, Allen & Unwin, London, 62; On the poetical, Ohio Univ Rev, 65; Sentimentality and the academic tradition, Col English, 4/76; The heritage of the New Criticism, Col English, 12/79; College teaching: The worst possible case, Philos Forum, summer 81; Teachers And Philosophers, Col English, Vol 56, 94; auth, Fighting for Words: Life in the Postmodern University, Essen, 99. **CONTACT ADDRESS** 50 Sunnyside Dr, Athens, OH 45701. **EMAIL** hswardso@atsbing.math.ohiou.edu

SWEENEY, JOHN ALBERT

PERSONAL Born 06/03/1925, Columbus, OH, m **DISCIPLINE** MUSICOLOGY, ETHNOMUSICOLOGY **EDUCATION** New York University, BA, 1949; Trinity College, London, LTCL, 1951; American Guild of Organists, AAGO, 1953; New York University, MA, 1953; State College of Music, Munich, Germany, graduate certificate, 1954; Free University, West Berlin, Germany, PhD, 1961; Johns Hopkins University, Ed, 1965; African Studies, University of Nairobi & Kenya, East Africa, graduate certificate, 1971. **CAREER** Morgan State University, professor of music, instruments, theory, musicology, ethnomusicology, 62; University of Maryland, Extension Program, USAF, Berlin, Germany, teacher music theory, 55-60; West Germany, guest lecturer, musicology, 54-61; New York City St Mark's, Morgan State University, 62-; New York, Munich, Baltimore, french hornist, bands, orchestras, 45-70; Music Education's National Conference; Society for Ethnomusicology; Morgan State University & Baltimore Area, advanced international studies. **HONORS AND AWARDS** Fulbright Scholar, Germany, 1953-54. **MEMBERSHIPS** Ping Council for Annual Black Music Week, Morgan State University; Advanced Council, Left Bank & Jazz Society, Baltimore; India Forum; Dedicated to Dissemination of Indian Culture; Organist, Union Baptist Church Elected to Following Honor Society; Mu Sigma, New York University, 1968; Phi Beta Kappa, New York University, 1949; Phi Delta Kappa, Johns Hopkins University, 1965. **SELECTED PUBLICATIONS** Published Anthem: "134th Psalm", 1951; Book: The Trumpets in the cntatas of J S Bach, 1961; Book Reviews; Article: "Guyanea & the African Diaspora", 1976. **CONTACT ADDRESS** Fine Arts, Morgan State Univ, 1700 E Cold Spring, Baltimore, MD 21239.

SWEENEY, MICHAEL S.

PERSONAL m, 1 child **DISCIPLINE** COMMUNICATION STUDIES **EDUCATION** Univ Nebr, BA, 80; Univ N Tex, MJ, 91; Phd, Univ Ohio, 96. **CAREER** Asst prof. **HONORS AND AWARDS** Pulitzer Prize, 86. **MEMBERSHIPS** Nebr Press Asn; Asn Edu Jour and Mass Commun. **RESEARCH** News writing; public affairs reporting and copy editing; mass media history. **SELECTED PUBLICATIONS** Auth, The Sound Historian; pubs on Ernie Pyle's most famous column, and death of Capt. Henry T. Waskow in World War II. **CONTACT ADDRESS** Dept of Communication, Utah State Univ, 3580 S Highway 91, Logan, UT 84321. **EMAIL** msweeney@wpo.hass.usu.edu

SWEENEY, SUSAN ELIZABETH

PERSONAL Born 03/07/1958, Hagerstown, MD, m, 1983 **DISCIPLINE** ENGLISH **EDUCATION** Mt Holyoke Col, BA, 80; Brown Univ, MA, 82; MFA, 85; PhD, 89. **CAREER** From Instr to Assoc Prof, Holy Cross Col, 87-. **HONORS AND AWARDS** Nat Endowment Humanities Grant, 93; Fac Fel, Holy Cross Col, 97; Fel, Five Col Women's Studies Res Ctr Fel, 97; Lilly Fel, 99. **MEMBERSHIPS** IVNS, MLA, NEMLA, ALA, SSNL. **RESEARCH** History of the novel, genre theory (detective fiction and Gothic romance), postmodernist fiction, feminist narratology, Vladimir Nabokov. **SELECTED PUBLICATIONS** Auth, "Anne Tyler's Invented Games: 'The Accidental Tourist' and 'Breathing Lessons'," Southern Quart 34.1 (95): 81-97; auth, "Mirror, Mirror, on the Wall: Gazing in Edith Wharton's 'Looking Glass'," Narrative 3.2 (95): 139-160; auth, "The Other Side of the Coin in Arthur Conan Doyle's 'The Red-Headed League'," Sherlock Holmes: Victorian Sleuth to Mod Hero, UP of Am (96): 37-63; coauth, "In League with Each Other: The Theory and Practice of Feminist Collaboration," Common Ground: Feminist Collaboration in the Acad, St Univ NY Pr (97): 63-79; auth, Triple Play: Poe, Borges, Auster and the Development of Detective Fiction, NEMLA Pr, 98; auth, "Fantasy, Folklore and Finite Numbers in Nabokov's 'Nursery Tale'," Slavis and E European J 43.3 (99): 511-529; auth, Detecting Texts: The Metaphysical Detective Story from Poe to Postmodernism, Univ Pa Pr (Philadelphia, PA), 99. **CONTACT ADDRESS** Dept English, Holy Cross Col, 1 College St, Worcester, MA 01610-2395. **EMAIL** ssweeney@holycross.edu

SWEET, NAN

DISCIPLINE BRITISH ROMANTICISM **EDUCATION** Univ Mich, AB; Univ Mo, MA; Univ Mich, PhD, 93. **CAREER** Instr, Univ Mo, Columbia, 66-68; instr, Webster Groves High Sch, St Louis, 76-81; sr lectr, Univ Mo, St Louis, 81-. **HONORS AND AWARDS** Jinx Walker Prize, Acad of Am Poets & Wash Univ, 81; Crse develop grant, Univ Mo-St Louis, 86; Rackham non-traditional fel, Univ Mich, 87-88; Rackham predoctoral fel, Univ Mich, 91-92; Heberle Awd, Dissertation 2nd Prize, Univ Mich; Lectr of Yr, Col of Arts and Sci, Univ Mo, Columbia. **MEMBERSHIPS** MLA; Nat Women's Stud Asn; North Am Soc for Stud of Romanticism; Col Eng Asn; Midwest MLA; Byron Soc; Keats-Shelley Asn. **RESEARCH** British history and culture. **SELECTED PUBLICATIONS** Auth, Classics for Ninth Graders: Solace and Status, Eng J 72.3, Mar 83; Thirty-One Ways to Avoid Book Reports, Eng J 73.4, Apr 84; History, Imperialism, and the Aesthetics of the Beautiful:Hemans and the Post-Napoleonic Moment, in At the Limits of Romanticism: Essays in Cultural, Feminist, and Materialist Criticism, eds, Mary A Favret and Nicola J Watson, Ind UP, 93. **CONTACT ADDRESS** Univ of Missouri, St. Louis, Saint Louis, MO 63121. **EMAIL** snlswee@umslvma.umsl.edu

SWEETSER, WESLEY DUAINE

PERSONAL Born 05/25/1919, National City, CA, m, 1942, 4 children **DISCIPLINE** ENGLISH **EDUCATION** Univ Colo, BA, 38, MA, 46, PhD(English lit), 58. **CAREER** Instr English, Univ Colo, 45-48; asst prof, Peru State Teachers Col, 48-50; assoc prof, US Air Force Acad, 58-63; asst prof air sci, Univ Nebr, 63-66; vis prof English, Nebr Wesleyan Univ, 66-67; assoc prof, State Univ NY Col Oswego, 67-69, prof, 69-82; RES & WRITING, 82- **MEMBERSHIPS** MLA; Arthur Machen Soc. **RESEARCH** Arthur Machen; Ralph Hodgson; colonial backgrounds in 19th century British literature (Australasia). **SELECTED PUBLICATIONS** Auth, Machen: A biographical study, Aylesford Rev, winter 59-60; Arthur Machen: Surface realities or essence of spirit, ELT, 64; Arthur Machen, Twayne, 64; coauth, A Bibiography of Arthur Machen, Univ Tex, 65; auth, Arthur Machen: A bibliography of writings about him, English Lit in Transition, 68; contribr, Thomas Hardy: An Annotated Biliography of Writings About Him, Northern Ill Univ, 73; Ralph Hodgson: A Bibliography, privately publ, 74 & rev & annotated, Garland, 80. **CONTACT ADDRESS** 52 Ridgeway Sites Ave, Oswego, NY 13126-6520.

SWENEY, JOHN R.

PERSONAL Born 11/25/1937, Shenandoah, IA, m, 1961, 3 children **DISCIPLINE** ENGLISH **EDUCATION** Colo Col, BA, 60; Claremont Grad Sch, MA, 62; Univ Wis, PhD, 68. **CAREER** Instr, Whitman Col, 62-64; Instr, Vis Prof, Univ Col of Cork, Ireland, 87-88, 92-93, 00-01; Asst Prof, Assoc Prof, Prof, Colby Col, 67- **HONORS AND AWARDS** Woodrow Wilson Fel, 60; NDEA Fel, 68. **RESEARCH** Restoration and 18th-century British literature. **SELECTED PUBLICATIONS** Articles in Language: New Directions, The Library, Philological Quarterly, Notes and Queries. **CONTACT ADDRESS** Dept English, Colby Col, 150 Mayflower Hill Dr, Waterville, ME 04901-4799. **EMAIL** jrsweney@colby.edu

SWENSON, EDWARD

DISCIPLINE MUSIC HISTORY **EDUCATION** Oberlin Col, BM; Univ Ky, MM; Cornell Univ, PhD. **CAREER** Prof. **SELECTED PUBLICATIONS** Auth, pubs on history of music. **CONTACT ADDRESS** Dept of Music History, Theory and Composition, Ithaca Col, 100 Job Hall, Ithaca, NY 14850. **EMAIL** swensone@ithaca.edu

SWERDLOW, DAVID G.

DISCIPLINE ENGLISH **EDUCATION** Ohio Univ, PhD **CAREER** Assoc prof. **HONORS AND AWARDS** Fel, Pa Coun Arts, 96; fulbright prof, am lit in peru; fel, va ctr for the creative arts; penn coun for the arts fel, poetry. **SELECTED PUBLICATIONS** Auth, The Last Hill and the Wild Trees, Ohio Rev; Self and Duende, Am Letters and Commentary. **CONTACT ADDRESS** Dept of Eng, Westminster Col, Pennsylvania, New Wilmington, PA 16172-0001.

SWETNAM, FORD

DISCIPLINE ENGLISH LITERATURE **EDUCATION** Cornell Univ, PhD, 67. **CAREER** Prof. **SELECTED PUBLICATIONS** Auth, Another Tough Hop and 301; co-ed, High Sky Over All: Idaho Fiction at the Centennial; auth, Ghostholders Know. **CONTACT ADDRESS** Dept of English and Philosophy, Idaho State Univ, Pocatello, ID 83209. **EMAIL** swetford@isu.edu

SWETNAM, SUSAN

PERSONAL Born 06/15/1950, Abingdon, PA, m, 1985 **DISCIPLINE** ENGLISH LITERATURE, AMERICAN LITERATURE, AMERICAN STUDIES **EDUCATION** Univ Mich, PhD, 79. **CAREER** Prof of Eng, Idaho State Univ. **HONORS AND AWARDS** Rackham Scholar, Univ of Mich; Phi Beta Kappa; Phi Kappa Phi; Distinguished Teacher, Idaho State Univ; Distinguished Public Servant, Idaho State Univ; Outstanding Res, Idaho State Univ. **RESEARCH** Fiction and Nonfiction narrative; personal essay; Intermountain West stud. **SELECTED PUBLICATIONS** Auth, Lives of the Saints in Southeast Idaho: An Introduction to Mormon Pioneer Life Story Writing; pubs in Tough Paradise, Idaho and the American West, Journal of the West, Frontiers: A Journal of Women

Studies, and Northwest Folklore; auth, Home Muontains: Reflections from a Western Middle Age, Washington State Univ Press, 00; auth, Ring of Fire: Writers of the Greater Yellowstone Region, Rendezvous, many popular national and regional magazines. **CONTACT ADDRESS** Dept of English and Philosophy, Idaho State Univ, Pocatello, ID 83209. **EMAIL** swetsusa@isu.edu

SWIDERSKI, SUZANNE M.
PERSONAL Born 06/05/1965, Milwaukee, WI, s **DISCIPLINE** EDUCATIONAL PSYCHOLOGY, ENGLISH **EDUCATION** BA, 87; MA, 90; M Ed, 93. **CAREER** Asst coord, St Norbert Col, 87-88; grad tutor, Loyola Univ, 88-89; instr, 89-90; coord, 90-91; coun, 92-93; fac, Heartland Comm Col, 93-95; asst prof, Loras Col, 95-. **HONORS AND AWARDS** NEH; Who's Who in Midwest, Am, World; Outstand People 20th Century. **MEMBERSHIPS** MCLCA; MWCA; NADE; NCTE; NWCA. **RESEARCH** Faculty development; teaching and learning; tutor training. **SELECTED PUBLICATIONS** Ed, contrb bibliographer, Tutor Training: An Annotated Bibliography of Theories, Principles, and Practices from 1989-1996 (MCLCA, 96); contr bibliogr, Annotated Research Bibliographies in Developmental Education: Tutoring (NCDE, 96); contr bibliogr, Conference on College Composition and Communication Bibliography of Composition Rhetoric, 95-98, 90-92, 88; rev of, "The Writing Center Resource Manual," Writing Lab NL (98): 12-13. **CONTACT ADDRESS** Dept English, Loras Col, 1450 Alta Vista St, Dubuque, IA 52001-4327.

SWIFT, CAROLYN RUTH
PERSONAL Born 11/10/1928, East Orange, NJ, 2 children **DISCIPLINE** DRAMA, RENAISSANCE & REFORMATION **EDUCATION** Univ Chicago, PbB, 48; Columbia Univ, MA, 50; Brown Univ, PhD(English), 73. **CAREER** Teacher English, Rosemary Hall, 50-52; teacher English & hist, Prospect Hill Sch, 52-53; teacher English, Joseph Case High Sch, 53-54 & Cranston High Sch, 54-56; from instr to asst prof, 65-73, ASSOC PROF ENGLISH, RI COL, 73-, Fac res grants, RI Col, 74-80; Nat Endow for Humanites summer stipend, 81. **MEMBERSHIPS** MLA; Northeast Mod Lang Asn; Women's Caucus Mod Lang; Shakespeare Asn. **RESEARCH** Shakespeare; John Lyly; intellectual history. **SELECTED PUBLICATIONS** Auth, The Shakespearean Wild, Geography, Genus, and Gender, Shakespeare Quart, Vol 44, 93. **CONTACT ADDRESS** Rhode Island Col, 50 Armstrong Ave, Providence, RI 02903.

SWIFT, LOUIS JOSEPH
PERSONAL Born 08/01/1932, Scranton, PA, m, 1964, 3 children **DISCIPLINE** LATIN LITERATURE AND PATRISTICS **EDUCATION** St Mary's Univ, Md, AB, 54; Pontif Gregorian Univ, STB, 56; Johns Hopkins Univ, MAT, 58, PhD(classics), 63. **CAREER** Chmn, Univ of Kentucky, 70-76; assoc prof, Univ of Kentucky, 70-82; prof, Univ of Kentucky, 82-; dir, Univ Studies Program, 86-; dean, Undergraduate Studies, 90-. **MEMBERSHIPS** Am Philol Asn; Arch Archaeol Inst Am; Class Asn Mid West & South; NAm Patristic Soc; AAUP. **RESEARCH** Latin literature; pastristics; ancient rhetoric. **CONTACT ADDRESS** Dept of Classics and Lit, Univ of Kentucky, 1077 Patterson Office Tower 0027, Lexington, KY 40506-0003. **EMAIL** lswift@pop.uky.edu

SWINDELL, WARREN C.
PERSONAL Born 08/22/1934, Kansas City, MO, m, 1967, 2 children **DISCIPLINE** MUSIC **EDUCATION** Lincoln Univ of Mo, BS Music Educ 56; Univ of Mich, MM, 64; Univ of Iowa, PhD Music Educ, 70. **CAREER** Central High Sch Hayti MO, band and choir dir 56-57, dir of musical act 59-60; Hubbard High Sch, dir of music act 60-61; Flint MI Public Schools, inst mus specialist 61-67; KY State Univ, chair/prof of music 70-79, prof of music 79-80; Indiana State Univ, Chair, Dir/Prof Ctr, Dept of African and African American Studies, 80-96; Prof Emeritus. **HONORS AND AWARDS** Numerous Service Awds NAACP 1978-94; NEH Summer Seminar for College Teachers Grant 1984; Faculty Rsch Grant Indiana State Univ 1985; IN State Univ Research Grant 1987-88; Amer Philosophical Society Research Grant 1988; Lilly Endowment Faculty Open Fellowship 1993-94; Caleb Mills Awd for Distinguished Teaching. **MEMBERSHIPS** Evaluator Natl Assoc of Schools of Music Accred 1977-78; screening panel KY Arts Commn Project 1977-79; chaired State, Div & Natl MENC meetings 1979-80; worshipful master, Prince Hall Lodge #16, 1991-92; president, Region V, National Council for Black Studies, 1989-91; secretary, Indiana Coalition of Blacks in Higher Education, 1992-93; first vp, Indiana Coalition of Blacks in Higher Educ, 1994-95; pres, Indiana Coalition, 1996-; Prince Hall Grand Lodge Jurisdiction of Indiana, chairman of masonic history & education; chairman, School of Instruction, Prince Hall Masons; Terre Haute, Indiana Branch NAACP, first vp 1995-96, pres, 1997. **CONTACT ADDRESS** Africana Studies, Indiana State Univ, Stalker Hall 204, Terre Haute, IN 47809. **EMAIL** abswin@ruby.indstate.edu

SWINDEN, KEVIN J.
PERSONAL Born 03/04/1970, Toronto, ON, Canada, m, 1998 **DISCIPLINE** MUSIC **EDUCATION** Univ W On, BM, 92; St Univ NYork Buffalo, PhD, 97. **CAREER** Vis asst prof, St Univ NY Buffalo, 97; vis asst prof, St Univ NY Potsdam, 98; asst prof, Univ Ms, 98- . **HONORS AND AWARDS** Thomas J. Clifton Mem Awd, 97 **MEMBERSHIPS** SMT; CUMS; SCSMT. **RESEARCH** Nineteenth century chromatic harmony; Bruckner, theory pedogogy. **SELECTED PUBLICATIONS** Auth, Bruckner's Perged Prelude-A dramatic revue of Wagner?, Music Anal, 99 **CONTACT ADDRESS** PO Box 6835, University, MS 38677. **EMAIL** kswinden@olemiss.edu

SWINSON, WARD
DISCIPLINE ENGLISH LITERATURE **EDUCATION** Northwestern Univ, BA; Univ Ill, MA, PhD. **CAREER** Assoc prof. **RESEARCH** 20th century American, British, and European Literature, especially Joyce and Nabokov. **SELECTED PUBLICATIONS** Auth, pubs on James Joyce, co-auth, monograph on Ezra Pound's China Adams Cantos. **CONTACT ADDRESS** Dept of English, Colorado State Univ, Fort Collins, CO 80523. **EMAIL** wswinson@lomar.colostate.edu

SWIONTKOWSKI, GALE
PERSONAL 2 children **DISCIPLINE** MODERN POETRY, ANGLO-IRISH LITERATURE **EDUCATION** Univ Bryn Mawr, PhD. **CAREER** Assoc prof, Fordham Univ. **RESEARCH** Psychological and feminist approaches to lit, mod and contemp poetry. **SELECTED PUBLICATIONS** Auth, A New Species of Man, Buchnell UP, 82; auth, The Psychic Struggle of the Narrative Ego in the Conclusion of Troylus and Creseyde, Philol Quart 72, 93; Rondo to Jazz: the Poetry of Michael O'Siadhail, Eire-Ireland 29, 94. **CONTACT ADDRESS** Dept of Eng, Fordham Univ, Fordham Rd, Bronx, NY 10458. **EMAIL** swiontkowski@fordham.edu

SWITZER, LES
PERSONAL m, 5 children **DISCIPLINE** COMMUNICATION **EDUCATION** Univ CA, Berkeley, BA, MA, 59; Univ Natal (Pietermaritzburg, South Africa), PhD, 72. **CAREER** Dept of Journalism & Broadcasting, CA State Univ, Los Angeles, 71-73, chair, 72-73; Dept of Journalism & Media Studies, Rhodes Univ, Grahamstown, South Africa, 73-82, chair, 79-82; School of Communication, Univ Houston, 83-, assoc dir, Telecommunications Res Inst, 85-86, dir grad studies, 92-93, head of Journalism Prog, 93-97; Herald Examiner, Los Angeles, 68-72; Natal Witness and World, Pietermaritzburg and Johannesburg, South Africa, 64-68; freelance journalist for British publications (London), 68, 81. **HONORS AND AWARDS** More than 35 individual grants and awards from Britain, South Africa and the United States for teaching and research activities. These include the NEH, Am Philos Soc, Am Coun of Learned Socs, South African Human Sciences Res Coun, and British Coun. Recipient of a Fulbright Senior Scholar Awd and a Distinguished Faculty Recognition Awd from the Houston City Council; joint appointments with communication and the african am studies prog, 83-86, and communication and hist, 86-91, univ houston. co-founder and co-director, center for critical cultural studies, univ houston, 90-96. am press inst, 96 (journalism educators s **MEMBERSHIPS** African Studies Asn; Asn for Journalism and Mass Communication. **RESEARCH** Journalism and media studies, development studies, cultural studies, southern African studies. **SELECTED PUBLICATIONS** Auth, The Black Press in South Africa and Lesotho: A Descriptive Bibliographic Guide 1836-1976, 79; Media and Dependency in South Africa, 85, 87; Power and Resistance in an African Society: The Ciskei Xhosa and the Making of South Africa, 93; South Africa's Alternative Press: Voices of Protest and Resistance, 1880-1960, South Africa's Resistence Press, 97; auth, Alternative Voices in the Test generation under Apartheid, Ohio Univ Press, 00. **CONTACT ADDRESS** School of Communication, Univ of Houston, Houston, TX 77204-3786. **EMAIL** lswitzer@uh.edu

SYED, JASMIN
DISCIPLINE CLASSICS **EDUCATION** Staatsexamen, PhD, 91. **CAREER** Asst prof, Stanford Univ. **RESEARCH** Latin lit; Roman cult hist; lit theory; gender in the ancient world. **SELECTED PUBLICATIONS** Auth, The Construction of Roman Identity in Vergil's Aeneid; Creating Roman Identity: Subjectivity and Self-Fashioning in Latin Literature, 97. **CONTACT ADDRESS** Stanford Univ, Bldg 20, Main Quad, Stanford, CA 94305.

SYLVESTRE, JEAN-GUY
PERSONAL Born 05/17/1918, Sorel, PQ, Canada **DISCIPLINE** LITERATURE **EDUCATION** Univ Ottawa, BA, 39, LPh, 40, MA, 41. **CAREER** Bk reviewer, Le Droit, Ottawa, 39-48; Wartime Info Bd, 44-45; Pvt secy Louis St. Laurent, 45-50; assoc librn, Libr Parliament, 56-68; Nat Librn Can, 68-83; pres, Can Inst Hist Microrepros, 83-86. **HONORS AND AWARDS** Fel, Royal Soc Can; DLS(hon), Univ Ottawa; DLitt(hon), Mt Allison Univ; LLD(hon), Univ Toronto; LLD(hon) Univ PEI; LLD(hon) Memorial Univ Nfld; LLD(hon) Concordia Univ; off, Order Can; comdr, Ordre internat du Bien public; Ordre du merite de Pologne; IFLA Medal; Outstanding Public Serv Awd. **MEMBERSHIPS** Can Libr Asn; Asn Sci Tech Doc; Ont Libr Asn; Can Asn Info Sci; past comt chmn, Gov Gen Lit Awards; past chmn, Can Writers Found; Academie Canadienne-francaise, 65-92; pres, World Poetry Conf, 67. **RESEARCH** Canadian literature/poetry **SELECTED PUBLICATIONS** Auth, Louis Francoeur, journaliste, 41; auth, Situation de la poesie canadienne, 42; auth, Anthologie de la poesie d'expression francaise, 43; auth, Poetes catholiques de la France contemporaine, 44; auth, Jules Laforge, 45; auth, Sondages, 45; Impressions de theatre, 50; auth, Panorama des lettres canadiennes francaises, 64; auth, Canadian Writers/Ecrivains canadiens, 64; auth, Un siecle de litterature canadienne, 67; auth, Guidelines for national libraries, 87. **CONTACT ADDRESS** 2286 Bowman Rd, Ottawa, ON, Canada K1H 6V6.

SYLVIE, GEORGE
PERSONAL Born 02/24/1954, Shreveport, LA, m, 1985, 2 children **DISCIPLINE** JOURNALISM **EDUCATION** La St Univ, BA, 76; Univ Missouri-Columbia, MA, 78; Univ Texas, PhD, 88. **CAREER** Assoc prof, Univ Tx, 92-; asst prof, Kent State Univ, 90-92; asst prof, La State Univ Shreveport, 87-90; Soc Sci Res assoc, Univ Tx, 87; Tchg asst & asst instr, Univ Tx, 84-86 **HONORS AND AWARDS** Outstanding Service Awd, Assoc for Educ in Journalism & Mass Communication, 97; Who's Who in Amer Educ, 92-93; Who's Who in Amer, 91; La St Univ, Shreveport Jour Fac Grant, 88-90; Univ Tx Fel, 83-85, 86-87; Ntl School Board Assoc Certificate of Merit, 81; News Media Awd, La Assoc of Educ, 79, 80. **RESEARCH** Media Management, Technology and the Future **SELECTED PUBLICATIONS** Coauth, Real-Time Journalism: Instantaneous Change for Newswriting, Newspaper Res Jour, 96; auth, Departmental Influences on Interdepartmental Cooperation in Daily Newspapers, Journalism and Mass Communication Quarterly, 96; coauth, Pagination Impact on Newspaper Design, Southwestern Mass Communication Jourl, 96; coauth, "Preserving Editorial Page Diversity," Mass Commun Rev (95); coauth, "Structural Analysis of Electronic Newspaper Market," J of Media Econ (98); coauth, Time, Change & The American Newspaper, Erlbaum Assocs, in press; coauth, Media Management: A Casebook Approach, Erlbaum Assocs, 2nd ed, 99. **CONTACT ADDRESS** Dept of Journalism, Univ of Texas, Austin, Austin, TX 78712. **EMAIL** g.sylvie@mail.utexas.edu

SYNDERGAARD, LARRY E.
PERSONAL Born 07/30/1936, Des Moines, IO, m, 1958, 2 children **DISCIPLINE** ENGLISH **EDUCATION** Iowa State Univ, BS, 59; Univ Wisc Madison, MS, 63; PhD, 70. **CAREER** Asst prof to prof, W Mich Univ, 68-. **MEMBERSHIPS** MLA; Medieval Acad; Soc for Advan of Scandinavian Study; Am Folklore Soc; AAUP; Assoc for Study of Lit and Environ; Int Ballad Comm. **RESEARCH** Oral-traditional and folk narrative, translation, Scandinavian traditional literatures. **SELECTED PUBLICATIONS** Auth, English Translations of the Scandinavian Medieval Ballads, Nordic Inst of Folklore, (Turku, Finland), 95. **CONTACT ADDRESS** Dept English, Western Michigan Univ, 1201 Oliver St, Kalamazoo, MI 49008-3804. **EMAIL** larry.syndergaard@wmich.edu

SYPHER, FRANCIS JACQUES
PERSONAL Born 11/04/1941, Hackensack, NJ, d, 1 child **DISCIPLINE** ENGLISH, COMPARATIVE LITERATURE **EDUCATION** Columbia Univ, AB, 63, MA, 64, PhD, 68. **CAREER** Precep, Eng, 65-68, Columbia Univ; asst prof, Eng, 68-75, SUNY, Albany; ed consul, 75-81, R.R. Bowker, NYU Press, & other publ; Fulbright Sr lectr, Amer lit, 81-83, Univ du Benin, Lome Togo, W Africa; asst to pres, 83-85, NY Schl of Inter Design, concurrent, adj prof, Eng, NY Univ; dir, 85-86, Amer Eng Lang Prog, Amer Cult Ctr, US Info Svc, Dakar Senegal, W Africa; Fulbright Sr Lectr, 86-88, Amer Lit, Univ Omar Bongo, Libreville Gabon, C Africa; writer, ed consul, 88-, NY. **HONORS AND AWARDS** NY St Regents Fel, 63-65; SUNY Res Found Awd, 74; Fulbright Sr Lectr, 81-83, 86-88; Pres Bronze Medal, 93, St Nicholas Soc NY. **MEMBERSHIPS** Art Stud League of NY; NY Genealogical and Biographical Soc; Friends of the Columbia Univ Lib. **RESEARCH** English & comparative lit; life and works of Letitia Elizabeth Landon, 1802-1838; NY history & biography. **SELECTED PUBLICATIONS** Auth, Stories of Africa, 89; ed, Works by Letitia Elizabeth Landon, 90-00; auth, The Yorkville Civic Council, 91; ed, The St. Nicholas Society, A 150 Year Record, 93; transl and ed, The Iskenius Letters, 94; ed, The Image of Irelande, Derricke, 98; ed, The Chronicle of the Society of Colonial Wars in the State of NY, 99; **CONTACT ADDRESS** FDR Station, PO Box 1125, New York, NY 10150-1125.

SZABO, LYNDA
PERSONAL Born 06/30/1959, Pittsburgh, PA, s **DISCIPLINE** ENGLISH **EDUCATION** Duquesne Univ, PhD, 98. **CAREER** Asst prof, Geneva Col. **MEMBERSHIPS** MLA. **RESEARCH** American Women Writers. **CONTACT ADDRESS** Dept English, Geneva Col, 3200 College Ave, Beaver Falls, PA 15010-3557.

SZANTO, GEORGE
DISCIPLINE COMMUNICATION STUDIES **EDUCATION** Darmouth Col, BA; Harvard Univ, PhD. **CAREER** Prof, McGill Univ. **HONORS AND AWARDS** Royal Soc of Canada, fel, 88; Winner, Silver Found Medal, Nat Magazine Awds, 87; Hugh MacLennan Prize for Fiction, 95. **RESEARCH** Cultural studies; artefactual analysis; Marxist cultural theory; propaganda theory; popular culture and intertextuality; Latin American culture; urbanization in Canada and America; Cana-

dian cultural institutions; narratology; dramaturgy. **SELECTED PUBLICATIONS** Auth, Inside the Statues of Saints, 96; auth, Friends & Marriages, 94; auth, The Underside of Stones, Harper and Row, 90; auth, Narrative Taste and Social Perspective: The Matter of Quality, 87. **CONTACT ADDRESS** Dept Communications, McGill Univ, 845 Sherbrooke St, Montreal, QC, Canada H3A 2T5. **EMAIL** gszanto@aol.com

SZARMACH, PAUL E.
DISCIPLINE ENGLISH & MEDIEVAL STUDIES **EDUCATION** Canisius Col, AB, 63; Harvard Univ, AM 64; PhD, 68. **CAREER** Tchg fel, Harvard Univ, 66;Instr, US Military Acad, 68-70; Asst prof, 70-75, assoc prof, 75-83; dir, Center for Medieval and Early Renaissance Studies, SUNY, 75-86, 88-92; prof, SUNY, 83-94; acting Vice-Povost, Graduate Studies and Res, SUNY, 86-87; Prof, Western Mich Univ, 94-. **MEMBERSHIPS** Member, Executive committee of Centers and Regional Asn (sub-committee of the Mediaeval Acadamy), 80-83; member, SUNY Res Foundation Board of Directors. **RESEARCH** Old English literature with special reference to Old English porse and its Latin backgrounds. **SELECTED PUBLICATIONS** Co-ed, ACTA 4: The Fourteenth Century, CEMERS, 77; ed, Aspects of Jewish Culture in the Middle Ages, SUNY Press, 78; The Old English Homily and Its Backgrounds, SUNY Press, 78; Vercelli Homilies IX-XXIII, Toronto Univ Press, 81; The Alliterative Tradition in the Fourteenth Century, Kent State Univ Press, 81; co-ed, Mediaevalia 6, Festschrift for Bernard F. Hupp, 80; An Introduction to the Mediaeval Mystics of Europe; SUNY Press, 84; Studies in Earlier Old English Prose, SUNY Press, 86; Sources of Anglo-Saxon Culture, Studies in Medieval Culture, 20, The Medieval Inst, 86; Sources of Anglo-Saxon Literary Culture: A Trial Version, Medieval and Renaissance Texts and Studies 74; Suffolk: Boydell and Brewer; 94; Holy Men and Holy Women: Old English Prose Saints' Lives and Their Contexts, SUNY Press, 96; gen ed, Medieval England: An Encyclopedia, Garland Publ, 98. **CONTACT ADDRESS** Dept Medieval Institute, Western Michigan Univ, 1903 W Michigan Ave, Kalamazoo, MI 49008. **EMAIL** paul.szarmach@wmich.edu

SZEGEDY-MASZAK, ANDREW
PERSONAL Born 07/10/1948 **DISCIPLINE** DRAMA **EDUCATION** Univ Mich, BA, 70, Profinceton Univ, MA, 72, PhD, 76. **CAREER** Instr, Wesleyan Univ, 73-77; Asst Prof, Wesleyan Univ, 77-80; Assoc Prof, Wesleyan Univ, 80-88; Prof, Wesleyan Univ, 88-; Jane A. Seney Prof, Wesleyan Univ, 92-; Vis Assoc Prof, UCLA, 85-87; Vis Assoc Prof, Dartmouth Col, 87; Vis prof, 89, 90, 91; Contribut ed, Archaeology Mag, 88-; Consultant-lect, NEH-sponsored proj, Cabrini Col, 89; Vis Prof, Yale Sch Drama, 96, 98. **HONORS AND AWARDS** Woodrow Wilson Fel, 70; Summer Inst, Am Socy Papyrologists, 70; NDEA/Profinceton Univ fels, 70-73; NEH Summer Sem SUNY-Buffalo, 76; Wesleyan Ctr Hum, fac fel, 78; Wesleyan Profoj Grant, 79; NEH Summer Sem, 81; NEH Transl Grant, 85; Guest Scholar, J. Paul Getty Mus, 85; Am Philol Asn Awd Excellence Tchng Clas, 86; Wesleyan Profoj Grant, 91; Wesleyan Univ Tchng Excellence Awd, 97; 250th Anniversary Vis Prof Distinguished Tchng, Profinceton Univ, 98-99. **SELECTED PUBLICATIONS** Auth, The Nomo Theophrastus, NY, 81. **CONTACT ADDRESS** Wesleyan Univ, Middletown, CT 06459.

SZEMAN, IMRE J.
PERSONAL Born 07/26/1968, Calgary, AB, Canada, M, 1996, 1 child **DISCIPLINE** ENGLISH, CULTURAL STUDIES **EDUCATION** Queens Univ, BA, 90; Univ Western Ont, MA, 93; Duke Univ, PhD, 98. **CAREER** Asst to assoc prof, McMaster Univ, 99-. **HONORS AND AWARDS** Gold Medal, Queen's Univ, 90; For Govt Award, Int Coun for Can Studies, 91; SSHRC Fel, 92-96, 97-99, 01-04; James B Duke Fel, 93-97; Myra and William Waldo Boone Fel, 97-98; John Charles Polanyi Prize, 00. **MEMBERSHIPS** MLA, Marxist Lit Group, Am Studies Asn, Am Comp Lit Asn. **RESEARCH** Critical and Cultural Theory, Globalization, Postcolonial Literature and Theory, Film, Contemporary visual Culture, History of Literary and Aesthetic Theory. **SELECTED PUBLICATIONS** Auth, "The Persistence of the Nation: Interdisciplinarity and Canadian Literary Criticism," Essays on Can Writing, (99); ed, Materializing Canada, Essays on Can Writing, (99); coed, Pierre Bourdieu: Fieldwork in Culture, Rowman and Littlefield, 00; auth, "The Rhetoric of Culture: Some Notes on Magazines, Canadian Culture and Globalization," Jour of Can Studies, (00); AUTH, "Belated of Isochronic?: Canadian Writing, Time and Globalization," Essays on Can Writing, (00); ed, Learning From Seattle, Rev of Educ/Pedagogy/Cult Studies, 01; auth, "Plundering the Empire: Globalization, Cultural Studies and Utopia," Rethinking Marxism, (01); auth, Zones of Instability: Literature, Postcolonialism and the Nation, Johns Hopkins Univ Pr, (forthcoming); coed, Anglophone Literatures and Global Changes, S Atlantic Quart, (forthcoming). **CONTACT ADDRESS** McMaster Univ, 1280 Main St W, Hamilton, ON, Canada L8S 4L9. **EMAIL** szeman@mcmaster.ca

SZITTYA, PENN
DISCIPLINE ENGLISH LITERATURE **EDUCATION** Univ NC, BA; Cornell Univ, PhD. **CAREER** Eng Dept, Georgetown Univ **RESEARCH** Medieval literature; Old and Middle English literature; Arthurian literature; medieval literary theory; medieval apocalyptic literature; medieval Icelandic literature; medieval Latin; patristic literature. **SELECTED PUBLICATIONS** Auth, Domesday Bokes: The Apocalypse in Medieval English Literary Culture, 91; The Trinity in Langland and Abelard, 89; The Antifraternal Tradition in Medieval Literature, 86; Metafiction: The Double Narration in Under Western Eyes, 81; The Living Stone and the Patriarchs: Typological Imagery in Andreas, 73; The Green Yeoman as Loathly Lady: The Friar's Parody of the Wife of Bath's Tale, 75. **CONTACT ADDRESS** English Dept, Georgetown Univ, 37th and O St, Washington, DC 20057.

SZUCHEWYCZ, BOHDAN G.
DISCIPLINE COMMUNICATIONS **EDUCATION** Univ Regina, BA, 80; Univ Toronto, MA, 81, PhD, 87, MLS, 89. **CAREER** Prof, Brock Univ. **RESEARCH** Ethnography of communication and discourse analysis. **SELECTED PUBLICATIONS** Auth, Evidentiality in ritual discourse: the social construction of religious meaning, Lang in Soc, 23, (94): 389-410; Where are you getting your God from? Conflicting Sources of Authority in Religious Discourse, Discours social/Soc Discourse 7, 95; Silence in ritual communication, Silence: Interdisciplinary Perspectives, Mouton de Gruyter, 97; co-auth, Discourses of exclusion: The Irish press and the Travelling People, 97. **CONTACT ADDRESS** Dept of Communications Studies, Brock Univ, 500 Glenridge Ave, Saint Catharines, ON, Canada L2S 3A1. **EMAIL** bszuchew@spartan.ac.brocku.ca

T

TABBI, JOSEPH
PERSONAL Born 05/04/1960, Buffalo, NY, s **DISCIPLINE** ENGLISH **EDUCATION** Cornell Univ, BS, BA, 83; Univ Toronto, MA, 84; PhD, 89. **CAREER** Assoc Prof, Univ Ill, 89-. **HONORS AND AWARDS** Fulbright Sr Scholar, Univ Hamburg, 84; Humanities Inst, Univ Ill, 98. **MEMBERSHIPS** SLS. **RESEARCH** American literature, literature and science, media theory. **SELECTED PUBLICATIONS** Auth, Postmodern Sublime: Technology and American Writing from Mailer to Cyberpunk, Cornell UP, 95; auth, Reading Matters: Narrative in the New Media Ecology, Cornell UP, 97. **CONTACT ADDRESS** Dept English, Univ of Illinois, Chicago, 601 S Morgan St, Chicago, IL 60607-7100. **EMAIL** jtabbi@uic.edu

TADIE, ANDREW A.
DISCIPLINE ENGLISH **EDUCATION** John Carroll Univ, BA, 66; Bradley Univ, MA, 67; St Louis Univ, PhD, 72. **CAREER** Eng, Seattle Univ. **RESEARCH** Seventeenth-century english literature; classical rhetoric; roman literature; G.K. Chesterton. **SELECTED PUBLICATIONS** Auth, The Popularization of English Deism: Lord Herbert of Cherbury's De Veritate and Sir William Davenant's The Siege of Rhodes, Acta Conventus Neo-Latini Bononesis, Paris: J Vrin, 85; coauth, A Problem of Audience: A Semiotical Approach to the Deistic Elements in The Siege of Rhodes, Semiotic Themes, Univ Kansas Press, 81; ed, Hakluyt's and Purchas Use of the Latin Version of Mandeville's Travels, Acta Conventus Neo-Latini Turonensis, Paris: J Vrin, 80; co-ed, Permanent Things, Eerdmans, 95; The Riddle of Joy, Eerdmans, 89, 2nd ed, 90; rev(s), William McFadden's Discovering the Comic: Studies in American Humor, 83-84; Castiglione: The Ideal and the Real in Renaissance Culture, The Hist, 85; introd to, Personal Recollections of Joan of Arc, Ignatius Press, 89. **CONTACT ADDRESS** Dept of Eng, Seattle Univ, 900 Broadway, Seattle, WA 98122-4460.

TADYCH, RENITA
PERSONAL Born 08/05/1934, Manitowoc, WI, s **DISCIPLINE** ENGLISH **EDUCATION** Silver Lake Col, BA, 60; Univ Dayton, MA, 72; Indiana Univ, Penn, PhD, 92. **CAREER** Elem edu, 13 yrs; sec edu, 16 yrs; prof, Silver Lake Col, 16 yrs. **HONORS AND AWARDS** Teach of Year, 66, 76; Who's Who, Am Edu, 98, 99. **MEMBERSHIPS** Wis Coun Teach Eng; Nat Coun Teach Eng. **RESEARCH** Shakespeare and literary criticism. **SELECTED PUBLICATIONS** Auth, "Reconstruction of Deconstruction," Wis Eng J (95). **CONTACT ADDRESS** Dept English, Silver Lake Col, 2406 South Alverno Rd, Manitowoc, WI 54220-9319. **EMAIL** srt@silver.sl.edu

TAKENAKA, MAKOTO
PERSONAL Born 07/01/1953, New Haven, CT, m, 1987, 2 children **DISCIPLINE** MUSIC **EDUCATION** ICU Tokyo, BA, 76; MEd, 78; Berklee Col Music, BM, 82. **CAREER** Assoc prof, Berklee, 89-; lectr, MIT, 88-90; lectr, Northeastern Univ, 88-92; lectr, Brandeis Univ, 97-90. **HONORS AND AWARDS** Magna Cum Laude, Berklee Col of Music, 82; concerts in Russia, Japan, Rumania, Hungary, England, Korea, & Costa Rica. **MEMBERSHIPS** Japan Asn of Greater Boston. **RESEARCH** Music, Jazz, Ethnic Music, Japanese. **SELECTED PUBLICATIONS** Auth, "Pianist Life in America," Harmonia (Tokyo, Japan), 97. **CONTACT ADDRESS** Dept Slavic & Eastern Lang, Boston Col, Chestnut Hill, 140 Commonwealth Ave, Chestnut Hill, MA 02467-3800. **EMAIL** takenama@bc.edu

TALIAFERRO, CHARLES
PERSONAL Born 08/25/1952, New York, NY, m, 1987 **DISCIPLINE** PHILOSOPHY & LITERATURE **EDUCATION** Univ Rhode Island, MA; Harvard Univ, MTS; Brown, MA & PhD, 94. **CAREER** Instr, Univ Mass, 82-84; instr, Univ Notre Dame, 84-85; vis scholar, Univ Oxford, 91-92; vis fel, Princeton Univ, 98-99; prof, philos, St. Olaf Col, 85-. **HONORS AND AWARDS** NEH fel, 91. **MEMBERSHIPS** Amer Philos Asn. **RESEARCH** Philosophy of mind; Philosophy of religion; Ethics. **SELECTED PUBLICATIONS** Auth, Praying with C. S. Lewis, St. Mary's Press, 98; auth, Contemporary Philosophy of Religion, Blackwell, 98; co-ed, A Companion to Philosophy of Religion, Blackwell, 97; auth, Consciousness and the Mind of God, Cambridge Univ Press, 94. **CONTACT ADDRESS** Dept. of Philosophy, St. Olaf Col, Northfield, MN 55057. **EMAIL** taliafer@stolaf.edu

TAMBURR, KARL
DISCIPLINE ENGLISH **EDUCATION** Princeton Univ, AB; VA Univ, MA; PhD. **CAREER** Prof, Sweet Briar Col. **HONORS AND AWARDS** Stu Govt Assn Excellence Tchg Awd, Sweet Briar Col, 93. **RESEARCH** Medieval lit; theology and iconography. **SELECTED PUBLICATIONS** Auth, articles on medieval drama and mysticism. **CONTACT ADDRESS** Sweet Briar Col, Sweet Briar, VA 24595.

TANDBERG, GERILYN
DISCIPLINE THEATRE **EDUCATION** Minot State, BS; Univ Minn, MA, PhD. **CAREER** Assoc prof, fac mem, Women's and Gender Stud dept, adj prof, Sch of Human Ecology, La State Univ. **SELECTED PUBLICATIONS** Published on the field of costume history in several journals. **CONTACT ADDRESS** Dept of Theatre, Louisiana State Univ and A&M Col, Baton Rouge, LA 70803. **EMAIL** gtandberg@home.com

TANKARD, JAMES WILLIAM
PERSONAL Born 06/20/1941, Newport News, VA, m, 1973, 3 children **DISCIPLINE** JOURNALISM **EDUCATION** VA Polytech Inst, BS 63; Univ NC, MA 65; Stanford Univ, PhD 70. **CAREER** Univ TX, Austin, vis asst prof 70; Univ WI, Madison, vis asst prof 70-71; Temple Univ, asst prof 71-72; Univ TX, Austin, asst prof 72-76, assoc prof 76-82, prof dept journalism 82-, Jesse H Jones Prof In Journalism, 89. **MEMBERSHIPS** Assn Edu in Jour Mass Commun; ICA; AAUP; **RESEARCH** Online journalism, inform graphics, sci reporting **SELECTED PUBLICATIONS** Samuel L Morison and the Government Crackdown on the Leaking of Classified Information, Journ Hist, 98; Propaganda Tests, in: Robert Cole, ed, The Ency of Propaganda, Sharpe Ref, 98; Expanding the News Frame: The Systems Theory Perspective, with Laura J Hendrickson, Jour Mass Comm Educator, 97; Communication Theories: Origins, Methods, Uses, with Werner J Severin, NT Longham, 97; Specificity and Imagery in Writing: Testing the Effects of Show, Don't tell, with Laura Hendrickson, Newspaper Res Journ, 96; Dorothy Thompson, in: Nancy Signorielli, ed, Women in Communication; Westport Ct, Greenwood Press, 96. **CONTACT ADDRESS** Dept of Journalism, Univ of Texas, Austin, Austin, TX 78712. **EMAIL** tankard@mail.utexas.edu

TANNER, JIM
DISCIPLINE ENGLISH LITERATURE **EDUCATION** Davidson Col, BA; Univ NC, MA, PhD. **CAREER** Assoc prof. **SELECTED PUBLICATIONS** Auth, pubs on rhetorical theory; stylistic analysis; composition pedagogy. **CONTACT ADDRESS** Dept of English, Colorado State Univ, Fort Collins, CO 80523-1773. **EMAIL** jtanner@vines.colostate.edu

TANNER, JOHN SEARS
PERSONAL Born 07/27/1950, Salt Lake City, UT, m, 1974, 5 children **DISCIPLINE** RENAISSANCE LITERATURE **EDUCATION** Brigham Young Univ, BA, 74; Univ Calif, Berkeley, PhD(English), 80. **CAREER** Teaching assoc Compos, Univ Calif, Berkeley, 78-80; vis instr, LDS Inst Relig, Berkeley, 77-79; asst prof Renaissance Lit & Rhet, Fla State Univ, 80-82; asst prof Renaissance Lit, Brigham Young Univ, 82-87, assoc prof to prof 87-92; Brigham Young Univ; from assoc prof to prof, 93-. **HONORS AND AWARDS** James Holly Hanford Award, 92: from the Milton Soc of Am for the most distinguished bk on John Milton published in 92; Honors prof of the year, Young Univ, distinguished lectr, Phi Kappa Phi, Young Univ; PA Christensen Lectr, Col of Humanities, Bringham Young Univ, 92-98; Fulbright Scholar to Brazil, 91. **MEMBERSHIPS** Milton Soc Am; MLA. **RESEARCH** Milton; Renaissance literature; religious literature and studies. **SELECTED PUBLICATIONS** Auth, The real world, Col English, 10/81; auth, Anxiety in Eden, Oxford UP, 92. **CONTACT ADDRESS** English Dept, Brigham Young Univ, 3146 Jkhb, Provo, UT 84602-0002. **EMAIL** john_tanner@byu.edu

TANNER, STEPHEN LOWELL
PERSONAL Born 04/18/1938, Ogden, UT, m, 1961, 3 children **DISCIPLINE** AMERICAN LITERATURE, LITERARY CRITICISM **EDUCATION** Univ Utah, BA, 62, MA, 64; Univ Wis, PhD (English), 69. **CAREER** From asst prof to assoc prof

English, Univ Idaho, 69-74; sr Fulbright lectr Am lit, Fed Univ Minas Gerais, Brazil, 74-76; assoc prof English, Univ Idaho, 76-78; assoc prof, 78-80, PROF ENGLISH, BRIGHAM YOUNG UNIV, 80-, Sr Fulbright lectr Am lit, Portugal, 79; Sr Fulbright lectr Am lit, Brazil, 83; Sr Fulbright lectr Am lit, Brazil, 89. **HONORS AND AWARDS** Ralph A. Britsch Humanities Prof of English, 95-; The Lionel Trilling Award, 99. **RESEARCH** American literature; literary criticism. **SELECTED PUBLICATIONS** Auth, Ken Kesey, 83; auth, Paul Elmer More: Literary Criticism as the History of Ideas, 87; Lionel Trilling, 88; auth, Ernest Haycox, 96. **CONTACT ADDRESS** Dept of English, Brigham Young Univ, Provo, UT 84601. **EMAIL** stephen_tanner@byu.edu

TANNER, WILLIAM EDWARD
PERSONAL Born 12/27/1937, Youngsport, TX **DISCIPLINE** BRITISH LITERATURE, RHETORIC **EDUCATION** Univ Tx, Austin, BA, 64; ETx State Univ, MA, 67; Univ Tulsa, PhD, 72. **CAREER** Instr French & English, Grayson County Col, 65-69; grad fel English & French, Univ Tulsa, 69-71; asst prof Humanities, Hendrix Col, 71-72; assoc prof English & chmn dept, Tex Col, 72-73; asst prof, 73-79, assoc prof English 85-99, prof English, 85-99, Tx Woman's Univ, prof emer, 99; Instr French, ETex State Univ, 68; writing consult Rhetoric, Commun Skills Ctr Col Teachers English, Augusta, Ga, 73 & Tex Col, 77-80; consult ed, English Tex, 80-. **HONORS AND AWARDS** Col English Asn Prof Achievement Awd, 94; Joe D Thomas Scholar Tchr, 94; Appreciation Awd Serv & Ldr Higher Educ, 94. **MEMBERSHIPS** NCTE; MLA; SCent Mod Lang Asn; Conf Col Compos & Commun; Milton Soc Am. **RESEARCH** Twentieth century rhetoric; bibliography; seventeenth-century British literature. **SELECTED PUBLICATIONS** Auth, The Arthurian Myth of Quest and Magic, ed Dallas: Caxton's Mod Arts Press, 93; Rhetorical Designs: A Teacher's Guide, ed Dallas: Caxton's Mod Arts Press, 94; Nonfiction Prose: A Special Issue of the CEA CRitic, ed Youngstown, OH:CEA, 98; Rhetoric and Technology in the Next Millennium, ed with Suzanne Webb, Caxton's Mod Arts Press, 98. **CONTACT ADDRESS** Dept of English & Speech, Texas Woman's Univ, PO Box 425829, Denton, TX 76204-5829. **EMAIL** wtanner@twu.edu

TANSELLE, GEORGE THOMAS
PERSONAL Born 01/29/1934, Lebanon, IN **DISCIPLINE** ENGLISH **EDUCATION** Yale Univ, BA, 55; Northwestern Univ, MA, 56; Northwestern, PhD, 59. **CAREER** Instr, 58-60, Chicago City Jr Col, Wright Br; from Asst Prof to Prof, 60-78, Univ Wis-Madison; Vice Pres, John Simon Guggenheim Mem Found, 78-; Mem, Planning Inst Comn Eng, Col Entrance Exam Bd, 61; Fel, Guggenheim, 69-70; Fel, Am Coun Learned Soc, 73-74; Fel, Nat Endow Humanities, 77-78; Mem Adv Comt, 70-73, Ctr Eds Am Authors; mem adv comt for drama for Bicentennial, 75-75, Kennedy Ctr; comt mem, 76-, Ctr for Scholarly Ed; mem, 76, Soviet-Am Symp Ed, Ind Univ; Adv, 77-, Ctr for the Bk, Libr Cong 76-8; Mem, 78-, North Am Comt for 18th Century Short Title Catalog; mem, comt on standards rare bk cataloging in machine readable form, 94-; Independent Res Libr Assn; bd dir & chmn, Ed Standards Comt, corp sec, 89-, Lit Classics US, Inc; mem adv comn, 80-92, N Am Imprints Prog; Hanes Lect, 81, Univ NC; mem adv coun, 80-, Rosenbach Mus & Lib; mem adv coun, 83-, Ind Univ Inst Adv Stud; mem fac, 84-, Sum Rare Bk Schl, mem adv bd, 85-94, Ctr for Amer Culture Stud, Columbia Univ; mem adv coun, 87-, Am Trust for the Brit Lib; lectr, 87, Rosenbach, Univ Pa; mem adv coun, 88-, Am Literary Manuscripts Proj; bd dir, 88-, 18th Century Short Title Catalogue/N Am Inc: chmn, 94-, Mark Twain Ed Proj, 91-, mem vis com, 88-92, Lilly Lib; mem adv bd, 90-, Ctr for Renaissance and Baroque Stud, Univ Md; mem adv com, 90-, Writings of J F Cooper. **HONORS AND AWARDS** Kiekhofer Tchng Awd, Univ Wisc, 63; Jenkins Awd in Bibliog, 73; Guggenheim fel, 69-70; Am Coun Learned Soc, fel, 73-74, NEH fel, 77-78; Laureate award, Am Printing Hist Assn, 87 . **MEMBERSHIPS** MLA; Bibliog Soc Am; Am Antiqn Soc; Mod Humanities Res Assn; London Bibliog Soc; Bibliog Soc Austrailia; Bibliog Soc Amer; Bibliog Soc Univ VA; Amer Antiquarian Soc; Melville Soc; Soc History of Authorship, Reading and Publishing; Phi Beta Kappa. **RESEARCH** American literature; analytical bibliography; publishing history. **SELECTED PUBLICATIONS** Auth, Royall Tyler, 67; auth, Guide to the Study of US Imprints, 71; auth, A Checklist of Eds of Moby Dick, 76; auth, Selected Studies in Bibliog, 79; auth, Textual Criticism since Greg, 87; auth, A Rationale of Textual Criticism, 89; auth, Textual Criticism and Scholarly Editing, 90; auth, The Life and Work of Fredson Bowers, 93; auth, Literature and Artifacts, 98. **CONTACT ADDRESS** John Simon Guggenheim Mem Found, 90 Park Ave, New York, NY 10016.

TAPPER, GORDON
DISCIPLINE ENGLISH, LITERATURE **EDUCATION** Colgate Univ, BA, 83; Columbia Univ, MA, 85; MPhil, 88; PhD, 00. **CAREER** Vis asst prof, Ctr Col, 99-01-. **HONORS AND AWARDS** Pres Fel, Columbia Univ, 85-88, 90-91. **MEMBERSHIPS** MLA. **RESEARCH** 20th-century literature and culture in the United States; American poetry; interdisciplinary approaches to modernism and post-modernism; contemporary art. **SELECTED PUBLICATIONS** Rev, "Contemporary Art," Zing Mag, citysearch.com (97-99); auth, "Introductory Essays on 20th-Century American Poets," American Literature: A Prentice Hall Anthology (91); auth, "Morton Minsky Reads the Bridge: Hart Crane and the Meaning of Burlesque," Ariz Quart (00). **CONTACT ADDRESS** 120 N 5th St, Danville, KY 40422-1416.

TARAN, LEONARDO
PERSONAL Born 02/22/1933, Galarza, Argentina, m, 1971, 1 child **DISCIPLINE** CLASSICS, ANCIENT PHILOSOPHY **EDUCATION** Princeton Univ, PhD, 62. **CAREER** Fel res, Inst Res Humanities, Univ Wis, 62-63; jr fel res, Ctr Hellenic Studies, 63-64; asst prof classics, Univ Calif, Los Angeles, 64-67; assoc prof, 67-71, chmn dept, 76-79, Prof, 71-87, Jay Prof Greek & Latin Langs, Columbia Univ, 87-; Am Philos Soc grant, 63, 71 & 75; fel Am Coun Learned Soc, 66-67, 71-72; Guggenheim Found fel, 75; mem Inst Advan Study, Princeton, 66-67 & 78-79; NEH fee. 1986-87. **MEMBERSHIPS** Am Philol Asn; Soc Ancient Greek Philos. **RESEARCH** Ancient philosophy; Greek literature. **SELECTED PUBLICATIONS** Auth, Parmenides, Princeton Univ, 65; Asclepius of Tralles: Commentary to Nicomachus' introduction to arithmetic, Am Philos Soc, 69; The creation myth in Plato's Timaeus, in Essays in Greek Philosophy, State Univ NY, 71; coauth, Eraclito, testimonianze e imitazioni, La Nuova Italia Editrice, 72; auth, Academica: Plato, Philip of Opus and the Pseudo-Platonic Epinomis, Am Philos Soc Memoirs, 75; Anonymous Commentary on Aristotle's de Interpretatione, Anton Hain, 78; Speusippus and Aristotle on homonymy and synonymy, Hermes, 106: 73-99; Speusippus of Athens, Leiden, Brill, 81. **CONTACT ADDRESS** Dept of Classics, Columbia Univ, 2960 Broadway, New York, NY 10027-6900. **EMAIL** lt1@columbia.edu

TARANOW, GERDA
PERSONAL Born New York, NY, s **DISCIPLINE** THEATRE HISTORY & ENGLISH **EDUCATION** NYork Univ, BA, 52; MA, 55; Yale Univ, PhD, 61. **CAREER** From instr to asst prof, Univ KY, 63-66; asst prof, Syracuse Univ, 66-67; from asst prof to assoc prof, 67-76, prof English, Conn Col, 76-; fel, Yale Univ, 62-63; NEH fel, 80-81, referee, 72-. **HONORS AND AWARDS** Delta Phi Alpha. **MEMBERSHIPS** MLA; Am Soc Theatre Res; Int Fed Theatre Res; Asn Recorded Sound Collections; Societe d'histoire du Theatre (France); Soc for Theatre Res (England). **RESEARCH** Shakespeare; drama; performance. **SELECTED PUBLICATIONS** Auth, Sarah Bernhardt: The Art Within the Legend, Princeton Univ, 72; The Bernhardt Hamlet: Culture and Context, Peter Lang, 97. **CONTACT ADDRESS** 292 Pequot Ave, Apt 2L, New London, CT 06320. **EMAIL** gtar@conncoll.edu

TARKOW, THEODORE A.
DISCIPLINE CLASSICAL STUDIES **EDUCATION** Oberlin Col, AB, 66; Univ Mich, MA, 67; Univ Mich, PhD, 71. **CAREER** Asst prof to prof, class studies, Univ Mo Columbia, 70-; assoc dean, col of arts and sci; Univ Mo Columbia, 82-. **HONORS AND AWARDS** Woodrow Wilson fel, 67; Amer Philos Asn award for excellence in teaching of the classics, 81; pres, Class Asn of Middlewest & South, 87. **MEMBERSHIPS** Amer Philol Asn; Archaeol Inst of Amer; Class Asn of Middlewest & South. **RESEARCH** Greek comedy & tragedy; Greek lyric poetry. **SELECTED PUBLICATIONS** Auth, Scan of Orestes, Rheinisches Mus fur Philol, 124; auth, Ainthes & the ghost of Aeschylus in Aristophanes Frogs, Traditio, 38; auth, Tyrtaeus 9D, L'antiquite Classique, 52; auth, Sight & Seeing in the Prometheus Board, Eranus, 89. **CONTACT ADDRESS** Univ of Missouri, Columbia, 317 Lowry Hall, Columbia, MO 65211. **EMAIL** tarkowt@missouri.edu

TARR, RODGER LEROY
PERSONAL Born 09/11/1941, Mercer, PA, m, 1982, 1 child **DISCIPLINE** NINETEENTH CENTURY ENGLISH LITERATURE **EDUCATION** Fla Southern Col, BA, 63; Kent State Univ, MA, 65; Univ SCar, PhD, 68. **CAREER** From asst prof to dist prof, Ill State Univ, 68-. **HONORS AND AWARDS** Res fel, Univ Edinburgh & Am Philos Soc res grant, 68-69; Fulbright Sr Res Scholar, Great Britain, 81; Nat Endowment for Humanities Sr Res Fel, 82. **MEMBERSHIPS** MLA **RESEARCH** Victorian novel and prose; bibliography. **CONTACT ADDRESS** Dept of English, Illinois State Univ, Normal, IL 61790-4240. **EMAIL** rtarr@ilstu.edu

TARRANT, RICHARD JOHN
PERSONAL Born 04/04/1945, New York, NY, m, 1968 **DISCIPLINE** CLASSICS **EDUCATION** Fordham Univ, BA, 66; Oxford Univ, DPhil, 72. **CAREER** From lectr to prof classics, Univ Toronto, 70-82; Prof Greek & Latin, Harvard Univ, 82-, Rev ed, Phoenix, Class Asn Can, 75-78, ed, 78-82. **MEMBERSHIPS** Am Philol Asn; Class Asn; Class Asn Can. **RESEARCH** Greek and Latin drama; Latin poetry; textual criticism. **SELECTED PUBLICATIONS** Auth, Greek and Latin Lyric Poetry in Translation, Am Philol Asn, 72; ed & auth, Seneca, Agamemnon, Cambridge Univ, 76; auth, Senecan drama and its antecedents, 78, The addressee of Virgil's eighth eclogue, 78 & Aeneas and the gates of sleep, 82, Harvard Studies Class Philol. **CONTACT ADDRESS** Dept of Greek & Latin, Harvard Univ, 319 Boylston Hall, Cambridge, MA 02138-3800.

TASCH, PETER ANTHONY
PERSONAL Born 11/28/1933, Brooklyn, NY, m, 1961, 3 children **DISCIPLINE** ENGLISH **EDUCATION** Bucknell Univ, AB, 54; Columbia Univ, MA, 59; Univ Edinburgh, dipl English studies, 60. **CAREER** Instr English, Western Md Col, 58-59 & Brooklyn Col, 60-61; from instr to asst prof, 64-72, ASSOC PROF ENGLISH, TEMPLE UNIV, 72-, Jr fel, Harvard Univ, 61-64, ed, Scriblerian & Kit-Cats, 68-; Danforth assoc, 81-. **MEMBERSHIPS** MLA; Am Soc 18th Century Studies. **RESEARCH** Restoration and 18th century drama; Kit-Cat and Scriblers Club members; 18th century novel. **SELECTED PUBLICATIONS** Ed, Fables of John Gay, Imprint Soc, 70; auth, The Dramatic Cobbler, Life of Isaac Bickerstaff, Bucknell Univ, 71; introd to Works of Issac Bickerstaff, 81; Works of George Colman, the Younger, Garland Press, 81. **CONTACT ADDRESS** Dept of English, Temple Univ, 1114 W Berks St, Philadelphia, PA 19122-6029.

TASSI, MARGUERITE
DISCIPLINE ENGLISH RENAISSANCE DRAMA **EDUCATION** Columbia Univ, BA; Univ Va, MA, Claremont Grad Sch, PhD. **CAREER** Instr, Middlebury Col; asst prof, Univ Nebr, Kearney. **RESEARCH** Views of painting in English Renaissance drama. **SELECTED PUBLICATIONS** Published articles on the theaters of Shakespeare and Beckett and on 19th-century English views of Florence. **CONTACT ADDRESS** Univ of Nebraska, Kearney, Kearney, NE 68849.

TATE, CLAUDIA
DISCIPLINE ENGLISH **EDUCATION** Univ Mich, AB, 68; Harvard Univ, MA, 71; PhD, 77. **HONORS AND AWARDS** NEH; Ford Foundation, ACLS Fel; Nat Humanities Ctr Fel. **SELECTED PUBLICATIONS** Auth, Domestic Allegories of Political Desire: The Black Heroines Text at the turn of the century, Oxford, 93; auth, Psychoanalysis and Black Novels: Desire and the Protocols of Race, Oxford, 98. **CONTACT ADDRESS** Dept English Dept English, Princeton Univ, 15 McCosh Hall, Princeton, NJ 08540.

TATE, GEORGE SHELDON
PERSONAL Born 09/07/1944, Santa Monica, CA, m, 1988, 6 children **DISCIPLINE** MEDIEVAL LITERATURE **EDUCATION** Brigham Young Univ, BA, 69; MA, 70; Cornell Univ, PhD(Medieval studies), 74. **CAREER** Asst prof, 74-79, assoc prof Comp Lit, Brigham Young Univ, 86-, Chmn dept, Humanities, Class & Comp Lit, 81-85, 96-00; assoc dean Gen Ed & Honors, 86-90; dean Gen Ed & Honors, 00-. **HONORS AND AWARDS** Fulbright Fel Ireland, 71-72; Marshall Fel Denmark, 73; P A Christensen Lectureship, 85-86; Karl G Maeser Gen Ed professorship, 93-96; Alcuin Fellowship, 98-01. **MEMBERSHIPS** Mediaeval Acad Am; Soc Advan Scand Studies; Int Soc for the Classical Tradition; Classical Assn of Middle West and South. **RESEARCH** Old Norse literature, 12th-Century Renaissance **SELECTED PUBLICATIONS** Ed, Liknarbraut: A Skaldic Drapa on the Cross, Univ Microfilms, 74; auth, Good Friday Liturgy and the Structure of Liknarbraut, Scand Studies, 78; Chiasmus as Metaphor: The Figura Crucis Tradition and The Dream of the Rood, Neuphilologische Mitteilungen, 78; The Cross as Ladder: Geisli 15-16 and Liknarbraut 34, Mediaeval Scand, 78; Halldor Laxness, the Mormons, and the Promised Land, Dialogue, 78; Fertility, ergi, and Violence in Laxdoela saga, Allegonca, 89; Undifferentiation and Violence: Girard and the Sagas, Epic and Epoch, ed Oberhelman, 94; The Rest After the Desert: Ending Confessions, JRMMRA, 95-96. **CONTACT ADDRESS** Dept of General Edu & Honors, Brigham Young Univ, 302 MSRB, Provo, UT 84602. **EMAIL** george_tate@byu.edu

TATUM, NANCY R.
PERSONAL Born 08/14/1930, Pittsburg, KS **DISCIPLINE** ENGLISH LITERATURE & HISTORY **EDUCATION** Univ Ark, BA, 52; Bryn Mawr Col, MA, 54, PhD, 60. **CAREER** Instr English & asst to dean, Lake Erie Col, 58-59; from instr to assoc prof, 60-69, Prof English, Washingotn Col, 69-, Ernest A Howard Prof, 79-99; Ernest A Howard, Prof Emerita, 99. **MEMBERSHIPS** MLA; Shakespeare Asn Am. **RESEARCH** Restoration drama; Shakespearean stage technique; seventeenth century English social and economic history. **CONTACT ADDRESS** Dept of English, Washington Col, 300 Washington Ave, Chestertown, MD 21620-1197.

TAVE, STUART MALCOLM
PERSONAL Born 04/10/1923, New York, NY, m, 1948, 4 children **DISCIPLINE** ENGLISH **EDUCATION** Columbia Univ, BA, 43; Harvard Univ, MA, 47; Oxford, DPhil(English), 50. **CAREER** Lectr English, Columbia Univ, 50-51; from instr to prof, 51-71, chemn dept, 72-78, master col div humanities & assoc dean col, 66-70, dean of humanities, 84-89,William Rainey Harper Prof English, 71-93, prof emer, Univ Chicago, 93-; Guggenheim fel, 59-60; vis assoc prof, Univ WI, 62 & Stanford Univ, 63; vis prof, Univ WA, 66; vis prof, WA Univ, 80 (Hurst prof); vis prof, Hawaii, 83 (Citizens prof); Am Coun Learned Soc fel, 70-71; Nat Endowment for Humanities fel, 78-79; Hurst prof, WA Univ, 80. **HONORS AND AWARDS** Quantrell Awd, Univ Chicago, 58; Laing Prize, Univ Chicago Press, 74; Hon D H L Ripon Col, 86; Ryerson lect, 91; Stuart Tave fel, 93-; Rockefeller Bellagio Residency, 98; Norman Ma-

clean, Fac Awd, 00. **MEMBERSHIPS** MLA. **RESEARCH** 18th and 19th century English literature. **SELECTED PUBLICATIONS** Auth, Amiable Humorist, Univ Chicago, 60; New Essays by De Quincey, Princeton Univ, 66; Some Words of Jane Austen, Univ Chicago, 73; ed, Bage's Hermsprong, PN State Univ, 82; Lovers, Clowns, and Fairies, Univ Chicago, 93. **CONTACT ADDRESS** 1050 E 59th St, Chicago, IL 60637-1476.

TAWA, NICHOLAS E.
PERSONAL Born 10/22/1923, Boston, MA, m, 1947, 2 children **DISCIPLINE** MUSICOLOGY **EDUCATION** Harvard Univ, BA, 45; Boston Univ, MA, 47; Harvard Univ, PhD, 74. **CAREER** Full Prof to 94, Prof Emeritus, Univ Mass-Boston, 94-. **HONORS AND AWARDS** Distinguished School Award, Univ Mass, 90 **MEMBERSHIPS** Sonneck Soc. **RESEARCH** Music in America. **SELECTED PUBLICATIONS** Auth, The Way to Tin Pan Alley: American Popular Song, 1886-1910, Schirmer, 90; auth, The Coming-of-Age of American Art Music, Greenwood, 91; auth, Mainstream Music of Early Twentieth-Century America: The Composers, Their Words, and Their Times, Greenwood, 92; auth, American Composers and Their Public: A Critical Look, Scarecrow, 95; auth, Arthur Foote: A Musician in the Frame of Time and Place, Scarecrow Press, 97; auth, Hifgh-Minded and Low-Down: Music in the Lives of americans, 1800-1861, Boston: Northeastern Univ Press, 00. **CONTACT ADDRESS** 69 Undine Rd., Boston, MA 02135-3811. **EMAIL** ntawa@worldnet.att.net

TAYLER, EDWARD W.
PERSONAL Born 03/13/1931, Berlin, Germany, m, 5 children **DISCIPLINE** ENGLISH LITERATURE **EDUCATION** Amherst Col, BA, 54; Stanford Univ, PhD, 60. **CAREER** Instructor, Stanford; vis prof, Princeton, Bread Loaf School of English; Columbia Univ, 60-; exec board of the English inst; dir, seventeenth-century division and the Milton general session, MLA; lecturer, Eichstatt (Germany), Fu Jen Univ (Taiwan), Huntington Libr, Illinois, Middlebury, Mount Holyoke (McGee Lecture), SMU, Univ of Calif (Davis, Los Angeles, Riverside), Virginia, West Point, Wesleyan; editorial boards of the Ben Jonson Jour and John Donne Jour. **HONORS AND AWARDS** Guggenheim fel, 68; grants, NEH-Huntington, 75, 83; great tchr award, Soc Older Grad, 85; Mark Van Doren award, 86; hon scholar, Milton Soc, 89; pres award for tchg, 96; distinguished service to the core curriculum, 98; exec bd, eng inst; ch, seventeenth-century div, mla. **MEMBERSHIPS** Renaissance Soc; Milton Soc; Spenser Soc; Acad Lit Stud. **SELECTED PUBLICATIONS** Auth, Nature and Art in Renaissance Literature, Columbia 64; auth, Literary Criticism of Seventeenth-Century England, Knopf, 67; auth, Milton's Poetry, Duqesne 79; auth, Donne's Idea of a Woman, Columbia, 91. **CONTACT ADDRESS** Dept of Eng, Columbia Univ, 609 Philosophy, New York, NY 10027.

TAYLOR, ARVILLA KERNS
PERSONAL Born 02/06/1931, San Antonio, TX **DISCIPLINE** RENAISSANCE & ENGLISH LITERATURE **EDUCATION** Univ Tex, Austin, BA, 51, MA, 53, PhD(English lit), 69. **CAREER** Instr hist, San Antonio Jr Col, 57; asst prof English, Colo State Univ, 65-66; asst prof, Wichita State Univ, 67-69; ASSOC PROF ENGLISH, MIDWESTERN UNIV, 69- **HONORS AND AWARDS** Tchg excellence awd. **MEMBERSHIPS** S Cent Mod Lang Asn; AAUP; SCRA; CCTE. **RESEARCH** Medieval and Renaissance as the same world order, comparative French, German, Spanish and English literature; man's limitations and potentials; Shakespeare and Conrad, existential heroes in action. **CONTACT ADDRESS** Dept of English, Midwestern Univ, 3410 Taft Blvd, Wichita Falls, TX 76308-2096. **EMAIL** ftaylora@mwsu.edu

TAYLOR, BEVERLY W.
PERSONAL Born 03/30/1947, Grenada, MS **DISCIPLINE** ENGLISH, LITERATURE **EDUCATION** Univ Miss, BA, 69; Duke Univ, MA, 70; PhD, 77. **CAREER** Instr, Memphis State Univ, 70-72; From Assoc Prof to Prof, Univ of NC Chapel Hill, 77-. **HONORS AND AWARDS** Am Philos Asn Grant; Am Coun of Learned Societies Grant; Nat Endowment for the Humanities Grant. **MEMBERSHIPS** MLA, Int Arthurian Soc, Victorians Inst, Nineteenth Century Studies Asn, Tennyson Soc. **RESEARCH** Arthurian Legend, Victorian Literature and Art. **SELECTED PUBLICATIONS** Auth, "Using the Visual Art to Teach 19th-Century Arthurian Literature," in Approaches to Teaching the Arthurian Tradition, MLA, 92; auth, "Victorian Camelot and the Pictorial Imagination," in Moderne Artusrezeption (Jahruhundert, Alfred Kummerle, 92), 18-20; auth, "'School-Miss Alfred' and 'Materfamilias': Female Sexuality and Poetic Voice in The Princess Aurora Leigh," in Gender and Discourse in Victorian Literature and Art (Northern Ill Univ, 92); ed, Gender and Discourse in Victorian Literature and Art, Northern Ill Univ, 92; auth, "Elizabeth Barrett Browning and the Annuals: Feminist Challenges to the 'Feminine'," Postscript (93); auth, "Elizabeth Barrett Browning's Subversion of the Gift Book Model," Studies in Browning and His Circle (93); auth, "Beatrix/Creatrix: Elizabeth Siddal as Muse and Creator," J of Pre-Raphaelite Studies (95); auth, "Female Savants: The Erotics of Knowledge in Pre-Raphaelite Art," in Collecting the Pre-Raphaelites (Scolar, 97); auth, "Re-Vamping Vivien: Reinventing Myth as Victorian Icon," in King Arthur's Modern Return (Garland, 98); auth, "Elizabeth Barrett Browning and the Romantic Child," in Studies n Browning and His Circle (00). **CONTACT ADDRESS** Dept English, Univ of No Carolina, Chapel Hill, CB 3520, Chapel Hill, NC 27599-2319. **EMAIL** btaylor@email.unc.edu

TAYLOR, BRYAN C.
DISCIPLINE COMMUNCATION STUDIES **EDUCATION** Univ Mass, BA, 83; Univ Utah, MA, 87, PhD, 91. **CAREER** Assoc prof. **MEMBERSHIPS** Speech Commun Asn, 87-; Western States Commun Asn, 85-. **RESEARCH** Organizational communication; interpretive research methods; critical theory; cultural studies. **SELECTED PUBLICATIONS** Auth, Make Bomb, Save World: Reflections on Dialogic Nuclear Ethnography, Jour Contemp Ethnography, 96; Revis(it)ing Nuclear History: Narrative Conflict at the Bradbury Science Museum, 96; Home Zero: Images of Home and Field in Nuclear-Cultural Studies, Western Jour Commun, 96; The Bomb in Pop Culture, 95; Visions of the Past: The challenge of film to our idea of hisfory (rev), 96. **CONTACT ADDRESS** Dept of Communication, Univ of Colorado, Boulder, Boulder, CO 80309. **EMAIL** taylorbc@stripe.colorado.edu

TAYLOR, CINDY
DISCIPLINE AMERICAN LITERATURE, WOMEN IN LITERATURE, SOUTHWESTERN LITERATURE **EDUCATION** Univ ID, BA, 77, MA, 79; Univ MN, PhD, 93. **CAREER** Asst prof, Univ of Southern Co. **RESEARCH** 20th century Am lit; women in lit; western lit; native Am lit; lit; environment. **SELECTED PUBLICATIONS** Auth, "Coming to Terms with the Image of the Mother in The Stone Angel," New Perspectives on Margaret Laurence, ed. Greta Coger (New York: Greenwood Press, 96); auth, "Claiming Female Space: Mary Austin's Western Landscapes," in The Big Empty: Essays on the Land as Narrative, ed. Leonard Engel (Alburquerque: Univ of New Mexico Press). **CONTACT ADDRESS** Dept of Eng, Univ of So Colorado, 2200 Bonforte Blvd, Pueblo, CO 81001-4901. **EMAIL** Ctaylor@meteor.uscolo.edu

TAYLOR, DANIEL JENNINGS
PERSONAL Born 09/01/1941, Covington, KY, m, 1966, 2 children **DISCIPLINE** CLASSICS, LINGUISTICS **EDUCATION** Lawrence Col, BA, 63; Univ Wash, MA, 65, PhD(classics), 70. **CAREER** From instr to asst prof classics, Univ Ill, Urbana, 68-74; asst prof, 74-78, Assoc Prof Classics, Lawrence Univ, 78-, Chmn Dept, 75-, Actg vpres & dean for Campus life, Lawrence Univ, 77-78, 79-80; Nat Endowment for Humanities fel, 80-81. **MEMBERSHIPS** Am Philol Asn; Am Class League; Archaeological Inst Am. **RESEARCH** Syntax of Greek and Latin; history of linguistics; Varro. **SELECTED PUBLICATIONS** Auth, Rationalism in language learning, Asn Dept Foreign Lang Bull, 72; Aspects of negation in classical Greek, Studies Ling Sci, 72; Declinatio: A Study of the Linguistic Theory of MT Varro, Amsterdam: John Benjamins, 74; Varro, De Lingua Latina, 76 & Two notes on Varro, 77, Am J of Philol; Varro's mathematical models of inflection, Trans & Proc Am Philol Asn, 77; Ordo in book ten of Varro's De Lingua Latina, Melanges Collart, 78; Palaemon's Pig, Historiographia Linguistica, 81. **CONTACT ADDRESS** 115 S Drew St, Appleton, WI 54911-5798.

TAYLOR, DONALD STEWART
PERSONAL Born 08/08/1924, Portland, OR, m, 1952, 3 children **DISCIPLINE** ENGLISH **EDUCATION** Univ CA, AB, 47, MA, 48, PhD, 50. **CAREER** Instr Eng, Northwestern Univ, 50-54; from instr to assoc prof, Univ WA, 54-68; prof eng, Univ OR, 68, actg head classics, 75-78. **HONORS AND AWARDS** Guggenheim fel, 72-73. **RESEARCH** Textual criticism; 18th century Eng lit; theory of lit hist. **SELECTED PUBLICATIONS** Auth, Catalytic rhetoric: Henry Green's theory of the modern novel, Criticism, 65; Complete Works of Chatterton, Clarendon, 71; R G Collingwood: art, craft and history, 6/73 & Literary criticism and historical inference, 76, Clio; Thomas Chatterton's Art: Experiments in Imagined History, Princeton Univ, 78; Johnson on the Metaphysicals, Eighteenth Century Life, 86. **CONTACT ADDRESS** Dept of Eng, Univ of Oregon, Eugene, OR 97403-1205. **EMAIL** dstaylor@oregon.uoregon.edu

TAYLOR, E. DENNIS
PERSONAL Born 02/26/1940, Baltimore, MD, m, 1966, 4 children **DISCIPLINE** ENGLISH **EDUCATION** Col of the Holy Cross, BA, 60; Yale Univ, PhD, 65. **CAREER** Instr, Bowdoin Col, 62-63; asst prof, Univ Calif Santa Barbara, 65-71; prof, Boston Col, 71-. **HONORS AND AWARDS** Mellon Fel, 81-82; Res Grant, Boston Col, 86-90; Macmillan/Hardy Soc Prize, 90; Fel, Erasmus Inst, Univ of Notre Dame, 00. **MEMBERSHIPS** MLA, Thomas Hardy Soc. **RESEARCH** Shakespeare and the Reformation, The Great Transition: Traditional to Free Verse. **SELECTED PUBLICATIONS** Auth, Hardy's Poetry 1860-1928, Macmillan (London), 81; auth, Hardy's Metres and Victorian Prosody, Oxford Univ Pr, 88; auth, Hardy's Language and Victorian Philology, Oxford Univ Pr, 93; ed, Jude the Obscure by Thomas Hardy, Penguin, 98. **CONTACT ADDRESS** Boston Col, Chestnut Hill, 24 Lawrence Ave, Chestnut Hill, MA 02467. **EMAIL** taylor@bc.edu

TAYLOR, GORDON OVERTON
PERSONAL Born 10/01/1938, Los Angeles, CA, m, 1964, 1 child **DISCIPLINE** ENGLISH, AMERICAN LITERATURE **EDUCATION** Harvard Univ, AB, 60; Univ Calif, Berkeley, MA, 62, PhD(Am Lit), 67. **CAREER** From instr English to lectr, Harvard Univ, 66-69; asst prof, Univ Calif, Berkeley, 69-76; assoc prof, 76-81, chmn, 81, prof English, grad fac Mod Lett, Univ Tulsa, 81-, chmn fac English Language & Literature, 82-, Chapman prof of Eng, 95-; John Simon Guggenheim Mem Found fel, 80-81; vis assoc prof English, Harvard Univ, Summer 81. **MEMBERSHIPS** MLA; AAUP; S Cent Mod Lang Asn. **RESEARCH** Nineteenth and 20th century American literature; American cultural history. **SELECTED PUBLICATIONS** Auth, The Passages of Thought: Psychological Representation in the American Novel, 1870-1900, Oxford Univ, 69; Of Adams and Aquarius, Am Lit, 3/74; American personal narrative of the war in Vietnam, Am Lit, 5/80; Voices from the veil: Black American autobiography, Georgia Rev, Summer 81; auth, Chapters of Experience: Modern American Autobiography, Macmillan/St. Martin's, 83; The Vietnam War & Postmodern Memory (guest ed.), special issue of Genre, Winter 88; The Country I Had Thought Was My Home: David Mura's Turning Japanese and Japanese American Narrative since World War II, Connotations, 6/97. **CONTACT ADDRESS** Fac English Lang & Lit, Univ of Tulsa, 600 S College, Tulsa, OK 74104-3189. **EMAIL** gordon-taylor@utulsa.edu

TAYLOR, HENRY
PERSONAL Born 06/21/1942, Loudoun County, VA, m, 1995, 2 children **DISCIPLINE** ENGLISH LITERATURE **EDUCATION** Univ VA, BA 65; Hollins Col, MA 66. **CAREER** Roanoke Col, instr, 66-68; Univ Utah, asst prof, 68-71; Amer Univ, assoc prof, prof, 71 to 76-; Univ Utah Writers Conf, dir 69-71; Hollins College, writer in res, 78; The Amer Univ MFA creative writ, co-dir, 82-; Amer Univ, ASP dir, 83-85; Wichita State Univ, dist poet in res, 94; Randolph-Macon Womens College, poet in res, 97. **HONORS AND AWARDS** Acad Amer Poets Prize; Rinetti Mem IT Essay Awd; Ralph W Collins Fel; NEH Fel; Witter Bynner Prize; NEA Fel; Pulitzer Prize In poetry 86; Doc Human Letters Shen College Con; Golden Crane Awd; ME Fest Poetry Slam Winner, 96, 98, 99; Dict Lit Biog Awd of Merit; Sm Press Bk Awd finalist; Who's Who In: Amer, S & SE, East, US Writers Editors and Poets, Emerging Leaders of Amer, the World; directory listings in: contemp auth, dictionary lit biog, contemp lit criticism, contemp auth autobiog series, oxford companion to twentieth-cent poetry, oxford comp to amer lit, contemporary poets. **SELECTED PUBLICATIONS** Auth, Understanding Fiction: Poems 1986-1996, Baton Rouge, Louisiana State Univ Press, 96; trans, Leaves From the Dry Tree, by Vladimir Levchev, NY, Cross Cult Comm, 96; auth, Compulsory Figures: Essays on Recent American Poets, BR, Louisiana State U Press, 92; The Horse Show At Midnight and an Afternoon of Pocket Billiards, BR, Louisiana State U Press, 92; auth, Brief Candles: 101 Clerihews, LSU, 00; trans, Black Book of the Endangered Species, Wordwales, DC, 99; trans, Sophocles' Electra, Penn Greek Drama Series, 98. **CONTACT ADDRESS** Dept of Literature, American Univ, Washington, DC 20016. **EMAIL** htaylor@american.edu

TAYLOR, HERMAN DANIEL
PERSONAL Born 02/26/1937, Yazoo City, MS, m **DISCIPLINE** MUSIC **EDUCATION** Chicago Musical Coll of Roosevelt Univ, BMus 1963; Univ of MI, MMus 1974, AMusD 1976. **CAREER** Southern Univ, instr of music 1963-67; Dillard Univ, instr of music 1969-73; Prairie View A&M Univ, assoc prof of music 1976-77; Dillard Univ, prof ofmusic 1977-. **HONORS AND AWARDS** Artist Fellowship Awd LA State Arts Council 1984; Performing from memory all the organ works of JS Bach in US & in Europe 1984-85; UNCF Disting Faculty Scholar 1985-86 **MEMBERSHIPS** State chmn Amer Guild of Organists; volunteer for the Heart Fund 1978-; asst club scout master 1984-85. **CONTACT ADDRESS** Professor of Music, Dillard Univ, 2601 Gentilly Blvd, New Orleans, LA 70122.

TAYLOR, JACQUELINE S.
PERSONAL Born 04/04/1951, Owensboro, KY, 2 children **DISCIPLINE** COMMUNICATION **EDUCATION** Georgtown Col, BA, 73; Univ TX, MA, 77, PhD, 80. **CAREER** Asst prof, 80-87, assoc prof, 87-92, full prof of Commun, DePaul Univ, 92-; assoc dean, Liberal Arts and Sciences, 95-99, dir, DePaul Humanities Center, 99-. **HONORS AND AWARDS** NEH summer grant, 88; hon fel, Women's Studies Res Center, Univ WI, Madison, July-Dec 93. **MEMBERSHIPS** Nat Commun Asn. **RESEARCH** Performing autobiography. **SELECTED PUBLICATIONS** Auth, Grace Paley: Illuminating the Dark Lives, Univ TX Press, 90; Performing the (Lesbian) Self: Teacher as Text, in Queer Words, Queer Images: Communication and the Construction of Homosexuality, R Jeffrey Ringer, ed, NY Univ Press, 94; Is There a Lesbian in this Text?: Sarton, Performance and Multicultural Pedagogy, Text and Performance Quart 15, Oct 95; with Lynn Miller, Editor's Introduction, special issue on Performing Autobiography, Text and Performance Quart, 17, Oct 97; Performing Commitment, in Readings in Cultural Contexts, Judith Martin, Tom Nakayama, and Lisa Flores, eds, Mayfield Pub Co, 98; Response to Strine's Essay, in Future of Performance Studies: The Next Millenium, ed Sheron Dailey, forthcoming; several other publications.

CONTACT ADDRESS Col of Liberal Arts and Sciences, DePaul Univ, 2320 N Kenmore, Chicago, IL 60614. **EMAIL** jtaylor@condor.depaul.edu

TAYLOR, JAMES R.

PERSONAL Born 12/13/1928, NB, Canada, m, 1966, 2 children **DISCIPLINE** COMMUNICATION **EDUCATION** Univ Penn, PhD 77; Mt Allison Univ, Sackville NB Canada, BA, MA. **CAREER** CBC, radio/tv producer, regional suprv pub affs productions, 56-66; Univ Penn, PhD stud, hd of Tv Lab, 66-70; Univ Montreal Canada, prof comm, 71-98. **HONORS AND AWARDS** Beaverbrook Overseas Sch. **MEMBERSHIPS** ICA; NCA; CCA; ACM. **RESEARCH** Communication theory; organization and communication; computerization of work. **SELECTED PUBLICATIONS** Auth, The Limits of Rationality: Asemiotic Reinterpretation of the Concept of speech Act, Stockholm Swed, 98; coauth, "A case of telecommuncations (mis) management," Management Communcation Quarterly, 12, (99), 580-599; coauth, "L'evolution du discours sur la qualite: d'une traduction a l'autre," Communcation et organisation, 15, (99), 39-68; coauth, "The procedural and rhetorical modesof te organizing dimension of communcation: discursive analysis of a Parliamentary Commission," Communication Rev, 3, (99), 65-101; auth, "What is organizational communciation?" Communication as a dialogic of text and conversation, Commun Rev, 3, (99); auth, "The other side of rationality: Socially distriburted cognition," Management Commun Quarterly, 13, (99), 317-326; coauth, The emergent organization: Communication as its site and surface, Mahwah, NJ: Lawrence Erlbaum Assoc, 00; auth, Is there a "Canadian approch to the studyof organizational communciation?, Millennium issue of the Can J of Commun; auth, What is an organization? Elelctronic J of Communication/La Revue Electronique de Commun, 00; coauth, "Association and dissociation in an ecological controversy: The great whale case," Norwood, NJ: Ablex, (00), 171-190; **CONTACT ADDRESS** Dept of Communication, Univ of Montreal, 3051 Cedar Ave, Montreal, QC, Canada H3Y 1Y8. **EMAIL** taylor@com.umontreal.ca

TAYLOR, JAMES SHEPPARD

PERSONAL Born 12/15/1943, Montgomery, AL, m, 1972, 2 children **DISCIPLINE** SPEECH **EDUCATION** Auburn Univ, BA, 65, MA, 66; Fla State Univ, PhD(speech), 68. **CAREER** Asst prof speech, NC State Univ, 68-69; asst prof, Auburn Univ, 69-73; assoc prof, 73-77, prof speech, Houston Baptist Univ, 77-, chmn dept, 73-98, dean, Arts & Humanities, 98-. **HONORS AND AWARDS** Teaching Excellence Awd, 76-77, 88-89; Sears Found Teaching Excellence and Campus Leadership Awd, 89-90; Piper Nominee, 88-89, 89-90. **MEMBERSHIPS** AAUP; Nat Commun Asn. **RESEARCH** Experimental persuasion; American public address; group dynamics. **SELECTED PUBLICATIONS** Coauth, William Huskisson and free trade, NC J Speech, 72; Loyalist propaganda in the sermons of Charles Inglis, 1770-1780, Western Speech, 73; Charles T Walker: The black spurgeon, Ga Speech J, 73. **CONTACT ADDRESS** Col of Arts and Humanities, Houston Baptist Univ, 7502 Fondren Rd, Houston, TX 77074-3298. **EMAIL** jtaylor@hbu.edu

TAYLOR, MARK

PERSONAL Born 03/13/1939, White Plains, NY, m, 2 children **DISCIPLINE** ENGLISH LITERATURE **EDUCATION** Yale Univ, AB, 61; City Univ New York, MA, 65, PhD(English), 69. **CAREER** Asst prof, 69-75, chmn dept, 78-82, assoc prof to prof English, Manhatten Col, 75-82, Poetry ed, Commonweal Mag, 72. **MEMBERSHIPS** Assoc of Literary Scholars and Critics. **RESEARCH** Shakespeare; the Renaissance; modern fiction. **SELECTED PUBLICATIONS** Auth, Baseball as myth, 5/72, History, humanism and Simone Weil, 8/73 & W H Auden's vision of Eros, 10/73, Commonweal; The Soul in Paraphrase: George Herbert's Poetics, Mouton, 74; War novels, 9/77, Words and idioms, 1/78 & On biography, 1/80, Commonwealth; Shakespeare's Darker Purpose, AMS Press, 82; Farther Privileges: Conflict and Change in Measure for Measure, Philological Quarterly, 73, 94. **CONTACT ADDRESS** Dept of English, Manhattan Col, 4513 Manhattan Coll, Bronx, NY 10471-4004. **EMAIL** mtaylor@manhatten.edu

TAYLOR, MICHAEL

PERSONAL Born 09/20/1959, Daytona Beach, FL, m, 1983, 3 children **DISCIPLINE** JOURNALISM **EDUCATION** Fla State Univ, BA, 80; Univ S C, MA, 89; Univ Ark, MFA, 96. **CAREER** Instr to Prof, Henderson State Univ, 91-. **HONORS AND AWARDS** Best Am Sports Writing, 95; Poetry Awd, Francis Marion Writer's Retreat, 90; Bread Loaf Scholarship, 89 **MEMBERSHIPS** Asn for Educ in Journalism and Mass Comm, Ark Press Asn, Nat Speleological Soc, NSS Pub Marketing Committee, Author's Guild. **SELECTED PUBLICATIONS** Auth, Amazing Caves: Journeys Into a Hidden Realm, Nat Geog Soc, forthcoming; auth, Dark Life: Marian Nanobacteria, Rock-Eating Cave Bugs, and Other Extreme Organisms of Inner Earth and Outer Space, Scribner Pub, 99; auth, Cave Passages: Roaming the Underground Wilderness, Scribner Pub, 96; auth, Lechuguilla: Jewel of the Underground, Speleo Projects, 91; auth, "Searching for DeSoto's Cross," Am Archeol, 00; auth, "Mars Polar Lander Found/" The Discovery Channel Online, 00; auth, "Explorers Probe Israeli Sub Mystery," The Discovery Channel Online, 00; auth, "What Went Wrong?," The Discovery Channel Online, 99; auth, "NASA to Review Mars Effort," The Discovery Channel Online, 99; auth, "Last Mars Lander Effort Tuesday,: The Discovery Channel Online, 99; auth, "NASA Not Giving Up, The Discovery Channel Online, 99; auth, "Landing Site Found, Still No Word," The Discovery Channel Online 99; auth, "No signal From Lander," The Discovery Channel Online, 99; auth, "Weather clear For Mars Landing," The Discovery Channel Online, 99; auth, "NASA's Landing Jitters Justified," The Discovery Channel Online 99; auth, "The art of chasing," Portfolio, 85; **CONTACT ADDRESS** Dept Comm Arts & Sci, Henderson State Univ, 1100 Henderson St, Arkadelphia, AR 71999-0001. **EMAIL** taylorm@hsu.edu

TAYLOR, ORLANDO L.

PERSONAL Born 08/09/1936, Chattanooga, TN, m, 1957 **DISCIPLINE** COMMUNICATIONS **EDUCATION** Hampton Institute, Hampton VA, BS, 1957; Indiana Univ, Bloomington IN, MA, 1960; Univ of Michigan, Ann Arbor MI, PhD, 1966. **CAREER** Indiana Univ, Bloomington IN, asst prof, 64-69; Center for Applied Linguistics, Washington DC, senior research fellow, 69-75; Univ of District of Columbia, Washington DC, prof, 70-73; Howard Univ, Washington DC, Prof, 73-; Dean of Communications, 85-. **HONORS AND AWARDS** Distinguished scholar award, Howard Univ, 1984; Awd of Appreciation, American Speech-Language-Hearing Association, 1990. **CONTACT ADDRESS** Sch of Communications, Howard Univ, Washington, DC 20059.

TAYLOR, SUSAN L.

DISCIPLINE WOMEN'S STUDIES, COMPOSITION **EDUCATION** Univ S Fla, BA, magna cum laude, 86; Fla State Univ, MA, 90, PhD, 94. **CAREER** Grad tchg asst, 87-93, vis instr, Fla State Univ, 93-94; lectr, 94-95, dir, Writing Ctr, 94-95, asst dir, freshman compos, 94-97, asst prof, 95-, dir, compos, Univ Nev, Las Vegas, 97-. **HONORS AND AWARDS** Eng Dept Excellence in Tchg Awd, 92, Univ Excellence in Tchg Awd, Fla State Univ, 93; State of Nev award for Distance Lrng, 96, 97. **MEMBERSHIPS** NCTE. **RESEARCH** Textbook selection. **SELECTED PUBLICATIONS** Auth, Time and Timelessness in Frank Waters' People of the Valley and Isak Dinesen's "The Blank Page," Stud in Frank Waters, 95; For a Good Time Type http://www.geekgirl.com.au/, Electronic Bk Rev, 96; Babes, BluBlockers, and Broncos, geekgirl, 96. **CONTACT ADDRESS** Dept English, Univ of Nevada, Las Vegas, PO Box 455011, Las Vegas, NV 89154-5011. **EMAIL** taylors@nevada.edu

TAYLOR, VELANDE P.

PERSONAL Born 09/10/1923, New York, NY, m, 1961 **DISCIPLINE** LITERATURE, PHILOSOPHY **EDUCATION** Hunter Col, BA, 44; Columbia Univ, MA, 45, PhD, 47. **CAREER** Instr, Paul Smiths Col, 46-47; asst prof, East Carolina Univ, 47-58; prof, head hum dept, Colorado Women's Col, 58-66; vis prof. St Mary's Univ, 66-69; prof, Middle Georgia Col, 69-72; prof, writer in residence and ed, Acad J, 74-84, Hong Kong Baptist Col; section ed, URAM J of Int Stud in the Philos of Understanding, 84-89; WordCraft by Lan, 93- ; ed, publ WordCraft Books, 96- . **HONORS AND AWARDS** Int Mark Twain Soc, 47, Order of the Dannebrog, 51; Freedom Found, 51, Bronze Medal, 52, Gold Medal, 53. **MEMBERSHIPS** APA; Acad of Am Poets; Grunewald Guild. **SELECTED PUBLICATIONS** Auth, Homilies in the Marketplace: Parables for Our Times, 96; Copper Flowers, 97, 99; Walking Songs, 97, 98; Tales from the Archetypal World, 98; Flowing Water, Singing Sand: The Metaphysics of Change, 99; Between the Lines, 99; auth, The Zodiac Affair, 00, gallery, 01. **CONTACT ADDRESS** #1008, Seattle, WA 98104-1273.

TAYLOR, WELFORD DUNAWAY

PERSONAL Born 01/03/1938, Caroline Co, VA, m, 1960 **DISCIPLINE** ENGLISH **EDUCATION** Univ Richmond, BA, 59, MA, 61; Univ MD, PhD, 66. **CAREER** Instr Eng, Richmond Prof Inst, 61-63; from instr to assoc prof, 64-73, prof eng, Univ Richmond, 73 chmn dept, 78-, James A Bostwick Ch Eng, 91. **RESEARCH** Amelie Rives; Sherwood Anderson; Am lit 1890 to the present. **SELECTED PUBLICATIONS** Ed, The Buck Fever Papers, Univ VA, 71; Virginia Authors Past and Present, VA Asn Tchr(s) Eng, 72; auth, Amelie Rives (Princess Troubetzkoy), Twayne, 73; ed, The Winesburg Eagle, Sherwood Anderson Soc, 75-86; Sherwood Anderson, Frederick Ungar, 77; Sherwood Anderson, J J Lankes and the Illustration of Perhaps Women, Waves, 81; ed, Our American Cousin, The Play that Changed History, Beacham, 90; The Newsprint Mask, Iowa State, 91; Robert Frost and J J Lakes: Riders on Pegasus, Dartmouth, 96; co-ed (with Charles E Modlin), Southern Odyssey: Selected Writings by Sherwood Anderson, Georgia, 97. **CONTACT ADDRESS** Dept of Eng, Univ of Richmond, Richmond, VA 23173-0002. **EMAIL** wtaylor@richmond.edu

TAYLOR-THOMPSON, BETTY E.

PERSONAL Born 02/06/1943, Houston, TX, m, 1985 **DISCIPLINE** ENGLISH **EDUCATION** Fisk Univ, Nashville TN, BA, 1963; Atlanta Univ, Atlanta GA, MLS, 1964; Howard Univ, Washington DC, MA, 1972, PhD, 1979. **CAREER** Washington DC Public Library, technology librarian, 69-72; Texas Southern Univ, Houston TX, instructor in English, 74-75; Houston Independent Schools, Houston TX, English teacher/librarian, 65-68, 82-84; Texas Southern Univ, Houston TX, assoc prof of English, 84-89, chair, Dept of English and Foreign Language, 89-91, associate professor of English, 91, Prof of English, currently. **HONORS AND AWARDS** National Endowment for the Humanities; University of Illinois at Urbanna, Institute for African Studies for the General Curriculum, Fellow; Director, Masterworks Seminar on the Harlem Reniassance; Phi Beta Kappa; National Endowment for the Humanities (NEH) Director; Masterwork Project on the Harlem Renaissance; Masterwork Project on African American Autobiographies; Study Grant on African and African American Women Writers; Director Focus Grant on Literature, Art and Music of the Harlem Renaissance; Participant, Literature and Modern Experience Institute, Accra Ghana; Tanzania, Study & Research, Fulbright Awd, summer 1997; Univ of Dar Es Saalam, Africa, Institute for Arts in Education, Humanities Scholar, summer 1997. **MEMBERSHIPS** Mem, College Language Assn, co-chair, Black Studies Comm; mem, National Council of Teachers of English; mem, Southern Conf of Modern Language Assn, sec of Afro-Amer Section; pres, Southern Conf of Afro-Amer Studies, 1990-92; Conference of College Teachers of English; American Literature Assn; Southern Conference of Afro-American Studies (past president); Natl College of Teachers of English; American Assn of University Women; Multi Ethnic Literature of the United States. **SELECTED PUBLICATIONS** Publications: Oxford Campanion to African American Literature, 1997; Essays: Grant and Proposal Writing Hand Book, 1997. **CONTACT ADDRESS** Dept of English and Foreign Language, Texas So Univ, 3100 Cleburne St, Houston, TX 77004.

TCHUDI, STEPHEN

PERSONAL m, 4 children **DISCIPLINE** ENGLISH LANGUAGE AND LITERATURE **EDUCATION** Hamilton Col, BA, 63; Northwestern Univ, MAT, 64, PhD, 67. **CAREER** Instr, Mich State Univ; prof, 90-, ch, dept Eng, Univ Nev, Reno; ed, Eng J; ed, Silver Sage. **HONORS AND AWARDS** Distinguished Fac Awd, Mich State Univ, 90; Mousel-Felter Awd, Univ Nev, Reno, 97. **MEMBERSHIPS** Past pres, NCTE; past pres, Nev State Coun of Tchr of Eng. **SELECTED PUBLICATIONS** Auth, Lock & Key: The Secrets of Locking Things Up, In, and Out, Scribner's, 93; The Interdisciplinary Teachers' Handbook with Stephen Lafer, Heinemann/Boynton Cook, 96; Science, Technology, and the American West, Halcyon, 97; coauth, The New Literacy, Jossey Bass, 96. **CONTACT ADDRESS** Dept of Eng, Univ of Nevada, Reno, Reno, NV 89557. **EMAIL** stuchu@powernet.net

TEAGUE, FRANCES NICOL

PERSONAL Born 01/16/1949, Toronto, ON, Canada, m, 1968 **DISCIPLINE** ENGLISH **EDUCATION** Rice Univ, BA, 70; Univ Tex, PhD(English), 75. **CAREER** Instr English, Univ Tex, 75-77; asst prof, 77-84, assoc prof, 84-91, Prof English, Univ GA, 91-, Am Coun Learned Soc grant-in-aid, 81. **HONORS AND AWARDS** Canada Counc doctoral fel, 74-75; Am Counc Learned Soc, grant-in-aid, summer 81; NEH fel, Folger Shakespeare Inst, summer 82; Assoc Col Res Libr travel grant, spring 85; Canadian Consulate fac res grant, 89-90; Sr fac teaching fel, Univ Ga, 95-96; Kappa Delta Epsilon Teaching Awd, 96-97. **MEMBERSHIPS** MLA; Shakespeare Asn Am; Southeastern Renaissance Conf **RESEARCH** Renaissance drama; theater history; women writers before 1700. **SELECTED PUBLICATIONS** Auth, The Curious History of Bartholomew Fair, Bucknell, 85; co-ed, One Touch of Shakespeare, The Letters of Joseph Crosby, Folger, 86; auth, Shakespeare's Speaking Properties, Bucknell, 91; ed, Acting Funny, Fairleigh Dickinson, 93; auth, Bathsua Makin, Woman of Learning, Bucknell, 98. **CONTACT ADDRESS** Dept of English, Univ of Georgia, 263 Park Hall, Athens, GA 30602-6205. **EMAIL** fteague@arches.uga.edu

TEBBEN, JOSEPH RICHARD

PERSONAL Born 11/26/1943, Columbus, OH, m, 1968, 6 children **DISCIPLINE** CLASSICS **EDUCATION** Duquesne Univ, BA, 65; Univ Pittsburgh, MA, 66; OH State Univ, PhD, 71. **CAREER** From instr to asst prof, 70-77, Assoc Prof Classics, OH State Univ, 77; Prof, Greek and Latin, OH State University, 99. **RESEARCH** Ancient Greek epic; Computing and class. **SELECTED PUBLICATIONS** Auth, A Course in Medical and Technical Terminology, Burgess, 79; Verba: A computer-assisted course in terminology, Class World, 75; Hesiod Konkordanz, 77 & Homer Konkordanz, 77, Georg Olms; Computer restoration of Greek diacritical symbols, Relo Rev, 77; Alkinoos and Phaiakian Security, Symbolae Osloenses, 91; Concordantia Homerica: Odyssea, Georg Olms, 94; Concordantia Homerica: Ilias, Georg Olms, 98. **CONTACT ADDRESS** Dept of Class, Ohio State Univ, Newark, 1179 University Dr, Newark, OH 43055-1797. **EMAIL** tebben.1@osu.edu

TEBBETTS, TERRELL L.

DISCIPLINE ENGLISH **EDUCATION** Hendrix Col, BA; Univ AR, MA, PhD. **CAREER** WC Brown Jr prof; fac, Lyon Col, 70-. **HONORS AND AWARDS** Ark Prof Yr awd, Coun Advan and Support of Educ & Carnegie Found, 92. **RESEARCH** Fiction of Faulkner; plays of Shakespeare. **SE-**

LECTED PUBLICATIONS Auth, Giving Jung a Crack at the Compsons. CONTACT ADDRESS Dept of Eng, Lyon Col, 300 Highland Rd, PO Box 2317, Batesville, AR 72503.

TEDARDS, DOUGLAS MANNING
PERSONAL Born 02/12/1944, Greenville, SC, 4 children **DISCIPLINE** COMPOSITION, AMERICAN POETRY **EDUCATION** Vanderbilt Univ, BA, 66; Univ Fla, MA, 68; Univ Pac, DA(English), 76. **CAREER** Instr, Paine Col, 70-72; lectr, Univ Calif, Santa Barbara, 78-81; assoc prof English, Univ Pac, 82-. **HONORS AND AWARDS** NEH Summer Fel. **MEMBERSHIPS** NCTE; CWP Advisory Board. **RESEARCH** The teaching of writing; modern American poetry. **SELECTED PUBLICATIONS** Auth, Hush Puppies (poem), Fla Quart, fall 69; Agrarian poet, Appalachian J, spring 78; Mothers of Fruition (poem), Ga Rev, spring 79; chapter, In: When Writing Teachers Teach Literature, Boynton/Cook, 95. **CONTACT ADDRESS** Dept of English, Univ of the Pacific, Stockton, 3601 Pacific Ave, Stockton, CA 95211-0197. **EMAIL** dtedards@uop.edu

TEDFORD, BARBARA WILKIE
PERSONAL Born 01/21/1936, Marshall, NC, m, 1958 **DISCIPLINE** ENGLISH **EDUCATION** Maryville Col, BA, 57; Univ TN, MA, 60; Univ Pittsburgh, PhD(English), 70. **CAREER** From instr to asst prof English, Davis & Elkins Col, 60-69; asst prof humanities, Robert Morris Col, 70-74; assoc prof to prof English, Glenville State Col, 75-98, RETIRED. **HONORS AND AWARDS** Phi Kappa Phi. **MEMBERSHIPS** SAtlantic MLA. **RESEARCH** Nineteenth and twentieth century English, Am, Russian, and Canadian lit. **SELECTED PUBLICATIONS** Auth, A Recipe for Satire and Civilization, Costerus Essays Eng & Am Lang & Lit, 72; Of Libraries and Salmon-colored Volumes: James's Reading of Turgenev through 1873, Resources Am Lit Study, 79; The Attitudes of Henry James and Ivan Turgenev toward the Russo-Turkish War, The Henry James Rev, 80; Flannery O'Connor and the Social Classes, Southern Lit J, 81; West Virginia Touches in Eudora Welty's Fiction, Southern Lit J, 86; Solving Crimes and Teaching English: Kate Fansler, Bull WV Asn Col English Teachers, 87; Confronting the Other in the Fiction of Julia Davis, Bull WV Asn Col Eng Teachers, 89; Ghostlier Demarcations, Keener Sounds: Elusiveness in Wallace Stevens' The Idea of Order at Key West, Bull WV Asn Col Eng Teachers, 90; Robertson Davis the Manipulator of the Salterton Trilogy, ERIC 91; ed Julia Davis, The Embassy Girls, WVUP, 92; Facade: An Enduring Icon of Modernism, Bull WV Asn Col Eng Teachers, 97. **CONTACT ADDRESS** PO Box 1121, Elkins, WV 26241. **EMAIL** btedford@neumedia.net

TEICHMANN, SANDRA G.
PERSONAL Born 06/13/1945, Salida, CO, m, 1983, 1 child **DISCIPLINE** ENGLISH **EDUCATION** Univ Colo, BA, 88; Vt Col, MFA, 90; Fla State Univ, PhD, 95. **CAREER** Asst Prof, W Tex A&M Univ, 95-. **SELECTED PUBLICATIONS** Ed, Woman of the Plains, Tex A&M Univ Press, 00. **CONTACT ADDRESS** Dept English, West Texas A&M Univ, Box 60965, Canyon, TX 79016. **EMAIL** steich0613@aol.com

TELLER, STEPHEN J.
DISCIPLINE ENGLISH LITERATURE **EDUCATION** Roosevelt Univ, BA; Univ Ill, MA, PhD. **CAREER** Prof. **RESEARCH** Chaucer, mythology, science fiction, film, world literature. **SELECTED PUBLICATIONS** Publ, articles on Shakespeare; bk rev(s). **CONTACT ADDRESS** Dept of Eng, Pittsburg State Univ, 1701 S Broadway St, Pittsburg, KS 66762. **EMAIL** steller@pittstate.edu

TEMPERLEY, NICHOLAS
PERSONAL Born Beaconsfield, England, m, 1960, 3 children **DISCIPLINE** MUSIC, MUSICOLOGY **EDUCATION** Royal Col of Music, London, ARCM, 52; Cambridge Univ, King's Col, MA, PhD, 59. **CAREER** Post-doctoral fel, Univ Il, 59-61; asst lect music, Cambridge Univ and fel of Clare Col, 61-66; asst prof music, Yale Univ, 66-67; assoc prof, 67-72, prof Music, Univ IL, 72-96, chair, musicology, 72-75, 92-96. **HONORS AND AWARDS** John Stewart of Rannoch Scholarship in Sacred Music, 53-57; Otto Kinkeldey Awd in Musicology, 80; Univ Scholar, Univ IL; Hon fel, Guild of Church Musicians. **MEMBERSHIPS** Am Musicology Soc; Royal Musical Asn; Midwest Victorian Asn; Hymn Soc of Am. **RESEARCH** Classical and early Romantic music; English music; rise and development of piano music and the art song; hymnology. **SELECTED PUBLICATIONS** Auth, Critical Edition of Berlioz, Symphonie fantastique, 71; The Music of the English Parish Church, 79; The Athlone History of Music in Britain, vol 5, The Romantic Age 1800-1914, 81; The London Pianoforte School, 20 vols, 82-85; The Lost Chord: Essays in Victorian Music; Haydn: The Creation; The Hymn Tune Index, 4 vols, 98. **CONTACT ADDRESS** Univ of Illinois, Urbana-Champaign, 1114 W Nevada, Urbana, IL 61801. **EMAIL** ntemp@uiuc.edu

TEMPLE, JUDY NOLTE
PERSONAL Born 03/14/1948, Omaha, NE, m, 1993, 2 children **DISCIPLINE** ENGLISH **EDUCATION** Univ Iowa, BA, 71; MA, 77; PhD, 87. **CAREER** Proj dir to fac member, Univ Ariz, 81-. **HONORS AND AWARDS** Reg Libr Asn Award, 88; Shambaugh Prize, 90; All-Campus Award, Univ Ariz, 01. **MEMBERSHIPS** W Lit Asn; W Hist Asn. **RESEARCH** Women's life writing, especially women's diaries; Dreams and visions writings of 'Baby Doe' Tabor. **SELECTED PUBLICATIONS** Ed, Open Space, City Places: Contemporary Writers on the Changing Southwest, Univ Ariz Press, 94; auth, "The Madwoman in the Cabin: The Dream Worlds of 'Baby Doe' Tabor, (forthcoming). **CONTACT ADDRESS** Dept English, Univ of Arizona, 445 Mod Lang Bldg, PO Box 210067, Tucson, AZ 85721. **EMAIL** jtemple@u.arizona.edu

TEMPLE, KATHRYN
DISCIPLINE ENGLISH LITERATURE **EDUCATION** Ga State Univ, BA; Emory Univ, MA, PhD. **CAREER** Eng Dept, Georgetown Univ **RESEARCH** 18th century British literature; 18th century popular culture; interactions between literature and law; history of intellectual property; feminist jurisprudence. **SELECTED PUBLICATIONS** Auth, pubs on eighteenth century authorship and "crimes of writing," the gothic, legal literature for women, recent developments in critical legal studies and critical race theory. **CONTACT ADDRESS** English Dept, Georgetown Univ, 37th and O St, Washington, DC 20057.

TENGER, ZEYNEP
DISCIPLINE LITERATURE **EDUCATION** Bosphorus Univ, BA, 80; Univ Minn, MA, 85; NYork Univ, PhD, 90. **CAREER** Teaching Asst, Univ Minn, 81-82; Instr, NY Univ, 86-90; Asst Prof, 90-96, Assoc Prof, Berry Col, 97-, Dir Honors Prog, 98-. **HONORS AND AWARDS** Univ Minn Res Fel, 80-81; Univ Minn Tuition Schol, 80-81; NY Univ Tuition Schol, 82-84; NY Univ Penfield Dissertation Fel, 89; Berry Col Travel Grants, 91-96; Berry Col Su Summer Stipend for Res, 92; Berry Col Fac Development Grant, 97; Berry Col Vulcan Teaching Excellence Awd, 97. **MEMBERSHIPS** Mod Lang Asn; Am Comp Lit Asn; Am Soc Eighteenth-Century Studies; SAtlantic Mod Lang Asn; SCentral Soc Eighteenth-Century Studies; NEastern Soc Eighteenth-Century Studies; Int Asn Philos & Lit. **SELECTED PUBLICATIONS** Coauth, Genius versus Capital: Mid-Eighteenth-Century Theories of Genius and Adam Smith's The Wealth of Nations, Mod Lang Quart, 6/94; Impartial Critic or Muses Handmaid: The Politics of Critical Practice in the Early Eighteenth Century, Essays in Lit, Spring 94; Politics of the Enlightenment: The Reaction to the French Revolution and Changes in Editorial Policies of the English Literary Periodical, Studies in Eighteenth-Century Cult 24, 95; Criticism Against Itself: Subverting Critical Authority in Late-Seventeenth Century England, Philol Quart 75, 96. **CONTACT ADDRESS** English Dept, Berry Col, Mount Berry, GA 30149.

TENNYSON, GEORG BERNHARD
PERSONAL Born 07/13/1930, Washington, DC, m, 1953, 2 children **DISCIPLINE** ENGLISH **EDUCATION** George Washington Univ, AB, 53, MA, 59; Princeton Univ, MA, 61, PhD(English), 63. **CAREER** Instr English, Univ NC, Chapel Hill, 62-64; from asst prof to assoc prof, 64-71, PROF ENGLISH, UNIV CALIF, LOS ANGELES, 71-, John Simon Guggenheim Mem Found fel, 70-71; ed, Nineteenth-Century Fiction, 71-74; ed, Nineteenth-Century Lit, 83-96. **MEMBERSHIPS** MLA; Philol Asn Pac Coast; Carlyle Soc; Res Soc Victorian Periodicals; Int Asn Univ Prof English. **RESEARCH** Victorian literature, Anglo-German literary relations, romantic to modern; religion and literature. **SELECTED PUBLICATIONS** Auth, Sartor Called Resartus, 65; auth, An Introduction to Drama, 69; auth, Carlyle and the Modern World, 72; coed, Religion and Modern Literature, 75; auth, Victorian Literature: Prose and Poetry, 76; auth, Nature and The Victorian Imagination, 77; auth, Victorian Devotional Poetry, 81; auth, Owen Barfield on C.S. Lewis, 90; auth, Owen Barfield: Man and Meaning, 96; ed, A Carlyle Reader, 3rd ed, 99; auth, A Barfield Reader, 99. **CONTACT ADDRESS** Dept of English, Univ of California, Los Angeles, Los Angeles, CA 90024.

TERPSTRA, VERN
PERSONAL Born 08/20/1927, Grand Rapids, MI, m, 1950, 2 children **DISCIPLINE** INTERNATIONAL BUSINESS, MARKETING **EDUCATION** BA 50, MBA 51, PhD 65, all Univ of Michigan. **CAREER** Prof of International Business Univ of Michigan 66-92, Asst Prof Marketing Wharton School 64-66, Dir Mormal School Congo 53-61. **HONORS AND AWARDS** Fellow-Academy of International Business; Fellow -Marketing Sci Institute;Fellow-Ford Foundation. **MEMBERSHIPS** Academy of International Business-President 70-72, Amer Marketing Assoc **RESEARCH** International Marketing, International Business, Cross Cultural Issues **SELECTED PUBLICATIONS** International Marketing 7th ed, Dryden Press, 97; International Dimensions of Marketing Kent 3rd ed, 93; Cultural Enviornment of International Business 3rd ed, Southwestern, 91; Lectures in International Marketing(Chinese) National Center for Management Development Dalian China, 86: Univ Educ for International Business AEIB 69; Amer Marketing in the Common Market Praeger, 67; Co-auth Comparative Analysis for International Marketing, Allyn&Bacon, 67; Co-auth Marketing Development in the European Economic Community, McGraw-Hill, 64; Co-auth, Patents and Progress, Irwin, 65. **CONTACT ADDRESS** Graduate School of Business, Univ of Michigan, Ann Arbor, Ann Arbor, MI 48109. **EMAIL** vterp@umich.edu

TERRELL, ROBERT L.
PERSONAL Born 07/19/1943, m **DISCIPLINE** JOURNALISM **EDUCATION** Morehouse Coll Atlanta, BA 1969; Univ CA Berkeley, MA 1971; Univ of CA Berkeley, PhD 1970. **CAREER** Publ poems short stories books 1967-; NY Post, reporter 1967-68; So Reg Council Atlanta, rsch writer 1968-69; Newsweek Mag, stringer 1968-69; Univ of CA,teaching asst 1969-70; Golden Gate Coll, instr 1969-71; San Francisco Chronicle, copy ed 1970; CA Jrnl Teacher Ed, asst prof 1971-76, ed 1972-73; OffRsch & Plnng, coord 1974-75; St Mary's Coll Morage CA, office experimental progs 1975-76; Stanford Univ, asst prof 1976; Univ of MO, assoc prof jrnlsm 1976-; School of Jrnlsm Univ of CA Berkeley, vstg prof 1979; Beijing Review Mag Beijing China, copy ed 1981-82; NY Univ Dept of Jrnlsm & Mass Commun, vstg prof 1985-86; Univ Nairobi School of Jrnlsm, fulbright prof 1984-85. **HONORS AND AWARDS** Fellowship CA State 1969-72, Grad Minority 1969-72, Fund for Peace 1970-71, NDEA 1971-74; Deans Fellowship Univ of CA 1974-75. **MEMBERSHIPS** Mem Amer Assoc Colls Teacher Ed, Amer Assoc Higher Ed, Amer Ed Rsch Assoc; bd dir CA Council Teacher Ed, Soc Coll & Univ; managing ed CA Jrnl Teacher Ed 1973; ed referee CA Jrnl Teacher Ed 1974-; adv screening comm commun Council for Intl Exchange of Scholars Fulbright Prog 1980-83. **CONTACT ADDRESS** Prof of News/Editing, Univ of Missouri, Columbia, 16 Walter Williams, Columbia, MO 65211.

TERRERO, IRENE
PERSONAL Born 03/12/1938, Venezuela, D, 2 children **DISCIPLINE** NEUROPSYCHOLOGY, NEUROLINGUISTICS **EDUCATION** Kendall Col, AA, 70; George Washington Univ, BA, 72; Northwestern Univ, MA, 74; Univ Paris, Doctorate, 83. **CAREER** Clinical Dir, Clinica de Lenguaje IT, Clinica de Idiomas IT, 74-00; res assoc, Gallandet Univ, 84-94; res assoc, Int Cendie Universidad Metropolitana, 89-98. **HONORS AND AWARDS** Phi Beta Kappa; Gallandet Univ, Res Awd Nomination; Ministry of Educ, Special Educ Honors, 90, 00. **MEMBERSHIPS** ASHA, AAUW, George Sand Lit Assoc. **RESEARCH** Linguistics, Languages, Neurlinguistics, Hearing Impaired, Special Education, Bilingual Education and Development. **CONTACT ADDRESS** 13895 Folkstone Cir, Wellington, FL 33414-7738. **EMAIL** ireneterrero@hotmail.com

TERRILL, ROBERT
PERSONAL Born 06/14/1961, San Jose, CA, m **DISCIPLINE** COMMUNICATION **EDUCATION** Northwestern Univ, PhD, 96; Univ Arkansas, MA, 92; San Jose State Univ, BA, 84. **CAREER** Asst Prof, Indiana Univ, 97-. **MEMBERSHIPS** National Communication Assoc. **RESEARCH** African-American Public Address; Film Criticism; Rhetorical Criticism. **SELECTED PUBLICATIONS** Auth, "Colonizing the Borderlands: Shifting Circumference in the Rhetoric of Malcolm X," Quarterly Journal of Speech, February, 00. **CONTACT ADDRESS** Dept Communication & Culture, Indiana Univ, Bloomington, 809 East 7th St, Bloomington, IN 47405-3937. **EMAIL** rterrill@indiana.edu

TERRY, JAMES L.
PERSONAL Born 09/12/1949, Terre Haute, IN **DISCIPLINE** LIBRARY SCIENCE; SOCIOLOGY **EDUCATION** Long Island Univ, MLS, 90; Purdue Univ, PhD, 88. **CAREER** Libr, Assoc Curator, New York Univ, 90-. **HONORS AND AWARDS** Louis Schneider Memorial Awd for Outstanding Dissertation, 88. **MEMBERSHIPS** Amer Libr Assoc; Amer Sociological Assoc. **RESEARCH** Political economy of information technology; information literacy; sociology of work and labor **SELECTED PUBLICATIONS** Auth, Authorship in College and Research Libraries revisited: Gender, Institutional Affiliation, Collaboration, College and Research Libraries, 96; auth, Automated Library Systems: A History of Constraints and Opportunities, Advances in Librarianship, 98. **CONTACT ADDRESS** Bobst Library, New York Univ, 70 Washington Sq S, New York, NY 10012. **EMAIL** terryj@elmer4.bobst.nyu.edu

TETEL, JULIE
DISCIPLINE ENGLISH LITERATURE **EDUCATION** UNC Chapel Hill, PhD, 80. **CAREER** Prof lit, Duke Univ. **RESEARCH** French, Ger, and Am theories of lang from the eighteenth through the twentieth centuries **SELECTED PUBLICATIONS** Auth, Linguistics in America 1769-1924: A Critical History, Routledge, 90; pubs on linguistic historiography. **CONTACT ADDRESS** Relig Dept, Duke Univ, Durham, NC 27706.

TETREAULT, RONALD
PERSONAL Born 12/31/1947, m, 1971, 2 children **DISCIPLINE** ENGLISH LITERATURE **EDUCATION** Univ Brit Columbia, BA, 69; Cornell Univ, MA, 72, PhD, 74. **CAREER** Lectr, Cornell Univ, 73-74; bibliog asst, Cornell Univ Lib, 74-75; asst prof, 75-81; assoc prof, 81-90; prof, 90-; fac assoc, 95-96. **RESEARCH** Romantic poetry (Wordsworth, Shelley, and Keats), radical writing 1790-1850, editing and electronic texts, humanities computing and educational technologies. **SELECTED PUBLICATIONS** Auth, "Shelley at the Opera," ELH: English Lit Hist, (81), 144-171; auth, The Poetry of Life, Shelley and Literary Form, Univ of Toronto Press, 87; auth, "Shelley among the Chartist," English Studies in Canada (90), 279-295;

auth, "Women and Words in Keats," The Mind in Creation: Essays in honour of Ross Woodman, McGill-Queens, 92; ed, Romanticism on the Net, (98), online publication. **CONTACT ADDRESS** Dept of Eng, Dalhousie Univ, Halifax, NS, Canada B3H 3J5. **EMAIL** tetro@is.dal.ca

TEUNISSEN, JOHN J.
DISCIPLINE ENGLISH LITERATURE **EDUCATION** Univ Saskatchewan, BA; Ma; Univ Rochester, PhD. **CAREER** Prof emer, Univ of Man, dept head, English Dept, Univ of Man, 72-77, 83-88, 89-92; Ed, Can Rev Am Stud, 77-86. **HONORS AND AWARDS** Cert of Excellence in Teaching, MLA of Am. **MEMBERSHIPS** MLA; Asn Can Univ Tchr English. **RESEARCH** Myth criticism; treatment of myth in literature. **SELECTED PUBLICATIONS** Coauth, A Key into the Language of America and Henry Miller's The World of Lawrence: A Passionate Appreciation (rev); ed, Other Worlds: Fantasy; Science Fiction Since 1939; Contexts: The Interdisciplinary Study of Literature. **CONTACT ADDRESS** Dept of English, Univ of Manitoba, 28 Trueman Walk, 625 Fletcher Argue Bldg, Winnipeg, MB, Canada R3T 5V5.

TEVEN, JASON
PERSONAL Born 05/28/1970, Chicago, IL **DISCIPLINE** COMMUNICATION STUDIES **EDUCATION** Carroll Col, BS, 93; Ill State Univ, MS, 95; W Va Univ, EdD, 98. **CAREER** TA, Ill State Univ, 93-95; instr, W Va Univ, 95-98; asst prof, NW Mo State Univ, 98-00; asst prof, W Tex A&M Univ, 00-. **HONORS AND AWARDS** Phi Kappa Phi, 98; William E. Vehse Awd, 97; Outstanding Teacher Awd, 00. **MEMBERSHIPS** Nat Commun Assoc, Int Commun Assoc, E Commun Assoc. **RESEARCH** Interpersonal, instructional, and nonverbal communication. **SELECTED PUBLICATIONS** Coauth, "The effects of office aesthetic quality on students' perceptions of teacher creditability and communicator style," Commun Res Reports 13, (96): 101-108; coauth, "The relationship of perceived teacher caring with student learning and teacher evaluation," Commun Educ 46, (97): 1-9; coauth, "Sibling relationships: Verbally aggressive messages and their effect on relational satisfaction," Commun Reports 11, (98): 179-186; coauth, Goodwill: A re-examination of the construct and its measurement," Commun Monogr 66, (99): 90-103; coauth, "A qualitative analysis of low-inference student perceptions of teacher caring and non-caring behaviors within the college classroom," Commun Res Reports 15, (99): 288-298; coauth, "Measuring tolerance for disagreement," Commun Res Reports 15, (99): 209-217; coauth, Mastering Public Speaking: Instructor's Resource manual and test bank, Allyn & Bacon, 00, auth, "The development of a teacher tolerance for disagreement measure," Iowa Jour of Commun, in press. **CONTACT ADDRESS** Dept Commun, West Texas A&M Univ, Box 60747, Canyon, TX 79016-0747. **EMAIL** jteven@hotmail.com

THADEN, BARBARA
PERSONAL Born 07/03/1955, New York, NY, m, 1981, 2 children **DISCIPLINE** BRITISH LITERATURE, AMERICAN LITERATURE **EDUCATION** Fla State Univ, BS, 77; MS, 81; Univ NC, PhD, 94. **CAREER** Teacher, Bainbridge High Sch, 78-80; Teacher, Hillside High Sch, 81-85; Tech Writer, Triangle Res Collab, 90-91, 94; Lectr, Univ NC, 94-96; Asst Prof, State Augustines Col, 97-. **HONORS AND AWARDS** Ford Found Fel, 89; Henry C McBay Res Fel, 99. **MEMBERSHIPS** MLA. **RESEARCH** Nineteenth-Century British fiction, contemporary African-American fiction. **SELECTED PUBLICATIONS** Auth, "Bakhtin, Dostoevsky and the Status of the T," Dostoevsky Studies, 8 (87): 199-207; auth, "Derrida in the Composition Class: Deconstructing Arguments," The Writing Instr, 7:3/4 (88): 131-137; auth, "Figure and Ground: The Receding Heroine in Jane Austen's Emma," S Atlantic Rev, 55:1 (90): 47-61; auth, New Essays on the Maternal Voice in the Nineteenth Century, Contemporary Res Pr (Dallas, TX), 95; auth, "Charles Johnson's 'Middle Passage' at Histoiographic Metafiction," Col English, 59:7 (97): 753-766; auth, The Maternal Voice in Victorian Fiction: Redefining the Patriarchal Family, Garland Pr (New York, NY), 97; auth, A Student Companion to Charlotte and Emily Bronte, Greenwood Pr (Westport, CT), forthcoming. **CONTACT ADDRESS** Dept Lib Arts, Saint Augustine's Col, 1315 Oakwood Ave, Raleigh, NC 27610-2247. **EMAIL** bzthaden@mindspring.com

THALER, DANIELLE
DISCIPLINE NINETEENTH CENTURY NOVEL; THEATRE **EDUCATION** Univ Toronto, PhD. **RESEARCH** Evolution of ideological discourse; genetic criticism; semiotics of drama; children's literature. **SELECTED PUBLICATIONS** Auth, La clinique de l'amour selon les freres Goncourt: Peuple, femme, hysterie, Editions Naaman, 86; Etait-il une fois? Litterature de jeunesse: panorama de la critique France-Canada, Toronto, Paratexte, 89; Jean-Come Nogues et les rites initiatiques, Rev francophone de Louisiane 5, 91-92; Ginette Anfousse et le jeu intertextuel, Can Children's Lit 72, 94. **CONTACT ADDRESS** Dept of French, Univ of Victoria, PO Box 3045 STN CSC, Victoria, BC, Canada V8W 3P4. **EMAIL** dthaler@uvic.ca

THAMELING, CARL L.
DISCIPLINE SPEECH COMMUNICATION **EDUCATION** Univ Louisville, BA, 79; Ind Univ, Bloomington, MA, 84, PhD, 90. **CAREER** Asst prof, Univ Col Cape Breton, 88-91; asst prof, Miami Univ, Ohio, 91-98; ASST PROF, NORTHEAST LA UNIV, 88-. **CONTACT ADDRESS** 3907 Harrison St., Monroe, LA 71203-4437. **EMAIL** CNThameling@alpha.nlu.edu

THATCHER, DAVID S.
DISCIPLINE ENGLISH LITERATURE **EDUCATION** Cambridge Univ, BA; Univ McMaster, MA; Univ Alberta, PhD. **CAREER** Prof, Univ of Victoria. **RESEARCH** Shakespeare; 20th-century British poetry. **SELECTED PUBLICATIONS** Auth, Nietzsche in England, Univ Toronto, 70; Musical Settings of Early and Mid-Victorian Literature: A Catalogue, Garland, 79; Musical Settings of British Romantic Literature, Garland, 82; A Shakespeare Music Catalogue, Oxford, Clarendon Press, 91; auth, Begging to Differ: Modes of Discrepancy in Shakespeare, New York, 99. **CONTACT ADDRESS** Dept of English, Univ of Victoria, PO Box 3070, Victoria, BC, Canada V8W 3W1.

THAYER, CALVIN G.
PERSONAL Born 06/19/1922, San Francisco, CA, m, 1944, 5 children **DISCIPLINE** ENGLISH RENAISSANCE **EDUCATION** Stanford Univ, BA, 43, Univ Calif, Berkeley, MA, 47, PhD(English), 51. **CAREER** Instr English, La State Univ, 50-51; from instr to prof, Univ Okla, 51-66; vis prof, 66-67, PROF ENGLISH, OHIO UNIV, 67-, Assoc ed, Bucknell Rev, 67-; ed consult, The Milton Quart, 67-; ed, Ohio Rev, 72. **RESEARCH** Medieval and Renaissance drama; 16th century nondramatic literature. **SELECTED PUBLICATIONS CONTACT ADDRESS** Dept of English, Ohio Univ, Athens, OH 45701.

THESING, WILLIAM BARNEY
PERSONAL Born 12/30/1947, St. Louis, MO, m, 1976, 1 child **DISCIPLINE** ENGLISH LITERATURE **EDUCATION** Unv Mo-St Louis, BA, 69; Ind Univ, Bloomington, MA, 70, PhD(-English), 77. **CAREER** Counter intel agent, US Army, Stuttgart, Ger, 70-73; assoc instr, Ind Univ, Bloomington, 75-77; instr, 77-79, asst prof english, Univ SC, Columbia, 79-89; prof, 89-. **HONORS AND AWARDS** SAtlantic Mod Lang Asn Studies Awd, 80. **MEMBERSHIPS** MLA. **RESEARCH** Victorian literature, especially poetry and criticism; city in literature. **SELECTED PUBLICATIONS** Auth, The London Muse: Victorian Poetic Responses to the City, The Univ of Ga Press (Athens), 82; auth, English Prose and Criticism, 1900-1950: A Guide to Information Sources, Gale Research Company (Detroit), 83; coauth, Conversations with South Carolina Poets, John F. Blair (Winston-Salem, NC), 86; ed, Executions and the British Experience from the Seventeeth to the Twentieth-Century: A Collection of Essays, McFarland (Jefferson, NC), 90; ed, Critical Essays on Edna St. Vincent Millay, Twayne (NYork), 93; ed, "British Short-Fiction Writers, 1880-1914: The Realist Tradition," in Dictionary of Literary Biography, Vol 135, Gale Research (Detroit), 94; coauth, "Indexes to Fiction in the Idler (1892-1911), in Victorian Fiction Research Guides, 23 (St. Lucia, Australia, Univ of Queensland, 94); ed, Robinson Jeffers and a Galaxy of Writers: Essays in Honor of William H. Nolte, Univ of SC (Columbia), 95; ed, "Victorian Women Poets," Doctionary of Literary Biography, Vol 199, Gale Research (Detroit), 99; ed, Caverns of the Night: Coal Mines in Art, Literature, and Film, Univ of SC (Columbia), 00. **CONTACT ADDRESS** Dept of English, Univ of So Carolina, Columbia, Columbia, SC 29208. **EMAIL** thesingw@gwm.sc.edu

THIEL, DIANE
DISCIPLINE ENGLISH **EDUCATION** Brown Univ, BA, 88; MFA, 90. **CAREER** Lecturer, Brown Univ, 90; Lecturer, Fla Intl Univ, 92-00; Lecturer, Univ Miami, 90-00. **HONORS AND AWARDS** Nicholas Roerich Poetry Prize, 00; New Millennium Writings Awd, 00; Robert Frost Awd, 99; Robinson Jeffers Awd, 98; Judith Siegel Pearson Awd, 90; Hackney Literary Awd, 90. **MEMBERSHIPS** Acad of Am Poets, Poetry Soc of Am, Assoc Writing Prog. **RESEARCH** Poetry; Languages; Cultural Studies: Fluency in Spanish, German, French (some Greek); Environmental issues. **SELECTED PUBLICATIONS** Auth, Echolocations, Story Line Press, 00; auth, Writing Your Rhythm: Using Nature, Culture, Form and Myth, Story Line Press, forthcoming; auth, Cleft in the Wall, Aralia Press, 99. **CONTACT ADDRESS** Dept English, Univ of Miami, PO Box 248145, Coral Gables, FL 33124-4632. **EMAIL** diane@dianethiel.net

THOMAS, AMY M.
DISCIPLINE ENGLISH **EDUCATION** Randolph-Macon, BA, 81; Univ Md, MA, 85; Duke, PhD, 91. **CAREER** Asst prof English, Mont State. **RESEARCH** Literature in Print; Literature in the Antebellum South. **SELECTED PUBLICATIONS** Fel Publ, Literature in Newsprint: Antebellum Family Newspapers and the uses of Reading, In: Reading Books: Essays on the Material Text and Literature, Univ Mass, 96. **CONTACT ADDRESS** Dept of English, Montana State Univ, Bozeman, Bozeman, MT 59717. **EMAIL** thomas@english.montana.edu

THOMAS, BROOK
PERSONAL Born 11/12/1947, Baltimore, MD, m, 1998, 1 child **DISCIPLINE** ENGLISH, LITERATURE **EDUCATION** Stanford Univ, BA, 70; Univ Calif Santa Barbara, MA, 71; PhD, 75. **CAREER** Vis asst prof, Univ Constance, 76; asst prof to assoc prof, Univ Haw, 76-85; assoc prof, Univ Mass, 82-88; prof, Univ Calif Irvine, 88-; vis prof, Univ Berlin, 91; vis prof, Univ Giesseny, 00. **HONORS AND AWARDS** Von Humboldt Fel; Woodrow Wilson Cen Fel; ACLS Fel; Sch Humanities Teaching Awd. **MEMBERSHIPS** MLA; ASA; Melville Soc. **RESEARCH** Law and literature; literature and the nation. **SELECTED PUBLICATIONS** Auth, James Joyce's 'Ulysses': A Book of Many Happy Returns; auth, Cross-Examinations of Law and Literature; auth, Cooper, Hawthorne, Stowe and Melville; auth, The New Historicism and Other Old Fashioned Topics; American Literary Realism and the Failed Promise of Contract; ed, Plussey vs. Ferguson: A Brief History with Documents; ed, Literature and the Nation; auth, Chinamen, US vs. Wong Kim Auk and the Question of Citizenship; auth, Citizen Hester: The Scarlet Letter as Civic Myth; auth, Inelectable Though Uneven: On Experimental Historical Narratives. **CONTACT ADDRESS** English Dept, Univ of California, Irvine, Irvine, CA 92607-0001. **EMAIL** bthomas@uci.edu

THOMAS, C. R.
PERSONAL Born 10/09/1938, Clarksburg, WV, d, 1 child **DISCIPLINE** ENGLISH **EDUCATION** WVa Univ, AB; MA; EdD; Calif Univ Pa, MEd; BS. **CAREER** From Instr to Prof, Calif Univ of Pa, 65-. **HONORS AND AWARDS** Penn Commonwealth Teaching Fel, 77; Distinguished Fac Awd for Excellence in Teaching, 77. **RESEARCH** Business Writing, persuasion, argumentation and social psychology. **SELECTED PUBLICATIONS** Auth, 23 plays; auth, The Other Way to Improve Your Writing: A Basic Writing Text; auth, Business Writing: A Course for Corporate Fast-Trackers, a Text for Business and Professional Career Tracks. **CONTACT ADDRESS** Dept English, California Univ of Pennsylvania, 250 University Ave, Box 36, California, PA 15419-1341.

THOMAS, CLARA M.
PERSONAL Born 05/22/1919, Strathroy, ON, Canada **DISCIPLINE** ENGLISH **EDUCATION** Univ Western Ont, BA, 41, MA, 44; Univ Toronto, PhD, 62; York Univ, DLitt, 86; Trent Univ, Dlitt, 91; Brock Univ, LLD, 92. **CAREER** Lectr, 61, prof, 69, Can Studies Res fel, York Univ Libr, 84-, Prof Emer English, York Univ 84-. **HONORS AND AWARDS** Northern Telecom Int Can Stud Prize, 89; Univ Western Ont Alumni Awd Merit, 95. **MEMBERSHIPS** Charter Secy, Drama Guild Can. **SELECTED PUBLICATIONS** Auth, Canadian Novelists 1920-45; auth, Love and Work Enough: The Life of Anna Jameson; auth, Margaret Laurence; auth, All My Sisters: Essays on Canadian Women Writers. **CONTACT ADDRESS** Dept English, York Univ, 4700 Keele St, 305H Scott Library, Toronto, ON, Canada M3J 1P 3.

THOMAS, DEBORAH ALLEN
PERSONAL Born 09/01/1943, Biddeford, ME, m, 1966, 1 child **DISCIPLINE** ENGLISH LITERATURE **EDUCATION** Brown Univ, AB, 65; Duke Univ, MA, 66; Univ Rochester, PhD(English), 72. **CAREER** Adj asst prof English, Fairleigh Dickinson Univ, Florham-Madison, 73-76; co adj asst prof, Rutgers Univ, Newark & New Brunswick, 76-80; asst prof English, Villanova Univ 80-84; from assoc prof to prof, 84-91. **HONORS AND AWARDS** National Merit Scholarship, 61-65; Phi Beta Kappa, 65; NEH Fel, 85-86; vis scholar, Harvard Univ, 85-86; fac research grants, Villanova Univ, summer 84, 87, 92. **MEMBERSHIPS** MLA; Northeast Victorian Studies Assn; Dickens Soc. **RESEARCH** Nineteenth century British literature; the novel; nineteenth-century British women writers. **SELECTED PUBLICATIONS** Auth, contribr, to the Christmas numbers of Household words and All the year round, 1850-1867 (2 parts), Dickensin, 9/73 & 1/74; The equivocal explanation of Dickens' George Silverman, In: Vol III, Dickens Studies Annual, Southern Ill Univ, 74; The chord of the Christmas season: Playing house at the Holly-Tree Inn, Dickens Studies Newslett, 12/75; ed, Dickens, Selected Short Fiction, Penguin, 76; auth, Dickens' Mrs Lirriper and the evolution of a feminine stereotype, In: Vol VI, Dickens Studies Annual, 77; auth, Dickens and the Short Story, Univ of Pa Pr, 82; Thackeray and Slavery, Ohio Univ Press, 93; Hard Times: A Fable of Fragmentation and Wholeness, Twayne-Simon & Schuster Macmillan, 97. **CONTACT ADDRESS** Dept of English, Villanova Univ, 800 Lancaster Ave, Villanova, PA 19085-1699. **EMAIL** deborah.thomas@villanova.edu

THOMAS, GARY CRAIG
PERSONAL Born 11/20/1944, Long Beach, CA **DISCIPLINE** GERMAN LITERATURE, MUSICOLOGY **EDUCATION** Univ Calif, Los Angeles, AB, 66; Harvard Univ, MA, 70, PhD, 73. **CAREER** Asst prof, Humanities & Ger, 71-91, Assoc Prof Cultural Studies & Ger, Univ Minn, Minneapolis, 91-. **MEMBERSHIPS** MLA; Am Soc Study 16th & 17th Century Ger Lit; Renaissance Soc Am; Am Guild Organists. **RESEARCH** Cultural Studies; musical-literary relations; queer theory. **SELECTED PUBLICATIONS** Auth, Philipp von Zesen's German Madrigals, Argenis, 78; Zesen, Rinckart and the Musical Origins of the Dactyl, Argenis, 78; Dance Music

and the Origins of the Dactylic Meter, in Daphins, Zeitschrift fur Mittlere Deutsche Literatur, 87; Die Aelbianische Musen-Lust, Peter Lang, 91; Musical Rhetoric and Politics in the Early German Lied, in Music and German Literature: Their Relationship since the Middle Ages, Camden House, 92; Philipp von Zesen's German Madrigals, in Daphnis: Zeitschrift fur Mittlere Deutsche Literatur, 92; co-ed, Queering the Pitch: The New Gay and Lesbian Musicology, Routledge, 93; Was George Frideric Handel Gay? - On Closet Questions and Cultural Politics, in Queering the Pitch: The New Gay and Lesbian Musicology, Routledge, 94. **CONTACT ADDRESS** Univ of Minnesota, Twin Cities, 9 Pleasant St. SE, 350 Folwell Hall, Minneapolis, MN 55455. **EMAIL** thoma002@tc.umn.edu

THOMAS, JEAN D'AMATO
PERSONAL Born 07/20/1945, Boston, MA, m, 1989, 3 children **DISCIPLINE** CLASSICAL TRADITION **EDUCATION** Tufts Univ, BA, 67; Middlebury Col, MA, 69; Johns Hopkins Univ, PhD, 76. **CAREER** Vis lectr, Univ Pittsburgh, 74-75; vis lectr Williams Col, 75-76; dir, Vergillian Soc of Am summer sessions, Rome, 78; asst prof, Univ So Calif, 76-81; dir, prof-in-charge, Intercollegiate Ctr for Class Stud, Rome, 82-83; adj asst prof, Brandeis Univ, 83; lectr, NEH funding, Summer Inst for High Sch Tchrs, 83, 84; adj instr, Univ Md, 87; humanist adm, NEH, 84-87; dir, lib arts progs for adults, Tufts Univ, 87-88; columnist, Natchitoches Times, 96- ; assoc prof, prof, Louisiana Scholars Col, Northwestern State Univ, 88-; co-dir, Athens in the Fifth Century, 92; co-dir Art and Science, 94; co-dir Companie Felix: Nature, Art and the Works of Men, 00. **HONORS AND AWARDS** Diss fel, AAU, 72; Am Council of Learned Soc fel, 77; NEH travel grant, 89; APA res grant, 91 Louisiana Endow Hum grant, 92; Il Premio Giornalistico Theodor Mommsen, 93; Athens in the Fifth Century, LEH funding, Summer Inst for High Sch Teachers, 92; Co-Dir, Art and Science LEH funding, 94; Co-Dir, Felix Nature, Art, and the Works of Men, NEH funding, 00. **MEMBERSHIPS** Am Philol Asn; Int Inst for Class Tradition; Louisiana Class Asn; Vergillian Soc Am. **RESEARCH** Classical tradition, both in literature and art and archaeology, as it applies to the Phlegraean Fields near Naples; the classical tradition in the United States. **SELECTED PUBLICATIONS** Auth, Cicero's Property in the Phlegraean Fields and Antiquarian Investigation in the Naples Area, VIATOR, 93; auth, The Apocryphal Lighthouse at Capo Miseno: A Creation of Medieval Scholarship, VIATOR, 96. **CONTACT ADDRESS** 332 Henry Ave, Natchitoches, LA 71457. **EMAIL** damato@alpha.nsula.edu

THOMAS, JOSEPH M.
PERSONAL Born 07/23/1954, Fort Worth, TX **DISCIPLINE** AMERICAN LITERATURE, CULTURE **EDUCATION** Univ Tex, BA, 77; MA, 84; Rutgers Univ, PhD, 94. **CAREER** TA, Univ of Tex, 81-83; vis prof, Rutgers Univ, 93-96; asst prof, Sam Houston State Univ, 96-00; asst dean, Pace Univ, 00-. **HONORS AND AWARDS** David L Kalstone Mem Awd; Fel, Univ of Tex, 81-82; Fel, Rutgers Univ, 85-89; Fel, Harvard Univ, 96; Fel, Sam Houston State Univ, 97, 98, 99. **MEMBERSHIPS** MLA, Am Lit Assoc, Nat Assoc for African Am Studies, Ralph Waldo Emerson Soc, Assoc for Documentary Editing, Nat Coun of Univ Res Admin. **RESEARCH** Nineteenth-Century American Writing and Culture, Early American writing and culture, African-American writing and culture, American Pragmatist tradition, Bibliography, research and textual editing, Composition and writing in the professions. **SELECTED PUBLICATIONS** Auth, "Peculiar Soil: Mining the Early American Imagination," Early Am Lit, (92); auth, "Figures of Habit in William James," New Eng Quart, (93); auth, ""Roughing It In Style: The 1993 Iowa-California Twain Edition," Review, (95); auth, "The Property of My Own Book: Emerson and the Literary Marketplace," New Eng Quart, (96); auth, "Late Emerson: Selected Poems and the Emerson Factory," ELH, (98); auth, "The Post-Abolitionist's Narrative: William Greenleaf Eliiot's The Story of Archer Alexander," New Eng Quart, (00); auth, "Ralph Waldo Emerson," Encycl of Am Studies, forthcoming. **CONTACT ADDRESS** Pace Univ, New York, One Pace Plaza, New York, NY 10038. **EMAIL** jthomas3@pace.edu

THOMAS, ORLAN E.
DISCIPLINE MUSIC HISTORY AND LITERATURE, MUSIC THEORY **EDUCATION** Univ NE, BME, MM; Eastman Sch Mus, DMA. **CAREER** Assoc prof Mus, TX Tech Univ. **SELECTED PUBLICATIONS** Auth, So You Want to Write a Song? Fundamentals of Songwriting. **CONTACT ADDRESS** Dept of Music, Texas Tech Univ, MS 2033, Lubbock, TX 79409. **EMAIL** othomas@ttacs.ttu.edu

THOMAS, PAUL R.
PERSONAL Born 11/30/1940, Takoma Park, MD, m, 1963, 4 children **DISCIPLINE** MEDIEVAL STUDIES, ENGLISH LITERATURE AND LANGUAGE **EDUCATION** Brigham Young Univ, BA, 64; Univ Va, MA, 67; Univ York, Eng, DPhil, 82. **CAREER** Instr, Church Col Haw, 67-72; asst prof, 72-76; asst prof, Vir Mil Inst, 77-78; asst prof, BYU, 80-94; assoc prof, 94-. **HONORS AND AWARDS** Huntington Lib Fel. **MEMBERSHIPS** MAA; EBS; NCS; UAAS; IRS; RMMRS. **RESEARCH** Chaucer studies; Middle English literature and language; Shakespeare; Medieval drama. **SELECTED PUBLICATIONS** Ed, A Reading of Beowulf, Chaucer Studio (Provo), 99; co-ed, The Poetics of Alliteration, Chaucer Stud (Provo), 00; auth, "Nun's Priest's Tale," in Masculinities in Chaucer, ed. Peter G Beidler (Woodbridge, Suffolk: Boydell and Brewer, 98). **CONTACT ADDRESS** Dept English, Brigham Young Univ, 3146 JKhb, Provo, UT 84602. **EMAIL** paul_thomas@byu.edu

THOMAS, STAFFORD H.
PERSONAL Born 08/09/1929, Lynchburg, VA, m, 1964, 2 children **DISCIPLINE** SPEECH **EDUCATION** Univ Colo, BA, 51; Univ Wyo, MA, 57; Univ Wash, PhD(Speech), 64. **CAREER** Asst prof, 64-77, assoc head dept, 67-70, assoc prof Speech, Univ Ill, Urbana, 77-. **HONORS AND AWARDS** Chancellors' Summer Instr Develop Awd, 65. **MEMBERSHIPS** Speech Commun Asn; Cent States Speech Commun Asn. **RESEARCH** Voice science; rhetoric and communication theory; speech and drama history. **SELECTED PUBLICATIONS** Auth, Effects of monotonous delivery on intelligibility, 6/69 & A terrorist's rhetoric: Citizen Lequinio's De L'eloquence, 3/72, Speech Monogr; Teaching segmental audience structure, Speech Teacher, 11/73; Parliamentary weakness in the French National Assemblies, 1789-1792, Southern Speech Commun J, fall 74; Teaching stagecraft through models, Commun Educ, 3/78. **CONTACT ADDRESS** Dept of Speech Commun, Univ of Illinois, Urbana-Champaign, 702 S Wright, Urbana, IL 61801-3631. **EMAIL** shthomas@uiuc.edu

THOMASON, WALLACE RAY
DISCIPLINE COMMUNICATION STUDIES **EDUCATION** Lamar Univ, BS, 85; Univ Tex, MA, 89, PhD, 92. **CAREER** Asst prof. **SELECTED PUBLICATIONS** Co-auth, Pauses, transition relevance and speaker change, Human Commun Res; Requests for demographic information in telephone calls to the cancer information service, Southern Jour Commun, Employment Interviewing and Post Bureaucracy, Jour Bus Tech Commun. **CONTACT ADDRESS** Dept of Communication, East Tennessee State Univ, PO Box 70717, Johnson City, TN 37614-0717.

THOMPSON, CHEVIA
DISCIPLINE LITERATURE **EDUCATION** Wash Univ, BA, 73; Wash Univ, MA, 75; Carnegie-Mellon Univ, PhD, 84. **CAREER** Prof, Md Inst Col of Art, 94-. **HONORS AND AWARDS** Carnegie-Mellon Univ Fel, 76-80; Int Woman of the Year Awd, Cambridge, 99; Individual Artist Awd, Cambridge, 99; Best Teachers in Am Awd, 00; Distinguished Black Marylander Awd, Towson Univ, 00. **SELECTED PUBLICATIONS** Auth, Catch the Fire, Riverhead Books/Berkeley Publ Group (New York, NY), 98; auth, "Art That Conceals and Reveals," Evening Sun Newspaper (98); auth, Crossing Into Fire, Maisonneuve Pr (Washington, DC), 00; auth, "Earl Lovelace," in The Concise Dict of World Lit Biog: African, Caribbean and Latin Am Writers, Bruccoli Clark (00); auth, Folk Realities and Bourgeoise Fantasies: 4 Maryland Artists in LINK: A Journal of the Arts in Baltimore and Beyond, 00. **CONTACT ADDRESS** Dept Lang & Lit, Maryland Inst, Col of Art, 1300 W Mt Royal Ave, Baltimore, MD 21217.

THOMPSON, CYNTHIA L.
PERSONAL Born 06/03/1943, Buffalo, NY **DISCIPLINE** CLASSICS IN GREEK NEW TESTAMENT **EDUCATION** Yale Univ, PhD, 73, MA, 68; Wellesley Col, BA, 66. **CAREER** Res, 73-75, Harvard Divinity School; Asst Prof of Classics & Religion, 75-80, Denison Univ, Granville, DH; Editor, 80-94, 97-, Westminster John Knox Press; Editor, 94-97, Fortress Press, Minneapolis, Philadelphia, Louisville. **HONORS AND AWARDS** Phi Beta Kappa **MEMBERSHIPS** APA, SBL. **RESEARCH** Women's Adornment in Greek-Roman World; Classical and Biblical Heritage. **SELECTED PUBLICATIONS** Auth, Hairstyles, Head Coverings and St Paul's Portraits From Roman Corinth, Biblical Archaeologist, 88; Rings of Gold-Neither Modest Nor Sensible, Bible Review, 93. **CONTACT ADDRESS** 39 Roslin St, #3, Dorchester, MA 02124. **EMAIL** cynthom@aol.com

THOMPSON, GARY
PERSONAL Born 08/18/1950, Oklahoma City, OK, m, 1971, 2 children **DISCIPLINE** AMERICAN & ENGLISH LITERATURE **EDUCATION** Rice Univ, BA, 73, MA, 75, PhD, 79. **CAREER** Asst Prof Eng, Saginaw Valley State Col, 79-82; Fulbright Prof, Marie Curie-Sklodowska Univ, Lublin, Poland, 82-84; Assoc Prof, 84-87, 88-89, Prof Eng, Saginaw Valley State Univ, 89-; Fulbright Prof, Univ Gdansk, Gdansk, Poland, 87-88; Asst ed, Green River Rev, 79-82, 84-86, ed, Polish Lit issue, 86. **HONORS AND AWARDS** MI Asn Governing Bds, 85. **MEMBERSHIPS** MLA; NCTE; CCCC. **RESEARCH** Nineteenth and twentieth century Am fiction; rhetoric and compos; media studies. **SELECTED PUBLICATIONS** Auth, Barth's letters and Hawke's passion, Mich Quart Rev, spring, 80; Doubles, Doppelgangers, and Twins in Mark Twain's Work, In: Mark Twain: Ritual Clown, Siena Col, 90; An Interview with Tadeusz Konwicki, Fiction Int, Spring 87; ed, Rhetoric through Media, Allyn & Bacon, 97; rev, "Kathleen E. Welch,_Electric Rhetoric_," CCC, 00; auth, "Pynchonian Pastiche," Beyond the Rainbow, Univ Press, forthcoming. **CONTACT ADDRESS** Dept of Eng, Saginaw Valley State Univ, 7400 Bay Rd, University Center, MI 48710-0001. **EMAIL** glt@tardis.svsu.edu

THOMPSON, GARY RICHARD
PERSONAL Born 12/11/1937, Los Angeles, CA, 4 children **DISCIPLINE** ENGLISH & AMERICAN LITERATURE **EDUCATION** San Fernando Valley State Col, BA, 59; Univ Southern Calif, MA, 60, PhD(English), 67. **CAREER** Teaching asst English, Univ Southern Calif, 62; instr, Ohio State Univ, 62-63; instr, Univ Calif, Los Angeles, 64-66; from instr to asst prof, Wash State Univ, 66-70, assoc prof, 71-75, chmn prog lit studies, 70-72; Prof English, Purdue Univ, 75-, Ed, Poe Studies, 68-79; ESQ: J Am Renaissance, 71-78; exchange prof, Universitat Hamburg, Germany, 84-85. **HONORS AND AWARDS** NDEA fel, 59-62; NEH fel, 73; Emerson Soc Prize, 89. **MEMBERSHIPS** MLA; Melville Soc Am; Hawthorne Soc; Poe Studies Asn, hon life mem; Am Lit Asn; Int Gothic Asn; Baltimore Poe Soc, life mem **RESEARCH** American romantic movement; Gothic tradition in literature; 19th century literature; Romance tradition; Narrative theory. **SELECTED PUBLICATIONS** Auth, Poe's readings of Pelham, Am Lit, 5/69; Unity, death & nothingness--Poe's romantic skepticism, PMLA, 3/70; ed, Great Short Works of Edgar Allan Poe, Harper & Row, 70, rev 74, HarperCollins, 90; auth, Themes, topics criticism, In: American Literary Scholarship: An Annual, Duke Univ, 71-73; co-ed, Ritual, Realism & Revolt: Major Traditions in the Drama, Scribner, 72; auth, Poe's Fiction: Romantic Irony in the Gothic Tales, Univ Wis, 73; ed, The Gothic Imagination: Essays in Dark Romanticism, Wash State Univ, 74; Edgar Allan Poe, In: Dictionary of Literary Biography, Gale, 79; ed, Romantic Gothic Tales, 1790-1840, Harper & Row, 79; co-ed, Ruined Eden of the present: Hawthorne, Melville, Poe, Critical Essays in Honor of Darrel Abel, Purdue Univ, 81; ed, Essays and Reviews of Edgar Allan Poe, Libr Am, 84; auth, Circumscribed Eden of Dreams: Dreamvision and Nightmare in Poe's Early Poetry, Enoch Pratt Libr & Baltimore Poe Soc, 84; auth, Edgar Allan Poe and the Writers of the Old South, In: Columbia Literary History of the U S, Columbia Univ, 88; auth, Development of Romantic Irony in the U S, Budapest Akademiai Kiado, 88; Romantic Arabesque, Contemporary Theory and Postmodernism, ESQ, 89; The Art of Authorial Presence: Hawthorne's Provincial Tales, Duke Univ, 93; Literary Politics and the Legitimate Sphere: Poe, Hawthorne, and the Tale Proper, Nineteenth-Century Literature, 94; co-auth, Neutral Ground: New Traditionalism and the American Romance Controversy, LSU, 98. **CONTACT ADDRESS** Dept of English, Purdue Univ, West Lafayette, West Lafayette, IN 47907-1968.

THOMPSON, HILARY
DISCIPLINE ENGLISH LITERATURE **EDUCATION** Univ Alberta, PhD, 72. **CAREER** Assoc prof emer, Acadia Univ. **MEMBERSHIPS** Children's Lit Asn. **RESEARCH** Art; literature; illustrated children's books; drama in education. **SELECTED PUBLICATIONS** Auth, Perspectives on Practice, Univ Victoria, 95; Children's Voices in Atlantic Literature and Culture, Guelph, 95; Warm is a Circle, Hantsport, 79; Fredericton, 82. **CONTACT ADDRESS** English Dept, Acadia Univ, Wolfville, NS, Canada B0P 1XO.

THOMPSON, JEWEL T.
PERSONAL Born Kinsale, VA, w, 1961, 2 children **DISCIPLINE** MUSIC THEORY AND COMPOSITION **EDUCATION** Virgina State Univ, BS, 56; Eastman Sch of Music of Univ of Rochester, MA, 60, PhD, 82. **CAREER** Asst prof, Virginia State Univ, 60-62; West Virginia Inst of Technology, 68-72; adjunct lect, Hunter Coll of City Univ of NY 72-75, adjunt asst prof, 75-85, asst prof 85-91, assoc prof 91-96, prof 96-. **HONORS AND AWARDS** Hattie M. Strong Found Fel; Ford Found Grant; Supreme Charitable Found of Ancient and Accepted Scottish Rite of Freemasonry Grant; Dame of Honour of the Grand Sovereign Dynastic Hospitalier of St John (Knights of Malta); Presidential Awd for Excellence in Service-Hunter Col. **MEMBERSHIPS** Amer Soc of Composers, Authors, and Publishers (ASCAP); Music Theory Society of NY State; The Amer Music Ctr. **RESEARCH** Analytical studies **SELECTED PUBLICATIONS** Auth, Samuel Coleridge-Taylor: The Development of His Compositional Style Metuelen, Scarecrow Press, 94; The International Dictionary of Black Composers, Five Critical Essays on Samuel Coleridge Taylor, Fitzroy/Dearborn Publishers, spring 99. **CONTACT ADDRESS** Hunter Col, CUNY, 695 Park Ave, New York, NY 10021. **EMAIL** wthompso@shiva.hunter.cuny.edu

THOMPSON, RAY
DISCIPLINE ENGLISH LITERATURE **EDUCATION** Queen's Univ, BA; Univ Mich, MA; Univ Alberta, PhD. **CAREER** Prof. **SELECTED PUBLICATIONS** Auth, pubs on Arthurian Legend. **CONTACT ADDRESS** English Dept, Acadia Univ, Wolfville, NS, Canada B0P 1XO. **EMAIL** ray.thompson@acadiau.ca

THOMPSON, ROGER C.
PERSONAL Born 11/08/1970, Santa Maria, CA, m, 1997 **DISCIPLINE** ENGLISH **EDUCATION** Baylor Univ, BA, 93; MA, 95; Tex Christ Univ, PhD, 99. **CAREER** Asst prof, Va Mil Inst, 99-. **HONORS AND AWARDS** SCMLA Inter Disc Group Humanities Prize, 98. **MEMBERSHIPS** MLA; RSA; Ralph Waldo Emerson Soc; ASHR. **RESEARCH** 19th-century American literature; history of rhetoric. **SELECTED PUBLICATIONS** Auth, Ralph Waldo Emerson and the American Kairos. **CONTACT ADDRESS** 487 Jacktown Rd, Lexington, VA 24450-4120. **EMAIL** thompsonrc@mail.vmi.edu

THOMSON, GEORGE HENRY
PERSONAL Born 07/22/1924, Bluevale, ON, Canada, m, 1956 **DISCIPLINE** BRITISH LITERATURE **EDUCATION** Univ Western Ont, BA, 47; Univ Toronto, MA, 48; PhD, 51. **CAREER** Lectr to assoc prof, Mt Allison Univ, 53-66; vis prof, Wayne State Univ, 66-67; prof, Univ of Ottawa, 69-89. **HONORS AND AWARDS** Can Coun Sr Fel, 67-68; Hilberry Publ Prize, Wayne State Univ Pr, 68. **MEMBERSHIPS** MLA, Virginia Woolf Soc, Can Numismatic Assoc. **RESEARCH** Dorothy Richardson, Modern British Novel. **SELECTED PUBLICATIONS** Auth, "The Trumpet-Major Chronicle," Nineteenth Century Fiction 17, (62): 45-56; auth, The Fiction of EM Forster, Wayne State Univ Pr, (Detroit), 67; auth, "A Forster Miscellany: Thoughts on the Uncollected Writings," Aspects of EM Forster: Essays and Recollections Written for his Ninetieth Birthday, ed Oliver Stallybrass, (London: Arnold, NY: Harcourt Brace, 69): 155-175; coed, Albergo Empedocle and Other Writings by DM Forster. Uncollected Writings, 1900-1915, Liveright (NY), 71; auth, "The Four Story Forms: Drama Film Comic Strips Narrative," Col Eng 37, (75): 265-280; coauth, "EM Forster's 'Life to Come': Description of the Manuscripts and Typescripts at King's College, Cambridge," Papers of the Bibliog Soc of Am 72, (78): 477-503; auth, "A Clean Well-Lighted Place: Interpreting the Original Text," Hemingway Rev 2, (83): 32-43; auth, A Reader's Guide to Dorothy Richardson's 'Pilgrimage', ELT Pr, (Greensboro, NC), 96; auth, Notes on 'Pilgrimage': Dorothy Richardson Annotated, ELT Pr, (Greensboro, NC), 99; auth, The Editions of Dorothy Richardson's 'Pilgrimage': A Comparison of Texts, ELT Pr, (Greensboro, NC), forthcoming. **CONTACT ADDRESS** 655 Echo Dr, Ottawa, ON, Canada K1S 1P2. **EMAIL** georgehthomson@compuserve.com

THONGTHIRAJ, DOOTSDEEMALACHANOK
PERSONAL Born 01/14/1971, Pasadena, CA, m **DISCIPLINE** ENGLISH **EDUCATION** UCLA, BS, 94; MA, 97; Can Philol, 98. **CAREER** Instr to teaching fel, UCLA, 95-. **HONORS AND AWARDS** Jean Stone Fel; Project 88 Fel; IACR Grant. **MEMBERSHIPS** MLA; AAAS; Phi Beta Kappa. **RESEARCH** Gender and ethnic studies; 19th and 20th-century American literature; Asian American literature; Southeast and Asian studies. **SELECTED PUBLICATIONS** Auth, "Toward a Movement Against Invisibility: Love Between Women in Thailand," in Desiring Asian Americans: Dimensions of the Gay Lesbian Experience, ed. Russell Leong (Routledge, 95); ed, "Voices From the Thum Thum Bowl," in Scaling the Chord (Multicultural Women Writers, forthcoming). **CONTACT ADDRESS** 2445 E Del Mar Blvd, Apt 340, Pasadena, CA 91107-4831. **EMAIL** thongthi@hotmail.com

THORN, ARLINE ROUSH
PERSONAL Born 11/22/1946, New Haven, WV, d, 1 child **DISCIPLINE** COMPARATIVE & ENGLISH LITERATURE **EDUCATION** Marshall Univ, AB, 67; Univ IL, Urbana, MA, 68, PhD, 71. **CAREER** From Instr to Assoc Prof, 71-79, prof eng, WVA State Col, 79-, Ch, Dept Eng, 86-94; Adj prof Eng, Marshall Univ Grad Col, 75-; mem, State Col System Bd Dir, 94-97. **HONORS AND AWARDS** Woodrow Wilson Inst on Interpreting Hum, 86; Citation as Outstanding Fac Mem, WVA Legislature, 89; Fulbright Seminar in Brazil, 93; First Prize, WVA Writers statewide competition, poetry, 96, 98. **MEMBERSHIPS** Am Comp Lit Asn; MLA; Asn for Integrative Studies. **RESEARCH** Women's studies; hist and theory of the novel; Holocaust Studies. **SELECTED PUBLICATIONS** Coauth, The veluminous word: McLuhan-D H Lawrence, Midwest Monogr, 71; The pivotal character in Dickens' novels, Papers WV a Asn Col Eng Tchr(s), spring 72; Shelley's Cenci as Tragedy, Costerus: Essays Eng Lit & Lang, 12/73; Harriette Arnow's mountain women, Bull WVA Asn Col Eng Tchr(s), 77; Feminine time in Dorothy Richardson's Pilgrimage, Int J Women's Studies, 78; How I became a historian, Kanawha Rev, 80; A mighty maze: Ulysses, Perspectives Contemp Lit, 80; co-ed, Origins: Texts for an Inquiry, Tapestry Press, 91; author of poems in Pikeville Rev, Southern Humanities Rev, and various anthologies. **CONTACT ADDRESS** Dept of Eng, West Virginia State Col, PO Box 1000, Institute, WV 25112-1000. **EMAIL** athorn@wvsvax.wvnet.edu

THORN, J. DALE
DISCIPLINE MASS COMMUNICATION **EDUCATION** Fla State Univ, PhD, 84. **CAREER** Prof in Residence, La State Univ; press secy to the Governor of La; assoc comnr, La Bd of Regents; area hd, PR, 93-97. **HONORS AND AWARDS** Ford Foundation/American Political Science Association award, 68; grant, Freedom Forum J prof publ prog, LSU coun on res; Bart Swanson Endowed Mem Professorship, 96-97. **RESEARCH** Media coverage and public relations impact on higher education desegregation litigation. **SELECTED PUBLICATIONS** Auth, Litigation Public Relations in the Civil Trial Setting, in Bus Res Yearbk, Vol. IV, UP of Am, 97; Media Mediocrity: A Perspective on Higher Education Desegregation News Coverage in the Second Reconstruction, in Kofi Lomotey and Charles Teddlie, eds, Readings on Equal Education, Vol 14, Forty Years After the Brown Decision: Social and Cultural Effects of School Desegregation, AMS Press, 97. **CONTACT ADDRESS** The Manship Sch of Mass Commun, Louisiana State Univ and A&M Col, Baton Rouge, LA 70803.

THORNDIKE, JONATHAN L.
PERSONAL Born 12/27/1959, Alma, MI, m, 1983, 2 children **DISCIPLINE** LITERATURE **EDUCATION** Alma Col, BA, 83; Mich State Univ, MA, 85; PhD, 89. **CAREER** Vis prof, Alma Col, 85-89; asst prof, Rocky Mtn Col, 89-91; assoc prof, Lakeland Col, 91-98; assoc prof, Belmont Univ, 98-. **HONORS AND AWARDS** NEH FEL, 94, 95, 01; Outstanding Fac Awd, Lakeland Col, 98; Lilly Endowment Fund, 00-03. **MEMBERSHIPS** MLA, Phi Beta Kappa; Alpha Chi. **SELECTED PUBLICATIONS** Ed, New Essays on James Joyce, Contemp Res Pr, 95; auth, Epperson vs. Arkansas, Enslow Pr, 99; auth, The Teapot Dome Scandal, Enslow Pr, 01. **CONTACT ADDRESS** Belmont Univ, 5028 Penbrook Dr, Franklin, TN 37069. **EMAIL** thorndikej@mail.belmont.edu

THORNTON, JERI
PERSONAL Born 03/20/1952, Tulsa, OK, d, 3 children **DISCIPLINE** EDUCATION, ENGLISH **EDUCATION** Univ Central Okla, BA, 85; MA, 87. **CAREER** From grad teaching asst to adj english prof, Univ of Okla, 87-93; dir of the Learning Ctr at Okla State Univ, 93-. **HONORS AND AWARDS** Delta Pi Honor Soc; Alpha Chi Honor Soc; Teaching Fel, Univ of Central Okla, 86-87; Outstanding English Grad Student, 87; Teaching Fel, Univ of Okla, 87-91; listed in Who's Who in Am Colleges and Universities, 91; Phi Theta Kappa; State-Wide Awd for Excellence (to The Learning Ctr), Okla Asn for the Improvement of Developmental Educ, 98; Outstanding Advisor, Phi theta Kappa, 99; listed in Who's Who Among America's Teachers, 00. **MEMBERSHIPS** Okla Global Educ Consortium, Okla Asn for the Improvement of Developmental Educ, Okla Asn of Community Col, Okla Asn of Instnl Res. **RESEARCH** English, Philosophy, Humanities, and Film. **SELECTED PUBLICATIONS** Auth, "The Learning Center: TLC for Students," Innovations Abstracts 17 (95); auth, "My Old House," What's Hot! (97); auth, "For the Love of it: Shakespeare and Love," What's Hot! (97). **CONTACT ADDRESS** Dept Humanities, Oklahoma State Univ, Oklahoma City, 900 N Portland Ave, Oklahoma City, OK 73107-6120. **EMAIL** tjeri@osuokc.edu

THORPE, JAMES
PERSONAL Born 08/17/1915, Aiken, SC, m, 1941, 3 children **DISCIPLINE** ENGLISH & AMERICAN LITERATURE **EDUCATION** The Citadel, AB, 36; Univ of NC, MA, 37; Harvard Univ, PhD, 41. **CAREER** Colonel, US Air Force, 41-46; instr to prof, Princeton Univ, Master of Grad Col, 46-66; dir, Huntington Libr & Art Gallery, 66-83, sr res assoc, Huntington Libr & Art Gallery, 66-99. **HONORS AND AWARDS** Litt D, Occidental Col, 68; LHD, Claremont Grad Sch, 68; LLD, The Citadel, 71; HHD, Univ Toledo, 77. **MEMBERSHIPS** Mod Lang Asn; Soc for Textual Scholar; Am Antiquarian Soc, Am Acad of Arts & Sci; Am Philos Soc. **RESEARCH** 17th century English lit; Contemporary Am lit; Hist of Huntington Library. **SELECTED PUBLICATIONS** Auth, Proverbs for Thinkers, Huntington Libr Press, 98; auth, Proverbs for Friends, Huntington Libr Press, 97; auth, A Pleasure of Proverbs, Huntington Libr Press, 96; auth, H. E. Huntington: A Short Biography, Huntington Libr Press, 96; auth, Henry Edwards Huntington: A Biography, Univ Calif Press, 94. **CONTACT ADDRESS** 20 Loeffler Rd, DuncasterT-320, Bloomfield, CT 06002.

THORPE, JUDITH M.
PERSONAL Born 03/19/1941, Fort Wayne, IN, m, 2000, 1 child **DISCIPLINE** COMMUNICATION **EDUCATION** Ball State Univ, BA, 63; MA, 76; Ohio State Univ, PhD, 86. **CAREER** Ohio State Univ, 84-86; Univ of Tenn Knoxville, 86-87; Univ of Wisc, 87-. **HONORS AND AWARDS** C-Span Fe, 90; AAUW Grant, 91; Acad of Television Arts and Sci Fac Sem, 92; Awd of Outstanding Scholarly Contribution, 92; AAUW Gift Scholar, 93; Awd, Univ Wis Oshkosh, 90, 94; Who's Who in America, 97; Nat Assoc of TelevisionProgrammers Fel Seminar, 00. **SELECTED PUBLICATIONS** Coauth, "Communication Training for Legal Professionals", J of the Tenn Speech Commun Assoc III.I, (87): 13-21; auth, "The Responsible Media Communicator: Guidelines for Consulting in the Information Age", J of the Tenn Speech Commun Assoc (87): 25-29; coauth, "Is Experiential Learning Effective in Teaching Organizational Communication Skills? Results of a Pilot Study Using Electronic Mail Instruction", Wis Commun Assoc J, (88): 20-37; coauth, "Chrysler's Success Story: Advertising as Anecdotes", J of Popular Cult 25.3 (91): 125-134; auth ""Writing for Media Commercials: Hitting the Target Audience", Feedback 32.1 (91): 17; auth, Media Criticism: Journeys in Interpretation, Kendall/Hunt, (Dubuque), 92; auth, "The Contribution of Marshall McLuhan to the Speech Communication Discipline When the Media is Not the Message", Canada Week Papers, Univ of Tenn, (94): 49-53; auth, Corporate Media: Communicating for an Organization, (forthcoming). **CONTACT ADDRESS** Dept Commun, Univ of Wisconsin, Oshkosh, 800 Algoma Blvd, Oshkosh, WI 54901-3551.

THORSON, CONNIE C.
PERSONAL Born 07/25/1940, Dallas, TX, m, 1970 **DISCIPLINE** ENGLISH LITERATURE OF THE RESTORATION AND EIGHTEENTH CENTURY; LIBRARY SCIENCE **EDUCATION** Univ AR, Fayetteville, BA, 62, MA, 64; Univ NM, Albuquerque, PhD (English), 70; Univ IL, Urbana, MS (Library Science), 77. **CAREER** Asst to Assoc prof, Head of Acquisitions, 79-90, Prof and Head of Reference and Aquisitions, 90-95, Prof Emerita, Univ NM, 95-; Dir of the Library and Prof, Allegheny Col, Meadville, PA, 95-. **HONORS AND AWARDS** Phi Kappa Phi; Beta Phi Mu; Lifetime Achievement Awd, South Central Soc for 18th-Century Studies, 94. **MEMBERSHIPS** Am Library Asn; Modern Lang Asn; Am Soc for 18th-Century Studies; SCSECS; MMLA; AAUP. **RESEARCH** Anti-Roman Catholic lit of the Restoration and eighteenth century; novel and drama, English and American; faculty status for Librarians. **SELECTED PUBLICATIONS** Auth, A Million Stars, 80; A Pocket Companion for Oxford, (1756), 89; The RFP Process: Effective Management of the Acquisition of Library Materials, 98. **CONTACT ADDRESS** 451 Hartz Ave., Meadville, PA 16335-1326. **EMAIL** cthorson@alleg.edu

THORSON, JAMES LLEWELLYN
PERSONAL Born 01/07/1934, Yankton, SD, m, 1970 **DISCIPLINE** ENGLISH AND AMERICAN LITERATURE **EDUCATION** Univ Nebr, BS, 56, MA, 61; Cornell Univ, PhD(English), 66. **CAREER** Instr English, Univ Nebr, 61-62; asst prof, 65-70, dir grad studies English, 69-71, ASSOC PROF ENGLISH, UNIV N MEX, 70-, Greater univ fund grant, Univ NMex, 67; sr Fulbright lectr English, Univ Macedonia, Yugoslavia, 71-72; vis tutor, English, Jesus Col, Oxford, 73, vis sr res fel, 76-77 and 80. **MEMBERSHIPS** AAUP; MLA; Friends of Bodleian Libr; Am Soc Eighteenth Century Studies. **RESEARCH** Restoration and 18th century English literature; bibliography; American literature. **SELECTED PUBLICATIONS** Auth, The Publication of Hudibras, Papers Bibliog Soc Am, 66; Samuel Butler, 1612-1680: A Bibliography, Bull Bibliog, 1/73; A Broadside by Samuel Butler, Bodleian Libr Rec, 2/74; Authorial Duplicity: A Warning to Editors, Anal Enumerative Bibliog, 3/79; The Expedition of Humphry Clinker, Oxford Mag, 5/82; Prior, Matthew An 'Epitaph,' Explicator, Vol 0051, 93; coauth, Academic Fredom: University of Texas of the Permian Basin, AAUP Bull, 6/79; ed, Yugoslav Perspectives on American Literature: An Anthology, Ardis, 80; The Expedition of Humphry Clinker, Norton, 82. **CONTACT ADDRESS** Dept of English, Univ of New Mexico, Albuquerque, 1 University Campus, Albuquerque, NM 87131-0001. **EMAIL** jthorson@unm.edu

THRALL, TREVOR
DISCIPLINE COMMUNICATION PROCESSES AND TECHNOLOGIES **EDUCATION** Univ MI, BA, 89; Mass Inst Technol, PhD, 96. **CAREER** Vis asst prof, Univ MI, 95-98. **SELECTED PUBLICATIONS** Auth, Public Perception of Interest Groups: How Journalistic Labeling Affects Interest Group Credibility, 1997 Annual Meeting Midwest Asn Public Opinion Res; Look Who's Talking: Elite Interest Group Dominance of the News, Am Polit Sci Asn, Mass Media Coverage of Interest Groups: Implications for Public Opinion, Annual Meeting Am Asn Public Opinion Res, Going Negative in '96, Wolverine Caucus; Competing Images of the Press, , Am Polit Sci Asn; The First Amendment and the Persian Gulf War, Gerald R. Ford Inst for Public Service; War and the Fourth Estate: Public Affairs from Vietnam to the Gulf, Am Polit Sci Asn; Return to Censorship? Government Control of the Press from Grenada to the Gulf, Annual Meeting, New Eng Pol Sci Asn. **CONTACT ADDRESS** Univ of Michigan, Ann Arbor, 515 E. Jefferson St, Ann Arbor, MI 48109-1316. **EMAIL** atthrall@umich.edu

THREATTE, LESLIE L.
PERSONAL Born 02/01/1943, Miami, FL **DISCIPLINE** CLASSICS **EDUCATION** Oberlin Col, BM and BA, 64; Harvard Univ, PhD, 69. **CAREER** Asst prof, Cornell Univ, 68-70; asst prof to prof, Univ of Calif at Berkeley, 70-. **HONORS AND AWARDS** NEH Summer Fel, 74; Guggenheim, 81; Inst for Advanced Study, 95. **MEMBERSHIPS** Am Philol Asn. **RESEARCH** Greek Epigraphy and Linguistics. **SELECTED PUBLICATIONS** Auth, Grammar of Attic Inscriptions Vol 1: Phonology, 80; auth, Grammar of Attic Inscriptions Vol 2: Morphology, 96. **CONTACT ADDRESS** Dept Classics, Univ of California, Berkeley, 7211 Dwinelle Hall, Berkeley, CA 94720-2520. **EMAIL** poovanna@earthlink.net

THRONE, BARRY
DISCIPLINE ENGLISH LITERATURE **EDUCATION** Univ Wis, PhD. **CAREER** Dept Eng, Queen's Univ **RESEARCH** Theatre history; Renaissance drama; feminist and reception theory. **SELECTED PUBLICATIONS** Auth, pubs on Shakespeare and the modern Canadian novel. **CONTACT ADDRESS** English Dept, Queen's Univ at Kingston, Kingston, ON, Canada K7L 3N6. **EMAIL** thorneb@post.queensu.ca

THUENTE, MARY HELEN
PERSONAL Born 03/21/1946, Chicago, IL, m, 1967, 2 children **DISCIPLINE** ENGLISH, IRISH LIT **EDUCATION** Clarke Col, BA, 67; Univ Kans, MA, 69, PhD, 73. **CAREER** Asst prof, 75-80, assoc prof, 80-94, prof, 94-, Ind Univ/Purdue Univ. **MEMBERSHIPS** MLA; Am Comt Irish Studies; Can Assn Irish Studies; Int Assn Study Irish Lit. **RESEARCH** Irish literature, hist. **SELECTED PUBLICATIONS** Auth, The Harp Re-Strung, 94. **CONTACT ADDRESS** Dept of English, Indiana Univ-Purdue Univ, Fort Wayne, 2101 Coliseum Blvd E, Fort Wayne, IN 46805-1445. **EMAIL** thuentem@ipfw.edu

THUNDY, ZACHARIAS P.
PERSONAL Born 09/28/1936, Changanacherry, India, m, 1983, 2 children **DISCIPLINE** ENGLISH, LINGUISTICS, MEDIEVAL STUDIES, INDOLOGY **EDUCATION** Pontif Athenaeum, India, BPh, 58; LPh, 59; BTh, 61; STL, 63; DePaul Univ, MA, 66; Univ Notre Dame, PhD(English), 69. **CAREER** Instr philos, Dharmaram Col, Bangalore, India, 63-64; from asst prof to assoc prof, 68-77, prof English, Northern Mich Univ, 77-, Am Inst Indian Studies sr fel, 74-75; Fulbright fel, 78-79; Joseph J. Malone fel, 93. **HONORS AND AWARDS** Citation & Medal, Mich Acad Sci, Arts & Lett, 77; Distinguised Fac Awd, 88; Killeen Lectr at St. Norbert Col, 00. **MEMBERSHIPS** MLA; Midwest Mod Lang Asn; Mich Acad; Medieval Asn of the Midwest; AAUP. **RESEARCH** Anthropological linguistics; American dialect survey; feminism in the Middle Ages; east-west relationship in literature and culture. **SELECTED PUBLICATIONS** Auth, Circumstance, Circumference, and Center, Hartford Studies Lit, 71; auth, Oaths in Germanic folklore, Folklore, 71; auth, Covenant in Anglo-Saxon Thought, Macmillan, 72; coed, Language and Culture, Northern Mich Univ, 73; auth, Beowulf and Jus diaboli, Christian Scholar's Rev, 73; coed, Chaucerian Problems and Perspectives, Univ Notre Dame, 78; auth, South Indian Folktales of Kadar, Meerut, & Berkeley, 83; auth, Buddha and Christ: Nativity Stories and Indian Traditions, Brill, 93; auth, Millennium: Apocalypse and Antichrist, Crosscultural Pub., 98. **CONTACT ADDRESS** 1414 North Ivy Rd. B4, South Bend, IN 46637-5690. **EMAIL** zthundy@nmu.edu

THURIN, SUSAN MOLLY SCHOENBAUER
PERSONAL Born 01/24/1942, Jordan, MN, m, 1969 **DISCIPLINE** ENGLISH LITERATURE **EDUCATION** Col St Benedict, BA, 63; IN Univ, Bloomington, MA, 66; Univ Wis-Milwaukee, PhD, 79. **CAREER** Teacher, Peace Corps, Liberia, W AFR, 63-65, teacher English, Marshall High Sch, Milwaukee, 66-67; teacher forms I & II, St Peter's Preparatory Sch, England, 67-68; instructor to assoc prof English, 68-85, Prof English, Univ WI-Stout, 86-; fac exchange, Beijing Institute of Light Industry, CNA, 86-87; lecturer, English dept, Univ Gothenburg, SWE, 89-90. **HONORS AND AWARDS** Thomas Hardy Summer School, Weymouth, England, 82; Univ WI System Faculty Col, 85, 94; NEH Summer Seminar: The Novel of Dickens, Univ of Rochester, NY, George H. Ford, 84; Ed Testing Service: Reader, AP test, Princeton, NJ, 86; NEH Summer Seminar: Culture and Soc in England, 1800-1900, Brown Univ, Roger Henkle and Perry Curtis, 89; Dahlgren Prof, 96-98. **MEMBERSHIPS** MLA; Midwest MLA; Nat Council of Teachers of English; TESOL; MVSA. **RESEARCH** Eighteenth and 19th century British novel; women in literature; travel literature. **SELECTED PUBLICATIONS** Auth, The Relationship between Dora and Agnes, Dickens Studies Newslett, 81; To Be Brought Up By Hand, Victorian Newslett, fall 83; The Accomplished Lady in the English Novel, Trans WI Acad of Sciences, Arts, and Letters, 84; The Madonna and the Child Wife in Romola, Tulsa Studies in Women's Lit, spring 85; The Seven Deadly Sins in Great Expectations, Dickens Studies Annual 15, ed Michael Timko, Fred Kaplan, and Edward Guiliano, NY: AMS Press, 86; Pickwick and Podsnap Abroad: Dicken's Pictures From Italy, Dickensian 83, summer 87; Travel and Tourism, Victorian Britain: An Encyclopedia, ed Sally Mitchell. NY: Garland Press, 88; China in Dickens, Dickens Quart, Sept 91; Virginia Woolf: Writing Through Manic-Depression, Kaleidoscope 24, winter/spring 92; Zhang Jie's Love Must Not Be Forgotten, Masterplots II: Women's Literature, Pasadena: Salem Press, 95; Annotated Bibliography of Great Expectations, Masterplots, Pasadena: Salem Press, 95; Michael Cotsell's Creditable Warriors, Carlyle Studies Annual 15, 95; Alison Blunt, Mary Kingsley and Maria Frawley, A Wider Range, Nineteenth Century Prose 23, spring 96; Constance Gordon Cumming, British Travel Writers, vol II, Dictionary of Literary Biography, ed, Barbara Brothers and Julia Gergits, Gale Research, 97; Victorian Travelers and the Opening of China, 1842-1907, OH Univ Press, 98. **CONTACT ADDRESS** Univ of Wisconsin, Stout, Menomonie, WI 54751-0790. **EMAIL** thurins@uwstout.edu

THYM, JURGEN
PERSONAL Born 07/02/1943, Bremervoerde, Germany, m, 1992 **DISCIPLINE** MUSICOLOGY **EDUCATION** Athenaeum Stade, Abitur, 63; Hochschule fuer Musik Berlin, Diploma Schulmusik, 67; Freie Universitaet Berlin, Diploma Hist, 69; Case Western Reserve Univ, PhD Musicology, 74. **CAREER** 73, Vis Instr, Oberlin Col-Conservatory; Eastman School of Music, Univ Rochester, Instr, 73, Asst Prof 74, Assoc Prof 80, Prof 89-, Ch Musicol 82-00. **HONORS AND AWARDS** Rayburn Wright Awd, 94; Deems-Taylor Awd, 83; Awd of American Music Library Association, 80, 78-79. **MEMBERSHIPS** Am Musicol Soc; Am Liszt Soc; Lyrica; Int Musicol Soc; Int Asn for Word and Music Studies. **RESEARCH** German Lied; Text/Music Relations; Beethoven; Analysis; Second Viennese School. **SELECTED PUBLICATIONS** Articles and Reviews in MLA Notes; Comparative Literature; J Music Theory; J Musicol Res; Fontes Artis Musicae; Am Choral Rev; Mendelssohn and Schumann Essays, ed Jon Finson and Larry Todd; German Lieder in the Nineteenth Century, ed Rufus Hallmark; Music Hist Through Sources, ed Alfred Mann; Translations of Kirnberger's Kunst des reinen Satzes in der Musik (with David Beach) and Schenker's Kontrapunkt (with John Rothgeb); Editions: Schoenberg Gesamtausgabe (4 v with Nikos Kokkinis), 100 Years of Eichendorff Songs. **CONTACT ADDRESS** Eastman Sch of Music, 26 Gibbs St, Rochester, NY 14604. **EMAIL** jthy@aol.com

TICHI, CECELIA
DISCIPLINE AMERICAN LITERATURE, WOMEN'S STUDIES **EDUCATION** UCLA, Davis, PhD. **CAREER** William R Kenan Jr Prof Eng, Vanderbilt Univ. **SELECTED PUBLICATIONS** Auth, New World, New Earth: Environmental Reform in American Literature from the Puritans through Whitman, 79; Shifting Gears: Technology, Literature, Culture in Modernist America; Electronic Hearth: Creating an American Television Culture, 91; High Lonesome: The American Culture of Country Music, 94. **CONTACT ADDRESS** Vanderbilt Univ, Nashville, TN 37203-1727.

TICK, JUDITH
PERSONAL Born 01/04/1943, Winthrop, m **DISCIPLINE** MUSIC HISTORY **EDUCATION** City Univ New York, PhD, 78. **CAREER** Asst-assoc prof music, Brooklyn Col, 75-91; prof, Northeastern Univ, 91-. **HONORS AND AWARDS** Humanities Fel, Nat Endowment for the Arts, 91; Rockefeller Found Nat Fel, 86. **MEMBERSHIPS** Sonneck Soc for Study of Am Music; Am Musicol Soc. **RESEARCH** Am music; hist of women in music. **SELECTED PUBLICATIONS** Ruth Crawford Seeger, A Composer's Search for American Music,Oxford Univ Press, 97; Charles Ives and Gender Ideology, in Musicology and Difference, UC Press, 93; Ruth Crawford's Spiritual Concept: The Sound Ideals of an Early American Modernist, JAMS, 91; Women and Music, New Grove Dictionary of Am Music, 86; Women Making Music, The Western Art Tradition 1150-1950, Univ Ill Press, 86; American Women Composers Before 1870, UMI, 83, Univ Rochester Press, 95. **CONTACT ADDRESS** Dept of Music, Northeastern Univ, 360 Huntington Ave, Boston, MA 02115.

TIDWELL, JOHN EDGAR
PERSONAL Born 12/13/1945, Independence, KS **DISCIPLINE** ENGLISH **EDUCATION** Washburn University, BA, English, 1969; Creighton University, MA, English, 1971; University of Minnesota, PhD, 1981; Yale University, visiting fellow, 1985-86. **CAREER** Atchison Neighborhood Center, Atchison, KS, director, 69-70; Maur Hill Catholic College Preparatory School, Atchison, KS, instructor, 69-70; Creighton University, instructor, 70-71; University of Nebraska at Omaha, instructor, 71-73, acting chairman of Black Studies Department, 72-73; St Olaf College, director of American Minority Studies, 73-74, instructor, 73-75; University of Minnesota, teaching associate II, 75-78; Carleton College, visiting instructor, Fall 1977, Spring 1979; University of Kentucky, assistant professor, 81-87; Miami University, assistant professor, 87-93, assoc prof, 93-. **HONORS AND AWARDS** American Lutheran Church Future Faculty Fellowship, 1975-77; Putnam Dana McMillan Fellowship, University of Minnesota, 1979; National Fellowships Fund Awd, 1978-81; NEH Fellowship for Independent Study and Research, 1985-86; several other fellowships and grants. **MEMBERSHIPS** Modern Language Association; Midwest Modern Language Association. **CONTACT ADDRESS** Department of English, Miami Univ, Oxford, OH 45056.

TIEMENS, ROBERT K.
DISCIPLINE COMMUNICATION STUDIES **EDUCATION** Univ Iowa, PhD, 62. **CAREER** Prof. **MEMBERSHIPS** Nat Commun Asn; Western States Commun Asn. **RESEARCH** Visual communication; media production. **SELECTED PUBLICATIONS** Auth, A Visual Analysis of the 1976 Presidential Debates, 78; The Visual Context of Argument: An Analysis of the September 25, 1988 Presidential Debate, Nat Commun Asn, 89; coauth, Children's Perceptions of Changes in Size of Television Images, Human Commun Res, 81; Television's Coverage of Jesse Jackson's Speech to the 1984 Democratic National Convention, Jour Broadcasting Elec Media, 88. **CONTACT ADDRESS** Dept of Communication, Univ of Utah, 100 S 1350 E, Salt Lake City, UT 84112. **EMAIL** R.Tiemens@m.cc.utah.edu

TIERNEY, JAMES EDWARD
PERSONAL Born 01/23/1935, Newark, NJ, m, 1995 **DISCIPLINE** ENGLISH LITERATURE **EDUCATION** Seton Hall Univ, BA, 56; Fordham Univ, MA, 64; New York Univ, PhD(English Lit), 69. **CAREER** From instr to asst prof English Lit, 68-75, from assoc prof to prof English, Univ MO-St Louis, 75-87; Nat Endowment for Humanities fel, 73-74; grants, Am Philos Soc, 76 & Am Coun Learned Soc, 77; Henry Huntington Libr fel, 76; bibliog ed, Eighteenth Century: A Current Bibliog, 78-; fel, inst res in Humanities, Univ Edinburgh, 82; prof emer, 00. **HONORS AND AWARDS** Univ of Missouri Research Board Grant, 93-94; UM-St Louis Research Office Grant, 94, 97; Fel Cen for Int Studies, UM-St Louis, 97. **MEMBERSHIPS** Bibliographical Soc of Am; East-Central Am Soc for Eighteenth-Century Stud; Soc for the Hist of Authorship, Reading, and Publishing; South Central Soc for Eighteenth-Century Stud. **RESEARCH** Eighteenth century British periodical, novel and drama. **SELECTED PUBLICATIONS** Auth, "Robert Dodsley: First Printer and Stationer to the Soc," Journal of the Royal Soc of the Arts, 83; auth, "A CD-ROM Subject Index to Pre-1800 British Periodicals," Journal of Newspaper and Periodical Hist, 8, (92): 56-62; auth, "Responses to Tyrants: Robert Dodsley to William Warburton and David Garrick,"in "Sent As A Gift,": Eight Correspondences for the Eighteenth Century, ed. Alan D. McKenzie, Athens, Geo, Georgia Univ Press, 93; auth, "Pre-1800 British Periodical Subject Index: An Update," East-Central Intelligencer, (95): 117-121; auth, "R. Dodsley, R. and J. Dodsley, J. Dodsley," in Dictionary of Literary Biography, 154, The British Literary Book Trade 1700-1820, eds., James K. Bracken and Joel Silver, Detroit, Washington, and London: Gale Res, (95): 106-122; auth, Advertisements for Books in London Newspapers, 1760-1785," Studies in Eighteenth-Century Culture, 30, (00): 153-64. **CONTACT ADDRESS** Dept of English, Univ of Missouri, St. Louis, 8001 Natural Bridge, Saint Louis, MO 63121-4499. **EMAIL** jetier@umsl.edu

TIESSEN, PAUL
DISCIPLINE GENDER POLITICS IN FILM; BRITISH MODERNISM **EDUCATION** WLU, BA; Alberta, MA, PhD. **CAREER** Prof **RESEARCH** British and Canadian modernism, film-and-literture studies cultural/media studies, Malcolm Lowry, Wyndham Lewis, Dorothy Richardson, Marshall McLuhan. **SELECTED PUBLICATIONS** Auth, and Apparently Incongruous Parts: The Worlds of Malcolm Lowry, Scarecrow Press, 90; The Letters of Malcolm Lowry and Gerald Noxon, 1940-1952 , UBC Press, 88; The Cinema of Malcolm Lowry: A Scholarly Edition of Lowry's Tender is the Night, UBC Press, 90; The 1940 Under the Volcano , MLR Editions Canada, 94; Co-ed, Joyce/Lowry: Critical Perspectives, UP of Kentucky, 97. **CONTACT ADDRESS** Dept of English, Wilfrid Laurier Univ, 75 University Ave W, Waterloo, ON, Canada N2L 3C5. **EMAIL** ptiessen@wlu.ca

TIGAY, JEFFREY HOWARD
PERSONAL Born 12/25/1941, Detroit, MI, m, 1965, 4 children **DISCIPLINE** BIBLICAL STUDIES, ANCIENT NEAR EASTERN LITERATURE **EDUCATION** Columbia Col, BA, 63; Jewish Theol Sem, Am, MHL, 66; Yale Univ, PhD(comp Blbl & Ancient Near East Studies), 71. **CAREER** From A.M Ellis asst prof to prof, Hebrew & Semitic Lang & Lit, Univ Pa, 71-; chair, Jewish Studies Program, Univ Pa, 95-98; vis assoc prof, Bible Jewish Theol Sem Am. **HONORS AND AWARDS** Lindback Awd for disting teaching, Univ of Pennsylvania; grantee, Nat Sci Found, 72; assoc, Univ Sem on Studies Hebrew Bible, Columbia Univ, 72; Am Coun Learned Soc fel, 75-76; fel, inst Advan Studies, Hebrew Univ, Jerusalem, 78-79; grant, Am Philos Soc, 80 & Am Coun Learned Soc, 80-81; Nat Endowment for Humanties summer res fel, 80; fel, Am Acad for Jewish Research, 80, 86; Mem Fedn Jewish Cult fel, 81-82; scholar-in-residence, Jewish Publication Soc of Am, 86-87; fel, Annenberg Res Institute, 91-92. **MEMBERSHIPS** Am Acad for Jewish Research, Am Schools of Oriental Res; Assoc for Jewish Studies; The Biblical Colloquium; Soc of Biblical Lit. **RESEARCH** Biblical literature and exegesis; comparative Biblical and ancient Near Eastern studies; ancient Judaism. **SELECTED PUBLICATIONS** Auth, The Evolution of the Gilgamesh Epic, Univ Pa Pr (Philadelphia), 82; auth/ed, Empirical Models for Biblical Criticism, Univ Pa Pr (Philadelphia), 85; auth, "You Shall Have No Other Gods," Israelite Religion in the Light of Hebrew Inscriptions, in Harvard Semitic Studies 31 (Atlanta: Scholars Pr, 86); co-ed, Studies in Midrash and Related Lit, Jewish Publication Soc (Philadelphia), 88; auth, The JPS Torah Commentary: Deuteronomy, Jewish Publication Soc of Am (Philadelphia), 96; co-ed, Tehilla le-Moshe, Biblical and Judaic Studies in Honor of Moshe Greenberg, Eisenbraun's (Winona Lake, Indiana), 97. **CONTACT ADDRESS** Dept Asian & Middle Eastern Studies, Univ of Pennsylvania, 847 Williams Hall, Philadelphia, PA 19104-6305. **EMAIL** jtigay@sas.upenn.edu

TIGER, VIRGINIA MARIE
PERSONAL Born 08/20/1940, Montreal, PQ, Canada, m, 1974, 1 child **DISCIPLINE** ENGLISH LITERATURE **EDUCATION** Univ Toronto, BA, 63; Univ BC, MA, 65, PhD, 71. **CAREER** Exten lectr lit, Univ BC, 64-66; from instr to asst prof, 70-75, assoc prof, 75-, prof eng, Rutgers Univ, Newark, 76, Dir Women's Studies, 75-78, dir, Grad Eng, ch Eng Dept, Assoc dean fac, Dean Instruction; Broadcaster, Can Broadcasting Corp, 64-67; Drama critic, Toronto Daily Star, 60-63; Doc Res & partic sex roles, Can TV, Toronto, 77; bk critic, Wash Post, 74-76; bk critic, Soho News, 77-80. **MEMBERSHIPS** MLA; Nat Women's Studies Asn; AAUP; Doris Lessing Soc. **RESEARCH** Mod Brit lit; women's studies; hist of the novel. **SELECTED PUBLICATIONS** Auth, Advertisements for Herself, Columbia Forum, spring 74; coauth, An Othello, Plays of the Open Space, Penguin, 74; auth, William Golding: The Dark Fields of Discovery, Calder & Boyars, 74; coauth, Everywoman, Random, 77; Inlaws/Outlaws: The language of women, In: Women's Language and Style, 78; Don's Lessing, G K Hall. **CONTACT ADDRESS** Dept of Eng, Rutgers, The State Univ of New Jersey, Newark, 360 King Blvd, Newark, NJ 07102-1897. **EMAIL** vtiger@andromeda.rutgers.edu

TILLIS, FREDERICK C.
PERSONAL Born 01/05/1930, Galveston, TX, m **DISCIPLINE** MUSIC **EDUCATION** Wiley College, BA 1949; Univ

of Iowa, MA, 1952, PhD, 1963. **CAREER** Wiley College, instructor/director of instrumental music, 49-51, assistant professor/chairman of the dept of music, 56-61, associate professor/chairman of the dept of music, 63-64; Grambling College, professor of music/head of theory dept, 64-67; Kentucky State University, professor/head of the music dept, 67-69; University of Massachusetts, associate professor of music, 70-73, professor of music theory and composition/director of Afro American music & jazz program, 73-, director of UMass jazz workshop, 74-80, director of fine arts center, 78-, associate chancellor for affirmative action and equal opportunity, 90-. **HONORS AND AWARDS** Recip United Negro Coll Fund Fellowship 1961-63; recip Rockefeller Fund Grant for Devl Compstn 1978; recip Nat Endowment for the Arts, Composers Grant 1979; Chancellor of the University of Massachusetts, Distinguished Lecturer, 1980; MA Cultural Council, Commonwealth Awd in organizational leadership, 1997. **MEMBERSHIPS** Music or DA board of dir, 1995; Chancellor's Executive Advisory Council, 1994-; ALANA Honor Society Board, 1994-; Faculty Senate Council on the Status of Minorities, 1984-; Academy of American Poets; American Composers Alliance; American Federation of Musicians; Broadcast Music Industry; Center for Black Music Research; International Association of Jazz Educators; Music Educators National Conference; TransAfrica Forum; American Music Center; Massachusetts Music Educators Association; United Negro College Fund. **SELECTED PUBLICATIONS** Composer of more than 120 compositions spanning both the European classical & jazz traditions; Albums: "Freedom," 1973; "Fantasy on a Theme by Julian Adderley," 1975; "The Music of Frederick Tillis, Vol I," 1979; "Quintet for Brass," 1980; "Kcor Variations," 1980; "Elegy," 1983; "Swing Low, Deep River," 1984; "Contrasts and Diversions: The Tillis-Holmes Jazz Duo," 1987; "Voices of Color," 1989; "Crucificion," 1990; "Paintings in Sound," 1990; "The Second Time Around: The Tillis-Holmes Jazz Duo," 1991; "Among Friends-The Billy Taylor Trio and Fred Tillis," 1992; author: In the Spirit and the Flesh, 1989; Images of Mind and Heart, 1991; In Celebration, 1993; Of Moons, Moods, Myths, and the Muse, 1994; "Free as a Feather," Jazz Educators Journal, Dec 1994; Harlem Echoes, 1995. **CONTACT ADDRESS** Director, Emeritus, Fine Arts Center, Univ of Massachusetts, Amherst, 129 Herter Hall, Amherst, MA 01003-3910. **EMAIL** fctillis@admin.umass.edu

TIMKO, MICHAEL
PERSONAL Born 08/16/1925, Garfield, NJ, m, 1947, 3 children **DISCIPLINE** ENGLISH LITERATURE **EDUCATION** Univ Mo, AB and BJ, 49, MA, 50; Univ Wis, PhD, 56. **CAREER** Instr English compos and lit, Univ Mo, 50-52; from instr to asst prof English lit, Univ Ill, 56-61; from asst prof to assoc prof English, 61-71, chmn dept, 72-78, PROF ENGLISH, QUEENS COL, NY, 71-; MEM GRAD FAC, GRAD CTR, CITY UNIV NEW YORK, 73-, DEP EXEC OFFICER, 78-, Mem bibliog comt and contrib ed, Victorian Studies, 63-66; chmn, Victorian comt, City Univ New York; ed, Dickens Studies Annual; fel, Inst Advan Studies, Edinburgh Univ, 82. **MEMBERSHIPS** MLA; Am Soc Theatre Res; English Inst; Browning Inst. **RESEARCH** Victorian literature; British and American drama; fiction. **SELECTED PUBLICATIONS** Auth, Ah, did you once see Browning plain?, Studies English Lit, autumn 66; Innocent Victorian: The Satiric Poetry of A H Clough, Ohio Univ, 66; Thirty-Eight Short Stories: An Introductory Anthology, Knopf, 68; Wordsworth's Ode and Arnold's Dover Beach: Celestial light and confused alarms, Cithara, 11/73; Arnold, Tennyson and the English idyl: Ancient criticism and modern poetry, Tex Studies Lit & Lang, spring 74; The Victorianism of Victorian literature, New Lit Hist, spring 75; The central wish: Human passion and cosmic love in Tennyson's Idyls, Victorian Poetry, spring 78; Arthur Hugh Clough: Palpable things and celestial fact, In: The Victorian Experience: The Poets, Ohio Univ Press, 82. **CONTACT ADDRESS** Dept of English, Queens Col, CUNY, 6530 Kissena Blvd, Flushing, NY 11367-1597.

TIMS, ALBERT R.
DISCIPLINE MASS COMMUNICATION STUDIES **EDUCATION** Univ Wis Madison, PhD. **CAREER** Assoc prof **SELECTED PUBLICATIONS** Auth, The Cultivation of Consumer Confidence: A Longitudinal Analysis of News Media Influence on Consumer Sentiment, Advances Consumer Res, 89; The Impact of the News Media on Public Opinion: American Presidential Election 1987-88, Int J Public Opinion Res, 89. **CONTACT ADDRESS** Mass Communication Dept, Univ of Minnesota, Twin Cities, 111 Murphy Hall, 206 Church St SE, Minneapolis, MN 55455. **EMAIL** timsx001@maroon.tc.umn.edu

TINKCOM, MATTHEW
DISCIPLINE ENGLISH LITERATURE **EDUCATION** Univ Ca, BA; Univ Tex, MA; Univ Pittsburgh, PhD. **CAREER** Eng Dept, Georgetown Univ **RESEARCH** Film, media and cultural studies; American studio film; avant-garde and experimental cinema. **SELECTED PUBLICATIONS** Auth, pubs in Cinema Jour, Film Quarterly. **CONTACT ADDRESS** English Dept, Georgetown Univ, 37th and O St, Washington, DC 20057.

TIPPENS, DARRYL L.
PERSONAL Born 05/30/1947, Elk City, OK, m, 1967, 2 children **DISCIPLINE** ENGLISH **EDUCATION** Okla Christian Univ, BA, 68; La State Univ, MA, 71, PhD, 73. **CAREER** JAMES W. CULP DISTING PORF ENG, ABILENE CHRISTIAN UNIV, 96-, pres, S Central Renaissance Conf, 91-92; TREAS, CONF ON CHRISTIANITY AND LIT, 95-99. **HONORS AND AWARDS** Who's Who in America 01; Alumnus of the Year, Okla. Christian Univ, 97; Wm M. Green Distinguished Scholar, Pepperdine Univ, 99; Graduate Prof of the Year, Abilene Christian Univ, 94. **RESEARCH** 17th Century British Literature; Shakespeare; poetry of Whet McDonald. **SELECTED PUBLICATIONS** Auth, Shadow and Light: Literature and The Life of Faith, ACU Press, 97. **CONTACT ADDRESS** Dept of English, Abilene Christian Univ, ACU Station, Box 28252, Abilene, TX 79699. **EMAIL** tippensd@acu.edu

TIRRO, FRANK PASCALE
PERSONAL Born 09/20/1935, Omaha, NE, m, 1961, 2 children **DISCIPLINE** MUSIC THEORY **EDUCATION** Univ NE, BME, 60; Northwestern Univ, MM, 61; Univ Chicago, PhD, 74. **CAREER** Tchr & chmn dept music, Univ Chicago Lab Schs, 61-70; vis lectr music hist, Univ KS, 72-73; asst prof, 73-74, assoc prof, 74-80, Dean Yale Sch Music & prof musicol, Yale Univ, 80, dir, Southeastern Inst Medieval & Renaissance Studies, 77-80. **HONORS AND AWARDS** Am Coun Learned Socs travel grant, 68; fel Villa I Tatti, Harvard Univ, 71-72; Duke Univ Res Coun grant, 75, 76 & 78. **MEMBERSHIPS** Am Musicol Soc; Int Musicol Soc; Int Soc Jazz Res; Medieval Acad Am; Renaissance Soc Am. **RESEARCH** Music of the Renaissance; hist of jazz; music theory. **SELECTED PUBLICATIONS** Auth, The silent theme tradition in jazz, Music Quart, 67; Jazz improvisation, Proc Sixth Int Cong Aesthetics, 68; Jazz, In: Dictionary of Contemporary Music, Dutton, 74; Constructive elements in jazz improvisation, J Am Musicol Soc, 74; Jazz: A History, Norton, 77, 2nd ed, 93; Lorenzo di Giacoma da Prato's organ at San Petronio and its use during the fifteenth and sixteenth centuries, Myron P Gilmore Festschrift, Sansoni, 78; The Humanities: Cultural Roots and Continuities, Houghton Mifflin, 80, 5th ed, 97; Royal 8 G VII: Strawberry Leaves, Single Arch, and Wrong-Way Lions, Music Quart, 81; La Stesura del Testo nei Manoscritti di Giovanni Spataro, Rivista Italiana di Musicologia, 80; Music of the Renaissance, Musical Quart, 82; Renaissance musical sources in the archive of San Petronio, Haensaler-Verlag, 86; Melody and the Markoff-Chain model, Leonard B Meyer Festschrift, 88; Culture and the cultivated mind, The Arts in Lutheran Higher Educ, 89; Music of the American dream, Eileen Southern Festschrift, 92; Censorship and the arts, Wittenberg Rev, 92; Medieval retentions in music of the 20th Century, Medievalism, 96; Living with jazz, Harcourt Brace, 96. **CONTACT ADDRESS** Sch of Music, Yale Univ, PO Box 208246, New Haven, CT 06520-8246. **EMAIL** frank.tirro@yale.edu

TISCHLER, HANS
PERSONAL Born 01/18/1915, Vienna, Austria, m, 1938, 4 children **DISCIPLINE** MUSIC HISTORY AND THEORY **EDUCATION** Vienna State Acad, MusB, 33, MusM, 36; Univ Vienna, PhD(musicol), 37. **CAREER** Prof music, Wesleyan Col, W Va, 45-47; assoc prof, Roosevelt Univ, 47-65; Prof Musicol, Ind Univ, Bloomington, 65-, Am Philos Soc grants, 55-56, 62-63, 64-65 and 81-82; guest prof musicol, Univ Chicago, 56-57; Roosevelt Univ res grant, 58; Guggenheim fel, 64-65; Chapelbrook Found and Ind Univ res grants, 65-66 and 69-70; guest prof musicol, Tel Aviv Univ, 72; Nat Endowment for Humanities fel, 75-76. **MEMBERSHIPS** Am Musicol Soc; Mediaeval Acad Am; Int Musicol Soc; Medieval Asn Midwest; AAUP. **RESEARCH** Medieval and 20th century music; music aesthetics; musical forms. **SELECTED PUBLICATIONS** Auth, The Perceptive Music Listener, Prentice-Hall, 55; Practical Harmony, Allyn and Bacon, 64; Structural Analysis of Mozart's Piano Concertos, Inst Mediaeval Music, 66; The Montpellier Codex, 3 vols, A-R Editions, 78; Complete Comparative Edition of the Earliest Motets, 3 vols, Yale Univ, 82; Complete Comparative Edition of the Parisian Two-Part Organa, Pendragon P, 88; The Earliest Motets: Their Style and Evolution, Inst of Mediaeval Music, 85; auth, Trouvere Lyrics with Melodies, Complete Comparative Edition, Amer. Institute of Musicology, 97; Interpreting the 'Roman De Fauvel' in Monophonic Song, Early Music, Vol 0021, 93; Mode, Modulation, and Transposition in Medieval Songs, J Musicology, Vol 0013, 95; Gace Brule and Melodic Formulas, Acta Musicologica, Vol 0067, 95; coauth and ed, Essays in Musicology for W Apel, Festschrift, 68; ed, Willi Apel: The History of Keyboard Music to 1700, Ind Univ, 73. **CONTACT ADDRESS** Sch of Music, Indiana Univ, Bloomington, 711 E 1st Street, Bloomington, IN 47401.

TISCHLER, NANCY MARIE
PERSONAL Born 03/20/1931, DeQueen, AR, m, 1958 **DISCIPLINE** LITERATURE **EDUCATION** Wilson Teachers Col, BS, 52; Univ Ark, MA, 54, PhD, 57. **CAREER** Asst, Univ Ark, 53-56; asst prof English, George Washington Univ, 56-62; assoc prof, Susquehanna Univ, 62-66; PROF HUMANITIES, PA STATE UNIV, CAPITOL CAMPUS, 66- **MEMBERSHIPS** MLA; Conf Christianity and Lit (pres, 70-72). **RESEARCH** Drama; modern novel; Southern literature. **SELECTED PUBLICATIONS** Auth, Tennessee Williams: Rebellious Puritan, Citadel, 61; Black Masks: Negro Characters in Modern Southern Fiction, Pa State Univ, 68; William Faulkner and the Southern Negro, In: Bear, Man and God, 2nd ed, 71; The distorted mirror, Tennessee Williams' Self-Portraits, Miss Quart, fall 72; Legacy of Eve, John Knox, 77; Dorothy L Sayers: A Pilgrim Soul, John Knox, 81. **CONTACT ADDRESS** Dept of Humanities, Pennsylvania State Univ, Harrisburg, The Capital Col, Middletown, PA 17057.

TISDALE, CELES
PERSONAL Born 07/31/1941, Salters, SC, m **DISCIPLINE** ENGLISH **EDUCATION** State Univ Coll/Buffalo, BS 1963, MS 1969, PhD 1991. **CAREER** PS 31 Buffalo, English teacher 1963-68; Woodlawn Jr High, English dept chmn 1968-69; WBEN TV, writer/producer 1969; WBFO-FM Radio, writer/announcer 1969-70; State Univ Coll Buffalo, English instructor 1969-72; WKBW TV, talk show host 1979-83; WKBW Radio, talk show host 1984-86; Erie Community Coll/City, prof of English. **HONORS AND AWARDS** NY State Univ Chancellors Awd for Teaching Excellence 1975; Man of Year, Business & Professional Women 1977; Media Awd Sickle Cell Assn 1978. **MEMBERSHIPS** Assoc dir Buffalo Urban league 1966-92; bd of dirs Artpark 1981-84; dir Adolescent Vocational Exploration 1985-88; Young Audiences, Inc, 1975-; Career Educator for Buffalo Urban League 1987-91. **CONTACT ADDRESS** Professor of English, Erie Comm Col, City, 121 Ellicott St, Buffalo, NY 14203.

TM, KING
PERSONAL Born 05/09/1929, Pittsburgh, PA, s **DISCIPLINE** RELIGIOUS STUDIES; THEOLOGY; ENGLISH **EDUCATION** Univ Pitts, BA, 51; Fordham Univ, MA, 59; Univ Strasbourg, DSR, 68. **CAREER** Asst prof, 68-74, assoc prof, 74-89, full prof, 89-, Georgetown Univ. **MEMBERSHIPS** Cosmos & Creation; Univ Fac for Life. **RESEARCH** Science and religion; Psychology and religion; History of spirituality. **SELECTED PUBLICATIONS** Auth, Sartre and the Sacred, Univ Chicago Press, 74; Teilhard's Mysticism of Knowing, Seabury, 81; Teilhard de Chardin, Glazier, 88; Enchantments, Religion and the Power of the Word, Sheed & Ward, 89; Merton: Mystic at the Center of America, Liturgical, 92; Jung's Four & Some Philosophers, Univ Notre Dame Press, 98; coed, Letters of Teilhard de Chardin and Lucile Swan, Georgetown Univ Press, 93. **CONTACT ADDRESS** Dept of Theology, Georgetown Univ, Washington, DC 20057. **EMAIL** kingt@gunet.georgetown.edu

TOBIAS, MICHAEL CHARLES
PERSONAL Born San Francisco, CA, m **DISCIPLINE** WRITER, DIRECTOR, PRODUCER, EXEC PRODUCER **EDUCATION** Univ of Calf, Santa Cruz, PhD. **CAREER** Asst prof of environment studies, adj asst prof of eng, Dartmouth Col, 79-80; vis assoc prof of humanities, Calif State Univ, Northridge, early 80s; Garey Carruthers Chair and vis prof of honors, Univ of NMex, Albuquerque, late 90s; vis prof of Environmental studies, Univ of Calif, Snata Barbara, spring 01; former exec producer for all Int Productions, Md Public Broadcasting; co-founder, CMM Studios, Mumbai, India; head of JMT Productions, Los Angeles. **HONORS AND AWARDS** Numerous film and some literary nominations and awards; "The Courage of Conscience Awd" from the Peace Abbey. **RESEARCH** Everything. **SELECTED PUBLICATIONS** Auth, A Parliment of Souls-In Search of Global Spirituality, KQED Books & Tapes, PBS, 95; auth, A Day in the Life of India, Harper Collins, 97; coauth, Kinship with Animals, Beyond Words Pub, 98; auth, Nature's Keepers-On the Frontlines of the Fight to Save Wildlife in America, John Wiley & Sons Pub, 98; ed, The Search of Reality-The Art of Documentary Filmmaking, Michael Wiese Pub, 98; auth, World War III, Continuum Pubs, 2nd ed, rev, updated, with foreward by Jane Goodall, 98; auth, The Adventures of Mr. Marigold, Artist's Proof, 01; director, The Cost of Cool, 01; director, producer, Images of Arizona, 01; coauth, A Parliament of Science, 01. **CONTACT ADDRESS** 2118 Wilshire Blvd #572, Santa Monica, CA 90403. **EMAIL** mctobias@aol.com

TOBIAS, RICHARD C.
PERSONAL Born 10/10/1925, Xenia, OH, w, 1949, 3 children **DISCIPLINE** ENGLISH **EDUCATION** Ohio State, BSc, 48; Ohio State, MA, 51: Ohio State, PhD, 57. **CAREER** Instr, Univ Colorado, 52-55; Instr, Ohio State, 55-57; Prof, Univ Pittsburgh, 57-. **MEMBERSHIPS** MLA. **RESEARCH** Nineteenth-century Britain, comedy as a genre, bibliography. **SELECTED PUBLICATIONS** Auth, Art of James Thurber, Ohio UP, 69; Auth, Shakespeare's Late Plays, Ohio UP, 74; Auth, T.E. Brown, Boston, 78; Auth, Bibliographies of Studies in Victorian Literature 1975-1984, Amis (NY), 91. **CONTACT ADDRESS** Dept English, Univ of Pittsburgh, 58 Cathedral of Learning, Pittsburgh, PA 15260-6100.

TOBIN, DANIEL
PERSONAL Born 01/13/1958, Brooklyn, NY, m **DISCIPLINE** 20TH CENTURY IRISH, BRITISH AND AMERICAN LITERATURE, POETRY **EDUCATION** Iona Col, BA, 80; Harvard Univ, MTS, 83; Warren Wilson Col, MFA, 90; Univ Virginia, PhD, 91. **CAREER** Assoc prof, 91- Carthage Col; assoc prof, 97-00, Schl of the Art Inst of Chicago; prog for

Writers, Warren Wilson Col, 00. **HONORS AND AWARDS** Fel, Univ Va; Commonwealth Marchant, a du Pont, Rotary Int; The Discovery Nation Awd; NEA Fellowships; Robert Penn Warren Awd; Donn Goodwin Poetry Prize; Irish American Cutural Institute. **MEMBERSHIPS** MLA; Assoc of Am Literary Scholars; Assoc Writing Programs. **RESEARCH** Irish poetry, american poetry. **SELECTED PUBLICATIONS** Auth, Where the World is Made, Passage to the Center: Imagination and the Sacred in the Poetry of Seamus Heary. **CONTACT ADDRESS** Dept of English, Carthage Col, 2001 Alford Dr, Kenosha, WI 53140. **EMAIL** tobindl@carthage.edu

TOBIN, FRANK J.
DISCIPLINE MEDIEVAL LITERATURE AND PHILOSOPHY, GERMAN **EDUCATION** Stanford Univ, PhD. **CAREER** Prof Ger, Univ Nev, Reno; ed bd, Studia Mystica and Mystic Quart. **RESEARCH** Translation of Mechthild von Magdeburg. **SELECTED PUBLICATIONS** Published major books on Meister Eckhart and on Mechthild von Magdeburg, numerous articles on the German Middle Ages, and a coauthored two-volume anthology of German literature. **CONTACT ADDRESS** Univ of Nevada, Reno, Reno, NV 89557. **EMAIL** tobinf@scs.unr.edu

TOBIN, THOMAS J.
PERSONAL Born 12/04/1971, Lackawanna, NY, m, 1997 **DISCIPLINE** ENGLISH LITERATURE **EDUCATION** Canisius Col, BA, 94; Ind State Univ, MA, 96; Duquesne Univ, PhD, 00. **CAREER** Instr Tech, Westmoreland County Community Col, 99-. **HONORS AND AWARDS** Hazel Tesh Pfennig Found Grant, 95; Ind State Univ Arts Endowment Fund Grant, 96; NEH Grant, 97; Hunkele Found Grant, 98; William Morris Soc Fel, 99. **MEMBERSHIPS** Am Libr Asn, Asn for Art Hist, Asn of Col and Res Libr, Asn for Interdisciplinary Study of the Arts, Int Soc for the Exdploration of Teaching Alternatives, Pre-Raphaelite Soc, William Morris Soc. **RESEARCH** Pre-Raphaelitism and 19th-century periodicals. **SELECTED PUBLICATIONS** Auth, "From Word to Icon: The Advent of Visuality," Rev of Pe-Raphaelite Soc, (96); auth, "Sexual Taboos, Catholic Views, and Critical Reviews: The Unspoken Words about Two Pre-Ralphaelite Paintings," Rev of the Pre-Ralphaelite Soc, (98); auth, "John ruskin's Defense of Pre-Ralphaelitism in the Periodical Press," Rev of the Pre-Raphaelite Soc, (00); auth, "Hunt, William Holman," "Burne-Jones, Edward," "Rossetti, Christina," Biographical Dict of Lit Influences, (Greenwood Pr, 00); ed, Worldwide Pre-Raphaelitism, SUNY Pr, (forthcoming), auth, Pre-Ralphaelitism: The Periodical Criticism, Ashgate Pr, (forthcoming). **CONTACT ADDRESS** William Morris Soc, 406 E Tenth Ave, Munhall, PA 15120. **EMAIL** webmaster@morrissociety.org

TODD, DENNIS
PERSONAL Born 08/04/1944, CA, m, 1 child **DISCIPLINE** ENGLISH LITERATURE **EDUCATION** Univ Ca, BA; Emory Univ, PhD. **CAREER** Eng Dept, Georgetown Univ **HONORS AND AWARDS** Clifford Prize, 92; Phi Beta Kappa. **MEMBERSHIPS** ASECS. **RESEARCH** Eighteenth century literature and culture; European encounters with New World cultures. **SELECTED PUBLICATIONS** Auth, Imagining Monsters, 95; pubs on Pope, Swift, Hogarth, Arbuthnot, and early science. **CONTACT ADDRESS** English Dept, Georgetown Univ, 37th and O St, Washington, DC 20057. **EMAIL** todd@qunet.georgetown.edu

TODD, LARRY
DISCIPLINE MUSIC **EDUCATION** Yale Univ, PhD. **CAREER** Musicol prof, Duke Univ. **RESEARCH** 19th century music and Mendelssohn. **SELECTED PUBLICATIONS** Ed, Schirmer Studies in Musical Genres and Repertories. **CONTACT ADDRESS** Dept of Music, Duke Univ, Mary Duke Biddle Music Bldg, Durham, NC 27706. **EMAIL** rltodd@duke.edu

TODD, WILLIAM B.
DISCIPLINE ENGLISH **EDUCATION** Lehigh, BA, 40, MA, 47; Univ Chicago, PhD, 49. **CAREER** Emer Prof English, Univ Tex, Austin. **HONORS AND AWARDS** LHD, Lehigh, 75. **RESEARCH** Sir Walter Scott. **SELECTED PUBLICATIONS** Coauth, Fel Publ, Scott's Commentary on The Journal of a Tour to the Hebrides with Samuel Johnson, Studies in Bibliog 48, 95; auth, A Bibliography of Edmund Burke, Rupert Harf-Davis, 64; A Directory of Printers and Others in London, London Print Hist Soc, 72; co-ed, The Writings and Speeches of Edmund Burke, Oxford, 61, 88. **CONTACT ADDRESS** Dept of English, Univ of Texas, Austin, Austin, TX 78712.

TOFT, ROBERT
DISCIPLINE MUSIC **EDUCATION** King's Col, PhD, 83. **CAREER** Prof, Univ of Western Ontario. **HONORS AND AWARDS** Ed, Studies in Music. **RESEARCH** 16th-century music; English lute-song; rhetoric and music; performance practices 16th to 19th centuries; opera in England170-1830; 1960s rock; the electric guitar and its music, (jazz, blues, rock). **SELECTED PUBLICATIONS** Auth, Aural Images of Lost Traditions: Sharps and Flats in the Sixteenth Century, Toronto: Univ of Toronto Press, 92; auth, Tune thy Musicke to thy Hart: The Art of Eloquent Singing in England 1597-1622, Toronto: Univ of Toronto Press, 93; auth, "The Expressive Pause: Punctuation, Rests, and Breathing in England 1770-1850," Performance Practice Review 7, (94): 199-232; auth, "The Vocal Appoggiatura in England c1780-c1830: A Regional Perspective Amidst a Pan-European Debate, Irish Musical Studies 5, (96): 336-55; auth, "Action and Singing in Late 18th and Early 19th Century England," Performance Practice Review 9, (96): 146-62; auth, The Promethean Fire of Eloquent Expression: Vocal Delivery in Handel's Oratorios in the Early 19th Century," Journal of Musicological Res, 17, (97): 23-52. **CONTACT ADDRESS** Dept of Music, Univ of Western Ontario, London, ON, Canada N6A 5B8. **EMAIL** rtoft@julian.uwo.ca

TOHER, MARK
DISCIPLINE CLASSICS **EDUCATION** Brown Univ, BA, 74, PhD, 85; Univ Oxford, BA, 76. **CAREER** Chemn, Dept of Classics, St George's Sch, 77-80; asst prof, 83-89, assoc prof, Classics, 89- , chemn dept, 91-94, Union College. **HONORS AND AWARDS** Phi Beta Kappa; Brown Univ Sr Scholarship, 74-76; dir of sem for NEH summer inst, 87; NEH summer inst, 88; NEH travel grant, 92; mem Managing Comm of Am School of Class Stud, Athens, 84- . **SELECTED PUBLICATIONS** Auth, The Tenth Table and the Conflict of the Orders, in Raaflaug, ed, Social Struggles in Archaic Rome: New Perspectives on the Roman Conflict of the Orders, Los Angeles, 86; auth, On the Terminal Date of Nicolaus' Universal History, Ancient Hist Bull, 87; auth, On the Use of Nicolaus' Historical Fragments, Class Antiquity, 89; auth, Augustus and the Evolution of Roman Historiography, in Raaflaub, ed, Between Republic and Empire: Interpretations of Augustus and His Principate, Los Angeles, 90; auth, Greek Funerary Legislation and the Two Spartan Funerals, in Flower, ed, Georgica: Studies in Honor of George Cawkwell, London, 91. **CONTACT ADDRESS** Dept of Classics, Union Col, New York, Schenectady, NY 12308.

TOKARCZYK, MICHELLE M.
PERSONAL Born 01/02/1953, Bronx, NY, m, 1979 **DISCIPLINE** ENGLISH **EDUCATION** Herbert Lehman Col, BA, 75; SUNY Stony Brook, MA, 78, PhD, 85. **CAREER** Asst prof, 85-86, Hofstra Col; asst prof, Rutgers Univ, 86-87; asst prof, 89-95, Assoc Prof, 95-, Goucher Col. **HONORS AND AWARDS** Susan Koppelman Awd, 94. **MEMBERSHIPS** NEMCA, MCA, ASA, CCC **RESEARCH** Gender and class intersections; Contemporary literature; Composition and literature. **SELECTED PUBLICATIONS** Ed, Working-Class Women in the Academy: Laborers in the Knowledge Factory, Univ Mass Press, 93; Getting the Job: The Adjunct Game, Concerns: Publication of the Women's Caucus of the Mod Lang Asn, 94; "The City, The Waterworks, and Writing: An Interview with E L Doctorow," Kenyon Rev, 95; rev "Lifting a Ton of Feathers: A Woman's Guide to Surviving in the Academic World," Jour Higher Educ, 95; The Waterworks, Lit Rev, 96; Talk the Talk: Differences in Working-Class and Academic Vocabularies, Uncommon Threads, 96; The Illusions of Postmodernism, Theory & Event, 97; auth, E.L. Doctorow's Skeptical Commitment, Peter Lang Press, 00. **CONTACT ADDRESS** Goucher Col, 1021 Dulaney Valley Rd, Baltimore, MD 21204. **EMAIL** mtokarcz@goucher.edu

TOLBERT, ELIZABETH D.
DISCIPLINE MUSIC HISTORY **EDUCATION** FL State Univ, BM; Univ CO, MM; Univ CA, PhD. **CAREER** Prof, John Hopkins Univ. **RESEARCH** Intercultural approaches to aesthetics; music theory; music cognition. **SELECTED PUBLICATIONS** Auth, pubs in Embodied Voices; World of Music; Notes; Ethnomusicology; Yearbook for Traditional Music. **CONTACT ADDRESS** Dept of Musicology, Johns Hopkins Univ, Baltimore, 1 E Mt Vernon Pl, Baltimore, MD 21202-2397.

TOLER, COLETTE
PERSONAL Born Pittsburgh, PA **DISCIPLINE** ENGLISH **EDUCATION** Seton Hill Col, BMus, 57; Univ Notre Dame, MA, 62, PhD, 65. **CAREER** From asst prof to assoc prof, 65-72, acad dean, 71-82, Prof English, Seton Hill Col, 73-, vis prof, Col Mt St Vincent, 68-69; mem task force higher educ Pa, Pa Dept Educ, 77-78; mem bd dirs, Southwestern Pa Higher Educ Coun, 77-; vis scholar, Cambridge Univ, 82- **MEMBERSHIPS** MLA **RESEARCH** Art and civilization in the fiction of Willa Cather; existential fiction; the American Twenties. **SELECTED PUBLICATIONS** Auth, Willa Cather's Vision of the Artist, in Personalist, autumn 64; Look On - Make No Sound, in Notre Dame English J, fall 64; Hemingway and Fitzgerald as Mirrors of the Twenties, in J Twenties, 72. **CONTACT ADDRESS** Dept of English, Seton Hill Col, 1 Seton Hill Dr, Greensburg, PA 15601-1599.

TOLES, GEORGE E.
DISCIPLINE ENGLISH LITERATURE **EDUCATION** State Univ NY Buffalo, BA; Univ Virg, MA; PhD. **CAREER** Prof **HONORS AND AWARDS** Ed, Mosaic. **RESEARCH** American films; theatre; and 19th and 20th century European and American fiction. **SELECTED PUBLICATIONS** Auth, pub(s) on William Faulkner, Charles Brockden Brown, Mark Twain, Frank Capra, Alfred Hitchcock, Judith Thompson, F. Scott Fitzgerald, James Agee, Marilynne Robinson, Anne Tyler, Jean Renoir, Tennessee Williams, Vittorio De Sica, Greta Garbo, Jean-Claude Lauzon, movie humiliation scenes and movie sentiment. **CONTACT ADDRESS** Dept of English, Univ of Manitoba, Winnipeg, MB, Canada R3T 2N2. **EMAIL** toles@cc.umanitoba.ca

TOLLERS, VINCENT LOUIS
PERSONAL Born 08/23/1939, Superior, WI, m, 1963, 2 children **DISCIPLINE** ENGLISH **EDUCATION** Univ Wis, Superior, BA, 61; Univ Colo, Boulder, MA, 65, PhD, 68. **CAREER** Asst prof English, Emporia State Univ, Emporia, 68-70; compiler, Abstracts English Studies, 72-80; compiler, MLA Int Bibliog, 74-79; ed, Lit Res, 76-85; vis lectr English, Matlock Col Educ, Eng, 76-77; from asst prof to Distinguished Service Prof English, State Univ NY Col, Brockport, 80-; Chemn, State Univ NY Col, Brockport, 80-83; proj dir, Ronald E McNair Post-baccalaureate Achievement Prog, 89-; proj dir, Col Sci & Technol Entry Prog, 98-. **MEMBERSHIPS** MLA; NCTE; CCCC; Nat Coun Educ Opportunity Asn; Am Asn Australian Lit Stud; Int Mentoring Asn; Nat Coun Undergrad Res. **RESEARCH** Victorian literature; bibliography; Bible studies; Australian studies. **SELECTED PUBLICATIONS** Ed, A Bibliography of Matthew Arnold, Pa State Univ, 74; auth, Eight New Arnold Letters, Arnoldian, 76; co-ed, The Bible in Its Literary Milieu: Contemporary Essays, W B Eerdmans, 79; Mapping of the Biblical Terrain, Bucknell Univ Press, 90; Guided Research in Freshman English, LRN, 81. **CONTACT ADDRESS** Dept of English, SUNY, Col at Brockport, 350 New Campus Dr, Brockport, NY 14420-2914. **EMAIL** vtollers@brockport.edu

TOLOMEO, DIANE
DISCIPLINE ENGLISH LITERATURE **EDUCATION** Univ Rochester, BA; Princeton Univ, MA, Phd. **CAREER** Assoc prof **RESEARCH** Biblical and modern literature; Anglo-Irish literature. **SELECTED PUBLICATIONS** Rev(s), Joyce Carol Oates, Amer Writers, Scribners, 80; auth, Anglo Irish Research, MLA, 83; Mapping the Biblical Terrain, Bucknell, Dictionary of Literary Biography, Yeats. **CONTACT ADDRESS** Dept of English, Univ of Victoria, PO Box 3070, Victoria, BC, Canada V8W 3W1. **EMAIL** dtolomeo@uvic.ca

TOLSON, NANCY D.
PERSONAL Born 07/04/1960, Detroit, MI, m, 1984, 3 children **DISCIPLINE** ENGLISH LITERATURE **EDUCATION** Madonna Univ, BA, 83; Univ Iowa, MA, 94; PhD, 98. **CAREER** TA, Univ of Iowa, 93-98; asst prof, Ill State Univ, 98-. **HONORS AND AWARDS** NEH, 99, 02; Ford Fel, 00; **MEMBERSHIPS** NCTE, Am Folklore Soc, Children's Lit Assoc, Int Reading Assoc, Assoc Black Acad Employees, Soc of children's Book Writers & Illustrators, Safundi. **RESEARCH** Black Children's Literature across the Diaspora, Tracing the folklore/mythology of Ananse across the Diaspora to study how slavery has affected the tales as well as the character, The art of Storytelling. **SELECTED PUBLICATIONS** Auth, "Regional Outreach and an Evolving Black Aesthetic", Children's Lit Assoc Quart, (96); auth, "Making Books Available: The Role of Early Libraries, Librarians, and Booksellers in the Promotion of African American Children's Literature," African Am Rev, (98); auth, Tales of Africa, Perfection Learning, 99; rev, of Oxford Book of Caribbean Short Stories, Rev of Contemp Fiction, (99); auth, "Brutal Honesty and Metaphorical Grace: The Blues Aesthetic in Black Children's Literature," Children's Lit Quarterly, (00); auth, "1st Day," Jour of the Assoc for Res on Mothering, (00); coauth, "African and African Voices and Experiences American Children's Book," Adventuring with Books, A Booklist for Pre-K-Grade 6, (00); auth, "Mothering Young Minds: African American Standard Bearers in Children's Literature," theafricanamerican.com, (00); ed, Don't Need an Interpreter: Black authors, illustrators and scholars speaking out on Black Children's Literature, Obsidian III/ Lit on the African Diaspora, 01; auth, "Searching for Self Within Black Children's Poetry," Five Owls, (01). **CONTACT ADDRESS** Dept English, Illinois State Univ, 2914 Coventry Ct, Bloomington, IL 61704. **EMAIL** ndtols2@ilstu.edu

TOMASULO, FRANK P.
DISCIPLINE FILM AND TELEVISION STUDIES **EDUCATION** Brooklyn Col, BA, 67; NYork Univ, MA, 73; UCLA, PhD, 86. **CAREER** Instr, NY Univ, UCLA, St Johns Univ, Ithaca Col, Cornell Univ, Univ Calif, Santa Cruz; assoc prof, ch, dept Commun, Ga State Univ, 91-94; ed, J of Film & Video. **HONORS AND AWARDS** NEH grant, Univ Calif, Berkeley; 1st prize, Scholarly Writing competition, Soc for Cinema Stud; Dana Awd for Scholarly Res, Ithaca Col. **RESEARCH** Italian film director Michelangelo Antonioni. **SELECTED PUBLICATIONS** Published over 40 academic articles, book chapters, reviews, interviews, and translations on film and television topics. **CONTACT ADDRESS** Georgia State Univ, Atlanta, GA 30303. **EMAIL** joufpt@panther.gsu.edu

TOMLIN, CAROL
PERSONAL Born 02/21/1960, United Kingdom **DISCIPLINE** ENGLISH **EDUCATION** Univ Woverhampton, BEd, 85; Univ Birmingham, MPhil, 88; Univ Reading, PhD, 95. **CAREER** Lecturer, Acton Col, 87-90; Lecturer, Univ East London, 90-96; Asst Prof, Bowie State Univ, 97-. **RESEARCH**

Educational experiences of African heritage students in both the U.S. and U.K. **SELECTED PUBLICATIONS** Auth, "God's Call and Overcoming," in Report for the Churches Commission for Racial Justice, (London, 95), 10-12; auth, "Black Pentecostal Churches in Britain," Journal of Diaspora, 96; auth, "Black Language Style in Sacred and Secular Context," Medgar Evers Col of Brooklyn. **CONTACT ADDRESS** Dept Eng & Lang, Bowie State Univ, 14000 Jericho Park Rd, Bowie, MD 20715-3319.

TOMPKINS, CYNTHIA MARGARITA
PERSONAL Born 01/30/1958, Cordoba, Argentina, s, 1 child **DISCIPLINE** LITERATURE **EDUCATION** Pa State Univ, MA, 85; PhD, 89. **CAREER** Instr, Dickinson Col, 88-89; asst prof, Univ Wisc, 89-92; asst prof to assoc prof, Ariz State Univ West, 92-99; assoc prof, Ariz State Univ Tempe, 99-. **HONORS AND AWARDS** Edwin Sparks Res Fel, Pa State Univ, 82; Fulbright Fel, Buenos Aires. **MEMBERSHIPS** AATSP; Am Asn of Teachers of Spanish and Portuguese; Am Comparative Lit Asn; LASA; MLA; SC/MLA. **RESEARCH** Latin American Women Writers; Film and cultural production; Postmodernism; Literary theory; Criticism and aesthetics; Comparative Literature; Translation Studies. **SELECTED PUBLICATIONS** Co-ed, Utopias, ojos azules, bocas suicidas: La narrativa de Alina Diaconu, Buenos Aires, 93; auth, "Intertextuality as Difference in Julieta Campos: El miedo de perder a Euridice: A Symptomatic Case of Latin American Post-Modernism," in The Postmodern in Latn and Latino American Cultural Narratives, (New York, 96), 153-180; auth, "Intertestualidad en Amatista (1989) y Cuando digo Magdalena (1992) de Alicia Steimberg," Hispamerica, (97): 197-201; auth, "Historiographic Metafiction or the Rewriting of History in Carmen Boullosa's Son vacas, somos puercos," in The Other Mirror: Women's Narrative in Mexico 1980-1995, (Greenwood Pub, 97), 85-98; auth, "Pasos bajo el agua y 'Bosquejo de alturas' de Alicia Kozameh; tortura, resistencia y secuelas," Chasqui, (98): 56-69; auth, "Aporia: la Vaca sagrada de Diamela Eltit," Explicacion de Textos Literarios, (99): 50-61; auth, "Representations of Gender, Race/Ethnicity and Subalternity in Marianne Eyde's La vida es una sola," Studies in Latin American Popular Culture, (forthcoming); co-ed, Dictionary of Latin American Women, Greenwood Press, 00. **CONTACT ADDRESS** Dept Lang & Lit, Arizona State Univ, PO Box 870202, Tempe, AZ 85287-0202. **EMAIL** cynthia.tompkins@asu.edu

TOMPKINS, JANE
DISCIPLINE ENGLISH LITERATURE **EDUCATION** Yale Univ, PhD, 66. **CAREER** Prof, Duke Univ. **RESEARCH** Am lit; popular cult; pedag. **SELECTED PUBLICATIONS** Auth, Sensational Designs: The Cultural Work of American Fiction, 1790-1860, Oxford, 85;), West of Everything, Oxford, 92; ed, Reader-Response Criticism: From Formalism to Post-Structuralism, Hopkins, 80. **CONTACT ADDRESS** Eng Dept, Duke Univ, Durham, NC 27706.

TOMPKINS, PHILLIP K.
DISCIPLINE COMMUNCATION STUDIES **EDUCATION** Univ Northern Colo, BA, 56; Univ Nebr, MA; 57; Purdue Univ, PhD, 62. **CAREER** Prof. **RESEARCH** Organizational communication; rhetorical literary and social theory; communication and control. **SELECTED PUBLICATIONS** Auth, A Note on Burke, Goethe, and the Jews, Quarterly Jour Speech, 95; Identification in the Self-Managing Organization: Characteristics of Target and Tenure, 94; Principles of Rigor in 'Qualitative' Research in Communication, Western Jour Commun, 94. **CONTACT ADDRESS** Dept of Communication, Univ of Colorado, Boulder, Boulder, CO 80309. **EMAIL** Phillip.Tompkins@Colorado.edu

TONGSON, KAREN L.
PERSONAL Born 08/23/1973, Manila, Philippines **DISCIPLINE** ENGLISH **EDUCATION** Univ Calif Los Angeles, BA, 95; Univ Calif Berkeley, PhD, 01. **HONORS AND AWARDS** Dr Warren Craig and Erile R thompson Prize, 95; Fel, Univ Calif, 96-97, 97-98; Mellon Fel, 99; Univ Calif Diss Fel, 01; Univ Calif Tvl Grant, 01. **MEMBERSHIPS** MLA, 19th Century Studies Assoc, Interdisciplinary 19th Century Studies, Int Assoc of Philos and Lit. **RESEARCH** 19th Century British Literature, Aesthetics and Nationalism, Style and Sexuality, Cosmopolitanism and Criticism, Queer Theory, Pilipino-American Short Fiction. **SELECTED PUBLICATIONS** Auth, "The Nether World of Neither World: Hybridization in the Literature of Wendy Rose," Am Indian Cult and Res Jour, (96); auth, "Thomas Carlyle and the Grain of the Voice," The Idea of Music in Victorian Fiction, ed Fuller and Lossef, (02). **CONTACT ADDRESS** Dept English, Univ of California, Berkeley, 322 Wheeler Hall, No 1030, Berkeley, CA 94703. **EMAIL** ktongson@uclink4.berkeley.edu

TONKIN, HUMPHREY R.
PERSONAL Born 12/02/1939, Truro, United Kingdom, m, 1983, 2 children **DISCIPLINE** ENGLISH, LINGUISTICS **EDUCATION** Cambridge Univ, BA, 62; Harvard Univ, MA, PhD, 62-66. **CAREER** Asst prof, assoc prof, v prov, co-od intl prog, mst Stouffer Col House, Univ Penn, 66-83; vis prof, Columbia Univ, 80-81; pres, SUNT Potsdam, 83-88; pres, Univ Hartford, 89-98; vis scholar, Yale Univ, 98-99; prof, Univ Hartford, 98-. **HONORS AND AWARDS** Knox Fel, 62-66; Guggenheim Fel, 74; Linback Awd, Dis Teach, 71; DLit, Univ Hart, 99. **MEMBERSHIPS** MLA; RSA; ACTFL; Spenser Soc; Milton Soc; CAAS; IASSM. **RESEARCH** Shakespeare and early modern English literature; English romantic poets; sociolinguistics and language policy and planning. **SELECTED PUBLICATIONS** Spenser's Courteous Pastoral, Oxford UP, 72; auth, The Faerie Queene, Unwin Hyman: Unwin Critical Library (London, 89); compiler, Sir Walter Raleigh: Elizabethan Bibliographies Supplements (London: Nether Press, 71); coauth, The World in the Curriculum, Change Magazine Press (New Rochelle, NY), 82; co-ed, Language in Religion (Lanham, MD: UP of Am, 89); ed and trans, Esperanto: Language, Literature and Community by Pierre Janton (Albany: SUNY Press, 93); ed, Esperanto, Interlinguistics and Planned Language (Lanham: UP of Am, 97); ed and trans, Maskerado: Dancing Around Death in Nazi Hungary by Tivadar Soros, Canongate (Edinburgh), 00; auth, "Esperanto and International Language Problems," Esperantic Stud (77). **CONTACT ADDRESS** Mortensen Lib, Univ of Hartford, West Hartford, CT 06117. **EMAIL** tonkin@mail.hartford.edu

TONN, ANKE
PERSONAL Born 02/03/1944, Hamburg, Germany, d, 2 children **DISCIPLINE** LIBRARY SCIENCE **EDUCATION** BA; MILS **CAREER** Nova Scotia Tech Univ; Memorial Univ of New Foundland; Tulane Univ; Asst prof, Nichols State Univ; Interlibrary Loans Librarian. **MEMBERSHIPS** ALA; ACRL; Louisiana Library Assoc. **RESEARCH** German literature; art history **SELECTED PUBLICATIONS** Auth, "Louisiana Library Association Bulletin," La Engl J 1 (99). **CONTACT ADDRESS** Ellender Memorial Library, Nicholls State Univ, Thibodaux, LA 70310. **EMAIL** el-at@nich-nsunet.nich.edu

TOOMBS, CHARLES PHILLIP
PERSONAL Born 12/02/1952, Indianapolis, IN, d **DISCIPLINE** LITERATURE **EDUCATION** Purdue University, West Lafayette, IN, BA, 1976, MA, 1978, MS, 1981, PhD, 1986. **CAREER** Purdue University, West Lafayette, Ind, graduate assistant, 76-81, graduate instuctor, 82-85; Indiana Univ Northwest, Gary, IN, visiting instructor, 85-86; California State Univ, Bakersfield, CA, asst prof, 86-88; Univ of Georgia, Athens, GA, Asst Prof, 88-; prof and chair, Africana Studies, San Diego St Univ. **HONORS AND AWARDS** Lilly Fellowship, University of Georgia, 1989-90; Howard G McCall Awd, Purdue U Black Cultural Center, 1978; First Place in Fiction and Poetry, Paul Robeson Literary Awds, 1976. **MEMBERSHIPS** Modern Language Association, Research Association of Minority Professors, Southern Conference on Afro-American Studies, National Council for Black Studies. **SELECTED PUBLICATIONS** "Joyce Carol Thomas," Dictionary of Literary Biography, 84; "Master Timothy," Indiana Experience, Indiana UP, 78; "Seven Haiku," High/Coo, 77. **CONTACT ADDRESS** Dept of Africana Studies, San Diego State Univ, 5500 Campanile Dr., San Diego, CA 92182. **EMAIL** ctoombs@mail.sdsu.edu

TORGOVNICK, MARIANNA DE MARCO
PERSONAL Born 08/31/1949, Brooklyn, NY, m, 1968, 2 children **DISCIPLINE** ENGLISH, COMPARATIVE LITERATURE **EDUCATION** NYork Univ, BA, 70; Columbia Univ, MA, 71; PhD, 75. **CAREER** Asst prof, Williams Col, 75-81; vis prof, Princeton Univ, 93; asst prof to prof, Duke Univ, 81-, assoc chair, 86-92, chair, 96-99, Dir, Duke in New York Arts Prog, 99. **HONORS AND AWARDS** John Simon Guggenheim Fel, 81; Cohen-Porter Vis Scholar, Tel Aviv Univ, 93; Winner, Am Book Awd for Crossing Ocean Parkway, 94; ed bd, Twentieth Century Literature, Religion, and the Arts; NEH Summer Seminar Grant, 97; numerous radio and television interviews, including in-depth Nat Public Radio Shows in New York, Washington, San Francisco, etc. **MEMBERSHIPS** Modern Lang Asn, Int Soc for the Study of Time. **RESEARCH** Twentieth-century literature and culture, contemporary America (U.S.), contemporary fiction, cultural criticism. **SELECTED PUBLICATIONS** Auth, Closure in the Novel, Princeton: Princeton Univ Press (81); auth, The Visual Arts, Pictorialism, and the Novel: James, Lawrence and Woolf, Princeton: Princeton Univ Press (85); auth, "Experimental Critical Writing," ADE Bull, 9, 6 (fall 90): 8-11; auth, "On Being White, Female, and Born in Bensonhurst," Partisan Rev, 57:3 (summer 90): 456-66; auth, Gone Primitive: Savage Intellects, Modern Lives, Chicago: Univ of Chicago Press (90, 91); auth, Eloquent Obsessions: Writing Cultural Criticism, Durham: Duke Univ Press (93); auth, Crossing Ocean Parkway: Readings by an Italian American Daughter, Chicago: Univ of Chicago Press (94); auth, Primitive Passions: Men, Women, and the Quest for Ecstasy, New York: Knopf (97). **CONTACT ADDRESS** Dept English, Duke Univ, PO Box 90015, Durham, NC 27708-0015. **EMAIL** Tor@Duke.edu

TORRES, HECTOR
DISCIPLINE CHICANO LITERATURE, LITERARY THEORY **EDUCATION** Univ Tex, PhD, 86. **CAREER** Instr, Univ NMex, 86-. **SELECTED PUBLICATIONS** Coauth, Dialogic Structure and Levels of Discourse in Steinbeck's The Grapes of Wrath, Ariz Quart, 89. **CONTACT ADDRESS** Dept of Lit, Univ of New Mexico, Albuquerque, Albuquerque, NM 87131. **EMAIL** hector@unm.edu

TORRES, LOUIS
PERSONAL Born 01/22/1938, Orange, NJ, m, 1987 **DISCIPLINE** PSYCHOLOGY, ENGLISH **EDUCATION** Rutgers Univ, BA, 60; Teachers Coll, Columbia Univ, 71. **CAREER** Teacher, Franklin School, NY City, 67-69; teacher, Indian Hills High School, NJ, 69-80; managing dir, William Carter Dance Ensemble, NY City, 80-82; teacher, Am Renaissance School, NY, 81-84; founder, ed, publ, Aristos, 82-91; co-ed, Publ, Aristos, 92-. **MEMBERSHIPS** Am Philos Asn; Am Soc for Aesthetics; Asn of Literary Scholars and Critics; Asn for Art Hist. **RESEARCH** Philosophy of Art. **SELECTED PUBLICATIONS** Auth, The New Dawn of Painting, ARISTOS, 86; The Child as Poet: An Insidious and Injurious Myth, Aristos, 88; Jack Schaefer, Teller of Tales, Aristos, 96; Jack Schaefer, Encycl of Frontier and Western Fiction, forthcoming; coauth, Ayn Rand's Philosophy of Art: A Critical Introduction, Aristos, 91-92; What Art Is: The Esthetic Theory of Ayn Rand, Open Court, 00. **CONTACT ADDRESS** Aristos, Radio City Station, PO Box 1105, New York, NY 10101.

TOSSA, WAJUPPA
PERSONAL Born 10/04/1950, Thatphanom, Thailand, s **DISCIPLINE** AMERICAN LITERATURE **EDUCATION** Drew Univ, PhD, 86. **CAREER** Asst prof, Humanities and Social Sci, Mahasavakham Univ, 78-98; vis prof, Center for Asian and Pacific Studies, Univ of Oregon, 98-99. **HONORS AND AWARDS** Witler Bynner Found for Poetry Awd, 85, 92, & 94; Fulbright Sr Scholar Grant, 91 & 98. **MEMBERSHIPS** Nat Storytelling Asn; Am Higher Ed Asn. **RESEARCH** Language and cultural preservation; storytelling; translation. **SELECTED PUBLICATIONS** Auth, Phya Khankhaak, The Toad King, a Translation: Fertility Myth into English Verse, Bucknell Univ, Press, 96; Phadaeng Nang Ai, A Translation of a Thai/Isan Folk Epic into English Verse, Bucknell Univ Press, 90. **CONTACT ADDRESS** Center for Asian and Pacific Studies, Univ of Oregon, 110 Gerlinger Hall, Eugene, OR 97403.

TOTH, BILL
PERSONAL Born 11/02/1944, Millfield, OH, s, 1 child **DISCIPLINE** ENGLISH AND AMERICAN LITERATURE **EDUCATION** BA, MA Calif State Univ, PhD The Union Institute **CAREER** Prof, 91-. **MEMBERSHIPS** Western Literature Asn, Asn for the Study of Literature and the evnironment. **RESEARCH** Nature writing, literature of the American West, modern drama, film. . **SELECTED PUBLICATIONS** 80+ bk reviews in bk(s) of the Southwest and Western American lit; auth, Poetry in Algonquin, other Humanities. **CONTACT ADDRESS** Dept of Humanities, Western New Mexico Univ, 1000 West College Ave., Silver City, NM 88061. **EMAIL** tothb@silver.wnmu.edu

TOTH, EMILY
DISCIPLINE LOUISIANA WRITERS **EDUCATION** Johns Hopkins Univ, PhD, 75. **CAREER** Prof, La State Univ; ed bd, Southern Stud; ed, Regionalism and the Female Imagination, 75-79. **HONORS AND AWARDS** Emily Toth Awd, 86; LEH res and publ grants, 90, 93; Cert of Commendation, Am Asn for State and Local Hist, 93; founder and ed, regionalism and the female imagination, 75-79 (formerly the kate chopin newsletter). **RESEARCH** Kate Chopin's papers; women's studies. **SELECTED PUBLICATIONS** Auth, Inside Peyton Place: The Life of Grace Metalious, 81; Daughters of New Orleans, 83; Women in Academia, The Acad's Handbk, 88; The Curse: A Cultural History of Menstruation, 88; Kate Chopin's New Orleans Years, New Orleans Rev, 88; A New Biographical Approach, in Approaches to Teaching Kate Chopin's "The Awakening", 88; Firing the Canon: The Fear That Literature is Fun, Earlhamite, 90; Kate Chopin: A Life of the Author of "The Awakening", 90; The Shadow of the First Biographer: The Case of Kate Chopin, Southern Rev, 90; Developing Political Savvy--Many Misadventures Later, Women's Stud Quart, 90; Kate Chopin on Divine Love and Suicide: Two Rediscovered Articles, Am Lit, 91; Ms. Mentor's Impeccable Advice for Women in Academica, 97; ed, Regionalism and Female Imagination, 85; A Vocation and a Voice by Kate Chopin, 91. **CONTACT ADDRESS** Dept of Eng, Louisiana State Univ and A&M Col, 236B Allen Hall, Baton Rouge, LA 70803. **EMAIL** etoth@unix1.sncc.lsu.edu

TOTOSY DE ZEPETNEK, STEVEN
PERSONAL Born 11/22/1950, Budapest, Hungary, m, 1976, 2 children **DISCIPLINE** COMMUNICATION, CULTURAL STUDIES **EDUCATION** Univ W Ont, BA, 80; Carleton Univ, MA, 83; Univ Ottawa, BEd, 84; Univ Albta, PhD, 89. **CAREER** Assoc dir, assoc, ed, adj to asst prof, Univ Albta, 94-00; ed, Purdue Univ, 00-. **MEMBERSHIPS** MLA, Can Comp Lit Assoc, Int Comp Lit Assoc, Am Comp Lit Assoc, Int Soc of Systems Sci, Int Assoc of Empirical Aesthetics. **RESEARCH** Literary and culture theories and application, (comparative) cultural studies, media and communication studies, comparative literature, the sociology of cultural participation and production, scholarly editing. **SELECTED PUBLICATIONS** Auth, Records of the Totosy de Zepetnek Family, Jozsef Attila Univ, (Szeged), 93; auth, The Social Dimensions of Fiction, Westdeutscher Verlag (Braunschweig), 93; ed, Postcolonial Literature: Theory and Practice, Can Rev of Comp Lit, 95; ed, East Asian Cultural and Historical Perspectives: Histories and Soci-

ety, Res Inst for Comp Lit, Univ of Albta (Edmonton), 97; auth, "Legitimizing the Study of Literature," Peking Univ Pr, (Beijing), 97); ed, Canadian Culture and Literatures. And a Taiwan Perspective, Res Inst for Comp Lit, Univ of Albta, (Edmonton), 98; auth, Comparative Literature: Theory, Method, Application, Rodopi, (Amsterdam-Atlanta, GA), 98; ed, Comparative Literature Now: Theories and Practice, Honore Champion, (Paris), 99; ed, Comparative Central European Culture, Purdue Univ Pr, (W Lafayette), 01. **CONTACT ADDRESS** Dept of Commun Studies, Northeastern Univ, 8 Sunset Rd, Winchester, MA 01890. **EMAIL** totosy@lib.purdue.edu

TOULOUSE, TERESA
DISCIPLINE EARLY AMERICAN LITERATURE **EDUCATION** Oberlin Col, BA, 72; Harvard Univ, PhD, 80. **CAREER** Engl, Tulane Univ. **SELECTED PUBLICATIONS** Auth, The Art of Prophesying: New England Sermons and the Shaping of Belief, Univ Ga Press, 87; Mary Rowlandson's Narrative and the 'New' Theories of Early American Literature, Amerikastudien/Amer Stud 36, 92; Mine Own Credit': Strategies of (E)Valuation in Rowlandson's Captivity Narrative, Amer Lit 64, 92; Mary Rowlandson and the Rhetoric of Ambiguity, Stud Puritan Amer Spirituality III, 92; co-ed, The Sermons of Ralph Waldo Emerson, Univ Mo Press, 90. **CONTACT ADDRESS** Dept of Eng, Tulane Univ, 6823 St Charles Ave, New Orleans, LA 70118. **EMAIL** toulouse@mailhost.tcs.tulane.edu

TOUMAZOU, MICHAEL K.
PERSONAL Born 12/11/1952, Famagusta, Cyprus, m, 1978, 3 children **DISCIPLINE** CLASSICS **EDUCATION** Marshall Col, BA, 77; Loyola Univ Chicago, MA, 80; Bryn Mawr Col, MA, 83, PhD, 87. **CAREER** Asst prof, classics, 87-93, Assoc Prof Classics, 93-, Dept Chair, 95-, Davidson Col. **HONORS AND AWARDS** Whiting Fnd fel, 86-87; NEH senior fel, 1994-95; Trustee of Cyprus Am Archeol Res Inst, 96-. **MEMBERSHIPS** Archeol Inst Am; Am Schs Oriental Res; Soc Promotion Hellenic Stud; Classical Asn Midwest & South; NC Class Asn. **RESEARCH** Classl & Cypriote Archeol **SELECTED PUBLICATIONS** Articles in Zeitsmrift fur Papyrologie und Epigraphic, 41, 81, Am J Archeol, 91-99, Bulletin de Correspondence Hellenique, J Field Archeol 25, 98; auth, Aspects of Burial Practices in Prehistoric Cypriote Site, c.7,000-25,000 B.C., Univ Mich, 87. **CONTACT ADDRESS** Dept of Classics, Davidson Col, Davidson, NC 28036. **EMAIL** mitoumazou@davidson.edu

TOWNS, SANNA NIMTZ
PERSONAL Born 10/12/1943, Hawthorne, NV, d **DISCIPLINE** ENGLISH **EDUCATION** Southern Univ, BA 1964; Teachers Coll Columbia Univ, MA 1967; Univ of Southern MS, PhD 1985. **CAREER** Amer Language Prog Columbia Univ, English lang instructo, 69-71; Office of Urban Affairs SUNY at Buffalo, prog coord, 73-75; Kuwait Univ, instructor & admin, 75-79; English Dept Univ of New Orleans, lang coord & instructor, 80-82, 85-86; Delgado Comm Coll, asst prof, asst chair, 86-87, chair, communication division, 87-92, Assoc Prof of English, 92-. **HONORS AND AWARDS** State of LA Bd of Regents Graduate Fellowship 1982-85; ; Black Achiever in Education, Dyrades YMCA, New Orleans, 1988-89; Fulbright-Hays Seminars Aboard Participant, American University in Cairo, 1988; Fulbright Scholar Awd, Comenius Univ, Bratislava, Slovakia, Jan-June 1994. **MEMBERSHIPS** Mem Natl Council of Teachers of English 1980-, LA Assoc of Developmental Educ 1981-, Phi Delta Kappa 1984-, South Central Modern Language Assoc 1986-; speaker New Orleans Museum of Art Speakers Bureau 1987; member, Delta Sigma Theta Sorority, 1962-; member, Conference on College Composition & Communications, 1980-. **SELECTED PUBLICATIONS** Article "Integrating Reading & Writing Instruction" in ERIC 1984. **CONTACT ADDRESS** English, Communication Div, Delgado Comm Col, 615 City Park Ave, New Orleans, LA 70119.

TOWNSEL, SYLVIANE
PERSONAL Born 12/03/1943, Moule, Guadeloupe, m, 1978, 1 child **DISCIPLINE** LITERATURE, SPANISH **EDUCATION** Emory Univ, BA; MA; PhD, 87. **CAREER** Asst prof, SUNY Oswego, 88-93; asst prof, Murray State, 93-94; asst prof Ball State Univ, 95-97; assoc prof, Albany State Univ, 97-. **HONORS AND AWARDS** Grant, Univ of Ga, 98; Grant, Univ of Haw, 00. **RESEARCH** Francophone Literature, Negritude, Colonization and Decolonization in French Antillean Literature, 20th Century French and Francophone Literature, 19th and 20th Century Spanish and Spanish American Literature. **SELECTED PUBLICATIONS** Auth, Negritude in French Caribbean Literature, 92; auth, "La Mujer en Secdun", 96. **CONTACT ADDRESS** Dept English and Lang, Albany State Univ, 504 College Dr, Albany, GA 31705-2717. **EMAIL** atownsel@asurams.edu

TOWNSEND, ANN
PERSONAL Born 12/05/1962, Pittsburgh, PA, m, 1987, 1 child **DISCIPLINE** POETRY, POETICS **EDUCATION** Denison Univ, BA, 85; Ohio State Univ, MA, 87; PhD, 91. **CAREER** From asst prof to assoc prof, Denison Univ, 93-; dir of Jonathan R. Reynolds Young Writers Workshop, Denison Univ, 95-. **HONORS AND AWARDS** "Discovery"/The Nation Prize; Pushcart Prize, Fel, Bread Loaf Writer's Confr; Individual Artist Grant, Ohio Arts Coun; Residency Grant, MacDowell Colony. **MEMBERSHIPS** Assoc Writing Prog, Poets & Writers, Acad of Am Poets, Poetry Soc of Am, Soc of Midland Authors. **RESEARCH** Twentieth-Century Poetry. **SELECTED PUBLICATIONS** Auth, Modern Lore, 95; auth, Holding Katherine, 96; auth, The Braille Words, 97; auth, Dime Store Erotics, 98. **CONTACT ADDRESS** Dept English, Denison Univ, Granville, OH 43023-1372. **EMAIL** townsend@denison.edu

TOWNSEND, ROBERT CAMPBELL
PERSONAL Born 06/05/1935, New Rochelle, NY, m, 1957, 3 children **DISCIPLINE** ENGLISH LITERATURE **EDUCATION** Princeton Univ, BA, 57; Cambridge Univ, MA, 59; Harvard Univ, PhD, 62. **CAREER** Teaching fel gen educ, Harvard Univ, 60-62; from instr to assoc prof, 62-76, Prof English, Amherst Col, 76- **MEMBERSHIPS** MLA **RESEARCH** Romantic and literary criticism; American literature and culture. **SELECTED PUBLICATIONS** Auth, John Worksworth and his brothers poetic development, PMLA, 3/66; W K Wimsatt's criticism, Mass Rev, winter 66; Cambridge English, Critical Surv, winter 67; Sherwood Andersen: A Biography, Houghton-Mifflin, 87; Manhood at Harvard: William James and Others, W.W. Norton, 96; author of numerous articles since 1967. **CONTACT ADDRESS** Dept of English, Amherst Col, Amherst, MA 01002-5000.

TRACE, JACQUELINE BRUCH
PERSONAL Born Buffalo, NY, 2 children **DISCIPLINE** RENAISSANCE LITERATURE, DRAMA, BLACK WOMEN WRITERS **EDUCATION** Bowling Green State Univ, BA, 57; OH Univ, MA, 59; Univ MA, PhD, 75. **CAREER** Prof lit, State Univ NY Fredonia, 78; dealer in bks. **MEMBERSHIPS** AAUW **RESEARCH** Historical influence on Shakespearean drama; the rhetoric of technical and business commun; hist of Niagara Frontier. **SELECTED PUBLICATIONS** Auth, "The supernatural element in Barbour's Bruce," Mass Studies English, spring 68; auth, "Shakespeare's bastard Faulconbridge: An early Tudor hero," Shakespeare Studies Vol XIII, 80; auth, Style and Strategy of the Business Letter, Prentice-Hall, 85; auth, "Dark Goddesses: Black Feminist Theology in Morrisons 'Beloved,'" Obsidian II, no 3, 91. **CONTACT ADDRESS** SUNY, Col at Fredonia, Fredonia, NY 14063-1143. **EMAIL** traceja@buffnet.net

TRACHTENBERG, ALAN
PERSONAL Born 03/22/1932, Philadelphia, PA, m, 1952, 3 children **DISCIPLINE** ENGLISH, AMERICAN STUDIES **EDUCATION** Temple Univ, AB, 54; Univ Minn, PhD(Am studies), 62. **CAREER** Instr English, Gen Col, Univ Minn, Minneapolis, 56-61; from instr to assoc prof, Pa State Univ, University Park, 61-69; assoc prof, 69-71, PROF AM STUDIES and ENGLISH, YALE UNIV, 72-, CHMN DEPT AM STUDIES, 80-, Am Coun Learned Soc grant-in-aid, 64-65, study fel, 68-69; fel, Ctr Adv Studies Behav Sci, 68-69. **MEMBERSHIPS** MLA; Am Studies Asn. **RESEARCH** American literature; American cultural history. **SELECTED PUBLICATIONS** Auth, Brooklyn Bridge: Fact and Symbol, Oxford, 65; The American scene: Versions of the city, Mass Rev, spring 67; The journey back: Myth and history in Tender is the Night, English Inst Essays, 68; ed, Democratic Vistas, 1860-1880, Braziller, 70; auth, The form of freedom in Huck Finn, Southern Rev, 71; ed, Memoirs of Waldo Frank, Univ Mass, 73. **CONTACT ADDRESS** Am Studies Prog, Yale Univ, P O Box 208302, New Haven, CT 06520-8302.

TRACY, ANN B.
DISCIPLINE ENGLISH **EDUCATION** Colby Univ, BA; Brown Univ, MA; Univ Toronto, PhD. **CAREER** Eng Dept, Plattsburgh State Univ **HONORS AND AWARDS** Disting tchg prof, 74. **RESEARCH** 18th and 19th-century lit; Renaissance lit; Gothic novel. **SELECTED PUBLICATIONS** Auth, bk on Gothic romance; several novels and short story collections. **CONTACT ADDRESS** SUNY, Col at Plattsburgh, 101 Broad St, Plattsburgh, NY 12901-2681.

TRACY, KAREN
DISCIPLINE COMMUNCATION STUDIES **EDUCATION** Pa State Univ, BA, 72; Bowling Green State Univ, MA, 74; Univ Wis, PhD, 81. **CAREER** Prof. **RESEARCH** Discourse analysis; facework and identity processes; language and social interaction; institutional discourse; dilematic and multiple goal perspectives. **SELECTED PUBLICATIONS** Auth, Action-implicative discourse analysis, Jour Lang Soc Psychol, 95; co-auth, Qualitative Contributions to the Empirical, 97. **CONTACT ADDRESS** Dept of Communication, Univ of Colorado, Boulder, Boulder, CO 80309. **EMAIL** Karen.Tracy@Colorado.edu

TRAINOR, CHARLES ROBERT
PERSONAL Born 08/16/1947, Stoneham, MA, s **DISCIPLINE** ENGLISH **EDUCATION** Dartmouth Col, BA, 69; Cambridge Univ, MA, 73; Yale Univ, PhD, 77. **CAREER** Asst prof, Ill Col, 77-82; prof, Siena Col, 82-. **HONORS AND AWARDS** Danforth Fel 73-77; Woodrow Wilson Fel, 73-77; Dunbaugh Distinguished Prof, 82. **MEMBERSHIPS** MLA. **RESEARCH** 18th-century English literature; drama. **SELECTED PUBLICATIONS** Auth, The Drama and Fielding's Novels, Garland, 88; auth, "The Irish Servant on the English Stage," Etudes Irland (93); auth, "Sam, Walter Lee, and the Powerless Black Male," Lit Ethnic Discrimination (99). **CONTACT ADDRESS** English Dept, Siena Col, 515 Loudon Rd, Loudonville, NY 12211-1462. **EMAIL** trainor@siena.edu

TRAISTER, BRYCE
PERSONAL Born 12/22/1967, Los Angeles, CA **DISCIPLINE** ENGLISH **EDUCATION** Univ Calif Berkeley, BA, 91; PhD, 96. **CAREER** Asst Prof, Univ W Ont, 96-. **MEMBERSHIPS** MLA; Am Studies Asn; Am Soc for Eighteenth Century Studies. **RESEARCH** American Literature and Culture to 1865; Religion and American Culture; Gender and American Culture. **SELECTED PUBLICATIONS** Aut? "Anne Hutchinson's 'Monstrous Birth' and the Feminization of antinomianism," Can Rev of Am Studies, (97): 133-158; auth, "Sentimental Medicine: Oliver Wendell Holmes and the Construction of Masculinity," Studies in Am Fiction, 99; auth, "Libertinism and Authorship in America's Early Republic," Am Lit, 00; auth, "Academic viagra: The Rise of Masculinity Studies," Am Quart, (00): 274-304. **CONTACT ADDRESS** Dept English, Univ W Ont, 916 William St, London, ON, Canada N5Y 3K7.

TRAUB, GEORGE WILLIAM
PERSONAL Born 01/30/1936, Chicago, IL, s **DISCIPLINE** THEOLOGY & LITERATURE, SPIRITUALITY **EDUCATION** Xavier Univ, BLitt, 58; West Baden Col, PhL, 61; Loyola Univ Chicago, MA, 68; Cornell Univ, PhD, 73. **CAREER** Instr English, Greek & Latin, Loyola Acad, Ill, 61-64; from Asst Prof to Assoc Prof English, 72-80; Dir Formation & Continuing Educ, Chicago Prov Soc of Jesus, 80-85; Jesuit Prof Theology & Dir Ignatian Programs, Xavier Univ, 87-; **MEMBERSHIPS** Coordrs for Mission & Identity, Assoc of Jesuit Cols and Univs. **RESEARCH** Ignatian sprituality; Jesuit history & education; theology and literature. **SELECTED PUBLICATIONS** Coauth, The Desert and the City: An Interpretation of the History of Christian Spirituality, Loyola Univ Press, 84; Do You Speak Ignatian? A Glossary. . . .Jesuit Circles: 5th ed, Xavier Univ, 00. **CONTACT ADDRESS** Xavier Univ, Ohio, 3800 Victory Pky, Cincinnati, OH 45207-5185. **EMAIL** traub@xu.edu

TRAVIS, MOLLY ABEL
DISCIPLINE TWENTIETH-CENTURY BRITISH AND AMERICAN LITERATURE **EDUCATION** Lamar Univ, BA, 72; Stephen F Austin State Univ, MA, 75; OH State Univ, PhD, 89. **CAREER** Assoc prof of Eng, Tulane Univ. **SELECTED PUBLICATIONS** Auth, Beloved and Middle Passage: Race, Narrative, and the Critic's Essentialism, Narrative 2.3, 94; auth, "Cybernetic Esthetics, Hypertext and the Future of Literature," in Mosiac 29.4, 96; auth, Reading Cultures: The Construction of Readers in the Twentieth Century, Southern Ill UP, 98. **CONTACT ADDRESS** Dept of Eng, Tulane Univ, 6823 St Charles Ave, New Orleans, LA 70118. **EMAIL** matravis@tulane.edu

TRAVIS, PETER W.
DISCIPLINE ENGLISH LITERATURE **EDUCATION** Univ Chicago, PhD, 72. **CAREER** Prof, Dartmouth Col. **RESEARCH** Lit theory; Brit lit; Brit Medieval lit. **SELECTED PUBLICATIONS** Auth, Deconstructing Chaucer's Retraction, Exemplaria, 91; The Social Body of the Dramatic Christ in Medieval England, ACTA, 87; Dramatic Design in the Chester Cycle, Univ Chicago P, 82; auth, "Chaucer's Chronographiae, the Confounded Reader, and Fourteenth-Century Measurements of Time," Disputatio 2 (97): 1-34; auth, "Chaucer's Helitropes and the Poetics of Metaphor," Speculum 72 (97): 399-427; auth, "Reading Chaucer Ab Ovo: Mock-Exemplum in the Nun's Priest's Tale," in The Performance of Medieval Culture, (98): 161-82. **CONTACT ADDRESS** Dept of English, Dartmouth Col, 6032 Sanborn House, Hanover, NH 03755. **EMAIL** Peter.W.Travis@dartmouth.edu

TRAVISANO, THOMAS J.
PERSONAL Born 12/14/1951, Livingston, NJ, m, 1981, 2 children **DISCIPLINE** ENGLISH **EDUCATION** Haverford Col, BA, 73; Univ Va, MA, 78; PhD, 81. **CAREER** Asst prof, Col of William and Mary, 80-82; asst prof to prof, Hartwick Col, 82-. **HONORS AND AWARDS** NEH Fel, 94-95; NEH Summer Seminar, 83, 00; Wandersee Scholar, Hartwick Col, 99-00. **MEMBERSHIPS** MLA; Am Lit Asn; Modernist Studies Asn; Elizabeth Bishop Soc. **RESEARCH** American literature; Modern and Contemporary American poetry; Nonfiction writing; Artistic Development. **SELECTED PUBLICATIONS** Co-ed, Gendered Modernisms: American Women Poets and their Readers, Univ Pa Press, 96; auth, Mid-century Quartet: Bishop, Lowell, Jarrell, Berryman and The Making of a Postmodern Aesthetic, Univ of Va Press, 99; ed, The Complete Letters of Elizabeth Bishop and Robert Lowell, Farrar, Straus and Giroux, (forthcoming) **CONTACT ADDRESS** Dept English, Hartwick Col, 28 State St, Oneonta, NY 13820-1311. **EMAIL** travisanot@hartwick.edu

TRAWICK, LEONARD MOSES
PERSONAL Born 07/04/1933, Decatur, AL, m, 1961, 2 children **DISCIPLINE** ENGLISH **EDUCATION** Univ of the South, BA, 55; Univ Chicago, MA, 57; Harvard Univ, PhD, 61. **CAREER** From instr to asst prof English, Columbia Univ, 61-69; assoc prof, 69-73, prof English, Cleveland State Univ, 73-98; prof Emeritus, 98; Ed, Gamut Jour, Cleveland State Univ, 80-92; Ed, Cleveland State Univ Poetry Centrer, 71-98. **HONORS AND AWARDS** James P Barry Ohioana Awd for Editorial Excellence, 91; Ohioana Poetry Awd for lifetime achievement in poetry, 94. **MEMBERSHIPS** MLA **RESEARCH** English romatic literature; American literature; poetics. **SELECTED PUBLICATIONS** Auth, Hazlitt, Reynolds and the ideal, Studies Romanticism, summer 65; Backgrounds of Romanticism, Ind Univ, 67; The present state of Blake studies, Studies Burke & His Time, winter 70-71; Beast Forms (poems), Cleveland State Univ, 71; Whittier's Snow-Bound: A poem about the imagination, Essays Lit, spring 74; Nature and art in Milton, Blake Newslett, winter 74; Blake's Empirical Occult, Wordsworth Circle, spring 77; Blake's German Connection, Colby Libr Quart, 12/77; Beastmorfs, Cleveland State Univ Poetry Center, 94. **CONTACT ADDRESS** Dept of English, Cleveland State Univ, 1983 E 24th St, Cleveland, OH 44115-2440. **EMAIL** l.trawick@csuohio.edu

TRAYLOR, ELEANOR W.
PERSONAL s **DISCIPLINE** ENGLISH **EDUCATION** Spelman College, BA; Atlanta University, MA; Catholic University, PhD. **CAREER** Department of Agriculture, Graduate School, English Department, chairperson, 66-67; Howard University, College of Fine Arts, adjunct prof, drama, 68-75; Hobart & William Smith Colleges, The Melvin Hill Professorship Chair, 79; Cornell University, visiting prof, literature, 79-80; Tougaloo College, visiting humanist, 82; Montgomery College, prof, English, 65-90; Howard Univ, professor, English, Humanities Department, chair, 90-93, Chair, Dept of English, 93-. **HONORS AND AWARDS** Midwest African-American Theatre Alliance, The Hazel Joan Bryant Recognition Awd, 1987; Peoples Congregational Church, The Black History Achievement Awd for contributions to the advancement & preservation of African-American Literature, 1989; Catholic University, The Alumni Achievement Awd, Literary criticism, 1989; The Marcus Garvey Memorial Foundation, The Larry Neal-Georgia Douglas Johnson Awd, literature and community service, 1989. **MEMBERSHIPS** The Larry Neal Cultural Series, designer, project director, 1984; Educators for the Advancement of American Literature in Public Schools, founder, 1984; College Language Association; Modern Language Association; Afro-American Museum Association, evaluator; The Smithsonian Institution, Program in Black American Culture, script writer; National Council of Teachers of English; National Endowment for the Humanities, panelist. **SELECTED PUBLICATIONS** Author, College Reading Skills, Random House, 1966; The Dream Awake: A Multi-Media Production, 1968; The Humanities and Afro-American Literature Tradition, 1988; Broad Sympathy: The Howard University Oral Tradition Reader, Simon and Schuster, 1996. **CONTACT ADDRESS** Department of English, Locke Hall, Rm 248, Howard Univ, Washington, DC 20059.

TREADGOLD, WARREN
PERSONAL Born 04/30/1949, Oxford, United Kingdom, m, 1982 **DISCIPLINE** HISTORY, CLASSICS **EDUCATION** Harvard Univ, AB, 70; PhD, 77. **CAREER** Lectr, UCLA, 77-78; Univ Munich, Free Univ Berlin, 78-80; 82-83; Lectr, Standford Univ, 80-82; asst prof, Hillsdale Col, 83-88; vis prof, Univ Calif at Berkeley, 86; asst prof, Fla Int Univ, 88-97; prof, St Louis Univ, 97- **HONORS AND AWARDS** Woodrow Wilson Int Center for Scholars Fel; NEH Fel (2); Visiting Fel, All Souls Col, Oxford; Alexander von Humboldt Fel; Outstanding Achievements and Performance awards, Fla Int Univ. **MEMBERSHIPS** AHA; Am Philos Assoc; Medieval Acad of Am; AAUP. **RESEARCH** Byzantine history and literature. **SELECTED PUBLICATIONS** Auth, The Nature of the Bibliotheas of Photrus, 80; auth, The Byzantine State Finances in the Eighth and Ninth Centures, 82; ed, Renaissances Before the Renaissance, 84; auth, The Byzantine Revivial, 88; auth, Byzantium and It's Army, 95; auth, A History of the Byzantine State and Society, 97; auth, A Concise History of Byzantium, 00. **CONTACT ADDRESS** Dept Hist, St. Louis Univ, 221 N Grand Boulevard, Saint Louis, MO 63103-2006. **EMAIL** treadgw@slu.edu

TREGGIARI, SUSAN M.
DISCIPLINE CLASSICS **EDUCATION** BA, 62; MA, 65; BLitt, 67; Oxford Univ, DLitt, 93. **CAREER** Anne T. and Robert M. Bass Prof Schl Hum and Sci; prof class/hist. **RESEARCH** Roman hist; Roman soc in the late Republic and Principate; lit, epigraphic and juristic sources. **SELECTED PUBLICATIONS** Auth, Roman Freedmen During the Late Republic, 69; Roman Marriage: Iusti Coniuges from the Time of Cicero to the Time of Ulpian, 91; Social Status And Social Legislation in the Cambridge Ancient History X, 96. **CONTACT ADDRESS** Stanford Univ, Bldg 20, Main Quad, Stanford, CA 94305.

TRELA, D. J.
PERSONAL Born Chicago, IL **DISCIPLINE** ENGLISH LITERATURE **EDUCATION** Univ Il Chicago, BA, 81; Univ Edinburgh, Scotland, PhD. **CAREER** Asst prof to assoc prof to prof, chair, asst dir to interim dir to dir, 89-, Roosevelt Univ. **HONORS AND AWARDS** Phi Beta Kappa; Phi Kappa Phi; Phi Eta Sigma; Univ Edinburgh Studentship, 81-84; NEH Travel to Collections Grant, 93; Roosevelt Univ res sabbatical, 93, 97; NEH Summer Stipend, 95; Univ Edinburgh Honorary Fel, 97; invited lectr, St. Joseph's Univ, Philadelphia, 97. **MEMBERSHIPS** Assoc of Governing Bds of Univ & Col; Amer Assoc of Univ Prof; Midwest Modern Lang Assoc; Modern Lang Assoc; Carlyle Soc; Midwest Victorian Stud Assoc; Res Soc for Victorian Per; Victorians Inst. **RESEARCH** British lit; Victorian prose & prose fiction; Victorian women writers espec Margaret Oliphant; Thomas Carlyle & Jane Welsh Carlyle: Victorian periodical lit & jour; race & lit; Scottish lit; bibliog & editing; literary criticism; gen educ courses; composition. **SELECTED PUBLICATIONS** Ed, Margaret Oliphant: Critical Essays on a Gentle Subversive, Assoc U Press, 95; coed; Victorian Urban Settings: The Nineteenth Century City and Its Contexts, Garland, 96; auth, Critical Response to Thomas Carlyle's Major Works, Greenwood Press, 97; auth, Margaret Oliphant: A Descriptive Bibliography, Locust Hill Press, 99; auth, Thomas Carlyle's Past and Present, Univ Calif Press, 00. **CONTACT ADDRESS** Sch of Liberal Stud, Roosevelt Univ, 430 S Michigan Ave, Chicago, IL 60605-1394. **EMAIL** jtrela@roosevelt.edu

TREMBATH, PAUL
DISCIPLINE ENGLISH LITERATURE **EDUCATION** Univ Wis, BA, MA; Univ Va, PhD. **CAREER** Assoc prof. **RESEARCH** Contemporary critical theory and its historical backgrounds. **SELECTED PUBLICATIONS** Auth, pubs in The Journal of Aesthetics and Art Criticism, Postmodern Culture Philosophy and Literature. **CONTACT ADDRESS** Dept of English, Colorado State Univ, Fort Collins, CO 80523. **EMAIL** ptrembath@vines.colostate.edu

TRENT, JIMMIE DOUGLAS
PERSONAL Born 11/17/1933, Lima, OK, m, 1969, 3 children **DISCIPLINE** SPEECH **EDUCATION** Emporia State Univ, BSEd, 55, MS, 59; Purdue Univ, PhD(speech), 66. **CAREER** Dir forensics, High Schs, Kans, 55-57; instr speech & dir forensics, Emporia State Univ, 57-60; instr speech, Purdue Univ, 60-62; asst prof, Eastern Ill Univ, 62-64; asst prof & dir masters degree prog, Wayne State Univ, 64-68, grad off & asst to dean col liberal arts, 68-69, assoc prof & chmn grad prog speech commun & theatre, 69-71; chmn dept, 71-82, Ed, Winning Orations, Interstate Oratorical Asn, 65-70; prof commun & theatre Miami Univ, 71-81; Prof of Commun, 81-99; vis scholar, Northwestern Univ, 82; Emer Prof of Commun, 99-. **HONORS AND AWARDS** Distinguished Service Awd, Speech Commun Asn Ohio, 80. **MEMBERSHIPS** Speech Commun Asn; Int Commun Asn; Interstate Oratorical Asn (exec secy, 64-70). **RESEARCH** Argumentation; leadership behavior; organizational communication. **SELECTED PUBLICATIONS** Auth, Small group discussions, In: Introduction to the Field of Speech, Scott, 65; Toulmon's model of an argument: An examination and extension, Quart J Speech, 68; coauth, Concepts in Communication, Allyn & Bacon, 73; auth, The rhetoric of the challenger: George Stanley McGovern, Cent State Speech J, spring 74; Personnel evaluation: Developing institutional support for a department, Asn Dept & Adminr Speech Commun Asn Bull, 1/74; Public relations education: An opportunity for speech communication, Commun Educ, 11/76; auth, The Ideal Candidate: A Study of the Desired Attributes of the Public and the Media Across Two Presidential Campaigns. Am Behavioral Sci, 93; auth, The Ideal Candidate Revisited, Am Behavioral Sci, 97; auth, CSCA and 50 Years of Communication Studies, Communications Studies, 00. **CONTACT ADDRESS** 101 County Club Ln, Oxford, OH 45056-1602. **EMAIL** trentjd@muohio.edu

TRENT, JUDITH
PERSONAL Born Grand Rapids, MI, m, 1961, 1 child **DISCIPLINE** COMMUNICATIONS **EDUCATION** Western Mich Univ, BS, 62; Univ Mich, MA, 68; PhD, 70. **CAREER** Instr, Belleville High School, 63-67; Director of Debate, Univ Mich, 67-69; Asst Prof, Youngstown State Univ, 70-71; Prof, Univ Dayton, 71-84; Prof and Assoc VP, Univ Cincinnati, 84-. **HONORS AND AWARDS** Fel, Am Coun on Educ, 83-84; Just Community Awd, Univ Cincinnati. **MEMBERSHIPS** Nat Comm Asn, Center for the Study of the Presidency, Central States Comm Asn, Eastern Comm Asn, Intl Comm Asn. **RESEARCH** Presidential Campaign Communication; Women in Politics. **SELECTED PUBLICATIONS** Auth, Political Campaign Communication: Principles and Practices, Praeger Pub, 00; auth, Communication: Views from the Helm for the Twenty-First Century, Allyn & Bacon, Inc, 98; auth, "The Beginning and the Early End," in The 1996 Presidential Campaign: A Communication Perspective, Praeger Pub, 98; auth, "Political Rhetoric," in Encyclopedia of Rhetoric and Composition, Garland Pub, 96; auth, "The Incumbent and His Challengers: Adapting to Prevailing Condition," in Presidential Campaign Discourse, 95; auth, "The Early Campaign of 1992: The Reluctant Candidates," in The 1992 Presidential Campaign: A Communication Perspective, Praeger Pub, 94; auth, "Acting Affirmatively: The Time is Now," CGS Communicator, (98): 1-6; auth, "The Ideal Candidate Revisited: A Study of the Desired Attributes of the Public and the Media Across Three Presidential campaigns," American Behavioral Scientist, (97): 1001-1019; auth, "The Ideal candidate: A Study of Perceived Attributes Across Two Presidential Campaigns," American Behavioral Scientist, (93): 225-239; auth, "Sex Still Counts: Women's Use of Televised Negative Advertising during the Decade of the 80s," Journal of Applied communication, (93): 21-40. **CONTACT ADDRESS** Dept Comm, Univ of Cincinnati, PO Box 210184, Cincinnati, OH 45221-0184. **EMAIL** Judith.Trent@uc.edu

TRICOMI, ALBERT HENRY
PERSONAL Born 12/30/1942, New York, NY, m, 1968, 3 children **DISCIPLINE** ENGLISH, DRAMA **EDUCATION** Columbia Col, AB, 64; Northwestern Univ, MA, 65, PhD(English), 69. **CAREER** Asst prof English, NC Cent Univ, 68-69; asst prof, 69-75, Assoc prof, English, State Univ NY Binghamton, 75-, vice provost, undergraduate studies, 93-98; prof, 76-. **HONORS AND AWARDS** Chancellor's award, Excellence in Teaching; FIPSE project dir for honors project in general education, 98-01. **MEMBERSHIPS** AAUP **RESEARCH** Shakespeare; Elizabethan-Jacobean drama and history; Renaissance literature. **SELECTED PUBLICATIONS** Auth, Anticourt Drama in England, 1603-1642, 89; auth , Reading Tudor-Stuart Texts, 94; ed, Contextualizing the Renaissance, 98. **CONTACT ADDRESS** Dept of English, SUNY, Binghamton, Binghamton, NY 13901. **EMAIL** atricomi@binghamton.edu

TRIECE, MARY
PERSONAL Born 02/27/1967, Lake Forest, IL **DISCIPLINE** SPEECH COMMUNICATION **EDUCATION** Univ of Tex, BBA, 90; MA, 92; PhD, 97. **CAREER** Asst instr to res asst, Univ of Tex Austin, 93-97; temp asst prof, Truman State Univ, 97-98; asst prof, Univ of Akron, 98-. **HONORS AND AWARDS** Jesse H. Jones Fel, 93-94; Fel, Univ of Akron, 99. **MEMBERSHIPS** Nat Commun Assoc. **RESEARCH** Rhetorical criticism, rhetorical theory, feminist criticism and theories, protest rhetoric, popular culture, labor history, Marxism. **SELECTED PUBLICATIONS** Coauth, "U.S. Presidency and Television", Museum of Broadcast Commun Encycl of Television, Fitzroy and Dearborn (Chicago), 97; auth, The Practical True Woman: Reconciling Women and Work in Popular Mail-Order Magazines, 1900-1920, Critical Studies in Mass Communication 16 (99): 42-62; auth, Rhetoric and Social Change: Women's Struggles for Economic and Political Equality, 1900-1917, Women's Studies in Communication, 00; auth, Protest and Popular Culture: Women in the American Labor Movement, Westview, (forthcoming). **CONTACT ADDRESS** Dept Commun, Univ of Akron, Kolbe Hall 108, Akron, OH 44325-1003. **EMAIL** mtriece@uakron.edu

TRIMBLE, JOHN RALSTON
PERSONAL Born 11/25/1940, Niagara Falls, ON, Canada, m, 1982, 5 children **DISCIPLINE** ENGLISH **EDUCATION** Princeton Univ, AB, 62; Univ Calif, Berkeley, MA, 64, PhD (English), 71. **CAREER** Asst prof, 70-77, from assoc prof to prof English, Univ Tex, Austin, 77-95; disting teaching prof, English; 95. **HONORS AND AWARDS** Jean Holloway Awd for Excellence in Teaching, Univ Tex, 75; Eyes of Texas Exc Awd, Univ Tex, 93; Charter member, Academy of Disting Teachers, Univ Tex, 95; Univ Tex Student Government Teaching Excelence Awd, 75; Univ Tex President's Associates Awd for Excellence in Teaching Composition, 80. **MEMBERSHIPS** NCTE. **RESEARCH** Composition and rhetoric; 18th-century English literature; American literature. **SELECTED PUBLICATIONS** Auth, Clarissa's Role in The Rape of the Lock, Tex Studies Lit & Lang, Winter 74; Writing with Style: Conversations on the Art of Writing, Prentice-Hall, 75, 2nd edition, 00. **CONTACT ADDRESS** Dept of English B 5000, Univ of Texas, Austin, Austin, TX 78712-1026. **EMAIL** trimble@mail.utexas.edu

TRIMMER, JOSEPH FRANCIS
PERSONAL Born 08/04/1941, Cortland, NY, m, 1966, 1 child **DISCIPLINE** AMERICAN LITERATURE & STUDIES **EDUCATION** Colgate Univ, BA, 63; Purdue Univ, MA, 66, PhD, 68. **CAREER** Tchg asst Eng, Purdue Univ, 65-68; asst prof, 68-72, assoc prof, 72-80, prof eng, Ball State Univ, 80, coordr gen educ eng,, 72, Adv ed, Alfred Publ Co, 78. **MEMBERSHIPS** MLA Conf Col Comp & Commun; Am Studics Asn. **RESEARCH** Am lit; Am studies; writing. **SELECTED PUBLICATIONS** Auth, Black American Notes on the Problem of Definition, Ball State Univ Monogr, 71; ed, A Casebook on Ralph Ellison's Invisible Man, Crowell, 72; auth, Ralph Ellison's Flying Home, Studies Short Fiction, spring 72; The Virginian: Novel and films, Ill Quart, 12/72; V K Ratliff: A portrait of the artist in motion, Mod Fiction Studies, winter 74; coauth, American Oblique: Writing About the American Experience, Houghton, 76; auth, Memoryscape: Jean Sheperd's midwest, Old Northwest, 12/76; ed, The National Book Award for Fiction: An Index to the First Twenty-Five Years, G K Hall, 78; Narration as Knowledge, Heinemann, 98; Fictions, Harcourt Brace, 98; Writing With a Purpose, Houghton Mifflin, 98. **CONTACT ADDRESS** Dept of Eng, Ball State Univ, 2000 W University, Muncie, IN 47306-0002. **EMAIL** jtrimmer@bsu.edu

TRIPP, BERNELL E.
DISCIPLINE MASS COMMUNICATIONS **EDUCATION** Univ Ala, BA, 82, MA, 89, PhD cand. **CAREER** Mass Comm, Univ Ala. **RESEARCH** 19th century Black press. **SELECTED PUBLICATIONS** Auth, The Antebellum Press, 1827-1861: Effective Abolitionist or Reluctant Reformer?; The Black Media, 1865-Present: Liberal Crusaders or Defenders of Tradition? In: Perspectives on Mass Communication History. **CONTACT ADDRESS** Dept of Journalism, Univ of Alabama, Tuscaloosa, PO Box 870172, Tuscaloosa, AL 34587-0172.

TROOST, LINDA V.
PERSONAL Born 06/08/1957, Washington, DC **DISCIPLINE** ENGLISH **EDUCATION** Smith Col, AB, 78; Univ Penn, PhD, 85. **CAREER** Asst prof, Wash Jefferson Col, 85-91; assoc prof, 91-. **HONORS AND AWARDS** NEH Summer Stipend; Res Fel, London. **MEMBERSHIPS** ASECS; MLA. **RESEARCH** 18th century drama in England; Jane Austen. **SELECTED PUBLICATIONS** Auth, "Jane Austen in Hollywood (Univ Press KY), 98. **CONTACT ADDRESS** Dept English, Washington and Jefferson Col, 60 S Lincoln St, Washington, PA 15301-4812. **EMAIL** ltroost@washjeff.edu

TROTTER, MARY
DISCIPLINE ENGLISH LITERATURE **EDUCATION** Northwestern Univ, PhD. **CAREER** Asst prof, TX Tech Univ. **RESEARCH** Mod Europ and Am drama; Irish studies; Northern Irish women playwrights. **SELECTED PUBLICATIONS** Publ articles on polit theatre in early 20th century and contemp Ireland. **CONTACT ADDRESS** Dept of English, Texas Tech Univ, Lubbock, TX 79409-5015. **EMAIL** M.Trotter@ttu.edu

TRUAX, ELIZABETH
PERSONAL Born New York, NY, w, 4 children **DISCIPLINE** ENGLISH **EDUCATION** Vassar Col, BA; Rutg Univ, MA; Univ S Cal, PhD. **CAREER** Instr, 66; asst prof, 68; assoc prof, 73; dept hd, 60-79; prof, 84-, Chapman Coll. **HONORS AND AWARDS** NEH, 82-83; IRS Fel, 79. **MEMBERSHIPS** SAA; RCSC; PAMLA. **SELECTED PUBLICATIONS** Auth, Metamorphosis In Shakespeare's Plays: A Pageant of Gods, Heroes, Maids and Monsters, Edwin Mellen Press (92); rev, The Index of Emblem Art Symposium, ed. Peter M Daly, 92; rev, The Index--Saturn: From Antiquity to the Renaissance, ed. Massimo Ciavolella, Amilcare Ab Iannucci, 93; auth, "Lucrece! What hath your conceited painter wrought?" in Shakespeare: Contemporary Critical Approaches, ed. Harry Garvin (Lewisburg: Burknell Univ Press, 80); auth, "Venus, Lucrece and Bess of Hardwick: Portraits to Please," in Shakespeare and the Arts, ed. Cecile Williamson Carey, Henry S Limouse (Washington, D.C.: Univ Press of Am, 83); auth, "Macbeth and Hercules: The Hero Bewitched," Comp Drama, 23 (90): 359-376. **CONTACT ADDRESS** Dept English, Chapman Univ, 333 North Glassell St, Orange, CA 92866-1011.

TRUE, MICHAEL D.
PERSONAL Born 11/08/1933, Oklahoma City, OK, m, 1958, 6 children **DISCIPLINE** ENGLISH & AMERICAN LITERATURE & PEACE STUDIES **EDUCATION** Univ Okla, BA, 55; Univ Minn, MA, 57; Duke Univ, PhD, 64. **CAREER** Lectr English, Duke Univ, 60-61; lectr Eng, NC Col Durham, 61; from instr to asst prof, Ind State Univ, 61-65; from asst prof to assoc prof, 65-74, prof English, 74-97, Assumption Col; vis lectr English & educ, Clark Univ, 68-78; prof nonfiction, Upper Midwest Writers Conf, 73-80; NEH fel, 76-77; vis scholar Am lit, Columbia Univ, 76-77; consult, Nat Humanities Fac, 77-; scheffer visiting prof of Religion, Colorado Col, 88, 90, 94, 99. **HONORS AND AWARDS** NEH fel, 76-77; Am Philos Soc grant, 79; F Andre Favat Awd, Mass Counc Tchrs English, 80; Peace Teacher of the Year, Consortium on Peace Res, Educ and Dev, 96; Fulbright lectr, India, 97-98; Peace stud Asn Lifetime Achievement Awd, 99. **MEMBERSHIPS** Peace Stud Asn; IPRA; MLA; NCTE. **RESEARCH** Am lit of World War I; Am art and culture; contemporary poetry; the nonviolent tradition in the U.S. **SELECTED PUBLICATIONS** Ed, Daniel Berrigan: Poetry, Drama, Prose, Orbis, 88; auth, Ordinary People: Family Life and Global Values, Orbis, 91; auth, To Construct Peace: 30 More Justice Seekers, Peacemakers, XXIII Publ, 92; auth, An Energy Field More Intense Than War: The Nonviolent Tradition and American Literature, Syracuse, 95; co-ed, The Frontiers of Nonviolence, IPRA, 98; coauth, "Who Needs Religion?" Erie, PA: Topics Press, 00. **CONTACT ADDRESS** 4 Westland St, Worcester, MA 01602. **EMAIL** mtrue@eve.assumption.edu

TRUJILLO, NICK L.
PERSONAL Born 12/14/1955, Pasadena, CA, m, 1985 **DISCIPLINE** COMMUNICATION **EDUCATION** Univ Utah, PhD 83. **CAREER** Purdue Univ, asst prof 82-84; Mich State Univ, vis asst prof, 84-85; S Methodist Univ, asst prof, 85-90; Calif State Univ Sacramento, prof 90-. **HONORS AND AWARDS** B Aubrey Fisher Awd; Quintus Wilson Alum Achv Awd. **MEMBERSHIPS** NCA; WSCA. **RESEARCH** Organizational Communication; Ethnography; Sport, Media and Society. **SELECTED PUBLICATIONS** Auth, The Meaning of Nolan Ryan, College Stn TX, TX A&M Univ Press, 94; auth, Shopping for Family, coauth, Qualitative Inq, 98; In Search of Naunny's Grave, Text and Performance Quart, 98; Fragments of Self at the Postmodern Bar, coauth, Jour of Contemporary Ethnography, 97; auth, Machine Missiles and Men: Images of the Male Body on ABC's Monday Night Football, Sociology of Sport Jour, 95; auth, Emotionality in the Field and in the Stands: Expressing Self Through Baseball, Jour of Sport and Social Issues, 94; auth, Qualitative Research in Organizational Communication, coauth, New Handbook of Organizational Comm, eds Fred Jablin, Linda Putnam, Newberry Pk CA, Sage, 00; From Wild Western Prodigy to the Ageless Wonder, The Mediated Revolution of Nolan Ryan, coauth, Heroes and Celebrities in American Culture, eds Robert Cathcart, Susan Drucker, Lanham MA, Hamilton, 94; auth, Five Reasons Why Nolan Ryan Should Not be Elected to the Hall of Fame, Elysian Fields Quart, 94; Remembering Nolan, A History of TX Baseball, 94. **CONTACT ADDRESS** Dept of Communication, California State Univ, Sacramento, 4125 Bruhn Ct, Sacramento, CA 95821. **EMAIL** nickt@csus.edu

TRUMPENER, KATIE
PERSONAL Born 04/10/1961, San Francisco, CA, m **DISCIPLINE** ENGLISH **EDUCATION** Univ Alberta, BA (honours), English, 82; Harvard Univ, AM, English and Amer Lit, 83; Stanford Univ, PhD, comparative lit, 90. **CAREER** Visiting asst prof, commun, Univ Iowa, 88; asst prof, German, 90-95, assoc prof, Germanic studies, comparative lit, English, cinema and media studies, 95-00, Univ of Chicago coeditor, Modern Philology, 98-; Full Prof, Germanic Studies Comparative Literature, English, Cinema and Media Studies, 00-. **HONORS AND AWARDS** Crawshay Prize, British Acad; ACLS Sr Scholarship; Mellon Postdoctoral Fellowship; MLA Prize for a First Book. **RESEARCH** 18th-20th century European Lit; 20th Germany; cinema. **SELECTED PUBLICATIONS** Auth, Bardic Nationalism: The Romantic Novel and the British Empire, 1997. **CONTACT ADDRESS** Dept. of Germanic Studies, Univ of Chicago, 1050 E. 59th St., Chicago, IL 60637. **EMAIL** ktrumpen@midway.uchicago.edu

TRYPHONOPOULOS, DEMETRES P. P.
PERSONAL Born 12/01/1956, Tripolis, Greece, m, 1980, 2 children **DISCIPLINE** 20TH CENTURY AMERICAN POETRY **EDUCATION** Univ West Ont, BA, 80, MA, 81, PhD, 88. **CAREER** Asst prof, Wilfrid Laurier Univ, 88-89; asst prof, Univ West Ont, 89-90; prof, Univ New Brunswick, 90-. **HONORS AND AWARDS** SSHRC Postdoct Fel, 89-90; SSHRC Fel, 93-96; UNB Merit Awd, 94. **MEMBERSHIPS** MLA. **RESEARCH** 20th-century American poetry; modernist poetry; poetry and prosody; modern Greek poetry. **SELECTED PUBLICATIONS** Auth, The Celestial Tradition: A Study of Ezra Pound's 'The Cantos', Wil Laur UP (Waterloo, ON), 92; co-ed, Pound's Letters to Olivia Rossetti Agresti, Univ IL Press (Champaign, IL), 98; auth, Pound a l'occulto: le radici esoteriche dei Cantos, Roma, 88; co-ed, Literary Modernism and the Occult Tradition, Nat Poetry Found, 96; co-ed, Fiddlehead Gold: An Anthology of Poetry and Fiction, Goose Lane, 96; co-ed, William Carlos Williams and Language, Nat Poetry Found, 99. **CONTACT ADDRESS** Eng Dept., Univ of New Brunswick, Fredericton, PO Box 4400, Fredericton, NB, Canada E3A 5A3. **EMAIL** demetres@unb.ca

TSAGARIS, ELLEN
DISCIPLINE ENGLISH **EDUCATION** Augustana Col, BA, 78; Univ Iowa, MA, 85; Univ Iowa, 85; Southern Illinois Univ, PhD, 1996. **CAREER** Program Coordinator, AK Col, 00; instr of English, Mary Crest International Univ, 99-00. **HONORS AND AWARDS** Dissertation Research Awd, Southern; Kappa; Sigma Delta Pi; Sigma Tau Delta. **MEMBERSHIPS** Modern Language Association; International Virginia Woolf Society; The Barbara Pym Society. **RESEARCH** Barbara Pym; Anna Rice; Tudor History; Romantic Literature; Rhetoric; Civil Rights; Employment Discrimination; Hispanic Studies. **SELECTED PUBLICATIONS** auth, "The Subversion of Romance in the Novels of Barbara Pym," The Popular Press, 98; auth, "He's not one of Them," The Gothic World of Anne Rice, Browne, Hoppenstand, eds, The Popular Press, 96; auth, "Men must be Manly and Women Womanly," Virginia Woolf, Pace University Press, 95. **CONTACT ADDRESS** Dept English, AIC Col, 1801 E Kimberly Rd, Davenport, IA 52807. **EMAIL** etsag1998@aol.com

TUCKER, CYNTHIA GRANT
PERSONAL Born 06/17/1941, New York, NY, m, 1966, 2 children **DISCIPLINE** COMPARATIVE LITERATURE, ENGLISH **EDUCATION** Denison Univ, BA, 63; Univ Iowa, PhD(comp lit), 67. **CAREER** Prof English, Univ Memphis; vstg fac, IA Summer Writing Festival, 99, 00; GTU in Berkeley, Summer 97, 99. **HONORS AND AWARDS** NEH prog gtants, 78-81; NEH fel for col teachers, 82; Schlesinger Lib res grants, 85, 94, 00; HW Durham Found grants, 95-98, 00. **MEMBERSHIPS** Unitarian Universalitst Hist Soc. **RESEARCH** Biography, Humor, Women's Studies, Women in Religion, Journals Diary Lit. **SELECTED PUBLICATIONS** Auth, Meredith's broken laurel: Modern Love and the Renaissance sonnet tradition, Victorian Poetry, 72; The Rilkean poet-lover and his laurel, Philol Quart, 74; Translation as resurrection: Rilke and Louise Labe, Mod Lang Notes, 74; Petrarchizing into the horrible: Baudelaire's Grotesque, Fr Rev, 75; Kate Freeman Clark: A Painter Rediscovered, Univ Press Miss, 81; Spirited Threads: The Writing and Art of Patricia Roberts Cline, Portland, OR, Sibyl Publications, Fall, 97; Prophetic Sisterhood: Liberal Women Ministers©1880-1930, 90, 95, 00; Healers in Harm's Way: Mary Collison, A Clergywoman in Christian Science, 85, 95. **CONTACT ADDRESS** Univ of Memphis, Patterson Hall, Memphis, TN 38152. **EMAIL** cgtucker@cc.memphis.edu

TUCKER, EDWARD L.
PERSONAL Born 11/19/1921, Crewe, VA, s **DISCIPLINE** ENGLISH **EDUCATION** Roanoke Col, BA, 46; Columbia Univ, MA, 47; Univ Ga, PhD, 57. **CAREER** Instr, Roanoke Col, 49-54; asst prof, Univ Richmond, 57-60; from asst prof to prof, Va Polytech Inst & State Univ, 60-. **HONORS AND AWARDS** Awded Emblem, Ctr for Scholarly Editions of the MLA. **MEMBERSHIPS** MLA, SAMLA, Edgar Allan Poe Soc. **RESEARCH** American (especially Southern) Literature. **SELECTED PUBLICATIONS** Auth, Richard Henry Wilde: His Life and Selected Poems, Univ Ga Press, 66; auth, Longfellow's John Endicott, Univ Press of Va, 86; auth, The Clemens-Johnston Reading of 17 January 1889, RALS (98); auth, The First Meeting of Thomas Nelson Page and Joel Chandler Harris, Miss Quart (99). **CONTACT ADDRESS** Dept English, Virginia Polytech Inst and State Univ, 100 Virginia Tech, Blacksburg, VA 24061-0001. **EMAIL** edtucke2@vt.edu

TUCKER, MARK
PERSONAL Born 10/25/1945, Natchez, MS, m, 1968 **DISCIPLINE** LIBRARY AND INFORMATION SCIENCE, HISTORY **EDUCATION** Lipscomb Univ, BA, 67; George Peabody Col Teach, Vanderbilt Univ, MLS, 68, EdS, 72; Univ Ill, Urbana-Champaign, PhD, 83. **CAREER** Head Librarian, Fred-Hardeman Univ, 68-71; ref librn, Wabash Col, 73-79; ref librn, Purdue Univ, 79-82; asst prof, libr sci, Purdue Univ, 79-85; sen ref librn, Purdue Univ, 82-90; assoc prof, libr sci, Purdue Univ, 85-89; PROF, LIBR SCI, 89-, HUM, SOC SCI, EDUC LIBRN, 90-, PURDUE UNIV. **HONORS AND AWARDS** Council on Library Resources Research Fellow, 90; Frederick B. Artz Research Grantee, Oberlin College Archives, 91; Grantee Committee on Institutional Cooperation, NEH, 91-94. **MEMBERSHIPS** American Library Asn; Sons of Confederate Veterans; Asn for the Bibliography of History; Asn of College and Research libraries; Disciples of Christ Historical Society; Society for Historians of the Guilded Age and Progressive Era; Southern Historical Asn; Friends of the Univ of Illinois Library; Phi Kappa Phi, Beta Phi Mu. **RESEARCH** Hist, biog, related to librarianship and higher educ. **SELECTED PUBLICATIONS** Auth, Sabin, Joseph (6 Dec 1821-5 June 1991), Am Nat Biography, 18: 168-69, Oxford Univ Press, 99; auth, Work, Monroe Nathan (1866-1945), in Notable Black American Men, 1262-66, Gale Research, 98; auth, Editor Untold Stories: Civil Rights, Libraries, and Black Librarianship, 98; auth, Wide Awakening: Political and Theological Impulses for Reading and Libraries at Oberlin College, 1883-1908, Univ Ill Occasional Papers, 207, 97; co-auth, Change and Tradition in Land Grant University Libraries, in For the Good of the Order: Essays Written in Honor of Edward G. Holley, JAI Press, 94; auth, American Library History: A Comprehensive Guide to the Literature, 89; auth, User Instruction in Academic Libraries: A Century of Selected Readings, 86; auth, co-ed, Reference Services and Library Education: Essays in Honor of Frances Neel Cheney, 83. **CONTACT ADDRESS** Hum, Soc Sci & Educ Libr, Purdue Univ, West Lafayette, Stewart Ctr, West Lafayette, IN 47907. **EMAIL** jmark@purdue.edu

TUCKER, MARTIN
PERSONAL Born 02/08/1928, Philadelphia, PA **DISCIPLINE** ENGLISH **EDUCATION** Wash Sq Col, NYork Univ, BA, 49; Univ Ariz, MA, 54; NYork Univ, PhD, 63. **CAREER** From asst prof to assoc prof, 58-69, PROF ENGLISH, LONG ISLAND UNIV, 69-, CHMN DEPT, 76-, Helene Wurlitzer Found grant, Taos, NMex, 56-57; grant, Long Island Univ, 64, ed, Confrontation Mag, 70; mem admis and scholar comt, British Univ summer sch prog, 65-; consult, col comprehensive test, Educ Testing Serv, 65-; co-moderator, Writers Alive, Brooklyn Acad Arts and Sci, 67-68; co-ed and consult, Belles-Lett English, Johnson Reprint Corp, 67-; fel creative writing, Ossabaw Island Proj, Ga, 68; ed, PEN Newslett, 73-78; MacDowell Colony residency grants, 77, 78 and 80. **HONORS AND AWARDS** Scholar Awd, Bread Loaf Writing Ctr, 59; Merit Awd, US Dept Health, Educ, Welfare, 72. **MEMBERSHIPS** MLA; African Studies Asn; PEN Club; Poetry Soc Am; Authors Guild. **RESEARCH** Contemporary British and American fiction; English and African literature; African prose fiction. **SELECTED PUBLICATIONS** Auth, Africa in Modern Literature, 68 & ed, The Critical Temper, 70 & 78, Ungar; Introd to Olive Schreiner's Undine, Johnson Reprint Corp, 72; auth, Wole Soyinka, Columbia Univ Forum, summer 73; Joseph Conrad, 76, contribr, World Literature Encycl, 76 & 80 & co-ed, Modern Commonwealth Literature, 77, Ungar; auth, Homes of Locks and Mysteries (poems), Dovetail Press, 82. **CONTACT ADDRESS** Dept of English, Long Island Univ, Brooklyn, Brooklyn, NY 11201.

TUERK, RICHARD
PERSONAL Born 07/10/1941, Baltimore, MD, m, 1963, 2 children **DISCIPLINE** LITERATURE **EDUCATION** Columbia Col, AB, 63; Johns Hopkins Univ, MA, 64, PhD, 67. **CA-**

REER Asst prof, Univ Calif Riverside, 67-72; Assoc prof to prof, Tx A&M Univ, 72- . **HONORS AND AWARDS** Piper Prof, Minnie Stevens Piper Found, 91; Honors Prof of the Year, E Tx St Univ, 85; H. M. Lafferty Distinguished Faculty Awd, Tx A&M Univ Commerce, 90. **MEMBERSHIPS** Amer Stud Assoc; Modern Lang Assoc; Popular Culture Assoc; MELUS; Amer Stud Assoc Tx; Tx Popular Culture Assoc. **RESEARCH** Amer lit; children's lit. **SELECTED PUBLICATIONS** Auth, What Side Was He On? Mike Gold During the Period of the Hitler-Stalin Pact, Modern Jewish Stud, 94; Michael Gold's Hoboken Blues: An Experiment that Failed, J of the Soc for the Study of Multi-Ethnic Lit of the US, 95; Dorothy's Adventures Underground, Baum Bugle, 96; Teaching Composition Via Distance Educ, 4th Annual Nat Distance Educ Conf 1997 Conf Proceedings, 97; Teaching Composition via Videoconferencing Using a Multi-Ethnic American Literature Reader, in Engines of Change: A Practical Guide for Using Technology to Teach American Culture, Amer Stud Assoc, 97. **CONTACT ADDRESS** Dept of Lit & Lang, Texas A&M Univ, Commerce, Box 3011, Commerce, TX 75429-3011. **EMAIL** Richard_Tuerk@tamu-commerce.edu

TURCO, LEWIS
PERSONAL Born 05/02/1934, Buffalo, NY, m, 1956, 2 children **DISCIPLINE** ENGLISH **EDUCATION** Univ Conn, BA, 59; Univ Iowa, MA, 62; Ashland Univ, LHD, 00; . **CAREER** Grad asst and part-time instr English, Univ Conn, 59; instr English, Fenn Col (Cleveland State Univ), 60-64, founder and dir, Cleveland Poetry Ctr, 61-64; asst prof, Hillsdale Col, 64-65; from asst prof to prof, 65-96, Poet-in-Residence, 95-, prof emeritus English, State Univ NY Col, Oswego, 96-, founder and dir Prog Writing Arts, 68-95; State Univ NY Res Found fac fels, 66, 67, 69, 71, 74 & 78; hon trustee, Theodore Roethke Mem Found, 68; vis prof, State Univ NY Col Potsdam, 68-69; State Univ NY Fac Exchange scholar, 76-; mem, Creative Writing Subcommittee Univ Awards Comt Res Found State Univ NY, 74-76, chm 76-77; Yaddo Found resident, 59 & 77; Bingham poet-in-residence, Univ Louisville, 82; writer-in-residence, Ashland Univ, 91. **HONORS AND AWARDS** Acad Am Poets Prize, Univ Iowa, 60; American Weave Chapbook Award, 62; Davidson Miscellany Fiction Prize, 69; Helen Bullis Prize, Poetry Northwest, 71; Nat Endowment for the Arts/PEN Syndicated Fiction Project Award, 83; Kans Quart/Kans Arts Comm First Poetry Award, 84-85; SUNY Col at Oswego President's Award for Schol and Creative Activity and Res, 85; Melville Cane Award in criticism of the Poetry Soc of Am, 86; Silverfish Rev Chapbook Award, 89; Cooper House Chapbook Award, 90; Distinguished Alumni Award, Alumni Asn of the Univ of Conn, 92; Meriden CT Hall of Fame, 93; Fac Enhancement Grant, SUNY Col at Oswego, 95; Bordighera Bilingual Poetry Prize, Bordighera, Inc, Purdue Univ, 97; John Ciardi Award for lifetime achievement in poetry from the National Italian American Foundation/Italian Americana (the Periodical), 99. **MEMBERSHIPS** Authors Guild; Poets & Writers; E.E. Cummings Soc. **RESEARCH** Writing arts; American and British poetry & poetics. **SELECTED PUBLICATIONS** Auth, First Poems, Golden Quill, 60; Awaken, Bells Falling: Poems 1959-1967, Univ Mo, 68; The Book of Forms: A Handbook of Poetics, Dutton, 68; Poetry: An Introduction Through Writing, Reston, 73; American Still Lifes (poems), Mathom, 81; The Compleat Melancholick, Bieler, 85; Emily Dickenson, Woman of Letters, Poems, and Centos from Lines in Emily Dickinson's Letters, Together with Essays, State Univ of NY, 93; auth, Bordello, poems, Grey Heron/Mathom, 96; Shaking the Family Tree, A Memoir, VIA Folios, 98; A Book of Fears, Bordighera, 98; auth, The Book of Literary Terms, auth, The Genres of Fiction, Drama, Nonfiction, Literary Criticism and Scholarship, Univ Press of New England, 99; auth, The Book of Forms: A Handbook of Poetics, 3rd ed, 00. **CONTACT ADDRESS** PO Box 161, Dresden, ME 04342-0161. **EMAIL** mathom@gwi.net

TURINO, THOMAS
DISCIPLINE MUSIC **EDUCATION** Colgate Univ, BA; Univ TX, PhD. **CAREER** Assoc prof, 87-, Univ IL Urbana Champaign. **HONORS AND AWARDS** Fulbright, Fel, Inter-Am Found, Fel, Tinker, Fel. **RESEARCH** Andean music, Latin American music, and the music of sountern Africa, also specializes in the semiotics of music and in theoretical issues of music and politics. **SELECTED PUBLICATIONS** Auth, Moving Away From Silence: The Music of the Peruvian Altiplano and the Experieence of Urban Migration, 93; auth, Nationalists, Cosmopolitans, and Popular Music in Zimbabwe, 00; coauth, Excursions in World Music. **CONTACT ADDRESS** Dept of Music, Univ of Illinois, Urbana-Champaign, E Gregory Dr, PO Box 52, Champaign, IL 61820. **EMAIL** t-turino@uiuc.edu

TURK, JUDY VAN SLYKE
DISCIPLINE COMMUNICATION **EDUCATION** Northwestern Univ, BSJ; Northern IL Univ, MA; Syracuse Univ, PhD. **CAREER** Dean & prof, Col of Communicationss and Media Sciences, Zayed Univ. **MEMBERSHIPS** Pres, Asn Educ Jour & Mass Commun, 94-95; Publ Rel Soc Am, Educ of the Yr, 92; former ch, Col Fellows, Publ Rel Soc Am. **RESEARCH** Agenda-setting theory applied to public rel(s); public rel(s) management. **SELECTED PUBLICATIONS** Coauth, leading introductory publ rel textbk; publ on, res interest. **CONTACT ADDRESS** United Arab Emirates, PO Box 19282, Dubai. **EMAIL** judy-turk@zu.ac.ae

TURLEY, HANS
PERSONAL Born 04/29/1956, Parkersburg, WV, p **DISCIPLINE** ENGLISH LITERATURE **EDUCATION** Univ Wash, BA, 89; MA, 91; PhD, 94. **CAREER** Instr, Univ of Wash, 95; asst prof, Tex Tech Univ, 96-98; asst prof, Univ of Conn, 98-. **HONORS AND AWARDS** Dorothy Collins Brown Fund, 93; Mellon, 94; Am Soc for Eighteenth Century Studies, 95, 97. **MEMBERSHIPS** MLA, NCTE, ASECS. **RESEARCH** 18th-Century British literature, LGBT studies, History of piracy. **SELECTED PUBLICATIONS** Auth, "Charlotte Charke and the Periodical Press," Introducing Charlotte Charke, (97); auth, "The Anomalous Fiction of Mary Hearne," Studies in the Novel, (98); auth, "Captain Singleton and the Search for Identity," 18th Cent Studies, (98); auth, Rum, Sodomy and the Lash, NY Univ Pr, (NY), 99; "Protestant Evangelism, British Imperialism," "Robinson Crusoe", in the New Imperial History, Cambridge Univ Pr, forthcoming. **CONTACT ADDRESS** Dept English, Univ of Connecticut, Storrs, Storrs, CT 06269-0001. **EMAIL** hans.turley@uconn.edu

TURNER, FREDERICK
PERSONAL Born 11/19/1943, East Haddon, England, m, 1966, 2 children **DISCIPLINE** ENGLISH **EDUCATION** Oxford Univ, BA, 65, MA, 67, PhD(English), 67. **CAREER** Asst prof English, Univ Calif, Santa Barbara, 67-72; ASSOC PROF ENGLISH, KENYON COL, 72-, Ed, Kenyon Rev. **MEMBERSHIPS** Fel Int Soc Study Time. **RESEARCH** Shakespeare; esthetics; philosophy in literature. **SELECTED PUBLICATIONS** Auth, Shakespeare and the Nature of Time, Oxford Univ, 70; Between Two Lives (poetry), Wesleyan Univ, 72; A structuralist analysis of Chaucer's Knight's Tale, Chaucer Rev, 74; Shakespeare's Romeo and Juliet, Hodder & Stoughton, 74; A Double Shadow (novel), Putnam's & Berkley, 78; Counter-Terra (poetry), Christopher's Bks, 78; Mighty poets in their misery dead, a polemic on the contemporary poetic scene, Mo Rev, fall 80; The Return (poetry), Countryman Press, 81. **CONTACT ADDRESS** Dept of English, Kenyon Col, Gambier, OH 43022.

TURNER, JEANINE W.
PERSONAL Born Louisville, KY, m, 1996 **DISCIPLINE** COMMUNICATION **EDUCATION** Univ of Dayton, BA, 87, MA, 93; Ohio State Univ, PhD, 96. **CAREER** Grad tchg assoc, Univ of Dayton, 92-93; Ohio State Univ, 93-96; adj res asst prof, Georgetown Univ Med Ctr, 97- ; asst prof, Georgetown Univ, 97- . **HONORS AND AWARDS** Outstanding Tchr Awd, Univ of Dayton, 93; Phi Kappa Phi Honor Soc. **MEMBERSHIPS** Acad of Mgt.; Nat Commun Asn; Asn for Bus Communicators; Int Commun Asn; Am Telemedicine Asn. **RESEARCH** Telemedicine; Virtual orgs; Commun tech adaption. **SELECTED PUBLICATIONS** Coauth, Product, process, and practice: Telecompetence in Telemedicine, Teleconference Mag, 4(16), 97; auth, The Effectiveness of Telemedicine in the Outpatient Pulmonary Clinic - Abstract, Am Jour of Respiratory and Critical Care Med, 153, 97; auth, Patient Satisfaction with Telemedicine in a Prison Environment: A Matter of Context, Jour of Telemedicine and Telecare; auth, The Effectiveness of Telemedicine in the Outpatient Pulmonary Clinic, Telemedicine Jour; auth, Teaching Mass Communication and Telecommunication, Teaching Communication: Theory, Research, and Methods, eds Jour. Daly, G. Friedrich, A. Vangelisti; auth, "Computer-based Telecommunication Among an Illness-Related Community: System Design, Service Delivery, and Early Use," Health Communication; auth, "The Ohio Telemedicine System for Prison Inmates," Telemedicine Jour; auth, "Economic Advantage of Telemedicine in a Corrections Environment," Telemedicine and Telehealth Networks; auth, "Telemedicine: An Alternative Method of Prison Inmate Care," Administrative Radiology Jour; auth, "Organizational Telecompetence: Creating the Virtual Organization," Telemedicine: Practicing in the Information Age. **CONTACT ADDRESS** School of Business, Georgetown Univ, G-04 Old North, Washington, DC 20057. **EMAIL** turnerjw@msb.edu

TURNER, MYRON M.
DISCIPLINE ENGLISH LITERATURE **EDUCATION** Univ NY, BA; Rutgers Univ, MA; Univ Wash, PhD. **CAREER** Sr Scholar, English, Prof, School of Art, Univ of Man (ret). **RESEARCH** Work of Philip Sidney; nature of poetic imagery and imagination in the 16th century. **SELECTED PUBLICATIONS** Auth, The River and the Window; 74; Things That Fly, 78; Rag Doll's Shadow, 80; pub(s) on Sidney, Spenser, Marlowe and American literature. **CONTACT ADDRESS** Dept of English, Univ of Manitoba, 381 University College, Winnipeg, MB, Canada R3T 5V5. **EMAIL** mturner@cc.umanitoba.ca

TURNER, PAIGE K.
PERSONAL Born Melford, OR, m, 2 children **DISCIPLINE** ORGANIZATIONAL COMMUNICATION **EDUCATION** Univ Ore, BS, 90; Purdue Univ, MS, 92; PhD, 98. **CAREER** Grad Teaching Asst, Purdue Univ, 90-96; adj prof, Seattle Pacific Univ, 97; asst prof, St Louis, 98-. **HONORS AND AWARDS** Top Three Paper Awd, Orgn Commun Div of the Speech Commun Asn; Top Four Paper Awd, Orgn and Professional Commun Div of the Central Speech Commun Asn, 95; Top Student Paper Awd, Orgn Commun Div of the Speech Commun Asn, 95; Alan H. Monroe Grad Scholar Awd, 95; Cheris Kramarae Dissertaion Awd, Orgn for the Study of Communication, Lang & Gender, 98. **MEMBERSHIPS** Nat Commun Asn, Int Commun Asn, Central States Commun Asn. **RESEARCH** Socialization, Midwifery. **SELECTED PUBLICATIONS** Coauth, "A social constructionist reconfiguration of metaphor analysis: An application of 'SCMA' to organizational socialization theorizing," commun Monographys 62 (95): 152-181; auth, "What if you don't: A response to Kramer and Miller," Commun Monographs (99): 382-389. **CONTACT ADDRESS** Dept Commun, Saint Louis Univ, 221 N Grand Blvd, Saint Louis, MO 63103-2006. **EMAIL** turnerp@slu.edu

TURNER, RICHARD CHARLES
PERSONAL Born 08/01/1944, Boston, MA, m, 1966, 3 children **DISCIPLINE** ENGLISH LITERATURE **EDUCATION** Boston Col, AB, 66; Emory Univ, MA, 68, PhD(English), 72. **CAREER** Asst prof, 70-78, assoc prof English, Ind Univ-Purdue Univ, Indianapolis, 78-85; prof, 85. **MEMBERSHIPS** MLA; Am Soc 18th Century Studies. **RESEARCH** Restoration and 18th century poetry and drama; literature and philanthropy. **SELECTED PUBLICATIONS** Auth, Ed, Taking Theoteeship Seriously, 95, Ken Folltee, 96. **CONTACT ADDRESS** Dept of English, Indiana Univ-Purdue Univ, Indianapolis, 1100 W Michigan St, Indianapolis, IN 46202-2880. **EMAIL** rturner@iupui.edu

TURNER, ROBERT KEAN
PERSONAL Born 11/30/1926, Richmond, VA, m, 1948, 2 children **DISCIPLINE** ENGLISH & DRAMA **EDUCATION** Va Mil Inst, BA, 47; Univ Va, MA, 49; PhD, 58. **CAREER** Instr to asst prof, Va Mil Inst, 57-62; assoc prof to prof emeritus, Univ Wis Milwaukee, 62-. **HONORS AND AWARDS** Guggenheim Fel, 83-84. **MEMBERSHIPS** MLA. **RESEARCH** Elizabethan and Jacobean drama. **SELECTED PUBLICATIONS** Auth, Shakespeare, The Winter's Tale, A New Varioriem Edition of Shakespeare, MLA, forthcoming. **CONTACT ADDRESS** 3202 Waterway Blvd, Isle of Palms, SC 29451. **EMAIL** junow149@hotmail.com

TURNER, ROBERT Y.
PERSONAL Born 02/19/1927, Marshalltown, IA **DISCIPLINE** ENGLISH **EDUCATION** Princeton Univ, AB, 49; Univ Chicago, AM, 51, PhD, 58. **CAREER** Instr, Dartmouth Col, 55-58; from instr to assoc prof, 58-74, grad chmn, 72-74 and 81-83, PROF ENGLISH, UNIV PA, 74-, Guggenheim Found fel, 74-75. **MEMBERSHIPS** Renaissance Soc Am; Shakespeare Asn Am; MLA. **RESEARCH** English Renaissance drama, including Shakespeare. **SELECTED PUBLICATIONS** **CONTACT ADDRESS** Dept of English, Univ of Pennsylvania, 210 S 34th St, Philadelphia, PA 19104.

TURNER, STEPHEN
PERSONAL Born 03/01/1951, Chicago, IL, m, 1990, 2 children **DISCIPLINE** SOCIOLOGY; PHILOSOPHY **EDUCATION** AB, 71, AM, 71, AM, 72, PhD, 75, Univ Missouri-Columbia. **CAREER** Visiting prof, 82, Notre Dame; Visiting Prof, 85, Virginia Poytech Inst; Visiting Prof, 87, Boston Univ; Asst Prof to Graduate Res prof, Univ South Florida, 75-; ch, Dept of Philos, 00-. **HONORS AND AWARDS** NEH Fel, 91-92; Fel, Swedish Collegium for Advanced Studies in the Social Sciences, 92 & 98; Honorary Visiting Prof, Univ Manchester, 96. **RESEARCH** History of social thought; philosophy of social science; science studies **SELECTED PUBLICATIONS** Auth, Sociological Explanition as Translation, 80; coauth, Max Weber and the Dispute over Reason and Value, 84; auth, The Search for a Methodology of Social Science: Durkheim, Weber, and the Nineteenth Century Problem of Cause, Probability, and Action, Boston Studies in Philosophy of Science, 86; Coauth, The Impossible Science: An Institutional Analysis of American Sociology, 90; Max Weber: The Lawyer as a Social Thinker, 94; Auth, The Social Theory of Practices: Tradition, Tacit Knowledge, and Presuppositions, 94. **CONTACT ADDRESS** Dept of Philosophy, Univ of So Florida, Tampa, FL 33620. **EMAIL** turner@chuma.cas.usf.edu

TUROW, JOSEPH G.
PERSONAL Born 04/05/1950, New York, NY, m, 3 children **DISCIPLINE** COMMUNICATIONS **EDUCATION** Univ of Pa, BA, 71, MA, 73, PhD, 76. **CAREER** From asst prof to assoc prof, Purdue Univ, 76-86; vis asst prof, UCLA, 80, 85; from assoc prof to prof, Univ of Pa, 86- ; ed bd mem, Jour of Broadcasting, 85-94, 97- , Crit Studies in Mass Commun, 84-89, 98- , Sage Annual Revs of Commun Res, 86- , Encycl of Advert, Commun Educ, 78-82; adv ed, Jour of Commun, 81-91, 96-99 , Ablex Commun Book Series, 88-91. **HONORS AND AWARDS** Phi Beta Kappa, 71; Dean's List With Distinction; Univ fel, 74-75; Diss Res Schol, 75-76; Dept Best Tchg Awd, 81, 83; Russel Nye Awd, Popular Cult Asn, for best article in Jour of Popular Cult, 82-83; Book of the Month Awd, Commun Booknotes, 84; Top Ten Mass Commun Div Paper, Int Commun Asn Confs, 81, 83, 84; Top Three Mass Commun Div Paper, Mass Commun and Speech Commun Asn Confs, 77, 84; Nat Endowment for the Hums Summer Stipend, Sen Div, 86, 94; App to the Nat Endowment for the Hums Summer Stipend Adv Comt, 87; Res grant, Pa Res Found, 88-89; App as a Commonwealth Speaker, Pa Hums Coun, 89, 91; Invited to teach a

master's session' at the annual Int Commun Asn Conf, 91; Elected to ch the Mass Commun Div of the Int Commun Asn, 93-97; Appointed to the Nat Endowment for Children's Educ Televison of the U.S. Dept of Commerce, 95-97; Co-recip of a major grant, Ford Found for res, 96. **MEMBERSHIPS** Int Commun Asn; Speech Commun Asn. **RESEARCH** Mass Media Industries; Marketing and the media. **SELECTED PUBLICATIONS** Auth, Getting Books to Children: An Exploration of Publisher-Market Relations, 79; Entertainment, Education, and the Hard Sell: Three Decades of Network Children's Television, 81; Media Industries: The Production of News and Entertainment, 84; Playing Doctor: Television, Storytelling, and Medical Power, 89; The Challenge of Inference in Interinstitutional Research on Mass Communication, Commun Res, 18:2, 91; On Conceptualizing Mass Communication, Jour of Broadcasting & Electronic Media, spring, 92; The Organizational Underpinnings of Contemporary Media Conglomerates, Commun Res 19:6, 92; Media Systems in Society: Understanding Industries, Strategies, and Power, 92; Hidden Conflicts and Journalistic Norms: The Case of Self Coverage, Jour of Commun 44:2, 94; Television Entertainment and the US Health Care Debate, The Lancet 347: 9010, 96; Breaking Up America: Advertising and the New Media World, 97; Media Today: An Introduction to Mass Communication, 98; ed, Careers in Mass Media, 84. **CONTACT ADDRESS** Annenberg Commun Sch, Univ of Pennsylvania, 3620 Walnut St, Philadelphia, PA 19104-6220. **EMAIL** jturow@pobox.asc.upenn.edu

TUTEN, NANCY
PERSONAL Born 08/27/1960, Charleston, SC, m, 1987, 2 children **DISCIPLINE** ENGLISH; AMERICAN LITERATURE **EDUCATION** Newberry Col, BA, 82; Univ S Carolina, MA, 85; PhD, 88. **CAREER** Prof English, Columbia Col, 88- . **HONORS AND AWARDS** Outstanding prof, S Atlantic Asn Dept English, 96. **MEMBERSHIPS** Mod Lang Asn; Pop Cult Asn S; Asn Res Mothering. **RESEARCH** American literature, Popular culture, Women's studies. **SELECTED PUBLICATIONS** Ed, Critical Essays on Galway Kinnell, G.K. Hall, (96); co-ed, The Robert Frost Encyclopedias, Greenwood Press, (00). **CONTACT ADDRESS** Dept English, Columbia Col, So Carolina, 1301 Columbia Col Dr, Columbia, SC 29203-5949. **EMAIL** ntuten@colacoll.edu

TUTTLE, JON
PERSONAL Born Salt Lake City, UT, m, 1997, 1 child **DISCIPLINE** ENGLISH **EDUCATION** Univ Utah, BS, 82; Univ NM, MA, 84, PhD, 89. **CAREER** Honors dir, 95-96, Francis Marion Univ; playwright-in-res, 98-, Trustus Theatre. **HONORS AND AWARDS** SC Acad of Auth Fel, SC Arts Comm Fel; numerous playwriting awards; phi kappa phi honor soc **MEMBERSHIPS** MLA; Dramatists Guild; Theatre Commun Group. **RESEARCH** Drama; playwriting. **SELECTED PUBLICATIONS** Auth, The Dramatic Climax and The Right Way to Write a Play, Carolina English Teacher, 95-96; auth, The Efficacy of Work: Arthur Miller and Camus' The Myth of Sisyphus, Amer Drama, 96; auth, Be What You Are: Identity and Morality in Edmond and Glengarry Glen Ross, Glengarry Glen Ross: Text and Performance, Garland Press, 96. **CONTACT ADDRESS** Dept of English, Francis Marion Univ, Florence, SC 29501-0547. **EMAIL** jtuttle@fmarion.edu

TUTTLETON, JAMES WESLEY
PERSONAL Born 08/19/1934, St. Louis, MO **DISCIPLINE** ENGLISH **EDUCATION** Harding Col, BA, 55; Univ NC, MA, 57, PhD(English), 63. **CAREER** Instr English, Clemson Univ, 56-59; instr, Univ NC, 62-63; from instr to asst prof, Univ Wis-Madison, 63-68; assoc prof, 68-74, PROF ENGLISH and CHMN DEPT, NY UNIV, 74-, Univ Wis res coun grant, 64 and 65; Am Philos Soc res grant, 66; Nat Endowment for Humanities fel, 67-68; co-ed, The Gotham Libr NY Univ Press, 74-. **MEMBERSHIPS** MLA; Am Studies Asn; Century Asn; Washington Irving Soc; Henry James Soc. **RESEARCH** American literature; English literature; American history. **SELECTED PUBLICATIONS** Auth, Aiken's Mr Arcularis, Am Imago, 63; Steinbeck in Russia, Mod Fiction Studies, 65; The novel of manners in America, Univ NC, 72; Thomas Wentworth Higginson, Twayne, 78; ed, Henry James's The American, Norton, 78; Seeing slightly red: Fitzgerald's May Day, In: The Short Stories of F Scott Fitzgerald, 82; ed, The Works of Washington Irving, The Libr Am Series, 82. **CONTACT ADDRESS** Dept of English, New York Univ, 19 University Pl, New York, NY 10003-4556.

TWINING, MARY ARNOLD
PERSONAL Born New York, NY, 2 children **DISCIPLINE** ENGLISH LITERATURE **EDUCATION** Ind Univ, PhD. **CAREER** Acting Chair, Doctor of Arts in Humanities and Undergraduate Humanities Programs; Dept Eng, Clark Atlanta Univ **RESEARCH** African and African American traditional cultures and orature; Native American oral and written literature; Sea island folklore and folklife; African American science fiction writers; Southern literature. **SELECTED PUBLICATIONS** Co-ed, Sea Island Roots: African Presence in the Carolinas and Georgia. **CONTACT ADDRESS** Clark Atlanta Univ, 223 James P Brawley Dr, SW, Atlanta, GA 30314. **EMAIL** marnoldtwining@hotmail.com

TWITCHELL, JAMES B.
PERSONAL Born 06/18/1943, Burlington, VT, m, 1967, 2 children **DISCIPLINE** ENGLISH **EDUCATION** Univ VT, AB, 66; MA, 68; Univ NCar, PhD, 71. **CAREER** Teaching Asst, Univ NCar, 68-70; Instructor, Duke Univ, 70-71; Asst Prof, Calif State Col, 71-73; Asst Prof to Alumni Prof, Univ Fla, 73-. **RESEARCH** Nineteenth-century English and American Literature; Romantic Painting; Development of Modern Horror; Sociology and Literature; American Popular Culture; History and Culture of Advertising; Commercial Culture. **SELECTED PUBLICATIONS** Auth, The Living Dead: The Vampire in Romantic Literature, Duke Univ Press, 80; auth, Romantic Horizons: Aspects of the Sublime in English Poetry and Painting 1770-1850, Univ MO Press, 83; auth, Dreadful Pleasures: An Anatomy of Modern Horror, Oxford Univ Press, 85; auth, Forbidden Partners: The Incest Taboo in Modern Culture, Columbia Univ Press, 86; auth, Preposterous Violence: Fables of Aggression in Modern Culture, Oxford Univ Press, 89; auth, Carnival Culture: The Trashing of Taste in America, Columbia Univ Press, 92; auth, Adcult USA: The Triumph of Advertising in America, Columbia Univ Press, 95; auth, For Shame: The Loss of Common Decency in American Culture, St Martin's Press, 97; auth, Lead Us Into Temptation: The Triumph of American Materialism, Columbia Univ Press, 99; auth, Twenty Ads That Shook The World: The Canon of Modern Advertising, 00. **CONTACT ADDRESS** Dept Eng, Univ of Florida, PO Box 117310, Gainesville, FL 32611-7310. **EMAIL** jtwitche@enlish.ufl.edu

TWOMBLY, ROBERT GRAY
PERSONAL Born 05/16/1935, New York, NY, m, 1960, 4 children **DISCIPLINE** ENGLISH **EDUCATION** Amherst Col, BA, 57; Yale Univ, PhD(English), 65. **CAREER** From instr to asst prof, 63-69, ASSOC PROF ENGLISH, UNIV TEX, AUSTIN, 69-, Soc Relig Higher Educ fel, 69-70. **MEMBERSHIPS** MLA; Soc Higher Educ. **RESEARCH** John Donne; 16th century religious literature; Shakespeare. **SELECTED PUBLICATIONS** Auth, The Rhetoric of Death and Knowledge, Library Chronicle Univ Tex-Austin, Vol 0026, 96. **CONTACT ADDRESS** Dept of English, Univ of Texas, Austin, 0 Univ of Texas, Austin, TX 78712-1026.

TWOMEY, MICHAEL
PERSONAL Born 12/23/1949, New York, NY, m, 1971, 2 children **DISCIPLINE** ENGLISH **EDUCATION** State Univ NYork, Albany, BA, 72; Boston Col, MA, 74; Cornell Univ, PhD, 79. **CAREER** Asst prof, Ithaca Col, 80-87, assoc prof, 87-96, prof, 96-, chair, dept English, 96-. **HONORS AND AWARDS** BA, magna cum laude, 72, MA, high honors, 74; Goethe Prize in Ger Lit, Cornell Univ, 75; Charles A. Dana Teaching Awd, Ithaca Col, 85; Phi Kappa Phi, 88; Sigma Tau Delta, 88; Fulbright Sr Lectr, English, Technical Univ of Dresden, Ger, 96-97. **MEMBERSHIPS** Medieval Acad of Am, Int Arthurian Soc. **RESEARCH** Middle English literature, medieval encyclopedias. **SELECTED PUBLICATIONS** In collaboration with Arthur Groos, Medieval Christian Literary Imagery: A Guide to Interpretation, by R. E. Kaske, Toronto Medieval Bibliographies, 11 (Toronto: Univ of Toronto press, 88); auth, "Cleanness, Peter Comestor, and the Revelationes Sancti Methodii," Mediaevalia, 11 (1989 for 1985), 203-17 (refereed); auth, "Cleanness 1057-64 and the Roman de la Rose," in Loyal Letters: Studies on Mediaevalia Groningana, 15 (Groningen: Egbert Forsten, 94), 167-86 (invited); auth, "Morgain la Fee in Sir Gawain and the Green Knight: From Troy to Camelot," in Text and Intertext in Medieval Arthurian Literature, ed Norris J. Lacy (New York: Garland, 96), 91-115 (invited); auth, "Towards a Reception History of Western Mediaeval Encyclopedias in England Before 1500," in Pre-Modern Encyclopaedic Texts: Proceedings of the Second COMERS Congress, Groningen, 1-4 July 1996, ed Peter Binkley (Leiden/NY/Cologne: Brill, 97), 329-62; auth, "The Pearl-/Gawain-Poet" and "Allegory and Related Symbolism" for Medieval England: An Encyclopedia, ed Joel Rosenthal, Paul E. Szarmach, and M. Teresa Tavormina (NY: Garland Press, 98, invited). **CONTACT ADDRESS** Dept English, Ithaca Col, 953 Danby Rd., Ithaca, NY 14850-7000. **EMAIL** twomey@ithaca.edu

TY, ELEANOR R.
PERSONAL Born 10/11/1958, Manila, Philippines, m, 1982, 3 children **DISCIPLINE** ENGLISH, WOMEN'S STUDIES **EDUCATION** Univ Toronto, BA, 81; McMaster Univ, MA, 82; PhD, 88. **CAREER** Asst prof, McMaster Univ, 89-90; asst prof, Brock Univ, 90-91; asst prof to prof, Wilfrid Laurier Univ, 91-. **HONORS AND AWARDS** Wilfrid Laurier Fel, 93; SSHRCC Res Grant, 94-97, 00-02; Grace Anderson Fel, 96. **MEMBERSHIPS** MLA, Assoc for Asian Am Studies, Can Soc for 18th Century Studies, Am Soc for 18th Century Studies. **RESEARCH** Narratives by Asian Canadian and Asian American Authors, Late Eighteenth Century Fiction, Feminist Theory and Women's Writing, Diasporic, Ethnic, and Minority Children. **SELECTED PUBLICATIONS** Auth, Unsex'd Revolutionaries: Five Women Novelists of the 1790s. Theory and Cult Series, Univ of Tor Pr, 93; ed, The Victim of Prejudice, by Mary Hays, 1799, Broadview Pr, (Peterborough and Lewiston, NY), 94; ed, Memoirs of Emma Courtney by Mary Hays 1796, Oxford World's Classics, (Oxford), 96; auth, Empowering the Feminine: The Narratives of Mary Robinson, Jane West, and Amelia Opie, 1796-1812, Univ of Toronto Pr, 98. **CONTACT ADDRESS** Dept English, Wilfrid Laurier Univ, Waterloo, ON, Canada N2L 3C5. **EMAIL** ety@wlu.ca

TYLER, CAROLE-ANNE
DISCIPLINE ENGLISH LITERATURE **EDUCATION** Williams Col, BA; Brown Col, MA, PhD, Eng. **HONORS AND AWARDS** Fel, Amer Coun Learned Soc, 91. **RESEARCH** Gender and sexuality, literary theory, cultural studies, 20th-Century fiction. **SELECTED PUBLICATIONS** Auth, "Boys Will Be Girls: The Politics of Gay Drag," Inside/Out: Lesbian Theories Gay Theories, 91; "Passing: Narcissism, Identity, and Difference," 94; "Death Masks," Rrose Is a Rrose Is a Rrose, cat, Guggenheim Museum exhib on gender performance in photography, 97. **CONTACT ADDRESS** Dept of Eng, Univ of California, Riverside, 1156 Hinderaker Hall, Riverside, CA 92521-0209. **EMAIL** caroleanne.tyler@ucr.edu

TYSON, NANCY JANE
PERSONAL Born 02/25/1949, South Bend, IN **DISCIPLINE** ENGLISH **EDUCATION** Marshall Univ, BA, 71; Ohio State Univ, MA, 73; PhD, 81. **CAREER** Lectr, Ohio State Univ, 78-81; asst prof, Univ Richmond, 81-84; asst prof, 84-90, assoc prof 90- , Univ S Fla, 84- . **HONORS AND AWARDS** USF Alumni Prof Awd, 86; USF Sr Class Outstanding prof award, 89; USF Outstanding Undergraduate Tchg Awd, 96. ALA "Choice" award for academic books, 83; (elected) Pres, Univ of S FLA Fac Senate, 00-01. **MEMBERSHIPS** Browning Inst; Mod Lang Asn; S Atlantic Mod Lang Asn; Res Soc Victorian Per; 19th Century Studies Asn; William Morris Soc; Popular Cult Asso. **RESEARCH** Victorian literature; bibliography and research methods for English studies; popular culture. **SELECTED PUBLICATIONS** Auth, Art and Society in the Late Prose Narratives of William Morris, Pre-Raphaelite Rev, 78; Eugene Aram: Literary History and Typology of the Scholar-Criminal, Shoe String Press, 83; Thackeray and Bulwer: Between the Lines in Barry Lyndon, English Lang Notes, 89; Altars to Attics: The State of Matrimony in Brontes Jane Eyre, Mistreated Mates: Family Violence in Life and Literature, Plenum, 91; Caliban in a Glass: Autoscopic Vision in The Picture of Dorian Gray, The Haunted Mind: The Supernatural in Victorian Literature, Scarecrow Pr, 99; Eugene Aram, New Dictionary of National Biography, Oxford UP, forthcoming. **CONTACT ADDRESS** English Dept, Univ of So Florida, 4202 E Fowler Ave., CPR 107, Tampa, FL 33620-5550. **EMAIL** tyson@chuma.cas.usf.edu

TYTELL, JOHN
PERSONAL Born 05/17/1939, Antwerp, Belgium, m, 1967 **DISCIPLINE** LITERATURE **EDUCATION** City Col New York, BA, 61; NYork Univ, MA, PhD(English), 68. **CAREER** Lectr, 63-68, from asst prof to assoc prof, 68-77, prof English, Queens Col, 77-, Nat Endowment for Humanities fel, 74; US Info Agency lectr, Asia, 75; U.S.I.A. lecturer in Asia, 75; vis prof Rutgers, spring 80, and Univ of Paris, 83. **HONORS AND AWARDS** PBK; Oscar Lloyd Meyerson Awd; Queens Col Presidential Research Awd, spring 92. **RESEARCH** Modern and contemporary American literature. **SELECTED PUBLICATIONS** Co-ed, The American Experience: A Radical Reader, Harper & Row, 70; Affinities: An Anthology of Stories, Crowell, 70; auth, Sexual Imagery in the Sacred and Secular Poems of Richard Crashaw, Lit & Psychol, 71; Frederick Rolfe and His Age, Studies Twentieth Century, fall 72; The Jamesian Legacy in The Good Soldier, Studies in Novel, 72; The Beat Generation and the Continuing American Revolution, Am Scholar, spring 73; Naked Angels: The Lives and Literature of the Beat Generation (also editions in Japanese & Ger), McGraw, 76 & 77; Epiphany in Chaos: Fragmentation in Modernism, In: Fragments, NY Lit Forum, 81; Ezra Pound: The Solitary Volcano, Doubleday, 87; Passionate Lives: D.H. Lawrence, F.Scott Fitzgerald, Henry Miller, Dylan Thomas, Sylvia Plath--In Love, Birch Lane Press, Carol Pub, 91; The Living Theatre: Art, Exile and Outrage, Grove press: NY, 95; auth, Paradise Outlaws: Remembering the Beats, William Morrow and Co., 99; and other articles and reviews. **CONTACT ADDRESS** Dept of English, Queens Col, CUNY, 6530 Kissena Blvd, Flushing, NY 11367-1597.

U

UEDA, MAKOTO
PERSONAL Born 05/20/1931, Ono, Japan, m, 1962, 2 children **DISCIPLINE** LITERATURE, AESTHETICS **EDUCATION** Kobe Univ, BLitt, 54; Univ Nebr, MA, 56; Univ Wash, PhD(comp lit), 61. **CAREER** Lectr Japanese, Univ Toronto, 61-62, from asst prof to prof, 62-71; PROF JAPANESE, STANFORD UNIV, 71-96. **RESEARCH** Japanese literature, including theatre; comparative literature, especially Japanese and Western; literary theory and criticism. **SELECTED PUBLICATIONS** Auth, Modern Japanese Poets and the Nature of Literature, Stanford Univ Press, 83; auth, The Mother of Dreams, Kodansha International, 86; auth, Basho and His Inerpreters, Stanford Univ Press, 92; auth, Modern Japanese Tanka, Columbia Univ Press, 96; auth, The Path of Flowering Thorn, Stanford Univ Press, 98; auth, Light Verse from the Floating World, Columbia Univ Press, 99. **CONTACT ADDRESS** 160 Formway Ct., Los Altos, CA 94022.

UFFELMAN, LARRY KENT
PERSONAL Born 12/25/1938, Burlington, IA, m, 1960, 2 children **DISCIPLINE** BIBLIOGRAPHY, VICTORIAN ENGLISH LITERATURE **EDUCATION** IL Wesleyan Univ, BA, 60; Univ IL, MA, 62; KS State Univ, PhD(English), 69. **CAREER** Instr English, Valparaiso Univ, 62-65; assoc prof, 69-76, prof English, Mansfield State Col, 76-; bibliogr, Res Soc Victorian Periodicals, 79-. **HONORS AND AWARDS** Cert of Excellence in Teaching, 79; Commonwealth Teaching Fel, 79; Distinguished Teaching Chair, 79; Distinguished Mentoring Cert, spring 94, fall 94, fall 96; grants of PA State System of Higher Ed Professional Development Comm, 90, 92, 95. **MEMBERSHIPS** Res Soc Victorian Periodicals. **RESEARCH** Victorian serial fiction; British poetry of World War I; Textual criticism and editing. **SELECTED PUBLICATIONS** Auth, Sutton Hoo: A Summary, Bull Kans Asn Teachers English, 69; Charles Hamilton Sorley: An Annotated Checklist, Serif, 73; Kingsley, the Poet, and the Press, Kans Quart, 75; coauth, Kingsley's Serial Novels: Yeast, Victorian Periodicals Newslett, 76; Charles Kingsley, G K Hall, 79; coauth, with Patrick Scott, Kingsley's Serial Novels II: The Water-Babies, Victorian Periodicals Rev, 19, 86; auth, Kingsley's Hypatia: Revisions in Context, Nineteenth-Century Lit 41, 86; Kingsley's Hereward the Wake: From Serial to Book, Victorian Inst J, 14, 86; Faust and Freshman Humanities, in Approaches to Teaching Goethe's Faust, ed Douglas J McMillan, NY: MLA, 87; Articles in Victorian Britain: An Encyclopedia, ed Sally Mitchell, NY: Garland, 88; contrib to Joseph Conrad: An Annotated Bibliography, ed Bruce Teets, NY: Garland, 90; ed, The Nineteenth-Century Periodical Press in Britain: A Bibliography of Modern Studies 1972-1987, Res Soc for Victorian Periodicals, 92; Victorian Periodicals: Research Opportunuites to Faculty-Undergraduate Research, Coun on Undergraduate Res Quart, June 95. **CONTACT ADDRESS** Dept of English, Mansfield Univ of Pennsylvania, Mansfield, PA 16933-1697. **EMAIL** luffelman@mnsfld.edu

UKPOKODU, PETER
DISCIPLINE THEATRE ARTS **EDUCATION** Univ Ibadan, BA, 77, MA, 79; Univ Kans, PhD, 85. **CAREER** Lect to Sr Lect, Univ of Benin, 85-90; asst prof, Univ of Kans, 90-96, assoc prof, 96-, chairperson, African & African-Am Studies Dept, 96-. **HONORS AND AWARDS** Distinguished Service, Univ Ibadan; Excellence in Teaching, Univ Kans; Golden Post Awd, World of Poetry, USA; Federal Government Scholar. **MEMBERSHIPS** Am Soc for Theatre Res, Asn for Theatre in Higher Ed, Int Fedn for Theatre Res, African Studies Asn, African Lit Asn, Asn of Literary Scholars and Critics. **RESEARCH** Theatre, dramatic literature, African culture. **SELECTED PUBLICATIONS** Auth, Socio-Political Theatre in Nigeria; auth, African Political Plays; auth, It Happened to the Blind Beggar; author of numerous articles and essays in The African-Am Encycl, The Drama Rev, Literary Griot, Theatre Annual, Theatre Res Int, Survey of Soc Scis. **CONTACT ADDRESS** Dept African & Afro-Am, Univ of Kansas, Lawrence, 104 Lippincott Hall, Lawrence, KS 66045-0001. **EMAIL** Ukpokodu@ukans.edu

ULANOV, BARRY
PERSONAL Born 04/10/1918, New York, NY, m, 1939, 4 children **DISCIPLINE** ENGLISH **EDUCATION** Columbia Univ, AB, 39, PhD(comp lit), 55. **CAREER** Instr English, Princeton Univ, 50-51; from instr to assoc prof, 51-66, chmn dept English, 67-72, chmn prof in the arts, 72-79, chmn dept relig, 73-74, PROF ENGLISH, BARNARD COL and ADJ PROF ENGLISH, COLUMBIA UNIV, 66-. Guggenheim fel, 62-63; Am Coun Learned Socs grant, 62-63. **HONORS AND AWARDS** Spiritual Life Awd, 63; O'Brien Awd for Distinguished Teaching, Newman Soc, 65; dlitt, villanova univ, 65. **MEMBERSHIPS** MLA; Mediaeval Acad Am; Cath Renaissance Soc (pres, 60-66); PEN Club; Asn Am Achievements. **RESEARCH** Relationship between literature and the arts; literature, theology and the drama; psychology and religion. **SELECTED PUBLICATIONS** Auth, Mapping the Territory, Jour Rel and Health, Vol 0033, 94; Truth and Method, Jour Rel and Health, Vol 0033, 94; Women in Jazz--Do they Belong, Down Beat, Vol 0061, 94; Spiritualism and the Foundations of Jung,C.G. Psychology, Jour Rel and Health, Vol 0033, 94; The Muse in the Machine--Computerizing the Poetry of Human Thought, Jour Rel and Health, Vol 0033, 94; Philosophical Issues in the Psychology of Jung,C.G., Jour Rel and Health, Vol 0033, 94; Seeing Straight with Crooked Lines, Jour Rel and Health, Vol 0033, 94; Nursing as Nourishment, Jour Rel and Health, Vol 0034, 95; Tough Minds and Open Hearts, Jour Rel and Health, Vol 0035, 96; co-ed, Jour Rel and Health, Vol 0034, 95; Composing the Soul--Reaches of Nietzsche Psychology, Jour Rel and Health, Vol 0034, 95; The Short-Circuit Syndrome, Jour Rel and Health, Vol 0034, 95; Nietzsche and Psychoanalysis, Jour Rel and Health, Vol 0034, 95; Culture, Anyone, Jour Rel and Health, Vol 0034, 95; The Nietzsche Legacy in Germany 1890-1990, Jour Rel and Health, Vol 0034, 95; Dumbing Down--Essays on the Strip-Mining of American Culture, Jour Rel and Health, Vol 0035, 96; Staying Awake--Consciousness and Conscience, Jour of Rel and Health, Vol 0035, 96; A Matter of Faith, Jour of Rel and Health, Vol 0035, 96; The Trinity--Augustine, Jour Rel and Health, Vol 0035, 96; Why Freud Was Wrong, Jour Rel and Health, Vol 0035, 96; Crucial Words, Crucial Attitudes, Jour Rel and Health, Vol 0035, 96; Childhood and Children--A Compendium of Customs, Superstitions, Theories, Profiles, and Facts, Jour Rel and Health, Vol 0036, 97; The Healing Syndrome, Jour Rel and Health, Vol 0036, 97; The Iconography of Job Through the Centuries--Artists as Biblical Interpreters, Jour Rel and Health, Vol 0036, 97; Surviving in a Drifting Culture, Jour Rel and Health, Vol 0036, 97; Spiritual Exercises, Jour Rel and Health, Vol 0036, 97. **CONTACT ADDRESS** Dept of English, Columbia Univ, 3061 Broadway, New York, NY 10027-5710.

ULEN, ELISA NEFERTARI
PERSONAL Born 12/22/1968, Philadelphia, PA, s **DISCIPLINE** ENGLISH **EDUCATION** Sarah Lawrence Col, BA, 90; Columbia Univ, MA, 95. **CAREER** Adj lectr, Hunter Col, 96-. **HONORS AND AWARDS** Nominated, Mellon Fels in the Humanities; Scholarship recipient: Sarah Lawrence Black Alumni Asn; Frederick Douglass Creative Arts Ctr Fel for Young African Am Fiction Writers, 95-97; the Fine Arts Work Ctr, Provincetown, full tuition residency scholarship, 99. **MEMBERSHIPS** Modern Lang Asn. **RESEARCH** Published writer--essays and articles concerning race, family, etc. **SELECTED PUBLICATIONS** Auth, Spirit's Returning Eye (novel); contribur, Am I the Last Virgin?: Ten African American Reflections on Sex and Love (97); contribur, Letters of Intent: Women Cross the Generations to Talk About Family, Work, Sex, Love, and the Future of Feminism 999); contribur, Sacred Fire: The QBR 100 Essential Black Books (99); contribur, Living Free Within Ourselves: Lessons for Black Authors (99). **CONTACT ADDRESS** Dept English, Hunter Col, CUNY, 695 Park Ave, New York, NY 10021-5024. **EMAIL** eisaulen@aol.com

ULERY, ROBERT W.
PERSONAL Born 04/02/1944, Goshen, IN, s **DISCIPLINE** CLASSICS, ITALIAN, GREEK **EDUCATION** Yale Univ, BA, 66; MA, 68; PhD, 71. **CAREER** Asst prof, Wake Forest Univ, 71-78; assoc prof, 78-89; prof, 89-. **HONORS AND AWARDS** Beinecke Rar Bk, vis Fel. **MEMBERSHIPS** APA; RSA; ACL; CAMWS; AANLS; IANLS; NAS. **RESEARCH** C Sallustius Crispus and Cornelius Tacitus; manuscript tradition; Nachleben. **SELECTED PUBLICATIONS** Auth, "Sallust," in Dictionary of Literary Biography, ed. Ward W Briggs (Detroit, 99); auth, "Cornelius Tacitus," in Catalogus Translationum et Commentariorum, eds. F Edward Cranz et al (Wash, DC, 86): 87-174. **CONTACT ADDRESS** Dept Classical Languages, Wake Forest Univ, PO Box 7343, Winston-Salem, NC 27109-7343. **EMAIL** ulery@wfu.edu

ULMER, WILLIAM A.
PERSONAL Born 05/05/1952, Plainfield, NJ, m, 1988, 2 children **DISCIPLINE** ENGLISH **EDUCATION** Gettysburg Col, BA; Univ Chicago, MA; Univ Va, PhD. **CAREER** Asst prof to prof, Univ Ala, 80-. **HONORS AND AWARDS** Col of Arts & Sciences Distinguished Teacing Fel; Alumni Asn Outstanding Commitment to Teaching Awd. **MEMBERSHIPS** Keats-Shelley Assoc; Wordsworth-Coleridge Assoc. **RESEARCH** British Romantic Literature. **SELECTED PUBLICATIONS** Auth, Shellyan Eros, Princeton, 90. **CONTACT ADDRESS** Dept English, Univ of Alabama, Tuscaloosa, PO Box 878244, Tuscaloosa, AL 35487-0244. **EMAIL** wulmer@english.as.ua.edu

UMEH, MARIE A.
PERSONAL Born 08/29/1947, Brooklyn, NY, m, 1976, 4 children **DISCIPLINE** ENGLISH **EDUCATION** St John's Univ, BA, 70; Syracuse Univ, MS, 72; Cornell Univ, MPS, 77; Univ Wis Madison, MA, 80; PhD, 81. **CAREER** Instr, SUNY Brockport and Oneonta, 72-75; asst instr, Cornell Univ, 76-77; lectr, chair, Anambra State Col, 82-89; sub assoc prof, Medgar Evers Col, CUNY, 89-90; assoc prof, CUNY, John Jay Col, 90-. **HONORS AND AWARDS** NEH, 91; PSC - CUNY Awd, 98, 99; Who's Who among Am Teachers, 98. **MEMBERSHIPS** AAUW, ALA, MLA, NYASA. **RESEARCH** Autobiography, Biography and Life Writing, African Literatures, Interdisciplinary Approaches to Culture and Society, Literary Criticism, Post Colonial Studies in Literature and Culture. **SELECTED PUBLICATIONS** Auth, Emerging Perspectives on Buchi Emecheta, 95; auth, Emerging Perspectives on Flora Nwapa, 97; coed, Who's Who in Contemporary Women's Writing, 01. **CONTACT ADDRESS** Dept English, John Jay Col of Criminal Justice, CUNY, 445 W 59 St, New York, NY 10019-1104. **EMAIL** msumeh@aol.com

UMLAND, REBECCA
PERSONAL Born 09/11/1954, Iowa City, IA, m, 1992, 1 child **DISCIPLINE** ENGLISH **EDUCATION** Univ Iowa, BA, 76; MA, 83; PhD, 85. **CAREER** Asst prof, Iowa State Univ, 86-89; asst to full prof, Univ of NE, 89-. **HONORS AND AWARDS** Pratt-Heins Distinguished Res Awd, Nebraska, 99; Outstanding Teaching Awd, 94; Honorary Member for Teaching Excellence, 92. **MEMBERSHIPS** Asn of Literary Scholars and Critics, Intl Arthurian Soc, Midwet Victorian Soc. **RESEARCH** Arthurian Literature, 19th Century British Literature, Film Studies. **SELECTED PUBLICATIONS** Auth, The Use of Arthurian Legend In Hollywood film: From Connecticut Yankees to Fisher Kings, Greenwood Press, 96; auth, "Down Among the Dead Men: The Lost Highways of David Lynch," Wrapped in Plastic 42, (99): 2-12; auth, "The King and I: Features of the Arthurian Legen in Twin Peaks" in Twin Peaks Revisited: Appraisals and Reappraisals of the Show that was Supposed to Change TV Forever, Wrapped in Plastic 31 (97); auth, "Unrequited Love in We Can Build You," in contemporary Critical Interpretations, Greenwood Press, (95): 127-141; auth, "The Snake in the Woodpile: Tennyson's Vivien as Victorian prostitute," in Culture and the King: The Social Implications of the Arthurian Legend, (94): 274-287; auth, "Tennyson's Hierarchy of Women in Idylls of the King," in History and community: Essays in victorian Medievalism, (92): 75-96. **CONTACT ADDRESS** Dept English, Univ of Nebraska, Kearney, 905 W 25th St, Kearney, NE 68845-4238. **EMAIL** umlandr@unk.edu

UMLAND, SAMUEL
PERSONAL Born 06/22/1954, Nebraska City, NE, m, 1992, 3 children **DISCIPLINE** ENGLISH **EDUCATION** Univ Nebr, Lincoln, BA, 79; MA, 81; PhD, 87. **CAREER** Asst prof, 88-91, assoc prof, 91-87, full prof, 97, Univ Nebr-Kearney. **HONORS AND AWARDS** Pres Grad Fel, 86-87. **MEMBERSHIPS** Int Arthurian Soc. **RESEARCH** Film, Science fiction studies. **SELECTED PUBLICATIONS** Ed, Philip K. Dick: Contemporary Critical Interpretations, Greenwood Press, (95). Coauth, The Use of Arthurian Legend in Hollywood Film: From Connecticut Yankees to Fisher Kings, Greenwood Press, (96); auth, "To Flee from Dionysus: Enthousiasmos from "Upon the Dull Earth" to VALIS," in Philip K. Dick: Contemporary Critical Interpretations: 81-99; coauth, "Down Among the Dead Men: The Lost Highways of David Lynch," Wrapped In Plastic 42 (Aug 99): 2-12. **CONTACT ADDRESS** Dept English, Univ of Nebraska, Kearney, 905 W 25 St, Kearney, NE 68845-4238. **EMAIL** umlands@unk.edu

UMPHLETT, WILEY LEE
PERSONAL Born 10/25/1931, Norfolk, VA, m, 1966, 3 children **DISCIPLINE** AMERICAN LIT **EDUCATION** Florida State Univ, PhD, Am Lit. **CAREER** Univ West Florida, admin, teacher, 30 years. **RESEARCH** Pop Culture; Social Aspects of Sports. **SELECTED PUBLICATIONS** Fantasizing the American Century: 100 Years of Escapist Culture; in progress; Creating the Big Game: John Heisman and the Intervention of American Football, Greenwood Press, 92; The Achievement of American Sport Literature: A Critical Appraisal, Fairleigh Dickenson UP, 91; numerous articles. **CONTACT ADDRESS** 7246-B Dogwood Ter, Pensacola, FL 32504. **EMAIL** joyceaone@aol.com

UNDERINER, TAMARA
DISCIPLINE THEATRE ARTS **EDUCATION** Univ Wash, PhD. **CAREER** Asst prof **SELECTED PUBLICATIONS** Auth, pubs on Latin American theatre, post-colonial theatre, 20th century American theatre, and dramatic literature. **CONTACT ADDRESS** Theatre Arts and Dance Dept, Univ of Minnesota, Twin Cities, 106 Norris Hall, 172 Pillsbury Dr SE, Minneapolis, MN 55455. **EMAIL** under009@tc.umn.edu

UNDERWOOD, RICHARD
DISCIPLINE ENGLISH LITERATURE **EDUCATION** Univ Mich, PhD, 70. **CAREER** Dept Eng, Clemson Univ **RESEARCH** Shakespeare; Milton; 17th century literature. **SELECTED PUBLICATIONS** Auth, The Two Nobel Kinsman and Its Beginnings, Salzburg, 93. **CONTACT ADDRESS** Clemson Univ, Clemson, SC 29634. **EMAIL** urichar@clemson.edu

UNDERWOOD, WILLARD A.
PERSONAL Born 08/14/1943, Fairmount, IL, m, 1975, 4 children **DISCIPLINE** SPEECH **EDUCATION** Ill State Univ, BS, 65, MS, 67; Bowling Green State Univ, PhD, 72. **CAREER** Asst prof, 75-76, assoc prof, Ariz State Univ, 76-81; lect, Univ NH, 84-85; asst prof, 85-88, Bethany Col, assoc prof, 88-91; prof, Okla Panhandle State Univ, 91-00; Trio Dir, Neosho County Community College, 00-. **HONORS AND AWARDS** Outstanding Educators of Am; Pi Kappa Delta. **MEMBERSHIPS** Nat Commun Asn; Central States Commun Asn; Okla Speech, Theatre and Commun Asn; Nat Educ Debate Asn. **RESEARCH** Health communication; intercultural communication; persuasion and argumentation; and social movements. **SELECTED PUBLICATIONS** Auth, Perceived Class and Ascribed Status of the Physically Disabled: A Case Study, in The Image of Class, Univ Southern Colo, 98; auth, Status Determination of Physically Different Members of Groups: Class Assigned by Others, The Image of Class, Univ Southern Colo, 98. **CONTACT ADDRESS** NEOSHO County Comm Col, 800 W. 14th St., Chanute, KS 66720. **EMAIL** underwoodwa@netscape.net

UNGER, DOUGLAS A.
PERSONAL Born 06/27/1952, Moscow, ID, d, 1 child **DISCIPLINE** ENGLISH **EDUCATION** Bachillerato Nacional, Argentina, 69; Univ Chicago, BA, 73; Univ Iowa, MFA, 77. **CAREER** Asst to assoc prof, Syracuse Univ, 83-91; prof, Univ of Nev Las Vegas, 91-. **HONORS AND AWARDS** Fel, Iowa Writers' Workshop, 75-76; PEN Ernest Hemingway Awd, 85; Soc of Midland Authors Awd, 85; Guggenheim Fel, 86. **MEMBERSHIPS** Assoc Writing Prog; Writers Guild of Aml **RE-**

SEARCH Latin American Studies, American Agrarian Fiction and Non-Fiction, International Terrorism, Contemporary Fiction. **SELECTED PUBLICATIONS** Auth, Leaving The Land, Harper & Row, 84; auth, El Yanqui, Harper & Row, 86; The Turkey War, Harper & Row, 88; Voices From Silence, Wyatt/St Martin's, 95. **CONTACT ADDRESS** Dept English, Univ of Nevada, Las Vegas, PO Box 455011, Las Vegas, NV 89154-5011. **EMAIL** dunger@nevada.edu

UNRAU, JOHN
PERSONAL Born 05/13/1941, Saskatoon, SK, Canada **DISCIPLINE** LITERATURE **EDUCATION** Univ Alta, BA, 62; Oxford Univ, BA, 65; MA; DPhil, 69. **CAREER** Asst prof to prof, York Univ, 69-. **HONORS AND AWARDS** Rhodes Scholar, 62-65; Robert Browning Res Studentship, Pembroke Col, 67-69; Can Coun Predoc Fel, 65-69; SSHRCC Res Fel; Atkinson Fel. **MEMBERSHIPS** Ruskin Soc; League of Can Poets; Saskatchewan Writers' Guild. **RESEARCH** Ruskin; Italian, especially Venetian architecture; Contemporary Canadian writers; Victorian poetry. **SELECTED PUBLICATIONS** Auth, The Balancings of the Clouds: Paintings of Mary Klassen, Windflower Pub, 91; auth, Iced Water (a collection of my poems), Salmon Books, 00; auth, "John Ruskin, Robert Venturi and Modernism in Architecture," in Ruskin and the Twentieth Century, Vercelli, 00; auth, "Elementi Gotici Nella Basilica Di San Marco, Alla Luce Degli Svolti Sugli Appunti Di Ruskin," in L'Architettura Gotica Veneziana, (Venice, 00), 253-266. **CONTACT ADDRESS** Sch of Arts and Letters, York Univ, 4700 Keele St, Toronto, ON, Canada M3J 1P3. **EMAIL** junrau@yorku.ca

UNSWORTH, JOHN M.
PERSONAL Born 01/24/1958, Northampton, MA, m, 1978, 3 children **DISCIPLINE** ENGLISH **EDUCATION** Amherst Col, BA, 80; Boston Univ, MA, 82; Univ Va, PhD,88. **CAREER** Asst prof, NCar State Univ, 89-93; assoc prof, Univ Va, 93-. **MEMBERSHIPS** MLA, Assoc for Computers and the Humanities. **RESEARCH** Humanities computing, contemporary American fiction, publishing. **SELECTED PUBLICATIONS** Auth, "The Book Market II," Columbia Hist of the Am Novel, (91); coed, Essays in Postmodern Culture, Oxford Univ Pr, 95; auth, "Electronic Scholarship," Lit Text in the Digital Age, (96); auth, "Living inside the operating system," Computer networking and scholarship in the 21st century, (96); auth, "The Importance of Failure," Jour of Electronic Publ, (97). **CONTACT ADDRESS** IATH, Univ of Virginia, Alderman Libr, Charlottesville, VA 22903. **EMAIL** jmu2m@virginia.edu

UPCHURCH, DAVID A.
PERSONAL Born 06/21/1947, New Castle, IN, m, 1985, 3 children **DISCIPLINE** ENGLISH **EDUCATION** Depauw Univ, BA, 69; Bread Loaf School English/Ball State Univ, MA, 77; Ball State Univ, PhD, 89. **CAREER** Ball State Univ, 90-. **HONORS AND AWARDS** Lambda 10th TAO; Phi Delta Kappa. **MEMBERSHIPS** MLA; MMLA. **RESEARCH** Oscar Wilde; Fin de Siecle (British); Twentieth Century British Literature. **SELECTED PUBLICATIONS** Auth, Wilde's Use of Irish Celtic Elements In the Picture of Dorian Gray, Peter Lang, 92; auth, "Northern Exposure and the Global Community" Journal of Popular Colture. **CONTACT ADDRESS** Dept English, Ball State Univ, 2000 W Univ Ave, Muncie, IN 47306-1022. **EMAIL** oodaupchutch@bsovc.bsu.edu

UPHAUS, ROBERT WALTER
PERSONAL Born 06/15/1942, East Orange, NJ, 3 children **DISCIPLINE** ENGLISH AND AMERICAN LITERATURE **EDUCATION** Calif State Col, Los Angeles, BA, 64; Univ Wash, MA, 66, PhD, 69. **CAREER** Instr English, Bellevue Community Col, 66-68; from asst prof to prof emeritus English, Mich State Univ, 68-; vis lectr English, Univ Leeds, 71-72. **MEMBERSHIPS** MLA; Am Soc 18th Century Studies. **RESEARCH** Shakespeare; 18th century English literature. **SELECTED PUBLICATIONS** Ed, American Protest in Perspective, Harper, 71; The Impossible Observer, 79; Beyond Tragedy, 81; auth, William Hazlitt, Twayne, 85; ed, The Idea of the Novel in the Eighteenth Century, Colleagues Press, 88; The 'Other' Eighteenth Century, Colleagues Press, 91. **CONTACT ADDRESS** Dept of English, Michigan State Univ, 201 Morrill Hall, East Lansing, MI 48824-1036. **EMAIL** uphaus@pilot.msu.edu

UPTON, LEE
PERSONAL Born 06/02/1953, St Johns, MI, m, 1989, 2 children **DISCIPLINE** ENGLISH **EDUCATION** Mich State Univ, BA, 78; Univ Mass Amherst, MFA, 81; State Univ NY Binghamton, PhD, 86. **CAREER** Vis asst prof, Lafayette Col, 86-78; asst prof, Grand Valley State Univ, 87-88; from asst prof to prof & writer in residence, Lafayette Col, 88-. **HONORS AND AWARDS** Pushcart Prize, 87; Winner, Nat Poetry Series, 88; Mary Louise Van Artsdalen Prize for Scholar, Lafayette Col, 93; Winner, Ga Contemporary Poetry Series, 95 & 99; Second Place Winner, Very Short Fiction Competition, 99. **SELECTED PUBLICATIONS** Auth, Jean Garrigue: A poetics of Plenitude, Farleigh Dickinson Univ Press, 91; auth, Obsession and Release: Rereading the Poetry of Louise Bogan, Bucknell Univ Press, 96; auth, Approximate Darling, Univ Ga Press, 96; auth, The Muse of Abandonment: Origin, Identity, Mastery in Five American Poets, Bucknell Univ Press, 98; auth, "Language in a Red Hat," Field 61 (99): 51-54; auth, "Disremembering, Dismembering," in Poets Reading: The FIELD Symposia, ed. David Walker (Oberlin Col Press, 99) 44-46; auth, "An Invitation to Wonder," in Poets Reading: The FIELD Symposia, ed. David Walker (Oberlin Col Press, 99), 201-202; auth, Civilian Histories, Univ Ga Press, 00; Auth, "Louise Gluck, 1943-," in Am Writers Supplement V, ed. Jay Parinia (NY: Scribner's, 00), 77-94. **CONTACT ADDRESS** Dept English, Lafayette Col, Easton, PA 18042. **EMAIL** uptonlee@lafayette.edu

URAIZEE, JOYA F.
PERSONAL Born 09/25/1961, Calcutta, India, M, 1988, 2 children **DISCIPLINE** ENGLISH **EDUCATION** St Xaviers Col, India, BA, 83; Baylor Univ, MA, 86; Purdue Univ, PhD, 94. **CAREER** Asst to assoc prof, St Louis Univ, 94-. **HONORS AND AWARDS** David Ross Fel, 91; Mellon Grant, 95, 97, 01. **MEMBERSHIPS** MLA, MWMLA, African Lit Asn. **RESEARCH** How women experience mass violence as r4epresented in postcolonial film and fiction, critiques of neocolonialism in African film, Nationalism in African fiction, postcolonial history, postcolonial feminist fiction. **SELECTED PUBLICATIONS** Auth, "Decolonizing the Mind: Paradigms for self definition in Nayantara Sahgal's Rich Like Us," Writing the Nation: Self and Country in the Post-Colonial Imagination, ed JC Hawley, (Rodopi, 96); auth, "Review of Black British Cultural Studies: A Reading, ed Houston A Baker, Manthia Diawara and Ruth Lindeborg, Readerly Writerly Texts 4.2 (97); auth, "Fragmented Borders and Female Boundary Markers in Buchi Emecheta's Destination Biafra," Jour of the MWMLA 30, (97): 1-2; auth, "She Walked Away Without Looking Back: Christophine and the Enigma of History in Jean Rhys' Wide Sargasso Sea," Clio 28, (99): 3; auth, "The Role of Ethics in the Undergraduate Curriculum," What's Ethics got to do With It? The Role of Ethics in Undergraduate, Graduate, and Professional Education at Saint Louis University, ed JF Kavanaugh and DJ Werner, (St Luis Univ Pr, 00); auth, "Buchi Emecheta and the Politics of Gender," Black women Writers Across Cultures: An Analysis of Their Contributions, ed VU James, JS Etim, MM James, AJ Njoh, (Int Scholars Publ, 00); auth, This is No Place for a Woman: Nadine Gordimer, Nayantara Sahgal, Buchi Emecheta and the Politics of Gender, Africa World Pr, 00; rev, of In Beautiful Disguises by Rajeev Balasubramanyam, Pacific Reader, (forthcoming). **CONTACT ADDRESS** Saint Louis Univ, 221 N Grand Blvd, Saint Louis, MO 63103. **EMAIL** uraizeej@slu.edu

URGO, JOSEPH R.
PERSONAL Born 01/29/1956, Hartford, CT, m, 1983, 1 child **DISCIPLINE** ENGLISH **EDUCATION** Haverford Col, BA, 78; Wesleyan Univ, MALS, 81; Brown Univ, MA, 85; PhD, 85. **CAREER** Vis asst prof, Syracuse Univ, 85-86; asst prof, Vanderbilt Univ, 86-89; asst prof to prof, chair, Bryant Col, 89-00; prof, chair, Univ of Miss, 00-. **HONORS AND AWARDS** Andrew W Mellon Fel, 86-89; Fulbright Awd, 92. **MEMBERSHIPS** MLA, Am Lit Assoc, William Faulkner Soc, Willa Cather Pioneer Mem and Educ Found. **RESEARCH** 19th and 20th century American Literature and Culture, professional issues in higher education. **SELECTED PUBLICATIONS** Auth, "Proletarian Literature and Feminism: the Gastonia Novels and Feminist Protest," Twentieth Century Literary Criticism Vol 54, Gale Res, (MI: Detroit, 85); auth, "Comedic Impulses and Societal Propriety: The Yippie! Carnival," Studies in Popular Cult X.1, (87); auth, Faulkner's Apocrypha: A Fable, Snopes, and the Spirit of Human Rebellion, Univ of Miss Pr, 89; auth, Novel Frames: Literature as Guide to Race, Sex, and History in American Culture, Univ of Miss Pr, 91; auth, "Faulkner Unplugged: Abortoposis and The Wild Palms," Faulkner and Gender: Faulkner and Yoknapatawpha, (94); auth, "Absalom, Absalom!: The Movie," Am Lit 62.1, (95); auth, Willa Cather and the Myth of American Migration, Ill Univ Pr, 95; auth, "The Affiliation Blues," Symploke 7:1-2, (00): 7-20; auth, "Willa Cather's Political Apprenticeship at McClure's Magazine," Willa Cather in New York, ed Merrill Skaggs, Fairleigh Dickinson Univ Pr, (NJ: Madison, 00). **CONTACT ADDRESS** Univ of Mississippi, 804 brentwood Cove, Oxfordm, MS 38655. **EMAIL** jurgo@olemiss.edu

URKOWITZ, STEVEN
PERSONAL Born 11/29/1941, New York, NY, m, 1966, 2 children **DISCIPLINE** ENGLISH **EDUCATION** City Col NY, BA, 64; MA, 68; Univ Chicago, PhD, 77. **CAREER** Teacher, New York Sec Schools, 63-68; instr, Barch Col, 72-76; instr, Medgar Evans Col, 78; instr, State Univ of NYork Maritime Col, 78-84; instr, , Hofstra Univ, 84-87; prof, CUNY, 87-. **HONORS AND AWARDS** NDH/Foger Library, Wash Dc, 90; Simon Rifkind Fel, City Col, 89; Nat Endowment for the Humanities Fel, 83-84. **MEMBERSHIPS** Alliance for Creative Theatre, Educ and Res; Columbia Univ Sem on Shakespeare. **RESEARCH** Shakespearean textual studies. **SELECTED PUBLICATIONS** Auth, "All things is handsome now: Murderers Nominated by Numbers in 2 Henry VI and Richard III," in Shakespeare's Speech-Headings: Speaking the Speech in Shakespeare's Plays, Newark, (97): 101-119; auth, "Two Versions of Romeo and Juliet 2.6 and Merry Wives of Windsor 5.2215-45: An Invitation to the Pleasures of Di(per)versity," in Elizabethan Theater: Essays in Honor of Samuel Schoenbaum, Univ Del Pres, (96): 222-238; auth, "Brother, Can You Spare a Paradigm?: Textual Generosity and the Printing of Shakespeare's Multiple-Text Plays by Contemporary Editors," Critical Survey 7, (95): 292-298; auth, "Back to Basics: Thinking about the HAMLET First Quarto," in The HAMLET First Published: Origins, Form, Intertextualites, Newark, (92): 257-291; auth, "Memorial Reconstruction," Shakespeare Newsletter 39; (89): 10; auth, "Peter Alexander's Textual Analysis of Shakespeare's Early Histories," English Literary Renaissance, 18, (88): 230-257; auth, "Good News about 'Bad' Quartos," in Bad Shakespeare, New York, (88): 189-206; auth, "Five Women eleven Ways: Changing Images of Shakespearean Characters in the Earliest Texts," in Images of Shakespeare: Proceedings of the Third Congress of the International Shakespeare Association, (88): 292-804; auth, "Reconsidering the Relationship of Quarto and folio Texts of Richard III," English Literary Renaissance, 16, (86): 442-466; auth, "Well-sayd olde Mole: Burying Three HAMLETs in Modern Editions," in Shakespeare Study Today: The Horace Howard Furness Memorial Lectures, New York: (86): 37-70. **CONTACT ADDRESS** Dept English, City Col, CUNY, 160 Convenant Ave, New York, NY 10031-9101. **EMAIL** SUrkowitz@aol.com

USCHER, NANCY
DISCIPLINE MUSIC **EDUCATION** Yale Univ, BA; Univ NYork, MA; PhD. **CAREER** Prof, Univ N Mex. **SELECTED PUBLICATIONS** Auth, The Schirmer Guide to Schools of Music; Conservatories Throughout the World; Your Own Way in Music: A Career and Resource Guide. **CONTACT ADDRESS** Music Dept, Univ of New Mexico, Albuquerque, 1805 Roma NE, Albuquerque, NM 87131. **EMAIL** muscher@unm.edu

UTZ, RICHARD J.
PERSONAL Born 01/30/1961, Amberg, Germany, m, 1989 **DISCIPLINE** ENGLISH LITERATURE **EDUCATION** Univ Regensburg, MA, 88; PhD, 90. **CAREER** Lectr, Univ Regensburg, 89-90; asst prof, Padagogische Hochschule, 90-91; asst prof, Univ Northern Iowa, 91-96; asst prof, Univ of Tubingen, 96-98; asst prof, prof, Univ Northern Iowa, 98-. **HONORS AND AWARDS** Outst Teach Awd, Col of Hum and Fine Arts, Univ of N Iowa, 95; Donald N. McKay Res Awd, 00; Regents Awd for Fac Excel, 01. **MEMBERSHIPS** Mediavistenverband, MLAA, New Chaucer Soc, John Gower Soc, Oswald von Wolkenstein Gesellschaft. **RESEARCH** Medieval English literature, language, and culture medievalism; theories of literary reception literature and travel; history of English studies, cultural nationalism. **SELECTED PUBLICATIONS** Auth, "Literarischer Nominalismus im Spatmittelalter: Eine Untersuchung zu Sprache Charakterzeichnung und Struktur," in Geoffrey Chaucer's 'Troilus and Criseyde' (Peter Lang, 90); ed, "Literary Nominalism and the Theory of Rereading Late Medieval Texts: A New Research Paradigm," (Edwin Mellen, 95"; ed, "Investigating the Unliterary: Six Readings of Edgar Rice Borroughs 'Tarzan of the Apes,'" (Ulrich Martzinek, 95); co-ed, The Late Medieval Epistle, Northwest UP, 96; co-ed, Constructions of Time in the Late Middle Ages, Northwest UP, 97; co-ed, Nominalism and Literary Discourse: New Perspectives, Rodopi, 97; co-ed, Medievalism in the Modern World: Essays in Honor of Leslie Workman, Brepols, 98; co-ed, Discourses of Power: Grammar and Rhetoric in the Late Middle Ages, Northwest UP, 00. **CONTACT ADDRESS** Eng Dept, Univ of No Iowa, Baker Hall 115, Cedar Falls, IA 50614-0502. **EMAIL** utz@uni.edu

V

VACCARO, JOSEPH
PERSONAL Born 02/07/1935, Cambridge, MA, m, 1963, 4 children **DISCIPLINE** MARKETING **EDUCATION** Boston Coll, BSBA, 57; Suffolk Univ, MBA, 69; Suffolk Univ Law Sch, JD, 76. **CAREER** Prof of marketing, 71-present, Suffolk Univ. **HONORS AND AWARDS** Dean's Teaching Awd; Certificate of recognition from Amer Marketing Assn; Amer Advertising Fedn; MA Press Assn; Faculty Advisor of the year award from Boston chapter of the Amer Marketing Assn; Hugh G. Wales Advisor of the Year from the Amer marketing Assn **MEMBERSHIPS** Amer Marketing Assn; Amer Advertising Fedn; Assn of Marketing Educators; Amer Acad of Advertising; Amer Assn of Advertising Agencies. **RESEARCH** Sales and sales management; advertising; marketing law; media planning; ethics; counter trade. **SELECTED PUBLICATIONS** Auth, Managing Sales Professionals - The Reality of Profitability, 95; Taking Advantage of Barter in Radio, The Journal of Services Marketing, 97; Assessing Attitudes and Opinions of Parents and Non-parent Adults Toward Television Exposure to Kids, Journal of Association of Marketing Educators, Spring 98. **CONTACT ADDRESS** 36 Oakwood Rd., Auburndale, MA 02466-2248. **EMAIL** jvaccaro@suffolk.edu

VAILAKIS, IVAN GORDON
PERSONAL Born Quito, Ecuador **DISCIPLINE** LATIN AMERICA LITERATURE **EDUCATION** Univ Calf Irvine, PhD, **CAREER** Prof, Univ Redlands. **RESEARCH** Contemporary Latin American Poetry. **SELECTED PUBLICATIONS** Auth, Colibries en el exilio, 97; Nuestrario, 87; pubs on Gabriela Mistral, Alicia Y¤nez Cossio, Sandra Cisneros, and

Helen Maria Viramontes. **CONTACT ADDRESS** History Dept, Univ of Redlands, 1200 E Colton Ave, Box 3090, Redlands, CA 92373-0999.

VALASKAKIS, GAIL
PERSONAL Born 05/09/1939, Ashland, WI **DISCIPLINE** COMMUNICATIONS **EDUCATION** Univ Wis, BS, 61; Cornell Univ, MA, 64; McGill Univ, PhD, 79. **CAREER** Lectr, comm arts, Loyola Col, 69-71, coordr Can studies, Loyola campus, 78-79; asst to assoc prof, 71-89, Prof Communication Stud, Concordia Univ, 89-, dir MA prog media stud, 82-84, ch, 83-85, dean arts & sci, 92-98. **MEMBERSHIPS** Can Commun Asn; Int Soc Intercultur Educ, Training & Res; Can Asn Suport Native Peoples; Native N Am Stud Inst (Montreal). **SELECTED PUBLICATIONS** Dir, Can J Commun, 86-89. **CONTACT ADDRESS** 3611 Marlowe Ave, Montreal, QC, Canada H4A 3L8.

VALENTI, PETER LOUIS
PERSONAL Born 01/12/1945, Springfield, MS, m, 1972, 2 children **DISCIPLINE** ENGLISH **EDUCATION** Westfield State Col, BA, 67; E Carolina Univ, MA, 70; Univ NC, Chapel Hill, PhD(English), 74. **CAREER** Instr English, Univ NC, Chapel Hill, 73-74; chmn, Dept English, Holmes High Sch, Edenton, NC, 74-75; asst prof, 75-81, assoc prof 82-88; prof, English, Fayetteville State Univ, 89-. **HONORS AND AWARDS** Dist Visit Prof, US Milit Acad, 91-92; Bd of Gov Awd for Excel In Teach, 96 **MEMBERSHIPS** MLA; SAtlantic Mod Lang Asn; Popular Cult Asn; Am Film Inst; Philol Asn Carolinas; CCCC; ASLE. **RESEARCH** Film; 17th-19th century English literature; 19th century American literature. **SELECTED PUBLICATIONS** Auth, Images of authority in Benito Cereno, CLA J, 3/78; The Film Blanc: Suggestions for a variety of fantasy, 1940-45, J Popular Film, 77-78; The ordering of God's providence: Law and landscape, In: The Pioneers, Studies Am Fiction, Vol VII, 78; The cultural hero in the World War II fantasy film, J Popular Film & TV, Vol VII, 79; Gatsby: Franklin and Hoppy, Notes Mod Am Lit, Vol 3, 79; The theological rhetoric of It's a Wonderful Life, Film Criticism, Vol V, 81; auth, Errol Flynn, Greenwood, 84; auth, The Treasure of the Sierra Madre: Spiritual Quest and Studio Patriarchy, Paulist, 92; auth, Visual Documentary in The Grapes of Wrath, Steinbeck and the Environment, Univ of Ala, 96; auth, Reading the Landscape: Writing a World, Harcourt Brace Col, 96. **CONTACT ADDRESS** Dept of English and Foreign Langs, Fayetteville State Univ, 1200 Murchison Rd, Fayetteville, NC 28301-4298. **EMAIL** pvalenti@uncfsu.edu

VALENTIS, MARY ARENSBERG
PERSONAL Born 06/27/1945, Albany, NY, m, 1991, 1 child **DISCIPLINE** ENGLISH AND AMERICAN LITERATURE **EDUCATION** CT College, BA, 67; SUNY Albany, MA, 74, PhD, 79. **CAREER** Lectr, 77 to 98-, SUNY Albany. **MEMBERSHIPS** MLA; ALS; Wallace Stevens Soc; Authors Guild. **RESEARCH** Literary theory; Psychoanalysis. **SELECTED PUBLICATIONS** Auth, Donne Che Non Hanno Paura De l Fucco, Frassinelli Pub, 97; auth, Die WUT Der Frauen, Knauer Pub, 96; coauth, Female Rage: Unlocking its secrets claiming its power, CSB div of Crown Pub, 94, Japanese edition, 96; Female Rage: How women can unlock their rage, Platkus Pub, 95; auth, Outing Rage, New Women Mag, 94; auth, Wallace Stevens and the Mythology of Gender, in: Wallace Stevens and the Feminine, ed, Melita Schawn, U of AL Press, 94. **CONTACT ADDRESS** Dept of English, SUNY, Albany, Albany, NY 12222. **EMAIL** mbvbooks@aol.comvalentis@csc.albany.edu

VALERIE M., BABB
DISCIPLINE ENGLISH **EDUCATION** CUNY Queen's Col, BA; SUNY Buffalo, MA, PhD. **CAREER** Georgetown Univ, prof. **RESEARCH** American studies; women's studies; American literature. **SELECTED PUBLICATIONS** Auth, Whiteness Visible: The Meaning of Whiteness in American Literature and Culture, 98. **CONTACT ADDRESS** Dept of English, Georgetown Univ, PO Box 571131, Washington, DC 20057-1131.

VALESIO, PAOLO
PERSONAL Born 10/14/1939, Bologna, Italy, m, 1963, 1 child **DISCIPLINE** RHETORICS, LITERARY THEORY; RELIGION AND LITERATURE. **EDUCATION** Univ Bologna, Dr Lett, 61, libero docente, 69. **CAREER** Asst, Inst Glottology, Univ Bologna, 61-62, 66-68; lectr Romance lang & lit, Harvard Univ, 68-70, assoc prof, 70-73; assoc prof Ital & dir prog, NY Univ, 73-74, prof, 74-76; Prof Ital, Yale Univ, 76-, Fel, Harvard Univ, 65-66. **HONORS AND AWARDS** Poetry Prize, Citta di San Vito al Tagliamento, 92; Guggenheim Fel, 94. **MEMBERSHIPS** Am Asn of Italian Studies; Dante Soc Am. **RESEARCH** Religion and literature. **SELECTED PUBLICATIONS** Auth, Novantiqua: Rhetorics as a Contemporary Theory, Indiana Univ Press (Bloomington, Indiana), 80; auth, Gabriele d'Annunzio: The Dark Flame, Yale Univ Press (New Haven/London), 92; auth, Nightchant: Selected Poems, trans Graziella Sidoli and Vanna Tessier, Edmonton: Snowapple Press, 95; Sonetos Profanos y Sacros, trans Taller de Traduccion Literaria de la Universidad di La Laguna, La Laguna, Tenerife: Ediciones Canarias, 96; auth, Piazza delle preghiere massacrate, Modena: Edizioni del Laboratorio, 99. **CONTACT ADDRESS** Dept of Ital, Yale Univ, PO Box 208311, New Haven, CT 06520-8311. **EMAIL** paolo.valesio@yale.edu

VALGEMAE, MARDI
PERSONAL Born 11/10/1935, Viljandi, Estonia, m, 1957, 2 children **DISCIPLINE** ENGLISH **EDUCATION** Rutgers Univ, BA, 57; Univ Calif, Los Angeles, MA, 62, PhD(English), 64. **CAREER** Asst prof English, Univ Calif, Los Angeles, 64-68; assoc prof, 68-75, prof English, Lehman Col, City Univ New York, 75-, Drama Ed, Mana, 64-; fac res grant, City Univ New York, 69-70; Am Coun Learned Soc Europ travel grant, 70, 81; dir The City and Humanities Program, 84-88; chmn Dept English, 88-97. **HONORS AND AWARDS** Criticism Prize, Estonian Writers' Union, 91; Visnapuu Prize, 96. **MEMBERSHIPS** MLA; Asn Advan Baltic Studies. **RESEARCH** Modern drama; Baltic studies. **SELECTED PUBLICATIONS** Auth, Socialist allegory of the absurd, Comp Drama, Spring 71; Expressionism and the new American drama, 20th Century Lit, 10/71; Accelerated Grimace: Expressionism in the American Drama of the 1920's, Southern Ill Univ, 72; co-ed, Baltic literature and linguistics, Asn Advan Baltic Studies, 73; contribr, Expressionism as an International Literary Phenomenon, Didier, Paris, 73; A Case Study of a Soviet Republic, 78 & Baltic Drama: A Handbook and Bibliography, 81, Westview; auth, Critical Essays on Edward Albee, Hall, Boston, 86; auth, Ikka teatrist moteldes, Theater on My Mind, Valis-Eesti & EMP, Stockholm, Sweden, 90; Linn ja teater, The City and the Theater, Vagabund, Tallinn, Estonia, 95; auth, Kaugekone, Long Distance, Vagabund, Tallinn, Estonia, 99. **CONTACT ADDRESS** Dept of English, Lehman Col, CUNY, 250 Bedford Park W, Bronx, NY 10468-1527. **EMAIL** mardival@mindspring.com

VALIHORA, KAREN
PERSONAL Born 04/08/1968, Ottawa, ON, Canada **DISCIPLINE** ENGLISH **EDUCATION** McGill Univ, BA, 90; MA, 92; Yale Univ, PhD, 00. **CAREER** Asst prof, York Univ, 97-. **MEMBERSHIPS** ASECS; MLA. **RESEARCH** Eighteenth-Century literature and philosophy. **CONTACT ADDRESS** Dept English, York Univ, 4700 Keele St, 208 Stong Col, Toronto, ON, Canada M3J 1P3. **EMAIL** valihora@yorku.ca

VALLETTA, CLEMENT LAWRENCE
PERSONAL Born 07/31/1938, Easton, PA **DISCIPLINE** AMERICAN CIVILIZATION, ENGLISH **EDUCATION** Univ Scranton, BA, 61; Univ Pa, MA, 62, PhD(Am Civilization), 68. **CAREER** From instr to assoc prof, 64-77, chmn dept, 71-80, prof English, King's Col, PA, 77-. **MEMBERSHIPS** MLA; Am Studies Asn; Am Folklore Soc; Christianity and Literature. **RESEARCH** Americanization of ethnic groups; influence of relativity physics in non-scientific aspects; American civilization, folk, rhetorical, literary aspects. **SELECTED PUBLICATIONS** Auth, Friendship and games in Italian American life, Keystone Folklore Quart, 70; Einstein, Edison and the conquest of irony, Cithara, 72; contrib, The ethnic experience in Pennsylvania, Bucknell Univ, 73; Studies in Italian American social history, Rowman & Littlefield, 75; auth, A study of Americanization in Carneta, Arno, 75; ed, Ethnic Drama: Video-Text and Study Guide, ERIC, 81; Pennsylavania History, 92; with Robert Paoletti In-Determindcy in Science and Discourse, Technical Writing and Communication, 95; Caring and Christian Irony in Ann Tyler's Novels, Repis Collage Proceedings, 96; A Christian Dispersion in Don DeLillo's The Names, Christianity and Literature, 98. **CONTACT ADDRESS** Dept of English, King's Col, 133 N River St, Wilkes-Barre, PA 18711-0801. **EMAIL** clvallet@kings.edu

VALLEY, DAVID B.
PERSONAL Born 09/12/1944, Rock Island, IL, m, 1990, 3 children **DISCIPLINE** SPEECH COMMUNICATION **EDUCATION** Univ of IL, PhD; IL St Univ, MS; Blackhawk Cmnty Col, AS **CAREER** 82-, Prof, S IL Univ **HONORS AND AWARDS** Tch Recog awd, 93 **MEMBERSHIPS** Nat Commun Asn; Cent Sts Speech Asn **RESEARCH** Parent-child conversation **SELECTED PUBLICATIONS** Auth, A History and Analysis of Democratic Presidential Nomination Acceptance Speeches to 1968, Univ Press of America, 88 **CONTACT ADDRESS** Dept of Speech Commun, So Illinois Univ, Edwardsville, Edwardsville, IL 62026-1772. **EMAIL** dvalley@siue.edu

VAN, THOMAS A.
PERSONAL Born 05/22/1938, New York, NY, m, 1963 **DISCIPLINE** ENGLISH, LINGUISTICS **EDUCATION** City Col New York, BA, 60; Duke Univ, MA, 63, PhD(English), 66. **CAREER** Instr English, Univ NC, Chapel Hill, 65-66; asst prof, Univ Ky, 66-70; Assoc Prof English, Univ Louisville, 70-, Chmn Dept, 80-. **MEMBERSHIPS** MLA; NCTE; Mediaeval Acad Am; fel NDEA. **RESEARCH** Dante; Chaucer; Shakespeare. **SELECTED PUBLICATIONS** Auth, False Texts and Disappearing Women in the Wife of Baths Prologue and Tale--An Analysis of the Thematic Development of Contradiction and Anomaly Between Teller and Tale in the Canterbury Tales of Chaucer, Geoffrey, Chaucer Rev, Vol 0029, 94. **CONTACT ADDRESS** Dept of English, Univ of Louisville, Louisville, KY 40208.

VAN APPLEDORN, MARY JEANNE
PERSONAL Born 10/02/1927, Holland, MI **DISCIPLINE** MUSIC THEORY, COMPOSITION **EDUCATION** Univ Rochester, Eastman Sch of Music, BM 48, MM theory 50, PhD music 66. **CAREER** Texas Tech Univ, Sch of Music, Paul Whitfield Horn Prof, 50-. **HONORS AND AWARDS** ASCAP, Stnd Panel Awds, Intl Trumpet Awd, Brit Trombone Asn Awd; will be listed in new grove dictionary of music and musicians. **MEMBERSHIPS** ASCAP; SCI. **RESEARCH** Musicology, Theory, Composition. **SELECTED PUBLICATIONS** Music of Enchantment, for native american flute, Colorado Springs CO, ZaloJP Pub, 98; Cycles of Moons and Tides, San Antonio TX, Southern Music Co, 98; Les Hommes Vides, Bryn Mawr PA, Hildegard Pub, 98; Passages, Warwick UK, Warwick Music, 97; numerous others. **CONTACT ADDRESS** School of Music, Texas Tech univ, Box 1583, Lubbock, TX 79408-1583. **EMAIL** a5sjm@techmail.admin.ttu.edu

VAN DOVER, JAMES K.
PERSONAL Born 01/01/1950, St. Louis, MO, m, 1979, 2 children **DISCIPLINE** ENGLISH **EDUCATION** Lafayette Col, AB, 72; Bryn Mawr Col, MA, 74, PhD, 78. **CAREER** Prof, Lincoln Univ, 78-. **HONORS AND AWARDS** Whiting Fel; Fulbright Professorships: Germany, 80-89, 88-89; China, 00; Lindback Awd for Tchg; Presidential Awd for Res. **RESEARCH** Am Literature; popular literature. **SELECTED PUBLICATIONS** Coauth, Isn't Justice Always Unfair? The Detective in Southern Literature, 96; auth, Centurions, Knights, Choirboys and Other Cops: The Fiction of Joseph Wambaugh, 95; auth, The Critical Response to Raymond Chandler, 95; auth, You Know My Method: The Science of the Detective, 94; auth, Polemical Pulps: The Novels of Sjowall and Wahloo, 93. **CONTACT ADDRESS** 212 Wilshire Ln, Newark, DE 19711. **EMAIL** vandover@lu.lincoln.edu

VAN EEMEREN, FRANS H.
PERSONAL Born 04/07/1946, Helmond, Netherlands **DISCIPLINE** DISCOURSE AND ARGUMENTATION STUDIES, RHETORIC **EDUCATION** Univ Amsterdam, PhD, 82. **CAREER** Full prof of Speech Commun, Argumentation Theory, and Rhetoric, Univ of Amsterdam; head of dept; former dean of the fac of Arts and former dean of the fac of Humanities; vis prof, New York Univ, 99-2000. **HONORS AND AWARDS** Res Awd, Am Forensic Asn, 93, 94; Medal of David the Invincible, Armenian Acad of Philos. **MEMBERSHIPS** Int Soc for the Study of Argumentation (ISSA), Nat Commun Asn (NCA), Int Commun Asn (ICA). **RESEARCH** Argumentation theory, rhetoric, discourse analysis. **SELECTED PUBLICATIONS** Coauth with R. Grootendorst, Speech Acts in Argumentative Discussions. A Theoretical Model for the Analysis of Discussions Directed towards Solving Conflicts of Opinion, Dorecht/Berlin: Foris/De Gruyter (84, Russian transl, 94); coauth with R. Grootendorst, Argumentation, Communication, and Fallacies. A Pragma-Dialectical Perspective, Hillsdale, NJ, Lawrence Erlbaum Assocs (92, Chinese transl, 92, Russian transl, 92, French transl, 92, Spanish transl, 99; coauth with R. Grootendorst, J. A. Blair and Ch. A Willard, eds, Argumentation Illuminated, Amsterdam: Sic Sat (92); coauth with R. Grootendorst, S. Jackson, and S. Jacobs, Reconstructing Argumentative Discourse, Tuscaloosa and London: The Univ of Ala Press, Studies in Rhetoric and Communication (93); co-ed with R. Grootendorst, Studies in Pragma-Dialectics, Amsterdam: Sic Sat (94); coauth with R. Grootendorst and A. F. Snoeck Henkemans, with J. A. Blair, R. H. Johnson, E. C. W. Krabbe, Ch. Plantin, D. N. Walton, Ch. A. Willard, J. Woods and D. Zarefsky, Fundamentals of Argumentation Theory. Handbook of Historical Backgrounds and Contemporary Developments, Mawhah, NJ: Lawrence Erlbaum Assocs (96, Dutch transl, 98); coauth with J. van Benthem, R. Grootendorst and F. Veltman, eds, Logic and argumentation, Amsterdam, etc: North-Holland, Koninklijke Nederlandse Akademie van Wetenschappen, Verhandelingen, Afd Letterkunde, Nieuwe Reeks, deel 1770 (96). **CONTACT ADDRESS** Discourse/Argumentation Studies, Inst von Neerlandoshik, Spuishaat 134, Amsterdam, VB, Netherlands 1012. **EMAIL** F.H.van.Eemeren@hum.uva.nl

VAN GELDEREN, ELLY
PERSONAL Born 09/24/1958, Geertruidenberg, Netherlands, m, 1985 **DISCIPLINE** ENGLISH **EDUCATION** Utrecht Univ, BA, 79; MA, 81; McGill Univ, PhD, 86. **CAREER** Instr, John Abbott Col, 86, 88, 90; lectr, McGill Univ, 89; vis asst prof, Queen's Univ, 89-90; asst prof, Univ Groningen, 90-95; asst prof, Ariz State Univ, 98-. **MEMBERSHIPS** Am Dialect Soc; Atlantic Provinces' Ling Asn; Intl Ling Asn; Ling Asn of Can and the U.S.; Ling Asn of the SW; Ling Asn of Great Britain; Ling Soc of India; Ling Soc of Am; Soc for Germanic Ling; Soc for the Study of the Indigenous Lang of the Am; Vereniging Taalwetenschap. **RESEARCH** Agreement; reflexives; Minimalism; Case. **SELECTED PUBLICATIONS** Auth, The Rise of functional Categories, Amsterdam, 93; auth, Verbal Agreement and the Grammar behind its 'Breakdown': Minimalist Feature Checking, Tbingen: Miemeyer, 97; co-ed, German: syntactic Problems - Problematic Syntax, Niemeyer, 97; auth, "Structures of Tense and Aspect," Ling Analysis, (97): 138-165; auth, "For to in the History of English," Am J of Germanic Lang and Lit, (98): 45-72; co-ed, Western Conference on Linguistics 1998 Proceedings, Fresno Univ Press, 99; auth, A History of English Reflexive Pronouns: Person, Self, and Interpretability, John Benjamins, 00; auth, "The Absence of Verb-movement and the Role of C: Some negative constructions in Shakespeare," Studia Ling, (00): 412-423; auth, "The Role of Person in the Loss of Verbal Agreement and of Pro-drop," in

Pathways of Change: Grammaticalization Processes in older English, (Berlin, 00), 187-206; auth, "Interpretable and Non-Interpretable Features Cross-linguistically," J of Formal, Computational & Cognitive Ling, 00. **CONTACT ADDRESS** Dept English, Arizona State Univ, Dept English, Tempe, AZ 85287-0302. **EMAIL** ellyvangelderen@asu.edu

VAN PELT, TAMISE
DISCIPLINE ENGLISH LITERATURE **EDUCATION** Univ Ill, PhD, 94. **CAREER** Asst prof. **RESEARCH** Critical and interpretive theories; pedagogy of theory; cybersubjectivity; virtual identity. **SELECTED PUBLICATIONS** Auth, The other Side of Desire: Lacan's Theory of the Registers, SUNY. **CONTACT ADDRESS** Dept of English and Philosophy, Idaho State Univ, Pocatello, ID 83209. **EMAIL** vantamis@isu.edu

VAN STEEN, GONDA ALINE HECTOR
PERSONAL Born 04/08/1964, Aalst, Belgium, m, 1996 **DISCIPLINE** CLASSICS **EDUCATION** Princeton Univ, MA, 93, PhD, 95. **CAREER** Asst Prof, 95-97, Cornell Univ; Asst Prof, Classic & Modern Greek, 97-, Univ of Ariz. **HONORS AND AWARDS** Undergrad full tuition fel Govt Belgium, Undergrad Dissertation Awd, J D & C T MacArthur Found Grant, Alexander Papamarkou Awd, Gennadeion Fel, AGTE Awd, Stanley J Seeger Fel, Mary Isabel Sibley Fel, MGSA PhD Dissertation Prize. **MEMBERSHIPS** APA, MGSA, MLA. **RESEARCH** Ancient & modern Greek drama, film & performance criticism, gender studies, language instruction, foreign studies program. **SELECTED PUBLICATIONS** Auth, Venom in Verse, Aristophanes in Modern Greece, Princeton Univ Press, 00; Destined to Be? - Tyche in Chariton's Chaereas and Callirhoe and in the Byzantine Romance of Kallimachos and Chrysorroi, in: L'Antiquite Classique, 88; Aristophanes Revival on the Modern Greek Stage, in: Dialogos, Hellenic Studies Review, Kings Coll London, 95; Aspects of Public Performance in Aristophanes' Acharnians, AC, 94. **CONTACT ADDRESS** Dept of Classics, Univ of Arizona, Mod Lang Bldg, Box 210067, Tucson, AZ 85721-0067. **EMAIL** gonda@u.arizona.edu

VANAUKEN, SHELDON
DISCIPLINE HISTORY, ENGLISH **EDUCATION** Oxford Univ, BLitt, 57. **CAREER** From asst prof to assoc prof, 48-73, Prof Hist and English, Lynchburg Col, 73- **RESEARCH** Nineteenth century England. **SELECTED PUBLICATIONS** Auth, Employment Law Survey, Denver Univ Law Rev, Vol 0072, 95. **CONTACT ADDRESS** 100 Breckenbridge, Lynchburg, VA 24501.

VANCE, JOHN ANTHONY
PERSONAL Born 08/09/1947, Oceanside, NY, m, 1974, 2 children **DISCIPLINE** ENGLISH LITERATURE **EDUCATION** Fla State Univ, BA, 74, MA, 75, PhD(English), 79. **MEMBERSHIPS** MLA; SAtlantic Mod Lang Asn; Am Soc 18th Century Studies; Southeastern Am Soc 18th Century Studies. **RESEARCH** Samuel Johnson and his circle; Restoration and 18th century drama. **CONTACT ADDRESS** Dept of English, Univ of Georgia, Athens, GA 30602-0001. **EMAIL** jvance@uga.edu

VANCE, WILLIAM LYNN
PERSONAL Born 04/19/1934, Dupree, SD **DISCIPLINE** ENGLISH & AMERICAN LITERATURE **EDUCATION** Oberlin Col, AB, 56; Univ Mich, MA, 57, PhD, 62. **CAREER** From assoc prof to prof, 62-73, assoc chmn dept, 72-73 & 81-83, chmn dept, 85-88, Prof English, Boston Univ, 73-, dir, Am Studies, 88-90. **HONORS AND AWARDS** Ralph Waldo Emerson Prize (Phi Beta Kappa), 90; Nat Book Critics Circle Awd Nomination, 90; guggenheim fel, 90-91; Doctor of Letters and Lit (hon), Univ S Dak, 92; Metcalf Cup and Prize, Excellence in Teaching, 92; NEH Distinguished teaching prof, 97-99. **MEMBERSHIPS** AAUP; ALSC; Soc Classic Tradition **RESEARCH** American literature and art; Italian culture. **SELECTED PUBLICATIONS** Co-ed, American Literature, Little, 70; co-ed, Imaginari a confronto, Jarsilio, Venice, 92; co-ed, The Faber Book of america, Faber, 92; auth, America's rome, 2 vol, Yale, 89; Selected articles: The comic element in Hawthorne's sketches, Studies in Romanticism, 3/64; Implications of form in The Sun Also Rises, The Twenties: Poetry and Prose, 66; Romance in The Octopus, Genre, 70; Tragedy and the tragic power of laughter: The Scarlet Letter and The House of the Seven Gables, Nathaniel Hawthorne Jour, 71; Dreiserian tragedy, Studies Novel, spring 72; Man or beast: The meaning of Cooper's The Prairie, PMLA, 3/74; Whitman's lonely orbit: Salut au Monde, Walt Whitman Rev, 79; Redefining Bostonian, In: The Bostonians: Painters of an Elegant Age: 1860-1930, Boston, Mus Fine Arts, 86; Seeing Italy: The realistic rediscovery by Twain, Howells, and James, In: The Lure of Italy: American Artists and the Italian Experience: 1760-1914, Boston, Mus Fine Arts and Abrams, 92; Stereotipi, differenze, e verita nel romanzo e nel racconto Americano sull'Italia, In: Imaginari a confronto, Venise, Marsilio, 92; Edit Wharton's Italian Mask: The Valley of Decision, In: The Cambridge Companion to Edith Wharton, Cambridge, 95; Guarda che cosa hai fatto, Cristoforo!, In: La Virtu e la liberta, Torino, Agnelli, 95; What legacy and whose? Arion, Fall 95-Winter 96; What they're saying about Whitman, Raritan, spring 97. **CONTACT ADDRESS** Dept of English, Boston Univ, 236 Bay State Rd, Boston, MA 02215-1403.

VANCIL, DAVID
DISCIPLINE COMMUNICATION STUDIES **EDUCATION** Wayne State Univ, BA, MA; Univ Ill, PhD. **CAREER** Prof. **RESEARCH** Classical rhetorical theory; argumentation and debate; persuasion. **SELECTED PUBLICATIONS** Auth, Rhetoric and Argumentation; The Evolution of Parliamentary Procedure in the Assembly of Ancient Athens, Parliamentary J, 96; Ethnic Conflict and the Limitations of Parliamentary Communication and Debate, Parliamentary J, 94; Managing Conflict with Parliamentary Procedure, Parliamentary J, 93; co-auth, The Myth of Viewer-Listener Disagreement in the First Kennedy-Nixon Debate, Central States Speech J, 89. **CONTACT ADDRESS** Speech Communication Dept, Colorado State Univ, Fort Collins, CO 80523. **EMAIL** dvancil@vines.colostate.edu

VANDE BERG, LEAH R.
PERSONAL Born, IA, m, 1985 **DISCIPLINE** COMMUNICATION STUDIES **EDUCATION** Univ Iowa, BA, 72, MA, 75, PhD, 81, **CAREER** Assoc Prof, Prof, 90 to 95-, Cal State Univ; Asst Prof, 85-90, S Meth Univ; Asst Prof, 81-85, NW Univ. **HONORS AND AWARDS** Phi Beta Kappa; B Aubrey Fisher Awd; **MEMBERSHIPS** NCA; WSCA; BEA; ORWAC, NASS. **RESEARCH** Television, media, cultural values; Images of women and men in the media and arts. **SELECTED PUBLICATIONS** Coed, Critical approaches to Television, Boston, Houghton Mifflin, 98; auth, The Sports Hero Meets Mediated Celebrity, in, L A Wenner, ed, Mediasport, London Routledge, 98; auth, Liminality: Worf as Metonymic Signifier of Racial Cultural and National Differences, in: Enterprise Zones: Critical Positions on Star Trek, T Harrison ed, et al, Boulder CO, Westview Press, 96; Aaron Spelling Dramedy and Moonlighting, in: Encyc of Television, ed H Newcomb, Chicago IL, Fitzroy Dearborn, 97; Living Room Pilgrimages: Television's Cynical Commemoration of the Assassination Anniversary of John Forthcoming; Kennedy, Comm Mono. 95; On Making A Difference: Samuel L Becker's Media and Society Criticism, IA J Comm, 93. **CONTACT ADDRESS** Communication Studies Dept, California State Univ, Sacramento, Sacramento, CA 95819-6070. **EMAIL** vandeberglr@csus.edu

VANDEN BOSSCHE, CHRIS R.
DISCIPLINE VICTORIAN LITERATURE, NONFICTION PROSE **EDUCATION** Univ Calif, Santa Cruz, PhD. **CAREER** Instr, Univ Notre Dame. **RESEARCH** The history of literature and authorship as a social institution in the 19th century. **SELECTED PUBLICATIONS** Auth, Carlyle and the Search for Authority; ed, Carlyle's Historical Essays and Past and Present. **CONTACT ADDRESS** Dept of English, Univ of Notre Dame, 211 Decio, Notre Dame, IN 46556. **EMAIL** VandenBossche.1@nd.edu

VANDER MEY, RANDALL J.
PERSONAL Born 06/04/1952, Grand Rapids, MI, m, 1993, 4 children **DISCIPLINE** 18TH AND 19TH CENTURY BRITISH LITERATURE **EDUCATION** Univ Iowa, PhD, 87. **CAREER** Asst prof, Dordt Col, 83-87; adj asst prof, Iowa State Univ, 87-90; assoc prof, Westmont Col, 90-. **HONORS AND AWARDS** Danforth Nat Teaching Fel, 74-78; First prize in fiction, Evangel Press Assn Nat Wrtg Competition, 80, 82; second prize in fiction, 77; Hopwood Awd in fiction, Univ Mich, 72; contrib ed, consult, the write source, 87-. **MEMBERSHIPS** MLA; NCTE **RESEARCH** Desire in Literature **SELECTED PUBLICATIONS** Auth, God Talk, InterVarsity Press, 93; Phrasing the Lord, New Man mag, 96; Poems in Potpourri; Christian and Literature; Raintown Review; Santa Barbara Review; the cresset, Mars Hill Review, et al. **CONTACT ADDRESS** Dept of Eng, Westmont Col, 955 La Paz Rd, Santa Barbara, CA 93108-1099. **EMAIL** vanderme@westmont.edu

VANDER PLOEG, SCOTT D.
PERSONAL Born 07/03/1957, Kokomo, IN, m, 1988, 2 children **DISCIPLINE** ENGLISH LITERATURE **EDUCATION** Purdue Univ, BA, 79, MA, 82; Univ Ky, PhD, 84. **CAREER** ASSOC PROF HUM, MADISONVILLE COMMUNITY COL, UNIV KY, 88-. **MEMBERSHIPS** John Donne Soc; KY Philological Assoc; MLA; Popular Culture Assoc; Int Assoc of the Fantastic in the Arts; Int Congress on Medieval Studies; Renaissance Soc of Am. **RESEARCH** Donne; Milton: Seventeenth Century Lit; Tudor Lit; Marlowe; Shakespeare; Chaucer; Contemporary Am Fiction; Creative writing; Gothic Lit; Sci-Fi/Fantasy; Popular Culture. **SELECTED PUBLICATIONS** Auth, Coping with LAN Syndrome, Networking Computer Composition Across Kentucky, 92; auth, Reflexive Self-Reference in Donne's 'The triple Foole', Kentucky Philological Review, 95; auth, Our Development as Professionals: A Tending of Conferences, Kentucky English Bulletin, 96; auth, Donne's 'Witchcraft by a Picture' as Evidence of a Performative Aesthetic, West Virginia Shakespeare and Renaissance Association Selected Papers, 96; auth, Mason's Characters Get Some College, Border States, 99; auth, Stoker's Dracula: A Neo-gothic Experiment?, in the Fantastic Vampire, 00; auth, Framing Wyatt's Poins, Kentucky Philological Review, 00. **CONTACT ADDRESS** Madisonville Comm Col, 2000 College Dr, Madisonville, KY 42431. **EMAIL** svander@pop.uky.edu

VANDERSEE, CHARLES ANDREW
PERSONAL Born 03/25/1938, Gary, IN, s **DISCIPLINE** AMERICAN LITERATURE **EDUCATION** Valparaiso Univ, BA, 60; Univ Calif, Los Angeles, MA, 61, PhD(English), 64. **CAREER** Asst prof, 64-70, dean Echols Scholars Prog, 73-97; assoc prof English, Univ Va, 70-, Bruern fel, Univ Leeds, 68-69; Am Coun Learned Soc fel, 72-73; Nat Endowment Humanities Ed grant, 77-82. **HONORS AND AWARDS** Woodrow Wilson grad fel, 60-61; Danforth grad fel, 60-64; Bruern fel, Univ Leeds, 68-69; Am Coun Learned Soc fel, 72-73; Nat Endowment Humanities res grat, 77-82; Phi Beta Kappa chapter award (with J.C. Levenson) for best fac scholarship, Univ Va, 83; Coolidge Colloquium fel, 88. **MEMBERSHIPS** ASA; MLA; Soc Values Higher Educ. **RESEARCH** American literature--19th century; Henry Adams; American identity. **CONTACT ADDRESS** Dept of English, Univ of Virginia, 219 Bryan Hall, P O Box 400121, Charlottesville, VA 22904-4121. **EMAIL** cav7w@virginia.edu

VANDERWERKEN, DAVID LEON
PERSONAL Born 10/29/1945, Canastota, NY, m, 1981, 3 children **DISCIPLINE** AMERICAN LITERATURE **EDUCATION** Colgate Univ, BA, 68; Rice Univ, MA, 73, PhD(English), 73. **CAREER** Assoc prof to prof English, Tex Christian Univ, 71-. **MEMBERSHIPS** MLA; SCent Mod Lang Asn; Col English Asn; Conf Col Teachers English; Popular Cult Asn. **RESEARCH** William Faulkner; modern American fiction in general; sports-centered literature. **SELECTED PUBLICATIONS** Auth, Trout fishing in America and the American tradition, Critique, 74; Dos Passos' Streets of Night: A Reconsideration, Markham Rev, 10/74; English 4503: Sports in Modern American Literature, Col Lit, spring 76; Manhattan Transfer: Dos Passos' Babel story, Am Lit, 5/77; USA: Dos Passos and the Old Words, Twentieth Century Lit, 5/77; The Americanness of The Moviegoer, Notes Miss Writers, summer 79; From Tackle to Teacher: James Whitehead's Joiner, NDak Quart, autumn 79; Dos Passos' Civil Religion, Res Studies, 12/80; auth, Faulkner's Literary Children: Patterns of Development, Lang, 97. **CONTACT ADDRESS** Dept of English, Texas Christian Univ, Box 297270, Fort Worth, TX 76129-0002. **EMAIL** D.Vanderwerken@tcu.edu

VANDIVER, ELIZABETH
DISCIPLINE CLASSICS **EDUCATION** Univ Tex, Austin, PhD, 90. **CAREER** Vis asst prof, 96-98; Univ of Maryland in January 00 from Northwestern Univ, 96-; assoce head, Willard Residential Col; co-organizer, 3-yr Colloquium on Translation in Context; **HONORS AND AWARDS** Am Philological Assoc "Excellence in Teaching Awd," 98 **RESEARCH** A Reader's Guide to Shakespeare's Mythology; 19th and 20th century British and American literature **SELECTED PUBLICATIONS** Auth, Heroes in Herodotus: The Interaction of Myth and History, Studien zur klassische philol, 91; Fireflies in a Jar, Sappho in Translation, Poetry in Rev, 96; Ex hoc ingrato gaudia amore tibi: Catullus' Unhappy Love and the Modern Reader, The New Engl Class Newsletter and J, 92; Greek Heroic Mythology and the Ritual Theory of Tragedy's Origin, Text and Presentation, 91; Sound Patterns in Catullus 84, Class J, 90. **CONTACT ADDRESS** Dept. of Classics, Univ of Maryland, Col Park, 2407 Marie Mount Hall, College Park, MD 20742. **EMAIL** ev23@umail.umd.edu

VANEGMOND, PETER
PERSONAL Born 10/25/1937, AL, w, 2 children **DISCIPLINE** ENGLISH **EDUCATION** Miss Col, BA, 59; Univ Miss, MA, 61; Univ NC, Chapel Hill, PhD, 66. **CAREER** Asst to assoc prof, Univ Md, 66-; vis prof, China Textile Inst, Shanghai, PRC, 87. **HONORS AND AWARDS** Fulbright-Hayes Prof, Austria, 68-69. **RESEARCH** American poetry, global ecology. **SELECTED PUBLICATIONS** Auth, Memoirs of T. B. Harnell (72); auth, The Critical Reception of Robert Frost (74); auth, Robert Frost: A Critical Evaluation (91). **CONTACT ADDRESS** Dept English, Univ of Maryland, Col Park, 3101 Susquehanna Hall, College Park, MD 20742-8800. **EMAIL** puane@wam.umd.edu

VANGELISTI, ANITA L.
PERSONAL Born Seattle, WA **DISCIPLINE** COMMUNICATION **EDUCATION** Univ of Wash, BA, 83; MA, 85; Univ of Tex at Aust, PhD, 89. **CAREER** Asst prof, Univ of Iowa, 89-91; asst prof to assoc prof, Univ of Tex at Austin, 91-. **HONORS AND AWARDS** Teaching Excellence Awd, Col of Commun; New Contribution Awd, International Soc for the Study of Personal Relationships; Dean's Fellow, Univ Tex, 00. **MEMBERSHIPS** Nat Commun Asn, Int Commun Asn, Am Psychol Asn, Int Soc for the Study of Personal Relationships. **RESEARCH** Interpersonal communication, family and relational communication, communication and emotion. **SELECTED PUBLICATIONS** Co-ed, Explaining Family Interactions, Sage (Thousand Oaks, CA), 95; co-ed, Teaching Communication: Theory, Research, and Methods, Lawrence Erlbaum (Mahwah, NJ), 90 & 99; coauth, "Family Portraits: Stories as Standards for Family Interaction," J of Soc and Personal Relationships 16 (99): 335-368; coauth, "Desire for Change in One's Partner as a Predictor of the Demand/Withdraw Pattern of Marital Communication," Commun Monographs 66 (99): 66-89; coauth, Interpersonal Communication and Human Relation-

ships, Allyn & Bacon (Boston, MA), 00; coauth, "Shame," Encyclopedia of Human Emotions, Macmillan (New York, NY), in press; coauth, "Communication, Relationships, and Health," Handbook of Language and Social Psychology, Wiley (New York, NY), in press; coauth, "Making Sense of Hurtful Interactions in Close Relationships: When Hurt Feelings Create Distance," Attribution, Communication Behavior, and Close Relationships, Cambridge Univ (New York), in press; coauth, "When Words Hurt: The Effects of Perceived Intentionality on Interpersonal Relationships," J of Soc and Person Relationships (in press). **CONTACT ADDRESS** Dept Commun Studies, Univ of Texas, Austin, Austin, TX 78712-1013. **EMAIL** a.vangelisti@mail.utexas.edu

VANN, JERRY DON
PERSONAL Born 01/17/1938, Weatherford, TX, m, 1958, 2 children **DISCIPLINE** ENGLISH **EDUCATION** Tex Christian Univ, BA, 59, MA, 60; Tex Technol Col, PhD(English), 67. **CAREER** From instr to Regent's Prof of English, Univ N Tex, 64-. **RESEARCH** Serialization of Dickens' novels; Victorian poetry; the English novel. **CONTACT ADDRESS** 811 W Oak, Denton, TX 76201. **EMAIL** vann@unt.edu

VANN, ROBERTA JEANNE
PERSONAL Born 12/17/1947, Indianapolis, IN, 1 child **DISCIPLINE** ENGLISH **EDUCATION** Ind Univ, AB, 70, MS, 73, PhD(English educ), 78. **CAREER** Instr teaching English as for lang, Haile Selaissie I Univ, Gondar, Ethiopia, 70-71; Fulbright lectr, Univ Gdansk, Poland, 74-76; asst prof English, 78-83, assoc prof, 83-91, prof 81-, dir intensive English & orientation prog, Iowa State Univ, 80-, Lang consult, US, Int Info Agency, 75-95. **MEMBERSHIPS** NCTE; Teaching English to Speakers Other Lang. **RESEARCH** Second language learning. **SELECTED PUBLICATIONS** Auth, Bilingual education today: The unresolved issues, Lang Arts, 2/78; Oral and written syntactic relationships in second language learning, In: On TESOL '79: The Learner in Focus, TESOL, 79; co-ed, Connections and Contrasts: Exploring Speaking and Writing Relationships & auth, Bridging the gap between oral and written communication in EFL, In: Connections and Contrasts, NCTE, 81. **CONTACT ADDRESS** English Dept, Iowa State Univ of Science and Tech, Ames, IA 50011-0002. **EMAIL** rvann@iastate.edu

VANNATTA, DENNIS
PERSONAL Born 11/21/1946, Appleton City, MO, m, 2 children **DISCIPLINE** CONTEMPORARY LITERATURE **EDUCATION** Univ Mo, PhD. **CAREER** English and Lit, Univ Ark **SELECTED PUBLICATIONS** Auth, E.H. Bates; The English Short Story, 1945-1980; Tennessee Williams; This Time, This Place; Prayers for the Dead. **CONTACT ADDRESS** Univ of Arkansas, Little Rock, 2801 S University Ave., Little Rock, AR 72204-1099. **EMAIL** dpvannatta@ualr.edu

VARADHARAJAN, ASHA
DISCIPLINE ENGLISH LITERATURE **EDUCATION** Univ Saskatchewan, PhD. **CAREER** Dept Eng, Queen's Univ **MEMBERSHIPS** Member of the Bush Program for excellence and diversity in teaching at the Univ of Minn, 94-95. **RESEARCH** Post-colonial and minority literatures; literary theory; cultural studies; race and gender theory; the Frankfurt School; theories of pedagogy and the politics of the institution. **SELECTED PUBLICATIONS** Auth, Exotic Parodies: Subjectivity in Adorno, Said, Spivak, Univ Minn, 95; Theory and Critical Practice, Univ Toronto, 94; Dissensus, Dissolution, and the Possibility of Community, Univ Toronto Quarterly, 97. **CONTACT ADDRESS** English Dept, Queen's Univ at Kingston, Kingston, ON, Canada K7L 3N6. **EMAIL** varadhar@qsilver.queensu.ca

VARDY, AGNES HUSZAR
PERSONAL Born 01/03/1943, Debrecen, Hungary, m, 1962, 3 children **DISCIPLINE** HUNGARIAN LITERATURE **EDUCATION** Ohio State Univ, BA, 64; Univ Pittsburgh, MA, 67; Univ Budapest, PhD, 70. **CAREER** Asst prof to full prof, Robert Morris Col, 71-. **HONORS AND AWARDS** Berzseny Literary Prize, Budapest, 92; Arpad Acad Gold Medal, 78. **MEMBERSHIPS** Intl PEN, Hungarian Writers' Fed. **RESEARCH** Central European Romanticism, Hungarian emigre literature, social-historical novel. **SELECTED PUBLICATIONS** Auth, Mimi, 99. **CONTACT ADDRESS** Dept Comm, Robert Morris Col, Pennsylvania, 600 5th Ave, Pittsburgh, PA 15219-3010.

VARNUM-GALLANT, BILLIE M.
PERSONAL Born 06/27/1951, Elberton, GA, m, 1982 **DISCIPLINE** ENGLISH, READING EDUCATION, COMMUNICATION ARTS **EDUCATION** Univ Ga, BA, 73; Med, 76; Ed S, 78; Ga State Univ, PhD, 84. **CAREER** Asst prof, Brenau Univ, 79-82; assoc prof, 82-85; prof, 85-. **HONORS AND AWARDS** LEAP Awd; Fac Mem of the Year; Who's Who Am Teach. **MEMBERSHIPS** NCTE. **RESEARCH** Business communication; composition; famous people who were English Majors; southern literature, **SELECTED PUBLICATIONS** Coauth, "Assessment Instrument: Personal Reflections from Multi-Disciplinary Perspectives," and "Assessment Instrument: Integrating Writing and Critical Thinking Competencies in the Humanities," in Assessing General Education Outcomes for the Individual Student: Performance Assessment-as-Learning Part 1 Designing and Implementing Performance Assessment Instruments, eds. Judeen Schute, Georgine Loaker (Alverno Coll: Writer's Choice, 94). **CONTACT ADDRESS** Dept Humanities, Brenau Univ, 204 Boulevard, Gainesville, FL 30501-3630.

VARONA, FEDERICO
PERSONAL Born 01/06/1946, Spain, m, 1984, 2 children **DISCIPLINE** COMMUNICATIONS STUDIES **EDUCATION** Univ Kansas, MA, 88; PhD, 91. **CAREER** Chemn and prof, Univ Sandriar, Guatemala, 81-86; assoc prof, San Jose State Univ, 91-; asst prof, San Jose State Univ, 91-97; assoc prof, San Jose State Univ, 97-. **HONORS AND AWARDS** Vis grant, USIA, 84; Fulbright Scholar, 86-90. **MEMBERSHIPS** Natl Commun Asn; Int Commun Asn; ADELIN (Spain); Western States Commun Asn. **RESEARCH** Organizational communications; intracultural communications. **SELECTED PUBLICATIONS** Auth, Un Estudio Comparativo de la Satisfaaccion con la Comunicacion y la Satifaccion con el trabajo en dos Companiaas Guatemaltecas, Cuadernos de Dia.logos de la Comunicacion, 28, (93): 1-16; auth, Conceptualizacion y Supervision de la Comunicacion y el Compromiso Organizacional, Dia.Logos de la Comunicacion, 35, (93): 68-77; auth, Las Auditorias de la Comunicacion Organizacional desde una Perspetiva Academica Estadounidense, Dia.logos de lal Comunicacion, 39, Lima, Peru, (94): 55-64; auth, Las Nuevas Tecnolgias de la Comunicacion: Impacto en la Cultura y la Ocmuncacion Organizacional, revista Comunicacion, 17, (94): 92-105; auth, Un Estudio Comparativo de la Satisfaccion con la Comunicacion y la satifaccion con el Tabajo en dos Companias Guatemaltecas, Revista de Ciencias de la Informacion, 10, (94): 125-144; auth, Comunicacion y Compromiso Organizacional, Comunicacion Interna, Informes, 45, (95): 1-12; auth, Las Nuevas Tecnolgias de la Comunicacion y su Impacto en la Cultrua y la Comunicacion Organizacional, Comunicacion Interna, Informes, 29, (95): 1-19; auth, "La comunicacion computarizada y su impacto en las organizaciones," CHASQUI, Revista Latinoamericana de Comunicaacion, no. 64, (98): 46-50; auth, "La ensenanza de la comunicacion empresarial en los Estados Unidos," La Comunicacion Interna en Espana, Guia Oficial, (99): 32-35; auth, "Communicacion Estrategica Interna,"Comunicacion Interna, Noticias, Ano XIV, no. 1889, 99. **CONTACT ADDRESS** Commun Studies Dept, San Jose State Univ, San Jose, CA 95192-0112. **EMAIL** fvarona@email.sjsu.edu

VARTABEDIAN, ROBERT A.
PERSONAL Born 08/27/1952, Fresno, CA, m, 1978, 2 children **DISCIPLINE** SPEECH COMMUNICATION **EDUCATION** CA State Univ, Fresno, BA, 74, CA Teaching Credential, 75; Wichita State Univ, MA, 80; Univ OK, PhD, 81. **CAREER** Graduate asst, part-time instr, CA State Univ, Fresno, 74-75, 77; res asst, Wichita State Univ, 77-78; grad asst, Univ OK, 78-80; asst prof, East Central OK State Univ, 80-81; Dir of forensics, 81-86, head, div of rhetoric and commun, 85-88, coord, grad studies in commun, 86-87, asst dean of graduate studies, Wichita State Univ, 87-88; head, dept of Art, Commun, & Theatre, 88-93, assoc prof, 88-92, prof, West TX A&M Univ, 92-; dean, Western Carolina Univ, Col Arts & Sciences. **HONORS AND AWARDS** Outstanding Teaching award, Univ OK, 80; Outstanding Dir of Forensics Awd, Univ UT, 83; President's Awd, Nat Intercollegiate Cross Examination Debate Asn, 86; Mortar Board Teaching Awd, Wichita State Univ, 88; Dean's nominee for Outstanding Graduate Fac Awd, WTAMU, 91, 93; Carnegie Found Prof of the Year, WTAMU, 94; Greek Council, Outstanding Fac Member Awd, WTAMU, 96; Univ Teaching Excellence Awd, WTAMU, 96; Univ Piper Professorship, WTAMU, 97. **MEMBERSHIPS** Am Forensic Asn; Central States Commun Asn; Cross Examination Debate Asn; Int Commun Asn; TX Speech Commun Asn; Nat Forensic Asn; Nat Commun Asn; West TX Speech Commun Asn. **RESEARCH** Presidential rhetoric; political communication; rhetorical criticism. **SELECTED PUBLICATIONS** Co-auth, Humor in the Workplace: A Communication Challenge, in Resources in Ed, 93; auth, Recruitment and Retention of Graduate Faculty at the Non-Doctoral Graduate Program, in Resources in Ed, 93; co-auth, Self-Disclosure and Decreased Persuasiveness of Political Speakers, in Resources in Ed, 94; auth, the Loud, Clear, and Transporting Voice of Oral Interpretation, in Resources in Ed, 95; co-auth, Self-Disclosure and Decreased Persuasiveness of Political Speakers, Speech Commun Annual, 10, 96; auth, Scholarly vs Non-Scholarly Print Sources, in Teaching Ideas for the Basic Communication Course; Audience Analysis, in Teaching Ideas for the Basic Communication Course; co-auth, Jones v. Clinton and the Apologetic Imperative, Speaker and Gavel. **CONTACT ADDRESS** Col of Arts & Sciences, Western Carolina Univ, Cullowhee, NC 28723. **EMAIL** vartabdn@wcu.edu

VASTA, EDWARD
DISCIPLINE MEDIEVAL LITERATURE **EDUCATION** Stanford Univ, PhD. **CAREER** Prof to prof emeritus, English, Univ Notre Dame. **RESEARCH** Bakhtinian approaches to medieval literature. **SELECTED PUBLICATIONS** Auth, The Spiritual Basis of Piers Plowman; ed, Interpretations of Piers Plowman and Chaucerian Problems and Perspectives. **CONTACT ADDRESS** Dept of English, Univ of Notre Dame, 517 Flanner Hall, Notre Dame, IN 46556. **EMAIL** edward.vasta.1@nd.edu

VATZ, RICHARD E.
PERSONAL Born 12/21/1946, Pittsburgh, PA, m, 1977, 2 children **DISCIPLINE** COMMUNICATIONS **EDUCATION** Univ Pittsburgh, BA, 69; MA, 70; PhD, 76. **CAREER** Instr to Full Prof, Towson Univ, 73-. **HONORS AND AWARDS** Thomas Szasz Awd, 94; Outstanding Teaching Awd, Towson Univ. **MEMBERSHIPS** Nat Comm Asn, Eastern Comm Asn. **RESEARCH** Political rhetoric, Rhetoric and psychiatry. **SELECTED PUBLICATIONS** Auth, "Psychobabble Revisited," Forbes Media Critic, 95; auth, "Hyperactivity?," Mothering 95; auth, "Overreacting to Attention Deficit Disorder," USA Today Magazine, 95; auth, "Rhetoric and Psychiatry," in Encyclopedia of Rhetoric and Composition, 96; auth, "Should We Destigmatize Mental Illness?," USA Today Magazine, 96; auth, "Better Late Than Never," Forbes Media Critic, 96; auth, "Is Mental Illness a Myth?," Abnormal Psychology, 96; auth, "PARITY: The New Buzzword in Mental Health," USA Today Magazine, 97; auth, "How Accurate Are Media Depictions of ADD?," USA Today Magazine, 97; auth, "Should Mental Illness Fall Under the Americans with Disabilities Act?," USA Today Magazine, 99; auth, "The Myth of the Rhetorical Situation," Contemporary Rhetorical Theory, 99; auth, "Dr. Kevorkian on the air: CBS and 60 Minutes Drop the Ball," USA Today Magazine, 99. **CONTACT ADDRESS** Dept Mass Comm, Towson State Univ, 8000 York Rd, Baltimore, MD 21252-0001. **EMAIL** rvatz@saber.towson.edu

VAUGHAN, VIRGINIA M.
PERSONAL Born 01/12/1947, Washington, DC, m, 1983 **DISCIPLINE** ENGLISH **EDUCATION** Univ Mich, BA, 68; MA, 70; PhD, 72. **CAREER** Asst Prof, Allegheny Col, 73-76; From Asst Prof to Prof, Clark Univ, 76-. **HONORS AND AWARDS** Phi Beta Kappa; O.B. Hardison Fel to Folger Shakespeare Libr, 87; Clark Univ Sr Fac Fel, 93; Andrea B. and Peter D. Klein '64 Distinguished Professorship, 00; Mellon Fel, Folger Libr, 01. **MEMBERSHIPS** MLA, Shakespeare Asn of Am. **RESEARCH** Shakespeare and Renaissance Drama. **SELECTED PUBLICATIONS** Auth, The Drama as Propaganda; A Study of the Troublesome Raigne of King John, Univ of Salzburg: Inst fur Englische Sprache and Literatur, 74; coauth, Othello: An Annotated Bibliography, Garland Publ (NY), 90; coauth, Othello: New Perspectives, Fairleigh Dickinson Univ Press (Cranbury, NJ), 91; coauth, Shakespeare's Caliban: A Cultural History, Cambridge Univ Press (Cambridge), 91, and Seidosha Press (Tokyo), 99; auth, Othello: A Contextual History, Cambridge Univ Press (Cambridge), 94, and in Shakespeare Criticism Yearbk (Detroit: Gale Res Press, 95), 330-338; auth, "Race Mattered: 'Othello' in Late Eighteenth-Century England," Shakespeare Surv 51 (98): 57-66; coauth, Critical Essays on Shakespeare's 'The Tempest'," G.K. Hall (NY), 98; coauth, Playing the Globe: Genre and Geography in English Renaissance Drama, Fairleigh Dickinson Univ Press (Cranbury, NJ), 98; coauth, The Tempest, Arden Ed Third Ser, Thomas Nelson and Sons Ltd (London), 99; auth, "Stephen Greenblatt and the New Historicism," in The Edinburgh Encyclopedia of Literary Criticism and Theory since 1940, ed. Julian Wolfreys (Edinburgh, forthcoming). **CONTACT ADDRESS** Dept English, Clark Univ, 950 Main St, Worcester, MA 01610-1400. **EMAIL** vvaughan@clarku.edu

VAUGHN, GARY LEE
PERSONAL Born 11/13/1951, Cincinnati, OH, d **DISCIPLINE** ENGLISH **EDUCATION** Univ Cincinnati, BA, 73; MA, 76. **CAREER** Instr in English, Univ of Cincinnati, 86-90; Asst Prof, Univ of Cincinnati, 90-. **MEMBERSHIPS** CCC, NCTE. **RESEARCH** Composition, Science Fiction, Mystery Fiction. **SELECTED PUBLICATIONS** Auth, "Fare From the Madding Crowd: The Lighter Side of Error in Student Writing", (99). **CONTACT ADDRESS** Dept Language Arts, Univ of Cincinnati, PO Box 210205, Cincinnati, OH 45221-0205. **EMAIL** vaughn@ucollege.uc.edu

VAUSE, DEBORAH
DISCIPLINE LITERATURE **EDUCATION** NC State Univ, BA; Univ NC at Chapel Hill, PhD. **SELECTED PUBLICATIONS** Area: the medieval monster; writer Stephen King. **CONTACT ADDRESS** York Col, Pennsylvania, 441 Country Club Road, York, PA 17403.

VAUSE, L. MIKEL
PERSONAL m, 4 children **DISCIPLINE** ENGLISH **EDUCATION** Bowling Green Univ, PhD. **CAREER** Vis scholar, University of Leeds, 96; Prof, Weber State Univ. **HONORS AND AWARDS** Crystal Crest Master Awd; The George & Beth Lowe Teaching Awd; The Continuing Ed Prof of the Yr Awd; Honors Cortez Prof Awd; dir, weber state univ honors prog. **MEMBERSHIPS** Weber Pathways; The Great West Trail Asn; Nat Undergrad Lit Conf (co-dir & founder); N Am Interdisciplinary Wilderness Conf, (co-dir & founder); Nat Advisory Bd for ASLE; MESA Advisory Bd. **SELECTED PUBLICATIONS** Auth, On Mountains and Mountaineers, Mountain n' Airs Books, 90; auth, Wilderness Tapestry, Univ of Nev Press, 92; auth, The Peregrine Reader, Gibbs M Smith, 97. **CONTACT ADDRESS** Dept of English, Weber State Univ, 2904 Univ Cir, Ogden, UT 84408-2904.

VAVRA, EDWARD
PERSONAL Born 04/06/1946, Endicott, NY, m, 1971, 1 child **DISCIPLINE** ENGLISH **EDUCATION** SUNY, BA, 67; Cornell Univ, MA, 74; PhD, 75. **CAREER** Assoc prof, Shenandoah Univ, 76-90; assoc prof, Pa Col of Tech, 90-. **MEMBERSHIPS** NCTE, AIEG, ASCD. **RESEARCH** Natural language development, The teaching of grammar. **SELECTED PUBLICATIONS** Auth, "On Not Teaching Grammar," English Journal, (96): 32-37; auth, "Welcome to the Shoe Store?" English Journal, (93): 81-84; auth, "Vygotsky and Grammar Instruction," Composition Chronicle, (90): 4-6; auth, "Grammar and Syntax: The Student's Perspective," English Journal, (87): 42-48; auth, "Professors Have Failed to Teach Evaluation," Chronicle of Higher Education, (86); auth, "Preposition Proposition," Instructor, 86; auth, "Review of What Makes Writing good," Teaching English in the Two-Year Col, (85): 318-320; auth, "Response to Patrick Hartwell," College English, (85): 647-649; auth, "The Unmentionable Politics of Fyodor Gladkov's Cement," Russian Language Journal, (84): 101-133; auth, "Meditations on the Teaching of Russian," AATSEEL Newsletter, 80. **CONTACT ADDRESS** Dept Interdisciplinary Studies, Pennsylvania Col of Tech, 1 Col Ave, Williamsport, PA 17701-5778. **EMAIL** evavra@sunlink.net

VEANER, ALLEN B.
PERSONAL Born 03/17/1929, Harrisburg, PA, m, 1983, 2 children **DISCIPLINE** LIBRARY, INFORMATION SCIENCE **EDUCATION** Gettysburg Col, BA, 49; Hebrew Un Col, BHL, 52; Simmons Col, MLS, 60; Hebrew Un Col, MA, 69; Harvard Univ, 57 **CAREER** Chaplain, 54-58, US Army; Cataloger, 57-59, Widener Lib, Harvard Univ; Spec, 59-64, Harvard; Head of Acquisit, 64-67, Stanford; Asst Dir, 67-77, Stanford; Libr, 77-83, Univ of CA, Santa Barbara; Principal, 83-91, Allen B. Veaner Assoc; Adj Asst Prof, 95-, Univ of AZ **HONORS AND AWARDS** Phi Beta kappa; Recipient of ACRL Awd, "Academic Res Librarian of the Year," 98. **MEMBERSHIPS** Am Lib Asn; Am Soc of Indexers **RESEARCH** Indexing **SELECTED PUBLICATIONS** Auth, Academic Librarianship in a Transformational Age: Program, Politics, and Personnel, Boston: G.K. Hall, 90 **CONTACT ADDRESS** PO Box 30786, Tucson, AZ 85751-0786. **EMAIL** veaner@worldnet.att.net

VECERA, GRANT
PERSONAL Born 06/19/1963, Indianapolis, IN, s **DISCIPLINE** ENGLISH **EDUCATION** Ind Univ, BA, 88; Univ Ark, MFA, 93. **CAREER** Instr, Univ of Ark, 89-93; adj instr, Ind Univ E, 94-95; assoc lectr, Ind Univ Purdue, 96-; assoc lectr, Butler Univ, 97-. **RESEARCH** Religious Studies, Post-Modern Cultural Studies, Eastern World Philosophy, Spirituality. **SELECTED PUBLICATIONS** Auth, "The Hole In My Chest", Birmingham Poetry Rev 13, (95): 43; auth, Two Ugly Robins", Lightning & Ash 1.1 (96): 13; auth, The Largemouth Bass", Blue Mesa Rev 1.8 (96): 181; auth, "Jar 899", A New Song 2.2 (97): 18; auth, "Warehouse", Eratica 2.4 (97): 31; auth, "Coin Laundry, Washington DC, June 97", Eratica 2.4 (97): 30; auth, "The Knowledge of Chicken Bones", Tinker's Shop 2.4 (97): 2; auth, "Adolescence", Birmingham Poetry Rev 20 (00): 39; auth, "Kitchen", Am Poets & Poetry, (forthcoming); auth, "Goldfish Sunday", The Silver Web: A Magazine of the Surreal, (forthcoming); **CONTACT ADDRESS** Dept English, Butler Univ, 4600 Sunset Ave, Indianapolis, IN 46208-3443. **EMAIL** gromet@indy.net

VELER, RICHARD
DISCIPLINE AMERICAN LITERATURE **EDUCATION** Wittenberg Univ, AB; Harvard Univ, MA; Ohio State Univ, PhD. **HONORS AND AWARDS** Woodrow Wilson fel, Harvard; Distinguished Tchng Award; General Sec, Wittenberg Univ; Chairperson, Engl dept; Pres, Col Eng Asn Ohio, Vis Prof, England. **RESEARCH** Mark Twain, Edgar Allan Poe, **SELECTED PUBLICATIONS** Area:Poe **CONTACT ADDRESS** Wittenberg Univ, Springfield, OH 45501-0720. **EMAIL** rveler@wittenberg.edu

VELIE, ALAN R.
PERSONAL Born 11/16/1937, New York, NY, m, 1962, 2 children **DISCIPLINE** ENGLISH **EDUCATION** Harvard Univ, BA, 59; Stanford Univ, MA, 66, PhD, 69. **CAREER** From instr to prof, 67-94, David Ross Boyd Prof English, Okla Univ, 94-, chmn dept, 78-82. **HONORS AND AWARDS** NEH fel, 73; Amoco Awd for Outstanding Teaching, 72; Baldwin Awd for Excellence in Classroom Instruction, 86; Mortarboard Honor Soc Outstanding Fac Mem, 88-89; Summer Fac Instructional Awd, 90. **MEMBERSHIPS** MLA; Am Folklore Soc. **RESEARCH** American Indian literature; Shakespeare; folklore. **SELECTED PUBLICATIONS** Co-ed, Blood and Knavery, Fairleigh Dickinson Univ Press, 73; auth, Shakespeare's Repentence Plays, The Search for an Adequate Form, Fairleigh Dickinson Univ Press, 73; co-ed, Appleseeds and Beercans, Goodyear, 74; auth, Shakespeare's use of folklore in The Merchant of Venice, Fabula, 76; Aztekisches Erzahlgut, in Enzyklopadie des Marchens, 76; The Dragon Killer, The Wild Man, and Hal, Fabula, 77; ed, American Indian Literature, Okla Univ Press, 79, rev ed, 91; Four American Indian Literary Masters, Okla Univ, 82; co-transl, Structural Semantics, Univ Nebr Press, 83; auth, The Lightning Within, Univ Nebr Press, 91; Native American Perspectives on Literature and History, Univ Okla Press, 95; author of numerous journal articles and book chapters. **CONTACT ADDRESS** Dept of English, Univ of Oklahoma, 760 Van Vleet Oval, Norman, OK 73019-2020. **EMAIL** alanvelie@ou.edu

VELIMIROVIC, MILOS
DISCIPLINE MUSIC HISTORY **EDUCATION** Harvard Univ, PhD. **CAREER** Dept Music, Va Univ **RESEARCH** Byzantine music; history of Slavonic music; history of Italian opera in the 18th century. **SELECTED PUBLICATIONS** Auth, The Melodies of the Ninth century Kanon for St. Demetrius, 84; Dr. Charles Burney and Russian Music, 93. **CONTACT ADDRESS** Dept of Music, Univ of Virginia, Charlottesville, VA 22903. **EMAIL** mmv@virginia.edu

VENARDE, BRUCE L.
PERSONAL Born 09/14/1962, Philadelphia, PA **DISCIPLINE** HISTORY, LITERATURE **EDUCATION** Swartmore Col, BA, 84; Harvard Univ, AM, 85, PhD, 92. **CAREER** Lectr, Harvard Univ, 92-95; vis asst prof, Tufts Univ, 94-96; asst prof, Univ Pittsburgh, 96-99, assoc prof, 99-. **MEMBERSHIPS** Medieval Acad of Am, Am Hist Asn. **RESEARCH** Medieval European history and culture, France, Christianity, Latin literature, gender and sexuality. **SELECTED PUBLICATIONS** Auth, " La reforme a Apt (X-XII siecles): Patrimoine, patronage et famille," Provence historique 38 (98): 131-147; auth, "Praesidentes Negotiis: Abbesses as Managers in Twelfth-Century France," in Samuel K. Cohn Jr. and Steven A. Epstein, eds, Portraits of Medieval and Renaissance Living: Essays in Memory of David Herlihy, Univ Mich Press (96); auth, Women's Monasticism and Medieval Society: Nunneries in France and England, 890-1215, Cornell Univ Press (97, paperback, 99); auth, "Drogo of Sint-Winoksbergen, Life of Godelieve, in Thomas F. Head, ed, Medieval Hagiography: An Anthology, Garland Pub (2000); auth, Robert of Arbrissel: A Reader, Cath Univ Press Am (forthcoming). **CONTACT ADDRESS** Dept Hist, Univ of Pittsburgh, WPHH 3M26, Pittsburgh, PA 15260. **EMAIL** bvenarde@pitt.edu

VENDLER, HELEN HENNESSY
PERSONAL Born 04/30/1933, Boston, MA, d, 1 child **DISCIPLINE** LITERATURE **EDUCATION** Emmanuel Col, AB 54; Harvard Univ, PhD 60. **CAREER** Harvard Univ, vis prof 81-85, prof 85-90, univ prof 90-; Boston Univ, assoc prof 66-69, prof 69-85; Smith Col, asst prof 64-66; Swarthmore and Haverford Colleges, lectr 63-64; Cornell Univ, inst 60-63; The New Yorker, poetry critic, 78-97. **HONORS AND AWARDS** Charles Stuart Parnell fel; Wilson Cen fel; several NEH; AAAL Awd; Guggenheim fel; honorary degrees from: ntl univ ireland; wabash col; univ cambridge; trinity col ireland; univ toronto; dartmouth col; bates col; univ ma; washington univ; fitchburg state univ; columbia univ; union col; univ hartford; kenyon col; univ oslo; smith col; ya **MEMBERSHIPS** MLA; AAAS; AAAL; APS. **RESEARCH** English and American **SELECTED PUBLICATIONS** Auth, Seamus Heaney, London Harper Collins, 98; The Art of Shakespeare's Sonnets, Cambridge MA, HUP, 97; Poems, Poets Poetry, Boston MA, Bedford Books, 96; The Breaking of Style: Hopkins, Heaney, Graham, Cambridge MA, HUP, 95; Soul Says: On Recent Poetry, Cambridge MA, HUP, 95. **CONTACT ADDRESS** Dept of English, Harvard Univ, Baker Center, Cambridge, MA 02138.

VENN, GEORGE
PERSONAL Born 10/12/1943, Tacoma, WA, d, 2 children **DISCIPLINE** ENGLISH, LITERATURE, WRITING **EDUCATION** Col Idaho, BA, 67; Univ Mont, MFA, 70. **CAREER** Prof, Eastern Ore Univ, 70-. **HONORS AND AWARDS** Andres Berger Awd in Poetry; Multiculture Pub Awd, NCTE; Stewart Holbrook Awd; Ore Book Awd; Ore Comm for the Humanities Fel; Pushcart Prize in Poetry; NEH Fel, Breadloaf Writer's Conf Fel. **MEMBERSHIPS** Western Lit Assoc; NCTE; PEN West; Poets and Writers; Ore Hist Soc. **RESEARCH** Wester/Northwestern Americana, Poetry and Poetics, Literary History, Regionalism, Professional Editing and Publishing, Eco-criticism, Conservation. **SELECTED PUBLICATIONS** Auth, "Excuses in Snow", The Kerf, (May 98): 22-23; auth, "Segues for Interstate 84", Hubbub, (Sept 98); auth, "A.J. Dickey Couldn't Run the Ends", Talking River Rev, (Winter 98): 117; auth, "Keynote for March 1", From a Writer's Hat, Eastern Ore Univ, (98): 99; auth, "Who Are Oregon's Writers?", OLA Quarterly 5.2 (99): 5-7; auth, "Singing the Silver Valley Cannonball", Idaho Yesterdays 43.3 (99): 3-12; auth, "On Burnside", Portland Lights: A Poetry Anthology, eds Nemirow and LaMorticella, Press 22 (Portland, 99): 17; auth, West of Paradise, Woodcraft of Ore, 99; auth, "Faith of our Fathers", World View and the American West: Essays in Honor of Barre Toelken, ed Polly Stewart, Utah State Univ Pr, (Logan, UT), (forthcoming). **CONTACT ADDRESS** Dept Arts and Sci, Eastern OR Univ, 1410 L Ave, La Grande, OR 97850-2899. **EMAIL** venng@eou.edu

VERDERBER, RUDOLPH FRANCIS
PERSONAL Born 08/07/1933, Cleveland, OH, m, 1973, 3 children **DISCIPLINE** SPEECH **EDUCATION** Bowling Green State Univ, BS, 55, MA, 56; Univ MO, Columbia, PhD, 62. **CAREER** From instr to assoc prof, 59-71, Prof Speech, Univ Cincinnati, 71. **MEMBERSHIPS** Nat Commun Asn; Cent States Speech Asn. **RESEARCH** Rhetoric and public address; argumentation and debate; interpersonal commun. **SELECTED PUBLICATIONS** Auth, An Invitation to Debate, Krieg, 71; The Challenge of Effective Speaking, 70, 73, 76, 79, 82, 85, 88, 91, 94, 97; Communicate!, 75, 78, 81, 84, 87, 90, 93, 96, 99; Inter-Act, 77, 80, 83, 86, 89, 92, 95, 98, Wadsworth. **CONTACT ADDRESS** Dept of Commun, Univ of Cincinnati, PO Box 210184, Cincinnati, OH 45221-0184. **EMAIL** rudolph.verderber@uc.edu

VERRICO, ROSE MAY
PERSONAL Born 05/01/1933, England, m, 1953, 2 children **DISCIPLINE** ENGLISH **EDUCATION** Univ Calif Irvine, BA, 88; Calif State Univ Fullerton, MA, 91; Univ Calif Irvine, TESOL, 96. **CAREER** Teaching asst, Calif State Univ Fullerton, 88-91; teaching asst to grad admin, Univ Calif Irvine, 91-. **MEMBERSHIPS** MLA; TESOL; ARA. **RESEARCH** English and comparative literature. **SELECTED PUBLICATIONS** Auth, "Detective Fiction and the Quest Hero," in Clues: A Journal of Detection (Bowling Green State Univ Pop Pr, 93); auth, "Women and the Problem of Bildung," Mid Atlantic Writers Rev (93). **CONTACT ADDRESS** 24641 Benjamin Cir, Dana Point, CA 92629-6013. **EMAIL** rmverric@uci.edu

VERSLUIS, ARTHUR
DISCIPLINE LITERATURE **EDUCATION** Univ Mich, PhD, 90. **CAREER** Prof, Washburn Univ, 90-94; Fulbright scholar, Univ Duesseldorf, 94-95; prof, Mich State Univ, 95-. **HONORS AND AWARDS** Hopwood Awd Lit. **MEMBERSHIPS** Am Acad Relig. **RESEARCH** American literature; American transcendentalism and Asian religions; Western esoteric traditions. **SELECTED PUBLICATIONS** Auth, Wisdom's Children: A Christian Esoteric Tradition, 99; auth, The Hermetic Book of Nature: An American Revolution in Consciousness, 97; auth, Gnosis and Literature, 96; auth, Theosophia: Hidden Dimensions of Christianity, 94; auth, Native American Traditions, 94; auth, American Transcendentalism and Asian Religions, 93. **CONTACT ADDRESS** Dept of Literature, Michigan State Univ, ATL Dept 235 Bessey Hall, East Lansing, MI 48824. **EMAIL** versluis@pilot.msu.edu

VEST, DAVID
DISCIPLINE COMMUNICATION STUDIES **EDUCATION** Monteith Col, PhB, Wayne State Univ, MSA; Central Mich Univ, PhD. **CAREER** Prof. **RESEARCH** Film theory and criticism; video production; quantitative methods. **SELECTED PUBLICATIONS** Auth, Prime-Time Pilots: A Content Analysis of Changes in Gender Representation, J Broadcasting Electronic Media, 94; co-auth, Electrical Engineers; Perceptions of Communication Training and Their Recommendations for Curricular Change: Results of a National Survey, 96; Enhancing Engineering Students' Communication Skills through Multimedia Instruction, J Engineering Edu, 95; Developing Online Writing Aids for Electrical Engineering Majors-a Progress Report, 95; Relating Communication Training to Workplace Requirements: The Perspective of New Engineers, 95. **CONTACT ADDRESS** Speech Communication Dept, Colorado State Univ, 202 Eddy Bldg, Fort Collins, CO 80523-1783. **EMAIL** dvest@vines.colostate.edu

VESTERMAN, WILLIAM
PERSONAL Born 02/08/1942, East Orange, NJ, m, 1964, 3 children **DISCIPLINE** ENGLISH **EDUCATION** Amherst Col, BA, 64; Rutgers Univ, PhD(English), 71. **CAREER** From instr to asst prof, 69-75, Assoc Prof English, Livingston Col, Rutgers Univ, 75-, Consult writing, Bell Lab, 75- **MEMBERSHIPS** Am Soc 18th Century Studies; Asn Teachers Tech Writing. **RESEARCH** Modernism; Vladimir Nabokov; eighteenth century. **CONTACT ADDRESS** Rutgers, The State Univ of New Jersey, New Brunswick, New Brunswick, NJ 08903.

VIATOR, TIMOTHY J.
PERSONAL Born 09/20/1956, Lafayette, LA **DISCIPLINE** LATE RENAISSANCE BRITISH LITERATURE, CONTEMPORARY DRAMA, LATINO LITERATURE **EDUCATION** Univ La, Lafayette, MA; BA; Auburn Univ, PhD. **CAREER** Assoc prof, Rowan Col of NJers. **RESEARCH** Plays of Colley Cibber. **SELECTED PUBLICATIONS** Articles in drama, theater history, comedy, and bibliography. **CONTACT ADDRESS** Rowan Univ, Glassboro, NJ 08028-1701. **EMAIL** viator@rowan.edu

VICKERS, ANITA M.
PERSONAL Born 10/25/1952, Chicago Heights, IL, s **DISCIPLINE** LITERATURE **EDUCATION** Purdue Univ, PhD, 92. **CAREER** Vis Instr, Purdue Univ 92-93; Asst/ Assoc Prof, Pa State Univ, 93-. **HONORS AND AWARDS** Purdue Res Found Grant, Purdue Univ, 89; Acad Achievement Grant, Purdue Univ, Sch of Lib Arts, 90; Phi Kappa Phi, 90; Res and Grad Studies Office Develop Grant, Penn State, 95; Outstanding Teacher Awd, Pa State Schuykill Campus, 97. **MEMBERSHIPS** MLA, NEMLA, PCA, MA-PCA, Soc of Early Americanists. **RESEARCH** American Literature of the Early Republic. **SELECTED PUBLICATIONS** Auth, "Ellis Peters," and "Josephine Tey," in Great Women Mystery Writers, ed. Kath-

leen Gregory Klein (Wesport, CT: Greenwood Press, 94), 279-283, 332-335; auth, "The Reaffirmation of African-American Dignity through the Oral Tradition in Zola Neale Hurton's 'Their Eyes Were Watching God'," CLA J 37 (94): 303-315; auth, "'Pray Madam, are you a Federalist?': Women's Rights and the Republican Utopia in 'Alcuin'," AM Studies 39-3 (98): 89-104; auth, "Social Corruption and the Subversion of the American Success Story in 'Arthur Mervyn'," PROSPECTS: An Annual J of Am Cultural Studies 23 (98): 129-145; auth, "Patriarchal and Political Authority in 'Wieland'," AUMLA: J of the Australasian Univ Lang and Lit Asn 90 (98): 1-19; auth, "The Role of Religion in the Cadfael Series," in Cordially Yours, Brother Cadfael, ed. Anne K. Kaler (Bowling Green, OH: Pop Press, 98), 11-25; auth, "Joel Barlow," in Encyclopedia of American Poetry: The Nineteenth Century, ed. Eric Haralson (Chicago and London: Fitzroy Dearborn Publ, 98), 21-24; rev, of "Buster Keaton's 'Sherlock Jr.'" ed by Andrew Horton, The Europ Legacy (forthcoming, 00); rev, of "Disease, Desire, and the Body in Victorian Women's Popular Novels," by Pamela K. Gilbert, The Europ Legacy (forthcoming, 00); auth, The New Nation: American Culture Through History," Greenwood Press (Westport, CT), forthcoming. **CONTACT ADDRESS** Dept English, Pennsylvania State Univ, Schuylkill, 200 Univ Dr, Schuylkill Haven, PA 17972-2208.

VICKERY, JOHN B.
PERSONAL Born 08/20/1925, Toronto, ON, Canada, m, 1975, 3 children **DISCIPLINE** ENGLISH **EDUCATION** Univ Toronto, BA, 47; Colgate Univ, MA, 49; Univ Wis, PhD, 55. **CAREER** Instr English, Univ Tenn, 54-56 and Northwestern Univ, 56-59; from asst prof to assoc prof, Purdue Univ, 59-65; vis prof, Calif State Col, Los Angeles, 65-66; assoc prof, 66-72, Prof English, Univ Calif, Riverside, 72-93, Vice-Chancellor for Faculty Relations and Academic Support, 83-93. **HONORS AND AWARDS** Guggenheim Found Fel, 75-76. **MEMBERSHIPS** MLA **RESEARCH** Modern literature. **SELECTED PUBLICATIONS** Auth, The Functions of Myth in Barth, John Chimera, Mod Fiction Stud, Vol 0038, 92; Ekphrasis, the Illusion of the Natural Sign, Mod Fiction Stud, Vol 0039, 93; auth, :The Aesthetics of Survival: Tillie Olson's 'Yonnondio,'" in American Literary Dimensions, Univ of Del (99): 99-111. **CONTACT ADDRESS** Dept of English, Univ of California, Riverside, Riverside, CA 92502. **EMAIL** john.vickery@ucr.edu

VICKROY, LAURIE
PERSONAL Born 10/31/1954, Milwaukee, WI, m, 1998 **DISCIPLINE** ENGLISH **EDUCATION** Univ Wis, BA; NYork Univ, MA; SUNY Binghamton, PhD. **CAREER** Asst prof to act dir to assoc prof, Bradley Univ, 90-. **HONORS AND AWARDS** Bradley Univ Res Awd, 93, 00; Lily Found Grant, 93-94; NEMLA Fel, 90; Dis Fel, SUNY, 88-89; NEH, 99. **MEMBERSHIPS** MLA; MMLA. **RESEARCH** Literature and trauma; literature and psychology; women writers; cultural studies; multicultural studies. **SELECTED PUBLICATIONS** Auth, "Ubu-en-proces: Jarry, Kristeva, and Semiotic Motility," Mod Lang Studies 21 (90); auth, "The Politics of Abuse: The Traumatized Child in Toni Morrison and Marguerite Duras," Mosaic 29 (96); auth, "The Force Outside, The Force Inside: Mother-Love and Regenerative Spaces in Sula and Beloved," Obsid (93); auth, "Filling the Void: Transference, Love, Being and Writing," in Marguerite Duras Lives On, ed. Janine Ricouart (UP America, 98); auth, "Beloved and Shoah: Witnessing the Unspeakable," Compar 23 (98); auth, "Elusive Redemptions: Trauma, Gender and Violence in Bastard Out of Carolina and Paco's Story," J Evol Psych (01); **CONTACT ADDRESS** 2010 W Kellogg Ave, Peoria, IL 60614. **EMAIL** vick@bradley.edu

VIDAL, HERNAN
PERSONAL Born 04/18/1937, Villa Alemana, Chile, m, 1962, 3 children **DISCIPLINE** SPANISH AMERICAN LITERATURE **EDUCATION** Univ Iowa, PhD(Span), 67. **CAREER** Instr English, Univ Chile, Temuco, 62-64; instr Span, Univ Iowa, 66-67; asst prof, Univ Va, 67-72; assoc prof, 72-80, PROF SPAN AND PORT AND DIR GRAD STUDIES, UNIV MINN, MINNEAPOLIS, 80-. **MEMBERSHIPS** Am Asn Teachers Span and Port; MLA. **RESEARCH** Spanish American novel and drama. **SELECTED PUBLICATIONS** Auth, Postmodernism, Postleftism, Neo-Avant-Gardism, the Case of Chiles Revista-De-Critica-Cultural, Boundary 2-Intl Jour Lit and Cult, Vol 0020, 93. **CONTACT ADDRESS** Univ of Minnesota, Twin Cities, 9 Pleasant St. SE, 34 Folwell Hall, Minneapolis, MN 55455.

VIERECK, PETER
PERSONAL Born 08/05/1916, New York, NY, m, 1972, 2 children **DISCIPLINE** POETRY, HISTORY **EDUCATION** Harvard Univ, BS, 37, AM, 39, PhD, 42. **CAREER** Instr hist and lit, Harvard Univ, 46-47; asst prof hist, Smith Col, 47-48; assoc prof, 48-49, assoc prof Europ and Russ hist, 49-55, alumni found prof Europ and Russ hist, 55-80, William R Kenan Jr Prof Hist, Mt Holyoke Col, 80-; Vis lectr, Smith Col, 48-49; Guggenheim fels, 49 and 55; vis lectr, Poet's Conf, Harvard Univ, 53 and Univ Calif, Berkeley, 57 and 64; Whittal lectr poetry, Libr Cong, 54 and 63; Fulbright prof Am poetry, Univ Florence, 55; Elliston poetry lectr, Univ Cincinnati, 56; US Dept State cult exchange poet, USSR, 61; Twentieth Century Fund travel and poetry res grant, Russia, 62; lectr poetry, City Col New York and New Sch Social Res, 64; dir poetry workshop, NY Writer's Conf, 65-67. **HONORS AND AWARDS** Garrison Prize for Poetry, Phi Beta Kappa, 36; Harvard Bowdoin Medal for Prose, 39; Tietjens Prize for Poetry, 48; Pulitzer Prize for Poetry, 49; dhl, olivet col, 59. **MEMBERSHIPS** AHA **RESEARCH** Modern European and Russian history; Anglo-American poetry; modern Russian culture. **SELECTED PUBLICATIONS** Metrics, Not Hour Hand, Parnassus Poetry In Rev, Vol 18, 93; My Seventy-Seventh Birthday, Parnassus Poetry Rev, Vol 18, 93; Slack A While, Parnassus Poetry Rev, Vol 18, 93; .. and Sometimes Not, Parnassus Poetry Rev, Vol 18, 93; Invocation, Parnassus Poetry Rev, Vol 18, 93; Threnody Reversals, Parnassus Poetry Rev, Vol 18, 93; Moon Ode, Parnassus Poetry Rev, Vol 18, 93; Second Moon Ode, Parnassus Poetry Rev, Vol 18, 93; Topsy Turvy, Parnassus Poetry Rev, Vol 18, 93; Why I Sometimes Believe in God, Parnassus Poetry Rev, Vol 18, 93; auth, Tide and Continuities, Poems New & Old, Univ of Ark, 95. **CONTACT ADDRESS** 12 Silver St., South Hadley, MA 01075.

VILLANUEVA, CELESTINO ALBERTO
PERSONAL Born 03/15/1949, Uruguay, m, 1994, 2 children **DISCIPLINE** LITERATURE **EDUCATION** Univ Tex Austin, BA, 94; Fla Intl Univ, MA, 97; PhD, 99. **CAREER** Asst instr to instr, Univ Tex Austin, 92-95; teaching asst, Fla Intl Univ, 95-99; asst prof, Univ Cen Fla, 99-. **HONORS AND AWARDS** Fulbright-Hays Grant, Peru, 00; Fla Intl Univ Grad Grant, 99; Teaching Merit Recog, 99; Outstanding Acad Achievement Awd, 98; 46th Ann Hon Day Col Scholar, Univ Tex, 94. **MEMBERSHIPS** Phi Kappa Phi; AAUP; MLA; AATSP. **RESEARCH** Spanish American poetry; Ibero American fiction; Spanish American culture and civilization. **CONTACT ADDRESS** 1097 Hollow Pine Dr, Oviedo, FL 32765-6161. **EMAIL** cvillanu@mail.ucf.edu

VILLANUEVA, VICTOR
PERSONAL Born 12/19/1948, Brooklyn, NY, m, 1980, 5 children **DISCIPLINE** ENGLISH **EDUCATION** Univ Wash, BA, 79, MA, 82, PhD, 86. **CAREER** Instr, 80, Big Bend Com Col; pre-dr assoc, 81-83, dir, ed opportunity prog, Engl, 84-85; Univ Wash; asst prof, 85-87, dir, greater Kansas City writing proj, 87, Univ Missouri; asst prof, 87-92, assoc prof, 92-95, N Arizona Univ; dir, composition, 95-00, assoc prof to prof, 95-; dept chair, 00-; Wash St Univ. **HONORS AND AWARDS** Richard A. Meade Awd for Distinguished Res in English Educ, Conference on English Educ, 94; David H. Russell Awd for Distinguished Res and Scholar in English, Nat Coun of Teachers of English, 95; Rhetorician of the Year, Young Rhetoricians Conference, 99; Martin Luther King, Jr. Distinguished Service Awd, fac, Wash State Univ, 99; Best Grad Seminar, English Grad Orgn, Wash State Univ, 00. **MEMBERSHIPS** Conference on Col Composition and Commun; Nat Coun of Teachers of English; Rhetoric Soc of Am. **RESEARCH** Literacy. **SELECTED PUBLICATIONS** Auth, Bootstraps: From an Am Academic of Color, NCTE (Urbana, Ohio), 93; ed, Cross Talk in Comp Theory: A Grad Reader, NCTE (Urbana, Ohio), 97; auth, Bare Bones Writing for Col, Longmans (NYork), forthcoming; co-ed, American Stwe: A Multicultural Guidebook, Mayfield (Mountain View, CA), forthcoming; auth, "The Politics of Literacy Across the Curriculum," in WAC for the New Millenium: Strategies for/or Continuing Writing Across the Curriculum Programs, eds. Susan McLeod, Eric Miraglia, Margot Soven, and Christopher Thaiss (Urbana: NCTE), forthcoming; auth, "On English Only: An Afterword," in Language Ideologies: Critical Perspectives on the Official English Movement, ed. Roseann Duenas Gonzalez (Urbana: NCTE), forthcoming; auth, "When the Multicultural Leaves the Race: Some Common Terms Reconsidered," The Relevance of English, eds. Robert P. Yagelski and Scott A. Leonard (Urbana: NCTE), forthcoming. **CONTACT ADDRESS** Dept of English, Washington State Univ, Pullman, WA 99164-5020. **EMAIL** victorv@wsu.edu

VINE, BRENT
DISCIPLINE CLASSICS **EDUCATION** Phillips Exeter Acad, Class Dipl, 69; Harvard Col, AB, 73; Harvard Univ, AM, 75, PhD, 82. **CAREER** Tchg fel, Harvard Univ, 74-80; vis instr, Tex Tech Univ, 81-82; sec, Mass Inst Tech, 82-83; instr, Phillips Acad, 83-86; asst prof, Yale Univ, 86-91; asst prof, Princeton Univ, 91-94; assoc prof, Princeton Univ, 91-94; Assoc Prof, UCLA, 95-. **SELECTED PUBLICATIONS** Auth, "On the 'Missing' Fourth Stanza of Catullus 51," Harvard Stud Class Philol 92; "On Phonetic Repetition in Moby-Dick," Lang and Style 22, 89; Gk. -isko: and Indo-European *-iske/o-, Hist Sprachforschung 106, 93; "Catullus 76.21: ut torpor in artus," Rheinisches Museum fur Philol 136, 94; "Greek opeas/ opear 'awl'," Glotta 72, 94/95; rev(s), J. Gager, "Curse Tablets and Binding Spells from the Ancient World," Bryn Mawr Class Rev 4, 91-94; comment on P. Keyser, review of J. Riddle, "Contraception and Abortion from the Ancient World to the Renaissance," Bryn Mawr Classl Rev 5, 95. **CONTACT ADDRESS** Dept of Classics, Univ of California, Los Angeles, PO Box 951436, Los Angeles, CA 90095-1436.

VINSON, MARK ALAN
PERSONAL Born 07/14/1958, Murray, KY, m, 1994 **DISCIPLINE** ENGLISH **EDUCATION** Univ Memphis, BA; BSE; MA; Univ Miss, Sp. Eng. **CAREER** Teaching asst, Univ Memphis & Univ Miss, 82-87; adj, Univ Memphis, 87-90; asst prof, Union Univ, 90-95; asst prof, Crichton Col, 95-; adj, Belhaven Col, 98-. **HONORS AND AWARDS** NEH Summer Sem, Vanderbilt Univ, 93. **MEMBERSHIPS** MLA, Am Dialect Soc. **RESEARCH** Dialectology, Faulkner. **CONTACT ADDRESS** Dept Arts & Sci, Crichton Col, PO Box 757830, Memphis, TN 38175-7830. **EMAIL** mavinson5@aol.com

VISCONTI, COLLEEN
PERSONAL Born 12/20/1963 **DISCIPLINE** COMMUNICATION **EDUCATION** Case Western Reserve Univ, BA, 86; Penn State Univ, MS, 88; Case Western Reserve Univ, PhD, 99. **CAREER** Instructor, Cleveland State Univ, 94-97; Asst Prof, Case Western Reserve Univ, 99-; asst Prof, Baldwin-Wallace Col, 94-. **HONORS AND AWARDS** Who's Who among Human Services Professionals, 92; Office of Educ Traineeship, Penn State Univ, 86-87; Nat Student Speech Lang and Hearing Asn Awd, Case Western Reserve Univ, 86; Greek Woman of the Year Awd, Case Western Reserve Univ, 86. **MEMBERSHIPS** Ohio Speech and Hearing Asn, Am Speech Lang and Hearing Asn, Nat Student Speech-Lang-Hearing Asn. **RESEARCH** Child Language Disorders; Relationship of Language and Cognition. **CONTACT ADDRESS** Dept Speech, Comm, Theatre, Baldwin-Wallace Col, 275 Eastland Rd, Berea, OH 44017-2005. **EMAIL** cviscont@bw.edu

VISER, VICTOR J.
DISCIPLINE COMMUNICATIONS **EDUCATION** Temple Univ, PhD. **CAREER** Asst prof, humanities, Penn State Univ. **MEMBERSHIPS** Int Comm Asn; Speech Comm Asn. **SELECTED PUBLICATIONS** Area: communication research. **CONTACT ADDRESS** Pennsylvania State Univ, Harrisburg, W356 Oldmsted Bldg., Penn State HBG, Middletown, PA 17057. **EMAIL** vjv1@psu.edu

VISOR, JULIA N.
PERSONAL Born New Albany, MS **DISCIPLINE** ENGLISH **EDUCATION** Illinois State University, Normal, IL, BS, 1971; Ohio University, Athens, OH, MA, 1975; Illinois State University, Normal, IL, DA, 1987. **CAREER** Cornell University, Ithaca, NY, residential area coordinator, 73-76; Illinois State University, Normal, IL, assistant director of residential life, 76-79, instructor of English, 79-80, 81-86, director, student support svcs, 80-81, assistant director, Univ Ctr for Learning Assistance, 86-90, assistant prof of English, 88-; Univ Ctr for Learning Assistance, associate director, 90-97, coordinator, 97-. **HONORS AND AWARDS** MAEOPP Distinguished Service Awd, MAEOPP, 1982; Outstanding Svc Awd, ISU Alumni Board of Directors, 1982; President's Awd, ILAEOPP, 1984; Ada Belle Clark Welsh Scholarship, ISU, 1985; Outstanding Svc Awd as co-editor, MAEOPP, 1989; David A Strand Diversity Achievement Awd, Illinois State University, 1995-96. **MEMBERSHIPS** President, Mid-America Assn of Educational Opportunity Program Personnel (MAEOPP), 1991-92; Mid-America Assn of Educational Opportunity Program Personnel, 1980-; Illinois Assn for Learning Assistance Professionals, 1986-; National Council of Teachers of English, 1979-; Illinois Assn of Educational Opportunity Program Personnel (ILAEOPP), 1980-; Natl Assn for Developmental Education, 1990-; Illinois Assn of Teachers of English: Modern Language Assn, 1997-. **CONTACT ADDRESS** Coordinator, Illinois State Univ, 4070 Illinois State University, Normal, IL 61761-4070.

VISWANATHAN, GAURI
PERSONAL Born Calcutta, India **DISCIPLINE** ENGLISH LITERATURE **EDUCATION** Univ Delhi, BA, 71, MA, 73; Columbia Univ, PhD, 85. **CAREER** Prof. **HONORS AND AWARDS** Ed bd, Interventions; Jouvert; S Asia Res; sr fel, Intl Inst, Amsterdam, 98; lect, Hum Res Ctr, Australian Nat Univ; Grants, fel Guggenheim; NEH; Mellon; Amer Inst Indian Stud; Harry Levin Prize, Am Comparative Literature Asn, 99; James Russell Lowell Prize, Modern Language Asn of Am; Amanda K. Coomaraswamy Prize Asn for Asian Studies, 00. **RESEARCH** Indian literature. **SELECTED PUBLICATIONS** Auth, Masks of Conquest: Literary Study and British Rule in India, Columbia UP: Faber, 89; auth, Outside the Fold: Conversion, Modernity, and Belief, Princeton UP, 98; Oxford UP, 98; auth, articles in Oxford Lit Rev, Yale Jour of Criticism; Comp Stud Soc and Hist; Stanford Hum Rev; Mod Lang Quart Critical Inquiry. **CONTACT ADDRESS** Dept of Eng, Columbia Univ, 2960 Broadway, New York, NY 10027-6902. **EMAIL** gv6@columbia.edu

VITTO, CINDY
DISCIPLINE BRITISH LITERATURE TO ROMANTICISM, AMERICAN ENGLISH GRAMMAR, CHAUCER **EDUCATION** Susquehanna Univ, BA; Duke Univ, MA; Rice Univ, PhD. **CAREER** Instr, Rowan Col of NJ. **RESEARCH** Medieval literature. **SELECTED PUBLICATIONS** Auth, The Virtuous Pagan in Middle English Literature; coed, The Rusted Hauberk: Feudal Ideals of Order and Their Declines. **CONTACT ADDRESS** Rowan Univ, Glassboro, NJ 08028-1701.

VLASOPOLOS, ANCA
PERSONAL Born 10/14/1948, Romania, m, 1972, 1 child **DISCIPLINE** ENGLISH **EDUCATION** Wayne State Univ, BA, 70; Univ Mich, MA, 71; PhD, 77. **CAREER** Instr to full prof, Wayne State Univ, 71-. **HONORS AND AWARDS** Woodrow Wilson Fel,; NDEA Fel; Phi Beta Kappa; Humanities Scholar (WSU); ACLS Travel fels; Presidential Awd for Excellence in Teaching, instructed 7 graduate courses in women's studies. **MEMBERSHIPS** Interdisciplinary 19th-century studies, Modern Lang Asn, Am Comp Lit Asn, Detroit Writer's Guild. **RESEARCH** Comparative literature, pseudo science in literature and culture, women's studies. **SELECTED PUBLICATIONS** Auth, The Symbolic Method of Coleridge, Baudelaire, and Yeats (83); auth, The Evidence of Spring (89); auth, Missing Members (90); auth, Through the Straits, At Lang (98); auth, No Return Address: H Menoir Displacement (2000). **CONTACT ADDRESS** Dept English, Wayne State Univ, 51 W Warren Ave, Detroit, MI 48201. **EMAIL** anca_vlasopolos@wayne.edu

VOGAN, NANCY F.
DISCIPLINE MUSIC **EDUCATION** Univ Rochester, MA, PhD. **CAREER** Prof. **RESEARCH** Hist of music instruction; hist of music in Canada. **SELECTED PUBLICATIONS** Auth, Music Education and Music Festivals: A Case Study, Can Music Edu, 94; co-auth, Music Education in Canada: A Historical Account, Univ Toronto, 91. **CONTACT ADDRESS** Mount Allison Univ, 63D York St, Sackville, NB, Canada E4L 1E4. **EMAIL** nvogan@mta.ca

VOGEL, NANCY
PERSONAL Born Lawrence, KS **DISCIPLINE** ENGLISH **EDUCATION** Univ Kans, BA & BS, 63, MA, 65, PhD, 71. **CAREER** Asst prof, 71-74, assoc prof, 74-77, prof Engish, Ft Hays State Univ, 78-. **HONORS AND AWARDS** President's Distinguished Scholar Award, 95; Interdisciplinary Fell, Menninger, 88. **MEMBERSHIPS** NCTE; ALAN; Kansas Humanities Council, Board, 88-92; Natl Adv Board, Gale's Authors and Artists for Young Adults. **RESEARCH** The pastoral tradition; the initiation theme; the arts. **SELECTED PUBLICATIONS** Auth, Exitus, the videotape that went to Boston: A momentary stay against confusion, Kans English, 12/72; Set theory: A paradigm pertinent to English education, English Educ, Winter 73; Robert Frost, Teacher, Phi Delta Kappa, 74; A post mortem on the death of the hired man, In: Frost: Centennial Essays, Univ Miss, 74; Academic travel, In: Improving Instruction, Ft Hays State Univ, 79; Poetry--Something Like a Star, ERIC; Felisa Rincon de Gautier: The Mayor of San Juan, Masterplots II: Juvenile and Young Adult Biography Series; Salem Press, 93; Maureen Daly, Writers for Young Adults, Scribner's 97; Contributor, The Robert Frost Encyclopedia, 00; auth, The Cambridge Guide to Children's Books in English, 01. **CONTACT ADDRESS** Dept of English, Fort Hays State Univ, 600 Park St, Hays, KS 67601-4009. **EMAIL** nvogel@tiger.fhsu.edu

VOGELER, MARTHA SALMON
PERSONAL Born New York, NY, m, 1962 **DISCIPLINE** ENGLISH LITERATURE, INTELLECTUAL HISTORY **EDUCATION** Jersey City State Col, BA, 46; Columbia Univ, MA, 52, PhD (English), 59. **CAREER** Lectr French Columbia Univ, 55-60; lectr, NY Univ, 56-59; instr, Vassar Col, 59-62; asst prof, Long Island Univ, 62-66; assoc prof, 69-73, Prof English, Calif State Univ, Fullerton, 73-; Am Coun Learned Soc grant, 67; Am Philos Soc grants, 67 and 70. **MEMBERSHIPS** MLA; AAUP; Tennyson Soc; Res Soc Victorian Periodicals; Pac Coast Conf British Studies. **RESEARCH** Victorian biography, aesthetics and religious thought. **SELECTED PUBLICATIONS** **CONTACT ADDRESS** Dept of English, California State Univ, Fullerton, Fullerton, CA 92831.

VOIGT, JOHN F.
PERSONAL Born 06/26/1939, Boston, MA, m, 1990, 2 children **DISCIPLINE** LIBRARY SCIENCE; EDUCATION; ENGLISH **EDUCATION** State Col at Boston, AB, 68; Simmons Col, MLS, 72. **CAREER** Libr dir, Berklee Col, 70-. **MEMBERSHIPS** ALA; MLA. **RESEARCH** Jazz music bibliography; free jazz. **SELECTED PUBLICATIONS** Coed, The New Grove Dictionary of Jazz, 88; auth, art, Printed Jazz Music: A Selected Bibliography, 91; coed, Dictionary of American Biography, 94; coed, Dictionary of American Biography, Suppl 9, 94, Suppl 10, 95; auth, art, Jazz Music: A Selective Bibliography, 96. **CONTACT ADDRESS** Berklee Col of Music, 150 Massachusetts Ave, Boston, MA 02115-2697. **EMAIL** jvoigt@berklee.edu

VOLOSHIN, BEVERLY R.
PERSONAL Born New Haven, CT, 1 child **DISCIPLINE** AMERICAN AND ENGLISH LITERATURE **EDUCATION** Univ Calif, Los Angeles, BA, 71; Univ Calif, Berkeley, MA, 73, PhD (English), 79. **CAREER** Teaching asst, Univ Calif, Berkeley, 72-74 and teaching assoc, 75-76; instr, 77-79, Asst Prof English, Univ Rochester, 79-. **MEMBERSHIPS** MLA; Am Studies Asn. **RESEARCH** The empiricist mode in american fiction; Melville; women novelists. **SELECTED PUBLICATIONS** **CONTACT ADDRESS** Dept English, Univ of Rochester, Rochester, NY 14627.

VON DASSANOWSKY, ROBERT
PERSONAL Born 01/28/1960, New York, NY, s **DISCIPLINE** GERMAN AND AUSTRIAN LITERATURE AND CULTURE, FILM **EDUCATION** Am Acad of Dramatic Arts, Pasadena, 77-78; Am Film Inst Conservatory Prof, Los Angeles, 79-81; Univ of Calif, Los Angeles, BA, 85, MA, 88, PhD, 92. **CAREER** Teaching assoc and fel, Dept of Germanic Langs, Univ Calif, Los Angeles, 89-92, vis asst prof of German, 92-93; asst prof of German, Univ Colo, Colorado Springs, 93-99, Head of German Prog, 93-, Dir, Film Studies, 97-, assoc prof of German and Film, 99-, interim chair, Dept of Visual and Performing Arts, 200-2001. **HONORS AND AWARDS** City of Los Angeles Cultural Affairs Grant Awd, 90, 91, 92; Univ of Colo, Colorado Springs Fac Res and Creative Proj Grant Awd, 94, 95, 97, 99; Univ Colo President's Fund for the Humanities Grant, 96; Univ of Colo, Colo Springs Letters, Arts and Sciences outstanding Fac Awd, 98. **MEMBERSHIPS** Austrian Am Film Asn, Int Alexander Lernet-Holenia Soc, PEN/USA West, Austrian PEN, MLA, IFP/West: Independent Features Proj, EPA: European Features Proj, Soc for Cinema Studies, AATG, Poets and Writers. **RESEARCH** 18th and 19th century German and Austrian Literature; Impressionism and Symbolism; First Republic Austrian and Weimar German Culture; Austrofascism; Third Reich and Exile culture; Second Republic Austrian, West German and GDR literature; Women's literature and Feminism; Postmodernism; Austrian, German, Italian, British and American film. **SELECTED PUBLICATIONS** Auth, Phantom Empires: The Novels of Alexander Lerner-Holenia and the Question of Postimperial Austrian Identity, Riverside: Ariadne (96); transl, Verses of a Marriage: Translation of Strophen einer Ehe by Hans Raimund, Los Angeles: Event Horizon (96); co-ed, Filmkunst No 154, Special Issue: Austria's Hollywood/Hollywood's Austria, Vienna: Osterreichische Gesellschaft fur Filmwissenschraft (97); auth, Telegrams from the Metropole: Selected Poetry 1980-1998, Salzburg: Poetry Salzburg/University of Salzburg Press (99); contribur ed, Gale Encyclopedia of Multicultural America, 2nd Ed, 3 vols, Farmington Hills: Gale Res (99); commentary to Leni Riefenstahl's Tag der Freiheit (1935), Short Vision DVD Series, Los Angeles (2000); auth, " 'A Mountain of a Ship': Locating the Bergfilm in James Cameron's 'Titanic', " Cinema J (fall 2000); contribur and ed adv, International Dictionary of Films and Filmmakers, 4th ed, St James Press (2000); co-exec producer, Semmelweis, Swinging Tree Productions/Belvedere Film (2001); transl, Mars in Aries: Translation of Mars im Widder by Alexander Lerner-Holenia, Los Angeles: Green Integer Series/Sun and Moon (2001). **CONTACT ADDRESS** Langs and Cultures, Univ of Colorado, Colorado Springs, 1420 Austin Bluffs Pkwy, Colorado Springs, CO 80918-3733. **EMAIL** Rvondass@mail.uccs.edu

VON FLOTOW, LUISE
PERSONAL Born 12/18/1951, St. Thomas, ON, Canada **DISCIPLINE** LITERATURE **EDUCATION** Univ London, BA, 74; Univ Windsor, MA, 85; Univ Mich, PhD, 91. **CAREER** Tchr, Univ Windsor, Univ Mich, 82-91; Res & tchg, Univ Marburg, Univ Freiburg, 87, 91; asst prof Translation Studies, Univ Ottawa, 96-. **HONORS AND AWARDS** SSHRC doctoral fel, 86-89; Translation Awd, 92; post-doctoral fel, 94-96; Translation Awd, 98. **RESEARCH** Quebec literature; East German literature; translation. **SELECTED PUBLICATIONS** Transl, L'Assassin de l'interieur/Diables d'espoir, by Anne Dandurand, (Montreal: Vehicule Press, 91); auth, "Translating Women of the Eighties: Eroticism, Anger, Ethnicity," Culture in Transit, ed. Sherry Simon, (Montreal: Vehicule Press, 95): 31-46.4.5; auth, "Weibliche Avantgarde, Zweisprachigkeit und Ubersetzung in Kanada", Literarische Polyphonie, Ubersetzung und Mehrsprachigkeit in der Literatur, eds. Johann Strutz and Peter Zima, (Tubingen: Gunter Narr Verlag, 96): 123-136; auth, "Mutual Pun-ishment? Feminist Wordplay in Transltion: Mary Daly in German", in Traductio: Essays on Punning and Translation, ed. Dirk Delabbastita, (Manchester: St. Jerome Press and Namur: Presses Universitaires de Namur, 97): 45-66; transl, Maude, by Suzanne Jacob, (Toronto: Guernica, 97); transl, Translation and Gender, Translating in an Era of Feminism, (Manchester: St. Jerome Press and Ottawa: Univ of Ottawa Press, 97); transl, "Hunger und Seide," by Herta Mueller in DELOS, vol. VIII, no 1-2, 98; transl, "Der Mann mit der Zuendholzschachtel," by Herta Mueller in TRANSLIT IV, 99; auth, "Translation Effects: How Beauvoir Talks about Sex in English," Contingent Loves, ed. Melnie Hawthorne, (Richmond: Univ Press of Virginia, 00); transl, Double Suspect, by Madeleine Monette, (Toronto: Guernica, 00). **CONTACT ADDRESS** Sch Translation & Interpretation, Univ of Ottawa, 70 Laurier, Ottawa, ON, Canada K1N 6N5. **EMAIL** vonfloto@aix1.uottawa.ca

VON FRANK, ALBERT J.
PERSONAL Born 09/05/1945, Mt Vernon, WA, m, 1972 **DISCIPLINE** ENGLISH **EDUCATION** Amherst, AB, 67; Univ Wisc, MA, 68; Univ Mo, PhD, 76. **CAREER** Prof English, American Studies, Wash State, Pullman. **RESEARCH** American studies, Ralph Waldo Emerson **SELECTED PUBLICATIONS** Fel Publ, The Trials of Anthony Burns, Harvard Univ, 98; auth, The Sacred Game: Provincialism and Frontier Consciousness in American Literature, Cambridge Univ, 85; The Complete Sermons of Ralph Waldo Emerson, Univ Mo, 4 vols, 88-91; The Poetry Notebooks of Ralph Waldo Emerson, Univ Mo, 86; An Emerson Chronology, G.K. Hall/Macmillan, 95. **CONTACT ADDRESS** Dept of English, Washington State Univ, Pullman, WA 99164-5020. **EMAIL** vonfrank@mail.wsu.edu

VON FRIEDERICHS-FITZWATER, MARLENE M.
PERSONAL Born 07/14/1939, Beatrice, NB, m, 1983, 4 children **DISCIPLINE** COMMUNICATION **EDUCATION** Westminster Col, BS; Univ Nebr, MA; Univ Utah, PhD. **CAREER** Dir, Health, Commun Res Inst, 88-; assoc clinical prof, Univ of Calif Davis, 87-; prof, Calif State Univ Sacramento 85-. **HONORS AND AWARDS** Fel, Univ of Nebr, Univ of Utah, 79-83; Woman of the Year, Am Biographical Inst Board of Int Res, 91; Outstanding Grantee, Sierra health Found, 91; Professional of the Year in Medicine, 91; Member, World Found of Successful Women 91; 1994 Annual Recognition Awd, Asn of Healing Health Care Projects; Lambda Pi Eta. **MEMBERSHIPS** Int Commun Assoc; Assoc for the Behav Sci and Med Educ; Assoc for Women in Sci; AAUP; Soc for Health Care Pub Relations and Marketing; Soc of Teachers for Family Med; Pub Relations Soc of Am; Balint Soc. **SELECTED PUBLICATIONS** Auth, "Support for the parents of children with cancer", Hospice of Salt Lake J, (82): 2-4; auth, The role of communication in the mourning process", Hospice of Salt Lake J, (83): 1-2; auth, "Relational control in the physician/patient relationship", Health Commun J 3.1 (91); auth, "Stories, power and healing", Sacramento Med Feb 91; auth, Narrative theory and its application in physician/patient communication", Health Commun J, (forthcoming); auth, "Communication and the dying process", Patient Care (forthcoming); coed, Special Issue, Health Commun J, (forthcoming); auth, "Building successful collaborations to improve family health", Public Health J, (forthcoming); auth, "Relational control and methodology and patient centered care", Health Commun J, (forthcoming); coed, Coding Methodologies in Health Communication, Sage Pub, (forthcoming). **CONTACT ADDRESS** Dept Commun Studies, California State Univ, Sacramento, 6000 J St, Sacramento, CA 95819-6070. **EMAIL** fitzwaterm@csus.edu

VONALT, LARRY
PERSONAL Born 01/10/1937, Angola, IN, m, 1976, 1 child **DISCIPLINE** ENGLISH AND AMERICAN LITERATURE **EDUCATION** Univ Denver, BA, 59; Univ Fla, MA, 61, PhD (English), 68. **CAREER** Instr English, Murray State Col, 61-63; interim instr, Univ Fla, 63-68; asst prof, Wesleyan Univ, 68-74; asst prof, 75-78, Assoc Prof English, Univ MO-Rolla, 78-. **MEMBERSHIPS** MLA **RESEARCH** Contemporary literature and eighteenth century English literature. **SELECTED PUBLICATIONS** Auth, An Interview with Harington, Donald, Chicago Rev, Vol 38, 93. **CONTACT ADDRESS** Humanities Dept, Univ of Missouri, Rolla, Rolla, MO 65401.

VOS, ALVIN
DISCIPLINE ENGLISH **EDUCATION** Calvin Col, BA, 65; Univ Chicago, MA, 66; PhD, 71. **CAREER** Asst prof, 70-77, assoc prof, 77-, dir undergrad prog, 83-98, fac, master, Hinman Col, 98-, Binghamton Univ (SUNY). **HONORS AND AWARDS** Chancellors award for excellence in teaching. **MEMBERSHIPS** MLA; Amer Acad Relig. **RESEARCH** English Renaissance. **SELECTED PUBLICATIONS** Trans and ed, Letters of Roger Ascham, New York and Berne, Peter Lang, 89; ed, Place and Displacement in the Renaissance, Binghamton, Medieval and Renaissance Texts and Studies, 95; auth, De copia and Classical Rhetoric, Class and Mod Lit, 7, pp 285-94, 87; Christopher Fry's Christian Dialectic in A Phoenix Too Frequent, Renaissance, 36, pp 230-42, 84; Good Matter and Good Utterance, The Character of English Ciceroianism, Studies in Eng Lit 1500-1900, 19, pp 3-18, 79; An Addition to the Biography of Janus Lascaris, Romance Notes, 19, pp 74-77, 78; Models and Methodologies in Renaissance Prose Stylistics, Studies in the Literary Imagination, 10, pp 1-15, 77; The Vita Longolii: Some Additional Considerations about Reginald Pole's Authorship, Renaissance Quart, 30, pp 324-333, 77; Form and Function in Roger Ascham's Prose, Philol Quart, 55, pp 305-322, 76; Humanistic Standards of Diction in the Inkhorn Controversy, Studies in Philol, 73, pp 376-396, 76. **CONTACT ADDRESS** English Dept., SUNY, Binghamton, Binghamton, NY 13902. **EMAIL** avos@binghamton.edu

VOS, NELVIN LEROY
PERSONAL Born 07/11/1932, Edgerton, MN, m, 1958, 3 children **DISCIPLINE** ENGLISH, THEOLOGY **EDUCATION** Calvin Col, AB, 54; Univ Chicago, AM, 55 PhD(theol & lit), 64. **CAREER** Instr English, Univ Chicago, AM; instr English, Unity Christian High Sch, 55-57; instr English, Calvin Col, 57-59; asst prof, Trinity Christian Col, 63-65; from assoc prof to prof English, Muhlenberg Col, 65-00; head dept, Muhlenberg Col, 76-87; VP and dean, Muhlenberg Col, 87-93; pres, Muhlenberg Col, 95-99; ex dir, Muhlenberg Col, 99-. **MEMBERSHIPS** MLA; Conf Christianity & Lit (secy, 65-67, pres, 68-70); Phi Beta Kap; Soc for Arts, Religion, and Contemp Culture. **RESEARCH** Comic theory; contemporary drama; theology and culture. **SELECTED PUBLICATIONS** Auth, The Drama of Comedy: Victim and Victor, 66; auth, For God's Sake Laugh, John Knox, 67; Versions of the Absurd Theater: Ionesco and Albee, Eerdmans, 68; The process of dying in the plays of Edward Albee, Educ Theatre J, 3/73; Monday's Minis-

tries, Fortress, 79; The Great Pendulum of Becoming: Images in Modern drama, Eerdmans, 80; auth, Seven Days a Week: Faith in Action, Fortress, 85; auth, Connections: Faith and Life, Fortress, 86, 97; auth, Where in the World Are You? Connecting Faith and Daily Life, Alban, 96; The Maestro: Giuseppi Hoschetti's Story, Nacci, 00. **CONTACT ADDRESS** Dept of English, Muhlenberg Col, 2400 W Chew St, Allentown, PA 18104-5586. **EMAIL** hlvos@gateway.net

VRETTOS, ATHENA
DISCIPLINE 19TH-CENTURY ENGLISH LITERATURE **EDUCATION** Vassar, BA; Univ Pa, MA, PhD. **CAREER** English, Case Western Reserve Univ. **SELECTED PUBLICATIONS** Auth or ed, Somatic Fictions: Imagining Illness in Victorian Culture. **CONTACT ADDRESS** Case Western Reserve Univ, 10900 Euclid Ave, Cleveland, OH 44106.

W

WAAGE, FREDERICK O.
PERSONAL Born 12/01/1943, Ithaca, NY, m, 1977, 2 children **DISCIPLINE** ENGLISH, FRENCH **EDUCATION** Princeton Univ, BA, 65; PhD, 71. **CAREER** Instr, Northwestern Univ, 68-71; Adj Asst Prof, Calif State Univ, 71-73; Asst Prof, Douglass Col, 74-77; Asst Prof, Col Misevicordia, 77-78; From Asst Prof to Prof, E Tenn State Univ, 78-. **MEMBERSHIPS** Popular Cult Asn, Mod Lang Asn, Asn for the Study of Lit and the Environ. **RESEARCH** Renaissance literature, popular culture, literature of the U S 1950's-1960's, authobiographies and memoirs, environmental writing. **SELECTED PUBLICATIONS** Auth, The White Devil Discover'd, Peter Lang Publ, 85; auth, Teaching Environmental Literature, Mod Lang Asn, 85; auth, "Warren's New Dawn," Souchen Quart, 31.4 (93); auth, "Traumatic Conformity: Robert Linduei's Narratives of Rebellion, JAC, 22.2 (99). **CONTACT ADDRESS** Dept English, East Tennessee State Univ, PO Box 23081, Johnson City, TN 37614-0001. **EMAIL** waage@etsu.edu

WACHOLDER, BEN ZION
PERSONAL Born 09/21/1924, Dzarow, Poland, m, 1993, 4 children **DISCIPLINE** ENGLISH LITERATURE; CLASSICS; HISTORY **EDUCATION** Yeshiva Univ, BA, 51; UCLA, PhD, 60. **CAREER** Prof, Hebrew Union Col, 56-98. **HONORS AND AWARDS** Pursuing the Text: Studies in Honor of Ben Zion Wacholder on the Occasion of his Seventieth Birthday **MEMBERSHIPS** Soc of Bibl Lit; Asoc of Jewish Studies **RESEARCH** Judaism during the second temple period; Hellenistic Judaism; Dead Sea Scrolls; Talmudic Studies; ancient historiography, ancient calendars **SELECTED PUBLICATIONS** auth, Nicolaus of Damascus, 62; auth, Eupolemus, 74; Essays in Jewish Chronology and Chronography, 84; The Dawn of Qumran, 84; A Preliminary Edition of the Unpublished Dead Sea Scrolls, 96. **CONTACT ADDRESS** 7648 Greenland Pl., Cincinnati, OH 45237. **EMAIL** ben648@aol.com

WACHTEL, ALBERT
PERSONAL Born 12/20/1939, Queens, NY, m, 1958, 7 children **DISCIPLINE** MODERN BRITISH & AMERICAN LITERATURE **EDUCATION** Queens Col, NYork, BA, 60; State Univ NYork Buffalo, PhD(English Lit), 68. **CAREER** Instr English, State Univ NY Buffalo, 63-66, asst to dean, 66-68; asst prof English, Univ Calif, Santa Barbara, 68-74; assoc prof, 74-78, prof English, Pitzer Col, 78-. **HONORS AND AWARDS** National Defense Education Act Fel 60-63; Creative Arts Inst Fel, 70; Danforth Assoc, 79; NEH grants, 86, 98. **MEMBERSHIPS** James Joyce Soc; MLA; Assoc of Am Scholars. **RESEARCH** Theory of tragedy; Shakespeare; modern fiction; Ancient Greek and Hebrew literature; literature and society. **SELECTED PUBLICATIONS** Auth, On Analogical Action, J Aesthet & Art Criticism, 63; The Boundaries of Narrative, J Aesthet Educ, 68; The Burden, 71 & The Genesis of Constructive Self-Destruction Dubliners, 74, Spectrum; Ripe for Peaching: Stephen Dedalus and the Chain of Command, James Joyce Quart, 76; A Clean Slate, 76 & Retreating Forward, 78, Moment; Cradle and all, Southern Rev, 82; Why Learn? Why Live?, 88; "It's Evolutionary and It's in the Bible," LA Times, 99; co-ed Modernism, 86; The Cracked Looking Glass, 92; Ham, Gettysburg Review, 96; A Malignant Metaphor, Wall Street Journal, 97; "From Cross to Swastika," Midstream (00). **CONTACT ADDRESS** Pitzer Col, 1050 N Mills Ave, Claremont, CA 91711-6101. **EMAIL** awachtel@pitzer.edu

WADDINGTON, MIRIAM
PERSONAL Born Winnipeg, MB, Canada **DISCIPLINE** ENGLISH **EDUCATION** Univ Toronto, BA, 39, MA, 68; Univ Pa, MSW, 45. **CAREER** Lectr & res advisor, McGill Sch Social Work, 45-48; case worker, Montreal, 48-60; supervisor, Family Svcs Agency, North York, 60-63; Prof English, York Univ, 64-90, prof emer, 83-. **HONORS AND AWARDS** J.I. Segal prize, 72, 86. **SELECTED PUBLICATIONS** Auth, Green World, 45; auth, The Season's Lovers, 58; auth, The Price of Gold, 76; auth, The Last Landscape, 92. **CONTACT ADDRESS** Dept of English, York Univ, North York, ON, Canada M3J 1P3.

WADDINGTON, RAYMOND B.
PERSONAL Born 09/27/1935, Santa Barbara, CA **DISCIPLINE** LITERATURE **EDUCATION** Stanford Univ, BA, 57; Rice Univ, PhD, 63. **CAREER** Instr, Univ of Houston, 61-62; Instr & asst prof, Univ of Ks, 62-65; from asst prof to prof, Univ of Wisc-Madison, 66-82; prof, Univ of Calif Davis, 82-. **HONORS AND AWARDS** Postdoctoral Fel in Humanities, John Hopkins Univ, 65-66; Inst for Res in the Humanities, Univ of Wisc-Madison, 71-72; Guggenheim fel, 72-73; NEH Fel, Newberry Libr, 78; NEH Sr Fel, 83. **MEMBERSHIPS** Milton Soc of Am, Renaissance Soc of Am, Sixteenth Century Studies Conf, British Art Medal Soc, Am Numis Soc. **RESEARCH** Renaissance literature, art, and culture, Shakespeare, Milton, iconography and rhetoric. **SELECTED PUBLICATIONS** Auth, The Mind's Empire, 74; co-ed, The Rhetoric of Renaissance Poetry, 74; auth, The Age of Milton, 80; auth, The Expulsion of the Jews, 94. **CONTACT ADDRESS** Dept English, Univ of California, Davis, 1 Shields Ave, Davis, CA 95616-5270. **EMAIL** rbwaddington@ucdavis.com

WADE, SETH
PERSONAL Born 11/12/1928, Decatur, KY, m, 1962, 3 children **DISCIPLINE** ENGLISH **EDUCATION** Univ Ky, AB, 52; La State Univ, MA, 54. **CAREER** Asst English, La State Univ, 52-53; asst, Univ Fla, 53-54; instr, Univ Ky, Northern Ctr, 54-55; teaching asst, Ohio State Univ, 57-59, asst instr, 59-60; mem fac, Western Ky State Col, 61-62; Asst Prof English, Pan Am Univ, 62-. **MEMBERSHIPS** NCTE **RESEARCH** Creative writing and modern poetry. **SELECTED PUBLICATIONS** Auth, Byzantium, New Eng Rev Middlebury Series, Vol 17, 95; Barn, New Eng Rev Middlebury Series, Vol 17, 95; The Conduit and Banjo Picker, Brown, Fleming, J Country Mus, Vol 17, 95; Turkish Bath, Poetry, Vol 168, 96; For my Mother, Am t The Poetry of Hamburger, Michael, Agenda, Vol 35, 97. **CONTACT ADDRESS** 1100 W Samano, Edinburg, TX 78539.

WADE-GAYLES, GLORIA JEAN
PERSONAL Born Memphis, TN, m, 1967 **DISCIPLINE** ENGLISH **EDUCATION** LeMoyne Coll, AB (Cum Laude with Distinction) 1959; Boston Univ Woodrow Wilson Fellow, AM 1962; George Washington Univ, doctoral work 1966-67; Emory Univ NEH Fellow, 1975; Emory Univ, PhD 1981. **CAREER** Spelman Coll, instructor of English 63-64; Howard Univ, instr of English 65-67; Morehouse Coll, asst prof 70-75; Emory Univ, graduate teaching fellow 75-77; Talladega Coll, asst prof 77-78; Spelman Coll, asst prof 84-90, prof, beginning 92; Dillard Univ, prof, currently. **HONORS AND AWARDS** Woodrow Wilson Fellowship 1959-62; Merrill Travel Grant to Europe The Charles Merril Found 1973; Danforth Fellow 1974; Faculty Awd of the Year Morehouse Coll 1975; mem Alpha Kappa Mu Natl Honor Soc; editor CLANOTES 1975-; poems published in, Essence, Black World, The Black Scholar, First World; articles published in, Callaloo, Liberator, The Atlantic Monthly; wrote the preface to " Sturdy Black Bridges" Doubleday 1979; author of "No Crystal Stair, Visions of Race and Sec in Black Women's Fiction 1946-1976" Pilgrim Press 1984 (won 1983 manuscript award); UNCF Mellon Rsch Grant 1987-88, Liaison with Natl Humanities Faculty; Presidential Awd for Scholarship, Spelman Coll, 1991; Named CASE Natl Prof of the Year, 1991; Dana Mentor, Spelmaoll, 1989-. **MEMBERSHIPS** Teacher COFO Freedom School/Valley View MS 1964; mem bd dir WETV 30 -WABE-FM 1976-77; sec Guardians for Quality Educ 1976-78; mem editorial bd of Callaloo 1977-80; exec bd Coll Language Assn 1977-80; mem NAACP, ASNLC, CORE; mem Alpha Kappa Alpha Sorority Inc; partner in Jon-Mon Consultants Inc; speech writer. **SELECTED PUBLICATIONS** Pushed Back to Strength, Beacon Press, 1993; My Soul Is a Witness, Beacon Press, Rooted Against the Wind, Beacon Press, 1996; Father Songs: Testimonies by African-American Sons and Daughters, Beacon Press, 1997; Author, Anointed to Fly, Harlem River, 1991. **CONTACT ADDRESS** Dillard Univ, 2601 Gentilly Blvd., New Orleans, LA 70122.

WADLINGTON, WARWICK PAUL
PERSONAL Born 05/02/1938, New Orleans, LA, m, 1995, 3 children **DISCIPLINE** ENGLISH **EDUCATION** US Mil Acad, BS, 61; Tulane Univ, MA, 66, PhD(English), 67. **CAREER** From asst prof to assoc prof, 67-78, prof English, Univ TX, Austin, 78-. **HONORS AND AWARDS** Bromberg Excellence in Teaching, Univ TX, Austin, 70; Kelleher Centennial Prof, 87-; Who's Who in America, 87-; President's Associates Teaching Excellence Awd, 86; Outstanding Graduate Teaching Awd, 96. **RESEARCH** American literature, modern literature. **SELECTED PUBLICATIONS** Auth, Pathos and Dreiser, Southern Rev, 71; Ishmael's Godly Gamesomeness, English Lit Hist, 72; contribr, Nathanael West: The Cheaters and the Cheated, Everett/Edwards, 73; auth, The Confidence Game in American Literature, Princeton Univ, 75; Deep Within the Reader's Eye, Wallace Stevens J, 78; The Sound and the Fury: A Logic of Tragedy, Am Lit, 81; Reading Faulknerian Tragedy, Cornell Univ Press, 87; As I Lay Dying: Stories Out of Stories, Simon & Schuster/Twayne, 92; Doing What Comes Culturally: Collective Action and the Discourse of Belief in Faulkner and Nathaniel West, in Faulkner, His Contemporaries, and His Posterity, Franke, 92; The Guns of Light in August: War and Peace in the Second Thirty Years War, in Faulkner in Cultural Context, Univ Press MS, 97. **CONTACT ADDRESS** Dept English, Univ of Texas, Austin, Austin, TX 78712-1026. **EMAIL** wadl@utexas.edu

WADSWORTH, SARAH A.
PERSONAL Born, CA **DISCIPLINE** ENGLISH **EDUCATION** Reed Col, BA; Univ NCar Chapel Hill, MA; Univ Minn, PhD. **CAREER** Lectr, Univ Minn Twin Cities, 00-01; vis asst prof, Carleton Col, 01-. **HONORS AND AWARDS** Univ Minn Fel, 99-00; A Garr Cranney Outstanding Diss Award, 00; Houghton Libr, Harvard Fel, 00-01; Leon Edel Prize, Henry James Rev, 01. **MEMBERSHIPS** MLA, MMLA, Soc for the Hist of Authorship, Reading, and Publ, Soc for the Study of Am Women Writers, Am Studies Asn, Popular Cult Asn. **RESEARCH** 19th-centry American literature, publishing history, 19th-century periodicals, library history, juvenile literature, gender and reading. **SELECTED PUBLICATIONS** Auth, "Revising Lives: Bernard Shaw and His Biographer," Biography 17.4 (94): 339-66; coauth, "The Making (and Remaking) of the Penny Magazine: An Electronic Edition of Charles Knight's 'The Commercial History of a Penny Magazine,'" Gutenberg Jahrbuch (97): 289-97; auth, "Charles Knight and Sir Francis Bond Head: Two Early Victorian Perspectives on Printing and the Allied Traces," Victorian Periodicals Rev 31.4 (98): 369-86; auth, "Nathaniel Hawthorne, Samuel Goodrich, and the Transformation of the Juvenile Literature Market," Nathaniel Hawthorne Rev 26.1 (00): 1-24; auth, "Louisa May Alcott, William t Adams, and the Rise of Gender-Specific Series Books," Lion and the Unicorn 25.1 (01): 17-46; auth, "Innocence Abroad: Henry James and the Re-Invention of the American Woman Abroad," Henry James Rev 22.2, (01): 107-27. **CONTACT ADDRESS** Dept English, Carleton Col, One N College St, Northfield, MN 55057.

WAGES, JACK D.
DISCIPLINE AMERICAN LITERATURE **EDUCATION** Univ TN, PhD, 68. **CAREER** Prof, TX Tech Univ, 68-. **SELECTED PUBLICATIONS** Auth, Seventy-Five Writers of the Colonial South. **CONTACT ADDRESS** Dept of English, Texas Tech Univ, Lubbock, TX 79409-5015. **EMAIL** J.Wages@ttu.edu

WAGNER, M. JOHN
PERSONAL Born 08/27/1917, Chicago, IL, m, 1954, 2 children **DISCIPLINE** ENGLISH **EDUCATION** Univ Chicago, BA, 39, MA, 40; Northwestern Univ, PhD (English), 56. **CAREER** Instr English, Northwestern Univ, 45-47, Ill Inst Technol, 51-52 and 55-56, Lake Forest Col, 52-55; asst prof, Humboldt State Col, 56-59, Univ Puget Sound, 59-62, Calif State Polytech Col Pomona, 62-64, from asst prof to assoc prof, 64-67, prof, 67-80, Emer Prof English and Chmn Dept, Calif State Univ, Fullerton, 80-. **RESEARCH** Eighteenth century English; fiction writing. **SELECTED PUBLICATIONS** Auth, Eminence Choices in 3 Musical Genres and Music Media Preferences, J Res Mus Educ, Vol 43, 95. **CONTACT ADDRESS** Dept of English, California State Univ, Fullerton, Fullerton, CA 92631.

WAGNER, MARK G.
PERSONAL Born Daterson, m, 1 child **DISCIPLINE** ENGLISH, LITERATURE **EDUCATION** Univ Mass, BA, 81; Boston Univ, MA, 91. **CAREER** Fac, Nichols Col; Correspondent, The Boston Globe, Worcester Telegram and Gazette. **HONORS AND AWARDS** Libris Poetry Prize. **SELECTED PUBLICATIONS** Auth, Silkheads, 96; auth, Monuments to Love and Dust - Poems, 00. **CONTACT ADDRESS** Dept Humanities and English, Nichols Col, PO Box 5000, Dudley, MA 01571-5000. **EMAIL** mthrshp1@aol.com

WAGNER, VERN
PERSONAL Born Broadview, MT, m, 1941, 3 children **DISCIPLINE** ENGLISH, AMERICAN LITERATURE **EDUCATION** Univ Wash, BA, 46, MA, 48, PhD (English), 50. **CAREER** Instr, Univ Wash, 50; prof and chmn dept lang, Nebr State Teachers Col, Chadron, 50-52; From asst prof to assoc prof, 52-71, Prof English, Wayne State Univ, 71-; Mem comt teacher training and qualification, NCTE, 57-; Fulbright prof, Univ Helsinki, 59-60; prof and dir, Am Studies Res Ctr, Hyderabad, India, 74-76; prof Am studies, Univ Indonesia, 80-81. **RESEARCH** Nineteenth and twentieth century American literature. **SELECTED PUBLICATIONS** Auth, Germs and Utopia and an Approach To 'Unveiling A Parallel', A Late Th-Century Feminist Utopian Novel By Jones, Alice, Ilgenfritz and Merchant, Ella, Genre Forms Discourse Cult, Vol 28, 95; Submachine Guns and Electronic Schoolmarms in a True Crime Western, Mod Fiction Studies, Vol 41, 95. **CONTACT ADDRESS** Dept of English, Wayne State Univ, Detroit, MI 48202.

WAGSTAFF, GRAYSON
PERSONAL Born 11/27/1963, South Boston, VA, s **DISCIPLINE** MUSICOLOGY AND MUSIC HISTORY **EDUCATION** James Madison Univ, BM; Univ TX, PhD. **CAREER** Music Dept, Univ of Ala; Catholic Univ of Am. **HONORS AND AWARDS** Fulbright Fel; Musicol adv, Gabrieli Consort and Players. **SELECTED PUBLICATIONS** Articles: Revista de Musicologea, Encomium Musicae, Musical Quart, Revised New Grove Dictionary. **CONTACT ADDRESS** Rome Sch of Music, Catholic Univ of America, Washington, DC 20064. **EMAIL** gwagstaf@music.cua.edu

WAHLSTROM, BILLIE J.
DISCIPLINE RHETORIC STUDIES **EDUCATION** Univ Mich, MA, PhD. **CAREER** Prof **RESEARCH** Design of distance learning materials; effects of new and emerging technologies; gender, ethics, and technology interactions. **SELECTED PUBLICATIONS** Auth, Designing a Research Program in Sientific and Technical Communication, 96; co-auth, The Rhetoric of Midwifery: Conflicts and Conversations in the Minnesota Home Birth Community in the 1990s, Quarterly J Speech, 96; Designing and Managing Virtual Learning Communities, 96. **CONTACT ADDRESS** Rhetoric Dept, Univ of Minnesota, Twin Cities, 64 Classroom Office Bldg, 1994 Buford Ave, Saint Paul, MN 55108. **EMAIL** bwahlstr@mailbox.mail.umn.edu

WAINER, ALEX
DISCIPLINE COMMUNICATIONS **EDUCATION** Valdasta State Univ, BFA, 88; Regent Univ, MA, 90, PhD, 96. **CAREER** Prof. **SELECTED PUBLICATIONS** Auth, Batman as Mythic Evocation Through Comics Technique, scholarly paper presented at the Popular Cult Asn Convention, Las Vegas, 96 & Willing Suspension of Belief: Faith and Unbelief in Classic Horror Films, Scheduled, presented at Speech Commun Asn convention in New Orleans, 94. **CONTACT ADDRESS** Dept of Communications, Milligan Col, PO Box 9, Milligan College, TN 37682. **EMAIL** awainer@milligan.edu

WAINGROW, MARSHALL
PERSONAL Born 03/26/1923, Bridgeport, CT, m, 1950, 3 children **DISCIPLINE** ENGLISH **EDUCATION** Harvard Univ, BS, 44; Univ Rochester, MA, 46; Yale Univ, PhD, 51. **CAREER** Instr English, Pa State Univ, 48-49; From instr to asst prof, Yale Univ, 52-59; Prof English, Claremont Grad Sch, 59-; Morse fel, Yale Univ, 56-57; Am Coun Learned Soc grant-in-aid, 63; Guggenheim fel, 70-71; Am Philos Soc grant, 72-73; vis prof, Univ Calif, Riverside, 73-74 and Univ Calif, Berkeley, 78. **MEMBERSHIPS** MLA; Am Soc 18th Century Studies. **RESEARCH** Eighteenth century literature; Boswell and Johnson. **SELECTED PUBLICATIONS** Auth, Source of Quotations Sought and Boswell, James and Cust, Francis, Cockayne, Query, Notes, Queries, Vol 41, 94. **CONTACT ADDRESS** Dept of English and Am Lit, Claremont Graduate Sch, Claremont, CA 91711.

WAINWRIGHT, JOHN A.
PERSONAL Born 05/12/1946, Toronto, ON, Canada **DISCIPLINE** ENGLISH **EDUCATION** Univ Toronto, BA, 69; Dalhousie Univ, MA, 73, PhD, 78. **CAREER** Prof English, Dalhousie Univ, 79-. **MEMBERSHIPS** Writers' Fedn NS; Writers' Union Can; PEN Can; Asn Can Univ Tchrs English. **SELECTED PUBLICATIONS** Auth, Moving Outward, 70; auth, The Requiem Journals, 76; auth, After the War, 81; auth, Flight of the Falcon: Scott's Journey to the South Pole 1910-12, 87; auth, World Enough and Time: Charles Bruce, A Literary Biography, 88; auth, Landscape and Desire: Poems Selected and New, 92; auth, A Deathful Ridge: A Novel of Everest, 97; ed, Notes for a Native Land, 69; ed, A Very Large Soul: Selected Letters from Margaret Lawrence to Canadian Writers, 95. **CONTACT ADDRESS** Dept of English, Dalhousie Univ, 1434 Henry St, Halifax, NS, Canada B3H 3J5. **EMAIL** darl@is.dal.ca

WAITH, EUGENE MERSEREAU
PERSONAL Born 12/29/1912, Buffalo, NY, m, 1939 **DISCIPLINE** ENGLISH LITERATURE **EDUCATION** Yale Univ, AB, 35, PhD (English), 39. **CAREER** From instr to assoc prof, 39-63, Prof English, Yale Univ, 63-; Secy, English Inst, 53-58, chmn, 62-63; mem exec comt, Am Soc Theatre Res, 78-81. **MEMBERSHIPS** MLA; Shakespeare Asn Am; Am Soc Theatre Res; English Inst. **RESEARCH** Shakespeare; 17th century drama; modern drama. **CONTACT ADDRESS** Dept of English, Yale Univ, New Haven, CT 06520. **EMAIL** eugene.waith@yale.edu

WAKEFIELD, ROBERT
DISCIPLINE COMMUNICATION **EDUCATION** Univ WY, BS, 67; Univ CO, MA, 71, PhD 76. **CAREER** Asst prof; fac adv, vox populi, stud video mag, TV/film Ad Club & TX High Sch Video Festival. **SELECTED PUBLICATIONS** Auth, Trail of the Jackasses, N Plains Press, 68; Schwiering And The West, N Plains Press, 73. **CONTACT ADDRESS** Dept of Commun, Univ of Texas, Pan American, 1201 W. University Dr, Edinburg, TX 78539. **EMAIL** Wakefield@PanAm.Edu

WAKOSKI, DIANE
PERSONAL Born 08/03/1937, Whittier, CA, m, 1982 **DISCIPLINE** ENGLISH **EDUCATION** Univ Berkley, BA, 60 **CAREER** Visiting Writer, Calif Inst Tech, 72; Visiting Writer, Univ Va, 72-73; Visiting Writer, Wilamette Univ, 73; Visiting Writer, Lake Forest Col, 74; Visiting Writer, Colo Col, 74; Visiting Writer, Univ Calif 74; Visiting Writer, Macalester Col, 75; Visiting Writer, Univ Wisc, 75; Visiting Writer, Hollins Col, 74; Visiting Writer, Univ WA, 78; Visiting Writer, Whitman Col, 76; Visiting Writer, Emory Univ, 80-81; Visiting Writer, Univ Haw, 78. **HONORS AND AWARDS** Cassandra Foundation Grant, NY, 70; Council Grant, 71-72; Guggenheim Fel, 72; NEA Grant, 73; MI Arts Council Grant, 88; MI Arts Foundation Awd, 89; Distinguished Fac Awd, MSU, 89; Univ Distinguished Prof, 90. **MEMBERSHIPS** PSA; Authors Guild; PEN. **RESEARCH** Contemporary American poetry. **SELECTED PUBLICATIONS** Auth, The Man Who Shook Hands, 78; auth, Cap of Darkness, 80; auth, The Magician's Feastletters, 82; auth, The collected Greed: Parts I-III, 84; auth, The Rings of Saturn, 86; auth, Emerald Ice: Selected Poems; auth, Medea the Sorceress, 91; auth, Jason the Sailor, 93; auth, The Emerald City of Las Vegas, 95; auth, Argonaut Rose, 98. **CONTACT ADDRESS** Dept Eng, Michigan State Univ, 201 Morrill Hall, East Lansing, MI 48824-1036. **EMAIL** wakoski@pilot.msu.edu

WAKS, LEAH
DISCIPLINE COMMUNICATION **EDUCATION** Univ MI, PhD, 91. **CAREER** Lectr, Univ MD. **RESEARCH** Commun behavior. **SELECTED PUBLICATIONS** Co-auth, The Social Construction of Attitudes Toward the Roles of Women and African Americans, Howard Jour Commun 2, 91. **CONTACT ADDRESS** Dept of Commun, Univ of Maryland, Col Park, 4229 Art-Sociology Building, College Park, MD 20742-1335. **EMAIL** leahwaks@wam.umd.edu

WALBANK, MICHAEL BURKE
PERSONAL Born 04/14/1933, Bristol, England, m, 1978 **DISCIPLINE** CLASSICS, ARCHEOLOGY **EDUCATION** Univ Bristol, BA, 54; Univ BC, MA, 65, PhD (classics), 70. **CAREER** Asst prof, 70-76, Assoc Prof Classics, Univ Calgary, 76-; Can Coun fels, 71-72 and 76-77; consult, BBCOpen Univ Prod, 78. **MEMBERSHIPS** Am Sch Class Studies Athens; Class Asn of Can; Archaeol Inst of Am; Soc Prom Hellenic Studies; Soc Prom of Roman Studies. **RESEARCH** Greek epigraphy; Greek archaeology; ancient science and technology. **SELECTED PUBLICATIONS** Auth, A Lex Sacra of the State and of the Deme of Kollytos, Hesperia, Vol 63, 94; Greek Inscriptions from the Athenian Agora in Lists of Names, Hesperia, Vol 63, 94; Greek Inscriptions from The Athenian-Agora in Building Records, Hesperia, Vol 64, 95; An Inscription from the Athenian Agora in Thasian Exiles at Athens, Hesperia, Vol 64, 95; Greek Inscriptions from the Athenian Agora Financial Documents, Hesperia, Vol 65, 96; Greek Inscriptions from the Athenian Agora, Hesperia, Vol 66, 97. **CONTACT ADDRESS** 14 Harcourt Rd SW, Calgary, AB, Canada T2V 5J1.

WALCHAK, KAROL L.
PERSONAL Born 06/16/1958, Alpena, MI, d, 2 children **DISCIPLINE** LITERATURE, LINGUISTICS **EDUCATION** Calif State Univ, Bakersfield, BA, 81; Calif State Univ, Sacramento, MA, 85; Univ Nev Reno, PhD, 95. **CAREER** Instr, Univ Nev Reno, 87-96; asst prof, Central Mich Univ, 96-. **HONORS AND AWARDS** Who's Who inAm Col and Univ, 90. **MEMBERSHIPS** TESOL; MITESOL; Medieval Soc of the Pacific; Phi Kappa Phi; Phi Beta Delta. **RESEARCH** Chaucer, John Lydate, sound and meaning, TESOL methodology, theory. **SELECTED PUBLICATIONS** auth, TESOL Methods and Approaches, Prentice-Hall. **CONTACT ADDRESS** Dept English, Central Michigan Univ, 100 W Preston Rd, Mount Pleasant, MI 48859-0001. **EMAIL** karol.walchak@cmich.edu

WALD, ALAN MAYNARD
PERSONAL Born 06/01/1946, Washington, DC, w, 1975, 2 children **DISCIPLINE** AMERICAN STUDIES, ENGLISH LITERATURE **EDUCATION** Antioch Col, BA, 69; Univ Calif, Berkeley, MA, 71, PhD(English), 74. **CAREER** Lectr English, San Jose State Univ, 74; teaching assoc, Univ Calif, Berkeley, 75; asst prof English Lit & Am Cult, Univ Mich, Ann Arbor, 75-, from assoc prof to prof, 81-86; Full Prof of English, 87-; Dir, Program in Am Culture, 00. **HONORS AND AWARDS** ACLS Natl Fel, 83-84; Beinecke llow, Yale, 89; Michigan Humanities fell, 85; Excellence in Research Awd from UM, 96; A Bartlett Giamatti Faculty fel at UM Instit for Humanities, 97-98; Guggenheim Fel, 99-00. **MEMBERSHIPS** MLA, ASA. **RESEARCH** American literary radicalism; Marxist aesthetics; the New York intellectuals. **SELECTED PUBLICATIONS** Auth, James T. Farrell: The Revolutionary Socialist Years, 78; auth, The Revolutionary Imagination, 83; auth, The New York Intellectuals, 87; The Responsibility of Intellectuals, 92; Writing From the Left, 94. **CONTACT ADDRESS** Dept of English, Univ of Michigan, Ann Arbor, 3187 Angell Hall, Ann Arbor, MI 48109-10003. **EMAIL** awald@umich.edu

WALDELAND, LYNNE M.
PERSONAL Born 06/13/1941, St. Paul, MN **DISCIPLINE** AMERICAN LITERATURE, FILM **EDUCATION** St Olaf Col, BA, 63; Purdue Univ, MA, 66, PhD, 70. **CAREER** Asst prof English, Albion Col, 69-70; assoc prof Am lit, 70-, asst prof for acad planning & develop, 86-, Northern Ill Univ; interim Exec VP and Provost, Northern Ill Univ, 99-. **MEMBERSHIPS** MLA; Midwest Mod Lang Assn; Am Assoc of Higher Ed; Soc for Coll & Univ Planning. **RESEARCH** Contemporary American writers; film adaptations of novels and stories; literature and photography. **SELECTED PUBLICATIONS** Auth, The Deep Sleep: The fifties in the novels of Wright Morris, Silhouettes on the Shade: Images of the Fifties Reexamined, Ball State Univ Press, 73; auth, John Cheever, G K Hall, 79; auth, Wright Morris: Bibliographical essay, Bibliography of Midwestern Literature, Univ Iowa Press, 81; auth, Plains Song: Women's voices in the fiction of Wright Morris, Critique, 82; auth, John Cheever's Bullet Park: A key to his thought and art, John Cheever: Critical Essays, G K Hall, 82; auth, "Women in the Fiction of John Cheever," The Critical Response to John Cheever, ed. Francis J. Bosha, Westport, Conn. Greenwood Press, 94. **CONTACT ADDRESS** Dept of English, No Illinois Univ, 1425 Lincoln Hwy, De Kalb, IL 60115-2825. **EMAIL** lwaldeland@niu.edu

WALDEN, DANIEL
PERSONAL Born 08/01/1922, Philadelphia, PA, m, 1957, 2 children **DISCIPLINE** ENGLISH **EDUCATION** CCNY, BA, 59; Columbia Univ, MA, 61; NYork Univ, PhD, 64. **CAREER** Lectr, Queens Col NY Univ, 60-63; Asst prof, Mich State Univ E Lansins, 63-66; prof to prof emer, Am Stud, 66-. **HONORS AND AWARDS** Univ Col, Mich State Univ, 65-66; res grant, Pa State Univ, 67-68; Truman Libr grnt, 67-68; Distinguished Svc. Awd, Soc Am Jewish Lit, 92; Distingushed MELUS Awd, 93; ALA Distinguished Awd, 97, 98. **MEMBERSHIPS** ALA, MLA, AM Studies Asn, Am Culture Asn, Soc for Utopian Studies, Soc Am Jewish Lit. **SELECTED PUBLICATIONS** co-ed, American Jewish Poets: The Roots and the Stems, 90; co-ed, Herbert Gold and Beyond, 91; co-ed, American Jewish Women Writers, 92; co-ed, The Changing Mosaic: Cahan to Malamud and Ozick, 93; co-ed, New Voices in and Old Tradition, 94; co-ed, Bernard Malamud's Literary Imagination: A New Look, 95; co-ed, The Tragedy of Joy, 96; co-ed, A Siginificant Pattern, 97; co-ed, The Resonance of Twoness, 98; co-ed, The Ties That Bind, 99. **CONTACT ADDRESS** Dept English, Pennsylvania State Univ, Univ Park, 116 Burrowes Bldg., University Park, PA 16802-6200. **EMAIL** dxw8@psu.edu

WALDOFF, LEON
PERSONAL Born 02/16/1935, Hattiesburg, MS, m, 1960, 1 child **DISCIPLINE** ENGLISH **EDUCATION** Northwestern Univ, BA, 57; Univ Mich, MA, 63, PhD (English), 67. **CAREER** From asst prof to prof, 67-, Univ Ill, Urbana; dir intro courses, 71-73; assoc head, 77-85; dir grad studies, 92-97; vis lctr, Univ Reading, Eng, 75-76. **MEMBERSHIPS** MLA; Keats-Shelley Asn Am; Wordsworth-Coleridge Assn. **RESEARCH** Romantic poetry; psychoanalytic criticism. **SELECTED PUBLICATIONS** Auth, From abandonment to skepticism in Keats, Essays Criticism, 71; auth, Quest for Father and Identity in The Rime of the Ancient Mariner, Psychanal Rev, 71; auth, Father-Son Conflict in Prometheus Unbound, Psychoanal Rev, 75; auth, Theme of Mutability in Ode to Psyche, PMLA, 77; auth, Porphyro's Imagination and Keats's Romanticism, JEGP, 77; auth, Psychological Determinism in Tess of the D'Ubervilles, Critical Approaches to Fiction of Hardy, Macmillan, 79; Keats and the Silent Work of Imagination, Uni Ill Press, 85; Keats's Identification with Wordsworth, Keats-Shelley J, 1989, Romantic Recognitions, American Imago, 90. **CONTACT ADDRESS** Univ of Illinois, Urbana-Champaign, 608 S Wright St, Urbana, IL 61801-3613. **EMAIL** lwaldoff@uiuc.edu

WALKER, ALBERT LYELL
PERSONAL Born 01/20/1907, Okla City, OK **DISCIPLINE** ENGLISH LITERATURE **EDUCATION** Park Col, AB, 29; State Univ Iowa, AM, 30, PhD, 36. **CAREER** Instr English, Univ Ark, 30-32; From instr to prof, 35-77, dir freshman English and chmn curric comt div sci and humanities, 42-59, chmn dept speech, 59-69, chmn dept English, 59-72, Emer Prof English, Iowa State Univ, 77-; Gen Educ Bd and Rockefeller fel, Univ Chicago, 40-41. **MEMBERSHIPS** NCTE; MLA **RESEARCH** Shakespeare, conventions of writing as modified and changed as plays increased and developments in his language and metaphor; modern American fiction, especially work and techniques of William Faulkner; theory of literature. **SELECTED PUBLICATIONS** Auth, Dialogue as a Strategy for Transformative Education, Relig Educ, Vol 91, 96. **CONTACT ADDRESS** Iowa State Univ of Science and Tech, Ames, IA 50010.

WALKER, ANDREW DAVID
DISCIPLINE CLASSICS **EDUCATION** Univ Wash, BA, 82; Univ NC, Chapel Hill, BA, 84, PhD, 93. **CAREER** Lectr, class, 91-92, Univ Va; lectr, class, Univ S Calif, 93-94. **MEMBERSHIPS** APA. **RESEARCH** Cultural stud; gender & comparative lit. **SELECTED PUBLICATIONS** Art, Eros and the Eye in the Love Letters of Philostratus, PCPS, 92; art, Enargeia and the Spectator in Greek Historiography, TPAP, 93; art, Lucan's Legends of the Fall, Ramus, 96; art, Oedipal Narratives and the Exilic Ovid, Ramus, 97. **CONTACT ADDRESS** 3444 Glenhurst Ave, Los Angeles, CA 90039. **EMAIL** adwalker@usc.edu

WALKER, BRENA B.
PERSONAL Born 10/16/1939, Summersville, GA, m, 1962, 2 children **DISCIPLINE** ENGLISH, RHETORIC, COMPOSITION **EDUCATION** Univ Mary Hardin-Baylor, BA, 61; Univ N Tex at Denton, MA, 65; Univ Tex at Austin, PhD, 74 **CAREER** Instr, Univ N Tex, 64-65; instr, N Greenville Col, 66-70; super of student teachers, Univ Tex at Austin, 71-73; prof, Anderson Col, 73-. **HONORS AND AWARDS** Teaching Fel,

Univ Tex at Austin. **MEMBERSHIPS** Nat Coun of Teachers of English, Am Asn of Univ Women. **RESEARCH** The Role of Narrative in Arts and Literature. **SELECTED PUBLICATIONS** Auth, "Reading as a Multi-Generational Activity," Delta Kappa Gamma Bullet 62.4 (96). **CONTACT ADDRESS** Dept Humanities, Anderson Col, 316 Boulevard, Anderson, SC 29621-4002. **EMAIL** brwalker@anderson-college.edu

WALKER, CHARLOTTE ZOE
PERSONAL Born 07/13/1935, New Orleans, LA, m, 3 children **DISCIPLINE** ENGLISH **EDUCATION** San Diego State Univ, BA, 57; Syracuse Univ, MA, 67; PhD, 72. **CAREER** Prof, eng & women's stud, 70-, SUNY Col at Oneonta; founder & co-ed, Phoebe: an Interdisciplinary Jour of Feminist Scholar, Theory & Aesthetics, SUNY Col at Oneonta, 88-92. **HONORS AND AWARDS** Chancellor's Awd, 75; Fel, NEH, 87; O. Henry Ward, 91; Honorable Mention, Best Am Short Stories, 93. **MEMBERSHIPS** Asn for the Study of Lit and Environment; Poetry Writers Asn. **RESEARCH** Environmental and nature writing; Women nature writers; Autobiography; Virginia Woolf; John Burroughs. **SELECTED PUBLICATIONS** Auth, "Dostoevsky's Azure Watch chain," Long Pond Review, 86; auth, "Fish," in Yellow Silk, 87; auth, "Sky come," in Field Guide to Outdoor Erotica, Solstice Press, 88; auth, "The Very Pineapple," The Georgia Review, 90; auth, "Goat's Milk," Ms, 92; auth, "The virgin of the rocks and the Mechanical Fat Lady," Ms, 94; auth, "Winds to End the drought," in Writing from the Catskills and A Little Beyond, Bright Hill Press, 97; auth, "The book Laid Upon the Landscape: Virginia Woolf's Dialogue with Nature," in Beyond Nature Writing, Univ Press VA, 00; ed, Sharp Eyes: John Burroughs and American Nature Writing, Syracuse Univ Press, 00; ed, The Art of Seeing Things: Selected Essays by John Burroughs, Syracuse Univ Press, 00. **CONTACT ADDRESS** Dept Eng, SUNY, Col at Oneonta, PO Box 4015, Oneonta, NY 13820-4015. **EMAIL** walkercz@oneonta.edu

WALKER, CHERYL
PERSONAL Born 11/07/1947, Evanston, IL, m, 1989, 2 children **DISCIPLINE** BRITISH; AMERICAN LITERATURE **EDUCATION** Wellesley Coll, BA, 69; Brandeis Univ, MA, 70; PhD, 73. **CAREER** Robert Bentley Publishing Co, 68, 70; poetry ed, 71-72, Modern Occasions; reader, 72, Wellesley Coll; managing ed, 72-73, Modern Occasions; assoc dir, 73-74, Federation of Organization for Professional Women, 73-74; teaching fell, summer 89, Telluride Summer Program; 78-79, 87, 90-93, chair, intercollegiat amer studies program, 84-85, chair, english dept, 85-86 dir, interdisciplinary program for freshman, chair, chair, 88-89, humanities programScripps Coll. **HONORS AND AWARDS** Resident Scholar, Rockefeller Villa Serbelloni, Bellagio, Italy, Jan 31-Mar 1, 1994; Mary W. Johnson Faculty Recognition Awd for Scholarly Achievement, 1995; dir, Scripps College Humanities Institute, 96-99; Mary W. Johnson Faculty Recognition Awd For Teaching, 98. **MEMBERSHIPS** MLA; ALA; Emily Dickinson Soc; Elizabeth Bishop Soc. **RESEARCH** Amer Women Poets; 19th century Native Amer writers. **SELECTED PUBLICATIONS** Auth, Indian Nation: Native American Literature and Nineteenth-Century Nationalisms, 97; The Whip Signature: Violence, Feminism, and Women Poets, in Gender and Genre: Essays on Women's Poetry, Late Romantics to Late Victorians 1830-1900, 98; Helen Hunt Jackson and Maria White Lowell in The Encyclopedia of American Poetry: The Nineteeth Century, 98; Nineteeth-Century American Women Poets Revisited, in Nineteeth-Century American Women Writers: A Critical Anthology, 98. **CONTACT ADDRESS** English Dept, Scripps Col, PO Box 1058, Claremont, CA 91711. **EMAIL** cwalker@scrippscol.edu

WALKER, DAVID
PERSONAL Born 09/14/1950, Richmond, VA, s **DISCIPLINE** ENGLISH **EDUCATION** Oberlin Col, BA, 72; Cornell Univ, MA, 76; PhD, 79. **CAREER** From asst prof to prof, Oberlin Col, 77-. **MEMBERSHIPS** MLA. **RESEARCH** Twentieth-Century Literature, Contemporary Poetry and Poetics, Creative Writing. **SELECTED PUBLICATIONS** Auth, The Transparent Lyric: Reading and Meaning in Stevens and Williams, Princeton Univ Press, 84; ed, A FIELD Guide to Contemporary Poetry and Poetics, Oberlin Col Press, 97; ed, Poets Reading: The FIELD Symposia, Oberlin Col Press, 99. **CONTACT ADDRESS** Dept English, Oberlin Col, 10 N Professor St, Oberlin, OH 44074-1053. **EMAIL** david.walker@oberlin.edu

WALKER, DAVID E.
PERSONAL Born 10/05/1938, Richmond, VA, m, 1964, 4 children **DISCIPLINE** COMMUNICATION STUDIES **EDUCATION** David Lipscomb Univ, AB, 60; Univ Flor, MA, 61; PhD, 69. **CAREER** Instr, Jack Univ, 63-65; prof, Mid Tenn Univ, 65-; coord, 98-. **HONORS AND AWARDS** Grad Fel, Univ Flor, 63-65; MTSU Gnts, 68, 77, 78, 88, 90, 92, 93, 94; Who's Who Am, World; Pres MTSU Fac Sen, 83-84. **MEMBERSHIPS** TCA; Pi Kappa Delta; Phi Kappa Phi; NEA; TEA; SPCA; CAS. **RESEARCH** Religious communication; American communication studies; Organizational communication. **SELECTED PUBLICATIONS** Auth, "Discrimination," Encyclopedia USA (95): 198-191; auth, "Dixie," Encyclopedia USA (95): 229-231; auth, "The Power of Feedback," Teaching for Success 7 (95): 3; auth, "None of the above: the rhetoric of Ross Perot," J Nontraditional Edu (95); auth, "John Donelson," Encyclopedia USA (96): 137-139; auth, "East Tennessee State University," Encyclopedia USA (98): 26-28; auth, "Eastern Orthodox Church," Encyclopedia USA (98): 61-64; auth, "Education, Antebellum South," Encyclopedia USA (99): 1-5; auth, "Electors, Presidential," Encyclopedia USA (99): 158-160. **CONTACT ADDRESS** Dept Speech, Theater, Middle Tennessee State Univ, 1301 E Main St, Murfreesboro, TN 37132-0001. **EMAIL** dwalker@mtsu.edu

WALKER, ETHEL PITTS
PERSONAL Born 02/04/1943, Tulsa, OK, m, 1977 **DISCIPLINE** DRAMA **EDUCATION** Lincoln Univ MO, BS Ed 1964; Univ of CO, MA Speech & Drama 1965; Univ of MO Columbia, PhD Theatre 1975. **CAREER** Southern Univ Baton Rouge LA, instr 1965-68; Lincoln Univ Jefferson City MO, asst prof 1968-77; Univ of IL Urbana, asst prof 1977-79; Laney Coll Oakland CA, instr 1979-80; African Amer Drama Co San Francisco, exec dir 1980-; Univ of CA Berkeley, asst prof 1988; Wayne State Univ, visiting asst prof 1988-89; San Jose State University, San Jose, CA, professor, theatre arts dept, 89-; Teacher/Scholar at SJSU, 99-00. **HONORS AND AWARDS** Ira Aldridge Scholarship 1963; Outstanding Ed 1974; Outstanding Instr Sr Class Lincoln Univ 1977; Best Actress Awd Lincoln Univ Stagecrafters 1963, Mother of the Year, Representative Teola Hunter of Michigan, 1989; "The Amer Negro Theatre" Black Amers in the Theatre; study, toured with Phelps/Stokes West African Heritage Seminar 1975; article "The Diction in Ed Bullins" In New Eng Winter, Encore 1977; Krigwa Players: A Theatre For, By, and About Black People in Theatre Journal 1989; directed, When the Jumbie Bird Calls at Bonstelle Theatre, Detroit MI 1989; director, To Be Young, Gifted And Black, 1991; "Incorporating African-American Theatre Into A Basic Theatre Course," Theatre Topic, Sept 1992; honorary lifetime membership, Black Theatre Network; Inducted into the Consortium of Doctors, 1993; 1st Arts in Education Awd-Afro Solo Theatre Festival, 99; Inducted in the Educational Theatre Association Hall of Fame-00; Outstanding Women Alumni of Lincoln University, Missouri. **MEMBERSHIPS** Mem 1984-85, chmn 1985- Amer Theatre Assoc, Natl Assoc of Dramatic & Speech Arts, Theta Alpha Phi Dramatic Frat, Speech Commun of Amer, Zeta Phi Beta; Third Baptist Church (San Fransisco), parents alliance, public relations dir; Children's Performance Center, pres of advisory council; Black Theatre Network, past pres 1985-88; member, Association for Theatre in Higher Education; past pres, California Educational Theatre Assn; pres, Legislative Action Coalition for Arts Education, Pres; The Consortium of Doctors. **SELECTED PUBLICATIONS** Coed, African American Scenebook. **CONTACT ADDRESS** San Jose State Univ, 1 Washington Square, San Jose, CA 95192-0098. **EMAIL** walker@mail.sjsu.edu

WALKER, JAMES
PERSONAL Born Bellefonte, PA, m **DISCIPLINE** MASS COMMUNICATIONS **EDUCATION** Univ IA, PhD. **CAREER** St Xavier Univ **MEMBERSHIPS** NCA; ICA; BEA; SSCA. **RESEARCH** Electronic media programming and promotion; media and sports **SELECTED PUBLICATIONS** Couth, The Remote Control in the New Media Environment, Praeger, 93; Television and the Remote Control: Grazing on a Vast Wasteland, Guilford, 96; The Broadcast Television Industry, Allyn & Bacon, 98. **CONTACT ADDRESS** Saint Xavier Univ, 3700 W 103rd Street, Chicago, IL 60655. **EMAIL** walker@sxu.edu

WALKER, JEANNE M.
PERSONAL Born 05/27/1944, Parkers Prairie, MN, m, 1982, 2 children **DISCIPLINE** ENGLISH **EDUCATION** Wheaton Col, BA, 66; Loyola Univ, MA, 69; Univ of Pa, PhD, 74. **CAREER** Haverford Col, 74-80; Univ of Del, 75-. **HONORS AND AWARDS** Fel, Univ of Del, 80; Res Fels, Univ of Del, 80, 83, 86, 91, 96, 00; Del State Arts Coun Grant, 82; Pa State Coun on the Arts Fels, 84, 87, 89, 91, 94; Del Humanities Forum Grant, 85; Fel, Center for Advan Study, 94; NEA Fel, 94; Pew Fel in the Arts, 98. **MEMBERSHIPS** Dramatists Guild of Am; CITA; Poets and Writers. **SELECTED PUBLICATIONS** Auth, "Failing Latin", Whetstone, Fall 89; auth, Coming Into History, Cleveland State Univ Pr, 90; auth, "Three Women", S Humanities Rev, Winter 91; auth, Stranger Than Fiction, Quart Rev of Fiction, 92; auth, "The Graduation", S Rev, Spring, 93; auth, Gaining Time, Copper Beech Pr, 97. **CONTACT ADDRESS** Dept English, Univ of Delaware, 42 Amstel Ave, Newark, DE 19716-2799. **EMAIL** jwalker@udel.edu

WALKER, JEFFREY
DISCIPLINE ENGLISH **EDUCATION** Shippenburg, BA, 68; Middlebury, MA, 71; Penn State, PhD, 77. **CAREER** Assoc prof English, Okla State. **RESEARCH** Collegiate literary culture in 18th century America. **CONTACT ADDRESS** RR 1, PO Box 476, Stillwater, OK 44074.

WALKER, KIM
DISCIPLINE MEDIA RESEARCH, TELEVISION PRODUCTION **EDUCATION** S Ill Univ, PhD. **CAREER** Telecommun consult, Ill Off Edu; McLuhan Prog Cult Tech, Univ Toronto; Amer Assn of Retired Persons; prof-. **HONORS AND AWARDS** TV award winning. Journey Into Literacy, 93; grants, Nat Assn Broadcasters; Intl Commun Assn; produced and directed, number of instructional and public aff prog(s). **SELECTED PUBLICATIONS** Publ, Commun Res Rpt; Commun Edu; Commun Monogr; Pub Pers Mgt; Jour Commun; Media Arts; Intl Jour Edu Telecommun. **CONTACT ADDRESS** Dept of Commun, Univ of Colorado, Colorado Springs, PO Box 7150, Colorado Springs, CO 80933-7150.

WALKER, NANCY A.
PERSONAL Born 09/05/1942, Shreveport, LA, m, 1976 **DISCIPLINE** ENGLISH **EDUCATION** La State Univ, BA, 64; Tulane Univ, MA, 66; Kent State Univ, PhD, 71. **CAREER** Fac mem, Stephens Col, 71-89; assoc prof to prof, Vanderbilt Univ, 89-. **HONORS AND AWARDS** Phi Kappa Phi, La State Univ, 64; Woodrow Wilson Fel, 64-65; Eng Speaking Union Fel, Oxford Univ, 65; NEH Summer Sem Fel, 81; Excellence in Teaching Awd, Stephens Col, 83; Omicron Delta Kappa, 92; Mary Jane Werthan Awd, Vanderbilt Univ, 95; Phi Beta Kappa, Vanderbilt Univ, 95; Mentor Awd, Margaret Cunninggim Women's Center, Vanderbilt Univ, 99. **MEMBERSHIPS** MLA; Am Studies Assoc, Am Humor Studies Assoc, Soc for the Study of Am Women Writers. **RESEARCH** American women's humor, women's autobiography, 19th Century Am women writers, Emily Dickinson, Kate Chopin, popular culture, Am literature and culture of the 1940s and 1950s. **SELECTED PUBLICATIONS** Auth, Redressing the Balance: American Women's Humor from the Colonial Period to the 1980s, UP of Miss, 88; auth, Feminist Alternatives: Irony and Fantasy in the Contemporary Novel by Women, UP of Miss, 90; ed, Communication: The Autobiography of Rachel Maddux, Univ of Tenn Pr, 91; ed, Kate Chopin's The Awakening, St. Martin's Pr Case Studies in Contemporary Criticism, 92; auth, Fanny Fern, Twayne, 92; auth, The Disobedient Writer: Women and Narrative Tradition, Univ of Tex Pr, 95; ed, Women's Magazines 1940-1960: Gender Roles and the Popular Pr, Bedford Books, 98; ed, What's So Funny? Essays on American Humor, Scholarly Res, 98; Auth, Shaping Our Mothers' World: American Women's Magazines, UP of Miss, 00; auth, Kate Chopin: A Literary Life, Macmillan, 00. **CONTACT ADDRESS** Dept English, Vanderbilt Univ, 2201 W End Ave., Nashville, TN 37235-0001. **EMAIL** nancy.a.walker@vanderbilt.edu

WALKER, PIERRE (PETER)
DISCIPLINE ENGLISH **EDUCATION** Univ Massachusetts, BA, 78; MA, 83, PhD, 89, Columbia Univ. **CAREER** Asst Prof, 89-93, Univ Minnesota (Duluth); Asst Prof, 93-97, Western Michigan Univ; Asst Prof, 97-98, Assoc Prof, 98-, Salem State Col. **SELECTED PUBLICATIONS** Auth, Reading Henry James in French Cultural Contexts, N Illinois UP, 95; auth, "Racial Protest, Identity, Words, and Form in Maya Angelou's, I Know Why the Caged Birds Sings," College Literature, 22:3, (95): 91-108; auth, Novels for Students, Gale Res, 98; auth, "Zoro Neale Hurston and the Post-Modern Self in Dust Tracks on a Road," African Am Review 32, (98): 387-99; ed, Henry James on Culture: Collected Essay on Politics, and the American Social Scene, U Nebraska P, 99; auth, "Adina: Henry Jame's Roman Allegory of Power and the Represenation of the Foreign," Henry James Review 21, (00): 14-26; auth, "Leon Edel and the Policing of the Henry James Letter," Henry James Rev 21, (00): 279-89. **CONTACT ADDRESS** English Dept, Salem State Col, Salem, MA 01970. **EMAIL** pwalker@salem.mass.edu

WALKER, ROBERT JEFFERSON
PERSONAL Born 04/22/1922, Gooding, ID, m, 1946, 2 children **DISCIPLINE** SPEECH, COMMUNICATION **EDUCATION** Univ Ill, BSEd, 46; Northwestern Univ, MA, 48; Wayne State Univ, PhD (mass commun), 66. **CAREER** Instr English and Speech, Kennedy-King Col, 46-48; asst prof speech and theatre, Chicago Teachers Col, 50-61; Prpf Speech, Northeastern Ill Univ, 61-. **MEMBERSHIPS** Int Commun Asn; Speech Commun Asn; Int Listening Asn. **RESEARCH** Interpersonal communication; mass media; organizational communication. **SELECTED PUBLICATIONS CONTACT ADDRESS** Dept of Speech and Performing Arts, Northeastern Illinois Univ, Chicago, IL 60625.

WALKER, RONALD GARY
PERSONAL Born 09/12/1945, Southgate, CA, m, 1967, 2 children **DISCIPLINE** ENGLISH AND AMERICAN LITERATURE **EDUCATION** Univ Redlands, BA, 67; Univ Calif, Los Angeles, MA, 68; Univ Md, College Park, PhD (English), 74. **CAREER** Instr, Barber-Scotia Col, 68-69; From instr to asst prof, 69-78, Assoc Prof English, Univ Houston, Victoria Campus. 78-; Chair Div Arts and Sci, 81-. **HONORS AND AWARDS** Fulbright lectr Am lit and mod lett, Univ Nacional Autonoma de Mexico, 80-81. **MEMBERSHIPS** MLA; Col English Asn; SCent Mod Lang Asn; Am Asn for Advanc of Humanities. **RESEARCH** The modern novel; theory of fiction; interdisciplinary studies (myth, ritual, art, film and literature). **SELECTED PUBLICATIONS** Auth, Seriation as stylistic norm in Graham Greene's The Heart of the Matter, Lang & Style, summer 73; Death in the sound of their name: Character motivation in Faulkner's Sartoris, Southern Humanities Rev,

summer 73; Infernal Paradise: Mexico and the Modern English Novel, Univ Calif, 78; The weight of the past: Toward a chronology of Under the Volcano, Malcolm Lowry Newsletter, fall 81; Aldous Huxley, In: Makers of Modern Culture, Routledge & Kegan Paul, London, 81; ed, D H Lawrence's The Plumed Serpent, Penguin English Libr, England, 82; El sueno que fracaso: Lawrence, Mexico y La serpiente emplumada, TEMAS (in press); D H Lawrence, In: Critical Survey of Long Fiction: Authors, Salem Press (in press). **CONTACT ADDRESS** Dept of English, Univ of Houston, Victoria, TX 77901.

WALKER-NIXON, DONNA
PERSONAL Born 03/08/1953, Denton, TX, m, 1991 **DISCIPLINE** ENGLISH **EDUCATION** Tarleton State Univ, BA, 74; Univ Nebr Omaha, MA, 76; Tex A&M univ, EdD, 79. **CAREER** Founding ed, Windhover; co-ed of New Tex Series; instr, Ranger Jr Col, 80-83; prof, Univ of Mary Hardin-Baylor, 83-85 & 89-; legal asst, Vial, Hamilton, 85-87; instr, Tex Tech Col, 87-89. **HONORS AND AWARDS** Univ of Mary Hardin-Baylor Fac Awd for Scholar, 96; Outstanding Alumnus in Arts & Sci, Tarleton State Univ, 00; listed in Who's Who of America's Teachers, 00. **MEMBERSHIPS** CCTF, SCMLA, MLA, TACWT. **RESEARCH** Creative Writing. **SELECTED PUBLICATIONS** Short stories have appeared in Tex Short Stories, Echoes, and Concho River Rev. **CONTACT ADDRESS** Dept English, Univ of Mary Hardin-Baylor, 900 College St, PO Box 8008, Belton, TX 76513-2578. **EMAIL** dwnixon@umhb.edu

WALKIEWICZ, EDWARD P.
DISCIPLINE 20TH CENTURY LITERATURE **EDUCATION** NMex, PhD, 80. **CAREER** Engl, Okla St Univ. **SELECTED PUBLICATIONS** Areas: Barth, Cheever, Joyce, Pound, and W. C. Williams. **CONTACT ADDRESS** Oklahoma State Univ, Stillwater, 101 Whitehurst Hall, Stillwater, OK 74078.

WALKOM, THOMAS L.
PERSONAL Born 08/17/1950, Kirkland Lake, ON, Canada **DISCIPLINE** COMMUNICATIONS **EDUCATION** Univ Toronto, BA, 73, MA, 74, PhD, 83. **CAREER** Lectr econ, Univ Guelph, 78-79; Globe & Mail, 81-89; Writer, Toronto Star 89-. **HONORS AND AWARDS** Winner, Nat News Awds (foreign reporting, 87, column-writing, 96). **SELECTED PUBLICATIONS** Auth, Rae Days: The Rise and Follies of the NDP, 94. **CONTACT ADDRESS** Toronto Star, 1 Yonge St, Toronto, ON, Canada M5E 1ES.

WALL, EAMONN
PERSONAL Born Enniscorthy, Ireland **DISCIPLINE** CREATIVE WRITING AND IRISH LITERATURE **EDUCATION** Univ Col, Dublin, BA; Univ Wis-Milwaukee, MA; CUNY Grad Sch, MPhil & PhD. **CAREER** Dir, Creighton Irish Summer Sch, Trinity Col, Dublin; Jefferson Smurfit Prof, Univ Mo-St Louis. **SELECTED PUBLICATIONS** Auth, The Tamed Goose, NY, Hale Press, 91; auth, Dyckman-200th Street, Galway, Ireland, Salmon Publ, 94; auth, Iron Mountain Road, Salmon, 97; auth, The Crosses, 00. **CONTACT ADDRESS** Dept of Eng, Univ of Missouri, Columbia, 8001 Natural Bridge Rd, Saint Louis, MO 63121-4499.

WALL, REBECCA A.
PERSONAL Born 02/25/1947, Asheboro, NC, d **DISCIPLINE** ENGLISH **EDUCATION** Wake Forest Univ, BA, 68; MA, 70; Univ NC, Greensboro, PhD, 80. **CAREER** Winston Salem State Univ, instr, 69-77; asst prof, 77-81; assoc prof, 81-99; prof, 99-. **HONORS AND AWARDS** Phi Beta Kappa; Doc Stud Assign, UNC Bd Gov; Excel Fel, UNC-E; Wilma Lassiter Mst Teach Awd. **MEMBERSHIPS** SAMLA; NCETA; NLTE; CCCC. **RESEARCH** Sarah Orne Jewett; late 19th C women writers. **SELECTED PUBLICATIONS** Auth, "Where Ever Prospect Pleases: Sarah Orne Jewett, South Berwick, and the Importance of Place, in Critical Essays on Sarah Orne Jewett, ed. Gwen L Nagel (B K Hall, 84). **CONTACT ADDRESS** Dept English, Languages, Winston-Salem State Univ, 601 S M L King Dr, Winston-Salem, NC 27110-0001. **EMAIL** wallr@wssumits.wssu.edu

WALL, WENDY
DISCIPLINE ENGLISH **EDUCATION** Univ Pa, PhD. **CAREER** Prof, Northwestern Univ. **HONORS AND AWARDS** Teaching Awd from Mortar Bd, 93. **RESEARCH** Renaissance poetry and drama. **SELECTED PUBLICATIONS** Auth, The Imprint of Gender: Authorship and Publication in the English Renaissance, 93; articles on, voyeurism and female authorship; co-ed, Renaissance Drama, with Jeffrey Masten. **CONTACT ADDRESS** Dept of English, Northwestern Univ, Univ Hall 215, 1897 Sheridan Rd, Evanston, IL 60208-2240. **EMAIL** w-wall@northwestern.edu

WALL, WILLIAM G.
PERSONAL Born 01/18/1950, Cortland, NY, m, 1997, 4 children **DISCIPLINE** ENGLISH **EDUCATION** Univ MA, PhD, 96. **CAREER** Prof Lit & Theol, Inst for Valsnaua Studies (Graduate Theological Union), 96-. **MEMBERSHIPS** AAR; ASECS; MLA; NSECS; Phi Kappa Phi; WSECS. **RESEARCH** Valsnaua lit; 17th century radical Christian lit; Hindutheology; 18th century poetry; Milton; Shakespeare; art of teaching. **SELECTED PUBLICATIONS** Auth, Proof Without Pain, Back to Godhead, 24:9-10, 89; The Dicken's Checklist, Dicken's Quart, 90-93; The Importance of Being Osric: Death, Fate and Foppery in Shakespeare's Hamlet, The Shakespearean Newsletter 42, winter 92; Mrs. Affery Flintwinch's Dreams: Reading and Remembering in Little Dorrit, Dickens Quart 10, 93; ISKCON's Response to Child Abuse: 1990-1998, ICJ 6, 98; Qualified Teachers, ICJ, forthcoming. **CONTACT ADDRESS** PO Box 1156, Alachua, FL 32616. **EMAIL** wwall@ivs.edu

WALLACE, CATHERINE MILES
PERSONAL Born 02/08/1950, Chicago, IL, m, 3 children **DISCIPLINE** ENGLISH, LITERATURE, RELIGION **EDUCATION** Northwestern Univ, MA, 73; Univ Mich, PhD, 77. **CAREER** Asst prof, Northwestern Univ, 76-82; writer in residence, Seabury-Western Theol Seminary. **HONORS AND AWARDS** Bk rev ed, Anglican Theol Rev; Lilly Found, Writer in Residence, 01-05. **MEMBERSHIPS** MLA; SBL; AAR; SCE; SSCS; The Authors Guild. **RESEARCH** Social ethics; social policy. **SELECTED PUBLICATIONS** Auth, The Design of Biographia Literaria, Allen/Unwin, 83; auth, For Fidelity: How Intimacy and Commitment Enrich Our Lives, Knopf, 98; auth, Dance Lessons, Moorehouse, 99. **CONTACT ADDRESS** Writer in Residence, Seabury-Western Theol Sem, 2122 Sheridan Rd, Evanston, IL 60201-2938. **EMAIL** books.atr@seabury.edu

WALLACE, JOHN MALCOLM
PERSONAL Born 02/28/1928, London, England **DISCIPLINE** ENGLISH LITERATURE **EDUCATION** Cambridge Univ, BA, 50, MA, 55; Johns Hopkins Univ, PhD, 60. **CAREER** Instr high sch, London, Eng, 52-54; instr English, Cornell Univ, 60-63; asst prof, Johns Hopkins Univ, 63-66, assoc prof, 66-67; Prof English, Univ Chicago, 67-; Fel, Guggenheim Found, 69-70; overseas fel, Churchill Col, Cambridge, 69-70; chmn, Renaissance Sem, Univ Chicago, 76-79; sr fel, Nat Endowment for Humanities, 80-81; sr res fel, William Andrews Clark Libr, Univ Calif, Los Angeles; vis prof lit and hist, Washington Univ, St Louis, fall, 81; William Andrews Clark Libr prof, Univ Calif Los Angeles, 81-82. **RESEARCH** Seventeenth century English literature and history. **SELECTED PUBLICATIONS** Auth, the Senecan Context of Coriolanus, Mod Philol, Vol 90, 93. **CONTACT ADDRESS** Dept of English, Univ of Chicago, 1050 E 59th St, Chicago, IL 60637.

WALLACE, NATHANIEL
PERSONAL Born 07/26/1948, Charleston, SC, m, 1979 **DISCIPLINE** COMMUNICATIONS **EDUCATION** Col Charleston, AB, 69; Rutgers Univ, MA, 75; PhD, 79. **CAREER** Lectr, Hebei Univ, China, 81-82; lectr, Jilin Univ, 82-83; lectr, Beijing Univ, 83-85; lectr, Univ of Md, 85-87; asst prof, Delaware Valley Col, 88-91; vis lectr, Univ of Konstanz, Ger, 94-95; assoc prof, SC State Univ, 91-. **HONORS AND AWARDS** NEH Fel, 90, 94-95; SC State Univ/Westinghouse Fac Grant, 95, 96; Camargo Residency Fel, France, 98. **MEMBERSHIPS** MLA; Am Assoc of Chinese Studies; Am Comp Lit Assoc; Renaissance Soc of Am; Soc of Am Mosaic Artists. **SELECTED PUBLICATIONS** Auth, "The Responsibilities of Madness: John Skelton, 'Speke Parrot', and Homeopathic Satire", Studies in Philology 82, (85): 60-80; auth, "Lost in Playto's Funhouse: Reflections on the Phaedrus and Derrida's La Pharmacie de Platon", De/Construction, eds Philip Buyck and Kris Humbeeck, Restant 15.4 (87): 229-45; auth, "The Darkened Vision of Renaissance Satire", Pa English 14.2 (90): 36-53; auth, "The Expatriate Malaise in China", San Jose Studies 16.2 (90): 52-62; auth, "Cultural Tropology in Romeo and Juliet", Studies in Philos 88, (91): 329-44; ed, "Literary Perspectives: An Anthology of Multicultural Currents in Western and Nonwesten Literature", Kendall/Hunt, (Dubuque, IA), 92; auth, "Architextual Poetics: The Hypnerotomachia and the Rise of the European Emblem", Emblematica 8.1 (94): 1-27; auth, "Mutability East and West: The Garden of Adonis and Longevity Mountain", Am J of Chinese Studies 3.1 (96): 1-21; auth, "Confrontations with Longevity in French and Chinese Literature", Comparative Literature Today: Theories and Practice, ed Steven Totosy de Zepetnek and Milan V Dimic, Honore Champion, (Paris, 99): 615-24; auth, "Cultural Dormancy and Collective Memory from the Book of Genesis to Aharon Appelfeld", The Conscience of Mankind, ed Elrud Ibsch, (forthcoming). **CONTACT ADDRESS** Dept Commun and Lang, So Carolina State Univ, 300 College St NE, PO Box 7486, Orangeburg, SC 29117-0001. **EMAIL** nwallace@scsu.edu

WALLACE, ROBERT
PERSONAL Born 03/20/1950, Baltimore, MD, d, 1982, 1 child **DISCIPLINE** CLASSICS **EDUCATION** Columbia Col, BA, 72; Oxford Univ, MA, 77; Harvard Univ, PhD, 84. **CAREER** Asso prof, Class dpt ch, Northwestern Univ,91-; master, Chapin Humanities Residential Col. **HONORS AND AWARDS** NEH Univ fel, 91-92; Keeley vis fel, Oxford, 01. **RESEARCH** Music, Philosophy, and Politics in 5th-Century Athens. **SELECTED PUBLICATIONS** Auth, The Areopagos Council, to 307 BC, Hopkins, 89; co-ed, Poet, Public and Performance in Ancient Greece, Hopkins, 97; Studies in Greco-Roman History 360-146 BC in Honor of Ernst Badian, Okla, 96; coauth, Harmonia Mundi: Music and Philosophy in the Ancient World, Quaderni Urbinati di Cultura Classica, 91. **CONTACT ADDRESS** Dept of Classics, Northwestern Univ, 1801 Hinman, Kresge 11, Evanston, IL 60208. **EMAIL** rwallace@nwu.edu

WALLACE, RONALD WILLIAM
PERSONAL Born 02/18/1945, Cedar Rapids, IA, m, 1968, 2 children **DISCIPLINE** MODERN LITERATURE **EDUCATION** Col Wooster, BA, 67; Univ Mich, MA, 68, PhD, 71. **CAREER** Assoc prof, 72-80, prof English & Dir Creative Writing, Univ of Wis-Madison, 80-; Am Coun Learned Soc fel comic novel, 75-76; Am Coun Learned Soc fel humor in poetry, 81. **HONORS AND AWARDS** Hopwood Awd for poetry, Univ Mich, 70; Scholarly Book Awd, Coun Wis Writers, 80. **MEMBERSHIPS** MLA; Poets & Writers; Acad Am Poets. **RESEARCH** Modern comic novel; contemporary poetry; humor. **SELECTED PUBLICATIONS** Auth, Henry James and the Comic Form, Univ Mich, 75; Installing the Bees (poems), Chowder, 77; Cucumbers (poems), Pendle Hill, 77; Never mind that the nag's a pile of bones: The modern comic novel and the comic tradition, Tex Studies Lit & Lang, 77; The Last Laugh: Form and Affirmation in the Contemporary American Comic Novel, 79; Plums, Stones, Kisses & Hooks (poems), 81; Babble and Doodle: Introducing Students to Poetry, Col English, 81; Tunes for Bears to Dance to (poems), Univ Pittsburgh Press, 83; God Be With the Clown: Humor in American Poetry, Univ Mo Press, 84; People and Day in the Sun (poems), Univ Pittsburgh Press, 87; The Makings of Happiness (poems), Univ Pittsburgh Press, 91; Time's Fancy (poems), Univ Pittsburgh Press, 94; The Uses of Adversity (poems), Univ Pittsburgh Press, 98; auth, Quick Bright Things: Stories, Mid-List Press, 00. **CONTACT ADDRESS** Dept of English, Univ of Wisconsin, Madison, 600 North Park St, Madison, WI 53706-1403. **EMAIL** rwallace@facstaff.wisc.edu

WALLACH, GERALDINE P.
DISCIPLINE SPEECH-LANGUAGE PATHOLOGY **EDUCATION** Long Island Univ, BA; NYork Univ, MA; CUNY, PhD. **CAREER** Speech, Emerson Col. **HONORS AND AWARDS** Fel, ASHA. **SELECTED PUBLICATIONS** Coed, Language Learning Disabilities of School-Age Children and Language Intervention Strategies and Academic Success. **CONTACT ADDRESS** Emerson Col, 100 Beacon Street, Boston, MA 02116-1596.

WALLACH, LUITPOLD
PERSONAL Born 02/06/1910, Munich, Germany, m, 1970 **DISCIPLINE** CLASSICS, MEDIEVAL LATIN **EDUCATION** Univ Tuebingen, DPhil(hist), 32; Cornell Univ, PhD (classics), 47. **CAREER** Asst prof classics, Hamilton Col, 51-52; asst prof hist, Univ Ore, 53; asst prof classics, Cornell Univ, 53-55; asst prof, Univ Okla, 55-57; asst prof, Harpur Col, 57-62; prof, Marquette Univ, 62-67; prof, 67-78, EMER PROF CLASSICS, UNIV ILL, URBANA, 78-; Fund Advan Educ fel, 52; Am Coun Learned Soc grant, 60; mem bd, Grad Sch, Marquette Univ, 63-67, fac fel, 67; Leo Baeck Inst fel, 67; assoc, Ctr Advan Studies, Univ Ill, 69-70. **HONORS AND AWARDS** Festschrift: Beitraege Luitpold Wallach Gewidmet, Hiersemann, Stuttgart, 75. **MEMBERSHIPS** Am Philol Asn; AHA; Mediaeval Acad Am. **RESEARCH** Philology; mediaeval Latin and history. **SELECTED PUBLICATIONS** Auth, Coercive Uses of Mandatory Reporting in Therapeutic Relationships, Behavioral Scis Law, Vol 11, 93. **CONTACT ADDRESS** Dept of Classics, Univ of Illinois, Chicago, Urbana, IL 61801.

WALLEN, MARTIN
DISCIPLINE BRITISH ROMANTICISM **EDUCATION** Vanderbilt, PhD, 85. **CAREER** Engl, Okla St Univ. **RESEARCH** British Romantic Poetry; continental philos - Schelling, Heidegger. **SELECTED PUBLICATIONS** Auth, Coleridge's Ancient Mariner: Texts and Revisions, 1798-1828, Station Hill Press, 93. **CONTACT ADDRESS** Oklahoma State Univ, Stillwater, 101 Whitehurst Hall, Stillwater, OK 74078.

WALLENSTEIN, BARRY
PERSONAL Born 02/13/1940, New York, NY, m, 1978, 2 children **DISCIPLINE** ENGLISH **EDUCATION** NYork Univ, PhD, 72. **CAREER** Prof, City Col NY. **HONORS AND AWARDS** CUNY Res Foundation Grand, 00; Res Fel, Hawthoruden Castle Scotland, 99. **MEMBERSHIPS** Poets House, Acad of Am Poets. **RESEARCH** Poetry, Poetic revision, Poetry in collaboration with music. **SELECTED PUBLICATIONS** Auth, A Measure of Conduct, Ridgeway Press, 99; auth, The Short Life of the Five Minute Dancer, Ridgeway Press, 93; auth, Love and Crush, Persea Books, 91; auth, Roller Coaster Kid, TY Crowell, 82; auth, Beast is a Wolf With Brown Fire, BOA Editions, 77; ed, Risions and Revisions: An Approach to Poetry, TY Crowell, 71; ed, Years of Protest: A Collection of American Writings from the 1930s, Pegasus, 67. **CONTACT ADDRESS** Dept English, City Col, CUNY, 160 Convent Ave, New York, NY 10031-9101. **EMAIL** barrywal23@aol.com

WALLER, GARY F.
PERSONAL Born 01/31/1944, Auckland, New Zealand, M, 1988, 3 children **DISCIPLINE** LITERATURE, CULTURAL STUDIES **EDUCATION** Auckland Univ, BA, 65; MA, 66, Univ Cambridge, PhD, 70. **CAREER** Lectr, Univ Auckland, 69-72; assoc prof, Dalhousie Univ, 72-78; prof, head, Wilfred Laurier Univ, 78-83; prof, head, Carnegie Mellon Univ, 83-92; dean, Univ Hartford, 92-95; VP Acad Affairs, SUNY Purchase Col, 95-. **HONORS AND AWARDS** Overseas Fel, Australian Nat Univ, 79; Guggenheim Fel, 88; Newberry Fel, 90. **MEMBERSHIPS** MLA. **RESEARCH** Shakespeare, Early Modern Culture, Curriculum and Pedagogy. **SELECTED PUBLICATIONS** Auth, Mary Sidney, Countess of Pembroke, Univ Salzburg, 77; auth, Lady Mary Worth's Pamphilia to Amphilanthus, Univ Salzburg, 79; auth, Dreaming America, LSU, 79; auth, Impossible Futures Indelible Pasts, Kellner McCaffrey, 83; auth, English Poetry of the Sixteenth Century, Longman, 85; auth, Reading Texts, Heath, 86; auth, Other Flights Always, Bargnton, 90; auth, Shakespeare's Comedies, Longman, 90; auth, The Sidney Family Romance, Wayne State Univ Pr, 93; auth, Edmund Spenser: A Literary Life, MacMillan, 95. **CONTACT ADDRESS** SUNY, Col at Purchase, 735 Anderson Hill Rd, Purchase, NY 10577-1402. **EMAIL** waller@purchase.edu

WALLING, WILLIAM
PERSONAL Born 12/19/1932, New York, NY, d, 2 children **DISCIPLINE** ROMANTICISM, AMERICAN LITERATURE, SHAKESPEARE **EDUCATION** Brooklyn Col, BA, 55; NYork Univ, MA, 62, PhD(English), 66. **CAREER** Lectr English, City Col New York, Uptown, 62-63; from instr to assoc prof, 65-74, chmn dept, 72-77, chmn dept Humanities, 75-77, prof English, Univ Col, Rutgers Univ, New Brunswick, 74-, Chief reader, Educ Testing Serv, 78-; Fulbright-Hays sr lectureship, 69-70. **MEMBERSHIPS** MLA; AAUP; Wordsworth Circle. **RESEARCH** Literature; art; film. **SELECTED PUBLICATIONS** Auth, Mary Shelley, Twayne, 72; Tradition and Revolution: Byron's vision of judgment, Wordsworth Circle, Autumn 72; Ralph Ellison's Invisible Man, Phylon, 3 & 6/73; Hegel, helas, Partisan Rev, 75; The glorious anxiety of motion: Jane Austen's Persuasion, Wordsworth Circle, Autumn 76; contribr, Candy in Context, NJ Lit Forum, Spring 78; contribr & translr, Jean Starobinski, Andre Chenier, In: Images of Romanticism, Yale Univ, 78; co-ed & contribr, Images of Romanticism, Yale Univ, 78. **CONTACT ADDRESS** Dept of English, Rutgers, The State Univ of New Jersey, New Brunswick, 510 George St, New Brunswick, NJ 08901-1167.

WALLIS, CARRIE G.
PERSONAL Born Clarksdale, MS, m, 1998 **DISCIPLINE** LIBRARY & INFORMATION SCIENCE **EDUCATION** Belhaven Col, BA, 98; Univ Alabama, MLS. **CAREER** Catalog and acquisitions librarian, Belhaven Col, 99-. **MEMBERSHIPS** Am Libr Asn; Special Libr Asn. **CONTACT ADDRESS** Warren A. Hood Library, Belhaven Col, 1500 Peachtree St., Jackson, MS 39202. **EMAIL** cokeefe3@slis.ua.edu

WALLS, LAURA DASSOW
PERSONAL Born 01/12/1955, Ketchikan, AK, m, 1982 **DISCIPLINE** ENGLISH **EDUCATION** Univ Washington, BA, 76; MA, 78; Indiana Univ, PhD, 92. **CAREER** Asst Prof, Lafayette Col, 92-97; Assoc Prof, 97-. **HONORS AND AWARDS** ACLS Fel, 96-97. **MEMBERSHIPS** MLA (Modern Language Assoc), Society for Literature and Science, History of Science Society, Thoreau Society, Emerson Society. **RESEARCH** Thoreau, Emerson, Transcendentatlism, 19th-Century Literature and Science. **SELECTED PUBLICATIONS** Auth, "'The Napoleon of Science': Alexander von Humboldt in Antebellum America", Nineteenth-Century Contexts 14 (90): 71-98; auth, "Walden as Feminist Manifesto" ISLE: Interdisciplinary Studies in Literature and Environment 1.1 (93): 137-44; auth, Seeing New Worlds: Henry David Thoreau and Nineteenth-Century Natual Science, Madison, Univ of Wisconsin Press, 95; auth, "Textbooks and Texts from the Brooks: Inventing Scientific Authority in America" American Quarterly, 49.1 (97): 1-25; auth, "Chains of Translation: On Being a Pacific Thoreauvian," American Studies of Scandinavia 29.1 (97): 1-17; also Nordlit 1 (97): 223-40; auth, "The Anatomy of Truth: Emerson's Poetic Science" Configurations: A Journal of Literature and Science 5.3 (97): 425-61; auth, "Rethinking Thoreau and the History of Amercian Ecology, " with Frank Egerton, The Concord Saunterer N.S. 5 (97): 4-20; auth, Material Faith: Thoreau on Science, ed. And auth of "Introduction: The Man Most Alive" NY: Houghton Mifflin, 99; auth, "Believing in Nature: Wilderness and Wildness in Thoreau's Science", Thoreau's Sense of Place: Essays in American Environmental Writing, ed, Richard Schneider, (Univ of Iowa Press, forthcoming 00); auth, "Romancing the Real: Thoreau's Technology of Inscription," The Oxford Guide to Henry David Thoreau, ed. William Cain (Oxford Univ Press: forthcoming 00). **CONTACT ADDRESS** Dept English, Lafayette Col, Lafayette College, Easton, PA 18042. **EMAIL** wallsl@atsmail.lafayette.edu

WALMSLEY, PETER
DISCIPLINE ENGLISH LITERATURE **EDUCATION** Univ Toronto, BA, MA; Cambridge Univ, PhD. **RESEARCH** British literature 1660-1800; histories of philosophy and science; 17th and 18th century philosophical writing. **SELECTED PUBLICATIONS** Auth, The Rhetoric of Berkeley's Philosophy and Thought, 90. **CONTACT ADDRESS** English Dept, McMaster Univ, 1280 Main St W, Hamilton, ON, Canada L8S 4L9. **EMAIL** walmsley@mcmaster.ca

WALSER, RICHARD
PERSONAL Born 10/23/1908, Lexington, NC **DISCIPLINE** AMERICAN LITERATURE **EDUCATION** Univ NC, AB, 29, AM, 33. **CAREER** Teacher high schs, 30-42; instr English, Univ NC, 46; From instr to prof, 46-70, Emer Prof English, NC State Univ, 70-; Guggenheim fel, 57-58. **HONORS AND AWARDS** Gold Medallion Awd, State of NC, 76. **MEMBERSHIPS** MLA **RESEARCH** Folklore; American humor; Thomas Wolf. **SELECTED PUBLICATIONS** Auth, Headbangers in The Worldwide Megabook of Heavy Metal Bands, Notes, Vol 50, 93; Out of Notes, Signification, Interpretation, and the Problem of Davis, Miles, Musical Quart, Vol 77, 93; Heavy Metal in a Cultural Sociology, Notes, Vol 49, 93; Disciplining Music in Musicology and Its Canons, Mus Letters, Vol 74, 93; A Passion for Polka in Old Time Ethnic Music in america, Am Music, Vol 12, 94; Theorizing the Body in african American Music, Black Mus Res J, Vol 14, 94; Rock and Popular Music in Politics, Policies, Institutions, Notes, Vol 51, 95; Heavy Metal Music and Response to Bjornberg, Alf Rev of Running with the Devil, Mus Letters, Vol 76, 95; Rhythm, Rhyme, and Rhetoric in The Music of Public Enemy, Ethnomusicology, Vol 39, 95; Its Not about a Salary in Rap, Race, and Resistance in Los Angeles, Ethnomusicology, Vol 39, 95; Kleist in Paris, AkzenteinZeitschrift Lit, Vol 43, 96; Adolescents and Their Music in If Its Too Loud, Youre Too Old, Notes, Vol 53, 96; Der Schriftsteller, AkzenteinZeitschrift Lit, Vol 43, 96; The Sex Revolts in Gender, Rebellion, and Rock NinRoll S, Notes, Vol 53, 97. **CONTACT ADDRESS** 3929 Arrow Drive, Raleigh, NC 27612.

WALSH, CHAD
PERSONAL Born 05/10/1914, South Boston, VA, m, 1938, 4 children **DISCIPLINE** ENGLISH **EDUCATION** Univ Va, AB, 38; Univ Mich, AM, 39, PhD, 43. **CAREER** Res analyst, US War Dept, 43-45; From asst prof to prof English, Beloit Col, 45-77, chmn dept, 62-70, writer-in-residence, 71-77; Retired. Asst priest, St Pauls Episcopal Church, Beloit, Wis, 48-77; vis distinguished prof English and religion, Juniata Col, 77-78. **HONORS AND AWARDS** DLitt, Rockford Col, 63 and St Norbert Col, 72. **RESEARCH** The preposition at the end of a clause in early Middle English; utopian and dystopian literature; relation between religion and the arts. **SELECTED PUBLICATIONS** Auth, The Factual Dark, Dekker, 49; C S Lewis: Apostle to the Skeptics, Macmillan, 49; Eden Two-Way, 54 & From Utopia to Nightmare, 62, Harper; The Psalm of Christ, Westminster, 63; The Unknowing Dance, Abelard, 64; The End of Nature, Swallow, 69; God at Large, Seabury, 71; The Literacy Legacy of C S Lewis, Harcourt, 79; Hang Me Up My Begging Bowl, Swallow, 81. **CONTACT ADDRESS** 745 Church St, Beloit, WI 53511.

WALSH, DENNIS
PERSONAL Born 10/27/1938, Carrington, ND, s, 2 children **DISCIPLINE** ENGLISH LITERATURE **EDUCATION** Univ Notre Dame, PhD, 73. **CAREER** Prof. **HONORS AND AWARDS** MA, Teacher, Fullbright Scholar. **RESEARCH** American Indian Literature. **SELECTED PUBLICATIONS** Auth, pubs in Studies in Short Fiction, The Journal of Technical Writing and Communication, and The American Indian Journal of Culture and Research; co-ed, The Idaho Stories and Far West Illustrations of Mary Hallock Foote. **CONTACT ADDRESS** Dept of English and Philosophy, Idaho State Univ, Pocatello, ID 83209. **EMAIL** walsdenn@isu.edu

WALSH, ELIZABETH
PERSONAL Born 05/30/1933, Cumberland, MD **DISCIPLINE** ENGLISH LITERATURE, MEDIEVAL STUDIES **EDUCATION** Manhattanville Col, BA, 55, MA, 63; Harvard Univ, PhD (English and Am lit), 73. **CAREER** Sec sch teacher English and related subjects, Acad of the Sacred Heart, Conn, 59-63 and Albany, NY, 64-67; dean freshman class, Manhattanville Col, 67; teaching fel English, Harvard Univ, 70-72, resident tutor, 72-73, instr, 73-74; asst prof, La State Univ, Baton Rouge, 74-75; asst prof, 75-77, Assoc Prof English, Univ San Diego, 77-83; Am Coun Learned Soc travel grant, 78; Assoc Prof English, 77-83; Prof 83-, Univ San Diego. **HONORS AND AWARDS** NEH Sem(s), 89, 96; NEH Inst 91; Vis scholar Harvard, 91-92; Univ Prof, USI, 96-97. **MEMBERSHIPS** MLA; Medieval Acad Am; Asn Scottish Lit Studies; Dante Soc Am; Medieval Asn Pac. **RESEARCH** The concept of the hero in epic and romance; cultural influences on fifteenth and sixteenth century Scottish literature; Chaucer and the Italian Tradition; Dante and the Renaissance. **SELECTED PUBLICATIONS** Ed., The Tale of Ralph the Coilyear, 89, (Peter Lang); auth, Higher of Learning (Peter Lang, 93). **CONTACT ADDRESS** Dept of English, Univ of San Diego, 5998 Alcala Park, San Diego, CA 92110-2492. **EMAIL** ewalsh@acusd.edu

WALSH, GRACE
PERSONAL Born 06/18/1910, St. Paul, MN **DISCIPLINE** SPEECH **EDUCATION** Wis State Col, BE, 32; Univ Wis, PhM, 39. **CAREER** Teacher, high sch, Wis, 32-42, 43-44 and Iowa, 42-43; prof, 45-80, Emer Prof Speech and Dir Forensics, Univ Wis-Eau Claire, 80-. **MEMBERSHIPS** Speech Commun Asn; Cent States Speech Asn; NEA; Am Forensic Asn. **RESEARCH** Intercollegiate discussion, debate and oratory. **SELECTED PUBLICATIONS** Tournaments for better or worse?, Speech Teacher; The Irish national debate championship, J Am Forensic Asn, spring 70; The case for Eau Claire, Forensic, 1/72. **CONTACT ADDRESS** Dept of Speech, Univ of Wisconsin, Eau Claire, Eau Claire, WI 54701.

WALSH, JONATHAN D.
DISCIPLINE 17TH AND 18TH CENTURY FRENCH THEATER AND PROSE **EDUCATION** Univ Calif, Santa Barbara, PhD. **CAREER** Fr, Wheaton Col. **RESEARCH** Psychoanalysis and literature; jealousy and symbolic exchange in the French novel; French moralists and philosophes. **SELECTED PUBLICATIONS** Publ, on Abbe Prevost, Marcel Proust and Enlightenment authors appear in Romance Quart and Esprit Createur. **CONTACT ADDRESS** Dept of Fr, Wheaton Col, Massachusetts, 26 East Main St, Norton, MA 02766. **EMAIL** jwalsh@wheatonma.edu

WALSH, MARY ELLEN
DISCIPLINE ENGLISH LITERATURE **EDUCATION** Univ Ariz, PhD, 71. **CAREER** Prof. **RESEARCH** Feminism; Western women's writing; institutional issues of race and gender. **SELECTED PUBLICATIONS** Auth, A Vast Landscape: Time in the Novels of Thornton Wilder; Angle of Repose and the Writing of Mary Hallock Foote: a Source Study; co-ed, The Idaho Stories and Far West Illustrations of Mary Hallock Foote. **CONTACT ADDRESS** Dept of English and Philosophy, Idaho State Univ, Pocatello, ID 83209. **EMAIL** walsmary@isu.edu

WALSH, PATRICK F.
PERSONAL Born North Adams, MA **DISCIPLINE** ENGLISH LITERATURE **EDUCATION** St. Francis Xavier Univ, BA, 58; Boston Col, MA, 67; Nat Univ Ireland, PhD, 73. **CAREER** Sr Eng Prof, Xavier Univ. **HONORS AND AWARDS** Univ Outreach Awd. **MEMBERSHIPS** Playwrights' Union Can. **RESEARCH** Modern drama; film; creative writing. **SELECTED PUBLICATIONS** Auth, The History of Antigonish; pubs about Ireland. **CONTACT ADDRESS** English Dept, St. Francis Xavier Univ, Antigonish, NS, Canada B2G 2W5. **EMAIL** pwalsh@stfx.ca

WALSH, THOMAS M.
DISCIPLINE RENAISSANCE ENGLISH LITERATURE **EDUCATION** Saint Louis Univ, PhD. **CAREER** Eng Dept, St Louis Univ. **HONORS AND AWARDS** Norman Foerster Awd, 81. **MEMBERSHIPS** Renaissance Society of America; Modern Language Association of America; International Society for the History of Rhetoric. **RESEARCH** Renaissance English Literature, Oral-Rhetorical Tradition, History of Rhetoric. **SELECTED PUBLICATIONS** Coauth, The Praise of Folly in Context: The Commentary of Gerardus Listrius, Renaissance Quart, 71; Mark Twain and the Art of Memory, Am Lit, 81. **CONTACT ADDRESS** English Dept, Saint Louis Univ, 221 N Grand Blvd, Saint Louis, MO 63103. **EMAIL** walshtm@slu.edu

WALTER, KAY
PERSONAL Born 07/21/1961, LaMarque, TX, m, 1997 **DISCIPLINE** ENGLISH **EDUCATION** Univ Ark, BA, 83; Univ Cen Ark, MA, 89; Tex AM Univ, PhD, 96. **CAREER** Instr, Univ Cen Ark, 89-90; asst teach, Tex AM Univ, 90-96; dir, writ netwk, Blinn Col, 96-99; instr, 99-00. **HONORS AND AWARDS** Piper Prof, BCHD, 98; BCPDC Trv Gnt; Diss Res Fel; ABWA Schlp; TAMU Grad Trv Gnt; Ernest Duke Awd; TAMU Dist Grad Awd. **MEMBERSHIPS** APA; BCPA; CMS; CLS; FRB; FSFB; MPA; ROF. **RESEARCH** Victorian Medievalism; Nineteenth-Century British literature; writing centers. **SELECTED PUBLICATIONS** Auth, "The Vicar's Villain," Philo Asn Louis (93): 157-61; auth, "William Morris, The Wood Beyond the World, and Changing Genres in Victorian England," Ark Philo Asn (95): 99-108; co-ed, "Cornish Ballads and Other Poems," by Robert Stephen Hawker (Delmar, NY: Scholars' Facsimiles & Reprints, 94). **CONTACT ADDRESS** Dept Humanities, Blinn Col, 902 College Ave, Brenham, TX 77833-4049. **EMAIL** kwalter@acmail.blinncol.edu

WALTERS, HUBERT EVERETT
PERSONAL Born 04/27/1933, Greenville, NC, d **DISCIPLINE** MUSIC EDUCATION **EDUCATION** NC Central Univ, BA 1951-55; vA State Univ, 1959; E Carolina Univ, MM 1963-65; Boston Univ, DMA (pending) 1969-; Boston University, School of Theology, pursing MDiv. **CAREER** TX Coll Tyler, TX, chrmn dept of Music 1965-66; Shaw Univ Raleigh, NC, asst prof Music 1966-69; Harvard Univ, lctr on Black Music 1970-74; Goddard Coll VT, lecturer on Black Music 1971-73; Boston State Coll, asst proj of Music 1971-82; Boston Coll, lecturer on Black Music 1982-; Univ of MA-Boston, asst prof of Music 1982-. **HONORS AND AWARDS** LO Kelly Awd Excell in Music NC Central Univ 1955; mem Pi Kappa Lambda; Natl Music Honor Soc; Martin Luther King, Jr flwshp

Awd from Woodrow Wilson Fdn 1969. **MEMBERSHIPS** V pres NC State Music Teachers 1963; mem Music Educators Natl Conf; mem Amer Choral Dir Assoc; Omega Psi Phi Frat; deacon Emmanuel Bapt Church; minister, Worship at Peoples Baptist Church, Boston MA. **CONTACT ADDRESS** Univ of Massachusetts, Boston, Harbor Campus Columbia Pt, Boston, MA 02125. **EMAIL** hubert.walters@umb.edu

WALTERSCHEID, KATHRYN A.
PERSONAL Born 08/16/1961, St Louis, MO, m, 1992 **DISCIPLINE** LITERATURE **EDUCATION** Fontbonne Col, BA, 83; Univ Mo St Louis, MA, 86; St Louis Univ, PhD, 91. **CAREER** Adj asst prof, St Louis Col, 91-98; lectr, Univ Mo, 98-. **HONORS AND AWARDS** Best Veteran Fac Award, Pierre Laclede Honors Col Student Asn, 97-98; Meritorious Serv Award, Disabled Student Union, 86. **MEMBERSHIPS** MLA; DHL Soc. **RESEARCH** Australian multicultural literature; Native American literature; Food in literature; Censorship. **SELECTED PUBLICATIONS** Auth, "Technology, Language, and Knowledge in DeLillo's Later Novels," Review, 92; auth, The Resurrection of the Body: Touch in D.H. Lawrence, Peter Lang, 93; auth, "Don Delillo and Daniel Boorstin: White Noise as an Illustration of Technology and Democracy," in Research in Philos And Technol, 94; auth, "Zora Neal Hurston," in Cavendish Encyclopedia of American Literature, Salem Press, (forthcoming); auth, "Marge Piercy," in Cavendish Encyclopedia of American Literature, Salem Press, (forthcoming); auth, "The Storyteller's Escape," in Masterplots II: Poetry, Rev Ed, Salem Press, (forthcoming). **CONTACT ADDRESS** Dept Lang and Lit, Univ of Missouri, St. Louis, 20 N Kingshighway Blvd, Saint Louis, MO 63108-1366. **EMAIL** walterscheidk@msx.umsl.edu

WALTON, JAMES E.
PERSONAL Born 09/13/1944, Bessemer, AL, m **DISCIPLINE** ENGLISH **EDUCATION** Andrews Univ, 1962-64; Kent State Univ, BS 1964-66; University of Akron, MA 1970-73, PhD 1973-78. **CAREER** Canton McKinley HS, english teacher 1967-70; Mount Union College, assoc prof of english 1970-. **MEMBERSHIPS** Dir Freedom House Project 1975; member Jaycees 1975; yearbook advisor Mount Union College 1975-83; board member Stark County Fair Housing Comm 1978-; board member Assoc for Better Community Development 1984-; member Alliance City Planning Commission 1984-. **SELECTED PUBLICATIONS** Poetry, essays Black Arts Society, Ohio State Univ 1971; essay English Language Arts Bulletin 1980; article Natl Council of Teachers of English 1980; essayModern Language Association 1985. **CONTACT ADDRESS** Dept English, California State Univ, Fresno, 5245 N Backer Ave, MS 98, Fresno, CA 93740-8001.

WALTON, JAMES H.
DISCIPLINE 18TH-CENTURY BRITISH LITERATURE **EDUCATION** Northwestern Univ, PhD. **CAREER** Prof, Univ Notre Dame. **RESEARCH** The child in English literature. **SELECTED PUBLICATIONS** Auth, The Romance of Gentility: Defoe's Heroes and Heroines; Margaret's Book. **CONTACT ADDRESS** Dept of English, Univ of Notre Dame, 356 O'Shaughnessy Hall, Notre Dame, IN 46556. **EMAIL** james.h.walton.1@nd.edu

WALTON, PRISCILLA L.
PERSONAL Born 03/02/1957, St Catharines, ON, Canada, m, 1994 **DISCIPLINE** ENGLISH **EDUCATION** McMaster Univ, BA, 80; BA, 84; MA, 85; Univ Toronto, PhD, 89. **CAREER** Asst prof, Univ Lethbridge, 89-91; asst prof to assoc prof, Carleton Univ, 91-98; vis scholar, Duke Univ, 97; prof, Carleton Univ, 98-. **HONORS AND AWARDS** Teaching Achievement Award, 00-01; SSHRC Res Grant, 92-95, 95-98, 99-02; Res Achievement Award, Carleton Univ, 97-98. **MEMBERSHIPS** MLA; ISNL; Henry James Soc; ASA; CAAS; ACUTE. **RESEARCH** Popular culture; detective texts; Henry James; American studies; Victorian studies. **SELECTED PUBLICATIONS** Auth, The Disruption of the Feminine in Henry James, Univ Toronto Pr, 92; auth, Patriarchal Desire and Victorian Discourse: A Lacanian Reading of Anthony Trollope's Palliser Novels, Univ Toronto Pr, 95; ed, The Portrait of A Lady, Everyman Paperbacks, 95; auth, What Then on Earth was I: Feminine Subjectivity and The Turn of the Screw, Bedford Bks, 95; ed, Canadian Review of American Studies, Univ Toronto Pr, 98; auth, "Form and Forum: The Agency of Detectives and the Venue of the Short Story," Narrative (98); auth, "Helen MacInnes," Mystery Writers (98); auth, Pop Can: Popular Culture in Canada, Prentice Hall, 99; auth, Border Crossings: Thomas King's Cultural Inversions, Univ Calif Pr, 01. **CONTACT ADDRESS** English Dept, Carleton Univ, 1125 Colonel By Dr, Ottawa, ON, Canada K1S 5B6. **EMAIL** pwalton@ccs.carleton.ca

WALZ, EUGENE P.
DISCIPLINE ENGLISH LITERATURE **EDUCATION** St. John Fisher Univ, BA; Univ Ind, MA; Univ Mass, PhD. **CAREER** Assoc prof **HONORS AND AWARDS** Pres, Film Studies Asn Can. **RESEARCH** Canadian films; film genres; screenwriting; American films of the 30s and 60s; cultural studies. **SELECTED PUBLICATIONS** Auth, pub(s) on Francois Truffaut, crime films, Canadian films, Manitoba films and filmmakers. **CONTACT ADDRESS** Dept of English, Univ of Manitoba, Winnipeg, MB, Canada R3T 2N2. **EMAIL** walz@cc.umanitoba.ca

WALZER, ARTHUR E.
DISCIPLINE RHETORIC STUDIES **EDUCATION** Univ Minn, MA, PhD. **CAREER** Assoc prof **RESEARCH** Rhetorical theory and criticism; 18th-century rhetorical theory; Aristotle's rhetoric; ethics and technical communication. **SELECTED PUBLICATIONS** Auth, The Meanings of 'Purpose', Rhet Rev, 91; Positivists, Postmodernists, Aristotelians, and the Challenger Disaster, Col English, 94; Rhetoric and Gender in Jane Austen's Persuasion, Col English, 95; coauth, The Challenger Disaster and the Revival of Rhetoric in Organizational Communication, Argumentation, 97; Aristotle's Rhetoric, Dialogism, and Contemorary Research in Composition, Rhet Rev, 97; auth, "Campbell on the Passions: A Rereading of the 'Philosophy of Rhetoric," Quart Jour of Speech 85 (99): 72-85; auth, Re-reading Aristotle's Rhetoric, Southern Illinois Univ Pr, 00. **CONTACT ADDRESS** Rhetoric Dept, Univ of Minnesota, Twin Cities, 64 Classroom Office Bldg, 1994 Buford Ave, Saint Paul, MN 55108. **EMAIL** awalzer@tc.umn.edu

WANCA-THIBAULT, MARYANNE
DISCIPLINE COMMUNICATIONS **EDUCATION** Univ Colo, BS, MA, PhD. **CAREER** Asst prof. **RESEARCH** Feminist issues as they affect organizations. **SELECTED PUBLICATIONS** Co-auth, Commun Interaction: A Practical Guide for Effective Skills, Observation, Analysis Presentation; Interactions Skills and Analysis: Workbook. **CONTACT ADDRESS** Commun Dept, Univ of Colorado, Colorado Springs, PO Box 7150, Colorado Springs, CO 80933-7150.

WANG, JENNIE
PERSONAL Born 03/19/1952, Shanghai, China **DISCIPLINE** ENGLISH **EDUCATION** San Francisco State Univ, BA, 83; Stanford Univ, MA, 84; State Univ NY Buffalo, PhD, 92. **CAREER** Instr, Shanghai Jiao-Tong Univ, 77-79; teaching fel, State Univ of NYork Buffalo, 87-91; Preceptor, Harvard Univ, 92-93; Res Assoc, Univ of Calif, Berkeley, 96; assoc prof, Univ of N Iowa, 93-. **RESEARCH** 20th century American literature, fiction; postmodern and postcolonial theories; Asian American Literature, American Orientalism; translation of Chinese literature in English; Chinese American writers and Chinese Diaspora writing; world literature, the novel, history of the novel, political philosophy, "love stories". **SELECTED PUBLICATIONS** Auth, "The Player's Song of Finnegans Wake: Translating Sound Sense", Jof Narrative Tech 21, (91): 212-23; auth, "To Wielderfight His Penisolate War: The Lover's Discourse in Postmodern Fiction", Critique: Studies in Contemp Fiction 34, (92): 63-79; auth, "Tripmaster Money: Kingston's Postmodern Representation of a New China Man", MELUS 20 (95): 101-114; auth, "Romantic Love and its Repudiation of Cultural Legacy: Faulkner's Silver Horn in Delta Autumn", Short Story 4.2 (96): 85-103; auth, "The Myth of Kingston's No Name Woman: Making Contextual and Intertextual Connections in Teaching Asian American Literature", CEA Critic 59, (96): 21-32; auth, Novelistic Love in the Platonic Tradition: Fielding, Faulkner and the Postmodernists, Lit and Philos Series, Rowman & Littlefield (Lanham, MA, Oxford, Eng), 97; transl, of "Smiles on Washington Square: A Love Story of Sorts", by Raymond Federman, Shanghai Trans Pub House, 99; transl, of "American Fiction Today: The Unreality of Reality", by Raymond Federman, East West Forum, (NY, 00) 32-37; auth, The Iron Curtain of Language: Maxine Hong Kingston and American Orientalism (forthcoming). **CONTACT ADDRESS** Dept English, Univ of No Iowa, PO Box 591094, San Francisco, CA 591094. **EMAIL** jennie.wang@uni.edu

WANG, JOAN PARSONS
PERSONAL Born 10/21/1925, Cincinnati, OH, w, 1947, 2 children **DISCIPLINE** ENGLISH, COMPARATIVE LITERATURE **EDUCATION** Radcliffe Col, AB, 47; Brown Univ, MA, 49; Ind Univ, PhD (comp lit), 64. **CAREER** Asst prof, 66-80, Assoc Prof English, Independent Studies Div, Sch Continuing Studies, Ind Univ, Bloomington, 80-. **HONORS AND AWARDS** Cert Merit, Nat Univ Exten Asn, 71 and 81. **MEMBERSHIPS** Nat Univ Exten Asn. **RESEARCH** Writing syllabi for independent study courses in English and world literature; modern European drama; women's studies. **CONTACT ADDRESS** Dept of English, Indiana Univ, Bloomington, 1 Ind Univ, Bloomington, IN 47405. **EMAIL** wang@indiana.edu

WANG, MASON YU-HENG
PERSONAL Born 05/07/1936, China, m, 1963, 3 children **DISCIPLINE** SHAKESPEARE, COMPARATIVE LITERATURE **EDUCATION** Nat Taiwan Univ, BA, 59; IN Univ, MA, 65, PhD(English), 72. **CAREER** Instr English, Cent MO State Col, 65-68; from instr to asst prof, 69-76, chmn dept, 74-78, assoc prof, 76-83, Prof English Saginaw Valley State Univ, 83-. **HONORS AND AWARDS** Fel, Li Foundation, 61-63; fel, Indiana Univ Foreign Student, 64-65; Natl Endowment for the Humanities Grant, Stanford Univ, 76; Natl Endowment for the Humanities Grant, Univ of Calif, Santa Cruz, 87; Correspondent, Intl Committee, World Shakespeare Bibliography, 92-. **MEMBERSHIPS** Shakespeare Asn Am. **RESEARCH** Shakespeare; comparative literature; Chinese literature. **SELECTED PUBLICATIONS** Auth, Burlesque and Irony in The Two Gentlemen of Verona, Shakespeare Newslett, 9/72; Review of Ten Poems and Lyrics by Mao Tse-tung, Green River Rev, 76; ed, Perspectives in Contemporary Chinese Literature, Green River Press, 83; tr & ed, Zhang Siyang, Hamlet's Melancholy, and Zhang Xiaoyang, Shakespeare and the Idea of Nature in the Renaissance, Shakespeare and the Triple Play, ed Sidney Homan, Bucknell Univ Press, 88; contrib & ed, Meng Xianqiang. A Historical .Survey of Shakespeare in China, Shakespeare Res Center of NE Normal Univ, 96; co-tr & ed, Meng Xianqiang. A Historical Survey of Shakespeare. **CONTACT ADDRESS** Dept of English, Saginaw Valley State Univ, 7400 Bay Rd, University Center, MI 48710-0001. **EMAIL** mywang@svsu.edu

WANG, QUN
PERSONAL Born 04/28/1956, Beijing, China, m, 1986, 2 children **DISCIPLINE** ENGLISH **EDUCATION** East China Normal Univ, BA, 79; MA, 82; Univ Ore, PhD, 90. **CAREER** From asst prof to assoc prof, Univ of Wis at River Falls, 90-95; from assoc prof to prof, Calif State Univ at Monterey Bay, 95-. **HONORS AND AWARDS** CSBLAC Ford Found Fel, 91; Univ of Wis Teaching Fel, 94; Calif State Univ Res Awd, 99. **MEMBERSHIPS** MLA, Race, Gender, and Class Asn, Soc for the Study of the Multi-Ethnic Lit of the U.S., Asn for Asian Am Studies, Arthur Miller Soc. **RESEARCH** Asian American literature and cultures, American ethnic literature and cultures. **SELECTED PUBLICATIONS** Auth, "The Tragedy of Ethical Bewilderment," The Achievement of Arthur Miller: New Essays, Contemp Res Press (Dallas, TX), 95; auth, "Asian American Short Stories: Dialoguing the Asian American Experience," Ethnicity and the American Short Story, Garland (New York), 97; co-ed, Race, Gender & Class: Asian American Voices, Southern Univ of New Orleans Press (New Orleans, LA), 97; auth, African American Playwright August Wilson: Vernacularizing the Blues on Stage, Edwin Mellen Press (Lewiston, NY), 99; auth, "Repositioning the Stars: Narratives of 20th Century Asian American Immigration," The Immigrant Experience in North American Literature: Carving out a Niche, Greenwood Press (Westport, CT), 99; auth, "Border Crossing, Cultural Negotiations, and the Authenticity of Asian American Voices," Passages 1.2 (99): 278-289; auth, "Positionality, Film, and Asian American Literature," Popular Culture Rev 10.2 (99): 65-77. **CONTACT ADDRESS** Dept Arts, Calif State Univ at Monterey Bay, 100 Campus Center, Seaside, CA 93955-8000. **EMAIL** qun_wang@monterey.edu

WANG, XIAO
PERSONAL Born 11/01/1962, China, m, 1997 **DISCIPLINE** COMPOSITION, RHETORIC **EDUCATION** Northwest Univ, BA, 83; St Cloud State, MA, 92; Ball State Univ, PhD, 97. **CAREER** Teacher, St. Cloud State, 90-92; instr, Ball State Univ, 92-97; instr, Ariz State, 97-98; prof, Broward Community Col, 98-. **HONORS AND AWARDS** Teaching Awd, Broward Community Col Educ Club, 00. **MEMBERSHIPS** MLA, NCTE, TYCA-SE. **RESEARCH** Contrastive Rhetoric, Freshman Composition, Basic Writing, Comparative Literature. **SELECTED PUBLICATIONS** Auth, Shirley's Heart, a Translation into Chinese, Northwestern Univ Newspaper, 90; auth, "On the Lake in St John's," Purposeful Writer, Allan and Bacon, 92; rev, of "Teaching K1 to 12 Students," Ind Writing Project Newsletter, (95); auth, Double-entry Notebook and Technical Writing Classes, Eric Clearing House, IN, 00; auth, Accommodating Features of Ebonics in Freshman Composition, Eric Clearing House, IN, 00. **CONTACT ADDRESS** Broward Comm Col, 9230 Langoon Pl, No 211, Ft lauderdale, FL 33324. **EMAIL** xwang@broward.cc.fl.us

WARD, ANNALEE R.
PERSONAL Born 09/23/1958, Denver, CO, m, 1982, 2 children **DISCIPLINE** COMMUNICATION **EDUCATION** Calvin Col, BA, 80; Colorado St Univ, MA, 82; Regent Univ, PhD, 97. **CAREER** Assoc prof, Trinity Christian Col, 85-. **HONORS AND AWARDS** Dean's list; Phi Kappa Phi Honor Soc; Faculty Awd; received relig commun assoc dissertation of the year; comprehensive exams, passed 'with distinction'. **MEMBERSHIPS** Nat Commun Assoc; Relig Commun Assoc; Popular Culture Assoc. **RESEARCH** Disney animated films; communication ethics. **SELECTED PUBLICATIONS** Rev, of " Foundational Concepts of Communication Theories," Commun Quarterly, 95; art, The Axiology of The Lion King's Mythic Narrative: Disney as Moral Educator, J of Popular Film & Television, 96; art, The Trouble with Disney Morality, The Banner, 95; chapter, The Christian Century, Popular Relig Magazines of the United States, 95. **CONTACT ADDRESS** Trinity Christian Col, 6601 W College Dr, Palos Heights, IL 60463. **EMAIL** ann.ward@trinity.edu

WARD, AUDREY L.
PERSONAL Born 01/17/1950, Durham, NC, m, 1977, 3 children **DISCIPLINE** ENGLISH **EDUCATION** Elon Col, BA, 72; North Carolina Cen Univ, MA; Univ North Carolina, PhD, 94. **CAREER** Coord, Mars Hill Col, 73-81; instr, Piedmont Comm Col, 81-82; instr, Durham Comm Col, 82-83; instr, Piedmont Comm Col, 83-89; instr, Duke Univ, 89-91; instr, acad adv, Shaw Univ, 89-91; asst prof, Bennett Col, 91-00. **HONORS AND AWARDS** Who's Who Am Teach; **MEMBERSHIPS** AERA; OCBHS; NCTE; AESA; BCIRB; SCTE;

CFSBD; NHESIB. **RESEARCH** Women's Narratives; African American Literature; cultural studies; Christian doctrines. **SELECTED PUBLICATIONS** Auth, Gender and Domination: The Narrative Works of Alice Walker, Alice Munro, Gloria Naylor, and Toni Morrison, Watermark Press, 90. **CONTACT ADDRESS** Dept English, Languages, Bennett Col, 900 E Washington St, Greensboro, NC 27401-3239. **EMAIL** audreywrd@aol.com

WARD, CAROL
DISCIPLINE ENGLISH LITERATURE **EDUCATION** Univ Tenn, PhD, 81. **CAREER** Dept Eng, Clemson Univ **RESEARCH** Film studies; women's literature. **SELECTED PUBLICATIONS** Auth, Rita Mae Brown, Twayne, 93; Rita Mae Brown, Reference Guide to American Literature, 94; Southern Landscape in Contemporary Film, Beyond the Stars: Locales in American Popular Film, 93; auth, Mae West: A Bio-Bibliography, Greenwood Press, 89. **CONTACT ADDRESS** Clemson Univ, 707 Strode, Clemson, SC 29634. **EMAIL** wardc@clemson.edu

WARD, CAROLE GENEVA
PERSONAL Born 01/14/1943, Phoenix City, AL **DISCIPLINE** ENGLISH, FILM **EDUCATION** CA State Univ at San Jose, BA 1965; MA 1973; Univ of CA, Grad Studies 1970; Intl Comm Coll, PhD; Univ of Ile-Ife Nigeria, 1970; Univ of Sci & Tech, 1970; Kumasi Ghana Forah Bay Coll Sierra Leone, 1970; Sorbonne, 1963. **CAREER** Ethnic Studies Laney Coll, chrwmn; Goddard Coll, mentor consult teacher for masters degree stud 1973-74; Laney Coll, 70-; CA Coll of Arts Cabrillo Coll, 70; Andrew Hill HS, 65-69; airline stewardess, 66-68. **HONORS AND AWARDS** Recip purchase award 27th Annual SF Art Festival 1973; alpha phi alpha award outstanding black woman for achvmnt & serv 1974; selec com chmn for Black Filmmakers Hall of Fame Paramount Theatre of the Arts; publ Images of Awareness Pan Africanist Mag 1973; Afro-Am Artists Bio-Biographical Dir Theres Dickason 1973; black artist on Art Vol 2 by Samella Lewis Ruth Waddy 1970. **MEMBERSHIPS** Mem Bay Area Black Artists 1972-; Nat Conf of Artists 1973-74. **CONTACT ADDRESS** Laney Col, 900 Fallon St, Oakland, CA 94607.

WARD, HERMAN M.
PERSONAL Born 03/11/1914, Jersey City, NJ, m, 1943, 4 children **DISCIPLINE** ENGLISH **EDUCATION** Montclair State Col, AB, 35; Princeton Univ, AM, 37, PhD, 40. **CAREER** Asst prof English, Jersey City State Col, 46-47; prof, 46-77, EMER PROF ENGLISH, TRENTON STATE COL, 77-; Fulbright fel, Anatolia Col, Greece, 52-53, Univ Iceland, 62-63; consult English, Princeton High Sch, 61-62; exchange prof, Univ Frankfurt, 66-67. **MEMBERSHIPS** NCTE **RESEARCH** Teaching of high school English; Irish and Greek literature; creative writing. **SELECTED PUBLICATIONS** Auth, Yankee Sailors in British Jails, Prisoners of War at Forton and Mill, 1777-1783, William Mary Quart, Vol 53, 96; Lincoln, Benjamin and the American Revolution, Va Quart Rev, Vol 72, 96; Escape in america, the British Convention Prisoners, 1777-1783, William Mary Quart, Vol 53, 96. **CONTACT ADDRESS** RD No 2, Belle Mead, NJ 08502.

WARD, JEAN M.
PERSONAL Born 01/14/1938, Eugene, OR, m, 1960, 2 children **DISCIPLINE** SPEECH **EDUCATION** Univ OR, BS, 60, MS, 64, PhD, 89. **CAREER** Teacher high sch, Fern Ridge Sch Dist, OR, 62-64; instr speech commun, 64-67, asst prof, 67-72, assoc prof, 72-79, prof commmun, Lewis & Clark Col, 80-, chp dept commun, 74-. **MEMBERSHIPS** Nat Speech Commun Asn; Nat Women's Studies Asn; Western Speech Asn. **RESEARCH** Women in American public address; protest rhetoric; American Studies. **SELECTED PUBLICATIONS** Ed, Dollars for Education, 72, co-ed, Democratic Alternatives, 74 & In Short Supply, 75, Nat Textbk; Pacific Northwest Women, 1815-1925, OSU Press, 95; auth, Yours for Liberty, OSU Press, 00. **CONTACT ADDRESS** Dept Commun, Lewis and Clark Col, 0615 SW Palatine Hill Rd, Portland, OR 97219-7879. **EMAIL** jean@lclark.edu

WARD, JERRY W.
PERSONAL Born 07/31/1943, Washington, DC, s **DISCIPLINE** ENGLISH **EDUCATION** Tougaloo Col, BS, 64; Ill Inst of Technol, MS, 66; Univ Va, PhD, 78. **CAREER** From Asst Prof to Prof, Tougaloo Col, 70-. **HONORS AND AWARDS** Nat Humanities Ctr Fel, 99-00. **MEMBERSHIPS** CLA, The Authors Guild, NCTE, MLA, OHA. **RESEARCH** Richard Wright, oral history, African-American literature. **SELECTED PUBLICATIONS** Auth, Redefining American Literary History, Mod Lang Asn (New York, NY), 90; auth, "Black Southern Voices, New Am Libr (92); auth, "Trouble the Water: 250 Years of African-American Poetry," Mentor (97). **CONTACT ADDRESS** Dept English, Tougaloo Col, 500 W County Line Rd, Tougaloo, MS 39174-9999. **EMAIL** jerryward31@hotmail.com

WARD, JOHN C.
PERSONAL Born 03/05/1944, Takoma PK, MD, m, 1967, 2 children **DISCIPLINE** ENGLISH LITERATURE **EDUCATION** Amherst Col, BA; Univ Va, MA, PhD. **CAREER** Fac, Kenyon Col, 70; vice pres, dean acad affairs, prof Eng, Centre Col, 90-. **HONORS AND AWARDS** Asst ed, Kenyon Rev; rdr, Jour Midwest MLA. **MEMBERSHIPS** Midwest MLA. **SELECTED PUBLICATIONS** Auth, poetry, literary biography, and literary criticism. **CONTACT ADDRESS** Centre Col, 600 W Walnut St, Danville, KY 40422. **EMAIL** wardj@centre.edu

WARD, TOM R.
DISCIPLINE MUSIC **EDUCATION** Univ Pittsburgh, MA, PhD. **CAREER** Prof, 69-, Univ IL Urbana Champaign. **MEMBERSHIPS** Am Musicol Soc. **RESEARCH** Music and liturgy in the Middle Ages and Renaissance; music and music theory in univ(s) of the fourteenth and fifteenth centuries. **SELECTED PUBLICATIONS** Auth, The Polyphonic Office Hymn 1400-1520: A Descriptive Catalog; pubs in Musica Disciplina; Journal of the American Musicological Society; Early Music History. **CONTACT ADDRESS** Dept of Music, Univ of Illinois, Urbana-Champaign, E Gregory Drive, PO Box 52, Champaign, IL 61820. **EMAIL** t-ward2@staff.uiuc.edu

WARDROPE, WILLIAM J.
PERSONAL Born 10/14/1962, San Antonio, TX, s **DISCIPLINE** SPEECH, COMMUNICATION **EDUCATION** Univ Central Okla, BA, 86; Okla State Univ, MA, 88; Univ Nebr, PhD, 95. **CAREER** Asst prof, Univ Central Okla, 92-98; asst prof, Stephen F. Austin State Univ, 98-99; Basic Commun Course Dir, Baruch Col, 99-2000. **HONORS AND AWARDS** Outstanding Young Col Teacher, Okla Speech Theatre Commun Asn, 94; Outstanding New Teacher, Central States Commun Asn, 96; Outstanding Business Commun Teacher, Asn for Business Commun (SW Region), 99; over 100 presentations at int, nat, and regional confs; taught over 15 different courses in 2 academic disciplines; numerous Awds for teaching and research. **MEMBERSHIPS** Asn for Business Commun, Nat Commun Asn, Phi Kappa Phi. **RESEARCH** Business, communication, gender communication, organizational studies **SELECTED PUBLICATIONS** Coauth, "Cooperative communication: enhancing group interaction through application," Refereed Proceedings of the Asn for Business Commun-SW (96); coauth, "A portrait of business communication: a content analysis of current syllabi," Refereed Proceedings of the Asn for Business Commun-SW (98); auth, "General education requirements of undergraduate business programs in Texas," Texas Bus Educ J, 7 (99): 166-172; auth, "Curricular profiles of communication departments in the United States," Commun Educ, 48 (99): 256-258; coauth, "Content of the business communication course: an analysis of coverage," Bus Commun Quart, 62 (99): 33-40. **CONTACT ADDRESS** Dept Speech, Baruch Col, CUNY, 17 Lexington Ave, New York, NY 10010-5518. **EMAIL** wardrope@prodigy.net

WARE, THOMAS C.
PERSONAL Born 04/07/1929, Louisville, KY, m, 1953, 5 children **DISCIPLINE** ENGLISH **EDUCATION** Univ Louisville, BA, 57; Univ NC, Chapel Hill, MA, 60, PhD (English), 69. **CAREER** From instr to asst prof, Univ Cincinnati, 62-67; asst prof, Univ Chattanooga, 67-69; assoc prof, 69-74, PROF ENGLISH and HEAD DEPT, UNIV TENN CHATTANOOGA, 74-; Nat Endowment for Humanities summer grants, Columbia Univ, 77 and 81. **MEMBERSHIPS** Asn Depts English; SAtlantic Mod Lang Asn. **RESEARCH** Anglo-Irish literature; British literature 1800-20; modern British novel. **SELECTED PUBLICATIONS** Auth, Naturalism in the European Novel in New Critical Perspectives, Eng Lit Transition, Vol 36, 93; coauth, Theodore O. Hare, Poet-Soldier of the Old South, Univ of Tenn Press, 98. **CONTACT ADDRESS** Dept of English, Univ of Tennessee, Chattanooga, Chattanooga, TN 37401. **EMAIL** tware@cecosun.utc.edu

WARE, TRACY
DISCIPLINE ENGLISH LITERATURE **EDUCATION** Univ Western Ontario, PhD. **CAREER** Dept Eng, Queen's Univ **HONORS AND AWARDS** W.J. Barnes Tchg Awd, 97. **RESEARCH** Canadian poetry; Canadian and Australian literary history; Romanticism past and present. **SELECTED PUBLICATIONS** Auth, Jean Baptiste, Can Poetry, 96 **CONTACT ADDRESS** English Dept, Queen's Univ at Kingston, Kingston, ON, Canada K7L 3N6. **EMAIL** tw5@qsilver.queensu.ca

WARKENTIN, GERMAINE
PERSONAL Born Toronto, ON, Canada **DISCIPLINE** ENGLISH **EDUCATION** Univ Toronto, BA, 55, PhD, 72; Univ Man, MA, 62. **CAREER** Freelance film critic, 53-64; ed, Canadian Newsreel, 54-57; lectr, United Col, Winnipeg, 58-59; lectr, Victoria Col, 70-72, asst prof, 72-76, assoc prof, 76-90, Prof English, Univ Toronto, 90-, dir, Ctr Reformation & Renaissance Studs, 85-90. **MEMBERSHIPS** Renaissance English Text Soc; Spencer Soc. **SELECTED PUBLICATIONS** Auth, James Reaney, Poems, 72; auth, Canadian Exploration Writing, in English: An Anthology, 93; auth, Ins and Outs of the Sidney family Library, in Times Lit Suppl, 85. **CONTACT ADDRESS** Dept of English, Victoria Col, Univ of Toronto, Toronto, ON, Canada M5S 1K9. **EMAIL** warkent@chass.utoronto.ca

WARKENTIN, LARRY R.
PERSONAL Born 08/14/1940, Reedley, CA, m, 1962, 2 children **DISCIPLINE** MUSIC **EDUCATION** Tabor Col, BA, 62; Calif St Univ, MA, 64; Univ So Ca, DMA, 67. **CAREER** Chmn, tchr, music dept, 66-, Fresno Pacific Univ. **HONORS AND AWARDS** Calif Music Tchrs, 1st place comp, 84; ASCAP, classical comp, 88-. **MEMBERSHIPS** Amer Soc of Composers Authors & Pub; Calif Music Tchrs Asn. **RESEARCH** Music composition; church music **SELECTED PUBLICATIONS** Auth, The Rise and Fall of Indian Music in California Missions, Univ of Texas Press, 81; auth, How Wondrous Great, Lorenz Music, OH, 90; auth, From the Hands, What does the Lord Require, Wonder of Wonders, When Grief is Raw, Hymnal: a Worship Book, Brethren Press, 92; art, Caring about Music in the Church, Dir Jour, 93; art, guest ed, Caring about Music in the Church, Direction Jour, 93; rev, On The Aisle, Fresno Bee, 88-95; auth, Huldrich Zwingli, Dict of Art, Macmillan, 96; auth, Alleluia, Moon of Hope Pub, 96; auth, When Grief is Raw, Covenant Hymnal, Covenant Press, 96; auth, Like Candle Flame, Lumina Music, 98. **CONTACT ADDRESS** Fresno Pacific Col, 1717 S Chestnut Ave, Fresno, CA 93702-9863. **EMAIL** lwarkent@fresno.edu

WARNER, JOHN M.
PERSONAL Born 04/30/1935, Haydenville, MA **DISCIPLINE** ENGLISH LITERATURE **EDUCATION** Univ Mass, BA, 56; Harvard Univ, MA, 60, PhD(English) lit), 64. **CAREER** From instr to asst prof, 62-71, assoc prof, 71-78, Prof English Lit, Drew Univ, 78-00. **MEMBERSHIPS** MLA. **RESEARCH** Eighteenth century novel; 20th century British literature; religion and literature. **SELECTED PUBLICATIONS** Auth, Smollet's development as a novelist, Novel, Vol V, 148-61; An epistemological view of the funtion of the interpolated stories in the fiction of Fielding and Smollett, Studies in Novel, Vol V, 271-83; The religious dimension of James's The Ambassadors, Essay Lit, Vol IV, 78-94; Belief and imagination in The Windhover, Hopkins Quart, Vol V, 127-135; Joyce's Grandfathers: Myth and History in Defoe, Smollett, Sterne, and Joyce, Univ Ga Press, 93. **CONTACT ADDRESS** 5 Webber Rd, Haydenville, MA 01039.

WARNER, MICHAEL D.
DISCIPLINE ENGLISH **CAREER** Asst prof English, Rutgers. **RESEARCH** English literature. **SELECTED PUBLICATIONS** Fel Publ, Textuality and Legitimacy in the Printed Constitution, Procs of AAS 97, 87; auth, Professionalization and the Rewards of Literature, 1875-1900, 85; Value, Agency, and Stephen Crane's 'The Monster,' Nineteenth-Century Fiction , 85; The Letters of the Republic: Publication and the Public Sphere in Eighteenth-Century America, Harvard Univ, 90; ed, Fear of a Queer Planet: Queer Politics and Social Theory, 93; co-ed, The Origins of Literary Studies in America, Routledge, 89; co-ed, The English Literatures of America, 1500-1800, Routledge, 97. **CONTACT ADDRESS** Dept of English, Rutgers, The State Univ of New Jersey, New Brunswick, New Brunswick, NJ 08903. **EMAIL** mwarner@interport.net.

WARNER, NICHOLAS OLIVER
PERSONAL Born 02/11/1950, San Francisco, CA, m, 3 children **DISCIPLINE** COMPARATIVE ; ENGLISH & AMERICAN LITERATURE **EDUCATION** Stanford Univ, BA, 72; Univ Calif, Berkeley, PhD, 77. **CAREER** Vis asst prof Eng, Oberlin Col, 78-80; asst prof Lit, Claremont McKenna Col, 80-86; assoc prof, Claremont McKenna Col, 86-94; full prof, Claremont McKenna Col, 94-. **HONORS AND AWARDS** Huntton Awd for Superior Tchg, 83, 84, 88, 90, 99; Graves fel in the Humanities. **MEMBERSHIPS** MLA; Am Asn Advan Slavic Studies; Am Studies Assoc. **RESEARCH** Literature and visual arts; 19th century British, Am & Russ lit. **SELECTED PUBLICATIONS** Auth, Blakes Moon-Ark symbolism, Blake Quart, fall 80; Spirits of America: Intoxication in 19th Century American Literature, Univ Oklahoma, 97; auth, "The Texture of Time in War & Peace," Slavic & East European Journal, 86. **CONTACT ADDRESS** Dept of Literature, Claremont McKenna Col, 850 Columbia Ave, Claremont, CA 91711-6420. **EMAIL** nwarner@mckenna.edu

WARNER, WILLIAM BEATTY
PERSONAL Born 02/03/1947, Montpelier, VT, m, 1971 **DISCIPLINE** ENGLISH LITERATURE, CRITICAL THEORY **EDUCATION** Univ Pa, BA, 68; Johns Hopkins Univ, MA, 74, PhD (English lit), 77. **CAREER** Asst prof, 77 79, ASSOC PROF ENGLISH LIT, STATE UNIV NY BUFFALO, 79-. **MEMBERSHIPS** MLA **SELECTED PUBLICATIONS** Auth, The play of fictions and succession of styles in Ulysses, James Joyce Quart, 2/78; Proposal and habitation: The temporality and authority of interpretation, Boundary 2, 7/78; Reading Clarissa: The Struggle of Interpretations, Yale Univ, 79. **CONTACT ADDRESS** SUNY, Buffalo, P O Box 604610, Buffalo, NY 14260-4610.

WARREN, CLAY
PERSONAL Born 08/11/1946, Lexington Park, MD, m, 1985, 2 children **DISCIPLINE** COMMUNICATION **EDUCATION** US Naval Acad, BS, 69; Univ Colo, MA, 73; PhD, 76. **CAREER** Asst Prof, Inst for Shipboard Edu, 77; Visiting Asst Prof, Univ Col of Cape Breton, 78; Asst Prof, Shepherd Col, 78-

79; Asst Prof, Univ Hawaii, 79-82; Sen Laerer, Intl People's Col, 82-84; Assoc Prof, Univ Col of Cape Breton, 84-90; Visiting Assoc Prof to Prof, George Washington Univ, 90-. **HONORS AND AWARDS** Undergrad Dept Advising Awd, George Washington Univ, 98; Grant, Grundtvig Foundation Board, 95-97; DMEF Fel, New York, 96, Morton Bender Awd for Teaching Excellence,00, Acad of Consciousness Studies Fel, 94, Rudolf Dreikurs Mem Scholar, Tompkins Instuture Research Fel, 87-89. **MEMBERSHIPS** Am Asn of Univ Prof, Folk Educ Asn of Am, Intl Soc for Intercultural Educ, Training & Res, Nat Comm Asn, N Am Soc of Adlerian Psychol. **SELECTED PUBLICATIONS** Ed, Democracy is Born in Conversations, Folk Education Association of America, 98; ed, Inner Visions, Outer Voices, Univ Col of Cape Breton Press, 88; auth, Coming Around, Budapest, 86; auth, "Writing in water: A life in folkhighschool education," Option: Journal of the Folk Education Association of America, (97): 1-10; auth, Beds of Strange, 90. **CONTACT ADDRESS** Dept Comm, The George Washington Univ, 2130 H St NW, Suite 707, Washington, DC 20052-0001. **EMAIL** claywar@gwu.edu

WARREN, JAMES PERRIN
PERSONAL Born 04/07/1954, TX, d, 2 children **DISCIPLINE** ENGLISH **EDUCATION** Auburn Univ, BA, 76; Yale Univ, MA, 80, MPhil, 81, PhD, 82. **CAREER** Teaching fel to instr, Yale Univ, 80-82; asst, Universite de Geneve, Switzerland, 82-84; asst prof to assoc prof to prof to chair, Washington & Lee Univ, 84-. **MEMBERSHIPS** American Studies Assoc; Religious Society of Friends. **RESEARCH** 19th-Century America literature, literature and environment. **SELECTED PUBLICATIONS** Auth, Walt Whitman's Language Experiment, Penn State Press, 90; auth, Reconstructing Language in Democratic Vistas, Walt Whitman: The Centennial Essays, Univ Iowa Press, 94; art, Reading Whitman's Post-War Poetry, Utopia in the Present Tense: Walt Whitman and the Language of the New World, Rome, 94; art, Reading Whitman's Post-War Poetry, Cambridge Companion to Walt Whitman, Cambridge Univ Press, 95; auth, Style and Techniques, Walt Whitman: An Encyclopedia, Garland, 98; auth, Culture of Eloquence: Oratory and Reform in Antebellum Armeica, Penn State Press, 99; auth, Contexts for Reading 'Song of the Redwood-Tree.'" Reading under the Sign of Nature, Univ of Idaho Press, 00. **CONTACT ADDRESS** Dept of English, Washington and Lee Univ, 448 Hollow Lane, Lexington, VA 24450. **EMAIL** warrenj@wlu.edu

WARREN, JOSEPH W.
PERSONAL Born 07/02/1949, Rocky Mount, NC, m, 1972 **DISCIPLINE** ENGLISH **EDUCATION** Oakwood Coll, BA (summa cum laude), 1971; Ohio State Univ, MA, 1973, PhD, 1982. **CAREER** Ohio State Univ, grad asst, 73-76; Lake Michigan Coll, adjunct professor, 78-80; Andrews Univ, assoc professor of English, 76-. **HONORS AND AWARDS** United Negro Coll Fund Fellowship, 1971; PhD, Fellowship, Ohio State Univ, 1971; Research Grant, Andrews Univ, 1984, 1992. **MEMBERSHIPS** Founder, Mid-Amer Network Marketing, Inc, 1984-; Inst for Christian Educ and Youth Devel, 1985-; cofounder, Scholastic Study Lab, Andrews Univ, 1984; founder, owner, Mid-Amer Premiere Brokerage, 1986-; founder, director, The Center for Building Self-Esteem in African-American Youth, 1990-. **CONTACT ADDRESS** Andrews Univ, Berrien Springs, MI 49103.

WARREN, JOYCE
PERSONAL Born Springfield, MA, m, 4 children **DISCIPLINE** ENGLISH **EDUCATION** Brown Univ, BA; MA; Columbia Univ, PhD, 81. **CAREER** Assoc Prof, Queens Col, 81-. **HONORS AND AWARDS** Phi Beta Kappa; NEH, 87. **MEMBERSHIPS** Mod Lang Asn; Am Lit Asn; Am Studies Asn. **RESEARCH** Nineteenth Century American literature. **CONTACT ADDRESS** Dept Eng, Queens Col, CUNY, 6530 Kissena Blvd, Flushing, NY 11367-1575. **EMAIL** joyce_warren@qc.edu

WARREN, LELAND EDDIE
PERSONAL Born 04/22/1944, Dublin, GA, m, 1967 **DISCIPLINE** ENGLISH LITERATURE **EDUCATION** Emory Univ, BA, 66; Univ Ga, MA, 68; Univ Ill, PhD(English), 76. **CAREER** Instr English, Col William & Mary, 69-72; asst prof, 76-81, from assoc prof to prof English, 81-87, Kansas State Univ; ed, The Eighteenth Century: A Current Bibliog, 76-; co ed, Eighteenth Centur Life, 81-95. **MEMBERSHIPS** MLA; Am Soc 18th Century Studies. **RESEARCH** Narrative theory; 18th century culture; satire. **SELECTED PUBLICATIONS** Auth, Wordsworth's conception of man: A study in apocalyptic vision, Southern Humanities Rev, 70; A sudden vision of life: DeQuincey's The English Mail Coach, Studies in Humanities, 72; The constant speaker: Aspects of conversation in Tristram Shandy, Univ Toronto Quart, 76; Fielding's problem and ours: Allworthy and authority in Tom Jones, Essays Lit, 78; History-As-Literature and the Narrative Stance of Henry Fielding, Clio, 79; Of the conversation of women: The female Quixote and the dream of perfection, Studies Eighteenth-Century Cult, 81. **CONTACT ADDRESS** Dept of English, Kansas State Univ, 106 Denison Hall, Manhattan, KS 66506-0701. **EMAIL** lwarren@ksu.edu

WARREN, NAGUEYALTI
PERSONAL Born 10/01/1947, Atlanta, GA, m, 3 children **DISCIPLINE** ENGLISH LITERATURE **EDUCATION** Fisk Univ, BA 1972; Simmons Coll, MA 1974; Boston Univ, MA 1974; Univ of Mississippi, PhD 1984. **CAREER** Northeastern Univ, instructor 1977-78; Univ of Calabar, lecturer 1979; Fisk Univ, asst prof and chairperson, Dept of English 1984-88; Emory University, assoc dean, assoc prof, 88-. **HONORS AND AWARDS** Golden Poet Awd World Poetry Assoc 1985; poetry published in the following The American Poetry Anthology, Mississippi Earthworks, Janus, Obsidian. **MEMBERSHIPS** Mem College Language Assoc, Modern Language Assoc, Natl Council of Teachers of English, Southern Conf on Afro-Amer Studies; advisory board member, W E B Du Bois Foundation. **RESEARCH** Alice Walker. **SELECTED PUBLICATIONS** Book: Lodestar and Other Night Lights, New York, Mellen, 1992; auth, Southern Mothers: Facts and Fictions in Southern Women's Writing, LSU Press, 99. **CONTACT ADDRESS** Emory Univ, 215 White Hall, Atlanta, GA 30322. **EMAIL** nwarren@emory.edu

WARREN, THOMAS
DISCIPLINE TECHNICAL WRITING **EDUCATION** Univ Kans, PhD, 74. **CAREER** Engl, Okla St Univ. **HONORS AND AWARDS** Inst Scientific & Technical Communicators; Soc Technical Comm; pres, erik j. visser fund found; ed, proceedings okla acad sci; past-pres, intecom; fel, asn tchs technical writing; soc technical comm. **RESEARCH** Cross-cultural communication; Communication theory; Document design, and graphics. **SELECTED PUBLICATIONS** Areas: cross-cultural communication, communication theory, document design, and graphics. **CONTACT ADDRESS** Oklahoma State Univ, Stillwater, 101 Whitehurst Hall, Stillwater, OK 74078.

WARTELLA, ELLEN A.
PERSONAL Born 10/16/1949, Kingston, PA, m, 1976, 2 children **DISCIPLINE** MASS COMMUNICATION **EDUCATION** Univ Pittsburgh, BA, 71; Univ Minn, MA, 74, PhD, 77. **CAREER** Instr, Univ Minn, 74, 75, 76; Asst Prof, Ohio State Univ, 76-79; Res Asst Prof, 79-83, Res Assoc Prof, 83-89, Univ Schol & Res Prof, Inst Commun Res, Univ Ill at Urbana-Champaign, 89-93; Vis Prof, Univ Calif - Santa Barbara, 92-93; Prof, Univ Tex-Austin, 93-. **HONORS AND AWARDS** NDEA Title IV Fel, Univ Minn, 71-74; Arnold O. Beckman Res Awd, Univ Ill, 83-84; Krieghbaum Under 40 Awd, Asn Educ Journalism & Mass Commun, 84; Res Awd, Ctr Population Options, 86-87; Fel, Int Commun Asn; Leadership Tex Class 1997; Educr of the Year, The Ad Soc, Austin Advertising Federation, 98. **MEMBERSHIPS** Int Commun Asn; Asn Educ Journalism & Mass Commun; Nat Commun Asn; Broadcast Educ Asn; Am Asn Public Opinion Res; Kappa Tau Alpha. **RESEARCH** Children and mass media. **SELECTED PUBLICATIONS** Co-ed, American Communication Research: The Remembered History, Lawrence Erlbaum, 96; The Audience and Its Landscape, Westview Press, 96; coauth, MediaMaking, Sage Publ, 98; author of numerous other books, book chapters, articles, and conference presentations. **CONTACT ADDRESS** Col of Communication, Univ of Texas, Austin, Austin, TX 78712-1094. **EMAIL** wartella@mail.utexas.edu

WASERMAN, MANFRED
PERSONAL Born 03/21/1933, Free City of Danzig, Poland, 1 child **DISCIPLINE** AMERICAN HISTORY, LIBRARY SCIENCE **EDUCATION** Univ Md, BA, 59, MA, 61; Cath Univ Am, MS, 63, PhD (hist), 82. **CAREER** Teacher hist, Prince Geofe's County, Md, Pub Sch, 60-62; librn, Library, Yale Univ, 63-65; Curator, Mod Manuscripts, Nat Libr Med, 65-. **MEMBERSHIPS** Am Asn Hist Med; AHA; Am Libr Asn; Oral Hist Asn. **RESEARCH** History of medicine and public health; history of child health care; primitive medicine and ethnology. **SELECTED PUBLICATIONS** Auth, Montefiore, Moses, A Hebrew Prayer Book, and Medicine in the Holy Land, Judaism, Vol 45, 96. **CONTACT ADDRESS** Hist Med Div, National Libr of Med, Bethesda, MD 20209.

WASHBURN, DENNIS
DISCIPLINE ASIAN AND MIDDLE EASTERN LANGUAGES AND LITERATURES **EDUCATION** Harvard Univ, BA, 76; Oxford Univ, MA, 79; Yale Univ, MPhil, PhD, 91. **CAREER** Asst prof, Dartmouth Col; Asst Prof, Conn Col, 87-91; Vis Instructor, Yale Univ, 89-90; Asst Prof, Harvard Univ, 91-92; Chair and Assoc Prof, Dartmouth, 92-; Dir of Japanese School, 00-. **HONORS AND AWARDS** Monbusho Scholar, Japanese Min Educ. **RESEARCH** Transition from Edo to Meiji lit; transl of moral categories in Meiji fiction. **SELECTED PUBLICATIONS** Auth, The Dilemma of the Modern in Japanese Fiction, Yale UP, 95; auth, "Toward A View from Nowhere: Perspective and Ethical Judgment in Fires on the Plain," Journal of Japanese Studies, 97; auth, "Structures of Emptiness: Kitsch, Nihilism and the Inauthentic in Mishima's Aesthetics, " in Studies in Modern Japanese Literature, 97; coed, Studies in Modern Japanese Literature, Univ of Mich, 97; coed, Between Word and Image: Essays on the Japanese Cineam, Cambridge Univ Pr, 00; auth, "The Arrest of Time: Sacred Trangressions of Vengeance Is Mine," in Between Word and Image: Essays on the Japanese Cinema, Cambridge Univ Pr, forthcoming. **CONTACT ADDRESS** Dartmouth Col, 3529 N Main St, #207, Hanover, NH 03755. **EMAIL** dennis.washburn@dartmouth.edu

WASHBURN, LAURA LEE
PERSONAL Born 09/30/1965, Virginia Beach, VA **DISCIPLINE** CREATIVE WRITING, POETRY **EDUCATION** Old Dominion Univ, BA, 87; Ariz State Univ, MFA, 90. **CAREER** Teach asst, Ariz State Univ, 88-90; fac assoc, 90-92; instr, Southwest Mo State Univ, 92-97; asst prof, Pittsburg State Univ, 97-. **HONORS AND AWARDS** Palanquin Chap Bk Prize; Wkg Schl, BWC. **RESEARCH** Poe. **SELECTED PUBLICATIONS** Auth, This Good Warm Place, March St Press; auth, Watching the Contortionists (Palanquin Press, USC). **CONTACT ADDRESS** Dept English, Pittsburg State Univ, 1701 S Broadway St, Pittsburg, KS 66762-5856.

WASHINGTON, DURTHY A.
PERSONAL Born 02/20/1948, Nuremberg, Germany, d, 1 child **DISCIPLINE** CONTEMPORARY AMERICAN LITERATURE; TECHNICAL WRITING **EDUCATION** San Diego State Univ, BA, 73; Univ Southern Calif, MS, 79; San Jose State Univ, MA, 86 **CAREER** Writer/Seminar Leader, Self-Employed, 93-; owner, Springs Seminarz; instr, Pikes Peak Comm Col, 98; instr, Col Univ, 92-96; instr, Univ Calif Santa Cruz, 93; instr, Univ Texas, 81-83 **HONORS AND AWARDS** Profiled in the Gazette, Colorado Springs major newspaper, 98; Best Feature Awd, Urban Spectrum News; 96; Awd for Excellence in Tech Writing, Soc Tech Comm, 91 **MEMBERSHIPS** Amer Libr Assoc; Colorado Libr Assoc; Colorado Lang Arts Soc; MELUS; Modern Lang Assoc; Ntl Coalition Independent Scholars; Phi Kappa Phi Ntl Honor Soc; Toni Morriosn Soc **RESEARCH** Technical Communication; American Ethnic Literature **SELECTED PUBLICATIONS** Auth, "Womanist of Feminist?: Black Women and the Women's Movement," African Amer Voice, 98; auth, "Swing Low: Black Men Writing," Bloomsbury Rev, 97; auth, "Bone Black: Memoirs of Girlhood," Bloomsbury Rev, 97 **CONTACT ADDRESS** 4581 Castlepoint Dr, Colorado Springs, CO 80917-1366. **EMAIL** durthy@aol.com

WASHINGTON, MARY HELEN
PERSONAL Born 01/21/1941, Cleveland, OH, s **DISCIPLINE** ENGLISH **EDUCATION** Notre Dame College, BA, 1962; University of Detroit, MA, 1966, PhD, 1976. **CAREER** High school teacher of English in Cleveland OH public schools, 62-64; St. John College, Cleveland, instructor in English, 66-68; Univ of Detroit, Detroit MI, asst prof of English, 72-75, director of Center for Black Studies, beginning 75; currently Assoc Prof of English, Boston Harbor College, Univ of Mass, Boston. **MEMBERSHIPS** National Council of Teachers of English, College Language Association, Michigan Black Studies Association. **SELECTED PUBLICATIONS** Richard Wright Award for Literary Criticism from Black World, 1974; anthologist, Memory of Kin: Stories About Family by Black Writers. **CONTACT ADDRESS** Dept of English, Univ of Massachusetts, Boston, Boston, MA 02125.

WASHINGTON, SARAH M.
PERSONAL Born 08/10/1942, Holly Hill, SC, d, 1967 **DISCIPLINE** ENGLISH **EDUCATION** Tuskegee Inst, Tuskegee AL, BS 1964; Univ of Illinois, Urbana IL, MS 1970, PhD 1980. **CAREER** Spartanburg District, Inman SC, English teacher, 64-65; Anderson Public Schools, Anderson SC, Eng teacher, 65-67; Sumter Schools, Sumter SC, social studies teacher, 67-68; AL State Univ, Montgomery AL, English instructor, 71-74; Univ of IL, Urbana IL, teaching asst, 74-80; SC State Coll, Orangeburg SC, English prof, 79-. **HONORS AND AWARDS** Sigma Tau Delta Natl Eng Honor Soc, 1981; field coordinator, Assessment Performance in Teaching, 1988-90; Scholar, Let's Talk About It, a national reading program. **MEMBERSHIPS** Pres, Orangeburg Branch, Assn of the Study of Afro-Amer Life & History, 1980-85; pres elect, 1991, chaplain, 1982-89, Phi Delta Kappa; mem, SC State Dept Writing Advisory Bd, 1983-89; mem, Amer Assn of Univ Women; reader, Natl Teachers Examination, 1989; Natl Council of Teachers of English; Natl Black Child Development Institute. **SELECTED PUBLICATIONS** Author of literary biog of Frank Horne, 1985; **CONTACT ADDRESS** Professor, English, So Carolina State Univ, PO Box 2034, Orangeburg, SC 29117.

WASHINGTON, VON HUGO, SR.
PERSONAL Born 03/09/1943, Albion, MI, m, 1974 **DISCIPLINE** DRAMA **EDUCATION** Western Michigan Univ, Kalamazoo, MI, BS, 1974, MA, 1975; Wayne State Univ, Detroit, MI, PhD, 1979. **CAREER** Univ of Michigan, Ann Arbor, MI, dir, black theatre, 75-77; Wayne State Univ, Detroit, MI, dir, black theatre, 79-88; Western Michigan Univ, Kalamazoo, MI, dir, multicultural & performance area, theatre, 88-, professor, currently. **HONORS AND AWARDS** Achievement Awd, Michigan Foundation for the Arts, 1984; Career Development Chair, Wayne State Univ, 1983; Carter G Woodson Education Awd, Wayne State Univ, 1984; Alumni Faculty Service Awd, Wayne State Univ, 1988; Best Actor, Detroit News, 1990. **MEMBERSHIPS** Black Theatre Network, 1986-96; artistic dir/co-founder; Afro-American Studio Theatre, Detroit, 1983-86; president/co-founder, Washington Prod Inc, 1992-. **CONTACT ADDRESS** Professor, Western Michigan Univ, PO Box 3253, Kalamazoo, MI 49003.

WASON, ROBERT W.
DISCIPLINE MUSIC **EDUCATION** Hartt Sch Music, MusB, 67, MusM, 69; Yale Univ, MPhil, 78, PhD, 81. **CAREER** Teaching Asst, 67-69, Piano Instr and Teaching Assoc, 69-70, Instr Theory/Compos, Hartt Sch Music, 70-76, 77-79; Teaching Asst, Yale Univ, 76-77; Lectr Music, Clark Univ, 80; Asst Prof, Univ N Texas, 81-83; Asst Prof to Assoc Prof, 83-97, Prof Music Theory, Eastman Sch Music, 97-; Heinrich Strobel Found Vis Prof, Univ Basel, 91; Vis Prof, Univ Brit Columbia, 92; Vis Prof, SUNY - Buffalo, 94. **HONORS AND AWARDS** Bronze Medal, Concours Int de Guitare, Radio France, 75; Fulbright Schol, 79-80; Paul Sacher Found Stipend, 89-90; NEH Fel Univ Teachers, 89-90; Guggenheim Fel, 90; UR Bridging Fel, 97; Special Opportunity Stipend, Arts and Cultural Coun Greater Rochester, 97; DAAD Study Visit, Ger Acad Exchange, 97. **SELECTED PUBLICATIONS** Auth, Viennese Harmonic Theory from Albrechtsberger to Schenker and Schoenberg, UMI Press, 85, repr U of R Press, 95; coauth, On Preparing Anton Webern's Early Songs for Performance: A Collaborators' Dialogue, Theory and Practice, vol 20, 95; auth, A Pitch-Class Motive in Webern's Op.3 George Lieder, Webern Studies, Cambridge Univ Press, 96; coauth, Die Harmonik des Jazz (forthcoming); author of several other articles, reviews, publications, and musical compositions. **CONTACT ADDRESS** Eastman Sch Music, Univ of Rochester, 26 Gibbs St., Rochester, NY 14604. **EMAIL** rwsn@theory.esm.rochester.edu

WASSER, HENRY H.
PERSONAL Born 04/13/1919, Pittsburgh, PA, m, 1942, 2 children **DISCIPLINE** LITERATURE **EDUCATION** Ohio State Univ, BA; MA; 40; Columbia Univ, PhD, 51. **CAREER** Teaching fel, George Wash Univ, 40-42; instr to assoc prof, CUNY, 46-66; prof and dean, Richmond Col CUNY, 66-73; prof and vp, Sacramento State Univ, 73-74; dir and pres, CUNY Acad of Humanities, 80-. **HONORS AND AWARDS** Fulbright Lectr, Univ Saconika; Fulbright Lectr, Univ Beugen and Oslo; Fulbright Lectr, Univ Aveiro; Award, Am Scand Found; Award, NEH; Award, Swedish Info Serv. **MEMBERSHIPS** MLA; Am Sociol Asn; Am Studies Asn; Soc of Higher Educ. **RESEARCH** Comparative higher education. **SELECTED PUBLICATIONS** Auth, Diversity in Higher Education, Germany, 99. **CONTACT ADDRESS** Grad Center, Graduate Sch and Univ Ctr, CUNY, 365 5th Ave, New York, NY 10816-4309. **EMAIL** s.wasser@worldnet.att.net

WASSERMAN, JERRY
PERSONAL Born 11/02/1945, Cincinnati, OH, m, 1982, 2 children **DISCIPLINE** ENGLISH **EDUCATION** Instr, Ill State Univ, 68-69; Prof, Univ BC, 72-. **HONORS AND AWARDS** Killam Teaching Prize, 98. **MEMBERSHIPS** Asn for Can Theatre Hist; Can Asn of Am Studies; Can Actors Equity Asn; Asn of Can Television and Radio Actors; Can Media Guild. **RESEARCH** Modern drama and theatre history, especially Canadian; The blues in/and African American and African Canadian literature. **SELECTED PUBLICATIONS** Ed, Twenty years at Play: A New Play Centre Anthology, Talonbooks, 90; auth, Modern Canadian Theatre: A Telecourse in 12 Acts, BC Open Learning Agency, 93; auth, "Daddy's Girls: Father-Daughter Incest and Canadian Plays by Women," Essays in Theatre, 95; auth, "'It's the Do-Gooders Burn My Ass': Modern Canadian Drama and the Crisis of Liberalism," Modern Drama, 00; auth, Modern Canadian Plays, 4th ed, Talonbooks, 01; auth, "Queen Bee, King Bee: The Color Purple and the Blues," Can Rev of Am Studies, 01. **CONTACT ADDRESS** Dept English, Univ of British Columbia, 3519 W 19th Ave, Vancouver, BC, Canada V6S 1Z1. **EMAIL** jerrywas@interchange.ubc.ca

WASSERMAN, JULIAN
PERSONAL Born 06/08/1948, Lubbock, TX **DISCIPLINE** MEDIEVAL LITERATURE **EDUCATION** Vanderbilt Univ, BA, 70; Southern Methodist Univ, MA, 72; Rice Univ, PhD (English), 75. **CAREER** From asst to assoc prof English, Univ Ark, Little Rock, 75-79; ASSOC PROF ENGLISH, UNIV ST THOMAS, 79-. **SELECTED PUBLICATIONS** Auth, Daddys Girls, Father Daughter Incest and Canadian Plays by Women, Essays in Theatre Etudes Theatrales, Vol 14, 95. **CONTACT ADDRESS** Dept of English, Univ of St. Thomas, Texas, Houston, TX 77006. **EMAIL** wasser@loyno.edu

WATERHOUSE, CAROLE
DISCIPLINE CREATIVE WRITING, JOURNALISM, 20TH CENTURY LITERATURE **EDUCATION** Univ Pittsburgh, MFA; OH Univ, PhD. **CAREER** Instr, CA State Univ PA; vol instr, State Correctional Inst, Pittsburgh. **RESEARCH** International film and lit. **SELECTED PUBLICATIONS** Auth, Without Wings; publ short stories in Mass Rev, Artful Dodge, Ball State Univ Forum, Ceilidh, Bassettown Rev, and Eureka Lit Mag. **CONTACT ADDRESS** California Univ of Pennsylvania, California, PA 15419. **EMAIL** waterhouse@cup.edu

WATERMAN, SUE A.
PERSONAL Born 09/06/1952, Pittsburgh, PA, m, 1978, 2 children **DISCIPLINE** LIBRARY SCIENCE **EDUCATION** Univ Mo, BA, 75; NYork Univ, MA, 78; Univ Mo, MLS, 92. **CAREER** Ref Libr, Community Col of Baltimore, 93-96; res serv libr, Johns Hopkins Univ, 96-. **HONORS AND AWARDS** Martinus Nijhoff Res Grant, Am Col, 01; Adj Fac of the Year, Community Col of Baltimore, 95; Jr Fel, Libr of Congress, 92-93. **MEMBERSHIPS** ALA; MLA; SHARP; Md Libr Asn. **RESEARCH** History of the Book; Cultures of Collecting. **SELECTED PUBLICATIONS** Auth, "Internet Resources in European Literature," Col and Res Libr News, 01; rev, "The History of reading in the West," in MLN (JHU Press), 01. **CONTACT ADDRESS** Eisenhower Libr, Johns Hopkins Univ, Baltimore, 3400 N Charles St, Baltimore, MD 21218-2608. **EMAIL** waterman@jhu.edu

WATERMEIER, DANIEL J.
DISCIPLINE THEATRE ARTS **EDUCATION** Univ IL, PhD, 68. **CAREER** Prof, Univ Toledo. **RESEARCH** Theatre hist; dramatic lit and criticism. **SELECTED PUBLICATIONS** Auth, Edwin Booth in Performance: The Mary Isabella Stone Commentaries, 90; Shakespeare Companies and Festivals: An International Guide, 95. **CONTACT ADDRESS** Dept of Theatre, Film and Dance, Univ of Toledo, Toledo, OH 43606. **EMAIL** danielwatermeier@pop3.utoledo.edu

WATERS, HAROLD A.
PERSONAL Born 11/08/1926, Wilmington, NC, m, 1989, 3 children **DISCIPLINE** POET, FRENCH **EDUCATION** Harvard Univ, AB, 49; Univ Paris, dipl & cert, 51; Univ WA, MA, 54, PhD(Romance lang), 56. **CAREER** From instr to asst prof mod lang, Col William & Mary, 55-60; asst prof Romance lang, Carleton Col, 60-62; from asst prof to assoc prof French, 62-69, Prof French, 69- , prof emeritus, Univ RI; Founder & coordr, Claudel Newslett, 68-72; assoc ed, Claudel Studies, 72-. **HONORS AND AWARDS** Betsy Colquitt Awd for Poetry, 98; BBC Contest for peoms on Africa, 80; Community Writers Asn Poetry Contest, 96; elected to Asn des Ecrivains de Langue Francasise, 98; Phi Beta Kappa, Rhode Island Beta Chapter--elected: Honorary Mem, 89; VP, 93-93; Pres, 93-94; Hist 96-98. **MEMBERSHIPS** Am Asn Tchrs Fr; AAUP; Northeast Mod Lang Asn; African Lit Asn; Acad of Am Poets; Asn Pour l' dtude des Litteratures Africainesdes. **RESEARCH** Black French lit; French soc theater; Claudel. **SELECTED PUBLICATIONS** Auth, Philosophic progression in Anouilh's plays, Symposium, summer 62; A propos de la seconde version de l'Echange, Rev Lett Mod annual Paul Claudel issue, 65; Paul Claudel, Twayne, 70; The heroic years of French Social Theater, Mod Lang Studies, spring 75; Black Theater in French: A Guide, Editions Naaman, 78; coauth, Today's English, Hatier-Nouvelles Editions Africaines, 79; auth, Theatre Noir, Three Continents, 88; Sengal, Poems on Africa, March St Pr, 00; 180 poems in various books, anthologies, magazines. **CONTACT ADDRESS** Box 233, Saunderstown, RI 02874. **EMAIL** hwa8559u@postoffice.uri.edu

WATERS, MICHAEL
PERSONAL Born 11/23/1949, New York, NY, m, 1999, 1 child **DISCIPLINE** AMERICAN LITERATURE **EDUCATION** SUNY-Brockport, BA, 71; MA, 72; U Iowa, MFA, 74; Ohio Univ, PhD, 77. **CAREER** Prof, Salisbury Univ, 78- ; vis prof, Univ of Athens, Greece, 81-82; writer-in Residence, Sweet Briar Col, 87-89; vis prof, Univ of Maryland, 95- . **HONORS AND AWARDS** Fel, Nat Endowment for the Arts, 84; Individual Artist Awds, Maryland State Arts Coun, 90, 92, 97; Pushcart Prizes, 84, 90; Towson State Univ Prizes for Lit, 85, 90; Lit Work-in-Progress Grants, Maryland State Arts Coun, 83, 85, 88, 89; Yaddo fels, 78, 80, 83, 84, 87, 92, 95; VA Ctr for Creative Arts Fels, 90, 91, 92, 94, 95, 97; MacDowell Colony Fels, 92, 94; Tyrone Guthrie Ctr Fel, 93; The Anderson Ctr for Interdisciplinary Studies Fel, 96; Individual Artist Awd, 01; Maryland State Arts Council, 01. **SELECTED PUBLICATIONS** Auth, Fish Light, 75; Not Just Any Death, 79; Anniversary of the Air, 85; The Burden Lifters, 89; Bountiful, 92; Green Ash, Red Maple, Black Gum, 97; auth, Parthenopi: New and Selected Poems, 01; ed, Contemporary American Poetry, 01; ed, A. Poulin, Jr.: Selected Poems, 01; ed, Perfect in Their Art: Poems on Boxing from Homer to Al:, 02. **CONTACT ADDRESS** Dept of English, Salisbury State Univ, Salisbury, MD 21801. **EMAIL** mgwaters@ssu.edu

WATERS, RICHARD L.
PERSONAL Born 10/07/1937, Golden City, MO, m, 1988, 5 children **DISCIPLINE** LIBRARY SCIENCE **EDUCATION** Univ Wash, MLIS, 66. **CAREER** Principal consultant Providence Associates, 79-. **MEMBERSHIPS** ALA; Texas Library Assoc. **RESEARCH** Public library service **SELECTED PUBLICATIONS** Editor, Public Library Quarterly **CONTACT ADDRESS** Providence Associates, 2501 Mesquite St., Denton, TX 76201-0898. **EMAIL** aneyeforit@sedona.net

WATERSTON, ELIZABETH H.
PERSONAL Born 04/18/1922, Montreal, PQ, Canada **DISCIPLINE** ENGLISH **EDUCATION** Univ Toronto, BA, 44, PhD, 50; Bryn Mawr Col, MA, 45. **CAREER** Asst prof, 45-47, assoc prof, Sir George Williams Col, 50-58, dept chair, 56-58; assoc prof, Univ W Ont, 58-67; assoc prof, 67-71, prof, 71-87, dept chair, 74-77, Prof Emer English Univ Guelph 89-. **MEMBERSHIPS** Founding mem, Asn Can Univ Tchrs English; Asn Can & Que Lit; founding & life mem, Asn Can Stud; edit bd mem, Scottish Tradition, English Stud Can; founder & ed Can Children's Lit; Nat pres, Humanities Asn Can, 77-79. **SELECTED PUBLICATIONS** Auth, Brush up Your Basics, 1981; auth, The Travelers: Canada to 1900, 89; auth, Gilbert Parker, 89; auth, Children's Literature in Canada, 92; auth, Kindling Spirit, 94; coauth, John Galt, 85; coauth, Silenced Sextet, 93; coauth, Writing a Life, 95; ed, Seats of the Mighty, 68; ed, Bogle Corbet, 76; ed, Some Scots, 82; co-ed, Selected Journals of L.M. Montgomery vol 1 85, vol 2 87, vol 3 92. **CONTACT ADDRESS** 535 Colborne St, London, ON, Canada N6B 2J7.

WATKINS, ANDREA
DISCIPLINE MUSIC **EDUCATION** Brigham Young Univ, BA; George Wash Univ, MA; Union Grad Sch, PhD. **CAREER** Prof. **SELECTED PUBLICATIONS** Co-author, Dancing Longer, Dancing Stronger, 90. **CONTACT ADDRESS** Music and Dance Dept, Univ of Massachusetts, Amherst, 720 Massachusetts Ave, Amherst, MA 01003.

WATKINS-GOFFMAN, LINDA
PERSONAL Born 02/24/1944, Greenwood, MO, m, 1980, 2 children **DISCIPLINE** ENGLISH **EDUCATION** Mississippi Univ, BA, 66; Hunter Col, MA, 73; NYork Univ, PhD, 86. **CAREER** Asst Prof, Jersey City State Col, 79-81; Adj Fac Member, William Patterson Col, 81-83; Assoc Prof, Hostos Cmty Col, 85-. **HONORS AND AWARDS** Prof Staff Congress Res Grant, 91-92, 92-93; Caribbean Exchange Res Grant, 91-92. **MEMBERSHIPS** NY TESOL; Intl TESOL; Nat Coun for the Teaching of Eng; MLA; NY Writing Cent Dir Asn; Soc for the Study of the Indigenous Lang of the Am. **SELECTED PUBLICATIONS** Co-auth, Thinking to Write: A Composing Process Approach to Writing, Maxwell MacMillan, 91; co-auth, "Putting Grammar in its place in the writing curriculum," Research in the Teaching of Developmental Education, 92; co-auth, Making Your Point: Writing the argumentative Essay, Heinle and Heinle Intl Pub Group, 93; co-auth, "An Experiment in Writing Across the Curriculum," Research in the Teaching of Developmental Education, 93; co-auth, Many Voices: A Reader for Developing Writers, Simon Schuster, 99; auth, "Bridging the Gap Between Native Language and Second Language Literacy Instruction: A Naturalistic Study," Bilingual Research Journal, 00; auth, Lives in Two Languages: An Exploration in Identity and Culture, Univ MI Press, 01; co-auth, "Developing Voice in Second Language Writing," Bilingual Research Journal, in press. **CONTACT ADDRESS** Dept Eng, Hostos Comm Col, 475 Grand Concourse, Bronx, NY 10451-5307. **EMAIL** liwho@mail.hostos.cuny.edu

WATSON, CHARLES N., JR.
PERSONAL Born 09/14/1939, Brooklyn, NY, d, 2 children **DISCIPLINE** ENGLISH **EDUCATION** Princeton Univ, AB, 61; Duke Univ, MA, 64; Duke Univ, PhD, 69. **CAREER** Asst Prof, Wash State Univ, 68-70; Asst Prof, Syracuse Univ, 70-75; Assoc Prof, Syracuse Univ, 75-82; Prof, Syracuse Univ, 82-. **MEMBERSHIPS** Mod Lang Asn, Melville Soc, Jack London Soc. **RESEARCH** American renaissance, American literary naturalism, environmental writing. **SELECTED PUBLICATIONS** Auth, The Novels of Jack London: A Reappraisal, Univ Wis Pr, 83; ed, The Son of the Wolf: Tales of the Far North, by Jack London, Oxford World Classics, 96. **CONTACT ADDRESS** Dept English, Syracuse Univ, Hall of Lang, Syracuse, NY 13244-1170. **EMAIL** cnwatson@syr.edu

WATSON, CRESAP SHAW
PERSONAL Born Ft Worth, TX, m, 1948, 3 children **DISCIPLINE** ENGLISH **EDUCATION** Brown Univ, BA, 49; Univ Dublin, Ireland, PhD (English), 53. **CAREER** From instr to asst prof English, La State Univ, 52-60; assoc prof and chmn dept English and speech, 60-72, PROF ENGLISH AND SPEECH, UNIV NEW ORLEANS, 72-; ED, LA ENGLISH J, 60-. **MEMBERSHIPS** NCTE; Col English Asn; SCent Mod Lang Asn. **RESEARCH** Anglo-Irish literature; modern fiction and drama; the novel. **SELECTED PUBLICATIONS** Auth, You Can Go Home Again, the Focus on Family in the Works of Foote, Horton, Mod Drama, Vol 39, 96. **CONTACT ADDRESS** Dept of English, Univ of New Orleans, New Orleans, LA 70122.

WATSON, JAMES GRAY
PERSONAL Born 06/16/1939, Balitmore, MD, m, 1963, 2 children **DISCIPLINE** AMERICAN & MODERN LITERATURE **EDUCATION** Bowdoin Col, AB, 61; Univ Pittsburgh, MA, 63, PhD(English), 68. **CAREER** Asst dean arts & sci, Univ Pittsburgh, 68-69; asst prof to prof English, Tulsa Univ, 69-. **MEMBERSHIPS** MLA; SCent Mod Lang Asn; Soc Study Southern Lit. **RESEARCH** William Faulkner; modern American literature; modernism. **SELECTED PUBLICATIONS** Auth, The Snopes Dilemma: Faulkner's Trilogy, Univ Miami, 70; William Faulkner, Letters and Fiction, Univ Texas, 87; ed, Thinjing of Home: William Faulkner's Letters to His Mother and Father, 1918-1925, WW Norton, 92; auth, essays on American literature in: Am Lit; Ariz Quart; Faulkner J; Falkner Stud; Miss Quart; Mod Fiction Studies; Mosaic; Southern Quart; Fifty Years of Yoknapatawpha, 79; New Directions in Faulkner Studies, 82; The Artist and His Masks: William Faulkner's Metafiction, 89; Faulkner, His Contemporaries and His Posterity, 92. **CONTACT ADDRESS** Dept of English, Univ of Tulsa, 600 S College, Tulsa, OK 74104-3126. **EMAIL** james-watson@utulsa.edu

WATSON, JEAN LOUISE
PERSONAL Born 06/20/1943, Albuquerque, NM, 2 children **DISCIPLINE** BRITISH AND CHILDREN'S LITERATURE **EDUCATION** Baylor Univ, BA, 65; Midwestern Univ, MA, 67; Ohio Univ, PhD (English), 75. **CAREER** Instr, Univ Nebr, 66-68; asst prof, Stonehill Col, 68-72, Gustavus Adolphus Col, 76-81; ASST PROF ENGLISH, MARSHALL UNIV, 81-; Fel, Summer Inst Women Higher Educ Admin, Bryn Mawr Col, summer, 79; vis scholar, Columbia Univ, 80-81. **MEMBERSHIPS** MLA; SAtlantic Mod Lang Asn; Midwest Victorian Studies Asn; Children's Lit Asn; Carolinas Symp Brit Studies. **RESEARCH** Coleridge's poetry and prose; th century British poetry and literature. **SELECTED PUBLICATIONS** Coauth, The perception of immortal beauty: Peter Quince at the Clavier, Col Lit, winter 75; auth, Shelley's witch: The naked conception, Concerning Poetry, spring 77; You are your own magician: A vision of integrity in the poetry of Marge Piercy, Mod Poetry Studies, winter 77; Of hunts and hunters: Atalanta in Calydon, Pre-Raphaelite Rev, 11/79; Apples and milkmaids: The visionary experience in Tennyson's The Holy Grail, Studia Mystica, summer 81. **CONTACT ADDRESS** Dept of English, Marshall Univ, Huntington, WV 25701.

WATSON, JOHN CLIFTON
PERSONAL Born 01/22/1954, Jersey City, NJ, m, 1994 **DISCIPLINE** JOURNALISM **EDUCATION** Rutgers Coll, BA, 1975; Rutgers Univ, School of Law, JD, 1980. **CAREER** Jersey City State Coll, writing instructor, 92-94; Rutgers Coll Newark, Journalish Instructor, 92-; The Jersey Journal, News Editor, Reporter, 75-. **HONORS AND AWARDS** North Jersey Press Assn, 1st Place Spot News Reporting Awd, 1983; NJ Press Assn, 1st Place Spot News Reporting Awd, 1983; Hudson County Newspaper Guild, Sports Writing Awd, 1983. **MEMBERSHIPS** Garden State Assn of Black Journalists, 1992-. **CONTACT ADDRESS** Jersey Journal Newspaper, 30 Journal Sq, 3rd Fl Newsroom, Jersey City, NJ 07306.

WATSON, REGINALD
PERSONAL Born 05/06/1963, Morristown, NJ, m, 1990, 1 child **DISCIPLINE** ENGLISH **EDUCATION** NCar Cent Univ, BA, 85; E Carolina Univ, MA, 91; Ind Univ, PhD, 98. **CAREER** Instructor, Lenoir Cmty Col, 89-90; Instructor, Martin Cmty Col, 90-91; Teaching Asst to Asst Prof, E Carolina Univ, 89-. **HONORS AND AWARDS** Sigma Tau Delta Honor Soc, 82-85; Alpha Kappa Mu Honor Soc, NC Cent Univ, 85; Fel Awd, UNC, 97-98. **MEMBERSHIPS** CAR; Delta Kappa; Golden Key Honor Soc. **RESEARCH** Post-colonial, African, African American, World, Caribbean, and Multi-cultural literatures; Cultural, Post-colonial criticism. **SELECTED PUBLICATIONS** Auth, Black Voices From the Past: A History Play About Black History, 93; auth, I've Seen the Mountain Top, But It Don't Look So Good, 96; auth, The Kwanzaa Story, 95; auth, "The Negative Male Imagery in the Works of Hurston and Walker," Penn State Univ Press, 98; auth, "Images of Blackness in the Works of charlotte and Emily Bronte," Morehouse Col, 99; auth, "Review of Winston James's Holding Aloft the Banner of Ethiopia: Caribbean Radicalism in Early Twentieth Century America," Contours, forthcoming. **CONTACT ADDRESS** Dept Eng, East Carolina Univ, 1000 E 5th St, Greenville, NC 27858-2502. **EMAIL** Watsonr@mail.ecu.edu

WATSON, ROBERT WINTHROP
PERSONAL Born 12/26/1925, Passaic, NJ, m, 1952, 2 children **DISCIPLINE** ENGLISH **EDUCATION** Williams Col, BA, 46; Johns Hopkins Univ, MA, 50, PhD(English), 55. **CAREER** Instr English, Williams Col, 46, 47-48, 52-53 & Johns Hopkins Univ, 50-52; from instr to assoc prof, 53-63, PROF ENGLISH, UNIV NC, GREENSBORO, 63-, Dir, Assoc Writing Prog, 67-72; vis prof, Calif State Univ, Northridge, 68-69. **HONORS AND AWARDS** Awd in Lit, Am Acad & Inst Arts & Lett, 77; Nat Endow Arts, 78. **MEMBERSHIPS** MLA **RESEARCH** Modern poetry and literature; poetics; the novel. **SELECTED PUBLICATIONS** Auth, A Paper Horse and Other Poems, 62 & Advantages of Dark(poems), 66, Atheneum; Three Sides of the Mirror, Putnam, 66; Christmas at Las Vegas-(poems), 71 & Selected Poems, 74, Atheneum; Lily Lang, St Martin's, 77, Island of Bones(poetry), Unicorn, 77; Night Blooming Cactus (poems), Atheneum, 80; auth, The Pendulum: New and Selected Poems, LSU Press, 95; auth, Betty Watson Paintings. **CONTACT ADDRESS** 9-D Fountain Manor Dr, Greensboro, NC 27405.

WATT, WILLIS M.
PERSONAL Born 12/20/1950, Ottawa, KS, m, 1970, 1 child **DISCIPLINE** COMMUNICATION **EDUCATION** Manhattan Christian Col, BS, 76; Ks St Univ, BS, 76, MA, 78, PhD, 80. **CAREER** Grad TA to instr, Ks St Univ, 76-80; asst prof, Iowa St Univ, 80-84; dir of forensics to chair, Ft Hays St Univ, 80-97; vice pres and dean, Manhattan Christian Col, Manhattan Ks, 97-00, adj assoc prof, Kansas State Univ. **HONORS AND AWARDS** Member, Mid-Amer Educ Hall of Fame, Ks City Comm Col; Ks Speech Comm Assoc Col Teacher of the Year, 96; Marquis' Who's Who in World, 97-99; Who's Who in Amer, 97-00; Who's Who in Educ, 97; Order of Highest Distinction, Pi Kappa Delta, Nat Debate/Speech Frat, 95; Ks Leadership Forum; editor, ks speech j; adv coun for acad aff, center for policy in higher educ, washington, dc; adv coun, leadership inst, ks st univ ed bd, privacy on campus, cphe, washington dc; adjudicator, region v, kennedy center-amer col theatre festival; theta alpha **RESEARCH** Leadership; intercultural commun; conflict mgt; orgn commun; relig drama and art. **SELECTED PUBLICATIONS** Coauth, Fundamentals of Oral Communication, McGraw-Hill, 97; auth, Three-Phase Process For Documenting And Evaluating Faculty Performance For Pay Increases, Promotion, And Tenure, The Department Chair: A Newsletter For Academic Administration, Anker Press, 96; auth, Leadership Ministries, Leadership Education: A Source Book Of Courses And Programs, Center For Creative Leadership, Greensboro, NC, 98; art, Using Mock Debates As Structured Learning Experiences To Teach Argument, The Forensic Educator, 98; art, Organizational Communication And Leadership: A Collaborative Philosophy Toward Teaching Leadership With Syllabus, The J of Leadership Stud, 97. **CONTACT ADDRESS** Communication Training Services, 2209 Terry Way, Manhattan, KS 66502-2643. **EMAIL** wmwatt@mccks.edu

WATTERS, DAVID HARPER
PERSONAL Born 12/28/1950, Hartford, CT, m, 1980 **DISCIPLINE** AMERICAN LITERATURE **EDUCATION** Dartmouth Col, AB, 72; Brown Univ, PhD(English), 79. **CAREER** Asst Prof English, Univ Nh, 78-, Panelist, NH Comn for the Arts Folk Arts Panel, 80- **MEMBERSHIPS** Asn Gravestone Studies. **RESEARCH** Early American literature and material culture; gravestones. **SELECTED PUBLICATIONS** Auth, Emerson, Dickenson and the atomic self, Emily Dickenson Bull, 77; co-ed, Increase Mather's New Jerusalem: Millennialism in late seventeenth century New England, Proceedings of the Am Antiquarian Soc, 77; auth, The Park and Whiting family stones revisited: The iconography of the church covenant, The Can Rev of Am Studies, 78; A priest to the temple, Puritan Gravestone Studies II, 79; Gravestones and historical archeology: A review essay, Markers: Asn for Gravestone Studies, 79-80; With Bodilie Eyes: Eschatological Themes in Puritan Literature and Gravestone Art, Univ Microfilm Int Res Press, 81; A Reading Of Taylor,Edward - Davis,Tm, William And Mary Quarterly, Vol 0052, 1995. **CONTACT ADDRESS** Dept of English, Univ of New Hampshire, Durham, 125 Technology Dr, Durham, NH 03824-4724. **EMAIL** dhw@christa.unh.edu

WATTS, ANN CHALMERS
PERSONAL Born 04/14/1938, Evanston, IL, m, 1962, 2 children **DISCIPLINE** ENGLISH **EDUCATION** Radcliffe Col, BA, 59; Yale Univ, PhD, 65. **CAREER** Asst prof English, Tufts Univ, 64-71; ASSOC PROF ENGLISH, RUTGERS UNIV, NEWARK, 71- . **MEMBERSHIPS** MLA; Mediaeval Acad Am. **RESEARCH** Old English literature; Middle English literature 19th century English and American literature. **SELECTED PUBLICATIONS** Auth, The Lyre and the Harp, Yale Univ, 69; Chaucerian selves, Chaucer Rev, 70; Amor Gloriae in Chaucer's House of Fame, J Medieval & Renaissance Studies, 73. **CONTACT ADDRESS** Dept of English, Rutgers, The State Univ of New Jersey, Newark, 360 Martin Luther King Jr Blvd, Newark, NJ 07102-1897.

WATTS, EMILY
PERSONAL Born 03/16/1936, Champaign, IL, m, 1958, 3 children **DISCIPLINE** LITERATURE **EDUCATION** Univ Ill at Urbana-Champaign, BA, 58; MA, 59; PhD, 63. **CAREER** From asst prof to prof, Univ Ill at Urbana-Champaign, 66-. **HONORS AND AWARDS** Woodrow Wilson Nat Fel, 58-59; John Simon Guggenheim Memorial Found Fel, 73-74. **MEMBERSHIPS** AAUP, Am Inst of Archaeol, Author's Guild of the Author's League of Am, Asn of Lit Scholars and Critics, Emily Dickinson Int Soc, Midwest MLA. **RESEARCH** Ernest Hemingway, Women's Literature, Poetry. **SELECTED PUBLICATIONS** Auth, Ernest Hemingway and the Arts, Univ Ill Press (Urbana, IL), 71; auth, The Poetry of American Women from 1632 to 1945, Univ Tex Press (Austin, TX), 77 & 78; auth, The Businessman in American Literature, Univ Ga Press (Athens, GA), 82 & 86. **CONTACT ADDRESS** Dept English, Univ of Illinois, Urbana-Champaign, 608 S Wright St, Urbana, IL 618001-3613.

WAUGH, BUTLER HUGGINS
PERSONAL Born 05/09/1934, Pittsburgh, PA, m, 1953, 6 children **DISCIPLINE** FOLKLORE, ENGLISH **EDUCATION** Washington & Jefferson Col, AB, 55; IN Univ, PhD, 59. **CAREER** Instr Eng, Univ KS, 59-61; from asst prof to assoc prof, Univ FL, 61-70; exec asst to pres, 69-70, dean col arts & sci, 70-76, prof eng, FL Int Univ, 70, Coordr hum & fine arts, State Univ Syst FL, 68-69. **MEMBERSHIPS** Am Folklore Soc; MLA; S Atlantic Mod Lang Asn. **RESEARCH** Mod Brit and Am poetry; comp folktale study; structural analysis of traditional lit. **SELECTED PUBLICATIONS** Auth, Negro tales of John Kendry, Midwest Folklore, 58; The child and the snake in North America, Norveg, 60; Deep and surface structure, SAtlantic Bull, 68. **CONTACT ADDRESS** Col Arts & Sci, Florida Intl Univ, 1 F I U South Campus, Miami, FL 33199-0001. **EMAIL** waugh@fiu.edu

WAUGH, CHARLES G.
PERSONAL Born 07/18/1943, Philadelphia, PA, m, 1968, 2 children **DISCIPLINE** COMMUNICATIONS AND PSYCHOLOGY **EDUCATION** Syracuse Univ, BS, 65; MA, 69; Kent State Univ, PhD, 82. **CAREER** Asst debate coach, teaching asst, Syracuse Univ, 665-66; instr, Ithaca Col, 67-69; teaching fel, Kent State Univ, 69-71; asst prof, Univ Maine at Augusta,71-78; Chairman, Div of Soc Sci, Univ Maine at Augusta, 74-76; pres fac assembly, Univ Maine at Augusta, 77-78; assoc prof, Univ Maine at Augusta, 78-81; prof, Univ Maine at Augusta, 81-; vp fac assembly, Univ Maine at Augusta, 97-98. **HONORS AND AWARDS** Unit citation, USCG, 66. **RESEARCH** Social interaction and influence; popular culture; mass media; Maine studies; Civil War. **SELECTED PUBLICATIONS** Coed, The Best Maine Stories, Lance Tapley, 86; co-compiled, Science Fiction and Fantasy Series and Sequels: Vol. 1, Garland Press, 86; co-compiled, Western Series and Sequels: A Reference Guide, Garland Press, 86; coed, Science Fiction: The Science Fiction Research Association Anthology, Harper & Row, 88; co-compiled, Women Writers: From Page to Screen: A Guide to the Literary Sources of British and American Feature Films, Garland Press, 90; coed, Wife or Spinster: Stories by Nineteenth Century Women, Yankee Books, 91; coed, A Distant War Comes Home: Maine in the Civil War, Down East, 96; coed, The Women's War in the South: Recollections and Reflections of the American Civil War, Cumberland House, 99; coed, The Price of Freedom: Slavery and the Civil War, Vols 1 &2, Cumberland House, 00; coauth, coed, Let's Talk: A Cognitive-Skills Approach to Interpersonal Communication, Kendal-Hunt, 01. **CONTACT ADDRESS** 5 Morrill St, Winthrop, ME 04364.

WAWRZYCKA, JOLANTA
PERSONAL Born, Poland, m, 1995, 1 child **DISCIPLINE** MODERN BRITISH AND IRISH LITERATURE; ANCIENT AND MODERN LITERARY THEORY AND **EDUCATION** Univ Wroclaw, Poland, MA, 80; Southern IL Univ, Carbondale, PhD, 87. **CAREER** Transl-interp, Univ Wroclaw, Poland;79-80; transl, Int Comput Med Ctr, Poland, 80-81; res fel, Southern IL Univ, Carbondale;81; writing tutor, Southern IL Univ, Carbondale, 82-84; vis scholar, World Inst of Phenomenol, Boston, 84; res asst, 83-84, tchg asst, 82-85, lectr, Southern IL Univ, Carbondale, 85-87; prof, Radford Univ, 87-; Russ instr, Radva Corp, Radford, Va, 90. **HONORS AND AWARDS** Dissertation res award, Southern IL Univ, 85; fel, Northwestern Univ, 88; RU Found grant; Italy, 90; NEH, Univ CA, Santa Cruz, 89; RU fac develop grant, Switz, 92; RU grad sch summer res grant, Switz, 93, 94; RU fac prof develop leave, 96. **MEMBERSHIPS** Mod Lang Asn, 84-; Midwest Mod Lang Asn, 85-90; ch, Slavic Div of Midwest MLA, 87-88; Int Zurich James Joyce Found, 87-; Am Lit Transl Asn, 89-92; Soc of Phenomenol and Lit, 89-; Am Conf for Irish Stud, 91-; Friends of the Zurich James Joyce Found, 92-. **RESEARCH** Philos; philos of lang; hist; semiotics; technology in academe. **SELECTED PUBLICATIONS** Auth, Rev of Czeslaw Milosz and the Insufficiency of Lyric by Donald Davie; J of Mod Lit, Vol 15, no 3; Rev of Conversations with Czeslaw Milosz by Ewa Czarnecka and Aleksander Fiut, J of Mod Lit, Vol 15, no 3; Rev of Joyce, Modernity and its Mediation, Christine van Boheemen, ed, James Joyce Quart, Vol 28, no 4; Transcultural Criticism: 'jingish janglage' Joyce in Polish, in Festschrift Fritz Senn, Liliput Press, 97; Photomorpheme: Semiotisizing in Camera Lucida, in Writing the Image After Roland Barthes, ed Jean-Michel Rabate, Univ Pa Press, 97; coed, Gender in Joyce. UP of Fla, 97; transl, Our Art: Our Passports, Jonesfilm Gp, Inc, 96; On Translations by Roman Ingarden Analecta Husserliana, Vol XXXIII; On Responsibility, Analecta Husserliana, Vol XXVII; cotransl, International Bibliography of Works by Roman Ingarden, Analecta Husserliana, Vol XXX. **CONTACT ADDRESS** Radford Univ, Radford, VA 24142. **EMAIL** jolanta@runet.edu

WAYNE, VALERIE
PERSONAL Born 08/02/1945, Chicago, IL, m, 1998, 1 child **DISCIPLINE** ENGLISH **EDUCATION** DePauw Univ, BA, philos, 66; Univ Chicago, MA, eng, 72, PhD, eng, 78. **CAREER** Teaching asst, philos, DePauw Univ, 64-65; teaching asst, humanities, Univ Chicago, 73-74; lectr, compos, Chicago State Univ, 74; lectr, compos, Univ Ill, 76-78; visiting asst prof, 78-79, asst prof, eng, 79-86, assoc prof, dir, undergrad honors eng prog, 88-91, eng, 86-93, prof, eng, 93-, dir, eng grad prog, 94-97, dir, UH London Abroad Prog, spring, 98, Univ Hawaii Manoa; visiting lectr, Univ Liverpool, Jan-May, 88; visiting scholar, Alice F. Holmes Inst, Univ Kans, 97. **HONORS AND AWARDS** Nat Endow for the Humanities, summer stipend, 92; Folger Inst Ctr for Shakespeare Studies, grant-in-aid, 88; Huntington Libr fel, 82; Woodrow Wilson Res grant for dissertation candidates in Women's Studies, 76; Phi Beta Kappa, 66; Alpha Lambda Delta, 64. **MEMBERSHIPS** Shakespeare Asn of Amer; Soc for the Study of Early Mod Women, Pres, 00, VP, 99; Mod Lang Asn; Renaissance Eng Text Soc; The Malone Soc. **RESEARCH** Shakespeare; Early modern women; Renaissance literature; Feminist theory; Textual editing. **SELECTED PUBLICATIONS** Ed, Anne Cooke Bacon, Part 2, Vol 1 of The Early Modern Englishwoman, Ashgata, 2000; auth, article, The Death of the Author: Anonymity's Allies and Swetnam the Women-hater, Maids and Mistresses, Cousins and Queens: Women's Alliances in Early Modern England, Oxford Univ Press, 99; auth, article, Shakespeare Wallah and Colonial Specularity, Shakespeare, the Movie, London, Routledge, 97; auth, article, Advice for Women from Mothers and Patriarchs, Women and Literature in Britain, 1500-1700, Cambridge Univ Press, 56-79, 96; ed, The Flower of Friendship: A Renaissance

Dialogue Contesting Marriage, Cornell Univ Press, 92; ed, The Matter of Difference: Materialist Feminist Criticism of Shakespeare, Harvester Wheatsheaf, Cornell Univ Press, 91; auth, article Historical Differences: Misogyny and Othello, Matter of Difference, 91; auth, article, Refashioning the Shrew, Shakespeare Studies 17, 159-87, 15. **CONTACT ADDRESS** Dept. of English, Univ of Hawaii, Manoa, 1733 Donaghho Rd, Honolulu, HI 96822. **EMAIL** vwayne@lava.net

WAZNAK, ROBERT P.
PERSONAL Born 02/05/1938, Scranton, PA, s **DISCIPLINE** RHETORIC **EDUCATION** Mt St Mary's Col, BA, 60, MA, 64; Temple Univ, PhD, 74. **CAREER** Asst prof Homiletics, St Mary's Sem & Univ, 68-69 & 80-84; vis prof Homiletics, Princeton Theol Sem, 77-78; Instr Homiletics, Cath Univ Am, 72-80; Prof Homiletics, Washington Theol Union, 80- ; CO-Ed New Theol Rev, 97- . **HONORS AND AWARDS** Univ Doctoral fel, Temple Univ, 70. **MEMBERSHIPS** Am Acad Homiletics; Cath Asn Tchrs Homiletics, Cath Theol Soc Am; Soc Homiletica. **RESEARCH** Homiletics; Media; Narrative theological; Biblical hermeneutics. **SELECTED PUBLICATIONS** Auth, Like Fresh Bread: Sunday Homilies in the Parish, Paulist Press, 93; The Catechism and the Sunday Homily, America, 94; Jean-Baptiste Massillon, The Concise Encyclo of Preaching, John Knox Press, 95; Heralds of Hope, Liturgy 90, 96; Preaching the Gospel in a Video Culture, Religious Rhetoric in a Video Culture, Sheed & Ward, 96; The Media as Saint-Maker and Devil's Advocate, America, 97; The Church and the Scientist in the New Millennium, New Theol Rev, 98; Anatomy of a Homily, New Theol Rev, 98; An Introduction to the Homily, The Liturgical Press, 98. **CONTACT ADDRESS** Washington Theol Union, 6896 Laurel Street, NW, Washington, DC 20012. **EMAIL** waznak@wtu.edu

WEALES, GERALD
PERSONAL Born 06/12/1925, Connersville, IN **DISCIPLINE** ENGLISH LITERATURE **EDUCATION** Columbia Col, AB, 49; Columbia Univ, AM, 50, PhD, 58. **CAREER** Instr English, GA Inst Technol, 51-53, Newark Col Engineering, 53-55 & Wayne State Univ, 55-56; asst prof, Brown Univ, 57-58; from asst prof to assoc prof, 58-67, Prof English, Univ PA, 67-, Lectr, Eng Inst, 59 & 63; Fulbright lectr, Sri Lanka, 79; Rockefeller Found, Residence Bellagio Study Ctr, 80; vis prof, Univ Hawaii, 81; Guggenheim fel, 81-82. **HONORS AND AWARDS** George Jean Nathan Awd, 64-65. **RESEARCH** Modern American and English drama. **SELECTED PUBLICATIONS** Auth, Religion in Modern English Drama, Univ Pa, 61; American Drama Since World War II, Harcourt, 62; ed, Edwardian Plays, Hill & Wang, 62; A Play and its Parts, Basic Bks, 64; The Complete Plays of William Wycherley, Doubleday Anchor, 66 & NY Univ, 67; auth, American Drama in the 1960's, Macmillian, 69; Clifford Odets, Playwright, Bobbs, 71. **CONTACT ADDRESS** Dept of English, Univ of Pennsylvania, Philadelphia, PA 19174.

WEARING, J. P.
PERSONAL Born Birmingham, England **DISCIPLINE** ENGLISH LITERATURE, THEATRE HISTORY **EDUCATION** Univ Wales, Swansea, BA, 67, PhD(English), 71; Univ Sask, MA, 68. **CAREER** Lectr English, Univ Alta, 71-74; asst prof, 74-77, assoc prof English, Univ Ariz, 77-84, Killam fel English, Univ Alta, 71-73; ed, Nineteenth Century Theatre Res, 72-; Guggenheim fel Theatre Hist, 78-79; prof English, Univ Ariz, 84-. **HONORS AND AWARDS** NEH Research Grant 87-91. **MEMBERSHIPS** Nineteenth Century Theatre Res; English Lit Transition. **RESEARCH** English theatre history; 19th and 20th century English drama; Shakespeare. **SELECTED PUBLICATIONS** Auth, Two early absurd plays in England, Mod Drama, 73; ed, The Collected Letters of Sir Arthur Pinero, Univ Minn, 74; auth, The London Stage 1890-1899: A Calendar of Plays and Players, Scarecrow, 76; The West End London Stage in the 1890's, Educ Theatre J, 77; coauth, English Drama and Theatre, 1800-1900, Gale Res, 78; auth, American and British Theatrical Biography: A Directory, Scarecrow, 78; Henry Arthur Jones: An Annotated Bibliography of Writings about Him, English Lit in Transition, 79; The London Stage 1900-1909: A Calendar of Plays and Players, Scarecrow, 81; The London Stage 1950-1959: A Calendar of Plays and Players, 2 vols, Metuchen, NJ & London: the Scarecrow Press, 93. **CONTACT ADDRESS** Dept of English, Univ of Arizona, 472 Modern Lang Bldg, PO Box 210067, Tucson, AZ 85721. **EMAIL** jpwearing@aol.com

WEASMER, JERIE
PERSONAL Born 12/28/1949, Clinton, IA, m, 1985, 4 children **DISCIPLINE** ENGLISH COMPOSITION STUDIES; ENG TEACHER PREPARATION; LITERACY **EDUCATION** Upper IA Col, BA, 71; Univ IA, MA, 88, Purdue Univ, PhD, 96. **CAREER** Eng Dept, Eastern Ill Univ **HONORS AND AWARDS** Univ Achievement in Contribution Award for Teaching, Res, & Serv, 98-99; Best Practices in Teaching Award, 97-98; HECA Grant, PIE21 96-97. **MEMBERSHIPS** Nat Coun Teachers Engl; Ill Asn Teachers Eng IL; Asn Teacher Educators; IL Philol Asn. **RESEARCH** Building teaching efficacy; teacher retention; interdisciplinary teaching. **SELECTED PUBLICATIONS** Auth, The Changemakers: Teachers as Active Agents for Change, Midwest Association of Teacher Educators Conference Proceedings, 96; coauth, A.M. Formative Assessment in Teacher Preparation, Clearing House, 97; Teaching is a Team Sport: Enhancing Collegial Roles, Kappa Delta Pi Record, 97; coauth, Teacher Preparation: A Revision Process Fostered by Formative Assessment, The Clearing House, 97; coauth, Teaching is a Team Sport: Enhancing Collegial Roles, Kappa Delta Pi Record, 97; coauth, Beat Burnout!: Strategies for Remaining Professionally Stimulated, Teaching Elementary Physical Education, 98; coauth, I Think I Can: The Role of Personal Teaching Efficacy in Effecting Change, The Clearing House, 98; auth, Collaborative Efforts toward Change: Infusing Technology into an American Literature Curriculum, Midwest Association of Teacher Educators Conference Proceedings, 98; coauth, Technology Partnership in Teaching and Learning, Eastern Education Journal 27, 98; coauth, Facilitating Success for New Teachers, Principal 78, 98; auth, Collaboration in Cyberspace, MATE Conference Proceedings, 99; coauth, Integrated Learning: Greater Than the Sum of Its Parts, Teaching Elementary Physical Education, 99; coauth, Programs in Practice: Peer Partnering for Change, Kappa Delta Pi Record, 36, 99; coauth, Preventing Baptism by Fire: Fostering Growth in New Teachers, The Clearing House, 00; coauth, At Center Stage: Strategies for Shifting Classroom Ownership, Middle School Journal, 00; coauth, Special Issue on Career Stages, The Clearing House: A Journal of Educational Strategies, Issues, and Ideas, forthcoming; coauth, Maintaining Job Satisfaction: Engaging Professionals as Active Participants, The Clearing House: A Journal of Educational Strategies, Issues, and Ideas, forthcoming; auth, A Gift of Time: Career History of a Prime Time Teacher, The Clearing House: A Journal of Educational Strategies, Issues, and Ideas, forthcoming; coauth, Who's the Boss: Affording Students Agency, Kappa Delta Pi Record, forthcoming. **CONTACT ADDRESS** Eastern Illinois Univ, 600 Lincoln Ave, Charleston, IL 61920-3099. **EMAIL** cfjrw1@eiu.edu

WEATHERBY, HAROLD L., JR.
DISCIPLINE RENAISSANCE AND VICTORIAN LITERATURE, SPENSER **EDUCATION** Yale Univ, PhD. **CAREER** Instr, Vanderbilt Univ. **SELECTED PUBLICATIONS** Auth, Cardinal Newman in His Age; The Keen Delight: The Christian Poet in the Modern World; Mirrors of Celestial Grace: Patristic Theology in Spenser's Allegory, 94. **CONTACT ADDRESS** Vanderbilt Univ, Nashville, TN 37203-1727.

WEATHERS, WINSTON
PERSONAL Born 12/25/1926, Pawhuska, OK **DISCIPLINE** ENGLISH, RHETORIC **EDUCATION** Univ Okla, BA, 50, MA, 51, PhD(English), 64. **CAREER** Asst prof English, Cottey Col, 51-54; from instr to prof English, 58-76, chairperson fac lett, 74-76, Grad Prof Mod Lett, Univ Tulsa, 76-. **RESEARCH** Rhetoric and style; poetics; William Blake. **SELECTED PUBLICATIONS** Auth, The Archetype and the Psyche, Univ Tulsa, 68; Messages From the Asylum, Joseph Nichols, 70; The Lonesome Game, David Lewis, 70; Indian and White: Sixteen Eclogues, Univ Nebr, 70; coauth, The New Strategy of Style, McGraw, 78; auth, An Alternate Style, Boynton/Cook, 80; Mezzo Cammin: Poems from the Middle of My Life, Joseph Nichols, 81; The Broken Word: Communication Pathos in Modern Literature, Gordon & Breach, 81; A 'Sacrament', Poetry, Vol 0162, 1993; 'On Entering The Hospice', Poetry, Vol 0162, 1993. **CONTACT ADDRESS** Grad Fac of Mod Lett, Univ of Tulsa, Tulsa, OK 74104.

WEAVER, GARY
DISCIPLINE INTERCULTURAL COMMUNICATION, ADAPTATION AND CONFLICT **EDUCATION** Am Univ, BA, MA, PhD. **CAREER** Prof, Am Univ; lect, Acad Educ Develop (AED), The Inst Int Educ (IIE); Ctr For Journalists. **HONORS AND AWARDS** Dir, Seminar Managing a Multicultural Workforce; Dir, The Fulbright Pre-Acad Prog, Dir, Community Studies Prog, Am Univ. **RESEARCH** Cross-cultural communications, contemporary social and political movements. **SELECTED PUBLICATIONS** Auth, The University and Revolution, Prentice-Hall, 69; Readings in Cross-Cultural Communication, Ginn Custom Publ, 87; Culture, Communication, and Conflict,Ginn Press, 94. **CONTACT ADDRESS** American Univ, 4400 Massachusetts Ave, Washington, DC 20016.

WEAVER, JACK WAYNE
PERSONAL Born 04/07/1932, Damascus, VA, m, 1957, 3 children **DISCIPLINE** ENGLISH LITERATURE **EDUCATION** Berea Col, BA, 54; Univ NC, Chapel Hill, MA, 59, PhD(English), 66. **CAREER** From asst prof to assoc prof English, Greensboro Col, 59-67; assoc prof, 67-72, coordr freshman English, 68-73, Prof English, Winthrop Col, 72-, Piedmont Univ Ctr res grant, 65-66; Greensboro Col res grant, 66-67; Winthrop Col res grant, 68 & 73. **MEMBERSHIPS** MLA; Southern Mod Lang Asn; AAUP Am Comt Irish Studies. **RESEARCH** Modern Irish literature; Romantic English poetry and criticism; English novel. **SELECTED PUBLICATIONS** Auth, Stage-management in the Irish theatre, English Lit Transition, 66; An exile's return, Eire, 68; Moore's name for Gogarty in Hail & Farewell, English Lit Transition, 71; AE's use of Blake in Irish Homestead, 76, J Irish Lit; Romanticism as source in Joyces's Portrait, S Atlantic Bull, 77; Moore's Use of Celtic Materials: What & How, English Lit Transition, 79; William Trevor, In: Dictionary of Irish Literature, 79; ed, Selected proceedings of the Scotch-Irish heritage festival at Winthrop College, 81. **CONTACT ADDRESS** 144 Brookwood Lane, Rock Hill, SC 29730.

WEBB, IGOR M.
PERSONAL Born 01/08/1941, Slovakia, m, 1990, 5 children **DISCIPLINE** ENGLISH **EDUCATION** Tufts Univ, AB, 63; Stanford Univ, MA, 66; PhD, 71. **CAREER** Assoc prof, Univ Mass, Boston, 77-78; Chair, Div of Humanities, Richmond Col, London, 79-86; Provost, Adelphi Univ, 86-97, prof of English, 97-. **HONORS AND AWARDS** Phi Beta Kappa, 63; Woodrow Wilson Fel, 63-64; Leverhulme Fel, 66-67; Res Grant, Univ of Mass, Boston, 73; Creative Writing Fel, NEH, 78. **RESEARCH** World literature; 19th and 20th century literature. **SELECTED PUBLICATIONS** Auth, "Thaw," in Anthology of Magazine Verse & Yearbook of American Poetry (84); auth, "The Herald and the Void: A Tribute to John Matthias" and invited contribution to ed Robert Achambeau, Word Play Place: Essays on the Poetry of John Matthias, Ohio State Univ Press and Swallow Press (98); auth, "Yvor Winters as Teacher," Partisan Rev (98); auth, Annotated Instructor's Edition: The Short Prose Reader, 9th ed, NY: McGraw-Hill (99); auth, "Socialism (1989)," Notre Dame Rev (99); auth, "Is It Excellence or False Equity?," Newsday (Sept 8, 99). **CONTACT ADDRESS** Dept English, Adelphi Univ, 1 South Ave, Garden City, NY 11530-4213. **EMAIL** Webb@Adelphi.edu

WEBB, LYNNE M.
PERSONAL Born 03/20/1951, Shamokin, PA, m, 1984, 3 children **DISCIPLINE** COMMUNICATION AND COMMUNITY DEVELOPMENT **EDUCATION** Pa State Univ, BS, 72; Univ Ore, MS, 75, PhD, 80. **CAREER** Instr, Berea Col, 78-80; vis assoc prof, Univ Hawaii, 90; assoc prof, Univ Fla, 80-91; assoc prof, Univ Memphis, 91-99; Prof., Univ Arkansas, 99-. **HONORS AND AWARDS** Who's Who in America; Who's Who of Amer Women; Who's Who in the South and Southwest; Who's Who in the Media and Commun; Who's Who in Amer Educ; Outreach award, Southern States Commun Asn, 97; top res paper award, 98, 90, 86; teaching award, Col of Liberal Arts & Sci, 89-90, 85-86, 83-84; teaching award, Alpha Lambda Delta, 86-87; American Communication Asn, 99-00. **MEMBERSHIPS** Intl Commun Asn; Nat Commun Asn; Southern States Commun Asn; Tenn Commun Asn. **RESEARCH** Commun theory; Interpersonal commun; Family commun; Commun and aging. **SELECTED PUBLICATIONS** Co-auth, Applied family commun res: Casting light upon the demon, Jour of Applied Commun Res, 95; co-auth, Maintaining effective interaction skills, Communication in Later Life, Butterworth-Heinemann, 95; co-auth, Socially constructing the aging experience: A review essay on the Handbook of Communication and Aging Research, Health Comm, 96; auth, Proactive collegiality: Stalking the demon where he lives, Spectra, 96; auth, A proactive stance, Connections, 95; Auth, Convention financing: Theft or misunderstanding, Connections, 97. **CONTACT ADDRESS** 417 Kimpel Hall, Fayetteville, AR 72701. **EMAIL** lynnewebb320@cs.com

WEBB, NANCY L.
PERSONAL Born Port Hueneme, CA **DISCIPLINE** ENGLISH **EDUCATION** Univ Florida, BA, 74; MA, 76; Northern Ill, PhD, 86. **CAREER** Grad teach asst, 74-76, adj asst prof, 78, Univ Florida; instr, 79-86, lectr, 86-87, ed, 87-92, Northern Ill Univ; asst prof, assoc prof, prof, Col of Du Page, 92-. **HONORS AND AWARDS** Women Leadshp Awd; Diss Compl Awd. **MEMBERSHIPS** STC; ATTW; Sigma Tau Delta. **RESEARCH** Technical writing. **SELECTED PUBLICATIONS** Co-ed, Index to Reviews of Bibliographical Publications: An International Annual vol V: 1980 (Troy, NY: Whitson Pub Co, 83); co-ed, Index to Reviews of Bibliographical Publications: An International Annual vol VI: 1981 (Troy, NY: Whitson Pub Co, 84). **CONTACT ADDRESS** Dept Communications, Col of DuPage, 425 22nd St, Glen Ellyn, IL 60137-6784. **EMAIL** webbna@cdnet.cod.edu

WEBB, RALPH, JR.
DISCIPLINE INTERPERSONAL COMMUNICATION **EDUCATION** Univ Wis, PhD, 65. **CAREER** Prof, Purdue Univ. **RESEARCH** Language; gender; intercultural communication; communication theory. **SELECTED PUBLICATIONS** Auth, Interpersonal Speech Communication: Principles and Practices, 75; Graduate Education in Speech Communication: Current Status and Future Directions, Commun Educ, 79. **CONTACT ADDRESS** Dept of Commun, Purdue Univ, West Lafayette, 1080 Schleman Hall, West Lafayette, IN 47907-1080.

WEBB, RUTH H.
DISCIPLINE CLASSICAL AND BYZANTINE RHETORIC AND EDUCATION **EDUCATION** Oxford Univ, MA, 86; London, PhD, 92. **CAREER** Asst prof, Princeton Univ. **RESEARCH** Literary narrative in late antique texts. **SELECTED PUBLICATIONS** Areas: Byzantine education, female entertainers,rhetorical ekphrasis. **CONTACT ADDRESS** Princeton Univ, 1 Nassau Hall, Princeton, NJ 08544. **EMAIL** rhwebb@princeton.edu

WEBER, CLIFFORD WHITBECK
PERSONAL Born 04/22/1943, Scranton, PA, m, 1967 **DISCIPLINE** CLASSICS **EDUCATION** Harvard Univ, AB, 65; Univ Calif, Berkeley, PhD, 75. **CAREER** Asst prof, 69-78, assoc prof classics, Kenyon Col, 78-89. **HONORS AND AWARDS** Harvard Col, Detur Prize for acad distinc, Louis Curtis Prize, Phi Beta Kappa; Kenyon Col Fac Develop Grants, 71, 72; NEH Sum Sem Grant at the Univ of Tex, 76. **MEMBERSHIPS** Am Philol Assn. **RESEARCH** Latin poetry. **SELECTED PUBLICATIONS** Art, Dodona Reneges: A Neglected Oxymoron in Georgics 1, Classical Philology, 91; auth, The Allegory of Virgil's Golden Bough, 95; art, Roscius and the Roscida Dea, Classical Quarterly, 96. **CONTACT ADDRESS** Kenyon Col, Ascension Hall, Gambier, OH 43022-9623. **EMAIL** weberc@kenyon.edu

WEBER, DONALD
PERSONAL Born 02/09/1951, Bronx, NY, m, 1973, 2 children **DISCIPLINE** AMERICAN LITERATURE **EDUCATION** State Univ NYork, BA, 72; Columbia Univ, MA, 73, PhD(English), 78. **CAREER** Adj lectr English, Lehman Col, City Univ New York, 73-78; asst prof, Univ Calif, Los Angeles, 78-81; Asst Prof English, Mt Holyoke Col, Mass, 81-. **RESEARCH** Puritanism in American literature; Jonathan Edwards; American religion and culture. **SELECTED PUBLICATIONS** Auth, Perry Miller and the recovery of Jonathan Edwards, introduction to Perry Miller, Jonathan Edwards, Univ Mass Press, 81; The question of the New England mind, New England Quart, 82; Hawthorne in His Own Time, Nathaniel Hawthorne J, 78 & 82. **CONTACT ADDRESS** Dept of English, Mount Holyoke Col, 50 College St, South Hadley, MA 01075-1461.

WEBSTER, GRANT T.
PERSONAL Born Fargo, ND, d, 2 children **DISCIPLINE** ENGLISH **EDUCATION** Carleton Col, BA, 54; Columbia Univ, MA, 58; Ohio St Univ, PhD, 63. **CAREER** Asst Instr, Ohio St Univ, 58-63; Asst Prof, Univ S Calif, 63-67; From Asst Prof to Prof, SUNY, 68-. **MEMBERSHIPS** MLA, ALSC. **RESEARCH** 18th Century literature, caricature, prints. **SELECTED PUBLICATIONS** Auth, The Republic of Letters: A History of Postwar American Literary Opinion, Johns Hopkins UP (Baltimore, MD), 79;auth, "American Literary Criticism: A Bibliographical Essay," Am Studies Int (81): 3-44; auth, "J Hillis Miller," Mod Am Critics Since 1955 (Detroit, MI: Gale Publ, 88), 221-231. **CONTACT ADDRESS** Dept English, SUNY, Binghamton, PO Box 6000, Binghamton, NY 13902-6000. **EMAIL** webster@binghamton.edu

WEBSTER, JAMES
DISCIPLINE MUSIC **EDUCATION** Harvard Col, BA, 63; Princeton Univ, MFA, 65; PhD, 74. **CAREER** Goldwin Smith prof. **HONORS AND AWARDS** Fulbright fel, 65-67; Alfred Einstein awd, Amer Musicol Soc, 77; Otto Kinkeldey awd, AMS, 92; NEH, sr res fel, 78-79, 99-00; Guggenheim fel, 92-93; ACLS fel, 99-00; Alexander von Humboldt Stiftung (Germany) fel, 00. **MEMBERSHIPS** Pres, Am Musicol Soc, 96-98; Int Musicol Soc; Soc Music Theory; Am Soc 18th-Century Stud; Am Acad of Arts and Sciences, 99-. **RESEARCH** Haydn; Mozart; Beethoven; Schubert; Brahms; opera buffa; analysis; theory of music; historiography; aesthetics. **SELECTED PUBLICATIONS** Auth, Haydn's Farewell Symphony and the Idea of Classical Style: Through-Composition and Cyclic Integration in his Instrumental Music, Cambridge Univ Press, 91; ed, Opera Buffa in Mozart's Vienna, Cambridge UP, 97; auth, The Analysis of Mozart's Arias, In Cliff Eisen, Mozart Studies, Oxford UP, 91; auth, The Form of the Finale of Beethoven's Ninth Symphony, Beethoven Forum, 92. **CONTACT ADDRESS** Dept of Music, Cornell Univ, 104 Lincoln Hall, Ithaca, NY 14853. **EMAIL** jcw4@cornell.edu

WEDBERG, LLOYD W.
PERSONAL Born 02/29/1924, Fremont, NE, m, 1945, 2 children **DISCIPLINE** MODERN GERMAN AND ENGLISH WRITING **EDUCATION** Univ Mich, BA, MA, PhD. **CAREER** Prof, 61-, Dean, Continuing Prof Educ, 82-91-. **HONORS AND AWARDS** Grant, Exxon Edu Found. **MEMBERSHIPS** AATG, MLA. **RESEARCH** 19th Century German Prose. **SELECTED PUBLICATIONS** Pub(s), 19th Century German Novelle; connections between the German Narrenschiff and Katherine Anne Porter's Ship of Fools; auth, The Theme of Loneliness in Theodor Storms Novellen, Mouton, 64. **CONTACT ADDRESS** Dept of Eng, Univ of Detroit Mercy, 4001 W McNichols Rd, PO BOX 19900, Detroit, MI 48219-0900. **EMAIL** wedbergsyl@aol.com

WEE, DAVID LUTHER
PERSONAL Born 01/20/1939, Madison, WI, m, 1961, 3 children **DISCIPLINE** ENGLISH **EDUCATION** St Olaf Col, BA, 61; Stanford Univ, MA, 65, PhD(English), 67. **CAREER** Asst prof, 65-71, sr fel & sr tutor, Paracollege, 71-72, ASSOC PROF ENGLISH, ST OLAF COL, 71-, Sr Tutor, Paracollege, 76-, Danforth assoc, St Olaf Col, 69-; sr commons room visitor, Mansfield Col, England, 73; adj prof English, Macalester Col, 78. **MEMBERSHIPS** AAUP **RESEARCH** Victorian literature. **SELECTED PUBLICATIONS** Auth, Studying the humanities: Heaven on earth?, Minn English J, 4/68; Athletics as a human experience, Event, 10/71; The temptation of Christ and the motif of divine duplicity in the Corpus Christi cycle drama, Mod Philol, 8/74. **CONTACT ADDRESS** Dept of English, St. Olaf Col, 1520 St Olaf Ave, Northfield, MN 55057-1099.

WEEKES, ANN
PERSONAL Born, Ireland, m, 3 children **DISCIPLINE** LITERATURE **EDUCATION** Univ Ariz, BA, 77; MA, 80; PhD, 86. **RESEARCH** Irish Literature - 20th Century, Maternal Representations - Native American and Irish Literature. **SELECTED PUBLICATIONS** Auth, Irish Women Writers: An Uncharted Tradition, Univ Pr of Ky, (Lexington), 90; auth, "The Creation of Students' Self Image: High Art and Popular Culture", Woman's Art J 13.2 (92); auth, Unveiling Treasures: Guide to Irish Women Writers, Attic Pr, (Dublin), 93; auth, "Ordinary Women: themes in Contemporary Fiction by Irish Women", Colby Quarterly 31.3, March 95; auth, "Molly Keane", Modern Irish Writers: A Bio-Critical Sourcebook, Greenwood Pub (Westport, CN), 97; auth, "Trackless Roads: Irish Nationalisms and Lesbian Writing", Border Crossings: Irish Women Writers and National Identity, Univ Of Ala Pr, 00; auth, "Figuring the Mother", Contemporary Irish Fiction, eds Michael Parker and Liam Harte, Macmillan, (London), 00; auth, "That ordinary thing--/a woman/worty of love: An Essay on Mary Dorcey", Irish Lit Suppl, (forthcoming); auth Hunting for Worms: The Birth of the Mother in Irish Twentieth-Century Fiction, Univ of Calif Pr, (forthcoming); auth, "Martyrs to Mistresses: The Mother Figures in Edna O'Brien's Fiction", Int Assoc for Study of Irish Lit, (forthcoming). **CONTACT ADDRESS** Dept Humanities, Univ of Arizona, PO Box 210076, Tucson, AZ 85721-0076. **EMAIL** aweekes @u.arizona.edu

WEGMANN-SANCHEZ, JESSICA M.
PERSONAL Born 08/24/1969, Boston, MA, m, 1998 **DISCIPLINE** ENGLISH **EDUCATION** Univ Albta, BA, 91; Univ Ill Urbana Champaign, MA, 93; PhD, 01. **CAREER** Instr, Univ Ill Urbana-Champaign, 91-99; instr, Grant MacEwan Col, 00-01. **HONORS AND AWARDS** Priscilla Hammond Mem Scholar, 90; Dr Geneva Misener Mem Scholar, 90; Louise McKinney Scholar, 88, 89, 90; Phi Kappa Phi, 94; Sir James Lougheed Award of Distinction, 95-96, 96-97; Gragg Fel, Univ Ill, 98. **MEMBERSHIPS** MLA, ACCUTE. **RESEARCH** Comparative Critical Race Theory, US and Canada Definitions of Race and Ethnicity in the Census and Legal Policy, African-American and African-Canadian Literatures, Native American and Aboriginal Canadian Literatures, American Literature, Immigration Law and Literatures of Immigration. **SELECTED PUBLICATIONS** Auth, "Ambrose in the Sources of Anglo-Saxon Literary Culture," Old English Newsletter, (93): auth, "Ambrose in Anglo-Saxon England with Pseudo-Ambrose and Ambrosiaster," Old English Newsletter, (97); auth, "Playing in the Dark with Longstreet'ts Georgia Scenes: Critical Reception and Reader Response to Treatments of Race and Gender," Southern Lit Jour, (97); auth, Medieval Iconography: A Research Guide, Garland, (NY), 98). **EMAIL** sanchezj@telusplanet.net

WEIDHORN, MANFRED
PERSONAL Born 10/10/1931, Vienna, Austria, m, 1969, 2 children **DISCIPLINE** ENGLISH **EDUCATION** Columbia Univ, BA, 54, PhD(English), 63; Univ Wis, MA, 57. **CAREER** Instr English, Univ Ala, 57-58, Brooklyn Col, 60-63; from asst prof to assoc prof, 63-73, prof English, Yeshiva Col, 73-, Danforth Assoc; prof English, Guterman, 88-. **HONORS AND AWARDS** Farrow Awd for Exellence in Churchill Studies, 98; Emmett Awd (for best essay), 99. **MEMBERSHIPS** Int Churchill Societies. **RESEARCH** Sir Winston Churchill; The Great Paradigm Shift in Culture. **SELECTED PUBLICATIONS** Auth, Dreams in 17th Century English Literature, Mouton, The Hague, 70; Richard Lovelace, Twayne, 70; Sword and Pen: A Survey of the Writings of Sir Winston Churchill, Univ NMex, 74; Turn Your Life Around, Prentice-Hall, 78; Sir Winston Churchill, Twayne, 79; Napoleon, Atheneum, 86; Churchill's Rhetoric and Political Dilemma, Univ Press of Am, 87; Robert E. Lee, Atheneum, 88; A Harmony of Interests, Fairleigh Dickinson, 92; Jackie Robinson, Atheneum, 93. **CONTACT ADDRESS** Dept of English, Yeshiva Univ, 500 W 185th St, New York, NY 10033-3299. **EMAIL** pegbw@aol.com

WEIGEL, RICHARD DAVID
PERSONAL Born 02/01/1945, Teaneck, NJ, m, 1968, 1 child **DISCIPLINE** HISTORY, CLASSICS **EDUCATION** Dickinson Col, BA, 66; Univ Del, MA, 68, PhD, 73. **CAREER** From instr to asst prof hist, Univ Del, 72-76; asst prof, Univ RI, 75; from Asst Prof to Assoc Prof, 76-84, Prof Hist, Western Ky Univ, 84-, Dept Head Hist, 98-. **HONORS AND AWARDS** Nat Endowment for Humanities summer sem grants, 77 & 80; Vis Schol, Wolfson Col, Oxford Univ, 93-; Am Acad in rome Advisory Coun, 94-. **MEMBERSHIPS** Am Philol Asn; Am Numismatic Soc; Assn Ancient Historians; Soc Prom Roman Studies; Royal Numismatic Soc. **RESEARCH** Roman Republic; ancient numismatics; Roman religion. **SELECTED PUBLICATIONS** Coauth, Peace in the Ancient World, McFarland, 81; auth, Lepidus: The Tarnished Triumvir, Routledge, 92; Roman History in the Age of Enlightenment: The Dassier Medals, Revue Numismatique 36, 95; Roman Coins: An Iconographical Approach, Annali dell Istituto di Numismatica 42, 95; auth, "Roman Republican Generals and the Vowing of Temples," Classica et Medievalia 49 (98); auth, "The Anonymous Quadrantes Reconsidered," Annotazioni Numismatich Suppl 11 (98); author of numerous other articles. **CONTACT ADDRESS** Dept of Hist, Western Kentucky Univ, 1 Big Red Way, Bowling Green, KY 42101-3576. **EMAIL** Richard.Weigel@wku.edu

WEIGEL, ROBERT G.
PERSONAL Born 03/24/1961, Ansbach, Germany, m, 2000 **DISCIPLINE** LITERATURE **EDUCATION** Univ at Albany, SUNY MA, 90; PhD, 92. **CAREER** Assoc Prof, Auburn Univ, 93. **MEMBERSHIPS** GSA- German Studies Assoc; AATG-American Assoc of Teachers of German. **RESEARCH** 20th Century German Literature; Culture; EXKE **SELECTED PUBLICATIONS** Auth, "Zurgeistigen Einheit Von Hermann Orochs Gerk Massenpsychologie Politologie Politologie Romane; auth, "Zerfall und aufbruch Profile der Osterreichischen Literatur im 20 Fahrhundert, Tubingen Francke, 00. **CONTACT ADDRESS** Dept Foreign Language, Auburn Univ, 6030 Haley Center, Auburn, AL 36849-2900. **EMAIL** weigerg@mail.auburn.edu

WEIGL, BRUCE
DISCIPLINE LITERATURE **EDUCATION** Univ Utah, PhD 79; Univ New Hampshire, MA 75; Oberlin Col, BA 74. **CAREER** Penn State Univ, prof, dir undergrad, dir MFA prog, 86-; Old Dominion Univ, prof, dir creat write, dir grad stud, 81-86; Univ Arkansas, prof, dir creat write, 79-81; Lorain Cnty Comm Col, inst, 76-77; Univ Utah, tchg fel, 77-79. **HONORS AND AWARDS** YADDO Found Fel; Acad Amer Poets Prize; Pushcart Prize; Breadloaf Fel; Tu Do Chien Kien Awd by Viet Vets of Amer; NEA Fel; Pulitzer Prize Nomin for SONG of NAPALM; Best Amer Poetry Prize; prof weigl's poetry has been translated into nine different languages. **RESEARCH** 20th Century Brit & Amer Poetry **SELECTED PUBLICATIONS** Auth, After the Others, TriQtly Books, Northwestern Univ Press, forthcoming; Wrestling Sharon: A Memoir, NY Grove, Atlantic Press, forthcoming; The Archeology of the Circle: New and Selected Poems, NY, Grove, Atlantic Press, 98; Angel Riding a Beast: Poems for America, translated with author, Liliana Ursu, Evanston, NUP, 98; Mountain River: Poetry from the Vietnam Wars: 1945-1995, coed, co-translated, Univ of Mass, 98; Between the Lines: Writings on War and its Social Consequences, coed, Boston Amherst, U of Mass Press, 96; Charles Simic: Essays on the Poetry, ed, Ann Arbor, U of Mich Press, 96; Poems from Captured Documents, co-trans, Amherst MA, U of Mass Press, 94. **CONTACT ADDRESS** Dept of Humanities, Lorain County Comm Col, 1005 N Abbe Rd, Elyria, OH 44035-1691.

WEIHE, EDWIN
DISCIPLINE ENGLISH **EDUCATION** Brown Univ, BA, 63; Univ IA, MA, 65, MFA, 66, PhD, 72. **CAREER** Eng, Seattle Univ. **RESEARCH** Am lit; Modism; fiction writing. **SELECTED PUBLICATIONS** Auth, I Can See a Man, poetry, Orphic Lute, 93; Merleau-Ponty's Doubt: The Wild of Nothing, Int Symp, Leuven, Belgium, 91, publ in Phenomelogia, 93; Her Birthday Suit, fiction, Arterial, 91; Her Dress, poem, Arterial, 91; Flannery O'Connor's Misfits, Inst forum, RWTH-Aachen, 93; Mystery of Flannery O'Connor, Amer Stud Prog, Katholieke Univ, Nijmegen, 93; Persephone, fiction, Fragments, 74; American Artificial Limb Co, fiction, Fragments, 73. **CONTACT ADDRESS** Dept of Eng, Seattle Univ, 900 Broadway, Seattle, WA 98122-4460. **EMAIL** eweihe@seattleu.edu

WEIL, ERIC A.
PERSONAL Born 06/19/1953, Bluefield, WV, m, 1979, 2 children **DISCIPLINE** ENGLISH **EDUCATION** Bowling Green State Univ, BS, 75; Univ NC, MFA, 79; PhD, 93. **CAREER** Adj Prof, High Point Univ, 93; Asst Prof, Shaw Univ, 93-. **HONORS AND AWARDS** Amon Liner Awd, Greensboro Rev, 80. **MEMBERSHIPS** MLA; Philol Asn of the Carolinas; NC Writers Network; Nat Coun of the Teachers of English. **SELECTED PUBLICATIONS** Auth, "An alchemical Freedom Flight: Linking the Manciple's tale," Medieval Perspectives, 91; auth, "Inner Light and Inner Lives: the Gospel According to Linda Beatrice Brown," NC Lit Rev, 92; auth, "The Fallen Philanthropist: Hollingsworth as the Center of the Blithedale Romance," Postscript, 93; auth, "Personal and Public: three First-Person Voices in African American Poetry," in The Furious Flowering of African American Poetry, Univ Press of Va, 99. **CONTACT ADDRESS** Dept English, Shaw Univ, 118 E South St, Raleigh, NC 27601. **EMAIL** eweil@shaw.edu

WEIL, HERBERT S.
DISCIPLINE ENGLISH LITERATURE **EDUCATION** Tulane Univ, BA; Stanford Univ, MA; PhD. **CAREER** Prof **RESEARCH** Psychology of audience and reader response; character; relations of performance to text; comparative literature; literature and art; film; modern fiction. **SELECTED PUBLICATIONS** Auth, pub(s) on Shakespeare's plays, Sophocles, modern drama, Alice Munro and Carol Shields. **CONTACT ADDRESS** Dept of English, Univ of Manitoba, Winnipeg, MB, Canada R3T 2N2. **EMAIL** hweil@cc.umanitoba.ca

WEIL, JUDITH R.
DISCIPLINE ENGLISH LITERATURE **EDUCATION** Univ Middlebury, BA; Stanford Univ, MA; PhD. **CAREER** Assoc prof, Univ of Manitoba. **RESEARCH** Social contexts of Renaissance literature; women's studies; traditions of literary criticism. **SELECTED PUBLICATIONS** Auth, Christopher Marlowe: Merlin's Prophet, Cambridge; co-ed, New Cambridge Henry IV Part One. **CONTACT ADDRESS** Dept of English, Univ of Manitoba, Winnipeg, MB, Canada R3T 2N2. **EMAIL** jweil@cc.umanitoba.ca

WEIMER, JOAN MYERS
PERSONAL Born 03/12/1936, Cambridge, MA, m, 1971, 3 children **DISCIPLINE** AMERICAN LITERATURE, WOMEN'S STUDIES, NON-FICTION WRITING **EDUCATION** Tufts Univ, AB, 57; Rutgers Univ, New Brunswick, MA, 64, PhD, 70. **CAREER** From instr to assoc prof, 68-82, prof eng, Drew Univ, 82, Vis scholar, Ctr Res Women, Stanford Univ, 78, 87; Vis scholar, Univ AZ, 96; Consulting ed, Legacy; Proj dir, State of NJ grant, 84-86; Producer/moderator, Women in the Center and Why They Belong There, 13-part television series, 83-84. **HONORS AND AWARDS** Phi Beta Kappa, 56; John H McGinnis Awd, Southwest Rev, 77; Semi-finalist, Nat Play Awd Competition of Nat Repertory Theater, 80; Res and travel grants, Drew Univ, 90-98. **MEMBERSHIPS** NJ Project on Curriculum Integration (mem, Advisory board); Central NJ/Masaya, Nicaragua Friendship City Project (corrdinating comt, 85; leader of delegation to Nicaragua, 1/87); Madison Area Chap Amnesty Int (co-founder, secy), 76-82; Westfield Area Comt for Hum Rights 63-66. **RESEARCH** Memoir; feminist criticism of lit; relationship between roles of mothers and polit repression and torture; machismo. **SELECTED PUBLICATIONS** Co-ed (with David R Weimer), Literature of America, America, 7 vol, McDougal, Littell, 73; The Belly Dancer and the Virgin: Mythic Women in Modern Egypt, Southwest Rev, winter 76; Magic in Brazil, North Am Rev, winter 76; The Mother, the Macho, and the State, Int Jour Women's Studies, 1/78; Co-auth (with David Weimer), Ready About, orig play, 78; Co-auth (with David Weimer), Pyramid, orig play, 79; The Story Tellers, orig play, 80; Mythic Parables of Female Power: Inanna, Demeter and Persephone and the Sleeping Beauty, Anima, fall 86; Women, Artists as Exiles in the Stories of Constance Fenimore Woolson, Legacy, fall 86; Individuation and Intimacy: Eleusis and the Sleeping Beauty, Anima, fall 88; Ed, Women Artists: Women Exiles: Miss Grief and Other Stories by Constance Fenimore Woolson, Rutgers Univ Press, 88; The Admiring Aunt and the Proud Salmon of the Pond: Constance Fenimore Woolson's Struggle with Henry James, In: Critical Essays on Constance Fenimore Woolson (Cheryl Torsney, ed), G K Hall, 92; But I'm Not Writing Fiction! And Other Autobiographical Fictions, Soundings, fall 93; Back Talk: Teaching Lost Selves to Speak, Random House, 94 and Univ Chicago Press, 95; Co-auth (with Phyllis Paullette), Back Talk, orig play, 95; Intimate Knowing: A Tale of a Haunted Biographer, Belles Lettres, summer 95; Life Stand Still Here, In: The Writer's Journal (Sheila Bender, ed), Dell 96. **CONTACT ADDRESS** Dept of Eng, Drew Univ, 36 Madison Ave, Madison, NJ 07940-1493. **EMAIL** jweimer@drew.edu

WEINBROT, HOWARD D.
PERSONAL Born 05/14/1936, New York, NY **DISCIPLINE** ENGLISH **EDUCATION** Antioch Col, BA, 58; Univ Chicago, MA, 59, PhD, 63. **CAREER** Instr English lit, Yale Univ, 63-66; from asst prof to assoc prof, Univ Calif, Riverside, 66-69; from Assoc Prof to Prof, 69-84, Ricardo Quintana Prof English, Univ Wis-Madison, 84-, William F. Vilas Res Prof, 87-. **HONORS AND AWARDS** NEH Sr Fel, 75-76; Huntington Libr Fel, 77; Newberry-Brit Acad Fel, 77-78; Huntington-NEH Fel, 83; Huntington-Brit Acad Fel, 84; Newberry-NEH Fel, 86; ACLS Travel Fel, 86; Humanities Inst Fel, Univ Wis, 87; Guggenheim Fel, 88-89; Mellon Prof, Inst Advanced Study, 93-94. **MEMBERSHIPS** Johnsonians; Am Soc 18th Century Studies, Johnson Soc Cent Region, Midwest ASECS; Scottish Studies Soc. **RESEARCH** Eighteenth century theory and practice of imitation and satire;18th century Anglo-classical and Anglo-French relations; Pope; Johnson; intellectual and literary history. **SELECTED PUBLICATIONS** Auth, The Formal Strain, Chicago, 69; ed, New Aspects of Lexicography, Southern Ill Univ, 72; co-ed, The Eighteenth-Century: A Current Bibliography, Philol Quart, 75; auth, Augustus Caesar in Augustan England, Princeton Univ, 78; Alexander Pope and the Traditions of Formal Verse Satire, Princeton Univ, 82; co-ed, Oxford Anthology of Poetry in English, 87; auth, Eighteenth Century Satire, Cambridge, 88; ed, Northrop Frye and 18th-Century Literature, Eighteenth-Century Studies, 91; auth, Britannia's Issue, Cambridge, 93; author numerous articles and reviews. **CONTACT ADDRESS** Dept of English, Univ of Wisconsin, Madison, 600 North Park St, Madison, WI 53706-1403. **EMAIL** weinbrot@facstaff.wisc.edu

WEINER, ANDREW DAVID
PERSONAL Born 06/29/1943, New York, NY, m, 1974, 4 children **DISCIPLINE** ENGLISH LITERATURE **EDUCATION** City Col NYork, AB, 66; Princeton Univ, PhD, 69. **CAREER** Asst prof, 69-74, assoc prof, 74-82, prof, 82, Univ Wis-Madison. **HONORS AND AWARDS** Nat Endowment for Univ of Wisc Grad School Summer Support, 70, 72, 73, 76, 77, 79, 80, 82, 86, 87; NEH younger scholar, 73-74. **MEMBERSHIPS** MLA; Spenser Soc; Rev Soc Am. **RESEARCH** Art history; Elizabethan literature; history of ideas. **SELECTED PUBLICATIONS** Coed and contrib, Graven Images 1, 94; coed and contrib, Graven Images 2: The Body, 95; coed and contrib, Madness, Melancholy and the Limits of the Self: Studies in Culture, Law, and the Sacred, Graven Images Vol 3, Madison: University of Wisconsin Law School, 96; coed and contrib, Burdens of Guilty Minds: Rape and Suicide in Shakespeare's Lucrece, Graven Images 2, 95; auth, Madness and the Limits of the Self in Shakespeare's King Lear, Madness, Melancholy and the Limits of the Self: Studies in Culture, Law, and the Sacred, Graven Images Volume 3, UW Law School, 96; coauth, Erasmus and Tyndale, Major Tudor Authors: A Bio-Critical Sourcebook, Greenwood Publishing, 97; auth, "'I Crave the Law:' Justice, Mercy, and the Law in The Merchant of Venice," Transgression, Punishment, Responsibility, Forgiveness: Studies in Culture, Law, and the Sacred (Graven Images 4) (Madison, Univ of Wis Law School, 98), 201-225. **CONTACT ADDRESS** Dept of English, Univ of Wisconsin, Madison, 600 North Park St, Madison, WI 53706-1403. **EMAIL** adweiner@facstaff.wisc.edu

WEINER, BRUCE I.
DISCIPLINE ENGLISH **EDUCATION** Princeton Univ, AB, 71; Univ PA, PhD, 78. **CAREER** Asst prof to prof, St Lawrence Univ, 78-. **HONORS AND AWARDS** Appointed Craig Prof of English, St. Lawrence Univ. **MEMBERSHIPS** MLA, Am Lit Asn, SHARP, Poe Studies Asn, Am Studies Asn. **RESEARCH** 19th century American literature and culture. **SELECTED PUBLICATIONS** Auth, The Most Noble of Professions: Poe and the Poverty of Authorship, Baltimore: Enoch Pratt Free Library and Edgar Allan Poe Soc (78); auth, "Poe's Subversion of Versimilitude," in The Naiad Voice: Essays on Poe's Satiric Hoaxing, ed Dannis W. Eddings, Assoc Faculty Press, 112-23 (83); auth, "The New York Mirror" and "The Democratic Review," in Am Lit Mags, ed Edward E. Chielens, NY: Greenwood Press (86); auth, "That Metaphysical Art: Mystery and Detection in Poe's Tales," in Poe and Our Times: Influences and Affinities, ed B. F. Fisher IV, Baltimore: Edgar Allan Poe Soc, 32-48 (86); auth, "Poe and the 'Blackwood's Magazine' Tale of Sensation," in Poe and Our Times: The Artist and His Milieu, ed B. F. Fisher IV, Baltimore: Enoch Pratt Free Library and Edgar Allan Poe Soc (78); auth, "Novels, Tales, and Problems of Form in 'The Narrative of Arthur Gordon Pym'," in Poe's Pym: Critical Explorations, ed Richard Kopley, Durham, NC: Duke Univ Press (92); auth, "Introduction," to Wiorks of Edgar Allan Poe, Wordsworth Poetry Library (95); auth, "Introduction," to The Scarlet Letter by Nathaniel Hawthorne, Wordsworth Am Classics (90); auth, "Poe and the Culture of American Magazines," in Perspectives on Poe, ed D. Ramakrishna, New Delhi: APC Pubs (96). **CONTACT ADDRESS** Dept English, St. Lawrence Univ, 1 Romoda Dr, Canton, NY 13617-1423. **EMAIL** bweiner@stlawu.edu

WEINER, ESTHA
DISCIPLINE ENGLISH, LITERATURE **EDUCATION** Sarah Lawrence Col, Bronxville, NY, BA; City Univ NY, MA. **CAREER** Writing Tutor, City Col of NY; Artist-in-Residence, Goddard Col, Vt; Playreading Teachers: YWCA Arts and Cult Dept, NY; Children's Drama Workshop Teacher, Sidewalks Theatre, NY; Lang/Comprehension Instr, Baruch Col; Poet-In-The-Sch; BZK Prod: Teaching Artist in Drama and Writing; Teachers and Writers Collab: Roster of Teaching Artists; Adj Prof, City Col of NY; Adj Prof, Marymount Mahattan Col. **HONORS AND AWARDS** Semi-Finalist, "Discovery" The Nation Prize; Shakespeare Speaker, NY Coun for the Humanities Speaker Series; Breadloaf Summer Writer's Conf: Poetry; Judge, Acad of Am Poets' Student Prize, City Col CUNY, WNYE Poetry Competition. **MEMBERSHIPS** MLA, Poetry Soc of Am, W.B. Yeats Soc, Poets House: "Friend of The House", Columbia Shakespeare Sem, AFTRA, SAG, Actors Equity, Acad of Am Poets, James Joyce Soc. **CONTACT ADDRESS** Dept English, City Col, CUNY, 138th St at Covent Ave, New York, NY 10031.

WEINER, NEAL O.
PERSONAL Born 07/24/1942, Baltimore, MD, 2 children **DISCIPLINE** PHILOSOPHY, CLASSICS **EDUCATION** St John's Col, Md, BA, 64; Univ Tex, PhD, 68. **CAREER** Asst prof philos, State Univ NY Col Old Westbury, 68-70; Assoc Prof Philos, Marlboro Col, 70-, Vis assoc prof philos, St Mary's Col, Notre Dame, IN, 77-78; tutor, Grad Inst St John's Col, NM, 78. **HONORS AND AWARDS** Wilson Fellow; Danforth Fellow. **MEMBERSHIPS** Am Philos Asn; Northern New Eng Philos Asn. **RESEARCH** Class philos; psychiatry and ethics. **SELECTED PUBLICATIONS** Auth, The Articulation of Thought, Marlboro Col, 86; The Harmony of the Soul, SUNY, 93 **CONTACT ADDRESS** Dept of Philos, Marlboro Col, General Delivery, Marlboro, VT 05344-9999.

WEINGAND, DARLENE E.
PERSONAL Born 08/13/1937, Oak Park, IL, m **DISCIPLINE** LIBRARY; INFORMATION STUDIES **EDUCATION** Univ Minnesota, PhD 80; Dominican Univ, MA 73; Elmhurst Col, BA 72. **CAREER** Univ Wisconsin Madison, asst, assoc, prof, 81 to 98-, fac dir, 81-, SLIS asst dir, 90-94, 97-; Curtin Univ W Aus, vis fel, 90; adj prof and member of Affiliate Graduate Fac, Univ of Hawaii Mano, 00-. **HONORS AND AWARDS** Dist Alum of the Yr, Dom U; ALISE res Gnt; Outstanding Achie Audio Apps; Fulbright lectshp; Contemporary Auth; Phi Delta Kappa; Beta Phi Mu. **MEMBERSHIPS** ALA; HLA. **RESEARCH** Cont EDU ; Mktg; Planning; Pub Lib; Library Futures; Tech Innovations; Dist EDU. **SELECTED PUBLICATIONS** Auth, Future Driven Library Marketing, ALA, 98; Customer Service Excellence: A Concise guide for Librarians, ALA, 97; Managing Today's Public Library, Lib Unlimited, 94; auth, Maarketing/Planning Library & Information Services, 2nd ed., Lib Unlimited, 99; auth, Administration of the Small Public Library, 4th ed, ALA, 01. **CONTACT ADDRESS** Dept of Information Studies, Univ of Wisconsin, Madison, 2550 Kuhio Ave, #2402, Honolulu, HI 96815. **EMAIL** weingand@lava.net

WEINHOUSE, LINDA
PERSONAL Born 03/22/1952, Brooklyn, NY, d, 5 children **DISCIPLINE** ENGLISH **EDUCATION** Brooklyn Col, BA, 72; Hunter Col, MA, 75; Hebrew Univ, PhD, 85. **CAREER** Prof, Community Col of Baltimore County, 90-. **HONORS AND AWARDS** Phi Beta Kappa; NEH Grant, 96, 99. **MEMBERSHIPS** MLA, Doris Lessing Soc. **RESEARCH** Post-colonial Female Writers, Bible as Literature. **SELECTED PUBLICATIONS** Auth, "The Urim and Thummim in Paradise Lost," Milton Quart, (77); auth, "The Paternal Gift of Narration: My Son's Story," Jour of Commonwealth Lit, (93); auth, "Alice Munro: Hard-Luck Stories or There is No Sexual Relation," Critique, (95); auth, "Faith and Fantasy - The Texts of the Jews," Medieval Encounters, (99). **CONTACT ADDRESS** 3211 Labryinth Rd, Baltimore, MD 21208-5616. **EMAIL** lweinhouse@ccbc.cc.md.us

WEINREICH, REGINA
PERSONAL Born 01/03/1949, Munich, Germany, m, 1984, 3 children **DISCIPLINE** ENGLISH **EDUCATION** CUNY, BA, 70; Univ Wis, MA, 72; NY Univ, PhD, 82. **CAREER** Lecturer, Brooklyn Col, 72-76; prof, School of Visual Arts, 76-. **MEMBERSHIPS** PEN, MLA, NY Women in Film & Television, Nat Book Critics Circle. **RESEARCH** Beat Generation, 20th Century literature and culture, Film holocaust. **SELECTED PUBLICATIONS** Auth, "Sister Act: A Reading of Jane Bowles's Puppet Play," in A Tawdry Place of Salvation: The Art of Jane Bowles, 97; auth, "Interview with Allen Ginsberg," Five Points; auth, The Spontaneous Poetics of Jack Kerouac: A Study of the fiction, Southern Ill Univ Press, 95; auth "Paul Bowle: The Complete Outsider," Conversations with Paul Bowles, Univ Press Miss, (93): 210-217; auth, "The Sinner Repents: Alan Ansen Talks to Regina Weinreich," The Review of Contemporary Fiction, (89): 199-209; auth, "Cuddling His Cats," American Book Review, (88(, cover; auth, "The Art of Fiction XCVI: Francine du Plessix Gray," The Paris Review, (87): 132-172; auth, "Why Mother Did It," New York Times Book Review, (87):12;auth, "Paul Bowles memoir in 'Aspects of Self: A Bowles Collage'," Twentieth Century Literature, (86): 267-274; auth, Visions of Kerouac," New York Times Book Review, (84):20. **CONTACT ADDRESS** Dept Humanities & Sci, School of Visual Arts, New York, 209 E 23rd St, New York, NY 10010-3901. **EMAIL** regbob@aol.com

WEINSTEIN, MARK A.
DISCIPLINE 19TH CENTURY BRITISH LITERATURE **EDUCATION** Cornell Univ, BA, 59; Yale Univ, MA, 60, PhD, 62. **CAREER** Lt, US Army, 62-64; instr, Bronx Community Col, 64-65; instr, 65-68, asst prof, Brooklyn Col, 68-70; assoc prof, 70-74, prof, Univ Nev, Las Vegas, 74-. **SELECTED PUBLICATIONS** Auth, Scott, Walter, Saint Ronan's Well, Vol 16 of The Edinburgh Ed of the Waverley Novels, ed, Mark A. Weinstein, 30 vols, Edinburgh UP and Columbia UP, 93-2003; The Manuscript of The Pirate, Princeton Univ Libr Chronicle, 58, 97. **CONTACT ADDRESS** Univ of Nevada, Las Vegas, Las Vegas, NV 89154. **EMAIL** weinstei@nevada.edu

WEINSTEIN, PHILIP MEYER
PERSONAL Born 07/08/1940, Memphis, TN, m, 1963, 2 children **DISCIPLINE** ENGLISH & AMERICAN LITERATURE **EDUCATION** Princeton Univ, AB, 62; Harvard Univ, MA, 66, PhD(English), 68. **CAREER** From instr to asst prof English, Harvard Univ, 68-71; asst prof, 71-74, assoc prof, 74 81, Prof English, Swarthmore Col, 81-, Chmn Dept, 80-. **MEMBERSHIPS** AAUP; MLA **RESEARCH** British fiction, Dickens through Joyce; American fiction, Hawthorne through Faulkner. **SELECTED PUBLICATIONS** Auth, Structure and collapse: A study of Bleak House, Dickens Studies, 68; The exploitative and protective imagination: Unreliable narration in The Sacred Fount, Harvard English Studies, 70; An interpretation of pastoral in The Winter's Tale, Shakespeare Quart, 71; Henry James and the Requirements of the Imagination, Harvard Univ, 71; Caddy Disparue: Exploring an episode common to Proust and Faulkner, Comp Lit Studies, 3/77; Precarious sanctuaries: Protection and exposure in Falkner's fiction, Studies Am Fiction, spring 79; Choosing between the Quick and the Dead: Three versions of Lady Chatterley's Lover, Mod Lang Quart, 82. **CONTACT ADDRESS** Dept of English Lit, Swarthmore Col, 500 College Ave, Swarthmore, PA 19081-1306.

WEINSTOCK, DONALD JAY
PERSONAL Born 09/02/1934, Chicago, IL, m, 1955 **DISCIPLINE** ENGLISH LITERATURE **EDUCATION** Univ Calif, Los Angeles, AB, 56, MA, 60, PhD(English), 68. **CAREER** Actg asst prof English, Univ Calif, Riverside, 65-68; lectr, Univ Calif, Los Angeles, 68-69; asst prof, 69-74, assoc prof, 74-80, prof English, Calif State Univ, Long Beach, 80-. **MEMBERSHIPS** MLA; Assn Poetry Ther. **RESEARCH** Victorian literature; psychological applications of poetry; contemporary African writing in English. **SELECTED PUBLICATIONS** Auth, The two swarms of locusts: Judgment by indirection, In: Things Fall Apart, Studies in Black Lit, Spring 71; The two Boer wars and the Jameson Raid: A checklist of novels in Dutch and Afrikaans, Spring 71 & The two Boer wars and the Jameson Raid: A checklist of novels in English, Spring 72; Poetry and the self, 78 & Poetry therapy: A bibliography, 79, ERIC; Jaggers in the country, NDak Quart, Summer 79; rev article Arthur Lerner, Poetry in the therapeutic experience, Maelstrom Rev, 80; Say not we are on a darkling plain: Clough's rejoinder to Dover Beach, Victorian Poetry, Spring 81. **CONTACT ADDRESS** Dept of English, California State Univ, Long Beach, 1250 N Bellflower, Long Beach, CA 90840-0001.

WEINSTOCK, JEFFREY A.
PERSONAL Born 01/24/1970, Washington, DC **DISCIPLINE** AMERICAN LITERATURE, CRITICAL THEORY **EDUCATION** Univ Pa, BA, 92; George Washington Univ, MA, 99; MPhil, 99; PhD, 99. **CAREER** Adj prof, George Washington Univ, 96-99; adj prof, Mt Vernon Col, 99; adj prof, Univ Conn, 99-00; vis asst prof, Trinity Col, 00; vis asst prof, Conn Col, 00-01; vis asst prof, Wesleyan Univ, 00-01; asst prof, Central Mich Univ, 01-. **HONORS AND AWARDS** George McClandish Hon Fel, 94-95; Univ Fel in Humanities, 94-98; Ray and Pat Browne Awd for Student Achievement, 95. **MEMBERSHIPS** MLA, Am Lit Assoc, Popular Cult Assoc, Int Assoc for the Fantastic in the Arts, Poe Studies Assoc, Edith Wharton Soc, Charlotte Perkins Gilman Soc, NEMLA. **RESEARCH** Ghosts, spectrality, monstrosity. **SELECTED PUBLICATIONS** Auth, "13 Ways of Looking at Donna Haraway," CEA Magazine, (94); auth, "Freaks in Space: 'Extraterrestrialism' and 'Deep-Space Multiculturalism,'" Freakery: Cultural Spectacles of the Extraordinary Body, (96); auth, "The Disappointed Bridge," Jour for the Fantastic in the Arts (97); auth, "This is not Foucault's Head," Post-Identity (97); auth, "Virus Culture," Studies in Popular Cult, (97); auth, "Introduction: Cultural Violences," Col Lit, (99); auth, "ZombieTV," Post-Identity, (99); auth, "Circumcising Dracula: The Vampire as Anti-Semitic Trope," Jour for the Fantastic in the Arts, (01); auth, "In Possession of the Letter: Kate Chopin's 'Her Letters,'" Studies in Am Fiction, (01); auth, "Mars Attacks! Wells, Welles, and Radio Panic or: The Story of the Century," Ordinary Reactions to Extraordinary Events, (01). **CONTACT ADDRESS** Dept English, Central Michigan Univ, Mount Pleasant, MI 48859. **EMAIL** drjeffrey@hotmail.com

WEINTRAUB, STANLEY
PERSONAL Born 04/17/1929, Philadelphia, PA, m, 1954, 3 children **DISCIPLINE** ENGLISH LITERATURE **EDUCATION** Pa State Col, West Chester, BS, 49; Temple Univ, MA, 51; PA State Univ, PhD(English), 56. **CAREER** From instr to prof English, 53-70, Res Prof, Pa State Univ, 70-, Dir Inst Arts & Humanistic Studies, 70-, Ed, Shaw Rev, 56-; Vis prof, Univ of Calif, 63, Univ of Hawaii, 73; Guggenheim fel, 68-69. **HONORS AND AWARDS** Nat Bk Awd nomination, 67, for Beardsley: A Biography; Guggenheim fel, 68-69; George Freedley Awd, Am Theatre Libr Asn, 71, for Journey to Heartbreak: The Crucible Years of Bernard Shw, 1914-1918; Freedoms Found Awd, 80, for The London Yankees: Portraits of Am Writers and Artists in London, 1894-1914; Distinguished Humanist Awd, Pennsylvania Humanities Counc, 85. **MEMBERSHIPS** MLA; Authors League of Am; Authors Guild; Int Asn for the Study of Anglo-Irish Lit. **RESEARCH** George Bernard Shaw; biographical writing; English literature since 1880. **SELECTED PUBLICATIONS** Auth, Journey to Heartbreak: The Crucible Years of Bernard Shaw, 1914-1918, Weybright, 71; auth, Whistler: A Biography, Weybright, 74; auth, Lawrence of Arabia: The Literary Impulse, Louisiana State Univ Press, 75; auth, Aubrey Beardsley: Imp of the Perverse, Pennsylvania State Univ Press, 76; auth, Four Rossettis: A Victorian Biography, Weybright, 77; auth, The London Yankees: Portraits of American Writers and Artists in London, 1894-1914, Harcourt, 79; auth, The Unexpected Shaw: Biographical Approaches to George Bernard Shaw and His Work, Ungar, 82; auth, A Stillness Heard round the World: The End of the Great War, November 1918, Dutton, 85; auth, Victoria: An Intimate Biography, Dutton, 87; auth, MacArthur's War: Korea and the Undoing of an American Hero, Free Press, 00. **CONTACT ADDRESS** 105 Ihlseng Cottage, University Park, PA 16802. **EMAIL** sqw4@psu.edu

WEISE, JUDITH ANDERSON
PERSONAL Born 11/04/1942, 1 child **DISCIPLINE** ENGLISH **EDUCATION** William Smith Col, BA, 63; Univ NC, Chapel Hill, MA, 66; Sunny Binghamton, Ph D, 71, **CAREER** Ed asst, Hearthside Press, New York, 64; asst prof English, Sunny Potsdam, 69-. **HONORS AND AWARDS** Fulbright Sr Scholar, 86; Phi Kappa Phi Hon Soc, 97; SUNY Distinguished Teaching Prof, 99. **MEMBERSHIPS** MLA; Old English Sect Mod Lang; Women's Caucus Mod Lang; United Univ Prof; Int Soc Anglo-Saxonists. **RESEARCH** _Beowulf_, Old English poetry **SELECTED PUBLICATIONS** Auth, "Ambuguity in Old English Poetry," Neophilologus, Vol 60, 79; Romancing Seyart Cecylie: Chaucer's Tell-Tale Lexicon, Style, in print. **CONTACT ADDRESS** Dept English, SUNY, Col at Potsdam, 44 Pierrepont Ave, Potsdam, NY 13676-2299. **EMAIL** Weiseja@potsdam.edu

WEISER, DAVID K.
PERSONAL Born 03/16/1944, Tel-Aviv, Israel, m, 1970, 4 children **DISCIPLINE** ENGLISH **EDUCATION** Brandeis Univ, BA, 96; Indiana Univ, PhD, 70. **CAREER** Lecturer/ Seminar Lecturer, Tel-Aviv Univ, 69-85; Assoc Prof, Tours Col, 85-88; Asst Prof, Hostos Community Col, 88-. **HONORS AND AWARDS** Research Awd, Tel-Aviv Univ, 83, PSCI CUNY Research Grant, 93. **RESEARCH** Shakespeare, American Poetry. **SELECTED PUBLICATIONS** Auth, Mind in Character: Shakespeare's Speaks in the Sonnets, Columbia Univ of Missouri Press, 87; auth, Jewish Sonnets, Targum Press, (Jerusalem and Southfield MI), 00. **CONTACT ADDRESS** Dept English, Hostos Community Col, 475 Grand Concourse, Bronx Bronx, NY 10451-5307.

WEISS, ALEXANDER
PERSONAL Born Tashkent, m, 1965, 2 children **DISCIPLINE** ENGLISH **EDUCATION** Univ Md, College Park, BA, 64, MA, 66; Univ Calif, Berkeley, PhD(English), 73. **CAREER** Asst dir col sem prog, Univ Calif, Berkeley, 74-76; from Asst Prof to Assoc Prof, 76-85, Prof English, Radford Univ, 86-. **MEMBERSHIPS** SAtlantic Mod Lang Asn; Southeastern Medieval Asn; New Chaucer Soc; Nat Asn Schol; Va Asn Schol; Asn Lit Schol and Critics. **RESEARCH** Middle English language and literature; Chaucer; Old English language and literature. **SELECTED PUBLICATIONS** Auth, Chaucer's early translations from French: The art of creative transformation, Proc Southeastern Medieval Convention, 81; Chaucer's Native Heritage, Peter Lang Publ, 85. **CONTACT ADDRESS** Dept of English, Radford Univ, PO Box 6935, Radford, VA 24142-6935. **EMAIL** aweiss@runet.edu

WEISS, MICHAEL L.
DISCIPLINE CLASSICS **EDUCATION** Univ PA, BA, 87; Univ Vienna, extra-mural stud, 91-92; Cornell Univ, PhD, 93. **CAREER** Asst prof, Univ NC, Chapel Hill. **RESEARCH** Class linguistics; Greek and Latin linguistics; Indo-Europ linguistics. **SELECTED PUBLICATIONS** Auth, Old Church Slavonic spodu and Avestan spada-, Die Sprache 35,1, 93; On the Non-Verbal Origin of the Greek Verb naefein," Historische Sprachforschung, 94; Life Everlasting: Latin iugis 'everflowing', Greek Igiaew 'healthy', Gothic ajukduKs 'eternity' and Avestan yauuaeji- 'living forever', Munchener Studien zur Sprachwissenschaft 55 (94), 96; An Oscanism in Catullus 53, Class Philol, 96; Greek muriow'countless,' Hittite muri- 'bunch (of fruit),' Historische Sprachforschung 96. **CONTACT ADDRESS** Univ of No Carolina, Chapel Hill, Chapel Hill, NC 27599. **EMAIL** mweiss@email.unc.edu

WEISS, PIERO
PERSONAL Born 01/26/1928, Trieste, Italy, d, 2 children **DISCIPLINE** MUSIC HISTORY **EDUCATION** Columbia Univ, AB, PhD. **CAREER** Prof, John Hopkins Univ. **SELECTED PUBLICATIONS** Auth, Letters of Composers Through Six Centuries, 67; co-auth, Music in the Western World: A History in Documents, 84. **CONTACT ADDRESS** Dept of Musicology, Johns Hopkins Univ, Baltimore, 1 E Mt Vernon Pl, Baltimore, MD 21202-2397.

WEISS, SUSAN FORSCHER
DISCIPLINE MUSIC HISTORY **EDUCATION** Goucher Col, BA; Smith Col, MA; Univ MD, PhD. **CAREER** Prof, John Hopkins Univ. **HONORS AND AWARDS** Epsilon Musicol Res Awd. **MEMBERSHIPS** Am Musicol Soc. **SELECTED PUBLICATIONS** Auth, pubs for Am and International Musicological Societies. **CONTACT ADDRESS** Dept of Musicology, Johns Hopkins Univ, Baltimore, 1 E Mt Vernon Pl, Baltimore, MD 21202-2397.

WEISS, SUSAN FORSCHER
PERSONAL Born 07/22/1944, New York, NY, m, 1967, 2 children **DISCIPLINE** MUSICOLOGY **EDUCATION** Goucher Col, BA, 65; Smith Col, MA, 67; Univ Md, PhD, 85. **CAREER** Chair, Music Dept, Garrison Forest Sch, 74-94; Faculty, Dept Musicol, Peabody Conserv of The Johns Hopkins Univ, 87-. **HONORS AND AWARDS** NEH Summer Stipend, 84; Cleveland Dodge Found Grant; ACLS Travel Grant, 86; Mu Phi Epsilon Res Contest Winner, 87; John M. Ward Fellow, 90; Short-term Fellow, 91; Distinguished Tchr Yr, 94; Provost's Awd for Distance Ed, JHU, 95. **MEMBERSHIPS** Chair, Acad Issues Subcomt of the Provost's Comt on Status of Women; Am Musicol Soc; Int Musicol Soc; Renaissance Soc of Am, Am Assoc of Univ Women; Fac Adv, Mu Phi Epsilon; AAUP. **RESEARCH** Medieval and Renaissance Music; Musical Pedagogy; Instruments and Instrumental Music; Musical Notation; use of computers in the study of early music; Musical Iconography. **SELECTED PUBLICATIONS** Musical Patronage of the Bentivoglio Signoria, 1465-1512, in Atti del XIV Congresso della Societa Internazionale de Musicologia, Transmissione e recezione delle forme di cultura musicale, Bologna, 87, vol 3, ch XI, p703-715;Bologna Q 18: Some Reflections on Content and Context, The Jour Am Musicol Soc,vol 41, 88,p63-101; What Do We Give Them This Time?, in Early Mus Am, vol. 1, no 2, wint 95, p20-24; Singing Along with Guido and Friends: Music In Manuscripts at the Walters Art Gallery, Bull of the Walters Art Gallery, Oct 96. **CONTACT ADDRESS** Peabody Conserv, Johns Hopkins Univ, Baltimore, 1 E Mt. Vernon, Baltimore, MD 21202. **EMAIL** sweiss@peabody.jhu.edu

WEISS, VICTORIA LOUISE
PERSONAL Born 07/21/1949, Cleveland, OH **DISCIPLINE** ENGLISH **EDUCATION** St Norbert Col, BA, 71; Lehigh Univ, MA, 74, PhD(English), 77. **CAREER** Asst Prof English, Oglethorpe Univ, 77-, Fac develop grant, Shell Oil Corp, 78. **MEMBERSHIPS** MLA **RESEARCH** Middle English literature, especially the relationship between history and literature; contemporary literature, especially experimental fiction. **SELECTED PUBLICATIONS** Auth, Form and meaning in Marguerite Duras' Moderato Cantabile, Critique, 74; Gawain's first failure: The beheading scene in Sir Gawain and the Green Knight, 76 & The Medieval knighting ceremony in Sir Gawain and the Green Knight, 11/78, Chaucer Rev; The Play World And The Real-World, Chivalry In 'Sir Gawain And The Green Knight', Philological Quarterly, Vol 0072, 1993; The Play World And The Real-World, Chivalry In 'Sir Gawain And The Green Knight', Philological Quarterly, Vol 0072, 1993; Grail Knight Or Boon Companion - The Inconsistent Sir-Bors Of Malory 'Morte Darthur', Studies In Philology, Vol 0094, 1997; Grail Knight Or Boon Companion - The Inconsistent Sir-Bors Of Malory 'Morte Darthur', Studies In Philology, Vol 0094, 1997. **CONTACT ADDRESS** Dept of English, Oglethorpe Univ, 4484 Peach Tree Rd, Atlanta, GA 30319-2797.

WEITZMAN, ARTHUR J.
PERSONAL Born 09/13/1933, m, 1982, 2 children **DISCIPLINE** ENGLISH **EDUCATION** Univ Chicago, BA, 56; MA, 57; NYork Univ, PhD, 64. **CAREER** Instructor, Brooklyn Col, 60-63; Asst Prof, Temple Univ, 63-69; Assoc Prof to Prof, Northeastern Univ, 69-. **HONORS AND AWARDS** Founder's Day Awd, NY Univ, 64; Res Awd, Temple Univ, 64, 66; Fel, NEH, 72-73; Mellon Fel, 76; Res Awd, Northeastern Univ, 93-94, 80-81. **MEMBERSHIPS** Mod Lang Asn; Am Soc for Eighteenth-Century Stud; Who's Who in Am Educ; Who's Who in the world; Who's Who in Am; Who's Who in the East. **SELECTED PUBLICATIONS** Auth, "Eighteenth-Century Views of Pope's Villa," Eighteenth-Century Life, 83; auth, "Pope's Poetry a Gift from the gods," Middlesex News, 89; auth, "After Riots, Caracas Crawls back to Normal," Middlesex News, 89; auth, "History Has New Meaning in the 80s," Middlesex News,, 89; auth, "Taking Aim at Canon Bashing," Middlesex News,, 90; auth, "Feminism's Fire Hurts on Campus," Middlesex News, 91; auth, "Confessions of an Eighteenth-Century Editor," Editor Notes, 94; auth, "The bitter Fruit of Diversity," Measure, 95; auth, "Orientalism," in Hanoverian England: An Encyclopedia, Garland Pub, 97; auth, "Scheherazade's Risk: Male Voyeurism and the Female Gambit in the Arabian Nights," in 1660-1850, AMS, in press. **CONTACT ADDRESS** Dept Eng, Northeastern Univ, 360 Huntington Ave, Boston, MA 02115-5005. **EMAIL** weitzman@neu.edu

WEIXLMANN, JOSEPH NORMAN
PERSONAL Born 12/16/1946, Buffalo, NY, m, 1982, 3 children **DISCIPLINE** ENGLISH **EDUCATION** Kansas State Univ, PhD, Eng, 73, MA, 70; Canisius Col, AB, 68. **CAREER** Dean, Col Arts and Sciences, Indiana State Univ, 92-; Assoc Dean, CAS, ISU, 87-92; Prof Eng, ISU, 83-; Assoc Prof Eng, ISU, 79-83; Asst Prof, 76-79; Asst Prof, Eng, Texas Tech Univ, 74-76; Inst Eng, Univ Oklahoma, 73-74. **HONORS AND AWARDS** NEH Fellow, 80-81; NEA Grants, 88-95; Lila Wallace, Readers Digest Fund Grants, 91, 92, 95; Am Lit Mag Awds, Ed Merit, 94-95; Intl Man of the Year Awd, Intl Biographical Cen, 93. **MEMBERSHIPS** Modern Language Asn; Col Lang Asn; Council of Editors of Learned Journals; Soc for Scholarly Pub; Soc for the Study of Multi-Ethnic Literature in the USA; Council of Col Arts and Sciences. **RESEARCH** African Am Lit and Culture; Contem Am Fic. **SELECTED PUBLICATIONS** Editor-in Chief, African Am Review, 76-; (Prin Ed with Chester J Fontenot) Black America Prose Theory, Greenwood, Penkevill, 84; (Prin Ed with Chester J Fontenot) Belief Versus Theory in Black America Literary Criticism, Greenwood, Penevill, 86; (Prin Ed with Houston A Baker Jr) Black Feminist Literature and Literary Theory, Greenwood, Penkevill, 88 . **CONTACT ADDRESS** Indiana State Univ, Stalker Hall 213, Terre Haute, IN 47809. **EMAIL** ascweix@amber.indstate.edu

WELBURN, RONALD GARFIELD
PERSONAL Born 04/30/1944, Berwyn, PA, m, 1988 **DISCIPLINE** ENGLISH **EDUCATION** Lincoln University, PA, BA, 1968; University of Arizona, MA, 1970; New York University, PhD, 1983. **CAREER** Syracuse University, Syracuse NY, asst prof of Afro-American studies, 70-75; Rutgers University, New Brunswick NJ, formerly affiliated with Institute for

Jazz Studies, asst prof of English, 83; Western Conn State Univ, Danbury, CT, Asst Prof of English, 87-. **HONORS AND AWARDS** Silvera Awd for poetry, Lincoln University, 1967 and 1968; fellow, Smithsonian Institute and Music Critics Association, 1975; Langston Hughes Legacy Certificate, Lincoln University, 1981. **MEMBERSHIPS** Board member, Eagle Wing Press, 1989-. **SELECTED PUBLICATIONS** Author of Peripheries: Selected Poems, 1966-1968, Greenfield Review Press, 1972; author of Heartland: Selected Poems, Lotus Press, 1981; author, Council Decisions: Poems, American Native Press Archives, 1991. **CONTACT ADDRESS** English Dept, Western Connecticut State Univ, 181 White St, Danbury, CT 06810.

WELCH, DENNIS MARTIN
PERSONAL Born 09/23/1944, Artesia, CA, m, 1966, 2 children **DISCIPLINE** ENGLISH & AMERICAN LITERATURE **EDUCATION** Loyola Univ, Los Angeles, BA, 67; Univ Southern Calif, MA, 69, PhD(English), 72. **CAREER** From instr to asst prof English, Gonzaga Univ, 71-74; assoc prof humanities, Clarkson Col Technol, 74-81; Assoc Prof English & Humanities, VA Polytechnic Inst, 81-. **MEMBERSHIPS** MLA; Northeast Mod Lang Asn. **RESEARCH** English Renaissance and Romantic Age; 20th century American. **SELECTED PUBLICATIONS** Auth, America and Atlantis: Blake's ambivalent millennialism, Blake Newslett, 72; The meaning of nothingness in Donne's Nocturnall upon St Lucies Day, Bucknell Rev, 76; Center, circumference, and vegetation imagery in the writings of Blake, Studies Philol, 78; In the throes of Eros: Blakes's early career, Mosaic, 78; Hickey as satanic force in The Iceman Cometh, Ariz Quart, 78; Blake's response to Wollstonecraft's original stories, Blake Quart, Vol 13; Distance and progress in In Memoriam, Victorian Poetry, Vol 18; Expressive theory and Blake's audience, PMLA, Vol 96. **CONTACT ADDRESS** Dept of English & Humanities, Virginia Polytech Inst and State Univ, 100 Virginia Tech, Blacksburg, VA 24061-0002.

WELCH, DONOVAN LEROY
PERSONAL Born 06/03/1932, Hastings, NE, m, 1953, 6 children **DISCIPLINE** ENGLISH **EDUCATION** Univ NE-Lincoln, PhD, 65. **CAREER** Prof English & Reynolds Distinguished Prof Poetry, Univ NE at Kearney, 60- **HONORS AND AWARDS** Pablo Neruda Awd Poetry; Best Prof: NE State Board Trustees, 90; Pratt-Heins Awd Distinguished Tchg, 89. **RESEARCH** Contemporary American poetry. **SELECTED PUBLICATIONS** Carved by Obadiah Verity, Press Col Col, 93; A Brief History of Feathers, A Slow Tempo Press, 96; Fire's Tongue in the Cavelle's End, Univ NE-Kearney, 96. **CONTACT ADDRESS** Donovan LeRoy Welch, 611 W 27, Kearney, NE 68847. **EMAIL** donovanwelch@aol.com

WELCH, OLGA MICHELE
PERSONAL Born 12/30/1948, Salisbury, NC, m **DISCIPLINE** COMMUNICATIONS **EDUCATION** Howard Univ, BA (Salutatorian), history/English/educ 1971; Univ of TN, MS deaf educ 1972, EdD educ admin & super 1977. **CAREER** The Model Secondary Sch for the Deaf, instructor 1972-73, The TN Sch for the Deaf, instructor 1973-75, supervising principal 1977-78; Univ of TN Dept of Spec Educ & Rehab, Assoc Prof & Dir 1978-, Professor Head, Dept of Counselig, Deafness and Human Services. **HONORS AND AWARDS** Phi Beta Kappa; Phi Delta Kappa; Phi Kappa Phi; Phi Alpha Theta; Dept Awd "Most Creative Dissertation Topic" Univ TN; appointment to the Natl Educ Adv Bd 1983; E C Merrill Distinguished Research Awd, 1990, 1992; Univ of TN, Chancellor's Awd, 1998. **MEMBERSHIPS** Council of Exceptional Children; Alexander Graham Bell Assn; Convention of Amer Instructors of the Deaf; Natl Educ Assn; Assn for Supervision & Curriculum Develop; Project HELP tutorial prog for disadvantaged students 1983; vice pres, Knoxville Chap Natl Black Women's Hook-Up 1980-81; Girl Scout neighborhood chmn "NightHawks" Neighborhood 1977-; Interdenominational Concert Choir 1975-; American Educational Research Assn; Co-dir, Project Excel. **RESEARCH** Curriculum development diversity, Career advancement mentoring. **CONTACT ADDRESS** CDHS, Univ of Tennessee, Knoxville, Claxton Addition, A204, Knoxville, TN 37996.

WELLS, COLIN
PERSONAL Born 11/15/1933, West Bridgeford, England, m, 1960, 2 children **DISCIPLINE** CLASSICAL STUDIES **EDUCATION** Univ Oxford, BA, MA, PhD. **CAREER** Prof and Chair, Univ Ottawa, 60; T Frank Murchison distinguished prof, 87-; dept ch. **HONORS AND AWARDS** Fellow of the Society of Antiquaries of London, Corresponding Member of the German Archaeological Institute; dir, sec can team excavations, carthage, tunisia, 76-86; dir, trinity univ excavations, 90-. **MEMBERSHIPS** Archaeological Institute of Am. **RESEARCH** Roman frontier studies, Roman, Africa. **SELECTED PUBLICATIONS** Auth, The German Policy of Augustus, 72; The Roman Empire, Harvard UP, 95. **CONTACT ADDRESS** Dept of Class, Trinity Univ, 715 Stadium Dr, San Antonio, TX 78212. **EMAIL** cwells@trinity.edu

WELLS, CORRI ELIZABETH
DISCIPLINE RHETORIC AND COMPOSITION **EDUCATION** Brigham Young Univ, BA, 77; Univ Houston, MA, 90; Univ TX at Arlington, PhD, 97. **CAREER** Adj fac, assoc dir, 1st Yr Composition, 95-97, grad tchg asst, 93-95 & instr, Univ TX at Arlington; adj fac, N Lake Col, Dallas Co Commun Col Dist 93-95; writing ctr asst, Northwest Campus, 92-93 & instr, Northeast Campus, 91-92, Tarrant Co Jr Col Dist; Instr, Extension Ctr, Salt Lake City & Tooele, 80 & grad tchg asst, Main Campus, Provo, 77-78, Brigham Young Univ. **MEMBERSHIPS** Nat Coun Tchrs Eng; Rhetoric Soc Am; MLA; Gorgias Soc. **SELECTED PUBLICATIONS** Auth, A Teacher's Guide to First Year English: Critical Reading, Thinking and Writing at the University of Texas at Arlington, 4th ed, Arlington, UTA Dept Engl, 96; Teaching Argument in the Computer Classroom, Instructor's Manual for Perspectives on Argument, By Nancy V. Wood, Englewood Cliffs, Prentice Hall, 95; Rev, Teaching Argument in the Computer Classroom & Teaching Students to Conduct Research Using Traditional and Online Sources, Instructor's Manual, 2nd ed Perspectives on Argument, 97; Toward a Poetics for Collecting Poetry by Women, Collection Building in Alternative Libr Lit, 6th ed, Jefferson, McFarland, 93. **CONTACT ADDRESS** Dept of Eng, Univ of Texas, Arlington, 203 Carlisle Hall, PO Box 19035, Arlington, TX 76019-0595.

WELLS, DANIEL ARTHUR
PERSONAL Born 10/16/1943, Adams, MA, m, 1966, 2 children **DISCIPLINE** AMERICAN LITERATURE **EDUCATION** Union Col, NYork, AB, 65; Duke Univ, MA, 68, PhD(English), 72. **CAREER** From asst prof to assoc prof, 70-81, prof English, Univ South FL, St Petersburg, 81-. **HONORS AND AWARDS** Teaching Awds. **MEMBERSHIPS** The Melville Soc; The Poe Soc. **RESEARCH** Nineteenth century American literature. **SELECTED PUBLICATIONS** Auth, Engraved Within the Hills: Further Perspectives on the Ending of Pym, Poe Studies, Vol 10, 6/77; An Index of American Writers and Selected British Writers in Duyckinck's Literary World, Studies Am Renaissance, 78; The Literary Index to American Magazines, 1815-65, Scarecrow Pre ss, 80; An Annotated Checklist of Twain Allusions in Harpers's Monthly, 1850-1900, Am Lit Realism, spring 84; Whitman Allusions in Harper's Monthly t o 1900, Walt Whitman Quart Rev, summer 86; Thoreau's Reputation in the Major Magazines, 1862-1900, Am Periodicals, vol 4, 94; The Literary Index to American Magazines, 1850-1900, Greenwood Press, 96; Mark Twain Allusions in the Boston Literary World, 1870-1904, Resources for Am Literary Study, summer 98. **CONTACT ADDRESS** Dept English, Univ of So Florida, 140 7th Ave S, Saint Petersburg, FL 33701-5016.

WELLS, WALTER
PERSONAL Born 12/13/1937, New York, NY, m, 1961, 3 children **DISCIPLINE** ENGLISH, AMERICAN STUDIES **EDUCATION** NYork Univ, BS, 60, MA, 63; Univ Sussex, DPhil, 71. **CAREER** Instr lang arts, CA State Polytech Col, 63-66; from asst prof to assoc prof, 67-77, prof English & Am Studies, 77-98, chmn Am Studies, 71-85, Prof Emeritus, CA State Univ, Dominguez Hills, 98-; gen consult ed in humanities, Educulture, Inc, 77-80. **RESEARCH** Twentieth century Am; narrative nonfiction; stylistics. **SELECTED PUBLICATIONS** Auth, Communications in Business, Wadsworth, 68, 2nd ed, 77; Tycoons and Locusts: A Regional Look at Hollywood Fiction of the 1930's, Southern IL Univ, 73; Mark Twain's Sure-Fire Programmed Guide to Backgrounds in American Literature, Educulture, 77-80. **CONTACT ADDRESS** Dept of English, California State Univ, Dominguez Hills, 1000 E Victoria, Carson, CA 90747-0005. **EMAIL** wwells@dhvx20.csudh.edu

WELLS, WILLIAM D.
DISCIPLINE MASS COMMUNICATION STUDIES **EDUCATION** Stanford Univ, MA, PhD. **CAREER** Prof **SELECTED PUBLICATIONS** Auth, Planning for R.O.I.: Effective Advertising Strategy, 88; co-auth, Consumer Behavior, 96; Advertising: Principles and Practices, 94; Consumer Behavior, 77; ed, Lifestyle and Psychographics, 72; co-ed, Measuring Advertising Effectiveness, 96; Attitude Research at Bay, 76. **CONTACT ADDRESS** Mass Communication Dept, Univ of Minnesota, Twin Cities, 111 Murphy Hall, 206 Church St SE, Minneapolis, MN 55455. **EMAIL** wells004@maroon.tc.umn.edu

WELSH, ALEXANDER
PERSONAL Born 04/29/1933, Albany, NY, d, 3 children **DISCIPLINE** ENGLISH **EDUCATION** Harvard Univ, AB, 54, MA, 57, PhD, 61. **CAREER** Instr, Yale Univ, 60-63, Asst Prof, 63-66, assoc prof, 66-67; prof, Univ of Pittsburgh, 67-72; Prof, Univ of Calif, 72-91; Emily Sanford Prof, Yale Univ, 91-. **HONORS AND AWARDS** Harvard Nat Scholar, 50-54; Phi Beta Kappa, 54; Frank Knox Fel, Edinburgh, 59-60; Guggenheim Fel, London, 69-70; National Endowment for the Humanities Fel, 77; Rockefeller Foundation Humanities Fel, Los Angeles & London, 84-85. **RESEARCH** Novel; 19th century stud; Shakespeare. **SELECTED PUBLICATIONS** Auth, The Hero of the Waverley Novels, New Haven: Yale Unive Press, 63 New York: Atheneum, 68. Princeton: Princeton Univ Press, 92; ed, Narrative Endings, Berkeley: Univ of California Press, 78; auth, The City of Dickens, Oxford: Claredon Press, 71, 73, Cambridge Harvard Univ Press, 86; auth, Reflections on the Hero as Quixote, Princeton: Princetown Univ Press, 81; auth, George Eliot and Blackmail, Cambridge: Harvard Univ Press, 81; auth, From Copyright to Copperfield, Cambridge: Harvard Univ Press, 87; auth, Strong Representations, Baltimore: Johns Hopkins Univ Press, 92; auth, Freud's Wishful Dream Book, Princeton: Princeton Univ Press, 94; auth, Dickens Redressed, New Haven: Yale Univ Press, 00; auth, Hamlet in his Modern Guises, Princeton: Princeton Univ Press, 01. **CONTACT ADDRESS** English Dept, Yale Univ, New Haven, CT 06520-8302.

WELSH, ANDREW
PERSONAL Born 11/20/1937, Pittsburgh, PA, m, 1971, 2 children **DISCIPLINE** ENGLISH LITERATURE **EDUCATION** Univ Pittsburgh, BS, 59, MA, 61, PhD(English), 70. **CAREER** Asst prof, 71-77, ASSOC PROF ENGLISH, RUTGERS UNIV, 77-, Mellon fel, Univ Pittsburgh, 74-75; Nat Endowment for Humanities fel, Univ Calif, Irvine, 77. **HONORS AND AWARDS** Melville Cane Awd, Poetry Soc Am, 78; James Russell Lowell Prize, Mod Lang Asn, 78. **MEMBERSHIPS** MLA; Mediaeval Acad Am; AAUP; CSANA; IAS/NAB. **RESEARCH** Medieval literature; folklore. **SELECTED PUBLICATIONS** Auth, Roots of Lyric, Princeton Univ, 78. **CONTACT ADDRESS** Dept of English, Rutgers, The State Univ of New Jersey, New Brunswick, 510 George St, New Brunswick, NJ 08901-1167. **EMAIL** awelsh@rci.rutgers.edu

WELSH, JAMES MICHAEL
PERSONAL Born 07/15/1938, Logansport, IN, m, 1960, 2 children **DISCIPLINE** LITERATURE **EDUCATION** Ind Univ, BA, 63; Univ Kans, MA, 65, PhD, 96. **CAREER** From Instr to Assoc Prof, 71-97, PROF ENGLISH, SALISBURY STATE UNIV, 97-; Co-founding ed, Lit/Film Quart, 72; assoc ed, Washington Rev of Arts, 76-77; East Coast ed, Am Classic Screen, 77-84. **HONORS AND AWARDS** Fulbright Fellowship, Romania, 94, 98. **MEMBERSHIPS** MLA; Brit Film Inst; Int'l Asn for Media & History (IAMHIST); Film and History League; Univ Film & Video Asn. Literature/Film Asn. **RESEARCH** Film history and theory; Literature and Film Asn. **SELECTED PUBLICATIONS** Auth, The sound of silents: An early Shrew, English J, 73; coauth, Ben Jonson: A Quadricentennial Bibliography, Scarecrow, 74; auth, To see it feelingly: King Lear through Russian eyes, Lit/Film Quart, 76; coauth, Peter Watkins: Therapeutic cinema and the repressive mind, Film & Hist, 77; auth, Beyond melodrama: Art, politics and State of Siege, Film Criticism, 77; The cinema of intimacy: Peter Watkins' Portrait of the Artist as a Young Munch, 1977 Film Studies Ann, Part 1, 77; coauth, His Majesty the American: The Cinema of Douglas Fairbanks, Sr, A S Barnes, 77; Able Gance, Twayne, 78; auth, Peter Watkins: A Guide to References and Resources, G.K. Hall, 86; coauth, The Encyclopedia of Novels into Film, Facts on File, 98; The Cinema of Tony Richardson: Essays and Interviews, SUNY Press, 99; auth, Novels into Films, Checkmark Books, 99; auth, Video Versions: Film Adaptations of Plays on Video, Greenwood Press, 00. **CONTACT ADDRESS** Dept of English, Salisbury State Univ, 1101 Camden Ave, Salisbury, MD 21801-6800. **EMAIL** jxwelsh@ssu.edu

WELTMAN, SHARON
PERSONAL Born Stanford, CT, m **DISCIPLINE** VICTORIAN POETRY AND PROSE **EDUCATION** Rutgers Univ, PhD, 92. **CAREER** Assoc prof, La State Univ; ed asst, Raritan Rev, 87-89. **HONORS AND AWARDS** Catherine Cantalupo Prize, 87; Catherine Moynahan Prize, 87; Marion Johnson fel, 88-89; Folger Libr Jr fel, 88; LSU summer grant, 93, 94; WGS Summer Inst grant, 95; LSU Arts and Sci res grant, 96; Finalist for Kurt Weill Foundation Awd for Best Article on Musical Theater in 98. Choice Magazine Outstanding Academic Book 1999. **RESEARCH** John Ruskin and gender; mythology and Victorian prose. **SELECTED PUBLICATIONS** Auth, The Least of It: Metaphor, Metamorphosis, and Synecdoche in Frost's 'The Subverted Flower,' The SC Rev, 89; Gender and the Architectonics of Metaphor in Ruskin's The Ethics of the Dust, Prose Stud, 93; auth "Gender and the Architectonics of Metaphor: Ruskin's Pathetic Fallacy in Ethics of the Dust," Prose Studies, 16.2 (93): 41-61; auth, "Performing Goblin Market," Essays on Trangressive Readings: Reading Over the Lines, ed Georgia Johnston, Lewiston, Queenston, Lampeter: The Edwin Mellen Press, (97): 121-143; auth, "Female and Malestrom: The Gender Vortex in Carlyle and Ruskin," Carlyle Annual 17 (97): 91-99; auth, "Be No More Housewives, But Queens': Queen Victoria and Ruskin's Domestic Mythology," Re-making Queen Victoria, ed, Margaret Homans and Adrienne Munich, Cambridge Univ Press, (97): 105-122; auth, "Mythic Language and Gender Subversion: The Case of Ruskin's Athena," Nineteenth-Century Literature 52.3 (97): 350-71; auth, "Myth and Gender in Ruskin's Science, " Ruskin and the Dawn of Modernism, ed Dinah Birch, Oxford Univ Press, 99. **CONTACT ADDRESS** Dept of Eng, Louisiana State Univ and A&M Col, 212R Allen Hall, Baton Rouge, LA 70803. **EMAIL** enwelt@unix1.sncc.lsu.edu

WENDLAND, ERNST R.
PERSONAL Born 10/14/1944, Washington, IA, m, 1971, 4 children **DISCIPLINE** AFRICAN LANGUAGES AND LITERATURE **EDUCATION** NW Col, BA, 68; Univ Wisc, MA, 75, PhD, 79; MST, 00. **CAREER** Instr, Lutheran Sem (Lusaka, Zambia), 68-; Lang coordr publ, Lutheran Church Cent Africa, 71-; transl adv, 75-96, transl consult, united bible soc, 96-; Vis Prof, U of Stellenbosch, South Africa **MEMBERSHIPS** New Testament Soc S Africa; Old Testament Soc S Africa **RESEARCH** Discourse, stylistic, and rhetorical analysis of Biblical and Bantu language texts, especially poetry, prophecy, and preaching. **SELECTED PUBLICATIONS** Ed, Discourse Perspectives on Hebrew Poetry in the Scriptures, United Bible Soc, 94; auth, The Discourse Analysis of Hebrew Prophetic Literature, Mellen Bibl Press, 95; Buku Loyera: An Introduction to the New Chichewa Bible Translation, Kachere Books, 98; Analyzing the Psalms, Summer Inst Ling, 98; auth, Preaching That Grabs the Heart, Kachere Books, 00. **CONTACT ADDRESS** Dept of State, 2310 Lusaka Place, Washington, DC 20521-2310. **EMAIL** wendland@zamnet.zm

WENDLING, RONALD CHARLES
PERSONAL Born 03/31/1939, Buffalo, NY, m, 1966, 2 children **DISCIPLINE** ENGLISH LITERATURE **EDUCATION** Fordham Univ, BA, 62, MA, 65; Case Western Reserve Univ, PhD(English), 70. **CAREER** Instr English, Canisius Col, 63-65 & St Joseph's Col, Pa, 65-66; from instr to asst prof, Hamilton Col, 69-72; asst prof, 72-81, from assoc prof to prof English, St Joseph's Univ, PA, 81-95. **HONORS AND AWARDS** Fac Merit Awd for Teaching, 96. **MEMBERSHIPS** MLA; Wordsworth Coleridge Assoc; Friends of Coleridge; North Am Soc for the Study of Romanticism, NASSR. **RESEARCH** Nineteenth century English literature; romantic poetry; Coleridge. **SELECTED PUBLICATIONS** Auth, Coleridge and the consistency of The Eolian Harp, Studies Romanticism, Fall 68; Dramatic reconciliation in Coleridge's conversation poems, Papers Lang & Lit, Spring 73; Coleridge's Progress To Christianity: Experience and Authority in Regigious Faith, Bucknell Univeristy Press, 95, auth, "Pater, Coleridge, and the Return of the Platraic," The Wordsworth Circle, Spring 99. **CONTACT ADDRESS** Dept of English, Saint Joseph's Univ, 5600 City Ave, Philadelphia, PA 19131-1395. **EMAIL** rwendlin@sju.edu

WENDORFF, LAURA C.
PERSONAL 1 child **DISCIPLINE** AMERICAN CULTURE **EDUCATION** Univ Wis, BA, 81; Univ Mich, MA, 84, PhD, 92. **CAREER** Tchg asst, Univ Mich, 83-84; asst prof, Univ Wis, 94-00; to assoc prof, 00-. **SELECTED PUBLICATIONS** Auth, Demonic Males: Apes and the Origins of Human Violence (rev), 98; Eric Heiden, Pierian, 88. **CONTACT ADDRESS** Dept of Humanities, Univ of Wisconsin, Platteville, 1 University Plaza, Platteville, WI 53818-3099. **EMAIL** wendorff@uwplatt.edu

WENZEL, JOSEPH WILFRED
PERSONAL Born 11/30/1933, Elkhart, IN, m, 1959, 2 children **DISCIPLINE** SPEECH COMMUNICATION **EDUCATION** Univ Ill, BS, 57, PhD(speech), 63; Northwestern Univ, MA, 58. **CAREER** Lectr speech, Hunter Col, City Univ NY, 60-63; from Asst Prof to Assoc Prof, 63-93, PROF Emeritus SPEECH COMM, UNIV ILL, URBANA, 94-. **HONORS AND AWARDS** Am Forensic Asn Res Awd. **MEMBERSHIPS** Nat Commun Asn; Am Forensic Asn; Int Soc Hist Rhetoric; Int Soc Study of Argumentation. **RESEARCH** Argumentation; rhetorical theory. **CONTACT ADDRESS** Dept of Speech Commun, Univ of Illinois, Urbana-Champaign, 702 S Wright, #244, Urbana, IL 61801-3631. **EMAIL** jwengel@uiuc.edu

WENZEL, SIEGFRIED
PERSONAL Born 08/20/1928, Bernsdorf, Germany, m, 1958, 4 children **DISCIPLINE** ENGLISH, MEDIEVAL LITERATURE **EDUCATION** Univ Parana, BA, 52; Ohio Univ, MA, 56; Ohio State Univ, PhD, 60. **CAREER** Instr English, Ohio State Univ, 59-60; from instr to prof English & comp lit, Univ NC, Chapel Hill, 60-75; Prof English, Univ Pa, 75-97, prof emer, 97-. **HONORS AND AWARDS** Am Coun Learned Soc fel, 64-65; Guggenheim fel, 68-69; Nat Endowment for Humanities fel, 75-76. **MEMBERSHIPS** MLA; Early English Text Soc; Mediaeval Acad Am. **RESEARCH** Medieval literature; Middle English and Chaucer; medieval Latin sermons. **SELECTED PUBLICATIONS** Auth, The Sin of Sloth, Univ NCar, 67; auth, Verses in Sermons, Mediaeval Acad of Am, 78; ed, Summa Virtutum de Remediis Anime, Univ of Athens Press, 84; auth, Preachers, Poets, and the Early English Lyric, Princeton Univ Press, 86; ed and transl, Fasciculus Morum, a Fourteenth-Century Preacher's Handbook, Pa State Univ Press, 89; auth, Macaronic Sermons: Bilingualism and Preaching in Late Medieval England, Univ of Mich Press, 94. **CONTACT ADDRESS** Dept of English, Univ of Pennsylvania, Philadelphia, PA 19104. **EMAIL** swenzel@gibbs.oit.unc.edu

WERGE, THOMAS
DISCIPLINE LITERATURE **EDUCATION** Cornell Univ, PhD. **CAREER** Prof, Univ Notre Dame; coed, Relig and Lit. **HONORS AND AWARDS** Sheedy Awd for Excellence in Tchg. **RESEARCH** The opposition and tension between gnostic and sacramental visions of experience. **SELECTED PUBLICATIONS** Wrote on Thomas Shepard, essays on Dante, Melville and Twain, and introductions to the writings of several Puritan writers, including William Bradford, Thomas Hooker and Shepard. **CONTACT ADDRESS** Dept of English, Univ of Notre Dame, 356 O'Shaughnessy Hall, Notre Dame, IN 46556. **EMAIL** thomas.a.werge.1@nd.edu

WERSTINE, PAUL
PERSONAL Born 01/12/1948, Galt, ON, Canada, m, 2 children **DISCIPLINE** ENGLISH **EDUCATION** Univ W Ont, BA, 70; MA, 71; Univ SC, PhD, 76. **CAREER** Asst prof to prof, Kings Col, 76-. **HONORS AND AWARDS** Fel, Can Coun, 73-76; Fel, SSHRCC, 82-83; Fel, Folger Shakespeare Libr, 85, 90; Mellon Fel, Huntington Libr, 89. **MEMBERSHIPS** MLA; Shakespeare Asn of Am; Bibliographical Soc of the Univ Va; Bibliographical Soc of the Univ N Ill Malone Soc; Asn of Can Col and Univ Teachers of English. **RESEARCH** Early modern English drama, especially Shakespeare; Editing; Editorial and textual theory. **SELECTED PUBLICATIONS** Auth, "Narratives about Printed Shakespeare Texts: Foul Papers and Bad Quartos," Shakespeare Quart, (90): 65-86; co-ed, The New Folger Library Shakespeare, New York, 92; auth, "Shakespeare," in Scholarly Editing: A Guide to Research, (New York, 95), 253-282; auth, "Plays in manuscript," in A New History of Early English Drama, (Columbia Univ Press, 97), 481-497. **CONTACT ADDRESS** Dept Mod Lang, King's Col, 266 Epworth Ave, London, ON, Canada N6A 2M3. **EMAIL** werstine@uwo.ca

WERTHEIM, ALBERT
PERSONAL Born 07/03/1940, New York, NY, m, 1968, 2 children **DISCIPLINE** ENGLISH **EDUCATION** Columbia Univ, AB, 61; Yale Univ, MA, 63, PhD(English), 65. **CAREER** From instr English to asst prof, Princeton Univ, 65-69; vis asst prof, 69-70, asst prof, 70-71, dir, overseas study prog, Hamburg, Ger, 74-75, assoc prof, 71-79, Prof English, Ind Univ, Bloomington, 79-, Folger Shakespeare Libr fel, 66; mem selection comt, George Jean Nathan drama critic award, 66-68; vis prof, Univ Hamburg, 77; Deutscher Akademischer Austauschdienst fel, 77; The Newberry Libr fel, 78; grant-in-aid, Am Philos Soc, 77; asst to dir, Berkeley Repertory Theatre, 82-83; Eli Lilly Found fac open fel, 82-83. **HONORS AND AWARDS** Frederic J Lieber Distinguished Teaching Awd, 81; Outstanding Teacher Awd, Ind Univ Student Alumni Asn, 81. **MEMBERSHIPS** Am Soc Theatre Res; MLA; Renaissance Soc Am; Am Theatre Asn; Eugene O'Neill Soc (pres, 82-84). **RESEARCH** Seventeenth century drama; Shakespeare; Modern British and American drama. **SELECTED PUBLICATIONS** Auth, Courtship and games in James Shirley's Hyde Park, Anglia, 72; The presentation of sin in Friar Bacon and Friar Bungay, Criticism, 74; Things climb upward to what they were before: The reteaching and regreening of Macbeth, In: Teaching Shakespeare, Princeton Univ, 77; James Shirley, In: A Survey and Bibliography of Recent Studies in English Renaissance Drama, Univ Nebr, 78; The unrestrained and the unconventional: Etherege's The Man of Mode, Lit, 80; Trevor Griffiths: Playwriting and politics, In: Essays on Contemporary British Drama, 81 & Arthur Miller: After the fall and after, In: Essays on Contemporary American Drama, 81, Max Hueber; The McCarthy era and the American theatre, Theatre J, 82; auth, The Dramatic Art of Athol Fugard: From South Africa to the World, Ind Univ Press, 00. **CONTACT ADDRESS** Dept of English, Indiana Univ, Bloomington, 1020 E Kirkwood Ave, 442 Ballantine Hall, Bloomington, IN 47405. **EMAIL** wertheim@indiana.edu

WERTHEIM, STANLEY CLAUDE
PERSONAL Born 11/11/1930, Warburg, Germany, m, 1963 **DISCIPLINE** ENGLISH **EDUCATION** NYork Univ, BA, 53, MA, 54, PhD(English), 63. **CAREER** Instr English, NY Univ, 55-61; from instr to asst prof, Fairleigh Dickinson Univ, 62-70; assoc prof, 70-78, chmn dept, 70-72, PROF ENGLISH, WILLIAM PATERSON UNIV, 78-, Assoc ed, Lit & Psychol, 68-75. **RESEARCH** Modern & late 19th cent Am lit; Stephen Crane. **SELECTED PUBLICATIONS** Ed, Studies in Maggie and George's Mother, Merrill, 70; coauth, Hawthorne, Melville, Stephen Crane: A Critical Bibliography, Free Press, 71; co-ed, The Correspondence of Stephen Crane, Columbia Univ Press, 88; co-auth, The Crane Log: A Documentary Life of Stephen Crane, Macmillan, 94; auth, A Stephen Crane Encyclopedia, Greenwood Press, 97; numerous essays and reviews on 19th and 20th cent Am authors; ed, Stephen Crane: A Photograph and a Letter, Black Sun Bks, 73; Stephen Crane remembered, Studies Am Fiction, Vol 4: 45-64, 76; H G Wells to Cora Crane: Some Letters and Corrections, Resources for Am Lit Study, fall 79; Libraries as Conserving Institutions, Manuscripts, spring 80; The Arthur Conan Dyle Mystery, Am Bk Collector, 1: 38-42. **CONTACT ADDRESS** Dept of Eng, William Paterson Col of New Jersey, 300 Pompton Rd, Wayne, NJ 07470-2152. **EMAIL** warburg@earthlink.net

WESLING, DONALD TRUMAN
PERSONAL Born 05/06/1939, Buffalo, NY, m, 1961, 3 children **DISCIPLINE** ENGLISH LITERATURE **EDUCATION** Harvard Univ, AB, 60, PhD, 65; Cambridge Univ, AB, 62, MA, 68. **CAREER** Tchng asst, 62-65, Harvard Univ; asst prof, 65-67, Univ Calif, San Diego; lectr, 67-70, Univ Essex; assoc prof, 70-80, prof, 80-, Univ Calif, San Diego; NEH younger humanist fel, 73-74. **HONORS AND AWARDS** Otto Salgo Prof, Budapest, 97-98 **MEMBERSHIPS** MLA; Amnesty Intl. **RESEARCH** Wordsworth & English Romanticism; modern English and American poetry; English prosody; Bakhtin studies. **SELECTED PUBLICATIONS** Auth, Wordsworth and the Adequacy of Landscape, Routledge, 70; auth, The Chances of Rhyme: Device and Modernity, Univ Calif Press, 80; auth, John Muir: To Yosemite and Beyond, Univ Wis Press, 80; auth, American Sentences: The History of West Seneca, New York, Black Mesa Press, 81; coauth, Literary Voice: The Calling of Jonah, SUNY Press, 95; auth, The Scissors of Meter, Univ Mich Press, 96. **CONTACT ADDRESS** Dept of Literature, Univ of California, San Diego, 9500 Gilman Dr, La Jolla, CA 92093. **EMAIL** dwesling@ucsd.edu

WESS, ROBERT
DISCIPLINE 18TH CENTURY BRITISH LITERATURE, THEORY **EDUCATION** Univ Chicago, BA, 63, MA, 66; PhD, 70. **CAREER** Engl, Oregon St Univ. **RESEARCH** Rhetoric. **SELECTED PUBLICATIONS** Auth, "The Probable and the Marvelous in Tom Jones," Modern Philology 68, (70): 32-45; auth, "Notes toward a Marxist Rhetoric," Buckness Rev 28, (83); 32-45; auth, Utopian Rhetoric in The Man of Mode, The Eighteenth Century: Theory and Interpretation, 86; Narrative as a Socially Symbolic Act: The Example of Clarissa, Papers in Comparative Studies 5, 87; 1670's Comedy and the Problem of Periodization, Restoration: Studies in English Literary Culture, 87; Kenneth Burke's 'Dialectic of Constitutions, 91; The Question of Truth Rhetorically Considered, 91; Kenneth Burke: Rhetoric, Subjectivity, Postmodernism, Cambridge UP, 96; ed, "Pentadic Terms and Master Tropes: Ontology of the Act and Epistemology of the Trope in A Grammer of Motives," Unending Conversations: Kenneth Burke, eds., Greig Henderson and David Cratis Williams, Southern Illinois UP, (01): 154-75. **CONTACT ADDRESS** Oregon State Univ, Corvallis, OR 97331-4501. **EMAIL** rwess@orst.edu

WEST, GRACE STARRY
PERSONAL Born 10/05/1946, Oklahoma City, OK, m, 1974, 4 children **DISCIPLINE** CLASSICS **EDUCATION** Scripps Col, BA, 68; Univ Calif, Los Angeles, CPhil, 72, PhD, 75. **CAREER** Univ of Dallas, 75- . **HONORS AND AWARDS** Fulbright full grant, 72-74, Univ Heidelberg. **MEMBERSHIPS** APA; Vergilian Soc; CAMWS; TCA; ACL; Nat Asn of Scholars. **RESEARCH** Greek and Roman literature and its survival to present times; teaching of Latin; myth; women in antiquity. **SELECTED PUBLICATIONS** Commentary, Cornelius Nepos, Dion, Bryn Mawr Commentaries, 85; commentary, Cicero, Pro Archia, Bryn Mawr Commentaries, 87; coauth, Four Texts on Socrates, rev ed, Cornell, 98. **CONTACT ADDRESS** Dept of Classics, Univ of Dallas, 1845 E Northgate Dr, Irving, TX 75062. **EMAIL** gwest@acad.udallas.edu

WEST, JAMES L. W., III
PERSONAL Born 11/15/1946, Roanoke, VA, d, 4 children **DISCIPLINE** ENGLISH **EDUCATION** Univ of SC, BA, 68, PhD, 71. **CAREER** Instr to prof, Virginia Tech, 71-86; prof, Penn State Univ, 86-. **HONORS AND AWARDS** Nat Hum. Ctr., 81-82; Guggenheim fel, 85-86; NEH fels, 94-95, 98-99; Fulbright Grants, 85-86, 89-90; distinguished prof eng, 92-00; fel inst arts & humanistic studies; edwin earle sparks prof of english, 00-. **MEMBERSHIPS** Soc for the Hist of Authorship, Reading and Publishing, Int Dreiser Soc; Bibliog Soc Am. **RESEARCH** Am literature; Lit biography; Scholarly editing; Hist of the book. **SELECTED PUBLICATIONS** Auth, The Making of This Side of Paradise, 83; American Authors and the Literary Marketplace since 1900, 88; William Styron, A Life, 98; ed, Theodore Dreiser, Jennie Gerhardt, Univ of Penn Press, 92; F. Scott Fitzgerald, This Side of Paradise, Trimalchio 00, Cambridge Univ Press, 95. **CONTACT ADDRESS** Dept of English, Pennsylvania State Univ, Univ Park, University Park, PA 16802. **EMAIL** jlw14@psu.edu

WEST, JOHN OLIVER
PERSONAL Born 01/01/1925, El Paso, TX, m, 1970, 1 child **DISCIPLINE** ENGLISH **EDUCATION** Miss Col, BA, 48; Tex Tech Col, MA, 51; Univ Tex, PhD(Am lit & folklore), 64. **CAREER** Teacher English & jour, Cent High Sch, Jackson, Miss, 48-50; hist & jour, Gardiner High Sch, Laurel, 51-52; asst prof English & jour & publicity dir, Miss Col, 52-53, assoc prof, 53-54; asst prof English, W Tex State Col, 56-57; instr English, Odessa Col, 57-59 & 60-63, dir pub relat, 59-60; assoc prof English & folklore, 63-65, head dept, 65-71, prof English, Univ Tex, El Paso, 65-. **MEMBERSHIPS** Am Folklore Soc. **RESEARCH** American folklore; southwestern United States history and literature. **SELECTED PUBLICATIONS** Auth, The Historian, the Folklorist, and Juan Diego, Southwest Folklore, winter 80; Cowboy Folk Humor, August House, 90; Cowboys Do the Damnedest Things, The Catch Pen, The Ranching Heritage Center, 91; Grutas in the Spanish Southwest, Hecho in Tex: Tex-Mex Folk Arts and Crafts, Tex Folklore Soc Pub, 91; Jose cisneros: An Artist's Journey, Tex Western Press, 93; Ned Buntline, Nineteenth Cent Western Am Writers: Dictionary of Lit Biog, Vol. 186; Gale Research, 97; ed, The American Folklore Newsletter, 70-78. **CONTACT ADDRESS** Dept of English, Univ of Texas, El Paso, 500 W University Ave, El Paso, TX 79968-0001. **EMAIL** jwest@utep.edu

WEST, MARK I.
PERSONAL Born 05/27/1955, Denver, CO, m, 1987, 1 child **DISCIPLINE** ENGLISH **EDUCATION** Franconia Col, BA, 75; Univ Wisc, Green Bay, MA, 80; Bowling Green State Univ, PhD, 83. **CAREER** Archivist, Menninger Foundation, 83-84; Univ of North Carolina at Charlotte, 84-; Full Prof, 96. **MEMBERSHIPS** Children's Literature Assoc. **RESEARCH** Children's Literature; Censorship. **SELECTED PUBLICATIONS** Auth, "Children, Culture & Controversy, 88; auth, 'Roald Dahl," 92; auth, "Wellsprings of Imagination: The Humes of Children's Authors, 92; auth, "Everyone's Guide to Children's Literature, 97; auth, "Trust Your Children: Voices Against Censorship in Children's Literature, 97; auth, "Psychoanalytic Responses to Children's Literature," 99. **CONTACT ADDRESS** Dept English, Univ of No Carolina, Charlotte, 9201 Univ City Boulevard, Charlotte, NC 28223-0001. **EMAIL** miwest@email.uncc.edu

WEST, MICHAEL DAVIDSON
PERSONAL Born 04/13/1937, Morristown, NJ, m, 1961, 1 child **DISCIPLINE** ENGLISH **EDUCATION** Harvard Univ, AB, 59, AM, 61, PhD, 65. **CAREER** Teaching fel English & humanities, Harvard Univ, 61-64; from instr English to asst prof, Wesleyan Univ, 64-72, res assoc 72-73; assoc prof English, 73-76, prof English, Univ of Pittsburgh, 76-. **HONORS AND AWARDS** First Prize, Cornell Classical Transl Contest, 71; cert excellence in teaching, Asn Depts English & MLA, 72; Sr fel, Wesleyan Ctr Humanities, 70; fel, Am Coun Learned Soc, 78-79; Fel, Newberry Libr, 85-86; NEH Fel, Huntington Libr, 85-86; Kate B. & Hall James Peterson Fel, Am Antiq Soc, 85; Hughes Awd & Thomas Awd (second), World Order of Narrative Poets, 86; DeGolyer Prize Essay, DeGolyer Inst for Am Studies, Southern Methodist Univ, 87; Hon Fel, Inst for Advanced Studies in the Humanities, Univ Edinburgh, 87; Northeast Mod Lang Asn/Ohio Univ Press Book Awd, 99; Fulbright Lecturer, Univ of Copenhagen, 00; NEMLA Special Anniv Awd, 00. **MEMBERSHIPS** MLA; Northeast Mod Lang Asn; Renaissance Soc Am. **RESEARCH** Renaissance English literature, especially Spenser, Shakespeare, and Dryden; comparative literature, especially influence of the classics on European heroic conventions; American literature, especially Thoreau and 19th century theories of language. **SELECTED PUBLICATIONS** Auth, Dryden's ambivalence as a translator of heroic themes, Huntington Libr Quart, 73; Scatology and eschatology: The heroic dimensions of Thoreau's wordplay, PMLA, 74; The internal dialogue of Shakespeare's Sonnet 146, Shakespeare Quart, 74; Prothalamia in Propertius and Spenser, Comp Lit, 74; The genesis and significance of Joyce's irony in A Painful Case, ELH, 77; Evaluating periodicals in English studies, Col English, 80; Reflection on Star Wars and Scholarly Reviewing, Lit Rev, 87; Spenser's Art of War: Chivalric Allegory, Military Technology, and the Elizabethan Mock-Heroic Sensibility, Ren Quart, 88; auth, Transcendental Wordplay: America's Romantic Punsters and the Search for the Language of Nature, Ohio Univ Press, 00. **CONTACT ADDRESS** Dept of English, Univ of Pittsburgh, 526 Cathedral/Learn, Pittsburgh, PA 15260-2504. **EMAIL** mikewest@pitt.edu

WEST, WILLIAM C., III
DISCIPLINE CLASSICS **EDUCATION** Univ NC, Chapel Hill, PhD. **CAREER** Prof, Univ NC, Chapel Hill. **RESEARCH** Greek prose; Greek historians. **SELECTED PUBLICATIONS** Auth, "Socrates as a Model of Civil Disobediece in the Writings of Martin Luther King, Jr." Classical Bulletin 76, 191; auth, The Public Archives in Fourth Century Athens, Greek, Roman, and Byzantine Stud 30, 89; M. Ulpius Domesticus and the Athletic Synod at Ephesus, Ancient Hist Bull 4.4, 90; The Decrees in Demosthenes' Against Leptines, Zeitschrift fur Papyrologie und Epigraphik 107, 95; New Light on an Opisthographic Lead Tablet in Chapel Hill, XI Int Cong of Greek and Latin Epigraphy, Ed Quasar, 99 **CONTACT ADDRESS** Univ of No Carolina, Chapel Hill, Chapel Hill, NC 27599. **EMAIL** wwest@email.unc.edu

WESTBROOK, ELLEN E.
DISCIPLINE ENGLISH **EDUCATION** Simmons, BA, 77; Univ Mich, MA, 79, PhD, 87. **CAREER** Asst prof English, Southern Miss Univ. **RESEARCH** Euro-Amer-Indian literature. **CONTACT ADDRESS** HC74, Box 622, Stafford, NH 03844-9269.

WESTERMEYER, PAUL
PERSONAL Born 03/28/1940, Cincinnati, OH, m, 1963, 4 children **DISCIPLINE** CHURCH MUSIC **EDUCATION** Univ Elmhurst, BA, 62; Lancaster Theol Sem, 65; Sch Sacred Mus, Union Theol Sem, SMM, 66; Univ Chicago, MA, 74, PhD, 78; additional study, Sch Cantorum; Concordia Theol Sem, 66; liturgical stud prog, Notre Dame, 69; Lutheran Gen Hospital, 83. **CAREER** Cantor, Ascension Lutheran Church, 82-90; ast pastor, Ascension Lutheran Church, 86-90; Vis prof, Yale Univ Inst Sacred Mus, 89-90; prof, dept ch, choir dir, organist, Elmhurst Col, 68-90; prof, 90-. **HONORS AND AWARDS** Pres, Hymn Society in the US & Canada, 98-00; National Chairman, Amer Guild of Organists, 91-98; Sears--Roebuck Awd Elmhurst College, for Teaching Excellence & Campus leadership, 90; Schaff Prize in church History, Lancaster Seminary, 65. **MEMBERSHIPS** Mem, Amer Choral Dir(s) Assn; Amer Guild of Organists; Amer Soc of Church Hist; Evangel and Reformed Hist Soc; Hymn Soc Am; Intl Arbeitsgemeinschaft fur Hymnologie; Liturgical Conf; Mercersburg Soc; N Amer Acad of Liturgy. **RESEARCH** Theology Music; Hymnody; Liturgy; 19th Century. **SELECTED PUBLICATIONS** Auth, With Tongues of Fire, 95; The Church Musician, 88. **CONTACT ADDRESS** Dept of Music, Luther Sem, 2481 Como Ave, Saint Paul, MN 55108. **EMAIL** pwesterm@luthersem.edu

WESTFAHL, GARY
PERSONAL Born 05/07/1951, Washington, DC, m, 1983, 2 children **DISCIPLINE** ENGLISH LITERATURE **EDUCATION** Carleton Col, BA, 73; Claremont Grad Univ, MA, 75, PhD, 86. **CAREER** Lectr, English Dept, Calif State Polytechnic Univ, Pomona, 80-85; lectr, English Dept, UC Riverside, 81-87; instr, English, Claremont Grad, 86-87; adj prof, Educ Progs in Corrections, Univ of LaVerne, 86- ; reading spec, Learning Ctr, UC Riverside, 87- . **HONORS AND AWARDS** Nominee, Pioneer Awd for best critical essay on science fiction, 95, 97. **MEMBERSHIPS** Sci Fic Res Asn; Science Fiction and Fantasy Writers of America. **RESEARCH** Science fiction; fantasy. **SELECTED PUBLICATIONS** Auth, Cosmic Engineers: A Study of Hard Science Fiction, Greenwood, 96; co-ed, Foods of the Gods: Eating and the Eaten in Fantasy and Science Fiction, Univ Georgia, 96; coed, Immortal Engines: Life Extension and Immortality in Science Fiction and Fantasy, Univ Georgia, 96; auth, Islands in the Sky: The Space Station Theme in Science Fiction Literature, Borgo, 96; co-ed, Science Fiction and Market Realities, Univ Georgia, 96; consult ed, Encyclopedia of Fantasy, St Martin's, 97; auth, Mechanics of Wonder: The Creation of the Idea of Science Fiction, Liverpool Univ Pr, 98; coed, Nursery Realms: Children in the Worlds of Science Fiction, Fantasy, and Horror, Univ Georgia Pr, 99; auth, Science Fiction, Children's Literature, and Popular Culture: Coming of Age in Fantasyland, Greenwood, 00; ed, Space and Beyond: The Frontier Theme in Science Fiction, Greenwood, 00; coed, Unearthly Visions: Approaches to Science Fiction and Fantasy Art, Greenwood, forthcoming; coed, No Cure for the Future: Diease and Medicine in Science Fiction and Fantasy, Greenwood, forthcoming, coed, Worlds Enough and Time: Explorations of Time in Science Fiction and Fantasy, Greenwood. Forthcoming, coed, Science Fiction, Canonization, Marginalization, and the Academy, Greenwood, forthcoming. **CONTACT ADDRESS** The Learning Ctr 052, Univ of California, Riverside, Riverside, CA 92521. **EMAIL** westfahl@pop.ucr.edu

WESTLING, LOUISE HUTCHINGS
PERSONAL Born 02/02/1942, Jacksonville, FL, m, 1975 **DISCIPLINE** ENGLISH, AMERICAN LITERATURE **EDUCATION** Randolph-Macon Woman's Col, BA, 64; Univ of Iowa, MA, 65; Univ of Ore, PhD, 74. **CAREER** Instr, Centre Col of Ky, 65-67; instr, Ore State Unive, 74-77; visiting asst prof, Honors Col, Univ of Ore, 78-81; INSTR, 81-84, ASST PROF, 85-88, ASSOC PROF, 88-94, PROF OF ENGLISH, 94-, DEPT HEAD, 94-97, UNIV OF ORE. **HONORS AND AWARDS** Clark Libr Fel, UCLA, 75; NEH Summer Inst, Univ of Tx at Austin, 90, Univ of Ore, 91; Fulbright Sr Lectureship, Univ of Heidelberg, Germany, 96. **MEMBERSHIPS** MLA; ALA; Asn for Study of Lit and Enviro.; PEN. **RESEARCH** 20th Century American Literature; Ecocriticism. **SELECTED PUBLICATIONS** Chair, Board of Eds, World Introduction to Literature, Prentic-Hall Pubs, 99; ed, Witness to Injustice, Univ Press of Miss, 95; ed, He Included Me: The Autobiography of Sarah Webb Rice, Univ of Ga Press, 89; auth, The Green Breast of the New World: Landscape, Gender, and American Fiction, Univ of Ga Press, 96; auth, Sacred Groves and Ravaged Gardens: The Fiction of Eudora Welty, Carson McCullers, and Flannery O'Connor, Univ of Ga Press, 85; auth, The Evolution of Michael Drayton's Idea, Institut fur Englische Sprache und Literatur, 74. **CONTACT ADDRESS** Dept of English, Univ of Oregon, Eugene, OR 97403. **EMAIL** lhwest@oregon.uoregon.edu

WESTON, RUTH DEASON
PERSONAL Born 07/26/1934, Hearne, TX, m **DISCIPLINE** ENGLISH **EDUCATION** Univ Houston, BA, 68; Univ Tulsa, MA, 75; BA, 79; PhD, 88. **CAREER** Instr, Tulsa Community Col, 74-88; vis lectr, Univ Tulsa, 98; prof, Oral Roberts Univ, 89-98; vis prof, US Mil Acad West Point, 93-94; vis assoc prof to adj prof, Univ Tulsa, 99. **HONORS AND AWARDS** Phoenix Awd Outstanding Achievement, 99; Oral Roberts Univ Outstanding Scholar, 90-91, 97-98; USMA Outstanding Civil Servant Awd, 93-94; Hon Soc, Phi Kappa Phi; Phi Delta Phi. **MEMBERSHIPS** MLA; SCMLA; SAMLA; SCCEA; CEA; SSSL; SSSS; ALA; Eudora Welty Soc. **RESEARCH** Southern American literature. **SELECTED PUBLICATIONS** Auth, Gothic Tradition and Narrative Techniques in the Fiction of Eudora Welty, LSU Pr, 94; auth, Barry Hannah, Postmodern Romantic, LSU Pr, 98. **CONTACT ADDRESS** 5374 E 26th Pl, Tulsa, OK 74114-4904. **EMAIL** rdweston@home.com

WESTREM, SCOTT D.
PERSONAL Born 12/26/1963, Minneapolis, MN, s **DISCIPLINE** ENGLISH **EDUCATION** Wheaton Col, BA, 75; Northwestern Univ, MA, 77; PhD, 85. **CAREER** Asst Prof to Assoc Prof, CUNY, 86-; Adj Assoc Prof, NYork Univ, 95-; Vis Prof, Univ Paris, 00. **HONORS AND AWARDS** Teacher of the Year, Lehman Col, 98; James Merrill Scholar-in-Residence, Conn, 96-97; Summer Study Awd, DAAD, 96; Res Awd, PSC/CUNY, 95-96; George and Eliza Gardner Howard Foundation Fel, 92-93; NEH Gel, Stanford Univ, 88 **SELECTED PUBLICATIONS** Auth, Broader Horizons: Johannes Witte de Hese's Itinerarius and Medieval Travel Narratives, in press; auth, Travel, Trade and Exploration in the Middle Ages: An Encyclopedia, Garland Pub, in press; auth, "Geography and Travel," in Companion to Chaucer, Blackwell Pub, in press; auth, "Dutch Discovery of the East Indies in the Fifteenth Century," in Publications of the American Association for Netherlands Studies, in press; auth, The Works of John Chalkhill, Princeton Univ Press, 99; auth, Learning from Legends on the Bell Library, Mappamundi, The James Ford Bell Lectures, 99; auth, "Against Gog and Magog," in Text and Territory: Geographical Imagination and the European Middle Ages, Univ Penn, 98; auth, The Imago mundi of Honorius Augustodunensis: Latin Text and English Translation, Commentary and Manuscript Census, Univ Minn Press; forthcoming; auth, William of Boldensele's Liber de quibusdam ultrmarinis partibus: A Critical Edition, English Translation and Commentary, forthcoming. **CONTACT ADDRESS** Dept English, Lehman Col, CUNY, 250 Bedford Park Blvd W, Bronx, NY 10468-1527. **EMAIL** sdwestrem@aol.com

WESTWATER, MARTHA E.
PERSONAL Born Boston, MA **DISCIPLINE** ENGLISH LITERATURE **EDUCATION** St John's Univ, BS, 57; MA, 62; Dalhousie Univ, PhD, 74. **CAREER** Prof, chair, Board of Governors, Senate, Mt St Vincent Univ, 72-98. **HONORS AND AWARDS** Soc Sci and Humanities Res Counc Awd, 74-77, 79-80, 81-89, 90-91; Teaching Awd of Excellence, Mt St Vincent Univ, 92; Hon Doctor of Humane Letters, Mt St Vincent Univ, 96. **MEMBERSHIPS** MLA, Children's Lit Assoc. **RESEARCH** Victorian Literature, Children's Literature. **SELECTED PUBLICATIONS** Auth, The Wilson Sisters: A Biographical Study of Upper Middle-Class Victorian Life, Ohio Univ Pr, (Athens, London), 84; auth, The Spasmodic Career of Sydney Dobell, Univ Pr of Am, (Lanham, London), 92; auth, Giant Despair Meets Hopeful: Kristevan Readings in Adolescent Literature, Univ of Albta Pr, (Edmonton), 00. **CONTACT ADDRESS** 50 Elm St, Wollaston, MA 02170-2913. **EMAIL** westwtrm@aol.com

WETHERBEE PHELPS, LOUISE
PERSONAL Born 08/05/1940, Greenville, MS, m, 1962, 3 children **DISCIPLINE** ENGLISH **EDUCATION** Vassar Col, BA, 62; Johns Hopkins Univ, MAT, 63; Cleveland State Univ, MA, 76; Case Western Reserve Univ, PhD, 80. **CAREER** Asst Prof, Univ Southern Calif, 79-86; Prof, Syracuse Univ, 86-. **HONORS AND AWARDS** Fel, Am Coun on Educ, 93-94. **MEMBERSHIPS** Conf on Col Composition & Comm, Nat Coun of Teachers of English, Mod Lang Asn, Writing Program Administrators, Am Asn of Higher Educ, Coalition of Women's Scholars in the Hist of Rhetoric and Composition. **RESEARCH** Composition theory and pedagogy, Rhetoric and hermeneutics, Writing program administration, Graduate pedagogy, Higher education reform. **SELECTED PUBLICATIONS** Auth, Composition as a Human Science: contributions to the Self-Understanding of a Discipline, Oxford, 88; auth, Feminine Principles and women's Experience in American composition and Rhetoric, Univ Pittsburgh, 95; auth, "Paths Not Taken: recovering History as alternate Future," History, Reflection, and Narrative: The Professionalization of composition, 1963-1983, Ablex, 99; auth, "Telling the Writing Program Its Own Story: A Tenth-Anniversary Speech," The Writing Program Administrator as Researcher: Inquiry in action and Reflection, Cook Heinemann, 99; auth, "Surprised by Response: Student, Teacher, Editor, Reviewer," Journal of advanced composition, 98; auth, "Becoming a Warrior: Lessons of the Feminist Workplace," Feminine Principles and Women's Experience in American composition and Rhetoric, Univ Pittsburgh, 95. **CONTACT ADDRESS** Writing Prog, Syracuse Univ, 239 H.B. Crouse, Syracuse, NY 13244-1160. **EMAIL** lwphelps@syr.edu

WEXLER, JOYCE
PERSONAL Born 02/26/1947, Chicago, IL, m, 1969, 2 children **DISCIPLINE** ENGLISH **EDUCATION** Univ Michigan, BA 68; Northwestern Univ, PhD 74. **CAREER** Loyola Univ, asst prof, assoc prof, assoc dean, prof, 80 to 98-, dir hon prog 86-; Barat College, lect 78-80. **HONORS AND AWARDS** Phi Beta Kappa; NDEA schshp; Woodrow Wilson Fel; Woodrow Wilson Diss Fel; IL Art Coun Essay Awd. **MEMBERSHIPS** MLA **RESEARCH** Modernism; cultural studies; psychoanalytic criticism; feminist criticism. **SELECTED PUBLICATIONS** Auth, Who Paid for Modernism? Art Money and the Fiction of Conrad, Joyce and Lawrence, Fayett, Univ Ark Press, 97; D. H. Lawrence Through a Postmodernist Lens, D. H. Law Rev, 97,98; Speaking Out: Dialogue and Over-determined Meaning, Style, 97; The Uncommon Language of Modernist Women Writers, Women's Studies, 96; Selling Sex as Art, in: Marketing Modernisms: Self Promotion, Canonization, Rereading, eds, J. H. Kevin, Dettmar and Steven Watt, Ann Arbor, Univ Mich Press, 96; Finnegans Wake: Breakthrough or Breakdown, Studies in Psychoanalytic Theory, 94; Requiem for Biography: The Case of Joseph Conrad, Conradiana, 94; Realism

and Modernists, Bad Reputation, Studies in the Novel 31, (99), 60-73. **CONTACT ADDRESS** English Dept, Loyola Univ, Chicago, 6525 N Sheridan Rd, Chicago, IL 60626. **EMAIL** jwexler@luc.edu

WEXMAN, VIRGINIA WRIGHT
PERSONAL Born 04/02/1941, Winnipeg, MB, Canada, m, 1960, 2 children **DISCIPLINE** ENGLISH, FILM **EDUCATION** Univ Chicago, BA, 70, MA, 71, PhD(English), 76. **CAREER** Lectr, 73-77, Asst Prof English, Univ Ill, Chicago Circle, 77-. **MEMBERSHIPS** MLA; Soc Cinema Studies. **RESEARCH** American film; American popular culture; the American novel. **SELECTED PUBLICATIONS** Auth, The role of structure in Tom Sawyer and Huckleberry Finn, Am Literary Realism: 2870-1910, spring 73; The Maltese Falcon from fiction to film, Libr Quart, 1/75; Macbeth and Polanski's theme of regression, Univ Dayton Rev, fall 78; coauth, A Reference Guide to Roman Polanski, 78 & A Reference Guide to Robert Altman, 79, Hall; auth, Roman Polanski: A Critical Guide, Twayne, 79; Stardom - Industry Of Desire - Gledhill,C, Film Quarterly, Vol 0046, 1992; Film As Art And Filmmakers As Artists - A Century Of Progress, Arachne, Vol 0002, 1995; auth, "The Family on the Land: Race and Nationhood in Silent Westerns," In The Birth of Whitenes Construction of Race in Silent Cinema, ed. Daniel Bernardi, (New Brunswick, NJ: Rutgers Univ Press, 96): 129-69; auth, "Portrait of a Body," Henry James Rev 18.2, (97): 184-86. **CONTACT ADDRESS** Dept of Eng, Univ of Illinois, Chicago, 2009/2714 Univ Hall, 601 S Morgan St, Chicago, IL 60607. **EMAIL** vwexman@uic.edu

WEYLER, KAREN A.
DISCIPLINE ENGLISH **EDUCATION** Center, BA, 88; Univ NC, MA, 90, PhD, 96. **CAREER** Vis asst prof English, Wake Forest. **RESEARCH** Early American fiction. **SELECTED PUBLICATIONS** Fel Publ, 'A Speculating Spirit': Trade, Speculation, and Gambling in Early American Fiction, Early Amer Lit 31.3, 96; auth, Melville's 'The Paradise of Bachelors and the Tartarus of Maids': A Dialogue About Experience, Understanding, and Truth, Studies in Short Fiction 31.3, 94); 'The Fruit of Unlawful Embraces': Sexual Transgression and Madness in Early American Sentimental Fiction, In: Sex and Sexuality in Early America, NYU, 97; Creating a Community of Readers: Mary Mebane's Exploitation of Difference in Mary and Mary, Wayfarer, South Quart vol 35.3, 97. **CONTACT ADDRESS** Dept of English, Box 7387, Wake Forest Univ, Reynolda Station, Winston-Salem, NC 27109-7387. **EMAIL** weylerKA@wfu.edu.

WHALEN, DAVID
PERSONAL Born 05/08/1960, m, 8 children **DISCIPLINE** ENGLISH **EDUCATION** Univ Kansas, BA, 82; MA, 84; PhD, 92. **CAREER** Asst prof, Abbey Col, Belmont, 92-94; asst prof, Hillside Col, 94-98; assoc prof, 98-. **HONORS AND AWARDS** Dougherty Teach Awd, 97; Bainter Prize, 95; Weaver Fel, 90; Salvatore Fel, 91. **MEMBERSHIPS** Phi Beta Kappa; NAS; ALSC; SCSA. **RESEARCH** Renaissance literature; Victorian non-fiction prose; John Henry Newman; educational philosophy. **SELECTED PUBLICATIONS** Auth, The Consolation of Rhetoric: John Henry Newman and the Realism of Personalist Thought, Catholic Schl Press, 94. **CONTACT ADDRESS** Dept English, Hillsdale Col, 33 East College St, Hillsdale, MI 49242-1205. **EMAIL** david.whalen@hillsdale.edu

WHARTON, LAWRENCE
PERSONAL Born 12/22/1946, Wichita Falls, m, 3 children **DISCIPLINE** FICTION WRITING **EDUCATION** Univ of UT, PhD, 75. **CAREER** Univ Ala **HONORS AND AWARDS** Senior Fulbright Lecture, Universidade Nova, Lisbon, Portugal, 1986-87. **SELECTED PUBLICATIONS** Auth, There Could Be No More to It, Tex A&M, 83; "Hard Work," Short Story, Fall 1999; "Slow Elk," Laurel Review, Vol. 14.2, 1980; "Have You Seen the Quarter Moon," 1976; "Rain City," Cutbank 3, 1970; "The Mercury of It All," Carolina Quarterly XXVI.3, 1979. **CONTACT ADDRESS** Univ of Alabama, Birmingham, 1400 University Blvd, Birmingham, AL 35294-1150. **EMAIL** lwharton@uah.edu

WHATLEY, ERIC GORDON
PERSONAL Born 07/16/1944, Blackburn, England, m, 1980, 2 children **DISCIPLINE** ENGLISH LITERATURE, LANGUAGE **EDUCATION** Oxford Univ, BA, 66; Harvard Univ, PhD(English), 73. **CAREER** Asst prof English, Lake Forest Col, 72-78, asst dean fac, 76-79; asst prof English, 80-84, assoc prof, 85-92, prof, Queens Col, NY, 93-; CUNY Grad Center, 89-. **HONORS AND AWARDS** Dir & fac fel, Newberry Libr Humanities Prog, Assoc Cols Midwest, 75-76; Nat Endowment for Humanities independent study fel, 79-80; Am Phil S oc grants, 75, 83; Nat Endowment for Humanities Res Tools grant (dir Paul Szarmach), 90-92; PSC-CUNY Res awards, 82-83, 85-87, 93, 97-98. **MEMBERSHIPS** Mediaeval Acad Am; Int Soc Anglo-Saxonists; Hagiography Soc N Am; Friends of the Saints. **RESEARCH** Old and Middle English hagiography; Medieval Latin hagiography. **SELECTED PUBLICATIONS** Auth, Cynewulf and Troy: A note on Cynewulf's Elene, Notes & Queries, 73; Bread and stone: Cynewulf's Elene 611-618, Neuphilol Mitteilungen, 75; Old English monastics and narrative art: Elene 1062, Mod Philol, 75; The Figure of Constantine the Great in Cynewulf's Elene, Traditio 37; The Middle English St Erkenwald in its liturgical context, Mediaevalia, 82; Opus dei, opus mundi: Patterns of Conflict in a Twelfth-century Miracle Collection, in Michael Sargent, ed, De cello in seculum, 89; The Saint of London: the Life and Miracles of St Erkenwald, 89; Acta Sanctorum, in Sources of Anglo-Saxon Literary Culture: A Trial Version, ed F Biggs et al, 90; Hagiography in Anglo-Saxon England: A Preliminary View from SASLC, Old English Newsletter, 90; with Jo Ann McNamara & John E Halborg, Sainted Women of the Dark Ages, 92; An Early Literary Quotation from the Inventio S. Crucis: a Note on Baudonivia's Vita S. Radegundis (BHL 7049), Analecta Bollandiana, 93; Late Old English Hagiography, ca 950-1150, in Hagiographies, ed Guy Philippart, 96; A Introduction to the Study of Old English Prose Hagiography: Sources and Resources, in Holy Men and Holy Women: Old English Prose Saints' Lives and Their Contexts, ed Paul E Szarmach, 96; Lost in Translation: Some Episodes in Old English Prose Saints' Lives, Anglo-Saxon England, 97. **CONTACT ADDRESS** Dept of English, Queens Col, CUNY, 6530 Kissena Blvd, Flushing, NY 11367-1597. **EMAIL** gwhatley@qc.edu

WHEATLEY, CHRISTOPHER J.
PERSONAL Born 10/19/1955, Buffalo, NY, s **DISCIPLINE** ENGLISH **EDUCATION** Univ Wash, BA, 78; Univ Wis, MA, 80; PhD, 87. **CAREER** Lect, Univ Wash, 86-88; Instr, Univ Tenn, 88-89; Prof, Cath Univ of Am, 89-. **HONORS AND AWARDS** Brit Coun Res Grant, 86; Fulbright Fel, 93-94. **MEMBERSHIPS** ASECS, Eighteenth-Century Ireland Soc. **RESEARCH** Drama. **SELECTED PUBLICATIONS** Auth, "'I hear the Irish are Naturally Brave': Dramatic Portrayals of the Irish Soldier in the Seventeenth and Eighteenth Centuries," The Irish Sword: J of the Military Hist Soc of Ireland, 19, vol 19, no 77 (95); auth, "Thornton Wilder, The Real and Theatrical Realism," Realism and the Am Dramatic Tradition, Univ Ala Pr (96): 139-155; auth, "'But Speak Everything in its Nature': Influence and Ethics in Durfey's Adaptations of Fletcher," J of English and Germanic Philol, 96 (96): 522-540; auth, Without God or Reason: The Plays of Thomas Shadwell and Secular Ethics in the Restoration, Bucknell Univ Pr, 93; auth, "Restoration Tragedy," in The Cambridge Companion to Restoration Drama (Cambridge: Cambridge Univ Pr, 00); **CONTACT ADDRESS** Dept English, Catholic Univ of America, 620 Michigan Ave NE, Washington, DC 20064-0001. **EMAIL** wheatley@cua.edu

WHEATLEY, EDWARD
PERSONAL Born 11/13/1957, Augusta, GA, m, 1984 **DISCIPLINE** ENGLISH **EDUCATION** Rhodes Col, BA, 79; Univ York, MA, 83; Univ Va, MA, 84; PhD, 90. **CAREER** Teacher, Col d'Enseignement General, Ivory Coast, 79-81; teacher, Khmer Resettlement Project, 82; asst to assoc prof, Hamilton Col, 90-. **HONORS AND AWARDS** Am Philos Soc Grant, 93; NEH Grant, 93; Mellon Fac Fel, 93-94. **MEMBERSHIPS** MLA, New Chaucer Soc, Early Book Soc. **RESEARCH** Manuscript and early book production, curricular texts and commentaries, disability studies. **SELECTED PUBLICATIONS** Auth, "A Selfless Ploughman and the Christ/Piers Conjunction in Langland's Piers Plowman," Notes and Queries, (93); auth, "Scholastic Commentary and Robert Henryson's 'Morall Fabillis,'" Modern Philol, (94); auth, "Commentary Displacing Text: the Nun's Priest's Tale and the Scholastic Fable Tradition," Studies in the Age of Chaucer, (96); auth, "The Aesopic Corpus Divided Against Itself, or a Literary Body and Its Members," Jour of the Early Book Soc, (99); auth, "'Modes of Representation' in Blackwell's Companion to Chaucer," Blackwell's, (00); auth, Mastering Aesop: Medieval Education, Chaucer, and His Followers, Univ Pr of Fla, 00. **CONTACT ADDRESS** Hamilton Col, New York, 198 College Hill Rd, Clinton, NY 13323. **EMAIL** ewheatle@hamilton.edu

WHEELER, ARTHUR M.
PERSONAL Born 11/20/1928, Toledo, OH, d, 3 children **DISCIPLINE** PHILOSOPHY; ENGLISH **EDUCATION** Bowling Green State Univ, BA, 51; Univ Chicago, MA, 53; Univ Wis, Madison, PhD, 58. **CAREER** Instr, 58-62, asst prof, 62-66, assoc prof, 66-70, prof, 70-91, Kent State Univ, Ohio; Retired. **HONORS AND AWARDS** Summer res grants, 66, 79; Sigma Tau Delta (English). **MEMBERSHIPS** AAUP; Amer Philos Assoc; Ohio Philos Assoc; Tri-State Philos Assoc; Soc for the Philos Study of Relig; Southern Soc for Philos and Psychol; Ohio Academy of Relig. **RESEARCH** Ethics; philos of relig; free will. **SELECTED PUBLICATIONS** Auth, On Lewis' Imperatives of Right, Phil Studies, 61; God and Myth, Hibbert Journal, 64; Are Theological Utterances Assertions?, Sophia, 69; Bliks as Assertions and as Attackable, Phil Studies, 74; Prima Facie and Actual Duty, Analysis, 77; On Moral Nose, Phil Quart, 77; Fiat Justitia, ruat Caelum, Ethics, 86. **CONTACT ADDRESS** 7686 Diagonal Rd., Kent, OH 44240.

WHEELER, BONNIE
PERSONAL Born Boston, MA **DISCIPLINE** MEDIEVAL STUDIES, ENGLISH **EDUCATION** Stonehill Col, AB, 66; Brown Univ, AM, 68; PhD, 71. **CAREER** Asst prof, Columbia Univ, 70-75; vis asst prof, Case Western Res Univ, 71-73; assoc prof and dir, S Methodist Univ, 75-. **HONORS AND AWARDS** Outstanding Teacher Award, SMU, 76, 80, 85, 87, 89, 91; Perrine Prize, Phi Beta Kappa, 88; Annual Alumni Asn Fac Award, 92; Maguire Center Fel, SMU, 98; Distinguished Prof, SMU, 98; Golden Key Soc, SMU, 99. **MEMBERSHIPS** Intl Courtly Lit Soc; The Medieval Acad of Am; New Chaucer Soc; Phi Beta Kappa; Soc Intl Arthurienne. **RESEARCH** Medieval literature; Medieval cultural studies. **SELECTED PUBLICATIONS** Auth, "The Prowess of Hands: Alchemical Psychology in Malory's Tale of sir Gareth," in Culture and the King: The Social Implication of Arthurian Literature, (Binghamton, 93); auth, "Romance and Parataxis and Malory: The Case of Sir Gawain's Reputation," in Arthurian Lit, Cambridge Univ Press, 93; ed, Feminea Medievalia I: Representations of the Feminine in the Middle Ages, Academia Press, 93; auth, "Trouthe without Consequences: Rhetoric and Gender in Chaucer's Franklin's Tale, in Feminea Medievalia I: Representations of the Feminine in the Middle Ages, Academia Press, 93; co-ed, Medieval Mothering, Garland, 96; co-auth, "Medieval Mothers, Medieval Motherers," in Medieval Mothering, Garland, 96; co-ed, Fresh Verdicts on Joan of Arc, Garland, 96; auth, "Joan of Arc's Sword in the Stone," in Fresh Verdicts on Joan of Arc, Garland, 96; co-ed, Becoming Male in the Middle Ages, Garland, 97; co-auth, "Becoming and Unbecoming," in Becoming Male in the Middle Ages, Garland 97; ed, Listening to Heloise: The Voice of a Twelfth-Century Woman, St. Martin's, 00; co-ed, The Malory Debate: The Texts of Le Morte Darthur, D.S. Brewer, 00; co-ed, On Arthurian Women: Essays in Memory of Maureen Fries, Scriptorium Press, 01. **CONTACT ADDRESS** Med Studies Prog, So Methodist Univ, 3225 University Blvd, Dallas, TX 75275-0432. **EMAIL** bwheeler@mail.smu.edu

WHEELER, RICHARD PAUL
PERSONAL Born 09/09/1943, Newton, IA, m, 1998, 3 children **DISCIPLINE** ENGLISH LITERATURE **EDUCATION** Cornell Col, BA, 65; State Univ NYork, Buffalo, MA, 67, PhD(English lit), 70. **CAREER** Asst prof, 69-75, assoc prof English Lit, Univ Ill, Urbana, 75-87, prof 87-. **MEMBERSHIPS** MLA; Shakespeare Asn Am. **RESEARCH** Modern British literature; Shakespeare; psychoanalytic criticism. **SELECTED PUBLICATIONS** Auth, The King and the Physician's Daughter, Comp Drama, winter 74; Poetry and Fantasy in Shakespeare's Sonnets 88-96, Lit & Psychol, 72; Marriage and Manhood in All's Well That Ends Well, Bucknell Rev, spring 74; Yeats's Second Coming: What Rough Beast?, Am Imago, fall 74; Intimacy and Irony in The Blind Man, summer 76 & Give and take in Tickets Please, fall 77, D H Lawrence Rev; Since First We Were Dissevered, In: Representing Shakespeare, Johns Hopkins Univ Press, 80; Shakespeare's Development and the Problem Comedies, Univ Calif Press, Berkeley, 81; Fantasy and History in The Tempest, in The Tempest, ed Nigel Wood, Buckingham: Open Univ Press, Theory and Practice Series, 95; coauth, The Whole Journey: Shakespeare's Power of Development, Univ of Calif press, 86; Ed, Creating Elizabethan Tragedy: The Theater of Marlowe and Kyd, Univ of Chicago press, 88. **CONTACT ADDRESS** Dept of English, Univ of Illinois, Urbana-Champaign, 608 S Wright St, Urbana, IL 61801-3613. **EMAIL** rpw@uiuc.edu

WHEELER, WAYNE R.
PERSONAL Born 03/17/1961, Tucson, AZ **DISCIPLINE** LIBRARY SCIENCE **EDUCATION** Northern Ariz Univ, BFA, 86; Univ Ariz, MLS, 89. **CAREER** Librn, Santa Cruz County Libr, 91-93; system librn, Luzern County Commun Col, 95-97; asst dir, Keystone Col, 97-. **MEMBERSHIPS** ALA; ACRL; SRRT; PALA; CRL; LIRT; NEPBC; CCAIT. **CONTACT ADDRESS** Miller Library, Keystone Col, One College Green, La Plume, PA 18440-0200. **EMAIL** wrwheeler@rocketmail.com

WHIDDEN, MARY BESS
DISCIPLINE ELIZABETHAN LITERATURE **EDUCATION** Univ Tex, PhD, 65. **CAREER** Instr, Univ NMex, 63-. **SELECTED PUBLICATIONS** Auth, Provincial Matters, 85. **CONTACT ADDRESS** Dept of Lit, Univ of New Mexico, Albuquerque, Albuquerque, NM 87131. **EMAIL** marybess@unm.edu

WHIPPLE, ROBERT DALE, JR.
PERSONAL Born, TX, m **DISCIPLINE** RHETORIC AND COMPOSITION **EDUCATION** TX Tech Univ, Lubbock, BA, 79; Univ TX at Austin, MA, 83; Miami Univ, Oxford, PhD, 90. **CAREER** Assoc prof 95; asst prof 90; assoc ch dept Eng 98- & dir, Compos 90-98, Creighton Univ; asst dir, Freshman Eng Col Compos, Miami Univ, 87-88; co-ed, NE Eng J, Creighton Univ, 91-95; adj prof, Birmingham-Southern Col, 89-90; lectr, Univ AL, 88-89; tchg fel, Miami Univ, 85-88; lectr, TX Tech Univ, 83-85; asst instr, Univ TX at Austin, 82-83; tchg asst, TX Tech Univ, 81. **HONORS AND AWARDS** Outstanding Advr Awd, Creighton Col Arts & Sci, 98; Nominee, Tchr for Tomorrow Awd, 97; US W Acad Technol & Develop fel, 95; Phi Kappa Phi Honor Soc, Miami Univ, 87; Sinclair fel, Miami Univ, 85; ed bd(s), engl j, 93-97, writing ctr j, 93-97 & h-rhetor discussion list and bk rev proj, 94-98; contrib bibliog, longmans bibliog of rhet & compos, 86, 87 & 88. **MEMBERSHIPS** Sec 92-93, ch 93-94 & Treas 94-95, Midwest Writing Ctr(s) Asn; Nat Coun Tchr(s) Eng; Nat Writing Ctr(s) Asn; Writing & Comput Asn, UK. **SELECTED PUBLICATIONS** Auth, Socratic Method and Writing Instruction, Lanham, UP Am, 97;

Larry McMurtry, The Last Picture Show, Lonesome Dove, & Comanche Moon, Encycl Popular Fiction, Beacham Press, 98; The World-Wide Web and Composition Theory, Theorizing Composition: A Critical Sourcebook of Theory and Scholarship in Contemporary Composition Studies, Westport, Greenwood Press, 98; The Press of Ideas: Readings for Writers on Print Culture and the Information Age by Julie Bates Dock, Kairos: A J Tchr(s) of Writing in Webbed Environments 2 1, 97; WEB Griffin, The Aviators, Men In Blue, & Semper Fi, Encycl Popular Fiction, Beacham Press, 96; ed, Native Heritage: American Indian Literature, Urbana, Nat Coun Tch(s) Engl, 94; Cather in the Classroom, Urbana, Nat Coun Tch(s) Engl, 92; rev, A History of Professional Writing Instruction in American Colleges: Years of Acceptance, Growth, and Doubt by Katherine H Adams, J Bus & Tech Commun 9 1, 95. **CONTACT ADDRESS** Dept of Eng, Creighton Univ, 2500 CA Plaza, Omaha, NE 68178. **EMAIL** whippl@creighton.edu

WHITAKER, ELAINE E.
PERSONAL Born 11/23/1942, Oklahoma City, OK, m, 1964, 3 children **DISCIPLINE** ENGLISH, LATE MEDIEVAL MANUSCRIPTS **EDUCATION** NYork Univ, PhD, 71. **CAREER** Adj to asst prof of humanities, Rhodes Col, 78-85; asst to assoc prof, English, Univ Alabama, 85-. **HONORS AND AWARDS** Univ Ala at Birmingham Tchr of Year, 97-98. **MEMBERSHIPS** Early Book Soc; Early English Text Soc; Medieval Acad Am; Soc Textual Scholar; NCTE. **RESEARCH** 15th Century British books; Composition/Rhetoric; Pedagogy. **SELECTED PUBLICATIONS** Auth, The Awakening Conscience in Brideshead Revisited, Evelyn Waugh Newsletter and Studies, 93; A Pedagogy to Address Plagiarism, Col Compos & Commun, 93; Reading the Paston Letters Medically, English Lang Notes, 93; auth, A Collaboration of Readers: Categorization of the Annotations in Copies of Caxton's Royal Book, Univ Mich Press, 94; John of Arderne and Chaucer's Physician, ANO: A Quart Jour of Short Articles, Notes, and Rev, 95; Traces of a Program of Illustration Specific to a Late Medieval Somme/Mirror Manuscripta, 95; coauth, Virtual Voices in "Letters Across Cultures," Computers and Composition, 98, Teacher Talk on E-Mail, Action in Teacher Education, 96. **CONTACT ADDRESS** Dept of English, Univ of Alabama, Birmingham, Birmingham, AL 35294-1260. **EMAIL** eew@uab.edu

WHITAKER, FAYE PAULI
PERSONAL Born 08/19/1941, Belleville, WI, m, 1970, 2 children **DISCIPLINE** ENGLISH LITERATURE **EDUCATION** Lakeland Col, AB, 63; Western Mich Univ, MA, 65; Northwestern Univ, PhD(English), 74. **CAREER** Instr English, Western Mich Univ, 64-67; instr, 70-74, asst prof English, Iowa State Univ, 74-91; assoc prof, 91; asst provost, 94; assoc provost, 00. **MEMBERSHIPS** MLA; **RESEARCH** Seventeenth century English poets; American Puritan poets; Renaissance drama; Biblical Lit. **CONTACT ADDRESS** Office of the Provost, Iowa State Univ of Science and Tech, 107 Beardshear Hall, Ames, IA 50011-2021. **EMAIL** fwhitake@iastate.edu

WHITAKER, ROSEMARY
DISCIPLINE ENGLISH LITERATURE **EDUCATION** Univ Okla, BM; Univ Tulsa, MA; Univ Okla, PhD. **CAREER** Prof. **RESEARCH** American women writers. **SELECTED PUBLICATIONS** Auth, pubs on Mari Sandoz and Helen Hunt Jackson. **CONTACT ADDRESS** Dept of English, Colorado State Univ, Fort Collins, CO 80523.

WHITAKER, THOMAS RUSSELL
PERSONAL Born 08/07/1925, Marquette, MI, m, 1950, 4 children **DISCIPLINE** ENGLISH **EDUCATION** Oberlin Col, AB, 49; Yale Univ, AM, 50; PhD, 53. **CAREER** From instr to prof, Oberlin Col, 52-64; teacher lit, Goddard Col, 64-66; prof English, Univ Iowa, 66-75; prof english, Yale Univ, 75-, chmn dept english, 79-. **HONORS AND AWARDS** Haskell fel, Oberlin Col, 58-59; Am Coun Learned Soc fel, 69-70; ed, Iowa Review, 74-77; Huntington fel Nat Endowment for Humanities, 81; Harbison Awd, Danforth Found, 72. **MEMBERSHIPS** MLA **RESEARCH** Twentieth century English and American literature; modern drama, continental, English and American. **SELECTED PUBLICATIONS** Auth, Swan and Shadow: Yeats's Dialogue with History, Univ NC, 64; William Carlos Williams, Twayne, 68; ed, Twentieth Century Interpretations of the Playboy of the Western World, Prentice-Hall, 69; auth, On speaking humanly, In: The Philosopher-Critic, Univ Tulsa, 70; Voices in the open: Wordsworth, Eliot and Stevens, Iowa Rev, 71; Since we have been a conversation, Clio, 76; Fields of Play in Modern Drama, Princeton Univ, 77; Sight Unseen - Beckett, Pinter, Stoppard, And Other Contemporary Dramatists On Radio, English Language Notes, 97. **CONTACT ADDRESS** Dept of English, Yale Univ, New Haven, CT 06520. **EMAIL** thomas.whitaker@yale.edu

WHITCHURCH, GAIL
PERSONAL Born 08/30/1952, Minneapolis, MN **DISCIPLINE** FAMILY STUDIES, COMMUNICATION STUDIES **EDUCATION** Univ Minn, BA, 74; MA, 81; Univ Del, PhD, 89. **CAREER** From asst prof to assoc prof, Indiana University-Purdue Univ Indianapolis, 93-. **HONORS AND AWARDS** Teaching Excellence Recognition Awd (Ind Univ Board of Trustees Awd), Ind Univ, 97 & 99. **MEMBERSHIPS** Nat Commun Asn, Nat Coun on Family Relations, Am Asn for Marriage and Family Therapy. **RESEARCH** Communication and families. **SELECTED PUBLICATIONS** Coauth, "Melding the objective and subjective sides of leadership: Behaviors and social judgments in decision-making groups," Commun Monographs 62 (95): 244-264; coauth, "Applied family communication research: Casting light upon the demon," J of Applied Commun Res 23 (95): 239-246; coauth, "Communication and emergent group leadership: Does content count?," Commun Res Reports 14 (97): 470-480; coauth, "Family Communication," in Handbook of Marriage and the Family, eds. M.B. Sussman, S.K. Steinmetz, & G.W. Peterson (NY: Plenum, 99), 687-704; coauth, "Big changes come with small packages: Communication processes in the transition to parenthood," in Case Studies in Interpersonal Communication: Processes and Problems, eds. D.O. Braithwaite & J.T. Wood (CA: ITP/Wadsworth, 00), 228-236; auth, "Violent critical incidents in four types of violent interspousal relationships," Marriage and Family Rev (in press). **CONTACT ADDRESS** Dept Commun, Indiana Univ-Purdue Univ, Indianapolis, 425 N University Blvd, Indianapolis, IN 46202-5140. **EMAIL** whig@iupui.edu

WHITE, CECIL R.
PERSONAL Born 10/15/1937, Hammond, IN, d, 2 children **DISCIPLINE** LIBRARY AND INFORMATION SCIENCE **EDUCATION** Southern IL Univ, BS in Ed, 59; Southwestern Baptist Theol Sem, M Div, 69; Univ North TX, MLS, 70, PhD, 83. **CAREER** Asst Dir of the Library, Southwestern Baptist Sem, 69-80; Dir of Libraries, Golden Gate Baptist Theol Sem, 80-87; Dir of the Library, West Oahu Col, 88-89; Special Projects Dir, North State Cooperative Library Asn, 89-90; Dir of the Library, St. Patrick's Seminary, 90-. **HONORS AND AWARDS** Who's Who in the West; Who's Who in Religion; Who's Who in America; Who's Who in the World; Lilly Found grantee, Am Theol Lib Asn; Beta Phi Mu Library Honorary Soc. **MEMBERSHIPS** Am Library Asn; Asn of Col and Res Librarians; Catholic Library Asn; Am Theol Library Asn. **RESEARCH** Theology; religion and social issues; ecumenism. **CONTACT ADDRESS** Dir, McKeon Memorial Library, St. Patrick's Sem, 320 Middlefield Rd., Menlo Park, CA 94025-3596. **EMAIL** stpats@ixnetcom.com

WHITE, CINDY H.
DISCIPLINE COMMUNCATION STUDIES **EDUCATION** Tex Tech Univ, BA, MA; Univ Ariz, PhD. **CAREER** Asst prof. **RESEARCH** Interpersonal communication. **SELECTED PUBLICATIONS** Co-auth, Research on nonverbal message production, 97; Interpersonal deception: XI. Relationship of suspicion to communication behaviors and perceptions, 96; Interpersonal deception: VII. Behavioral profiles of falsification, concealment, and equivocation, Jour Lang Soc Psychol, 96. **CONTACT ADDRESS** Dept of Communication, Univ of Colorado, Boulder, Boulder, CO 80309. **EMAIL** Cindy.White@Colorado.edu

WHITE, CYNTHIA
PERSONAL Born Philadelphia, PA, m, 1992, 1 child **DISCIPLINE** CLASSICS **EDUCATION** Chestnut Hill Col, BA, 76; Villanova Univ, MA, 78; Cath Univ Am, PhD, 91. **CAREER** Asst prof, Cath Univ Am, 86-91; asst prof, assoc prof, Univ Ariz, 91-. **HONORS AND AWARDS** NEH, Medieval Pilg, 99; AM Acad Rome, Cen Hellen Stud Fel, 97; Wakonse Teach Awd, 96; CAMWS Awd. Comm Promo Latin, 95; Rome Prize, 88-89; Fulbright Res Grnt, Italy, 88-89; ACL McKinlay Scholar, 88. **MEMBERSHIPS** APA; ACL; CAMWS; NAPS; APS, Vergillian Soc. **RESEARCH** Greek and Latin Epithalamia; patristic and medieval Latin; medieval pilgrimage; Latin pedagogy; iopography of Rome. **SELECTED PUBLICATIONS** Auth, "De Raptu Proserpinae in the Church Fathers: The Sacrum Mysterium of Marriage," in Kaina; kai; Palaiav: Festschrift for Thomas P. Halton (Wash: DC, Cath Univ Am Press, 98): 244-269; auth, "Agnes," "Catherine of Alexandria," "Cecilia" "Eustochium," "Gervasius and Protasius," in Encycl of Early Christ, ed. E. Ferguson (Garland Pub Inc, 97); auth, "Music in the Latin Classroom," Teach Guide Adv Place Cour in Latin (01); auth, "Docere Docentes: Training New Teachers in an Ancient Discipline," in Latin for the 21st Century: From Concept to Classroom, ed. Richard A. LaFleur (Glenview, IL: Scott Foresman, Addison Wesley, 97). **CONTACT ADDRESS** Dept Classics, Univ of Arizona, ML371, Tucson, AZ 85712. **EMAIL** ckwhite@u.arizona.edu

WHITE, DEBORAH
DISCIPLINE ROMANTICISM AND CONTEMPORARY LITERARY THEORY **EDUCATION** Yale Univ, BA, 82, MPhil, 87, PhD, 93. **CAREER** Assoc prof. **RESEARCH** Romantic theories of imagination. **SELECTED PUBLICATIONS** Pubs on Shelley, DeMan, and Freud. **CONTACT ADDRESS** Dept of Eng, Columbia Col, New York, 2960 Broadway, New York, NY 10027-6902.

WHITE, DONALD JERRY
PERSONAL Born 06/05/1946, Anderson, IN, m, 1967, 1 child **DISCIPLINE** RENAISSANCE & MEDIEVAL LITERATURE **EDUCATION** Barton Col, AB, 68; Univ Ill, Urbana, AM, 72, PhD(English), 77. **CAREER** Asst prof, Albertson Col Idaho, 75-78; asst prof, Eureka Col, 78-80; asst prof, assoc prof, prof English, Cent Mo State Univ, 80-. **HONORS AND AWARDS** Hon Woodrow Wilson Fellow, 68; Phi Kappa Phi National Honor Soc, 73; Phi Beta Delta Honor Soc for International Scholars, 94. **MEMBERSHIPS** MLA; Shakespeare Asn Am; Renaissance Soc Am; Medieval Acad Am. **RESEARCH** Renaissance drama; Shakespeare; Medieval drama. **SELECTED PUBLICATIONS** Auth, Irony and the three temptations in Philaster, Thoth, spring 75; Richard Edwards' Damon and Pithias: A Critical, Old Spelling Edition, Garland Press, 80; contribr, William Blake, John Bunyan, Dante, Holy Grail, C S Lewis, and John Milton, In: Abingdon Dictionary of Living Religions, Abingdon, 81; Early English Drama: Everyman to 1580, G. K. Hall, 86; Richard Edwards, in Elizabethen Dramatists, ed Fredson Bowers, Dictionary of Literary Biography 62, Bruccoli, 87; Contrib, World Shakespeare Bibliography (1988-present). **CONTACT ADDRESS** Dept of English, Central Missouri State Univ, Warrensburg, MO 64093-5046. **EMAIL** jwhite@cmsu1.cmsu.edu

WHITE, DONNA R.
PERSONAL Born 10/06/1955, Walton Beach, FL **DISCIPLINE** ENGLISH **EDUCATION** Ark Tech Univ, BA, 76; Univ Tex Austin, MA, 83; Univ Minn, PhD, 91. **CAREER** Asst prof, Clemson Univ, 92-98; vis lectr to asst prof, Ark Tech Univ, 99-. **HONORS AND AWARDS** Ore Humanities Ctr, 96; NEH, 93, 94; Nat Welsh Am Found, 89; Univ Minn English Dept Fel, 86; Mythopoeic Scholar Award, 99. **MEMBERSHIPS** MLA; CLA; SCBWI. **RESEARCH** Children's literature; young adult literature; Celtic studies; fantasy and science fiction. **SELECTED PUBLICATIONS** Auth, A Century of Welsh Myth in Children's Literature, Greenwood Pr, 98; auth, Dancing With Dragons: Ursula LeGuin and the Critics, Camden House, 99. **CONTACT ADDRESS** English Dept, Arkansas Tech Univ, Russellville, AR 72801. **EMAIL** milliew@mail.cswnet.com

WHITE, DOUGLAS HOWARTH
PERSONAL Born 08/26/1929, Omaha, NE, m, 1964 **DISCIPLINE** ENGLISH **EDUCATION** Univ Omaha, BA, 51; Univ Nebr, MA, 54; Univ Chicago, PhD, 63. **CAREER** Instr English, Coe Col, 57-59; from instr to asst prof, Ill Inst Technol, 60-67; from asst prof to assoc prof, 67-78, Prof English, Loyola Univ, Chicago, 78-, Nat Endowment for Humanities fel, 67-68; Newberry Libr-Brit Acad fel, 76. **MEMBERSHIPS** MLA; Am Soc 18th Cent Studies. **RESEARCH** Eighteenth century literature; intellectual history of 18th century England. **SELECTED PUBLICATIONS** Auth, Pope and the Context of Controversy The Manipulation of Ideas in an Essay on Man, Univ Chicago, 70; Swift and the definition of man, Mod Philol, Vol 73, No 4, 5/76. **CONTACT ADDRESS** Dept of English, Loyola Univ, Chicago, 6525 N Sheridan Rd, Chicago, IL 60626-5385.

WHITE, EDWARD MICHAEL
PERSONAL Born 08/16/1933, Brooklyn, NY, m, 1976, 2 children **DISCIPLINE** ENGLISH **EDUCATION** NYork Univ, BA, 55; Harvard Univ, MA, 56, PhD, 60. **CAREER** From instr Eng to asst prof, Wellesley Col, 60-65; assoc prof, 65-69, chmn freshman compos, 65-66, chmn dept Eng, 66-76, prof Eng, 69-98, prof emer eng, CA State Univ, San Bernardino, 98-; sr lectr Eng, Univ AZ, 98; Pres, CA State Univ & Col Eng Coun, 73-75; consult, Eng testing & measurement writing ability to many schs and col, 73-; coordr, Eng testing prog & consult, credit by evaluation, CA State Univ & Cols, 76-80; dir, CA State Univ & Cols freshman Eng equivalency exam, 73-; dir, Nat Inst Educ res in effective tchg. **MEMBERSHIPS** MLA; NCTE; Soc for Values Higher Educ; Conf Col Compos & Commun; AAUP. **RESEARCH** Eng and Am fiction; compos; Eng testing, particularly direct measurement of writing ability. **SELECTED PUBLICATIONS** Auth, Thackeray's contribution to Fraser's magazine, Studies Bibliog, 66; A critical theory of Mansfield Park, Studies English Lit, fall 67; The Writer's Control of Tone, 70 & The Pop Culture Tradition, 72, Norton; Equivalency testing in freshman English, Bull Asn Dept English, 3/73; Freedom is restraint: The pedagogical problem of Jane Austen, San Jose Studies, 2/76; Racial minorities and writing skills assessment in the California State University and Colleges, Col English, 3/81; Teaching and Assessing Writing, Jossey-Bass, 85, 2nd ed, 94; Developing Successful College Writing Programs, Jossey-Bass, 89; Assigning, Responding, Evaluating: A Writing Teacher's Guide, 3rd ed, St Martins, 95; Inquiry: A Cross Cultural Reader, Prentice Hall, 93, Composition in the 21st Century: Crisis and Change, Southern Ill Univ Press, 96; Writing Assessment: Politics, Policies, Practices, MLA, 96. **CONTACT ADDRESS** 3045 W Brenda Loop, Flagstaff, AZ 86001. **EMAIL** ewhite@csusb.edu

WHITE, FRED D.
PERSONAL Born 08/06/1943, Los Angeles, CA, 2 children **DISCIPLINE** COMPOSITION **EDUCATION** Univ Minn, BA, 67, MA, 74; Univ Iowa, PhD, 80. **CAREER** Assoc prof English, Santa Clara Univ, 80-; Instr English, Lakewood Community Col, 74-75 & Anoka-Ramsey Community Col, 76-77. **HONORS AND AWARDS** Brutocao Awd for Teaching Excellence, 97. **MEMBERSHIPS** MLA; Conf Col Compos & Commun. **RESEARCH** Composition theory and pedagogy; interrelationships of the literary and scientific imagination. **SE-**

LECTED PUBLICATIONS Auth, Whitman's cosmic spider, Walt Whitman Rev, 77; Robert Sheckley, in Twentieth Century Science-Fiction Writers, St Martin's, 81; Releasing the self: Teaching journal writing to freshmen, Writing Instr, summer 82; Albee's hunger artist: The Zoo Story as a parable of the writer vs society, Ariz Quart, 83; Science, Discourse, & Authorial Responsibility, San Jose Studies, 84; The Writer's Art, Wadsworth, 86; Poetic Responses to Einstein, San Jose Studies, 89; Science and the Human Spirit, Wadsworth, 89; Science in the Poetry of Emily Dickinson, Col Lit, 92; Rachel Carson: Encounters with the Primal Mother, NDak Quart, 91; Communicating Technology, Harper Collins, 96. **CONTACT ADDRESS** Dept of English, Santa Clara Univ, 500 El Camino Real, Santa Clara, CA 95053-0001.

WHITE, JAMES P.
PERSONAL Born 09/28/1940, Wichita Falls, TX, m, 1961, 1 child **DISCIPLINE** ENGLISH **EDUCATION** Univ Tex, BA; Vanderbilt Univ, MA; Brown Univ, MA. **CAREER** Asst Prof, Univ Tex, 73-78; Dir, Univ S Calif, 79-81; Prof, Univ S Ala, 82-. **HONORS AND AWARDS** Guggenheim Fel; Fulbright Fel. **MEMBERSHIPS** AWP, Gulf Coast Asn of Creative Writing Teachers, Tex Asn of Creative Writing Teachers. **RESEARCH** Fiction, literary biography, Christopher Islewood. **SELECTED PUBLICATIONS** Auth, Birdsong, A Novel, Copper Beach Pr, Brown Univ; auth, Persian Oven, A Novella, Methuen Pr, London; auth, California Exit, A Novella, Methuen Pr, London; auth, The 9th Car, G P Putnam's. **CONTACT ADDRESS** Dept English, Univ of So Alabama, 307 University Blvd N, Mobile, AL 36688-3053. **EMAIL** james@americanartists.org

WHITE, JOHN D.
PERSONAL Born 07/23/1948, Benham, KY **DISCIPLINE** MUSIC; PHILOSOPHY **EDUCATION** Univ Ky, BM, 70; Univ Idaho, MM, 72; Univ Iowa, PhD, 77. **CAREER** Sabbatical replacement, Willamette Univ, spring, 74; asst prof, 76-78, interim chair, 78-79, assoc prof, 78-80, dept chair, fall, 80, Western Wy Community Col, driver, Webb's Trucking, spring, 81; assoc prof, Benedict Col, 81-82; assoc prof, Chattahoochee Valley State Community Col, 82-83; grad study in philos, Univ Ky, spring, 84; lectr, Okla State Univ, 84-85; grad asst, Univ Tex Austin, 85-86; grad study in philos, Univ Iowa, spring, 87; assoc prof, Col of the Ozarks, 87-88; pianist, Univ Iowa, 88-89; prof, philos/humanities, Talladega Col, 89-. **SELECTED PUBLICATIONS** Auth, The Pythagorean Derivation and Theories of Truth, 96; auth, The Substance Argument, 95; auth, The Confluence of Deism, African Creation Myth, and Thomas Hobbes, 94; auth, Philosophy of Law, 94; auth, The Origin of Number, 93; auth, The Antigone Effect, 92; auth, Belief System Internal Inconsistency, 91; auth, The Maker's Mind Model in Aesthetics, 91; auth, The Analysis of Law and the Nesting of the Philosophy of History in the History of Empiricism, 88; auth, Some Remarks on Some Remarks on Logical Form, 87; auth, Considerations on Infinity Derived from Spinozist Theory, 87; auth, Empiricism, Hume, Quantum Mechanics, and Universe Models, 86. **CONTACT ADDRESS** Dept. of Philosophy, Talladega Col, Campus Box 165, Talladega, AL 35160.

WHITE, LANA
PERSONAL Born 08/01/1939, Canyon, TX, m, 1960, 1 child **DISCIPLINE** ENGLISH **EDUCATION** West TX State Univ, BA, 60; MA, 64; Texas Christian Univ, PhD, 83. **CAREER** Teacher, TX Pub Sch's, 60-81; fel, TX Christian Univ, 81-83; prof, West Texas AM Univ, 83-. **HONORS AND AWARDS** Fel, TX Christ Univ; Innov Teach of Year Awd. **MEMBERSHIPS** NCTE; Intl Asn Improv Mother Tongue Edu; Worchester's Group, Chld Lit. **RESEARCH** Teaching the English Language; the shaping of consciences of children through literature. **SELECTED PUBLICATIONS** Ed, contrb, Language Awareness: A History and Implementations, Amsterdam Univ Press, 00; contrb, Text, Culture and National Identity in Children's Literature, NORDINFO 44 (99). **CONTACT ADDRESS** Dept English Languages, West Texas A&M Univ, 7408 Bayswater Rd, Amarillo, TX 79119.

WHITE, PETER
DISCIPLINE AMERICAN LITERATURE **EDUCATION** Pa State Univ, PhD, 76. **CAREER** Instr, 76-, dir, grad stud Eng, 93-95, assoc dean, Col Arts and Sci, Univ NMex. **SELECTED PUBLICATIONS** Auth, The Lore of New Mexico, 88. **CONTACT ADDRESS** Univ of New Mexico, Albuquerque, Albuquerque, NM 87131. **EMAIL** plwhite@unm.edu

WHITE, ROBERT A.
PERSONAL Born 05/23/1943, Danbury, CT, s **DISCIPLINE** THEATER ARTS **EDUCATION** Wagner Col, BA, 66; Dartmouth Col, MALS, 78; Antioch Univ, MA, 93; Union Inst, PhD, 98. **CAREER** Instr, Baltimore Community Col, 68-69; instr, Broward Community Col, 81-83; instr, Blue Ridge Community Col, 84-87; asst prof, dir of theater studies, artistic dir of the Morrison Playhouse, and artistic dir of the sch for gifted students in the arts, Brevard Col, 91-. **HONORS AND AWARDS** Listed in Who's Who Among Am College and University Professors, 95 & 96; Stanbach Awd, Brevard Col, 96. **MEMBERSHIPS** Southeastern Theatre Confr, Writer's Guild. **RESEARCH** Theatre History, Symbolism, Philosophy. **SELECTED PUBLICATIONS** Auth, White Tie; Top Hat and No Tails; auth, Remission; auth, Who Shall Hang His Head in Shame? **CONTACT ADDRESS** Dept Fine Arts, Brevard Col, 400 N Broad St, Brevard, NC 28712-3306. **EMAIL** bobaw@brevard.edu

WHITE, ROBERTA
DISCIPLINE BRITISH LITERATURE **EDUCATION** Albion Col, BA; Univ Chicago, MA; Stanford Univ, PhD. **CAREER** Fac, 67; Charles J. Luellen Prof and chr Dept Eng; chr, Hum Div. **HONORS AND AWARDS** Dir, writer-in-res prog, Centre Col. **RESEARCH** Modern British literature, Irish literature, Virginia Woolf, John Milton, and 17th-century poetry. **SELECTED PUBLICATIONS** Auth, articles on modern contemporary writers including John Berryman, Margaret Atwood; contrib, Mother Puzzles, Greenwood Press. **CONTACT ADDRESS** Centre Col, 600 W Walnut St, Danville, KY 40422. **EMAIL** whiter@centre.edu

WHITEAKER, JANET FAYE
PERSONAL Born, TN, s **DISCIPLINE** ENGLISH **EDUCATION** Tenn Tech Univ, BA, 72; MA, 81; Appalachian State Univ, Certificate, 92. **CAREER** Instr to asst prof and prog leader, Tenn Tech Univ, 85-. **HONORS AND AWARDS** Res Grant, Tenn Tech Univ. **MEMBERSHIPS** MLA; NADE; TNADE; AHEAD TNAHEAD; CWPA; NCTE; NEA; TEA; AAUP; AAUW; WHET. **RESEARCH** The effects of intermittent central suppression of vision on academic skills; Methods of assisting under prepared students; Intervention strategies to aid student retention. **SELECTED PUBLICATIONS** Auth, "Earthlings are a strange lot," in Poetry of the Millennium, 00; co-auth, Developing College Skills in Writing, 3rd ed, Boston, 00; co-auth, "Identifying and reversing intermittent central suppression in students with low rending comprehension as a method of improving student performance in reading," J of Vision Develop, (00): 131-137; co-auth, "Identifying and Reversing intermittent central suppression to improve reading," in Research and Teaching in Developmental Education, (01): 93-95; auth, Writer's Stylebook, 4th ed, Boston, 01. **CONTACT ADDRESS** Acad Develop Prog, Tennessee Tech Univ, 1380 S Maple Ave, Cookeville, TN 38506-6203. **EMAIL** jwhiteaker@tntech.edu

WHITELEY, PATRICK
PERSONAL Born 04/29/1953, Wilkes-Barre, PA **DISCIPLINE** ENGLISH **EDUCATION** Calif State Univ at Long Beach, BA, 75; MA, 78; Univ Calif at Riverside, PhD, 83. **CAREER** Lectr, Univ Calif at Santa Barbara, 84-89; prof, Northern State Univ, 89-. **RESEARCH** Law and Literature. **SELECTED PUBLICATIONS** Auth, Knowledge and Experimental Realism in Conrad, Lawrence, and Woolf, 87; auth, "The Social Framework of Knowledge: Muriel Spark's The Prime of Miss Jean Brodic," Mosaic, 96; auth, "Perspective and Indeterminacy in Charles Tomlinson's Verse," Arachne, 98. **CONTACT ADDRESS** Dept English & Lang, No State Univ, 1200 S Jay St, Aberdeen, SD 57401-7155. **EMAIL** whitelep@northern.edu

WHITEMAN, D. BRUCE
PERSONAL Born 06/18/1952, Toronto, ON, Canada, m, 1973, 2 children **DISCIPLINE** ENGLISH LITERATURE & LIBRARIANSHIP **EDUCATION** Trent Univ, BA, 75; Univ Toronto, MA, 77, MLS, 79. **CAREER** Librn, 79-88, McMaster Univ; dept head, 88-96, McGill Univ; head librn, 96-, William Andrews Clark Mem Libr, UCLA. **MEMBERSHIPS** Amer Libr Assoc; Bibliog Soc Amer; Bibliog Soc Canada; SHARP Grober Club, Zaworcuo Club. **RESEARCH** Canadian literary history; descriptive bibliography; history of the book; forgery. **SELECTED PUBLICATIONS** Coauth, A Bibliography of Macmillan of Canada Imprints, 1906-1980, Dundern Press, 85; auth, The Letters of John Sutherland, ECW Press, 92; auth, Scholarly Publishing in Canada and Canadian Bibliography: Selected Papers on Two Themes, Assoc for Canadian Stud, 93; auth, Lasting Impressions: A Short History of English Publishing in Quebec, Vehicule Press, 94; auth, J.E.H. MacDonald, Quarry Press, 95. **CONTACT ADDRESS** William Andrews Clark Mem Lib, Univ of California, Los Angeles, 2520 Cimarron St, Los Angeles, CA 90018-2019. **EMAIL** whiteman@humnet.UCLA.edu

WHITING, STEVEN
PERSONAL Born 07/11/1953, Chicago, IL, m, 2 children **DISCIPLINE** MUSICOLOGY **EDUCATION** Univ Ill, PhD 91. **CAREER** Ed A-R Editions (Madison), 85-89; vis lectr, Univ Ill, 89-91; asst prof of Musical, Univ Mich, 92-99, to assoc prof 99-; dir Centre for Europ Studies, 98-; dir Int Inst, 00-. **HONORS AND AWARDS** Phi Beta Kappa. **MEMBERSHIPS** Am Musical Soc. **RESEARCH** 18th-century music; Beethoven; Satie; musical narratology. **SELECTED PUBLICATIONS** Satie the Bohemian: From Cabaret to Concert Hall, Oxford Univ Press, 99; Erik Satie, Neuf chansons de cabaret et de caf conc, pour chant et piano, Edition etablie et prefacee par Steven Moore Whiting. Paris: Editions Salabert, 96, pl. nos. E. A.S. 19340-49, 19350; Symmetry and Process in Two Variation Works by Beethoven, Katachi U Symmetry, ed T. Ogawa et al., 301-5. Tokyo, Springer-Verlag, 96; Music on Montmartre, In The Spirit of Montmartre: Cabarets, Humor, and the Avant-Garde, 1875-1905, ed Phillip Dennis Cate & Mary Shaw, 159-97. New Brunswick, NJ: Rutgers Univ Press, 96; Erik Satie and Vincent Hyspa: Notes on a Collaboration; Music & Letters 77, 96:64-91; Three Marchen-Medieval, Musical, and Modern: Fouque's Undine, Mozart's Die Zauberflote, and Hoffmann's Der goldne Topf; Symmetry: Culture and Science 7, 96: 361-76; Musical Parody and Two 'oeuvres posthumes' of Erik Satie: The 'Reverie du pauvre' and the 'Petite musique de clown triste.'41 Revue de Musicologie 81 (95): 215-34.Carl Dahlhaus, Albrecht Riethmuller, and Alexander L. Ringer, eds., Beethoven: Interpretationen seiner Werke, 2 vols. Laaber: Laaber-Verlag, 94, 1:600-603, 2:404-8, 443-64. (Articles on seven of Beethoven's variation works for piano.)Alexander L. Ringer, Musik als Geschichte: Gesammelte Aufsatze. Herausgegeben von Albrecht Riethmuller und Steven Moore Whiting, Laaber: Laaber-Verlag, 93; Computers and Scholarly Publication, Mod Music Librarianship: In Honor of Ruth Watanabe, edited by Alfred Mann, 133-36, New York: Pendragon, 89; 'Hoert ihr wohl': Zu Funktion und Programm von Beethovens Chorfantasie, Archiv fur Musikwissenschaft 45, 88:132-47; Pianos, In Bruno Nettl, The Western Impact on World Music, 51-54, New York: Schirmer, 85. **CONTACT ADDRESS** Sch of Music, Univ of Michigan, Ann Arbor, Ann Arbor, MI 48109-2085. **EMAIL** stevenmw@umich.edu

WHITLARK, JAMES S.
DISCIPLINE WORLD LITERATURE **EDUCATION** Univ Chicago, PhD, 76. **CAREER** Prof, TX Tech Univ. **RESEARCH** Relig in lit. **SELECTED PUBLICATIONS** Auth, Illuminated Fantasy: From Blake's Visions to Recent Graphic Fiction, Assoc UP, 88; Behind the Great Wall: A Post-Jungian Approach to Kafkaesque Literature, Assoc UP, 91; coed, The Literature of Emigration and Exile, TX Tech, 92. **CONTACT ADDRESS** Texas Tech Univ, Lubbock, TX 79409-5015. **EMAIL** ditjw@ttacs.ttu.edu

WHITMAN, ROBERT F.
PERSONAL Born 07/09/1925, Boston, MA, m, 1956, 2 children **DISCIPLINE** ENGLISH **EDUCATION** Cornell Univ, AB, 49; Harvard Univ, MA, 51; PhD, 56. **CAREER** Instr, Princeton, 55-60; asst prof to prof, Univ of Pittsburgh, 60-88; chair, 67-72. **HONORS AND AWARDS** NEH Res Fel, 72-73. **MEMBERSHIPS** MLA, Malone Soc. **RESEARCH** Play Theory as it relates to theater. **SELECTED PUBLICATIONS** Auth, "Beatrice's Pernicious Mistake," The Cenci, (59); auth, The Play Readers Handbook, Bobbs-Merrill, (Indianapolis, NY), 66; auth, Beyond Melancholy: John Webster and the Tragedy of Darkness, (Salzburg), 73; auth, Shaw and The Play of Ideas, Cornell Univ Press, 77; auth, "Shaw Listens to the Actors," in Shaw, (Penn State Univ Press, 83). **CONTACT ADDRESS** 2101 Belmont Rd, Ann Arbor, MI 48104-2819.

WHITNEY, CHARLES C.
DISCIPLINE EARLY MODERN DRAMA, SEVENTEENTH CENTURY, SIXTEENTH CENTURY, LITERARY THEORY **EDUCATION** San Francisco State Col, BA, 69; CUNY, PhD, 77. **CAREER** Asst prof, Penn State Univ, 81-86; vis assoc prof, St Bonaventure Univ, 87-88; assoc prof, Univ Nev, Las Vegas, 88-. **HONORS AND AWARDS** A W Mellon fel in the Hum, CUNY, 78-79; NEH summer sem, Yale Univ, 79; NEH summer sem, Huntington Libr, 83; NEH summer inst, Newberry Libr, 86; sem fel, Folger Inst, 86; Choice Mag Outstanding Acad Bk Sel, 87; vis fac mem, NEH summer inst, Univ Fla, 90; Am Philos Soc grant, Guildhall Libr, London, 97. **RESEARCH** Theater audiences of Shakespeare and his contemporary dramatists. **SELECTED PUBLICATIONS** Auth, Francis Bacon and Modernity, Yale 86; "Francis Bacon's--Instauratio--: Dominion of and over Humanity," Journal of the History of Ideas 50, (89; auth "Festivity and Topicality in the Coventy Scene of Henry IV, Eng Lit Renaissance 24 (94); "Usually in the Weakening Daies: Playgoing Apprentices, Journeymen, and Servants in Guild Records, 1582-92," Shakespeare Quarterly 50 (99); "Toward a Theory of Early Modern Audience Response," Shakespeare and Modernity, ed. Hugh Grady, (Routledge, 00). **CONTACT ADDRESS** Dept of Eng, Univ of Nevada, Las Vegas, 4505 Maryland Pky, PO Box 455011, Las Vegas, NV 89154-5011. **EMAIL** whitney@nevada.edu

WICK, AUDREY
DISCIPLINE RHETORIC AND COMPOSITION, MINORITY LITERATURE, FEMINIST LITERARY CRITICISM **EDUCATION** OH State Univ, BA, 75; Univ TX at Arlington, MA, 90, PhD, 96. **CAREER** Dir, 1st-Yr Eng & assoc dir, 91-94, Univ TX at Arlington; ch, Freshman Eng Comt & Grad Tchg Asn Comt, 92-96; mem, Curric Task Force, 92-96, Dept Goals Comt, 94-96, Travel Comt, 94-96, Rhetoric Curric Comt, 93-96, Freshman Eng Comt, 88-91 & Comt for Curric Design Prog in Freshman & Sophomore Eng, 85-87; co ch, Freshman Eng Comt, 91; res asst to dir Freshman Eng, 88-89. **MEMBERSHIPS** Pres, Gorgias Soc, 87; Univ TX at Arlington Current: Mod Lang Soc; Writing Prog Admin; Rhetoric Soc Am; Nat Coun Tchrs Engl; Gorgias Soc. **SELECTED PUBLICATIONS** Auth, Rhetoric: Concepts, Definitions, Boundaries, an anthology, The Feminist Sophistic Enterprise: From Euripides to the Vietnam War, 95; Rhetoric Society Quarterly, The Feminist Sophistic Enterprise: From Euripides to the Vietnam War, 92; Tulsa Studies in Women's Lit, Book Rev(s), 91. **CONTACT ADDRESS** Dept of Eng, Univ of Texas, Arlington, 203 Carlisle Hall, PO Box 19035, Arlington, TX 76019-0595.

WICK, ROBERT L.
PERSONAL Born 12/06/1938, Sioux City, IA, m, 1964, 3 children **DISCIPLINE** FINE ARTS; ENGLISH; LIBRARY SCIENCE **EDUCATION** Univ SD, BFA, 61, MA, 64; Univ Denver, MALS, 71. **CAREER** Band dir, Gregory High Sch, 61-63; prof, Sioux Falls Col, 64-69; libr, Metropolitan St Col, Denver Co, 71-78; Bibliogr, Univ Co Denver, 78- . **HONORS AND AWARDS** Excellence in Teaching Awd, Univ Co Denver, 88; Excellence in Svc Awd, Univ Co Denver, 93; Excellence in Res Awd, Univ of Co, 97. **MEMBERSHIPS** Modern Lang Soc; Modern Libr Assoc. **RESEARCH** Biography; electronic music bibliogr; music ref bibliogr. **SELECTED PUBLICATIONS** Auth, A Library/Media Marriage That Works, Medium, 76; Denver's Dining Delights: A Midwinter Guide to Mile-High Eating, Amer Libr, 93; The Literature of electronic and computer Music: A Basic Library Collection, Choice, 93; Electronic and Computer Music: An Annotated Bibliography, Greenwood Press, 97; ed, ARBA - Guide to Biographical Resources, Libr Unlimited Press, 98. **CONTACT ADDRESS** Univ of Colorado, Denver, 3398 S Oneida Way, Denver, CO 80224-2832. **EMAIL** bwick@castle.cudenver.edu

WICKERT, MAX ALBRECHT
PERSONAL Born 05/26/1938, Augsburg, Germany, d, 1 child **DISCIPLINE** ENGLISH & AMERICAN LITERATURE **EDUCATION** St Bonaventure Univ, BA, 58; Yale Univ, MA, 59, PhD, 65. **CAREER** From instr English to asst prof, Nazareth Col Rochester, 61-66; asst prof, 66-70, Assoc Prof English, State Univ NY Buffalo, 70-; Dir, Outriders Poetry Prog, Buffalo, NY, 71-. **HONORS AND AWARDS** New Poets Rev Prize, 80; NEH Fel, 86. **RESEARCH** Anglo-German literary relations; 19th century aesthetics; history and criticism of opera; translation of Italian verse. **SELECTED PUBLICATIONS** Auth, Structure and ceremony in Spenser's Epithalamion, ELH, 6/68; various poems in Poetry, Choice, Works & Mich Quart Rev, 69-82; transl various poems by Georg Trakl in Chicago Rev, Choice, Extensions & Malahat Rev, 69-; co-transl, 1001 Ways to Live Without Working, Er"ffnungen, Vienna, 71; auth, All the Weight of the Still Midnight (poems), Outriders, 72; Dismemberment of Orpheus: Operatic myth goes underground, Salmagundi, 5/77; Myth and meaning in early opera, Opera J, 4/78; Pat Sonnets, Street Press, 00. **CONTACT ADDRESS** Dept of English, SUNY, Buffalo, P O Box 604610, Buffalo, NY 14260-4610. **EMAIL** wickert@acsu.buffalo.edu

WICKES, GEORGE
PERSONAL Born 01/06/1923, Antwerp, Belgium, m, 1975, 4 children **DISCIPLINE** ENGLISH **EDUCATION** Univ Toronto, BA, 44; Columbia Univ, MA, 49; Univ Calif, PhD, 54. **CAREER** Asst secy, Belgian-Am Educ Found, 47-49; exec officer, US Educ Found, Belgium, 52-54; instr English, Duke Univ, 54-57; from asst prof to prof, Harvey Mudd Col & Claremont Grad Sch, 57-70; Prof English & Comp Lit, Univ Ore, 70-93, dir, Comp Lit Prog, 74-77, Head Dept English, 76-83; Prof Emeritus, 93-, Fulbright lectr, France, 62-63, 66 & 78; US Info Serv lectr, Europe, 69 & Africa, 78 & 79; vis prof, Univ Rouen, 70, Univ Tubingen, 81, Univ Heidelberg, 96; adv ed, Northwest Rev. **HONORS AND AWARDS** Am Philos Soc grant, 71; sr fel, Ctr Twentieth Century Studies, Univ Wis-Milwaukee, 71; Am Coun Learned Soc grant, 72; Nat Endowment for Arts creative writing fel, 73; Camargo Fel, 72-93. **MEMBERSHIPS** MLA; PEN. **RESEARCH** Renaissance poetry; modern literature; comparative literature. **SELECTED PUBLICATIONS** Ed, Durrell-Miller Correspondence, Dutton, 63; Masters of Modern British Fiction, Macmillan, 63; Henry Miller and the Critics, Southern Ill Univ, 63; Aldous Huxley at UCLA: A Catalogue of the Manuscripts in the Aldous Huxley Collection, Univ Calif Libr, 64; Henry Miller, Univ Minn, 66; Americans in Paris, Doubleday, 69; The Amazon of Letters, Putnam, 76; transl, The Memoirs of Frederic Mistral, New Directions, 86; ed, Henry Miller, Letters to Emil, New Directions, 89; Henry Miller and James Laughlin, Selected Letters, Norton, 95. **CONTACT ADDRESS** Dept of English, Univ of Oregon, Eugene, OR 97403-1205.

WIDDICOMBE, RICHARD TOBY
PERSONAL Born 04/12/1955, Salisbury, England, m, 1979 **DISCIPLINE** ENGLISH AND AMERICAN LITERATURE **EDUCATION** Cambridge Univ, BA, 77, MA, 81; Univ CA, Irvine, MA, 79, PhD, 84. **CAREER** Vis lect, Univ CA, Santa Barbara, 84-86, lect, 86-89; asst prof, NY Inst of Technology, 89-92; asst prof, 92-95, assoc prof, Univ AK, Anchorage, 95-, chair, dept English, 95-97. **HONORS AND AWARDS** Arthur E Lewis Awd, 89; AAUP Awd, 92; Several fac research and travel awards, 92-; Who's Who Among America's Teachers, 96, 98. **MEMBERSHIPS** Modern Lang of Am; Soc for Utopian Studies. **RESEARCH** 19th and 20th century Am lit; bibliographical and textual studies. **SELECTED PUBLICATIONS** Auth, Edward Bellamy: An Annotated Bibliography of Secondary Criticism, Garland Pub, 88; A Few Soiled Flowers': Nathanael West and Greek Tragedy, English Lang Notes 30-3, March 93; America and the Americans in 1833-1834, Fordham Univ Press, 95; Reply to Neil Easterbrook, Extrapolation, forthcoming; four entries on Edward Bellamy in Le Dictionnaire de l'Utopie, Slatkine, forthcoming 00; A Reader's Guide to Raymond Chandler, Greenwood Press, forthcoming 01; auth, Simply Shakespeare, Addison Wesley Longman, forthcoming, 01. **CONTACT ADDRESS** Dept of English, Univ of Alaska, Anchorage, Anchorage, AK 99508. **EMAIL** afrtw@uaa.alaska.edu

WIDER, SARAH ANN
PERSONAL Born 06/07/1959, Albuquerque, NM **DISCIPLINE** AMERICAN RENAISSANCE, MUSIC AND LITERATURE **EDUCATION** Univ NM, BA, 81; Cornell Univ, MA, PhD, 84, 86. **CAREER** Assoc prof, Colgate Univ, 86. **MEMBERSHIPS** Phi Beta Kappa; Phi Kappa Phi; The Emerson Society. **RESEARCH** Emerson, congregation response to early 19th century Am sermons. **SELECTED PUBLICATIONS** Auth, Anna Tilden, Unitarian Culture and the Problem of Self-Representation, Georgia, 97; auth, The Critical Reception of Emerson: Unsettling All Things, Camden House, 00. **CONTACT ADDRESS** Dept of Eng, Colgate Univ, 13 Oak Drive, Hamilton, NY 13346. **EMAIL** swider@mail.colgate.edu

WIEBE, MEL
DISCIPLINE ENGLISH LITERATURE **EDUCATION** Univ Manitoba, PhD. **CAREER** Dept Eng, Queen's Univ **HONORS AND AWARDS** Ed, Disraeli Project, 83-. **RESEARCH** Victorian age; scholarly editing. **SELECTED PUBLICATIONS** Auth, "Benjamin Disraeli Letters," Vols. I, II; gen ed, "Benjamin Disraeli Letters," Vols. III, IV, V, VI, University of Toronto Press; author of articles on Tennysonm Hardy and Disraeli, in "Book Collector," "English Studies in Canada," "Victorian Periodicals Review;" contri of three articles to the "New Dictionary of National Biograpnhy, Oxford. **CONTACT ADDRESS** English Dept, Queen's Univ at Kingston, Kingston, ON, Canada K7L 3N6. **EMAIL** wiebem@qsilver.queensu.ca

WIECEK, WILLIAM MICHAEL
PERSONAL Born 01/31/1938, Cleveland, OH, m, 2000, 3 children **DISCIPLINE** UNITED STATES LEGAL & CONSTITUTIONAL HISTORY **EDUCATION** Cath Univ Am, BA, 59; Harvard Univ, LLB, 62; Univ Wis-Madison, PhD(hist), 68. **CAREER** From asst prof to assoc prof, 68-77, Prof Hist, Univ MO-Columbla, 77-85; Congdon Prof of Publoc Law & Prof of Hist, Syracuse Univ Col of Law, 85-. **HONORS AND AWARDS** Phi Beta Kappa **MEMBERSHIPS** Orgn Am Historians; Am Law Inst; Am Historical Asn. **RESEARCH** American legal and constitutional development; slavery; U.S. Supreme Court. **SELECTED PUBLICATIONS** Auth, The reconstruction of federal judicial power, 1863-1875, Am J Legal Hist, 69; The great writ and reconstruction: The Habeas Corpus Act of 1867, J Southern Hist, 70; The Guarantee Clause of the US Constitution, Cornell Univ, 72; Somerset: Lord Mansfield and the legitimacy of slavery in the Anglo-American World, Univ Chicago Law Rev, 74; The law of slavery and race in the thirteen mainland colonies of British America, William & Mary Quart, 77; The Sources of Antislavery Constitutionalism in America, 1760-1848, Cornell Univ Press; Equal Justice Under Law: Constitutional Development, 1835-1875, Harper & Row; auth, Lost World of Classical Legal Thought, Oxford Univ Press, 98. **CONTACT ADDRESS** Col of Law, Syracuse Univ, Syracuse, NY 13244. **EMAIL** wmwiecek@law.syr.edu

WIEGENSTEIN, STEVE
PERSONAL Born 08/23/1955, Ironton, MO, m, 1982, 1 child **DISCIPLINE** COMMUNICATION **EDUCATION** Univ Mo-Columbia, BJ, 76, MA, 81, PhD, 87. **CAREER** Adv, radio station, 99-01; assoc prof & adv stud newspaper, Culver-Stockton Col, 96- & asst prof, 92-96, granted tenure, 96; asst prof, Drury Col, Springfield, 88-92; stud newspaper adv, 88-92; yearbk adv, 89-92; actg adv, radio station, 90-91; instr, Engl & Jour, Centenary Col La, Shreveport, 85-88; news ed, Wayne Co Jo Banner, Piedmont, 76-79. **HONORS AND AWARDS** MO Governor's Awd Excellence Tchg, 96; Huggins Grad Scholar, Univ MO, 82-85; Univ MO Dept Engl Awd Excellence Tchg, 81; DR Francis fel, Univ MO, 79-80; who's who in the midwest, who's who in am educ. **MEMBERSHIPS** Col Media Advisers, MO Col Media Asn, elected liaison to MO Press Asn, 96; Soc Prof Jour; Nat Icarian Heritage Soc; AAUP, Local Chap Sec/Treas 89-90 & pres, 90-91; bd dir, Lit Vol(s) Am, Shreveport Chap, 87-88. **SELECTED PUBLICATIONS** Auth, "Understanding the Human Drama of Your Community," in The Responsible Reporter, 2nd ed., (Vision Press, 97); auth, "The Sedition Act of 1798" and "Customized License Plates," in Ready Reference: Censorship, (Salem Press, 98); auth, "Rethinking Don Marquqis" presented to Midwest Conference on Film, Literature and Language, 99; auth, "Nature Travel in Ghana" in Transitions Abroad, 00; auth, The Academic Novel and the Academic Ideal: John Williams' Stoner, McNeese Rev 33, 94; The Image of Nature in Annie Dillard's The Living, in The Image of Nature: Selected Papers, Univ Southern CO, 93; Naturalism, Literary History, and The Story of a Country Town, Univ MS Stud in Eng, NS 7, 89; The Media and/in Politics, address to Quincy, Ill, Rotary Club, 96; Signs and Wonders, short story, NE Rev 22 2, 94; Jailer's Experiences Become 'Prison Rhymes,' Ozarks Mountaineer, 91; Commemorating the Trail of Tears, Ozarks Mountaineer, 89; The Trouble with Women, short story, Oxford Mag, 89; The End of the World, short story, Kans Quart 20:3, 88; Why Miss Elizabeth Never Joined the Shakespeare Club, short story, La Lit, 87; Bill Burkens and Peter Krull, short story, Beloit Fiction J, 86; ed & wrote critical preface to 2 previously unpubl plays by Tennessee Williams, "Beauty is the Word" and "Hot Milk at Three in the Morning," MO Review 7:3, Summer 1984. **CONTACT ADDRESS** Dept of Commun, Culver-Stockton Col, 1 College Hill, Canton, MO 63435-1299. **EMAIL** swiegenstein@culver.edu

WIEMANN, JOHN M.
PERSONAL Born 07/11/1947, New Orleans, LA, m, 1969, 2 children **DISCIPLINE** INTERPERSONAL COMMUNICATION **EDUCATION** Loyola Univ (La), AB, 69; Purdue Univ, MS, 73, PhD(commun), 75. **CAREER** Employee rels specialist, Int Bus Machines Corp, 69-71; grad instr commun, Purdue Univ, 71-75; asst prof human commun, Rutgers Univ, 75-77; Asst Prof Commun Studies, Univ Calif, Santa Barbara, 77-, Res Assoc, Instrnl Develop, Measurement & Res Ctr, Purdue Univ, 73-74; vis scholar, Col Commun, Univ Tex, Austin, fall 80; W K Kellogg Found nat fel, 80-83. **HONORS AND AWARDS** Industry Awd Outstanding Applied Res, Orgn Commun Div, Int Commun Asn, 74; Outstanding Res Report, Interpersonal Commun Div, Int Commun Asn, 76. **MEMBERSHIPS** Int Commun Asn; Speech Commun Asn; AAAS; Am Educ Res Asn; Am Psychol Asn. **RESEARCH** Effective interpersonal communication; nonverbal communication; organizational communication & development. **SELECTED PUBLICATIONS CONTACT ADDRESS** Commun Studies Prog, Univ of California, Santa Barbara, 552 University Rd, Santa Barbara, CA 93106-0001.

WIENEN, MARK VAN
DISCIPLINE ENGLISH **EDUCATION** Calvin Col, BA, 86; Univ Ill Urbana -Champaign, MA, 88; PhD, 92. **CAREER** Vis Asst Prof, Univ of Southern Maine, 94-95; Asst Prof, Augustana Col, SDak, 96-. **MEMBERSHIPS** MLA, Am Studies Asn. **RESEARCH** Modern Poetry, Literary Criticism and Theory, American Literature. **SELECTED PUBLICATIONS** Auth, Partisans and Poets: The Political Work of American Poetry in the Great War, Cambridge Univ Press (NY), 97. **CONTACT ADDRESS** Dept English, Augustana Col, So Dakota, 2001 S Summit Ave, Sioux Falls, SD 57197-0001. **EMAIL** vwienen@inst.angie.edu

WIENER, HARVEY SHELBY
PERSONAL Born 04/07/1940, Brooklyn, NY, m, 1965, 3 children **DISCIPLINE** ENGLISH, AMERICAN LITERATURE **EDUCATION** Brooklyn Col, BS, 61, MA, 68; Fordham Univ, PhD, English, 71. **CAREER** Asst, 70, Fordham Univ; Instr, 70-71, prof, English, 71-, Queensborough Comm Col, CUNY; prof, English, LaGuardia, CUNY, 71-; adj asst prof, 70-72, Brooklyn Col; NEH Fel, 72-73; vis asst prof, 74-, SUNY, Stony Brook; vis Assoc prof, Eng, 76-77, PA St Univ; Dean, AC AF CUNY; Vice Provost, Adelphi Univ, Vis Pres, 97-, Marymount-Manhattan Col. **HONORS AND AWARDS** Phi Beta Kappa **MEMBERSHIPS** MLA; NCTE; Conf Col Compos & Comm. **RESEARCH** 17th cent non-dramatic lit; Shakespeare; 20th cent Amer novel. **SELECTED PUBLICATIONS** Auth, Science or providence: Towards knowledge in the New Atlantis, Enlightenment Essays, 72; auth, Creating Compositions, McGraw-Hill, 6th ed; auth, Media Compositions: Preludes to Writing, Col English, 2/74; auth, Bacon and Poetry: A View of the New Atlantis, Anglia, 76; auth, Any Child Can Write, McGraw-Hill, 78; auth, The Writing Room, Oxford, 81; auth, The Short Prose Reader, McGraw-Hill, 8th ed, 97. **CONTACT ADDRESS** 309 Clearview Lane, Massapequa, NY 11758. **EMAIL** Hswien@aol.com

WIESENFARTH, JOSEPH JOHN
PERSONAL Born 08/20/1933, Brooklyn, NY, m, 1971, 1 child **DISCIPLINE** ENGLISH & AMERICAN LITERATURE **EDUCATION** Cath Univ Am, BA, 56, PhD, 62; Univ Detroit, MA, 59. **CAREER** Asst prof Eng, La Salle Col, 62-64; from asst prof to assoc prof, Manhattan Col, 64-70; assoc prof, 70-76, prof eng, Univ WI, Madison, 76-, Sally Mead Hands-Bascom, prof, 92-00; prof, Nathan S. Blount, 94-00; Emeritus prof, 00; Nat Endowment for Hum, fel, 67-68; Inst Res Hum, fel, 74-75, fulbright fel, 82-83; chair eng dept, 83-86, 89-92; assoc dean, grd sch, 95-96; assoc dean, letters & sci, 97. **HONORS AND AWARDS** Chancellors award disting tch, 79; cath univ Am award for outstand ach field of resear scholar, 96. **MEMBERSHIPS** MLA; Jane Austen Soc; Henry James Soc; Ford Jadox Ford Soc; Katherine Anne Porter Soc. **RESEARCH** The Eng novel; George Eliot; Henry James; Ford Madox Ford; Katherine Ann Porter; lit theory. **SELECTED PUBLICATIONS** Auth, Henry James and the Dramatic Analogy, Fordham Univ, 63; auth, The Errand of Form: An Essay of Jane Austen's Art, 67; auth, George Eliot's Mythmaking, Carl Winter, Heidelberg, W Ger, 77; auth, Gothic Manners and the Classic English Novel, 88; The Good Soldier on Parade, Rev, 97; ed, george Eliot: A Writers Notebook 1854-1879; ed, Ford Madox Ford and the Arts, Contemp Liter 89. **CONTACT ADDRESS** Dept of Eng, Univ of Wisconsin, Madison, 600 North Park St, Madison, WI 53706-1403. **EMAIL** jjwiesen@facstaff.wisc.edu

WIESENTHAL, CHRISTINE
DISCIPLINE ENGLISH LITERATURE **EDUCATION** Univ Manitoba, BA; MA; Univ Alberta, PhD. **CAREER** Assoc prof, Univ of Alberta, 00-. **RESEARCH** Victorian literature; nineteenth century British and American fiction and poetry; critical theory; contemporary poetry. **SELECTED PUBLICATIONS** Auth, Figuring Madness in Nineteenth Century Fiction, Mac-

millan, 97. **CONTACT ADDRESS** Dept of English, Univ of Alberta, 3-5 Humanities Centre, Edmonton, AB, Canada T6G 2E5. **EMAIL** christine.wiesenthal@ualberta.ca

WIGAL, GRACE J.
DISCIPLINE LEGAL RESEARCH AND WRITING **EDUCATION** Marshall Univ, BA, 72, MA, 76; W Va Univ Col Law, JD, 89. **CAREER** Instr, Col Law, 90; dir, Legal Res and Wrtg Prog, 92; dir, Acad Support Prog, 93; dir, Appellate Advocacy Prog; act dir, -. **HONORS AND AWARDS** W Va Law Rev Lit award, 89. **MEMBERSHIPS** Order of the Coif. **SELECTED PUBLICATIONS** Ed, W V Law Rev; Auth, bk(s), articles, on legal issues that arise in the medical and construction settings. **CONTACT ADDRESS** Law Sch, West Virginia Univ, Morgantown, PO Box 6009, Morgantown, WV 26506-6009.

WIGGINS, JACQUELINE D.
DISCIPLINE MUSIC EDUCATION **EDUCATION** Univ IL, Ed D, 92. **CAREER** Public school music teacher, 72-94; coordinator of Music Ed, Oakland Univ, Rochester, MI, 94-. **MEMBERSHIPS** MENC; NASM; AERA. **RESEARCH** Creative process and connections to cognitive process. **SELECTED PUBLICATIONS** Auth, Children's Strategies for Solving Compositional Problems with Peers, J of Res in Music Ed, vol 42, no 3, 94; Teacher-Research in a General Music Classroom: Effects on the Teacher, Bul of the Coun for Res in Music Ed, no 123, winter 94/95; Building Structural Understanding: Sam's Story, The Quart J of Music-Teaching and Learning, vol 6, no 3, 96; with Karen Bodoin, Painting a Big Soup: Teaching and Learning in a Second Grade General Music Classroom, J of Res in Music Ed, vol 46, no 2, 98; auth, Composition in the Clasroom, MENC, 90; auth, Synthesizers in the Elem Music Classroom, MENC, 91; auth, Teaching for Musical Understanding, McGraw-Hill, 01. **CONTACT ADDRESS** Dept of Music, Theatre and Dance, Oakland Univ, Rochester, MI 48063. **EMAIL** jwiggins@oakland.edu

WIGNALL, DENNIS L.
PERSONAL Born 05/31/1943, Salt Lake City, UT, m, 1988, 3 children **DISCIPLINE** HUMAN COMMUNICATION **EDUCATION** Univ of Denver, PhD, 93. **CAREER** 31 years as adjunct faculty at: Univ of CO-Denver, Metro State Col of Denver, Regis Univ, Front Range Community Col, Univ of Northern CO, Int Univ, Univ of Denver. **HONORS AND AWARDS** Recipient of multiple awards: teaching excellence. **MEMBERSHIPS** Nat Commun Asn (life member); Int Commun Asn (assoc member); Western States Commun Asn (assoc member); CO Speech Commun Asn (member). **RESEARCH** Human commun and the influence of ....and the internet. **CONTACT ADDRESS** Department of Communication, C-159, Saginaw Valley State Univ, 7400 Bay Road, University Center, MI 48710. **EMAIL** dwignall@svsu.edu

WIGODSKY, MICHAEL M.
PERSONAL Born 05/23/1935, Houston, TX **DISCIPLINE** CLASSICS **EDUCATION** Univ of Texas, BA, 57; Princeton Univ, MA, 59; PhD, 64. **CAREER** Prof Emer, Stanford Univ. **RESEARCH** Latin poetry; Hellenistic and Roman philos. **SELECTED PUBLICATIONS** Auth, Vergil and Early Latin Poetry, 72; Horace's Miser (Sat. 1.1.108) and Aristotelian Self-love, 80; The Alleged Impossibility of Philosophical Poetry, in Philodemus and Poetry, 94. **CONTACT ADDRESS** Stanford Univ, Bldg 20, Main Quad, Stanford, CA 94305. **EMAIL** wigodsky@leland.stanford.edu

WIKANDER, MATTHEW H.
PERSONAL Born 03/21/1950, Philadelphia, PA, m, 1980 **DISCIPLINE** ENGLISH **EDUCATION** Williams Col, BA, 70; Christ's Col Cambridge, BA, 72; MA, 79; Univ Mich, PhD, 75. **CAREER** Postdoctoral Lect, Univ Mich, 75-78; Asst Prof, Columbia Univ, 78-87; From Assoc Prof to Prof, Univ Toledo, 87-. **HONORS AND AWARDS** Marshall Scolar, 70-72; ACLS Grant-in-Aid, 89; NEH Summer Fel, 90; Outstanding Res Awd, Univ Toledo, 93; Newberry Libr Short Term Fel, 96 . **MEMBERSHIPS** MLA, SAA, ASTR. **SELECTED PUBLICATIONS** Auth, The Play of Truth and State, Johns Hopkins UP, 86; auth, Prines to Act, Johns Hopkins UP, 93; contributing auth, The Cambridge Companion to O'Neill, 98; contributing auth, The Cambridge Companion to Shaw, 98. **CONTACT ADDRESS** Dept English, Univ of Toledo, 2801 W Bancroft St, Toledo, OH 43606-3328. **EMAIL** mwikand@uoft02.utoledo.edu

WILCOX, DEAN
PERSONAL Born 04/20/1964, Mt. Kisco, NY, m, 1987, 1 child **DISCIPLINE** THEATRE HISTORY, THEORY, AND CRITICISM **EDUCATION** Glasboro State College (now Rowan Univ), NJ, BA (Theatre Arts), 86; Univ SC, MFA (Lighting Design), 89; Univ WA School of Drama, Seattle, PhD (Theatre Hist, Theory, and Criticism), 94. **CAREER** Teaching asst, Dept of Drama, Univ WA, 91-94; lect, Theatre Hist, Univ CA, San Diego, spring 95; vis asst prof, Dartmouth Col, June-Aug 98; Asst Prof, Theatre Histroy, Theory, and Criticism, TX Tech Univ, 96-. **HONORS AND AWARDS** Univ WA Fowler Graduate travel grant, 93; Univ WA Grad School Dissertation Fel, 93; Mellon Postdoctoral Fel at Cornell Univ, 95-96; accepted to Teaching Academy at TX Tech Univ, April 98. **MEMBERSHIPS** Asn of Theatre in Higher Ed; Int Federation for Theatre Res; Am Soc for Theatre Res; Am Soc for Aesthetics. **RESEARCH** Performance studies; postmodernism; semiotics; deconstruction; design hist and theory; chaos theory; performance art. **SELECTED PUBLICATIONS** Auth, book review of Phillip B. Zarilli's Acting (Re)Considered and Mariellen R. Sanford's Happenings and Other Acts, Theatre Survey, Vol 37, no 2, Nov 96; Political Allegory or Multimedia Extravaganza? A Historical Reconstruction of the Opera Company of Boston's Intolleranza, Theatre Survey, Vol 37, no 2, Nov 96; What Does Chaos Theory Have to Do with Art?, Modern Drama, Vol XXXIX, no 4, winter 96; book review of Alma Law and Mel Gordon's Meyerhold, Eisenstein and Biomechanics, Theatre Res Int, Vol 22, no 2, Autumn 97; book review of Marvin Carlson's Performance: A Critical Introduction and Richard Schechner's The Future of Ritual, Theatre Survey, Vol 38, no 2, Nov 97; Karen Finley's Hymen, Theatre Res Int, Vol 22, no 1, spring 97; A Complex Tapestry of Text and Imagery: Karen Finley, The American Chestnut, Cornell University, May 10, 1996, The Jour of Dramatic Theory and Criticism, Vol XII, no 1, fall 97; book review of Colin Counsell's Signs of Performance and Walter Gropius' The Theatre of the Bauhaus, Theatre Jour, Vol 50, no 3, Oct 98; book review of William Demastes' Theatre of Chaos: Beyond Absurdism, Into Orderly Disorder, Theatre Survey, Vol 39, no 2, Nov 98; book review of Arthur Holmberg's The Theatre of Robert Wilson, Theatre Res Int, Vol 23, no 3, Autumn 98; book review of Jonathan Kalb's The Theatre of Heiner Muller, Theatre Res Int, forthcoming; The Historical Nature of Time: Dramatic Criticism and New Historicism, Theatre Insight, forthcoming. **CONTACT ADDRESS** Dept of Theatre and Dance, Texas Tech Univ, Box 42061, Lubbock, TX 79409-2061. **EMAIL** thdea@ttu.edu

WILCOX, DENNIS LEE
PERSONAL Born 03/31/1941, Rapid City, SD, m, 1969 **DISCIPLINE** PUBLIC RELATIONS, AFRICAN AFFAIRS **EDUCATION** Univ Denver, BA, 63; Univ IA, MA, 66; Univ MO, PhD, 74. **CAREER** Reporter, Daily Sentinel, Grand Junction, CO, 63-64; ed, OH State Univ Publ, 66-68; reporter, Congwer Legis News Serv, Columbus, 67-68; dir pub rel, Ketchum Inc, Pittsburgh, 68-71; public rel officer, Chapman Col Semester at Sea, 71-72; Public rel prof, San Jose State Univ, 74. **HONORS AND AWARDS** Rex Harlow Awd, 82; PRSA outstanding educator, 84; East-West Center fel, 86; vis prof, Rhodes Univ, South Africa, 86; vis prof, Chulalongkorn Univ, Thailand, 87; vis prof, Queensland Univ, Australia, 89; Fulbright scholar, Univ Botswana, 94-95. **MEMBERSHIPS** Asn Educ Jour; Pub Rel Soc Am; Int Pub Rel Asn; Intl Asn Bus Comm; Arthur Page Soc; SF Round Table. **RESEARCH** Public rel, organizational commun, nat media policy. **SELECTED PUBLICATIONS** Auth, English Language Dailies Abroad, Gale, 67; Mass Media in Black Africa, Praeger, 75; auth, Effective Public Relations Writing, John Wiley, 82; auth, Public Relations Writing & Media Techniques, 4th ed, Longman, forthcoming; auth, Public Relations Strategies & Tactics, 6th ed, Longman, 00. **CONTACT ADDRESS** Sch of Jour, San Jose State Univ, 1 Washington Sq, San Jose, CA 95192-0055. **EMAIL** wilcox@jmc.sjsu.edu

WILDBERG, CHRISTIAN
PERSONAL Born 02/12/1957, Flensburg, Germany, m, 1997, 1 child **DISCIPLINE** CLASSICS, ANCIENT PHILOSOPHY **EDUCATION** Cambridge Univ, PhD, 84; Marburg Univ, MTh, 85. **CAREER** Res Fellow, 84-87, Caius Coll Cambridge; Vis Lectr, 87-88, Univ of TX at Austin; Asst Prof, 88-94, Freie Univ Berlin; Res Fellow, 95-96, Center for Hellenic Studies, Washington; Assoc Prof of Classics 96-, Princeton Univ. **HONORS AND AWARDS** Res Grant-DFG; Res grant, Howard Found. **MEMBERSHIPS** Amer Philos Assoc; Amer Philo Assoc; **RESEARCH** Aristotle, Neoplatonism, Tragedy. **SELECTED PUBLICATIONS** Auth, Philoponus against Aristotle on the Eternity of the World, London, Duckworth, 87; John Philoponus Criticism of Aristotle's Theory of Aether, Peripatio vol 6, pp 274, Berlin, NY, 88; Simplicius against Philpopnus on the Eternity of the World, London, Duckworth, pp 95-135, 91; Hyperesie und Epiphanie, Zur Bedeutung und Funkiton der Gotter in den Dramen des Euripdes, in prog; Aristoteles, DeCaelo, Translation, into German and Commentary, in prog. **CONTACT ADDRESS** Dept of Classics, Princeton Univ, 108 East Pyne, Princeton, NJ 08544. **EMAIL** wildberg@princeton.edu

WILDE, ALAN
PERSONAL Born 05/26/1929, New York, NY **DISCIPLINE** ENGLISH, AMERICAN LITERATURE **EDUCATION** NYork Univ, BA, 50, MA, 51; Harvard Univ, PhD, 58. **CAREER** From instr English to asst prof, Williams Col, 58-64; assoc prof, 64-67, Prof English, Temple Univ, 67-, Grad Chmn, 75-, Scholar, NY Univ, 50-51 & Harvard Univ, 51-52, teaching fel, 54-58; Fulbright fel, Univ Paris, 52-53. **HONORS AND AWARDS** Lindback Found Awd for Distinguished Teaching, 75. **MEMBERSHIPS** MLA; AAUP **RESEARCH** Modern novel; British literature between the wars; contemporary American fiction. **SELECTED PUBLICATIONS** Auth, Art and Order: A Study of E M Forster, NY Univ, 64; The illusion of St Mawr: Technique and vision in D H Lawrence's novel, PMLA, 3/64; Christopher Isherwood, Twayne, 71; Language and surface: Isherwood and the thirties, Contemp Lit, autumn 75; Barthelme unfair to Kierkegaard: Some thoughts on modern and postmodern irony, boundary 2, fall 76; Desire and consciousness: The anironic Forster, Novel, winter 76; Modernism and the Aesthetics of Crisis, Contemporary Lit, winter 79; Horizons of Assent: Modernism, Postmodernism, and the Ironic Imagination, Johns Hopkins Univ, 81; The Once And Future Novel - Letters To Iwp-L-Muri@Ucsbuxa.Bitnet, Anq-A Quarterly Journal Of Short Articles Notes And Reviews, Vol 0005, 1992; The Vanishing Subject, Early Psychology And Literary Modernism - Ryan,J, Modern Fiction Studies, Vol 0039, 1993. **CONTACT ADDRESS** Dept of English, Temple Univ, Philadelphia, PA 19122.

WILDER, GEORGIA LEE
PERSONAL Born 08/06/1963, Canada **DISCIPLINE** RENAISSANCE LITERATURE, 17TH CENTURY LITERATURE, DRAMA **EDUCATION** Univ of Toronto, BA, 94; MA, 95; PhD, 00. **CAREER** Instr, Univ of Toronto, 00-. **MEMBERSHIPS** MLA, ACCUTE. **RESEARCH** 17th Century: Antinomianism and heresiography, Judaic women and crypto-Judaicism, Early Modern Women's Wriring, Milton, Shakespeare, Spectorship as Dramatic Theory. **SELECTED PUBLICATIONS** Auth, "John Taylor and the Parliament of Women (1640): An Attribution," Notes and Queries, (01). **CONTACT ADDRESS** 96 Manning Ave, Toronto, ON, Canada M6J 2K5. **EMAIL** gwilder@chass.utoronto.ca

WILE, KIP
DISCIPLINE MUSIC **EDUCATION** Clark Univ, BA; Univ Chicago, MA, PhD. **CAREER** Asst prof, Sam Houston State Univ, 95-. **HONORS AND AWARDS** M. Giles Whiting dissertation fel. **MEMBERSHIPS** Mem, TSMT exec bd. **RESEARCH** Music of late 19th- and early 20th-century Russia and France. **SELECTED PUBLICATIONS** Auth, Communication and Interaction in Stravinsky's Scherzo Fantastique 1907-8, Ind Theory Rev. **CONTACT ADDRESS** Dept of Music, Sam Houston State Univ, PO Box 2208 SHSU, Huntsville, TX 77341-2208. **EMAIL** mus_kdw@shsu.edu

WILEY, RAYMOND A.
PERSONAL Born 10/30/1923, New York, NY, m, 1948, 8 children **DISCIPLINE** GERMAN, MYTHOLOGY & CLASSICAL LITERATURE **EDUCATION** Fordham Univ, AB, 46, MA, 48; Goethe Inst, Munich, cert, 56; Syracuse Univ, PhD(humanities), 66. **CAREER** Instr Ger & English, Boston Col, 47-48; from instr to assoc prof Ger, 48-71, dir lang lab, 70-77, actg chm dept mod lang, 76, actg chm dept classics, 76-78, Prof , 71-89, Adjunct Prof Emeritus Foreign Lang & Lit, Le Moyne Col, 89-, chm, Dept For Lang & Lit, 86-89. **HONORS AND AWARDS** Fordharn Univ Encaenia award, 56; Fulbright Summer Teachers Awd to Germany, 56; NEH Summer Seminar, Stanford Univ, 80. **MEMBERSHIPS** Am Asn Teachers Ger. **RESEARCH** The Correspondence between John Mitchell Kemble and Jakob Grimm, 1832-52; 19th century German-English literary relations; Teutonic mythology; Biography of Alford J. Williams (1896-1958), Aircraft Pilot. **SELECTED PUBLICATIONS** Auth, Four unpublished letters of Jacob Grimm to John Mitchell Kemble, 1832-40, J English & Ger Philol, 7/68; ed, John Mitchell Kemble and Jacob Grimm, a Correspondence: 1832-1852, Brill, Leiden, 71; auth, From letters to life, Heights Mag, Le Moyne Col, fall 71; The German-American verse of Dr Franz Lahmeyer, Ger-Am Studies, spring 74; ed, Austausch, Cent NY Chap Am Asn Teachers Ger Newslett, Vols 1-5, 70-74; auth, Dear Harriet: Fanny Kemble's View of Centennial America, Pa Gazette, 7/76; Anglo-Saxon Kemble, The Life and Works of John Mitchell Kemble 1807-57: Philologist, Historian, Archaeologist, Brit Archaeol Rec, No 72: Anglo-Saxon Studies Archaeol & Hist, I: 165-273; ed, John Mitchell Kemble's Review of Jacob Grimm's Deutsche Grammatik, State Univ NY Ctr Medieval & Early Renaissance Studies, 81; transl, On the Origin of Language, Leiden, Brill, 84; auth, Tints and Texts, A Comparison of the Nibelungenlied's MS Illustrations with Its Narrative, Acta, X, 86; Grimm's Grammar Gains Ground in England, In: The Grimm Brothers & The Germanic Past, J. Benjamins, 90; auth, Science in Fiction: Aviation in Nevil Shute's Works, pub on web at http://web.lemoyne.edu/~wileyra/shutelif.htm. **CONTACT ADDRESS** Dept of Foreign Lang, Le Moyne Col, 1419 Salt Springs Rd., Syracuse, NY 13214-1300. **EMAIL** oparay@juno.com

WILKENS, ANN
PERSONAL Born 01/23/1944, Portsmouth, NH, m, 1966, 2 children **DISCIPLINE** CLASSICS **EDUCATION** Wellesley Col, BA, 66; Univ Pittsburgh, MA, 75; PhD, 90. **CAREER** Instr, Vasser col, 78-79; lecturer, Univ Pittsburgh, 86-94; lecturer, Winchester Thurston, 80-87; asst prof to assoc prof, Duquesne Univ, 94-. **HONORS AND AWARDS** Teach of the Year Awd; AAUW; Apple for the Tchr Awd; Mellon Fel; Tchg Asstshps and Felshps; Thomas Lawrence Fel; Presidential Sch awd; Noble K Dick Gnt; NEH. **MEMBERSHIPS** Am Philol Inst, Am Inst of Archaeol, Classical Asn of Midwest & S, Classical Asn of Atl States. **RESEARCH** Classical tradition. **SELECTED PUBLICATIONS** Auth, Villain or Hero: Sallust's Portrayne of Catiline; auth, "Sallust's Tullianum: Reality, De-

scription and Beyond," in Rome and Her Monuments, Carducci Press, 00; auth, "Bernini and Ovid: Expanding the concept of Metamorphosis," in International Journal of the Classical Tradition, Vol 29. **CONTACT ADDRESS** Dept Classics, Duquesne Univ, 600 Forbes Ave, Pittsburgh, PA 15282-0001. **EMAIL** wilkins@duq2.cc.duq.edu

WILKENS, KENNETH G.
PERSONAL Born 01/17/1921, MN, m, 1981, 3 children **DISCIPLINE** RHETORIC, PUBLIC ADDRESS **EDUCATION** Northwestern Univ, PhD, 54. **CAREER** Asst Prof, St Olaf Coll, 47-56; prof, Univ Tex, 56-58; prof, Speech, St. Olaf Coll, 58-86. **HONORS AND AWARDS** Melvin Jones Fellow, Internatl Assoc of Lions. **MEMBERSHIPS** Speech Commun Asn; Speech Asn Minn. **RESEARCH** Rhetoric/Public address. **CONTACT ADDRESS** 1111 W 2nd St, Northfield, MN 55057.

WILKERSON, MARGARET BUFORD
PERSONAL Born 04/03/1938, Los Angeles, CA, m, 3 children **DISCIPLINE** DRAMATIC ART **EDUCATION** Univ of Redlands, BA History (magna cum laude) 1959; UCLA, Teachers Cred 1960-61; Univ Of CA Berkeley, MA Dramatic Art 1967, PhD Dramatic Art 1972. **CAREER** YWCA Youngstown OH, adlt pgm dir 1959-60; YWCA Los Angeles, adlt pgm dir 1960-62; Jordan HS LA CA, drama/engl tchr 1962-66; English Dept Dramatic Art Dept, lctr 1968-74; Dept Afro-Am Studies UC Berkeley, lctr 1976-83; Ctr for Study Ed & Adv of Women, dir 1975-83; Univ of CA Berkeley African American Studies Dept, prof and chair, 88-94; The Ford Foundation, program officer (gender, Ethnicity & Identity in Higher Education), 98-; Univ of CA Berkeley, chair/dir, Dramatic Art Dept Ctr for Theater Arts, 95-98; The Ford Foundation, Dir, Media Arts & Culture, 00-. **HONORS AND AWARDS** Hon dr/Humane Letters Univ of Redlands 1980; humanities flwshp Rockefeller Fndtn 1982-83; sr postdoctoral flwshp Natl Rsrch Cncl/Ford Found 1983-84; Ford Flwshp/Dissertation Ford Fndtn 1970; otstndng black alumna Univ of CA Berkeley Black Alumni Club 1976; Kellogg Lecturer Am Cncl on Ed 1980; co-editor Black Scholar theatre issue & other publs; author of "9 Plays by Black Women" New Amer Library 1986; Honoree, Equal Rights Advocates, 1989; College of Fellows of the American Theatre/JF Kennedy Ctr for Performing Arts, 1990; Awd for Exemplary Educational Leadersip/Black Caucus of American Assn of Higher Education, 1990; Profile of Excellence, KGO-TV, San Francisco, 1990; Association of American Theatre, Career Achievement Awd for Outstanding Educator, 1996; Black Theatre Network Lifetime Membership Awd. **MEMBERSHIPS** V pres/adm Am Theatre Asso 1983-85; chair Black Theatre Prog/ Am Theatre Asso 1979-83; adv bd Bus & Prof Womens Fndtn 1983-; consult Am Cncl on Ed Natl Identification Prog for Womdn Adms 1980-83; panelist Natl Rsrch Cncl/Lhumanitgies Doct Comm 1983-; consult CA Arts Cncl 1984-; mem Natl Cncl of Negro Women; mem Univ of CA Berkeley Black Alumni Club; mem NAACP; founder/dir Kumoja Players 1971-75; bd of trustees, San Francisco Theological Seminary, 1987-97; Assoc of Theatre in Higher Education, chair, Awards Comm, 1996-98; Bd of Trustees, U. of Redlands, and Mills College, 99-. **CONTACT ADDRESS** Director, EMAC Division, Ford Foundation, 320 E 43rd St, New York, NY 10017. **EMAIL** m.wilkerson@fordfound.org

WILKIE, BRIAN
DISCIPLINE ROMANTIC POETRY **EDUCATION** Univ Wisc, PhD. **CAREER** English and Lit, Univ Ark. **SELECTED PUBLICATIONS** Auth, Romantic Poets and Epic Tradition, Wisc, 65; Blake's 'Four Zoas': The Design of a Dream, Harvard, 78; Blake's Thel and Oothoon, Engl Lit Studies, 90; Structural Layering in Jane Austen's Problem Novels, Nineteenth-Century Lit, 92; Jane Austen: Amor and Amoralism, JEGP, 92; Literature of the Western World, Macmillan, 96. **CONTACT ADDRESS** Univ of Arkansas, Fayetteville, Fayetteville, AR 72701.

WILKIE, NANCY C.
PERSONAL Born 12/27/1942, Milwaukee, WI, m **DISCIPLINE** GREEK ARCHEOLOGY, CLASSICS **EDUCATION** Stanford Univ, AB, 64; Univ Minn, MA, 67, PhD(Greek), 75. **CAREER** Instr classics, Macalester Col, 72-75; adj instr, 74-75, adj asst prof classics, 75-79, Prof Classics & Socioanthrop, Carleton Col, 79-, Field dir, Phocis-Doris Exped, Loyola Univ, Chicago, 77-80; Dir, Grevena Project, 88-. **MEMBERSHIPS** Archaeol Inst Am, Pres, 98-; Am Philol Asn; Soc Prof Archaeologists; Soc Am Archaeol; Register of Professional Archaeologists. **RESEARCH** Prehistoric Greek archaeology; archeological sampling. **SELECTED PUBLICATIONS** Auth, The Nichoria Tholos & Area-IV-6, Hesperia, 75; Area I, Evacuations at Nichoria in Southwest Greece, Vol I, Minn, 78; Early Helladic Pottery from Phokis and Doris, Teiresias, 79; Shaft Graves at Nichoria, Temple Univ Aegean Symp, 81; ed. With W.D.E. Coulson Contributions to Aegean Archaeology, CAS, U of MN, 85; auth, Excavations at N. Choria. Vol 2 (U of MN Press) editor with W.A. McDonald, 92; The Earliest Farmers In Macedonia, Antiquity, Vol 0071, 1997; **CONTACT ADDRESS** Carleton Col, 1 N College St, Northfield, MN 55057-4044. **EMAIL** nwilkie@carleton.edu

WILKINS, LEONA B.
PERSONAL Born 02/09/1922, Winston-Salem, NC **DISCIPLINE** MUSIC EDUCATION **EDUCATION** NC Central Univ, BA 1941; Univ MI, MMus 1944, PhD 1971; Sorbonne Univ Paris, France, cert 1968. **CAREER** Raleigh NC, teacher 1942-44; St Louis, teacher 1952-55; Detroit, teacher 1955-64; Bluefield State, 44-45; Hampton Inst, 45-48; TN State Univ, 48-52; E MI Univ 1964-68; Temple Univ, 68-72; Northwestern Univ, assoc prof 1972-; Northwestern Univ, assoc prof emeritus, 88-; Trinity Episcopal Church, Chicago, IL, dir, children's music educ, 90-. **HONORS AND AWARDS** Consult Silver Burdett Music Series 1970-71. **MEMBERSHIPS** Mem Music Educ Conf; Intl Soc of Music Educators; Amer Assn of Univ Profs, Am Orff-Schulwerk Assn; Coll Music Soc; Alpha Kappa Alpha; mem Bicentennial Commn for MENC 1974-76; Comn for Revision of Natl Tchrs Exam for Music Educ 1974-75; consult IL State Arts Plan; Comn for Revision of Music Objectives for Natl Assessment of Educ Progress Task Force; Role of the Arts Comm USOE; MENC; consult Evanston Public School Dist 65. **CONTACT ADDRESS** Sch of Music, Northwestern Univ, Evanston, IL 60201.

WILKINSON, KENTON
PERSONAL Born 06/03/1961, Ann Arbor, MI, m, 1986, 2 children **DISCIPLINE** COMMUNICATION **EDUCATION** Univ Colo, Boulder, BA, 86; Univ Calif, Berkeley, MA, 91; Univ Tex, Austin, PhD, 95. **CAREER** Asst prof, Inst Tecnologico de Monterrey, 94-96; asst prof, Univ Tex at San Antonio, 96-. **HONORS AND AWARDS** Space Across Borders, Dartmouth Col; External Fel, Dartmouth Fall 2000 Humanities Inst. **MEMBERSHIPS** Int Commun Asn, Inter-University Prog for Latino Res, Am Asn of Univ Professors. **RESEARCH** International Communication (specializing in Spanish- and Portuguese-language media), Ethnic-Oriented Media and Political Communication in the United States, New Communication Technologies in Disadvantaged Populations. **SELECTED PUBLICATIONS** Co-ed, Communication Technology Update 1993-1994, Technol Futures, Inc. (Austin, TX), 93; co-ed, Mass Media and Free Trade: NAFTA and the Cultural Industries, Univ Tex Press (Austin, TX), 96. **CONTACT ADDRESS** Dept English, Classics & Philos, Univ of Texas, San Antonio, 6900 N Loop 1604 W, San Antonio, TX 78249-1130. **EMAIL** kwilkinson@utsa.edu

WILL, BARBARA E.
DISCIPLINE ENGLISH LITERATURE **EDUCATION** Duke Univ, PhD, 93. **CAREER** Asst prof, Dartmouth Col. **RESEARCH** Contemp Am lit; women writers. **SELECTED PUBLICATIONS** Auth, 1990 Rencontres Gertrude Stein (film), Univ Geneva; Pound's Feminine Other: A Reading of Canto XXIX, Paideuma, 90; auth, Gertrude Stein, Modernism, and the Problem of Genius. **CONTACT ADDRESS** Dept of English, Dartmouth Col, 6032 Sanborn House, Hanover, NH 03755. **EMAIL** Barbara.E.Will@dartmouth.edu

WILLARD, BARB
DISCIPLINE COMMUNICATION STUDIES **EDUCATION** Fla State Univ, BS; MS; Univ Iowa, PhD. **CAREER** Asst Prof. **RESEARCH** Oral reading; rhetoric of social movements, women and communication. **SELECTED PUBLICATIONS** Auth, Performing Nature: The Bioregional Enactment of the Biotic Community, J NW Commun Asn, 97; Theory and Practice in the Speaking Lab: Speech Assignments and Rhetorical Assumptions, Iowa J Commun, 95. **CONTACT ADDRESS** Dept of Commun, DePaul Univ, 1 E Jackson, Chicago, IL 60604. **EMAIL** bwillard@wppost.depaul.edu

WILLARD, CHARLES A.
DISCIPLINE COMMUNICATIONS **EDUCATION** KS State Tchr Col, BA, 67; Univ IL, MA, 68, PhD, 72. **CAREER** Prof; ch, Univ KS. **RESEARCH** Argumentation, persuasion and soc knowledge. **SELECTED PUBLICATIONS** Auth, Argumentation and the Social Grounds of Knowledge; Theory of Argumentation; Liberalism and the Problem of Knowledge: A New Rhetoric for Modern Democracy. **CONTACT ADDRESS** Dept of Commun, Univ of Louisville, 2301 S 3rd St, Louisville, KY 40292. **EMAIL** cawill01@ulkyvm.louisville.edu

WILLARD, THOMAS SPAULDING
PERSONAL Born 11/25/1944, Richmond, VA, m, 1976, 2 children **DISCIPLINE** ENGLISH **EDUCATION** George Wash Univ, BA, 67; MA, 70; Univ Toronto, PhD, 78. **MEMBERSHIPS** MLA. **RESEARCH** Teaching of literature, including Shakespeare and the Bible **SELECTED PUBLICATIONS** Ed, Visionary Tactics: Essays on Northrop Frye's Criticism, 92; ed, Jean D'Espagnet, the Summary of Physics Restored, 00. **CONTACT ADDRESS** Dept English, Univ of Arizona, PO Box 210067, Tucson, AZ 85721-0067. **EMAIL** willard@u.arizona.edu

WILLERTON, CHRISTIAN WILLIAM
PERSONAL Born 08/16/1947, Borger, TX, m, 1969, 3 children **DISCIPLINE** VICTORIAN & MODERN LITERATURE **EDUCATION** TX Christian Univ, BA, 69; Univ NC, Chapel Hill, MA, 70, PhD, 79. **CAREER** Instr, 70-73, asst prof, 76-81, assoc prof, 81-85, Prof Eng, Abilene Christian Univ, 85. **MEMBERSHIPS** Nat Coun Tchr(s) Eng; Conf Christianity & Lit; Pater Soc; Electronic Lit Org. **RESEARCH** Hypertext. **SELECTED PUBLICATIONS** Auth, John Payne, In: Dict of Literary Biography, #35; Reginald Gibbons, In: Dict of Literary Biography, #120; auth, Londale Hotel (hypertext), In: Behind the Lines. **CONTACT ADDRESS** Dept of Eng, Abilene Christian Univ, ACU Box 28242, Abilene, TX 79699-8242. **EMAIL** willerto@nicanor.acu.edu

WILLETTS, ELIZABETH M.
PERSONAL Born 11/19/1969, Toms River, NJ, s **DISCIPLINE** THEATRE ARTS **EDUCATION** Rutgers Univ, BA, 92; Montclair Univ, MA, 94; Drew Univ, DLH. **CAREER** Adj prof, Brookdale Col, 94-96; adj prof, Monmouth Univ, 98; lecturer, Ocean Co Col, 95-. **HONORS AND AWARDS** Grad Assistantship, Montclair State; Newark Star Ledger's Best comic Actress, Who's Who Among Am Women. **MEMBERSHIPS** OCPGA, AAUW, NOW. **RESEARCH** Shakespearean literature, French Absurdist theatre genres; Dramaturgy. **SELECTED PUBLICATIONS** Auth, Museum Peace, auth, Sibling Rivalry. **CONTACT ADDRESS** Dept Humanities, Ocean County Col, PO Box 2001, Toms River, NJ 08754-2001. **EMAIL** bethwil@hometowncomm.com

WILLEY, EDWARD
DISCIPLINE ENGLISH LITERATURE **EDUCATION** Univ NC, PhD, 68. **CAREER** Dept Eng, Clemson Univ **RESEARCH** 17th and 18th century literature. **SELECTED PUBLICATIONS** Auth, Matriarchs, Re: Arts & Letters, 95; Neoclassic, Re: Arts & Letters, 95; 1940s Southern Circus, Crossroads: Jour Southern Cult. **CONTACT ADDRESS** Clemson Univ, 605 Strode, Clemson, SC 29634. **EMAIL** wedward@clemson.edu

WILLHEIM, IMANUEL
DISCIPLINE MUSIC **EDUCATION** St Scholastica Col, BM; Northwestern Univ, MM, Univ Ill, MA, PhD. **CAREER** Prof emer, Hartt School Music. **SELECTED PUBLICATIONS** Auth, pubs on aesthetics of music & history of performance practices. **CONTACT ADDRESS** Hartt Sch Music, Univ of Hartford, 200 Bloomfield Ave, West Hartford, CT 06117.

WILLIAMS, BRUCE
DISCIPLINE FILM THEORY, HISTORY, HISPANIC LANGUAGES & LITERATURES **EDUCATION** Univ Calif-Los Angeles, PhD, 86. **CAREER** Assoc prof. **RESEARCH** Film theory and cinema history and aesthetics. **SELECTED PUBLICATIONS** Publ on res interest. **CONTACT ADDRESS** Dept of Language and Cultures, William Paterson Col of New Jersey, 300 Pompton Rd., Wayne, NJ 07470. **EMAIL** williamsb@wpunj.edu

WILLIAMS, CARMALETTA M.
PERSONAL Born 02/17/1951, MO, d, 2 children **DISCIPLINE** ENGLISH **EDUCATION** Univ Mo Kansas City, BA, 83; MA, 85; Univ Kans, PhD, 01. **CAREER** Assoc prof, Johnson County Community Col, 88-. **HONORS AND AWARDS** Carnegie Found; Johnson County Community College Distinguished Svc Award; Burlington Norther-Sante Fe Railroad Fac Achievement Award; Fulbright Hays Award; Innovation of the Year Award, League for Innovation. **MEMBERSHIPS** MLA, Col Lang Asn, Community Col Humanities Asn. **RESEARCH** African American Migration. **SELECTED PUBLICATIONS** Auth, "A Teacher Becoming: An Interview with Carmaletta M Williams, Kans English, (99); auth, "Legacy of the Harlem Renaissance, "Cottonwood, (00); auth, "Lacey's Longing," AmerAsian Jour, (01). **CONTACT ADDRESS** 12345 College Blvd, Overland Park, KS 66210-1283. **EMAIL** cwilliam@jccc.net

WILLIAMS, DANIEL E.
DISCIPLINE ENGLISH **EDUCATION** Univ Wash, BA, 73; Univ Denver, MA, 76, 84, PhD, 80. **CAREER** Assoc prof English, Univ Miss. **RESEARCH** The theft of authorship. **CONTACT ADDRESS** Dept of English, Univ of Mississippi, University, MS 38677.

WILLIAMS, DAVID E.
PERSONAL Born 09/14/1963, Heath, OH, m, 1990, 1 child **DISCIPLINE** RHETORIC **EDUCATION** Otterbein Col, BA; Northern Ill Univ, MA; Ohio Univ, 90. **CAREER** Visiting asst prof, Kent State, 90-91; Asst/Prof, dir Forensic Prog, Tx Tech, 91-. **MEMBERSHIPS** Nat Commun Asn. **RESEARCH** American temperance movement; crisis communication. **SELECTED PUBLICATIONS** Auth, The Question of Audience in Forensic Education, The Southern J of Forensics, 98; auth, Over-quantification in Public Address Events, The Southern J of Forensics, 97; auth, Impromptu Speaking, Understanding Forensics: Direction, Coaching and Performing Competitive Individual Events, Ally & Bacon, in press; auth, Educational Criteria in Forensics: An Argument for Lincoln-Douglas Debate, Nat Forensic J, 96; auth, The Drive for Prohibition: A Transition from Social Reform to Legislative Reform, The Southern Commun J, 96; coauth, Teaching Honors Public Speaking, Basic Commun Course Annual, 98; Introducing Par-

liamentary Debate in the Public Speaking Course, Teaching the Public Speaking Course, Kendall/Hunt, 97; coauth, Introducing Parliamentary Debate in the Argumentation and Debate Course, The Forensic, 96; coauth, Judging the Space/Time Case in Parliamentary Debate, Southern Forensic J, 96; coauth, Burkian Counternature and the Vigilant Response: An Anticipatory model of Crisis Management and Technology, Commun in Crisis: Theory and Application. **CONTACT ADDRESS** Dept of Commun Studies, Texas Tech Univ, Lubbock, TX 79409-3080. **EMAIL** mqdav@ttacs.ttu.edu

WILLIAMS, EDWIN W.

PERSONAL Born 06/22/1936, Belzoni, MS, m, 1997, 2 children **DISCIPLINE** ENGLISH **EDUCATION** Millsaps Col, BA, 58; Duke Univ, MDiv, 62; Univ NC Chapel Hill, PhD, 72. **CAREER** Asst prof, 65-67, Bibl Stud, Brevard Col; asst prof, 72-78, asst dean, 78-79, assoc prof, 78-85, prof, engl, 85-89, prof emeritus, 99-, E Tenn St Univ. **RESEARCH** James Joyce, Irish Stud, Victorian period. **CONTACT ADDRESS** Dept of English, East Tennessee State Univ, PO Box 70683, Johnson City, TN 37614. **EMAIL** williaew@Access.ETSU.Edu

WILLIAMS, EMILY A.

PERSONAL Born, VA, m **DISCIPLINE** BRITISH LITERATURE, CARIBBEAN POETRY **EDUCATION** Saint Paul's Col, BA, 77; Va Commonwealth Univ, MA, 90; Clark Atlanta Univ, DAH, 97. **CAREER** Information Officer/Regional Grants Coordr, Va Commission for the Arts, 80-85; Arts Grants Prog Coordr, Ga Coun for the Arts, 86-87; Grants Dir, City of Atlanta Bureau of Cultural Affairs, 87-91; instr, English and Speech, Clark Atlanta Univ, 91-92; continuing ed instr, Spelman Col, 94-95, lectr, 95-96; instr, English, Morehouse Col, 92-96, asst prof, 97-. **HONORS AND AWARDS** Morehouse Col Fac Res grant for book publication, 97-98, 99-2000; Chair's Awd for Exemplary Service to the Dept of English, 98-99; Scholar-in-residence, New York Univ Fac Resource Network, summer 99; Summer Scholar, New York Univ Fac Resource Network, 98; Fulbright Scholar, Univ of the West Indies, Kingston, Jamaica, 2000-2001; listed in Contemporary Authors. **MEMBERSHIPS** Col Lang Asn, Charles Chestnutt Asn, Popular Culture Asn, Alpha Kappa Mu Nat Honor Soc, Saint Paul's Col Alumni Asn, Va Commonwealth Univ Alumni Asn, Delta Sigma Theta Sorority. **RESEARCH** Anglophone Caribbean literature, Francophone Caribbean literature, post-colonial studies. **SELECTED PUBLICATIONS** Auth, "Destiny," (poem) Richmond Quart (82); auth, "Keep the Candle Burning: Morehouse College into the 21st Century," J of African Am Men (95); auth, "Whose Words Are These? Lost Identity and Search for Self in Brathwaite's Poetry," CLA J (96); interview, "Harryette Mullen: The Queen of Hip Hyperbole Speaks Out," African Am Rev (2000); auth, Poetic Negotiation of Identity in the Works of Edward Kamau Brathwaite, Claire Harris, Olive Senior, and David Dabydeen, New York: Mellon Press (99); interview, "Claire Harris: A Caribbean Writer Speaks From Canada," conducted July 99 in Calgary, Alberta, Can (forthcoming 2000); auth, A Guide to Anglophone Caribbean Poetry, 1970-2000, Greenwood Press (2001). **CONTACT ADDRESS** Dept English, Morehouse Col, 830 Westview Dr SW, Atlanta, GA 30314-3773. **EMAIL** ewill35001@aol.com

WILLIAMS, FREDERICK

PERSONAL Born Denver, CO **DISCIPLINE** CLASSICAL GREEK, LATIN LANGUAGE, LITERATURE **EDUCATION** Univ Tex, BA, 65; Univ Col, MA, 72; Cornell Univ, PhD, 76. **CAREER** Instr, Converse Col, 68-71; asst prof, Cornell Univ, 76-77; asst prof, assoc prof, dir, SIU Carbondale,77-. **HONORS AND AWARDS** SIUC Teach of Yr Awd, 84. **MEMBERSHIPS** APA **RESEARCH** Performance translations of Greek and Roman drama; elementary language instruction; Greek and Latin poetry. **SELECTED PUBLICATIONS** Auth, Elementary Classical Greek, SIU Press, 83, rev ed 91; auth, A Cry of Kings: Six Greek Dramas in Modern English, Stipes, 99; auth, "Neapolitanus II.C.32: a New Source for the Text of Pausanias," Scrip 36 (82): 190-218; auth, "Odysseus' Homecoming as a Parody of Homeric Formal Welcomes," Classic World 79 (86): 395-97; co-auth, "Lewes at Colonus: an Early Victorian View of Translation from the Greek," Mod Lang Rev 82 (87): 293-312. **CONTACT ADDRESS** Dept For Lang and Lit, So Illinois Univ, Carbondale, Carbondale, IL 62901-4521. **EMAIL** rickw@siu.edu

WILLIAMS, GARETH D.

PERSONAL Born 05/29/1965, Wales, s **DISCIPLINE** CLASSICS **EDUCATION** Cambridge Univ England, BA 86. **CAREER** Columbia Univ, asst prof, 95-98. **MEMBERSHIPS** APA **RESEARCH** Silven Latin; Pros and Poetry. **SELECTED PUBLICATIONS** Auth, Banished Voices: Readings in Ovid's Exile Poetry, Cambridge, 94. **CONTACT ADDRESS** Dept of Classics, Columbia Univ, 614 Hamilton Hall, MC 2861, New York, NY 10027. **EMAIL** gdw5@columbia.edu

WILLIAMS, GARY

PERSONAL Born 05/06/1947, m, 1970, 2 children **DISCIPLINE** ENGLISH **EDUCATION** Washington Univ. (St. Louis) AB, 69; Cornell, MA, PhD, 73. **CAREER** Prof English, Univ Idaho. **HONORS AND AWARDS** Phi Beta Kappa, 69. **RESEARCH** James Fenimore Cooper; Julia Ward Howe; 19th Century American Literature. **SELECTED PUBLICATIONS** Fel Publ, Edition of Cooper's Notions of the Americans, SUNY, 91; auth, Hungry Heart: The Literary Emergence of Julia Ward Howe, Amherst: U. Mass Press, 99. **CONTACT ADDRESS** Dept of English, Univ of Idaho, Moscow, ID 83844-1102. **EMAIL** jwg@uidaho.edu.

WILLIAMS, GEORGE W.

PERSONAL Born 10/10/1922, Charleston, SC, m, 1953, 3 children **DISCIPLINE** ENGLISH **EDUCATION** Yale Univ, BA, 47; Univ Vir, MA, 49; PhD, 54. **CAREER** Asst prof to assoc prof to prof to emer to chmn, Duke Univ, 57-; vis prof, West Point, 82-83. **HONORS AND AWARDS** Guggenheim Fel, 77-78; Outstanding Prof, 66; John Hurt Fisher Awd, SAMLA, 01. **MEMBERSHIPS** MLA; SAMLA; SE Ren Conf. **RESEARCH** Shakespeare; bibliography; textual criticism. **SELECTED PUBLICATIONS** Ed, The Changling, 66; co-ed, King Henry VI, pts 2 and 3, 67; ed, Complete Poetry of Richard Crashaw, 70; co-ed, Renaissance Papers, 16 vol, 60-70, 91-96; ed, Jacob Eckhard's Choirmaster's Book of 1809, 71; auth, "The Year's Contribution to Shakespeare's Studies: Textual Studies," Shakespeare Surv (78-82); gen ed, The Arden Shakespeare, 10 vols, 99; contrb ed, The Dramatic Works in the Beaumont and Fletcher Canon, 10 vols, 66-96; auth, St Michael's, Charleston 1751-1951, 51, 01. **CONTACT ADDRESS** English Dept, Duke Univ, PO Box 90015, Durham, NC 27708-0015.

WILLIAMS, HAZEL BROWNE

PERSONAL Born Kansas City, MO, w **DISCIPLINE** ENGLISH **EDUCATION** Univ of KS, AB 1927; Univ of KS, MA 1929; Columbia Univ, MA 1943; Pi Lambda Theta; NYork Univ, PhD 1953; Univ of Berlin, Kappa Delta Pi foreign study 1930; Alpha Kappa Alpha Foreign fellowship. **CAREER** Univ of MO KC, prof emeritus english educ; Southern Univ, visiting lectr 1967; Atlanta Univ, 46-47; Vienna Austria, fulbright exchange teacher 1956-57; TN A&I State Univ, prof 1953-56; NY Univ, instr 1948-51; Louisville Muni Coll, asst prof 1932-42; KC MO Public Schools, english teacher 1927-32. **MEMBERSHIPS** Life mem NCTE; Internatl Soc of Gen Semantics; inst for Gen Semantics; MLA, AAUP; Phi Beat Kappa; Gr Assn of Chappers; MO State Tchrs Assn Golden Heritage; mem NAACP; mem KC NAACP Exec Bd; YWCA; life mem Univ of MO KC Friends of the Library; Univ of KS Alumni Assn. **CONTACT ADDRESS** School of Education, Univ of Missouri, Kansas City, Kansas City, MO 64110.

WILLIAMS, HELEN ELIZABETH

PERSONAL Born 12/13/1933, Timmonsville, SC **DISCIPLINE** LIBRARY SCIENCE **EDUCATION** Morris College, BA 1954; Phoenix College, Certificate 1959; Atlanta Univ, MSLS 1960; Queens College, Certificate 1966; Univ of IL-Urbana, CAS 1969; Univ of Wis-Madison, PhD 1983. **CAREER** Williams Memorial High School, St George, SC, teacher/librarian 1955-57; Carver High School, Spindale, NC, teacher/librarian 1957-58; Percy Julian Elem Sch, librarian 1959-60; Brooklyn Public Library, librarian 1960-62; Mt Vernon Public Library, librarian 1963-64; Jenkins Hill High School,librarian/teacher 1964-66; Westchester Co Library System, librarian 1966; White Plains City Public Schools, librarian 1966-68, 69-73; Bro-Dart Inc, library consultant 1976-81; Univ of MD, College Park, MD, lecturer 1981-83, professor 1983-. **HONORS AND AWARDS** Beta Phi Mu Intl Library Sci Honor Frat 1960-; Fellow Higher Education Act 1966; Fellow Natl Defense Educ Act 1967-68; Fellow Comm on Institutional Cooperation 1973-76; Book Reviewer School Library Journal 1981-; Disting Alumnus Awd Morris Coll 1985; Disting Alumni of the Year Citation Natl Assoc for Equal Oppor in Higher Educ 1986; Fulbright Professorship, University of the South Pacific, Suva, FIJI 1988-89; editor "The High/Low Consensus," Bro-Dart Publishing Co 1980; editor "Independent Reading, K-3" Bro-Dart Publishing Co 1980; editor Books By African American Authros and Illustrators for Children and Young Adults, American Library Assn. **MEMBERSHIPS** Mem Library Adminis and Managerial Assoc 1977-80; mem Black Caucus of the Amer Library Assoc 1977-; mem MD Educ Media Organization 1981-; mem Amer Library Assoc 1977-; mem Amer Assoc of School Librarians; mem Young Adults Serv Div; mem Assoc of Library Services to Children; member National Council of Negro Women, Inc 1990-. **CONTACT ADDRESS** Professor of Librarianship, Univ of Maryland, Col Park, Hornbake Bldg Rm 4105, College Park, MD 20742.

WILLIAMS, JEFF

PERSONAL Born 12/14/1958, Long Island, NY, d **DISCIPLINE** ENGLISH **EDUCATION** State Univ NYork, BA, 84; PhD, 90. **CAREER** Instr, SUNY, 84-89; Adj Prof, Mercy Col, 90; Asst Prof to Assoc Prof, East Carolina Univ, 90-98; Asst Prof to Assoc prof, Univ of Mo, 98-. **HONORS AND AWARDS** Res Awd, Univ Mo, 00; Big 12 Fel, Univ Okla, 99; Res Awd, ECU Col of Arts, 96; NEH Grant for Summer Seminar, 95; Scholarship, Dartmouth Col, 92, 89. **MEMBERSHIPS** MLA, MMLA, MLG, SSNL, SCE, ASA, AAUP, Radical Caucus, Joseph Conrad Soc. **RESEARCH** Literary and Critical Theory; The History of Criticism; The Novel; Modern British Literature; contemporary American Literature and Culture; Cultural Studies. **SELECTED PUBLICATIONS** Auth, Theory and the Novel: Narrative Reflexivity in the British tradition, Cambridge Univ Press, 98; ed, PC Wars: Politics and Theory in the academy, Routledge Press, 95; co-ed, The Norton anthology of Literary Theory and criticism, Norton & Co., forthcoming; ed, The Institution of Literature, SUNY Press, forthcoming; auth, The Theory Market: Criticism and the University, Univ Minn Press, forthcoming; auth, "The New Belletrism," Critics and Criticism, (99): 414-442; auth, "Conrad and the Problem of Professionalism," in approaches to Teaching Conrad's Heart of Darkness and The Secret Sharer, MLA, forthcoming; auth, "The Issue of corporations: Richard Powers' Gain," Cultural Logic, 00; auth, "Brave new University," College English, (99): 742-751; auth, Education in the global Economy: The Rhetoric of Reform, Lawrence Erlbaum, 99. **CONTACT ADDRESS** Dept English, Univ of Missouri, Columbia, 107 Tate Hall, Columbia, MO 65211-1500. **EMAIL** williamsjeff@missouri.edu

WILLIAMS, JOHN ALFRED

PERSONAL Born 12/05/1925, Jackson, MS, m, 3 children **DISCIPLINE** AFRICAN-AMERICAN LITERATURE **EDUCATION** Syracuse Univ, BA 1950, Grad Sch, 1950-51. **CAREER** Col of the Virgin Islands, lecturer black lit 1968; CUNY, lecturer creative writing 1968-69; Sarah Lawrence Col, guest writer 1972-73; Univ of CA Santa Barbara, regents lecturer 1973; CUNY LaGuardia Comm Col, disting prof 1973-78; Univ of HI, vstg prof 1974; Boston Univ, vstg prof 1978-79; Exxon vstg prf New York Univ 1986-87; Rutgers Univ, prof of Engl 1979-93, Paul Robeson Prof of English, 90-93; Bard Ctr, fellow, 94-95. **HONORS AND AWARDS** Syracuse Univ, DLih, 1995; Univ Mass, Dartmouth, DLih, 1978; Natl Inst of Arts and Letters, 1962; Syracuse Univ, Centenial Medal, Outstanding Achievement, 1970; Natl Endowment for the Arts, 1977; US Observer, 23rd Premio Casa Awd, 1985, Disting Writer Awd, Middle Atlantic Writers, 1987; NJ Lit Hall of Fame, Michael Awd, 1987; Drama: Last Flight from Ambo Ber, 1981; August Forty-Five, 1991: Vangui (libreto), 1999; Safari West, 1998, American Book Awd, 1983, 1998. **MEMBERSHIPS** Columnist, stringer, spec assignment, staff The Natl Leader, Progressive Herald, Assoc Negro Press, The Age, The Defender, Post-Standard, The Tribune, The Courier; Holiday Magazine Europe 1965-66; corresp Newsweek Africa 1964-65; dir of info Amer Comm on Africa 1957, spec events WOV NY 1957; corresp Ebony-Jet Spain 1958-59; WNET-TV writer, narrator on location Nigeria, Spain, 1964-65; bd of dir Coord Council Literary Mags 1983-85; bd of dir Jrnl of African Civilizations 1980-;contrib ed Politicks 1977, Amer Jnrl 1972-74; ed bd Audience Mag 1970-72; contrib ed Herald-Tribune Book Week 1963-65; asst to publ Abelard Schuman 1957-58; editor & publ Negro Mkt Newsletter 1956-57. **SELECTED PUBLICATIONS** Auth, Africa, Her History, Lands & People, Cooper Square Pr, 63; auth, Flashbacks: A 20-Year Diary of Article Writing, Doubleday, 73; auth, Minorities in the City, Harper & Row, 75; auth, !Click Song, Houghton Mifflin, 82; auth, The Berhama Account, New Horizon Pr, 85; auth, Jacob's Ladder, Thunder's Mouth Pr, 87; auth, If I Stop I'll Die: The Comedy and Tragedy of Richard Pryor, Thunder's Mouth Pr, 91; ed, Bridges: Lit Across Cultures, McGraw-Hill, 94; ed, Street Guide to African Am in Paris, 2nd ed, CEAA (Paris), 96; auth, Clifford's Blues, Coffee House Pr, 99; ed, Introduction to Lit, 2nd ed, McGraw-Hill, 94. **CONTACT ADDRESS** Barbara Hogenson Agency, 165 West End Ave, New York, NY 10024.

WILLIAMS, JOHN HOWARD

PERSONAL Born 11/19/1946, Louisville, KY, m, 1969, 2 children **DISCIPLINE** FRENCH LANGUAGES & LITERATURE, CLASSICS **EDUCATION** David Lipscomb Col, BA, 67; Univ Wis-Madison, MA, 68, PhD(French), 72. **CAREER** Instr French, Tenn Technol Univ, 68-69; Fulbright advan teaching fel Am lit, Univ Besancon, 71-72; asst prof French, Eastern Ky Univ, 72-74; asst prof, 74-76, assoc prof, 76-82, Prof French & Chmn Dept, Abilene Christian Univ, 82-. **MEMBERSHIPS** MLA; Am Asn Teachers Fr. **RESEARCH** Contemporary French culture; 16th century French Poetry. **CONTACT ADDRESS** Abilene Christian Univ, Station Box 824, Abilene, TX 79601.

WILLIAMS, JOHN S.

DISCIPLINE ENGLISH LITERATURE **EDUCATION** Cornell Col, BA, 58; Univ Chicago, MA, 61, PhD, 69. **CAREER** Prof, Univ Pacific . **SELECTED PUBLICATIONS** Auth, publ(s) on Faulkner, Sartre, Dostoevsky, and Jerzy Kosinski. **CONTACT ADDRESS** Eng Dept, Univ of the Pacific, Stockton, Pacific Ave, PO Box 3601, Stockton, CA 95211.

WILLIAMS, JOSEPH M.

PERSONAL Born 08/18/1933, Cleveland, OH, m, 1960, 2 children **DISCIPLINE** ENGLISH, LINGUISTICS **EDUCATION** Miami Univ, BA, 55, MA, 60; Univ Wis, PhD(English), 66. **CAREER** Instr English, Miami Univ, 59-60; from instr to assoc prof, 65-76, Prof English, Univ Chicago, 76-, Consult med writing, Am Med Asn, 66. **MEMBERSHIPS** MLA; Lang Soc Am; Col English Asn. **RESEARCH** Stylistics; rhetoric; generative grammars. **SELECTED PUBLICATIONS CONTACT ADDRESS** Dept of English, Univ of Chicago, 5845 Ellis Av, Chicago, IL 60637-1476.

WILLIAMS, KENNY J.
DISCIPLINE ENGLISH LITERATURE **EDUCATION** PA Univ, PhD, 61. **CAREER** Prof, Duke Univ. **SELECTED PUBLICATIONS** Auth, Prairie Voices: A Literary History of Chicago from the Frontier to 1893, Townsend, 80; A Storyteller for a City: Sherwood Anderson s Chicago, Northern Ill, 88; co-ed, Chicago s Public Wits, LSU, 83. **CONTACT ADDRESS** Eng Dept, Duke Univ, Durham, NC 27706.

WILLIAMS, LINDA F.
PERSONAL Born 08/02/1954, Greenwood, SC, s **DISCIPLINE** MUSIC **EDUCATION** Univ Mich MA, 76; Ind Univ, PhD, 95. **CAREER** Univ of Pittsburgh, 85-87; Univ of Zimbabwe Col of Music, 92-93; Mt. Hozyoke Col, 94-96; Bates Col, 96-. **HONORS AND AWARDS** Fulbright Grant: Zimbabwe, Africa, 92, National Endowment for The Humanities, 99. **MEMBERSHIPS** Society for African Studies Asn, Center for Black Music Research, International Jazz Archives. **RESEARCH** The Study of Transatlantic Influences of African American Music in Africa (Both West Africa and South Africa). **SELECTED PUBLICATIONS** Auth, Bibliographic Entry in African Music: A Bibliographical Guide to the Traditional, Popular, Art, and Liturgical Musics of Sub-Saharan Africa by John Gray, 97; auth, "Radical Empiricism: Double Vision and Negotiation," New Directions: Readings in African Diaspora Music, 1: 84-95; auth, "Straight-Fashioned Melodies"--The Transatlantic Interplay of American Music in Zimbabwe American Music, 15:285-304; rev, "Africa in Scott Joplin's Music," New Directions: Readings in African Disapora Music, Lems-Dworkin Publisher, 2: 71-74; auth, "A Joyful Noise: African American Music During the Civil Rights Movement," The Movement Revisited, National Endowment for the Arts Foundation, 99; rev, "A Day for the Hunter, A Day for the Prey: Popular Music and Power in Haiti, Gage Averill (Chicago: Univ of Chicago Press), American Ethnologist 26 (97); rev, "Music Modernity, and the Global Imagination: South Africa and the West, Veit Erlmann, (New York: Oxford Univ Press), 99; Quarterly Journal of the Music Library Assoc (forthcoming, Dec. 99); auth, Who Will Revere the Black Woman? Anthology of African American Female Musicians, Garland Publishing, Inc. (New York, New York); auth, "Reconciling Divergent Possibilities Through Radical Empiricism," International Jaxx Archives Journal, Univ of Pittsburgh International Academy of Jazz; auth, "Stepping Into Zimbabwe," Social Change and Development, Mambo Press (Gweru, Zimbabwe). **CONTACT ADDRESS** Dept Music, Bates Col, 75 Russell St, Lewiston, ME 04240-6044. **EMAIL** lwilliam@bates.edu

WILLIAMS, MELVIN GILBERT
PERSONAL Born 11/07/1937, Collingswood, NJ, m, 1958, 3 children **DISCIPLINE** ENGLISH **EDUCATION** Univ PA, AB, 60, MA, 61; Univ MA, PhD, 73, dr minis, Hartford seminary. **CAREER** From instr to asst prof, 61-73, assoc prof eng, Am Int Col, 73-, interim pastor, United Church of Christ in MA, CT; prof ch, dept Eng commun, 89. **HONORS AND AWARDS** Ordained Minister, United Church of Christ, certified spec in edu United Church of Christ. **MEMBERSHIPS** MLA; New Eng MLA; Col English Asn; Conf Christianity & Lit. **RESEARCH** Bible as lit; relig and lit; African Am Lit. **SELECTED PUBLICATIONS** Auth, Martin Luther: Portraits in prose, Christian Century, 10/67; Samuel Johnson and the concrete universal, 3-4/72 & Black literature: A stereophonic experience for monophonic students, 3/77, CEA Critic; The Psalms as literature, Christianity & Lit, summer 73; The Last Word, Boston, 73; The Gospel according to Simple, spring 77 & Black literature vs Black studies: Three lynchings, fall 77, Black Am Lit Forum. **CONTACT ADDRESS** Dept of Eng, American Intl Col, 1000 State St, Springfield, MA 01109-3151. **EMAIL** revdrmel@aol.com

WILLIAMS, PENNY
PERSONAL m, 1 child **DISCIPLINE** JOURNALISM **EDUCATION** CA State Univ Northridge, BA, 80; SUNY Buffalo, MS, 91; PhD, 98. **CAREER** Co-anchor/reporter, KCSN-FM, 77-79; anchor/reporter/producer/assignment ed/shooter, KNAZ-TV, 80; gen assignment reporter and anchor, WAVY-TV, 80-82; gen assignment/med reporter and anchor, WGRZ-TV, 82-87; weekend anchor/reporter, WBEN-AM, 87-88; asst prof, Buffalo State Col, 88-95; publ affairs host and prod, WUTV, 91-93; asst prof, St Bonaventure Univ, 95-. **HONORS AND AWARDS** NY AP Broadcasters' Awd; tv journalist; fac adviser, wsbu-fm; internship coord for the sch of journalism and ma commun. **MEMBERSHIPS** Buffalo Broadcasters' Assn, Radio-Television News Dirs Assoc; Soc Prof Journalists. **RESEARCH** Broadcast media, commun, and journalism. **SELECTED PUBLICATIONS** Auth, articles on broadcast journalism for Communicator, and an article on electronic database reporting for SPJ's Quill. **CONTACT ADDRESS** St. Bonaventure Univ, Saint Bonaventure, NY 14778. **EMAIL** pwilliam@sbu.edu

WILLIAMS, PETER
DISCIPLINE MUSIC **EDUCATION** Cambridge Univ, PhD. **CAREER** Musicol prof, Duke Univ. **HONORS AND AWARDS** Center Performance Pract Studies dir. **SELECTED PUBLICATIONS** Auth, The Organ Music of J.S. Bach. **CONTACT ADDRESS** Dept of Music, Duke Univ, Mary Duke Biddle Music Bldg, Durham, NC 27706.

WILLIAMS, PHILIP F. C.
PERSONAL Born, AR, m, 1990, 1 child **DISCIPLINE** CHINESE LITERATURE **EDUCATION** UCLA, MA, 81, PhD, 85. **CAREER** Vis asst prof, Chinese, 86, UCLA; contract escort, Chinese interpreter, 86-96, US Dept of St, Office of Language Svcs; asst prof, Chinese, 86-92, Ariz St Univ; post doc res fel, 90-91, Fairbank Center for East Asian Research, Harvard Univ; asst prof, 91-92 Univ of Vermont; assoc prof, Chinese Literature and Interdisciplinary Humanities, 93-99, Ariz St Univ; prof, Chinese Literature and Interdisciplinary Humanities, Ariz St Univ, 00-. **HONORS AND AWARDS** Phi Beta Kappa, 78; UCLA Alumni Asn Awd for Academic Achievement, 81; Humanities Res Awd, AZ St Univ, 89; Svc Awd, AZ St Univ, 97; Pres Southwest Conf on Asian Stud, 96-97. **MEMBERSHIPS** Council of Conf Member of the Asn for Asian Stud; Exec Bd Mem of the Southwest Conf on Asian Stud; Exec Comm of the Am Asn for Chinese Comparative Lit; AZ Beta Chapter of the Phi Beta Kappa Honorary Soc. **RESEARCH** Chinese literature and society, esp in 20th century; Chinese language and cultural history. **SELECTED PUBLICATIONS** Auth, Village Echoes: The Fiction of Wu Zuxiang, Westview Press, 93; auth, Chinese the Easy Way, Hauppauge, NY Barron's Ed Series, 99; auth, Selected Papers of the 1997 Southwest Conference on Asian Studies, Tempe: Southwest Conf on Asian Stud, 98. **CONTACT ADDRESS** Dept of Languages and Lit, Arizona State Univ, PO Box 870202, Tempe, AZ 85287-0202. **EMAIL** pfwms@juno.com

WILLIAMS, ROLAND L.
PERSONAL Born Philadelphia, PA, m **DISCIPLINE** ENGLISH **EDUCATION** Univ Pa, BA; PhD. **CAREER** Lectr, Univ Delaware, 88-89; instr, Oh State Univ, 90-93; adj prof, Otterbein Col, 94; asst prof, Oh State Univ, 93-95; vis asst prof, Haverford Col, 99-00; asst prof, Temple Univ, 95-. **HONORS AND AWARDS** Penn-in-London Fel; Macarthur Fel; Fontaine Fel; ACA Artist Res; Outstand Teach Awd; Sum res Fel; NEH Stp. **MEMBERSHIPS** ASA; CLA; MLA; NAAAS. **SELECTED PUBLICATIONS** Auth, African American Autobiography and the Quest for Freedom, Greenwood Press (Westport, Conn), 00; auth, Black from Reel to Reel: An Analysis of Black Buddies on the Silver Screen, in progress; auth, The Groundskeeper, in progress; "Briton Hammon," The Oxford Companion to African American Literature, OUP (NY), 97; auth, "All God's Dangers," The Oxford Companion to African American Literature, OUP (NY), 97; rev, Ten Is the Age of Darkness: The Black Bildungsroman, by Geta LeSeur, Res Afr Lit 28 (97); rev, Things of Darkness: Economies of Race and Gender in Early Modern England, by Kim Hall, Res Afr Lit 29 (98); rev, An Enchanting Darkness: The American Vision of Africa in the 20th Century, by D Hickey and K Wylie, Res Afr Lit 29 (98); rev, Woodholme: A Black Man's Story of Growing Up Alone, by Dewayne Wick- ham, Afr Am Rev 33 (99): 174; auth, "John Marrant," African American Writers, 1745-1945, Greenwood Press (Westport Conn), 99. **CONTACT ADDRESS** Dept English, Haverford Col, 370 Lancaster Ave, Haverford, PA 19041-1336. **EMAIL** rwilli00@nimbus.ocis.temple.edu

WILLIAMS, SEAN
PERSONAL Born 08/17/1959, Berkeley, CA, m, 1984, 1 child **DISCIPLINE** MUSIC; ETHNOMUSICOLOGY **EDUCATION** Univ Cal-Berkeley, BA, 81; Univ Wash, MA, 85, PhD, 90. **CAREER** Columbia Univ, asst Prof, 90-91, Evergreen State Col, Mem Fac, 91-; Managing Ed, Asian Mus J, 96-. **HONORS AND AWARDS** Fulbright-Hays Doctoral Dissertation fel; Ford Found Dissertation fel. **MEMBERSHIPS** Soc Ethnomusicology, reg ch, 83-84, 98-99; Soc Asian Music. **RESEARCH** Music & language; music and urbanization; popular music; issues of race, class and gender, identity and ethnicity in music; Sundanese (Indonesian) music; Irish music. **SELECTED PUBLICATIONS** Co-ed & author several articles, The Garland Encyclopedia of World Music, Southeast Asia, v4, Garland Publishing, 98; Constructing Gender in Sundanese Music, in Yearbook for Traditional Music, v30, 98; Competition in the Sundanese Performing Arts of West Java, Indonesia, in Current Musicology, v62, 98; World Beat: Modern Colonialism or Indigenous Synthesis? ReView 17/1:31, 95; Our Laughter Balances Our Tears: Humor in Sundanese Arts, Balungan 5/2, 93; The Urbanization of Tembang Sunda, an Aristocratic Musical Genre of West Java, Indonesia, Univ Wash, 90; Current Developments in Sundanese Popular Music, Asian Music 21/1, 90; auth, "The Voice of the Ancestral Ship: Highland Music of West Java," Oxford University Press, 01. **CONTACT ADDRESS** Evergreen State Col, 2700 Evergreen Pky NW, Olympia, WA 98505. **EMAIL** williams@evergreen.edu

WILLIAMS, SUSAN
PERSONAL Born 01/07/1963, Atlanta, GA, m, 1998, 1 child **DISCIPLINE** ENGLISH **EDUCATION** Yale Univ, BA, 85, MA, 89, PhD, 91. **CAREER** Assoc prof English, Ohio State. **MEMBERSHIPS** Modern Lang Assoc; Phi Beta Kappa; Society for the History of authorship, Reading and Publishing; Research Society for American Periodicals. **RESEARCH** 19th century American literature; Female authorship and print culture. **SELECTED PUBLICATIONS** Auth, Confounding Images: Photography and Portraiture in Antebellium American Literature, 97; coed, Reciprocal Influences: Literary Production, Consumption and Distribution in America, 99; articles in American Quarterly, Nineteenth-Century Literature; New England Quarterly, & others. **CONTACT ADDRESS** Dept of English, Ohio State Univ, Columbus, 164 W 17th Ave., Columbus, OH 43210-1370. **EMAIL** Williams.488@osu.edu

WILLIAMS, SUZANNE HURST
DISCIPLINE COMMUNICATION ARTS **EDUCATION** Marquette Univ, BA, 79; Univ Wis, MA, 82, PhD, 87. **CAREER** Tchg asst, Univ WI; 84-87; lectr, Univ WI, 83-84; prof, 87-. **HONORS AND AWARDS** Charlene Wackman summer scholar, Univ WI, 84; tchg award for grad stud, Univ WI, 84; outstanding female grad stud, Univ WI, 87; fac develop summer stipend, 90; dir, summer media inst, 91; co-coord, trinity fac summer sem, 92; vice ch, 89-90, ch, 90-92, broadcast edu assn; convention coord, broadcast edu assn, 94; co-ch, speech commun assn, 95; newsletter ed, soc animation stud, 94-97; bd dir(s), broadcast edu as **MEMBERSHIPS** Mem, Broadcast Edu Assn; Intl Commun Assn; Speech Commun Assn; Soc for Animation Stud; Tex Assn Broadcast Educators. **SELECTED PUBLICATIONS** Auth, Video Production Switchers, Special Effects Generators, and Digital Video Effects, Broadcast Tech Update, Focal Press, 97; Sustaining Program, Encycl of TV, Fitzroy Dearborn Publ, 97; The Howdy Doody Show, Encycl of TV, Fitzroy Dearborn Publ, 97;Captain Video and His Video Rangers, Encycl of TV, Fitzroy Dearborn Publ, 97; co-auth, The Encyclopedia of Television, Fitzroy Dearborn Publ, 97. **CONTACT ADDRESS** Dept of Commun, Trinity Univ, 715 Stadium Dr, San Antonio, TX 78212.

WILLIAMS, TONY
PERSONAL Born 01/11/1946, Swansea, Wales, m, 1991 **DISCIPLINE** CINEMA STUDIES **EDUCATION** Manchester Univ, 67-73; Warwick Univ, PhD, theology, 76-77, MA, film studies. **CAREER** Southern IL Univ, assoc prof, eng, 84-. **HONORS AND AWARDS** Jack London Found Man of the Year, 89. **MEMBERSHIPS** Soc for Cinema Studies. **RESEARCH** Am Film Genres; Hong Kong Cin; Brit Cin; Lit Naturalism; Jack London; James Jones. **SELECTED PUBLICATIONS** Auth, Jack London: The Movies, Los Angeles, 92; Vietnam War films: over 600, feature made for TV, pilot and short movies, 1939-1992, Tony Williams, Jean-Jacques Malo, eds, Jefferson NC, McFarland & Co Inc, 94; Hearths of Darkness: The Family in the American Horror Film, Cranbury NJ, Farleigh Dickinson Univ Press, 96; Larry Cohen: The Radical Allegories of an Independent Filmmaker, Jefferson NC, McFarland &co, 97; Jack London's Sea Wolf, screen play by Robert Rossen, ed by Rocco Fumento and Tony Williams, Carbobale IL, SO Univ IL Press, 98; numerous articles. **CONTACT ADDRESS** Dept English, So Illinois Univ, Carbondale, Carbondale, IL 62901. **EMAIL** tonyw@siu.edu

WILLIAMS, WILLIAM PROCTOR
PERSONAL Born 09/01/1939, Glade, KS, m, 1984, 2 children **DISCIPLINE** ENGLISH **EDUCATION** Kans State Univ, BA, 61, MA, 64, PhD(English), 68. **CAREER** Instr freshman rhet, Kans State Univ, 66-67; from asst prof to assoc prof, 67-78, PROF ENGLISH, NORTHERN ILL UNIV, 78-, Am Philos Soc fel, 72-73; Newberry Libr fel, 74; Am Coun Learned Soc grant, 75 & 79; Nat Endowment for Humanities res grant, 78; dir, Grad Studies English, Northern Ill Univ, 78-81, actg assoc dean res, Grad Sch, 82. **MEMBERSHIPS** Bibliog Soc England; Malone Soc **RESEARCH** Bibliography and textual studies; Renaissance English literature; Shakespeare **SELECTED PUBLICATIONS** Auth, The Stationers-Company Archives--An Account of the Records, 1554-1984, 18th Century Stud, Vol 0027, 93; The Reception of Shakespeare in the 18th Century France and Germany, 18th Century Stud, Vol 0026, 93; Shakespeare Domesticated--The 18th Century Editions, 18th Century Stud, Vol 0026, 93; Early Cambridge Theaters, Notes and Queries, Vol 0042, 95; The Cambridge Illustrated History of British Theater, Notes and Queries, Vol 0043, 96; The Elizabethan Theater XIII, Notes and Queries, Vol 0043, 96; Winter Fruit--English Drama 1642-1660, Notes and Queries, Vol 0044, 97. **CONTACT ADDRESS** Dept English, No Illinois Univ, 1425 W Lincoln Hwy, Dekalb, IL 60115-2825. **EMAIL** wwilliam@niu.edu

WILLIAMS-HACKETT, LAMARA
PERSONAL Born 01/17/1967, Inkster, MI, m, 1997 **DISCIPLINE** JOURNALISM; LIBRARY SCIENCE **EDUCATION** Alcorn State Univ, BA, 96; La State Univ, MLIS, 97. **CAREER** Librn, Univ Iowa Libr, 98-. **HONORS AND AWARDS** ACRL, 99; Nat Conference Scholar Recipient. **MEMBERSHIPS** Am Libr Asn; Asn Col & Res Libr; New Members Roundtable. **RESEARCH** Current events; African Am hist; women's hist; African American women's hist. **CONTACT ADDRESS** 1680 Oneal Ln, Apt 204, Baton Rouge, LA 70816-1626. **EMAIL** lamara-williams-hackett@uiowa.edu

WILLIAMSON, CRAIG B.
PERSONAL Born 08/26/1943, Lafayette, IN, 4 children **DISCIPLINE** ENGLISH **EDUCATION** Stanford Univ, BA; 65; Harvard Univ, MA, 66; Univ Penn, PhD, 72. **CAREER** Asst prof, assoc prof, prof, assoc prof, Swarthmore Col, 73-. **HONORS AND AWARDS** NEH, 74, 81, 83; ACLS, 75; Woodrow Wilson Fel, 65, 82; Danforth Fel, 69; Phi Beta Kappa; Columbia Trans Prize. **MEMBERSHIPS** MLA. **RESEARCH** Old English language and literature; medieval literature; intertextu-

ality; modern poetry and film. **SELECTED PUBLICATIONS** Auth, African Wings, Citadel (69); ed, trans, Selected Poems/ Poesie Choisies of Leopold Senghor (Rex Collings, 76); ed and comm, The Old English Riddles of the Exeter Book, NC UP, 77; trans and comm, A Feast of Creatures: Anglo-Saxon Riddle-Songs (Univ Penn Press, 83). **CONTACT ADDRESS** Eng Dept., Swarthmore Col, Swarthmore, PA 19081. **EMAIL** cwillial@swarthmore.edu

WILLIAMSON, J. W.
PERSONAL Born 03/17/1944, Dallas, TX, m, 1985 **DISCIPLINE** ENGLISH LITERATURE **EDUCATION** Wayland College, BA, 66; Univ Utah, MA, 68, PhD, 70. **CAREER** Appalachian State Univ, 70-, Prof 78-; ed, Appalachian Journal, 72-00. **HONORS AND AWARDS** Thomas Wolfe Literary Awd; W.D. Weatherford Awd. **MEMBERSHIPS** Appalachian Studies Asn. **RESEARCH** Appalachian Literature; Appalachian Imagery in Amer Popular Culture. **SELECTED PUBLICATIONS** Auth, Southern Mountaineers in Silent Films, McFarland, 94; coed, Interviewing Appalachia: The Appalachian J Interviews, Univ Tenn Press, 94; Hillbillyland: What the Movies Did to the Mountains and the Mountains Did to the Movies, Univ NC Press, 95. **CONTACT ADDRESS** Center for Appalachian Studies, Appalachian State Univ, Boone, NC 28608. **EMAIL** williamsonjw@appstate.edu

WILLIAMSON, JANE LOUISE
PERSONAL Born St. Louis, MO **DISCIPLINE** ENGLISH LITERATURE **EDUCATION** Wash Univ, AB, 58; Bryn Mawr Col, MA, 60, PhD, 63. **CAREER** Instr Eng, Univ WI, Madison, 63-64; asst prof, Univ MO, St Louis, 64-66; asst prof, Univ CA, Santa Barbara, 66-67; asst prof, 67-69, assoc prof eng, Univ MO, St Louis, 69, chemn dept, 72-75, 94-99, chemn Univ Senate, 76-77. **HONORS AND AWARDS** Amoco Awd for Outstanding Tchr in the Hum, Univ MO, 74; Outstanding Academic Bks List, Am Libr Asn, for Charles Kemble. **MEMBERSHIPS** MLA; Am Soc Theatre Res; Soc Theatre Res, Eng; Shakespeare Asn Am; AAUP. **RESEARCH** Shakespeare and Elizabethan drama; theatre hist. **SELECTED PUBLICATIONS** Auth, Charles Kemble, Man of the Theatre, Univ Nebr, 70; The Duke and Isabella on the mod stage, In: The Triple Bond, PA State Univ, 75. **CONTACT ADDRESS** Dept of Eng, Univ of Missouri, St. Louis, 8001 Natural Bridge, Saint Louis, MO 63121-4499.

WILLIAMSON, JANICE
PERSONAL Born Brandon, MB, Canada **DISCIPLINE** ENGLISH **EDUCATION** Carleton Univ, BA, 75; York Univ, MA, 81, PhD, 87. **CAREER** Asst prof, 87-91, Assoc Prof, Univ Alberta, 91-. **HONORS AND AWARDS** The Pushcart Prize, 89; bp nichol Chapbook Awd, 96. **MEMBERSHIPS** Acad Women's Asn, Univ Alta; Writers' Union Can. **RESEARCH** Canadian women's writing, feminist cultural studies and popular culture. **SELECTED PUBLICATIONS** Coauth, Dangerous Goods: Feminist Visual Art Practices, Edmonton Art Gallery, 90; auth, Tell Tale signs: fictions, Turnstone Press, 91; auth, Altitude X 2, disOrientation Press, 92; co-ed, Women's Writing and the Literary Institution, in Canada/Quebec, (U of A Res Institution for Comparatice Literature, 92); ed, Sounding Differences: Conversations with Seventeen Canadian Women Writers, UTP, 93; auth, A Boy Named, arsonist auntie, 96; auth, Crybaby!, NeWest Press, 98. **CONTACT ADDRESS** Dept of English, Univ of Alberta, Edmonton, AB, Canada T6G 2E5. **EMAIL** janice.williamsom@ualberta.ca

WILLIAMSON, JOHN STEWART
PERSONAL Born 04/29/1908, Bisbee, AZ, m, 1947, 2 children **DISCIPLINE** ENGLISH LITERATURE **EDUCATION** Eastern NMex Univ, BA & MA, 57; Univ Colo, PhD, 64. **CAREER** Instr, 57-59, NMex Mil Inst; from asst prof to prof, 60-77, Eastern NMex Univ, dir,77-80, Inst for Lib & Fine Arts;. **HONORS AND AWARDS** Grand Master Awd, Sci Fiction Writers of Am, 76; lhd, eastern nmex univ, portales. **MEMBERSHIPS** Sci Fiction Writers of Am (pres, 78-79); Am Assn for Adv of Sci; Sci Fiction Res Assn. **RESEARCH** Science fiction; H G Wells. **SELECTED PUBLICATIONS** Auth, Mazeway, 90; coauth, The Singers of Time, 91; auth, Beachhead, 92; auth, Demon Moon, 94; auth, The Black Sun, 96; auth, The Silicon Dagger, 99. **CONTACT ADDRESS** Box 761, Portales, NM 88130-0761. **EMAIL** jack.williamson@enmu.edu

WILLIAMSON, KEITH
DISCIPLINE INTERPERSONAL COMMUNICATION, COMMUNICATION THEORY **EDUCATION** Temple Univ, PhD. **CAREER** Asst prof, Director of the Basic Course. Chair Depart Speech Commun,Wichita State Univ. **SELECTED PUBLICATIONS** Publ, Communication Education; co-auth, Leading Interpersonal Communication Textbook. **CONTACT ADDRESS** Wichita State Univ, 1845 Fairmont, Wichita, KS 67260-0062. **EMAIL** williamson@elliott.es.twsu.edu

WILLIAMSON, MARILYN LAMMERT
PERSONAL Born 09/06/1927, Chicago, IL, m, 1950, 1 child **DISCIPLINE** ENGLISH **EDUCATION** Vassar Col, BA, 49; Univ Wis, MA, 50; Duke Univ, PhD(English), 56. **CAREER** Instr English, Duke Univ, 55-56 & 59; instr, NC State Univ, 57-58 & 61-62; from asst prof to assoc prof, Oakland Univ, 65-72; chmn dept English, 72-74, assoc dean Col Lib Arts, 74-79, PROF ENGLISH, WAYNE STATE UNIV, 72-, DIR WOMEN'S STUDIES, 76-, CHMN DEPT, 81-, Fel, Radcliffe Inst, Harvard Univ, 69-70. **MEMBERSHIPS** MLA; Asn Depts of English (pres, 76); Renaissance Soc Am; Shakespeare Asn. **RESEARCH** Shakespeare; Renaissance drama; women's studies. **SELECTED PUBLICATIONS** Auth, A Reading of Milton's Twenty-third Sonnet, Milton Studies, 72; co-ed, Essays in the Renaissance in Honor of Allan H Gilbert, S Atlantic Quart, 72; auth, Infinite Variety: Antony and Cleopatra in Renaissance Drama and Earlier Tradition, Lawrence Verry, 74; The courtship of Katherine and the second tetralogy, Criticism, 75; Who's Afraid of Mrs Barbauld? The Blue Stockings and Feminism, Int J Women's Studies, 80; ed, Female Poets of Great Britain, Wayne State Univ Press, 81; auth, Romeo and Death, Shakespeare Studies, 81; Doubling, Women's Anger and Genre, Women's Studies, 82. **CONTACT ADDRESS** Women's Studies, Wayne State Univ, 431 State Hall, Detroit, MI 48202-1308.

WILLIAMSON-IGE, DOROTHY KAY
PERSONAL Born 04/18/1950, Parma, MO, m **DISCIPLINE** SPEECH, DRAMA **EDUCATION** Southeast Missouri State Univ, BS, Speech, 1971; Central Missouri State Univ, MA, Speech Comm, 1973; Ohio State Univ, PhD, Speech, 1980. **CAREER** Webster Grove Schools, speech & drama teacher, 71-77; DOD Dependents Schools, drama teacher, 77-78; Bowling Green State Univ, faculty & field exper coord, 80-84; Indiana Univ NW, faculty, 85-. **HONORS AND AWARDS** Academic Scholarship Certificate Southeast Missouri State Univ, 1970; (Civilian) Intl Talent Search Judge, US Military, Ramstein, Germany, Air Force Base, 1978; TV, radio, newspaper interviews and keynote speeches, papers, consultantships in Midwest US, Africa, Caribbean & Europe, 1978-; published over 20 articles & book chapters on communication education for minorities, the handicapped and women, 1981-87; Third World Peoples Awd, Bowling Green State Univ, 1984; Department Head, Community WPA; Acting Department Head, Minority Studies. **MEMBERSHIPS** Public adv bd, Bowling Green State Univ, 1980-83; assoc, Ohio State Univ Black Alumni, 1980-; Phi Delta Kappa, 1980-; speech comm, assoc black caucus pres, legislative council, Black Oppor Task Force, 1981-87; State of Ohio Bd Redesign of Educ Programs, 1982; pres, Women Investing Together & program chairperson, Human Relations Comm, Bowling Green State Univ, 1984; TV radio newspaper interviews, keynote speeches, papers & consultantships in Midwest USA, Africa, Caribbean & Europe. **CONTACT ADDRESS** Communications Dept, Indiana Univ, Northwest, 3400 Broadway, Gary, IN 46408.

WILLIS, DEBORAH
DISCIPLINE ENGLISH LITERATURE **EDUCATION** Univ Calif-Berkeley; BA, MA, PhD. **CAREER** Prof, Univ Calif, Riverside. **RESEARCH** Shakespeare; Renaissance drama; Cultural studies. **SELECTED PUBLICATIONS** Auth, "The Tempest and Colonial Discourse," Stud Eng Lit 1500-1900, 89; Malevolent Nurture: Witch-hunting and Maternal Power in Early Modern England, Cornell Univ Press, 95. **CONTACT ADDRESS** Dept of Eng, Univ of California, Riverside, 1156 Hinderaker Hall, Riverside, CA 92521-0209.

WILLIS, GLADYS JANUARY
PERSONAL Born 02/29/1944, Jackson, MS, m **DISCIPLINE** ENGLISH **EDUCATION** Jackson State Univ, BA 1965; Bryn Mawr Coll, Independent Study 1966; Michigan State Univ, MA 1967; Princeton Univ, PhD 1973; Lutheran Theological Seminary, Philadelphia PA, MDiv 1996. **CAREER** Cheyney State Univ, instructor, English, 67-68; Rider Coll, instructor, English, 68-70; City University of New York, asst prof, English 1973-76; Pennsylvania Human Relations Commn, educ representative 1976-77; Lincoln Univ, assoc prof, chair 1977-84, prof, dept chair 1977-; First Redemption Evangelical Church, asst pastor, 92-. **HONORS AND AWARDS** Woodrow Wilson Natl Fellowship, Woodrow Wilson Natl Fellowship Found 1966-67; Princeton Univ Fellow, Princeton Univ 1970-73; author, The Penalty of Eve; John Milton and Divorce New York, Peter Lang 1984; Ordained Chaplain 1988; Outstanding Young Women of America, 1978; Lindback Distinguished Teachers Awd, Lincoln Univ, 1984; Service Awd, Lincoln Univ, 1992. **MEMBERSHIPS** Founder, dir Coll Preparatory Tutorial 1974; mem, bd of dir Philadelphia Christian Academy 1977-, Natl Council of Teachers of English; reviewer Middle States Assn. **CONTACT ADDRESS** English Dept, Lincoln Univ, Pennsylvania, Lincoln University, PA 19352.

WILLIS, PATRICIA CANNON
PERSONAL Born 09/21/1938, Chicago, IL, m, 1972 **DISCIPLINE** AMERICAN LITERATURE **EDUCATION** Barat Col, BA, 64; Univ Chicago, AM, 66; PhD, 72. **CAREER** Curator, Rosenbach Museum and Libr, Philadelphia, 75-87; curator, Beinecke Libr, Yale Univ, 87-. **HONORS AND AWARDS** Univ Fel, 68, 69; NEH Younger Humanist, 72; Assoc of Univ Women Fel, 71. **MEMBERSHIPS** MLA; Ct Acad of Arts and Sci. **RESEARCH** Modernist literature; Native American literature **SELECTED PUBLICATIONS** Auth, Complete Prose of Marianne Moore, Viking, 87; auth, Vision into Verse, Rosenback, 87. **CONTACT ADDRESS** Curator, Yale Univ, Beinecke Libr, PO Box 208240, New Haven, CT 06520-8240. **EMAIL** patricia.willis@yale.edu

WILLIS, PAUL J.
PERSONAL Born 11/08/1955, Fullerton, CA, m, 1979, 2 children **DISCIPLINE** ENGLISH **EDUCATION** Wash State Univ, PhD, 85. **CAREER** Asst prof, Houghton Col, 85-88; assoc prof, Westmont Col, 88-. **HONORS AND AWARDS** Individual artist award for poetry, The Arts Fund of Santa Barbara, 97; choice award for The Stolen River, Christianity Today Critics', 92; work included in Best American Poetry, 96 and Best Spiritual Writing, 99. **MEMBERSHIPS** Conf on Christianity and Lit; Asn for the Study of Lit & Environment. **RESEARCH** Literature and the environment; renaissance literature; Shakespeare; Milton. **SELECTED PUBLICATIONS** Auth, The Stolen River, Crossway Bk(s), 92; No Clock in the Forest: An Alpine Tale, Crossway Bk(s), 91; auth, Poison Oak, Mille Grazie Press, 99. **CONTACT ADDRESS** Dept of Eng, Westmont Col, 955 La Paz Rd, Santa Barbara, CA 93108-1099. **EMAIL** willis@westmont.edu

WILLIS, RESA
DISCIPLINE ENGLISH LITERATURE **EDUCATION** SW MO State Univ, BA; Univ AR, MA, Univ Tulsa, PhD. **CAREER** Prof lit, 80, Drury Col. **RESEARCH** Biog. **SELECTED PUBLICATIONS** Auth, Mark and Livy: The Love Story of Mark Twain and the Woman Who Almost Tamed Him, Atheneum, 92. **CONTACT ADDRESS** Eng Dept, Drury Col, N Benton, PO Box 900, Springfield, MO 65802. **EMAIL** rwillis@lib.drury.edu

WILLIS, SUSAN
DISCIPLINE ENGLISH LITERATURE **EDUCATION** Univ CA San Diego, PhD, 77. **CAREER** Prof, Duke Univ. **SELECTED PUBLICATIONS** Auth, Specifying: Black Women Writing the American Experience, Univ Wis, 87; A Primer For Daily Life, Routledge, 90; co-auth, Inside the Mouse: Work and Play at Walt Disney World, Duke, 95. **CONTACT ADDRESS** Eng Dept, Duke Univ, Durham, NC 27706.

WILLIS, SUSAN
PERSONAL Born 08/23/1947, Nashville, TN **DISCIPLINE** ENGLISH **EDUCATION** Emory Univ, BA (with honors), 69; Univ of Va, MA, 70, PhD, 74. **CAREER** Tchg asst to adjunct instr, Univ of Va, 70-74; asst prof Eng, Univ of Minn, 74-78; Prof Eng, Auburn Univ, Montgomery, 78-; Dramaturg, Alabama Shakespeare Festival, 85-. **HONORS AND AWARDS** Phi Beta Kappa; Mortar Board; Phi Kappa Phi. **MEMBERSHIPS** MLA; SAMLA; Shakespeare Asn of Am; Lit Managers & Dramaturgs of the Americas. **RESEARCH** Shakespeare in production. **SELECTED PUBLICATIONS** Auth, The BBC Shakespeare Plays: Making the Televised Canon, Univ of NC Press, 91; numerous articles on Shakespeare in production, W.H. Auden, fantasy lit, and dramaturgy; extensive writing for the Ala Shakespeare Festival. **CONTACT ADDRESS** 621 Felder Ave, Montgomery, AL 36106. **EMAIL** swillis@edla.aum.edu

WILLMOTT, GLENN ALLAN
PERSONAL Born 04/12/1963, Toronto, ON, Canada, m, 1995, 1 child **DISCIPLINE** ENGLISH **EDUCATION** Univ Toronto, BA, 87; Duke Univ, MA, 89; PhD, 92. **CAREER** Asst prof, Dalhousie Univ, 93-95; asst prof to assoc prof, Queen's Univ, 95-. **HONORS AND AWARDS** SSHRCC Res Grant, 97-00. **MEMBERSHIPS** MLA; ACS; ACSUS; ACCUTE. **RESEARCH** Modernity; Canadian literature in English. **SELECTED PUBLICATIONS** Auth, McLuhan or Modernism in Reverse, Univ Tor Pr, 96; auth, "Bad Multiplicity," Ess Can Writ 71 (00): 37-47; auth, "Canadian Resentment," New Lit Hist 32 (01): 133-156; auth, Unreal Country: Modernity and the Canadian Novel in English, McGill/Queen's UP, (forthcoming). **CONTACT ADDRESS** English Dept, Queen's Univ at Kingston, Kingston, ON, Canada K7L 3N6. **EMAIL** gw12@post.queens.ca

WILLS, DAVID
DISCIPLINE CINEMA AND FILM THEORY, LITERARY THEORY, 20TH CENTURY LITERATURE **EDUCATION** Univ Sorbonne, Nouvelle-Paris III, Doctorat, 79. **CAREER** Prof, La State Univ; prof and chair, SUNY, Albany. **SELECTED PUBLICATIONS** Auth, Screen/Play: Derrida and Film Theory, 89; Writing Pynchon: Strategies in Fictional Analysis, 90; Deconstruction and the Visual Arts, 94; Prosthesis, 95. **CONTACT ADDRESS** Dept of Lang, Lit and Cult, SUNY, Albany, 1400 Wash Ave, Albany, NY 12222-0001. **EMAIL** dwills@cas.albany.edu

WILLS, JACK CHARLES
PERSONAL Born 12/10/1936, Beaver, WV, m, 1958, 2 children **DISCIPLINE** ENGLISH **EDUCATION** WVa Univ, BSF, 60; Univ Del, MA, 63, PhD(English), 66. **CAREER** Asst prof English, Va Polytech Inst, 66-67 & Westhampton Col, Univ Richmond, 67-71; assoc prof, 71-74, Prof English, Fair-

mont State Col, 74-, Nat Endowment for Humanities summer sem, 79. **HONORS AND AWARDS** William A Boram Awd, Teaching Excellence, 97-98. **MEMBERSHIPS** Bronte Soc; MLA; S Atlantic Mod Lang Asn; Byron Soc; Soc Study Social Lit **RESEARCH** Eighteenth and 19th century novel, especially Charlotte Bronte; romantic period, 18th century; Southern literature. **SELECTED PUBLICATIONS** Auth, The shrine of truth: An approach to the works of Charlotte Bronte, Bronte Soc Trans, 70; The Deserted Village, Ecclesiastes, and the enlightenment, Enlightenment Essays, fall-winter, 73; The narrator of the Deserted Village: A reconsideration, WVa Univ Philol Papers, 12/75; The enchanted rocks at Uncle Billy Basham's, 75 & An unnamed Ballad, 77, WVA Folklore J; Lord Byron and 'Poor Dear Sherry', Richard Brinsley Sheridan, In: Lord Byron and His Contemporaries: Essays from the Sixth International Byron Seminar, Univ Delaware Press, 82; The theme of education and communication in Journey to the Western Islands of Scotland, Bull West Va Asn Col English Teachers, fall, 89; Villette and The Marble Faun, Studies in the Novel, fall, 93. **CONTACT ADDRESS** Dept of English, Fairmont State Col, 1201 Locust Ave, Fairmont, WV 26554-2470. **EMAIL** jcwills1@aol.edu

WILLS, JEFFREY
DISCIPLINE CLASSICS **EDUCATION** Harvard Univ, PhD, 88 **CAREER** Assoc Prof, 88-99, Univ of WI. **HONORS AND AWARDS** Fulbright Scholar, Ukraine, 97-98 **RESEARCH** Latin Literature **CONTACT ADDRESS** Dept of Classics, 212 N Broom St, Madison, WI 53703. **EMAIL** wills@ucef.org

WILLUMSON, GLENN GARDNER
PERSONAL Born 06/22/1949, Glendale, CA, m, 1970, 2 children **DISCIPLINE** ART HISTORY; ENGLISH **EDUCATION** St. Mary's Col, BA, 71; Univ Calif Davis, MA, 84; Univ Calif Santa Barbara, PhD, 88. **CAREER** Teacher, Calif Secondary Sch, 71-81; cur, Amer Art and Photog, Getty Res Inst, 88-92; affil prof, Dept of Art Hist, Pa State, 93-; Senior Cur, Palmer Mus of Art, Pa State, 92-. **HONORS AND AWARDS** Nat Endow for the Humanities fel, 97-98; Haynes fel, Huntington Libr, fac res grant, 94; J. Paul Getty Publ grant, 91; Annette Baxter prize, Amer studies, 87; Kress found fel, 87; Nat Writing Proj fel, 87; teaching resources grant, 84. **MEMBERSHIPS** Col Art Asn; Amer Studies Asn; Asn of Hist of Amer Art; Asn of Univ Mus and Galleries. **RESEARCH** History of photography; American art. **SELECTED PUBLICATIONS** Auth, "The Shifting Audience of the University Museum," Museum International; auth, The Getty Research Institute: Materials for a New Photo-History, Hist of Photog, XXII, 1, 31-39, Spring, 98; auth, Clement Greenberg, Encycl of World Bio, Jan, 95; auth, A Family Album: Portraits by John Sloan, Amer Art Rev, 116-117, June-July, 94; auth, Collecting with a Passion: Selections from the Pincus Collection of Contemporary Art, Univ Pk, Palmer Mus of Art, 93; auth, Silver Salts and Blueprints, London Times Lit Suppl, 19 Mar, 93; auth, W. Eugene Smith and the Photographic Essay, NY, Cambridge Univ Press, 92; essays, Van Dyck's Iconographie, Mus Plantin-Moretus, Stedelijk Prenteenkabinet, 376-387, 91; auth, Alfred Hart: Photographer of the Transcontinental Railroad, Hist of Photog, XII, 1, 61-75, Jan-Mar, 88. **CONTACT ADDRESS** Palmer Museum of Art, Pennsylvania State Univ, Univ Park, University Park, PA 16802-2507. **EMAIL** ggw2@psu.edu

WILMETH, DON B.
PERSONAL Born 12/15/1939, Houston, TX, m, 1963, 1 child **DISCIPLINE** THEATRE HISTORY, POPULAR CULTURE **EDUCATION** Abilene Christian Col, BA, 61; Univ AR, MA, 62; Univ IL, PhD, 64. **CAREER** Asst prof theatre, Eastern NM Univ, 64-65, head dept drama, 65-67; from asst prof to The Asa Messer Prof, theatre & English, Brown Univ, 67-, actg chmn theatre arts prog, 72-73, exec officer, Theatre Arts Dept, 73-, Chmn Dept, 79-87, 98-01; honorary curator, H. Adrian Smith Collection of Conjuring Books & Magiciana (In Brown Special Collections); consult, Asn Col & Res Libr, 70-; theatre ed, Intellect Mag, 74-; bk rev ed, The Theatre J, 78-80; assoc ed, Mod Lang Studies, 80; coordr, Grad Prog in Theatre Studies, 87-95; consult, Libr Congress Am theatre project, 92-94; Vis Schol, Osaka Univ and Japan Found, Summer 93; Selection Comt, Robert Lewis Medal for Lifetime Achievement in Theater Res, 94-99; O.R. and Eva Mitchell Distinguished Vis Prof, Trinity Univ, 95; Dean, Col Fels Am Theatre, 96-98; Corresponding Schol, Shaw Festival, Ontario, 98. **HONORS AND AWARDS** Eastern NM Univ res grants, 66-68; George Freedley Theatre Bk Awd, Theatre Libr Asn, 71-72; Bernard Hewitt Awd, 81, 99; Guggenheim fel, 82; Outstanding Theatre Alum, Univ Arkansas, 98; Special Awd, New England Theatre Conference, 98; Betty Jean Jones Awd, 99; Special Jury Awd, Theatre Libr Asn, 99; ma, brown univ, 70. **MEMBERSHIPS** Theatre Libr Asn (vpres, 81); Am Theatre Asn; Am Soc Theatre Res (pres 91-94, secy 95-01); Int Fedn Theatre Res (exec comt 94-97); New Engl Theatre Conf; Am Theatre & Drama Soc (exec bd 95-99). **RESEARCH** Popular entertainment; life and art of the 19th century actor, G F Cooke; Am theatre of the 19th century. **SELECTED PUBLICATIONS** Contribr, Drama/theatre, In: Books for College Libraries, 2nd ed, Am Libr Asn, 74; auth, The American Stage to World War I, 78 & American and English Popular Entertainment, 80, Gale Res Co; The Language of American Popular Entertainment, 81 & Variety Entertainment and Outdoor Amusements, 82, Greenwood Press; co-ed, Plays by William Hooker Gillette, Cambridge Univ Press, 83; auth, Mud Show: American Tent Circus Life, Univ NMex Press, 88; co-ed and contribr, Cambridge Guide to World Theatre, Cambridge Univ Press, 88; contribr, Theatre in the Colonies and United States, 1750-1915: A Documentary History, Cambridge Univ Press, 96; co-ed, The Cambridge Guide to the American Theatre, Cambridge Univ Press, 93; auth, Staging the Nation: Plays from the American Theatre, 1787-1909, Bedford Bks, 98; co-ed, The Cambridge History of American Theatre, Beginnings to 1870, Cambridge Univ Press, 98, vol 2, 99, vol 3, 00. . **CONTACT ADDRESS** Dept of Theatre Arts, Brown Univ, 1 Prospect St, Providence, RI 02912-9127. **EMAIL** donwilmeth@brown.edu

WILSON, BLAKE
PERSONAL Born 05/16/1952, Spokane, WN, m, 2 children **DISCIPLINE** MUSICOLOGY **EDUCATION** Univ Calif, Berkeley, BA, 79; Ind Univ, MM, 82, PhD, 87. **CAREER** Asst prof, Colby Col, 88-89; asst prof, Vanderbilt Univ, 89- 93; from asst prof to assoc prof music, Dickinson Col, 93-; dept chemn, Dickinson Col, 99-. **HONORS AND AWARDS** Phi Beta Kappa; Fulbright Fel for res, Florence, Italy, 85; Villa I Tatti Fel, Harvard Center for Italian Renaissance Studies, Florence, Italy, 97-98. **MEMBERSHIPS** Am Musicological Soc; Int Machaut Soc; Soc for Confraternity Studies. **RESEARCH** Music of Renaissance Italy, especially Florence; music & rhetoric; improvisatory & oral traditions; Italian confraternities. **SELECTED PUBLICATIONS** Auth, Music and Merchants: The Laudesi Companies of Republican Florence, Clarendon Pr (Oxford), 92; auth, The Florence Laudario: An Editon of Florence, Biblioteca Nazionale Centrale, Banco Rari 18, A-R Editions (Madison, Wis), 95; auth, "Madrigal, Lauda, and Local Culture in Trecento Florence," J of Musicology 15 (97): 137-177; auth, "Song collections in Early Renaissance Florence: the Cantasi come Tradition and its Manuscript Sources," Recercare 10 (98): 69-104; auth, "Rhetorica and Music; I. Middle Ages and Renaissance," and "Lauda," New Grove Dictionary of Music and Musicians, 7th ed, McMillan/Norton, forthcoming. **CONTACT ADDRESS** Music Dept, Dickinson Col, Carlisle, PA 17013. **EMAIL** wilson@dickinson.edu

WILSON, CHARLES E., JR.
PERSONAL Born 12/08/1961, Carrollton, GA, s **DISCIPLINE** AFRICAN AMERICAN LITERATURE **EDUCATION** W Ga Univ, BA; N Ca State Univ, MA; Univ Ga, PhD. **CAREER** Engl, Old Dominion Univ. **HONORS AND AWARDS** NEH Seminar, 93, 98. **SELECTED PUBLICATIONS** Area: Black Manhood; Race, Class, and Gender in Southern Fiction; Intersection of Past and Present in the South. **CONTACT ADDRESS** Old Dominion Univ, 4100 Powhatan Ave, Norfolk, VA 23058. **EMAIL** CWilson@odu.edu

WILSON, DANA
PERSONAL Born Lakewood, OH, m, 2 children **DISCIPLINE** MUSIC **EDUCATION** Bowdoin Col, BA; Univ Conn, MA; Eastman Sch Music, PhD. **CAREER** Prof. **HONORS AND AWARDS** Sudler, Ostwald, ITG Composition Prizes. **SELECTED PUBLICATIONS** Co-auth, Contemporary Choral Arranging, Prentice Hall, 86. **CONTACT ADDRESS** Dept of Music History, Theory and Composition, Ithaca Col, 100 Job Hall, Ithaca, NY 14850. **EMAIL** wilson@ithaca.edu

WILSON, DOUGLAS B.
PERSONAL Born 08/19/1930, Denver, CO, m, 1956, 4 children **DISCIPLINE** ENGLISH **EDUCATION** Williams Col, BA, 52; Oxford Univ, MA, 62; Harvard Univ, PhD, 67. **CAREER** Instructor to Asst Prof, Williams Col, 64-68; Asst Prof to Prof, Univ Denver, 68-99. **HONORS AND AWARDS** NEH Summer Sem, Stanford, 82. **MEMBERSHIPS** N Am Sco for Study of Romanticism; PMLA; Asn for Scholars & Critics. **RESEARCH** Wordsworth; Coleridge; Keats and Shakespeare. **SELECTED PUBLICATIONS** Auth, "Reading the Urn: Death in Keat's Arcadia", in Studies in English Literature, 85; auth, "The Dreaming Imagination: Coleridge, Keats and Wordsworth," in Adam's Dream: Coleridge, Keats, and the Romantic Imagination, (Univ MO Press, 90), 58-80; auth, The Romantic Dream: Wordsworth and the Poetics of the Unconscious, Univ NE Press, 93; auth, "Reading the Urn: Death in Keat's Arcadia", in Contexts for Criticism, (Mayfield Pub Co, 94), 166-178. **CONTACT ADDRESS** 2551 E Floyd Ave, Englewood, CO 80110. **EMAIL** dwilson@du.edu

WILSON, DOUGLAS LAWSON
PERSONAL Born 11/10/1935, St. James, MN, m, 1957, 2 children **DISCIPLINE** ENGLISH **EDUCATION** Doane Col, AB, 57; Univ Pa, AM, 59; PhD, 64. **CAREER** Asst instr English, Univ Pa, 59-61; from instr to asst prof, 61-69, assoc prof, 69-79, Prof English, Knox Col, Ill, 79-96, Dir Libr, 72-91; Saunders dir, Int Center for Jefferson Studies, 94-98; co-dir, Lincoln Studies Center, Know Col, 98-. **HONORS AND AWARDS** Res grant, Am Philos Soc, 80; res grant, Am Coun of Learned Soc, 81, 85; fel, Huntington Libr, 81, 91, 92; fel, Nat Endowment for the Humanities, 82-83; fel, Newberry Libr, 85-86; fel, Mass Hist Soc, 99; Lincoln Diploma of Honor, Lincoln Mem. Univ, 00. **MEMBERSHIPS** Asn for Documentary Editing. **RESEARCH** Abraham Lincoln; Thomas Jefferson; Nineteenth-century American culture. **SELECTED PUBLICATIONS** Auth, "A Most Abandoned Hypocrite," Am Heritage (94); auth, Jefferson's Books, Monticello Monogr, 96; auth, Lincoln Before Washington: New Perspectives on the Illinois Years, Univ Ill Press, 97; coed, Herndon's Informants: Letters, Interviews, and Statements about Abraham Lincoln, Univ Ill Press, 98; auth, Honor's Voice: The Transformation of Abraham Lincoln, Knopf, 98; auth, "Lincoln's Affair of Honor," The Atlantic Monthly (98); coed, Jefferson Abroad, The Mod Libr, 99; auth, "Keeping Lincoln's Secrets," The Atlantic Monthly (00); auth, "Jefferson and Bolingbroke: Some Notes on the Question of Influence;" in Religion and Political Culture in Jefferson's Virginia, ed. Garrett Ward Sheldon and Daniel L. Dreisbach (00); auth, "Collaborating with the Past: Remarks on Being Awarded the Lincoln Prize," in Accepting the Lincoln Prize: Two Historians Speak (00). **CONTACT ADDRESS** Lincoln Studies Center, Knox Col, Illinois, Galesburg, IL 61401. **EMAIL** dwilson@knox.edu

WILSON, GRACE G.
PERSONAL Born 06/15/1948, Pittsburgh, PA, m, 1975, 3 children **DISCIPLINE** ENGLISH **EDUCATION** Smith Col, BA, 70; Univ Pa, MA, 73; PhD, 80. **CAREER** Instr, Muskingum Col, 74-75; asst prof, Wilmington Col, 75-79; adj, Col of New Rochelle, 84-92; asst prof, Elizabeth City State Univ, 92-96; adj, instr, Col of the albemarle, 98-. **HONORS AND AWARDS** NDEA Fel, 70-74. **MEMBERSHIPS** Int Arthurian Soc, MLA. **RESEARCH** Early Scottish Historical Literature, Developmental English and Reading. **SELECTED PUBLICATIONS** Auth, "Amonges Othere Wordes Wyse: The Medieval Seneca and the Canterbury Tales," Chaucer Rev 29, (93): 135-45; auth, "History and the Common Reader? Robert Lindsay of Pitscottie's Chronicles," Forum for Mod Lang Studies 29, (93): 97-110; auth, "Robert Henryson", British Writers, Scribners, in press. **CONTACT ADDRESS** Col of the Albemarle, 500 W Main St, Elizabeth City, NC 27909. **EMAIL** gwilson@albemarle.cc.nc.us

WILSON, HUGH F.
DISCIPLINE ENGLISH **EDUCATION** Johns Hopkins Univ, BA; Univ Chicago, MA; PhD, 91. **CAREER** Instr, Chicago State Univ, 78; instr, Roosevelt Univ, 79; vis asst prof, Kenyon Col, 90-92; asst prof, Tex Tech Univ, 93-00; asst prof, SUNY Plattsburgh, 00-. **HONORS AND AWARDS** Woodrow Wilson Fel, 70; Ford Found Fel, 70-75; NEH Fel, 92; Breck Award, RMMRA Conf, 00. **MEMBERSHIPS** Shakespeare Asn of Am, Milton Soc of Am, John Donne Soc, MLA, Am Soc for 18th Century Studies, Rocky Mountain Medieval Renaissance Asn, Renaissance Eng Text Soc, Milton Transcription Proj. **RESEARCH** Renaissance or Early Modern Literature, especially Shakespeare, Milton, and Donne, Tudor-Stuart Drama and Poetry. **SELECTED PUBLICATIONS** Auth, "Nineteenth Century British Literary Biographers," Dict of Lit Biog, Vol 144, ed Steven Serafin, (Detroit: Gale Group, 94); 188-203; auth, "Unraveling the Snarled Chronology of Milton's Earliest Lives," Milton Quart 32.2, (98): 57-71; auth, "The Publication of Paradise Lost, The Occasion of the First Edition: Censorship and Resistance," Milton Studies 37, (99): 18-41; auth, "Shakespeare's The Taming of the Shrew and the Possible Traces of Spanish Influence: Or, Exemplary Tales, and Picaresque Fictions," Sedera: Yearbook of the Span Soc for Eng Renaissance Studies 9, (99): 233-55; auth, "Morbus Satanicus: The Psychomachia of the Seven Deadly Sins in Ben Jonson's 'On My First Sonne,'" Ben Jonson Jour 7, (00): 325-342; auth, "Ann Southwell, Metaphysical Poet," Quidditas (forthcoming). **CONTACT ADDRESS** Dept English, SUNY, Col at Plattsburgh, Plattsburgh, NY 12901. **EMAIL** hwilson@together.net

WILSON, JOHN H.
PERSONAL Born 06/20/1936, Binghamton, NY **DISCIPLINE** ENGLISH **EDUCATION** Col Holy Cross, AB, 58; Yale Univ, MA, 60, PhD(English), 66. **CAREER** From instr to asst prof, 61-72, ASSOC PROF ENGLISH, COL HOLY CROSS, 72-. **RESEARCH** Middle English literature; 18th century literature. **SELECTED PUBLICATIONS** Auth, Nell Gwyn: Royal Mistress, McCosh Bkstore, 52; ed, Six Restoration Plays, HM Publ, 59; co-ed, City Politiques, Univ Nebr, 67; auth, Ordeal of Mr Pepys's Cler, Ohio State Univ, 72; All the King's Ladies: Actresses of the Resoration, Univ Chicago, 74; Court Satires of the Restoration, Ohio State Univ, 76. **CONTACT ADDRESS** 142 Wheelock Ave, Millbury, MA 01527. **EMAIL** jwilson@holycross.edu

WILSON, JOHN H.
PERSONAL Born 09/26/1961, Erie, PA, s **DISCIPLINE** ENGLISH, LITERATURE **EDUCATION** Univ Mich, BA, 84; MA, 84; PhD, 88. **CAREER** Assoc Prof, Dakota Wesleyen Univ, 89-00; Lecturer, Eastern Michigan Univ, 88-89; Teaching Asst, Univ of Michigan, Ann Arbor, 83-88. **HONORS AND AWARDS** C.A. Patrides Memorial Fel, 88; META Fel, 83-88; Rackham Dissertation Grant, 87. **MEMBERSHIPS** Assoc of Literary Scholars and Critics; Institute for Evolutionary Psychology. **RESEARCH** Evelyn Waugh; Modern British Fiction; Film; Japan. **SELECTED PUBLICATIONS** Auth, "What Happened in U.S. History?" Tokyo: Eifousha, 00; auth, " Evelyn Waugh: a Literary Biography, 1903-1924," Madison, NJ: Fairleigh Dickinson UP, 96; auth, "An Internal Invitation to Enjoy British Authors," Tokyo: Eihowsha, 97. **CONTACT**

ADDRESS Dept Humanities, Dakota Wesleyan Univ, 1200 West University Ave, Mitchell, SD 57301-4358. **EMAIL** jowilson@dwu.edu

WILSON, JOHN HAROLD
PERSONAL Born 02/11/1900, Springfield, OH **DISCIPLINE** ENGLISH **EDUCATION** Oberlin Col, AB, 22; Syracuse Univ, AM, 24; Ohio State Univ, PhD, 27. **CAREER** Instr English, Syracuse Univ, 22-24; from instr to prof, 24-68, EMER PROF ENGLISH, OHIO STATE UNIV, 68-, Vis prof, Univ Tenn, 36 & 38; Guggenheim fel, 50- **MEMBERSHIPS** MLA **RESEARCH** The influence of Beaumont and Fletcher on restoration drama; court wits of the restoration; early 17th century plays. **SELECTED PUBLICATIONS** Auth, All the King's Ladies, Chicago Univ, 58; Private Life of Mr Pepys, Farrar, Straus, 59; Mr Goodman the Player, Univ Pittsburgh, 64; A Preface to Restoration Drama, Houghton, 65; ed, Crowne's City Politiques, Univ Nebr, 67; auth, Mr Pepys' Clerk, 72 & Restoration Court Satires, 76, Ohio State Univ. **CONTACT ADDRESS** Dept of English, Ohio State Univ, Columbus, Columbus, OH 43210.

WILSON, JOSEPH P.
DISCIPLINE CLASSICS **EDUCATION** Univ Toledo, BA; Univ IA, PhD. **CAREER** Assoc prof, Univ of Scranton. **RESEARCH** Greek and Latin poetry; Greek tragedy; 20th-century Italian Women's Writing; Roman hist; Roman law. **SELECTED PUBLICATIONS** Auth, Defending an Unwed Stepmother: Catullus 64.402, The Death of Lucan: Suicide and Execution in Tacitus, The Hero and the City: An Interpretation of Sophocles' Oedipus at Colonus. **CONTACT ADDRESS** Dept of For Lang(s) and Lit(s), Univ of Scranton, Scranton, PA 18510.

WILSON, KEITH G.
PERSONAL Born 12/15/1945, London, England **DISCIPLINE** ENGLISH **EDUCATION** Magdalene Col, Cambridge Univ, BA, 67, MA, 70; Queen's Univ, MA, 69, PhD, 73. **CAREER** Lectr, Royal Univ Malta, 72-74; instr, Carleton Univ, 74-76; asst prof, 76-82, assoc prof, 82-90, dir grad stud Eng, 85-87, Prof English, Univ Ottawa, 90-, Chmn Dept, 96-. **HONORS AND AWARDS** Ont grad fel, 69-70; Can Coun doctoral fel, 70-72; SSHRCC & Univ Ottawa res grants, 80, 81, 86, 88, 93, 94. **MEMBERSHIPS** Asn Can Univ Tchrs Eng; Thomas Hardy Soc; Victorian Stud Asn; Soc Theatre Res; Cambridge Soc; vice pres(Can), Thomas Hardy Soc N Am, 97-. **RESEARCH** 19th & 20th century literature; Thomas Hardy. **SELECTED PUBLICATIONS** Auth, Thomas Hardy on Stage, 95; ed, The Mayor of Casterbridge (Thomas Hardy), 97; ed adv bd, Eng Lit Transition, 90-; ed adv bd, Eng Stud Can, 93-. **CONTACT ADDRESS** English Dept, Univ of Ottawa, 70 Laurier Ave E, Ottawa, ON, Canada K1N 6N5. **EMAIL** kwilson@rohcg.on.ca

WILSON, L. AUSTIN
DISCIPLINE ENGLISH **EDUCATION** Univ SC, PhD. **CAREER** Dept Eng, Millsaps Col **SELECTED PUBLICATIONS** Contribur, Mississippi Writers: Reflections of Childhood and Youth, vol 1 & 2. **CONTACT ADDRESS** Dept of English, Millsaps Col, 1701 N State St, Jackson, MS 39210.

WILSON, LAURIE J.
DISCIPLINE COMMUNICATIONS **EDUCATION** Brigham Young Univ, BA, 79; MA, 82; Am Univ, PhD, 88. **CAREER** Assoc Prof to Prof and Dept Chair, Brigham Young Univ, 89-. **HONORS AND AWARDS** Fel, Pub Relations Soc of Am, 98; Pyramid of Honor, BYU, 98; Maeser Awd, BYU, 97; IABC Awd, Chicago, 97; Teaching Excellence Awd, BYU, 94-97. **MEMBERSHIPS** Broadcast Educ Asn; Radio and Television News Dir Asn; Pub Relations Soc of Am; PRSA Col of Fel; Asn for Educators in Journalism and Mass Comm; Intl Comm Asn; Asn of Latter-Day Saint Pub Relations Prof; Intl Acad of Business Disciplines. **SELECTED PUBLICATIONS** Auth, "Placing Community-Oriented Policing in the Broader Realm of Community Cooperation," The Police Chief, (95): 127-128; co-auth, Public Relations Program Management, Kendall/Hunt Pub, 96; auth, Strategic Program Planning for Effective Public Relations Campaigns, 3rd ed, Kendall/Hunt Pub, 97; co-auth, "The Effect of time on the Perceptions of Relationship Dimensions and Behavior of Members of a Key Public: Monitoring and Predicting Organization-Public Relationships," Journal of Public Relations Research, 99; auth, A Matrix approach to Solving Public Relations Problems: A Desktop Reference for strategic Matrix Planning and the Development of communication Tactics, Tittle & Pyne Comm, 99; auth, "Extending strategic Planning to Communications Tactics," in Handbook of Public relations, Sage Pub, forthcoming; auth, "Relationships Within communities: Public relations for the Next Century," in Handbook of Public Relations, Sage Pub, forthcoming. **CONTACT ADDRESS** Dept Comm, Brigham Young Univ, E-509 HFAC, Provo, UT 84602. **EMAIL** laurie_wilson@byu.edu

WILSON, LISA MARIE
PERSONAL Born 02/17/1968, Syracuse, NY, s **DISCIPLINE** ENGLISH **EDUCATION** Univ Rochester, BA, 90; Univ Buffalo, MA, 94; PhD, 99. **CAREER** Vis asst prof, Murray State Univ, 99-00; instr, Winona State Univ, 00-. **HONORS AND AWARDS** NEH, 89; Phi Beta Kappa; Joseph O'Connor Grad Study Prize, 90; Pres Fel, 90-95; Mark Diamond Res Grant, 95; Grad Asst, Office of President, Univ at Buffalo, 95-97. **MEMBERSHIPS** MLA, N Am Soc for the Study of Romanticism. **RESEARCH** 18th and 19th Century British Literature, Authorship, Romantics, Gothic, Women Writers. **SELECTED PUBLICATIONS** Auth, "Monk Lewis as Literary Lion," Romanticism on the Net, ed Frederick S Frank, (97); auth, MG 'Monk' Lewis," The Age of Romanticism and Revolution: An Oxford Companion to British Culture, ed Iain McCalman, (Oxford Univ Pr, 99): 582-583. **CONTACT ADDRESS** 119 Kansas St, Apt 4, Winona, MN 55987. **EMAIL** lwilson17@aolcom

WILSON, NORMA CLARK
PERSONAL Born 01/30/1946, Clarksville, TN, m, 1973, 2 children **DISCIPLINE** AMERICAN & BRITISH LITERATURE **EDUCATION** TN Technol Univ, BA, 68; Austin Peay State Univ, MA, 70; Univ OK, PhD, 78. **CAREER** Instr commun, comp & lit, Western OK State Univ, 77-78; prof eng, Univ SD, 78. **HONORS AND AWARDS** Ch, SD Hum Coun, 97-99. **MEMBERSHIPS** SD Peace and Justice Ctr; NOW; SD Resources Coalition. **RESEARCH** Contemp Am Indian lit; contemp Am poetry; contemp lit. **SELECTED PUBLICATIONS** Auth, Wild Iris, Point Riders Press, 78; Old ones have passed here: The poetry of Lance Henson, A: J Contemp Lit Contemp Lit, Vol 4, No 2; Turtles and learning to be a human: An interview with Linda Hogan, English Notes, Vol 26, No 1; Lost in a Dream, Dakota Woman, & Splendid Woman (poems), NDak Quart, Vol 48, No 4; Heartbeat: Within the Visionary Tradition, Walt Whitman of Mickle Street, Univ Tenn Press, 94; Outlook for survival, Denver Quart, Vol 14, No 4; Joy Harjo, Linda Henderson Hogan, Wendy Rose, Roberta Hill Whiteman, entries in: Handbook of Native American Literature, Garland, 96; Nesting in the Ruins, In: English Postcoloniality: Literatures from Around the World, Greenwood Press, 96; Ceremony: from Alienation to Reciprocity, In: Teaching American Ethnic Literatures, Univ NMex Press, 96; coed, One-Room Country School: South Dakota Stories, Brookings, SD: SD Humanities Foundation 98. **CONTACT ADDRESS** Dept of Eng, Univ of So Dakota, Vermillion, 414 E Clark St, Vermillion, SD 57069-2390. **EMAIL** nwilson@usd.edu

WILSON, REBECCA A.
PERSONAL Born 06/18/1944, St. Petersburg, FL, 2 children **DISCIPLINE** LIBRARY SCIENCE, BRITISH LITERATURE **EDUCATION** PA St Univ, Ded, 97; FL St Univ, MSLS, 67, BA, 66 **CAREER** Assoc Dir, 95-, Asst Dir, 87-95, Act Dir, 93-94, Susquehanna Univ; Site Librn, 85-87, PA St Univ; Ref Librn, 83-84, St Col of Arts and Sci; Ref Librn, 82-83, St Lawrence Univ; Map Librn, 80-81, Micronesian Area Res Ctr; Ref Librn, 70-75, St Clair County Commun Col; Ref Librn, 69-70, Univ of S FL **HONORS AND AWARDS** Res, Inst Tech Grants, 94, 95; ELCA admin study grants, 91-92 **MEMBERSHIPS** Am lib Assoc; PA Lib Assoc **SELECTED PUBLICATIONS** Auth, Students' Use of the Internet for Course-Related Research: Factors Which Account for Use or Non-use, PA St Univ, 97; Index to the Readex Microfilm Collection of Early American Newspapers, Readex Corp, 91 **CONTACT ADDRESS** 11 Linda Lane, Selinsgrove, PA 17870-1157. **EMAIL** wilsonb@susqu.edu

WILSON, ROBERT F.
PERSONAL Born 01/12/1939, Detroit, MI, m, 1995, 2 children **DISCIPLINE** ENGLISH **EDUCATION** Wayne State Univ, BA, 61; Univ Wis, MA, 62; PhD, 65. **CAREER** Asst prof, Temple Univ, 65-66; asst prof, Univ Mich Ann Arbor, 66-73, assoc prof to prof, Univ Mich Kansas City, 74-; Chair, Univ Mich Kansas City, 75-90; assoc Dean, Univ Mich Kansas City, 79-80. **HONORS AND AWARDS** All-Student Asn Teaching Awd, 75, UMKC; Deans Reg Fac Teaching Awd, UMKC, 99. **MEMBERSHIPS** Shakespeare Assoc of Am, Int Shakespeare Assoc. **RESEARCH** Shakespeare, Shakespeare on film, literary criticism. **SELECTED PUBLICATIONS** Ed, Entering the Maze: Shakespeare's Art of Beginning, Peter Lang, 95; ed, Shakespeare in Hollywood, 1929-1956, Fairleigh Dickinson, UP, 00. **CONTACT ADDRESS** Dept English, Univ of Missouri, Kansas City, 5100 Rockhill Rd, Kansas City, MO 64110-2446. **EMAIL** willsonr@umkc.edu

WILSON, ROBERT H.
PERSONAL Born 01/21/1928, Des Moines, IA, m, 1963 **DISCIPLINE** AMERICAN LITERATURE **EDUCATION** State Univ Iowa, BA, 48, MA, 50. **CAREER** From instr to asst prof, 54-73, dir grad asst & exten courses English, 67, chmn tenured fac, 74-75, ASSOC PROF ENGLISH, NORTHERN ILL UNIV, 73-, DIR UNDERGRAD STUDIES, 76-, Consult, Price-Waterhouse, 70; consult writing, Farm Credit Admin, Washington, DC, 77- **MEMBERSHIPS** MLA; Midwest Mod Lang Asn. **RESEARCH** American fiction; American drama since 1920. **CONTACT ADDRESS** Dept of English, No Illinois Univ, De Kalb, IL 60115.

WILSON, ROBERT J.
PERSONAL Born 09/29/1952, Niskayuna, NY **DISCIPLINE** ENGLISH **EDUCATION** Iona Col, BA, 74; Fordham Univ, MS, 78; NY Univ, MA, 84; CUNY Graduate Center, PhD, 00. **CAREER** Teacher, Sacred Heart Sch, NY, 74-75; teacher, Bergen Cath HS, NJ, 75-78; teacher, Sacred Heart HS, NY, 78-83; teacher, Suffern HS, NY, 83-91, 92-, ed asst, Fordham Univ, 84-85. **HONORS AND AWARDS** Fordham Univ Fel, 84-85; NEH Fel, 87, 00, 01-02; Excellence Award in Teaching, 99. **MEMBERSHIPS** Am Soc of Geolinguistics, Dict Soc of N Am, Int Ling Asn, Manuscript Soc, MLA, Nat Asn of Scholars, NAACP, New Chaucer Soc, Soc for the Hist of Authorship, Reading, and Publishing, Yonkers Hist Soc. **RESEARCH** Constitutional law, US Supreme Court, law and literature, history of the English language, textual scholarship, lexicography. **SELECTED PUBLICATIONS** Auth, "The Viking Linguistic Legacy," Verbatim, (85); auth, Ramapo Central School District Research Guide, Ramapo Central Sch Dist, 96; auth, "Censorship, Anti-Semitism, and The Merchant of Venice," Eng Jour, (97); auth, "Editing a Secondary School Research Manual," Eng Record, (97); auth, "Two Previously Unidentified Windows at St Mary's Church, Yonkers," Yonkers Hist, (98); auth, "On Academic prospects for the new century," PMLA, (00); auth, Constitutional Law and the English Teacher, NEH, (forthcoming). **CONTACT ADDRESS** Suffern High Sch, 49 Viola Rd, Suffern, NY 10901. **EMAIL** wilsonb@ramnet.k12.ny.us

WILSON, SHARON ROSE
PERSONAL Born 05/13/1941, Denver, CO, s, 1 child **DISCIPLINE** ENGLISH **EDUCATION** Colo State Col, BA, 63; Purdue Univ, MA, 67; Univ Wis, Madison, PhD, 76. **CAREER** Instr to assoc prof, Univ Northern Colo, 70-84, Dir, Writing Minor, 85-88, prof, 85-. **HONORS AND AWARDS** Fulbright Exchange Teacher, Middlesex Polytechnic, London, England, 78-79; Honors Prog Awd, UNC, 83; Int Affairs Awd, 91, 93; Who's Who in the West, 95-; Contemporary Authors, 95-; Col Scholar, Arts and Sciences, UNC, spring 96; Co-honor, Best Atwood Book, Int Margaret Atwood Soc, 97; Outstanding Fac, Disability Access Ctr & PRIDE, 99. **MEMBERSHIPS** Modern Lang Asn, Maragaret Atwood Soc, Doris Lessing Soc, Samuel Beckett Soc, Maragret Laurence Soc, Int Asn for Fantastic in the Arts, Popular Culture Asn, Nat Fulbright Asn, Western States Women's Studies Asn, Women's Caucus of Modern Lang Asn. **RESEARCH** Postcolonial Metafiction by Women; Literary work of Maragaret Atwood, Doris Lessing, Samuel Beckett; camera images in literature; narcissism in literature and film; self-conscious Novels; feminist literary criticism; Canadian literature; folklore in literature. **SELECTED PUBLICATIONS** Auth, The Self-Conscious Narrator and His Twentieth-Century Faces, Ann Arbor, Mich: Univ Microfilms (76); auth, Margaret Atwood's Fairy-Tale Sexual Politics, co-pub, Jackson: Univ Press of Miss (93) and Toronto: ECW, (94); coed, Approaches to Teaching Atwood's The Handmaid's Tale and Other Works, NY: Modern Langs Asn (96); auth, "Beyond Colonization: The Handmaid's Tale as a Postmodern and Postcolonial Metafiction," The Handmaid's Tale, M. Atwood, ed, Marta Dvorak, Paris: Ellipses (98); auth, "Mythological Intertexts in Maragaret Atwood's Work," Margaret Atwood: Works and Impact, ed Reingard Nischik, Columbia, SC: Camden House/Boydell and Brewer (2000); Auth, "The Artist's Marriage to Death in Bodily Harm," Rpt Margaret Atwood, ed and intro by Harold Bloom, Modern Critical Views, Philadelphia: Chelsea House (2000): 49-70. **CONTACT ADDRESS** Dept English, Univ of No Colorado, 501 20th St, Greeley, CO 80639-0001.

WILSON, STEVEN M.
PERSONAL Born 03/30/1960, Ft Sill, OK, m, 1982, 2 children **DISCIPLINE** CREATIVE WRITING, AMERICAN LITERATURE **EDUCATION** Univ Okla, BA, 82; Tex Christian Univ, MA, 84; Wichita State Univ, MFA, 87. **CAREER** Assoc Prof, Southwest Tex State Univ, 87-. **HONORS AND AWARDS** Fulbright Fel, 94-95; Honor Prof of the Year, 99. **MEMBERSHIPS** Fulbright Asn, Assoc Writing Prog. **RESEARCH** Beat Generation, transcendentalism, American protest literature. **SELECTED PUBLICATIONS** Auth, Allegory Dance; auth, The Singapore Express; auth, The Anatomy of water: A Sampling of Contemporary American Prose Poetry. **CONTACT ADDRESS** Dept Creative Writing & Am Lit, Southwest Texas State Univ, 601 University Dr, San Marcos, TX 78666-4685. **EMAIL** sw13@swt.edu

WILSON, STEVEN R.
PERSONAL Born 10/26/1960, Lincoln, IL, m, 1992, 6 children **DISCIPLINE** COMMUNICATION **EDUCATION** Western IL Univ, BA 82; Indiana Univ, MA 84; Purdue Univ, PhD 89. **CAREER** Northwestern Univ, assoc, 98-; Northern IL, assoc, 94-98; Michigan State Univ, asst, asst, assoc prof, 88-94. **MEMBERSHIPS** NCA; ICA; APA; INPR; ISSPR **RESEARCH** Persuasion; family violence; conflict and negotiation; social cognition and communication. **SELECTED PUBLICATIONS** Auth, Identity implications of influence goals: A revised analysis of face-threatening acts and applications to seeking compliance with same sex friends, coauth, Hum Comm Res, 98; Regulative communication strategies within mother-child interactions: Implications for the study of reflection-enhancing parental communication, coauth, Res on Lang and Soc Interaction, 97; Attribution complexity and actor observer bias, coauth, Jour of Soc Behavior and Personality; 97; Developing theories of persuasive message production: The Next generation, in: J. O. Greene, ed, Message Production: Advances in communication theory, Hillsdale NJ, Law Erlbaum, 97; Communication discipline and physical child abuse, in: Parents

Children Communication: Frontiers of Theory and Research, eds, T. J. Socha G. H. Stamp, Mahwah NJ, Law Erlbaum, 95. **CONTACT ADDRESS** Dept of Communication Studies, Northwestern Univ, 1815 Chicago Ave, Evanston, IL 60208-1340. **EMAIL** s-wilson2@nwu.edu

WILT, DAVID E.
PERSONAL Born 11/05/1955, Washington, DC **DISCIPLINE** RADIO, TV, FILM. **EDUCATION** Univ MD, BA 77, MA 80, MLS 85, PhD 91. **CAREER** Univ MD, Circulation Librarian, 86-. **RESEARCH** Pop culture and society; cinema and hist. **SELECTED PUBLICATIONS** Poster Art from the Golden Age of Mexican Cinema, contr, Agrasanchez Film Archive-IMCINE-Univ of Guadalajara, 97; Mondo Macabro, Titan books, UK, 97; Encyclopedia of Physical Sciences and Engineering Information Sources, 2d, Co ed, Gale Research, 96; Hollywood War Films, 1937-1945, with Michael Shull, McFarland 7 Co, 96; Mexican Fantasy Films, Cinefantastique, 96; The Baron of Terror: Abel Salazar, Filmfax, 96; Los Vampiros, Imagi-Movies, 94. **CONTACT ADDRESS** 4812B College Park Av # 12, College Park, MD 20740. **EMAIL** dw45@umail.umd.edu

WILT, JUDITH
PERSONAL Born 09/17/1941, Pittsburgh, PA **DISCIPLINE** ENGLISH LITERATURE **EDUCATION** Duquesne Univ, BA, 67; Ind Univ, PhD(English), 72. **CAREER** Asst prof English, Princeton Univ, 72-78; assoc prof, 78-82, PROF ENGLISH, BOSTON COL, 82- **HONORS AND AWARDS** AAUW fel, 78-79; NEH summer seminar, 91. **MEMBERSHIPS** MLA **RESEARCH** British fiction; women's studies **SELECTED PUBLICATIONS** Auth, The Readable People of George Meredith, Princeton Univ, 75; Ghosts of the Gothic: Austen, Eliot and Lawrence, Princeton Univ, 80; Secret Leaves: The Novels of Walter Scott, Univ Chicago, 85; Abortion, Choice and Contemporary Fiction: The Armageddon of the Maternal Instinct, Univ Chicago, 91. **CONTACT ADDRESS** Dept of English, Boston Col, Chestnut Hill, 140 Commonwealth Ave, Chestnut Hill, MA 02167-3800. **EMAIL** judith.wilt@bc.edu

WILTSHIRE, SUSAN FORD
PERSONAL Born 10/13/1941, Amarillo, TX, m, 1969, 2 children **DISCIPLINE** CLASSICS **EDUCATION** Univ Texas, Austin, BA, 63; Columbia Univ, MA, 64, PhD, 67. **CAREER** Asst prof classics, Univ Ill, Champaign-Urbana, 67-69; asst prof English & dir Honors Program, Fisk Univ, 69-71; asst prof to prof classics, 71- , chair Dept of Class Stud, Vanderbilt Univ. **HONORS AND AWARDS** Phi Beta Kappa; Woodrow Wilson Fel, Dissertation Fel, 63-64, 66-67; Madison Sarratt Prize for Excellence in Undergrad Tchg, 79; Phi Beta Kappa Assoc Lctr Panel, 91-92, 92-93; listed in Contemp Auth; Alex Haley Mem Awd, 93; Overall Awd of Excellence, So Books Competition, 98. **MEMBERSHIPS** Nat Coun on Hum; Am Philol Asn; Class Asn of the Middle West and South; Overseers' Comm to Visit the Dept of Classics, Harvard Univ, 96-99; Int Bonhoeffer Soc. **RESEARCH** Latin poetry; Greek epic and drama; the classical tradition in America. **SELECTED PUBLICATIONS** Auth, Public and Private in Vergil's Aeneid, (Massachusetts), 89; auth, Greece, Rome, and the Bill of Rights, (Oklahoma), 92; auth, Seasons of Grief and Grace: A Sister's Story of AIDS, Vanderbilt, 94; coauth, Classical Nashville: Athens of the South, Vanderbilt, 96; auth, Athena's Disguises: Mentors in Everyday Life, John Knox, 98; ed, Prairie Laureate: The Collected Poems of Robert Lee Brothers, Eakin, 98. **CONTACT ADDRESS** Vanderbilt Univ, PO Box 18 Station B, Nashville, TN 37235. **EMAIL** Susan.F.Wiltshire@vanderbilt.edu

WIMSATT, JAMES I.
PERSONAL Born 09/25/1927, Detroit, MI, m, 1991, 3 children **DISCIPLINE** ENGLISH **EDUCATION** Univ Mich, BA, 50; Wayne State Univ, MA, 59; Duke Univ, PhD(English), 64. **CAREER** Instr, Univ Tenn, 63-64; asst prof, Tex Christian Univ, 64-66; from asst prof to prof, Univ NC, Greensboro, 66-77; PROF ENGLISH, UNIV TEX, AUSTIN, 77-, Fels, Duke Univ & Univ NC Coop Prog in Humanities, 70-71; Am Coun Learned Soc fel, 74-75; Guggenheim fel, 81-82; Temple prof, emer, 94-. **MEMBERSHIPS** Mediaeval Acad Am; New Chaucer Soc. **RESEARCH** Chaucer; Middle English literature; Old French literature. **SELECTED PUBLICATIONS** Auth, Rhyme-Reason, Chaucer-Pope, Icon-Symbol, Mod Lang Quart, Vol 0055, 94; John Duns-Scotus, Charles Sanders Pine, and Geoffrey Chasiceis Portrayal of the Canterbury Pilgrims; Rhyme, the Icons of Sound, and the Middle English 'Pearl', Style, Vol 0030, 96; Chaucer and Hio French Contemporaries, U Toronto Press, 91. **CONTACT ADDRESS** Dept of English, Univ of Texas, Austin, Austin, TX 78712.

WIMSATT, MARY ANN
PERSONAL Born Miami, FL **DISCIPLINE** ENGLISH **EDUCATION** Stetson Univ, AB, 57; Duke Univ, MA, 58; PhD, 64. **CAREER** Instr, Tex Christian Univ, 65-66; Instr, Guilford Col, 67-69; Asst Prof, Greensboro Col, 69-74; Asst Prof, Elon Col, 76-79; From Asst Prof to Assoc Prof, Southwest Tex State Univ, 79-90; Prof, Univ SC, 90-. **HONORS AND AWARDS** Phi Beta Kappa; Nat Endowment Humanities Younger Humanist Fel, 72-73; Nat Endowment Humanities Sen Fel, 85-86. **MEMBERSHIPS** MLA, SAMLA, ALA, SSSL. **RESEARCH** American and Southern literature. **SELECTED PUBLICATIONS** Auth, "Gail Godwin, the South and the Canons," Southern Lit J, 27 (95): 86-95; co-ed, Southern Women Writers, Gale Res, Inc (Detroit, MI), 95; ed, Tales of the South by William Gilmore Simms, Univ SC Pr (Columbia, SC), 96; auth, "The Professional Author in the South: William Gilmore Simms and Antebellum Literary Publishing," in The Professions of Authorship: Essays in Hon of Matthew J. Bruccoli (Columbia: Univ SC Pr, 96); auth, "Region, Time and Memory: 'The Optimist's Daughter' as Southern Renascence Fiction," in The Late Novels of Eudora Welty (Columbia: Univ SC Pr, 98); auth, "The Old Order Undermined: Daughters, Mothers and Grandmothers in Katherine Anne Porter's Miranda Tales," in Southern Mothers (Baton Rouge: La St UP, 99). **CONTACT ADDRESS** Dept English, Univ of So Carolina, Columbia, Columbia, SC 29208.

WINANS, ROBERT B.
DISCIPLINE ENGLISH **EDUCATION** Cornell, BA, 64; Univ NYork, MA, 65, PhD, 72. **CAREER** Asst prof English, Gettysburg. **RESEARCH** Folklore, minstrel shows. **SELECTED PUBLICATIONS** Fel Publ, A Descriptive Checklist of Book Catalogues Separately Printed in America, 1639-1800, AAS, 81; auth, The Folk, the Stage, and the Five-String Banjo in Nineteenth-Century America, Jour of Amer Folklore 89, 76; 'Sadday Night and Sunday Too': The Uses of Slave Songs in the WPA Ex-Slave Narratives for Historical Study, NJ Folklore 7, 82; Bibliography and the Cultural Historian: Notes on the Eighteenth-Century Novel, Printing and Society in Early America, 83; Early Minstrel Show Music, In: Musical Theater in America: Papers and Proceedings of the Conference on Musical Theater in America, 84; The Early Minstrel Show, New World Records, NW 338, 85. **CONTACT ADDRESS** Dept of English, Gettysburg Col, Gettysburg, PA 17325.

WINCHATZ, MICHAELA R.
PERSONAL Born 01/04/1967, Summit, NJ, m, 1992 **DISCIPLINE** SPEECH COMMUNICATION **EDUCATION** Rutgers Col, BA, 88; Ludwig-Maximilians Univ, Germany, MA, 92; Univ of Washington, PhD, 97. **CAREER** Asst Prof, 97-, Southern Illinois University-Carbondale. **HONORS AND AWARDS** Alice Schlimmbach Alumnae Soc Scholar stud in Germany, Rutgers Univ, 86; Class of 1920 Merit Scholar, Rutgers Univ, 88; Fulbright Full Grant, 90-91, renewal grant, 91-92; DAAD Annual Grant to Germany, 95-96; Humanities Dissertation Fel, Univ of Washington, 96; Joint Womens Stud and Univ Womens Prof Advancement Juried Comp Res Awd, 97; Southern Illinois Univ Dean's Appreciation Awd, 00; ed asst, quarterly jour of speech, 97. **MEMBERSHIPS** NCA, WSCA. **RESEARCH** Ethnography of commun; ethnographic fieldwork methods; intercultural commun; interpersonal commun; conversation analysis. **SELECTED PUBLICATIONS** Coauth, Reading Ella CaraDelorias Waterlily for Cultured Speech, Iowa Jour of Comm, 97; Coauth, Acting Out Our Minds Incorporating Behavior into Models of Stereotype Based Expectancies for Cross Cultural Interactions, Comm Mono, 97; auth, "Social Meanings in German Interactions: An Ethnographic Analysis of the Second-Person Pronoun Sie," Res on Lang and Social Interaction, 01. **CONTACT ADDRESS** Dept of Speech Commun, So Illinois Univ, Carbondale, Dept of Speech Communication, Mailcode 6605, Carbondale, IL 62901-6605. **EMAIL** winchatz@siu.edu

WINCHELL, DONNA
DISCIPLINE ENGLISH LITERATURE **EDUCATION** Tex Christian Univ, PhD, 83. **CAREER** Dept Eng, Clemson Univ **RESEARCH** Rhetoric and composition. **SELECTED PUBLICATIONS** Auth, Cries of Outrage: Three Novelists' Use of History, Miss Quart, 96; Alice Walker, Dictionary of Literary Biography, 94; Tracing the Motherlines, Miss Quart, 93; Alice Walker: Biographical and Bibliographic Beginning, Notes on Tchg Eng, 93; The Wound and the Fiddle Bow, SC Rev, 93. **CONTACT ADDRESS** Clemson Univ, Clemson, SC 29634. **EMAIL** winched@clemson.edu

WINCHELL, MARK
DISCIPLINE ENGLISH LITERATURE **EDUCATION** Vanderbilt Univ, PhD, 78. **CAREER** Dept Eng, Clemson Univ **RESEARCH** American literature and literary criticism. **SELECTED PUBLICATIONS** Auth, The Myth is the Message, or, Why Streetcar Keeps Running, Confronting Streetcar, Greenwood, 92; Rod Serling's Requiem for a Heavyweight: A Drama for Its Time, Studies Am Drama, 1945-The Present, 93; South of Boston, Sewanee Rev, 95; Come Back to the Locker Room Ag'in, Brick Honey, Miss Quart, 93. **CONTACT ADDRESS** Clemson Univ, 307 Strode, Clemson, SC 29634. **EMAIL** ixtlan@clemson.edu

WINDERL, CARL A.
DISCIPLINE ENGLISH **EDUCATION** Trevecca Nazarene Col, BA; Univ Chicago, MA; NYork Univ, PhD. **CAREER** Eng Dept, Eastern Nazarene Col **RESEARCH** Gerard Manley Hopkins. **SELECTED PUBLICATIONS** Area: poems. **CONTACT ADDRESS** Eastern Nazarene Col, 23 East Elm Ave, Quincy, MA 02170-2999.

WINDERL, RONDA RICE
DISCIPLINE MEDIA STUDIES **EDUCATION** Olivet Nazarene Univ, BA; Emerson Col, MA; NYork Univ, PhD. **CAREER** Eng Dept, Eastern Nazarene Col **HONORS AND AWARDS** Chair, Div Arts & Letters; Chair, Dept Comm Arts; Prod/Dir, Theatre Prog. **SELECTED PUBLICATIONS** Area: the influence of Western theatre on contemporary Japanese theatre. **CONTACT ADDRESS** Eastern Nazarene Col, 23 East Elm Ave, Quincy, MA 02170-2999.

WINDHAUSER, JOHN W.
DISCIPLINE MASS COMMUNICATION **EDUCATION** Ohio Univ, PhD, 75. **CAREER** Ed, Col Press Rev; ed bd, Jour Quart, Newspaper Res J; prof, mem, grad fac, area hd, polit commun, La State Univ. **RESEARCH** Health and political communications. **SELECTED PUBLICATIONS** Auth, How the Metropolitan Press Covered the 1970 General Election Campaigns in Ohio, in Jour Quart, 75; coauth, Reliability of Six Techniques for the Content Analysis of Local Coverage, in Jour Quart, 79; The Media in the 1984 and 1988 Presidential Campaign; the Editorial Process; Coverage by the Prestige Press of the 1988 Presidential Campaign, in Jour Quart, 89; What Children Saw in 16 Years: A Nutrient Analysis of Foods in Television Advertisements, in FASEB J, 94. **CONTACT ADDRESS** The Manship Sch of Mass Commun, Louisiana State Univ and A&M Col, Baton Rouge, LA 70803. **EMAIL** jrwill@lsu.edu

WINDHOLZ, ANNE
DISCIPLINE ENGLISH **EDUCATION** Univ Colo, BA, 84; Univ Ill, MA, 85; Univ Ill, PhD, 90. **CAREER** Grad Teaching Asst, Univ Ill, 86-90; Asst Prof, Roanoke Col, 90-96; From Asst Prof to Assoc Prof, Augustana Col, 96-. **HONORS AND AWARDS** Andrew W. Mellon Fel Humanities; Phi Kappa Phi, Nat Endowment Humanities Summer Fel, Univ Mich, 96. **MEMBERSHIPS** MLA, Res Soc for Victorian Periodicals, Midwest Victorian Studies Asn, MMLA. **RESEARCH** Victorian literature and culture, Nineteenth and early Twentieth-Century British and American fiction, women writers, gender and imperialism, transatlanticism, Victorian periodicals, the 1890s. **SELECTED PUBLICATIONS** Auth and rev, articles and reviews in Victorian Studies, Victorian Periodicals Rev; auth, essays in "Brit Short Fiction Writers: The Realist Tradition, Nineteenth-Century Brit Women Writers, The 1890s: An Encycl of Brit Lit, Art and Cult. **CONTACT ADDRESS** Dept English, Augustana Col, So Dakota, 2001 S Summit Ave, Sioux Falls, SD 57197-0001. **EMAIL** windholz@inst.augie.edu

WINEAPPLE, BRENDA
PERSONAL Born 02/05/1949, Boston, MA, m **DISCIPLINE** ENGLISH AND AMERICAN LITERATURE **EDUCATION** Brandeis Univ, BA; Univ of Wis at Madison, PhD. **CAREER** Vis prof, NYU, 97; co-dir, biography seminar, NYU; Washington Irving Prof of Modern Literary and Hist Studies, Union Col, 94-. **HONORS AND AWARDS** Am Coun of Learned Societies Fel, 97-98; Guggenheim Fel, 91; Donald C. Gallop Fel, Yale Univ, 91; Nat Endowment of the Humanities Fel, 87, 00. **MEMBERSHIPS** New York Institute for the Humanities; MLA; Am Studies Asn; Columbia Univ Seminar in Am Civilization. **RESEARCH** Biography; American literature; women's studies. **SELECTED PUBLICATIONS** Auth, Sister, Brother: Gertrude and Leo Stein, Johns Hopkins Univ Press, 97; Genet: A Biography of Genet Flanner, Houghton Mifflin, 89; The Conqueror's Hat: Poetry and Biography, Parnassus, 98; Gertrude Stein and the Lost Ark: A Woman's a Woman IS, Am Scholar, 98; Mourning Becomes Biography, Am Image, 97/98; Gertrude Stein Reads JAMA, J of the Am Medical Asn, 96; Biography and Transgression, Graven Images, 98; Hawthorne, American Literary Scholarship, Duke, 99; Lying Dreams, That Obscure Object of Desire, Routledge, 99; Introduction, The Wings of the Dove, Signet, 99; Introduction, The Scarlet Letter, Signet, 00; The Transformations, Parnassus, 00 **CONTACT ADDRESS** English Dept, Union Col, New York, Schenectady, NY 12308. **EMAIL** wineappb@union.edu

WING, NATHANIEL
DISCIPLINE 19TH AND 20TH CENTURY LITERATURE, LITERARY THEORY **EDUCATION** Haverford Col, BA, 59; Columbia Univ, MA, 62; PhD, 68. **CAREER** Chair, Dept of French and Italian, 85-93; prof, dept of French and Italian, 85-; assoc dir, Ctr of Fr and Francophone Stud, 93-98, La State Univ. **HONORS AND AWARDS** Fulbright scholar, Universite d'Aix en Provence, 62-63; Louisiana Endowment for the Humanities/ Nat Endowment for the Humanities grant, 88; Louisiana Endowment for the Humanities grant, 95. **MEMBERSHIPS** Am Asn of Teachers of French; Am Asn of Univ profs; MLA. **SELECTED PUBLICATIONS** Auth, Present Appearance: Aspects of Poetic Structure in Rimbaud's 'Illuminations
Univ of Mississippi Press, 74; auth, The Limits of Narrati
Essays on Baudelaire, Falubert, Rimbaud, and Mallarme, C
bridge Univ Press, 86; auth, "Reading Simplicity: Flau
'Un Coeur simple,'" Nineteenth Century Fr Stud 21.1
93): 88-101; auth, "Ecriture et relation dans les
d'Edouard Glissant," in Horizons d'Edouard Glissan
Favre and A. De Brito (J&D Editions, 92), 295-30
laire's 'Frisson fraternal:' Horror and Encahntment
leaux parisiens,'" Neophilologus LXXXI.1 (97)
"Androgyny, Hysteria, and the Poet in Baudelai

Fanfarlo," Romance Quarterly 45.3 (98): 143-153. **CONTACT ADDRESS** Dept of Fr Grad Stud, Louisiana State Univ and A&M Col, Baton Rouge, LA 70803. **EMAIL** nwing@lsu.edu

WINKLER, CAROL
DISCIPLINE SPEECH COMMUNICATION **EDUCATION** Univ Md, PhD, 87. **CAREER** Assoc prof, ch, dept Commun, Ga State Univ, 94-. **HONORS AND AWARDS** Mortarboard Distinguished Prof Awd. **MEMBERSHIPS** Exec Comt, Southern Speech Commun Asn; Legis Coun, Speech Commun Asn. **RESEARCH** Visual communication. **SELECTED PUBLICATIONS** Wrote three books and published more than forty articles in political debates, visual communication, and presidential foreign policy rhetoric. **CONTACT ADDRESS** Georgia State Univ, Atlanta, GA 30303. **EMAIL** cwinkler@gsu.edu

WINKLER, MARTIN M.
PERSONAL Born 05/24/1952, Germany **DISCIPLINE** CLASSICS **EDUCATION** Univ of Southern CA, PhD, 82 **CAREER** Lectr, Univ CA-Riverside, 81-82; asst prof, Univ Utah, 82-83; asst prof, Univ Wisconsin-Madison, 83-87; asst prof, Bucknell Univ, 87-89; assoc prof, prof, 89-, George Mason Univ **HONORS AND AWARDS** Mellon Found post doctoral research fel, 89-90 **MEMBERSHIPS** Amer Assoc of Univ Profs; Amer Philological Assoc; Classical Assoc of the Middle West and South; Vergician Soc of Amer **RESEARCH** Roman satire; classical tradion; classics and cinema **SELECTED PUBLICATIONS** Ed, Classics and Cinema, 91; auth, Der lateinische Eulenspiegel des Ioannes Nemius: Text und Ubersetzung, Kommentar und Untersuchungen, 95; Alogia and emphasis in Juvenal's Fourth Satire, Ramus: Critical Studies in Greek and Roman Literature, 95; Cinema and the Fall of Rome, Transactions of the American Philological Association, 95; Homeric Kleos and the Western Film, Syllecta Classica, 96; The Roman Empire in American Cinema After 1945, The Classical Journal, 98. **CONTACT ADDRESS** Dept of Modern and Classical Languages, George Mason Univ, Fairfax, 4400 Univ Dr., Fairfax, VA 22030. **EMAIL** mwinkler@gmu.edu

WINNER, ANTHONY
PERSONAL Born 08/17/1931, New York, NY, m, 1964, 1 child **DISCIPLINE** ENGLISH, COMPARATIVE LITERATURE **EDUCATION** Harvard Univ, AB, 53, PhD, 62; Columbia Univ, MA, 54. **CAREER** Instr English, Univ Pa, 61-63 & Hunter Col, 63-65; asst prof, 65-68, ASSOC PROF ENGLISH, UNIV VA, 68-. **MEMBERSHIPS** MLA **RESEARCH** The novel; realism; character in fiction. **SELECTED PUBLICATIONS** Auth, Adjustment, tragic humanism, and Italy, Studi Americani, 61; co-transl, Ugo Foscolo, Last letters of Jacopo Ortis, In: Great European Short Novels, 68 & ed, Great European Short Novels, 68, Perennial Libr, Harper; Characters in the Twilight: Hardy, Zola, and Chekhov, Univ Va, 81. **CONTACT ADDRESS** Dept of English, Univ of Virginia, 219 Bryan Hall, Charlottesville, VA 22903.

WINNER, VIOLA HOPKINS
PERSONAL Born 03/13/1928, Cleveland, OH, m, 1964, 1 child **DISCIPLINE** AMERICAN LITERATURE **EDUCATION** Oberlin Col, BA, 49; NYork Univ, MA, 53, PhD, 60. **CAREER** Instr, 54-57, Adelphi Univ; instr, Hunter Col, 60-64; asst prof, 65-72, Univ Va; prof, 73-76, Sweet Briar Col; ed assoc, 77-, Letters Henry Adams, Univ Va; NEH sr fel, 72-73. **MEMBERSHIPS** Am Studies Assn; MLA. **RESEARCH** Henry James; American fiction; literature and the visual arts. **SELECTED PUBLICATIONS** Auth, On Faulkner's The Hamlet: A Study in Meaning and Form, Accent, 55; auth, Glori-ani and the Tides of Taste, 19th Century Fiction, 63; auth, Henry James and the Visual Arts, Univ Va, 70; ed, Edith Wharton's Fast and Loose, Univ Press of Va, 77; contribr, American Fiction: Historical and Critical Essays, Northeastern Univ, 77; auth, Thackeray and Richard Doyle, the Wayward Artist of the Newcomes, Harvard Libr Bull, 4/78. **CONTACT ADDRESS** 950 Locust Ave, Charlottesville, VA 22901.

WINSECK, DWAYNE
DISCIPLINE POLITICAL ECONOMY OF COMMUNICATION, MEDIA HISTORY **EDUCATION** Univ Oregon, PhD. **CAREER** Instr, universities in the People's Rep of China; US; Turkish Rep of N Cyprus; UK; assoc prof, Carleton Univ. **RESEARCH** Communication policy, theories of democracy and global communication. **SELECTED PUBLICATIONS** Co-ed, Democratizing Communication?: Comparative Perspectives on Information and Power, Hampton Press, 97; Media in Global Context, Edward Arnold, 97; Reconvergence: A Political Economy of Telecommunications in Canada, Hampton Press, 98. **CONTACT ADDRESS** Dept of Commun, Carleton Univ, 1125 Colonel By Dr, Ottawa, ON, Canada K1S 5B6. **EMAIL** dwayne_winseck@carleton.ca

WINSHIP, MICHAEL B.
DISCIPLINE ENGLISH **EDUCATION** Harvard, AB, 71; Simmons, MS, 82; Oxford, DPhilos, 89. **CAREER** Asst prof English, Univ Tex, Austin; ed, Bibliog of Amer Lit. **RESEARCH** Literary publishing. **SELECTED PUBLICATIONS** Auth, Bibliography of American Literature vols 7-9, Yale Univ, 83-91; American Literary Publishing in the Mid-Nineteenth Century: The Business of Ticknor and Fields, Cambridge Univ, 85; Publishing in America, Procs of the AAS 96, 86; Hermann Ernst Ludewig, Columbia Univ, 86; Ticknor and Fields: The Business of American Literary Publishing in the 19th Century, Hanes Fdn. and Univ NC Libr, 92; Epitome and Selective Index, North Amer Press, 95. **CONTACT ADDRESS** Dept of English, Univ of Texas, Austin, Austin, TX 78712-1164.

WINSHIP, PETER
PERSONAL Born Pensacola, FL, m, 1966, 2 children **DISCIPLINE** HISTORY; LITERATURE (18TH -20TH CENTURIES-EUROPE) **EDUCATION** Harvard, AB, 64, LLB, 68; London Univ, London Sch of Economics and political sci, LLM, 73. **CAREER** Lectr, 70-72, Addis Ababa Univ; 74-present, Southern Methodist Univ **MEMBERSHIPS** American Law Inst. **RESEARCH** Legal history; Comparative law; International law **SELECTED PUBLICATIONS** Auth, The U.N. Sales Convention and the Emerging Caselaw, in EMPTIO-VENDITIO INTER NATIONES: IN ANERKENNUNG FUR LEHRTATIGKEIT KARL HEINZ NEUMAYER, 97; auth, Selected Security Interests in the United States, Emerging Financial Markets and Secured Transactions, Kluwer, 98; auth, Karl Llewellyn in Rome, 98. **CONTACT ADDRESS** Dallas, TX 75275-0116. **EMAIL** pwinship@mail.smu.edu

WINSTON, MATHEW
PERSONAL Born 10/03/1942, New York, NY, d, 2 children **DISCIPLINE** ENGLISH **EDUCATION** Cornell Univ, BA, 64; Harvard Univ, MA, 65; PhD, 72. **CAREER** Asst prof, Columbia Univ, 70-79; asst prof, Col William and Mary, 79-83; assoc prof, Univ Ala, 83. **MEMBERSHIPS** SAMLA; SRC; Shakespeare Asn; Marlowe Soc; CUSR. **RESEARCH** Renaissance drama; Sixteenth-Century English Literature; Contemporary Literature. **SELECTED PUBLICATIONS** Auth, "Gendered Nostalgia in The Duchess of Malfi," Renaissance Papers (98): 103-113; auth, "Christopher Marlowe," Major Tudor Authors: A Bio-Critical Sourcebook, ed. Alan Hager (NY: Greenwood Press,97): 335-342; auth, "The Incoherent Self in Contemporary Comedy," Modern Drama 29 (86): 388-402; auth, "'Craft against Vice': Morality Play Elements in Measure for Measure," Shakespeare Studies 14 (81): 229-248; auth, "Black Humor: To Weep with Laughing," Comedy: New Perspectives, ed. Maurice Charney (NY Literary Forum, 78): 31-43; auth, "Watt's First Footnote," J Mod Lit 6 (77): 69-82; auth, "Edward Albee: A Delicate Balance," Das amerikanische Drama der Gecrenwart, ed. Herbert Grabes (Kronberg: Athenaeum, 76: 29-43; auth, "The Ethics of Contemporary Black Humor," Colorado Quart 24 (76): 275-288; auth, "Lolita and the Dangers of Fiction," Twentieth Century Lit 21; (75): 421-427. **CONTACT ADDRESS** Dept English, Univ of Alabama, Tuscaloosa, PO Box 870244, Tuscaloosa, AL 35487-0244. **EMAIL** mwinston@bama.ua.edu

WINTER, DARIA PORTRAY
PERSONAL Born 09/07/1949, Washington, DC **DISCIPLINE** ENGLISH **EDUCATION** Hampton Inst, BS, English educ, 1972; Univ of Virginia, MA, English, 1973; George Washington Univ, PhD program, 1988-89. **CAREER** DC Office of Bicentennial Programs, asst to exec dir, 75-76; UDC Coop Extension Program, education specialist, 76-77; Univ of the District of Columbia, instructor of English, 77-97, Asst Prof of English, 95-; Mayor of District of Columbia, general assistant, 92-95; Southeastern Univ, asst prof of English; Univ of District of Columbia Lorton Coll Prison Program, faculty, 98. **HONORS AND AWARDS** Appreciation Awd, University of District of Columbia Student NEA, 1984; Appreciation Awd in Support of Public Education, from superintendent, Floretta McKenzie, 1983; Outstanding Service Awd; Distinguished Public Service Awd, 1994; Univ of the District of Columbia, College of Liberal and Fine Arts, Image Awd, 1996; Steering Committee of DC, Reclaim Our Youth Awd, 1996. **MEMBERSHIPS** Alternate natl committeewoman DC Dem State Comm 1980-92; NEA Standing Comm on Higher Educ 1981-87; vice chair DC Democratic State Comm 1984-92; Democratic Natl Comm 1984-92; delegate to Democratic Convention 1984, 1988, 1992; Modern Language Assn, Coll Language Assn; NCTE; editor, Newsletter Natl Educ Assn Black Caucus 1987-89; Public Defender Service Bd of Trustees, 1988-92, commissioner, 1987-; District Statehood Commn, 1979-92; vice chair, DNC Eastern Region Caucus, 1988-92; bd mem, DC Juvenile Justice Advisory Group; bd mem, United Planning Organization; mem appointed by Pres Wm Clinton, Presidential Rank Commssion, 1994; chairperson, Univ of the District of Columbia Advocacy Committee, 1996; chairperson, DC Juvenile Justice Advisory Group, 1998. **CONTACT ADDRESS** Univ of District of Columbia, 4200 Connecticut Ave NW, Bldg 52, Rm 409, Washington, DC 20008.

WINTER, KARI J.
PERSONAL Born 10/18/1960, Minneapolis, MN, m, 1 child **DISCIPLINE** ENGLISH **EDUCATION** Ind Univ, BA, 81; Univ Minn, PhD, 90. **CAREER** Tchng asst, 84-90, Univ Minn; asst prof, 90-92, Fisk Univ; asst prof, 92-97, assoc prof, 97-, Univ Vt. **HONORS AND AWARDS** Tchng Awd Fel, 87-88, Univ Minn; Doct Diss Fel, Univ Minn, 88; Choice Outstanding Acad Book; Univ Vt Comm on Res & Scholars Sum Grant, 93; Tchng Awd, Golden Key Natl Honor Soc, 95; Univ Vt Instruct Incentive Grants, 93-94, 96-97. **MEMBERSHIPS** Modern Lang Assn; Amer Stud Assn; New Eng Amer Stud Assn. **RESEARCH** Amer Indian Lit; African-Amer Lit; feminist theory. **SELECTED PUBLICATIONS** Auth, Subjects of Slavery, Agents of Change: Women and Power in Gothic Novels and Slave Narratives, 1790-1865, Univ Ga Press, 92. **CONTACT ADDRESS** Dept of English, Univ of Vermont, Burlington, VT 05405. **EMAIL** Kwinter@zoo.uvm.edu

WINTER, THOMAS NELSON
PERSONAL Born 01/27/1944, Lansing, MI, m, 1964, 2 children **DISCIPLINE** CLASSICS **EDUCATION** Mich State Univ, BA, 64; Northwestern Univ, MA, 65, PhD, 68. **CAREER** Guest lectr, Adler Planetarium, 66; asst prof, 68-70, actg hd, Classics Div, Univ Hawaii, 69; asst prof, 70-75, assoc prof, Univ Nebr, Lincoln, 76-. **HONORS AND AWARDS** Merit Increment for Excellence in Tchg and Res, Univ Hawaii, 69; NEH summer sem, Am Acad Rome, 78; Parents Assn Award for Serv to Stud, Univ Nebr, Lincoln, 95, 96. **MEMBERSHIPS** APA, CAMWS, ACL, EAA, AOPA. **RESEARCH** Circumstantial case-assignment in the Latin of Caesar. **SELECTED PUBLICATIONS** Auth, When Quod is 'Which' and When Quod is 'Because', Class Outlook 72, 95. **CONTACT ADDRESS** Univ of Nebraska, Lincoln, 233 Andrews Hall, Lincoln, NE 68855-0337. **EMAIL** twinter1@unl.edu

WINTERS, DONALD
PERSONAL Born 04/15/1945, Albany, NY, m, 1969, 1 child **DISCIPLINE** AMERICAN CULTURE, POETRY **EDUCATION** Long Beach State Univ, BA, 68; Univ Mich, MA, 70; Univ Minn, PhD, 81. **CAREER** Instr, Col of St Francis, 89, 91; Instr, Minn Community and Tech Col. **HONORS AND AWARDS** Diss Fel, 80-81; Ralph Gabriel Diss Awd, 82; NEH Summer Sem, Yale Univ, 86. **MEMBERSHIPS** Am Studies Assoc; Minn Educ Assoc; Community Col Humanities Assoc. **RESEARCH** I.W.W. and radical labor history, popular culture, rock music, music and poetry of Bob Dylan. **SELECTED PUBLICATIONS** Auth, Soul of the Wobblies, greenwood Pr, 85; auth, "Covington Hall: The Utopian Vision of a Wobbly Poet", Labor's Heritage 4.2, 92. **CONTACT ADDRESS** Dept Humanities, Minneapolis Comm and Tech Col, 1501 Hennepin Ave, Minneapolis, MN 55403-1710.

WINTON, CALHOUN
PERSONAL Born 01/21/1927, Ft Benning, GA, m, 1948, 2 children **DISCIPLINE** ENGLISH **EDUCATION** Univ of the South, BA, 48; Vanderbilt Univ, MA, 50; Princeton Univ, MA, 54, PhD(English), 55. **CAREER** Ford Found teaching fel, Dartmouth Col, 54-55, instr English, 55-57; asst prof, Univ Va, 57-60; Winterthur asst prof, Univ Del, 60-64, assoc prof, 64-67, coordr Winterthur Grad Prog Early Am Cult, 61-67; prof English, Univ SC, 67-75, chmn dept, 70-75, dir grad studies, 68-70; actg chmn dept, 76-77, dir Grad Studies, 76-79, PROF ENGLISH, UNIV MD, 75-97, Am Philos Soc grant, 60; Am Coun Learned grant, 63; Guggenheim fel, 65-66; Fulbright lectureship, Turkey, 79-80; Prof Emer, 97-. **HONORS AND AWARDS** John Carter Brown Library Fel, 95. **MEMBERSHIPS** MLA; Conf Brit Studies, Am Studies Asn, Am Soc 18th Century Studies, S Atlantic Mod Lang Asn, Am Antiquarian Soc. **RESEARCH** Colonial American literature, 18th century literature. **SELECTED PUBLICATIONS** auth, John Gay and the London Theatre, 93; auth, Genre and Generic--Change in English Comedy, 1660-1710, Scriblerian and the Kit-Cats, Vol 0027, 94; auth, Colonial Book in the Atlantic World, 99. **CONTACT ADDRESS** Dept of English, Univ of Maryland, Col Park, College Park, MD 20742-0001. **EMAIL** cw41@umail.umd.edu

WION, PHILIP KENNEDY
PERSONAL Born 09/06/1941, Bellefonte, PA, m, 1967, 2 children **DISCIPLINE** ENGLISH LITERATURE **EDUCATION** Swarthmore Col, BA, 63; Yale Univ, MA, 64, PhD(English), 67. **CAREER** Asst prof, 67-72, assoc prof English, Univ Pittsburgh, 72-. **MEMBERSHIPS** NCTE; AAUP; Am Fedn Teachers. **RESEARCH** Sixteenth century English literature; psychoanalytic criticism. **SELECTED PUBLICATIONS** Auth, Marlowe's Doctor Faustus, the Oedipus Complex, and the Denial of Death, Colby Libr Quart, XVI: 190-204; The Absent Mother in Emily Bronte's Wuthering Heights, American Imago, XLII, No 2, pp 143-64. **CONTACT ADDRESS** Dept of English, Univ of Pittsburgh, 526 Cathedral/Learn, Pittsburgh, PA 15260-2504. **EMAIL** pwion@pitt.edu

WISNESKI, RICHARD
PERSONAL Born 09/03/1968, New York, NY, s **DISCIPLINE** ENGLISH **EDUCATION** SUNY, BA, 90; Mich State Univ, MA, 92; PhD, 97. **CAREER** Teaching Asst, Mich State Univ, 92-96; Adj Asst Prof to Lecturer, Univ Mich, 96-. **HONORS AND AWARDS** Dissertation Completion Fel, MSU, 97; Res Excellence Fund, PURA, 00. **MEMBERSHIPS** MLA, NCTE, Soc for Early Americanists. **RESEARCH** Revolutionary War Letters and Diaries from non-colonials; Representations of Creole Identities in Early American Drama; Publication and Reception of travel narratives from early nationalist era. **CONTACT ADDRESS** Dept English, Univ of Michigan, Flint, 303 E Kearsley St, Flint, MI 48502-1907. **EMAIL** wisneski@pilot.msu.edu

WITEMEYER, HUGH
DISCIPLINE VICTORIAN AND MODERN BRITISH AND AMERICAN LITERATURE **EDUCATION** Princeton Univ, PhD, 66. **CAREER** Instr, Univ NMex, 73-. **SELECTED PUBLICATIONS** Auth, Pound/Williams: Selected Letters of Ezra Pound and William Carlos Williams, 96; coed, Ezra Pound and Senator Bronson Cutting: A Political Correspondence 1930-1935, 95. **CONTACT ADDRESS** Univ of New Mexico, Albuquerque, Albuquerque, NM 87131. **EMAIL** hughwit@unm.edu

WITHERELL, ELIZABETH H.
PERSONAL Born 08/15/1948, Columbus, OH, m, 1969, 1 child **DISCIPLINE** ENGLISH **EDUCATION** Univ Mich, BA, 69; Univ Wis, MA, 72; PhD, 79. **CAREER** Textual asst, ed, lectr, Princeton Univ, 74-83; ed, curator, lectr, Univ Calif, Santa Barbara, 83-98; ed, adj prof, Northern Ill Univ, 99-. **HONORS AND AWARDS** NEH, 81-87, 88. **MEMBERSHIPS** MLA, Asn for Documentary Editing, Bibliog Soc of Am, Soc for Textual Scholar, Thoreau Soc. **RESEARCH** Henry David Thoreau, Transcendentalism, Science and Literature, Book Studies. **SELECTED PUBLICATIONS** Coed, Henry D Thoreau, A Week on the Concord and Merrimack Rivers, Princeton Univ Pr, 80; coed, Henry D Thoreau, Journal 1: 1837-1844, Princeton Univ Pr, 81; auth, "Thoreau's Watershed Season as a Poet: The Hidden Fruits of the Summer and Fall of 1841," Studies in the Am Renaissance 1990, ed Joel Myerson, (Univ Pr of Va, 90); auth, "The Availability of Thoreau's Texts and Manuscripts from 1862 to the Present," Thoreau's World and Ours, ed Edmund A Schofield and Robet C Baron, (Golden, CO: N Am Pr, 93); auth, "Thoreau as Poet," Cambridge Companion to Henry David Thoreau, ed Joel Myerson, (Cambridge Univ Pr, 95); auth, "Prospects for the Study of Henry David Thoreau," Prospects for Am Lit Study, ed Richard Kopley, (NY Univ Pr, 97); ed, Thoreau: Collected Essays and Poems, Libr of Am, 01. **CONTACT ADDRESS** No Illinois Univ, Founders Mem Libr, Dekalb, IL 60115. **EMAIL** witherell @niu.edu

WITKE, E. C.
PERSONAL Born 09/22/1931, Los Angeles, CA, m, 1975 **DISCIPLINE** CLASSICAL AND MEDIEVAL LATIN LITERATURE **EDUCATION** UCLA, BA, 53; Harvard Univ, AM, 57, PhD, 62. **CAREER** Asst prof, Univ Chicago, 62-63; asst to assoc prof Univ Cal Berkeley, 63-70; prof SUNY Binghamton, 70-71; prof, Univ Mich, 71-01. **HONORS AND AWARDS** Am Acad Rome Prize, 60-62. **MEMBERSHIPS** Am Philol Asn; Medieval Acad Am; Soc for the Promotion of Roman Stud (life member). **RESEARCH** Classical tradition in Middle Ages; Medieval theology; Erasmus. **SELECTED PUBLICATIONS** Auth, Enarratio Catulliana, Mnemosyne Supplementa, Leiden, 68; Latin Satire: The Structure of Persuasion, Leiden, 70; Numen Litterarum: The Old and the New in Latin Poetry from Constantine to Gregory the Great, Leiden & Cologne, 71; Horace's Roman Odes: A Critical Examination, Mnemosyne Supplementa, Leiden, 83; auth, Resident in Claassical Studies, Am Academy in Rome, 97-98. **CONTACT ADDRESS** Dept of Classical Studies, Univ of Michigan, Ann Arbor, Ann Arbor, MI 48109. **EMAIL** frchas@umich.edu

WITMER, DIANE F.
PERSONAL Born Pasadena, CA, d, 1 child **DISCIPLINE** COMMUNICATION ARTS & SCIENCES **EDUCATION** Univ of La Verne, BS, 80; Univ S Cal, MS, 89, MA, 93, PhD, 94. **CAREER** Instr, 90, Univ of La Verne; Instr, 90-91 & 92-94, dept of comm, Cal State Univ, Fullerton; researcher, 92, Nat Acad of Sci, Wash DC; Asst Lectr, 91-94, Univ S Cal, LA; Asst Prof, Communication, 94-97, Purdue Univ, IN; Assoc Prof, 97-, Cal State Univ, Fullerton. **HONORS AND AWARDS** Dept Honors 4.0/4.0 gpa, Univ La Verne, 2 Protos Awds, Top Four Paper Awd, Who's Who in; of Amer Women, in America, in the West & in the Midwest. **MEMBERSHIPS** CIOR, ICA, NCA, PRSA, WSCA. **RESEARCH** Computer-mediated communications, organizational communications & public relations. **SELECTED PUBLICATIONS** Auth, Understanding the Human Communication Process, Study Guide, Englewood CO, Jones Intl Ltd, 98; Public Relations, Study Guide, Englewood CO, Jones Intl Ltd, 97; Human Communications, Study Guide, Englewood CO, Jones Intl Ltd, 97; co-auth, From Paper-and-Pencil to Screen-and-Keyboard, Toward a Methodology for Survey Research on the Internet, in: Doing Internet Research, ed, S Jones, forthcoming; Practicing Safe Computing, Why People engage in Risky Computer-mediated Communication, in: Network and Netplay, Virtual Groups on the Internet, eds, F Sudweeks, M L McLaughlin & S Rafaeli, Menlo Park CA, AAAI/MIT Press, 98; Risky Business, Do People Feel Safe in Sexually Explicit Online Communication? in: J of Computer-Mediated Communication, 97. **CONTACT ADDRESS** Dept of Communications, California State Univ, Fullerton, Box 6846, Fullerton, CA 92834-6846. **EMAIL** dwitmer@fullerton.edu

WITT, DORIS
PERSONAL Born Dade City, FL **DISCIPLINE** ENGLISH **EDUCATION** Center Col, BA, 84; Univ Va, MA, 77; PhD, 95. **CAREER** Asst Prof, Univ Iowa, 95-. **HONORS AND AWARDS** Dissertation Awd, Commonwealth Ctr for Literacy. **MEMBERSHIPS** Mod Lang Asn, Asn for the Study of Food and Soc, Am Studies Asn. **RESEARCH** 20th Century US Multiethnic literature and culture, especially African-American literature and culture; Food and culture; Space exploration and culture. **SELECTED PUBLICATIONS** Auth, Black Hunger: Food and the Politics of US Identity, Oxford Univ Press, 99. **CONTACT ADDRESS** Dept English, The Univ of Iowa, 308 English Philosophy Bld, Iowa City, IA 52242-1408. **EMAIL** doris-witt@uiowa.edu

WITT, ROBERT WAYNE
PERSONAL Born 03/26/1937, Scottsville, KY **DISCIPLINE** SEVENTEETH CENTURY LITERATURE **EDUCATION** Georgetown Col, BA, 59; Univ Miss, MA, 61, PhD(English), 70. **CAREER** Instr English, Univ Miss, 65-70; asst prof, 70-75, assoc prof, 75-80, prof English, Eastern KY Univ, 80-. **MEMBERSHIPS** MLA; South Atlantic Mod Lang Asn. **RESEARCH** Dramatic literature and non-dramatic poetry of the 17th century. **SELECTED PUBLICATIONS** Auth, Building a pillar of fame, Univ Miss Studies in English, 72; Kipling as representative of the counter-aesthetes Kipling J, 70; Yeats, Plato, and the editors, T S Eliot Newslett, 74; Caliban upon Plato, Victorian Poetry, 75; Mirror Within A Mirror: Ben Jonson and the Play-Within, 75 & Of Comfort and Despair: Shakespeare's Sonnet Sequence, 79, Salzburg: Institut fur Englische Sprache und Literatur; Reason is not enough: Hamlet's recognition, Hamlet Studies, 81; On Faulkner and Verbena, Southern Literary Journal, 94; Montague or Capulet, Utstart Crow, 95; "The Duel in Hamlet as a Play-Within," Hamlet Studies, 98. **CONTACT ADDRESS** Dept of English, Eastern Kentucky Univ, 521 Lancaster Ave, Richmond, KY 40475. **EMAIL** engwitt@acs.eku.edu

WITTEBOLS, JAMES H.
PERSONAL Born 08/22/1955, Mt. Clemens, MI, s **DISCIPLINE** COMMUNICATION **EDUCATION** Cent Mich Univ, BA, 77; Wa St Univ, MA, 79, PhD, 83. **CAREER** Educ res, Washington DC, 85-87; asst prof to chair to assoc prof to prof, 87-. **MEMBERSHIPS** AEJMC; ICA. **RESEARCH** Political communication; politics of popular culture. **SELECTED PUBLICATIONS** Auth, Words and Worlds of Terror: Context and Meaning of a Media Buzzword, Etc: A Review of General Semantics, 91; art, Media and the Institutional Perspective: U. S. and Canadian Coverage of Terrorism, Polit Commun & Persuasion, 92; art, News and the Institutional Perspective: Sources in Terror Stories, Canadian J of Commun, 95; art, News from the Noninstitutional World: US and Canadian Coverage of Social Protest, Polit Commun, 96; auth, Watching M*A*S*H, Watching America: A Critical Analysis and Episode Guide, McFarland Publ, 98. **CONTACT ADDRESS** Commun Studies Dept, Niagara Univ, 64 Greenfield St, NY 14109. **EMAIL** jhw@niagara.edu

WITTIG, JOSEPH SYLVESTER
PERSONAL Born 08/18/1939, Pittsburgh, PA, m, 1969 **DISCIPLINE** ENGLISH, MEDIEVAL STUDIES **EDUCATION** Wheeling Col, BA, 63; Univ Scranton, MA, 65; Cornell Univ, PhD(English, medieval studies), 69. **CAREER** Asst prof, 69-76, assoc prof, 76-88, prof, English, Univ NCar-Chapel Hill, 88- . **MEMBERSHIPS** MLA; Mediaeval Acad Am; New Chaucer Soc; AAUP; Southern Atlantic Mod Lang Asn. **RESEARCH** Middle English literature; Old English literature; medieval studies. **SELECTED PUBLICATIONS** Auth, Homiletic fragment II and the Epistle to the Ephesians, Traditio, 69; auth, The Aeneas-Dido allusion in Chretien's Erec et Enide, Comp Lit, 70; Piers Plowman B, Passus IX-XII: Elements in the design of the inward journey, Traditio, 72; The dramatic and rhetorical development of Long Will's Pilgrimage, Neuphilologische Mitteilungen, 76; auth, Figural Narrative in Cynewulf's Juliana, Anglo-Saxon England, No 4; auth, William Langland Revisted, NY, 97. **CONTACT ADDRESS** Dept of English, Univ of No Carolina, Chapel Hill, Chapel Hill, NC 27514. **EMAIL** jwittog@unc.edu

WITTREICH, JOSEPH ANTHONY, JR
PERSONAL Born 07/23/1939, Cleveland, OH, s **DISCIPLINE** ENGLISH **EDUCATION** Univ Louisville, BA, 61; MA, 62; W Res Univ, PhD, 66. **CAREER** Asst prof to prof, Univ Wisc, 66-76; prof, Univ Md, 77-88; prof, Grad Center CUNY, 88-. **HONORS AND AWARDS** Fel, Am Philos Soc; Fel, NEH; Fel, Folger Shakespeare Libr; Fel, Henry E. Huntington Libr; Fel, John Simon Guggenheim Found. **MEMBERSHIPS** Renaissance Soc of Am; Milton Soc of Am; Spenser Soc; MLA. **RESEARCH** Milton and the Romantics. **SELECTED PUBLICATIONS** Auth, Angel of Apocalypse: Blake's Idea of Milton; auth, Visionary Poetics: Milton's Tradition and His Legacy; auth, Image of Horror: History, Prophecy and Apocalypse in 'King Lear'; auth, Interpreting Samson Agonistes; auth, Feminist Milton; auth, The Truths of Poetry: Reinterreting Samson Agonistes. **CONTACT ADDRESS** 25 Central Park W, New York, NY 10023-7253. **EMAIL** jwittreich@gc.cuny.edu

WLATER, OTIS M.
PERSONAL Born 04/20/1921, Chicago, IL, d **DISCIPLINE** CLASSICAL RHETORIC **EDUCATION** Northwestern Univ, PhD, 48. **CAREER** Prof of Commun, Univ of Pittsburgh, 58-84. **HONORS AND AWARDS** Phi Kappa Phi **MEMBERSHIPS** Nat Commun Asn. **RESEARCH** Classical rhetoric. **SELECTED PUBLICATIONS** Auth, Speaking Intelligently: Communication for Problem Solving, Macmillan Pub Co., 76; The Improvement of Attitute Research, J of Social Psychol, 51; Toward an Analysis of Motivation, Quart J of Speech, 55; On Views of Rhetoric, Whether Conservative or Progressive, Quart J of Speech, 63; The Value of the Classics in Rhetoric, Col Composition and Commun, 98; Plato's Idea of Rhetoric for Contemporary Students, Col Composition and Commun, 84; The Measurement of Ethos, Northwestern Univ, 84; coauth, Toward an Analysis of Ethics for Rhetoric, Quart J of Speech, 55. **CONTACT ADDRESS** 1115 Kenoyer Dr., Bellingham, WA 98226-2333.

WOHLGELERNTER, MAURICE
PERSONAL Born 02/13/1921, Poland, m, 1948, 3 children **DISCIPLINE** AMERICAN LITERATURE, ENGLISH **EDUCATION** Yeshiva Univ, BA, 41; Columbia Univ, MA, 46; PhD, 61. **CAREER** Asst prof to adj prof to prof, Yeshiva Univ, 55-92; prof, CUNY Baruch Col, 70-92-; adj prof, NYork Univ, 92-. **HONORS AND AWARDS** NEH; Vir Cen Creative Arts Writing Fel. **MEMBERSHIPS** MLA; NAS; PEN; ALSC. **RESEARCH** Modern English; Irish; American literature. **SELECTED PUBLICATIONS** Auth, Israel Zangwill: A Study, Columbia UP, 64; auth, Jewish Writers, Irish Writers: Selected Essays on the Love of Words, Trans Pub, 00; auth, Frank O'Connor: An Introduction, Columbia UP, 77; ed, History, Religion, and American Democracy, Transaction Pub (NJ), 93. **CONTACT ADDRESS** English Dept, Baruch Col, CUNY, PO Box 411, New York, NY 10010. **EMAIL** rebesther@aol.com

WOJCIK, DANIEL
PERSONAL Born 12/21/1955, Detroit, MI **DISCIPLINE** ENGLISH; FOLKLORE **EDUCATION** BA, anthrop, Univ Calif Santa Barbara, 78; MA, folklore and myth, Univ Calif Los Angeles, 86; PhD, folklore and myth, Univ Calif Los Angeles, 92. **CAREER** Asst prof, 91-97, assoc prof, 97-, dept of eng, Univ Ore. **HONORS AND AWARDS** Amer Acad of Relig individual res grant, 96; summer res award, Office of Res and Sponsored Prog, Univ Ore, 95; Arnold Rubin award, Fowler Mus of Cultural Hist, Univ Calif Los Angeles, 90. **MEMBERSHIPS** Amer Acad of Relig; Amer Culture Asn; Amer Folklore Soc; Amer Studies Asn; Calif Folklore Soc; Intl Soc for Contemp Legend Res; Popular Culture Asn. **RESEARCH** Millennialist movements and apocalyptic beliefs; Contemporary American folklore; Popular culture; Subcultures and youth cultures; Body art; Popular religion. **SELECTED PUBLICATIONS** Auth, The End of the World As We Know It: Faith, Fatalism, and Apocalypse in America, NY Univ Press, 97; article, Embracing Doomsday: Faith, Fatalism, and Apocalyptic Beliefs in the Nuclear Age, Western Folklore, 55, no 4, 297-330, 96; article, Polaroids from Heaven: Photography, Folk Religion, and the Miraculous Image Tradition at a Marian Apparition Site, Jour of Amer Folklore, 109, no 432, 129-148, 96; auth, Punk and Neo-Tribal Body Art, Folk Art and Artists Series, Univ Press of Miss, 95. **CONTACT ADDRESS** English and Folklore Studies, Univ of Oregon, 1286 University of Oregon, Eugene, OR 97403-1286. **EMAIL** dwojcik@oregon.uoregon.edu

WOLAK, WILLIAM J.
DISCIPLINE THEATRE ARTS **EDUCATION** CT State Col, BA; St Louis Univ, MA; Tulane Univ, PhD. **CAREER** Prof, Univ Pacific. **HONORS AND AWARDS** UOP. **SELECTED PUBLICATIONS** Auth, The Inspector General (rev); The Servant of Two Masters (rev). **CONTACT ADDRESS** Dept of Theatre Arts, Univ of the Pacific, Stockton, Pacific Ave, PO Box 3601, Stockton, CA 95211.

WOLF, DONALD
PERSONAL Born 04/12/1924, Sandpoint, ID, m, 1955, 1 child **DISCIPLINE** ENGLISH **EDUCATION** Lehigh Univ, BS, 48, MA, 52; Columbia Univ, PhD, 60. **CAREER** Instr English, Lehigh Univ, 50-52; from instr to asst prof, 53-70, PROF ENGLISH, ADELPHI UNIV, 70-, CHMN DEPT, 75-. **RESEARCH** Romantic and Victorian English literature. **SELECTED PUBLICATIONS** Auth, 'Law and Order' Creator-Executive Producer Wolf, Dick + An Interview--Its the Writing, Stupid, Television Quart, Vol 0028, 97. **CONTACT ADDRESS** Dept of English, Adelphi Univ, Garden City, NY 11530.

WOLF, EUGENE KENDRICK
PERSONAL Born 05/25/1939, New York, NY, m, 1964, 2 children **DISCIPLINE** MUSICOLOGY **EDUCATION** Univ Rochester, BMus, 61; NYork Univ, MA, 64, PhD, 72. **CAREER** Lectr fine arts, Syracuse Univ, 67-72, asst prof, 72-73; asst prof, 73-75, chmn dept, 77-80, Assoc Prof Music, Univ PA, 75-83, Prof, 83-98; Rev ed, J Am Musicol Soc, 72-77; Guggenheim fel, 75-76; Am Coun Learned Soc fel, 81-82; emer prof, 98-. **HONORS AND AWARDS** Alfred Einstein Award, Am Musicol Soc, 75. **MEMBERSHIPS** Am Musicol Soc; Int Musicol Soc. **RESEARCH** Early classical symphony; 18th century musicology. **SELECTED PUBLICATIONS** Auth, Studies on Richter, Franz, Xaver Church Music 1709-1789, Notes, Vol 0051, 94; Newly Identified Manuscripts of Opera and Related Works From Mannheim + 18th-Century Electoral Court Music, J Amer Musicol Soc, Vol 0047, 94; The 18th-Century Symphony, Notes, Vol 0052, 96; Studies on the Musical Relations Be-

tween Mannheim, Bohemia and Moravia in the Late 18th and Early 19th Centuries, Notes, Vol 0052, 96. **CONTACT ADDRESS** Dept of Music, Univ of Pennsylvania, 201 S 34th St, Philadelphia, PA 19104-6313. **EMAIL** ewolf@sas.upenn.edu

WOLF, MARK J. P.
PERSONAL Born 05/21/1967, Milwaukee, WI, s **DISCIPLINE** CINEMA STUDIES, MEDIA STUDIES, MASS COMMUNICATION **EDUCATION** Univ Southern Calif, BA, 90; MA, 92; PhD, 95. **CAREER** Teaching asst, Univ Southern Calif, 90-94; grad readership, Univ Southern Calif, 94; res asst, Univ Southern Calif, 95; from adj prof to asst prof, Concordia Univ Wis, 95-; adj prof, Univ Wis, 97. **HONORS AND AWARDS** U.S.C. Outstanding Student Scholar; Phi Kappa Phi Res Mentorship Awd, 93; Associates Scholar, USC Sch of Cinema/Television, 94; George Cukor Scholar, USC Sch of Cinema/Television, 94. **MEMBERSHIPS** Golden Key Nat Honor Soc, Soc for Cinema Studies, Christians in the Visual Arts. **RESEARCH** Cinema, Moving Imagery, Documentary, Video Games, Sub-Created Worlds, Plausibility, History, Digital Technology, New Media, Animation, Graphic Design, Art, Animation (Traditional, experimental, & computer), Science Fiction, Narrative Theory, Game Structure & Design, Recreational Mathematics. **SELECTED PUBLICATIONS** Auth, "In the Frame of Roger Rabbit: Visual Compositing in Film," The Velvet Light Trap 36 (95): 45-59; rev, of "Animating Culture" and "Disney Discourse," Film Quart Vol 50 (96); auth, "Inventing Space: The Use of On-screen and Off-screen Space in Video Games," Film Quart Vol 51 (97): 11-23; rev, of "Virtual Subcreation," World (97): 23; auth, "Subjunctive Documentary: Computer Imaging and Simulation," in Collecting Visible Evidence, eds. Michael Renov and Jane Gaines (MN: Univ Minn Press, 00); auth, "A Brief History of Morphing," in Meta-Morphing: Visual Transformation and the Culture of Quick Change, ed. Vivian Sobchack (MN: Univ Minn Press, 00); auth, Abstracting Reality: Art, Communication, and Cognition in the Digital Age, Univ Press of Am, forthcoming. **CONTACT ADDRESS** Dept Commun, Concordia Univ, Wisconsin, 12800 N Lake Shore Dr, Mequon, WI 53097-2418. **EMAIL** mark.wolf@cuw.edu

WOLFE, ETHYLE RENEE
PERSONAL Born 03/14/1919, Burlington, VT, m, 1954 **DISCIPLINE** CLASSICAL LANGUAGES AND LITERATURE **EDUCATION** Univ Vt, BA, 40, MA, 42; NYork Univ, PhD, 50. **CAREER** Lectr classics, eve session, 47-49, from instr to assoc prof, 49-67, acting chmn dept classics & comp lit, 62-63, chmn, 67-72, Prof Classics, Brooklyn Col, 68-, Dean Sch Humanities, 71-, Assoc ed, Class World, 65-70; co-ed, Am Class Rev, 70-. **MEMBERSHIPS** Am Philol Asn; Archaeol Inst Am; Am Soc Papyrologists. **RESEARCH** Latin poetry; Greek tragedy; papyrology. **SELECTED PUBLICATIONS** Auth, The Brooklyn College Core Curriculum, Arethusa, Vol 0027, 94; Cicero 'De Oratore' and the Liberal Arts Tradition in America, Class World, Vol 0088, 95. **CONTACT ADDRESS** Brooklyn Col, CUNY, Brooklyn, NY 11210.

WOLFE, GARY KENT
PERSONAL Born 03/24/1946, Sedalia, MO, m, 1966 **DISCIPLINE** LITERATURE **EDUCATION** Univ Kans, BA, 68; Univ Chicago, MA, 69, PhD(English), 71. **CAREER** Danforth tutor humanities, Univ Chicago, 70-71; asst prof, 71-77, ASSOC PROF HUMANITIES, ROOSEVELT UNIV, 77-82, DEAN COL CONTINUING EDUC, 82-90, prof himanities and english, 83-; contrib ed, Locus magazine, 92-. **HONORS AND AWARDS** Eaton Award, 81; Pilgrim Award 86, IAFA Distinguished Scholar Award, 98. **MEMBERSHIPS** Sci Fiction Res Asn; Int Conf on Fantastic. **RESEARCH** Science fiction and fantastic literature; film and television; adult continuing education. **SELECTED PUBLICATIONS** Auth, Vonnegut and the metaphor of science fiction, J Popular Cult, spring 72; The limits of science fiction, Extrapolation, 12/72; David Lindsay and George MacDonald, Studies Scottish Lit, 10/74; Symbolic fantasy, Genre, 9/75; Mythic structures in Cordwainer Smith's The Game of Rat and Dragon, Sci Fiction Studies, 7/77; The Known and the Unknown: The Iconography of Science Fiction, Kent State Univ Press, 79; David Lindsay, Starmont House, 82; coauth, Elements of Research, Alfred Pub Co, 79; auth, Critical Terms for Science Fiction and Fantasy, 86; auth, Harlam Ellison, with Ellen Weil, 01. **CONTACT ADDRESS** Roosevelt Univ, 430 S Michigan Ave, Chicago, IL 60605. **EMAIL** gwolfe@roosevelt.edu

WOLFE, RALPH HAVEN
PERSONAL Born 06/23/1931, Weston, OH **DISCIPLINE** ENGLISH **EDUCATION** Bowling Green State Univ, BS, 51, MA, 56; Ind Univ, PhD(English), 60. **CAREER** Instr English, Bowling Green State Univ, 60-61; asst prof, Monmouth Col, Ill, 61-62; assoc prof, Ind State Univ, Terre Haute, 62-69; asst chmn dept, 69-76, PROF ENGLISH, BOWLING GREEN STATE UNIV, 69-, Vis assoc prof, Bowling Green State Univ, 67-69. **MEMBERSHIPS** MLA **RESEARCH** English and American literature; drama. **SELECTED PUBLICATIONS** Coauth, The Ohio Roots of Gish, Dorothy and Gish, Lillian, J Popular Film and Television, Vol 0022, 94. **CONTACT ADDRESS** Dept of English, Bowling Green State Univ, Bowling Green, OH 43403.

WOLFENSOHN, JAMES DAVID
PERSONAL Born 12/01/1933, Sydney, Australia, m, 1961, 3 children **DISCIPLINE** MULTILATERAL DEVELOPMENT BANKING, PERFORMING ARTS **EDUCATION** Univ of Sydney, BA & LLB; Harvard Grad School of Business, MBA. **CAREER** Australian Olympic Fencing Team, 56; lawyer, Allen Allen & Hemsley; board mem to chmn emer, Carnegie Hall, board mem 70-80, chmn, 80-91, chmn emer; chmn of the board of trustees, 90-96, chmn emer, John F. Kennedy Center for the Performing Arts, 96-; head of investment banking, exec partner, Salomon Brothers; exec deputy chmn and managing dir, Schroders Ltd; pres, J. Henry Schroders Banking Corp; managing dir, Darling & Co; Pres and CEO, James D. Wolfensohn Inc., Pres, World Bank Group, 95-; Chmn of the Bd, Inst for Advanced Study at Princeton Univ. **HONORS AND AWARDS** David Rockefeller Prize, Museum of Modern Art; Honorary Knighthood, 95; decorated by the governments of Australia, France, Germany, Morocco, and Norway. **MEMBERSHIPS** Am Acad of Arts and Sci; Am Philos Soc. **CONTACT ADDRESS** 1818 H St NW, Washington, DC 20433.

WOLFF, CYNTHIA GRIFFIN
PERSONAL Born St. Louis, MO, m, 1988, 2 children **DISCIPLINE** ENGLISH AND AMERICAN LITERATURE **EDUCATION** Radcliffe Col, BA, 58; Harvard Univ, PhD(English), 65. **CAREER** Instr English, Boston Univ, 63-64; instr, Queens Col, NY, 65-68; asst prof, Manhattanville Col, 68-71; assoc prof, Univ Mass, Amherst, 71-76, dir honors prog, 72-74, prof, 76-80; PROF LIT, MASS INST TECHNOL, 80-84; Class of 1922 Prof of Humanities, 84-. **MEMBERSHIPS** MLA; Am Studies Asn. **RESEARCH** English and American fiction; 19th and early 20th century American literature; psychology and literature; biography. **SELECTED PUBLICATIONS** Auth, Lily Bart and the Drama of Feminity + Wharton, Edith 'House of Mirth', Amer Lit Hist, Vol 0006, 94; Masculinity in 'Uncle Toms Cabin' + Stowe, Harriet, Beecher, American Literature, American Quart, Vol 0047, 95; Passing Beyond the Middle Passage, Brown, Henry, Box Translations of Slavery, Mass Rev, Vol 0037, 96; Un Utterable Longing + Chopin, Kate--The Discourse of Feminine Sexuality in the 'Awakening', Stud in Amer Fiction, Vol 0024, 96. **CONTACT ADDRESS** Dept of English, Massachusetts Inst of Tech, 77 Massachusetts Ave, Cambridge, MA 02139.

WOLFF, FLORENCE I.
PERSONAL Born Pittsburgh, PA, 7 children **DISCIPLINE** SPEECH COMMUNICATION **EDUCATION** Temple Univ, BS, 41; Duquesne Univ, MA, 67; Univ Pittsburgh, PhD, 69. **CAREER** Sec tchr bus educ & Eng, Charleroi Sr High Sch, 41-46, Pub & Pvt High Schs, 56-60 & Cent Dist Cath High Sch, 61-69; from Instr to Prof Speech Commun, 70-89, Prof Emeritus Commun, Univ Dayton, 89; Dir, Wolff Innovative Training System - conducts management training seminars for corporations, the military, and law enforcement. **HONORS AND AWARDS** Inductee, Int Listening Asn Hall of Fame; Teachers Awds, 79-96; Selected as Ohio Professor of the Year with the CASE (Council for Administration and Study of Education); Silver CASE Awd. **MEMBERSHIPS** Relig Speech Commun Asn (exec secy, 78-81, 2nd vpres, 82, 1st vpres, 83); Int Listening Asn; Speech Commun Asn; hon mem Nat Forensic League. **RESEARCH** Listening; oral interpretation; public address. **SELECTED PUBLICATIONS** Auth, A survey of evaluative criteria for faculty promotion in college and university speech departments, Speech Teacher, 11/71; A teacher oriented eclectic review of recent interpersonal and small group communication research, Speech Asn Minn J, 5/75; Student evaluation of college and university speech communication courses and faculty: A survey, Speech Teacher, 9/75; A 1977 Survey: General insights into the status of listening course offerings in selected colleges and universities, NC J Speech Commun, winter 79; A lector's nightmare: Professional tips for proclaiming the word, Today's Parish, 9/80; A unique synthesized motivational evaluation strategy for assessing high school students' speech performance: An instructional unit, Ohio Speech J, 80; Re-creative bible reading, Relig Commun Today, 9/80; Perceptive Listening, Holt, Rinehart & Winston, 2nd ed, 93. **CONTACT ADDRESS** Dept of Commun, Univ of Dayton, 300 College Park, Dayton, OH 45469-1410.

WOLFF, GEORGE
DISCIPLINE ENGLISH **EDUCATION** Wash Univ, BA, 58; MA, 59; Mich State Univ, PhD, 66. **CAREER** Instr, Pa State Univ, 62-63; prof, Univ Cincinnati, 66-. **HONORS AND AWARDS** Elizabeth Clark Fel, Wash Univ, Centennial Review Fel, Mich State Univ. **RESEARCH** The Cyberpunk Movement. **SELECTED PUBLICATIONS** Auth, Theodore Roethke, Twayne, 81. **CONTACT ADDRESS** Dept of Humanities & Soc Sci, Clermont Col, 4200 Clermont College Dr, Batavia, OH 45103-1748. **EMAIL** george.wolff@uc.edu

WOLGAST, ELIZ H.
PERSONAL Born 02/27/1929, NJ, m, 1949, 2 children **DISCIPLINE** ENGLISH; PHILOSOPHY **EDUCATION** Cornell Univ, BA, 50, MA, 52; Univ Wash, PhD, 55. **CAREER** Univ Calif Davis, 66-67; Calif State Hayward, 68-97; visiting prof, Dartmouth Col, 75-76; Univ Wales, Lampeter, 95, 96. **HONORS AND AWARDS** AAUW fel, 58; ACLS fel, 70; NEH fel, 78, 88; Finnish Acad fel, 92; Rockefeller Bellagio fel, 88. **MEMBERSHIPS** APA. **RESEARCH** Wittgenstein; Ethics; Epistemology. **SELECTED PUBLICATIONS** Auth, "Personal Identity", Philos Invest, 99; auth, Democracy: The Message from Athens, Consequences of Modernity in Contemporary Legal Theory, Dunker & Humbolt, 98; auth, Mental Causes and the Will, Philos Investigations, Winter, 97; auth, Moral Paradigms, Philos, Spring, 95; auth, Individualism and Democratic Citizenship, Democrazia e Diritto, Summer, 94; auth, The Demands of Public Reason, Columbia Law Rev, Oct, 94; auth, Primitive Reactions, Philos Investigations, Oct, 94; auth, Ethics of an Artificial Person: Lost Responsibility in Professions and Organizations, Stanford Univ Press, 92; auth, La Grammatica della Giustizia, Riuniti, Italy, 91; auth, The Grammar of Justice, Cornell Univ Press, 87; auth, Equality and the Rights of Women, Cornell Univ Press, 80; auth, Paradoxes of Knowledge, Cornell Univ Press, 77. **CONTACT ADDRESS** 1536 Olympus Av., Berkeley, CA 94708. **EMAIL** ewolgast@csuhayward.edu

WOLLAEGER, MARK A.
DISCIPLINE 20TH-CENTURY BRITISH LITERATURE **EDUCATION** Yale Univ, PhD. **CAREER** Instr, dir, col writing prog, Vanderbilt Univ. **RESEARCH** Modernism; postcolonial literature and theory; film; Conrad; Forster; Joyce; Woolf. **SELECTED PUBLICATIONS** Auth, Joseph Conrad and the Fictions of Skepticism, Stanford Univ Press, 90; co-ed Joyce and the Subject of History, Mich, 96. **CONTACT ADDRESS** Vanderbilt Univ, Nashville, TN 37203-1727.

WOLOCH, GEORGE MICHAEL
PERSONAL Born 06/01/1934, Akron, OH **DISCIPLINE** CLASSICS **EDUCATION** Yale Univ, BA, 56; Oxford Univ, BA, 60, MA, 63; Johns Hopkins Univ, PhD(classics), 66. **CAREER** Instr Latin, Pomfret Sch, 56-57; lectr sch gen studies, Brooklyn Col, 61; instr classics, McGill Univ, 61-63; jr instr, Johns Hopkins Univ, 63-64; asst prof, 66-70, Assoc Prof Classics, McGill Univ, 70-, Res assoc, Ctr Medieval Studies, Univ Calif, Los Angeles, 70; Can Coun leave fel, 70-71; hon cur, McGill Univ Coin Collection. **MEMBERSHIPS** Am Philol Asn; Class Asn Can; fel Royal Numis Soc. **RESEARCH** Roman cities; Ostrogothic Italy, AD 489-552; Ammianus Marcellinus. **SELECTED PUBLICATIONS** Auth, Mediterranean Cities, Phoenix-J Class Asn Can, Vol 0046, 92; Emperors and Gladiators, Amer Hist Rev, Vol 0099, 94. **CONTACT ADDRESS** Dept of Classics, McGill Univ, 855 Sherbrooke St W, Montreal, QC, Canada H3A 2T5.

WOLPER, ROY S.
PERSONAL Born 07/07/1931, Pittsburgh, PA, m, 1995, 2 children **DISCIPLINE** ENGLISH **EDUCATION** Univ Pittsburgh, MA, 52, MA, 59, PhD, 65. **CAREER** Instr Eng lit, Carnegie Inst Technol, 61-64 & Univ Pittsburgh, 64-65; asst prof, Univ Sask, 65-67; from asst prof to assoc prof, 67-75, prof eng, lit, Temple Univ, 75-99, Co-ed, The Scriblerian; Nat Endowment for Arts fel, creative writing, 74-75. **HONORS AND AWARDS** Option Awd, Doubleday & Co. **MEMBERSHIPS** MLA; Northeastern Mod Lang Asn; Am Soc 18th Century Studies. **RESEARCH** The Scriblerians; Voltaire; Jews in 18th century lit. **SELECTED PUBLICATIONS** Auth, Johnson's neglected muse: The drama, Studies in Eighteenth Century, 68; Candide, gull in the garden?, Eighteenth Century Studies, 69; The rhetoric of gunpowder and the idea of progress, J Hist Ideas, 70; Zadig, a grim comedy?, Romanic Rev, 74; The final foolishness of Babouc: The dark center of Le Monde comme il va, Mod Lang Rev, 75; The lustful Jew in the eighteenth century: A sympathetic stereotype?, Proc 6th World Congr Jewish Studies, 77; Voltaire's Contes: A reconsideration, Forum, 78; The toppling of Jeannot, Studies on Voltaire and the Eighteenth Century, 80. **CONTACT ADDRESS** Dept of Eng, Temple Univ, 1114 W Berks St, Philadelphia, PA 19122-6029. **EMAIL** rwolper@dellnet.com

WOLVERTON, ROBERT E.
PERSONAL Born 08/04/1925, Indianapolis, IN, m, 1952, 4 children **DISCIPLINE** CLASSICS **EDUCATION** Hanover Col, AB, 48; Univ MI, MA, 49; Univ NC, PhD(Latin, Greek & ancient hist), 54. **CAREER** Asst prof classics, Univ GA, 54-59; from asst to assoc prof classics & hist, Tufts Univ, 59-62; assoc prof classics & dir hon prog, FL State Univ, 62-67; assoc dean grad col, Univ Ill, 67-69; dean grad sch, Miami Univ, OH, 69-72; prof classics & pres, Col of Mt St Josephs on the OH, 72-77; Prof Classics & Educ Leadership & Vpres Acad Affairs, MS State Univ, 77-86, Title IV consult-reader of langs, NDEA, 67-72; consult-reviewer admin, NCent Asn Cols & Schs, 67-77; instr personnel mgt, Main Event Mgt Inc, 76-; mem exec comt, Nat Coun Chief Acad Officers, 81-; Head dept. For Lang, Miss State Univ, 91-96. **HONORS AND AWARDS** Alumni Achievement Awd, Hanover Col, 71; hon life pres, Am Class League, 77, Outstanding Tchr Awd, 91; John Grisham Master Tchr, 91; littd, col of mt st joseph on the oh, 77. **MEMBERSHIPS** Am Class League (pres, 72-76); Am Philol Asn; Class Asn Mid West & South; Am Asn Higher Educ. **RESEARCH** Administration in higher educ; class mythology; etymology. **SELECTED PUBLICATIONS** Auth, Classical Elements in English Words, 66 & An Outline of Classical Mythology, 67, Littlefield; contribr, Graduate Programs and Admission Manu-

al, 4 vols, Grad Record & Exam Bd & Coun Grad Schs USA, 71 & 72; auth, The future of classics, Class Outlook, 76; contrib auth & translr, A Life of George Washington, in Latin Prose, George Washington Univ, 76; The future of graduate studies in the humanities, Nat Forum, 79; contribr, Mythological References, Arete Publ, 80. **CONTACT ADDRESS** Dept of Foreign Langs, Mississippi State Univ, PO Drawer FL, Mississippi State, MS 39762. **EMAIL** REW1@RA.MSSTATE.EDU

WOLVIN, ANDREW D.
PERSONAL Born Columbus, NE, m, 2 children **DISCIPLINE** ORGANIZATIONAL COMMUNICATION AND COMMUNICATION EDUCATION **EDUCATION** Purdue Univ, PhD, 68. **CAREER** Prof, Univ MD. **HONORS AND AWARDS** Lilly Teaching Fel; Eastern Commun; Assoc Distinguished Teaching Fel. **MEMBERSHIPS** International Listening Assoc; Nat Commun Assoc; Assoc of Business Commun. **RESEARCH** The study of listening behavior. **SELECTED PUBLICATIONS** Co-auth, Listening, 5th edn, Brown, 96; auth, Business Communication in a Changing World, St. Martins, 97; Communicating: A Social and Career Focus, 8th edn, Houghton-Mifflin, 01. **CONTACT ADDRESS** Dept of Commun, Univ of Maryland, Col Park, 211 Skinner Building, College Park, MD 20742-1335. **EMAIL** awolvin@deans.umd.edu

WOMACK, MORRIS M.
DISCIPLINE CLASSICAL RHETORIC, SPEECH **EDUCATION** Butler Univ, BA, Butler Univ, BD, 58; Wayne State Univ, PhD, 67. **CAREER** Prof, Mich Christian Col, 59-66; REGISTRAR, PROF SPEECH, MICH CHRISTIAN COL, 67-; minister, Church of Christ, 47-. **CONTACT ADDRESS** 409 Vista Dorado Ln, Oak Park, CA 91377. **EMAIL** womack@pepperdine.edu

WOMACK, WHITNEY
PERSONAL Born 08/30/1970, s **DISCIPLINE** ENGLISH **EDUCATION** Univ Mo at Columbia, AB, 91; MA, 93; Purdue Univ, PhD, 99. **CAREER** Asst prof, Miami Univ of Ohio, 98-. **HONORS AND AWARDS** Purdue Res Fel; British Women Writers Asn Grad Student Awd; Pew Teaching Leadership Awd; Phi Beta Kappa. **MEMBERSHIPS** MLA, NCTE, AAUP, British Women Writers Asn, Midwest Victorian Studies Asn. **RESEARCH** Nineteenth-Century British Literature and Culture, Nineteenth-Century American Literature and Culture, Women's Literature and Feminist Studies, Transatlantic Studies. **SELECTED PUBLICATIONS** Auth, "Elizabeth Siddal," in DLB: Victorian Women Writers Vol 199 (MI: The Gale Group, 98). **CONTACT ADDRESS** Dept Humanities & English, Miami Univ, Hamilton, 1601 Peck Blvd, Hamilton, OH 45011-3316. **EMAIL** womackwa@muohio.edu

WONG, TIMOTHY C.
PERSONAL Born 01/24/1941, Hong Kong, China, m, 1970, 3 children **DISCIPLINE** CHINESE LITERATURE **EDUCATION** St Mary's Col, BA, 63; Univ Hawaii, MA, 68; Stanford Univ, PhD, 75. **CAREER** Asst prof, 74-79, assoc prof, 79-85, prof, 95-, Arizona St Univ; assoc prof, 85-95, Ohio St Univ. **HONORS AND AWARDS** ACLS grants, 77, 81-82. **MEMBERSHIPS** Asn for Asian Studies; Am Oriental Soc; Chinese Lang Teachers Asn. **RESEARCH** Traditional Chinese fiction and narratology **SELECTED PUBLICATIONS** Wu Chingtzu, Boston, 78. **CONTACT ADDRESS** Center for Asian Studies, Arizona State Univ, PO Box 871702, Tempe, AZ 85287-1702. **EMAIL** twong@asu.edu

WOOD, ANDELYS
PERSONAL Born 10/01/1947, Randolph, VT **DISCIPLINE** ENGLISH **EDUCATION** Middlebury Col, AB, 69; Indiana Univ, PhD, 74. **CAREER** Vis Asst Prof, Univ of Oklahoma, 75-76; Instr, St Mary's Col of Maryland, 77; Asst Prof, Union Col, 77-81; Asst Prof, Union Col, 81-85; Prof, Union Col, 85-, English Dept Chair, 97-. **HONORS AND AWARDS** James Still Fel, 84; Excellence in Research Awd, Union College, 94-96; Exemplary Teacher Awd, 97; Excellence in Teaching Awd, Union College, 98. **MEMBERSHIPS** Modern Language Assoc; American Assoc of Univ Prof; Kentucky Philological Assoc; Children's Literature Assoc. **RESEARCH** 19th and 20th century British Literature; British Children's Literature since 1945; Shakespeare in performance. **SELECTED PUBLICATIONS** Author of several articles. **CONTACT ADDRESS** Dept English & Languages, Union Col, Kentucky, 310 College St, Barbourville, KY 40906-1410. **EMAIL** acwood@unionky.edu

WOOD, BARBARA
DISCIPLINE COMMUNICATION STUDIES **EDUCATION** Univ of Wis, BS, 63; MS, 64; PhD, 66. **CAREER** Prof, Univ Il at Chicago, 96-. **HONORS AND AWARDS** Silver Circle Awds for Excellence in Teaching, vote of the sr classes, 76, 79, 83, 87, 90. **RESEARCH** Communication competence and language, dev of functional communication of children and youth, assessing communication behaviors in educational and business settings, communication training and dev in a culturally diverse work place. **SELECTED PUBLICATIONS** Auth, pubs on communication behaviors; communication training. **CONTACT ADDRESS** Dept of Commun, Univ of Illinois, Chicago, 1030 N State St, #30C, Chicago, IL 60610. **EMAIL** bwood@uic.edu

WOOD, CAROL L.
PERSONAL Born 07/18/1949, Fayetteville, AR, m, 1972, 1 child **DISCIPLINE** LINGUISTICS, LITERATURE **EDUCATION** Univ Ark, BA; MA; PhD. **CAREER** From assoc prof to prof, McNeese State Univ, 87-. **HONORS AND AWARDS** Shearman Prof of Liberal Arts, 98-99; project assistance grants, Calcasieu Arts & Humanities Coun, 98-99; Humanist of the Year, Calcasieu Arts & Humanities Coun, 99-00; artist's minigrants, La Div of the Arts, 99-00. **MEMBERSHIPS** Hist Harp Soc. **RESEARCH** Literature and Music (especially harp) of the Medieval Period. **SELECTED PUBLICATIONS** Auth, An Overview of Welsh Poetry Before the Norman conquest, Edwin Mellen Press, 96; auth, The Chaucer Songbook, Mel Bay, 00. **CONTACT ADDRESS** Dept Lang Arts, McNeese State Univ, PO Box 92655, Lake Charles, LA 70605. **EMAIL** woodharp@hotmail.com

WOOD, GERALD CARL
PERSONAL Born 03/22/1944, Valparaiso, IN, d, 2 children **DISCIPLINE** BRITISH LITERATURE, FILM STUDY **EDUCATION** Wabash Col, AB, 66; Univ Fla, PhD, 71. **CAREER** Prof English, Carson-Newman Col, 71-, Vis scholar, Univ Iowa, 79-80; vis assoc prof English, Univ Tn-Knoxville, 82. **MEMBERSHIPS** MLA; S Atlantic Mod Lang Asn; Byron Soc. **RESEARCH** Writings of Lord Byron; film studies; theories of comedy. **SELECTED PUBLICATIONS** Auth, Nature and narrative in Byron's Prisoner of Chillon, Keats-Shelley J, 75; Lord Byron, the metaphor of the climates and Don Juan, Byron J, 78; Francois Truffaut's Day for Night and the life of art in contemporary film, Interpretations: Studies Lang & Lit, 78; And Now..who knows: The Nature or Mystery in Horton Foote's The Young Man From Atlanta, S Atlantic Mod Lang Asn, Atlanta, Ga, 95; Old Beginnings and Roads to Home: Horton Foote and Mythic Realism, Christianity and Lit, 96; Horton Foote's Politics of Intimacy, J Am Drama and Theatre, 97; Ed, Horton Foote: A Casebook, Garland, 98; Horton Foote and the Theatre of Intimacy, La State Univ, 99. **CONTACT ADDRESS** Dept English, Carson-Newman Col, P O Box 71971, Jefferson City, TN 37760. **EMAIL** gwood@cn.edu

WOOD, JULIA T.
PERSONAL Born 08/26/1950, Bethesda, MD, m, 1975 **DISCIPLINE** COMMUNICATION **EDUCATION** Pa State Univ, PhD, 75. **CAREER** PROF, UNIV NC, CHAPEL HILL, 75-. **HONORS AND AWARDS** Research and Teaching Awds. **CONTACT ADDRESS** Univ of No Carolina, Chapel Hill, CB 3285, Chapel Hill, NC 27599. **EMAIL** jwood1@email.unc.edu

WOOD, NANCY
DISCIPLINE ENGLISH **EDUCATION** Univ OR, Eugene, BA, 56; Cornell Univ, MA, 63; Rutgers Univ, PhD, 72. **CAREER** Prof, 96-, prof & ch, 94-96, assoc prof & ch, 93-94, assoc prof, ch & dir freshman Eng, 92-93, assoc prof, actg ch, & dir freshman Eng, 91 & assoc prof and dir freshman Eng, 89-90, Univ TX at Arlington; vis scholar, Cambridge Univ, 97; founder & dir, Study Skills and Tutorial Serv, 73-89; dir, Study Skills and Tutorial Services, 80-81, Study Skills Couns in Freshman Serv Off, 72-73 & instr, 68-72, Univ TX at El Paso; mem Ed Staff, Partisan Rev Magazine, Rutgers Univ, 63-64; instr, 59, 60 & 61 and tchg asst, 58-62, Cornell Univ; Judging, most outstanding article in the 92 vol, J Develop Educ, 93; sec & mem, Exec Bd, Nat Asn Develop Educ, 90-92; pres, TX Asn Develop Educ, 88-89; pres-elect & prog ch, Annual Conf Acad Support Prog, El Paso, 88; mem, Adv Coun, Nat Asn Develop Educ, 88-89; reg rep, TX Asn Develop Educ, 86-87; mem ch, TADE, 86-87; coordr, Chp(s) Nat Conf Col Reading and Learning Asn, 85; mentor, 2 CRLA conf, 85 & 87. **HONORS AND AWARDS** Hon mem, Sigma Tau Delta, Engl Honor Soc, 89, Certificate of Appreciation, 96; hon mem, Golden Key Nat Honor Soc, 89; Certificate Merit for Adv, Am Coun Testing/Nat Acad Adv Asn, 86; Distinguished Achievement Awd, UT El Paso, 84; 1st annual Mortar Bd Achievement Awd, 74. **MEMBERSHIPS** Asn Dep Eng; MLA; Coun Writing Prog Admin; Conf Col Tchrs Eng TX; Nat Coun Tchrs Eng; Int Reading Asn; Nat Reading Conf; Nat Asn Develop Educ; TX Asn Develop Educ; Col Reading and Learning Asn; Nat Acad Adv Asn, hon mem. **SELECTED PUBLICATIONS** Auth, Perspectives on Argument with Instructor's Manual, NJ, Prentice Hall, 95. 2nd ed, 97; Strategies for College Reading and Thinking with Instructor's Manual, NY, McGraw Hill, 91; Improving Reading with Instructor's Manual, NY, Holt, Rinehart, & Winston, 84; College Reading and Study Skills: A Guide to Improving Academic Communication, NY, Holt, Rinehart, & Winston, 78, 2nd ed, with Instructor's Manual, 82, 3rd ed with Instructor's Manual, 86, 4th ed with Instructor's Manual, 91, 5th ed College Reading and Study Skills: Learning, Thinking, Making Connections with Instructorl/4s Manual, 96; College Reading Instruction as Reflected by Current Reading Textbooks, J Col Reading and Learning, 97; Codifying Literacy: Identifying and Measuring Reading Competencies in Statewide Basic Skills Assessment Programs, J Col Reading and Learning, Vol XXXII, 89; Reading Tests and Reading Assessment, J Develop Educ, Vol 13, 89; Standardized Reading Tests and the Postsecondary Reading Curriculum, J Reading, Vol XXXII, 88. **CONTACT ADDRESS** Dept of Eng, Univ of Texas, Arlington, 203 Carlisle Hall, PO Box 19035, Arlington, TX 76019-0595.

WOOD, RUTH
DISCIPLINE ENGLISH LITERATURE **EDUCATION** Bowling Green State Univ, MA; Univ MN, PhD. **CAREER** Prof, Univ of WI. **RESEARCH** Portfolio assessment. **SELECTED PUBLICATIONS** Auth, Lolita in Peyton Place. **CONTACT ADDRESS** Eng Dept, Univ of Wisconsin, River Falls, S 3rd St, PO Box 410, River Falls, WI 54022-5001.

WOOD, SUSAN H.
PERSONAL Born 12/20/1963, Columbus, OH, s **DISCIPLINE** ENGLISH **EDUCATION** Carleton Col, BA, 86; Wash Univ, St Louis, AM, 88; Univ Tenn, PhD, 94. **CAREER** Adj instr, 88-89, Tourism Chinese Culture U, Yangmingshan; grad tchng assoc, 89-94, Univ Tenn; lectr, eng, 94-97, UNLV; instr, eng, 97-, Louisiana St Univ. **RESEARCH** historical novel, 19th century women authors, Chinese & Japanese lit, 18th century lit, the novel, world/multicultural. **CONTACT ADDRESS** Dept of English, Louisiana State Univ and A&M Col, Baton Rouge, LA 70803. **EMAIL** swood@unix1.sncc.lsu.edu

WOODALL, NATALIE JOY
DISCIPLINE ENGLISH **EDUCATION** SUNY Albany, BA, 68; MA, 69; PhD, 72; Admin Cert, 83; Syracuse Univ, MA, 92; PhD, 94. **CAREER** Teacher, Fairport High School, 72-82; dept chair, Oswego City Sch District, 82-91; adj instr, SUNY Oswego; instr, Syracuse Univ, 91-94; teacher, W Middle Sch, Auburn NY, 94--95; vis asst prof, W Carolina Univ, 95-96; correspondent to sen correspondent, Oswego, 97-. **HONORS AND AWARDS** Outstanding Young Women of Am, 71; Woodrow Wilson Dissertation Fel, 71-72; Outstanding Leaders in Elementary and Secondary Educ, 76; World Who's Who of Women, 79; Intl Who's Who in Educ, 79; Newspaper Fund Teacher Fel Award, 82; 2000 Outstanding Scholars of the 21st Century, 01. **MEMBERSHIPS** Am Philol Asn; MLA; Nat Coalition of Indep Scholars; Prof Asn of Diving Instr. **SELECTED PUBLICATIONS** Auth, "Jane Barlow" The Eighteen Nineties: An Encyclopedia of British Literature, Art and Culture, 92; co-auth, "Parody and the Character of Ulysses," Mythology: From Ancient to Post-Modern, 92; auth, "Milton's Vergilian Mottoes of 1637 and 1645," in Spokesperson Milton: Voices in Contemporary Criticism, 94; auth, "Landscape as Dystopia in Gambaro's La Malasangre," in Renaming the Landscape, 94; auth, "Women are Knights-Errant to the Last," in Reinventing the Middle Ages and the Renaissance, 98; auth, "Elizabeth Robins," in an Encyclopedia of British Women Writers, 99. **CONTACT ADDRESS** 2450 County Rte 7, Oswego, NY 13126-5706.

WOODARD, EMORY H., IV
PERSONAL Born 08/20/1971, Wilmington, DE, m, 1997 **DISCIPLINE** COMMUNICATIONS **EDUCATION** Univ Va, BA, 93; Univ Pa, MA, 95; PhD, 98. **CAREER** Teaching Asst to Lecturer, Univ Pa, 94-. **HONORS AND AWARDS** Outstanding Student Awd for Jewish Life, 92; James McDonald Awd for Social Justice, JAAR, 92; Outstanding Academic Achievement Awd, Col of Arts and Sci, 92; Nat Col Comm Arts Awd, 93; Omicron Delta Kappa, 93; Distinguished Student Awd, 93; George Tucker Fac Cup, Univ Va, 93; Comm Honor Soc, 93; Top Student Paper Awd, 95; Competitive Paper Awd, 96. **SELECTED PUBLICATIONS** Auth, "Interactive Media--Communicating Technologies for the 21st Century," Media Development, 94; co-auth, "Growing Pains: Children's Television in the New Regulatory Environment," The annals of the American Academy of Political and Social Science, 98; co-auth, "The Developmental Implications of Commercial Broadcaster' Educational Offerings," Journal of applied Developmental Psychology, in press; co-auth, "The Prosocial Effects of Television," Handbook of Children's Television Research, Sage Pub, in press; co-auth, "The Positive Effects of Television on Children's Social Interactions," Meta-Analyses of Media Effects, Lawrence Erlbaum, in press; co-auth, The State of Children's Television: Economic, Regulatory and Social Forces that Shape What Children See Today, Univ Chicago Press, forthcoming. **CONTACT ADDRESS** Dept Comm, Univ of Pennsylvania, 3620 Walnut St, Philadelphia, PA 19104-6220. **EMAIL** EWoodard@asc.upenn.edu

WOODBRIDGE, JOHN M.
PERSONAL Born 01/26/1929, New York, NY, m, 1975, 3 children **DISCIPLINE** ENGLISH AND ARCHITECTURE **EDUCATION** Amherst Col, AB, 51; Princeton Univ, MFA, archit, 56. **CAREER** Archit, Princeton Univ Archaeol expedition to Morgantina, Sicily, 56; Holden Egan Wilson & Corser, NY and Wash DC, 56-57; archit, John Funk, San Francisco, 57-58; John Lyon Reid and Partners, San Francisco, 57-58; assoc partner, Skidmore Owings & Merrill, 59-73; pres adv coun on Penn Ave, chief of design, 63-64, staff dir, 65-66, Pennsylvania Ave Development Corp, exec dir, 73-77; vpres, Braccia Joe & Woodbridge, 77-80; cons, Stoller Partners, Berkeley, 80-82; adjunct partner, Sprankle Lynd & Sprague, 82-91. **HONORS AND AWARDS** Phi Beta Kappa, 50; AIA Student Medal, 56; fel, Amer Inst of Archit, 74; Fed Design Achievement Awd, 88. **MEMBERSHIPS** AIA. **RESEARCH** Spanish colonial architectural history especially Mexico; Architectural history in Europe and U.S. **SELECTED PUBLICATIONS** Coauth,with Sally B. Woodbridge, San Francisco Architecture, San Francisco, Chronicle Books, 92; with Sally B. Woodbridge, Architec-

ture San Francisco, San Francisco, 101 Prod, 82; with David Gebhard, Roger Montgomery, Robert Winter and Sally B. Woodbridge, A Guide to the Architecture of San Francisco and Northern California, Salt Lake City, Peregrine Smith, 73; with Sally B. Woodbridge and Philip Thiel, Buildings of the Bay Area, NY, Grove Press, 60; auth, The Bay Area Style, Casabella 232, Oct 59; For the Cathedral of St. John the Divine, Relig Bldgs for Today, NY, F. W. Dodge, 57. **CONTACT ADDRESS** 19772 - 8th St. E, Sonoma, CA 95476. **EMAIL** jwoodbridge@peoplepo.com

WOODBRIDGE, LINDA
PERSONAL Born 03/23/1945, Chelsea, MA, m, 1994, 2 children **DISCIPLINE** ENGLISH **EDUCATION** UCLA, BA, 66; MA, 68; PhD, 70. **CAREER** Asst prof to prof, Univ of Albta; prof, Pa State Univ, 94-. **HONORS AND AWARDS** McCall Prof, 90; Acad Women's Assoc Awd, 92; Rutherford Teaching Awd, 94; NEH Fel, 01; Fel, Folger Shakespear Libr, 01-02. **MEMBERSHIPS** MLA, Shakespeare Assoc of Am. **RESEARCH** Shakespeare, English Renaissance Literature. **SELECTED PUBLICATIONS** Auth, Women and the English Renaissance: Literature and the Nature of Womankind, 1540-1620, Univ of Ill Pr, (Urbana, Chicago), 84; auth, Shakespeare: A Selective Bibliography of Criticism, Locust Hill Pr, (W Cornwall, CT), 88; auth, True Rites and Maimed Rites: Ritual and Anti-Ritual in the Age of Shakespeare, Univ of Ill Pr, (Urbana, Chicago), 92; auth, The Scythe of Saturn: Shakespeare and Magical Thinking, Univ of Ill Pr, 94; auth, Vagrancy, Homelessness, and English Renaissance Literature, Univ of Ill Pr, 01. **CONTACT ADDRESS** Dept English, Pennsylvania State Univ, Univ Park, 117 Burrowes Bldg, University Park, PA 16802-6200. **EMAIL** lxw18.@psu.edu

WOODELL, HAROLD
DISCIPLINE ENGLISH LITERATURE **EDUCATION** Univ UC, PhD, 74. **CAREER** Dept Eng, Clemson Univ **RESEARCH** American literature; Southern literature. **SELECTED PUBLICATIONS** Auth, All the King's Men: The Search for a Usable Past, 93; Archibald Rutledge, A Literary Map of South Carolina. **CONTACT ADDRESS** Clemson Univ, 811 Strode, Clemson, SC 29634. **EMAIL** wcharle@clemson.edu

WOODMANSEE, MARTHA
DISCIPLINE LITERARY THEORY **EDUCATION** Northwestern Univ, BA; Stanford Univ, MA, PhD. **CAREER** English, Case Western Reserve Univ. **SELECTED PUBLICATIONS** Auth or ed, The Author, Art and the Market: Rereading the History of Aesthetics; The Construction of Authorship: Textual Appropriation in Law and Literature; Erkennen und Deuten: Essays sur Literature und Literaturtheorie. **CONTACT ADDRESS** Case Western Reserve Univ, 10900 Euclid Ave, Cleveland, OH 44106.

WOODRESS, JAMES
PERSONAL Born 07/07/1916, Webster Groves, MO, m, 1940 **DISCIPLINE** AMERICAN LITERATURE **EDUCATION** Amherst Col, AB, 38; NYork Univ, AM, 43; Duke Univ, PhD, 50. **CAREER** Asst news ed, Sta KWK, St Louis, Mo, 38-40; radio writer, United Press Asn, NYC, 40-43; asst, Duke Univ, 47-49, vis lectr & res assoc, 54-55; instr English, Grinnell Col, 49-50; from asst prof to assoc prof, Butler Univ, 50-58; from assoc to prof, San Fernando Valley State Col, 58-66, chmn dept, 58-63, dean sch lett & sci, 63-65; chmn dept, 70-74, PROF ENGLISH, UNIV CALIF, DAVIS, 66-87, Fund Advan Educ fel, 52-53; Guggenheim fel, 56-57; secy, Am lit group, MLA, 61-65; Fulbright lectr, France, 62-63, Italy, 65-66; vis prof, Univ Paris, 74-75 & 83. **HONORS AND AWARDS** Am Lit Scholarship, 65-69, 75-77, 79, 81, 87. **MEMBERSHIPS** MLA; AAUP **RESEARCH** American civilization. **SELECTED PUBLICATIONS** Auth, Howells and Italy, 52; auth, Booth Tarkington: Gentleman from Indiana, 55; auth, Dissertations in Am Lit, 57, 62, 68; auth, A Yankee's Odyssey: The Life of Joel Barlow, 58; auth, Willa Cather: Her Life and Art, 70; ed, Eight American Authors, 71; auth, American Fiction, 1900-1950, Litt D Univ, Nebr, 74; ed, Cather's The Troll Garden, 83; ed, Critical Essays on Walt Whitman, 83; ed, Willa Cather: A Literary Life, 87. **CONTACT ADDRESS** Dept of English, Univ of California, Davis, 892 W Harrison Ave., Claremont, CA 91711.

WOODRING, CARL
PERSONAL Born 08/29/1919, Terrell, TX, m, 1942 **DISCIPLINE** ENGLISH LITERATURE **EDUCATION** Rice Inst, AB, 40, AM, 42; Harvard Univ, AM, 47, PhD, 49. **CAREER** Asst, Rice Inst & Harvard Univ; from instr English to prof English lit, Univ Wis, 48-61; prof, 61-76, GEORGE EDWARD WOODBERRY PROF OF LIT, COLUMBIA UNIV, 76-, Fels, Fund Avan Educ & Guggenheim Found, 55, Am Coun Learned Soc, 65. **HONORS AND AWARDS** Christian Gauss Prize, Nat Phi Beta Kappa, 71; Vis Scholar, Phi Beta Kappa, 74-75. **MEMBERSHIPS** MLA; Int Asn Univ Prof English; Asn Depts English (pres, 71); Keats-Shelley Asn Am; Acad Lit Studies. **RESEARCH** Nineteenth century English literature. **SELECTED PUBLICATIONS** Auth, Victorian Samplers: William and Mary Howitt, Univ Kans, 52; Politics in the Poetry of Coleridge, Univ Wis, 61; Prose of the Romantic Period, Houghton, 61; Wordsworth, Houghton, 65 & Harvard Univ, 68; Virginia Woolf, Columbia Univ, 66; Politics in English Romantic Poetry, Harvard Univ 70. **CONTACT ADDRESS** Dept of English & Comp Lit, Columbia Univ, New York, NY 10027.

WOODS, ALAN LAMBERT
PERSONAL Born 11/23/1942, Philadelphia, PA, m, 1967, 1 child **DISCIPLINE** THEATRE HISTORY **EDUCATION** Columbia Univ, AB, 64; Univ Southern Calif, MA, 69, PhD(theatre), 72. **CAREER** Lectr drama, Univ Southern Calif, 68-71; instr theatre, Long Beach City Col, 71-72; asst prof to assoc prof Theatre, Ohio State Univ, 72-, Lectr theatre, Calif State Univ, Los Angeles, 70; ed, Theatre Studies, 72-77; coordr res panel Comt Instnl Coop, 73-; lectr, Am Asn Health, Phys Educ & Recreation, 74; co-ed, Educ Theatre J, Univ Col Theatre Asn, 78-80; mem, res comn Am Theatre Asn, 78 & exec comt, Am Soc Theatre Res, 76-78, 89-92; visiting prof, Ind Univ, 78-79; dir, Lawrence and Lee Theatre Res Inst, 79-; pres, Ohio Theatre Alliance, 90-91. **HONORS AND AWARDS** Fel, Col of the Am Theatre, 96. **MEMBERSHIPS** Am Theatre Asn; Am Soc Theatre Res. **RESEARCH** Ancient theatre; 19th century popular theatre; theatre historiography. **SELECTED PUBLICATIONS** Coauth, A note on the symmetry of Delphi, Theatre Surv, 5/72; auth, Popular theatre in Los Angeles, Players, 5/73; A quantification approach to popular American theatre, Res in Educ, 1/74; James J Corbett, theatrical star, J Sports Hist, 76; Theatre historiography, Ohio Speech J, 76; Reconstructions of performances, Copenhagen, Royal Libr, 76; Frederick B Warde, tragedian, Educ Theatre J, 77; The Ohio Theatre, 80; Selected Plays of Jerome Lawrence and Robert E. Lee, Ohio State Univ Press, 95. **CONTACT ADDRESS** Dept of Theatre, Ohio State Univ, Columbus, 1089 Drake Union, 1849 Cannon Dr, Columbus, OH 43210-1266. **EMAIL** woods.1@osu.edu

WOODS, DAVID L.
PERSONAL Born 07/23/1932, San Jose, CA, m, 1998 **DISCIPLINE** COMMUNICATION **CAREER** Dalewood Enterprises, Inc, 87-; Marshall Univ, 97-; Shepherd College, 94-95; Univ Virginia, 67-83; George Washington Univ, 65-82, 86-88; spec Asst Chf Naval Material, Dir Naval sci tech info, 65 to 93-, US Navy Civl; Univ Maryland, 59-67; Aerospace Elec Firms, 59-65; US Navy, 56-59; Ohio State Univ,55-56; Lehigh Univ, 54-55, Stanford Univ, 53-54; US Naval Reserve, 49-87. **HONORS AND AWARDS** Navy Superior Civl Ser Medal; ROA Ntl Pres; United Way Honor; Republican candidate for WV House of Delegates; republican candidate for wv house of delegates. **MEMBERSHIPS** SAR, NCA, AFCEA, USNI, SHT, NRA, NERA. **RESEARCH** Military signals and signal systems; Mass media and society; Early broadcasting; Radio drama; Broadway musicals. **SELECTED PUBLICATIONS** Auth, A History of Tactical Communication Techniques, Arno Press; Signaling and Communications at Sea, Arno Press; The Development of Visual Signals on Land or Sea; US Navy Speakers Guide; Outstanding Navy Speeches; Quotable Navy Quotes. **CONTACT ADDRESS** RR #1, Box 161, Middleway, WV 25430-9726. **EMAIL** dwoods7807@aol.com

WOODS, JEANNIE MARLIN
PERSONAL Born 10/06/1947, Shreveport, LA, m, 1973 **DISCIPLINE** THEATER **EDUCATION** Univ Idaho, BA, 70; Hunter College, MA, 87; CUNY, MPh, 88, PhD, 89. **CAREER** From artistic dir to prof, Winthrop Univ, 89-, Winthrop Univ. **HONORS AND AWARDS** Diss Fel, CUNY, 88-89; Outstanding Jr Prof, 95; Fulbright Sch, 98-99. **MEMBERSHIPS** ATHE. **RESEARCH** The artistic process of the stage dir; Connections between Asian and Western theater in performance. **SELECTED PUBLICATIONS** Auth, Maureen Stapleton: A Bio-Bibliography, Westport CT, Greenwood Press, 92; auth, Theater to Change Men's Souls, the Artistry of Adrian Hall, Univ Delaware Press, 93; stage directing, The Sea, by Edward Bond, Winthrop Univ, 95; stage directing, As You Like It, by Wm Shakespeare, Winthrop Univ, 96; stage directing,The Way of the World, by Congreve, Winthrop U, 97; stage directing, On the Verge, by Eric Overmyer, Newstage Ensemble, 97; stage directing, The Complete Works of Wllm Shakespeare, abridged, by Adam Long, Daniel Singer, Jeff Borgeson, Newstage SCAC Tour, 97, 98; stage directing: The Fantasticks, Blowing Rock Stage Co, 98; co-trans, The Bride and Her Double, by Chi-Mei Wang, (Taiwan: Yuan Liou Pr, 00). **CONTACT ADDRESS** Dept of Theater and Dance, Winthrop Univ, 115 Johnson Hall, Rock Hill, SC 29733. **EMAIL** woodsj@winthrop.edu

WOODS, WILLIAM FORRESTERE
PERSONAL Born 02/03/1942, Syracuse, NY, m, 1967, 2 children **DISCIPLINE** RHETORIC, COMPOSITION **EDUCATION** Dartmouth Col, BA, 64; Univ Chicago, MA, 67; Ind Univ, PhD, 75. **CAREER** Instr, Cleveland State Univ, 67-69; asst prof, 75-80, assoc to prof english, Wichita State Univ, 80-. **MEMBERSHIPS** MLA; NCTE **RESEARCH** Medieval literature; 19th and 20th century history of composition teaching; Middle English narrative poetry; Chaucer. **SELECTED PUBLICATIONS** Auth, Private and Public Space in the 'Millers Tale' + Merging Metaphors of Personal, Domestic, and Societal Domains in the Concentric Narrative Movement of the 'Canterbury Tales' by Chaucer, Geoffrey, Chaucer Rev, 94; The Logic of Deprivation in the 'Reeves Tale' + Chaucer, Geoffrey, Chaucer Review, 95; Society and Nature in the 'Cooks Tale', Papers on Lang and Lit, 96. **CONTACT ADDRESS** Dept English, Wichita State Univ, 641 Lindquist Hall, Wichita, KS 67208.

WOODS, WILLIE G.
PERSONAL Born Yazoo City, MS, s **DISCIPLINE** ENGLISH **EDUCATION** Shaw Univ Raleigh NC, BA Ed 1965; Duke Univ Durham NC, MEd 1968; Temple Univ PA, PA State Univ, NYork Univ, attended; Indiana University of Pennsylvania, Indiana, PA, PhD English, 1995. **CAREER** Berry O'Kelly School, language arts teacher 65-67; Preston School, 5th grade teacher 67-69, adult ed teacher 68-69; Harrisburg Area Comm Coll, Prof English/ed 69-, dir acad found prog, 83-87, asst dean of Academic Foundations and Basic Education Division, 87-89, asst dean of Social Science, Public Services, and Basic Education Division, 89-92. **HONORS AND AWARDS** Cert of Merit for Community Serv Harrisburg 1971; Meritorious Faculty Contrib Harrisburg 1977; Outstanding Serv Awd PA Black Conf on Higher Ed 1980; Central Reg Awd for Serv PA Black Conf on Higher Ed 1982; Alpha Kappa Alpha Sor Outstanding Comm Serv Awd Harrisburg 1983; YMCA Youth Urban Serv Volunteer of the Year Awd 1983; Alpha Kappa Alpha Sor Basileus' Awd for Excellence as Comm Chair 1985; Administrative Staff Merit Awd, Harrisburg Area Comm College, 1986; Outstanding Service Awd, Black StudentUnion at Harrisburg Area Comm College, 1989; tribute for outstanding contributions to Harrisburg Area Comm College and to comm-at-large, HACC Minority Caucus, 1989; Alpha Kappa Mu Natl Hon Soc; Brooks Dickens Mem Awd in Education. **MEMBERSHIPS** Bd of mgrs Camp Curtin Branch of Harrisburg YMCA 1971-79; rep council 1972-, sec 1977-79, assoc ed 1981-, PA Black Conf on Higher Ed; exec bd 1978-, council chairperson 1981-82, Western Reg Act 101 Dir Council; bd of dir Alternative Rehab Comm Inc 1978-; bd of dir 1979-, charter mem sec 1981-82, treas 1982-83, PA Assoc of Devel Ed; bd of dir 1981-, sec 1984-85, Dauphin Residences Inc; bd of advisors 1981-, chairperson, acting chairperson, bd sec Youth Urban Serv Harrisburg YMCA; inst rep Natl Council on Black Amer Affairs of the Amer Assoc of Comm & Jr Coll 1983-. **CONTACT ADDRESS** Acting Vice President, Faculty and Instruction, Harrisburg Area Comm Col, One HACC Dr, Harrisburg, PA 17110-2999.

WOODSON, LINDA
PERSONAL Born 10/14/1943, Clifton, TX, m, 1983, 1 child **DISCIPLINE** RHETORIC, LITERATURE **EDUCATION** TX Christian Univ, BS, PhD. **CAREER** Prof taught at, TX Tech Univ, Southern Methodist Univ & TX Christian Univ; mem, Nominating Comt, Conf Col Composition and Commun, 85 & Exec Coun of CCTE; admin exp as, Coordr of Composition, UTSA, 86-98; Division Dir., 98-present, served as, dir Core Curric, UTSA. **HONORS AND AWARDS** Co-developed, R-WISE, Functional Skills Reading and Writing Tutor, 92. **RESEARCH** Contemp rhetorical theory; hist of rhetoric; compos theory; tchg of compos; tech writing and other kinds of writing; Am lit and the lit of TX and the Southwest. **SELECTED PUBLICATIONS** Auth, A Handbook of Rhetorical Terms, NCTE, 79; From Cases to Composition, Scott Foresman, 82; The Writer's World, HBJ, 85; essay in, Sacred Violence: A Reader's Companion to Cormac McCarthy, Tex Western Press, 95; coauth, Writing in Three Dimensions, Allyn and Bacon, 96; publ in, Style, Col Composition and Commun, JAEPL, Freshman Engl News. **CONTACT ADDRESS** Col of Fine Arts and Hum, Univ of Texas, San Antonio, 6900 N Loop 1604 W, San Antonio, TX 78249. **EMAIL** lwoodson@utsa.edu

WOODSON, THOMAS
PERSONAL Born 04/24/1931, Hartford, CT, m, 1963, 3 children **DISCIPLINE** ENGLISH, AMERICAN LITERATURE **EDUCATION** Yale Univ, BA, 53; MA, 56, PhD(English), 63. **CAREER** Instr English, Williams Col, 59-62; asst instr, Yale Univ, 62-63; from asst prof to assoc prof, 63-74, chmn comp lit, 74-78, Prof English, Ohio State Univ, 74-, Fulbright lectr, Univ Pau, France, 68-69; vis assoc prof English & Am studies, Yale Univ, 69-70. **HONORS AND AWARDS** House of the Seven Gables Hawthorne Awd, 91. **MEMBERSHIPS** MLA; Hawthorne Soc; Thoreau Soc. **RESEARCH** American fiction and Renaissance; style and stylistics. **SELECTED PUBLICATIONS** Ed, Twentieth Century Interpretations of the Fall of the House of Usher, Prentice-Hall , 69; auth, Thoreau on poverty and Magnanimity, Publ Mod Lang Asn Am, 1/70; auth, The loss and recovery of 19th-century American literature, Bull Midwest Mod Lang Asn, 74; ed, The French and Italian Notebooks, Nathaniel Hawthorne, Ohio State Press, 80; ed, The Letters, Nathaniel Hawthorne, Ohio State Press, 4 vols, 84-87; auth, In Respect to Egotism, Amer Lit, Vol 0064, 92; ed, Miscellaneous Prose and Verse, Nathaniel Hawthorne, Ohio State Press, 94; auth, Salem in The House of the Seven Gables, Critical Essays on Hawthorne's House of the Seven Gales, G.K. Hall, 95; Beyond the Classroom, Cithara Essays in the Judeochristian Tradition, Vol 0036, 96; ed, The English Notebooks, Nathaniel Hawthorne, Ohio State Press, 2 vols, 97. **CONTACT ADDRESS** 741 Lincrest Dr., Westerville, OH 43081-2436. **EMAIL** twoodson@columbus.rr.com

WOODWARD, CAROLYN
DISCIPLINE THEORY, 18TH-CENTURY BRITISH LITERATURE, AND FEMINIST STUDIES **EDUCATION** Univ Wash, PhD, 87. **CAREER** Instr, Univ NMex, 87-. **RESEARCH** 18th-century cultural deviance and experimental fiction. **SELECTED PUBLICATIONS** Auth, 'My Heart S o Wrapt': Lesbian Disruptions in 18th-Century British Literature,

Signs, 93; Who Wrote The Cry: a Fable for Our Times, 18th-Century Fiction, 96. **CONTACT ADDRESS** Univ of New Mexico, Albuquerque, Albuquerque, NM 87131. **EMAIL** woodward@unm.edu

WOODWARD, PAULINE
DISCIPLINE ENGLISH LANGUAGE AND LITERATURE **EDUCATION** Boston Univ, AB; Univ Hartford, MA; Tufts Univ, PhD. **CAREER** Eng Dept, Endicott Col **RESEARCH** 20th century traditions in Am Lit, concentrating on the works of Asian Am, Native Am, black Am, and Chicanos. **SELECTED PUBLICATIONS** Auth, study of Louise Erdich's fiction in American Writers: Supplement IV, Scribner's/Macmillan. **CONTACT ADDRESS** Endicott Col, 376 Hale St, Beverly, MA 01915.

WOODWARD, STEVEN P.
PERSONAL Born 07/03/1964, Broadstairs, Britain, m, 2000 **DISCIPLINE** ENGLISH LITERATURE **EDUCATION** Queen's Univ, BA, 85; Ryerson Polytechnic Univ, BAA, 90; Univ of Toronto, MA, 92; PhD, 01. **CAREER** Asst prof, Nipissing Univ, 99-01; adj, Univ of Toronto, 01. **MEMBERSHIPS** MLA, Children's Lit Soc, Walter de la Mare Soc. **RESEARCH** Modern British Literature, Children's Literature, Film. **SELECTED PUBLICATIONS** Auth, ""Playing with Words, Speaking with Guns: The Case of Grosse Pointe Blank," Bang Bang, Shoot Shoot!, eds John Sakeris and Murray Pomerance, (98); auth, "She's Murder: Pretty Poisons and Bad Seeds," Sugar, Spice, and Everything Nice, ed Murray Pomerance, (01); auth, "No Safe Place: Gender and Space in Polanski's Recent Films," Ladies and Gentlemen, Boys and Girls, ed Frances Gateward and Murray Pomerance, (01). **CONTACT ADDRESS** 642 Adelaide St W, Toronto, ON, Canada M6J 1A9. **EMAIL** woodward@chass.utoronto.ca

WOOLF, LEONARD
PERSONAL Born 03/27/1916, Baltimore, MD, m, 1944, 1 child **DISCIPLINE** ENGLISH **EDUCATION** Johns Hopkins Univ, BS, 52; Univ Md, MEd, 51, DEd, 59. **CAREER** Chmn dept English, Jr High Sch, Md, 50-54; teacher, Baltimore Polytech Inst, 54-56; English specialist, Baltimore City Pub Schs, 56-63; supvr English, Anne Arundel County Publ Schs, 63-66; assoc prof sec educ & coordr English Educ, 66-73, prof English, 73-80, Emer Prof Sec Educ, Univ MD, College Park, 80-, Consult, English for foreign internes, Church Home & Hosp, 60-61; consult, US Off Educ, 65- **HONORS AND AWARDS** Distinguished Service Awd, Phi Delta Kappa, 72 & Md Coun Teachers English, 73. **RESEARCH** Secondary education; reading, especially literature for slow learner. **SELECTED PUBLICATIONS** Auth, Conrad, Joseph Vision + From the Monks House Papers of Woolf, Leonard, Engl Lit in Transition 1880-1920, Vol 0036, 93; Alive or Dead, Hunting the Highbrow, Cambridge Quart, Vol 0024, 95. **CONTACT ADDRESS** Col of Educ, Univ of Maryland, Col Park, College Park, MD 20742.

WOOLLEY, JAMES
PERSONAL Born 07/19/1944, Shelbyville, KY **DISCIPLINE** ENGLISH **EDUCATION** Wake Forest Univ, BA, 66; Univ Chicago, MA, 67, PhD, 72. **CAREER** From instr to asst prof English, Marquette Univ, 71-74; asst prof English, Univ Pa, 74-80; from asst prof English to Frank Lee and Edna M Smith prof English, 80-; head, dept English, 93-97, clerk of fac, 97-, Lafayette Col; Am Coun Learned Socs res fel, 77. **HONORS AND AWARDS** Summer fac fel, 75; sum res fel, 83; Jones Fac lectr, 90; Jones Awd for Tchg and Scholarship, 91; Student Government Awd for Superior Tchg, 94; Lindback Found Awd for Distinguished Tchg, 95. **MEMBERSHIPS** MLA; Am Soc Eighteenth Century Studies; Bibliog Soc; AAUP; Asn for Computers and the Hum; Asn for Documentary Ed; Br Soc for Eighteenth Century Stud; Eighteenth-Century Ireland Soc; Soc for Textual Scholarship; Soc for the Hist of Authorship, Reading, and Publ. **RESEARCH** Eighteenth-century British and Irish literature and social history; bibliography; satire. **SELECTED PUBLICATIONS** Swift's Later Poems, Garland, 88; co-ed and contribur, Swift and His Contexts, AMS, 89; ed, The Intelligencer by Jonathan Swift and Thomas Sheridan, Oxford, 92; auth, "The Canon of Swift's Poems: The Case of An Apology to the Lady Carteret," in Reading Swift, Wilhelm Fink, 93; auth, "Annotation: Some Guiding Considerations," East-Central Intelligencer, 94; coauth, "The Full Text of Swift's On Poetry: A Rapsody," Swift Stud, 94; auth, "Sarah Harding as Swift's Printer," in Walking Naboth's Vineyard: New Studies of Swift, Notre Dame, 95; auth, "Writing Libels on the Germans: Swift's Wicked Treasonable Libel," in Swift: The Enigmatic Dean, Stauffenburg, 98. **CONTACT ADDRESS** Dept of English, Lafayette Col, Easton, PA 18042-1781. **EMAIL** woolleyj@lafayette.edu

WOOTEN, CECIL W.
DISCIPLINE CLASSICS **EDUCATION** Davidson Col, AB, 67; Univ NC, Chapel Hill, MA, 68; Middlebury Col and Univ Paris, AM, 73; Univ NC, Chapel Hill, PhD, 72. **CAREER** Prof, Univ NC, Chapel Hill. **RESEARCH** Greek and Latin rhetoric and oratory; the ancient novel. **SELECTED PUBLICATIONS** Auth, The Elusive 'Gay' Teenagers of Classical Antiquity, The High Schl J 77, 93/94; The Peripatetic Tradition in the Literary Essays of Dionysius of Halicarnassus, in Peripatetic Rhetoric after Aristotle, eds, W. Fortenbaugh and D. Mirhady, New Brunswick, 94. **CONTACT ADDRESS** Univ of No Carolina, Chapel Hill, Chapel Hill, NC 27599. **EMAIL** cwwooten@email.unc.edu

WORK, JAMES
DISCIPLINE ENGLISH LITERATURE **EDUCATION** Colo State Univ, BA, MA; Univ NMex, PhD. **CAREER** Prof. **HONORS AND AWARDS** Excellence Tchg Awd, 92. **MEMBERSHIPS** Western Lit Asn; Western Writers of Am. **RESEARCH** Western American literature. **SELECTED PUBLICATIONS** Auth, Following Where the River Begins; auth, Ride South to Purgatory; auth, The Tobermory Manuscript; auth, Ride West to Dawn; ed, Prose and Poetry of the American West; ed, Gunfight!; ed, Shane: The Critical Edition. **CONTACT ADDRESS** Dept of English, Colorado State Univ, Fort Collins, CO 80523.

WORLEY, DAVID W.
PERSONAL Born 07/03/1950; Herrin, IL, m, 1999 **DISCIPLINE** COMMUNICATION **EDUCATION** Western Ill Univ, BA, 91; Southern Ill Univ, MS, 93; PhD, 96. **CAREER** Teaching asst, Southern Ill Univ, 91-95, instr, 95-96; asst prof, Basic Course Dir, Ind State Univ, 96-. **HONORS AND AWARDS** Nominated for Outstanding Dissertation Awd, SIU-C, 97; Excellence in Education, Col of Arts and Scis, Ind State Univ, 98; Outstanding New Teacher Awd, Central States Commun Asn, 2000. **MEMBERSHIPS** Nat Commun Asn, Phi Kappa Phi, Nat Commun Educ Asn, Central States Commun Asn, Golden Key Honor Soc. **RESEARCH** Communication with persons with disabilities; classroom communication; ethics and communication; communication education. **SELECTED PUBLICATIONS** Auth, "Using feature films to teach interpersonal communication," in Teaching Ideas for the basic course, Vol 2, eds L. & B. Hugenberg, Dubuque, IA: Kendall/Hunt (98); auth, "Communication and students with disabilities on college campuses," in Handbook of communication and people with disabilities: Research and application, eds D. Braithwaite & T. Thompson, Mahwah, NJ: Earlbaum (99); auth, ":Learning by doing: Activities in the basic course," in Teaching ideas for the basic course III, eds, L. & B. Hugenberg, Dubuque, IA: Kendall/Hunt (99); auth, "Pencils and impromptus," in Teaching ideas for the basic course III, eds, L. & B. Hugenberg, Dubuque, IA: Kendall/Hunt (99); auth, "Organizational, explanatory and application functions of the textbook," Commun Educ, 48 (99): 323-324; auth, "An acrostic approach to teaching public speaking in the basic hybrid communication course," Basic Communication Annual, 12 (2000); coauth, "The discipline of communication in higher education: Mutually defining and reciprocal relationships," J of the Asn for Commun Admin, 29 (2000): 26-39. **CONTACT ADDRESS** Dept Commun, Indiana State Univ, 210 N 7th St, Erickson Hall, Terre Haute, IN 47809-0001. **EMAIL** cmworley@ruby.indstate.edu

WORTH, FABIENNE ANDRE
PERSONAL Born 05/24/1944, Lyon, France, m, 1967, 2 children **DISCIPLINE** FRENCH LITERATURE, CINEMA **EDUCATION** Univ NC, Chapel Hill, BA, 70, MA, 73, PhD(comp lit), 79. **CAREER** Vis lectr, 78-79, Vis Lectr French Lit, Duke Univ, 80-, Instr, French Cinema Arts Sch, Carrboro, NC, 80. **MEMBERSHIPS** MLA; Am Asn Teachers Fr; Am Comp Lit Asn. **RESEARCH** History and the novel; authorship in the cinema. **SELECTED PUBLICATIONS** Auth, Le Sacre Et Le Sida--Representations of Sexuality and Their Contradictions in France, 1971-1996, a Perspective from Across the Atlantic, Temps Modernes, Vol 0052, 97. **CONTACT ADDRESS** 209 Pritchard Ave, Chapel Hill, NC 27514.

WORTH, GEORGE JOHN
PERSONAL Born 06/11/1929, Vienna, Austria, m, 1951, 2 children **DISCIPLINE** ENGLISH **EDUCATION** Univ Chicago, AB, 48, AM, 51; Univ Ill, PhD(English), 54. **CAREER** Instr English, Univ Ill, 54-55; from instr to assoc prof, 55-65, from asst chmn dept to assoc chmn dept, 61-63, chmn dept, 63-79, Prof English, Univ Kans, 65-, Am Philos Soc grant, 62. **MEMBERSHIPS** Midwest Mod Lang Asn: MLA; Int Asn Univ Prof English; Dickens Soc. **RESEARCH** Victorian fiction. **SELECTED PUBLICATIONS** Auth, Dickens on Literature, Dickens Quart, Vol 0009, 92; The Dickens Aesthetic, Dickens Quart, Vol 0009, 92; The Companion to 'Oliver Twist', Dickens Quart, Vol 0010, 93; Dickens, Charles and the Image of Woman, Dickens Quart, Vol 0011, 94; Life as History, J Engl and Ger Philol, Vol 0094, 95; Stephen, Leslie Life in Letters, a Bibliographical Study, 19th Century Prose, Vol 0022, 95; Muscular Christianity, Embodying the Victorian Age, 19th Century Prose, Vol 0023, 96; Oliphant, Margaret, J Engl and Ger Philol, Vol 0096, 97; Dickens, Charles, Dickens Quart, Vol 0014, 97, **CONTACT ADDRESS** Dept of English, Univ of Kansas, Lawrence, Lawrence, KS 66045. **EMAIL** GJWorth@aol.com

WORTHAM, THOMAS
PERSONAL Born 12/05/1943, Liberal, KS **DISCIPLINE** ENGLISH **EDUCATION** Marquette Univ, AB, 65; IN Univ, PhD (English), 70. **CAREER** Asst prof, 70-76, assoc prof, 76-82, Prof English, Univ CA, Los Angeles, 82-, vice chair, dir of Undergrad Studies, 92-97, Chair, 97-; Fulbright lect, Univ Warsaw, Poland, 76-77; Ed, Nineteenth-Century Lit, 83-; member, ed bd, The Collected Works of Ralph Waldo Emerson, Harvard Univ Press, 96-. **HONORS AND AWARDS** Regent's Faculty Fel in the Humanities, Univ CA, 71; Grants-in-Aid of Res, Am Philos Soc, 76, 81; Sr fel, Am Coun of Learned Socs, 83-84; travel grants, NEH, 85-86, 88-89. **MEMBERSHIPS** MLA; Asn for Documentary Editing; Soc for Textual Scholarship; Int Asn of Univ Profs of English. **RESEARCH** 19th-Century Am lit and culture; textual scholarship and criticism. **SELECTED PUBLICATIONS** Auth, Co-compiler, Am Literary Manuscripts, 2nd ed, Univ GA Press, 77; James Russell Lowell's The Bigelow Papers (first series): A Critical Edition, Northern IL Univ Press, 77; Letters of W. D. Howells: 1892-1901, Twayne, 81; The Early Prose Writings of William Dean Howells, OH Univ Press, 90; ed, My Mark Twain by W. D. Howells, Dover, 97; ed, Mark Twain's Some Chapters from My Autobiography, Dover, 99; ed, The Poems of Ralph Waldo Emerson, Harvard Univ Press, forthcoming. **CONTACT ADDRESS** Dept of English, Univ of California, Los Angeles, Box 951530, Los Angeles, CA 90095-1530. **EMAIL** wortham@humnet.ucla.edu

WORTHEN, THOMAS
PERSONAL Born 08/18/1937, Salt Lake City, UT, 4 children **DISCIPLINE** CLASSICS **EDUCATION** Univ Utah, BA, 59; Univ Wash, MA, 63, PhD, 68. **CAREER** Lectr, 65-68, asst prof, 68-72, Assoc Prof to Assoc Prof Emer Greek, Univ Ariz, 72-. **MEMBERSHIPS** AAS (HAD div); AAAS. **RESEARCH** Greek science and proto science. **SELECTED PUBLICATIONS** Auth, Pneumatic Action in the Klepsydra and Empedocles' Account of Breathing, Isis, 70; Note on Ajax 494-5, Class Philol, 72; co-auth, The Thucydides Syndrome: A New Hypothesis for the Cause of Plague of Athens, NEJM, 86; rev, English Words from latin and Greek Elements by Donald Ayers, Univ Ariz Press, 86; Ideas of Sky in Archaic Greek Poetry, Glotta, 88; The Myth of Replacement: Stars, Gods and Order in the Univers, Univ Ariz Press, 91; contribr, Stalking the Second Tier, An Occasional Paper on Neglected Problems in Science Education, Res Corp, 91; Eclipses by the Semester, Griffith Observer, 93; Pleiades and Hesperides, Vistas in Astronomy, 95; Herodotos's Report on Thales' Eclipes, Electronic Antiquity, 97. **CONTACT ADDRESS** Dept of Classics, Univ of Arizona, 371 Modern Languages Bldg, PO Box 210067, Tucson, AZ 85721-0067. **EMAIL** tdw@u.arizona.edu

WORTHINGTON, IAN
PERSONAL Born 03/19/1958, Lytham Lanes, United Kingdom, m, 1996, 1 child **DISCIPLINE** CLASSICS, ANCIENT HISTORY **EDUCATION** Univ Hull, BA, 79; Univ Durham, MA, 81; Monash Univ, PhD, 87. **CAREER** Lectr, Univ New England, 88-92; sr lectr, Univ Tasmania, 93-97; prof, Univ Mo Columbia, 98-. **RESEARCH** Greek History, Alexander the Great, Greek Oratory. **SELECTED PUBLICATIONS** Auth, "[Plutarch], X.Or. 848e: A Loeb Mistranslation and Its Effect on Hyperides' Entry Into Athenian Political Life," Electronic Antiquity 3.2 (95); ed, Voice Into Text. Orality and Literacy in Ancient Greece, Brill, 96; rev, of "Theopompus of Chios, History and Rhetoric in the Fourth Century BC," by M. Flower, Classical Rev 46 (96): 179; rev, of "Faces of Power. Alexander's Image and Hellenistic Politics," by A. Stewart, Classical J 91 (96): 210-211; auth, "Alexander the Great and the 'Interests of Historical Accuracy': A Reply," Ancient Hist Bull 13.4 (99): 121-127; auth, "How 'Great' was Alexander?," Ancient Hist Bull 13.2 (99): 39-55; auth, Greek Orators Volume 2: Dinarchus and Hyperides, Aris & Phillips, 99; rev, of "Thucydides and Ancient Simplicity," by G. Crane, Classical Rev 49 (99): 368-369; **CONTACT ADDRESS** Dept Hist, Univ of Missouri, Columbia, 101 Read Hall, Columbia, MO 65211-7500. **EMAIL** worthingtoni@missouri.edu

WORTMAN, WILLIAM A.
PERSONAL Born 09/19/1940, Council Bluffs, IA, m, 1966, 2 children **DISCIPLINE** ENGLISH **EDUCATION** Wesleyan Univ, BA, 62; Univ Neb, MA, 65; Case West Res Univ, PhD, 72; Columbia Univ, MS, 75. **CAREER** Hum librn, Miami Univ, 75-. **HONORS AND AWARDS** Beta Phi Mu; Who's Who in Am. **MEMBERSHIPS** Am Library Asn; Mod Lang Asn; Soc for the Hist of Authorship, Reading, and Publishing. **RESEARCH** Hist of printing and publishing, lib collections and info services. **SELECTED PUBLICATIONS** Auth, Collection Management: Background and Principles, 89; auth, Collection Management, 93; auth, A Guide to Serial Bibliographies for the Modern Literatures, 95; ed, Literature in English: Aguide for Librarians, 00. **CONTACT ADDRESS** King Library, Miami Univ, 4879 Somerville Rd, Oxford, OH 45056. **EMAIL** wortmawa@muohio.edu

WOSK, JULIE
PERSONAL Born 06/05/1944, Chicago, IL, m, 2000 **DISCIPLINE** ENGLISH, ART HISTORY **EDUCATION** Wash Univ, St Louis, BA, 66; Harvard Univ, MAT, 67; Univ Wis, PhD, 74. **CAREER** Prof, SUNY Maritime Col, 75-. **HONORS AND AWARDS** Phi Beta Kappa; Mortar Board; NEH Fel in Art Hist; Sloan Found Grant. **MEMBERSHIPS** Soc for the Hist of Technol, Col Art Asn, Int Comt for the Hist of Technol, Soc for Lit and Sci. **RESEARCH** Art and technology; literature and technology; representations of women and machines; society for literature and science. **SELECTED PUBLICATIONS** Auth, Breaking Frame: Technology and the Visual Arts in the

Nineteenth Century, Rutgers Univ Press (92); auth, "Manhole Covers and the Myths of Am," Design Book Rev (MIT Press) (winter/spring 95); auth, "Brunel Meets Brubelleschi," Am Heritage of Invention and Technology (summer 95); auth, "Mutant Materials in Contemporary Design," Design Issues (spring 96); auth, Women and the Machine: Representations from the Spinning Wheel to the electronic Age, Oxford Univ Press (2001). **CONTACT ADDRESS** Dept Humanities, SUNY, Maritime Col, 6 Pennyfield Ave, Bronx, NY 10465-4127.

WRIGHT, AUSTIN M.
PERSONAL Born 09/06/1922, NY, m, 1950, 3 children **DISCIPLINE** ENGLISH **EDUCATION** Harvard Univ, MA, 43; Univ Chicago, MA, 48; PhD, 59. **CAREER** Instr, Augustana Col, 48-50; teacher, Wright Jr Col, 55-60; asst prof, Univ Chicago, 60-62; asst prof to assoc prof to prof to emer, Univ Cincinnati, 62-93. **HONORS AND AWARDS** Cohen Awd, Univ Cinci, 67; George Rieve Scholar Awd, 73; Whiting Writers Awd, 85. **MEMBERSHIPS** PEN; MLA; AG. **RESEARCH** Creative writing; critical theory; 20th-century American fiction. **SELECTED PUBLICATIONS** Auth, Campfire Eyes, 69; auth, The Marbey Mythology, 77; auth, The Formal Principle in the Novel, 82; auth, Recalcitrance, Faulkner and the Professors, 90; auth, Tony and Susan, 93; auth, After Gregory, 94; auth, Telling Time, 95; Disciple, 97. **CONTACT ADDRESS** 601 Maple Trace, Cincinnati, OH 45246. **EMAIL** austin.wright@uc.edu

WRIGHT, DEBORAH KEMPF
PERSONAL Born 03/10/1949, South Bend, IN, m, 1975 **DISCIPLINE** ENGLISH LITERATURE **EDUCATION** Univ Evansville, BA, 71; Miami Univ, MA, 73, PhD(English), 80. **CAREER** Grad asst res, 71-72, grad asst English, 72-teaching fel, 73-76, diss fel, 76-77, instr, 77, Asst Prof English, Miami Univ, 80-, Fel, William Andrews Clark Mem Libr, Univ Calif, Los Angeles, 82. **MEMBERSHIPS** Col English Asn; Johnson Soc Cent Region; Midwest Branch Am Soc 18th Century Studies; Midwest Mod Lang Asn; MLA. **RESEARCH** Matthew Prior, 18th century English poet and diplomatist; Robert Sidney, Earl of Leicester, English Renaissance poet. **SELECTED PUBLICATIONS** Auth, An Autobiographical Ballad by Prior, Matthew, Brit Libr J, Vol 0018, 92. **CONTACT ADDRESS** 1033 Cedar Dr, Oxford, OH 45056.

WRIGHT, GEORGE THADDEUS
PERSONAL Born 12/17/1925, Staten Island, NY, m, 1955 **DISCIPLINE** ENGLISH **EDUCATION** Columbia Univ, AB, 46, MA, 47; Univ Calif, Berkeley, PhD, 57. **CAREER** Lectr English, Univ Calif, Berkeley, 56-67; vis asst prof, NMex Highlands Univ, summer 57; instr, Univ Ky, 57-59, asst prof, 59-60; asst prof, San Francisco State Col, 60-61; assoc prof, Univ Tenn, 61-68; chmn dept, 74-77, prof English, Univ Minn, Minneapolis, 68-89, Regents prof, 89-93, Emeritus 93-. **HONORS AND AWARDS** Fulbright lectr Am lit, Univ Aix-Marseille, 64-66, Univ Thessaloniki, Greece, 77-78; ed, Univ Minn pamphlets on Am writers, 68-; NEH grant, summer 81; NEH fel, 84-85; Guggenheim fel, 82, William Riley Parker Prize, MLA, 74 & 81. **MEMBERSHIPS** MLA; Shakespeare Asn, T S Eliot Society, ALSC. **RESEARCH** English and American poetry; modernist lit; Shakespeare. **SELECTED PUBLICATIONS** Auth, The Poet in the Poem, Univ CA Pess, 60; auth, W.H. Auden, Twayne, 69; rev. ed, 81; auth, "The Lyric Present: Simple Present Verbs in English Poems, PMLA, 74; auth, "Hendiadys and Hamlet, PMLA, 81; auth, "Wyatt's Decasyllabic Line, Studies in Philogy, 85; auth, Shakespeare's Metrical Art, Univ of CA Press, 88; auth, Sustained Stages and States: T S Eliot's Peculiar Personae in: T S Eliot Annual, 90; Voices that Figure in Four Quartets, in The Placing of T S Eliot, Univ Missouri, 91; An Almost Oral Art: Shakespeare's Language on Stage and Page, Shakespeare Quart, 92; Blank Verse in the Jacobean Theater: Language that Vanishes, Language that Keeps, in: The Elizabethan Theatre XII, 93; cont, New Princeton Encyclopedia of Poetry and Poetics, 93; Troubles of a Professional Meter Reader, in: Shakespeare Reread, Cornell Univ, 94; Hearing the Measures, Style, 97; auth, "The Silent Speech of Shakespeare's Sonnets, in Shakespeare and the Twentieth Century, 98; auth, Aimless Life: Poems, 1961-95, 99; auth, "Hearing Shakespeare's Dramatic Verse, in a Companion to Shakespeare, 99. **CONTACT ADDRESS** 2617 West Crown King Dr, Tucson, AZ 85741. **EMAIL** twright@u.arizona.edu

WRIGHT, H. BUNKER
PERSONAL Born 03/26/1907, Woodstock, IL, m, 1931, 1 child **DISCIPLINE** ENGLISH LITERATURE **EDUCATION** Northwestern Univ, BS, 30; AM, 31, PhD, 37. **CAREER** Asst English, Northwestern Univ, 31-35, instr, 35-38; from instr to prof, 38-74, chmn dept, 56-59, dean grad sch, 59-69, Emer Prof English, Miami Univ, 74-, Lectr, Univ Cincinnati, 39-55; chmn Midwest Conf Grad Studies & Res, 65-66; ed, Prior Proj, 74-; fel, Huntington Libr, 82. **MEMBERSHIPS** MLA; Midwest Mod Lang Asn; Am Soc 18th Century Studies; Midwest Am Soc 18th Century Studies; Johnson Soc Cent Region. **RESEARCH** English literature and history of the 17th and 18th centuries; unpublished correspondence, literary and diplomatic; Matthew Prior. **SELECTED PUBLICATIONS** Auth, An Autobiographical Ballad by Prior,Matthew, Brit Lib Jour, Vol 0018, 92. **CONTACT ADDRESS** 1033 Cedar Dr, Oxford, OH 45056.

WRIGHT, JANIS
PERSONAL Born 10/03/1963, San Diego, CA, m, 1999 **DISCIPLINE** LITERATURE; SPEECH COMMUNICATION **EDUCATION** Umboldt State Univ, BA, 86; Univ Tex-Austin, MA, 90. **CAREER** Sale mgr. Confetti/Entertainment One, 89-90; instr, Santa Rosa Jr Col, 91- ; co-founder, Assoc Commun Trainers & Speakers, 95- ; instr, Napa Valley Col, 00- . **HONORS AND AWARDS** Marjorie Davison Parker fel, 86-87, Shell grant, 86-87, Prof Dev Awd, 87-88, Univ Texas-Austin; Youth 2000 Mentor Part Awd, 98; Redwood Awd, 99. **MEMBERSHIPS** Sonoma County Dept Health's Prev Div Media Literacy Coalition & Planning Comt. **RESEARCH** Researching and writing a book. **SELECTED PUBLICATIONS** Co-auth, "Forms of Discourse in Moral Conflict: A Case Study", (87); auth, "Adapting th Novels of Larry McMurtry for Stage: Leaving Cheyenne in Production", (96). **CONTACT ADDRESS** Dept Commun, Santa Rosa Junior Col, 1501 Mendocino Ave, Santa Rosa, CA 95401-4332.

WRIGHT, JOSEPHINE
PERSONAL Born 09/05/1942, Detroit, MI, s **DISCIPLINE** MUSIC HISTORY AND LITERATURE **EDUCATION** Univ Mo, BM, Pius XII Acad, Italy, MM; Univ Mo, MA; NYork Univ, PhD. **CAREER** Instr, Harvard Univ; York Col; City Univ NY; prof, Col of Wooster, 81-00; prof music and the Josephine Lincoln Morris Prof Black Studies, 00-. **HONORS AND AWARDS** Ed, New Music, The Black Perspective in Mus, 79-90; Amer Mus, 93-97; ed, Garland Publ's new Music In African American Culture series, 95-. **SELECTED PUBLICATIONS** Auth, articles in Amer Mus; The Black Perspective in Mus; Black Mus Res Newsletter; The New Grove Dictionary of Mus and Musicians; The New Grove Dictionary of Amer Mus; The New Grove Dictionary of Opera, Notes, and Women's Studies Quart; ed, Ignatius Sancho, 1729-1780: An Early African Composer in England, Garland Press, 81; co-author African-American Traditions in Song, Sermon, Tale, and Dance: An Annotated Bibliography, Greenwood Press, 90; principal ed, New Perspectives in Music: Essays in Honor of Eileen Southern, Harmonie Park Press, 91. **CONTACT ADDRESS** Dept of Mus, The Col of Wooster, Wooster, OH 44691. **EMAIL** jwright@acs.wooster.edu

WRIGHT, MICHELLE M.
PERSONAL Born 10/31/1968, Rome, Italy **DISCIPLINE** ENGLISH, LITERATURE **EDUCATION** Oberlin Col, BA, 88; Univ Mich, PhD, 97. **CAREER** Asst prof, Carnegie Mellon Univ, 97-00; asst prof, Macalester Col, 01-. **HONORS AND AWARDS** Mellon Min Fel, 90-97; Rackham Merit Fel, 92-96; Rackham Predoct Fel, 96-97; McCandless Career Dev Chair, 97-00; Phi Kappa Phi; CAUSE Res Grnt; Falk Human Awd; Postdoct Res Awd. **MEMBERSHIPS** MLA, CAAR, ASA, EAAS. **RESEARCH** Literature and theory from the African Diaspora. **SELECTED PUBLICATIONS** Auth, Alas! Poor Richard, NYU Press, 99; auth, "Nigger Peasants from France," Callaloo 22 (99); auth, "Primitive Viewers, Complex Spectacle," J African Art ('01): 13-14; auth, "Tampering with the Goods" (Mediated Identities Press, 01); auth, "Racism and Technology," Switch: J of Tech (01); auth, Missing Persons: The search for Postcolonial Subjects in the African Diaspora, Duke Univ Press, forthcoming. **CONTACT ADDRESS** Eng Dept., Macalester Col, 1600 Grand Ave, Saint Paul, MN 55105. **EMAIL** wright@macalester

WRIGHT, ROBERT L.
PERSONAL Born 05/23/1920, Connersville, IN, m, 1944, 1 child **DISCIPLINE** LANGUAGES AND LITERATURES; FOLK SONG **EDUCATION** Defiance, BA, 43; Univ Minn, MA, 47; Columbia's Harvard, SU, 47-49; Teachers Col, EdD, 55; postdoc study, Stockholm, 57-58. **CAREER** Emer Prof Thought and Language, Mich State Univ; US Navy, active duty 43-46, 51-53 (from seamen to lieutenant-commander) **HONORS AND AWARDS** Mich State Univ Book Award; Swodish Gov't Fel, 57-58; Fel, Int Inst Arts and Letters, 61; MSU Bk Award, 63; Am Philosophical Soc grantee, 66-67, 69-70, 71-73; Huntington Lib Follow, 69; Fel, Am Antiquarian Soc, 74; Mich State Imov Distinguished Fac Award, 81; Doriance Col Alumni Achievement Award, 81. **MEMBERSHIPS** MLA; Am Folklore Soc; Canadian Folk Music Soc; Soc AAU; Scand in Study, etc. **RESEARCH** Ballads and songs, emigrant ballads. **CONTACT ADDRESS** 274 Oakland Dr., East Lansing, MI 48823-4747.

WRIGHT, ROOSEVELT R., JR.
PERSONAL Born 07/24/1943, Elizabeth City, NC, s **DISCIPLINE** COMMUNICATIONS **EDUCATION** Elizabeth City State Univ, BS 1964; North Carolina Central Univ, MA 1969; Virginia State University, CGS, 1970; Syracuse Univ, PhD 1992. **CAREER** SI Newhouse School of Comm, assoc prof, radio/TV, 75-; NBC Radio Div WRC/WKYS Washington, acc exec 1974-75; Howard Univ Washington, DC, adj prof radio TV 1974-75; WTNJ Radio Trenton, NJ, gen manager 1973-74; North Carolina Central Univ, asst prof ed media 1972-73; WDNC-AM/FM Durham, NC, announcer radio engr 1972-73; Elizabeth City State Univ, asso dir ed media 1968-69; DC State Coll Dover, dir ed media 1969-70; WNDR Radio Syracuse, announcer radio engr 1970-72; WLLE Radio Raleigh, NC, program dir 1973-74; WOLF Radio Syracuse, NY, chief engineer 1980-84. **HONORS AND AWARDS** Soldier of the Quarter 32AADC AUS 1967; Doctoral Flwsp Syracuse Univ 1970-72; Men's Day Awd Mt Lebanon AMEZ Ch Eliz City 1974, 1997; Upward Bound Prog Awd LeMoyne Coll Syracuse 1977; Ed Media & Speaker Awd NC Ed Media Assn 1977; Natl Council of Negro Women Communications Awd 1984, 1994; Syracuse Univ Pan Hellenic Council Awd 1986, 1987, 1989, 1990; Outstanding Mass Media Teacher Awd 1987-91; Naval Achievement Medal 1987, 1997; Keynote Speaker Awd, NAACP Jefferson Co Chapter, Watertown, NY 1989; Comm Serv Awd, Syracuse Univ 1988; consulting editor, "Cobblestone Magazine, History of Radio", 1988; Naval Commendation Medal, 1992, 1993, 1995; US Navy Campus Liaison Officer of the Year, 1992. **MEMBERSHIPS** Historian Chi Pi Chap Omega Psi Phi Frat 1975-95; radio com mem Natl Assn of Educ Broadcasters 1976-80; adv Natl Acad of TV Arts & Scis Syracuse Chpt 1976-80; public affairs officer natl naval Officers Assoc 1983-85; chmn communications comm Amer Heart Assoc New York 1985-87; CEO WJPZ-FM Syracuse NY; US naval liaison officer, Syracuse Univ, 1981-; steward AME Zion Church; public affairs officer, US Navy, Great Lakes Cruise 1985-; mem communications comm, United Way of Onondaga County 1988-; bd mem Hiawatha Council Boy Scout of America, 1992-. **CONTACT ADDRESS** Schl of Publ Comms, Syracuse Univ, Syracuse, NY 13244-0003. **EMAIL** rrwright@mailbox.syr.edu

WRIGHT, STEPHEN CALDWELL
PERSONAL Born 11/11/1946, Sanford, FL, s **DISCIPLINE** ENGLISH **EDUCATION** St Petersburg Jr Coll, AA, 1967; FL Atlantic Univ, BA, 1969; Atlanta Univ, MA, 1972; Indiana Univ of Pennslyvania, PhD, 1983. **CAREER** Seminole County School Bd, teacher, 69-70; Seminole Comm Coll, professor, 72-. **HONORS AND AWARDS** Morgan State Univ, Distinguished Authors Series Awd, 1998; Illinois Poet Laureate, Illinois Salutes Awd, 1992; Gwendolyn Brooks Poetry Prize, 1984; Univ of South FL, First Superior Poet Awd, 1969. **MEMBERSHIPS** Zora Festival of Arts & Humanities, national planning comm, 1989-99; Boys & Girls Club, chair, advisory council, 1993-96; Gwendolyn Brooks Writers Assn of FL, founder & pres, 1987-; Revelry Poetry Journal, editor, 1987-; Florida Div of Cultural Affairs Literary Organizations Panel, panelist, 1996-98. **SELECTED PUBLICATIONS** First Statement, poetry collection, 1983; Poems In Movement, poetry collection, 1984; Making Symphony: New & Selected Poems, 1987; "Pearl," New Visions: Fiction by Florida Writers, 1989; Inheritance, poetry collection, 1992; Editor "On Gwendolyn Brooks: Reliant Contemplation," 1995. **CONTACT ADDRESS** Prof, English Dept, Seminole Comm Col, 100 Weldon Blvd, Sanford, FL 32773.

WRIGHT, TERRENCE C.
DISCIPLINE PHENOMENOLOGY AND CONTEMPORARY PHILOSOPHIES OF LITERATURE AND AESTHETICS **EDUCATION** St Vincent Col, BA; Villanova Univ, MA; Bryn Mawr Col, PhD. **CAREER** Fac, Mt Saint Mary's Col, 89-. **RESEARCH** Theories of interpretation in art and literature and the nature of poetic expression. **SELECTED PUBLICATIONS** Publ on, relationship between poetry and philos. **CONTACT ADDRESS** Dept of Philosophy, Mount Saint Mary's Col and Sem, 16300 Old Emmitsburg Rd, Emmitsburg, MD 21727-7799. **EMAIL** wright@msmary.edu

WRIGHT, THOMAS L.
PERSONAL Born 12/19/1925, Hattiesburg, MS **DISCIPLINE** MEDIEVAL LITERATURE **EDUCATION** Tulane Univ, BA, 49, MA, 51, PhD, 60. **CAREER** Asst prof English, Auburn Univ, 60-61; assoc prof, Tex Christian Univ, 62-64; assoc prof, 64-75, Prof English, Auburn Univ, 64-. **MEMBERSHIPS** Mediaeval Acad Am; MLA; Int Arthurian Soc. **RESEARCH** Arthurian romance; Chaucer. **SELECTED PUBLICATIONS** Auth, The Life of Chaucer,Geoffrey--A Critical Biography, So Hum Rev, Vol 0028, 94; Chaucer,Geoffrey, So Hum Rev, Vol 0028, 94. **CONTACT ADDRESS** Dept of English, Auburn Univ, Auburn, AL 36830.

WROBEL, ARTHUR
PERSONAL Born 07/14/1940, Jamaica, NY, 1 child **DISCIPLINE** AMERICAN AND ENGLISH LITERATURE **EDUCATION** Queens Col, NYork, AB, 62; Univ NC, MA, 64, PhD(English), 68. **CAREER** Grad asst freshman compos, Univ NC, 64-68; asst prof, 68-75, Assoc Prof Am Lit, Univ KY, 75-, Ed, Anq. **MEMBERSHIPS** Am Lit Group; MLA; Popular Cult Asn. **RESEARCH** Nineteenth century American poetry and fiction. **SELECTED PUBLICATIONS** Auth, The Great Gatsby and Modern Times, Anq-Quart Jour of Short Articles Notes and Rev(s), Vol 0008, 95. **CONTACT ADDRESS** Dept of English, Univ of Kentucky, 500 S Limestone St, Lexington, KY 40506-0003. **EMAIL** wrobel@pop.uky.edu

WULFF, DONALD H.
PERSONAL Born 08/05/1944, Billings, MT, d, 2 children **DISCIPLINE** SPEECH COMMUNICATION **EDUCATION** Univ Mont, MA, 75; Univ Wash, PhD, 85. **CAREER** Instruct Develop Specialist, 85-88; asst dir, 99-92, assoc dir, Center for Instruct Develop and Res, Univ Wash Seattle, 92-. **HONORS AND AWARDS** Distinguished tchg Awd, Univ Wash, 84;

Univ Wash Tchg Acad, 98-. **MEMBERSHIPS** Nat Commun Asn; Prof Orgn Develop network; Am Asn for Higher Educ; Am Educ Res Asn. **RESEARCH** Teaching Effectiveness/ Student Learning; The development of graduate teaching assistants as future professors. **SELECTED PUBLICATIONS** Auth, The Case of worrisome workload, Learning from students: Early term student feedback in higher education, 94; coauth, Working Effectively with Graduate Assistants, 96; Professional development for consultants at the University Washington's Center for Instructional Development and Research, Practically speaking: A sourcebook for instructional consultants in higher education, 97; Engaging students in learning in the communication classroom, forthcoming. **CONTACT ADDRESS** Center for Instructional Development and Research, Univ of Washington, Box 351725, Seattle, WA 98195-1725. **EMAIL** wulff@cidr.washington.edu

WUTZ, MICHAEL
PERSONAL m, 2 children **DISCIPLINE** ENGLISH **EDUCATION** Julius-Maximilians Univ Wurzburg, Ger, BA, 83; Univ Mont, MA, 86; Emory Univ, PhD, 91. **CAREER** TA, Univ of Mont, 85-86; TA to vis asst prof, Emory Univ, 87-92; asst to assoc prof, Weber State Univ, 92-. **HONORS AND AWARDS** DAD Fel, 83-84; Fel, Inst of Int Educ, 88-89; Fel, Dartmouth Col, 91; Can Studies Res Grant, 94; Ralph M. Nye Honors Prof, 96; New Prof of the Year Honors, 96; NEH Summer Sem, 97; Phi Kappa Phi. **MEMBERSHIPS** MLA; Soc for Lit and Sci; Rocky Mountain MLA; Deutsche Shakespeare Gesellschaft. **SELECTED PUBLICATIONS** Auth, "Hawthorne's Drowne: Felix Culpa Exculpated", Studies in Am Fiction 18.2 (Fall 90): 99-110; auth, "The Word and the Self in the Ambassadors", Style 25.1 (Spring 91): 89-103; auth, "The Energetics of Tarr: The Vortex-Machine Kreisler", Mod Fiction Studies 38.4 (Winter 92): 845-869; auth, "An Interview with E.L. Doctorow", Weber Studies: An Interdisciplinary Humanities J 11.1 (94): 6-15; auth, "The Thermodynamics of Gender: The Case of D.H. Lawrence", Mosaic: A J for the Interdisciplinary Study of Lit 28.2 (95): 83-108; coauth, "Narrative in the New Media Ecology", Am Studies 41.3 (96): 445-464; ed, Science, Technology & the Arts Special Issue, Weber Studies, Jan 97; coed, Reading Matters: Narrative in the New Media Ecology, Cornell Univ Pr, 97; auth, "Archaic Mechanics, Anarchic Meaning: Malcolm Lowry and the Technology of Narrative", Reading Matters, Cornell Univ Pr, (97): 53-75; auth, "Modern Discontinuities", Summer 98; transl, Gramophone, Film, Typewriter by Friedrich Kittler, Stanford Univ Pr, (Mar 99). **CONTACT ADDRESS** Dept English, Weber State Univ, 3750 Harrison Blvd, Ogden, UT 84408-0001. **EMAIL** mwutz@weber.edu

WYATT, DAVID M.
PERSONAL Born 10/07/1948, Lynwood, CA, m, 1991, 3 children **DISCIPLINE** ENGLISH **EDUCATION** Yale Univ, BA 70; Univ Calif Berkeley, PhD 75. **CAREER** Univ Maryland, prof 89-, assoc prof 87-89; VA Found for Hum and Pub Policy, prog assoc, 82-87; Princeton Univ, vis prof, 84-85; Univ Virginia, asst prof, 75-82. **HONORS AND AWARDS** NEH Summer Stipend, 80; two res fel, Huntington Library; Phi Beta Kappa Book Prize, Univ of Virginia, 87. **RESEARCH** American West; 19th and 20th Century American Literature. **SELECTED PUBLICATIONS** Auth, Prodigal Sons: A Study in Authorship and Authority, Johns Hopkins, 75; auth, The Fall into Eden: Landscape and Imagination in California, Cambridge, 86; auth, Editions: Bret Harte: Sselected Stories and Sketches, Oxford World Classics; auth, New Essays on the Grapes of Wrath, Cambridge, 92; auth, John Steinbeck's East of Eden, Viking, 93; auth, Five Fires: Race and the Making of California, Addison-Wesley, 97; auth, Out of the Sixties: Storytelling and the Vietnam Generation, Cambridge Univ Press, 93. **CONTACT ADDRESS** Dept of English, Univ of Maryland, Col Park, 115 Rothery Rd, Charlottesville, VA 22903. **EMAIL** dw58@umail.umd.edu

WYATT, WILLIAM F.
PERSONAL Born 07/14/1932, Medford, MA, m, 1989, 3 children **DISCIPLINE** CLASSICS **EDUCATION** Bowdoin Col, AB; Harvard Univ, PhD 62. **CAREER** Univ Washington, asst prof, assoc prof, 60-67; Brown Univ, assoc prof, prof, 67 to 98. **RESEARCH** Homer; Linguistics. **SELECTED PUBLICATIONS** Auth, Several books, many articles and reviews. **CONTACT ADDRESS** Dept of Classics, Brown Univ, Providence, RI 02912. **EMAIL** william_wyatt_jr@brown.edu

WYCZYNSKI, PAUL
PERSONAL Born 06/29/1921, Zelgoszcz, Poland **DISCIPLINE** LITERATURE **EDUCATION** Univ Lille, LL, 49, DES, 50; Univ Ottawa, PhD, 57. **CAREER** Dir-fondateur, Centre de recherche en litterature canadienne-francaise, 58-73, prof agrege 60-64, prof titulaire, 64-70, Prof Titulaire De Recherche, Univ Ottawa, 70-. **HONORS AND AWARDS** Prof de l'annee, Univ Ottawa, 68; DLitt(hon), Univ Laurentienne, 78; Killam res fel, 84; Prix Champlain, 86; DLitt(hon), Univ Guelph, 89; Ordre des francophones d'Amerique, 88; DL(hon), Univ Laval, 89; Chevalier de l'ordre des arts et des lettres de France, 90; off, Order Can, 93; DL(hon), Univ Kulv (Poland), 96. **MEMBERSHIPS** Royal Soc Can; Asn de litterature comparee; Soc des ecrivains canadiens-francais; Soc francaise d'histoire d'outremer; Inst polonias des arts et des sciences en Amerique du Nord; Asn Can Profs. **RESEARCH** French Canadian literature; Emile Nelligan; Francois-Xavier Garneau. **SELECTED PUBLICATIONS** Auth, "Albert laberge, La Scouine," Montreal, P. U.M., (86), 301; coauth, Dictionnaire des auteurs de langue francaise en Amerique de Nord, en collaboration avec Reginald hamel et John E. Hare, Nontreal, Fides,26, (89), 1364; auth, Nelligan, 1879-1941, Montreal, Fides, (90), 635; coauth, "Emile Nelligan: Poesies completes 1896-1941," en collaboration avec Rejena Robidoux, Montreal, fides, (91), 646; auth, "Emile Nelligan," Poemes autographes, Motreal, Fides, (91), 176; auth, "Semper Fidelis," Ottawa, Parafii sw. Jacka Odrowaza, (97), 84. **CONTACT ADDRESS** Univ of Ottawa, Pavillon Simard, Local 200, C.P. 450, Succ. A, Ottawa, ON, Canada K1N 6N5.

WYKE, CLEMENT HORATIO
PERSONAL Born 12/22/1934, Port-of-Spain, Trinidad, m, 1964, 2 children **DISCIPLINE** ENGLISH **EDUCATION** Univ Man, BA Hons, 63, MA & cert educ, 65; Univ Toronto, PhD(English), 70. **CAREER** Lectr English, Med Hat Col, Univ Calgary, 65-67; teaching asst, Univ Toronto, 68-70; sr instr lang & commun, Cambrian Col, 70-71; asst prof English 71-76, Assoc Prof English, Univ Winnipeg, 77-, Teaching fel, Govt Ont, Univ Toronto, 68-69 & 69-70. **MEMBERSHIPS** Asn Can Teachers English; Can Asn Commonwealth Lit & Lang Studies. **RESEARCH** Seventeenth century literature; Donne, Bunyan and Milton. **SELECTED PUBLICATIONS** Auth, Voice and Identity in Selvon,Sam Late Short-Fiction, Ariel-Rev Intl Eng Lit, Vol 0027, 96. **CONTACT ADDRESS** Univ of Winnipeg, 515 Portage Ave, Winnipeg, MB, Canada R3B 2E9. **EMAIL** clement.wyke@uwinnipeg.ca

WYKES, DAVID
PERSONAL Born 01/14/1941, England, m, 1963, 1 child **DISCIPLINE** ENGLISH LITERATURE **EDUCATION** Univ VA, PhD, 72. **CAREER** Prof, Dartmouth Col. **HONORS AND AWARDS** Phi Beta Kappa. **RESEARCH** Brit lit. **SELECTED PUBLICATIONS** Auth, Evelyn Waugh: Literary Life, Macmillan, UK, 99. **CONTACT ADDRESS** Dept English, Dartmouth Col, 3529 N Main St, #207, Hanover, NH 03755. **EMAIL** david.wykes@dartmouth.edu

WYLDER, DELBERT E.
PERSONAL Born 10/05/1923, Jerseyville, IL, m, 1965, 2 children **DISCIPLINE** ENGLISH **EDUCATION** Univ Iowa, BA, 48, MFA, 50, PhD(English), 68. **CAREER** Asst prof English, Bemidji State Col, 68-69; prof lit, Southwest Minn State Univ, 69-77; Prof English & Chmn Dept, Murray State Univ, 77-. **MEMBERSHIPS** MLA; AAUP; Western Lit Asn (pres, 67); Am Studies Asn; Asn Dept English. **RESEARCH** Ernest Hemingway; Western American literature; modern American literature. **SELECTED PUBLICATIONS CONTACT ADDRESS** Dept of English, Murray State Univ, Murray, KY 42071.

WYLIE, HAL
PERSONAL Born 09/16/1935, New York, NY, m, 1971, 5 children **DISCIPLINE** FRENCH AND AFRICAN LITERATURE **EDUCATION** Univ Ariz, BA, 57; Stanford Univ, MA, 61, PhD(French & humanities), 65. **CAREER** Asst ed, Agr Experiment Station, Univ Ariz, 57-59; Asst Prof French, Univ Tex, Austin, 64-; Assoc Prof, French, Univ Texas, 80-. **MEMBERSHIPS** African Lit Asn; Am Asn Teachers Fr. **RESEARCH** Caribbean and African literature. **SELECTED PUBLICATIONS** Auth, World Literature Today; auth, The Gar, Literary Review, 71-80; auth, Contemporary African Literature, Three Continents Press, 83; auth, African Literature 1988: New Masks, Three Continents, 91; auth, Cosmopolitan Conde, or Unscrambling the Worlds, World Lit Today, Vol 0067, 93; auth, Multicultralism and Hybridit in African Literature, Africa World Press, 00. **CONTACT ADDRESS** Dept of French, Univ of Texas, Austin, Austin, TX 78712. **EMAIL** hwylie@mail.utexas.edu

WYMAN, LINDA LEE
PERSONAL Born 04/01/1937, Rockford, IL **DISCIPLINE** ENGLISH LITERATURE **EDUCATION** Southern Methodist Univ, AB, 58; Univ MoColumbia, MA, 60; George Peabody Col, PhD(English), 71. **CAREER** Instr English, Western Ky Univ, 60-65; assoc prof, Motlow State Community Col, 71-74; assoc prof, 75-80, prof English, Lincoln Univ, 80-. **HONORS AND AWARDS** CASE Missouri Prof of the Year, 90; Governor's Awd for Excellence in Teaching, 96; Dean's Awd for Excellence in Teaching, 97. **MEMBERSHIPS** MLA; NCTE; Missouri Assoc of Teachers of English MATE; T S Eliot Soc. **RESEARCH** T S Eliot's plays; modern poetry; the teaching of English. **SELECTED PUBLICATIONS** Auth, Concerning the relevance of Falconers (poem), 3/71, Anthologizing (poem), 5/73 & How plot and sub-plot unite in Marlowe's Faustus, 11/74, CEA Critic; CEA Forum; Murder in the Cathedral: The plot of diction, Mod Drama, 6/76; Poetry for those who need it and can't read it, Notes on Teaching English, 5/78; Common Liberation: The idea of salvation in T S Eliot's plays, Christianity & Lit, Summer 80; On Teaching Murder in the Cathedral, in Approaches to Teaching Eliot's Poetry and Plays, ed J Brooker, MLA, 88; Language as Plot in The Family Reunion, in The Placing of T S Eliot, ed, J Brooker, UMissouri P, 91. **CONTACT ADDRESS** Dept of English, Lincoln Univ, Missouri, 820 Chestnut St, Jefferson City, MO 65101-3500. **EMAIL** wymanl@lincolnu.edu

WYNN, DIANNA
PERSONAL Born 11/16/1963, Phoenix, AZ, m, 1989 **DISCIPLINE** SPEECH COMMUNICATION **EDUCATION** Cerritos Col, AA, 83; Calif State Univ at Fullerton, BA, 85; Univ N Tex, MS, 88. **CAREER** Assoc prof, Prince George's Community Col, 89-97; instr, Midland Col, 97-. **HONORS AND AWARDS** Outstanding Teacher of the Year, Prince George Community Col, 96. **MEMBERSHIPS** Nat Commun Asn, Southern Speech Commun Asn, Eastern Commun Asn, Tex Speech Commun Asn. **RESEARCH** Argumentation, small group communication, legal communication, public speaking, interpersonal communication. **SELECTED PUBLICATIONS** Auth, "Dacum: A National Database Justifying the Study of Speech Communication," J of the Asn of Commun Admin (95); auth, The Future of Communication Education in the Community, J of the Asn of Commun Admin, forthcoming; auth, Working in Groups: Communication Principles and Strategies 2nd edition, Houghton-Mifflin, forthcoming; auth, The Fundamentals of communication: Challenges, Chokes, and Consequences, Houghton-Mifflin, forthcoming. **CONTACT ADDRESS** Dept Lang and Fine Arts, Midland Col, 3600 N Garfield St, Midland, TX 79705-6329.

WYSS, HILARY W.
PERSONAL Born 02/04/1965, New York, NY, m **DISCIPLINE** AMERICAN LITERATURE, AMERICAN STUDIES **EDUCATION** Hamil Col, BA, 86; Univ NCar, MA, 91; PhD, 98. **CAREER** Asst prof, Aub Col, 98-. **HONORS AND AWARDS** Phi Beta Kappa; Teach Fel, Princeton; Sr Teach Fel, UNC; Diss Res Fel, UNC; Ruth, Lincoln Ekstrom Fel; Holman Diss Awd; Fac Ment Gnt; Comp Res Gnt. **MEMBERSHIPS** MLA; SEA; ASA. **RESEARCH** Colonial Native American writing. **SELECTED PUBLICATIONS** Rev of, "The Indian Captivity Narrative 1550-1900, by Kathryn Zabelle Derounian-Stodola and James Levernier, Ear Am Lit 29 (94); auth, " 'Things That Do Accompany Salvation': Colonialism, Conversion, and Cultural Exchange," in Experience Mayhew's Indian Converts, Ear Am Lit (98); auth, "William Apess, Mary Jemison, and Narratives of Racial Identity," Am Ind Quart 23 (99); auth, Writing Indians: Literacy, Christianity, and Narrative Community in Early America, Univ Mass Press, forthcoming. **CONTACT ADDRESS** Dept English, Auburn Univ, 9030 Haley Center, Montgomery, AL 36849-2900. **EMAIL** wysshil@mail.auburn.edu

Y

YAHNKE, ROBERT EUGENE
PERSONAL Born 09/11/1947, Green Bay, WI, m, 1975 **DISCIPLINE** FILM STUDY, VIDEO PRODUCTION, AND THE ARTS **EDUCATION** Univ Wis-Madison, BA, 69, MA, 71, PhD, 75. **CAREER** Asst prof, 76-82, Assoc prof, 82-90; prof film, hum & arts, Gen Col, Univ MN, 90. **MEMBERSHIPS** MN Gerontological Soc; Nat Assoc of Developmental Educ; Am Educ Res Assoc. **RESEARCH** Tchg film and the arts to developmental students **SELECTED PUBLICATIONS** Ed, A Time of Humanities: An Oral History Recollections of David H Stevens as Director of the Division of the Humanities, Rockefeller Foundation, 1930-1950, Wis Acad Sci, Arts & Lett, 76; The Great Circle of Life: A Resource Guide to Films and Videos on Aging, Wilkins & Wilkins, 88; co-auth (with Richard M Eastman), co-auth (with Richard M Eastman), Aging in Literature, ALA, 90; Literature and Gerontology: A Research Guide, Greenwood, 95. **CONTACT ADDRESS** Univ of Minnesota, Twin Cities, 25/ Appleby Hall, 128 Pleasa, Minneapolis, MN 55455-0434. **EMAIL** yahnk001@umn.edu

YALKUT, CAROLYN
DISCIPLINE ENGLISH **EDUCATION** Columbia Univ, AB, 74; Johns Hopkins Univ, MA, 75; Univ Denver, PhD, 84. **CAREER** Asst prof, Le Moyne Col, 84-87; asst prof, SUNY Albany 87-96; Dir of Jour, SUNY, 87-99; Dir of English Honors, SUNY, 99-. **HONORS AND AWARDS** First Prize, Acad of Am Poets, 82; Residency, Ucross Found Artists Colony, 83; Machlachlan Prize for Poetry, 87; Fel, Va Ctr for the Creative Arts, 86; United Univ Prof New Fac Develop Awd, 87; Univ at Albany Awd, 88-89, 92; Nuala McGann Drescher Awd, 93-94. **MEMBERSHIPS** MLA; Poets and Writers; Dramatists Guild. **SELECTED PUBLICATIONS** Auth, "The Solace of Summer is the Solstice", Poet and Critic, (Sept 83): 4; auth, "A Friend of the Family Tells the Story to a Neighbor", Washington Jewish Week, (Dec 83): 26; auth, "The Literature Listener", "The Literature of Baseball", Webster Rev, (Spring 85): 77-79; auth, "Dolcezza", West Hills Rev, (Summer 87): 22-24; auth, "Yoking Erogenous Ideas by Violence Together", Northeast J, (88): 24; auth, "Everywoman's Journalist: Gloria Steinem Writes About Changing America", Writers, (Fall 88): 3; auth, "Big Boy", New Works Theatre Group, Saragota Springs, NY, (Nov 90); auth, "H.L. Mencken" and "Norman Mailer", St James Guide to Biography, St James Pr, (Chicago), 91; auth, "Etymology", Confrontation, (95): 334-35; auth, Egocentric

and Invisible: Innovation and Tradition in American Journalism, Univ of Miss Pr, (forthcoming). **CONTACT ADDRESS** Dept English, SUNY Albany, 1400 Washington Ave, Albany, NY 12222-0100. **EMAIL** jrnalism@csc.albany.edu

YAMAMOTO, TRAISE
PERSONAL Born 08/06/1961, San Jose, CA, 2 children **DISCIPLINE** ASIAN AMERICAN LITERATURE AND CULTURE **EDUCATION** San Jose State Univ, BA; Univ Wash, MFA, MA, PhD. **CAREER** Prof, Univ Calif, Riverside, 94-. **HONORS AND AWARDS** Exec bd, Assn Asian Amer Stud; assoc dir, Ctr Asian Pacific Am. **RESEARCH** Poetry, race and gender theory, autobiography studies, and British and American Modernism. **SELECTED PUBLICATIONS** Auth, Between the Lines; "Different Silences: The Poetics and Politics of Location," The Intimate Critique, Duke Univ Press, 93; auth, Masking Selves, Making Subjects: Japanese American Women, Identity, and the Body, Univ of CA Press, 99. **CONTACT ADDRESS** Dept of Eng, Univ of California, Riverside, Riverside, CA 92521-0323. **EMAIL** traise.yamamoto@ucr.edu

YANCY, KATHLEEN BLAKE
PERSONAL Born 07/05/1950, San Mateo, CA, m, 1973, 2 children **DISCIPLINE** ENGLISH: RHETORIC AND WRITING **EDUCATION** VA Tech, BA, 72, MA, 77, Purdue Univ, PhD, 83. **CAREER** Tchr in MD; TA, 77-83; Dir, Off Writing Rev, Purdue Univ, 87-90; Assoc Prof & Dir, Writing Project, Dept of English, UNC, Charlotte, 90-99; Roy Pearce Prof of Professional Communication, Clemson Univ, 99-. **MEMBERSHIPS** NCTE, CCCC, WPA. **RESEARCH** Writing assessor; electronic writing (theory and practice). **SELECTED PUBLICATIONS** Ed, Portfolios in the Writing Classroom: An Introduction, NCTE, 92; Still Hopeful After All These Years: Teachers as Agents of Change, Lang Arts J of MI, 93; Ed, Voices on Voice: Perspectives, Definitions, Inquiry, NCTE, 94; Contrib, New directions in Portfolio Assessment: Reflective Practice, CriticalTheory, and Large-scale Scoring, Make Haste Slowly: Portfolios and New Teaching assistants, Heinemann, 94; Contr, When Writing Teachers Teach Literature, Portfolios, Literature, and Learning: Story as a Way of Constructing the World, Heinemann, 95; Contr, Portfolios in the Writing Classroom: Policy and Practice, Promise and Peril, Dialogue, Interplay, and Discovery, Erlbaum Assoc, 96; Reflecting on Reflection: Notes on Developing a Reflective Frame of Mind, Iowa Eng Bul, 96; Ed, Situating Portfolios: Four Perspectives, Utah St Univ Press, 97; Ed, Assessing Writing across the Curriculum: Diverse Methods and Practices, Ablex, 97; Auth, Reflection in the writing Classroom, Utah St Univ Press, 98; Contr, The Theory and Practice of Grading Writing, Construction, Deconstruction, and (Over) Determination: A Foucaultian Analysis of Grades, SUNY Press, 98; Ed. "Self Assessner and Development in Writing," Hampton Press, 00. **CONTACT ADDRESS** Dept of English, Clemson Univ, Clemson, SC 29434. **EMAIL** kbyancey@clemson.edu

YANCY, PRESTON MARTIN
PERSONAL Born 10/18/1938, Sylvester, GA, m **DISCIPLINE** COMMUNICATIONS **EDUCATION** Morehouse Coll, BA 1959; Univ of Richmond, MH 1968; Syracuse Univ, MSS 1974, PhD 1979. **CAREER** USAF, civilian supply clerk 1959-61; US Dept of Defense, civilian supply clerk 1961-69; VA Union Univ, professor 1969-, vice pres for academic affairs, 94-97; Richmond Free Press, columnist 1992-94, 97-. **HONORS AND AWARDS** Emory O Jackson Best Column Awds 1975-78, 1980; Doctoral Grants Ford Found 1973-75; Doctoral Grants United Negro Coll Fund 1978-79; Post Doctoral Grants United Negro Coll Fund 1981-84. **MEMBERSHIPS** Columnist, Richmond Afro-Amer Newspaper 1967-71, 1974-82; Assoc for the Study of Afro Amer Life and History; member, Langston Hughes Society 1981-91; treasurer, Urban League of Greater Richmond, 1996-. **SELECTED PUBLICATIONS** Auth, The Afro-Amer Short Story Greenwood Press 1986. **CONTACT ADDRESS** Professor, Communications, Virginia Union Univ, 1500 N Lombardy, Richmond, VA 23220-1711.

YANDELL, CATHY M.
PERSONAL Born 12/27/1949, Anadarko, OK, m, 1974, 2 children **DISCIPLINE** LITERATURE **EDUCATION** Univ of NMex, BA, 71; Univ Calif, Berkeley, MA, 73; PhD, 77. **CAREER** Teaching asst, Univ of Calif Berkeley, 71-75; lectrice, Ecole Nat de Statistique et Admin Econ, 75-76; acting instr, Univ of Calif Berkeley, 76-77; from asst prof to W.I. And Hulda F. Daniell Prof of Lang, Lit and Culture, Carleton Col, 77-. **HONORS AND AWARDS** NEH res grant, 94-95; listed in Who's Who in Am, 95-. **MEMBERSHIPS** MLA, Soc Fransaise desl'Etrdes du Seizieme Siecle, Renaissance Soc of Am, AATF, Women in French, Sixteenth-Century Studies. **RESEARCH** French Sixteenth-Century Poetry, Dialogue, pedagogy and authority, rhetoric, gender. **SELECTED PUBLICATIONS** Auth, "Corps and Corpus: Montaigne's 'Sur des vers de Virgile,'" Montaigne: A Collection of Essays: Language and Meaning, Garland (New York, NY), 95; auth, "Carpe Diem Revisited: Ronsard's Temporal Ploys," The Sixteenth Century J 28: 4 (97): 1281-1298; auth, "Raconter le temps: la reflexivite dans Les Miseres de la femme mariee de Nicole Estienne," Dans les miroirs de l'ecriture: La reflexivite dans les textes des femmes erivains sous l'ancien regime, Univ of Montreal Press (Montreal), 98; "'L'habit ne fait pas la nonne': Controversy and Authority in Anne de Marquests," Mediaevalia 22 (99): 157-180; auth, "Carpe Diem," The Feminist Encyclopedia of French Literature, Greenwood Pub (Westport, CT), 99; coauth, Vagabondages litteraires: initiation a la litterature d'expression francais," McGraw-Hill (New York, NY), 96; auth, Carpe Corpus: Time and Gender in Early Modern France, Univ of Del Press (Newark, NJ) and Assoc Univ Presses (London, Eng), 00. **CONTACT ADDRESS** Dept Romance Lang, Carleton Col, 1 N College St, Northfield, MN 55057-4001. **EMAIL** cyandell@carleton.edu

YANG, XIAOBIN
PERSONAL Born Shanghai, China **DISCIPLINE** CHINESE LITERATURE **EDUCATION** Yale Univ, PhD, 96. **CAREER** Adj prof, Fairfield Univ, 97-98; Croft Asst Prof, Univ Miss, 98-. **RESEARCH** Chinese Literature and Culture, Poetry, Comparative Literature, Literary Theory. **SELECTED PUBLICATIONS** Auth, Across the Sunlight Zone, Modern Poetry Soc, 94; auth, Negative Aesthetics: Literary Theory and Cultural Criticism of the Frankfurt School, 95 & 99; auth, History and Rhetoric: On Contemporary Chinese Literature, 99. **CONTACT ADDRESS** Dept Modern Lang, Univ of Mississippi, University, MS 38667-9999.

YANNATOS, JAMES
PERSONAL Born 03/13/1929, New York, NY, m, 1959, 2 children **DISCIPLINE** MUSIC **EDUCATION** Yale Univ, BM, 51, MM, 52; Univ of Iowa, PhD, 61. **CAREER** SENIOR LECTR/MUSIC DIR, HARVARD-RADCLIFFE ORCHESTRA, 64-. **HONORS AND AWARDS** Fulbright Grant; Wooley Fel; Ditson Awd; New England Artists Awd; Virgil Thomson Found Grant. **MEMBERSHIPS** BMI. **RESEARCH** Composing. **SELECTED PUBLICATIONS** Performances: Concerto for String Quartet and Orchestra, 96, CD in 99; Variations: Solo Contra Bass, 98; Haiku Cycle (voice & chamber ensemble), 95; Concerto for percussion ensemble (..of Things Past and Present), 96; Bach-anale (suite for 2 pianos), 97; Piano Trio, 95. **CONTACT ADDRESS** Dept of Music, Harvard Univ, 9 Stearns St., Cambridge, MA 02138. **EMAIL** yannatos@fas.harvard.edu

YANNELLA, DONALD
PERSONAL Born 05/12/1934, New York, NY, m, 1959, 5 children **DISCIPLINE** ENGLISH **EDUCATION** Fordham Univ, BS, 56; MA, 63; PhD, 71. **CAREER** Adj asst prof, Westchester Community Col, 64; prof, Rowan Univ, 64-81; 83-91; prof, Univ of Southern Miss, 81-83; prof, Barat Col, 91-. **HONORS AND AWARDS** NEH Fel, 78-79; Merit Awd, Glassboro State Col, 79-80, 85-86. **MEMBERSHIPS** AAUP; MLA; Melville Soc; Nat Project Center for Film and the Humanities. **RESEARCH** American literature. **SELECTED PUBLICATIONS** Coauth, American Prose to 1820, Gale, (Detroit), 79; coauth, "The Endless, Winding Way in Melville: New Charts by Kring and Carey", Melville Soc, 81; auth, Ralph Waldo Emerson, Twayne-Simon & Schuster, 82; auth, "Herman Melville: Damned in Paradise: A Companion Guide, Film Co, (Washington, DC), 85; coauth, The Perfect Prodigy: Melville on the Birth of Malcolm, NY Public Libr, 86; coed, The Piazza Tales and Other Prose Pieces, 1839-1860, The Writings of Herman Melville 9, Northwestern Univ Pr, 87; coauth, Herman Melville's Malcolm Letter: Man's Final Lore, Fordham Univ Pr, (NY), 92; auth, "Evert Augustus Duyckinck", "Fred Gray", "Cornelius Mathews", Walt Whitman Encyclopedia, eds James LeMaistre and Doanld Kummins, Garland (NY), 98; auth, New Essays on Billy Budd, Cambridge Univ Pr, (forthcoming). **CONTACT ADDRESS** Dept English, Barat Col, 700 E Westleigh Rd, Lake Forest, IL 60045-3263.

YARDLEY, J. C.
DISCIPLINE CLASSICS **EDUCATION** St Andrews, MA, 66, PhD, 76; Oxford, BA, 70. **CAREER** Asst, Assoc to Prof, 69-88, Univ of Calgary; Prof, Chr, 88-, Univ of Ottawa. **HONORS AND AWARDS** Pres, Class Assoc of Can, 94-96. **MEMBERSHIPS** CAC; Amer Philos Assoc. **RESEARCH** Roman Poetry; The Alexander Hist; Justin. **SELECTED PUBLICATIONS** Auth, Quintus Curtis Rufus, Penguin Classics, 84; Justin, Scholars Press, 94; Justin 11-12, Oxford Univ Press, 97. **CONTACT ADDRESS** Dept Classic Studies, Univ of Ottawa, Ottawa, ON, Canada K1N 6N5. **EMAIL** JCYard@AIX1.UOTTAWA.ca

YARUSS, J. SCOTT
PERSONAL Born 12/01/1967, Downey, CA, m, 1989, 2 children **DISCIPLINE** SPEECH-LANGUAGE PATHOLOGY **EDUCATION** Syracuse Univ, MS, 91, PhD, 94. **CAREER** Co-dir, Stuttering Center Western Pa; asst prof, Northwestern Univ, 94-98; asst prof, Univ Pittsburgh, PA, 98-. **HONORS AND AWARDS** Carol Prutting Editor's Awd, Amer Speech Lang Hearing Assn. **MEMBERSHIPS** Amer Speech Lang Hearing Assn, International Fluency Asn. **RESEARCH** Stuttering; fluency disorders; child phenology. **CONTACT ADDRESS** 4033 Forbes Tower, Pittsburgh, PA 15260. **EMAIL** jsyaruss@csd.upmc.edu

YEAGER, ROBERT FREDERICK
PERSONAL Born 03/07/1948, San Jose, CA **DISCIPLINE** MEDIEVAL ENGLISH LITERATURE **EDUCATION** Stanford Univ, BA, 70; Oxford Univ, MA, 72; Yale Univ, MPhil & PhD(English lit), 76. **CAREER** Instr, Yale Univ, 74-76 & Wesleyan Univ, 75-76; Asst Prof English, Warren Wilson Col, 76-, Am Coun Learned Soc fel, 82-83; Mellon fac fel, Harvard Univ, 82-83; fel, Inst Advan Studies, Univ Edinburgh, 83. **MEMBERSHIPS** MLA; SAtlantic Mod Lang Asn; Mediaeval Acad Am; New Chaucer Soc; John Gower Soc. **RESEARCH** Old English language and literature; Middle English literature; John Gower's poetry. **SELECTED PUBLICATIONS** Auth, The Origins of Beowulf and the Pre-Viking Kingdom of East-Anglia, Medium Aevum, Vol 0064, 95; Studies in Troilus--Chaucer Text, Meter and Diction, Medium Aevum, Vol 0065, 96. **CONTACT ADDRESS** Dept of English, Warren Wilson Col, Swannanoa, NC 28778.

YEARSLEY, DAVID
DISCIPLINE MUSIC **EDUCATION** Harvard Univ, AB, 87; Stanford Univ, MA, 90, PhD, 94. **CAREER** Asst prof **HONORS AND AWARDS** First prize, Bruges Int Organ Competition, 94; top prize, Schnitger Int Organ Competition, 91. **MEMBERSHIPS** Amer Musicol Soc. **RESEARCH** J. S. Bach; 17th- and early 18th-century aesthetics and criticism; keyboard music before 1750; the occult in 18th-century music. **SELECTED PUBLICATIONS** Auth, JS Bach, Cambridge Guide to the Organ. **CONTACT ADDRESS** Dept of Music, Cornell Univ, 104 Lincoln Hall, Ithaca, NY 14853. **EMAIL** dgy2@cornell.edu

YEAZELL, RUTH BERNARD
PERSONAL Born 04/04/1947, New York, NY, d **DISCIPLINE** ENGLISH **EDUCATION** Swarthmore Col, BA, 67; Yale Univ, MPhil, 70, PhD, 71. **CAREER** Asst prof, 71-75, Boston Univ; asst prof, 75-77, assoc prof, 77-80, prof, 80-91, UCLA; prof, 91-, Chace Family prof, 95-, Yale Univ; dir, 96- Lewis Walpole Lib; chair, Yale Univ, 00. **HONORS AND AWARDS** Phi Beta Kappa, 67; Woodrow Wilson Fel, 67-68; Guggenheim Fel, 79-80; NEH Senior Fel, 88-89; Presidents Research Rel, Univ of Cali, 88-89; Harvey L Eby Awd for the Art of Teaching, UCLA, 90; Fel, Whitney Humanities Center, Yale Univ, 92-95. **MEMBERSHIPS** ASELS, MLA. **RESEARCH** British & Amer novel; hist of gender & sexuality; lit & visual arts. **SELECTED PUBLICATIONS** Auth, Language and Knowledge in the Late Novels of Henry James, Univ of Chicago Press, 76, Paper, 80; auth, The Death and Letters of Alice James, Univ of California Press, 81, Paper, 83, Rpt, Exact Change Press, 97; auth, Fictions of Modesty: Women and Courtship in the English Novel, Univ Of Chicago Press, 91; auth, Harems of the Mind: Passages of Western Art and Literature, Yale Univ Press, 00; ed, Sex, Politics, and Science in the Nineteenth-Century Novel: Selected Papers from the English Institute, 1983-1984, Johns Hopkins Univ Press, 86; Paper, 90; ed, Henry James: A Collection of Critical Essays, Prentice-Hall, 94; American Literary History; Columbia Literary History of the United States; Critical Inquiry; Criticism. **CONTACT ADDRESS** Dept of English, Yale Univ, PO Box 208302, New Haven, CT 06520-8302. **EMAIL** ruth.yeazell@yale.edu

YEHUDA, SIMONE N.
PERSONAL Born 12/04/1943, Cambridge, MA, m, 1999, 2 children **DISCIPLINE** COMPARATIVE LITERATURE, CREATIVE WRITING **EDUCATION** Bennington Col, BA, 65; Columbia Univ, MA, 67; Union Inst, PhD, 99. **CAREER** Playwt res, Attic Th, 82-86; dir, Ann Arbor Rep Th, 86-90; prof, Siena Hts Univ, 93-. **HONORS AND AWARDS** Cir Schls, Un Inst, 99; NEH Sem, 97; MCA Creat Ach Awd, 83; Who's Who in US Writ, Eds, Poets. **MEMBERSHIPS** MLA; AAUW; Dram Guild; SWGW; DAPFW; DCW; **RESEARCH** Women's studies; film studies; theater studies; multiculturalism; Judaic studies; playwriting; screenwriting; poetry; memoir; creative non-fiction. **SELECTED PUBLICATIONS** Auth, Lifting Water, Crowfoot Press (79); auth, Thaw, Horizon Press (74). **CONTACT ADDRESS** Dept Humanities, Siena Heights Univ, 1247 East Siena Hts Dr, Adrian, MI 49221-1755. **EMAIL** syehuda@sienahts.edu

YELIN, LOUISE
PERSONAL Born 12/01/1945, NJ, m, 1978, 1 child **DISCIPLINE** ENGLISH, LITERATURE **EDUCATION** Bryn Mawr Col, AB, 67; Columbia Univ, MA, 69; PhD, 77. **CAREER** Asst prof, Hostos Community Col, 77-79; vis prof to asst prof to assoc prof to prof, Purchase Col SUNY, 80-. **HONORS AND AWARDS** SUNY Chancellor's Awd, 97; UUP Fac Development Awd; Greenwood Humanities Development Awd; Pres Awd, 89; Dickens's Soc Prize, 79. **MEMBERSHIPS** MLA; ADE; ACLA. **RESEARCH** 20th-century literature in English; postcolonial literature. **SELECTED PUBLICATIONS** Auth, "Deciphering the Academy Hieroglyph: Marxist Literary Theory and the Practice of Basic Writing," J Basic Writing 5 (78): 13-29; auth, "Strategies for Survival: Florence and Edith in Domby and Son," Victoria Studies 22 (79): 297-320; auth, "Fifty Years of Reading: A Reception Study of The Man Who Loved Children," Contemporary Lit 31 (90): 472-498; auth, "'Buffoon Odyssey?': Christina Stead's For Love Alone and the Writing of Exile," in Postcolonial Conditions: Exiles, Migra-

tions and Nomalisms (Yale Pre Studies, 93): 183-203; auth, "Caryl Phillips," Scrib Brit Auth (99): 379-94; auth, "Christina Stead," Scrib Brit Auth (97): 459-78; auth, From the Margins of Empire: Christine Stead, Doris Lessing, Nadine Gordimer, Cornell up, 98; auth, "Decolonizing the Novel: Nadine Gordimer's A Sport of Nature and British Literary Traditions," in Decolonizing Tradition: New Views of Twentieth Century British Literary Canons, ed. Karen Lawrence (Urbana: Univ Ill Pr, 99): 191-211; auth, "Representing the Nineteen thirties: Capitalism, Phallocracy and the Politics of the Popular Front in the House of All Nations," in The Mastic Phrase: Critical Essays on Stead, ed. M. Harris (Univ Queensland Pr, 00). **CONTACT ADDRESS** Humanities Dept, SUNY, Col at Purchase, 735 Anderson Hill Rd, Purchase, NY 10577. **EMAIL** louise.yelin@purchase.edu

YELLIN, JEAN FAGAN
PERSONAL Born 09/19/1930, Lansing, MI, m, 1948, 3 children **DISCIPLINE** AMERICAN LITERATURE AND STUDIES **EDUCATION** Roosevelt Univ, BA, 51; Univ Ill, Urbana, MA, 63, PhD(English), 69. **CAREER** Asst prof, 68-74, assoc prof, 74-80, Prof to distinguished prof emer, English & Dir, New York City Humanities Prog, Pace Univ, 80-. **HONORS AND AWARDS** Nat Endowment for Humanities younger humanist fel, 74-75; guest lectr, Univ Heidelberg, Sorbonne Nouvelle, Univ East Anglia, Univ Sussex, 75, 76; Nat Humanities Inst, Yale Univ, fel, 76-77; fels, Nat Endowment for Humanities, 78, Smithsonian Inst, Nat Collection of Fine Arts, 78-79 & Am Asn Univ Women, 81-82; proj dir, Nat Endowmnet for Humanities demonstration grant, Pace Univ, 79-81. **MEMBERSHIPS** MLA; Am Studies Asn; Asn Studies Afro-Am Life & Hist; Nat Women's Studies Asn. **RESEARCH** American literature and culture; women's studies; radical literature. **SELECTED PUBLICATIONS** Auth, Jacobs, Harriet Family History, Amer Lit, Vol 0066, 94; Written By Herself--Literary Production by African-American Women, 1746-1892, African Amer Rev, Vol 0030, 96. **CONTACT ADDRESS** 38 Lakeside Dr, New Rochelle, NY 10801.

YENSER, STEPHEN I.
PERSONAL Born 11/03/1941, Wichita, KS, 1 child **DISCIPLINE** ENGLISH **EDUCATION** Wichita State Univ, BA, 63; Univ Wis, MS, 65; PhD, 69. **CAREER** Vis lectr, Univ Baghdad, 65-66; asst prof, UCLA, 69-75; Fulbright prof, Univ de Pau, 70-71; assoc prof, UCLA, 75-81; Fulbright prof, Univ Athens, 75-76; prof, UCLA, 81-. **HONORS AND AWARDS** Pushcart Prize, 00; Dis Alum , Wichita State Univ, 96; Bernard F. Connors Prize for Poetry, 95; Walt Whitman Awd Acad Am Poets, 92; Harvey L. Eby Awd, Art of Teach, 89; Ingram Merrill Awd, Poetry, 81; Discovery/Nation Poetry Awd, 80; UC Regents' Fac Fel, Creat Arts, 74; Vilas Fel, Univ Wis, 63-64, 68-69. **SELECTED PUBLICATIONS** Co-ed, Circle to Circle, Univ Calif Press, 75; auth, The Consuming Myth, Harvard UP, 87; auth, The Fire in All Things, La State UP, 93; auth, Collected Poems of James Merrill, Alfred Knopf, 01; auth, A Boundless Field, Univ Mich Press, 01. **CONTACT ADDRESS** Eng Dept., Univ of California, Los Angeles, Los Angeles, CA 90095-1530. **EMAIL** yenser@humnet.ucla.edu

YERKES, DAVID
DISCIPLINE ANGLO-SAXON LANGUAGE AND LITERATURE **EDUCATION** Yale Univ, 71; Oxford Univ, BA, 73 Dphil, 76. **CAREER** Prof, 77-. **MEMBERSHIPS** Mem, London Medieval Soc; Medieval Acad; Soc Text Scholar. **SELECTED PUBLICATIONS** Auth, An Old English Thesaurus; Syntax and Style in Old English; The Old English Life of Machutus. **CONTACT ADDRESS** Dept of Eng, Columbia Col, New York, 2960 Broadway, New York, NY 10027-6902.

YETMAN, MICHAEL G.
PERSONAL Born 08/16/1939, New York, NY, m, 1963, 3 children **DISCIPLINE** ROMANTIC AND VICTORIAN LITERATURE **EDUCATION** St Peter's Col, NJ, BS, 61; Univ Notre Dame, MA, 62, PhD(English), 67. **CAREER** Instr English, St Mary's Col, Ind, 65-68; asst prof, 68-73, Assoc Prof English, Purdue Univ, West Lafayette, 73-. **MEMBERSHIPS** MLA **RESEARCH** Modern literature. **SELECTED PUBLICATIONS** Auth, In Xanadu, Mass Rev, Vol 0035, 94. **CONTACT ADDRESS** Dept of English, Purdue Univ, West Lafayette, West Lafayette, IN 47907-1968.

YEZZO, DOMINICK
PERSONAL Born 06/21/1947, Manhattan, NY, m, 2 children **DISCIPLINE** ENGLISH **EDUCATION** CUNY, BA, MA, JD. **CAREER** Teacher, Nassau Community Col; attorney at law, Garden City, NY. **HONORS AND AWARDS** Distinguished Service Cross, Air Medal, Army Commendation. **MEMBERSHIPS** Vietnam Veterans of Am; Ital Am Lang Assoc. **SELECTED PUBLICATIONS** Auth, A GI's Vietnam Diary, Franklyn Waub, (NY), 74. **CONTACT ADDRESS** Dept English, Nassau Comm Col, 1 Education Dr, Garden City, NY 11530-6719.

YINGLING, JULIE
PERSONAL Born 02/19/1948, Washington, DC **DISCIPLINE** SPEECH COMMUNICATION **EDUCATION** Univ Denver, PhD, 81. **CAREER** Asst prof, Univ WI, 81-85; assoc prof, Univ Northern CO, 85-88; vis assoc prof, Univ IA, 93-94; prof, Humboldt State Univ, 88-98. **MEMBERSHIPS** Int Network on Personal Relationships; Nat Commun Asn; Western States Commun Asn. **RESEARCH** Commun development in children; relational commun. **SELECTED PUBLICATIONS** Auth, Does That Mean No? Negotiating Protoconversations in Infany-Caregiver Pairs, Res on Lang and Social Interaction, vol 24, 91; Childhood: Talking the Mind Into Existence, in D R Vocate, ed, Intrapersonal Communication: Different Voice, Different Minds, Lawrence Erlbaum Assocs, 94; Constituting Friendship in Talk and Metatalk, J of Social and Personal Relationships, 11 (3), 94; Development as the Context of Student Assessment, in S Morreale & M Brooks, eds, 1994 SCA summer conference: Proceedings and prepared remarks, The Speech Commun Asn, 94; The First Relationship: Infant-Parent Communication, in T J Socha & G H Stamp, eds, Parents, Children and Communication: Frontiers of Theory and Research, Lawrence Erlbaum Assocs, 95; Resource review of Children Communication: The First 5 Years, by B B Haslett & W Samter, and Normal Conversation Aquisition: An Animated Database of Behaviors, Version 1-0 for Macintosh and Windows by K S Retherford, in Communication Education, 98; auth, Vergal responses of children and their supportive providers in a pedatric oncology unit," J of Health Commun, vol 5, (00). **CONTACT ADDRESS** 1850 Lime Ave, McKinleyville, CA 95519. **EMAIL** jmy2@axe.humboldt.edu

YOCOM, MARGARET ROSE
PERSONAL Born 01/23/1948, Pottstown, PA **DISCIPLINE** FOLKLORE, ENGLISH LITERATURE **EDUCATION** Univ Pa, BA, 70; Univ Mass, Amherst, MA, 73; PhD, 80. **CAREER** Asst prof eng & folklore, George Mason Univ, 77-, consult folklife, Festival Am Folklife, Smithsonian Inst, 75-85; consult, Eskimo Heritage Prog of Nome, Alaska, 83-84; consult folklife, Rangeley Lakes Region Logging Mus, 84-. **MEMBERSHIPS** Am Folklore Soc; Oral Hist Asn; Mid Atlantic Folklife Asn (treas, 81-83); Northeast Folklore Asn. **RESEARCH** Family folklore and fieldwork; material culture; folk narrative; women's folklore. **SELECTED PUBLICATIONS** Auth, "Cut my teeth on a spud!, Rodney Richard, Mad Whittler from Rangeley, Maine," Chip Chats, 94; auth, "What is Culture? and Ethics from a Folklorist's Perspective," in Cultural Reporter: Reporter's Handbook (Tom Snyder Prod and Smithsonian Inst, 95); auth, "Marie Campbell," in American Folklore: An Encyclopedia (Garland Publ, 96) and in Notable American Women Folklorists (Am Folklore Soc, 97); auth, "Woodcarving," in American Folklore: An Encyclopedia (Garland Publ, 96); auth, The Yellow Ribboning of the USA: Contested Meanings in the Construction of a Political Symbol, Western Folklore, 96; auth, "Family Folklore," in Folklore: An Encyclopedia of Beliefs, Customs, Tales, Music, and Art (ABC-CLIO, 97); auth, " Women's Folklife," in Encyclopedia of New England Culture, (Yale Univ Press, forthcoming); auth, "If We Don't Joke With Each Other, We Won't Have No Fun, Will We? Storytelling in the Richard Family of Rangeley, Maine," in Traditional Storytelling Today (ABC-CLIO, 99); auth, Exuberance in Control: Dialogic Discourse in the Repertoire of Wood Carver and Storyteller William Richard, Northeast Folklore, 00; coauth, "Just Call Me Sandy, Son:" Poet Jeep Wilcox's Tribute to Sandy Ives, Northeast Folklore, 00. **CONTACT ADDRESS** Dept of Eng, George Mason Univ, Fairfax, 4400 University Dr, MSN 3E4, Fairfax, VA 22030-4444. **EMAIL** myocom@gmu.edu

YODER, DON
PERSONAL Born Mediapolis, IA **DISCIPLINE** ORGANIZATIONAL COMMUNICATION **EDUCATION** Iowa State Univ, BA, 73; Univ Nebr, MA, 75; Ohio State Univ, PhD, 82. **CAREER** Instr, Iowa State Univ; asst, assoc prof, Creighton Univ; assoc prof, chp, Univ Dayton, 89. **RESEARCH** Motivation in communications; conflict management; communnunication education. **SELECTED PUBLICATIONS** Co-author, Creating Competent Communication. **CONTACT ADDRESS** Dept of Commun, Univ of Dayton, 300 Col Park, Dayton, OH 75062. **EMAIL** Yoder@udayton.edu

YOKE, CARL B.
PERSONAL Born 03/23/1937, Clarksburg, WV, m, 1973, 3 children **DISCIPLINE** ENGLISH **EDUCATION** Ohio Wesleyan Univ, 55-56; Kent State Univ, BS, 59, MA, 61; Univ Wisc, 61-62; Case Western Reserve Univ, 62-68. **CAREER** Dir, Euclid Acacdemic Center, 65-66; several mid-mgt postions, Kent State; assoc prof, Kent State Univ, 74-; founder, ed, pub, of J of the Fantastic in the Arts, 86-98; assoc ed, Extrapolation, 79-86. **HONORS AND AWARDS** Academic Scholar, Ohio Wesleyan; assistantship, Kent State; PhD Fel, Univ Wisc; ACPRA Nat Awd; nominated for PushCast Awd; nominated from Peabody Awd; listed in several Who's Who, Dict of Int Biog, Encycl of Sci Fiction, et al; Cleveland Found grant. **MEMBERSHIPS** IAFA, MLA, CCC, NCTE. **RESEARCH** Fantasy and science fiction literature, psychology and fiction. **SELECTED PUBLICATIONS** Auth, A Guide to Rober Zelazny; auth, Death of the Srpent; auth, Zelazny & Norton; auth, Phoenix from the Ashhes; auth, The Future That Wasn't (2000); author of over 100 critical articles, 95 radio shows, newspaper articles, PR material, and numerous reviews. **CONTACT ADDRESS** Dept English, Kent State Univ, Trumbull, 4314 Mahoning Ave NW, Warren, OH 44483-1931.

YORDON, JUDY E.
PERSONAL Born 11/06/1946, Chicago, IL **DISCIPLINE** PERFORMANCE STUDIES **EDUCATION** Northeastern Ill Univ, BA, 68; Northwestern Univ, MA, 70; Southern Ill Univ, PhD, 77. **CAREER** Teacher, Hayt Elem School, 69; instructor, Northeast Mo St Univ, 70-74; grad asst, Southern Ill Univ, 74-76; distinguished prof, Ball State Univ, 77-. **HONORS AND AWARDS** Creative Endeavor Awd, 89; Dean's Teaching Awd, 95; Leslie Irene Coger Performance Awd, 96; Invited to teach in Japan, 96; Distinguished Prof, 97. **MEMBERSHIPS** Nat Commun Asn, Phi Kappa Phi. **RESEARCH** Shakespeare in Performance, Analyzing Literature for Solo Performance, Adapting Non-Dramatic Literature for the Stage. **SELECTED PUBLICATIONS** Auth, Roles in Interpretation, 4th ed, McGraw-Hill, 82; auth, Experimental Theatre: Creating and Staging Tests, Waveland Press. **CONTACT ADDRESS** Dept of Theatre & Dance, Ball State Univ, 2000 West University Ave, Muncie, IN 47306-1022. **EMAIL** judy@ecicnet.org

YORK, LORRAINE
PERSONAL Born London, ON, Canada **DISCIPLINE** ENGLISH **EDUCATION** McMaster Univ, BA, 81, MA, 82, PhD, 85. **CAREER** Asst prof, McGill Univ, 85-88; asst prof, 88-91, Assoc Prof, Mcmaster Univ, 91-. **HONORS AND AWARDS** Tchr Awd Hum, McMaster Students Union. **MEMBERSHIPS** MLA; Asn Can Col Univs Tchrs Eng; Asn Can Stud US. **RESEARCH** Nineteenth- and twentieth-century Canadian Literature; Feminist theory; Alice Munro; Timothy Findley; visual arts; women's collaborative narrative. **SELECTED PUBLICATIONS** Auth, The Other Side of Dailiness: Photography in the Works of Alice Munroe, Timothy Findley, Michael Ondaatji and Margaret Laurence, 88; auth, Front Lines: The Fiction of Timothy Findley, 91; auth, Various Atwoods: Essays on the Later Poems, Short Fiction and Novels, 95. **CONTACT ADDRESS** Dept of English, McMaster Univ, Hamilton, ON, Canada L8S 4L5. **EMAIL** yorkl@mcmaster.ca

YOUM, K. H.
PERSONAL Born 09/06/1952, South Korea, m, 1980, 2 children **DISCIPLINE** JOURNALISM AND LAW **EDUCATION** Southern Ill Univ, PhD, 85; Yale Law Sch, MSL, 98. **CAREER** Prof, Ariz State Univ, 96- . **HONORS AND AWARDS** Most Productive Scholar in J and Mass Commun in U.S. **MEMBERSHIPS** EAJMC; ICA. **RESEARCH** Media law; press freedom; international journalism. **SELECTED PUBLICATIONS** Press Freedom and Judicial Review in South Korea, Stanford J Int Law, 94; Suing U.S. Media in Foreign Countries, Hastings Comm/ENT Law J, 94; Media Countersuits in Libel Law, Hastings Comm/ENT Law J, 95 Press Law in South Korea, 96; Neutral Repartage Doctrine, Commun Law and Policy, 98. **CONTACT ADDRESS** Cronkite School of Journalism and Telecom., Arizona State Univ, Tempe, AZ 85287-1305.

YOUNG, ARLENE
DISCIPLINE ENGLISH LITERATURE **EDUCATION** Univ Manitoba, BA; MA; Cornell Univ, PhD. **CAREER** Asst prof. **RESEARCH** Victorian lit and culture; representations of class and gender; writing by and about women and members of the lower middle class. **SELECTED PUBLICATIONS** Auth, pub(s) on nineteenth century British and American novels; auth, Culture, Class and Gender in the Victorian Novel: Gentlemen, Gents and Working Women. **CONTACT ADDRESS** Dept of English, Univ of Manitoba, Winnipeg, MB, Canada R3T 2N2. **EMAIL** adyoung@cc.umanitoba.ca

YOUNG, ARTHUR P.
PERSONAL Born 06/05/1943, Washington, DC, d, 3 children **DISCIPLINE** ENGLISH LITERATURE **EDUCATION** Miami Univ, PhD, 71. **CAREER** Dept Eng, Clemson Univ **RESEARCH** Professional communication; composition, romantic literature. **SELECTED PUBLICATIONS** Auth, Monograph: Writing Across the Curriculum, Blair Resources for Teaching Writing, Prentice Hall, 94; Writing Across the Curriculum, Skriving ved Universitetet (Writing at the University), Univ Tromso Press, 94; The Wonder of Writing Across the Curriculum, Lang Lrng Across Disciplines, 94; Recalling James Britton, Eng Int, 95; coauth, Portfolios in the Disciplines: Sharing Knowledge in the Contact Zone, New Directions in Portfolio Assessment, Heinemann Boynton/Cook, 94; Resisting Writing/Resisting Writing Teachers, The Subject is Writing, Boynton/Cook Heinemann, 93; ed, Programs and Practices: Writing Across the Secondary Curriculum, Boynton/Cook Heinemann, 94; When Writing Teachers Teach Literature: Bringing Writing to Reading, Boynton,Cook Heinemann, 95; Critical Theory and the Teaching of Literature: Politics, Curriculum, Pedagogy, Nat Coun Tchrs Eng, 96. **CONTACT ADDRESS** Clemson Univ, 616 Strode, Clemson, SC 29634-0523. **EMAIL** apyoung@clemson.edu

YOUNG, C.
PERSONAL Born 07/07/1970, OH, s **DISCIPLINE** INTERPERSONAL COMMUNITY **EDUCATION** Bowling Green State Univ, BA, 92; MA, 95; Univ Birmingham England, M Soc Sci; 96; BGSU, PhD, 00. **CAREER** Graduate Teaching Asst, BGSU, 95; Research Asst, BGSU, 95; Adjunct, Lakeland Community Col, 97-98; Adjunct, John Carrol Univ, 97. **HONORS**

AND AWARDS Doctoral Fellowship-non service, 99-00, Funding for Doctoral Research, 99-00, Nominated for Graduate Student Teaching Asst, 95. **MEMBERSHIPS** National Communication Assoc (NCA), International Communication Assoc (ICA), Central States Communication (CSCA). **RESEARCH** Inter Cultural Communication, Gender/Sexuality, Organizational Communication. **SELECTED PUBLICATIONS** Auth, Queer Theory Meets Rhetorical Criticism, Journal of the Wisconsin Communication Assoc.; auth, The Buddy System, in Teaching ideas for the Basic Course, ed. L. Hugenberg and B. Hugenberg; auth, Cultural Diversity in Organizations, Gonzalez, A. Willis, J. Young, Co., ed. P.Y. Buyers, 96; auth, Organizational Communication: Theory and Behavior, (Boston: Allyn and Bacon), 284-304; auth, Coming Out Stories: Readers Guide to Gay and Lesbian Studies, Fitzroy Dearborn Publishers. **CONTACT ADDRESS** Dept Interpersonal Community, Bowling Green State Univ, 313 West Hall, BGSU, Bowling Green, OH 43403-0001. **EMAIL** cyoung@bgnet.bgsu.edu

YOUNG, CYNTHIA A.
PERSONAL Born 10/16/1969, Cleveland, OH **DISCIPLINE** AFRICANA STUDIES, COMPARATIVE LITERATURE **EDUCATION** Columbia Univ, BA, 91; Yale Univ, PhD, 99. **CAREER** Asst Prof, SUNY Binghamton, 98-. **CONTACT ADDRESS** Dept Comp Lit, SUNY, Binghamton, PO Box 6000, Binghamton, NY 13902-6000. **EMAIL** cyoung@binghamton.edu

YOUNG, DAVID
DISCIPLINE LITERATURE **EDUCATION** Carleton Col, BA, 58; Yale Univ, MA, 59, PhD, 65. **CAREER** Ch, Oberlin's Danenburg Oberlin-in-London Prog; Longman prof, 61. **RESEARCH** Modern poets, creative writing, renaissance drama. **SELECTED PUBLICATIONS** Au, Night Thoughts and Henry Vaughan (poetry); trans, The Book of Fresh Beginnings: Selected Poems of Rainer Maria Rilke; The Action to the Word: Structure and Style in Shakespearean Tragedy (criticism); co-ed, FIELD, Oberlin Col Press; Models of the Universe (an anthology of prose poems). **CONTACT ADDRESS** Dept of Eng, Oberlin Col, Rice 30, Oberlin, OH 44074. **EMAIL** David_Young@qmgate.cc.oberlin.edu

YOUNG, DAVID CHARLES
PERSONAL Born 12/09/1937, Lincoln, NE, m, 1958, 3 children **DISCIPLINE** CLASSICS **EDUCATION** Univ Nebr, BA, 59; Univ Iowa, MA, 60 , PhD(classics), 63. **CAREER** From asst prof to assoc prof, 63-72, chmn dept, 68-72, Prof Classics, Univ Calif, Santa Barbara, 72- **MEMBERSHIPS** Am Philol Asn. **RESEARCH** Greek poetry, especially choral lyric. **SELECTED PUBLICATIONS** Auth, Myths About the Ancient Games, Archaeol, Vol 0049, 96. **CONTACT ADDRESS** Dept of Classics, Univ of California, Santa Barbara, Santa Barbara, CA 93106.

YOUNG, ELIZABETH BELL
PERSONAL Born 07/02/1929, Durham, NC, m **DISCIPLINE** SPEECH **EDUCATION** NC Central U, BA 1948, MA 1950; OH St U, PhD 1959. **CAREER** Catholic Univ of America, D.C., graduate school prof 1966-79; Barber Scotia Coll NC; Talladega Coll AL; VA State Coll; OH State Univ; FL A&M Univ; Fayetteville State Univ NC; Howard Univ Wash DC; Univ of MD, Eastern Shore; Princess Anne, MD; Univ of the DC, Dept Speech Science (communications) & English, univ prof & chmn 1949-84; Natl & Intl Organizations & Universities, Consultant & Lectr, 81-; Congressional Staff Aide, 80, 87-91, Staff aide US House of Reps (Office of Congressman Walter E Fauntroy), 80, 87-91; Lecturer & Consultant US Govt (Office of Ed) 1981-87; Field Reader & Team Reviewer, US St Dept Promotion Panelist 1980-. **HONORS AND AWARDS** Fel Am Speech, Lang, Hearing Asso 1980; Otstndng Alumni Awd OH St Univ 1976; publ Journal Articles in Field of Communications & Made Over 450 Speeches in US; Pioneer in field of speech Pathology & Audiology; 1st African-American to receive PhD in Speech Science; 1st African-American to obtain dual certification in Speech Pathology and Audiology; 1st African-American to obtain PhD from Ohio State Univ in communications and speech science, and started 1st certified speech & learning clinics in historically black colleges and universities. **MEMBERSHIPS** Mem of Bd (Public Mem Asso) 1979-; mem bd of dir Washington Ctr Music Thrpy Clinic; mem adv bd United Negro Clg Fund 1979-82; mem Congressional Adv B D on Educ 1979-82; mem Alpha Kappa Alpha Sor 1946-; bd mem Clinical Cert Am Speech-L & H Assn 1979-83; bd dir Handicapped Intervention Prog for High Risk Infants Wash DC 1978-87. **RESEARCH** Intelligibility and English as a Second Language. **CONTACT ADDRESS** Consultant, 8104 W Beach Dr NW, Washington, DC 20012.

YOUNG, ELIZABETH V.
PERSONAL Born 09/27/1962, Ithaca, NY **DISCIPLINE** ENGLISH **EDUCATION** Cornell Univ, BA, 84; Univ MI, PhD, 89. **CAREER** Assoc prof, CSULB. **HONORS AND AWARDS** Phi Beta Kappa, Cornell, 84. **MEMBERSHIPS** MLA; ASECS; AAUW; NEA. **RESEARCH** Restoration and 18th-century poetry; women writers in England and America. **SELECTED PUBLICATIONS** Auth, Engendering Response: Staging in Introductory Shakespeare Courses, with Mimi Hotchkiss, Proceedings of the CA State Univ Shakespeare Conference, 91; Aphra Behn, Gender, and Pastoral, Studies in English Lit, 33-3, 93; Images of Women in Early Modern England and America, with Patricia Cleary, Am Soc for Eighteenth-Century Studies Teaching Competition: Three Courses, 95; Aphra Behn's Elegies, Genre, 28 1-2, 95; Eve (poem), Phoebe, 7 1-2, 95; Pleasure(poem), Amaranth, 2, 96; Fireflies and Containment(poems), Folio, summer 96; Tabula Rasa and Saguaro-(poems), Frontiers, 17-3, 96; Some Current Publications, Restoration, 96; Aphra Behn and Anne Bradstreet (entries in reference work), Feminist Writers, St James Press, 96; The Farming of a Verse': Storytelling in the Classroom, Reflections, 3 1, 98; Aphra Behn's Horace, Restoration, forthcoming. **CONTACT ADDRESS** Dept of English, California State Univ, Long Beach, Long Beach, CA 90840. **EMAIL** evyoung@csulb.edu

YOUNG, JAMES A.
PERSONAL Born 07/08/1941, Toledo, OH, m, 1988, 2 children **DISCIPLINE** HISTORY, COMMUNICATION **EDUCATION** Ohio Univ, BA, 63; Univ Toledo, MA, 66; Case Western Res, PhD, 71. **CAREER** Instr, Cleveland State Univ, 67-68; asst prof, Edinboro Univ, 69-86; adj fac, Union Lead Acad, 80-95; dir, Penn Soc Serv Union, 86-95; dir Disloc Worler Cen, 95-96; div chmn, Cen Penn Col, 97-. **HONORS AND AWARDS** CWRU Fel, 69; NEH Fel, 80; NDEA Fel, 68; Emeritus, Edinboro Univ. **MEMBERSHIPS** MLA;' AHA; ASA; SIHS; Penn Labor Hist Soc; ITA. **RESEARCH** American labor and social history; history of ideas; European labor and left history; global communications. **SELECTED PUBLICATIONS** Auth, Workin' on the Railroad: Multimedia Interactive Presentation Project, 01; auth, "W.H. Auden and D. H. Lawrence: A Journey in Ideas," in W. H. Auden: A Legacy, ed. David G. Izzo (01); auth of biographies of 'Clarence Darrow,' 'Agnes Smedley,' 'Norman Thomas,' 'George Seldes,' and 'Joseph Freeman,' in Advocates and Activists Who Shaped the 20th Century (01, 02). **CONTACT ADDRESS** 2038 Susquehanna St, Harrisburg, PA 17102-2120. **EMAIL** jimyoung@centralpenn.edu

YOUNG, JANE J.
PERSONAL d, 1 child **DISCIPLINE** ENGLISH, LITERATURE **EDUCATION** City Col, BA, 62; Harvard Univ, MA, 63; NY Univ, PhD, 96. **CAREER** Asst to the Acad Dean, Bor of Manhattan Community Col, 66-68; Chair of the Bor of Manhattan Community Col Curric Committee, -; Inst to Full Prof, Bor of Manhattan Community Col, 68-. **HONORS AND AWARDS** Bard Scholar For the Lit Division, 69; Phi Beta Kappa, 62; Full Fel for PhD, Harvard Univ, 62-; Prizes for Essay, Short Story and Poetry, City Col. **MEMBERSHIPS** Nat Coun of Teachers of English, D.H. Lawrence Soc, Asn of Lit Critics and Scholars. **RESEARCH** Film, Literature. **SELECTED PUBLICATIONS** Auth, D.H. Lawrence Screen: Re-Visioning Prose Style in the Films of "The Rocking Horse Winner," Sons and Lovers and Woman in Love, Peter Lang Publ (NY), 99; auth, Anger, Envy and Sweet Revenge, Redrock Press (NY), forthcoming. **CONTACT ADDRESS** Dept English, Borough of Manhattan Comm Col, CUNY, 199 Chambers St, New York, NY 10007-1044.

YOUNG, KAY
PERSONAL m, 1983, 1 child **DISCIPLINE** ENGLISH LITERATURE **EDUCATION** Harvard Univ, PhD, 92. **CAREER** Asst Prof, Eng, Univ Calif, Santa Barbara. **RESEARCH** Victorian fiction; Hollywood films of the '30s and '40s; Relationship of narrative to architect, philos, music, and dance. **SELECTED PUBLICATIONS** Auth, "Hollywood, 1934: 'Inventing' Romantic Comedy," Look Who's Laughing: Studies in Gender and Comedy, 94; "'Everyday a Little Death': Stephen Sondheim's Unmusicaling of Marriage," Ars Lyrica, 94. **CONTACT ADDRESS** Dept of Eng, Univ of California, Santa Barbara, Santa Barbara, CA 93106-7150. **EMAIL** kayyoung@humanitas.ucsb.edu

YOUNG, MICHAEL
PERSONAL Born 05/21/1957, Pittsburgh, PA, s **DISCIPLINE** ENGLISH LITERATURE **EDUCATION** Duquesne Univ, BA, 80; Kansas State Univ, MA, 83; Univ Cincinnati, PhD, 89. **CAREER** Vis prof, Univ of Nebr Lincoln, 89-92; asst prof, Davis and Elkins Col, 92-95; adj prof, Robert Morris Col, 95-; adj prof, La Roche Col, 96-. **HONORS AND AWARDS** Grad Scholarship, Univ of Cincinnati, 85-89; William C. Boyce Awd, Univ of Cincinnati, 88; Recognition Awd, Univ of Nebr, 91; Grants, Univ of Nebr, 91, 92; Fac Enrichment Grant, Govt of Can, 94. **MEMBERSHIPS** MLA; AWP; RUCTE. **RESEARCH** Writing American Literature, Shakespeare, Canadian Literature, Popular Culture. **SELECTED PUBLICATIONS** Auth, Prairie Wind Sonnet", River of Dreams, 95; auth, "All the Class' a Stage: Connecting Shakespeare With the Students's World Through Performance", Shakespeare and the Classroom, 96; auth, "Editing an Aery Nothing into Local Animation: The HBO Shakespeare Series", Shakespeare and the Classroom 98; auth, "On to All The Western Stars", A Hero Bourne, 99; auth, "Changing the Shape of the Poet's World and Work", Assoc Writing Prog Pedagogy Papers, 99; auth, "Canadian Literature of the Sea", Encycl of Am Lit of the Sea and Great Lakes, Greenwood, (forthcoming); coauth, "Ann Beattie", Reader's Companion to Short Fiction in English, Greenwood (forthcoming); auth, "Teaching Text and Performance Through Soundscripting", Approaches to Teaching Hamlet, MLA, (forthcoming); auth, "Canada: Diaries and Letters to 1900", in Encycl of Life Writing, Fitzroy Dearborn Pub, (forthcoming), auth, "Myths and Titanic: Teaching our Students the World of Classic Myths from the deck of Cameron's ship", Ky English Bull (forthcoming). **CONTACT ADDRESS** Dept Humanities, La Roche Col, 9000 Babcock Blvd, Pittsburgh, PA 15237-5808. **EMAIL** youngm1@laroche.edu

YOUNG, RICHARD E.
PERSONAL Born 07/12/1932, Owosso, MI, m, 1983, 5 children **DISCIPLINE** ENGLISH LITERATURE, RHETORIC **EDUCATION** Univ MI, BA, 54 PhD, 64; Univ CT, MA, 56. **CAREER** From instr to prof Eng, Col Engineering, Univ MI, Ann Arbor, 58-78, chmn dept hum, 71-76; prof eng & rhetoric, chmn dept, Carnegie Mellon Univ, 78, Mem staff, Ctr Res Lang & Lang Behavior, 64-68; consult, NDEA Inst, 65-68; Educ prof Develop Act Inst, 68-70; Nat Endowment for Humanities grant, 71-72; Nat Adv Comt, Formative Evaluation Res Assoc, 77-78; dir fels in residence, Nat Endowment for Humanities, 78; Nat Endowment for the Humanities Summer Sem grants, 77, 79 & 81. **HONORS AND AWARDS** Distinguished Serv Awd, Col Engineering, Univ MI, Ann Arbor, 68; LHD, St Edwards Univ, 80; E D Smith Distinguished Tchg Awd, 93; Thomas S. Becker Ch, Eng, 93; prof Emeritus, 98; lhd, st edward's univ, 80. **MEMBERSHIPS** NCTE; Conf Col Compos & Commun; Speech Commun Asn; Mod Lang Asn; Rhetoric Soc Am. **RESEARCH** Rhetoric; lit; linguistics. **SELECTED PUBLICATIONS** Auth, Toward a modern theory of rhetoric: A tagmemic contribution, Harvard Educ Rev, fall 65; The psychological reality of the paragraph, J Verbal Learning & Verbal Behavior, 69; coauth, Rhetoric: Discovery and Change, Harcourt, 70; contribr, Invention: A Topographical Survey, Teaching Composition, Tex Christian Univ, 76; contribr, Paradigms and problems: Needed research in rhetorical invention, research on composing, NCTE, 78; auth, Arts, crafts, gifts, and knacks: Some disharmonics in the New Rhetoric, Visible Lang, 80. **CONTACT ADDRESS** Dept of Eng, Carnegie Mellon Univ, 5000 Forbes Ave, Pittsburgh, PA 15213-3890.

YOUNG, ROBERT VAUGHAN
PERSONAL Born 06/20/1947, Marianna, FL, m, 1968, 5 children **DISCIPLINE** RENAISSANCE ENGLISH, COMPARATIVE LITERATURE **EDUCATION** Rollins Col, BA, 68; Yale Univ, 71, PhD(English), 72. **CAREER** Asst prof, 72-79; Visiting prof & Acting Chair English, Chistendom Coll, 79-80; Assoc Prof, 80-86 Prof English NC State, 87-; Visiting Prof & Acting Dept Chair, Franciscan Univ of Steubenville, 91-93; Dir Grad Prog, English NC State, 98-. **HONORS AND AWARDS** Southeastern Inst Medieval and Ren Studies Fellow, 79; Fulbright Fellow Belguim. 83; ACLS Fellow 86-87; Fulbright Fellow Belgium, 00. **MEMBERSHIPS** NAS, ALSC, Ren Soc of Am, Shakespeare Assoc of Am, John Donne Society, Fellowship of Am School, Conf on Christianity and Literature. **RESEARCH** Comparative literature of Baroque Age, especially English, Latin and Spanish; neo-Latin rhetorical studies, especially Justus Lipsius; contemporary moral & social issues. **SELECTED PUBLICATIONS** Auth, Richard Crashaw and the Spanish Golden Age, Yale, 82; auth, At War with The Word, ISI, 99; auth, Doctrine and Devotion in 17th -Century Literature, Boydell & Brewer, 00; auth, A Student's Guide to Literature, ISI, 00; ed and transl, Justus Lipsius Principles of Letter-Writing, with M.T. Hester, Southern Ill, 96; ed, John Donne Journal, with M.T. Hester, 82. **CONTACT ADDRESS** Dept of English, No Carolina State Univ, English NC State U Raleigh, 8105, Raleigh, NC 27695-8105. **EMAIL** vyoung@social.chass.ncsu.edu

YOUNGER, KELLY
PERSONAL Born 06/28/1972 **DISCIPLINE** ENGLISH **EDUCATION** Loyola Marymount Univ, BA, 94; Loyola Univ Chicago, MA, 96; Nat Univ Ireland, Univ Col Dublin, PhD, 99. **CAREER** Teaching fel, Loyola Univ Chicago, 95-96; part-time lectr, Loyola Marymount Univ, 97-98; vis asst prof and asst dir of Honors, Loyola Marymount Univ, 98-. **HONORS AND AWARDS** Fr. Alfres Kilp Service Awd, 93; Daniel T. Mitchell Writing Awd, 94; Frank Sullivan Short Story Awd, 94; Presidential Citation of Loyola Marymount Univ, 94; Ratmunde McKay Awd, 94; Jesuit Soc of Chicago, Full Scholar Awd, 94; Rotary Int Ambassadorial Scholar, 96; Highest Honors Placement, Drama Studies Centre, Univ Col Dublin, 99; Text Consult for Prentice-Hall's Drama: Classical to Contemporary (forthcoming), 99; Univ Calif Summer Res Sem, with Judith Butler, 99; Distinguished English Prof of the Year, 2000. **MEMBERSHIPS** Modern Lang Asn, Asn for the Psychoanalysis of Culture and Soc, Alpha Sigma Nu Jesuit Honors Soc, Sigma Tau Delta English Honors Soc. **SELECTED PUBLICATIONS** Auth, The Kiss as Threshold: a comparative view of three medieval texts," The Criterion (94); auth, "Pull for Exit," Attic Salt (94); auth, "My Grandmother's Map," National Poetry Anthology (94); auth, "A Liberal Dose of a Liberal Education," Int Mag of Sigma Chi (spring 96); auth, "Pinter is a Liar and a Cheat: A Review of the Pinter Festival '97," Irish Theatre Forum (autumn 97); auth, "Lady Gregory's Ingredients (excerpt)," Galway Advertiser (July 31, 97); auth, "Lady Gregory's Ingredients," Irish Theatre Forum (spring 98); auth, "Brendan Kennelly's Greek Trilogy-An Interview with the Author," Irish

Theatre Forum (summer 98); auth, "Louis MacNeice's Agamemnon: The Long Goodbye," Pages, vol 5 (98); auth, "Yeats and his Oedipus: 'a naitonless man, aye'," genres (forthcoming); auth, "A Kind of Ireland: Pinter Across the Pond," The Pinter Rev (forthcoming). **CONTACT ADDRESS** Dept English, Loyola Marymount Univ, Los Angeles, CA 90045-8215.

YOWELL, ROBERT L.
PERSONAL Born 07/16/1941, St. Louis, MO, m, 1966, 2 children **DISCIPLINE** SPEECH AND THEATRE **EDUCATION** Southeast Mo State Univ; AB, St Louis Univ, MA, 68; Bowling Green State Univ PhD, 72. **CAREER** Chair, theatre and dance, Univ Ark Little Rock, 73-81; chair, theatre and dance, Univ Birmingham, 81-88; chair, theatre, Calif State Univ, San Bernadino, 88-93; prof, theatre, Northern Ariz Univ, 93-. **HONORS AND AWARDS** ACTF, Kennedy Ctr, nat finalist; Oblesik award, Birmingham, Ala; Teacher of the Year Awd, 99-00; School of performing Arts. **MEMBERSHIPS** Nat Comm Asn; Amer Col Theatre Festival. **RESEARCH** New play development; Drama as a learning medium. **SELECTED PUBLICATIONS** Interview, with playwright Octavio Solis, Eric Montana Love Story, Nancy & Charlie Russell, Pancakes are forbidden, new play develop. **CONTACT ADDRESS** School of Performing Arts, No Arizona Univ, Box 6040, Flagstaff, AZ 86011-6040. **EMAIL** robert.yowell@nau.edu

YUAN, YUAN
PERSONAL Born 03/02/1957, Jinan, China, m, 1983, 2 children **DISCIPLINE** LITERATURE, WRITING **EDUCATION** Shandong Univ, BA, 81; MA, 84; Univ Wis at Milwaukee, PhD, 92. **CAREER** Researcher, Shandong Univ, 85-90; from asst prof to prof, Calif State Univ at San Marcos, 91-; chair, Calif State Univ at San Marcos Literature and Writing Dept, 99-00. **HONORS AND AWARDS** Fulbright Scholar, 85-90; res grants, Calif State Univ, 92-93 & 94-95; multicultural grants, Calif State Univ at San Marcos, 92-93 & 94-95; Fac Development Grant, Calif State Univ at San Marcos, 93-95. **MEMBERSHIPS** MLA, Asn of Interdisciplinary Study of Art, Int Asn of the Fantastic in Art & Lit, Int Asn of Univ Professors. **RESEARCH** Modern and Postmodern Fiction and Culture, Critical Theories, Twentieth-century Comparative Literature, Post-Colonial Discourse, American Literature, Ethnic Studies. **SELECTED PUBLICATIONS** Transl, "The Adventure of Asper March," by Saul Bellow, 92; auth, Discourse of Fantasy: Theoretical and Fictional Perspectives, Hollowbrook Publ, 94; ed, J of the Fantastic in Arts: Special Issue on Dream and Narrative Space, 96. **CONTACT ADDRESS** Dept Arts & Sci, California State Univ, San Marcos, 333 S Twin Oaks Valley, San Marcos, CA 92096-0001. **EMAIL** yuan@csusm.edu

YUDIN, FLORENCE L.
PERSONAL Born 01/26/1937, Brooklyn, NY **DISCIPLINE** SPANISH, LITERATURE **EDUCATION** Brooklyn Col, BA, 58; Univ IL, Urbana, MA, 60, PhD, 64. **CAREER** From instr to asst prof Span, Univ MI, Ann Arbor, 64-69; asst prof, Dartmouth Col, 69-71; assoc prof, 71-74, chmn dept mod lang, 71-76, Prof Span, FL Int Univ, 74-98, Publ subsidy, FL Int Univ Found, 74. **HONORS AND AWARDS** Fla Int Univ Found, Publ Subvention, 74; Excellence in Tchg Awd, FL Int Univ, 87; Acad Affairs Res Competition, Summer A, 90; Latin Am and Caribbean Affairs Center, Res Support, fall 90, spring 91; Excellence in Res Awd, FL Int Univ, 95; Latin Am and Caribbean Center: Publ Subvention, 97. **MEMBERSHIPS** MLA; Midwest Mod Lang Asn. **RESEARCH** Contemp Span poetry; contemp Eng poetry; 17th & 20th century Span lit. **SELECTED PUBLICATIONS** Auth, The novela corta as comedia: Lope's Las Fortunas de Diana, Bull Hisp Studies, 68; Theory and practice of the novela comdiesca, Romanishche Forsch, 69; Earth words, 74 & Whose House of books, 74, Caribbean Rev; The Vibrant Silence in Jorge Guillen's Aire Nuestro, Univ NC, 74; The dark silence in Lorca's poetry, Garcia Lorca Rev, 78; The Yes and the No of Lorca's Ocean, The World of Nature in the Works of Federico Garcia Lorca, 80; Lawrence Durrell's Songs to Syntax, Lang and Style, 83; The Dialectical Failiure in Neruda's Las furias y las penas, Hispania, 3/85; The Poetry of Jorge Guillen, In: Contemporary World Writers, St James Press, 86; The Dark Canticles in Jorge Guillen's Y otros poemas, Hispania, 12/87; From Synthesis to Continuity: Jorge Guillen's Y otros poemas, In: Jorge Guillen Aire nuestro, Anthropos, 10/91; Rozando el paraiso (Poety in Spanish), Thesaurus, Brazil, 95; Nightglow: Borges' Poetics of Blindness, Catedra de Poetica Fray Luis de Leon, Salamanca, Spain, 97. **CONTACT ADDRESS** Dept of Mod Lang, Florida Intl Univ, 1 F I U Univ Park Campus, Miami, FL 33199.

Z

ZACHARIAS, GREG
DISCIPLINE 19TH-CENTURY AMERICAN LITERATURE AND WRITING **EDUCATION** NYork Univ, BA, MA, PhD. **CAREER** Ch & co-dir, MA prog Liberal Stud, 96; dir, Ctr Henry James Stud, Creighton & co-gen ed, Complete Letters of Henry James, 96; taught at, Hofstra Univ, Cooper Union NY City & NY Univ. **SELECTED PUBLICATIONS** Publ on, Milton, Mark Twain, Henry James. **CONTACT ADDRESS** Dept of Eng, Creighton Univ, 2500 CA Plaza, CA 304D, Omaha, NE 68178. **EMAIL** gwzach@creighton.edu

ZACHER, CHRISTIAN KEELER
PERSONAL Born 03/06/1941, St. Louis, MO, m, 1967, 2 children **DISCIPLINE** ENGLISH LITERATURE, MEDIEVAL STUDIES **EDUCATION** Col of the Holy Cross, BA, 63; Univ Calif, Riverside, MA, 65, PhD(English), 69. **CAREER** Teaching asst English, Univ Calif, Riverside, 64-67; asst prof, 68-74, Assoc Prof English, Ohio State Univ, 74-. **MEMBERSHIPS** MLA; Mediaeval Acad Am; Soc Hist Discoveries; AAUP. **RESEARCH** Medieval English and Latin literature; medieval and Renaissance travel literature. **SELECTED PUBLICATIONS** Co-ed, Critical Studies of Sir Gawain and the Green Knight, Univ Notre Dame, 68; auth, Curiosity and Pilgrimage: The Literature of Discovery in Fourteenth-Century England, Johns Hopkins Univ, 76. **CONTACT ADDRESS** Dept of English, Ohio State Univ, Columbus, 164 W 17th Ave, Columbus, OH 43210-1326.

ZACKEL, FRED
PERSONAL Born 07/16/1946, m, 1980, 2 children **DISCIPLINE** ENGLISH **EDUCATION** Bowling Green State Univ, BA, 71; Sonoma State Univ, MA, 91; Bowling Green State Univ, PhD, 95. **CAREER** Adj Instr, Santa Rosa Jr Col, 91-92; Grad Teacher, Bowling Green State Univ, 92-94; Instr, Bowling Green State Univ, 94-96; Adj Instr, Univ Findlay, 96; Adj Instr, Owens Community Col, 97; Asst Prof, Bowling Green State Univ, 96-. **HONORS AND AWARDS** Grad Fel, Bowling Green State Univ, 92-94; ABD Instr Awd, Bowling Green State Univ, 94-95. **RESEARCH** The novel, Twentieth-Century American and British fiction, creative writing, American postmodern fiction, the detective in literature, California culture, movies and myth. **SELECTED PUBLICATIONS** Auth, "Sunday School" A short story, Getting By: Stories of Working Lives, Bottom Dog Pr (96); auth, "Poor Man" A short story, The Heartlands Today: The Urban Midwest Anthology, vol 7, Firelands Writing Ctr Midwest Publ (97); rev, "Elmore Leonard - Out of Sight," Encycl of Popular Fiction, vol 12 (Washington, DC: Beacham Publ, 98); auth, "Your POV or mine," Exquisite Corpse: A J of Letters and Life, Cyber Corpse 2 (99); auth, "The Snake Lies!" Exquisite Corpse: A J of Letters and Life (00); auth, "Ross Macdonald," in The Dict of Lit Biog (Columbia, SC: Bruccoli Clark Layman, 00); auth, "Elmore Leonard," in The Dict of Lit Biog (Columbia, SC: Bruccoli Clark Layman, 00). **CONTACT ADDRESS** Dept English, Bowling Green State Univ, 1001 E Wooster St, Bowling Green, OH 43403-0001. **EMAIL** fzackel@bgnet.bgsu.edu

ZAFERSON, WILLIAM S.
PERSONAL Born 02/10/1925, Greece, m, 1955 **DISCIPLINE** PHILOSOPHY; CLASSICAL LANGUAGES & LITTERATURE **EDUCATION** Univ Athens, BA, 52, PhD, 76; Univ Chicago, MA, 65. **CAREER** Asst prof, philos, Univ Upper Iowa, Fayette, 66-68; prof philos, marymount Col, 68-70; prof philos, St Mary's Univ, 70-72. **HONORS AND AWARDS** Magna Cum Laude, 76; A. Daniel Shorey fel, Univ Chicago. **MEMBERSHIPS** Am Asn Learned Soc; APA; AAUP; NRTA; Univ of Chicago Alumni Asn; National Asn of Scholars Who's Who in Am; Who Who in the World 18th Edition, 01; Goethe-Institut Chicago; The Swedish Cultural Society in Am-Chicago Chapter; Center for Scandinavian Studies. **RESEARCH** Ancient Greek mythology; original Greek texts of Hesiod, Homer, Pindar; the Greek tragedians; Plato; Aristotle; Plotimes; he Bible; Epictetus; Heraclitus. **SELECTED PUBLICATIONS** Auth, The Meaning of Metempsychosis, 65; auth, The Universe, Its Elements and Justice, 74; auth, A Hymn to Health, 75; auth, The Platonic View of Moral Law and the Influence of the Tragedians on Plato's Thoughts, 76; auth, The Songs of the Muses for Gods and Men, 97; Auth, Poem & Music Hephaetus, 99, 00. **CONTACT ADDRESS** PO Box 1551, Chicago, IL 60690.

ZAFREN, HERBERT C.
PERSONAL Born 08/25/1925, Baltimore, MD, m, 1951, 2 children **DISCIPLINE** LIBRARY SCIENCE **EDUCATION** Johns Hopkins Univ, BA, 44; Baltimore Hebrew Col, diploma, 44; Univ Mich, AMLS, 50; **CAREER** Librn, 50-91, dir of libr, 66-94, dir emeritus, 94- , prof Jewish Bibl, 68-95, prof emeritus, 95- , Hebrew Union Col Jewish Inst Relig; exec dir, 56-80, co-dir, 80-96, dir, 96- , Am Jewish Periodical Ctr. **HONORS AND AWARDS** Phi Beta Kappa; Beta Phi Mu. **MEMBERSHIPS** ALA; Asn of Jewish Libr; Coun of Archives and Res Libr in Jewish Stud; Am Hist Asn; World Union of Jewish Stud. **RESEARCH** Library science; history of Hebrew printing. **SELECTED PUBLICATIONS** Auth, Was Gutenberg Jewish? And Other Conundrums: Exploring the Margins of Jewish Bibliography, Council of Archives and Research Libraries in Jewish Studies, 97; coauth, Vilnius Judaica: Still Portrait - Dynamic Reality: Report of the CARLJS Delegation on Its Survey of Judaica in Vilnius, 97; auth, Hebrew Printing by and for Frankfurt Jews -- to 1800, in, Grozinger, ed, Judische Kultur in Frankfurt am Main von den Anfangen bis zur Gegenwart, Harrassowitz, 97. **CONTACT ADDRESS** 3863 Middleton Drive, Cincinnati, OH 45220-1126. **EMAIL** hzafren@huc.edu

ZAGANO, PHYLLIS
PERSONAL Born New York, NY **DISCIPLINE** RELIGION; LITERATURE **EDUCATION** Marymount Col, BA, 69; Boston Univ, MS, 70; C.W. Post Center of Long Island Univ, MA, 72; St. John's Univ, MA, 90; State Univ New York Stony Brook, PhD **CAREER** Boston Univ, 88-99. **MEMBERSHIPS** Am Acad Rel, co-chair, Roman Catholic Studies; Am Cath Philos Assoc; Am Jour Historians Assoc; Col Theol Soc; Soc Study Christian Spirituality; Spiritual Directors Int **SELECTED PUBLICATIONS** Ed, The Nuclear Arms Debate, New York: The Hudson River Press, 83; ed, Religion and Public Policy: A Directory of Organizations and People, The Rockford Institute (Rockford, Illinois), 87; coed, The Social Impact of the Mass Media, Ginn Press (Needham, MA), 91; ed, Woman to Woman: An Anthology of Women's Spiritualities, The Liturgical Press (Collegeville, MN), 93; auth, On Prayer, Paulist Press (Mahwah, NJ), 94; auth, Ita Ford: Missionary Martyr, Paulist Press (Mahwah, NJ), 96; co-ed, The Exercise of the Primacy: Continuing the Dialogue, Crossroad/Herder (New York), 98; co-ed, Things New and Old: Essays on the Theology of Elizabeth A. Johnson, New York: Crossroad/Herder, 98; ed, Twentieth-Century Apostles: Christian Spirituality in Action, The Liturgical Press (Collegiate, MN), 99; auth, Holy Saturday: An Argument for the Restoration of the Female Diaconate in the Catholic Church, Herder & Herder (New York), 00. **CONTACT ADDRESS** 250 E 63rd St, New York, NY 10021. **EMAIL** pzagano@interport.net

ZAGARELL, SANDRA ABELSON
PERSONAL Born 08/12/1943, Washington, DC, d **DISCIPLINE** LITERATURE **EDUCATION** City Col NYork, BA, 65; Columbia Univ, MA, 67; PhD, 76. **CAREER** Instr, Purdue Univ, 69-71; asst wissen, Berlin, 75-79; asst prof to assoc prof to prof, Oberlin Univ, 79-. **HONORS AND AWARDS** Florence Howe Awd, Vis Scholar CLCS, Harvard Univ, 90-91; NEW Res Grant, 88; Vis Scholar Henry A. Murray Ctr, Radcliffe Col, 85-96; Fel Mary I. Bunting Inst, Radcliffe Col, 95-86. **MEMBERSHIPS** MLA; ASA; SSAWW; NAWWSG. **SELECTED PUBLICATIONS** Auth, "Crosscurrents: Registers of Nordicism, Community and Culture in Jewett's Country of the Pointed First," Yale J Crit (97): 355-70; auth, "Troubling Regionalism: Native, Cosmopolitan, Jewett's Deephaven," ALH 10 (98): 639-63; ed, intro, "A New England Nun," by Mary E. Wilkins Freeman, Penguin, 00; ed, The Heath Anthology of American Literature, Houghton Mifflin, 01; auth, "Strenuous Artistry: Elizabeth Stoddard's The Morgesons," in The Cambridge Companion to 19th Century American Women's Writing, eds. Dale Bauer, Phillip Gould (Cambridge Univ Pr, 01) . **CONTACT ADDRESS** English Dept, Oberlin Col, Oberlin, OH 44074-1355. **EMAIL** sandra.zagarell@oberlin.edu

ZAHARNA, RHONDA S.
PERSONAL Born, TX, m, 1956 **DISCIPLINE** COMMUNICATIONS **EDUCATION** Georgetown Univ, BS, 78; Columbia Univ, MEd, 82; EdD, 87. **CAREER** From Asst Prof to Prof, Am Univ, 90-. **HONORS AND AWARDS** Fulbright Sen Scholar; Senate Res Competition Awd, Am Univ; Curric Develop Grant, Am Univ; Top Paper, IICICA. **MEMBERSHIPS** ICA, ECA, IABD, AEJMC. **RESEARCH** International public communication. **SELECTED PUBLICATIONS** Auth, "The Palestinian Leadership and the American Media: Changing Images, Conflicting Results," in The Mid E and the Am Media (Chicago: Greenwood Pr, 95), 37-49; auth, "Media Information or Media Bias?" Palestine Aid Soc (95): 7; auth, "Managing Cross-Cultural Challenges: A Pre-K Lesson for Training in the Gaza Strip," J of Management Develop 15 (96): 80-92; auth, "Final Status: A Communication Perspective," Palestine-Isreal J of Polit, Econ and Cult 3 (97): 123-128; auth, Proposal Writing Handbook, An-Najah Nat Univ, 97; auth, Toolbox of Communication Skills: A Workbook for School Educators, Palestinian Ministry of Educ, 97. **CONTACT ADDRESS** Dept Commun, American Univ, 4400 Mass Ave NW, Washington, DC 20016. **EMAIL** zaharna@american.edu

ZAHAROPOULOS, THIMIOS
PERSONAL Born Amalias, Greece, 2 children **DISCIPLINE** BROADCASTING, MASS MEDIA THEORY **EDUCATION** S Ill Univ-Carbondale, BS, MA, PhD. **CAREER** Assoc prof, 85-86, 88; dept chair, 97. **HONORS AND AWARDS** Fulbright Awd, 94-95 **MEMBERSHIPS** ICA; AESMC; World Communication **RESEARCH** International Communication **SELECTED PUBLICATIONS** Publ, "Mass Media in Greece," articles on intl news flow and intercultural commun. **CONTACT ADDRESS** Mass Media, Washburn Univ of Topeka, Topeka, KS 66621. **EMAIL** thimios@washburn.edu

ZAHORSKI, KENNETH
PERSONAL Born 10/23/1939, Cedarville, IN, m, 1962, 2 children **DISCIPLINE** ENGLISH, SPEECH **EDUCATION** Univ Wis-River Falls, BS, 61; Ariz State Univ, MA, 63; Univ Wis, PhD(English), 67. **CAREER** Asst prof English, Univ Wis-Eau Claire, 67-69; asst prof, 69-71, asoc prof, 71-80, prof English, St Norbert Col, 80-, dir of faculty development, 84-, consultant and sr assoc, CIC, 94-. **HONORS AND AWARDS** Outstanding Teacher of the Year Awd, St Norbert Col, 74; Outstanding Alumnus Awd, Univ Wis-River Falls, 75; Distinguished Scholar Awd, St Norbert Col, 87; Sears Roebuck Found, Teaching Excellence and Campus Leadership Awd, 91. **MEMBERSHIPS** MLA; NCTE; AAUP; Col English Asn. **RESEARCH** Renaissance Drama; modern drama; Fantasy literature; higher education. **SELECTED PUBLICATIONS** Co-ed, Visions of

Wonder: An Anthology of Christian Fantasy, Avon Bks, 81; Fantasists on Fantasy, Avon, 84; Visions and Imaginings, Acad Chicago Pubs, 92; auth, Peter S Beagle, Starmont Press, 88; The Sabbatical Mentor, Anker Pub Co, 94; auth, Reconsidering Faculty Rules and Rewards, CIC Press, 99. **CONTACT ADDRESS** Dept of English, St. Norbert Col, 100 Grant St, De Pere, WI 54115-2099. **EMAIL** zahokj@mail.snc.edu

ZAKAHI, WALTER R.
PERSONAL Born 02/05/1956, Monterrey, Mexico, m, 1983, 2 children **DISCIPLINE** COMMUNICATION **EDUCATION** Bradley Univ, BA, 78; Bowling Green State Univ, MA, 79; PhD, 82. **CAREER** Asst prof, Rutgers Univ, 82-85; asst prof to assoc prof, W Va Univ, 85-91; assoc prof to prof, NMex State Univ, 91-. **HONORS AND AWARDS** Golden Key Honor Soc, 99. **MEMBERSHIPS** Nat Commun Assoc; Western Commun Assoc; Int Network on Personal Relationships. **RESEARCH** Interpersonal communication, sex role stereotyping, presidential debates, loneliness. **SELECTED PUBLICATIONS** Auth, "The effects of loneliness on perceptions of interaction: A cross lag panel study", Commun Res Reports 3, (86): 94-99; auth, "Gender differences and loneliness", Communication, gender, and sex roles in diverse interaction contexts, eds L Stewart and S Ting-Toomey, Albex, (Norwood, 87): 11-17; coauth, "The influence of communication competence upon roommate satisfaction", Western Speech Commun Assoc J 52, (88): 135-146; coauth, "A test of the perceptions of the target's loneliness and gender orientation on self disclosure", Commun Quarterly 36, (88): 109-101; coauth, "Physical attractiveness as a contributing factor to loneliness: An exploratory study", Psychol Reports (88): 747-751; coauth, "a comparison of teacher and student perceptions of immediacy and learning: Monitoring process and product", Commun Educ 39, (90): 353-368; coauth, "Televised presidential debates and candidate images", Candidate Images in presidential election campaigns, Praeger, 95; coauth, "Loneliness and Interpersonal decoding skills", Commun Quarterly 43, (95): 75-85; coauth, "Women who tell and men who ask: Perceptions of men and women departing from gender stereotypes during initial interaction", Sex Roles 34, (96): 767-786; coauth, "Adult attachment and strategic relational communication: Love schemes and affinity seeking", Commun Reports 13, (00): 11-19. **CONTACT ADDRESS** Dept Commun Arts, New Mexico State Univ, PO Box 30001, Las Cruces, NM 88003-8001.

ZALACAIN, DANIEL
PERSONAL Born 12/15/1948, Havana, Cuba, m, 1976, 1 child **DISCIPLINE** LATIN AMERICAN LITERATURE & THEATRE **EDUCATION** Wake Forrest Univ, BA, 71; Univ NC, Chapel Hill, MA, 72, PhD, 76. **CAREER** Asst prof Span lang & lit & bus Span, Northern IL Univ, 77-80; Asst Prof Span Lang & Lit & Bus Span, Seton Hall Univ, 80. **MEMBERSHIPS** Am Asn Tchr(s) Span & Port; MLA. **RESEARCH** Latin Am theatre of the absurd; Span for business careers; Latin Am myths. **SELECTED PUBLICATIONS** Auth, Rene Marques, del absurdo a la realidad, Latin Am Theatre Rev, fall 78; El arte dramatico en Cuculcan, Explicacion textos lit, 78; Calabar: O elogio da traicao, Chasqui: Rev Lit Latinoam, 2/79; Falsa alarma: Vanguardia del absurdo, Romance Notes, 80; El tiempo, tema fundamental en la obra de Rene Marques, Ky Romance Quart, 80; El personae fuera del juego en el teatro de Griselda Gambaro, Rev Estudios Hispanicos, 5/80; Los recursos dramaticos en Soluna, Latin Am Theatre Rev, spring 81; La Antigona de Sanchez: Recreacion puertorriquena del mito, Explicacion Textos Lit, 81. **CONTACT ADDRESS** Dept of Mod Lang, Seton Hall Univ, So Orange, 400 S Orange Ave, South Orange, NJ 07079-2697.

ZANTS, EMILY
PERSONAL Born 08/03/1937, Tulsa, OK **DISCIPLINE** FRENCH LITERATURE; FILM **EDUCATION** Stanford Univ, BA, 58; Columbia Univ, MA, 61, PhD(French), 65; Barch, U of HI, 85. **CAREER** Instr French, Brooklyn Col, 65-67; asst prof, Univ Calif, Davis, 67-72; assoc prof, 72-80, Prof French Lang & Lit, Univ Hawaii, Manoa, 80-96. **HONORS AND AWARDS** Mabelle McLeod Lewis Awd, Stanford Univ, 72. **MEMBERSHIPS** Santa Fe Cir. **RESEARCH** The novel; Flaubert; Proust, film. **SELECTED PUBLICATIONS** Auth, The Aesthetics of the New Novel in France, Univ Colo, 68; Dialogue, Diderot and the new novel in France, 18th Century Studies, winter 68; The relation of Epiphany to description in the modern French novel, Comp Lit Studies, winter 69; Proust and the new novel in France, PMLA, 1/73; auth, Chaos Theory, Complexity, Cinema, and the Evolution of the French Novel, Vthe Edwin Mellen Press (Lewiston), 96; auth, Bertrand Tavernier: Fractured Narrative and Bourgeois Values, Scarecrow Press (Lanham, Md), 99; auth, Creative Encounters with French Film, 2nd edition Edwin Mellen Press (Lewiston), 00. **CONTACT ADDRESS** 7 Camdel Prado, Santa Fe, NM 87501. **EMAIL** emily@ezdigitaldesign.com

ZASLAW, NEAL
PERSONAL Born 06/28/1939, New York, NY, m, 1962, 2 children **DISCIPLINE** MUSIC **EDUCATION** Harvard Col, BA, 61; Juilliard Sch, MS, 63; Columbia Univ, MA, 65, PhD, 70. **CAREER** Herbert Gussman prof of music. **HONORS AND AWARDS** Nat Endowment for the Humanities fel; Amer Coun Learned Societies fel; Martha Baird Rockefeller Fund for Music, fel; Oesterreichische Ehrenkreuz fuer Wissenschaft u Kunst. **MEMBERSHIPS** Amer Musicol Soc; Music Libr Asn; Early Music Am; Royal Musical Asn; Gesellschaft fuer Musikforschung; Soc francaise de musicol; Int Musicol Soc; ed, Der neue Koechel. **RESEARCH** European music of the 17th and 18th centuries; performance practice; French baroque music; Mozart; history of the orchestra. **SELECTED PUBLICATIONS** Auth, Mozart as a Working Stiff, in JM Morris, On Mozart, Cambridge, 94; Mozart's European Orchestras, Musicol Australia, 94; Ornaments for Corelli's Violin Sonatas, Op 5, Early Music, 96; Audiences for Mozart's Symphonies during His Lifetime, Israel Stud in Musicol, 96; Waiting for Figaro, in S. Sadie, Wolfgang Amade Mozart: Essays on His Life and His Music, Oxford, 97; The Breitkopf Firm's Relations with Leopold and Wolfgang Mozart, Bach Perspectives, 96; Contexts for Mozart's Piano Concertos, in N. Zaslaw, Mozart's Piano concertos: Text, Context, Performance, Mich, 96; The Adagio in F major, K Anhang 206a = A65, in S. Brandenburg, Haydn, Mozart and Beethoven, Oxford, 97. **CONTACT ADDRESS** Dept of Music, Cornell Univ, Lincoln Hall, Ithaca, NY 14853. **EMAIL** naz2@cornell.edu

ZATLIN, LINDA GERTNER
PERSONAL Born 11/28/1938, New York, NY, d, 1960, 2 children **DISCIPLINE** VICTORIAN LITERATURE, LITERATURE AND SOCIETY **EDUCATION** Univ Md, BA, 60; Emory Univ, MA, 64, PhD(English), 74. **CAREER** Instr English, Ga Inst Technol, 67; instr, 67-70, asst prof, 74-78, Assoc Prof English, Morehouse Col, 78-, Lectr Human Valuen in Med, 80-, Vis asst prof, Emory Univ, 74; Fulbright fel, 81; United Negro Col Fund-Mellon Found Grant, 82; consult, Atlanta Bur Jewish Educ, 80- & Dept Educ Curric Serv, State Ga, 81-; Inst, Medicine and Literature, Emory Univ School of Medicine, 82-83; Prof, Dept of English, Morehouse Col, 83-; Consultant, Aubrey Beardsley, Princeton Univ, 98; Co-Curator Aubrey Beardsley, 98; Consultant, Oscar Wilde Death Centenary Exhibition, The British Library, 00. **HONORS AND AWARDS** Wallerstein Grant, 00-01; Mott Grant, 99; Sr Advisory Council, Nineteenth-Century Studies Asn, 99; Historians of British Art Best Book Awd for 97; Friends of the Princeton Univ Library Fellowship, 98; Mellon Fellow, Harry Ransom Humanities Research Ctr, 97; National Endowment of the Humanities Summer Stipend, 97; Newberry Library Fellowship, 97; W.A. Clark Memorial Library Short-Term Fellowship, 96; Phi Beta Kappa (honorary), 94; Bibliographical Society of America Fellowship, 94; Beardsley Consultant, Sotheby's, 93; NYU Facutly Scholar in Residence & Davis Fellow, 93, 94; Ota Memorial Museum of Art (Tokyo) Grant for Research on Ukiyo-e, 90-91; Dana Fellow, Emory Univ, 90-91; Faculty Mentor, Dana Foundation Scholars, Program, 89-91; faculty Mentor, Ford Foundation Scholars Program, 86-89; United Negro Col Fund-Mellon Foundation Grants, 82, 84-85, 86. **MEMBERSHIPS** MLA; Southeastern Nineteenth-Century Studies Asn (sec-treas, 80-82, vpres, 82-84); SAtlantic Mod Lang Asn; AAUP; Soc Study Multi Ethnic Lit; Southeastern Nineteenth-Century Studies Asn, 84-88; Southeastern College Art Conference, 86-. **RESEARCH** 1890s, Aubrey Beardsley. **SELECTED PUBLICATIONS** Auth, The Nineteenth-Century Anglo-Jewish Novel, Boston: G.K.Hall, 81; auth, "The Absence of Heroism in the Anglo-Jewish Novel," In Perspectives on Nineteenth-Century Heroism, ed. Sara Putzell and David Leonard, Madrid: Studia Huamnitatis, (82): 146-64; auth, "The Anglo-Jewish Novel," "Grace Aguilar," "Benjamin Farjeion," "Israel Zangwil," In Victorian Britain: An Encyclopedia, ed. Sally Mitchell, (New York: Garland Press), 28 (88): 29-51; auth, "Aubrey Beardsley and Felicien Rops," IN Reconsidering Aubrey beardsley, ed. Robert Langenfeld, UMI Research Press, (89): 167-205; auth, Aubrey Beardsley and Victorian Sexual Politics (Oxford: Clarendon, 90); auth, "Amy Levy," In The 1890s: An Encyclopedia, ed. G.A. Cevasco (NY: Garland Press, 93); auth, "The Story of a Confession Album': The Literary Precursor of Aubrey Beardsley's Fascination with Triangles," In Transforming Genres: New Approaches to British Fiction, 1890-1901, eds. Meri-Jane Rochelson & Nikki Manos, New York: St Martin's Press, (94): 237-60; auth, "Aubrey Beardsley, John Lane, The Yellow Book, and Archival Material," Journal of the 1890s Society (Oxford, England: Privately Printed for the 1890s Society; auth, Aubrey Beardsley: A Centenary Tribute (Obur Biazurten: seikimatsu geijutsu no hana) with Simon Wilson, Tate Gallery), Tokyo: Art Life, 98; auth, "Oscar Wilde, Aubrey Beardsley, and the Making of Salome: Research in the Nex Millenium," forthcoming, The Journal of Victorian Culture, England. **CONTACT ADDRESS** 1735 Peachtree St, NE, Apt 129, Atlanta, GA 30309. **EMAIL** lzatlin@morehouse.edu

ZAVARZADEH, MAS'UD
PERSONAL Born 05/17/1938, Tehran, Iran **DISCIPLINE** LITERARY & CRITICAL THEORY **EDUCATION** Tehran Univ, BA, 63; Univ Nottingham, dipl English studies, 64; Univ Birmingham, MA, 66; Ind Univ, Bloomington, PhD, 73. **CAREER** From asst prof to assoc prof lit theory, Univ Ore, Eugene, 71-77; Prof English, Syracuse Univ, 78-82, Prof 82-; Nat Endowment Humanities res fel, 77-78; Nat Humanities Ctr fel, 81-82. **MEMBERSHIPS** MLA; Semiotic Soc Am; NCTE; Can Semiotic Res Asn. **RESEARCH** Critical theory. **SELECTED PUBLICATIONS** Auth, Mythopeic Reality, auth, Seeing Films Politically; coauth, Theory, Postmodernity, opposition; coauth, Theory as Resistance. **CONTACT ADDRESS** Dept of English, Syracuse Univ, Syracuse, NY 13244.

ZEBOUNI, SELMA
DISCIPLINE 17TH CENTURY LITERATURE **EDUCATION** La State Univ, PhD, 63. **CAREER** Assoc prof, La State Univ. **SELECTED PUBLICATIONS** Auth, Dyrden, A Study in Heroic Characterization, 65; Presentation, representation: Le Classicisme au carrefour, in l'Esprit Createur, 93; Mimesis et sublime: Boileau, Kant, Derrida, in Cahiers du dix-septieme, 94. **CONTACT ADDRESS** Dept of Fr Grad Stud, Louisiana State Univ and A&M Col, Baton Rouge, LA 70803. **EMAIL** szeboun@lsu.edu

ZEGURA, ELIZABETH CHESNEY
PERSONAL Born 09/07/1949, Knoxville, TN, m, 1983, 1 child **DISCIPLINE** RENAISSANCE LITERATURE, FRENCH, ITALIAN **EDUCATION** Bryn Mawr Col, AB, 71; Duke Univ, MA, 74, PhD, 76. **CAREER** Instr, Davidson Col, 75-76; asst prof, DePauw Univ, 81-82; vis asst prof, 78-80, lectr, 85, 87-88, sr lectr, 89-, Univ of Ariz. **HONORS AND AWARDS** AB (magna cum laude), Bryn Mawr, 71; NDEA Fel, Duke Univ. **MEMBERSHIPS** Renaissance Soc of Am. **RESEARCH** Renaissance Literature: Rabelais, Ariosto, Marguerite de Navarre. **SELECTED PUBLICATIONS** Auth, The Countervoyage of Rabelais and Ariosto: A Comparative Reading of Two Renaissance Mock Epics, Duke Univ Press, 82; coauth, Rabelais Revisited, MacMillan/Twayne, 93. **CONTACT ADDRESS** Dept of French and Italian, Univ of Arizona, 556 Modern Lang Bldg, Tucson, AZ 85721. **EMAIL** zegurae@u.arizona.edu

ZEIGER, MELISSA F.
DISCIPLINE ENGLISH LITERATURE **EDUCATION** Cornell Univ, PhD, 86. **CAREER** Assoc prof, Dartmouth Col. **RESEARCH** Am and Brit lit, women's lit. **SELECTED PUBLICATIONS** Auth, Beyond Consolation: Death, Sexuality, and the Changing Shapes of Elegy, Cornell UP, 96; 'A Muse Funereal': The Critique of Elegy in Swinburne's 'Ave atque Vale,' Victorian Poetry, 86. **CONTACT ADDRESS** Dept of English, Dartmouth Col, 6032 Sanborn House, Hanover, NH 03755. **EMAIL** Melissa.F.Zeiger@dartmouth.edu

ZEITLIN, MICHAEL
PERSONAL Born 01/30/1957, Detroit, MI, d, 1 child **DISCIPLINE** ENGLISH **EDUCATION** Univ Toronto, BA, 79; MA, 80; PhD, 88. **CAREER** Asst to assoc prof, Univ of Brit Colum, 90-. **HONORS AND AWARDS** Fel, Res Grant, Soc Sci and Humanities Fel; Izzak Walton Killam Mem Grant. **MEMBERSHIPS** MLA, William Faulkner Soc. **RESEARCH** American Literature, Psychoanalysis. **SELECTED PUBLICATIONS** Auth, "Versions of the Primal Scene: Faulkner and Ulysses," MOSAIC 22, (89): 63-77; auth, "Faulkner's Pylon: The City in the Age of Mechanical Reproduction," Can Rev of Am Studies 22, (91): 229-240; auth, "Father-Murder and Father-Rescue: The Post-Freudian Allegories of Donald Barthelme," Contemp Lit 34 (93): 182-203; auth, "The Passion of Margaret Powers: A Psychoanalytic Reading of Soldiers' Pay," Miss Quart 46, (93): 351-372; auth, "Faulkner and Psychoanalysis: The Elmer Case," Faulkner and Psychology: Faulkner and Yoknapatawpha, 1991, eds Donald Kartiganer and Ann J Abadie, Univ Pr of Miss, (Jackson, 94): 219-241; auth, "Pylon, Joyce, and Faulkner's Imagination," Faulkner and the Artist: Faulkner and Yoknapatawpha, 1993, eds Donald Kartiganer and Ann J Abadie, Univ Pr of Miss, (Jackson, 96): 181-207; auth, "The Ego Psychologists in Lacan's Theory," Am Imago: Studies in Psychoanalysis and Culture 54.2, (97): 209-232; auth, "Returning to Freud and 'The Sound and the Fury,'" Faulkner Jour 13, (98): 55-74; auth, "Psychoanalysis and the Postmodern Subject: The Question of a Metapsychology", Postmodern Times: A Critical Guide to the Contemporary, eds Thomas Carmichael and Alison Lee, N Ill Univ Pr, (00): 15-40; auth, "Meconnaissance and (the Shadowy Indefinite Shape of) Truth in 'If I Forget Thee, Jerusalem,'' Etudes faulkneriennes III: Faulkner, the Major Years, eds Andre Bleikasten, Michael Gresset, Nichole Moulinoux, Francois Pitavy, Presses Univ de Rennes, 01. **CONTACT ADDRESS** Dept English, Univ of British Columbia, 397 - 1873 East Mall, Vancouver, BC, Canada V6T 1Z1. **EMAIL** mzeitlin@interchange.ubc.ca

ZEITZ, EILEEN
PERSONAL Born 05/26/1948, Chicago, IL, m, 2 children **DISCIPLINE** SPANISH AMERICAN LITERATURE **EDUCATION** Univ Ill, Urbana-Champaign, PhD. **CAREER** Instr to prof, Univ Minn, Duluth. **HONORS AND AWARDS** NEA Creative Writing Fel, 80-81; Horace T. Morse, Minn Alumni Assoc Awd (Execellence in Teaching), 97. **MEMBERSHIPS** MLA, MMLA, LASA, Asoc Int de Hsipanistas, ASCD, AATSP. **RESEARCH** Spanish American prose fiction. **SELECTED PUBLICATIONS** Published critical articles on a variety of Spanish American prose fiction writers, and a critical book on the novels of the Uruguayan writer Mario Benedetti; she also has published two books of creative fiction--short stories and poetry--in Spanish. **CONTACT ADDRESS** Univ of Minnesota, Duluth, Duluth, MN 55812-2496. **EMAIL** ezeitz@d.umn.edu

ZENDER, KARL FRANCIS
PERSONAL Born 09/10/1937, Portsmouth, OH, m, 1968, 2 children **DISCIPLINE** ENGLISH **EDUCATION** Case Inst Technol, BS, 59; Western Reserve Univ, MA, 62; Univ Iowa, PhD, 70. **CAREER** Instr English, Univ Iowa, 65-66; from instr to asst prof, Wash Univ, St Louis, 66-73; from Lectr to Assoc Prof, 73-89, prof English, Univ Calif, Davis, 89-; from Actg Chair to Chair, Dept English, 93-98. **MEMBERSHIPS** MLA **RESEARCH** Faulkner and Southern literature; Renaissance drama; 20th century American literature. **SELECTED PUBLICATIONS** Auth, A hand of poker: Game and ritual in Faulkner's Was, Studies Short Fiction, 74; The death of Young Siward: Providential order and tragic loss in Macbeth, Tex Studies Lang & Lit, 75; The function of Propertius in Jonson's Poetaster, Papers Lang & Lit, 75; contribr, William Faulkner, In: American Literary Scholarship, Duke Univ, annual, 74, 75, 80, 81; auth, The unveiling of the Goddess in Cynthia's Revels, J English & Ger Philol, 78; Reading in The Bear, Faulkner Studies, 80; Faulkner at forty: The artist at home, Southern Rev, 81; Faulkner and the Power of Sound, PMLA, 84; The Coming of the Days: William Faulkner, the South, and the Modern World, Rutgers, 89; author of numerous other essays and reviews. **CONTACT ADDRESS** Dept of English, Univ of California, Davis, Davis, CA 95616-5200. **EMAIL** kfzender@ucdavis.edu

ZEUSCHNER, RAYMOND F.
PERSONAL Born 02/23/1945, Chicago, IL, m, 1967, 2 children **DISCIPLINE** SPEECH COMMUNICATION **EDUCATION** Univ Calif Berkeley, AB, 66; San Francisco State Univ, MA, 68; Univ Calif at Los Angeles, PhD, 73. **CAREER** Assoc prof, Calif State Univ Northridge, 74-80; prof, Calif Polytech State Univ, 80-. **HONORS AND AWARDS** Distinguished Services, Phi Ro Pi. **MEMBERSHIPS** NCA, WCSA, CSCA. **RESEARCH** Small group communication, debate, public speaking, communication studies. **SELECTED PUBLICATIONS** Auth, Communication Today, Allyn & Bacon; auth, The Debater's Guide, S Ill Univ Press. **CONTACT ADDRESS** Dept Speech Communication, California Polytech State Univ, San Luis Obispo, 1 Grand Ave, San Luis Obispo, CA 93407-9000. **EMAIL** rzeuschn@calpoly.edu

ZHANG, WEIHAU
PERSONAL Born 07/09/1957, Liaoning, People's Republic of China, m, 1984, 1 child **DISCIPLINE** AFRICAN AMERICAN LITERATURE AND CULTURE, ASIAN AMERICAN LITERATURE AND CULTURE **EDUCATION** Northeast Normal Univ, China, BA, 82; Nankai Univ, China, MA, 84; SUNY, DA, 96. **CAREER** Instr, Nankai Univ, 84-89; instr, Swarthmore Col, 89-90; adj prof, SUNY, 94-96; prof, Savannah Col of Art and Design, 96-. **HONORS AND AWARDS** Grants, SUNY. **MEMBERSHIPS** MLA, Soc for the Study of the Multi-Ethnic Lit of the US, TESOL, African Am Lit and Cult Soc. **RESEARCH** African American literature and culture, Asian American Literature and Culture, Interdisciplinary approaches to multiethnic literature. **SELECTED PUBLICATIONS** Auth, "Ann Petry's 'The Narrows,'" Masterplots II: Am Fiction, Salem Pr, (94); auth, "Nikki Giovanni's 'Gemini: An Extended Autobiographical Statement on My First Twenty-Five Years of Being a Black Poet,'" Masterplots II: Women's Lit, (95); auth, "Alice Walker's 'Her Sweet Jerome'" and "Bienvenida Santos's Immigration Blues," Masterplots II: Short Story, Salem Pr, (96); auth, "Cynthia Kadohata," Writers of Multicultural Fiction for Young Adults, Greenwood, (CT: Westport, 96); auth, Claiming B(l)ack Manhood, Claiming Souls: Male Portraiture in Novels by Alice Walker, Toni Morrison, and Gloria Naylor: A Womanist Reading, Univ Microfilm, (Ann Arbor), 97; auth, "Letter to the Editor: Who Shall Teach African American Literature?" PMLA 114, (99); rev, of "Becoming Madame Mao," by Anchee Min, Campus Chronicle, (01); rev, of "God, Dr. Buzzard, and the Bolito Man: A Saltwater Geechee Talks About Life on Sapelo Island," Campus Chronicle, (01). **CONTACT ADDRESS** Savannah Col of Art and Design, Kiah Hall, PO Box 3146, Savannah, GA 31402-3146. **EMAIL** wzhant@scad.edu

ZHENG, JIANQING
DISCIPLINE CREATIVE WRITING, MODERN LITERATURE **EDUCATION** Huazhong Teachers Univ, BA, 81; Univ Southern Miss, MA, 93, PhD, 96. **CAREER** Asst prof, Univ Wisc, 87-91; asst prof, Miss Valley State Univ, 96-. **MEMBERSHIPS** Acad of Am Poets, Miss Philol Asn. **RESEARCH** Ezra Pound's employment of Chinese images, modern writers with China. **SELECTED PUBLICATIONS** Auth, "Ezra Pound's Adaptation of Chinese Poems," POMPA (99); auth, The Dozen Tongues, Red Moon Press; auth, "Ezra Pound and Chinese Images," J of Univ Wisc (99); auth of poetry in Miss Rev, Antigonish Rev, and others. **CONTACT ADDRESS** Dept English, Mississippi Valley State Univ, 14000 Hwy 82 W, Itta Bena, MS 38941-1400. **EMAIL** jqzheng@hotmail.com

ZHOU, JIAN-ZHONG
PERSONAL Born 03/06/1963, Beijing, China, m, 1992, 3 children **DISCIPLINE** PHYSICS; LIBRARY & INFORMATION SCIENCE **EDUCATION** Beijing Normel Univ, BS, 85; Dominican Univ, MLIS, 90; Univ Del, MBA, 96. **CAREER** Info spec, Chinese Acad Science, 85-88; proj copy cataloger, Am Libr Asn, 88-89; intern librn, Northwestern Univ, 89-90; science librn, Univ Del, 90-. **MEMBERSHIPS** Am Libr Asn; Asn Col Res Libs; Libr & Info Technol Asn; Patent & Trademark Depostitory Libr Asn; Chinese-Am Librn Asn. **RESEARCH** Hi-tech and the libraries; organization and the retrieval of information in the web-based system; cost and the quality of electronic publications; copyright and the fair use of scholarly information; establishing of a good market for the intellectual properties. **SELECTED PUBLICATIONS** Ed and compiler, Research Report of the Institute of Physics, Chinese Academia Sinica, 85-88; auth, art, The Development of Library and Information Technologies in Southeast Asia, 97; auth, art, A New Subclass for Library of Congress Classification, QF: Computer Science, 98; auth, art, The Interlibrary Loan Cost Studies and Copyright Fees, 99; auth, art, The Internet, the World Wide Web, Library Web Browsers and Library Web Servers, 00. **CONTACT ADDRESS** 10 Woodward Dr, Wilmington, DE 19808. **EMAIL** joezhou@udel.edu

ZIAREK, EWA
DISCIPLINE LITERATURE **EDUCATION** SUNY, Buffalo, PhD. **CAREER** Instr, assoc prof, Univ Notre Dame. **RESEARCH** Modernism, comparative fiction, critical theory. **SELECTED PUBLICATIONS** Auth, The Rhetoric of Failure: Deconstruction of Skepticism, Reinvention of Modernism. **CONTACT ADDRESS** Dept of English, Univ of Notre Dame, 356 O'Shaughnessy Hall, Notre Dame, IN 46556. **EMAIL** ewa.ziarek.1@nd.edu

ZIAREK, KRZYSZTOF
DISCIPLINE LITERATURE **EDUCATION** SUNY, Buffalo, PhD. **CAREER** Instr, Univ Notre Dame. **HONORS AND AWARDS** NEH fel; ACLS fel. **RESEARCH** The interrelations between literature and philosophy. **SELECTED PUBLICATIONS** Auth, Inflected Language: Toward a Hermeneutics of Nearness. Heidegger, Levinas, Stevens, Celan. **CONTACT ADDRESS** Univ of Notre Dame, Notre Dame, IN 46556.

ZIEGELMUELLER, GEORGE W.
PERSONAL Born 07/28/1930, Speedway City, IN, w, 1965, 1 child **DISCIPLINE** COMMUNICATION **EDUCATION** DePauw Univ, BA, 53; Southern Ill Univ, MA, 54; Northwestern Univ, PhD, 61. **CAREER** Grad asst, Southern Ill Univ, 52-54; grad asst, Northwestern Univ, 54-57; from instr to distinguished prof, Wayne State Univ, 57-97; fac, Wake Forest Col, 59; fac, Univ Mass, 69 & 80; fac, Univ NC, 73; fac, Univ Vt, 75; fac, Baylor Univ, 78; fac, Gonzaga Univ, 80. **HONORS AND AWARDS** Outstanding Young Teacher of Speech Awd, Central States Speech Asn, 61; Distinguished Fac Advisory Awd, Omicron Delta Kappa, 65; Debate Coach of the Year Awd, Emory Univ Barkely Forum, 68; Distinguished Alumni Awd, Delta Sigma Rho-Tau Kappa Alpha, 74; Distinguished Member Awd, Am Forensic Asn, 81; President's Excellence in Teaching Awd, Wayne State Univ, 83; Alumni Fac Service Awd, Wayne State Univ, 83; Debate Coach of the Year, Wake Forest Univ, 86; Coach of the Year, Univ Ut, 91; Col of FPCA Service Awd, Wayne State Univ, 96; Keele Awd for Outstanding Service, Nat Debate Tournament, 99; Ziegelmueller Outstanding Dir of Debate Awd, Nat Debate Tournament, 99; Donald H. Ecroyd Awd for Outstanding Commun Teacher in Higher Educ, Nat Commun Asn, 99; "One of the Ten Most Influential Persons in Forensics". Goden Anniversary Awd, Am Forensics Asn, 99; Elice Howard Awd for Outstanding Contribution to High Sch Forensics, Mich High Sch Forensic Asn, 00. **MEMBERSHIPS** Mich Asn of Speech Commun, Central States Commun Asn, Nat Commun Asn, Am Forensic Asn, Nat Forensic Asn. **RESEARCH** Argumentation theory and contemporary debate. **SELECTED PUBLICATIONS** Coauth, Advancing in Debate: Skills and Concepts, Clark, 94; coauth, "The Power of the Voice," Detroit Monthly (July, 95); auth, "The National Debate Tournament Through a Half Century of Argument," Argumentation and Advocacy (Winter, 96); coauth, Argumentation: Inquiry & Advocacy, Allyn & Bacon, 97; auth, "The Detroit Experience," Contemporary Argumentation and Debate Vol 19 (98); auth, "The National Debate Tournament: A Test of the AFA's Professionalism," Argumentation and Advocacy (Summer, 00). **CONTACT ADDRESS** Dept Commun, Wayne State Univ, 585 Manoogian Hall, Detroit, MI 48202-3919. **EMAIL** aa4248@wayne.edu

ZIEGLER, DHYANA
PERSONAL Born 05/05/1949, New York, NY, s **DISCIPLINE** ENGLISH **EDUCATION** Baruch Coll CUNY BA Program, BS (Cum Laude) 1981; Southern IL Univ-Carbondale, MA 1983, PhD 1985. **CAREER** Essence Magazine, market researcher 1972-75; Rosenfeld Sirowitz & Lawson, copywriter & radio producer 1974-75; Patten and Guest Productions NY, regional mgr 1976-79; WNEW TV, internship desk asst & production asst; Seton Hall Univ, counselor for high school students 1979-81; Baruch Coll CUNY, English tutor & instructor for writing workshops 1979-81; Westside Newspaper, reporter 1980-; CBS TV Network, production intern 1980-81; Southern IL Univ Dept of Radio & Television, lab instructor 1981-83; Jackson State Univ Dept of Mass Comm, asst prof 1984-85; Univ of TN-Knoxville Dept of Broadcasting, asst prof of broadcasting 1985-90, assoc professor, 90-. **HONORS AND AWARDS** Seek Scholarship Awds for Academic & Service 1979-81 Baruch Coll; Rita Leeds Service Awd 1981 Baruch Coll; Sheldon Memorial Awd Baruch Coll 1981; Scrippt-Howard Awd Baruch Coll 1981; United Press Intl Outstanding Achievement Radio Documentary 1982; Dept of Radio and TV SIUC Outstanding Radio Production Awd 1982-83; Grad Dean's Doctoral Fellowship 1983-84; Paul Robinson's Roby Scholar Awd Black Affairs Council 1984; Certificate of Merit Awd Southern IL Univ Broadcasting Serv 1984; Ebony Bachelorette 1985; Seek Alumni Awd Baruch Coll 1985; numerous publications and other professional works; Outstanding Faculty Member of the Year, Coll of Communications, UTK, 1987-88; Chancellor's Citation for Service, Univ of TN Knoxville, 1988; Faculty Research Awd, 1992; Chancellor Citation for Extraordinary Service, 1992; State of Tennessee Governor's Awd for Outstanding Achievement, 1991; Consortium of Doctors Awd, 1991. **MEMBERSHIPS** Natl Political Congress of Black Women; Delta Sigma Theta Sor Inc; Phi Delta Kappa; grad fellow Post Doctoral Acad of Higher Educ; Speech Comm Assn; pres & founder Blacks in Communications Alliance; Natl Cncl of Negro Women Inc; legislative council Southern IL Univ Alumni Assn; panelist Metro Black Media Coalition Conference 1984, Southern IL Univ/Blacks in Communications Alliance 1985, Natl Black Media Coalition Conf 1985; speaker/consultant US Armed Forces Azores Portugal 1986; chmn/public relations, Kiwanis Club of Knoxville, 1988-; Southern Regional Devel Educ Project Coord, Delta Sigma Theta, 1988-; Women in Communications, Inc, vice pres of develop, pres-elect 1989, pres 1990-91;Society of Professional Journalists, 1988-. **SELECTED PUBLICATIONS** Co-author, Thunder and Silence: The Mass Media in Africa; several book chapters and journal articles, MaxRobinson, Jr, Turbulent Life of a Media phet, Journal of Black Studies, 1989, Challenging Racism in the Classrom: Paving the Road to the Future/Thoughts and Action-The Journal of the Natl Educ Assn, 1989; articles, "Women and Minorities on Network Television News," Journal of Broadcasting, Spring 1990, "Teaching Television News: A Classroom Newsroom Model," Feedback, Spring 1990. **CONTACT ADDRESS** Univ of Tennessee, Knoxville, 295 Communications Bldg, Knoxville, TN 37996.

ZIFF, LARZER
PERSONAL Born 10/02/1927, Holyoke, MA, m, 1952, 4 children **DISCIPLINE** AMERICAN LITERATURE **EDUCATION** Univ Chicago, MA, 50, PhD, 55; Oxford Univ, MA, 72. **CAREER** Test constructor English, Educ Testing Serv, 51-52; lectr humanities, Univ Chicago, 52-53, dir spec prog, 53-56; from asst prof to prof English, Univ Calif, Berkeley, 56-72; lectr Am lit, Oxford Univ, 72-78; prof English, Univ Pa, 78-81; Caroline Donovan Prof English, Johns Hopkins Univ, 81-, Huntington Libr fel, 57; Univ Calif pres fel, 58; Fulbright lectr, Univ Copenhagen, 59-60; Am Coun Learned Soc fel, 63-64; Nat Coun Teachers English distinguished lectr, 66-67; mem comt, Am Studies Int Exchange Persons, 66-; Nat Endowment for Humanities sr fel, 67-68; univ lectr Am lit & fel, Exeter Col, Oxford, 73-78; Guggenheim fel, 77-78. **HONORS AND AWARDS** Christian Gauss Awd, 67; Ford Found lectr, Univs of Poland, 60; Fulbright lectr, Univ Sussex, 64. **MEMBERSHIPS** MLA; Am Studies Asn; Am Antiquarian Society; Soc Am Historians. **RESEARCH** Colonial American culture; modern American literature; 19th century culture. **SELECTED PUBLICATIONS** Auth, The Genteel Tradition and the Sacred Rage--High Culture Versus Democracy in Adams, James, and Santayana, Amer Lit, Vol 0064, 92; Franklin, Benjamin, Edwards, Jonathan, and the Representation of American Culture, Jour Amer Hist, Vol 0081, 94; The Cambridge History of American Literature, Vol 1, 1590-1820, Mod Lang Quart, Vol 0056, 95; Conquest and Recovery in Early Writings from America, Amer Lit, Vol 0068, 96; Memoirs--Editorship of Chicago Review--1940s, Chicago Rev, Vol 0042, 96; Voicing America--Language, Literary Farm, and the Origins of the United-States, William and Mary Quart, Vol 0054, 97. **CONTACT ADDRESS** Dept of English, Johns Hopkins Univ, Baltimore, 3400 N Charles St, Baltimore, MD 21218-2680.

ZIMBARDO, ROSE A.
PERSONAL Born 05/29/1932, m, 1957, 1 child **DISCIPLINE** ENGLISH **EDUCATION** Brooklyn Col, AB, 56; Yale Univ, MA, 57, PhD, 60. **CAREER** From instr to assoc prof English, City Col NY, 60-72, grant, 62; Assoc Prof English, State Univ NY, Stony Brook, 72- **MEMBERSHIPS** English Inst; MLA. **RESEARCH** Restoration literature; Shakespeare; modern drama. **SELECTED PUBLICATIONS** **CONTACT ADDRESS** Dept of English, SUNY, Stony Brook, Stony Brook, NY 11790.

ZIMMERMAN, EVERTETT
DISCIPLINE EIGHTEENTH-CENTURY BRITISH LITERATURE **EDUCATION** Temple Univ, PhD, 66. **CAREER** Prof, Eng, Univ Calif, Santa Barbara. **HONORS AND AWARDS** John Simon Guggenheim Mem Fel , 89; Dir, NEH Summer Sem for Col Teachers, 83. **MEMBERSHIPS** MLA; Am Soc for Eighteenth-Century Studies. **RESEARCH** Satire, nove, historiography. **SELECTED PUBLICATIONS** Auth, Defoe and the Novel, Univ Calif, 75; Swift's Narrative Satires, Cornell, 83; auth, The Boundaries of Fiction, Cornell, 96. **CONTACT ADDRESS** Dept of Eng, Univ of California, Santa Barbara, Santa Barbara, CA 93106-7150. **EMAIL** ezimmer@humanitas.ucsb.edu

ZIMMERMAN, FRANKLIN B.
PERSONAL Born 06/20/1923, Wauneta, KS, m, 1957, 4 children **DISCIPLINE** MUSIC HISTORY & LITERATURE **EDUCATION** Univ Southern Calif, BA, 49, MA, 52, PhD, 58; Oxford Univ, BLitt, 56; Univ Pa, AM, 70. **CAREER** Asst prof music, Crane Dept Music, State Univ NY Teachers Col, Potsdam, 58-60; vis assoc prof, Sch Music, Univ Southern Calif, 60-61, assoc prof, 61-64, chm dept music hist & lit, 60-64; prof music, Dartmouth Col, 64-66; prof music, dir pro musica & div music hist & musicol, Univ Ky, 67-68; Chm Dept Music & Dir Pro Musica, Univ PA, 68-, Conductor & performer, var concerts in US & England, 38-; lectr, var orgn, 58-; Am Coun Learned Soc fel, London, 59-60, grant, Univ Calif, Los Angeles, 63; Dartmouth Col Res & Publ Fund grant, 64; sr res fel, Univ Calif, Los Angeles, 68; dir, Pa Pro Musica, 71- **HONORS AND AWARDS** Gold Medal for Musicol, Arnold Bax Found, 60; Ben Franklin technolol grant for visible music soundscapes, 98; ma, dartmouth col, 66 & univ pa, 71. **MEMBERSHIPS** Am Musicol Soc; Int Musicol Soc; Royal Music Asn; Renaissance Soc Am; Col Music Soc. **RESEARCH** Purcell; Baroque music; Handel. **SELECTED PUBLICATIONS** Auth, A Purcell Iconography, Henricksen, London, 58; Henry Purcell, 1659-1695: An Analytical Catalogue of his Music, 63 & Henry Purcell, 1659-1695: His Life and Times, 67, MacMillan, London; Henry Purcell, 1659-1695: A Thematic Index to His Complete Works, 73 & G F Handel: Thematic and First-Line Indexes to His Complete Works, Vienna House, 73-74; The Anthems of Henry Purcell, Am Choral Found, 73; Louis Grabu's Albion & Albanius, In: The Works of John Dryden, Vol XV, Univ Calif, 75; The William Kennedy Gostling Manuscript: A Primary Source for the Anthems of Henry Purcell, John Blow, Univ Tex, Austin, 77; auth, Invented Visible Music Soundscapes. **CONTACT ADDRESS** 225 South 42nd St, Apt. 1A, Philadelphia, PA 19104. **EMAIL** fzimmer3@maie.sas.upenn.edu

ZIMMERMAN, MICHAEL
PERSONAL Born 07/29/1937, North Adams, MA, m, 4 children **DISCIPLINE** JOYCE, AMERICAN LITERATURE **EDUCATION** Columbia Univ, Ba, 59, MA, 60, PhD(English), 63. **CAREER** Lectr English, Columbia Col, Columbia Univ, 61-62, preceptor, Sch Gen Studies, 62-63; from actg instr to asst prof, Univ Calif, Berkeley, 63-68; from lectr to assoc prof, 68-69, prof English, San Francisco State Univ, 74-, Fulbright lectr, Japan, 67-68; ed, Dialogue: J Psychoanal Perspectives, 78-. **MEMBERSHIPS** Philol Asn Pac Coast. **RESEARCH** Nineteenth and 20th century American literature; James Joyce. **SELECTED PUBLICATIONS** Auth, Literary Revivalism in America, Am Quart, spring 68; Sociological Criticism, of the 1930's, Harper, 73; Stephen's Mothers in Ulysses, Pac Coast Philol, 4/75; James Joyce's Mothers, Dialogue, spring, 78. **CONTACT ADDRESS** Dept of English, San Francisco State Univ, 1600 Holloway Ave, San Francisco, CA 94132-1740. **EMAIL** mzimman@sfsu.edu

ZIOLKOWSKI, ERIC JOZEF
PERSONAL Born 12/28/1958 **DISCIPLINE** RELIGION; LITERATURE **EDUCATION** Dartmouth Col, BA, 80; Univ Chicago, MA, 81; Univ Chicago, PhD, 87 **CAREER** Asst prof Comparative Literature, Univ Wisconsin Madison, 87-88; asst prof Religion, Lafayette Col, 88-94; assoc prof Religion, Lafayette Col, 94-. **HONORS AND AWARDS** Fel, Soc Arts Relig Cult, 97-; Thomas Roy and Lura Forrest Jones Awd for Superior Teaching, 98 **MEMBERSHIPS** Amer Acad Relig; Amer Assoc Univ Prof; Amnesty Int **RESEARCH** Religion and Literature, History of Religion, Philosophy of Religion **SELECTED PUBLICATIONS** Ed, A Museum of Faiths: Histories and Legacies of the 1893 World's Parliament of Religions, Scholars Press, 93; auth, The Sanctification of Don Quixote: From Hidalgo to Priest, Penn St Univ, 91; "Religion and Literature and the History of Religions: Grounds for Alliance." Jour Lit Theol, 98; "Sancho Panza and Nemi's Priest: Reflections on Myth and Literature." Myth and Method, 96; auth, Evil Children in Religion, Literature, and Art: The Bad Boys of Bethel, Macmillan Press, 00. **CONTACT ADDRESS** Dept Relig, Lafayette Col, Easton, PA 18042. **EMAIL** ziolkowe@lafayette.edu

ZIOLKOWSKI, JAN M.
PERSONAL Born 11/17/1956, New Haven, CT, m, 1978, 3 children **DISCIPLINE** ENGLISH **EDUCATION** Princeton Univ, AB, 78; Cambridge Univ, PhD, 82. **CAREER** Asst Prof to Prof, Harvard Univ, 81-. **HONORS AND AWARDS** Guggenheim Fel; Fel, Am Coun for Learned Soc; Phi Beta Kappa Teaching Prize; NEH Summer Stipend; Am Acad Fel, Rome; Marshall Scholar. **MEMBERSHIPS** Am Comparative Literature Asn, Am Philol Asn, Asn of Literary Scholars and Critics, Dante Soc of Am, Medieval Acad of Am, Medieval Latin Asn of N Am, Mod Lang Asn. **RESEARCH** Medieval literature; Latin literature; Comparative literature. **SELECTED PUBLICATIONS** Ed, Obscenity: Social Control and Artistic Creation in the European Middle Ages, Leiden, 98; ed, The Cambridge Songs (Carmina cantabrigiensia), New York, 94; ed, Nigel of Canterbury, The Passion of St. Lawrence, Epigrams, and Marginal Poems, Leiden, 94; auth, Talking animals: Medieval Latin Beast Poetry, Philadelphia, 93; ed, On Philology, University park, 90. **CONTACT ADDRESS** Dept English, Harvard Univ, G-04 Boylston Hall, Cambridge, MA 02138.

ZIRIN, RONALD A.
DISCIPLINE CLASSICS **EDUCATION** Princeton Univ, PhD, 67; Univ Buffalo, PhD, 85. **CAREER** Assoc prof emer, Fac, 66; prof, present, SUNY Buffalo. **RESEARCH** Linguistics; mythology; Sanskrit; applications of psychoanalysis to Classical traditions. **SELECTED PUBLICATIONS** Auth, The Phonological Basis of Latin Prosody, Mouton, 70; articles on Greek and Latin linguistics. **CONTACT ADDRESS** Dept Classics, SUNY, Buffalo, 705 Clemens Hall, Buffalo, NY 14260.

ZLOGAR, LAURA
DISCIPLINE ENGLISH LITERATURE **EDUCATION** Marquette Univ, MA, PhD. **CAREER** Prof, Univ of WI. **RESEARCH** 19th century Brit lit; African-Am lit; ethnic Am women writers. **SELECTED PUBLICATIONS** Auth, pubs on Amiri Baraka, Toni Morrison, Amy Tan, Charles Chesnutt, and Paule Marshall. **CONTACT ADDRESS** Eng Dept, Univ of Wisconsin, River Falls, S 3rd St, PO Box 410, River Falls, WI 54022-5001. **EMAIL** lauralee.zlogar@uwrf.edu

ZLOTNICK, JOAN C.
PERSONAL Born 07/14/1942, New York, NY, m, 1963, 2 children **DISCIPLINE** AMERICAN & URBAN LITERATURE **EDUCATION** Brooklyn Col, BA, 63; Hunter Col, MA, 65; New York Univ, PhD, 69. **CAREER** From lectr to asst prof, 64-77, assoc prof English, 77-84, prof English, Brooklyn Col, City Univ New York, 77- **HONORS AND AWARDS** Founders Day Awd, New York Univ, 70. **RESEARCH** Jewish literature; women's literature; New York literature. **SELECTED PUBLICATIONS** Auth, The medium is the message, or is it: A study of Nathanael West's comic strip novel, J Popular Cult, 8/71; Abraham Cahan: A Neglected Realist in Am Jewish Arch, 71; The Damnation of Thereon Ware, with a Backward Glance at Hawthorne, Markham Rev, 71; Day of the locust, a night at the movies?: Nathanael West's Hollywood novel, Film Libr Quart, winter 73; Nathanael West and the pictorial imagination, Western Am Lit, 11/74; Influence or coincidence: A comparative study of The Beast in the Jungle and A Painful Case, Colby Libr Quart, 6/75; Dubliners in Winesburg, Ohio: A note on Joyce's 'The Sisters' and Anderson's 'The Philosopher', Studies in Short Fiction, fall 75; Malamud's The Assistant: Of Frank, Morris, and St Francis, Studies in Am-Jewish Lit, winter, 75; The inflation of the negative: A study of Nathanael West's use (and abuse) of literary sources, Descant, winter 76; Of Dubliners and Ohioans: A Comparative Study of Joyce's Dubliners and Anderson's Winesburg Ohio, Ball State Univ Forum, 76; The Day of the Locust: Comparing John Schlessinger's Film and Nathanial West's Novel, Filmograph, 76; Portrait of an American City: The Novelists' New York, Kennikat Press, 82; Musings from the Brooklyn Bridge: The Brooklyn Bridge as Literary Inspiration, New Brooklyn Quart, 83; The Chosen Borough: Chaim Potok's Brooklyn, Studies in American Jewish Literature, 84; A Woman's Will: Kate Chopin on Selfhood, Wifehood, and Motherhood, Markham Rev, 68. **CONTACT ADDRESS** Dept English, Brooklyn Col, CUNY, 2901 Bedford Ave, Brooklyn, NY 11210-2813.

ZLOTSKY, ANDRES
PERSONAL Born 07/25/1958, Buenos Aires **DISCIPLINE** COMPARATIVE LITERATURE, ENGLISH **EDUCATION** Univ Amsterdam, Propedeutic, 88; Doctorandus, 92; SUNY, MA, 97; PhD, 01. **CAREER** TA to lectr, SUNY, 93-01. **HONORS AND AWARDS** Univ of Amsterdam, 87-92; Excellence in Teaching Awd, 98; SUNY, 93-99; Univ Honors Lectr, 99, 00. **MEMBERSHIPS** MLA. **RESEARCH** UFO Phenomenon, Popular Culture, Media Studies, Psychoanalysis, Semiotics, Science Fiction. **SELECTED PUBLICATIONS** Ed, Psychoanalysis and the Debate on Abortion: Dossier on Contempt, Umbr(a), 95; transl, The Flirtatious Remark, Umbr(a, 96); auth, Antigone and the Real: Two Reflections on the Notion of Coherence, Umbr (a), 96; auth, Supposed Science, Alleged fiction; Patterns of Distortion in the Transmission of Cultural paradigms in the Twenty Century, SUNY, 01. **CONTACT ADDRESS** Dept Comp Lit, SUNY, Buffalo, 638 Clemens Hall, Buffalo, NY 14214-3001. **EMAIL** zlotsky@acsu.buffalo.edu

ZOCH, LYNN M.
PERSONAL Born, NY **DISCIPLINE** COMMUNICATION **EDUCATION** St Lawrence Univ, BA; Syracuse Univ, MS, PhD. **CAREER** Taught at Univ W FL & Syracuse Univ, From Asst to assoc prof, dir, Master's deg progs, Univ SC, 93-; **RESEARCH** Organizational boundary spanning and organizational crisis management. **SELECTED PUBLICATIONS** Publ in Publ Rel Quart, Jour Educ & Small Gp Res; chap in Beyond the Velvet Ghetto. **CONTACT ADDRESS** Col of Journalism & Mass Commun, Univ of So Carolina, Columbia, Carolina Coliseum rm 4010D, Columbia, SC 29208. **EMAIL** lynn.zoch@usc.jour.sc.edu

ZOLBROD, PAUL GEYER
PERSONAL Born 12/10/1932, Pittsburgh, PA, m, 1967, 2 children **DISCIPLINE** LITERARY CRITICISM, LINGUISTICS **EDUCATION** Univ Pittsburgh, BA, 58, MA, 62, PhD(English), 67. **CAREER** Instr English, Univ Pittsburgh, Titusville, 63-64; from instr to assoc prof 64-77, Prof English, Allegheny Col, Meadville, 77-, Fel, Univ NMex, 71-72; consult, Public Broadcasting Northwest Pa, 76-78; Res fel, Nat Endowment Humanities, 78-79. **MEMBERSHIPS** MLA; AAUP; NCTE; Northwest Mod Lang Asn; Soc Am Indian Studies. **RESEARCH** Renaissance literature; ethnopoetics; linguistics. **SELECTED PUBLICATIONS** Auth, The Wind in a Jar, Amer Indian Cult and Res Jour, Vol 0018, 94; Saanii-Dahataal--The Women Are Singing, Amer Indian Cult and Res Jour, Vol 0018, 94. **CONTACT ADDRESS** Dept of English, Allegheny Col, Park Ave, Meadville, PA 16335.

ZOMPETTI, JOSEPH P.
PERSONAL Born 10/27/1970, Indianapolis, IN, s **DISCIPLINE** COMMUNICATION **EDUCATION** Wayne State Univ, PhD, 98. **CAREER** Asst prof, Mercer Univ, 98- . **HONORS AND AWARDS** Fulbright scholar. **MEMBERSHIPS** Nat Commun Asoc; Speech Pedag. **RESEARCH** Labor rhetoric; postcolonialism; speech pedagogy. **SELECTED PUBLICATIONS** Auth, Developing a Critical Speech Pedagogy, Mich Asoc of Speech Commun J, 96; auth, Toward a Gramscian Critical Rhetoric, Western J Commun, 97; auth, Reading Postcolonial Identity: The Rhetoric of Devolution from Sri Lanka's President, Chandrika Kumaratunga, Howard J Commun, 97; co-auth with S.J. Berkowitz and S. Aonuma, Transforming the Quest for Meaning: A Case Study in Public Argument, 1997 Proceedings of the SCA/AFA Conference on Argumentation, 98. **CONTACT ADDRESS** Communications Dept, Mercer Univ, Macon, 1400 Coleman Ave, Macon, GA 31207-0001. **EMAIL** zompetti_jp@mercer.edu

ZUCKER, ALFRED JOHN
PERSONAL Born 09/25/1940, Hartford, CT, m, 1966, 6 children **DISCIPLINE** ENGLISH, HISTORY **EDUCATION** Valley Col Los Angeles, AA, 60; Univ Calif at Los Angeles, AB English, 62; AB Speech, 62; MA Speech, 63; CSULA, MA English, 67, CSULB, MA Hist, 99, Univ Calif at Los Angeles, PhD, 67. **CAREER** Lectr, Los Angeles City Col, 62-68; Lectr, CSULA, 66-68; Prof, Chemn of English Dept, Chemn of the Humanities Div, Acad Senate Pres, Los Angeles Southwest Col, 68-88; Prof, Chemn English Dept, Los Angeles Valley Col, 88-. **HONORS AND AWARDS** Les Savants, Tau Alpha Epsilon, Phi Theta Kappa, Phi Kappa Phi, Phi Delta Kappa, Phi Beta Kappa. **MEMBERSHIPS** Emily Dickinson Soc. **RESEARCH** 19th Century American Literature, 19th Century American History. **CONTACT ADDRESS** English Dept, Los Angeles Valley Col, PO Box 3308, Palos Verdes, CA 90274.

ZUCKER, DAVID HARD
PERSONAL Born 05/27/1938, Cleveland, OH, m, 1997, 2 children **DISCIPLINE** ENGLISH & AMERICAN LITERATURE **EDUCATION** Oberlin Col, BA, 60; Syracuse Univ, MA, 64, PhD(English), 68. **CAREER** Asst ed, Columbia Encycl, 60-62; asst prof English, Washington & Lee Univ, 68-71; from asst prof to assoc prof, 71-78, prof English, Quinnipiac Col, 78-. **HONORS AND AWARDS** NEH Summer Seminars. **MEMBERSHIPS** Asn of Literary Scholars & Critics. **RESEARCH** Elizabethan drama; autobiography; fiction and poetry. **SELECTED PUBLICATIONS** Co-ed, Selected Essays of Delmore Schwartz, Univ Chicago, 70; auth, Stage and Image in the Plays of Christopher Marlowe, Univ Salzburg, 72; An American Elegist: The Poetry of Horace Gregory, 73, Mod Poetry Studies; Self and History in Delmore Schwartz, Iowa Rev, 78. **CONTACT ADDRESS** Dept of English, Quinnipiac Col, 275 Mt Carmel Ave, Hamden, CT 06518-1908. **EMAIL** davidzucker@quinnipac.edu

ZUCKERMAN, MARY ELLEN
PERSONAL Born 01/10/1954, Gainsville, FL, m, 1988, 2 children **DISCIPLINE** MARKETING **EDUCATION** Simmons Col, BA, 76; Columbia Univ Grad School of Business, MBA, 82; Columbia Univ Graduate School of Arts & Sci, PhD, 87. **CAREER** Res Fel, Freedom Forum Media Studies Center, 89-90; vis assoc prof, McGill Univ, 90-91; asst prof, 85-90, Prof and Head, School of Business, SUNY Geneseo, 90-; vis prof, Advertising Ed Found Prog, Time Inc, summer, 96. **HONORS AND AWARDS** Found grant, 87 & 89, mid-career summer fel, Geneseo Found, 94; Spencer Found Grant, 92-94; Who's Who in the East; res fel, Gannett Center for Media Studies, 89-90; Nuala Drescher Leave Awd, 89-90; NEH Travel to Collections Grant, 89; PDQWL Travel Grant Awd, SUNY Union, 89; fac advisor res grant, Am Marketing Asn, 88. **SELECTED PUBLICATIONS** Auth, Encyclopaedia of Women in Journalism, in progress; A History of Mass Circulation Women's Magazines in the U.S., Greenwood Press, 98; From Voting with the Ballot to Voting with the Pocketbook: The Good Citizenship and Pro-Advertising Campaigns in the Woman's Home Companion 1920-1934, Am Periodicals, fall 95; McCall's, Family Circle, Woman's Day, Women's Periodicals in the United States, Greenwood Press, 95; The Career of Mrs. Christine Frederick, presented at the Org of Am Hist, spring 94; rev, Magazines for Millions: Gender and Commerce in the Ladies' Home Journal and The Saturday Evening Post 1880-1910, Business Hist Rev, 95. **CONTACT ADDRESS** Dept of Marketing, SUNY, Col at Geneseo, 206-C Welles, Geneseo, NY 14454.

ZUKER, JOEL
DISCIPLINE FILM STUDIES **EDUCATION** NYork Univ, MA, PhD. **CAREER** Taught crse(s) in film, NYU, Saint Peters

Col, Rutgers & Hunter; instr, Hunter Univ, 72-; have lect or presented papers at colleges, Utah, Fla, Mont, NH, Vermont & Ohio. **HONORS AND AWARDS** PSC-CUNY grants. **RESEARCH** Films of Mel Brooks. **SELECTED PUBLICATIONS** Auth, on Ralph Steiner: Filmmaker and Photographer, Arno Press; bk(s) on, Arthur Penn, G.K Hall & Francis Coppola, G.K. Hall. **CONTACT ADDRESS** Dept of Education, Hunter Col, CUNY, 695 Park Ave, New York, NY 10021.

ZULAUF, SANDER W.
PERSONAL Born 11/05/1946, Paterson, NJ, m, 1979, 3 children **DISCIPLINE** ENGLISH **EDUCATION** Indiana Univ, Bloomington, Indiana, MA, 73; Gettysburg Col, Gettysburg, PA, 68. **CAREER** Prof of English, County Col of Morris, Randolph, NJ, 73-; Editor, Journal of New Jersey Poets, 89-. **HONORS AND AWARDS** Poet Laureate, Diocese of Newark, 99-01; Climp Literary Journal Institute Honoree, Atlanta, 99; NEH Fellow, Princeton, 87; Author, County College of Morris Alma Mater, 87; NEH Research Fel, 77; Graeff English Prize, 68. **MEMBERSHIPS** Academy of Amer Poets; Poetry Society of America; Poets House, NYC; Associated Writing Programs; Kenneth Burke Society; Thoreau Society. **RESEARCH** American Poetry. **SELECTED PUBLICATIONS** Auth, "Succasunna New Jersey," Poems, Breaking Point, Inc., 87; auth, "Index of American Periodical Verse," Founding Editor, 71-80; auth, "Tristram Shandy," Writers Guild of America, 94. **CONTACT ADDRESS** Dept English, County Col of Morris, 214 Center Grove Rd, Randolph, NJ 07869-2007. **EMAIL** szulauf@ccm.edu

ZURAKOWSKI, MICHELE M.
PERSONAL Born 03/06/1960, Bay City, MI, m, 1982, 1 child **DISCIPLINE** SPEECH COMMUNICATION **EDUCATION** Univ Minn, PhD, 92. **CAREER** Asst Prof Speech Commun, Col St. Catherine, 94-, Dept Chair, 94-. **MEMBERSHIPS** NCA; CSCA; CTAM. **RESEARCH** Women and public address; birth control rhetoric. **SELECTED PUBLICATIONS** Auth, "Interiors" as Interdisciplinary Text: A Case Analysis Using Film to Integrate Classroom Discussion of Interpersonal and Mass Mediated Meanings, Mich Asn Speech Commun J, 94; From Doctors and Lawyers to Wives and Mothers: Enacting "Feminine Style" and Changing Abortion Rights Arguments, Women's Studies in Communication, Spring 94; Ti-Grace Atkinson, Women Public Speakers in the United States, 1925-1993: A Bio-Critical Sourcebook, Greenwood Press, 94; Modeling Rhetorical Criticism, The Speech Commun Teacher 11, 97. **CONTACT ADDRESS** Speech Communication Dept, Col of St. Catherine, 2004 Randolph Ave., Saint Paul, MN 55105. **EMAIL** mmzurakowski@stkate.edu

ZURLO, JOHN A.
PERSONAL Born 10/07/1941, Takoma Park, MO, m **DISCIPLINE** ENGLISH **EDUCATION** Univ Tex Arlington BA, 63; SUNY Stony Brook, MA, 74; Univ Tex Arlington, MA, 75; East Tex State Univ, EdD, 83. **CAREER** Prof, Tarrant County Col, 92-. **HONORS AND AWARDS** Fel, Yaddo Artist Colony, 86; Humanities Scholar, St Mary's, OH, 88; Int Who's Who in Poetry and Poets, 99. **MEMBERSHIPS** Nat Peace Corps Assoc; World Affairs Counc of Greater Fort Worth; Okla Writers Fedn Inc. **RESEARCH** China - History and Culture, West Africa - History and Culture. **SELECTED PUBLICATIONS** Auth, Japan: Superpower of the Pacific, 91; auth, China: the Dragon Awakes, Dillon Pr, 94. **CONTACT ADDRESS** Dept Fine Arts, Tarrant County Junior Col, 1200 Tcjc Pky, Arlington, TX 76018-2907. **EMAIL** libai@tcjc.cc.tx.us

ZWEIG, ELLEN
PERSONAL Born 01/27/1947, Chicago, IL **DISCIPLINE** CONTEMPORARY POETRY AND POETICS **EDUCATION** Columbia Univ, MFA, 70; Univ Mich, BA, 67, PhD(English), 80. **CAREER** Lectr Interdisciplinary Art, San Francisco Univ, 80-, Res fel poetics & ling, Mass Inst Technol, summer 81; writer-in-residence, Griffith Univ, Australia, summer 82. **MEMBERSHIPS** MLA **RESEARCH** Contemporary poetry; performance art; history of interdisciplinary art. **SELECTED PUBLICATIONS** Auth, Presence and Resistance--Postmodernism and Cultural Politics in Contemporary American Performance, Amer Bk Rev, Vol 0016, 94; Acting-Out--Feminist Performances, Amer Bk Rev, Vol 0016, 94; Mendicant Erotics Sydney, a Performance for Radio, Tdr-Drama Rev-Jour Performance Stud, Vol 0040, 96. **CONTACT ADDRESS** 201 Ridgeway #2, Oakland, CA 94611.

ZWERDLING, ALEX
PERSONAL Born 06/21/1932, Breslau, Germany, m, 1969, 1 child **DISCIPLINE** ENGLISH **EDUCATION** Cornell Univ, BA, 53; Princeton Univ, MA, 56, PhD(English), 60. **CAREER** Instr English, Swarthmore Col, 57-61; from asst prof to assoc prof, 61-73, Prof English, Univ Calif, Berkeley, 73-86, Am Coun Learned Soc study fel, 64-65; Ctr Advanced Studies Behav Sci fel, 64-65; Nat Endowment for Humanities fel, 73-74; vis prof English, Northwestern Univ, 77; Guggenheim fel, 77-78; consult fel panel, Nat Endowment Humanities, 77-81; Prof, George Washington Univ, 86-88; Dir, Univ Calif Educ Abroad Prog, Britain and Ireland, 96-98. **HONORS AND AWARDS** Guggenheim Fel, 86-88; Distinguished Prof English, Letters and Science Alumni, Univ Calif, Berkeley, 86-; Bay Area Book Reviews Awd in Arts and Letters, 87; Nat Humanities Ctr, 89-90; Woodrow Wilson Int Ctr for Scholars Fel, 91-92; Nat Humanities Ctr Fel, 92-93. **MEMBERSHIPS** MLA **RESEARCH** Modern literature; contemporary literature; literature and politics. **SELECTED PUBLICATIONS** Auth, Yeats and the Heroic Ideal (N.Y., 1965; London, 1966); auth, Orwell and the Left (New Haven-London, 74; Tokyo, 1982); auth, Virginia Woolf and the Real World (Berkely, Los Angeles-London) 86; auth, Improvised Europeans: American Literary Expatriates and the Siege of London, (New York), 98. **CONTACT ADDRESS** Dept of English, Univ of California, Berkeley, Berkeley, CA 94720. **EMAIL** alexzw@uclink4.berkeley.edu

ZWICKER, HEATHER S.
PERSONAL Born 04/29/1966, Edmonton, AB, Canada **DISCIPLINE** ENGLISH **EDUCATION** Univ Albta, BA, 88; Stanford Univ, PhD, 93. **CAREER** Asst to assoc prof, Univ Albta, 93-. **HONORS AND AWARDS** Harriet Winspear-Sheila Watson Res Fel, 93; SSHRCC Fel, 96-99; Fac of Arts Teaching Award, 99; Rutherford Award for Excellence in Undergraduate Teaching, 99. **MEMBERSHIPS** MLA, Assoc of Commonwealth Lit and Lang Studies, Can Lesbian and Gay Studies Assoc. **RESEARCH** Postcolonial fiction and theory, feminist studies, cultural studies, queer theory, contemporary African, Canadian and Northern Irish literature, the Troubles. **SELECTED PUBLICATIONS** Auth, "Canadian Women of Colour: Marlene Nourbese Philip, Beatrice Culleton and Joy Kogawa Fight Their Way Home," Canadian Women Writing Fiction, ed Mickey Pearlman, (Univ Pr Miss, 93); auth, Gendered Troubles: Refiguring 'Women' in Northern Ireland," Genders 19, (94); auth, "Between Mater and Matter: Radical Novels by Republican Women," Reclaiming Gender: Transgressive Identities in Modern Ireland, ed Marilyn Cohen and Nancy Curtin, (St Martins Pr, 99); auth, "Daphne Marlatt's Ana Historic: Queering the Postcolonial Nation," ARIEL 30:2 (99); auth, "The Nervous Collusion's of Nation and Gender: Tsitsi Dangarembga's Challenge to Fanon," Critical Perspectives on Tsitsi Dangarembga, ed Jeannette Treiber and Elizabeth Willey, (Africa World Pr, 00); auth, "Multiculturalism: Pied Piper of Nationalism (And Joy Kogawa's Ambivalent Antiphony)," ARIEL, (01). **CONTACT ADDRESS** Dept English, Univ of Alberta, 3-5 Humanities Centre, Edmonton, AB, Canada T6G 2E5. **EMAIL** heather.zwicker@ualberta.ca

ZWICKER, STEVEN NATHAN
PERSONAL Born 06/04/1943, San Diego, CA, m, 1965, 4 children **DISCIPLINE** SEVENTEENTH CENTURY LITERATURE **EDUCATION** Univ Calif, Los Angeles, BA, 65; Brown Univ, PhD(English), 69. **CAREER** Assoc Prof English, Wash Univ, 69-, Taft fel, Univ Cincinnati, 70-71. **MEMBERSHIPS** MLA **RESEARCH** Seventeenth century political poetry; typology; political history. **SELECTED PUBLICATIONS** Auth, The king and Christ: Figural imagery in Dryden's Restoration panegyrics, Philol Quart, 71; Dryden's Political Poetry: The typology of King and Nation, Brown Univ, 72; Models of governance in Marvell's The First Anniversary, Criticism, 74; Politics and panegyric, In: Essays in Literary Figuralism, Princeton Univ, 77. **CONTACT ADDRESS** Dept of English, Washington Univ, 1 Brookings Dr, Saint Louis, MO 63130-4899.

ZYCHOWICZ, JAMES L.
PERSONAL Born 12/13/1955, Toledo, OH **DISCIPLINE** MUSICOLOGY **EDUCATION** Univ Toledo, BME, 77; Bowling Green State Univ, MM, 81; Univ Cincinnati, PhD, 88. **CAREER** Dean of Stud, mus tchr, Holy Spirit Seminary, Ohio, 81-83; teach asst, Univ Cincinnati, Col-Conserv Mus, 84-86; Dir Mus Engraving, A-R Editions, Madison, 88-92; Dir Prod Svcs, 92-93; Exec Dir, 93-97; Dir Sales Marketing, Mng Ed,Computer Mus and Digital Audio Series, 97-99; Series Ed, Computer Mas and Digital Audio Series, 99-. **HONORS AND AWARDS** Fulbright Scholar, Vienna, 86-87. **MEMBERSHIPS** Am Musicol Soc; Am Musicol Soc, Midwest Ch; Int Gustav Mahler Gesellschaft; Kurt Weill Found Mus; Carl-Maria-von-Weber Ausgabe, Detmold, Ger Mem. **RESEARCH** Musicology: Nineteenth-century music, including music of Gustav Mahler, Carl- Maria von Weber; sketch and manuscript studies; also music of Kurt Weill; opera studies. **SELECTED PUBLICATIONS** Ed, The Seventh Symphony of Gustav Mahler: A Symposium, Univ Cincinnati, 91; Ed, Ein schlechter Jasager: Considerations on the Finale to Mahler's Seventh Symphony, in The Seventh Symphony of Gustav Mahler: A Symposium, Univ Cincinnati, 91, pp 98-106; Liszt and Mahler: Perspectives on a Difficult Relationship, in Jour Am Liszt Soc, vol 36, 94,pp 1-18; The Odyssey of Kurt Weill's 'Ulysses Africanus,' The Am Mus Res Ctr Jour, vol 4, 94,pp 77-97; Music Manuscripts in the Bibliotheque Musicale Gustav Mahler, Paris, Fontes Artis Mus, vol 41, no 3, pp279-95 Toward an Ausgabe letzter Hand: The Publication and Revision of Mahler's Fourth Symphony, Jour Musicol, vol 12, 95, pp260-72; Mozart by Mahler, in Neue Forschungen zu Gustav Mahler und seiner Zeit: Festschrift Henry-Louis de La Grange zum 70. Geburtstag, Berne: Peter Lang, 97, p381-412. **CONTACT ADDRESS** 803 E. Gorham St., Madison, WI 53703. **EMAIL** JZychowicz@aol.com

ZYTARUK, GEORGE J.
DISCIPLINE ENGLISH **EDUCATION** BA, Univ Alberta; BEd, MA, PhD, Dlitt. **CAREER** Prof Nipissing Univ, 67-92; Prof Emer, 92-. **HONORS AND AWARDS** Founding pres, Nipissing Univ, 1967, **RESEARCH** D.H. Lawrence. **SELECTED PUBLICATIONS** Ed, D.H. Lawrence's letters; ed, Correspondence of Jessie Chambers. **CONTACT ADDRESS** Dept of English, Nipissing Univ, 100 College Dr, Box 5002, North Bay, ON, Canada P1B 8L7. **EMAIL** georgez@einstein.unipissing.ca

Geographic Index

Azusa
Griesinger, Emily
Shoemaker, Melvin H.

Bakersfield
Flachmann, Michael C.
Kleinsasser, Jerome

Balboa Island
Leedom, Tim C.

Bel Air
Bouler, Steven W.

Belmont
Gavin, Rosemarie Julie

Berkeley
Adelman, Janet Ann
Ahmadi, Shahwali
Altieri, Charles F.
Anderson, William Scovil
Bagdikian, Ben Haig
Bloom, Robert
Booth, Stephen
Christ, Carol Tecla
Christian, Barbara T.
Coolidge, John Stanhope
Countryman, L. Wm
Crews, Frederick
Crocker, Richard Lincoln
Friedman, Donald M.
Holub, Robert C.
Kirk-Duggan, Cheryl Ann
Knapp, Robert C.
Lesser, Wendy
Long, Anthony A.
Marcus, Sharon
Melia, Daniel Frederick
Middleton, Anne Louise
Murgia, Charles Edward
Nagler, Michael Nicholas
Ogden, Dunbar Hunt
Parsons, Jedediah David
Richardson, Anne
Richmond, Hugh M.
Richmond, Velma Bourgeois
Rosenberg, Marvin
Scheiffele, Eberhard
Scott, Peter Dale
Sloane, Thomas O.
Stroud, Ronald Sidney
Threatte, Leslie L.
Tongson, Karen L.
Wolgast, Eliz H.
Zwerdling, Alex

Campbell
Nichols, Patricia Causey

Canoga Park
Levy, William Turner

Carson
Geller, Lila Belle
Ravitz, A.
Wells, Walter

Chico
Downes, David Anthony
Karman, James

Chula Vista
Benkendorf, Ray R.

Claremont
Bellman, Samuel Irving
Elsbree, Langdon
Farrell, John C.
Greene, Gayle Jacoba
Groves, Jeffrey D.
Lohrli, Anne
Martin, Jay
Mezey, Robert
Redfield, Marc
Rice, Albert R.
Sellery, J'nan Morse
Wachtel, Albert
Waingrow, Marshall
Walker, Cheryl
Warner, Nicholas Oliver
Woodress, James

Cupertino
Bogus, Diane Adamz
Splitter, Randolph N.

Dana Point
Verrico, Rose May

Davis
Carter, Everett
Ferguson, Margaret Williams
Gilbert, Sandra Mortola
Grossman, George S.
Hays, Peter L.
Hoffman, Michael Jerome
Levin, Richard A.
Major, Clarence
Sarlos, Robert Karoly
Schaeffer, Peter Moritz-Friedrich
Schleiner, Winfried H.
Stewart, John Othneil
Waddington, Raymond B.
Zender, Karl Francis

Dominguez Hills
Ravitz, Abe C.

El Dorado Hills
Schlachter, Gail Ann

Encinitas
Beyer, David W.
Fisher, Edith Maureen

Fresno
Adams, Katherine L.
Bloom, Melanie
Bluestein, Gene
Bochin, Hal William
Carmichael, Carl W.
Faderman, Lillian
Fraleigh, Douglas
Levine, Philip
Rosenthal, Judith Ann
Walton, James E.
Warkentin, Larry R.

Fullerton
Axelrad, Arthur Marvin
Cummings, Sherwood
Jaskoski, Helen
Myers, Mitzi
Sayre, Shay
Vogeler, Martha Salmon
Wagner, M. John
Witmer, Diane F.

Glendora
Salwak, Dale F.

Hayward
Barrett, Eileen
Doyle, Jacqueline
Fuchs, Jacob
Hammerback, John C.

Irvine
Beevi, Mariam
Brown, Homer O.
Donlan, Walter
Folkenflik, Robert
Fuller, M. A.
Menton, Seymour
Newsom, Robert
Rieckmann, Jens
Rowe, John Carlos
Sutton, Dana Ferrin
Thomas, Brook

Kenington
Michaels, Leonard

Kentfield
Robertson-Gutierrez, Noel D.

La Jolla
Cancel, Robert
Cole, Mike
Cox, Stephen D.
Davis, Susan
Dijkstra, Bram
Engestrom, Yrjo
Falk, Thomas Heinrich
Foster, Frances Smith
Gaffney, Floyd
Hallin, Daniel C.
Hartouni, Valerie
Horwitz, Robert
Humphries, Tom
Keyssar, Helene
Mosshammer, Alden Adams
Mukerji, Chandra
Pasler, Jann C.
Rafael, Vicente
Schiller, Anita R.
Smarr, Janet L.
Wesling, Donald Truman

La Mirada
Lewis, Todd Vernon

Laguna Beach
Krieger, Murray

Loma Linda
Baker, Delbert Wayne

Long Beach
Aspiz, Harold
Cargile, Aaron C.
Domingo-Foraste, Douglas
Locklin, Gerald Ivan
May, Charles Edward
Samuelson, David N.
Weinstock, Donald Jay
Young, Elizabeth V.

Los Altos
Ueda, Makoto

Los Angeles
Allmendinger, Blake
Ando, Clifford
Band, Arnold J.
Banet-Weiser, Sarah
Banta, Martha
Baswell, Christopher C.
Behdad, Ali
Beniger, James R.
Berst, Charles A.
Blank, David L.
Borsch, Frederick Houk
Boyle, Thomas Coraghessan
Braudy, Leo
Braunmuller, A. R.
Brier, Peter A.
Burwick, Frederick
Cheng, Meiling
Cheung, King-Kok
Colley, Nathaniel S.
Cooper, Marilyn Marie
Dane, Joseph A.
Diaz, Roberto Ignacio
Dutton, William H.
Dyck, Andrew R.
Eubanks, Rachel Amelia
Fisher, Walter R.
Fitch, Noel Filey
Free, Katherine B.
Freeman, Donald C.
Friedman, Philip Allan
Frischer, Bernard D.
Fulk, Janet
Garrett, James M.
Gilliland-Swetland, Anne J.
Goldberg, Sander M.
Grassian, Esther Stampfer
Green, Lawrence Donald
Gurval, Robert Alan
Harley, Maria Anna
Hayles, Katherine N.
Houston, Velina H.
Kelly, Henry Ansgar
Kipling, Gordon L.
Kolb, Gwin Jack
Komar, Kathleen Lenore
Ladefoged, Peter
Lanham, Richard Alan
Lattimore, Steven
Lazar, Moshe
Lewis, Jayne Elizabeth
Lincoln, Kenneth
Maniquis, Robert Manuel
Mellor, Anne Kostelanetz
Mellor, Ronald
Middlebrook, Geoffrey C.
Morgan, Kathryn A.
Nagy, Joseph F.
Naiditch, P. G.
Novak, Maximillian E.
Nussbaum, Felicity
Packer, Barbara Lee
Passamaneck, Stephen Maurice
Pecora, Vincent P.
Perez-Torres, Rafael
Post, Jonathan F. S.
Quintero, Ruben
Richlin, Amy
Roper, Alan
Rosenthal, Margaret F.
Roston, Murray
Rowe, Karen E.
Roy, Alice M.
Schor, Hilary
Schwartz, Jeff L.
Sellin, Paul R.
Sharpe, Jenny
Sheats, Paul Douglas
Shuger, Debora
Smith, Jeffrey A.
Stockwell, Robert Paul
Tennyson, Georg Bernhard
Vine, Brent
Walker, Andrew David
Whiteman, D. Bruce
Wortham, Thomas
Yenser, Stephen I.
Younger, Kelly

Los Gatos
Rogers, Franklin R.

Lucerne
Rising, Catharine C.

Malibu
Buchanan, Raymond W.
Casey, Michael W.
Casmir, Fred L.
Clegg, Cyndia Susan
Fulmer, Constance M.
Holmes, David
Lowry, David

McKinleyville
Yingling, Julie

Menlo Park
White, Cecil R.

Merced
Cabezut-Ortiz, Delores

Mill Valley
McCoy, Gary W.

Mission Viejo
Heffernan, William A.

Modesto
Morris, Bernard E.

Monterey
Nitsche, Richard

Moorpark
Kairschner, Anne J.

Moraga
Beran, Carol L.
Fleming, John

Mount View
Brennan, Mary Alethea

Napa
Francoz, Marion

Northridge
Armer, Alan A.
Attias, Bernardo
Clendenning, John
Goss, James
Johnson, DeWayne Burton
Klotz, Marvin
Marlane, Judith
Peters, John U.
Solomon, Jack

Oak Park
Womack, Morris M.

Oakland
Abinader, Elmaz
Adisa, Opal P.
Bloch, Chana
Hart, Thomas Joel
Kahn, Madeleine
Milowicki, Edward John
Ratcliffe, Stephen
Scheinberg, Cynthia
Strychacz, Thomas
Ward, Carole Geneva
Zweig, Ellen

Orange
Nakell, Martin E.
Schneider, Matthew T.
Truax, Elizabeth

Palo Alto
Balsamo, Anne
Ginsberg, Lesley

Palos Verdes
Zucker, Alfred John

Pasadena
Brandler, Marcielle
Brennan, Linda
Clark, Justus Kent
King, Roberta R.
Mandel, Oscar
Shin, Andrew
Smallenburg, Harry Russell
Thongthiraj, Dootsdeemalachanok

Playa del Rey
Mahoney, John Francis

Pomona
Carrier, Rebecca
Morsberger, Robert E.
Smith, David Richard

Rancho Palos Verdes
Sayers, Kari

Rancho Santa Fe
McDonald, Marianne

Redlands
Musmann, Klaus
Vailakis, Ivan Gordon

Reedley
Borofka, David

Reseda
James, Woodrow C.

Riverside
Axelrod, Steven Gould
Bredbeck, Gregory W.
Brett, Philip
Briggs, John C.
Childers, Joseph W.
Devlin, Kimberly J.
Dunn, Robert P.
Elliott, Emory B.
Essick, Robert N.
Fabricant, Carole
Fagundo, Ana Maria
Ganim, John Michael
Gillis, Catherine L.
Haggerty, George E.
Hornby, Richard
King, Ben L.
Kinney, Katherine
Kronenfeld, Judith Z.
Lopez, Tiffany Ana
Mileur, Jean-Pierre
Morton, Carlos
Quin, Carolyn L.
Roy, Parama
Stewart, Stanley N.
Tyler, Carole-Anne
Vickery, John B.
Westfahl, Gary
Willis, Deborah
Yamamoto, Traise

Rocklin
Fishman, Jerry

Rohnert Park
Abernethy, Cecil Emory
Gale, Richard A.
Haslam, Gerald William
Raskin, Jonah
Rust, Ezra Gardner

Rohnert Pk
Allen, Julia M.

Sacramento
Agosta, Lucien
Bankowsky, Richard James
Madden, David
Trujillo, Nick L.
Vande Berg, Leah R.
Von Friederichs-Fitzwater, Marlene M.

San Bernardino
Barnes, Ronald Edgar
Burgess, Michael

COLORADO

CONNECTICUT

Geographic Index

Killingworth
Sampson, Edward C.

Middletown
Abelove, Henry
O'Hara, James J.
Reeve, F. D.
Roberts, Michael
Rose, Phyllis Davidoff
Stowe, William
Szegedy-Maszak, Andrew

Mystic
Hartman, Charles O.

New Britain
Bonaccorso, Richard L.
Gigliotti, Gilbert L.

New Haven
Anderson, Michael John
Avram, Wesley D.
Babcock, Robert
Bers, Victor
Bloom, Harold
Brisman, Leslie
Bromwich, David
Chang, Kang-I S.
Cole, Susan Letzler
Deresiewicz, William
Dimock, Wai Chee
Eder, Doris Leonora
Elwood, William R.
Forte, Allen
Franklin, Ralph William
French, Richard Frederic
Garvey, Sheila Hickey
Hollander, John
Holley, Sandra Cavanaugh
Krasner, David
Lawler, Traugott
Lewis, Perciles
Matthews, John F.
Metlitzki, Dorothee
Nelihaus, Tobin
Parks, Stephen Robert
Perlis, Vivian
Peterson, Linda H.
Robinson, Fred C.
Russell, Tilden A.
Solodow, Joseph B.
Stambovsky, Phillip
Stepto, Robert Burns
Tirro, Frank Pascale
Trachtenberg, Alan
Valesio, Paolo
Waith, Eugene Mersereau
Welsh, Alexander
Whitaker, Thomas Russell
Willis, Patricia Cannon
Yeazell, Ruth Bernard

New London
Bleeth, Kenneth Alan
Evans, Robley Jo
Held, Dirk
Taranow, Gerda

Orchard Branford
Palisca, Claude Victor

South Windsor
Bradley, James Robert

Storrs
Bloom, Lynn Z.
Carlson, Eric Walter
Charters, Ann D.
Chow, Karen
Gatta, John J.
Gibson, Margaret
Gilbert, Harvey R.
Hamilton, Mark A.
Higonnet, Margaret R.
Hollenberg, Donna Krolik
Jacobus, Lee Andre
Liles, Betty Z.
Molette, Carlton Woodard, II
Nelson, Marilyn
Peterson, Richard Scot
Robb, Michael P.
Roberts, Thomas J.
Stern, Milton R.
Turley, Hans

Waterbury
Macleod, Glen

West Hartford
Azzara, Christopher D.
Blume, Donald Thomas
Braus, Ira
Ellis, Donald
Ghnassia, Jill Dix
Jamil, S. Selina
Katz, Sandra
Miller, Patrick
Mori, Akane
Roderick, John M.
Saunders, T. Clark
Seabury, Marcia
Stanley, William Chad
Stull, William L.
Tonkin, Humphrey R.
Willheim, Imanuel

West Haven
Emma, Ronald David
Marx, Paul
Sloane, David Edward Edison

West Simsbury
Stevenson, Catherine Barnes

Westport
Greeley, June-Ann T.

Willimantic
Anderson, Celia Catlett
Jacobik, Gray
Mama, Raouf
Molette, Barbara J.

Windham
Murphy, Brenda C.

Woodbridge
Kimnach, Wilson H.

DELAWARE

Dover
Nielsen, Michael
Pelzer, Linda C.

Newark
Beasley, Jerry Carr
Brock, Dewey Heyward
Calhoun, Thomas O.
Courtright, John A.
Cox, Roger Lindsay
Dawson, Carl
Dee, Juliet L.
Detenber, Benjamin H.
Donaldson-Evans, Mary P.
Gates, Barbara Timm
Goodman, Susan
Grossman, Jonathan H.
Halio, Jay L.
Haslett, Betty J.
Henderson, Carol E.
Hogan, Robert
Horowitz, Sara R.
Leitch, Thomas
Martin, Ronald Edward
McInnis, Judy B.
Mcleod, Douglas M.
Mell, Donald Charles
Merrill, Thomas F.
Pauly, Thomas Harry
Pavitt, Charles
Perse, Elizabeth M.
Peterson, Larry
Pifer, Ellen
Safer, Elaine Berkman
Samter, Wendy
Scott, Bonnie Kime
Signorielli, Nancy
Van Dover, James K.
Walker, Jeanne M.

Wilmington
Zhou, Jian-Zhong

DISTRICT OF COLUMBIA

Washington
Abraham, Daniel
Arnez, Nancy L.
Aufderheide, Patricia
Austin, Bobby William
Babb, Valerie M.
Barlow, William
Bennett, Betty T.
Betz, Paul F.
Blair, Carole
Blair, P.
Boswell, Jackson Campbell
Boyd, Linda F. Wharton
Brady, Leo
Broderick, John Caruthers
Captain, Yvonne
Cardaci, Paul F.
Cima, Gay Gibson
Claydon, Margaret
Cole, John Y., Jr.
Collins, Michael J.
Comor, Edward
Corrigan, Maureen
Crane, Milton
Crowley, Kelley M. Wickham
Farr, Judith Banzer
Fernandes, James
Fisher, Leona W.
Fisk, Deborah Payne
Fort, Keith
Fox, Pamela
Fox, Stephen D.
Gewanter, David
Glavin, John
Gopalan, Lalitha
Gunzerath, David
Hall, Kim
Hammer, Mitchell R.
Hendrix, Jerry
Hirsh, John Campion
Holmer, Joan Ozark
Ingebretsen, Edward J.
Irvine, Martin
Jackson, Mary E.
Jamme, Albert W. F.
Jorgens, Jack J.
Kadlec, David
Kaplan, Lindsay
Kent, Carol Fleisher
Lanouette, William John
Larson, Charles Raymond
Leche, Emma Jean Ghee
Levy, Anita B.
Loesberg, Jonathan
Mack, Michael
Maddox, Lucy
Mahony, Robert E. P.
Malek, Abbas
Mann, Thomas J.
Mason, Abelle
Matabane, Paula W.
McAleavey, David Willard
McCann, Richard
Miller, Jeanne-Marie A.
Mitchell, Angelyn
Mowlana, Hamid
Moyer, Kermit W.
Noble, Marianne K.
O'Brien, George
O'Connor, Michael P.
O'Connor, Patricia E.
O'Donnell, Anne M.
Ortiz, Ricardo
Pfordresher, John P.
Pike, David
Pinkett, Harold Thomas
Pope, Rebecca A.
Prevots, Naima
Ragussis, Michael
Reilly, John M.
Reusher, Jay
Ribeiro, Alvaro
Robinson, Amy
Rosenblatt, Jason Philip
Roy, Abhik
Rubenstein, Roberta
Salamon, Linda B.
Schlossman, David A.
Schwartz, Henry J.
Schwartz, Richard B.
Sendry, Joseph M.
Sha, Richard
Shahid, Irfan Arif
Shanks, Hershel
Shulman, Jeffrey
Siegel, Joel E.
Sitterson, Joseph
Slakey, Roger L.
Slevin, James
Smith, Bruce Ray
Snyder, Susan Brooke
Solomon, Julie R.
Stack, Richard
Sten, Christopher W.
Stetz, Margaret
Sutton, Sharyn
Szittya, Penn
Taylor, Henry
Taylor, Orlando L.
Temple, Kathryn
Tinkcom, Matthew
Tm, King
Todd, Dennis
Traylor, Eleanor W.
Turner, Jeanine W.
Valerie M., Babb
Wagstaff, Grayson
Warren, Clay
Waznak, Robert P.
Weaver, Gary
Wendland, Ernst R.
Wheatley, Christopher J.
Winter, Daria Portray
Wolfensohn, James David
Young, Elizabeth Bell
Zaharna, Rhonda S.

FLORIDA

Alachua
Wall, William G.

Boca Raton
Budd, Michael
Rice, Julian
Smith, Voncile Marshall

Boynton Beach
Fine, Africa R.

Coral Gables
Benstock, Shari
Freeman, Kathryn S.
Guttenberg, Barnett
Kelleghan, Fiona
McCarthy, Patrick A.
Palmeri, Frank
Russo, John Paul
Suzuki, Mihoko
Thiel, Diane

Dania
Skellings, Edmund

Davie
Grow, Lynn

Daytona Beach
Glassman, Steve

DeLand
Kaivola, Karen
McCoy, Ken W.
Pearson, John H.

Destin
Beavers, Myrtle B.

Fairfield
Douglas, Jane Yellowlees

Fort Myers
Golian, Linda Marie
Klemt, Barbara
Sullivan, Brad

Ft Lauderdale
Doan, James E.
Wang, Xiao

Gainesville
Cailler, Bernadette Anne
Carnell, Corbin Scott
Clark, Ira
Derrick, Clarence
Dickison, Sheila Kathryn
Duckworth, Alistair Mckay
Gilbert, Pamela K.
Gordon, Andrew
Hartigan, Karelisa V.
Hill-Lubin, Mildred Anderson
Holland, Norman N.
Kershner, R. Brandon
Kushner, David Z.
McKeen, William
Miller, D. Gary
Nelson, Marie
New, Melvyn
Page, Judith W.
Paris, Bernard J.
Schmidt, Patricia Lois
Schulz, Geralyn
Shoaf, R. Allen
Smith, F. Leslie
Smith, Julian
Smith, Stephanie A.
Sussman, Lewis Arthur
Twitchell, James B.
Varnum-Gallant, Billie M.

Jacksonville
Baron, Mary K.
Clines, Raymond H.
Gibson, Richard J.
Harmon, Gary L.
Stanton, Robert J.

Key West
Elwood, William N.

Lake Worth
Dilgen, Regina M.

Lakeland
Bruce, Alexander
Lott, Raymond

Leesburg
Sligh, Gary Lee

Lutz
Smith, Elton Edward

Madison
Mc Cauley, Barbara L.

Maitland
Sinclair, Gail

Melbourne
Matar, Nabil
Slaughter, Beverley

Miami
Casines, Gisela P.
Clarke, Robert F.
Johnson, Kenneth E.
Judd, Catherine
Robinson, Christine A.
Samra, Risà Jana
Schwartz, Richard A.
Sugg, Richard Peter
Waugh, Butler Huggins
Yudin, Florence L.

North Miami
Dufresne, John

Opa Locka
Ross, Marilyn J.

Orange Park
McClain, E.

Orlando
De Lorme, Denise
Dombrowski, Paul M.
Hubbard, Susan S.
Schiffhorst, Gerald Joseph

Oviedo
Adicks, Richard R.
Villanueva, Celestino Alberto

Pensacola
Auter, Philip J.
Dews, Carlos L.
Maddock, Lawrence H.
McLeod, Stephen G.
Umphlett, Wiley Lee

Saint Petersburg
Brooker, Jewel Spears
Dunlap, Karen F. Brown
Meinke, Peter
Wells, Daniel Arthur

Sainte Augustine
Horner, Carl S., III

Sanford
Wright, Stephen Caldwell

Davis, Lennard J.
Davis, Phoebe Stein
Dik, Helma
Faraone, Christopher
Fennell, Francis L.
Fields, Beverly
Fiscella, Joan B.
Fish, Stanley E.
Floyd, Samuel A., Jr.
Foster, Verna A.
Frantzen, Allen J.
Friedrich, Paul
Fromm, Gloria Glikin
Gans, Bruce
Gardiner, Judith Kegan
Gariepy, Margo R.
Garrigan, Kristine O.
Gasienica-Byrcyn, Anna Zofia
Georgalas, Robert N.
Good, Jacquelyn Fox
Gossett, Philip
Gossett, Suzanne
Graff, Gerald E.
Greeley, Andrew M.
Guenther, Barbara J.
Hall, Jonathan M.
Hardy, John Edward
Hoover, Paul
Hoover, Polly
Howard, C. Jeriel
Hulse, Clark
Janangelo, Joseph
Jay, Paul
Johnson, W. Ralph
Johnston, Mark D.
Jones, Richard A.
Jones, Steven
Kaminski, Thomas
Keenan, J. G.
Kendrick, Christopher
Kolb, Gwin Jackson
Koptak, Paul E.
Krause, David H.
Lazarus, Cathy Lynn
Leer, Norman Robert
Leighton, Lauren Gray
Lieb, Michael J.
Lightfoot, Jean Harvey
Lind, Rebecca
Livatino, Melvin W.
Lucas, James L.
Lukacher, Ned
Mann, Harveen Sachdeva
Marshall, Donald G.
Messbarger, Paul Robert
Messenger, Christian Karl
Mitchell, W. J. Thomas
Musgrove, Laurence E.
Nabholtz, John R.
Nims, John Frederick
O'Donnell, Thomas G.
Oliker, Michael A.
Pavel, Thomas
Phillips, Gene D.
Poston, Lawrence S.
Potee, Nanette
Pullin, Nicolas G.
Ramsey, John T.
Ranes, Barbara
Redfield, James M.
Rinehart, Lucy
Robinson, Edward A.
Robinson, Rochelle
Rocks, James E.
Shea, John Stephen
Sheasby, R.
Stern, Richard G.
Sternberg, Joel
Strier, Richard
Tabbi, Joseph
Tave, Stuart Malcolm
Taylor, Jacqueline S.
Trela, D. J.
Trumpener, Katie
Walker, James
Walker, Robert Jefferson
Wallace, John Malcolm
Wexler, Joyce
Wexman, Virginia Wright
White, Douglas Howarth
Willard, Barb
Williams, Joseph M.
Wolfe, Gary Kent
Wood, Barbara
Zaferson, William S.

De Kalb
Abbott, Craig Stephens
Berkowitz, Gerald Martin
Burwell, Rose Marie
Court, Franklin Edward
Giles, James Richard
Johannesen, Richard Lee
Mellard, James Milton
Self, Robert Thomas
Shesgreen, Sean Nicholas
Waldeland, Lynne M.
Wilson, Robert H.

Decatur
Detmer-Groebel, Emily
Rozema, Hazel J.

Deerfield
Baxter, Harold J.
Graddy, William E.

Dekalb
Baker, William
Bryan, Ferald J.
Day, Michael
Kipperman, Mark
Knapp, John V.
Williams, William Proctor
Witherell, Elizabeth H.

Edwardsville
Bukalski, Peter J.
Meyering, Sheryl L.
Murphy, Patrick D.
Petry, Alice Hall
Ragen, Brian A.
Richardson, Betty
Schmidt, Barbara Quinn
Springer, Carl P. E.
Spurgeon, Dickie A.
Valley, David B.

Eureka
Logsdon, Loren
Schwab, Allen

Evanston
Appel, Alfred, Jr.
Breslin, Paul
Brkkila, Betsy
Cheah, Pheng
Cirillo, Albert
Citron, Michelle
Dubey, Madhu
Eldred, Katherine O.
Evans, Lawrence
Froula, Christine
Garrison, Daniel H.
Gibbons, Reginald
Goodnight, G. Thomas
Griswold, Wendy
Harris, Robert Allen
Herbert, Christopher
Kinzie, Mary
Lassner, Phyllis
Law, Jules
Lipking, Lawrence
Manning, Susan
Marshall, David
Monoson, S. Sara
Mueller, Martin
Mulcaire, Terry
Newman, Barbara J.
Packer, James
Reginald, Allen
Rumold, Rainer
Schwartz, Regina
Schwarzlose, Richard A.
Schwoch, James J.
Stern, Julia
Styan, John Louis
Wall, Wendy
Wallace, Catherine Miles
Wallace, Robert
Wilkins, Leona B.
Wilson, Steven R.

Galesburg
Wilson, Douglas Lawson

Glen Ellyn
Chu, Mike S.
Pierson, Steven J.
Webb, Nancy L.

Glencoe
Kotler, Philip

Grayslake
Roeske, Paulette
Rosenberg, Judith

Jacksonville
Decker, Philip H.
Metcalf, Allan Albert

Joliet
Chilton, H. Randolph
Marzec, Marcia Smith

Lake Forest
Schneiderman, Davis A.
Yannella, Donald

Lebanon
Brailow, David Gregory
Greenfield, John R.

Lincoln
Shaw, Wayne Eugene
Sullivan, James

Lisle
Komechak, Michael E.

Macomb
Chu, Felix T.
Colvin, Daniel Lester
Conger, Syndy Mcmillen
Dallinger, Judith M.
Dunlap, Isaac H.
Edwards, Janis
Frazer, June
Frazer, Timothy C.
Hallwas, John Edward
Harrison, Leland Bruce
Helm, Thomas Eugene
Lee, Jai Hyon
Mann, John Stuart
Mann, Karen Berg
Na'allah, Abdul-Rasheed

Monmouth
De Young, James

Naperville
Kanwar, Anju

Normal
Baldwin, John R.
Beck, Ann R.
Brosnahan, Leger
Burt, Susan Meredith
Carr, Robin
Dammers, Richard H.
De Santis, Christopher
Harris, Charles Burt
Hulit, Lloyd
Kagle, Steven Earl
McLaughlin, Robert
Mullenix, Elizabeth Reitz
Nourie, Alan Raymond
Pancrazio, James
Poole, John R.
Shields, John Charles
Snyder, David W.
Tarr, Rodger Leroy
Visor, Julia N.

Oglesby
Lynch, Rose Marie

Palatine
Johnson, Richard F.

Palos Heights
Ward, Annalee R.

Palos Hills
Porter, Joyce K.

Park Forest
Mc Master, Michele

Payson
House, Kay S.

Peoria
Cheng, Hong
Claussen, Ernest Neal
Stein, Kevin J.
Vickroy, Laurie

Quincy
Schweda, Donald Norman
Sparks, Sherry L.

River Forest
Froehlich, Charles Donald
Jenne, Natalie R.
McGinty, Carolyn
Rohman, Chad

River Grove
Brackett, Mary Virginia
Latham, Angela

Rock Island
Huse, Nancy Lyman

Rockford
Hesselgrave, David J.
Lee, Hsiao-Hung
LeFew-Blake, Penelope

Springfield
Jackson, Jacqueline Dougan

Urbana
Adelman, Gary S.
Baron, Dennis
Baym, Nina
Calder, William M., III
Campbell, Jackson Justice
Carringer, Robert L.
Cole, Howard Chandler
Dean, Tim
Douglas, George Halsey
Dussinger, John Andrew
Friedman, John Block
Garrett, Peter
Goldsmith, Daena J.
Guibbory, Achsah
Hurt, James Riggins
Jacobson, Howard
Kay, W. David
Klein, Joan Larsen
Kramer, Dale Vernon
Lieberman, Laurence
Lorbe, Ruth Elisabeth
Michelson, Bruce
Mullin, Michael A.
Nelson, Cary Robert
Nettl, Bruno
Sansone, David
Scanlan, Richard T.
Shapiro, Michael
Stein, Arnold
Stillinger, Jack
Sullivan, Zohreh Tawakuli
Temperley, Nicholas
Thomas, Stafford H.
Waldoff, Leon
Wallach, Luitpold
Watts, Emily
Wenzel, Joseph Wilfred
Wheeler, Richard Paul

Wauconda
Bolchazy, Ladislaus J.

Western
Hawkinson, Kenneth S.

Wheaton
Hein, Rolland Neal
Madigan, Mary
Ryken, Leland

Wilmette
Lu, Xing L.

INDIANA

Anderson
Chapman, Virginia
Rhule, Imogene G.
Robertson, Patricia C.

Bloomington
Anderson, Judith H.
Bannon, Cynthia J.
Beaty, Frederick L.
Brown, A. Peter
Buelow, George John
Burnim, Mellonee Victoria
Christ, Matthew R.
Curtin, Michael
David, Alfred
Eakin, Paul John
Fletcher, Winona Lee
Forker, Charles Rush
Franklin, James L.
Glowacki, Kevin T.
Gray, Donald
Hansen, William F.
Jensen, H. James
Johnston, Kenneth R.
Justus, James Huff
Klotman, Phyllis Rauch
Leach, Eleanor W.
Lochrie, Karma D.
Lohmann, Christoph Karl
Long, Timothy
Mathiesen, Thomas J.
Maultsby, Portia K.
Nagle, Betty Rose
Naremore, James
Nord, David P.
Nordloh, David Joseph
Scalabrini, Massimo
Shipps, Anthony Wimberly
Sobrer, Josep Miquel
Sperry, Stuart M.
Terrill, Robert
Tischler, Hans
Wang, Joan Parsons
Wertheim, Albert

Crawford
Danby, Judd G.

Crawfordsville
Baker, Donald Whitelaw
Fisher, James
Gomez, Gilberto
Herzog, Tobey C.

Evansville
Baer, William
Brown, Arthur A.
Carson, Michael
Haegert, John
Hemminger, William
Longmire, Samuel
McMullan, Margaret
McMullen, Margaret
Richardson, Donald
Sands, Helen R.
Shiller, Dana
Snow, Helena

Fort Wayne
Blythe, Stuart
Brennan, John P.
Carr, Steven A.
Crismore, Avan G.
Thuente, Mary Helen

Gary
Barr, Alan Philip
Buckley, William Kermit
Williamson-Ige, Dorothy Kay

Goshen
Davis, Todd Fleming

Greencastle
Huffman, Carl A.
Sununu, Andrea

Hammond
Boiarsky, Carolyn
Casto-Urios, Jose
Fewer, Colin D.
Selig, Robert L.

Hanover
Clark, George Peirce
Eden, Melissa
Fearnow, Mark
Jobe, Steve

Indianapolis
Baetzhold, Howard George
Blair, Rebecca S.
Broman, Per F.
Dick, Robert C.
Eller, Jonathan R.
Feinman, Paul I.
Fong, Bobby
Gentry, Marshall Bruce
Goering, Elizabeth
Hamilton, Sharon J.
Kooreman, Thomas Edward
Kovacik, Karen
Leeper, Jill M.
Saffire, Paula Reiner
Schmidt, Steven J.
Shaughnessy, Edward

IOWA

KANSAS

KENTUCKY

Howard, Leigh Anne
Mann, David D.
Miller, Robert H.
Mullen, Karen A.
Rothenbusch, Esther H.
Slavin, Arthur J.
Van, Thomas A.
Willard, Charles A.

Madisonville
Vander Ploeg, Scott D.

Murray
Cella, Charles Ronald
Cohen, Michael Martin
Osborne, Carol D.
Wylder, Delbert E.

Newport
Adams, Susan S.
Alberti, John
Bechtel, Judith A.
Forman, Sandra

Richmond
Benson, Richard Lee
Carney, Virginia I.
Culross, Jack Lewis
Dean, Margaret J.
Hill, Ordelle Gerhard
Kopacz, Paula D.
Myers, Marshall
Shearon, Forrest Bedford
Stephens, Jessica
Witt, Robert Wayne

Williamsburg
Fish, Thomas Edward

Wilmore
Joly, Ralph Robert
Simmons, Donald B.

LOUISIANA

Baton Rouge
Babin, James L.
Borck, Jim Springer
Bradford, Clinton W.
Brind'Amour, Lucie
Carmona, Vicente
Carrithers, Gale
Cassidy, Jane W.
Catano, James
Clarke, William M.
Coldiron, Anne E. B.
Cope, Kevin
Cowan, Bainard
Crump, Rebecca
d'Hemecourt, Jules
Daniels, LeAnne
Demastes, William
Doty, Gresdna Ann
Edgeworth, Robert J.
Euba, Femi
Fischer, John Irwin
Fletcher, Alan D.
Fogel, Daniel Mark
Freedman, Carl H.
Garay, Mary Sue
Garay, Ronald
Gellrich, Jesse M.
Gellrich, Michelle
Gourdine, A. K. M.
Hamilton, John Maxwell
Harbin, Bill J.
Honeycutt, James M.
Jensen, Katharine
Kennedy, J. Gerald
Kronick, Joseph
Kurpius, David
Lane, Pinkie Gordon
Leupin, Alexandre
Liggett, Sarah
Looser, Devoney K.
Lowe, John
Madden, David
Masse, Michelle
Mattingly, Carol
May, John Richard
Mayo, Charles M.
McMahon, Robert
Michie, Elsie B.
Mickelson, Sig
Moore, Don
Moreland, Richard
Nardo, Anna
Nelson, Richard Alan
Oliver, Elizabeth L.
Olney, James
Perlmutter, David
Prenshaw, Peggy
Ragsdale, J. Donald
Reid, Panthea
Richardson, Malcolm
Ross, Billy I.
Sandiford, Keith
Schierling, Stephen P.
Shiflett, Orvin Lee
Smith, David J.
Stanford, Donald Elwin
Stone, Gregory
Suchy, Patricia
Tandberg, Gerilyn
Thorn, J. Dale
Toth, Emily
Weltman, Sharon
Williams-Hackett, Lamara
Windhauser, John W.
Wing, Nathaniel
Wood, Susan H.
Zebouni, Selma

Hammond
Bettagere, Ramesh N.
Laurent, Dianna V.

Lafayette
Arehole, S.
Dorwick, Keith
Fackler, Herbert Vern
Iskander, Sylvia W.
Laudun, John
Petitjean, Thomas D., Jr
Raffel, Burton
Riehl, Joseph E.

Lake Charles
Goins, Scott
Marcello, Leo L.
Nesanovich, Stella
Wood, Carol L.

Leesville
Norman, Paralee Frances

Monroe
Kauffman, Bette J.
McClelland, John Fleming
Steckline, C. Turner
Thameling, Carl L.

Natchitoches
Green, Suzanne Disheroon
Jarred, Ada D.
Thomas, Jean D'Amato

New Orleans
Ahearn, W. Barry
Baron, John H.
Berlin, Netta
Bonner, Thomas, Jr.
Boyd, Anne E.
Cohen, Joseph
Collins, Richard W.
Cooley, Peter John
Cotton, William Theodore
Cummings, Anthony M.
Desai, Gaurav Gajanan
Dixon, Nancy J.
Draper, David E.
Engel, Kirsten H.
Eskew, Harry Lee
Ewell, Barbara Claire
Gelderman, Carol W.
Harpham, Geoffrey Galt
Hazlett, John D.
Holditch, William Kenneth
Koritz, Amy
Lackey, Kris L.
Liuzza, Roy
Major, Wilfred E.
Mark, Rebecca
Mosier, John
Nair, Supryia M.
Olivera, Otto H.
Pizer, Donald
Qian, Zhaoming
Reiss, Benjamin D.
Simmons, Joseph Larry
Skinner, Robert Earle
Snare, Gerald
Spaeth, Barbette S.
Stewart, Maaja Agur
Taylor, Herman Daniel
Toulouse, Teresa
Towns, Sanna Nimtz
Travis, Molly Abel
Wade-Gayles, Gloria Jean
Watson, Cresap Shaw

Ruston
Leissner, Debra
Robbins, Kenneth

Shreveport
Alexander, Bryan
Guerin, Wilfred Louis
Labor, Earle G.
Leitz, Robert C.

Thibodaux
Bello, Richard S.
Davis, Albert J.
Fletcher, Marie
Tonn, Anke

MAINE

Bar Harbor
Carpenter, William Morton

Brunswick
Boyd, Barbara Weiden

Cape Neddick
Hapgood, Robert

Castine
Booth, Philip

Dresden
Turco, Lewis

Farmington
Flint, Allen Denis
Franson, J. Karl

Harborside
Miner, Thelma Smith
Miner, Ward L.

Lewiston
Williams, Linda F.

Machias
Huggins, Cynthia

New Gloucester
Eckersley, L. Lynnette

Norway
Kuritz, Paul

Orono
Hatlen, Burton Norval
Jacobs, Naomi
Langellier, Kristin M.
Peterson, Eric E.
Rogers, Deborah D.

Portland
Gish, Nancy K.
McGrath, Francis C.
Shedletsky, Leonard Jerald

Presque Isle
Petress, Kenneth C.

South Andover
Rosenwald, John

South Berwick
Olbricht, Thomas H.

Standish
Rielly, Edward J.

Waterville
Bassett, Charles Walker
Clogan, Paul Maurice
Lepley, Doug
O'Neill, Kerill
Roisman, Hanna M.
Sweney, John R.

Winthrop
Waugh, Charles G.

York Beach
Davison, Nancy R.

York Harbor
Henderson, Charles, Jr.

MARYLAND

Annapolis
Barbera, Andre
Culham, Phyllis
Fleming, Bruce E.
Gilliland, C. Herbert
Jason, Philip K.

Arnold
Lefcowitz, Barbara

Baltimore
Bett, Richard
Bowman, Leonard Joseph
Cameron, Sharon
Carruthers, Virginia
Crockett, Bryan L.
Davisson, Mary H. T.
Douglas, Paul H.
Faulcon, Clarence Augustus, II
Fitzpatrick, Carolyn H.
Fitzpatrick, Vincent D.
Fleishman, Avrom
Gibson, Stephanie
Hahn, H. George
Hall, Tom
Harrison, Daphne Duval
Hawthorne, Lucia Shelia
Irmscher, Christoph
Irwin, John Thomas
Kaplan, Nancy
Kelley, Delores G.
Kleinman, Neil
Korenman, Joan Smolin
Macksey, Richard Alan
Matanle, Stephen
Mc Glamery, Gayla
McKusick, James C.
Moulthrop, Stuart
Nagele, Rainer
Oden, Gloria
Pfefferle, W. T.
Roller, Matthew B.
Roome, Dorothy M.
Scheye, Thomas Edward
Sheffey, Ruthe G.
Spitzer, John
Stephens, Charles Ralph
Sweeney, John Albert
Thompson, Chevia
Tokarczyk, Michelle M.
Tolbert, Elizabeth D.
Vatz, Richard E.
Waterman, Sue A.
Weinhouse, Linda
Weiss, Piero
Weiss, Susan Forscher
Weiss, Susan Forscher
Ziff, Larzer

Bethesda
Levine, Molly Myerowitz
Linton, Calvin Darlington
Waserman, Manfred

Bowie
English, Daylanne K.
Onwumechili, Chukwuka
Ransome, Cora
Tomlin, Carol

Burtonsville
Rothfeld, Anne

Chestertown
Deprospo, Richard Chris
Tatum, Nancy R.

College Park
Achinstein, Sharon
Auerbach, Jonathan
Barry, Jackson Granville
Bauer, Ralph R.
Bryer, Jackson R.
Cai, Deborah A.
Caramello, Charles
Davis, Johnetta Garner
Donawerth, Jane L.
Fink, Edward L.
Fraistat, Neil R.
Freedman, Morris
Freimuth, Vicki S.
Gaines, Robert N.
Gillespie, Patti P.
Hiebert, Ray Eldon
Holton, William Milne
Isaacs, Neil D.
Kelly, R. Gordon
Klumpp, James F.
Lawson, Lewis Allen
Lee, Hugh Ming
Leonardi, Susan J.
Lightfoot, David
McCaleb, Joseph L.
Niles, Lyndrey Arnaud
Parks, Sheri L.
Parry-Giles, Trevor
Peterson, Carla L.
Rutherford, Charles Shepard
Rutledge, Steven H.
Sherman, William H.
Staley, Gregory A.
Sthele, Eva
Vandiver, Elizabeth
Vanegmond, Peter
Waks, Leah
Williams, Helen Elizabeth
Wilt, David E.
Winton, Calhoun
Wolvin, Andrew D.
Woolf, Leonard

Emmitsburg
Craft, William
Dorsey, Peter
Ducharme, Robert
Gandal, Keith
Hamel, Mary
Heath, William
Wright, Terrence C.

Frederick
Caminals-Heath, Roser

Frostburgh
Lutz, Mary Anne

Gaithersburg
Garson, Helen S.

La Plata
Klink, William

Lanham Seabrook
Kari, Daven Michael

New Market
Mintz, Lawrence E.

Parkville
Dunn, E. Catherine

Princess Anne
Hedgepeth, Chester Melvin, Jr.
Keenan, Richard Charles

Rockville
Goldenberg, Myrna
Okechukwu, Chinwe C.

Salisbury
Waters, Michael
Welsh, James Michael

Silver Spring
Irving, Kartina M.
Moore, Robert Henry
Null, Elisabeth M.

Takoma Park
Giron, Robert L.
Loizeaux, Elizabeth Bergmann

Towson
Bergman, David L.
Chen, Ni
Faller, Greg
Flippen, Charles
Gissendanner, John M.
Hedges, William Leonard
Leahy, David G.
Lev, Peter
McElreath, Mark
McGrain, John W.

Ann Arbor
Bailey, Richard Weld
Bauland, Peter Max
Billick, David Joseph
Bornstein, George J.
Brater, Enoch
Britton, Allen Perdue
Collins, Derek B.
Crawford, Richard
Eby, Cecil Degrotte
Faller, Lincoln B.
Frier, Bruce W.
Gernes, Todd Steven
Gikandi, Simon E.
Gonzalez, John M.
Hayes-Scott, Fairy Cesena
Ingram, William
Jensen, Ejner Jacob
Johnson, Lemuel A.
Knott, John R.
Konigsberg, Ira
Kucich, John Richard
Kuznets, Lois R.
Looker, Mark S.
Mackey, Barbara S.
Malm, William P.
McIntosh, James Henry
Patterson, Willis Charles
Perkins, Barbara M.
Porter, J. I.
Rabkin, Eric S.
Super, Robert Henry
Terpstra, Vern
Thrall, Trevor
Wald, Alan Maynard
Whiting, Steven
Whitman, Robert F.
Witke, E. C.

Berkley
Price, Danielle E.

Berrien Springs
Warren, Joseph W.

Big Rapids
Green, Lon C.
Russell, David L.

Dearborn
Berkove, Lawrence Ivan
Lee, Dorothy A. H.
Limbacher, James L.
Linn, William Joseph
Rietz, John
Spinelli, Emily L.
Summers, Claude Joseph

Detroit
Aguirre, Robert D.
Barry, Michael
Bolz, Barbara J.
Boyd, Melba J.
Byars, Jackie L.
Calarco, N. Joseph
Crabtree, Clarie
Culik, Hugh
Dause, Charles A.
Dicks, Vivian I.
Farrow, J. G.
Freeman, John
Holley, Robert P.
Kelly, Justin J.
Koontz, Christian
Kowalczyk, Richard L.
Lahey, Christine
Latta, Susan M.
Lauer, Janice M.
Leland, Christopher
Levine, Bernard
Liebler, Michael L.
Madgett, Naomi Long
Marotti, Arthur Francis
McKendrick, Norman G.
McNamee, Kathleen
Mehaffey, Karen Rae
Mika, Joseph John
Miller, Jay
Powell, Ronald R.
Reed, John R.
Rombes, Nicholas
Ronnick, Michele Valerie
Sabino, Osvaldo R.
Scrivener, Michael Henry
Sheridan, Jennifer A.
Spinelli, Donald C.
Vlasopolos, Anca
Wagner, Vern
Wedberg, Lloyd W.
Williamson, Marilyn Lammert
Ziegelmueller, George W.

East Lansing
Athanason, Arthur Nicholas
Bresnahan, Roger J. Jiang
Bunge, Nancy Liddell
Donakowski, Conrad L.
Fernandez, Ramona E.
Fishburn, Katherine Richards
Fogel, Jerise
Francese, Joseph
Gochberg, Donald S.
Goodson, Alfred Clement
Greenberg, Bradley
Hudson, Robert Vernon
Julier, Laura S.
Landrum, Larry N.
LeBlanc, Albert
Lunde, Erik Sheldon
Mcguire, Philip Carroll
Meiners, Roger K.
Miller, Vernon D.
Noverr, Douglas Arthur
Paananen, Victor N.
Seadle, Michael S.
Shafer, Gregory
Sowards, Steven W.
Stockman, Ida J.
Uphaus, Robert Walter
Versluis, Arthur
Wakoski, Diane
Wright, Robert L.

Farmington Hills
Ali, Schari M.

Flint
Friesen, Lauren
Wisneski, Richard

Grand Rapids
Eberle, Gary M.
Jefchak, Andrew Timothy
Romanowski, William D.
Sandberg, Stephanie L.
Saupe, Karen E.
Schultze, Quentin J.

Hancock
Anderson, Laurie

Hillsdale
Discenza, Nicole Guenther
Whalen, David

Holland
Cox, John D.
Dove, Linda L.
Huttar, Charles Adolph
Pannapacker, William Albert
Peckham, Joel

Houghton
Gill, Glenda E.
Selfe, Richard J.
Sullivan, Dale L.

Kalamazoo
Bailey, Thomas Cullen
Borden, Sandra L.
Brinkley, Ellen H.
Carey-Webb, Allen
Davidson, Clifford Oscar
Dybek, Stuart
Gianakaris, Constantine John
Gibson, Melissa K.
Haight, Robert C.
Heller, Janet
Johnston, Arnold
Jones, Leander Corbin
Joslin, Katherine
Phillips, Romeo Eldridge
Saillant, John D.
Syndergaard, Larry E.
Szarmach, Paul E.
Washington, Von Hugo, Sr.

Kentwood
Sivier, Evelyn M.

Lansing
Fox, Hugh B.
McGiveron, Rafeeq O.

Livonia
Eyster, Kevin Irenies
Kearly, Peter R.
Schneider, Barbara J.

Marquette
Cantrill, James G.
Heldreth, Leonard Guy
Jones, James H.
Leuthold, Steven M.
Livingston, James L.
Payant, Katherine B.
Rose, Toby
Schiffer, James M.

Midland
Serum, Robert W.

Mount Pleasant
Alton, Anne
Apter, Ronnie
Buerkel-Rothfuss, Nancy
Craig, J. Robert
Dornan, Reade W.
Fulton, Henry Levan
Haines, Annette L.
Hughes, Diana L.
Kochhar-Lindgren, Gray M.
McCluskey, James J.
Murphy, Sean P.
Orlik, Peter B.
Pfeiffer, John R.
Root, Robert L., Jr.
Steffel, Susan B.
Walchak, Karol L.
Weinstock, Jeffrey A.

Okemos
Roberto, Anthony J.

Rochester
Eberwein, Jane Donahue
Fitzsimmons, Thomas
Horning, Alice S.
Murphy, Brian
Papazian, Mary A.
Sudol, Ronald A.
Wiggins, Jacqueline D.

Roscommon
La Femina, Gerard

Sault Ste. Marie
Fields, Polly Stevens

Spring Arbor
Daigle-Williamson, Marsha A.

University Center
Braddock, Robert Cook
Clark, Basil Alfred
Munn, Paul T.
Ramet, Carlos
Thompson, Gary
Wang, Mason Yu-Heng
Wignall, Dennis L.

Univesity Center
Riegle, Rosalie G.

West Bloomfield
Bertman, Stephen

Ypsilanti
Burlingame, Lori
Cross, Gilbert B.
Duncan, Jeffrey Light
Eiss, Harry Edwin
Geherin, David J.
George, Laura J.
Holoka, James P.
Knapp, James A.
McGlynn, Paul Dumon
Perkins, George
Shuter, Bill
Staal, Arie
Stevens, Lizbeth Jane

MINNESOTA

Apple Valley
O'Sullivan, Michael K.

Bemidji
Blackwood, Roy E.
Evans, Deanna G.
Mathewson, Dave L.

Collegeville
Drekonja, Otmar Maximilian
Freeman, Christopher Edward

Duluth
Adams, Stephen J.
Bock, Carol A.
Bock, Martin F.
Cole, Eve Browning
Hagen, Patricia
Linn, Michael D.
Lips, Roger C.
Zeitz, Eileen

Edina
Nash, Elizabeth

Mankato
Cronn-Mills, Daniel
Davis, Terry
Larsson, Donald
Lindberg, John

Marshall
Pichaske, David

Minneapolis
Babcock, William
Bales, Kent
Belifiore, Elizabeth S.
Brennan, Timothy A.
Brewer, Daniel
Brewer, Maria Minich
Browne, Donald R.
Cardamone, Donna
Chang, Tsan-Kuo
Clayton, Tom
Crain, Patricia
Faber, Ronald
Fang, Irving E.
Firchow, Peter Edgerly
Garcia, Hazel F. Dicken
Gidmark, Jill B.
Gillmor, Donald M.
Griffin, Edward M.
Hancher, Charles Michael
Hirsch, Gordon D.
Johnson, Willie J.
Kendall, Calvin B.
Kraabel, Alf Thomas
Krevans, Nita
Kuftinec, Sonja
Lardinois, Andre P. M. H.
Laudon, Robert Tallant
Lee, Chin-Chuan
Leyasmeyer, Archibald I.
Liu, Catherine
Malandra, William
Matsen, William
McNaron, Toni Ann Hurley
Norwood, James
Reed, Peter J.
Roberts, Nancy L.
Ross, Donald
Schwartz, Dona B.
Scott, Robert Lee
Sonkowsky, Robert Paul
Southall, Geneva H.
Sugnet, Charles Joseph
Thomas, Gary Craig
Tims, Albert R.
Underiner, Tamara
Vidal, Hernan
Wells, William D.
Winters, Donald
Yahnke, Robert Eugene

Moorehead
Larson, George S.

Moorhead
Buckley, Joan
Hanson, Colan T.
Iverson, Stanley
Sprunger, David A.

Northfield
Achberger, Karen Ripp
Barbour, John D.
Boling, Becky
Buckstead, Richard C.
Carpenter, Scott
Dust, Patrick
Freier, Mary P.
Groton, Anne H.
Kowalewski, Michael J.
May, James M.
Morral, Frank R.
Posfay, Eva
Reece, Steve
Soule, George
Strand, Dana
Taliaferro, Charles
Wadsworth, Sarah A.
Wee, David Luther
Wilkens, Kenneth G.
Wilkie, Nancy C.
Yandell, Cathy M.

Owatonna
Lyda, Paul

Rochester
Penniston, Joyce K.

Roseville
Gross, Alan G.
Sauter, Kevin O.

Saint Cloud
Dillman, Richard H.
Roman-Morales, Belen

Saint Paul
Baer, Joel H.
Brown, Carole Ann
Duin, Ann Hill
Frazier, Leta J.
Gaskill, Gayle
Glancy, Diane
Griffin, Michael S.
Gurak, Laura J.
Hensley, Carl Wayne
Hicks, Patrick
Jensen, J. Vernon
Lay, Mary M.
MacKenzie, Raymond
McDowell, Earl E.
McFarland, Douglas D.
Mikelonis-Paraskov, Victoria M.
Mulcahy, Gregory
Philipon, Daniel J.
Pollard, Tanya Louise
Reece, Debra J.
Reichardt, Mary R.
Scanlan, Thomas
Smith, L. Ripley
St. Amant, Kirk R.
Wahlstrom, Billie J.
Walzer, Arthur E.
Westermeyer, Paul
Wright, Michelle M.
Zurakowski, Michele M.

Saint Peter
Flory, Marleen Boudreau
Flory, Stewart Gilman
Freiert, William K.

Wayzata
Howe, Sondra Wieland

Winona
Carducci, Jane
Cowgill, Kent
Grawe, Paul H.
Hayes, Douglas W.
Nichols, James
Wilson, Lisa Marie

MISSISSIPPI

Clinton
Fant, Gene C., Jr.
Lytal, Billy D.
Miller, David G.

Columbus
Smith, Gail K.

Hattiesburg
Bradley, Doris P.
Clark, Mark E.
Harvey, Tamara
Kolin, Philip
Langstraat, Lisa R.
Lares, Jameela
Meyer, John
Polk, Noel E.
Sims, James Hylbert

Holly Springs
Chapman, Norman

Blackwood
Murphey, Kathleen

Caldwell
Kramer, Jennifer

Camden
Barbarese, J. T.
Bowden, Betsy
Cornelia, Marie E.
Fitter, Chris
Lutz, William
Martin, Timothy
Mccolley, Diane K.
Sill, Geoffrey M.
Singley, Carol J.

Cranford
Pizzo, Joseph S.

Dayton
Adickes, Sandra Elaine

Edison
Manogue, Ralph Anthony

Elizabeth
Siegel, Adrienne

Englewood
Lee, William L.

Glassboro
Coulombe, Joseph L.
Doskow, Minna
Grupenhoff, Richard
Haba, James
Kaleta, Kenneth C.
Patrick, Barbara
Penrod, Diane
Viator, Timothy J.
Vitto, Cindy

Hackettstown
Grigsby, Bryon L.

Hewitt
Mollenkott, Virginia Ramey

Highland Park
Edmunds, Lowell

Hoboken
Foster, Edward H.

Iselin
Caffrey, Raymond T.

Jackson
Cappucci, Paul R.

Jersey City
Finn, Margaret R.
Hamilton, Harlan
Kharpertian, Theodore
Luhr, William
Lynch, Thomas Patrick
Mintz, Kenneth A.
Schmidtberger, Loren F.
Watson, John Clifton

Lakewood
Chinery, Mary
Holian, Gail

Lawrenceville
Mcleod, Alan L.
Onyshkevych, Larissa M. L. Z.

Lebanon
Callander, Marilyn Berg

Lodi
Castellitto, George

Madison
Bicknell, John W.
Cummins, Walter M.
Goodman, Michael B.
Green, Martin
Keyishian, Harry
Lenz, John Richard
Skaggs, Merrill Maguire
Steiner, Joan Elizabeth
Weimer, Joan Myers

Mahwah
Alaya, Flavia M.

Maplewood
Higgins, William E.

Montclair
Metcalf, William E.
Mintz, Donald
Newman, Geoffrey W.

Morristown
Marlin, John
Sand, R. H.

New Brunswick
Adams, Kimberly V.
Attridge, Derek
Barnett, Louise
Belton, John
Blumenthal, Eileen
Bodel, John
Chandler, Daniel Ross
Charney, Maurice Myron
Crane, Susan
Crozier, Alice Cooper
Davidson, Harriet
DeKoven, Marianne
Diamond, Elin
Dowling, William C.
Edwards, Brent Hayes
Flitterman-Lewis, Sandy
Fortenbaugh, William Wall
Galperin, William
George, Kearns
Gibson, Donald Bernard
Gliserman, Martin
Gossy, Mary S.
Guetti, James L.
Habib, M. A. Rafey
Harris, Daniel A.
Hoffman, Tyler B.
Jehlen, Myra
Lears, T. J. Jackson
Levine, George L.
Lyons, Bridget G.
Maman, Marie
Matro, Thomas G.
McClure, John
McKeon, Michael
Mull, Donald L.
Ostriker, Alicia
Qualls, Barry V.
Robbins, Bruce
Roberts, Brian
Ruben, Brent David
Ryan, Robert M.
Smith, Carol Hertzig
Stauffer, George B.
Stroffolino, Chris
Vesterman, William
Walling, William
Warner, Michael D.
Welsh, Andrew

New Jersey
Avins, Styra

Newark
Baker, David
Coppola, Nancy
Crew, Louie
Foley, Barbara
Franklin, H. Bruce
Hadas, Rachel
Heffernan, Carol F.
Hirschberg, Stuart
Kimmelman, Burt
Lamay, J. Leo
Leubsdorf, John
Lyngstad, Sverre
Miller, Gabriel
Tiger, Virginia Marie
Watts, Ann Chalmers

Newton
Carducci, Eleanor

Paramus
Kievitt, F. David
Sadock, Geoffrey

Piscataway
Ellis, Katherine

Pomona
Schwartz, Mimi J.

Princeton
Aarsleff, Hans
Bartow, Charles L.
Drewry, Cecelia Hodges
Dubrovsky, Gertrude
Fagles, Robert
Fantham, Elaine
Howarth, William L.
Jeffery, Peter
Kaster, Robert A.
Keaney, John J.
Knoepflmacher, U. C.
Kosar, Anthony J.
Leaver, Robin A.
Litz, Arthur Walton
Ludwig, Richard Milton
Makino, Yasuko
Martin, Janet Marion
Martinez, Yolanda
McLaughlin, Kevin P.
Morrison, Simon
Mulvihill, Maureen E.
Rampersad, Arnold
Rigolot, Francois
Schor, Esther
Showalter, Elaine
Tate, Claudia
Webb, Ruth H.
Wildberg, Christian

Randolph
Levy, Stephen
Zulauf, Sander W.

Somerville
Bezanson, Mark

South Orange
Gray, Jeffrey
MacPhee, Laurence Edward
Zalacain, Daniel

Summit
Jooma, Minaz
Sherry, Lee F.

Teaneck
Becker, John
Gordon, Lois G.
Manganaro, Elise Salem
Rye, Marilyn
Shapiro, Susan

Toms River
Willetts, Elizabeth M.

Trenton
Halpern, Sheldon
Konkle, Lincoln Ernest
Sethi, Robbie Clipper
Sullivan, Jack R.

Union
Crew, H.
Mulling, Sylvia S.

Upper Montclair
Brewton, Butler E.
Gencarelli, Thomas F.

Wayne
Araujo, Luisa
Hand, Sally Nixon
Liu, T.
Radford, Gary P.
Wertheim, Stanley Claude
Williams, Bruce

West Long Branch
Dell, Chad E.

NEW MEXICO

Albuquerque
Aleman, Jesse
Bartlett, Lee
Beene, Lynn Dianne
Block, Steven
Damico, Helen
Dunaway, David K.
Fischer, Michael
Fleming, Robert
Fresch, Cheryl
Gaines, Barry
Gibson, Dirk C.
Gish, Robert F.
Harrison, Gary
Hermann, Richard
Johnson-Sheehan, Richard
Lindskold, Jane M.
Mares, E. A.
Marquez, Antonio
Martin, Wanda
Martinez, Nancy Conrad
McPherson, David
Melada, Ivan
Morris, David B.
Power, Mary
Sanders, Scott P.
Schaefer, Richard J.
Shultis, Christopher
Smith, Pat Clark
Thorson, James Llewellyn
Torres, Hector
Uscher, Nancy
Whidden, Mary Bess
White, Peter
Witemeyer, Hugh
Woodward, Carolyn

Gallup
Dyc, Gloria

Las Cruces
Crabtree, Robbin D.
Zakahi, Walter R.

Mankato
Mink, Joanna

Portales
Berne, Stanley
Williamson, John Stewart

Santa Fe
Clubbe, John
Zants, Emily

Silver City
Gutierrez, Donald
Juszcyk, Frank
Toth, Bill

NEW YORK

Albany
Barlow, Judith Ellen
Barnard, Sylvia
Burian, Jarka Marsano
Cooren, Francois
Fetterley, Judith
Hartman, C.
Hill, Mike K.
Joris, Pierre
Kendall, Kathleen E.
Laroche, Roland Arthur
Lawrence, Samuel G.
Maclean, Hugh Norman
Morehead, Joseph Hyde
Noller, David K.
Pohlsander, Hans Achim
Salomon, Herman Prins
Sanders, Robert E.
Smith, Karen A.
Strelka, Joseph Peter
Valentis, Mary Arensberg
Wills, David
Yalkut, Carolyn

Amherst
LaHood, Marvin John

Annandale
Sourian, Peter

Aurora
Bogel, Fredric V.
Burroughs, Catherine

Ballston Spa
Barba, Harry

Bayside
Camus, Raoul F.

Binghamton
Brackett, David
Carpenter, Charles Albert
Fajardo, Salvador J.
Freimarck, Vincent
Glenny, Sharon
Hanson, John
Levin, Saul
Lincoln, Harry B.
Reardon, Colleen
Silverberg, Carol
Spanos, William
Tricomi, Albert Henry
Vos, Alvin
Webster, Grant T.
Young, Cynthia A.

Brockport
Anderson, Floyd D.
Crume, Alice L.
Gemmett, Robert J.
Hale, David George
Madden, Kate
Maier, John
Marchant, Peter L.
Reed, Bill
Tollers, Vincent Louis

Bronx
Antush, John V.
Arzoomanian, Ralph Sarkis
Barnes, Sue
Blot, David
Boon, Kevin A.
Boyle, Frank T.
Bullaro, Grace Russo
Clowers, Marsha L.
Dobson, Joane
Erler, Mary C.
Fergenson, Laraine R.
Frank, Mortimer Henry
Giannone, Richard
GoGwilt, Christopher
Hall, N. John
Hallett, Charles A.
Hill, W. Speed
Kearns, Francis E.
Kiernan, Robert F.
Kligerman, Jack
Kubis, Theresa S.
Losada, Luis Antonio
Mbabuike, Michael C.
Penella, Robert J.
Pirraglia, Elvira
Pitchford, Nicola
Rowe, Joyce A.
Stadler, Eva Maria
Strate, Lance
Swiontkowski, Gale
Taylor, Mark
Valgemae, Mardi
Watkins-Goffman, Linda
Westrem, Scott D.
Wosk, Julie

Bronx Bronx
Weiser, David K.

Bronxville
Bodling, Kurt A.
Krupat, Arnold
Lauinger, Joseph

Brooklyn
Ashley, Leonard R. N.
Baumbach, Jonathan
Beckson, Karl
Bernard, Kenneth
Black, Nancy BreMiller
Browne, William Francis
Bruffee, Kenneth Allen
Doloff, Steven
Erickson, Gregory T.
Filer, Malva Esther
Fjelde, Rolf Gerhard
Fox, Robert Charles
Fry, Katherine G.
Gargan, William M.
Gelernt, Jules
Greaves, Gail-Ann
Halpern, Martin
Hirsch, Julia
Kelly, Ernece Beverly
Kitts, Thomas M.
Kleinberg, Seymour
Kotzin, Joshua Boaz
Kramer, Maurice
Langley, Stephen G.
Leiter, Samuel Louis
Lvovich, Natasha
Martinez, Inez A.
McLaughlin, Andree Nicola
Meyler, Joan Bernadette
O'Malley, Susan Gushee

Geographic Index

Lake Prescott, Anne
Lamb, Margaret
Leibowitz, Herbert
Levin, Jonathan
Lin, Yi-chun Tricia
Lippman, Edward
Lockridge, Laurence Shockley
Loney, Glenn Meredith
Low, Anthony
Low, Lisa
Lowrie, Michele
Lubetski, Edith
Macchiarulo, Louis
Macovski, Michael
Magnuson, Paul Andrew
Mapp, Edward C.
Marcus, Steven
Margolies, Alan
Margulies, Ivone
Marincola, John
Mason, Bobbie Ann
Maynard, John Rogers
Meisel, Perry H.
Mendelson, Edward
Middendorf, John Harlan
Miller, Daisy Sophia
Miller, Edwin Haviland
Miller, Joshua L.
Minkoff, Harvey
Mohsen, Raed
Morris, Virginia Baumgartner
Morrison, Toni
Mueller, Claus
Munker, Dona Feldman
Neaman, Judith S.
Nixon, Rob
Nunes, Zita
O'Conell, Robert J.
O'Meally, Robert
Oppenheimer, Paul
Pappano, Margaret
Parisi, Peter
Parker, Mary
Parker-Starbuck, Jennifer
Penceal, Bernadette Whitley
Perkins, Leeman Lloyd
Peters, Francis Edward
Peters, Julie
Peterson, R. G.
Phillips, Louis
Pinedo, Isabel
Poirier, Richard
Prescott, Anne L.
Prior, Sandra Pierson
Quigley, Austin E.
Quigley, Austin F.
Rajagopal, Arvind
Ricke, Joseph M.
Ringer, Mark
Rollyson, Carl E., Jr.
Romm, James S.
Rosenberg, John D.
Rosenthal, Michael
Rubin, Andrew M.
Said, Edward
Saloman, Ora Frishberg
Scaglione, Aldo
Scammell, Michael
Schaafsma, David
Scharffenberger, Elizabeth Watson
Schechner, Richard
Scheeder, Louis
Scherzinger, M.
Schirmeister, Pamela J.
Schmemann, S.
Schoen, Carol Bronston
Seidel, Michael Alan
Seymour, Deborah M.
Shapiro, James S.
Sharma, Vishnu
Shugrue, Michael F.
Sicker, Philip
Siegel, Paul N.
Silver, Carole Greta
Silverman, Kenneth Eugene
Simmons, Diane
Slade, Carole
Snyder, Emery
Spivak, Gayatri Chakravorty
Stade, George
Stimpson, Catharine R.
Stuber, Florian
Swann, Brian
Sypher, Francis Jacques
Tanselle, George Thomas
Taran, Leonardo
Tayler, Edward W.
Terry, James L.
Thomas, Joseph M.
Thompson, Jewel T.
Torres, Louis
Tuttleton, James Wesley
Ulanov, Barry
Ulen, Elisa Nefertari
Umeh, Marie A.
Urkowitz, Steven
Viswanathan, Gauri
Wallenstein, Barry
Wardrope, William J.
Wasser, Henry H.
Weidhorn, Manfred
Weiner, Estha
Weinreich, Regina
White, Deborah
Wilkerson, Margaret Buford
Williams, Gareth D.
Williams, John Alfred
Wittreich, Joseph Anthony, Jr
Wohlgelernter, Maurice
Woodring, Carl
Yerkes, David
Young, Jane J.
Zagano, Phyllis
Zuker, Joel

Newburgh
Cotter, James Finn
Saldivar, Toni

Niagara Univ
Pinti, Daniel J.

North Syracuse
Boudreau, Gordon V.

Nyack
Isang, S. Akpan

Oakdale
Poppiti, Kim

Oakland Gardens
Fonesca, Terezinha

Old Westbury
Hobson, Christopher
Reynolds, David S.

Oneonta
Beattie, Thomas Charles
Devlin, James E.
Lilly, Paul R., Jr.
Meanor, Patrick
Morgan, Eileen M.
Travisano, Thomas J.
Walker, Charlotte Zoe

Oswego
Fisher, John C.
Hill, David
Knapp, John A., II
Loe, Thomas Benjamin
Loveridge-Sanbonmatsu, Joan
Messere, Frank
O'Shea, Edward
Schaber, Bennet
Smith, John Kares
Sweetser, Wesley Duaine
Woodall, Natalie Joy

Pittsford
Albright, Daniel

Plains
Larson, Richard Leslie

Plattsburgh
Burde, Edgar J.
Butterfield, Bruce A.
Corodimas, Peter
Davis, Ron
Groth, Janet
Johnston, Paul
Kiefer, Lauren
Kutzer, M. Daphne
Levitin, Alexis
Morrissey, Thomas J.
Shout, John
Tracy, Ann B.
Wilson, Hugh F.

Pleasantville
Anstendig, Linda
Coupe, Lynda

Port Washington
Muller, Gilbert Henry
Schroeder, Christopher L.

Potsdam
Brady, Owen E.
Coleman, Mark
Funston, Judith
Johnson-Eilola, Johndan
Ratliff, Gerald Lee
Serio, John N.
Subramanian, Jane M.
Weise, Judith Anderson

Poughkeepsie
DeMaria, Robert, Jr.
Foster, Donald W.
Imbrie, Ann Elizabeth
Libin, Kathryn
Mann, Brian
Pisani, Michael

Purchase
Grebstein, Sheldon Norman
Lemire, Elise V.
Waller, Gary F.
Yelin, Louise

Quaker Street
Black, Steve

Ridgewood
Constantinou, Constantia

Riverdale
Brennan, Anne Denise
Noone, Pat
Smith, Barbara

Rochester
Baldo, Jonathan
Bleich, David
Cartwright, Lisa
Cherchi-Usai, Paolo
Dooley, Deborah
Eaves, Morris
Freedman-Baum, Roselyn L.
Gollin, Richard M.
Grella, George
Gross, Kenneth
Hahn, Thomas George O'Hara
Haverly, Thomas
Higley, Sarah
Howard, Hubert Wendell
Ishman, Sybil R.
Johnson, James William
Kegl, Rosemary
Kowalke, Kim H.
Levy, Anita
Lipscomb, Drema Richelle
Locke, Ralph Paul
London, Bette
Longenbach, James
Lupack, Alan
Lylak, Eugene
Madigan, Mark J.
Mann, Alfred
Marvin, Elizabeth W.
McKenzie, Stanley D.
Michael, John
Middleton, Joyce Irene
Peck, Russell A.
Ramsey, Jarold
Rodowick, David N.
Rosenthal, Peggy
Shuffelton, Frank
Sullivan, Mary C., RSM
Thym, Jurgen
Voloshin, Beverly R.
Wason, Robert W.

Rushville
Kane, Peter

Saint Bonaventure
Farrow, Anthony
Martine, James John
Williams, Penny

Sanborn
Liu, Yu

Saratoga Springs
Boyers, Robert
Cahn, Victor L.
Casey, James Galligami
Ciancio, Ralph Armando
Goldensohn, Barry
Lewis, Thomas Spottswood Wellford
Porter, David H.
Roth, Phyllis Ann
Simon, Linda

Schenectady
Mace, Sarah
Scullion, Scott
Sorum, Christina Elliott
Toher, Mark
Wineapple, Brenda

Selden
Becker, Lloyd George

Sound Beach
Elkin, Robert Terrell

Southampton
Ganesan, Indira
Garcia-Gomez, Jorge
Haynes, Jonathan

Sparkill
McCarthy, Gerald

Staten Island
Feola, Maryann
Seminara, Gloria
Simpson, Peter P.

Stone Ridge
Corrales, Edwin

Stony Brook
Beaufort, Anne
Bottigheimer, Ruth B.
Burner, David B.
Czerwinski, Edward J.
Davidson, Cynthia A.
Fuller, Sarah
Gardaphe, Fred L.
Godfrey, Aaron W.
Goldenberg, Robert
Huffman, Clifford Chalmers
Levin, Richard L.
Levine, Richard Allan
Manning, Peter J.
Sanders, Ivan
Scheps, Walter
Sprinker, Michael
Zimbardo, Rose A.

Suffern
Bay, Libby
Wilson, Robert J.

Syracuse
Bonesteel, Margaret D.
Butler, Katharine G.
Comstock, George Adolphe
Crowley, John W.
Doherty, Karen A.
Echeruo, Michael
Edwards, Mary Louise
Hovendick, Kelly B.
Lambert, Gregg
Lloyd, David T.
Milac, Metod M.
Milosky, Linda M.
Novelli, Cornelius
Olin-Ammentorp, Julie
Phillips, Kendall R.
Prieve, Beth A.
Shires, Linda M.
Shoemaker, Pamela J.
Sternlicht, Sanford
Watson, Charles N., Jr.
Wetherbee Phelps, Louise
Wiecek, William Michael
Wiley, Raymond A.
Wright, Roosevelt R., Jr.
Zavarzadeh, Mas'ud

Tarrytown
Goldin, Milton

Teaneck
Dick, Bernard F.

Troy
Halloran, Stephen Michael

Utica
Bergmann, Frank
Gifford, James J.
Labuz, Ronald
Nassar, Eugene Paul
Searles, George J.

Valhalla
Costanzo, William Vincent
Courage, Richard A.

Vestal
Jackson, Allan Stuart
Manso, Leira Annette

Wayne
Rosen, Robert Charles

West Point
Hartle, Anthony E.

Williamsville
Glazier, Loss Pequeno

NORTH CAROLINA

Asheville
Malicote, S.
McGlinn, Jeanne
Mills, Sophie J.
Moseley, Merritt

Banner Elk
Joslin, Michael E.

Black Mountain
Matin, A. Michael

Boone
Dorgan, Howard
Hay, Fred J.
Rupp, Richard
Williamson, J. W.

Brevard
White, Robert A.

Chapel Hill
Anderson, Thomas Jefferson
Blansfield, Karen C.
Breen, Marcus
Broughton, Thomas Robert Shannon
Calhoun, Richard James
Connor, Carolyn
Dessen, Alan Charles
Dessen, Cynthia Sheldon
Eaton, Charles Edward
Eble, Connie C.
Emerson, Everett
Finson, Jon William
Flora, Joseph M.
Grossberg, Lawrence
Haar, James
Harris, Trudier
Hobson, Fred C.
Houston, George W.
Jackson, Blyden
Linderski, Jerzy
Mack, Sara
McGowan, John P.
Moran, Barbara B.
Pollock, Della
Powers, Doris Bosworth
Race, William H.
Raper, Julius R.
Rust, Richard Dilworth
Schultz, Heidi M.
Shaw, Donald Lewis
Smith, Rebekah M.
Smither, Howard Elbert
Stadter, Philip Austin
Strauss, Albrecht Benno
Taylor, Beverly W.
Weiss, Michael L.
West, William C., III
Wittig, Joseph Sylvester
Wood, Julia T.
Wooten, Cecil W.
Worth, Fabienne Andre

Charlotte
Crane, Jon
Davis, Christopher
Doerfel, Marya L.
Gaide, Tanure
Gavran, James Holt

Geographic Index

Elyria
Owens, Suzanne
Weigl, Bruce

Gambier
Bennett, Robert E.
Finke, L. A.
Heuchemer, Dane
Klein, William Francis
McCulloh, William Ezra
Sharp, Ronald Alan
Turner, Frederick
Weber, Clifford Whitbeck

Granville
Baker, David Anthony
Miller, Gill Wright
Townsend, Ann

Hamilton
Friedenberg, Robert Victor
Inness, Sherrie A.
Krafft, John M.
Womack, Whitney

Highland Hills
Badal, James J.

Hudson
Dyer, Joyce

Huron
Currie, William W.
Smith, Larry

Kent
Andrews, Larry Ray
Apseloff, Marilyn Fain
Bank, Rosemarie Katherine
Davis, Thomas M.
Dooley, Allan C.
Fontes, Manuel D.
Fried, Lewis Fredrick
Hakutani, Yoshinobu
Hassler, Donald M.
Krause, Sydney Joseph
Larson, Orville K.
Marovitz, Sanford E.
McCormick, Edgar Lindsley
Rubin, Rebecca B.
Wheeler, Arthur M.

Kirtland
Johnston, Stanley Howard

Lancaster
Killoran, Helen

Lima
Anspaugh, Kelly C.
Hellmann, John M.

Marietta
O'Donnell, Mabry Miller

New Concord
Schultz, William J.

Newark
Loucks, James F.
Tebben, Joseph Richard

North Canton
Horvath, Brooke

Oberlin
Albright, Ann Cooper
Alexander, Pamela
Erwin, Joanne
Ganzel, Dewey Alvin
Gorfain, Phyllis
Goulding, Daniel J.
Helm, James Joel
Jones, Nicholas
Koch, Christian Herbert
Lubben, Joseph
Plank, Steven E.
Rogers, Lynne
Rothstein, William
Walker, David
Young, David
Zagarell, Sandra Abelson

Orrville
Johanyak, Debra L.

Oxford
Branch, Edgar Marquess
Brock, James W.
Clark, James Drummond
Coakley, Jean Alexander
Dolan, Frances E.
Erlich, Richard D.
Fox, Alice
Fritz, Donald Wayen
Fryer, Judith
Frymier, Ann Bainbridge
Fuller, Mary J.
Harwood, Britton James
Rose, Peter Wires
Sosnoski, James Joseph
Tidwell, John Edgar
Trent, Jimmie Douglas
Wortman, William A.
Wright, Deborah Kempf
Wright, H. Bunker

Painesville
Lunardi, Egidio

Pepper Pike
Glavac, Cynthia
Podis, Joanne

Portsmouth
Dillard, J. L.
Field, Michael J.
Powell, Michael

Salem
Figg, Kristen Mossler

Shaker Heights
Miller, Clement Albin

Shaker Hts
Giannetti, Louis Daniel

Springfield
Ashworth, Suzanne M.
Davis, Robert Leigh
Dixon, Mimi S.
Faber, J. Arthur
Inboden, Robin L.
Jones, Mary Ellen
Otten, Terry Ralph
Veler, Richard

Steubenville
Lyons, Declan P.
Sunyoger, Mary Ann

Toledo
Barden, Thomas
Dessner, Lawrence Jay
Gregory, Elmer Richard
Kydd, Elspeth
Manheim, Michael
Many, Paul
Moskovitz, Marc
Riebling, Barbara
Rudolph, Robert Samuel
Smith, David Quintin
Watermeier, Daniel J.
Wikander, Matthew H.

Toronto
Marbais, Peter C.

University Heights
Nevin, Thomas R.

Warren
Yoke, Carl B.

Westerville
Eisenstein, Paul S.
Woodson, Thomas

Wilberforce
Fleissner, Robert F.

Willoughby
Coughlin, Robert M.

Wooster
Bostdorff, Denise M.
Christianson, Paul
Frye, Joanne S.
Grace, Nancy
Herring, Henry
Holliday, Vivian Loyrea
Shostak, Debra
Stewart, Larry
Wright, Josephine

Yellow Springs
Filemyr, Ann
Hussman, Lawrence
Rinehart, John

Youngstown
Bowers, Bege K.
Brown, Steven
Harrison, W. Dale
Issac, Megan
Shale, Rick

OKLAHOMA

Ada
Sukholutskaya, Mara

Bethany
Bracken, Pamela

Chickasha
Brown, Brenda

Claremore
Dial-Driver, Emily

Cleveland
Rollins, Peter

Edmond
Hayes, Kevin J.
Lehman, Paul Robert
Lewis, Gladys S.

Enid
Bowers, Paul

Norman
Byre, Calvin S.
Dharwadker, Aparna
Fears, J. Rufus
Friedrich, Gustav William
Gross, David Stuart
Leitch, Vincent B.
Lewis, Mitchell R.
Purinton, Jeffrey S.
Velie, Alan R.

Oklahoma City
Thornton, Jeri

Shawnee
Hall, Larry Joe

Stillwater
Anderson, Eric Gary
Austin, Linda
Batteiger, Richard P.
Berkeley, David Shelley
Broadhead, Glenn J.
Decker, William
Grubgeld, Elizabeth
Leavell, Linda
Leff, Leonard J.
Lewis, Lisa
Mayer, Robert
Walker, Jeffrey
Walkiewicz, Edward P.
Wallen, Martin
Warren, Thomas

Tahlequah
Baker, Terri M.

Tulsa
de Almeida, Hermione
Deller, David C.
Latham, Sean
Palma, Ronald B.
Rapp, M. H. Kris
Sullivan, Paula
Taylor, Gordon Overton
Watson, James Gray
Weathers, Winston
Weston, Ruth Deason

Weatherford
Jones, Jill T.
Jones, Robin A.

OREGON

Albany
Jensen, Peter

Ashland
Maltz, Diana F.

Brookings
McCarren, Vincent Paul

Corvallis
Ahearn, Kerry
Anderson, Chris
Barbour, Richmond
Campbell, Elizabeth
Collins, Vicki
Copek, Peter Joseph
Daniels, Richard
Daugherty, Tracy
Davison, Neil
Ede, Lisa
Frank, Robert
Helle, Anita
Johnson, Simon
Leeson, Ted
Lewis, Jon
Oriard, Michael
Robinson, David
Schwartz, Robert Barnett
Wess, Robert

Eugene
Alley, Henry Melton
Bergquist, Peter
Biles, Zachary P.
Boren, James Lewis
Bowditch, Lowell
Brown, James Dale
Clark, Suzanne
Coleman, Edwin Leon, II
Dugaw, Dianne M.
Epple, Juan Armando
Frank, David A.
Grudin, Robert
Love, Glen A.
McLucas, Anne Dhu
Taylor, Donald Stewart
Tossa, Wajuppa
Westling, Louise Hutchings
Wickes, George
Wojcik, Daniel

La Grande
Venn, George

Marylhurst
Maiers, Joan

McMinnville
Drake, Barbara
Konick, Steve

Medford
Barret, Harold

Monmouth
Baker, Robert Samuel

Newberg
Ankeny, Rebecca T.

Pendleton
Grover, Dorys Crow

Portland
Callahan, John Francis
Carafiol, Peter
Cooper, John Rex
Covert, James Thayne
Fortier, Jan Marie
Giarelli, Andrew
Gradin, Sherrie L.
Hancock, Virginia
Hillis, Rick
Hunt, Steven B.
Knapp, Robert Stanley
Nicholson, Nigel
Sawaya, Francesca
Soldati, Joseph Arthur
Steinman, Lisa M.
Ward, Jean M.

Salem
Eddings, Dennis Wayne
Knorr, Ortwin

PENNSYLVANIA

Allentown
Fletcher, LuAnn McCracken
Prettiman, C. A.
Pulham, Carol Ann
Vos, Nelvin Leroy

Altoona
Petrulionis, Sandra H.

Ambler
Morse, Josiah Mitchell

Aston
McDonnell, Clare I.

Beaver Falls
Copeland, Robert M.
Szabo, Lynda

Bethlehem
Beidler, Peter Grant
Fifer, Elizabeth
Phillips, C. Robert, III
Stinson, Robert William

Bloomsburg
Bertelsen, Dale A.
Brasch, Walter Milton
Fuller, Lawrence Benedict
Smith, Riley Blake

Blue Bell
Scheponik, Peter C.

Bryn Athyn
Gladish, Robert Willis

Bryn Mawr
Bernstein, Carol L.
Burlin, Robert B.
Dean, Susan Day
Dickerson, Gregory Weimer
Kramer, Joseph Elliot

California
Korcheck, Robert
Murdick, William
Pagen, Michele A.
Thomas, C. R.
Waterhouse, Carole

Carlisle
Bullard, Truman
Johnston, Carol Ann
Lockhart, Philip N.
Nichols, Ashton
Rosen, Kenneth Mark
Schiffman, Joseph
Wilson, Blake

Chester
Danford, Robert E.
LeStourgeon, Diana E.

Collegeville
Decatur, Louis Aubrey
Lionarons, Joyce T.

Dallas
Blanchard, Scott
Johnson, Jeffrey

Doylestown
Corbett, Janice
Kuehl, Linda Kandel
Schmidt, Jack

Drexel Hill
Lent, John Anthony

Du Bois
Evans, Dale Wilt
McCarthy, William B.

Dunmore
Daniels, Marilyn
Dolis, John
Smith, Gayle Leppin

East Stroudsburg
Meyers, Ronald J.

Easton
Lusardi, James P.
Upton, Lee
Walls, Laura Dassow
Woolley, James
Ziolkowski, Eric Jozef

Edinboro
Drane, James Francis
Howell, Allen C.

Elkins Park
Puchek, Peter A.

Ellwood City
Lambert, Lynda J.

Erie
Baldwin, Dean
Minot, Walter
O'Leary, Brian Eugene

Gettysburg
Barnes, Dorothy
Fredrickson, Robert Stewart
Winans, Robert B.

Glenside
Bracy, William

Greensburg
Toler, Colette

Grove City
Kring, Hilda Adam

Gwynedd Valley
Duclow, Donald F.

Hanover
Capps, Jack L.

Harrisburg
Graham, Theodora Rapp
Qi, Shouhua
Woods, Willie G.
Young, James A.

Haverford
Gillis, Daniel J.
Knauer, Georg Nicolaus
Russo, Joseph Anthony
Williams, Roland L.

Hazleton
Kemmerer, Kathleen
Price, Alan

Huntingdon
Doyle, Esther M.

Indiana
Ault, C. Thomas
Kilwein-Guevara, Maurice A.
Murphy, Patrick Dennis
Rodriguez, Lydia H.
Shafer, Ronald G.
Slater, Thomas J.

Johnstown
Mock, Michele L.

Kutztown
Huang, Guiyou
Laubach, David C.
Newman, Arnold E.
Nigro, August John
Okafor, Dubem

La Plume
Wheeler, Wayne R.

Lancaster
Farber, Jay Joel
Grushow, Ira
Pinsker, Sanford S.
Steinbrink, Jeffrey

Latrobe
Clough, Wulfstan

Lewisburg
Baumwoll, Dennis
Holzberger, William George
Padilla, Mark
Payne, Michael

Lincoln University
Rowe, Patsy Baxter
Willis, Gladys January

Lock Haven
Coltrane, Robert
Hybels, Saundra
Jenkins, Charles M.

Lumberville
Fallon, Robert Thomas

Mansfield
Gertzman, Jay Albert
Hindman, Kathleen Behrenbruch
Uffelman, Larry Kent

McKeesport
Frushell, Richard Clayton

Meadville
Nesset, Kirk
Rose, Judith
Thorson, Connie C.
Zolbrod, Paul Geyer

Media
Kessler, Carol
Markley, Arnold A.
McMullen, Wayne
Sorkin, Adam J.

Middletown
Johnson, Patricia E.
Tischler, Nancy Marie
Viser, Victor J.

Millersville
Carballo, Robert
Duncan, Bonnie I.
Hopkins, Leroy Taft, Jr.
Miller, Steven Max
Schneller, Beverly
Shields, Kenneth

Monaca
Gall, John
Marshall, Cynthia

Munhall
Tobin, Thomas J.

New Kensington
Rubin, L.

New Wilmington
Horvath, Cary W.
Macky, Nancy
McTaggart, William
Perkins, James Ashbrook
Pitman, Grover A.
Sprow, Richard
Swerdlow, David G.

Newton
Huberman, Elizabeth Lyle

Newtown
Bursk, Christopher
Freeman, James A.

Newtown Square
Myrsiades, Linda

Philadelphia
Baker, C. Edwin
Beckman, Richard
Bentman, Raymond
Bernstein, Lawrence F.
Butler, James Albert
Cappella, Joseph N.
Cohen, Eileen Z.
Curran, Stuart Alan
DeLaura, David Joseph
Donahue, Thomas John
DuPlessis, Rachel Blau
Feeney, Joseph John
Frye, Roland Mushat
Fusco, Richard A.
Gilman, Owen W.
Graham, A. John
Greenberg, Robert M.
Greenburg, Mark Lawrence
Harty, Kevin John
Himelstein, Morgan Y.
Hoffman, Daniel
Hunt, John Dixon
Jackson, Arlene M.
Karcher, Carolyn Lury
Korshin, Paul J.
Lebofsky, Dennis Stanley
Letzring, Monica
Levitt, Morton Paul
Lucid, Robert Francis
Lyons, Timothy James
Mallin, Dea Z.
Mannino, Mary Ann V.
Marsilio, Maria S.
Mazer, Cary M.
Mellen, Joan
Meyer, Leonard B.
Mitchell, Sally
Mitchell-Boyask, Robin N.
Morris, Francis J.
Nishimura-Jensen, Julie M.
Norberg, Peter
O'Donnell, James J.
Orvell, Miles
Paglia, Camille
Parker, Jo Alyson
Perelman, Bob
Railton, Benjamin A.
Rainey, Penelope
Richetti, John J.
Samway, Patrick H.
Soven, Margot
Steiner, Wendy Lois
Tasch, Peter Anthony
Tigay, Jeffrey Howard
Turner, Robert Y.
Turow, Joseph G.
Weales, Gerald
Wendling, Ronald Charles
Wenzel, Siegfried
Wilde, Alan
Wolf, Eugene Kendrick
Wolper, Roy S.
Woodard, Emory H., IV
Zimmerman, Franklin B.

Pittsburgh
Arac, Jonathan
Arnett, Ronald C.
Avery, Harry Costas
Bernstein, Jane
Brockmann, Stephen
Carr, Stephen Leo
Clack, Jerry
Davis, Nathan T.
Downing, David
Edwards, Clark
Flower, Linda S.
Floyd, Edwin Douglas
Gaichas, Lawrence Edward
Glazener, Nancy K.
Groch, John R.
Hamilton, Carol Van der Veer
Hart, John Augustine
Hayes, Ann Louise
Helfand, Michael S.
Hopper, Paul
Howard, Susan K.
Knapp, James Franklin
Knapp, Peggy Ann
Kurland, Stuart M.
Labriola, Albert C.
Landy, Marcia
Lenz, William Ernest
Liu, Yameng
Martin, Sean Elliot
Masters, Hilary
Mcshea, William Patrick
Miller, Andrew M.
Newberry, Frederick
Newberry, Ruth E.
Newmyer, Stephen Thomas
Olsen, Lester C.
Root, Deane Leslie
Seitz, James E.
Shumway, David R.
Smethurst, Mae J.
St. Clair, Gloriana
Steinberg, Erwin Ray
Straub, Kristina
Tobias, Richard C.
Vardy, Agnes Huszar
Venarde, Bruce L.
West, Michael Davidson
Wilkens, Ann
Wion, Philip Kennedy
Yaruss, J. Scott
Young, Michael
Young, Richard E.

Pottstown
Bender, Henry V.

Reading
Cacicedo, Alberto Jesus
Feinstein, Sandy
Law, Richard
Peemoeller, Helen C.

Saint Davids
Bittenbender, J. Christopher
Cherry, Caroline Lockett
Morgan, Betsy

Schuykill Haven
Vickers, Anita M.

Scranton
Beal, Rebecca S.
Casey, Ellen Miller
DeRitter, Jones
Friedman, Michael D.
Gougeon, Len G.
Wilson, Joseph P.

Selinsgrove
Chabora, Pamela
Wilson, Rebecca A.

Sharon
Berland, Kevin Joel

Shavertown
Lennon, J. Michael

Shippensburg
Brofman, Mikita
McFarland, Katharine

Slippery Rock
Bass, Eben E.
Crafton, Robert E.
Curry, Elizabeth R.
Egan, Mary Joan
Lasarenko, Jane
McIlvaine, Robert Morton
Stewart, Thomas D.

Springfield
Malsbary, Gerald Henry

State College
Anderson, Roland F.
Bell, Bernard W.
Lyon, Janet W.
Pfaff, Daniel W.

Swarthmore
Blackburn, Thomas
Devin, Lee
Marissen, Michael
North, Helen Florence
Schmidt, Peter Jarrett
Skelnar, Robert John
Weinstein, Philip Meyer
Williamson, Craig B.

Uniontown
Hovanec, Evelyn Ann

University Park
Afifi, Walid A.
Astroff, Roberta J.
Begnal, Michael Henry
Benson, Thomas W.
Bialostosky, Don
Brasfield, James
Brockman, William S.
Broyles, Michael
Buckalew, Ronald Eugene
Cheney, Patrick
Clausen, Christopher
Ebbitt, Wilma Robb
Eckhardt, Caroline Davis
Engel, David M.
Hale, Thomas Albert
Hecht, Michael L.
Hogan, J. Michael
Holmes, Charlotte
Hume, Kathryn
Hume, Robert David
Jackson, Ronald, II
Kiernan, Michael Terence
Lankewish, Vincent A.
Lougy, Robert E.
Meserole, Harrison Talbot
Miller-Day, Michelle
Morrisson, Mark S.
Mulford, Carla J.
Oliver, Mary Beth
Secor, Robert Arnold
Walden, Daniel
Weintraub, Stanley
West, James L. W., III
Willumson, Glenn Gardner
Woodbridge, Linda

Upper Black Eddy
Regney, Gabrielle

Verona
Matthews, Jack

Villanova
Cherry, Charles L.
Delano, Sterling F.
Greene, Thomas R.
Heitzmann, William Ray
Hunt, John M., Jr.
Kinney, Joseph
Kirschke, James J.
Shyles, Leonard C.
Thomas, Deborah Allen

Washington
Troost, Linda V.

West Chester
Lavasseur, David G.

West Mifflin
Milne, Christopher

Wilkes-Barre
Bedford, Bonnie C.
Fields, Darin E.
Napieralski, Edmund Anthony
Valletta, Clement Lawrence

Williamsport
Vavra, Edward

York
Abudu, Gabriel
Barr, Jeanine R.
Collison, Gary L.
Jones, Edward T.
McGhee, James
Siegel, Gerald
Sutton, Jane
Vause, Deborah

PUERTO RICO

Bayamon
Guzman-Merced, Rosa Maria

Humacao
Darhower, Martin L.

Mayaguez
Hunt, Anthony

Rio Piedras
Pena, Juan A.

RHODE ISLAND

Adamsville
Lawrence, Elizabeth Atwood

Bristol
Hollingsworth, Anthony L.

Kingston
Chen, Guo-Ming
Culatta, Barbara
Gullason, Thomas Arthur
Jacobs, Dorothy Hieronymus
Ketrow, Sandra M.
Kovarsky, Dana
Kunz, Don
Maclaine, Allan Hugh
Miles, Libby
Stein, Karen F.

Providence
Barbour, Brian Mich
Blasing, Mutlu Ko
Boegehold, Alan
Curran, Sonia T
deBoo, Edwar

Delasanta, Rodney
Denniston, Dorothy L.
Fornara, Charles William
Gordon-Seifert, Catherine
Hennedy, John Francis
Hirsch, David Harry
Kahn, Coppelia
Konstan, David
McMunn, Maradith T.
Putnam, Michael C. J.
Raaflaub, Kurt A.
Reddy, Maureen T.
Robinson, William Henry
Rosenberg, Bruce
Scanlan, J. T.
Schapiro, Barbara
Scholes, Robert
Singh, Amritjit
Spilka, Mark
Stevens, Earl Eugene
Swift, Carolyn Ruth
Wilmeth, Don B.
Wyatt, William F.

Saunderstown
Waters, Harold A.

Smithfield
Kozikowski, Stanley John

Wakefield
Coffin, Tristram Potter

SOUTH CAROLINA

Aiken
Mack, S. Thomas
Roy, Emil L.

Allendale
Chilcote, Wayne L.

Anderson
Walker, Brena B.

Beaufort
Eby, Carl P.
Flannagan, Roy C.

Central
Marrus, Francine E.

Charleston
Heisser, David C. R.
Holbein, Woodrow Lee
Hunt, Caroline C.
Hutchisson, James M.
Leon, Philip Wheeler
Leonard, James S.
Reisman, Rosemary C.
Shields, David S.

Clemson
Andreas, James, Sr.
Barfield, Ray
Bell, Kimberly
Bennett, Alma
Bzdyl, Donald G.
Chapman, Wayne K.
Charney, Mark
Daniell, Beth
Dettmar, Kevin
Hilligoss, Susan
Howard, Tharon
Jacobi, Martin
Koon, G. W.
Longo, Bernadette
Lovitt, Carl
Morrissey, Lee J.
Palmer, Barton
Rollin, Lucy
Shilstone, Frederick William
Sparks, Elisa Kay
Underwood, Richard
Ward, Carol
Willey, Edward
Winchell, Donna
Winchell, Mark
Woodell, Harold
Yancy, Kathleen Blake
Young, Arthur P.

Clinton
McCabe, Nancy

Columbia
Briggs, Ward W.
Bruccoli, Matthew J.
Cowart, David
Davis, Marianna White
Dickey, James
Dillon, Bert
Edmiston, William F.
Elfe, Wolfgang Dieter
Farrar, Ronald
Feldman, Paula R.
Franklin, Benjamin
Grant, August E.
Greiner, Donald James
Hark, Ina Rae
Hynes, Jennifer
Layman, Richard
Lewis, Kevin
Little, Greta D.
Mathisen, Ralph Whitney
Myerson, Joel Arthur
Nolan, Edward Francis
Roy, G(eorge) Ross
Scott, Mary Jane W.
Scott, Patrick G.
Thesing, William Barney
Tuten, Nancy
Wimsatt, Mary Ann
Zoch, Lynn M.

Due West
Christie, N. Bradley

Florence
Tuttle, Jon

Greenville
Allen, Gilbert Bruce
Dobson, Jeannie S.
Gingery, Gail Alvah
Hill, Philip George
Horton, Ronald A.
Kindall, Susan Carol
Kuehmann, Karen Marie
Parker, Mark M.
Radel, Nicholas F.
Rogers, William E.

Greenwood
Bethel, Elizabeth Rauh

Hilton Head
Stehle, Cheryl F.

Holly Hill
Morant, Mack Bernard

Isle of Palms
Turner, Robert Kean

Newberry
O'Shea, Michael J.

Orangeburg
Harris, Gil W.
Johnson, Alex C.
Ratliff, Peggy S.
Wallace, Nathaniel
Washington, Sarah M.

Rock Hill
Click, J. William
Weaver, Jack Wayne
Woods, Jeannie Marlin

Spartanburg
Bullard, John Moore
Carson, Warren Jason, Jr.
Crosland, Andrew Tate
Shand, Rosa
Stevenson, John Weamer

Tigerville
Collier, Cheryl

SOUTH DAKOTA

Aberdeen
Hastings, A. Waller
Ruud, Jay
Whiteley, Patrick

Brookings
Bareiss, Warren J.
Brandt, Bruce E.
Evans, David Allan
Marken, Jack Walter

Huron
Meyer, Kenneth John

Madison
Johnson, Eric

Mitchell
Wilson, John H.

Sioux Falls
Huseboe, Arthur R.
Wienen, Mark Van
Windholz, Anne

Spearfish
Salomon, David A.

Vermillion
Cherry, Paul
Cunningham, Frank Robert
Gasque, Thomas J.
Moyer, Ronald L.
Rude, Roberta N.
Sebesta, Judith Lynn
Shen, Fuyuan
Wilson, Norma Clark

Yankton
Neville, Mary Eileen

TENNESSEE

Athens
Fisher, Nancy
Folks, Jeffrey J.
Gowdy, Anne R.

Chattanooga
Jackson, Richard P.
McClary, Ben Harris
Sachsman, David B.
Ware, Thomas C.

Clarksville
Joyce, Donald Franklin
Lester, James

Cleveland
Kailing, Joel

Collegedale
Byrd, R.
Dick, Donald
McClarty, Wilma King- Doering
Morrison, Robert R.

Cookeville
Bode, Robert Francis
Burduck, Michael L.
Clougherty, Robert, Jr.
Deese, Helen R.
Slotkin, Alan
Whiteaker, Janet Faye

Dyerburg
Griffin, Larry D.

Franklin
Harrington, E. Michael
Thorndike, Jonathan L.

Gallatin
Flynn, David

Henderson
Fulkerson, Raymond Gerald

Hermitage
Moser, Harold Dean

Jackson
Mc Millin, Barbara C.

Jefferson City
Wood, Gerald Carl

Johnson City
Bonnyman-Stanley, Isabel
Brown, Dan
Harris, William Styron, Jr.
Hilliard, Jerry
Hines, Randy
Kirkwood, William
Mooney, Jack
Nelson, Ardis L.
Ralston, Steven
Roberts, Charles
Schneider, Valerie Lois
Sherrill, Catherine Anne
Shields, Bruce E.
Slagle, Judith Baily
Thomason, Wallace Ray
Waage, Frederick O.
Williams, Edwin W.

Knoxville
Adams, Percy Guy
Ashdown, Paul George
Bates, Benjamin J.
Cox, Don Richard
Craig, Christopher P.
Drake, Robert Y., Jr.
Ensor, Allison R.
Evelev, John
Finneran, Richard John
Fisher, John Hurt
Fuller, Homer Woodrow
Gesell, Geraldine C.
Howard, Herbert
Koski, Cheryl A.
Leggett, B. J.
Maland, Charles J.
Martin, Susan D.
Nappa, Christopher
Rutledge, Harry Carraci
Sutherland, Elizabeth H.
Welch, Olga Michele
Ziegler, Dhyana

Martin
Alexander, Lynn M.
Buchanan, Carl J.
Graves, Roy Neil

Memphis
Bensman, Marvin R.
Burgos, Fernando
Carlson, Thomas Clark
Dameron, John Lasley
Entzminger, Robert L.
Evans, David Huhn
Fulton, DoVeanna S.
Kriegel, Abraham David
Lasslo, Andrew
MacNealy, Mary Sue
Moore, Charles B.
Ranta, Richard R.
Shaffer, Brian W.
Shaheen, Naseeb
Sick, David
Stagg, Louis Charles
Tucker, Cynthia Grant
Vinson, Mark Alan

Milligan College
Wainer, Alex

Morristown
Eichelman, Sarah M.

Murfreesboro
Brantley, William
Clark, Bertha Smith
Hutcheson, Thom
Ostrowski, Carl
Sherman, Theodore
Sullivan, Sheila J.
Walker, David E.

Nashville
Allen, Harriette Louise
Bell, Vereen M.
Bowen, Barbara C.
Church, Dan M.
Clayton, Jay
Cockrell, Dale
Cyrus, Cynthia
Davis, Thadious
Elledge, Paul
Enterline, Lynn
Felton, Sharon
Girgus, Sam B.
Goddu, Teresa
Gottfried, Roy K.
Griffith, Larry D.
Halperin, John
Hassel, R. Chris, Jr
Hudson, Robert J.
Insignares, Harriette B.
Jrade, Cathy L.
Kezar, Dennis
Kreyling, Michael
Landes, W. Daniel
Lee, Douglas
Mack, Robert
Marcus, Leah S.
McFague, Sallie
Mckoy, Sheila Smith
Nathanson, Leonard
Plummer, John F.
Schoenfield, Mark
Schwarz, Kathryn
Sullivan, Walter L.
Tichi, Cecelia
Walker, Nancy A.
Weatherby, Harold L., Jr.
Wiltshire, Susan Ford
Wollaeger, Mark A.

Sewanee
Bates, Scott
Core, George
Grammer, John M.

Signal Mountain
Conwell, David

Sneedville
Dodson, Danita Joan

TEXAS

Abilene
Barton, Gay
Clayton, Lawrence Ray
Ellis, Laura
Haire, Carol
Hamner, Robert Daniel
Richardson, Charles R.
Shankle, Nancy
Tippens, Darryl L.
Willerton, Christian William
Williams, John Howard

Alpine
De Ortego Y Gasca, Felipe
Nelson, Barbara J.

Amarillo
White, Lana

Arlington
Alaimo, Stacy
Barros, Carolyn
Cohen, Philip G.
Kellner, Hans
Kolko, Beth E.
Reddick, Robert J.
Roemer, Kenneth M.
Wells, Corri Elizabeth
Wick, Audrey
Wood, Nancy
Zurlo, John A.

Ashland
Inge, M. Thomas

Austin
Antokoletz, Elliott Maxim
Behague, Gerard
Bertelsen, Lance
Bremen, Brian A.
Brokaw, John W.
Bruster, Douglas
Bump, Jerome Francis Anthony
Cable, Thomas Monroe
Carter, Joseph Coleman
Cloud, Dana L.
Cook, Erwin
Davis, Donald G., Jr.
Dell' Antonio, Andrew
Dryden, M.
Duban, James
Erdener, Yildiray
Erlmann, Veit
Faigley, Lester
Farrell, John P.
Flowers, Betty Sue
Friedman, Alan
Gagarin, Michael
Galinsky, Karl
Garrison, James Dale
Ghose, Zulfikar Ahmed
Gillam, Ronald G.
Goff, Barbara E.

Goosman, Stuart
Graham, Don B.
Green, Douglass Marshall
Harris, Elizabeth Hall
Hart, Roderick P.
Herring, Phillip F.
Hilfer, Tony
Hubbard, Thomas K.
Jensen, Robert W.
Klawitter, George
Knapp, Mark L.
Langford, Gerald
Lukenbill, Willis B.
Mackay, Carol Hanbery
MacNeil, Anne
Malof, Joseph Fetler
McCombs, Maxwell E.
Meritt, Lucy Shoe
Moldenhauer, Joseph John
Moore, T. J.
Moragne e Silva, Michele
Neeld, Elizabeth Harper
Nethercut, William Robert
Newton, Adam Zachary
Olasky, Marvin N.
Oliphant, Dave
Rainwater, Catherine
Rossman, Charles R.
Ruszkiewicz, John Joseph
Scheick, William J.
Shelmerdine, Cynthia Wright
Shumway, Nicolas
Slate, Joseph Evans
Slawek, Stephen
Staley, Thomas F.
Stott, William Merrell
Sutherland, William Owen Sheppard
Sylvie, George
Tankard, James William
Todd, William B.
Trimble, John Ralston
Twombly, Robert Gray
Vangelisti, Anita L.
Wadlington, Warwick Paul
Wartella, Ellen A.
Wimsatt, James I.
Winship, Michael B.
Wylie, Hal

Baytown
Adams, Dale Talmadge

Beaumont
Hawkins, Emma
Roth, Lane
Saur, Pamela S.

Belton
Howard, Diane
Shelburne, D. Audell
Walker-Nixon, Donna

Borger
Strecker, Judy

Brenham
Dietrich, Wilfred O.
Walter, Kay

Bryan
Gangotena, Margarita
Machann, Virginia

Canyon
Bradley, Jerry W.
Dudt, Charmazel
Furnish, Shearle
Teichmann, Sandra G.
Teven, Jason

College Station
Atkins, Stephen E.
Beasley, Vanessa B.
Berthold, Dennis A.
Cannon, Garland
Christensen, Paul N.
Clark, William Bedford
Conrad, Charles R.
Dickson, Donald R.
Dorsey, Leroy
Gibson, Claude Louis
Goodman, Jennifer Robin
Hannah, James R.
Harner, James L.
Kallendorf, Craig William
Kern-Foxworth, Marilyn L.
Loving, Jerome M.
Machann, Clinton J.
Marshall, Alicia A.
McCann, Janet P.
Medhurst, Martin J.
Miller, Katherine I.
Myers, David G.
Poole, Marshall Scott
Portales, Marco
Putnam, Linda L.
Rigsby, Enrique D.
Rimal, Rajiv Nath
Ritter, Kurt
Salazar, Abran J.
Self, Charles C.
Sharf, Barbara F.
Street, Richard L., Jr.

Colleyville
Hawkes, Lory

Commerce
Duchovnay, Gerald
Fulkerson, Richard P.
Grimshaw, James
Tuerk, Richard

Corinth
Hise, Pat J.

Dallas
Bradley, Jacqueline
Murfin, Ross C.
Spiegelman, Willard Lester
Wheeler, Bonnie
Winship, Peter

Denton
Bean, Judith M.
Emery, Sarah W.
Kesterson, David B.
Kobler, Jasper Fred
La Forte, Robert Sherman
Nahrgang, Wilbur Lee
Reynolds, Richard Clay
Shillingsburg, Peter Leroy
Tanner, William Edward
Vann, Jerry Don
Waters, Richard L.

Edinburg
La Prade, Douglas E.
Wade, Seth
Wakefield, Robert

El Paso
Bledsoe, Robert Terrell
Leach, Joseph
Louden, Bruce
Ross, David
Small, Ray
West, John Oliver

Fort Worth
Alter, Judy
Daniel, Lee A.
Erisman, Fred Raymond
Hughes, Linda K.
King, Paul E.
Newsom, Douglas Ann
Perez, Frank E.
Shepard, Alan
Sherwood, Steven E.
Stripling, Mahala Yates
Vanderwerken, David Leon

Gainesville
McDaniel, Gerald

Galveston
Curley, Stephen J.
Jones, Anne Hudson
Streeter, Donald

Garland
Hufman, Melody J.

Georgetown
Gleason, Paul W.
Saenger, Michael B.

Houston
Adams, Leslie Kennedy
Benremouga, Karima
Berger, Sidney L.
Bernard, John
Brown-Guillory, Elizabeth
Carmichael, Sheleigh
Chance, Jane
Cunningham, Merrilee A.
Dirst, Matthew
Ford, Thomas Wellborn
Grob, Alan
Hawes, William K.
Huston, John Dennis
Kanellos, Nicolas
Levander, Caroline Field
Lindahl, Carl
Lomas, Ronald Leroy
Mackie, Hilary S.
Markos, Louis
Mieszkowski, Gretchen
Mikics, David
Minter, David Lee
Naficy, Hamid
Natunewicz, Mary Ann T.
Oby, Jason B.
Patten, Robert Lowry
Phillips, Robert
Pollock, James
Rothman, Irving N.
Schiff, Frederick
Skura, Meredith Anne
Switzer, Les
Taylor, James Sheppard
Taylor-Thompson, Betty E.
Wasserman, Julian

Huntsville
Coers, Donald V.
Dowdey, Diane
Mallard, Harry
Parotti, Phillip
Richardson, Don
Ruffin, Paul
Wile, Kip

Hurst
Stripling, Luther

Irving
West, Grace Starry

Kerrville
Breeden, David M.
Keeble, Robert L.
Sullivan, Claudia N.

Kingsville
Elkins, Michael R.

Laredo
Farrokh, Faridoun
Mitchell, Thomas R.
Soto, Gilberto D.

Lubbock
Ashby, Clifford
Aycock, Wendell M.
Barker, Thomas T.
Barkley, Heather S.
Breslin, Linda
Brown, Lady
Carter, Locke
Ceniza, Sherry
Clarke, Bruce Cooper
Conrad, Bryce D.
Crowell, Douglas E.
Cutter, Paul F.
Davis, Dale W.
Davis, Kenneth Waldron
Dickson, John H.
Dragga, Sam A.
George, Edward
Harrienger, Myrna J.
Higdon, David Leon
Hobbs, Wayne
Kemp, Fred O.
Ketner, Kenneth Laine
Kuriyama, Constance
Langford, Thomas
McDonald, Walter Robert
Purinton, Marjean D.
Rickly, Rebecca
Rude, Carolyn D.
Rude, Donald W.
Samson, John W.
Santos, Jose Andre
Schoenecke, Michael Keith
Shaw, Patrick W.
Thomas, Orlan E.
Trotter, Mary
Van Appledorn, Mary Jeanne
Wages, Jack D.
Whitlark, James S.
Wilcox, Dean
Williams, David E.

Marshall
Ellison, Robert

McAllen
Evans, James L.

Midland
Wynn, Dianna

Nacogdoches
Abernethy, Francis Edward
Duncan, Kirby Luther
Gaston, Edwin W., Jr
Johnson, Bobby Harold

Odessa
Simpson, Megan B.

Pasadena
Kinnebrew, Mary Jane

Prairie View
Shine, Theodis

Richardson
Cohen, Milton
Gossin, Pamela
Haynes, Cynthia
Kratz, Dennis
Michaelson, Pat
Nelsen, Robert
Ozsvath, Zsuzsanna
Redman, Tim
Schulte, Rainer
Simpson, Michael

San Antonio
Allen, Mark
Andrea, Bernadette D.
Barker, Wendy
Bernstein, Mark H.
Blanchard, Robert O.
Burton, Joan
Carey, Catherine
Caver, Christine
Christ, William G.
Craven, Alan
Fisher, Judith Law
Hill, L. Brooks
Hovey, Kenneth
Huesca, Robert
Humphries, Bettye
Larson, Doran
Levitt, Steven R.
Lopez, Debbie
Lyons, Bonnie
Matthews, Rebecca
McBride, Margaret
Mendoza, Louis
Pearce, James
Perry, John
Reesman, J. C.
Rodriguez, Clemencia
Romano, Susan
Spinks, C. William
Wells, Colin
Wilkinson, Kenton
Williams, Suzanne Hurst
Woodson, Linda

San Macros
Rosenberg, Teya

San Marcos
Beebe, Steven A.
Bell-Metereau, Rebecca
Blair, John
Brunson, Martha Luan
Chase Hankins, June
Chavkin, Allan
England, Michael Timothy
Grayson, Nancy Jane
Hennessy, Michael
Laird, Edgar
Lochman, Daniel
Marron, Maria B.
Monroe, Debra
Nelson, Claudia B.
Nelson, David C.
Peirce, Kate L.
Rao, Sandhya
Renfro, Paula C.
Renfro, R. Bruce
Ronan, Clifford J.
Salem, Philip
Skerpan-Wheeler, Elizabeth P.
Wilson, Steven M.

Seguin
Bittrich, Louis Edward

Sherman
Cape, Robert W., Jr.
Moore, William Hamilton

Station
Costa, Richard Hauer

Stephenville
Martin, William Bizzell

Tomball
Dernovsek, Vera

Tyler
Eidenmuller, Michael
Rogers, Jack E.
Scherb, Victor I.

Vernon
Farber, Jimmie D.

Victoria
Walker, Ronald Gary

Waco
Barge, J. Kevin
Collmer, Robert George
Davis, William V.
Hunt, Maurice A.
Kelly, S.
Lahaie, Scott
Lemaster, Jimmie R.
Nordling, John G.
Patterson, Bob E.
Ray, Robert H.
Rennie, Mairi C.
Smith, Diane E.

Wichita Falls
Brown, Harry Matthew
Hoggard, James Martin
Smith, Evans L.
Taylor, Arvilla Kerns

UTAH

Cedar City
Aton, James M.
Heuett, Brian L.
Lee, William David

Ceder City
Lee, David

Logan
Bakker, Jan
Chung, Younsook Na
Derry, James
Pease, Ted
Siporin, Steve
Smitten, Jeffrey
Sweeney, Michael S.

Ogden
Krantz, Mary Diane F.
Vause, L. Mikel
Wutz, Michael

Orem
McDonald, R.

Provo
Christiansen, Nancy Lee
Cracroft, Richard Holton
Duerden, Richard Y.
Geary, Edward Acord
Hart, Edward Leroy
Murphy, John J.
Oaks, Harold Rasmus
Parry, Joseph D.
Paxman, David B.
Shumway, Larry V.
Tanner, John Sears
Tanner, Stephen Lowell
Tate, George Sheldon
Thomas, Paul R.
Wilson, Laurie J.

Salt Lake City
Aggeler, Geoffrey
Alexander, Denn
Bergstrom, Mar

Council, Norman Briggs
Donavin, Georgiana
Hess, William Huie
Hollstein, Milton C.
Holmes, Michael E.
Knapp, Gerhard Peter
McPhail, Mark L.
Mujcinovic, Fatima
Oravec, Christine
Revell, Donald
Samuels, Wilfred D.
Sillars, Malcolm O.
Steensma, Robert Charles
Tiemens, Robert K.

VERMONT

Barton
Hoagland, Edward

Bennington
Glazier, Lyle Edward
Newman, Lea Bertani Vozar
Sandy, Stephen

Burlington
Bailly, Jacques A.
Guitar, Barry
Gutman, Stanley T.
Huddle, David R.
McCauley, Rebecca J.
Prelock, Patricia A.
Roberts, Julie
Rosa, Alfred
Rothwell, Kenneth Sprague
Winter, Kari J.

Castleton
Gershon, Robert
Holmes, Burnham

Colchester
Balutansky, Kathleen M.
Kaplan, Carey
Lewis, Nathaniel
Niemi, Robert
Reiss, John
Smith, Lorrie

Cornwall
Littlefield, David J.

Lincoln
Shattuck, Roger

Marlboro
Weiner, Neal O.

Middlebury
Carney, Raymond
Elder, John
McWilliams, John P.
Millier, Brett

Northfield
Liberman, Terri

Norwich
Conley, Katharine

Poultney
Christensen, Laird E.

Saint George
Manchel, Frank

Washington
Dates, Jannette Lake
George, Luvenia A.
Subryan, Carmen

VIRGINIA

Alexandria
Edwards, Don R.
McVeigh, Paul J.

Annandale
...die, William F.

Arlington
Hering, Frank G.
Schurman, Lydia Cushman

Ashland
Daugherty, Gregory Neil
McCaffrey, Daniel

Big Stone Gap
Quillen, Rita S.

Blacksburg
Anderson, Linda
Barr, Marleen Sandra
Becker, Andrew S.
Fine, Elizabeth C.
Fowler, Virginia C.
Graham, Peter W.
Hasselman, Margaret
Mann, Jeffrey A.
Mcallister, Matthew P.
Norstedt, Johann A.
Riley, Sam G.
Saffle, Michael
Stahl, John D.
Stubbs, John C.
Sulloway, Alison G.
Tucker, Edward L.
Welch, Dennis Martin

Bridgewater
Pierson, Jeffery A.

Bristol
Pridgen, Allen

Buena Vista
Cluff, Randall

Charlottesville
Arata, Stephen D.
Barolsky, Paul
Battestin, Martin Carey
Blotner, Joseph Leo
Cantor, Paul Arthur
Casey, John Dudley
Chase, Karen S.
Clay, Jenny Strauss
Courtney, Edward
Cushman, Stephen B.
Cusick, Suzanne G.
DeVeaux, Scott
Feldman, Jessica R.
Felski, Rita
Fry, Donald K.
Gaunt, Kyra D.
Hudson, G. Elizabeth
Kovacs, P. David
Lang, Cecil Y.
Langbaum, Robert
Levenson, Jacob Clavner
Loach, Donald
Malone, Dumas
Maus, Fred Everett
Maus, Katharine E.
McClymonds, Marita P.
Miller, John F.
Nohrnberg, James Carson
Nolan, Barbara
Picker, John
Picker, Martin
Ramazani, Jahan
Unsworth, John M.
Vandersee, Charles Andrew
Velimirovic, Milos
Winner, Anthony
Winner, Viola Hopkins
Wyatt, David M.

Emory
Reid, Robert L.

Fairfax
Bateson, Mary Catherine
Brown, Lorraine Anne
Brown, Stephen Jeffry
Foster, John Burt
Gras, Vernon W.
Irvine, Lorna Marie
Jann, Rosemary
Kelley, Michael Robert
Lont, Cynthia M.
Roman-Mendoza, Esperanza
Rowan, Katherine E.
Starosta, William J.
Winkler, Martin M.
Yocom, Margaret Rose

Falls Church
Moore, Robert Hamilton

Ferrum
Hardt, John S.

Fredericksburg
Rochelle, Warren Gary

Hampden-Sydney
Arieti, James Alexander
Simpson, Hassell Algernon

Hampton
Brown, Jessie Lemon
Long, Thomas L.
Porter, Michael LeRoy

Harrisonburg
Anderson, Steven D.
Arthur, Thomas H.
Cohen, Ralph Alan
Gabbin, Joanne Veal
Hawthorne, Mark D.
Hoskins, Robert V.
King, Thomas L.
McGuire, Charles
Nickels, Cameron C.

Lexington
Craun, Edwin David
Emmitt, Helen
Gentry, Thomas Blythe
Hodges, Louis Wendell
Keen, Suzanne
Stuart, Dabney
Thompson, Roger C.
Warren, James Perrin

Lynchburg
Hanenkrat, Frank Thomas
Hostetler, Theodore J.
Isaac, Lily
Isaac, Samuel
Vanauken, Sheldon

Newport News
Hines, James Robert

Norfolk
Altegoer, Diana B.
Aycock, Roy E.
Bazin, Nancy Topping
Bing, Janet M.
Card, James Van Dyck
Carroll, William
Cirrone, Steven F.
Comfort, Juanita R.
Cooper, Virginia W.
Dandridge, Rita Bernice
Davis, Katie Campbell
Edgerton, Gary R.
Habib, Imitiaz
Hassencahl, Frances J.
Heller, Dana
Hoffmann, Joyce
Jackson, Kathy Merlock
Jacobs, Edward
Metzger, David
Moorti, Sujata
Mourao, Manuela
Neff, Joyce
Pearson, Michael
Raisor, Philip
Richards, Jeffrey H.
Shores, David Lee
Slane, Andrea
Wilson, Charles E., Jr.

Petersburg
Norris, Ethel Maureen

Radford
Adams, Lynn
Baker, Moira
Christianson, Scott
Du Plessis, Eric
Edwards, Grace Toney
Gainer, Kim
Gallo, Louis
Guruswamy, Rosemary
Kovarik, Bill
Kranidis, Rita
Lanier, Parks
Poe, Elizabeth
Poland, Tim
Riddle, Rita Sizemore
Samson, Donald
Saperstein, Jeff
Secreast, Donald
Siebert, Hilary
Wawrzycka, Jolanta
Weiss, Alexander

Richmond
Berry, Boyd Mcculloch
Coppedge, Walter Raleigh
Cornis-Pope, Marcel H.
Dance, Daryl Cumber
Griffin, Claudius Williams
Gruner, Elisabeth
Hilliard, Raymond Francis
Jones, Suzanne W.
Kinney, James Joseph
Longest, George Calvin
McMurtry, Josephine
Meeker, Michael W.
Morse, Charlotte Cook
Neumann, Frederick
Priebe, Richard K.
Taylor, Welford Dunaway
Yancy, Preston Martin

Roanoke
Fallon, Jean
Keyser, Elizabeth

Staunton
Reich, Robert D.

Sweet Briar
Aiken, Ralph
Dabney, Ross H.
Evans-Grubbs, Judith
Mares, Cheryl
Piepho, Lee
Tamburr, Karl

Williamsburg
Baron, James
Blank, Paula Carin
Bongie, Chris
Catron, Louis E.
Donahue, John F.
Donaldson, Scott
Hart, Henry W.
Hutton, William E.
Jones, Ward
Meyers, Terry L.
Nettels, Elsa
Pinson, Hermine Dolorez
Potkay, Adam S.
Preston, Katherine K.
Reilly, Linda
Scholnick, Robert James

Willis
Smith, Michael W.

Winchester
Daddario, Gina
Jacobs, John T.

Wise
Benke, Robin Paul
Miller, Laura

Woodbridge
Hintz, Suzanne S.

Wytheville
Jones, Dan Curtis

WASHINGTON

Auburn
Lowe, Walter G.

Bellevue
Korolenko, A. Michael
Skillman, Judith

Bellingham
Buckland, Roscoe Lawrence
Guess, Carol A.
McDonald, Kelly M.
Skinner, Knute R.
Wlater, Otis M.

Big Harbor
Neufeldt, Leonard N.

Cheney
Gerber, Sanford E.
Hendryx-Bedalov, P.
Lester, Mark
Lindholdt, Paul
Smith, Grant William

College Place
Dickinson, Loren

Des Moines
McColley, Kathleen

Ellenberg
McIntyre, Jerilyn S.

Ellensburg
Benton, Robert Milton
Halperin, Mike
Olson, Steven
Powell, Joseph E.
Schactler, Carolyn
Schneider, Christian Immo

Kirkland
Inslee, Forrest
MacDonald, Margaret Read

Olympia
Williams, Sean

Pullman
Burbick, Joan
Chermak, Gail D.
Condon, William
Delahoyde, Michael
Ehrstine, John
Faulkner, Thomas Corwin
Fulton, Richard Delbert
Gillespie, Diane F.
Gorsevski, Ellen
Hammond, Alexander
Harris, Laurilyn J.
Hellegers, Desiree
Hyde, Virginia Crosswhite
Jankowski, Theodora
Johnson, Jeanne M.
Kennedy, George E.
Kiessling, Nicolas
Law, Richard G.
Linden, Stanton J.
McLeod, Susan
Ong, Rory J.
Reed, T. V.
Roman, Camille
Sherard, Tracey
Sitko, Barbara
Smith, Shawn M.
Villanueva, Victor
Von Frank, Albert J.

Richland
Orr, Leonard

Seattle
Aanerud, Rebecca J.
Adelman, Mara
Alexander, Edward
Allen, Carolyn J.
Bernard, J. W.
Blau, Herbert
Bliquez, Lawrence J.
Bosmajian, Hamida H.
Bullon-Fernandez, Maria
Carlsen, James Caldwell
Ceccarelli, Leah M.
Clauss, James
Cobb, Jerry
Cumberland, Sharon L.
Dunn, Richard John
Eichenlaub, Constance
Ewald, Owen M.
Fearn-Banks, Kathleen
Gastil, John Webster
Griffith, Malcolm A.
Harmon, Daniel P.
Heilman, Robert Bechtold
Iyer, Nalini
Kaplan, Sydney Janet
Korg, Jacob
Leigh, David J.
Matchett, William H.
Mccracken, David
McElroy, Colleen J.
Moody, Joycelyn K.
Pascal, Paul
Philpott, Jeffrey S.
Post, Robert M.

Winnipeg
Amabile, George
Arnason, David E.
Bucknell, Brad
Cahill, Jane
Cooley, Dennis O.
de Toro, Fernando
Donatelli, Joseph M. P.
Egan, Rory Bernard
Finnegan, Robert Emmett
Golden, Mark
Groome, Margaret
Heidenreich, Rosmarin
Hoople, Robin P.
Johnson, Christopher G.
Kroetsch, Robert P.
Layman, Lewis M.
Lenoski, Daniel S.
Moss, Laura
Muller, Adam
O'Kell, Robert P.
Ogden, John T.
Rempel, John W.
Shields, Carol
Smith, Brenda Austin
Snyder, Stephen W.
Teunissen, John J.
Toles, George E.
Turner, Myron M.
Walz, Eugene P.
Weil, Herbert S.
Weil, Judith R.
Wyke, Clement Horatio
Young, Arlene

NEW BRUNSWICK

Douglas
Cogswell, Frederick W.

Fredericton
Beyea, Marion
Dalzell, Alexander
Doerksen, Daniel William
Tryphonopoulos, Demetres P. P.

Moncton
Ohlhauser, Jon B.

Sackville
Bamford, Karen V.
Lapp, Robert Keith
Lochhead, Douglas Grant
MacMillan, Carrie H.
Stark, James A.
Vogan, Nancy F.

NEWFOUNDLAND

Saint John's
Clark, Raymond John
Miller, Elizabeth A.
O'Dea, Shane
Pitt, David G.
Rompkey, Ronald G.

NOVA SCOTIA

Antigonish
O'Brien, Kevin
Walsh, Patrick F.

Halifax
Anthony, Geraldine
Darby, Barbara
Gantar, Jure
Greenfield, Bruce R.
Maitzen, Rohan Amanda
Ross, Trevor T.
Schotch, Peter K.
Silverberg, Mark A.
Tetreault, Ronald
Wainwright, John A.

Pointe-de-l'Eglise
Knutson, Susan

ambro Head
Connell, Kathleen

Wolfville
Callon, Gordon
Davies, Gwendolyn
Fink, Robert J.
Quema, Anne
Thompson, Hilary
Thompson, Ray

ONTARIO

Arnprior
Collins, Robert G.

Downsview
Feltes, Norman Nicholas

Guelph
Cyr, Mary
Davis, Marie
Graham, Kenneth Wayne
Keefer, Janice Kulyk
Marshall, Linda Edith
Matthews, Victor J.
Rooke, Constance M.
Rubio, Mary H.
Spring, Howard

Haileybury
Gold, Joseph

Hamilton
Adamson, Joseph
Ballstadt, Carl P. A.
Bishop, Allan
Blewett, David
Bowerbank, Sylvia
Brennan, Anthony
Clark, David L.
Coldwell, Joan
Coleman, Daniel
Donaldson, Jeffery
Ferns, John
Goellnicht, Donald
Granofsky, Ronald
Hall, Frederick A.
Hyman, Roger L.
John, Brian
King, James
Lee, Alvin A.
Maqbool, Aziz
McKay, Alexander G.
Morton, Richard E.
O'Brien, Susie
O'Connor, Mary E.
Ostovich, Helen
Paul, George Mackay
Savage, Anne
Silcox, Mary
Szeman, Imre J.
Walmsley, Peter
York, Lorraine

Kingston
Berg, Maggie
Carpenter, Mary
Clark, George
Colwell, Frederic
Dick, Susan M.
Finlayson, John
Hamilton, Albert C.
Hanson, Elizabeth
James, William Closson
Jolly, Rosemary J.
Jones, Mark
Kilpatrick, Ross S.
King, Shelley
Lobb, Edward
Lock, F. P.
Logan, George
Moffatt, John
Monkman, Leslie G.
Murray, Laura
Pierce, John
Rae, Patricia
Rasula, Jed
Robinson, Laura
Rogers, Phil
Schlick, Yael
Schroeder, Frederic M.
Skarbarnicki, Anne
Soderlind, Sylvia
Stevens, Paul
Straznicky, Marta
Streight, Irwin
Throne, Barry
Varadharajan, Asha
Ware, Tracy
Wiebe, Mel
Willmott, Glenn Allan

London
Auksi, Peter
Avotins, Ivars
Bailey, Terence
Barsky, Robert
Bentley, D. M. R.
Brydon, Diana
Carmichael, Thomas
Davey, Frank W.
Esterhammer, Angela
Farber, Carole
Gerber, Douglas E.
Green, Richard F.
Grier, James
Groden, Michael
Hair, Donald S.
Harvey, Elizabeth D.
Hieatt, Allen Kent
Kreiswirth, Martin
Neville, Don
Rajan, Balachandra
Rajan, Tilottama
Ross, Catherine S.
Semmens, Richard
Toft, Robert
Traister, Bryce
Waterston, Elizabeth H.
Werstine, Paul

Manotick
Morley, Patricia

Mississauga
Astington, John H.

North Bay
Janzen, Lorraine
Kooistra, John
Kruk, Laurie
Plumstead, William
Zytaruk, George J.

North York
Doob, Penelope
Faas, Ekbert
Godard, Barbara J.
Herren, Michael W.
Lennox, John W.
Rowland, Beryl
Waddington, Miriam

Ottawa
Bird, Roger A.
Chari, V. K.
Chartier, Yves
Dorland, Michael
Dornan, Christopher
Edwards, Mary-Jane
Gillingham, Bryan R.
Gillmor, Alan
Gnarowski, Michael
Henighan, Thomas J.
Jeffrey, David Lyle
Keillor, Elaine
Loiselle, Andre
Macdonald, Robert Hugh
Manganiello, Dominic
Marks, Laura U.
McMullen, Lorraine
Merkely, Paul B.
Mosco, Vincent
Noonan, James S.
O'Brien, Charles
Panek, Jennifer Marie
Perrakis, Phyllis J.
Shepherd, John
Smart, Patricia
Staines, David
Sylvestre, Jean-Guy
Thomson, George Henry
Von Flotow, Luise
Walton, Priscilla L.
Wilson, Keith G.
Winseck, Dwayne
Wyczynski, Paul
Yardley, J. C.

Peterborough
Conolly, Leonard W.
Moss, John E.
Neufeld, James Edward

Port Hope
Montagnes, Ian

Portland
Killam, G. Douglas

Saint Catharines
Baxter-Moore, Nick
Bredin, Marian
Debly, Patricia
Dyer, Klay
Grant, Barry Keith
Irons, Glenwood H.
Leach, Jim
Miller, Mary Jane
Preston, Joan M.
Sivell, John
Sloniowski, Jeannette
Spearey, Susan
Szuchewycz, Bohdan G.

Saint Catherines
Nicks, Joan P.
Parker, Richard W.
Sauer, Elizabeth

Sault Ste. Marie
Grace, Dominick M.

Scarborough
Irwin, Eleanor

Sudbury
Gerry, Thomas M. F.
Hengen, Shannon
Krajewski, Bruce
Orr, Marilyn
Parker, Douglas
Schell, Richard
Steven, Laurence

Thunder Bay
Colton, Glenn
Forbes, Joyce
Mamoojee, Abdool-Hack

Toronto
Adolph, Robert
Atwood, Margaret
Baird, John D.
Bakker, Barend H.
Barnes, Timothy David
Bartel, Lee R.
Beck, Roger L.
Beckwith, John
Bewell, Alan J.
Burgess, Jonathan
Cameron, Elspeth M.
Clivio, Gianrenzo Pietro
Cohen, Derek M.
Cohen, Judith
Collie, Michael J.
Conacher, Desmond J.
Cook, Eleanor
Corkin, Jane
Corman, Brian
Courtney, Richard
Domville, Eric W.
Duffy, Dennis
Elliott, Thomas G.
Embleton, Sheila
Frank, Roberta
Grant, John Neilson
Grant, Judith A. S.
Gregory, Michael J. P.
Grosskurth, Phyllis M.
Halewood, William H.
Hanke, Robert
Heller, Deborah
Hoeniger, Frederick J. D.
Hughes, Andrew
Hutcheon, Linda
Imboden, Roberta
Innes, Christopher
Jackson, Heather J.
Jackson, James Robert de Jager
Johnston, Alexandra F.
Kuin, Roger
Lancashire, Anne C.
Lancashire, Ian
Lary, Nikita
Lee, M. Owen
Leland, Charles Wallace
Lesk, Andrew J.
Levenson, Jill
Macpherson, Jay
Maniates, Maria Rika
Marinelli, Peter V.
Mason, H. J.
McDonough, C. J.
Mount, Nick James
Mulhallen, Karen
Murray, Heather
Nikolova, Irena N.
O'Grady, Jean
Parry, Hugh
Pothecary, Sarah
Rigg, Arthur George
Rutherford, Paul F. W.
Sabiston, Elizabeth
Sol, Adam
Sullivan, Rosemary
Thomas, Clara M.
Unrau, John
Valihora, Karen
Walkom, Thomas L.
Warkentin, Germaine
Wilder, Georgia Lee
Woodward, Steven P.

Waterloo
Campbell, Jane
Chamberlin, John
Comensoli, Viviana
DiCenzo, Maria
Downey, James
Doyle, James
Enns, Leonard
Evans, Joan
Fletcher, Judith
Fogel, Stan
Forsyth, Phyllis
Froese Tiessen, Hildi
Gray, Laura
Greene, Gordon K.
Harris, Randy Allen
Hinchcliffe, Peter
Hull, Kenneth
Jewinski, Edwin
Jones, Charlene Diehl
Macnaughton, William Robert
McCormack, Eric
McGee, Christopher Edward
Moore, Michael
O'Dell, Leslie
Russell, Anne
Santosuosso, Alma
Shakinovsky, Lynn
Smith, Rowland
Tiessen, Paul
Ty, Eleanor R.

West Hill Scarborough
Brown, Russell Morton

Willowdale
Copeland, David Robert

Windsor
Atkinson, Colin B.
Bebout, Linda J.
Bird, Harold Wesley
Brandt, Di
Davison, Carol Margaret
de Villers, Jean-Pierre
Dilworth, Thomas
Ditsky, John M.
Harder, Bernhard D.
Herendeen, Wyman H.
Janzen, Henry David
Klein, Owen
Kovarik, Edward
Mackendrick, Louis King
MacLeod, Alistair
Quinsey, Katherine M.
Ruggles, Myles A.
Smedick, Lois Katherine
Stevens, Peter S.
Straus, Barrie Ruth

Winnipeg
Schnitzer, Deborah